Cambridge English Pronouncing Dictionary

Daniel Jones

18TH EDITION

Edited by
Peter Roach
Jane Setter
John Esling

CAMBRIDGE
UNIVERSITY PRESS

CAMBRIDGE
UNIVERSITY PRESS

University Printing House, Cambridge CB2 8BS, United Kingdom

One Liberty Plaza, 20th Floor, New York, NY 10006, USA

477 Williamstown Road, Port Melbourne, VIC 3207, Australia

4843/24, 2nd Floor, Ansari Road, Daryaganj, Delhi – 110002, India

79 Anson Road, #06–04/06, Singapore 079906

Cambridge University Press is part of the University of Cambridge.

It furthers the University's mission by disseminating knowledge in the pursuit of education, learning and research at the highest international levels of excellence.

www.cambridge.org
Information on this title: www.cambridge.org/9780521152556

First published by J. M. Dent & Sons Ltd 1917
First published by Cambridge University Press 1991
This edition published 2011
20 19 18 17 16 15 14 13 12 11 10 9 8

Printed in Great Britain by CPI Group (UK) Ltd, Croydon CR0 4YY

A catalogue record for this publication is available from the British Library

ISBN 978-052-115255-6 Paperback with CD-ROM
ISBN 978-052-115253-2 Paperback
ISBN 978-052-176575-6 Hardback

Editors' preface to the 18th Edition

The *English Pronouncing Dictionary* has been in use for over 90 years, and during that time it has become established as a classic work of reference, both for native speakers of English wanting an authoritative guide to pronunciation, and for users of English as a foreign or second language all over the world. The dictionary was first published in 1917, perhaps the greatest work of the greatest of British phoneticians, Daniel Jones (born in 1881). Jones was Professor of Phonetics at University College London from 1921 until his retirement in 1949. He was still an occasional visitor to the department in 1967 when Peter Roach was there as a postgraduate student of phonetics, though he died in December of that year. The last edition of the *English Pronouncing Dictionary* in which Jones was directly involved was the 12th, and the 13th was substantially revised by A.C. Gimson, his successor as Professor of Phonetics at University College. From the 13th edition, Gimson was assisted by Dr. Susan Ramsaran, and in her preface to the 14th edition she notes that they had been making plans for a 15th edition at the time of Gimson's death. After this, the publishing rights were acquired from the original publishers, J.M. Dent & Sons, by Cambridge University Press.

With the publication of the 15th edition in 1997, which saw a massive injection of 18,000 new words, the *English Pronouncing Dictionary* entered the computer age. All the entries were converted into a computer database, making the process of updating and adding to previous editions much more efficient. American pronunciations were included for the first time. The 16th edition added information panels explaining phonetic terminology and explaining the relationship between spelling and pronunciation. The other major recent development for the *English Pronouncing Dictionary* was the creation of an electronic version, which gives both British and American spoken pronunciations for every word in the dictionary. For linguists and learners of English there is also the ability to search on both alphabetic and phonetic characters, and to record the user's own voice and compare it with the spoken pronunciation.

In the course of preparing the 18th edition, a thorough revision of the dictionary and of the recordings has resulted in several thousand alterations and improvements. In addition, we have made some changes to the transcription conventions, most notably in the treatment of triphthongs and in the preferring of /tʃ/ and /dʒ/ over /tj/ and /dj/ in words such as 'tune' and 'dune' in accordance with contemporary pronunciation.

As a new study aid, we have included in this edition a collection of short essays specially written by leading figures in phonetics and pronunciation teaching. These essays, with the general title of *The world of pronunciation*, are to be found on page xx.

Above all, the aim of the dictionary is to include information which is relevant to the needs of contemporary users and which is presented in the clearest possible way. This aim has informed both the choice of vocabulary covered and the range of pronunciations shown. The process of updating continues with each new edition, and we are fortunate to have the use of the Cambridge International Corpus, which currently contains around 1.5 billion words of written and transcribed spoken texts from a variety of genres. This corpus informs all Cambridge dictionaries, and gives us clear, empirical evidence for new words (general and proper nouns) which have come to prominence since the last edition.

PETER ROACH
JANE SETTER
JOHN ESLING

Acknowledgements

Senior Commissioning Editor
Colin McIntosh

Project manager
Elizabeth Walter

Global Corpus Manager
Ann Fiddes

Database management
Daniel Perrett

Electronic project management
Clare Tunstall

Proofreading
Lucy Hollingworth
Patrick Phillips
Judith Willis

Design
Boag Associates
Claire Parson

Series Cover Design
Andrew Oliver

Typesetting
Data Standards Limited

Production
Chris Williams

We were very glad to be able to work again with Liz Walter of Cambridge Lexicography and Language Services, who has played a vital editorial role in all editions of this dictionary since the 15th, and who guided our work with her usual patience and insight. Nobuo Yuzawa, of Utsunomiya University, read the revised Introduction and gave us valuable advice and criticism. Finally, Jack Windsor Lewis and Francis Nolan gave us helpful answers to difficult questions.

The front cover shows a spectrogram of the word 'Cambridge' as pronounced by Peter Roach.

Contents

Introduction

1 What is a pronouncing dictionary?

1.1 Why do we need pronunciation dictionaries?

The simple answer is that the spelling of English is so unreliable as a guide to pronunciation that we need something better. English spelling has evolved over many centuries, but has never been reformed. If it worked as well as the writing systems used for languages such as Finnish or Italian we would know from the spelling exactly how a word should be pronounced, and there would be no point in producing a special dictionary for pronunciations. If at some time in the future the English-speaking world agrees to reform the way English is written, there will probably no longer be a need for our dictionary.

It is very important to remember that in this dictionary we are not trying to tell you how English *ought* to be pronounced; we are presenting how we believe some native speakers of English actually *do* pronounce the words.

This dictionary is designed to provide information on the current pronunciation of approximately 80,000 English words and phrases. For each entry, a British and an American pronunciation is shown. The dictionary provides much essential information that is not usually available in a general dictionary, such as the pronunciation of proper names, the pronunciation of all inflected forms of each word, and a large amount of detail about variant pronunciations. In addition, the electronic versions of the dictionary allow the reader to listen to the British and American pronunciation of a word.

1.2 Can I use the dictionary if I don't know anything about phonetics?

All the information on pronunciation is written using special phonetic symbols based on those of the International Phonetic Association. There is a full explanation of these inside the front cover.

1.3 What is the CD-ROM for?

All the words and all the transcriptions that are in the printed dictionary are also included on the CD-ROM. You can type in any word in the dictionary and see its entry. In addition, with this facility you can listen to a pronunciation of each word (spoken by a British or American voice), then if you wish you can record your own voice and compare it with our version. You can also search for any combination of letters or IPA symbols.

2 The sounds of English

In this section we set out the sounds and the sound structures of the two accents of English (one British and one American) that are the basis of the dictionary. We describe the phonemes and their allophones, then look at syllable structure.

The accent of British English that we describe in this dictionary is called *BBC pronunciation*, since it is the accent most often heard in the speech of newsreaders and announcers on serious channels of the BBC (see Section 3.1 for discussion of the choice of accent); it is also sometimes referred to in this section as *BBC English* or *BBC accent*, often shortened to *BBC*. The corresponding accent of American English is called *General American*, often shortened to *GA*. Many writers have noted that although British and American accents sound very different from each other, the set of sounds (phonemes) used by each is remarkably similar. The differences lie elsewhere. A familiar case is the word 'tomato', where British speakers say /təˈmɑː.təʊ/ and American speakers say /təˈmeɪ.t̬oʊ/; British and American speakers both use the phonemes /ɑː/ and /eɪ/ in speaking English, but in the case of 'tomato' they make a different phonemic choice.

To explain one of the most important differences we need to introduce the term *rhotic*. A rhotic accent is one in which the phoneme /r/ is found at the end of syllables as well as at the beginning. In such an accent it is usual for /r/ to be pronounced wherever the letter 'r' occurs in the spelling, so that 'car' is pronounced /kɑːr/ and 'cart' is pronounced /kɑːrt/. Most American accents are rhotic; the British accent described in this dictionary (BBC pronunciation) is *non-rhotic*, though many other accents that can be heard in Britain are rhotic. It is very noticeable in the General American accent that vowels when followed by /r/ are strongly affected ('coloured') by the tongue position required for the production of /r/. The tip of the tongue is curled backwards, in a shape that is called *retroflex*.

2.1 Vowels and diphthongs

It is standard practice in phonetics to represent the quality of vowels and diphthongs by placing them in a four-sided figure often known as the *Cardinal Vowel quadrilateral*. This device is used in the vowel descriptions in the following section.

2.1.1 British English

British English (BBC pronunciation) is generally described as having short vowels, long vowels, and diphthongs. There are said to be seven short vowels, five long ones, and eight diphthongs. At the end of this section some attention is also given to triphthongs. Each vowel symbol is given a corresponding key-word[1].

- Short vowels:
  ɪ e æ ʌ ɒ ʊ
  k**i**t dr**e**ss tr**a**p str**u**t l**o**t f**oo**t

The vowel /æ/, classified as a short vowel, is nevertheless considerably longer than the other short vowels before /b, d, g, dʒ, m, n, ŋ/.

In addition, there is the 'schwa' vowel /ə/ which only occurs in weak syllables.

ə ə
anoth**er**

Two additional vowels, /i/ and /u/, are introduced later (Section 3.11).

- Long vowels:
  iː ɑː ɔː uː ɜː
  fl**ee**ce p**al**m th**ou**ght g**oo**se n**ur**se

- Diphthongs:
  eɪ aɪ ɔɪ əʊ
  f**a**ce pr**i**ce ch**oi**ce g**oa**t
  aʊ ɪə eə ʊə
  m**ou**th n**ear** squ**are** c**ure**

These vowels and diphthongs may be placed in the vowel quadrilateral (based on the Cardinal Vowel diagram) as shown in Figs. 1 – 3. It should be noted that though each vowel (or diphthong starting-point) is marked with a circle, it is misleading to think of this as a precise target; the circle represents the area within which the typical vowel pronunciation falls.

[1] The key-words used here for vowels and diphthongs were devised by Professor J.C. Wells and are widely used throughout the world as a standard set.

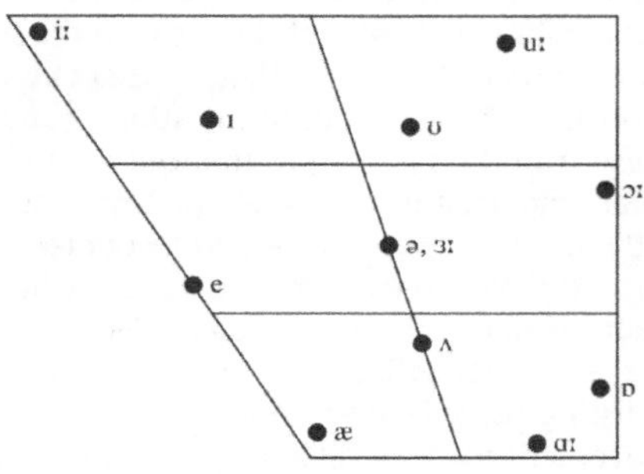

Fig. 1 BBC English pure vowels

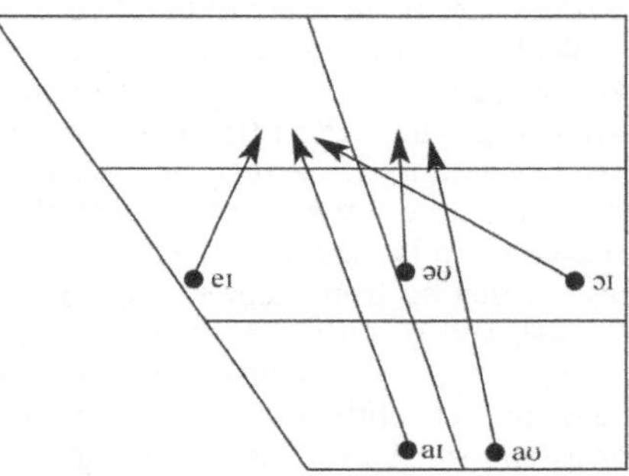

Fig. 2 BBC English closing diphthongs

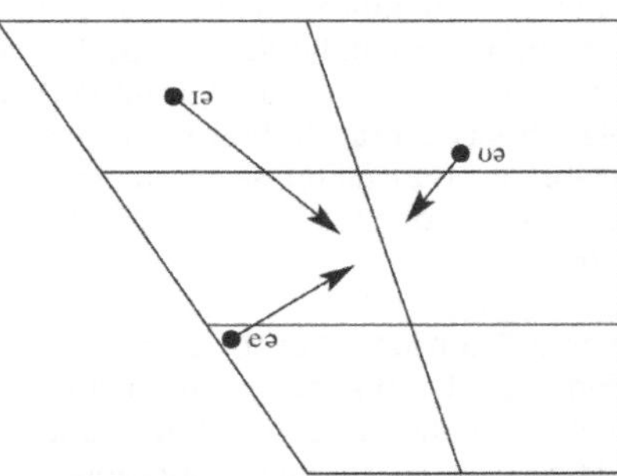

Fig. 3 BBC English centring diphthongs

- Triphthongs:

We need to consider the special case of diphthongs followed by a schwa; examples of these are 'layer' /leɪə^{r}/; 'fire' /faɪə^{r}/. The full set is as shown below:

/eɪə/ 'player'
/aɪə/ 'fire'
/ɔɪə/ 'loyal'
/əʊə/ 'grower'
/aʊə/ 'power'

Such sequences are sometimes referred to as

triphthongs; they are not phonemes of English, but combinations of diphthongs with the schwa (/ə/) vowel. However, they present unique problems: in BBC pronunciation many of these triphthongs are pronounced with such a small movement in vowel quality that it is difficult for foreign learners to recognize them; for example, the name 'Ireland', which is traditionally transcribed /ˈaɪə.lənd/, frequently has an initial syllable which sounds virtually indistinguishable from /ɑː/, with just a small movement towards /ɪ/ and then towards /ə/ at the end. Some triphthongs are pronounced like single syllables, as in the example just given, while others are more likely to be divided into two syllables (in the list above we have not marked syllable divisions). We usually find the two-syllable pronunciation (i) when the schwa is a separate morpheme (e.g. '-er' in 'buyer' /baɪ.əʳ/), (ii) when the word is thought to be foreign (this includes many biblical names originating from Hebrew, e.g. 'Messiah' /məˈsaɪ.ə/), and (iii) when a word is not used very frequently, e.g. 'cyanosis' /ˌsaɪ.əˈnəʊ.sɪs/. Where we feel a triphthong may be pronounced either as two syllables or as one, we give one pronunciation with a syllable division and an alternative with a one-syllable pronunciation. In the single-syllable case the middle vowel is printed in italic to indicate that in this reduced pronunciation the middle vowel may be very much reduced or even elided (omitted); for example, 'briar', /ˈbraɪ.əʳ, bra*ɪ*əʳ/; where the one-syllable pronunciation seems more likely, that pronunciation is given first: 'fire' is /fa*ɪ*əʳ, ˈfaɪ.əʳ/.

Before an /r/ consonant at the beginning of a following syllable, the distinction between a diphthong and the corresponding triphthong seems to be neutralized, most noticeably in the case of /aɪ/ and /aʊ/ plus /ə/ – it seems that 'Irish', 'irate', 'Maori' may be pronounced as /ˈa*ɪ*ə.rɪʃ/, /a*ɪ*əˈreɪt/, /ˈma*ʊ*ə.ri/ or as /ˈaɪ.rɪʃ/, /aɪˈreɪt/, /ˈmaʊ.ri/ with no regular distinction made in pronunciation. This is because the glide from /ɪ/ or /ʊ/ to /r/ sounds similar to a schwa. In general, the practice of this dictionary is to transcribe such cases as /aɪə/, /aʊə/; the middle vowel is not printed in italic, to make the transcription less complicated, but it should be understood that the middle vowel in this context may also be considerably weakened.

Speakers of American English are less likely to reduce a triphthong to a single-syllable glide, and this fact is reflected in the transcriptions given.

A few comments on variation in individual vowels and vowel symbols are needed.

i. The length of vowels and diphthongs is very much reduced when they occur in syllables closed by the voiceless or fortis consonants /p, t, k, tʃ, f, θ, s, ʃ/. Thus /iː/ in 'beat' has only about half the length of /iː/ in 'bead' or 'bee'; similarly /eɪ/ in 'place' is much reduced in length compared with /eɪ/ in 'plays' or 'play'. It is important to remember this in talking about 'long' and 'short' vowels.

ii. The quality of /æ/ is more open than it used to be, and the symbol /a/ might be considered a suitable alternative. We have retained the /æ/ symbol partly because it is phonetically appropriate for the corresponding American vowel.

iii. The vowel /ʌ/ used to be a back vowel in the early years of this dictionary, and the symbol was chosen for this reason. Nowadays it is no longer a back vowel, but a central one. Alternative symbols could be considered in the future.

iv. Among younger speakers, the vowels /uː, ʊ, u/ have moved to a more front quality, with less lip rounding, particularly when preceded by /j/ as in 'use'.

v. Among the diphthongs, there seems to be a progressive decline in the use of /ʊə/, with /ɔː/ taking its place (for example, the pronunciation of the word 'poor' as /pɔː/ is increasingly common). The other centring diphthongs also seem to be moving towards a pronunciation more like a long vowel, so that /ɪə/ sounds like [ɪː] and /eə/ sounds like [ɛː] in some speakers.

2.1.2 American English

In American English we do not find the difference between long and short vowels described above, and the vowel system is commonly described as having lax vowels, tense vowels, and diphthongs. Lax vowels, which correspond to British short vowels, are said to be made with less oral tension and do not usually end syllables. The /ɒ/ vowel of British pronunciation is not found in General American. The length of a vowel in American English is principally conditioned by the environment in which it occurs. However, we have retained the length mark on the tense vowels /iː, ɑː, ɔː, uː/ and the retroflex vowel /ɝː/

in order to mark their relationship to the English long vowels.

Vowels preceding /r/ are notably influenced by rhotic colouring. The retroflex vowels /ɝː/ and /ɚ/ are among those features that noticeably distinguish American English pronunciation from BBC pronunciation. All vowels occurring before /r/ within a syllable are likely to become 'r-coloured' to some extent.

- Lax vowels:

ɪ	e	æ	ʌ	ʊ
kit	dress	trap	strut	foot

In addition, there is the schwa vowel and its retroflex counterpart:

about	mother
ə	ɚ

Two other vowels, /i/ and /u/, are introduced below (Section 3.11).

- tense vowels:

iː	ɑː	ɔː	uː	ɝː
fleece	palm	thought	goose	nurse

- Diphthongs:

eɪ	aɪ	ɔɪ	oʊ	aʊ
face	price	choice	goat	mouth

The above vowels and diphthongs may be placed in a vowel quadrilateral as was done for British English (BBC) vowels above. In most cases the positions of the American vowels are so similar to the British ones that the vowel diagrams given (Figs 1 – 3 above) will serve to show the American values, with a few exceptions:

i. There are no centring diphthongs in GA; the equivalents of the BBC vowels shown in Fig. 3 are /ɪr/ (for /ɪə/), /er/ (for eə) and /ʊr/ (for /ʊə/).

ii. There are no contexts in which the /ɜː/ ('nurse') vowel occurs in GA without a following /r/, and we represent this vowel as /ɝː/.

iii. There is no /ɒ/ vowel in GA.

iv. The diphthong in the word 'home' has for many years been represented as /əʊ/ for British pronunciation, but in earlier editions of this and others of Jones' works the symbolization was /oʊ/, indicating a rounded initial vowel. This is still the preferred transcription for the GA diphthong in American books and papers. Therefore, in order to preserve compatibility with other works, we have chosen to use /əʊ/ for BBC English and /oʊ/ for GA. The starting point of /oʊ/ is similar to that of /ɔɪ/, but less back.

v. The GA /æ/ vowel is somewhat closer than BBC /æ/, and seems to be evolving into an even closer vowel. Although it is used in the same words as those with /æ/ in BBC pronunciation, we frequently find /e/ in GA instead. Thus 'marry' is often pronounced /ˈmer.i/, the same pronunciation that can be seen also for 'merry' and 'Mary' (though in some other dialects of US English, notably New York City, there are three different vowels in 'Mary': /ˈmeɪ.ri/, 'merry' /ˈmer.i/, 'marry' /ˈmær.i/). The /æ/ vowel is also found in most of the words which in BBC have /ɑː/ when there is no letter 'r' in the spelling and there is a fricative consonant following the vowel, (e.g. 'pass', 'ask').

vi. The quality of American /ɑː/ is similar to the BBC /ɑː/ vowel; it is used in some of the words which have /ɑː/ in BBC pronunciation when there is no letter 'r' in the spelling (e.g. 'father', 'calm'). It also replaces the BBC short /ɒ/ vowel in many words (e.g. 'hot', 'top', 'bother'): 'bother' rhymes with 'father'.

vii. GA /ɔː/ is more open in quality than BBC /ɔː/. It is used in some words where BBC pronunciation has /ɔː/ (e.g. 'fault', 'wall'), and is also found as a possible pronunciation of words which have the short /ɒ/ in BBC pronunciation, e.g. 'long', 'dog'.

viii. GA /uː/ is similar to BBC /uː/, though slightly more back, but it is also used where BBC has /juː/ after alveolar consonants (e.g. 'new', 'duty').

ix. As explained previously, many GA vowels have 'r-colouring' when they occur before the consonant /r/. Although there are some words where /ɑː/ occurs without this colouring (e.g. 'bra', 'palm'), there are many words like 'car', 'cart' where the /r/ following the /ɑː/ causes the vowel to sound almost like /r/ itself.

2.2 Consonants

2.2.1 British English (BBC pronunciation)

- Plosives:

p	t	k	b	d	g
pin	**t**in	**k**in	**b**in	**d**in	**g**ive

- Affricates:

tʃ	dʒ
chain	**J**ane

- Fricatives:
  f v θ ð
  fine **v**ine **th**ink **th**is
  s z ʃ ʒ h
  seal **z**eal **sh**ip mea**s**ure **h**ow
- Nasals:
  m n ŋ
  su**m** su**n** su**ng**
- Approximants:
  l r w j
  light **r**ight **w**et **y**et

These consonants (which are common to British and American pronunciation) can be arranged as shown below in the form of a table. The layout of the symbols follows that of the chart of the International Phonetic Alphabet: the horizontal axis corresponds to the place of articulation of the consonant, with the left side of the chart corresponding to the part of the vocal tract furthest from the larynx (i.e. the lips), while the right side is the nearest to the larynx (the place for glottal consonants). From top to bottom are the various types of consonant ('manners of articulation'). Within each box, where there are two consonants which differ only in voicing, they are placed side by side with the voiceless one to the left.

Some explanatory comments about the different consonants are needed.

i. Certain types of consonant have a distinction such as that between /t/ and /d/; this is commonly classed as a distinction between voiceless and voiced consonants, but the distinction is in fact much more complex. Consonants usually classed as voiceless are /p, t, k, f, θ, s, ʃ, tʃ/, with voiced partners /b, d, g, v, ð, z, ʒ, dʒ/. The sound /h/ is also classed as voiceless. Since the presence or absence of voicing is often less important than some other phonetic features, it has been suggested that instead the terms *fortis* (equivalent to voiceless) and *lenis* (equivalent to voiced) should be used. These terms imply that the main distinguishing factor is the amount of energy used in the articulation (fortis consonants being made with greater energy than lenis). They are not used in this dictionary, since the usefulness of this terminology is uncertain. Some of the characteristics of the two types of consonant are set out below.

ii. /p, t, k/ are typically accompanied by aspiration (i.e. an interval of breath before the following vowel onset), especially when initial in a stressed syllable. Thus, 'pin' is distinguished from 'bin' very largely by the aspiration accompanying /p/. However, in the syllable-initial sequences /sp-, st-, sk-/, /p, t, k/ lack such aspiration. When /l/, /j/, /w/, or /r/ immediately follow /p, t, k/, they are devoiced and are pronounced as fricatives. Another characteristic of /p, t, k/ that is not marked in transcriptions is glottalization; when one of these consonants is followed by another consonant it is now usual to find that a glottal closure precedes the /p/, /t/, or /k/, particularly if the syllable in which they occur is stressed. Thus the pronunciation of 'captain', 'rightful', 'Yorkshire', which are phonemically /ˈkæp.tɪn/, /ˈraɪt.f^{ə}l/, /ˈjɔːk.ʃə/, could be shown (using the symbol [ʔ] for glottal closure) as [ˈkæʔp.tɪn], [ˈraɪʔt.fl], [ˈjɔːʔk.ʃə]. This glottalization also occurs in the case of /tʃ/, e.g. 'butcher' /bʊtʃ.ə^{r}/, [bʊʔtʃ.ə]. When /p/, /t/, /k/, or /tʃ/ occur at the end of a word before a pause they are often glottalized. A related phenomenon can be called 'glottal replacement': younger speakers, in particular, now often pronounce a glottal stop *instead of* /t/ at the end of a stressed syllable preceding an unstressed syllable (e.g. 'getting better' [geʔ.ɪŋ beʔ.ə]), but

Table of English Consonants

	Bilabial	*Labio-dental*	*Dental*	*Alveolar*	*Post-alveolar*	*Palatal*	*Velar*	*Glottal*
Plosive	p b			t d			k g	
Affricate					tʃ dʒ			
Fricative		f v	θ ð	s z	ʃ ʒ		(x)	h
Nasal	m			n			ŋ	
Lateral approximant				l				
Approximant	w				r	j		

though some prominent British politicians have adopted this, it is at present not regarded as acceptable BBC pronunciation.

iii. As noted in the section on vowels and diphthongs above, voiceless consonants have a shortening effect on sounds preceding them within a syllable. Thus in the words 'right' and 'ride' (/raɪt/ and /raɪd/) the diphthong is noticeably shorter in the first word than in the second; in the words 'bent' and 'bend' (/bent/ and /bend/), both the vowel /e/ and the nasal consonant /n/ are shorter in the first word. This length difference is not always easy to observe in connected speech.

iv. The consonant /l/ has two different allophones in BBC pronunciation, the so-called 'clear' and 'dark' allophones. The 'clear' one (which has an /iː/-like quality) occurs before vowels, the 'dark' one (which has an /uː/-like quality) before consonants or before a pause. One aspect of the pronunciation of /l/ is becoming much more widespread: in contexts where a 'dark /l/' would be expected, many speakers produce instead a vowel similar to /ʊ/ (for example, in 'hill', 'help'). This is sometimes referred to as '/l/-vocalization'; it has been known to writers on English phonetics for a long time, but has recently become much more widespread.

v. The consonants /ʃ/, /ʒ/, /tʃ/, /dʒ/, /r/ are usually accompanied by lip rounding.

2.2.2 American English

The consonant phonemes of the American English model may be represented by the same scheme used for British English above. Similarly, many of the distinguishing phonetic traits discussed for BBC pronunciation hold for General American as well: initial /p, t, k/ are normally aspirated except when immediately preceded by /s/. Glottalization that precedes the plosives /p, t, k, tʃ/ occurs often in rapid speech. There are, of course, numerous phonetic and phonological differences between British and American English, as there are within regional and social varieties. A few differences are important enough to be mentioned here:

- The 'tapped' medial /t/ following a stressed syllable (as in 'butter', 'water', 'enter') is transcribed as t̬. This sound is the norm in General American pronunciation; it is usually voiced in conversational speech, but may be devoiced in formalizing environments or in lower-frequency words (which are not shown as tapped in the dictionary). The tap may also occur after /l/ (e.g. 'filter' /ˈfɪl.t̬ɚ/), and in this case it is usually voiceless. Since tapping of /t/ after /l/ is not a standard feature of GA, it is not shown in the dictionary.

- Another is phonological, and has already been introduced: the presence (in American English) of postvocalic /r/ (as in 'farmer' /ˈfɑːr.mɚ/), making GA a rhotic accent.

- It should also be noted that the difference between 'clear' and 'dark' /l/ is much less marked in GA than in BBC pronunciation, so that even prevocalic /l/ in American pronunciation sounds dark to English ears. The pronunciation known as '/l/-vocalization', described above in relation to BBC pronunciation, is widely found in contemporary American pronunciation too.

2.3 English syllables

Although vowels and consonants are presented here as the basic building blocks of speech, it is important to remember that each language has its own individual ways of combining those sounds into larger units called syllables. English syllable structure is more complex than that of most of the world's languages. For a description of English syllable structure see Roach (2009), Chapter 8, and more advanced works referred to there. Almost all English syllables have a vowel as their central element, and in the case of an utterance like 'ah' /ɑː/ there is no consonant present. A syllable may have an initial consonant followed by a vowel, e.g. 'bee' /biː/, or a vowel followed by a final consonant, e.g. 'ought' /ɔːt/ (BBC), /ɑːt/ (GA); however, if an English syllable contains one of the 'short' or 'tense' vowels /ɪ, e, æ, ʌ, ɒ, ʊ/ the syllable must end with at least one consonant. Many syllables have an initial and a final consonant, e.g. 'bat' /bæt/. Even with simple syllables like these we must observe certain rules and regularities: for example, the velar nasal /ŋ/ cannot begin a syllable, and the consonant /h/ cannot end one. The rules and regularities become much more complex when we consider syllables containing consonant clusters, that is sequences containing more than one consonant. We find English syllables beginning with two consonants (e.g. 'ski' /skiː/) or three (e.g. 'straw' /strɔː/ (BBC), /strɑː/ (GA)), and syllables ending with two consonants (e.g. 'eats' /iːts/), three (e.g. 'risked' /rɪskt/) or four (e.g. 'sixths'

/sɪksθs/). A detailed study shows that only certain combinations of consonants are possible, while other combinations would result in a word that could not be accepted as English, e.g. /zkɑːðh/.

3 How the CEPD is organized

This dictionary contains a huge amount of information, and we have to use many conventions and devices to compress it all into one book; many of these date back to the original edition of the dictionary published in 1917, but a number of others have been introduced in later editions. Therefore, if you are going to understand fully all the information you see in the dictionary, you need to understand how it is presented. In addition, we need to explain our policy and practice on such matters as the pronunciation of foreign words, optional sounds, changes in pronunciation that we think are in progress now, differences between younger and older speakers, variability in stress patterns and many other matters.

At the end of this section, on page xxxii, there is a double-page display of examples showing how the dictionary entries appear.

3.1 Whose pronunciation is represented?

A pronouncing dictionary must base its recommendations on one or more *models*. A pronunciation model is a carefully chosen and defined accent of a language. In the first edition of this dictionary (1917), Daniel Jones described the type of pronunciation recorded as "that most usually heard in everyday speech in the families of Southern English persons whose menfolk have been educated at the great public boarding-schools". Accordingly, he felt able to refer to his model as 'Public School Pronunciation' (PSP). In later editions, e.g. that of 1937, he added the remark that boys in boarding schools tend to lose their markedly local peculiarities, whereas this is not the case for those in day schools. He had by 1926, however, abandoned the term PSP in favour of 'Received Pronunciation' (RP). The type of speech he had in mind had for centuries been regarded as a kind of standard, having its base in the educated pronunciation of London and the Home Counties (the counties surrounding London). Its use was not restricted to this region, however, being characteristic by the nineteenth century of upper-class speech throughout the country. The editor of the 13th and 14th edition of this dictionary, A.C. Gimson, commented in 1977 "Such a definition of RP is hardly tenable today", and went on "If I have retained the traditional, though imprecise, term 'received pronunciation', it is because the label has such wide currency in books on present-day English and because it is a convenient name for an accent which remains generally acceptable and intelligible within Britain".

For recent editions of this dictionary a more broadly based and accessible model accent for British English is represented, and pronunciations for a broadly equivalent accent of American English have been added. The archaic name Received Pronunciation is no longer used. The model used for British English is what is referred to as BBC English; this is the pronunciation of professional speakers who are employed by the BBC as newsreaders and announcers on BBC1 and BBC2 television, the World Service and BBC Radio 3 and 4, as well as many commercial broadcasting organizations such as ITN. Of course, one finds differences between such speakers – individual broadcasters all have their own personal characteristics, and an increasing number of broadcasters with Scottish, Welsh, and Irish accents are employed. However, the accent described here is typical of broadcasters with an English accent, and there is a useful degree of consistency in the broadcast speech of these speakers. Their speech does not carry for most people the connotations of high social class and privilege that PSP and RP have had in the past. An additional advantage in concentrating on the accent of broadcasters is that it is easy to gain access to examples, and the quality of the sound that one can record is usually of a very high standard.

For American English, the selection also follows what is frequently heard from professional voices on national network news and information programmes, and we refer to it as 'General American'. Broadly speaking, this covers those speakers of American English who do not have an accent from New England or the southern states. However, it should be remembered that even national broadcast media with professionally trained voices have speakers with some regionally marked features.

3.2 How are the pronunciations chosen?

It is important to remember that the pronunciation of English words is not governed by a strict set of rules; many words have more than one pronunciation, and the speaker's choice of which to use depends on a wide range of factors. These include the degree of formality, the speaker's age, the amount of background noise, the speed of utterance, the speaker's perception of the listener, and the frequency with which the speaker uses the word. If such variation did not exist, most of the work of compiling a pronouncing dictionary could be done easily by means of one of the available computer programs that convert English spelling into a phonemic transcription. Ultimately, however, the decisions about which pronunciation to recommend, which pronunciations have dropped out of use, and so on, have been based on our intuitions as professional phoneticians and observers of the pronunciation of English (particularly broadcast English) over many years. The opinion of many colleagues and acquaintances has also been a valuable source of information.

The pronunciation of any language is constantly changing, and a dictionary such as this one should reflect such changes. However, there is an understandable reluctance among users of phonemic transcription to change the symbols used too frequently, as this causes existing teaching materials and textbooks to become out of date.

In general, a pronunciation typical of a more casual, informal style of speaking is given for common words, and a more careful pronunciation for uncommon words. In real life, speakers tend to articulate most carefully when listeners are likely to have difficulty in recognizing the words they hear. When more than one pronunciation of a word is given, the order of the alternatives is important. The first pronunciation given is believed to be the most usual one, although the distance between the alternatives may vary, with some alternant forms rivalling the first-given in perceived frequency while others may be a more distant second.

3.3 Pronunciation of foreign words

Many of the words in an English dictionary are of foreign origin. It is very important to be aware that in this dictionary we do not attempt to give phonetic transcriptions of how those foreign words are pronounced by native speakers of the languages they come from. The primary aim of the dictionary is to list pronunciations likely to be used by educated speakers of English, and to use an 'authentic' pronunciation would in most circumstances be quite inappropriate (pronouncing 'Paris' as [pæʁˈiː], or 'Copenhagen' as [kʰøb̥ənˈhaʊ̯ˀn], for example). In some cases the information is unnecessary (very few English speakers would attempt, or even recognize, an authentic pronunciation of a word from a non-European language), while in other cases it is difficult to establish what the authentic original was. Many African place names, for example, have reached us after being adapted by British, French, or Portuguese colonists. Place names in Spain may be pronounced in different ways according to their regional affiliation, so that the name 'Barcelona' might be given a Catalan or a Castilian Spanish pronunciation, while other Spanish names are different according to whether they originate in Spain or South America. Words and names of foreign origin are therefore given in what is felt to be the pronunciation likely to be used among educated speakers of English. In some cases it is possible to identify an alternative pronunciation which represents an attempt to pronounce in a manner closer to the supposed original. This is marked by first indicating the language which the speaker would be aiming at, then giving the pronunciation, using where necessary additional phonetic symbols not required for the phonemic transcription of English. For example, the word 'bolognese' is widely used to refer to a sauce served with pasta; most speakers of English are not aware that this word originates from the name of the Italian city of Bologna. The word is given in the dictionary as /ˌbɒl.əˈneɪz/ for BBC pronunciation and as /ˌboʊ.ləˈniːz/ for General American; for speakers of both groups, a pronunciation aimed at being nearer to the Italian original would be /ˌbɒl.əˈnjeɪ.zeɪ/ (though this would still be quite different from the pronunciation that would be produced by an Italian speaker). To indicate that this last pronunciation is aimed at sounding Italian, it is marked in the entry as: *as if Italian* /ˌbɒl.əˈnjeɪ.zeɪ/. In a few cases it has been necessary to mark separate British and American pronunciations for such words, as the degree and style of Anglicization of any given word may vary between British and American English.

We need to look at how non-English sounds in words taken from other languages are adapted for use by English speakers. The number of such sounds is small, since most foreign words and names are Anglicized in such a way that they are pronounced entirely with English phonemes. However, we find the voiceless velar fricative [x] in the Celtic languages of Scotland, Ireland, and Wales in words such as 'loch' and names such as 'Cwmbach'. The same sound is often used by English speakers for the German sound which is written 'ch' (e.g. 'Bach' [bɑːx]) and the Spanish sound spelt 'j' (e.g. 'Badajoz' [ˌbæd.əˈxɒθ]). The voiceless lateral fricative [ɬ] is found (always represented in spelling with 'll') in Welsh words and names such as 'Llanberis'; we give the pronunciation of this sound as /*h*l/ to indicate that it may be pronounced either as a voiceless [ɬ] (as some British English speakers do), or alternatively as a voiced one: thus /*h*lænˈber.ɪs/. The dictionary lists a few names with more than one of these sounds (e.g. 'Llanelli', 'Llangollen'). Most non-Welsh speakers are unlikely to pronounce more than one [ɬ] sound in a word, so we give the pronunciation as /θl/ for 'll' sounds after the initial one.

The other case which needs special attention is the pronunciation of French nasalized vowels. Many English speakers attempt to produce something similar to the French vowels /ɛ̃/, /ɑ̃/, /ɔ̃/, /œ̃/ in words such as '**vin**', 'restaur**ant**', 'b**on**', 'Lebr**un**'. Although most speakers do not get close to the French vowels, the principle adopted here is to use English vowel symbols with added nasalization. The equivalents are:

French	*English*
ɛ̃	æ̃
ɑ̃	ɑ̃ː
ɔ̃	ɔ̃ː
œ̃	ɜ̃ː

3.4 Regional accents

A pronouncing dictionary that systematically presented the pronunciations of a range of regional accents of English, all described on equal terms, would be very valuable, but it would be very much bigger than the present volume. In the case of some place names, information about local pronunciations has been retained or added as well as 'official' broadcasting ones, but the other words are given only in the standard accents chosen for British and American English.

3.5 Usage notes

Usage notes are given where extra information is needed for a full understanding of how alternative pronuncations are used. For example, entries for the so-called 'weak form words' such as 'there' or 'her' show how different pronunciation possibilities are used. General rules for prefixes and suffixes are shown at their own entries, as well as in the entries for words containing them.

In addition, a different form of usage note is given at many entries which have interesting, unusual, or controversial pronunciations.

3.6 Syllable divisions

Although native speakers find little difficulty in dividing words into syllables, it seems that learners of English have trouble in doing so. Descriptions of stress and rhythm are usually expressed in terms of syllables, and so it is helpful to have polysyllabic words clearly broken up into their constituent syllables. The syllabified transcription of a polysyllabic word is usually easier to read and interpret than an undivided one. In addition, the dictionary is likely to be of interest to the field of speech and language technology, where syllable divisions can be useful in developing automatic speech and language analysis systems.

A dot **.** is used to divide syllables, in accordance with the recommendations of the International Phonetic Association. These may be read in the IPA Handbook (International Phonetic Association 1999). However, this is not used where a stress mark ˈ or ˌ occurs, as these are effectively also syllable division markers. No completely satisfactory scheme of syllable division can be produced – all sets of rules will throw up some cases which cannot be dealt with properly. The principles used in this edition are set out below. This requires some discussion of *phonotactics*, the study of permissible phoneme sequences.

As far as possible, syllables should not be divided in a way that goes against what is known of English syllable structure. The 'Maximal Onset Principle', which is widely recognized in contemporary phonology, is followed as far as possible. This means that syllables should be divided in such a way that as many consonants as possible are assigned to the beginning of the syllable to the right (if one thinks in terms of how they are written in transcription), rather than to the end of the syllable to the left. However, when this would result in a syllable ending with a stressed /ɪ/, /e/, /æ/, /ʌ/, /ɒ/ or /ʊ/, it is considered that this would constitute a violation of English phonotactics, and the first (or only) intervocalic consonant is assigned to the preceding syllable; thus the word 'better' is divided /ˈbet.əʳ/ (BBC), /ˈbeţ.ɚ/ (GA), whereas 'beater' is divided

/ˈbiː.təʳ/ (BBC), /ˈbiː.t̬ɚ/ (GA). In the case of unstressed short vowels, /e/, /æ/, /ʌ/, and /ɒ/ are also prevented from appearing in syllable-final position; however, unstressed /ɪ/ and /ʊ/ are allowed the same 'privilege of occurrence' as /ə/ when a consonant begins a following syllable, and may therefore occur in final position in unstressed syllables except pre-pausally. Thus in a word such as 'develop', the syllable division is /dɪˈvel.əp/.

Notwithstanding the above, words in compounds are not normally re-divided syllabically in a way that does not agree with perceived word boundaries. For example, 'hardware' could in theory be divided /ˈhɑː.dweəʳ/ (BBC), /ˈhɑːr.dwer/ (GA), but we believe most readers would find this counter-intuitive and would prefer /ˈhɑːd.weəʳ/ (BBC), /ˈhɑːrd.wer/ (GA). This principle applies to open, closed, and hyphenated compounds.

3.7 The phoneme principle

The basic principle of our transcriptions is, as in all previous editions, phonemic. This means that a small set of symbols is used to represent the sounds that can be shown to be distinctive in English, so that replacing one phoneme by another can change the identity of a word. We do not usually add phonetic detail such as the presence of glottal stops, aspiration or vowel devoicing. It is usual to put slant brackets before and after symbols representing phonemes (e.g. the word 'cat' is represented phonemically as /kæt/). When non-phonemic symbols *are* used, the convention is to use square brackets (e.g. the glottal stop is represented as [ʔ]). In entries in the dictionary itself, however, we do not use these brackets; this is in order to keep the information simple, and because we are able to use colour to distinguish between alphabetic and phonetic symbols. Only in explanatory material do we use slant or square brackets. For an explanation of the principle of the phoneme and some of the problems associated with it, see Roach (2009), Chapters 5 and 13. The use of phonemic transcription in works on pronunciation (including this one) has remained in the 'realist' tradition established by Jones, while approaches to the phoneme by theoretical phonologists have changed radically during recent decades and become much more abstract. There are a few exceptions to our general use of the phoneme principle that should be mentioned here, however. One is the use, mentioned above, of the [̬] diacritic in American pronunciations to indicate the voicing and 'tapping' of /t/ in words such as 'getting' /ˈget̬.ɪŋ/, and 'better' /ˈbet̬.ɚ/. This is an important feature of American pronunciation, but speakers of British English find it difficult to apply the rule which determines when /t/ is voiced and/or tapped. Another exception to the phoneme principle is the use of the symbols i and u, the use of which is explained below. Finally, it is necessary to use a number of special symbols which are not normally used for English phonemes. This set includes some nasalized vowels used particularly in some words taken from French, the [x] sound found in Scottish words such as 'loch', and some sounds not usually found in English which are used in certain exclamations and interjections.

3.8 Stress

Stress patterns present one of the most difficult problems in a pronouncing dictionary. One reason for this is that many polysyllabic words have more than one possible stress pattern, and one must consider carefully which should be recommended. Secondly, the stress of many words changes in different contexts, and it is necessary to indicate how this happens. Thirdly, there is no straightforward way to decide on how many different levels of stress are recognizable. The minimum possible range is two: stressed and unstressed. This is inadequate for representing English words in a pronouncing dictionary: a word such as 'controversial' clearly has stress(es) on the first and third syllables, and equally clearly has stronger stress on the third syllable than on the first. It is therefore necessary to recognize an intermediate level of stress ('secondary'). In this dictionary, primary stress (the strongest level of stress) is marked with ˈ and secondary stress with ˌ. Syllables which do not have primary or secondary stress are unstressed, and are not marked. The transcription of the word 'controversial', therefore, is /ˌkɒn.trəˈvɜː.ʃəl/ (BBC), /ˌkɑːn.trəˈvɝː.ʃəl/ (GA).

Here are some further points about the marking of stress:

i. Where more than one stress pattern is possible, the preferred pronunciation is given first and then alternatives are listed. Many dictionaries use the convention of representing stress patterns using dashes to represent syllables: thus the two possible patterns for 'cigarette' (ˌcigaˈrette and ˈcigarette) can be shown as ˌ– – ˈ – and ˈ– – –. This convention, which is sometimes referred to (incorrectly) as 'Morse Code', is used in this work for short words, since it is economical on space. However, in longer words users are likely to find it difficult to interpret. In the planning of an earlier edition of our dictionary, an experiment was carried out to test this, and it was found that readers (both native speakers and non-native speakers of English) take less time to read word stress patterns when the whole word is given, rather than just a 'dashes and dots' pattern (Stromberg and Roach, 1993). Consequently, words of more than three syllables are given in full when alternative stress patterns are being given.

ii. The most common case of variable stress placement caused by context is what is usually nowadays known as 'stress shift'. As a general rule, when a word of several syllables has a stress near the end of the word, and is followed by another word with stress near its beginning, there is a tendency for the stress in the first word to move nearer the beginning if it contains a syllable there that is capable of receiving stress. For example, the word 'academic' in isolation usually has the stress on the penultimate syllable /-ˈdem-/. However, when the word 'year' follows, the stress is often found to move to the first syllable /æk-/. The whole phrase 'academic year' will have its primary stress on the word 'year', so the resulting stress pattern will be ˌacademic ˈyear. To make this process easier to understand, the dictionary gives specific examples in each case where stress shift is possible except where certain prefixes such as 'un-' produce hundreds of such cases. In general, this shift is not obligatory: it would not be a mispronunciation to say acaˌdemic ˈyear. However, it is undoubtedly widespread and in some cases is found almost without exception.

iii. Secondary stresses have only limited occurrence after a primary stress: such a secondary stress is only marked in closed or hyphenated compound words where the second element is polysyllabic (e.g. ˈfishˌmonger).

iv. Stress assignment on prefixes:

a. Many words contain a prefix such as con-, de-, im-, in- that is considered to be inseparable from the stem that follows; in such words, secondary stress is not usually applied to the prefix where the following (i.e. second) syllable is stressed, for example in 'intoxicate' /ɪnˈtɒk.sɪ.keɪt/ (BBC), /ɪnˈtɑːk.sə.keɪt/ (GA).

b. However, where the prefix is separable, as in 'decolonize', the pronunciation may be given with a secondary stress, as /ˌdiːˈkɒl.ə.naɪz/ (BBC), /ˌdiːˈkɑː.l.ə.naɪz/ (GA); in words such as 'impossible', a variant showing secondary stress on the prefix is listed, as follows: /ɪmˈpɒs.ə.bᵊl, ˌɪm-/ (BBC), /ɪmˈpɑː.sə.bᵊl, ˌɪm-/ (GA).

c. In all other cases, primary or secondary stress is applied to the prefix where appropriate. Notes are given in the dictionary to outline the pronunciation of each affix.

v. In the case of words which do not have a prefix but have a stressed second syllable preceded by a syllable with a full vowel (e.g. 'shampoo', 'Chinese') the first syllable is usually treated as unstressed, though in some cases capable of receiving primary stress through stress shift.

3.9 Assimilation

Assimilation is a process found in all languages which causes speech sounds to be modified in a way which makes them more similar to their neighbours. A well-known example is that of English alveolar consonants such as /t/, /d/, /n/, which, when they are followed by a consonant which does not have alveolar place of articulation, tend to adopt the place of articulation of the following consonant. Thus the /t/ at the end of 'foot' /fʊt/ changes to /p/ when followed by /b/ in the word 'football', giving the pronunciation /ˈfʊp.bɔːl/. A similar case is the assimilation of /s/ to a following /ʃ/ or /j/, resulting in the pronunciation of 'this ship' as /ðɪʃ.ʃɪp/ and 'this year' as /ðɪʃ.jɪəʳ/ (BBC), /ðɪʃ.jɪr/ (GA). This assimilation can be considered to be optional. The assimilation of /n/ is a rather special case: many English words begin with the prefixes 'in-' and 'un-', and in a number of cases the /n/ of these prefixes is followed by a consonant which is not alveolar. In some cases it seems to be normal that the /n/ is regularly assimilated to the place of articulation of the following consonant (e.g. 'inquest' /ˈɪŋ.kwest/), while in others this assimilation is optional (e.g. 'incapable' may be /ɪnˈkeɪ.pə.bᵊl/ or /ɪŋˈkeɪ.pə.bᵊl/). Where it is clear that the prefix is attached to a word that exists independently, so that prefix and stem are easily separable, the assimilation is normally treated as optional. When it seems more like an integral part of the word, the assimilation is shown as obligatory. Although the optional assimilation of /n/ is also found in American pronunciation, we do not repeat the transcription of the alternative, in order to reduce duplication; we give only the unassimilated version for American pronunciation, and it should be assumed that the assimilation shown for British pronunciation is found equally in American.

3.10 Treatment of /r/

As mentioned above, the accent used for British English is classed as non-rhotic – the phoneme /r/ is not usually pronounced except when a vowel follows it. The American pronunciations, on the other hand, do show a rhotic accent, and in general in the accent described, /r/ is pronounced where the letter r is found in the spelling.

It is necessary to show, in BBC pronunciation entries, cases of *potential* pronunciation of /r/, mainly in word-final position; in other words, it is necessary to indicate, in a word such as 'car', that though the word when said in isolation does not have /r/ in the pronunciation (/kɑː/), there is a potential /r/ which is realized if a vowel follows (e.g. in 'car owner'). This is indicated by giving the transcription as /kɑːʳ/, where the superscript /r/ indicates the potential for pronunciation. This is traditionally known as 'linking r'.

A controversial question is that of so-called 'intrusive r', where the phoneme /r/ is pronounced when no 'r' is seen in the spelling. For example, the phrase 'India and Pakistan' may be pronounced with /r/ at the end of the name 'India', thus /ˌɪn.di.ər.ənˌpɑːk.ɪˈstɑːn/, US /-ˈpæk.ɪ.stæn/. Intrusive /r/ is most frequently found after /ə/, as in the above example, after /ɪə/ (e.g. at the end of 'idea' in 'the idea of it' /ði.aɪˈdɪər.əv.ɪt/), occasionally after /ɑː/ (e.g. at the end of 'Shah' in 'Shah of Persia' /ˌʃɑːr.əvˈpɜː.ʒə/, US /-ˈpɝː-/) and after /ɔː/ (e.g. at the end of 'law' in 'law and order' /ˌlɔːr.ənˈɔː.də/, US /ˌlɑːr.ənˈɔːr.dɚ/). All of these examples can be called 'inter-word' cases. Final /ə/ or /ɪə/ (without a letter 'r' in the spelling) are by far the most frequently found contexts for intrusive /r/, and almost all of these cases involve words whose spelling form ends in letter 'a' (see the examples with 'India' and 'idea' above); these contexts are the nearest we find to full acceptability of intrusive /r/ as BBC pronunciation. However, we also find *word-internal* intrusive /r/, usually when a suffix is added to a stem that ends with /ə, ɪə, ɑː/ or /ɔː/; thus the verb 'to saw' can have a form such as 'sawing', and while the pronunciation given in this dictionary is /ˈsɔː.ɪŋ/, US /ˈsɑː.ɪŋ/, the pronunciation /ˈsɔː.rɪŋ/, US /ˈsɑː.rɪŋ/, containing intrusive /r/, is also heard.

Although intrusive /r/ is certainly found in the speech of some speakers of the accent described, it is still judged by many people to be 'substandard', and it has become a matter of legend that the BBC receives many complaints every time a newsreader is heard to pronounce 'law and order' as 'loranorder'. It remains safer not to recommend this pronunciation to foreign learners, and it is not marked in this dictionary.

3.11 Use of the symbols i and u

There are many places in present-day British and American English where the distinction between /ɪ/ and /iː/ is neutralized. For example, the final vowel of 'city' and 'seedy' seems to belong neither to the /ɪ/ phoneme nor to /iː/. The symbol /i/ is used in this case. It is not, strictly speaking, a phoneme symbol, and therefore the slant brackets / / that we use for phoneme symbols may be thought inappropriate. However, since the symbol frequently appears among phonemic symbols in the dictionary it is simpler and more convenient to use these brackets. A parallel argument can be made for the distinction between /ʊ/ and /uː/ (with a corresponding 'neutralized' symbol /u/), though this is needed much less frequently. This issue, and the issues which follow, are discussed in detail in Roach (2009), pp. 66–68.

i. In word-final position, /ɪ/ and /ʊ/ do not occur. Word-final, close vowels are transcribed with /i/ and /u/ if weak and unstressed. Word-final /iː/ and /uː/ are possible both with stress ('grandee', 'bamboo') and without ('Hindi', 'argue'), although in the unstressed case it is often not possible to draw a clear line between /iː/ and /i/, or between /uː/ and /u/.

ii. In compounds such as 'busybody' and names such as 'Merryweather', /i/ is permitted to occur word-medially, e.g. 'busybody' is transcribed /ˈbɪz.iˌbɒd.i/ (BBC), /ˈbɪz.iˌbɑː.di/ (GA) and 'Merryweather' as /ˈmer.iˌweð.əʳ (BBC), /ˈmer.iˌweð.ɚ/ (GA). Separable prefixes comprising more than one syllable, such as 'poly-', 'anti-' are usually transcribed with final

/i/ even when a consonant follows, e.g. 'polyvalent' /ˌpɒl.iˈveɪ.lənt/ (BBC) /ˈpɑː.li.veɪ.lənt/ (GA), 'antibacterial' /ˌænti.bækˈtɪə.ri.əl/ (BBC) /ˌæn.ţi.bækˈtɪr.i.əl/ (GA), though some words like 'polythene' and 'polytechnic' have come to be treated as single-morpheme words and are transcribed here as /ˈpɒl.ɪ.θiːn/ (BBC) /ˈpɑː.lɪ.θiːn/ (GA), /ˌpɒl.ɪˈtek.nɪk/ (BBC) /ˌpɑː.lɪˈtek.nɪk/ (GA). When morphemes are added to words ending in /i/ such as 'hurry' /ˈhʌr.i/, 'study' /ˈstʌd.i/ the /i/ is retained so that 'hurried' is pronounced /ˈhʌr.id/ and 'studies' /ˈstʌd.iz/. In most other cases word-medially, /ɪ/ is used when the vowel is unstressed, unless a vowel follows (see below).

iii. The vowel symbols /ɪ/ and /ʊ/ only occur in front of another vowel symbol if they form part of a composite (diphthong or triphthong) phoneme symbol (e.g. /ɪə, ʊə/). Otherwise /i/ or /u/ is used (e.g. 'studying' /ˈstʌd.i.ɪŋ/, 'influenza' /ˌɪn.fluˈen.zə/.

iv. A matter related to this decision concerns words ending in '-ier', '-eer', '-ia'. The words 'reindeer' and 'windier' (comparative form of 'windy') do not have identical pronunciations in their final syllables; 'reindeer' is transcribed as /ˈreɪn.dɪəʳ/ (BBC), /ˈreɪn.dɪr/ (GA) and 'windier' as /ˈwɪn.di.əʳ/ (BBC), /ˈwɪn.di.ɚ/ (GA). The latter transcription indicates a different (closer) vowel quality in the second syllable of 'windier', and implies a pronunciation with three rather than two syllables. The long vowels /iː/ and /uː/ may also occur before other vowels, but only when in a stressed syllable (e.g. 'skiing' /ˈskiː.ɪŋ/, 'canoeing' /kəˈnuː.ɪŋ/).

3.12 Syllabic consonants

Syllabic consonants are frequently found in English pronunciation: these are cases where instead of an expected vowel-plus-consonant sequence, the consonant alone (usually one of /m, n, ŋ, l, r/) is pronounced with the rhythmical value of a syllable. (See Roach, 2009, pp. 68–71). The main problem here is to explain when and where these syllabic consonants occur. The most frequently found case is where an item may have three possible pronunciations: (i) a schwa vowel followed by a non-syllabic consonant, (ii) a syllabic consonant not preceded by schwa or (iii) a non-syllabic consonant not preceded by schwa. For example, 'lightening' may be (i) /ˈlaɪ.tə.nɪŋ/, (ii) /ˈlaɪ.tn̩.ɪŋ/ or (iii) /ˈlaɪt.nɪŋ/. In this dictionary, such items are transcribed as /ˈlaɪ.tᵊn.ɪŋ/ and /ˈlaɪt.nɪŋ/, the first representing cases (i) and (ii), in which there are three syllables, and the second representing only the two-syllable pronunciation. The use of superscript schwa in words such as /ˈlaɪ.tᵊn.ɪŋ/ should be interpreted as meaning that the schwa may be pronounced, or may be omitted while giving its syllabic character to the following consonant. In both cases, the transcription indicates that the word has three syllables.

Syllabic nasals are not usual where they would result in a nasal-plosive-syllabic nasal sequence (e.g. 'London', 'abandon' normally contain a schwa vowel in the final syllable).

3.13 Optional sounds: elision and epenthesis

There are many occasions when sounds which are present in words pronounced on their own, or in slow, careful speech, are not found in a different style of speech. This is known as *elision*, and this dictionary does not show all possible elisions in order to avoid adding a large number of additional pronunciations that are typical of casual speech. However, some cases are very noticeable and need to be indicated in the transcriptions. We use italic print for symbols to indicate that they represent a sound that may be omitted or pronounced very weakly. One clear example is that we often do not pronounce a plosive in between two other consonants if the following consonant is a plosive: thus the /d/ in 'handball' is often omitted, and the dictionary shows the pronunciation as /ˈhæn*d*.bɔːl/. This is an example of the simplification of consonant clusters.

There are also some less general cases which only apply in certain contexts: for example, some speakers pronounce words such as 'lunch' and 'French' with a final /ntʃ/ while others have final /nʃ/. We transcribe these with /n*tʃ*/, thus /lʌn*tʃ*, fren*tʃ*/. This is a case of an insertion or deletion that is restricted to a particular phonological environment; if we regard the /t/ here as an extra consonant that is inserted by some speakers, we say that the /t/ is *epenthetic*, that is, this is a case of epenthesis. Speakers are usually consistent in using one or other of the alternative pronunciations in such cases.

3.14 /tʃ/ and /dʒ/

In words like 'tune' and 'dune', where earlier editions have recommended /tjuːn/ and /djuːn/ for BBC pronunciation, it now seems

/tʃuːn/ and /dʒuːn/ are more widely used and these pronunciations are given priority for most such words, with the /tj/ and /dj/ pronunciations as second choice. There are many words with 'tu' and 'du' in their spelling where this choice applies, such as 'institute' /ˈɪnt.stɪ.tʃuːt/, 'reduce' /rɪˈdʒuːs/. American pronunciation usually has /tuːn/, /duːn/, /ˈɪnt.stɪ.tuːt/, /rɪˈduːs/, but we give /tjuːn/, /djuːn/, /ˈɪnt.stɪ.tjuːt/, /rɪˈdjuːs/ as alternative pronunciations for GA since we do not believe that the /tʃ/ and /dʒ/ pronunciations have become as widespread in America.

4 References

International Phonetic Association (1999) *Handbook of the International Phonetic Association*, Cambridge University Press.

Roach, P. (2009) *English Phonetics and Phonology* (4th edition), Cambridge University Press.

Stromberg, K. and Roach, P. (1993) 'The representation of stress-patterns in pronunciation dictionaries: "Morse-code" vs. orthographic marking', *Journal of the International Phonetic Association*, vol. 23.3, pp. 55–584.

The world of pronunciation

Pronunciation in spontaneous speech

Richard Cauldwell

Richard Cauldwell authors, designs, and publishes electronic materials for the online study of listening and pronunciation. His first publication Streaming Speech: Listening and Pronunciation for Advanced Learners of English *won a British Council Innovations in ELT award in 2004. His publications make a unique use of recordings of spontaneous speech: for listening, there is a focus on the fast, messy, and heavily accented sections; for pronunciation, tidy extracts of spontaneous speech are used as the pronunciation model.*

This dictionary provides guidance for optimally clear pronunciation. It does so by means of the citation form (CF) – which is given both in phonemic transcription and (in the electronic version) in a soundfile. The phonemic transcription contains symbols for segments, syllables, stresses (primary and secondary), and unstressed syllables. The soundfile contains a performance in which all these features are clearly delineated and perceptible, with the initial and final segments uninterfered with by contact with other words. The soundfile adds a pitch contour ending with a falling tone.

The optimal clarity of the CF is however rare in spontaneous speech, because speech does not consist of a sequence of isolated words spoken slowly, with falling tone, as if they are an answer to the question 'How do you say this word?'. On the contrary, the normal state of words in spontaneous speech is that they are joined together into multi-word rhythmic bursts – speech units – which are streamlike in nature, which have continually varying properties of speed, volume, pitch height, and tone. Syllables may be dropped, primary and secondary stresses may become imperceptible, and the initial, medial, and final segments may all vary according to the relationship the word has with its neighbours.

This leads to a situation where language learners – having mastered a CF – believe they know everything they need to know about a word's pronunciation, but are mystified when they cannot hear it when it occurs in spontaneous speech. In the words of one learner "I believe I need to learn what the word sounds like when it is used in the sentence. Because sometimes when a familiar word is used in a sentence, I couldn't catch it. Maybe it changes somewhere when it is used in a sentence." (Goh 1997, p. 366). The CF soundshape is not the only soundshape that a word has – so the information about the CF requires supplementing by other information to help learners master the range of soundshapes that words can have in spontaneous speech.

The learner quoted above thought that the word changes "in the sentence" – it would be more helpful to say that the soundshape of a word varies with its position in a speech unit. I will demonstrate this using the word 'collaboration' first on its own, and then in combination with other words in a two-prominence speech unit. In CEPD, the phonemic transcription is /kəˌlæb.ᵊrˈeɪ.ʃᵊn/ and there is a soundfile which lasts 0.9 seconds, giving a speed of 5.5 syllables per second, 70 words per minute. The word has five syllables, with two of them receiving word-stress: secondary stress on the second syllable, and primary stress in the fourth syllable.

If we transfer the transcription to a table, and remove the syllable marks and full stops, allowing one syllable per cell, we get the word displayed in the five-part pattern of a two prominence speech unit as follows:

1:

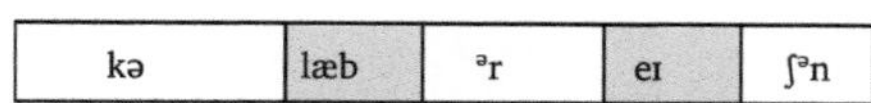

kə	læb	ᵊr	eɪ	ʃᵊn

Example 1 shows each syllable in a separate cell: white cells denote unstressed syllables, the shaded cells denote stressed syllables, with the primary stress shown in the fourth cell. The important thing to note is that these cells comprise a pattern – a five-part pattern – of alternating unstressed and stressed syllables. With this five-part pattern we can investigate two other soundshapes that 'collaboration' can have in spontaneous speech, by adding words to the pattern, while retaining only two prominent syllables.

In example 2 the words 'in' and 'with teachers' are added around 'collaboration' in the five-part pattern, but in order to accommodate them, the first syllable 'col-' has to share the space in the first cell with 'in', and its fourth and fifth syllables '-a-tion' have to move left into the middle cell in order to allow room for the word 'teachers' to occupy the last two cells.

2:

in col	LAB	oration with	TEACH	ers

Now that we have added extra words to this pattern, the shaded cells no longer represent the location of stresses in a single word, they represent prominences at the level of the speech unit, with the syllables in the white cells being non-prominent. So in example 2 we are looking at an utterance in which the speaker has highlighted the words 'collaboration' and 'teachers' by making one syllable prominent in each word.

Because only two prominences are available in the five part pattern, the final three syllables of 'collaboration' have to fit between '-LAB-' and the other available shaded cell, which 'TEACH-' occupies. These final three syllables thus become non-prominent, thereby losing the primary stress which it would have in the CF version.

In spontaneous speech, it is not the location of word-level secondary and primary stresses which are the main shapers of the rhythm of the speech unit, but rather the speaker's choice, at the moment of speaking, of which syllables to make prominent and which to make non-prominent. Syllables which are stressed in the CF, may become non-prominent in spontaneous speech, thus changing the soundshape of a word dramatically.

In example 3, the words on either side of 'collaboration' are made prominent, resulting in all its syllables becoming non-prominent:

3:

in	CLOSE	collaboration with	TEACH	ers

With 'close' and the first syllable of 'teacher' prominent, the six syllables of the inter-prominence gap ('collaboration with') all become non-prominent, including those syllables which carry primary and secondary stress in the CF.

What we have seen is that one of the patterns of spontaneous speech (a speech unit with the five-part pattern) can result in words having soundshapes which are dramatically different from the CF. It is therefore important to realize that the CF – while a very important tool in modelling the spoken language to learners, should be supplemented by an engagement with the soundshape-changing patterns of spontaneous speech.

References:

Goh, C. (1997). Metacognitive awareness and second language listeners. *ELT Journal 51*(4), 361–369.

http://www.speechinaction.com

Pronunciation for English as a Lingua Franca
Jennifer Jenkins

Jennifer Jenkins is Chair of Global Englishes at the University of Southampton where she lectures and supervises in the fields of World Englishes and English as a Lingua Franca, and directs a Global Englishes Research Group for staff and doctoral students. She has been conducting research into English as a Lingua Franca with a particular focus on accent-related issues for over two decades, and is the author of many articles and books on the subject, including The Phonology of English as an International Language *(OUP, 2000) and* English as a Lingua Franca: Attitude and Identity *(OUP, 2007).*

During the past two decades, a new phenomenon has emerged in English language use: that of English as a Lingua Franca, or ELF for short. ELF (which is also known sometimes as 'English as an International Language', or EIL) is an additionally acquired kind of English that serves as a means of intercultural communication among speakers who come from different first languages. Because the majority of the world's English speakers are non-native – there are thought to be up to two billion non-native English speakers contrasted with 350 million native speakers – most ELF use does not involve native English speakers at all. And if native English speakers do take part in ELF communication, they soon realize that its linguistic forms, as well as the kinds of skills they need to communicate successfully in ELF settings, are often different from those they have always known as 'standard British' or 'standard (North) American' English. To give just two examples, ELF users, even if they know the grammar rule, generally prefer not to put an –s on the 3rd person singular in the present tense. Hence, they may say "she think" rather than "she think<u>s</u>". They also tend to regularize uncountable nouns according to the principles of pluralization relating to countable nouns, so that in ELF communication we may hear a speaker say "some advice<u>s</u>" rather than "some advice", "<u>an</u> information" instead of "<u>a piece of</u> information", and the like.

However, the most widespread impact of ELF research so far has been in the field of pronunciation, and the way in which the research has begun to influence orientations towards standard (native) English pronunciation accents, particularly Received Pronunciation (RP) and General American (GA), for communication in ELF settings. Although it is too early yet to consider its findings definitive, research conducted into pronunciation in ELF interactions has revealed three particularly interesting findings. Firstly, depending on who is speaking with whom, certain pronunciation features of RP and GA accents seem often to be necessary in order that pronunciation is not an obstacle to intelligible speech. These pronunciation features are often referred to collectively as the 'Lingua Franca Core'. They consist primarily of approximations (i.e. near pronunciations) of most distinctive RP/GA consonant sounds except for /θ/ and /ð/; consonant clusters in word-initial and medial (but not word-final) position; the distinctions between short and long vowel, sounds such as /ɪ/ contrasted with /iː/; and the placement of nuclear stress within word groups, that is, the placement of the strongest syllable stress in a group of words on the most important syllable for the speaker's meaning.

The second particularly interesting finding of ELF pronunciation research is that outside the areas covered by the Lingua Franca Core, many other features that ELF speakers habitually use instead of native English features (often as a result of transfer from their first languages) do not seem to cause intelligibility problems in ELF communication. These can therefore be considered 'non-core' (or non-important) areas for ELF. They consist mainly of the following:

- vowel quality (as contrasted with vowel length), in other words the difference between, for example, /æ/ and /ʌ/ as in RP 'c<u>a</u>t' and 'c<u>u</u>t';
- the consonant sounds /θ/ and /ð/, which ELF speakers regularly substitute with /s/ and /z/, or /t/ and /d/;
- the features of connected speech, especially elision (i.e. omitting sounds such as the second 'o' in 'chocolate'), assimilation (e.g. producing the first /t/ in 'whi<u>t</u>e paint' as /p/), and weak forms (e.g. ELF speakers are more likely to pronounce the vowel in the word 'but' with its full quality /ʌ/ rather than with schwa, /ə/ as most native English speakers do, and in fact ELF research has revealed that weak forms can be more likely to lower intelligibility in ELF communication);

- word stress; and pitch direction and change.

In addition, while most varieties of native English are said to be stress-timed at least in the sense that native English speakers lengthen stressed syllables and weaken or 'collapse' unstressed syllables in the stream of speech, most ELF speakers use a more syllable-timed English, and find this more intelligible.

Finally, as well as – and probably more important than – these 'core' and 'non-core' pronunciation features, ELF research has shown that accommodation is a key ELF pronunciation skill. Accommodation, or more specifically, its strategy of convergence, refers to speakers' ability to adjust aspects of their speech such as pronunciation, speed, pitch, and so on, to make it more like that of their addressee. Speakers do this for both affective reasons (to show liking for the addressee) and for communicative efficiency reasons (to make their speech more intelligible to their addressee).

In the case of ELF pronunciation, research has demonstrated how ELF speakers often try to adjust their pronunciation in order to bring it closer to the expectations of their addressees, regardless of whether this 'closeness' makes a feature less or more like that of an RP or GA accent. Although accommodation involves normal communication strategies that we can all perform to some extent, the skill requires further developing for ELF communication, where the range of addressees is potentially so vast and varied. A key point in this respect is that as well as developing the ability to adjust their pronunciation, ELF speakers need to become familiar with a range of non-native English accents rather than purely with a range of native English accents. Further details of the Lingua Franca Core and non-core features, along with discussions of accommodation, can be found in Jenkins 2000, and of teaching issues related to it in Walker 2010.

On the other hand, we must not lose sight of the fact that by no means all non-native users of English communicate in English mainly with other non-native users. In this respect, it needs to be emphasized that ELF pronunciation goals are not intended as a replacement for RP and GA, but to complement them. For those non-native English speakers who interact mainly with native speakers, the need to be able to pronounce and understand English with a nearish-RP or near-GA accent remains a priority.

References:

Jenkins, J. 2000. *The Phonology of English as an International Language*. Oxford: Oxford University Press.

Walker, R. 2010. *Teaching the Pronunciation of English as a Lingua Franca*. Oxford: Oxford University Press.

The Daniel Jones legacy

Jack Windsor Lewis

Jack Windsor Lewis graduated in Medieval English at Cardiff but after studies at the Department of Phonetics at University College London, where he still works on summer courses, began mainly teaching English for non-mothertongue speakers. He has lectured at over eighty universities in many countries staying longest at Tehran, Oslo, Brussels, and especially Leeds, near where he now lives. His over 100 publications have included numerous articles and books. His Concise Pronouncing Dictionary of British and American English *was the first substantial pronunciation dictionary to give equal treatment to both varieties. His website is www.yek.me.uk.*

The publication in 1917 by Daniel Jones of the very first edition of his EPD, his *English Pronouncing Dictionary*, marked the beginning of a whole new epoch in the history of the teaching and learning of the English language. No single work even approaching its excellence, its authority, its fullness and clarity of setting out of its information had ever appeared before. It was immediately recognized as indispensable especially by all the leading figures in the field of EFL (English as a Foreign Language). For generations the simple question "What does Jones say?" was to be probably more often asked than any other by teachers of English all over the world.

Daniel Jones had written probably more books on the pronunciation of English than any other writer. They were about to culminate in his masterly *Outline of English Phonetics* of 1918 which he harmonized completely with the EPD. What became famously known as the International Phonetic Association had in 1888 drawn up its Alphabet, a very carefully chosen set of recommended phonetic symbols which have ever since become more and more universally respected and more widely adopted. These the EPD has always employed with great faithfulness and effectiveness incorporating only slight changes of detail over the years. In particular a small set of preferences was reconsidered in 1977 by A. C. Gimson, Jones's most highly regarded colleague, who took over from him the editorship of the EPD for its 13th edition which appeared early in 1967. He was to became a successor to Jones as Professor of Phonetics at University College London. Jones died at the end of 1967 at the age of 86.

The achievement of providing information in that 1917 first edition on over 50,000 words (not counting their variant forms or their many plural and past-tense inflections) can easily be underestimated. Also the difficulty of forming opinions on which of two or more variants should regarded as the predominant usage, and so to be recommended for adoption by EFL learners, can also easily be underrated. He had no radio or television and hardly any gramophone recordings that he could turn to to check on his impressions. Even speech soundtracks in cinemas did not begin until the mid 1920s. He had only the evidence of his own contacts and of friends and colleagues on whose powers of observation he could rely to help him.

The International Phonetic Association had its origins mainly in a group of European teachers of English with a variety of new ideas on how their work should best be done often summarized as the 'direct method'. They revolutionized language teaching not least by the especially high value they placed on the use of phonetic transcriptions in the teaching of pronunciation. The one sort of book they most needed for that purpose was the very thing that the EPD provided. There had been plenty of dictionaries of and/or with pronunciations in the previous century but they were almost all highly unreliable either from being grossly out of touch with current usages or from being revised by writers whose competence to make phonetic observations was highly questionable. The most complete work available, John Walker's *Critical Pronouncing Dictionary* had been revised repeatedly but so very inadequately as to be left still containing large numbers of obsolete usages.

The great *Oxford English Dictionary* (OED) which had begun publication in 1884 had by 1917 progressed only as far as the letter S. Its earlier volumes had already come to have numerous pronunciations that Jones had to reject as out of date such as the stressings of *advertise, alcove, ancillary, anaesthetist*. The wisdom of the simplicity of Jones's choice of symbols for his transcriptions could be seen by anyone who compared it with those of the OED which would by their daunting complexity strike terror into the heart of any ordinary user. Over the following almost one century of the EPD's existence it has been possible to observe Jones and his successors regularly from one edition to the next updating the entries in order to keep the EPD abreast of the many changes that inevitably occur with the passage of time. The many past editions of the EPD are to this day prized by scholars as providing records in their pages of the demise of many usages and the arrival on the scene of large numbers of new pronunciations and new words. The great twenty-volume second edition of the OED which is now undergoing the long process of being revised online often acknowledges the authority of the EPD in its accounts of the pronunciations of many of its entries.

A sometime member of Jones's staff at UCL, Harold Palmer, along with two colleagues, produced in 1926 a very modest (less than a fifth of the number of entries in EPD) *Dictionary of English Pronunciation with American Variants*, which was published in England. The most major change to the EPD took place in 1997, when for the first time American pronunciations were supplied alongside the British ones for every entry. When the EPD had been first published the teaching of English pronunciation meant simply and automatically the least regionalized accent of the United Kingdom. It was only in the 1930s that the teaching of the similarly least localized pronunciations of the United States of America began to gain the importance that it now has for millions of learners where the influence of the USA has now become established. It was not until 1944 that Americans produced a work comparable to the EPD. This was the *Pronouncing Dictionary of American English* (PDAE), whose senior editor John S. Kenyon had studied with Daniel Jones at UCL and, unlike most other American scholars, followed him in using the International Phonetic Association's alphabet. The PDAE Preface acknowledged that Professor Jones had "placed all later lexicographers under inescapable obligation to him". Unfortunately the PDAE has never undergone any serious revision, so that the present edition of EPD provides a much more complete and up-to-date account of General/Network American English than can be found in any American single-volume dictionary of pronunciations.

References:

Jones, D. (1917) *English Pronouncing Dictionary*, Dent.

Kenyon, J.S. and Knott, T.A. (1953) *A Pronouncing Dictionary of American English*, (2nd Edition), G. & C. Merriam & Co.

Palmer, H.E., Victor Martin, J. and Blandford., F.G. (1926) *A Dictionary of English Pronunciation*, Heffer.

Walker, J. (1791) *A Critical Pronouncing Dictionary*.

Teaching and learning pronunciation

Jonathan Marks

Jonathan Marks lives in Poland and works as a freelance teacher trainer, writer, and translator. He has a particular interest in pronunciation and how it can be integrated into general language teaching methodology. He is the author of English Pronunciation in Use Elementary *(CUP 2007) and co-author of a forthcoming teachers' resource book on pronunciation. He is a founder member and the current Coordinator of the Pronunciation Special Interest Group of IATEFL (the International Association of Teachers of English as a Foreign Language).*

Teachers of English vary in their attitudes to pronunciation, and in how much pronunciation work they include in lessons. Some feel that pronunciation is relatively unimportant, or that learners will simply pick it up as they learn the language. Others would like to give learners more help with pronunciation, but feel that their own knowledge is inadequate. Coursebooks also vary in how much attention they give to pronunciation, and how much support they give teachers in this area; coverage of pronunciation is sometimes limited to a couple of square inches at the end of a unit. Because of these factors, pronunciation is often neglected.

When learners are asked about their goals and priorities, on the other hand, they often say that pronunciation is very important. Good pronunciation is a key part of confidence in speaking a language, and poor pronunciation is the first barrier to communication; no matter how much English you know, you won't be able to make use of your knowledge if other people can't understand you.

What is 'good' pronunciation? Traditionally, the assumed target for pronunciation learning was a standard British or American accent. But these accents are difficult to acquire, at least for adult learners, and probably unnecessary for most learners. In many cases, a more appropriate and achievable alternative is to consider what is needed for international intelligibility – see the essay by Jennifer Jenkins. Nevertheless, some learners do want to achieve a native-like accent, and teachers should help them to do so.

How and when should teachers include pronunciation work in their lessons? Probably the best approach is simply to integrate a concern for pronunciation into every lesson. If you're introducing the vocabulary of town facilities, make sure learners can pronounce the items accurately: the correct sounds in *museum*, the correct stress in *shopping centre*, etc. If they make mistakes with these items in a later practice activity, correct them. Similarly, if you're teaching conditionals, teach the weak forms of *would have* and *wouldn't have*, or if you're teaching phrases such as *whenever you like*, *whoever you ask*, *whatever they said*, teach them with the words linked together and with this rhythm: xXxxX.

In more open-ended activities, listen for pronunciation mistakes and correct any that stand out or are likely to cause confusion. For example, in a discussion activity about cooking, if *oven* is consistently pronounced /əʊvən/, it would be appropriate to correct this.

As well as integrating pronunciation into other work, it is also sometimes useful to include specific pronunciation activities. For example, if you notice that your learners are consistently failing to distinguish between /p/ and /b/, you might decide to include an activity to practise hearing and producing the difference between minimal pairs such as *pear* and *bear*.

Whichever pronunciation they aim at for their own speech, it is important for learners to have substantial and wide experience of *listening* to different varieties of English, for two reasons. Firstly, the pronunciation of English varies enormously in different parts of the world (even in Britain, in fact!) and secondly, whatever the variety is, words in spontaneous speech are subject to reductions in pronunciation which can make them unrecognizable to the unpractised ear – see the essays by Linda Shockey and Richard Cauldwell.

Is it important to use phonemic transcription in teaching English? Some teachers find it an unnecessary complication, especially for learners who are already facing the task of learning a new writing system, the Roman alphabet. But many of the symbols, especially those for consonant sounds, are identical to those used in alphabetic spelling, and the task of learning the other symbols can be made easier by introducing them gradually.

The idea of an alphabetic writing system is that one letter represents one sound; the spelling of English is probably the worst example of such a system, which is why phonemic transcription is so useful to learners. Many of them are confused by groups of words such as *wear*, *where*, *were*, *we're*, *wore*, *war* – these can all sound confusingly similar, and the spellings do not help to clarify the similarities and differences. But the transcriptions reveal that *wear* and *where* are pronounced identically, as are *wore* and *war*, while *we're* has the same vowel sound as *near*, etc.

Learners can include in their personal vocabulary records the transcriptions of words they are unsure of, and group words according to similarity of pronunciation – e.g. *thirty*, *worse*, *surf*, *journey*, *heard*, *prefer*.

Once they are familiar with the symbols, and the habit of checking pronunciation in a dictionary, they will have acquired a powerful means of independent learning. If they find the unfamiliar word *weir* in a text, reference to a general learner's dictionary will immediately show that it has the same pronunciation as *we're*. Reference to a specialized pronunciation dictionary such as the EPD will give them access to the pronunciations of less common words, including place names such as *Welwyn* or *Widecombe,* and the sound recordings such as those on the EPD CD-ROM add valuable information.

The relationship between pronunciation and spelling in English is, for many words, more predictable than often supposed. If the word *wrought* appears in a text during a lesson and the learners ask about its pronunciation, the teacher can simply give the correct pronunciation. But there is also an opportunity to use the question to foster independent learning:

The teacher invites suggestions from the class and writes them on the board. Learners should realize that the *w* will be silent, by analogy with *write*, *wrong*, etc. Their suggestions might include /rɔːt/, /rəʊt/, /ruːt/, /rʌft/, /rɒft/. When asked to justify these suggestions, they might refer to *thought*, *although*, *through*, *enough*, and *cough*; the teacher should acknowledge that these are all reasonable hypotheses. Learners will be able to think of further examples of *-ought* pronounced as /ɔːt/ (*bought*, *fought*), but not as /əʊt/, /ʌft/, etc. They could even vote for the best suggestion! Finally, they can check the actual pronunciation in their dictionaries.

It would clearly be tedious and time-consuming to follow this procedure with every new word, but if they do it periodically, learners will gradually acquire the habits of predicting the pronunciation of unknown words by analogy with known ones, and using a dictionary to check. These twin strategies will build their independence and confidence in dealing with pronunciation.

The BBC, its Pronunciation Unit, and 'BBC English'

Catherine Sangster

Catherine Sangster is the co-ordinator of the BBC Pronunciation Unit, where she has worked as a pronunciation linguist since 2003. She studied linguistics and phonetics at the Universities of Oxford, Massachusetts, and Leeds. Her doctoral research, in the field of sociophonetics, was about inter- and intra-speaker variation in Liverpool English. Her ongoing linguistic interests include phonetics, accents and dialects, lexicography, sociolinguistic and idiolectal variation and change, anglicization, language and gender/sexuality, dialect coaching, and accent performance. She is the co-editor of the Oxford BBC Guide to Pronunciation.

The British Broadcasting Corporation is the largest broadcasting organization in the world. Its aim since it was founded in the 1920s is "to inform, educate, and entertain". It is a public service broadcaster funded by a licence fee that is paid by UK households. This funding is used to provide services including eight national TV channels, ten national radio stations, and an extensive website. The BBC has a great influence on British culture, including its language. Perhaps because of its long history, its public status and the way it is funded, many people in the UK and around the world feel that the BBC has a particular responsibility to uphold standards in its broadcasts, including standards in language and pronunciation.

Learners of English are likely to find it useful to listen to the BBC to improve their comprehension and pronunciation and to widen their vocabulary. For those who live outside the UK, there are various ways to listen to and watch the BBC's programmes. With a broadband internet connection, you can access a wide range of radio and television programmes online from anywhere in the world using the BBC iPlayer (www.bbc.co.uk/iplayer). The iPlayer allows users to listen to or watch programmes streamed live as they are being broadcast, or for up to a week afterwards. You can also download podcasts of BBC radio programmes onto your computer or MP3 player; these are soundfiles which you can keep permanently (www.bbc.co.uk/podcasts). Certain BBC channels are available via digital and satellite networks around the world, and the BBC World Service broadcasts on short wave radio in thirty-two languages including English.

In the early days of the BBC, phonetics experts played an active role in advising on standards in language and pronunciation, through the Advisory Committee on Spoken English. This committee, which existed from 1926 until the Second World War, included among its members Professors Arthur Lloyd James and Daniel Jones, the latter being the person who originally compiled the *English Pronouncing Dictionary* and edited it until its 12th edition; other members were the playwright George Bernard Shaw and the poet laureate Robert Bridges. This Advisory Committee deliberated on pronunciations, and published a series of booklets called *Broadcast English* to help broadcasters with them. The first of these booklets made recommendations on "words of doubtful pronunciation", and others dealt with English, Scottish, Welsh, and Northern Irish place names, British family names, and foreign place names.

After the Second World War, Jones and Lloyd James continued to be advisors to the BBC until their deaths, and the Advisory Committee evolved into a Pronunciation Unit. This is a service that can be used by BBC broadcasters in order "to ensure that pronunciations used on the BBC are accurate and consistent". The Pronunciation Unit is staffed by a small team of phoneticians whose job it is to research and advise on pronunciations in all languages for any sort of programme. Typical pronunciation requests include medical and scientific terms, words and phrases in foreign languages, unfamiliar vocabulary, and long lists of names for major events such as sports championships and general elections. Advice is given in both written and spoken form directly to programme makers who ask for the Unit's help. Pronunciations are added to a computer database containing over 200,000 names, words, and phrases, coded using IPA and also phonetic spellings which are considered simpler for non-specialists to interpret, and which (being plain text) can more easily be added to scripts, teleprompters and screen messages for broadcasters to read. The database is accessible within the BBC and also features a synthesizer which creates a spoken version of the pronunciation so that the user can hear as well as see the advice.

Sometimes pronunciations change over time. There are several words in English which can be pronounced in more than one way, as you can see in this dictionary (try looking at entries for words like *research*, *controversy*, *cervical*). Often, when two pronunciations are possible, one is the more traditional or conservative form, and the other, often more popular one is newer. When asked to advise on words like this, where two or more forms are listed in pronouncing dictionaries, neither pronunciation is considered incorrect and so the Pronunciation Unit does not enforce one over the other. Another change which happens over time and is particularly relevant to the BBC is the level of anglicization used in, for example, names of cities and countries. Often, an older more anglicized pronunciation is replaced by a newer pronunciation which is closer to the original language (examples are *Kenya, Majorca, Ossetia*). Bearing in mind the BBC's potential influence, the Pronunciation Unit wishes neither to bring changes about nor to hold them back once underway, so these matters are carefully considered and weighed up before a recommendation is given.

When advising on pronunciations in English, the Pronunciation Unit concentrates on recommending the correct sounds and stress, not on any particular accent. Although BBC broadcasters are expected to speak fluently and clearly, there is not (and never was) an official BBC pronunciation standard; its broadcasters speak English with a range of accents. In spite of this, the term 'BBC English' is often used as a synonym for Received Pronunciation (Roach, 2004) and for the sort of accent described in dictionaries like this one (see the Introduction to this dictionary, Sections 3.1 and 3.2). Of course, in the early years of broadcasting, the announcers and newsreaders heard on the BBC did speak with this sort of accent, but this would be better viewed as a by-product of the restricted social group from which BBC employees was drawn at that time, rather than a matter of deliberate policy. Even in the most formal broadcasting contexts such as reading the news or announcing programmes, many accents can now be heard. These include not just different regional accents from within the UK, but also from around the world. This is felt to be important for the BBC because it means that the voices that the BBC's broad audience hear in its broadcasts are as diverse as their own voices.

Reference:

Roach, Peter (2004): 'Illustrations of the IPA. British English: Received Pronunciation', *Journal of the International Phonetic Association*, vol. 34.2, pp.239–245.

Shortcuts in casual English pronunciation

Linda Shockey

Linda Shockey has studied phonetics both in the USA, where she earned her academic qualifications, and in the UK, where she has taught and researched since 1977. She has written on aspects of the pronunciation of informal English in several different accents, based on both auditory and instrumental techniques.

A pronouncing dictionary is essential to the learner and even to the native speaker of a language, but it has to be borne in mind that entries are 1) often based on formal pronunciation of a word in isolation and 2) transcribed with a small number of symbols which reflect the linguistic structure of the word but leave out some of the phonetic detail.

Words are only rarely spoken as isolated utterances in real life. In unselfconscious casual English, the pronunciation of words can be remarkably different from what you find in the dictionary: many shortcuts are taken by native speakers of the language which, if met unexpectedly, can be confusing to others. For example, I was asked [stɪɣoˈnʌp]? by a person who wanted to know if the lift was "still going up". Anyone who takes a close look at spontaneous English conversation is soon convinced that this is neither unusual nor extreme.

Native speakers of most (if not all) varieties of English use shortcuts in their speech, but they rarely acknowledge it, presumably because 1) the shortcuts are made subconsciously, so the speakers are not aware of any difference from the citation form and 2) even if they are pointed out, speakers are reluctant to admit that they are using them because they worry about producing 'sloppy speech'. Nevertheless, the streamlining undeniably occurs, and not only in speech produced at a fast rate, despite the common belief that shortcuts are a feature of rapid speech.

There are two factors which give English a tendency to shortcuts: one is the complex sequences of consonants used to construct English syllables and the other is the enormous contrast between stressed and unstressed syllables.

1) Most human languages allow only very simple syllables, with one or two consonants at the beginning and at most one consonant at the end. CV (one consonant and one vowel) is a universal syllabic template: nearly all languages allow it, and some allow nothing else. English is one of only a few languages which allow words like 'scrimped' (CCCVCCC). Articulation moves in the direction of streamlining these clusters, especially the final ones: the beginnings of syllables (onsets) in English are much more resistant to reduction in casual speech than the ends of syllables. There are dozens of reductions which appear syllable-finally, for example, 't' can be pronounced as [ʔ] as in 'boathouse' [ˈbəʊʔhaʊs] or 'hot sauce' [hɒʔˈsɔːs]

The substitute for 't' here is the glottal stop, which is often regarded as substandard by linguistic purists, but which is used even in formal situations by speakers of a great many accents of English. It is regarded as a simplification because it doesn't call any of the normal articulators such as the tongue or lips into play, but is made by the vocal cords alone: it is, of course, still a consonant.

Consonant clusters are especially vulnerable at the ends of syllables, especially when the following syllable begins with a consonant:

first base	[fɜːsˈbeɪs]
cold plate	[kəʊlˈpleɪt]
act normal	[ækˈnɔːməl]
band master	[ˈbænmɑːstə] (or [ˈbæmmɑːstə])

Loss of final consonants is most evident in the word 'and' (see below) and a few other small function words.

When there is a final 'nt' cluster, the vowel preceding the 'n' can be nasalized and the 'n' not articulated:

paint [pẽĩt] (or [pẽĩʔ])
can't [kɑ̃ːt] (or [kɑ̃ːʔ])

While initial consonants are generally stable in casual speech, initial [ð] is often not fully articulated as a voiced dental fricative when preceded by an alveolar sound (n, l, t, d, s, z). Instead, it takes on the quality of the preceding consonant while retaining some of its dental quality. The sound to which it has assimilated can be longer than usual:

scan the papers	[skæn̪ːə ...]
feel this way	[fiːl̪ːɪs ...]
hit the note	[hɪt̪ːəˈnəʊt]

Most treatises on English pronunciation note that initial 'h' may not be clearly pronounced in utterances such as 'That's his sister', but the absence of a fully-articulated initial [ð] is mentioned only rarely.

Word-initial 'y'-type sounds can combine with a previous word-final t, d, s or z to create a new sound with friction:

that you said	[ðətʃəˈsed]
guess your weight	[ˌgeʃːəˈweɪt]
said 'yes'	[seˈdʒes]

This by no means covers all possible consonantal shortcuts in English, but gives a sample of what can be expected.

2) The great difference between stressed and unstressed syllables in English is most noticeable in the vowels, though there are some consonantal effects as well. Everyone knows that unstressed vowels move towards what might be called a neutral quality, but few mention that unstressed vowels can virtually disappear. For example, it is not at all unusual to hear;

to see	[tʰsiː]
potato	[pʰteɪtəʊ]
support	[sːpɔːt]
eggs and bacon	[egzm̩beɪkn̩]
alone	[lːəʊn]

The word 'and' is very susceptible to reduction, varying from [ænd, ənd, æn, ənn, ə̃] to the 'm' seen in the example above.

This suppression of unstressed vowels can work across word boundaries as well, which can make the division between words hard to specify:

he's **got a new** car [gɒtn̩juː]

The major effect of stress on consonants is that many of them achieve less closure after a stressed vowel. 'Tapping' is an example, where a sound which resembles a very short 'd' occurs in place of 't' between vowels:

later	[ˈleɪɾə]
British	[ˈbrɪɾɪʃ]

(In the dictionary, t̬ is used instead of the tap symbol [ɾ]) .

Tapping is normally thought of as a feature of American accents, but is found for 't', though less frequently, in many accents of British English, especially in common words such as 'British'.

A more common occurrence in the south-eastern UK is that /p, b, t, d/ and /k, g/ do not achieve full closure after a stressed vowel and before an unstressed one, causing fricative-like sounds with no noticeable release. Some write the resulting 't' sound as a retroflex 's' ([ʂ]):

matter	[ˈmæʂə]
meeting	[ˈmiːʂɪŋ]

While each of these shortcuts is easy to unravel, having several of them in the same utterance can create effects which are surprising for the uninitiated, e.g.:

'And that's not all that's the matter'.

Expected:	[ændˈðæts nɒt ˈɔːl ðəts ðə mætə]
Actual:	[n̩ˈæs nɒɾ ˈɔːl̥ːətʂːə ˈmæʂə]

Normally, those who speak English natively can make sense of this and similar utterances without thinking, but even they sometimes need more context to say for sure whether they have heard 'sport' or 'support'.

As mentioned in the first paragraph, many of these shortcuts would be difficult to represent in a pronouncing dictionary because they require extra symbols and extra knowledge on the part of the user, but an awareness of them is crucial to understanding naturally produced conversational English. Consulting the dictionary is important, but being alert to variation from the idealized form – using your ears as well as your eyes – is also essential.

Reference:

Shockey, L (2003) *Sound Patterns of Spoken English*, Blackwell.

Guide to the Dictionary

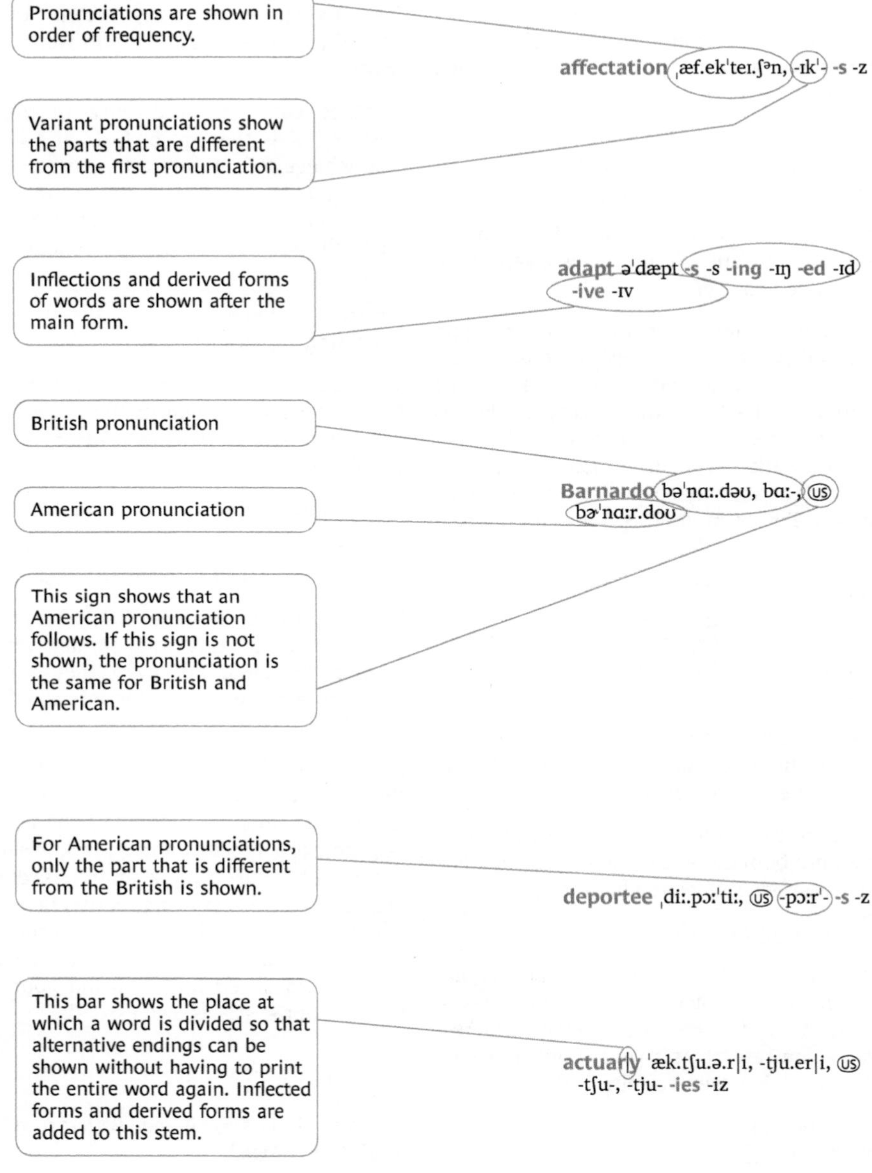
Pronunciations are shown in order of frequency.
Variant pronunciations show the parts that are different from the first pronunciation.
affectation ˌæf.ekˈteɪ.ʃən, -ɪkˈ- -s -z
Inflections and derived forms of words are shown after the main form.
adapt əˈdæpt -s -s -ing -ɪŋ -ed -ɪd -ive -ɪv
British pronunciation
American pronunciation
This sign shows that an American pronunciation follows. If this sign is not shown, the pronunciation is the same for British and American.
Barnardo bəˈnɑː.dəʊ, bɑː-, US bɚˈnɑːr.doʊ
For American pronunciations, only the part that is different from the British is shown.
deportee ˌdiː.pɔːˈtiː, US -pɔːrˈ- -s -z
This bar shows the place at which a word is divided so that alternative endings can be shown without having to print the entire word again. Inflected forms and derived forms are added to this stem.
actuar|y ˈæk.tʃu.ə.r|i, -tju.er|i, US -tʃu-, -tju- -ies -iz

Stress patterns are shown for common compounds and idioms.

apple ˈæp.əl **-s** -z ˈ**apple** ˌ**blossom**; ˈ**apple** ˌ**butter**; ˌ**apple** ˈ**sauce** (US) ˈ**apple** ˌ**sauce**; ˈ**apple** ˌ**tree**; **the** ˌ**apple of one's** ˈ**eye**

In some words the stress moves according to the position of the word. This is called *stress shift*, and is indicated with an example.

Adriatic ˌeɪ.driˈæt.ɪk, (US) -ˈæţ- *stress shift:* ˌ**Adriatic** ˈ**Sea**

Glosses indicate where pronunciations differ according to meaning.

Aden *in Yemen:* ˈeɪ.dən, (US) ˈɑː-, ˈeɪ- *in Aberdeenshire:* ˈæd.ən

Words which can be used with or without a capital letter are shown like this.

advent, A~ ˈæd.vent, -vənt **-s** -s ˈ**Advent** ˌ**calendar**

A semicolon indicates that the alternatives that follow cannot be added to the pronunciation given earlier.

adenoidectom|y ˌæd.ə.nɔɪˈdek.tə.m|i, -ɪn.ɔɪˈ-, (US) -ən.ɔɪˈ-; (US) ˌæd.nɔɪˈ- **-ies** -iz

Variant spellings of the word are shown.

Italic symbols indicate that a sound is optional.

Acheulean, Acheulian əˈ*t*ʃuː.li.ən

THE INTERNATIONAL PHONETIC ALPHABET (revised to 2005)

CONSONANTS (PULMONIC)

	Bilabial	Labiodental	Dental	Alveolar	Postalveolar	Retroflex	Palatal	Velar	Uvular	Pharyngeal	Glottal
Plosive	p b			t d		ʈ ɖ	c ɟ	k ɡ	q ɢ		ʔ
Nasal	m	ɱ		n		ɳ	ɲ	ŋ	ɴ		
Trill	ʙ			r					ʀ		
Tap or Flap		ⱱ		ɾ		ɽ					
Fricative	ɸ β	f v	θ ð	s z	ʃ ʒ	ʂ ʐ	ç ʝ	x ɣ	χ ʁ	ħ ʕ	h ɦ
Lateral fricative				ɬ ɮ							
Approximant		ʋ		ɹ		ɻ	j	ɰ			
Lateral approximant				l		ɭ	ʎ	ʟ			

Where symbols appear in pairs, the one to the right represents a voiced consonant. Shaded areas denote articulations judged impossible.

CONSONANTS (NON-PULMONIC)

Clicks		Voiced implosives		Ejectives	
ʘ	Bilabial	ɓ	Bilabial	ʼ	Examples:
ǀ	Dental	ɗ	Dental/alveolar	pʼ	Bilabial
ǃ	(Post)alveolar	ʄ	Palatal	tʼ	Dental/alveolar
ǂ	Palatoalveolar	ɠ	Velar	kʼ	Velar
ǁ	Alveolar lateral	ʛ	Uvular	sʼ	Alveolar fricative

VOWELS

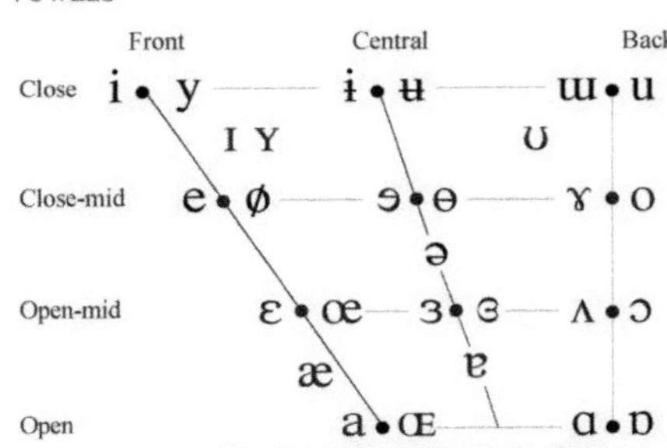

Where symbols appear in pairs, the one to the right represents a rounded vowel.

OTHER SYMBOLS

ʍ Voiceless labial-velar fricative

w Voiced labial-velar approximant

ɥ Voiced labial-palatal approximant

ʜ Voiceless epiglottal fricative

ʢ Voiced epiglottal fricative

ʡ Epiglottal plosive

ɕ ʑ Alveolo-palatal fricatives

ɺ Voiced alveolar lateral flap

ɧ Simultaneous ʃ and x

Affricates and double articulations can be represented by two symbols joined by a tie bar if necessary. k͡p t͡s

SUPRASEGMENTALS

ˈ Primary stress

ˌ Secondary stress ˌfoʊnəˈtɪʃən

ː Long eː

ˑ Half-long eˑ

◌̆ Extra-short ĕ

| Minor (foot) group

‖ Major (intonation) group

. Syllable break ɹi.ækt

‿ Linking (absence of a break)

DIACRITICS Diacritics may be placed above a symbol with a descender, e.g. ŋ̊

◌̥	Voiceless	n̥ d̥	◌̤	Breathy voiced	b̤ a̤	◌̪	Dental	t̪ d̪
◌̬	Voiced	s̬ t̬	◌̰	Creaky voiced	b̰ a̰	◌̺	Apical	t̺ d̺
ʰ	Aspirated	tʰ dʰ	◌̼	Linguolabial	t̼ d̼	◌̻	Laminal	t̻ d̻
◌̹	More rounded	ɔ̹	ʷ	Labialized	tʷ dʷ	◌̃	Nasalized	ẽ
◌̜	Less rounded	ɔ̜	ʲ	Palatalized	tʲ dʲ	ⁿ	Nasal release	dⁿ
◌̟	Advanced	u̟	ˠ	Velarized	tˠ dˠ	ˡ	Lateral release	dˡ
◌̠	Retracted	e̠	ˤ	Pharyngealized	tˤ dˤ	◌̚	No audible release	d̚
◌̈	Centralized	ë	◌̴	Velarized or pharyngealized	ɫ			
◌̽	Mid-centralized	e̽	◌̝	Raised	e̝ (ɹ̝ = voiced alveolar fricative)			
◌̩	Syllabic	n̩	◌̞	Lowered	e̞ (β̞ = voiced bilabial approximant)			
◌̯	Non-syllabic	e̯	◌̘	Advanced Tongue Root	e̘			
˞	Rhoticity	ɚ a˞	◌̙	Retracted Tongue Root	e̙			

TONES AND WORD ACCENTS

LEVEL			CONTOUR		
e̋ or	˥	Extra high	ě or	˩˥	Rising
é	˦	High	ê	˥˩	Falling
ē	˧	Mid	e᷄	˧˥	High rising
è	˨	Low	e᷅	˩˨	Low rising
ȅ	˩	Extra low	e᷈	˧˦˧	Rising-falling
↓		Downstep	↗		Global rise
↑		Upstep	↘		Global fall

Pronouncing the letter A

→ *See also* **AE, AEO, AI/AY, AU/AW**

The vowel letter **a** has two main strong pronunciations linked to spelling: a 'short' pronunciation /æ/ and a 'long' pronunciation /eɪ/. In the 'short' pronunciation, the **a** is usually followed by a consonant which closes the syllable, or a double consonant before another vowel, e.g.:

tap	tæp
tapping	ˈtæp.ɪŋ

The 'long' pronunciation usually means the **a** is followed by a single consonant and then a vowel, e.g.:

tape	teɪp
taping	ˈteɪ.pɪŋ

When there is an **r** in the spelling, the strong pronunciation is one of three possibilities: /ɑː/ Ⓤⓢ /ɑːr/, /eə/ Ⓤⓢ /er/ or /æ/ Ⓤⓢ /e/, /æ/, e.g.:

car	kɑːʳ Ⓤⓢ kɑːr
care	keəʳ Ⓤⓢ ker
carry	kær.i Ⓤⓢ ker.i, kær.i

In addition

There are other vowel sounds associated with the letter **a**, e.g.:

ɑː	father /ˈfɑː.ðəʳ/ Ⓤⓢ /ˈfɑː.ðɚ/
ɑː Ⓤⓢ æ	bath /bɑːθ/ Ⓤⓢ /bæθ/
ɒ Ⓤⓢ ɑː	swan /swɒn/ Ⓤⓢ /swɑːn/
ɔː Ⓤⓢ ɑː, ɔː	walk /wɔːk/ Ⓤⓢ /wɑːk/
	warm /wɔːm/ Ⓤⓢ /wɔːrm/

And, in rare cases:

e	many /ˈmen.i/

In weak syllables

The vowel letter **a** is realized with the vowels /ə/ and /ɪ/ in weak syllables, and may also not be pronounced at all in British English, due to compression, e.g.:

above	əˈbʌv
village	ˈvɪl.ɪdʒ
necessary	ˈnes.ə.sri Ⓤⓢ -ser.i

a *indefinite article: strong form:* eɪ; *weak form:* ə
Note: Weak-form word. The strong form /eɪ/ is used mainly for contrast (e.g. 'This is *a* solution, but not the only one.'). The weak form only occurs before consonants, and is usually pronounced /ə/. In rapid speech, when /ə/ is preceded by a consonant, it may combine with a following /l/, /n/, or /r/ to produce a syllabic consonant (e.g. 'got a light' /ˌɡɒt.əlˈlaɪt/ Ⓤⓢ /ˌɡɑːt̬.əˈlaɪt/; 'get another' /ˌget.n̩ˈʌð.əʳ/ Ⓤⓢ /-ɚ/).

a, A *the letter:* eɪ **-'s** -z

A-1 ˌeɪˈwʌn *stress shift:* ˌ**A-1 conˈdition**

A4 ˌeɪˈfɔːʳ, Ⓤⓢ -ˈfɔːr *stress shift:* ˌ**A4 ˈpaper**

AA ˌeɪˈeɪ *stress shift:* ˌ**AA patˈrol**

AAA *Amateur Athletics Association:* ˌθriːˈeɪz, ˌeɪ.eɪˈeɪ *American Automobile Association:* ˌtrɪp.əlˈeɪ

Aachen ˈɑː.kən

aah ɑː

Aalborg ˈɑːl.bɔːɡ, Ⓤⓢ ˈɑːl.bɔːrɡ, ˈɔːl-

aardvark ˈɑːd.vɑːk, Ⓤⓢ ˈɑːrd.vɑːrk **-s** -s

aardwol|f ˈɑːd.wʊl|f, Ⓤⓢ ˈɑːrd- **-ves** -vz

Aarhus ˈɑː.hʊs, Ⓤⓢ ˈɑːr-, ˈɔːr-

Aaron ˈeə.rən, Ⓤⓢ ˈer.ən, ˈær-

ab, Ab æb

AB ˌeɪˈbiː

ab- ˈæb, əb
Note: Prefix. Examples include **abnegate** /ˈæb.nɪ.ɡeɪt/, in which it is stressed, and **abduct** /əbˈdʌkt/, where it is unstressed.

Abacha əˈbætʃ.ə, Ⓤⓢ -ˈbɑːtʃ-

aback əˈbæk

Abaco ˈæb.ə.kəʊ, Ⓤⓢ -koʊ

abacus ˈæb.ə.kəs **-es** -ɪz

Abadan ˌæb.əˈdɑːn, -ˈdæn

Abaddon əˈbæd.ən

abaft əˈbɑːft, Ⓤⓢ -ˈbæft

abalone æb.əˈləʊ.ni, Ⓤⓢ -ˈloʊ-

abandon əˈbæn.dən **-s** -z **-ing** -ɪŋ **-ed** -d **-ment** -mənt

à bas æˈbɑː, Ⓤⓢ æ-, ɑː-

abas|e əˈbeɪs **-es** -ɪz **-ing** -ɪŋ **-ed** -t **-ement** -mənt

abash əˈbæʃ **-es** -ɪz **-ing** -ɪŋ **-ed** -t

abatab|le əˈbeɪ.tə.b|əl, Ⓤⓢ -t̬ə- **-ly** -li

a|bate ə|ˈbeɪt **-bates** -ˈbeɪts **-bating** -ˈbeɪ.tɪŋ, Ⓤⓢ -ˈbeɪ.t̬ɪŋ **-bated** -ˈbeɪ.tɪd, Ⓤⓢ -ˈbeɪ.t̬ɪd **-batement/s** -ˈbeɪt.mənt/s

abat(t)is ˈæb.ə.tɪs, -tiː, Ⓤⓢ -ə.t̬ɪs, əˈbæt̬.ɪs **-es** ˈæb.ə.tɪ.sɪz, Ⓤⓢ -t̬ɪ-, əˈbæt̬.ɪ.sɪz *alternative plural:* ˈæb.ə.tiːz, Ⓤⓢ -t̬iːz, əˈbæt̬.iːz

abattoir ˈæb.ə.twɑːʳ, Ⓤⓢ -twɑːr, -twɔːr **-s** -z

abaxial əˈbæk.si.əl, æbˈæk-

Abba ˈæb.ə

abbac|y ˈæb.ə.s|i **-ies** -iz

Abbado əˈbɑː.dəʊ, Ⓤⓢ -doʊ

Abbas ˈæb.əs, əˈbæs

Abbassid, Abbasid əˈbæs.ɪd **-s** -z

abbé ˈæb.eɪ, Ⓤⓢ ˈæb.eɪ, -ˈ- **-s** -z

abbess ˈæb.es, -ɪs, Ⓤⓢ -əs **-es** -ɪz

Abbeville *in France:* ˈæb.viːl, Ⓤⓢ ˌæbˈviːl *in US:* ˈæb.ɪ.vɪl

abbey, A~ ˈæb.i **-s** -z

Abbie ˈæb.i

abbot, A~ ˈæb.ət **-s** -s

Abbotsford ˈæb.əts.fəd, Ⓤⓢ -fɚd

abbotship ˈæb.ət.ʃɪp **-s** -s

Abbott ˈæb.ət **-s** -s ˌ**Abbott and Cosˈtello**

abbrevi|ate əˈbriː.vi|.eɪt **-ates** -eɪts **-ating** -eɪ.tɪŋ, Ⓤⓢ -eɪ.t̬ɪŋ **-ated** -eɪ.tɪd, Ⓤⓢ -eɪ.t̬ɪd **-ator/s** -eɪ.təʳ/z, Ⓤⓢ -eɪ.t̬ɚ/z

abbreviation əˌbriː.viˈeɪ.ʃən **-s** -z

abbreviatory əˈbriː.vi.ə.tri, əˌbriː.viˈeɪ.tər.i, Ⓤⓢ əˈbriː.vi.ə.tɔːr.i

Abbs æbz

Abby ˈæb.i

abc, ABC ˌeɪ.biːˈsiː **-'s** -z

Abdera æbˈdɪə.rə, Ⓤⓢ -ˈdɪr.ə

abdicant ˈæb.dɪ.kənt **-s** -s

abdi|cate ˈæb.dɪ|.keɪt **-cates** -keɪts **-cating** -keɪ.tɪŋ, Ⓤⓢ -keɪ.t̬ɪŋ **-cated** -keɪ.tɪd, Ⓤⓢ -keɪ.t̬ɪd **-cator/s** -keɪ.təʳ/z, Ⓤⓢ -keɪ.t̬ɚ/z

abdication ˌæb.dɪˈkeɪ.ʃən, -dəˈ- **-s** -z

Abdiel ˈæb.dɪəl, Ⓤⓢ -di.əl

abdomen ˈæb.də.mən, -men; æbˈdəʊ.mən, Ⓤⓢ ˈæb.də.mən, æbˈdoʊ- **-s** -z

abdominal æbˈdɒm.ɪ.nəl, əb-, -ˈdəʊ.mɪ-, Ⓤⓢ -ˈdɑː.mə- **-ly** -i

abducent əbˈdʒuː.sənt, æb-, -ˈdjuː-, Ⓤⓢ æbˈduː-, -ˈdjuː-

abduct əbˈdʌkt, æb- **-s** -s **-ing** -ɪŋ **-ed** -ɪd **-or/s** -əʳ/z, Ⓤⓢ -ɚ/z

A

abduction əbˈdʌk.ʃən, æb- -s -z
Abdul ˈæb.dʊl
Abdulla(h) æbˈdʌl.ə, əb-, -ˈdʊl-
Abe eɪb
abeam əˈbiːm
abecedarian ˌeɪ.biː.siːˈdeə.ri.ən, ⓊⓈ -ˈder.i-
à Becket əˈbek.ɪt
abed əˈbed
Abednego ˌæb.edˈniː.gəʊ, əˈbed.nɪ.gəʊ, ⓊⓈ -goʊ
Abel ˈeɪ.bəl
Abelard ˈæb.ə.lɑːd, ˈ-ɪ-, ⓊⓈ -lɑːrd
Abelmeholah ˌeɪ.bəl.miˈhəʊ.lə, -məˈ-, ⓊⓈ -ˈhoʊ-
Abenaki ˌæb.əˈnæk.i, ⓊⓈ ˌɑː.bəˈnɑː.ki, ˌæb.əˈ-, -ˈnæk.i -s -z
Aberavon ˌæb.əˈræv.ən, ⓊⓈ -ɚˈæv-
Abercanaid ˌæb.əˈkæn.aɪd, ⓊⓈ ˌ-ɚ-
Abercarn ˌæb.əˈkɑːn, ⓊⓈ -ɚˈkɑːrn
Aberconway ˌæb.əˈkɒn.weɪ, ⓊⓈ -ɚˈkɑːn-
Aberconwy ˌæb.əˈkɒn.wi, ⓊⓈ -ɚˈkɑːn-
Abercorn ˈæb.ə.kɔːn, ⓊⓈ -ɚ.kɔːrn
Abercrombie, Abercromby ˈæb.ə.krɒm.bi, -krʌm-; ˌæb.əˈkrɒm.bi, -ˈkrʌm-, ⓊⓈ -ɚ.krɑːm-, -ɚˈkrɑːm-
Aberdare ˌæb.əˈdeər, ⓊⓈ -ɚˈder
Aberdeen ˌæb.əˈdiːn, ⓊⓈ -ɚˈ- **-shire** -ʃər, -ʃɪər, ⓊⓈ -ʃɚ, -ʃɪr *stress shift:* ˌ**Aberdeen** ˈ**station**
Aberdonian ˌæb.əˈdəʊ.ni.ən, ⓊⓈ -ɚˈdoʊ- -s -z
Aberdour ˌæb.əˈdaʊ.ər, -ˈdaʊər, ⓊⓈ -ɚˈdaʊ.ɚ
Aberdovey ˌæb.əˈdʌv.i, ⓊⓈ -ɚˈ-
Aberfan ˌæb.əˈvæn, ⓊⓈ -ɚˈ-
Abergavenny *place:* ˌæb.ə.gəˈven.i, ⓊⓈ ˌæb.ɚ- *family name:* ˌæb.əˈgen.i, ⓊⓈ -ɚˈ-
Abergele ˌæb.əˈgel.i, ⓊⓈ -ɚˈ-
Aberkenfig ˌæb.əˈken.fɪg, ⓊⓈ -ɚˈ-
Abernathy ˌæb.əˈnæθ.i, ⓊⓈ ˈæb.ɚ.næθ-
Abernethy ˌæb.əˈneθ.i, -ˈniː.θi, ⓊⓈ ˈæb.ɚˈneθ.i
aberran|t æbˈer.ən|t, əˈber-; ˈæb.ə.rən|t **-ce** -*t*s **-cy** -*t*.si
aber|rate ˈæb.ə|.reɪt **-rates** -reɪts **-rating** -reɪ.tɪŋ, ⓊⓈ -reɪ.t̬ɪŋ **-rated** -reɪ.tɪd, ⓊⓈ -reɪ.t̬ɪd
aberration ˌæb.əˈreɪ.ʃən -s -z
Abersychan ˌæb.əˈsɪk.ən, ⓊⓈ -ɚˈ-
Abert ˈeɪ.bɜːt, -bət, ⓊⓈ -bɝːt, -bɚt
Abertillery ˌæb.ə.tɪˈleə.ri, -təˈ-, ⓊⓈ -ɚ.təˈler.i
Abertridwr ˌæb.əˈtrɪd.ʊər, ⓊⓈ -ʊr
Aberystwyth ˌæb.əˈrɪs.twɪθ
a|bet ə|ˈbet **-bets** -ˈbets **-betting** -ˈbet.ɪŋ, ⓊⓈ -ˈbet̬.ɪŋ **-betted** -ˈbet.ɪd, ⓊⓈ -ˈbet̬.ɪd **-bettor/s** -ˈbet.ər/z, ⓊⓈ -ˈbet̬.ɚ/z **-betment** -ˈbet.mənt
abeyance əˈbeɪ.ən*t*s
abhor əbˈhɔːr, əˈbɔːr, ⓊⓈ æbˈhɔːr, əb- -s -z **-ring** -ɪŋ **-red** -d **-rer/s** -ər/z, ⓊⓈ -ɚ/z
abhorren|ce əbˈhɒr.ən|*t*s, əˈbɒr-, ⓊⓈ æbˈhɔːr-, əb- **-t** -t
Abia *biblical name:* əˈbaɪ.ə *city:* ˈæb.i.ə
Abiathar əˈbaɪ.ə.θər, ⓊⓈ -θɚ
abid|e əˈbaɪd **-es** -z **-ing** -ɪŋ **-ed** -ɪd **abode** əˈbəʊd, ⓊⓈ -ˈboʊd
Abidjan ˌæb.iːˈdʒɑːn, -ɪˈ-
abigail, A~ ˈæb.ɪ.geɪl -s -z
Abilene *in Syria:* ˌæb.ɪˈliː.ni, -əˈ- *in US:* ˈæb.ə.liːn
abilit|y əˈbɪl.ə.t|i, -ɪ.t|i, ⓊⓈ -ə.t̬|i **-ies** -iz
-ability əˈbɪl.ə.ti, -ɪ.ti, ⓊⓈ -ə.t̬i
Note: Suffix. Words containing **-ability** always exhibit primary stress as shown above, e.g. **taxability** /ˌtæk.səˈbɪl.ə.ti/ ⓊⓈ /-ə.t̬i/.
Abimelech əˈbɪm.ə.lek
Abingdon ˈæb.ɪŋ.dən
Abinger ˈæb.ɪn.dʒər, ⓊⓈ -dʒɚ
Abington ˈæb.ɪŋ.tən
ab initio ˌæb.ɪˈnɪʃ.i.əʊ, -əˈ-, -ˈnɪs-, ⓊⓈ -oʊ
abiogenesis ˌeɪ.baɪ.əʊˈdʒen.ə.sɪs, ˈ-ɪ-, ⓊⓈ -oʊˈ-
Abiola ˌæb.iˈəʊ.lə, ⓊⓈ -ˈoʊ-
abiotic ˌeɪ.baɪˈɒt.ɪk, ⓊⓈ -ˈɑː.t̬ɪk
abject ˈæb.dʒekt, ⓊⓈ ˈæb.dʒekt, -ˈ- **-ly** -li **-ness** -nəs, -nɪs
abjection æbˈdʒek.ʃən
abjudi|cate æbˈdʒuː.dɪ|.keɪt, əb-, ⓊⓈ -də- **-cates** -keɪts **-cating** -keɪ.tɪŋ, ⓊⓈ -keɪ.t̬ɪŋ **-cated** -keɪ.tɪd, ⓊⓈ -keɪ.t̬ɪd
abjuration ˌæb.dʒʊˈreɪ.ʃən, -dʒəˈ-, -dʒʊəˈ-, ⓊⓈ -dʒəˈ-, -dʒʊˈ- -s -z
abjur|e əbˈdʒʊər, æb-, -ˈdʒɔːr, ⓊⓈ -ˈdʒʊr **-es** -z **-ing** -ɪŋ **-ed** -d **-er/s** -ər/z, ⓊⓈ -ɚ/z
ablat|e əˈbleɪt, æbˈleɪt, ˌæbˈleɪt **-es** -s **-ing** -ɪŋ, ⓊⓈ ˌæbˈleɪ.t̬ɪŋ **-ed** -ɪd, ⓊⓈ ˌæbˈleɪ.t̬ɪd
ablation əˈbleɪ.ʃən, æbˈleɪ-, ⓊⓈ ˌæb-
ablatival ˌæb.ləˈtaɪ.vəl
ablative ˈæb.lə.tɪv, ⓊⓈ -t̬ɪv -s -z
ablaut ˈæb.laʊt -s -s
ablaze əˈbleɪz
ab|le ˈeɪ.b|əl **-ler** -əl.ər, -lər, ⓊⓈ -əl.ɚ, -lɚ **-lest** -əl.əst, -ləst, -əl.ɪst, -lɪst **-ly** -əl.i, -li
-able ə.bəl
Note: Suffix. Does not normally affect stress patterning, e.g. **knowledge** /ˈnɒl.ɪdʒ/ ⓊⓈ /ˈnɑː.lɪdʒ/, **knowledgeable** /ˈnɒl.ɪ.dʒə.bəl/ ⓊⓈ /ˈnɑː.lɪ-/; **rely** /rɪˈlaɪ/, **reliable** /rɪˈlaɪ.ə.bəl/. In some cases, however, the stress patterning may change, e.g. **admire** /ədˈmaɪər/ ⓊⓈ /-ˈmaɪ.ɚ/, **admirable** /ˈæd.mər.ə.bəl/.
able-bodied ˌeɪ.bəlˈbɒd.id, ⓊⓈ ˈeɪ.bəlˌbɑː.did, ˌeɪ.bəlˈbɑː- *stress shift, British only:* ˌ**able-bodied** ˈ**person**
Ablett ˈæb.lət, -lɪt
ablution əˈbluː.ʃən -s -z
-ably ə.bli
Note: Suffix. Behaves as **-able** above.
Abnaki æbˈnæk.i, ⓊⓈ -ˈnɑː.ki -s -z
abneg|ate ˈæb.nɪ.g|eɪt, -neg|.eɪt, -nə.g|eɪt **-ates** -eɪts **-ating** -eɪ.tɪŋ, ⓊⓈ -eɪ.t̬ɪŋ **-ated** -eɪ.tɪd, ⓊⓈ -eɪ.t̬ɪd
abnegation ˌæb.nɪˈgeɪ.ʃən, -negˈeɪ-, -nəˈgeɪ- -s -z
Abner ˈæb.nər, ⓊⓈ -nɚ
abnormal æbˈnɔː.məl, əb-, ⓊⓈ -ˈnɔːr- **-ly** -i
abnormalit|y ˌæb.nɔːˈmæl.ə.t|i, -ɪ.t|i, ⓊⓈ -nɔːrˈmæl.ə.t̬|i **-ies** -iz
abnormit|y æbˈnɔː.mə.t|i, əb-, -mɪ-, ⓊⓈ -ˈnɔːr.mə.t̬|i **-ies** -iz
abo ˈæb.əʊ, ⓊⓈ -oʊ -s -z
ABO ˌeɪ.biːˈəʊ, ⓊⓈ -ˈoʊ
aboard əˈbɔːd, ⓊⓈ -ˈbɔːrd
abode əˈbəʊd, ⓊⓈ -ˈboʊd -s -z
abolish əˈbɒl.ɪʃ, ⓊⓈ -ˈbɑː.lɪʃ **-es** -ɪz **-ing** -ɪŋ **-ed** -t **-er/s** -ər/z, ⓊⓈ -ɚ/z
abolition ˌæb.əˈlɪʃ.ən -s -z
abolition|ism ˌæb.əˈlɪʃ.ən|.ɪ.zəm **-ist/s** -ɪst/s
abomas|um ˌæb.əʊˈmeɪ.s|əm, ⓊⓈ -oʊˈ- **-a** -ə
A-bomb ˈeɪ.bɒm, ⓊⓈ -ˌbɑːm -s -z
abominab|le əˈbɒm.ɪ.nə.b|əl, -ən.ə-, ⓊⓈ -ˈbɑː.mɪ- **-ly** -li **-leness** -əl.nəs, -nɪs
abomi|nate əˈbɒm.ɪ|.neɪt, ˈ-ə-, ⓊⓈ -ˈbɑː.mɪ- **-nates** -neɪts **-nating** -neɪ.tɪŋ, ⓊⓈ -neɪ.t̬ɪŋ **-nated** -neɪ.tɪd, ⓊⓈ -neɪ.t̬ɪd
abomination əˌbɒm.ɪˈneɪ.ʃən, -əˈ-, ⓊⓈ -ˌbɑː.mɪˈ- -s -z
à bon marché æˌbɔ̃ː.mɑːˈʃeɪ, -ˌbɒn-, ⓊⓈ -ˌbõʊn.mɑːrˈ-
aboriginal, A~ ˌæb.əˈrɪdʒ.ən.əl, -ɪ.nəl -s -z **-ly** -i
aborigine, A~ ˌæb.əˈrɪdʒ.ən.i, -ɪ.ni -s -z
a|bort ə|ˈbɔːt, ⓊⓈ -ˈbɔːrt **-borts** -ˈbɔːts, ⓊⓈ -ˈbɔːrts **-borting** -ˈbɔː.tɪŋ, ⓊⓈ -ˈbɔːr.t̬ɪŋ **-borted** -ˈbɔː.tɪd, ⓊⓈ -ˈbɔːr.t̬ɪd
aborticide əˈbɔː.tɪ.saɪd, ⓊⓈ -ˈbɔːr.t̬ə-
abortifacient əˌbɔː.tɪˈfeɪ.ʃi.ənt, -ʃənt, ⓊⓈ -ˌbɔːr.t̬əˈ-
abortion əˈbɔː.ʃən, ⓊⓈ -ˈbɔːr- -s -z **-ist/s** -ɪst/s
abortive əˈbɔː.tɪv, ⓊⓈ -ˈbɔːr.t̬ɪv **-ly** -li **-ness** -nəs, -nɪs
Aboukir ˌæb.uːˈkɪər, -ʊˈ-, ⓊⓈ -ˈkɪr
abound əˈbaʊnd -s -z **-ing** -ɪŋ **-ed** -ɪd
about əˈbaʊt
about-fac|e əˌbaʊtˈfeɪs **-es** -ɪz **-ing** -ɪŋ **-ed** -d
about-turn əˌbaʊtˈtɜːn, ⓊⓈ -ˈtɝːn -s -z
above əˈbʌv
above-board əˌbʌvˈbɔːd, ⓊⓈ əˈbʌv.bɔːrd
aboveground əˌbʌvˈgraʊnd, ⓊⓈ əˈbʌv.graʊnd
above-mentioned əˌbʌvˈmen.tʃənd, ⓊⓈ -ˈment.ʃənd *stress shift:* **a**ˌ**bove-mentioned** ˈ**person**
ab ovo ˌæbˈəʊ.vəʊ, ⓊⓈ -ˈoʊ.voʊ
abracadabra ˌæb.rə.kəˈdæb.rə -s -z

A

abrad|e əˈbreɪd -es -z -ing -ɪŋ -ed -ɪd

Abraham ˈeɪ.brə.hæm, -həm *as a biblical name in Britain often also:* ˈɑː-

Abrahams ˈeɪ.brə.hæmz

Abram ˈeɪ.brəm, -bræm *as a biblical name in Britain often also:* ˈɑː-

Abramovich əˈbræm.ə.vɪtʃ, æbˈræm-

abrasion əˈbreɪ.ʒᵊn -s -z

abrasive əˈbreɪ.sɪv, -zɪv -ly -li -s -z

abreact ˌæb.riˈækt -s -s -ing -ɪŋ -ed -ɪd

abreaction ˌæb.riˈæk.ʃᵊn

abreast əˈbrest

abridg|e əˈbrɪdʒ -es -ɪz -ing -ɪŋ -ed -d

abridg(e)ment əˈbrɪdʒ.mənt -s -s

abroad əˈbrɔːd, (US) -ˈbrɑːd, -ˈbrɔːd

abro|gate ˈæb.rəʊ|.ɡeɪt, (US) -rə- -gates -ɡeɪts -gating -ɡeɪ.tɪŋ, (US) -ɡeɪ.t̬ɪŋ -gated -ɡeɪ.tɪd, (US) -ɡeɪ.t̬ɪd

abrogation ˌæb.rəʊˈɡeɪ.ʃᵊn, (US) -rəˈ- -s -z

A'Brook əˈbrʊk

abrupt əˈbrʌpt -er -əʳ, (US) -ɚ -est -ɪst, -əst -ly -li -ness -nəs, -nɪs

abruption əˈbrʌp.ʃᵊn

Abruzzi əˈbrʊt.si, -ˈbruːt-, (US) -ˈbruːt-

ABS ˌeɪ.biːˈes

Absalom ˈæb.sᵊl.əm

abscess ˈæb.ses, -sɪs -es -ɪz

abscis|e æbˈsaɪz, əb- -es -ɪz -ing -ɪŋ -ed -d

abscisin æbˈsɪs.ɪn

absciss|a æbˈsɪs|.ə, əb- -ae -i -as -əz

abscission æbˈsɪʃ.ᵊn, -ˈsɪʒ- -s -z

abscond æbˈskɒnd, əb-, (US) -ˈskɑːnd -s -z -ing -ɪŋ -ed -ɪd -er/s -əʳ/z, (US) -ɚ/z

Abse ˈæb.si, -zi

abseil ˈæb.seɪl, -saɪl -s -z -ing -ɪŋ -ed -d

absenc|e ˈæb.sᵊnts -es -ɪz

absent adj ˈæb.sᵊnt -ly -li **ˌabsent without ˈleave**

ab|sent v æb|ˈsent, əb- -sents -ˈsents -senting -ˈsen.tɪŋ, (US) -ˈsen.t̬ɪŋ -sented -ˈsen.tɪd, (US) -ˈsen.t̬ɪd

absentee ˌæb.sᵊnˈtiː, -senˈ- -s -z -ism -ɪ.zᵊm *stress shift, see compounds:* **ˌabsentee ˈballot; ˌabsentee ˈlandlord**

absentia æbˈsen.ti.ə, -ˈsent.ʃi-, (US) -ˈsent.ʃə, ˈ-ʃi.ə

absent-minded ˌæb.sᵊntˈmaɪn.dɪd -ly -li -ness -nəs, -nɪs *stress shift:* **ˌabsent-minded ˈperson**

absinth(e) ˈæb.sæ̃θ, -sɪntθ

absolut|e ˌæb.səˈluːt, -ljuːt, ˈæb.sᵊl.uːt, -juːt, (US) ˌæb.səˈluːt, ˈ--- -es -s -est -ɪst, -əst -ness -nəs, -nɪs

absolutely ˌæb.səˈluːt.li, -ˈljuːt-, (US) ˌæb.səˈluːt-, ˈæb.sə.luːt- *stress shift:* **ˌabsolutely ˈfabulous**

absolution ˌæb.səˈluː.ʃᵊn, -ˈljuː-, (US) -ˈluː- -s -z

absolut|ism ˈæb.sᵊl.uː.t|ɪ.zᵊm, -juː-, (US) -sə.luː.t̬|ɪ- -ist/s -ɪst/s

absolutive ˌæb.səˈluː.tɪv, -ˈljuː-, (US) -ˈluː.t̬ɪv

absolv|e əbˈzɒlv, -ˈsɒlv, (US) -ˈzɑːlv, -ˈsɑːlv, -ˈzɔːlv, -ˈsɔːlv -es -z -ing -ɪŋ -ed -d -er/s -əʳ/z, (US) -ɚ/z

absorb əbˈzɔːb, -ˈsɔːb, (US) -ˈsɔːrb, -ˈzɔːrb -s -z -ed -d -edly -ɪd.li, -əd.li -able -ə.bᵊl

absorbency əbˈzɔː.bᵊnt.si, -ˈsɔː-, (US) -ˈsɔːr-, -ˈzɔːr-

absorbent əbˈzɔː.bənt, -ˈsɔː-, (US) -ˈsɔːr-, -ˈzɔːr- -ly -li

absorbing əbˈzɔː.bɪŋ, -ˈsɔː-, (US) -ˈsɔːr-, -ˈzɔːr- -ly -li

absorption əbˈzɔːp.ʃᵊn, -ˈsɔːp-, (US) -ˈsɔːrp-, -ˈzɔːrp-

absorptive əbˈzɔːp.tɪv, -ˈsɔːp-, (US) -ˈsɔːrp-, -ˈzɔːrp-

abstain æbˈsteɪn, əb- -s -z -ing -ɪŋ -ed -d -er/s -əʳ/z, (US) -ɚ/z

abstemious æbˈstiː.mi.əs, əb- -ly -li -ness -nəs, -nɪs

abstention æbˈsten.tʃᵊn, əb-, (US) -ˈstent.ʃᵊn -s -z

abstergent æbˈstɜː.dʒᵊnt, əb-, (US) -ˈstɝː- -s -s

abstinen|ce ˈæb.stɪ.nən|ts, -stə- -t -t

abstract n, adj ˈæb.strækt -s -s

abstract v æbˈstrækt, əb- -s -s -ing -ɪŋ -ed/ly -ɪd/li

abstraction æbˈstræk.ʃᵊn, əb- -s -z

abstraction|ism æbˈstræk.ʃᵊn|.ɪ.zᵊm, əb- -ist/s -ɪst/s

abstract|ly ˈæb.strækt|.li, əbˈstrækt-, æbˈ- -ness -nəs, -nɪs

abstrict əbˈstrɪkt, æb- -s -s -ing -ɪŋ -ed -ɪd

abstriction əbˈstrɪk.ʃᵊn, æb-

abstruse æbˈstruːs, əb- -ly -li -ness -nəs, -nɪs

absurd əbˈzɜːd, -ˈsɜːd, (US) -ˈsɝːd, -ˈzɝːd -est -ɪst, -əst -ly -li -ness -nəs, -nɪs

absurd|ism əbˈzɜː.d|ɪ.zᵊm, -ˈsɜː-, (US) -ˈsɝː-, -ˈzɝː- -ist -ɪst

absurdit|y əbˈzɜː.də.t|i, -ˈsɜː-, -dɪ-, (US) -ˈsɝː.də.t̬|i, -ˈzɝː- -ies -iz

ABTA ˈæb.tə

Abu ˈɑː.buː, ˈæb.uː

Abu Dhabi ˌæb.uːˈdɑː.bi, ˌɑː.buː-, -ˈdæb.i, (US) ˌɑː.buːˈdɑː.bi

Abu Ghraib ˌæb.uːˈɡreɪb

Abuja əˈbuː.dʒə

abulia əˈbuː.li.ə, eɪ-, -ˈbjuː-

abundance əˈbʌn.dənts

abundant əˈbʌn.dənt -ly -li

Abu Nidal ˌæb.uː.niːˈdɑːl, ˌɑː.buː-, -ˈdæl, (US) ˌɑː.buː-

Abury ˈeɪ.bᵊr.i, (US) -ber-, -bɚ-

abus|e n əˈbjuːs -es -ɪz

abus|e v əˈbjuːz -es -ɪz -ing -ɪŋ -ed -d -er/s -əʳ/z, (US) -ɚ/z

Abu Simbel ˌæb.uːˈsɪm.bᵊl, -bel, (US) ˌɑː.buːˈ-

abusive əˈbjuː.sɪv, -zɪv -ly -li -ness -nəs, -nɪs

a|but ə|ˈbʌt -buts -ˈbʌts -butting -ˈbʌt.ɪŋ, (US) -ˈbʌt̬.ɪŋ -butted -ˈbʌt.ɪd, (US) -ˈbʌt̬.ɪd -buttal -ˈbʌt.ᵊl, (US) -ˈbʌt̬.ᵊl

abutilon əˈbjuː.tɪ.lən, -lɒn, (US) -t̬ə.lɑːn, -lən -s -z

abutment əˈbʌt.mənt -s -s

abutter əˈbʌt.əʳ, (US) -ˈbʌt̬.ɚ -s -z

abuzz əˈbʌz

Abydos əˈbaɪ.dɒs, -dəs; ˈæb.ɪ.dɒs, (US) əˈbaɪ.dɑːs; (US) ˈæb.ɪ-

abysm əˈbɪz.ᵊm -s -z

abysmal əˈbɪz.mᵊl -ly -i

abyss əˈbɪs -es -ɪz

abyssal əˈbɪs.ᵊl

Abyssini|a ˌæb.ɪˈsɪn.i|.ə, -əˈ- -an/s -ən/z

AC, a/c (US abbrev. for **air conditioning**) ˌeɪˈsiː

-ac æk, ək

a/c (abbrev. for **account**) əˈkaʊnt

acacia əˈkeɪ.ʃə, ˈ-si.ə, (US) ˈ-ʃə -s -z

academe, A~ ˈæk.ə.diːm

academia ˌæk.əˈdiː.mi.ə

academic ˌæk.əˈdem.ɪk -s -s *stress shift, see compound:* **ˌacademic ˈyear**

academic|al ˌæk.əˈdem.ɪ.k|ᵊl -als -ᵊlz -ally -ᵊl.i, -li

academician əˌkæd.əˈmɪʃ.ᵊn, ˌæk.ə.dəˈ-, -dɪˈ-, (US) ˌæk.ə.dəˈ-, əˌkæd- -s -z

academicism ˌæk.əˈdem.ɪ.sɪ.zᵊm, ˈ-ə-

academism əˈkæd.ə.mɪ.zᵊm

academ|y əˈkæd.ə.m|i -ies -iz **Aˌcademy Aˈward**

Acadi|a əˈkeɪ.di|.ə -an/s -ən/z

acajou ˈæk.ə.ʒuː -s -z

acanth|us əˈkænt.θ|əs -i -aɪ -uses -ə.sɪz -ine -aɪn

a cap(p)ella ˌæ.kəˈpel.ə, -kæpˈel-, (US) ˌɑː.kəˈpel-

Acapulco ˌæk.əˈpʊl.kəʊ, (US) ˌæk.əˈpuːl.koʊ, ˌɑː.kəˈ-, -ˈpʊl-

acarid ˈæk.ᵊr.ɪd -s -z

acarolog|y ˌæk.əˈrɒl.ə.dʒ|i, (US) -ˈrɑː.lə- -ist/s -ɪst/s

acarpel(l)ous ˌeɪˈkɑː.pᵊl.əs, (US) -ˈkɑːr-

acarpous ˌeɪˈkɑː.pəs, (US) -ˈkɑːr-

ACAS, Acas ˈeɪ.kæs

acatalectic ˌeɪ.kæt.əˈlek.tɪk, əˌkæt-, (US) -kæt̬.əˈ- -s -s *stress shift:* **ˌacatalectic ˈverse, aˌcatalectic ˈverse**

acatalepsy ˌeɪˈkæt.ə.lep.si, əˈkæt-, (US) -ˈkæt̬.ə-

acataleptic ˌeɪ.kæt.əˈlep.tɪk, əˌkæt-, (US) -kæt̬.əˈ-

Accad ˈæk.æd

Accadi|a əˈkeɪ.di|.ə, ækˈeɪ- -an/s -ən/z

acced|e əkˈsiːd, æk- -es -z -ing -ɪŋ -ed -ɪd -er/s -əʳ/z, (US) -ɚ/z

accelerando ækˌsel.əˈræn.dəʊ, ək-, əˌtʃel-, (US) -ˈrɑːn.doʊ

accelerant əkˈsel.ə.rᵊnt, æk-, (US) -ɚ.ənt -s -s

accele|rate əkˈsel.ə|.reɪt, æk- -rates -reɪts -rating -reɪ.tɪŋ, (US) -reɪ.t̬ɪŋ -rated -reɪ.tɪd, (US) -reɪ.t̬ɪd

acceleration əkˌsel.əˈreɪ.ʃᵊn, æk- -s -z

A

accelerative əkˈsel.ə.rə.tɪv, æk-, (US) -ɚ.ə.t̬ɪv

accelerator əkˈsel.ə.reɪ.təʳ, æk-, (US) -t̬ɚ -s -z

accelerometer əkˌsel.əˈrɒm.ɪ.təʳ, æk-, ˈ-ə-, (US) -ˈrɑː.mə.t̬ɚ -s -z

accent n ˈæk.sᵊnt, (US) -sent -s -s

ac|cent v ək|ˈsent, æk-, (US) æk-, ək- -cents -ˈsents -centing -ˈsen.tɪŋ, (US) -ˈsen.t̬ɪŋ -cented -ˈsen.tɪd, (US) -ˈsen.t̬ɪd

accentual əkˈsen.tʃu.əl, æk-, -tju- -ly -i

accentu|ate əkˈsen.tʃu.eɪt, æk-, -tju- -ates -eɪts -ating -eɪ.tɪŋ, (US) -eɪ.t̬ɪŋ -ated -eɪ.tɪd, (US) -eɪ.t̬ɪd

accentuation əkˌsen.tʃuˈeɪ.ʃᵊn, æk-, -tjuˈ- -s -z

accept əkˈsept, æk- -s -s -ing -ɪŋ -ed -ɪd -er/s -əʳ/z, (US) -ɚ/z -or/s -əʳ/z, (US) -ɚ/z

acceptability əkˌsep.təˈbɪl.ə.ti, æk-, -ɪ.ti, (US) -ə.t̬i

acceptab|le əkˈsep.tə.b|ᵊl, æk- -ly -li -leness -ᵊl.nəs, -nɪs

acceptanc|e əkˈsep.tᵊnts, æk- -es -ɪz

acceptant əkˈsep.tᵊnt, æk- -s -s

acceptation ˌæk.sepˈteɪ.ʃᵊn -s -z

access, A~® ˈæk.ses -es -ɪz -ing -ɪŋ -ed -t

accessar|y əkˈses.ᵊr|.i, æk- -ies -iz

accessibility əkˌses.əˈbɪl.ə.ti, æk-, -ɪˈ-, -ɪ.ti, (US) -ə.t̬i

accessible əkˈses.ə.bᵊl, æk-, ˈ-ɪ-

accession əkˈseʃ.ᵊn, æk- -s -z

accessit ækˈses.ɪt -s -s

accessoriz|e, -is|e əkˈses.ᵊr.aɪz, (US) -ə.raɪz -es -ɪz -ing -ɪŋ -ed -d

accessor|y əkˈses.ᵊr|.i, æk- -ies -iz

acciaccatur|a əˌtʃæk.əˈtʊə.r|ə, (US) ɑːˌtʃɑː.kəˈtʊr|.ə -as -əz -e -eɪ, -iː

accidence ˈæk.sɪ.dᵊnts, -sə-

accident ˈæk.sɪ.dᵊnt, -sə- -s -s **ˈaccident-ˌprone**

accidental ˌæk.sɪˈden.tᵊl, -səˈ-, (US) -t̬ᵊl -ly -i

accidia ækˈsɪd.i.ə

accidie ˈæk.sɪ.di, -sə-

accipiter ækˈsɪp.ɪ.təʳ, ək-, -ə.təʳ, (US) -ə.t̬ɚ -s -z

acclaim əˈkleɪm -s -z -ing -ɪŋ -ed -d

acclamation ˌæk.ləˈmeɪ.ʃᵊn -s -z

acclamatory əˈklæm.ə.tᵊr.i, (US) -ə.tɔːr.i

acclimatation əˌklaɪ.məˈteɪ.ʃᵊn

acclima|te ˈæk.lɪ.meɪ|t, -lə-; əˈklaɪ.mə|t, (US) ˈæk.lə.meɪ|t; (US) əˈklaɪ.mə|t -tes -ts -ting -tɪŋ, (US) -t̬ɪŋ -ted -tɪd, (US) -t̬ɪd

acclimation ˌæk.lɪˈmeɪ.ʃᵊn

acclimatization, -isa- əˌklaɪ.mə.taɪˈzeɪ.ʃᵊn, -tɪˈ-, (US) -t̬əˈ-

acclimatiz|e, -is|e əˈklaɪ.mə.taɪz, -mɪ- -es -ɪz -ing -ɪŋ -ed -d

acclivit|y əˈklɪv.ə.t|i, ækˈlɪv-, -ɪt|i, (US) -t̬|i -ies -iz

accolade ˈæk.ə.leɪd, ˌ--ˈ- -s -z

accommo|date əˈkɒm.ə|.deɪt, (US) -ˈkɑː.mə- -dates -deɪts -dated -de.tɪd, (US) -deɪ.t̬ɪd -dator/s -deɪ.təʳ/z, (US) -deɪ.t̬ɚ/z -dative/ly -deɪ.tɪv/li, (US) -deɪ.t̬ɪv/li

accommodating əˈkɒm.ə.deɪ.tɪŋ, (US) əˈkɑː.mə.deɪ.t̬ɪŋ -ly -li

accommodation əˌkɒm.əˈdeɪ.ʃᵊn, (US) əˌkɑː.məˈ- -s -z

accompaniment əˈkʌm.pᵊn.ɪ.mənt -s -s

accompanist əˈkʌm.pə.nɪst -s -s

accompan|y əˈkʌm.pə.n|i -ies -iz -ying -i.ɪŋ -ied -id -yist/s -i.ɪsts -ier/s -i.əʳ/z, (US) -i.ɚ/z

accomplic|e əˈkʌm.plɪs, -ˈkɒm-, (US) -ˈkɑːm-, -ˈkʌm- -es -ɪz

accomplish əˈkʌm.plɪʃ, -ˈkɒm-, (US) -ˈkɑːm-, -ˈkʌm- -es -ɪz -ing -ɪŋ -ed -t

accomplishment əˈkʌm.plɪʃ.mənt, -ˈkɒm-, (US) -ˈkɑːm-, -ˈkʌm- -s -s

accord əˈkɔːd, (US) -ˈkɔːrd -ed -ɪd -ing -ɪŋ -s -z

accordan|ce əˈkɔː.dᵊn|ts, (US) -ˈkɔːr- -t -t

according əˈkɔː.dɪŋ, (US) -ˈkɔːr- -ly -li

accordion əˈkɔː.di.ən, (US) -ˈkɔːr- -s -z

accost əˈkɒst, (US) -ˈkɑːst -s -s -ing -ɪŋ -ed -ɪd

accouchement əˈkuːʃ.mɑ̃ːŋ, (US) -mɑːnt, ˌæk.uːʃˈmɑ̃ː

accoucheur ˌæk.uːˈʃɜːʳ, əˈkuː.ʃɜːʳ, (US) ˌæk.uːˈʃɝː -s -z

accoucheus|e ˌæk.uːˈʃɜːz, əˈkuː.ʃɜːz, (US) ˌæk.uːˈʃɜːz -es -ɪz

ac|count ə|ˈkaʊnt -counts -ˈkaʊnts -counting -ˈkaʊn.tɪŋ, (US) -ˈkaʊn.t̬ɪŋ -counted -ˈkaʊn.tɪd, (US) -ˈkaʊn.t̬ɪd **aˈccount ˌbook**

accountability əˌkaʊn.təˈbɪl.ə.ti, -ɪ.ti, (US) -t̬əˈbɪl.ə.t̬i

accountab|le əˈkaʊn.tə.b|ᵊl, (US) -t̬ə- -ly -li -leness -ᵊl.nəs, -nɪs

accountancy əˈkaʊn.tənt.si, (US) -t̬ənt-

accountant əˈkaʊn.tənt -s -s

accout|er əˈkuː.t|əʳ, (US) -t̬|ɚ -ers -əz, (US) -ɚz -ering -ᵊr.ɪŋ -ered -əd, (US) -ɚd -erment/s -ə.mənt/s, (US) -ɚ-

accout|re əˈkuː.t|əʳ, (US) əˈkuː.t̬|ɚ -res -əz -ring -ᵊr.ɪŋ -red -əd, (US) -ɚd -rement/s -rə.mənt/s, -ə.mənt/s, (US) -ɚ.mənt/s

Accra əˈkrɑː, ækˈrɑː

accred|it əˈkred|.ɪt -its -ɪts -iting -ɪ.tɪŋ, (US) -ɪ.t̬ɪŋ -ited -ɪ.tɪd, (US) -ɪ.t̬ɪd

accreditation əˌkred.ɪˈteɪ.ʃᵊn, (US) -əˈ-

accre|te əˈkriː|t, ækˈriː|t -tes -ts -ting -tɪŋ, (US) -t̬ɪŋ -ted -tɪd, (US) -t̬ɪd

accretion əˈkriː.ʃᵊn, ækˈriː- -s -z

accretive əˈkriː.tɪv, ækˈriː-, (US) əˈkriː.t̬ɪv

Accrington ˈæk.rɪŋ.tən

accrual əˈkruː.əl, -ˈkrʊəl, (US) -ˈkruː.əl

accru|e əˈkruː -es -z -ing -ɪŋ -ed -d

accruement əˈkruː.mənt

accultur|ate əˈkʌl.tʃᵊr|.eɪt, ækˈʌl-, (US) -tʃə.r|eɪt -ates -eɪts -ating -eɪ.tɪŋ, (US) -eɪ.t̬ɪŋ -ated -eɪ.tɪd, (US) -eɪ.t̬ɪd

acculturation əˌkʌl.tʃᵊrˈeɪ.ʃᵊn, ækˌʌl-, (US) -tʃəˈreɪ-

accumben|t əˈkʌm.bən|t -cy -t.si

accumu|late əˈkjuː.mjə|.leɪt, -mjʊ- -lates -leɪts -lating -leɪ.tɪŋ, (US) -leɪ.t̬ɪŋ -lated -leɪ.tɪd, (US) -leɪ.t̬ɪd -lator/s -leɪ.təʳ/z, (US) -leɪ.t̬ɚ/z

accumulation əˌkjuː.mjəˈleɪ.ʃᵊn, -mjʊˈ- -s -z

accumulative əˈkjuː.mjə.lə.tɪv, -mjʊ-, (US) -t̬ɪv

accuracy ˈæk.jə.rə.si, -jʊ-, (US) -jɚ.ə-, -jʊ.rə-

accurate ˈæk.jə.rət, -jʊ-, -rɪt, (US) -jɚ.ət, -jʊ.rət, -rɪt -ly -li -ness -nəs, -nɪs

accursed əˈkɜː.sɪd, -ˈkɜːst, (US) əˈkɝːst, -ˈkɝː.səd -ly -li

accusal əˈkjuː.zᵊl -s -z

accusation ˌæk.jʊˈzeɪ.ʃᵊn, -jəˈ- -s -z

accusatival əˌkjuː.zəˈtaɪ.vᵊl

accusative əˈkjuː.zə.tɪv, (US) -t̬ɪv -s -z

accusativity əˌkjuː.zəˈtɪv.ə.ti, -ɪ.ti, (US) -ə.t̬i

accusatory əˈkjuː.zə.tᵊr.i; ˌæk.jʊˈzeɪ-, -jəˈ-, -tri, (US) əˈkjuː.zə.tɔːr.i

accus|e əˈkjuːz -es -ɪz -ing/ly -ɪŋ/li -ed -d -er/s -əʳ/z, (US) -ɚ/z

accustom əˈkʌs.təm -s -z -ing -ɪŋ -ed/ness -d/nəs, -nɪs

AC/DC ˌeɪ.siːˈdiː.siː

ac|e eɪs -es -ɪz

acedia əˈsiː.di.ə

Aceldama əˈkel.də.mə, -ˈsel-; ˌæk.elˈdɑː-, (US) əˈsel.də-

-aceous ˈeɪ.ʃəs, ˈeɪ.ʃi.əs

Note: Suffix. Words containing **-aceous** always exhibit primary stress as shown above, e.g. **herbaceous** /hɜːˈbeɪ.ʃəs/ (US) /hɚ-/.

acephalous əˈsef.ᵊl.əs, ˌeɪ-, -ˈkef-, (US) eɪˈsef-, ə-

acequia əˈseɪ.ki.ə, -ˈsiː- -s -z

acer|bate ˈæs.ə.|beɪt, (US) ˈ-ɚ- -bates -beɪts -bating -beɪ.tɪŋ, (US) -beɪ.t̬ɪŋ -bated -beɪ.tɪd, (US) -beɪ.t̬ɪd

acerbic əˈsɜː.bɪk, æsˈɜː-, (US) əˈsɝː- -ally -ᵊl.i, -li

acerbity əˈsɜː.bə.ti, -bɪ-, (US) əˈsɝː.bə.t̬i

Acestes əˈses.tiːz, -ˈkes-

acetabul|um ˌæs.ɪˈtæb.jə.l|əm, -jʊ- -ums -əmz -a -ə -ar -əʳ, (US) -ɚ

acetaldehyde ˌæs.ɪˈtæl.dɪ.haɪd, -də-

acetaminophen əˌsiː.təˈmɪn.ə.fən, ˌæs.ɪ-, (US) ˌæs.ɪ.t̬əˈ-; (US) əˌsiː.t̬əˈ-, -ˌset̬.əˈ-

acetate ˈæs.ɪ.teɪt, ˈ-ə- -s -s

acetic əˈsiː.tɪk, æsˈiː-, -ˈet.ɪk, (US) əˈsiː.t̬ɪk **aˌcetic ˈacid**

acetif|y əˈsiː.tɪ.f|aɪ, ˈ-tə-, æsˈiː-, -ˈset.ɪ-, (US) -ˈset̬.ɪ-, -ˈset̬.ə- -ies -aɪz -ying -aɪ.ɪŋ -ied -aɪd

acetone ˈæs.ɪ.təʊn, ˈ-ə-, (US) -toʊn

acetose ˈæs.ɪ.təʊs, ˈ-ə-, -təʊz, (US) -toʊs

acetous ˈæs.ɪ.təs, ˈ-ə-, (US) ˈæs.ɪ.t̬əs; (US) əˈsiː-

acetum əˈsiː.təm, (US) -t̬əm

acetyl ˈæs.ɪ.taɪl, ˈ-ə-, -tɪl; əˈsiː-, -taɪl, (US) æˈset̬.əl, -iːl; (US) əˈsiː.t̬əl

acetyl|ate əˈset.ɪ.l|eɪt, -əl|.eɪt, (US) -ˈset̬.ə.l|eɪt, -ˈsiː.t̬ə- **-ates** -eɪts **-ating** -eɪ.tɪŋ, (US) -eɪ.t̬ɪŋ **-ated** -eɪ.tɪd, (US) -eɪ.t̬ɪd

acetylation əˌset.ɪˈleɪ.ʃən, -əlˈeɪ-, (US) -ˌset̬.əˈleɪ-

acetylcholine ˌæs.ɪ.taɪlˈkəʊ.liːn, ˌ-ə-, (US) əˌsiː.t̬əlˈkoʊ-, -ˌset̬.əlˈ-; (US) ˌæs.ə.t̬əlˈ-

acetylene əˈset.ɪ.liːn, -əl.iːn, (US) -ˈset̬.ə.liːn

Achae|a əˈkiː|.ə **-an/s** -ən/z

Achaia əˈkaɪ.ə

Achates əˈkeɪ.tiːz, -ˈkɑː-, (US) -t̬iːz

ach|e eɪk **-es** -s **-ing/ly** -ɪŋ/li **-ed** -t **-er/s** -ər/z, (US) -ɚ/z

Achebe əˈtʃeɪ.bi

Achernar ˈeɪ.kə.nɑːr, (US) -kɚ.nɑːr

Acheron ˈæk.ə.rɒn, -rən, (US) -rɑːn

Acheson ˈætʃ.ɪ.sən, ˈ-ə-

Acheulean, Acheulian əˈtʃuː.li.ən

à cheval ˌæ.ʃəˈvæl

achiev|e əˈtʃiːv **-es** -z **-ing** -ɪŋ **-ed** -d **-able** -ə.bəl **-er/s** -ər/z, (US) -ɚ/z

achievement əˈtʃiːv.mənt **-s** -s

Achil(l) ˈæk.ɪl

Achilles əˈkɪl.iːz **Aˌchilles ˈheel** (US) **Aˈchilles ˌheel**

Achille Serre ˌæʃ.ɪlˈseər, -iːlˈ-, (US) -ˈser

Achin əˈtʃiːn

Achish ˈeɪ.kɪʃ

achondro|plasia əˌkɒn.drəʊ|ˈpleɪ.zi.ə, -ʒə, (US) -ˌkɑːn.drə|ˈpleɪ.ʒi.ə, ˌeɪ- **-plastic** -ˈplæs.tɪk

achoo əˈtʃuː, (US) əˈtʃuː, ˈæ.tʃuː

Achray əˈkreɪ, əˈxreɪ

achromatic ˌæk.rəʊˈmæt.ɪk, ˌeɪ.krəʊ-, (US) ˌæk.rəˈmæt̬- **-ally** -əl.i, -li *stress shift:* **ˌachromatic ˈlens**

achromatism əˈkrəʊ.mə.tɪ.zəm, ˌeɪ-, (US) -ˈkroʊ-

achromatiz|e, -is|e əˈkrəʊ.mə.taɪz, ˌeɪ-, (US) -ˈkroʊ- **-es** -ɪz **-ing** -ɪŋ **-ed** -d

achromatous əˈkrəʊ.mə.təs, ˌeɪ-, (US) -ˈkroʊ.mə.t̬əs

achtung ˈɑːx.tʊŋ, ˈæx-, (US) ˈɑːx-, ˈɑːk-

achy ˈeɪ.ki

acicul|a əˈsɪk.jʊ.l|ə, -jə- **-ae** -i **-ar** -ə

acid ˈæs.ɪd **-s** -z **-ly** -li **-ness** -nəs, -nɪs ˈ**acid ˌdrop**; ˌ**acid ˈrain**; ˌ**acid ˈtest**; ˈ**acid ˌtest**

acidhead ˈæs.ɪd.hed **-s** -z

acidic əˈsɪd.ɪk

acidif|y əˈsɪd.ɪ.f|aɪ, ˈ-ə-, æsˈɪd- **-ies** -aɪz **-ying** -aɪ.ɪŋ **-ied** -aɪd

acidity əˈsɪd.ə.ti, æsˈɪd-, -ɪ.ti, (US) -ə.t̬i

acidiz|e, -is|e ˈæs.ɪ.daɪz **-es** -ɪz **-ing** -ɪŋ **-ed** -d

acidophilus ˌæs.ɪˈdɒf.ɪ.ləs, -əl.əs, (US) -ˈdɑː.fəl.əs

acidosis ˌæs.ɪˈdəʊ.sɪs, (US) -ˈdoʊ-

acidu|late əˈsɪd.jʊ|.leɪt, æsˈɪd-, -jə-, -ˈsɪdʒ.ʊ-, ˈ-ə- **-lates** -leɪts **-lating** -leɪ.tɪŋ, (US) -leɪ.t̬ɪŋ **-lated** -leɪ.tɪd, (US) -leɪ.t̬ɪd

acidulous əˈsɪdʒ.ə.ləs, æsˈɪdʒ-, ˈ-ʊ-, -ˈsɪd.jə-, ˈ-jʊ-

acin|ose ˈæs.ɪ.n|əʊs, -n|əʊz, (US) -n|oʊs, -n|oʊz **-ous** -əs

acin|us ˈæs.ɪ.n|əs **-i** -aɪ

Acis ˈeɪ.sɪs

ack-ack ˌækˈæk *stress shift:* **ˌack-ack ˈgun**

ackee ˈæk.i **-s** -z

Ackerley ˈæk.əl.i, (US) -ɚ.li

Ackerman(n) ˈæk.ə.mən, -mæn, (US) ˈ-ɚ-

Ackland ˈæk.lənd

acknowledg|e əkˈnɒl.ɪdʒ, æk-, (US) -ˈnɑː.lɪdʒ **-es** -ɪz **-ing** -ɪŋ **-ed** -d **-eable** -ə.bəl

acknowledg(e)ment əkˈnɒl.ɪdʒ.mənt, æk-, (US) -ˈnɑː.lɪdʒ- **-s** -s

Ackroyd ˈæk.rɔɪd

Ackworth Moor Top ˌæk.wəθˌmɔːˈtɒp, (US) -wɚθˌmʊrˈtɑːp

Acland ˈæk.lənd

ACLU ˌeɪ.siː.elˈjuː

acme ˈæk.mi **-s** -z

acne ˈæk.ni

Acol *road in London, system of bridge playing:* ˈæk.əl *in Kent:* ˈeɪ.kɒl, (US) -kɑːl

acolyte ˈæk.əl.aɪt, (US) -ə.laɪt **-s** -s

Acomb ˈeɪ.kəm

Aconcagua ˌæk.ɒnˈkæg.wə, -ɒŋˈ-, (US) ˌɑː.kənˈ-, -kəŋˈ-, -kɑː.gwə

aconite ˈæk.ə.naɪt **-s** -s

acorn ˈeɪ.kɔːn, (US) -kɔːrn **-s** -z ˈ**acorn ˌsquash**

acotyledon əˌkɒt.ɪˈliː.dən, ˌeɪ-, -əlˈiː-, (US) -ˌkɑː.t̬əˈliː- **-s** -z

acouchi əˈkuː.ʃi, (US) ɑːˈkuː.ʃi, ə-

acoustic əˈkuː.stɪk **-s** -s **-ally** -əl.i, -li

acoustician ˌæ.kuːˈstɪʃ.ən **-s** -z

acoustooptic əˌkuː.stəʊˈɒp.tɪk, (US) -stoʊˈɑːp- **-s** -s **-al** -əl

ac|quaint ə|ˈkweɪnt **-quaints** -ˈkweɪnts **-quainting** -ˈkweɪn.tɪŋ, (US) -ˈkweɪn.t̬ɪŋ **-quainted** -ˈkweɪn.tɪd, (US) -ˈkweɪn.t̬ɪd

acquaintanc|e əˈkweɪn.tənts **-es** -ɪz

acquaintanceship əˈkweɪn.tənts.ʃɪp, -tənt.ʃɪp **-s** -s

acquest əˈkwest **-s** -s

acquiesc|e ˌæk.wiˈes **-es** -ɪz **-ing** -ɪŋ **-ed** -t **-ence** -ənts **-ent/ly** -ənt/li

acquir|e əˈkwaɪər, -ˈkwaɪ.ər, (US) -ˈkwaɪ.ɚ **-es** -z **-ing** -ɪŋ **-ed** -d **-ement/s** -mənt/s **-able** -ə.bəl

acquisition ˌæk.wɪˈzɪʃ.ən, -wə- **-s** -z

acquisitive əˈkwɪz.ə.tɪv, ˈ-ɪ-, (US) -ə.t̬ɪv **-ly** -li **-ness** -nəs, -nɪs

acquit əˈkwɪt **-s** -s **-ting** -ɪŋ, (US) əˈkwɪt̬.ɪŋ **-ted** -ɪd, (US) əˈkwɪt̬.ɪd

acquittal əˈkwɪt.əl, (US) -ˈkwɪt̬- **-s** -z

acquittance əˈkwɪt.ənts

acre, A~ ˈeɪ.kər, (US) -kɚ **-s** -z

acreag|e ˈeɪ.kər.ɪdʒ, ˈ-krɪdʒ **-es** -ɪz

acrid ˈæk.rɪd **-ly** -li **-ness** -nəs, -nɪs

acridine ˈæk.rɪ.diːn, -daɪn

acridity əˈkrɪd.ə.ti, ækˈrɪd-, -ɪ.ti, (US) -ə.t̬i

Acrilan® ˈæk.rɪ.læn, -rə-

acrimonious ˌæk.rɪˈməʊ.ni.əs, -rəˈ-, (US) -ˈmoʊ- **-ly** -li **-ness** -nəs, -nɪs

acrimon|y ˈæk.rɪ.mə.n|i, -rə-, (US) -moʊ- **-ies** -iz

acritical ˌeɪˈkrɪt.ɪ.kəl, (US) -ˈkrɪt̬.-

acritude ˈæk.rɪ.tʃuːd, -rə-, -tjuːd, (US) -tuːd, -tjuːd

acro- ˈæk.rəʊ; əˈkrɒ, (US) ˈæk.rə, -roʊ; (US) əˈkrɑː

Note: Prefix. Either takes primary or secondary stress on the first syllable, e.g. **acrosome** /ˈæk.rəʊ.səʊm/ (US) /-rə.soʊm/, **acrosomal** /ˌæk.rəʊˈsəʊ.məl/ (US) /-rəˈsoʊ-/, or primary stress only on the second syllable, e.g. **acropolis** /əˈkrɒp.ə.lɪs/ (US) /-ˈkrɑː.pə-/.

acrobat ˈæk.rə.bæt **-s** -s

acrobatic ˌæk.rəˈbæt.ɪk, (US) -ˈbæt̬- **-s** -s **-ally** -əl.i, -li *stress shift:* **ˌacrobatic ˈleap**

acrobatism ˈæk.rə.bæt.ɪ.zəm, ˌæk.rəˈbæt-, (US) ˈæk.rə.bæt̬-, ˌæk.rəˈbæt̬-

acrogen ˈæk.rəʊ.dʒən, -dʒen, (US) -roʊ-, -rə- **-s** -z

acrolect ˈæk.rəʊ.lekt, (US) -roʊ-, -rə- **-s** -s **-al** -əl

acrolith ˈæk.rəʊ.lɪθ, (US) -roʊ-, -rə- **-s** -s

acromegalic ˌæk.rəʊ.mɪˈgæl.ɪk, -məˈ-, (US) -roʊ-

acromegaly ˌæk.rəʊˈmeg.əl.i, (US) -roʊˈ-

acromion əˈkrəʊ.mi.ən, (US) -ˈkroʊ- **-s** -z

acronym ˈæk.rəʊ.nɪm, (US) -rə- **-s** -z

acropetal əˈkrɒp.ɪ.təl, (US) -ˈkrɑː.pə.t̬əl **-ly** -i

acrophob|ia ˌæk.rəʊˈfəʊ.b|i.ə, (US) -rəˈfoʊ- **-ic** -ɪk

acropolis, A~ əˈkrɒp.ə.lɪs, (US) -ˈkrɑː.pə- **-es** -ɪz

acrosomal ˌæk.rəʊˈsəʊ.məl, (US) -rəˈsoʊ-

acrosome ˈæk.rəʊ.səʊm, (US) -rə.soʊm

across əˈkrɒs, (US) -ˈkrɑːs

across-the-board əˌkrɒs.ðəˈbɔːd, (US) -ˌkrɑːs.ðəˈbɔːrd

acrostic əˈkrɒs.tɪk, (US) -ˈkrɑː.stɪk **-s** -s

Acrux ˈeɪ.krʌks

acrylic əˈkrɪl.ɪk, ækˈrɪl- **-s** -s

act ækt **-s** -s **-ing** -ɪŋ **-ed** -ɪd **get ˌin on the ˈact**; **ˌget one's ˈact together**

ACT ˌeɪ.siːˈtiː

acta ˈæk.tə

Actaeon ˈæk.ti.ən, (US) ækˈtiː-

ACTH ˌeɪ.siː.tiːˈeɪtʃ, ækθ

actinic ækˈtɪn.ɪk **-ly** -li

actinide ˈæk.tɪn.aɪd **-s** -z

actinism ˈæk.tɪn.ɪz.əm

actinium ækˈtɪn.i.əm

A

action ˈæk.ʃᵊn **-s** -z **-ing** -ɪŋ **-ed** -d ˈ**action** ˌ**man**; ˈ**action** ˌ**stations**

actionable ˈæk.ʃᵊn.ə.bᵊl

action-packed ˌæk.ʃᵊnˈpækt *stress shift:* ˌ**action-packed** ˈ**movie**

Actium ˈæk.ti.əm

activable ˈæk.tɪv.ə.bᵊl

acti|vate ˈæk.tɪ|.veɪt **-vates** -veɪts **-vating** -veɪ.tɪŋ, (US) -veɪ.t̬ɪŋ **-vated** -veɪ.tɪd, (US) -veɪ.t̬ɪd **-vator/s** -veɪ.təʳ/z, (US) -veɪ.t̬ɚ/z

activation ˌæk.tɪˈveɪ.ʃᵊn

active ˈæk.tɪv **-ly** -li **-ness** -nəs, -nɪs

activ|ism ˈæk.tɪ.v|ɪ.zᵊm **-ist/s** -ɪst/s

activit|y ækˈtɪv.ə.t|i, -ɪ.t|i, (US) -ə.t̬|i **-ies** -iz

activiz|e ˈæk.tɪ.vaɪz **-es** -ɪz **-ing** -ɪŋ **-ed** -d

Acton ˈæk.tən

actor ˈæk.təʳ, (US) -tɚ **-s** -z

actress ˈæk.trəs, -trɪs **-es** -ɪz

Acts ækts

actual ˈæk.tʃu.əl, -tju-, -tʃᵊl, -tʃʊl, (US) -tʃu.əl, -tju.əl, -tʃᵊl, -tʃʊl **-ly** -i

actualit|y ˌæk.tʃuˈæl.ə.t|i, -tju-, -ɪ.t|i, (US) -tʃuˈæl.ə.t̬|i, -tju- **-ies** -iz

actualiz|e, -is|e ˈæk.tʃu.ə.laɪz, -tju-, -ʃu-, (US) -tʃu-, -tju- **-es** -ɪz **-ing** -ɪŋ **-ed** -d

actuarial ˌæk.tʃuˈeə.ri.əl, -tju-, (US) -tʃuˈer.i-, -tju-

actuar|y ˈæk.tʃu.ə.r|i, -tju.er|i, (US) -tʃu-, -tju- **-ies** -iz

actu|ate ˈæk.tʃu|.eɪt, -tju-, (US) -tʃu-, -tju- **-ates** -eɪts **-ating** -eɪ.tɪŋ, (US) -eɪ.t̬ɪŋ **-ated** -eɪ.tɪd, (US) -eɪ.t̬ɪd

actuation ˌæk.tʃuˈeɪ.ʃᵊn, -tjuˈ-, (US) -tʃuˈ-, -tjuˈ- **-s** -z

Act-Up ˌæktˈʌp

acuity əˈkjuː.ə.ti, -ɪt.i, (US) -ə.t̬i

.ac.uk dɒtˌeɪ.siː.dɒt.juˈkeɪ, ˌdɒt.eɪ.siːˌdɒt-; ˌækˈʌk, (US) dɑːtˌeɪ.siː.dɑːt.juˈkeɪ, ˌdɑːt.eɪ.siːˌdɑːt-; (US) ˌækˈʌk

acumen ˈæk.jʊ.mən, -jə-, -men, (US) əˈkjuː.mən, ˈæk.jə-

acupressure ˈæk.jʊ.preʃ.əʳ, -jə-, (US) -ɚ

acupunctur|e ˈæk.jʊ.pʌŋk.tʃəʳ, -jə-, (US) -tʃɚ **-ist/s** -ɪst/s

a|cute ə|ˈkjuːt **-cuter** -ˈkjuː.təʳ, (US) -ˈkjuː.t̬ɚ **-cutest** -ˈkjuː.tɪst, -təst, (US) -ˈkjuː.t̬ɪst, -t̬əst **-cutely** -ˈkjuːt.li **-cuteness** -ˈkjuːt.nəs, -nɪs aˌ**cute** ˈ**angle**

acyl ˈæs.ɪl **-s** -z

ad æd **-s** -z

AD (abbrev. for **Anno Domini**) ˌeɪˈdiː, ˌæn.əʊˈdɒm.ɪ.naɪ, (US) ˌeɪˈdiː, ˌæn.oʊˈdɑː.mə.niː, -ˈdoʊ-, -naɪ

ad- ˈæd, əd

Note: Prefix. Examples include **adjective** /ˈædʒ.ɪk.tɪv/, in which it is stressed, and **admonish** /ədˈmɒn.ɪʃ/ (US) /-ˈmɑː.nɪʃ/, where it is unstressed.

Ada ˈeɪ.də

ADA ˌeɪ.diːˈeɪ

adactylous ˌeɪˈdæk.tɪ.ləs

adag|e ˈæd.ɪdʒ **-es** -ɪz

adagio əˈdɑː.dʒi.əʊ, ˈ-ʒi-, (US) -ˈdɑː.dʒoʊ, -dʒi.oʊ **-s** -z

Adair əˈdeəʳ, (US) -ˈder

Adalbert ˈæd.ᵊl.bɜːt, (US) -bɝːt

Adam ˈæd.əm ˌ**Adam's** ˈ**apple** (US) ˈ**Adam's** ˌ**apple**

adamant ˈæd.ə.mənt **-ly** -li

adamantine ˌæd.əˈmæn.taɪn, (US) -tiːn, -taɪn, -tᵊn

adamite, A~ ˈæd.ə.maɪt **-s** -s

Adams ˈæd.əmz

adamsite ˈæd.əm.zaɪt

Adamson ˈæd.əm.sᵊn

Adamthwaite ˈæd.əm.θweɪt

Adana ˈɑː.də.nə; əˈdɑː-

Adapazari ˌɑː.dəˈpɑː.zᵊr.i, (US) -ˌpɑː.zəˈriː

adapt əˈdæpt **-s** -s **-ing** -ɪŋ **-ed** -ɪd **-ive** -ɪv

adaptability əˌdæp.təˈbɪl.ə.ti, -ɪt.i, (US) -ə.t̬i

adaptable əˈdæp.tə.bᵊl **-ness** -nəs, -nɪs

adaptation ˌæd.æpˈteɪ.ʃᵊn, -əpˈ- **-s** -z

adapter əˈdæp.təʳ, (US) -tɚ **-s** -z

adaption əˈdæp.ʃən, ædˈæp- **-s** -z

adaptive əˈdæp.tɪv, ædˈæp- **-ly** -li

adaptor əˈdæp.təʳ, (US) -tɚ **-s** -z

Adare əˈdeəʳ, (US) -ˈder

Adar Sheni ɑːˌdɑːˈʃeɪ.ni, (US) -ˌdɑːrˈ-

ADC ˌeɪ.diːˈsiː

Adcock ˈæd.kɒk, (US) -kɑːk

add æd **-s** -z **-ing** -ɪŋ **-ed** -ɪd

ADD ˌeɪ.diːˈdiː

Addams ˈæd.əmz

addax ˈæd.æks **-es** -ɪz

added-value ˌæd.ɪdˈvæl.juː *stress shift:* ˌ**added-value** ˈ**costs**

addend əˈdend, ædˈend, (US) ˈæd.end; (US) əˈdend **-s** -z

addend|um əˈden.d|əm, ædˈen- **-a** -ə

adder ˈæd.əʳ, (US) -ɚ **-s** -z ˈ**adder's** ˌ**tongue**

adderwort ˈæd.ə.wɜːt, (US) -ɚ.wɝːt, -wɔːrt

addict **n** ˈæd.ɪkt **-s** -s

addict **v** əˈdɪkt **-s** -s **-ing** -ɪŋ **-ed/ness** -ɪd/nəs, -nɪs

addiction əˈdɪk.ʃᵊn **-s** -z

addictive əˈdɪk.tɪv **-ly** -li **-ness** -nəs, -nɪs

Addington ˈæd.ɪŋ.tən

Addis ˈæd.ɪs

Addis Ababa ˌæd.ɪsˈæb.ə.bə, -ˈɑːb-

Addiscombe ˈæd.ɪ.skəm

Addison ˈæd.ɪ.sən

addition əˈdɪʃ.ᵊn **-s** -z

additional əˈdɪʃ.ᵊn.ᵊl **-ly** -i

additive ˈæd.ə.tɪv, ˈ-ɪ-, (US) -ə.t̬ɪv **-s** -z

addl|e ˈæd.ᵊl **-es** -z **-ing** -ɪŋ, ˈæd.lɪŋ **-ed** -d

addleheaded ˌæd.ᵊl|ˈhed.ɪd, (US) ˈæd.ᵊl|ˌhed- *stress shift, British only:* ˌ**addleheaded** ˈ**person**

Addlestone ˈæd.ᵊl.stən

add-on ˈæd.ɒn, (US) -ɑːn **-s** -z

address **n** əˈdres, (US) ˈæd.res, əˈdres **-es** -ɪz aˈ**ddress** ˌ**book** (US) ˈ**address** ˌ**book**

address **v** əˈdres **-es** -ɪz **-ing** -ɪŋ **-ed** -t

addressable əˈdres.ə.bᵊl

addressee ˌæd.resˈiː **-s** -z

Addressograph® əˈdres.ə.grɑːf, -græf, (US) -oʊ.græf, -ə- **-s** -s

adduc|e əˈdʒuːs, -ˈdjuːs-, ædˈjuːs, (US) əˈduːs, -ˈdjuːs **-es** -ɪz **-ing** -ɪŋ **-ed** -t **-er/s** -əʳ/z, (US) -ɚ/z **-ible** -ə.bᵊl, -ɪ.bᵊl

adducent əˈdʒuː.sᵊnt, -ˈdjuː-, (US) -ˈduː-, -ˈdjuː-

adduct əˈdʌkt **-s** -s **-ing** -ɪŋ **-ed** -ɪd **-ive** -ɪv

adduction əˈdʌk.ʃᵊn

adductor əˈdʌk.təʳ, (US) -tɚ **-s** -z

Ade eɪd

-ade eɪd, ɑːd

Note: Suffix. Generally carries primary stress, e.g. **lemonade** /ˌlem.əˈneɪd/, but see individual entries. For instance, **escapade** is also /ˈes.kə.peɪd/. In words derived from French it is often pronounced /-ɑːd/, e.g. **roulade** is /ruːˈlɑːd/.

Adeane əˈdiːn

Adel ˈæd.ᵊl

Adela *English name:* ˈæd.ɪ.lə, ˈ-ə- *foreign name:* əˈdeɪ.lə

Adelaide ˈæd.ᵊl.eɪd, -ɪ.leɪd, (US) -ə.leɪd

Adele əˈdel

Adelina ˌæd.ɪˈliː.nə, -ᵊlˈiː-, (US) -əˈliː-

Adeline ˈæd.ɪ.liːn, -ᵊl.iːn, -aɪn, (US) -ə.laɪn, -liːn

Adelphi əˈdel.fi

Aden *in Yemen:* ˈeɪ.dᵊn, (US) ˈɑː-, ˈeɪ- *in Aberdeenshire:* ˈæd.ᵊn

Adenauer ˈæd.ᵊn.aʊ.əʳ, ˈɑː.dᵊn-, (US) -ɚ

adenoid ˈæd.ᵊ.nɔɪd, -ɪn.ɔɪd, (US) -ᵊn.ɔɪd; (US) ˈæd.nɔɪd **-s** -z

adenoidal ˌæd.ᵊˈnɔɪ.dᵊl, -ɪnˈɔɪ-, (US) -ᵊnˈɔɪ-; (US) ædˈnɔɪ-

adenoidectom|y ˌæd.ᵊ.nɔɪˈdek.tə.m|i, -ɪn.ɔɪˈ-, (US) -ᵊn.ɔɪˈ-; (US) ˌæd.nɔɪˈ- **-ies** -iz

adenoma ˌæd.ɪˈnəʊ.mə, -əˈ-, (US) -ˈnoʊ- **-s** -z **-tous** -təs, (US) -t̬əs

adenosine ædˈen.əʊ.siːn, əˈden-; ˌæd.ɪˈnəʊ-, (US) əˈden.ə.siːn, -sᵊn

adept **n** ˈæd.ept, əˈdept, ædˈept **-s** -s

adept **adj** əˈdept, ædˈept; ˈæd.ept, (US) əˈdept **-ly** -li

adequacy ˈæd.ɪ.kwə.si, ˈ-ə-

adequate ˈæd.ɪ.kwət, ˈ-ə-, -kwɪt **-ly** -li **-ness** -nəs, -nɪs

adessive əˈdes.ɪv, ædˈes-

à deux æˈdɜː

ADHD ˌeɪ.diː.eɪtʃˈdiː

adher|e ədˈhɪəʳ, æd-; əˈdɪəʳ, (US) ədˈhɪr, æd- **-es** -z **-ing** -ɪŋ **-ed** -d **-er/s** -əʳ/z, (US) -ɚ/z

adheren|ce ədˈhɪə.rᵊn|ts, æd-, -ˈher.ᵊn|ts; əˈdɪə.rᵊn|ts, (US) ədˈhɪr.ᵊn|ts, æd- **-t/s** -t/s

adhesion ədˈhiː.ʒən, æd-; əˈdiː- **-s** -z

adhesive ədˈhiː.sɪv, æd-, -zɪv; əˈdiː.sɪv, -zɪv **-ly** -li **-ness** -nɪs, -nəs
ad hoc ˌædˈhɒk, -ˈhəʊk, (US) -ˈhɑːk, -ˈhoʊk
ad hominem ˌædˈhɒm.ɪ.nəm, ˈ-ə-, -nem, (US) -ˈhɑː.mə.nəm, -nem
adiabatic ˌeɪ.daɪ.əˈbæt.ɪk, ˌæd.aɪ.ə-, (US) ˌæd.i.əˈbæţ-; (US) ˌeɪ.daɪ.əˈ- **-ally** -əl.i, -li
Adidas® ˈæd.ɪ.dæs; əˈdiː.dəs, (US) əˈdiː.dəs
Adie ˈeɪ.di
adieu əˈdjuː; *as if French:* ædˈjɜː; (US) əˈduː, -ˈdjuː
adieus, adieux əˈdjuː, -ˈdjuːz; *as if French:* ædˈjɜː; (US) əˈduːz, -ˈdjuːz
Adige ˈæd.ɪ.dʒeɪ, (US) ˈɑː.di.dʒeɪ, -ə
ad infinitum ˌæd.ɪn.fɪˈnaɪ.təm, (US) ˌæd.ɪn.fɪˈnaɪ.ţəm, ˌɑːd-
adios ˌæd.iˈɒs, (US) ˌɑː.diˈoʊs, ˌæd.iˈ-
adipocere ˌæd.ɪ.pəʊˈsɪəʳ, (US) ˈæd.ə.poʊ.sɪr, -pə-
adipose ˈæd.ɪ.pəʊs, -pəʊz, (US) -ə.poʊs
adiposity ˌæd.ɪˈpɒs.ə.ti, -ɪ.ti, (US) -əˈpɑː.sə.ţi
Adirondack ˌæd.ɪˈrɒn.dæk, -əˈrɒn-, (US) -ˈrɑːn- **-s** -s
adit ˈæd.ɪt **-s** -s
adjacency əˈdʒeɪ.sənt.si
adjacent əˈdʒeɪ.sənt **-ly** -li
adjectival ˌædʒ.ɪkˈtaɪ.vəl, -ekˈ-, -əkˈ- **-ly** -i
adjective ˈædʒ.ɪk.tɪv, -ek-, -ək- **-s** -z
adjoin əˈdʒɔɪn **-s** -z **-ing** -ɪŋ **-ed** -d
adjourn əˈdʒɜːn, (US) -ˈdʒɝːn **-s** -z **-ing** -ɪŋ **-ed** -d **-ment/s** -mənt/s
adjudg|e əˈdʒʌdʒ, ædʒˈʌdʒ, (US) əˈdʒʌdʒ **-es** -ɪz **-ing** -ɪŋ **-ed** -d **-ment/s** -mənt/s
adjudi|cate əˈdʒuː.dɪ|.keɪt, -də- **-cates** -keɪts **-cating** -keɪ.tɪŋ, (US) -keɪ.ţɪŋ **-cated** -keɪ.tɪd, (US) -keɪ.ţɪd
adjudication əˌdʒuː.dɪˈkeɪ.ʃən, -dəˈ- **-s** -z
adjudicator əˈdʒuː.dɪ.keɪ.təʳ, -də-, (US) -ţɚ **-s** -z
adjunct ˈædʒ.ʌŋkt **-s** -s **-ly** -li; əˈdʒʌŋkt.li
adjunction əˈdʒʌŋk.ʃən, ædʒˈʌŋk-
adjunctival ˌædʒ.ʌŋkˈtaɪ.vəl
adjuration ˌædʒ.əˈreɪ.ʃən, -ʊəˈ-, -ɔːˈ-, (US) -əˈ- **-s** -z
adjur|e əˈdʒʊəʳ, -ɔːʳ, (US) -dʒʊr **-es** -z **-ing** -ɪŋ **-ed** -d
adjust əˈdʒʌst **-s** -s **-ing** -ɪŋ **-ed** -ɪd **-able** -ə.bəl **-er/s** -əʳ/z, (US) -ɚ/z
adjustment əˈdʒʌst.mənt **-s** -s
adjutage ˈædʒ.ʊ.tɪdʒ; əˈdʒuː-
adjutan|cy ˈædʒ.ʊ.tən|t.si, ˈ-ə- **-t/s** -t/s
Adkins ˈæd.kɪnz
Adkinson ˈæd.kɪn.sən
Adlai ˈæd.leɪ
Adler ˈæd.ləʳ, ˈɑːd.ləʳ, (US) -lɚ
ad-lib ˌædˈlɪb **-s** -z **-bing** -ɪŋ **-bed** -d
Adlington ˈæd.lɪŋ.tən
ad|man ˈæd.mæn, -mən **-men** -men, -mən
admass ˈæd.mæs
admeasur|e ædˈmeʒ.əʳ, əd-, (US) -ɚ, -ˈmeɪ.ʒɚ **-es** -z **-ing** -ɪŋ **-ed** -d **-ement/s** -mənt/s
Admetus ædˈmiː.təs, (US) -ţəs
admin ˈæd.mɪn
administer ədˈmɪn.ɪ.stəʳ, -ə-, (US) -stɚ, æd- **-s** -z **-ing** -ɪŋ **-ed** -d
administr|able ədˈmɪn.ɪ.str|ə.bəl, ˈ-ə-, (US) əd-, æd- **-ant/s** -ənt/s
admini|strate ədˈmɪn.ɪ|.streɪt, ˈ-ə-, (US) əd-, æd- **-strates** -streɪts **-strating** -streɪ.tɪŋ, (US) -streɪ.ţɪŋ **-strated** -streɪ.tɪd, (US) -streɪ.ţɪd
administration ədˌmɪn.ɪˈstreɪ.ʃən, -əˈ-, (US) əd-, æd- **-s** -z
administrative ədˈmɪn.ɪ.strə.tɪv, ˈ-ə-, -streɪ-, (US) əd-, æd- **-ly** -li
administrator ədˈmɪn.ɪ.streɪ.təʳ, ˈ-ə-, (US) -ţɚ, æd- **-s** -z **-ship/s** -ʃɪp/s
administra|trix ədˈmɪn.ɪ.streɪ|.trɪks, ˈ-ə-, (US) əd-, æd- **-trixes** -trɪk.sɪz **-trices** -trɪ.siːz
admirab|le ˈæd.mər.ə.b|əl **-ly** -li **-leness** -əl.nəs, -nɪs
admiral ˈæd.mər.əl, -mɪ.rəl **-s** -z
admiralt|y, A~ ˈæd.mər.əl.t|i, -mɪ.rəl-, (US) -t|i **-ies** -iz
admiration ˌæd.məˈreɪ.ʃən, -mɪˈ-
admir|e ədˈmaɪəʳ, -ˈmaɪ.əʳ, (US) -ˈmaɪ.ɚ, æd- **-es** -z **-ing/ly** -ɪŋ/li **-ed** -d **-er/s** -əʳ/z, (US) -ɚ/z
admissibility ədˌmɪs.əˈbɪl.ə.ti, æd-, -ɪˈ-, -ɪ.ti, (US) -ə.ţi
admissibl|e ədˈmɪs.ə.b|əl, æd-, -ɪ- **-y** -i
admission ədˈmɪʃ.ən, æd- **-s** -z
ad|mit əd|ˈmɪt **-mits** -ˈmɪts **-mitting** -ˈmɪt.ɪŋ, (US) -ˈmɪţ.ɪŋ **-mitted/ly** -ˈmɪt.ɪd/li, (US) -ˈmɪţ.ɪd/li
admittanc|e ədˈmɪt.ənts **-es** -ɪz
admix ædˈmɪks, əd- **-es** -ɪz **-ing** -ɪŋ **-ed** -t
admixture ədˈmɪks.tʃəʳ, æd- **-s** -z
admonish ədˈmɒn.ɪʃ, æd-, (US) -ˈmɑː.nɪʃ **-es** -ɪz **-ing/ly** -ɪŋ/li **-ed** -t **-ment/s** -mənt/s
admonition ˌæd.məˈnɪʃ.ən **-s** -z
admonitory ədˈmɒn.ɪ.tər.i, æd-, (US) -ˈmɑː.nə.tɔːr-
Adnams ˈæd.nəmz
ad nauseam ˌædˈnɔː.zi.æm, -si-, -əm, (US) -ˈnɑː-, -ˈnɔː-
adnominal ˌædˈnɒm.ɪn.əl, (US) -ˈnɑːm- **-s** -z
ado əˈduː
adobe, A~® əˈdəʊ.bi, ædˈəʊ-, (US) -ˈdoʊ- **-s** -z
adolescence ˌæd.əlˈes.ənts, -əʊˈles-, (US) -əˈles-
adolescent ˌæd.əlˈes.ənt, -əʊˈles-, (US) -əˈles- **-s** -s
Adolf ˈæd.ɒlf, (US) ˈeɪ.dɑːlf, ˈæd.ɑːlf
Adolphus əˈdɒl.fəs, (US) -ˈdɑːl-
Adonai ˈæd.əʊ.naɪ, (US) ˌɑː.dəˈnaɪ, -doʊˈ-, -ˈnɔɪ
Adonais ˌæd.əʊˈneɪ.ɪs, (US) -əˈ-
Adonijah ˌæd.əʊˈnaɪ.dʒə, (US) -əˈ-
Adonis əˈdəʊ.nɪs, -ˈdɒn.ɪs, (US) -ˈdɑː.nɪs, -ˈdoʊ-
adopt əˈdɒpt, (US) -ˈdɑːpt **-s** -s **-ing** -ɪŋ **-ed** -ɪd **-ive** -ɪv **-er/s** -əʳ/z, (US) -ɚ/z
adoption əˈdɒp.ʃən, (US) -ˈdɑːp- **-s** -z
adoptionism əˈdɒp.ʃən.ɪ.zəm, (US) -ˈdɑːp-
adorab|le əˈdɔː.rə.b|əl, (US) -ˈdɔːr.ə- **-ly** -li **-leness** -əl.nəs, -nɪs
adoration ˌæd.əˈreɪ.ʃən, -ɔːˈ-, (US) -əˈreɪ- **-s** -z
ador|e əˈdɔːʳ, (US) -ˈdɔːr **-es** -z **-ing/ly** -ɪŋ/li **-ed** -d **-er/s** -əʳ/z, (US) -ɚ/z
adorn əˈdɔːn, (US) -ˈdɔːrn **-s** -z **-ing** -ɪŋ **-ed** -d **-ment/s** -mənt/s
Adorno əˈdɔː.nəʊ, (US) -ˈdɔːr.noʊ
ADP ˌeɪ.diːˈpiː
Adrastus əˈdræs.təs
adrenal əˈdriː.nəl aˌdrenal ˈgland
adrenalin(e) əˈdren.əl.ɪn, (US) -ə.lɪn
adrenocortical əˌdriː.nəʊˈkɔː.tɪ.kəl, (US) -noʊˈkɔːr.ţɪ-, -ˌdren.oʊˈ-, -əˈ-
adrenocorticotroph|ic əˌdriː.nəʊˌkɔː.tɪ.kəʊˈtrɒf|.ɪk, (US) -noʊˌkɔːr.ţɪ.koʊˈtroʊ.f|ɪk, -ˌdren.oʊˌ-, -əˌ-, -ˈtrɑː- **-in** -ɪn
Adria ˈeɪ.dri.ə
Adrian ˈeɪ.dri.ən
Adriana ˌeɪ.driˈɑː.nə, ˌædri-
Adrianople ˌeɪ.dri.əˈnəʊ.pəl, ˌæd.ri-, (US) -ˈnoʊ-
Adrianopolis ˌeɪ.dri.əˈnɒp.əl.ɪs, ˌæd.ri-, (US) -ˈnɑː.pəl-
Adriatic ˌeɪ.driˈæt.ɪk, (US) -ˈæţ- *stress shift:* ˌAdriatic ˈSea
Adrienne ˌeɪ.driˈen, ˌæd.riˈ-; ˈeɪ.dri.ən, ˈæd.ri-
adrift əˈdrɪft
adroit əˈdrɔɪt **-est** -ɪst, -əst **-ly** -li **-ness** -nəs, -nɪs
ADSL ˌeɪ.diː.esˈel
adsorb ædˈzɔːb, əd-, -ˈsɔːb, (US) -ˈsɔːrb, -ˈzɔːrb **-s** -z **-ing** -ɪŋ **-ed** -d
adsorbent ædˈzɔː.bənt, ədˈ-, -ˈsɔː-, (US) -ˈsɔːr-, -ˈzɔːr-
adsorption ædˈzɔːp.ʃən, ədˈ-, -ˈsɔːp-, (US) -ˈsɔːrp-, -ˈzɔːrp-
adsorptive ædˈzɔːp.tɪv, ədˈ-, -ˈsɔːp-, (US) -ˈsɔːrp-, -ˈzɔːrp-
adsum ˈæd.sʌm, -sʊm, -səm
aduki əˈduː.ki, ædˈ- aˈduki ˌbean
adularia ˌædʒ.ʊˈleə.ri.ə, ˌæd.jəˈ-, ˌædʒ.ʊˈ-, (US) ˌædʒ.ʊˈler.i-, ˌæd.jəˈ-
adu|late ˈædʒ.ə|.leɪt, ˈædʒ.ʊ-, ˈæd.jʊ-, ˈ-jə-, (US) ˈædʒ.ə-, ˈæd.jə-, ˈ-ə- **-lates** -leɪts **-lating** -leɪ.tɪŋ, (US) -leɪ.ţɪŋ **-lated** -leɪ.tɪd, (US) -leɪ.ţɪd
adulation ˌæd.jʊˈleɪ.ʃən, -jəˈ-, ˌædʒ.ʊˈ-, -əˈ-, (US) ˌædʒ.əˈ-, ˌæd.jəˈ-, -əˈ- **-s** -z
adulatory ˌæd.jʊˈleɪ.tər.i, -jəˈ-, ˌædʒ.ʊˈ-, -əˈ-; ˈæd.jʊ.leɪ-, -jə-, ˈædʒ.ʊ-, ˈ-ə-, -tər.i, (US) ˈædʒ.əl.ə.tɔːr-, ˈæd.jəl-, -əl-
Adullam əˈdʌl.əm **-ite/s** -aɪt/s
adult ˈæd.ʌlt, əˈdʌlt, (US) əˈdʌlt, ˈæd.ʌlt **-s** -s ˌadult eduˈcation
adulterant əˈdʌl.tər.ənt **-s** -s
adulter|ate əˈdʌl.tər|.eɪt, (US) -tə.r|eɪt **-ates** -eɪts **-ating** -eɪ.tɪŋ, (US) -eɪ.ţɪŋ **-ated** -eɪ.tɪd, (US) -eɪ.ţɪd **-ator/s** -eɪ.təʳ/z, (US) -eɪ.ţɚ/z

Pronouncing the letters AE

The vowel digraph **ae** is a fairly low-frequency spelling. In some cases, the American spelling of words containing **ae** omits the **a**, e.g. in *aesthetic*, which is spelt in American English as *esthetic*.

The pronunciation of the digraph in strong syllables depends on whether or not it is followed by an **r** in the spelling. If so, the pronunciation is /eə/ (US) /er/, e.g:

aeroplane ˈeə.rə.pleɪn (US) ˈer.ə-

When not followed by **r**, the pronunciation is most usually one of /iː/, /ɪ/, or /e/, the latter being most common in American English pronunciation, e.g.:

Caesar ˈsiː.zəʳ (US) -zɚ
aesthetic iːsˈθet.ɪk, ɪs- (US) esˈθeţ-

In addition

Other vowel sounds associated with the digraph **ae** include /æ/, for Old English names, e.g.:

Aethelstan ˈæθ.ᵊl.stən

In weak syllables

The vowel digraph is realized with the vowels /ə/ and /ɪ/ in weak syllables, e.g.:

gynaecology ˌgaɪ.nəˈkɒl.ə.dʒi, -nɪˈ- (US) -ːkɑː.lə-

adulteration əˌdʌl.tᵊrˈeɪ.ʃᵊn, (US) -təˈreɪ- **-s** -z
adulterer əˈdʌl.tᵊr.əʳ, (US) -tɚ.ɚ **-s** -z
adulteress əˈdʌl.tᵊr.es, -ɪs, -əs, (US) -tɚ-, ˈ-trɪs **-es** -ɪz
adulterous əˈdʌl.tᵊr.əs, (US) ˈ-tɚ.əs **-ly** -li
adulter|y əˈdʌl.tᵊr|.i, (US) ˈ-tɚ|.i **-ies** -iz
adulthood ˈæd.ʌlt.hʊd, əˈdʌlt-, (US) əˈdʌlt-
adum|brate ˈæd.ʌm|.breɪt, -əm- **-brates** -breɪts **-brating** -breɪ.tɪŋ, (US) -breɪ.ţɪŋ **-brated** -breɪ.tɪd, (US) -breɪ.ţɪd
adumbration ˌæd.ʌmˈbreɪ.ʃᵊn, -əm- **-s** -z
Adur ˈeɪ.dəʳ, (US) -dɚ
ad valorem ˌæd.vəˈlɔː.rem, -vælˈɔː-, -rəm, (US) -vəˈlɔːr.əm
advanc|e ədˈvɑːnts, (US) -ˈvænts, æd- **-es** -ɪz **-ing** -ɪŋ **-ed** -t **-ement/s** -mənt/s **adˌvance ˈnotice; adˌvance ˈpayment; Adˈvanced ˌLevel**
advantag|e ədˈvɑːn.tɪdʒ, (US) -ˈvæn.ţɪdʒ, æd- **-es** -ɪz
advantageous ˌæd.vənˈteɪ.dʒəs, -vɑːnˈ-, -vænˈ-, (US) -vænˈ-, -vənˈ- **-ly** -li **-ness** -nəs, -nɪs
adven|e ædˈviːn, əd- **-es** -z **-ing** -ɪŋ **-ed** -d
advent, A~ ˈæd.vent, -vənt **-s** -s ˈ**Advent ˌcalendar**
Adventism ˈæd.ven.tɪ.zᵊm, -vən-, (US) -vən-
Adventist ˈæd.ven.tɪst, -vən-, (US) -vən-; (US) ədˈven-
adventitious ˌæd.vənˈtɪʃ.əs, -ven- **-ly** -li
adventive ædˈven.tɪv, (US) -ţɪv **-ly** -li
advent|ure ədˈven.tʃ|əʳ, (US) -tʃ|ɚ, æd- **-ures** -əz, -ɚz **-uring** -ᵊr.ɪŋ **-ured** -əd, -ɚd **-urer/s** -ᵊr.əʳ/z, (US) -ɚ.ɚ/z **-uress/es** -ᵊr.əs/ɪz, -ə.res/ɪz **adˌventure ˈplayground**
adventuresome ədˈven.tʃə.sᵊm, (US) -tʃɚ-, æd-
adventurous ədˈven.tʃᵊr.əs, (US) əd-, æd- **-ly** -li **-ness** -nəs, -nɪs
adverb ˈæd.vɜːb, (US) -vɝːb **-s** -z
adverbial ədˈvɜː.bi.əl, æd-, (US) -ˈvɝː- **-ly** -i

adversarial ˌæd.vəˈseə.ri.əl, -vɜːˈ-, (US) -vɚˈser.i- **-ly** -i
adversar|y ˈæd.və.sᵊr|.i, ədˈvɜː-, (US) ˈæd.vɚ.ser- **-ies** -iz
adversative ədˈvɜː.sə.tɪv, æd-, (US) -ˈvɝː.sə.ţɪv
adverse ˈæd.vɜːs, -ˈ-, əd-, (US) ædˈvɝːs, ˈ-- **-ly** -li
adversit|y ədˈvɜː.sə.t|i, -sɪ-, (US) -ˈvɝː.sə.ţ|i, æd- **-ies** -iz
advert n ˈæd.vɜːt, (US) -vɝːt **-s** -s
ad|vert v əd|ˈvɜːt, æd-, (US) -ˈvɝːt **-verts** -ˈvɜːts, (US) -ˈvɝːts **-verting** -ˈvɜː.tɪŋ, (US) -ˈvɝː.ţɪŋ **-verted** -ˈvɜː.tɪd, (US) -ˈvɝː.ţɪd
advertenc|e ədˈvɜː.tᵊnts, (US) -ˈvɝː-, æd- **-y** -i
advertent ədˈvɜː.tᵊnt, (US) -ˈvɝː-, æd- **-ly** -li
advertis|e, -iz|e ˈæd.və.taɪz, (US) -vɚ- **-es** -ɪz **-ing** -ɪŋ **-ed** -d **-er/s** -əʳ/z, (US) -ɚ/z
advertisement, -ize- ədˈvɜː.tɪs.mənt, -tɪz-, -təs-, -təz-, (US) ˌæd.vɚˈtaɪz.mənt; (US) ədˈvɝː.ţəs-, -ţəz- **-s** -s
advertorial ˌæd.vəˈtɔː.ri.əl, (US) -vɚˈtɔːr.i-
advic|e ədˈvaɪs, (US) əd-, æd- **-es** -ɪz
advisability ədˌvaɪ.zəˈbɪl.ə.ti, ˈ-ɪ-, (US) -ə.ţi, æd-
advisab|le ədˈvaɪ.zə.b|ᵊl, (US) əd-, æd- **-ly** -li **-leness** -ᵊl.nəs, -nɪs
advis|e ədˈvaɪz, (US) əd-, æd- **-es** -ɪz **-ing** -ɪŋ **-ed** -d **-edly** -ɪd.li **-edness** -ɪd.nəs, -nɪs
advisement ədˈvaɪz.mənt
adviser, advisor ədˈvaɪ.zəʳ, (US) -zɚ, æd- **-s** -z
advisor|y ədˈvaɪ.zᵊr|.i, (US) əd-, æd- **-ies** -iz **adˈvisory ˌbody**
advocaat ˈæd.vəʊ.kɑː, -kɑːt, (US) -voʊ-
advocacy ˈæd.və.kə.si
advocate n ˈæd.və.kət, -keɪt, -kɪt **-s** -s
advo|cate v ˈæd.və|.keɪt **-cates** -keɪts **-cating** -keɪ.tɪŋ, (US) -keɪ.ţɪŋ **-cated** -keɪ.tɪd, (US) -keɪ.ţɪd **-cator/s** -keɪ.təʳ/z, (US) -keɪ.ţɚ/z
advocation ˌæd.vəˈkeɪ.ʃᵊn
advowson ədˈvaʊ.zᵊn **-s** -z
Adwa ˈɑː.dwə

Adwick le Street ˌæd.wɪk.lɪˈstriːt
Adye ˈeɪ.di
adynamia ˌeɪ.daɪˈneɪ.mi.ə, ˌæd.ɪˈ-
adynamic ˌeɪ.daɪˈnæm.ɪk, ˌæd.aɪˈ-, -ɪˈ-
adz|e, adz ædz **-es** -ɪz **-ing** -ɪŋ **-ed** -d
adzuki ædˈzuː.ki **adˈzuki ˌbean**
aedile ˈiː.daɪl **-s** -z **-ship/s** -ʃɪp/s
Aeetes iːˈiː.tiːz
Aegean iːˈdʒiː.ən, ɪˈ-
Aegeus ˈiː.dʒi.əs, (US) ˈiː.dʒi.əs, ˈiː.dʒuːs
Aegina iːˈdʒaɪ.nə, ɪˈdʒaɪ-
aegis ˈiː.dʒɪs
Aegisthus iːˈdʒɪs.θəs, ɪˈdʒɪs-
aegrotat ˈaɪ.grəʊ.tæt, ˈiː-, (US) -groʊ- **-s** -s
Aegyptus iːˈdʒɪp.təs
Aelfric ˈæl.frɪk
Aemilius iːˈmɪl.i.əs, ɪˈmɪl-
Aeneas iːˈniː.əs, ɪˈniː-, -æs
Aeneid ˈiː.ni.ɪd, iːˈniː.ɪd, ɪˈ- **-s** -z
Aeneus ˈiː.ni.əs, iːˈniː-, ɪ-
Aeoli|a iːˈəʊ.li|.ə, (US) -ˈoʊ- **-an/s** -ən/z
Aeolic iːˈɒl.ɪk, -ˈəʊ.lɪk, (US) -ˈɑː.lɪk
Aeolus ˈiː.əʊ.ləs, (US) ˈ-ə-
aeon ˈiː.ən, -ɒn, (US) -ɑːn **-s** -z
aera|te eəˈreɪ|t, ˈ--, (US) erˈeɪ|t **-tes** -ts **-ting** -tɪŋ, (US) -ţɪŋ **-ted** -tɪd, (US) -ţɪd **-tor/s** -təʳ/z, (US) -ţɚ/z
aeration eəˈreɪ.ʃᵊn, (US) erˈeɪ-
aerial ˈeə.ri.əl, (US) ˈer.i- **-s** -z **-ly** -i
aerie ˈɪə.ri, ˈeə-, (US) ˈer.i, ˈɪr-, ˈeɪ.ri **-s** -z
aerif|y ˈeə.rɪ.faɪ, ˈ-rə-, (US) ˈer.ɪ-, ˈer.ə- **-ies** -z **-ying** -ɪŋ **-ied** -aɪd
Aer Lingus® ˌeəˈlɪŋ.gəs, (US) ˌer-
aero ˈeə.rəʊ, (US) ˈer.oʊ
aero- ˈeə.rəʊ; eəˈrɒ, (US) ˈer.oʊ, ˈer.ə; (US) erˈɑː
Note: Prefix. Either takes primary or secondary stress on the first syllable, e.g. **aerolite** /ˈeə.rəʊ.laɪt/ (US) /ˈer.oʊ.laɪt/ **aerodynamic** /ˌeə.rəʊ.daɪˈnæm.ɪk/ (US) /ˌer.oʊ.daɪˈnæm.ɪk/, or primary stress on the second syllable, e.g. **aerology** /eəˈrɒl.ə.dʒi/ (US) /erˈɑː.lə-/.
aeroballistics ˌeə.rəʊ.bəˈlɪs.tɪks, (US) ˌer.oʊ-

A

Pronouncing the letters AEO

The vowel letter combination **aeo** is of low frequency, and is often spelt **eo** in American English. It has two pronunciations associated with it:

i'ɒ (US) i'ɑː archaeology /ˌɑː.ki'ɒl.ə.dʒi/ (US) /ˌɑːr.ki'ɑː.lə-/
iəʊ (US) ioʊ, iə palaeotype /'pæl.i.əʊ.taɪp/ (US) /'peɪ.li.oʊ-, -ə-/

aerobatic ˌeə.rəʊ'bæt.ɪk, (US) ˌer.oʊ'bæţ- **-s** -s **-ally** -əl.i, -li
aerobe 'eə.rəʊb, (US) 'er.oʊb **-s** -z
aerobic eə'rəʊ.bɪk, (US) er'oʊ- **-s** -s
aerodrome 'eə.rə.drəʊm, (US) 'er.ə.droʊm **-s** -z
aerodynamic ˌeə.rəʊ.daɪ'næm.ɪk, -dɪ'-, (US) ˌer.oʊ-, ˌer.ə- **-s** -s **-ally** -əl.i, -li *stress shift:* **ˌaerodynamic 'fairing**
aerodyne 'eə.rəʊ.daɪn, (US) 'er.oʊ-, '-ə- **-s** -z
Aeroflot® 'eə.rəʊ.flɒt, (US) 'er.ə.flɑːt, -floʊt
aerofoil 'eə.rəʊ.fɔɪl, (US) 'er.ə-, '-oʊ- **-s** -z
aerogram, aerogramme 'eə.rəʊ.græm, (US) 'er.oʊ-, '-ə- **-s** -z
aerolite 'eə.rəʊ.laɪt, (US) 'er.ə- **-s** -s
aerolith 'eə.rəʊ.lɪθ, (US) 'er.ə-, '-oʊ- **-s** -s
aerological ˌeə.rəʊ'lɒdʒ.ɪ.kəl, (US) ˌer.oʊ'lɑː.dʒɪ-, ˌer.ə-
aerologist eə'rɒl.ə.dʒɪst, (US) er'ɑː.l.ə- **-s** -s
aerolog|y eə'rɒl.ə.dʒ|i, (US) er'ɑː.lə- **-ist/s** -ɪst/s
aeronaut 'eə.rə.nɔːt, (US) 'er.ə.nɑːt, -nɔːt **-s** -s
aeronautic ˌeə.rə'nɔː.tɪk, (US) ˌer.ə'nɑː.ţɪk, -'nɔː- **-s** -s **-al** -əl
aerophone 'eə.rəʊ.fəʊn, (US) 'er.ə.foʊn, '-oʊ- **-s** -z
aeroplane 'eə.rə.pleɪn, (US) 'er.ə- **-s** -z
Aerosmith 'eə.rəʊ.smɪθ, (US) 'e.roʊ-
aerosol 'eə.rə.sɒl, (US) 'er.ə.sɑːl **-s** -z
aerospace 'eə.rəʊ.speɪs, (US) 'er.oʊ-, '-ə-
aerostat 'eə.rəʊ.stæt, (US) 'er.ə-, '-oʊ- **-s** -s
Aertex® 'eə.teks, (US) 'er-
aery adj 'eə.ri, (US) 'er.i, 'eɪ.ə.ri
aer|y n 'ɪə.r|i, 'eə-, (US) 'er|.i, 'ɪr-, 'eɪ|.ri **-ies** -iz
Aeschines 'iː.skɪ.niːz, -skə.niːz, (US) 'es.kə-, 'iː.skə-
Aeschylus 'iː.skɪ.ləs, -skə.ləs, (US) 'es.kə-, 'iː.skə-
Aesculapi|us ˌiː.skjʊ'leɪ.pi|.əs, (US) ˌes.kjə'-, -kə'- **-an** -ən
Aesop 'iː.sɒp, (US) -sɑːp, -səp
aesthete 'iːs.θiːt, (US) 'es- **-s** -s
aesthetic iːs'θet.ɪk, ɪs-, es-, (US) es'θeţ-, ɪs- **-s** -s **-al** -əl **-ally** -əl.i, -li
aesthetic|ism iːs'θet.ɪ.s|ɪ.zəm, ɪs-, es-, (US) es-, ɪs- **-ist/s** -ɪst/s
aestival iː'staɪ.vəl, (US) 'es.tə-, es'taɪ-
Aethelstan 'æθ.əl.stən, -stæn
aether 'iː.θər, (US) -θɚ
aetiolog|y ˌiː.ti'ɒl.ə.dʒ|i, (US) -ţi'ɑː.lə- **-ist/s** -ɪst/s
Aetna 'et.nə
afar ə'fɑːr, (US) -'fɑːr
afeard ə'fɪəd, (US) -'fɪrd
affability ˌæf.ə'bɪl.ə.ti, -ɪ.ti, (US) -ə.ţi
affab|le 'æf.ə.b|əl **-ly** -li **-leness** -əl.nəs, -nɪs
affair ə'feər, (US) -'fer **-s** -z
affect v ə'fekt **-s** -s **-ing/ly** -ɪŋ/li **-ed** -ɪd
affect n 'æf.ekt **-s** -s
affectation ˌæf.ek'teɪ.ʃən, -ɪk'- **-s** -z
affected ə'fek.tɪd **-ly** -li **-ness** -nəs, -nɪs
affection ə'fek.ʃən **-s** -z
affectionate ə'fek.ʃən.ət, -ɪt **-ly** -li **-ness** -nəs, -nɪs
affective ə'fek.tɪv, æf'ek-
affenpinscher 'æf.ənˌpɪn.tʃər, (US) -ˌpɪnt.ʃɚ **-s** -z
afferent 'æf.ər.ənt
affettuoso əˌfet.ju'əʊ.səʊ, æfˌet-, -zəʊ, (US) əˌfet.ju'oʊ.soʊ, æfˌet-, -ˌetʃ.u'-
affianc|e ə'faɪ.ənts **-es** -ɪz **-ing** -ɪŋ **-ed** -t
affiant ə'faɪ.ənt **-s** -s
affich|e æf'iːʃ, ə'fiːʃ **-es** -ɪz
affidavit ˌæf.ɪ'deɪ.vɪt, -ə'- **-s** -s
affili|ate ə'fɪl.i|.eɪt **-ates** -eɪts **-ating** -eɪ.tɪŋ, (US) -eɪ.ţɪŋ **-ated** -eɪ.tɪd, (US) -eɪ.ţɪd
affiliation əˌfɪl.i'eɪ.ʃən **-s** -z
affinit|y ə'fɪn.ə.t|i, -ɪt|i, (US) -ə.ţ|i **-ies** -iz
affirm ə'fɜːm, (US) -'fɝːm **-s** -z **-ing** -ɪŋ **-ed** -d **-able** -ə.bəl
affirmation ˌæf.ə'meɪ.ʃən, (US) -ɚ'- **-s** -z
affirmative ə'fɜː.mə.tɪv, (US) -'fɝː.mə.ţɪv **-ly** -li **afˌfirmative 'action**
affirmatory ə'fɜː.mə.tər.i, (US) -'fɝː.mə.tɔːr-
affix n 'æf.ɪks **-es** -ɪz
affix v ə'fɪks, 'æf.ɪks **-es** -ɪz **-ing** -ɪŋ **-ed** -d
affixation ˌæf.ɪk'seɪ.ʃən
affixture æf'ɪks.tʃər, (US) -tʃɚ, æf'ɪks-
afflatus ə'fleɪ.təs, (US) -ţəs
Affleck 'æf.lek
afflict ə'flɪkt **-s** -s **-ing** -ɪŋ **-ed** -ɪd **-ive** -ɪv
affliction ə'flɪk.ʃən **-s** -z
affluence 'æf.lu.ənts
affluent 'æf.lu.ənt
affluenza ˌæf.lu'en.zə
afflux 'æf.lʌks **-es** -ɪz
afford ə'fɔːd, (US) -'fɔːrd **-s** -z **-ing** -ɪŋ **-ed** -ɪd
affordab|le ə'fɔː.də.b|əl, (US) -'fɔːr- **-ly** -li
afforest ə'fɒr.ɪst, æf'ɒr-, (US) ə'fɔːr.əst **-s** -s **-ing** -ɪŋ **-ed** -ɪd
afforestation æfˌɒr.ɪ'steɪ.ʃən, əˌfɒr-, -ə'-, (US) əˌfɔːr.ə'- **-s** -z
affray ə'freɪ **-s** -z
affricate 'æf.rɪ.kət, -rə-, -kɪt, -keɪt, (US) -kɪt **-s** -s
affricated 'æf.rɪ.keɪ.tɪd, -rə-, (US) -ţɪd
affrication ˌæf.rɪ'keɪ.ʃən, -rə'-
affricative æf'rɪk.ə.tɪv, ə'frɪk-, (US) -ţɪv **-s** -z
af|fright ə|'fraɪt **-frights** -'fraɪts **-frighting** -'fraɪ.tɪŋ, (US) -'fraɪ.ţɪŋ **-frighted/ly** -'fraɪ.tɪd/li, (US) -'fraɪ.ţɪd/li
af|front ə|'frʌnt **-fronts** -'frʌnts **-fronting** -'frʌn.tɪŋ, (US) -'frʌn.ţɪŋ **-fronted** -'frʌn.tɪd, (US) -'frʌn.ţɪd
Afghan 'æf.gæn **-s** -z **ˌAfghan 'hound**
afghani æf'gæn.i, -'gɑː.ni **-s** -z
Afghanistan æf'gæn.ɪ.stɑːn, '-ə-, -stæn; æfˌgæn.ɪ'stɑːn, -ə'-, -'stæn, (US) æf'gæn.ə.stæn, -stɑːn
aficionado əˌfɪʃ.i.ən'ɑː.dəʊ, -ˌfɪs-; *as if Spanish:* æfˌɪθ.jə'nɑː.dəʊ; (US) əˌfɪʃ.i.ə'nɑː.doʊ, -ˌfɪs-, -ˌfiː.si- **-s** -z
afield ə'fiːld
afire ə'faɪər, -'faɪ.ər, (US) -'faɪ.ɚ
aflame ə'fleɪm
aflatoxin ˌæf.lə'tɒk.sɪn, (US) -'tɑːk.sən
AFL-CIO eɪ.efˌel.siː.aɪ'əʊ, (US) -'oʊ
afloat ə'fləʊt, (US) -'floʊt
aflutter ə'flʌt.ər, (US) -'flʌţ.ɚ
afoot ə'fʊt
afore ə'fɔːr, (US) -'fɔːr
aforementioned ə'fɔː.men.tʃənd, əˌfɔː'men-, (US) ə'fɔːr.ment.ʃənd
aforesaid ə'fɔː.sed, (US) -'fɔːr-
aforethought ə'fɔː.θɔːt, (US) -'fɔːr.θɑːt, -θɔːt
aforetime ə'fɔː.taɪm, (US) -'fɔːr-
a fortiori ˌeɪ.fɔː.ti'ɔː.raɪ, ˌɑː-, -ri, (US) ˌeɪ.fɔːr.ţi'ɔːr.i, -ʃi'-, -aɪ
afoul ə'faʊl
afraid ə'freɪd
A-frame 'eɪ.freɪm **-s** -z
afreet 'æf.riːt, ə'friːt **-s** -s
afresh ə'freʃ
Afric 'æf.rɪk
Afric|a 'æf.rɪ.k|ə **-an/s** -ən/z
African-American ˌæf.rɪ.kən.ə'mer.ɪ.kən **-s** -z
Africander ˌæf.rɪ'kæn.dər, (US) -dɚ **-s** -z
Africanist 'æf.rɪ.kə.nɪst **-s** -s
Africanization, -isa-

ˌæf.rɪ.kə.naɪˈzeɪ.ʃᵊn, -rə-, -nɪˈ-, (US) -nəˈ-
Africaniz|e, -is|e ˈæf.rɪ.kə.naɪz **-es** -ɪz **-ing** -ɪŋ **-ed** -d
Africanus ˌæf.rɪˈkɑː.nəs, -ˈkeɪ-
Afridi æfˈriː.di, əˈfriː- **-s** -z
Afrikaans ˌæf.rɪˈkɑːnts, -rəˈkɑːnts, -rɪkˈɑːnz, -rəˈkɑːnz
Afrikaner ˌæf.rɪˈkɑː.nəʳ, (US) -nɚ **-s** -z
afrit ˈæf.riːt, əˈfriːt **-s** -s
Afro ˈæf.rəʊ, (US) -roʊ **-s** -z
Afro- ˌæf.rəʊ, (US) ˌæf.roʊ
Note: Prefix. Normally carries secondary stress on the first syllable, e.g. **Afro-American** /ˌæf.rəʊ.əˈmer.ɪ.kən/ (US) /-roʊ-/.
Afro-American ˌæf.rəʊ.əˈmer.ɪ.kən, (US) -roʊ- **-s** -z
Afro-Asian ˌæf.rəʊˈeɪ.ʃᵊn, -ʒᵊn, (US) -roʊˈeɪ.ʒᵊn, -ʃᵊn **-s** -z
Afro-Asiatic ˌæf.rəʊ.eɪ.ʃiˈæt.ɪk, -siˈ-, -ʒiˈ-, -ziˈ-, (US) -roʊ.eɪ.ʒiˈæt̬-, -ʃiˈ-
Afro-Caribbean ˌæf.rəʊ.kær.ɪˈbiː.ən, (US) -roʊ.ker-, -kær-; (US) -kəˈrɪb.i- **-s** -z
aft ɑːft, (US) æft
after ˈɑːf.təʳ, (US) ˈæf.tɚ ˌ**after** ˈ**all**; *TM:* ˌ**After** ˈ**Eights**
after- ˈɑːf.tə, (US) ˈæf.tɚ
Note: Prefix. Words containing **after-** usually carry primary stress on the first syllable, e.g. **afterglow** /ˈɑːf.tə.gləʊ/ (US) /ˈæf.tɚ.gloʊ/, but there are exceptions, including **afternoon** /ˌɑːf.təˈnuːn/ (US) /ˌæf.tɚ-/.
afterbirth ˈɑːf.tə.bɜːθ, (US) ˈæf.tɚ.bɝːθ **-s** -s
after-burner ˈɑːf.təˌbɜː.nəʳ, (US) ˈæf.tɚˌbɝː.nɚ **-s** -z
aftercare ˈɑːf.tə.keəʳ, (US) ˈæf.tɚ.ker
after-crop ˈɑːf.tə.krɒp, (US) ˈæf.tɚ.krɑːp **-s** -s
aftereffect ˈɑːf.təʳ.ɪˌfekt, -əˌfekt, (US) ˈæf.tɚ- **-s** -s
afterglow ˈɑːf.tə.gləʊ, (US) ˈæf.tɚ.gloʊ **-s** -z
after-hours ˌɑːf.təʳˈaʊəz, -ˈaʊ.əz, (US) ˈæf.tɚˌaʊ.ɚz, ˌ--ˈ- *stress shift:* ˌ**after-hours** ˈ**drinking**
afterli|fe ˈɑːf.tə.laɪ|f, (US) ˈæf.tɚ- **-ves** -vz
aftermath ˈɑːf.tə.mɑːθ, -mæθ, (US) ˈæf.tɚ.mæθ **-s** -s
afternoon ˌɑːf.təˈnuːn, (US) ˌæf.tɚˈ- **-s** -z *stress shift, see compounds:* ˌ**afternoon** ˈ**tea**; **good** ˌ**after**ˈ**noon**
afterpiec|e ˈɑːf.tə.piːs, (US) ˈæf.tɚ- **-es** -ɪz
afters ˈɑːf.təz, (US) ˈæf.tɚz
after-sales ˌɑːf.təˈseɪlz, (US) ˌæf.tɚˈ- *stress shift:* ˌ**after-sales** ˈ**service**
aftershave ˈɑːf.tə.ʃeɪv, (US) ˈæf.tɚ- **-s** -z
aftershock ˈɑːf.tə.ʃɒk, (US) ˈæf.tɚ.ʃɑːk **-s** -s
aftertaste ˈɑːf.tə.teɪst, (US) ˈæf.tɚ- **-s** -s
afterthought ˈɑːf.tə.θɔːt, (US) ˈæf.tɚ.θɑːt, -θɔːt **-s** -s
afterward ˈɑːf.tə.wəd, (US) ˈæf.tɚ.wɚd **-s** -z
AFTRA ˈæf.trə
Aga® ˈɑː.gə
Agadir ˌæg.əˈdɪə, (US) ˌɑː.gəˈdɪr, ˌæg.əˈ-
Agag ˈeɪ.gæg
again əˈgen, -ˈgeɪn, (US) əˈgen
against əˈgentst, -ˈgeɪntst, (US) əˈgentst
Aga Khan ˌɑː.gəˈkɑːn
Agamemnon ˌæg.əˈmem.nən, -nɒn, (US) -nɑːn, -nən
agamete eɪˈgæm.iːt, əˈ-, (US) ˌæg.əˈmiːt **-s** -s
Agana ɑːˈgɑː.nə, -njə, (US) -njə
agape **adj, adv** əˈgeɪp
agape **n** ˈæg.ə.pi, -peɪ, (US) ɑːˈgɑː.peɪ, ˈɑː.gə- **-s** -z
agar *jelly:* ˈeɪ.gɑːʳ, -əʳ, (US) -gɑːr, ˈɑː-, -gɚ
Agar *family name:* ˈeɪ.gəʳ, -gɑːʳ, (US) -gɚ, -gɑːr
agar-agar ˌeɪ.gəʳˈeɪ.gəʳ, -gɑːʳˈ-, -gɑːʳ, (US) -gɚˈeɪ.gɚ, ˌɑː.gɚˈɑː-, -gɑːrˈ-, -gɑːr
agaric **n** ˈæg.ə.rɪk; əˈgær.ɪk, (US) ˈæg.ɚ.ɪk; (US) əˈger-, -ˈgær- **-s** -s
agaric **adj** ægˈær.ɪk, əˈgær-
Agassi ˈæg.ə.si
Agassiz ˌæg.əˈsiː, (US) ˈæg.ə.si
agate *stone:* ˈæg.ət, -gɪt **-s** -s
Agate *surname:* ˈeɪ.gət, ˈæg.ət
Agatha ˈæg.ə.θə
Agathocles əˈgæθ.əʊ.kliːz, (US) ˈ-ə-
agave əˈgɑː.vi, -ˈgeɪ-, ˈæg.ɑː-, ˈæg.eɪ-, -veɪ, (US) əˈgɑː- **-s** -z
agaze əˈgeɪz
ag|e eɪdʒ **-es** -ɪz **-(e)ing** -ɪŋ **-ed** -d ˌ**age of con**ˈ**sent**; ˈ**golden** ˌ**age**
-age ɪdʒ, ɑːʒ
Note: Suffix. Normally pronounced /-ɪdʒ/, e.g. **advantage** /ədˈvɑːn.tɪdʒ/ (US) /-ˈvæn.t̬ɪdʒ/, which is unstressed, but in words of French origin it is often /-ɑːʒ/, which may be stress-bearing; see for example, **corsage**, in which it has both stressed and unstressed variants.
aged **adj** *old:* ˈeɪ.dʒɪd *of the age of:* eɪdʒd
agedness ˈeɪdʒ.ɪd.nəs, -nɪs
Agee ˈeɪ.dʒiː
age|ism ˈeɪdʒ.|ɪ.zᵊm **-ist/s** -ɪst/s
ageless ˈeɪdʒ.ləs, -lɪs
agelong ˈeɪdʒ.lɒŋ, (US) -lɑːŋ, -lɔːŋ
agenc|y ˈeɪ.dʒᵊnt.s|i **-ies** -iz
agenda əˈdʒen.də **-s** -z
agendum əˈdʒen.dəm **-s** -z
agene ˈeɪ.dʒiːn
agenesis ˌeɪˈdʒen.ə.sɪs, ˈ-ɪ-
agent ˈeɪ.dʒᵊnt **-s** -s ˌ**Agent** ˈ**Orange**
agentival ˌeɪ.dʒᵊnˈtaɪ.vᵊl
agentive ˈeɪ.dʒᵊn.tɪv
agent(s) provocateur(s) ˌæʒ.ɑ̃ː.prəˌvɒk.əˈtɜːʳ, ˌæʒ.ɒŋ-, (US) ˌɑːʒ.ɑ̃ː.proʊˌvɑː.kəˈtɝː, -tʊr
age-old ˌeɪdʒˈəʊld, (US) ˈeɪdʒ.oʊld *stress shift, British only:* ˌ**age-old** ˈ**city**
-ageous ˈeɪ.dʒəs
Note: Suffix. Words containing **-ageous** are normally stressed on the penultimate syllable, e.g. **advantageous** /ˌæd.vənˈteɪ.dʒəs/ (US) /-vænˈ-/.
Ager ˈeɪ.dʒəʳ, (US) -dʒɚ
Agesilaus əˌdʒes.ɪˈleɪ.əs, ædʒˌes-, (US) -əˈ-
Agfa® ˈæg.fə
aggie, A~ ˈæg.i **-s** -z
aggiornamento əˌdʒɔː.nəˈmen.təʊ, (US) -ˌdʒɔːr.nəˈmen.toʊ
agglomerate **n, adj** əˈglɒm.ᵊr.ət, -ɪt, (US) -ˈglɑː.mɚ- **-s** -s
agglomer|ate **v** əˈglɒm.ᵊr|.eɪt, (US) -ˈglɑː.mə.r|eɪt **-ates** -eɪts **-ating** -eɪ.tɪŋ, (US) -eɪ.t̬ɪŋ **-ated** -eɪ.tɪd, (US) -eɪ.t̬ɪd
agglomeration əˌglɒm.əˈreɪ.ʃᵊn, (US) -ˌglɑː.məˈ- **-s** -z
agglutinate **adj** əˈgluː.tɪ.nət, -ɪt, (US) -tᵊn.ət
agglutin|ate **v** əˈgluː.tɪ.n|eɪt, (US) -tᵊn|.eɪt **-ates** -eɪts **-ating** -eɪ.tɪŋ, (US) -eɪ.t̬ɪŋ **-ated** -eɪ.tɪd, (US) -eɪ.t̬ɪd
agglutination əˌgluː.tɪˈneɪ.ʃᵊn, (US) -tᵊnˈeɪ- **-s** -z
agglutinative əˈgluː.tɪ.nə.tɪv, -eɪ.tɪv, (US) -tᵊn.eɪ.t̬ɪv
agglutinin əˈgluː.tɪ.nɪn, (US) -tᵊn.ɪn
aggrandiz|e, -is|e əˈgræn.daɪz **-es** -ɪz **-ing** -ɪŋ **-ed** -d
aggrandizement, -ise- əˈgræn.dɪz.mənt, (US) -dɪz-, -daɪz-
aggra|vate ˈæg.rə|.veɪt **-vates** -veɪts **-vating/ly** -veɪ.tɪŋ/li, (US) -veɪ.t̬ɪŋ/li **-vated** -veɪ.tɪd, (US) -veɪ.t̬ɪd
aggravation ˌæg.rəˈveɪ.ʃᵊn **-s** -z
aggregate **n, adj** ˈæg.rɪ.gət, -rə.gət, -gɪt **-s** -s
aggre|gate **v** ˈæg.rɪ|.geɪt, -rə- **-gates** -geɪts **-gating** -geɪ.tɪŋ, (US) -geɪ.t̬ɪŋ **-gated** -geɪ.tɪd, (US) -geɪ.t̬ɪd
aggregation ˌæg.rɪˈgeɪ.ʃᵊn, -rəˈ- **-s** -z
aggregative ˈæg.rɪ.gə.tɪv, -rə-
aggregator ˈæg.rɪ.geɪ.təʳ, (US) -t̬ɚ **-s** -z
aggress əˈgres, ægˈres **-es** -ɪz **-ing** -ɪŋ **-ed** -t
aggression əˈgreʃ.ᵊn, ægˈreʃ- **-s** -z
aggressive əˈgres.ɪv, ægˈres- **-ly** -li **-ness** -nəs, -nɪs
aggressor əˈgres.əʳ, ægˈres-, (US) -ɚ **-s** -z
aggriev|e əˈgriːv **-es** -z **-ing** -ɪŋ **-ed** -d
aggro ˈæg.rəʊ, (US) -roʊ
aghast əˈgɑːst, (US) -ˈgæst
agil|e ˈædʒ.aɪl, (US) -ᵊl **-ist** -əst, -ɪst **-ely** -li
agility əˈdʒɪl.ə.ti, -ɪ.ti, (US) -ə.t̬i
agin əˈgɪn
Agincourt ˈædʒ.ɪn.kɔːʳ, -kɔːt, -kʊəʳ, (US) -kɔːrt
agiotage ˈædʒ.ə.tɪdʒ, ˈædʒ.i.əʊ-,

A

Pronouncing the letters **AI, AY**

The vowel letter digraphs **ai** and **ay** are similar in that their most common pronunciation is /eɪ/, e.g.:

day	deɪ
daily	ˈdeɪ.li

However, in days of the week, **ay** is also frequently pronounced /i/, e.g.:

Monday	ˈmʌn.di

When followed by an **r** in the spelling, **ai** and **ay** are pronounced as /eə/ (US) /er/, e.g.:

air	eəʳ (US) er
Ayr	eəʳ (US) er

In addition

There are other vowel sounds associated with the digraphs **ai** and **ay**, e.g.:

e	said, says /sed, sez/
æ	plait /plæt/
aɪ	aisle /aɪl/

And, in rare cases:

eɪ.ɪ	archaic /ɑːˈkeɪ.ɪk/ (US) /ɑːr-/

In weak syllables

The vowel digraphs **ai** and **ay** are realized with the vowels ɪ and i in weak syllables respectively, and **ai** may also result in a schwa vowel or a syllabic consonant, e.g.:

bargain	ˈbɑː.gɪn (US) ˈbɑːr-
Murray	ˈmʌr.i (US) ˈmɜː-
Britain	ˈbrɪt.ᵊn

-tɑːʒ, (US) ˈædʒ.i.ə.tɪdʒ; (US) ˌæʒ.əˈtɑːʒ
ag|ism ˈeɪ.dʒ|ɪ.zᵊm **-ist/s** -ɪst/s
agi|tate ˈædʒ.ɪ|.teɪt, ˈ-ə- **-tates** -teɪts **-tating** -teɪ.tɪŋ, (US) -teɪ.t̬ɪŋ **-tated** -teɪ.tɪd, (US) -teɪ.t̬ɪd **-tator/s** -teɪ.təʳ/z, (US) -teɪ.t̬ɚ/z
agitation ˌædʒ.ɪˈteɪ.ʃᵊn, -əˈ- **-s** -z
agitato ˌædʒ.ɪˈtɑː.təʊ, (US) -t̬oʊ
agitprop ˈædʒ.ɪt.prɒp, (US) -prɑːp
Aglaia əˈglaɪ.ə, -ˈgleɪ-
aglow əˈgləʊ, (US) -ˈgloʊ
AGM ˌeɪ.dʒiːˈem
agnail ˈæg.neɪl **-s** -z
agnate ˈæg.neɪt
agnation ægˈneɪ.ʃᵊn
Agnes ˈæg.nəs, -nɪs
Agnew ˈæg.njuː, (US) -nuː, -njuː
Agni ˈæg.ni
agnomen ægˈnəʊ.men, -mən, (US) -ˈnoʊ- **-s** -z
agnostic ægˈnɒs.tɪk, əg-, (US) -ˈnɑː.stɪk **-s** -s
agnosticism ægˈnɒs.tɪ.sɪ.zᵊm, əg-, -tə-, (US) -ˈnɑː.stɪ-, -stə-
Agnus Dei ˌæg.nəsˈdeɪ.i, -nʊs-, -ˈdiː.aɪ **-s** -z
ago əˈgəʊ, (US) -ˈgoʊ
agog əˈgɒg, (US) -ˈgɑːg, -ˈgɔːg
a go-go, à go-go əˈgəʊ.gəʊ, (US) -ˈgoʊ.goʊ
-agogue ə.gɒg, (US) ə.gɑːg, ə.gɔːg
Note: Suffix. Normally unstressed, e.g. **pedagogue** /ˈped.ə.gɒg/ (US) /-gɑːg/.
agone əˈgɒn, (US) -ˈgɑːn
agonist ˈæg.ə.nɪst **-s** -s
Agonistes ˌæg.əʊˈnɪs.tiːz, (US) -əˈ-
agonistic ˌæg.əʊˈnɪs.tɪk, (US) -əˈ- **-s** -s **-ally** -ᵊl.i, -li
agoniz|e, -is|e ˈæg.ə.naɪz **-es** -ɪz **-ing/ly** -ɪŋ/li **-ed** -d
agon|y ˈæg.ə.n|i **-ies** -iz ˈ**agony** ˌ**aunt**; ˈ**agony** ˌ**column**
agor|a ˈæg.ə.r|ə, -ɒr|.ə, ˌæg.əˈr|ɑː, (US) ˈæg.ə.r|ə, -ɔːr|.ə **-ae** -iː **-as** -əz
agoraphob|ia ˌæg.ᵊr.əˈfəʊ.b|i.ə, -ɔː.rəˈ-, (US) -ɚ.əˈfoʊ-; (US) əˌgɔːr.əˈ- **-ic/s** -ɪk/s
agouti əˈguː.ti, (US) -t̬i **-s** -z
Agra ˈɑː.grə, ˈæg.rə
agrarian əˈgreə.ri.ən, (US) -ˈgrer.i- **-s** -z **-ism** -ɪ.zᵊm
agree əˈgriː **-s** -z **-ing** -ɪŋ **-d** -d
agreeab|le əˈgriː.ə.b|ᵊl **-ly** -li **-leness** -ᵊl.nəs, -nɪs
agreement əˈgriː.mənt **-s** -s
agribusiness ˈæg.riˌbɪz.nɪs, -nəs **-es** -ɪz
Agricola əˈgrɪk.əʊ.lə, (US) -ᵊl.ə
agricultural ˌæg.rɪˈkʌl.tʃᵊr.ᵊl, -rəˈ- **-ist/s** -ɪst/s
agriculture ˈæg.rɪ.kʌl.tʃəʳ, -rə-, (US) -tʃɚ
agriculturist ˌæg.rɪˈkʌl.tʃᵊr.ɪst, -rəˈ- **-s** -s
Agrigento ˌæg.rɪˈdʒen.təʊ, (US) -toʊ
agrimony ˈæg.rɪ.mə.ni, -rə-, (US) -moʊ-
Agrippa əˈgrɪp.ə
Agrippina ˌæg.rɪˈpiː.nə, -rəˈ-
agro- ˈæg.rəʊ; əˈgrɒ, (US) ˈæg.roʊ, -rə; (US) əˈgrɑː
Note: Prefix. Either takes primary or secondary stress on the first syllable, e.g. **agrobiology** /ˌæg.rəʊ.baɪˈɒl.ə.dʒi/ (US) /-roʊ.baɪˈɑː.lə-/, or primary stress on the second syllable, e.g. **agronomy** /əˈgrɒn.ə.mi/ (US) /-ˈgrɑː.nə-/.
agrobiologic ˌæg.rəʊ.baɪ.əˈlɒdʒ.ɪk, (US) -roʊ.baɪ.əˈlɑː.dʒɪk **-al** -ᵊl **-ally** -ᵊl.i, -li
agrobiology ˌæg.rəʊ.baɪˈɒl.ə.dʒi, (US) -roʊ.baɪˈɑː.lə-
agrochemical ˌæg.rəʊˈkem.ɪ.kᵊl, (US) -roʊˈ- **-s** -z
agrolog|y əˈgrɒl.ə.dʒ|i, ægˈ-, (US) əˈgrɑː.lə- **-ist/s** -ɪst/s
agronomics ˌæg.rəˈnɒm.ɪks, (US) -ˈnɑː.mɪks
agronom|y əˈgrɒn.ə.m|i, (US) -ˈgrɑː.nə- **-ist/s** -ɪst/s
agrotourism ˈæg.rəʊˌtʊə.rɪ.zᵊm, -ˌtɔː-, ˌæg.rəʊˈtʊə.rɪ.zᵊm, -ˈtɔː-, (US) -roʊ.tʊr.ɪ-
aground əˈgraʊnd
Aguascalientes ˌæg.wɑːs.kæl.iˈen.tes, (US) ˌɑː.gwɑːs.kælˈjen.tes, -iˈen-
ague ˈeɪg.juː **-s** -z
Aguecheek ˈeɪg.juː.tʃiːk
Aguilera ˌæg.wɪˈleə.rə, (US) -ler.ə, ˌɑː.g.jəˈ-
Agulhas əˈgʌl.əs
Agutter ˈæg.ə.təʳ; əˈgʌt.əʳ, (US) əˈgʌt̬.ɚ; (US) ˈæg.ə.t̬ɚ
ah ɑː
aha ɑːˈhɑː, əˈhɑː
Ahab ˈeɪ.hæb
Ahasuerus eɪˌhæz.juˈɪə.rəs, əˌhæz-, (US) -ˈɪr.əs
Ahaz ˈeɪ.hæz
Ahaziah ˌeɪ.həˈzaɪ.ə
ahead əˈhed
aheap əˈhiːp
ahem mˈʔm̥m, ʔm̥m, əˈhem

> Note: Interjection. The spelling attempts to represent a clearing of the throat to attract attention. The pronunciation /əˈhem/ represents the spelling pronunciation of this word.

Ahenobarbus əˌhen.əʊˈbɑː.bəs, (US) -oʊˈbɑːr-, -ˌhiː.noʊˈ-
Ahern(e) əˈhɜːn, (US) -ˈhɝːn
A'Hern ˈeɪ.hɜːn, (US) -hɝːn
Ahimsa ɑːˈhɪm.sɑː, (US) ə-
ahistorical ˌeɪ.hɪˈstɒr.ɪ.kᵊl, (US) -ˈstɔːr-
Ahithophel əˈhɪθ.əʊ.fel, (US) ˈ-ə-
Ahmadabad ˈɑː.mə.də.bæd, (US) -bɑːd
Ahmadinejad ˌɑː.məˈdɪn.ə.ʒæd, ˌæx-, -ˈdiː.nə-, -dʒæd, -ʒɑːd
Ahmed ˈɑː.med
ahold əˈhəʊld, (US) -hoʊld
ahoy əˈhɔɪ
ai ˈɑː.i, aɪ
AI ˌeɪˈaɪ
Aicken ˈeɪ.kᵊn
aid eɪd **-s** -z **-ing** -ɪŋ **-ed** -ɪd **-er/s** -əʳ/z, (US) -ɚ/z ˌ**aid and aˈbet**

A

Aïda, Aida aɪˈiː.də, ɑː-
Aidan ˈeɪ.dᵊn
aide eɪd **-s** -z
aide(s)-de-camp ˌeɪd.dəˈkɑ̃ː, (US) -ˈkæmp
Aideed aɪˈdiːd
aide(s)-mémoire ˌeɪd.memˈwɑː, (US) -ˈwɑːr
aid|-man ˈeɪd|.mən, -mæn **-men** -men, -mən
AIDS, Aids eɪdz
aigrette ˈeɪ.gret, eɪˈgret **-s** -s
aiguille ˌeɪˈgwiː, -ˈgwiːl, (US) ˌeɪˈgwiːl, ˈ-- **-s** -z
Aiken ˈeɪ.kᵊn
aikido ˌaɪˈkiː.dəʊ, ˈaɪ.kɪ-, (US) ˌaɪˈkiː.doʊ
Aikin ˈeɪ.kɪn, -kᵊn
Aikman ˈeɪk.mən
ail eɪl **-s** -z **-ing** -ɪŋ **-ed** -d
ailanthus ˌaɪˈlænt.θəs **-es** -ɪz
Aileen ˈeɪ.liːn, (US) aɪˈliːn
aileron ˈeɪ.lᵊr.ɒn, (US) ˈeɪl.ə.rɑːn **-s** -z
Ailesbury ˈeɪlz.bᵊr.i, (US) -ber-
ailment ˈeɪl.mənt **-s** -s
Ailred ˈeɪl.red, ˈaɪl-
Ailsa ˈeɪl.sə
ailurophile aɪˈljʊə.rəʊ.faɪl, eɪ-, (US) -ˈlʊr.ə-, ˈ-oʊ- **-s** -z
ailurophobe aɪˈljʊə.rəʊ.fəʊb, eɪ-, (US) -ˈlʊr.ə.foʊb, ˈ-oʊ- **-s** -z
ailurophobia aɪˌljʊə.rəʊˈfəʊ.bi.ə, eɪ-, (US) -ˌlʊr.əˈfoʊ-, ˌ-oʊ-
aim eɪm **-s** -z **-ing** -ɪŋ **-ed** -d
aimless ˈeɪm.ləs, -lɪs **-ly** -li **-ness** -nəs, -nɪs
Ainger ˈeɪn.dʒəʳ, (US) -dʒɚ
Ainsley, Ainslie ˈeɪnz.li
Ainsworth ˈeɪnz.wəθ, -wɜːθ, (US) -wɚθ, -wɝːθ
ain't eɪnt
Aintree ˈeɪn.triː
Ainu ˈaɪ.nuː **-s** -z
aïoli, aioli aɪˈəʊ.li, eɪˈ-, ˈ---, (US) -ˈoʊ-, ˈ---
air eəʳ, (US) er **-s** -z **-ing/s** -ɪŋ/z **-ed** -d **ˈair ˌforce; ˈair hoˌstess; ˈair ˌletter; ˈair ˌpocket; ˈair ˌraid; ˈair ˌrifle; ˈair ˌroute; ˈair ˌterminal; ˌair traffic conˈtrol; ˌair traffic conˈtroller; ˌclear the ˈair**
airbag ˈeə.bæg, (US) ˈer- **-s** -z
airbase ˈeə.beɪs, (US) ˈer- **-s** -ɪz
airbed ˈeə.bed, (US) ˈer- **-s** -z
air-boat ˈeə.bəʊt, (US) ˈer.boʊt **-s** -s
airborne ˈeə.bɔːn, (US) ˈer.bɔːrn
airbrake ˈeə.breɪk, (US) ˈer- **-s** -s
airbrick ˈeə.brɪk, ˈer-
airbridg|e ˈeə.brɪdʒ, (US) ˈer- **-es** -ɪz
airbrush ˈeə.brʌʃ, (US) ˈer- **-es** -ɪz **-ing** -ɪŋ **-ed** -d
air-burst ˈeə.bɜːst, (US) ˈer.bɝːst **-s** -s
airbus, A~® ˈeə.bʌs, (US) ˈer- **-es** -ɪz
air-check ˈeə.tʃek, (US) ˈer- **-s** -s
air-condition ˈeə.kənˌdɪʃ.ᵊn, ˌeə.kənˈdɪʃ-, (US) ˈer.kənˌdɪʃ- **-s** -z **-ing** -ɪŋ **-ed** -d **-er/s** -əʳ/z, (US) -ɚ/z
air-cool ˈeə.kuːl, (US) ˈer- **-s** -z **-ing** -ɪŋ **-ed** -d
aircraft ˈeə.krɑːft, (US) ˈer.kræft
aircraft|man ˈeə.krɑːft|.mən, (US) ˈer.kræft- **-men** -mən
aircraft|woman ˈeə.krɑːft|ˌwʊm.ən, (US) ˈer.kræft- **-women** -ˌwɪm.ɪn
aircrew ˈeə.kruː, (US) ˈer- **-s** -z
Aird eəd, (US) erd
airdate ˈeə.deɪt, (US) ˈer- **-s** -s
Airdrie ˈeə.dri, (US) ˈer-
Airdrieonian ˌeə.driˈəʊ.ni.ən, (US) ˌer.driˈoʊ- **-s** -z
airdrome ˈeə.drəʊm, (US) ˈer.droʊm **-s** -z
air-drop ˈeə.drɒp, (US) ˈer.drɑːp **-s** -s **-ping** -ɪŋ **-ped** -t
air-dr|y ˈeə.dr|aɪ, (US) ˈer- **-ies** -z **-ing** -ɪŋ **-ied** -d
Aire eəʳ, (US) er
Airedale ˈeə.deɪl, (US) ˈer- **-s** -z
air-engine ˈeəʳ.en.dʒɪn, (US) ˈer- **-s** -z
airer ˈeə.rəʳ, (US) ˈer.ɚ **-s** -z
Airey ˈeə.ri, (US) ˈer.i
airfare ˈeə.feəʳ, (US) ˈer.fer **-s** -z
airfield ˈeə.fiːld, (US) ˈer- **-s** -z
airfleet ˈeə.fliːt, (US) ˈer-
airflow ˈeə.fləʊ, (US) ˈer.floʊ **-s** -z
air-foil ˈeə.fɔɪl, (US) ˈer- **-s** -z
airgraph ˈeə.grɑːf, -græf, (US) ˈer.græf **-s** -s
airgun ˈeəˌgʌn, (US) ˈer- **-s** -z
airhead ˈeə.hed, (US) ˈer- **-s** -z
airi|ly ˈeə.rᵊ|l.i, -rɪ|l.i, (US) ˈer- **-ness** -nəs, -nɪs
airing ˈeə.rɪŋ, (US) ˈer.ɪŋ **-s** -z **ˈairing ˌcupboard**
air-kiss ˈeə.kɪs, (US) ˈer- **-es** -ɪz **-ing** -ɪŋ **-ed** -t
airless ˈeə.ləs, -lɪs, (US) ˈer-
Airlie ˈeə.li, (US) ˈer-
airlift ˈeə.lɪft, (US) ˈer- **-s** -s **-ing** -ɪŋ **-ed** -ɪd
airlin|e ˈeə.laɪn, (US) ˈer- **-es** -z **-er/s** -əʳ/z, (US) -ɚ/z
airlock ˈeə.lɒk, (US) ˈer.lɑːk **-s** -s
airmail ˈeə.meɪl, (US) ˈer- **-s** -z
air|man ˈeə|.mən, -mæn, (US) ˈer- **-men** -mən, -men
airmarshal ˈeəˌmɑː.ʃᵊl, (US) ˈerˌmɑːr-
airmobile ˈeə.məʊ.biːl, (US) ˈerˌmoʊ.bᵊl
airplane ˈeə.pleɪn, (US) ˈer- **-s** -z
airplay ˈeə.pleɪ, (US) ˈer-
airport ˈeə.pɔːt, (US) ˈer.pɔːrt **-s** -s
air-sea ˌeəˈsiː, (US) ˌer- *stress shift, see compound:* **ˌair-sea ˈrescue**
airship ˈeə.ʃɪp, (US) ˈer- **-s** -s
airshow ˈeə.ʃəʊ, (US) ˈer.ʃoʊ **-s** -z
airsick ˈeə.sɪk, (US) ˈer- **-ness** -nəs, -nɪs
airspace ˈeə.speɪs, (US) ˈer-
airspeed ˈeə.spiːd, (US) ˈer- **-s** -z
airstream ˈeə.striːm, (US) ˈer-
airstrike ˈeə.straɪk, (US) ˈer- **-s** -s
airstrip ˈeə.strɪp, (US) ˈer- **-s** -s
airtight ˈeə.taɪt, (US) ˈer-
airtime ˈeə.taɪm, (US) ˈer-
air-to-air ˌeə.tuˈeəʳ, (US) ˌer.t̬əˈer, -tuˈ- *stress shift:* **ˌair-to-air ˈmissile**
air-to-ground ˌeə.təˈgraʊnd, (US) ˌer.t̬ə-
air-to-surface ˌeə.təˈsɜː.fɪs, (US) ˌer.t̬əˈsɝː.fəs *stress shift:* **ˌair-to-surface ˈmissile**
Airtours® ˈeə.tɔːz, -tʊəz, (US) ˈer.tʊrz
air traffic ˈeəˌtræf.ɪk, (US) ˈer-
airwave ˈeə.weɪv, (US) ˈer- **-s** -z
airway ˈeə.weɪ, (US) ˈer- **-s** -z
air|woman ˈeə|ˌwʊm.ən, (US) ˈer- **-women** -ˌwɪm.ɪn
airworth|y ˈeəˌwɜː.ð|i, (US) ˈerˌwɝː- **-iness** -i.nəs, -i.nɪs
air|y, A~ ˈeə.r|i, (US) ˈer|.i **-ier** -i.əʳ, (US) -i.ɚ **-iest** -i.əst, -i.ɪst **-ily** -ᵊ.li, -ɪ.li **-iness** -ɪ.nəs, -ɪ.nɪs
airy-fairy ˌeə.riˈfeə.ri, (US) ˌer.iˈfer.i *stress shift:* **ˌairy-fairy ˈconcept**
Aisha aɪˈiː.ʃə
Aislaby ˈeɪz.lə.bi; *locally:* ˈeɪ.zᵊl.bi
aisle aɪl **-s** -z **-d** -d
aitch eɪtʃ **-es** -ɪz

> Note: The pronunciation /heɪtʃ/ is a common non-standard pronunciation of 'aitch'. In Northern Ireland it is considered a shibboleth, being particularly associated with Catholic speakers.

aitchbone ˈeɪtʃ.bəʊn, (US) -boʊn **-s** -z
Aitchison ˈeɪ.tʃɪ.sᵊn
Aith eɪθ
Aitken ˈeɪt.kɪn, -kən
Aix eɪks, eks
Aix-en-Provence ˌeɪks.ɑ̃ːm.prəˈvɑ̃ːns, ˌeks-, (US) -ɑːn.proʊˈvɑ̃ːs
Aix-la-Chapelle ˌeɪks.lɑː.ʃæpˈel, ˌeks-, -ʃəˈpel, (US) -ʃɑːˈpel
Aix-les-Bains ˌeɪks.leɪˈbæ̃ŋ, ˌeks-
Ajaccio əˈʒæk.si.əʊ, əˈdʒæs.i.əʊ, (US) ɑːˈjɑː.tʃoʊ, -tʃi.oʊ
ajar əˈdʒɑːʳ, (US) -dʒɑːr
Ajax *cleaning substance ®:* ˈeɪ.dʒæks *football team:* ˈaɪ.æks
ajutage ˈædʒ.ʊ.tɪdʒ, əˈdʒuːt-, (US) ˈædʒ.ə.t̬ɪdʒ, əˈdʒuː-
AKA, aka ˌeɪ.keɪˈeɪ, ˈæk.ə
Akaba ˈæk.ə.bə
Akabusi ˌæk.əˈbuː.si
Akahito ˌæk.əˈhiː.təʊ, (US) ˌɑː.kəˈhiː.toʊ
Akbar ˈæk.bɑːʳ, (US) -bɑːr
akela ɑːˈkeɪ.lə
Akerman ˈæk.ə.mən, (US) ˈ-ɚ-
Akers ˈeɪ.kəz, (US) -kɚz
Akhmatova əkˈmɑː.tə.və, ˌɑːk.məˈtəʊ-, (US) ʌkˈmɑː.tə.və, ˌɑːk.məˈtoʊ-
Akihito ˌæk.iˈhiː.təʊ, (US) ˌɑː.kiˈhiː.toʊ
akimbo əˈkɪm.bəʊ, (US) -boʊ
akin əˈkɪn
Akkad ˈæk.æd, (US) ˈæk.æd, ˈɑː.kɑːd
Akkadian əˈkeɪ.di.ən, (US) -ˈkeɪ-, -ˈkɑː- **-s** -z
Akond of Swat *former title of the*

Wali of Swat territory in Pakistan: əˌkuːnd.əvˈswɒt, ⓤⓢ -ˈswɑːt *name in poem by Edward Lear:* ˌæk.ənd.əvˈswɒt, ⓤⓢ -ˈswɑːt
Akron ˈæk.rɒn, -rən, ⓤⓢ -rən
Akrotiri ˈæk.rəʊˈtɪə.ri, ⓤⓢ ˌɑːk.roʊˈtɪr.i
Akroyd ˈæk.rɔɪd
Al æl
AL ˌeɪˈel
al- ˈæl, əl
Note: Prefix. Examples include **allocate** /ˈæl.ə.keɪt/, in which it is stressed, and **allure** /əˈljʊəʳ/ ⓤⓢ /-ˈlʊr/, where it is unstressed.
-al əl
Note: Suffix. When forming a noun, **-al** does not normally affect the stress pattern, e.g. **arouse** /əˈraʊz/, **arousal** /əˈraʊ.zəl/. In forming adjectives, however, the resulting item is usually either stressed one or two syllables before the suffix, e.g. **abdomen** becomes **abdominal** /æbˈdɒm.ɪ.nəl/ ⓤⓢ /-ˈdɑː.mə-/, **adjective** becomes **adjectival** /ˌædʒ.ɪkˈtaɪ.vəl/.
à la ˈæl.ɑː, ˈɑː.lɑː, ⓤⓢ ˈɑː.lɑː, ˈɑː.lə, ˈæl.ə
Ala. (abbrev. for **Alabama**) ˌæl.əˈbæm.ə, -ˈbɑː.mə, ⓤⓢ -ˈbæm.ə
Alabama ˌæl.əˈbæm.ə, -ˈbɑː.mə, ⓤⓢ -ˈbæm.ə
alabaster, A~ ˌæl.əˈbæs.təʳ, -ˈbɑː.stəʳ, ˈæl.ə.bæs.təʳ, -bɑː.stəʳ, ⓤⓢ ˈæl.ə.bæs.tɚ
à la carte ˌæl.əˈkɑːt, ˌɑː.lɑːˈ-, ⓤⓢ ˌɑː.ləˈkɑːrt, ˌæl.əˈ-
alack əˈlæk
alackaday əˌlæk.əˈdeɪ, əˈlæk.əˈdeɪ
alacrity əˈlæk.rə.ti, -rɪ.ti, ⓤⓢ -t̬i
Aladdin əˈlæd.ɪn, ⓤⓢ -ən **Aˌladdin's ˈcave**
Alagoas ˌæl.əˈgəʊ.əs, ⓤⓢ -ˈgoʊ-
à la grecque ˌæl.əˈgrek, ˌɑː.lɑːˈ-, ⓤⓢ ˌɑː.ləˈ-, ˌæl.əˈ-
Alain *man's name:* ælˈæ̃ːn *woman's name:* əˈleɪn
Alain-Fournier ˌæl.æ̃nˈfɔː.ni.eɪ; *as if French:* -fʊəˈnjeɪ; ⓤⓢ -ˌæ̃n.fɔːrˈnjeɪ
Alameda ˌæl.əˈmeɪ.də
Alamein ˈæl.ə.meɪn
Alamo ˈæl.ə.məʊ, ⓤⓢ -moʊ
à la mode ˌæl.əˈməʊd, ˌɑː.lɑː-, -ˈmɒd, ⓤⓢ ˌɑː.ləˈmoʊd, ˌæl.əˈ-
Alamogordo ˌæl.ə.məˈgɔː.dəʊ, ⓤⓢ -ˈgɔːr.doʊ
Alan ˈæl.ən
Alana əˈlɑː.nə, -ˈlæn.ə
aland adv əˈlænd
Aland *islands:* ˈɑː.lənd, ˈɔː-
à l'anglaise ˌæl.ɑ̃ːŋˈgleɪz, ˌɑː.lɑ̃ːŋˈ-, -ˈglez
alanine ˈæl.ə.naɪn, -niːn
alar ˈeɪ.ləʳ, -lɑːʳ, ⓤⓢ -lɚ
Alaric ˈæl.ə.rɪk
alarm əˈlɑːm, ⓤⓢ -ˈlɑːrm **-s** -z **-ing/ly** -ɪŋ/li **-ed** -d **aˈlarm ˌclock**
alarmist əˈlɑː.mɪst, ⓤⓢ -ˈlɑːr- **-s** -s
alarum əˈlær.əm; -ˈlɑː.rəm, -ˈleə-, ⓤⓢ -ˈler.əm, -ˈlɑːr- **-s** -z
alas əˈlæs, -ˈlɑːs, ⓤⓢ -ˈlæs
Alasdair ˈæl.ə.stəʳ, -steəʳ, ⓤⓢ -stɚ
Alask|a əˈlæs.k|ə **-an/s** -ən/z
Alastair ˈæl.ə.stəʳ, -steəʳ, ⓤⓢ -stɚ, -ster
Alastor əˈlæs.tɔːʳ, ælˈæs-, ⓤⓢ -tɔːr, -tɚ
alate ˈeɪ.leɪt **-s** -s
alb ælb **-s** -z
Alba ˈæl.bə
albacore ˈæl.bə.kɔː, ⓤⓢ -kɔːr **-s** -z
Alba Longa ˌæl.bəˈlɒŋ.gə, ⓤⓢ -ˈlɑːŋ.gə, -ˈlɔːŋ-
Alban ˈɔːl.bən, ˈɒl-, ⓤⓢ ˈɑːl-
Albani ælˈbɑː.ni, ⓤⓢ ɑːl-, ɔːl-
Albani|a ælˈbeɪ.ni|.ə, ɔːl- **-an/s** -ən/z
Albany *in London:* ˈɔːl.bə.ni, ˈɒl-, ˈæl-, ⓤⓢ ˈɑːl-, ˈɔːl- *in Australia:* ˈæl.bə.ni, ⓤⓢ ˈɑːl.bə-, ˈɔːl- *in US:* ˈɔːl.bə.ni, ˈɒl-, ⓤⓢ ˈɑːl-
Albarn ˈɔːl.bɑːn, ˈɒl-, ⓤⓢ ˈɑːl.bɑːrn
albatross ˈæl.bə.trɒs, ⓤⓢ -trɑːs, -trɔːs **-es** -ɪz
albedo ælˈbiː.dəʊ, ⓤⓢ -doʊ **-(e)s** -z
Albee ˈɔːl.biː, ˈæl-, ⓤⓢ ˈɑːl-, ˈɔːl-, ˈæl-
albeit ɔːlˈbiː.ɪt, ⓤⓢ ɔːl-, ɑːl-
Albemarle ˈæl.bə.mɑːl, -bɪ-, ⓤⓢ -mɑːrl
Alberic ˈæl.bə.rɪk
Alberich ˈæl.bə.rɪk, -rɪx, ⓤⓢ -rɪk
Albers ˈæl.bɜːz, ˈɔːl.bəz, ⓤⓢ ˈæl.bɝːz, ˈɑːl.bɚz
albert, A~ ˈæl.bət, ⓤⓢ -bɚt **-s** -s **ˌAlbert ˈHall**
Alberta ælˈbɜː.tə, ⓤⓢ -ˈbɝː.t̬ə
albertite ˈæl.bə.taɪt, ⓤⓢ -bɚ-
Alberto ælˈbɜː.təʊ, ⓤⓢ -ˈbɝː.t̬oʊ
Alberton ˈæl.bə.tən, ⓤⓢ -bɚ-
albescen|ce ælˈbes.ən|ts **-t** -t
Albi ˈæl.bi
Albigenses ˌæl.bɪˈgent.siːz, -bɪˈdʒent-
albinism ˈæl.bɪ.nɪ.zəm
albino ælˈbiː.nəʊ, ⓤⓢ -ˈbaɪ.noʊ **-s** -z
Albinoni ˌæl.bɪˈnəʊ.ni, ⓤⓢ -ˈnoʊ-
Albinus ælˈbiː.nəs
Albion ˈæl.bi.ən
Albrecht ˈæl.brekt, -brext, ⓤⓢ ˈɑːl.brekt
Albright ˈɔːl.braɪt, ˈɒl-, ⓤⓢ ˈɑːl-, ˈɔːl-
Albrighton ˈɔː.braɪ.tən, ˈɔːl-, ˈɒl-, ⓤⓢ ˈɑːl-
Albrow ˈɔːl.braʊ, ⓤⓢ ˈɑːl-
Albufeira ˌæl.buˈfeə.rə, ⓤⓢ ˌɑːl.buːˈfeɪ.rə
Albula ˈæl.bjʊ.lə, ⓤⓢ ˈɑːl.buː-, -bjuː-
album ˈæl.bəm **-s** -z
albumen ˈæl.bjʊ.mən, -men, -mɪn, ⓤⓢ ælˈbjuː.mən
albumin ˈæl.bjʊ.mɪn, -bjə.mɪn, ⓤⓢ ælˈbjuː.mən
albuminoid ælˈbjuː.mɪ.nɔɪd **-s** -z
albuminous ælˈbjuː.mɪ.nəs
albuminuria ˌæl.bjuː.mɪˈnjʊə.ri.ə, ⓤⓢ -ˈnʊr.i-, -ˈnjʊr-
Albuquerque ˌæl.bəˈkɜː.ki, ˈæl.bəˌkɜː-, ⓤⓢ ˈæl.bəˌkɝː-; *esp. for person:* ˌ--ˈ--
Albury ˈɔːl.bər.i, ˈɒl-, ⓤⓢ ˈɔːl-, ˈɑːl-
Alcaeus ælˈsiː.əs
alcaic, A~ ælˈkeɪ.ɪk **-s** -s
alcalde ælˈkæl.deɪ, -di, ⓤⓢ -ˈkɑːl.di, -deɪ **-s** -z
Alcan® ˈæl.kæn
Alcatraz ˈæl.kə.træz, ˌ--ˈ-
Alcazar *Spanish palace:* ˌæl.kəˈzɑː, ⓤⓢ ˈæl.kə.zɑːr; ⓤⓢ ælˈkæz.ɚ *music hall:* ælˈkæz.əʳ, ⓤⓢ -ɚ
Alcester ˈɔːl.stəʳ, ˈɒl-, ⓤⓢ ˈɔːl.stɚ, ˈɑːl-
Alcestis ælˈses.tɪs
alchemic ælˈkem.ɪk **-al** -əl
alchemist ˈæl.kə.mɪst, -kɪ- **-s** -s
alchemy ˈæl.kə.mi, -kɪ-
Alcibiades ˌæl.sɪˈbaɪ.ə.diːz
Alcinous ælˈsɪn.əʊ.əs, ⓤⓢ ˈ-oʊ-
Alcmene ælkˈmiː.niː
Alcock ˈɔːl.kɒk, ˈæl-, ˈɒl-, ⓤⓢ ˈɑːl.kɑːk, ˈæl-, ˈɔːl-
alcohol ˈæl.kə.hɒl, ⓤⓢ -hɑːl **-s** -z
alcoholic ˌæl.kəˈhɒl.ɪk, ⓤⓢ -ˈhɑː.lɪk **-s** -s *stress shift:* **ˌalcoholic ˈdrink**
alcoholism ˈæl.kə.hɒl.ɪ.zəm, ⓤⓢ -hɑː.lɪ-
Alconbury ˈɔːl.kən.bər.i, ˈɔː-, ˈɒl-, -kəm-, -bri, ⓤⓢ ˈɔːl.kən.ber.i, ˈɑːl-, -bɚ-
alcopop ˈæl.kəʊ.pɒp, ⓤⓢ -koʊ.pɑːp **-s** -s
Alcott ˈɔːl.kət, ˈɒl-, -kɒt, ⓤⓢ ˈɑːl.kɑːt, ˈæl-, -kət
alcove ˈæl.kəʊv, ˈɒl-, ⓤⓢ ˈæl.koʊv **-s** -z **-d** -d
Alcuin ˈæl.kwɪn, ˈɒl-, ⓤⓢ ˈæl-
Alcyone ælˈsaɪ.ə.ni
Aldborough ˈɔːld.bər.ə, ˈɒl-; *locally:* ˈɔː.brə, ⓤⓢ ˈɔːld.bɚ.oʊ, ˈɑːld-
Aldbury ˈɔːld.bər.i, ˈɒl-, ⓤⓢ ˈɔːld.ber-, ˈɑːld-, -bɚ-
Alde ɔːld, ⓤⓢ ɔːld, ɑːld
Aldebaran ælˈdeb.ə.rən, -ræn
Aldeburgh ˈɔːld.bər.ə, ˈɒl-, ⓤⓢ ˈɔːld.bɚ.ə, ˈɑːld-
aldehyde ˈæl.dɪ.haɪd, -də- **-s** -z
Alden ˈɔːl.dən, ˈɒl-, ⓤⓢ ˈɔːl-, ˈɑːl-
Aldenham ˈɔːld.ən.əm, ˈɒld-, ⓤⓢ ˈɔːld-, ˈɑːld-
al dente ælˈden.teɪ, ɑːl-
alder, A~ ˈɔːl.dəʳ, ˈɒl-, ⓤⓢ ˈɔːl.dɚ, ˈɑːl- **-s** -z
Alderley Edge ˌɔːl.də.liˈedʒ, ˌɒl-, ⓤⓢ ˌɔːl.dɚ-, ˌɑːl-
alder|man, A~ ˈɔːl.də|.mən, ˈɒl-, ⓤⓢ ˈɔːl.dɚ-, ˈɑːl- **-men** -mən, -men
aldermanic ˌɔːl.dəˈmæn.ɪk, ˌɒl-, ⓤⓢ ˌɔːl.dɚˈ-, ˌɑːl-
Aldermaston ˈɔːl.də.mɑː.stən, ⓤⓢ ˈɔːl.dɚ-, ˈɑːl-
aldern ˈɔːl.dən, ˈɒl-, -dɜːn, ⓤⓢ ˈɔːl.dɚn, ˈɑːl-
Alderney ˈɔːl.də.ni, ˈɒl-, ⓤⓢ ˈɔːl.dɚ-, ˈɑːl-
Aldersgate ˈɔːl.dəz.geɪt, ˈɒl-, -gɪt, ⓤⓢ ˈɔːl.dɚz-, ˈɑːl-
Aldershot ˈɔːl.də.ʃɒt, ˈɒl-, ⓤⓢ ˈɔːl.dɚ.ʃɑːt, ˈɑːl-
Alderson ˈɔːl.də.sən, ˈɒl-, ⓤⓢ ˈɔːl.dɚ-, ˈɑːl-
Alderton ˈɔːl.də.tən, ˈɒl-, ⓤⓢ ˈɔːl.dɚ-, ˈɑːl-

A

Aldgate ˈɔːl*d*.geɪt, ˈɒl-, -gɪt, US ˈɔːl*d*-, ˈɑːl*d*-
Aldhelm ˈɔːld.helm, ˈɒl-, US ˈɔːld-, ˈɑːld-
Aldi® ˈæl.di, US ˈɑːl-
Aldine ˈɔːl.daɪn, ɒl-, -diːn, US ˈɔːl-, ˈɑːl-
Aldington ˈɔːl.dɪŋ.tən, ˈɒl-, US ˈɔːl-, ˈɑːl-
Aldis(s) ˈɔːl.dɪs, ˈɒl-, US ˈɔːl-, ˈɑːl-
Aldous ˈɔːl.dəs, ˈɒl-, US ˈɔːl.dəs, ˈɑːl-, ˈæl-
Aldred ˈɔːl.drɪd, ˈɒl-, -dred, US ˈɔːl-, ˈɑːl-
Aldrich ˈɔːl.drɪtʃ, ˈɒl-, -drɪdʒ, US ˈɔːl-, ˈɑːl-
Aldridge ˈɔːl.drɪdʒ, ˈɒl-, US ˈɔːl-, ˈɑːl-
Aldrin ˈɔːl.drɪn, ˈɒl-, US ˈɔːl-, ˈɑːl-
Aldsworth ˈɔːldz.wəθ, ˈɒl-, -wɜːθ, US ˈɔːldz.wɚθ, ˈɑːldz-, -wɝːθ
Aldus ˈɔːl.dəs, ˈɒl-, ˈæl-, US ˈɔːl-, ˈɑːl-
Aldwych ˈɔːld.wɪtʃ, ˈɒld-, US ˈɔːld-, ˈɑːld-
ale, A~ eɪl **-s** -z
aleatoric ˌæl.i.əˈtɒr.ɪk, ˌeɪ.li-, US -ˈtɔːr-, -ˈtɑːr- **-ally** -əl.i, -li
aleatory ˈeɪ.li.ə.tər.i, ˌæl.iˈeɪ.tər.i, US ˈeɪ.li.ə.tɔːr-
Alec(k) ˈæl.ɪk, -lek
Alecto əˈlek.təʊ, US -toʊ
Aled ˈæl.ed, -ɪd
alehou|se ˈeɪl.haʊ|s **-ses** -zɪz
Alemannic ˌæl.ɪˈmæn.ɪk, -əˈ-
alembic əˈlem.bɪk **-s** -s
Alençon ˈæl.ɑ̃n.sɔ̃ːŋ, US əˈlen.sən; US ˌæl.ɑːnˈsoʊn
Aleppo əˈlep.əʊ, ælˈep-, US -oʊ
a|lert ə|ˈlɜːt, US -ˈlɝːt **-lerts** -ˈlɜːts, US -ˈlɝːts **-lertly** -ˈlɜːt.li, US -ˈlɝːt.li **-lertness** -ˈlɜːt.nəs, -nɪs, US -ˈlɝːt.nəs, -nɪs **-lerting** -ˈlɜː.tɪŋ, US -ˈlɝː.t̬ɪŋ **-lerted** -ˈlɜː.tɪd, US -ˈlɝː.t̬ɪd
Alessandria ˌæl.ɪˈsæn.dri.ə, -esˈ-, US ˌæl.əˈsæn-, ˌɑː.ləˈsɑːn-
Alessi əˈles.i
Alethea ˌæl.əˈθiː.ə; əˈliː.θi-; ˈæl.ɪ.θi-, US ˌæl.ɪˈθiː.ə; US əˈliː.θi-
alethic ælˈiː.θɪk, əˈliː-
Aletsch ˈæl.ɪtʃ, ˈɑː.lɪtʃ, -letʃ, US ˈɑː.letʃ
Aleut əˈljuːt, -luːt; ˈæl.juːt, -uːt, US əˈluːt; US ˈæl.juːt, -i.uːt **-s** -s
Aleutian əˈljuː.ʃən, -ˈluː-, US -ˈluː-
A-level ˈeɪˌlev.əl **-s** -z
alewi|fe ˈeɪl.waɪ|f **-ves** -vz
Alex ˈæl.ɪks
Alexander ˌæl.ɪgˈzɑːn.dər, -egˈ-, -əgˈ-, -ˈzæn-, -ɪkˈsɑːn-, US -ˈzæn.dɚ **Alexˈander techˌnique**
Alexandra ˌæl.ɪgˈzɑːn.drə, -egˈ-, -əgˈ-, -ˈzæn-, -ɪkˈsɑːn-, US -ˈzæn-
Alexandria ˌæl.ɪgˈzɑːn.dri.ə, -əgˈ-, -ˈzæn-, -ɪkˈsɑːn-, US -ˈzæn-
alexandrian ˌæl.ɪgˈzɑːn.dri.ən, -egˈ-, -əgˈ-, -ˈzæn-, -ɪkˈsɑːn-, US -ˈzæn- **-s** -z
Alexandrina ˌæl.ɪg.zænˈdriː.nə, -eg-, -əg-ˈ, -zɑːnˈ-, -ɪk.sɑːnˈ-
alexandrine ˌæl.ɪgˈzæn.draɪn, -egˈ-, -əgˈ-, -ˈzɑːn-, -ɪkˈsɑːn-, US -ˈzæn.drɪn, -ˈzæn.draɪn **-s** -z
alexia ˌeɪˈlek.si.ə, ə-, US ə-
Alexis əˈlek.sɪs
Alf ælf
alfalfa ˌælˈfæl.fə
Alfa Romeo® ˌæl.fə.rəʊˈmeɪ.əʊ, US -roʊˈmeɪ.oʊ
Alfie ˈæl.fi
Alfonso ælˈfɒn*t*.səʊ, -ˈfɒn.zəʊ, US -ˈfɑːn*t*.soʊ, -ˈfɑːn.zoʊ
Alford ˈɔːl.fəd, ˈɒl-, US ˈɔːl.fɚd, ˈɑːl-
Alfred ˈæl.frɪd, -frəd
Alfreda ælˈfriː.də
Alfredian ælˈfriː.di.ən
alfresco, al fresco ælˈfres.kəʊ, US -koʊ
Alfreton ˈɔːl.frɪ.tən, ˈɒl-, US ˈɔːl.frɪ.tən, ˈɑːl-
Alfric ˈæl.frɪk
Alfriston ˈæl.frɪ.stən, ˈɔːl-
al|ga ˈæl|.gə **-gae** -dʒiː, -dʒaɪ, -giː, -gaɪ
Algarve ælˈgɑːv, ˈæl.gɑːv, US ɑːlˈgɑːr.və
algebra ˈæl.dʒɪ.brə, -dʒə- **-s** -z
algebraic ˌæl.dʒɪˈbreɪ.ɪk, -dʒəˈ- **-al** -əl **-ally** -əl.i, -li *stress shift:* **ˌalgebraic ˈsum**
algebraist ˌæl.dʒɪˈbreɪ.ɪst, -dʒəˈ- **-s** -s
Algeciras ˌæl.dʒɪˈsɪə.rəs, -dʒəˈ-, -dʒesˈɪə-, -ˈsɪr.əs, US -ˈsɪr.əs
Alger ˈæl.dʒər, US -dʒɚ
Algeri|a ælˈdʒɪə.ri|.ə, US -ˈdʒɪr.i- **-an/s** -ən/z
Algerine ˌæl.dʒəˈriːn
Algernon ˈæl.dʒə.nən, -nɒn, US -dʒɚ.nɑːn, -nən
Algiers ælˈdʒɪəz, US -ˈdʒɪrz
Algoa ælˈgəʊ.ə, US -ˈgoʊ-
Algol, ALGOL ˈæl.gɒl, US -gɑːl
Algonquian ælˈgɒŋ.kwi.ən, -ki.ən, US -ˈgɑːŋ-, -ˈgɔːŋ-
Algonquin ælˈgɒŋ.kwɪn, -kɪn, US -ˈgɑːn-, -ˈgɔːŋ-
algorism ˈæl.gər.ɪ.zəm
algorithm ˈæl.gər.ɪ.ðəm **-s** -z
algorithmic ˌæl.gəˈrɪð.mɪk *stress shift:* **ˌalgorithmic deˈsign**
Algren ˈɔːl.grɪn, ˈɒl-, US ˈɔːl-, ˈɑːl-
Algy ˈæl.dʒi
Alhambra *in Spain:* ælˈhæm.brə, əl-; əˈlæm- *in California:* ælˈhæm.brə
Ali *girl's name:* ˈæl.i; *boy's name and surname:* ˈɑː.li, ɑːˈli
alias ˈeɪ.li.əs, -æs **-es** -ɪz
Ali Baba ˌæl.iˈbɑː.bɑː, ˌɑː.li-, -bə
alibi ˈæl.ɪ.baɪ **-s** -z
Alicante ˌæl.ɪˈkæn.teɪ, -ti, US -ti, -teɪ
Alice ˈæl.ɪs **ˌAlice ˈSprings; ˌAlice in ˈWonderland**
Alicia əˈlɪs.i.ə, -ˈlɪʃ.ə, US -ˈlɪʃ.ə, -i.ə
Alick ˈæl.ɪk
alien ˈeɪ.li.ən **-s** -z **-ing** -ɪŋ **-ed** -d **-age** -ɪdʒ
alienable ˈeɪ.li.ən.ə.bəl
alie|nate ˈeɪ.li.ə|.neɪt **-nates** -neɪts **-nating** -neɪ.tɪŋ, US -neɪ.t̬ɪŋ **-nated** -neɪ.tɪd, US -neɪ.t̬ɪd **-nator/s** -neɪ.tər/z, US -neɪ.t̬ɚ/z
alienation ˌeɪ.li.əˈneɪ.ʃən **-s** -z
alien|ism ˈeɪ.li.ə.n|ɪ.zəm **-ist/s** -ɪst/s
a|light ə|ˈlaɪt **-lights** -ˈlaɪts **-lighting** -ˈlaɪ.tɪŋ, US -ˈlaɪ.t̬ɪŋ **-lighted** -ˈlaɪ.tɪd, US -ˈlaɪ.t̬ɪd
align əˈlaɪn **-s** -z **-ing** -ɪŋ **-ed** -d
alignment əˈlaɪn.mənt, -ˈlaɪm-, US -ˈlaɪn- **-s** -s
alike əˈlaɪk
aliment ˈæl.ɪ.mənt **-s** -s
alimental ˌæl.ɪˈmen.təl, US -t̬əl
alimentary ˌæl.ɪˈmen.tər.i, ˈ-tri, US -t̬ər.i, ˈ-tri **aliˌmentary caˈnal** US **aliˈmentary caˌnal**
alimentation ˌæl.ɪ.menˈteɪ.ʃən
alimon|y ˈæl.ɪ.mə.n|i, US -moʊ- **-ies** -iz
alin|e *= align:* əˈlaɪn **-es** -z **-ing** -ɪŋ **-ed** -d
Aline *woman's name:* ælˈiːn, əˈliːn; ˈæl.iːn
A-line ˈeɪ.laɪn
alineation əˌlɪn.iˈeɪ.ʃən **-s** -z
Alington ˈæl.ɪŋ.tən
Ali Pasha ˌæl.iˈpɑː.ʃə, ˌɑː.li-, -ˈpæʃ.ə, US ˌɑː.liˈpɑː.ʃɑː, ˌæl.iˈ-
aliqu|ant ˈæl.ɪ.kw|ənt **-ot** -ɒt, US -ɑːt
Alisha əˈlɪʃ.ə
Alison ˈæl.ɪ.sən
Alissa əˈlɪs.ə
Alistair, Alister ˈæl.ɪ.stər, US -stɚ
alit əˈlɪt
Alitalia® ˌæl.ɪˈtæl.i.ə, ˌɑː.liˈtɑː.li-, US -jə
alive əˈlaɪv
Alix ˈæl.ɪks
alizarin əˈlɪz.ə.rɪn
alkahest ˈæl.kə.hest
alkalescen|ce ˌæl.kəlˈes.ən|*t*s, US -kəˈles- **-cy** -*t*.si **-t** -t
alkali ˈæl.kəl.aɪ, US -kə.laɪ **-(e)s** -z
alkalic ˌælˈkæl.ɪk
alkali|fy ˌælˈkæl.ɪ.f|aɪ, -ə.faɪ **-ies** -aɪz **-ying** -aɪ.ɪŋ **-ied** -aɪd
alkaline ˈæl.kəl.aɪn, US -kə.laɪn
alkalinity ˌæl.kəlˈɪn.ə.ti, -ɪ.ti, US -kəˈlɪn.ə.t̬i
alkalization, -isa- ˌæl.kəl.aɪˈzeɪ.ʃən, -ɪˈ-, US -əˈ-
alkaliz|e, -is|e ˈæl.kəl.aɪz, US -kə.laɪz **-es** -ɪz **-ing** -ɪŋ **-ed** -d
alkaloid ˈæl.kəl.ɔɪd, US -kə.lɔɪd **-s** -z **-al** -əl
alkane ˈæl.keɪn **-s** -z
Alka Seltzer® ˌæl.kəˈselt.sər, US ˈæl.kəˌselt.sɚ
alkene ˈæl.kiːn **-s** -z
Alkoran ˌæl.kɒrˈɑːn, -kɔːˈrɑːn, -kəˈrɑːn, US -kɔːrˈɑːn, -kəˈrɑːn, -ˈræn
alk|y ˈæl.k|i **-ies** -iz
alkyl ˈæl.kɪl, US -kəl **-s** -z
alkyne ˈæl.kaɪn **-s** -z
all ɔːl, US ɔːl, ɑːl **ˌall ˈfours; ˌall ˈright**
alla breve ˌæl.əˈbreɪ.veɪ, -vi, US ˌɑː.ləˈbreɪ.vi, -veɪ
Allah ˈæl.ə, -ɑː; əˈlɑː, ælˈɑː

Allahabad ˌæl.ə.həˈbɑːd, -ˈbæd
all-American ˌɔːl.əˈmer.ɪ.kᵊn, US ˌɔːl-, ˌɑːl-
Allan ˈæl.ən
Allan-a-Dale ˌæl.ən.əˈdeɪl
Allandale ˈæl.ən.deɪl
allantois əˈlæn.təʊ.ɪs, US -toʊ- **allantoides** əˌlænˈtəʊ.ɪ.diːz, US ˌæl.ənˈtoʊ.ə-
Allard ˈæl.ɑːd, -əd, US -ɑːrd, -ɚd
Allardice, Allardyce ˈæl.ə.daɪs, US ˈ-ɚ-
allargando ˌæl.ɑːˈgæn.dəʊ, US ˌɑː.lɑːrˈgɑːn.doʊ
allative ˈæl.ə.tɪv, US -t̬ɪv
allay əˈleɪ **-s** -z **-ing** -ɪŋ **-ed** -d
All-Bran® ˈɔːl.bræn, US ˈɔːl-, ˈɑːl-
Allbright ˈɔːl.braɪt, ˈɒl-, US ˈɔːl-, ˈɑːl-
all-clear ˌɔːlˈklɪəʳ, US ˌɔːlˈklɪr, ˌɑːl-
Allcock ˈɔːl.kɒk, US ˈɔːl.kɑːk, ˈɑːl-
all-comers ˈɔːlˌkʌm.əz, US ˈɑːlˌkʌm.ɚz
Allcroft ˈɔːl.krɒft, ˈɒl-, US ˈɔːl.krɑːft, ˈɑːl-
allegation ˌæl.ɪˈgeɪ.ʃᵊn, -əˈ-, -egˈeɪ- **-s** -z
alleg|e əˈledʒ **-es** -ɪz **-ing** -ɪŋ **-ed** -d
allegedly əˈledʒ.ɪd.li, -əd-
Alleghany, Allegheny ˌæl.ɪˈgeɪ.ni, -əˈ-, US -əˈ-
allegian|ce əˈliː.dʒᵊn|ts **-ces** -sɪz **-t** -t
allegoric ˌæl.ɪˈgɒr.ɪk, -əˈgɒr-, US -ˈgɔːr- **-al** -ᵊl **-ally** -ᵊl.i, -li
allegorist ˈæl.ɪ.gə.rɪst, ˈ-ə-, US -gɔːr.ɪst **-s** -s
allegoriz|e, -is|e ˈæl.ɪ.gə.raɪz, ˈ-ə-, US -gɔː-, -gə- **-es** -ɪz **-ing** -ɪŋ **-ed** -d
allegor|y ˈæl.ɪ.gə.r|i, ˈ-ə-, US -gɔːr|.i **-ies** -iz
allegretto ˌæl.ɪˈgret.əʊ, -əˈ-, US -ˈgret̬.oʊ **-s** -z
Allegri ælˈeg.ri, -ˈeɪ.gri
allegro əˈleg.rəʊ, ælˈeg-, -ˈeɪ.grəʊ, US -ˈleg.roʊ, -ˈleɪ.groʊ **-s** -z
Allein(e) ˈæl.ɪn
allele ˈæl.iːl **-s** -z
allelic əˈliː.lɪk
allelism əˈliː.li.zᵊm
alleluia, A~ ˌæl.ɪˈluː.jə, -əˈ- **-s** -z
allemande ˈæl.ə.mɑːnd, -mænd, -mɒnd, US -mænd, -mɑːnd, -mæn, -mən **-s** -z
all-embracing ˌɔːl.ɪmˈbreɪ.sɪŋ, -emˈ-, US ˌɔːl.emˈ-, ˌɑːl-, -ɪmˈ- *stress shift:* ˌ**all-embracing** ˈ**theory**
Allen ˈæl.ən, -ɪn ˈ**Allen** ˌ**key**; ˈ**Allen** ˌ**wrench**
Allenby ˈæl.ən.bi
Allendale ˈæl.ən.deɪl, -ɪn-
Allende aɪˈend.eɪ, -ii, US ɑːˈjen.deɪ, ɑːl-
Allentown ˈæl.ən.taʊn, -ɪn-
allergen ˈæl.ə.dʒen, -dʒən, US ˈ-ɚ- **-s** -z
allergenic ˌæl.əˈdʒen.ɪk, US -ɚˈ-
allergic əˈlɜː.dʒɪk, US -ˈlɝː-
allergist ˈæl.ə.dʒɪst, US ˈ-ɚ- **-s** -s
allerg|y ˈæl.ə.dʒ|i, US ˈ-ɚ- **-ies** -iz
Allerton ˈæl.ə.tᵊn, US ˈ-ɚ.tən
allevi|ate əˈliː.vi|.eɪt **-ates** -eɪts **-ating** -eɪ.tɪŋ, US -eɪ.t̬ɪŋ **-ated** -eɪ.tɪd, US -eɪ.t̬ɪd **-ator/s** -eɪ.təʳ/z, US -eɪ.t̬ɚ/z
alleviation əˌliː.viˈeɪ.ʃᵊn
alley ˈæl.i **-s** -z ˈ**alley** ˌ**cat**
Alleyn ˈæl.ɪn
Alleyne ælˈiːn, ˈæl.ɪn, ælˈeɪn
Alleynian əˈleɪ.ni.ən, ælˈeɪ- **-s** -z
alleyway ˈæl.i.weɪ **-s** -z
All Fools' Day ˌɔːlˈfuːlz.deɪ, US ˌɔːl-, ˌɑːl- **-s** -z
Allhallows ˌɔːlˈhæl.əʊz, US -oʊz, ˌɑːl-
allianc|e əˈlaɪ.ənts **-es** -ɪz
allicin ˈæl.ə.sɪn, ˈ-ɪ-
allied ˈæl.aɪd
Allies ˈæl.aɪz
alligator ˈæl.ɪ.geɪ.təʳ, US -t̬ɚ **-s** -z
all-important ˌɔːl.ɪmˈpɔː.tᵊnt, US ɔːl.ɪmˈpɔːr-, ɑːl- *stress shift:* ˌ**all-important** ˈ**meeting**
all-in ˌɔːlˈɪn, US ˌɔːl-, ˌɑːl- *stress shift:* ˌ**all-in** ˈ**wrestling**
all-inclusive ˌɔːl.ɪŋˈkluː.sɪv, US -ɪnˈ-, ˌɑːl-, -ɪŋˈ-
allineation əˌlɪn.iˈeɪ.ʃᵊn, ælˌɪn- **-s** -z
Allingham ˈæl.ɪŋ.əm
all-in-one ˌɔːl.ɪnˈwʌn, US ˌɑːl- *stress shift:* ˌ**all-in-one sham**ˈ**poo**
Allison ˈæl.ɪ.sᵊn
alliter|ate əˈlɪt.ᵊr|.eɪt, ælˈɪt-, US əˈlɪt̬.ə.r|eɪt **-ates** -eɪts **-ating** -eɪ.tɪŋ, US -eɪ.t̬ɪŋ **-ated** -eɪ.tɪd, US -eɪ.t̬ɪd
alliteration əˌlɪt.əˈreɪ.ʃᵊn, ælˌɪt-, US əˌlɪt̬- **-s** -z
alliterative əˈlɪt.ᵊr.ə.tɪv, ælˈɪt-, -eɪ-, US əˈlɪt̬.ᵊr.ə.t̬ɪv, -ə.reɪ.t̬ɪv
Allman ˈɔːl.mən, US ˈɔːl-, ˈɑːl-
all-nighter ˌɔːlˈnaɪ.təʳ, US -t̬ɚ, ˌɑːl- **-s** -z
Alloa ˈæl.əʊ.ə, US -oʊ.ə
Allobroges əˈlɒb.rə.dʒiːz, ælˈɒb-, -rəʊ-, US əˈlɑː.broʊ-
allo|cate ˈæl.ə|.keɪt **-cates** -keɪts **-cating** -keɪ.tɪŋ, US -keɪ.t̬ɪŋ **-cated** -keɪ.tɪd, US -keɪ.t̬ɪd
allocation ˌæl.əˈkeɪ.ʃᵊn **-s** -z
allocution ˌæl.əˈkjuː.ʃᵊn **-s** -z
allodi|al əˈləʊ.di|.əl, US -ˈloʊ- **-um** -əm
allogeneic ˌæl.əʊ.dʒəˈniː.ɪk, -ˈneɪ-, US ˌ-ə-, ˌ-oʊ- **-ally** -ᵊl.i, -li
allomorph ˈæl.əʊ.mɔːf, US -ə.mɔːrf, -oʊ- **-s** -s
Allon ælˈɒn
allopath ˈæl.əʊ.pæθ, US ˈ-ə-, ˈ-oʊ- **-s** -s
allopathic ˌæl.əʊˈpæθ.ɪk, US -əˈ-, -oʊˈ-
allopath|y əˈlɒp.ə.θ|i, ælˈɒp-, US əˈlɑː.pə- **-ist/s** -ɪst/s
allophone ˈæl.əʊ.fəʊn, US -ə.foʊn, -oʊ- **-s** -z
allophonic ˌæl.əʊˈfɒn.ɪk, US -əˈfɑː.nɪk *stress shift:* ˌ**allophonic** ˈ**variant**
all-or-nothing ˌɔːl.ɔːˈnʌθ.ɪŋ, -əˈ-, -ˈnɒθ-, US -ɔːrˈnʌθ.ɪŋ, ˌɑːl-, -ɚˈ- *stress shift:* ˌ**all-or-nothing** ˈ**gamble**
al|lot əˈl|ɒt, US -ˈlɑːt **-lots** -ˈlɒts, US -ˈlɑːts **-lotting** -ˈlɒt.ɪŋ, US -ˈlɑː.t̬ɪŋ **-lotted** -ˈlɒt.ɪd, US -ˈlɑː.t̬ɪd
allotment əˈlɒt.mənt, US -ˈlɑːt- **-s** -s
allotone ˈæl.əʊ.təʊn, US -ə.toʊn **-s** -z
allotrope ˈæl.ə.trəʊp, US -troʊp **-s** -s
allotropic ˌæl.əˈtrɒp.ɪk, US -ˈtrɑː.pɪk
allotropy ælˈɒt.rə.pi, əˈlɒt-, US əˈlɑː.trə-
all-out ˌɔːlˈaʊt, US ˌɔːl-, ˌɑːl- *stress shift:* ˌ**all-out** ˈ**effort**
allow əˈlaʊ **-s** -z **-ing** -ɪŋ **-ed** -d
allowab|le əˈlaʊ.ə.b|ᵊl **-ly** -li **-leness** -ᵊl.nəs, -nɪs
allowanc|e əˈlaʊ.ənts **-es** -ɪz **-ing** -ɪŋ **-ed** -t
Alloway ˈæl.ə.weɪ
allowedly əˈlaʊ.ɪd.li, -əd-
alloy n ˈæl.ɔɪ **-s** -z
alloy v əˈlɔɪ **-s** -z **-ing** -ɪŋ **-ed** -d
all-powerful ˌɔːlˈpaʊ.ə.fᵊl, -ˈpaʊə-, -fʊl, US -ˈpaʊɚ-, ˌɑːl- *stress shift:* ˌ**all-powerful** ˈ**monarch**
all-purpose ˌɔːlˈpɜː.pəs, US ˌɔːlˈpɝː-, ˌɑːl- *stress shift:* ˌ**all-purpose** ˈ**knife**
all-round ˌɔːlˈraʊnd, US ˌɔːl-, ˌɑːl- *stress shift:* ˌ**all-round** ˈ**athlete**
all-rounder ˌɔːlˈraʊn.dəʳ, US -dɚ, ɑːl- **-s** -z
All Saints' Day ˌɔːlˈseɪntsˌdeɪ, US ˌɔːl-, ˌɑːl- **-s** -z
Allsop(p) ˈɔːl.sɒp, US ˈɔːl.sɑːp, ˈɑːl-
allsorts ˈɔːl.sɔːts, US -sɔːrts, ˈɑːl-
All Souls' Day ˌɔːlˈsəʊlzˌdeɪ, US ˌɔːlˈsoʊlz-, ɑːl- **-s** -z
allspice ˈɔːl.spaɪs, US ˈɔːl-, ˈɑːl-
all-star ˈɔːl.stɑːʳ, US ˈɔːl.stɑːr, ˈɑːl-
all-time ˌɔːlˈtaɪm, US ˈɔːl.taɪm, ˈɑːl- *stress shift, British only, see compound:* ˌ**all-time** ˈ**greats**
allud|e əˈluːd, -ˈljuːd, US -ˈluːd **-es** -z **-ing** -ɪŋ **-ed** -ɪd
Allum ˈæl.əm
allur|e əˈljʊəʳ, -ˈlʊəʳ, -ˈljɔːʳ, US -ˈlʊr **-es** -z **-ing/ly** -ɪŋ/li **-ed** -d **-ement/s** -mənt/s
allusion əˈluː.ʒᵊn, əˈljuː-, US -ˈluː- **-s** -z
allusive əˈluː.sɪv, -ˈljuː-, US -ˈluː- **-ly** -li **-ness** -nəs, -nɪs
alluvi|al əˈluː.vi|.əl, -ˈljuː-, US -ˈluː- **-a** -ə
alluvion əˈluː.vi.ən, -ˈljuː-, US -ˈluː- **-s** -z
alluvi|um əˈluː.vi|.əm, -ˈljuː-, US -ˈluː- **-ums** -əmz **-a** -ə
Allworth ˈɔːl.wəθ, -wɜːθ, US -wɚθ, ˈɑːl-, -wɝːθ
Allworthy ˈɔːlˌwɜː.ði, US -ˌwɝː-, ɑːl-
all|y n ˈæl.aɪ, əˈlaɪ **-ies** -z
all|y v əˈl|aɪ, ælˈ|aɪ; ˈæl|.aɪ **-ies** -aɪz **-ying** -aɪ.ɪŋ **-ied** -aɪd
Note: **Allied** is usually pronounced /ˈæl.aɪd/ when attributive.
Ally ˈæl.i
-ally əl.i, li
Note: Suffix. Words containing **-ally**

are stressed in the same manner as adjectives containing **-al**. Where the word ends **-ically**, two forms are possible, e.g. **musically** is either /ˈmjuː.zɪ.kəl.i/ or /ˈmjuː.zɪ.kli/.

Allyson ˈæl.ɪ.sən
Alma ˈæl.mə
Alma-Ata ˌæl.mɑː.əˈtɑː, ælˌmɑː-, ˌɑːl.məˈɑː.tə
Almack ˈɔːl.mæk, ˈɒl-, (US) ˈɔːl-, ˈɑːl-
almagest ˈæl.mə.dʒest **-s** -s
al-Maliki ælˈmæl.ɪ.ki, əlˈ-
alma mater, (A M) ˌæl.məˈmɑː.təʳ, -ˈmeɪ.təʳ, (US) -ˈmɑː.t̬ɚ, ˌɑːl- **-s** -z
almanac(k) ˈɔːl.mə.næk, ˈɒl-, ˈæl-, (US) ˈɔːl-, ˈɑːl-, ˈæl- **-s** -s
almandine ˈæl.mən.diːn, -dɪn **-s** -z
Almanzor ælˈmæn.zɔːʳ, -zəʳ, (US) -zɔːr, -zɚ
Alma-Tadema ˌæl.məˈtæd.ɪ.mə
Almeida ælˈmiː.də, -ˈmeɪ-, (US) -ˈmeɪ-
Almería ˌæl.məˈri.ə
Almesbury ˈɑːmz.bər.i, (US) -ber-, -bɚ-
almight|y, A~ ɔːlˈmaɪ.t|i, (US) -t̬|i, ɑːl- **-ily** -əl.i, -ɪ.li **-iness** -ɪ.nəs, -ɪ.nɪs
Almodovar ˌæl.məˈdəʊ.vɑːʳ, -ˈdɒ-, (US) -ˈdoʊ.vɑːr
Almon ˈæl.mən
almond, A~ ˈɑː.mənd, (US) ˈɑː-, ˈɑːl-, ˈæl- **-s** -z

> Note: The pronunciation /ˈɑːl.mənd/ is also heard in British pronunciation; it is considered to be a case of spelling pronunciation.

Almondbury ˈæl.mənd.bər.i, ˈɑː-, ˈɔː-, (US) ˈæl.mənd.ber.i, ˈɑː-, ˈɑːl-, -bɚ-
Almondsbury ˈɑː.məndz.bər.i; *locally also:* ˈeɪmz.bər.i, (US) ˈɑː.məndz.ber.i, ˈɑːl-, -bɚ-
almoner ˈɑː.mə.nəʳ, ˈæl-, (US) ˈæl.mə.nɚ, ˈɑː-, ˈɑːl- **-s** -z
almonr|y ˈɑː.mən.r|i, ˈæl-, (US) ˈæl-, ˈɑː-, ˈɑːl- **-ies** -iz
almost ˈɔːl.məʊst, -məst, (US) ˈɔːl.moʊst, ˈɑːl-
alms ɑːmz
almsgiv|er ˈɑːmzˌgɪv|əʳ, (US) -ˌgɪv|ɚ **-ers** -əz, (US) -ɚz **-ing** -ɪŋ
almshou|se ˈɑːmz.haʊ|s **-ses** -zɪz
Alne ɔːn
Alness ˈɔːl.nɪs, ˈæl-
Alnmouth ˈæln.maʊθ, ˈeɪl-
Alnwick ˈæn.ɪk
aloe ˈæl.əʊ, (US) -oʊ **-s** -z
aloe vera ˌæl.əʊˈvɪə.rə, (US) -oʊˈvɪr.ə
aloft əˈlɒft, (US) -ˈlɑːft
aloha əˈləʊ.hə, ælˈəʊ-, -hɑː, -ə, (US) əˈloʊ.hɑː
alone əˈləʊn, (US) -ˈloʊn **-ness** -nəs, -nɪs
along əˈlɒŋ, (US) -ˈlɑːŋ, -ˈlɔːŋ
alongside əˌlɒŋˈsaɪd, (US) əˈlɑːŋ.saɪd, -ˈlɔːŋ-, -ˌ-ˈ-
Alonso əˈlɒnt.səʊ, -ˈlɒn.zəʊ, (US) -ˈlɑːnt.soʊ, -ˈlɑːn.zoʊ
aloof əˈluːf **-ness** -nəs, -nɪs
alopecia ˌæl.əʊˈpiː.ʃə, -ˈ-ʃi.ə, (US) -əˈ-, -oʊˈ-
aloud əˈlaʊd
Aloysius ˌæl.əʊˈɪʃ.əs, -ˈɪs.i.əs, (US) ˌæl.oʊˈɪʃ-, -ˈɪs.i.əs, -əˈwɪʃ.əs, -i.əs
alp, A~ ælp **-s** -s
alpaca ælˈpæk.ə **-s** -z
Alpen® ˈæl.pən
alpenglow ˈæl.pən.gləʊ, (US) -gloʊ
alpenhorn ˈæl.pən.hɔːn, -pɪn-, (US) -hɔːrn **-s** -z
alpenstock ˈæl.pən.stɒk, -pɪn-, (US) -stɑːk **-s** -s
Alperton ˈæl.pə.tən, (US) -pɚ-
alpha ˈæl.fə **-s** -z **ˈalpha ˌparticle; ˈalpha ˌray; ˈalpha ˌrhythm; ˈalpha ˌwave**
alphabet ˈæl.fə.bet **-s** -s
alphabetic ˌæl.fəˈbet.ɪk, (US) -ˈbet̬- *stress shift:* **ˌalphabetic ˈwriting**
alphabetic|al ˌæl.fəˈbet.ɪ.k|əl, (US) -ˈbet̬- **-ally** -əl.i, -li **ˌalphabetical ˈorder; alphaˌbetical ˈorder**
alphabeticiz|e, -is|e ˌæl.fəˈbet.ɪ.saɪz, (US) -ˈbet̬.ə- **-es** -ɪz **-ing** -ɪŋ **-ed** -d
alphabetization, -isa- ˌæl.fə.bet.aɪˈzeɪ.ʃən, -ɪˈ-, (US) -bet̬.əˈ-
alphabetiz|e, -is|e ˈæl.fə.bet.aɪz, -bə.taɪz, -bɪ-, (US) -bə.taɪz **-es** -ɪz **-ing** -ɪŋ **-ed** -d
Alpha Centauri ˌæl.fə.senˈtɔː.ri, -kenˈ-, -ˈtaʊ-, (US) -senˈtɔːr.i
Alphaeus ælˈfiː.əs
alphanumeric ˌæl.fə.njuːˈmer.ɪk, (US) -nuːˈ-, -njuːˈ- **-al** -əl **-ally** -əl.i, -li *stress shift:* **ˌalphanumeric ˈcode**
Alphonse ælˈfɒnts, ˈ--, (US) ælˈfɑːnts, -ˈfɔːnts, ˈ--
Alphonso ælˈfɒnt.səʊ, -ˈfɒn.zəʊ, (US) -ˈfɑːnt.soʊ, -ˈfɑːn.zoʊ
alpine, A~ ˈæl.paɪn
alpin|ism ˈæl.pɪ.n|ɪ.zəm **-ist/s** -ɪst/s
Alps ælps
Al-Qaida, Al Qaeda ˌælˈkaɪ.də; ˌæl.kɑːˈiː.də, (US) ˌælˈkeɪ.də, ˌɑːl-; (US) ˌɑːlˈkaɪ.ə.də
already ɔːlˈred.i, (US) ɔːl-, ɑːl- *stress shift:* **ˌalready ˈhere**
Alresford ˈɔːlz.fəd, ˈɔːls-, ˈɑːlz-, ˈɑːls-, (US) -fɚd
Alrewas ˈɔːl.rəs, -rə.wəs
alright ɔːlˈraɪt, (US) ɔːl-, ɑːl-
Alsace ælˈsæs, -ˈzæs
Alsace-Lorraine ælˌsæs.lɒrˈeɪn, -ˈzæs, (US) -loʊˈreɪn, -ˌseɪs-, -ləˈ-
Alsager ˈɔːl.sɪ.dʒəʳ, -sə.dʒəʳ, ɔːlˈseɪ.dʒəʳ, (US) ˈɔːl.sə.dʒɚ, ˈɑːl-, ɔːlˈseɪ.dʒɚ, ɑːl-
Alsatia ælˈseɪ.ʃə, ˈ-ʃi.ə
alsatian, A~ ælˈseɪ.ʃən **-s** -z
also ˈɔːl.səʊ, (US) ˈɔːl.soʊ, ˈɑːl-
Alsop(p) ˈɔːl.sɒp, ˈɒl-, -səp, (US) ˈɔːl.sɑːp, ˈɑːl-
also-ran ˈɔːl.səʊˌræn, (US) ˈɔːl.soʊ.ræn, ˈɑːl- **-s** -z
Alston ˈɔːl.stən, ˈɒl-, (US) ˈɔːl-, ˈɑːl-
alt ælt, ɔːlt, (US) ælt, ɑːlt
Altai ɑːlˈtaɪ
Altaic ælˈteɪ.ɪk
Altair ˈæl.teəʳ, -ˈ-, (US) ælˈter, -ˈtær, -ˈtaɪr
altar ˈɔːl.təʳ, ˈɒl-, (US) ˈɔːl.tɚ, ˈɑːl- **-s** -z **ˈaltar ˌboy; ˈaltar ˌrail**
altarpiec|e ˈɔːl.tə.piːs, ˈɒl-, (US) ˈɔːl.tɚ-, ˈɑːl- **-es** -ɪz
AltaVista® ˌæl.təˈvɪs.tə, ˌɔːl-, (US) ˌɑːl-, ˌæl-
altazimuth ælˈtæz.ɪ.məθ **-s** -s
Altdorf ˈælt.dɔːf, (US) ˈɑːlt.dɔːrf, ˈælt-
alter ˈɔːl.təʳ, ˈɒl-, (US) ˈɔːl.tɚ, ˈɑːl- **-s** -z **-ing** -ɪŋ **-ed** -d **-able** -ə.bəl **-ant/s** -ənt/s
alteration ˌɔːl.tərˈeɪ.ʃən, ˌɒl-, (US) ˌɔːl.təˈreɪ-, ˌɑːl- **-s** -z
alterative ˈɔːl.tər.ə.tɪv, ˈɒl-, -tər.eɪ-, (US) ˈɔːl.tə.reɪ.t̬ɪv, ˈɑːl-, -tɚ.ə-
alter|cate ˈɔːl.tə|.keɪt, ˈɒl-, (US) ˈɔːl.tɚ-, ˈɑːl- **-cates** -keɪts **-cating** -keɪ.tɪŋ, (US) -keɪ.t̬ɪŋ **-cated** -keɪ.tɪd, (US) -keɪ.t̬ɪd
altercation ˌɔːl.təˈkeɪ.ʃən, ˌɒl-, (US) ˌɔːl.tɚˈ-, ˌɑːl- **-s** -z
alter ego ˌɔːl.tərˈiː.gəʊ, ˌɒl-, ˌæl-, -ˈeg.əʊ, (US) ˌɔːl.tɚˈiː.goʊ, ˌɑːl- **-s** -z
alternanc|e ɔːlˈtɜː.nənts, ˈɒl-, (US) ˈɔːl.tɝː-, ˈɑːl- **-es** -ɪz
alternant ɔːlˈtɜː.nənt, ɒl-, (US) ˈɔːl.tɝː-, ˈɑːl- **-s** -s
alternate adj ɔːlˈtɜː.nət, ɒl-, -nɪt, (US) ɔːlˈtɝː-, ɑːl-; (US) ˈɔːl.tɚ-, ˈɑːl- **-ly** -li **-ness** -nəs, -nɪs
alter|nate v ˈɔːl.tə|.neɪt, ˈɒl-, (US) ˈɔːl.tɚ-, ˈɑːl- **-nates** -neɪts **-nating** -neɪ.tɪŋ, (US) -neɪ.t̬ɪŋ **-nated** -neɪ.tɪd, (US) -neɪ.t̬ɪd
alternation ˌɔːl.təˈneɪ.ʃən, ˌɒl-, (US) ˌɔːl.tɚˈ-, ˌɑːl- **-s** -z
alternative ɔːlˈtɜː.nə.tɪv, ɒl-, (US) ɔːlˈtɝː.nə.t̬ɪv, ɑːl- **-s** -z **-ly** -li **alˌternative ˈmedicine**
alternator ˈɔːl.tə.neɪ.təʳ, (US) ˈɔːl.tɚ.neɪ.t̬ɚ, ˈɑːl-, ˈæl- **-s** -z
Althea ˈæl.θi.ə, (US) ælˈθiː-
Althorp ˈɔːl.θɔːp, ˈɒl-, -trəp, (US) ˈɔːl.θɔːrp, ˈɑːl-

> Note: Viscount Althorp pronounces /ˈɔːl.trəp/.

although ɔːlˈðəʊ, (US) ɔːlˈðoʊ, ɑːl-
Althusser ˌæl.tʊˈseə, (US) ˌɑːl.tuːˈser
altimeter ˈæl.tɪ.miː.təʳ, ˈɔːl-, ˈɒl-; ælˈtɪm.ɪ-, (US) ælˈtɪm.ə.t̬ɚ, ˈæl.tə.miː- **-s** -z
altimetry ælˈtɪm.ə.tri, ɔːl-, ɒl-, ˈ-ɪ-, (US) ælˈtɪm.ə-
altissimo ælˈtɪs.ɪ.məʊ, (US) -moʊ, ɑːl-
altitude ˈæl.tɪ.tʃuːd, ˈɔːl-, ˈɒl-, -tjuːd, (US) ˈæl.tə.tuːd, -tjuːd **-s** -z
Altman ˈɔːlt.mən, (US) ˈɔːlt-, ˈɑːlt-
alto ˈæl.təʊ, ˈɒl-, (US) ˈæl.toʊ **-s** -z
altogether ˌɔːl.təˈgeð.əʳ, (US) -ɚ, ˌɑːl- *stress shift:* **ˌaltogether ˈmarvellous**
Alton ˈɔːl.tən, ˈɒl-, (US) ˈɔːl-, ˈɑːl-
Altona ˈæl.təʊ.nə, (US) ɑːlˈtoʊ-
Altoona ælˈtəʊ.nə, (US) -ˈtuː-
alto-relievo, alto-rilievo

ˌæl.təʊ.rɪˈliː.vəʊ, ⓊⓈ -toʊ.rəˈliː.voʊ, ˌɑːl-
Altrincham ˈɔːl.trɪŋ.əm, ˈɒl-, ⓊⓈ ˈɔːl-, ˈɑːl-
altru|ism ˈæl.tru|.ɪ.zəm **-ist/s** -ɪst/s
altruistic ˌæl.truˈɪs.tɪk **-ally** -əl.i, -li *stress shift:* **ˌaltruistic ˈaction**
alum, A~ ˈæl.əm **-s** -z
alumina əˈluː.mɪ.nə, ælˈuː-, -ˈljuː-, ⓊⓈ əˈluː-
aluminium ˌæl.jəˈmɪn.i.əm, -jʊˈ-, -əˈ-, ˈ-jəm *stress shift:* **ˌaluminium ˈfoil**
aluminiz|e, -is|e əˈluː.mɪ.naɪz, əˈljuː-, ⓊⓈ -ˈluː- **-es** -ɪz **-ing** -ɪŋ **-ed** -d
aluminous əˈluː.mɪ.nəs, -ˈljuː-, ⓊⓈ -ˈluː-
aluminum əˈluː.mɪ.nəm, -ˈljuː-, ⓊⓈ -ˈluː-
alumn|a əˈlʌm.n|ə **-ae** -iː
alumn|us əˈlʌm.n|əs **-i** -aɪ
Alun ˈæl.ɪn
Alva ˈæl.və
Alvar ˈæl.vɑːʳ, -vəʳ, ⓊⓈ -vɑːr, -vɚ
Alvarez ælˈvɑː.rez; ˈæl.və-, ⓊⓈ ˈæl.və.rez; ⓊⓈ ˈɑːl.vɑː.reθ
Alvary ˈæl.vər.i
alveolar ˌæl.viˈəʊ.ləʳ; ælˈviː.ə-; ˈæl.vi-, ⓊⓈ ælˈviː.ə.lɚ **-s** -z
alveolate ælˈviː.ə.lət, -lɪt, -leɪt, ⓊⓈ -lɪt
alveole ˈæl.vi.əʊl, ⓊⓈ -oʊl **-s** -z
alveol|us ˌæl.viˈəʊ.l|əs; ælˈviː.ə-; ˈæl.vi.ə-, ⓊⓈ ælˈviː.ə- **-i** -aɪ, -iː
Alverstone ˈɔːl.və.stən, ˈɒl-, ⓊⓈ ˈɔːl.vɚ-, ˈɑːl-
Alvescot ˈæl.vɪ.skɒt, -skət; *locally:* ˈɔːl.skət, ⓊⓈ -skɑːt
Alveston ˈæl.vɪ.stən
Alvey ˈæl.vi
Alvin ˈæl.vɪn
alway ˈɔːl.weɪ, ˈɑːl-
always ˈɔːl.weɪz, -wəz, -wɪz, ⓊⓈ ˈɔːl-, ˈɑːl-
Alwyn ˈæl.wɪn, ˈɔːl-
Alyn ˈæl.ɪn, -ən
Alyson ˈæl.ɪ.sən
Alyssa ælˈɪs.ə
alyssum ˈæl.ɪ.səm
Alzheimer ˈælts.haɪ.məʳ, ⓊⓈ ˈɑːlts.haɪ.mɚ, ˈælts- **ˈAlzheimer's diˌsease**
am *strong form:* æm; *weak forms:* əm, m
Note: Weak-form word. The strong form /æm/ is used for emphasis (e.g. 'I **am** going to leave.'), for contrast (e.g. 'I know what I **am** and am **not** capable of.') and in final position (e.g. 'That's who I am.'). The weak form is usually /əm/ (e.g. 'How am I going to pay?' /ˌhaʊ.əm.aɪˌgəʊ.ɪŋ.təˈpeɪ/ ⓊⓈ /-goʊ.ɪŋ.t̬əˈ-/), but after 'I' /aɪ/ it is frequently shortened to /m/ (e.g. 'I am (I'm) here' /aɪmˈhɪəʳ/ ⓊⓈ /aɪmˈhɪr/).
a.m., AM ˌeɪˈem
A&M eɪ.əndˈem
AMA ˌeɪ.emˈeɪ
Amabel ˈæm.ə.bel
Amadeus ˌæm.əˈdeɪ.əs, ⓊⓈ ˌɑː.məˈdeɪ.ʊs, -əs
Amadis ˈæm.ə.dɪs
amadou ˈæm.ə.duː
amah ˈɑː.mə, ˈæm.ɑː, ⓊⓈ ˈɑː.mɑː **-s** -z
Amahl ˈæm.ɑːl, ⓊⓈ əˈmɑːl
amain əˈmeɪn
Amalekite əˈmæl.ə.kaɪt, ˈ-ɪ-, ⓊⓈ ˌæm.əˈlek.aɪt; ⓊⓈ əˈmæl.ə.kaɪt **-s** -s
Amalfi əˈmæl.fi, æmˈæl-, ⓊⓈ əˈmæl-, -ˈmɑːl
amalgam əˈmæl.gəm **-s** -z
amalga|mate əˈmæl.gə|.meɪt **-mates** -meɪts **-mating** -meɪ.tɪŋ, ⓊⓈ -meɪ.t̬ɪŋ **-mated** -meɪ.tɪd, ⓊⓈ -meɪ.t̬ɪd
amalgamation əˌmæl.gəˈmeɪ.ʃən **-s** -z
Amalia əˈmɑː.li.ə, æmˈɑː-, ⓊⓈ əˈmeɪl.jə
Amalth(a)ea ˌæm.əlˈθiː.ə
Aman ˈæm.ən, ⓊⓈ ˈeɪ.mən
Amanda əˈmæn.də
amandine əˈmæn.daɪn; ˌɑː.mənˈdiːn, ⓊⓈ ˌɑː.mənˈdiːn, ˌæm.ənˈ-
amanuens|is əˌmæn.juˈent.s|ɪs **-es** -iːz
Amara əˈmɑː.rə
amaranth ˈæm.ər.ænθ, ⓊⓈ -ə.rænθ **-s** -s
amaranthine ˌæm.ərˈænt.θaɪn, ⓊⓈ -əˈrænt.θɪn, -θiːn, -θaɪn
amaretto, A~ ˌæm.ərˈet.əʊ, ⓊⓈ -əˈret̬.oʊ
Amarillo ˌæm.ərˈɪl.əʊ, ⓊⓈ -əˈrɪl.oʊ
amaryllis, A~ ˌæm.ərˈɪl.ɪs, ⓊⓈ -əˈrɪl- **-es** -ɪz
Amasis əˈmeɪ.sɪs
amass əˈmæs **-es** -ɪz **-ing** -ɪŋ **-ed** -t
amateur ˈæm.ə.təʳ, -tɜːʳ, -tʃʊəʳ, -tʃəʳ, -tjəʳ; ˌæm.əˈtɜːʳ, ⓊⓈ ˈæm.ə.tjɚ, -tjʊr, -t̬ɚ, -tɝː **-s** -z **ˌamateur draˈmatics**
Note: The final British form is not used attributively.
amateurish ˈæm.ə.tər.ɪʃ, -tɜː.rɪʃ, -tʃʊə-, -tʃɔː-, -tʃər.ɪʃ, -tjər-, ⓊⓈ ˌæm.əˈtɝː.ɪʃ, -ˈtjʊr- **-ly** -li **-ness** -nəs, -nɪs
amateurism ˈæm.ə.tər.ɪ.zəm, -tɜː.rɪ-, -tʃʊə-, -tjʊə-, -tʃɔː-, -tjɔː-, -tʃər.ɪ-, -tjər-, ⓊⓈ ˈæm.ə.tʃɚ.ɪ-, -tjʊ.rɪ-, -t̬ɚ.ɪ-
Amati əˈmɑː.ti, æmˈɑː-, ⓊⓈ -t̬i **-s** -z
amatol ˈæm.ə.tɒl, ⓊⓈ -tɑːl
amatory ˈæm.ə.tər.i, ⓊⓈ -tɔːr-
amaurosis ˌæm.ɔːˈrəʊ.sɪs, ⓊⓈ -ˈroʊ-
amaz|e əˈmeɪz **-es** -ɪz **-ed** -d **-edly** -ɪd.li **-edness** -ɪd.nəs, -nɪs **-ement/s** -mənt/s
amazing əˈmeɪ.zɪŋ **-ly** -li
amazon, A~ ˈæm.ə.zən, ⓊⓈ -zɑːn **-s** -z
Amazonia ˌæm.əˈzəʊ.ni.ə, ⓊⓈ -ˈzoʊ-
amazonian, A~ ˌæm.əˈzəʊ.ni.ən, ⓊⓈ -ˈzoʊ-
amazonite ˈæm.ə.zə.naɪt **-s** -s
ambassador æmˈbæs.ə.dəʳ, ⓊⓈ -dɚ **-s** -z
ambassadorial æmˌbæs.əˈdɔː.ri.əl, ˌæm.bæs-
ambassadress æmˈbæs.ə.drəs, -drɪs, -dres, ⓊⓈ -drəs **-es** -ɪz
Ambato æmˈbɑː.təʊ, ɑːm-, ⓊⓈ -toʊ
amber, A~ ˈæm.bəʳ, ⓊⓈ -bɚ
ambergris ˈæm.bə.griːs, ⓊⓈ -bɚ.grɪs
amberjack ˈæm.bə.dʒæk, ⓊⓈ -bɚ- **-s** -s
ambi- ˈæm.bɪ, ˈæm.bi; æmˈbɪ
Note: Prefix. Normally either takes primary or secondary stress on the first syllable, e.g. **ambient** /ˈæm.bi.ənt/, **ambidextrous** /ˌæm.bɪˈdek.strəs/, or primary stress on the second syllable, e.g. **ambivalence** /æmˈbɪv.əl.ənts/.
ambianc|e ˈæm.bi.ənts, -ɑ̃ːnts, ⓊⓈ ˈæm.bi.ənts, ˌɑːm.biˈɑːnts **-es** -ɪz
ambidexter ˌæm.bɪˈdek.stəʳ, ⓊⓈ -stɚ **-s** -z
ambidexterity ˌæm.bɪ.dekˈster.ə.ti, -ɪ.ti, ⓊⓈ -ə.t̬i
ambidextrous ˌæm.bɪˈdek.strəs
ambienc|e ˈæm.bi.ənts, -ɑ̃ːnts, ⓊⓈ ˈæm.bi.ənts, ˌɑːm.biˈɑːnts **-es** -ɪz
ambient ˈæm.bi.ənt
ambiguit|y ˌæm.bɪˈgjuː.ə.t|i, -ɪ.t|i, ⓊⓈ -bəˈgjuː.ə.t̬|i **-ies** -iz
ambiguous æmˈbɪg.ju.əs **-ly** -li **-ness** -nəs, -nɪs
Ambiorix æmˈbaɪ.ə.rɪks, ⓊⓈ -ɚ.ɪks, -oʊ.rɪks
ambit ˈæm.bɪt **-s** -s
ambition æmˈbɪʃ.ən **-s** -z
ambitious æmˈbɪʃ.əs **-ly** -li **-ness** -nəs, -nɪs
ambivalen|ce æmˈbɪv.əl.ən|ts **-t/ly** -t/li
ambl|e, A~ ˈæm.bəl **-es** -z **-ing** -ɪŋ, ˈæm.blɪŋ **-ed** -d **-er/s** -əʳ/z, ˈ-bləʳ/z, ⓊⓈ ˈ-bəl.ɚ/z, ˈ-blɚ/z
Ambler ˈæm.bləʳ, ˈ-bəl.əʳ, ⓊⓈ ˈ-blɚ, ˈ-bəl.ɚ
Ambleside ˈæm.bəl.saɪd
amboyna, A~ æmˈbɔɪ.nə
Ambree ˈæm.bri
Ambridge ˈæm.brɪdʒ
Ambrose ˈæm.brəʊz, -brəʊs, ⓊⓈ -broʊz
ambrosi|a æmˈbrəʊ.zi|.ə, -ʒ|ə, ⓊⓈ -ˈbroʊ.ʒ|ə **-al** -əl **-ally** -əl.i **-an** -ən
Ambrosius æmˈbrəʊ.zi.əs, -ʒəs, ⓊⓈ -ˈbroʊ.ʒəs
ambsace ˈeɪm.zeɪs, ˈæm-
ambulance ˈæm.bjə.lənts, -bjʊ.lənts, -bə- **-s** -ɪz **-man** -mæn **-men** -men **-woman** -ˌwʊm.ən **-women** -ˌwɪm.ɪn
ambulance-chaser ˈæm.bjə.læntsˌtʃeɪ.səʳ, -bjʊ-, ⓊⓈ -sɚ **-s** -z
ambulant ˈæm.bjə.lənt, -bjʊ.lənt
ambu|late ˈæm.bjə|.leɪt, -bjʊ- **-lates** -leɪts **-lating** -leɪ.tɪŋ, ⓊⓈ -leɪ.t̬ɪŋ **-lated** -leɪ.tɪd, ⓊⓈ -leɪ.t̬ɪd
ambulation ˌæm.bjəˈleɪ.ʃən, -bjʊˈ- **-s** -z

A

ambulator|y ˌæm.bjəˈleɪ.tər|.i, -bjʊ-; ˈæm.bjə.lə-, -bjʊ-, (US) ˈæm.bjə.lə.tɔːr-, -bjʊ- **-ies** -iz
ambuscad|e ˌæm.bəˈskeɪd **-es** -z **-ing** -ɪŋ **-ed** -ɪd
ambush ˈæm.bʊʃ **-es** -ɪz **-ing** -ɪŋ **-ed** -t
ameb|a əˈmiː.b|ə **-as** -əz **-ae** -iː **-ic** -ɪk
Amelia əˈmiː.li.ə, (US) -ˈmiːl.jə, -ˈmiː.li.ə
amelior|ate əˈmiː.li.ər|.eɪt, (US) -ˈmiː.li.ə.r|eɪt, -ˈmiːl.jə- **-ates** -eɪts **-ating** -eɪ.tɪŋ, (US) -eɪ.t̬ɪŋ **-ated** -eɪ.tɪd, (US) -eɪ.t̬ɪd
amelioration əˌmiː.li.ərˈeɪ.ʃən, (US) -ˌmiː.li.əˈreɪ-, -ˌmiːl.jəˈ- **-s** -z
ameliorative əˈmiː.li.ər.ə.tɪv, -eɪ-, (US) -ˈmiː.li.ə.reɪ.t̬ɪv, -ˈmiːl.jə-
amen ˌɑːˈmen, ˌeɪ- **-s** -z
amenability əˌmiː.nəˈbɪl.ə.ti, -ɪ.ti, (US) -ə.t̬i
amenab|le əˈmiː.nə.b|əl, (US) -ˈmiː.nə-, -ˈmen.ə- **-ly** -li **-leness** -əl.nəs, -nɪs
Amen Corner ˌeɪ.menˈkɔː.nər, (US) -ˈkɔːr.nɚ
amend əˈmend **-s** -z **-ing** -ɪŋ **-ed** -ɪd
amendatory əˈmen.də.tər.i, (US) -tɔː.ri
amendment əˈmend*.*mənt **-s** -s
amenit|y əˈmiː.nə.t|i, -ˈmen.ə-, -ɪ.t|i, (US) əˈmen.ə.t̬|i **-ies** -iz
amenorrh(o)ea ˌeɪ.men.əˈriː.ə, ˌæm.en-, (US) ˌeɪ.men-
Amerasian ˌæm.əˈreɪ.ʃən, -ʒən, (US) -əˈreɪ.ʒən, -ʃən **-s** -z
amerc|e əˈmɜːs, (US) -ˈmɝːs **-es** -ɪz **-ing** -ɪŋ **-ed** -t **-ement/s** -mənt/s
America əˈmer.ɪ.kə **-s** -z
American əˈmer.ɪ.kən **-s** -z **-ist/s** -ɪst/s **AˌmericanˈExˈpress**®
Americana əˌmer.ɪˈkɑː.nə, (US) -ˈkæn.ə, -ˈkɑː.nə
Americanese əˌmer.ɪ.kəˈniːz, (US) -ˈniːz, -ˈniːs
american|ism, A~ əˈmer.ɪ.kə.n|ɪ.zəm **-isms** -ɪ.zəmz **-ist/s** -ɪst/s
americanization, -isa-, A~ əˌmer.ɪ.kə.naɪˈzeɪ.ʃən, -nɪˈ-, (US) -nəˈ-
americaniz|e, -is|e, A~ əˈmer.ɪ.kə.naɪz **-es** -ɪz **-ing** -ɪŋ **-ed** -d
americium ˌæm.əˈrɪs.i.əm, -ˈrɪʃ-
Amerindian ˌæm.əˈrɪn.di.ən **-s** -z
Amersham ˈæm.ə.ʃəm, (US) -ɚ-
Amery ˈeɪ.mər.i
Ames eɪmz
Amesbury ˈeɪmz.bər.i, (US) -ber.i
Ameslan ˈæm.ɪ.slæn
amethyst ˈæm.ə.θɪst, -ɪ.θɪst **-s** -s
amethystine ˌæm.əˈθɪs.taɪn, -ɪˈ-, (US) -tən, -taɪn, -tɪn, -tiːn
Amex ˈæm.eks
AMF ˌeɪ.emˈef
Amharic æmˈhær.ɪk, (US) -ˈhær-, -ˈhɑːr-
Amherst ˈæm.əst, -hɜːst, (US) -ɚst, -hɝːst
amiability ˌeɪ.mi.əˈbɪl.ə.ti, -ɪ.ti, (US) -ə.t̬i
amiab|le ˈeɪ.mi.ə.b|əl **-ly** -li **-leness** -əl.nəs, -nɪs
amicability ˌæm.ɪ.kəˈbɪl.ə.ti, -ɪ.ti, (US) -ə.t̬i
amicab|le ˈæm.ɪ.kə.b|əl, əˈmɪk- **-ly** -li **-leness** -əl.nəs, -nɪs
amic|e ˈæm.ɪs **-es** -ɪz
Amice ˈeɪ.mɪs
Amicus ˈæm.ɪ.kəs
amid əˈmɪd
amide ˈæm.aɪd, ˈeɪ.maɪd, (US) ˈæm.aɪd, -əd **-s** -z
amidships əˈmɪd.ʃɪps
amidst əˈmɪdst, -ˈmɪtst
Amiel ˈæm.i.əl, ˈeɪ.mi-
Amiens *French city:* ˈæm.jæ̃ŋ, -i.ɑ̃ː, -i.ənz *Shakespearean character:* ˈæm.i.ənz *street in Dublin:* ˈeɪ.mi.ənz
Amies ˈeɪ.miz
amiga, A~® əˈmiː.gə, (US) əˈmiː.gə, ɑː- **-s** -z
amigo əˈmiː.gəʊ, (US) -goʊ, ɑː- **-s** -z
Amin ɑːˈmiːn, æmˈiːn
amino əˈmiː.nəʊ, æmˈiː-, (US) -noʊ **aˌmino ˈacid; aˈmino ˌacid**
amir əˈmɪər, (US) -ˈmɪr **-s** -z
Amis ˈeɪ.mɪs
Amish ˈɑː.mɪʃ, ˈæm.ɪʃ, ˈeɪ.mɪʃ, (US) ˈɑː-, ˈæm.ɪʃ
amiss əˈmɪs
amitosis ˌæm.ɪˈtəʊ.sɪs, (US) -ˈtoʊ-
amitotic ˌæm.ɪˈtəʊ.tɪk, (US) -ˈtoʊ.t̬ɪk
amity ˈæm.ɪ.ti, -ə.ti, (US) -ə.t̬i
Amlwch ˈæm.lʊk, -lʊx
Amman əˈmɑːn, (US) ɑːˈmɑːn
Ammanford ˈæm.ən.fəd, (US) -fɚd
ammeter ˈæm.iː.tər, -ɪ.tər, (US) -t̬ɚ **-s** -z
ammo ˈæm.əʊ, (US) -oʊ
Ammon ˈæm.ən, -ɒn, (US) -ən
ammonia əˈməʊ.ni.ə, (US) -ˈmoʊ.njə
ammoniac əˈməʊ.ni.æk, (US) -ˈmoʊ-
ammoniacal ˌæm.əʊˈnaɪ.ə.kəl, -əˈ-
ammoniated əˈməʊ.ni.eɪ.tɪd, (US) -ˈmoʊ.ni.eɪ.t̬ɪd
ammonification əˌməʊ.nɪ.fɪˈkeɪ.ʃən, -nə-, -fəˈ-, (US) -mɑː-, -moʊ-
ammonif|y əˈməʊ.nɪ|.faɪ, -nə-, (US) -ˈmɑː-, -ˈmoʊ- **-ies** -aɪz **-ying** -aɪ.ɪŋ **-ied** -aɪd **-ier/s** -aɪ.ər/z, (US) -aɪ.ɚ/z
ammonite, A~ ˈæm.ə.naɪt **-s** -s
ammonium əˈməʊ.ni.əm, (US) -ˈmoʊ-
Ammons ˈæm.ənz
ammunition ˌæm.jəˈnɪʃ.ən, -jʊˈ-, (US) -jəˈ-
amnesia æmˈniː.zi.ə, -ʒə, (US) -ʒə
amnesiac æmˈniː.zi.æk, (US) -ʒi- **-s** -s
amnesic æmˈniː.zɪk, -sɪk **-s** -s
amnest|y ˈæm.nə.st|i, -nɪ- **-ies** -iz **ˌAmnesty Interˈnational**
amniocentesis ˌæm.ni.əʊ.senˈtiː.sɪs, -sənˈ-, (US) -oʊ-
amniotic ˌæm.niˈɒt.ɪk, (US) -ˈɑː.t̬ɪk *stress shift:* **ˌamniotic ˈmembrane**
Amoco® ˈæm.ə.kəʊ; əˈməʊ-, (US) ˈæm.ə-
amoeb|a əˈmiː.b|ə **-ae** -iː **-as** -əz **-ic** -ɪk
amoebiasis ˌæm.iːˈbaɪ.ə.sɪs, -ɪˈ-
amok əˈmɒk, -ˈmʌk, (US) -ˈmʌk, -ˈmɑːk
Amon ˈɑː.mən
among əˈmʌŋ
amongst əˈmʌŋst
Amon-Ra ˌɑː.mənˈrɑː
amontillado, A~ əˌmɒn.tiˈjɑː.dəʊ, -tɪˈlɑː-, (US) -ˌmɑːn.təˈlɑː.doʊ **-s** -z
amoral ˌeɪˈmɒr.əl, æmˈɒr-, (US) ˌeɪˈmɔːr- **-ly** -li
amorality ˌeɪ.mərˈæl.ɪ.ti, (US) -mɔːrˈæl.ə.t̬i
Amoretti ˌæm.əˈret.i, (US) -ˈret̬-, ˌɑː.məˈ-
amorett|o ˌæm.əˈret|.əʊ, (US) -ˈret̬|.oʊ, ˌɑː.məˈ- **-i** -i
amorist ˈæm.ər.ɪst **-s** -s
Amorite ˈæm.ər.aɪt, (US) -ə.raɪt **-s** -s
amorous ˈæm.ər.əs **-ly** -li **-ness** -nəs, -nɪs
amorph|ism əˈmɔː.f|ɪ.zəm, (US) -ˈmɔːr- **-ous** -əs
amortizable, -isa- əˈmɔː.taɪ.zə.bəl, (US) ˌæm.ɔːrˈtaɪ-
amortization, -isa- əˌmɔː.taɪˈzeɪ.ʃən, -tɪˈ-, (US) æmˌɔːr.t̬əˈ- **-s** -z
amortiz|e, -is|e əˈmɔː.taɪz, (US) æmˈɔːr- **-es** -ɪz **-ing** -ɪŋ **-ed** -d
amortizement, -ise- əˈmɔː.tɪz.mənt, (US) ˈæm.ɚˌtaɪz.mənt, əˈmɔːr.t̬ɪz.mənt
Amory ˈeɪ.mər.i
Amos ˈeɪ.mɒs, (US) -məs
a|mount ə|ˈmaʊnt **-mounts** -ˈmaʊnts **-mounting** -ˈmaʊn.tɪŋ, (US) -ˈmaʊn.t̬ɪŋ **-mounted** -ˈmaʊn.tɪd, (US) -ˈmaʊn.t̬ɪd
amour əˈmʊər, æmˈʊər, əˈmɔːr, æmˈɔːr, (US) əˈmʊr, æmˈʊr **-s** -z
amour-propre ˌæm.ʊəˈprɒp.rə, (US) ˌɑː.mʊrˈproʊ.prə, ˌæm.ʊrˈ-
Amoy əˈmɔɪ, æmˈɔɪ
amp æmp **-s** -s
ampelopsis ˌæm.pɪˈlɒp.sɪs, (US) -ˈlɑːp-
amperage ˈæm.pər.ɪdʒ, -per-, -peə.rɪdʒ, (US) ˈæm.prɪdʒ, -pɪ.rɪdʒ
ampère, ampere, A~ ˈæm.peər, (US) -pɪr, -per **-s** -z
ampersand ˈæm.pə.sænd, (US) -pɚ- **-s** -z
amphetamine æmˈfet.ə.miːn, -mɪn, (US) -fet̬- **-s** -z
amphi- ˈæm*p*.fɪ; æmˈfɪ, (US) ˈæm*p*.fɪ, -fə; (US) æmˈfɪ
Note: Prefix. Either takes primary or secondary stress on the first syllable, e.g. **amphibrach** /ˈæm*p*.fɪ.bræk/, **amphibiotic** /ˌæm*p*.fɪ.baɪˈɒt.ɪk/ (US) /-ˈɑː.t̬ɪk/, or primary stress on the second syllable, e.g. **amphibian** /æmˈfɪb.i.ən/.
amphibi|a æmˈfɪb.i|ə **-ous** -əs
amphibian æmˈfɪb.i.ən **-s** -z

A

amphibiotic ˌæmp.fɪ.baɪˈɒt.ɪk, (US) -ˈɑː.t̬ɪk
amphibole ˈæmp.fɪ.bəʊl, (US) -boʊl
amphibology ˌæmp.fɪˈbɒl.ə.dʒi, (US) -ˈbɑː.lə-
amphiboll|y æmˈfɪb.ə.l|i **-ies** -iz
amphibrach ˈæmp.fɪ.bræk **-s** -s
Amphictyon æmˈfɪk.ti.ən **-s** -z
amphictyonic æmˌfɪk.tiˈɒn.ɪk, (US) -ˈɑː.nɪk
amphimacer æmˈfɪm.ɪ.səʳ, (US) -ə.sɚ
Amphion æmˈfaɪ.ən
Amphipolis æmˈfɪp.ə.lɪs
amphitheatre, amphitheater ˈæmp.fɪˌθɪə.təʳ, (US) -fəˌθiː.ə.t̬ɚ **-s** -z
Amphitrite ˌæmp.fɪˈtraɪ.ti, (US) -t̬i
Amphitryon æmˈfɪt.ri.ən
amphor|a ˈæmp.fᵊr|.ə **-ae** -iː **-as** -əz
amphoric æmˈfɒr.ɪk, (US) -ˈfɔːr-
amphoteric ˌæmp.fəʊˈter.ɪk, (US) -fəˈ-
ampicillin ˌæm.pɪˈsɪl.ɪn, (US) -pəˈ-
amp|le ˈæm.p|ᵊl **-ler** -ləʳ, (US) -lɚ **-lest** -ləst, -lɪst **-ly** -li **-leness** -ᵊl.nəs, -nɪs
Ampleforth ˈæm.pᵊl.fɔːθ, -fəθ
amplification ˌæm.plɪ.fɪˈkeɪ.ʃᵊn, -plə-, -fəˈ- **-s** -z
amplificatory ˌæm.plɪ.fɪˈkeɪ.tᵊr.i, -plə-, ˈ-tri, (US) æmˈplɪf.ɪ.kə.tɔːr.i
amplifier ˈæm.plɪ.faɪ.əʳ, (US) -ɚ **-s** -z
amplif|y ˈæm.plɪ.f|aɪ, ˈ-plə- **-ies** -aɪz **-ying** -aɪ.ɪŋ **-ied** -aɪd
amplitude ˈæm.plɪ.tʃuːd, -tjuːd, (US) -tuːd, -tjuːd **-s** -z
ampoule ˈæm.puːl **-s** -z
Amps æmps
Ampthill ˈæmpt.*h*ɪl
ampule ˈæm.pjuːl, (US) -pjuːl, -puːl **-s** -z
ampull|a æmˈpʊl|.ə **-ae** -iː
ampu|tate ˈæm.pjə|.teɪt, ˈæm.pjʊ- **-tates** -teɪts **-tating** -teɪ.tɪŋ, (US) -teɪ.t̬ɪŋ **-tated** -teɪ.tɪd, (US) -teɪ.t̬ɪd
amputation ˌæm.pjəˈteɪ.ʃᵊn, ˌæm.pjʊˈ- **-s** -z
amputee ˌæm.pjəˈtiː, -pjʊˈ- **-s** -z
Amram ˈæm.ræm
Amritsar æmˈrɪt.səʳ, -sɑːʳ, (US) -sɚ
Amsterdam ˌæmp.stəˈdæm, ˈ--ˌ-, (US) ˈæmp.stɚ.dæm
Note: In British English, the latter form is used when attributive.
Amstrad® ˈæm.stræd
Amtrak® ˈæm.træk
amuck əˈmʌk
amulet ˈæm.jʊ.lət, -jə-, -let, -lɪt **-s** -s
Amundsen ˈɑː.mənd.sᵊn, -mʊnd-
Amur əˈmʊəʳ, æmˈʊəʳ, ˈæm.ʊəʳ, (US) ɑːˈmʊr
amus|e əˈmjuːz **-es** -ɪz **-ing/ly** -ɪŋ/li **-ingness** -ɪŋ.nəs, -nɪs **-ed** -d
amusement əˈmjuːz.mənt **-s** -s **aˈmusement arˌcade; aˈmusement ˌpark**
Amway® ˈæm.weɪ
Amy ˈeɪ.mi
Amyas ˈeɪ.mi.əs
amygdalin əˈmɪg.də.lɪn, æmˈɪg-
amygdaloid əˈmɪg.də.lɔɪd
amyl ˈæm.ɪl, -əl **-s** -z
amylase ˈæm.ɪ.leɪz, ˈ-ə-, -leɪs
amylic æmˈɪl.ɪk, əˈmɪl-
amytal ˈæm.ɪ.tæl, (US) -tɑːl
an *strong form:* æn; *weak form:* ᵊn
Note: Weak-form word. The strong form /æn/ is used mainly for contrast (e.g. 'This is **an** ideal, but it's not **the** ideal.'). The weak form is usually /ən/ (e.g., 'make an excuse' /ˌmeɪk.ən.ɪkˈskjuːs/); in rapid speech, and particularly after an alveolar or palatoalveolar consonant, it may be pronounced as a syllabic /n̩/ (e.g. 'find an example' /ˌfaɪnd.n̩.ɪgˈzɑːm.pᵊl/ (US) /-ˈzæm-/).
an- ˈæn, ən
Note: Prefix. When used as a negative prefix, **an-** is normally /æn-/, e.g. **anaerobic** /ˌæn.əˈrəʊ.bɪk/ (US) /-erˈoʊ-/, but in some items it may be reduced, e.g. **anomaly** /əˈnɒm.ə.li/ (US) /-ˈnɑː.mə-/. Otherwise, it contains /æ/ when stressed, e.g. **anaerobe** /ˈæn.ə.rəʊb/ (US) /-roʊb/, and /ə/ when unstressed, e.g. **annul** /əˈnʌl/.
ana, A~ ˈɑː.nə
ana- ˈæn.ə, əˈnæ
Note: Prefix. Either takes primary or secondary stress on the first syllable, e.g. **anagram** /ˈæn.ə.græm/, **anatomic** /ˌæn.əˈtɒm.ɪk/, or primary stress on the second syllable, e.g. **anachronism** /əˈnæk.rə.nɪ.zᵊm/.
Anabapt|ism ˌæn.əˈbæp.t|ɪ.zᵊm **-ist/s** -ɪst/s
anabas|is əˈnæb.ə.s|ɪs **-es** -iːz
anabi|osis ˌæn.ə.baɪ|ˈəʊ.sɪs, (US) -ˈoʊ- **-otic** -ˈɒt.ɪk, (US) -ˈɑː.t̬ɪk
anabolic ˌæn.əˈbɒl.ɪk, (US) -ˈbɑː.lɪk *stress shift, see compound:* **ˌanabolic ˈsteroid**
anabolism əˈnæb.əʊ.lɪ.zᵊm, (US) -ᵊl.ɪ-
anachronism əˈnæk.rə.nɪ.zᵊm **-s** -z
anachronistic əˌnæk.rəˈnɪs.tɪk **-ally** -ᵊl.i, -li
anachronous əˈnæk.rə.nəs **-ly** -li
Anacin® ˈæn.ə.sɪn
anacoluth|on ˌæn.ə.kəʊˈluː.θ|ɒn, -ˈljuː-, -θ|ᵊn, (US) -kəˈluː.θ|ᵊn **-a** -ə
anaconda ˌæn.əˈkɒn.də, (US) -ˈkɑːn- **-s** -z
Anacreon əˈnæk.ri.ən, (US) -ɑːn, -ən
anacrus|is ˌæn.əˈkruː.s|ɪs **-es** -iːz
Anadin® ˈæn.ə.dɪn
anadiplosis ˌæn.ə.dɪˈpləʊ.sɪs, (US) -ˈploʊ-
anaemia əˈniː.mi.ə
anaemic əˈniː.mɪk
anaerobe ˈæn.ə.rəʊb, ˈæn.ɪ-, (US) -roʊb **-s** -z
anaerobic ˌæn.eəˈrəʊ.bɪk, -əˈ-, (US) -erˈoʊ-, -əˈroʊ-
anaesthesia ˌæn.əsˈθiː.zi.ə, -ɪsˈ-, -iːsˈ-, -ʒi-, ˈ-ʒə, (US) ˌæn.əsˈθiː.ʒə
anaesthesiology ˌæn.əsˌθiː.ziˈɒl.ə.dʒi, -ɪsˌ-, -iːsˌ-, -ʒiˈ-, (US) -ziˈɑː.lə-
anaesthetic ˌæn.əsˈθet.ɪk, -ɪsˈ-, -iːsˈ-, (US) -ˈθet̬- **-s** -s **-ally** -ᵊl.i, -li *stress shift:* **ˌanaesthetic ˈmask**
anaesthetist əˈniːs.θə.tɪst, ænˈiːs-, -θɪ-, (US) əˈnes.θə.t̬ɪst **-s** -s
anaesthetiz|e, -is|e əˈniːs.θə.taɪz, ænˈiːs-, -θɪ-, (US) əˈnes- **-es** -ɪz **-ing** -ɪŋ **-ed** -d
anaglyph ˈæn.ə.glɪf **-s** -s
anagram ˈæn.ə.græm **-s** -z
anagrammatic ˌæn.ə.grəˈmæt.ɪk, (US) -ˈmæt̬- **-al** -ᵊl **-ally** -ᵊl.i, -li
Anaheim ˈæn.ə.haɪm
Anaïs ˌæn.aɪˈiːs
anal ˈeɪ.nᵊl **-ly** -i
analects ˈæn.ə.lekts
analeptic ˌæn.əˈlep.tɪk
analgesia ˌæn.əlˈdʒiː.zi.ə, -ælˈ-, -si-, (US) ˈ-ʒə
analgesic ˌæn.əlˈdʒiː.zɪk, -ælˈ-, -sɪk
analog ˈæn.ə.lɒg, (US) -lɑːg, -lɔːg **-s** -z
analogic ˌæn.əˈlɒdʒ.ɪk, (US) -ˈlɑː.dʒɪk **-al** -ᵊl **-ally** -ᵊl.i, -li
analogist əˈnæl.ə.dʒɪst **-s** -s
analogous əˈnæl.ə.gəs **-ly** -li **-ness** -nəs, -nɪs
analogue ˈæn.ə.lɒg, (US) -lɑːg, -lɔːg **-s** -z
analog|y əˈnæl.ə.dʒ|i **-ies** -iz
analphabetic ˌæn.æl.fəˈbet.ɪk, (US) -ˈbet̬- **-al** -ᵊl **-ally** -ᵊl.i, -li
anal-retentive ˌeɪ.nᵊl.rɪˈten.tɪv, (US) -t̬ɪv
analysable ˌæn.ᵊlˈaɪ.zə.bᵊl, (US) -əˈlaɪ-, ˈæn.ə.laɪ-
analysand əˈnæl.ɪ.sænd, ˈ-ə- **-s** -z
analys|e, -yz|e ˈæn.ᵊl.aɪz, -ə.laɪz **-es** -ɪz **-ing** -ɪŋ **-ed** -d
analys|is əˈnæl.ə.s|ɪs, -ɪ.s|ɪs **-es** -iːz
analyst ˈæn.ᵊl.ɪst, (US) -ə.lɪst **-s** -s
analytic ˌæn.ᵊlˈɪt.ɪk, (US) -əˈlɪt̬- **-s** -s **-al** -ᵊl **-ally** -ᵊl.i, -li *stress shift:* **ˌanalytic ˈmind**
analyzable ˌæn.ᵊlˈaɪ.zə.bᵊl, (US) -əˈlaɪ-, ˈæn.ə.laɪ-
analyz|e, -ys|e ˈæn.ᵊl.aɪz, -ə.laɪz **-es** -ɪz **-ing** -ɪŋ **-ed** -d
anamorphosis ˌæn.əˈmɔː.fə.sɪs; -mɔːˈfəʊ-, (US) -ˈmɔːr.fə-; (US) -mɔːrˈfoʊ-
Anand ˈɑː.nənd
Ananias ˌæn.əˈnaɪ.əs
anap(a)est ˈæn.ə.piːst, -pest, (US) -pest **-s** -s
anap(a)estic ˌæn.əˈpes.tɪk, -ˈpiː.stɪk, (US) -ˈpes.tɪk
anaphor ˈæn.ə.fɔːʳ, -fəʳ, (US) -fɔːr **-s** -z
anaphora əˈnæf.ᵊr.ə **-s** -z
anaphoric ˌæn.əˈfɒr.ɪk, (US) -ˈfɔːr- *stress shift:* **ˌanaphoric ˈreference**
anaphrodisiac ˌæn.æf.rəʊˈdɪz.i.æk, (US) -roʊˈ- **-s** -s
anaptyctic ˌæn.əpˈtɪk.tɪk, -æpˈ-
anaptyxis ˌæn.əpˈtɪk.sɪs, -æpˈ-
Anapurna ˌæn.əˈpɜː.nə, -ˈpʊə-, (US) -ˈpɝː-, -ˈpʊr-
anarch ˈæn.ɑːk, (US) -ɑːrk **-s** -s

A

anarchic əˈnɑː.kɪk, ænˈɑː-, US ænˈɑːr-, əˈnɑːr- **-al** -əl **-ally** -əl.i, -li
anarchism ˈæn.ə.kɪ.zəm, -ɑː-, US -ɚ-, -ɑːr-
anarchist ˈæn.ə.kɪst, -ɑː-, US -ɚ-, -ɑːr- **-s** -s
anarchistic ˌæn.əˈkɪs.tɪk, -ɑːˈ-, US -ɚˈ-, -ɑːrˈ- *stress shift:* ˌ**anarchistic** ˈ**views**
anarchy ˈæn.ə.ki, -ɑː-, US -ɚ-, -ɑːr-
Anastasia *English Christian name:* ˌæn.əˈsteɪ.zi.ə, ˈ-ʒə, US ˈ-ʒə *foreign name:* ˌæn.əˈstɑː.zi.ə, US ˈ-ʒə
Anastasius ˌæn.əˈstɑː.zi.əs, -ˈsteɪ-, US ˈ-ʒəs
anastigmat əˈnæs.tɪg.mæt, ænˈæs-; ˌæn.əˈstɪg-, US əˈnæs.tɪg-; US ˌæn.əˈstɪg- **-s** -s
anastigmatic ˌæn.ə.stɪgˈmæt.ɪk; əˌnæs.tɪgˈ-, US əˌnæs.tɪgˈmæţ-; US ˌæn.ə.stɪgˈmæţ-
anastomosis ˌæn.ə.stəˈməʊ.sɪs, US -ˈmoʊ-
anastrophe əˈnæs.trə.fi, ænˈæs- **-s** -z
anathema əˈnæθ.ə.mə, ænˈ-, ˈ-ɪ- **-s** -z
anathematization, -isa- əˌnæθ.ə.mə.taɪˈzeɪ.ʃən, ænˌæθ-, -tɪˈ-, US -ţəˈ- **-s** -z
anathematiz|e, -is|e əˈnæθ.ə.mə.taɪz, ænˈ-, ˈ-ɪ- **-es** -ɪz **-ing** -ɪŋ **-ed** -d
Anatole ˈæn.ə.təʊl, US -toʊl
Anatoli|a ˌæn.əˈtəʊ.li|.ə, US -ˈtoʊ- **-an/s** -ən/z
anatomic ˌæn.əˈtɒm.ɪk, US -ˈtɑː.mɪk **-al** -əl **-ally** -əl.i, -li *stress shift:* ˌ**anatomic** ˈ**diagram**
anatomist əˈnæt.ə.mɪst, US -ˈnæţ- **-s** -s
anatomiz|e, -is|e əˈnæt.ə.maɪz, US -ˈnæţ- **-es** -ɪz **-ing** -ɪŋ **-ed** -d
anatom|y əˈnæt.ə.m|i, US -ˈnæţ- **-ies** -iz
Anaxagoras ˌæn.ækˈsæg.ə.rəs, -ræs, US -ɚ.əs
ANC ˌeɪ.enˈsiː
-ance ənts
Note: Suffix. When attached to a free stem, **-ance** does not change the stress pattern of the word, e.g. **admit** /ədˈmɪt/, **admittance** /ədˈmɪt.ənts/. In other cases, the stress may be on the penultimate or antepenultimate syllable, e.g. **reluctance**/rɪˈlʌk.tənts/, **brilliance** /ˈbrɪl.i.ənts/ US /ˈ-jənts/. There are exceptions; see individual entries.
ancestor ˈæn.ses.təʳ, -sɪ.stəʳ, -sə-, US -ses.tɚ **-s** -z
ancestral ænˈses.trəl
ancestress ˈæn.ses.trəs; -sɪ.strəs, -ses.trɪs, US -ses.trɪs **-es** -ɪz
ancestr|y ˈæn.ses.tr|i, -sɪ.str|i, -sə-, US -ses.tr|i **-ies** -iz
Anchises ænˈkaɪ.siːz, æŋˈ-
anch|or ˈæŋ.k|əʳ, US -k|ɚ **-ors** -əz, US -ɚz **-oring** -ər.ɪŋ **-ored** -əd, US -ɚd
anchorag|e, A~ ˈæŋ.kər.ɪdʒ **-es** -ɪz
anchoress ˈæŋ.kər.ɪs, -es, -əs **-es** -ɪz
anchoret ˈæŋ.kər.et, -ɪt **-s** -s
anchorhold ˈæŋ.kə.həʊld, US -kɚ.hoʊld **-s** -z
anchorite ˈæŋ.kər.aɪt, US -kə.raɪt **-s** -s
anchor|man ˈæŋ.kə|.mæn, -mən, US -kɚ- **-men** -men, -mən
anchorperson ˈæŋ.kəˌpɜː.sən, US -kɚˌpɝː-
anchor|woman ˈæŋ.kə|ˌwʊm.ən, US -kɚˌ- **-women** -ˌwɪm.ɪn
anchov|y ˈæn.tʃə.v|i, ænˈtʃəʊ-, US ˈæn.tʃoʊ-, -ˈ-- **-ies** -iz
ancien(s)-régime(s) ˌɑ̃ːnt.si.æ̃n.reɪˈʒiːm, ˌɑːnt-, ɒnt.sjæn-, US ˌɑːnt.si.æn-
ancient ˈeɪn.tʃənt, US ˈeɪnt.ʃənt **-est** -ɪst, -əst **-ly** -li **-s** -s ˌ**ancient** ˈ**Greek**; ˌ**ancient** ˈ**history**
ancillar|y ænˈsɪl.ər|.i, US ˈænt.sə.ler- **-ies** -iz
ancipit|al ænˈsɪp.ɪ.t|əl, US -ţ|əl **-ous** -əs
Ancona æŋˈkəʊ.nə, US ænˈ-, ɑːnˈ-, -ˈkoʊ-
Ancram ˈæŋ.krəm
Ancren Riwle ˌæŋ.krɪnˈriː.u.li, -krenˈ-, -krənˈ-, -lə
-ancy ənt.si
Note: Suffix. Words containing **-ancy** are stressed in a similar way to those containing **-ance**; see above.
and *strong form:* ænd; *weak forms:* ənd, ən, nd, n, m, ŋ
Note: Weak-form word. The strong form /ænd/ is used for emphasis (e.g. 'The price included bed **and** breakfast.'), for contrast (e.g. 'It's not trick **and** treat, it's trick **or** treat.') or for citation (e.g. 'You should not begin a sentence with *and*.'). There are several weak pronunciations. In slow, careful speech the pronunciation may be /ənd/, but is more often /ən/ (e.g. 'Come and see.' /ˌkʌm.ənˈsiː/). In more rapid speech, when it occurs between consonants, the pronunciation may be a syllabic nasal consonant with a place of articulation assimilated to the neighbouring consonants (e.g. 'cut and dried' /ˌkʌt.n̩ˈdraɪd/; 'thick and creamy' /ˌθɪk.ŋ̍ˈkriː.mi/; 'up and back' /ˌʌp.m̩ˈbæk/).
Andalusi|a ˌæn.dəˈluː.si|.ə, -zi-, -luˈsiː|.ə, US -ˈluː.ʒ|ə, ˈ-ʒi|.ə, -ʃi- **-an** -ən
Andaman ˈæn.də.mæn, -mən
andante ænˈdæn.teɪ, -ti, US ɑːnˈdɑːn.teɪ, ænˈdæn.ţi **-s** -z
andantino ˌæn.dænˈtiː.nəʊ, US ˌɑːn.dɑːnˈtiː.noʊ, ˌæn.dænˈ-
Andean ænˈdiː.ən, ˈæn.di.ən
Anderlecht ˈæn.də.lekt, US -dɚ-
Andersen, Anderson ˈæn.də.sən, US -dɚ-
Anderton ˈæn.də.tən, US -dɚ-
Andes ˈæn.diːz
Andhra Pradesh ˌæn.drə.prɑːˈdeʃ, -prəˈ-, ˌɑːn-, -ˈdeɪʃ
andiron ˈæn.daɪ.ən, -daɪən, US -daɪ.ɚn **-s** -z
Andizhan ˈæn.dɪ.ʒæn, US ˈɑːn.dɪ.ʒɑːn, ˈæn.dɪ.ʒæn
Andorra ænˈdɔː.rə, -ˈdɒr.ə, US -ˈdɔːr.ə
Andorra la Vella ænˌdɔː.rə.ləˈveɪ.jə, US -ˌdɔːr.ə.lɑːˈveɪl.jə
Andover ˈæn.dəʊ.vəʳ, US -doʊ.vɚ
Andow ˈæn.daʊ
Andrade ˈæn.dreɪd, -drɑːd
Andrassy ænˈdræs.i
Andre, André ˈɑ̃ːn.dreɪ, ˈɑːn-, ˈæn-, US ˈɑːn.dreɪ, ˈæn-, ˈɑ̃ː-
Andrea ˈæn.dri.ə; ænˈdreɪ.ə, US ˈæn.dri.ə, ˈɑːn-; US ænˈdreɪ.ə, ɑːn-
Andrea del Sarto ænˌdreɪ.ə.delˈsɑː.təʊ, US ɑːnˌdreɪ.ə.delˈsɑːr.ţoʊ, æn-
Andreas ˈæn.dri.əs, -dri.æs; ænˈdreɪ.əs, US ɑːnˈdreɪ.əs, æn-
Andrei ˈæn.dreɪ, ˈɒn-, US ˈɑːn.dreɪ, ˈæn-, ˈɑ̃ː-
Andrew ˈæn.druː
Andrewartha *Cornish family:* ænˈdruː.θə *Plymouth family:* ænˈdruː.ə.θə, ˌæn.druˈɒθ.ə, US ˌæn.druˈɑːr.θə
Andrews, Andrewes ˈæn.druːz
Andrex® ˈæn.dreks
Andria ˈæn.dri.ə, US ˈæn-, ˈɑːn-
andro- ˈæn.drəʊ; ænˈdrɒ, US ˈæn.drə, -droʊ; US ænˈdrɑː
Note: Prefix. Either takes primary or secondary stress on the first syllable, e.g. **androgen** /ˈæn.drəʊ.dʒən/ US /-drə-/ **androgenic** /ˌæn.drəʊˈdʒen.ɪk/ US /-drəˈ-/, or primary stress on the second syllable, e.g. **androgynous** /ænˈdrɒdʒ.ən.əs/ US /-drɑː.dʒən.əs/.
androcentric ˌæn.drəʊˈsen.trɪk, US -drəˈ-
Androcles ˈæn.drəʊ.kliːz, US -drə-
Androclus ænˈdrɒk.ləs, US -ˈdrɑː.kləs
androeci|um ænˈdriː.si|.əm, US -ʃi-, -si- **-ia** -ə
androgen ˈæn.drəʊ.dʒən, -dʒen, -dʒɪn, US -drə-, -droʊ- **-s** -z
androgenic ˌæn.drəʊˈdʒen.ɪk, US -drəˈ-, -droʊˈ-
androgynous ænˈdrɒdʒ.ɪ.nəs, -ən.əs, US -ˈdrɑː.dʒən.əs
androgyny ænˈdrɒdʒ.ɪ.ni, -ən.i, US -ˈdrɑː.dʒən.i
android ˈæn.drɔɪd **-s** -z
Andromache ænˈdrɒm.ə.ki, US -ˈdrɑː.mə-
Andromeda ænˈdrɒm.ɪ.də, -ə.də, US -ˈdrɑː.mə-
Andronicus *Byzantine emperors and other figures in ancient history:* ˌæn.drəˈnaɪ.kəs, ænˈdrɒn.ɪ.kəs, US ˌænˈdrɑː.nə- *in Shakespeare's* **Titus Andronicus**: ænˈdrɒn.ɪ.kəs, US -ˈdrɑː.nɪ-

A

Andropov ˈæn.drə.pɒf; æn'drɒp.ɒf, -əf, (US) ɑːnˈdrɔː.pɑːv, -ˈdroʊ-, -pəf
Andros ˈæn.drɒs, (US) -ˈdrɑːs
Andvari ænˈdwɑː.ri, (US) ɑːn-
Andy ˈæn.di
-ane eɪn
Note: Suffix. Does not normally affect word stress, e.g. **alkane** /ˈæl.keɪn/.
anecdotage ˈæn.ɪk.dəʊ.tɪdʒ, -ək-, (US) -doʊ.t̬ɪdʒ
anecdotal ˌæn.ɪkˈdəʊ.təl, -ək-, (US) -ˈdoʊ.t̬əl
anecdote ˈæn.ɪk.dəʊt, -ək-, (US) -doʊt **-s** -s
anecdotic ˌæn.ɪkˈdəʊ.tɪk, -ek-, -ək-, -ˈdɒt-, (US) -ɪkˈdɑː.t̬ɪk **-al** -əl **-ally** -əl.i, -li
anechoic ˌæn.ɪˈkəʊ.ɪk, -ekˈəʊ-, -əˈkəʊ-, (US) -əˈkoʊ-, -ɪˈ-, -ekˈoʊ- *stress shift:* ˌ**anechoic** ˈ**chamber**
anelectric ˌæn.ɪˈlek.trɪk, -əˈlek- **-s** -s
anelectrode ˌæn.ɪˈlek.trəʊd, -əˈlek-, (US) -troʊd **-s** -z
anemia əˈniː.mi.ə
anemic əˈniː.mɪk
anemometer ˌæn.ɪˈmɒm.ɪ.təʳ, -ə.təʳ, (US) -ˈmɑː.mə.t̬ɚ **-s** -z
anemometric ˌæn.ɪ.məʊˈmet.rɪk, (US) -moʊˈ-
anemometry ˌæn.ɪˈmɒm.ə.tri, ˈ-ɪ-, (US) -ˈmɑː.mə-
anemone əˈnem.ə.ni **-s** -z
anemoscope əˈnem.ə.skəʊp, (US) -skoʊp **-s** -s
anent əˈnent
aneroid ˈæn.ə.rɔɪd, -ɪ.rɔɪd **-s** -z
anesthesia ˌæn.əsˈθiː.zi.ə, -ɪsˈ-, -iːsˈ-, -ʒi-, ˈ-ʒə, (US) ˈ-ʒə
anesthesiolog|y ˌæn.əsˌθiː.ziˈɒl.ə.dʒ|i, -ɪsˌ-, -iːsˌ-, -ʒiˈ-, (US) -ziˈɑː.lə- **-ist/s** -ɪst/s
anesthetic ˌæn.əsˈθet.ɪk, -ɪsˈ-, -iːsˈ-, (US) -θet̬- **-s** -s **-ally** -əl.i, -li *stress shift:* ˌ**anesthetic** ˈ**mask**
anesthetist əˈniːs.θə.tɪst, ænˈiːs-, -θɪ-, (US) əˈnes.θə.t̬ɪst **-s** -s
anesthetiz|e, -is|e əˈniːs.θə.taɪz, ænˈiːs-, -θɪ-, (US) əˈnes.θə- **-es** -ɪz **-ing** -ɪŋ **-ed** -d
aneurin əˈnjʊr.ɪn, -ˈnjʊə.rɪn, (US) ˈæn.jɚ.ɪn, -jʊ.rɪn
Aneurin əˈnaɪə.rɪn, (US) -ˈnaɪ-
aneurism ˈæn.jʊə.rɪ.zəm, (US) ˈæn.jɚ.ɪ-, -jʊ.rɪ- **-s** -z
aneurismal ˌæn.jʊəˈrɪz.məl, (US) -jəˈ-, -jʊˈ-
aneurysm ˈæn.jʊə.rɪ.zəm, (US) -jɚ.ɪ-, -jʊ.rɪ- **-s** -z
aneurysmal ˌæn.jʊəˈrɪz.məl, (US) -jəˈ-, -jʊˈ-
anew əˈnjuː, (US) -ˈnuː, -ˈnjuː
Anfield ˈæn.fiːld
anfractuosity ˌæn.fræk.tʃuˈɒs.ə.ti, -tjuˈ-, -ɪ.ti, (US) -tʃuˈɑː.sə.t̬i, -tjuˈ-
anfractuous ænˈfræk.tʃu.əs, -tju-, (US) -tʃu-
angel, A~ ˈeɪn.dʒəl **-s** -z ˈ**angel** ˌ**dust**
Angela ˈæn.dʒəl.ə, -dʒɪ.lə
Angeleno ˌæn.dʒəlˈiː.nəʊ, (US) -dʒəˈliː.noʊ
Angeles ˈæn.dʒəl.iːz, -dʒɪ.liːz, -liz, -lis, (US) -dʒəl.əs, -dʒə.liːz
angelfish ˈeɪn.dʒəl.fɪʃ **-es** -ɪz
angel-food cake ˌeɪn.dʒəlˈfuːdˌkeɪk, (US) ˈeɪn.dʒəlˌfuːd-
angelic ænˈdʒel.ɪk **-al** -əl **-ally** -əl.i, -li
angelica, A~ ænˈdʒel.ɪ.kə
Angelico ænˈdʒel.ɪ.kəʊ, (US) -koʊ
Angelina ˌæn.dʒəlˈiː.nə, -dʒelˈ-, (US) -dʒəˈliː-, -dʒelˈiː-
Angelo ˈæn.dʒəl.əʊ, -dʒɪ.ləʊ, (US) -dʒə.loʊ
Angelou ˈæn.dʒəl.uː, (US) -dʒə.luː, -loʊ
angelus, A~ ˈæn.dʒəl.əs, -dʒɪ.ləs **-es** -ɪz
ang|er ˈæŋ.g|əʳ, (US) -g|ɚ **-ers** -əz, (US) -ɚz **-ering** -ər.ɪŋ **-ered** -əd, (US) -ɚd
Angers ɑ̃ːnˈʒeɪ
Angevin ˈæn.dʒɪ.vɪn, -dʒə-
Angharad æŋˈhær.əd, æn-; ˈæŋ.ər-, (US) æŋˈher-, æn-, -ˈhær-
Angie ˈæn.dʒi
Angier ˈæn.dʒɪəʳ
angina ænˈdʒaɪ.nə **-s** -z
angiogram ˈæn.dʒi.əʊ.græm, (US) -ə-, -oʊ- **-s** -z
angiographic ˌæn.dʒi.əʊˈgræf.ɪk, (US) -əˈ-, -oʊˈ-
angiography ˌæn.dʒiˈɒg.rə.fi, (US) -ˈɑː.grə-
angioplasty ˈæn.dʒi.əʊ.plæs.ti, (US) -ə-, -oʊ-
angiosperm ˈæn.dʒi.əʊ.spɜːm, (US) -ə.spɝːm, -oʊ- **-s** -z
Angkor Thom ˌæŋ.kɔːˈtɔːm, (US) -kɔːrˈtɑːm
angl|e, A~ ˈæŋ.gəl **-es** -z **-ing** -ɪŋ, ˈ-glɪŋ **-ed** -d
Anglepoise® ˈæŋ.gəl.pɔɪz ˌ**Anglepoise** ˈ**lamp** (US) ˈ**Anglepoise** ˌ**lamp**
angler ˈæŋ.gləʳ, -gəl.əʳ, (US) ˈ-glɚ, -gəl.ɚ **-s** -z
Anglesea ˈæŋ.gəl.si, -siː
Anglesey ˈæŋ.gəl.si, -siː
Angli|a ˈæŋ.gli|.ə **-an/s** -ən/z
Anglican ˈæŋ.glɪ.kən **-s** -z **-ism** -ɪzəm
anglice ˈæŋ.glɪ.si, -glə-
anglicism ˈæŋ.glɪ.sɪ.zəm, -glə- **-s** -z
anglicist ˈæŋ.glɪ.sɪst, -glə- **-s** -s
anglicization, -isa- ˌæŋ.glɪ.saɪˈzeɪ.ʃən, -glə-, -sɪˈ-, (US) -səˈ-
angliciz|e, -is|e ˈæŋ.glɪ.saɪz, -glə- **-es** -ɪz **-ing** -ɪŋ **-ed** -d
angling ˈæŋ.glɪŋ, -gəl.ɪŋ
Anglo ˈæŋ.gləʊ, (US) -gloʊ **-s** -z
Anglo- ˈæŋ.gləʊ, (US) ˈæŋ.gloʊ, -glə
Note: Prefix. Words containing **anglo-** normally carry either primary or secondary stress on the first syllable, e.g. **anglophobe** /ˈæŋ.gləʊ.fəʊb/ (US) /-glə.foʊb/, **anglophobia** /ˌæŋ.gləʊˈfəʊ.bi.ə/ (US) /-gləˈfoʊ-/. Where the prefix is used to mean 'English and ...', it usually carries secondary stress, and the diphthong in the second syllable is only rarely reduced to /ə/, e.g. **Anglo-French** /ˌæŋ.gləʊˈfrentʃ/ (US) /-gloʊˈ-/.
Anglo-American ˌæŋ.gləʊ.əˈmer.ɪ.kən, (US) -gloʊ- **-s** -z
Anglo-French ˌæŋ.gləʊˈfrentʃ, (US) -gloʊˈ-
Anglo-Indian ˌæŋ.gləʊˈɪn.di.ən, (US) -gloʊ-
Anglo-Irish ˌæŋ.gləʊˈaɪə.rɪʃ, (US) -gloʊˈaɪ-
anglomania ˌæŋ.gləʊˈmeɪ.ni.ə, (US) -gləˈ-, -gloʊˈ-, -njə
Anglo-Norman ˌæŋ.gləʊˈnɔː.mən, (US) -gloʊˈnɔːr-
anglophile, A~ ˈæŋ.gləʊ.faɪl, (US) -glə-, -gloʊ- **-s** -z
anglophilia ˌæŋ.gləʊˈfɪl.i.ə, (US) -gləˈ-, -gloʊˈ-
anglophobe ˈæŋ.gləʊ.fəʊb, (US) -glə.foʊb, -gloʊ- **-s** -z
anglophobia ˌæŋ.gləʊˈfəʊ.bi.ə, (US) -gləˈfoʊ-, -gloʊˈ-
anglophone ˈæŋ.gləʊ.fəʊn, (US) -glə.foʊn, -gloʊ- **-s** -z
Anglo-Saxon ˌæŋ.gləʊˈsæk.sən, (US) -gloʊˈ- **-s** -z
Anglo-Saxondom ˌæŋ.gləʊˈsæk.sən.dəm, (US) -gloʊˈ-
Anglo-Saxonism ˌæŋ.gləʊˈsæk.sən.ɪ.zəm, (US) -gloʊˈ- **-s** -z
Angmering ˈæŋ.mə.rɪŋ
Angol|a æŋˈgəʊ.l|ə, (US) -ˈgoʊ-, æn- **-an/s** -ən/z
angora, A~ *cat, rabbit, cloth:* æŋˈgɔː.rə, (US) -ˈgɔːr.ə, æn- **-s** -z
Angora *old form of* **Ankara** *in Turkey:* ˈæŋ.gə.rə, æŋˈgɔː.rə, (US) æŋˈgɔːr.ə, æn-
angostura, A~ ˌæŋ.gəsˈtʃʊə.rə, -gɒsˈtʃʊə-, -ˈtjʊə-, -ˈstjɔː-, (US) -gəˈstʊr.ə, -ˈstjʊr- ˌ**Angostura** ˈ**bitters**®
Angoulême ɑ̃ːŋ.guˈlem
angr|y ˈæŋ.gr|i **-ier** -i.əʳ, (US) -i.ɚ **-iest** -i.əst, -i.ɪst **-ily** -əl.i, -ɪ.li **-iness** -ɪ.nəs, -ɪ.nɪs ˌ**angry young** ˈ**man**
angst æŋkst, (US) æŋkst, ɑːŋkst **-y** -i
angstrom ˈæŋk.strəm **-s** -z
Anguill|a æŋˈgwɪl|.ə **-an/s** -ən/z
anguine ˈæŋ.gwɪn
anguish ˈæŋ.gwɪʃ **-es** -ɪz **-ing** -ɪŋ **-ed** -t
angular ˈæŋ.gjə.ləʳ, -gjʊ-, (US) -lɚ **-ly** -li **-ness** -nəs, -nɪs
angularit|y ˌæŋ.gjəˈlær.ə.t|i, -gjʊ-, -ɪ.t|i, (US) -ˈler.ə.t̬|i, -ˈlær- **-ies** -iz
angulate ˈæŋ.gjə.leɪt, -gjʊ-, -lɪt, -lət
angulated ˈæŋ.gjə.leɪ.tɪd, -gjʊ-, (US) -t̬ɪd
Angus ˈæŋ.gəs
Angustura ˌæŋ.gəsˈtʃʊə.rə, -ˈtjʊə-,

A

-ˈtʃɔː-, -ˈtjɔː-, -ˈstʊr.ə, (US) -ˈstʊr.ə, -ˈstjʊr.ə
anharmonic ˌæn.hɑːˈmɒn.ɪk, (US) -hɑːrˈmɑː.nɪk *stress shift:* ˌ**anharmonic** ˈ**system**
anhungered ənˈhʌŋ.gəd, æn-, (US) -gɚd
anhydride ænˈhaɪ.draɪd **-s** -z
anhydrite ænˈhaɪ.draɪt
anhydrous ænˈhaɪ.drəs
anil ˈæn.ɪl
anile ˈeɪ.naɪl, ˈæn.aɪl
aniline ˈæn.ɪ.liːn, -lɪn, -laɪn, (US) -lɪn, -liːn, -laɪn
anility ænˈɪl.ə.ti, əˈnɪl-, -ɪ.ti, (US) -ə.ţi
anima ˈæn.ɪ.mə
animadversion ˌæn.ɪ.mædˈvɜː.ʃən, -mədˈ-, -ʒən, (US) -ˈvɝː.ʒən, -ʃən **-s** -z
animad|vert ˌæn.ɪ.mæd|ˈvɜːt, -mədˈ-, (US) -ˈvɝːt **-verts** -ˈvɜːts, (US) -ˈvɝːts **-verting** -ˈvɜː.tɪŋ, (US) -ˈvɝː.ţɪŋ **-verted** -ˈvɜː.tɪd, (US) -ˈvɝː.ţɪd
animal ˈæn.ɪ.məl, ˈ-ə- **-s** -z
animalcule ˌæn.ɪˈmæl.kjuːl **-s** -z
animalism ˈæn.ɪ.məl.ɪ.zəm
animalistic ˌæn.ɪ.məlˈɪs.tɪk, (US) -məˈlɪs-, -məlˈ-
animate adj ˈæn.ɪ.mət, -mɪt, -meɪt
ani|mate v ˈæn.ɪ|.meɪt, ˈ-ə- **-mates** -meɪts **-mating** -meɪ.tɪŋ, (US) -meɪ.ţɪŋ **-mated/ly** -meɪ.tɪd/li, (US) -meɪ.ţɪd/li
animation ˌæn.ɪˈmeɪ.ʃən, -əˈ- **-s** -z
animator ˈæn.ɪ.meɪ.təʳ, ˈ-ə-, (US) -ţɚ **-s** -z
animatronic ˌæn.ɪ.məˈtrɒn.ɪk, ˌ-ə-, (US) -ˈtrɑː.nɪk **-s** -s
anim|ism ˈæn.ɪ.m|ɪ.zəm, ˈ-ə- **-ist/s** -ɪst/s
animosit|y ˌæn.ɪˈmɒs.ə.t|i, -əˈ-, -ɪ.t|i, (US) -ˈmɑː.sə.ţ|i **-ies** -iz
animus ˈæn.ɪ.məs
anion ˈæn.aɪ.ən **-s** -z
anis ˈæn.iːs, -i; ænˈiːs, (US) ˈæn.iːs, ˈɑː.niːs, -i; (US) ænˈiːs, ɑːˈniːs
anise ˈæn.ɪs, ænˈiːs
aniseed ˈæn.ɪ.siːd, ˈ-ə-
anisette ˌæn.ɪˈset, -əˈ-, -ˈzet
anisometric ænˌaɪ.səʊˈmet.rɪk, (US) -soʊˈ-
anisotropic ˌæn.aɪ.səʊˈtrɒp.ɪk, -ˈtrəʊ.pɪk, (US) -soʊˈtrɑː.pɪk, -ˈtroʊ- **-ally** -əl.i, -li
anisotropism ˌæn.aɪˈsɒt.rə.pɪ.zəm, (US) -ˈsɑː.trə-
anisotropy ˌæn.aɪˈsɒt.rə.pi, (US) -ˈsɑː.trə-
Aniston ˈæn.ɪ.stən
Anita əˈniː.tə, (US) -ţə
Anjou ɑ̃ːnˈdʒuː, ɑːnˈ-
Ankara ˈæŋ.kər.ə, (US) ˈæŋ-, ˈɑːŋ-
ankerite ˈæŋ.kər.aɪt, (US) -kə.raɪt
ankh ɑːŋk, æŋk **-s** -s
ankle ˈæŋ.kəl **-s** -z ˈ**ankle** ˌ**sock**
anklet ˈæŋ.klət, -klɪt **-s** -s
Ann æn
anna, A~ ˈæn.ə **-s** -z
Annaba ænˈɑː.bə
Annabel ˈæn.ə.bel
Annabella ˌæn.əˈbel.ə
Annagh ænˈɑː, ˈæn.ɑː
Annakin ˈæn.ə.kɪn
annalist ˈæn.əl.ɪst **-s** -s
annals ˈæn.əlz
Annaly ˈæn.ə.li
Annam ænˈæm, ˈæn.æm
Annamese ˌæn.əˈmiːz
Annan ˈæn.ən
Annandale ˈæn.ən.deɪl
Annapolis əˈnæp.əl.ɪs, ænˈæp-
Annapurna ˌæn.əˈpɜː.nə, -ˈpʊə-, (US) -ˈpɝː-, -ˈpʊr-
Ann Arbor ˌænˈɑː.bə, (US) -ˈɑːr.bɚ
Annas ˈæn.æs, -əs
annatto əˈnæt.əʊ, ænˈæt-, (US) əˈnɑː.toʊ, əˈnæt.oʊ
Anne æn
anneal əˈniːl **-s** -z **-ing** -ɪŋ **-ed** -d
Anneka ˈæn.ɪ.kə, -ə.kə
annelid ˈæn.ə.lɪd **-s** -z
Annesley ˈænz.li
Annett ˈæn.ɪt, -ət
Annette əˈnet, ænˈet, (US) əˈnet
annex n ˈæn.eks **-es** -ɪz
annex v əˈneks, ænˈeks **-es** -ɪz **-ing** -ɪŋ **-ed** -t **-ment/s** -mənt/s
annexation ˌæn.ekˈseɪ.ʃən, -ɪkˈ- **-s** -z
annex|e ˈæn.eks **-es** -ɪz
Annfield Plain ˌæn.fiːldˈpleɪn
Annie ˈæn.i
Annigoni ˌæn.ɪˈgəʊ.ni, (US) -ˈgoʊ-
annihi|late əˈnaɪ.ɪ|.leɪt, ˈ-ə-, (US) ˈ-ə- **-lates** -leɪts **-lating** -leɪ.tɪŋ, (US) -leɪ.ţɪŋ **-lated** -leɪ.tɪd, (US) -leɪ.ţɪd **-lator/s** -leɪ.təʳ/z, (US) -leɪ.ţɚ/z
annihilation əˌnaɪ.ɪˈleɪ.ʃən, -əˈ-, (US) -əˈ- **-s** -z
Anning ˈæn.ɪŋ
Anniston ˈæn.ɪ.stən
anniversar|y ˌæn.ɪˈvɜː.sər|.i, (US) -ˈvɝː- **-ies** -iz
anno Domini, A~ ˌæn.əʊˈdɒm.ɪ.naɪ, (US) -oʊˈdɑː.mə.niː, -ˈdoʊ-, -naɪ
anno|tate ˈæn.əʊ|.teɪt, (US) ˈ-ə-, ˈ-oʊ- **-tates** -teɪts **-tating** -teɪ.tɪŋ, (US) -teɪ.ţɪŋ **-tated** -teɪ.tɪd, (US) -teɪ.ţɪd **-tator/s** -teɪ.təʳ/z, (US) -teɪ.ţɚ/z **-tative** -teɪ.tɪv, (US) -teɪ.ţɪv
annotation ˌæn.əʊˈteɪ.ʃən, (US) -əˈ-, -oʊˈ- **-s** -z
announc|e əˈnaʊnts **-es** -ɪz **-ing** -ɪŋ **-ed** -t **-ement/s** -mənt/s
announcer əˈnaʊnt.səʳ, (US) -sɚ **-s** -z
annoy əˈnɔɪ **-s** -z **-ing/ly** -ɪŋ/li **-ed** -d
annoyanc|e əˈnɔɪ.ənts **-es** -ɪz
annual ˈæn.ju.əl **-s** -z **-ly** -i
annualiz|e, -is|e ˈæn.ju.əl.aɪz, æn.julˌ-, (US) -ə.laɪz **-es** -ɪz **-ing** -ɪŋ **-ed** -d
annuit|y əˈnjuː.ə.t|i, -ɪ.t|i, (US) -ˈnuː.ə.ţ|i, -ˈnjuː- **-ies** -iz **-ant/s** -ənt/s
annul əˈnʌl **-s** -z **-ling** -ɪŋ **-led** -d
annular ˈæn.jə.ləʳ, -jʊ-, (US) -lɚ
annu|late ˈæn.jə|.leɪt, ˈ-jʊ- **-lated** -leɪ.tɪd, (US) -leɪ.ţɪd
annulet ˈæn.jʊ.lət, ˈ-jə-, -lɪt **-s** -s
annulment əˈnʌl.mənt **-s** -s
annul|us æn.jə.l|əs, ˈ-jʊ- **-uses** -əs.ɪz **-i** -aɪ, -iː
annum ˈæn.əm
annunci|ate əˈnʌnt.si|.eɪt, -ʃi- **-ates** -eɪts **-ating** -eɪ.tɪŋ, (US) -eɪ.ţɪŋ **-ated** -eɪ.tɪd, (US) -eɪ.ţɪd
annunciation, A~ əˌnʌnt.siˈeɪ.ʃən **-s** -z
annus mirabilis, A~ ˌæn.əs.mɪˈrɑː.bəl.ɪs, -məˈ-, (US) ˌɑː.nəs-, ˌæn.əs-
anode ˈæn.əʊd, (US) -oʊd **-s** -z
anodiz|e, -is|e ˈæn.əʊ.daɪz, (US) ˈ-oʊ-, ˈ-ə- **-es** -ɪz **-ing** -ɪŋ **-ed** -d
anodyne ˈæn.əʊ.daɪn, (US) ˈ-oʊ-, ˈ-ə- **-s** -z
a|noint ə|ˈnɔɪnt **-noints** -ˈnɔɪnts **-nointing** -ˈnɔɪn.tɪŋ, (US) -ˈnɔɪn.ţɪŋ **-nointed** -ˈnɔɪn.tɪd, (US) -ˈnɔɪn.ţɪd **-nointment/s** -ˈnɔɪnt.mənt/s
anomalous əˈnɒm.ə.ləs, (US) -ˈnɑː.mə- **-ly** -li
anomal|y əˈnɒm.ə.l|i, (US) -ˈnɑː.mə- **-ies** -iz
anomie ˈæn.ɒm.iː, (US) ˈæn.ə.mi
anon, A~ əˈnɒn, (US) -ˈnɑːn
anonym ˈæn.ə.nɪm, -ɒn.ɪm, (US) -ə.nɪm **-s** -z
anonymity ˌæn.əˈnɪm.ə.ti, -ɒnˈɪm-, -ɪ.ti, (US) -əˈnɪm.ə.ţi
anonymiz|e, -is|e əˈnɒn.ɪ.maɪz, ˈ-ə-, (US) -ˈnɑː.nə- **-es** -ɪz **-ing** -ɪŋ **-ed** -d
anonymous əˈnɒn.ɪ.məs, ˈ-ə-, (US) -ˈnɑː.nə- **-ly** -li
anopheles əˈnɒf.ɪ.liːz, ˈ-ə-, (US) -ˈnɑː.fə-
anorak ˈæn.ər.æk, (US) -ə.ræk **-s** -s
anorectic ˌæn.ərˈek.tɪk, (US) -əˈrek- **-s** -s
anorexia ˌæn.ərˈek.si.ə, (US) -əˈrek- **ano**ˌ**rexia ner**ˈ**vosa**
anorexic ˌæn.ərˈek.sɪk, (US) -əˈrek- **-s** -s
anosmia ænˈɒz.mi.ə, -ˈnɒs-, (US) ænˈɑːz-, -ˈɑːs-
another əˈnʌð.əʳ, (US) -ɚ
A N Other ˌeɪ.enˈʌð.əʳ, (US) -ɚ
Anouilh ˈæn.uː.iː, ˌæn.uːˈiː, (US) ɑːˈnuː.jə, ænˈuː-, -iː; (US) ˌɑː.nuːˈiː, ˌæn.uːˈ-
anoxia ænˈɒk.si.ə, eɪˈnɒk-, (US) ænˈɑːk-
ansaphone, ansafone, A~® ˈɑːnt.sə.fəʊn, (US) ˈæn.sə.foʊn **-s** -z
anschauung, A~ ˈæn.ʃaʊ.ʊŋ, (US) ˈɑːn.ʃaʊ.əŋ
anschluss, A~ ˈæn.ʃlʊs, (US) ˈɑːn-, ˈæn-
Ansell ˈænt.səl
Anselm ˈænt.selm
anserine ˈænt.sə.raɪn, -riːn, -rɪn
Ansley ˈænz.li
Anson ˈænt.sən
Ansonia ænˈsəʊ.ni.ə, (US) -ˈsoʊ-, ˈ-njə
Ansted ˈænt.sted, -stɪd
Anster ˈænt.stəʳ, (US) -stɚ
Anstey ˈænt.sti
Anston ˈænt.stən
Anstruther ˈænt.strʌð.əʳ, (US) -ɚ

answ|er ˈɑːnt.s|əʳ, (US) ˈænt.s|ɚ **-ers** -əz, (US) -ɚz **-ering** -ər.ɪŋ **-ered** -əd, (US) -ɚd **-erer/s** -ər.əʳ/z, (US) -ɚ.ɚ/z ˈ**answering maˌchine**

answerability ˌɑːnt.sər.əˈbɪl.ə.ti, -ɪ.ti, (US) ˌænt.sɚ.əˈbɪl.ə.t̬i

answerab|le ˈɑːnt.sər.ə.b|əl, (US) ˈænt- **-ly** -li

answerphone ˈɑːnt.sə.fəʊn, (US) ˈænt.sɚ.foʊn **-s** -z

ant ænt **-s** -s ˈ**ant ˌlion**

ant- ˈænt

Note: Prefix. Where **ant-** is attached to a free stem it often carries secondary stress, e.g. **antacid** /ˌænˈtæs.ɪd/. In other cases it may take primary, secondary, or no stress at all, e.g. **antonym** /ˈæn.tə.nɪm/ (US) /-tən.ɪm/, **antonymic** /ˌæn.təˈnɪm.ɪk/, **antonymous** /ænˈtɒn.ɪ.məs/ (US) /-ˈtɑː.nə-/.

-ant ənt

Note: Suffix. Words containing **-ant** are stressed in a similar way to those containing **-ance**; see above.

Antabuse® ˈæn.tə.bjuːs, -bjuːz

antacid ˌænˈtæs.ɪd **-s** -z

Antaeus ænˈtiː.əs, -ˈteɪ-

antagonism ænˈtæg.ən.ɪ.zəm **-s** -z

antagonist ænˈtæg.ən.ɪst **-s** -s

antagonistic ænˌtæg.ənˈɪs.tɪk, ˌæn.tæg.ənˈ-, (US) -əˈnɪs- **-ally** -əl.i, -li

antagoniz|e, -is|e ænˈtæg.ən.aɪz, (US) -ə.naɪz **-es** -ɪz **-ing** -ɪŋ **-ed** -d

Antalya ænˈtæl.jə, (US) ˌɑːn.təlˈjɑː, ˌæn-

Antananarivo ˌæn.təˌnæn.əˈriː.vəʊ, (US) -voʊ

Antarctic ænˈtɑːk.tɪk, (US) -ˈtɑːrk-, -ˈtɑːr.t̬ɪk **Antˌarctic ˈCircle**; **Antˌarctic ˈOcean**

Antarctica ænˈtɑːk.tɪ.kə, (US) -ˈtɑːrk-, -ˈtɑːr.t̬ɪ-

Antares ænˈteə.riːz, (US) -ˈter.iːz

ant-bear ˈænt.beəʳ, (US) -ber **-s** -z

ante ˈæn.ti, (US) -t̬i **-s** -z **-ing** -ɪŋ **-d** -d

ante- ˈæn.tɪ, (US) -t̬ə

Note: Prefix. Words containing **ante-** carry either primary or secondary stress on the first syllable, e.g. **antechamber** /ˈæn.tɪˌtʃeɪm.bəʳ/ (US) /-t̬əˌtʃeɪm.bɚ/, **antenatal** /ˌæn.tɪˈneɪ.təl/ (US) /-t̬əˈneɪ.t̬əl/.

anteater ˈæntˌiː.təʳ, (US) -t̬ɚ **-s** -z

antebellum ˌæn.tɪˈbel.əm, (US) -t̬əˈ-

antecedence ˌæn.tɪˈsiː.dənts, ˈæn.tɪ.siː-, (US) ˌæn.t̬əˈsiː-

antecedent ˌæn.tɪˈsiː.dənt, (US) -t̬əˈ- **-s** -s **-ly** -li

antechamber ˈæn.tɪˌtʃeɪm.bəʳ, (US) -t̬əˌtʃeɪm.bɚ **-s** -z

antechapel ˈæn.tɪˌtʃæp.əl, (US) -t̬ə- **-s** -z

ante|date ˌæn.tɪˈdeɪt, (US) ˈæn.t̬ə|.deɪt **-dates** -ˈdeɪts, (US) -deɪts **-dating** -ˈdeɪ.tɪŋ, (US) -deɪ.t̬ɪŋ **-dated** -ˈdeɪ.tɪd, (US) -deɪ.t̬ɪd

antediluvi|an ˌæn.tɪ.dɪˈluː.vi|.ən, -dəˈ-, -daɪˈ-, -ˈljuː-, (US) -t̬ə.dəˈluː- **-ans** -ənz **-al** -əl **-ally** -əl.i

antelope ˈæn.tɪ.ləʊp, (US) -t̬əl.oʊp **-s** -s

antemeridian ˌæn.tɪ.məˈrɪd.i.ən, (US) -t̬ə-

ante meridiem ˌæn.tɪ.məˈrɪd.i.əm, (US) -t̬ə-

antenatal ˌæn.tɪˈneɪ.təl, (US) -t̬əˈneɪ.t̬əl

antenn|a ænˈten|.ə **-ae** -iː **-as** -əz **-al** -əl **-ary** -ər.i

Antenor ænˈtiː.nɔːʳ, (US) -nɔːr

antenuptial ˌæn.tɪˈnʌp.ʃəl, -tʃəl, (US) -t̬əˈ-

antepenult ˌæn.tɪ.pɪˈnʌlt, -penˈʌlt, -pəˈnʌlt, (US) ˌæn.t̬əˈpiː.nʌlt; (US) -pɪˈnʌlt **-s** -s

antepenultimate ˌæn.tɪ.pəˈnʌl.tɪ.mət, -pɪˈnʌl-, -penˈʌl-, -tə-, -mɪt, (US) -t̬ə.pɪˈnʌl.tə.mət **-s** -s

anteprandial ˌæn.tɪˈpræn.di.əl, (US) -t̬əˈ-

anterior ænˈtɪə.ri.əʳ, (US) -ˈtɪr.i.ɚ **-ly** -li

anteroom ˈæn.tɪ.rʊm, -ruːm, (US) -t̬ə.ruːm, -rʊm **-s** -z

Anthea ˈænt.θi.ə, (US) ænˈθiː-

ant-heap ˈænt.hiːp **-s** -s

antheli|on æntˈhiː.li|.ən, æntˈθiː- **-ons** -ənz **-a** -ə

anthelix æntˈhiː.lɪks, æntˈθiː- **-es** -ɪz

anthem ˈænt.θəm **-s** -z

anthemic ænˈθem.ɪk, (US) ænˈθiː.mɪk, -ˈθem-

anther ˈænt.θəʳ, (US) -θɚ **-s** -z

anthill ˈænt.hɪl **-s** -z

anthological ˌænt.θəˈlɒdʒ.ɪ.kəl, (US) -ˈlɑː.dʒɪ-

anthologist ænˈθɒl.ə.dʒɪst, (US) -ˈθɑː.lə- **-s** -s

anthologiz|e, -is|e ænˈθɒl.ə.dʒaɪz, (US) -ˈθɑː.lə- **-es** -ɪz **-ing** -ɪŋ **-ed** -d

antholog|y ænˈθɒl.ə.dʒ|i, (US) -ˈθɑː.lə- **-ies** -iz

Anthon ˈæn.tɒn, (US) ˈænt.θən, ˈæn.tɑːn

Anthony ˈæn.tə.ni, ˈænt.θə.ni, (US) ˈæn.θə.ni, ˈæn.tə.ni

> Note: The pronunciation with /θ/ is becoming more frequently used by British speakers; it has usually been considered a case of spelling pronunciation.

anthracite ˈænt.θrə.saɪt

anthracitic ˌænt.θrəˈsɪt.ɪk, (US) -ˈsɪt̬-

anthrax ˈænt.θræks

anthropic ænˈθrɒp.ɪk, (US) -ˈθrɑː.pɪk **-al** -əl

anthropo- ˌænt.θrəʊ.pəʊ; ˌænt.θrəʊˈpɒ, (US) ˌænt.θrə.pə, ˈ-θroʊ-, -poʊ; (US) ˌænt.θrəˈpɑː

Note: Prefix. Words containing **anthropo-** normally exhibit secondary stress on the first syllable, e.g. **anthropomorphic** /ˌænt.θrəʊ.pəʊˈmɔː.fɪk/ (US) /-θrə.pəˈmɔːr-/, but may also have primary stress on the third syllable, e.g., **anthropology** /ˌænt.θrəʊˈpɒl.ə.dʒi/ (US) /-θrəˈpɑː.lə-/.

anthropocentric ˌænt.θrəʊ.pəʊˈsen.trɪk, (US) -θrə.pəˈ-, -poʊˈ-

anthropocentrism ˌænt.θrəʊ.pəʊˈsen.trɪ.zəm, (US) -θrə.pəˈ-, -poʊˈ-

anthropoid ˈænt.θrəʊ.pɔɪd, (US) -θrə-, -θroʊ- **-s** -z

anthropoidal ˌænt.θrəʊˈpɔɪd.əl, (US) -θrəˈ-, -θroʊˈ-

anthropological ˌænt.θrəʊ.pəˈlɒdʒ.ɪ.kəl, (US) ˌ-θrə-, ˌ-θroʊ-, -ˈlɑː.dʒɪ- **-ly** -i

anthropologist ˌænt.θrəʊˈpɒl.ə.dʒɪst, (US) ˌ-θrə-, ˌ-θroʊ-, -ˈpɑː.lə- **-s** -s

anthropology ˌænt.θrəʊˈpɒl.ə.dʒi, (US) -θrəˈpɑː.lə-, -θroʊˈ-

anthropometric ˌænt.θrəʊ.pəʊˈmet.rɪk, (US) -θrə.pəˈ-, -θroʊ-, -poʊˈ-

anthropometry ˌænt.θrəʊˈpɒm.ə.tri, ˈ-ɪ-, (US) -θrəˈpɑː.mə-, -θroʊˈ-

anthropomorph|ic ˌænt.θrə.pəʊˈmɔː.f|ɪk, (US) -pəˈmɔːr-, -poʊˈ- **-ous** -əs

anthropomorph|ism ˌænt.θrə.pəʊˈmɔː.f|ɪ.zəm, (US) -pəˈmɔːr-, -poʊˈ- **-ist/s** -ɪst/s

anthropomorphiz|e, -is|e ˌænt.θrəʊ.pəʊˈmɔː.faɪz, (US) -θrə.pəˈmɔːr-, -θroʊ-, -poʊ- **-es** -ɪz **-ing** -ɪŋ **-ed** -d

anthropomorphosis ˌænt.θrəʊ.pəʊ.mɔːˈfəʊ.sɪs, (US) -θrə.pə.mɔːrˈfoʊ-, -θroʊ-, -poʊ-

anthropopha|gus ˌænt.θrəʊˈpɒf.ə|.gəs, (US) -θrəˈpɑː.fə- **-gi** -dʒaɪ, -gaɪ, (US) -dʒaɪ

anthropopha|gy ˌænt.θrəʊˈpɒf.ə|.dʒi, (US) -θrəˈpɑː.fə- **-gous** -gəs

anthroposoph|y ˌænt.θrəʊˈpɒs.ə.f|i, (US) -θrəˈpɑː.sə- **-ist/s** -ɪst/s

anti ˈæn.ti, (US) -t̬i, -taɪ **-s** -z

anti- ˈæn.ti; ænˈtɪ, (US) -t̬i, -taɪ; (US) ænˈtɪ

Note: Prefix. Numerous compounds may be formed by prefixing **anti-** to other words. Most often, these compounds carry primary or secondary stress on the first syllable, e.g. **antihero** /ˈæn.tiˌhɪə.rəʊ/ (US) /-t̬iˌhɪr.oʊ/, **anti-icer** /ˌæn.tiˈaɪ.səʳ/ (US) /-t̬iˈaɪ.sɚ/, but there are also cases in which the second syllable takes the primary stress, e.g. **antinomy** /ænˈtɪn.ə.mi/.

anti-abortion ˌæn.ti.əˈbɔː.ʃən, (US) -t̬i.əˈbɔːr-, -taɪ- **-ist/s** -ɪst/s

anti-ageing ˌæn.tiˈeɪ.dʒɪŋ, (US) -t̬i-, -taɪ-

anti-aircraft ˌæn.tiˈeə.krɑːft, ⓊⓈ -t̬iˈer.kræft, -taɪˈ-

anti-American ˌæn.ti.əˈmer.ɪ.kən, ⓊⓈ -t̬i-, -taɪ-

antibacterial ˌæn.ti.bækˈtɪə.ri.əl, ⓊⓈ -t̬i.bækˈtɪr.i-, -taɪ-

antiballistic ˌæn.ti.bəˈlɪs.tɪk, ⓊⓈ -t̬i-, -taɪ-

Antibes ɑːnˈtiːb, æn-, ɒnˈ-, ⓊⓈ ɑːnˈ-

antibiosis ˌæn.ti.baɪˈəʊ.sɪs, ⓊⓈ -t̬i.baɪˈoʊ-, -taɪ-

antibiotic ˌæn.ti.baɪˈɒt.ɪk, ⓊⓈ -t̬i.baɪˈɑː.t̬ɪk, -taɪ- **-s** -s

antibod|y ˈæn.tiˌbɒd|.i, ⓊⓈ -t̬iˌbɑː.d|i, -taɪˌ- **-ies** -iz

antic ˈæn.tɪk, ⓊⓈ -t̬ɪk **-s** -s

anticatholic ˌæn.tiˈkæθ.əl.ɪk, ⓊⓈ -t̬iˈ-, -taɪˈ- **-s** -s

anti-choice ˌæn.tiˈtʃɔɪs, ⓊⓈ -t̬iˈ-, -taɪˈ-

antichrist, A~ ˈæn.ti.kraɪst, ⓊⓈ -t̬i-, -taɪ- **-s** -s

antichristian *opposing Christianity:* ˌæn.tiˈkrɪs.tʃən, -ˈkrɪʃ-, ⓊⓈ -t̬iˈ-, -taɪˈ- *pertaining to Antichrist:* ˈæn.tiˌkrɪʃ.tʃən, ⓊⓈ -t̬iˌ-, -taɪˌ- **-s** -z

anticipant ænˈtɪs.ɪ.pənt, ˈ-ə- **-s** -s

antici|pate ænˈtɪs.ɪ|.peɪt, ˈ-ə-, ⓊⓈ ˈ-ə- **-pates** -peɪts **-pating** -peɪ.tɪŋ, ⓊⓈ -peɪ.t̬ɪŋ **-pated** -peɪ.tɪd, ⓊⓈ -peɪ.t̬ɪd **-pative/ly** -peɪ.tɪv/li, ⓊⓈ -peɪ.t̬ɪv/li

anticipation ænˌtɪs.ɪˈpeɪ.ʃən, -əˈ-; ˌæn.tɪ.sɪˈ-, -səˈ-, ⓊⓈ ænˌtɪs.əˈ- **-s** -z

anticipator|y ænˌtɪs.ɪˈpeɪ.tər|.i, -əˈ-; ˌæn.tɪ.sɪˈ-, -səˈ-, ⓊⓈ ænˈtɪs.ə.pə.tɔːr- **-ily** -əl.i, -ɪ.li

anticiz|e, -is|e ˈæn.tɪ.saɪz, ⓊⓈ -t̬ɪ-, -taɪ- **-es** -ɪz **-ing** -ɪŋ **-ed** -d

anticlerical ˌæn.tiˈkler.ɪ.kəl, ⓊⓈ -t̬iˈ-, -taɪˈ- **-ism** -ɪ.zəm **-ist/s** -ɪst/s

anticlimactic ˌæn.ti.klaɪˈmæk.tɪk, -klɪˈ-, ⓊⓈ -t̬i.klaɪˈ-, -taɪ- **-ally** -əl.i, -li

anticlimatic ˌæn.ti.klaɪˈmæt.ɪk, -klɪˈ-, ⓊⓈ -t̬i.klaɪˈmæt̬-, -taɪ- **-al** -əl **-ally** -əl.i, -li

anticlimax ˌæn.tiˈklaɪ.mæks, ⓊⓈ ˌæn.t̬iˈklaɪ-, -taɪˈ- **-es** -ɪz

anticline ˈæn.ti.klaɪn, ⓊⓈ -t̬i- **-s** -z

anticlockwise ˌæn.tiˈklɒk.waɪz, ⓊⓈ -t̬iˈklɑːk-, -taɪˈ- *stress shift:* ˌ**anticlockwise** ˈ**action**

anticoagulant ˌæn.ti.kəʊˈæg.jʊ.lənt, -jə-, ⓊⓈ -t̬i.koʊˈæg.jə-, -taɪ- **-s** -s

anticommunist ˌæn.tiˈkɒm.jə.nɪst, ⓊⓈ -t̬iˈkɑː-, -taɪˈ-

anticonsumer|ism ˌæn.ti.kənˈsjuː.mər|.ɪ.zəm, -ˈsuː-, ⓊⓈ -t̬i.kənˈsuː- **-ist/s** -ɪst/s

anticonvulsant ˌæn.ti.kənˈvʌl.sənt, ⓊⓈ -t̬i-, -taɪ- **-s** -s

anticonvulsive ˌæn.ti.kənˈvʌl.sɪv, ⓊⓈ -t̬i-, -taɪ- **-s** -z

anticyclone ˌæn.tiˈsaɪ.kləʊn, ˈæn.ti.saɪ-, ⓊⓈ ˌæn.t̬iˈsaɪ.kloʊn, -taɪˈ- **-s** -z

anticyclonic ˌæn.ti.saɪˈklɒn.ɪk, ⓊⓈ -t̬i.saɪˈklɑː.nɪk, -taɪ-

antidepressant ˌæn.ti.dɪˈpres.ənt, -dəˈ-, ⓊⓈ -t̬i-, -taɪ- **-s** -s

antidotal ˌæn.tɪˈdəʊ.təl, ˈæn.tɪ.dəʊ-, ⓊⓈ ˈæn.t̬ɪ.doʊ-

antidote ˈæn.tɪ.dəʊt, ⓊⓈ -t̬ɪ.doʊt **-s** -s

Antietam ænˈtiː.təm, ⓊⓈ -t̬əm

antifebrile ˌæn.tiˈfiː.braɪl, -ˈfeb.raɪl, ⓊⓈ -t̬iˈfiː.brɪl, -taɪˈ-, -ˈfeb.rɪl, -rəl

anti-federal ˌæn.tiˈfed.ər.əl, ⓊⓈ -t̬iˈ-, -taɪˈ- **-ism** -ɪ.zəm **-ist/s** -ɪst/s

antifreeze ˈæn.ti.friːz, ⓊⓈ -t̬i-

antigen ˈæn.tɪ.dʒən, -dʒen, ⓊⓈ -t̬ɪ- **-s** -z

Antigone ænˈtɪg.ə.ni

Antigonus ænˈtɪg.ə.nəs

Antigu|a ænˈtiː.g|ə, ⓊⓈ -gw|ə, -g|ə; ⓊⓈ -ˈtɪg.w|ə, ˈ-|ə **-an/s** -ən/z

antihel|ix ˌæn.tiˈhiː.l|ɪks, ⓊⓈ -t̬iˈ-, -taɪˈ- **-ixes** -ɪk.sɪz **-ices** -ɪ.siːz, -ˈhel.ɪs.iːz

antihero ˈæn.tiˌhɪə.rəʊ, ⓊⓈ -t̬iˌhiːr.oʊ, -taɪ- **-es** -z

antiheroic ˌæn.ti.hɪˈrəʊ.ɪk, -həˈ-, -herˈəʊ-, ⓊⓈ -t̬i.hɪˈroʊ-, -taɪ-

antiheroine ˈæn.tiˌher.əʊ.ɪn, ⓊⓈ -t̬iˌher.oʊ-, -taɪ- **-s** -z

antihistamine ˌæn.tiˈhɪs.tə.miːn, -mɪn, ⓊⓈ -t̬iˈ- **-s** -z

anti-icer ˌæn.tiˈaɪ.sər, ⓊⓈ -t̬iˈaɪ.sɚ **-s** -z

anti-inflammatory ˌæn.ti.ɪnˈflæm.ə.tər.i, ⓊⓈ -t̬i.ɪnˈflæm.ə.tɔːr-, -taɪ-

Anti-Jacobin ˌæn.tiˈdʒæk.ə.bɪn, -ɒb.ɪn, ⓊⓈ -t̬iˈdʒæk.ə.bɪn, -taɪˈ-

antiknock ˌæn.tiˈnɒk, ⓊⓈ ˈæn.t̬iˌnɑːk, -taɪˈ- **-ing** -ɪŋ

Antilles ænˈtɪl.iːz

antilock ˌæn.tiˈlɒk, ⓊⓈ -t̬iˈlɑːk, -taɪˈ- *stress shift:* ˌ**antilock** ˈ**brakes**

anti-locking ˌæn.tiˈlɒk.ɪŋ, ⓊⓈ -t̬iˈlɑː.kɪŋ

antilog ˌæn.tiˈlɒg, ⓊⓈ ˈæn.t̬i.lɑːg, -lɔːg **-s** -z

antilogarithm ˌæn.tiˈlɒg.ə.rɪ.ðəm, -θəm, ⓊⓈ -t̬iˈlɑː.gɚ.ɪ.ðəm, -ˈlɔː- **-s** -z

antilog|y ænˈtɪl.ə.dʒ|i **-ies** -iz

antimacassar ˌæn.ti.məˈkæs.ər, ⓊⓈ -t̬i.məˈkæs.ɚ **-s** -z

Antimachus ænˈtɪm.ə.kəs

antimatter ˈæn.tiˌmæt.ər, ⓊⓈ -t̬iˌmæt̬.ɚ, -taɪˌ-

anti-missile ˌæn.tiˈmɪs.aɪl, ⓊⓈ -t̬iˈmɪs.əl, -taɪˈ-

antimonarchical ˌæn.ti.mɒnˈɑː.kɪ.kəl, -məˈnɑː-, ⓊⓈ -t̬i.məˈnɑːr-, -taɪ-

antimonarchist ˌæn.tiˈmɒn.ə.kɪst, ⓊⓈ -t̬iˈmɑː.nɚ-, -taɪˈ-, -nɑːr- **-s** -s

antimonial ˌæn.tɪˈməʊ.ni.əl, ⓊⓈ -t̬ɪˈmoʊ- **-s** -z

antimonic ˌæn.tɪˈmɒn.ɪk, ⓊⓈ -t̬ɪˈmɑː.nɪk

antimony ˈæn.tɪ.mə.ni, ænˈtɪm.ə-, ⓊⓈ ˈæn.t̬ə.moʊ-

antinode ˈæn.ti.nəʊd, ⓊⓈ -t̬i.noʊd

antinomian ˌæn.tɪˈnəʊ.mi.ən, ⓊⓈ -t̬ɪˈnoʊ-, -taɪˈ- **-s** -z

antinomic ˌæn.tɪˈnɒm.ɪk, ⓊⓈ -t̬ɪˈnɑː.mɪk **-al** -əl **-ally** -əl.i, -li

antinom|y ænˈtɪn.ə.m|i **-ies** -iz

Antinous ænˈtɪn.əʊ.əs, ⓊⓈ -oʊ-

antinovel ˈæn.tiˌnɒv.əl, ⓊⓈ -t̬iˌnɑː.vəl, -taɪˌ- **-s** -z

antinuclear ˌæn.tiˈnjuː.kli.ə, ⓊⓈ -t̬iˈnuː-, -taɪˈ-, -ˈnjuː-

Antioch ˈæn.ti.ɒk, ⓊⓈ -t̬i.ɑːk

Antiochus ænˈtaɪ.ə.kəs

Antioquia ˌæn.ti.əʊˈkiː.ə, ⓊⓈ -t̬i.əˈ-; ⓊⓈ ɑːnˈtjoʊ.kjɑː

antioxidant ˌæn.tiˈɒk.sɪ.dənt, ⓊⓈ -t̬iˈɑːk-, -taɪˈ- **-s** -s

Antipas ˈæn.tɪ.pæs, ⓊⓈ -t̬ɪ-

antipasti ˌæn.tɪˈpæs.ti, ⓊⓈ ˌæn.t̬ɪˈpɑː.sti, ˌɑːn.t̬ɪˈ-, -ˈpæs.ti

antipasto ˌæn.tiˈpæs.təʊ, ⓊⓈ ˌæn.t̬iˈpɑː.stoʊ, ˌɑːn-, -ˈpæs.toʊ **-s** -z

Antipater ænˈtɪp.ə.tər, ⓊⓈ -t̬ɚ

antipathetic ˌæn.tɪ.pəˈθet.ɪk, ænˌtɪp.əˈ-, ⓊⓈ ˌæn.t̬ɪ.pəˈθet̬.ɪk, ænˌtɪ.pəˈ- **-al** -əl **-ally** -əl.i, -li

antipath|y ænˈtɪp.ə.θ|i **-ies** -iz

anti-personnel ˌæn.tiˌpɜː.sənˈel, ⓊⓈ -t̬iˌpɝː-, -taɪˌ-

antiperspirant ˌæn.tiˈpɜː.spər.ənt, -spɪ.rənt, ⓊⓈ -t̬iˈpɝː.spɚ.ənt, -taɪˈ- **-s** -s

Antipholus ænˈtɪf.ə.ləs

antiphon ˈæn.tɪ.fən, -fɒn, ⓊⓈ -t̬ə.fɑːn, -fən **-s** -z

antiphonal ænˈtɪf.ə.nəl **-s** -z

antiphoner ænˈtɪf.ən.ər, ⓊⓈ -ɚ **-s** -z

antiphonic ˌæn.tɪˈfɒn.ɪk, ⓊⓈ -t̬ɪˈfɑː.nɪk **-al** -əl **-ally** -əl.i, -li

antiphon|y ænˈtɪf.ə.n|i **-ies** -iz

antipodal ænˈtɪp.ə.dəl

antipodean, A~ ænˌtɪp.əʊˈdiː.ən, ˌæn.tɪp-, ⓊⓈ -əˈ-

antipodes ænˈtɪp.ə.diːz

antipope ˈæn.ti.pəʊp, ⓊⓈ -t̬i.poʊp **-s** -s

antipyretic ˌæn.ti.paɪəˈret.ɪk, -pɪˈret-, ⓊⓈ -t̬i.paɪˈret̬-, -taɪ- **-s** -s

antiquarian ˌæn.tɪˈkweə.ri.ən, ⓊⓈ -t̬əˈkwer.i- **-s** -z **-ism** -ɪ.zəm

antiquar|y ˈæn.tɪ.kwər|.i, ⓊⓈ -t̬ə.kwer- **-ies** -iz

anti|quate ˈæn.tɪ|.kweɪt, ⓊⓈ -t̬ə- **-quates** -kweɪts **-quating** -kweɪ.tɪŋ, ⓊⓈ -kweɪ.t̬ɪŋ **-quated** -kweɪ.tɪd, ⓊⓈ -kweɪ.t̬ɪd

antique ænˈtiːk **-s** -s **-ly** -li **-ness** -nəs, -nɪs

antiquit|y ænˈtɪk.wə.t|i, -wɪ-, ⓊⓈ -wə.t̬|i **-ies** -iz

anti-racial|ism ˌæn.tiˈreɪ.ʃəl|.ɪ.zəm, -ʃi.ə.l|ɪ-, ⓊⓈ -t̬iˈreɪ.ʃəl|.ɪ-, -taɪˈ- **-ist/s** -ɪst/s

anti-rac|ism ˌæn.tiˈreɪ.s|ɪ.zəm, ⓊⓈ -t̬iˈ-, -taɪˈ- **-ist/s** -ɪst/s

anti-retroviral ˌæn.tiˌret.rəʊˈvaɪə.rəl, ⓊⓈ -t̬iˌret.roʊˈ-, -taɪ-

antirrhinum ˌæn.tɪˈraɪ.nəm, -təˈ-, ⓊⓈ -t̬əˈ- **-s** -z

antiscorbutic ˌæn.ti.skɔːˈbjuː.tɪk, ⓊⓈ -t̬i.skɔːrˈbjuː.t̬ɪk, -taɪ- **-s** -s

anti-Semite ˌæn.tiˈsiː.maɪt, -ˈsem.aɪt, US -t̬iˈsem.aɪt, -taɪˈ- **-s** -s
anti-Semitic ˌæn.ti.sɪˈmɪt.ɪk, -səˈ-, US -t̬i.səˈmɪt̬-, -taɪ- *stress shift:* ˌ**anti-Semitic** ˈ**views**
anti-Semitism ˌæn.tiˈsem.ɪ.tɪ.zᵊm, ˈ-ə-, US -t̬iˈsem.ə-, -taɪˈ-
antisepsis ˌæn.tiˈsep.sɪs, US -t̬əˈ-
antiseptic ˌæn.tiˈsep.tɪk, US -t̬əˈ- **-s** -s **-ally** -ᵊl.i, -li *stress shift:* ˌ**antiseptic** ˈ**lozenge**
antiser|um ˌæn.tiˈsɪə.r|əm, US -t̬iˈsɪr|.əm, -taɪˈ- **-ums** -əmz **-a** -ə
antislavery ˌæn.tiˈsleɪ.vᵊr.i, US -t̬i-, -taɪ-
antisocial ˌæn.tiˈsəʊ.ʃᵊl, US -t̬iˈsoʊ-, -taɪˈ- **-ly** -i
antisocialist ˌæn.tiˈsəʊ.ʃᵊl.ɪst, US -t̬iˈsoʊ-, -taɪˈ- **-s** -s
anti-spam ˌæn.tiˈspæm, US -t̬i-, -taɪ-
antistatic ˌæn.tiˈstæt.ɪk, US -t̬iˈstæt̬-, -taɪˈ- *stress shift:* ˌ**antistatic** ˈ**cloth**
Antisthenes ænˈtɪs.θə.niːz, -θɪ-
antistrophe ænˈtɪs.trə.fi **-s** -z
antistrophic ˌæn.tɪˈstrɒf.ɪk, US -t̬əˈstrɑː.fɪk
anti-tank ˌæn.tiˈtæŋk, US -t̬iˈ-, -taɪˈ-
anti-terror|ist ˌæn.tiˈter.ᵊr|.ɪst, US -t̬i-, -taɪ- **-ists** -ɪsts **-ism** -ɪzm
antithes|is ænˈtɪθ.ə.s|ɪs, ˈ-ɪ- **-es** -iːz
antithetic ˌæn.tɪˈθet.ɪk, US -t̬əˈθet̬.ɪk **-al** -ᵊl **-ally** -ᵊl.i, -li
antitox|ic ˌæn.tiˈtɒk.|sɪk, US -t̬iˈtɑːk-, -taɪˈ- **-in/s** -sɪn/z
antitrust ˌæn.tiˈtrʌst, US -t̬iˈ-, -taɪˈ-
antiviral ˌæn.tiˈvaɪə.rᵊl, US -t̬iˈvaɪ-, -taɪˈ-
anti-virus ˌæn.tiˈvaɪə.rəs, US -t̬iˈvaɪ-, -taɪ-
anti-vivisection ˌæn.tiˌvɪv.ɪˈsek.ʃᵊn, US -t̬iˈvɪv.ɪ.sek-, -taɪˈ- **-ist/s** -ɪst/s
antiwar ˌæn.tiˈwɔː, US -t̬iˈwɔːr, -taɪˈ-
antler ˈænt.ləʳ, US -lɚ **-s** -z **-ed** -d
Antofagasta ˌæn.tə.fəˈgæs.tə
Antoine ɑːnˈtwæn, ɒnˈ-, US ˈæn.twɑːn; US ˈɑːn-
Antoinette ˌɑːn.twɑːˈnet, ˌæn-, -twəˈ-, US ˌæn.twəˈ-, ˌɑːn-
Anton ˈæn.tɒn, US -tɑːn
Antonia ænˈtəʊ.ni.ə, US -ˈtoʊ-; US ˌæn.toʊˈniː-
Antonine ˈæn.tə.naɪn **-s** -z
Antoninus ˌæn.təʊˈnaɪ.nəs
Antonio ænˈtəʊ.ni.əʊ, US -ˈtoʊ.ni.oʊ
Antonius ænˈtəʊ.ni.əs, US -ˈtoʊ-
Antony ˈæn.tə.ni, US -tᵊn.i
antonym ˈæn.tə.nɪm, US -tᵊn.ɪm **-s** -z
antonymic ˌæn.təˈnɪm.ɪk, US -tᵊnˈɪm-
antonymous ænˈtɒn.ɪ.məs, ˈ-ə-, US -ˈtɑː.nə-
antonymy ænˈtɒn.ɪ.mi, ˈ-ə-, US -ˈtɑː.nə-
Antrim ˈæn.trɪm
Antrobus ˈæn.trə.bəs
Antron ˈæn.trɒn, US -trɑːn
antr|um ˈæn.tr|əm **-ums** -əmz **-a** -ə
antsy ˈænt.si
Antwerp ˈæn.twɜːp, US -twɝːp
ANU ˌeɪ.enˈjuː
Anubis əˈnjuː.bɪs, US -ˈnuː-, -ˈnjuː-
anuresis ˌæn.jʊəˈriː.sɪs, -jə-, US -juˈ-, -jəˈ-
anuria ænˈjuː.ri.ə, -ˈjɔː-, US -ˈjʊr.i-
anus ˈeɪ.nəs **-es** -ɪz
anvil ˈæn.vɪl, US -vᵊl, -vɪl **-s** -z
Anwar ˈæn.wɑːʳ, US ˈɑːn.wɑːr, ˈæn-
Anwick ˈæn.ɪk, US -wɪk
anxiet|y æŋˈzaɪ.ə.t|i, æŋg-, -ɪt|.i, US -ə.t̬|i **-ies** -iz
anxious ˈæŋ*k*.ʃəs **-ly** -li **-ness** -nəs, -nɪs
any *normal form:* ˈen.i; *occasional weak form:* ə.ni; *occasional weak form after t or d:* ᵊn.i
Note: The usual pronunciation is /ˈen.i/, but when the word follows immediately after a strongly stressed word it may be weakened to /ə.ni/ (e.g. 'Have you got any change?' /hæv.juˌgɒt.ə.niˈtʃeɪndʒ/ US /-ˌgɑːt̬-/). In more rapid speech, and when preceded by an alveolar consonant, the first syllable may be reduced to syllabic /n̩/ (e.g. 'Got any more?' /ˌgɒt.n̩.iˈmɔːʳ/ US /ˌgɑːt̬.n̩.iˈmɔːr/).
anybody ˈen.iˌbɒd.i, -bə.di, US -ˌbɑː.di
anyhow ˈen.i.haʊ
anymore ˌen.iˈmɔːʳ, US -ˈmɔːr
anyone ˈen.i.wʌn, -wən, -wɒn, US -wʌn, -wən
anyplace ˈen.i.pleɪs
anyroad ˈen.i.rəʊd, US -roʊd
anything ˈen.i.θɪŋ
anytime ˈen.i.taɪm
anyway ˈen.i.weɪ **-s** -z
anywhere ˈen.i.*h*weəʳ, US -*h*wer
anywise ˈen.i.waɪz
Anzac ˈæn.zæk **-s** -s ˈ**Anzac** ˌ**Day**
Anzio ˈæn.zi.əʊ, US -oʊ
AOB ˌeɪ.əʊˈbiː, US -oʊˈ-
Aoife ˈiː.fə
A-OK, A-Okay ˌeɪ.əʊˈkeɪ, US -oʊˈ-
AOL® ˌeɪ.əʊˈel, US -oʊ-
A-one ˌeɪˈwʌn, -ˈwɒn, US -ˈwʌn *stress shift:* ˌ**A-one con**ˈ**dition**
Aoni|a eɪˈəʊ.ni|.ə, US -ˈoʊ- **-an/s** -ən/z
aorist ˈeɪ.ə.rɪst, ˈeə.rɪst, US ˈeɪ.ə- **-s** -s
aort|a eɪˈɔː.t|ə, US -ˈɔːr.t̬|ə **-as** -əz **-ae** -iː **-al** -ᵊl **-ic** -ɪk
Aosta ɑːˈɒs.tə, US -ˈɔː.stə, -ˈoʊ-
Aouita aʊˈiː.tə, US -t̬ə
apace əˈpeɪs
Apache əˈpætʃ.i **-s** -z
apart əˈpɑːt, US -ˈpɑːrt **-ness** -nəs, -nɪs
apartheid əˈpɑː.taɪt, -taɪd, -teɪd, -teɪt, -ˈpɑːt.heɪt, -heɪd, -haɪt, US -ˈpɑːr.teɪt, -taɪt
apartment əˈpɑːt.mənt, US -ˈpɑːrt- **-s** -s aˈ**partment** ˌ**block**; aˈ**partment** ˌ**house**
apathetic ˌæp.əˈθet.ɪk, US -ˈθet̬- **-al** -ᵊl **-ally** -ᵊl.i, -li *stress shift:* ˌ**apathetic** ˈ**voters**
apath|y ˈæp.ə.θ|i **-ies** -iz
ap|e eɪp **-es** -s **-ing** -ɪŋ **-ed** -t
Apelles əˈpel.iːz
Apemantus æp.ɪˈmæn.təs, US -t̬əs
Apennines ˈæp.ə.naɪnz, -en.aɪnz
aperçu ˌæp.ɜːˈsjuː, -əˈ-, -ˈsuː, US -ɚˈsuː, ˌɑː.pɚˈ- **-s** -z
aperient əˈpɪə.ri.ənt, US -ˈpɪr.i- **-s** -s
aperiodic ˌeɪ.pɪə.riˈɒd.ɪk, US -pɪr.iˈɑː.dɪk
aperiodicity ˌeɪ.pɪə.ri.əˈdɪs.ə.ti, -ɪ.ti, US -pɪr.i.əˈdɪs.ə.t̬i
aperitif əˌper.əˈtiːf, æpˌer-, -ɪˈ-, əˈper.ə.tɪf, US ɑːˌper.ɪˈ-, -əˈ- **-s** -s
aperture ˈæp.ə.tʃəʳ, -tjəʳ, -tʃʊəʳ, -tjʊəʳ, US -ɚ.tʃʊr, -tʃɚ **-s** -z
aper|y ˈeɪ.pə.r|i **-ies** -iz
apeshit ˈeɪp.ʃɪt
apex, APEX, A~ ˈeɪ.peks **-es** -ɪz
aphaeresis æfˈɪə.rə.sɪs, əˈfɪə-, -rɪ-, US əˈfer.ə-
aphasia əˈfeɪ.zi.ə, æfˈeɪ-, eɪˈfeɪ-, -ʒi.ə, -ʒə, US əˈfeɪ.ʒə, -ʒi.ə
aphasic əˈfeɪ.zɪk, æfˈeɪ-, eɪˈfeɪ-, US əˈfeɪ-
apheli|on æfˈiː.li.|ən **-a** -ə
apheresis æfˈɪə.rə.sɪs, əˈfɪə-, -rɪ-, US əˈfer.ə-
aphes|is ˈæf.ə.s|ɪs, ˈ-ɪ- **-es** -iːz
aphid ˈeɪ.fɪd, US ˈeɪ.fɪd, ˈæf.ɪd, -əd **-s** -z
aphidian eɪˈfɪd.i.ən, æfˈɪd- **-s** -z
aph|is ˈeɪ.f|ɪs, ˈæf|.ɪs **-ides** -ɪ.diːz **-ises** -ɪ.sɪz
aphonia eɪˈfəʊ.ni.ə, æfˈəʊ-, əˈfəʊ-, US eɪˈfoʊ-
aphonic eɪˈfɒn.ɪk, æfˈɒn-, əˈfɒn-, US eɪˈfɑː.nɪk
aphony ˈæf.ə.ni
aphorism ˈæf.ᵊr.ɪ.zᵊm, -ɒr-, US ˈ-ɚ- **-s** -z
aphorist ˈæf.ᵊr.ɪst, -ɒr-, US ˈ-ɚ- **-s** -s
aphoristic ˌæf.ᵊrˈɪs.tɪk, -ɒrˈ-, US -əˈrɪs- **-ally** -ᵊl.i, -li
aphoriz|e, -is|e ˈæf.ᵊr.aɪz, -ɒr-, US -ə.raɪz **-es** -ɪz **-ing** -ɪŋ **-ed** -d **-er/s** -əʳ/z, US -ɚ/z
Aphra ˈæf.rə
aphrodisiac ˌæf.rəʊˈdɪz.i.æk, US -rəˈ-, -roʊˈ-, -ˈdiː.zi- **-s** -s
aphrodisian ˌæf.rəʊˈdɪz.i.ən, US -rəˈdiː.zi-, -roʊˈ-, -ˈdɪz.i-, -ˈdɪʒ.ən **-s** -z
Aphrodite ˌæf.rəʊˈdaɪ.ti, US -rəˈdaɪ.t̬i, -roʊˈ-
aphtha ˈæf.θə
Apia ɑːˈpiː.ə
apian ˈeɪ.pi.ən
apiarian ˌeɪ.piˈeə.ri.ən, US -ˈer.i- **-s** -z
apiarist ˈeɪ.pi.ə.rɪst **-s** -s
apiar|y ˈeɪ.pi.ə.r|i, US -er|.i **-ies** -iz
apical ˈæp.ɪ.kᵊl, ˈeɪ.pɪ- **-ly** -i
apices (alternative plural of **apex**) ˈeɪ.pɪ.siːz, ˈæp.ɪ-
apiculture ˈeɪ.pɪ.kʌl.tʃəʳ, US -tʃɚ
apiece əˈpiːs

apis ˈeɪ.pɪs
Apis ˈɑː.pɪs, ˈeɪ-
apish ˈeɪ.pɪʃ **-ly** -li **-ness** -nəs, -nɪs
aplenty əˈplen.ti, (US) -t̬i
aplomb əˈplɒm, æpˈlɒm, (US) əˈplɑːm, -ˈplʌm
apn(o)ea æpˈniː.ə, ˈæp.ni.ə
apn(o)eic æpˈniː.ɪk
apocalyps|e, A~ əˈpɒk.ə.lɪps, (US) -ˈpɑː.kə- **-es** -ɪz
apocalypt|ic əˌpɒk.əˈlɪp.t|ɪk, (US) -ˌpɑː.kəˈ- **-ist/s** -ɪst/s **-ical** -ɪ.kᵊl *stress shift:* **aˌpocalyptic ˈvision**
apocope əˈpɒk.əʊ.pi, (US) -ˈpɑː.kə- **-s** -z
apocryph|a, A~ əˈpɒk.rɪ.f|ə, -rə-, (US) -ˈpɑː.krə- **-al** -ᵊl
apocryphal əˈpɒk.rɪ.fəl, -rə-, (US) -ˈpɑː.krə-
apodeictic ˌæp.əʊˈdaɪk.tɪk, (US) -əˈ-, -oʊˈ- **-al** -ᵊl **-ally** -ᵊl.i, -li
apodictic ˌæp.əʊˈdɪk.tɪk, (US) -əˈ-, -oʊˈ- **-al** -ᵊl **-ally** -ᵊl.i, -li
apodos|is əˈpɒd.ə.s|ɪs, (US) -ˈpɑː.də- **-es** -iːz
apogee ˈæp.əʊ.dʒiː, (US) -ə- **-s** -z
apolitical ˌeɪ.pəˈlɪt.ɪ.kᵊl, (US) -ˈlɪt̬.-
Apollinaire əˌpɒl.ɪˈneəʳ, (US) -ˌpɑː.lɪˈner
Apollinaris əˌpɒl.ɪˈnɑː.rɪs, -ˈeə-, (US) -pɑː.lɪˈner.ɪs
Apollo əˈpɒl.əʊ, (US) -ˈpɑː.loʊ
Apollodorus əˌpɒl.əˈdɔː.rəs, (US) -ˌpɑː.ləˈdɔːr.əs
Apolloni|a ˌæp.əˈləʊ.ni.|ə, -ɒlˈəʊ-, (US) -əˈloʊ- **-an** -ən **-us** -əs
Apollos əˈpɒl.əs, (US) -ˈpɑː.ləs
Apollyon əˈpɒl.i.ən, (US) -ˈpɑː.li-
apologetic əˌpɒl.əˈdʒet.ɪk, (US) -ˌpɑː.ləˈdʒet̬.ɪk **-al** -ᵊl **-ally** -ᵊl.i, -li **-s** -s
apologia ˌæp.əˈləʊ.dʒə, ˈ-dʒi.ə, (US) -ˈloʊ- **-s** -z
apologist əˈpɒl.ə.dʒɪst, (US) -ˈpɑː.lə- **-s** -s
apologiz|e, -is|e əˈpɒl.ə.dʒaɪz, (US) -ˈpɑː.lə- **-es** -ɪz **-ing** -ɪŋ **-ed** -d **-er/s** -əʳ/z, -ɚ/z
apologue ˈæp.əʊ.lɒg, (US) -ə.lɑːg **-s** -z
apolog|y əˈpɒl.ə.dʒ|i, (US) -ˈpɑː.lə- **-ies** -iz
apophthegm ˈæp.ə.θem **-s** -z
apoplectic ˌæp.əˈplek.tɪk **-al** -ᵊl **-ally** -ᵊl.i, -li
apoplex|y ˈæp.ə.plek.s|i **-ies** -iz
aposiopes|is ˌæp.ə.saɪ.əʊˈpiː.s|ɪs, əˌpɒs.i.əʊˈ-, (US) ˌæp.oʊ.saɪ.oʊˈ-, -ə.saɪ.əˈ- **-es** -iːz
apostas|y əˈpɒs.tə.s|i, (US) -ˈpɑː.stə- **-ies** -iz
apostate əˈpɒs.teɪt, -tɪt, -tət, (US) -ˈpɑː.steɪt, -stɪt, -stət **-s** -s
apostatic ˌæp.əʊˈstæt.ɪk, (US) -əˈstæt̬- **-al** -ᵊl
apostatiz|e, -is|e əˈpɒs.tə.taɪz, (US) -ˈpɑː.stə- **-es** -ɪz **-ing** -ɪŋ **-ed** -d
a posteriori ˌeɪ.pɒsˌter.iˈɔː.raɪ, ˌɑː-, -ˌtɪə.riˈ-, -riː, (US) ˌeɪ.pɑːˌstɪr-
apostil əˈpɒs.tɪl, (US) -ˈpɑː.stɪl **-s** -z
apostle əˈpɒs.ᵊl, (US) -ˈpɑː.sᵊl **-s** -z **-ship** -ʃɪp
apostolate əˈpɒs.tə.lət, -lɪt, -leɪt, (US) -ˈpɑː.stə.lɪt, -leɪt **-s** -s
apostolic ˌæp.əˈstɒl.ɪk, (US) -ˈstɑː.lɪk **-al** -ᵊl **-ally** -ᵊl.i, -li
apostolicism ˌæp.əˈstɒl.ɪ.sɪ.zᵊm, (US) -ˈstɑː.lɪ-
apostrophe əˈpɒs.trə.fi, (US) -ˈpɑː.strə- **-s** -z
apostrophiz|e, -is|e əˈpɒs.trə.faɪz, (US) -ˈpɑː.strə- **-es** -ɪz **-ing** -ɪŋ **-ed** -d
apothecar|y əˈpɒθ.ə.kᵊr.|i, ˈ-ɪ-, (US) -ˈpɑː.θə.ker.i **-ies** -iz
apothegm ˈæp.ə.θem **-s** -z
apothegmatic ˌæp.ə.θegˈmæt.ɪk, (US) -ˈmæt̬- **-al** -ᵊl
apotheos|is əˌpɒθ.iˈəʊ.s|ɪs, ˌæp.əʊ.θiˈ-, (US) əˌpɑː.θiˈoʊ-, ˌæp.əˈθiː.ə- **-es** -iːz
apotheosiz|e, -is|e əˈpɒθ.i.əʊ.saɪz, ˌæp.əˈθiː.əʊ.saɪz, (US) əˈpɑː.θi.oʊ-, ˌæp.əˈθiː.ə- **-es** -ɪz **-ing** -ɪŋ **-ed** -d
app æp **-s** -s
appal əˈpɔːl, (US) -ˈpɔːl, -ˈpɑːl **-s** -z **-ling/ly** -ɪŋ/li **-led** -d
Appalachi|a ˌæp.əˈleɪ.ʃ|ə, ˈ-tʃ|ə, ˈ-ʃi|.ə, (US) -ˈleɪ.tʃi-, -ˈlætʃ.i.ə, -ˈleɪ.tʃ|ə, -ˈlætʃ|.ə **-an/s** -ən/z
appall əˈpɔːl, (US) -ˈpɔːl, -ˈpɑːl **-s** -z **-ing/ly** -ɪŋ/li **-ed** -d
Appaloosa ˌæp.əˈluː.sə
appanag|e ˈæp.ə.nɪdʒ **-es** -ɪz
apparat ˌæp.əˈrɑːt, (US) ˌɑː.pəˈ-, ˈæp.ə.ræt **-s** -s
apparatchik ˌæp.əˈrætʃ.ɪk, -ˈræt.tʃɪk, -ˈrɑːt-, -ˈrɑː.tʃɪk, (US) ˌɑː.pəˈrɑː.tʃɪk, -ˈrɑːt.tʃɪk **-s** -s **-i** -i
apparatus ˌæp.ᵊrˈeɪ.təs, -ˈæt.əs, (US) -əˈræt̬.əs **-es** -ɪz
apparel əˈpær.ᵊl, (US) -ˈper-, -ˈpær- **-s** -z **-ling** -ɪŋ **-led** -d
apparent əˈpær.ᵊnt, -ˈpeə.rᵊnt, (US) -ˈper.ᵊnt, -ˈpær- **-ly** -li **-ness** -nəs, -nɪs
apparition ˌæp.ᵊrˈɪʃ.ᵊn, (US) -əˈrɪʃ- **-s** -z
apparitor əˈpær.ɪ.təʳ, (US) -ˈper.ɪ.t̬ɚ, -ˈpær- **-s** -z
appassionata əˌpæs.i.əˈnɑː.tə, -ˌpæs.jəˈ-, (US) -ˌpɑː.si.əˈnɑː.t̬ə, -ˌpæs.i-
appeal əˈpiːl **-s** -z **-ing** -ɪŋ **-ed** -d **-er/s** -əʳ/z, (US) -ɚ/z **ApˈpeaI ˌCourt**
appealing əˈpiː.lɪŋ **-ly** -li **-ness** -nəs, -nɪs
appear əˈpɪəʳ, (US) -ˈpɪr **-s** -z **-ing** -ɪŋ **-ed** -d **-er/s** -əʳ/z, (US) -ɚ/z
appearanc|e əˈpɪə.rᵊnts, (US) -ˈpɪr.ᵊnts **-es** -ɪz
appeas|e əˈpiːz **-es** -ɪz **-ing/ly** -ɪŋ/li **-ed** -d **-able** -ə.bᵊl
appeasement əˈpiːz.mənt **-s** -s
appellant əˈpel.ənt **-s** -s
appellate əˈpel.ət, æpˈel-, -eɪt, -ɪt, (US) -ɪt
appellation ˌæp.əˈleɪ.ʃᵊn, -ɪˈ-, -elˈeɪ- **-s** -z
appellation contrôlée *as if French:* ˌæp.el.æsˌjɔ̃ːŋ.kɔ̃ːn.trəʊˈleɪ; ˌæp.elˌæs.jɔ̃ːŋ-, -kɒnˈtrəʊ.leɪ, (US) ˌæp.elˌɑː.sjoʊn.kɑːn.troʊˈleɪ
appellative əˈpel.ə.tɪv, æpˈel-, (US) -t̬ɪv **-ly** -li **-ness** -nəs, -nɪs
append əˈpend **-s** -z **-ing** -ɪŋ **-ed** -ɪd
appendag|e əˈpen.dɪdʒ **-es** -ɪz
appendant əˈpen.dənt **-s** -s
appendectom|y ˌæp.enˈdek.tə.m|i **-ies** -iz
appendicitis əˌpen.dɪˈsaɪ.tɪs, -dəˈ-, -təs, (US) -t̬ɪs, -t̬əs
appendicular ˌæp.enˈdɪk.jʊ.ləʳ, -ənˈ-, -ɪnˈ-, -jə-, (US) -ju.lɚ
append|ix əˈpen.d|ɪks **-ixes** -ɪk.sɪz **-ices** -ɪ.siːz
appercep|tion ˌæp.əˈsep.|ʃᵊn, (US) -ɚˈ- **-tive** -tɪv
Apperley ˈæp.ə.li, (US) -ɚ-
appertain ˌæp.əˈteɪn, (US) -ɚˈ- **-s** -z **-ing** -ɪŋ **-ed** -d
appertinent əˈpɜː.tɪ.nənt, æpˈɜː-, (US) əˈpɝː.tᵊn.ənt
appeten|ce ˈæp.ɪ.tᵊn|ts **-cy** -t.si **-t** -t
appetite ˈæp.ɪ.taɪt, ˈ-ə-, (US) ˈ-ə- **-s** -s
appetizer, -iser ˈæp.ɪ.taɪ.zəʳ, ˈ-ə-, (US) -ə.taɪ.zɚ **-s** -z
appetizing, -isi- ˈæp.ɪ.taɪ.zɪŋ, ˈ-ə-, (US) ˈ-ə- **-ly** -li
Appi|an ˈæp.i|.ən **-us** -əs
applaud əˈplɔːd, (US) -ˈplɑːd, -ˈplɔːd **-s** -z **-ing/ly** -ɪŋ/li **-ed** -ɪd **-er/s** -əʳ/z, -ɚ/z
applause əˈplɔːz, (US) -ˈplɑːz, -ˈplɔːz
apple ˈæp.ᵊl **-s** -z **ˈapple ˌblossom; ˈapple ˌbutter; ˌapple ˈsauce** (US) **ˈapple ˌsauce; ˈapple ˌtree; the ˌapple of one's ˈeye**
Appleby ˈæp.ᵊl.bi
apple-cart ˈæp.ᵊl.kɑːt, (US) -kɑːrt
Appledore ˈæp.ᵊl.dɔːʳ, (US) -dɔːr
Appleford ˈæp.ᵊl.fəd, (US) -fɚd
Applegate ˈæp.ᵊl.geɪt, -gɪt
applejack ˈæp.ᵊl.dʒæk
apple-pie ˌæp.ᵊlˈpaɪ **-s** -z *stress shift, see compounds:* **in ˌapple-pie ˈorder;** *British only:* **ˌapple-pie ˈbed**
Appleseed ˈæp.ᵊl.siːd
applet ˈæp.lət, -let **-s** -s
Appleton ˈæp.ᵊl.tən, (US) -tən
appliable əˈplaɪ.ə.bᵊl **-ness** -nəs, -nɪs
applianc|e əˈplaɪ.ənts **-es** -ɪz
applicability ˌæp.lɪ.kəˈbɪl.ə.ti, əˌplɪk-, -ɪ.ti, (US) -ə.t̬i
applicab|le əˈplɪk.ə.b|ᵊl, ˈæp.lɪ- **-ly** -li **-leness** -ᵊl.nəs, -nɪs
applicant ˈæp.lɪ.kənt, -lə- **-s** -s
applicate ˈæp.lɪ.kət, -lə-, -kɪt, -keɪt
application ˌæp.lɪˈkeɪ.ʃᵊn, -ləˈ- **-s** -z
applicator ˈæp.lɪ.keɪ.təʳ, -lə-, (US) -t̬ɚ **-s** -z
appliqué æpˈliː.keɪ, əˈpliː-; ˈæp.lɪ.keɪ, (US) ˈæp.lə.keɪ, -lɪ- **-s** -z **-ing** -ɪŋ **-d** -d
appl|y əˈpl|aɪ **-ies** -aɪz **-ying** -aɪ.ɪŋ **-ied** -aɪd
appoggiatura əˌpɒdʒ.əˈtʊə.rə, -i.əˈ-, -ˈtjʊə-, (US) əˌpɑː.dʒəˈtʊr.ə **-s** -z
ap|point əˈ|pɔɪnt **-points** -ˈpɔɪnts

-pointing -ˈpɔɪn.tɪŋ, Ⓤⓢ -ˈpɔɪn.t̬ɪŋ -pointed -ˈpɔɪn.tɪd, Ⓤⓢ -ˈpɔɪn.t̬ɪd
appointee əˌpɔɪnˈtiː, ˌæp.ɔɪnˈ- -s -z
appointive əˈpɔɪn.tɪv, Ⓤⓢ -t̬ɪv
appointment əˈpɔɪnt.mənt -s -s
Appomattox ˌæp.əˈmæt.əks, Ⓤⓢ -ˈmæt̬-
ap|port ə|ˈpɔːt, Ⓤⓢ -ˈpɔːrt -ports -ˈpɔːts, Ⓤⓢ -ˈpɔːrts -porting -ˈpɔː.tɪŋ, Ⓤⓢ -ˈpɔːr.t̬ɪŋ -ported -ˈpɔː.tɪd, Ⓤⓢ -ˈpɔːr.t̬ɪd
apportion əˈpɔː.ʃən, Ⓤⓢ -ˈpɔːr- -s -z -ing -ɪŋ -ed -d -ment/s -mənt/s
appos|e əˈpəʊz, æpˈəʊz, Ⓤⓢ əˈpoʊz -es -ɪz -ing -ɪŋ -ed -d
apposite ˈæp.ə.zɪt, -zaɪt, Ⓤⓢ -zɪt -ly -li -ness -nəs, -nɪs
apposition ˌæp.əˈzɪʃ.ən -s -z
appositional ˌæp.əˈzɪʃ.ən.əl
appraisal əˈpreɪ.zəl -s -z
apprais|e əˈpreɪz -es -ɪz -ing -ɪŋ -ed -d -er/s -ər/z, Ⓤⓢ -ɚ/s -able -ə.bəl
appraisee ˌæp.reɪˈziː, -ˈ--, Ⓤⓢ ˌæ.preɪˈziː, ˌə- -s -z
appraisement əˈpreɪz.mənt -s -s
appreciab|le əˈpriː.ʃə.b|əl; ˈ-ʃi.ə.b|əl, -si.ə-, Ⓤⓢ ˈ-ʃə-, ˈ-ʃi.ə- -ly -li
appreci|ate əˈpriː.ʃi|.eɪt, -si-, Ⓤⓢ -ʃi- -ates -eɪts -ating/ly -eɪ.tɪŋ/li, Ⓤⓢ -eɪ.t̬ɪŋ/li -ated -eɪ.tɪd, Ⓤⓢ -eɪ.t̬ɪd -ator/s -eɪ.təʳ/z, Ⓤⓢ -eɪ.t̬ɚ/z
appreciation əˌpriː.ʃiˈeɪ.ʃən, -siˈ-, Ⓤⓢ -ʃiˈ- -s -z
appreciative əˈpriː.ʃə.tɪv; ˈ-ʃi.ə.tɪv, ˈ-si-, Ⓤⓢ əˈpriː.ʃə.t̬ɪv; Ⓤⓢ ˈ-ʃi.ə-, -eɪ- -ly -li -ness -nəs, -nɪs
appreciatory əˈpriː.ʃi.ə.tər.i, -ʃi.eɪ-, -si.ə-, Ⓤⓢ ˈ-ʃə.tɔːr.i, ˈ-ʃi.ə.tɔːr.i
apprehend ˌæp.rɪˈhend, -rəˈ- -s -z -ing -ɪŋ -ed -ɪd
apprehensibility ˌæp.rɪˌhent.səˈbɪl.ə.ti, -rə-, -sɪˈ-, -ɪ.ti, Ⓤⓢ -ə.t̬i
apprehensible ˌæp.rɪˈhent.sə.bəl, -rəˈ-, -sɪ-
apprehension ˌæp.rɪˈhen.tʃən, -rəˈ-, Ⓤⓢ -ˈhent.ʃən -s -z
apprehensive ˌæp.rɪˈhent.sɪv, -rəˈ- -ly -li -ness -nəs, -nɪs
apprentic|e əˈpren.tɪs, Ⓤⓢ -t̬ɪs -es -ɪz -ing -ɪŋ -ed -t
apprenticeship əˈpren.tɪ.ʃɪp, -tɪs-, Ⓤⓢ -t̬əs.ʃɪp, -t̬ə- -s -s
appris|e, -iz|e əˈpraɪz -es -ɪz -ing -ɪŋ -ed -d -er/s -əʳ/z, Ⓤⓢ -ɚ/z
appro ˈæp.rəʊ, Ⓤⓢ -roʊ
approach əˈprəʊtʃ, Ⓤⓢ -ˈproʊtʃ -es -ɪz -ing -ɪŋ -ed -t
approachability əˌprəʊ.tʃəˈbɪl.ə.ti, -ɪ.ti, Ⓤⓢ -ˌproʊ.tʃəˈbɪl.ə.t̬i
approachable əˈprəʊ.tʃə.bəl, Ⓤⓢ -ˈproʊ-
appro|bate ˈæp.rəʊ|.beɪt, Ⓤⓢ -rə- -bates -beɪts -bating -beɪ.tɪŋ, Ⓤⓢ -beɪ.t̬ɪŋ -bated -beɪ.tɪd, Ⓤⓢ -beɪ.t̬ɪd -bative -beɪ.tɪv, Ⓤⓢ -beɪ.t̬ɪv
approbation ˌæp.rəʊˈbeɪ.ʃən, Ⓤⓢ -rəˈ-, -roʊˈ- -s -z
approbatory ˌæp.rəʊˈbeɪ.tər.i, Ⓤⓢ əˈproʊ.bə.tɔːr-
appropriate adj əˈprəʊ.pri.ət, -ɪt, Ⓤⓢ -ˈproʊ- -ly -li -ness -nəs, -nɪs
appropri|ate v əˈprəʊ.pri|.eɪt, Ⓤⓢ -ˈproʊ- -ates -eɪts -ating -eɪ.tɪŋ, Ⓤⓢ -eɪ.t̬ɪŋ -ated -eɪ.tɪd, Ⓤⓢ -eɪ.t̬ɪd -ator/s -eɪ.təʳ/z, Ⓤⓢ -eɪ.t̬ɚ/z
appropriation əˌprəʊ.priˈeɪ.ʃən, Ⓤⓢ -ˌproʊ- -s -z
approval əˈpruː.vəl -s -z
approv|e əˈpruːv -es -z -ing/ly -ɪŋ/li -ed -d -er/s -əʳ/z, Ⓤⓢ -ɚ/z -able -ə.bəl
approx (abbrev. for **approximate/ly**) əˈprɒk.sɪ.mət/li, -sə-, -mɪt/li, Ⓤⓢ -ˈprɑːk-
approximant əˈprɒk.sɪ.mənt, -sə-, Ⓤⓢ -ˈprɑːk- -s -s
approximate adj əˈprɒk.sɪ.mət, -sə-, -mɪt, Ⓤⓢ -ˈprɑːk- -ly -li
approxi|mate v əˈprɒk.sɪ|.meɪt, -sə-, Ⓤⓢ -ˈprɑːk- -mates -meɪts -mating -meɪ.tɪŋ, Ⓤⓢ -meɪ.t̬ɪŋ -mated -meɪ.tɪd, Ⓤⓢ -meɪ.t̬ɪd
approximation əˌprɒk.sɪˈmeɪ.ʃən, -səˈ-, Ⓤⓢ -ˌprɑːk- -s -z
approximative əˈprɒk.sɪ.mə.tɪv, -sə-, Ⓤⓢ -ˈprɑːk.sə.mə.t̬ɪv
appui æpˈwiː, əˈpwiː
appuls|e æpˈʌls, əˈpʌls, ˈæp.ʌls -es -ɪz
appurtenan|ce əˈpɜː.tɪ.nən|ts, -tən.ən|ts, Ⓤⓢ -ˈpɝː.tən.ən|ts -ces -t.sɪz -t -t
APR ˌeɪ.piːˈɑːʳ, Ⓤⓢ -ˈɑːr
Apr. (abbrev. for **April**) ˈeɪ.prəl, -prɪl
après ˈæp.reɪ, Ⓤⓢ ˌɑːˈpreɪ, æpˈreɪ
après-ski ˌæp.reɪˈskiː, Ⓤⓢ ˌɑː.preɪˈ-, ˌæp.reɪˈ- *stress shift:* **ˌaprès-ski ˈdrinks**
apricot ˈeɪ.prɪ.kɒt, Ⓤⓢ -kɑːt, ˈæp.rɪ- -s -s
April ˈeɪ.prəl, -prɪl -s -z **ˌApril ˈFools' ˌDay**
a priori ˌeɪ.praɪˈɔː.raɪ, ˌɑː.priːˈɔː.ri, Ⓤⓢ ˌɑː.priːˈɔːr.aɪ, ˌeɪ-, -i
apriority ˌeɪ.praɪˈɒr.ə.ti, -ɪ.ti, Ⓤⓢ -ˈɔːr.ə.t̬i
apron ˈeɪ.prən -s -z -ed -d **ˈapron ˌstrings**
apropos ˌæp.rəˈpəʊ, Ⓤⓢ -ˈpoʊ
aps|e æps -es -ɪz
apsidal ˈæp.sɪ.dəl
Apsley ˈæp.sli
apt æpt -er -əʳ, Ⓤⓢ -ɚ -est -ɪst, -əst -ly -li -ness -nəs, -nɪs
apter|al ˈæp.tər|.əl -ous -əs
apteryx ˈæp.tər.ɪks -es -ɪz
aptitude ˈæp.tɪ.tʃuːd, -tə-, -tjuːd, Ⓤⓢ -tuːd, -tjuːd -s -z
Apuli|a əˈpjuː.li|.ə -an/s -ən/z
apyretic ˌeɪ.paɪəˈret.ɪk; ˌæp.aɪəˈ-, Ⓤⓢ -paɪˈret̬-
aqua ˈæk.wə, Ⓤⓢ ˈɑːk-
aqua-aerobics ˌæk.wə.eəˈrəʊ.bɪks, Ⓤⓢ ˌɑː.kwə.erˈoʊ-, ˌæk.wə-
aquacultural ˌæk.wəˈkʌl.tʃər.əl, Ⓤⓢ ˌɑː.kwəˈ-, ˌæk.wəˈ-
aquaculture ˈæk.wəˌkʌl.tʃəʳ, Ⓤⓢ ˈɑː.kwəˌkʌl.tʃɚ, ˈæk.wəˌ-
aqua fortis ˌæk.wəˈfɔː.tɪs, Ⓤⓢ ˌɑː.kwəˈfɔːr.t̬ɪs, ˌæk.wəˈ-
Aqua-Lung® ˈæk.wə.lʌŋ, Ⓤⓢ ˈɑː.kwə-, ˈæk.wə- -s -z
aquamarine ˌæk.wə.məˈriːn, ˈæk.wə.mə.riːn, Ⓤⓢ ˌɑː.kwə.məˈriːn, ˌæk.wə- -s -z
aquaplan|e ˈæk.wə.pleɪn, Ⓤⓢ ˈɑː.kwə-, ˈæk.wə- -es -z -ing -ɪŋ -ed -d
aqua regia ˌæk.wəˈriː.dʒi.ə, Ⓤⓢ ˌɑː.kwəˈ-, ˌæk.wəˈ-
aquarell|e ˌæk.wəˈrel, Ⓤⓢ ˌɑː.kwəˈ-, ˌæk.wəˈ- -es -z -ist/s -ɪst/s
aquarist ˈæk.wə.rɪst, Ⓤⓢ əˈkwer.ɪst -s -s
aquari|um əˈkweə.ri.|əm, Ⓤⓢ -ˈkwer.i- -ums -əmz -a -ə
Aquari|us əˈkweə.ri.|əs, Ⓤⓢ -ˈkwer.i- -an/s -ən/z
Aquascutum® ˌæk.wəˈskjuː.təm, Ⓤⓢ ˌɑː.kwəˈskuː.t̬əm, ˌæk.wəˈ-
aquatic əˈkwæt.ɪk, -ˈkwɒt-, Ⓤⓢ -ˈkwæt̬-, -ˈkwɑː.t̬ɪk -s -s -ally -əl.i, -li
aquatint ˈæk.wə.tɪnt, Ⓤⓢ ˈɑː.kwə-, ˈæk.wə- -s -s
aquatube ˈæk.wə.tʃuːb, -tjuːb, Ⓤⓢ ˈɑː.kwə.tuːb, ˈæk.wə-, -tjuːb -s -z
aquavit ˈæk.wə.vɪt, -viːt, Ⓤⓢ ˈɑː.kwə.viːt
aqua vitae ˌæk.wəˈviː.taɪ, -ˈvaɪ.tiː, Ⓤⓢ ˌɑː.kwəˈvaɪ.t̬iː, ˌæk.wəˈ-
aqueduct ˈæk.wɪ.dʌkt, -wə- -s -s
aqueous ˈeɪ.kwi.əs, ˈæk.wi- -ly -li
aquifer ˈæk.wɪ.fəʳ, -wə.fəʳ, Ⓤⓢ ˈɑː.kwə.fɚ, ˈæk.wə- -s -z
Aquila ˈæk.wɪ.lə, -wə-; əˈkwɪl.ə
aquilegia ˌæk.wɪˈliː.dʒə, -wə-, -ˈliː.dʒi.ə -s -z
aquiline ˈæk.wɪ.laɪn, -wə-, Ⓤⓢ -lən
Aquinas əˈkwaɪ.nəs, ækˈwaɪ-, -næs
Aquino əˈkiː.nəʊ, Ⓤⓢ -noʊ
Aquitaine ˌæk.wɪˈteɪn, -wəˈteɪn, ˈ---
Aquitania ˌæk.wɪˈteɪ.ni.ə
aquiver əˈkwɪv.əʳ, Ⓤⓢ -ɚ
ar- əˈr; ˈær, Ⓤⓢ əˈr; Ⓤⓢ ˈer, ˈær
Note: Prefix. Examples include **arrogate** /ˈær.əʊ.geɪt/ Ⓤⓢ /ˈer.ə-/, in which it is stressed, and **array** /əˈreɪ/, where it is unstressed.
-ar əʳ, ɑːʳ, Ⓤⓢ ɚ, ɑːr
Note: Suffix. Normally pronounced /-əʳ/ Ⓤⓢ /-ɚ/, e.g. **molecular** /məʊˈlek.jə.ləʳ/ Ⓤⓢ /məˈlek.jə.lɚ/.
Arab ˈær.əb, Ⓤⓢ ˈer-, ˈær- -s -z
Arabella ˌær.əˈbel.ə, Ⓤⓢ ˌer-, ˌær-
arabesque ˌær.əˈbesk, Ⓤⓢ ˌer-, ˌær- -s -s -d -t
Arabi|a əˈreɪ.bi|.ə -an/s -ən/z
Arabic *of Arabia:* ˈær.ə.bɪk, Ⓤⓢ ˈer-, ˈær- *name of ship:* ˈær.ə.bɪk; əˈræb-, Ⓤⓢ ˈer.ə-, ˈær-; Ⓤⓢ əˈræb-
arabis ˈær.ə.bɪs, Ⓤⓢ ˈer-, ˈær-
Arabist ˈær.ə.bɪst, Ⓤⓢ ˈer-, ˈær- -s -s
arable ˈær.ə.bəl, Ⓤⓢ ˈer-, ˈær-
Araby ˈær.ə.bi, Ⓤⓢ ˈer-, ˈær-
Aracaju əˌræk.əˈʒuː, Ⓤⓢ ɑːˌrɑː.kəˈʒuː
Arachne əˈræk.ni

A

arachnid ə'ræk.nɪd **-a** -ə **-s** -z
arachnoid ə'ræk.nɔɪd **-s** -z
arachnologist ˌær.æk'nɒl.ə.dʒɪst, -ək'-, (US) ˌer.ək'nɑː.lə-, ˌær- **-s** -s
arachnopho|bia əˌræk.nəʊ'fəʊ.|bi.ə, (US) -nə'foʊ-, -noʊ'- **-bic** -bɪk
Arafat 'ær.ə.fæt, (US) 'er-, 'ær-
Arafura ˌær.ə'fʊə.rə, (US) ˌɑːr.ə'fʊr.ə
Aragon 'ær.ə.gən, (US) 'er.ə.gɑːn, 'ær-, -gən
aragonite ə'ræg.ən.aɪt; 'ær.ə.gən-, (US) ə'ræg.ən-; (US) 'er.ə.gən-, 'ær-
Aral 'ɑː.rəl, 'ær.əl, -æl, (US) 'er.əl, 'ær-
Araldite® 'ær.əl.daɪt, (US) 'er-, 'ær-
Aram *biblical name:* 'eə.ræm, -rəm, (US) 'er.æm, 'ær-, 'eɪ.rəm, 'ɑːr.əm *surname:* 'eə.rəm, (US) 'er.əm, 'ær-
Aramaean ˌær.ə'miː.ən, (US) ˌer-, ˌær-
Arama|ic ˌær.ə'meɪ|.ɪk, (US) ˌer-, ˌær- **-ism** -ɪ.zəm
Aramean ˌær.ə'miː.ən, (US) ˌer-, ˌær- **-s** -z
aramid 'ær.ə.mɪd, (US) 'er-, 'ær- **-s** -z
Aramite 'ær.ə.maɪt, (US) 'er-, 'ær- **-s** -s
Aran 'ær.ən, (US) 'er-, 'ær-
Arapaho ə'ræp.ə.həʊ, (US) -hoʊ
Ararat 'ær.ə.ræt, (US) 'er-, 'ær-
Araucani|a ˌær.ɔː'keɪ.ni|.ə, (US) ˌer-, ˌær-, -ɑː'-; (US) əˌraʊ.kɑː'niː|.ə **-an/s** -ən/z
araucaria ˌær.ɔː'keə.ri.ə, (US) ˌer.ɔː'ker.i-, ˌær-, -ɑː'- **-s** -z
Arawak 'ær.ə.wæk, -wɑːk, (US) 'ɑːr.ə.wɑːk; (US) 'ær.ə.wæk, 'er- **-s** -s
Arber 'ɑː.bər, (US) 'ɑːr.bɚ
Arberry 'ɑː.bər.i, (US) 'ɑːr.ber-
Arbil 'ɑː.bɪl, (US) 'ɑːr-
arbiter 'ɑː.bɪ.tər, (US) 'ɑːr.bɪ.t̬ɚ **-s** -z
arbitrage *arbitration:* 'ɑː.bɪ.trɪdʒ, (US) 'ɑːr- *of stocks, etc.:* 'ɑː.bɪ.trɑːʒ, 'ɑː.bɪ.trɪdʒ, (US) 'ɑːr.bɪ.trɑːʒ
arbitrageur ˌɑː.bɪ.trɑː'ʒɜːr, (US) 'ɑːr.bɪ.trɑː.ʒɚ **-s** -z
arbitrament ɑː'bɪt.rə.mənt, (US) ɑːr- **-s** -s
arbitrarily ˌɑː.bɪ'treə.rəl.i, -rɪ.li, 'ɑː.bɪ.trər.əl.i, (US) ˌɑːr.bə'trer.əl-
arbitrar|y 'ɑː.bɪ.trər|.i, (US) 'ɑːr.bə.trer- **-iness** -ɪ.nəs, -ɪ.nɪs
arbi|trate 'ɑː.bɪ|.treɪt, (US) 'ɑːr.bə|.treɪt **-trates** -treɪts **-trating** -treɪ.tɪŋ, (US) -treɪ.t̬ɪŋ **-trated** -treɪ.tɪd, (US) -treɪ.t̬ɪd
arbitration ˌɑː.bɪ'treɪ.ʃən, (US) ˌɑːr.bə'- **-s** -z
arbitrator 'ɑː.bɪ.treɪ.tər, (US) 'ɑːr.bə.treɪ.t̬ɚ **-s** -z
Arblay 'ɑː.bleɪ, (US) 'ɑːr-
arbor *tree:* 'ɑː.bɔːr, -bər, (US) 'ɑːr.bɚ *axle, shaft:* 'ɑː.bər, (US) 'ɑːr.bɚ **-s** -z
Arbor 'ɑː.bər, (US) 'ɑːr.bɚ **'Arbor ˌDay**
arboraceous ˌɑː.bər'eɪ.ʃəs, -bɔː'reɪ-, (US) ˌɑːr.bə'reɪ-, -bɔː'-
arbore|al ɑː'bɔː.ri|.əl, (US) ɑːr'bɔːr.i- **-ous** -əs
arborescen|ce ˌɑː.bər'es.ən|ts, -bɔː'res-, (US) ˌɑːr.bə'res-, -bɔː'- **-t** -t
arbore|tum ˌɑː.bər'iː.|təm, -bɔː'riː-, (US) ˌɑːr.bə'riː.t̬əm, -bɔː'- **-tums** -təmz, (US) -t̬əmz **-ta** -tə, (US) -t̬ə
arboriculture 'ɑː.bər.ɪˌkʌl.tʃər, -bɔː-; ɑːr'bɔːr.ɪ-, (US) 'ɑːr.bɚ.ɪˌkʌl.tʃɚ
arborization, -isa- ˌɑː.bər.aɪ'zeɪ.ʃən, -bɔː.raɪ'-, -rɪ'-, (US) ˌɑːr.bɚ.ə'-, -bɔːr-
arboriz|e, -is|e 'ɑː.bər.aɪz, (US) 'ɑːr.bə.raɪz **-es** -ɪz **-ing** -ɪŋ **-ed** -d
arbor-vitae ˌɑː.bə'viː.taɪ, -bɔː-, -'vaɪ-, -tiː, (US) ˌɑːr.bɚ'vaɪ.t̬iː, -'viː- **-s** -z
arbour 'ɑː.bər, (US) 'ɑːr.bɚ **-s** -z
Arbroath ɑː'brəʊθ, (US) ɑːr'broʊθ
Arbus 'ɑː.bəs, (US) 'ɑːr-
Arbuthnot(t) ɑː'bʌθ.nət, ə'bʌθ-, (US) ɑːr-, -nɑːt
arbutus ɑː'bjuː.təs, (US) ɑːr'bjuː.t̬əs **-es** -ɪz
arc, A~ ɑːk, (US) ɑːrk **-s** -s **-(k)ing** -ɪŋ **-(k)ed** -t **'arc ˌlamp; 'arc ˌlight**
arcade ɑː'keɪd, (US) ɑːr- **-s** -z
Arcadi|a ɑː'keɪ.di|.ə, (US) ɑːr- **-an/s** -ən/z
Arcady 'ɑː.kə.di, (US) 'ɑːr-
arcane ɑː'keɪn, (US) ɑːr-
arcan|um ɑː'keɪ.n|əm, (US) ɑːr- **-a** -ə
arch adj ɑːtʃ, (US) ɑːrtʃ **-est** -ɪst, -əst **-ly** -li **-ness** -nəs, -nɪs
arch n, v ɑːtʃ, (US) ɑːrtʃ **-es** -ɪz **-ing** -ɪŋ **-ed** -t
arch- ɑːtʃ, ɑːk, (US) ɑːrtʃ, ɑːrk
Note: Prefix. Words containing **arch-** normally carry secondary stress on the first syllable, e.g. **archbishop** /ˌɑːtʃ'bɪʃ.əp/ (US) /ˌɑːrtʃ-/, with the exception of **archangel** /ɑː'keɪn.dʒəl/ (US) /'ɑːr-/.
-arch ɑːk, ək, (US) ɑːrk, ɚk
Note: Suffix. Normally /-ɑːk/ (US) /-ɑːrk/, e.g. **oligarch** /'ɒl.ɪ.gɑːk/ (US) /'ɑː.lɪ.gɑːrk/, but /-ək/, (US) /-ɚk/ is preferred in some words, e.g. **monarch** /'mɒn.ək/ (US) /'mɑː.nɚk -nɑːrk/.
archaean, A~ ɑː'kiː.ən, (US) ɑːr-
archaeo- ˌɑː.ki.əʊ; ˌɑː.ki'ɒ, (US) -ə; (US) ˌɑːr.ki'ɑː
Note: Prefix. Words containing **archaeo-** normally carry secondary stress on the first syllable, and in the items which follow have primary stress on the third syllable, e.g. **archaeology** /ˌɑː.ki'ɒl.ə.dʒi/ (US) /ˌɑːr.ki'ɑː.lə-/, with the exception of **archaeological**.
archaeologic|al ˌɑː.ki.ə'lɒdʒ.ɪ.k|əl, (US) ˌɑːr.ki.ə'lɑː.dʒɪ- **-ally** -əl.i, -i
archaeologist ˌɑː.ki'ɒl.ə.dʒɪst, (US) ˌɑːr.ki'ɑː.lə- **-s** -s
archaeology ˌɑː.ki'ɒl.ə.dʒi, (US) ˌɑːr.ki'ɑː.lə-
archaeopteryx ˌɑː.ki'ɒp.tər.ɪks, (US) ˌɑːr.ki'ɑːp- **-es** -ɪz
archaic ɑː'keɪ.ɪk, (US) ɑːr- **-ally** -əl.i, -li
archaism ɑː'keɪ.ɪ.zəm, 'ɑː.keɪ-, (US) 'ɑːr.ki-, -keɪ- **-s** -z
archangel ɑː'keɪn.dʒəl, 'ɑː.keɪn-, (US) 'ɑːr.keɪn- **-s** -z
Archangel 'ɑː.keɪn.dʒəl, ˌɑː'keɪn-, (US) 'ɑːr.keɪn-
archbishop ˌɑːtʃ'bɪʃ.əp, (US) ˌɑːrtʃ- **-s** -s *stress shift:* **ˌArchbishop of 'Canterbury**
archbishopric ˌɑːtʃ'bɪʃ.ə.prɪk, (US) ˌɑːrtʃ- **-s** -s
Archbold 'ɑːtʃ.bəʊld, (US) 'ɑːrtʃ.boʊld
Archdale 'ɑːtʃ.deɪl, (US) 'ɑːrtʃ-
archdeacon ˌɑːtʃ'diː.kən, (US) ˌɑːrtʃ- **-s** -z
archdeaconr|y ˌɑːtʃ'diː.kən.r|i, (US) ˌɑːrtʃ- **-ies** -iz
archdioces|e ˌɑːtʃ'daɪ.ə.sɪs, (US) ˌɑːrtʃ- **-es** -ɪz
archducal ˌɑːtʃ'dʒuː.kəl, -'djuː-, (US) ˌɑːrtʃ'duː-, -'djuː-
archduchess ˌɑːtʃ'dʌtʃ.ɪs, -əs, (US) ˌɑːrtʃ- **-es** -ɪz
archduch|y ˌɑːtʃ'dʌtʃ.|i, (US) ˌɑːrtʃ- **-ies** -iz
archduke ˌɑːtʃ'dʒuːk, -'djuːk, (US) ˌɑːrtʃ'duːk, -'djuːk **-s** -s *stress shift:* **ˌArchduke 'Ferdinand**
archdukedom ˌɑːtʃ'dʒuːk.dəm, -'djuːk-, (US) ˌɑːrtʃ'duːk-, -'djuːk **-s** -z
Archelaus ˌɑː.kɪ'leɪ.əs, -kə'-, (US) ˌɑːr-
archenem|y ˌɑːtʃ'en.ə.m|i, -ɪ.m|i, (US) ˌɑːrtʃ- **-ies** -iz
archeo- ˌɑː.ki.əʊ; ˌɑː.ki'ɒ, (US) ˌɑːr.ki.ə; (US) ˌɑːr.ki'ɑː
Note: Prefix. See **archaeo-**.
archeologic|al ˌɑː.ki.ə'lɒdʒ.ɪ.k|əl, (US) ˌɑːr.ki.ə'lɑː.dʒɪ- **-ally** -əl.i, -li
archeologist ˌɑː.ki'ɒl.ə.dʒɪst, (US) ˌɑːr.ki'ɑː.lə- **-s** -s
archeology ˌɑː.ki'ɒl.ə.dʒi, (US) ˌɑːr.ki'ɑː.lə-
archeopteryx ˌɑː.ki'ɒp.tə.rɪks, (US) ˌɑːr.ki'ɑːp- **-es** -ɪz
archer, A~ 'ɑː.tʃər, (US) 'ɑːr.tʃɚ **-s** -z
archery 'ɑː.tʃər.i, (US) 'ɑːr-
archetypal ˌɑː.kɪ'taɪ.pəl, 'ɑː.kɪˌtaɪ-, (US) ˌɑːr.kɪ'taɪ-
archetype 'ɑː.kɪ.taɪp, (US) 'ɑːr- **-s** -s
archetypic|al ˌɑː.kɪ'tɪp.ɪ.k|əl, (US) ˌɑːr.kə'- **-ally** -əl.i, -li *stress shift:* **ˌarchetypical 'incident**
archfiend ˌɑːtʃ'fiːnd, (US) ˌɑːrtʃ- **-s** -z
arch-heretic ˌɑːtʃ'her.ə.tɪk, '-ɪ-, (US) ˌɑːrtʃ'her.ə- **-s** -s
Archibald 'ɑː.tʃɪ.bɔːld, -bəld, (US) 'ɑːr.tʃə.bɔːld, -bɑːld
-archic ɑː.kɪk, (US) ɑːr.kɪk
Archie 'ɑː.tʃi, (US) 'ɑːr-
Archilochus ɑː'kɪl.ə.kəs, (US) ɑːr-
archimandrite ˌɑː.kɪ'mæn.draɪt, (US) ˌɑːr.kə'- **-s** -s
archimedean ˌɑː.kɪ'miː.di.ən, -miː'diː.ən, (US) ˌɑːr.kə- *stress shift:* **ˌarchimedean 'screw**
Archimedes ˌɑː.kɪ'miː.diːz, (US) ˌɑːr.kə'-
archipelago ˌɑː.kɪ'pel.əg.əʊ, (US) ˌɑːr.kə'pel.ə.goʊ **-(e)s** -z

A

archiphoneme ˌɑː.kɪˈfəʊ.niːm, (US) ˈɑːr.kɪˌfoʊ-, ˌɑːr.kɪˈfoʊ- **-s** -z
architect ˈɑː.kɪ.tekt, (US) ˈɑːr.kə- **-s** -s
architectonic ˌɑː.kɪ.tekˈtɒn.ɪk, (US) ˌɑːr.kə.tekˈtɑː.nɪk **-s** -s
architectural ˌɑː.kɪˈtek.tʃər.əl, (US) ˌɑːr.kəˈ- **-ly** -i
architecture ˈɑː.kɪ.tek.tʃər, (US) ˈɑːr.kə.tek.tʃɚ
architrave ˈɑː.kɪ.treɪv, (US) ˈɑːr.kə- **-s** -z **-d** -d
archival ɑːˈkaɪ.vəl, (US) ɑːr-
archive ˈɑː.kaɪv, (US) ˈɑːr- **-s** -z
archivist ˈɑː.kɪ.vɪst, (US) ˈɑːr.kaɪ-, -kə- **-s** -s
archon ˈɑː.kən, -kɒn, (US) ˈɑːr.kɑːn **-s** -z
arch-prelate ˌɑːtʃˈprel.ət, -ɪt, (US) ˌɑːrtʃ- **-s** -s
arch-priest ˌɑːtʃˈpriːst, (US) ˌɑːrtʃ- **-s** -s *stress shift:* **ˌarch-priest's ˈceremony**
arch-traitor ˌɑːtʃˈtreɪ.tər, (US) ˌɑːrtʃˈtreɪ.t̬ɚ **-s** -z *stress shift:* **ˌarch-traitor ˈclique**
archway, A~ ˈɑːtʃ.weɪ, (US) ˈɑːrtʃ- **-s** -z
archwise ˈɑːtʃ.waɪz, (US) ˈɑːrtʃ-
Archytas ɑːˈkaɪ.təs, -tæs, (US) ɑːrˈkaɪ.t̬əs
Arcite ˈɑː.saɪt, (US) ˈɑːr-
Arcot ˈɑː.kɒt, (US) ˈɑːr.kɑːt
arctic, A~ ˈɑːk.tɪk, (US) ˈɑːrk-; (US) ˈɑːr.t̬ɪk **ˌArctic ˈCircle; ˌArctic ˈOcean**
Arcturus ɑːkˈtʃʊə.rəs, -ˈtjʊə-, -ˈtʃɔː-, -ˈtjɔː-, (US) ɑːrkˈtʊr.əs
arcuate ˈɑː.kju.ət, -eɪt, -ɪt, (US) ˈɑːr-
arcuated ˈɑː.kju.eɪ.tɪd, (US) ˈɑːr.kju.eɪ.t̬ɪd
Arcy ˈɑː.si, (US) ˈɑːr-
-ard əd, ɑːd, (US) ɚd, ɑːrd
Note: Suffix. In frequently occurring words, normally /-əd/ (US) /-ɚd/, e.g. **wizard** /ˈwɪz.əd/ (US) /-ɚd/, but may also be /-ɑːd/ (US) /-ɑːrd/, e.g. **brassard** /ˈbræs.ɑːd/, (US) /-ɑːrd/. See individual items.
Ardagh ˈɑː.də, -dɑː, (US) ˈɑːr-
Ardèche ɑːˈdeʃ, (US) ɑːr-
Ardee ɑːˈdiː, (US) ɑːr-
Arden ˈɑː.dən, (US) ˈɑːr-
ardency ˈɑː.dənt.si, (US) ˈɑːr-
Ardennes ɑːˈden, -denz, (US) ɑːr-
ardent ˈɑː.dənt, (US) ˈɑːr- **-ly** -li
Arding ˈɑː.dɪŋ, (US) ˈɑːr-
Ardingly ˈɑː.dɪŋ.laɪ, ˌ--ˈ-, (US) ˈɑːr.dɪŋ-, ˌ--ˈ-
Ardleigh, Ardley ˈɑːd.li, (US) ˈɑːrd-
Ardoch ˈɑː.dɒk, -dɒx, (US) ˈɑːr.dɑːk
ardo(u)r ˈɑː.dər, (US) ˈɑːr.dɚ
Ardrishaig ɑːˈdrɪʃ.ɪg, -eɪg, (US) ɑːr-
Ardrossan ɑːˈdrɒs.ən, (US) ɑːrˈdrɑː.sən
Ards ɑːdz, (US) ɑːrdz
Arduin ˈɑː.dwɪn, (US) ˈɑːr-
arduous ˈɑː.dʒu.əs, -dju-, (US) ˈɑːr.dʒu- **-ly** -li **-ness** -nəs, -nɪs
Ardwick ˈɑː.dwɪk, (US) ˈɑːr-
are (from **be**) *strong form:* ɑːr, (US) ɑːr; *weak form:* ər, (US) ɚ; *occasional weak form before vowels:* r
Note: Weak-form word. The strong form /ɑːr/ (US) /ɑːr/ is used for emphasis (e.g. 'You **are** stupid.'), for contrast (e.g. 'You **are** rich, but you **aren't** handsome.') and in final position (e.g. 'Here you are.'). The weak form is usually /ər/ (US) /ɚ/ (e.g. 'These are mine.' /ˌðiːz.əˈmaɪn/ (US) /-ɚˈ-/; 'These are old.' /ˌðiːz.ərˈəʊld/ (US) /-ɚˈoʊld/), but when the weak form precedes a vowel, as in the last example, it often happens that the word is pronounced as a syllabic /r̩/ (e.g. /ˌðiːz.r̩ˈəʊld/ (US) /-ˈoʊld/).
are n *surface measure:* ɑːr, (US) ɑːr **-s** -z
area ˈeə.ri.ə, (US) ˈer.i- **-s** -z **ˈarea ˌcode**
areca əˈriː.kə; ˈær.ɪ-, (US) əˈriː.kə; (US) ˈær.ɪ-, ˈer- **-s** -z
arena əˈriː.nə **-s** -z
Arendt ˈær.ənt, ˈɑː.rənt, (US) ˈɑːr.ənt, ˈer-
aren't ɑːnt, (US) ɑːrnt
areol|a əˈriː.əl|.ə, ærˈiː- **-as** -əz **-ae** -iː
areometer ˌær.iˈɒm.ɪ.tər, ˌeə.riˈ-, ˈ-ə-, (US) ˌer.iˈɑː.mə.t̬ɚ, ˌær- **-s** -z
areometry ˌær.iˈɒm.ə.tri, ˌeə.riˈ-, ˈ-ɪ-, (US) ˌer.iˈɑː.mə-, ˌær-
Areopagite ˌær.iˈɒp.ə.gaɪt, -dʒaɪt, (US) ˌer.iˈɑː.pə-, ˌær- **-s** -s
Areopagitic ˌær.i.ɒp.əˈdʒɪt.ɪk, -ˈgɪt-, (US) ˌer.iˌɑː.pəˈdʒɪt̬-, ˌær- **-a** -ə
Areopagus ˌær.iˈɒp.ə.gəs, (US) ˌer.iˈɑː.pə-, ˌær-
Arequipa ˌær.ɪˈkiː.pə, -ekˈiː-, (US) ˌɑː.rəˈkiː-, ˌer.əˈ-, ˌær-
Ares ˈeə.riːz, (US) ˈer.iːz
arête ærˈet, əˈret
Aretha əˈriː.θə
Arethusa ˌær.ɪˈθjuː.zə, -eθˈjuː-, (US) ˌɑːr.əˈθuː-
Arezzo ærˈet.səʊ, əˈret-, (US) ɑːˈret.soʊ
Arfon ˈɑː.vən, -vɒn, (US) ˈɑːr-, -fən
Argand ˈɑː.gænd, -gənd, (US) ˌɑːrˈgɑːnd, -ˈgænd **-s** -z *stress shift, US only, see compound:* **ˌArgand ˈdiagram**
argent, A~ ˈɑː.dʒənt, (US) ˈɑːr-
Argentina ˌɑː.dʒənˈtiː.nə, -dʒenˈ-, (US) ˌɑːr-
argentine, A~ ˈɑː.dʒən.taɪn, (US) ˈɑːr.dʒən.taɪn, -tiːn, -tɪn
Argentinian ˌɑː.dʒənˈtɪn.i.ən, (US) ˌɑːr- **-s** -z
argillaceous ˌɑː.dʒɪˈleɪ.ʃəs, (US) ˌɑːr.dʒəˈ-
Argive ˈɑː.gaɪv, (US) ˈɑːr- **-s** -z
Argo ˈɑː.gəʊ, (US) ˈɑːr.goʊ
argol ˈɑː.gɒl, -gəl, (US) ˈɑːr.gɑːl, -gəl
Argolis ˈɑː.gəl.ɪs, (US) ˈɑːr-
argon ˈɑː.gɒn, -gən, (US) ˈɑːr.gɑːn
Argonaut ˈɑː.gə.nɔːt, (US) ˈɑːr.gə.nɑːt, -nɔːt **-s** -s
Argonautic ˌɑː.gəˈnɔː.tɪk, (US) ˌɑːr.gəˈnɑː.t̬ɪk, -ˈnɔː-
Argos ˈɑː.gɒs, (US) ˈɑːr.gɑːs, -gəs
argos|y ˈɑː.gə.s|i, (US) ˈɑːr.gə.s|i **-ies** -iz
argot ˈɑː.gəʊ, (US) ˈɑːr.goʊ, -gət **-s** -z
arguab|le ˈɑːg.ju.ə.b|əl, (US) ˈɑːrg- **-ly** -li
argu|e ˈɑːg.juː, (US) ˈɑːrg- **-es** -z **-ing** -ɪŋ **-ed** -d **-er/s** -ər/z, (US) -ɚ/z
argument ˈɑːg.jə.mənt, -jʊ-, (US) ˈɑːrg.jə-, -jʊ- **-s** -s
argumental ˌɑːg.jəˈmen.təl, -jʊ-, (US) ˌɑːrg.jəˈmen.t̬əl, -jʊˈ-
argumentation ˌɑːg.jə.menˈteɪ.ʃən, -jʊ-, -mən-, (US) ˌɑːrg.jə-, -jʊ- **-s** -z
argumentative ˌɑːg.jəˈmen.tə.tɪv, -jʊ-, (US) ˌɑːrg.jəˈmen.t̬ə.t̬ɪv, -jʊˈ- **-ly** -li **-ness** -nəs, -nɪs
argus, A~ ˈɑː.gəs, (US) ˈɑːr- **-es** -ɪz
argy-bargy ˌɑː.dʒiˈbɑː.dʒi, (US) ˌɑːr.dʒiˈbɑːr-
Argyle ɑːˈgaɪl, (US) ɑːr-, ˈ-- *stress shift:* **ˌArgyle ˈtartan**
Argyllshire ɑːˈgaɪl.ʃər, -ʃɪər, (US) ɑːrˈgaɪl.ʃɚ, -ʃɪr
aria ˈɑː.ri.ə, (US) ˈɑːr.i- **-s** -z
Ariadne ˌær.iˈæd.ni, (US) ˌær-, ˌer-
Arian ˈeə.ri.ən, (US) ˈer.i-, ˈær- **-s** -z **-ism** -ɪ.zəm
-arian ˈeə.ri.ən, (US) ˈer.i-, ˈær-
Note: Suffix. Always carries primary stress, e.g. **grammarian** /grəˈmeə.ri.ən/ (US) /-ˈmer.i-/.
arid ˈær.ɪd, (US) ˈer-, ˈær- **-ly** -li **-ness** -nəs, -nɪs
aridity ærˈɪd.ə.ti, əˈrɪd-, -ɪ.ti, (US) erˈɪd.ə.t̬i, ær-
ariel, A~ ˈeə.ri.əl, (US) ˈer.i- **-s** -z
Aries ˈeə.riːz, -ri.iːz, (US) ˈer.iːz
arietta ˌær.iˈet.ə, ˌɑː.riˈ-, (US) ˌɑːr.iˈet̬-, ˌær.iˈ-, ˌer- **-s** -z
aright əˈraɪt
-arily ər.ə.li, -ɪ.li; ˈer.əl.i, -ɪ.li, (US) er.ə.li, ær-
Note: Suffix. The stress pattern of words containing **-arily** in British English is either unaffected by the affix, or primary stress moves to the antepenultimate syllable, in which case it contains a full vowel, e.g. **momentarily** /ˈməʊ.mən.tər.əl.i, -ɪ.li; ˌməʊ.mənˈter-/. In American English, **-arily** normally has a full vowel, but the antepenultimate syllable may or may not take primary stress, e.g. **momentarily** /ˈmoʊ.mən.ter.əl.i, ˌmoʊ.mənˈter-/. See individual entries.
Arimathaea ˌær.ɪ.məˈθiː.ə, (US) ˌer.ə-, ˌær-
Arion əˈraɪ.ən, ærˈaɪ.ən, (US) əˈraɪ.ən
arioso ˌɑː.riˈəʊ.səʊ, ˌær.iˈ-, -zəʊ, (US) ˌɑːr.iˈoʊ.soʊ
Ariosto ˌær.iˈɒs.təʊ, (US) ˌɑːr.iˈɑː.stoʊ, ˌer-, ˌær-, -ˈɔː-, -ˈoʊ-
aris|e əˈraɪz **-es** -ɪz **-ing** -ɪŋ
arisen əˈrɪz.ən
Aristaeus ˌær.ɪˈstiː.əs, -əˈ-, (US) ˌer.əˈ-, ˌær-
Aristarchus ˌær.ɪˈstɑː.kəs, (US) ˌer.əˈstɑːr-, ˌær-

A

Aristide ˌær.ɪˈstiːd, ⓤⓢ ˌer-, ˌær-
Aristides ˌær.ɪˈstaɪ.diːz, ⓤⓢ ˌer.əˈ-, ˌær-
aristo əˈrɪs.təʊ, ⓤⓢ -toʊ **-s** -z
aristocrac|y ˌær.ɪˈstɒk.rə.s|i, ⓤⓢ ˌer.əˈstɑː.krə-, ˌær- **-ies** -iz
aristocrat ˈær.ɪ.stə.kræt; əˈrɪs.tə-, ⓤⓢ əˈrɪs-; ⓤⓢ ˈer.ə.stə-, ˈær- **-s** -s
aristocratic ˌær.ɪ.stəˈkræt.ɪk, ⓤⓢ əˌrɪs.təˈkræţ.ɪk; ⓤⓢ ˌer.ə.stəˈ-, ˌær- **-al** -əl **-ally** -əl.i, -li *stress shift, British:* **ˌaristocratic ˈairs**; *stress shift, US:* **aˌristocratic ˈairs, ˌaristocratic ˈairs**
Aristophanes ˌær.ɪˈstɒf.ə.niːz, ⓤⓢ ˌer.əˈstɑː.fə-, ˌær-
aristophanic ˌær.ɪ.stəˈfæn.ɪk, -tɒfˈæn-, ⓤⓢ ˌer.ə.stəˈ-, ˌær-
aristotelian, A~ ˌær.ɪ.stɒtˈiː.li.ən, -stəˈtiː-, ⓤⓢ ˌer.ə.stəˈtiː-, ˌær- **-s** -z
Aristotle ˈær.ɪ.stɒt.əl, ⓤⓢ ˈer.ə.stɑː.ţəl, ˈær-
Aristoxenus ˌær.ɪˈstɒk.sɪ.nəs, -sə.nəs, ⓤⓢ ˌer.əˈstɑːk.sə-, ˌær-
arithmetic n əˈrɪθ.mə.tɪk, -mɪ- **-s** -s
arithmetic adj ˌær.ɪθˈmet.ɪk, ⓤⓢ ˌer.ɪθˈmeţ-, ˌær- **-al** -əl **-ally** -əl.i, -li **ˌarithmetic ˈmean**
arithmetician əˌrɪθ.məˈtɪʃ.ən, -mɪˈ-; ˌær.ɪθ-, ⓤⓢ əˌrɪθ.məˈ- **-s** -z
-arium ˈeə.ri.əm, ⓤⓢ ˈer.i-
Note: Suffix. Always carries primary stress, e.g. **solarium** /səʊˈleə.ri.əm/ ⓤⓢ /soʊˈler.i-, ⓤⓢ sə-/.
Arius ˈeə.ri.əs; əˈraɪ-, ⓤⓢ ˈer.i-, ˈær-
Ariz. (abbrev. for **Arizona**) ˌær.ɪˈzəʊ.nə, ⓤⓢ ˌer.ɪˈzoʊ-, ˌær-, -əˈ-
Arizona ˌær.ɪˈzəʊ.nə, ⓤⓢ ˌer.ɪˈzoʊ-, ˌær-, -əˈ-
Arjuna ɑːˈʒuː.nə, ⓤⓢ ɑːr-, ɜː-
ark, A~ ɑːk, ⓤⓢ ɑːrk **-s** -s
Ark. (abbrev. for **Arkansas**) ˈɑː.kən.sɔː; ɑːˈkæn.zəs, ⓤⓢ ˈɑːr.kən.sɑː, -sɔː; ⓤⓢ ɑːrˈkæn.zəs
Arkan ˈɑː.kæn, ⓤⓢ ˈɑːr-
Arkansas *US state:* ˈɑː.kən.sɔː, ⓤⓢ ˈɑːr.kən.sɑː, -sɔː; *river:* ɑːˈkæn.zəs, ⓤⓢ ɑːrˈkæn.zəs
Arkhangelsk ˌɑː.kæŋˈgelsk, ⓤⓢ ɑːrˈkɑːn.gelsk
Arklow ˈɑː.kləʊ, ⓤⓢ ˈɑːr.kloʊ
Arkwright ˈɑː.kraɪt, ⓤⓢ ˈɑːr-
Arlen ˈɑː.lən, ⓤⓢ ˈɑːr-
Arlene ˈɑː.liːn, ⓤⓢ ɑːrˈliːn
Arlington ˈɑː.lɪŋ.tən, ⓤⓢ ˈɑːr-
arm ɑːm, ⓤⓢ ɑːrm **-s** -z **-ing** -ɪŋ **-ed** -d **cost an ˌarm and a ˈleg; ˌkeep someone at ˌarm's ˈlength; ˌarmed to the ˈteeth**
armada, A~ ɑːˈmɑː.də, ⓤⓢ ɑːrˈ- **-s** -z
Armadale ˈɑː.mə.deɪl, ⓤⓢ ˈɑːr-
armadillo ˌɑː.məˈdɪl.əʊ, ⓤⓢ ˌɑːr.məˈdɪl.oʊ **-s** -z
Armado ɑːˈmɑː.dəʊ, ⓤⓢ ɑːrˈmɑː.doʊ
Armageddon ˌɑː.məˈged.ən, ⓤⓢ ˌɑːr-
Armagh ˌɑːˈmɑː, ⓤⓢ ˌɑːr-
Armagnac ˈɑː.mə.njæk, ⓤⓢ ˈɑːr-, ˌ--ˈ-
Armah ˈɑː.mə, ⓤⓢ ˈɑːr-
Armalite® ˈɑː.məl.aɪt, ⓤⓢ ˈɑːr.mə.laɪt
armament ˈɑː.mə.mənt, ⓤⓢ ˈɑːr- **-s** -s
Armani ˌɑːˈmɑː.ni, ⓤⓢ ˌɑːr-
Armatrading ˌɑː.məˈtreɪ.dɪŋ, ⓤⓢ ˌɑːr.məˈtreɪ-
armature ˈɑː.mə.tʃəʳ, -tjəʳ, -tʃʊəʳ, -tjʊəʳ, ⓤⓢ ˈɑːr.mə.tʃɚ **-s** -z
armband ˈɑːm.bænd, ⓤⓢ ˈɑːrm- **-s** -z
armchair ˈɑːm.tʃeəʳ, -ˈ-, ⓤⓢ ˈɑːrm.tʃer **-s** -z
armed ɑːmd, ⓤⓢ ɑːrmd **ˌarmed ˈrobbery**
Armeni|a ɑːˈmiː.ni|.ə, ⓤⓢ ɑːr- **-an/s** -ən/z
Armfield ˈɑːm.fiːld, ⓤⓢ ˈɑːrm-
armful ˈɑːm.fʊl, ⓤⓢ ˈɑːrm- **-s** -z
armhole ˈɑːm.həʊl, ⓤⓢ ˈɑːrm.hoʊl **-s** -z
armiger, A~ ˈɑː.mɪ.dʒəʳ, ⓤⓢ ˈɑːr.mɪ.dʒɚ **-s** -z
Armin ˈɑː.mɪn, ⓤⓢ ˈɑːr-
arm-in-arm ˌɑːm.ɪnˈɑːm, ⓤⓢ ˌɑːrm.ɪnˈɑːrm
Arminian ɑːˈmɪn.i.ən, ⓤⓢ ɑːr- **-s** -z
Armistead ˈɑː.mɪ.sted, -stɪd, ⓤⓢ ˈɑːr-
armistic|e ˈɑː.mɪ.stɪs, ⓤⓢ ˈɑːr.mə- **-es** -ɪz **ˈArmistice ˌDay**
Armitage ˈɑː.mɪ.tɪdʒ, -mə-, ⓤⓢ ˈɑːr.mə.ţɪdʒ
armless ˈɑːm.ləs, -lɪs, ⓤⓢ ˈɑːrm-
armlet ˈɑːm.lət, -lɪt, ⓤⓢ ˈɑːrm- **-s** -s
armload ˈɑːm.ləʊd, ⓤⓢ ˈɑːrm.loʊd **-s** -z
armlock ˈɑːm.lɒk, ⓤⓢ ˈɑːrm.lɑːk **-s** -s
arm|or ˈɑː.m|əʳ, ⓤⓢ ˈɑːr.m|ɚ **-ors** -əz, ⓤⓢ -ɚz **-oring** -əʳ.ɪŋ **-ored** -əd, ⓤⓢ -ɚd **ˌarmored ˈvehicle**
armorer ˈɑː.məʳ.əʳ, ⓤⓢ ˈɑːr.mɚ.ɚ **-s** -z
armorial ɑːˈmɔː.ri.əl, ⓤⓢ ɑːrˈmɔːr.i-
Armoric ɑːˈmɒr.ɪk, ⓤⓢ ɑːrˈmɔːr-
Armoric|a ɑːˈmɒr.ɪ.k|ə, ⓤⓢ ɑːrˈmɔːr- **-an/s** -ən/z
armor-pla|te ˌɑː.məˈpleɪ|t, ˈ---, ⓤⓢ ˈɑːr.mɚ.pleɪ|t **-tes** -ts **-ting** -tɪŋ, ⓤⓢ -ţɪŋ **-ted** -tɪd, ⓤⓢ -ţɪd
armor|y ˈɑː.məʳ|.i, ⓤⓢ ˈɑːr- **-ies** -iz
arm|our, A~ ˈɑː.m|əʳ, ⓤⓢ ˈɑːr.m|ɚ **-ours** -əz, ⓤⓢ -ɚz **-ouring** -əʳ.ɪŋ **-oured** -əd, ⓤⓢ -ɚd **ˌarmoured ˈvehicle**
armourer ˈɑː.məʳ.əʳ, ⓤⓢ ˈɑːr.mɚ.ɚ **-s** -z
armour-pla|te ˌɑː.məˈpleɪ|t, ˈ---, ⓤⓢ ˈɑːr.mɚ.pleɪ|t **-tes** -ts **-ting** -tɪŋ, ⓤⓢ -ţɪŋ **-ted** -tɪd, ⓤⓢ -ţɪd
Note: The latter British form is used attributively.
armour|y ˈɑː.məʳ|.i, ⓤⓢ ˈɑːr- **-ies** -iz
armpit ˈɑːm.pɪt, ⓤⓢ ˈɑːrm- **-s** -s
armrest ˈɑːm.rest, ⓤⓢ ˈɑːrm- **-s** -s
arms ɑːmz, ⓤⓢ ɑːrmz **ˈarms conˌtrol; ˈarms ˌrace; ˌup in ˈarms**
Armstead ˈɑːm.sted, -stɪd, ⓤⓢ ˈɑːrm-
Armstrong ˈɑːm.strɒŋ, ⓤⓢ ˈɑːrm.strɑːŋ, -strɔːŋ
Armthorpe ˈɑːm.θɔːp, ⓤⓢ ˈɑːrm.θɔːrp
arm-twisting ˈɑːmˌtwɪs.tɪŋ, ⓤⓢ ˈɑːrm-
arm|y ˈɑː.m|i, ⓤⓢ ˈɑːr- **-ies** -iz
army-corps *sing.:* ˈɑː.mi.kɔːʳ, ⓤⓢ ˈɑːr.mi.kɔːr *plural:* -kɔːz, ⓤⓢ -kɔːrz
Arnald ˈɑː.nəld, ⓤⓢ ˈɑːr-
Arndale ˈɑːn.deɪl, ⓤⓢ ˈɑːrn-
Arne ɑːn, ⓤⓢ ɑːrn
Arnfield ˈɑːn.fiːld, ⓤⓢ ˈɑːrn-
Arnhem ˈɑː.nəm, ˈɑːn.həm, ⓤⓢ ˈɑːr.nəm, ˈɑːrn.hem
arnica ˈɑː.nɪ.kə, ⓤⓢ ˈɑːr-
Arno ˈɑː.nəʊ, ⓤⓢ ˈɑːr.noʊ
Arnold ˈɑː.nəld, ⓤⓢ ˈɑːr- **-son** -sən
Arnot(t) ˈɑː.nət, -nɒt, ⓤⓢ ˈɑːr.nət, -nɑːt
aroma əˈrəʊ.mə, ⓤⓢ -ˈroʊ- **-s** -z
aromatherap|y əˌrəʊ.məˈθer.ə.p|i, ⓤⓢ -ˌroʊ- **-ist/s** -ɪst/s
aromatic ˌær.əʊˈmæt.ɪk, ⓤⓢ ˌer.əˈmæţ-, ˌær- **-s** -s *stress shift:* **ˌaromatic ˈoils**
arose (from **arise**) əˈrəʊz, ⓤⓢ -ˈroʊz
around əˈraʊnd
arousal əˈraʊ.zəl **-s** -z
arous|e əˈraʊz **-es** -ɪz **-ing** -ɪŋ **-ed** -d
arpeggio ɑːˈpedʒ.i.əʊ, -ˈpedʒ.əʊ, ⓤⓢ ɑːrˈpedʒ.i.oʊ, -ˈpeʒ-, -ˈpedʒ.oʊ **-s** -z
arpeggione ɑːˌpedʒ.iˈəʊ.neɪ, ˌɑː.pedʒˈəʊ-, -ni, ⓤⓢ ɑːrˌpedʒ.iˈoʊ-, ˌɑːr pedʒˈoʊ- **-s** -z
arquebus ˈɑː.kwɪ.bəs, -kwə.bəs, -bʌs, ⓤⓢ ˈɑːr- **-es** -ɪz
Arquette ɑːˈket, ⓤⓢ ɑːr-
arr (abbrev. for **arranged by**) əˈreɪndʒdˌbaɪ (abbrev. for **arrives, arrival**) əˈraɪvz; -ˈraɪ.vəl
arrack ˈær.ək, ⓤⓢ ˈer-, ˈær-; ⓤⓢ əˈræk
arraign əˈreɪn **-s** -z **-ing** -ɪŋ **-ed** -d **-er/s** -əʳ/z, ⓤⓢ -ɚ/z **-ment/s** -mənt/s
Arran ˈær.ən, ⓤⓢ ˈer-, ˈær-
arrang|e əˈreɪndʒ **-es** -ɪz **-ing** -ɪŋ **-ed** -d **-er/s** -əʳ/z, ⓤⓢ -ɚ/z
arrangement əˈreɪndʒ.mənt **-s** -s
arrant ˈær.ənt, ⓤⓢ ˈer-, ˈær- **-ly** -li
arras *wall hanging:* ˈær.əs, ⓤⓢ ˈer-, ˈær- **-es** -ɪz
Arras *French town:* ˈær.əs, -æs, ⓤⓢ ˈer-, ˈær-
Arrau əˈraʊ; ˈær.aʊ, ⓤⓢ əˈraʊ
array əˈreɪ **-s** -z **-ing** -ɪŋ **-ed** -d
arrear əˈrɪəʳ, ⓤⓢ -ˈrɪr **-s** -z **-age** -ɪdʒ
arrest əˈrest **-s** -s **-ing** -ɪŋ **-ed** -ɪd **-ment/s** -mənt/s
arrestable əˈres.tə.bəl
arrestation ˌær.esˈteɪ.ʃən, ⓤⓢ ˌer-, ˌær-; ⓤⓢ əˌresˈ- **-s** -z
arrhythm|ia əˈrɪð.m|i.ə **-ic** -ɪk **-ical** -ɪ.kəl **-ically** -ɪ.kəl.i, -ɪ.kli
Arrian ˈær.i.ən, ⓤⓢ ˈer-, ˈær-
arrière-ban ˌær.i.eəˈbæn, ⓤⓢ -erˈbɑːn, -ˈbæn **-s** -z
arrière pensée ˌær.i.eəˈpɑ̃ːnt.seɪ, -pɑːntˈseɪ, ⓤⓢ -er.pɑːnˈseɪ

A

arris ˈær.ɪs, ⓊⓈ ˈer-, ˈær- **-es** -ɪz
arrival əˈraɪ.vᵊl **-s** -z
arriv|e əˈraɪv **-es** -z **-ing** -ɪŋ **-ed** -d
arrivederci ˌær.i.vəˈdeə.tʃi, ⓊⓈ əˌriː.vəˈder-
arriviste ˌær.iːˈviːst, ⓊⓈ ˌer-, ˌær- **-s** -s
arroganc|e ˈær.ə.gənts, ⓊⓈ ˈer-, ˈær- **-y** -i
arrogant ˈær.ə.gənt, ⓊⓈ ˈer-, ˈær- **-ly** -li
arro|gate ˈær.əʊ|.geɪt, ⓊⓈ ˈer.ə-, ˈær- **-gates** -geɪts **-gating** -geɪ.tɪŋ, ⓊⓈ -geɪ.t̬ɪŋ **-gated** -geɪ.tɪd, ⓊⓈ -geɪ.t̬ɪd
arrogation ˌær.əʊˈgeɪ.ʃᵊn, ⓊⓈ ˌer.əˈ-, ˌær- **-s** -z
arrogative əˈrɒg.ə.tɪv, ⓊⓈ -ˈrɑː.gə.t̬ɪv
arrondissement ˌær.ɒn-ˈdiː.sᵊm.ɑ̃ːŋ, ⓊⓈ erˌɑːn.diːsˈmɑːn, ær-; ⓊⓈ əˌrɑːn- **-s** -s
arrow ˈær.əʊ, ⓊⓈ ˈer.oʊ, ˈær- **-s** -z **ˈarrow ˌhead**
arrowroot ˈær.əʊ.ruːt, ⓊⓈ ˈer.oʊ-, ˈær-
Arrowsmith ˈær.əʊ.smɪθ, ⓊⓈ ˈer.oʊ-, ˈær-
arrowwood ˈær.əʊ.wʊd, ⓊⓈ ˈer.oʊ-, ˈær-
arroyo əˈrɔɪ.əʊ, ⓊⓈ -oʊ **-s** -z
ars ɑːz, ⓊⓈ ɑːrz
ars|e ɑːs, ⓊⓈ ɑːrs, æs **-es** -ɪz

> Note: In US dictionaries, **arse** is usually listed as a variant of **ass**, which is pronounced /æs/. **Arse** is normally a British spelling.

arsed ɑːst, ⓊⓈ ɑːrst
arsehole ˈɑːs.həʊl, ⓊⓈ ˈɑːrs.hoʊl **-s** -z
arse-licker ˈɑːsˌlɪk.əʳ, ⓊⓈ ˈɑːrsˌlɪk.ɚ **-s** -z
arsenal, A~ ˈɑː.sᵊn.ᵊl, ⓊⓈ ˈɑːr- **-s** -z
arsenate ˈɑː.sᵊn.eɪt, -sɪ.neɪt, -nɪt, -nət, ⓊⓈ ˈɑːr- **-s** -s
arsenic n ˈɑː.sᵊn.ɪk, ⓊⓈ ˈɑːr-
arsenic adj ɑːˈsen.ɪk, ⓊⓈ ɑːr- **-al** -ᵊl
arsenide ˈɑː.sᵊn.aɪd, ⓊⓈ ˈɑːr- **-s** -z
arsenite ˈɑː.sᵊn.aɪt, -sɪ.naɪt, ⓊⓈ ˈɑːr-
ars|is ˈɑː.s|ɪs, ⓊⓈ ˈɑːr- **-es** -iːz
arson ˈɑː.sᵊn, ⓊⓈ ˈɑːr-
arsonist ˈɑː.sᵊn.ɪst, ⓊⓈ ˈɑːr- **-s** -s
art, A~ n ɑːt, ⓊⓈ ɑːrt **-s** -s **ˈart ˌgallery; ˌarts and ˈcrafts; ˈart ˌschool**
art (from **be**) *normal form:* ɑːt, ⓊⓈ ɑːrt; *occasional weak form:* ət, ⓊⓈ ɚt
Artaxerxes ˌɑː.təˈzɜːk.siːz, -təkˈsɜːk-, -təgˈzɜːk-, ˈɑː.tə.zɜːk-, -tək.sɜːk-, -təg.zɜːk-, ⓊⓈ ˌɑːr.t̬əˈzɝːk-
Art Deco ˌɑːtˈdek.əʊ, ˌɑːˈ-, ⓊⓈ ˌɑːrtˈde.koʊ, ˌɑːr-, -ˈdeɪ.koʊ, -deɪˈkoʊ
artefact ˈɑː.tɪ.fækt, -tə.fækt, ⓊⓈ ˈɑːr.t̬ə- **-s** -s
Artemis ˈɑː.tɪ.mɪs, -tə.mɪs, ⓊⓈ ˈɑːr.t̬ə-
Artemus ˈɑː.tɪ.məs, -tə.məs, ⓊⓈ ˈɑːr.t̬ɪ-
arterial ɑːˈtɪə.ri.əl, ⓊⓈ ɑːrˈtɪr.i-
arteriolar ɑːˌtɪə.riˈəʊ.ləʳ, ⓊⓈ ɑːrˌtɪr.iˈoʊ.lɚ
arteriol|e ɑːˈtɪə.ri.əʊl, ⓊⓈ ɑːrˈtɪr.i.oʊl **-es** -z
arteriosclerosis ɑːˌtɪə.ri.əʊ.skləˈrəʊ.sɪs, -sklɪəˈ-, ⓊⓈ ɑːrˌtɪr.i.oʊ.skləˈroʊ.səs
arteritis ˌɑː.tᵊrˈaɪ.tɪs, -tɪˈraɪ-, -təs, ⓊⓈ ˌɑːr.t̬əˈraɪ.t̬ɪs, -t̬əs
arter|y ˈɑː.tᵊr|.i, ⓊⓈ ˈɑːr.t̬ɚ- **-ies** -iz
artesian ɑːˈtiː.zi.ən, -ʒᵊn, ⓊⓈ ɑːrˈtiː.ʒᵊn **arˌtesian ˈwell**
Artex® ˈɑː.teks, ⓊⓈ ˈɑːr-
artful ˈɑːt.fᵊl, -fʊl, ⓊⓈ ˈɑːrt- **-ly** -i **-ness** -nəs, -nɪs **ˌArtful ˈDodger**
arthouse ˈɑːtˌhaʊs, ⓊⓈ ˈɑːrt-
arthritic ɑːˈθrɪt.ɪk, ⓊⓈ ɑːrˈθrɪt̬.ɪk **-s** -s
arthritis ɑːˈθraɪ.tɪs, -təs, ⓊⓈ ɑːrˈθraɪ.t̬ɪs, -t̬əs
arthropod ˈɑː.θrə.pɒd, ⓊⓈ ˈɑːr.θrə.pɑːd **-s** -z
arthroscope ˈɑː.θrə.skəʊp, ⓊⓈ ˈɑːr.θrə.skoʊp **-s** -s
arthroscopic ˌɑː.θrəˈskɒp.ɪk, ⓊⓈ ˌɑːr.θrəˈskɑː.pɪk
arthroscopy ɑːˈθrɒs.kə.pi, ⓊⓈ ɑːrˈθrɑː.skə-
Arthur ˈɑː.θəʳ, ⓊⓈ ˈɑːr.θɚ
Arthurian ɑːˈθjʊə.ri.ən, -ˈθʊə-, ⓊⓈ ɑːrˈθʊr.i-, -ˈθɝː-
artichoke ˈɑː.tɪ.tʃəʊk, ⓊⓈ ˈɑːr.t̬ə.tʃoʊk **-s** -s
articl|e ˈɑː.tɪ.kᵊl, ⓊⓈ ˈɑːr.t̬ɪ- **-es** -z **-ing** -ɪŋ, -klɪŋ **-ed** -d
articular ɑːˈtɪk.jə.ləʳ, -jʊ-, ⓊⓈ ɑːrˈtɪk.jə.lɚ
articulate adj ɑːˈtɪk.jə.lət, -jʊ-, -lɪt, ⓊⓈ ɑːrˈtɪk.jə.lət **-ly** -li **-ness** -nəs, -nɪs
articu|late v ɑːˈtɪk.jə|.leɪt, -jʊ-, ⓊⓈ ɑːrˈtɪk.jə- **-lates** -leɪts **-lating** -leɪ.tɪŋ, ⓊⓈ -leɪ.t̬ɪŋ **-lated** -leɪ.tɪd, ⓊⓈ -leɪ.t̬ɪd **-lator/s** -leɪ.təʳ/z, ⓊⓈ -leɪ.t̬ɚ/s **arˌticulated ˈlorry**
articulation ɑːˌtɪk.jəˈleɪ.ʃᵊn, -jʊˈ-, ⓊⓈ ɑːrˌtɪk.jəˈ- **-s** -z
articulatory ɑːˈtɪk.jə.lə.tᵊr.i, -jʊ-; ɑːˌtɪk.jəˈleɪ-, -jʊˈ-, ⓊⓈ ɑːrˈtɪk.jə.lə.tɔːr-
artifact ˈɑː.tɪ.fækt, ⓊⓈ ˈɑːr.t̬ə- **-s** -s
artific|e ˈɑː.tɪ.fɪs, ⓊⓈ ˈɑːr.t̬ə- **-es** -ɪz
artificer ɑːˈtɪf.ɪ.səʳ, ⓊⓈ ɑːrˈtɪf.ə.sɚ **-s** -z
artificial ˌɑː.tɪˈfɪʃ.ᵊl, ⓊⓈ ˌɑːr.t̬əˈ- **-ly** -i **-ness** -nəs, -nɪs *stress shift, see compounds:* **ˌartificial insemiˈnation; ˌartificial inˈtelligence; ˌartificial respiˈration**
artificialit|y ˌɑː.tɪˌfɪʃ.iˈæl.ə.t|i, -ɪ.t|i, ⓊⓈ ˌɑːr.t̬əˌfɪʃ.iˈæl.ə.t̬|i **-ies** -iz
artificializ|e, -is|e ˌɑː.tɪˈfɪʃ.ᵊl.aɪz, ⓊⓈ ˌɑːr.t̬ə- **-es** -ɪz **-ing** -ɪŋ **-ed** -d
artiller|y ɑːˈtɪl.ᵊr|.i, ⓊⓈ ɑːr- **-ies** -iz **-ist/s** -ɪst/s
artillery|-man ɑːˈtɪl.ᵊr.i|.mən, -mæn, ⓊⓈ ɑːrˈ- **-men** -mən, -men
artisan ˌɑː.tɪˈzæn, -təˈzæn, ˈ---, ⓊⓈ ˈɑːr.t̬ə.zᵊn, -sᵊn **-s** -z
artist ˈɑː.tɪst, ⓊⓈ ˈɑːr.t̬əst, -t̬ɪst **-s** -s
artiste ɑːˈtiːst, ⓊⓈ ɑːr- **-s** -s
artistic ɑːˈtɪs.tɪk, ⓊⓈ ɑːr- **-al** -ᵊl **-ally** -ᵊl.i, -li
artistry ˈɑː.tɪ.stri, ⓊⓈ ˈɑːr.t̬ə-, -t̬ɪ-
artless ˈɑːt.ləs, -lɪs, ⓊⓈ ˈɑːrt- **-ly** -li **-ness** -nəs, -nɪs
Art Nouveau ˌɑːt.nuːˈvəʊ, ˌɑː-, ˌ-ˈ--, ⓊⓈ ˌɑːrt.nuːˈvoʊ, ˌɑːr-
Artois ɑːˈtwɑː, ˈ--, ⓊⓈ ɑːr-
arts|man ˈɑːts|.mæn, ⓊⓈ ˈɑːrts- **-men** -men
artsy ˈɑːt.si, ⓊⓈ ˈɑːrt-
artsy-craftsy ˌɑːt.siˈkrɑːft.si, ⓊⓈ ˌɑːrt.siˈkræft-
artwork ˈɑːt.wɜːk, ⓊⓈ ˈɑːrt.wɝːk
arty ˈɑː.ti, ⓊⓈ ˈɑːr.t̬i
arty-crafty ˌɑː.tiˈkrɑːf.ti, ⓊⓈ ˌɑːrt.iˈkræf-
arty-farty ˌɑː.tiˈfɑː.ti, ⓊⓈ ˌɑːr.t̬iˈfɑːr.t̬i *stress shift:* **ˌarty-farty ˈperson**
Arub|a əˈruː.b|ə **-an/s** -ən/z
arugula əˈruː.gᵊl.ə, -gjʊ.lə, -gjᵊl.ə **-s** -z
arum ˈeə.rəm, ⓊⓈ ˈer- **-s** -z
Arun ˈær.ᵊn, ⓊⓈ ˈer-, ˈær-
Arundel ˈær.ᵊn.dᵊl; əˈrʌn-, ⓊⓈ ˈer.ᵊn-, ˈær-; ⓊⓈ əˈrʌn-
Arundell ˈær.ᵊn.del, -dᵊl, ⓊⓈ ˈer-, ˈær-
Arveragus ɑːˈver.ə.gəs, ⓊⓈ ɑːr-
-ary ᵊr.i, ⓊⓈ er.i, ɚ.i
Note: Suffix. When added to a free stem, **-ary** does not normally affect the stress pattern, e.g. **imagine** /ɪˈmædʒ.ɪn/, **imaginary** /ɪˈmæʒd.ɪ.nᵊr.i/ ⓊⓈ /-ə.ner-/. Otherwise words containing **-ary** normally carry stress one or two syllables before the suffix, e.g. **centenary** /senˈtiː.nᵊr.i, -ˈten.ᵊr-/ ⓊⓈ /ˈsen.tᵊn.er-, ⓊⓈ senˈten.ᵊr-/, **culinary** /ˈkʌl.ɪ.nᵊr.i/ ⓊⓈ /-ə.ner-/. There are exceptions; see individual entries.
Aryan ˈeə.ri.ən, ˈɑː-, ⓊⓈ ˈer.i-, ˈær-, ˈɑːr- **-s** -z **-ism** -ɪ.zᵊm
arytenoid ˌær.ɪˈtiː.nɔɪd, -rəˈtiː-; ærˈɪt.ᵊn.ɔɪd, ⓊⓈ əˈrɪt.ᵊn-; ⓊⓈ ˌer.ɪˈtiː.nɔɪd, ˌær- **-s** -z
as conj *strong form:* æz; *weak form:* əz
Note: Weak-form word. The strong form /æz/ is used in contrastive or coordinative constructions (e.g. 'as and when it's ready'), and in sentence-final position (e.g. 'That's what I bought it as.'). Quite frequently the strong form is found when the word occurs in initial position in a sentence if the following word is not stressed (e.g. 'As I was saying, ...'). The weak form is /əz/ (e.g. 'as good as gold' /əzˌgʊd.əzˈgəʊld/ ⓊⓈ /-ˈgoʊld/).
as n *coin:* æs **-es** -ɪz
AS (abbrev. for **airspeed** or **Anglo-Saxon** or **antisubmarine**) ˌeɪˈes
Asa *biblical name:* ˈeɪ.sə, ˈɑː.sə *as modern first name:* ˈeɪ.zə

asaf(o)etida ˌæs.əˈfet.ɪ.də, -ˈfiː.tɪ-, (US) -ˈfeţ.ə-
a.s.a.p., ASAP ˌeɪ.es.eɪˈpiː, ˈeɪ.sæp
Asaph ˈæs.əf
ASAT ˈeɪ.sæt
asbest|ic æsˈbes.t|ɪk, əs-, æz-, əz- **-ous** -əs
asbestos æsˈbes.tɒs, æz-, əs-, əz-, -təs, (US) -təs
asbestosis ˌæs.besˈtəʊ.sɪs, ˌæz-, -bɪs-, (US) -ˈtoʊ-
ASBO ˈæz.bəʊ, (US) -boʊ **-s** -z
Ascalon ˈæs.kə.lɒn, -lən, (US) -lɑːn
Ascanius æsˈkeɪ.ni.əs
ascend əˈsend, æsˈend **-s** -z **-ing** -ɪŋ **-ed** -ɪd
ascendan|ce əˈsen.dən|*t*s, æsˈen- **-cy** -*t*.si **-t** -t
ascenden|ce əˈsen.dən|*t*s, æsˈen- **-cy** -*t*.si **-t** -t
ascender əˈsen.dəʳ, (US) -dɚ **-s** -z
ascension, A~ əˈsen.*t*ʃᵊn, (US) -ˈsent.ʃᵊn **-s** -z **Aˈscension ˌDay**
ascensional əˈsen.*t*ʃᵊn.ᵊl, (US) -ˈsent.ʃᵊn-
ascent əˈsent, æsˈent **-s** -s
ascertain ˌæs.əˈteɪn, (US) -ɚˈ- **-s** -z **-ing** -ɪŋ **-ed** -d **-ment** -mənt **-able** -ə.bᵊl
ascetic əˈset.ɪk, æsˈet-, (US) əˈseţ.ɪk **-al** -ᵊl **-ally** -ᵊl.i, -li **-s** -s
asceticism əˈset.ɪ.sɪ.zᵊm, æsˈet-, (US) əˈseţ.ə-
Asch æʃ
Ascham ˈæs.kəm
ASCII ˈæs.kiː, -ki
Asclepius əˈskliː.pi.əs, æsˈkliː-
ascorbate əˈskɔː.beɪt, æsˈkɔː-, (US) əˈskɔːr- **-s** -s
ascorbic əˈskɔː.bɪk, æsˈkɔː-, (US) əˈskɔːr- **aˌscorbic ˈacid**
ascot *item of clothing:* ˈæs.kət, (US) -kɑːt, -kət **-s** -s
Ascot *place in Berkshire:* ˈæs.kət, (US) -kɑːt
ascrib|e əˈskraɪb **-es** -z **-ing** -ɪŋ **-ed** -d **-able** -ə.bᵊl
ascription əˈskrɪp.ʃᵊn, æsˈkrɪp-
ascriptive əˈskrɪp.tɪv
Asda® ˈæz.də
asdic ˈæz.dɪk **-s** -s
-ase eɪz, eɪs
Note: Suffix. Does not normally affect stress pattern, e.g. **amylase** /ˈæm.ɪ.leɪz/.
ASEAN ˈæs.i.æn, ˈɑː.si.ɑːn
asepsis ˌeɪˈsep.sɪs, ə-, æsˈep-
aseptic ˌeɪˈsep.tɪk, ə-, æˈsep- **-s** -s
asexual ˌeɪˈsek.ʃʊəl, -ʃu.əl, -sjʊəl, -ʃᵊl, (US) -ʃu.əl **-ly** -i
asexuality ˌeɪ.sek.ʃuˈæl.ə.ti, -sjuˈ-, -ɪ.ti, (US) -ʃuˈæl.ə.ţi
Asgard ˈæs.gɑːd, ˈæz-, (US) -gɑːrd, ˈɑːs-, ˈɑːz-
Asgill ˈæs.gɪl, ˈæz-
ash, A~ æʃ **-es** -ɪz **ˈash ˌcan; ˌAsh ˈWednesday**
asham|ed əˈʃeɪm|d **-edly** -ɪd.li **-edness** -ɪd.nəs, -nɪs
Ashanti əˈʃæn.ti, æʃˈ-, (US) əˈʃæn-, -ˈʃɑːn- **-s** -z
Ashbee ˈæʃ.bi
Ashbery ˈæʃ.bᵊr.i, (US) -ber-
Ashbourne ˈæʃ.bɔːn, (US) -bɔːrn
Ashburne ˈæʃ.bɜːn, (US) -bɝːn
Ashburnham æʃˈbɜː.nəm, (US) -ˈbɝː-
Ashburton æʃˈbɜː.tᵊn, (US) -ˈbɝː-
Ashbury ˈæʃ.bᵊr.i, (US) -ber-, -bɚ-
Ashby ˈæʃ.bi
Ashby-de-la-Zouch ˌæʃ.bi.də.lɑːˈzuːʃ, -del.əˈ-
ashcan ˈæʃ.kæn **-s** -z
Ashcombe ˈæʃ.kəm
Ashcroft ˈæʃ.krɒft, (US) -krɑːft
Ashdod ˈæʃ.dɒd, (US) -dɑːd
Ashdown ˈæʃ.daʊn
Ashe æʃ
ashen ˈæʃ.ᵊn
Asher ˈæʃ.əʳ, (US) -ɚ
asher|y ˈæʃ.ᵊr|.i **-ies** -iz
Ashfield ˈæʃ.fiːld
Ashford ˈæʃ.fəd, (US) -fɚd
Ashington ˈæʃ.ɪŋ.tən
Ashkenazy, Ashkenazi ˌæʃ.kəˈnɑː.zi, -kɪˈnɑː-, (US) ɑːʃ-
Ashkhabad ˌɑːʃ.kəˈbɑːd, (US) ˌɑːʃ.kɑːˈbɑːd
Ashland ˈæʃ.lənd
ashlar ˈæʃ.ləʳ, -lɑːʳ, (US) -lɚ
Ashley, Ashlee, Ashleigh ˈæʃ.li
Ashman ˈæʃ.mən
Ashmole ˈæʃ.məʊl, (US) -moʊl
Ashmolean æʃˈməʊ.li.ən, æʃ.məʊˈliː.ən, (US) -ˈmoʊ.li-
Ashmore ˈæʃ.mɔːʳ, (US) -mɔːr
ashore əˈʃɔːʳ, (US) -ˈʃɔːr
Ashover ˈæʃ.əʊ.vəʳ, (US) -oʊ.vɚ
ashpan ˈæʃ.pæn **-s** -z
ashram ˈæʃ.rəm, -ræm **-s** -z
Ashtaroth ˈæʃ.tə.rɒθ, (US) -rɑːθ, -rɔːθ
Ashton ˈæʃ.tᵊn
Ashton-in-Makerfield ˌæʃ.tᵊn.ɪnˈmeɪ.kə.fiːld, (US) -kɚ-
Ashton-under-Lyne ˌæʃ.tᵊnˌʌn.dəˈlaɪn, -ˈʌn.dəˌlaɪn, (US) -ʌn.dɚˈ-, -ˈʌn.dɚˌ-
Ashtoreth ˈæʃ.tə.reθ, -tɒr.eθ, (US) -tə.reθ
ashtray ˈæʃ.treɪ **-s** -z
Ashurbanipal ˌæʃ.ɜːˈbɑː.nɪ.pæl, -pᵊl, (US) ˌɑː.ʃʊrˈbɑː.nɪ.pɑːl
Ashwell ˈæʃ.wel, -wᵊl
Ashworth ˈæʃ.wəθ, -wɜːθ, (US) -wɚθ, -wɝːθ
ash|y ˈæʃ.|i **-ier** -i.əʳ, (US) -i.ɚ **-iest** -i.əst, -i.ɪst **-iness** -ɪ.nəs, -ɪ.nɪs
Asia ˈeɪ.ʒə, -ʃə, (US) ˈeɪ.ʒə **ˌAsia ˈMinor**
Asian ˈeɪ.ʒᵊn, -ʃᵊn, (US) ˈeɪ.ʒᵊn, -ʃᵊn **-s** -z **ˌAsian ˈflu**
Asiatic ˌeɪ.ziˈæt.ɪk, ˌeɪ.si-, ˌeɪ.ʒi-, ˌeɪ.ʃi-, (US) ˌeɪ.ʒiˈæţ.ɪk, -ʃiˈ- **-s** -s *stress shift:* **ˌAsiatic ˈorigin**
aside əˈsaɪd **-s** -z
Asimov ˈæz.ɪ.mɒf, ˈæs-, ˈ-ə-, -mɒv, (US) ˈæz.ə.mɑːf, -mɑːv
asinine ˈæs.ɪ.naɪn, -ə.naɪn
asininit|y ˌæs.ɪˈnɪn.ə.t|i, -əˈnɪn-, -ɪ.t|i, (US) -əˈnɪn.ə.ţ|i **-ies** -iz
ask ɑːsk, (US) æsk **-s** -s **-ing** -ɪŋ **-ed** -t

Note: /æks/ is a commonly heard non-standard pronunciation, particularly among Black speakers in the UK, the US, and the Caribbean area.

askance əˈskæn*t*s, -ˈskɑːn*t*s, (US) əˈskæn*t*s
Aske æsk
Askelon ˈæs.kɪ.lən, -kə.lən, -lɒn, (US) -kə.lɑːn
Askern ˈæs.kɜːn, -kən, (US) -kɝːn, -kɚn
askew əˈskjuː
Askew ˈæs.kjuː
Askey ˈæs.ki
Askrigg ˈæs.krɪg
Askwith ˈæs.kwɪθ
Aslam ˈæz.ləm
aslant əˈslɑːnt, (US) -ˈslænt
asleep əˈsliːp
ASLEF, Aslef ˈæz.lef
Asmara æsˈmɑː.rə, æz-, (US) -ˈmɑːr.ə
Asmodeus æsˈməʊ.di.əs, (US) ˌæz.moʊˈdiː-, ˌæs-, -məˈ-

Note: For British English, the name must be pronounced /ˌæs.məʊˈdiː.əs/ in Milton's 'Paradise Lost', iv, 168.

asocial ˌeɪˈsəʊ.ʃᵊl, (US) -ˈsoʊ-
Asoka əˈʃəʊ.kə, əˈsəʊ-, (US) -ˈsoʊ-
asp æsp, ɑːsp, (US) æsp **-s** -s
asparagus əˈspær.ə.gəs, (US) -ˈsper-, -ˈspær-
aspartame əˈspɑː.teɪm; ˈæs.pə-, (US) ˈæs.pɚ-; (US) əˈspɑːr-
Aspasia æsˈpeɪ.zi.ə, əˈspeɪ-, -ʒə, (US) -ʒə
ASPCA ˌeɪ.esˌpiː.siːˈeɪ
aspect ˈæs.pekt **-s** -s
aspectable æsˈpek.tə.bᵊl
aspectual əˈspek.tʃu.əl, æsˈpek-, -tju-, (US) -tʃu-
Aspel(l) ˈæs.pᵊl
aspen, A~ ˈæs.pən **-s** -z
asper ˈæs.pəʳ, (US) -pɚ
asperg|e əˈspɜːdʒ, æsˈpɜːdʒ, (US) əˈspɝːdʒ **-es** -ɪz **-ing** -ɪŋ **-ed** -d
Asperger ˈæs.pɜː.dʒəʳ, (US) -pɝː.dʒɚ **ˈAsperger's ˌsyndrome**
asperges, A~ æsˈpɜː.dʒiːz, əˈspɜː-, (US) əˈspɝː-
aspergill ˈæs.pə.dʒɪl, (US) -pɚ- **-s** -z
asperit|y æsˈper.ə.t|i, əˈsper-, -ɪ.t|i, (US) -ə.ţ|i **-ies** -iz
Aspern ˈæs.pɜːn, (US) -pɝːn
aspers|e əˈspɜːs, æsˈpɜːs, (US) əˈspɝːs **-es** -ɪz **-ing** -ɪŋ **-ed** -t
aspersion əˈspɜː.ʃᵊn, æsˈpɜː-, (US) əˈspɝː.ʒᵊn, -ʃᵊn **-s** -z
asphalt n ˈæs.fælt, -fɔːlt, -fəlt, (US) -fɑːlt, -fɔːlt **-s** -s **ˌasphalt ˈjungle**
asphal|t v ˈæs.fæl|t, æsˈfæl|t, (US) ˈæs.fɑːl|t, -fɔːl|t **-ts** -ts **-ting** -tɪŋ, (US) -ţɪŋ **-ted** -tɪd, (US) -ţɪd
asphaltic æsˈfæl.tɪk, (US) -ˈfɑːl.tɪk, -ˈfɔːl-
asphodel ˈæs.fə*ʊ*.del, (US) -fə- **-s** -z

asphyxia əsˈfɪks.i.ə, æs-

asphyxiant əsˈfɪk.si.ənt, æsˈ- -s -s

asphyxi|ate əsˈfɪk.si|.eɪt, æs- -ates -s -ating -eɪ.tɪŋ, (US) -eɪ.t̬ɪŋ -ated -eɪ.tɪd, (US) -eɪ.t̬ɪd -ator/s -eɪ.təʳ/z, (US) -eɪ.t̬ɚ/z

asphyxiation əsˌfɪk.siˈeɪ.ʃən, æs- -s -z

asphyx|y æsˈfɪk.s|i -ies -iz

aspic ˈæs.pɪk

aspidistra ˌæs.pɪˈdɪs.trə, (US) -pəˈ- -s -z

Aspinall ˈæs.pɪ.nɔːl, -nəl

Aspinwall ˈæs.pɪn.wɔːl, (US) -wɔːl, -wɑːl

aspirant ˈæs.pɪ.rənt; əˈspaɪə-, (US) ˈæs.pɚ.ənt, -pɪ.rənt -s -s

aspirate n, adj ˈæs.pər.ət, -pɪ.rət-, -rɪt -s -s

aspir|ate v ˈæs.pər.|eɪt, -pɪ.r|eɪt, (US) -pə.r|eɪt, -pɪ- -ates -eɪts -ating -eɪ.tɪŋ, (US) -eɪ.t̬ɪŋ -ated -eɪ.tɪd, (US) -eɪ.t̬ɪd -ator/s -eɪ.təʳ/z, (US) -eɪ.t̬ɚ/z

aspiration ˌæs.pərˈeɪ.ʃən, -pɪˈreɪ-, (US) -pəˈreɪ-, -pɪˈ- -s -z

aspirational ˌæs.pərˈeɪ.ʃən.əl, -pɪˈreɪ-, (US) -pəˈreɪ-, -pɪˈ- -ly -i

aspir|e əˈspaɪəʳ, -ˈspaɪ.əʳ, (US) -spaɪ.ɚ -es -z -ing/ly -ɪŋ/li -ed -d -er/s -əʳ/z, (US) -ɚ/z

aspirin ˈæs.prɪn, ˈ-pər.ɪn -s -z

aspirine ˈæs.pər.iːn, -pɪ.riːn, (US) -pə.riːn, -pɪ- -s -z

asplenium æsˈpliː.ni.əm, əˈspliː- -s -z

Asquith ˈæs.kwɪθ

ass æs -es -ɪz

assaf(o)etida ˌæs.əˈfet.ɪ.də, -ˈfiː.tɪ-, (US) -ˈfet̬.ə-

assagai ˈæs.ə.gaɪ -s -z

assai æsˈaɪ

assail əˈseɪl -s -z -ing -ɪŋ -ed -d -able -ə.bəl -ant/s -ənt/s

Assam æsˈæm, ˈæs.æm

Assamese ˌæs.əˈmiːz, -æmˈiːz, (US) -əˈmiːz, -ˈmiːs

Assange æsˈɑ̃ːndʒ, -ˈændʒ, əˈsɑ̃ːndʒ, -ˈsændʒ

assassin əˈsæs.ɪn, (US) -ən -s -z

assassi|nate əˈsæs.ɪ|.neɪt, ˈ-ə- -nates -neɪts -nating -neɪ.tɪŋ, (US) -neɪ.t̬ɪŋ -nated -neɪ.tɪd, (US) -neɪ.t̬ɪd -nator/s -neɪ.təʳ/z, (US) -neɪ.t̬ɚ/z

assassination əˌsæs.ɪˈneɪ.ʃən, -əˈ- -s -z

assault əˈsɔːlt, -ˈsɒlt, (US) -ˈsɔːlt, -ˈsɑːlt -s -s -ing -ɪŋ, (US) əˈsɔːl.t̬ɪŋ -ed -ɪd, (US) əˈsɔːl.t̬ɪd -er/s -əʳ/z, (US) əˈsɔːl.t̬ɚ/z **asˌsault and ˈbattery; asˈsault ˌcourse**

assay n əˈseɪ; ˈæs.eɪ, (US) ˈæs.eɪ; (US) əˈseɪ -s -z

assay v əˈseɪ, æsˈeɪ -s -z -ing -ɪŋ -ed -d -er/s -əʳ/z, (US) -ɚ/z

Assaye æsˈeɪ

assegai ˈæs.ə.gaɪ, ˈ-ɪ-, (US) ˈ-ə- -s -z

assemblag|e əˈsem.blɪdʒ -es -ɪz

assembl|e əˈsem.bəl -es -z -ing -ɪŋ, ˈ-blɪŋ -ed -d -er/s -əʳ/z, ˈ-bləʳ/z, (US) ˈ-bəl.ɚ/z, -blɚ/z

assembl|y əˈsem.bl|i -ies -iz **asˈsembly ˌline; asˈsembly ˌroom; asˈsembly ˌlanguage**

assembly|man əˈsem.bli|.mæn, -mən -men -men, -mən

assembly|woman əˈsem.bli|ˌwʊm.ən -women -ˌwɪm.ɪn

assen|t əˈsen|t, æsˈen|t -ts -ts -ting/ly -tɪŋ/li, (US) -t̬ɪŋ/li -ted -tɪd, (US) -t̬ɪd

Asser ˈæs.əʳ, (US) -ɚ

as|sert ə|ˈsɜːt, (US) -ˈsɝːt -serts -ˈsɜːts, (US) -ˈsɝːts -serting -ˈsɜː.tɪŋ, (US) -ˈsɝː.t̬ɪŋ -serted -ˈsɜː.tɪd, (US) -ˈsɝː.t̬ɪd -serter/s -ˈsɜː.təʳ/z, (US) -ˈsɝː.t̬ɚ/s -sertor/s -ˈsɜː.təʳ/z, (US) -ˈsɝː.t̬ɚ/z -sertable -ˈsɜː.tə.bəl, (US) -ˈsɝː.t̬ə.bəl

assertion əˈsɜː.ʃən, (US) -ˈsɝː- -s -z

assertive əˈsɜː.tɪv, (US) -sɝː.t̬ɪv -ly -li -ness -nəs, -nɪs **asˈsertiveness ˌtraining**

assess əˈses -es -ɪz -ing -ɪŋ -ed -t -or/s -əʳ/z, (US) -ɚ/z -able -ə.bəl

assessment əˈses.mənt -s -s

asset ˈæs.et, -ɪt -s -s

asset-stripp|ing ˈæs.etˌstrɪp|.ɪŋ -er/s -əʳ/z, (US) -ɚ/z

assev|er æsˈev|.əʳ, əˈsev-, (US) -ɚ -ers -əz, (US) -ɚs -ering -ər.ɪŋ -ered -əd, (US) -ɚd

assever|ate əˈsev.ər|.eɪt, æsˈev-, (US) -ə.r|eɪt -ates -eɪts -ating -eɪ.tɪŋ, (US) -eɪ.t̬ɪŋ -ated -eɪ.tɪd, (US) -eɪ.t̬ɪd

asseveration əˌsev.əˈreɪ.ʃən, æsˌev- -s -z

asshole ˈɑːs.həʊl, ˈæs-, (US) ˈæs.hoʊl -s -z

Note: Chiefly US; see note at **arse**.

assibi|late əˈsɪb.ɪ|.leɪt, æsˈɪb-, ˈ-ə- -lates -leɪts -lating -leɪ.tɪŋ, (US) -leɪ.t̬ɪŋ -lated -leɪ.tɪd, (US) -leɪ.t̬ɪd

assibilation əˌsɪb.ɪˈleɪ.ʃən, æsˌɪb-, -əˈ- -s -z

assiduit|y ˌæs.ɪˈdʒuː.ə.t|i, -ˈdjuː-, -ɪ.t|i, (US) -ˈduː.ə.t̬|i, -ˈdjuː- -ies -iz

assiduous əˈsɪdʒ.u.əs, -ˈsɪd.ju-, (US) -ˈsɪdʒ.u- -ly -li -ness -nəs, -nɪs

assign əˈsaɪn -s -z -ing -ɪŋ -ed -d -er/s -əʳ/z, (US) -ɚ/z -able -ə.bəl

assignat *as if French:* ˌæs.ɪnˈjɑː; æs.ɪgˈnæt -s -z, -s

assignation ˌæs.ɪgˈneɪ.ʃən -s -z

assignee ˌæs.aɪˈniː, -ɪˈniː, (US) əˌsaɪˈniː, ˌæs.əˈ- -s -z

assignment əˈsaɪn.mənt, -ˈsaɪm-, (US) -ˈsaɪn- -s -s

assimilable əˈsɪm.əl.ə.bəl, -ɪ.lə-

assimil|ate əˈsɪm.ɪ.l|eɪt, -əl|.eɪt, (US) -ə.l|eɪt -ates -eɪts -ating -eɪ.tɪŋ, (US) -eɪ.t̬ɪŋ -ated -eɪ.tɪd, (US) -eɪ.t̬ɪd

assimilation əˌsɪm.ɪˈleɪ.ʃən, -əlˈeɪ-, (US) -əˈleɪ- -s -z

assimilative əˈsɪm.ɪ.lə.tɪv, -əl.ə-, -ə.leɪ-, (US) -ə.leɪ.t̬ɪv, -lə-

assimilatory əˈsɪm.ɪ.lə.tər.i, -əl.ə-; əˌsɪm.ɪˈleɪ-, -əˈ-, (US) əˈsɪm.əl.ə.tɔːr-

Assiniboine əˈsɪn.ɪ.bɔɪn, -ə.bɔɪn -s -z

Assisi əˈsiː.si, -zi, -ˈsɪs.i

assist əˈsɪst -s -s -ing -ɪŋ -ed -ɪd -er/s -əʳ/z, (US) -ɚ/z

assistanc|e əˈsɪs.tənts -es -ɪz

assistant əˈsɪs.tənt -s -s

Assiut æsˈjuːt, (US) ɑːˈsjuːt

assiz|e əˈsaɪz -es -ɪz -er/s -əʳ/z, (US) -ɚ/z

assoc (abbrev. for **associated**) əˈsəʊ.ʃi.eɪ.tɪd, -si-, (US) -ˈsoʊ.ʃi.eɪ.t̬ɪd, -si-

associable əˈsəʊ.ʃi.ə.bəl, -ʃə-, -si.ə-, (US) -ˈsoʊ-

associate n əˈsəʊ.ʃi.ət, -si.ət, (US) -ˈsoʊ.ʃi.ɪt, -si-, -ət -s -s

associ|ate v əˈsəʊ.ʃi|.eɪt, -si-, (US) -ˈsoʊ- -ates -eɪts -ating -eɪ.tɪŋ, (US) -eɪ.t̬ɪŋ -ated -eɪ.tɪd, (US) -eɪ.t̬ɪd

association əˌsəʊ.ʃiˈeɪ.ʃən, -siˈ-, (US) -ˌsoʊ- -s -z

associative əˈsəʊ.ʃi.ə.tɪv, -si-, (US) -ˈsoʊ-

assonanc|e ˈæs.ən.ənts -es -ɪz

assonant ˈæs.ən.ənt -s -s

asson|ate ˈæs.ən|.eɪt, (US) -ə.n|eɪt -ates -eɪts -ating -eɪ.tɪŋ, (US) -eɪ.t̬ɪŋ -ated -eɪ.tɪd, (US) -eɪ.t̬ɪd

as|sort ə|ˈsɔːt, (US) -ˈsɔːrt -sorts -ˈsɔːts, (US) -ˈsɔːrts -sorting -ˈsɔː.tɪŋ, (US) -ˈsɔːr.t̬ɪŋ -sorted -ˈsɔː.tɪd, (US) -ˈsɔːr.t̬ɪd

assortment əˈsɔːt.mənt, (US) -ˈsɔːrt- -s -s

Assouan æsˈwæn, ɑːˈswæn, -ˈswɑːn, (US) ˈæs.wɑːn, ˈɑː.swɑːn *stress shift, British only, see compound:* **ˌAssouan ˈDam**

asst (abbrev. for **assistant**) əˈsɪs.tənt

assuag|e əˈsweɪdʒ -es -ɪz -ing -ɪŋ -ed -d -ement -mənt

assum|e əˈsjuːm, -ˈsuːm, (US) -ˈsuːm -es -z -ing/ly -ɪŋ/li -ed -d -edly -ɪd.li, -əd- -able -ə.bəl -ably -ə.bli

assumpsit əˈsʌmp.sɪt

assumption, A~ əˈsʌmp.ʃən -s -z

assumptive əˈsʌmp.tɪv

assuranc|e əˈʃɔː.rənts, -ˈʃʊə-, (US) -ˈʃʊr.ənts, -ˈʃɝː- -es -ɪz

assur|e əˈʃɔːʳ, -ˈʃʊəʳ, (US) -ˈʃʊr, -ˈʃɝː -es -z -ing -ɪŋ -ed -d -edly -ɪd.li, -əd- -edness -d.nəs, -nɪs -er/s -əʳ/z, (US) -ɚ/z

Assyri|a əˈsɪr.i|.ə -an/s -ən/z

assyriologist, A~ əˌsɪr.iˈɒl.ə.dʒɪst, (US) -ˈɑː.lə- -s -s

assyriology, A~ əˌsɪr.iˈɒl.ə.dʒi, (US) -ˈɑː.lə-

Astaire əˈsteəʳ, (US) -ˈster

Astarte æsˈtɑː.ti, (US) əˈstɑːr.t̬i

astatine ˈæs.tə.tiːn, -tɪn

Astbury ˈæst.bər.i, (US) -ber-

aster ˈæs.təʳ, (US) -tɚ -s -z

asterisk ˈæs.tər.ɪsk -s -s -ing -ɪŋ -ed -t

> Note: the pronunciation /ˈæs.tər.ɪks/ is now widely heard in Britain, perhaps as a result of confusion with the name of the cartoon character Asterix.

asterism ˈæs.tər.ɪ.zəm -s -z

Asterix ˈæs.tᵊr.ɪks
astern əˈstɜːn, (US) -ˈstɝːn
asteroid ˈæs.tᵊr.ɔɪd, (US) -tə.rɔɪd **-s** -z
asthenia æsˈθiː.ni.ə
asthenic æsˈθen.ɪk **-al** -ᵊl
asthma ˈæsθ.mə, ˈæs.mə, (US) ˈæz.mə
asthmatic æsθˈmæt.ɪk, æsˈmæt.ɪk, (US) æzˈmæţ- **-al** -ᵊl **-ally** -ᵊl.i, -li **-s** -s
Asti ˈæs.ti, -tiː, (US) ˈɑː.sti
astigmatic ˌæs.tɪɡˈmæt.ɪk, (US) -ˈmæţ-
astigmatism əˈstɪɡ.mə.tɪ.zᵊm, æsˈtɪɡ-
astir əˈstɜːʳ, (US) -ˈstɝː
Asti Spumante ˌæs.ti.spuˈmæn.ti, -teɪ, (US) ˌɑː.sti.spuˈmɑːn-, ˌæs.ti-
Astle ˈæs.tᵊl, ˈæs.ᵊl
Astley ˈæst.li
Aston ˈæs.tᵊn *TM:* ˌ**Aston** ˈ**Martin**; ˌ**Aston** ˈ**Villa**
astonish əˈstɒn.ɪʃ, (US) -ˈstɑː.nɪʃ **-es** -ɪz **-ed/ly** -t/li
astonishing əˈstɒn.ɪ.ʃɪŋ, (US) -ˈstɑː.nɪ- **-ly** -li
astonishment əˈstɒn.ɪʃ.mənt, (US) -ˈstɑː.nɪʃ-
Astor ˈæs.təʳ, -tɔːʳ, (US) -tɚ
Astoria əˈstɔː.ri.ə, æsˈtɔː-, (US) əˈstɔːr.i-, æsˈtɔːr-
astound əˈstaʊnd **-s** -z **-ing/ly** -ɪŋ **-ed** -ɪd
Astra® ˈæs.trə
Astraea æsˈtriː.ə
astragal ˈæs.trə.ɡᵊl **-s** -z
astrakhan, A~ ˌæs.trəˈkæn, -kɑːn
astral ˈæs.trᵊl **-ly** -i
astray əˈstreɪ
Astrid ˈæs.trɪd
astride əˈstraɪd
astring|e əˈstrɪndʒ **-es** -ɪz **-ing** -ɪŋ **-ed** -d
astringency əˈstrɪn.dʒənt.si
astringent əˈstrɪn.dʒənt **-s** -s **-ly** -li
astro- ˈæs.trəʊ; əˈstrɒ, (US) ˈæs.troʊ, ˈ-trə; (US) əˈstrɑː
Note: Prefix. Either takes primary or secondary stress on the first syllable, e.g. **astrolabe** /ˈæs.trəʊ.leɪb/ (US) /-trə-/, **astronomic** /ˌæs.trəˈnɒm.ɪk/ (US) /-ˈnɑː.mɪk/, or primary stress on the second syllable, e.g. **astronomy** /əˈstrɒn.ə.mi/ (US) /əˈstrɑː.nə-/.
astrobiology ˌæs.trəʊ.baɪˈɒl.ə.dʒi, (US) -troʊ.baɪˈɑː.lə-, -trə-
astrodome ˈæs.trəʊ.dəʊm, (US) -troʊ.doʊm, -trə- **-s** -z
astrolabe ˈæs.trəʊ.leɪb, (US) -troʊ-, -trə- **-s** -z
astrologer əˈstrɒl.ə.dʒəʳ, æsˈ-, (US) əˈstrɑː.lə.dʒɚ **-s** -z
astrologic ˌæs.trəˈlɒdʒ.ɪk, (US) -ˈlɑː.dʒɪk **-al** -ᵊl **-ally** -ᵊl.i, -li
astrologist əˈstrɒl.ə.dʒɪst, æsˈ-, (US) əˈstrɑː.lə- **-s** -s
astrology əˈstrɒl.ə.dʒi, æsˈ-, (US) əˈstrɑː.lə-
astromet|er əˈstrɒm.ɪ.t|əʳ, æsˈtrɒm-, -ə.t|əʳ, (US) əˈstrɑː.mə.ţ|ɚ **-ers** -əz, (US) -ɚz **-ry** -ri
astronaut ˈæs.trə.nɔːt, (US) -nɑːt, -nɔːt **-s** -s
astronautic|al ˌæs.trəˈnɔː.tɪ.k|ᵊl, (US) -trəˈnɑː.ţɪ-, -ˈnɔː- **-s** -s
astronomer əˈstrɒn.ə.məʳ, æsˈ-, (US) əˈstrɑː.nə.mɚ **-s** -z
astronomic ˌæs.trəˈnɒm.ɪk, (US) -ˈnɑː.mɪk **-al** -ᵊl **-ally** -ᵊl.i, -li *stress shift:* ˌ**astronomic** ˈ**increase**
astronom|y əˈstrɒn.ə.m|i, æsˈ-, (US) əˈstrɑː.nə- **-ies** -iz
Astrophil ˈæs.trəʊ.fɪl, (US) -troʊ-, -trə-
astrophysical ˌæs.trəʊˈfɪz.ɪ.kᵊl, (US) -troʊˈ-, -trəˈ-
astrophysicist ˌæs.trəʊˈfɪz.ɪ.sɪst, (US) -troʊˈ-, -trəˈ- **-s** -s
astrophysics ˌæs.trəʊˈfɪz.ɪks, (US) -troʊˈ-, -trəˈ-
Astros ˈæs.trəʊz, (US) -troʊz
astroturf, A~® ˈæs.trəʊ.tɜːf, (US) -troʊ.tɝːf, -trə-
Asturias æsˈtʊə.ri.æs, əˈstʊə-, -ˈstjʊə-, -əs, (US) əˈstʊr.i-
astu|te əˈstʃuː|t, æsˈtʃuː|t, -ˈtjuː|t, (US) əˈstuː|t, -ˈstjuː|t **-ter** -təʳ, (US) -ţɚ **-test** -tɪst, -təst, (US) -ţɪst, -ţəst **-tely** -t.li **-teness** -t.nəs, -t.nɪs
Astyanax əˈstaɪ.ə.næks, æsˈtaɪ-
astylar eɪˈstaɪ.ləʳ, -lɑːʳ, (US) -lɚ
Asunción əˌsʊnt.siˈəʊn, -ˈɒn, (US) ɑːˌsuːnt.siˈoʊn, ˌɑː.suːnt-
asunder əˈsʌn.dəʳ, (US) -dɚ
Aswan æsˈwæn, ɑːˈswæn, -swɑːn, (US) ˈæs.wɑːn, ˈɑː.swɑːn *stress shift, British only, see compound:* ˌ**Aswan** ˈ**Dam**
asyllabic ˌeɪ.sɪˈlæb.ɪk, -səˈ-, (US) -sɪˈ- *stress shift:* ˌ**asyllabic** ˈ**vowel**
asylum əˈsaɪ.ləm **-s** -z **aˈsylum** ˌ**seeker**
asymmetric ˌeɪ.sɪˈmet.rɪk, ˌæs.ɪˈ-, -səˈ- **-al** -ᵊl **-ally** -ᵊl.i, -li *stress shift:* ˌ**asymmetric** ˈ**bars**
asymmetry eɪˈsɪm.ə.tri, æsˈɪm-, ˈ-ɪ-
asymptote ˈæs.ɪmp.təʊt, (US) -toʊt **-s** -s
asymptotic ˌæs.ɪmpˈtɒt.ɪk, (US) -ˈtɑː.ţɪk **-al** -ᵊl **-ally** -ᵊl.i, -li *stress shift:* ˌ**asymptotic** ˈ**curve**
asyndet|on æsˈɪn.dɪ.t|ən, əˈsɪn-, (US) əˈsɪn.də.t|ɑːn, ˌeɪ- **-a** -ə
at prep *strong form:* æt; *weak form:* ət
Note: Weak-form word. The strong form is /æt/, and is used mainly in sentence-final position (e.g. 'What are you playing at?'). It may also be used in sentence-initial position. The weak form is /ət/ (e.g. 'She's at home.' /ʃiz.ətˈhəʊm/ (US) /-ˈhoʊm/).
at n *currency:* ɑːt, æt
at- ət, ˌæt
Note: Prefix. Examples include **attestation** /ˌæt.esˈteɪ.ʃᵊn/ (US) /æţ-/, in which it is stressed, and **attest** /əˈtest/, where it is unstressed.
Atalanta ˌæt.əˈlæn.tə, (US) ˌæţ.əˈlæn.ţə
Atall ˈæt.ɔːl
Atari® əˈtɑː.ri, (US) -ˈtɑːr.i
Atatürk ˈæt.ə.tɜːk, ˌ--ˈ-, (US) ˈæţ.ə.tɝːk
atavism ˈæt.ə.vɪ.zᵊm, (US) ˈæţ-
atavistic ˌæt.əˈvɪs.tɪk, (US) ˌæţ.əˈ- **-ally** -ᵊl.i, -li *stress shift:* ˌ**atavistic** ˈ**feelings**
ataxia əˈtæk.si.ə, ætˈæk-, eɪˈ-
atax|y əˈtæk.s|i, eɪ- **-ies** -iz **-ic** -ɪk
Atbara ætˈbɑː.rə, (US) -ˈbɑːr.ə
ATC ˌeɪ.tiːˈsiː
Atchison ˈætʃ.ɪ.sᵊn, ˈeɪ.tʃɪ-, (US) ˈætʃ.ɪ-
ate (from **eat**) et, eɪt, (US) eɪt
Ate n ˈɑː.ti, ˈeɪ-, (US) ˈɑː-
-ate eɪt, ət, ɪt
Note: Suffix. When forming a verb, **-ate** is always pronounced with a full vowel, and the verb itself is usually stressed two syllables before the suffix, e.g. **demonstrate** /ˈdem.ən.streɪt/, unless it is a word containing two syllables, in which case the suffix normally carries primary stress in British English, e.g. **rotate** /rəʊˈteɪt/ (US) /ˈroʊ.teɪt/, /-ˈ-/. In nouns, **-ate** is normally pronounced /-ət/ or /-ɪt/, e.g. **climate** /ˈklaɪ.mət, -mɪt/, but where the noun is a chemical term it generally has a full vowel, e.g. **nitrate** /ˈnaɪ.treɪt, -trɪt/ (US) /-treɪt/. There are numerous exceptions; see individual entries.
A-team ˈeɪˌtiːm
atelic əˈtel.ɪk, ætˈel.ɪk, -iː.lɪk, (US) ˌeɪˈtiː.lɪk, ˌætˈiː-, -ˈel.ɪk
atelier əˈtel.i.eɪ, ˈæt.el-, ˈæt.ə.li-, -jeɪ, (US) əˈtᵊl.jeɪ, ætˈel-; (US) ˌæt.elˈjeɪ **-s** -z
a tempo ˌɑːˈtem.pəʊ, (US) -poʊ
Atfield ˈæt.fiːld
Athabasca ˌæθ.əˈbæs.kə
Athaliah ˌæθ.əˈlaɪ.ə
Athanasian ˌæθ.əˈneɪ.zi.ən, ˈ-ʒən, -si.ən, -ʒi-, (US) -ʒən
Athanasius ˌæθ.əˈneɪ.zi.əs, ˈ-ʒəs, -si.əs, -ʒi-, (US) -ʒəs
Athawes ˈæt.hɔːz, ˈæθ.ɔːz, (US) ˈæţ.hɑːz, -hɔːz, ˈæθ.ɑːz, -ɔːz
atheism ˈeɪ.θi.ɪ.zᵊm
atheist ˈeɪ.θi.ɪst **-s** -s
atheistic ˌeɪ.θiˈɪs.tɪk **-al** -ᵊl **-ally** -ᵊl.i, -li *stress shift:* ˌ**atheistic** ˈ**culture**
atheling, A~ ˈæθ.ə.lɪŋ **-s** -z
Athelney ˈæθ.ᵊl.ni
Athelstan ˈæθ.ᵊl.stən; *as if Old English:* ˈæð.ᵊl.stɑːn
Athelston ˈæθ.ᵊl.stən
Athena əˈθiː.nə
Athenaeum ˌæθ.ɪˈniː.əm, -əˈ- **-s** -z
Athene əˈθiː.ni, -niː
Athenian əˈθiː.ni.ən **-s** -z
Athenry ˌæθ.ənˈraɪ, -ɪnˈ-
Athens ˈæθ.ᵊnz, -ɪnz
Atherley ˈæθ.ə.li, (US) ˈ-ɚ-
atherosclerosis

A

ˌæθ.ə.rəʊ.skləˈrəʊ.sɪs, -sklerˈəʊ-, sklɪrˈ-, US -roʊ.skləˈroʊ.səs
atherosclerotic ˌæθ.ə.rəʊ.skləˈrɒt.ɪk, -sklerˈɒt-, -sklɪrˈ-, US -roʊ.skləˈrɑː.t̬ɪk
Atherston ˈæθ.ə.stən, US ˈ-ɚ-
Atherstone ˈæθ.ə.stəʊn, -stən, US -ɚ.stoʊn, -stən
Atherton ˈæθ.ə.tən, US ˈ-ɚ.t̬ən
athirst əˈθɜːst, US -ˈθɝːst
Athlestaneford ˈel.ʃən.fəd, US -fɚd
athlete ˈæθ.liːt **-s** -s ˌ**athlete's** ˈ**foot** US ˈ**athlete's** ˌ**foot**

> Note: the non-standard pronunciation /ˈæθ.ə.liːt/ is sometimes heard in the UK.

athletic æθˈlet.ɪk, əθ-, US -ˈlet̬.ɪk **-al** -əl **-ally** -əl.i, -li **-s** -s
athleticism æθˈlet.ɪ.sɪ.zəm, əθ-, ˈ-ə-, US -ˈlet̬.ə-
Athlone æθˈləʊn, US -ˈloʊn *stress shift:* ˌ**Athlone** ˈ**Press**
Athol ˈæθ.əl, -ɒl, US -ɑːl, -əl
Atholl, Athole ˈæθ.əl
Athos ˈæθ.ɒs, ˈeɪ.θɒs, US ˈæθ.ɑːs, ˈeɪ.θɑːs; US ˈæθ.oʊs
athwart əˈθwɔːt, US -ˈθwɔːrt
Athy əˈθaɪ
-ation ˈeɪ.ʃən
Note: Suffix. Always carries primary stress, e.g. **demonstration** /ˌdem.ənˈstreɪ.ʃən/.
atishoo əˈtɪʃ.uː
-ative ə.tɪv, eɪ-, US ə.t̬ɪv, eɪ-
Note: Suffix. Words containing **-ative** are normally stressed one or two syllables before the suffix, e.g. **ablative** /ˈæb.lə.tɪv/ US /-t̬ɪv/, **operative** /ˈɒp.ər.ə.tɪv/ US /ˈɑː.pɚ.ə.t̬ɪv/. See individual entries for exceptions.
Atkins ˈæt.kɪnz
Atkinson ˈæt.kɪn.sən
Atlanta ətˈlæn.tə, æt-, US -t̬ə
atlantean ˌæt.lænˈtiː.ən, -lənˈ-; ətˈlæn.ti-, æt-, US ˌæt.lænˈtiː-, -lənˈ-
Atlantes *statues:* ətˈlæn.tiːz, æt- *in Ariosto's 'Orlando Furioso':* ətˈlæn.tes, æt-
Atlantic ətˈlæn.tɪk, æt-, US -t̬ɪk Atˌlantic ˈ**City**
Atlantis ətˈlæn.tɪs, æt-, US -t̬ɪs
atlas, A~ ˈæt.ləs **-es** -ɪz
ATM ˌeɪ.tiːˈem **-s** -z
atman, A~ ˈɑːt.mən
atmometer ætˈmɒm.ɪ.təʳ, ˈ-ə-, US -ˈmɑː.mə.t̬ɚ **-s** -z
atmosphere ˈæt.məs.fɪəʳ, US -fɪr **-s** -z
atmospheric ˌæt.məsˈfer.ɪk, US -ˈfer-, -ˈfɪr- **-s** -s **-al** -əl **-ally** -əl.i, -li *stress shift:* **atmospheric** ˈ**pressure**
Atocha əˈtɒtʃ.ə, ætˈɒtʃ-, US əˈtɑːtʃ.ə
atoll ˈæt.ɒl; əˈtɒl, US ˈæt.ɑːl, ˈeɪ.tɑːl, -tɔːl **-s** -z
atom ˈæt.əm, US ˈæt̬- **-s** -z
atomic əˈtɒm.ɪk, US -ˈtɑː.mɪk **-s** -s **-ally** -əl.i, -li **aˌtomic** ˈ**energy**
atom|ism ˈæt.ə.m|ɪ.zəm, US ˈæt̬- **-ist/s** -ɪst/s
atomistic ˌæt.əˈmɪs.tɪk, US ˌæt̬-
atomization, -isa- ˌæt.ə.maɪˈzeɪ.ʃən, -mɪˈ-, US ˌæt̬.ə.məˈ-
atomiz|e, -is|e ˈæt.ə.maɪz, US ˈæt̬- **-es** -ɪz **-ing** -ɪŋ **-ed** -d **-er/s** -əʳ/z, US -ɚ/z
atonal eɪˈtəʊ.nəl, ə-, ætˈəʊ-, US eɪˈtoʊ-, ætˈoʊ- **-ism** -ɪ.zəm **-ly** -i
atonality ˌeɪ.təʊˈnæl.ə.ti, ə-, ˌæt.əʊˈ-, -ɪ.ti, US ˌeɪ.toʊˈnæl.ə.t̬i, ˌæt.oʊˈ-
aton|e əˈtəʊn, US -ˈtoʊn **-es** -z **-ing/ly** -ɪŋ/li **-ed** -d **-er/s** -əʳ/z, -ɚ/z
atonement əˈtəʊn.mənt, -ˈtoʊm-, US -ˈtoʊn- **-s** -s
atonic eɪˈtɒn.ɪk, ə-, ætˈɒn-, US eɪˈtɑː.nɪk, ætˈɑː- **-s** -s
atony ˈæt.ən.i, US ˈæt̬-
atop əˈtɒp, US -ˈtɑːp
-ator ə.təʳ, eɪ.təʳ, US ə.t̬ɚ, eɪ.t̬ɚ
Note: Suffix. Words containing **-ator** behave similarly to verbs containing **-ate**, e.g. **demonstrator** /ˈdem.ən.streɪ.təʳ/ US /-t̬ɚ/.
-atory ə.tər.i, eɪ-, US ə.tɔːr.i
Note: Suffix. The pronunciation differs between British and American English. In British English, the penultimate syllable is always reduced, but the antepenultimate syllable may be stressed, and in either case may be pronounced with a full vowel, e.g. **articulatory** /ɑːˈtɪk.jə.lə.tər.i, -jʊ-; ɑːˌtɪk.jəˈleɪ-, -jʊˈ-/. In American English, the penultimate syllable is pronounced with a full vowel (but does not carry primary stress), e.g. **articulatory** /ɑːrˈtɪk.jə.lə.tɔːr.i/.
ATP ˌeɪ.tiːˈpiː
atrabilious ˌæt.rəˈbɪl.i.əs, US ˈ-jəs
Atreus ˈeɪ.tri.əs, -tri.uːs, -truːs
atri|um ˈeɪ.tri.|əm, ˈæt.ri-, US ˈeɪ.tri- **-a** -ə **-ums** -əmz
atrocious əˈtrəʊ.ʃəs, US -ˈtroʊ- **-ly** -li **-ness** -nəs, -nɪs
atrocit|y əˈtrɒs.ə.t|i, -ɪ.t|i, US -ˈtrɑː.sə.t̬|i **-ies** -iz
atrophic əˈtrɒf.ɪk, ætˈrɒf-, US əˈtrɑː.fɪk
atroph|y ˈæt.rə.f|i **-ies** -iz **-ying** -i.ɪŋ **-ied** -id
atropine ˈæt.rə.pɪn, -piːn
Atropos ˈæt.rə.pɒs, -pəs, US -pɑːs
AT&T® ˌeɪ.tiː.əndˈtiː
attaboy ˈæt.ə.bɔɪ, US ˈæt̬-
attach əˈtætʃ **-es** -ɪz **-ing** -ɪŋ **-ed** -t **-able** -ə.bəl
attaché əˈtæʃ.eɪ, ætˈæʃ-, US ˌæt̬.əˈʃeɪ, əˈtæʃ.eɪ **-s** -z **atˈtaché** ˌ**case** US **attaˈché** ˌ**case atˈtaché** ˌ**case**
attachment əˈtætʃ.mənt **-s** -s
attack əˈtæk **-s** -s **-ing** -ɪŋ **-ed** -t **-er/s** -əʳ/z, -ɚ/z
attain əˈteɪn **-s** -z **-ing** -ɪŋ **-ed** -d **-able** -ə.bəl
attainability əˌteɪ.nəˈbɪl.ə.ti, -ɪ.ti, US -ə.t̬i
attainder əˈteɪn.dəʳ, US -dɚ **-s** -z
attainment əˈteɪn.mənt, -ˈteɪm-, US -ˈteɪn- **-s** -s
at|taint ə|ˈteɪnt **-taints** -ˈteɪnts **-tainting** -ˈteɪn.tɪŋ, US -ˈteɪn.t̬ɪŋ **-tainted** -ˈteɪn.tɪd, US -ˈteɪn.t̬ɪd
attar ˈæt.əʳ, US ˈæt̬.ɚ, -ɑːr
attempt əˈtempt **-s** -s **-ing** -ɪŋ **-ed** -ɪd **-er/s** -əʳ/z, US -ɚ/z **-able** -ə.bəl
Attenborough ˈæt.ən.bər.ə, -əm-, -ˌbʌr.ə, US -ən.bɚ.oʊ
attend əˈtend **-s** -z **-ing** -ɪŋ **-ed** -ɪd **-er/s** -əʳ/z, US -ɚ/z
attendanc|e əˈten.dənts **-es** -ɪz
attendant əˈten.dənt **-s** -s
attendee ə.tenˈdiː, ˌæt.en- **-s** -z
attention əˈten.tʃən **-s** -z
attentive əˈten.tɪv, US -t̬ɪv **-ly** -li **-ness** -nəs, -nɪs
attenuate adj əˈten.ju.ɪt, -ət, -eɪt
attenu|ate v əˈten.ju|.eɪt **-ates** -eɪts **-ating** -eɪ.tɪŋ, US -eɪ.t̬ɪŋ **-ated** -eɪ.tɪd, US -eɪ.t̬ɪd
attenuation əˌten.juˈeɪ.ʃən **-s** -z
attenuator əˈten.ju.eɪ.təʳ, US -t̬ɚ **-s** -z
Atterbury ˈæt.ə.bər.i, US ˈæt̬.ɚ.ber.i, -bɚ-
Attercliffe ˈæt.ə.klɪf, US ˈæt̬.ɚ-
attest əˈtest **-s** -s **-ing** -ɪŋ **-ed** -ɪd **-or/s** -əʳ/z, US -ɚ/z **-able** -ə.bəl
attestation ˌæt.esˈteɪ.ʃən, US ˌæt̬- **-s** -z
Attfield ˈæt.fiːld
attic ˈæt.ɪk, US ˈæt̬- **-s** -s
Attica ˈæt.ɪ.kə, US ˈæt̬-
atticism ˈæt.ɪ.sɪ.zəm, US ˈæt̬- **-s** -z
atticiz|e, -is|e ˈæt.ɪ.saɪz, US ˈæt̬- **-es** -ɪz **-ing** -ɪŋ **-ed** -d
Attila əˈtɪl.ə; ˈæt.ɪ.lə, US əˈtɪl.ə; US ˈæt̬.ɪ.lə
attir|e əˈtaɪəʳ, -ˈtaɪ.əʳ, US -ˈtaɪ.ɚ **-es** -z **-ing** -ɪŋ **-ed** -d **-ement** -mənt
Attis ˈæt.ɪs, US ˈæt̬-
attitude ˈæt.ɪ.tʃuːd, -tjuːd, US ˈæt̬.ə.tuːd, -tjuːd **-s** -z
attitudinal ˌæt.ɪˈtʃuː.dɪ.nəl, -ˈtjuː-, US ˌæt̬.əˈtuː.dən.əl, -ˈtjuː-
attitudinarian ˌæt.ɪ.tʃuː.dɪˈneə.ri.ən, -tjuː-, US ˌæt̬.əˌtuː.dɪˈner.i-, -ˌtjuː- **-s** -z
attitudiniz|e, -is|e ˌæt.ɪˈtʃuː.dɪ.naɪz, -ˈtjuː-, US ˌæt̬.əˈtuː.dən.aɪz, -ˈtjuː- **-es** -ɪz **-ing** -ɪŋ **-ed** -d **-er/s** -əʳ/z, -ɚ/z
Attleborough ˈæt.əl.bər.ə, -ˌbʌr.ə, US ˈæt̬.əl.bɚ.oʊ
Attlee ˈæt.liː
Attock əˈtɒk, US -ˈtɑːk
attorn əˈtɜːn, US -ˈtɝːn **-s** -z **-ing** -ɪŋ **-ed** -d
attorney əˈtɜː.ni, US -ˈtɝː- **-s** -z aˌ**ttorney** ˈ**general**
attorney-at-law əˌtɜː.ni.ətˈlɔː, US -ˌtɝː.ni.ətˈlɑː, -ˈlɔː **attorneys-at-law** əˌtɜː.niz.ətˈlɔː, US -ˌtɝː.niz.ətˈlɑː, -ˈlɔː

A

Pronouncing the letters AU, AW

The vowel-letter combinations **au** and **aw** are similar in that their most common pronunciation is /ɔː/ (US) /ɑː/, e.g.:

sauce sɔːs (US) sɑːs
saw sɔː (US) sɑː

However, there is more variation in the case of **au**.

When followed by **gh** in the spelling realized as /f/, it is pronounced as /ɑː/ (US) /æ/, e.g.:

laugh lɑːf (US) læf

The combination **au** may also be pronounced as /ɒ/ (US) /ɑː/, e.g.:

Australia ɒsˈtreɪ.li.ə (US) ɑːˈstreɪ-
because bɪˈkɒz (US) -ˈkɑːz

In addition

Other sounds associated with the combinations **au** are:

əʊ (US) oʊ chauffeur /ˈʃəʊ.fər/ (US) /ʃoʊˈfɝː/

And, in rare cases:

eɪ gauge /geɪdʒ/

In weak syllables

The vowel combinations **au** and **aw** are realized with the vowel /ə/ in weak syllables, and **au** may also result in a syllabic consonant or an elided vowel, e.g.:

awry əˈraɪ
restaurant ˈres.tər.ɔ̃ːŋ, ˈ-trɔ̃ːŋ (US) -tə.rɑːnt, ˈ-trɑːnt

attorneyship əˈtɜː.ni.ʃɪp, (US) -ˈtɝː- -s -s
attract əˈtrækt -s -s -ing/ly -ɪŋ/li -ed -ɪd -or/s -ər/z, (US) -ɚ/z -able -ə.bəl
attractability əˌtræk.təˈbɪl.ə.ti, -ɪ.ti, (US) -ə.ţi
attraction əˈtræk.ʃən -s -z
attractive əˈtræk.tɪv -ly -li -ness -nəs, -nɪs
attributable əˈtrɪb.jə.tə.bəl, -jʊ-, (US) -jə.ţə-
attribute n ˈæt.rɪ.bjuːt -s -s
attri|bute v əˈtrɪ|.bjuːt -butes -bjuːts -buting -bjʊ.tɪŋ, (US) -bjə.ţɪŋ, -bjuː- -buted -bjʊ.tɪd, (US) -bjə.ţɪd, -bjuː-
attribution ˌæt.rɪˈbjuː.ʃən -s -z
attributive əˈtrɪb.jə.tɪv, -jʊ-, (US) -jə.ţɪv -ly -li
attrition əˈtrɪʃ.ən, ætˈrɪʃ-
attun|e əˈtʃuːn, əˈtjuːn, ætʃˈuːn, ætˈjuːn, (US) əˈtuːn, -ˈtjuːn -es -z -ing -ɪŋ -ed -d
Attwell ˈæt.wel, -wəl
ATV ˌeɪ.tiːˈviː -s -z
Atwater ˈæt.wɔː.tər, (US) -wɑː.ţɚ, -wɔː-
At(t)wood ˈæt.wʊd
atypical ˌeɪˈtɪp.ɪ.kəl
aubade əʊˈbɑːd, (US) oʊ- -s -z
auberg|e əʊˈbeəʒ, -ˈbɜːʒ, (US) oʊˈberʒ -es -ɪz
aubergine ˈəʊ.bə.ʒiːn, -dʒiːn, (US) ˈoʊ.bɚ- -s -z
Auberon ˈɔː.bə.rən, ˈəʊ-, -rɒn, ˌ--ˈ-, (US) ˈɑː.bə.rɑːn, ˈɔː-
aubretia ɔːˈbriː.ʃə, -ʃi.ə, (US) ɑː-, ɔː-
Aubrey ˈɔː.bri, (US) ˈɑː-, ˈɔː-
aubrietia ɔːˈbriː.ʃə, -ʃi.ə, (US) ɑː-, ɔː- -s -z
auburn, A~ ˈɔː.bən, -bɜːn, (US) ˈɑː.bɚn, ˈɔː-
Auchindachie ˌɔː.kɪnˈdæk.i, -xɪnˈdæx-, (US) ˌɑː.kɪnˈdæk-, ˌɔː-
Auchinleck ˌɔː.kɪnˈlek, -xɪnˈ-, ˈ---, (US) ˌɑː.kɪnˈlek, ˌɔː-, ˈ---
Auchmuty ɔːkˈmjuː.ti, (US) ɑːk-, ɔːk-
Auchtermuchty ˌɔːk.təˈmʌk.ti, ˌɒk.tə-, ˌɔːx.təˈmʌx.ti, ˌɒx.tə-, (US) ˌɑːk.tɚˈmʌk-, ˌɔːk-
Auckland ˈɔːk.lənd, (US) ˈɑːk-, ˈɔːk-
au contraire ˌəʊ.kɒnˈtreər, (US) ˌoʊ.kɑːnˈtrer
au courant əʊˈkʊr.ɑ̃ːŋ, (US) ˌoʊ.kuːˈrɑːn
auction ˈɔːk.ʃən, ˈɒk-, (US) ˈɑːk.ʃən, ˈɔːk- -s -z -ing -ɪŋ -ed -d
auctionary ˈɔːk.ʃən.ər.i, ˈɒk-, (US) ˈɑːk.ʃən.er-, ˈɔːk-
auctioneer ˌɔːk.ʃənˈɪər, ˌɒk-, (US) ˌɑːk.ʃəˈnɪr, ˌɔːk- -s -z -ing -ɪŋ -ed -d
audacious ɔːˈdeɪ.ʃəs, (US) ɑː-, ɔː- -ly -li -ness -nəs, -nɪs
audacit|y ɔːˈdæs.ə.t|i, -ɪ.t|i, (US) ɑːˈdæs.ə.ţ|i, ɔː- -ies -iz
Audelay ˈɔːd.leɪ, (US) ˈɑːd-, ˈɔːd-
Auden ˈɔː.dən, (US) ˈɑː-, ˈɔː-
Audenshaw ˈɔː.dən.ʃɔː, (US) ˈɑː.dən.ʃɑː, ˈɔː-, -ʃɔː
Audi® ˈaʊ.di, (US) ˈaʊ-, ˈɑː-
audibility ˌɔː.dəˈbɪl.ə.ti, -dɪˈ-, -ɪ.ti, (US) ˌɑː.dəˈbɪl.ə.ţi, ˌɔː-
audib|le ˈɔː.də.b|əl, ˈ-dɪ-, (US) ˈɑː.də-, ˈɔː- -ly -li -leness -əl.nəs, -nɪs
audienc|e ˈɔː.di.ənts, (US) ˈɑː-, ˈɔː- -es -ɪz
audio ˈɔː.di.əʊ, (US) ˈɑː.di.oʊ, ˈɔː-
audiocassette ˌɔː.di.əʊ.kəˈset, (US) ˌɑː.di.oʊ-, ˌɔː- -s -s
audiologist ˌɔː.diˈɒl.ə.dʒɪst, (US) ˌɑː.diˈɑː.lə-, ˌɔː- -s -s
audiology ˌɔː.diˈɒl.ə.dʒi, (US) ˌɑː.diˈɑː.lə-, ˌɔː-
audiometer ˌɔː.diˈɒm.ɪ.tər, -ə.tər, (US) ˌɑː.diˈɑː.mə.ţɚ, ˌɔː- -s -z
audiometry ˌɔː.diˈɒm.ə.tri, ˈ-ɪ-, (US) ˌɑː.diˈɑː.mə-, ˌɔː-
audiotape ˈɔː.di.əʊ.teɪp, (US) ˈɑː.di.oʊ-, ˈɔː- -s -s
audio-typ|ing ˈɔː.di.əʊˌtaɪ.p|ɪŋ, (US) ˈɑː.di.oʊ-, ˈɔː- -ist/s -ɪst/s
audio-visual ˌɔː.di.əʊˈvɪʒ.u.əl, -ˈvɪz.ju-, (US) ˌɑː.di.oʊˈvɪʒ.ju-, ˌɔː-
audiphone ˈɔː.dɪ.fəʊn, (US) ˈɑː.dɪ.foʊn, ˈɔː- -s -z
au|dit ˈɔː|.dɪt, (US) ˈɑː-, ˈɔː- -dits -dɪts -diting -dɪ.tɪŋ, (US) -də.ţɪŋ -dited -dɪ.tɪd, (US) -də.ţɪd
audition ɔːˈdɪʃ.ən, (US) ɑː-, ɔː- -s -z -ing -ɪŋ -ed -d
auditor ˈɔː.dɪt.ər, (US) ˈɑː.də.ţɚ, ˈɔː- -s -z
auditori|um ˌɔː.dɪˈtɔː.ri|.əm, (US) ˌɑː.dəˈtɔːr.i-, ˌɔː- -ums -əmz -a -ə
auditorship ˈɔː.dɪt.ə.ʃɪp, (US) ˈɑː.də.ţɚ-, ˈɔː- -s -s
auditor|y ˈɔː.dɪ.tər|.i, (US) ˈɑː.də.tɔːr-, ˈɔː- -ies -iz
Audley ˈɔːd.li, (US) ˈɑːd-, ˈɔːd-
Audrey ˈɔː.dri, (US) ˈɑː-, ˈɔː-
Audubon ˈɔː.də.bɒn, ˈ-djə-, -bən, (US) ˈɑː.də.bɑːn, ˈɔː-, -bən
au fait ˌəʊˈfeɪ, (US) ˌoʊ-
Aufidius ɔːˈfɪd.i.əs, (US) ɑː-, ɔː-
Aufklärung ˈaʊf.kleə.rʊŋ, (US) -kler.ʊŋ
Auf Wiedersehen ˌaʊfˈviː.də.zeɪn, -zeɪ.ən, (US) -ˈviː.dɚ-
Aug. (abbrev. for **August**) ˈɔː.gəst, (US) ˈɑː-, ˈɔː-
Augean ɔːˈdʒiː.ən, (US) ɑː-, ɔː-
Augeas ɔːˈdʒiː.æs, (US) ɑː-, ɔː-
Augener ˈaʊ.gən.ər, (US) -ɚ
auger ˈɔː.gər, (US) ˈɑː.gɚ, ˈɔː- -s -z
Aughrim ˈɔː.grɪm, (US) ˈɑː-, ˈɔː-
aught ɔːt, (US) ɑːt, ɔːt
Aughton *Humberside, S. Yorks & Nr. Ormskirk, Lancashire:* ˈɔː.tən, (US) ˈɑː-, ˈɔː- *Nr. Lancaster, Lancashire:* ˈæf.tən
Augie ˈɔː.gi, (US) ˈɑː-, ˈɔː-
augment n ˈɔːg.mənt, (US) ˈɑːg-, ˈɔːg- -s -s
aug|ment v ɔːg|ˈment, (US) ɑːg-, ɔːg- -ments -ˈments -menting -ˈmen.tɪŋ, (US) -ˈmen.ţɪŋ -mented -ˈmen.tɪd, (US) -ˈmen.ţɪd -mentable -ˈmen.tə.bəl, (US) -ˈmen.ţə.bəl
augmentation ˌɔːg.menˈteɪ.ʃən, -mənˈ-, (US) ˌɑːg-, ˌɔːg- -s -z
augmentative ɔːgˈmen.tə.tɪv, (US) ɑːgˈmen.ţə.ţɪv, ɔːg-
au gratin əʊˈgræt.æ̃ŋ, (US) oʊˈgrɑː.tən, -ˈgræt.ən
Augsburg ˈaʊgz.bɜːg, ˈaʊks-, -bʊəg, (US) ˈɑːgz.bɝːg, ˈɔːgz-, -bʊrg
aug|ur ˈɔː.g|ər, (US) ˈɑː.g|ɚ, ˈɔː- -urs -əz, (US) -ɚz -uring -ər.ɪŋ -ured -əd, (US) -ɚd
augural ˈɔː.gjʊ.rəl, -jər.əl, (US) ˈɑː.gjɚ.əl, ˈɔːg-

A

augur|y ˈɔːg.jʊ.r|i, -jər.|i, (US) ˈɑːg.jɚ|.i, ˈɔːg- **-ies** -iz
august **adj** ɔːˈgʌst, (US) ɑː-, ɔː-, ˈ-- **-est** -ɪst, -əst **-ly** -li **-ness** -nəs, -nɪs
August **n** ˈɔː.gəst, (US) ˈɑː-, ˈɔː- **-s** -s
ˌ**August Bank** ˈ**Holiday**
August|a ɔːˈgʌs.t|ə, ə-, (US) əˈ-, ɑːˈ-, ɔːˈ- **-an** -ən
Augustine ɔːˈgʌs.tɪn, ə-, (US) ɑː-, ɔː-; (US) ˈɑː.gə.stiːn, ˈɔː-
Augustinian ˌɔː.gəˈstɪn.i.ən, (US) ˌɑː-, ˌɔː-
Augustus ɔːˈgʌs.təs, ə-, (US) ə-, ɑː-, ɔː-
auk ɔːk, (US) ɑːk, ɔːk **-s** -s
aul|a ˈɔː.l|ə, ˈaʊ-, (US) ˈɑː-, ˈɔː- **-ae** -iː, -aɪ, -eɪ
auld, A~ ɔːld, (US) ɑːld, ɔːld
auld lang syne ˌɔːld.læŋˈsaɪn, -zaɪn, (US) ˌɑːld-, ˌɔːld-
Aumerle ɔːˈmɜːl, (US) ɑːˈmɝːl, ɔː-
au naturel ˌəʊ.nætʃ.ʊˈrel, (US) ˌoʊ.nætʃ.əˈrel; (US) -nɑː.tuˈ-
Aungier ˈeɪn.dʒər, (US) -dʒɚ
Aung San Suu Kyi ˌaʊŋ.sæn.suːˈtʃiː
aunt ɑːnt, (US) ænt, ɑːnt **-s** -s

> Note: Although **aunt** is generally /ænt/ in American English, regional and social subgroups have persistent /ɑːnt/.

auntie, aunty ˈɑːn.ti, (US) ˈæn.t̬i, ˈɑːn- **-s** -z
au pair ˌəʊˈpeər, (US) oʊˈper **-s** -z
aura ˈɔː.rə, (US) ˈɔːr.ə **-s** -z
aural ˈɔː.rəl, ˈaʊ-, (US) ˈɔːr.əl **-ly** -i
aurate ˈɔː.reɪt, -rɪt, (US) ˈɔːr.eɪt **-s** -s
aureate ˈɔː.ri.eɪt, -ət, -ɪt, (US) ˈɔːr.i-
Aureli|a ɔːˈriː.li.|ə **-an** -ən **-us** -əs
aureola ɔːˈriː.ə.lə, (US) ˌɔːr.iˈoʊ- **-s** -z
aureole ˈɔː.ri.əʊl, (US) ˈɔːr.i.oʊl **-s** -z
aureomycin ˌɔː.ri.əʊˈmaɪ.sɪn, (US) ˌɔːr.i-
au revoir ˌəʊ.rəvˈwɑːr, -rɪvˈ-, (US) ˌoʊ.rəvˈwɑːr
auricle ˈɔː.rɪ.kəl, ˈɒr.ɪ-, (US) ˈɔːr.ɪ- **-s** -z
auricula ɔːˈrɪk.jə.lə, ɒrˈɪk-, -jʊ-, (US) ɔːˈrɪk.jə- **-s** -z
auricular ɔːˈrɪk.jə.lər, ɒrˈɪk-, -jʊ-, (US) ɔːˈrɪk.jə.lɚ **-ly** -li
auricu|late ɔːˈrɪk.jə|.lət, -jʊ-, -lɪt, -leɪt, (US) -jə- **-lated** -leɪ.tɪd, (US) -leɪ.t̬ɪd
Auriel ˈɔː.ri.əl, (US) ˈɔːr.i-
auriferous ɔːˈrɪf.ər.əs
Auriga ɔːˈraɪ.gə
Aurignacian ˌɔː.rɪgˈneɪ.ʃən, -ʃi.ən, (US) ˌɔːr.ɪg-
aurist ˈɔː.rɪst, (US) ˈɔːr.ɪst **-s** -s
aurochs ˈɔː.rɒks, ˈaʊ-, (US) ˈɔːr.ɑːks, ˈaʊ.rɑːks **-es** -ɪz
auror|a, A~ ɔːˈrɔː.r|ə, ə-, (US) -ˈrɔːr|.ə **-as** -əz **-al** -əl
aurora australis ɔːˌrɔː.rə.ɒsˈtreɪ.lɪs, ə-, -ˈtrɑː-, (US) -ˌrɔːr.ə.ɔːˈstreɪ-
aurora borealis ɔːˌrɔː.rə.bɒr.iˈeɪ.lɪs, ə-, -ˈɑː.lɪs, (US) -ˌrɔːr.ə.bɔːr.iˈæl.ɪs, -ˈɑː.lɪs
Auschwitz ˈaʊʃ.wɪts; *as if German:* -vɪts
auscul|tate ˈɔː.skəl|.teɪt, ˈɒs.kəl-, -kʌl-, (US) ˈɑː.skəl-, ˈɔː- **-tates** -teɪts **-tating** -teɪ.tɪŋ, (US) -teɪ.t̬ɪŋ **-tated** -teɪ.tɪd, (US) -teɪ.t̬ɪd
auscultation ˌɔː.skəlˈteɪ.ʃən, ˌɒs.kəlˈ-, -kʌlˈ-, (US) ˌɑː.skəl-, ˌɔː- **-s** -z
auscultator ˈɔː.skəl.teɪ.tər, ˈɒs.kəl-, -kʌl-, (US) ˈɑː.skəl.teɪ.t̬ɚ, ˈɔː- **-s** -z
auspic|e ˈɔː.spɪs, ˈɒs.pɪs, (US) ˈɑː.spɪs, ˈɔː- **-es** -ɪz
auspicious ɔːˈspɪʃ.əs, ɒsˈpɪʃ-, (US) ɑːˈspɪʃ-, ɔː- **-ly** -li **-ness** -nəs, -nɪs
Aussie ˈɒz.i, (US) ˈɑː.zi, ˈɔː-, -si **-s** -z
Austell ˈɔː.stəl, ˈɒs.təl; *local Cornish pronunciation:* ˈɔː.səl, (US) ˈɑː.stəl, ˈɔː-
Austen ˈɒs.tɪn, ˈɔː.stɪn, (US) ˈɑː.stɪn, ˈɔː-
Auster ˈɔː.stər, ˈɒs.tər, (US) ˈɑː.stɚ, ˈɔː-
auster|e ɒsˈtɪər, ɔːˈstɪər, (US) ɑːˈstɪr, ɔː- **-er** -ər, -ɚ **-est** -ɪst, -əst **-ely** -li **-eness** -nəs, -nɪs
austerit|y ɒsˈter.ə.t|i, ɔːˈster-, -ɪ.t|i, (US) ˈɑː.ster.ə.t̬|i, ˈɔː- **-ies** -iz
Austerlitz ˈɔː.stə.lɪts, ˈaʊ-, (US) ˈɑː.stɚ-, ˈɔː-
Austin ˈɒs.tɪn, ˈɔː.stɪn, (US) ˈɑː.stɪn, ˈɔː- **-s** -z
austral ˈɒs.trəl, ˈɔː.strəl, (US) ˈɑː.strəl, ˈɔː-
Australasi|a ˌɒs.trəˈleɪ.ʒ|ə, ˌɔː.strə-, -zi|.ə, -ʃi|.ə, -ʃ|ə, (US) ˌɑː.strəˈ-, ˌɔː- **-an/s** -ən/z
Australi|a ɒsˈtreɪ.li|.ə, ɔːˈstreɪ-, (US) ɑːˈstreɪl.j|ə, ɔː- **-an/s** -ən/z
australopithecus ˌɒs.trə.ləʊˈpɪθ.ɪ.kəs, ˌɔː.strə-, -ə.kəs, (US) ˌɑː.strə.loʊˈ-, ˌɔː-
Austri|a ˈɒs.tri|.ə, ˈɔː.stri|-, (US) ˈɑː.stri|-, ˈɔː- **-an/s** -ən/z
Austro- ɒs.trəʊ, ɔː.strəʊ, (US) ɑː.stroʊ, ɔː-
Note: Prefix. Behaves as **Anglo-**.
Austro-German ˌɒs.trəʊˈdʒɜː.mən, ˌɔː.strəʊˈ-, (US) ˌɑː.stroʊˈdʒɝː-, ˌɔː-
Austro-Hungarian ˌɒs.trəʊ.hʌŋˈgeə.ri.ən, ˌɔː.strəʊ-, (US) ˌɑː.stroʊ.hʌŋˈger.i-, ˌɔː-
Austronesi|a ˌɒs.trəʊˈniː.ʒ|ə, ˌɔː.strəʊˈ-, -zi|.ə, -si|.ə, -ʃ|ə, (US) ˌɑː.stroʊˈ-, ˌɔː- **-an/s** -ən/z
autarchic ɔːˈtɑː.kɪk, (US) ɑːˈtɑːr-, ɔː- **-al** -əl
autarch|y ˈɔː.tɑː.k|i, (US) ˈɑː.tɑːr-, ˈɔː- **-ies** -iz
autarkic ɔːˈtɑː.kɪk, (US) ɑːˈtɑːr-, ɔː- **-al** -əl
Auteuil əʊˈtɜː.i, (US) oʊˈtuː.i, -ˈtɜː.i
authentic ɔːˈθen.tɪk, (US) ɑːˈθen.t̬ɪk, ɔː- **-al** -əl **-ally** -əl.i, -li
authenti|cate ɔːˈθen.tɪ|.keɪt, (US) ɑːˈθen.t̬ɪ-, ɔː- **-cates** -keɪts **-cating** -keɪ.tɪŋ, (US) -keɪ.t̬ɪŋ **-cated** -keɪ.tɪd, (US) -keɪ.t̬ɪd **-cator/s** -keɪ.tər/z, (US) -keɪ.t̬ɚ/z
authentication ɔːˌθen.tɪˈkeɪ.ʃən, -təˈ-, (US) ɑːˌθen.t̬ɪˈ-, ɔː- **-s** -z
authenticit|y ˌɔː.θenˈtɪs.ə.t|i, -θənˈ-, -ɪ.t|i, (US) ˌɑː.θenˈtɪs.ə.t̬|i, ˌɔː- **-ies** -iz
author ˈɔː.θər, (US) ˈɑː.θɚ, ˈɔː- **-s** -z **-ing** -ɪŋ **-ed** -d
authoress ˈɔː.θər.es, -ɪs, -əs; ˌɔː.θərˈes, (US) ˈɑː.θɚ.ɪs, ˈɔː-, -əs **-es** -ɪz
authorial ɔːˈθɔː.ri.əl, (US) ɑːˈθɔːr.i-, ɔː-
authoritarian ˌɔː.θɒr.ɪˈteə.ri.ən, ɔːˌθɒr-, -əˈ-, (US) əˌθɔːr.əˈter.i-, ɑː-, ɔː- **-s** -z
authoritarianism ɔːˌθɒr.ɪˈteə.ri.ə.nɪ.zəm, -əˈ-, (US) əˌθɔːr.əˈter.i-, ɑː-, ɔː-
authoritative ɔːˈθɒr.ɪ.tə.tɪv, ə-, ˈ-ə-, -teɪ-, (US) əˈθɔːr.ə.teɪ.t̬ɪv, ɑː-, ɔː- **-ly** -li **-ness** -nəs, -nɪs
authorit|y ɔːˈθɒr.ə.t|i, ə-, -ɪ.t|i, (US) əˈθɔːr.ə.t̬|i, ɑː-, ɔː- **-ies** -iz
authorization, -isa- ˌɔː.θər.aɪˈzeɪ.ʃən, -ɪˈ-, (US) ˌɑː.θɚ.əˈ-, ˌɔː- **-s** -z
authoriz|e, -is|e ˈɔː.θər.aɪz, (US) ˈɑː-, ˈɔː- **-es** -ɪz **-ing** -ɪŋ **-ed** -d **-able** -ə.bəl
authorship ˈɔː.θə.ʃɪp, (US) ˈɑː.θɚ-, ˈɔː-
autism ˈɔː.tɪ.zəm, (US) ˈɑː.tɪ-, ˈɔː-
autistic ɔːˈtɪs.tɪk, (US) ɑː-, ɔː-
auto ˈɔː.təʊ, (US) ˈɑː.t̬oʊ, ˈɔː- **-s** -z
auto- ˈɔː.təʊ; ɔːˈtɒ, (US) ˈɑː.t̬oʊ, ˈ-t̬ə-, ɔː-; (US) ɑːˈtɑː, ɔː-
Note: Prefix. Either takes primary or secondary stress on the first syllable. e.g. **autocue** /ˈɔː.təʊ.kjuː/ (US) /ˈɑː.t̬oʊ-, ɔː-/, **autogenic** /ˌɔː.təʊˈdʒen.ɪk/ (US) /ˌɑː.t̬oʊˈdʒen-, ɔː-/, or primary stress on the second syllable, e.g. **automaton** /ɔːˈtɒm.ə.tən/ (US) /ɑːˈtɑː.mə-, ɔː-, -tɑːn/.
autobahn ˈɔː.təʊ.bɑːn, ˈaʊ-, (US) ˈɑː.t̬oʊ-, ˈɔː- **-s** -z
autobiographer ˌɔː.tə.baɪˈɒg.rə.fər, (US) ˌɑː.t̬ə.baɪˈɑː.grə.fɚ, ˌɔː- **-s** -z
autobiographic ˌɔː.təˌbaɪ.əʊˈgræf.ɪk, (US) ˌɑː.t̬əˌbaɪ.əˈ-, ˌɔː- **-al** -əl **-ally** -əl.i, -li
stress shift: ˌ**autobiographic** ˈ**novel**
autobiograph|y ˌɔː.tə.baɪˈɒg.rə.f|i, (US) ˌɑː.t̬ə.baɪˈɑː.grə-, ˌɔː- **-ies** -iz
autocade ˈɔː.təʊ.keɪd, (US) ˈɑː.t̬oʊ-, ˈɔː-
auto-car ˈɔː.təʊ.kɑːr, (US) ˈɑː.t̬oʊ.kɑːr, ˈɔː- **-s** -z
autochthon ɔːˈtɒk.θən, -θɒn, (US) ɑːˈtɑːk.θən, ɔː- **-s** -z
autochthonous ɔːˈtɒk.θən.əs, (US) ɑːˈtɑːk-, ɔː-
autoclav|e ˈɔː.təʊ.kleɪv, (US) ˈɑː.t̬oʊ-, ˈɔː- **-es** -z **-ing** -ɪŋ **-ed** -d
autocrac|y ɔːˈtɒk.rə.s|i, (US) ɑːˈtɑː.krə-, ɔː- **-ies** -iz
autocrat ˈɔː.tə.kræt, (US) ˈɑː.t̬ə-, ˈɔː- **-s** -s
autocratic ˌɔː.təˈkræt.ɪk, (US) ˌɑː.t̬əˈkræt̬-, ˌɔː- **-al** -əl **-ally** -əl.i, -li

stress shift: ˌ**autocratic** ˈ**government**

autocross ˈɔː.təʊ.krɒs, ⓊⓈ ˈɑː.t̬oʊ.krɑːs, ˈɔː-

autocue, A~® ˈɔː.təʊ.kjuː, ⓊⓈ ˈɑː.t̬oʊ-, ˈɔː- **-s** -z

auto-da-fé ˌɔː.təʊ.dɑːˈfeɪ, ˌaʊ-, ⓊⓈ ˌɑː.t̬oʊ.dəˈ-, ˌɔː- **-s** -z

autodestruct ˌɔː.təʊ.dɪˈstrʌkt, -dəˈ-, ⓊⓈ ˌɑː.t̬oʊ-, ˌɔː- **-s** -s **-ing** -ɪŋ **-ed** -ɪd

autodidact ˌɔː.təʊˈdaɪ.dækt, ⓊⓈ ˌɑː.t̬oʊ-, ˌɔː- **-s** -s

autodidactic ˌɔː.təʊ.daɪˈdæk.tɪk, -dɪˈ-, ⓊⓈ ˌɑː.t̬oʊ-, ˌɔː-

autoerotic ˌɔː.təʊ.ɪˈrɒt.ɪk, -əˈrɒt-, ⓊⓈ ˌɑː.t̬oʊ.ɪˈrɑː.t̬ɪk, ˌɔː- *stress shift:* ˌ**autoerotic** ˈ**fantasy**

autoerot|ism ˌɔː.təʊ.ˈer.ə.t|ɪ.zᵊm; -ɪˈrɒt|.ɪ-, ⓊⓈ ˌɑː.t̬oʊ.ɪˈrɑː.t̬|ɪ-, ˌɔː- **-icism** -ɪ.sɪ.zᵊm, ⓊⓈ -ə.sɪ.zᵊm

autogam|ous ɔːˈtɒg.ə.m|əs, ⓊⓈ ɑːˈtɑː.gə-, ɔː- **-y** -i

autogenesis ˌɔː.təʊˈdʒen.ə.sɪs, ˈ-ɪ-, ⓊⓈ ˌɑː.t̬oʊˈdʒen.ə-, ˌɔː-

autogenetic ˌɔː.təʊ.dʒᵊnˈet.ɪk, ⓊⓈ ˌɑː.t̬oʊ.dʒəˈnet̬-, ˌɔː-

autogenic ˌɔː.təʊˈdʒen.ɪk, ⓊⓈ ˌɑː.t̬oʊˈ-, ˌɔː-

autogenous ɔːˈtɒdʒ.ɪ.nəs, ˈ-ə-, ⓊⓈ ɑːˈtɑː.dʒɪ-, ɔː- **-ly** -li

autogiro ˌɔː.təʊˈdʒaɪə.rəʊ, ⓊⓈ ˌɑː.t̬oʊˈdʒaɪ.roʊ, ˌɔː- **-s** -z

autograph ˈɔː.tə.grɑːf, -græf, ⓊⓈ ˈɑː.t̬ə.græf, ˈɔː- **-s** -s **-ing** -ɪŋ **-ed** -d

autographic ˌɔː.təʊˈgræf.ɪk, ⓊⓈ ˌɑː.t̬oʊ, ˌɔː- **-al** -ᵊl **-ally** -ᵊl.i, -li

autography ɔːˈtɒg.rə.fi, ⓊⓈ ɑːˈtɑː.grə-, ɔː-

autogyro ˌɔː.təʊˈdʒaɪə.rəʊ, ⓊⓈ ˌɑː.t̬oʊˈdʒaɪ.roʊ, ˌɔː- **-s** -z

Autoharp® ˈɔː.təʊ.hɑːp, ⓊⓈ ˈɑː.t̬oʊ.hɑːrp, ˈɔː-

auto-immun|e ˌɔː.təʊ.ɪˈmjuːn, ⓊⓈ ˌɑː.t̬oʊ-, ˌɔː- **-ity** -ə.ti, -ɪ.ti, ⓊⓈ -ə.t̬i

autolexic|al ˌɔː.təʊˈlek.sɪ.k|ᵊl, ⓊⓈ ˌɑː.t̬oʊˈlek-, ˌɔː- **-ally** -ᵊl.i, -li

autolock ˈɔː.təʊ.lɒk, ⓊⓈ ˈɑː.t̬oʊ.lɑːk, ˈɔː-

Autolycus ɔːˈtɒl.ɪ.kəs, ⓊⓈ ɑːˈtɑː.lɪ-, ɔː-

automaker ˈɔː.təʊˌmeɪ.kəʳ, ⓊⓈ ˈɑː.t̬oʊˌmeɪ.kɚ, ˈɔː- **-s** -z

automat, A~® ˈɔː.tə.mæt, ⓊⓈ ˈɑː.t̬ə-, ˈɔː-

auto|mate ˈɔː.tə|.meɪt, ⓊⓈ ˈɑː.t̬ə-, ˈɔː- **-mates** -meɪts **-mating** -meɪ.tɪŋ, ⓊⓈ -meɪ.t̬ɪŋ **-mated** -meɪ.tɪd, ⓊⓈ -meɪ.t̬ɪd

automatic ˌɔː.təˈmæt.ɪk, ⓊⓈ ˌɑː.t̬əˈmæt̬-, ˌɔː- **-al** -ᵊl **-ally** -ᵊl.i, -li *stress shift, see compound:* ˌ**automatic** ˈ**pilot**

automation ˌɔː.təˈmeɪ.ʃᵊn, ⓊⓈ ˌɑː.t̬əˈ-, ˌɔː-

automat|ism ɔːˈtɒm.ə.t|ɪ.zᵊm, ⓊⓈ ɑːˈtɑː.mə.t̬|ɪ-, ɔː- **-ist/s** -ɪst/s

automat|on ɔːˈtɒm.ə.t|ᵊn, ⓊⓈ ɑːˈtɑː.mə-, ɔː-, -t|ɑːn **-ons** -ᵊnz, ⓊⓈ -ᵊnz, -ɑːnz **-a** -ə

automobile ˈɔː.tə.məʊ.biːl, ˌɔː.tə.məʊˈbiːl, ⓊⓈ ˈɑː.t̬ə.moʊ.biːl, ˈɔː-, ˌɑː.t̬ə.moʊˈbiːl, ˌɔː-, ˌɑː.t̬əˈmoʊ-, ˈɔː- **-s** -z

automotive ˌɔː.təˈməʊ.tɪv, ⓊⓈ ˌɑː.t̬əˈmoʊ.t̬ɪv, ˌɔː-

autonomic ˌɔː.təˈnɒm.ɪk, ⓊⓈ ˌɑː.t̬əˈnɑː.mɪk, ˌɔː- *stress shift:* ˌ**autonomic** ˈ**reflex**

autonomous ɔːˈtɒn.ə.məs, ⓊⓈ ɑːˈtɑː.nə-, ɔː-

autonom|y ɔːˈtɒn.ə.m|i, ⓊⓈ ɑːˈtɑː.nə-, ɔː- **-ies** -iz

autonym ˈɔː.tə.nɪm, ⓊⓈ ˈɑː.t̬ə-, ˈɔː- **-s** -z

auto-pilot ˈɔː.təʊˌpaɪ.lət, ⓊⓈ ˈɑː.t̬oʊ-, ˈɔː- **-s** -s

autops|y ˈɔː.tɒp.s|i, -təp-, ɔːˈtɒp.s|i, ⓊⓈ ˈɑː.tɑːp-, ˈɔː-, -t̬əp- **-ies** -iz

autoroute ˈɔː.təʊ.ruːt, ⓊⓈ ˈɑː.t̬oʊ-, ˈɔː-, -raʊt **-s** -s

autosegment ˈɔː.təʊ.seg.mənt, ⓊⓈ ˈɑː.t̬oʊ-, ˈɔː- **-s** -s

autosegmental ˌɔː.təʊ.segˈmen.tᵊl, ⓊⓈ ˌɑː.t̬oʊ.segˈmen.t̬ᵊl, ˌɔː- **-ly** -i

autosug|gestion ˌɔː.təʊ.sə|ˈdʒes.tʃᵊn, -ˈdʒeʃ-, ⓊⓈ ˌɑː.t̬oʊ.səgˈ-, ˌɔː- **-gestive** -ˈdʒes.tɪv

autotroph ˈɔː.təʊ.trɒf, ⓊⓈ ˈɑː.t̬oʊ.trɑːf, ˈɔː-, -troʊf

autotyp|e ˈɔː.təʊ.taɪp, ⓊⓈ ˈɑː.t̬oʊ-, ˈɔː- **-es** -s **-ing** -ɪŋ **-ed** -t

autotypography ˌɔː.təʊ.taɪˈpɒg.rə.fi, ⓊⓈ ˌɑː.t̬oʊ.taɪˈpɑː.grə-, ˌɔː-

autoworker ˈɔː.təʊˌwɜː.kəʳ, ⓊⓈ ˈɑː.t̬oʊˌwɝː.kɚ, ˈɔː- **-s** -z

autumn, A~ ˈɔː.təm, ⓊⓈ ˈɑː.t̬əm, ˈɔː- **-s** -z

autumnal ɔːˈtʌm.nᵊl, ⓊⓈ ɑː-, ɔː- **-ly** -i

Auvergne əʊˈveən, -ˈvɜːn, ⓊⓈ oʊˈvern, -ˈvɝːn

Auxerre əʊˈseəʳ, əʊkˈseəʳ, ⓊⓈ oʊˈser

auxiliar|y ɔːgˈzɪl.i.əʳ|.i, ɔːkˈsɪl-, -jᵊr|.i, ⓊⓈ ɑːgˈzɪl.jᵊr.i, ɔːg-, ˈ-i.er|.i **-ies** -iz

auxin ˈɔːk.sɪn, ⓊⓈ ˈɑːk-, ˈɔːk-

AV ˌeɪˈviː

Ava ˈɑː.və, ˈeɪ.və, ⓊⓈ ˈeɪ-

avail əˈveɪl **-s** -z **-ing/ly** -ɪŋ/li **-ed** -d

availability əˌveɪ.ləˈbɪl.ə.ti, -ɪ.ti, ⓊⓈ -ə.t̬i

availab|le əˈveɪ.lə.b|ᵊl **-ly** -li **-leness** -ᵊl.nəs, -nɪs

avalanch|e ˈæv.ᵊl.ɑːntʃ, ⓊⓈ -æntʃ **-es** -ɪz

Avalon ˈæv.ᵊl.ɒn, ⓊⓈ -ə.lɑːn

avant-courier ˌæv.ɑ̃ːŋˈkʊr.i.eɪ, ⓊⓈ ˌɑː.vɑːnt-, ˌæv.ɑːnt- **-s** -z

avant-garde ˌæv.ɑ̃ːŋˈgɑːd, ⓊⓈ ˌɑː.vɑːntˈgɑːrd, ˌæv.ɑːnt-; ⓊⓈ əˌvɑːnt-

avarice ˈæv.ᵊr.ɪs

avaricious ˌæv.ᵊrˈɪʃ.əs, ⓊⓈ -əˈrɪʃ- **-ly** -li **-ness** -nəs, -nɪs

avast əˈvɑːst, ⓊⓈ əˈvæst

avatar ˈæv.ə.tɑːʳ, ˈ---, ⓊⓈ ˈæv.ə.tɑːr **-s** -z

avaunt əˈvɔːnt, ⓊⓈ -ˈvɑːnt, -ˈvɔːnt

AVC ˌeɪ.viːˈsiː

ave *prayer:* ˈɑː.veɪ, -viː **-s** -z

Ave. (abbrev. for **avenue**) ˈæv.ə.njuː, ˈ-ɪ-, æv, ⓊⓈ ˈæv.ə.nuː, ˈ-ɪ-, -njuː

Avebury ˈeɪv.bᵊr.i, ⓊⓈ -ber-, -bɚ-

Aveley ˈeɪv.li

Aveline ˈæv.ə.laɪn, -liːn

Aveling ˈeɪv.lɪŋ

Ave Maria ˌɑː.veɪ.məˈriː.ə, -viː- **-s** -z

Ave Maria Lane ˌɑː.vi.mə.riː.əˈleɪn; *formerly:* ˌeɪ.vi.məˌraɪ.əˈleɪn

aveng|e əˈvendʒ **-es** -ɪz **-ing** -ɪŋ **-ed** -d **-er/s** -əʳ/z, ⓊⓈ -ɚ/z **-eful** -fʊl

avenue ˈæv.ə.njuː, ˈ-ɪ-, ⓊⓈ -nuː, -njuː **-s** -z

aver əˈvɜːʳ, ⓊⓈ -ˈvɝː **-s** -z **-ring** -ɪŋ **-red** -d **-ment/s** -mənt/s

averag|e ˈæv.ᵊr.ɪdʒ, ˈ-rɪdʒ **-es** -ɪz **-ing** -ɪŋ **-ed** -d **-ely** -li

averse əˈvɜːs, ⓊⓈ -ˈvɝːs **-ly** -li **-ness** -nəs, -nɪs

aversion əˈvɜː.ʃᵊn, -ʒᵊn, ⓊⓈ -ˈvɝː.ʒᵊn, -ʃᵊn **-s** -z

a|vert ə|ˈvɜːt, ⓊⓈ -ˈvɝːt **-verts** -ˈvɜːts, ⓊⓈ -ˈvɝːts **-verting** -ˈvɜː.tɪŋ, ⓊⓈ -ˈvɝː.t̬ɪŋ **-verted** -ˈvɜː.tɪd, ⓊⓈ -ˈvɝː.t̬ɪd **-vertible** -ˈvɜː.tə.bᵊl, -tɪ-, ⓊⓈ -ˈvɝː.t̬ə.bᵊl

Avery ˈeɪ.vᵊr.i, ˈeɪv.ri

Aves ˈeɪ.viːz

Avesta əˈves.tə

avgolemono ˌæv.gəʊˈlem.ə.nəʊ, ⓊⓈ ˌɑːv.goʊˈlem.ə.noʊ

Avia® ˈeɪ.vi.ə, ⓊⓈ əˈviː-

avian ˈeɪ.vi.ən **-s** -z

aviarist ˈeɪ.vi.ᵊr.ɪst **-s** -s

aviar|y ˈeɪ.vi.ᵊr|.i, ⓊⓈ -er- **-ies** -iz

aviation ˌeɪ.viˈeɪ.ʃᵊn

aviator ˈeɪ.vi.eɪ.təʳ, ⓊⓈ -t̬ɚ **-s** -z

Avice ˈeɪ.vɪs

Avicenna ˌæv.ɪˈsen.ə

aviculture ˈeɪ.vɪˌkʌl.tʃəʳ, ˈæv.ɪ-, ⓊⓈ -tʃɚ

avid ˈæv.ɪd **-ly** -li

avidity əˈvɪd.ə.ti, ævˈɪd-, -ɪ.ti, ⓊⓈ -ə.t̬i

Aviemore ˈæv.i.mɔːʳ, ˌ--ˈ-, ⓊⓈ ˌæv.iˈmɔːr

Avignon ˈæv.i.njɔ̃ːŋ, ⓊⓈ ˌæv.iːˈnjõʊn, -ˈnjɑːn

avionic ˌeɪ.viˈɒn.ɪk, ⓊⓈ -ˈɑː.nɪk **-s** -s *stress shift:* ˌ**avionic** ˈ**system**

Avis® ˈeɪ.vɪs

Aviva® əˈviː.və

Avoca əˈvəʊ.kə, ⓊⓈ -ˈvoʊ-

avocado ˌæv.əˈkɑː.dəʊ, ⓊⓈ -doʊ, ɑː.vəˈ- **-s** -z

avocation ˌæv.əʊˈkeɪ.ʃᵊn, ⓊⓈ -əˈ-, -oʊˈ- **-s** -z

avocet ˈæv.əʊ.set, ⓊⓈ ˈ-ə- **-s** -s

Avoch ɔːk, ɔːx

Avogadro ˌæv.əʊˈgæd.rəʊ, -ˈgɑː.drəʊ, ⓊⓈ -əˈgɑː.droʊ, ˌɑː.vəˈ-, -ˈgæd.roʊ

avoid əˈvɔɪd **-s** -z **-ing** -ɪŋ **-ed** -ɪd

avoidab|le əˈvɔɪ.də.b|ᵊl **-ly** -li

avoidanc|e əˈvɔɪ.dᵊnts **-es** -ɪz

avoirdupois ˌæv.ə.dəˈpɔɪz, ˌæv.wɑː.djuˈpwɑː, ⓊⓈ ˌæv.ɚ.dəˈpɔɪz, ˈæv.ɚ.dəˌpɔɪz

Avon *in Avon:* ˈeɪ.vᵊn, (US) -vɑːn, -vᵊn, ˈæv.ᵊn *in Devon:* ˈæv.ᵊn *in Aberdeenshire:* ɑːn *trademark:* ˈeɪ.vɒn, (US) -vɑːn
Avondale ˈeɪ.vᵊn.deɪl, (US) ˈeɪ.vᵊn-, ˈæv.ᵊn-
Avonmouth ˈeɪ.vᵊn.maʊθ, -vᵊm-, (US) -vᵊn-
Avory ˈeɪ.vᵊr.i, (US) ˈeɪv.ri
avow əˈvaʊ **-s** -z **-ing** -ɪŋ **-ed** -d **-edly** -ɪd.li, -əd-
avowal əˈvaʊ.əl **-s** -z
Avril ˈæv.rɪl, -rəl
avuncular əˈvʌŋ.kjə.ləʳ, -kjʊ-, (US) -lɚ **-ly** -li
AWACS ˈeɪ.wæks
a|wait ə|ˈweɪt **-waits** -ˈweɪts **-waiting** -ˈweɪ.tɪŋ, (US) -ˈweɪ.t̬ɪŋ **-waited** -ˈweɪ.tɪd, (US) -ˈweɪ.t̬ɪd
awak|e əˈweɪk **-es** -s **-ing** -ɪŋ **-ed** -t **awoke** əˈwəʊk, (US) -ˈwoʊk
awaken əˈweɪ.kᵊn **-s** -z **-ing/s** -ɪŋ/z **-ed** -d **-ment/s** -mənt/s
awakening n əˈweɪ.kᵊn.ɪŋ **-s** -z
award əˈwɔːd, (US) -ˈwɔːrd **-s** -z **-ing** -ɪŋ **-ed** -ɪd **-able** -ə.bᵊl
award-winning əˈwɔːdˌwɪn.ɪŋ, (US) -ˈwɔːrdˌ-
aware əˈweəʳ, (US) -ˈwer **-ness** -nəs, -nɪs
awash əˈwɒʃ, (US) -ˈwɑːʃ, -ˈwɔːʃ
away əˈweɪ
aw|e, A~ ɔː, (US) ɑː, ɔː **-es** -z **-(e)ing** -ɪŋ **-ed** -d
awe-inspiring ˈɔː.ɪn.spaɪə.rɪŋ, (US) ˈɑː-, ˈɔː- **-ly** -li
aweless ˈɔː.ləs, -lɪs, (US) ˈɑː-, ˈɔː- **-ness** -nəs, -nɪs
awesome ˈɔː.səm, (US) ˈɑː-, ˈɔː- **-ly** -li **-ness** -nəs, -nɪs
awe-stricken ˈɔːˌstrɪk.ᵊn, (US) ˈɑː-, ˈɔː-
awe-struck ˈɔː.strʌk, (US) ˈɑː-, ˈɔː-
awful *terrible:* ˈɔː.fᵊl, -fʊl, (US) ˈɑː-, ˈɔː- *inspiring awe:* ˈɔː.fʊl, (US) ˈɑː-, ˈɔː- **-ness** -nəs, -nɪs
awfully ˈɔː.fᵊl.i, -fʊl-, (US) ˈɑː-, ˈɔː-
awhile əˈ*h*waɪl
awkward ˈɔː.kwəd, (US) ˈɑː.kwɚd, ˈɔː- **-est** -ɪst, -əst **-ly** -li **-ness** -nəs, -nɪs **-ish** -ɪʃ
awl ɔːl, (US) ɔːl, ɑːl **-s** -z
awn ɔːn, (US) ɑːn, ɔːn **-s** -z **-ed** -d
awning ˈɔː.nɪŋ, (US) ˈɑː-, ˈɔː- **-s** -z
awoke (from **awake**) əˈwəʊk, (US) -ˈwoʊk
awoken əˈwəʊ.kᵊn, (US) -ˈwoʊ-
AWOL, Awol ˈeɪ.wɒl, (US) -wɑːl
Awooner əˈwuː.nəʳ, (US) -nɚ
awry əˈraɪ
aw-shucks ɔːˈʃʌks, (US) ɑːˈ-, ɔːˈ-
Axa® ˈæk.sə
ax|e, ax æks **-es** -ɪz **-ing** -ɪŋ **-ed** -t **have an ˈaxe to ˌgrind**
axel, A~ ˈæk.sᵊl **-s** -z
axes (plural of **axis**) ˈæk.siːz
axes (plural of **axe**) ˈæk.sɪz
Axholm(e) ˈæks.*h*əʊm, -əm, (US) -*h*oʊm
axial ˈæk.si.əl **-ly** -i
axil ˈæk.sɪl, -sᵊl **-s** -z
axill|a ækˈsɪl.|ə **-ae** -iː **-as** -əz **-ar** -əʳ, (US) -ɚ **-ary** -ᵊr.i
axiom ˈæk.si.əm **-s** -z
axiomatic ˌæk.si.əˈmæt.ɪk, (US) -ˈmæt̬- **-al** -ᵊl **-ally** -ᵊl.i, -li
ax|is ˈæk.s|ɪs **-es** -iːz
axle ˈæk.sᵊl **-s** -z **-d** -d
axle-tree ˈæk.sᵊl.triː **-s** -z
Axminster ˈæks.mɪn.stəʳ, (US) -stɚ **-s** -z
axolotl ˈæk.sə.lɒt.ᵊl, (US) ˈæk.sə.lɑː.t̬ᵊl **-s** -z
axon ˈæk.sɒn, (US) -sɑːn **-s** -z
ay aɪ, eɪ **-es** -z
ayah ˈaɪ.ə, ˈɑː.jə **-s** -z
ayatollah ˌaɪ.əˈtɒl.ə, (US) -ˈtoʊ.lə; (US) -toʊˈlɑː **-s** -z
Ayckbourn ˈeɪk.bɔːn, (US) -bɔːrn
Aycliffe ˈeɪ.klɪf
aye *ever:* eɪ *yes:* aɪ **-s** -z
aye-aye ˈaɪ.aɪ **-s** -z
Ayenbite of Inwyt ˌeɪ.ən.baɪt.əvˈɪn.wɪt
Ayer eəʳ, (US) er
Ayers eəz, (US) erz **ˌAyers ˈRock**
Ayesha aɪˈiː.ʃə
Aylesbury ˈeɪlz.bᵊr.i, (US) -ber-, -bɚ-
Aylesford ˈeɪlz.fəd, ˈeɪls-, (US) -fɚd
Ayling ˈeɪ.lɪŋ
Aylmer ˈeɪl.məʳ, (US) -mɚ
Aylsham ˈeɪl.ʃəm
Aylward ˈeɪl.wəd, (US) -wɚd
Aylwin ˈeɪl.wɪn
Aymer ˈeɪ.məʳ, (US) -mɚ
Ayot ˈeɪ.ət
Ayr eəʳ, (US) er **-shire** -ʃəʳ, -ʃɪəʳ, (US) -ʃɚ, -ʃɪr
Ayre eəʳ, (US) er **-s** -z
Ayrton ˈeə.tᵊn, (US) ˈer-
Ayscough ˈæs.kə, ˈæsk.juː, ˈeɪ.skəf, ˈeɪz.kɒf, (US) ˈæs.kjuː
Ayscue ˈeɪ.skjuː, (US) ˈæs.kjuː
Ayton, Aytoun ˈeɪ.tᵊn
ayurved|a ˌaɪ.ʊəˈveɪ.d|ə, ɑː-, -ˈviː-, (US) ˌɑː.jʊrˈveɪ- **-ic** -ɪk
A-Z ˌeɪ.təˈzed, (US) -t̬əˈziː
azalea əˈzeɪ.li.ə, (US) -ˈzeɪl.jə **-s** -z
Azani|a əˈzeɪ.ni|.ə **-an/s** -ən/z
Azariah ˌæz.əˈraɪ.ə
Azerbaijan ˌæz.ə.baɪˈdʒɑːn, -ˈʒɑːn, (US) ˌɑː.zɚ-, ˌæz.ɚ- **-i/s** -i/z
azimuth ˈæz.ɪ.məθ, ˈ-ə- **-s** -s
Aziz əˈziːz, -ˈzɪz
Aznavour ˈæz.nə.vɔːʳ, -vʊəʳ, (US) ˌ--ˈvɔːr, -ˈvʊr
azodye ˈeɪ.zəʊ.daɪ, ˈæz.əʊ-, (US) -zoʊ- **-s** -z
azoic əˈzəʊ.ɪk, æzˈəʊ-, eɪˈzəʊ-, (US) əˈzoʊ-, eɪ-
Azores əˈzɔːz, (US) ˈeɪ.zɔːrz; (US) əˈzɔːrz

> Note: It is customary to pronounce /əˈzɔː.rɪz/ (US) /-ˈzɔːr.ɪz/ (or /-ˈzɔː.rez/ (US) /-ˈzɔːr.ez/) in reciting Tennyson's poem 'The Revenge'.

azote əˈzəʊt, æzˈəʊt; ˈæz.əʊt, ˈeɪ.zəʊt, (US) ˈæz.oʊt, ˈeɪ.zoʊt; (US) əˈzoʊt
azotic əˈzɒt.ɪk, æzˈɒt-, eɪˈzɒt-, (US) əˈzɑː.t̬ɪk
Azov ˈɑː.zɒv, ˈeɪ-, ˈæz.ɒv, (US) ˈɑː.zɑːf, ˈeɪ-, ˈæz.ɑːf, -ɔːf
AZT ˌeɪ.zedˈtiː, (US) -ziːˈ-
Aztec ˈæz.tek **-s** -s
azure ˈæz.jʊəʳ, ˈeɪ.zjʊəʳ, ˈæʒ.əʳ, ˈeɪ.ʒəʳ, əˈzjʊəʳ, əˈzjʊəʳ, (US) ˈæʒ.ɚ, ˈeɪ.ʒɚ
azygous əˈzaɪ.gəs, æzˈaɪ-, ˌeɪˈzaɪ-, (US) ˌeɪˈzaɪ-

B

Pronouncing the letter B

The consonant **b** is most often realized as /b/, e.g.:

boy	bɔɪ
grab	græb

In addition

b can be silent, or have a zero realization. There are two combinations in which this can occur: **bt** and **mb**.

bt is either word-medial or word-final, e.g.:

doubt	daʊt
subtle	ˈsʌt.ᵊl © ˈsʌṭ.ᵊl

Words containing **mb** in which **b** is silent have the **mb** in word-final position, except where an inflection is added, e.g.:

bomb	bɒm © bɑːm
bombing	ˈbɒm.ɪŋ © ˈbɑː.mɪŋ

However, the appearance of **bt** and **mb** does not necessarily indicate a silent **b**. In the case of **mb**, the **b** is pronounced if it occurs inside a morpheme or unit of meaning. Compare:

number = arithmetical value	ˈnʌm.bəʳ © ˈnʌm.bɚ
number = comparative of *numb*	ˈnʌm.əʳ © ˈnʌm.ɚ

For **bt**, the **b** is not silent if part of a prefix. Compare:

subtract	səbˈtrækt
subtle	ˈsʌt.ᵊl © ˈsʌṭ.l

b, B biː -ˈs -z
B2B ˌbiː.təˈbiː, © -ṭə-
B2C ˌbiː.təˈsiː, © -ṭə-
ba beɪ -s -z
BA ˌbiːˈeɪ
baa bɑː, © bæ, bɑː -s -z -ing -ɪŋ -ed -d
Baader-Meinhof ˌbɑː.dəˈmaɪn.hɒf, © -dɚˈmaɪn.hɑːf, -hoʊf
Baal ˈbeɪ.ᵊl; *Jewish pronunciation:* bɑːl
BAAL bɑːl
baa-lamb ˈbɑː.læm, © ˈbɑː-, ˈbæ- -s -z
baas n *master:* bɑːs -es -ɪz
baas (from **baa**) bɑːz, © bæz, bɑːz
baaskaap ˈbɑːs.kæp, © -kɑːp
Ba'ath bɑːθ, © bɑːθ, bæθ -ist/s -ɪst/s
Bab bɑːb
baba ˈbɑː.bɑː, -bə -s -z
Babar ˈbɑː.bɑːʳ, © bəˈbɑːr; © ˈbæb.ɑːr, ˈbɑː.bɑːr
Babbage ˈbæb.ɪdʒ
babbit, B~ ˈbæb.ɪt -s -s
babbl|e ˈbæb.ᵊl -es -z -ing -ɪŋ, ˈbæb.lɪŋ -ed -d -er/s -əʳ/z, ˈ-ləʳ/z, © ˈ-ᵊl.ɚ/z, ˈ-lɚ/z -ement/s -mənt/s
Babcock ˈbæb.kɒk, © -kɑːk
babe beɪb -s -z
babel, B~ ˈbeɪ.bᵊl, © ˈbeɪ-, ˈbæb.ᵊl -s -z
Babington ˈbæb.ɪŋ.tən
Bab|ism ˈbɑː.b|ɪ.zᵊm -ist/s -ɪst/s -ite -aɪt
Babi Yar ˌbɑː.biˈjɑːʳ, © -ˈjɑːr *stress shift:* ˌ**Babi Yar** ˈ**massacre**
babka ˈbɑːb.kə -s -z
baboo, B~ ˈbɑː.buː -s -z
baboon bəˈbuːn, © bæbˈuːn, bəˈbuːn -s -z
Babs bæbz
babu, B~ ˈbɑː.buː -s -z
babushka bæbˈuːʃ.kə, bəˈbuːʃ-, -ˈbʊʃ- -s -z
bab|y, B~ ˈbeɪ.b|i -ies -iz -ying -i.ɪŋ -ied -id ˈ**baby** ˌ**boom**; ˈ**baby** ˌ**boomer**; ˈ**baby** ˌ**carriage**; ˌ**baby** ˈ**grand**; ˈ**baby** ˌ**talk**; **throw the** ˌ**baby out with the** ˈ**bath water**
Babycham® ˈbeɪ.bi.ʃæm
Babygro® ˈbeɪ.bi.grəʊ, © -groʊ -s -z
babyhood ˈbeɪ.bi.hʊd
babyish ˈbeɪ.bi.ɪʃ -ly -li -ness -nəs, -nɪs
Babylon ˈbæb.ɪ.lɒn, -ə-, -lən, © -lɑːn
Babyloni|a ˌbæb.ɪˈləʊ.ni|.ə, -əˈ-, © -ˈloʊ- -an/s -ən/z
baby|sit ˈbei.bi|.sɪt -sitter/s -ˌsɪt.əʳ/z, © -ˌsɪṭ.ɚ/z -sits -sɪts -sitting -ˌsɪt.ɪŋ, © -ˌsɪṭ.ɪŋ -sat -sæt
Bacall bəˈkɔːl, © -ˈkɔːl, -ˈkɑːl
Bacardi® bəˈkɑː.di, © -ˈkɑːr- -s -z
baccalaureate ˌbæk.əˈlɔː.ri.ət, -ɪt, © -ˈlɔːr.i-, -ɪt -s -s
baccarat ˈbæk.ə.rɑː, ˌ--ˈ-, © ˌbæk.əˈrɑː, ˌbɑː.kəˈ-, ˈ---
Bacchae ˈbæk.iː
bacchanal ˈbæk.ə.nᵊl; ˌbæk.əˈnæl, © ˌbæk.əˈnæl -s -z
bacchanali|a ˌbæk.əˈneɪ.li|.ə, © -jə -an/s -ən/z
bacchant ˈbæk.ənt -s -s
bacchante bəˈkæn.ti, bəˈkænt, © -ˈkænt; © -ˈkæn.ti, -ˈkɑːn- -s -z, -s
bacchic ˈbæk.ɪk
Bacchus ˈbæk.əs, © ˈbæk.əs, ˈbɑː.kəs
Bacchylides bækˈɪl.ɪ.diːz, bəˈkɪl-
baccy ˈbæk.i
bach *Welsh term of address:* bɑːk; *as if Welsh:* bɑːx; © bɑːk
Bach *German composer:* bɑːk; *as if German:* bɑːx; © bɑːk *English surname:* beɪtʃ, bætʃ
Bacharach ˈbæk.ə.ræk
Bache beɪtʃ
bachelor, B~ ˈbætʃ.ᵊl.əʳ, -ɪ.ləʳ, © -ᵊl.ɚ -s -z -hood -hʊd -ship -ʃɪp ˌ**Bachelor of** ˈ**Arts**; ˌ**Bachelor of** ˈ**Science**; ˈ**bachelor** ˌ**girl**
baciliform bəˈsɪl.ɪ.fɔːm, bæsˈɪl-, © bəˈsɪl.ə.fɔːrm
bacillary bəˈsɪl.ᵊr.i, bæsˈɪl-, © bəˈsɪl-
bacill|us bəˈsɪl.|əs, bæsˈɪl-, © bəˈsɪl- -i -aɪ, -iː
back, B~ bæk -s -s -ing -ɪŋ -ed -t ˈ**Back** ˌ**Bay**; ˌ**back** ˈ**door** *stress shift:* ˌ**back door** ˈ**deal** ˌ**back** ˈ**garden**; ˌ**back of be**ˈ**yond**; ˌ**back** ˈ**seat**; ˌ**back seat** ˈ**driver**; ˈ**back** ˌ**talk**; ˌ**back** ˈ**yard** *stress shift:* ˌ**back yard** ˈ**special**; **have one's** ˌ**back to the** ˈ**wall**; ˌ**put someone's** ˈ**back up**; ˌ**turn one's** ˈ**back on someone/ something**
backache ˈbæk.eɪk -s -s
backbeat ˈbæk.biːt
backbench ˌbækˈbentʃ -es -ɪz *stress shift:* ˌ**backbench** ˈ**speaker**
backbencher ˌbækˈben.tʃəʳ, © -tʃɚ -s -z *stress shift:* ˌ**backbencher** ˈ**vote**
backbi|ting ˈbækˌbaɪ|.tɪŋ, © -ṭɪŋ -ter/s -təʳ/z, © -ṭɚ/z
backboard ˈbæk.bɔːd, © -bɔːrd -s -z
backbone ˈbæk.bəʊn, © -boʊn -s -z
backbreaker ˈbækˌbreɪ.kəʳ, © -kɚ -s -z
backbreaking ˈbækˌbreɪ.kɪŋ -ly -li
backchat ˈbæk.tʃæt
back|cloth ˈbæk|.klɒθ, © -klɑːθ

B

-cloths -klɒθs, -klɒðz, US -klɑːθs, -klɑːðz
backcomb ˈbæk.kəʊm, ˌ-ˈ-, US ˈbæk.koʊm -s -z -ing -ɪŋ -ed -d
back|date ˌbækˈdeɪt, US ˈbæk|.deɪt -dates -ˈdeɪts, US -deɪts -dating -ˈdeɪ.tɪŋ, US -deɪ.t̬ɪŋ -dated -ˈdeɪ.tɪd, US -deɪ.t̬ɪd *stress shift:* **ˌbackdated ˈcheque**
backdrop ˈbæk.drɒp, US -drɑːp -s -s
backer ˈbæk.əʳ, US -ɚ -s -z
backfield ˈbæk.fiːld
backfill ˈbæk.fɪl -s -z -ing -ɪŋ -ed -d
backfir|e ˌbækˈfaɪəʳ, -ˈfaɪ.əʳ, ˈ--, US ˌbækˈfaɪ.ɚ, ˈ-- -es -z -ing -ɪŋ -ed -d
back-formation ˈbæk.fɔːˌmeɪ.ʃən, US -fɔːrˌ- -s -z
backgammon ˈbæk.gæm.ən, ˌ-ˈ--
background ˈbæk.graʊnd -s -z **ˈbackground ˌnoise; ˌbackground ˈnoise** US **ˈbackground ˌnoise**
backhand ˈbæk.hænd -s -z
backhanded ˌbækˈhænd.ɪd -ly -li -ness -nəs, -nɪs *stress shift, see compound:* **ˌbackhanded ˈcompliment**
backhander ˌbækˈhænd.əʳ, US -ɚ -z -z
backhoe ˈbæk.həʊ, US -hoʊ -s -z
Backhouse ˈbæk.haʊs
backing ˈbæk.ɪŋ -s -z
backlash ˈbæk.læʃ
backless ˈbæk.ləs, -lɪs
back|light ˈbæk|.laɪt -lights -laɪts -lighting -ˌlaɪ.tɪŋ, US -ˌlaɪ.t̬ɪŋ -lighted -ˌlaɪ.tɪd, US -ˌlaɪ.t̬ɪd **backlit** ˈbæk.lɪt
backlist ˈbæk.lɪst -s -s -ing -ɪŋ -ed -ɪd
backlog ˈbæk.lɒg, US -lɑːg, -lɔːg -s -z
backpack ˈbæk.pæk -s -s -ing -ɪŋ -ed -d -er/s -əʳ/z, US -ɚ/z
back-pedal ˌbækˈped.əl, ˈ-ˌ--, US ˈbæk.ped- -s -z -(l)ing -ɪŋ -(l)ed -d
backrest ˈbæk.rest -s -s
backroom ˌbækˈrʊm, -ˈruːm, ˈ--, US ˌbækˈruːm, -ˈrʊm, ˈ-- **ˈbackroom ˌboy**
backscratcher ˈbækˌskrætʃ.əʳ, US -ɚ -s -z
backsheesh, backshish ˌbækˈʃiːʃ, ˈ--
backside ˌbækˈsaɪd, ˈ--, US ˈ-- -s -z
backslap ˈbæk.slæp -s -s -ping -ɪŋ -ped -t -per/s -əʳ/z, US -ɚ/z
backslash ˈbæk.slæʃ -es -ɪz
backslid|e ˈbæk.slaɪd -es -z -ing -ɪŋ -er/s -əʳ/z, US -ɚ/z **backslid** ˈbæk.slɪd
backspac|e ˈbæk.speɪs -es -ɪz -ing -ɪŋ -ed -t
backspin ˈbæk.spɪn
back-stabb|er ˈbækˌstæb|.əʳ, US -ɚ -ers -əz, US -ɚz -ing -ɪŋ
backstage ˌbækˈsteɪdʒ *stress shift:* **ˌbackstage ˈpass**
backstairs ˌbækˈsteəz, US ˌbækˈsterz *stress shift:* **ˌbackstairs ˈgossip**
backstay ˈbæk.steɪ -s -z
backstitch ˈbæk.stɪtʃ -es -ɪz -ing -ɪŋ -ed -t
backstop ˈbæk.stɒp, US -stɑːp -s -s -ping -ɪŋ -ped -t
backstrap ˈbæk.stræp -s -s
backstreet ˈbæk.striːt -s -s
backstroke ˈbæk.strəʊk, US -stroʊk
back-to-back ˌbæk.təˈbæk *stress shift:* **ˌback-to-back ˈhouse**
backtrack ˈbæk.træk -s -s -ing -ɪŋ -ed -t
backup ˈbæk.ʌp -s -s
backward ˈbæk.wəd, US -wɚd -ly -li -ness -nəs, -nɪs -s -z **ˌbend over ˈbackwards**
backwash ˈbæk.wɒʃ, US -wɑːʃ, -wɔːʃ -es -ɪz
backwater ˈbækˌwɔː.təʳ, US -ˌwɑː.t̬ɚ, -ˌwɔː- -s -z
backwoods ˈbæk.wʊdz
backwoods|man ˌbækˈwʊdz|.mən, ˈ-ˌ-- -men -mən, -men
backyard ˌbækˈjɑːd, US -jɑːrd *stress shift:* **ˌbackyard ˈwrestling**
bacon, B~ ˈbeɪ.kən **ˌbring home the ˈbacon**
Baconian beɪˈkəʊ.ni.ən, bəˈkəʊ-, US -ˈkoʊ- -s -z
bacteria bækˈtɪə.ri.ə, US bækˈtɪr.i.ə
bacterial bækˈtɪə.ri.əl, US bækˈtɪr.i.əl
bacteriological bækˌtɪə.ri.əˈlɒdʒ.ɪ.kəl, US -ˌtɪr.i.əˈlɑː.dʒɪ-
bacteriolog|y bækˌtɪə.riˈɒl.ə.dʒ|i, US -ˌtɪr.iˈɑː.lə- -ist/s -ɪst/s
bacteriophag|e bækˈtɪə.ri.əʊ.feɪdʒ, US -ˈtɪr.i.ə- -es -ɪz
bacterium bækˈtɪə.ri.əm, US bækˈtɪr.i.əm
Bactri|a ˈbæk.tri|.ə -an/s -ən/z
Bacup ˈbeɪ.kəp
bad bæd **ˌbad ˈblood; ˌbad ˈlanguage; ˌbad ˈnews; ˌbad ˈtemper; go from ˌbad to ˈworse**
Badajoz ˌbæd.əˈhɒs; *as if Spanish:* ˌbæd.əˈxɒθ; US ˌbɑː.dɑːˈhoʊz, -ðɑːˈhoʊθ
badass ˈbæd.æs -ed -t
Badcock ˈbæd.kɒk, US -kɑːk
Baddeley ˈbæd.əl.i
baddie ˈbæd.i -s -z
Baddiel bəˈdɪəl, bædˈɪəl
baddish ˈbæd.ɪʃ
baddly ˈbæd|.i -ies -iz
bade (from **bid**) bæd, beɪd
Badedas® ˈbæd.ɪ.dæs; bəˈdeɪ.dəs
Badel bəˈdel
Baden ˈbɑː.dən
Baden-Powell ˌbeɪ.dənˈpaʊ.əl, -ˈpəʊ.əl, -ˈpəʊ.ɪl, -ˈpəʊ.el, US -ˈpoʊ.əl, -ˈpaʊ.əl
Baden-Württemberg ˌbɑː.dənˈvɜː.təm.bɜːg, US -ˈvɝː.təm.bɝːg
Bader ˈbɑː.dəʳ, ˈbeɪ-, US -dɚ
badg|e bædʒ -es -ɪz -ing -ɪŋ -ed -d
badg|er, B~ ˈbædʒ|.əʳ, US -ɚ -ers -əz, US -ɚz -ering -ər.ɪŋ -ered -əd, US -ɚd
badger-baiting ˈbædʒ.əˌbeɪ.tɪŋ, US -ɚˌbeɪ.t̬ɪŋ
badger-dog ˈbædʒ.ə.dɒg, US -ɚ.dɑːg, -dɔːg -s -z
Bad Godesberg ˌbɑːdˈgəʊ.dəz.bɜːg, -ˈgəʊdz-, -beəg, US -ˈgoʊ.dəz.bɝːg
Badham ˈbæd.əm
badinage ˈbæd.ɪ.nɑːʒ, -nɑːdʒ, ˌ--ˈ-
badlands ˈbæd.lændz
badly ˈbæd.li
badly-off ˌbæd.liˈɒf, US -ˈɑːf *stress shift:* **ˌbadly-off ˈstudent**
badminton, B~ ˈbæd.mɪn.tən
bad-mouth ˈbæd.maʊθ -s -z -ing -ɪŋ -ed -d
badness ˈbæd.nəs, -nɪs
Badoit® ˈbæd.wɑː, -ˈ-, US bɑːˈdwɑː
bad-tempered ˌbædˈtem.pəd, US ˈbædˌtem.pɚd -ly -li -ness -nəs, -nɪs *stress shift, British only:* **ˌbad-tempered ˈperson**
Baedeker ˈbeɪ.dek.əʳ, ˈbaɪ-, -dɪ.kəʳ, US ˈbeɪ.də.kɚ, ˈbaɪ- -s -z
Baez ˈbaɪ.ez, -ˈ-
Baffin ˈbæf.ɪn **ˌBaffin ˈBay; ˌBaffin ˈIsland**
baffl|e ˈbæf.əl -es -z -ing/ly -ɪŋ/li, ˈ-lɪŋ -ed -d -er/s -əʳ/z, ˈ-ləʳ/z, US ˈ-əl.ɚ/z, ˈ-lɚ/z -ement -mənt
BAFTA, Bafta ˈbæf.tə
bag bæg -s -z -ging -ɪŋ -ged -d -ger/s -gəʳ/z, US -gɚ/z **ˈbag ˌlady; ˌbag of ˈbones**
bagatelle ˌbæg.əˈtel -s -z
Bagdad *in Iraq:* ˌbægˈdæd, ˈ--, US ˈbæg.dæd *in Tasmania, Florida:* ˈbæg.dæd
Bagehot ˈbædʒ.ət, ˈbæg-
bagel ˈbeɪ.gəl -s -z
bag-for-life ˌbæg.fəˈlaɪf, US -fɚ ˈ-
bagful ˈbæg.fʊl -s -z
baggag|e ˈbæg.ɪdʒ -es -ɪz
Baggie® ˈbæg.i -s -z
bagg|y ˈbæg.|i -ier -i.əʳ, US -i.ɚ -iest -i.ɪst, -i.əst -ily -əl.i, -ɪ.li -iness -ɪ.nəs, -ɪ.nɪs
Baghdad bægˈdæd, ˈ--, US ˈbæg.dæd
Bagheera bægˈɪə.rə, bəˈgɪə-, US bəˈgɪr.ə
Bagley ˈbæg.li
Bagnall ˈbæg.nəl, -nɔːl
Bagnell ˈbæg.nəl
bagnio ˈbæn.jəʊ, ˈbɑː.njəʊ, US ˈbɑː.njoʊ, ˈbæn.joʊ -s -z
Bagnold ˈbæg.nəʊld, US -noʊld
Bagot ˈbæg.ət
bagpip|e ˈbæg.paɪp -es -s -er/s -əʳ/z, US -ɚ/z
bags bægz -es -ɪz -ing -ɪŋ -ed -d
Bagshaw(e) ˈbæg.ʃɔː, US -ʃɑː, -ʃɔː
Bagshot ˈbæg.ʃɒt, US -ʃɑːt
bags|y ˈbæg.z|i -ies -iz -ing -ɪŋ -ied -id

B

baguette, baguet bæɡˈet, bəˈɡet **-s** -s
Bagworthy ˈbædʒ.ər.i
bah bɑː, (US) bɑː, bæ
bahadur bəˈhɑː.dəʳ, (US) -dɚ **-s** -z
Baha'i bəˈhaɪ, bɑː-, -ˈhɑː.i, -ˈhaɪ.i **-s** -z
Baha|ism bəˈhaɪ|.ɪ.zəm, bɑː-, -ˈhɑː- **-ist/s** -ɪst/s
Bahama bəˈhɑː.mə **-s** -z
Bahamian bəˈheɪ.mi.ən, -ˈhɑː- **-s** -z
Bahasa bəˈhɑː.sə
Bahawalpur bɑːˈhɑː.wəl.pʊəʳ, bə-, (US) -pʊr
Bahia bəˈhiː.ə
Bahrain, Bahrein bɑːˈreɪn **-i** -i
baht bɑːt **-s** -s
baignoire ˈbeɪn.wɑːʳ, (US) benˈwɑːr, beɪn- **-s** -z
Baikal ˈbaɪ.kæl, -kɑːl, -ˈ-
bail beɪl **-s** -z **-ing** -ɪŋ **-ed** -d **-er/s** -əʳ/z, (US) -ɚ/z
bailable ˈbeɪ.lə.bəl
bail-bond ˈbeɪl.bɒnd, -ˈ-, (US) ˈbeɪl.bɑːnd **-s** -z
bail-bonds|man ˈbeɪlˌbɒndz|.mən, (US) -ˌbɑːndz- **-men** -mən
Baildon ˈbeɪl.dən
bailee ˌbeɪˈliː **-s** -z
bailey, B~ ˈbeɪ.li
bailie, B~ ˈbeɪ.li **-s** -z
bailiff ˈbeɪ.lɪf **-s** -s
bailiwick ˈbeɪ.lɪ.wɪk **-s** -s
Baillie ˈbeɪ.li
Baillieu ˈbeɪ.ljuː, (US) ˈbeɪl.juː
Bailly ˈbeɪ.li
bailment ˈbeɪl.mənt **-s** -s
bailout ˈbeɪl.aʊt **-s** -s
Baily ˈbeɪ.li
Bain beɪn
Bainbridge ˈbeɪn.brɪdʒ, ˈbeɪm-, (US) ˈbeɪn-
Baines beɪnz
bain-marie ˌbæn.məˈriː; *as if French:* bæ̃m-; (US) ˌbæn- **-s** -z
Baird beəd, (US) berd
bairn beən, (US) bern **-s** -z
Bairstow ˈbeə.stəʊ, (US) ˈber.stoʊ
bait beɪt **-s** -s **-ing** -ɪŋ, (US) ˈbeɪ.t̬ɪŋ **-ed** -ɪd, (US) ˈbeɪ.t̬ɪd
bai|za ˈbaɪ|.zə, (US) -zɑː **-zas** -zəz
baiz|e beɪz **-es** -ɪz
Baja California ˌbɑː.hɑː.kæl.ɪˈfɔː.njə, (US) -əˈfɔːr-
bak|e beɪk **-es** -s **-ing** -ɪŋ **-ed** -t **ˌbaked Aˈlaska; ˌbaked ˈbeans; ˈbaking ˌpowder; ˈbaking ˌsoda**
bakehou|se ˈbeɪk.haʊ|s **-ses** -zɪz
Bakelite® ˈbeɪ.kəl.aɪt, (US) ˈbeɪ.kə.laɪt, ˈbeɪk.laɪt
baker, B~ ˈbeɪ.kəʳ, (US) -kɚ **-s** -z
Bakerloo ˌbeɪ.kəlˈuː, (US) -kɚˈluː
Bakersfield ˈbeɪ.kəz.fiːld, (US) -kɚz-
baker|y ˈbeɪ.kər|.i **-ies** -iz
Bakewell ˈbeɪk.wel, -wəl
Bakke ˈbɑː.ki
baklava ˈbæk.lə.vɑː, ˈbɑː.klə-; *as if Greek:* ˌ--ˈ- **-s** -z
baksheesh ˌbækˈʃiːʃ, ˈ--
Baku bækˈuː, (US) bɑːˈkuː
Bakunin bəˈkuː.nɪn, bɑː-, (US) bɑːˈkuːn.jɪn, bə-
Bala ˈbæl.ə
balaam, B~ ˈbeɪ.læm, -ləm **-s** -z
balaclava, B~ ˌbæl.əˈklɑː.və, ˌbɑː.ləˈ- **-s** -z
Balakirev bəˈlæk.ɪ.rev, -ˈlɑː.kɪ-, (US) ˌbɑː.lɑːˈkɪr.jef
balalaika ˌbæl.əˈlaɪ.kə **-s** -z
balanc|e ˈbæl.ənts **-es** -ɪz **-ing** -ɪŋ **-ed** -t **ˈbalancing ˌact; ˌbalance of ˈpayments; ˈbalance ˌsheet**
Balanchine ˈbæl.ən.tʃiːn, ˌ--ˈ-, (US) ˈbæl.ənt.ʃiːn
Balatka bəˈlæt.kə, (US) -kɑː, -ˈlɑːt-
Balaton ˈbæl.ə.tɒn; *as if Hungarian:* ˈbɒl.ɒt.ɒn; (US) ˈbɑː.lɑː.tɑːn
Balboa bælˈbəʊ.ə, (US) -ˈboʊ-
Balbriggan bælˈbrɪɡ.ən
Balbus ˈbæl.bəs
Balchin ˈbɔːl.tʃɪn, ˈbɒl-, (US) ˈbɔːl-, ˈbɑːl-
balcon|y ˈbæl.kə.n|i **-ies** -iz
bald bɔːld, (US) bɔːld, bɑːld **-er** -əʳ, (US) -ɚ **-est** -ɪst, -əst **-ing** -ɪŋ **-ish** -ɪʃ **-ly** -li **-ness** -nəs, -nɪs **ˌbald ˈeagle**
baldachin, baldaquin ˈbɔːl.də.kɪn, (US) ˈbɔːl-, ˈbɑːl- **-s** -z
Balder ˈbɔːl.dəʳ, ˈbɒl-, (US) ˈbɔːl.dɚ, ˈbɑːl-
balderdash ˈbɔːl.də.dæʃ, ˈbɒl-, (US) ˈbɔːl.dɚ-, ˈbɑːl-
baldfaced ˌbɔːldˈfeɪst, (US) ˈbɔːld.feɪst, ˈbɑːld- *stress shift, British only:* **ˌbaldfaced ˈliar**
bald-headed ˌbɔːldˈhed.ɪd, (US) ˌbɔːld-, ˌbɑːld- *stress shift:* **ˌbald-headed ˈman**
Baldock ˈbɔːl.dɒk, (US) ˈbɔːl.dɑːk, ˈbɑːl-
baldric, B~ ˈbɔːl.drɪk, ˈbɒl-, (US) ˈbɔːl-, ˈbɑːl- **-s** -s
Baldry ˈbɔːl.dri, (US) ˈbɔːl-, ˈbɑːl-
Baldwin ˈbɔːld.wɪn, (US) ˈbɔːld-, ˈbɑːld-
bald|y ˈbɔːl.d|i, (US) ˈbɔːl-, ˈbɑːl- **-ies** -iz
bal|e, B~ beɪl **-es** -z **-ing** -ɪŋ **-ed** -d
Bale, Bâle *in Switzerland:* bɑːl
Baleares ˌbæl.iˈɑː.rɪz, (US) ˌbɑː.liˈ-, ˌbæl.iˈ-
Balearic ˌbæl.iˈær.ɪk, (US) ˌbɑː.liˈ-, ˌbæl.iˈ-, -ˈer-
baleen bəˈliːn, bælˈiːn **-s** -z
baleful ˈbeɪl.fəl, -fʊl **-ly** -i **-ness** -nəs, -nɪs
baler ˈbeɪ.ləʳ, (US) -lɚ **-s** -z
Balfour ˈbæl.fəʳ, -fɔːʳ, (US) -fɚ, -fɔːr
Balguy ˈbɔːl.ɡi, (US) ˈbɔːl-, ˈbɑːl-
Balham ˈbæl.əm
Bali ˈbɑː.li, (US) ˈbɑː.li, ˈbæl.i
Balinese ˌbɑː.lɪˈniːz, (US) ˌbɑː.ləˈ-, ˌbæl.əˈ-
Baliol ˈbeɪ.li.əl
balk bɔːlk, bɔːk, (US) bɔːk, bɑːk **-s** -s **-ing** -ɪŋ **-ed** -t
Balkan ˈbɔːl.kən, bɒl-, (US) ˈbɔːl-, ˈbɑːl- **-s** -z
Balkanization, -isa- ˌbɔːl.kə.naɪˈzeɪ.ʃən, ˌbɒl-, -nɪˈ-, (US) ˌbɔːl.kə.nəˈ-, ˌbɑːl-
Balkaniz|e, -is|e ˈbɔːl.kə.naɪz, ˈbɒl-, (US) ˈbɔːl-, ˈbɑːl- **-es** -ɪz **-ing** -ɪŋ **-ed** -d
Balkhash bælˈkæʃ, (US) bɑːlˈkɑːʃ, bæl-, -ˈkæʃ
ball, B~ bɔːl, (US) bɔːl, bɑːl **-s** -z **ˌball and ˈchain; ˌball ˈbearing; ˈball ˌboy; ˈball ˌgame; ˈball ˌgirl; ˈball ˌpark; ˌon the ˈball; ˌset the ball ˈrolling; ˌset the ˈball ˌrolling**
ballad ˈbæl.əd **-s** -z
ballade bælˈɑːd, bəˈlɑːd **-s** -z
balladeer ˌbæl.əˈdɪəʳ, (US) -ˈdɪr **-s** -z
ball-and-socket ˌbɔːl.əndˈsɒk.ɪt, (US) ˌbɑːl.əndˈsɑː.kɪt, ˌbɔːl-
Ballantine, Ballantyne ˈbæl.ən.taɪn
Ballantrae ˌbæl.ənˈtreɪ
Ballarat ˌbæl.əˈræt, ˈ---
Ballard ˈbæl.əd, -ɑːd, (US) -ɚd, -ɑːrd
ballast ˈbæl.əst **-s** -s
Ballater ˈbæl.ə.təʳ, (US) -t̬ɚ
ballcarrier ˈbɔːlˌkær.i.əʳ, (US) -ˌker.i.ɚ, ˈbɑːl-, -ˌkær- **-s** -z
ballcock ˈbɔːl.kɒk, (US) ˈbɔːl.kɑːk, ˈbɑːl- **-s** -s
Balleine bælˈen
ballerina ˌbæl.ərˈiː.nə, (US) -əˈriː- **-s** -z
Ballesteros ˌbæl.ɪˈstɪə.rɒs, ˌbaɪ.ɪˈ-, -əˈ-, -ˈsteə-, (US) ˌbaɪ.əˈster.oʊs, ˌbæl-
ballet ˈbæl.eɪ, (US) bælˈeɪ, ˈ-- **-s** -z **ˈballet ˌdancer**
balletic bælˈet.ɪk, bəˈlet-, (US) bəˈlet̬.ɪk
balletomane ˈbæl.ɪ.təʊ.meɪn, -et.əʊ-, (US) bəˈlet̬.ə- **-s** -z
ballgown ˈbɔːl.ɡaʊn, (US) ˈbɔːl-, ˈbɑːl- **-s** -z
Ballingry bəˈlɪŋ.ɡri
Balliol ˈbeɪ.li.əl
ballistic bəˈlɪs.tɪk **-s** -s
balloon bəˈluːn **-s** -z **-ing** -ɪŋ **-ed** -d **-ist/s** -ɪst/s **go ˌdown/ˌover like a ˌlead baˈlloon**
ball|ot ˈbæl|.ət **-ots** -əts **-oting** -ə.tɪŋ, (US) -ə.t̬ɪŋ **-oted** -ə.tɪd, (US) -ə.t̬ɪd **ˈballot ˌbox; ˈballot ˌpaper; ˈballot ˌrigging**
ballpark ˈbɔːl.pɑːk, (US) -pɑːrk, ˈbɑːl- **ˌball-park ˈfigure**
ballplayer ˈbɔːlˌpleɪ.əʳ, (US) -ɚ, ˈbɑːl- **-s** -z
ball|point ˈbɔːl|.pɔɪnt, (US) ˈbɔːl-, ˈbɑːl- **-points** -pɔɪnts **-pointed** -ˌpɔɪn.tɪd, (US) -ˌpɔɪn.t̬ɪd **ˌball-point ˈpen**
ballroom ˈbɔːl.rʊm, -ruːm, (US) ˈbɔːl.ruːm, -rʊm, ˈbɑːl- **-s** -z **ˌballroom ˈdancing** (US) **ˈballroom ˌdancing**
balls-up ˈbɔːlz.ʌp, (US) ˈbɔːlz-, ˈbɑːlz-
balls|y ˈbɔːl.z|i, (US) ˈbɔːl-, ˈbɑːl- **-ier** -i.əʳ, (US) -i.ɚ **-iest** -i.əst, -i.ɪst
bally ˈbæl.i
Ballycastle ˌbæl.iˈkɑː.səl, (US) -ˈkæs.əl
Ballyclare ˌbæl.iˈkleəʳ, (US) -ˈkler
ballyhoo ˌbæl.iˈhuː, (US) ˈ---
Ballymena ˌbæl.iˈmiː.nə
Ballymoney ˌbæl.iˈmʌn.i

balm bɑːm **-s** -z
Balm(e) bɑːm
Balmain ˈbæl.mæ̃ŋ, -ˈ-, (US) ˈbæl.meɪn, -ˈ-
Balmer ˈbɑː.məʳ, (US) ˈbɑːl.mɚ, ˈbɑː-
Balmoral bælˈmɒr.əl, (US) -ˈmɔːr-
balm|y ˈbɑː.m|i **-ier** -i.əʳ, (US) -i.ɚ **-iest** -i.ɪst, -i.əst **-ily** -əl.i, -ɪ.li **-iness** -ɪ.nəs, -ɪ.nɪs
Balniel bælˈniːl
Balogh ˈbæl.ɒg, (US) -ɑːg
baloney bəˈləʊ.ni, (US) -ˈloʊ-
Baloo bəˈluː
balsa ˈbɔːl.sə, ˈbɒl-, (US) ˈbɔːl-, ˈbɑːl- **ˈbalsa ˌwood**
balsam ˈbɔːl.səm, ˈbɒl-, (US) ˈbɔːl-, ˈbɑːl- **-s** -z
balsamic bɔːlˈsæm.ɪk, bɒl-, (US) bɔːl-, bɑːl- **balˌsamic ˈvinegar**
Balta ˈbæl.tə, (US) ˈbæl-, ˈbɑːl-
Balthazar ˌbæl.θəˈzɑːʳ, ˈ---; bælˈθæz.əʳ, (US) ˌbæl.θəˈzɑːr, ˈ---; (US) bælˈθeɪ.zɚ

> Note: In Shakespeare, normally /ˌbæl.θəˈzɑːʳ, ˈ---/ (US) /ˌbæl.θəˈzɑːr, (US) ˈ---/.

balti, B~ ˈbɔːl.ti, ˈbɒl-, (US) ˈbɔːl-, ˈbɑːl-, ˈbʌl-
Baltic ˈbɔːl.tɪk, ˈbɒl-, (US) ˈbɔːl-, ˈbɑːl- **ˌBaltic ˈSea; ˌBaltic ˈStates**
Baltimore ˈbɔːl.tɪ.mɔːʳ, ˈbɒl-, (US) ˈbɔːl.tə.mɔːr, ˈbɑːl-, -mɚ **-s** -z
Baluchistan bəˌluː.tʃɪˈstɑːn, bælˌuː-, -kɪˈ-, -ˈstæn, (US) -tʃəˈstæn, -ˈstɑːn
baluster ˈbæl.ə.stəʳ, (US) -stɚ **-s** -z **-ed** -d
balustrade ˌbæl.əˈstreɪd, (US) ˈ--- **-s** -z
Balzac ˈbæl.zæk, (US) ˈbɔːl-, ˈbɑːl-, ˈbæl-
Bamako ˌbæm.əˈkəʊ, (US) ˌbæm.əˈkoʊ, ˌbɑː.mə-
Bambi ˈbæm.bi
bambin|o bæmˈbiː.n|əʊ, (US) bæmˈbiː.n|oʊ, bɑːm- **-os** -əʊz, (US) -oʊz **-i** -i
bamboo bæmˈbuː **-s** -z
bamboozl|e bæmˈbuː.zəl **-es** -z **-ing** -ɪŋ, -ˈbuːz.lɪŋ **-ed** -d
Bamborough ˈbæm.bər.ə, (US) -bɚ.oʊ
Bamburgh ˈbæm.bər.ə, (US) -bɚ.ə
Bamfield ˈbæm.fiːld
Bamford ˈbæm.fəd, (US) -fɚd
ban **n,v** *prohibit:* bæn **-s** -z **-ning** -ɪŋ **-ned** -d
ban **n** *Romanian money:* bæn, (US) bɑːn **bani** ˈbɑː.ni
banal bəˈnɑːl, bænˈɑːl, -ˈnæl
banalit|y bəˈnæl.ə.t|i, bænˈæl-, -ɪ.t|i, (US) -ə.t̬|i **-ies** -iz
banana bəˈnɑː.nə, (US) -ˈnæn.ə **-s** -z **baˌnana reˈpublic; baˈnana ˌskin; baˌnana ˈsplit**
Banaras bəˈnɑː.rəs, (US) -ˈnɑːr.əs
Banbridge ˈbæn.brɪdʒ, ˈbæm-, (US) ˈbæn-
Banbury ˈbæn.bər.i, ˈbæm-, (US) ˈbæn.ber-, -bɚ-
bancassurance ˈbæŋ.kəˌʃɔː.rənts, -ˌʃʊə-, (US) ˈbæŋ.kəˌʃʊr.ents
Banchory ˈbæŋ.kər.i
Bancroft ˈbæŋ.krɒft, (US) ˈbæn.krɑːft, ˈbæŋ-
band bænd **-s** -z **-ing** -ɪŋ **-ed** -ɪd **ˈband ˌshell**
Banda ˈbæn.də, (US) ˈbɑːn-, ˈbæn-
bandag|e ˈbæn.dɪdʒ **-es** -ɪz **-ing** -ɪŋ **-ed** -d
Band-Aid®, band-aid ˈbænd.eɪd **-s** -z
bandan(n)a bænˈdæn.ə **-s** -z
Bandaranaike ˌbæn.dər.əˈnaɪ.ɪ.kə, -ˈnaɪ.kə, (US) ˌbɑːn-
Bandar Seri Begawan ˌbæn.də.ser.i.bəˈgɑː.wən, -beˈ-, -bɪˈ-, -ˈgaʊ.ən, (US) ˌbɑːn.dɚ-
B and B ˌbiː.əndˈbiː, -əmˈ-, (US) -əndˈ- **-s** -z
bandbox ˈbænd.bɒks, (US) -bɑːks **-es** -ɪz
bandeau ˈbæn.dəʊ; *as if French:* bɑ̃nˈdəʊ; (US) bænˈdoʊ **bandeaux** ˈbæn.dəʊ, -dəʊz; *as if French:* bæ̃nˈdəʊ; (US) bænˈdoʊ, -doʊz
banderole ˈbæn.dər.əʊl, (US) -də.roʊl **-s** -z
bandicoot ˈbæn.dɪ.kuːt **-s** -s
bandit ˈbæn.dɪt **-s** -s **-ry** -ri
bandleader ˈbændˌliː.dəʳ, (US) -dɚ **-s** -z
bandmaster ˈbændˌmɑː.stəʳ, (US) -ˌmæs.tɚ **-s** -z
bandog ˈbæn.dɒg, (US) -dɑːg, -dɔːg **-s** -z
bandoleer, bandolier ˌbæn.dəlˈɪəʳ, (US) -dəˈlɪr **-s** -z
bands|man ˈbændz|.mən **-men** -mən, -men
bandstand ˈbænd.stænd **-s** -z
Bandung ˈbæn.dʊŋ, -ˈ-, (US) ˈbɑːn-, ˈbæn-
bandwagon ˈbændˌwæg.ən **-s** -z
bandwidth ˈbænd.wɪtθ, -wɪdθ, (US) ˈbænd.wɪtθ, -wɪdθ, -wɪθ **-s** -s
band|y ˈbæn.d|i **-ier** -i.əʳ, (US) -i.ɚ **-iest** -i.ɪst, -i.əst **-ies** -iz **-ying** -i.ɪŋ **-ied** -id
bandy-legged ˌbæn.diˈlegd, -ˈleg.ɪd, -ˈleg.əd *stress shift:* **ˌbandy-legged ˈchild**
bane beɪn **-s** -z
baneful ˈbeɪn.fəl, -fʊl **-ly** -i **-ness** -nəs, -nɪs
Banff bænf **-shire** -ʃəʳ, -ʃɪəʳ, (US) -ʃɚ, -ʃɪr
Banfield ˈbæn.fiːld
bang bæŋ **-s** -z **-ing** -ɪŋ **-ed** -d **go ˌoff with a ˈbang**
Bangalore ˌbæŋ.gəˈlɔːʳ, (US) ˈbæŋ.gə.lɔːr, ˌ--ˈ-
banger ˈbæŋ.əʳ, (US) -ɚ **-s** -z
Banger ˈbeɪn.dʒəʳ, (US) -dʒɚ
Bangkok bæŋˈkɒk, (US) ˈbæŋ.kɑːk, -ˈ- *stress shift, British only:* **ˌBangkok ˈtemple**
Bangladesh ˌbæŋ.gləˈdeʃ, -ˈdeɪʃ, (US) ˌbæŋ.gləˈdeʃ, ˌbɑːŋ-
Bangladeshi ˌbæŋ.gləˈdeʃ.i, -ˈdeɪ.ʃi, (US) ˌbæŋ.gləˈdeʃ-, ˌbɑːŋ- **-s** -z
bangle ˈbæŋ.gəl **-s** -z **-d** -d
bang-on ˌbæŋˈɒn, (US) ˈbæŋ.ɑːn
Bangor *in Wales:* ˈbæŋ.gəʳ, (US) -gɚ *in US:* ˈbæŋ.gɔːʳ, -gəʳ, (US) -gɔːr, -gɚ
Bangui ˌbɑːŋˈgiː, (US) ˌbɑːŋ-
bang-up ˌbæŋˈʌp, (US) ˈ--
Banham ˈbæn.əm
bani (plural of **ban**) ˈbɑː.ni
banian ˈbæn.i.ən, ˈ-jæn **-s** -z
banish ˈbæn.ɪʃ **-es** -ɪz **-ing** -ɪŋ **-ed** -t **-ment/s** -mənt/s
banister, B~ ˈbæn.ɪ.stəʳ, (US) -ə.stɚ **-s** -z
Banja Luka ˌbæn.jəˈluː.kə, (US) ˌbɑː.njəˈ-
banjo ˈbæn.dʒəʊ, -ˈ-, (US) ˈbæn.dʒoʊ **-(e)s** -z
Banjul bænˈdʒuːl, (US) ˈbɑːn.dʒuːl
bank bæŋk **-s** -s **-ing** -ɪŋ **-ed** -t **ˈbank aˌccount; ˈbank ˌcard; ˈbank ˌclerk; ˌbank ˈholiday; ˈbank ˌmanager; ˈbank ˌrate; ˈbank ˌstatement; ˌBank of ˈEngland**
bankability ˌbæŋ.kəˈbɪl.ə.ti, -ɪ.ti, (US) -ə.t̬i
bankable ˈbæŋ.kə.bəl
banker ˈbæŋ.kəʳ, (US) -kɚ **-s** -z
Bankes bæŋks
Bankhead ˈbæŋk.hed
banknote ˈbæŋk.nəʊt, (US) -noʊt **-s** -s
bankroll ˈbæŋk.rəʊl, (US) -roʊl **-s** -z **-ing** -ɪŋ **-ed** -d
bankrupt ˈbæŋk.rʌpt, -rəpt **-s** -s **-ing** -ɪŋ **-ed** -ɪd
bankruptc|y ˈbæŋk.rʌpt.s|i, -rəpt- **-ies** -iz
Banks bæŋks
banksia ˈbæŋk.si.ə **-s** -z
Ban-Lon® ˈbæn.lɒn, (US) -lɑːn
Bann bæn
Bannatyne ˈbæn.ə.taɪn
banner, B~ ˈbæn.əʳ, (US) -ɚ **-s** -z
Bannerman ˈbæn.ə.mən, (US) ˈ-ɚ-
Banning ˈbæn.ɪŋ
bannister, B~ ˈbæn.ɪ.stəʳ, (US) -ə.stɚ **-s** -z
bannock ˈbæn.ək **-s** -s
Bannockburn ˈbæn.ək.bɜːn, (US) -bɝːn, -bɚn
Bannon ˈbæn.ən
banns bænz
banoffee, banoffi bəˈnɒf.i, (US) -ˈnɑː.fi **baˌnoffee ˈpie**
banque|t ˈbæŋ.kwɪ|t, (US) -kwə|t, -kwɪ|t **-ts** -ts **-ting** -tɪŋ, (US) -t̬ɪŋ **-ted** -tɪd, (US) -t̬ɪd **ˈbanquet ˌroom; ˈbanqueting ˌhall**
banquette bæŋˈket **-s** -s
Banquo ˈbæŋ.kwəʊ, (US) -kwoʊ
banshee ˈbæn.ʃiː, -ˈ- **-s** -z
Banstead ˈbænt.stɪd, -sted
bant bænt **-s** -s **-ing** -ɪŋ, (US) ˈbæn.t̬ɪŋ **-ed** -ɪd, (US) ˈbæn.t̬ɪd
bantam, B~ ˈbæn.təm, (US) -t̬əm **-s** -z

B

bantamweight ˈbæn.təm.weɪt, Ⓤⓢ -t̬əm-
bant|er ˈbæn.t|əʳ, Ⓤⓢ -t̬|ɚ **-ers** -əz, Ⓤⓢ -ɚz **-ering** -ər.ɪŋ **-ered** -əd, Ⓤⓢ -ɚd
Banting ˈbæn.tɪŋ, Ⓤⓢ -t̬ɪŋ
bantling ˈbænt.lɪŋ **-s** -z
Bantry ˈbæn.tri
Bantu ˌbænˈtuː, ˌbɑːn-, ˈ--, Ⓤⓢ ˈbæn.tuː
bantustan, B~ ˌbæn.tuˈstɑːn, ˌbɑːn-, -ˈstæn
banyan ˈbæn.jæn, -ni.ən, ˈ-jən, Ⓤⓢ ˈ-jən, ˈ-jæn **-s** -z
Banyard ˈbæn.jɑːd, Ⓤⓢ -jɑːrd
banzai bænˈzaɪ, bɑːn-, ˈ--, Ⓤⓢ bɑːnˈzaɪ, ˈ--
baobab ˈbeɪ.əʊ.bæb, Ⓤⓢ ˈ-oʊ-, ˈbɑː- **-s** -z
bap bæp **-s** -s
baptism ˈbæp.tɪ.zəm **-s** -z ˌ**baptism of** ˈ**fire**
baptismal bæpˈtɪz.məl **-ly** -i
baptist, B~ ˈbæp.tɪst **-s** -s ˌ**John the** ˈ**Baptist**
baptister|y ˈbæp.tɪ.stər|.i **-ies** -iz
baptistr|y ˈbæp.tɪ.str|i **-ies** -iz
baptiz|e, -is|e bæpˈtaɪz, Ⓤⓢ ˈ-- **-es** -ɪz **-ing** -ɪŋ **-ed** -d
bar, B~ bɑːʳ, Ⓤⓢ bɑːr **-s** -z **-ring** -ɪŋ **-red** -d ˈ**bar** ˌ**code;** ˈ**bar** ˌ**graph;** ˈ**bar** ˌ**meal;** ˈ**bar** ˌ**staff**
Barabbas bəˈræb.əs
Barack ˈbæ.rək, -ræk; bəˈræk, -ˈrɑːk, Ⓤⓢ -ˈrɑːk
barb bɑːb, Ⓤⓢ bɑːrb **-s** -z **-ing** -ɪŋ **-ed** -d
Barbadian bɑːˈbeɪ.di.ən, -dʒən, Ⓤⓢ bɑːr- **-s** -z
Barbados bɑːˈbeɪ.dɒs, -dəs, Ⓤⓢ bɑːrˈbeɪ.doʊs
Barbara ˈbɑː.bər.ə, ˈ-brə, Ⓤⓢ ˈbɑːr-
barbarian bɑːˈbeə.ri.ən, Ⓤⓢ bɑːrˈber.i- **-s** -z
barbaric bɑːˈbær.ɪk, Ⓤⓢ bɑːrˈber-, -ˈbær- **-ally** -əl.i, -li
barbarism ˈbɑː.bər.ɪ.zəm, Ⓤⓢ ˈbɑːr- **-s** -z
barbarit|y bɑːˈbær.ə.t|i, -ɪ.t|i, Ⓤⓢ bɑːrˈber.ə.t̬|i, -ˈbær- **-ies** -iz
barbariz|e, -is|e ˈbɑː.bər.aɪz, Ⓤⓢ ˈbɑːr- **-es** -ɪz **-ing** -ɪŋ **-ed** -d
Barbarossa ˌbɑː.bərˈɒs.ə, Ⓤⓢ ˌbɑːr.bəˈroʊ.sə, -ˈrɑː-
barbarous ˈbɑː.bər.əs, Ⓤⓢ ˈbɑːr- **-ly** -li **-ness** -nəs, -nɪs
Barbary ˈbɑː.bər.i, Ⓤⓢ ˈbɑːr- ˌ**Barbary** ˈ**ape;** ˌ**Barbary** ˈ**Coast**
barbate ˈbɑː.beɪt, -bɪt, -bət, Ⓤⓢ ˈbɑːr-
barbated ˈbɑː.beɪ.tɪd, -bɪ-, -bə-; bɑːˈbeɪ-, Ⓤⓢ bɑːrˈbeɪ.t̬ɪd
Barbauld ˈbɑː.bəld, Ⓤⓢ ˈbɑːr-
barbecu|e ˈbɑː.bɪ.kjuː, -bə-, Ⓤⓢ ˈbɑːr- **-es** -z **-ing** -ɪŋ **-ed** -d
barbed bɑːbd, Ⓤⓢ bɑːrbd ˌ**barbed** ˈ**wire**
barbell ˈbɑː.bel, Ⓤⓢ ˈbɑːr- **-s** -z
barber, B~ ˈbɑː.bəʳ, Ⓤⓢ ˈbɑːr.bɚ **-s** -z
barberr|y ˈbɑː.bər|.i, Ⓤⓢ ˈbɑːr.ber|.i **-ies** -iz
barbershop ˈbɑː.bə.ʃɒp, Ⓤⓢ ˈbɑːr.bɚ.ʃɑːp **-s** -s ˌ**barbershop quar**ˈ**tet**
barbette bɑːˈbet, Ⓤⓢ bɑːr- **-s** -s
barbican, B~ ˈbɑː.bɪ.kən, Ⓤⓢ ˈbɑːr.bə- **-s** -z
barbie, B~ ˈbɑː.bi, Ⓤⓢ ˈbɑːr- ˈ**Barbie** ˌ**doll**®
Barbirolli ˌbɑː.bɪˈrɒl.i, -bəˈ-, Ⓤⓢ ˌbɑːr.bəˈrɑː.li
barbitone ˈbɑː.bɪ.təʊn, Ⓤⓢ ˈbɑːr.bə.toʊn **-s** -z
barbiturate bɑːˈbɪtʃ.ər.ət, -ˈbɪt.jʊ.rət, -jər.ət, -ɪt, -eɪt, Ⓤⓢ bɑːrˈbɪtʃ.ər.ət, -eɪt **-s** -s
barbituric ˌbɑː.bɪˈtʃʊə.rɪk; ˌbɑːˈbɪt.jʊ-, -jər.ɪk, Ⓤⓢ ˌbɑːr.bəˈtʃʊr.ɪk, -ˈtʊr- **barbi**ˌ**turic** ˈ**acid**
Barbour® ˈbɑː.bəʳ, Ⓤⓢ ˈbɑːr.bɚ **-s** -z
Barbuda bɑːˈbjuː.də, Ⓤⓢ bɑːrˈbuː-, -ˈbjuː-
barbule ˈbɑː.bjuːl, Ⓤⓢ ˈbɑːr- **-s** -z
barbwire ˈbɑːb.waɪ.əʳ, Ⓤⓢ ˈbɑːrb.waɪ.ɚ
Barca ˈbɑː.kə, Ⓤⓢ ˈbɑːr-
barcarol(l)e ˌbɑː.kəˈrəʊl, -ˈrɒl, ˈ---, Ⓤⓢ ˈbɑːr.kə.roʊl **-s** -z
Barcelona ˌbɑː.səlˈəʊ.nə, -sɪˈləʊ-, Ⓤⓢ ˌbɑːr.səˈloʊ-
Barchester ˈbɑː.tʃes.təʳ, -tʃɪ.stəʳ, Ⓤⓢ ˈbɑːr.tʃə.stɚ, -tʃes.tɚ
Barclay ˈbɑː.kli, -kleɪ, Ⓤⓢ ˈbɑːr- **-'s** -z
Barclaycard® ˈbɑː.kli.kɑːd, -kleɪ-, Ⓤⓢ ˈbɑːr.kli.kɑːrd
bar code ˈbɑː.kəʊd, Ⓤⓢ ˈbɑːr.koʊd **-s** -z
Barcroft ˈbɑː.krɒft, Ⓤⓢ ˈbɑːr.krɑːft
bard, B~ bɑːd, Ⓤⓢ bɑːrd **-s** -z **-ic** -ɪk
Bardell bɑːˈdel; ˈbɑː.dəl, -del, Ⓤⓢ bɑːrˈdel; Ⓤⓢ ˈbɑːr.dəl, -del

> Note: In Dickens's 'The Pickwick Papers' generally pronounced /bɑːˈdel/ Ⓤⓢ /bɑːr-/.

bardolatry bɑːˈdɒl.ə.tri, Ⓤⓢ bɑːrˈdɑː.lə-
Bardolph ˈbɑː.dɒlf, Ⓤⓢ ˈbɑːr.dɑːlf
Bardot bɑːˈdəʊ, Ⓤⓢ bɑːrˈdoʊ
Bardsey ˈbɑːd.si, Ⓤⓢ ˈbɑːrd-
Bardsley ˈbɑːdz.li, Ⓤⓢ ˈbɑːrdz-
Bardswell ˈbɑːdz.wəl, -wel, Ⓤⓢ ˈbɑːrdz-
Bardwell ˈbɑːd.wəl, -wel, Ⓤⓢ ˈbɑːrd-
bar|e beəʳ, Ⓤⓢ ber **-er** -əʳ, Ⓤⓢ -ɚ **-est** -ɪst, -əst **-es** -z **-ing** -ɪŋ **-ed** -d
bareback ˈbeə.bæk, Ⓤⓢ ˈber- **-ed** -t
Barebones ˈbeə.bəʊnz, Ⓤⓢ ˈber.boʊnz
barefaced beəˈfeɪst, Ⓤⓢ ˈber.feɪst **-ly** -li, -ɪd.li **-ness** -nəs, -nɪs *stress shift, British only:* ˌ**barefaced** ˈ**liar**
barefoot beəˈfʊt, Ⓤⓢ ˈber.fʊt *stress shift, British only:* ˌ**barefoot** ˈ**child**
barefooted ˌbeəˈfʊt.ɪd, Ⓤⓢ ˈber.fʊt̬- *stress shift, British only:* ˌ**barefooted** ˈ**child**
barehanded ˌbeəˈhæn.dɪd, Ⓤⓢ ˈberˌhæn- *stress shift, British only:* ˌ**barehanded** ˈ**warrior**
bare-headed ˌbeəˈhed.ɪd, Ⓤⓢ ˈberˌhed- *stress shift, British only:* ˌ**bare-headed** ˈ**worshippers**
Bareilly bəˈreɪ.li
bare-legged ˌbeəˈlegd, -ˈleg.ɪd, Ⓤⓢ ˈberˌleg.ɪd, -legd *stress shift, British only:* ˌ**bare-legged** ˈ**child**
bare|ly ˈbeə|.li, Ⓤⓢ ˈber- **-ness** -nəs, -nɪs
Barenboim ˈbær.ən.bɔɪm, ˈbɑːr-, Ⓤⓢ ˈber-, ˈbær-
Barents ˈbær.ənts, Ⓤⓢ ˈber-, ˈbær-
barf bɑːf, Ⓤⓢ bɑːrf **-s** -s **-ing** -ɪŋ **-ed** -t
Barfield ˈbɑː.fiːld, Ⓤⓢ ˈbɑːr-
bar|fly ˈbɑː|.flaɪ, Ⓤⓢ ˈbɑːr- **-flies** -flaɪz
Barfoot ˈbɑː.fʊt, Ⓤⓢ ˈbɑːr-
bargain ˈbɑː.gɪn, -gən, Ⓤⓢ ˈbɑːr- **-s** -z **-ing** -ɪŋ **-ed** -d **-er/s** -əʳ/z, Ⓤⓢ -ɚ/z ˌ**bargain** ˈ**basement;** ˈ**bargain** ˌ**hunter**
barg|e bɑːdʒ, Ⓤⓢ bɑːrdʒ **-es** -ɪz **-ing** -ɪŋ **-ed** -d
bargee bɑːˈdʒiː, ˈ--, Ⓤⓢ bɑːrˈdʒiː **-s** -z
barge|man ˈbɑːdʒ|.mən, -mæn, Ⓤⓢ ˈbɑːrdʒ- **-men** -mən, -men
bargepole ˈbɑːdʒ.pəʊl, Ⓤⓢ ˈbɑːrdʒ.poʊl **-s** -z
Barger ˈbɑː.dʒəʳ, Ⓤⓢ ˈbɑːr.dʒɚ
Bargh bɑːdʒ, bɑːf, Ⓤⓢ bɑːrdʒ, bɑːrf
Bargoed ˈbɑː.gɔɪd, Ⓤⓢ ˈbɑːr-
Bargrave ˈbɑː.greɪv, Ⓤⓢ ˈbɑːr-
Barham *surname:* ˈbær.əm, ˈbɑː.rəm, Ⓤⓢ ˈber-, ˈbær-, ˈbɑːr.əm *in Kent:* ˈbær.əm, Ⓤⓢ ˈber-, ˈbær-
Bari ˈbɑː.ri, Ⓤⓢ ˈbɑːr.i
Baring ˈbeə.rɪŋ, ˈbær.ɪŋ, Ⓤⓢ ˈber.ɪŋ, ˈbær-
Baring-Gould ˌbeə.rɪŋˈguːld, Ⓤⓢ ˌber.ɪŋˈ-
barista bɑːˈriː.stə, -ˈɪs.tə, Ⓤⓢ -ˈriː.stə **-s** -z
baritone ˈbær.ɪ.təʊn, Ⓤⓢ ˈber.ə.toʊn, ˈbær- **-s** -z
barium ˈbeə.ri.əm, Ⓤⓢ ˈber.i-, ˈbær- ˌ**barium** ˈ**meal**
bark bɑːk, Ⓤⓢ bɑːrk **-s** -s **-ing** -ɪŋ **-ed** -t **-er/s** -əʳ/z, Ⓤⓢ -ɚ/z ˌ**bark up the wrong** ˈ**tree;** ˌ**their** ˌ**bark is** ˌ**worse than their** ˈ**bite**
barkeep ˈbɑː.kiːp, Ⓤⓢ ˈbɑːr- **-s** -s **-er/s** -əʳ/z, Ⓤⓢ -ɚ/z
Barker ˈbɑː.kəʳ, Ⓤⓢ ˈbɑːr.kɚ
Barking ˈbɑː.kɪŋ, Ⓤⓢ ˈbɑːr-
Barkston ˈbɑːk.stən, Ⓤⓢ ˈbɑːrk-
barley ˈbɑː.li, Ⓤⓢ ˈbɑːr- ˈ**barley** ˌ**sugar;** ˈ**barley** ˌ**water;** ˌ**barley** ˈ**wine**
barleycorn, B~ ˈbɑː.li.kɔːn, Ⓤⓢ ˈbɑːr.li.kɔːrn **-s** -z
Barlow(e) ˈbɑː.ləʊ, Ⓤⓢ ˈbɑːr.loʊ
barm bɑːm, Ⓤⓢ bɑːrm
barmaid ˈbɑː.meɪd, Ⓤⓢ ˈbɑːr- **-s** -z

B

bar|man ˈbɑː|.mən, -mæn, (US) ˈbɑːr- **-men** -mən, -men
Barmby ˈbɑːm.bi, (US) ˈbɑːrm-
Barmecide ˈbɑː.mɪ.saɪd, (US) ˈbɑːr.mə-
bar mi(t)zvah bɑːˈmɪts.və, (US) bɑːr- **-s** -z
Barmouth ˈbɑː.məθ, (US) ˈbɑːr-
barm|y ˈbɑː.m|i, (US) ˈbɑːr- **-ier** -i.əʳ, (US) -i.ɚ **-iest** -i.ɪst, -i.əst **-iness** -ɪ.nəs, -ɪ.nɪs
barn bɑːn, (US) bɑːrn **-s** -z ˈ**barn** ˌ**dance;** ˌ**barn** ˈ**door**
Barnabas ˈbɑː.nə.bəs, -bæs, (US) ˈbɑːr-
Barnaby ˈbɑː.nə.bi, (US) ˈbɑːr-
barnacle ˈbɑː.nə.kəl, (US) ˈbɑːr- **-s** -z
Barnard ˈbɑː.nəd, -nɑːd, (US) ˈbɑːr.nɚd; (US) bɑːrˈnɑːrd
Barnardiston ˌbɑː.nəˈdɪs.tən, (US) ˌbɑːr.nɚˈ-
Barnardo bəˈnɑː.dəʊ, bɑː-, (US) bɚˈnɑːr.doʊ
Barnby ˈbɑːn.bi, ˈbɑːm-, (US) ˈbɑːrn-
Barnes bɑːnz, (US) bɑːrnz
Barnet(t) ˈbɑː.nɪt, (US) bɑːrˈnet, ˈ--
barney, B~ ˈbɑː.ni, (US) ˈbɑːr- **-s** -z
Barnfield ˈbɑːn.fiːld, (US) ˈbɑːrn-
Barnham ˈbɑː.nəm, (US) ˈbɑːr-
Barnicott ˈbɑː.nɪ.kət, -kɒt, (US) ˈbɑːr.nə.kɑːt, -nɪ-, -kət
Barnoldswick bɑːˈnəʊldz.wɪk; *locally also:* ˈbɑː.lɪk, (US) bɑːrˈnoʊldz.wɪk
Barnsley ˈbɑːnz.li, (US) ˈbɑːrnz-
Barnstaple ˈbɑːn.stə.pəl; *locally also:* -bəl, (US) ˈbɑːrn.stə.pəl
barnstorm ˈbɑːn.stɔːm, (US) ˈbɑːrn.stɔːrm **-s** -z **-ing** -ɪŋ **-ed** -d **-er/s** -əʳ/z, (US) -ɚ/z
Barnum ˈbɑː.nəm, (US) ˈbɑːr-
barnyard ˈbɑːn.jɑːd, (US) ˈbɑːrn.jɑːrd **-s** -z
Baroda bəˈrəʊ.də, (US) -ˈroʊ-
barograph ˈbær.əʊ.grɑːf, -græf, (US) ˈber.ə.græf, ˈbær- **-s** -s
Barolo bəˈrəʊ.ləʊ, (US) -ˈroʊ.loʊ
Barolong ˌbɑː.rəʊˈləʊŋ, ˌbær.əʊ-, -ˈlɒŋ, (US) ˌbɑːr.əˈloʊŋ
barometer bəˈrɒm.ɪ.təʳ, -ə.təʳ, (US) -ˈrɑː.mə.t̬ɚ **-s** -z
barometric ˌbær.əʊˈmet.rɪk, (US) ˌber.əˈ-, ˌbær- **-al** -əl **-ally** -əl.i, -li
barometry bəˈrɒm.ə.tri, ˈ-ɪ-, (US) -ˈrɑː.mə-
baron, B~ ˈbær.ən, (US) ˈber-, ˈbær- **-s** -z
baronag|e ˈbær.ən.ɪdʒ, (US) ˈber-, ˈbær- **-es** -ɪz
baroness, B~ ˈbær.ən.es, -ɪs, -əs; ˌbær.ənˈes, (US) ˈber.ən.əs, ˈbær- **-es** -ɪz
baronet ˈbær.ən.ət, -ɪt, -et, ˌbær.ənˈet, (US) ˈber.ən.ət, ˈbær-, -ɪt **-s** -s
baronetag|e ˈbær.ə.nə.tɪdʒ, -nɪ-, ˌbær.əˈnet.ɪdʒ, (US) ˈber.ə.nə.t̬ɪdʒ, ˈbær- **-es** -ɪz
baronetc|y ˈbær.ə.nət.s|i, -nɪt-, -net-, (US) ˈber-, ˈbær- **-ies** -iz
baronial bəˈrəʊ.ni.əl, (US) -ˈroʊ-
baron|y ˈbær.ən|.i, (US) ˈber-, ˈbær- **-ies** -iz
baroque bəˈrɒk, bærˈɒk, (US) bəˈroʊk, bærˈoʊk, -ˈɑːk
baroscope ˈbær.əʊ.skəʊp, (US) ˈber.ə.skoʊp, ˈbær- **-s** -s
baroscopic ˌbær.əʊˈskɒp.ɪk, (US) ˌber.əˈskɑː.pɪk, ˌbær-
Barossa bəˈrɒs.ə, (US) -ˈrɑː.sə **Ba**ˌ**rossa** ˈ**Valley**
barouch|e bəˈruːʃ, bærˈuːʃ, (US) bəˈruːʃ **-es** -ɪz
barperson ˈbɑːˌpɜː.sən, (US) ˈbɑːrˌpɝː- **-s** -z
barque bɑːk, (US) bɑːrk **-s** -s
Barquisimeto ˌbɑː.kɪ.sɪˈmeɪ.təʊ, (US) ˌbɑːr.kə.səˈmeɪ.toʊ
Barr bɑːʳ, (US) bɑːr
Barra ˈbær.ə, (US) ˈber-, ˈbær-
barrack ˈbær.ək, (US) ˈber-, ˈbær- **-s** -s **-ing** -ɪŋ **-ed** -t
Barraclough ˈbær.ə.klʌf, (US) ˈber-, ˈbær-
barracouta ˌbær.əˈkuː.tə, (US) ˌber.əˈkuː.t̬ə, ˌbær-, -də **-s** -z
barracuda ˌbær.əˈkjuː.də, -ˈkuː-, (US) ˌber.əˈkuː-, ˌbær-
barrag|e ˈbær.ɑːdʒ, (US) bəˈrɑːdʒ **-es** -ɪz
barramund|a ˌbær.əˈmʌn.d|ə, (US) ˌber-, ˌbær- **-as** -əz **-i** -i **-is** -ɪs
Barranquilla ˌbær.əŋˈkiː.ə, (US) ˌbɑːr.ɑːnˈkiː.jɑː, ˌber-, ˌbær-
Barrat(t) ˈbær.ət, (US) ˈber-, ˈbær-
barratry ˈbær.ə.tri, (US) ˈber-, ˈbær-
barre bɑːʳ, (US) bɑːr **-s** -z
barrel ˈbær.əl, (US) ˈber-, ˈbær- **-s** -z **-(l)ing** -ɪŋ **-(l)ed** -d
barrel-organ ˈbær.əlˌɔː.gən, (US) ˈber.əlˌɔːr-, ˈbær- **-s** -z
barren ˈbær.ən, (US) ˈber-, ˈbær- **-est** -ɪst, -əst **-ly** -li **-ness** -nəs, -nɪs
Barrett ˈbær.ət, -et, -ɪt, (US) ˈber-, ˈbær-
barrette bəˈret, bɑː-, (US) bəˈret **-s** -s
Barrhead ˈbɑː.hed, (US) ˈbɑːr-
barricad|e ˌbær.ɪˈkeɪd, -əˈ-, ˈ---, (US) ˈber.ə.keɪd, ˈbær-, ˌ--ˈ- **-es** -z **-ing** -ɪŋ **-ed** -ɪd
Barrie ˈbær.i, (US) ˈber-, ˈbær-
barrier, B~ ˈbær.i.əʳ, (US) ˈber.i.ɚ, ˈbær- **-s** -z ˌ**Great** ˌ**Barrier** ˈ**Reef**
barring ˈbɑː.rɪŋ, (US) ˈbɑːr.ɪŋ
Barrington ˈbær.ɪŋ.tən, (US) ˈber-
barrio ˈbær.i.əʊ, (US) ˈbɑːr.i.oʊ, ˈber-, ˈbær- **-s** -z
barrister ˈbær.ɪ.stəʳ, (US) ˈber.ɪ.stɚ, ˈbær- **-s** -z
barrister-at-law ˌbær.ɪ.stəʳ.ətˈlɔː, (US) ˌber.ə.stɚ.ətˈlɑː, ˌbær-, -ˈlɔː **barristers-at-law** ˌbær.ɪ.stəz.ətˈlɔː, (US) ˌber.ə.stɚz.ətˈlɑː, ˌbær-, -ˈlɔː
Barron ˈbær.ən, (US) ˈber-, ˈbær-
barroom ˈbɑː.rʊm, -ruːm, (US) ˈbɑːr.ruːm, -rʊm **-s** -z
barrow, B~ ˈbær.əʊ, (US) ˈber.oʊ, ˈbær- **-s** -z
Barrow-in-Furness ˌbær.əʊ.ɪnˈfɜː.nɪs, -nes, -nəs, (US) ˌber.oʊ.ɪnˈfɝː-, ˌbær-
Barry ˈbær.i, (US) ˈber-, ˈbær-
Barrymore ˈbær.i.mɔːʳ, (US) ˈber.i.mɔːr, ˈbær-
Barsetshire ˈbɑː.sɪt.ʃəʳ, -ʃɪəʳ, -set-, -sət-, (US) ˈbɑːr.sɪt.ʃɚ, -ʃɪr
barstool ˈbɑː.stuːl, (US) ˈbɑːr- **-s** -z
Barstow ˈbɑː.stəʊ, (US) ˈbɑːr.stoʊ
bart, B~ bɑːt, (US) bɑːrt **-s** -s
bartend ˈbɑː.tend, (US) ˈbɑːr- **-s** -z **-ing** -ɪŋ **-ed** -ɪd
bartender ˈbɑːˌten.dəʳ, (US) ˈbɑːrˌten.dɚ **-s** -z
bart|er, B~ ˈbɑː.t|əʳ, (US) ˈbɑːr.t̬|ɚ **-ers** -əz, (US) -ɚz **-ering** -ər.ɪŋ **-ered** -əd, (US) -ɚd
Barth bɑːθ, (US) bɑːrθ
Barthelme ˈbɑː.təl.meɪ, (US) ˈbɑːr.t̬əl-
Barthes bɑːt, (US) bɑːrt
Bartholomew bɑːˈθɒl.ə.mjuː, bəˈ-, (US) bɑːrˈθɑː.lə-, bɚ-

> Note: This ancient name has had a variety of pronunciations in British English. The older form /ˈbɑː.təl.mi/ has been supplanted by the pronunciations given above, which are closer to the spelling.

Bartle ˈbɑː.təl, (US) ˈbɑːr.t̬əl
Bartleby ˈbɑː.təl.bi, (US) ˈbɑːr.t̬əl-
Bartlett ˈbɑːt.lət, -lɪt, (US) ˈbɑːrt-
Bartók ˈbɑː.tɒk, (US) ˈbɑːr.tɑːk
Bartoli bɑːˈtəʊ.li, (US) bɑːrˈtoʊ.li
Bartolommeo ˌbɑː.tɒl.əˈmeɪ.əʊ, (US) ˌbɑːr.tɑː.ləˈmeɪ.oʊ
Bartolozzi ˌbɑː.təˈlɒt.si, (US) ˌbɑːr.t̬əˈlɑːt-
Barton ˈbɑː.tən, (US) ˈbɑːr-
Bartram ˈbɑː.trəm, (US) ˈbɑːr-
Bart's bɑːts, (US) bɑːrts
bartsia ˈbɑːt.si.ə, (US) ˈbɑːrt-
Baruch *biblical name:* ˈbɑː.rʊk, ˈbeə-, -rək, (US) bəˈruːk; (US) ˈbɑːr.uːk, ˈber- *modern surname:* bəˈruːk
Barugh bɑːf, (US) bɑːrf
Barum ˈbeə.rəm, (US) ˈber.əm
Barwick *in the UK:* ˈbær.ɪk, (US) ˈber.ɪk, ˈbær- *in the US:* ˈbɑː.wɪk; ˈbær.ɪk, (US) ˈbɑːr.wɪk
Baryshnikov bəˈrɪʃ.nɪ.kɒf, bærˈɪʃ-, -kəf, (US) bəˈrɪʃ.nɪ.kɔːf, bɑːˈ-, -kɑːf
barysphere ˈbær.ɪ.sfɪəʳ, (US) ˈber.ɪ.sfɪr, ˈbær- **-s** -z
baryton ˈbær.ɪ.tɒn, (US) ˈber.ə.tɑːn, ˈbær- **-s** -z
barytone ˈbær.ɪ.təʊn, (US) ˈber.ə.toʊn, ˈbær- **-s** -z
basal ˈbeɪ.səl
basalt ˈbæs.ɔːlt; -əlt; bəˈsɔːlt, -ˈsɒlt, (US) bəˈsɔːlt, -ˈsɑːlt; (US) ˈbeɪ.sɔːlt, -sɑːlt
basaltic bəˈsɔːl.tɪk, -ˈsɒl-, (US) bəˈsɔːl.tɪk, -ˈsɑːl-
Basan ˈbeɪ.sæn
bascule ˈbæs.kjuːl **-s** -z
bas|e beɪs **-es** -ɪz **-er** -əʳ, (US) -ɚ **-est** -ɪst, -əst **-ely** -li **-eness** -nəs, -nɪs

-ing -ɪŋ -ed -t ˌbase ˈmetal; ˈbase ˌrate
baseball ˈbeɪs.bɔːl, (US) -bɔːl, -bɑːl ˈbaseball ˌbat; ˈbaseball ˌcap
baseboard ˈbeɪs.bɔːd, (US) -bɔːrd -s -z
baseborn ˈbeɪs.bɔːn, (US) -bɔːrn
Baseden ˈbeɪz.dən
Basel ˈbɑː.zəl
baseless ˈbeɪs.ləs, -lɪs -ly -li -ness -nəs, -nɪs
baseline ˈbeɪs.laɪn -s -z
base|man ˈbeɪs|.mən, -mæn -men -mən, -men
basement ˈbeɪs.mənt -s -s
bases (plural of **base**) ˈbeɪ.sɪz (plural of **basis**) ˈbeɪ.siːz
Basford *in Nottinghamshire:* ˈbeɪs.fəd, (US) -fɚd *in Staffordshire:* ˈbæs.fəd, (US) -fɚd
bash bæʃ -es -ɪz -ing -ɪŋ -ed -t
Basham ˈbæʃ.əm
Bashan ˈbeɪ.ʃæn
Bashford ˈbæʃ.fəd, (US) -fɚd
bashful ˈbæʃ.fəl, -fʊl -lest -ɪst, -əst -ly -i -ness -nəs, -nɪs
basho ˈbæʃ.əʊ, (US) bɑːˈʃoʊ -s (US) -z
basic, B~ ˈbeɪ.sɪk -s -s -ally -əl.i, -li
BASIC, Basic ˈbeɪ.sɪk
basicity beɪˈsɪs.ə.ti, bə-, -ɪ.ti, (US) -ə.t̬i
Basie ˈbeɪ.si, -zi
basil, B~ ˈbæz.əl, -ɪl, (US) ˈbeɪ.zəl, -səl; (US) ˈbæz.əl
basilar ˈbæz.ɪ.ləʳ, ˈbæs-, -əl.əʳ, (US) -ɪ.lɚ, -əl.ɚ ˌbasilar ˈmembrane
Basildon ˈbæz.əl.dən
basilect ˈbæz.ɪ.lekt, ˈ-ə-, (US) ˈbæz.ə-, ˈbeɪ.sə- -s -s -al -əl
basilic|a bəˈzɪl.ɪ.k|ə, -ˈsɪl-, (US) -ˈsɪl- -as -əz -an -ən
basilisk ˈbæz.ə.lɪsk, ˈ-ɪ-, (US) ˈbæs-, ˈbæz- -s -s
basin ˈbeɪ.sən -s -z
basinet ˈbæs.ɪ.net; ˈ-ə-; -nɪt; ˌbæs.ɪˈnet -s -s
Basinger ˈbeɪ.sɪŋ.gəʳ, ˈbæs.ɪn.dʒəʳ, (US) ˈbeɪ.sɪŋ.gɚ, ˈbæs.ɪn.dʒɚ
Basingstoke ˈbeɪ.zɪŋ.stəʊk, (US) -stoʊk
bas|is ˈbeɪ.s|ɪs -es -iːz
bask bɑːsk, (US) bæsk -s -s -ing -ɪŋ -ed -t
Basker ˈbɑː.skəʳ, (US) ˈbæs.kɚ
Baskervill(e) ˈbæs.kə.vɪl, (US) -kɚ-
basket ˈbɑː.skɪt, (US) ˈbæs.kət -s -s -ful/s -fʊl/z ˈbasket ˌcase; put all one's ˌeggs in one ˈbasket
basketball ˈbɑː.skɪt.bɔːl, (US) ˈbæs.kət.bɔːl, -bɑːl
basketry ˈbɑː.skɪ.tri, (US) ˈbæs.kə-
basketwork ˈbɑː.skɪt.wɜːk, (US) ˈbæs.kət.wɝːk
Baskin-Robbins® ˌbæs.kɪnˈrɒb.ɪnz, (US) -ˈrɑː.bɪnz
Basle bɑːl
basmati bəˈsmɑː.ti, bæsˈmɑː-, bəz-, bæz-
bas mi(t)zvah ˌbæsˈmɪts.və, (US) ˌbɑːs- -ing -ɪŋ -ed -d
Basnett ˈbæz.nɪt, -nət, -net
Basotho bəˈsuː.tuː, -ˈsəʊ.təʊ, (US) -ˈsoʊ.toʊ
basque, B~ bæsk, bɑːsk, (US) bæsk -s -s
Basra(h) ˈbæz.rə, ˈbʌz-, ˈbæs-, (US) ˈbɑːz.rə, ˈbæs-, ˈbæz-, ˈbɑːs-
bas-relief ˌbɑː.rɪˈliːf, ˌbæs-, ˌbɑːs-, -rəˈliːf -s -s
bass, B~ *fish, fibre, beer:* bæs
bass *in music:* beɪs -es -ɪz ˌbass clariˈnet; ˌbass ˈclef; ˌbass ˈdrum; ˌbass guiˈtar
Bassanio bəˈsɑː.ni.əʊ, bæsˈɑː-, (US) -oʊ
Bassenthwaite ˈbæs.ən.θweɪt
basset ˈbæs.ɪt, (US) -ət -s -s ˈbasset ˌhorn; ˈbasset ˌhound
Basset(t) ˈbæs.ɪt, (US) -ət
Basseterre bæsˈteəʳ, (US) -ˈter
Bassey ˈbæs.i
bassinet(te) ˌbæs.ɪˈnet, -əˈ- -s -s
Bassingbourne ˈbæs.ɪŋ.bɔːn, (US) -bɔːrn
bassist ˈbeɪ.sɪst -s -s
bass|o ˈbæs|.əʊ, (US) -oʊ, ˈbɑː.s|oʊ -os -z -i -iː
bassoon bəˈsuːn -s -z -ist/s -ɪst/s
basswood ˈbæs.wʊd
bast, B~ bæst
Bastable ˈbæs.tə.bəl
bastard ˈbɑː.stəd, ˈbæs.təd, (US) ˈbæs.tɚd -s -z -y -i
bastardiz|e, -is|e ˈbɑː.stə.daɪz, ˈbæs.tə-, (US) ˈbæs.tɚ- -es -ɪz -ing -ɪŋ -ed -d
bast|e beɪst -es -s -ing -ɪŋ -ed -ɪd
bastille, B~ bæsˈtiːl -s -z
bastinado ˌbæs.tɪˈnɑː.dəʊ, -ˈneɪ-, (US) -doʊ -es -z -ing -ɪŋ -ed -d
bastion ˈbæs.ti.ən, (US) ˈ-tʃən, ˈ-ti.ən -s -z -ed -d
Basuto bəˈsuː.təʊ, -ˈzuː-, (US) -toʊ -s -z
Basutoland bəˈsuː.təʊ.lænd, -ˈzuː-, (US) -toʊ-
bat bæt -s -s -ting -ɪŋ, (US) ˈbæt̬.ɪŋ -ted -ɪd, (US) ˈbæt̬.ɪd
Ba'taan bəˈtɑːn, (US) -ˈtæn, -ˈtɑːn
Batavia bəˈteɪ.vi.ə
batboy ˈbæt.bɔɪ -s -z
batch bætʃ -es -ɪz
Batchelar, Batchelor ˈbætʃ.əl.əʳ, -ɪ.ləʳ, (US) -əl.ɚ
bat|e, B~ beɪt -es -s -ing -ɪŋ, (US) ˈbeɪ.t̬ɪŋ -ed -ɪd, (US) ˈbeɪ.t̬ɪd
Bateman ˈbeɪt.mən -s -z
Bates beɪts
Bateson ˈbeɪt.sən
Batey ˈbeɪ.ti, (US) -t̬i
bath v bɑːθ, (US) bæθ -s -s -ing -ɪŋ -ed -t
ba|th, B~ n bɑː|θ, (US) bæ|θ -ths -ðz ˌBath ˈbun; ˈBath ˌbun; ˌbath ˈchair; ˈbath ˌcube; ˈbath ˌmat; ˈbath ˌsalts; ˈBath ˌstone; ˌBath ˈOliver
bath|e beɪð -es -z -ing -ɪŋ -ed -d ˈbathing ˌbeauty; ˈbathing ˌcostume; ˈbathing ˌsuit
bather ˈbeɪ.ðəʳ, (US) -ðɚ -s -z
bathetic bəˈθet.ɪk, bæθˈet-, (US) bəˈθet̬-
Bathgate ˈbɑː.θ.geɪt, (US) ˈbæθ-
bathhou|se ˈbɑːθ.haʊ|s, (US) ˈbæθ- -ses -zɪz
bathmat ˈbɑːθ.mæt, (US) ˈbæθ- -s -s
Batho ˈbæθ.əʊ, ˈbeɪ.θəʊ, (US) ˈbæθ.oʊ, ˈbeɪ.θoʊ
batholite ˈbæθ.əʊ.laɪt, (US) ˈ-ə- -s -s
batholith ˈbæθ.əʊ.lɪθ, (US) ˈ-ə- -s -s
bathos ˈbeɪ.θɒs, (US) -θɑːs
bathrobe ˈbɑːθ.rəʊb, (US) ˈbæθ.roʊb -s -z
bathroom ˈbɑːθ.rʊm, -ruːm, (US) ˈbæθ.ruːm, -rʊm -s -z
Bathsheba ˈbæθ.ʃɪ.bə; bæθˈʃiː-
bathtub ˈbɑːθ.tʌb, (US) ˈbæθ- -s -z
Bathurst ˈbæθ.ɜːst, -əst, -hɜːst, ˈbɑː.θɜːst, -θəst, ˈbɑːθ.hɜːst, (US) ˈbæθ.ɝːst, -hɝːst
bathyscaphe ˈbæθ.ɪ.skæf -s -s
bathysphere ˈbæθ.ɪ.sfɪəʳ, (US) -sfɪr -s -z
batik bætˈiːk; ˈbæt.ɪk, (US) bəˈtiːk; (US) ˈbæt̬.ɪk
batiste bætˈiːst, bəˈtiːst
Batley ˈbæt.li
batman *oriental weight:* ˈbæt.mən -s -z
bat|man *military:* ˈbæt|.mən -men -mən
Batman® ˈbæt.mæn
baton ˈbæt.ɒn; -ən, (US) bəˈtɑːn -s -z
Baton Rouge ˌbæt.ənˈruːʒ
bats bæts
bats|man ˈbæts|.mən -men -mən
battalion bəˈtæl.i.ən, ˈ-jən, (US) ˈ-jən -s -z
Battambang ˈbæt.əm.bæŋ, (US) ˈbæt̬-
battels ˈbæt.əlz, (US) ˈbæt̬-
batten, B~ ˈbæt.ən -s -z -ing -ɪŋ -ed -d
Battenberg ˈbæt.ən.bɜːg, -əm-, (US) -ən.bɝːg ˈBattenberg ˌcake
batt|er ˈbæt|.əʳ, (US) ˈbæt̬|.ɚ -ers -əz, (US) -ɚz -ering -ər.ɪŋ -ered -əd, (US) -ɚd ˈbattering ˌram
Battersby ˈbæt.əz.bi, (US) ˈbæt̬.ɚz-
Battersea ˈbæt.ə.si, (US) ˈbæt̬.ɚ-
batter|y ˈbæt.ər|.i, (US) ˈbæt̬- -ies -iz ˈbattery ˌacid
batting n ˈbæt.ɪŋ, (US) ˈbæt̬.ɪŋ ˈbatting ˌaverage; ˈbatting ˌorder
Battishill ˈbæt.ɪ.ʃɪl, -ʃəl, (US) ˈbæt̬-
battl|e, B~ ˈbæt.əl, (US) ˈbæt̬- -es -z -ing -ɪŋ, ˈbæt.lɪŋ -ed -d -er/s -əʳ/z, ˈ-ləʳ/z, (US) ˈ-əl.ɚ/z, ˈ-lɚ/z ˈbattle ˌcry; ˌBattle of ˈBritain; ˌbattle ˈroyal; ˈbattle ˌstations
battleax|e, battle-ax ˈbæt.əl.æks, (US) ˈbæt̬- -es -ɪz
battledore, battledoor ˈbæt.əl.dɔːʳ, (US) ˈbæt̬.əl.dɔːr -s -z
battledress ˈbæt.əl.dres, (US) ˈbæt̬-
battlefield ˈbæt.əl.fiːld, (US) ˈbæt̬- -s -z
battleground ˈbæt.əl.graʊnd -s -z
battlement ˈbæt.əl.mənt, (US) ˈbæt̬- -s -s -ed -ɪd, (US) -mən.t̬ɪd
battleship ˈbæt.əl.ʃɪp, (US) ˈbæt̬- -s -s

battue bæt'uː, -'juː **-s** -z
batt|y 'bæt.|i, (US) 'bæţ- **-ier** -i.əʳ, (US) -i.ɚ **-iest** -i.ɪst, -i.əst
Battye 'bæt.i, (US) 'bæţ-
Batumi bɑː'tuː.mi
batwing 'bæt.wɪŋ ˌ**batwing 'sleeve**
bauble 'bɔː.bəl, (US) 'bɑː-, 'bɔː- **-s** -z
Baucis 'bɔː.sɪs, (US) 'bɑː-, 'bɔː
Baudelaire 'bəʊ.də.leəʳ, ˌ--'-, (US) ˌboʊ.də'ler, ˌboʊd'ler
Baudouin 'bəʊ.dwæ̃ŋ, (US) boʊ'dwɑːn
Bauer baʊ.əʳ, (US) baʊ.ɚ
Baugh bɔː, (US) bɑː, bɔː
Baughan bɔːn, (US) bɑːn, bɔːn
Bauhaus 'baʊ.haʊs
baulk bɔːk, bɔːlk, (US) bɑːk, bɔːk **-s** -s **-ing** -ɪŋ **-ed** -t
Baum *US name:* bɔːm, (US) bɑːm, bɔːm *German name:* baʊm
bauxite 'bɔːk.saɪt, (US) 'bɑːk-, 'bɔːk-
Bavari|a bə'veə.ri|.ə, (US) -'ver.i- **-an/s** -ən/z
bawbee bɔː'biː, '--, (US) 'bɑː.biː, 'bɔː-, -'- **-s** -z
bawd bɔːd, (US) bɑːd, bɔːd **-s** -z **-ry** -ri
Bawden 'bɔː.dən, (US) 'bɑː-, 'bɔː-
bawd|y 'bɔː.d|i, (US) 'bɑː-, 'bɔː- **-ier** -i.əʳ, (US) -i.ɚ **-iest** -i.ɪst, -i.əst **-ily** -əl.i, -ɪ.li **-iness** -ɪ.nəs, -ɪ.nɪs '**bawdy ˌhouse**
bawl bɔːl, (US) bɑːl, bɔːl **-s** -z **-ing** -ɪŋ **-ed** -d **-er/s** -əʳ/z, (US) -ɚ/z
Bax bæks
Baxandall 'bæk.sən.dɔːl, (US) -dɔːl, -dɑːl
Baxter 'bæk.stəʳ, (US) -stɚ
bay, B~ beɪ **-s** -z **-ing** -ɪŋ **-ed** -d '**bay ˌleaf;** ˌ**Bay of 'Pigs;** '**bay ˌtree;** ˌ**bay 'window**
bayard, B~ *horse:* 'beɪ.əd, (US) 'beɪ.ɚd **-s** -z
Bayard *surname:* 'beɪ.ɑːd, (US) -ɑːrd *airship:* 'beɪ.ɑːd, -'-; 'beɪ.əd, (US) 'beɪ.ɚd; (US) 'beɪ.ɑːrd **-s** -z
bayberr|y 'beɪ.bər|.i, (US) -ˌber- **-ies** -iz
Bayer® 'beɪ.əʳ, (US) -ɚ, ber
Bayeux baɪ'jɜː, beɪ-, (US) 'beɪ.juː, 'baɪ- *stress shift, British only: see compound:* ˌ**Bayeux 'Tapestry**
Bayley 'beɪ.li
Bayliss 'beɪ.lɪs
Baylor 'beɪ.ləʳ, (US) -lɚ
Bayly 'beɪ.li
Baynes beɪnz
Baynham 'beɪ.nəm
Baynton 'beɪn.tən, (US) -tən
bayone|t 'beɪ.ə.nə|t, -nɪ|t, -ne|t; ˌbeɪ.ə'ne|t, (US) ˌbeɪ.ə'ne|t, '--- **-ts** -ts **-t(t)ing** -tɪŋ, (US) -ţɪŋ **-t(t)ed** -tɪd, (US) -ţɪd
Bayonne *in France:* baɪ'ɒn, (US) beɪ'oʊn, -'ɑːn, -'ɔːn *in New Jersey:* beɪ'əʊn, (US) -'oʊn, -'joʊn
bayou 'baɪ.uː, -əʊ, (US) -juː, -joʊ **-s** -z
Bayreuth baɪ'rɔɪt, '--
bay-rum ˌbeɪ'rʌm
bay-salt 'beɪ.sɔːlt, -sɒlt, (US) -sɑːlt
Bayston Hill ˌbeɪ.stən'hɪl
Bayswater 'beɪzˌwɔː.təʳ, (US) -ˌwɑː.ţɚ, -ˌwɔː-
bazaar bə'zɑːʳ, (US) -'zɑːr **-s** -z
Bazalgette 'bæz.əl.dʒɪt, -dʒet
bazooka bə'zuː.kə **-s** -z
BBC ˌbiː.biː'siː
BC ˌbiː'siː
BCG ˌbiː.siː'dʒiː
bdellium 'del.i.əm, bə'del-
be *strong form:* biː; *weak form:* bi
being 'biː.ɪŋ **been** biːn, bɪn, (US) bɪn
Note: Weak-form word. The strong form /biː/ is used contrastively, e.g. 'the **be** all and **end** all' and in sentence-final position, e.g. 'What'll it be?'. The weak form is /bi/, e.g. 'It'll be opening soon' /ɪt.əl.bi'əʊ.pən.ɪŋˌsuːn/ (US) /-'oʊ-/. See note at **been** for further weak-form information.
be- bɪ, bə
Note: Prefix. Words containing **be-** are always stressed on the second syllable, e.g. **friend** /frend/, **befriend** /bɪ'frend/.
Bea biː
beach, B~ biːtʃ **-es** -ɪz **-ing** -ɪŋ **-ed** -t '**beach ˌball;** '**beach ˌbum**
beachchair 'biːtʃ.tʃeəʳ, (US) -tʃer **-s** -z
beachcomber, B~ 'biːtʃˌkəʊ.məʳ, (US) -ˌkoʊ.mɚ **-s** -z
beachfront 'biːtʃ.frʌnt **-s** -s
beachhead 'biːtʃ.hed **-s** -z
beach-la-mar, Beach-la-Mar ˌbiːtʃ.lə'mɑːʳ, (US) -'mɑːr
beachwear 'biːtʃ.weəʳ, (US) -wer
beachy, B~ 'biː.tʃi ˌ**Beachy 'Head**
beacon 'biː.kən **-s** -z
Beaconsfield *place in Buckinghamshire:* 'bek.ənz.fiːld *title of Benjamin Disraeli:* 'biː.kənz.fiːld
bead biːd **-s** -z **-ing/s** -ɪŋ/z **-ed** -ɪd **-er/s** -əʳ/z, (US) -ɚ/z
beadle, B~ 'biː.dəl **-s** -z
Beadon 'biː.dən
beadwork 'biːd.wɜːk, (US) -wɝːk
bead|y 'biː.d|i **-ier** -i.əʳ, (US) -i.ɚ **-iest** -i.ɪst, -i.əst **-iness** -ɪ.nɪs, -ɪ.nəs
beagle 'biː.gəl **-s** -z
beak biːk **-s** -s **-ed** -t
beaker 'biː.kəʳ, (US) -kɚ **-s** -z
Beal(e) biːl
beam biːm **-s** -z **-ing** -ɪŋ **-ed** -d '**beam ˌengine**
beam-ends ˌbiːm'endz, '--
beamer 'biː.məʳ, (US) -ɚ **-s** -z
Beaminster 'bem.ɪnt.stəʳ; *locally also:* 'bem.ɪ.stəʳ, (US) -stɚ
Beamish 'biː.mɪʃ
beam|y 'biː.m|i **-ily** -əl.i, -ɪ.li **-iness** -ɪ.nɪs, -ɪ.nəs
bean biːn **-s** -z ˌ**full of 'beans;** ˌ**spill the 'beans**
beanbag 'biːn.bæg, 'biːm-, (US) 'biːn- **-s** -z
beanfeast 'biːn.fiːst **-s** -s **-er/s** -əʳ/z, (US) -ɚ/z
beanie 'biː.ni **-s** -z
beano, B~ 'biː.nəʊ, (US) -noʊ **-s** -z
beanpole 'biːn.pəʊl, 'biːm-, (US) 'biːn.poʊl **-s** -z
beanshoot 'biːn.ʃuːt **-s** -s
beansprout 'biːn.spraʊt **-s** -s
beanstalk 'biːn.stɔːk, (US) -stɔːk, -stɑːk **-s** -s
bear beəʳ, (US) ber **-s** -z **-ing/s** -ɪŋ/z **bore** bɔːʳ, (US) bɔːr **borne** bɔːn, (US) bɔːrn '**bear ˌgarden**
bearab|le 'beə.rə.b|əl, (US) 'ber.ə- **-ly** -li **-leness** -əl.nəs, -əl.nɪs
bear-baiting 'beəˌbeɪ.tɪŋ, (US) 'berˌbeɪ.ţɪŋ
beard, B~ bɪəd, (US) bɪrd **-s** -z **-ing** -ɪŋ **-ed** -ɪd
Bearder 'bɪə.dəʳ, (US) 'bɪr.dɚ
beardless 'bɪəd.ləs, -lɪs, (US) 'bɪrd-
Beardsley 'bɪədz.li, (US) 'bɪrdz-
Beare bɪəʳ, (US) bɪr
bearer 'beə.rəʳ, (US) 'ber.ɚ **-s** -z
bearhug 'beə.hʌg, (US) 'ber- **-s** -z
bearing n 'beə.rɪŋ, (US) 'ber.ɪŋ **-s** -z
bearing rein 'beə.rɪŋ.reɪn, (US) 'ber.ɪŋ- **-s** -z
bearish 'beə.rɪʃ, (US) 'ber.ɪʃ **-ly** -li **-ness** -nəs, -nɪs
béarnaise, B~ ˌbeə'neɪz, -'nez, (US) ˌber'neɪz, ˌbeɪ.ɑːr'-, ˌbeɪ.ɚ'-
Bearsden beəz'den, (US) berz-
bearskin 'beə.skɪn, (US) 'ber- **-s** -z
Bearsted 'bɜː.sted, 'beə.sted, (US) 'bɝː-, 'ber-
Beasant 'beɪ.zənt
Beasley 'biːz.li
beast biːst **-s** -s ˌ**beast of 'burden**
beastie 'biː.sti **-s** -z
beastings 'biː.stɪŋz
beastl|y 'biːst.l|i **-ier** -i.əʳ, (US) -i.ɚ **-iest** -i.ɪst, -i.əst **-iness** -ɪ.nəs, -i.nɪs
beat biːt **-s** -s **-ing/s** -ɪŋ/z, (US) 'biː.ţɪŋ/z **-en** -ən, (US) 'biː.ţən **-er/s** -əʳ/z, (US) 'biː.ţɚ/z ˌ**beat about the 'bush;** '**Beat Geneˌration**
beatific ˌbiː.ə'tɪf.ɪk **-al** -əl **-ally** -əl.i, -li
beatification biˌæt.ɪ.fɪ'keɪ.ʃən, ˌ-ə-, -fə'-, (US) -ˌæţ.ə- **-s** -z
beatif|y bi'æt.ɪ.f|aɪ, '-ə-, (US) -'æţ.ɪ-, -'æţ.ə- **-ies** -aɪz **-ying** -aɪ.ɪŋ **-ied** -aɪd
beatitude, B~ bi'æt.ɪ.tʃuːd, '-ə-, -tjuːd, (US) -'æţ.ə.tuːd, -tjuːd **-s** -z
Beatles 'biː.təlz, (US) -ţəlz
beatnik 'biːt.nɪk **-s** -s
Beaton 'biː.tən, (US) -ţən
Beatrice 'bɪə.trɪs, (US) 'biː.ə-
Beatrix 'bɪə.trɪks, (US) 'biː.ə-
Beattie 'biː.ti, (US) -ţi, 'beɪ-
Beattock 'biː.tək, (US) -ţək
Beatty 'biː.ti, (US) 'beɪ.ţi, 'biː-
beat-up ˌbiːt'ʌp *stress shift:* ˌ**beat-up 'car**
beau, B~ bəʊ, (US) boʊ **-s** -z ˌ**Beau 'Brummell**
Beauchamp 'biː.tʃəm
Beauclerc(k) 'bəʊ.kleəʳ, (US) 'boʊ.kler, -klɝːk
Beaufort *in South Carolina:* 'bjuː.fət, -fɔːt, (US) 'bjuː.fɚt *other senses:* 'bəʊ.fət, -fɔːt, (US) 'boʊ.fɚt

beau(x) geste(s), B~ G~ ˌbəʊˈʒest, (US) ˌboʊ-
Beauharnais ˌbəʊ.ɑːˈneɪ, (US) ˌboʊ.ɑːr-
Beaujolais ˈbəʊ.ʒəl.eɪ, -ʒɒl.eɪ, (US) ˌboʊ.ʒəˈleɪ
Beaujolais nouveau ˌbəʊ.ʒəˌleɪ.nuːˈvəʊ, -ʒɒlˌeɪ-, (US) ˌboʊ.ʒəˌleɪ.nuːˈvoʊ
Beaulieu *in Hampshire:* ˈbjuː.li *US family name:* ˈbəʊ.juː, (US) ˈboʊ-, ˈboʊl- *in France:* bəʊˈljɜː, (US) boʊ-
Beaumarchais ˈbəʊ.mɑːˌʃeɪ, ˌ--ˈ-, (US) ˌboʊ.mɑːrˈʃeɪ
Beaumaris bəʊˈmær.ɪs, bjuː-, (US) boʊˈmer-, -ˈmær-
beau(x) monde(s) bəʊˈmɒnd, (US) ˌboʊˈmɑːnd
Beaumont ˈbəʊ.mənt, -mɒnt, (US) ˈboʊ-, -mɑːnt
Beaune bəʊn, (US) boʊn
Beauregard ˈbəʊ.rɪ.gɑːd, (US) ˈboʊ.rə.gɑːrd
beaut bjuːt **-s** -s
beauteous ˈbjuː.ti.əs, (US) -t̬i- **-ly** -li **-ness** -nəs, -nɪs
beautician bjuːˈtɪʃ.ən **-s** -z
beautification ˌbjuː.tɪ.fɪˈkeɪ.ʃən, -tə-, -fəˈ-, (US) -t̬ə-
beautiful ˈbjuː.tɪ.fəl, -tə-, -fʊl, (US) -t̬ə- **-ly** -i
beautif|y ˈbjuː.tɪ.f|aɪ, -tə-, (US) -t̬ɪ-, -t̬ə- **-ies** -aɪz **-ying** -aɪ.ɪŋ **-ied** -aɪd **-ier/s** -aɪ.əʳ/z, (US) -aɪ.ɚ/z
beaut|y ˈbjuː.t|i, (US) -t̬|i **-ies** -iz ˈ**beauty** ˌ**contest;** ˈ**beauty** ˌ**mark;** ˈ**beauty** ˌ**parlo(u)r;** ˈ**beauty** ˌ**sleep;** ˈ**beauty** ˌ**spot**
Beauvoir ˈbəʊv.wɑː, (US) boʊvˈwɑːr
beaux-arts bəʊˈzɑːʳ, (US) boʊˈzɑːr
Beaux' Stratagem ˌbəʊzˈstræt.ə.dʒəm, (US) ˌboʊzˈstræt̬-
Beavan, Beaven ˈbev.ən
beaver, B~ ˈbiː.vəʳ, (US) -vɚ **-s** -z
Beaverbrook ˈbiː.və.brʊk, (US) -vɚ-
Beavis ˈbiː.vɪs
Beazley ˈbiːz.li
Bebb beb
Bebington ˈbeb.ɪŋ.tən
Bebo ˈbiː.bəʊ, (US) -boʊ
bebop ˈbiː.bɒp, (US) -bɑːp **-per/s** -əʳ/z, (US) -ɚ/z
becalm bɪˈkɑːm, bə- **-s** -z **-ing** -ɪŋ **-ed** -d
became (from **become**) bɪˈkeɪm, bə-
because bɪˈkɒz, bə-, -ˈkəz; *colloquially also:* kɒz, kəz, (US) bɪˈkɑːz, bə-, -ˈkʌz, -ˈkəz, kəz

> Note: The form /bɪˈkəz/ or /bə-/ is unusual in having a stressed schwa vowel. This is found only in a few phrases, most commonly in 'because of the/a ...'. The abbreviation of this word, with the pronunciation /kəz/ (also /kɒz/ in British English), is often spelt **'cos**.

Beccles ˈbek.əlz
bechamel, béchamel ˌbeɪ.ʃəˈmel, ˌbeʃ.əˈ- *stress shift:* ˌ**bechamel** ˈ**sauce**
Becher ˈbiː.tʃəʳ, (US) -tʃɚ
Bechstein ˈbek.staɪn **-s** -z
Bechuana ˌbetʃ.uˈɑː.nə **-s** -z **-land** -lænd
beck, B~ bek **-s** -s ˌ**beck and** ˈ**call**
Becke bek
Beckenbauer ˈbek.ən.baʊ.əʳ, (US) -baʊ.ɚ
Beckenham ˈbek.ən.əm
Becker ˈbek.əʳ, (US) -ɚ
Becket(t) ˈbek.ɪt
Beckford ˈbek.fəd, (US) -fɚd
Beckham ˈbek.əm
Beckinsale ˈbek.ɪn.seɪl
Beckles ˈbek.əlz
Beckley ˈbek.li
beckon ˈbek.ən **-s** -z **-ing** -ɪŋ **-ed** -d
Beckton ˈbek.tən
Beckwith ˈbek.wɪθ
Becky ˈbek.i
becloud bɪˈklaʊd, bə- **-s** -z **-ing** -ɪŋ **-ed** -ɪd
becom|e bɪˈkʌm, bə- **-es** -z **-ing** -ɪŋ **became** bɪˈkeɪm, bə-
becoming bɪˈkʌm.ɪŋ, bəˈ- **-ly** -li **-ness** -nəs, -nɪs
Becontree ˈbek.ən.triː
becquerel, B~ ˌbek.əˈrel; ˈbek.ə.rel, -rəl **-s** -z
bed bed **-s** -z **-ding** -ɪŋ **-ded** -ɪd ˈ**bed** ˌ**rest;** ˌ**bed and** ˈ**breakfast;** ˌ**get out of** ˌ**bed on the** ˌ**wrong** ˈ**side**
BEd biːˈed
bedad bɪˈdæd, bə-
Bedale ˈbiː.dəl, -deɪl
Bedales ˈbiː.deɪlz
bedaub bɪˈdɔːb, bə-, (US) -ˈdɑːb, -ˈdɔːb **-s** -z **-ing** -ɪŋ **-ed** -d
bedazzl|e bɪˈdæz.əl, bə- **-es** -z **-ing** -ɪŋ **-ed** -d
bedbug ˈbed.bʌg **-s** -z
bedchamber ˈbedˌtʃeɪm.bəʳ, (US) -bɚ **-s** -z
bedclothes ˈbed.kləʊðz, -kləʊz, (US) -kloʊðz, -kloʊz
Beddau ˈbeð.aɪ
bedder ˈbed.əʳ, (US) -ɚ **-s** -z
Beddgelert beðˈgel.ət, bed-, beɪð-, -ɜːt, (US) -ɚt
bedding **n** ˈbed.ɪŋ
Beddoes ˈbed.əʊz, (US) -oʊz
beddy-bye ˈbed.i.baɪ **-s** -z
Bede biːd
bedeck bɪˈdek, bə- **-s** -s **-ing** -ɪŋ **-ed** -t
Bedel ˈbiː.dəl; bɪˈdel, bə-
bedel(l) bedˈel, bɪˈdel, bə- **-s** -z
Bedevere ˈbed.ɪ.vɪəʳ, ˈ-ə-, (US) -ə.vɪr
bedevil bɪˈdev.əl, bə- **-s** -z **-(l)ing** -ɪŋ **-(l)ed** -d
bedevilment bɪˈdev.əl.mənt, bə-
bedew bɪˈdʒuː, -ˈdjuː, bə-, (US) -ˈduː, -ˈdjuː **-s** -z **-ing** -ɪŋ **-ed** -d
bedfellow ˈbedˌfel.əʊ, (US) -oʊ **-s** -z
Bedford ˈbed.fəd, (US) -fɚd **-shire** -ʃəʳ, -ʃɪəʳ, (US) -ʃɚ, -ʃɪr
bedim bɪˈdɪm, bə- **-s** -z **-ming** -ɪŋ **-med** -d
Bedingfield ˈbed.ɪŋ.fiːld
Bedivere ˈbed.ɪ.vɪəʳ, ˈ-ə-, (US) -ə.vɪr
bedizen bɪˈdaɪ.zən, bə-, -ˈdɪz.ən **-s** -z **-ing** -ɪŋ **-ed** -d
bedjacket ˈbedˌdʒæk.ɪt **-s** -s
bedlam, B~ ˈbed.ləm
Bedlamite ˈbed.lə.maɪt **-s** -s
bedlinen ˈbedˌlɪn.ɪn, -ən, (US) -ən
bedmaker ˈbedˌmeɪ.kəʳ, (US) -kɚ **-s** -z
Bedouin ˈbed.u.ɪn **-s** -z
bedpan ˈbed.pæn **-s** -z
bedpost ˈbed.pəʊst, (US) -poʊst **-s** -s
bedraggl|e bɪˈdræg.əl, bə- **-es** -z **-ing** -ɪŋ **-ed** -d
bedridden ˈbedˌrɪd.ən
bedrock ˈbed.rɒk, (US) -rɑːk **-s** -s
bedroll ˈbed.rəʊl, (US) -roʊl **-s** -z
bedroom ˈbed.rʊm, -ruːm, (US) -ruːm, -rʊm **-s** -z
Beds. (abbrev. for **Bedfordshire**) bedz; ˈbed.fəd.ʃəʳ, -ˌʃɪəʳ, (US) bedz; (US) ˈbed.fɚd.ʃɚ, -ˌʃɪr
bedside ˈbed.saɪd ˌ**bedside** ˈ**manner;** ˌ**bedside** ˈ**table**
bedsit ˈbed.sɪt **-s** -s
bedsitter ˌbedˈsɪt.əʳ, ˈ-ˌ--, (US) ˌbedˈsɪt̬.ɚ, ˈ-ˌ-- **-s** -z
bedsore ˈbed.sɔːʳ, (US) -sɔːr **-s** -z
bedspread ˈbed.spred **-s** -z
bedstead ˈbed.sted **-s** -z
bedstraw ˈbed.strɔː, (US) -strɑː, -strɔː **-s** -z
bedtime ˈbed.taɪm
Bedwas ˈbed.wæs
Bedwell ˈbed.wel, -wəl
bed-wetting ˈbedˌwet.ɪŋ, (US) -t̬ɪŋ
Bedworth ˈbed.wəθ, (US) -wɚθ
bee, B~ biː **-s** -z ˈ**bee** ˌ**sting;** **have a** ˈ**bee in one's** ˌ**bonnet;** **the** ˌ**bee's** ˈ**knees**
Beeb biːb
Beeby ˈbiː.bi
beech, B~ biːtʃ **-es** -ɪz **-en** -ən
Beecham ˈbiː.tʃəm ˌ**Beecham's** ˈ**Powders**®
Beecher ˈbiː.tʃəʳ, (US) -tʃɚ
Beeching ˈbiː.tʃɪŋ
beechnut ˈbiːtʃ.nʌt **-s** -s
beechwood ˈbiːtʃ.wʊd
bee eater ˈbiːˌiː.təʳ, (US) -t̬ɚ **-s** -z
beef **n** biːf **-s** -s **beeves** biːvz
beef **v** biːf **-s** -s **-ing** -ɪŋ **-ed** -t
beefalo ˈbiː.fəl.əʊ, (US) -fə.loʊ **-(e)s** -z
beefburger ˈbiːfˌbɜː.gəʳ, (US) -ˌbɜːː.gɚ **-s** -z
beefcake ˈbiːf.keɪk **-s** -s
beefeater, B~ ˈbiːfˌiː.təʳ, (US) -t̬ɚ **-s** -z
beefsteak ˈbiːf.steɪk, -ˈ- **-s** -s
beef|y ˈbiː.f|i **-ier** -i.əʳ, (US) -i.ɚ **-iest** -i.ɪst, -i.əst **-ily** -əl.i, -ɪ.li **-iness** -ɪ.nəs, -ɪ.nɪs
beehive ˈbiː.haɪv **-s** -z
bee-keep|ing ˈbiːˌkiː.p|ɪŋ **-er/s** -əʳ/z, (US) -ɚ/z
beeline ˈbiː.laɪn **-s** -z
Beelzebub biːˈel.zɪ.bʌb, -zə-
Beemer ˈbiː.məʳ, (US) -mɚ
been (from **be**) biːn, bɪn, (US) bɪn
Note: Weak-form word, British

English. The pronunciation /bɪn/ may be used optionally as a weak form corresponding to /biːn/, e.g. 'Jane's been invited' /ˈdʒeɪnz.bɪn.ɪnˌvaɪ.tɪd/ (US) /-t̬ɪd/. In American English, /biːn/ does not usually occur.
beep biːp **-s** -s **-ing** -ɪŋ **-ed** -t
beeper ˈbiː.pəʳ, (US) -pɚ **-s** -z
beer, B~ bɪəʳ, (US) bɪr **-s** -z ˈ**beer** ˌ**garden**; ˈ**beer** ˌ**mat**
Beerbohm ˈbɪə.bəʊm, (US) ˈbɪr.boʊm
Beersheba ˌbɪəˈʃiː.bə, ˈbɪə.ʃɪ-, (US) ˌbɪrˈʃiː-, ˌber-
beer|y ˈbɪə.r|i, (US) ˈbɪr|.i **-ier** -i.əʳ, (US) -i.ɚ **-iest** -i.ɪst, -i.əst **-ily** -əl.i, -ɪ.li **-iness** -ɪ.nəs, -ɪ.nɪs
Beesl(e)y ˈbiːz.li
beestings ˈbiː.stɪŋz
Beeston ˈbiː.stən
beeswax ˈbiːz.wæks
beeswing ˈbiːz.wɪŋ
beet biːt **-s** -s
Beetham ˈbiː.θəm
Beethoven *composer:* ˈbeɪt.əʊ.vən, ˈbeɪt.həʊ-, (US) ˈbeɪ.toʊ- *London street:* ˈbiːt.həʊ.vən, ˈbiː.təʊ-, (US) ˈbiː.toʊ-
beetl|e ˈbiː.təl, (US) -t̬əl **-es** -z **-ing** -ɪŋ, ˈbiːt.lɪŋ **-ed** -d
Beeton ˈbiː.tən
beetroot ˈbiːt.ruːt **-s** -s
beeves (plural of **beef**) biːvz
befall bɪˈfɔːl, bə-, (US) -ˈfɔːl, -ˈfɑːl **-s** -z **-ing** -ɪŋ **-en** -ən
befell (from **befall**) bɪˈfel, bə-
befit bɪˈfɪt, bə- **-s** -s **-ting/ly** -ɪŋ/li, (US) -ˈfɪt̬.ɪŋ/li **-ted** -ɪd, (US) -ˈfɪt̬.ɪd
before bɪˈfɔːʳ, bə-, (US) -ˈfɔːr
beforehand bɪˈfɔː.hænd, bə-, (US) -ˈfɔːr-
before-mentioned bɪˈfɔːˌmen.tʃənd, -ˌ-ˈ--, (US) bəˈfɔːrˌmen-
beforetime bɪˈfɔː.taɪm, bə-, (US) -ˈfɔːr-
befoul bɪˈfaʊl, bə- **-s** -z **-ing** -ɪŋ **-ed** -d
befriend bɪˈfrend, bə- **-s** -z **-ing** -ɪŋ **-ed** -ɪd
befuddl|e bɪˈfʌd.əl, bə- **-es** -z **-ing** -ɪŋ, -ˈfʌd.lɪŋ **-ed** -d
befuddlement bɪˈfʌd.əl.mənt, bə-
beg beg **-s** -z **-ging** -ɪŋ **-ged** -d
begad bɪˈgæd, bə-
began (from **begin**) bɪˈgæn, bə-
begat (from **beget**) bɪˈgæt, bə-
beget bɪˈget, bə- **-s** -s **-ting** -ɪŋ, (US) -ˈget̬.ɪŋ **begat** bɪˈgæt, bə- **begot** bɪˈgɒt, bə-, (US) -ˈgɑːt **begotten** bɪˈgɒt.ən, bə-, (US) -ˈgɑː.tən
Begg beg
beggar ˈbeg.əʳ, (US) -ɚ **-s** -z **-ing** -ɪŋ **-ed** -d
beggarl|y ˈbeg.əl|.i, (US) -ɚ.l|i **-iness** -ɪ.nəs, -ɪ.nɪs
beggar-my-neighbour ˌbeg.ə.mɪˈneɪ.bəʳ, -maɪˈ-, (US) -ɚ.maɪˈneɪ.bɚ
beggarweed ˈbeg.ə.wiːd, (US) ˈ-ɚ- **-s** -z
beggary ˈbeg.ər.i
Beggs begz
begin bɪˈgɪn, bə- **-s** -z **-ning/s** -ɪŋ/z
Begin ˈbeɪ.gɪn
beginner bɪˈgɪn.əʳ, bə-, (US) -ɚ **-s** -z
Begley ˈbeg.li
begone bɪˈgɒn, bə-, (US) -ˈgɑːn
begonia bɪˈgəʊ.ni.ə, bə-, (US) -ˈgoʊ.njə **-s** -z
begorra bɪˈgɒr.ə, bə-, (US) -ˈgɔːr.ə
begot (from **beget**) bɪˈgɒt, bə-, (US) -ˈgɑːt **-ten** -ən, (US) -ˈgɑː.t̬ən
begrim|e bɪˈgraɪm, bə- **-es** -z **-ing** -ɪŋ **-ed** -d
begrudg|e bɪˈgrʌdʒ, bə- **-es** -ɪz **-ing** -ɪŋ **-ed** -d
beguil|e bɪˈgaɪl, bə- **-es** -z **-ing/ly** -ɪŋ/li **-ed** -d
beguine bɪˈgiːn
begum, B~ ˈbeɪ.gəm **-s** -z
begun (from **begin**) bɪˈgʌn, bə-
behalf bɪˈhɑːf, bə-, (US) -ˈhæf
Behan ˈbiː.ən
behav|e bɪˈheɪv, bə- **-es** -z **-ing** -ɪŋ **-ed** -d
behavio(u)r bɪˈheɪ.vjəʳ, bə-, (US) -vjɚ **-s** -z
behavio(u)ral bɪˈheɪ.vjər.əl, bə-, (US) -vjɝː.əl
behavio(u)r|ism bɪˈheɪ.vjər|.ɪ.zəm, bə- **-ist/s** -ɪst/s
behead bɪˈhed, bə- **-s** -z **-ing** -ɪŋ **-ed** -ɪd
beheld (from **behold**) bɪˈheld, bə-
behemoth, B~ bɪˈhiː.mɒθ, bə-, -məθ, (US) -mɑːθ, -məθ; (US) ˈbiː.ə.məθ **-s** -s
behest bɪˈhest, bə- **-s** -s
behind bɪˈhaɪnd, bə-
behindhand bɪˈhaɪnd.hænd, bə-
behind-the-scenes bɪˌhaɪnd.ðəˈsiːnz, (US) bə- *stress shift:* ˌ**behind-the-scenes** ˈ**tour**
Behn ben
behold bɪˈhəʊld, bə-, (US) -ˈhoʊld **-s** -z **-ing** -ɪŋ **beheld** bɪˈheld, bə- **beholder/s** bɪˈhəʊl.dəʳ/z, bə-, (US) -ˈhoʊl.dɚ/z
beholden bɪˈhəʊl.dən, bə-, (US) -ˈhoʊl-
behoof bɪˈhuːf, bə-
behoov|e bɪˈhuːv, bə- **-es** -z **-ing** -ɪŋ **-ed** -d
behov|e bɪˈhəʊv, bə-, (US) -ˈhoʊv **-es** -z **-ing** -ɪŋ **-ed** -d
Behrens ˈbeə.rənz, (US) ˈber.ənz
Behrman ˈbeə.mən, (US) ˈber-
Beiderbecke ˈbaɪ.də.bek, (US) -dɚ-
beige beɪʒ
Beighton ˈbeɪ.tən, ˈbaɪ-
beignet ˈbeɪ.njeɪ, -ˈ-, (US) ˌbeɪˈnjeɪ **-s** -z
Beijing ˌbeɪˈdʒɪŋ
being ˈbiː.ɪŋ **-s** -z
Beira ˈbaɪ.rə, (US) ˈbeɪ-
Beirut beɪˈruːt
Beit baɪt
Beith *surname:* biːθ *place in Scotland:* biːð
Bejam® ˈbiː.dʒæm
bejan ˈbiː.dʒən **-s** -z
bejesus, bejezus bɪˈdʒiː.zəz, bə-, -zəs
bejewel bɪˈdʒuː.əl **-s** -z **-(l)ing** -ɪŋ **-(l)ed** -d
bel bel **-s** -z
belabo(u)r bɪˈleɪ.bəʳ, bə-, (US) -bɚ **-s** -z **-ing** -ɪŋ **-ed** -d
Belarius bɪˈleə.ri.əs, bə-, -ˈlɑː-, (US) -ˈler.i-
Belarus ˌbel.əˈruːs, ˌbjel- **-ian** -ruːs.i.ən, -rus.i.ən, -ru.ʃən
Belasco bɪˈlæs.kəʊ, bə-, (US) -koʊ
belated bɪˈleɪ.tɪd, bə-, (US) -t̬ɪd **-ly** -li **-ness** -nəs, -nɪs
belay bɪˈleɪ, bə- **-s** -z **-ing** -ɪŋ **-ed** -d
bel canto ˌbelˈkæn.təʊ, (US) -toʊ
belch, B~ beltʃ **-es** -ɪz **-ing** -ɪŋ **-ed** -t **-er/s** -əʳ/z, (US) -ɚ/z
Belcher ˈbel.*t*ʃəʳ, (US) -*t*ʃɚ
beldam(e) ˈbel.dəm **-s** -z
beleagu|er bɪˈliː.g|əʳ, bə-, (US) -g|ɚ **-ers** -əz, (US) -ɚz **-ering** -ər.ɪŋ **-ered** -əd, (US) -ɚd **-erer/s** -əʳ/z, (US) -ɚ/z
Belém bəˈlem, belˈem
belemnite ˈbel.əm.naɪt **-s** -s
Belfast belˈfɑːst, ˈ--, (US) ˈbel.fæst, ˌ-ˈ-
belfr|y ˈbel.fr|i **-ies** -iz
Belgian ˈbel.dʒən **-s** -z
Belgic ˈbel.dʒɪk
Belgium ˈbel.dʒəm
Belgrade belˈgreɪd, (US) ˈ-- *stress shift, British only:* ˌ**Belgrade** ˈ**streets**
Belgrano belˈgrɑː.nəʊ, (US) -noʊ
Belgrave ˈbel.greɪv
Belgravia belˈgreɪ.vi.ə
Belial ˈbiː.li.əl
bel|ie bɪˈl|aɪ, bə- **-ies** -aɪz **-ying** -aɪ.ɪŋ **-ied** -aɪd
belief bɪˈliːf, bə- **-s** -s
believab|le bɪˈliː.və.b|əl, bə- **-ly** -li
believ|e bɪˈliːv, bə- **-es** -z **-ing/ly** -ɪŋ/li **-ed** -d
believer bɪˈliː.vəʳ, bə-, (US) -vɚ **-s** -z
belike bɪˈlaɪk, bə-
Belinda bəˈlɪn.də, bɪ-
Belisha bəˈliː.ʃə, bɪ- **Be**ˌ**lisha** ˈ**beacon**
belittl|e bɪˈlɪt.əl, bə-, (US) -ˈlɪt̬- **-es** -z **-ing** -ɪŋ, -ˈlɪt.lɪŋ **-ed** -d
Belize bəˈliːz, belˈiːz
bell, B~ bel **-s** -z **-ing** -ɪŋ **-ed** -d ˈ**bell** ˌ**jar**; ˈ**bell** ˌ**pepper**; ˈ**bell** ˌ**tent**; ˈ**bell** ˌ**tower**
Bella ˈbel.ə
belladonna ˌbel.əˈdɒn.ə, (US) -ˈdɑː.nə
Bellamy ˈbel.ə.mi
Bellatrix ˈbel.ə.trɪks, bəˈleɪ-, (US) ˈbel.ə-
bell-bottom ˈbelˌbɒt.əm, (US) -ˌbɑː.t̬əm **-s** -z **-ed** -d
bellboy ˈbel.bɔɪ **-s** -z
belle, B~ bel **-s** -z ˌ**Southern** ˈ**belle**; ˌ**belle of the** ˈ**ball**
belle époque ˌbel.eɪˈpɒk, (US) -ˈpɑːk
Belle Isle ˌbelˈaɪl
Bellerophon bəˈler.ə.fən, bɪ-, (US) -fən, -fɑːn

belles lettres ˌbelˈlet.rə

Bellevue ˌbelˈvjuː, ˈ--, US ˈbel.vjuː

Bellew ˈbel.juː

bellhop ˈbel.hɒp, US -hɑːp -s -s

bellicose ˈbel.ɪ.kəʊs, ˈ-ə-, -kəʊz, US -koʊs -ly -li

bellicosity ˌbel.ɪˈkɒs.ə.ti, -ɪ.ti, US -əˈkɑː.sə.t̬i

belligeren|ce bəˈlɪdʒ.ᵊr.ən*t*|s, bɪ- -cy -si

belligerent bəˈlɪdʒ.ᵊr.ənt, bɪ- -s -s -ly -li

Bellingham *in Northumberland:* ˈbel.ɪn.dʒəm *surname:* ˈbel.ɪn.dʒəm, -ɪŋ.əm, -hæm *in London:* ˈbel.ɪŋ.əm *in the US:* ˈbel.ɪŋ.hæm

Bellini belˈiː.ni, bəˈliː-

bell|man ˈbel|.mən, -mæn -men -mən, -men

Belloc ˈbel.ɒk, US -ɑːk

Bellot ˈbel.əʊ, US belˈoʊ

bellow, B~ ˈbel.əʊ, US -oʊ -s -z -ing -ɪŋ -ed -d

bell-pull ˈbel.pʊl -s -z

bell-push ˈbel.pʊʃ -es -ɪz

bellringer ˈbelˌrɪŋ.əʳ, US -ɚ -s -z

Bellshill belzˈhɪl

Bellsouth ˌbelˈsaʊθ

bellwether ˈbelˌweð.əʳ, US -ɚ -s -z

bell|y ˈbel|.i -ies -iz -ying -i.ɪŋ -ied -id **ˈbelly ˌbutton; ˈbelly ˌdance; ˈbelly ˌflop; ˈbelly ˌlaugh**

bellyach|e ˈbel.i.eɪk -es -s -ing -ɪŋ -ed -t

bellyful ˈbel.i.fʊl -s -z

belly-up ˌbel.iˈʌp

Belmarsh ˈbel.mɑːʃ, US -mɑːrʃ

Belmont ˈbel.mɒnt, -mənt, US -mɑːnt

Belmopan ˌbel.məʊˈpæn, US -moʊˈ-

Belo Horizonte ˌbeɪ.ləʊ.hɒr.ɪˈzɒn.ti, US -loʊ.hɔːr.əˈzɑːn-, ˌbel.oʊ-

belong bɪˈlɒŋ, bə-, US -ˈlɑːŋ, -ˈlɔːŋ -s -z -ing/s -ɪŋ/z -ed -d

Belorussi|a ˌbel.əʊˈrʌʃ|.ə, ˌbjel-, -ˈruː.si|-, US -oʊˈ-, -əˈ- -an/s -ən/z

beloved *used predicatively:* bɪˈlʌvd, bə- *used attributively or as a noun:* bɪˈlʌv.ɪd, bə-, -ˈlʌvd

below bɪˈləʊ, bə-, US -ˈloʊ

Bel Paese ˌbel.pɑːˈeɪ.zeɪ, -zi, US -zi

Belper ˈbel.pəʳ, US -pɚ

Belsen ˈbel.sᵊn

Belsham ˈbel.ʃəm

Belshaw ˈbel.ʃɔː, US -ʃɑː, -ʃɔː

Belshazzar belˈʃæz.əʳ, US -ɚ

Belsize ˈbel.saɪz

Belstead ˈbel.stɪd, -sted

belt, B~ belt -s -s -ing/s -ɪŋ/z, US ˈbel.t̬ɪŋ -ed -ɪd, US ˈbel.t̬ɪd **beˌlow the ˈbelt**

Beltingham ˈbel.tɪn.dʒəm

Belton ˈbel.tən

beltway ˈbelt.weɪ -s -z

Beluchistan bəˈluː.tʃɪ.stɑːn, bɪ-, -stæn; bəˌluː.tʃɪˈstɑːn, bə-, -kɪˈ-, -ˈstæn

beluga bəˈluː.gə, bɪˈ-, belˈuː- -s -z

belvedere, B~ ˈbel.və.dɪəʳ, -vɪ-, ˌ--ˈ-, US ˈbel.və.dɪr, ˌ--ˈ- -s -z

Belvoir ˈbiː.vəʳ, US -vɚ

bema ˈbiː.mə -s -z -ta -tə, US -t̬ə

Bembridge ˈbem.brɪdʒ

bemoan bɪˈməʊn, bə-, US -ˈmoʊn -s -z -ing -ɪŋ -ed -d

bemus|e bɪˈmjuːz, bə- -es -ɪz -ing -ɪŋ -ed -d -ement -mənt

Ben ben

Benares bɪˈnɑː.rɪz, bə-, benˈɑː-, US bəˈnɑːr.iːz

Benbecula benˈbek.jʊ.lə, bem-, -jə-, US ben-

Benbow ˈben.bəʊ, ˈbem-, US ˈben.boʊ

bench bentʃ -es -ɪz

bencher ˈben.*t*ʃəʳ, US -*t*ʃɚ -s -z

Benchley ˈben*t*ʃ.li

benchmark ˈben*t*ʃ.mɑːk, US -mɑːrk -s -s -ing -ɪŋ

bend bend -s -z -ing -ɪŋ -ed -ɪd **bent** bent **bendable** ˈben.də.bᵊl **ˌround the ˈbend**

Bendall ˈben.dᵊl, -dɔːl, US -dᵊl, -dɔːl, -dɑːl

bender, B~ ˈben.dəʳ, US -dɚ -s -z

Bendix® ˈben.dɪks

bendroflumethiazide ˌben.drəʊˌfluː.mɪˈθaɪ.ə.zaɪd, US -droʊ-

bend|y ˈben.d|i -ier -i.əʳ, US -i.ɚ -iest -i.ɪst, -i.əst -iness -ɪ.nəs, -ɪ.nɪs

beneath bɪˈniːθ, bə-

Benedicite ˌben.ɪˈdaɪ.sɪ.ti, -ˈdiː.tʃɪ-, -tʃə-, -teɪ, US -əˈdɪs.ə.t̬i, ˌbeɪ.neɪˈdiː.tʃiː.teɪ -s -z

Benedick ˈben.ɪ.dɪk, ˈ-ə- -s -s

Benedict ˈben.ɪ.dɪkt, ˈ-ə-

benedictine *liqueur:* ˌben.ɪˈdɪk.tiːn, -əˈ- -s -z

Benedictine *monk:* ˌben.ɪˈdɪk.tɪn, -əˈ-, -taɪn, US -tɪn, -tiːn -s -z

> Note: Members of the Order pronounce /-tɪn/.

benediction ˌben.ɪˈdɪk.ʃᵊn, -əˈ- -s -z

Benedictus ˌben.ɪˈdɪk.təs, -əˈ-, -tʊs -es -ɪz

benefaction ˌben.ɪˈfæk.ʃᵊn, -əˈ-, US ˌben.əˈfæk-, ˈben.ə.fæk- -s -z

benefactive ˈben.ɪ.fæk.tɪv, -ə-; ˌben.ɪˈfæk-, -əˈ-, US ˈben.ə.fæk-, ˌben.əˈfæk-

benefactor ˈben.ɪ.fæk.təʳ, ˈ-ə-, US -tɚ -s -z

benefactress ˈben.ɪ.fæk.trəs, ˈ-ə-, -trɪs; ˌben.ɪˈfæk-, -əˈ-, US ˈben.ə.fæk- -es -ɪz

benefic bɪˈnef.ɪk

benefic|e ˈben.ɪ.fɪs, ˈ-ə- -es -ɪz -ed -t

beneficen|ce bɪˈnef.ɪ.sᵊn|*t*s, bə- -t/ly -t/li

beneficial ˌben.ɪˈfɪʃ.ᵊl, -əˈ- -ly -li -ness -nəs, -nɪs

beneficiar|y ˌben.ɪˈfɪʃ.ᵊr|.i, -əˈ- -ies -iz

bene|fit ˈben.ɪ|.fɪt, ˈ-ə- -fits -fɪts -fit(t)ing -fɪ.tɪŋ, US -fɪ.t̬ɪŋ -fit(t)ed -fɪ.tɪd, US -fɪ.t̬ɪd

Benelux ˈben.ɪ.lʌks

Benenden ˈben.ən.dən

Benet ˈben.ɪt

Bene't ˈben.ɪt

Benét *US surname:* benˈeɪ, US bəˈneɪ, benˈeɪ

Benetton® ˈben.ɪ.tᵊn, ˈ-ə-, -tɒn, US -ə.t̬ən, -tɑːn

benevolence bɪˈnev.ᵊl.ən*t*s, bə-

benevolent bɪˈnev.ᵊl.ənt, bɪ- -ly -li

Benfleet ˈben.fliːt

BEng ˌbiːˈendʒ

Bengal ˌbeŋˈgɔːl, ˌben-, US -ˈgɔːl; US ˈbeŋ.gᵊl, ˈben- -s -z *stress shift, British only:* **ˌBengal ˈtiger**

Bengalese ˌbeŋ.gᵊlˈiːz, ˌben-, -gɔːˈ-, US -gəˈliːz, -ˈliːs

Bengali beŋˈgɔː.li, ben- -s -z

Bengasi beŋˈgɑː.zi, ben-

Benge bendʒ

Benghazi beŋˈgɑː.zi, ben-

Ben-Gurion benˈgʊə.ri.ən, beŋ-, -ˈgʊr.i-, US -ˈgʊr.i-, ˌben.gʊrˈjɑːn

Benham ˈben.əm

Ben-Hur benˈhɜːʳ, US -ˈhɝː

Benidorm ˈben.ɪ.dɔːm, ˈ-ə-, US -dɔːrm

benighted bɪˈnaɪ.tɪd, bə-, US -t̬ɪd

benign bɪˈnaɪn, bə- -est -ɪst, -əst -ly -li

benignancy bɪˈnɪg.nən*t*.si, bə-

benignant bɪˈnɪg.nənt, bə- -ly -li

Benigni bəˈniː.ni

benignity bɪˈnɪg.nə.ti, bə-, -nɪ-, US -nə.t̬i

Benin benˈiːn, bɪˈniːn, bə-

Bening ˈben.ɪŋ

benison ˈben.ɪ.sᵊn, ˈ-ə-, -zᵊn -s -z

Benis(s)on ˈben.ɪ.sᵊn, ˈ-ə-

Benítez benˈiː.tez, bəˈniː-, US ˈ-tez, -t̬ez

Benito benˈiː.təʊ, bəˈniː-, US bəˈniː.t̬oʊ

Benjamin ˈben.dʒə.mɪn, -mən

Benjamite ˈben.dʒə.maɪt -s -s

Benn ben

Bennet(t) ˈben.ɪt

Bennette benˈet, bəˈnet

Ben Nevis ˌbenˈnev.ɪs

Bennington ˈben.ɪŋ.tən

Benny ˈben.i

Bensham ˈben*t*.ʃəm

Bensley ˈbenz.li

Benson ˈben*t*.sᵊn

Benstead ˈben*t*.stɪd, -sted

bent, B~ (from **bend**) bent -s -s

Bentham ˈben.təm, ˈben*t*.θəm, US ˈben*t*.θəm -ism -ɪ.zᵊm -ite/s -aɪt/s

benthic ˈben*t*.θɪk

Bentinck ˈben.tɪŋk

Bentine benˈtiːn, ˈ--

Bentley ˈbent.li -s -z

Benton ˈben.tən

bentwood ˈbent.wʊd

benumb bɪˈnʌm, bə- -s -z -ing -ɪŋ -ed -d

Benvolio benˈvəʊ.li.əʊ, US -ˈvoʊ.li.oʊ

Benz benz, bents

Benzedrine® ˈben.zɪ.driːn, -zə-, -drɪn

B

benzene, benzine ˈben.ziːn, -ˈ-
benzoate ˈben.zəʊ.eɪt, (US) -zoʊ-
benzoic benˈzəʊ.ɪk, (US) -ˈzoʊ-
benzoin ˈben.zəʊ.ɪn, -ˈ--, (US) ˈben.zoʊ-, benˈzoʊ-
benzol ˈben.zɒl, (US) -zɑːl
benzoline ˈben.zəʊ.liːn, (US) -zə-
benzyl ˈben.zɪl, (US) -ziː.əl, -zᵊl
Beowulf ˈbeɪ.əʊ.wʊlf, ˈbiː-, (US) ˈbeɪ.ə.wʊlf
beque|ath bɪˈkwiː|ð, bə-, -ˈkwiː|θ **-ths** -ðz, -θs **-thing** -ðɪŋ **-thed** -ðd, -θt
bequest bɪˈkwest, bə- **-s** -s
be|rate bɪ|ˈreɪt, bə-, bɪ- **-rates** -ˈreɪts **-rating** -ˈreɪ.tɪŋ, (US) -ˈreɪ.t̬ɪŋ **-rated** -ˈreɪ.tɪd, (US) -ˈreɪ.t̬ɪd
Berber ˈbɜː.bəʳ, (US) ˈbɝː.bɚ **-s** -z
berceuse beəˈsɜːz, (US) berˈsuz, -ˈsɜːz
Bere bɪəʳ, (US) bɪr
Berea bəˈriː.ə, bɪ-, (US) bə-
bereav|e bɪˈriːv, bə-, (US) bɪ- **-es** -z **-ing** -ɪŋ **-ed** -d
bereavement bɪˈriːv.mənt, bə- **-s** -s
bereft bɪˈreft, bə-
Berengaria ˌber.ᵊŋˈgeə.ri.ə, -ɪŋˈ-, -eŋˈ-, (US) -ˈger.i-
Berenice *in ancient Egypt, etc.:* ˌber.ɪˈnaɪ.si, -ki, -ˈniː.tʃeɪ *opera by Handel:* ˌber.ɪˈniː.tʃi *modern name:* ˌber.əˈniːs, -ɪˈ-
Berenson ˈber.ᵊnt.sən
Beresford ˈber.ɪs.fəd, -ɪz-, (US) -fɚd
beret ˈber.eɪ, -i, (US) bəˈreɪ **-s** -z
berg, B~ bɜːg, beəg, (US) bɝːg **-s** -z
bergamot ˈbɜː.gə.mɒt, -mət, (US) ˈbɝː.gə.mɑːt **-s** -s
Bergen ˈbɜː.gən, ˈbeə-, (US) ˈbɝː-
Berger *English surname:* ˈbɜː.dʒəʳ, (US) ˈbɝː.dʒɚ *US surname:* ˈbɜː.gəʳ, (US) ˈbɝː.gɚ
Bergerac ˈbɜː.ʒə.ræk, (US) ˌbɝː.ʒəˈræk, -ˈrɑːk
Bergkamp ˈbɜːg.kæmp, (US) ˈbɝːg-, -kɑːmp
Bergman ˈbɜːg.mən, (US) ˈbɝːg-
Bergson ˈbɜːg.sən, (US) ˈberg-, ˈbɝːg-
Bergsonian bɜːgˈsəʊ.ni.ən, (US) bergˈsoʊ-, bɝːg-
beribboned bɪˈrɪb.ᵊnd, bə-
beriberi ˌber.ɪˈber.i
Bering ˈbeə.rɪŋ, ˈber-, (US) ˈber.ɪŋ
ˌBering ˈStrait
Berio ˈber.i.əʊ, (US) -oʊ
Berisford ˈber.ɪs.fəd, (US) -fɚd
berk bɜːk, (US) bɝːk **-s** -z
Berkeleian bɑːkˈliː.ən, (US) ˈbɝː.kli.ən
Berkeley *in England:* ˈbɑː.kli, (US) ˈbɑːr-, ˈbɝː- *in US:* ˈbɜː.kli, (US) ˈbɝː-
berkelium bɜːˈkiː.li.əm, (US) ˈbɝː.kli.əm, bɝːˈkliː.əm
Berkhamsted, Berkhampstead ˈbɜː.kəmp.stɪd, -sted, (US) ˈbɝː-

> Note: The usual British pronunciation is /ˈbɜː-/, but the form /ˈbɑː-/ is used by some residents.

Berkley ˈbɜː.kli, (US) ˈbɝː-
Berkoff ˈbɜː.kɒf, (US) ˈbɝː.kɑːf
Berks. (abbrev. for **Berkshire**) bɑːks, ˈbɑːk.ʃəʳ, -ˌʃɪəʳ, (US) bɝːks; (US) ˈbɝːk.ʃɚ, -ˌʃɪr
Berkshire ˈbɑːk.ʃəʳ, -ʃɪəʳ, (US) ˈbɝːk.ʃɚ, -ʃɪr
Berlin *in Germany:* bɜːˈlɪn, (US) bɝː- *stress shift, British only, see compound:* **ˌBerlin ˈWall** *surname:* ˈbɜː.lɪn, -ˈ-, (US) ˈbɝː-, -ˈ- *town in US:* ˈbɜː.lɪn, (US) ˈbɝː-
Berliner bɜːˈlɪn.əʳ, (US) bɚˈlɪn.ɚ **-s** -z
Berlioz ˈbeə.li.əʊz, ˈbɜː-, (US) ˈber.li.oʊz
Berlitz bɜːˈlɪts, ˈ--, (US) ˈbɝː.lɪts, ˌ-ˈ-
Berlusconi ˌbɜː.lʊˈskəʊ.ni, ˌbeə-, (US) ˌbɝː.lʊˈskoʊ-, ˌber-
Bermondsey ˈbɜː.mənd.zi, (US) ˈbɝː-
Bermuda bəˈmjuː.də, (US) bɚ- **-s** -z
Berˌmuda ˈshorts; Berˌmuda ˈtriangle
Bern bɜːn, beən, (US) bɝːn
Bernadette ˌbɜː.nəˈdet, (US) ˌbɝː-
Bernard *first name:* ˈbɜː.nəd, (US) ˈbɝː.nɚd *surname:* bɜːˈnɑːd, bəˈ-; ˈbɜː.nəd, (US) bɚˈnɑːrd; (US) ˈbɝː.nɚd
Berne bɜːn, beən, (US) bɝːn
Berners ˈbɜː.nəz, (US) ˈbɝː.nɚz
Bernese bɜːˈniːz, (US) bɝː-, -ˈniːs *stress shift:* **ˌBernese ˈOberland**
Bernhardt ˈbɜːn.hɑːt, (US) ˈbɝːn.hɑːrt
Bernice *biblical name:* bɜːˈnaɪ.si, (US) bɚ- *modern name:* ˈbɜː.nɪs, bɜːˈniːs, (US) ˈbɝː-; (US) bɚˈniːs
Bernie ˈbɜː.ni, (US) ˈbɝː-
Bernini bɜːˈniː.ni, bə-, (US) bɚ-, ber-
Bernoulli bɜːˈnuː.ji, bəˈ-, -li, (US) bɚˈnuː.li
Bernstein ˈbɜːn.staɪn, -stiːn, (US) ˈbɝːn-
Berol® ˈbiː.rɒl, -rəʊl, (US) -rɑːl, -roʊl
Berowne bəˈrəʊn, (US) -ˈroʊn
Berra ˈber.ə
Berridge ˈber.ɪdʒ
berr|y, B~ ˈber|.i **-ies** -iz
Berryman ˈber.i.mæn, -mən
berserk bəˈzɜːk, -ˈsɜːk, (US) bɚˈsɝːk, -ˈzɝːk **-s** -s
Bert bɜːt, (US) bɝːt
Bertelsmann® ˈbɜː.tᵊlz.mæn, -mən, (US) ˈbɝː.t̬ᵊlz-
berth n bɜːθ, (US) bɝːθ **-s** -s, bɜːðz, (US) bɝːðz
berth v bɜːθ, (US) bɝːθ **-s** -s **-ing** -ɪŋ **-ed** -t
Bertha ˈbɜː.θə, (US) ˈbɝː-
Bertie *first name:* ˈbɜː.ti, (US) ˈbɝː.t̬i *surname:* ˈbɑː.ti, ˈbɜː-, (US) ˈbɑːr.t̬i, ˈbɝː-
Bertolucci ˌbɜː.təʊˈluː.tʃi, -təˈ-, -ˈlʊtʃ.i, (US) ˌbɝː.t̬əˈluː.tʃi, ˌber-
Bertram ˈbɜː.trəm, (US) ˈbɝː-
Bertrand ˈbɜː.trənd, (US) ˈbɝː-
Berwick ˈber.ɪk **-shire** -ʃəʳ, -ʃɪəʳ, (US) -ʃɚ, -ʃɪr
Berwick-on-Tweed ˌber.ɪk.ɒnˈtwiːd, (US) -ɑːnˈ-
beryl, B~ ˈber.ᵊl, -ɪl, (US) -ᵊl **-s** -z
beryllium bəˈrɪl.i.əm, berˈɪl-, (US) bəˈrɪl-
Besançon bəˈzɑ̃ːn.sɔ̃ːŋ, (US) -ˈzɑ̃ːn.sõʊn
Besant ˈbes.ᵊnt, ˈbez-; bɪˈzænt, bə-
beseech bɪˈsiːtʃ, bə- **-es** -ɪz **-ing/ly** -ɪŋ/li **-ed** -t **besought** bɪˈsɔːt, bə-, (US) -ˈsɑːt, -ˈsɔːt
beseem bɪˈsiːm, bə- **-s** -z **-ing** -ɪŋ **-ed** -d
beset bɪˈset, bə- **-s** -s **-ting** -ɪŋ, (US) -ˈset̬.ɪŋ
Beshear beʃˈɪəʳ, bəˈʃɪər, (US) beʃˈɪr
beshrew bɪˈʃruː, bə-
beside bɪˈsaɪd, bə- **-s** -z
besieg|e bɪˈsiːdʒ, bə- **-es** -ɪz **-ing** -ɪŋ **-ed** -d **-er/s** -əʳ/z, (US) -ɚ/z
Besley ˈbez.li
besmear bɪˈsmɪəʳ, bə-, (US) -ˈsmɪr **-s** -z **-ing** -ɪŋ **-ed** -d
besmirch bɪˈsmɜːtʃ, bə-, (US) -ˈsmɝːtʃ **-es** -ɪz **-ing** -ɪŋ **-ed** -t
besom ˈbiː.zᵊm **-s** -z
besotted bɪˈsɒt.ɪd, bə-, (US) -ˈsɑː.t̬ɪd **-ly** -li **-ness** -nəs, -nɪs
besought (from **beseech**) bɪˈsɔːt, bə-, (US) -ˈsɑːt, -ˈsɔːt
bespangl|e bɪˈspæŋ.gᵊl, bəˈspæŋ- **-es** -z **-ing** -ɪŋ, ˈ-glɪŋ **-ed** -d
bespatt|er bɪˈspæt|.əʳ, bə-, (US) -ˈspæt̬|.ɚ **-ers** -əz, (US) -ɚz **-ering** -ᵊr.ɪŋ **-ered** -əd, (US) -ɚd
bespeak bɪˈspiːk, bə- **-s** -s **-ing** -ɪŋ **bespoke** bɪˈspəʊk, bə-, (US) -ˈspoʊk **bespoken** bɪˈspəʊ.kᵊn, bə-, (US) -ˈspoʊ-
bespectacled bɪˈspek.tə.kᵊld, -tɪ.kᵊld
besprinkl|e bɪˈsprɪŋ.kᵊl, bə- **-es** -z **-ing** -ɪŋ, ˈ-klɪŋ **-ed** -d
Bess bes
Bessacarr ˈbes.ə.kəʳ, (US) -kɚ
Bessarabia ˌbes.əˈreɪ.bi.ə
Bessborough ˈbez.bᵊr.ə, (US) -bɚ.oʊ
Bessemer ˈbes.ɪ.məʳ, ˈ-ə-, (US) -mɚ
Besses o' th' Barn ˌbes.ɪz.əðˈbɑːn, (US) -ˈbɑːrn
Bessette bəˈset
Bessie ˈbes.i
best, B~ best **-s** -s **-ing** -ɪŋ **-ed** -ɪd **ˌbest ˈman; ˌmake the ˈbest of ˌsomething; the ˌbest of ˈboth ˈworlds** (US) **the ˌbest of ˌboth ˈworlds**
bestial ˈbes.ti.əl, ˈbiː.sti-, (US) ˈbes.tʃᵊl, ˈbiːs-, -ti.əl **-ly** -i **-ism** -ɪ.zᵊm
bestialit|y ˌbes.tiˈæl.ə.t|i, ˌbiː.stiˈ-, -ɪ.t|i, (US) ˌbes.tʃiˈæl.ə.t̬|i, ˌbiːs- **-ies** -iz
bestiar|y ˈbes.ti.ᵊr|.i, ˈbiː.sti-, (US) -tʃi.er|.i **-ies** -iz
bestir bɪˈstɜːʳ, bə-, (US) -ˈstɝː **-s** -z **-ring** -ɪŋ **-red** -d
bestow bɪˈstəʊ, bə-, (US) -ˈstoʊ **-s** -z **-ing** -ɪŋ **-ed** -d
bestowal bɪˈstəʊ.əl, bə-, (US) -ˈstoʊ- **-s** -z
bestrew bɪˈstruː, bə- **-s** -z **-ing** -ɪŋ **-ed** -d **bestrewn** bɪˈstruːn, bə-

bestrid|e bɪˈstraɪd, bə- **-es** -z **-ing** -ɪŋ **bestrode** bɪˈstrəʊd, bə-, ⓊⓈ -ˈstroʊd **bestridden** bɪˈstrɪ.dᵊn, bə-

bestseller ˌbestˈsel.əʳ, ⓊⓈ -ɚ **-s** -z *stress shift:* **ˌbestseller ˈlistings**

best-selling ˌbestˈsel.ɪŋ *stress shift:* **ˌbest-selling ˈbook**

Beswick ˈbez.ɪk

bet, B~ bet **-s** -s **-ting** -ɪŋ, ⓊⓈ ˈbeţ.ɪŋ **-ted** -ɪd, ⓊⓈ ˈbeţ.ɪd **ˌhedge one's ˈbets**

beta ˈbiː.tə, ⓊⓈ ˈbeɪ.ţə **-s** -z

beta-blocker ˈbiː.təˌblɒk.əʳ, ⓊⓈ ˈbeɪ.ţəˌblɑː.kɚ **-s** -z

beta-carotene ˌbiː.təˈkær.ə.tiːn, ⓊⓈ ˌbeɪ.ţəˈker-

betak|e bɪˈteɪk, bə- **-es** -s **-ing** -ɪŋ **betook** bɪˈtʊk, bə- **betaken** bɪˈteɪ.kᵊn, bə-

betel ˈbiː.tᵊl, ⓊⓈ -ţᵊl **-nut/s** -nʌt/s

Betelgeuse, Betelgeux ˈbet.ᵊl.dʒɜːz, ˈbiː.tᵊl-, -dʒuːz, ⓊⓈ ˈbeţᵊl.dʒuːs, ˈbiː.ţ.ᵊl-, -dʒɜːz

bête noire ˌbetˈnwɑːʳ, ⓊⓈ -ˈnwɑːr, ˌbeɪt- **bêtes noires** ˌbetˈnwɑːʳ, -ˈnwɑːz, ⓊⓈ -nwɑːr, beɪt-, -nwɑːrz

Beth beθ

Bethany ˈbeθ.ᵊn.i

Bethel ˈbeθ.ᵊl

Bethell ˈbeθ.ᵊl, bəˈθel

Bethesda beθˈez.də, bɪˈθez-, bə-, ⓊⓈ bəˈθez-, bɪ-

bethink bɪˈθɪŋk, bə- **-s** -s **-ing** -ɪŋ **bethought** bɪˈθɔːt, bə-, ⓊⓈ -ˈθɑːt, -ˈθɔːt

Bethlehem ˈbeθ.lɪ.hem, -lə-, ⓊⓈ -lə.hem, -həm

Bethnal ˈbeθ.nᵊl

bethought (from **bethink**) bɪˈθɔːt, bə-, ⓊⓈ -ˈθɑːt, -ˈθɔːt

Bethsaida beθˈseɪ.də, -ˈsaɪ-

Bethune *surname:* ˈbiː.tᵊn, ⓊⓈ bəˈθuːn *in names of streets, etc.:* beθˈjuːn, bɪˈθjuːn, bə-, ⓊⓈ bəˈθuːn, -ˈθjuːn

betid|e bɪˈtaɪd, bə- **-es** -z

betimes bɪˈtaɪmz, bə-

Betjeman ˈbetʃ.ə.mən

betoken bɪˈtəʊ.kᵊn, bə-, ⓊⓈ -ˈtoʊ- **-s** -z **-ing** -ɪŋ **-ed** -ᵊnd

betony ˈbet.ə.ni

betook (from **betake**) bɪˈtʊk, bəˈtʊk

betray bɪˈtreɪ, bə- **-s** -z **-ing** -ɪŋ **-ed** -d **-er/s** -əʳ/z, ⓊⓈ -ɚ/z

betrayal bɪˈtreɪ.əl, bə- **-s** -z

betro|th bɪˈtrəʊ|ð, bə-, -ˈtrəʊ|θ, ⓊⓈ -ˈtroʊ|ð, -ˈtrɑː|θ **-ths** -ðz, -θs **-thing** -ðɪŋ, -θɪŋ **-thed** -ðd, -θt

> Note: In British English, the voiceless version is unlikely before **-ing**.

betrothal bɪˈtrəʊ.ðᵊl, bə-, ⓊⓈ -ˈtroʊ-, -θᵊl **-s** -z

Betsy ˈbet.si

Bette bet; ˈbet.i, ⓊⓈ bet; ⓊⓈ ˈbeţ.i

Betteley ˈbet.ᵊl.i, ⓊⓈ ˈbeţ-

bett|er ˈbet|.əʳ, ⓊⓈ ˈbeţ|.ɚ **-ers** -əz, ⓊⓈ -ɚz **-ering** -ᵊr.ɪŋ **-ered** -əd, ⓊⓈ -ɚd **for ˌbetter or (for) ˈworse**

betterment ˈbet.ə.mənt, ⓊⓈ ˈbeţ.ɚ-

betting ˈbet.ɪŋ, ⓊⓈ ˈbeţ- **-s** -z **ˈbetting ˌshop**

bettor ˈbet.əʳ, ⓊⓈ ˈbeţ.ɚ **-s** -z

Bettws ˈbet.əs, ⓊⓈ ˈbeţ-

Bettws-y-Coed ˌbet.ə.siˈkɔɪd, -ʊ.siˈ-, -kəʊ.ɪd, -əd, ⓊⓈ ˌbeţ.ə.siˈkɔɪd

Betty ˈbet.i, ⓊⓈ ˈbeţ-

between bɪˈtwiːn, bə-

betweentimes bɪˈtwiːn.taɪmz, bə-

betwixt bɪˈtwɪkst, bə-

Beulah ˈbjuː.lə

Bevan ˈbev.ᵊn

bevel ˈbev.ᵊl **-s** -z **-(l)ing** -ɪŋ **-(l)ed** -d

Beven ˈbev.ᵊn

beverag|e ˈbev.ᵊr.ɪdʒ, ˈ-rɪdʒ **-es** -ɪz

Beveridge ˈbev.ᵊr.ɪdʒ, ˈ-rɪdʒ

Beverley ˈbev.ᵊl.i, ⓊⓈ -ɚ.li

Beverly ˈbev.ᵊl.i, ⓊⓈ -ɚ.li **ˌBeverly ˈHills**

Bevin ˈbev.ɪn

Bevis ˈbiː.vɪs, ˈbev.ɪs

bevv|y ˈbev|.i **-ies** -iz **-ied** -id

bev|y ˈbev|.i **-ies** -iz

bewail bɪˈweɪl, bə- **-s** -z **-ing** -ɪŋ **-ed** -d

beware bɪˈweəʳ, bə-, ⓊⓈ -ˈwer

Bewdley ˈbjuːd.li

bewhiskered bɪˈ*h*wɪs.kəd, bə-, ⓊⓈ -kɚd

Bewick(e) ˈbjuː.ɪk

bewigged bɪˈwɪgd, bə-

bewild|er bɪˈwɪl.d|əʳ, bə-, ⓊⓈ -d|ɚ **-ers** -əz, ⓊⓈ -ɚz **-ering/ly** -ᵊr.ɪŋ/li **-ered** -əd, ⓊⓈ -ɚd **-erment/s** -ə.mənt/s, ⓊⓈ -ɚ.mənt/s

bewitch bɪˈwɪtʃ, bə- **-es** -ɪz **-ing/ly** -ɪŋ/li **-ed** -t **-ment/s** -mənt/s

Bewley ˈbjuː.li

Bexhill beksˈhɪl *stress shift:* **ˌBexhill ˈstation**

Bexley ˈbek.sli

Bexleyheath ˌbek.slɪˈhiːθ

Bey beɪ **-s** -z

Beynon ˈbaɪ.nən, ˈbeɪ-

Beyonce biˈɒnt.seɪ, beɪ-, ⓊⓈ -ˈɑːnt-

beyond biˈɒnd, ⓊⓈ -ˈjɑːnd

Beyrout(h) beɪˈruːt

bezant ˈbez.ᵊnt **-s** -s

bezel ˈbez.ᵊl **-s** -z

Béziers ˈbez.i.eɪ

bezique bɪˈziːk, bə-

BFPO ˌbiː.ef.piːˈəʊ, ⓊⓈ -ˈoʊ

Bhagavad-Gita ˌbæg.ə.vədˈgiː.tə, ˌbʌg-, -vædˈ-, ⓊⓈ ˌbɑː.gə.vɑːdˈ-

bhagwan, B~ ˈbæg.wɑːn

bhaji ˈbɑː.dʒi **-s** -z

bhang bæŋ

bhangra ˈbæŋ.grə, ˈbɑːŋ-

bhindi ˈbɪn.di

Bhopal bəʊˈpɑːl, ⓊⓈ boʊ-

Bhutan buːˈtɑːn, -ˈtæn

Bhutanese ˌbuː.təˈniːz

Bhutto ˈbuː.təʊ, ˈbʊt.əʊ, ⓊⓈ ˈbuː.ţoʊ

bi- baɪ

Note: Prefix. Words containing **bi-** normally take secondary stress, but sometimes primary stress, on the first syllable, e.g. **bimetallic** /ˌbaɪ.metˈæl.ɪk/, **biped** /ˈbaɪ.ped/, or primary stress on the second syllable, e.g. **biathlete** /baɪˈæθ.liːt/.

Biafr|a biˈæf.r|ə, baɪˈ- **-an/s** -ən/z

Bialystok biˈæl.ɪ.stɒk; ˈ-ə-; ˌbiː.əˈlɪs.tɒk, ⓊⓈ biˈɑː.lə.stɑːk, -ˈæl.ə-

Bianca biˈæŋ.kə, ⓊⓈ -ˈæŋ-, -ˈɑːŋ-

biannual baɪˈæn.ju.əl **-s** -z **-ly** -li

Biarritz ˌbɪəˈrɪts, ˈ--, ⓊⓈ ˌbiː.əˈrɪts, ˈ---

bias ˈbaɪ.əs **-(s)es** -ɪz **-(s)ing** -ɪŋ **-(s)ed** -t

biathlete baɪˈæθ.liːt **-s** -s

biathlon baɪˈæθ.lən, -lɒn, ⓊⓈ -lɑːn **-s** -z

biaxal baɪˈæk.sᵊl

biaxial baɪˈæk.si.əl

bib bɪb **-s** -z

Bibby ˈbɪb.i

bibelot ˈbɪb.ləʊ, -ᵊl.əʊ, ⓊⓈ -ə.loʊ, ˈbiː.bloʊ **-s** -z

Bible ˈbaɪ.bᵊl **-s** -z **ˈBible ˌBelt**

Bible-basher ˈbaɪ.bᵊlˌbæʃ.əʳ, ⓊⓈ -ɚ **-s** -z

Bible-bashing ˈbaɪ.bᵊlˌbæʃ.ɪŋ

biblic|al ˈbɪb.lɪ.k|ᵊl **-ally** -ᵊl.i, -li

biblio- ˈbɪb.li.əʊ; ˌbɪb.liˈɒ, ⓊⓈ ˈbɪb.li.ə, -oʊ; ⓊⓈ ˌbɪb.liˈɑː-

Note: Prefix. Normally takes either primary or secondary stress on the first syllable, e.g. **bibliophile** /ˈbɪb.li.əʊ.faɪl/ ⓊⓈ /-ə-/, **bibliomania** /ˌbɪb.li.əʊˈmeɪ.ni.ə/ ⓊⓈ /-əˈ-/, or secondary stress on the first syllable, with primary stress occurring on the third syllable, e.g. **bibliography** /ˌbɪb.liˈɒg.rə.fi/ ⓊⓈ /-ˈɑː.grə-/.

bibliograph|y ˌbɪb.liˈɒg.rə.f|i, ⓊⓈ -ˈɑː.grə- **-ies** -iz **-er/s** -əʳ/z, ⓊⓈ -ɚ/z

bibliolat|ry ˌbɪb.liˈɒl.ə.t|ri, ⓊⓈ -ˈɑː.lə- **-er/s** -əʳ/z, ⓊⓈ -ɚ/z

bibliomania ˌbɪb.li.əʊˈmeɪ.ni.ə, ⓊⓈ -əˈ-, -oʊˈ-, -njə

bibliomaniac ˌbɪb.li.əʊˈmeɪ.ni.æk, ⓊⓈ -əˈ-, -oʊˈ- **-s** -s

bibliophile ˈbɪb.li.əʊ.faɪl, ⓊⓈ -ə-, -oʊ- **-s** -z

bibulous ˈbɪb.jə.ləs, -jʊ- **-ly** -li

Bic® bɪk

bicameral baɪˈkæm.ᵊr.ᵊl **-ism** -ɪ.zᵊm

bicarb ˈbaɪ.kɑːb, ⓊⓈ baɪˈkɑːrb

bicarbonate baɪˈkɑː.bᵊn.ət, -eɪt, -ɪt, ⓊⓈ -ˈkɑːr- **-s** -s **biˌcarbonate of ˈsoda**

bice baɪs

Bice ˈbiː.tʃi; baɪs

bicentenar|y ˌbaɪ.senˈtiː.nᵊr|.i, -sᵊnˈ-, -ˈten.ᵊr-, ⓊⓈ baɪˈsen.tᵊn.er|.i; ⓊⓈ ˌbaɪ.senˈten.ᵊr- **-ies** -iz

bicentennial ˌbaɪ.senˈten.i.əl, -sənˈ- **-s** -z

biceps ˈbaɪ.seps

Bicester ˈbɪs.təʳ, ⓊⓈ -tɚ

bichloride baɪˈklɔː.raɪd, ⓊⓈ -ˈklɔːr.aɪd

bichromate baɪˈkrəʊ.meɪt, -met, -mɪt, (US) -ˈkroʊ-
bick|er ˈbɪk|.əʳ, (US) -ɚ **-ers** -əz, (US) -ɚz **-ering/s** -ᵊr.ɪŋ/z **-ered** -əd, (US) -ɚd **-erer/s** -ᵊr.əʳ/z, (US) -ɚ.ɚ/z
Bickerstaff(e) ˈbɪk.ə.stɑːf, (US) -ɚ.stæf
Bickersteth ˈbɪk.ə.steθ, -stɪθ, (US) ˈ-ɚ-
Bickerton ˈbɪk.ə.tᵊn, (US) ˈ-ɚ-
Bickford ˈbɪk.fəd, (US) -fɚd
bickie ˈbɪk.i **-s** -z
Bickleigh, Bickley ˈbɪk.li
Bicknell ˈbɪk.nᵊl
bicoastal baɪˈkəʊ.stᵊl, (US) -ˈkoʊ-
bicuspid baɪˈkʌs.pɪd **-s** -z
bicyc|le ˈbaɪ.sɪ.k|ᵊl, -sə- **-les** -ᵊlz **-ling** -lɪŋ **-led** -ᵊld
bicyclist ˈbaɪ.sɪ.klɪst, -sə- **-s** -s
bid bɪd **-s** -z **-ding** -ɪŋ **-der/s** -əʳ/z, (US) -ɚ/z **bade** bæd, beɪd **bidden** ˈbɪd.ən
biddable ˈbɪd.ə.bᵊl
bidder, B~ ˈbɪd.əʳ, (US) -ɚ **-s** -z
Biddle ˈbɪd.ᵊl
Biddulph ˈbɪd.ʌlf, -ᵊlf
bidd|y, B~ ˈbɪd|.i **-ies** -iz
bid|e, B~ baɪd **-es** -z **-ing** -ɪŋ **-ed** -ɪd
Bideford ˈbɪd.ɪ.fəd, (US) -fɚd
Biden ˈbaɪ.dᵊn
bidet ˈbiː.deɪ, (US) bɪˈdeɪ, biː- **-s** -z
bidialectal ˌbaɪ.daɪ.əˈlek.tᵊl
bidialectalism ˌbaɪ.daɪ.əˈlek.tᵊl.ɪ.zᵊm
Bidwell ˈbɪd.wel
Bielefeld ˈbiː.lə.felt, -feld
biennial baɪˈen.i.əl **-ly** -i
bier bɪəʳ, (US) bɪr **-s** -z
Bierce bɪəs, (US) bɪrs
biff bɪf **-s** -s **-ing** -ɪŋ **-ed** -t
Biffen ˈbɪf.ɪn, -ən
bifocal baɪˈfəʊ.kᵊl, (US) ˈbaɪˌfoʊ-, -ˈ-- **-s** -z
bifur|cate ˈbaɪ.fə.keɪt, -fɜː-, (US) -fɚ- **-cates** -keɪts **-cating** -keɪ.tɪŋ, (US) -keɪ.t̬ɪŋ **-cated** -keɪ.tɪd, (US) -keɪ.t̬ɪd
bifurcation ˌbaɪ.fəˈkeɪ.ʃᵊn, -fɜːˈ-, (US) -fɚˈ- **-s** -z
big bɪg **-ger** -əʳ, (US) -ɚ **-gest** -ɪst, -əst **-ness** -nəs, -nɪs **ˌBig ˈApple; ˌBig ˈBang; ˌBig ˈBen; ˌbig ˈbusiness; ˌBig ˈDipper; ˌbig ˈgame; ˌbig ˈscreen; ˌbig ˈwheel; ˌhit the ˈbig ˌtime**
bigamist ˈbɪg.ə.mɪst **-s** -s
bigamous ˈbɪg.ə.məs **-ly** -li
bigam|y ˈbɪg.ə.m|i **-ies** -iz
Bigelow ˈbɪg.ᵊl.əʊ, -ɪ.ləʊ, (US) -ə.loʊ
Bigfoot ˈbɪg.fʊt
Bigge bɪg
biggie ˈbɪg.i
Biggin ˈbɪg.ɪn
biggish ˈbɪg.ɪʃ
Biggles ˈbɪg.ᵊlz
Biggleswade ˈbɪg.ᵊlz.weɪd
Biggs bɪgz
biggl|y ˈbɪg|.i **-ies** -iz
Bigham ˈbɪg.əm
bighead ˈbɪg.hed **-s** -z
bigheaded ˌbɪgˈhed.ɪd, -əd, (US) ˈ-ˌ-- **-ly** -li **-ness** -nəs, -nɪs *stress shift:* **ˌbigheaded ˈbully**
bighorn ˈbɪg.hɔːn, (US) -hɔːrn **-s** -z
bight baɪt **-s** -s **-ing** -ɪŋ, (US) ˈbaɪ.t̬ɪŋ **-ed** -ɪd, (US) ˈbaɪ.t̬ɪd
big-league ˈbɪg.liːg
Biglow ˈbɪg.ləʊ, (US) -loʊ
Bignell ˈbɪg.nᵊl
big|ot ˈbɪg|.ət **-ots** -əts **-oted** -ə.tɪd, (US) -ə.t̬ɪd
bigotr|y ˈbɪg.ə.tr|i **-ies** -iz
bigraph ˈbaɪ.grɑːf, -græf, (US) -græf **-s** -s
Big Sur ˌbɪgˈsɜːʳ, (US) -ˈsɝː
big-ticket ˌbɪgˈtɪk.ɪt
big-time ˈbɪg.taɪm **-er/s** -əʳ/z, (US) -ɚ/z
bigwig ˈbɪg.wɪg **-s** -z
Bihar bɪˈhɑːʳ, biː-, (US) -ˈhɑːr
bijou ˈbiː.ʒuː, -ˈ-
bik|e baɪk **-es** -s **-ing** -ɪŋ **-ed** -t
biker, B~ ˈbaɪ.kəʳ, (US) -kɚ **-s** -z
bikini, B~ bɪˈkiː.ni, bə- **-s** -z
Biko ˈbiː.keʊ, (US) -koʊ
bilabial n, adj baɪˈleɪ.bi.əl **-s** -z **-ly** -i
bilateral baɪˈlæt.ᵊr.ᵊl, ˈ-rᵊl, (US) -ˈlæt̬.ɚ.ᵊl **-y** -i **-ness** -nəs, -nɪs
Bilbao bɪlˈbaʊ, -ˈbɑː.əʊ, (US) -ˈbɑː.oʊ, -ˈbaʊ
bilberr|y ˈbɪl.bᵊr|.i, (US) -ber- **-ies** -iz
Bilborough ˈbɪl.bᵊr.ə, (US) -bɚ.oʊ
Bilbrough ˈbɪl.brə, (US) -broʊ
bilb|y ˈbɪl.bi **-ies** -iz
Bildungsroman ˈbɪl.dʊŋz.rəʊ.mɑːn, (US) -roʊ- **-s** -z **-e** -ə
bile baɪl
bilg|e bɪldʒ **-es** -ɪz **-ing** -ɪŋ **-ed** -d **ˈbilge ˌpump; ˈbilge ˌwater**
bilgy ˈbɪl.dʒi
bilharzia bɪlˈhɑː.zi.ə, -ˈhɑːt.si-, (US) -ˈhɑːr.zi-
biliary ˈbɪl.i.ᵊr.i
bilingual baɪˈlɪŋ.gwᵊl **-s** -z **-ly** -i **-ism** -ɪ.zᵊm *stress shift, see first compound:* **ˌbilingual ˈsecretary, biˌlingual ˈsecretary**
bilious ˈbɪl.i.əs, (US) ˈ-jəs, ˈ-i.əs **-ly** -li **-ness** -nəs, -nɪs
bilirubin ˌbɪl.ɪˈruː.bɪn
biliteral baɪˈlɪt.ᵊr.ᵊl, ˈ-rᵊl, (US) -ˈlɪt̬.ɚ.ᵊl **-ly** -i
bilk bɪlk **-s** -s **-ing** -ɪŋ **-ed** -t
bill, B~ bɪl **-s** -z **-ing** -ɪŋ **-ed** -d **ˌbill of ˈfare; ˌfit the ˈbill**
billable ˈbɪl.ə.bᵊl
billabong ˈbɪl.ə.bɒŋ, (US) -bɑːŋ, -bɔːŋ **-s** -z
billboard ˈbɪl.bɔːd, (US) -bɔːrd **-s** -z
Billericay ˌbɪl.əˈrɪk.i
bille|t ˈbɪl|.ɪt, -ət, (US) -ət **-ts** -ts **-ting** -tɪŋ, (US) -t̬ɪŋ **-ted** -tɪd, (US) -t̬ɪd
billet-doux ˌbɪl.eɪˈduː **billets-doux** ˌbɪl.eɪˈduː, -duːz
billfold ˈbɪl.fəʊld, (US) -foʊld **-s** -z
billhook ˈbɪl.hʊk **-s** -s
billiard ˈbɪl.jəd, ˈ-i.əd, (US) ˈ-jɚd **-s** -z **ˈbilliard ˌball; ˈbilliard ˌcue; ˈbilliard ˌroom; ˈbilliard ˌtable**
Billie ˈbɪl.i
Billie-Jean ˌbɪl.iˈdʒiːn
Billing ˈbɪl.ɪŋ **-s** -z
Billinge ˈbɪl.ɪndʒ
Billingham ˈbɪl.ɪŋ.*h*əm
Billinghurst ˈbɪl.ɪŋ.hɜːst, (US) -hɝːst
Billingsgate ˈbɪl.ɪŋz.geɪt
Billington ˈbɪl.ɪŋ.tən
billion ˈbɪl.jən, -i.ən, (US) -jən **-s** -z
billionaire ˌbɪl.jəˈneəʳ, ˌ-i.əˈ-, (US) -jəˈner **-s** -z
billionth ˈbɪl.jənθ, ˈ-i.ənθ, (US) ˈ-jənθ **-s** -s
billow ˈbɪl.əʊ, (US) -oʊ **-s** -z **-ing** -ɪŋ **-ed** -d **-y** -i
billposter ˈbɪlˌpəʊ.stəʳ, (US) -ˌpoʊ.stɚ **-s** -z
billsticker ˈbɪlˌstɪk.əʳ, (US) -ɚ **-s** -z
bill|y, B~ ˈbɪl|.i **-ies** -iz **ˈbilly ˌcan; ˈbilly ˌclub; ˈbilly ˌgoat**
billycock ˈbɪl.i.kɒk, (US) -kɑːk **-s** -s
billy-o ˈbɪl.i.əʊ, (US) -oʊ
Biloxi bɪˈlʌk.si, bə-, -ˈlɒk-, (US) -ˈlɑːk-, -ˈlʌk-
Bilston(e) ˈbɪl.stən
Bilton ˈbɪl.tᵊn
biltong ˈbɪl.tɒŋ, (US) -tɑːŋ, -tɔːŋ
bimbo ˈbɪm.bəʊ, (US) -boʊ **-(e)s** -z
bimestrial baɪˈmes.tri.əl
bimetallic ˌbaɪ.metˈæl.ɪk, -mɪˈtæl-, -mə-
bimetall|ism baɪˈmet.ᵊl|.ɪ.zᵊm, (US) -ˈmet̬- **-ist/s** -ɪst/s
bimolecular ˌbaɪ.məˈlek.jə.ləʳ, -jʊ-, (US) -lɚ
bimonthl|y baɪˈmʌntθ.l|i **-ies** -iz
bin bɪn **-s** -z **-ning** -ɪŋ **-ned** -d
binar|y ˈbaɪ.nᵊr|.i **-ies** -iz **ˌbinary ˈnumber**
binaural baɪˈnɔː.rᵊl, bɪ-, (US) -ˈnɔːr.ᵊl
Binchy ˈbɪn.tʃi, (US) ˈbɪnt.ʃi
bind baɪnd **-s** -z **-ing** -ɪŋ **bound** baʊnd
binder ˈbaɪn.dəʳ, (US) -dɚ **-s** -z
binder|y ˈbaɪn.dᵊr|.i **-ies** -iz
bindi ˈbɪn.di
bindweed ˈbaɪnd.wiːd
Binet ˈbiː.neɪ, (US) bɪˈneɪ
Binet-Simon ˌbiː.neɪˈsaɪ.mən, (US) bɪˌneɪ.siˈmoʊn
Bing bɪŋ
bing|e bɪndʒ **-es** -ɪz **-(e)ing** -ɪŋ **-ed** -d **ˈbinge ˌdrinker; ˈbinge ˌdrinking**
Bingen ˈbɪŋ.ən
Bingham ˈbɪŋ.əm
Bingley ˈbɪŋ*g*.li
bingo ˈbɪŋ.gəʊ, (US) -goʊ
Bink(e)s bɪŋks
bin Laden ˌbɪnˈlɑː.dᵊn
bin|man ˈbɪn|.mæn, ˈbɪm-, -mən, (US) ˈbɪn- **-men** -men, -mən
binnacle ˈbɪn.ə.kᵊl **-s** -z
Binney, Binnie ˈbɪn.i
Binns bɪnz
Binoche bɪˈnɒʃ, biː-, (US) -noʊʃ
binocular adj baɪˈnɒk.jə.ləʳ, bɪ-, bə-, -jʊ-, (US) -ˈnɑː.kjə.lɚ, -kjʊ-
binoculars n bɪˈnɒk.jə.ləz, baɪ-, bə-, -jʊ-, (US) -ˈnɑː.kjə.lɚz, -kjʊ-
binomial baɪˈnəʊ.mi.əl, (US) -ˈnoʊ- **-s** -z **-ly** -i

B

Binste(a)d ˈbɪn.stɪd, -sted
bint bɪnt -s -s
Binyon ˈbɪn.jən
bio- ˈbaɪ.əʊ; baɪˈɒ, (US) ˈbaɪ.oʊ, -ə; (US) baɪˈɑː
Note: Prefix. Normally carries primary or secondary stress on the first syllable, e.g. **biodata** /ˈbaɪ.əʊ.deɪ.tə/ (US) /-oʊ.deɪ.t̬ə/, **biographic** /ˌbaɪ.əʊˈɡræf.ɪk/ (US) /-əˈ-/, or primary stress on the second syllable, e.g. **biographer** /baɪˈɒɡ.rə.fəʳ/ (US) /-ˈɑː.ɡrə.fɚ/. There are exceptions; see individual entries.
biochemic|al ˌbaɪ.əʊˈkem.ɪ.k|əl, (US) -oʊˈ- -als -əlz -ally -əl.i, -li
biochemist ˌbaɪ.əʊˈkem.ɪst, (US) -oʊˈ- -s -s -ry -ri
biocoenosis ˌbaɪ.əʊ.sɪˈnəʊ.sɪs, -siːˈ-, (US) -oʊ.sɪˈnoʊ-
biodata ˈbaɪ.əʊˌdeɪ.tə, -ˌdɑː-, (US) -oʊˌdeɪ.t̬ə, -ˌdɑː-, -ˌdæt̬.ə
biodegradability ˌbaɪ.əʊ.dɪˌɡreɪ.dəˈbɪl.ɪ.ti, -dəˌɡreɪ-, -ə.ti, (US) -oʊ.dɪˌɡreɪ.dəˈbɪl.ə.t̬i, -də-
biodegradab|le ˌbaɪ.əʊ.dɪˈɡreɪ.də.b|əl, -dəˈ-, (US) -oʊ- -ly -li
biodegradation ˌbaɪ.əʊˌdeg.rəˈdeɪ.ʃən, (US) ˌ-oʊ-
biodegrad|e ˌbaɪ.əʊ.dɪˈɡreɪd, -dəˈ-, (US) -oʊ- -es -z -ing -ɪŋ -ed -ɪd
biodiesel ˈbaɪ.əʊˌdiː.zəl, (US) -oʊˌdiː.səl, -zəl
biodiversity ˌbaɪ.əʊ.daɪˈvɜː.sə.ti, -dɪˈ-, -sɪ-, (US) -oʊ.dɪˈvɝː.sə.t̬i, -daɪˈ-
bioenergy ˈbaɪ.əʊˌen.ə.dʒ|i, (US) -oʊˌen.ɚ-
bioengineer ˌbaɪ.əʊ.en.dʒɪˈnɪəʳ, -dʒəˈ-, (US) -oʊ.en.dʒɪˈnɪr, -dʒəˈ- -s -z
bioengineering ˌbaɪ.əʊˌen.dʒɪˈnɪə.rɪŋ, -dʒəˈ-, (US) -oʊˌen.dʒɪˈnɪr.ɪŋ, -dʒəˈ-
bioethanol ˌbaɪ.əʊˈeθ.ə.nɒl, -ˈiː.θə-, (US) -oʊˈeθ.ə.nɑːl, -noʊl
bioethics ˈbaɪ.əʊˌeθ.ɪks, (US) -oʊ-
biofeedback ˌbaɪ.əʊˈfiːd.bæk, (US) -oʊˈ-
biofuel ˈbaɪ.əʊˌfjuː.əl, -ˌfjʊəl, (US) -oʊˌfjuː.əl, -ˌfjuːl -s -z
biogenesis ˌbaɪ.əʊˈdʒen.ə.sɪs, ˈ-ɪ-, (US) -oʊˈ-
biogenetic ˌbaɪ.əʊ.dʒəˈnet.ɪk, -dʒɪˈ-, (US) -oʊ.dʒəˈnet̬- -ally -əl.i, -li
biogenic ˌbaɪ.əʊˈdʒen.ɪk, (US) -oʊˈ-
biograph ˈbaɪ.əʊ.ɡrɑːf, -ɡræf, (US) -oʊ.ɡræf -s -s
biographer baɪˈɒɡ.rə.fəʳ, (US) -ˈɑː.ɡrə.fɚ -s -z
biographic ˌbaɪ.əʊˈɡræf.ɪk, (US) -əˈ- -al -əl -ally -əl.i, -li
biograph|y baɪˈɒɡ.rə.f|i, (US) -ˈɑː.ɡrə- -ies -iz
biolinguistics ˌbaɪ.əʊ.lɪŋˈɡwɪs.tɪks, (US) ˌ-oʊ-
biologic ˌbaɪ.əˈlɒdʒ.ɪk, (US) -ˈlɑː.dʒɪk
biologic|al ˌbaɪ.əˈlɒdʒ.ɪ.k|əl, (US) -ˈlɑː.dʒɪ- -ally -əl.i, -li **bioˌlogical ˈclock; bioˌlogical ˈwarfare**
biologist baɪˈɒl.ə.dʒɪst, (US) -ˈɑː.lə- -s -s
biology baɪˈɒl.ə.dʒi, (US) -ˈɑː.lə-
biomass ˈbaɪ.əʊˌmæs, (US) -oʊˌ-
biome ˈbaɪ.əʊm, (US) -oʊm
biomedical ˌbaɪ.əʊˈmed.ɪ.kəl, (US) -oʊˈ-
biometric ˌbaɪ.əʊˈmet.rɪk, (US) -oʊˈ- -s -s -al -əl
biometry baɪˈɒm.ə.tri, ˈ-ɪ-, (US) -ˈɑː.mə-
bionic baɪˈɒn.ɪk, (US) -ˈɑː.nɪk -s -s
biophysicist ˌbaɪ.əʊˈfɪz.ɪ.sɪst, -oʊˈ- -s -s
biophysic|s ˌbaɪ.əʊˈfɪz.ɪk|s, (US) -oʊˈ- -al -əl
biopic ˈbaɪ.əʊ.pɪk, (US) -oʊ- -s -s
biops|y ˈbaɪ.ɒp.s|i, (US) -ɑːp- -ies -iz
biorhythm ˈbaɪ.əʊˌrɪð.əm, (US) -oʊˌ- -s -z
bioscope ˈbaɪ.əʊ.skəʊp, (US) -oʊ.skoʊp -s -s
biosecurity ˌbaɪ.əʊ.sɪˈkjʊə.rə.ti, sə-, -ˈkjɔː-, -ɪ.ti, (US) -oʊ.səˈkjʊr.ə.t̬i
biosphere ˈbaɪ.əʊ.sfɪəʳ, (US) -ə.sfɪr, ˈ-oʊ- -s -z
biotech ˈbaɪ.əʊ.tek, (US) -oʊ-
biotechnology ˌbaɪ.əʊ.tekˈnɒl.ə.dʒi, (US) -oʊ.tekˈnɑː.lə-
bioterrorism ˌbaɪ.əʊˈter.ər.ɪ.zəm, (US) -oʊˌ-
biotope ˈbaɪ.əʊ.təʊp, (US) -oʊ.toʊp -s -s
biparous ˈbɪp.ər.əs
bipartisan baɪˈpɑː.tɪ.zæn; ˌbaɪ.pɑː.tɪˈzæn, -zən, (US) baɪˈpɑːr.t̬ə.zən
bipartite baɪˈpɑː.taɪt, (US) baɪˈpɑːr- *stress shift:* **ˌbipartite ˈtreaty**
biped ˈbaɪ.ped -s -z
bipedal baɪˈpiː.dəl, -ˈped.əl, (US) -ˈped.əl -ism -ɪ.zəm
biplane ˈbaɪ.pleɪn -s -z
bipod ˈbaɪ.pɒd, (US) -pɑːd -s -z
bipolar baɪˈpəʊ.ləʳ, (US) -ˈpoʊ.lɚ
bipolarity ˌbaɪ.pəʊˈlær.ɪ.ti, -ə.ti, (US) -poʊˈler.ə.t̬i, -ˈlær-
biquadratic ˌbaɪ.kwɒdˈræt.ɪk, -kwəˈdræt-, (US) -kwɑːˈdræt̬.ɪk -s -s
birch, B~ bɜːtʃ, (US) bɝːtʃ -es -ɪz -ing -ɪŋ -ed -t
Birchall ˈbɜː.tʃɔːl, -tʃəl, (US) ˈbɝː.tʃɔːl, -tʃɑːl, -tʃəl
Birchenough ˈbɜː.tʃɪ.nʌf, (US) ˈbɝː-
Bircher ˈbɜː.tʃəʳ, (US) ˈbɝː.tʃɚ
Birchwood ˈbɜːtʃ.wʊd, (US) ˈbɝːtʃ-
Bircotes ˈbɜː.kəʊts, (US) ˈbɝː.koʊts
bird, B~ bɜːd, (US) bɝːd -s -z **ˈbird cage; ˈbird ˌdog; ˈbird ˌfancier; ˈbird ˌflu; ˌbird of ˈparadise; ˌbird of ˈprey; ˌkill two ˌbirds with ˌone ˈstone**
bird-brain ˈbɜːdˌbreɪn, (US) ˈbɝːd-
bird-brained ˈbɜːdˌbreɪnd, (US) ˈbɝːd-
birdhou|se ˈbɜːd.haʊ|s, (US) ˈbɝːd- -ses -zɪz
birdie ˈbɜː.di, (US) ˈbɝː- -s -z -d -d
birdlike ˈbɜːd.laɪk, (US) ˈbɝːd-
birdlime ˈbɜːd.laɪm, (US) ˈbɝːd-
birdseed ˈbɜːd.siːd, (US) ˈbɝːd-
Birds Eye® ˈbɜːdz.aɪ, (US) ˈbɝːdz-
bird's-eye n, adj ˈbɜːdz.aɪ, (US) ˈbɝːdz- -s -z **ˌbird's-eye ˈview**
bird's-nest ˈbɜːdz.nest, (US) ˈbɝːdz- -s -s -ing -ɪŋ -ed -ɪd **ˌbird's nest ˈsoup**
birdsong ˈbɜːd.sɒŋ, (US) ˈbɝːd.sɑːŋ, -sɔːŋ
birdwatch|ing ˈbɜːdˌwɒtʃ|.ɪŋ, (US) ˈbɝːdˌwɑː.tʃ|ɪŋ, -ˌwɔː- -er/s -əʳ/z, (US) -ɚ/z
bireme ˈbaɪ.riːm, -ˈ-, (US) baɪˈriːm -s -z
biretta bɪˈret.ə, (US) -ˈret̬- -s -z
Birgit ˈbɜː.ɡɪt, ˈbɪə-, (US) ˈbɝː-, -ɡiːt
biriani ˌbɪr.iˈɑː.ni -s -z
Birkbeck *surname:* ˈbɜː.bek, ˈbɜːk-, (US) ˈbɝː-, ˈbɝːk- *college in London:* ˈbɜːk.bek, (US) ˈbɝːk-
Birkenau ˈbɜː.kən.aʊ, (US) ˈbɝː-
Birkenhead ˌbɜː.kənˈhed, ˈ---, (US) ˌbɝː.kənˈhed, ˈ---
Birkenstocks® ˈbɜː.kən.stɒks, (US) ˈbɝː.kən.stɑːks
Birkett ˈbɜː.kɪt, (US) ˈbɝː-
Birkin ˈbɜː.kɪn, (US) ˈbɝː-
Birley ˈbɜː.li, (US) ˈbɝː-
Birling ˈbɜː.lɪŋ, (US) ˈbɝː-
Birmingham *place in UK:* ˈbɜː.mɪŋ.əm, (US) ˈbɝː- *places in US:* ˈbɜː.mɪŋ.hæm, (US) ˈbɝː-

> Note: In the UK, locally also /ˈbɜː.mɪŋ.ɡəm/. American speakers often use the /-hæm/ pronunciation for the British city, though this is regarded as a mispronunciation in the UK.

Birnam ˈbɜː.nəm, (US) ˈbɝː-
Birney ˈbɜː.ni, (US) ˈbɝː-
Biro® ˈbaɪə.rəʊ, (US) ˈbaɪ.roʊ -s -z
Biron ˈbaɪə.rən

> Note: /bɪˈruːn/ in 'Love's Labour's Lost'.

birr bɜːʳ, (US) bɝː **birrotch** ˈbɜː.rɒtʃ, (US) ˈbɝː.ɑːtʃ
Birrell ˈbɪr.əl
birrotch (plural of **birr**) ˈbɜː.rɒtʃ, (US) ˈbɝː.ɑːtʃ
Birstall ˈbɜː.stɔːl, (US) ˈbɝː.stɔːl, -stɑːl
Birt bɜːt, (US) bɝːt
birth bɜːθ, (US) bɝːθ -s -s **ˈbirth cerˌtificate; ˈbirth conˌtrol; ˈbirthing ˌcenter**
birthday ˈbɜːθ.deɪ, -di, (US) ˈbɝːθ.deɪ -s -z **ˈbirthday ˌcake; ˈbirthday ˌcard; ˈbirthday ˌparty; ˈbirthday ˌpresent; in one's ˈbirthday ˌsuit**
birthmark ˈbɜːθ.mɑːk, (US) ˈbɝːθ.mɑːrk -s -s
birthplac|e ˈbɜːθ.pleɪs, (US) ˈbɝːθ- -es -ɪz
birthrate ˈbɜːθ.reɪt, (US) ˈbɝːθ- -s -s
birthright ˈbɜːθ.raɪt, (US) ˈbɝːθ- -s -s
Birtwistle ˈbɜː.twɪ.səl, (US) ˈbɝː-
biryani ˌbɪr.iˈɑː.ni -s -z
bis bɪs
Biscay ˈbɪs.keɪ, -ki **ˌBay of ˈBiscay**

B

biscuit ˈbɪs.kɪt **-s** -s ˈ**biscuit** ˌ**barrel**
bisect baɪˈsekt, (US) ˈbaɪ.sekt, -ˈ- **-s** -s **-ing** -ɪŋ **-ed** -ɪd
bisection baɪˈsek.ʃᵊn **-s** -z
bisector baɪˈsek.təʳ, (US) -tɚ **-s** -z
bisexual baɪˈsek.ʃuəl, -ʃu.əl, -sjuəl, -sjʊ.əl, (US) -ʃu.əl
bisexuality baɪˌsek.ʃuˈæl.ɪ.ti, ˌbaɪ-, -sjuˈæl-, -ə.ti, (US) -ʃuˈæl.ə.ţi
bishop, B~ ˈbɪʃ.əp **-s** -s
bishopric ˈbɪʃ.ə.prɪk **-s** -s
Bishopsgate ˈbɪʃ.əps.geɪt, -gɪt
Bishop's Stortford ˌbɪʃ.əpsˈstɔːt.fəd, -ˈstɔː-, (US) -ˈstɔːrt.fɚd, -ˈstɔːr-
Bishopstoke ˈbɪʃ.əp.stəʊk, (US) -stoʊk
Bishopston ˈbɪʃ.əp.stən
Bishopton ˈbɪʃ.əp.tən
Bisley ˈbɪz.li **-s** -z
Bismarck ˈbɪz.mɑːk, (US) -mɑːrk
bismuth ˈbɪz.məθ
bison ˈbaɪ.sᵊn **-s** -z
Bispham *surname:* ˈbɪs.fəm, ˈbɪs.pəm *place:* ˈbɪs.pəm
bisque biːsk, bɪsk, (US) bɪsk **-s** -s
Bissau bɪsˈaʊ
Bissell ˈbɪs.ᵊl
Bissett ˈbɪs.ɪt, ˈbɪz-
bissextile bɪˈsek.staɪl, ˈ-stɪl, (US) -stᵊl, -staɪl **-s** -z
bister ˈbɪs.təʳ, (US) -tɚ
Bisto® ˈbɪs.təʊ, (US) -toʊ
bistour|y ˈbɪs.tᵊr|.i **-ies** -iz
bistre ˈbɪs.təʳ, (US) -tɚ
bistro, bistrot ˈbiː.strəʊ, ˈbɪs-, (US) -stroʊ **-s** -z
bisulph|ate baɪˈsʌl.f|eɪt, -f|ɪt, -f|ət, (US) -f|eɪt **-ite** -aɪt
bit bɪt **-s** -s ˌ**bits and** ˈ**pieces;** ˌ**take the** ˌ**bit between one's** ˈ**teeth**
bitch bɪtʃ **-es** -ɪz **-ing** -ɪŋ **-ed** -d
bitch|y ˈbɪtʃ|.i **-iness** -ɪ.nəs, -ɪ.nɪs **-ier** -i.əʳ, (US) -i.ɚ **-iest** -i.ɪst, -i.əst
bit|e baɪt **-es** -s **-ing** -ɪŋ, (US) ˈbaɪ.ţɪŋ **bit** bɪt **bitten** ˈbɪt.ᵊn **biter/s** ˈbaɪ.təʳ/z, (US) -ţɚ/z ˌ**bite off** ˌ**more than one can** ˈ**chew;** ˌ**bite one's** ˈ**tongue;** ˌ**bite someone's** ˈ**head off;** ˌ**bite the** ˈ**bullet;** ˌ**bite the** ˈ**dust;** ˌ**bite the** ˌ**hand that** ˈ**feeds one**
bite-sized ˈbaɪt.saɪzd
Bithell ˈbɪθ.ᵊl, bɪˈθel
Bithynia bɪˈθɪn.i.ə, baɪ-
bitmap ˈbɪt.mæp **-s** -s
Bitola ˈbiː.təʊ.lə, (US) -toʊ-, -ţᵊl.ə
Bitolj ˈbiː.təʊ.ljə, (US) -toʊ-, -ţᵊl.jə
bitten (from **bite**) ˈbɪt.ᵊn ˌ**once** ˌ**bitten twice** ˈ**shy**
bitt|er ˈbɪt|.əʳ, (US) ˈbɪţ|.ɚ **-erer** -ᵊr.əʳ, (US) -ɚ.ɚ **-erest** -ᵊr.ɪst, -əst **-erly** -ə.li, (US) -ɚ.li **-erness** -ə.nəs, -nɪs, (US) -ɚ.nəs, -nɪs **to the** ˌ**bitter** ˈ**end**
bittern ˈbɪt.ən, -ɜːn, (US) ˈbɪţ.ɚn **-s** -z
bitters ˈbɪt.əz, (US) ˈbɪţ.ɚz
bittersweet ˈbɪt.ə.swiːt, ˌ--ˈ-, (US) ˈbɪţ.ɚ.swiːt
bitt|y ˈbɪt|.i, (US) ˈbɪţ- **-ier** -i.əʳ, (US) -i.ɚ **-iest** -i.ɪst, -i.əst **-iness** -ɪ.nəs, -ɪ.nɪs
bitumen ˈbɪtʃ.ə.mən, ˈ-ʊ-, -mɪn, (US) bɪˈtuː.mən, baɪ-, -ˈtjuː- **-s** -z
bituminous bɪˈtʃuː.mɪ.nəs, bə-, -ˈtjuː-, -mə-, (US) -ˈtuː-, -ˈtjuː-
bivalen|ce baɪˈveɪ.lən|*t*s, (US) baɪˈveɪ.lən|*t*s, ˈbaɪ.veɪ- **-cy** -*t*.si **-t** -t
bivalve ˈbaɪ.vælv **-s** -z
bivouac ˈbɪv.u.æk, (US) -u.æk, ˈ-wæk **-s** -s **-king** -ɪŋ **-ked** -t
bi-weekl|y baɪˈwiː.kl|i **-ies** -iz *stress shift:* ˌ**bi-weekly** ˈ**journal**
bizarre bɪˈzɑːʳ, bə-, (US) -ˈzɑːr **-ly** -li **-ness** -nəs, -nɪs
Bizerte, Bizerta bɪˈzɜː.tə, (US) -ˈzɝː-
Bizet ˈbiː.zeɪ, (US) -ˈ-
Bjork, Björk bjɔːk, bjɜːk, biˈɔːk, (US) bjɔːrk
Bjorn, Björn bjɔːn, bjɜːn; biˈɔːn, -ˈɜːn, (US) bjɔːrn, bjɝːn
BL ˌbiːˈel
blab blæb **-s** -z **-bing** -ɪŋ **-bed** -d **-ber/s** -əʳ/z, (US) -ɚ/z
blabb|er ˈblæb|.əʳ, (US) -ɚ **-ers** -əz, (US) -ɚz **-ering** -ᵊr.ɪŋ **-ered** -əd, (US) -ɚd
blabber|mouth ˈblæb.ə|.maʊθ, (US) ˈ-ɚ- **-mouths** -maʊðz, -maʊθs
Blaby ˈbleɪ.bi
Blachford ˈblæʃ.fəd, (US) -fɚd
black, B~ blæk **-s** -s **-er** -əʳ, (US) -ɚ **-est** -ɪst, -əst **-ish** -ɪʃ **-ly** -li **-ness** -nəs, -nɪs **-ing** -ɪŋ **-ed** -t ˌ**black** ˈ**belt;** ˌ**black** ˈ**box;** ˌ**black** ˈ**eye;** ˌ**Black** ˈ**Forest;** ˌ**Black Forest** ˈ**gateau;** ˌ**black** ˈ**hole;** ˌ**black** ˌ**hole of Cal**ˈ**cutta;** ˌ**black** ˈ**ice;** ˌ**black** ˈ**magic;** ˌ**black** ˈ**market;** ˌ**black** ˈ**pepper;** ˌ**black** ˈ**pudding;** ˌ**Black** ˈ**Rod;** ˌ**black** ˈ**treacle;** ˌ**black and** ˈ**blue;** ˌ**black and** ˈ**tan;** ˌ**black and** ˈ**white;** ˌ**black** ˌ**sheep of the** ˈ**family**
Blackadder ˈblækˌæd.əʳ, ˌ-ˈ--, (US) ˈblækˌæd.ɚ
blackamoor ˈblæk.ə.mɔːʳ, (US) -mʊr **-s** -z
blackball v ˈblæk.bɔːl, (US) -bɔːl, -bɑːl **-s** -z **-ing** -ɪŋ **-ed** -d
blackbeetle ˌblækˈbiː.tᵊl, (US) ˈblækˌbiː.ţᵊl **-s** -z
blackberr|y ˈblæk.bᵊr|.i, -ˌber-, (US) -ˌber- **-ies** -iz **-ying** -i.ɪŋ **-ied** -id
BlackBerr|y® ˈblæk.bᵊr|.i, -ˌber-, (US) -ˌber- **-ies** -iz **-ying** -i.ɪŋ **-ied** -id
blackberrying ˈblæk.bᵊr.i.ɪŋ, -ˌber-, (US) -ˌber-
blackbird ˈblæk.bɜːd, (US) -bɝːd **-s** -z
blackboard ˈblæk.bɔːd, (US) -bɔːrd **-s** -z
black box ˌblækˈbɒks, (US) -ˈbɑːks **-es** -ɪz
blackboy ˈblæk.bɔɪ **-s** -z
Blackburn(e) ˈblæk.bɜːn, (US) -bɝːn
blackcap ˈblæk.kæp **-s** -s
blackcock ˈblæk.kɒk, (US) -kɑːk **-s** -s
blackcurrant ˌblækˈkʌr.ᵊnt, (US) ˈblækˌkɝː- **-s** -s *stress shift, British only:* ˌ**blackcurrant** ˈ**pie**
Blackdown ˈblæk.daʊn
blacken ˈblæk.ᵊn **-s** -z **-ing** -ɪŋ **-ed** -d
Blackett ˈblæk.ɪt
black-eyed ˌblækˈaɪd *stress shift:* ˌ**black-eyed** ˈ**peas**
black|fly ˈblæk|.flaɪ **-flies** -flaɪz
Black|foot ˈblæk|.fʊt **-feet** -fiːt
Blackford ˈblæk.fəd, (US) -fɚd
Blackfriars ˌblækˈfraɪəz, -ˈfraɪ.əz, (US) -ˈfraɪ.ɚz *stress shift:* ˌ**Blackfriars** ˈ**Bobby**
blackgame ˈblæk.geɪm **-s** -z
blackguard ˈblæg.ɑːd, ˈ-əd, (US) -ɑːrd, -ɚd **-s** -z **-ly** -li
blackhead ˈblæk.hed **-s** -z
Blackheath ˌblækˈhiːθ *stress shift:* ˌ**Blackheath** ˈ**Harriers**
Blackie ˈblæk.i, ˈbleɪ.ki, (US) ˈblæk.i
blacking n ˈblæk.ɪŋ **-s** -z
blackjack ˈblæk.dʒæk **-s** -s
blacklead n ˈblæk.led
blacklead v ˌblækˈled, ˈ-- **-s** -z **-ing** -ɪŋ **-ed** -ɪd
blackleg ˈblæk.leg **-s** -z
Blackley *Manchester:* ˈbleɪ.kli *surname:* ˈblæk.li
blacklist ˈblæk.lɪst **-s** -s **-ing** -ɪŋ **-ed** -ɪd
blackmail ˈblæk.meɪl **-s** -z **-ing** -ɪŋ **-ed** -d **-er/s** -əʳ/z, (US) -ɚ/z
Blackman ˈblæk.mən
Black Maria ˌblæk.məˈraɪ.ə
Blackmoor, Blackmore ˈblæk.mɔːʳ, (US) -mɔːr
blackout ˈblæk.aʊt **-s** -s
Blackpool ˈblæk.puːl
Blackpudlian ˌblækˈpʌd.li.ən **-s** -z
Blackrock ˈblæk.rɒk, (US) -rɑːk
Blackshirt ˈblæk.ʃɜːt, (US) -ʃɝːt **-s** -s
blacksmith ˈblæk.smɪθ **-s** -s
Blackston ˈblæk.stᵊn
Blackstone ˈblæk.stəʊn, -stᵊn, (US) -stoʊn, -stᵊn
blackthorn, B~ ˈblæk.θɔːn, (US) -θɔːrn **-s** -z
blacktop ˈblæk.tɒp, (US) -tɑːp **-s** -s **-ping** -ɪŋ **-ped** -t
Blackwall ˈblæk.wɔːl, (US) -wɔːl, -wɑːl
blackwater, B~ ˈblækˌwɔː.təʳ, (US) -ˌwɑː.ţɚ, -ˌwɔː-
Blackwell ˈblæk.wel, -wᵊl
Blackwood *surname:* ˈblæk.wʊd *place in Gwent:* ˌblækˈwʊd
bladder ˈblæd.əʳ, (US) -ɚ **-s** -z
bladderwort ˈblæd.ə.wɜːt, (US) -ɚ.wɝːt, -wɔːrt **-s** -s
bladderwrack ˈblæd.ᵊr.æk
blade bleɪd **-s** -z
Bladon ˈbleɪ.dᵊn
blaeberr|y ˈbleɪ.bᵊr|.i, (US) -ber- **-ies** -iz
Blaenau Ffestiniog ˌblaɪ.naɪ.fesˈtɪn.i.ɒg, ˌbleɪ.ni-, (US) -ɑːg
Blaenau Gwent ˌblaɪ.naɪˈgwent, ˌbleɪ.ni-
Blaenavon blaɪˈnæv.ᵊn
Blagojevich bləˈgɔɪ.ə.vɪtʃ
blah-blah ˈblɑː.blɑː, ˌ-ˈ-
Blahnik ˈblɑː.nɪk
Blaikie ˈbleɪ.ki
Blaikley ˈbleɪ.kli

blain bleɪn -s -z

Blair bleəʳ, (US) bler -ite/s -aɪt/s -ism -ɪ.zᵊm

Blair Atholl ˌbleəʳˈæθ.ᵊl, (US) ˌbler-

Blairgowrie ˌbleəˈgaʊə.ri, (US) ˌbler-

Blaise bleɪz

Blake bleɪk

Blakelock ˈbleɪ.klɒk, (US) -klɑːk

Blakely ˈbleɪ.kli

Blakeney ˈbleɪk.ni

Blakey ˈbleɪ.ki

Blakiston ˈblæk.ɪ.stᵊn, ˈbleɪ.kɪ-

blamab|le ˈbleɪ.mə.b|ᵊl -ly -li -leness -ᵊl.nəs, -nɪs

blam|e bleɪm -es -z -ing -ɪŋ -ed -d

blameless ˈbleɪm.ləs, -lɪs -ly -li -ness -nəs, -nɪs

blameworth|y ˈbleɪmˌwɜː.ð|i, (US) -ˌwɝː- -iness -ɪ.nəs, -ɪ.nɪs

Blamires bləˈmaɪ.əz, (US) -ˈmaɪ.ɚz

Blanc in **Mont Blanc** blɑ̃ːŋ, (US) blɑ̃ːŋ, blɑːŋk

blanch blɑːntʃ, (US) blæntʃ -es -ɪz -ing -ɪŋ -ed -t

Blanchard ˈblæn.tʃəd, -tʃɑːd, (US) ˈblænt.ʃɚd, -ʃɑːrd

Blanche blɑːntʃ, (US) blæntʃ

Blanchett ˈblɑːn.tʃɪt, (US) ˈblæn-

Blanchflower ˈblɑːntʃ.flaʊ.əʳ, (US) ˈblæntʃ.flaʊ.ɚ

blancmang|e bləˈmɒndʒ, -ˈmɒ̃ːnʒ, (US) -ˈmɑːndʒ -es -ɪz

blanco ˈblæŋ.kəʊ, (US) -koʊ

bland, B~ blænd -er -əʳ, (US) -ɚ -est -ɪst, -əst -ly -li -ness -nəs, -nɪs

Blandford ˈblænd.fəd, (US) -fɚd

blandish ˈblæn.dɪʃ -es -ɪz -ing -ɪŋ -ed -t

blandishment ˈblæn.dɪʃ.mᵊnt -s -s

Blandy ˈblæn.di

Blaney ˈbleɪ.ni

blank **n, adj, v** blæŋk -s -s -er -əʳ, (US) -ɚ -est -ɪst, -əst -ly -li -ness -nəs, -nɪs -ing -ɪŋ -ed -t **ˌblank ˈcheque/check; ˌblank ˈverse**

blan|ket ˈblæŋ|.kɪt -kets -kɪts -keting -kɪ.tɪŋ, (US) -kɪ.t̬ɪŋ -keted -kɪ.tɪd, (US) -kɪ.t̬ɪd

Blankley ˈblæŋ.kli

blanquette ˌblɒŋˈket, ˌblæŋ-, ˌblɑ̃ːŋ-, (US) ˌblɑːŋ- -s -s

Blantyre blænˈtaɪ.əʳ, -ˈtaɪəʳ, ˈ--, (US) blænˈtaɪ.ɚ

> Note: In Malawi the preferred stress pattern is /ˈ--/.

blar|e bleəʳ, (US) bler -es -z -ing -ɪŋ -ed -d

blarney, B~ ˈblɑː.ni, (US) ˈblɑːr-

blasé ˈblɑː.zeɪ, blɑːˈzeɪ, (US) -ˈ-

blasphem|e ˌblæsˈfiːm, ˌblɑːs-, (US) ˈblæs.fiːm -es -z -ing/ly -ɪŋ/li -ed -d -er/s -əʳ/z, (US) -ɚ/z

blasphemous ˈblæs.fə.məs, ˈblɑːs-, -fɪ-, (US) ˈblæs- -ly -li

blasphem|y ˈblæs.fə.m|i, ˈblɑːs-, -fɪ-, (US) ˈblæs- -ies -iz

blast blɑːst, (US) blæst -s -s -ing -ɪŋ -ed -ɪd **ˈblast ˌfurnace**

blastoderm ˈblæs.təʊ.dɜːm, (US) -tə.dɝːm -s -z

blast-off ˈblɑːst.ɒf, (US) ˈblæst.ɑːf -s -s

blatancy ˈbleɪ.tᵊnt.si

blatant ˈbleɪ.tᵊnt -ly -li

Blatchford ˈblætʃ.fəd, (US) -fɚd

blath|er ˈblæð|.əʳ, (US) -ɚ -ers -əz, (US) -ɚz -ering -ᵊr.ɪŋ -ered -əd, (US) -ɚd

Blawith *in Cumbria:* ˈblɑː.ð *road in Harrow:* ˈbleɪ.wɪθ

blaxploitation ˌblæk.splɔɪˈteɪ.ʃᵊn

Blaydes bleɪdz

Blaydon ˈbleɪ.dᵊn

blaz|e bleɪz -es -ɪz -ing -ɪŋ -ed -d

blazer ˈbleɪ.zəʳ, (US) -zɚ -s -z

Blazes ˈbleɪ.zɪz

Blazey ˈbleɪ.zi

blazon ˈbleɪ.zᵊn; *in original heraldic sense also:* ˈblæz.ᵊn -s -z -ing -ɪŋ -ed -d

bleach bliːtʃ -es -ɪz -ing -ɪŋ -ed -t **ˈbleaching ˌpowder**

bleachers ˈbliː.tʃəz, (US) -tʃɚz

bleak bliːk -er -əʳ, (US) -ɚ -est -ɪst, -əst -ly -li -ness -nəs, -nɪs

Bleakley ˈbliː.kli

blear blɪəʳ, (US) blɪr

blear|y ˈblɪə.r|i, (US) ˈblɪr|.i -ier -i.əʳ, (US) -i.ɚ -iest -i.ɪst, (US) -i.əst -ily -ᵊl.i, -ɪ.li -iness -ɪ.nəs, -ɪ.nɪs

bleary-eyed ˌblɪə.riˈaɪd, (US) ˈblɪr.i.aɪd- *stress shift, British only:* **ˌbleary-eyed ˈchild**

Bleasdale ˈbliːz.deɪl

Bleasedale ˈbliːz.deɪl

bleat bliːt -s -s -ing -ɪŋ, (US) ˈbliː.t̬ɪŋ -ed -ɪd, (US) ˈbliː.t̬ɪd

bleb bleb -s -z

bled (from **bleed**) bled

Bledisloe ˈbled.ɪ.sləʊ, (US) -sloʊ

bleed bliːd -s -z -ing -ɪŋ -er/s -əʳ/z, (US) -ɚ/z bled bled

bleeding-edge ˌbliː.dɪŋˈedʒ

bleep bliːp -s -s -ing -ɪŋ -ed -t

bleeper ˈbliː.pəʳ, (US) -pɚ -s -z

blemish ˈblem.ɪʃ -es -ɪz -ing -ɪŋ -ed -t

blench, B~ blentʃ -es -ɪz -ing -ɪŋ -ed -t

Blencowe ˈbleŋ.kəʊ, (US) -koʊ

blend blend -s -z -ing -ɪŋ -ed -ɪd

blende blend

blender ˈblen.dəʳ, (US) -dɚ -s -z

Blenheim ˈblen.ɪm, -əm

Blenkinsop ˈbleŋ.kɪn.sɒp, (US) -sɑːp

Blennerhassett ˌblen.əˈhæs.ɪt, (US) ˈblen.ɚ.hæs-

Blériot ˈbler.i.əʊ, (US) ˌbler.iˈoʊ, ˈ--- -s -z

bless bles -es -ɪz -ing -ɪŋ -ed -t blest blest

blessed **adj** ˈbles.ɪd, -əd -ly -li -ness -nəs, -nɪs

blessing ˈbles.ɪŋ -s -z **a ˌblessing in disˈguise**

Blessington ˈbles.ɪŋ.tən

blest (from **bless**) blest

Bletchley ˈbletʃ.li

bleth|er ˈbleð|.əʳ, (US) -ɚ -ers -əz, (US) -ɚz -ering -ᵊr.ɪŋ -ered -əd, (US) -ɚd

blew (from **blow**) bluː

Blewett, Blewitt ˈbluː.ɪt

Blickling ˈblɪk.lɪŋ

Bligh blaɪ

blight blaɪt -s -s -ing -ɪŋ, (US) ˈblaɪ.t̬ɪŋ -ed -ɪd, (US) ˈblaɪ.t̬ɪd

blighter ˈblaɪ.təʳ, (US) -t̬ɚ -s -z

Blighty ˈblaɪ.ti, (US) -t̬i

blimey ˈblaɪ.mi

blimp blɪmp -s -s -ish -ɪʃ

blind blaɪnd -er -əʳ, (US) -ɚ -est -ɪst, -əst -ly -li -ness -nəs, -nɪs -s -z -ing -ɪŋ -ed -ɪd **ˌblind ˈdate; ˈblind ˌside; ˈblind ˌspot; as ˌblind as a ˈbat; (a ˌcase of) the ˌblind ˌleading the ˈblind; ˌturn a ˌblind ˈeye (to)**

blinder ˈblaɪn.dəʳ, (US) -dɚ -s -z

blindfold ˈblaɪnd.fəʊld, (US) -foʊld -s -z -ing -ɪŋ -ed -ɪd

blinding ˈblaɪn.dɪŋ -ly -li

blindman's-buff ˌblaɪnd.mænzˈbʌf

blindsid|e ˈblaɪnd.saɪd -s -z -ing -ɪŋ -ed -ɪd

blindworm ˈblaɪnd.wɜːm, (US) -wɝːm -s -z

blini ˈblɪn.i, ˈbliː.ni -s -z

blink blɪŋk -s -s -ing -ɪŋ -ed -t

blinker ˈblɪŋ.kəʳ, (US) -kɚ -s -z -ed -d

blip blɪp -s -s -ping -ɪŋ -ped -t

bliss, B~ blɪs

Blissett ˈblɪs.ɪt

blissful ˈblɪs.fᵊl, -fʊl -ly -i -ness -nəs, -nɪs

blist|er ˈblɪs.t|əʳ, (US) -t|ɚ -ers -əz, (US) -ɚz -ering -ᵊr.ɪŋ -ered -əd, (US) -ɚd

BLit(t) ˌbiːˈlɪt

blith|e blaɪð -er -əʳ, (US) -ɚ -est -ɪst, -əst -ely -li -eness -nəs, -nɪs

Blithedale ˈblaɪð.deɪl

blithering ˈblɪð.ᵊr.ɪŋ

blithesome ˈblaɪð.səm -ly -li -ness -nəs, -nɪs

blitz blɪts -es -ɪz -ing -ɪŋ -ed -t

blitzkrieg ˈblɪts.kriːg -s -z

Blix blɪks

Blixen ˈblɪk.sᵊn

blizzard ˈblɪz.əd, (US) -ɚd -s -z

bloat bləʊt, (US) bloʊt -s -s -ing -ɪŋ, (US) ˈbloʊ.t̬ɪŋ -ed/ness -ɪd/nəs, -nɪs, (US) ˈbloʊ.t̬ɪd/nəs, -nɪs

bloater ˈbləʊ.təʳ, (US) ˈbloʊ.t̬ɚ -s -z

blob blɒb, (US) blɑːb -s -z

blobb|y ˈblɒb|.i, (US) ˈblɑː.b|i -ier -i.əʳ, (US) -i.ɚ -iest -i.ɪst, -ɪ.əst

bloc blɒk, (US) blɑːk -s -s

Bloch blɒk; *as if German:* blɒx; (US) blɑːk

block, B~ blɒk, (US) blɑːk -s -s -ing -ɪŋ -ed -t -er/s -əʳ/z, (US) -ɚ/z **ˌblock ˈbooking; ˌblock ˈcapitals**

blockad|e blɒkˈeɪd, bləˈkeɪd, (US) blɑːˈkeɪd -es -z -ing -ɪŋ -ed -ɪd -er/s -əʳ/z, (US) -ɚ/z

blockag|e ˈblɒk.ɪdʒ, (US) ˈblɑː.kɪdʒ -es -ɪz

blockbust|er ˈblɒkˌbʌs.t|əʳ, (US) ˈblɑːkˌbʌs.t|ɚ -ers -əz, (US) -ɚz -ering -ᵊr.ɪŋ

blockhead ˈblɒk.hed, (US) ˈblɑːk- -s -z

blockhou|se ˈblɒk.haʊ|s, (US) ˈblɑːk- **-ses** -zɪz

Blodwen ˈblɒd.wɪn, -wen, (US) ˈblɑːd-

Bloemfontein ˈbluːm.fən.teɪn, -fɒn-, (US) -fɑːn-

Blofeld ˈbləʊ.felt, -feld, (US) ˈbloʊ-

blog blɒg, (US) blɑːg, blɔːg **-s** -z **-ging** -ɪŋ **-ged** -d **-ger/s** -əʳ/z, (US) -ɚ/z

blogosphere ˈblɒg.ə.sfɪəʳ, (US) ˈblɑː.gə.sfɪr

Blois *town in France:* blwɑː *surname:* blɔɪs

bloke bləʊk, (US) bloʊk **-s** -s **-ish/ly** -ɪʃ/li

Blom blɒm, (US) blɑːm

Blomefield ˈbluːm.fiːld

Blomfield ˈblɒm.fiːld, ˈblʊm-, ˈblʌm-, ˈbluːm-, (US) ˈblɑːm-, ˈblʊm-, ˈblʌm-, ˈbluːm-

blond(e) blɒnd, (US) blɑːnd **-s** -z

Blondel(l) ˈblʌn.dᵊl, ˈblɒn-; blɒnˈdel, (US) blɑːnˈdel; (US) ˈblɑːn.dᵊl, ˈblʌn-

Blondin ˈblɒn.dɪn; *as if French:* blɔ̃ːnˈdæ̃ŋ; (US) blɑːnˈdæn

blood blʌd **-s** -z **-ing** -ɪŋ **-ed** -ɪd **ˈblood ˌcell; ˈblood ˌdonor; ˈblood ˌgroup; ˈblood ˌmoney; ˈblood ˌpoisoning; ˈblood ˌpressure; ˌblood reˈlation; ˈblood ˌsport; ˈblood ˌtest; ˈblood transˌfusion; ˈblood ˌvessel; ˌblood is thicker than ˈwater; get ˌblood out of a ˈstone; in ˌcold ˈblood**

bloodba|th ˈblʌd.bɑː|θ, (US) -bæ|θ **-ths** -ðz

bloodcurdling ˈblʌdˌkɜː.dᵊl.ɪŋ, -ˌkɜːd.lɪŋ, (US) -ˌkɝː.dᵊl.ɪŋ, -ˌkɝːd.lɪŋ **-ly** -li

bloodhound ˈblʌd.haʊnd **-s** -z

bloodied ˈblʌd.id

bloodless ˈblʌd.ləs, -lɪs **-ly** -li **-ness** -nəs, -nɪs

bloodletting ˈblʌdˌlet.ɪŋ, (US) -ˌlet̬.ɪŋ

bloodline ˈblʌd.laɪn

blood-red ˌblʌdˈred *stress shift:* **ˌblood-red ˈlips**

bloodshed ˈblʌd.ʃed

bloodshot ˈblʌd.ʃɒt, (US) -ʃɑːt

bloodstain ˈblʌd.steɪn **-s** -z **-ed** -d

bloodstock ˈblʌd.stɒk, (US) -stɑːk

bloodstone ˈblʌd.stəʊn, (US) -stoʊn **-s** -z

bloodstream ˈblʌd.striːm **-s** -z

bloodsucker ˈblʌdˌsʌk.əʳ, (US) -ɚ **-s** -z

bloodthirst|y ˈblʌdˌθɜː.st|i, (US) -ˌθɝː- **-ier** -i.əʳ, (US) -i.ɚ **-iest** -i.ɪst, -i.əst **-ily** -ᵊl.i, -ɪ.li **-iness** -ɪ.nəs, -ɪ.nɪs

blood|y ˈblʌd|.i **-ier** -i.əʳ, (US) -i.ɚ **-iest** -i.ɪst, -i.əst **-ily** -ᵊl.i, -ɪ.li **-iness** -ɪ.nəs, -ɪ.nɪs **ˌBloody ˈMary**

bloody-minded ˌblʌd.iˈmaɪn.dɪd *stress shift:* **ˌbloody-minded ˈperson**

bloom, B~ bluːm **-s** -z **-ing** -ɪŋ **-ed** -d

Bloomberg ˈbluːm.bɜːg, (US) -bɝːg

bloomer, B~ ˈbluː.məʳ, (US) -mɚ **-s** -z

Bloomfield ˈbluːm.fiːld

Bloomingdale ˈbluː.mɪŋ.deɪl **-'s** -z

Bloomington ˈbluː.mɪŋ.tən

Bloomsbury ˈbluːmz.bᵊr.i, (US) -ber-, -bɚ-

bloop bluːp **-s** -s **-ing** -ɪŋ **-ed** -t

blooper ˈbluː.pəʳ, (US) -pɚ **-s** -z

Blore blɔːʳ, (US) blɔːr

blossom, B~ ˈblɒs.ᵊm, (US) ˈblɑː.sᵊm **-s** -z **-ing** -ɪŋ **-ed** -d

blot blɒt, (US) blɑːt **-s** -s **-ting** -ɪŋ, (US) ˈblɑː.t̬ɪŋ **-ted** -ɪd, (US) ˈblɑː.t̬ɪd

blotch blɒtʃ, (US) blɑːtʃ **-es** -ɪz **-ing** -ɪŋ **-ed** -t

blotch|y ˈblɒtʃ|.i, (US) ˈblɑː.tʃ|i **-ier** -i.əʳ, (US) -i.ɚ **-iest** -i.ɪst, -i.əst **-ily** -ᵊl.i, -ɪ.li **-iness** -ɪ.nəs, -ɪ.nɪs

blotter ˈblɒt.əʳ, (US) ˈblɑː.t̬ɚ **-s** -z

blotting ˈblɒt.ɪŋ, (US) ˈblɑː.t̬ɪŋ **ˈblotting ˌpaper**

blotto ˈblɒt.əʊ, (US) ˈblɑː.t̬oʊ

Blount blʌnt, blaʊnt

blous|e blaʊz, (US) blaʊs **-es** -ɪz

blouson ˈbluː.zɒn, (US) -sɑːn, ˈblaʊ-, -zɑːn **-s** -z

blow, B~ bləʊ, (US) bloʊ **-s** -z **-ing** -ɪŋ **blew** bluː **blown** bləʊn, (US) bloʊn **blowed** bləʊd, (US) bloʊd **blower/s** ˈbləʊ.əʳ/z, (US) ˈbloʊ.ɚ/s

blow-by-blow ˌbləʊ.baɪˈbləʊ, (US) ˌbloʊ.baɪˈbloʊ *stress shift:* **ˌblow-by-blow acˈcount**

blow|dry ˈbləʊ|.draɪ, (US) ˈbloʊ- **-dries** -draɪz **-drying** -ˌdraɪ.ɪŋ **-dried** -draɪd **-drier/s** -ˌdraɪ.əʳ/z, (US) -ˌdraɪ.ɚ/z

blowfl|y ˈbləʊ.fl|aɪ, (US) ˈbloʊ- **-ies** -aɪz

blowgun ˈbləʊ.gʌn, (US) ˈbloʊ- **-s** -z

blowhard ˈbləʊ.hɑːd, (US) ˈbloʊ.hɑːrd **-s** -z

blowhole ˈbləʊ.həʊl, (US) ˈbloʊ.hoʊl **-s** -z

blowlamp ˈbləʊ.læmp, (US) ˈbloʊ- **-s** -s

blown (from **blow**) bləʊn, (US) bloʊn

blowout ˈbləʊ.aʊt, (US) ˈbloʊ- **-s** -s

blowpipe ˈbləʊ.paɪp, (US) ˈbloʊ- **-s** -s

blows|y ˈblaʊ.z|i **-ier** -i.əʳ, (US) -i.ɚ **-iest** -i.ɪst, -i.əst **-ily** -ᵊl.i, -ɪ.li **-iness** -ɪ.nəs, -ɪ.nɪs

blowtorch ˈbləʊ.tɔːtʃ, (US) ˈbloʊ.tɔːrtʃ **-es** -ɪz

blow|y ˈbləʊ|.i, (US) ˈbloʊ- **-ier** -i.əʳ, (US) -i.ɚ **-iest** -i.ɪst, -i.əst **-ily** -ᵊl.i, -ɪ.li **-iness** -ɪ.nəs, -ɪ.nɪs

blowz|y ˈblaʊ.z|i **-ier** -i.əʳ, (US) -i.ɚ **-iest** -i.ɪst, -i.əst **-ily** -ᵊl.i, -ɪ.li **-iness** -ɪ.nəs, -ɪ.nɪs

Blox(h)am ˈblɒk.səm, (US) ˈblɑːk-

BLT ˌbiː.elˈtiː

blub blʌb **-s** -z **-bing** -ɪŋ **-bed** -d

blubb|er ˈblʌb|.əʳ, (US) -ɚ **-ers** -əz, (US) -ɚz **-ering** -ᵊr.ɪŋ **-ered** -əd, (US) -ɚd **-erer/s** -ᵊr.əʳ/z

bludgeon ˈblʌdʒ.ᵊn **-s** -z **-ing** -ɪŋ **-ed** -d

blu|e bluː **-es** -z **-er** -əʳ, (US) -ɚ **-est** -ɪst, -əst **-(e)ing** -ɪŋ **-ed** -d **ˌblue ˈcheese; ˈblue ˌjay; ˈblue ˌlaw; ˌblue ˈmovie; ˈblue ˌtit; ˌout of the ˈblue**

Bluebeard ˈbluː.bɪəd, (US) -bɪrd

bluebell ˈbluː.bel **-s** -z

blueberr|y ˈbluː.bᵊr|.i, -ˌber-, (US) -ˌber- **-ies** -iz

bluebird ˈbluː.bɜːd, (US) -bɝːd **-s** -z

blue-blooded ˌbluːˈblʌd.ɪd, (US) ˈ-ˌ-- *stress shift, British only:* **ˌblue-blooded ˈmonarch**

bluebottle ˈbluːˌbɒt.ᵊl, (US) -ˌbɑː.t̬ᵊl **-s** -z

blue-chip ˈbluː.tʃɪp

bluecoat ˈbluː.kəʊt, (US) -koʊt **-s** -s

blue-collar ˌbluːˈkɒl.əʳ, (US) ˈbluːˌkɑː.lɚ *stress shift, British only:* **ˌblue-collar ˈworker**

blue-eyed ˌbluːˈaɪd, ˈ-- *stress shift, British only: see compound:* **ˌblue-eyed ˈboy**

bluegrass ˈbluː.grɑːs, (US) -græs

bluejacket ˈbluːˌdʒæk.ɪt **-s** -s

bluejay ˈbluː.dʒeɪ **-s** -z

bluejeans, blue jeans ˌbluːˈdʒiːnz, (US) ˈ--

blueness ˈbluː.nəs, -nɪs

blue-pencil ˌbluːˈpent.sᵊl, -sɪl, (US) ˈ-ˌ-- **-s** -z **-(l)ing** -ɪŋ **-(l)ed** -d

blueprint ˈbluː.prɪnt **-s** -s

blue-sky ˌbluːˈskaɪ *stress shift:* **ˌblue-sky reˈsearch**

bluestocking ˈbluːˌstɒk.ɪŋ, (US) -ˌstɑː.kɪŋ **-s** -z

bluesy ˈbluː.zi

Bluetooth® ˈbluː.tuːθ

Bluett ˈbluː.ɪt

bluey ˈbluː.i

bluff blʌf **-s** -s **-er** -əʳ, (US) -ɚ **-est** -ɪst, -əst **-ly** -li **-ness** -nəs, -nɪs **-ing** -ɪŋ **-ed** -t

bluish ˈbluː.ɪʃ

Blum bluːm

Blume bluːm

Blumenthal ˈbluː.mən.tɑːl

Blundell ˈblʌn.dᵊl; blʌnˈdel

Blunden ˈblʌn.dən

blund|er ˈblʌn.d|əʳ, (US) -d|ɚ **-ers** -əz, (US) -ɚz **-ering** -ᵊr.ɪŋ **-ered** -əd, (US) -ɚd **-erer/s** -ᵊr.əʳ/z, (US) -ɚ.ɚ/z

blunderbuss ˈblʌn.də.bʌs, (US) -dɚ- **-es** -ɪz

Blunkett ˈblʌŋ.kɪt

Blunn blʌn

blunt, B~ blʌnt **-er** -əʳ, (US) ˈblʌn.t̬ɚ **-est** -ɪst, -əst, (US) ˈblʌn.t̬ɪst, -t̬əst **-ly** -li **-ness** -nəs, -nɪs **-s** -s **-ing** -ɪŋ, (US) ˈblʌn.t̬ɪŋ **-ed** -ɪd, (US) ˈblʌn.t̬ɪd **ˌblunt ˈinstrument**

blur, B~ blɜːʳ, (US) blɝː **-s** -z **-ring** -ɪŋ **-red** -d

blurb blɜːb, (US) blɝːb **-s** -z

blurt blɜːt, (US) blɝːt **-s** -s **-ing** -ɪŋ, (US) ˈblɝː.t̬ɪŋ **-ed** -ɪd, (US) ˈblɝː.t̬ɪd

blush blʌʃ **-es** -ɪz **-ing/ly** -ɪŋ/li **-ed** -t

blusher ˈblʌʃ.əʳ, (US) -ɚ **-s** -z

blust|er ˈblʌs.t|əʳ, (US) -t|ɚ **-ers** -əz, (US) -ɚz **-ering/ly** -ᵊr.ɪŋ/li **-ered** -əd, (US) -ɚd **-erer/s** -ᵊr.əʳ/z, (US) -ɚ.ɚ/z

B

bluster|y ˈblʌs.tᵊr|.i **-iness** -ɪ.nəs, -ɪ.nɪs
Blu-Tack® ˈbluː.tæk
Bly blaɪ
Blyth blaɪð, blaɪθ, blaɪ
Blythborough ˈblaɪ.bᵊr.ə, (US) -bɚ.oʊ
Blythe blaɪð
Blyton ˈblaɪ.tᵊn
B-movie ˈbiːˌmuː.vi **-s** -z
BMus ˌbiːˈmʌz
BMW® ˌbiː.emˈdʌb.ᵊl.ju
BMX ˌbiː.emˈeks *stress shift, see compound:* ˌ**BMX** ˈ**bike**
bn (abbrev. for **billion**) ˈbɪl.jən, ˈ-i.ən, (US) ˈ-jən
Bo bəʊ, (US) boʊ
BO ˌbiːˈəʊ, (US) -ˈoʊ
boa bəʊ.ə, (US) boʊ.ə **-s** -z
Boadicea ˌbəʊ.dɪˈsiː.ə, -dəˈ-, (US) ˌboʊ.də-
Boag bəʊg; ˈbəʊ.æg, -əg, (US) boʊg
Boal bəʊl, (US) boʊl
Boanas ˈbəʊ.nəs, (US) ˈboʊ-
Boanerges ˌbəʊ.əˈnɜː.dʒiːz, (US) ˌboʊ.əˈnɝː-
boar bɔːʳ, (US) bɔːr **-s** -z
board bɔːd, (US) bɔːrd **-s** -z **-ing** -ɪŋ **-ed** -ɪd ˈ**board** ˌ**game**; ˈ**boarding** ˌ**house**; ˈ**boarding** ˌ**pass**; ˈ**boarding** ˌ**school**; ˌ**go by the** ˈ**board**
boarder ˈbɔː.dəʳ, (US) ˈbɔːr.dɚ **-s** -z
boardroom ˈbɔːd.rʊm, -ruːm, (US) ˈbɔːrd.ruːm, -rʊm **-s** -z
boardwalk ˈbɔːd.wɔːk, (US) ˈbɔːrd.wɔːk, -wɑːk **-s** -s
boarish ˈbɔː.rɪʃ, (US) ˈbɔːr.ɪʃ
Boas ˈbəʊ.æz, -əz, -æs, -əs, (US) ˈboʊ-
Boase bəʊz, (US) boʊz
boast bəʊst, (US) boʊst **-s** -s **-ing/ly** -ɪŋ/li **-ed** -ɪd **-er/s** -əʳ/z, (US) -ɚ/z
boastful ˈbəʊst.fᵊl, -fʊl, (US) ˈboʊst- **-ly** -li **-ness** -nəs, -nɪs
boat bəʊt, (US) boʊt **-s** -s **-er/s** -əʳ/z, (US) ˈboʊ.t̬ɚ/z ˈ**boat** ˌ**race**; ˈ**boat** ˌ**train**; ˌ**burn one's** ˈ**boats**
Boateng ˈbwɑː.teŋ, ˈbəʊ-, (US) ˈbwɑː-, ˈboʊ-
boathook ˈbəʊt.hʊk, (US) ˈboʊt- **-s** -s
boathou|se ˈbəʊt.haʊ|s, (US) ˈboʊt- **-ses** -zɪz
boating ˈbəʊ.tɪŋ, (US) ˈboʊ.t̬ɪŋ
boatload ˈbəʊt.ləʊd, (US) ˈboʊt.loʊd **-s** -z
boat|man ˈbəʊt|.mən, (US) ˈboʊt- **-men** -mən, -men
boatswain ˈbəʊ.sᵊn, ˈbəʊt.sweɪn, (US) ˈboʊ.sᵊn **-s** -z
boatyard ˈbəʊt.jɑːd, (US) ˈboʊt.jɑːrd **-s** -z
Boaz ˈbəʊ.æz, (US) ˈboʊ-
bob, B~ bɒb, (US) bɑːb **-s** -z **-bing** -ɪŋ **-bed** -d
Bobbie ˈbɒb.i, (US) ˈbɑː.bi
bobbin ˈbɒb.ɪn, (US) ˈbɑː.bɪn **-s** -z
bobbl|e ˈbɒb.ᵊl, (US) ˈbɑː.bᵊl **-es** -z **-ing** -ɪŋ **-ed** -d
bobb|y, B~ ˈbɒb|.i, (US) ˈbɑː.b|i **-ies** -iz ˈ**bobby** ˌ**pin**
bobbysox ˈbɒb.i.sɒks, (US) ˈbɑː.bi.sɑːks **-er/s** -əʳ/z, (US) -ɚ/z
bobcat ˈbɒb.kæt, (US) ˈbɑːb- **-s** -s
Bobo Dioulasso ˌbəʊ.bəʊ.djuˈlæs.əʊ, (US) ˌboʊ.boʊ.djuˈlæs.oʊ
bobolink ˈbɒb.ə.lɪŋk, (US) ˈbɑː.bə- **-s** -s
bobsled ˈbɒb.sled, (US) ˈbɑːb- **-s** -z **-ding** -ɪŋ **-ded** -ɪd
bobsleigh ˈbɒb.sleɪ, (US) ˈbɑːb- **-s** -z
bobstay ˈbɒb.steɪ, (US) ˈbɑːb- **-s** -z
bobtail ˈbɒb.teɪl, (US) ˈbɑːb- **-s** -z
Boca Raton ˌbəʊ.kə.rəˈtəʊn, (US) ˌboʊ.kə.rəˈtoʊn
Boccaccio bɒkˈɑː.tʃi.əʊ, bəˈkɑː-, bɒkˈætʃ.i.əʊ, bəˈkætʃ-, (US) boʊˈkɑː.tʃi.oʊ
Boccherini ˌbɒk.ᵊrˈiː.ni, (US) ˌbɑː.kəˈriː-, ˌboʊ-
Boche(s) bɒʃ, (US) bɑːʃ, bɔːʃ
Bochum ˈbəʊ.kᵊm, (US) ˈboʊ-
bod bɒd, (US) bɑːd **-s** -z
bodacious bəʊˈdeɪ.ʃəs, (US) boʊ- **-ly** -li
Boddington ˈbɒd.ɪŋ.tən, (US) ˈbɑː.dɪŋ-
Boddy ˈbɒd.i, (US) ˈbɑː.di
bod|e, B~ bəʊd, (US) boʊd **-es** -z **-ing** -ɪŋ **-ed** -ɪd
bodega, B~ bəˈdeɪ.gə, bɒdˈeɪ-, (US) boʊˈdeɪ- **-s** -z
Boden ˈbəʊ.dᵊn, (US) ˈboʊ-
Bodey ˈbəʊ.di, (US) ˈboʊ-
bodg|e bɒdʒ, (US) bɑːdʒ **-es** -ɪz **-ing** -ɪŋ **-ed** -d
bodger ˈbɒdʒ.əʳ, (US) ˈbɑː.dʒɚ **-s** -z
Bodiam ˈbəʊ.di.əm, (US) ˈboʊ-
bodic|e ˈbɒd.ɪs, (US) ˈbɑː.dɪs **-es** -ɪz
Bodie ˈbəʊ.di, (US) ˈboʊ-
-bodied -ˈbɒd.id, (US) -ˈbɑː.did
Note: Suffix. Always carries primary stress unless used attributively, e.g. **full-bodied** /ˌfʊlˈbɒd.id/ (US) /-ˈbɑː.did/, ˌ**full-bodied** ˈ**wine**.
bodily ˈbɒd.ᵊl.i, -ɪ.li, (US) ˈbɑː.d- ˌ**bodily** ˈ**function**
bodkin, B~ ˈbɒd.kɪn, (US) ˈbɑːd- **-s** -z
Bodleian ˈbɒd.li.ən, bɒdˈliː-, (US) ˈbɑːd.li.ən, bɑːdˈliː-
Bodley ˈbɒd.li, (US) ˈbɑːd-
Bodmin ˈbɒd.mɪn, (US) ˈbɑːd-
Bodnant ˈbɒd.nænt, (US) ˈbɑːd-
bod|y ˈbɒd|.i, (US) ˈbɑː.d|i **-ies** -iz ˈ**body** ˌ**bag**; ˈ**body** ˌ**builder**; ˈ**body** ˌ**building**; ˈ**body** ˌ**language**; ˈ**body** ˌ**snatcher**; **keep** ˌ**body and soul to**ˈ**gether**; **over** ˌ**my** ˌ**dead** ˈ**body**
bodyboard ˈbɒd.i.bɔːd, (US) ˈbɑː.di.bɔːrd **-ing** -ɪŋ **-s** -z
bodyguard ˈbɒd.i.gɑːd, (US) ˈbɑː.di.gɑːrd **-s** -z
bodysuit ˈbɒd.i.suːt, -sjuːt, (US) ˈbɑː.di.suːt **-s** -s
bodysurf ˈbɒd.i.sɜːf, (US) ˈbɑː.di.sɝːf **-s** -s **-ing** -ɪŋ **-ed** -t **-er/s** -əʳ/z, (US) -ɚ/z
bodywarmer ˈbɒd.iˌwɔː.məʳ, (US) ˈbɑː.diˌwɔːr.mɚ **-s** -z
bodywork ˈbɒd.i.wɜːk, (US) ˈbɑː.di.wɝːk
Boeing® ˈbəʊ.ɪŋ, (US) ˈboʊ-
Boeoti|a biˈəʊ.ʃ|ə, -ʃi|.ə, (US) -ˈoʊ.ʃ|ə **-an/s** -ən/z
Boer ˈbəʊ.əʳ, bɔːʳ, bʊəʳ, (US) bɔːr, ˈboʊ.ɚ, bʊr **-s** -z
Boethius bəʊˈiː.θi.əs, (US) boʊ-
boeuf bourguignon ˌbɜːfˌbʊə.giːˈnjɔ̃ːŋ, -ˌbɔː-, -gɪˈ-, (US) ˌbɜːfˌbʊr.giːˈnjõʊn
boff bɒf, (US) bɑːf **-s** -s **-ing** -ɪŋ **-ed** -t
boffin, B~ ˈbɒf.ɪn, (US) ˈbɑː.fɪn **-s** -z
Bofors ˈbəʊ.fəz, (US) ˈboʊ.fɔːrz, -fɔːrs
bog bɒg, (US) bɑːg, bɔːg **-s** -z **-ging** -ɪŋ **-ged** -d
Bogan ˈbəʊ.gᵊn, (US) ˈboʊ-
Bogarde ˈbəʊ.gɑːd, (US) ˈboʊ.gɑːrd
Bogart ˈbəʊ.gɑːt, (US) ˈboʊ.gɑːrt
Bogdan ˈbɒg.dæn, (US) ˈbɑːg-, ˈbɔːg-
Bogdanovich bɒgˈdæn.ə.vɪtʃ, (US) bɑːgˈdɑː.n-, bɔːg-
bogey ˈbəʊ.gi, (US) ˈboʊ- **-s** -z
bogey|man ˈbəʊ.gi|.mæn, (US) ˈboʊ- **-men** -men
boggl|e ˈbɒg.ᵊl, (US) ˈbɑː.gᵊl **-es** -z **-ing** -ɪŋ, ˈ-lɪŋ, (US) ˈ-glɪŋ **-ed** -d **-er/s** -əʳ/z, ˈ-ləʳ/z, (US) ˈbɑː.gᵊl.ɚ/z, ˈbɑːg.lɚ/z
bogg|y ˈbɒg|.i, (US) ˈbɑː.g|i **-ier** -i.əʳ, (US) -i.ɚ **-iest** -i.ɪst, -i.əst **-iness** -ɪ.nəs, -ɪ.nɪs
bogie ˈbəʊ.gi, (US) ˈboʊ- **-s** -z ˈ**bogie** ˌ**engine**; ˈ**bogie** ˌ**wheel**
Bognor ˈbɒg.nəʳ, (US) ˈbɑːg.nɚ, ˈbɔːg- ˌ**Bognor** ˈ**Regis**
bog-oak ˌbɒgˈəʊk, ˈ--, (US) ˈbɑːg.oʊk, ˈbɔːg-
BOGOF ˈbɒg.ɒf, (US) ˈbɑː.gɑːf
Bogota *in Columbia:* ˌbɒg.əʊˈtɑː, ˌbəʊ.gə-, (US) ˌboʊ.gəˈtɑː, ˈ--- *in New Jersey:* bəˈgəʊ.tə, (US) -ˈgoʊ.t̬ə
bogstandard ˌbɒgˈstæn.dəd, (US) ˈbɑːgˌstæn.dɚd, ˈbɔːg-
bogus ˈbəʊ.gəs, (US) ˈboʊ-
bog|y ˈbəʊ.g|i, (US) ˈboʊ- **-ies** -iz
bohea bəʊˈhiː, (US) boʊ-
Bohème bəʊˈem, -ˈeɪm, (US) boʊ-
Bohemia bəʊˈhiː.mi.ə, (US) boʊ-
bohemian, B~ bəʊˈhiː.mi.ən, (US) boʊ- **-s** -z
Böhm bɜːm
Bohn bəʊn, (US) boʊn
Bohr bɔːʳ, (US) bɔːr
Bohun ˈbəʊ.ən, buːn, (US) ˈboʊ-, buːn

> Note: /buːn/ in Shaw's 'You never can tell'.

boil bɔɪl **-s** -z **-ing** -ɪŋ **-ed** -d ˈ**boiling** ˌ**point**
boiler ˈbɔɪ.ləʳ, (US) -lɚ **-s** -z ˈ**boiler** ˌ**suit**
boilermaker ˈbɔɪ.ləˌmeɪ.kəʳ, (US) -lɚˌmeɪ.kɚ **-s** -z
boilerplate ˈbɔɪ.lə.pleɪt, (US) -lɚ- **-s** -s
boil-in-the-bag ˌbɔɪl.ɪn.ðəˈbæg *stress shift:* ˌ**boil-in-the-bag** ˈ**meal**
boing bɔɪŋ
Boipatong ˌbɔɪ.pəˈtɒŋ, -pætˈɒŋ, (US) ˈbɔɪ.pə.tɑːŋ, -tɔːŋ
Bois bɔɪs, bwɑː

B

Boise ˈbɔɪ.zi, ˈbɔɪ.si
boisterous ˈbɔɪ.stər.əs **-ly** -li **-ness** -nəs, -nɪs
Boker ˈbəʊ.kər, (US) ˈboʊ.kɚ
Bokhara bəʊˈkɑː.rə, (US) boʊˈkɑːr.ə
Bolan ˈbəʊ.lən, (US) ˈboʊ-
bolas ˈbəʊ.ləs, -læs, (US) ˈboʊ- **-es** -ɪz
bold bəʊld, (US) boʊld **-er** -ər, (US) -ɚ **-est** -ɪst, -əst **-ly** -li **-ness** -nəs, -nɪs
bold-face ˌbəʊldˈfeɪs, (US) ˈboʊld.feɪs, ˈboʊl- **-d** -t *stress shift, British only:* ˌ**bold-face** ˈ**type**
Boldon ˈbəʊl.dən, (US) ˈboʊl-
Boldre ˈbəʊl.dər, (US) ˈboʊl.dɚ
bole bəʊl, (US) boʊl **-s** -z
bolero *dance:* bəˈleə.rəʊ, bɒlˈeə-, -ˈlɪə-, (US) bəˈler.oʊ, boʊ- *garment:* ˈbɒl.ə.rəʊ, (US) bəˈler.oʊ **-s** -z
bolet|us bəʊˈliː.t|əs, (US) boʊˈliː.ţ|əs **-uses** -ə.sɪz **-i** -aɪ
Boleyn bəʊˈlɪn; bʊ-; -ˈliːn, (US) ˈbʊ.lɪn, bʊˈlɪn
Bolingbroke ˈbɒl.ɪŋ.brʊk, (US) ˈbɑː.lɪŋ-, ˈboʊ-
Bolinger ˈbɒl.ɪn.dʒər, ˈbəʊ.lɪn-, (US) ˈbɑː.lən.dʒɚ
Bolitho bəˈlaɪ.θəʊ, bɒlˈaɪ-, (US) bəˈlaɪ.θoʊ
bolivar *money:* bɒlˈiː.vɑːr; ˈbɒl.ɪ.vər, (US) boʊˈliː.vɑːr; (US) ˈbɑː.lə.vɚ **-s** -z
Bolívar *S. American general:* ˈbɒl.i.vɑːr; bɒlˈiː-, (US) ˈboʊ.lə.vɑːr *places in US:* ˈbɒl.ɪ.vər, ˈ-ə-, -vɑːr, (US) ˈbɑː.lə.vɚ
bolivares (alternative plural of **bolivar**) ˌbɒl.ɪˈvɑː.reɪz, (US) boʊˌliː.vɑːˈreɪs; (US) ˌboʊ.lɪˈvɑːr.es
Bolivi|a bəˈlɪv.i|.ə, bɒlˈɪv-, (US) bəˈlɪv-, boʊ- **-an/s** -ən/z
bolivia|no bəʊˌlɪv.iˈɑː|.nəʊ, bɒlˌɪv-; ˌbəʊ.lɪ.viˈ-, ˌbɒl.ɪv-, (US) bəˌlɪv.iˈɑː.noʊ, boʊ- **-nos** -nɒs, (US) -noʊs
boll bəʊl, bɒl, (US) boʊl **-s** -z **-ed** -d ˌ**boll** ˈ**weevil** (US) ˈ**boll** ˌ**weevil**
Böll bɜːl, (US) bɜːl, boʊl
bollard ˈbɒl.ɑːd, -əd, (US) ˈbɑː.lɚd **-s** -z
Bolling ˈbəʊ.lɪŋ, (US) ˈboʊ-
Bollinger ˈbɒl.ɪn.dʒər, (US) ˈbɑː.lən.dʒɚ
Bollington ˈbɒl.ɪŋ.tən, (US) ˈbɑː.lɪŋ-
bollix ˈbɒl.ɪks, (US) ˈbɑː.lɪks **-es** -ɪz **-ing** -ɪŋ **-ed** -t
bollocking ˈbɒl.ə.kɪŋ, (US) ˈbɑː.lə-
bollocks ˈbɒl.əks, (US) ˈbɑː.ləks
Bollywood ˈbɒl.i.wʊd, (US) ˈbɑː.li-
bolo ˈbəʊ.ləʊ, (US) ˈboʊ.loʊ **-s** -z
bologna *sausage:* bəˈləʊ.ni, (US) -ˈloʊ-
Bologna *city:* bəˈlɒn.jə, bɒlˈɒn-, -ˈləʊ.njə, -ni.ə, (US) bəˈloʊ.njə, -ˈlɑː-
bolognaise ˌbɒl.əˈneɪz, -ˈnjeɪz, (US) ˌboʊ.ləˈnjeɪz
Bolognese ˌbɒl.əˈneɪz; *as if Italian:* -ˈnjeɪ.zeɪ; (US) ˌboʊ.ləˈniːz, -ˈnjiːz
bolometer bəʊˈlɒm.ɪ.tər, ˈ-ə-, (US) boʊˈlɑː.mə.ţɚ **-s** -z
boloney bəˈləʊ.ni, (US) -ˈloʊ-
Bolshevik ˈbɒl.ʃə.vɪk, -ʃɪ-, (US) ˈboʊl-, ˈbɑːl- **-s** -s
Bolshev|ist ˈbɒl.ʃə.v|ɪst, -ʃɪ-, (US) ˈboʊl-, ˈbɑːl- **-ism** -ɪ.zəm
bolshie ˈbɒl.ʃi, (US) ˈboʊl-, ˈbɑːl- **-s** -z
Bolshoi, Bolshoy bɒlˈʃɔɪ, ˈ--, (US) ˈboʊl.ʃɔɪ, ˈbɑːl-; (US) boʊlˈʃɔɪ
bolsh|y ˈbɒl.ʃ|i, (US) ˈboʊl-, ˈbɑːl- **-ies** -z **-ier** -i.ər, (US) -i.ɚ **-iest** -i.ɪst, -i.əst
Bolsover *surname, street in London:* ˈbɒl.səʊ.vər, (US) ˈboʊl.soʊ.vɚ *in Derbyshire:* ˈbəʊl.zəʊ.vər; ˈbəʊl.səʊ-, (US) ˈboʊl.zoʊ.vɚ
bolst|er ˈbəʊl.st|ər, (US) ˈboʊl.st|ɚ **-ers** -əz, (US) -ɚz **-ering** -ər.ɪŋ **-ered** -əd, (US) -ɚd
bolt, B~ bəʊlt, (US) boʊlt **-s** -s **-ing** -ɪŋ, (US) ˈboʊl.ţɪŋ **-ed** -ɪd, (US) ˈboʊl.ţɪd ˌ**bolt** ˈ**upright**
bolter, B~ ˈbəʊl.tər, (US) ˈboʊl.ţɚ **-s** -z
bolt-hole ˈbəʊlt.həʊl, (US) ˈboʊlt.hoʊl **-s** -z
Bolton ˈbəʊl.tən, (US) ˈboʊl-
Bolton-le-Sands ˌbəʊl.tən.ləˈsændz, -lɪˈ-, (US) ˌboʊl.tən-
bolus ˈbəʊ.ləs, (US) ˈboʊ- **-es** -ɪz
Bolzano bɒltˈzɑː.nəʊ, (US) boʊltˈsɑː.noʊ, boʊlˈzɑː-
bomb bɒm, (US) bɑːm **-s** -z **-ing/s** -ɪŋ/z **-ed** -d ˌ**bomb dis**ˈ**posal** ˌ**unit**; ˈ**bomb di**ˌ**sposal** ˌ**unit**
bombard **n** ˈbɒm.bɑːd, (US) ˈbɑːm.bɑːrd **-s** -z
bombard **v** bɒmˈbɑːd, (US) bɑːmˈbɑːrd **-s** -z **-ing** -ɪŋ **-ed** -ɪd **-ment/s** -mənt/s
bombardier ˌbɒm.bəˈdɪər, (US) ˌbɑːm.bəˈdɪr **-s** -z
bombardon ˈbɒm.bə.dən; bɒmˈbɑː-, (US) ˈbɑːm.bɚ-; (US) bɑːmˈbɑːr- **-s** -z
bombasine ˈbɒm.bə.ziːn, -siːn, ˌ--ˈ-, (US) ˌbɑːm.bəˈziːn
bombast ˈbɒm.bæst, (US) ˈbɑːm-
bombastic bɒmˈbæs.tɪk, (US) bɑːm- **-ally** -əl.i, -li
Bombay ˌbɒmˈbeɪ, (US) ˌbɑːm- *stress shift, see compound:* ˌ**Bombay** ˈ**duck**
bombe bɒm, bɒmb, (US) bɑːm **-s** -z
bomber ˈbɒm.ər, (US) ˈbɑː.mɚ **-s** -z
bombshell ˈbɒm.ʃel, (US) ˈbɑːm- **-s** -z
bombsite ˈbɒm.saɪt, (US) ˈbɑːm- **-s** -s
Bompas ˈbʌm.pəs
bon bɔ̃ːŋ, (US) bɔ̃ːn
bona fid|e ˌbəʊ.nəˈfaɪ.d|i, -d|eɪ, (US) ˌboʊ.nəˈ- **-es** -iːz, -eɪz
bonanza bəˈnæn.zə **-s** -z
Bonapart|e ˈbəʊ.nə.pɑːt, (US) ˈboʊ.nə.pɑːrt **-ist/s** -ɪst/s
Bonar ˈbɒn.ər, ˈbəʊ.nər, (US) ˈbɑː.nɚ, ˈboʊ-
bonbon ˈbɒn.bɒn, ˈbɒm-, (US) ˈbɑːn.bɑːn **-s** -z
Bonchurch ˈbɒn.tʃɜːtʃ, (US) ˈbɑːn.tʃɝːtʃ
bond, B~ bɒnd, (US) bɑːnd **-s** -z **-ing** -ɪŋ **-ed** -ɪd ˈ**bond** ˌ**holder**
bondage ˈbɒn.dɪdʒ, (US) ˈbɑːn-
Bondi *in Australia:* ˈbɒn.daɪ, (US) ˈbɑːn- ˌ**Bondi** ˈ**Beach** *mathematician:* ˈbɒn.di, (US) ˈbɑːn-
bondmaid ˈbɒnd.meɪd, (US) ˈbɑːnd- **-s** -z
bond|man ˈbɒnd|.mən, (US) ˈbɑːnd- **-men** -mən, -men
bonds|man ˈbɒndz|.mən, (US) ˈbɑːndz- **-men** -mən, -men
bonds|woman ˈbɒndz|ˌwʊm.ən, (US) ˈbɑːndz- **-women** -ˌwɪm.ɪn
bond|woman ˈbɒnd|ˌwʊm.ən, (US) ˈbɑːnd- **-women** -ˌwɪm.ɪn
bon|e, B~ bəʊn, (US) boʊn **-es** -z **-ing** -ɪŋ **-ed** -d **-er/s** -ər/z, (US) -ɚ/z **-eless** -ləs, -lɪs ˈ**bone** ˌ**marrow**; ˈ**bone** ˌ**meal**; ˌ**chilled to the** ˈ**bone**; **have a** ˈ**bone to pick with** ˌ**someone**; ˌ**make no** ˈ**bones about something**
bone-dry ˌbəʊnˈdraɪ, (US) ˌboʊn- *stress shift:* ˌ**bone-dry** ˈ**desert**
bonehead ˈbəʊn.hed, (US) ˈboʊn- **-s** -z
bonesetter ˈbəʊnˌset.ər, (US) ˈboʊnˌseţ.ɚ **-s** -z
bone-shaker ˈbəʊnˌʃeɪ.kər, (US) ˈboʊnˌʃeɪ.kɚ **-s** -z
Bo'ness bəʊˈnes, (US) boʊ-
bonfire ˈbɒn.faɪər, -faɪ.ər, (US) ˈbɑːn.faɪ.ɚ **-s** -z ˈ**Bonfire** ˌ**Night**
bong bɒŋ, (US) bɑːŋ, bɔːŋ **-s** -z
bongo ˈbɒŋ.gəʊ, (US) ˈbɑːŋ.goʊ **-(e)s** -z ˈ**bongo** ˌ**drum**
Bonham ˈbɒn.əm, (US) ˈbɑː.nəm
Bonham-Carter ˌbɒn.əmˈkɑː.tər, (US) ˌbɑː.nəmˈkɑːr.ţɚ
bonhomie ˈbɒn.ɒm.i, -ə.mi, -miː, ˌ--ˈ-, (US) ˌbɑː.nəˈmiː, ˈ---
Boniface ˈbɒn.ɪ.feɪs, -fæs, (US) ˈbɑː.nɪ-
Bonifacio ˌbɒn.iˈfæʃ.i.əʊ, -ˈfæs-, (US) ˌboʊ.niˈfɑː.ʃoʊ, ˈ-ʃi.oʊ
Bonington ˈbɒn.ɪŋ.tən, (US) ˈbɑː.nɪŋ.ţən
bonk bɒŋk, (US) bɑːŋk, bɔːŋk **-s** -s **-ing** -ɪŋ **-ed** -t
bonkbuster ˈbɒŋkˌbʌs.tər, (US) ˈbɑːŋkˌbʌstɚ **-s** -z
bonkers ˈbɒŋ.kəz, (US) ˈbɑːŋ.kɚz, ˈbɔːŋ-
bon(s) mot(s) ˌbɔ̃ːmˈməʊ, (US) ˌbɔ̃ːnˈmoʊ
Bonn bɒn, (US) bɑːn
Bonnard ˈbɒn.ɑːr, (US) bɑːˈnɑːr, bɔː-
Bonner ˈbɒn.ər, (US) ˈbɑː.nɚ
bonn|et ˈbɒn|.ɪt, (US) ˈbɑː.n|ɪt **-ets** -ɪts **-eting** -ɪ.tɪŋ, (US) -ɪ.ţɪŋ **-eted** -ɪ.tɪd, (US) -ɪ.ţɪd
Bonnett ˈbɒn.ɪt, (US) ˈbɑː.nɪt
Bonnie ˈbɒn.i, (US) ˈbɑː.ni
bonn|y ˈbɒn|.i, (US) ˈbɑː.n|i **-ier** -i.ər, (US) -i.ɚ **-iest** -i.ɪst, -i.əst **-ily** -əl.i, -ɪ.li **-iness** -ɪ.nəs, -ɪ.nɪs
Bono ˈbəʊ.nəʊ, ˈbɒn.əʊ, (US) ˈboʊ.noʊ, ˈbɑː-
bonsai ˈbɒn.saɪ, (US) ˌbɑːnˈsaɪ, ˌboʊn- **-s** -z
Bonsor ˈbɒnt.sər, -zər, (US) ˈbɑːnt.sɚ, -zɚ
bonus ˈbəʊ.nəs, (US) ˈboʊ- **-es** -ɪz

B

bon(s) vivant(s) ˌbɔ̃ːŋ.vi.ˈvɑ̃ːŋ, ⓊⓈ ˌbɑːn.viːˈvɑːnt, ˌbɔ̃ː-
bon(s) viveur(s) ˌbɔ̃ːŋ.viˈvɜːʳ, ⓊⓈ ˌbɑːn.viːˈvɝː
bon voyage ˌbɔ̃ːŋ.vɔɪˈɑːʒ, -vwaɪˈ-, ⓊⓈ ˌbɑːn.vwaɪˈ-, -vɔɪˈ-
bon|y ˈbəʊ.n|i, ⓊⓈ ˈboʊ- **-ier** -i.əʳ, ⓊⓈ -i.ɚ **-iest** -i.ɪst, -i.əst **-iness** -ɪ.nəs, -ɪ.nɪs
bonz|e bɒnz, ⓊⓈ bɑːnz **-es** -ɪz
bonzer ˈbɒn.zəʳ, ⓊⓈ ˈbɑːn.zɚ
boo buː **-s** -z **-ing** -ɪŋ **-ed** -d **-er/s** -əʳ/z, ⓊⓈ -ɚ/z ˌ**couldn't say** ˌ**boo to a** ˈ**goose**
boob buːb **-s** -z **-ing** -ɪŋ **-ed** -d
boo-boo ˈbuː.buː **-s** -z
boob|y ˈbuː.b|i **-ies** -iz **-yish** -i.ɪʃ ˈ**booby** ˌ**prize;** ˈ**booby** ˌ**trap**
boodle, B~ ˈbuː.dəl
booger ˈbuː.gəʳ, ˈbʊg.əʳ, ⓊⓈ ˈbʊg.ɚ, ˈbuː.gɚ **-s** -z
boogey|man ˈbʊg.i|.mæn, ˈbuː.gi- **-men** -men
boog|ie ˈbuː.g|i, ⓊⓈ ˈbʊg.|i, ˈbuː.g|i **-ies** -iz **-ieing** -i.ɪŋ **-ied** -id
boogie-woogie ˌbuː.giˈwuː.gi, ˈbuː.giˌwuː-, ˌbʊg.iˈwʊg.i
boohoo ˌbuːˈhuː **-s** -z **-ing** -ɪŋ **-ed** -d
book bʊk **-s** -s **-ing** -ɪŋ **-ed** -t **-er/s** -əʳ/z, ⓊⓈ -ɚ/z ˈ**book** ˌ**club;** ˈ**book** ˌ**token;** ˌ**bring someone to** ˈ**book; in someone's** ˈ**good/bad** ˌ**books; in someone's** ˌ**good/**ˌ**bad** ˈ**books**
bookable ˈbʊk.ə.bəl
bookbind|er ˈbʊkˌbaɪn.d|əʳ, ⓊⓈ -d|ɚ **-ers** -əz, ⓊⓈ -ɚz **-ing** -ɪŋ
bookcas|e ˈbʊk.keɪs **-es** -ɪz
bookend ˈbʊk.end **-s** -z
Booker ˈbʊk.əʳ, ⓊⓈ -ɚ
Bookham ˈbʊk.əm
bookie ˈbʊk.i **-s** -z
booking ˈbʊk.ɪŋ **-s** -z ˈ**booking** ˌ**office**
bookish ˈbʊk.ɪʃ **-ly** -li **-ness** -nəs, -nɪs
bookkeep|er ˈbʊkˌkiː.p|əʳ, ⓊⓈ -p|ɚ **-ers** -əz, ⓊⓈ -ɚz **-ing** -ɪŋ
bookland ˈbʊk.lænd
book-learning ˈbʊkˌlɜː.nɪŋ, ⓊⓈ -ˌlɝː-
booklet ˈbʊk.lət, -lɪt **-s** -s
bookmak|er ˈbʊkˌmeɪ.k|əʳ, ⓊⓈ -k|ɚ **-ers** -əz, ⓊⓈ -ɚz **-ing** -ɪŋ
book|man ˈbʊk|.mən, -mæn **-men** -mən, -men
bookmark ˈbʊk.mɑːk, ⓊⓈ -mɑːrk **-s** -s **-ing** -ɪŋ **-ed** -t **-er/s** -əʳ/z, ⓊⓈ -ɚ/z
bookmobile ˈbʊk.məʊˌbiːl, ⓊⓈ -mə-, -moʊ- **-s** -z
bookplate ˈbʊk.pleɪt **-s** -s
booksell|er ˈbʊkˌsel|.əʳ, ⓊⓈ -ɚ **-ers** -əz, ⓊⓈ -ɚz **-ing** -ɪŋ
booksheI|f ˈbʊk.ʃel|f **-ves** -vz
bookshop ˈbʊk.ʃɒp, ⓊⓈ -ʃɑːp **-s** -s
bookstall ˈbʊk.stɔːl, ⓊⓈ -stɔːl, -stɑːl **-s** -z
bookstand ˈbʊk.stænd **-s** -z
bookstore ˈbʊk.stɔːʳ, ⓊⓈ -stɔːr **-s** -z
bookwork ˈbʊk.wɜːk, ⓊⓈ -wɝːk
bookworm ˈbʊk.wɜːm, ⓊⓈ -wɝːm **-s** -z
Boolean ˈbuː.li.ən **-s** -z
boom buːm **-s** -z **-ing** -ɪŋ **-ed** -d ˈ**boom** ˌ**box**
boomerang ˈbuː.mər.æŋ, ⓊⓈ -mə.ræŋ **-s** -z **-ing** -ɪŋ **-ed** -d
boomlet ˈbuːm.lət, -lɪt **-s** -s
boon buːn **-s** -z
Boon(e) buːn
boondock ˈbuːn.dɒk, ⓊⓈ -dɑːk **-s** -s
boondoggl|e ˈbuːnˌdɒg.əl, ⓊⓈ -ˌdɑː.gəl, -ˌdɔː- **-es** -z **-ing** -ɪŋ, ˌ-lɪŋ, ⓊⓈ -ˌdɑː.gəl.ɪŋ, -ˌdɔː-, ˌ-glɪŋ **-ed** -d **-er/s** -əʳ/z, ˌ-ləʳ/z, ⓊⓈ -ˌdɑː.gəl.ɚ/z, -ˌdɔː-, ˌ-glɚ/z
boonies ˈbuː.niz
boor bɔːʳ, bʊə, ⓊⓈ bʊr **-s** -z
Boord bɔːd, ⓊⓈ bɔːrd
boorish ˈbɔː.rɪʃ, ˈbʊə-, ⓊⓈ ˈbʊr.ɪʃ **-ly** -li **-ness** -nəs, -nɪs
Boosey ˈbuː.zi
boost buːst **-s** -s **-ing** -ɪŋ **-ed** -ɪd
booster ˈbuː.stəʳ, ⓊⓈ -stɚ **-s** -z
boot, B~ buːt **-s** -s **-ing** -ɪŋ, ⓊⓈ ˈbuː.t̬ɪŋ **-ed** -ɪd, ⓊⓈ ˈbuː.t̬ɪd ˈ**boot** ˌ**sale;** ˌ**put the** ˈ**boot in;** ˌ**too** ˌ**big for one's** ˈ**boots**
bootblack ˈbuːt.blæk **-s** -s
bootee ˌbuːˈtiː; ˈbuː.ti, ⓊⓈ ˈbuː.t̬i **-s** -z
Boötes bəʊˈəʊ.tiːz, ⓊⓈ boʊˈoʊ-
booth, B~ buːð, buːθ **-s** -z, -s
Boothby ˈbuːð.bi
Boothe buːð
Boothroyd ˈbuːθ.rɔɪd, ˈbuːð-
bootie ˈbuː.ti, ⓊⓈ -t̬i **-s** -z
bootjack ˈbuːt.dʒæk **-s** -s
bootlac|e ˈbuːt.leɪs **-es** -ɪz
Bootle ˈbuː.təl, ⓊⓈ ˈbuː.t̬əl
bootleg ˈbuːt.leg **-s** -z **-ging** -ɪŋ **-ged** -d
bootlegger ˈbuːtˌleg.əʳ, ⓊⓈ -ɚ **-s** -z
bootless ˈbuːt.ləs, -lɪs **-ly** -li **-ness** -nəs, -nɪs
Boots® buːts
boots sing *hotel servant:* buːts **plur** buːts, ˈbuːt.sɪz
bootstrap ˈbuːt.stræp **-s** -s **-ping** -ɪŋ **-ped** -t
booty ˈbuː.ti, ⓊⓈ -t̬i
bootylicious ˌbuː.tiˈlɪʃ.əs, ⓊⓈ -t̬i-
booz|e buːz **-es** -ɪz **-ing** -ɪŋ **-ed** -d **-er/s** -əʳ/z, ⓊⓈ -ɚ/z
booze-up ˈbuːz.ʌp **-s** -s
booz|y ˈbuː.z|i **-ier** -i.əʳ, ⓊⓈ -i.ɚ **-iest** -i.ɪst, -i.əst **-ily** -əl.i, -ɪ.li
bop bɒp, ⓊⓈ bɑːp **-s** -s **-ping** -ɪŋ **-ped** -t **-py** -i
Bo-peep ˌbəʊˈpiːp, ⓊⓈ ˌboʊ-
Bophuthatswana ˌbɒp.uː.tætˈswɑː.nə, ˌboʊ.puː-, -tətˈ-, ⓊⓈ ˌboʊ.puː.tɑːtˈswɑː-, -t̬ətˈ-
boracic bəˈræs.ɪk, bɒrˈæs-, ⓊⓈ bəˈræs-, bɔː-
borage ˈbɒr.ɪdʒ, ˈbʌr-, ⓊⓈ ˈbɔːr-
Borat ˈbɔː.ræt, ⓊⓈ ˈbɔːr.æt
borate ˈbɔː.reɪt, -rɪt, -rət, ⓊⓈ ˈbɔːr.eɪt, -ɪt, -ət **-s** -s
borax ˈbɔː.ræks, ⓊⓈ ˈbɔːr.æks
borborygmus ˌbɔː.bəˈrɪg.məs, ⓊⓈ ˌbɔːr-
Bord bɔːd, ⓊⓈ bɔːrd
Bordeaux bɔːˈdəʊ, ⓊⓈ bɔːrˈdoʊ
bordello bɔːˈdel.əʊ, ⓊⓈ bɔːrˈdel.oʊ **-s** -z
Borden ˈbɔː.dən, ⓊⓈ ˈbɔːr.dən
bord|er ˈbɔː.d|əʳ, ⓊⓈ ˈbɔːr.d|ɚ **-ers** -əz, ⓊⓈ -ɚz **-ering** -ər.ɪŋ **-ered** -əd, ⓊⓈ -ɚd **-erer/s** -ər.əʳ/z, ⓊⓈ -ɚ.ɚ/z
borderland ˈbɔː.dəl.ænd, ⓊⓈ ˈbɔːr.dɚ.lænd **-s** -z
borderline ˈbɔː.dəl.aɪn, ⓊⓈ ˈbɔːr.dɚ.laɪn **-s** -z
Borders ˈbɔː.dəz, ⓊⓈ ˈbɔːr.dɚz
Bordon ˈbɔː.dən, ⓊⓈ ˈbɔːr-
bordure ˈbɔː.djʊəʳ, ⓊⓈ ˈbɔːr.djɚ, -dʒɚ **-s** -z
bore (from **bear**) bɔːʳ, ⓊⓈ bɔːr
bor|e bɔːʳ, ⓊⓈ bɔːr **-es** -z **-ing** -ɪŋ **-ed** -d
borealis ˌbɒr.iˈɑː.lɪs, ˌbɔː.riˈ-, -ˈeɪ-, ⓊⓈ ˌbɔːr.iˈæl.ɪs, -ˈeɪ.lɪs
Boreas ˈbɒr.i.æs, ˈbɔː.ri-, -əs, ⓊⓈ ˈbɔːr.i-
boredom ˈbɔː.dəm, ⓊⓈ ˈbɔːr-
Boreham ˈbɔː.rəm, ⓊⓈ ˈbɔːr.əm
Borehamwood ˌbɔː.rəmˈwʊd, ⓊⓈ ˌbɔːr.əm-
borehole ˈbɔː.həʊl, ⓊⓈ ˈbɔːr.hoʊl **-s** -z
borer ˈbɔː.rəʳ, ⓊⓈ ˈbɔːr.ɚ **-s** -z
Borg bɔːg, ⓊⓈ bɔːrg
Borges ˈbɔː.ges, -xes, ⓊⓈ ˈbɔːr.hes
Borgia ˈbɔː.*dʒ*i.ə, -*dʒ*ə, ⓊⓈ ˈbɔːr.*dʒ*ə
boric ˈbɔː.rɪk, ˈbɒr.ɪk, ⓊⓈ ˈbɔːr.ɪk ˌ**boric** ˈ**acid**
Boris ˈbɒr.ɪs, ⓊⓈ ˈbɔːr-
Borland ˈbɔː.lənd, ⓊⓈ ˈbɔːr-
borlotti, B~ bɔːˈlɒt.i, ⓊⓈ bɔːrˈlɑː.t̬i
born bɔːn, ⓊⓈ bɔːrn
born-again ˌbɔːn.əˈgen, -ˈgeɪn, ⓊⓈ ˌbɔːrn.əˈgen *stress shift, see compound:* ˌ**born-again** ˈ**Christian**
borne (from **bear**) bɔːn, ⓊⓈ bɔːrn
Borneo ˈbɔː.ni.əʊ, ⓊⓈ ˈbɔːr.ni.oʊ
Borodin ˈbɒr.ə.dɪn, ⓊⓈ ˈbɔːr-
boron ˈbɔː.rɒn, ⓊⓈ ˈbɔːr.ɑːn
borough ˈbʌr.ə, ⓊⓈ ˈbɝː.oʊ, -ə **-s** -z
borrow, B~ ˈbɒr.əʊ, ⓊⓈ ˈbɑːr.oʊ **-s** -z **-ing/s** -ɪŋ/z **-ed** -d **-er/s** -əʳ/z, ⓊⓈ -ɚ/z
Borrowash ˈbɒr.əʊ.wɒʃ, ⓊⓈ ˈbɑːr.oʊ.wɑːʃ, -wɔːʃ
Borrowdale ˈbɒr.ə.deɪl, ⓊⓈ ˈbɑːr-
Bors bɔːs, ⓊⓈ bɔːrs
borsch bɔːʃ, ⓊⓈ bɔːrʃ
borscht bɔːʃt, ⓊⓈ bɔːrʃt
borstal, B~ ˈbɔː.stəl, ⓊⓈ ˈbɔːr- **-s** -z
borstch bɔːʃ, bɔːstʃ, bɔːʃtʃ, ⓊⓈ bɔːrʃt
Borthwick ˈbɔːθ.wɪk, ⓊⓈ ˈbɔːrθ-
Borwick ˈbɒr.ɪk, ⓊⓈ ˈbɔːr.wɪk
borzoi ˈbɔː.zɔɪ, -ˈ-, ⓊⓈ ˈbɔːr- **-s** -z
Bosanquet ˈbəʊ.zən.ket, -kɪt, ⓊⓈ ˈboʊ-
boscag|e ˈbɒs.kɪdʒ, ⓊⓈ ˈbɑːs- **-es** -ɪz
Boscastle ˈbɒs.kɑː.səl, -kæs.əl, ⓊⓈ ˈbɑː.skæs.əl
Boscawen bɒsˈkəʊ.ən; -ɪn; -ˈkɔː-; ˈbɒs.kwɪn, ⓊⓈ bɑːˈskoʊ.ən; ⓊⓈ ˈbɑː.skwɪn

Bosch bɒʃ, (US) bɑːʃ
bosh bɒʃ, (US) bɑːʃ
Bosham ˈbɒz.əm, ˈbɒs-, ˈbɒʃ-, (US) ˈbɑː.zəm, -səm
Bosher ˈbəʊ.ʃəʳ, (US) ˈboʊ.ʃɚ
bosky ˈbɒs.ki, (US) ˈbɑː.ski
bos'n, bo's'n ˈbəʊ.sᵊn, (US) ˈboʊ- **-s** -z
Bosni|a ˈbɒz.ni|.ə, (US) ˈbɑːz- **-an/s** -ən/z
Bosnia-Herzegovina ˌbɒz.ni.əˌhɜːt.səˈgɒv.ɪ.nə; -gəʊˈviː-, (US) ˌbɑːz.ni.əˌhert.sə.goʊˈviː.nə, -gəˈ-
bosom ˈbʊz.ᵊm **-s** -z **-y** -i
Bosphorus ˈbɒs.fᵊr.əs, -pᵊr-, (US) ˈbɑːs.fɚ-, ˈbɑː.spɚ-
Bosporus ˈbɒs.pᵊr.əs, (US) ˈbɑː.spɚ-
boss, B~ bɒs, (US) bɑːs **-es** -ɪz **-ing** -ɪŋ **-ed** -t
bossa nova ˌbɒs.əˈnəʊ.və, (US) ˌbɑː.səˈnoʊ-
boss-eyed ˌbɒsˈaɪd, (US) ˈbɑːs.aɪd *stress shift:* **ˌboss-eyed ˈcat**
Bossuet ˈbɒs.u.eɪ, (US) ˈbɑː.sweɪ
boss|y ˈbɒs|.i, (US) ˈbɑː.s|i **-ier** -i.əʳ, (US) -i.ɚ **-iest** -i.ɪst, -i.əst **-ily** -ᵊl.i, -ɪ.li **-iness** -ɪ.nəs, -ɪ.nɪs
Bostik® ˈbɒs.tɪk, (US) ˈbɑː.stɪk
Bostock ˈbɒs.tɒk, (US) ˈbɑː.stɑːk
Boston ˈbɒs.tᵊn, (US) ˈbɑː.stᵊn, ˈbɔː-
Bostonian bɒsˈtəʊ.ni.ən, (US) bɑːˈstoʊ-, bɔː- **-s** -z
Bostridge ˈbɒs.trɪdʒ, (US) ˈbɑː.strɪdʒ
bosun ˈbəʊ.sᵊn, (US) ˈboʊ- **-s** -z
Boswell ˈbɒz.wəl, -wel, (US) ˈbɑːz-
Bosworth ˈbɒz.wəθ, -wɜːθ, (US) ˈbɑːz.wɚθ, -wɝːθ
botanic bəˈtæn.ɪk, bɒtˈæn-, (US) bəˈtæn- **-al** -ᵊl **-ally** -ᵊl.i, -li **boˌtanic ˈgarden**
botanist ˈbɒt.ᵊn.ɪst, (US) ˈbɑː.tᵊn- **-s** -s
botaniz|e, -is|e ˈbɒt.ᵊn.aɪz, (US) ˈbɑː.tᵊn- **-es** -ɪz **-ing** -ɪŋ **-ed** -d
botany ˈbɒt.ᵊn.i, (US) ˈbɑː.tᵊn- **ˌBotany ˈBay**
botch bɒtʃ, (US) bɑːtʃ **-es** -ɪz **-ing** -ɪŋ **-ed** -t **-er/s** -əʳ/z, (US) -ɚ/z
botch-up ˈbɒtʃ.ʌp, (US) ˈbɑːtʃ- **-s** -s
both bəʊθ, (US) boʊθ
Botha ˈbəʊ.tə, (US) ˈboʊ.t̬ə
Botham ˈbəʊ.θəm, ˈbɒð.əm, (US) ˈboʊ.θəm, ˈbɑː.ðəm
both|er ˈbɒð|.əʳ, (US) ˈbɑː.ð|ɚ **-ers** -əz, (US) -ɚz **-ering** -ᵊr.ɪŋ **-ered** -əd, (US) -ɚd
botheration ˌbɒð.ᵊrˈeɪ.ʃᵊn, (US) ˌbɑː.ðəˈreɪ-
bothersome ˈbɒð.ə.sᵊm, (US) ˈbɑː.ðɚ-
Bothnia ˈbɒθ.ni.ə, (US) ˈbɑːθ-
Bothwell ˈbɒθ.wᵊl, ˈbɒð-, -wel, (US) ˈbɑːθ-, ˈbɑːð-
both|y ˈbɒθ|.i, bɒð-, (US) ˈbɑː.θ|i, -ð|i **-ies** -iz
botnet ˈbɒt.net, (US) ˈbɑːt- **-s** -s
Botolph ˈbɒt.ɒlf, -ᵊlf, (US) ˈbɑː.tɑːlf
Botox® ˈbəʊ.tɒks, (US) ˈboʊ.tɑːks
botrytis bɒtˈraɪ.tɪs, (US) boʊˈtraɪ.t̬əs
Botswana bɒtˈswɑː.nə, (US) bɑːt-
Botticelli ˌbɒt.ɪˈtʃel.i, (US) ˌbɑː.t̬əˈ- **-s** -z
bottl|e ˈbɒt.ᵊl, (US) ˈbɑː.t̬ᵊl **-es** -z **-ing** -ɪŋ, ˈ-lɪŋ, (US) ˈbɑː.t̬ᵊl.ɪŋ, ˈbɑːt.lɪŋ **-ed** -d **-er/s** -əʳ/z, ˈ-ləʳ/z, (US) ˈbɑː.t̬ᵊl.ɚ/z, ˈbɑːt.lɚ/z **ˈbottle ˌbank**
bottle-green ˌbɒt.ᵊlˈgriːn, (US) ˌbɑː.t̬ᵊlˈ- *stress shift:* **ˌbottle-green ˈjacket**
bottleneck ˈbɒt.ᵊl.nek, (US) ˈbɑː.t̬ᵊl- **-s** -s
bottle-nos|e ˈbɒt.ᵊl.nəʊz, (US) ˈbɑː.t̬ᵊl.noʊz **-es** -ɪz **-ed** -d
bottle-wash|er ˈbɒt.ᵊlˌwɒʃ.əʳ, (US) ˈbɑː.t̬ᵊlˌwɑː.ʃɚ **-ers** -əz, (US) -ɚs **-ing** -ɪŋ
bottom, B~ ˈbɒt.əm, (US) ˈbɑː.t̬əm **-s** -z **-ing** -ɪŋ **-ed** -d
Bottome bəˈtəʊm, (US) -ˈtoʊm
bottomless ˈbɒt.əm.ləs, -lɪs, (US) ˈbɑː.t̬əm-
Bottomley ˈbɒt.əm.li, (US) ˈbɑː.t̬əm-
bottomry ˈbɒt.əm.ri, (US) ˈbɑː.t̬əm-
botulism ˈbɒtʃ.ə.lɪ.zᵊm, -ʊ-; ˈbɒt.jʊ-, ˈ-jə-, (US) ˈbɑː.tʃə-
Bouaké ˈbwɑː.keɪ
Boucicault ˈbuː.si.kəʊ; *as if French:* ˌ--ˈ-; (US) ˈbuː.si.koʊ, -kɑːlt
bouclé ˈbuː.kleɪ, (US) -ˈ-
Boudicca ˈbuː.dɪ.kə, ˈbəʊ-, (US) buːˈdɪk.ə
boudoir ˈbuːd.wɑːʳ, (US) ˈbuːd.wɑːr, ˈbʊd- **-s** -z
bouffant ˈbuː.fɑ̃ːŋ, -fɒnt, (US) buːˈfɑːnt, ˈ--
bougainvillaea ˌbuː.gᵊnˈvɪl.i.ə, (US) -i.ə, ˈ-jə **-s** -z
Bougainville ˈbuː.gᵊn.vɪl, -viːl
bougainvillea ˌbuː.gᵊnˈvɪl.i.ə, (US) -i.ə, ˈ-jə **-s** -z
bough baʊ **-s** -z
Bough bɒf, (US) bɑːf
Boughey ˈbəʊ.i, (US) ˈboʊ-
bought (from **buy**) bɔːt, (US) bɑːt, bɔːt
Boughton ˈbɔː.tᵊn, ˈbaʊ-, (US) ˈbɑː.tᵊn, ˈbɔː-, ˈbaʊ-
bougie ˈbuː.dʒiː, -ˈ- **-s** -z
bouillabaisse ˌbuː.jəˈbes, ˌbwiː-, -jɑːˈ-, -ˈbeɪs, ˈ---
bouillon ˈbuː.jɔ̃ːŋ, ˈbwiː-, -jɒn, (US) ˈbʊl.jɑːn, ˈbuː-, -jən
Boulanger ˌbuː.lɑ̃ːnˈʒeɪ, ˈ---
Boulby ˈbəʊl.bi, (US) ˈboʊl-
boulder ˈbəʊl.dəʳ, (US) ˈboʊl.dɚ **-s** -z
Bouler ˈbuː.ləʳ, (US) -lɚ
boules buːl
boulevard ˈbuː.lə.vɑːd, -lɪ-, ˈbuːl.vɑːʳ, (US) ˈbʊl.ə.vɑːrd **-s** -z
Boulez ˈbuː.lez, -leɪ, (US) buːˈlez
Boulogne bʊˈlɔɪn, bə-, (US) -ˈloʊn, -ˈlɔɪn
Boult bəʊlt, (US) boʊlt
Boulter ˈbəʊl.təʳ, (US) ˈboʊl.tɚ
Boulton ˈbəʊl.tᵊn, (US) ˈboʊl-
bounc|e baʊnts **-es** -ɪz **-ing** -ɪŋ **-ed** -t
bouncer, B~ ˈbaʊnt.səʳ, (US) -sɚ **-s** -z
bounc|y ˈbaʊnt.s|i **-ier** -i.əʳ, (US) -i.ɚ **-iest** -i.ɪst, -i.əst
bound baʊnd **-s** -z **-ing** -ɪŋ **-ed** -ɪd
boundar|y ˈbaʊn.dᵊr|.i **-ies** -iz
bounden ˈbaʊn.dən **ˌbounden ˈduty**
bounder ˈbaʊn.dəʳ, (US) -dɚ **-s** -z
Bounderby ˈbaʊn.də.bi, (US) -dɚ-
boundless ˈbaʊnd.ləs, -lɪs **-ly** -li **-ness** -nəs, -nɪs
bounteous ˈbaʊn.ti.əs, -tʃəs, (US) -t̬i.əs **-ly** -li **-ness** -nəs, -nɪs
bountiful ˈbaʊn.tɪ.fᵊl, -tə-, -fʊl, (US) -t̬ə-, -t̬ɪ- **-ly** -i **-ness** -nəs, -nɪs
bount|y ˈbaʊn.t|i, (US) -t̬|i **-ies** -iz **ˈbounty ˌhunter**
bouquet bʊˈkeɪ; bəʊ-; ˈbuː.keɪ, (US) boʊˈkeɪ, buː- **-s** -z
bouquet(s) garni(s) bʊˌkeɪ.gɑːˈniː, ˌbuː.keɪ-, (US) ˌboʊ.keɪ.gɑːrˈ-
bourbon *drink:* ˈbɜː.bən, ˈbʊə-, (US) ˈbɝː- *biscuit:* ˈbɔː.bən, ˈbʊə-, -bɒn, (US) ˈbɝː- **-s** -z
Bourbon *French royal house:* ˈbʊə.bən, ˈbɔː-, -bɒn, (US) ˈbʊr.bən, -bɔːn **-s** -z
Bourchier ˈbaʊ.tʃəʳ, (US) -tʃɚ
Bourdillon bəˈdɪl.i.ən, bɔː-, -ˈdɪl.ən, (US) bɔːrˈdɪl.jən, bɚ-
bourdon ˈbɔː.dᵊn, ˈbʊə-, (US) ˈbʊr-, ˈbɔːr- **-s** -z
bourgeois *middle class:* ˈbɔː.ʒwɑː, ˈbʊəʒ-, (US) ˈbʊrʒ- *printing type:* bɜːˈdʒɔɪs, (US) bɝː-
bourgeoisie ˌbɔː.ʒwɑːˈziː, ˌbʊəʒ-, -wəˈ-, (US) ˌbʊrʒ-
Bourke bɜːk, (US) bɝːk
bourn(e) bɔːn, bʊən, (US) bɔːrn, bʊrn **-s** -z
Bourne bɔːn, bʊən; *as surname also:* bɜːn, (US) bɔːrn, bʊrn, bɝːn
Bournemouth ˈbɔːn.məθ, (US) ˈbɔːrn-
Bournville ˈbɔːn.vɪl, (US) ˈbɔːrn-
bourrée ˈbʊr.eɪ, ˈbʊə.reɪ, (US) bʊˈreɪ **-s** -z
bours|e, B~ bʊəs, bɔːs, (US) bʊrs, bɔːrs **-es** -ɪz
boustrophedon ˌbuː.strəˈfiː.dᵊn, ˌbaʊ-, -dɒn, (US) -dɑːn
bout baʊt **-s** -s
boutique buːˈtiːk **-s** -s
Boutros-Ghali ˌbuː.trɒsˈgɑː.li, (US) -troʊsˈ-
Bouverie ˈbuː.vᵊr.i
bouzouki bʊˈzuː.ki, bə-, buː- **-s** -z
Bovary ˈbəʊ.vᵊr.i, (US) ˈboʊ-
Bovey *place:* ˈbʌv.i *surname:* ˈbuː.vi, ˈbəʊ-, ˈbʌv.i, (US) ˈbuː.vi, ˈboʊ-, ˈbʌv.i
Bovey Tracey ˌbʌv.iˈtreɪ.si
Bovill ˈbəʊ.vɪl, (US) ˈboʊ-
bovine ˈbəʊ.vaɪn, (US) ˈboʊ-, -viːn
Bovingdon ˈbʌv.ɪŋ.dən, ˈbɒv-, (US) ˈbʌv-, ˈbɑː.vɪŋ-

> Note: Locally /ˈbʌv-/.

Bovington ˈbɒv.ɪŋ.tən, (US) ˈbɑː.vɪŋ-
Bovis ˈbəʊ.vɪs, (US) ˈboʊ-
Bovril® ˈbɒv.rɪl, -rəl, (US) ˈbɑːv-

B

bovver ˈbɒv.əʳ, ˈbɑː.vɚ ˈ**bovver** ˌ**boot**; ˈ**bovver** ˌ**boy**
bow n *bending, fore end of ship:* baʊ -s -z
bow, B~ n *for shooting, etc., knot:* bəʊ, (US) boʊ -s -z ˌ**bow** ˈ**tie**; ˌ**bow** ˈ**window**
bow v *bend body:* baʊ *in playing the violin, etc.:* bəʊ, (US) boʊ -s -z -ing/s -ɪŋ/z -ed -d
Bowater ˈbəʊˌwɔː.təʳ, (US) ˈboʊˌwɑː.t̬ɚ, -ˌwɔː-
Bowden ˈbəʊ.dən, ˈbaʊ-, (US) ˈboʊ-, ˈbaʊ-
Bowdler ˈbaʊd.ləʳ, (US) ˈboʊd.lɚ, ˈbaʊd-
bowdlerism ˈbaʊd.lər.ɪ.zəm, (US) ˈboʊd-, ˈbaʊd- -s -z
bowdlerization, -isa- ˌbaʊd.lər.aɪˈzeɪ.ʃən, -ɪˈ-, (US) ˌboʊd.lɚ.əˈ-, ˌbaʊd-
bowdleriz|e, -is|e ˈbaʊd.lər.aɪz, (US) ˈboʊd.lə.raɪz, ˈbaʊd- -es -ɪz -ing -ɪŋ -ed -d
Bowdoin, Bowdon ˈbəʊ.dən, (US) ˈboʊ-
bowel ˈbaʊ.əl -s -z
Bowen ˈbəʊ.ɪn, (US) ˈboʊ-
bower, B~ ˈbaʊ.əʳ, (US) ˈbaʊ.ɚ -s -z
Bowering ˈbaʊ.ə.rɪŋ, (US) ˈbaʊ.ɚ.ɪŋ
bowery, B~ ˈbaʊ.ə.ri, (US) ˈbaʊ.ɚ.i, ˈbaʊ.ri
Bowes bəʊz, (US) boʊz
Bowie ˈbaʊ.i, ˈbəʊ-, (US) ˈboʊ-, ˈbuː-
bowie-kni|fe ˈbəʊ.i.naɪ|f, ˈbuː-, (US) ˈboʊ-, ˈbuː- -ves -vz
Bowker ˈbaʊ.kəʳ, (US) -kɚ
bowl bəʊl, (US) boʊl -s -z -ing -ɪŋ -ed -d ˈ**bowling** ˌ**alley**; ˈ**bowling** ˌ**green**
Bowland ˈbəʊ.lənd, (US) ˈboʊ-
bow-legged bəʊˈlegd, -ˈleg.ɪd, -əd, (US) boʊ- *stress shift:* ˌ**bow-legged** ˈ**child**
bowler, B~ ˈbəʊ.ləʳ, (US) ˈboʊ.lɚ -s -z
Bowles bəʊlz, (US) boʊlz
bowline ˈbəʊ.lɪn, (US) ˈboʊ- -s -z
Bowling ˈbəʊ.lɪŋ, (US) ˈboʊ-
bow|man, B~ ˈbəʊ|.mən, (US) ˈboʊ- -men -mən, -men
Bowmer ˈbəʊ.məʳ, (US) ˈboʊ.mɚ
Bown baʊn
Bowness bəʊˈnes, (US) boʊ-
Bowra ˈbaʊ.rə
Bowring ˈbaʊ.rɪŋ
bowshot ˈbəʊ.ʃɒt, (US) ˈboʊ.ʃɑːt -s -s
bowsprit ˈbəʊ.sprɪt, ˈbaʊ-, (US) ˈbaʊ-, ˈboʊ- -s -s
bowstring ˈbəʊ.strɪŋ, (US) ˈboʊ- -s -z
Bowtell bəʊˈtel, (US) boʊ-
bow-wow interj *sound made by a dog:* ˌbaʊˈwaʊ -s -z **n** *dog:* ˈbaʊ.waʊ -s -z
bowyer, B~ ˈbəʊ.jəʳ, (US) ˈboʊ.jɚ
box, B~ bɒks, (US) bɑːks -es -ɪz -ing -ɪŋ -ed -t ˌ**box** ˈ**bed**; ˈ**box** ˌ**cloth**; ˌ**box** ˈ**junction**; ˈ**box** ˌ**number**; ˈ**box** ˌ**office**; ˌ**boxed** ˈ**set**; ˈ**box** ˌ**score**; ˈ**box** ˌ**seat**
boxcar ˈbɒks.kɑːʳ, (US) ˈbɑːks.kɑːr -s -z
boxer, B~ ˈbɒk.səʳ, (US) ˈbɑːk.sɚ -s -z ˈ**boxer** ˌ**shorts**
boxing ˈbɒk.sɪŋ, (US) ˈbɑːk- ˈ**Boxing** ˌ**Day**; ˈ**boxing** ˌ**glove**; ˈ**boxing** ˌ**match**
Boxmoor ˈbɒks.mɔːʳ; *also locally:* -ˈ-, (US) ˈbɑːks.mʊr, -mɔːr
boxroom ˈbɒks.rʊm, -ruːm, (US) ˈbɑːks.ruːm, -rʊm -s -z
boxwood ˈbɒks.wʊd, (US) ˈbɑːks-
box|y ˈbɒk.s|i, (US) ˈbɑːk- -iness -ɪ.nəs, -ɪ.nɪs
boy bɔɪ -s -z ˌ**boy** ˈ**scout** (US) ˈ**boy** ˌ**scout**
boyar ˈbɔɪ.əʳ, -ɑːʳ; ˈbəʊ.jɑːʳ, -ˈ-, (US) boʊˈjɑːr; (US) ˈbɔɪ.ɚ -s -z
Boyce bɔɪs
boyco|tt, B~ ˈbɔɪ.kɒ|t, -kə|t, (US) -kɑː|t -tts -ts -tting -tɪŋ, (US) -t̬ɪŋ -tted -tɪd, (US) -t̬ɪd -tter/s -təʳ/z, (US) -t̬ɚ/z
Boyd bɔɪd
Boyer ˈbwaɪ.eɪ; ˈbɔɪ.əʳ, (US) bɔɪˈeɪ; (US) ˈbɔɪ.ɚ
Boyet ˈbɔɪ.et, -ˈ-, (US) bwɑːˈjeɪ
boyfriend ˈbɔɪ.frend -s -z
boyhood ˈbɔɪ.hʊd -s -z
boyish ˈbɔɪ.ɪʃ -ly -li -ness -nəs, -nɪs
Boyle bɔɪl
Boyne bɔɪn
boyo ˈbɔɪ.əʊ, (US) -oʊ -s -z
boysenberr|y ˈbɔɪ.zən.bər|.i, -ˌber-, (US) -ˌber- -ies -iz
Boyson ˈbɔɪ.sən
Boyton ˈbɔɪ.tən
Boyzone ˈbɔɪ.zəʊn, (US) -zoʊn
Boz bɒz, (US) bɑːz

> Note: This pen name of Charles Dickens was originally pronounced /bəʊz/ (US) /boʊz/, but this pronunciation is not often heard now.

bozo ˈbəʊ.zəʊ, (US) ˈboʊ.zoʊ -s -z
BP ˌbiːˈpiː
BPhil ˌbiːˈfɪl
BR ˌbiːˈɑːʳ, (US) -ˈɑːr
bra brɑː -s -z
braai braɪ -s -z -ing -ɪŋ -ed -d
Brabant brəˈbænt; ˈbræb.ənt
Brabantio brəˈbæn.ti.əʊ, bræbˈæn-, -tʃi-, (US) brəˈbæn.t̬i.oʊ, -ˈbænt.ʃi-
Brabazon ˈbræb.ə.zən, (US) -zɑːn
Brabham ˈbræb.əm
Brabourne *place:* ˈbreɪ.bɔːn, (US) -bɔːrn *family name:* ˈbreɪ.bən, ˈbreɪ.bɔːn, (US) -bɚn, -bɔːrn
brac|e, B~ breɪs -es -ɪz -ing -ɪŋ -ed -t
Bracebridge ˈbreɪs.brɪdʒ
bracelet ˈbreɪs.lət, -lɪt -s -s
brach brætʃ, (US) brætʃ, bræk -es -ɪz
brachial ˈbreɪ.ki.əl, (US) ˈbreɪ-, ˈbræk.i-
brachy- ˈbræk.i
brachycephalic ˌbræk.i.səˈfæl.ɪk, -sɪˈ-
brack bræk -s -s
bracken ˈbræk.ən
Brackenbury ˈbræk.ən.bər.i, (US) -ber-
Brackenridge ˈbræk.ən.rɪdʒ
brack|et ˈbræk|.ɪt -ets -ɪts -eting -ɪ.tɪŋ, (US) -ɪ.t̬ɪŋ -eted -ɪ.tɪd, (US) -ɪ.t̬ɪd
brackish ˈbræk.ɪʃ -ness -nəs, -nɪs
Brackley ˈbræk.li
Bracknell ˈbræk.nəl
brad, B~ bræd -s -z
bradawl ˈbræd.ɔːl, (US) -ɑːl, -ɔːl -s -z
Bradbury ˈbræd.bər.i, ˈbræb-, (US) -ber-
Braddon ˈbræd.ən
Braden ˈbreɪ.dən
Bradfield ˈbræd.fiːld
Bradford ˈbræd.fəd, (US) -fɚd
Bradgate ˈbræd.geɪt, -gɪt
Bradlaugh, Bradlaw ˈbræd.lɔː, (US) -lɑː, -lɔː
Bradley ˈbræd.li
Bradman ˈbræd.mən
Bradshaw ˈbræd.ʃɔː, (US) -ʃɑː, -ʃɔː
Bradstreet ˈbræd.striːt
Bradwardine ˈbræd.wə.diːn, (US) -wɚ-
Brady ˈbreɪ.di
bradycardia ˌbræd.iˈkɑː.di.ə, (US) -ˈkɑːr-
brae breɪ -s -z
Braemar breɪˈmɑːʳ, (US) -ˈmɑːr *stress shift:* ˌ**Braemar** ˈ**games**
brag bræg -s -z -ging/ly -ɪŋ/li -ged -d
Bragg bræg
braggadocio ˌbræg.əˈdəʊ.tʃi.əʊ, (US) -ˈdoʊ- -s -z
braggart ˈbræg.ət, -ɑːt, (US) -ɚt -s -s
Braham ˈbreɪ.əm
Brahe ˈbrɑː.hə, -ə, -hi
brahma, B~ *god:* ˈbrɑː.mə *breed of fowl or cattle:* ˈbreɪ.mə, (US) ˈbrɑː-, ˈbreɪ-, ˈbræm.ə -s -z
Brahman ˈbrɑː.mən -s -z -ism -ɪ.zəm
Brahmaputra ˌbrɑː.məˈpuː.trə
brahmin, B~ ˈbrɑː.mɪn -s -z -ism -ɪ.zəm
brahminical ˌbrɑːˈmɪn.ɪ.kəl
Brahms brɑːmz
braid, B~ breɪd -s -z -ing -ɪŋ -ed -ɪd
brail breɪl -s -z
Braille breɪl
Brailsford ˈbreɪls.fəd, (US) -fɚd
brain, B~ breɪn -s -z -ing -ɪŋ -ed -d ˈ**brain** ˌ**damage**; ˈ**brain** ˌ**death**; ˈ**brain** ˌ**drain**
brain|child ˈbreɪn|.tʃaɪld -children -ˌtʃɪl.drən
Braine breɪn
brainless ˈbreɪn.ləs, -lɪs -ness -nəs, -nɪs
brainsick ˈbreɪn.sɪk
brainstorm ˈbreɪn.stɔːm, (US) -stɔːrm -s -z -ing -ɪŋ -ed -d
brainstorming ˈbreɪnˌstɔː.mɪŋ, (US) -ˌstɔːr-
brainteaser ˈbreɪnˌtiː.zəʳ, (US) -zɚ -s -z
Braintree ˈbreɪn.triː, -tri
brainwash ˈbreɪn.wɒʃ, (US) -wɑːʃ, -wɔːʃ -es -ɪz -ing -ɪŋ -ed -t

B

brainwave ˈbreɪn.weɪv **-s** -z
brain|y ˈbreɪ.n|i **-ier** -i.əʳ, US -i.ɚ **-iest** -i.ɪst, -i.əst
brais|e breɪz **-es** -ɪz **-ing** -ɪŋ **-ed** -d
Braithwaite ˈbreɪ.θweɪt
brak|e breɪk **-es** -s **-ing** -ɪŋ **-ed** -t ˈ**brake** ˌ**fluid**; ˈ**brake** ˌ**light**
Brakenridge ˈbræk.ən.rɪdʒ
Bram bræm
Bramah ˈbrɑː.mə, ˈbræm.ə
Bramall ˈbræm.ɔːl, US -ɔːl, -ɑːl
bramble ˈbræm.bəl **-s** -z ˈ**bramble** ˌ**bush**
Brambler ˈbræm.bləʳ, US -blɚ
brambly ˈbræm.bli
Bramhall ˈbræm.hɔːl, US -hɔːl, -hɑːl
Bramley ˈbræm.li **-s** -z
Brampton ˈbræmp.tən
Bramwell ˈbræm.wel, -wəl
bran, B~ bræn ˌ**bran** ˈ**mash**; ˌ**bran** ˈ**pie**
Branagh ˈbræn.ə
branch, B~ brɑːntʃ, US bræntʃ **-es** -ɪz **-ing** -ɪŋ **-ed** -t
branchi|a ˈbræŋ.ki|.ə **-ae** -iː
branchial ˈbræŋ.ki.əl
branchiate ˈbræŋ.ki.eɪt, -ət
Brancusi bræŋˈkuː.zi, US bræn-, brɑːŋ-
brand, B~ brænd **-s** -z **-ing** -ɪŋ **-ed** -ɪd ˈ**brand** ˌ**name**; ˌ**brand** ˈ**new**; ˈ**branding** ˌ**iron**
Brandeis ˈbræn.daɪs
Brandenburg ˈbræn.dən.bɜːg, US -bɝːg ˌ**Brandenburg** ˈ**Gate**
Brandi ˈbræn.di
brandish ˈbræn.dɪʃ **-es** -ɪz **-ing** -ɪŋ **-ed** -t
Brando ˈbræn.dəʊ, US -doʊ
Brandon ˈbræn.dən
Brandram ˈbræn.drəm
Brandreth ˈbræn.drɪθ, -drəθ, -dreθ
Brandt brænt
brand|y, B~ ˈbræn.d|i **-ies** -iz **-ied** -id **-ying** -i.ɪŋ ˌ**brandy** ˈ**butter** US ˈ**brandy** ˌ**butter**; ˈ**brandy** ˌ**snap**
brank bræŋk **-s** -s
Branksome ˈbræŋk.səm
Branson ˈbrænt.sən
Branston ˈbrænt.stən
brant brænt **-s** -s
Brant brɑːnt, US brænt
brant|-goose brænt|ˈguːs **-geese** -ˈgiːs
Braque brɑːk, bræk
Brasenose ˈbreɪz.nəʊz, US -noʊz
brash bræʃ **-er** -əʳ, US -ɚ **-est** -ɪst, -əst **-es** -ɪz **-ly** -li **-ness** -nəs, -nɪs
Brasher ˈbreɪ.ʃəʳ, US -ʃɚ
brasier ˈbreɪ.zi.əʳ, ˈ-ʒəʳ, US ˈ-ʒɚ **-s** -z
Brasilia brəˈzɪl.i.ə, US -i.ə, ˈ-jə
Brasov ˈbræʃ.ɒv, US ˈbrɑː.ʃɔːv
brass brɑːs, US bræs **-es** -ɪz ˌ**brass** ˈ**band**; ˌ**brass** ˈ**knuckles**; ˌ**brass** ˈ**monkey**; ˌ**brassed** ˈ**off**
brassard ˈbræs.ɑːd, -ˈ-, US ˈbræs.ɑːrd; US brəˈsɑːrd **-s** -z
brasserie ˈbræs.ər.i, US ˌbræs.əˈriː **-s** -z
Brassey ˈbræs.i
brassica ˈbræs.ɪ.kə **-s** -z
brassière ˈbræs.i.əʳ, ˈbræz-, US brəˈzɪr **-s** -z
Brasso® ˈbrɑː.səʊ, US ˈbræs.oʊ
brass-rubbing ˈbrɑːsˌrʌb.ɪŋ, US ˈbræs-
brass|y, brass|ie *golf club:* ˈbrɑː.s|i, US ˈbræs|.i **-ies** -iz
brass|y adj ˈbrɑː.s|i, US ˈbræs|.i **-ier** -i.əʳ, US -i.ɚ **-iest** -i.ɪst, -i.əst
Brasted ˈbreɪ.stɪd, ˈbræs.tɪd
brat bræt **-s** -s ˈ**brat** ˌ**pack**
Bratislava ˌbræt.ɪˈslɑː.və, US ˌbrɑː.t̬ɪˈ-
Bratsk brætsk, brɑːtsk, US brɑːtsk
Brattleboro ˈbræt.əl.bər.ə, US ˈbræt̬.əl.bɚ.oʊ
Braughing ˈbræf.ɪŋ
Braun brɔːn, braʊn, US brɑːn, brɔːn, braʊn

> Note: The trademark is pronounced /brɔːn/ in British English, /brɑːn, brɔːn/ in American English.

Braunton ˈbrɔːn.tən, US ˈbrɑːn-, ˈbrɔːn-
Brautigan ˈbraʊ.tɪ.gən, ˈbrɔː-, ˈbræt.ɪ-, US ˈbrɑː.t̬ɪ-, ˈbrɔː-
bravado brəˈvɑː.dəʊ, US -doʊ **-(e)s** -z
brav|e breɪv **-er** -əʳ, US -ɚ **-est** -ɪst, -əst **-ely** -li **-es** -z **-ing** -ɪŋ **-ed** -d
Braveheart ˈbreɪv.hɑːt, US -hɑːrt
braver|y ˈbreɪ.vər|.i **-ies** -iz
Bravington ˈbræv.ɪŋ.tən
bravo brɑːˈvəʊ, ˈ--, US ˈbrɑː.voʊ, -ˈ- **-(e)s** -z

> Note: Always /ˈ--/ in the ICAO alphabet.

bravura brəˈvjʊə.rə, -ˈvjɔː-, -ˈvʊə-, US -ˈvjʊr.ə, -ˈvʊr-
brawl brɔːl, US brɑːl, brɔːl **-s** -z **-ing** -ɪŋ **-ed** -d **-er/s** -əʳ/z, US -ɚ/z
brawn brɔːn, US brɑːn, brɔːn
Brawne brɔːn, US brɑːn, brɔːn
brawn|y ˈbrɔː.n|i, US ˈbrɑː-, ˈbrɔː- **-ier** -i.əʳ, US -i.ɚ **-iest** -i.ɪst, -i.əst **-iness** -ɪ.nəs, -ɪ.nɪs
Braxton ˈbræk.stən
bray, B~ breɪ **-s** -z **-ing** -ɪŋ **-ed** -d
Braybrooke ˈbreɪ.brʊk
Brayley ˈbreɪ.li
braz|e breɪz **-es** -ɪz **-ing** -ɪŋ **-ed** -d
brazen ˈbreɪ.zən **-ly** -li **-ness** -nəs, -nɪs
brazen-faced ˌbreɪ.zənˈfeɪst *stress shift:* ˌ**brazen-faced** ˈ**child**
brazier ˈbreɪ.zi.əʳ, ˈ-ʒəʳ, US ˈ-ʒɚ **-s** -z
Brazier ˈbreɪ.ʒəʳ, US -ʒɚ
Brazil *country:* brəˈzɪl *English surname:* ˈbræz.ɪl, -əl; brəˈzɪl **Braˈzil** ˌ**nut**
Brazilian brəˈzɪl.i.ən, US -jən **-s** -z
Brazzaville ˈbræz.ə.vɪl, ˈbrɑː.zə-
breach briːtʃ **-es** -ɪz **-ing** -ɪŋ **-ed** -t ˌ**breach of the** ˈ**peace**
bread bred **-s** -z **-ed** -ɪd ˈ**bread** ˌ**basket**; ˌ**bread and** ˈ**butter**
Breadalbane *Earl:* brəˈdɔːl.bɪn, brɪ-, -bən, US -ˈdɔːl-, -ˈdɑːl- *place:* brəˈdæl.bɪn, -ˈdɔːl-, -bən, US -ˈdæl-, -ˈdɔːl-, -ˈdɑːl-
breadboard ˈbred.bɔːd, US -bɔːrd **-s** -z
breadbox ˈbred.bɒks, US -bɑːks **-es** -ɪz
breadcrumb ˈbred.krʌm **-s** -z
breadfruit ˈbred.fruːt **-s** -s
breadline ˈbred.laɪn
breadth bretθ, bredθ **-s** -s
breadth|ways ˈbretθ|.weɪz, ˈbredθ- **-wise** -waɪz
breadwinner ˈbredˌwɪn.əʳ, US -ɚ **-s** -z
break breɪk **-s** -s **-ing** -ɪŋ **broke** brəʊk, US broʊk **broken** ˈbrəʊ.kən, US ˈbroʊ- ˌ**breaking and** ˈ**entering**
breakable ˈbreɪ.kə.bəl **-s** -z
breakag|e ˈbreɪ.kɪdʒ **-es** -ɪz
breakaway ˈbreɪ.kə.weɪ **-s** -z
break-danc|ing ˈbreɪkˌdɑːnt.s|ɪŋ, US -ˌdænt- **-er/s** -əʳ/z, US -ɚ/z
breakdown ˈbreɪk.daʊn **-s** -z
breaker ˈbreɪ.kəʳ, US -kɚ **-s** -z
break-even ˌbreɪkˈiː.vən
breakfast ˈbrek.fəst **-s** -s **-ing** -ɪŋ **-ed** -ɪd
break-in ˈbreɪk.ɪn **-s** -z
breakneck ˈbreɪk.nek
breakout ˈbreɪk.aʊt **-s** -s
Breakspear ˈbreɪk.spɪəʳ, US -spɪr
breakthrough ˈbreɪk.θruː **-s** -z
breakup ˈbreɪk.ʌp **-s** -s
breakwater ˈbreɪkˌwɔː.təʳ, US -ˌwɑː.t̬ɚ, -ˌwɔː- **-s** -z
bream, B~ briːm, US briːm, brɪm **-s** -z
Breamore ˈbrem.əʳ, US -ɚ
breast brest **-s** -s **-ing** -ɪŋ **-ed** -ɪd ˌ**make a** ˌ**clean** ˈ**breast of some-thing**
breastbone ˈbrest.bəʊn, US -boʊn **-s** -z
breast-feed ˈbrest.fiːd **-s** -z **-ing** -ɪŋ **breast-fed** ˈbrest.fed
Breaston ˈbriː.stən
breastplate ˈbrest.pleɪt **-s** -s
breaststroke ˈbrest.strəʊk, US -stroʊk
breastwork ˈbrest.wɜːk, US -wɝːk **-s** -s
breath breθ **-s** -s ˈ**breath** ˌ**test**; ˌ**take someone's** ˈ**breath away**; ˌ**waste one's** ˈ**breath**
breathalyz|e, -ys|e ˈbreθ.əl.aɪz, US -ə.laɪz **-es** -ɪz **-ed** -d **-ing** -ɪŋ **-er/s** -əʳ/z, US -ɚ/z
breath|e briːð **-es** -z **-ing** -ɪŋ **-ed** -d ˈ**breathing** ˌ**room**; ˈ**breathing** ˌ**space**; ˌ**breathe** ˌ**down some-one's** ˈ**neck**
breathed *obsolete phonetic term:* breθt, briːðd
breather ˈbriː.ðəʳ, US -ðɚ **-s** -z
breathiness ˈbreθ.i.nəs, -nɪs
breathless ˈbreθ.ləs, -lɪs **-ly** -li **-ness** -nəs, -nɪs
breathtaking ˈbreθˌteɪ.kɪŋ **-ly** -li

B

breath|y ˈbreθ|.i **-ier** -i.əʳ, ⓊⓈ -i.ɚ **-iest** -i.ɪst, -i.əst **-iness** -ɪ.nəs, -ɪ.nɪs
Brebner ˈbreb.nəʳ, ⓊⓈ -nɚ
Brechin ˈbriː.kɪn, -xɪn, ⓊⓈ -kɪn
Brecht brekt; *as if German:* brext **-ian** -i.ən
Breckenridge, -kin- ˈbrek.ən.rɪdʒ, -ɪn-
Brecknock ˈbrek.nɒk, -nək, ⓊⓈ -nɑːk **-shire** -ʃəʳ, -ʃɪəʳ, ⓊⓈ -ʃɚ, -ʃɪr
Brecon ˈbrek.ən ˌ**Brecon** ˈ**Beacons**
bred (from **breed**) bred
Bredbury ˈbred.bər.i, ˈbreb-, ⓊⓈ ˈbred.ber-, -bɚ-
Bredon ˈbriː.dən
bree briː
breech n briːtʃ **-es** -ɪz **-ed** -t ˈ**breech** ˌ**birth**; ˌ**breech** ˈ**birth** ⓊⓈ ˈ**breech** ˌ**birth**
breeches *trousers:* ˈbrɪtʃ.ɪz, ˈbriː.tʃɪz
breeching ˈbrɪtʃ.ɪŋ, ˈbriː.tʃɪŋ **-s** -z
breech-loader ˈbriːtʃˌləʊ.dəʳ, ⓊⓈ -ˌloʊ.dɚ **-s** -z
breed briːd **-s** -z **-ing** -ɪŋ **bred** bred ˈ**breeding** ˌ**ground**
breeder ˈbriː.dəʳ, ⓊⓈ -dɚ **-s** -z ˈ**breeder re**ˌ**actor**
breeks briːks
breez|e briːz **-es** -ɪz **-ing** -ɪŋ **-ed** -d
breez|y ˈbriː.z|i **-ier** -i.əʳ, ⓊⓈ -i.ɚ **-iest** -i.ɪst, -i.əst **-ily** -əl.i, -ɪ.li **-iness** -ɪ.nəs, -ɪ.nɪs
Bremen *in Germany:* ˈbreɪ.mən, ⓊⓈ ˈbrem.ən, ˈbreɪ.mən *in US:* ˈbriː.mən, ˈbrem.ən
Bremerhaven ˈbreɪ.məˌhɑː.vən, ⓊⓈ ˈbrem.ɚ-, ˈbreɪ.mɚ-
Bremner ˈbrem.nəʳ, ⓊⓈ -nɚ
Bren bren
Brenda ˈbren.də
Brendan ˈbren.dən
Brendel ˈbren.dəl
Brendon ˈbren.dən
Brennan ˈbren.ən
Brenner ˈbren.əʳ, ⓊⓈ -ɚ
Brent brent
Brentford ˈbrent.fəd, ⓊⓈ -fɚd
brent|-goose ˌbrent|ˈguːs **-geese** -giːs
Brenton ˈbren.tən
Brentwood ˈbrent.wʊd
bre'r, br'er, B~ breəʳ, brɜːʳ, ⓊⓈ brer, brɜː
Brereton ˈbrɪə.tən, ⓊⓈ ˈbrɪr-
Brescia ˈbreʃ.ə, ˈbreɪ.ʃə, ⓊⓈ ˈbreʃ.ɑː, ˈbreɪ.ʃɑː
Breslau ˈbrez.laʊ, ˈbres-
Brest brest
Bret(t) bret
brethren ˈbreð.rən, -rɪn
Breton ˈbret.ɒn, -ən; *as if French:* bretˈɔ̃ːŋ; ⓊⓈ ˈbret.ən **-s** -z
Bretwalda bretˈwɔːl.də, -ˈwɒl-, ˈ---, ⓊⓈ -ˈwɑːl-, -ˈwɔːl-
Breughel ˈbrɔɪ.gəl, ˈbrɜː-, ˈbruː-; *as if Dutch:* -xəl; ⓊⓈ ˈbruː.gəl, ˈbrɔɪ-, ˈbrɔː-
breve briːv, ⓊⓈ briːv, brev **-s** -z
brev|et ˈbrev|.ɪt **-ets** -ɪts **-eting** -ɪ.tɪŋ, ⓊⓈ -ɪ.t̬ɪŋ **-eted** -ɪ.tɪd, ⓊⓈ -ɪ.t̬ɪd
breviar|y ˈbrev.i.ər|.i, ˈbriː.vi-, ⓊⓈ -er|.i, -ɚ|.i **-ies** -iz
breviate ˈbriː.vi.ət, -ɪt **-s** -s
brevier brəˈvɪəʳ, brɪ-, ⓊⓈ -ˈvɪr
brevity ˈbrev.ə.ti, -ɪ.ti, ⓊⓈ -ə.t̬i
brew, B~ bruː **-s** -z **-ing** -ɪŋ **-ed** -d
brewer, B~ ˈbruː.əʳ, ⓊⓈ -ɚ **-s** -z ˌ**brewer's** ˈ**yeast**
brewer|y ˈbruː.ər|.i, ⓊⓈ ˈbruː.ɚ|.i, ˈ-r|i **-ies** -iz
brewpub ˈbruː.pʌb **-s** -z
Brewster ˈbruː.stəʳ, ⓊⓈ -stɚ
Brezhnev ˈbreʒ.nef, -njef, ⓊⓈ -nef, -nev
Brian ˈbraɪ.ən

> Note: /ˈbriː.ən/ in Ireland.

Bria(n)na briˈæn.ə
Brianne briˈæn
briar ˈbraɪ.əʳ, braɪəʳ, ⓊⓈ ˈbraɪ.ɚ **-s** -z
Briareus ˌbraɪˈeə.ri.əs, ⓊⓈ -ˈer.i-
brib|e braɪb **-es** -z **-ing** -ɪŋ **-ed** -d **-er/s** -əʳ/z, ⓊⓈ -ɚ/z
briber|y ˈbraɪ.bər|.i **-ies** -iz
bric-à-brac ˈbrɪk.əˌbræk
Brice braɪs
brick brɪk **-s** -s ˈ**brick** ˌ**dust**; ˈ**brick** ˌ**field**
brickbat ˈbrɪk.bæt **-s** -s
brickie ˈbrɪk.i **-s** -z
brick-kiln ˈbrɪk.kɪln **-s** -z

> Note: The pronunciation /-kɪl/ was a traditional pronunciation used by those concerned with the working of kilns.

bricklay|er ˈbrɪkˌleɪ|.əʳ, ⓊⓈ -ɚ **-ers** -əz, ⓊⓈ -ɚz **-ing** -ɪŋ
brickmak|er ˈbrɪkˌmeɪ|.kəʳ, ⓊⓈ -kɚ **-ers** -əz, ⓊⓈ -ɚz **-ing** -ɪŋ
brickwork ˈbrɪk.wɜːk, ⓊⓈ -wɝːk
bricolage ˌbrɪk.əʊˈlɑːʒ, ˈ---, ⓊⓈ ˌbriː.koʊˈlɑːʒ, ˌbrɪk.oʊˈ-
bridal ˈbraɪ.dəl
bride braɪd **-s** -z
bridegroom ˈbraɪd.grʊm, -gruːm, ⓊⓈ -gruːm, -grʊm **-s** -z
Brideshead ˈbraɪdz.hed
bridesmaid ˈbraɪdz.meɪd **-s** -z
brides|man ˈbraɪdz|.mən **-men** -mən, -men
bride-to-be ˌbraɪd.təˈbiː **brides-to-be** ˌbraɪdz.təˈbiː
Bridewell ˈbraɪd.wel, -wəl
bridg|e, B~ brɪdʒ **-es** -ɪz **-ing** -ɪŋ **-ed** -d ˌ**burn one's** ˈ**bridges**
bridgeable ˈbrɪdʒ.ə.bəl
bridgehead ˈbrɪdʒ.hed **-s** -z
Bridgeman ˈbrɪdʒ.mən
Bridgend ˌbrɪdʒˈend, ˈ--
Bridgenorth ˈbrɪdʒ.nɔːθ, -ˈ-, ⓊⓈ ˈbrɪdʒ.nɔːrθ, -ˈ-
Bridgeport ˈbrɪdʒ.pɔːt, ⓊⓈ -pɔːrt
Bridger ˈbrɪdʒ.əʳ, ⓊⓈ -ɚ
Bridges ˈbrɪdʒ.ɪz
Bridget ˈbrɪdʒ.ɪt
Bridgetown ˈbrɪdʒ.taʊn
Bridgewater ˈbrɪdʒˌwɔː.təʳ, ⓊⓈ -ˌwɑː.t̬ɚ, -ˌwɔː-
bridgework ˈbrɪdʒ.wɜːk, ⓊⓈ -wɝːk
Bridgnorth ˈbrɪdʒ.nɔːθ, ˌ-ˈ-, ⓊⓈ ˈbrɪdʒ.nɔːrθ, ˌ-ˈ-
Bridgwater ˈbrɪdʒˌwɔː.təʳ, ⓊⓈ -ˌwɑː.t̬ɚ, -ˌwɔː-
bridie, B~ ˈbraɪ.di **-s** -z
bridl|e ˈbraɪ.dəl **-es** -z **-ing** -ɪŋ, ˈbraɪd.lɪŋ **-ed** -d ˈ**bridle** ˌ**path**
bridleway ˈbraɪ.dəl.weɪ **-s** -z
Bridlington ˈbrɪd.lɪŋ.tən
bridoon brɪˈduːn **-s** -z
Bridport ˈbrɪd.pɔːt, ⓊⓈ -pɔːrt
brie, B~ briː
brief briːf **-s** -s **-er** -əʳ, ⓊⓈ -ɚ **-est** -ɪst, -əst **-ly** -li **-ness** -nəs, -nɪs **-ing/s** -ɪŋ/z **-ed** -t
briefcas|e ˈbriːf.keɪs **-es** -ɪz, -əz
briefless ˈbriː.fləs, -flɪs
brier ˈbraɪ.əʳ, braɪəʳ, ⓊⓈ ˈbraɪ.ɚ **-s** -z
Brierfield ˈbraɪ.ə.fiːld, ⓊⓈ ˈbraɪ.ɚ-
Brierley ˈbraɪ.ə.li, ˈbrɪə-, ⓊⓈ ˈbraɪ.ɚ-, ˈbrɪr-
Briers ˈbraɪ.əz, braɪəz, ⓊⓈ ˈbraɪ.ɚz
brig brɪg **-s** -z
brigade brɪˈgeɪd, brə- **-s** -z
brigadier ˌbrɪg.əˈdɪəʳ, ⓊⓈ -ˈdɪr **-s** -z *stress shift, see compound:* ˌ**brigadier** ˈ**general**
Brigadoon ˌbrɪg.əˈduːn
brigand ˈbrɪg.ənd **-s** -z **-age** -ɪdʒ
brigantine ˈbrɪg.ən.tiːn, -taɪn **-s** -z
Briges ˈbrɪdʒ.ɪz
Brigg brɪg **-s** -z
Brigham ˈbrɪg.əm
Brighouse ˈbrɪg.haʊs
bright, B~ braɪt **-er** -əʳ, ⓊⓈ ˈbraɪ.t̬ɚ **-est** -ɪst, -əst, ⓊⓈ ˈbraɪ.t̬ɪst, -t̬əst **-ly** -li **-ness** -nəs, -nɪs
brighten ˈbraɪ.tən **-s** -z **-ing** -ɪŋ **-ed** -d
Brightlingsea ˈbraɪt.lɪŋ.siː
Brighton ˈbraɪ.tən
brights braɪts
Brigid ˈbrɪdʒ.ɪd
Brigit ˈbrɪdʒ.ɪt
Brignell ˈbrɪg.nəl
Brigstock(e) ˈbrɪg.stɒk, ⓊⓈ -stɑːk
brill, B~ brɪl **-s** -z
brillian|ce ˈbrɪl.i.ənt|s, ⓊⓈ ˈ-jənt|s **-cy** -si
brilliant ˈbrɪl.i.ənt, ⓊⓈ ˈ-jənt **-s** -s **-ly** -li **-ness** -nəs, -nɪs
brilliantine ˈbrɪl.i.ən.tiːn, ⓊⓈ ˈ-jən-
-d -d
Brillo® ˈbrɪl.əʊ, ⓊⓈ -oʊ
Brillo pad® ˈbrɪl.əʊˌpæd, ⓊⓈ -oʊˌ-
brim brɪm **-s** -z **-ming** -ɪŋ **-med** -d
brimful ˌbrɪmˈfʊl, ˈ--
brimstone ˈbrɪm.stəʊn, ⓊⓈ -stoʊn
Brind brɪnd
Brindisi ˈbrɪn.dɪ.si, -də-, -zi
brindle, B~ ˈbrɪn.dəl **-s** -z **-d** -d
brine braɪn
bring brɪŋ **-s** -z **-ing** -ɪŋ **brought** brɔːt, ⓊⓈ brɑːt, brɔːt **bringer/s** ˈbrɪŋ.əʳ/z, ⓊⓈ -ɚ/z
brinjal ˈbrɪn.dʒəl
brink, B~ brɪŋk **-s** -s
brinkmanship ˈbrɪŋk.mən.ʃɪp
brinksmanship ˈbrɪŋks.mən.ʃɪp
Brinks-Mat® ˌbrɪŋksˈmæt
Brinsley ˈbrɪnz.li

B

brin|ly ˈbraɪ.n|i **-ier** -i.əʳ, ⓤⓢ -i.ɚ **-iest** -i.ɪst, -i.əst **-iness** -ɪ.nəs, -ɪ.nɪs
Bri-Nylon® ˌbraɪˈnaɪ.lɒn, ⓤⓢ -lɑːn
brio ˈbriː.əʊ, ⓤⓢ -oʊ
brioch|e briˈɒʃ, -ˈəʊʃ, ⓤⓢ -ˈoʊʃ, -ˈɑːʃ **-es** -ɪz
Briony ˈbraɪ.ə.ni
briquet(te) brɪˈket **-s** -s
Brisbane ˈbrɪz.bən, ⓤⓢ -bən, -beɪn

> Note: /ˈbrɪz.bən/ is the pronunciation in Australia.

Briscoe ˈbrɪs.kəʊ, ⓤⓢ -koʊ
brisk brɪsk **-er** -əʳ, ⓤⓢ -ɚ **-est** -ɪst, -əst **-ly** -li **-ness** -nəs, -nɪs
brisket ˈbrɪs.kɪt **-s** -s
bristl|e ˈbrɪs.ᵊl **-es** -z **-ing** -ɪŋ, ˈbrɪs.lɪŋ **-ed** -d
brist|ly ˈbrɪs|.ᵊl.i, ˈbrɪs|.li **-liness** -ᵊl.ɪ.nəs, ˈbrɪs|.li-, -nɪs
Bristol ˈbrɪs.tᵊl
Bristow(e) ˈbrɪs.təʊ, ⓤⓢ -toʊ
Brit brɪt **-s** -s
Brit. (abbrev. for **Britain**) brɪt; ˈbrɪt.ᵊn
Brit. (abbrev. for **British**) brɪt; ˈbrɪt.ɪʃ, ⓤⓢ brɪt; ⓤⓢ ˈbrɪţ.ɪʃ
Britain ˈbrɪt.ᵊn
Britannia brɪˈtæn.jə, ˈ-i.ə, ⓤⓢ ˈ-jə
Britannic brɪˈtæn.ɪk **-a** -ə
britches ˈbrɪtʃ.ɪz, -əz
Briticism ˈbrɪt.ɪ.sɪ.zᵊm, ⓤⓢ ˈbrɪţ- **-s** -z
British ˈbrɪt.ɪʃ, ⓤⓢ ˈbrɪţ- **-er/s** -əʳ/z, ⓤⓢ -ɚ/z ˌ**British** ˈ**English**; ˌ**British** ˈ**Isles**; ˌ**British** ˈ**Summer** ˌ**Time**
Britishism ˈbrɪt.ɪ.ʃɪ.zᵊm, ⓤⓢ ˈbrɪţ- **-s** -z
British Leyland® ˌbrɪt.ɪʃˈleɪ.lənd, ⓤⓢ ˌbrɪţ-
Britling ˈbrɪt.lɪŋ
Britney ˈbrɪt.ni
Britomart ˈbrɪt.əʊ.mɑːt, ⓤⓢ -oʊ.mɑːrt
Briton ˈbrɪt.ᵊn **-s** -z
Britpop ˈbrɪt.pɒp, ⓤⓢ -pɑːp
Britt brɪt
Brittain ˈbrɪt.ᵊn; brɪˈteɪn, ⓤⓢ ˈbrɪt.ᵊn; ⓤⓢ brɪˈteɪn
Brittan ˈbrɪt.ᵊn
Brittany ˈbrɪt.ᵊn.i
Britten ˈbrɪt.ᵊn
brittl|e ˈbrɪt.ᵊl, ⓤⓢ ˈbrɪţ- **-er** -əʳ, ⓤⓢ -ɚ **-est** -ɪst, -əst **-eness** -nəs, -nɪs
Brittney ˈbrɪt.ni
Britton ˈbrɪt.ᵊn
Britvic® ˈbrɪt.vɪk
Brixham ˈbrɪk.sᵊm
Brixton ˈbrɪk.stᵊn
Brize Norton ˌbraɪzˈnɔː.tᵊn, ⓤⓢ -ˈnɔːr-
Brno ˈbɜː.nəʊ; *as if Czech:* ˈbɚ-; ⓤⓢ ˈbɝː.noʊ
bro brəʊ, ⓤⓢ broʊ **-s** -z
broach brəʊtʃ, ⓤⓢ broʊtʃ **-es** -ɪz **-ing** -ɪŋ **-ed** -t
broad brɔːd, ⓤⓢ brɑːd, brɔːd **-er** -əʳ, ⓤⓢ -ɚ **-est** -ɪst, -əst **-ly** -li **-ness** -nəs, -nɪs ˌ**broad** ˈ**bean**
Broad brɔːd, ⓤⓢ brɑːd, brɔːd **-s** -z
broadband ˈbrɔːd.bænd, ⓤⓢ ˈbrɑːd-, ˈbrɔːd-
Broadbent ˈbrɔːd.bent, ⓤⓢ ˈbrɑːd-, ˈbrɔːd-
broadbrimmed ˌbrɔːdˈbrɪmd, ⓤⓢ ˌbrɑːd-, ˌbrɔːd- *stress shift:* ˌ**broadbrimmed** ˈ**hat**
broadcast ˈbrɔːd.kɑːst, ⓤⓢ ˈbrɑːd.kæst, ˈbrɔːd- **-s** -s **-ing** -ɪŋ **-er/s** -əʳ/z, ⓤⓢ -ɚ/z
broadcloth ˈbrɔːd.klɒθ, ⓤⓢ ˈbrɑːd.klɑːθ, ˈbrɔːd-
broaden ˈbrɔː.dᵊn, ⓤⓢ ˈbrɑː-, ˈbrɔː- **-s** -z **-ing** -ɪŋ **-ed** -d
broad-gauge ˈbrɔːd.geɪdʒ, ⓤⓢ ˈbrɑːd-, ˈbrɔːd-
Broadhurst ˈbrɔːd.hɜːst, ⓤⓢ ˈbrɑːd.hɝːst, ˈbrɔːd-
Broadlands ˈbrɔːd.ləndz, ⓤⓢ ˈbrɑːd-, ˈbrɔːd-
broadloom ˈbrɔːd.luːm, ⓤⓢ ˈbrɑːd-, ˈbrɔːd-
broad-minded ˌbrɔːdˈmaɪn.dɪd, ⓤⓢ ˌbrɑːd-, ˌbrɔːd-, ˈ-ˌ-- **-ness** -nəs, -nɪs *stress shift, British only:* ˌ**broadminded** ˈ**person**
Broadmoor ˈbrɔːd.mɔːʳ, ⓤⓢ ˈbrɑːd.mʊr, ˈbrɔːd-, -mɔːr
broadsheet ˈbrɔːd.ʃiːt, ⓤⓢ ˈbrɑːd-, ˈbrɔːd- **-s** -s
broadside ˈbrɔːd.saɪd, ⓤⓢ ˈbrɑːd-, ˈbrɔːd- **-s** -z
Broadstairs ˈbrɔːd.steəz, ⓤⓢ ˈbrɑːd.sterz, ˈbrɔːd-
broadsword ˈbrɔːd.sɔːd, ⓤⓢ ˈbrɑːd.sɔːrd, ˈbrɔːd- **-s** -z
Broadwater ˈbrɔːdˌwɔː.təʳ, ⓤⓢ ˈbrɑːdˌwɑː.ţɚ, -ˌwɔː-
Broadway ˈbrɔːd.weɪ, ⓤⓢ ˈbrɑːd-, ˈbrɔːd-
Broadwood ˈbrɔːd.wʊd, ⓤⓢ ˈbrɑːd-, ˈbrɔːd- **-s** -z
Brobdingnag ˈbrɒb.dɪŋ.næg, ⓤⓢ ˈbrɑːb-
Brobdingnagian ˌbrɒb.dɪŋˈnæg.i.ən, ⓤⓢ ˌbrɑːb- **-s** -z
brocade brəʊˈkeɪd, ⓤⓢ broʊ- **-s** -z **-d** -ɪd
brocard ˈbrəʊ.kəd, -kɑːd, ⓤⓢ ˈbroʊ.kɚd, ˈbrɑː-, -kɑːrd **-s** -z
broccoli ˈbrɒk.ᵊl.i, -aɪ, ⓤⓢ ˈbrɑː.kᵊl-
broch brɒk; brɒx; ⓤⓢ brɑːk
brochette brɒʃˈet, ⓤⓢ broʊˈʃet **-s** -s
brochure ˈbrəʊ.ʃəʳ, -ʃʊəʳ, brɒʃˈʊəʳ, brəˈʃʊəʳ, ⓤⓢ broʊˈʃʊr **-s** -z
brock, B~ brɒk, ⓤⓢ brɑːk **-s** -s
Brocken ˈbrɒk.ᵊn, ⓤⓢ ˈbrɑː.kᵊn
Brockenhurst ˈbrɒk.ᵊn.hɜːst, ⓤⓢ ˈbrɑː.kᵊn.hɝːst
Brocket ˈbrɒk.ɪt, ⓤⓢ ˈbrɑː.kɪt
Brocklehurst ˈbrɒk.ᵊl.hɜːst, ⓤⓢ ˈbrɑː.kᵊl.hɝːst
Brockley ˈbrɒk.li, ⓤⓢ ˈbrɑː.kli
Brockman ˈbrɒk.mən, ⓤⓢ ˈbrɑːk-
Brockovich ˈbrɒk.ə.vɪtʃ, ⓤⓢ ˈbrɑː.kə-
Brockwell ˈbrɒk.wəl, -wel, ⓤⓢ ˈbrɑː.kwəl, -kwel
Broderick ˈbrɒd.ᵊr.ɪk, ⓤⓢ ˈbrɑː.dᵊr-
broderie anglaise ˌbrəʊ.dᵊr.iˈɑ̃ː*ŋ*.gleɪz, ˌbrɒd.ᵊr-, -ˈglez, -ɑ̃ːŋˈgleɪz, -ˈglez, ⓤⓢ ˌbroʊ.də.riː.ɑːŋˈgleɪz
Brodie ˈbrəʊ.di, ⓤⓢ ˈbroʊ-
Brodrick ˈbrɒd.rɪk, ⓤⓢ ˈbrɑː.drɪk
Brogan ˈbrəʊ.gᵊn, ⓤⓢ ˈbroʊ-
brogue brəʊg, ⓤⓢ broʊg **-s** -z
broil brɔɪl **-s** -z **-ing** -ɪŋ **-ed** -d
broiler ˈbrɔɪ.ləʳ, ⓤⓢ -lɚ **-s** -z
broke (from **break**) brəʊk, ⓤⓢ broʊk
brok|e v brəʊk, ⓤⓢ broʊk **-es** -s **-ing** -ɪŋ **-ed** -t
Broke brʊk
broken ˈbrəʊ.kᵊn, ⓤⓢ ˈbroʊ- **-ly** -li
broken-down ˌbrəʊ.kᵊnˈdaʊn, ⓤⓢ ˌbroʊ- *stress shift:* ˌ**broken-down** ˈ**car**
broken-hearted ˌbrəʊ.kᵊnˈhɑː.tɪd, ⓤⓢ ˌbroʊ.kᵊnˈhɑːr.ţɪd *stress shift:* ˌ**broken-hearted** ˈ**suitor**
broker ˈbrəʊ.kəʳ, ⓤⓢ ˈbroʊ.kɚ **-s** -z **-ing** -ɪŋ **-ed** -d
brokerag|e ˈbrəʊ.kᵊr.ɪdʒ, ⓤⓢ ˈbroʊ- **-es** -ɪz
broll|y ˈbrɒl|.i, ⓤⓢ ˈbrɑː.l|i **-ies** -iz
bromate ˈbrəʊ.meɪt, ⓤⓢ ˈbroʊ- **-s** -s
brome brəʊm, bruːm, ⓤⓢ broʊm **-s** -z
Brome brəʊm, bruːm, ⓤⓢ broʊm, bruːm
bromeliad brəʊˈmiː.li.æd, ⓤⓢ broʊ-
Bromfield ˈbrɒm.fiːld, ⓤⓢ ˈbrɑːm-
Bromham ˈbrɒm.əm, ⓤⓢ ˈbrɑː.məm
bromic ˈbrəʊ.mɪk, ⓤⓢ ˈbroʊ-
bromide ˈbrəʊ.maɪd, ⓤⓢ ˈbroʊ- **-s** -z
bromine ˈbrəʊ.miːn, -mɪn, ⓤⓢ ˈbroʊ-
Bromley ˈbrɒm.li, ˈbrʌm-, ⓤⓢ ˈbrɑːm-
Brompton ˈbrɒm*p*.tən, ˈbrʌm*p*-, ⓤⓢ ˈbrɑːm*p*-
Bromsgrove ˈbrɒmz.grəʊv, ⓤⓢ ˈbrɑːmz.groʊv
Bromwich *in place names:* ˈbrɒm.ɪtʃ, ˈbrʌm-, -ɪdʒ, ⓤⓢ ˈbrɑː.m.wɪtʃ *surname:* ˈbrʌm.ɪdʒ, ⓤⓢ -wɪtʃ
Bromyard ˈbrɒm.jɑːd, -jəd, ⓤⓢ ˈbrɑːm.jɑːrd, -jɚd
bronchi|a ˈbrɒŋ.ki|.ə, ˈbrɒn-, ⓤⓢ ˈbrɑːŋ-, ˈbrɑːn- **-ae** -iː
bronchial ˈbrɒŋ.ki.əl, ˈbrɒn-, ⓤⓢ ˈbrɑːŋ-, ˈbrɑːn-
bronchiole ˈbrɒŋ.ki.əʊl, ˈbrɒn-, ⓤⓢ ˈbrɑːŋ.ki.oʊl, ˈbrɑːn- **-s** -z
bronchitic brɒŋˈkɪt.ɪk, brɒn-, ⓤⓢ brɑːŋˈkɪţ-, brɑːn-
bronchitis brɒŋˈkaɪ.tɪs, brɒn-, -təs, ⓤⓢ brɑːŋˈkaɪ.ţɪs, brɑːn-, -ţəs
broncho-pneumonia ˌbrɒŋ.kəʊ.njuːˈməʊ.ni.ə, ˌbrɒn-, -njʊˈ-, ⓤⓢ ˌbrɑːŋ.koʊ.nuːˈmoʊ.njə, ˌbrɑːn-, -njuːˈ-
bronch|us ˈbrɒŋ.k|əs, ˈbrɒn-, ⓤⓢ ˈbrɑːŋ-, ˈbrɑːn- **-i** -iː, -aɪ
bronco ˈbrɒŋ.kəʊ, ⓤⓢ ˈbrɑːŋ.koʊ **-s** -z
Bronson ˈbrɒn*t*.sən, ⓤⓢ ˈbrɑːn*t*-
Bronstein ˈbrɒn.stiːn, ⓤⓢ ˈbrɑːn-

Bronte, Brontë ˈbrɒn.teɪ, -ti, (US) ˈbrɑːn.teɪ, -t̬i

brontosaur ˈbrɒn.tə.sɔːʳ, (US) ˈbrɑːn.t̬ə.sɔːr **-s** -z

brontosaur|us ˌbrɒn.təˈsɔː.r|əs, (US) ˌbrɑːn.t̬əˈsɔːr|.əs **-uses** -ə.sɪz **-i** -aɪ

Bronwen ˈbrɒn.wen, -wɪn, (US) ˈbrɑːn-

Bronx brɒŋks, (US) brɑːŋks ˌ**Bronx** ˈ**cheer**

bronz|e brɒnz, (US) brɑːnz **-es** -ɪz **-ing** -ɪŋ **-ed** -d **-y** -i ˈ**Bronze** ˌ**Age**

bronzer ˈbrɒn.zəʳ, (US) ˈbrɑːn.zɚ **-s** -z

brooch brəʊtʃ, (US) broʊtʃ, bruːtʃ **-es** -ɪz

brood bruːd **-s** -z **-ing** -ɪŋ **-ed** -ɪd

brood|y ˈbruː.d|i **-ily** -əl.i, -ɪ.li **-iness** -ɪ.nəs, -ɪ.nɪs

brook brʊk **-s** -s **-ing** -ɪŋ **-ed** -t

Brook(e) brʊk **-s** -s

Brooker ˈbrʊk.əʳ, (US) -ɚ

Brookfield ˈbrʊk.fiːld

Brookland ˈbrʊk.lənd **-s** -z

brooklet ˈbrʊk.lət, -lɪt **-s** -s

Brookline ˈbrʊk.laɪn

Brooklyn ˈbrʊk.lɪn, (US) -lɪn, -lən ˌ**Brooklyn** ˈ**Bridge**

Brookner ˈbrʊk.nəʳ, (US) -nɚ

Brooks brʊks

Brookside ˈbrʊk.saɪd

Brooksmith ˈbrʊk.smɪθ

Brookwood ˈbrʊk.wʊd

broom bruːm, brʊm **-s** -z

Broom(e) bruːm

Broomfield ˈbruːm.fiːld, ˈbrʊm-

broomstick ˈbruːm.stɪk, ˈbrʊm- **-s** -s

Brophy ˈbrəʊ.fi, (US) ˈbroʊ-

Bros. ˈbrʌð.əz, (US) ˈbrʌð.ɚz; brɒs

Broseley ˈbrəʊz.li, (US) ˈbroʊz-

Brosnahan ˈbrɒz.nə.hən, ˈbrɒs-, (US) ˈbrɑːz-, ˈbrɑːs-

Brosnan ˈbrɒz.nən, (US) ˈbrɑːz-

broth brɒθ, (US) brɑːθ **-s** -s

brothel ˈbrɒθ.əl, (US) ˈbrɑː.θəl **-s** -z

brother ˈbrʌð.əʳ, (US) -ɚ **-s** -z

brotherhood ˈbrʌð.ə.hʊd, (US) ˈ-ɚ- **-s** -z

broth|er-in-law ˈbrʌð|.əʳ.ɪn.lɔː, (US) -ɚ.ɪn.lɑː, -lɔː **-ers-in-law** -əz.ɪn.lɔː, (US) -ɚz.ɪn.lɑː, -lɔː

brotherl|y ˈbrʌð.əl|.i, (US) -ɚ.l|i **-iness** -ɪ.nəs, -ɪ.nɪs

Brotton ˈbrɒt.ən, (US) ˈbrɑː.tən

Brough brʌf

brougham ˈbruː.əm, bruːm, (US) broʊm, ˈbruː.əm, bruːm **-s** -z

Brougham brʊm, bruːm; ˈbruː.əm, ˈbrəʊ-, (US) brʊm, bruːm, ˈbruː.əm, ˈbroʊ-

Brougham and Vaux ˌbrʊm.əndˈvɔːks, (US) -ˈvɑːks, -ˈvɔːks

brought (from **bring**) brɔːt, (US) brɑːt, brɔːt

Broughton *in Northamptonshire:* ˈbraʊ.tən *all others in England:* ˈbrɔː.tən, (US) ˈbrɑː-, ˈbrɔː-

brouhaha ˈbruː.hɑː.hɑː **-s** -z

brow braʊ **-s** -z

brow|beat ˈbraʊ|.biːt **-beats** -biːts **-beating** -biː.tɪŋ, (US) -biː.t̬ɪŋ **-beaten** -biː.tən, (US) -biː.t̬ən

brown, B~ braʊn **-s** -z **-er** -əʳ, (US) -ɚ **-est** -ɪst, -əst **-ness** -nəs, -nɪs **-ing** -ɪŋ **-ed** -d ˌ**brown** ˈ**ale;** ˌ**brown** ˈ**Betty;** ˌ**brown** ˈ**bread;** ˌ**brown** ˈ**owl;** ˌ**brown** ˈ**sauce;** ˌ**brown** ˈ**sugar**

brown-bag ˌbraʊnˈbæg **-s** -z **-ging** -ɪŋ **-ged** -d

Browne braʊn

Brownfield ˈbraʊn.fiːld

Brownhills ˈbraʊn.hɪlz

Brownian ˈbraʊ.ni.ən ˌ**Brownian** ˈ**motion** (US) ˈ**Brownian** ˌ**motion;** ˌ**Brownian** ˈ**movement** (US) ˈ**Brownian** ˌ**movement**

brownie, B~ ˈbraʊ.ni **-s** -z ˈ**Brownie** ˌ**Guide;** ˈ**brownie** ˌ**point**

browning, B~ ˈbraʊ.nɪŋ

brownish ˈbraʊ.nɪʃ

Brownjohn ˈbraʊn.dʒɒn, (US) -dʒɑːn

Brownlee, Brownlie ˈbraʊn.li

Brownlow ˈbraʊn.ləʊ, (US) -loʊ

brown-nos|e ˌbraʊnˈnəʊz, (US) -ˈnoʊz **-es** -ɪz **-ing** -ɪŋ **-ed** -d

brownout ˈbraʊn.aʊt **-s** -s

Brownrigg ˈbraʊn.rɪg

brownshirt, B~ ˈbraʊn.ʃɜːt, (US) -ʃɝːt **-s** -s

Brownsmith ˈbraʊn.smɪθ

Brownson ˈbraʊn.sən

brownstone ˈbraʊn.stəʊn, (US) -stoʊn **-s** -z

brows|e, B~ braʊz **-es** -ɪz **-ing** -ɪŋ **-ed** -d

browser ˈbraʊ.zəʳ, (US) -zɚ **-s** -z

Broxbourne ˈbrɒks.bɔːn, (US) ˈbrɑːks.bɔːrn

Broxburn ˈbrɒks.bɜːn, (US) ˈbrɑːks.bɝːn

Brubeck ˈbruː.bek

Bruce bruːs

brucellosis ˌbruː.sɪˈləʊ.sɪs, -səˈ-, (US) -ˈloʊ-

Bruch brʊk; *as if German:* brʊx

Bruckner ˈbrʊk.nəʳ, (US) -nɚ

Brueg(h)el ˈbrɔɪ.gəl, ˈbrɜː-, ˈbruː-; *as if Dutch:* -xəl; (US) ˈbruː.gəl, ˈbrɔɪ-, ˈbrɔː-

Bruges bruːʒ

bruin, B~ ˈbruː.ɪn, (US) ˈbruː.ɪn **-s** -z

bruis|e bruːz **-es** -ɪz **-ing** -ɪŋ **-ed** -d

bruiser ˈbruː.zəʳ, (US) -zɚ **-s** -z

bruit bruːt **-s** -s **-ing** -ɪŋ, (US) ˈbruː.t̬ɪŋ **-ed** -ɪd, (US) ˈbruː.t̬ɪd

Brum brʌm

Brumaire bruːˈmeəʳ, (US) -ˈmer

brumb|y ˈbrʌm.b|i **-ies** -iz

brume bruːm

brummagem, B~ ˈbrʌm.ə.dʒəm

Brummel ˈbrʌm.əl

Brummie ˈbrʌm.i

brunch brʌntʃ **-es** -ɪz

Brunei bruːˈnaɪ, ˈ--, (US) bruːˈnaɪ

Brunel bruːˈnel

brunette, brunet bruːˈnet **-s** -s

Brünnhilde brʊnˈhɪl.də, ˈ-ˌ--

Brunning ˈbrʌn.ɪŋ

Bruno ˈbruː.nəʊ, (US) -noʊ

Brunswick ˈbrʌnz.wɪk

brunt brʌnt

Brunton ˈbrʌn.tən

bruschetta brʊˈsket.ə, -ˈʃet-, (US) -ˈsket̬-, bruːˈʃet̬.ə

> Note: The pronunciation with /-ˈʃet-/ is widespread but does not correspond to the Italian original; it may be a form of spelling pronunciation.

brush brʌʃ **-es** -ɪz **-ing** -ɪŋ **-ed** -t

brush-off ˈbrʌʃ.ɒf, (US) -ɑːf **-s** -s ˌ**give someone the** ˈ**brush-off**

brushstroke ˈbrʌʃ.strəʊk, (US) -stroʊk **-s** -s

brushwood ˈbrʌʃ.wʊd

brushwork ˈbrʌʃ.wɜːk, (US) -wɝːk

brusque bruːsk, brʊsk, brʌsk, (US) brʌsk **-ly** -li **-ness** -nəs, -nɪs

Brussels ˈbrʌs.əlz ˌ**brussels** ˈ**sprout(s)** (US) ˈ**brussels** ˌ**sprout(s)**

brut, B~® bruːt

brutal ˈbruː.təl, (US) -t̬əl **-ly** -i

brutalit|y bruːˈtæl.ə.t|i, -ɪ.t|i, (US) -ə.t̬|i **-ies** -iz

brutaliz|e, -is|e ˈbruː.təl.aɪz, (US) -t̬əl- **-es** -ɪz **-ing** -ɪŋ **-ed** -d

brute bruːt **-s** -s

brutish ˈbruː.tɪʃ, (US) -t̬ɪʃ **-ly** -li **-ness** -nəs, -nɪs

Brutnell ˈbruːt.nel, -nəl

Bruton ˈbruː.tən, (US) -tən

Brutus ˈbruː.təs, (US) -t̬əs

bruv brʌv

Bryan ˈbraɪ.ən **-s** -z

Bryant ˈbraɪ.ənt

Bryce braɪs

Brydon ˈbraɪ.dən

Bryers ˈbraɪ.əz, braɪəz, (US) ˈbraɪ.ɚz

Brylcreem® ˈbrɪl.kriːm **-ed** -d

Brymbo ˈbrɪm.bəʊ, ˈbrʌm-, (US) ˈbrɪm.boʊ

Bryn brɪn

Bryncoch brɪnˈkɒx, (US) -ˈkoʊx

Brynhild ˈbrɪn.hɪld

Brynmawr *in Wales:* brɪnˈmaʊ.əʳ, brɪm-, (US) -ˈmaʊ.ɚ

Bryn Mawr *in US:* brɪnˈmɔːʳ, (US) -ˈmɑːr

Brynmor ˈbrɪn.mɔːʳ, ˈbrɪm-, (US) ˈbrɪn.mɔːr

bryony, B~ ˈbraɪ.ə.ni

Bryson ˈbraɪ.sən

BS ˌbiːˈes

BSc ˌbiː.esˈsiː

BSE ˌbiː.esˈiː

B-side ˈbiː.saɪd **-s** -z

BSkyB ˌbiː.skaɪˈbiː

BST ˌbiː.esˈtiː

BT ˌbiːˈtiː

bub bʌb **-s** -z

bubbl|e ˈbʌb.əl **-es** -z **-ing** -ɪŋ, ˈbʌb.lɪŋ **-ed** -d ˌ**bubble-and-**ˈ**squeak;** ˈ**bubble** ˌ**bath;** ˈ**bubble** ˌ**gum;** ˈ**bubble** ˌ**wrap**

Bubblejet® ˈbʌb.əl.dʒet

bubbly ˈbʌb.əl.i, -li

Buber ˈbuː.bəʳ, (US) -bɚ

B

bubo ˈbjuː.bəʊ, ˈbuː-, (US) -boʊ **-es** -z
bubonic bjuːˈbɒn.ɪk, buː-, (US) -ˈbɑː.nɪk **buˌbonic ˈplague**
Bucaramanga ˌbʊk.ær.əˈmæŋ.gə, ˌbuː-, ˈ-gɑː
buccal ˈbʌk.əl
buccaneer ˌbʌk.əˈnɪəʳ, (US) -ˈnɪr **-s** -z
Buccleuch bəˈkluː
Bucephalus bjuːˈsef.əl.əs
Buchan ˈbʌk.ən, ˈbʌx-
Buchanan bjuːˈkæn.ən, bə-
Bucharest ˌbuː.kəˈrest, ˌbjuː-, ˌbʊk.əˈ-, ˈ---, (US) ˈbuː.kə.rest, ˈbjuː-
Buchel ˈbjuː.ʃəl
Buchenwald ˈbuː.kən.væld; *as if German:* ˈbʊx.ən.vælt; (US) ˈbuː.kən.wɑːld, -wɔːld
Büchner ˈbuːk.nəʳ; *as if German:* ˈbuːx-; (US) ˈbʊk.nɚ, ˈbuːk-
buck, B~ bʌk **-s** -s **-ing** -ɪŋ **-ed** -t **ˌbuck's ˈfizz; ˌbuck ˈteeth; ˌpass the ˈbuck**
buckboard ˈbʌk.bɔːd, (US) -bɔːrd **-s** -z
buck|et ˈbʌk|.ɪt **-ets** -ɪts **-eting** -ɪ.tɪŋ, (US) -ɪ.t̬ɪŋ **-eted** -ɪ.tɪd, (US) -ɪ.t̬ɪd **ˌkick the ˈbucket**
bucketful ˈbʌk.ɪt.fʊl **-s** -z
bucketload ˈbʌk.ɪt.ləʊd, (US) -loʊd **-s** -z
Buckhaven ˈbʌkˌheɪ.vən
buckhorn ˈbʌk.hɔːn, (US) -hɔːrn
Buckhurst ˈbʌk.*h*ɜːst, (US) -*h*ɝːst
Buckie ˈbʌk.i
Buckingham ˈbʌk.ɪŋ.əm **-shire** -ʃəʳ, -ʃɪəʳ, (US) -ʃɚ, -ʃɪr **ˌBuckingham ˈPalace**
Buckland ˈbʌk.lənd
buckl|e, B~ ˈbʌk.əl **-es** -z **-ing** -ɪŋ, ˈbʌk.lɪŋ **-ed** -d
buckler ˈbʌk.ləʳ, (US) -lɚ **-s** -z
Buckley ˈbʌk.li
Buckmaster ˈbʌkˌmɑː.stəʳ, (US) -ˌmæs.tɚ
Bucknall ˈbʌk.nəl
Bucknell ˈbʌk.nəl; bʌkˈnel
Bucknill ˈbʌk.nɪl, -nəl
buck-passing ˈbʌkˌpɑː.sɪŋ, (US) -ˌpæs.ɪŋ
buckram ˈbʌk.rəm **-s** -z
Bucks. (abbrev. for **Buckinghamshire**) bʌks; ˈbʌk.ɪŋ.əm.ʃəʳ, -ˌʃɪəʳ, (US) bʌks; (US) ˈbʌk.ɪŋ.əm.ʃɚ, -ˌʃɪr
buckshee ˌbʌkˈʃiː, ˈ--
buckshot ˈbʌk.ʃɒt, (US) -ʃɑːt
buckskin ˈbʌk.skɪn **-s** -z
Buckston ˈbʌk.stən
buckwheat ˈbʌk.*h*wiːt
bucolic bjuːˈkɒl.ɪk, (US) -ˈkɑː.lɪk **-al** -əl **-ally** -əl.i, -li
Buczacki bʊˈtʃæt.ski, bjuː-
bud, B~ bʌd **-s** -z **-ding** -ɪŋ **-ded** -ɪd **ˌnip something in the ˈbud**
Budapest ˌbjuː.dəˈpest, ˌbuː-, (US) ˈbuː.də.pest; (US) ˌbuː.dəˈpeʃt
Budd bʌd
Buddha ˈbʊd.ə, (US) ˈbuː.də, ˈbʊd.ə
Buddh|ism ˈbʊd|.ɪ.zəm, (US) ˈbuː.d|ɪ-, ˈbʊd|.ɪ- **-ist/s** -ɪst/s
Buddhistic bʊˈdɪs.tɪk, (US) buː-, bʊ-
budding ˈbʌd.ɪŋ
Buddle ˈbʌd.əl, ˈbʊd-
buddleia ˈbʌd.li.ə, (US) bədˈliː-; (US) ˈbʌd.li- **-s** -z
budd|y ˈbʌd|.i **-ies** -iz
Bude bjuːd
budg|e, B~ bʌdʒ **-es** -ɪz **-ing** -ɪŋ **-ed** -d
Budgens® ˈbʌdʒ.ənz
budgerigar ˈbʌdʒ.ər.ɪ.gɑːʳ, (US) -gɑːr **-s** -z
budg|et ˈbʌdʒ|.ɪt **-ets** -ɪts **-eting** -ɪ.tɪŋ, (US) -ɪ.t̬ɪŋ **-eted** -ɪ.tɪd, (US) -ɪ.t̬ɪd
budgetary ˈbʌdʒ.ɪ.tər.i, ˈ-ə-, (US) -ter.i
budgie ˈbʌdʒ.i **-s** -z
Budleigh ˈbʌd.li
Budweiser® ˈbʌd.waɪ.zəʳ, (US) -zɚ
Buenos Aires ˌbweɪ.nɒsˈaɪə.rez, -nəs-, -riːz, -rɪs, (US) ˌbweɪ.nəsˈer.iːz, -noʊsˈ-, ˌboʊ.nəsˈ-, -aɪ.riːz
buff bʌf **-s** -s **-ed** -d **-ing** -ɪŋ
buffalo, B~ ˈbʌf.əl.əʊ, (US) -ə.loʊ **-es** -z **ˌBuffalo ˈBill**
buffer ˈbʌf.əʳ, (US) -ɚ **-s** -z **-ing** -ɪŋ **-ed** -d **ˈbuffer ˌzone**
buffet n *blow:* ˈbʌf.ɪt *refreshment, sideboard:* ˈbʊf.eɪ, ˈbʌf-, -i, (US) bʌˈfeɪ, buː- **-s** -s
buff|et v *hit against:* ˈbʌf|.ɪt **-ets** -ɪts **-eting** -ɪ.tɪŋ, -ə.tɪŋ, (US) -ɪ.t̬ɪŋ, -ə.t̬ɪŋ **-eted** -ɪ.tɪd, -ə.tɪd, (US) -ɪ.t̬ɪd, -ə.t̬ɪd
Buffett ˈbʌf.ɪt
buffo ˈbuː.fəʊ, (US) -foʊ **-s** -z
buffoon bəˈfuːn, bʌfˈuːn, (US) bəˈfuːn **-s** -z
buffooner|y bəˈfuː.nər|.i, bʌfˈuː-, (US) bəˈfuː- **-ies** -iz
Buffs bʌfs
Buffy ˈbʌf.i
bug bʌg **-s** -z **-ging** -ɪŋ **-ged** -d
Bug *river:* buːg
bugaboo ˈbʌg.ə.buː **-s** -z
Buganda buːˈgæn.də
Bugatti bjʊˈgæt.i, bʊ-, (US) -ˈgɑː.t̬i, -ˈgæt̬.i
bugbear ˈbʌg.beəʳ, (US) -ber **-s** -z
bug-eyed ˌbʌgˈaɪd, (US) ˈ-- *stress shift, British only:* **ˌbug-eyed ˈmonster**
bugg|er ˈbʌg|.əʳ, (US) -ɚ **-ers** -əz, (US) -ɚz **-ering** -ər.ɪŋ **-ered** -əd, (US) -ɚd
buggery ˈbʌg.ər.i
Buggins ˈbʌg.ɪnz
Buggs bjuːgz, bʌgz
bugg|y ˈbʌg|.i **-ies** -iz
bugl|e, B~ ˈbjuː.gəl **-es** -z **-ing** -ɪŋ, ˈbjuː.glɪŋ **-ed** -d
bugler ˈbjuː.gləʳ, (US) -glɚ **-s** -z
bugloss ˈbjuː.glɒs, (US) -glɑːs
Bugner ˈbʌg.nəʳ, (US) -nɚ
Bugs Bunny ˌbʌgzˈbʌn.i
Buick® ˈbjuː.ɪk **-s** -s
build bɪld **-s** -z **-ing/s** -ɪŋ/z **built** bɪlt **ˈbuilding soˌciety**
builder ˈbɪl.dəʳ, (US) -dɚ **-s** -z
build-up ˈbɪld.ʌp **-s** -s
built (from **build**) bɪlt
Builth bɪlθ
built-in ˌbɪltˈɪn, (US) ˈbɪlt.ɪn *stress shift, British only:* **ˌbuilt-in ˈmicrophone**
built-up ˌbɪltˈʌp *stress shift:* **ˌbuilt-up ˈarea**
Buist bjuːst, ˈbjuː.ɪst
Buitoni® bjuːˈtəʊ.ni, bwiː-, (US) -ˈtoʊ-
Bujumbura ˌbuː.dʒəmˈbʊə.rə, -dʒʊmˈ-, (US) -ˈbʊr.ə
Bukowski bjʊˈkɒf.ski, bjuː-, -ˈkaʊ-, (US) bjuːˈkaʊ-
Bulawayo ˌbʊl.əˈweɪ.əʊ, ˌbuː.lə-, (US) -oʊ
bulb bʌlb **-s** -z
bulbous ˈbʌl.bəs
bulbul ˈbʊl.bʊl **-s** -z
Bulford ˈbʊl.fəd, (US) -fɚd
Bulgakov bʊlˈgɑː.kɒf, (US) -kɔːf, -kɔːv
bulgar ˈbʌl.gəʳ, ˈbʊl-, (US) -gɚ **ˈbulgar ˌwheat**
Bulgar ˈbʌl.gɑːʳ, ˈbʊl-, -gəʳ, (US) -gɑːr, -gɚ **-s** -z
Bulgari|a bʌlˈgeə.ri|.ə, (US) -ˈger.i- **-an/s** -ən/z
bulg|e bʌldʒ **-es** -ɪz **-ing** -ɪŋ **-ed** -d
Bulger ˈbʊl.dʒəʳ, ˈbʌl-, (US) -dʒɚ
bulgur ˈbʊl.gəʳ, (US) -gɚ
bulg|y ˈbʌl.dʒ|i **-iness** -ɪ.nəs, -ɪ.nɪs
bulim|ia bʊˈlɪm|.i.ə, buː-, bjuː-, -ˈliː.m|i-, (US) bjuːˈliː.m|i-, buː- **-ic/s** -ɪk/s **buˌlimia nerˈvosa**
Bulins ˈbjuː.lɪnz
bulk bʌlk **-s** -s **-ing** -ɪŋ **-ed** -t
bulkhead ˈbʌlk.hed **-s** -z
Bulkington ˈbʌl.kɪŋ.tən
bulk|y ˈbʌl.k|i **-ier** -i.əʳ, (US) -i.ɚ **-iest** -i.ɪst, -i.əst **-ily** -əl.i, -ɪ.li **-iness** -ɪ.nəs, -ɪ.nɪs
bull, B~ bʊl **-s** -z **-ing** -ɪŋ **-ed** -d **ˌbull ˈterrier; ˈbull's ˌeye; like a ˌbull in a ˈchina shop; take the ˌbull by the ˈhorns**
bullac|e ˈbʊl.ɪs **-es** -ɪz
Bullard ˈbʊl.ɑːd, -əd, (US) -ɑːrd, -ɚd
bull-baiting ˈbʊlˌbeɪ.tɪŋ, (US) -t̬ɪŋ
bull-cal|f ˈbʊlˌkɑː|f, ˌ-ˈ-, (US) ˈbʊl.kæ|f **-ves** -vz
bulldog ˈbʊl.dɒg, (US) -dɑːg, -dɔːg **-s** -z
bulldoz|e ˈbʊl.dəʊz, (US) -doʊz **-es** -ɪz **-ing** -ɪŋ **-ed** -d
bulldozer ˈbʊlˌdəʊ.zəʳ, (US) -ˌdoʊ.zɚ **-s** -z
Bulleid ˈbʊl.iːd
Bullen ˈbʊl.ən, -ɪn
Buller ˈbʊl.əʳ, ˈbʌl-, (US) -ɚ
bullet ˈbʊl.ɪt, -ət **-s** -s
bulletin ˈbʊl.ə.tɪn, ˈ-ɪ-, (US) -ə.t̬ɪn **-s** -z **ˈbulletin ˌboard**
bullet-proof ˈbʊl.ɪt.pruːf **ˌbullet-proof ˈvest**
bullfight ˈbʊl.faɪt **-s** -s
bullfight|er ˈbʊlˌfaɪ.t|əʳ, (US) -t̬|ɚ **-ers** -əz, (US) -ɚz **-ing** -ɪŋ
bullfinch ˈbʊl.fɪntʃ **-es** -ɪz
bullfrog ˈbʊl.frɒg, (US) -frɑːg, -frɔːg **-s** -z
bullheaded ˌbʊlˈhed.ɪd, (US) ˈ-ˌ-- **-ly** -li **-ness** -nəs, -nɪs *stress shift, British only:* **ˌbullheaded ˈperson**
bullhorn ˈbʊl.hɔːn, (US) -hɔːrn **-s** -z
bullion ˈbʊl.i.ən, ˈ-jən, (US) ˈ-jən

B

bullish ˈbʊl.ɪʃ **-ly** -li **-ness** -nəs, -nɪs
Bullman ˈbʊl.mən
bullock, B~ ˈbʊl.ək **-s** -s
Bullokar ˈbʊl.ə.kɑːr, -kər, (US) -kɑːr
Bullough ˈbʊl.əʊ, (US) -oʊ
bullpen ˈbʊl.pen **-s** -z
bullring ˈbʊl.rɪŋ **-s** -z
bullrush ˈbʊl.rʌʃ **-es** -ɪz
bull|shit ˈbʊl|.ʃɪt **-shits** -ʃɪts **-shitting** -ˌʃɪt.ɪŋ, (US) -ˌʃɪţ.ɪŋ **-shitted** -ˌʃɪt.ɪd, (US) -ˌʃɪţ.ɪd
bullshitter ˈbʊlˌʃɪt.ər, (US) -ˌʃɪţ.ɚ **-s** -z
bull|y ˈbʊl|.i **-ies** -iz **-ying** -i.ɪŋ **-ied** -id
Bulmer ˈbʊl.mər, (US) -mɚ
bulrush ˈbʊl.rʌʃ **-es** -ɪz
Bulstrode ˈbʊl.strəʊd, ˈbʌl.strəʊd, (US) -stroʊd
Bultitude ˈbʊl.tɪ.tʃuːd, -tjuːd, ˈbʌl-, ˈ-tə-, (US) -tuːd, -tjuːd
bulwark ˈbʊl.wək, ˈbʌl-, -wɜːk, (US) -wɚk, -wɝːk **-s** -s
Bulwer ˈbʊl.wər, (US) -wɚ
Bulwer-Lytton ˌbʊl.wəˈlɪt.ən, (US) -wɚˈlɪţ-
bum bʌm **-s** -z **-ming** -ɪŋ **-med** -d
bumbag ˈbʌm.bæg **-s** -z
bumbl|e ˈbʌm.bəl **-es** -z **-ing** -ɪŋ, ˈbʌm.blɪŋ **-ed** -d **-er/s** -ər/z, ˈ-blər/z, (US) ˈ-bəl.ɚ/z, ˈ-blɚ/z
bumblebee ˈbʌm.bəl.biː **-s** -z
bumboat ˈbʌm.bəʊt, (US) -boʊt **-s** -s
bumf bʌmpf
Bumford ˈbʌm.fəd, (US) -fɚd
bumkin ˈbʌmp.kɪn **-s** -z
bummaree ˌbʌm.əˈriː, ˈ---, (US) ˈbʌm.ə.riː **-s** -z
bummer ˈbʌm.ər, (US) -ɚ **-s** -z
bump bʌmp **-s** -s **-ing** -ɪŋ **-ed** -t
bumper ˈbʌm.pər, (US) -pɚ **-s** -z **ˈbumper ˌcar; ˈbumper ˌsticker; ˌbumper to ˈbumper**
bumph bʌmpf
bumpkin ˈbʌmp.kɪn **-s** -z
bumptious ˈbʌmp.ʃəs **-ly** -li **-ness** -nəs, -nɪs
Bumpus ˈbʌm.pəs
bump|y ˈbʌm.p|i **-ier** -i.ər, (US) -i.ɚ **-iest** -i.ɪst, -i.əst **-ily** -əl.i, -ɪ.li **-iness** -ɪ.nəs, -ɪ.nɪs
bun bʌn **-s** -z **have a ˈbun in the ˌoven**
Bunce bʌnts
bunch, B~ bʌntʃ **-es** -ɪz **-ing** -ɪŋ **-ed** -t
buncombe, B~ ˈbʌŋ.kəm
Bundesbank ˈbʊn.dəz.bæŋk
Bundesrat ˈbʊn.dəz.rɑːt
Bundestag ˈbʊn.dəz.tɑːg; *as if German:* -də.ztɑːk; (US) -dəz.tɑːg
bundl|e ˈbʌn.dəl **-es** -z **-ing** -ɪŋ, ˈbʌnd.lɪŋ **-ed** -d
bung bʌŋ **-s** -z **-ing** -ɪŋ **-ed** -d
bungalow ˈbʌŋ.gəl.əʊ, (US) -oʊ **-s** -z
Bungay ˈbʌŋ.gi
Bunge ˈbʌŋ.i
bunged-up ˌbʌŋdˈʌp *stress shift:* **ˌbunged-up ˈnose**
bungee ˈbʌn.dʒi **ˈbungee ˌjumping**
bungl|e ˈbʌŋ.gəl **-es** -z **-ing** -ɪŋ, ˈbʌŋ.glɪŋ **-ed** -d **-er/s** -ər/z, ˈ-glər/z, (US) ˈ-gəl.ɚ/z, ˈ-glɚ/z
bunion ˈbʌn.jən **-s** -z
bunk bʌŋk **-s** -s **-ing** -ɪŋ **-ed** -t
bunk|er, B~ ˈbʌŋ.k|ər, (US) -k|ɚ **-ers** -əz, (US) -ɚz **-ering** -ər.ɪŋ **-ered** -əd, (US) -ɚd
bunkhou|se ˈbʌŋk.haʊ|s **-ses** -zɪz
bunkum ˈbʌŋ.kəm
Bunnett ˈbʌn.ɪt
bunn|y ˈbʌn|.i **-ies** -iz
Bunsen ˈbʌnt.sən, (US) -sɪn **ˌBunsen ˈburner** (US) **ˈBunsen ˌburner**
bunt bʌnt **-s** -s
Bunter ˈbʌn.tər, (US) -ţɚ
bunting, B~ ˈbʌn.tɪŋ, (US) -ţɪŋ **-s** -z
Bunty ˈbʌn.ti, (US) -ţi
Buñuel ˌbuː.njuˈel, ˈ---; ˌbuːnˈwel, ˌbʊn-, (US) ˌbuːnˈwel, ˌbʊn-
Bunyan ˈbʌn.jən
buoy bɔɪ, (US) bɔɪ, ˈbuː.i **-s** -z **-ing** -ɪŋ **-ed** -d
buoyancy ˈbɔɪ.ənt.si, (US) ˈbɔɪ-, ˈbuː.jənt-
buoyant ˈbɔɪ.ənt, (US) ˈbɔɪ-, ˈbuː.jənt **-ly** -li
BUPA ˈbuː.pə, ˈbjuː-
bur bɜːr, (US) bɝː **-s** -z
Burbage ˈbɜː.bɪdʒ, (US) ˈbɝː-
Burberr|y® ˈbɜː.bər|.i, (US) ˈbɝː.ber-, -bɚ- **-y's** -iz **-ies** -iz
burbl|e ˈbɜː.bəl, (US) ˈbɝː- **-es** -z **-ing** -ɪŋ, ˈ-blɪŋ **-ed** -d
Burbridge ˈbɜː.brɪdʒ, (US) ˈbɝː-
Burbury ˈbɜː.bər.i, (US) ˈbɝː.ber-, -bɚ-
Burch bɜːtʃ, (US) bɝːtʃ
Burchell, Burchall ˈbɜː.tʃəl, (US) ˈbɝː-
Burchill ˈbɜː.tʃəl, -tʃɪl, (US) ˈbɝː-
Burco ˈbɜː.kəʊ, (US) ˈbɝː.koʊ
burden, B~ ˈbɜː.dən, (US) ˈbɝː- **-s** -z **-ing** -ɪŋ **-ed** -d
burdensome ˈbɜː.dən.səm, (US) ˈbɝː-
Burdett ˈbɜː.det, -ˈ-, (US) bɝːˈdet, ˈ--
Burdett-Coutts ˌbɜː.detˈkuːts, -ˌ-ˈ-, (US) bɝːˌdetˈ-
burdock ˈbɜː.dɒk, (US) ˈbɝː.dɑːk **-s** -s
Burdon ˈbɜː.dən, (US) ˈbɝː-
Bure bjʊər, (US) bjʊr
bureau ˈbjʊə.rəʊ, ˈbjɔː-, bjʊəˈrəʊ, (US) ˈbjʊr.oʊ, -ˈ- **-s** -z
bureaucrac|y bjʊəˈrɒk.rə.s|i, bjəˈ-, bjɔːˈ-, (US) bjʊˈrɑː.krə- **-ies** -iz
bureaucrat ˈbjʊə.rəʊ.kræt, ˈbjɔː-, (US) ˈbjʊr.ə- **-s** -s
bureaucratic ˌbjʊə.rəʊˈkræt.ɪk, ˌbjɔː-, (US) ˌbjʊr.əˈkræţ- **-ally** -əl.i, -li
bureaux (alternative plural of **bureau**) ˈbjʊə.rəʊ, ˈbjɔː-, -rəʊz; ˌbjʊəˈrəʊ, -ˈrəʊz, (US) ˈbjʊr.oʊ, -oʊz
burette, buret bjʊəˈret, (US) bjʊrˈet **-s** -s
Burford ˈbɜː.fəd, (US) ˈbɝː.fɚd
burg bɜːg, (US) bɝːg **-s** -z
Burgar ˈbɜː.gər, (US) ˈbɝː.gɚ
Burg|e bɜːdʒ, (US) bɝːdʒ **-es** -ɪz
burgee ˈbɜː.dʒiː, -ˈ-, (US) ˈbɝː.dʒi **-s** -z
burgeon ˈbɜː.dʒən, (US) ˈbɝː- **-s** -z **-ing** -ɪŋ **-ed** -d
burger ˈbɜː.gər, (US) ˈbɝː.gɚ **-s** -z
burgess, B~ ˈbɜː.dʒəs, -dʒɪs, -dʒes, (US) ˈbɝː- **-es** -ɪz
burgh ˈbʌr.ə, (US) bɝːg, ˈbɝː.oʊ, -ə **-s** -z
Burgh bɜːg, (US) bɝːg *in Suffolk:* bɜːg; ˈbʌr.ə, (US) bɝːg; (US) ˈbɝː.oʊ, -ə *Baron, Heath in Surrey, place in Lincolnshire:* ˈbʌr.ə, (US) ˈbɝː.oʊ, -ə *Burgh-by-Sands:* brʌf
Burghclere ˈbɜː.kleər, (US) ˈbɝː.kler
burgher ˈbɜː.gər, (US) ˈbɝː.gɚ **-s** -z
Burghersh ˈbɜː.gəʃ, (US) ˈbɝː.gɚʃ
Burghley ˈbɜː.li, (US) ˈbɝː-
burglar ˈbɜː.glər, (US) ˈbɝː.glɚ **-s** -z
burglariz|e ˈbɜː.glər.aɪz, (US) ˈbɝː.glə.raɪz **-es** -ɪz **-ing** -ɪŋ **-ed** -d
burglar|y ˈbɜː.glər|.i, (US) ˈbɝː- **-ies** -iz
burgl|e ˈbɜː.gəl, (US) ˈbɝː- **-es** -z **-ing** -ɪŋ, ˈ-glɪŋ **-ed** -d
burgomaster ˈbɜː.gəʊˌmɑː.stər, (US) ˈbɝː.gəˌmæs.tɚ **-s** -z
Burgos ˈbʊə.gɒs, (US) ˈbʊr.gɑːs
Burgoyne ˈbɜː.gɔɪn, -ˈ-, (US) bɝːˈgɔɪn, ˈ--
burgund|y, B~ ˈbɜː.gən.d|i, (US) ˈbɝː- **-ies** -iz
burial ˈber.i.əl **-s** -z **ˈburial ˌground; ˈburial ˌplace**
burin ˈbjʊə.rɪn, (US) ˈbʊr.ɪn, ˈbɝː- **-s** -z
burk bɜːk, (US) bɝːk **-s** -s
burk|e, B~ bɜːk, (US) bɝːk **-es** -s **-ing** -ɪŋ **-ed** -t
Burkina Faso bɜːˌkiː.nəˈfæs.əʊ, (US) bʊrˌkiː.nəˈfɑː.soʊ
burlap ˈbɜː.læp, (US) ˈbɝː-
Burleigh ˈbɜː.li, (US) ˈbɝː-
burlesqu|e bɜːˈlesk, (US) bɝː- **-es** -s **-ing** -ɪŋ **-ed** -t
Burley ˈbɜː.li, (US) ˈbɝː-
Burling ˈbɜː.lɪŋ, (US) ˈbɝː-
Burlington ˈbɜː.lɪŋ.tən, (US) ˈbɝː-
burl|y, B~ ˈbɜː.l|i, (US) ˈbɝː- **-ier** -i.ər, (US) -i.ɚ **-iest** -i.ɪst, -i.əst **-iness** -ɪ.nəs, -ɪ.nɪs
Burma ˈbɜː.mə, (US) ˈbɝː-
Burmah ˈbɜː.mə, (US) ˈbɝː-
Burman ˈbɜː.mən, (US) ˈbɝː- **-s** -z
Burmese bɜːˈmiːz, (US) bɝː-, -ˈmiːs
burn bɜːn, (US) bɝːn **-s** -z **-ing** -ɪŋ **-ed** -d **burnt** bɜːnt, (US) bɝːnt
Burnaby ˈbɜː.nə.bi, (US) ˈbɝː-
Burnand bɜːˈnænd, bə-, (US) bɚ-
Burne bɜːn, (US) bɝːn
burner ˈbɜː.nər, (US) ˈbɝː.nɚ **-s** -z **ˌput something on a/the ˌback ˈburner**
burnet, B~ ˈbɜː.nɪt, (US) ˈbɝː- **-s** -s
Burnett bɜːˈnet, bə-; ˈbɜː.nɪt, (US) bɚˈnet; (US) ˈbɝː.nɪt
Burney ˈbɜː.ni, (US) ˈbɝː-
Burnham ˈbɜː.nəm, (US) ˈbɝː-
Burnham-on-Crouch ˌbɜː.nəm.ɒnˈkraʊtʃ, (US) ˌbɝː.nəm.ɑːnˈ-
Burnham-on-Sea ˌbɜː.nəm.ɒnˈsiː, (US) ˌbɝː.nəm.ɑːnˈ-

B

burnish ˈbɜː.nɪʃ, (US) ˈbɝː- **-es** -ɪz **-ing** -ɪŋ **-ed** -t **-er/s** -əʳ/z, (US) -ɚ/z
Burnley ˈbɜːn.li, (US) ˈbɝːn-
burnous, burnouse bɜːˈnuːs, (US) bɚ- **-es** -ɪz
burnout ˈbɜːn.aʊt, (US) ˈbɝːn-
Burns bɜːnz, (US) bɝːnz
Burnside ˈbɜːn.saɪd, (US) ˈbɝːn-
burnt (from **burn**) bɜːnt, (US) bɝːnt ˌ**burnt** ˈ**offering**
Burntisland ˌbɜːntˈaɪ.lənd, (US) ˌbɝːnt-
burnt-out ˌbɜːntˈaʊt, (US) ˌbɝːnt- *stress shift:* ˌ**burnt-out** ˈ**case**
Burntwood ˈbɜːnt.wʊd, (US) ˈbɝːnt-
burp bɜːp, (US) bɝːp **-s** -s **-ing** -ɪŋ **-ed** -t
burqa ˈbɜː.kə, (US) ˈbɝː- **-s** -z
burr, B~ bɜːʳ, (US) bɝː **-s** -z
Burrell ˈbʌr.əl, ˈbɜːr-
Burridge ˈbʌr.ɪdʒ, (US) ˈbɝː-
burrito bəˈriː.təʊ, bʊrˈiː-, (US) bəˈriː.t̬oʊ **-s** -z
Burrough(e)s ˈbʌr.əʊz, (US) ˈbɝː.oʊz
burrow ˈbʌr.əʊ, (US) ˈbɝː.oʊ **-s** -z **-ing** -ɪŋ **-ed** -d
Burrows ˈbʌr.əʊz, (US) ˈbɝː.oʊz
Burry Port ˌbʌr.iˈpɔːt, (US) ˌbɝː.iˈpɔːrt
Bursa ˈbɜː.sə, (US) bʊrˈsɑː, bɝː-
bursar ˈbɜː.səʳ, (US) ˈbɝː.sɚ, -sɑːr **-s** -z
bursarship ˈbɜː.sə.ʃɪp, (US) ˈbɝː.sɚ-, -sɑːr- **-s** -s
bursar|y ˈbɜː.sər|.i, (US) ˈbɝː- **-ies** -iz
Burscough Bridge ˌbɜː.skəʊˈbrɪdʒ, (US) ˌbɝː.skoʊˈ-
Bursledon ˈbɜː.zəl.dən, (US) ˈbɝː-
Burslem ˈbɜːz.ləm, (US) ˈbɝːz-
burst bɜːst, (US) bɝːst **-s** -s **-ing** -ɪŋ
Burt bɜːt, (US) bɝːt
burthen ˈbɜː.ðən, (US) ˈbɝː- **-s** -z
burton, B~ ˈbɜː.tən, (US) ˈbɝː-
Burundi bʊˈrʊn.di, bə- **-an/s** -ən/z
Burwash ˈbɜː.wɒʃ; *locally also:* ˈbʌr.əʃ, (US) ˈbɝː.wɑːʃ, -wɔːʃ
bur|y v ˈber|.i **-ies** -iz **-ying** -i.ɪŋ **-ied** -id
Bury *place:* ˈber.i *surname:* ˈbjʊə.ri, ˈber.i, (US) ˈbʊr.i, ˈber-
bus bʌs **-(s)es** -ɪz **-(s)ing** -ɪŋ **-(s)ed** -t ˈ**bus con**ˌ**ductor;** ˈ**bus** ˌ**stop**
busbar ˈbʌs.bɑːʳ, (US) -bɑːr **-s** -z
busboy ˈbʌs.bɔɪ **-s** -z
busb|y ˈbʌz.b|i **-ies** -iz
Busch bʊʃ
bush, B~ bʊʃ **-es** -ɪz **-ing** -ɪŋ **-ed** -t ˈ**bush** ˌ**baby;** ˌ**beat about the** ˈ**bush**
bushel ˈbʊʃ.əl **-s** -z
Bushell ˈbʊʃ.əl, (US) ˈbʊʃ.əl, bʊˈʃel
Bushey ˈbʊʃ.i
Bushire buːˈʃɪəʳ, (US) buːˈʃɪr
bush-league ˈbʊʃ.liːg **-s** -z
bush|man, B~ ˈbʊʃ|.mən **-men** -mən, -men
Bushmills ˈbʊʃ.mɪlz, -ˈ-
Bushnell ˈbʊʃ.nəl, (US) -nəl, -nel
bushranger ˈbʊʃˌreɪn.dʒəʳ, (US) -dʒɚ **-s** -z
bushwhack ˈbʊʃ.*h*wæk **-s** -s **-ing** -ɪŋ **-ed** -t
bushwhacker ˈbʊʃˌ*h*wæk.əʳ, (US) -ɚ **-s** -z
bush|y, B~ ˈbʊʃ|.i **-ier** -i.əʳ, (US) -i.ɚ **-iest** -i.ɪst, -i.əst **-ily** -əl.i, -ɪ.li **-iness** -ɪ.nəs, -ɪ.nɪs
business ˈbɪz.nɪs, -nəs **-es** -ɪz ˌ**mind one's** ˌ**own** ˈ**business**
businesslike ˈbɪz.nɪs.laɪk, -nəs-
business|man ˈbɪz.nɪs|.mən, -nəs-, -mæn **-men** -men, -mən
business|person ˈbɪz.nɪs|ˌpɜː.sən, -nəsˌ- **-people** -ˌpiː.pəl
business-to-business ˌbɪz.nɪs.təˈbɪz.nɪs
business-to-consumer ˌbɪz.nɪs.tə.kənˈsjuː.məʳ, -ˈsuː-, (US) -ˈsuː.mɚ
business|woman ˈbɪz.nɪs|ˌwʊm.ən, -nəsˌ- **-women** -ˌwɪm.ɪn
busk, B~ bʌsk **-s** -s **-ing** -ɪŋ **-ed** -t **-er/s** -əʳ/z, (US) -ɚ/z
buskin ˈbʌs.kɪn **-s** -z **-ed** -d
bus|man ˈbʌs|.mən, -mæn **-men** -mən, -men ˌ**busman's** ˈ**holiday**
Busoni buːˈzəʊ.ni, bjuː-, -ˈsəʊ-, (US) bʊˈzoʊ.ni, bjuː-
buss, B~ bʌs **-es** -ɪz **-ing** -ɪŋ **-ed** -t
bust bʌst **-s** -s **-ing** -ɪŋ **-ed** -ɪd
bustard ˈbʌs.təd, (US) -tɚd **-s** -z
buster, B~ ˈbʌs.təʳ, (US) -tɚ **-s** -z
bustier ˈbʌs.ti.əɪ, ˈbʊs-, ˈbuː.sti-, (US) ˈbuː.sti.eɪ, ˈbʊs.tjeɪ **-s** -z
bustl|e ˈbʌs.əl **-es** -z **-ing** -ɪŋ, ˈbʌs.lɪŋ **-ed** -d
bust-up ˈbʌst.ʌp **-s** -s
bust|y ˈbʌs.t|i **-ier** -i.əʳ, (US) -i.ɚ **-iest** -i.ɪst, -i.əst **-iness** -ɪ.nəs, -ɪ.nɪs
bus|y ˈbɪz|.i **-ies** -ɪz **-ying** -i.ɪŋ **-ied** -ɪd **-ier** -i.əʳ, (US) -i.ɚ **-iest** -i.ɪst, -i.əst **-ily** -əl.i, -ɪ.li ˈ**busy** ˌ**signal**
busybod|y ˈbɪz.iˌbɒd|.i, (US) -ˌbɑː.d|i **-ies** -iz
busyness ˈbɪz.i.nəs, -nɪs
but *strong form:* bʌt; *weak form:* bət
Note: Weak-form word. The strong form /bʌt/ is used contrastively (e.g. **ifs** and **buts**) and in sentence-final position (e.g. 'It's anything but'). The weak form is /bət/ (e.g. 'It's good but expensive' /ɪtsˌgʊd.bət.ɪkˈspent.sɪv/).
butane ˈbjuː.teɪn, (US) ˈbjuː.teɪn, -ˈ-
butch, B~ bʊtʃ
butch|er, B~ ˈbʊtʃ|.əʳ, (US) -ɚ **-ers** -əz, (US) -ɚz **-ering** -ər.ɪŋ **-ered** -əd, (US) -ɚd
butcher|y ˈbʊtʃ.ər|.i **-ies** -iz
Bute bjuːt **-shire** -ʃəʳ, -ʃɪəʳ, (US) -ʃɚ, -ʃɪr
Buthelezi ˌbuː.təˈleɪ.zi
butler, B~ ˈbʌt.ləʳ, (US) -lɚ **-s** -z
Butlin ˈbʌt.lɪn **-s** -z
butt, B~ bʌt **-s** -s **-ing** -ɪŋ, (US) ˈbʌt̬.ɪŋ **-ed** -ɪd, (US) ˈbʌt̬.ɪd
Butte bjuːt
butt-end ˈbʌt.end **-s** -z
butt|er ˈbʌt|.əʳ, (US) ˈbʌt̬|.ɚ **-ers** -əz, (US) -ɚz **-ering** -ər.ɪŋ **-ered** -əd, (US) -ɚd ˈ**butter** ˌ**bean;** ˈ**butter** ˌ**dish;** ˈ**butter** ˌ**knife;** ˌ**butter wouldn't** ˌ**melt in his/her** ˈ**mouth**
butterball ˈbʌt.ə.bɔːl, (US) ˈbʌt̬.ɚ.bɔːl, -bɑːl **-s** -z
buttercup ˈbʌt.ə.kʌp, (US) ˈbʌt̬.ɚ- **-s** -s
butterfat ˈbʌt.ə.fæt, (US) ˈbʌt̬.ɚ-
Butterfield ˈbʌt.ə.fiːld, (US) ˈbʌt̬.ɚ-
butterfinger|s ˈbʌt.əˌfɪŋ.gə|z, (US) ˈbʌt̬.ɚˌfɪŋ.gɚ|z **-ed** -d
butterfl|y ˈbʌt.ə.fl|aɪ, (US) ˈbʌt̬.ɚ- **-ies** -aɪz
Butterick ˈbʌt.ər.ɪk, (US) ˈbʌt̬-
Butterleigh, Butterley ˈbʌt.əl.i, (US) ˈbʌt̬.ɚ.li
Buttermere ˈbʌt.ə.mɪəʳ, (US) ˈbʌt̬.ɚ.mɪr
buttermilk ˈbʌt.ə.mɪlk, (US) ˈbʌt̬.ɚ-
butternut ˈbʌt.ə.nʌt, (US) ˈbʌt̬.ɚ- **-s** -s
butterscotch ˈbʌt.ə.skɒtʃ, (US) ˈbʌt̬.ɚ.skɑːtʃ
Butterwick ˈbʌt.ər.ɪk, -ə.wɪk, (US) ˈbʌt̬.ɚ.ɪk, -wɪk
Butterworth ˈbʌt.ə.wəθ, -wɜːθ, (US) ˈbʌt̬.ɚ.wɚθ, -wɝːθ
butter|y ˈbʌt.ər|.i, (US) ˈbʌt̬- **-ies** -iz
buttock ˈbʌt.ək, (US) ˈbʌt̬- **-s** -s
button, B~ ˈbʌt.ən **-s** -z **-ing** -ɪŋ **-ed** -d
button-down ˌbʌt.ənˈdaʊn *stress shift:* ˌ**button-down** ˈ**collar**
buttoned-down ˌbʌt.əndˈdaʊn
buttonhol|e ˈbʌt.ən.həʊl, (US) -hoʊl **-es** -z **-ing** -ɪŋ **-ed** -d
buttonhook ˈbʌt.ən.hʊk **-s** -s
buttress, B~ ˈbʌt.rəs, -rɪs **-es** -ɪz **-ing** -ɪŋ **-ed** -d
butt|y ˈbʌt|.i, (US) ˈbʌt̬- **-ies** -iz
butut buːˈtuːt
butyric bjuːˈtɪr.ɪk, (US) bjuː-
buxom ˈbʌk.səm **-ness** -nəs, -nɪs
Buxtehude ˌbʊk.stəˈhuː.də, ˈbʊk.stəˌhuː.də
Buxton ˈbʌk.stən
buy baɪ **-s** -z **-ing** -ɪŋ **bought** bɔːt, (US) bɑːt, bɔːt
buyable ˈbaɪ.ə.bəl
buyback ˈbaɪ.bæk **-s** -s
buyer ˈbaɪ.əʳ, (US) -ɚ **-s** -z
buyout ˈbaɪ.aʊt **-s** -s
Buzfuz ˈbʌz.fʌz
buzz bʌz **-es** -ɪz, -əz **-ing** -ɪŋ **-ed** -d
buzzard ˈbʌz.əd, (US) -ɚd **-s** -z
buzzer ˈbʌz.əʳ, (US) -ɚ **-s** -z
buzzword ˈbʌz.wɜːd, (US) -wɝːd **-s** -z
bwana ˈbwɑː.nə
by *normal form:* baɪ; *occasional weak forms:* bɪ, bə
Note: Weak-form word. The strong form is /baɪ/. The weak forms /bɪ, bə/ are rarely used, but can be found occasionally, particularly in measurements (e.g. 'two by three' /ˌtuː.bəˈθriː/).
by-and-by ˌbaɪ.ənd̬ˈbaɪ, -əm-, (US) -ənd̬ˈ-
Byard ˈbaɪ.əd, (US) ˈbaɪ.ɚd
Byars ˈbaɪ.əz, (US) ˈbaɪ.ɚz

Byas(s) ˈbaɪ.əs
Byatt ˈbaɪ.ət
Bydgoszcz ˈbɪd.gɒʃt; *as if Polish:* -gɒʃtʃ; (US) -gɔːʃtʃ
bye, B~ baɪ **-s** -z
bye-bye n *sleep:* ˈbaɪ.baɪ **-s** -z
bye-bye exclamation *goodbye:* ˌbaɪˈbaɪ, bə-, bʌbˈaɪ; ˈbaɪ.baɪ, ˈbʌb.aɪ
byelaw ˈbaɪ.lɔː, (US) -lɑː, -lɔː **-s** -z
by-election ˈbaɪ.ɪˌlek.ʃən, -əˌ- **-s** -z
Byelorussi|a ˌbjel.əʊˈrʌʃ|.ə, ˌbel-, -ˈruː.si-, (US) -oʊˈ-, -əˈ- **-an/s** -ən/z
Byers ˈbaɪ.əz, (US) ˈbaɪ.ɚz
Byfleet ˈbaɪ.fliːt
Byford ˈbaɪ.fəd, (US) -fɚd
bygone ˈbaɪ.gɒn, (US) -gɑːn **-s** -z
Bygraves ˈbaɪ.greɪvz
bylaw ˈbaɪ.lɔː, (US) -lɑː, -lɔː **-s** -z
Byles baɪlz
byline ˈbaɪ.laɪn **-s** -z
Byng bɪŋ
Bynoe ˈbaɪ.nəʊ, (US) -noʊ
BYO ˌbiː.waɪˈəʊ, (US) -ˈoʊ
bypass ˈbaɪ.pɑːs, (US) -pæs **-es** -ɪz **-ing** -ɪŋ **-ed** -d
bypa|th ˈbaɪ.pɑː|θ, (US) -pæ|θ **-ths** -ðz
byplay ˈbaɪ.pleɪ
by-product ˈbaɪˌprɒd.ʌkt, -əkt, (US) -ˌprɑː.dəkt **-s** -s
Byrd bɜːd, (US) bɝːd
byre ˈbaɪ.əʳ, (US) ˈbaɪ.ɚ **-s** -z
Byrne bɜːn, (US) bɝːn
byroad ˈbaɪ.rəʊd, (US) -roʊd **-s** -z
Byrom ˈbaɪ.rəm
Byron ˈbaɪə.rən
Byronic baɪˈrɒn.ɪk, (US) -ˈrɑː.nɪk **-ally** -əl.i, -li
Bysshe bɪʃ
bystander ˈbaɪˌstæn.dəʳ, (US) -dɚ **-s** -z
bystreet ˈbaɪ.striːt **-s** -s
byte baɪt **-s** -s
Bythesea ˈbaɪθ.siː, ˈbɪð.ə.siː
byway ˈbaɪ.weɪ **-s** -z
byword ˈbaɪ.wɜːd, (US) -wɝːd **-s** -z
Byzantian bɪˈzæn.ti.ən, baɪ-, bə-, ˈ-*t*ʃən, (US) bɪˈzæn.ti.ən, bə-, baɪ-, -ˈzænt.ʃən
Byzantine bɪˈzæn.taɪn, baɪ-, bə-, -tiːn; ˈbɪz.ən-, (US) ˈbɪz.ən.tiːn, -taɪn
Byzantium bɪˈzæn.ti.əm, baɪ-, bə-, ˈ-*t*ʃəm, (US) bɪˈzæn.ti.əm, bə-, baɪ-, -ˈzænt.ʃəm

C

Pronouncing the letter C

→ *See also* **CC, CCH, CH, CK, CQU**

The consonant letter **c** has four pronunciations: /s/, /k/, /ʃ/, and /tʃ/.

Before the vowel letters **i**, **e** or **y** (when functioning as a vowel letter), it is pronounced as /s/, e.g.:

specific	spəˈsɪf.ɪk
cell	sel
cycle	ˈsaɪ.kəl

In suffixes **-cial**, **-cious**, **-ciate**, **-cient** and their derivatives, **c** is realized as /ʃ/, e.g.:

social	ˈsəʊ.ʃəl (US) ˈsoʊ-
vicious	ˈvɪʃ.əs

In most other situations, **c** is pronounced as /k/, e.g.:

cat	kæt
critic	ˈkrɪt.ɪk (US) ˈkrɪt̬-

In addition

C can be silent. There are two occasions when this can occur:

the combination **ct** in some words, and in British place names such as *Leicester*, e.g.:

Leicester	ˈles.təʳ (US) -tɚ
indict	ɪnˈdaɪt

An exceptional pronunciation for **c** is /tʃ/ in some words borrowed from Italian, e.g.:

cello	ˈtʃel.əʊ (US) -oʊ
Cinquecento	ˌtʃɪŋ.kweɪˈtʃen.təʊ (US) -toʊ

A final exception:

Caesar	ˈsiː.zəʳ (US) -zɚ

c, C siː -ˈs -z
ca (abbrev. for **circa**) ˈsɜː.kə, (US) ˈsɝː-
CAA ˌsiː.eɪˈeɪ
cab kæb -s -z
CAB ˌsiː.eɪˈbiː
cabal kəˈbæl, kæbˈæl, (US) kəˈbɑːl, -ˈbæl -s -z
cabala, C~ kəˈbɑː.lə, kæbˈɑː-
cabalism ˈkæb.ə.lɪ.zəm
cabalistic ˌkæb.əˈlɪs.tɪk -al -əl -ally -əl.i, -li
caballero ˌkæb.əˈleə.rəʊ, -ˈljeə-, (US) -ˈler.oʊ, -əlˈjer- -s -z
cabana kəˈbɑː.nə, (US) -ˈbæn.ə, -ˈbɑː.nə, -njə -s -z
cabaret ˈkæb.ə.reɪ, ˌ--ˈ-, (US) ˌkæb.əˈreɪ, ˈ--- -s -z
cabbag|e ˈkæb.ɪdʒ -es -ɪz ˈ**cabbage** ˌ**rose**
cabbala, C~ kəˈbɑː.lə, kæbˈɑː- -s -z
cabbal|ism ˈkæb.ə.l|ɪ.zəm -ist/s -ɪst/s
cabbalistic ˌkæb.əˈlɪs.tɪk -al -əl -ally -əl.i, -li
cabb|ie, cabb|y ˈkæb|.i -ies -iz
cabdriver ˈkæbˌdraɪ.vəʳ, (US) -vɚ -s -z
Cabell ˈkæb.əl
caber ˈkeɪ.bəʳ, (US) -bɚ -s -z
Cabernet Sauvignon ˌkæb.ə.neɪˈsəʊ.vi.njɔ̃ːŋ, -njɒn, (US) -ɚˌneɪ.soʊ.viːˈnjoʊn
cabin ˈkæb.ɪn -s -z ˈ**cabin** ˌ**boy;** ˈ**cabin** ˌ**cruiser;** ˈ**cabin** ˌ**fever**
cabinet, C~ ˈkæb.ɪ.nət, -ə-, -nɪt -s -s ˈ**Cabinet** ˌ**Minister;** ˌ**Cabinet** ˈ**Minister**
cabinetmak|er ˈkæb.ɪ.nətˌmeɪ.k|əʳ, -nɪt-, (US) -k|ɚ -ers -əz, (US) -ɚz -ing -ɪŋ
cabl|e, C~ ˈkeɪ.bəl -es -z -ing -ɪŋ, ˈ-blɪŋ -ed -d ˈ**cable** ˌ**car;** ˌ**cable** ˈ**television;** ˌ**cable teleˈvision**
cablecast ˈkeɪ.bəl.kɑːst, (US) -kæst -s -s -ing -ɪŋ -er/s -əʳ/z, (US) -ɚ/z
cablegram ˈkeɪ.bəl.græm -s -z
cab|man ˈkæb|.mən -men -mən, -men
caboodle kəˈbuː.dəl
caboos|e kəˈbuːs -es -ɪz
Caborn ˈkeɪ.bɔːn, (US) -bɔːrn
Cabot ˈkæb.ət
cabotage ˈkæb.ə.tɑːʒ, -tɪdʒ
Cabrini kəˈbriː.ni
cabriole ˈkæb.ri.əʊl, (US) -oʊl -s -z
cabriolet ˈkæb.ri.əʊ.leɪ, ˌkæb.ri.əʊˈleɪ, (US) ˌkæb.ri.əˈleɪ -s -z
cabstand ˈkæb.stænd -s -z
ca-ca ˈkɑː.kɑː
cacao kəˈkaʊ, kækˈaʊ; kəˈkɑː.əʊ, kækˈɑː-, -ˈeɪ-, (US) kəˈkɑː.oʊ, kækˈɑː.oʊ -s -z
cachalot ˈkæʃ.ə.lɒt, (US) -lɑːt, -loʊ -s -s, -z
cach|e kæʃ -es -ɪz
cachepot ˈkæʃ.pəʊ, ˌkæʃˈpɒt, (US) ˈkæʃ.pɑːt, -poʊ -s -s, -z
cachet ˈkæʃ.eɪ, (US) -ˈ- -s -z
cachinnat|e ˈkæk.ɪ.neɪt, ˈ-ə- -es -s -ing -ɪŋ -ed -ɪd
cachinnation ˌkæk.ɪˈneɪ.ʃən
cachou kæʃˈuː, kəˈʃuː; ˈkæʃ.uː -s -z
cachucha kəˈtʃuː.tʃə -s -z
cacique kæsˈiːk, kəˈsiːk -s -s
cack-handed ˌkækˈhæn.dɪd, ˈ--- -ly -li -ness -nəs, -nɪs
cackl|e ˈkæk.əl -es -z -ing -ɪŋ, ˈ-lɪŋ -ed -d -er/s -əʳ/z, ˈ-ləʳ/z, (US) ˈ-əl.ɚ/z, ˈ-lɚ/z
cacoepy kækˈəʊ.ɪ.pi, -ep.i, (US) -ˈoʊ.ə-
cacographic ˌkæk.əʊˈgræf.ɪk, (US) -oʊˈ-, -əˈ- -al -əl
cacography kækˈɒg.rə.fi, kəˈkɒg-, (US) kəˈkɑː.grə-
cacology kækˈɒl.ə.dʒi, kəˈkɒl-, (US) kəˈkɑː.lə-
cacophonic ˌkæk.əʊˈfɒn.ɪk, (US) -oʊˈfɑː.nɪk, -əˈ- -al -əl -ally -əl.i, -li
cacophonous kəˈkɒf.ə.nəs, kækˈɒf-, (US) kəˈkɑː.fə-
cacophon|y kəˈkɒf.ə.n|i, kækˈɒf-, (US) kəˈkɑː.fə- -ies -iz
cactus ˈkæk.təs -es -ɪz **cacti** ˈkæk.taɪ
cacuminal kækˈjuː.mɪ.nəl, kəˈkjuː-, (US) kəˈkjuː.mə- -s -z
cad kæd -s -z
CAD kæd
cadaster kəˈdæs.təʳ, (US) -tɚ
cadastral kəˈdæs.trəl
cadastre kəˈdæs.təʳ, (US) -tɚ
cadaver kəˈdɑː.vəʳ, -ˈdeɪ-, -ˈdæv.əʳ, (US) -ˈdæv.ɚ -s -z
cadaveric kəˈdæv.ə.rɪk, (US) -ɚ.ɪk
cadaverous kəˈdæv.ər.əs -ness -nəs, -nɪs
Cadbury ˈkæd.bər.i, (US) ˈkæd.ber.i, -bɚ-
Cadby ˈkæd.bi, ˈkæb-
CAD/CAM ˈkæd.kæm
Caddell kəˈdel
Caddick ˈkæd.ɪk
caddie ˈkæd.i -s -z
caddis ˈkæd.ɪs ˈ**caddis** ˌ**fly**
caddish ˈkæd.ɪʃ -ly -li -ness -nəs, -nɪs
cadd|y ˈkæd|.i -ies -iz -ying -i.ɪŋ -ied -ɪd
cade, C~ keɪd -s -z
Cadell ˈkæd.əl, kəˈdel
cadenc|e ˈkeɪ.dənts -es -ɪz
cadency ˈkeɪ.dənt.si
cadenza kəˈden.zə -s -z
Cader Idris ˌkæd.əʳˈɪd.rɪs, (US) -ɚˈ-

C

cadet kəˈdet -s -s **caˈdet ˌcorps**
cadetship kəˈdet.ʃɪp -s -s
cadg|e kædʒ -es -ɪz -ing -ɪŋ -ed -d -er/s -əʳ/z, (US) -ɚ/z
cadi ˈkɑː.di, ˈkeɪ- -s -z
Cadillac® ˈkæd.ɪ.læk, -əl.æk, (US) -ə.læk, -əl.æk -s -s
Cadiz *in Spain:* kəˈdɪz; *as if Spanish:* ˈkæd.ɪθ; (US) kəˈdɪz; (US) ˈkeɪ.dɪz *in Phillipines:* ˈkɑː.diːs, (US) kəˈdɪz; (US) ˈkeɪ.dɪz *in the US:* kædˈɪz; ˈkeɪ.dɪz, (US) kəˈdɪz; (US) ˈkeɪ.dɪz
Cadman ˈkæd.mən
Cadmean ˈkæd.mi.ən, kædˈmiː-, (US) kædˈmiː-
cadmic ˈkæd.mɪk
cadmium ˈkæd.mi.əm, ˈkæb-, (US) ˈkæd-
Cadmus ˈkæd.məs
Cadogan kəˈdʌg.ən
cadre ˈkɑː.dəʳ, ˈkeɪ-, -drə, (US) ˈkɑː.d.reɪ, ˈ-.dri -s -z
caduce|us kəˈdʒuː.si|.əs, -ˈdjuː-, (US) -ˈduː-, -ˈdjuː-, -ʃ|əs -i -aɪ
Cadwallader kædˈwɒl.ə.dəʳ, (US) -ˈwɑː.lə.dɚ
CAE ˌsiː.eɪˈiː
caec|um ˈsiː.k|əm -a -ə
Caedmon ˈkæd.mən
Caen kɑ̃ːn, (US) kɑːn
Caerleon kɑːˈliː.ən, kə-, -ˈlɪən, (US) kɑːr-
Caernarvon, Caernarfon kəˈnɑː.vən, (US) kɑːrˈnɑːr- -shire -ʃəʳ, -ʃɪəʳ, (US) -ʃɚ, -ʃɪr
Caerphilly keəˈfɪl.i, kɑː-, kəˈfɪl-, (US) kɑːr-
Caesar ˈsiː.zəʳ, (US) -zɚ -s -z
Caesarea ˌsiː.zəˈriː.ə
caesarean, caesarian **n, adj** *way of having a baby:* sɪˈzeə.ri.ən, sə-, (US) sɪˈzer.i- -s -z **caeˌsarean ˈsection**
Caesarean **adj** *of Caesarea:* ˌsiː.zəˈriː.ən *of Caesar:* siːˈzeə.ri.ən, sɪ-, (US) sɪˈzer.i-
caesium ˈsiː.zi.əm
caesura sɪˈzjʊə.rə, siː-, -ˈzjɔː-, -ˈʒʊə-, (US) səˈzʊr.ə, -ˈʒʊr- -s -z
café, cafe ˈkæf.eɪ, (US) kæfˈeɪ, kəˈfeɪ -s -z
cafeteria ˌkæf.əˈtɪə.ri.ə, -ɪˈ-, (US) -ˈtɪr.i- -s -z
cafetière, cafetiere ˌkæf.əˈtjeəʳ, (US) -ˈtjer -s -z
caff kæf -s -s
caffein ˈkæf.iːn, -eɪn, (US) kæfˈiːn
caffeinated ˈkæf.ɪ.neɪ.tɪd, ˈ-ə-, (US) -ə.neɪ.t̬ɪd
caffeine ˈkæf.iːn, -eɪn, (US) kæfˈiːn
caftan ˈkæf.tæn, (US) -tæn, -tən -s -z
cag|e, C~ keɪdʒ -es -ɪz -ing -ɪŋ -ed -d
cager ˈkeɪ.dʒəʳ, (US) -dʒɚ -s -z
cag|ey ˈkeɪ.dʒ|i -ier -i.əʳ, (US) -i.ɚ -iest -i.ɪst, -i.əst -ily -əl.i, -ɪ.li -iness -ɪ.nəs, -ɪ.nɪs
Cagliari ˌkæl.jiˈɑː.ri, ˈkæl.jə.ri, (US) ˈkɑː.l.jɑːr.i, -jɚ-
Cagliostro kæl.jiˈɒs.trəʊ, (US) kɑːlˈjɔː.stroʊ
Cagney ˈkæg.ni
cagoule kəˈguːl, kægˈuːl -s -z
cag|y ˈkeɪ.dʒ|i -ier -i.əʳ, (US) -i.ɚ -iest -i.ɪst, -i.əst -ily -əl.i, -ɪ.li -iness -ɪ.nəs, -ɪ.nɪs
Cahal kəˈhæl, ˈkæ.həl
Cahan kɑːn
Cahill ˈkɑː.hɪl, ˈkeɪ.hɪl
Cahoon kəˈhuːn, kæ-
cahoots kəˈhuːts
CAI ˌsiː.eɪˈaɪ
Caiaphas ˈkaɪ.ə.fæs, -fəs
Caicos ˈkeɪ.kɒs, -kəs, (US) -kəs
Caillard ˈkaɪ.ɑːʳ, (US) -ɑːr
caiman ˈkeɪ.mən, ˈkaɪ-, -mæn, (US) ˈkeɪ- -s -z
Cain(e) keɪn
caique, caïque kaɪˈiːk, kɑː-, (US) kɑːˈiːk -s -s
Caird keəd, (US) kerd
Cairene ˈkaɪə.riːn, (US) ˈkaɪ-, -ˈ-
cairn keən, (US) kern -s -z
cairngorm, C~ ˌkeənˈgɔːm, ˌkeəŋ-, ˈ--, (US) ˈkern.gɔːrm -s -z
Cairns keənz, (US) kernz
Cairo *in Egypt:* ˈkaɪə.rəʊ, (US) ˈkaɪ.roʊ *in the US:* ˈkeə.rəʊ, (US) ˈker.oʊ
caisson ˈkeɪ.sɒn, -sən; *sometimes in engineering:* kəˈsuːn, (US) ˈkeɪ.sən, -sɑːn -s -z
Caister ˈkeɪ.stəʳ, (US) -stɚ
Caister-on-Sea ˌkeɪ.stəʳ.ɒnˈsiː, (US) -stɚ.ɑːnˈ-
Caistor ˈkeɪ.stəʳ, (US) -stɚ
Caithness ˈkeɪθ.nes, -nəs; keɪθˈnes
caitiff ˈkeɪ.tɪf, (US) -t̬ɪf -s -s
Caitlin, Caitlín ˈkeɪt.lɪn, ˈkæt.lɪn
Caius *Roman name, character in Shakespeare's Merry Wives:* ˈkaɪ.əs, ˈkeɪ.əs; *as if Latin:* ˈgaɪ- *Cambridge college:* kiːz
cajol|e kəˈdʒəʊl, (US) -ˈdʒoʊl -es -z -ing -ɪŋ -ed -d -er/s -əʳ/z, (US) -ɚ/z
cajoler|y kəˈdʒəʊ.lər|.i, (US) -ˈdʒoʊ- -ies -iz
Cajun ˈkeɪ.dʒən -s -z
cak|e keɪk -es -s -ing -ɪŋ -ed -t **(sell/go) like ˌhot ˈcakes** (US) **(sell/go) like ˈhot ˌcakes; ˌhave one's ˌcake and ˈeat it** (US) **ˌhave one's ˌcake and ˌeat it ˈtoo**
cakewalk ˈkeɪk.wɔːk, (US) -wɑːk, -wɔːk -s -s
Cakovec ˈtʃæk.əʊ.vets, (US) -oʊ-
CAL kæl, ˌsiː.eɪˈel
Calabar ˌkæl.əˈbɑːʳ, ˈ---, (US) ˈkæl.ə.bɑːr, ˌ--ˈ-
calabash ˈkæl.ə.bæʃ -es -ɪz, -əz
calaboos|e ˈkæl.ə.buːs, –ˈ- -es -ɪz
calabrese ˈkæl.ə.briːs, -briːz
Calabri|a kəˈlæb.ri|.ə, kælˈæb-, -ˈɑː.bri|-, (US) kəˈleɪ.bri|-, -ˈlɑː- -an/s -ən/z
Calais ˈkæl.eɪ, (US) kælˈeɪ
calamari ˌkæl.əˈmɑː.ri, (US) -ˈmɑːr.i
calamine ˈkæl.ə.maɪn
calamitous kəˈlæm.ɪ.təs, -ə.təs, (US) -ə.t̬əs -ly -li -ness -nəs, -nɪs
calamit|y kəˈlæm.ə.t|i, -ɪ.t|i, (US) -ə.t̬|i -ies -iz **Caˌlamity ˈJane**
calamus ˈkæl.ə.məs
calash kəˈlæʃ -es -ɪz
calcareous kælˈkeə.ri.əs, (US) -ˈker.i-, -ˈkær- -ness -nəs, -nɪs
calceolaria ˌkæl.si.əˈleə.ri.ə, (US) -ˈler.i-, -ˈlær- -s -z
calces ˈkæl.siːz
Calchas ˈkæl.kæs
calciferol kælˈsɪf.ə.rɒl, (US) -roʊl, -rɑːl
calciferous kælˈsɪf.ər.əs
calcification ˌkæl.sɪ.fɪˈkeɪ.ʃən, -sə-, -fəˈ-
calcifug|e ˈkæl.sɪ.fjuːdʒ -es -ɪz
calcif|y ˈkæl.sɪ.f|aɪ, -sə- -ies -aɪz -ying -aɪ.ɪŋ -ied -aɪd
calcination ˌkæl.sɪˈneɪ.ʃən, -səˈ-
calcin|e ˈkæl.saɪn, -sɪn -es -z -ing -ɪŋ -ed -d
calcite ˈkæl.saɪt -s -s
calcium ˈkæl.si.əm
Calcot(t) ˈkɔːl.kət, ˈkɒl-, ˈkæl-, -kɒt, (US) ˈkɔːl.kɑːt, ˈkɑːl-, ˈkæl-

> Note: In Calcot Row, Berkshire, the pronunciation is /ˈkæl.kət/.

calculab|le ˈkæl.kjə.lə.b|əl, -kjʊ-, (US) -kjə- -ly -li
calcu|late ˈkæl.kjə|.leɪt, -kjʊ-, (US) -kjə- -lates -leɪts -lating -leɪ.tɪŋ, (US) -leɪ.t̬ɪŋ -lated -leɪ.tɪd, (US) -leɪ.t̬ɪd
calculation ˌkæl.kjəˈleɪ.ʃən, -kjʊˈ-, (US) -kjəˈ- -s -z
calculative ˈkæl.kjə.lə.tɪv, -kjʊ-, (US) -kjə.lə.t̬ɪv
calculator ˈkæl.kjə.leɪ.təʳ, -kjʊ-, (US) -kjə.leɪ.t̬ɚ -s -z
calcul|us ˈkæl.kjə.l|əs, -kjʊ-, (US) -kjə- -uses -ə.sɪz -i -aɪ
Calcutt ˈkæl.kʌt
Calcutta kælˈkʌt.ə, (US) -ˈkʌt̬-
Caldecote ˈkɔːl.dɪ.kət, ˈkɒl-, -də-, (US) ˈkɑːl.də.koʊt, ˈkɔːl-, -kət
Caldecott ˈkɔːl.də.kət, ˈkɒl-, -dɪ-, -kɒt, (US) ˈkɑːl.də.kɑːt, ˈkɔːl-, -kət
Calder ˈkɔːl.dəʳ, ˈkɒl-, (US) ˈkɔːl.dɚ, ˈkɑːl-
caldera kælˈdeə.rə, ˈkɔːl.də.rə, (US) kælˈder.ə
Calderon *English name:* ˈkɔːl.də.rən, ˈkɒl-, ˈkæl-, (US) ˈkɔːl.də.rɑːn, ˈkɑːl- *Spanish name:* ˌkæl.dəˈrɒn, -deɪˈ-, (US) ˌkɑːl.ðəˈrɔːn, -ðeɪˈ-
Caldicot(t) ˈkɔːl.dɪ.kɒt, ˈkɒl-, -də-, -kət, (US) ˈkɑːl.də.kɑːt, ˈkɔːl-, -kət
caldron ˈkɔːl.drən, ˈkɒl-, (US) ˈkɑːl-, ˈkɔːl- -s -z
Caldwell ˈkɔːld.wəl, ˈkɒld-, -wel, (US) ˈkɔːld-, ˈkɑːld-
Caleb ˈkeɪ.leb, -lɪb, -ləb
Caledon ˈkæl.ɪ.dən, ˈ-ə-
Caledoni|a ˌkæl.ɪˈdəʊ.ni|.ə, -əˈ-, (US) -ˈdoʊ- -an/s -ən/z
calefaction ˌkæl.ɪˈfæk.ʃən, -əˈ-
calefactor|y ˌkæl.ɪˈfæk.tər|.i, -əˈ-, -tr|i -ies -iz
calendar ˈkæl.ən.dəʳ, -ɪn-, (US) -dɚ -s -z
calend|er ˈkæl.ən.d|əʳ, -ɪn-, (US) -d|ɚ

-ers -əz, (US) -ɚz -ering -ər.ɪŋ -ered -əd, (US) -ɚd
calends ˈkæl.ɪndz, -endz, -əndz, (US) ˈkæl.ɪndz, ˈkeɪ.lɪndz, -lendz, -ləndz
calendula kəˈlen.dʒə.lə, ˈ-djə-, kælˈen-, -dʒʊ-, -djʊ-, (US) -dʒə- -s -z
calenture ˈkæl.ən.tʃʊəʳ, -ɪn-, -tjʊəʳ, -tʃəʳ, (US) -tʃɚ, -tʃʊr -s -z
cal|f kɑː|f, (US) kæ|f -ves -vz ˌ**calf's-foot ˈjelly**
calfskin ˈkɑːf.skɪn, (US) ˈkæf-
Calgary ˈkæl.gᵊr.i
Calhoun kælˈhuːn, -ˈhəʊn, kəˈhuːn, (US) kælˈhuːn, -ˈhoʊn, kəˈhuːn
Cali ˈkɑː.li
Caliban ˈkæl.ɪ.bæn, ˈ-ə-, -bən
caliber ˈkæl.ɪ.bəʳ, ˈ-ə-, (US) ˈkæl.ə.bɚ -s -z
Calibra® kəˈliː.brə
cali|brate ˈkæl.ɪ|.breɪt, ˈ-ə- -brates -breɪts -brating -breɪ.tɪŋ, (US) -breɪ.t̬ɪŋ -brated -breɪ.tɪd, (US) -breɪ.t̬ɪd
calibration ˌkæl.ɪˈbreɪ.ʃᵊn, -əˈ-
calibrator ˈkæl.ɪ.breɪ.təʳ, ˈ-ə-, (US) -t̬ɚ -s -z
calibre ˈkæl.ɪ.bəʳ, ˈ-ə-, (US) ˈkæl.ə.bɚ -s -z
calicle ˈkæl.ɪ.kᵊl -s -z
calico ˈkæl.ɪ.kəʊ, ˈ-ə-, (US) -koʊ -(e)s -z
Calicut ˈkæl.ɪ.kət, ˈ-ə-, -kʌt
calif ˈkeɪ.lɪf, ˈkæl.ɪf -s -s
Calif. (abbrev. for **California**) ˌkæl.ɪˈfɔː.ni.ə, -əˈ-, ˈ-njə, (US) -əˈfɔːr.njə, -ni.ə
Californi|a ˌkæl.ɪˈfɔː.ni|.ə, -əˈ-, ˈ-nj|ə, (US) ˌkæl.əˈfɔːr.nj|ə, -ni|.ə -an/s -ən/z
californium ˌkæl.ɪˈfɔː.ni.əm, -əˈ-, (US) -əˈfɔːr-
Caligula kəˈlɪg.jʊ.lə, -jə-
calipash ˈkæl.ɪ.pæʃ
calipee ˈkæl.ɪ.piː, ˌ--ˈ-
caliper ˈkæl.ɪ.pəʳ, (US) -ə.pɚ -s -z
caliph ˈkeɪ.lɪf, ˈkæl.ɪf -s -s
caliphate ˈkæl.ɪ.feɪt, ˈkeɪ.lɪ-, -fɪt, -fət, (US) ˈkeɪ.lɪ.fət, ˈkæl.ɪ.feɪt -s -s
calisthenic ˌkæl.ɪsˈθen.ɪk, -əsˈ-, (US) -əsˈ- -s -s
Calisto kəˈlɪs.təʊ, (US) -toʊ
cal|ix ˈkeɪ.l|ɪks, ˈkæl|.ɪks -ices -ɪs.iːz
calk kɔːk, (US) kɔːk, kɑːk -s -s -ing -ɪŋ -ed -t
calkin ˈkæl.kɪn, ˈkɔː-, (US) ˈkɔː-, ˈkɑː- -s -z
call kɔːl, (US) kɔːl, kɑːl -s -z -ing -ɪŋ -ed -d ˈ**call ˌgirl**
Callaghan ˈkæl.ə.hən, -hæn, -gən, (US) -hæn
Callahan ˈkæl.ə.hæn, -hən, (US) -hæn
Callan ˈkæl.ən
Callander ˈkæl.ən.dəʳ, (US) -dɚ
callanetics® ˌkæl.əˈnet.ɪks, (US) -ˈnet̬-
Callao kəˈjaʊ, (US) kəˈjɑː.oʊ
Callas ˈkæl.əs, -æs
callback ˈkɔːl.bæk, (US) ˈkɔːl-, ˈkɑːl-
callboy ˈkɔːl.bɔɪ, (US) ˈkɔːl-, ˈkɑːl- -s -z
Callcott ˈkɔːl.kət, ˈkɒl-, (US) ˈkɔːl.kɑːt, ˈkɑːl-
Callender ˈkæl.ɪn.dəʳ, -ən-, (US) -dɚ
caller ˈkɔː.ləʳ, (US) ˈkɔː.lɚ, ˈkɑː- -s -z
Caller ˈkæl.əʳ, (US) -ɚ
Callie *surname:* ˈkɔː.li, (US) ˈkɔː-, ˈkɑː- *girl's name:* ˈkæl.i
calligraphic ˌkæl.ɪˈgræf.ɪk, -əˈ- -al -ᵊl -ally -ᵊl.i, -li
calligraph|y kəˈlɪg.rə.f|i, kælˈɪg- -ist/s -ɪst/s -er/s -əʳ/z, (US) -ɚ/z
call-in ˈkɔːl.ɪn, (US) ˈkɑːl-, ˈkɔːl- -s -z
calling ˈkɔː.lɪŋ, (US) ˈkɔː-, ˈkɑː- -s -z ˈ**calling ˌcard**
Calliope kəˈlaɪ.ə.pi, kælˈaɪ.ə-
calliper ˈkæl.ɪ.pəʳ, (US) -ə.pɚ -s -z
callipygian ˌkæl.ɪˈpɪdʒ.i.ən, -əˈ-, (US) -əˈ-
callipygous ˌkæl.ɪˈpaɪ.gəs, -əˈ-, (US) -əˈ-
Callisthenes kælˈɪs.θə.niːz, kəˈlɪs-, (US) kəˈlɪs-
callisthenic ˌkæl.ɪsˈθen.ɪk -s -s
Callistratus kælˈɪs.trə.təs, kəˈlɪs-, (US) kəˈlɪs-
callosit|y kælˈɒs.ə.t|i, kəˈlɒs-, -ɪt|.i, (US) kəˈlɑː.sə.t̬|i -ies -iz
callous ˈkæl.əs -ly -li -ness -nəs, -nɪs -ed -t
callow, C~ ˈkæl.əʊ, (US) -oʊ -er -əʳ, (US) -ɚ -est -ɪst, -əst
Calloway ˈkæl.ə.weɪ
call-up ˈkɔːl.ʌp, (US) ˈkɔːl-, ˈkɑːl-
callus ˈkæl.əs -es -ɪz -ed -t
calm kɑːm, (US) kɑːlm -s -z -er -əʳ, (US) -ɚ -est -ɪst, -əst -ly -li -ness -nəs, -nɪs -ing -ɪŋ -ed -d
calmative ˈkæl.mə.tɪv, ˈkɑː.mə-, (US) ˈkɑː.mə.t̬ɪv, ˈkæl- -s -z
calmodulin kəlˈmɒd.jə.lɪn, kælˈ-, -jʊ-, (US) kælˈmɑː.dʒə-, -dʒʊ-
Calne kɑːn
calomel ˈkæl.əʊ.mel, (US) -ə.mel, -məl
calor ˈkæl.əʳ, (US) -ɚ ˈ**Calor ˌgas**
caloric kəˈlɒr.ɪk; ˈkæl.ᵊr-, (US) kəˈlɔːr-
calorie ˈkæl.ᵊr.i -s -z
calorific ˌkæl.əˈrɪf.ɪk, -ɔːˈ-, (US) -əˈ-
calorification kəˌlɒr.ɪ.fɪˈkeɪ.ʃᵊn, -fəˈ-; ˌkæl.ə.rɪ-, ˌkæl.ɔː-, ˌkæl.ɒr.ɪ-, (US) kəˌlɔːr.ɪ-, kælˌɔːr-
calorimeter ˌkæl.əˈrɪm.ɪ.təʳ, -ɔːˈ-, -ɒrˈɪm-, ˈ-ə-, (US) -əˈrɪm.ə.t̬ɚ -s -z
calorimetry ˌkæl.əˈrɪm.ə.tri, -ɔːˈ-, -ɒrˈɪm-, ˈ-ɪ-, (US) -əˈrɪm.ə-
calotte kəˈlɒt, (US) -lɑːt -s -s
Calpurnia ˌkælˈpɜː.ni.ə, (US) -ˈpɝː-
calque kælk -s -s
Calshot ˈkæl.ʃɒt, (US) -ʃɑːt
Calthorpe *district in Birmingham:* ˈkæl.θɔːp, (US) -θɔːrp *surname:* ˈkɔːl.θɔːp, ˈkɒl-, ˈkæl.θɔːp, (US) ˈkɔːl.θɔːrp, ˈkɑːl-, ˈkæl-
Calton *in Edinburgh:* ˈkɔːl.tᵊn, (US) ˈkɔːl-, ˈkɑːl- *in Glasgow:* ˈkɑːl.tᵊn
caltrop ˈkæl.trəp, -trɒp -s -s
calumet ˈkæl.jʊ.met, (US) ˈkæl.jə.met, -mɪt; (US) ˌkæl.jəˈmet -s -s
calumni|ate kəˈlʌm.ni|.eɪt -ates -eɪts -ating -eɪ.tɪŋ, (US) -eɪ.t̬ɪŋ -ated -eɪ.tɪd, (US) -eɪ.t̬ɪd -ator/s -eɪ.təʳ/z, (US) -eɪ.t̬ɚ/z
calumniation kəˌlʌm.niˈeɪ.ʃᵊn -s -z
calumn|y ˈkæl.əm.n|i -ies -iz
calvados, C~ ˈkæl.və.dɒs, (US) ˌkæl.vəˈdoʊs, ˌkɑːl-
calvar|y, C~ ˈkæl.vᵊr|.i -ies -iz
calv|e kɑːv, (US) kæv -es -z -ing -ɪŋ -ed -d
Calverley *surname:* ˈkæl.vᵊl.i, (US) -vɚ.li *place in West Yorkshire:* ˈkɑː.və.li, ˈkɔːv.li, (US) ˈkɑː.vɚ-, ˈkɔːv-
Calvert ˈkæl.vɜːt, -vət, ˈkɔːl.vət, (US) ˈkæl.vɝːt, -vɚt
Calverton ˈkæl.və.tᵊn, ˈkɔːl-, (US) ˈkæl.vɚ.t̬ən
calves'-foot ˈkɑːvz.fʊt, (US) ˈkævz-
Calvin ˈkæl.vɪn
Calvin|ism ˈkæl.vɪ.n|ɪ.zᵊm, -və- -ist/s -ɪst/s
Calvinistic ˌkæl.vɪˈnɪs.tɪk, -vəˈ- -al -ᵊl -ally -ᵊl.i, -li
ca|lx kæl|ks -ces -siːz -xes -k.sɪz
Calydon ˈkæl.ɪ.dᵊn, ˈ-ə-
calypso, C~ kəˈlɪp.səʊ, (US) -soʊ -(e)s -z
ca|lyx ˈkeɪ|.lɪks, ˈkæ|l.ɪks -lyces -lɪ.siːz -lyxes -lɪk.sɪz
calzone kælˈzəʊ.ni; *as if Italian:* kæltˈsəʊ.neɪ; (US) kælˈzoʊ.ni, -ˈzoʊn -s -z
cam, C~ kæm -s -z
CAm (abbrev. for **Central America**) ˌsen.trᵊl.əˈmer.ɪ.kə
CAM kæm
Camalodunum ˌkæm.ə.ləʊˈdjuː.nəm, (US) -loʊˈduː-, -ˈdjuː-
camaraderie ˌkæm.əˈrɑː.dᵊr.i, -ˈræd.ᵊr-, -iː, (US) ˌkæm.əˈrɑː.dɚ.i, ˌkɑː.məˈ-, -ˈræd.ɚ-
Camargue kæmˈɑːg, kəˈmɑːg, (US) kəˈmɑːrg
camarilla ˌkæm.əˈrɪl.ə -s -z
Camay® kæmˈeɪ
camber, C~ ˈkæm.bəʳ, (US) -bɚ -s -z
Camberley ˈkæm.bᵊl.i, (US) -bɚ.li
Camberwell ˈkæm.bə.wel, -wəl, (US) -bɚ-
cambial ˈkæm.bi.əl
cambium ˈkæm.bi.əm
Cambodi|a ˌkæmˈbəʊ.di|.ə, (US) -ˈboʊ- -an/s -ən
Camborne ˈkæm.bɔːn, -bən, (US) -bɔːrn
Cambray ˈkɑ̃ːm.breɪ, ˈkɒm-, (US) kɑːmˈbreɪ
Cambri|a ˈkæm.bri|.ə -an/s -ən/z
cambric ˈkæm.brɪk, ˈkeɪm-
Cambridge ˈkeɪm.brɪdʒ -shire -ʃəʳ, -ʃɪəʳ, (US) -ʃɚ, -ʃɪr
Cambs. (abbrev. for **Cambridgeshire**) kæmbz; ˈkeɪm.brɪdʒ.ʃəʳ, -ʃɪəʳ, (US) kæmbz; (US) ˈkeɪm.brɪdʒ.ʃɚ, -ʃɪr
Cambyses kæmˈbaɪ.siːz
camcorder ˈkæmˌkɔː.dəʳ, (US) -ˌkɔːr.dɚ -s -z
Camden ˈkæm.dən
came (from **come**) keɪm

C

C

camel ˈkæm.əl **-s** -z
Camelford ˈkæm.əl.fəd, (US) -fɚd
camelhair ˈkæm.əl.heəʳ, (US) -her
camel(l)ia, C~ kəˈmiː.li.ə, -ˈmel.i-, (US) -ˈmiː.li.ə, -ˈmiː.ljə **-s** -z
Camelot ˈkæm.ə.lɒt, ˈ-ɪ-, (US) -lɑːt
Camembert ˈkæm.əm.beəʳ, (US) -ber
cameo ˈkæm.i.əʊ, (US) -oʊ **-s** -z **ˈcameo ˌrole**
camera ˈkæm.rə, ˈkæm.ər.ə **-s** -z
cameral ˈkæm.ər.əl
camera|man ˈkæm.rə|.mæn, kæm.ər.ə-, -mən **-men** -men
camera obscura ˌkæm.ər.ə.əbˈskjʊə.rə, ˌkæm.rə-, -ɒbˈ-, (US) -əbˈskjʊr.ə
camera-shy ˈkæm.rə.ʃaɪ, ˈkæm.ər.ə-
camera|woman ˈkæm.rə|ˌwʊm.ən, -ər.ə-ˌ **-women** -ˌwɪm.ɪn
Camero kəˈmeə.rəʊ, (US) -ˈmer.oʊ
Cameron ˈkæm.ər.ən, ˈkæm.rən
Cameronian ˌkæm.ərˈəʊ.ni.ən, (US) -ˈoʊ- **-s** -z
Cameroon ˌkæm.əˈruːn, ˈ--- **-s** -z
camiknickers ˈkæm.iˌnɪk.əz, ˌkæm.iˈnɪk-, (US) ˈkæm.iˌnɪk.ɚz
Camilla kəˈmɪl.ə
Camille kəˈmiːl, -ˈmɪl
camis|e kəˈmiːz **-es** -ɪz
camisole ˈkæm.ɪ.səʊl, (US) -soʊl **-s** -z
Camlachie kæmˈlæk.i, -ˈlæx-
Cammell Laird ˌkæm.əlˈleəd, (US) -ˈlerd
camomile ˈkæm.əʊ.maɪl, (US) -ə.miːl
Camorra kəˈmɒr.ə, (US) -ˈmɔːr-
camouflag|e ˈkæm.ə.flɑːʒ, ˈ-ʊ-, (US) -flɑːdʒ **-es** -ɪz **-ing** -ɪŋ **-ed** -d
Camoys kəˈmɔɪz
camp, C~ kæmp **-s** -s **-ing** -ɪŋ **-ed** -t **-y** -i ˌ**camp ˈbed, ˈcamp ˌbed; ˌCamp ˈDavid; ˈcamp ˌfollower; ˈcamp ˌstool**
Campagna kæmˈpɑː.njə, (US) -njɑː, kəmˈpæn.jə
campaign kæmˈpeɪn **-s** -z **-ing** -ɪŋ **-ed** -d **-er/s** -əʳ/z, (US) -ɚ/z
campanile ˌkæm.pəˈniː.leɪ, (US) -leɪ, -li **-s** -z
campanolog|y ˌkæm.pəˈnɒl.ə.dʒ|i, (US) -ˈnɑː.lə- **-ist/s** -ɪst/s
campanula kəmˈpæn.jʊ.lə, kæm-, -jə- **-s** -z
Campari® kæmˈpɑː.ri, (US) -ˈpɑːr.i
Campbell ˈkæm.bəl **-s** -z
Campbellite ˈkæm.bəl.aɪt, (US) -bə.laɪt **-s** -s
Campbeltown ˈkæm.bəl.taʊn
Campden ˈkæmp.dən
Campeche kæmˈpiː.tʃi
camper ˈkæm.pəʳ, (US) -pɚ **-s** -z **ˈcamper ˌvan**
Camperdown ˈkæm.pə.daʊn, (US) -pɚ-
campfire ˈkæmp.faɪəʳ, -faɪ.əʳ, (US) -faɪ.ɚ **-s** -z
campground ˈkæmp.graʊnd **-s** -z
camphire ˈkæmp.faɪ.əʳ, (US) -faɪ.ɚ
camphor ˈkæmp.fəʳ, (US) -fɚ **-s** -z
camphor|ate ˈkæmp.fə.r|eɪt **-ates** -eɪts **-ating** -eɪ.tɪŋ, (US) -eɪ.t̬ɪŋ **-ated** -eɪ.tɪd, (US) -eɪ.t̬ɪd ˌ**camphorated ˈoil**
camphoric kæmˈfɒr.ɪk, (US) -ˈfɔːr-
camping ˈkæm.pɪŋ
campion, C~ ˈkæm.pi.ən **-s** -z
Camps kæmps
campsite ˈkæmp.saɪt **-s** -s
campus ˈkæm.pəs **-es** -ɪz
CAMRA ˈkæm.rə
camshaft ˈkæm.ʃɑːft, (US) -ʃæft **-s** -s
Camus kæmˈuː, (US) kæmˈuː, kɑːˈmuː, kə-
can n kæn **-s** -z **ˈcan ˌopener; (ˌopen a) ˌcan of ˈworms; ˌcarry the ˈcan**
can v *put in cans:* kæn **-s** -z **-ning** -ɪŋ **-ned** -d
can auxil. v *strong form:* kæn; *weak forms:* kən, kn̩, kŋ̍
Note: Weak-form word. The strong form /kæn/ is used for emphasis (e.g. 'You **can** do it'), and for contrast (e.g. 'I don't know if he can or he can't'). It is also used finally in a sentence (e.g. 'I don't know if I can'). The form /kŋ/ occurs only before words beginning with /k/ or /g/.
Cana ˈkeɪ.nə
Canaan ˈkeɪ.nən, -ni.ən; *Jewish pronunciation:* kəˈneɪ.ən
Canaanite ˈkeɪ.nə.naɪt, -ni.ə-; *Jewish pronunciation:* kəˈneɪ.ə.naɪt **-s** -s
Canada ˈkæn.ə.də
Canadian kəˈneɪ.di.ən **-s** -z
Canadiens kəˈneɪ.di.ənz, -ˌneɪ.diˈenz
canaille kəˈneɪəl, -naɪ, (US) kəˈneɪl
canal kəˈnæl **-s** -z
Canaletto ˌkæn.əlˈet.əʊ, (US) -əˈlet̬.oʊ
canalization, -isa- ˌkæn.əl.aɪˈzeɪ.ʃən, -ɪˈ-, (US) -əˈ-
canaliz|e, -is|e ˈkæn.əl.aɪz, (US) -ə.laɪz **-es** -ɪz **-ing** -ɪŋ **-ed** -d
Cananite ˈkæn.ə.naɪt, ˈkeɪ.nə- **-s** -s
canapé ˈkæn.ə.peɪ **-s** -z
canard ˈkæn.ɑːd, kəˈnɑːd, kænˈɑːd, (US) kəˈnɑːrd **-s** -z
canar|y, C~ kəˈneə.r|i, (US) -ˈner|.i **-ies** -iz **Caˈnary ˌIslands**
canasta kəˈnæs.tə
canaster kəˈnæs.təʳ, (US) -tɚ **-s** -z
Canaveral kəˈnæv.ər.əl
Canberra ˈkæn.bər.ə, ˈkæm-, (US) ˈkæn.ber-, -bɚ-
cancan ˈkæn.kæn, ˈkæŋ- **-s** -z
cancel ˈkænt.səl **-s** -z **-(l)ing** -ɪŋ **-(l)ed** -d
cancell|ate ˈkænt.səl|.eɪt, -sɪ.l|eɪt, (US) -sə.l|eɪt **-ates** -eɪts **-ating** -eɪ.tɪŋ, (US) -eɪ.t̬ɪŋ **-ated** -eɪ.tɪd, (US) -eɪ.t̬ɪd
cancellation ˌkænt.səlˈeɪ.ʃən, -sɪˈleɪ-, (US) -səˈleɪ- **-s** -z
cancellous ˈkænt.səl.əs
cancer, C~ ˈkænt.səʳ, (US) -sɚ **-s** -z
Cancerean, Cancerian kænˈsɪə.ri.ən, -ˈseə-, (US) -ˈser.i-, -ˈsɪr- **-s** -z
cancerous ˈkænt.sər.əs
cancroid ˈkæŋ.krɔɪd
Candace kænˈdeɪ.si, ˈkæn.dɪs, -dəs
candela kænˈdel.ə, -ˈdeɪ.lə, -ˈdiː- **-s** -z
candelabr|a ˌkæn.dəlˈɑː.br|ə, -dɪˈlɑː-, -ˈlæb.r|ə, (US) -dəˈlɑː.br|ə, -ˈlæb.r|ə **-as** -əz **-um** -əm
Canderel® ˌkæn.dərˈel, ˈ---
candescen|ce kænˈdes.ən|ts **-t** -t
Candia ˈkæn.di.ə
Candice ˈkæn.dɪs, -diːs
candid ˈkæn.dɪd **-ly** -li **-ness** -nəs, -nɪs
Candida ˈkæn.dɪ.də
candida|cy ˈkæn.dɪ.də|.si **-cies** -siz
candidate ˈkæn.dɪ.dət, -deɪt, -dɪt **-s** -s
candidature ˈkæn.dɪ.də.tʃəʳ, ˈ-də-, -deɪ-, -dɪtʃ.əʳ, (US) ˈkæn.də.də.tʃʊr, -tʃɚ **-s** -z
Candide kɑ̃ːnˈdiːd, (US) kɑːn-, kæn-
candidias|is ˌkæn.dɪˈdaɪ.ə.s|ɪs, -dəˈ- **-es** -iːz
candle ˈkæn.dəl **-s** -z ˌ**burn the ˌcandle at ˌboth ˈends**
candlelight ˈkæn.dəl.laɪt
candle-lit ˈkæn.dəl.lɪt ˌ**candle-lit ˈdinner**
Candlemas ˈkæn.dəl.məs, -mæs
candlepower ˈkæn.dəl.paʊ.əʳ, -paʊəʳ, (US) -paʊɚ **-s** -z
candlestick ˈkæn.dəl.stɪk **-s** -s
candlewick ˈkæn.dəl.wɪk
can-do ˌkænˈduː
cando(u)r ˈkæn.dəʳ, (US) -dɚ
cand|y, C~ ˈkæn.d|i **-ies** -iz **-ying** -i.ɪŋ **-ied** -id
candy-ass ˈkæn.di.æs, -ɑːs, (US) -æs
candyfloss ˈkæn.di.flɒs, (US) -flɑːs
candytuft ˈkæn.di.tʌft
can|e, C~ keɪn **-es** -z **-ed** -d **-ing** -ɪŋ ˌ**cane ˈsugar; ˈcane ˌsugar**
Canford ˈkæn.fəd, (US) -fɚd
Canham ˈkæn.əm
canicular kəˈnɪk.jə.ləʳ, kænˈɪk-, -jʊ-, (US) -jə.lɚ
canine ˈkeɪ.naɪn, ˈkæn.aɪn, (US) ˈkeɪ.naɪn **-s** -z
Canis ˈkeɪ.nɪs, ˈkæn.ɪs
canister ˈkæn.ɪ.stəʳ, (US) -ə.stɚ **-s** -z
cank|er ˈkæŋ.k|əʳ, (US) -k|ɚ **-ers** -əz, (US) -ɚz **-ering** -ər.ɪŋ **-ered** -əd, (US) -ɚd
cankerous ˈkæŋ.kər.əs
canna ˈkæn.ə **-s** -z
cannabis ˈkæn.ə.bɪs
Cannan ˈkæn.ən
cannelloni ˌkæn.əlˈəʊ.ni, -ɪˈləʊ-, (US) -əˈloʊ-
canner|y ˈkæn.ər|.i **-ies** -iz
Cannes kæn, kænz, (US) kæn, kænz, kɑːn ˌ**Cannes ˈFilm ˌFestival**
cannibal ˈkæn.ɪ.bəl, ˈ-ə- **-s** -z
cannibalism ˈkæn.ɪ.bəl.ɪ.zəm, ˈ-ə-
cannibalistic ˌkæn.ɪ.bəlˈɪs.tɪk, ˌ-ə-, (US) -bəˈlɪs-
cannibaliz|e, -is|e ˈkæn.ɪ.bəl.aɪz,

ˈ-ə-, (US) -bə.laɪz -es -ɪz -ing -ɪŋ -ed -d
cannikin ˈkæn.ɪ.kɪn, (US) ˈ-ə- -s -z
Canning ˈkæn.ɪŋ
Cannizzaro ˌkæn.ɪˈzɑː.rəʊ, -əˈ-, (US) -roʊ
Cannock ˈkæn.ək
cannon, C~ ˈkæn.ən -s -z -ing -ɪŋ -ed -d **ˈcannon ˌfodder**
cannonad|e ˌkæn.əˈneɪd -es -z -ing -ɪŋ -ed -ɪd
cannonball ˈkæn.ən.bɔːl, (US) -bɔːl, -bɑːl -s -z -ing -ɪŋ -ed -d
cannoneer ˌkæn.əˈnɪəʳ, (US) -ˈnɪr -s -z
cannonry ˈkæn.ən.ri
cannonshot ˈkæn.ən.ʃɒt, (US) -ʃɑːt -s -s
cannot ˈkæn.ɒt, -ət, (US) ˈkæn.ɑːt, kəˈnɑːt
Note: This word is usually contracted to /kɑːnt/ (US) /kænt/. See **can't**.
cannul|a ˈkæn.jə.l|ə, -jʊ-, (US) -jə- -ae -iː, -aɪ -as -əz
cann|y ˈkæn|.i -ier -i.əʳ, (US) -i.ɚ -iest -i.ɪst, -i.əst -ily -ᵊl.i, -ɪ.li -iness -ɪ.nəs, -ɪ.nɪs
canoe kəˈnuː -s -z -ing -ɪŋ -d -d
canoeist kəˈnuː.ɪst -s -s
canon ˈkæn.ən -s -z **ˌcanon ˈlaw**
Canonbury ˈkæn.ən.bᵊr.i, -əm-, (US) -ən.ber-, -bɚ-
canoness ˌkæn.əˈnes, ˈkæn.ə.nɪs, -nes, (US) ˈkæn.ə.nəs -es -ɪz
Canongate ˈkæn.ən.geɪt, -əŋ-
canonic kəˈnɒn.ɪk, kænˈɒn-, (US) kəˈnɑː.nɪk -al/s -ᵊl/z -ally -ᵊl.i, -li
canonization, -isa- ˌkæn.ə.naɪˈzeɪ.ʃᵊn, -nɪˈ-, (US) -nəˈ- -s -z
canoniz|e, -is|e ˈkæn.ə.naɪz -es -ɪz -ing -ɪŋ -ed -d
canonr|y ˈkæn.ən.r|i -ies -iz
canoodl|e kəˈnuː.dᵊl -es -z -ing -ɪŋ, -ˈnuːd.lɪŋ -ed -d
Canopus kəˈnəʊ.pəs, (US) -ˈnoʊ-
canop|y ˈkæn.ə.p|i -ies -iz
Canossa kəˈnɒs.ə, kænˈɒs-, (US) kəˈnɑː.sə
canst (from **can**) *strong form:* kænst; *weak form:* kənst
cant, C~ kænt -s -s -ing -ɪŋ -ed -ɪd -er/s -əʳ/z, (US) -ɚ/z
can't (= **can not**) kɑːnt, (US) kænt
Cantab. ˈkæn.tæb
cantabile kænˈtɑː.bɪ.leɪ, -bə-
Cantabria kænˈtæb.ri.ə, (US) -ˈteɪ.bri-
Cantabrian kænˈtæb.ri.ən, (US) -ˈteɪ.bri-
Cantabrigian ˌkæn.təˈbrɪdʒ.i.ən -s -z
cantaloup(e) ˈkæn.tə.luːp, (US) -t̬ə.loʊp -s -s
cantankerous ˌkænˈtæŋ.kᵊr.əs, kən- -ly -li -ness -nəs, -nɪs
cantata kænˈtɑː.tə, kən-, (US) kənˈtɑː.t̬ə -s -z
cantatrice ˌkæn.təˈtriːs; *as if French:* ˌkɑ̃ːn.tætˈriːs; (US) ˌkɑːn.təˈtriːs -s -ɪz
canteen kænˈtiːn -s -z *stress shift:* ˌ**canteen ˈfood**
cant|er, C~ ˈkæn.t|əʳ, (US) -t̬|ɚ -ers -əz, (US) -ɚz -ering -ᵊr.ɪŋ -ered -əd, (US) -ɚd
Canterbury ˈkæn.tə.bᵊr.i, -ber-, (US) -t̬ɚ.ber-, -bɚ- **ˌCanterbury ˈTales**
cantharides kænˈθær.ɪ.diːz, kənt-, (US) -ˈθer-, -ˈθær-
canticle ˈkæn.tɪ.kᵊl, (US) -t̬ə- -s -z
Canticles ˈkæn.tɪ.kᵊlz, (US) -t̬ə-
cantilena ˌkæn.tɪˈleɪn.ə, (US) -t̬əˈ-
cantilever ˈkæn.tɪ.liː.vəʳ, -tə-, (US) -t̬ə.liː.vɚ, -lev.ɚ -s -z
Cantire kænˈtaɪ.əʳ, (US) -ˈtaɪ.ɚ
Cantling ˈkænt.lɪŋ
canto ˈkæn.təʊ, (US) -toʊ -s -z
canton n *Swiss state:* ˈkæn.tɒn, ˌ-ˈ-, (US) ˈkæn.tɑːn, -tᵊn, kænˈtɑːn *in heraldry:* ˈkæn.tən -s -z
canton v *divide into portions or districts:* kænˈtɒn, (US) -ˈtɑːn -s -z -ing -ɪŋ -ed -d
Canton *in China:* ˌkænˈtɒn, (US) -ˈtɑːn *in Wales, surname, place in US:* ˈkæn.tən, (US) -tᵊn
Cantona ˈkæn.tə.nɑː
cantonal ˈkæn.tə.nᵊl, kænˈtəʊ.nᵊl, (US) ˈkæn.tə.nᵊl, kænˈtɑː.nəl
Cantonese ˌkæn.təˈniːz, -tɒnˈiːz, (US) -tᵊnˈiːz, -ˈiːs
cantor ˈkæn.tɔːʳ, (US) -tɚ, -tɔːr -s -z
cantoris kænˈtɔː.rɪs, (US) -ˈtɔːr.ɪs
cantus ˈkæn.təs, (US) -t̬əs
can't've (= can not have) ˈkɑːnt.ᵊv, (US) ˈkænt.ᵊv
Cantwell ˈkænt.wel
Canty ˈkæn.ti, (US) -t̬i
Canuck kəˈnʌk -s -s
Canute kəˈnjuːt, (US) -ˈnuːt, -ˈnjuːt
canvas ˈkæn.vəs -es -ɪz
canvasback ˈkæn.vəs.bæk -s -s
canvass ˈkæn.vəs -es -ɪz -ing -ɪŋ -ed -t -er/s -əʳ/z, (US) -ɚ/z
Canvey ˈkæn.vi
canyon ˈkæn.jən -s -z -ing -ɪŋ -ed -d
Canyonlands ˈkæn.jən.lændz
canzone kæntˈsəʊ.neɪ, kænˈzəʊ-, (US) kænˈzoʊ.ni, kɑːntˈsoʊ.neɪ -s -z
canzonet ˌkæn.zəʊˈnet, kænˈzəʊ- -s -s
caoutchouc ˈkaʊ.tʃʊk, -tʃuːk, -tʃuː, -ˈ-
cap kæp -s -s -ping -ɪŋ -ped -t
CAP ˌsiː.eɪˈpiː
capabilit|y ˌkeɪ.pəˈbɪl.ə.t|i, -ɪ.t|i, (US) -ə.t̬|i -ies -iz
capab|le ˈkeɪ.pə.b|ᵊl -ly -li -leness -ᵊl.nəs, -nɪs
capacious kəˈpeɪ.ʃəs -ly -li -ness -nəs, -nɪs
capacitance kəˈpæs.ɪ.tᵊnts, (US) ˈ-ə.t̬ənts
capaci|tate kəˈpæs.ɪ|.teɪt, (US) ˈ-ə- -tates -teɪts -tating -teɪ.tɪŋ, (US) -teɪ.t̬ɪŋ -tated -teɪ.tɪd, (US) -teɪ.t̬ɪd
capacitor kəˈpæs.ɪ.təʳ, ˈ-ə-, (US) -ə.t̬ɚ -s -z
capacit|y kəˈpæs.ə.t|i, -ɪ.t|i, (US) -ə.t̬|i -ies -iz
cap-à-pie ˌkæp.əˈpiː
caparison kəˈpær.ɪ.sᵊn, (US) -ˈper.ə-, -ˈpær- -s -z -ing -ɪŋ -ed -d
cape, C~ keɪp -s -s -d -t **ˌCape Caˈnaveral; ˌCape ˈCod; ˌCape ˈHorn; ˌCape of Good ˈHope; ˈCape ˌProvince; ˌcaped cruˈsader**
Capel *surname, places in Kent and Surrey:* ˈkeɪ.pᵊl *in Wales:* ˈkæp.ᵊl
Capel Curig ˌkæp.ᵊlˈkɪr.ɪg
Capell ˈkeɪ.pᵊl
capel(l)et ˈkæp.ə.let, -lɪt -s -s
Capello kəˈpel.əʊ, kæpˈel-, (US) -oʊ
caper *bird:* ˈkæp.əʳ, (US) -ɚ -s -z
cap|er ˈkeɪ.p|əʳ, (US) -p|ɚ -ers -əz, (US) -ɚz -ering -ᵊr.ɪŋ -ered -əd, (US) -ɚd -erer/s -ᵊr.əʳ/z, (US) -ɚ.ɚ/z
capercailzie, capercaillie ˌkæp.əˈkeɪ.li, -ˈkeɪ.lji, -ˈkeɪl.zi, (US) -ɚˈkeɪ.li, -ˈkeɪl.ji, -zi -s -z
Capernaum kəˈpɜː.ni.əm, (US) -ˈpɝː-
Cape Town, Capetown ˈkeɪp.taʊn
Cape Verde ˌkeɪpˈvɜːd, -ˈveəd, (US) -vɝːd
Capgrave ˈkæp.greɪv
capias ˈkeɪ.pi.æs, -pjæs, -pjəs, (US) ˈkeɪ.pi.əs -es -ɪz
capillarity ˌkæp.ɪˈlær.ə.ti, -əˈ-, -ɪ.ti, (US) -ˈler.ə.t̬i, -ˈlær-
capillary kəˈpɪl.ᵊr.i, (US) ˈkæp.ə.ler-
capital ˈkæp.ɪ.tᵊl, (US) -ə.t̬ᵊl -s -z -ly -i **ˌcapital ˈletter; ˌcapital ˈpunishment**
capitalism ˈkæp.ɪ.tᵊl.ɪ.zᵊm, kəˈpɪt.ᵊl-, kæpˈɪt-, (US) ˈkæp.ə.t̬ᵊl-
capitalist ˈkæp.ɪ.tᵊl.ɪst, kəˈpɪt.ᵊl-, kæpˈɪt-, (US) ˈkæp.ə.t̬ᵊl- -s -s
capitalistic ˌkæp.ɪ.tᵊlˈɪs.tɪk, (US) -ə.t̬əˈlɪs- -ally -ᵊl.i, -li
capitalization, -isa- ˌkæp.ɪ.tᵊl.aɪˈzeɪ.ʃᵊn, kæpˌɪt.ᵊl-, kəˌpɪt-, -ɪˈ-, (US) ˌkæp.ə.t̬ᵊl.əˈ- -s -z
capitaliz|e, -is|e ˈkæp.ɪ.tᵊl.aɪz, kæpˈɪt.ᵊl-, kəˈpɪt-, (US) ˈkæp.ə.t̬ə.laɪz -es -ɪz -ing -ɪŋ -ed -d
capitation ˌkæp.ɪˈteɪ.ʃᵊn, (US) -əˈ- -s -z
capitol, C~ ˈkæp.ɪ.tᵊl, (US) -ə.t̬ᵊl -s -z **ˌCapitol ˈHill**
capitoline, C~ kəˈpɪt.əʊ.laɪn, (US) ˈkæp.ə.t̬ə.laɪn, -liːn
capitular kəˈpɪtʃ.ə.ləʳ, -ˈpɪt.jə-, -ˈpɪtʃ.ʊ-, -ˈpɪt.jʊ-, (US) -ˈpɪtʃ.ᵊl.ɚ, ˈ-ʊ- -s -z
capitular|y kəˈpɪtʃ.ə.lə.r|i, -ˈpɪt.jʊ-, -ˈpɪtʃ.ʊ-, -ˈpɪt.jʊ-, ˈ-ə-, (US) -ˈpɪtʃ.ə.ler|.i, ˈ-ʊ- -ies -iz
capitu|late kəˈpɪtʃ.ə|.leɪt, -ˈpɪt.jə-, -ˈpɪtʃ.ʊ-, -ˈpɪt.jʊ-, (US) -ˈpɪtʃ.ə|.leɪt, ˈ-ʊ- -lates -leɪts -lating -leɪ.tɪŋ, (US) -leɪ.t̬ɪŋ -lated -leɪ.tɪd, (US) -leɪ.t̬ɪd
capitulation kəˌpɪtʃ.əˈleɪ.ʃᵊn, -ˌpɪt.jəˈ-, -ˌpɪtʃ.ʊˈ-, -ˌpɪt.jʊˈ-, (US) -ˌpɪtʃ.əˈ-, -ˌpɪt.jʊˈ- -s -z
capitul|um kəˈpɪtʃ.ə.l|əm, -ˈpɪt.jə-, -ˈpɪtʃ.ʊ-, ˈ-ˈpɪt.jʊ-, (US) -ˈpɪtʃ.ə- -a -ə
capo *for guitar:* ˈkæp.əʊ, ˈkeɪ.pəʊ, (US) ˈkeɪ.poʊ *criminal chieftain:* ˈkɑː.pəʊ, ˈkæp.əʊ, (US) ˈkɑː.poʊ, ˈkæp.oʊ -s -z

capoeira ˌkæp.əʊˈeɪ.rə, -uˈ-; kæpˈweɪ.rə, -ˈweər.ə, (US) ˌkɑː.poʊˈeɪ.rə, -ˈer.ə; (US) kɑːˈpweɪ.rə, -ˈer.ə
capon ˈkeɪ.pən, -pɒn, (US) -pɑːn, -pᵊn **-s** -z
Capone kəˈpəʊn, keɪ-, (US) kəˈpoʊn
capot kəˈpɒt, (US) -ˈpɑːt **-s** -s **-ting** -ɪŋ, (US) -ˈpɑː.t̬ɪŋ **-ted** -ɪd, (US) -ˈpɑː.t̬ɪd
capote kəˈpəʊt, (US) -ˈpoʊt **-s** -s
Capote kəˈpəʊ.ti, (US) -ˈpoʊ.t̬i
Cappadoci|a ˌkæp.əˈdəʊ.si|.ə, -ʃi|.ə, -ʃ|ə, (US) -ˈdoʊ.ʃ|ə **-an/s** -ən/z
Capper ˈkæp.əʳ, (US) -ɚ
cappuccino ˌkæp.ʊˈtʃiː.nəʊ, -əˈ-, (US) ˌkæp.əˈtʃiː.noʊ, ˌkɑː.pəˈ- **-s** -z
Capra ˈkæp.rə
Capri kæpˈriː, kəˈpriː
Capriati ˌkæp.riˈɑː.ti, (US) -ˈɑː.t̬i, ˌkɑːp-
capric ˈkæp.rɪk
capriccio kəˈprɪtʃ.i.əʊ, -ˈpriː.tʃi-, (US) -ˈpriː.tʃoʊ **-s** -z
capriccioso kəˌprɪtʃ.iˈəʊ.zəʊ, -ˌpriː.tʃiˈ-, -səʊ, (US) ˌkɑː.priːˈtʃoʊ.soʊ, -tʃiˈoʊ-; (US) kəˌpriː-
capric|e kəˈpriːs **-es** -ɪz
capricious kəˈprɪʃ.əs **-ly** -li **-ness** -nəs, -nɪs
Capricorn ˈkæp.rɪ.kɔːn, (US) -rə.kɔːrn
Capricornus ˌkæp.rɪˈkɔː.nəs, (US) -rəˈkɔːr-
capriol|e ˈkæp.ri.əʊl, (US) -oʊl **-es** -z **-ing** -ɪŋ **-ed** -d
capsicum ˈkæp.sɪ.kəm
capsiz|e kæpˈsaɪz, (US) ˈ--, -ˈ- **-es** -ɪz **-ing** -ɪŋ **-ed** -d
capstan ˈkæp.stən **-s** -z
capsular ˈkæp.sjʊ.ləʳ, -sjə-, (US) -sə.lɚ, -sjʊ-
capsule ˈkæp.sjuːl, (US) -sᵊl, -sjʊl **-s** -z
captain ˈkæp.tɪn, (US) -tᵊn **-s** -z **-ing** -ɪŋ **-ed** -d
captainc|y ˈkæp.tɪn.s|i, -tən- **-ies** -iz
caption ˈkæp.ʃᵊn **-s** -z **-ing** -ɪŋ **-ed** -d
captious ˈkæp.ʃəs **-ly** -li **-ness** -nəs, -nɪs
capti|vate ˈkæp.tɪ|.veɪt, (US) -tə- **-vates** -veɪts **-vating** -veɪ.tɪŋ, (US) -veɪ.t̬ɪŋ **-vated** -veɪ.tɪd, (US) -veɪ.t̬ɪd
captivation ˌkæp.tɪˈveɪ.ʃᵊn, (US) -təˈ-
captive ˈkæp.tɪv **-s** -z
captivit|y kæpˈtɪv.ə.t|i, -ɪ.t|i, (US) -ə.t̬|i **-ies** -iz
captor ˈkæp.təʳ, -tɔːʳ, (US) -tɚ, -tɔːr **-s** -z
capt|ure ˈkæp.tʃ|əʳ, (US) -tʃ|ɚ **-ures** -əz, (US) -ɚz **-uring** -ᵊr.ɪŋ **-ured** -əd, (US) -ɚd
Capua ˈkæp.ju.ə
capuch|e kəˈpuːʃ, -ˈpuːtʃ **-es** -ɪz
capuchin, C~ ˈkæp.jʊ.tʃɪn, -ʃɪn; kəˈpuː-, (US) ˈkæp.jʊ.tʃɪn, -jə-, -ʃɪn; (US) kəˈpjuː- **-s** -z
Capulet ˈkæp.jʊ.let, -jə-, -lət, -lɪt
capybara ˌkæp.ɪˈbɑː.rə, (US) -ˈbɑːr.ə **-s** -z
car kɑːʳ, (US) kɑːr **-s** -z ˈ**car aˌlarm**; ˈ**car ˌferry**; ˈ**car ˌpark**; ˈ**car ˌpool**; ˈ**car ˌport**; ˈ**car ˌwash**
Cara ˈkɑː.rə, (US) ˈker.ə, ˈkær-, ˈkɑːr-
carabineer ˌkær.ə.bɪˈnɪəʳ, (US) ˌker.ə.bɪˈnɪr, ˌkær- **-s** -z
carabiner ˌkær.əˈbiː.nəʳ, (US) ˌker.əˈbiː.nɚ, ˌkær- **-s** -z
carabinieri ˌkær.ə.bɪnˈjeə.ri, (US) ˌker.ə.bənˈjer.i, ˌkær-
caracal ˈkær.ə.kæl, (US) ˈker-, ˈkær- **-s** -z
Caracas kəˈræk.əs, -ˈrɑː.kəs, (US) -ˈrɑː.kəs
caracole ˈkær.ə.kəʊl, (US) ˈker.ə.koʊl, ˈkær- **-s** -z
Caractacus kəˈræk.tə.kəs
Caradoc kəˈræd.ək; ˈkær.ə.dɒk, (US) ˈker.ə.dɑːk, ˈkær-; (US) kəˈræd.ək
carafe kəˈræf, -ˈrɑːf **-s** -s
carambola ˌkær.əmˈbəʊ.lə, (US) ˌker.əmˈboʊ-, ˌkær- **-s** -z
caramel ˈkær.ə.mᵊl, -mel, (US) ˈkɑːr.mᵊl; (US) ˈker.ə-, ˈkær- **-s** -z
carameliz|e, -is|e ˈkær.ə.mᵊl.aɪz, -mel-, (US) ˈkɑːr.mə.laɪz, ˈker.ə-, ˈkær- **-es** -ɪz **-ing** -ɪŋ **-ed** -d
Caran d'Ache® ˌkær.ᵊnˈdæʃ, (US) ˌkɑːr.ɑːnˈdɑːʃ
carapac|e ˈkær.ə.peɪs, (US) ˈker-, ˈkær- **-es** -ɪz
carat ˈkær.ət, (US) ˈker-, ˈkær- **-s** -s
Caratacus kəˈræt.ə.kəs, (US) -ˈræt̬-
Caravaggio ˌkær.əˈvædʒ.i.əʊ, ˌkɑː.rəˈ-, -ˈvɑː.dʒi-, (US) ˌker.əˈvɑː.dʒi.oʊ, ˌkær-
caravan ˈkær.ə.væn, ˌ--ˈ-, (US) ˈker.ə.væn, ˈkær- **-s** -z **-ning** -ɪŋ
caravansar|y ˌkær.əˈvæn.sᵊr|.i, (US) ˌker-, ˌkær- **-ies** -iz
caravanserai ˌkær.əˈvæn.sᵊr.aɪ, -eɪ, -i, (US) ˌker-, ˌkær- **-s** -z
caravel ˈkær.ə.vel, ˌ--ˈ-, (US) ˈker.ə.vel, ˈkær- **-s** -z
caraway ˈkær.ə.weɪ, (US) ˈker-, ˈkær- **-s** -z ˈ**caraway ˌseed**
Carbery ˈkɑː.bᵊr.i, (US) ˈkɑːr.ber-, -bɚ-
carbide ˈkɑː.baɪd, (US) ˈkɑːr- **-s** -z
carbine ˈkɑː.baɪn, (US) ˈkɑːr.biːn, -baɪn **-s** -z
carbineer ˌkɑː.bɪˈnɪəʳ, -bəˈ-, (US) ˌkɑːr.bəˈnɪr **-s** -z
carbohydrate ˌkɑː.bəʊˈhaɪ.dreɪt, -drɪt, (US) ˌkɑːr.boʊˈhaɪ.dreɪt, -bəˈ- **-s** -s
carbolic kɑːˈbɒl.ɪk, (US) kɑːrˈbɑː.lɪk **carˌbolic ˈacid**
carbon ˈkɑː.bᵊn, (US) ˈkɑːr- **-s** -z **ˌcarbon ˈcopy** (US) ˈ**carbon ˌcopy**; **ˌcarbon diˈoxide**
carbonaceous ˌkɑː.bəʊˈneɪ.ʃəs, (US) ˌkɑːr.bəˈ-
carbonade ˌkɑː.bəˈneɪd, ˈ---, (US) ˌkɑːr.bəˈneɪd **-s** -z
carbonara ˌkɑː.bəˈnɑː.rə, (US) ˌkɑːr.bəˈnɑːr.ə
carbonate n ˈkɑː.bᵊn.eɪt, -ɪt, -ət, (US) ˈkɑːr- **-s** -s
carbon|ate v ˈkɑː.bᵊn|.eɪt, (US) ˈkɑːr- **-ates** -eɪts **-ating** -eɪ.tɪŋ, (US) -eɪ.t̬ɪŋ **-ated** -eɪ.tɪd, (US) -eɪ.t̬ɪd
carbon|-date ˌkɑː.bᵊn|ˈdeɪt, (US) ˌkɑːr- **-dates** -ˈdeɪts **-dating** -ˈdeɪ.tɪŋ, (US) -ˈdeɪ.t̬ɪŋ **-dated** -ˈdeɪ.tɪd, (US) -ˈdeɪ.t̬ɪd
carbonic kɑːˈbɒn.ɪk, (US) kɑːrˈbɑː.nɪk
carboniferous ˌkɑː.bəˈnɪf.ᵊr.əs, (US) ˌkɑːr-
carbonization, -isa- ˌkɑː.bᵊn.aɪˈzeɪ.ʃᵊn, -ɪˈ-, (US) ˌkɑːr.bᵊn.əˈ-
carboniz|e, -is|e ˈkɑː.bᵊn.aɪz, (US) ˈkɑːr- **-es** -ɪz **-ing** -ɪŋ **-ed** -d
carbonnade ˌkɑː.bᵊnˈeɪd, -ˈɑːd, ˈ---, (US) ˌkɑːr.bᵊnˈeɪd **-s** -z
carbonyl ˈkɑː.bə.nɪl, -naɪl, (US) ˈkɑːr-, -niːl **-s** -z
Carborundum® ˌkɑː.bᵊrˈʌn.dəm, (US) ˌkɑːr.bɚ-
carboxyl kɑːˈbɒk.sɪl, -saɪl, (US) kɑːrˈbɑːk.sᵊl
carboy ˈkɑː.bɔɪ, (US) ˈkɑːr- **-s** -z
carbuncle ˈkɑː.bʌŋ.kᵊl, (US) ˈkɑːr- **-s** -z
carburation ˌkɑː.bjəˈreɪ.ʃᵊn, -bjʊˈ-, (US) ˌkɑːr.bə-, -bjə-
carburetter, carbure(t)tor ˌkɑː.bjəˈret.əʳ, -bjʊˈ-, ˈkɑː.bjə.ret.ə, (US) ˈkɑːr.bə.reɪ.t̬ɚ, -bjə- **-s** -z
carburization, -isa- ˌkɑː.bjə.raɪˈzeɪ.ʃᵊn, -bjʊ-, -rɪˈ-, (US) ˌkɑːr.bɚ.əˈ-, -bjɚ-
carburiz|e, -is|e ˈkɑː.bjə.raɪz, -bjʊ-, (US) ˈkɑːr.bɚ-, -bjɚ- **-es** -ɪz **-ing** -ɪŋ **-ed** -d
carcanet ˈkɑː.kə.net, -nɪt, (US) ˈkɑːr- **-s** -s
carcas|e ˈkɑː.kəs, (US) ˈkɑːr- **-es** -ɪz
carcass ˈkɑː.kəs, (US) ˈkɑːr- **-es** -ɪz
Carcassonne ˌkɑː.kəˈsɒn, (US) ˌkɑːr.kəˈsoʊn, -ˈsɔːn
Carchemish ˈkɑː.kə.mɪʃ, -kɪ-; kɑːˈkiː-, (US) ˈkɑːr.kə-; (US) kɑːrˈkiː-
carcinogen kɑːˈsɪn.ə.dʒᵊn, -dʒen; ˈkɑː.sɪ.nə-, -sᵊn.ə-, (US) kɑːrˈsɪn.ə-; (US) ˈkɑːr.sᵊn.ə- **-s** -z
carcinogenic ˌkɑː.sɪ.nəʊˈdʒen.ɪk, -sᵊn.əʊˈ-, (US) ˌkɑːr.sᵊn.oʊˈ-; (US) kɑːrˌsɪn-
carcinom|a ˌkɑː.sɪˈnəʊ.m|ə, (US) ˌkɑːr.sᵊnˈoʊ- **-as** -əz **-ata** -ə.tə, (US) -ə.t̬ə
car-crash ˈkɑː.kræʃ, (US) ˈkɑːr-
Carcroft ˈkɑː.krɒft, (US) ˈkɑːr.krɑːft
card kɑːd, (US) kɑːrd **-s** -z **-ing** -ɪŋ **-ed** -ɪd ˈ**card ˌindex**; ˈ**card ˌkey**; **put one's ˌcards on the ˈtable**
cardamom, cardamum ˈkɑː.də.məm, (US) ˈkɑːr-, -mɑːm **-s** -z
cardboard ˈkɑːd.bɔːd, (US) ˈkɑːrd.bɔːrd
card-carrying ˈkɑːdˌkær.i.ɪŋ, (US) ˈkɑːrdˌker-, -ˌkær-
Cardenden ˌkɑː.dənˈden, ˈ---, (US) ˌkɑːr-
Cardew ˈkɑː.djuː, (US) ˈkɑːr.duː

cardholder ˈkɑːdˌhəʊl.dəʳ, US ˈkɑːrdˌhoʊl.dɚ -s -z
cardiac ˈkɑː.di.æk, US ˈkɑːr- ˌ**cardiac aˈrrest**
cardiacal kɑːˈdaɪ.ə.kəl, US kɑːr-
Cardiff ˈkɑː.dɪf, US ˈkɑːr-
cardigan ˈkɑː.dɪ.gən, US ˈkɑːr- -s -z
Cardigan ˈkɑː.dɪ.gən, US ˈkɑːr- -shire -ʃəʳ, -ʃɪəʳ, US -ʃɚ, -ʃɪr
Cardin ˈkɑː.dæ̃ŋ, -dæn, US kɑːrˈdæn
cardinal ˈkɑː.dɪ.nəl, -dən.əl, US ˈkɑːr- -s -z ˌ**cardinal ˈnumber; ˌcardinal ˈpoint; ˌcardinal ˈrule; ˌcardinal ˈvowel**
cardio- ˈkɑː.di.əʊ, ˌkɑː.diˈɒ, US ˈkɑːr.di.oʊ, ˈ-di.ə, ˌkɑːr.diˈɑː
Note: Prefix. Normally takes either primary or secondary stress on the first syllable, e.g. **cardiogram** /ˈkɑː.di.əʊ.græm/ US /ˈkɑːr.di.oʊ-/, **cardiovascular** /ˌkɑː.di.əʊˈvæs.kjə.ləʳ/ US /ˌkɑːr.di.oʊˈvæs.kjə.lɚ/, or primary stress on the third syllable, e.g. **cardiology** /ˌkɑː.diˈɒl.ə.dʒi/ US /ˌkɑːr.diˈɑː.lə-/.
cardiogram ˈkɑː.di.əʊ.græm, US ˈkɑːr.di.oʊ-, -di.ə- -s -z
cardiograph ˈkɑː.di.əʊ.grɑːf, -græf, US ˈkɑːr.di.oʊ.græf, -di.ə- -s -s
cardiography ˌkɑː.diˈɒg.rə.fi, US ˌkɑːr.diˈɑː.grə-
cardioid ˈkɑː.di.ɔɪd, US ˈkɑːr- -s -z
cardiological ˌkɑː.di.əʊˈlɒdʒ.ɪ.kəl, US ˌkɑːr.di.əˈlɑː.dʒɪ-
cardiolog|y ˌkɑː.diˈɒl.ə.dʒ|i, US ˌkɑːr.diˈɑː.lə- -ist/s -ɪst/s
cardiometer ˌkɑː.diˈɒm.ɪ.təʳ, -mə-, US ˌkɑːr.diˈɑː.mə.t̬ɚ -s -z
cardiopulmonary ˌkɑː.di.əʊˈpʌl.mən.ər.i, -ˈpʊl-, US ˌkɑːr.di.oʊˈpʊl.mə.ner-, -ˈpʌl-
cardiovascular ˌkɑː.di.əʊˈvæs.kjə.ləʳ, -kjʊ-, US ˌkɑːr.di.oʊˈvæs.kjə.lɚ, -əˈ-
cardoon kɑːˈduːn, US kɑːr- -s -z
cardphone ˈkɑːd.fəʊn, US ˈkɑːrd.foʊn -s -z
cardpunch ˈkɑːd.pʌntʃ, US ˈkɑːrd- -es -ɪz
cardsharp ˈkɑːd.ʃɑːp, US ˈkɑːrd.ʃɑːrp -s -z -er/s -əʳ/z, US -ɚ/z
Cardwell ˈkɑːd.wəl, -wel, US ˈkɑːrd-
card|y, card|ie ˈkɑː.d|i, US ˈkɑːr- -ies -iz
Cardy ˈkɑː.di, US ˈkɑːr-
car|e keəʳ, US ker -es -z -ing -ɪŋ -ed -d -er/s -əʳ/z, US -ɚ/z
careen kəˈriːn -s -z -ing -ɪŋ -ed -d
career kəˈrɪəʳ, US -ˈrɪr -s -z -ing -ɪŋ -ed -d **caˈreers adˌvisor; caˈreers ˌoffice**
careerist kəˈrɪə.rɪst, US -ˈrɪr.ɪst -s -s
carefree ˈkeə.friː, US ˈker-
careful ˈkeə.fəl, -fʊl, US ˈker- -lest -ɪst -ly -i -ness -nəs, -nɪs
caregiver ˈkeəˌgɪv.əʳ, US ˈkerˌgɪv.ɚ -s -z
careless ˈkeə.ləs, -lɪs, US ˈker- -ly -li -ness -nəs, -nɪs
caress kəˈres -es -ɪz -ing/ly -ɪŋ/li -ed -t
caret ˈkær.ət, -ɪt, -et, US ˈker-, ˈkær- -s -s
caretaker ˈkeəˌteɪ.kəʳ, US ˈkerˌteɪ.kɚ -s -z ˌ**caretaker ˈgovernment** US ˈ**caretaker ˌgovernment**
Carew kəˈruː; ˈkeə.ri, US kəˈruː; US ˈker.u, -i
careworn ˈkeə.wɔːn, US ˈker.wɔːrn
Carey ˈkeə.ri, US ˈker.i, ˈkær-
carfare ˈkɑː.feəʳ, US ˈkɑːr.fer -s -z
Carfax ˈkɑː.fæks, US ˈkɑːr-
Cargill ˈkɑː.gɪl, -ˈ-, US ˈkɑːr.gɪl, -ˈ-
cargo ˈkɑː.gəʊ, US ˈkɑːr.goʊ -(e)s -z
carhop ˈkɑː.hɒp, US ˈkɑːr.hɑːp -s -s
Caria ˈkeə.ri.ə, US ˈker.i-
Carib ˈkær.ɪb, US ˈker-, ˈkær- -s -z
Caribbean ˌkær.ɪˈbiː.ən, -ə-; kəˈrɪb.i.ən, US ˌker.ɪˈbiː-, ˌkær-; US kəˈrɪb.i-
Caribbees ˈkær.ɪ.biːz, US ˈker-, ˈkær-
caribou, C~ ˈkær.ɪ.buː, US ˈker-, ˈkær- -s -z
caricatur|e ˈkær.ɪ.kə.tʃʊəʳ, -tʃɔːʳ, -tjʊəʳ, -tjɔːʳ; ˌkær.ɪ.kəˈtʃʊəʳ, -ˈtʃɔːʳ, -ˈtjʊəʳ, US ˈker.ə.kə.tʃʊr, ˈkær-, -tʊr, -tʃɚ -es -z -ing -ɪŋ -ed -d
caricaturist ˈkær.ɪ.kə.tʃʊə.rɪst, -tʃɔː-, -tjʊə-, -tjɔː-; ˌkær.ɪ.kəˈtʃʊə.rɪst, -ˈtʃɔː-, -ˈtjʊə-, US ˈker.ə.kə.tʃʊr.ɪst, ˈkær-, -tʊr-, -tʃɚ- -s -s
caries ˈkeə.riːz, -ri.iːz, US ˈker.iːz, -i.iːz
carillon kærˈɪl.jən, kəˈrɪl-, -ɒn; ˈkær.ɪ.ljən, -əl.jən, -ɒn, US ˈker.ə.lɑːn, ˈkær- -s -z
Carinthia kəˈrɪnt.θi.ə, kærˈɪnt-, US kəˈrɪnt-
carious ˈkeə.ri.əs, US ˈker.i-
Carisbrooke ˈkær.ɪs.brʊk, -ɪz-, US ˈker-, ˈkær-
carjack ˈkɑː.dʒæk, US ˈkɑːr- -s -s -ing/s -ɪŋ/z -ed -t -er/s -əz, US -ɚz
Carl kɑːl, US kɑːrl
Carla ˈkɑː.lə, US ˈkɑːr-
Carle kɑːl, US kɑːrl -s -z
Carless ˈkɑː.ləs, US ˈkɑːr-
Carleton ˈkɑːl.tən, US ˈkɑːrl-
Carlile kɑːˈlaɪl, US kɑːr-
Carlin ˈkɑː.lɪn, US ˈkɑːr-
Carling ˈkɑː.lɪŋ, US ˈkɑːr-
Carlingford ˈkɑː.lɪŋ.fəd, US ˈkɑːr.lɪŋ.fɚd
Carlisle kɑːˈlaɪl; *locally:* ˈ--, US kɑːrˈlaɪl, kɚˈ-; US ˈkɑːr.laɪl
Carlist ˈkɑː.lɪst, US ˈkɑːr- -s -s
Carlos ˈkɑː.lɒs, US ˈkɑːr.ləs, -loʊs
Carlovingian ˌkɑː.ləʊˈvɪn.dʒi.ən, -dʒən, US ˌkɑːr.ləˈ-
Carlow ˈkɑː.ləʊ, US ˈkɑːr.loʊ
Carlsbad ˈkɑːlz.bæd, US ˈkɑːrlz-
Carlsberg® ˈkɑːlz.bɜːg, US ˈkɑːrlz.bɝːg -s -z
Carlson ˈkɑːl.sən, US ˈkɑːrl-
Carlsruhe ˈkɑːlzˌruː.ə, US ˈkɑːrlz-
Carlton ˈkɑːl.tən, US ˈkɑːrl-
Carluccio kɑːˈluː.tʃi.əʊ, US kɑːrˈluː.tʃi.oʊ
Carluke kɑːˈluːk, US kɑːr-
Carly ˈkɑː.li, US ˈkɑːr-
Carlyle kɑːˈlaɪl, ˈ--, US kɑːrˈlaɪl, ˈ--
carmaker ˈkɑːˌmeɪ.kəʳ, US ˈkɑːrˌmeɪ.kɚ -s -z
car|man ˈkɑː|.mən, US ˈkɑːr- -men -mən, -men
Carmarthen kəˈmɑː.ðən, US kɑːrˈmɑːr- -shire -ʃəʳ, -ʃɪəʳ, US -ʃɚ, -ʃɪr
Carmel ˈkɑː.mel, -məl, kɑːˈmel, US ˈkɑːr.mel, -məl; US kɑːrˈmel

> Note: The form /kɑːˈmel/ US /kɑːr-/ is preferred for the city in California.

Carmelite ˈkɑː.məl.aɪt, -mɪ.laɪt, -mel.aɪt, US ˈkɑːr.mə.laɪt, -mɪ-, -mel.aɪt -s -s
Carmen ˈkɑː.men, -mən, US ˈkɑːr-
Carmichael kɑːˈmaɪ.kəl, ˈ---, US ˈkɑːr.maɪ-
Carmina Burana ˌkɑː.mɪ.nə.bəˈrɑː.nə, kɑːˌmiː-, -bjʊˈ-, -bʊˈ-, US kɑːrˌmiː.nə.bəˈ-
carminative ˈkɑː.mɪ.nə.tɪv, -mə-, US ˈkɑːr.mə.nə.t̬ɪv -s -z
carmine ˈkɑː.maɪn, -mɪn, US ˈkɑːr-
Carnaby ˈkɑː.nə.bi, US ˈkɑːr- ˈ**Carnaby ˌStreet**
Carnac ˈkɑː.næk, US kɑːrˈnæk
carnage ˈkɑː.nɪdʒ, US ˈkɑːr-
Carnaghan ˈkɑː.nə.gən, -hən, US ˈkɑːr.nə.hæn
carnal ˈkɑː.nəl, US ˈkɑːr- -ly -i
carnality kɑːˈnæl.ə.ti, -ɪ.ti, US kɑːrˈnæl.ə.t̬i
Carnarvon kəˈnɑː.vən, US kɑːrˈnɑːr-
Carnatic kɑːˈnæt.ɪk, US kɑːrˈnæt̬-
carnation, C~ kɑːˈneɪ.ʃən, US kɑːr- -s -z
Carné kɑːˈneɪ, US kɑːr-
Carnegie kɑːˈneg.i, -ˈneɪ.gi, -ˈniː-; ˈkɑː.nə.gi, US ˈkɑːr.nə.gi; US kɑːrˈneɪ-, -ˈneg.i, -ˈniː.gi **Carˌnegie ˈHall**
carnelian kɑːˈniː.li.ən, kə-, US kɑːr-, -ˈniːl.jən -s -z
carnet ˈkɑː.neɪ, US kɑːrˈneɪ -s -z
Carney ˈkɑː.ni, US ˈkɑːr-
Carnforth ˈkɑːn.fɔːθ, -fəθ, US ˈkɑːrn.fɔːrθ, -fɚθ
carnival ˈkɑː.nɪ.vəl, US ˈkɑːr.nə- -s -z
carnivore ˈkɑː.nɪ.vɔːʳ, -nə-, US ˈkɑːr.nə.vɔːr -s -z
carnivorous kɑːˈnɪv.ər.əs, US kɑːr-
Carnochan ˈkɑː.nə.kən, -nɒk.ən, -nɒx-, US ˈkɑːr.nə.kən, -nɑː.kən
Carnoustie kɑːˈnuː.sti, US kɑːr-
carob ˈkær.əb, US ˈker-, ˈkær- -s -z
carol, C~ ˈkær.əl, US ˈker-, ˈkær- -s -z -(l)ing -ɪŋ -(l)ed -d ˈ**carol ˌsinger**

C

Carole ˈkær.ᵊl, (US) ˈker-, ˈkær-
Carolina ˌkær.ᵊlˈaɪ.nə, (US) ˌker.əˈlaɪ-, ˌkær-
Caroline ˈkær.ᵊl.aɪn, -ɪn, (US) ˈker.ə.laɪn, ˈkær-, -ᵊl.ɪn
carolus, C~ ˈkær.ᵊl.əs, (US) ˈker-, ˈkær- **-es** -ɪz
Carolyn ˈkær.ᵊl.ɪn, (US) ˈker-, ˈkær-
carotene ˈkær.ə.tiːn, (US) ˈker-, ˈkær-
carotid kəˈrɒt.ɪd, (US) -ˈrɑː.t̬ɪd **-s** -z
carotin ˈkær.ə.tɪn, (US) ˈker-, ˈkær-
carousal kəˈraʊ.zᵊl **-s** -z
carous|e kəˈraʊz **-es** -ɪz **-ing** -ɪŋ **-ed** -d **-er/s** -əʳ/z, (US) -ɚ/z
carousel ˌkær.əˈsel, -ʊˈ-, (US) ˈker.ə.sel, ˈkær-, ˌ--ˈ- **-s** -z
carp kɑːp, (US) kɑːrp **-s** -s **-ing** -ɪŋ **-ed** -t **-er/s** -əʳ/z, (US) -ɚ/z
carpaccio kɑːˈpætʃ.i.əʊ, -ˈpætʃ.əʊ, (US) kɑːrˈpɑː.tʃ.oʊ
carpal ˈkɑː.pᵊl, (US) ˈkɑːr- **-s** -z
Carpathian kɑːˈpeɪ.θi.ən, (US) kɑːr- **-s** -z
carpe diem ˌkɑː.peɪˈdiː.em, -piˈ-, (US) ˌkɑːr.peɪˈ-, -piˈ-
carpel ˈkɑː.pᵊl, -pel, (US) ˈkɑːr- **-s** -z
Carpentaria ˌkɑː.pᵊnˈteə.ri.ə, -penˈ-, -pᵊmˈ-, (US) ˌkɑːr.pᵊnˈter.i-
carpent|er, C~ ˈkɑː.pᵊn.t|əʳ, -pɪn-, (US) ˈkɑːr.pᵊn.t̬|ɚ **-ers** -əz, (US) -ɚz **-ering** -ᵊr.ɪŋ **-ered** -əd, (US) -ɚd
carpentry ˈkɑː.pᵊn.tri, -pɪn-, (US) ˈkɑːr.pᵊn-
carp|et ˈkɑː.p|ɪt, (US) ˈkɑːr.p|ət **-ets** -ɪts, (US) -əts **-eting** -ɪ.tɪŋ, (US) -ə.t̬ɪŋ **-eted** -ɪ.tɪd, (US) -ə.t̬ɪd **ˈcarpet ˌbroom; ˈcarpet ˌslipper; ˈcarpet ˌsweeper**
carpetbag ˈkɑː.pɪt.bæg, (US) ˈkɑːr.pət- **-s** -z **-ging** -ɪŋ
carpetbagger ˈkɑː.pɪtˌbæg.əʳ, (US) ˈkɑːr.pətˌbæg.ɚ **-s** -z
carpet-bomb ˈkɑː.pɪt.bɒm, (US) ˈkɑːr.pət.bɑːm **-s** -z **-ing** -ɪŋ **-ed** -d
carport ˈkɑː.pɔːt, (US) ˈkɑːr.pɔːrt **-s** -s
carp|us ˈkɑː.p|əs, (US) ˈkɑːr- **-i** -aɪ, -iː
Carr kɑːʳ, (US) kɑːr
carrag(h)een ˈkær.ə.giːn, –ˈ-, (US) ˈker.ə.giːn, ˈkær-
Carrara kəˈrɑː.rə, (US) kəˈrɑːr.ə
Carrauntoohill ˌkær.ənˈtuː.hᵊl, (US) ˌker-, ˌkær-
carraway ˈkær.ə.weɪ, (US) ˈker-, ˈkær- **-s** -z
Carrhae ˈkær.iː, (US) ˈker-, ˈkær-
carriag|e ˈkær.ɪdʒ, (US) ˈker-, ˈkær- **-es** -ɪz **ˈcarriage ˌclock**
carriageway ˈkær.ɪdʒ.weɪ, (US) ˈker-, ˈkær- **-s** -z
carrick, C~ ˈkær.ɪk, (US) ˈker-, ˈkær-
Carrickfergus ˌkær.ɪkˈfɜː.gəs, (US) ˌker.ɪkˈfɝː-, ˌkær-
Carrie ˈkær.i, (US) ˈker-, ˈkær-
carrier ˈkær.i.əʳ, (US) ˈker.i.ɚ, ˈkær- **-s** -z **ˈcarrier ˌbag; ˈcarrier ˌpigeon**
Carrington ˈkær.ɪŋ.tən, (US) ˈker-, ˈkær-
carrion ˈkær.i.ən, (US) ˈker-, ˈkær- **ˌcarrion ˈcrow** (US) **ˈcarrion ˌcrow**
Carroll ˈkær.ᵊl, (US) ˈker-, ˈkær-
Carron ˈkær.ᵊn, (US) ˈker-, ˈkær-
carrot ˈkær.ət, (US) ˈker-, ˈkær- **-s** -s
carroty ˈkær.ə.ti, (US) ˈker.ə.t̬i, ˈkær-
carrousel ˌkær.əˈsel, -ʊˈ-, (US) ˌker.əˈsel, ˌkær-, ˈ--- **-s** -z
Carruthers kəˈrʌð.əz, (US) -ɚz
carr|y ˈkær|.i, (US) ˈker-, ˈkær- **-ies** -iz **-ying** -i.ɪŋ **-ied** -id **-ier/s** -i.əʳ/z, (US) -i.ɚ/z
carryall ˈkær.i.ɔːl, (US) ˈker.i.ɔːl, ˈkær-, -ɑːl **-s** -z
carrycot ˈkær.i.kɒt, (US) ˈker.i.kɑːt, ˈkær- **-s** -s
carryings-on ˌkær.i.ɪŋzˈɒn, (US) ˌker.i.ɪŋzˈɑːn, ˌkær-
carry-on ˈkær.i.ɒn, (US) ˈker.i.ɑːn, ˈkær- **-s** -z
carryout ˈkær.i.aʊt, (US) ˈker-, ˈkær- **-s** -s
Carse kɑːs, (US) kɑːrs
Carshalton kɑːˈʃɔːl.tᵊn, kəˈ-; *old-fashioned local pronunciation:* keɪsˈhɔː.tᵊn, (US) kɑːrˈʃɔːl-, kɚ-, -ˈʃɑːl-
carsick ˈkɑː.sɪk, (US) ˈkɑːr- **-ness** -nəs, -nɪs
Carson ˈkɑː.sᵊn, (US) ˈkɑːr-
Carstairs ˈkɑː.steəz, ˌ-ˈ-, (US) ˈkɑːr.sterz
cart, C~ kɑːt, (US) kɑːrt **-s** -s **-ing** -ɪŋ, (US) ˈkɑːr.t̬ɪŋ **-ed** -ɪd, (US) ˈkɑːr.t̬ɪd **-er/s** -əʳ/z, (US) ˈkɑːr.t̬ɚ/z **put the ˌcart before the ˈhorse**
Carta ˈkɑː.tə, (US) ˈkɑːr.t̬ə
cartage ˈkɑː.tɪdʒ, (US) ˈkɑːr.t̬ɪdʒ
Cartagena ˌkɑː.təˈgeɪ.nə, (US) ˌkɑːr.t̬əˈdʒiː.nə, -ˈheɪ-, -ˈgeɪ-
carte, C~ kɑːt, (US) kɑːrt
carte blanche ˌkɑːtˈblɑ̃ːntʃ, (US) ˌkɑːrtˈblɑːnʃ, -ˈblæntʃ
cartel kɑːˈtel, (US) kɑːr- **-s** -z
Carter ˈkɑː.təʳ, (US) ˈkɑːr.t̬ɚ
Carteret *surname:* ˈkɑː.tə.ret, -rɪt, (US) ˈkɑːr.t̬ɚ.ɪt *US place name:* ˌkɑː.təˈret, (US) ˌkɑːr.t̬əˈ-
Cartesian kɑːˈtiː.zi.ən, -ʒᵊn, (US) kɑːrˈtiː.ʒᵊn **-ism** -ɪ.zᵊm
Carthage ˈkɑː.θɪdʒ, (US) ˈkɑːr-
Carthaginian ˌkɑː.θəˈdʒɪn.i.ən, (US) ˌkɑːr- **-s** -z
cart-hors|e ˈkɑːt.hɔːs, (US) ˈkɑːrt.hɔːrs **-es** -ɪz
Carthusian kɑːˈθjuː.zi.ən, -ˈθuː-, (US) kɑːrˈθuː.ʒᵊn, -ˈθjuː- **-s** -z
Cartier ˈkɑː.ti.eɪ, (US) ˌkɑːr.tiˈeɪ; (US) kɑːrˈtjeɪ
Cartier-Bresson ˌkɑː.ti.eɪˈbres.ɔ̃ːn, (US) ˌkɑːr.tjeɪ.breɪˈsõʊn, -bresˈõʊn
cartilag|e ˈkɑː.tɪ.lɪdʒ, -tᵊl.ɪdʒ, (US) ˈkɑːr.t̬ᵊl.ɪdʒ **-es** -ɪz
cartilaginous ˌkɑː.tɪˈlædʒ.ɪ.nəs, -tᵊlˈædʒ-, -ᵊn.əs, (US) ˌkɑːr.təˈlædʒ.ᵊn.əs
carting ˈkɑː.tɪŋ, (US) ˈkɑːr.t̬ɪŋ
Cartland ˈkɑːt.lənd, (US) ˈkɑːrt-
cartload ˈkɑːt.ləʊd, (US) ˈkɑːrt.loʊd **-s** -z
Cartmel(e) ˈkɑːt.mel, -mᵊl, (US) ˈkɑːrt-
cartographic ˌkɑː.təʊˈgræf.ɪk, (US) ˌkɑːr.t̬əˈ- **-ally** -ᵊl.i, -li
cartograph|y kɑːˈtɒg.rə.f|i, (US) kɑːrˈtɑː.grə- **-er/s** -əʳ/z, (US) -ɚ/z
cartomancy ˈkɑː.təʊ.mænt.si, (US) ˈkɑːr.t̬ə-
carton ˈkɑː.tᵊn, (US) ˈkɑːr- **-s** -z
cartoon kɑːˈtuːn, (US) kɑːr- **-s** -z **-ist/s** -ɪst/s
cartouch|e, cartouch kɑːˈtuːʃ, (US) kɑːr- **-es** -ɪz
cartridg|e ˈkɑː.trɪdʒ, (US) ˈkɑːr- **-es** -ɪz **ˈcartridge ˌpaper**
cartwheel ˈkɑːt.hwiːl, (US) ˈkɑːrt- **-s** -z **-ing** -ɪŋ **-ed** -d
cartwright, C~ ˈkɑːt.raɪt, (US) ˈkɑːrt- **-s** -s
caruncle ˈkær.əŋ.kᵊl; kəˈrʌŋ-, (US) kəˈrʌŋ-, kerˈʌŋ-, kær- **-s** -z
Carus ˈkeə.rəs, (US) ˈker.əs, ˈkɑːr-
Caruso kəˈruː.zəʊ, -səʊ, (US) -soʊ, -zoʊ
Caruthers kəˈrʌð.əz, (US) -ɚz
carv|e kɑːv, (US) kɑːrv **-es** -z **-ing/s** -ɪŋ/z **-ed** -d **ˈcarving ˌknife**
carver, C~ ˈkɑː.vəʳ, (US) ˈkɑːr.vɚ **-s** -z
carver|y ˈkɑː.vᵊr|.i, (US) ˈkɑːr- **-ies** -iz
Carville ˈkɑː.vɪl, (US) ˈkɑːr-
Carwardine ˈkɑː.wə.diːn, (US) ˈkɑːr.wɚ-
carwash ˈkɑː.wɒʃ, (US) ˈkɑːr.wɑːʃ, -wɔːʃ **-es** -ɪz
Cary *surname:* ˈkeə.ri, (US) ˈker.i *first name:* ˈkær.i, (US) ˈker.i, ˈkær-
caryatid ˌkær.iˈæt.ɪd, ˈkær.i.ə.tɪd, (US) ˌker.iˈæt̬.ɪd, ˌkær-; (US) kəˈraɪ.ə.t̬ɪd **-s** -z **-es** -iːz
Caryll ˈkær.ɪl, -ᵊl, (US) ˈker-, ˈkær-
Carysfort ˈkær.ɪs.fɔːt, -əs-, (US) ˈker.ɪs.fɔːrt, ˈkær-
Casablanca ˌkæs.əˈblæŋ.kə, (US) ˌkæs.əˈblæŋ.kə, ˌkɑː.səˈblɑːŋ.kə
Casals kəˈsæls, (US) -ˈsɑːlz, -ˈsælz
Casamassima ˌkæs.əˈmæs.ɪ.mə
Casanova ˌkæs.əˈnəʊ.və, ˌkæz-, (US) ˌkæs.əˈnoʊ-, ˌkæz-
Casaubon kəˈsɔː.bᵊn; ˈkæz.ə.bɒn, -ɔː-, (US) kəˈsɑː.bᵊn, -ˈsɔː-; (US) ˈkæz.ə.bɑːn
casbah, C~ ˈkæz.bɑː, (US) ˈkæz.bɑː, ˈkɑːz- **-s** -z
cascad|e kæsˈkeɪd **-es** -z **-ing** -ɪŋ **-ed** -ɪd
cascara kæsˈkɑː.rə, kəˈskɑː-, (US) kæsˈker.ə, -ˈkær- **-s** -z
cascarilla ˌkæs.kəˈrɪl.ə
cas|e, C~ keɪs **-es** -ɪz **-ing** -ɪŋ **-ed** -t **ˈcase ˌending; ˌcase ˈhistory; ˈcase ˌknife; ˈcase ˌlaw; ˈcase ˌshot; ˈcase ˌstudy**
casebook ˈkeɪs.bʊk **-s** -s
casein ˈkeɪ.siːn, -siː.ɪn, (US) -siː.ɪn, -siːn
caseload ˈkeɪs.ləʊd, (US) -loʊd **-s** -z
casemate ˈkeɪs.meɪt **-s** -s
casement ˈkeɪs.mənt **-s** -s
Casement ˈkeɪs.mənt
casern kəˈzɜːn, (US) -ˈzɝːn **-s** -z
casework ˈkeɪs.wɜːk, (US) -wɝːk **-er/s** -əʳ/z, (US) -ɚ/z
Casey ˈkeɪ.si
cash, C~ kæʃ **-es** -ɪz **-ing** -ɪŋ **-ed** -t **-less** -ləs, -lɪs **ˈcash ˌcrop; ˈcash**

ˌdesk; ˈcash disˌpenser; ˈcash ˌflow; ˈcash maˌchine; ˈcash ˌregister
cash-and-carry ˌkæʃ.ənd'kær.i, -əŋˈ-, (US) -ənd'ker-, -ˈkær-
cashback ˈkæʃ.bæk
cashbook ˈkæʃ.bʊk -s -s
cashbox ˈkæʃ.bɒks, (US) -bɑːks -es -ɪz
cashew ˈkæʃ.uː; -ˈ-, kəˈʃuː, (US) ˈkæʃ.uː; (US) kəˈʃuː -s -z ˈcashew ˌnut; caˈshew ˌnut (US) caˈshew ˌnut
cashier n kæʃˈɪəʳ, kəˈʃɪəʳ, (US) kæʃˈɪr -s -z
cashier v kəˈʃɪəʳ, kæʃˈɪəʳ, (US) kəˈʃɪr, kæʃˈɪr -s -z -ing -ɪŋ -ed -d
cash-in-hand ˌkæʃ.ɪnˈhænd *stress shift:* ˌcash-in-hand ˈpayment
cashless ˈkæʃ.ləs, -lɪs
cashmere *fabric:* ˈkæʃ.mɪəʳ, ˌ-ˈ-, (US) ˈkæʒ.mɪr, ˈkæʃ- -s -z
Cashmere *place:* ˈkæʃ.mɪəʳ, ˌ-ˈ-, (US) ˈkæʃ.mɪr -s -z
Cashmore ˈkæʃ.mɔːʳ, (US) -mɔːr
cashpoint ˈkæʃ.pɔɪnt -s -s
cash-strapped ˈkæʃ.stræpt
Casimir ˈkæs.ɪ.mɪəʳ, (US) -ə.mɪr
casing ˈkeɪ.sɪŋ -s -z
casino kəˈsiː.nəʊ, (US) -noʊ -s -z
Casio® ˈkæs.i.əʊ, (US) -oʊ
cask kɑːsk, (US) kæsk -s -s -ing -ɪŋ -ed -t
casket ˈkɑː.skɪt, (US) ˈkæs.kɪt -s -s
Caslon ˈkæz.lən, -lɒn, (US) -lən, -lɑːn
Caspar ˈkæs.pəʳ, -pɑːʳ, (US) -pɚ
Caspian ˈkæs.pi.ən
casque kæsk, kɑːsk, (US) kæsk -s -s
Cass kæs
Cassandra kəˈsæn.drə, -ˈsɑːn-
Cassani kəˈsɑː.ni
cassareep ˈkæs.ə.riːp
cassata kəˈsɑː.tə, kæsˈɑː-, (US) kəˈsɑː.t̬ə
cassation kæsˈeɪ.ʃən, kəˈseɪ- -s -z
Cassatt kəˈsæt
cassava kəˈsɑː.və
Cassavetes ˌkæs.əˈviː.tiːz, (US) -t̬iːz
Cassel(l) ˈkæs.əl
casserol|e ˈkæs.ər.əʊl, (US) -ə.roʊl -es -z -ing -ɪŋ -ed -d
cassette kəˈset, kæsˈet, (US) kəˈset -s -s casˈsette reˌcorder
cassia ˈkæs.i.ə
Cassidy ˈkæs.ə.di, -ɪ.di, (US) -ə.di
Cassie ˈkæs.i
Cassio ˈkæs.i.əʊ, (US) -oʊ
Cassiopeia ˌkæs.i.əʊˈpiː.ə; *as name of constellation also:* ˌkæs.iˈəʊ.pi-, (US) ˌkæs.i.əˈpiː-
cassis kæsˈiːs, ˈ--, (US) kæsˈiːs
Cassius ˈkæs.i.əs, (US) ˈkæʃ.əs, ˈkæs.i-
Cassivelaunus ˌkæs.ɪ.vɪˈlɔː.nəs, ˌ-ə-, -vəˈ-, (US) -ɪ.vəˈlɑː-, -ˈlɔː-
cassock ˈkæs.ək -s -s -ed -t
cassoulet ˈkæs.u.leɪ, ˈ---, (US) ˌkæs.uˈleɪ -s -z
cassowar|y ˈkæs.ə.weə.r|i, -wə-, (US) -wer|.i -ies -iz
Cass Timberlane ˌkæsˈtɪm.bə.leɪn, (US) -bɚ-
cast kɑːst, (US) kæst -s -s -ing -ɪŋ ˌcast-ˈiron
Castali|a kæsˈteɪ.li|.ə, (US) -li|.ə, -ˈteɪl.j|ə -an/s -ən/z
castanet ˌkæs.təˈnet -s -s
castaway ˈkɑː.stə.weɪ, (US) ˈkæs.tə- -s -z
caste kɑːst, (US) kæst -s -s
Castel Gandolfo ˌkæs.tel.gænˈdɒl.fəʊ, (US) -ˈdɑːl.foʊ, -ˈdɔːl-
castellated ˈkæs.tə.leɪ.tɪd, -tɪ-, -tel.eɪ-, (US) -tə.leɪ.t̬ɪd
Castelnau ˈkɑː.səl.nɔː, -nəʊ, (US) ˈkæs.əl.nɔː, -noʊ
caster ˈkɑː.stəʳ, (US) ˈkæs.tɚ -s -z ˈcaster ˌsugar
Casterbridge ˈkɑː.stə.brɪdʒ, (US) ˈkæs.tɚ-
casti|gate ˈkæs.tɪ|.geɪt, -tə|.geɪt, (US) -tə- -gates -geɪts -gating -geɪ.tɪŋ, (US) -geɪ.t̬ɪŋ -gated -geɪ.tɪd, (US) -geɪ.t̬ɪd -gator/s -geɪ.təʳ/z, (US) -geɪ.t̬ɚ/z
castigation ˌkæs.tɪˈgeɪ.ʃən, -təˈ-, (US) -təˈ- -s -z
Castile kæsˈtiːl
Castilian kæsˈtɪl.i.ən, kəˈstɪl-, (US) -i.ən, -jən -s -z
casting ˈkɑː.stɪŋ, (US) ˈkæs.tɪŋ -s -z ˈcasting ˌcouch; ˈcasting ˌnet; ˌcasting ˈvote
castl|e, C~ ˈkɑː.səl, (US) ˈkæs.əl -es -z -ing -ɪŋ -ed -d
Castlebar ˌkɑː.səlˈbɑːʳ, (US) ˌkæs.əlˈbɑːr
Castleford ˈkɑː.səl.fəd, (US) ˈkæs.əl.fɚd
Castlemaine ˈkɑː.səl.meɪn, (US) ˈkæs.əl-
Castlenau ˈkɑː.səl.nɔː, (US) ˈkæs.əl.nɑː, -nɔː
Castlerea(gh) ˈkɑː.səl.reɪ, ˌ--ˈ-, (US) ˈkæs.əl-
Castleton ˈkɑː.səl.tən, (US) ˈkæs.əl.tən
Castlewellan ˌkɑː.səlˈwel.ən, (US) ˌkæs.əlˈ-
cast-off ˈkɑːst.ɒf, ˌ-ˈ-, (US) ˈkæst.ɑːf -s -s
castor, C~ ˈkɑː.stəʳ, ˈkæs.təʳ, (US) ˈkæs.tɚ -s -z ˌcastor ˈoil; ˈcastor ˌsugar
cas|trate kæs|ˈtreɪt, (US) ˈ-- -trates -ˈtreɪts, (US) -treɪts -trating -ˈtreɪ.tɪŋ, (US) -treɪ.t̬ɪŋ -trated -ˈtreɪ.tɪd, (US) -treɪ.t̬ɪd
castration kæsˈtreɪ.ʃən -s -z
castrat|o kæsˈtrɑː.t|əʊ, (US) -t|oʊ -i -iː
Castries kæsˈtriːz, -ˈtriːs
Castro ˈkæs.trəʊ, (US) -troʊ
Castrol® ˈkæs.trɒl, (US) -trɑːl, -troʊl
casual ˈkæʒ.ju.əl, -zju-, (US) ˈ-uː- -ly -i ˌcasual ˈsex
casualt|y ˈkæʒ.ju.əl.t|i, ˈkæz-, (US) ˈkæʒ.uː- -ies -iz
casuarina ˌkæz.juəˈriː.nə, ˌkæʒ-, (US) ˌkæʒ.u.əˈriː- -s -z
casuist ˈkæz.ju.ɪst, ˈkæʒ-, (US) ˈkæʒ.u- -s -s
casuistic ˌkæz.juˈɪs.tɪk, ˌkæʒ-, (US) ˌkæʒ.uˈ- -al -əl
casuistry ˈkæz.ju.ɪ.stri, ˈkæʒ-, (US) ˈkæʒ.u-
casus belli ˌkɑː.sʊsˈbel.iː, ˌkeɪ.səsˈbel.aɪ, (US) ˌkeɪ.səsˈbel.i, ˌkɑː-
Caswell ˈkæz.wəl, -wel, (US) ˈkæz-, ˈkæs-
cat kæt -s -s ˈcat ˌburglar; ˌcat's ˈwhiskers; let the ˌcat out of the ˈbag; play ˌcat and ˈmouse with; set the ˌcat among the ˈpigeons
CAT kæt ˈCAT ˌscan
cata- ˈkæt.ə, (US) ˈkæt̬.ə, kəˈtæ
Note: Prefix. This usually takes primary or secondary stress on the first syllable, e.g. **catalogue** /ˈkæt.ə.lɒg/ (US) /ˈkæt̬.ə.lɑːg/, or on the second syllable, e.g. **catastrophe** /kəˈtæs.trə.fi/.
catabolic ˌkæt.əˈbɒl.ɪk, (US) ˌkæt̬.əˈbɑː.lɪk -ally -əl.i, -li
catabolism kəˈtæb.əl.ɪ.zəm
catachresis ˌkæt.əˈkriː.sɪs, (US) ˌkæt̬.əˈ-
cataclysm ˈkæt.ə.klɪ.zəm, (US) ˈkæt̬- -s -z
cataclysmal ˌkæt.əˈklɪz.məl, (US) ˌkæt̬.əˈ- -ly -li
cataclysmic ˌkæt.əˈklɪz.mɪk, (US) ˌkæt̬.əˈ- -ally -əl.i, -li
catacomb ˈkæt.ə.kuːm, -kəʊm, (US) ˈkæt̬.ə.koʊm -s -z
catafalque ˈkæt.ə.fælk, (US) ˈkæt̬.ə.fælk, -fɔːlk, -fɑːlk -s -s
Catalan ˌkæt.əˈlæn, ˈ---, -lən, (US) ˈkæt̬.ə.læn, -əl.ən -s -z
catalectic ˌkæt.əˈlek.tɪk, (US) ˌkæt̬.əˈlek.tɪk
catalepsy|y ˈkæt.ə.lep.s|i, (US) ˈkæt̬.ə- -ies -iz
cataleptic ˌkæt.əˈlep.tɪk, (US) ˌkæt̬.əˈ-
catalexis ˌkæt.əˈlek.sɪs, (US) ˌkæt̬.ə-
catalog ˈkæt.əl.ɒg, (US) ˈkæt̬.ə.lɑːg, -lɔːg -s -z -ing -ɪŋ -ed -d -er/s -əʳ/z, (US) -ɚ/z -ist/s -ɪst/s
catalogu|e ˈkæt.əl.ɒg, (US) ˈkæt̬.ə.lɑːg, -lɔːg -es -z -ing -ɪŋ -ed -d -er/s -əʳ/z, (US) -ɚ/z -ist/s -ɪst/s
Cataloni|a ˌkæt.əˈləʊ.ni|.ə, -nj|ə, (US) ˌkæt̬.əˈloʊ-, -nj|ə -an/s -ən/z
catalpa kəˈtæl.pə -s -z
Catalunya ˌkæt.əˈluː.njə, (US) ˌkæt̬-
catalysis kəˈtæl.ə.sɪs, ˈ-ɪ-
catalyst ˈkæt.əl.ɪst, (US) ˈkæt̬- -s -s
catalytic ˌkæt.əˈlɪt.ɪk, (US) ˌkæt̬ˈə- *stress shift, see compound:* ˌcatalytic conˈverter
catamaran ˌkæt.ə.məˈræn, ˈkæt.ə.mə.ræn, (US) ˌkæt̬.ə.məˈræn -s -z
Catania kəˈtɑː.ni.ə, -njə
cataphora kəˈtæf.ər.ə
cataphoric ˌkæt.əˈfɒr.ɪk, (US) ˌkæt̬.əˈfɔːr-
cataplasm ˈkæt.ə.plæz.əm, (US) ˈkæt̬- -s -z

cata|pult ˈkæt.ə|.pʌlt, US ˈkæţ- **-pults** -pʌlts **-pulting** -pʌl.tɪŋ, US -pʌl.ţɪŋ **-pulted** -pʌl.tɪd, US -pʌl.ţɪd
cataract ˈkæt.ər.ækt, US ˈkæţ.ər.ækt **-s** -s
catarrh kəˈtɑːr, kætˈɑːr, US kəˈtɑːr **-s** -z **-al** -əl
catastas|is kəˈtæs.tə.s|ɪs **-es** -iːz
catastrophe kəˈtæs.trə.fi **-s** -z
catastrophic ˌkæt.əˈstrɒf.ɪk, US ˌkæţ.əˈstrɑː.fɪk **-ally** -əl.i, -li
catatonia ˌkæt.əˈtəʊ.ni.ə, US ˌkæţ.əˈtoʊ-
catatonic ˌkæt.əˈtɒn.ɪk, US ˌkæţ.əˈtɑː.nɪk
catawba, C~ kəˈtɔː.bə, US -ˈtɔː-, -ˈtɑː-
catbird ˈkæt.bɜːd, US -bɝːd **-s** -z
catboat ˈkæt.bəʊt, US -boʊt **-s** -s
catcall ˈkæt.kɔːl, US -kɔːl, -kɑːl **-s** -z **-ing** -ɪŋ **-ed** -d
catch kætʃ **-es** -ɪz **-ing** -ɪŋ **caught** kɔːt, US kɑːt, kɔːt
catch-22, C~ ˌkætʃˌtwen.tiˈtuː, US -ţiˈ-
catchall ˈkætʃ.ɔːl, US -ɔːl, -ɑːl **-s** -z
catcher ˈkætʃ.ər, US -ɚ **-s** -z
catching ˈkætʃ.ɪŋ
catchment ˈkætʃ.mənt **-s** -s ˈ**catchment** ˌ**area**
catchpenn|y ˈkætʃ.pen|.i **-ies** -iz
catchphras|e ˈkætʃ.freɪz **-es** -ɪz
catchpole, C~ ˈkætʃ.pəʊl, US -poʊl **-s** -z
catchword ˈkætʃ.wɜːd, US -wɝːd **-s** -z
catch|y ˈkætʃ|.i **-ier** -i.ər, US -i.ɚ **-iest** -i.ɪst, -i.əst **-iness** -ɪ.nəs, -ɪ.nɪs
catechism ˈkæt.ə.kɪ.zəm, ˈ-ɪ-, US ˈkæţ.ə- **-s** -z
catechist ˈkæt.ə.kɪst, ˈ-ɪ-, US ˈkæţ.ə- **-s** -s
catechiz|e, -is|e ˈkæt.ə.kaɪz, ˈ-ɪ-, US ˈkæţ.ə- **-es** -ɪz **-ing** -ɪŋ **-ed** -d **-er/s** -ər/z, US -ɚ/z
catechu ˈkæt.ə.tʃuː, ˈ-ɪ-, US ˈkæţ.ə.tʃuː, -kjuː
catechumen ˌkæt.ɪˈkjuː.men, -əˈ-, -mɪn, US ˌkæţ.əˈkjuː.mən **-s** -z
categoric|al ˌkæt.əˈgɒr.ɪ.k|əl, -ɪˈ-, US ˌkæţ.əˈgɔːr- **-ally** -əl.i, -li
categorization, -isa- ˌkæt.ə.gər.aɪˈzeɪ.ʃən, ˌ-ɪ-, -ɪˈ-, US ˌkæţ.ə.gɚ.əˈ- **-s** -z
categoriz|e, -is|e ˈkæt.ə.gər.aɪz, ˈ-ɪ-, US ˈkæţ.ə.gə.raɪz **-es** -ɪz **-ing** -ɪŋ **-ed** -d
categor|y ˈkæt.ə.gər|.i, ˈ-ɪ-, US ˈkæţ.ə.gɔːr- **-ies** -iz
catenar|y kəˈtiː.nər|.i **-ies** -iz
caten|ate ˈkæt.ɪ.n|eɪt, ˈ-ə-, US ˈkæt.ən|.eɪt **-ates** -eɪts **-ating** -eɪ.tɪŋ, US -eɪ.ţɪŋ **-ated** -eɪ.tɪd, US -eɪ.ţɪd
catenation ˌkæt.ɪˈneɪ.ʃən, -əˈ-, US ˌkæt.ənˈeɪ- **-s** -z
catenative kəˈtiː.nə.tɪv
cateniz|e, -is|e ˈkæt.ɪ.naɪz, ˈ-ə-, US ˈkæt.ən.aɪz **-es** -ɪz **-ing** -ɪŋ **-ed** -d
cat|er, C~ ˈkeɪ.t|ər, US -ţ|ɚ **-ers** -əz, US -ɚz **-ering** -ər.ɪŋ **-ered** -əd, US -ɚd **-erer/s** -ər.ər/z, US -ɚ.ɚ/z
Caterham ˈkeɪ.tər.əm, US -ţɚ-
Caterina ˌkæt.ərˈiː.nə, US ˌkæţ-
caterpillar ˈkæt.ə.pɪl.ər, US ˈkæţ.ɚ.pɪl.ɚ, ˈ-ə- **-s** -z
caterwaul ˈkæt.ə.wɔːl, US ˈkæţ.ɚ-, -wɑːl **-s** -z **-ing** -ɪŋ **-ed** -d
Catesby ˈkeɪts.bi
catfish ˈkæt.fɪʃ **-es** -ɪz
Catford ˈkæt.fəd, US -fɚd
catgut ˈkæt.gʌt
Cathar ˈkæθ.ɑːr, US -ɑːr **-ism** -ɪ.zəm **-ist/s** -ɪst/s
Catharine ˈkæθ.ər.ɪn, ˈkæθ.rɪn
cathars|is kəˈθɑː.s|ɪs, kæθˈɑː-, US kəˈθɑːr- **-es** -iːz
cathartic kəˈθɑː.tɪk, kæθˈɑː-, US kəˈθɑːr.ţɪk **-s** -s
Cathay kæθˈeɪ, kəˈθeɪ
Cathcart ˈkæθ.kət, -kɑːt; kæθˈkɑːt, kəθ-, US ˈkæθ.kɑːrt, -kɚt; US kæθˈkɑːrt, kəθ-
cathead ˈkæt.hed **-s** -z
cathedra kəˈθiː.drə, -ˈθed.rə, US kəˈθiː.drə, ˈkæθ.ə- **-s** -z
cathedra (in phrase **ex cathedra**) kəˈθiː.drə, kæθˈed.rɑː, kəˈθed-
cathedral kəˈθiː.drəl **-s** -z
Cather ˈkæð.ər, US -ɚ
Catherine ˈkæθ.ər.ɪn, ˈkæθ.rɪn ˈ**catherine** ˌ**wheel**
catheter ˈkæθ.ɪ.tər, ˈ-ə-, US -ə.ţɚ **-s** -z
catheterization, -isa- ˌkæθ.ɪ.tər.aɪˈzeɪ.ʃən, ˌ-ə-, -ɪˈ-, US -ə.ţɚ.əˈ-
catheteriz|e, -is|e ˈkæθ.ɪ.tər.aɪz, ˈ-ə-, US ˈ-ə.ţɚ- **-es** -ɪz **-ing** -ɪŋ **-ed** -d
cathetometer ˌkæθ.ɪˈtɒm.ɪ.tər, -əˈ-, ˈ-ə-, US -əˈtɑː.mə.ţɚ **-s** -z
cathex|is kəˈθek.s|ɪs, kæθˈek- **-es** -iːz
Cathleen ˈkæθ.liːn, -ˈ-, US -ˈ-, ˈ--
cathode ˈkæθ.əʊd, US -oʊd **-s** -z ˌ**cathode** ˈ**ray**; ˌ**cathode-**ˈ**ray** ˌ**tube**
catholic, C~ ˈkæθ.əl.ɪk **-s** -s
catholicism, C~ kəˈθɒl.ɪ.sɪ.zəm, ˈ-ə-, US -ˈθɑː.lə-
catholicity, C~ ˌkæθ.əʊˈlɪs.ə.ti, -ɪ.ti, US ˌkæθ.əˈlɪs.ə.ţi
catholiciz|e, -is|e kəˈθɒl.ɪ.saɪz, ˈ-ə-, US -ˈθɑː.lə- **-es** -ɪz **-ing** -ɪŋ **-ed** -d
Cathy ˈkæθ.i
Catiline ˈkæt.ɪ.laɪn, -əl.aɪn, US -ɪ.laɪn, ˈ-ə-
cation ˈkæt.aɪ.ən **-s** -z
catkin ˈkæt.kɪn **-s** -z
catlike ˈkæt.laɪk
catmint ˈkæt.mɪnt
catnap ˈkæt.næp **-s** -s **-ping** -ɪŋ **-ped** -t
catnip ˈkæt.nɪp
Cato ˈkeɪ.təʊ, US -ţoʊ
cat-o'-nine-tails ˌkæt.əˈnaɪn.teɪlz, US ˌkæţ-
Cator ˈkeɪ.tər, US -ţɚ
Catriona kəˈtriː.ə.nə, kætˈriː-, -ˈtriː.nə, ˌkæt.riˈəʊ.nə, US ˌkæt.riˈoʊ-
cat's-cradle ˌkætsˈkreɪ.dəl, US ˌ-ˈ--, ˈ-ˌ--
cat's-eye ˈkæts.aɪ **-s** -z
Catshill kætsˈhɪl *stress shift:* ˌ**Catshill** ˈ**stores**
Catskill ˈkæt.skɪl
catsuit ˈkæt.suːt, -sjuːt, US -suːt **-s** -s
catsup ˈkæt.səp, ˈkætʃ.əp, ˈketʃ.əp **-s** -s
Cattell kætˈel, kəˈtel
Catterick ˈkæt.ər.ɪk, US ˈkæţ-
Cattermole ˈkæt.ə.məʊl, US ˈkæţ.ɚ.moʊl
catter|y ˈkæt.ər|.i, US ˈkæţ- **-ies** -iz
cattish ˈkæt.ɪʃ, US ˈkæţ-
cattle ˈkæt.əl, US ˈkæţ- ˈ**cattle** ˌ**grid**; ˈ**cattle** ˌ**market**; ˈ**cattle** ˌ**pen**; ˈ**cattle** ˌ**truck**
cattle-show ˈkæt.əl.ʃəʊ, US ˈkæţ.əl.ʃoʊ **-s** -z
catt|y ˈkæt|.i, US ˈkæţ- **-ier** -i.ər, US -i.ɚ **-iest** -i.ɪst, -i.əst **-ily** -əl.i, -ɪ.li **-iness** -ɪ.nəs, -ɪ.nɪs
Catullus kəˈtʌl.əs
catwalk ˈkæt.wɔːk, US -wɑːk, -wɔːk **-s** -s
Caucasi|a kɔːˈkeɪ.ʒ|ə; -ʒi|.ə, -zi-, US kɑːˈkeɪ.ʒ|ə, kɔː-, -ʃ|ə **-an/s** -ən/z
Caucasus ˈkɔː.kə.səs, -zəs, US ˈkɑː-, ˈkɔː-
caucus ˈkɔː.kəs, US ˈkɑː-, ˈkɔː- **-es** -ɪz
caudal ˈkɔː.dəl, US ˈkɑː-, ˈkɔː-
caudate ˈkɔː.deɪt, US ˈkɑː-, ˈkɔː-
caudillo kaʊˈdiː.əʊ, kɔːˈdɪl-, -jəʊ, US kaʊˈdiː.joʊ, -ˈdɪl- **-s** -z
Caudine ˈkɔː.daɪn, US ˈkɑː-, ˈkɔː-
caudle, C~ ˈkɔː.dəl, US ˈkɑː-, ˈkɔː-
caught (from **catch**) kɔːt, US kɑːt, kɔːt
caul kɔːl, US kɑːl, kɔːl **-s** -z
cauldron ˈkɔːl.drən, ˈkɒl-, US ˈkɑːl-, ˈkɔːl- **-s** -z
Caulfield ˈkɔːl.fiːld, ˈkɔː-, US ˈkɑːl-, ˈkɔːl-, ˈkɑː-, ˈkɔː-
cauliflower ˈkɒl.ɪ.flaʊər, -ˌflaʊ.ər, US ˈkɑː.ləˌflaʊ.ɚ, ˈkɔː- **-s** -z ˌ**cauliflower** ˈ**ear**
caulk kɔːk, US kɑːk, kɔːk **-s** -s **-ing** -ɪŋ **-ed** -t
caulker ˈkɔː.kər, US ˈkɑː.kɚ, ˈkɔː- **-s** -z
causal ˈkɔː.zəl, US ˈkɑː-, ˈkɔː- **-ly** -i
causality kɔːˈzæl.ə.ti, -ɪ.ti, US kɑːˈzæl.ə.ţi, kɔː-
causa mortis ˌkaʊ.səˈmɔː.tɪs, -zəˈ-, US -mɔːr.ţɪs
causation kɔːˈzeɪ.ʃən, US kɑː-, kɔː-
causative ˈkɔː.zə.tɪv, US ˈkɑː.zə.ţɪv, ˈkɔː- **-ly** -li
caus|e kɔːz, US kɑːz, kɔːz **-es** -ɪz **-ing** -ɪŋ **-ed** -d
cause(s) célèbre(s) ˌkɔːz.selˈeb.rə, ˌkəʊz-, -səˈleb-, -ˈleɪ.brə, US ˌkɑːz.səˈleb.rə, ˌkɔːz-, ˌkoʊz-
causeless ˈkɔːz.ləs, -lɪs, US ˈkɑːz-, ˈkɔːz- **-ly** -li
causerie ˈkəʊ.zər.i, -iː, US ˌkoʊ.zəˈriː **-s** -z
causeway ˈkɔːz.weɪ, US ˈkɑːz-, ˈkɔːz- **-s** -z
caustic ˈkɔː.stɪk, ˈkɒs.tɪk, US

Pronouncing the letters CC

The consonant digraph **cc** has two pronuncations: /ks/ and /k/.

Before the vowel letters **i** or **e**, it is pronounced as /ks/, e.g.:

accident ˈæk.sɪ.dᵊnt

In most other situations, **cc** is pronounced as /k/, e.g.:

acclaim əkˈleɪm

In addition

The word *flaccid* has two possible pronunciations: /ˈflæk.sɪd/, /ˈflæs.ɪd/

Words borrowed from Italian may have /tʃ/, e.g.:

cappuccino ˌkæp.uˈtʃiː.nəʊ (US) -əˈtʃiː.noʊ

ˈkɑː.stɪk, ˈkɔː- **-al** -ᵊl **-ally** -ᵊl.i, -li **ˌcaustic ˈsoda**

causticity kɔːˈstɪs.ə.ti, kɒsˈtɪs-, -ɪ.ti, (US) kɑːˈstɪs.ə.ţi, kɔː-

cauterization, -isa- ˌkɔː.tᵊr.aɪˈzeɪ.ʃᵊn, -ɪˈ-, (US) ˌkɑː.ţɚ.əˈ-, ˌkɔː- **-s** -z

cauteriz|e, -is|e ˈkɔː.tᵊr.aɪz, (US) ˈkɑː.ţə.raɪz, ˈkɔː- **-es** -ɪz **-ing** -ɪŋ **-ed** -d

cauter|y ˈkɔː.tᵊr|.i, (US) ˈkɑː.ţɚ-, ˈkɔː- **-ies** -iz

Cauthen ˈkɔː.θᵊn, (US) ˈkɑː-, ˈkɔː-

caution ˈkɔː.ʃᵊn, (US) ˈkɑː-, ˈkɔː- **-s** -z **-ing** -ɪŋ **-ed** -d **-er/s** -əʳ/z, (US) -ɚ/z **ˈcaution ˌmoney; throw ˌcaution to the ˈwind**

cautionary ˈkɔː.ʃᵊn.ᵊr.i, -ʃᵊn.ri, (US) ˈkɑː.ʃᵊn.er-, ˈkɔː- **ˌcautionary ˈtale**

cautious ˈkɔː.ʃəs, (US) ˈkɑː-, ˈkɔː- **-ly** -li **-ness** -nəs, -nɪs

cavalcade ˌkæv.ᵊlˈkeɪd, ˈ--- **-s** -z

cavalier ˌkæv.ᵊlˈɪəʳ, (US) -əˈlɪr **-s** -z

Cavalleria Rusticana kəˌvæl.əˌriː.ə.rʊs.tɪˈkɑː.nə, ˌkæv.ᵊl-, -ˌrɪə-

cavalr|y ˈkæv.ᵊl.r|i **-ies** -iz

cavalry|man ˈkæv.ᵊl.ri|.mən, -mæn **-men** -mən, -men

Cavan ˈkæv.ᵊn

Cavanagh ˈkæv.ə.nə

Cavanaugh ˈkæv.ə.nɔː, (US) -nɑː, -nɔː

cavatina ˌkæv.əˈtiː.nə **-s** -z

cave *beware:* ˈkeɪ.vi

cav|e, C~ n, v keɪv **-es** -z **-ing** -ɪŋ **-ed** -d **-er/s** -əʳ/z, (US) -ɚ/z **ˈcave ˌdweller**

caveat ˈkæv.i.æt, ˈkeɪ.vi-, (US) ˈkæv.i-, ˈkeɪ.vi-, ˈkɑː- **-s** -s

caveat emptor ˌkæv.i.ætˈemp.tɔːʳ, ˌkeɪ.vi-, -təʳ, (US) -tɔːr, ˌkɑː-, -ɑːtˈ-, -tɚ

Cavell ˈkæv.ᵊl, kəˈvel

> Note: The family of Nurse Edith Cavell pronounces /ˈkæv.ᵊl/.

cave|man ˈkeɪv|.mæn **-men** -men

Cavendish ˈkæv.ᵊn.dɪʃ

cavern ˈkæv.ᵊn, -ɜːn, (US) -ɚn **-s** -z

cavernous ˈkæv.ᵊn.əs, (US) -ɚn- **-ly** -li

Caversham ˈkæv.ə.ʃəm, (US) ˈ-ɚ-

cave|woman ˈkeɪv|ˌwʊm.ən **-women** -ˌwɪm.ɪn

caviar(e) ˈkæv.i.ɑːʳ, ˌ--ˈ-, (US) ˈkæv.i.ɑːr

cavil ˈkæv.ᵊl, -ɪl **-s** -z **-(l)ing** -ɪŋ **-(l)ed** -d **-(l)er/s** -əʳ/z, (US) -ɚ/z

cavit|y ˈkæv.ə.t|i, -ɪ.t|i, (US) -ə.ţ|i **-ies** -iz

ca|vort kə|ˈvɔːt, (US) -ˈvɔːrt **-vorts** -ˈvɔːts, (US) -ˈvɔːrts **-vorting** -ˈvɔː.tɪŋ, (US) -ˈvɔːr.ţɪŋ **-vorted** -ˈvɔː.tɪd, (US) -ˈvɔːr.ţɪd

cav|y ˈkeɪ.v|i **-ies** -iz

caw kɔː, (US) kɑː, kɔː **-s** -z **-ing** -ɪŋ **-ed** -d

Cawdor ˈkɔː.dəʳ, -dɔːʳ, (US) ˈkɑː.dɚ, ˈkɔː-, -dɔːr

Cawdrey ˈkɔː.dri, (US) ˈkɑː-, ˈkɔː-

Cawley ˈkɔː.li, (US) ˈkɑː-, ˈkɔː-

Cawse kɔːz, (US) kɑːz, kɔːz

Caxton ˈkæk.stᵊn

cay kiː, keɪ **-s** -z

cayenne, C~ keɪˈen, (US) kaɪ-, keɪ- *stress shift:* **ˌcayenne ˈpepper**

Cayley ˈkeɪ.li

cayman, C~ ˈkeɪ.mən **-s** -z **ˈCayman ˌIslands**

Cazenove ˈkæz.ᵊn.əʊv, (US) -oʊv

CB ˌsiːˈbiː

CBC ˌsiː.biːˈsiː

CBE ˌsiː.biːˈiː

CBI ˌsiː.biːˈaɪ

CBS ˌsiː.biːˈes *stress shift:* **ˌCBS ˈrecords**

cc ˌsiːˈsiː

CCTV ˌsiː.siː.tiːˈviː *stress shift:* **CCTˌV ˈfootage**

CD ˌsiːˈdiː **-s** -z **ˌCˈD ˌplayer**

CDC ˌsiː.diːˈsiː

CDI ˌsiː.diːˈaɪ

Cdr. (abbrev. for **commander**) kəˈmɑːn.dəʳ, (US) -ˈmæn.dɚ

CD-ROM ˌsiː.diːˈrɒm, (US) -ˈrɑːm **-s** -z

CD-RW ˌsiː.diː.ɑːˈdʌb.ᵊl.juː, (US) -ɑːrˈ-

CDT ˌsiː.diːˈtiː

ceas|e siːs **-es** -ɪz **-ing** -ɪŋ **-ed** -t

cease-fire ˈsiːs.faɪəʳ, -faɪ.əʳ, (US) -faɪ.ɚ

ceaseless ˈsiː.sləs, -slɪs **-ly** -li **-ness** -nəs, -nɪs

Ceauşescu ˌtʃaʊˈʃes.kuː

Cebu sɪˈbuː

Cecil ˈses.ᵊl, -ɪl, ˈsɪs.ᵊl, -ɪl, (US) ˈsiː.sᵊl, ˈses.ᵊl

> Note: The family name of the Marquess of Exeter and that of the Marquess of Salisbury is /ˈsɪs.ᵊl, -ɪl/.

Cecile sesˈiːl, ˈ--, ˈses.ɪl, -ᵊl, (US) sɪˈsiːl

Cecilia sɪˈsiː.li.ə, sə-, -ˈsɪl.i-, (US) -ˈsiːl.jə, -ˈsɪl-

Cecily ˈses.ɪ.li, ˈsɪs-, -ᵊl.i, (US) ˈses-

cec|um ˈsiː.k|əm **-a** -ə

cedar ˈsiː.dəʳ, (US) -dɚ **-s** -z

ced|e siːd **-es** -z **-ing** -ɪŋ **-ed** -ɪd

cedi ˈsiː.di **-s** -z

cedilla səˈdɪl.ə, sɪ- **-s** -z

Cedric ˈsed.rɪk, ˈsiː.drɪk

Ceefax® ˈsiː.fæks

Cefn-Mawr ˌkev.ᵊnˈmaʊ.əʳ, (US) -ˈmaʊ.ɚ

CEGB ˌsiː.iː.dʒiːˈbiː

ceilidh ˈkeɪ.li **-s** -z

ceiling ˈsiː.lɪŋ **-s** -z

celadon ˈsel.ə.dɒn, -dən, (US) -dɑːn

celandine ˈsel.ən.daɪn, -diːn **-s** -z

Celanese® ˌsel.əˈniːz, (US) -ˈniːz, -ˈniːs

celeb səˈleb, sɪ- **-s** -z

Celebes selˈiː.biz, səˈliː-, sɪ-, (US) ˈsel.ə.biːz, səˈliː.biz

celebrant ˈsel.ə.brᵊnt, ˈ-ɪ- **-s** -s

cele|brate ˈsel.ə|.breɪt, ˈ-ɪ- **-brates** -breɪts **-brating** -breɪ.tɪŋ, (US) -breɪ.ţɪŋ **-brated** -breɪ.tɪd, (US) -breɪ.ţɪd **-brator/s** -breɪ.təʳ/z, (US) -breɪ.ţɚ/z

celebration ˌsel.əˈbreɪ.ʃᵊn, -ɪˈ- **-s** -z

celebratory ˌsel.əˈbreɪ.tᵊr.i, -ɪˈ-; -tri; ˈsel.ɪ.brə-, ˈ-ə-, (US) ˈsel.ə.brə.tɔːr.i; (US) səˈleb.rə-

celebrit|y səˈleb.rə.t|i, sɪ-, -rɪ-, (US) səˈleb.rə.ţ|i **-ies** -iz

celeriac səˈler.i.æk, sɪ-; ˈsel.ᵊr-

celerity səˈler.ə.ti, sɪ-, -ɪ.ti, (US) -ə.ţi

Celeron® ˈsel.ᵊr.ɒn, (US) -ɑːn

celery ˈsel.ᵊr.i

celeste, C~ səˈlest, sɪ- **-s** -s

celestial, C~ səˈles.ti.əl, sɪ-, (US) ˈ-tʃᵊl **-ly** -i

celestine ˈsel.ə.staɪn, ˈ-ɪ-, -stɪn

Celestine ˈsel.ə.staɪn, ˈ-ɪ-; sɪˈles.taɪn, sə-, -tɪn, -tiːn **-s** -z

Celia ˈsiː.li.ə

celiac ˈsiː.li.æk

celibacy ˈsel.ə.bə.si, ˈ-ɪ-

celibatarian ˌsel.ə.bəˈteə.ri.ən, ˌ-ɪ-, (US) -ˈter.i- **-s** -z

celibate ˈsel.ə.bət, ˈ-ɪ-, -bɪt **-s** -s

Céline selˈiːn, seɪˈliːn

cell sel **-s** -z

cellar ˈsel.əʳ, (US) -ɚ **-s** -z

cellarage ˈsel.ᵊr.ɪdʒ

cellarer ˈsel.ᵊr.əʳ, (US) -ɚ **-s** -z

cellaret ˌsel.ᵊrˈet, ˈsel.ᵊr.et, (US) ˌsel.ɚˈet **-s** -s

cellarist ˈsel.ᵊr.ɪst **-s** -s

cellar|man ˈsel.ə|.mən, -mæn, (US) -ɚ- **-men** -mən, -men

Cellini tʃelˈiː.ni, tʃɪˈliː-, tʃə-

cellist ˈtʃel.ɪst **-s** -s

Pronouncing the letters CCH

The consonant letter combination **cch** only has one possible realization: /k/, e.g.:

saccharine ˈsæk.ərɪn

C

cellmate ˈsel.meɪt **-s** -s
Cellnet® ˈsel.net
cello ˈtʃel.əʊ, ⓊⓈ -oʊ **-s** -z
Cellophane® ˈsel.ə.feɪn
cellphone ˈsel.fəʊn, ⓊⓈ -foʊn **-s** -z
cellular ˈsel.jə.lər, -jʊ-, ⓊⓈ -lɚ **ˌcellular ˈphone; ˌcellular ˈradio**
cellule ˈsel.juːl **-s** -z
cellulite ˈsel.jə.laɪt, -jʊ-
celluloid, C~ ˈsel.jə.lɔɪd, -jʊ-
cellulose ˈsel.jə.ləʊs, -jʊ-, -ləʊz, ⓊⓈ -loʊs
Celsius ˈsel.si.əs, ⓊⓈ ˈsel.si.əs, -ʃəs
celt *axe:* selt **-s** -s
Celt *people, tribe:* kelt, selt *member of football or baseball team:* selt **-s** -s
Celtic *people, tribe:* ˈkel.tɪk, ˈsel.tɪk *in names of football or baseball teams:* ˈsel.tɪk *Sea:* ˈkel.tɪk **-s** -z
cembal|o ˈtʃem.bə.l|əʊ, ˈsem-, ⓊⓈ -l|oʊ **-os** -əʊz, ⓊⓈ -oʊz **-i** -iː
cement sɪˈment, sə- **-s** -s **-ing** -ɪŋ **-ed** -ɪd **ceˈment-ˌmixer**
cementation ˌsiː.menˈteɪ.ʃən **-s** -z
cementium sɪˈmen.ʃi.əm, sə-, ˈ-ti-, ⓊⓈ -ţi-
cemeter|y ˈsem.ə.tr|i, ˈ-ɪ-, ⓊⓈ -ə.ter|.i **-ies** -iz
Cenci ˈtʃen.tʃi
CENELEC ˈsen.ɪ.lek, ˈ-ə-
cenematics ˌsen.ɪˈmæt.ɪks, -əˈ-, ⓊⓈ -ˈmæţ-
cenetics səˈnet.ɪks, sɪ-, ⓊⓈ -ˈneţ-
CEng (abbrev. for **Chartered Engineer**) ˌsiːˈendʒ; ˌtʃɑː.tədˌen.dʒɪˈnɪər, -dʒəˈ-, ⓊⓈ ˌsiːˈendʒ, ˌtʃɑːr.ţədˌen.dʒɪˈnɪr, -dʒəˈ-
Cenis səˈniː, senˈiː
cenobite ˈsiː.nə.baɪt, ˈsen.ə-, ⓊⓈ ˈsen.ə- **-s** -s
cenotaph ˈsen.əʊ.tæf, -tɑːf, ⓊⓈ -ə.tæf **-s** -s
cens|e sents **-es** -ɪz **-ing** -ɪŋ **-ed** -t
censer ˈsent.sər, ⓊⓈ -sɚ **-s** -z
cens|or ˈsent.s|ər, ⓊⓈ -s|ɚ **-ors** -əz, ⓊⓈ -ɚz **-oring** -ər.ɪŋ **-ored** -əd, ⓊⓈ -ɚd
censorial sentˈsɔː.ri.əl, ⓊⓈ -ˈsɔːr.i- **-ly** -i
censorian sentˈsɔː.ri.ən, ⓊⓈ -ˈsɔːr.i-
censorious sentˈsɔː.ri.əs, ⓊⓈ -ˈsɔːr.i- **-ly** -li **-ness** -nəs, -nɪs
censorship ˈsent.sə.ʃɪp, ⓊⓈ -sɚ- **-s** -s
censurable ˈsent.sjər.ə.bəl, -ʃər-, ⓊⓈ -ʃɚ-
cens|ure ˈsent.ʃ|ər, -sj|ər, ⓊⓈ ˈsent.ʃ|ɚ **-ures** -əz, ⓊⓈ -ɚz **-uring** -ər.ɪŋ **-ured** -əd, ⓊⓈ -ɚd
census ˈsent.səs **-es** -ɪz **ˈcensus ˌpaper**
cent sent **-s** -s
centage ˈsen.tɪdʒ
cental ˈsen.təl **-s** -z
centaur ˈsen.tɔːr, ⓊⓈ -tɔːr **-s** -z
Centaur|us senˈtɔː.r|əs, ⓊⓈ -ˈtɔːr|.əs **-i** -aɪ, -iː
centaur|y ˈsen.tɔː.r|i, ⓊⓈ -tɔːr|.i **-ies** -iz
centavo senˈtɑː.vəʊ, ⓊⓈ -voʊ **-s** -z
centenarian ˌsen.tɪˈneə.ri.ən, -təˈ-, ⓊⓈ -tənˈer.i- **-s** -z
centenar|y senˈtiː.nər|.i, sən-, -ˈten.ər-, ⓊⓈ ˈsen.tən.er-; ⓊⓈ senˈten.ər- **-ies** -iz
centennial senˈten.i.əl, sən- **-s** -z **-ly** -i
cent|er ˈsen.t|ər, ⓊⓈ -ţ|ɚ **-ers** -əz, ⓊⓈ -ɚz **-ering** -ər.ɪŋ **-ered** -əd, ⓊⓈ -ɚd **ˌcenter of ˈgravity; ˌcenter ˈstage**
centerboard ˈsen.tə.bɔːd, ⓊⓈ -ţɚ.bɔːrd **-s** -z
center-field ˌsen.təˈfiːld, ⓊⓈ -ţɚˈ- **-s** -z **-er/s** -ər/z, ⓊⓈ -ɚ/z
centerfold ˈsen.tə.fəʊld, ⓊⓈ -ţɚ.foʊld **-s** -z
center-forward ˌsen.təˈfɔː.wəd, ⓊⓈ -ţɚˈfɔːr.wɚd **-s** -z
center-|half ˌsen.tə|ˈhɑːf, ⓊⓈ -ţɚ|ˈhæf **-halves** -ˈhɑːvz, ⓊⓈ -ˈhævz
centerpiec|e ˈsen.tə.piːs, ⓊⓈ -ţɚ- **-es** -ɪz
centesimal senˈtes.ɪ.məl, ˈ-ə- **-ly** -i
centesim|o senˈtes.ɪ.m|əʊ, ˈ-ə-, ⓊⓈ -m|oʊ **-i** -aɪ, -iː **-os** -əʊz, ⓊⓈ -oʊz
centi- ˈsen.tɪ, ⓊⓈ -ţə
Note: Prefix. Carries stress on first syllable, e.g. **centipede** /ˈsen.tɪ.piːd/ⓊⓈ /-ţə
centigrade ˈsen.tɪ.greɪd, ⓊⓈ -ţə-
centigram(me) ˈsen.tɪ.græm, ⓊⓈ -ţə- **-s** -z
centilitre, centiliter ˈsen.tɪˌliː.tər, ⓊⓈ -ţəˌliː.ţɚ **-s** -z
centime ˈsɑ̃ːn.tiːm, ˈsɔ̃ːn-, ˈsɑːn-; -ˈ-, ⓊⓈ ˈsɑːn-, ˈsen-, -ˈ- **-s** -z
centimetre, centimeter ˈsen.tɪˌmiː.tər, ⓊⓈ -ţəˌmiː.ţɚ **-s** -z
centimo ˈsen.tɪ.məʊ, ⓊⓈ -moʊ **-s** -z
centipede ˈsen.tɪ.piːd, ⓊⓈ -ţə- **-s** -z
centipois|e ˈsen.tɪ.pɔɪz, ⓊⓈ -ţə- **-es** -ɪz
centner ˈsent.nər, ⓊⓈ -nɚ **-s** -z
cento ˈsen.təʊ, ⓊⓈ -toʊ **-s** -z
CENTO ˈsen.təʊ, ⓊⓈ -toʊ
central, C~ ˈsen.trəl **-ly** -i **ˌCentral ˌAfrican Reˈpublic; ˌCentral Aˈmerica; ˌCentral ˈDaylight ˌTime; ˌcentral ˈheating; ˌcentral reserˈvation; ˌCentral ˈStandard ˌTime**
centralism ˈsen.trəl.ɪ.zəm
centralist ˈsen.trəl.ɪst **-s** -s
centrality senˈtræl.ə.ti, -ɪ.ti, ⓊⓈ -ə.ţi
centralization, -isa- ˌsen.trəl.aɪˈzeɪ.ʃən, -ɪˈ-, ⓊⓈ -əˈ-
centraliz|e, -is|e ˈsen.trəl.aɪz **-es** -ɪz **-ing** -ɪŋ **-ed** -d
cent|re ˈsen.t|ər, ⓊⓈ -ţ|ɚ **-res** -əz, ⓊⓈ -ɚz **-ring** -ər.ɪŋ **-red** -əd, ⓊⓈ -ɚd **ˌcentre of ˈgravity; ˌcentre ˈstage**
centreboard ˈsen.tə.bɔːd, ⓊⓈ -ţɚ.bɔːrd **-s** -z
centre-field ˌsen.təˈfiːld, ⓊⓈ -ţɚ- **-s** -z **-er/s** -ər/z, ⓊⓈ -ɚ/z
centrefold ˈsen.tə.fəʊld, ⓊⓈ -ţɚ.foʊld **-s** -z
centre-forward ˌsen.təˈfɔː.wəd, ⓊⓈ -ţɚˈfɔːr.wɚd **-s** -z
centre-|half ˌsen.tə|ˈhɑːf, ⓊⓈ -ţɚ|ˈhæf **-halves** -ˈhɑːvz, ⓊⓈ -ˈhævz
centrepiec|e ˈsen.tə.piːs, ⓊⓈ -ţɚ- **-es** -ɪz
Centrepoint ˈsen.tə.pɔɪnt, ⓊⓈ -ţɚ-
centre-spread ˌsen.təˈspred, ⓊⓈ -ţɚ- *stress shift:* **ˌcentre-spread ˈpicture**
centric ˈsen.trɪk **-al** -əl **-ally** -əl.i, -li
Centrica® ˈsen.trɪk.ə
centrifugal ˌsen.trɪˈfjuː.gəl, -trəˈ-, senˈtrɪf.jʊ-, -jə-, ⓊⓈ senˈtrɪf.jə.gəl, ˈ-ə-, -juː-
centrifug|e ˈsen.trɪ.fjuːdʒ, -trə-, ⓊⓈ -trə- **-es** -ɪz **-ing** -ɪŋ **-ed** -d
centriole ˈsen.tri.əʊl, ⓊⓈ -oʊl **-s** -z
centripetal ˌsen.trɪˈpiː.təl, ˈ-ə-, senˈtrɪ.pɪ-, ⓊⓈ senˈtrɪ.pə.ţəl
centr|ism ˈsen.tr|ɪ.zəm **-ist/s** -ɪst/s
centro- ˈsen.trəʊ, ⓊⓈ ˈsen.trə
centr|um ˈsen.tr|əm **-a** -ə
centumvirate senˈtʌm.vɪ.rət, -və-, -rɪt, ⓊⓈ senˈtʌm.vɚ.ət, ken-, -vɪ.rət **-s** -s
Centumviri senˈtʌm.vɪ.riː, ⓊⓈ ˈsen.təm.vɪ-, ˈken.tʊm-, -raɪ
centuple ˈsen.tʃʊ.pəl, -tjʊ-, -tʃə-, -tjə-; senˈtʃuː-, -ˈtjuː-, ⓊⓈ ˈsen.ţə-; ⓊⓈ senˈtuː-, -ˈtjuː-
centurion senˈtʃʊə.ri.ən, -ˈtjʊə-, -ˈtʃɔː-, -ˈtjɔː-, ⓊⓈ -ˈtʊr.i-, -ˈtjʊr- **-s** -z
centur|y ˈsen.tʃər|.i **-ies** -iz
CEO ˌsiː.iːˈəʊ, ⓊⓈ -ˈoʊ
cep sep **-s** -s
cèpe sep **-s** -s
cephalic sefˈæl.ɪk, sɪf-, səˈfæl-, kefˈæl-, kɪf-, ⓊⓈ səˈfæl.ɪk
Cephalonia ˌsef.əˈləʊ.ni.ə, ⓊⓈ -ˈloʊ-
cephalopod ˈsef.əl.əʊ.pɒd, ⓊⓈ -ə.pɑːd **-s** -z
cephalopoda ˌsef.əˈlɒp.ə.də, ⓊⓈ -ˈlɑː.pə-
cephalous ˈsef.əl.əs
Cephas ˈsiː.fæs
Cepheid ˈsiː.fi.ɪd, ˈsef.i- **-s** -z
Cepheus ˈsiː.fi.əs, -fjəs
ceramic səˈræm.ɪk, sɪ-, kɪ-, kə-, ⓊⓈ səˈræm- **-s** -s
ceramicist səˈræm.ɪ.sɪst, sɪ-, ˈ-ə-, ⓊⓈ səˈræm.ə- **-s** -s
ceramist ˈser.ə.mɪst, səˈræm.ɪst **-s** -s
cerastes səˈræs.tiːz, sɪ-, ⓊⓈ sə-
cerate ˈsɪə.reɪt, -rɪt, -rət, ⓊⓈ ˈsɪr.eɪt, -ɪt **-s** -s
Cerberus ˈsɜː.bər.əs, ⓊⓈ ˈsɜː-
cercari|a sɜːˈkeə.ri|.ə, ⓊⓈ sɚˈker.i- **-ae** -iː
cer|e sɪər, ⓊⓈ sɪr **-es** -z **-ing** -ɪŋ **-ed** -d

C

Pronouncing the letters CH

The consonant digraph **ch** has three main pronunciations: /tʃ/, /k/, and /ʃ/. Before the letter **r**, **ch** is always realized as /k/, e.g.:

Christmas ˈkrɪst.məs
anachronism əˈnæk.rə.nɪ.zəm

However, there is no reliable way of predicting whether **ch** will be pronounced as /tʃ/, /k/, or /ʃ/ in most other situations by looking at the spelling alone, e.g.:

chap tʃæp
stomach ˈstʌm.ək
champagne ʃæmˈpeɪn

In general, /k/ words are those originating from Greek (e.g. *chaos, chorus*). Words containing /ʃ/ are usually late borrowings from French (e.g. *champagne, chauffeur*).

The remainder, pronounced /tʃ/, are more long-established, often being common everyday words (e.g. *lunch, chew*).

In addition

Occasionally, **ch** is pronounced /dʒ/, as in British placenames such as *Greenwich* /ˈgren.ɪdʒ/ and *Norwich* /ˈnɒr.ɪdʒ/.

Words from Scots ending **ch** may be pronounced /x/, but can also have the realization /k/, e.g.:

loch lɒk, lɒx (US) lɑːk, lɑːx

In the case of *yacht* **ch** is silent:

yacht jɒt (US) jɑːt

cereal ˈsɪə.ri.əl, (US) ˈsɪr.i- **-s** -z
cerebell|um ˌser.ɪˈbel|.əm, -əˈ-, (US) -əˈ- **-ums** -əmz **-a** -ə
Cerebos® ˈser.ə.bɒs, ˈ-ɪ-, (US) -bɑːs
cerebral ˈser.ə.brᵊl, ˈ-ɪ-; səˈriː-, sɪ-, (US) ˈser.ə-; (US) səˈriː- **-s** -z ˌ**cerebral** ˈ**palsy**
cere|brate ˈser.ə|.breɪt, ˈ-ɪ-, (US) ˈ-ə- **-brates** -breɪts **-brating** -breɪ.tɪŋ, (US) -breɪ.t̬ɪŋ **-brated** -breɪ.tɪd, (US) -breɪ.t̬ɪd
cerebration ˌser.əˈbreɪ.ʃᵊn, -əˈ-, (US) -əˈ- **-s** -z
cerebr|um səˈriː.br|əm, sɪ-; ser.ɪ-, ˈ-ə-, (US) ˈser.ə-; (US) səˈriː- **-a** -ə **-ums** -əmz
Ceredigion ˌker.əˈdɪg.i.ɒn, -ɪˈ-, (US) -ɑːn
cerement ˈsɪə.mənt, ˈser.ə.mənt, (US) ˈsɪr.mənt **-s** -s
ceremonial ˌser.ɪˈməʊ.ni.əl, -əˈ-, (US) -əˈmoʊ- **-s** -z **-ly** -i **-ism** -ɪ.zᵊm
ceremonious ˌser.ɪˈməʊ.ni.əs, -əˈ-, (US) -əˈmoʊ- **-ly** -li **-ness** -nəs, -nɪs
ceremon|y ˈser.ɪ.mə.n|i, ˈ-ə-, (US) ˈ-ə.moʊ.n|i **-ies** -iz
Ceres ˈsɪə.riːz, (US) ˈsɪr.iːz
cerif ˈser.ɪf **-s** -s
cerise səˈriːz, sɪ-, -ˈriːs, (US) sə-
cerium ˈsɪə.ri.əm, (US) ˈsɪr.i-
ceroplastic ˌsɪə.rəʊˈplæs.tɪk, -ˈplɑː.stɪk, (US) ˈsɪr.oʊ.plæs-, ˈser-
cert sɜːt, (US) sɝːt **-s** -s
certain ˈsɜː.tᵊn, -tɪn, (US) ˈsɝː- **-ly** -li
certaint|y ˈsɜː.tᵊn.t|i, -tɪn-, (US) ˈsɝː- **-ies** -iz
certes ˈsɜː.tiːz, -tɪz, sɜːts, (US) ˈsɝː.tiːz
certifiab|le ˌsɜː.tɪˈfaɪ.ə.b|ᵊl, -təˈ-, ˈsɜː.tɪ.faɪ-, -tə-, (US) ˈsɝː.t̬ə.faɪ- **-ly** -li
certificate n səˈtɪf.ɪ.kət, sɜː-, ˈ-ə-, -kɪt, (US) sɚ- **-s** -s
certifi|cate v səˈtɪf.ɪ|.keɪt, sɜː-, ˈ-ə-, (US) sɚ- **-cates** -keɪts **-cating** -keɪ.tɪŋ, (US) -keɪ.t̬ɪŋ **-cated** -keɪ.tɪd, -kə.tɪd, -kɪ-, (US) -keɪ.t̬ɪd
certification *act of certifying:* ˌsɜː.tɪ.fɪˈkeɪ.ʃᵊn, -fəˈ-, (US) ˌsɝː.t̬ə- *providing with a certificate:* ˌsɜː.tɪ.fɪˈkeɪ.ʃᵊn, səˌtɪ-, -fəˈ-, (US) ˌsɝː.t̬ə- **-s** -z
certificatory səˈtɪf.ɪ.kə.tᵊr.i, sɜː-, -keɪ-, -tri, (US) sɚˈtɪf.ɪ.kə.tɔːr.i
certif|y ˈsɜː.tɪ.f|aɪ, -tə-, (US) -t̬ɪ-, -t̬ə- **-ies** -aɪz **-ying** -aɪ.ɪŋ **-ied** -aɪd **-ier/s** -aɪ.əʳ/z, (US) -aɪ.ɚ/z ˌ**certified** ˈ**mail**
certiorari ˌsɜː.ʃi.ɔːˈreə.raɪ, -ti.əˈ-, -ˈrɑː.ri, (US) ˌsɝː.ʃi.əˈrer.i, -ˈrɑːr- **-s** -z
certitude ˈsɜː.tɪ.tʃuːd, -tjuːd, (US) ˈsɝː.t̬ə.tuːd, -tjuːd
cerulean səˈruː.li.ən, sɪ-, (US) səˈruː-
cerumen səˈruː.men, sɪ-, -mən, (US) səˈruː-
Cervantes sɜːˈvæn.tiːz, -tɪz, (US) sɚ-
cervical səˈvaɪ.kᵊl, sɜː-; ˈsɜː.vɪ-, (US) ˈsɝː.vɪ- **cer**ˌ**vical** ˈ**smear**; ˌ**cervical** ˈ**smear** (US) ˌ**cervical** ˈ**smear**
cervine ˈsɜː.vaɪn, (US) ˈsɝː-
cer|vix ˈsɜː|.vɪks, (US) ˈsɝː- **-vices** -vɪs.iːz **-vixes** -vɪk.sɪz
César ˈseɪ.zɑːʳ, -zəʳ, (US) seɪˈzɑːr
cesarean, cesarian sɪˈzeə.ri.ən, sə-, (US) səˈzer.i- **-s** -z **ce**ˌ**sarean** ˈ**section**
Cesarewitch *Russian prince:* sɪˈzɑː.rə.vɪtʃ, sə-, (US) -ˈzɑːr.ə- *race:* sɪˈzær.ə.wɪtʃ; -ˈzɑː.rə-, -rɪ-, (US) -ˈzɑːr.ə-
Cesario siːˈzɑː.ri.əʊ, -ˈzær.i-, (US) -ˈzɑːr.i.oʊ
cesium ˈsiː.zi.əm
cess ses **-es** -ɪz
cessation sesˈeɪ.ʃᵊn, sɪˈseɪ-, sə- **-s** -z
cession ˈseʃ.ᵊn **-s** -z
Cessna® ˈses.nə
cesspit ˈses.pɪt **-s** -s
cesspool ˈses.puːl **-s** -z
c'est la vie ˌseɪ.læˈviː, -lɑːˈ-, -ləˈ-
cestui que trust ˌses.twiː.kiːˈtrʌst **-s** -s
cestui que vie ˌses.twiː.kiːˈviː **-s** -z
cestuis que trust ˌses.twiːz.kiːˈtrʌst
cestuis que vie ˌses.twiːz.kiːˈviː
cestus ˈses.təs **-es** -ɪz
Cetacea sɪˈteɪ.ʃə, sə-, -ʃi.ə, -si.ə, (US) -ʃə
cetacean sɪˈteɪ.ʃᵊn, sə-, -ʃi.ən, -si.ən, (US) -ʃᵊn **-s** -z
cetaceous sɪˈteɪ.ʃəs, sə-, -ʃi.əs, -si.əs, (US) -ʃəs
cetane ˈsiː.teɪn
Cetewayo ketʃˈwaɪ.əʊ, ˌket.iˈwaɪ-, -wɑː.jəʊ, (US) -ˈwaɪ.oʊ
Ceuta ˈsjuː.tə, seɪˈuː.tə, (US) ˈseɪ.uː.t̬ə
Cévennes sevˈen, səˈven, sɪ-, -venz, (US) seɪˈven
ceviche səˈviː.tʃeɪ, sevˈiː-, -tʃiː
Ceylon sɪˈlɒn, sə-, (US) sɪˈlɑːn, seɪ-
Ceylonese ˌsel.əˈniːz, ˌsiː.lə-, (US) ˌsiː.ləˈniːz, ˌseɪ-, -ˈniːs
Cézanne seɪˈzæn, sɪ-, sezˈæn, (US) seɪˈzɑːn
cf. (abbrev. for **compare**) kəmˈpeəʳ, kənˈfɜːʳ; ˌsiːˈef, (US) kəmˈper, kənˈfɝː; (US) ˌsiːˈef
CFC ˌsiː.efˈsiː **-s** -z
cg (abbrev. for **centigramme, centigram**) ˈsen.tɪ.græm, (US) -t̬ə-
Chablis ˈʃæb.liː, -bli, -ˈ-, (US) ʃæbˈli, ʃɑːˈbli
Chabrier ˈʃæb.ri.eɪ, ˈʃɑː.bri-, –ˈ-, (US) ˌʃɑː.briˈeɪ
cha-cha ˈtʃɑː.tʃɑː **-s** -z **-ing** -ɪŋ **-ed** -d
cha-cha-cha ˌtʃɑː.tʃɑːˈtʃɑː **-s** -z
chaconne ʃækˈɒn, ʃəˈkɒn, (US) ʃɑːˈkɑːn, ʃækˈɑːn, -ˈɔːn **-s** -z
chacun à son goût ˌʃæk.ɜːnˌɑː.sɔ̃ːŋˈguː, -æ.sɒŋˈ-, (US) ʃɑːˌkuːnˌɑː.sɑːnˈ-, ʃækˌuːn-, -sɔːnˈ-
chad, C~ tʃæd **-s** -z **-ian/s** -i.ən/z
Chadband ˈtʃæd.bænd
Chadderton ˈtʃæd.ə.tᵊn, (US) -ɚ.t̬ən
chador ˈtʃɑː.dɔːʳ, ˈtʃʌd.ɔːʳ, -dəʳ, (US) ˈtʃʌd.ɚ **-s** -z
Chadwick ˈtʃæd.wɪk
chaf|e tʃeɪf **-es** -s **-ing** -ɪŋ **-ed** -t
chafer ˈtʃeɪ.fəʳ, (US) -fɚ **-s** -z
chaff tʃæf, tʃɑːf, (US) tʃæf **-s** -s **-ing/ly** -ɪŋ/li **-ed** -t
chaff|er ˈtʃæf|.əʳ, (US) -ɚ **-ers** -əz, (US) -ɚz **-ering** -ᵊr.ɪŋ **-ered** -əd, (US) -ɚd
Chaffey ˈtʃeɪ.fi
chaffinch ˈtʃæf.ɪntʃ **-es** -ɪz
chaff|y ˈtʃæf|.i, ˈtʃɑː.f|i, (US) ˈtʃæf|.i **-iness** -ɪ.nəs, -ɪ.nɪs
chafing-dish ˈtʃeɪ.fɪŋ.dɪʃ **-es** -ɪz
Chagall ʃægˈæl, ʃəˈgæl, -gɑːl, (US) ʃəˈgɑːl
chagrin n ˈʃæg.rɪn, -rᵊn, (US) ʃəˈgrɪn
chagrin v ˈʃæg.rɪn, ʃəˈgriːn, (US) ʃəˈgrɪn **-s** -z **-ing** -ɪŋ **-ed** -d

Chaim haɪm, xaɪm
chain tʃeɪn -s -z -ing -ɪŋ -ed -d ˈ**chain** ˌ**gang;** ˌ**chain** ˈ**letter;** ˈ**chain** ˌ**mail;** ˌ**chain re**ˈ**action;** ˈ**chain** ˌ**store**
chainless ˈtʃeɪn.ləs, -lɪs
chain-link ˈtʃeɪn.lɪŋk ˌ**chain-link** ˈ**fence**
chainsaw ˈtʃeɪn.sɔː, ⓊⓈ -sɑː, -sɔː -s -z -ing -ɪŋ -ed -d
chain-smok|e ˈtʃeɪn.sməʊk, ⓊⓈ -smoʊk -es -s -ing -ɪŋ -ed -t -er/s -əʳ/z, ⓊⓈ -ɚ/z
chainstitch ˈtʃeɪn.stɪtʃ
chainwork ˈtʃeɪn.wɜːk, ⓊⓈ -wɝːk
chair tʃeəʳ, ⓊⓈ tʃer -s -z -ing -ɪŋ -ed -d
chairlift ˈtʃeə.lɪft, ⓊⓈ ˈtʃer- -s -s
chair|man ˈtʃeə|.mən, ⓊⓈ ˈtʃer- -men -mən
chairmanship ˈtʃeə.mən.ʃɪp, ⓊⓈ ˈtʃer- -s -s
chairperson ˈtʃeəˌpɜː.sᵊn, ⓊⓈ ˈtʃerˌpɝː- -s -z
chair|woman ˈtʃeə|ˌwʊm.ən, ⓊⓈ ˈtʃer- -women -ˌwɪm.ɪn
chais|e ʃeɪz, ⓊⓈ ʃeɪz, tʃeɪs -es -ɪz
chaise(s) longue(s) ˌʃeɪzˈlɒŋ, ˌʃez-, -ˈlɒŋg, -ˈlɔ̃ːŋg, ⓊⓈ ˌʃeɪzˈlɔːŋ, ˌtʃeɪs-, -ˈlɑːŋ

> Note: a common British mispronunciation is /-lɒndʒ/

chakra ˈtʃæk.rə, ⓊⓈ ˈtʃɑː.krə, ˈtʃæk.rə -s -z
Chalcedon ˈkæl.sɪ.dᵊn, -dɒn, ⓊⓈ -sə.dɑːn
chalcedony kælˈsed.ᵊn.i, ⓊⓈ kælˈsed.ᵊn.i, ˈkæl.sə.doʊ.ni
chalcedonyx ˌkæl.sɪˈdɒn.ɪks, ⓊⓈ -ˈdɑː.nɪks; ⓊⓈ kælˈsed.ᵊn.ɪks -es -ɪz
Chalcis ˈkæl.sɪs
chalcography kælˈkɒg.rə.fi, ⓊⓈ -ˈkɑː.grə-
Chalde|a kælˈdiː|.ə, kɔːl-, ⓊⓈ kæl- -an/s -ən/z
Chaldee ˈkæl.diː, ˈkɔːl-, -ˈ-, ⓊⓈ ˈkæl- -s -z
chaldron ˈtʃɔːl.drᵊn, ⓊⓈ ˈtʃɔːl-, ˈtʃɑːl- -s -z
chalet ˈʃæl.eɪ, ˈʃæl.i, ⓊⓈ ʃælˈeɪ -s -z
Chalfont *in Buckinghamshire:* ˈtʃæl.fənt, -fɒnt; *old-fashioned:* ˈtʃɑː-, ⓊⓈ -fɑːnt
chalic|e ˈtʃæl.ɪs -es -ɪz -ed -t
chalk, C~ tʃɔːk, ⓊⓈ tʃɔːk, tʃɑːk -s -s -ing -ɪŋ -ed -t ˈ**chalk** ˌ**pit;** **as** ˌ**different as** ˌ**chalk and** ˈ**cheese**
chalkboard ˈtʃɔːk.bɔːd, ⓊⓈ -bɔːrd, ˈtʃɑːk- -s -z
Chalker ˈtʃɔː.kəʳ, ⓊⓈ ˈtʃɔː.kɚ, ˈtʃɑː-
chalkface ˈtʃɔːk.feɪs, ⓊⓈ ˈtʃɔːk-, ˈtʃɑːk-
Chalkley ˈtʃɔːk.li, ⓊⓈ ˈtʃɔːk-, ˈtʃɑːk-
chalkstone ˈtʃɔːk.stəʊn, ⓊⓈ ˈtʃɔːk.stoʊn, ˈtʃɑːk- -s -z
chalk|y ˈtʃɔː.k|i, ⓊⓈ ˈtʃɔː-, ˈtʃɑː- -ier -i.əʳ, ⓊⓈ -i.ɚ -iest -i.ɪst, -i.əst -ily -ᵊl.i, -ɪ.li -iness -ɪ.nəs, -ɪ.nɪs
challeng|e ˈtʃæl.ɪndʒ, -əndʒ -es -ɪz -ing -ɪŋ -ed -d -er/s -əʳ/z, ⓊⓈ -ɚ/z
Challenor ˈtʃæl.ə.nəʳ, ˈ-ɪ-, ⓊⓈ -ə.nɚ
challis, C~ ˈʃæl.ɪs, ˈʃæl.i
Challoner ˈtʃæl.ə.nəʳ, ⓊⓈ -nɚ
Chalmers ˈtʃɑː.məz, ˈtʃæl-, ⓊⓈ -mɚz
Chaloner ˈtʃæl.ə.nəʳ, ⓊⓈ -nɚ
chalybeate kəˈlɪb.i.ət, -ɪt, -eɪt
chamber ˈtʃeɪm.bəʳ, ⓊⓈ -bɚ -s -z -ed -d ˈ**chamber** ˌ**music;** ˈ**chamber** ˌ**pot**
chamberlain ˈtʃeɪm.bᵊl.ɪn, -ən, ⓊⓈ -bɚ.lɪn -s -z
Chamberlain ˈtʃeɪm.bᵊl.ɪn, -ən, -eɪn, ⓊⓈ -bɚ.lɪn
chamberlainship ˈtʃeɪm.bᵊl.ɪn.ʃɪp, -ən-, ⓊⓈ -bɚ.lɪn- -s -s
chambermaid ˈtʃeɪm.bə.meɪd, ⓊⓈ -bɚ- -s -z
Chambers ˈtʃeɪm.bəz, ⓊⓈ -bɚz
Chambourcy® ʃæmˈbʊə.si, -ˈbɔː-, ⓊⓈ ˌʃɑːm.bʊrˈsiː
chambray ˈʃæm.breɪ
chambré ˈʃɑ̃ːm.breɪ, ⓊⓈ ʃɑːmˈbreɪ
chameleon kəˈmiː.li.ən, ⓊⓈ -li.ən, -ˈmiːl.jən -s -s
chamfer ˈʃæmp.fəʳ, ˈtʃæmp-, ⓊⓈ -fɚ -s -z
chamois **sing** *goat-antelope:* ˈʃæm.wɑː, ⓊⓈ ˈʃæm.i, ʃæmˈwɑː **plur** ˈʃæm.wɑːz, ⓊⓈ ˈʃæm.iz, ʃæmˈwɑːz *leather:* ˈʃæm.i ˈ**chamois** ˌ**leather,** ˌ**chamois** ˈ**leather**
chamomile ˈkæm.ə.maɪl, ⓊⓈ -miːl, -maɪl
Chamonix ˈʃæm.ə.niː, -ɒn.iː, ⓊⓈ ˌʃæm.əˈniː
champ tʃæmp -s -s -ing -ɪŋ -ed -t
champagne, C~ ʃæmˈpeɪn -s -z *stress shift:* ˌ**champagne** ˈ**socialist**
champaign ˈtʃæm.peɪn -s -z
champers ˈʃæm.pəz, ⓊⓈ -pɚz
champerty ˈtʃæm.pə.ti, -pɜː-, ⓊⓈ -pɚ.t̬i
champignon ˈʃæm.piː.njɔ̃ː, ˈʃɑ̃ːm-, ˌ--ˈ-; ⓊⓈ ˌʃæm.pinˈjɔːn, -ˈjɑːn -s -z
champion, C~ ˈtʃæm.pi.ən, ⓊⓈ -pi.ən, -pjən -s -z -ing -ɪŋ -ed -d
championship ˈtʃæm.pi.ən.ʃɪp, ⓊⓈ ˈtʃæm.pi.ən.ʃɪp, -pjən- -s -s
Champlain *French explorer:* ʃæmˈpleɪn; ʃɔ̃ːŋˈplɑ̃ːŋ, ⓊⓈ ʃæmˈpleɪn; ⓊⓈ ʃɑ̃ːˈplɑ̃ːŋ *lake in US:* ʃæmˈpleɪn
Champneys ˈtʃæmp.niz
Champs Elysées ˌʃɑ̃ːnz.elˈiː.zeɪ, ˌʃɔ̃ːnz-, ⓊⓈ ˌʃɑːnz.eɪ.liːˈzeɪ
chanc|e tʃɑːnts, ⓊⓈ tʃænts -es -ɪz -ing -ɪŋ -ed -t -er/s -əʳ/z, ⓊⓈ -ɚ/z
chancel ˈtʃɑːnt.sᵊl, ⓊⓈ ˈtʃænt- -s -z
chanceller|y ˈtʃɑːnt.sᵊl.ᵊr|.i, ⓊⓈ ˈtʃænt- -ies -iz
chancellor, C~ ˈtʃɑːnt.sᵊl.əʳ, -sɪ.ləʳ, ⓊⓈ ˈtʃænt- -s -z -ship/s -ʃɪp/s ˌ**chancellor of the ex**ˈ**chequer**
Chancellorsville ˈtʃɑːnt.sᵊl.əz.vɪl, ⓊⓈ ˈtʃænt.sᵊl.ɚz-
chancer|y, C~ ˈtʃɑːnt.sᵊr|.i, ⓊⓈ ˈtʃænt- -ies -iz
chancre ˈʃæŋ.kəʳ, ⓊⓈ -kɚ
chancroid ˈʃæŋ.krɔɪd -s -z
chanc|y ˈtʃɑːnt.s|i, ⓊⓈ ˈtʃænt- -ier -i.əʳ, ⓊⓈ -i.ɚ -iest -i.ɪst, -i.əst
chandelier ˌʃæn.dəˈlɪəʳ, -dɪˈ-, ⓊⓈ -ˈlɪr -s -z
Chandigarh ˌtʃæn.dɪˈgɜːʳ, ˌtʃʌn-, -ˈgɑːʳ, ˈ---, ⓊⓈ -ˈgɝː, -ˈgɑːr
chandler, C~ ˈtʃɑːnd.ləʳ, ⓊⓈ ˈtʃænd.lɚ -s -z
Chandos ˈʃæn.dɒs, ˈtʃæn.dɒs, ⓊⓈ -dɑːs

> Note: **Chandos Street** in London is generally pronounced with /ˈtʃæn-/.

Chanel ʃəˈnel, ʃænˈel
Chaney ˈtʃeɪ.ni
Chang tʃæŋ
chang|e tʃeɪndʒ -es -ɪz -ing -ɪŋ -ed -d -er/s -əʳ/z, ⓊⓈ -ɚ/z
changeability ˌtʃeɪn.dʒəˈbɪl.ə.ti, -ɪ.ti, ⓊⓈ -ə.t̬i
changeab|le ˈtʃeɪn.dʒə.b|ᵊl -ly -li -leness -ᵊl.nəs, -ᵊl.nɪs
changeful ˈtʃeɪndʒ.fᵊl, -fʊl -ly -i -ness -nəs, -nɪs
changeless ˈtʃeɪndʒ.ləs, -lɪs
changeling ˈtʃeɪndʒ.lɪŋ -s -z
changeover ˈtʃeɪndʒˌəʊ.vəʳ, ⓊⓈ -ˌoʊ.vɚ -s -z
Chang Jiang ˌtʃæŋ.dʒiˈæŋ, ⓊⓈ ˌtʃɑːŋ.dʒiˈɑːŋ, ˌtʃæŋ-, -ˈæŋ
channel ˈtʃæn.ᵊl -s -z -(l)ing -ɪŋ -(l)ed -d ˈ**Channel** ˌ**Islands;** ˌ**Channel** ˈ**Tunnel**
channelization, -isa- ˌtʃæn.ᵊl.aɪˈzeɪ.ʃᵊn, -ɪˈ-, ⓊⓈ -əˈ-
channeliz|e, -is|e ˈtʃæn.ᵊl.aɪz, ⓊⓈ -ə.laɪz -es -ɪz -ing -ɪŋ -ed -d
Channell ˈtʃæn.ᵊl
Channing ˈtʃæn.ɪŋ
Channon ˈtʃæn.ən, ˈʃæn.ən
chanson ˈʃɑ̃ːn.sɔ̃ːŋ, -sɒn, -ˈ-, ⓊⓈ ʃɑ̃ːnˈsoʊn, -ˈsɑːn, -ˈsɔːn -s -z
chant, C~ tʃɑːnt, ⓊⓈ tʃænt -s -s -ing -ɪŋ, ⓊⓈ ˈtʃæn.t̬ɪŋ -ed -ɪd, ⓊⓈ ˈtʃæn.t̬ɪd -er/s -əʳ/z, ⓊⓈ ˈtʃæn.t̬ɚ/z
Chantal ʃɑ̃ːnˈtɑːl, ʃæn-, -tæl, ⓊⓈ ʃɑːnˈtɑːl
Chantelle ʃɑ̃ːnˈtel, ʃæn-, ⓊⓈ ʃɑːnˈtel, ʃæn-
Chanter ˈtʃɑːn.təʳ, ⓊⓈ ˈtʃæn.t̬ɚ
chanterelle ˌʃɑ̃ːn.təˈrel, ˌʃæn-, ˌtʃæn-, ⓊⓈ ˌʃæn.t̬əˈ-, ˌʃɑːn- -s -z
chanteus|e ʃɑ̃ːnˈtɜːz, ʃɑːn-, ⓊⓈ ʃɑ̃ːnˈtuːz, ʃæn-, -ˈtuːs -es -ɪz
chantey ˈʃæn.ti, ˈtʃæn-, ˈtʃɑːn-, ⓊⓈ ˈʃæn.t̬i -s -z
chanticleer, C~ ˈtʃɑːn.tɪ.klɪəʳ, ˈtʃænt-, ˈʃɑːn-, -tə-, ˌ--ˈ-, ⓊⓈ ˈtʃæn.t̬ə.klɪr, ˈʃæn- -s -z
Chantilly *in France:* ʃænˈtɪl.i, ʃɑ̃ːn-, ⓊⓈ ʃænˈtɪl.i; ⓊⓈ ˌʃɑːn.tiˈjiː
Chantrey ˈtʃɑːn.tri, ⓊⓈ ˈtʃæn-
chantr|y ˈtʃɑːn.tr|i, ⓊⓈ ˈtʃæn- -ies -iz
chant|y ˈtʃɑːn.t|i, ⓊⓈ ˈtʃæn.t̬|i -ies -iz
Chanukah ˈhʌn.ʊ.kə, ˈhæn-, ˈxʌn-, ⓊⓈ ˈhɑː.nə.kə, ˈxɑː-, -nʊ.kɑː

chaos ˈkeɪ.ɒs, ⓤⓢ -ɑːs
chaotic keɪˈɒt.ɪk, ⓤⓢ -ˈɑː.t̬ɪk **-ally** -əl.i, -li
chap tʃæp **-s** -s **-ping** -ɪŋ **-ped** -t
chapat(t)i tʃəˈpɑː.ti, -ˈpæt.i **-(e)s** -z
chapbook ˈtʃæp.bʊk **-s** -s
chape tʃeɪp **-s** -s
chapeau ˈʃæp.əʊ, -ˈ-, ⓤⓢ ʃæpˈoʊ **-s** -z
chapeaux (alternative plural of **chapeau**) ˈʃæp.əʊ, -əʊz, ⓤⓢ ʃæpˈoʊ, -ˈoʊz
chapel ˈtʃæp.əl **-s** -z
Chapel-en-le-Frith ˌtʃæp.əl.ən.ləˈfrɪθ, -en.ləˈ-
chapelr|y ˈtʃæp.əl.r|i **-ies** -iz
Chapeltown ˈtʃæp.əl.taʊn
chaperon|e, chaperon ˈʃæp.ər.əʊn, ⓤⓢ -ə.roʊn **-es** -z **-ing** -ɪŋ **-ed** -d **-age** -ɪdʒ
chapfallen ˈtʃæpˌfɔː.lən, ⓤⓢ -ˌfɔː-, -ˌfɑː-
chaplain ˈtʃæp.lɪn **-s** -z
chaplainc|y ˈtʃæp.lɪnt.s|i, -lənt- **-ies** -iz
chaplet ˈtʃæp.lət, -lɪt, -let **-s** -s
Chaplin ˈtʃæp.lɪn
Chapman ˈtʃæp.mən
Chapone ʃəˈpəʊn, ⓤⓢ -poʊn
Chappaquiddick ˌtʃæp.əˈkwɪd.ɪk
Chappell ˈtʃæp.əl
chappie, chappy ˈtʃæp.i **-s** -z
Chapple ˈtʃæp.əl
chapstick ˈtʃæp.stɪk **-s** -s
chapter ˈtʃæp.təʳ, ⓤⓢ -tɚ **-s** -z ˈ**chapter** ˌ**house**; ˌ**chapter and** ˈ**verse**
Chapultepec tʃəˈpuːl.təˌpek, -ˈpʊl-
char tʃɑːʳ, ⓤⓢ tʃɑːr **-s** -z **-ring** -ɪŋ **-red** -d
charabanc ˈʃær.ə.bæŋ, -bɑ̃ːŋ, ⓤⓢ -bæŋ **-s** -s
character ˈkær.ək.təʳ, -ɪk-, ⓤⓢ ˈker.ək.tɚ, ˈkær- **-s** -z
characteristic ˌkær.ək.təˈrɪs.tɪk, -ɪk-, ⓤⓢ ˌker.ək-, ˌkær- **-s** -s **-al** -əl **-ally** -əl.i, -li
characterization, -isa- ˌkær.ək.tər.aɪˈzeɪ.ʃən, -ɪk-, -ɪˈ-, ⓤⓢ ˌker.ək.tɚ.əˈ-, ˌkær- **-s** -z
characteriz|e, -is|e ˈkær.ək.tər.aɪz, -ɪk-, ⓤⓢ ˈker.ək.tə.raɪz, ˈkær- **-es** -ɪz **-ing** -ɪŋ **-ed** -d
characterless ˈkær.ək.tə.ləs, -ɪk-, -lɪs, ⓤⓢ ˈker.ək.tɚ-, ˈkær- **-ness** -nəs, -nɪs
charade ʃəˈrɑːd, ⓤⓢ -ˈreɪd **-s** -z
charbroil ˈtʃɑː.brɔɪl, ⓤⓢ ˈtʃɑːr- **-s** -z **-ing** -ɪŋ **-ed** -d
charcoal ˈtʃɑː.kəʊl, ⓤⓢ ˈtʃɑːr.koʊl
chard, C~ tʃɑːd, ⓤⓢ tʃɑːrd
Chardin ˈʃɑː.dæ̃ŋ, -ˈ-, ⓤⓢ ʃɑːrˈdæ̃n
chardonnay, C~ ˈʃɑː.dən.eɪ, ⓤⓢ ˈʃɑːr-, ˌ--ˈ- **-s** -z
char|e tʃeəʳ, ⓤⓢ tʃer **-es** -z **-ing** -ɪŋ **-ed** -d
charg|e tʃɑːdʒ, ⓤⓢ tʃɑːrdʒ **-es** -ɪz **-ing** -ɪŋ **-ed** -d ˈ**charge** ˌ**card**
chargeab|le ˈtʃɑː.dʒə.b|əl, ⓤⓢ ˈtʃɑːr- **-ly** -li **-leness** -əl.nəs, -nɪs
chargé(s) d'affaires *sing:* ˌʃɑː.ʒeɪ.dæfˈeəʳ, -dəˈfeəʳ, ⓤⓢ ˌʃɑːr.ʒeɪ.dəˈfer, -dæfˈer; *plural:* -z
charger ˈtʃɑː.dʒəʳ, ⓤⓢ ˈtʃɑːr.dʒɚ **-s** -z
chargrilled ˈtʃɑː.grɪld, ⓤⓢ ˈtʃɑːr-
Charing Cross ˌtʃær.ɪŋˈkrɒs, ˌtʃeər-, ⓤⓢ ˌtʃer.ɪŋˈkrɑːs, ˌtʃær-
chariot ˈtʃær.i.ət, ⓤⓢ ˈtʃer-, ˈtʃær- **-s** -s
charioteer ˌtʃær.i.əˈtɪəʳ, ⓤⓢ ˌtʃer.i.əˈtɪr, ˌtʃær- **-s** -z
charisma kəˈrɪz.mə
charismatic ˌkær.ɪzˈmæt.ɪk, ⓤⓢ ˌker.ɪzˈmæt̬-, ˌkær-
charitab|le ˈtʃær.ɪ.tə.b|əl, ˈ-ə-, ⓤⓢ ˈtʃer-, ˈtʃær- **-ly** -li **-leness** -əl.nəs, -nɪs
charit|y, C~ ˈtʃær.ɪ.t|i, -ə.t|i, ⓤⓢ ˈtʃer.ə.t̬|i, ˈtʃær- **-ies** -iz
charivari ˌʃɑː.rɪˈvɑː.ri, ⓤⓢ ʃəˌrɪv.əˈriː; ⓤⓢ ˌʃɑː.rɪˈvɑː.ri, ˌʃɪv.əˈriː **-s** -z
charivaria ˌʃɑː.rɪvˈɑː.ri.ə, ⓤⓢ ˌʃɑːr.ɪˈvɑːr.i-
charlad|y ˈtʃɑːˌleɪ.d|i, ⓤⓢ ˈtʃɑːr- **-ies** -iz
charlatan ˈʃɑː.lə.tən, -tæn, ⓤⓢ ˈʃɑːr.lə.tən **-s** -z
charlatanism ˈʃɑː.lə.tən.ɪ.zəm, ⓤⓢ ˈʃɑːr.lə.tən-, -t̬ə.nɪ- **-s** -z
charlatanry ˈʃɑː.lə.tən.ri, ⓤⓢ ˈʃɑːr.lə.tən-, -t̬ən-
Charlbury ˈtʃɑːl.bər.i, ⓤⓢ ˈtʃɑːrl.ber.i, -bɚ-
Charlecote ˈtʃɑːl.kəʊt, ⓤⓢ ˈtʃɑːrl.koʊt
Charlemagne ˈʃɑː.lə.meɪn, -maɪn, ˌ--ˈ-, ⓤⓢ ˈʃɑːr.lə.meɪn
Charlemont ˈtʃɑː.lɪ.mənt, ˈtʃɑːl.mənt, ⓤⓢ ˈtʃɑːr.lɪ.mənt, ˈtʃɑːrl.mənt
Charlene ˈtʃɑː.liːn, ˈʃɑː-, ʃɑːˈliːn, ⓤⓢ ʃɑːrˈliːn, ˈ--
Charleroi ˈʃɑː.lə.rɔɪ; *as if French:* ˌʃɑː.ləˈrwɑː; ⓤⓢ ˈʃɑːr-
Charles tʃɑːlz, ⓤⓢ tʃɑːrlz
Charleston ˈtʃɑːl.stən, ⓤⓢ ˈtʃɑːrl-
Charlestown ˈtʃɑːlz.taʊn, ⓤⓢ ˈtʃɑːrlz-
Charlesworth ˈtʃɑːlz.wəθ, -wɜːθ, ⓤⓢ ˈtʃɑːrlz.wɚθ, -wɝːθ
Charleville ˈʃɑː.lə.vɪl, ⓤⓢ ˈʃɑːr-
Charley ˈtʃɑː.li, ⓤⓢ ˈtʃɑːr- ˈ**charley** ˌ**horse**
charlie, C~ ˈtʃɑː.li, ⓤⓢ ˈtʃɑːr- **-s** -z
charlock ˈtʃɑː.lɒk, ⓤⓢ ˈtʃɑːr.lɑːk
charlotte, C~ ˈʃɑː.lət, ⓤⓢ ˈʃɑːr- **-s** -s
Charlottenburg ʃɑːˈlɒt.ən.bɜːg, ⓤⓢ ʃɑːrˈlɑː.tən.bɝːg
Charlottesville ˈʃɑː.ləts.vɪl, ⓤⓢ ˈʃɑːr-
Charlton ˈtʃɑːl.tən, ⓤⓢ ˈtʃɑːrl-
charm tʃɑːm, ⓤⓢ tʃɑːrm **-s** -z **-ed** -d **-ing** -ɪŋ **-er/s** -əʳ/z, ⓤⓢ -ɚ/z **-less/ly** -ləs/li, -lɪs.li
Charmaine ʃɑːˈmeɪn, ⓤⓢ ʃɑːr-
Charmian ˈtʃɑː.mi.ən, ˈʃɑː-, ˈkɑː-, ⓤⓢ ˈtʃɑːr-, ˈʃɑːr-, ˈkɑːr-
Charmin® ˈtʃɑː.mɪn, ⓤⓢ ˈʃɑːr-
charming ˈtʃɑː.mɪŋ, ⓤⓢ ˈtʃɑːr- **-ly** -li
charnel ˈtʃɑː.nəl, ⓤⓢ ˈtʃɑːr- ˈ**charnel** ˌ**house**
Charnock ˈtʃɑː.nɒk, -nək, ⓤⓢ ˈtʃɑːr.nɑːk
Charnwood ˈtʃɑːn.wʊd, -wəd, ⓤⓢ ˈtʃɑːrn-
Charolais *sing:* ˈʃær.ə.leɪ, ⓤⓢ ˌʃɑːr.əˈleɪ *plur:* ˈʃær.ə.leɪ, -leɪz, ⓤⓢ ˌʃɑːr.əˈleɪ, -ˈleɪz
Charon ˈkeə.rən, -rɒn, ⓤⓢ ˈker.ən
Charpentier ʃɑːˈpɑ̃ːn.ti.eɪ, ⓤⓢ ʃɑːrˌpɑ̃ːn.tiˈeɪ, -ˈtjeɪ
Charrington ˈtʃær.ɪŋ.tən, ⓤⓢ ˈtʃer-, ˈtʃær-
chart tʃɑːt, ⓤⓢ tʃɑːrt **-s** -s **-ing** -ɪŋ, ⓤⓢ ˈtʃɑːr.t̬ɪŋ **-ed** -ɪd, ⓤⓢ ˈtʃɑːr.t̬ɪd
chart|er, C~ ˈtʃɑː.t|əʳ, ⓤⓢ ˈtʃɑːr.t̬|ɚ **-ers** -əz, ⓤⓢ -ɚz **-ering** -ər.ɪŋ **-ered** -əd, ⓤⓢ -ɚd **-erer/s** -ər.əʳ/z, ⓤⓢ -ɚ.ɚ/z ˈ**charter** ˌ**flight**; ˌ**chartered a**ˈ**ccountant**
Charterhouse ˈtʃɑː.tə.haʊs, ⓤⓢ ˈtʃɑːr.t̬ɚ-
Charteris ˈtʃɑː.təz, -tər.ɪs, ⓤⓢ ˈtʃɑːr.t̬ɚ.ɪs
charterpart|y ˈtʃɑː.təˌpɑː.t|i, ⓤⓢ ˈtʃɑːr.t̬ɚˌpɑːr.t̬|i **-ies** -iz
chart|ism, C~ ˈtʃɑː.t|ɪ.zəm, ⓤⓢ ˈtʃɑːr.t̬|ɪ- **-ist/s** -ɪst/s
Chartres ˈʃɑː.trə; ʃɑːt, ⓤⓢ ˈʃɑːr.trə; ⓤⓢ ʃɑːrt
Chartreuse® ʃɑːˈtrɜːz, ⓤⓢ ʃɑːrˈtruːz
Chartwell ˈtʃɑːt.wel, -wəl, ⓤⓢ ˈtʃɑːrt-
char|woman ˈtʃɑː|ˌwʊm.ən, ⓤⓢ ˈtʃɑːr- **-women** -ˌwɪm.ɪn
char|y ˈtʃeə.r|i, ⓤⓢ ˈtʃer|.i **-ier** -i.əʳ, ⓤⓢ -i.ɚ **-iest** -i.ɪst, -i.əst **-ily** -əl.i, -ɪ.li **-iness** -ɪ.nəs, -ɪ.nɪs
Charybdis kəˈrɪb.dɪs
Chas tʃæz, tʃɑːlz, ⓤⓢ tʃæz, tʃɑːrlz
chas|e, C~ tʃeɪs **-es** -ɪz **-ing** -ɪŋ **-ed** -t **-er/s** -əʳ/z, ⓤⓢ -ɚ/z
chasm ˈkæz.əm **-s** -z
chassé ˈʃæs.eɪ, ⓤⓢ -ˈ- **-s** -z
chasseur ʃæsˈɜːʳ, ⓤⓢ -ˈɝː **-s** -z
chassis *sing:* ˈʃæs.i, -iː, ⓤⓢ ˈtʃæs-, ˈʃæs- *plur:* ˈʃæs.iz, -iːz, ⓤⓢ ˈtʃæs-, ˈʃæs-
chaste tʃeɪst **-ly** -li **-ness** -nəs, -nɪs
chasten ˈtʃeɪ.sən **-s** -z **-ing** -ɪŋ **-ed** -d
chastis|e tʃæsˈtaɪz, ⓤⓢ ˈ-- **-es** -ɪz **-ing** -ɪŋ **-ed** -d
chastisement tʃæsˈtaɪz.mənt, ˈtʃæs.tɪz-, ⓤⓢ ˈtʃæs.taɪz-, -ˈ-- **-s** -s
chastiser tʃæsˈtaɪ.zəʳ, ⓤⓢ -zɚ **-s** -z
chastity, C~ ˈtʃæs.tə.ti, -tɪ-, ⓤⓢ -tə.t̬i ˈ**chastity** ˌ**belt**
chasuble ˈtʃæz.jʊ.bəl, -jə-, ⓤⓢ -jə-, ˈ-ə- **-s** -z
chat tʃæt **-s** -s **-ting** -ɪŋ, ⓤⓢ ˈtʃæt̬.ɪŋ **-ted** -ɪd, ⓤⓢ ˈtʃæt̬.ɪd ˈ**chat** ˌ**show**
Chataway ˈtʃæt.ə.weɪ, ⓤⓢ ˈtʃæt̬-
château ˈʃæt.əʊ, -ˈ-, ⓤⓢ ʃætˈoʊ **-s** -z
chateaubriand, C~ ˌʃæt.əʊ.briˈɑ̃ːnd, ˌʃæt.əʊˈbriː-, ʃætˈəʊ-, ⓤⓢ ˌʃæt.oʊ.briˈɑ̃ːnd, ˌʃɑː.toʊ- **-s** -z
Châteauneuf-du-Pape ˌʃæt.əʊˌnɜːf.djuˈpæp, ⓤⓢ -oʊˌnɜːf.du-, -dju-, -ˈpɑːp

châteaux (plural of **château**) ˈʃæt.əʊ, -əʊz, -ˈ-, Ⓤⓢ ʃætˈoʊ, -ˈoʊz
chatelain ˈʃæt.əl.eɪn, -æ̃ŋ, Ⓤⓢ ˈʃæt̬.ə.leɪn **-s** -z
chatelaine ˈʃæt.əl.eɪn, Ⓤⓢ ˈʃæt̬.ə.leɪn **-s** -z
Chater ˈtʃeɪ.təʳ, Ⓤⓢ -tɚ
Chatham ˈtʃæt.əm, Ⓤⓢ ˈtʃæt̬-
chatline ˈtʃæt.laɪn **-s** -z
chatroom ˈtʃæt.ruːm, -rʊm **-s** -z
Chatsworth ˈtʃæts.wəθ, -wɜːθ, Ⓤⓢ -wɚθ, -wɝːθ
Chattanooga ˌtʃæt.ənˈuː.gə, Ⓤⓢ ˌtʃæt̬.əˈnuː-, ˌtʃæt.ənˈuː-
chattel ˈtʃæt.əl, Ⓤⓢ ˈtʃæt̬- **-s** -z
chatt|er ˈtʃæt|.əʳ, Ⓤⓢ ˈtʃæt̬|.ɚ **-ers** -əz, Ⓤⓢ -ɚz **-ering** -ər.ɪŋ **-ered** -əd, Ⓤⓢ -ɚd **-erer/s** -ər.əʳ/z, Ⓤⓢ -ɚ.ɚ/z ˈ**chattering** ˌ**classes**
chatterbox ˈtʃæt.ə.bɒks, Ⓤⓢ ˈtʃæt̬.ɚ.bɑːks **-es** -ɪz
Chatteris ˈtʃæt.ər.ɪs
Chatterley ˈtʃæt.əl.i, Ⓤⓢ ˈtʃæt̬.ɚ.li
Chatterton ˈtʃæt.ə.tən, Ⓤⓢ ˈtʃæt̬.ɚ-
Chatto ˈtʃæt.əʊ, Ⓤⓢ -oʊ, ˈtʃæt̬-
chatt|y ˈtʃæt|.i, Ⓤⓢ ˈtʃæt̬|.i **-ier** -i.əʳ, Ⓤⓢ -i.ɚ **-iest** -i.ɪst, -i.əst **-ily** -əl.i, -ɪ.li **-iness** -ɪ.nəs, -ɪ.nɪs
Chatwin ˈtʃæt.wɪn
Chaucer ˈtʃɔː.səʳ, Ⓤⓢ ˈtʃɑː.sɚ, ˈtʃɔː-
Chaucerian tʃɔːˈsɪə.ri.ən, Ⓤⓢ tʃɑːˈsɪr.i-, tʃɔː-, -ˈser-
chaudfroid ˈʃəʊ.fwɑː, -frwɑː, Ⓤⓢ ˈʃoʊ-
Chaudhuri ˈtʃaʊ.dər.i
chauffer ˈtʃɔː.fəʳ, Ⓤⓢ ˈtʃɑː.fɚ, ˈtʃɔː- **-s** -z
chauffeur ˈʃəʊ.fəʳ, ʃəʊˈfɜːʳ, Ⓤⓢ ʃoʊˈfɝː **-s** -z **-ing** -ɪŋ **-ed** -d
Chauncey ˈtʃɔːnt.si, Ⓤⓢ ˈtʃɑːnt-, ˈtʃɔːnt-
chauvin|ism ˈʃəʊ.vɪ.n|ɪ.zəm, -və-, Ⓤⓢ ˈʃoʊ- **-ist/s** -ɪst/s
chauvinistic ˌʃəʊ.vɪˈnɪs.tɪk, -vəˈ-, Ⓤⓢ ˌʃoʊ- **-ally** -əl.i, -li
chav tʃæv **-s** -z **-vy** -i
Chavez ˈtʃæv.es, Ⓤⓢ ˈʃɑː.vez, ˈtʃɑː-, -ves
Chaworth ˈtʃɑː.wəθ, -wɜːθ, Ⓤⓢ -wɚθ, -wɝːθ
Chayefsky tʃaɪˈef.ski
Che tʃeɪ
Cheadle ˈtʃiː.dəl
Cheam tʃiːm
cheap tʃiːp **-er** -əʳ, Ⓤⓢ -ɚ **-est** -ɪst, -əst **-ly** -li **-ness** -nəs, -nɪs ˌ**cheap** ˈ**shot**
cheapen ˈtʃiː.pən **-s** -z **-ing** -ɪŋ **-ed** -d
cheapie ˈtʃiː.pi **-s** -z
cheap-jack ˈtʃiːp.dʒæk **-s** -s
cheapo ˈtʃiː.pəʊ, Ⓤⓢ -poʊ **-s** -z
cheap-rate ˌtʃiːpˈreɪt *stress shift:* ˌ**cheap-rate** ˈ**call**
Cheapside ˈtʃiːp.saɪd, tʃiːpˈsaɪd
cheapskate ˈtʃiːp.skeɪt **-s** -s
cheat tʃiːt **-s** -s **-ing** -ɪŋ, Ⓤⓢ ˈtʃiː.t̬ɪŋ **-ed** -ɪd, Ⓤⓢ ˈtʃiː.t̬ɪd
Cheatham ˈtʃiː.təm, Ⓤⓢ -t̬əm
Chechen ˌtʃetʃˈen **-s** -z *stress shift:* ˌ**Chechen** ˈ**fighters**
Chechenia ˈtʃetʃ.ni.ɑː, -ni.ə; tʃetʃ.ɪˈnjɑː, Ⓤⓢ -ni.ə
Chechnya ˈtʃetʃ.ni.ə, -ni.ɑː; tʃetʃ.ɪˈnjɑː, Ⓤⓢ -ni.ə
check tʃek **-s** -s **-ing** -ɪŋ **-ed** -t ˈ**checking ac**ˌ**count**
checkbook ˈtʃek.bʊk **-s** -s
check|er, C~ ˈtʃek|.əʳ, Ⓤⓢ -ɚ **-ers** -əz, Ⓤⓢ -ɚz **-ering** -ər.ɪŋ **-ered** -əd, Ⓤⓢ -ɚd
checkerboard ˈtʃek.ə.bɔːd, Ⓤⓢ -ɚ.bɔːrd **-s** -z
checkers ˈtʃek.əz, Ⓤⓢ -ɚz
check-in ˈtʃek.ɪn **-s** -z ˈ**check-in** ˌ**desk**
Checkland ˈtʃek.lənd
checklist ˈtʃek.lɪst **-s** -s
checkma|te ˈtʃek.meɪ|t, ˌ-ˈ- **-tes** -ts **-ting** -tɪŋ, Ⓤⓢ -t̬ɪŋ **-ted** -tɪd, Ⓤⓢ -t̬ɪd
checkout ˈtʃek.aʊt **-s** -s
checkpoint ˈtʃek.pɔɪnt **-s** -s ˌ**Checkpoint** ˈ**Charlie**
checkrein ˈtʃek.reɪn **-s** -z
checkroom ˈtʃek.rʊm, -ruːm, Ⓤⓢ -ruːm, -rʊm **-s** -z
checkup ˈtʃek.ʌp **-s** -s
cheddar, C~ ˈtʃed.əʳ, Ⓤⓢ -ɚ **-s** -z **-ing** -ɪŋ **-ed** -d
cheek tʃiːk **-s** -s **-ing** -ɪŋ **-ed** -t ˌ**turn the other** ˈ**cheek**
cheekbone ˈtʃiːk.bəʊn, Ⓤⓢ -boʊn **-s** -z
Cheeke tʃiːk
cheek|y ˈtʃiː.k|i **-ier** -i.əʳ, Ⓤⓢ -i.ɚ **-iest** -i.ɪst, -i.əst **-ily** -əl.i, -ɪ.li **-iness** -ɪ.nəs, -ɪ.nɪs
cheep tʃiːp **-s** -s **-ing** -ɪŋ **-ed** -t
cheer tʃɪəʳ, Ⓤⓢ tʃɪr **-s** -z **-ing** -ɪŋ **-ed** -d
cheerful ˈtʃɪə.fəl, -fʊl, Ⓤⓢ ˈtʃɪr- **-ly** -i **-ness** -nəs, -nɪs
cheerio ˌtʃɪə.riˈəʊ, Ⓤⓢ ˌtʃɪr.iˈoʊ **-s** -z
Cheerios® ˈtʃɪə.ri.əʊz, Ⓤⓢ ˈtʃɪr.i.oʊz
cheerleader ˈtʃɪəˌliː.dəʳ, Ⓤⓢ ˈtʃɪrˌliː.dɚ **-s** -z
cheerless ˈtʃɪə.ləs, -lɪs, Ⓤⓢ ˈtʃɪr- **-ly** -li **-ness** -nəs, -nɪs
cheer|y ˈtʃɪə.r|i, Ⓤⓢ ˈtʃɪr|.i **-ier** -i.əʳ, Ⓤⓢ -i.ɚ **-iest** -i.ɪst, -i.əst **-ily** -əl.i, -ɪ.li **-iness** -ɪ.nəs, -ɪ.nɪs
chees|e tʃiːz **-es** -ɪz **-ed** -d ˌ**cheesed** ˈ**off**
cheeseboard ˈtʃiːz.bɔːd, Ⓤⓢ -bɔːrd **-s** -z
cheeseburger ˈtʃiːzˌbɜː.gəʳ, Ⓤⓢ -ˌbɝː.gɚ **-s** -z
cheesecake ˈtʃiːz.keɪk **-s** -s
cheesecloth ˈtʃiːz.klɒθ, Ⓤⓢ -klɑːθ
Cheeseman ˈtʃiːz.mən
cheesemonger ˈtʃiːzˌmʌŋ.gəʳ, Ⓤⓢ -gɚ, -ˌmɑːŋ- **-s** -z
cheeseparing ˈtʃiːzˌpeə.rɪŋ, Ⓤⓢ -ˌper.ɪŋ
Cheesewright ˈtʃiːz.raɪt, ˈtʃez-
chees|y ˈtʃiː.z|i **-ier** -i.əʳ, Ⓤⓢ -i.ɚ **-iest** -i.ɪst, -i.əst **-iness** -ɪ.nəs, -ɪ.nɪs
cheetah ˈtʃiː.tə, Ⓤⓢ -t̬ə **-s** -z
Cheetham ˈtʃiː.təm, Ⓤⓢ -t̬əm
Cheever ˈtʃiː.vəʳ, Ⓤⓢ -vɚ
chef ʃef **-s** -s
chef d'équipe ˌʃef.dekˈiːp
chef(s) d'oeuvre, chef(s)-d'oeuvre ˌʃeɪˈdɜː.vrə, -əʳ, Ⓤⓢ ˌʃeɪˈdɜː.v.rə, -ˈdɝːv
Cheke tʃiːk
Chekhov ˈtʃek.ɒf, -ɒv, Ⓤⓢ -ɑːf, -ɔːf, -ɑːv
chela ˈtʃeɪ.lə, ˈtʃiː.lə **-s** -z
chela|te ˈkiː.leɪ|t, ˈtʃiː-, Ⓤⓢ ˈkiː.leɪ|t **-tes** -ts **-ting** -tɪŋ, Ⓤⓢ -t̬ɪŋ **-ted** -tɪd, Ⓤⓢ -t̬ɪd
chelation kiːˈleɪ.ʃən, kə-, tʃiː-, kɪ-
Chelmer ˈtʃel.məʳ, Ⓤⓢ -mɚ
Chelmsford ˈtʃelmz.fəd, ˈtʃelmps-; *old-fashioned local pronunciations:* ˈtʃemz-, ˈtʃɒmz-, Ⓤⓢ -fɚd
Chelsea ˈtʃel.si ˌ**Chelsea** ˈ**bun**; ˈ**Chelsea** ˌ**bun**; ˌ**Chelsea** ˈ**pensioner**
Chelsey ˈtʃel.si
Cheltenham ˈtʃel.tən.əm
Chelyabinsk tʃelˈjɑː.bɪnsk
chemic ˈkem.ɪk
chemical ˈkem.ɪ.kəl **-ly** -i **-s** -z ˌ**chemical engi**ˈ**neering**; ˌ**chemical** ˈ**warfare**
chemis|e ʃəˈmiːz **-es** -ɪz
chemist ˈkem.ɪst **-s** -s
chemistry ˈkem.ɪ.stri, -ə-
Chemnitz ˈkem.nɪts
chemo ˈkiː.məʊ, ˈkem.əʊ, Ⓤⓢ ˈkiː.moʊ, ˈkem.oʊ
chemotherapy ˌkiː.məʊˈθer.ə.pi, ˌkem.əʊ-, Ⓤⓢ ˌkiː.moʊˈ-, ˌkem.oʊˈ-
Chen tʃen
Chenevix ˈtʃen.ə.vɪks, ˈʃen.ə.vɪks
Cheney ˈtʃeɪ.ni, ˈtʃiː-, Ⓤⓢ ˈtʃeɪ-
Chengdu ˌtʃʌŋˈduː, ˌtʃeŋ-
Chenies *in Buckinghamshire:* ˈtʃeɪ.niz *street in London:* ˈtʃiː.niz
chenille ʃəˈniːl
Chennai ˈtʃen.aɪ, -ˈ-
cheongsam ˌtʃɒŋˈsæm, tʃiˌɒŋ-, Ⓤⓢ ˌtʃɔːŋ-, ˌtʃɑːŋ- **-s** -z
Cheops ˈkiː.ɒps, Ⓤⓢ -ɑːps
Chepstow ˈtʃep.stəʊ, Ⓤⓢ -stoʊ
cheque tʃek **-s** -s ˈ**cheque** ˌ**card**
chequebook ˈtʃek.bʊk **-s** -s
chequecard ˈtʃek.kɑːd, Ⓤⓢ -kɑːrd **-s** -z
chequ|er ˈtʃek|.əʳ, Ⓤⓢ -ɚ **-ers** -əz, Ⓤⓢ -ɚz **-ering** -ər.ɪŋ **-ered** -əd, Ⓤⓢ -ɚd
Chequers ˈtʃek.əz, Ⓤⓢ -ɚz
Cher ʃeəʳ, Ⓤⓢ ʃer
Cherbourg ˈʃeə.bʊəg, ʃɜː-, -bɔːg, -bɜːg, Ⓤⓢ ˈʃer.bʊrg, -bʊr, -ˈ-
Cherie ʃəˈriː, ˈʃer.i
cherish ˈtʃer.ɪʃ **-es** -ɪz **-ing** -ɪŋ **-ed** -t
Cheriton ˈtʃer.ɪ.tən
Chernobyl tʃɜːˈnəʊ.bəl, tʃə-, -ˈnɒb.əl, -ɪl, Ⓤⓢ tʃɚˈnoʊ.bəl
Chernomyrdin ˌtʃɜː.nəˈmɪə.dɪn, ˌtʃeə-, -ˈmɜː-, -dən, Ⓤⓢ ˌtʃɝː.nəˈmɪr-, -noʊˈ-, ˌtʃer-, -ˈmɝː-
Cherokee ˈtʃer.ə.kiː, ˌ--ˈ- **-s** -z
cheroot ʃəˈruːt **-s** -s
cherr|y, C~ ˈtʃer|.i **-ies** -iz ˌ**cherry** ˈ**brandy**; ˌ**cherry** ˈ**pie**; ˌ**cherry to**ˈ**mato**
cherrystone ˈtʃer.i.stəʊn, Ⓤⓢ -stoʊn **-s** -z

C

chersonese ˈkɜː.sə.niːs, -niːz, ˌ--ˈ-, (US) ˌkɝː.səˈniːz, -niːs
Chertoff ˈtʃɜː.tɒf, (US) ˈtʃɝː.tɑːf
Chertsey ˈtʃɜːt.si, (US) ˈtʃɝːt-
cherub ˈtʃer.əb **-s** -z
cherubic tʃəˈruː.bɪk, tʃerˈuː-, (US) tʃəˈruː- **-ally** -əl.i, -li
cherubim ˈtʃer.ə.bɪm, ˈ-ʊ-
Cherubini ˌker.ʊˈbiː.niː, -əˈ-, -ni
chervil ˈtʃɜː.vɪl, -vəl, (US) ˈtʃɝː-
Cherwell ˈtʃɑː.wəl, -wel, (US) ˈtʃɑːr-
Cheryl ˈtʃer.əl, ˈʃer-, -ɪl, (US) ˈʃer.əl
Chesapeake ˈtʃes.ə.piːk
Chesebro, Chesebrough ˈtʃiːz.brə
Chesham ˈtʃeʃ.əm; *old-fashioned local pronunciation:* ˈtʃes-
Cheshire ˈtʃeʃ.əʳ, -ɪəʳ, (US) -ɚ, -ɪr **ˌCheshire ˈcat; ˌCheshire ˈcheese**
Cheshunt ˈtʃes.ənt, ˈtʃeʃ-
Chesil ˈtʃez.əl **ˌChesil ˈBank; ˌChesil ˈBeach**
Chesney ˈtʃes.ni, ˈtʃez.ni
Chesnutt ˈtʃes.nʌt
chess tʃes
chessboard ˈtʃes.bɔːd, (US) -bɔːrd **-s** -z
chess|man ˈtʃes|.mæn, -mən **-men** -men, -mən
chest tʃest **-s** -s **-ed** -ɪd **ˌchest of ˈdrawers**
Chester ˈtʃes.təʳ, (US) -tɚ
chesterfield, C~ ˈtʃes.tə.fiːld, (US) -tɚ- **-s** -z
Chester-le-Street ˌtʃes.tə.lɪˈstriːt, ˈ---ˌ-, (US) -tɚ-
Chesterton ˈtʃes.tə.tən, (US) -tɚ.t̬ən
chestnut ˈtʃes.nʌt, ˈtʃest- **-s** -s
chest|y ˈtʃes.t|i **-ier** -i.əʳ, (US) -i.ɚ **-iest** -i.ɪst, -i.əst **-ily** -əl.i, -ɪ.li **-iness** -ɪ.nəs, -ɪ.nɪs
Chetham ˈtʃet.əm
chetrum ˈtʃet.rʊm, -rəm
Chettle ˈtʃet.əl, (US) ˈtʃet̬-
Chetwode ˈtʃet.wʊd
Chetwynd ˈtʃet.wɪnd
cheval-glass ʃəˈvæl.glɑːs, (US) -glæs **-es** -ɪz
chevalier ˌʃev.əˈlɪəʳ, (US) -ˈlɪr **-s** -z
Chevalier *surname:* ʃəˈvæl.i.eɪ, ʃɪ-, (US) -i.eɪ, -jeɪ
Chevening ˈtʃiːv.nɪŋ
Cheves tʃiːvz
Chevette® ʃəˈvet, ʃevˈet **-s** -s
Cheviot *hills, sheep:* ˈtʃiː.vi.ət, ˈtʃev.i-, ˈtʃɪv.i-, (US) ˈʃev.i- *cloth:* ˈtʃev.i.ət, (US) ˈʃev-
Chevis ˈtʃev.ɪs
Chevrolet® ˈʃev.rə.leɪ, ˌ--ˈ-, (US) ˌʃev.rəˈleɪ **-s** -z
chevron ˈʃev.rən, -rɒn, (US) -rən **-s** -z
chev|y, C~ ˈtʃev|.i **-ies** -iz **-ying** -i.ɪŋ **-ied** -id
Chevy ˈʃev.i
chew tʃuː **-s** -z **-ing** -ɪŋ **-ed** -d **ˈchewing ˌgum**
chew|y ˈtʃuː|.i **-ier** -i.əʳ, (US) -i.ɚ **-iest** -i.ɪst, -i.əst **-iness** -ɪ.nəs, -ɪ.nɪs
Cheyenne ˌʃaɪˈæn, -ˈen, (US) -ˈen, -ˈæn
Cheyne ˈtʃeɪ.ni, tʃeɪn
Cheyney ˈtʃeɪ.ni
chez ʃeɪ
chi *Greek letter:* kaɪ *energy:* tʃiː
Chiang Kai-Shek ˌtʃæŋ.kaɪˈʃek, (US) ˌtʃæŋ-, ˌdʒæŋ-
Chiang Mai tʃiˌæŋˈmaɪ, (US) ˌdʒɑːŋˈmaɪ, tʃiˌɑːŋ-
chianti, C~ kiˈæn.ti, (US) -ˈɑːn.t̬i, -ˈæn-
Chiantishire kiˈæn.ti.ʃəʳ, -ʃɪəʳ, (US) -ˈɑːn.t̬i.ʃɚ, -ˈæn-, -ʃɪr
Chiapas tʃiˈæp.əs, (US) -ˈɑː.pəs
chiaroscuro kiˌɑː.rəˈskjʊə.rəʊ, -rɒsˈkʊə-, (US) -ˌɑːr.əˈskjʊr.oʊ
chias|ma kaɪˈæz|.mə **-mata** -mə.tə, (US) -mə.t̬ə **-mas** -məz
chiasmus kaɪˈæz.məs
chic ʃiːk, ʃɪk
Chicago ʃɪˈkɑː.gəʊ, ʃə-, (US) -goʊ, -ˈkɔː-
chican|e ʃɪˈkeɪn, ʃə- **-es** -z **-ing** -ɪŋ **-ed** -d **-er/s** -əʳ/z, (US) -ɚ/z
chicaner|y ʃɪˈkeɪ.nəʳ|.i, ʃə- **-ies** -iz
chicano tʃɪˈkɑː.nəʊ, (US) -noʊ **-s** -z
Chichele ˈtʃɪtʃ.əl.i, -ɪ.li
Chichén Itzá tʃiˌtʃen.ɪtˈsɑː, (US) -iːtˈ-
Chichester ˈtʃɪtʃ.ɪ.stəʳ, ˈ-ə-, (US) -stɚ
chi-chi ˈʃiː.ʃiː
chick, C~ tʃɪk **-s** -s
chickabidd|y ˈtʃɪk.əˌbɪd|.i **-ies** -iz
chickadee ˈtʃɪk.əˌdiː, ˌ--ˈ- **-s** -z
Chickasaw ˈtʃɪk.ə.sɔː, (US) -sɔː, -sɑː **-s** -z
chicken ˈtʃɪk.ɪn, -ən **-s** -z **-ing** -ɪŋ **-ed** -d **ˈchicken ˌfeed; ˌchicken ˈKiev; ˌdon't count your ˌchickens before they ˈhatch**
chickenhearted ˌtʃɪk.ɪnˈhɑː.tɪd, -ənˈ-, -təd; ˈtʃɪk.ɪnˌhɑː-, -ənˌ-, (US) ˌtʃɪk.ɪnˈhɑːr.t̬ɪd, -ənˈ-, -t̬əd
chickenpox ˈtʃɪkɪnˌpɒks, (US) -ˌpɑːks
chickenshit ˈtʃɪk.ɪn.ʃɪt, -ən- **-s** -s
Chicklets® ˈtʃɪk.ləts, -lɪts
chickpea ˈtʃɪk.piː **-s** -z
chickweed ˈtʃɪk.wiːd
Chiclayo tʃiˈklɑː.jəʊ, (US) -joʊ
chicory ˈtʃɪk.ər.i
Chiddingly ˈtʃɪd.ɪŋˌlaɪ, ˌ--ˈ-
chid|e tʃaɪd **-es** -z **-ing** -ɪŋ **-ed** -ɪd **chid** tʃɪd **chidden** ˈtʃɪd.ən
chief tʃiːf **-s** -s **-ly** -li **ˌchief inˈspector; ˌchief of ˈstaff**
chieftain ˈtʃiːf.tən, -tɪn **-s** -z
chieftanc|y ˈtʃiːf.tənt.s|i, -tɪnt- **-ies** -iz
chiff-chaff ˈtʃɪf.tʃæf **-s** -s
chiffon ˈʃɪf.ɒn, ʃɪˈfɒn, (US) ʃɪˈfɑːn **-s** -z
chiffon(n)ier ˌʃɪf.əˈnɪəʳ, -ni.eɪ; *as if French:* ˌʃiː.fɔ̃ːˈnje; (US) -ˈnɪr **-s** -z
chignon ˈʃiː.njɒn, -njɒŋ, -njɔ̃ː; *old-fashioned:* ʃɪˈnɒn, (US) ˈʃiː.njɑːn **-s** -z
Chigwell ˈtʃɪg.wel, -wəl
chihuahua, C~ tʃɪˈwɑː.wə, tʃə-, ʃɪ-, ʃə-, -wɑː **-s** -z
chilblain ˈtʃɪl.bleɪn **-s** -z
child, C~ tʃaɪld **children** ˈtʃɪl.drən **ˈchild aˌbuse; ˌchild ˈbenefit; ˈchild's ˌplay; ˌchild ˈprodigy; ˌchild supˈport**
childbearing ˈtʃaɪldˌbeə.rɪŋ, (US) -ˌber.ɪŋ
childbed ˈtʃaɪld.bed
childbirth ˈtʃaɪld.bɜːθ, (US) -bɝːθ
childcare ˈtʃaɪld.keəʳ, (US) -ker
Childe tʃaɪld
Childermas ˈtʃɪl.də.mæs, -məs, (US) -dɚ.mæs
Childers ˈtʃɪl.dəz, (US) -dɚz
childhood ˈtʃaɪld.hʊd **ˌchildhood ˈsweetheart**
childish ˈtʃaɪl.dɪʃ **-ly** -li **-ness** -nəs, -nɪs
childless ˈtʃaɪld.ləs, -lɪs **-ness** -nəs, -nɪs
childlike ˈtʃaɪld.laɪk
childmind|er ˈtʃaɪldˌmaɪn.d|əʳ, (US) -d|ɚ **-ers** -əz, (US) -ɚz **-ing** -ɪŋ
childproof ˈtʃaɪld.pruːf
children (from **child**) ˈtʃɪl.drən **ˈchildren's ˌhome**
Childs tʃaɪldz
Chile ˈtʃɪl.i, ˈtʃiː.leɪ
Chilean ˈtʃɪl.i.ən, tʃɪˈliː.ən, (US) tʃɪˈliː-, ˈtʃɪl.i- **-s** -z
chili ˈtʃɪl.i **-s** -z
chiliad ˈkɪl.i.æd, ˈkaɪ.li-, -əd **-s** -z
chili|asm ˈkɪl.i|.æz.əm **-ast/s** -æst/s
chilidog ˈtʃɪl.i.dɒg, (US) -dɑːg, -dɔːg **-s** -z
chill tʃɪl **-s** -z **-ing/ly** -ɪŋ/li **-ed** -d **-ness** -nəs, -nɪs **-er** -əʳ, (US) -ɚ
chillax tʃɪˈlæks
chiller ˈtʃɪl.əʳ, (US) -ɚ **-s** -z
chilli ˈtʃɪl.i **-es** -z **ˈchilli ˌpepper; ˈchilli ˌpowder**
chilli con carne ˌtʃɪl.i.kɒnˈkɑː.neɪ, -kɒŋˈ-, -kənˈ-, -kəŋˈ-, -ni, (US) -kɑːnˈkɑːr.ni, -kənˈ-
Chillingham ˈtʃɪl.ɪŋ.əm
Chillingly ˈtʃɪl.ɪŋ.li
Chillingworth ˈtʃɪl.ɪŋ.wəθ, -wɜːθ, (US) -wɚθ, -wɝːθ
Chillon ʃiˈlɒn, -ˈjɒn; ˈʃɪl.ən, -ɒn, (US) ʃəˈlɑːn, ʃɪ-; (US) ˈʃɪl.ən; (US) ʃiˈjoʊn

> Note: In Byron's 'Castle of Chillon' it is usual to pronounce /ˈʃɪl.ən/ or /ˈʃɪl.ɒn/ (US) /-ɑːn/.

chill|y ˈtʃɪl|.i **-ier** -i.əʳ, (US) -i.ɚ **-iest** -i.ɪst, -i.əst **-iness** -ɪ.nəs, -ɪ.nɪs
Chiltern ˈtʃɪl.tən, (US) -tɚn **ˌChiltern ˈHills; ˌChiltern ˈHundreds**
Chilton ˈtʃɪl.tən
chimaera kaɪˈmɪə.rə, kɪ-, kə-, ʃɪ-, ʃə-, -ˈmeə-; ˈkɪm.ər.ə, (US) kaɪˈmɪr.ə, kɪ- **-s** -z
Chimborazo ˌtʃɪm.bəˈrɑː.zəʊ, ˌʃɪm-, -bɒrˈɑː-, (US) -bəˈrɑː.zoʊ
chim|e tʃaɪm **-es** -z **-ing** -ɪŋ **-ed** -d **-er/s** -əʳ/z, (US) -ɚ/z
chimera kaɪˈmɪə.rə, kɪ-, kə-, ʃɪ-, ʃə-, -ˈmeə-; ˈkɪm.ər.ə, (US) kaɪˈmɪr.ə, kɪ- **-s** -z
chimere tʃɪˈmɪəʳ, ʃɪ-, kɪ-, kaɪ-, (US) -ˈmɪr **-s** -z
chimeric kaɪˈmer.ɪk, kɪ-, kə- **-al** -əl **-ally** -əl.i, -li
Chimkent tʃɪmˈkent
chimney ˈtʃɪm.ni **-s** -z **ˈchimney ˌbreast; ˈchimney ˌpot; ˈchimney**

ˌstack; ˈchimney ˌsweep; ˈchimney ˌsweeper

chimneypiec|e ˈtʃɪm.ni.piːs **-es** -ɪz

chimp tʃɪmp **-s** -s

chimpanzee ˌtʃɪm.pənˈziː, -pænˈ-, (US) tʃɪmˈpæn.zi, ˌtʃɪm.pənˈzi **-s** -z

chin tʃɪn **-s** -z ˌchin-ˈdeep

china, C~ ˈtʃaɪ.nə ˈchina ˌclay; ˌchina ˈclay; like a ˌbull in a ˈchina shop

China|man ˈtʃaɪ.nə|.mən **-men** -mən

Chinatown ˈtʃaɪ.nə.taʊn

chinchilla tʃɪnˈtʃɪl.ə **-s** -z

Chindit ˈtʃɪn.dɪt **-s** -s

chin|e tʃaɪn **-es** -z **-ing** -ɪŋ **-ed** -d

Chinese tʃaɪˈniːz, (US) -ˈniːz, -ˈniːs *stress shift, see compounds:* ˌChinese ˈgooseberry; ˌChinese ˈlantern; ˌChinese ˈrestaurant

Chingford ˈtʃɪŋ.fəd, (US) -fɚd

chink, C~ tʃɪŋk **-s** -s **-ing** -ɪŋ **-ed** -t

Chinkie, Chinky ˈtʃɪŋ.ki

chinless ˈtʃɪn.ləs, -lɪs ˌchinless ˈwonder

Chinnock ˈtʃɪn.ək

Chinnor ˈtʃɪn.əʳ, (US) -ɚ

chino ˈtʃiː.nəʊ, (US) -noʊ **-s** -z

Chinook tʃɪˈnʊk, -ˈnuːk, (US) ʃəˈnʊk, tʃə-

chinstrap ˈtʃɪn.stræp **-s** -s

chintz tʃɪnts **-es** -ɪz **-y** -i

chinwag ˈtʃɪn.wæg **-s** -s **-ging** -ɪŋ

Chios ˈkiː.ɒs, ˈhiː-, (US) -ɑːs

chip tʃɪp **-s** -s **-ping** -ɪŋ **-ped** -t ˈchip ˌshop; have a ˈchip on one's ˌshoulder

chipboard ˈtʃɪp.bɔːd, (US) -bɔːrd

chipmunk ˈtʃɪp.mʌŋk **-s** -s

chipolata ˌtʃɪp.əlˈɑː.tə, (US) -əˈlɑː.t̬ə **-s** -z

Chipp tʃɪp

Chippendale ˈtʃɪp.ən.deɪl **-s** -z

Chippenham ˈtʃɪp.ən.əm

chipper ˈtʃɪp.əʳ, (US) -ɚ

Chipperfield ˈtʃɪp.ə.fiːld, (US) -ɚ-

Chippewa ˈtʃɪp.ɪ.wɑː, -wə **-s** -z

chippie ˈtʃɪp.i **-s** -z

Chipping ˈtʃɪp.ɪŋ

Chipping Sodbury ˌtʃɪp.ɪŋˈsɒd.bər.i, (US) -ˈsɑːd.ber-, -bɚ-

chipp|y ˈtʃɪp|.i **-ier** -i.əʳ, (US) -i.ɚ **-iest** -i.ɪst, -i.əst **-iness** -ɪ.nəs, -ɪ.nɪs

Chips tʃɪps

Chiquita tʃɪˈkiː.tə, (US) -t̬ə

Chirac ˈʃɪə.ræk, ʃiˈræk, (US) ʃəˈrɑːk, ʃɪˈræk

Chirk tʃɜːk, (US) tʃɝːk

chirograph ˈkaɪə.rəʊ.grɑːf, -græf, (US) ˈkaɪ.rə.græf **-s** -s

chirographer kaɪəˈrɒg.rə.fəʳ, (US) kaɪˈrɑː.grə.fɚ **-s** -z

chirographic ˌkaɪə.rəʊˈgræf.ɪk, (US) ˌkaɪ.roʊˈ-

chirographist kaɪəˈrɒg.rə.fɪst, (US) kaɪˈrɑː.grə- **-s** -s

chirography kaɪəˈrɒg.rə.fi, (US) kaɪˈrɑː.grə-

chiromancer ˈkaɪə.rəʊ.mænt.səʳ, (US) ˈkaɪ.roʊ.mænt.sɚ **-s** -z

chiromancy ˈkaɪə.rəʊ.mænt.si, (US) ˈkaɪ.roʊ-

Chiron ˈkaɪə.rən, (US) ˈkaɪ-

chiropodist kɪˈrɒp.ə.dɪst, ʃɪ-, tʃɪ-, (US) kɪˈrɑː.pə-, kaɪ-, ʃɪ- **-s** -s

chiropody kɪˈrɒp.ə.di, ʃɪ-, tʃɪ-, (US) kɪˈrɑː.pə-, kaɪ-, ʃɪ-

chiropractic ˌkaɪə.rəʊˈpræk.tɪk, (US) ˌkaɪ.roʊˈ-, ˈkaɪ.roʊ.præk-

chiropractor ˈkaɪə.rəʊ.præk.təʳ, (US) ˈkaɪ.roʊ.præk.tɚ **-s** -z

chirp tʃɜːp, (US) tʃɝːp **-s** -s **-ing** -ɪŋ **-ed** -t

chirp|y ˈtʃɜː.p|i, (US) ˈtʃɝː- **-ier** -i.əʳ, (US) -i.ɚ **-iest** -i.ɪst, -i.əst **-ily** -əl.i, -ɪ.li **-iness** -ɪ.nəs, -ɪ.nɪs

chirr tʃɜːʳ, (US) tʃɝː **-s** -z **-ing** -ɪŋ **-ed** -d

chirrup ˈtʃɪr.əp, (US) ˈtʃɪr-, ˈtʃɝː- **-s** -s **-ing** -ɪŋ **-ed** -t

chisel ˈtʃɪz.əl **-s** -z **-(l)ing** -ɪŋ **-(l)ed** -d **-(l)er/s** -əʳ/z, (US) -ɚ/z

Chisholm ˈtʃɪz.əm

Chislehurst ˈtʃɪz.əl.hɜːst, (US) -hɝːst

Chiswick ˈtʃɪz.ɪk

chit tʃɪt **-s** -s

chit-chat, chitchat ˈtʃɪt.tʃæt

chitin ˈkaɪ.tɪn, -tən, (US) -tən

Chittagong ˈtʃɪt.ə.gɒŋ, (US) ˈtʃɪt̬.ə.gɑːŋ, -gɔːŋ

Chittenden ˈtʃɪt.ən.dən

chitterling ˈtʃɪt.əl.ɪŋ, (US) ˈtʃɪt̬.ɚ.lɪŋ **-s** -z

Chitty ˈtʃɪt.i, (US) ˈtʃɪt̬-

chivalric ˈʃɪv.əl.rɪk, (US) ʃɪˈvæl-; (US) ˈʃɪv.əl-

chivalrous ˈʃɪv.əl.rəs **-ly** -li **-ness** -nəs, -nɪs

chivalry ˈʃɪv.əl.ri

chive tʃaɪv **-s** -z

Chivers ˈtʃɪv.əz, (US) -ɚz

chivv|y ˈtʃɪv|.i **-ies** -iz **-ying** -i.ɪŋ **-ied** -id

chiv|y ˈtʃɪv|.i **-ies** -iz **-ying** -i.ɪŋ **-ied** -id

chlamid|ia, chlamyd|ia kləˈmɪd|.i.ə **-iae** -i.i **-ial** -i.əl

chlamy|s ˈklæm.ɪ|s, ˈkleɪ.mɪ|s **-des** -diːz

Chloe, Chloë ˈkləʊ.i, (US) ˈkloʊ-

chloral ˈklɔː.rəl, (US) ˈklɔːr.əl

chloramine ˈklɔː.rə.miːn; -mɪn, (US) ˈklɔːr.ə.miːn, ˌ-ˈ-; (US) klɔːˈræm.iːn, -ɪn

chlorate ˈklɔː.reɪt, -rɪt, (US) ˈklɔːr.eɪt, -ɪt **-s** -s

chloric ˈklɔː.rɪk, ˈklɒr.ɪk, (US) ˈklɔːr.ɪk

chloride ˈklɔː.raɪd, (US) ˈklɔːr.aɪd **-s** -z

chlori|nate ˈklɔː.rɪ|.neɪt, ˈklɒr.ɪ-, (US) ˈklɔːr.ɪ- **-nates** -neɪts **-nating** -neɪ.tɪŋ, (US) -neɪ.t̬ɪŋ **-nated** -neɪ.tɪd, (US) -neɪ.t̬ɪd

chlorine ˈklɔː.riːn, (US) ˈklɔːr.iːn, -ɪn

Chloris ˈklɔː.rɪs, ˈklɒr.ɪs, (US) ˈklɔːr.ɪs

chlorite ˈklɔː.raɪt, (US) ˈklɔːr.aɪt **-s** -s

chloro- ˈklɔː.rəʊ, ˈklɒr.əʊ, (US) ˈklɔːr.ə, ˈ-oʊ

chlorodyne ˈklɔː.rə.daɪn, ˈklɒr.ə-, (US) ˈklɔːr.ə-

chlorofluorocarbon ˌklɔː.rəʊˌflɔː.rəʊˈkɑː.bən, ˌklɒr.əʊ-, -ˌflʊə-, (US) ˌklɔːr.oʊˌflɔːr.oʊˈkɑːr-, -ˌflʊr- **-s** -z

chloroform ˈklɔː.rə.fɔːm, ˈklɒr.ə-, (US) ˈklɔːr.ə.fɔːrm **-s** -z **-ing** -ɪŋ **-ed** -d

Chloromycetin® ˌklɔː.rəʊ.maɪˈsiː.tɪn, ˌklɒr.əʊ-, (US) ˌklɔːr.oʊ.maɪˈsiː.tən

chlorophyl(l) ˈklɔː.rə.fɪl, ˈklɒr.ə-, (US) ˈklɔːr.ə-

chlorophyllose ˌklɔː.rəˈfɪl.əʊs, ˌklɒr.əˈ-, (US) ˌklɔːr.əˈfɪl.oʊs

chloroplast ˈklɒr.ə.plɑːst, -plæst, (US) ˈklɔːr.ə.plæst

chlorous ˈklɔː.rəs, (US) ˈklɔːr.əs

Cho tʃəʊ, (US) tʃoʊ

Choate tʃəʊt, (US) tʃoʊt

choc tʃɒk, (US) tʃɑːk **-s** -s

chocc|y ˈtʃɒk|.i, (US) tʃɑːk- **-ies** -iz

choc-ic|e ˈtʃɒk.aɪs, (US) ˈtʃɑːk- **-es** -ɪz

chock tʃɒk, (US) tʃɑːk **-s** -s ˌchock-ˈfull

chock-a-block ˌtʃɒk.əˈblɒk, ˈ---, (US) ˈtʃɑːk.ə.blɑːk

chocker, chocka ˈtʃɒk.əʳ, (US) ˈtʃɑː.kɚ

chocoholic, chocaholic ˌtʃɒk.əˈhɒl.ɪk, (US) ˌtʃɑː.kəˈhɑː.lɪk **-s** -s

chocolate ˈtʃɒk.əl.ət, -ɪt, ˈ-lət, -lɪt, (US) ˈtʃɑːk.lət, ˈtʃɔːk-, ˈtʃɑː.kəl.ət, ˈtʃɔː-, -ɪt **-s** -s ˌchocolate ˈcake; ˈchocolate ˌcake; ˌchocolate chip ˈcookie; ˈdrinking ˌchocolate

Choctaw ˈtʃɒk.tɔː, (US) ˈtʃɑːk.tɔː, -tɑː

choic|e tʃɔɪs **-es** -ɪz **-er** -əʳ, (US) -ɚ **-est** -ɪst, -əst **-ely** -li **-eness** -nəs, -nɪs

choir kwaɪəʳ, ˈkwaɪ.əʳ, (US) ˈkwaɪ.ɚ **-s** -z ˈchoir ˌscreen

choirboy ˈkwaɪə.bɔɪ, ˈkwaɪ.ə-, (US) ˈkwaɪ.ɚ- **-s** -z

choirmaster ˈkwaɪəˌmɑː.stəʳ, ˈkwaɪ.ə-, (US) ˈkwaɪ.ɚˌmæs.tɚ **-s** -z

chok|e tʃəʊk, (US) tʃoʊk **-es** -s **-ing** -ɪŋ **-ed** -t

choker ˈtʃəʊ.kəʳ, (US) ˈtʃoʊ.kɚ **-s** -z

chok|y ˈtʃəʊ.k|i, (US) ˈtʃoʊ- **-ier** -i.əʳ, (US) -i.ɚ **-iest** -i.ɪst, -i.əst **-iness** -ɪ.nəs, -ɪ.nɪs

Cholderton ˈtʃəʊl.də.tən, (US) ˈtʃoʊl.dɚ.t̬ən

choler ˈkɒl.əʳ, (US) ˈkɑː.lɚ

cholera ˈkɒl.ər.ə, (US) ˈkɑː.lɚ-

choleraic ˌkɒl.əˈreɪ.ɪk, (US) ˌkɑː.ləˈ-

choleric ˈkɒl.ər.ɪk; kɒlˈer-, (US) ˈkɑː.lɚ-; (US) kəˈler-

cholesterol kəˈles.tər.ɒl, kɒlˈes-, -əl, (US) kəˈles.tə.rɑːl, -rɔːl, -roʊl

choliamb ˈkəʊ.li.æmb, (US) ˈkoʊ- **-s** -z

choliambic ˌkəʊ.liˈæm.bɪk, (US) ˌkoʊ-

choline ˈkəʊ.liːn, (US) ˈkoʊ-, -lɪn

Cholmeley ˈtʃʌm.li

Cholmondeley ˈtʃʌm.li

Cholsey ˈtʃəʊl.zi, ˈtʃɒl.si, (US) ˈtʃoʊl-

Chomley ˈtʃʌm.li

chomp tʃɒmp, (US) tʃɑːmp **-s** -s **-ing** -ɪŋ **-ed** -t

Chomsky ˈtʃɒmp.ski, (US) ˈtʃɑːmp- **-an** -ən
Chon tʃəʊn, (US) tʃoʊn
chondroitin kɒnˈdrɔɪ.tɪn, (US) kɑːnˈdrɔɪt.ən
Chongquing ˌtʃʊŋˈtʃɪŋ
Choo tʃuː
choo-choo ˈtʃuː.tʃuː **-s** -z
chook tʃʊk **-s** -s
choos|e tʃuːz **-es** -ɪz **-ing** -ɪŋ **chose** tʃəʊz, (US) tʃoʊz **chosen** ˈtʃəʊ.zən, (US) ˈtʃoʊ- **chooser/s** ˈtʃuː.zər/z, (US) -zɚ/z
choos|y, choos|ey ˈtʃuː.z|i **-ier** -i.ər, (US) -i.ɚ **-iest** -i.ɪst, -i.əst **-iness** -ɪ.nəs, -ɪ.nɪs
chop tʃɒp, (US) tʃɑːp **-s** -s **-ping** -ɪŋ **-ped** -t ˈ**chopping** ˌ**board**; ˌ**chop** ˈ**suey**
chop-chop ˌtʃɒpˈtʃɒp, (US) ˌtʃɑːpˈtʃɑːp
chophou|se ˈtʃɒp.haʊ|s, (US) ˈtʃɑːp- **-ses** -zɪz
Chopin ˈʃɒp.æ̃ŋ, ˈʃəʊ.pæ̃ŋ, -pæŋ, (US) ˈʃoʊ.pæn; (US) ʃoʊˈpæ̃n
chopper ˈtʃɒp.ər, (US) ˈtʃɑː.pɚ **-s** -z
chopp|y ˈtʃɒp|.i, (US) ˈtʃɑː.p|i **-ier** -i.ər, (US) -i.ɚ **-iest** -i.ɪst, -i.əst **-ily** -əl.i, -ɪ.li **-iness** -ɪ.nəs, -ɪ.nɪs
chopstick ˈtʃɒp.stɪk, (US) ˈtʃɑːp- **-s** -s
chop-suey ˌtʃɒpˈsuː.i, (US) ˌtʃɑːp-
choral ˈkɔː.rəl, (US) ˈkɔːr.əl **-ly** -i
chorale kɒrˈɑːl, kəˈrɑːl, kɔː-, (US) kəˈræl, -ˈrɑːl **-s** -z
chord kɔːd, (US) kɔːrd **-s** -z
chordate ˈkɔː.deɪt, -dɪt, -dət, (US) ˈkɔːr-
chore tʃɔːr, (US) tʃɔːr **-s** -z
chorea kɒrˈɪə, kɔːˈrɪə, kə-, (US) kəˈriː.ə, kɔːrˈiː-
choreograph ˈkɒr.i.ə.grɑːf, ˈkɔː.ri-, -græf, (US) ˈkɔːr.i.ə.græf **-s** -s **-ing** -ɪŋ **-ed** -t
choreographer ˌkɒr.iˈɒg.rə.fər, ˌkɔː.ri-, (US) ˌkɔːr.iˈɑː.grə.fɚ **-s** -z
choreographic ˌkɒr.i.əʊˈgræf.ɪk, ˌkɔː.ri-, (US) ˌkɔːr.i.əˈ-
choreography ˌkɒr.iˈɒg.rə.fi, ˌkɔː.ri-, (US) ˌkɔːr.iˈɑː.grə-
choriamb ˈkɒr.i.æmb, ˈkɔː.ri-, (US) ˈkɔːr.i- **-s** -z
choriambic ˌkɒr.iˈæm.bɪk, ˌkɔː.ri-, (US) ˌkɔːr.iˈ-
choric ˈkɒr.ɪk, (US) ˈkɔːr-
chorion ˈkɔː.ri.ən, -ɒn, (US) ˈkɔːr.i.ɑːn **-s** -z
chorionic ˌkɔː.riˈɒn.ɪk, (US) ˌkɔːr.iˈɑː.nɪk
chorister ˈkɒr.ɪ.stər, (US) ˈkɔːr.ɪ.stɚ **-s** -z
chorizo tʃəˈriː.zəʊ, tʃɒrˈiː-, -səʊ, (US) tʃəˈriː.zoʊ, tʃoʊ-, -soʊ **-s** -z

> Note: A common mispronunciation is /tʃəˈrɪt.səʊ/ (US) /-soʊ/.

Chorley ˈtʃɔː.li, (US) ˈtʃɔːr-
Chorleywood ˌtʃɔː.liˈwʊd, (US) ˌtʃɔːr-
choroid ˈkɔː.rɔɪd, (US) ˈkɔːr.ɔɪd
chortl|e ˈtʃɔː.təl, (US) ˈtʃɔːr.t̬əl **-es** -z **-ing** -ɪŋ, ˈtʃɔːt.lɪŋ, (US) ˈtʃɔːr.t̬əl.ɪŋ, ˈtʃɔːrt.lɪŋ **-ed** -d
chorus ˈkɔː.rəs, (US) ˈkɔːr.əs **-es** -ɪz **-ing** -ɪŋ **-ed** -t
chose **n** *legal term:* ʃəʊz, (US) ʃoʊz
chose (from **choose**) tʃəʊz, (US) tʃoʊz
chosen (from **choose**) ˈtʃəʊ.zən, (US) ˈtʃoʊ-
Chosen *Japanese name for Korea:* ˌtʃəʊˈsen, (US) ˌtʃoʊ-
Chou En-lai ˌtʃəʊ.enˈlaɪ, ˌdʒəʊ-, (US) ˌdʒoʊ-
chough tʃʌf **-s** -s
choux ʃuː ˌ**choux** ˈ**pastry**
chow tʃaʊ **-s** -z
chow-chow ˌtʃaʊˈtʃaʊ, ˈ-- **-s** -z
chowder ˈtʃaʊ.dər, (US) -dɚ **-s** -z
Chowles tʃəʊlz, (US) tʃoʊlz
chow mein ˌtʃaʊˈmeɪn
chrestomath|y kresˈtɒm.ə.θ|i, (US) -ˈtɑː.mə- **-ies** -iz
Chrétien de Troyes kreɪˌtjæ̃n.dəˈtrwɑː
Chris krɪs **-'s** -ɪz
chrism ˈkrɪz.əm
chrisom ˈkrɪz.əm **-s** -z
Chrissie ˈkrɪs.i
Christ kraɪst **-s** -s
Christa ˈkrɪs.tə
Christabel ˈkrɪs.tə.bel, -bəl
Christadelphian ˌkrɪs.təˈdel.fi.ən **-s** -z
Christchurch ˈkraɪst.tʃɜːtʃ, (US) -tʃɝːtʃ
Christdom ˈkraɪst.dəm
christen ˈkrɪs.ən **-s** -z **-ing** -ɪŋ **-ed** -d
Christendom ˈkrɪs.ən.dəm
christening ˈkrɪs.ən.ɪŋ **-s** -z
Christensen ˈkrɪs.tən.sən
Christi (in **Corpus Christi**) ˈkrɪs.ti
Christian ˈkrɪs.tʃən, ˈkrɪʃ-; ˈkrɪs.ti.ən, (US) ˈkrɪs.tʃən, -ti.ən **-s** -z ˈ**Christian** ˌ**name**; ˌ**Christian** ˈ**Science**; ˌ**Christian** ˈ**Scientist**
Christiana ˌkrɪs.tiˈɑː.nə, (US) -tiˈæn.ə, -tʃiˈ-, -ˈɑː.nə
Christiania ˌkrɪs.tiˈɑː.ni.ə, (US) -tiˈæn.i-, -tʃiˈ-, -ˈɑː.ni-
Christianism ˈkrɪs.tʃən.ɪ.zəm, ˈkrɪʃ-; ˈkrɪs.ti.ə.nɪ-, (US) ˈkrɪs.tʃən.ɪ-, -ti.ə.nɪ-
Christianity ˌkrɪs.tiˈæn.ə.ti, -ˈtʃæn-, -ɪ.ti, (US) -tʃiˈæn.ə.t̬i, -tiˈ-
christianiz|e, -is|e, C~ ˈkrɪs.tʃə.naɪz, ˈkrɪʃ-; ˈkrɪs.ti.ə-, (US) ˈkrɪs.tʃə- **-es** -ɪz **-ing** -ɪŋ **-ed** -d
christianly, C~ ˈkrɪs.tʃən.li, ˈkrɪʃ-; ˈkrɪs.ti.ən-, (US) ˈkrɪs.tʃən-
Christie ˈkrɪs.ti **-'s** -z
Christina krɪˈstiː.nə
Christine ˈkrɪs.tiːn, krɪˈstiːn
Christlike ˈkraɪst.laɪk **-ness** -nəs, -nɪs
Christmas ˈkrɪst.məs, (US) ˈkrɪs- **-es** -ɪz ˈ**Christmas** ˌ**box**; ˈ**Christmas** ˌ**cake**; ˈ**Christmas** ˌ**card**; ˌ**Christmas** ˈ**Day**; ˌ**Christmas** ˈ**Eve**; ˈ**Christmas** ˌ**present**; ˌ**Christmas** ˈ**pudding**; ˈ**Christmas** ˌ**tree**
Christmassy ˈkrɪst.mə.si, (US) ˈkrɪs-
Christmastide ˈkrɪst.məs.taɪd, (US) ˈkrɪs-
Christminster ˈkraɪst.mɪnt.stər, ˈkrɪst-, (US) -stɚ
Christobel ˈkrɪs.tə.bel
Christophe krɪˈstɒf; ˈkrɪs.tɒf, (US) kriːˈstɑːf, krɪ-, -ˈstɔːf
christophene ˈkrɪs.tə.fiːn **-s** -z
Christopher ˈkrɪs.tə.fər, (US) -fɚ
Christopherson krɪˈstɒf.ə.sən, (US) -ˈstɑː.fɚ-
Christy ˈkrɪs.ti
chroma ˈkrəʊ.mə, (US) ˈkroʊ-
chromate ˈkrəʊ.meɪt, -mɪt, (US) ˈkroʊ- **-s** -s
chromatic krəʊˈmæt.ɪk, (US) kroʊˈmæt̬-, krə- **-ally** -əl.i, -li
chromaticity ˌkrəʊ.məˈtɪs.ə.ti, -ɪ.ti, (US) ˌkroʊ.məˈtɪs.ə.t̬i
chromatin ˈkrəʊ.mə.tɪn, (US) ˈkroʊ-
chromatogram ˈkrəʊ.mə.tə.græm, krəʊˈmæt.ə-, (US) kroʊˈmæt̬.ə- **-s** -z
chromatographic ˌkrəʊ.mə.təˈgræf.ɪk, krəʊˌmæt.əˈ-, (US) kroʊˌmæt̬.ə-
chromatography ˌkrəʊ.məˈtɒg.rə.fi, (US) ˌkroʊ.məˈtɑː.grə-
chrome krəʊm, (US) kroʊm
chrom|ic ˈkrəʊ.m|ɪk, (US) ˈkroʊ- **-ous** -əs
chromite ˈkrəʊ.maɪt, (US) ˈkroʊ- **-s** -s
chromium ˈkrəʊ.mi.əm, (US) ˈkroʊ-
chromolithograph ˌkrəʊ.məʊˈlɪθ.əʊ.grɑːf, -græf, (US) ˌkroʊ.moʊˈlɪθ.ə.græf **-s** -s
chromolithography ˌkrəʊ.məʊ.lɪˈθɒg.rə.fi, (US) ˌkroʊ.moʊ.lɪˈθɑː.grə-
chromosomal ˌkrəʊ.məˈsəʊ.məl, (US) ˌkroʊ.məˈsoʊ-
chromosome ˈkrəʊ.mə.səʊm, (US) ˈkroʊ.mə.soʊm **-s** -z
chromosphere ˈkrəʊ.mə.sfɪər, (US) ˈkroʊ.mə.sfɪr **-s** -z
chromotype ˈkrəʊ.məʊ.taɪp, (US) ˈkroʊ.moʊ-
chronic ˈkrɒn.ɪk, (US) ˈkrɑː.nɪk **-al** -əl **-ally** -əl.i, -li
chronicl|e ˈkrɒn.ɪ.kəl, (US) ˈkrɑː.nɪ- **-es** -z **-ing** -ɪŋ, -klɪŋ **-ed** -d **-er/s** -klər/z, (US) -klɚ/z
Chronicles ˈkrɒn.ɪ.kəlz, (US) ˈkrɑː.nɪ-
chrono- ˈkrɒn.əʊ, ˈkrəʊ.nəʊ, krəˈnɒ, (US) ˈkrɑː.noʊ, ˈkroʊ.noʊ, ˈ-nə, krəˈnɑː

Note: Prefix. This may take primary or secondary stress on the first syllable (e.g. **chronograph** /ˈkrɒn.əʊ.grɑːf/ (US) /ˈkrɑː.nə.græf/) or primary stress on the second syllable (e.g. **chronometer** /krəˈnɒm.ɪ.tər/ (US) /krəˈnɑː.mə.t̬ɚ/).

chronogram ˈkrɒn.əʊ.græm, ˈkrəʊ.nəʊ-, (US) ˈkrɑː.nə-, ˈkroʊ-, ˈ-noʊ- **-s** -z
chronograph ˈkrɒn.əʊ.grɑːf,

ˈkrəʊ.nəʊ-, -græf, US ˈkrɑː.nə.græf, ˈkroʊ-, ˈ-noʊ- -s -s
chronologic ˌkrɒn.əʊˈlɒdʒ.ɪk, ˌkrəʊn-, US ˌkrɑː.nəˈlɑː.dʒɪk, ˌ-noʊ-, ˌkroʊ- -al -əl -ally -əl.i, -li
chronolog|y krəˈnɒl.ə.dʒ|i, krɒnˈɒl-, US krəˈnɑː.lə-, krɑː- -ies -iz -ist/s -ɪst/s
chronometer krəˈnɒm.ɪ.təʳ, krɒnˈɒm-, -ə.təʳ, US krəˈnɑː.mə.t̬ɚ, krɑː- -s -z
chronometric ˌkrɒn.əʊˈmet.rɪk, ˌkrəʊ-, US ˌkrɑː.nəˈ-, ˌ-noʊ-, ˌkroʊ- -al -əl -ally -əl.i, -li
chronometry krəˈnɒm.ə.tri, krɒnˈɒm-, ˈ-ɪ-, US krəˈnɑː.mə-, krɑː-
chrysalid ˈkrɪs.əl.ɪd -s -z
chrysalides krɪˈsæl.ɪ.diːz, krə-, ˈ-ə-
chrysalis ˈkrɪs.əl.ɪs -es -ɪz
chrysanth krɪˈsæntθ, krə-, -ˈzæntθ -s -s
chrysanthemum krɪˈsæntθ.ə.məm, krə-, -ˈzæntθ-, ˈ-ɪ- -s -z
chryselephantine ˌkrɪs.el.ɪˈfæn.taɪn, -əˈ-, US -taɪn, -tiːn, -tɪn
Chrysler® ˈkraɪz.ləʳ, US ˈkraɪs.lɚ -s -z
chrysolite ˈkrɪs.əʊ.laɪt, US ˈ-ə- -s -s
chrysopras|e ˈkrɪs.əʊ.preɪz, US ˈ-ə- -es -ɪz
Chrysostom ˈkrɪs.ə.stəm, US ˈkrɪs.ə.stəm, krɪˈsɑː-
Chryston ˈkraɪ.stən
chthonian ˈθəʊ.ni.ən, ˈkθəʊ-, US ˈθoʊ-
chthonic ˈθɒn.ɪk, ˈkθɒn-, US ˈθɑː.nɪk
chub tʃʌb -s -z
Chubb tʃʌb
chubb|y ˈtʃʌb|.i -ier -i.əʳ, US -i.ɚ -iest -i.ɪst, -i.əst -ily -əl.i, -ɪ.li -iness -ɪ.nəs, -ɪ.nɪs
chuck, C~ tʃʌk -s -s -ing -ɪŋ -ed -t ˈ**chuck ˌwagon**
chuckl|e ˈtʃʌk.əl -es -z -ing -ɪŋ, ˈ-lɪŋ -ed -d
Chudleigh ˈtʃʌd.li
chuff tʃʌf -s -s -ing -ɪŋ -ed -t
Chuffey ˈtʃʌf.i
chug tʃʌg -s -z -ging -ɪŋ -ged -d
chugalug ˈtʃʌg.ə.lʌg -s -z -ging -ɪŋ -ged -d
chukka ˈtʃʌk.ə -s -z
chukker ˈtʃʌk.əʳ, US -ɚ -s -z
chum tʃʌm -s -z -ming -ɪŋ -med -d
Chumbi ˈtʃʊm.bi
chumm|y ˈtʃʌm|.i -ier -i.əʳ, US -i.ɚ -iest -i.ɪst, -i.əst -ily -əl.i, -ɪ.li -iness -ɪ.nəs, -ɪ.nɪs
chump tʃʌmp -s -s
chund|er ˈtʃʌn.d|əʳ, US -d|ɚ -ers -əz, US -ɚz -ering -ər.ɪŋ -ered -əd, US -ɚd
Chungking ˌtʃʊŋˈkɪŋ, ˌtʃʌŋ-, US ˌtʃʊŋˈkɪŋ, ˌtʃʌŋ-, ˌdʒʊŋ-, ˌdʒʌŋ-, -ˈgɪŋ *stress shift:* ˌ**Chungking** ˈ**Mansions**
chunk tʃʌŋk -s -s
chunk|y ˈtʃʌŋ.k|i -ier -i.əʳ, US -i.ɚ -iest -i.ɪst, -i.əst -ily -əl.i, -ɪ.li -iness -ɪ.nəs, -ɪ.nɪs
Chunnel ˈtʃʌn.əl
chunt|er ˈtʃʌn.t|əʳ, US -t̬|ɚ -ers -əz, US -ɚz -ering -ər.ɪŋ -ered -əd, US -ɚd
church, C~ tʃɜːtʃ, US tʃɝːtʃ -es -ɪz ˌ**Church of** ˈ**England**
Churchdown ˈtʃɜːtʃ.daʊn, US ˈtʃɝːtʃ-

> Note: An old local pronunciation /ˈtʃəʊ.zən/ is preserved in the name of a hill nearby, which is now written **Chosen**.

churchgo|er ˈtʃɜːtʃˌgəʊ|.əʳ, US ˈtʃɝːtʃˌgoʊ|.ɚ -ers -əz, US -ɚz -ing -ɪŋ
Churchill ˈtʃɜː.tʃɪl, US ˈtʃɝː-
Churchillian tʃɜːˈtʃɪl.i.ən, US tʃɝː-
church|man, C~ ˈtʃɜːtʃ|.mən, US ˈtʃɝːtʃ- -men -mən
churchwarden ˌtʃɜːtʃˈwɔː.dən, US ˌtʃɝːtʃˈwɔːr- -s -z *stress shift:* ˌ**churchwarden** ˈ**pipe**
church|woman ˈtʃɜːtʃ|ˌwʊm.ən, US ˈtʃɝːtʃ- -women -ˌwɪm.ɪn
church|y ˈtʃɜː.tʃ|i, US ˈtʃɝː- -ier -i.əʳ, US -i.ɚ -iest -i.ɪst, -i.əst -ily -əl.i, -ɪ.li -iness -ɪ.nəs, -ɪ.nɪs
churchyard *outside church:* ˈtʃɜːtʃ.jɑːd, US ˈtʃɝːtʃ.jɑːrd -s -z
Churchyard *surname:* ˈtʃɜː.tʃəd, US ˈtʃɝː.tʃɚd
churl tʃɜːl, US tʃɝːl -s -z
churlish ˈtʃɜː.lɪʃ, US ˈtʃɝː- -ly -li -ness -nəs, -nɪs
churn tʃɜːn, US tʃɝːn -s -z -ing -ɪŋ -ed -d
chute ʃuːt -s -s
Chute tʃuːt
Chuter ˈtʃuː.təʳ, US -t̬ɚ
chutney ˈtʃʌt.ni -s -z
chutzpa(h) ˈhʊt.spɑː, ˈxʊt-, -spə
Chuzzlewit ˈtʃʌz.əl.wɪt
chyle kaɪl
chyme kaɪm
CIA ˌsiː.aɪˈeɪ
ciabatta tʃəˈbæt.ə, -ˈbɑː.tə
Cian ˈkiː.ən
ciao tʃaʊ
Ciara ˈkɪə.rə, US ˈkɪr.ə
Ciaran ˈkɪə.rən, US ˈkɪr.ən
Ciba-Geigy® ˌsiː.bəˈgaɪ.gi
Cibber ˈsɪb.əʳ, US -ɚ
cibori|um sɪˈbɔː.ri|.əm, sə-, US -ˈbɔːr.i- -ums -əmz -a -ə
cicada sɪˈkɑː.də, -ˈkeɪ-, US -ˈkeɪ-, -ˈkɑː- -s -z
cicala sɪˈkɑː.lə -s -z
cicatric|e ˈsɪk.ə.trɪs -es -ɪz
cicatrix ˈsɪk.ə.trɪks; səˈkeɪ-, sɪ- **cicatrices** ˌsɪk.əˈtraɪ.siːz; səˈkeɪ.trɪ-, sɪ-
cicatriz|e, -is|e ˈsɪk.ə.traɪz -es -ɪz -ing -ɪŋ -ed -d
cicel|y, C~ ˈsɪs.əl|.i, -ɪ.l|i -ies -iz
Cicero ˈsɪs.ər.əʊ, US -ə.roʊ
cicerone ˌtʃɪtʃ.əˈrəʊ.ni, ˌsɪs.əˈ-, ˌtʃiː.tʃəˈ-, US ˌsɪs.əˈroʊ- -s -z
Ciceronian ˌsɪs.ərˈəʊ.ni.ən, US -əˈroʊ- -s -z
cicisbe|o ˌtʃɪtʃ.ɪzˈbeɪ|.əʊ, US sɪˈsɪs.biː|.oʊ -i -iː
Cid sɪd
CID ˌsiː.aɪˈdiː
-cidal ˈsaɪ.dəl
-cide saɪd
cider ˈsaɪ.dəʳ, US -dɚ -s -z ˈ**cider-ˌcup**
cig sɪg -s -z
cigar sɪˈgɑːʳ, sə-, US -ˈgɑːr -s -z **ciˈgar-ˌshaped**
cigarette ˌsɪg.ərˈet, ˈ---, US ˈsɪg.ə.ret, ˌ--ˈ- -s -s **cigaˈrette ˌholder** US ˈ**cigarette ˌholder; cigaˈrette ˌlighter** US ˈ**cigarette ˌlighter**
cigarillo ˌsɪg.əˈrɪl.əʊ, US -oʊ -s -z
cigg|y, cigg|ie ˈsɪg|.i -ies -iz
cilantro sɪˈlæn.trəʊ, sə-, US -ˈlɑːn.troʊ, -ˈlæn-
cilia ˈsɪl.i.ə
ciliary ˈsɪl.i.ər.i, US -er-
cilic|e ˈsɪl.ɪs -es -ɪz
Cilicia sɪˈlɪʃ.i.ə, -ˈlɪs-, US səˈlɪʃ.ə
cilium ˈsɪl.i.əm
Cilla ˈsɪl.ə
Ciller ˈsɪl.əʳ, US -ɚ
Cimabue ˌtʃɪm.əˈbuː.eɪ, ˌtʃiː.məˈ-, -i
Cimmeri|an sɪˈmɪə.ri|.ən, US -ˈmɪr.i- -i -aɪ
C-in-C ˌsiː.ɪnˈsiː -s -z
cinch sɪntʃ -es -ɪz -ing -ɪŋ -ed -d
cinchona sɪŋˈkəʊ.nə, US -ˈkoʊ-, sɪn- -s -z
cinchonic sɪŋˈkɒn.ɪk, US -ˈkɑː.nɪk, sɪn-
Cincinnati ˌsɪnt.sɪˈnæt.i, -səˈ-, US -ˈnæt̬-
Cincinnatus ˌsɪnt.sɪˈnɑː.təs, -ˈneɪ-, US -ˈnæt̬.əs, -ˈnɑː.t̬əs, -ˈneɪ-
cincture ˈsɪŋk.tʃəʳ, US -tʃɚ -s -z
cinder ˈsɪn.dəʳ, US -dɚ -s -z ˈ**cinder ˌblock;** ˈ**cinder ˌpath;** ˈ**cinder ˌtrack**
Cinderella ˌsɪn.dərˈel.ə
Cinderford ˈsɪn.də.fəd, US -dɚ.fɚd
Cindy ˈsɪn.di
cine- ˈsɪn.i
cinecamera ˈsɪn.iˌkæm.ər.ə, -ˌkæm.rə, ˌsɪn.iˈkæm- -s -z
cinefilm ˈsɪn.i.fɪlm -s -z
cinema ˈsɪn.ə.mə, ˈ-ɪ-, -mɑː, US -mə -s -z
cinemago|er ˈsɪn.ə.məˌgəʊ|.əʳ, ˈ-ɪ-, US -goʊ|.ɚ -ers -əz, US -ɚz -ing -ɪŋ
CinemaScope® ˈsɪn.ə.mə.skəʊp, ˈ-ɪ-, US -skoʊp -s -s
cinematic ˌsɪn.ɪˈmæt.ɪk, -əˈ-, US -əˈmæt̬- -ally -əl.i, -li
cinematograph ˌsɪn.ɪˈmæt.ə.grɑːf, -əˈ-, -græf, US -əˈmæt̬.ə.græf -s -s
cinematographic ˌsɪn.ɪ.mæt.əˈgræf.ɪk, ˌ-ə-; sɪ.nɪˌmæt-, US ˌsɪn.əˌmæt̬- -al -əl -ally -əl.i, -li
cinematograph|y

C

ˌsɪn.ɪ.məˈtɒg.rə.f|i, ˌ-ə-, (US) -ə.məˈtɑː.grə- **-er/s** -əʳ/z, (US) -ɚ/z

cinema verité ˌsɪn.ɪ.mɑːˈver.ɪ.teɪ, ˌ-ə-, -ə.məˈ-, (US) ˌsɪn.ɪ.mɑː.ver.əˈteɪ, -məˈver.ə.teɪ

cine-projector ˈsɪn.i.prəˌdʒek.təʳ, (US) -tɚ **-s** -z

Cinerama® ˌsɪn.əˈrɑː.mə, -ɪˈ-, (US) -əˈrɑː-, -ˈræm.ə

cineraria ˌsɪn.əˈreə.ri.ə, (US) -ˈrer.i- **-s** -z

cinerari|um ˌsɪn.əˈreə.ri|.əm, (US) -ˈrer.i- **-a** -ə

cinerary ˈsɪn.ə.rᵊr.i, (US) -rer-

cineration ˌsɪn.əˈreɪ.ʃᵊn

cinnabar ˈsɪn.ə.bɑːʳ, (US) -bɑːr

cinnamon ˈsɪn.ə.mən

cinque, C~ sɪŋk **ˈCinque ˌPorts**

Cinquecento® ˌtʃɪŋ.kweɪˈtʃen.təʊ, -kwɪˈ-, (US) -toʊ

cinquefoil ˈsɪŋk.fɔɪl

Cinzano® tʃɪnˈzɑː.nəʊ, sɪn-, tʃɪntˈsɑː-, sɪntˈsɑː-, (US) -noʊ

ciph|er ˈsaɪ.f|əʳ, (US) -f|ɚ **-ers** -əz, (US) -ɚz **-ering** -ᵊr.ɪŋ **-ered** -əd, (US) -ɚd **ˈcipher ˌkey**

Cipriani ˌsɪp.riˈɑː.ni; *as if Italian:* ˌtʃiː.pri-

circa ˈsɜː.kə, (US) ˈsɝː-

circadian sɜːˈkeɪ.di.ən, sə-, (US) sɚ-; (US) ˌsɝː.kəˈdiː.ən

Circassi|a sɜːˈkæs.i|.ə, sə-, -ˈkæʃ|.ə, -i|.ə, (US) sɚ- **-an/s** -ən/z

Circe ˈsɜː.si, (US) ˈsɝː-

circl|e ˈsɜː.kᵊl, (US) ˈsɝː- **-es** -z **-ing** -ɪŋ, ˈ-klɪŋ, (US) ˈ-kᵊl.ɪŋ, ˈ-klɪŋ **-ed** -d

circlet ˈsɜː.klət, -klɪt, (US) ˈsɝː- **-s** -s

circuit ˈsɜː.kɪt, (US) ˈsɝː- **-s** -s **-ry** -ri **ˈcircuit ˌbreaker; ˈcircuit ˌtraining**

circuitous səˈkjuː.ɪ.təs, sɜː-, ˈ-ə-, (US) sɚˈkjuː.ə.t̬əs **-ly** -li **-ness** -nəs, -nɪs

circular ˈsɜː.kjə.ləʳ, -kjʊ-, (US) ˈsɝː.kjə.lɚ **-s** -z **ˈcircular ˌsaw; ˌcircular ˈsaw**

circularity ˌsɜː.kjəˈlær.ə.ti, -kjʊˈ-, -ɪ.ti, (US) -kjəˈler.ə.t̬i, -ˈlær-

circulariz|e, -is|e ˈsɜː.kjə.lᵊr.aɪz, -kjʊ-, (US) ˈsɝː.kjə.lə.raɪz **-es** -ɪz **-ing** -ɪŋ **-ed** -d

circu|late ˈsɜː.kjə|.leɪt, -kjʊ-, (US) ˈsɝː.kjə- **-lates** -leɪts **-lating** -leɪ.tɪŋ, (US) -leɪ.t̬ɪŋ **-lated** -leɪ.tɪd, (US) -leɪ.t̬ɪd **-lator/s** -leɪ.təʳ/z, (US) -leɪ.t̬ɚ/z

circulation ˌsɜː.kjəˈleɪ.ʃᵊn, -kjʊˈ-, (US) ˌsɝː- **-s** -z

circulatory ˌsɜː.kjəˈleɪ.tᵊr.i, -kjʊˈ-, -tri; ˈsɜː.kjə.lə-, -kjʊ-, (US) ˈsɝː.kjə.lə.tɔːr.i

circum- ˈsɜː.kəm, səˈkʌm, (US) ˈsɝː.kəm, sɚˈkʌm

Note: Prefix. This may have primary or secondary stress on the first syllable, e.g. **circumstance** /ˈsɜː.kəm.stɑːnts/ (US) /ˈsɝ.kəm.stæns/ or on the second syllable, e.g. **circumference** /səˈkʌmp.fᵊr.ᵊnts/ (US) /sɚ-/.

circumambient ˌsɜː.kəmˈæm.bi.ənt, (US) ˌsɝː-

circumambu|late ˌsɜː.kəmˈæm.bjə|.leɪt, -bjʊ-, (US) ˌsɝː.kəmˈæm.bjə- **-lates** -leɪts **-lating** -leɪ.tɪŋ, (US) -leɪ.t̬ɪŋ **-lated** -leɪ.tɪd, (US) -leɪ.t̬ɪd

circumcis|e ˈsɜː.kəm.saɪz, (US) ˈsɝː- **-es** -ɪz **-ing** -ɪŋ **-ed** -d

circumcision ˌsɜː.kəmˈsɪʒ.ᵊn, (US) ˌsɝː- **-s** -z

circumferenc|e səˈkʌmp.fᵊr.ᵊnts, (US) sɚ- **-es** -ɪz

circumferential səˌkʌmp.fᵊˈren.tʃᵊl, (US) sɚˌkʌmp.fɚˈrent.ʃᵊl

circumflex ˈsɜː.kəm.fleks, (US) ˈsɝː- **-es** -ɪz

circumlocution ˌsɜː.kəm.ləˈkjuː.ʃᵊn, (US) ˌsɝː- **-s** -z

circumlocutory ˌsɜː.kəm.ləˈkjuː.tᵊr.i, -tri; -ˈlɒk.jʊ-, (US) ˌsɝː.kəmˈlɑː.kjʊ.tɔːr.i

circumnavi|gate ˌsɜː.kəmˈnæv.ɪ|.geɪt, (US) ˌsɝː- **-gates** -geɪts **-gating** -geɪ.tɪŋ, (US) -geɪ.t̬ɪŋ **-gated** -geɪ.tɪd, (US) -geɪ.t̬ɪd **-gator/s** -geɪ.təʳ/z, (US) -geɪ.t̬ɚ/z

circumnavigation ˌsɜː.kəmˌnæv.ɪˈgeɪ.ʃᵊn, (US) ˌsɝː- **-s** -z

circumpolar ˌsɜː.kəmˈpəʊ.ləʳ, (US) ˌsɝː.kəmˈpoʊ.lɚ

circumscrib|e ˈsɜː.kəm.skraɪb, ˌ--ˈ-, (US) ˈsɝː-, ˌ--ˈ- **-es** -z **-ing** -ɪŋ **-ed** -d

circumscription ˌsɜː.kəmˈskrɪp.ʃᵊn, (US) ˌsɝː- **-s** -z

circumspect ˈsɜː.kəm.spekt, (US) ˈsɝː- **-ly** -li **-ness** -nəs, -nɪs

circumspection ˌsɜː.kəmˈspek.ʃᵊn, (US) ˌsɝː-

circumstanc|e ˈsɜː.kəm.stænts, -stənts, -stɑːnts, (US) ˈsɝː.kəm.stænts, -stənts **-es** -ɪz **-ed** -t

circumstantial ˌsɜː.kəmˈstæn.tʃᵊl, (US) ˌsɝː.kəmˈstænt.ʃᵊl- **-ly** -i **ˌcircumstantial ˈevidence**

circumstantiality ˌsɜː.kəmˌstæn.tʃiˈæl.ə.ti, -ɪ.ti, (US) ˌsɝː.kəmˌstænt.ʃiˈæl.ə.t̬i

circumstanti|ate ˌsɜː.kəmˈstæn.tʃi|.eɪt, (US) ˌsɝː.kəmˈstænt.ʃi|- **-ates** -eɪts **-ating** -eɪ.tɪŋ, (US) -eɪ.t̬ɪŋ **-ated** -eɪ.tɪd, (US) -eɪ.t̬ɪd

circumvallation ˌsɜː.kəm.vəˈleɪ.ʃᵊn, -vælˈeɪ-, (US) ˌsɝː- **-s** -z

circum|vent ˌsɜː.kəm|ˈvent, ˈ--|-, (US) ˌsɝː- **-vents** -ˈvents **-venting** -ˈven.tɪŋ, (US) -ˈven.t̬ɪŋ **-vented** -ˈven.tɪd, (US) -ˈven.t̬ɪd

circumvention ˌsɜː.kəmˈven.tʃᵊn, (US) ˌsɝː.kəmˈvent.ʃᵊn **-s** -z

circus, C~ ˈsɜː.kəs, (US) ˈsɝː- **-es** -ɪz

Cirencester ˈsaɪə.rᵊn.ses.təʳ, ˈsɪs.ɪ.təʳ, -stəʳ, (US) ˈsaɪ.rᵊn.ses.tɚ

> Note: The pronunciation most usually heard locally is /ˈsaɪə.rᵊn.ses.təʳ/, or /-tər/.

cirque sɜːk, sɪək, (US) sɝːk **-s** -s

cirrhosis sɪˈrəʊ.sɪs, sə-, (US) səˈroʊ-

cirrocumulus ˌsɪr.əʊˈkjuː.mjə.ləs, -mjʊ-, (US) -oʊˈkjuː.mjə-

cirrostratus ˌsɪr.əʊˈstrɑː.təs, -ˈstreɪ-, (US) -oʊˈstreɪ.t̬əs, -ˈstræt̬.əs

cirrus ˈsɪr.əs

CIS ˌsiː.aɪˈes

Cisalpine sɪˈsæl.paɪn

Cisco® ˈsɪs.kəʊ, (US) -koʊ

Ciskei sɪˈskaɪ, ˈsɪs.kaɪ, (US) ˈsɪs.kaɪ

Cissie ˈsɪs.i

cissoid ˈsɪs.ɔɪd **-s** -z

cissy, C~ ˈsɪs.i

cist sɪst **-s** -s

Cistercian sɪˈstɜː.ʃᵊn, sə-, (US) -ˈstɝː- **-s** -z

cistern ˈsɪs.tən, (US) -tɚn **-s** -z

cistus ˈsɪs.təs **-es** -ɪz

citadel ˈsɪt.ə.del, -dᵊl, (US) ˈsɪt̬- **-s** -z

citation saɪˈteɪ.ʃᵊn **-s** -z

citatory ˈsaɪ.tə.tᵊr.i, ˈsɪ-, -tri; saɪˈteɪ-, (US) ˈsaɪ.t̬ə.tɔːr.i

cit|e saɪt **-es** -s **-ing** -ɪŋ, (US) ˈsaɪ.t̬ɪŋ **-ed** -ɪd, (US) ˈsaɪ.t̬ɪd

cithar|a ˈsɪθ.ᵊr|.ə **-ae** -iː

cither ˈsɪθ.əʳ, (US) -ɚ, ˈsɪð- **-s** -z

Citibank® ˈsɪt.i.bæŋk, (US) ˈsɪt̬-

Citigroup ˈsɪt.i.gruːp, (US) ˈsɪt̬-

citizen ˈsɪt.ɪ.zᵊn, ˈ-ə-, (US) ˈsɪt̬- **-s** -z **ˌcitizen's arˈrest**

citizenry ˈsɪt.ɪ.zᵊn.ri, ˈ-ə-, (US) ˈsɪt̬-

citizenship ˈsɪt.ɪ.zᵊn.ʃɪp, ˈ-ə-, (US) ˈsɪt̬-

citole ˈsɪt.əʊl, sɪˈtəʊl, (US) ˈsɪt.oʊl, sɪˈtoʊl **-s** -z

citrate ˈsɪt.reɪt, ˈsaɪ.treɪt, -trɪt **-s** -s

citric ˈsɪt.rɪk **ˌcitric ˈacid**

citrine sɪˈtriːn, sə-

Citroën® ˈsɪt.rəʊ.ən, ˈsɪt.rᵊn, (US) ˌsɪt.roʊˈen, ˈsɪt.roʊn **-s** -z

citron ˈsɪt.rᵊn **-s** -z

citronella ˌsɪt.rᵊnˈel.ə, (US) -rəˈnel-

citrous ˈsɪt.rəs

citrus ˈsɪt.rəs **-es** -ɪz **ˈcitrus ˌfruit**

cittern ˈsɪt.ɜːn, -ən, (US) ˈsɪt̬.ɚn **-s** -z

cit|y, C~ ˈsɪt|.i, (US) ˈsɪt̬|.i **-ies** -iz **ˌcity ˈfather; ˌcity ˈgent; ˌcity ˈhall; ˌcity ˈslicker** (US) **ˈcity ˌslicker**

city-dweller ˈsɪt.iˌdwel.əʳ, (US) ˈsɪt̬.iˌdwel.ɚ **-s** -z

city-state ˌsɪt.iˈsteɪt, (US) ˌsɪt̬-

citywide ˌsɪt.iˈwaɪd, (US) ˌsɪt̬- *stress shift, British only:* **ˌcitywide ˈmeetings**

Ciudad Bolívar θjuˌdɑːd.bɒlˈiː.vɑːʳ, θiː.uˌdɑːd-, (US) sjuːˌdɑːd.boʊˈliː.vɑːr, ˌsiː.uː-

Ciudad Guayana θjuˌdɑːd.gwaɪˈjɑː.nə, θiː.uˌdɑːd-, (US) sjuːˌdɑːd.gəˈ-, ˌsiː.uː-, -gwəˈ-, -gwɑːˈ-

Ciudad Juárez θjuˌdɑːdˈhwɑː.rez, θiː.u-, -ˈwɑː-, (US) sjuːˌdɑːdˈhwɑː.r.es, ˌsiː.uː-, -ˈwɑː.r.ez

civet ˈsɪv.ɪt **-s** -s

civic ˈsɪv.ɪk **-s** -s **ˌcivic ˈcentre** (US) **ˈcivic ˌcenter**

civil ˈsɪv.ᵊl, -ɪl **-ly** -i **ˌcivil deˈfence; ˌcivil disoˈbedience; ˌcivil engiˈneer; ˌcivil engiˈneering; ˌcivil**

Pronouncing the letters CK

The consonant digraph **ck** only has one possible realization in English words: /k/, e.g.:

sock sɒk (US) sɑːk

C

ˈ**liberty**; ˌ**civil** ˈ**rights** ˌ**movement**; ˌ**civil** ˈ**servant**; ˌ**civil** ˈ**service**; ˌ**civil** ˈ**war**
civilian sɪˈvɪl.i.ən, sə-, (US) ˈ-jən -s -z
civilit|y sɪˈvɪl.ə.t|i, sə-, -ɪ.t|i, (US) -ə.ţ|i -ies -iz
civilizable, -isa- ˈsɪv.ɪ.laɪ.zə.bᵊl, ˈ-ə-
civilization, -isa- ˌsɪv.ᵊl.aɪˈzeɪ.ʃᵊn, -ɪ.laɪˈ-, -lɪˈ-, (US) -ᵊl.əˈ- -s -z
civiliz|e, -is|e ˈsɪv.ᵊl.aɪz, -ɪ.laɪz, (US) -ə.laɪz, ˈ-ɪ- -es -ɪz -ing -ɪŋ -ed -d
civitas ˈsɪv.ɪ.tæs, ˈkɪv-
civv|y ˈsɪv|.i -ies -iz ˈ**civvy** ˌ**street**
CJD ˌsiː.dʒeɪˈdiː
cl (abbrev. for **centilitre/s**) *singular:* ˈsen.tɪˌliː.təʳ, (US) -ţəˌliː.ţɚ; *plural:* -z
clack klæk -s -s -ing -ɪŋ -ed -t
Clackmannan klækˈmæn.ən -shire -ʃəʳ, -ʃɪəʳ, (US) -ʃɚ, -ʃɪr
Clacton ˈklæk.tən
clad klæd
cladding ˈklæd.ɪŋ
cladistics kləˈdɪs.tɪks, klædˈɪs-
Claggart ˈklæg.ət, (US) -ɚt
Claiborne ˈkleɪ.bɔːn, (US) -bɔːrn
claim kleɪm -s -z -ing -ɪŋ -ed -d
claimant ˈkleɪ.mənt -s -s
claimer ˈkleɪ.məʳ, (US) -mɚ -s -z
clairaudien|ce ˌkleəˈrɔː.di.ən|ts, (US) ˌklerˈɑː-, -ˈɔː- -t -t
Claire kleəʳ, (US) kler
Clairol® ˈkleə.rɒl, (US) ˈkler.ɑːl
clairvoyan|ce ˌkleəˈvɔɪ.ənt|s, (US) ˌkler- -cy -si
clairvoyant ˌkleəˈvɔɪ.ənt, (US) ˌkler- -s -s
clam klæm -s -z -ming -ɪŋ -med -d
clamant ˈkleɪ.mənt, ˈklæm.ənt -ly -li
clambake ˈklæm.beɪk -s -s
clamb|er ˈklæm.b|əʳ, (US) -b|ɚ -ers -əz, (US) -ɚz -ering -ᵊr.ɪŋ -ered -əd, (US) -ɚd
clamm|y ˈklæm|.i -ier -i.əʳ, (US) -i.ɚ -iest -i.ɪst, -i.əst -ily -ᵊl.i, -ɪ.li -iness -ɪ.nəs, -ɪ.nɪs
clam|or ˈklæm|.əʳ, (US) -ɚ -ors -əz, (US) -ɚz -oring -ᵊr.ɪŋ -ored -əd, (US) -ɚd -orer/s -ᵊr.əʳ/z, (US) -ɚ.ɚ/z
clamorous ˈklæm.ᵊr.əs -ly -li -ness -nəs, -nɪs
clam|our ˈklæm|.əʳ, (US) -ɚ -ours -əz, (US) -ɚz -ouring -ᵊr.ɪŋ -oured -əd, (US) -ɚd -ourer/s -ᵊr.əʳ/z, (US) -ɚ.ɚ/z
clamp klæmp -s -s -ing -ɪŋ -ed -t
clampdown ˈklæmp.daʊn -s -z
clan klæn -s -z
clandestine klænˈdes.tɪn, -taɪn, ˈklæn.dɪs-, (US) klænˈdes.tɪn -ly -li
clang klæŋ -s -z -ing -ɪŋ -ed -d
clanger ˈklæŋ.əʳ, (US) -ɚ -s -z
clangor ˈklæŋ.gəʳ, -əʳ, (US) -ɚ, -gɚ
clangorous ˈklæŋ.gᵊr.əs, -ᵊr-, (US) ˈ-ɚ-, -gɚ- -ly -li
clangour ˈklæŋ.gəʳ, -əʳ, (US) -ɚ, -gɚ
clank klæŋk -s -s -ing -ɪŋ -ed -t
Clanmaurice klænˈmɒr.ɪs, klæm-, (US) -ˈmɔːr-, -ˈmɑːr-
Clanmorris klænˈmɒr.ɪs, klæm-, (US) klænˈmɔːr-
clannish ˈklæn.ɪʃ -ly -li -ness -nəs, -nɪs
Clanricarde klænˈrɪk.əd, (US) -ɚd
clanship ˈklæn.ʃɪp
clans|man ˈklænz|.mən -men -mən
clap klæp -s -s -ping -ɪŋ -ped -t ˌ**clapped** ˈ**out** *stress shift:* ˌ**clapped-out** ˈ**car**
clapboard ˈklæp.bɔːd, (US) -bɔːrd; (US) ˈklæb.ɚd -s -z
Clapham ˈklæp.ᵊm ˌ**Clapham** ˈ**omnibus**
clapometer klæpˈɒm.ɪ.təʳ, (US) -ˈɑː.mə.ţɚ -s -z
clapper ˈklæp.əʳ, (US) -ɚ -s -z
clapperboard ˈklæp.ə.bɔːd, (US) -ɚ.bɔːrd -s -z
Clapton ˈklæp.tən
claptrap ˈklæp.træp
claque klæk -s -s
Clara ˈklɑː.rə, ˈkleə-, (US) ˈkler.ə, ˈklær-
clarabella, C~ ˌklær.əˈbel.ə, (US) ˌkler-, ˌklær- -s -z
Clare kleəʳ, (US) kler
Clarel ˈkleə.rᵊl, (US) ˈkler.ᵊl, ˈklær.ᵊl; (US) kləˈrel
Claremont ˈkleə.mɒnt, -mənt, (US) ˈkler.mɑːnt
Clarence ˈklær.ᵊnts, (US) ˈkler-, ˈklær-
Clarenc(i)eux ˈklær.ᵊn.suː, -sjuː, (US) ˈkler-, ˈklær-
clarendon, C~ ˈklær.ᵊn.dən, (US) ˈkler-, ˈklær-
claret ˈklær.ət, -ɪt, (US) ˈkler-, ˈklær- -s -s
Clarges ˈklɑː.dʒɪz, -dʒəz, (US) ˈklɑːr-
Clarice ˈklær.ɪs, (US) ˈkler-, ˈklær-; (US) klerˈiːs, klær-
Claridge ˈklær.ɪdʒ, (US) ˈkler-, ˈklær- -'s -ɪz
clarification ˌklær.ɪ.fɪˈkeɪ.ʃᵊn, ˌ-ə-, -fəˈ-, (US) ˌkler-, ˌklær- -s -z
clari|fy ˈklær.ɪ|.faɪ, ˈ-ə-, (US) ˈkler-, ˈklær- -fies -faɪz -fying -faɪ.ɪŋ -fied -faɪd -fier/s -faɪ.əʳ/z, (US) -faɪ.ɚ/z
Clarina kləˈraɪ.nə
clarinet ˌklær.ɪˈnet, -əˈ-, (US) ˌkler-, ˌklær- -s -s
clarinet(t)ist ˌklær.ɪˈnet.ɪst, -əˈ-, (US) ˌkler.əˈneţ-, ˌklær- -s -s
clarion ˈklær.i.ən, (US) ˈkler-, ˈklær- -s -z ˈ**clarion** ˌ**call**
Clarissa kləˈrɪs.ə, klærˈɪs-, (US) kləˈrɪs-
clarity ˈklær.ə.ti, -ɪ.ti, (US) ˈkler.ə.ţi, ˈklær-
Clark(e) klɑːk, (US) klɑːrk
clarkia ˈklɑː.ki.ə, (US) ˈklɑːr- -s -z
Clarkson ˈklɑːk.sᵊn, (US) ˈklɑːrk-
Clarrie ˈklær.i, (US) ˈkler-, ˈklær-
Clary ˈkleə.ri, (US) ˈkler.i, ˈklær-
clash klæʃ -es -ɪz -ing -ɪŋ -ed -t
clasp klɑːsp, (US) klæsp -s -s -ing -ɪŋ -ed -t ˈ**clasp** ˌ**knife**
class klɑːs, (US) klæs -es -ɪz -ing -ɪŋ -ed -t ˈ**class** ˌ**system**; ˈ**class** ˌ**war**; ˌ**class** ˈ**war**
class-conscious ˈklɑːsˌkɒn.*t*ʃəs, ˌ-ˈ--, (US) ˈklæsˌkɑːn*t*.ʃəs -ness -nəs, -nɪs
classic ˈklæs.ɪk -s -s
classic|al ˈklæs.ɪ.k|ᵊl -ally -ᵊl.i, -li -alness -ᵊl.nəs, -nɪs ˌ**classical** ˈ**music**
classicism ˈklæs.ɪ.sɪ.zᵊm, ˈ-ə- -s -z
classicist ˈklæs.ɪ.sɪst, ˈ-ə- -s -s
classifiable ˈklæs.ɪ.faɪ.ə.bᵊl, ˌklæs.ɪˈfaɪ-, (US) ˈklæs.ə.faɪ-
classification ˌklæs.ɪ.fɪˈkeɪ.ʃᵊn, ˌ-ə-, -fəˈ-, (US) ˌ-ə- -s -z
classificatory ˌklæs.ɪ.fɪˈkeɪ.tᵊr.i, ˌ-ə-, -tri; ˈklæs.ɪ.fɪ.kə-, ˈ-ə-, (US) ˈklæs.ə.fɪ.kə.tɔːr.i; (US) kləˈsɪf.ə-
classi|fy ˈklæs.ɪ|.faɪ, ˈ-ə- -fies -faɪz -fying -faɪ.ɪŋ -fied -faɪd -fier/s -faɪ.əʳ/z, (US) -faɪ.ɚ/z ˌ**classified** ˈ**ad** (US) ˈ**classified** ˌ**ad**; ˌ**classified** ˌ**infor**ˈ**mation**
class|ism ˈklɑː.s|ɪ.zᵊm, (US) ˈklæs|.ɪ- -ist/s -ɪst/s
classless ˈklɑːs.ləs, -lɪs, (US) ˈklæs- -ness -nəs, -nɪs
class|man ˈklɑːs|.mæn, -mən, (US) ˈklæs- -men -men, -mən
classmate ˈklɑːs.meɪt, (US) ˈklæs- -s -s
classroom ˈklɑːs.rʊm, -ruːm, (US) ˈklæs.ruːm, -rʊm -s -z
classwork ˈklɑːs.wɜːk, (US) ˈklæs.wɝːk
class|y ˈklɑː.s|i, (US) ˈklæs|.i -ier -i.əʳ, (US) -i.ɚ -iest -i.ɪst, -i.əst -ily -ᵊl.i, -ɪ.li -iness -ɪ.nəs, -ɪ.nɪs
clatt|er ˈklæt|.əʳ, (US) ˈklæţ|.ɚ -ers -əz, (US) -ɚz -ering -ᵊr.ɪŋ -ered -əd, (US) -ɚd
Claud(e) klɔːd, (US) klɑːd, klɔːd
Claudette klɔːˈdet, (US) klɑː-, klɔː-
Claudi|a ˈklɔː.di|.ə, ˈklaʊ-, (US) ˈklɑː-, ˈklɔː-, ˈklaʊ- -an -ən
Claudine klɔːˈdiːn, (US) klɑː-, klɔː-
Claudio ˈklaʊ.di.əʊ, ˈklɔː-, (US) ˈklɑː.di.oʊ, ˈklɔː-, ˈklaʊ-
Claudius ˈklɔː.di.əs, (US) ˈklɑː-, ˈklɔː-
claus|e klɔːz, (US) klɑːz, klɔːz -es -ɪz -al -ᵊl
Clausewitz ˈklaʊ.sə.vɪts, -zə-
claustral ˈklɔː.strᵊl, (US) ˈklɑː-, ˈklɔː-
claustrophob|ia ˌklɔː.strəˈfəʊ.b|i.ə, ˌklɒs.trə-, (US) ˌklɑː.strəˈfoʊ-, ˌklɔː- -ic -ɪk
clave (archaic past of **cleave**) kleɪv
clavecin ˈklæv.ɪ.sɪn, -ə.sɪn, ˈ-ɪ- -s -z
Claverhouse ˈkleɪ.və.haʊs, (US) -vɚ-
Clavering ˈkleɪ.vᵊr.ɪŋ, ˈklæv.ᵊr-
clavichord ˈklæv.ɪ.kɔːd, (US) -kɔːrd -s -z

clavicle ˈklæv.ɪ.kəl -s -z
clavicular kləˈvɪk.jʊ.ləʳ, klævˈɪk-, -jə-, ⓤⓢ -jə.lɚ
clavier *keyboard:* ˈklæv.i.əʳ; klævˈɪəʳ, kləˈvɪəʳ, ⓤⓢ ˈklæv.i.ɚ; ⓤⓢ kləˈvɪr *instrument:* kləˈvɪəʳ, klævˈɪəʳ, ⓤⓢ ˈklæv.i.ɚ; ⓤⓢ kləˈvɪr -s -z
claw klɔː, ⓤⓢ klɑː, klɔː -s -z -ing -ɪŋ -ed -d
clawback ˈklɔː.bæk, ⓤⓢ ˈklɑː-, ˈklɔː- -s -s
Claxton ˈklæk.stən
clay, C~ kleɪ -s -z ˌ**clay** ˈ**pigeon**
Clayden, Claydon ˈkleɪ.dən
clayey ˈkleɪ.i
Clayhanger ˈkleɪ.hæŋ.əʳ, ⓤⓢ -ɚ
claymore ˈkleɪ.mɔːʳ, ⓤⓢ -mɔːr -s -z
Clayton ˈkleɪ.tən
Clayton-le-Moors ˌkleɪ.tən.liˈmɔːʳ, ⓤⓢ -ˈmɔːr
clean kliːn -s -z -ing -ɪŋ -ed -d -est -ɪst, -əst -ly -li -ness -nəs, -nɪs
clean-cut ˌkliːnˈkʌt, ˌkliːŋ-, ⓤⓢ ˌkliːn- *stress shift:* ˌ**clean-cut** ˈ**image**
cleaner ˈkliː.nəʳ, ⓤⓢ -nɚ -s -z
cleanliness ˈklen.lɪ.nəs, -nɪs
cleanl|y ˈkliːn.l|i -ier -i.əʳ, ⓤⓢ -i.ɚ -iest -i.ɪst, -i.əst
cleans|e klenz -es -ɪz -ing -ɪŋ -ed -d -er/s -əʳ/z, ⓤⓢ -ɚ/z -able -ə.bəl
cleanshaven ˌkliːnˈʃeɪ.vən *stress shift:* ˌ**cleanshaven** ˈ**chin**
clean-up ˈkliːn.ʌp -s -s
clear klɪəʳ, ⓤⓢ klɪr -er -əʳ, ⓤⓢ -ɚ -est -ɪst, -əst -ly -li -ness -nəs, -nɪs -s -z -ing -ɪŋ -ed -d ˌ**clear-**ˈ**headed** ⓤⓢ ˈ**clear-**ˌ**headed** *stress shift, British only:* ˌ**clear-headed** ˈ**thinking** ˌ**clear-**ˈ**sighted** ⓤⓢ ˈ**clear-**ˌ**sighted** *stress shift, British only:* ˌ**clear-sighted** ˈ**planning**
clearage ˈklɪə.rɪdʒ, ⓤⓢ ˈklɪr.ɪdʒ
clearanc|e ˈklɪə.rənts, ⓤⓢ ˈklɪr.ənts -es -ɪz ˈ**clearance** ˌ**sale**
clear-cut ˌklɪəˈkʌt, ⓤⓢ ˌklɪr- *stress shift:* ˌ**clear-cut** ˈ**difference**
clearing-hou|se ˈklɪə.rɪŋ.haʊ|s, ⓤⓢ ˈklɪr.ɪŋ- -ses -zɪz
clearout ˈklɪə.raʊt, ⓤⓢ ˈklɪr- -s -s
clearway ˈklɪə.weɪ, ⓤⓢ ˈklɪr- -s -z
Cleary ˈklɪə.ri, ⓤⓢ ˈklɪr.i
cleat kliːt -s -s
Cleator Moor ˌkliː.təˈmɔːʳ, ⓤⓢ -tɚˈmɔːr
cleavag|e ˈkliː.vɪdʒ -es -ɪz
cleav|e kliːv -es -z -ing -ɪŋ -ed -d **clove** kləʊv, ⓤⓢ kloʊv **cleft** kleft **cloven** ˈkləʊ.vən, ⓤⓢ ˈkloʊ- **clave** kleɪv
cleaver, C~ ˈkliː.vəʳ, ⓤⓢ -vɚ -s -z
Cleckheaton klekˈhiː.tən, ⓤⓢ -ṭən
Clee kliː
cleek kliːk -s -s -ing -ɪŋ -ed -t
Cleese kliːz
Cleethorpes ˈkliː.θɔːps, ⓤⓢ -θɔːrps
clef klef -s -s
cleft kleft -s -s ˌ**cleft** ˈ**palate**
cleg kleg -s -z
Clegg kleg
Cleland ˈklel.ənd, ˈkliː.lənd
Clem klem
clematis ˈklem.ə.tɪs; klɪˈmeɪ.tɪs, klə-, klemˈeɪ-, ⓤⓢ ˈklem.ə.ṭəs; ⓤⓢ kləˈmæṭ.əs, -ˈmɑː.ṭəs
Clemence ˈklem.ənts
Clemenceau ˈklem.ən.səʊ, -ɑ̃ːn-, ⓤⓢ -soʊ
clemency ˈklem.ənt.si
Clemens ˈklem.ənz
clement, C~ ˈklem.ənt -ly -li
Clementi klɪˈmen.ti, klə-, klemˈen-, ⓤⓢ -ṭi
Clementina ˌklem.ənˈtiː.nə
clementine, C~ ˈklem.ən.tiːn, -taɪn, ⓤⓢ -taɪn, -tiːn -s -z
Clements ˈklem.ənts
Clemo ˈklem.əʊ, ⓤⓢ -oʊ
Clemson ˈklemp.sən, ⓤⓢ ˈklem.zən
clench klentʃ -es -ɪz -ing -ɪŋ -ed -t
Cleo ˈkliː.əʊ, ⓤⓢ -oʊ
Cleobury *places in Shropshire:* ˈklɪb.ər.i, ˈkleb-, ˈklɪə.bər-, ⓤⓢ -er-, ˈ-ɚ- *surname:* ˈkləʊ.bər.i, ˈkliː-, ⓤⓢ ˈkloʊ.ber-, ˈkliː-, -bɚ-
Cleopatra ˌkliː.əˈpæt.rə, -ˈpɑː.trə, ⓤⓢ ˌkli.oʊˈpæt.rə, -əˈ-, -ˈpeɪ.trə, -ˈpɑː-
clepsydr|a ˈklep.sɪ.dr|ə, klepˈsɪd.r|ə, ⓤⓢ ˈklep.sɪ.dr|ə -ae -iː
clerestor|y ˈklɪə.stɔː.r|i, -stə-, ⓤⓢ ˈklɪr.stɔːr|.i -ies -iz
clergy ˈklɜː.dʒi, ⓤⓢ ˈklɝː-
clergy|man ˈklɜː.dʒɪ|.mən, ⓤⓢ ˈklɝː- -men -mən
clergy|woman ˈklɜː.dʒɪ|ˌwʊm.ən, ⓤⓢ ˈklɝː- -women -ˌwɪm.ɪn
cleric ˈkler.ɪk -s -s
clerical ˈkler.ɪ.kəl -s -z -ly -i
Clerides klerˈiː.diːz, kləˈriː-, ⓤⓢ klerˈiː.ðiːz, -diːz
clerihew, C~ ˈkler.i.hjuː, ˈ-ə-, ⓤⓢ ˈ-ə- -s -z
clerisy ˈkler.ə.si, ˈ-ɪ-, ⓤⓢ ˈ-ə-
clerk, C~ klɑːk, ⓤⓢ klɝːk -s -s
Clerke klɑːk, ⓤⓢ klɝːk, klɑːrk
Clerkenwell ˈklɑː.kən.wel, -wəl, ⓤⓢ ˈklɝː-, ˈklɑːr-
clerkship ˈklɑːk.ʃɪp, ⓤⓢ ˈklɝːk- -s -s
Clermont *towns in Ireland, village in Norfolk:* ˈkleə.mɒnt, -mənt, ⓤⓢ ˈkler.mɑːnt *in US:* ˈkleə.mɒnt, ˈklɜː-, ⓤⓢ ˈkler.mɑːnt, ˈklɝː-
Clermont-Ferrand ˌkleə.mɔ̃ːn.ferˈɑ̃ːŋ, ⓤⓢ ˌkler.mɑːn.ferˈɑ̃ːn
Clery ˈklɪə.ri, ⓤⓢ ˈklɪr.i
Clevedon ˈkliːv.dən
Cleveland ˈkliːv.lənd
Cleveleys ˈkliːv.liz
clev|er ˈklev|.əʳ, ⓤⓢ -ɚ -erer -ər.əʳ, ⓤⓢ -ɚ.ɚ -erest -ər.ɪst, -əst -erly -əl.i, ⓤⓢ -ɚ.li -erness -ə.nəs, -nɪs, ⓤⓢ -ɚ.nəs, -nɪs -erish -ər.ɪʃ ˈ**clever** ˌ**clogs; too** ˌ**clever by** ˈ**half**
clever-dick ˈklev.ə.dɪk, ⓤⓢ ˈ-ɚ- -s -s
Cleverdon ˈklev.ə.dən, ⓤⓢ ˈ-ɚ-
Cleves kliːvz
clew kluː -s -z -ing -ɪŋ -ed -d
Clews kluːz
Cley klaɪ, kleɪ
cliché ˈkliː.ʃeɪ, -ˈ-, ⓤⓢ -ˈ- -s -z -d -d
click klɪk -s -s -ing -ɪŋ -ed -t
clickable ˈklɪk.ə.bəl
client ˈklaɪ.ənt -s -s
clientage ˈklaɪ.ən.tɪdʒ
clientele ˌkliː.ɑ̃ːnˈtel, -ɑːnˈ-, -ənˈ-, ⓤⓢ ˌklaɪ.ənˈtel, ˌkliː-, -ɑːnˈ- -s -z
client-server ˌklaɪ.əntˈsɜː.vəʳ, ⓤⓢ -ˈsɝː.vɚ *stress shift:* ˌ**client-server** ˈ**systems**
cliff klɪf -s -s
Cliff(e) klɪf
cliffhanger ˈklɪfˌhæŋ.əʳ, ⓤⓢ -ɚ -s -z
Clifford ˈklɪf.əd, ⓤⓢ -ɚd
clifftop ˈklɪf.tɒp, ⓤⓢ -tɑːp -s -s
clift, C~ klɪft -s -s
Clifton ˈklɪf.tən
climacteric klaɪˈmæk.tər.ɪk; ˌklaɪ.mækˈter-, ⓤⓢ klaɪˈmæk.tɚ.ɪk; ⓤⓢ ˌklaɪ.mækˈter-, -ˈtɪr- -s -s
climacterical ˌklaɪ.mækˈter.ɪ.kəl
climactic klaɪˈmæk.tɪk -al -əl -ally -əl.i, -li
climate ˈklaɪ.mət, -mɪt -s -s
climatic klaɪˈmæt.ɪk, ⓤⓢ -ˈmæṭ- -al -əl -ally -əl.i, -li
climatolog|y ˌklaɪ.məˈtɒl.ə.dʒ|i, ⓤⓢ -ˈtɑː.lə- -ist/s -ɪst/s
climax ˈklaɪ.mæks -es -ɪz -ing -ɪŋ -ed -t
climb klaɪm -s -z -ing -ɪŋ -ed -d -able -ə.bəl ˈ**climbing** ˌ**frame**
climb-down ˈklaɪm.daʊn -s -z
climber ˈklaɪ.məʳ, ⓤⓢ -mɚ -s -z
clime klaɪm -s -z
clinch, C~ klɪntʃ -es -ɪz -ing -ɪŋ -ed -t -er/s -əʳ/z, ⓤⓢ -ɚ/z
cline, C~ klaɪn -s -z
cling klɪŋ -s -z -ing -ɪŋ **clung** klʌŋ
cling film ˈklɪŋ.fɪlm
clingstone ˈklɪŋ.stəʊn, ⓤⓢ -stoʊn -s -z
cling|y ˈklɪŋ|.i -ier -i.əʳ, ⓤⓢ -i.ɚ -iest -i.ɪst, -i.əst -iness -ɪ.nəs, -ɪ.nɪs
clinic ˈklɪn.ɪk -s -s -al -əl -ally -əl.i, -li
clinician klɪˈnɪʃ.ən, ⓤⓢ klɪ-, klə- -s -z
Clinique® klɪˈniːk
clink klɪŋk -s -s -ing -ɪŋ -ed -t
clinker, C~ ˈklɪŋ.kəʳ, ⓤⓢ -kɚ -s -z
clinometer klaɪˈnɒm.ɪ.təʳ, klɪ-, ˈ-ə-, ⓤⓢ -ˈnɑː.mə.ṭɚ -s -s
clinometric ˌklaɪ.nəʊˈmet.rɪk, ˌklɪn.əʊˈ-, ⓤⓢ -noʊˈ-
clinometry klaɪˈnɒm.ə.tri, klɪ-, ˈ-ɪ-, ⓤⓢ klaɪˈnɑː.mə-
Clint klɪnt
Clinton ˈklɪn.tən, ⓤⓢ ˈklɪn.tən, -tən
Clio ˈkliː.əʊ, ˈklaɪ-, ⓤⓢ -oʊ
clip klɪp -s -s -ping -ɪŋ -ped -t ˈ**clip** ˌ**joint**
clipboard ˈklɪp.bɔːd, ⓤⓢ -bɔːrd -s -z
clip-clop ˈklɪp.klɒp, ⓤⓢ -klɑːp -s -s -ping -ɪŋ -ped -t
clipper ˈklɪp.əʳ, ⓤⓢ -ɚ -s -z
clippie ˈklɪp.i -s -z
clipping ˈklɪp.ɪŋ -s -z
clique kliːk, ⓤⓢ kliːk, klɪk -s -s -y -i
cliquish ˈkliː.kɪʃ, ⓤⓢ ˈkliː.kɪʃ, ˈklɪk.ɪʃ -ly -li -ness -nəs, -nis
cliqu|y ˈkliː.k|i, ⓤⓢ ˈkliː.k|i, ˈklɪk|.i

-ier -i.əʳ, US -i.ɚ -iest -i.ɪst, -i.əst -iness -ɪ.nəs, -ɪ.nɪs
Clissold ˈklɪs.əld, -əʊld, US -oʊld
Clitheroe ˈklɪð.ə.rəʊ, US -roʊ
clitic ˈklɪt.ɪk, US ˈklɪţ- -s -s
clitoral ˈklɪt.ər.əl, US ˈklɪţ.ɚ-, ˈklaɪ.ţɚ-
clitoridectom|y ˌklɪt.ər.ɪˈdek.tə.m|i, US ˌklɪt- -ies -iz
clitor|is ˈklɪt.ər|.ɪs, US ˈklɪţ.ɚ|.əs, ˈklaɪ.ţɚ-; US klɪˈtɔːr- -ic -ɪk
Clive klaɪv
Cliveden ˈklɪv.dən, ˈkliːv-
cloa|ca kləʊˈeɪ|.kə, US kloʊ- -cae -kiː, -siː, US -siː, -kiː -cal -kəl
cloak, C~ kləʊk, US kloʊk -s -s -ing -ɪŋ -ed -t
cloak-and-dagger ˌkləʊk.ənˈdæg.əʳ, US ˌkloʊk.ənˈdæg.ɚ
cloakroom ˈkləʊk.rʊm, -ruːm, US ˈkloʊk.ruːm, -rʊm -s -z
clobb|er ˈklɒb|.əʳ, US ˈklɑː.b|ɚ -ers -əz, US -ɚz -ering -ər.ɪŋ -ered -əd, US -ɚd
cloch|e klɒʃ, kləʊʃ, US kloʊʃ -es -ɪz
clock klɒk, US klɑːk -s -s -ing -ɪŋ -ed -t ˈ**clock** ˌ**face; put the** ˈ**clock** ˌ**back**
clock-watch|ing ˈklɒkˌwɒtʃ|.ɪŋ, US ˈklɑːkˌwɑː.tʃ|ɪŋ, -ˌwɔː- -er/s -əʳ/z, US -ɚ/z
clockwise ˈklɒk.waɪz, US ˈklɑːk-
clockwork ˈklɒk.wɜːk, US ˈklɑːk.wɝːk
clod klɒd, US klɑːd -s -z -dy -i
clodhopp|ing ˈklɒdˌhɒp|.ɪŋ, US ˈklɑːdˌhɑː.p|ɪŋ -er/s -əʳ/z, US -ɚ/z
Cloete kləʊˈiː.ti; ˈkluː.ti, US ˈkluː.ţi; US kloʊˈiː.ţi
clog klɒg, US klɑːg, klɔːg -s -z -ging -ɪŋ -ged -d
clogg|y ˈklɒg|.i, US ˈklɑː.g|i -ier -i.əʳ, US -i.ɚ -iest -i.ɪst, -i.əst -ily -əl.i, -ɪ.li -iness -ɪ.nəs, -ɪ.nɪs
Clogher ˈklɒ.həʳ, ˈklɒx.əʳ, ˈklɔː-, klɔːʳ, US ˈklɑː.hɚ, -xɚ
cloisonné klwɑːˈzɒn.eɪ, klwʌzˈɒn-; ˌklɔɪ.zəˈneɪ, US ˌklɔɪ.zəˈneɪ
cloist|er ˈklɔɪ.st|əʳ, US -st|ɚ -ers -əz, US -ɚz -ering -ər.ɪŋ -ered -əd, US -ɚd
cloistral ˈklɔɪ.strəl
clonal ˈkləʊ.nəl, US ˈkloʊ- -ly -i
clon|e kləʊn, US kloʊn -es -z -ing -ɪŋ -ed -d
Clonmel ˈklɒn.mel, -ˈ-, US ˈklɑːn.mel, -ˈ-
Clooney ˈkluː.ni
clos|e v kləʊz, US kloʊz -es -ɪz -ing -ɪŋ -ed -d -er/s -əʳ/z, US -ɚ/z ˌ**closed** ˈ**book;** ˌ**closed** ˈ**circuit** *stress shift:* ˌ**closed circuit** ˈ**television;** ˌ**closed** ˈ**shop**
clos|e n *end:* kləʊz, US kloʊz -es -ɪz
clos|e adj *near:* kləʊs, US kloʊs -er -əʳ, US -ɚ -est -ɪst, -əst -ely -li -eness -nəs, -nɪs ˌ**close** ˈ**quarters;** ˌ**close** ˈ**season**
close-cut ˌkləʊsˈkʌt, US ˌkloʊs-
closefisted ˌkləʊsˈfɪs.tɪd, US ˌkloʊs- *stress shift:* ˌ**closefisted** ˈ**miser**
close-grained ˌkləʊsˈgreɪnd, US ˌkloʊs- *stress shift:* ˌ**close-grained** ˈ**wood**
close-hauled ˌkləʊsˈhɔːld, US ˌkloʊsˈhɔːld, -ˈhɑːld *stress shift:* ˌ**close-hauled** ˈ**sailing**
close-knit ˌkləʊsˈnɪt, US ˌkloʊs- *stress shift:* ˌ**close-knit** ˈ**family**
closely ˈkləʊ.sli, US ˈkloʊ-
closely-guarded ˌkləʊ.sliˈgɑː.dɪd, US ˌkloʊ.sliˈgɑːr- *stress shift:* ˌ**closely-guarded** ˈ**secret**
close-set ˌkləʊsˈset, US ˌkloʊsˈ- *stress shift:* ˌ**close-set** ˈ**eyes**
clos|et ˈklɒz|.ɪt, US ˈklɑː.z|ɪt -ets -ɪts -eting -ɪ.tɪŋ, US -ɪ.ţɪŋ, ˈ-ə- -eted -ɪ.tɪd, US -ɪ.ţɪd, ˈ-ə- **come** ˌ**out of the** ˈ**closet**
close-up ˈkləʊs.ʌp, US ˈkloʊs- -s -s
closure ˈkləʊ.ʒəʳ, US ˈkloʊ.ʒɚ -s -z
clot klɒt, US klɑːt -s -s -ting -ɪŋ, US ˈklɑː.ţɪŋ -ted -ɪd, US ˈklɑː.ţɪd ˌ**clotted** ˈ**cream**
cloth klɒθ, US klɑːθ -s klɒθs, klɒðz, US klɑːθs, klɑːðz ˈ**cloth** ˌ**yard; cut one's** ˌ**coat according to one's** ˈ**cloth**
cloth|e kləʊð, US kloʊð -es -z -ing -ɪŋ -ed -d **clad** klæd
cloth-eared ˌklɒθˈɪəd, US ˌklɑːθˈɪrd *stress shift:* ˌ**cloth-eared** ˈ**listener**
clothes kləʊðz, US kloʊðz ˈ**clothes** ˌ**brush;** ˈ**clothes** ˌ**hanger**

> Note: The pronunciation without /ð/ used to be widespread but has been overtaken by pronunciation with /ð/.

clotheshors|e ˈkləʊðz.hɔːs, US ˈkloʊðz.hɔːrs -es -ɪz
clothesline ˈkləʊðz.laɪn, US ˈkloʊðz- -s -z
clothespeg ˈkləʊðz.peg, US ˈkloʊðz- -s -z
clothespin ˈkləʊðz.pɪn, US ˈkloʊðz- -s -z
clothier ˈkləʊ.ði.əʳ, US ˈkloʊ.ði.ɚ -s -z
Clothilde klɒtˈɪld, ˈ--, US kloʊˈtɪl.də
clothing ˈkləʊ.ðɪŋ, US ˈkloʊ-
Clotho ˈkləʊ.θəʊ, US ˈkloʊ.θoʊ
cloud klaʊd -s -z -ing -ɪŋ -ed -ɪd ˈ**cloud-**ˌ**capped**
cloudberr|y ˈklaʊd.bər|.i, ˈklaʊb-, -ber-, US ˈklaʊd.ber- -ies -iz
cloudburst ˈklaʊd.bɜːst, US -bɝːst -s -s
cloud-cuckoo-land ˌklaʊdˈkʊk.uː.lænd, US -ˈkuː.kuː-, -ˈkʊk.ʊ-
Cloudesley ˈklaʊdz.li
cloudless ˈklaʊd.ləs, -lɪs -ly -li -ness -nəs, -nɪs
cloudware ˈklaʊd.weəʳ, US -wer
cloud|y ˈklaʊ.d|i -ier -i.əʳ, US -i.ɚ -iest -i.ɪst, -i.əst -ily -əl.i, -ɪ.li -iness -ɪ.nəs, -ɪ.nɪs
clough klʌf -s -s
Clough *surname:* klʌf, kluː *in Ireland:* klɒx, US klʌf
Clouseau kluːˈsəʊ, ˈ--, US kluːˈzoʊ, ˈ--
clout klaʊt -s -s -ing -ɪŋ, US ˈklaʊ.ţɪŋ -ed -ɪd, US ˈklaʊ.ţɪd
clove n kləʊv, US kloʊv -s -z
clov|e (from **cleave**) kləʊv, US kloʊv -en -ən
Clovelly kləˈvel.i
cloven ˈkləʊ.vən, US ˈkloʊ- ˌ**cloven-**ˈ**footed** *stress shift:* ˌ**cloven-footed** ˈ**beast**
clover, C~ ˈkləʊ.vəʳ, US ˈkloʊ.vɚ -s -z
clover|leaf ˈkləʊ.və|.liːf, US ˈkloʊ.vɚ- -leafs -liːfs -leaves -liːvz
Clovis ˈkləʊ.vɪs, US ˈkloʊ-
Clow kləʊ, US kloʊ, klaʊ
Clowes *in Norfolk:* kluːz *surname:* klaʊz, kluːz
clown klaʊn -s -z -ing -ɪŋ -ed -d
Clowne klaʊn
clownish ˈklaʊ.nɪʃ -ly -li -ness -nəs, -nɪs
cloy klɔɪ -s -z -ing/ly -ɪŋ/li -ed -d
cloze kləʊz, US kloʊz
club klʌb -s -z -bing -ɪŋ -bed -d ˌ**club** ˈ**moss** US ˈ**club** ˌ**moss;** ˌ**club** ˈ**sandwich;** ˌ**club** ˈ**soda**
clubbable ˈklʌb.ə.bəl
clubber ˈklʌb.əʳ, US -ɚ -s -z
club|foot ˌklʌb|ˈfʊt, ˈ--, US ˈ-- -feet -ˈfiːt, US -fiːt
clubfooted ˌklʌbˈfʊt.ɪd, ˈ---, US ˈklʌbˌfʊţ.ɪd
clubhou|se ˈklʌb.haʊ|s -ses -zɪz
clubland ˈklʌb.lænd, -lənd
club|man ˈklʌb|.mən, -mæn -men -mən, -men
Club Med ˌklʌbˈmed
Club Méditerranée® ˌklʌbˌmed.ɪ.ter.əˈneɪ
club-room ˈklʌb.rʊm, -ruːm, US -ruːm, -rʊm -s -z
cluck klʌk -s -s -ing -ɪŋ -ed -t
clu|e kluː -es -z -(e)ing -ɪŋ -ed -d ˌ**clued** ˈ**up**
clueless ˈkluː.ləs, -lɪs -ness -nəs, -nɪs
Cluj kluːʒ
clumber, C~ ˈklʌm.bəʳ, US -bɚ -s -z
clump klʌmp -s -s -ing -ɪŋ -ed -t
clumpy ˈklʌm.pi
clums|y ˈklʌm.z|i -ier -i.əʳ, US -i.ɚ -iest -i.ɪst, -i.əst -ily -əl.i, -ɪ.li -iness -ɪ.nəs, -ɪ.nɪs
Clun klʌn
clunch klʌntʃ
clung (from **cling**) klʌŋ
clunk klʌŋk -s -s -ing -ɪŋ -ed -t
clunk|y ˈklʌŋ.k|i -ier -i.əʳ, US -i.ɚ -iest -i.ɪst, -i.əst
clust|er ˈklʌs.t|əʳ, US -t|ɚ -ers -əz, US -ɚz -ering -ər.ɪŋ -ered -əd, US -ɚd
clutch klʌtʃ -es -ɪz -ing -ɪŋ -ed -t ˈ**clutch** ˌ**bag**
clutt|er ˈklʌt|.əʳ, US ˈklʌţ|.ɚ -ers -əz, US -ɚz -ering -ər.ɪŋ -ered -əd, US -ɚd

Clutterbuck ˈklʌt.ə.bʌk, US ˈklʌţ.ɚ-
Clutton ˈklʌt.ən, US ˈklʌţ-
Clwyd ˈkluː.ɪd
Clwydian kluˈɪd.i.ən
Clydach ˈklɪd.ək, ˈklʌd-, -əx, US -ək
Clyde klaɪd
Clydebank ˈklaɪd.bæŋk, -ˈ-
Clydesdale ˈklaɪdz.deɪl -s -z
Clydeside ˈklaɪd.saɪd
Clym klɪm
clyster ˈklɪs.təʳ, US -tɚ -s -z
Clytemnestra ˌklaɪ.təmˈnes.trə, ˌklɪt.əmˈ-, -ɪmˈ-, -emˈ-, -ˈniː.strə, US ˌklaɪ.ţəmˈnes.trə
Clytie *in Greek mythology:* ˈklɪt.i.iː, ˈklaɪ.tiː, US ˈklaɪ.ţi.iː, ˈklɪţ.i.iː *modern first name, chignon:* ˈklaɪ.ti, -tiː, US ˈklaɪ.ţi, klɪˈʃiː.ə
cm (abbrev. for **centimetre/s**) *singular:* ˈsen.tɪˌmiː.təʳ, US -ţəˌmiː.ţɚ; *plural:* -z
c'mon kəˈmɒn, US kəˈmɑːn
CNBC ˌsiː.en.biːˈsiː
CND ˌsiː.enˈdiː
Cnidus ˈnaɪ.dəs, ˈknaɪ-
CNN ˌsiː.enˈen
C-note ˈsiː.nəʊt, US -noʊt -s -s
Cnut kəˈnjuːt, knuːt
CO ˌsiːˈəʊ, US -ˈoʊ
co- kəʊ, US koʊ
Note: Prefix. May carry primary stress in a mathematical term such as **cosine** /ˈkəʊ.saɪn/, US /ˈkoʊ.saɪn/, secondary stress as in **co-axial** /ˌkəʊˈæk.si.əl/, US /ˌkoʊˈæk.si.əl/ or no stress as in **cooperate** /kəʊˈɒp.ər.eɪt, US /koʊˈɑː.pə.reɪt/.
c/o (abbrev. for **care of**) ˈkeəʳ.ɒv, US ˈker.ɑːv, -əv
c/o (abbrev. for **carried over**) ˌkær.idˈəʊ.vəʳ, US ˌker.idˈoʊ.vɚ, ˌkær-
Co. (abbrev. for **company**) kəʊ, ˈkʌm.pən.i, US koʊ, ˈkʌm.pən.i
coach kəʊtʃ, US koʊtʃ -es -ɪz -ing -ɪŋ -ed -t ˈ**coach** ˌ**horse**; ˈ**coach** ˌ**house**; ˈ**coach** ˌ**party**; ˈ**coach** ˌ**station**
coach|man ˈkəʊtʃ|.mən, -mæn, US ˈkoʊtʃ- -men -mən
coachwork ˈkəʊtʃ.wɜːk, US ˈkoʊtʃ.wɝːk
coac|tion kəʊˈæk|.ʃən, US koʊ- -tive -tɪv
coadjacent ˌkəʊ.əˈdʒeɪ.sənt, US ˌkoʊ-
coadjutant kəʊˈædʒ.ʊ.tənt, ˈ-ə-, US koʊˈædʒ.ə.ţənt -s -s
coadjutor kəʊˈædʒ.ʊ.təʳ, ˈ-ə-, US koʊˈædʒ.ə.ţɚ -s -z
co-administrator ˌkəʊ.ədˈmɪn.ɪ.streɪ.təʳ, US ˌkoʊ.ædˈmɪn.ɪ.streɪ.ţɚ, -ədˈ- -s -z
coagulant kəʊˈæg.jə.lənt, -jʊ-, US koʊˈæg.jə- -s -s
coagu|late kəʊˈæg.jə|.leɪt, -jʊ-, US koʊˈæg.jə- -lates -leɪts -lating -leɪ.tɪŋ, US -leɪ.ţɪŋ -lated -leɪ.tɪd, US -leɪ.ţɪd
coagulation kəʊˌæg.jəˈleɪ.ʃən, -jʊˈ-, US koʊˌæg.jəˈ-
coal kəʊl, US koʊl -s -z -ing -ɪŋ -ed -d ˈ**coal** ˌ**bed**; ˈ**coal** ˌ**black**; ˈ**coal** ˌ**bunker**; ˈ**coal** ˌ**scuttle**; ˈ**coal** ˌ**tar**; ˌ**haul someone over the** ˈ**coals**
coalesc|e kəʊ.əˈles, kəʊə-, US koʊ.ə- -es -ɪz -ing -ɪŋ -ed -t
coalescen|ce kəʊ.əˈles.ən|ts, kəʊə-, US koʊ.ə- -t -t
coalfac|e ˈkəʊl.feɪs, US ˈkoʊl- -es -ɪz
coalfield ˈkəʊl.fiːld, US ˈkoʊl- -s -z
coalhole ˈkəʊl.həʊl, US ˈkoʊl.hoʊl -s -z
coalhou|se ˈkəʊl.haʊ|s, US ˈkoʊl- -ses -zɪz
Coalite® ˈkəʊ.laɪt, US ˈkoʊ-
coalition kəʊ.əˈlɪʃ.ən, kəʊə-, US koʊ.ə- -s -z
coal|man ˈkəʊl|.mən, -mæn, US ˈkoʊl- -men -men, -mən
coalmine ˈkəʊl.maɪn, US ˈkoʊl- -s -z
coalminer ˈkəʊlˌmaɪ.nəʳ, US ˈkoʊlˌmaɪ.nɚ -s -z
coalpit ˈkəʊl.pɪt, US ˈkoʊl- -s -s
Coalville ˈkəʊl.vɪl, US ˈkoʊl-
coanchor ˌkəʊˈæŋ.kəʳ, US ˌkoʊˈæŋ.kɚ -s -z
coars|e kɔːs, US kɔːrs -er -əʳ, US -ɚ -est -ɪst, -əst -ely -li -eness -nəs, -nɪs ˈ**coarse** ˌ**fishing**; ˌ**coarse** ˈ**fishing**
coarse-grained ˌkɔːsˈgreɪnd, US ˈkɔːrs.greɪnd *stress shift:* ˌ**coarse-grained** ˈ**picture**
coarsen ˈkɔː.sən, US ˈkɔːr- -s -z -ing -ɪŋ -ed -d
coarticulation ˌkəʊ.ɑː.tɪ.kjəˈleɪ.ʃən, -jʊˈ-, US ˌkoʊ.ɑːr.tɪ.kjəˈ-
coast kəʊst, US koʊst -s -s -ing -ɪŋ -ed -ɪd
coastal ˈkəʊs.təl, US ˈkoʊs-
coaster ˈkəʊ.stəʳ, US ˈkoʊ.stɚ -s -z
coastguard ˈkəʊst.gɑːd, US ˈkoʊst.gɑːrd -s -z
coastline ˈkəʊst.laɪn, US ˈkoʊst- -s -z
coastwise ˈkəʊst.waɪz, US ˈkoʊst-
coat kəʊt, US koʊt -s -s -ing -ɪŋ -ed -ɪd ˈ**coat** ˌ**check**; ˈ**coat** ˌ**hanger**; ˌ**coat of** ˈ**arms**; ˈ**coat** ˌ**room**; ˈ**coat** ˌ**tail(s)**; ˌ**cut one's** ˌ**coat according to one's** ˈ**cloth**
Coatbridge ˈkəʊt.brɪdʒ, US ˈkoʊt-
coati kəʊˈɑː.ti, US koʊˈɑː.ţi -s -z
coating ˈkəʊ.tɪŋ, US ˈkoʊ.ţɪŋ -s -z
Coat(e)s kəʊts, US koʊts
coauthor kəʊˈɔː.θəʳ, ˈ---, US koʊˈɑː.θɚ, -ˈɔː- -s -z -ing -ɪŋ -ed -d
coax kəʊks, US koʊks -es -ɪz -ing/ly -ɪŋ/li -ed -t -er/s -əʳ/z, US -ɚ/z
co-axial ˌkəʊˈæk.si.əl, US ˌkoʊ- -ly -i
cob kɒb, US kɑːb -s -z
Cobain kəʊˈbeɪn, US ˈkoʊ-, ˌkoʊˈbeɪn
cobalt ˈkəʊ.bɔːlt, -bɒlt, US ˈkoʊ.bɔːlt, -bɑːlt
Cobb(e) kɒb, US kɑːb
cobber ˈkɒb.əʳ, US ˈkɑː.bɚ -s -z
Cobbett ˈkɒb.ɪt, US ˈkɑː.bɪt
cobbl|e ˈkɒb.əl, US ˈkɑː.bəl -es -z -ing -ɪŋ, ˈ-lɪŋ, US ˈkɑː.bəl.ɪŋ, ˈ-blɪŋ -ed -d
Cobbleigh ˈkɒb.li, US ˈkɑː.bli
cobbler ˈkɒb.ləʳ, ˈkɒb.əl.əʳ, US ˈkɑː.blɚ -s -z
cobblestone ˈkɒb.əl.stəʊn, US ˈkɑː.bəl.stoʊn -s -z
Cobbold ˈkɒb.əʊld, -əld, US ˈkɑː.boʊld
Cobden ˈkɒb.dən, US ˈkɑːb-
Cobh kəʊv, US koʊv
Cobham ˈkɒb.əm, US ˈkɑː.bəm
Coblenz kəʊˈblents, ˈkəʊ.blents, US ˈkoʊ-
cobnut ˈkɒb.nʌt, US ˈkɑːb- -s -s
COBOL, Cobol ˈkəʊ.bɒl, US ˈkoʊ.bɔːl, -bɑːl
cobra ˈkəʊ.brə, ˈkɒb.rə, US ˈkoʊ.brə -s -z
Coburg ˈkəʊ.bɜːg, US ˈkoʊ.bɝːg -s -z
cobweb ˈkɒb.web, US ˈkɑːb- -s -z
coca ˈkəʊ.kə, US ˈkoʊ.kə -s -z
Coca-Cola® ˌkəʊ.kəˈkəʊ.lə, US ˌkoʊ.kəˈkoʊ-
cocaine kəʊˈkeɪn, US koʊ-, ˈ--
coccal ˈkɒk.əl, US ˈkɑː.kəl
coccid ˈkɒk.sɪd, US ˈkɑːk-
cocciferous kɒkˈsɪf.ər.əs, US kɑːk-
coccoid ˈkɒk.ɔɪd, US ˈkɑː.kɔɪd
coccus ˈkɒk.əs, US ˈkɑː.kəs **cocci** ˈkɒk.aɪ, ˈkɒk.saɪ, US ˈkɑːk.saɪ
coccyx ˈkɒk.sɪks, US ˈkɑːk- -es -ɪz **coccyges** -saɪ.dʒiːz
Cochabamba ˌkəʊ.tʃəˈbæm.bə, US ˌkoʊ.tʃəˈbɑːm-
Cochin ˈkəʊ.tʃɪn, ˈkɒtʃ.ɪn, US ˈkoʊ.tʃɪn, ˈkɑː-
Cochin-China ˌkəʊ.tʃɪnˈtʃaɪ.nə, ˌkɒtʃ.ɪn-, US ˌkoʊ.tʃɪnˈ-, ˌkɑː-
cochineal ˌkɒtʃ.ɪˈniːl, -əˈ-, ˈ---, US ˈkɑː.tʃə.niːl, ˌ--ˈ-
Cochise kəʊˈtʃiːs, US koʊ-, -ˈtʃiːz
cochle|a ˈkɒk.li|.ə, US ˈkɑː.k-, ˈkoʊk- -as -əz -ae -iː -ar -əʳ, US -ɚ
Cochran(e) ˈkɒk.rən, ˈkɒx-, US ˈkɑːk-
cock kɒk, US kɑːk -s -s -ing -ɪŋ -ed -t
cockade kɒkˈeɪd, US kɑːˈkeɪd -s -z
cock-a-doodle-doo ˌkɒk.ə.duː.dəlˈduː, US ˌkɑːk-
cock-a-hoop ˌkɒk.əˈhuːp, US ˌkɑːk-
Cockaigne kɒkˈeɪn, kəˈkeɪn, US kɑːˈkeɪn
cock-a-leekie ˌkɒk.əˈliː.ki, US ˌkɑːk-
cockalorum ˌkɒk.əˈlɔː.rəm, US ˌkɑː.kəˈlɔːr.əm -s -z
cockamamie ˌkɒk.əˈmeɪ.mi, US ˈkɑː.kə.meɪ-
cock-and-bull ˌkɒk.əndˈbʊl, -əmˈ-, US ˌkɑːk.ənd- *stress shift, British only, see compound:* ˌ**cock-and-bull** ˈ**story** US ˌ**cock-and-**ˈ**bull** ˌ**story**
cockateel, cockatiel ˌkɒk.əˈtiːl, US ˌkɑː.kəˈ- -s -z

cockatoo ˌkɒk.əˈtuː, (US) ˈkɑː.kə.tuː **-s** -z
cockatric|e ˈkɒk.ə.traɪs, -trɪs, -trəs, (US) ˈkɑː.kə- **-es** -ɪz
Cockaygne kɒkˈeɪn, kəˈkeɪn, (US) kɑːˈkeɪn
Cockburn ˈkəʊ.bɜːn, -bən, (US) ˈkoʊ.bɝːn
cockchafer ˈkɒkˌtʃeɪ.fəʳ, (US) ˈkɑːkˌtʃeɪ.fɚ **-s** -z
Cockcroft ˈkəʊk.krɒft, ˈkɒk.*k*rɒft, (US) ˈkɑːk.*k*rɑːft, ˈkoʊ.krɑːft
cockcrow ˈkɒk.krəʊ, (US) ˈkɑːk.kroʊ
Cocke *place:* kɒk, (US) kɑːk *surname:* kəʊk, kɒk, (US) koʊk, kɑːk
Cockell ˈkɒk.əl, (US) ˈkɑː.kəl
cocker, C~ ˈkɒk.əʳ, (US) ˈkɑː.kɚ **-s** -z ˌ**cocker** ˈ**spaniel**
cockerel ˈkɒk.ər.əl, (US) ˈkɑː.kɚ- **-s** -z
Cockerell ˈkɒk.ər.əl, (US) ˈkɑː.kɚ-
Cockermouth ˈkɒk.ə.məθ, -maʊθ; *locally:* -məθ, (US) ˈkɑː.kɚ-
cockeye ˈkɒk.aɪ, (US) ˈkɑːk.aɪ **-d** kɒkˈaɪd, (US) ˈkɑːk.aɪd *stress shift, British only:* ˌ**cockeyed** ˈ**optimist**
cock|fight ˈkɒk|.faɪt, (US) ˈkɑːk- **-fights** -faɪts **-fighting** -ˌfaɪ.tɪŋ, (US) -ˌfaɪ.t̬ɪŋ
Cockfosters ˌkɒkˈfɒs.təz, ˈ-ˌ--, (US) ˈkɑːkˌfɑː.stɚz, ˌ-ˈ--
cockhors|e ˌkɒkˈhɔːs, (US) ˈkɑːk.hɔːrs **-es** -ɪz
cockl|e, C~ ˈkɒk.əl, (US) ˈkɑː.kəl **-es** -z **-ing** -ɪŋ, ˈ-lɪŋ, (US) ˈkɑː.kəl.ɪŋ, ˈ-klɪŋ **-ed** -d
cockleshell ˈkɒk.əl.ʃel, (US) ˈkɑː.kəl- **-s** -z
cockney, C~ ˈkɒk.ni, (US) ˈkɑːk- **-s** -z
cockneyism ˈkɒk.ni.ɪ.zəm, (US) ˈkɑːk- **-s** -z
cockpit ˈkɒk.pɪt, (US) ˈkɑːk- **-s** -s
cockroach ˈkɒk.rəʊtʃ, (US) ˈkɑːk.roʊtʃ **-es** -ɪz
Cockroft ˈkɒk.rɒft, ˈkəʊ.krɒft, (US) ˈkɑː.krɑːft, ˈkoʊ-
cockscomb ˈkɒk.skəʊm, (US) ˈkɑːk.skoʊm **-s** -z
Cocksedge ˈkɒk.sɪdʒ, ˈkɒs.ɪdʒ, -edʒ, ˈkəʊ.sɪdʒ, (US) ˈkɑːk.sɪdʒ, ˈkɑː-, ˈkoʊ-, -sedʒ
Cockshott ˈkɒk.ʃɒt, (US) ˈkɑːk.ʃɑːt
cocksh|y ˈkɒk.ʃ|aɪ, (US) ˈkɑːk- **-ies** -aɪz
cockspur, C~ ˈkɒk.spɜːʳ, -spəʳ, (US) ˈkɑːk.spɝː **-s** -z
cocksure ˌkɒkˈʃʊəʳ, -ˈʃɔːʳ, (US) ˌkɑːkˈʃʊr, -ˈʃɝː
cocktail ˈkɒk.teɪl, (US) ˈkɑːk- **-s** -z ˈ**cocktail** ˌ**dress**; ˈ**cocktail** ˌ**lounge**; ˈ**cocktail** ˌ**party**; ˈ**cocktail** ˌ**stick**
cock-up ˈkɒk.ʌp, (US) ˈkɑːk- **-s** -s
Cockwood ˈkɒk.wʊd, (US) ˈkɑːk-

> Note: There exists also a local pronunciation /ˈkɒk.ʊd/ (US) /ˈkɑː.kʊd/.

cock|y ˈkɒk|.i, (US) ˈkɑː.k|i **-ier** -i.əʳ, (US) -i.ɚ **-iest** -i.ɪst, -i.əst **-ily** -əl.i, -ɪ.li **-iness** -ɪ.nəs, -ɪ.nɪs
cocky-leeky ˌkɒk.iˈliː.ki, (US) ˌkɑː.ki-
coco ˈkəʊ.kəʊ, (US) ˈkoʊ.koʊ **-s** -z
cocoa ˈkəʊ.kəʊ, (US) ˈkoʊ.koʊ **-s** -z ˈ**cocoa** ˌ**butter**
cocoanut ˈkəʊ.kə.nʌt, (US) ˈkoʊ- **-s** -s
co-conspirator ˌkəʊ.kənˈspɪr.ə.təʳ, ˈ-ɪ-, (US) ˌkoʊ.kənˈspɪr.ə.t̬ɚ **-s** -z
coconut ˈkəʊ.kə.nʌt, (US) ˈkoʊ- **-s** -s ˌ**coconut** ˈ**ice**; ˈ**coconut** ˌ**shy**
cocoon kəˈkuːn **-s** -z **-ing** -ɪŋ **-ed** -d
Cocos ˈkəʊ.kəs, -kɒs, (US) ˈkoʊ.koʊs, -kəs
cocotte kəˈkɒt, kəʊ-, kɒkˈɒt, (US) koʊˈkɑːt **-s** -s
Cocteau ˈkɒk.təʊ, (US) kɑːkˈtoʊ
Cocytus kəʊˈsaɪ.təs, (US) koʊˈsaɪ.t̬əs
cod, C~ kɒd, (US) kɑːd **-s** -z **-ding** -ɪŋ **-ded** -ɪd ˌ**cod-liver** ˈ**oil**
COD ˌsiː.əʊˈdiː, (US) -oʊˈ-
coda ˈkəʊ.də, (US) ˈkoʊ- **-s** -z
Coddington ˈkɒd.ɪŋ.tən, (US) ˈkɑː.dɪŋ-
coddl|e ˈkɒd.əl, (US) ˈkɑː.dəl **-es** -z **-ing** -ɪŋ, ˈ-lɪŋ, (US) ˈkɑː.dəl.ɪŋ, ˈkɑːd.lɪŋ **-ed** -d
cod|e kəʊd, (US) koʊd **-es** -z **-ing** -ɪŋ **-ed** -ɪd **-er/s** -əʳ/z, (US) -ɚ/s
co-defendant ˌkəʊ.dɪˈfen.dənt, -dəˈ-, (US) ˌkoʊ- **-s** -s
codeine ˈkəʊ.diːn, (US) ˈkoʊ-
co-determination ˌkəʊ.dɪˌtɜː.mɪˈneɪ.ʃən, -də-, (US) ˌkoʊ.dɪˌtɝː-, -də-
cod|ex ˈkəʊ.d|eks, (US) ˈkoʊ- **-exes** -ek.sɪz, -səz **-ices** -ɪ.siːz, ˈkɒd.ɪ.siːz, (US) ˈkoʊ.də.siːz, ˈkɑː-
codger ˈkɒdʒ.əʳ, (US) ˈkɑː.dʒɚ **-s** -z
codicil ˈkəʊ.dɪ.sɪl, ˈkɒd.ɪ-, ˈ-ə-, (US) ˈkɑː.də.səl, -sɪl **-s** -z
codicillary ˌkəʊ.dɪˈsɪl.ər.i, ˌkɒd.ɪˈ-, (US) ˌkɑː.dəˈ-
Codicote ˈkəʊ.dɪ.kəʊt, ˈkɒd.ɪ.kət, (US) ˈkoʊ.dɪ.koʊt, ˈkɑː.dɪ.kət
codification ˌkəʊ.dɪ.fɪˈkeɪ.ʃən, -də-, -fəˈ-, (US) ˌkɑː-, ˌkoʊ- **-s** -z
codi|fy ˈkəʊ.dɪ|.faɪ, -də-, (US) ˈkɑː-, ˈkoʊ- **-fies** -faɪz **-fying** -faɪ.ɪŋ **-fied** -faɪd
codling ˈkɒd.lɪŋ, (US) ˈkɑːd- **-s** -z
codpiec|e ˈkɒd.piːs, (US) ˈkɑːd- **-es** -ɪz
Codrington ˈkɒd.rɪŋ.tən, (US) ˈkɑːd-
Codsall ˈkɒd.səl, (US) ˈkɑːd-
codswallop ˈkɒdzˌwɒl.əp, (US) ˈkɑːdzˌwɑː.ləp, -ˌwɔː-
Cody ˈkəʊ.di, (US) ˈkoʊ-
Coe kəʊ, (US) koʊ
coed ˌkəʊˈed, (US) ˈkoʊ.ed **-s** -z *stress shift, British only:* ˌ**coed** ˈ**school**
Coed kɔɪd
coeducation ˌkəʊ.edʒ.ʊˈkeɪ.ʃən, -ed.jʊˈ-, (US) ˌkoʊ.edʒ.ʊˈ-, -əˈ-
coeducational ˌkəʊ.edʒ.ʊˈkeɪ.ʃən.əl, -ed.jʊˈ-, -ˈkeɪʃ.nəl, (US) ˌkoʊ.edʒ.əˈ- **-ly** -li
coefficient ˌkəʊ.ɪˈfɪʃ.ənt, -əˈfɪʃ-, (US) ˌkoʊ- **-s** -s
coelacanth ˈsiː.lə.kæn*t*θ **-s** -s
coeliac ˈsiː.li.æk
coenobite ˈsiː.nəʊ.baɪt, (US) ˈsen.ə- **-s** -s
coequal ˌkəʊˈiː.kwəl, (US) ˌkoʊ- **-ly** -i
coequality ˌkəʊ.ɪˈkwɒl.ə.ti, -ɪ.ti, (US) ˌkoʊ.iːˈkwɑː.lə.t̬i
coerc|e kəʊˈɜːs, (US) koʊˈɝːs **-es** -ɪz **-ing** -ɪŋ **-ed** -t
coercib|le kəʊˈɜː.sə.b|əl, -sɪ-, (US) koʊˈɝː.sɪ-, -sə- **-ly** -li
coercion kəʊˈɜː.ʃən, (US) koʊˈɝː.ʒən, -ʃən
coercionist kəʊˈɜː.ʃən.ɪst, (US) koʊˈɝː.ʒən-, -ʃən- **-s** -s
coercive kəʊˈɜː.sɪv, (US) koʊˈɝː- **-ly** -li
co-eternal ˌkəʊ.ɪˈtɜː.nəl, (US) ˌkoʊ.ɪˈtɝː-
Coetzee kuːtˈsɪə, -ˈsiː, (US) -ˈsiː.ə, -ˈsiː
Coeur de Lion ˌkɜː.dəˈliː.ɔ̃ː*ŋ*, -dəlˈiː-, -ɒn, (US) ˌkɝː.dəˈliː.ən, -ˈlaɪ.ən
coeval kəʊˈiː.vəl, (US) koʊ- **-s** -z
co-executor ˌkəʊ.ɪɡˈzek.jʊ.təʳ, -eɡˈ-, -jə-; -ɪkˈsek-, -ekˈ-, (US) ˌkoʊ.ɪɡˈzek.juː.t̬ɚ, -eɡˈ- **-s** -z
co-exist ˌkəʊ.ɪɡˈzɪst, -eɡˈ-, -əɡˈ-; -ɪkˈsɪst, -ekˈ-, -əkˈ-, (US) ˌkoʊ.ɪɡˈzɪst, -eɡˈ- **-s** -s **-ing** -ɪŋ **-ed** -ɪd
co-existen|ce ˌkəʊ.ɪɡˈzɪs.tən|*t*s, -eɡˈ-, -əɡˈ-; -ɪkˈsɪs-, -ekˈ-, -əkˈ-, (US) ˌkoʊ.ɪɡˈ-, -eɡˈ- **-t** -t
co-extend ˌkəʊ.ɪkˈstend, -ekˈ-, -əkˈ-, (US) ˌkoʊ.ɪkˈ-, -ekˈ- **-s** -z **-ing** -ɪŋ **-ed** -ɪd
co-extension ˌkəʊ.ɪkˈsten.*t*ʃən, -ekˈ-, -əkˈ-, (US) ˌkoʊ.ɪkˈ-, -ekˈ- **-s** -z
co-extensive ˌkəʊ.ɪkˈsten*t*.sɪv, -ekˈ-, -əkˈ-, (US) ˌkoʊ.ɪkˈ-, -ekˈ-
Coey ˈkəʊ.i, (US) ˈkoʊ-
C of E (abbrev. for **Church of England**) ˌsiː.əvˈiː
coffee ˈkɒf.i, (US) ˈkɑː.fi, ˈkɔː- **-s** -z ˈ**coffee** ˌ**bar**; ˈ**coffee** ˌ**bean**; ˈ**coffee** ˌ**break**; ˈ**coffee** ˌ**cup**; ˈ**coffee** ˌ**mill**; ˈ**coffee** ˌ**table**
coffeehou|se ˈkɒf.i.haʊ|s, (US) ˈkɑː.fi-, ˈkɔː- **-ses** -zɪz
coffee klatch, coffee klatsch ˈkɒf.iˌklætʃ, (US) ˈkɑː.fi-, ˈkɔː-
coffeemaker ˈkɒf.iˌmeɪ.kəʳ, (US) ˈkɑː.fiˌmeɪ.kɚ, ˈkɔː- **-s** -z
coffeepot ˈkɒf.i.pɒt, (US) ˈkɑː.fi.pɑːt, ˈkɔː- **-s** -s
coffer ˈkɒf.əʳ, (US) ˈkɑː.fɚ, ˈkɔː- **-s** -z
cofferdam ˈkɒf.ə.dæm, (US) ˈkɑː.fɚ-, -dəm **-s** -z
Coffey ˈkɒf.i, (US) ˈkɑː.fi, ˈkɔː-
coffin, C~ ˈkɒf.ɪn, (US) ˈkɔː.fɪn, ˈkɑː- **-s** -z **-ing** -ɪŋ **-ed** -d
cog kɒɡ, (US) kɑːɡ, kɔːɡ **-s** -z **-ging** -ɪŋ **-ged** -d
cogen|ce ˈkəʊ.dʒən*t*|s, (US) ˈkoʊ- **-cy** -si
Cogenhoe ˈkʊk.nəʊ, (US) -noʊ
cogent ˈkəʊ.dʒənt, (US) ˈkoʊ- **-ly** -li
Coggeshall *in Essex:* ˈkɒɡ.ɪ.ʃəl; ˈkɒk.səl, (US) ˈkɑː.ɡɪ.ʃəl, ˈkɔː-; (US) ˈkɑːk.səl *surname:* ˈkɒɡ.zɔːl, (US) ˈkɑːɡ.zɔːl, ˈkɔːɡ-, -zɑːl
Coggin ˈkɒɡ.ɪn, (US) ˈkɑː.ɡɪn, ˈkɔː-
Coghill ˈkɒɡ.ɪl, -hɪl, (US) ˈkɑː.ɡɪl, ˈkɔː-, ˈkɑːɡ.hɪl, ˈkɔːɡ-
cogi|tate ˈkɒdʒ.ɪ|.teɪt, ˈ-ə-, (US)

ˈkɑː.dʒə- **-tates** -teɪts **-tating** -teɪ.tɪŋ, ⓤⓢ -teɪ.t̬ɪŋ **-tated** -teɪ.tɪd, ⓤⓢ -teɪ.t̬ɪd **-tator/s** -teɪ.təʳ/z, ⓤⓢ -teɪ.t̬ɚ/z
cogitation ˌkɒdʒ.ɪˈteɪ.ʃᵊn, -əˈ-, ⓤⓢ ˌkɑː.dʒəˈ- **-s** -z
cogitative ˈkɒdʒ.ɪ.tə.tɪv, ˈ-ə-, -teɪ-, ⓤⓢ ˈkɑː.dʒə.teɪ.t̬ɪv
cogito ergo sum ˌkɒg.ɪ.təʊˌɜː.gəʊˈsʊm, ⓤⓢ ˌkɑː.giː.toʊˌer.goʊˈsʌm, ˌkoʊ.gə-, -dʒiː-, -ˌɜː-, -ˈsʊm
cognac ˈkɒn.jæk, ⓤⓢ ˈkoʊ.njæk **-s** -s
cognate ˈkɒg.neɪt, -ˈ-, ⓤⓢ ˈkɑːg.neɪt, ˈkɔːg- **-s** -s
cognation kɒgˈneɪ.ʃᵊn, ⓤⓢ kɑːg-, kɔːg-
cognition kɒgˈnɪʃ.ᵊn, ⓤⓢ kɑːg-, kɔːg- **-s** -z
cognitive ˈkɒg.nə.tɪv, -nɪ-, ⓤⓢ ˈkɑːg.nə.t̬ɪv, ˈkɔːg-
cognizable, -isa- ˈkɒg.nɪ.zə.bᵊl, ˈkɒn.ɪ-; kɒgˈnaɪ-, ⓤⓢ ˈkɑːg.nɪ-, ˈkɔːg-, ˈkɑː-, kɑːgˈnaɪ-, kɔːg-
cognizanc|e, -isa- ˈkɒg.nɪ.zᵊnts, ˈkɒn.ɪ-; kɒgˈnaɪ-, ⓤⓢ ˈkɑːg.nə-, ˈkɔːg-, ˈkɑː- **-es** -ɪz
cognizant, -isa- ˈkɒg.nɪ.zᵊnt, ˈkɒn.ɪ-; kɒgˈnaɪ-, ⓤⓢ ˈkɑːg.nə-, ˈkɔːg-, ˈkɑː-
cognomen kɒgˈnəʊ.men, -mən, ⓤⓢ kɑːgˈnoʊ-, kɔːg- **-s** -z
cognominal kɒgˈnəʊ.mɪ.nᵊl, -ˈnɒm.ɪ-, ⓤⓢ kɑːgˈnɑː.mə-, kɔːg-
cognoscent|e ˌkɒn.jəʊˈʃen.t|i, ˌkɒg.nəʊˈ-, -ˈsen-, ⓤⓢ ˌkɑːg.nəˈʃen.t̬|i, ˌkɔːg-, ˌkɑː.njəˈ- **-i** -iː, -i
cognovit kɒgˈnəʊ.vɪt, ⓤⓢ kɑːgˈnoʊ-, kɔːg- **-s** -s
cogwheel ˈkɒg.wiːl, -hwiːl, ⓤⓢ ˈkɑːg-, ˈkɔːg- **-s** -z
cohab|it kəʊˈhæb|.ɪt, ⓤⓢ koʊ- **-its** -ɪts **-iting** -ɪ.tɪŋ, ⓤⓢ -ɪ.t̬ɪŋ **-ited** -ɪ.tɪd, ⓤⓢ -ɪ.t̬ɪd
cohabitant kəʊˈhæb.ɪ.tᵊnt, ⓤⓢ koʊˈhæb.ɪ.t̬ᵊnt **-s** -s
cohabitation kəʊˌhæb.ɪˈteɪ.ʃᵊn, ˌkəʊ.hæb-, ⓤⓢ koʊˌhæb-
cohabitee ˌkəʊ.hæb.ɪˈtiː, kəʊˌhæb.ɪˈtiː, ⓤⓢ ˌkoʊ- **-s** -z
co-heir ˌkəʊˈeəʳ, ˈ--, ⓤⓢ ˈkoʊ.er, -ˈ- **-s** -z
co-heiress ˌkəʊˈeə.res, -rɪs, -rəs, ˌ--ˈ-, ⓤⓢ ˈkoʊ.er.əs, ˌ-ˈ-- **-es** -ɪz
Cohen ˈkəʊ.ɪn, -ən, ⓤⓢ ˈkoʊ.ən
coher|e kəʊˈhɪəʳ, ⓤⓢ koʊˈhɪr **-es** -z **-ing** -ɪŋ **-ed** -d
coheren|ce kəʊˈhɪə.rᵊnt|s, ⓤⓢ koʊˈhɪr.ᵊnt|s **-cy** -si
coherent kəʊˈhɪə.rᵊnt, ⓤⓢ koʊˈhɪr.ᵊnt **-ly** -li
cohesion kəʊˈhiː.ʒᵊn, ⓤⓢ koʊ-
cohesive kəʊˈhiː.sɪv, -zɪv, ⓤⓢ koʊ- **-ly** -li **-ness** -nəs, -nɪs
Cohn kəʊn, ⓤⓢ koʊn
Cohn-Bendit ˌkəʊnˈben.dɪt, ˌkəʊm-, ⓤⓢ ˌkoʊn-
cohort ˈkəʊ.hɔːt, ⓤⓢ ˈkoʊ.hɔːrt **-s** -s
COHSE ˈkəʊ.zi, ⓤⓢ ˈkoʊ-
coif **n** kɔɪf **-s** -s
coif **v** kwɑːf **-s** -s **-fing** -ɪŋ **-fed** -t
coiffé ˈkwɑː.feɪ, ˈkwɒf.eɪ, ˈkwæf-, -ˈ-, ⓤⓢ kwɑːˈfeɪ **-s** -z **-ing** -ɪŋ **-d** -d
coiffeur kwɑːˈfɜːʳ, kwɒfˈɜːʳ, kwæf-, ⓤⓢ kwɑːˈfɝː **-s** -z
coiffeus|e kwɑːˈfɜːz, kwɒfˈɜːz, kwæf-, ⓤⓢ kwɑːˈfɜːz **-es** -ɪz
coiffure kwɒˈfjʊəʳ, kwɒfˈjʊəʳ, kwæf-, ⓤⓢ kwɑːˈfjʊr **-s** -z
coign kɔɪn **-s** -z
coil kɔɪl **-s** -z **-ing** -ɪŋ **-ed** -d
Coimbra ˈkwɪm.brə, ˈkwiːm-
coin kɔɪn **-s** -z **-ing** -ɪŋ **-ed** -d **-er/s** -əʳ/z, ⓤⓢ -ɚ/z
coinag|e ˈkɔɪ.nɪdʒ **-es** -ɪz
coin-box ˈkɔɪn.bɒks, ˈkɔɪm-, ⓤⓢ ˈkɔɪn.bɑːks **-es** -ɪz
coincid|e ˌkəʊ.ɪnˈsaɪd, -ənˈ-, ⓤⓢ ˌkoʊ- **-es** -z **-ing** -ɪŋ **-ed** -ɪd
coincidenc|e kəʊˈɪnt.sɪ.dᵊnts, ⓤⓢ koʊ- **-es** -ɪz
coincidental kəʊˌɪnt.sɪˈden.tᵊl, ˌkəʊ.ɪn-, ⓤⓢ koʊˌɪnt.sɪˈden.t̬ᵊl **-ly** -i
co-inheritor ˌkəʊ.ɪnˈher.ɪ.təʳ, ˈ-ə-, ⓤⓢ ˌkoʊ.ɪnˈher.ə.t̬ɚ **-s** -z
coinsurance ˌkəʊ.ɪnˈʃʊə.rᵊnts, -ˈʃɔː-, ⓤⓢ ˌkoʊ.ɪnˈʃʊr.ᵊnts, -ˈʃɜː-
coinsur|e ˌkəʊ.ɪnˈʃʊəʳ, -ˈʃɔːʳ, ⓤⓢ ˌkoʊ.ɪnˈʃʊr, -ˈʃɝː **-es** -z **-ing** -ɪŋ **-ed** -d **-er/s** -əʳ/z, ⓤⓢ -ɚ/z
Cointreau® ˈkwɒn.trəʊ, ˈkwɑːn-, ˈkwæn-, ⓤⓢ ˈkwɑːn.troʊ
coir kɔɪ.əʳ, ⓤⓢ kɔɪr
coition kəʊˈɪʃ.ᵊn, ⓤⓢ koʊ-
coit|us ˈkəʊ.ɪ.t|əs, ˈkɔɪ.t|əs, ⓤⓢ ˈkoʊ.ə.t̬|əs **-al** -ᵊl **-ally** -ᵊl.i
coitus interruptus ˌkəʊ.ɪ.təs.ɪn.təˈrʌp.təs, ˌkɔɪ-, ⓤⓢ ˌkoʊ.ə.t̬əs.ɪn.t̬əˈ-
coke kəʊk, ⓤⓢ koʊk
Coke *surname:* kəʊk, kʊk, ⓤⓢ koʊk
Coke® kəʊk, ⓤⓢ koʊk
Coker ˈkəʊ.kəʳ, ⓤⓢ ˈkoʊ.kɚ
col kɒl, ⓤⓢ kɑːl **-s** -z
Col. (abbrev. for **Colonel**) ˈkɜː.nᵊl, ⓤⓢ ˈkɝː-
cola ˈkəʊ.lə, ⓤⓢ ˈkoʊ-
colander ˈkʌl.ən.dəʳ, ˈkɒl-, ⓤⓢ ˈkʌl.ən.dɚ, ˈkɑː.lən- **-s** -z
Colbert kɒlˈbeəʳ, ⓤⓢ kɔːlˈber, koʊl-
Colby ˈkəʊl.bi, ˈkɒl-, ⓤⓢ ˈkoʊl-
colcannon kəlˈkæn.ən, ˈkɒl.kæn-, ⓤⓢ kəlˈkæn.ən, ˈkɑːl.kæn-
Colchester ˈkəʊl.tʃɪ.stəʳ, -tʃə-, ⓤⓢ ˈkoʊl.tʃes.tɚ
colchicum ˈkɒl.tʃɪ.kəm, -kɪ-, ⓤⓢ ˈkɑːl-
Colchis ˈkɒl.kɪs, ⓤⓢ ˈkɑːl-
Colclough ˈkɒl.klʌf, ˈkəʊl-, ˈkəʊ.kli, ⓤⓢ ˈkɑːl.klʌf, ˈkoʊl-, ˈkoʊ.kli
cold kəʊld, ⓤⓢ koʊld **-s** -z **-er** -əʳ, ⓤⓢ -ɚ **-est** -ɪst, -əst **-ly** -li **-ness** -nəs, -nɪs ˌ**cold** ˈ**comfort**; ˈ**cold** ˌ**cream**; ˌ**cold** ˈ**feet**; ˈ**cold** ˌ**frame**; ˈ**cold** ˌ**sore**; ˌ**cold** ˈ**storage**; ˌ**cold** ˈ**turkey**; ˌ**cold** ˈ**war**; ˌ**cold** ˈ**water**; **blow** ˌ**hot and** ˈ**cold**
cold-blooded ˌkəʊldˈblʌd.ɪd, ⓤⓢ ˌkoʊld- **-ly** -li **-ness** -nəs, -nɪs *stress shift:* ˌ**cold-blooded** ˈ**killer**
cold-call **v** ˈkəʊld.kɔːl, ⓤⓢ ˈkoʊld-, -kɑːl **-s** -z **-ing** -ɪŋ **-ed** -d
cold-hearted ˌkəʊldˈhɑː.tɪd, ⓤⓢ ˌkoʊldˈhɑːr.t̬ɪd **-ness** -nəs, -nɪs
coldish, C~ ˈkəʊl.dɪʃ, ⓤⓢ ˈkoʊl-
Colditz ˈkəʊl.dɪts, ⓤⓢ ˈkoʊl-, ˈkɑːl-
Coldplay ˈkəʊld.pleɪ, ⓤⓢ ˈkoʊld-
cold-should|er ˌkəʊldˈʃəʊl.d|əʳ, ⓤⓢ ˌkoʊldˈʃoʊl.d|ɚ **-ers** -əz, ⓤⓢ -ɚz **-ering** -ᵊr.ɪŋ **-ered** -əd, ⓤⓢ -ɚd
Coldstream ˈkəʊld.striːm, ⓤⓢ ˈkoʊld-
cole, C~ kəʊl, ⓤⓢ koʊl **-s** -z
Colebrook(e) ˈkəʊl.brʊk, ⓤⓢ ˈkoʊl-
Coleby ˈkəʊl.bi, ⓤⓢ ˈkoʊl-
Coleclough ˈkəʊl.klaʊ, -klʌf, ⓤⓢ ˈkoʊl-
Coleen kɒlˈiːn, ˈ--, ⓤⓢ kɑːˈliːn, koʊˈliːn
Coleford ˈkəʊl.fəd, ⓤⓢ ˈkoʊl.fɚd
Coleman ˈkəʊl.mən, ⓤⓢ ˈkoʊl-
Colenso kəˈlen.zəʊ, ⓤⓢ -zoʊ
coleopter|a ˌkɒl.iˈɒp.tᵊr|.ə, ⓤⓢ ˌkɑː.liˈɑːp- **-al** -ᵊl
Coleraine kəʊlˈreɪn, ⓤⓢ koʊl-
Coleridge ˈkəʊ.lᵊr.ɪdʒ, ⓤⓢ ˈkoʊ-
Coles kəʊlz, ⓤⓢ koʊlz
Coleshill ˈkəʊlz.hɪl, ⓤⓢ ˈkoʊlz-
coleslaw ˈkəʊl.slɔː, ⓤⓢ ˈkoʊl.slɑː, -slɔː
Colet ˈkɒl.ɪt, ⓤⓢ ˈkɑː.lɪt
cole-tit ˈkəʊl.tɪt, ⓤⓢ ˈkoʊl- **-s** -s
Colette kɒlˈet, kəˈlet, ⓤⓢ koʊˈlet, kɑː-
coley, C~ ˈkəʊ.li, ⓤⓢ ˈkoʊ- **-s** -z
Colgan ˈkɒl.gən, ⓤⓢ ˈkɑːl-
Colgate® ˈkəʊl.geɪt, ˈkɒl-, -gət, -gɪt, ⓤⓢ ˈkoʊl.geɪt
colic ˈkɒl.ɪk, ⓤⓢ ˈkɑː.lɪk **-ky** -i
Colin ˈkɒl.ɪn, ⓤⓢ ˈkɑː.lɪn
Colindale ˈkɒl.ɪn.deɪl, -ən-, ⓤⓢ ˈkɑː.lɪn-, -lən-
Coling ˈkəʊ.lɪŋ, ⓤⓢ ˈkoʊ-
coliseum, C~ ˌkɒl.ɪˈsiː.əm, -əˈ-, ⓤⓢ ˌkɑː.ləˈ-
colitis kɒlˈaɪ.tɪs, kəʊˈlaɪ-, -təs, ⓤⓢ koʊˈlaɪ.t̬ɪs, kə-, -t̬əs
collabor|ate kəˈlæb.ᵊr|.eɪt, kɒlˈæb-, ⓤⓢ kəˈlæb.ə.r|eɪt **-ates** -eɪts **-ating** -eɪ.tɪŋ, ⓤⓢ -eɪ.t̬ɪŋ **-ated** -eɪ.tɪd, ⓤⓢ -eɪ.t̬ɪd
collaboration kəˌlæb.ᵊˈreɪ.ʃᵊn, kɒlˌæb-, ⓤⓢ kəˌlæb- **-s** -z
collaborative kəˈlæb.ᵊr.ə.tɪv, kɒlˈæb-, ⓤⓢ kəˈlæb.ɚ.ə.t̬ɪv, -rə.t̬ɪv **-ly** -li
collaborator kəˈlæb.ᵊr.eɪ.təʳ, kɒlˈæb-, ⓤⓢ kəˈlæb.ə.reɪ.t̬ɚ **-s** -z
collag|e kɒlˈɑːʒ, kəˈlɑːʒ; ˈkɒl.ɑːʒ, ⓤⓢ kəˈlɑːʒ, kɑː-, koʊ- **-es** -ɪz
collagen ˈkɒl.ə.dʒən, -dʒɪn, ⓤⓢ ˈkɑː.lə-
collagenic ˌkɒl.əˈdʒen.ɪk, ⓤⓢ ˌkɑː.ləˈ-
collagenous kəˈlædʒ.ɪ.nəs, ˈ-ə-
collaps|e kəˈlæps **-es** -ɪz **-ing** -ɪŋ **-ed** -t
collapsible kəˈlæp.sə.bᵊl, -sɪ-
coll|ar ˈkɒl|.əʳ, ⓤⓢ ˈkɑː.l|ɚ **-ars** -əz, ⓤⓢ -ɚz **-aring** -ᵊr.ɪŋ **-ared** -əd, ⓤⓢ -ɚd ˌ**hot under the** ˈ**collar**

C

collarbone ˈkɒl.ə.bəʊn, (US) ˈkɑː.lɚ.boʊn **-s** -z
Collard ˈkɒl.əd, (US) ˈkɑː.lɚd
coll|ate kəˈl|eɪt, kɒlˈ|eɪt, (US) kəˈl|eɪt, koʊ-, kɑː- **-ates** -eɪts **-ating** -eɪ.tɪŋ, (US) -eɪ.t̬ɪŋ **-ated** -eɪ.tɪd, (US) -eɪ.t̬ɪd **-ator/s** -eɪ.təʳ/z, (US) -eɪ.t̬ɚ/z
collateral kəˈlæt.ər.əl, kɒlˈæt-, (US) kəˈlæt̬- **-s** -z **-ly** -i
collation kəˈleɪ.ʃən, kɒlˈeɪ-, (US) kɑːˈleɪ-, kə-, koʊ- **-s** -z
colleague ˈkɒl.iːg, (US) ˈkɑː.liːg **-s** -z
collect n ˈkɒl.ekt, -ɪkt, (US) ˈkɑːl.ekt, -ɪkt **-s** -s
collect v kəˈlekt **-s** -s **-ing** -ɪŋ **-ed** -ɪd
collectable kəˈlek.tə.bəl **-s** -z
collectanea ˌkɒl.ekˈteɪ.ni.ə, -ˈtɑː-, (US) ˌkɑː.lekˈ-
collected kəˈlek.tɪd, -təd **-ly** -li **-ness** -nəs, -nɪs
collectible kəˈlek.tə.bəl, -tɪ- **-s** -z
collection kəˈlek.ʃən **-s** -z
collective kəˈlek.tɪv **-ly** -li **coˌllective ˈbargaining**
collectiv|ism kəˈlek.tɪ.v|ɪ.zəm, (US) -tə- **-ist/s** -ɪst/s
collectivity ˌkɒl.ekˈtɪv.ɪ.ti, kəˌlek-, -ə.ti, (US) ˌkɑː.lekˈtɪv.ə.t̬i, kəˌlekˈ-
collectivization, -isa- kəˌlek.tɪ.vaɪˈzeɪ.ʃən, -tə-, -vɪˈ-, (US) -tɪ.vəˈzeɪ-
collectiviz|e, -is|e kəˈlek.tɪ.vaɪz, -tə- **-es** -ɪz **-ing** -ɪŋ **-ed** -d
collector kəˈlek.təʳ, (US) -tɚ **-s** -z **coˈllector's ˌitem; coˌllector's ˈitem**
colleen, C~ ˈkɒl.iːn; *in Ireland:* -ˈ-, (US) kɑːˈliːn, ˈ-- **-s** -z
colleg|e, C~ ˈkɒl.ɪdʒ, (US) ˈkɑː.lɪdʒ **-es** -ɪz **ˈCollege ˌBoard; ˌcollege ˈtry**
collegian kəˈliː.dʒi.ən, kɒlˈiː-, ˈ-dʒən, (US) kəˈliː.dʒən, ˈ-dʒi.ən **-s** -z
collegiate kəˈliː.dʒi.ət, kɒlˈiː-, -dʒət, (US) kəˈliː.dʒɪt, -dʒi.ɪt
Colles ˈkɒl.ɪs, -əs, (US) ˈkɑː.lɪs
collet, C~ ˈkɒl.ɪt, -ət, (US) ˈkɑː.lɪt **-s** -s
Collett ˈkɒl.ɪt, -et, -ət, (US) ˈkɑː.lɪt
Colley ˈkɒl.i, (US) ˈkɑː.li
collid|e kəˈlaɪd **-es** -z **-ing** -ɪŋ **-ed** -ɪd
collie, C~ ˈkɒl.i, (US) ˈkɑː.li **-s** -z
collier, C~ ˈkɒl.i.əʳ, ˈ-jəʳ, (US) ˈkɑːl.jɚ **-s** -z
collier|y ˈkɒl.jə.r|i, -i.ər|.i, (US) ˈkɑːl.jɚ|.i **-ies** -iz
colli|gate ˈkɒl.ɪ|.geɪt, ˈ-ə-, (US) ˈkɑː.lə- **-gates** -geɪts **-gating** -geɪ.tɪŋ, (US) -geɪ.t̬ɪŋ **-gated** -geɪ.tɪd, (US) -geɪ.t̬ɪd
colligation ˌkɒl.ɪˈgeɪ.ʃən, -əˈ-, (US) ˌkɑː.ləˈ-
colli|mate ˈkɒl.ɪ|.meɪt, ˈ-ə-, (US) ˈkɑː.lə- **-mates** -meɪts **-mating** -meɪ.tɪŋ, (US) -meɪ.t̬ɪŋ **-mated** -meɪ.tɪd, (US) -meɪ.t̬ɪd
collimation ˌkɒl.ɪˈmeɪ.ʃən, -əˈ-, (US) ˌkɑː.ləˈ-
collimator ˈkɒl.ɪ.meɪ.təʳ, ˈ-ə-, (US) ˈkɑː.lə.meɪ.t̬ɚ **-s** -z
collinear kɒlˈɪn.i.əʳ, kəʊˈlɪn-, (US) kəˈlɪn.i.ɚ, kɑː-
Collingham ˈkɒl.ɪŋ.əm, (US) ˈkɑː.lɪŋ-
Collings ˈkɒl.ɪŋz, (US) ˈkɑː.lɪŋz
Collingwood ˈkɒl.ɪŋ.wʊd, (US) ˈkɑː.lɪŋ-
Collins ˈkɒl.ɪnz, (US) ˈkɑː.lɪnz
Collinson ˈkɒl.ɪn.sən, -ən-, (US) ˈkɑː.lɪn-
Collis ˈkɒl.ɪs, (US) ˈkɑː.lɪs
collision kəˈlɪʒ.ən **-s** -z **coˈllision ˌcourse**
collo|cate ˈkɒl.əʊ|.keɪt, (US) ˈkɑː.lə- **-cates** -keɪts **-cating** -keɪ.tɪŋ, (US) -keɪ.t̬ɪŋ **-cated** -keɪ.tɪd, (US) -keɪ.t̬ɪd
collocation ˌkɒl.əʊˈkeɪ.ʃən, (US) ˌkɑː.ləˈ- **-s** -z
collodi|on kəˈləʊ.di|.ən, (US) -ˈloʊ- **-um** -əm
colloid ˈkɒl.ɔɪd, (US) ˈkɑː.lɔɪd **-s** -z
colloidal kəˈlɔɪ.dəl, kɒlˈɔɪ-, (US) kəˈlɔɪ-
collop ˈkɒl.əp, (US) ˈkɑː.ləp **-s** -s
colloquial kəˈləʊ.kwi.əl, (US) -ˈloʊ- **-ly** -i **-ism/s** -ɪ.zəm/z
colloquium kəˈləʊ.kwi.əm, (US) -ˈloʊ-
colloqu|y ˈkɒl.ə.kw|i, (US) ˈkɑː.lə- **-ies** -iz
collotype ˈkɒl.əʊ.taɪp, (US) ˈkɑː.lə- **-s** -s
Colls kɒlz, (US) kɑːlz
collud|e kəˈluːd, -ljuːd, (US) -ˈluːd **-es** -z **-ing** -ɪŋ **-ed** -ɪd **-er/s** -əʳ/z, (US) -ɚ/z
collusion kəˈluː.ʒən, -ˈljuː-, (US) -ˈluː- **-s** -z
collusive kəˈluː.sɪv, -ˈljuː-, (US) -ˈluː- **-ly** -li
Collyns ˈkɒl.ɪnz, (US) ˈkɑː.lɪnz
collywobbles ˈkɒl.iˌwɒb.əlz, (US) ˈkɑː.liˌwɑː.bəlz
Colman ˈkəʊl.mən, ˈkɒl-, (US) ˈkoʊl-, ˈkɑːl-
Colnaghi kɒlˈnɑː.gi, (US) kɑːl-
Colnbrook ˈkəʊln.brʊk, ˈkəʊn-, (US) ˈkoʊln-, ˈkoʊn-
Colne kəʊn, kəʊln, (US) koʊn, koʊln
Colney ˈkəʊ.ni, (US) ˈkoʊ-
Colo. (abbrev. for **Colorado**) ˌkɒl.ərˈɑː.dəʊ, (US) ˌkɑː.ləˈræd.oʊ, -ˈrɑː.doʊ
cologne, C~ kəˈləʊn, (US) -ˈloʊn **-s** -z
Colombi|a kəˈlɒm.bi|.ə, -ˈlʌm-, (US) -ˈlʌm- **-an/s** -ən/z
Colombo kəˈlʌm.bəʊ, -ˈlɒm-, (US) -ˈlʌm.boʊ
colon *punctuation, part of intestine:* ˈkəʊ.lɒn, -lən, (US) ˈkoʊ.lən **-s** -z
cola ˈkəʊ.lə, (US) ˈkoʊ-
colon, colón *currency:* kɒlˈɒn, kəˈlɒn, (US) kəˈloʊn **-s** -z **-es** -es, -əs
colonel, C~ ˈkɜː.nəl, (US) ˈkɝː- **-s** -z **ˌColonel ˈBlimp**
colonelc|y ˈkɜː.nəl.s|i, (US) ˈkɝː- **-ies** -iz
colonelship ˈkɜː.nəl.ʃɪp, (US) ˈkɝː- **-s** -s
colonial kəˈləʊ.ni.əl, (US) -ˈloʊ- **-s** -z
colonial|ism kəˈləʊ.ni.ə.l|ɪ.zəm, (US) -ˈloʊ- **-ist/s** -ɪst/s
colonist ˈkɒl.ə.nɪst, (US) ˈkɑː.lə- **-s** -s
colonization, -isa- ˌkɒl.ə.naɪˈzeɪ.ʃən, -nɪˈ-, (US) ˌkɑː.lə.nəˈ-
coloniz|e, -is|e ˈkɒl.ə.naɪz, (US) ˈkɑː.lə- **-es** -ɪz **-ing** -ɪŋ **-ed** -d **-er/s** -əʳ/z, (US) -ɚ/z
colonnade ˌkɒl.əˈneɪd, (US) ˌkɑː.ləˈ- **-s** -z
colonoscope kəʊˈlɒn.əʊ.skəʊp, (US) koʊˈlɑː.nə.skoʊp, kə- **-s** -s
colonoscop|y ˌkəʊ.ləˈnɒs.kə.p|i, (US) ˌkoʊ.ləˈnɑː.skə- **-ies** -iz
Colonus kəˈləʊ.nəs, (US) -ˈloʊ-
colon|y ˈkɒl.ə.n|i, (US) ˈkɑː.lə- **-ies** -iz
colophon ˈkɒl.ə.fən, -fɒn, (US) ˈkɑː.lə.fən, -fɑːn **-s** -z
col|or ˈkʌl|.əʳ, (US) -ɚ **-ors** -əz, (US) -ɚz **-oring** -ər.ɪŋ **-ored/s** -əd/z, (US) -ɚd/s **-orer/s** -ər.əʳ/z, (US) -ɚ.ɚ/z **-orist/s** -ər.ɪst/s
colorab|le ˈkʌl.ər.ə.b|əl **-ly** -li
Colorado ˌkɒl.ərˈɑː.dəʊ, (US) ˌkɑː.ləˈræd.oʊ, -ˈrɑː.doʊ *stress shift, see compounds:* **ˌColorado ˈbeetle; ˌColorado ˈSprings**
colorant ˈkʌl.ər.ənt **-s** -s
coloration ˌkʌl.əˈreɪ.ʃən
coloratura ˌkɒl.ər.əˈtjʊə.rə, -ˈtʊə-, (US) ˌkʌl.ɚ.əˈtʊr.ə, ˌkɑː.lɚ-, -ˈtjʊr-
color|-blind ˈkʌl.ə|.blaɪnd, (US) ˈ-ɚ- **-blindness** -ˌblaɪnd.nəs, -nɪs
colorcast ˈkʌl.ə.kɑːst, (US) -ɚ.kæst **-s** -s **-ing** -ɪŋ **-ed** -ɪd
color-coded ˈkʌl.əˌkəʊ.dɪd, (US) -ɚˌkoʊ-
colorfast ˈkʌl.ə.fɑːst, (US) -ɚ.fæst **-ness** -nəs, -nɪs
colorful ˈkʌl.ə.fəl, -fʊl, (US) ˈ-ɚ- **-ly** -i
colorific ˌkɒl.əˈrɪf.ɪk, ˌkʌl-, (US) ˌkʌl.ɚˈ-
coloring ˈkʌl.ər.ɪŋ, (US) ˈkʌl.ɚ- **-s** -z
Colorization® ˌkɒl.ə.raɪˈzeɪ.ʃən, ˌkʌl-, -rɪˈ-, (US) ˌkʌl.ɚ.ɪˈ-
colorless ˈkʌl.ə.ləs, -lɪs, (US) ˈ-ɚ- **-ly** -li **-ness** -nəs, -nɪs
colossal kəˈlɒs.əl, (US) -ˈlɑː.səl **-ly** -i
colosseum, C~ ˌkɒl.əˈsiː.əm, (US) ˌkɑː.ləˈ-
Colossian kəˈlɒs.i.ən, -ˈlɒʃ.i.ən, -ˈlɒʃ.ən, (US) -ˈlɑː.ʃən **-s** -z
coloss|us kəˈlɒs|.əs, (US) -ˈlɑː.s|əs **-i** -aɪ **-uses** -ə.sɪz
colostom|y kəˈlɒs.tə.m|i, kɒlˈɒs-, (US) kəˈlɑː.stə- **-ies** -iz
colostrum kəˈlɒs.trəm, kɒlˈɒs-, (US) kəˈlɑː.strəm
col|our ˈkʌl|.əʳ, (US) -ɚ **-ours** -əz, (US) -ɚz **-ouring** -ər.ɪŋ, (US) -ɚ.ɪŋ **-oured/s** -əd/z, (US) -ɚd/s **-ourer/s** -ər.əʳ/z, (US) -ɚ.ɚ/z **-ourist/s** -ər.ɪst/s
colourab|le ˈkʌl.ər.ə.b|əl **-ly** -li
colourant ˈkʌl.ər.ənt **-s** -s
colouration ˌkʌl.əˈreɪ.ʃən
colour|-blind ˈkʌl.ə|.blaɪnd, (US) ˈ-ɚ- **-blindness** -ˌblaɪnd.nəs, -nɪs
colourcast ˈkʌl.ə.kɑːst, (US) -ɚ.kæst **-s** -s
colour-coded ˈkʌl.əˌkəʊ.dɪd, (US) -ɚˌkoʊ-
colourfast ˈkʌl.ə.fɑːst, (US) -ɚ.fæst **-ness** -nəs, -nɪs
colourful ˈkʌl.ə.fəl, -fʊl, (US) ˈ-ɚ- **-ly** -i

C

colouring ˈkʌl.ər.ɪŋ **-s** -z
colourless ˈkʌl.ə.ləs, -lɪs, (US) ˈ-ɚ- **-ly** -li **-ness** -nəs, -nɪs
colourway ˈkʌl.ə.weɪ, (US) -ɚ- **-s** -z
colporteur ˈkɒl.pɔː.tər, ˌkɒl.pɔːˈtɜːr, (US) ˈkɑːl.pɔːr.t̬ɚ, ˌkɑːl.pɔːrˈtɝː **-s** -z
colposcope ˈkɒl.pə.skəʊp, (US) ˈkɑːl.pə.skoʊp **-s** -s
colposcopic ˌkɒl.pəˈskɒp.ɪk, (US) ˌkɑːl.pəˈskɑː.pɪk
colposcopy kɒlˈpɒs.kə.pi, (US) kɑːlˈpɑː.skə-
Colquhoun kəˈhuːn
Cols. (abbrev. for **Colonels**) ˈkɜː.nəlz, (US) ˈkɝː-
Colson ˈkəʊl.sən, (US) ˈkoʊl-
Colston ˈkəʊl.stən, (US) ˈkoʊl-
colt kəʊlt, (US) koʊlt **-s** -s
coltish ˈkəʊl.tɪʃ, (US) ˈkoʊl.tɪʃ **-ly** -li **-ness** -nəs, -nɪs
Coltrane kɒlˈtreɪn, kəʊl-, (US) ˈkoʊl.treɪn
coltsfoot ˈkəʊlts.fʊt, (US) ˈkoʊlts- **-s** -s
colubrine ˈkɒl.jʊ.braɪn, -brɪn, (US) ˈkɑː.lə-, ˈkɑːl.jə-
Columba kəˈlʌm.bə
columbari|um ˌkɒl.əmˈbeə.ri|.əm, (US) ˌkɑː.ləmˈber.i- **-ums** -əmz **-a** -ə
Columbi|a kəˈlʌm.bi|.ə **-an/s** -ən/z
Columbiad kəˈlʌm.bi.æd
columbine, C~ ˈkɒl.əm.baɪn, (US) ˈkɑː.ləm- **-s** -z
Columbo kəˈlʌm.bəʊ, (US) -boʊ
Columbus kəˈlʌm.bəs
column ˈkɒl.əm, (US) ˈkɑː.ləm **-s** -z **-ed** -d
column|al kəˈlʌm.n|əl **-ar** -ər, (US) -ɚ
columnist ˈkɒl.əm.nɪst, -ə.mɪst, (US) ˈkɑː.ləm.nɪst, -lə.mɪst **-s** -s
colure kəˈljʊər, -ˈlʊər; ˈkəʊ.ljʊər, -lʊər, (US) koʊˈlʊr, kə-; (US) ˈkoʊ.lʊr **-s** -z
Colwyn ˈkɒl.wɪn, (US) ˈkɑːl- ˌ**Colwyn** ˈ**Bay**
Colyton ˈkɒl.ɪ.tən, (US) ˈkɑː.lɪ.t̬ən
colza ˈkɒl.zə, (US) ˈkɑːl-
com- ˈkɒm, kəm, ˈkʌm, (US) ˈkɑːm, kəm
Note: Prefix. This may carry primary or secondary stress, e.g. **combat** /ˈkɒm.bæt/ (US) /ˈkɑːm.bæt/ or be unstressed, e.g. **complete** /kəmˈpliːt/. The pronunciation ˈkʌm- is old-fashioned.
coma *deep sleep:* ˈkəʊ.mə, (US) ˈkoʊ- **-s** -z *tuft:* ˈkəʊ.m|ə, (US) ˈkoʊ- **-as** -əz **-ae** -iː
Coma Berenices ˌkəʊ.məˌber.əˈnaɪ.siːz, (US) ˌkoʊ.məˌber.əˈ-
Comanche kəˈmæn.tʃi, kəʊ-, (US) kə- **-s** -z
Comaneci ˌkɒm.əˈnetʃ, -ˈnetʃ.i, (US) ˌkoʊ.mə.ˈniː.tʃ, -ˈnetʃ.i
comatose ˈkəʊ.mə.təʊs, -təʊz, (US) ˈkoʊ.mə.toʊs, ˈkɑː-
comb kəʊm, (US) koʊm **-s** -z **-ing/s** -ɪŋ/z **-ed** -d
combat n ˈkɒm.bæt, ˈkʌm-, -bət, (US) ˈkɑːm.bæt **-s** -s
comba|t v ˈkɒm.bæ|t, ˈkʌm-, -bə|t; kəmˈbæ|t, (US) kəmˈbæ|t, kɑːm-; (US) ˈkɑːm.bæ|t **-ts** -ts **-(t)ting** -tɪŋ, (US) -t̬ɪŋ **-(t)ted** -tɪd, (US) -t̬ɪd
combatant ˈkɒm.bə.tənt, ˈkʌm-; kəmˈbæt.ənt, (US) kəmˈbæt.ənt; (US) ˈkɑːm.bə.tənt **-s** -s
combative ˈkɒm.bə.tɪv, ˈkʌm-; kəmˈbæt.ɪv, (US) kəmˈbæt̬.ɪv; (US) ˈkɑːm.bə.t̬ɪv **-ly** -li **-ness** -nəs, -nɪs
combe, C~ kuːm, kəʊm, (US) kuːm, koʊm **-s** -z
comber *combing machine:* ˈkəʊ.mər, (US) ˈkoʊ.mɚ *fish:* ˈkɒm.bər, (US) ˈkɑːm.bɚ **-s** -z
combination ˌkɒm.bɪˈneɪ.ʃən, -bəˈ-, (US) ˌkɑːm.bəˈ-, -bɪˈ- **-s** -z **combiˈnation** ˌ**lock**; ˌ**combiˈnation** ˌ**room**
combinative ˈkɒm.bɪ.nə.tɪv, -bə-, -neɪ-, (US) ˈkɑːm.bə.neɪ.t̬ɪv, -nə-; (US) -bɪ-, kəmˈbaɪ.nə.t̬ɪv
combinatorial ˌkɒm.bɪ.nəˈtɔː.ri.əl, -bən.əˈ-, (US) ˌkɑːm.bə.nəˈtɔːr.i-; (US) -bɪn.əˈ-; (US) kəmˌbaɪ-
combinatory ˈkɒm.bɪ.nə.tər.i, -tri; ˌkɒm.bɪˈneɪ-, (US) ˈkɑːm.bə.nə.tɔːr.i, -bɪ-; (US) kəmˈbaɪ-
combine n ˈkɒm.baɪn; kəmˈbaɪn, (US) ˈkɑːm.baɪn **-s** -z
combin|e v *join:* kəmˈbaɪn *harvest:* ˈkɒm.baɪn, (US) ˈkɑːm- **-es** -z **-ing** -ɪŋ **-d** -d ˌ**combine** ˈ**harvester**
combo ˈkɒm.bəʊ, (US) ˈkɑːm.boʊ **-s** -z
Combs kəʊmz, kuːmz, (US) koʊmz
combust kəmˈbʌst **-s** -s **-ing** -ɪŋ **-ed** -ɪd **-er/s** -ər/z, (US) -ɚ/z
combustibility kəmˌbʌs.təˈbɪl.ə.ti, -tɪˈ-, -ɪ.ti, (US) -ə.t̬i
combustible kəmˈbʌs.tə.bəl, -tɪ- **-ness** -nəs, -nɪs
combustion kəmˈbʌs.tʃən **-s** -z **comˈbustion** ˌ**engine**
Comcast ˈkɒm.kɑːst, (US) ˈkɑːm.kæst
com|e kʌm **-es** -z **-ing/s** -ɪŋ/z **came** keɪm
come-at-able ˌkʌmˈæt.ə.bəl, (US) -ˈæt̬-
comeback ˈkʌm.bæk **-s** -s
Comecon ˈkɒm.ɪ.kɒn, (US) ˈkɑː.mɪ.kɑːn
comedian kəˈmiː.di.ən **-s** -z
comedic kəˈmiː.dɪk **-ally** -əl.i, -li
comedienne kəˌmiː.diˈen, ˌkɒm.iː-, (US) kəˌmiː- **-s** -z
comedown ˈkʌm.daʊn, ˌ-ˈ-, (US) ˈ-- **-s** -z
comed|y ˈkɒm.ə.d|i, ˈ-ɪ-, (US) ˈkɑː.mə- **-ies** -iz
come-hither ˌkʌmˈhɪð.ər, (US) ˌkʌmˈhɪð.ɚ *stress shift:* ˌ**come-hither** ˈ**look**
comel|y ˈkʌm.l|i **-ier** -i.ər, (US) -i.ɚ **-iest** -i.ɪst, -i.əst **-iness** -ɪ.nəs, -ɪ.nɪs
Comenius kəˈmeɪ.ni.əs, kɒmˈeɪ-, -ˈiː-, (US) kəˈmiː-
come-on ˈkʌm.ɒn, (US) -ɑːn **-s** -z
comer ˈkʌm.ər, (US) -ɚ **-s** -z
-comer ˌkʌm.ər, (US) -ɚ
comestible kəˈmes.tə.bəl, -tɪ- **-s** -z
comet ˈkɒm.ɪt, (US) ˈkɑː.mɪt **-s** -s **-ary** -ər.i, (US) -er.i
come-uppanc|e kʌmˈʌp.ənts **-es** -ɪz
comfit ˈkʌm.fɪt, ˈkɒm-, (US) ˈkʌm-, ˈkɑːm- **-s** -s
com|fort ˈkʌmp|.fət, (US) -fɚt **-forts** -fəts, (US) -fɚts **-forting/ly** -fə.tɪŋ/li, (US) -fɚ.t̬ɪŋ/li **-forted** -fə.tɪd, (US) -fɚ.t̬ɪd **-forter/s** -fə.tər/z, (US) -fɚ.t̬ɚ/z ˈ**comfort** ˌ**station**
comfortab|le ˈkʌmpf.tə.b|əl, ˈkʌmp.fə.tə-, (US) ˈkʌmp.fɚ.t̬ə-, ˈkʌmpf.tə- **-ly** -li
comforter ˈkʌmp.fə.tər, (US) -fɚ.t̬ɚ **-s** -z
comfortless ˈkʌmp.fət.ləs, -lɪs, (US) -fɚt-
comfrey ˈkʌmp.fri
comf|y ˈkʌmp.f|i **-ier** -i.ər, (US) -i.ɚ **-iest** -i.ɪst, -i.əst **-ily** -əl.i, -ɪ.li **-iness** -ɪ.nəs, -ɪ.nɪs
comic ˈkɒm.ɪk, (US) ˈkɑː.mɪk **-s** -s ˈ**comic** ˌ**book**; ˈ**comic** ˌ**strip**; ˌ**comic** ˈ**strip**
comic|al ˈkɒm.ɪ.k|əl, (US) ˈkɑː.mɪ- **-ally** -əl.i, -li **-alness** -əl.nəs, -nɪs
Cominform ˈkɒm.ɪn.fɔːm, -ən-, ˌ--ˈ-, (US) ˈkɑː.mən.fɔːrm
Comintern ˈkɒm.ɪn.tɜːn, -ən-, ˌ--ˈ-, (US) ˈkɑː.mən.tɝːn
comity ˈkɒm.ɪ.ti, -ə.ti, (US) ˈkɑː.mə.t̬i, ˈkoʊ-
comma ˈkɒm.ə, (US) ˈkɑː.mə **-s** -z
command kəˈmɑːnd, (US) -ˈmænd **-s** -z **-ing** -ɪŋ **-ed** -ɪd
commandant ˈkɒm.ən.dænt, -dɑːnt, ˌ--ˈ-, (US) ˈkɑː.mən.dænt, -dɑːnt **-s** -s
commandantship ˌkɒm.ənˈdænt.ʃɪp, -ˈdɑːnt-, ˈkɒm.ən.dænt.ʃɪp, -dɑːnt-, (US) ˈkɑː.mən.dænt-, -dɑːnt- **-s** -s
commandeer ˌkɒm.ənˈdɪər, (US) ˌkɑː.mənˈdɪr **-s** -z **-ing** -ɪŋ **-ed** -d
commander kəˈmɑːn.dər, (US) -ˈmæn.dɚ **-s** -z
commander-in-chief kəˌmɑːn.də.rɪnˈtʃiːf, (US) -ˌmæn.dɚ-
commanders-in-chief kəˌmɑːn.dəz.ɪnˈtʃiːf, (US) -ˌmænd.ɚz-
commandership kəˈmɑːn.də.ʃɪp, (US) -ˈmæn.dɚ- **-s** -s
commanding kəˈmɑːn.dɪŋ, (US) -ˈmæn- **-ly** -li
commandment kəˈmɑːnd.mənt, -ˈmɑːm-, (US) -ˈmænd- **-s** -s
commando kəˈmɑːn.dəʊ, (US) -ˈmæn.doʊ **-(e)s** -z
Comme des Garçons ˌkɒm.deɪ.gɑːˈsɔ̃ːŋ, ˌkɒm.deɪˈgɑː.sɔːŋ, (US) ˌkɑːm.deɪ.gɑːrˈsõʊn
commedia dell'arte kɒmˌeɪ.di.ə.delˈɑː.teɪ, kəˌmeɪ-, -ˌmed.i-, (US) kəˌmeɪ.di.ə.delˈɑːr.t̬i

comme il faut ˌkɒm.iːlˈfəʊ, US ˌkʌm.iːlˈfoʊ, ˌkɑːm-

commemo|rate kəˈmem.ə|.reɪt -rates -reɪts -rating -reɪ.tɪŋ, US -reɪ.t̬ɪŋ -rated -reɪ.tɪd, US -reɪ.t̬ɪd -rator/s -reɪ.təʳ/z, US -reɪ.t̬ɚ/z

commemoration kəˌmem.əˈreɪ.ʃᵊn -s -z

commemorative kəˈmem.ᵊr.ə.tɪv, -eɪ-, US -ə.t̬ɪv, -eɪ- -ly -li

commenc|e kəˈments -es -ɪz -ing -ɪŋ -ed -t

commencement kəˈments.mənt -s -s

commend kəˈmend -s -z -ing -ɪŋ -ed -ɪd

commendab|le kəˈmen.də.b|ᵊl -ly -li -leness -ᵊl.nəs, -nɪs

commendation ˌkɒm.enˈdeɪ.ʃᵊn, -ənˈ-, US ˌkɑː.mənˈ- -s -z

commendatory kəˈmen.də.tᵊr.i, -tri; ˌkɒm.enˈdeɪ-, -ənˈ-, US kəˈmen.də.tɔːr.i

commensal kəˈment.sᵊl

commensalism kəˈment.sᵊl.ɪ.zᵊm

commensurability kəˌment.ʃᵊr.əˈbɪl.ə.ti, -ʃʊ.rə-, -sjᵊr.ə-, -ɪ.ti, US -sɚ.əˈbɪl.ə.t̬i, -ʃɚ-

commensurab|le kəˈment.ʃᵊr.ə.b|ᵊl, -ʃʊ.rə-, -sjᵊr.ə-, US -sɚ.ə-, -ʃɚ- -ly -li -leness -ᵊl.nəs, -nɪs

commensurate kəˈment.ʃᵊr.ət, -ʃʊ.rət, -sjᵊr.ət, -ɪt, US -sɚ.ət, -ʃɚ- -ly -li -ness -nəs, -nɪs

comment n ˈkɒm.ent, US ˈkɑː.ment -s -s

commen|t v ˈkɒm.en|t, -ən|t; kɒmˈent, kəˈmen|t, US ˈkɑː.men|t -ts -ts -ting -tɪŋ, US -t̬ɪŋ -ted -tɪd, US -t̬ɪd

commentar|y ˈkɒm.ən.tᵊr|.i, -tr|i, US ˈkɑː.mən.ter|.i -ies -iz

commen|tate ˈkɒm.ən|.teɪt, -en-, US ˈkɑː.mən- -tates -teɪts -tating -teɪ.tɪŋ, US -teɪ.t̬ɪŋ -tated -teɪ.tɪd, US -teɪ.t̬ɪd

commentator ˈkɒm.ən.teɪ.təʳ, -en-, US ˈkɑː.mən.teɪ.t̬ɚ -s -z

commerce ˈkɒm.ɜːs, US ˈkɑː.mɝːs

commercial kəˈmɜː.ʃᵊl, US -ˈmɝː- -s -z -ly -i

commercialese kəˌmɜː.ʃᵊlˈiːz, US -ˌmɝː.ʃəˈliːz

commercial|ism kəˈmɜː.ʃᵊl|.ɪ.zᵊm, US -ˈmɝː- -ist/s -ɪst/s

commerciality kəˌmɜː.ʃiˈæl.ə.ti, -ɪ.ti, US -ˌmɝː.ʃiˈæl.ə.t̬i

commercialization, -isa- kəˌmɜː.ʃə.laɪˈzeɪ.ʃᵊn, -lɪˈ-, US -mɝː.ʃə.ləˈ-

commercializ|e, -is|e kəˈmɜː.ʃᵊl.aɪz, US -ˈmɝː.ʃə.laɪz -es -ɪz -ing -ɪŋ -ed -d

commie ˈkɒm.i, US ˈkɑː.mi -s -z

commi|nate ˈkɒm.ɪ|.neɪt, US ˈkɑː.mə- -nates -neɪts -nating -neɪ.tɪŋ, US -neɪ.t̬ɪŋ -nated -neɪ.tɪd, US -neɪ.t̬ɪd

commination ˌkɒm.ɪˈneɪ.ʃᵊn, US ˌkɑː.məˈ- -s -z

comminatory ˈkɒm.ɪ.nə.tᵊr.i, -neɪ-, -tri, US ˈkɑː.mɪ.nə.tɔːr.i; US kəˈmɪn.ə-

commingl|e kɒmˈɪŋ.gᵊl, kəˈmɪŋ-, US kəˈmɪŋ-, kɑː- -es -z -ing -ɪŋ, ˈ-glɪŋ -ed -d

commi|nute ˈkɒm.ɪ.njuːt, US ˈkɑː.mə.nuːt, -njuːt -nutes -njuːts, US -nuːts, -njuːts -nuting -njuː.tɪŋ, US -nuː.t̬ɪŋ, -njuː- -nuted -njuː.tɪd, US -nuː.t̬ɪd, -njuː-

comminution ˌkɒm.ɪˈnjuː.ʃᵊn, US ˌkɑː.məˈnuː-, -ˈnjuː-

commis ˈkɒm.i, -ɪs, US ˌkɑːˈmi *stress shift, American only, see compound:* **ˈcommis ˌchef; ˌcommis ˈchef**

commiser|ate kəˈmɪz.ᵊr|.eɪt, kɒmˈɪz-, US kəˈmɪz- -ates -eɪts -ating -eɪ.tɪŋ, US -eɪ.t̬ɪŋ -ated -eɪ.tɪd, US -eɪ.t̬ɪd

commiseration kəˌmɪz.ᵊrˈeɪ.ʃᵊn, kɒmˌɪz-, US kəˌmɪz- -s -z

commissar ˌkɒm.ɪˈsɑːʳ, -əˈ-, ˈ---, US ˈkɑː.mə.sɑːr -s -z

commissarial ˌkɒm.ɪˈseə.ri.əl, -əˈ-, -ˈsɑː-, -ˈsær.i-, US ˌkɑː.məˈser.i-

commissariat ˌkɒm.ɪˈseə.ri.ət, -əˈ-, -ˈsɑː-, -ˈsær.i-, -æt, US ˌkɑː.məˈser-

commissar|y ˈkɒm.ɪ.sᵊr|.i, kəˈmɪs.ᵊr-, US ˈkɑː.mə.ser- -ies -iz

commission kəˈmɪʃ.ᵊn -s -z -ing -ɪŋ -ed -d -er/s -əʳ/z, ˈ-nəʳ/z, US ˈ-ᵊn.ɚ/z, ˈ-nɚ/z **comˈmission ˌagent; comˌmissioned ˈofficer**

commissionaire kəˌmɪʃ.ᵊnˈeəʳ, US -ˈer -s -z

commissive kəˈmɪs.ɪv, ˈkɒm.ɪ.sɪv, US kəˈmɪs-

commissure ˈkɒm.ɪ.sjʊəʳ, ˈ-ə-, -ʃʊəʳ, US ˈkɑː.mə.ʃʊr -s -z

com|mit kə|ˈmɪt -mits -s -mitting -ˈmɪt.ɪŋ, US -ˈmɪt̬.ɪŋ -mitted -ˈmɪt.ɪd, US -ˈmɪt̬.ɪd -mitter/s -ˈmɪt.əʳ/z, US -ˈmɪt̬.ɚ/z

commitment kəˈmɪt.mənt -s -s

committal kəˈmɪt.ᵊl, US -ˈmɪt̬- -s -z

committee *council:* kəˈmɪt.i, US -ˈmɪt̬- **comˈmittee ˌmeeting** *one committed:* ˌkɒm.ɪˈtiː, US ˌkɑː.mɪˈtiː -s -z

committor ˌkɒm.ɪˈtɔːʳ, kəˈmɪt.əʳ, US ˌkɑː.mɪˈt̬ɔːr; US kəˈmɪt̬.ɚ -s -z

commixture kəˈmɪks.tʃəʳ, US -tʃɚ -s -z

commode kəˈməʊd, US -ˈmoʊd -s -z

commodious kəˈməʊ.di.əs, US -ˈmoʊ- -ly -li -ness -nəs, -nɪs

commodit|y kəˈmɒd.ə.t|i, -ɪ.t|i, US -ˈmɑː.də.t̬|i -ies -iz

commodore ˈkɒm.ə.dɔːʳ, US ˈkɑː.mə.dɔːr -s -z

Commodus ˈkɒm.ə.dəs, US ˈkɑː.mə-

common ˈkɒm.ən, US ˈkɑː.mən -s -z -er -əʳ, US -ɚ -est -ɪst, -əst -ly -li -ness -nəs, -nɪs **ˌcommon deˈnominator; ˌCommon ˈMarket; ˈcommon ˌroom; ˌcommon ˈsense; ˈcommon ˌtouch**

commonage ˈkɒm.ə.nɪdʒ, US ˈkɑː.mə-

commonality ˌkɒm.əˈnæl.ə.ti, -ɪ.ti, US ˌkɑː.məˈnæl.ə.t̬i

commonalt|y ˈkɒm.ə.nᵊl.t|i, US ˈkɑː.mə- -ies -iz

Commondale ˈkɒm.ən.deɪl, US ˈkɑː.mən-

commoner ˈkɒm.ə.nəʳ, US ˈkɑː.mə.nɚ -s -z

common-law ˌkɒm.ənˈlɔː, US ˈkɑː.mən.lɑː, -lɔː *stress shift, British only:* **ˌcommon-law ˈwife**

common-or-garden ˌkɒm.ən.ɔːˈgɑː.dᵊn, -əˈgɑː-, US ˌkɑː.mən.ɔːrˈgɑːr-

commonplac|e ˈkɒm.ən.pleɪs, -əm-, US ˈkɑː.mən- -es -ɪz

commons, C~ ˈkɒm.ənz, US ˈkɑː.mənz

commonsense ˌkɒm.ənˈsents, US ˌkɑː.mənˈ-

commonsensical ˌkɒm.ənˈsent.sɪ.kᵊl, US ˌkɑː.mənˈ-

commonwealth, C~ ˈkɒm.ən.welθ, US ˈkɑː.mən- -s -s

commotion kəˈməʊ.ʃᵊn, US -ˈmoʊ- -s -z

communal ˈkɒm.jʊ.nᵊl, -jə-; kəˈmjuː-, US kəˈmjuː-; US ˈkɑː.mjə- -ly -i

communard, C~ ˈkɒm.jʊ.nɑːd, ˌkɒm.jʊˈnɑː, US ˈkɑː.mjʊ.nɑːrd, -nɑːr -s -z

commune n ˈkɒm.juːn, US ˈkɑː.mjuːn -s -z

commun|e v kəˈmjuːn -es -z -ing -ɪŋ -ed -d

communicab|le kəˈmjuː.nɪ.kə.b|ᵊl -ly -li -leness -ᵊl.nəs, -nɪs

communicant kəˈmjuː.nɪ.kənt -s -s

communi|cate kəˈmjuː.nɪ|.keɪt, -nə- -cates -keɪts -cating -keɪ.tɪŋ, US -keɪ.t̬ɪŋ -cated -keɪ.tɪd, US -keɪ.t̬ɪd -cator/s -keɪ.təʳ/z, US -keɪ.t̬ɚ/z

communication kəˌmjuː.nɪˈkeɪ.ʃᵊn, -nəˈ- -s -z

communicative kəˈmjuː.nɪ.kə.tɪv, -nə-, -keɪ-, US -nə.keɪ.t̬ɪv, -kə- -ly -li -ness -nəs, -nɪs

communion kəˈmjuː.ni.ən, US -njən -s -z

communiqué kəˈmjuː.nɪ.keɪ, kɒmˈjuː-, -nə-, US kəˌmjuː.nɪˈkeɪ, kəˈmjuː.nɪ.keɪ -s -z

commun|ism ˈkɒm.jə.n|ɪ.zᵊm, -jʊ-, US ˈkɑː.mjə- -ist/s -ɪst/s

communit|y kəˈmjuː.nə.t|i, -nɪ-, US -nə.t̬|i -ies -iz **comˈmunity ˌcentre; comˈmunity ˌchest** US **community ˈchest; comˈmunity ˌcollege**

commutability kəˌmjuː.təˈbɪl.ə.ti, -ɪ.ti, US -t̬əˈbɪl.ə.t̬i

commutable kəˈmjuː.tə.bᵊl, US -t̬ə-

commu|tate ˈkɒm.jʊ|.teɪt, US ˈkɑː.mjə- -tates -teɪts -tating -teɪ.tɪŋ, US -teɪ.t̬ɪŋ -tated -teɪ.tɪd,

Ⓤⓢ -teɪ.t̬ɪd **-tator/s** -teɪ.təʳ/z, Ⓤⓢ -teɪ.t̬ɚ/z
commutation ˌkɒm.jʊˈteɪ.ʃən, Ⓤⓢ ˌkɑː.mjəˈ- **-s** -z
commutative kəˈmjuː.tə.tɪv, ˈkɒm.jʊ.teɪ-, Ⓤⓢ ˈkɑː.mjə.teɪ.t̬ɪv, kəˈmjuː.t̬ə- **-ly** -li
com|mute kə|ˈmjuːt **-mutes** -ˈmjuːts **-muting** -ˈmjuː.tɪŋ, Ⓤⓢ -ˈmjuː.t̬ɪŋ **-muted** -ˈmjuː.tɪd, Ⓤⓢ -ˈmjuː.t̬ɪd
commuter kəˈmjuː.təʳ, Ⓤⓢ -t̬ɚ **-s** -z
Como ˈkəʊ.məʊ, Ⓤⓢ ˈkoʊ.moʊ
Comorin ˈkɒm.ə.rɪn, Ⓤⓢ ˈkɑː.mɚ.ɪn
Comoros ˈkɒm.ə.rəʊz, Ⓤⓢ ˈkɑː.mə.roʊz
comose ˈkəʊ.məʊs, -məʊz, -ˈ-, Ⓤⓢ ˈkoʊ.moʊs
compact n ˈkɒm.pækt, Ⓤⓢ ˈkɑːm- **-s** -s
compact adj, v kəmˈpækt, Ⓤⓢ kəm-, kɑːm- **-er** -əʳ, Ⓤⓢ -ɚ **-est** -ɪst, -əst **-ly** -li **-ness** -nəs, -nɪs **-s** -s **-ing** -ɪŋ **-ed** -ɪd *stress shift, see compound:* **ˌcompact ˈdisc/ˌcompact ˈdisk**
compactor kəmˈpæk.təʳ; ˈkɒm.pæk-, Ⓤⓢ kəmˈpæk.tɚ; Ⓤⓢ ˈkɑːm.pæk- **-s** -z
companion kəmˈpæn.jən **-s** -z **-ship** -ʃɪp
companionab|le kəmˈpæn.jə.nə.b|əl **-ly** -li **-leness** -əl.nəs, -nɪs
companionate kəmˈpæn.jə.nət, -nɪt
companionway kəmˈpæn.jən.weɪ **-s** -z
compan|y ˈkʌm.pə.n|i **-ies** -iz
Compaq® ˈkɒm.pæk, Ⓤⓢ ˈkɑːm-
comparability ˌkɒm.pər.əˈbɪl.ə.ti; kəmˌpær-, -ɪ.ti, Ⓤⓢ ˌkɑːm.pɚ.əˈbɪl.ə.t̬i
comparab|le ˈkɒm.pər.ə.b|əl, Ⓤⓢ ˈkɑːm-; Ⓤⓢ kəmˈper.ə-, -ˈpær- **-ly** -li **-leness** -əl.nəs, -nɪs
comparative kəmˈpær.ə.tɪv, Ⓤⓢ -ˈper.ə.t̬ɪv, -ˈpær- **-s** -z **-ly** -li
compar|e kəmˈpeəʳ, Ⓤⓢ -per **-es** -z **-ing** -ɪŋ **-ed** -d
comparison kəmˈpær.ɪ.sən, Ⓤⓢ -ˈper-, -ˈpær- **-s** -z
compartment kəmˈpɑːt.mənt, Ⓤⓢ -ˈpɑːrt- **-s** -s
compartmentalization, -isa- ˌkɒm.pɑːtˌmen.təl.aɪˈzeɪ.ʃən, -ɪˈ-, Ⓤⓢ kəm.pɑːrtˌmen.t̬əl.əˈ-, ˌkɑːm-
compartmentaliz|e, -is|e ˌkɒm.pɑːtˈmen.təl.aɪz, Ⓤⓢ kəm.pɑːrtˈmen.t̬ə.laɪz, ˌkɑːm- **-es** -ɪz **-ing** -ɪŋ **-ed** -d
compass ˈkʌm.pəs, Ⓤⓢ ˈkʌm-, ˈkɑːm- **-es** -ɪz **-ing** -ɪŋ **-ed** -t
compassion kəmˈpæʃ.ən
compassionate kəmˈpæʃ.ən.ət, -ɪt **-ly** -li **-ness** -nəs, -nɪs
compatibility kəmˌpæt.əˈbɪl.ə.ti, -ɪˈ-, -ɪ.ti, Ⓤⓢ -ˌpæt̬.əˈbɪl.ə.t̬i
compatib|le kəmˈpæt.ə.b|əl, ˈ-ɪ-, Ⓤⓢ -ˈpæt̬- **-ly** -li **-leness** -əl.nəs, -nɪs
compatriot kəmˈpæt.ri.ət, kɒm-, -ˈpeɪ.tri-, Ⓤⓢ kəmˈpeɪ.tri-, kɑːm- **-s** -s
compeer ˈkɒm.pɪəʳ, -ˈ-, Ⓤⓢ ˈkɑːm.pɪr; Ⓤⓢ -ˈ-, kəm- **-s** -z
compel kəmˈpel **-s** -z **-ling/ly** -ɪŋ/li **-led** -d **-lable** -ə.bəl
compendious kəmˈpen.di.əs **-ly** -li **-ness** -nəs, -nɪs
compendi|um kəmˈpen.di|.əm **-ums** -əmz **-a** -ə
compen|sate ˈkɒm.pən|.seɪt, -pen-, Ⓤⓢ ˈkɑːm- **-sates** -seɪts **-sating** -seɪ.tɪŋ, Ⓤⓢ -seɪ.t̬ɪŋ **-sated** -seɪ.tɪd, Ⓤⓢ -seɪ.t̬ɪd
compensation ˌkɒm.pənˈseɪ.ʃən, -pen-, Ⓤⓢ ˌkɑːm- **-s** -z
compensative kəmˈpent.sə.tɪv, ˌkɒm.pənˈseɪ-, Ⓤⓢ kəmˈpent.sə.t̬ɪv, ˈkɑːm.pən.seɪ-
compensatory ˌkɒm.pənˈseɪ.tər.i, -tri; kəmˈpent.sə-; ˈkɒm.pen.seɪ-, -pən-, Ⓤⓢ kəmˈpent.sə.tɔːr.i
comper|e, compèr|e ˈkɒm.peəʳ, Ⓤⓢ ˈkɑːm.per **-es** -z **-ing** -ɪŋ **-ed** -d
com|pete kəmˈpiːt **-petes** -ˈpiːts **-peting** -ˈpiː.tɪŋ, Ⓤⓢ -ˈpiː.t̬ɪŋ **-peted** -ˈpiː.tɪd, Ⓤⓢ -ˈpiː.t̬ɪd
competen|ce ˈkɒm.pɪ.tənt|s, -pə-, Ⓤⓢ ˈkɑːm- **-cies** -siz **-cy** -si
competent ˈkɒm.pɪ.tənt, -pə-, Ⓤⓢ ˈkɑːm.pɪ.t̬ənt, -pə- **-ly** -li
competition ˌkɒm.pəˈtɪʃ.ən, -pɪˈ-, Ⓤⓢ ˌkɑːm- **-s** -z
competitive kəmˈpet.ɪ.tɪv, ˈ-ə-, Ⓤⓢ -ˈpet̬.ə.t̬ɪv **-ly** -li **-ness** -nəs, -nɪs
competitor kəmˈpet.ɪ.təʳ, ˈ-ə-, Ⓤⓢ -ˈpet̬.ə.t̬ɚ **-s** -z
compilation ˌkɒm.pɪˈleɪ.ʃən, -pəˈ-, -paɪˈ-, Ⓤⓢ ˌkɑːm.pəˈ- **-s** -z
compil|e kəmˈpaɪl **-es** -z **-ing** -ɪŋ **-ed** -d **-er/s** -əʳ/z, Ⓤⓢ -ɚ/z
complacen|ce kəmˈpleɪ.sənt|s **-cy** -si
complacent kəmˈpleɪ.sənt **-ly** -li
complain kəmˈpleɪn **-s** -z **-ing** -ɪŋ **-ed** -d **-er/s** -əʳ/z, Ⓤⓢ -ɚ/z
complainant kəmˈpleɪ.nənt **-s** -s
complaint kəmˈpleɪnt **-s** -s
complaisance kəmˈpleɪ.zənts, Ⓤⓢ -sənts
complaisant kəmˈpleɪ.zənt, Ⓤⓢ -sənt **-ly** -li
compleat kəmˈpliːt
complement n ˈkɒm.plɪ.mənt, -plə-, Ⓤⓢ ˈkɑːm- **-s** -s
comple|ment v ˈkɒm.plɪ|.ment, ˌkɒm.plɪ|ˈment, Ⓤⓢ ˈkɑːm.plɪ- **-ments** -ments, -ˈments, Ⓤⓢ -ments **-menting** -men.tɪŋ, -ˈmen.tɪŋ, Ⓤⓢ -men.t̬ɪŋ **-mented** -men.tɪd, -ˈmen.tɪd, Ⓤⓢ -men.t̬ɪd
complemental ˌkɒm.plɪˈmen.təl, Ⓤⓢ ˌkɑːm.plɪˈmen.t̬əl
complementary ˌkɒm.plɪˈmen.tər.i, -pləˈ-, ˈ-tri, Ⓤⓢ ˌkɑːm.pləˈmen.t̬ɚ.i, ˈ-tri
complementation ˌkɒm.plɪ.menˈteɪ.ʃən, -plə-, -mənˈ-, Ⓤⓢ ˌkɑːm-
complementiser, -izer ˈkɒm.plɪ.men.taɪ.zəʳ, -plə-, -mən-, Ⓤⓢ ˈkɑːm.plə.mən.taɪ.zɚ, -men- **-s** -z
com|plete kəm|ˈpliːt **-pletest** -ˈpliː.tɪst, -təst, Ⓤⓢ -ˈpliː.t̬ɪst, -t̬əst **-pletely** -ˈpliːt.li **-pleteness** -ˈpliːt.nəs, -nɪs **-pletes** -ˈpliːts **-pleting** -ˈpliː.tɪŋ, Ⓤⓢ -ˈpliː.t̬ɪŋ **-pleted** -ˈpliː.tɪd, Ⓤⓢ -ˈpliː.t̬ɪd
completion kəmˈpliː.ʃən
complex adj ˈkɒm.pleks, kəmˈpleks, Ⓤⓢ kɑːmˈpleks, kəm-; Ⓤⓢ ˈkɑːm.pleks
complex n ˈkɒm.pleks, Ⓤⓢ ˈkɑːm- **-es** -ɪz
complexion kəmˈplek.ʃən **-s** -z **-ed** -d
complexit|y kəmˈplek.sə.t|i, -sɪ-, Ⓤⓢ -sə.t̬|i **-ies** -iz
complianc|e kəmˈplaɪ.ənts **-es** -ɪz
compliant kəmˈplaɪ.ənt **-ly** -li
compli|cate ˈkɒm.plɪ|.keɪt, Ⓤⓢ ˈkɑːm.plə- **-cates** -keɪts **-cating** -keɪ.tɪŋ, Ⓤⓢ -keɪ.t̬ɪŋ **-cated** -keɪ.tɪd, Ⓤⓢ -keɪ.t̬ɪd
complication ˌkɒm.plɪˈkeɪ.ʃən, -pləˈ-, Ⓤⓢ ˌkɑːm.pləˈ- **-s** -z
complicit kəmˈplɪs.ɪt
complicity kəmˈplɪs.ə.ti, -ɪ.ti, Ⓤⓢ -ə.t̬i
compliment n ˈkɒm.plɪ.mənt, -plə-, Ⓤⓢ ˈkɑːm.plə- **-s** -s
compli|ment v ˈkɒm.plɪ|.ment, -plə-, ˌkɒm.plɪ|ˈment, Ⓤⓢ ˈkɑːm.plə- **-ments** -ments, -ˈments, Ⓤⓢ -ments **-menting** -men.tɪŋ, -ˈmen.tɪŋ, Ⓤⓢ -men.t̬ɪŋ **-mented** -men.tɪd, -ˈmen.tɪd, Ⓤⓢ -men.t̬ɪd
complimentarily ˌkɒm.plɪˈmen.tər.əl.i, -plə-, -ɪ.li, Ⓤⓢ ˌkɑːm.plə.menˈter-; Ⓤⓢ -ˈmen.t̬ɚ-
complimentar|y ˌkɒm.plɪˈmen.tər|.i, -pləˈ-, ˈ-tr|i, Ⓤⓢ ˌkɑːm.pləˈmen.t̬ɚ|.i, ˈ-tr|i **-ies** -iz
complin ˈkɒm.plɪn, Ⓤⓢ ˈkɑːm- **-s** -z
compline ˈkɒm.plɪn, -plaɪn, Ⓤⓢ ˈkɑːm- **-s** -z
compl|y kəmˈpl|aɪ **-ies** -aɪz **-ying** -aɪ.ɪŋ **-ied** -aɪd **-ier/s** -aɪ.əʳ/z, Ⓤⓢ -aɪ.ɚ/z
compo ˈkɒm.pəʊ, Ⓤⓢ ˈkɑːm.poʊ
component kəmˈpəʊ.nənt, Ⓤⓢ -ˈpoʊ- **-s** -s
componential ˌkɒm.pəʊˈnen.tʃəl, Ⓤⓢ ˌkɑːm.pəˈ- **ˌcompoˌnential aˈnalysis**
com|port kəm|ˈpɔːt, Ⓤⓢ -ˈpɔːrt **-ports** -ˈpɔːts, Ⓤⓢ -ˈpɔːrts **-porting** -ˈpɔː.tɪŋ, Ⓤⓢ -ˈpɔːr.t̬ɪŋ **-ported** -ˈpɔː.tɪd, Ⓤⓢ -ˈpɔːr.t̬ɪd
comportment kəmˈpɔːt.mənt, Ⓤⓢ -ˈpɔːrt-
compos|e kəmˈpəʊz, Ⓤⓢ -ˈpoʊz **-es** -ɪz **-ing** -ɪŋ **-ed** -d
compos|ed kəmˈpəʊz|d, Ⓤⓢ -ˈpoʊz|d **-edly** -ɪd.li, -əd.li **-edness** -ɪd.nəs, -d.nəs, -nɪs
composer kəmˈpəʊ.zəʳ, Ⓤⓢ -ˈpoʊ.zɚ **-s** -z

C

composite ˈkɒm.pə.zɪt, -sɪt, -zaɪt, -saɪt, (US) kəmˈpɑː.zɪt **-ly** -li **-ness** -nəs, -nɪs
composition ˌkɒm.pəˈzɪʃ.ən, (US) ˌkɑːm- **-s** -z
compositor kəmˈpɒz.ɪ.təʳ, (US) -ˈpɑː.zɪ.t̬ɚ **-s** -z
compos mentis ˌkɒm.pəsˈmen.tɪs, -pɒs-, (US) ˌkɑːm.pəsˈmen.t̬əs
compost ˈkɒm.pɒst, (US) ˈkɑːm.poʊst **-s** -s **-ing** -ɪŋ **-ed** -ɪd ˈ**compost** ˌ**heap**
composure kəmˈpəʊ.ʒəʳ, (US) -ˈpoʊ.ʒɚ
compote ˈkɒm.pɒt, -pəʊt, (US) ˈkɑːm.poʊt **-s** -s
compound **n, adj** ˈkɒm.paʊnd, (US) ˈkɑːm- **-s** -z ˌ**compound** ˈ**fracture**
compound **v** kəmˈpaʊnd, kɒm-; ˈkɒm.paʊnd, (US) kɑːmˈpaʊnd, kəm-; (US) ˈkɑːm.paʊnd **-s** -z **-ing** -ɪŋ **-ed** -ɪd **-able** -ə.bəl
comprehend ˌkɒm.prɪˈhend, -prəˈ-, (US) ˌkɑːm- **-s** -z **-ing** -ɪŋ **-ed** -ɪd
comprehensibility ˌkɒm.prɪ.hent.səˈbɪl.ə.ti, -prə-, -sɪˈ-, -ɪ.ti, (US) ˌkɑːm.prə.hent.səˈbɪl.ə.t̬i, -prɪ-
comprehensib|le ˌkɒm.prɪˈhent.sə.b|əl, -prəˈ-, -sɪ-, (US) ˌkɑːm- **-ly** -li **-leness** -əl.nəs, -nɪs
comprehension ˌkɒm.prɪˈhen.tʃən, -prəˈ-, (US) ˌkɑːm.prɪˈhent.ʃən, -prəˈ-
comprehensive ˌkɒm.prɪˈhent.sɪv, -prəˈ-, (US) ˌkɑːm.prə-, -prɪ- **-s** -z **-ly** -li **-ness** -nəs, -nɪs **compreˈhensive** ˌ**school**
compress **n** ˈkɒm.pres, (US) ˈkɑːm- **-es** -ɪz
compress **v** kəmˈpres **-es** -ɪz **-ing** -ɪŋ **-ed** -t **-or/s** -əʳ/z, (US) -ɚ/z
compressibility kəmˌpres.əˈbɪl.ə.ti, -ɪˈ-, -ɪ.ti, (US) -ə.t̬i
compressible kəmˈpres.ə.bəl, ˈ-ɪ- **-ness** -nəs, -nɪs
compression kəmˈpreʃ.ən **-s** -z **-al** -əl
compressive kəmˈpres.ɪv
compris|e kəmˈpraɪz **-es** -ɪz **-ing** -ɪŋ **-ed** -d **-able** -ə.bəl
compromis|e ˈkɒm.prə.maɪz, (US) ˈkɑːm- **-es** -ɪz **-ing/ly** -ɪŋ/li **-ed** -d **-er/s** -əʳ/z, (US) -ɚ/z
Comptometer® ˌkɒmpˈtɒm.ɪ.təʳ, ˈ-ə-, (US) ˌkɑːmpˈtɑː.mə.t̬ɚ **-s** -z
Compton ˈkɒm*p*.tən, ˈkʌm*p*-, (US) ˈkɑːm*p*-

> Note: For British English, as a surname more often /ˈkʌm*p*-/, as a place name more often /ˈkɒm*p*-/. The London street is generally /ˈkɒm*p*-/.

Compton-Burnett ˌkɒmp.tən.bɜːˈnet, -ˈbɜː.nɪt, (US) ˌkɑːmp.tən.bɝːˈnet
comptroller kənˈtrəʊ.ləʳ, kəmp-, kɒmp-, (US) kənˈtroʊ.lɚ, kəmp-, kɑːmp-; (US) ˈkɑːmp.troʊ- **-s** -z

> Note: The pronunciation with /kəmp-/ is a spelling pronunciation that is an alternative to the traditional pronunciation with /kən/.

compulsion kəmˈpʌl.ʃən
compulsive kəmˈpʌl.sɪv **-ly** -li
compulsor|y kəmˈpʌl.sər|.i **-ily** -əl.i, -ɪ.li
compunction kəmˈpʌŋ*k*.ʃən
compunctious kəmˈpʌŋ*k*.ʃəs
compurgation ˌkɒm.pɜːˈgeɪ.ʃən, (US) ˌkɑːm.pɚˈ-
computability kəmˌpjuː.təˈbɪl.ə.ti, ˌkɒm.pjʊ-, -ɪ.ti, (US) kəmˌpjuː.t̬əˈbɪl.ə.t̬i
computable kəmˈpjuː.tə.bəl; ˈkɒm.pjʊ-, (US) kəmˈpjuː.t̬ə-
computation ˌkɒm.pjəˈteɪ.ʃən, -pjʊˈ-, (US) ˌkɑːm.pjəˈ- **-s** -z
computational ˌkɒm.pjəˈteɪ.ʃən.əl, -pjʊˈ-, -ˈteɪʃ.nəl, (US) ˌkɑːm- **-ly** -i **compuˌtational linˈguistics**
computator ˈkɒm.pjə.teɪ.təʳ, -pjʊ-, (US) ˈkɑːm.pjə.teɪ.t̬ɚ **-s** -z
com|pute kəm|ˈpjuːt **-putes** -ˈpjuːts **-puting** -ˈpjuː.tɪŋ, (US) -ˈpjuː.t̬ɪŋ **-puted** -ˈpjuː.tɪd, (US) -ˈpjuː.t̬ɪd
computer kəmˈpjuː.təʳ, (US) -t̬ɚ **-s** -z **comˈputer** ˌ**game**; **comˌputer** ˈ**programmer**; **comˌputer aided deˈsign**
computerate kəmˈpjuː.tər.ət, (US) -t̬ɚ-
computerization, -isa- kəmˌpjuː.tər.aɪˈzeɪ.ʃən, -ɪˈ-, (US) -t̬ɚ.əˈ-
computeriz|e, -is|e kəmˈpjuː.tər.aɪz, (US) -t̬ə.raɪz **-es** -ɪz **-ing** -ɪŋ **-ed** -d
computist kəmˈpjuː.tɪst, (US) -t̬ɪst **-s** -s
comrade ˈkɒm.reɪd, ˈkʌm-, -rɪd, (US) ˈkɑːm.ræd, -rəd **-s** -z **-ship** -ʃɪp
Comsat® ˈkɒm.sæt, (US) ˈkɑːm- **-s** -s
Comte kɔ̃ːnt, kɔːnt, kɒnt, (US) kɔ̃ːnt, koʊnt
Comus ˈkəʊ.məs, (US) ˈkoʊ-
Comyn ˈkʌm.ɪn
con kɒn, (US) kɑːn **-s** -z **-ning** -ɪŋ **-ned** -d ˈ**con** ˌ**man**; ˈ**con** ˌ**trick**
con- kɒn, kən, (US) kɑːn, kən
Note: Prefix. This may carry primary or secondary stress, e.g. **concept** /ˈkɒn.sept/ (US) /ˈkɑːn-/, or may be unstressed, e.g. **consume** /kənˈsjuːm/ (US) /kənˈsuːm/.
Conakry ˌkɒn.əˈkriː, ˈkɒn.ə.kri, (US) ˈkɑː.nə.kri
Conall ˈkɒn.əl, (US) ˈkɑː.nəl
Conan *personal name:* ˈkəʊ.nən, ˈkɒn.ən, (US) ˈkoʊ.nən, ˈkɑː- *place in Scotland:* ˈkɒn.ən, ˈkəʊ.nən, (US) ˈkɑː-, ˈkoʊ-

> Note: The members of the family of Sir Arthur Conan Doyle pronounce /ˈkəʊ.nən/.

Conant ˈkɒn.ənt, (US) ˈkoʊ.nənt
conation kəʊˈneɪ.ʃən, (US) koʊ-
conative ˈkəʊ.nə.tɪv, (US) ˈkoʊ.nə.t̬ɪv
Concannon kɒnˈkæn.ən, kɒŋ-, (US) kɑːn-
concaten|ate kənˈkæt.ən|.eɪt, kəŋ-, kɒn-, kɒŋ-, ˈ-ɪ-, (US) kənˈkæt̬-, kɑːn- **-ates** -eɪts **-ating** -eɪ.tɪŋ, (US) -eɪ.t̬ɪŋ **-ated** -eɪ.tɪd, (US) -eɪ.t̬ɪd
concatenation kənˌkæt.əˈneɪ.ʃən, kəŋ-, kɒn-, kɒŋ-, -ɪˈ-; ˈkɒn.kæt-, ˈkɒŋ-, (US) kənˌkæt̬.əˈ-; (US) ˌkɑːn.kæt̬- **-s** -z
concave kɒŋˈkeɪv, kəŋ-, kɒn-, kən-; ˈkɒŋ.keɪv, (US) kɑːnˈkeɪv, ˈkɑːn- *stress shift:* ˌ**concave** ˈ**lens**
concavit|y kɒnˈkæv.ə.t|i, kən-, kɒŋ-, kəŋ-, -ɪ.t|i, (US) kɑːnˈkæv.ə.t̬|i **-ies** -iz
conceal kənˈsiːl **-s** -z **-ing** -ɪŋ **-ed** -d **-able** -ə.bəl **-er/s** -əʳ/z, (US) -ɚ/z
concealment kənˈsiːl.mənt **-s** -s
conced|e kənˈsiːd **-es** -z **-ing** -ɪŋ **-ed** -ɪd
conceit kənˈsiːt **-s** -s
conceited kənˈsiː.tɪd, (US) -t̬ɪd **-ly** -li **-ness** -nəs, -nɪs
conceivab|le kənˈsiː.və.b|əl **-ly** -li **-leness** -əl.nəs, -nɪs
conceiv|e kənˈsiːv **-es** -z **-ing** -ɪŋ **-ed** -d
concele|brate kɒnˈsel.ə|.breɪt, kən-, ˈ-ɪ-, (US) kən-, kɑːn- **-brates** -breɪts **-brating** -breɪ.tɪŋ, (US) -breɪ.t̬ɪŋ **-brated** -breɪ.tɪd, (US) -breɪ.t̬ɪd
concelebration ˌkɒn.sel.əˈbreɪ.ʃən, -ɪˈ-; kənˌsel-, (US) kənˌsel-; (US) ˌkɑːn.sel- **-s** -z
concent kənˈsent, kɒn-, (US) kən-
concent|er kɒnˈsen.t|əʳ, (US) kənˈsen.t̬|ɚ, kɑːn- **-ers** -əz, (US) -ɚz **-ering** -ər.ɪŋ **-ered** -əd, (US) -ɚd
concen|trate ˈkɒnt.sən|.treɪt, -sɪn-, -sen-, (US) ˈkɑːnt.sən- **-trates** -treɪts **-trating** -treɪ.tɪŋ, (US) -treɪ.t̬ɪŋ **-trated** -treɪ.tɪd, (US) -treɪ.t̬ɪd
concentration ˌkɒnt.sənˈtreɪ.ʃən, -sɪnˈ-, -senˈ-, (US) ˌkɑːnt.sənˈ- **-s** -z **concenˈtration** ˌ**camp**
concentrative ˈkɒnt.sən.treɪ.tɪv, -sɪn-, -sen-, (US) ˈkɑːnt.sən.treɪ.t̬ɪv; (US) kənˈsen.trə-
concent|re kɒnˈsen.t|əʳ, (US) kənˈsen.t̬|ɚ, kɑːn- **-res** -əz, (US) -ɚz **-ring** -rɪŋ **-ering** -ər.ɪŋ **-red** -əd, (US) -ɚd
concentric kənˈsen.trɪk, kɒn-, (US) kən- **-ally** -əl.i, -li
Concepción kənˌsep.siˈəʊn, ˌkɒn.sep-, (US) kən-, kɑːn-, -ˈoʊn
concept ˈkɒn.sept, (US) ˈkɑːn- **-s** -s

C

conception kənˈsep.ʃən -s -z
conceptual kənˈsep.tʃu.əl, -ʃu-, -tju-, (US) -tʃu-, -tju- -ly -i
conceptualization, -isa- kənˌsep.tʃu.ə.laɪˈzeɪ.ʃən, -ʃu-, -tju-, -ɪˈ-, (US) -tʃu.əl.əˈ-, -tju-
conceptualiz|e, -is|e kənˈsep.tʃu.ə.laɪz, -ʃu-, -tju-, -tʃʊ.laɪz, -tʃə-, (US) -tʃu.ə-, -tju.ə- -es -ɪz -ing -ɪŋ -ed -d
conceptually kənˈsep.tʃu.ə.li, -ʃu-, -tju-, (US) -tʃu-, -tju-
conceptus kənˈsep.təs -es -ɪz
concern kənˈsɜːn, (US) -ˈsɝːn -s -z -ing -ɪŋ -ed -d -ment/s -mənt/s
concern|ed kənˈsɜːn|d, (US) -ˈsɝːn|d -edly -ɪd.li -edness -ɪd.nəs, -d.nəs, -nɪs
con|cert v kən|ˈsɜːt, (US) -ˈsɝːt -certs -ˈsɜːts, (US) -ˈsɝːts -certing -ˈsɜː.tɪŋ, (US) -ˈsɝː.t̬ɪŋ -certed -ˈsɜː.tɪd, (US) -ˈsɝː.t̬ɪd
concert n *musical entertainment:* ˈkɒn.sət, (US) ˈkɑːn.sɚt -s -s
concert, C~ n *union:* ˈkɒn.sɜːt, -sət, (US) ˈkɑːn.sɚt -s -s
concerti (plural of **concerto**) kənˈtʃeə.ti, kɒn-, -ˈtʃɜː-, (US) -ˈtʃer.t̬i
concertina ˌkɒnt.səˈtiː.nə, (US) ˌkɑːnt.sɚˈ- -s -z -ing -ɪŋ -ed -d
concertino ˌkɒn.tʃəˈtiː.nəʊ, (US) ˌkɑːn.tʃɚˈtiː.noʊ -s -z
concerto kənˈtʃeə.təʊ, -ˈtʃɜː-, (US) -ˈtʃer.t̬oʊ -s -z **concerti** kənˈtʃeə.ti, -ˈtʃɜː-, (US) -ˈtʃer.t̬i
concerto grosso kənˌtʃeə.təʊˈgrɒs.əʊ, kɒn-, -ˌtʃɜː-, (US) kənˌtʃer.t̬oʊˈgroʊ.soʊ, kɑːn- **concerti grossi** kənˌtʃeə.tiˈgrɒs.i, kɒn-, -ˌtʃɜː-, (US) -ˌtʃer.t̬iˈgroʊ.si, kɑːn-
concession kənˈseʃ.ən -s -z
concessionaire kənˌseʃ.ənˈeər, (US) -ˈer -s -z
concessional kənˈseʃ.ən.əl, ˈ-nəl, (US) -ən.əl -ly -i
concessionary kənˈseʃ.ən.ər.i, -ən.ri, (US) -ən.er.i
concessive kənˈses.ɪv -ly -li
conch kɒntʃ, kɒŋk, (US) kɑːŋk, kɑːntʃ **conches** ˈkɒn.tʃɪz, (US) ˈkɑːn.tʃɪz **conchs** kɒŋks, (US) kɑːŋks
concha ˈkɒŋ.kə, (US) ˈkɑːŋ-, ˈkɔːŋ- -s -z
conchie ˈkɒn.tʃi, (US) ˈkɑːn- -s -z
Conchobar ˈkɒŋ.kə.vər, ˈkɒn.u.ər, krəˈxʊər, (US) ˈkɑː.nu.ɚ, ˈkɑːŋ.koʊ.ɚ, ˈkɔːŋ-
conchoid ˈkɒŋ.kɔɪd, (US) ˈkɑːn- -s -z
conchologist kɒŋˈkɒl.ə.dʒɪst, (US) kɑːŋˈkɑː.lə-, kɔːŋ- -s -s
conchology kɒŋˈkɒl.ə.dʒi, (US) kɑːŋˈkɑː.lə-, kɔːŋ-
concierge ˌkɒn.siˈeəʒ, ˌkɔːn-, ˌkɔ̃ːn-, ˈ---, (US) koʊnˈsjerʒ, kɑːn-, -siˈerʒ -s -ɪz
concili|ate kənˈsɪl.i|.eɪt -ates -eɪts -ating -eɪ.tɪŋ, (US) -eɪ.t̬ɪŋ -ated -eɪ.tɪd, (US) -eɪ.t̬ɪd
conciliation kənˌsɪl.iˈeɪ.ʃən
conciliative kənˈsɪl.i.ə.tɪv, -eɪ-, (US) -eɪ.t̬ɪv
conciliator kənˈsɪl.i.eɪ.tər, (US) -t̬ɚ -s -z
conciliatory kənˈsɪl.i.ə.tər.i, -eɪ-, -tri; kənˌsɪl.iˈeɪ-, (US) kənˈsɪl.i.ə.tɔːr.i
concis|e kənˈsaɪs -er -ər, (US) -ɚ -est -ɪst, -əst -ely -li -eness -nəs, -nɪs
concision kənˈsɪʒ.ən -s -z
conclave ˈkɒŋ.kleɪv, ˈkɒn-, (US) ˈkɑːn- -s -z
conclud|e kənˈkluːd, kəŋ-, (US) kən- -es -z -ing -ɪŋ -ed -ɪd
conclusion kənˈkluː.ʒən, kəŋ-, (US) kən- -s -z
conclusive kənˈkluː.sɪv, kəŋ-, (US) kən- -ly -li -ness -nəs, -nɪs
concoct kənˈkɒkt, kəŋ-, (US) kənˈkɑːkt -s -s -ing -ɪŋ -ed -ɪd -er/s -ər/z, (US) -ɚ/z
concoction kənˈkɒk.ʃən, kəŋ-, (US) kənˈkɑːk- -s -z
concomitan|ce kənˈkɒm.ɪ.tənt|s, kəŋ-, ˈ-ə-, (US) kənˈkɑː.mə.t̬ənt|s -cy -si
concomitant kənˈkɒm.ɪ.tənt, kəŋ-, ˈ-ə-, (US) kənˈkɑː.mə.t̬ənt -ly -li
concord, C~ n ˈkɒŋ.kɔːd, ˈkɒn-, (US) ˈkɑːn.kɔːrd, ˈkɑːŋ-, ˈkɔːŋ- -s -z
concord v kənˈkɔːd, kəŋ-, (US) kənˈkɔːrd -s -z -ing -ɪŋ -ed -ɪd
Concord *place in the US, type of grape:* ˈkɒŋ.kəd, (US) ˈkɑːŋ.kɚd
concordanc|e kənˈkɔː.dənts, kəŋ-, (US) kənˈkɔːr- -es -ɪz -ing -ɪŋ -ed -d
concordant kənˈkɔː.dənt, kəŋ-, (US) kənˈkɔːr- -ly -li
concordat kɒnˈkɔː.dæt, kɒŋ-, kən-, kəŋ-, (US) kənˈkɔːr- -s -s
Concorde ˈkɒŋ.kɔːd, ˈkɒn-, (US) ˈkɑːn.kɔːrd -s -z
concours|e ˈkɒŋ.kɔːs, ˈkɒn-, -kʊəs, (US) ˈkɑːn.kɔːrs -es -ɪz
concrete n, adj ˈkɒŋ.kriːt, ˈkɒn-, (US) ˈkɑːn- ˌ**concrete** ˈ**jungle**
con|crete v *cover with concrete:* ˈkɒŋ|.kriːt, ˈkɒn-, (US) ˈkɑːn- *solidify:* kən|ˈkriːt, kəŋ-, (US) kən- -cretes -ˈkriːts -creting -ˈkriː.tɪŋ, (US) -ˈkriː.t̬ɪŋ -creted -ˈkriː.tɪd, (US) -ˈkriː.t̬ɪd
concrete|ly kɒŋˈkriːt|.li, kɒn-, (US) kɑːn- -ness -nəs, -nɪs
concretion kənˈkriː.ʃən, kəŋ-, kɒn-, (US) kən-, kɑːn- -s -z
concretiz|e, -is|e ˈkɒŋ.kriː.taɪz, ˈkɒn-, -krɪ-, (US) ˈkɑːn.kriː-, kɑːnˈkriː.taɪz, kɑːŋ- -es -ɪz -ing -ɪŋ -ed -d
concubinage kɒnˈkjuː.bɪ.nɪdʒ, kɒŋ-, kən-, kəŋ-, (US) kənˈkjuː.bə-, kɑːn-
concubine ˈkɒŋ.kjʊ.baɪn, ˈkɒn-, -kjə-, (US) ˈkɑːŋ-, ˈkɑːn- -s -z
concupiscen|ce kənˈkjuː.pɪ.sən|ts, kəŋ-, kɒn-, kɒŋ-, (US) kɑːn-, kənˈkjuː.pə- -t -t
concur kənˈkɜːr, kəŋ-, (US) -ˈkɝː -s -z -ring -ɪŋ -red -d
concurren|ce kənˈkʌr.ənt|s, kəŋ-, (US) kən- -cy -si
concurrent kənˈkʌr.ənt, kəŋ-, (US) kən- -ly -li
concuss kənˈkʌs, kəŋ-, (US) kən- -es -ɪz -ing -ɪŋ -ed -t
concussion kənˈkʌʃ.ən, kəŋ-, (US) kən- -s -z
condemn kənˈdem -s -z -ing -ɪŋ -ed -d -able -nə.bəl
condemnation ˌkɒn.demˈneɪ.ʃən, -dəmˈ-, (US) ˌkɑːn- -s -z
condemnatory kənˈdem.nə.tər.i, -tri; ˌkɒn.demˈneɪ-, -dəmˈ-, (US) kənˈdem.nə.tɔːr.i
condensation ˌkɒn.denˈseɪ.ʃən, -dənˈ-, (US) ˌkɑːn- -s -z
condens|e kənˈdents -es -ɪz -ing -ɪŋ -ed -t -able -ə.bəl **conˌdensed** ˈ**milk**
condenser kənˈden.sər, (US) -sɚ -s -z
condescend ˌkɒn.dɪˈsend, -dəˈ-, (US) ˌkɑːn- -s -z -ing -ɪŋ -ed -ɪd
condescending ˌkɒn.dɪˈsen.dɪŋ, -dəˈ-, (US) ˌkɑːn- -ly -li
condescension ˌkɒn.dɪˈsen.ʃən, -dəˈ-, (US) ˌkɑːn-
condign kənˈdaɪn, kɒn-, (US) kənˈdaɪn, ˈkɑːn.daɪn -ly -li -ness -nəs, -nɪs
condiment ˈkɒn.dɪ.mənt, (US) ˈkɑːn.də- -s -s
condition kənˈdɪʃ.ən -s -z -ing -ɪŋ -ed -d
conditional kənˈdɪʃ.ən.əl, ˈ-nəl -ly -i
conditioner kənˈdɪʃ.ən.ər, ˈ-nər, (US) ˈ-ən.ɚ, ˈ-nɚ -s -z
condo ˈkɒn.dəʊ, (US) ˈkɑːn.doʊ -s -z
condol|e kənˈdəʊl, (US) -ˈdoʊl -es -z -ing -ɪŋ -ed -d -ement/s -mənt/s
Condoleezza ˌkɒn.dəˈliː.zə, (US) ˌkɑːn-
condolenc|e kənˈdəʊ.lənts, (US) -ˈdoʊ- -es -ɪz
condolent kənˈdəʊ.lənt, (US) -ˈdoʊ-
condom ˈkɒn.dɒm, -dəm, (US) ˈkɑːn.dəm, ˈkʌn- -s -z
condominium ˌkɒn.dəˈmɪn.i.əm, (US) ˌkɑːn.dəˈ- -s -z
Condon ˈkɒn.dən, (US) ˈkɑːn-
condonation ˌkɒn.dəʊˈneɪ.ʃən, (US) ˌkɑːn.doʊˈ- -s -z
condon|e kənˈdəʊn, (US) -ˈdoʊn -es -z -ing -ɪŋ -ed -d
condor, C~ ˈkɒn.dɔːr, -dər, (US) ˈkɑːn.dɚ, -dɔːr -s -z
conduc|e kənˈdʒuːs, -ˈdjuːs, (US) -ˈduːs, -ˈdjuːs -es -ɪz -ing -ɪŋ -ed -t -ement/s -mənt/s
conducive kənˈdʒuː.sɪv, -ˈdjuː-, (US) -ˈduː-, -ˈdjuː- -ly -li -ness -nəs, -nɪs
conduct n ˈkɒn.dʌkt, -dəkt, (US) ˈkɑːn- -s -s
conduct v kənˈdʌkt -s -s -ing -ɪŋ -ed -ɪd
conductance kənˈdʌk.tənts
conductibility kənˌdʌk.təˈbɪl.ə.ti, -tɪˈ-, -ɪ.ti, (US) -ə.t̬i
conductible kənˈdʌk.tə.bəl, -tɪ-
conduction kənˈdʌk.ʃən
conductive kənˈdʌk.tɪv
conductivity ˌkɒn.dʌkˈtɪv.ə.ti, -dəkˈ-, -ɪ.ti, (US) ˌkɑːn.dʌkˈtɪv.ə.t̬i

conductor kənˈdʌk.təʳ, (US) -tə -s -z
conductress kənˈdʌk.trəs, -trɪs -es -ɪz
conduit ˈkɒn.dʒu.ɪt, ˈkʌn-, -du-, -dju-, -dɪt, (US) ˈkɑːn.du.ɪt, -dɪt -s -s
Conduit *street:* ˈkɒn.dɪt, ˈkʌn-, (US) ˈkɑːn-
Condy ˈkɒn.di, (US) ˈkɑːn-
condyle ˈkɒn.dɪl, -daɪl, (US) ˈkɑːn- -s -z
cone kəʊn, (US) koʊn -s -z
Conestoga ˌkɒn.əˈstəʊ.gə, (US) ˌkɑː.nəˈstoʊ- **Conesˈtoga ˌwagon**
coney, C~ ˈkəʊ.ni, (US) ˈkoʊ- -s -z **ˌConey ˈIsland** *stress shift:* **ˌConey Island ˈresident**
confab ˈkɒn.fæb; kɒnˈfæb, kən-, (US) ˈkɑːn.fæb -s -z
confabu|late kənˈfæb.jʊ|.leɪt, kɒn-, (US) kənˈfæb.jə- -lates -leɪts -lating -leɪ.tɪŋ, (US) -leɪ.t̬ɪŋ -lated -leɪ.tɪd, (US) -leɪ.t̬ɪd
confabulation kənˌfæb.jʊˈleɪ.ʃən, kɒn-, (US) kənˌfæb.jəˈ- -s -z
confect n ˈkɒn.fekt, (US) ˈkɑːn- -s -s
confect v kənˈfekt -s -s -ing -ɪŋ -ed -ɪd
confection kənˈfek.ʃən -s -z -ing -ɪŋ -ed -d -er/s -əʳ/z, (US) -ə/z
confectionery kənˈfek.ʃən.ər.i, -ʃən.ri, (US) -er-
confederac|y, C~ kənˈfed.ər.ə.s|i -ies -iz
confederate, C~ n, adj kənˈfed.ər.ət, -ɪt -s -s
confede|rate v kənˈfed.ə|.reɪt -rates -reɪts -rating -reɪ.tɪŋ, (US) -reɪ.t̬ɪŋ -rated -reɪ.tɪd, (US) -reɪ.t̬ɪd
confederation kənˌfed.əˈreɪ.ʃən -s -z
confer kənˈfɜːʳ, (US) -ˈfɝː -s -z -ring -ɪŋ -red -d -rable -ə.bəl -ment -mənt
conferenc|e ˈkɒn.fər.ənts, (US) ˈkɑːn.fə- -es -ɪz -ing -ɪŋ
conferral kənˈfɜː.rəl, (US) -ˈfɝː.əl -s -z
confess kənˈfes -es -ɪz -ing -ɪŋ -ed -t -edly -ɪd.li
Confessio Amantis kɒnˌfes.i.əʊ.əˈmæn.tɪs, kən-, (US) kɑːnˌfes.i.oʊ.əˈmɑːn-
confession kənˈfeʃ.ən -s -z
confessional kənˈfeʃ.ən.əl, ˈ-nəl -s -z
confessor kənˈfes.əʳ, kɒn-, (US) kənˈfes.ə -s -z

> Note: In British English, some Catholics used to use the pronunciation /kɒnˈfes.ɔːʳ/ for the sense of 'Father Confessor'.

confetti kənˈfet.i, kɒn-, (US) kənˈfet̬-
confidant(e) ˈkɒn.fɪ.dænt, -fə-, -dənt; ˌkɒn.fɪˈdænt, -ˈdɑːnt, (US) ˈkɑːn.fə.dænt, -dɑːnt, ˌ--ˈ- -s -s
confid|e kənˈfaɪd -es -z -ing/ly -ɪŋ/li -ed -ɪd -er/s -əʳ/z, (US) -ə/z
confidenc|e ˈkɒn.fɪ.dənts, -fə-, (US) ˈkɑːn.fə- -es -ɪz
confident ˈkɒn.fɪ.dənt, -fə-, (US) ˈkɑːn.fə- -ly -li
confidential ˌkɒn.fɪˈden.tʃəl, (US) ˌkɑːn.fəˈdent.ʃəl -ly -i
confidentiality ˌkɒn.fɪ.den.tʃiˈæl.ə.ti, -fə-, -ɪ.ti, (US) ˌkɑːn.fə.dent.ʃiˈæl.ə.t̬i
configuration kənˌfɪg.əˈreɪ.ʃən, ˌkɒn.fɪg-, -jəˈ-, (US) kənˌfɪg.jəˈ- -s -z
config|ure kənˈfɪg|.əʳ, -j|əʳ, (US) -j|ə -ures -əz, (US) -əz -uring -ər.ɪŋ -ured -əd, (US) -əd
confine n ˈkɒn.faɪn, (US) ˈkɑːn- -s -z
confin|e v kənˈfaɪn -es -z -ing -ɪŋ -ed -d
confinement kənˈfaɪn.mənt -s -s
confirm kənˈfɜːm, (US) -ˈfɝːm -s -z -ing -ɪŋ -ed -d -er/s -əʳ/z, (US) -ə/z
confirmation ˌkɒn.fəˈmeɪ.ʃən, (US) ˌkɑːn.fəˈ- -s -z
confirma|tive kənˈfɜː.mə|.tɪv, (US) -ˈfɝː.mə|.t̬ɪv -tory -tər.i, -tri, (US) -tɔːr.i
confi|scate ˈkɒn.fɪ|.skeɪt, -fə-, (US) ˈkɑːn.fə-, -fɪ- -scates -skeɪts -scating -skeɪ.tɪŋ, (US) -skeɪ.t̬ɪŋ -scated -skeɪ.tɪd, (US) -skeɪ.t̬ɪd -scator/s -skeɪ.təʳ/z, (US) -skeɪ.t̬ə/z
confiscation ˌkɒn.fɪˈskeɪ.ʃən, -fəˈ-, (US) ˌkɑːn.fəˈ-, -fɪ- -s -z
confiscatory kənˈfɪs.kə.tər.i, kɒn-, -tri; ˌkɒn.fɪˈskeɪ-, -fəˈ-, ˈkɒn.fɪ.skeɪ-, -fə-, (US) kənˈfɪs.kə.tɔːr.i
confit kɒnˈfiː, (US) koʊn-, kɔ̃ːn- -s -z
confiteor, C~ kɒnˈfɪt.i.ɔːʳ, kən-, ˈ-eɪ-, (US) kənˈfɪt̬.i.ɔːr, -ˈfiː.t̬i- -s -z
confiture ˈkɒn.fɪ.tjʊəʳ, -tjɔːʳ, (US) ˈkɑːn.fə.tʃʊr, -tjʊr -s -z
conflagration ˌkɒn.fləˈgreɪ.ʃən, (US) ˌkɑːn- -s -z
con|flate kən|ˈfleɪt, kɒn-, (US) kən- -flates -ˈfleɪts -flating -ˈfleɪ.tɪŋ, (US) -ˈfleɪ.t̬ɪŋ -flated -ˈfleɪ.tɪd, (US) -ˈfleɪ.t̬ɪd
conflation kənˈfleɪ.ʃən, kɒn-, (US) kən-
conflict n ˈkɒn.flɪkt, (US) ˈkɑːn- -s -s
conflict v kənˈflɪkt -s -s -ing -ɪŋ -ed -ɪd
confluenc|e ˈkɒn.flu.ənts, (US) ˈkɑːn- -es -ɪz
confluent ˈkɒn.flu.ənt, (US) ˈkɑːn- -s -s -ly -li
conform kənˈfɔːm, (US) -ˈfɔːrm -s -z -ing -ɪŋ -ed -d -er/s -əʳ/z, (US) -ə/z
conformability kənˌfɔː.məˈbɪl.ə.ti, -ɪ.ti, (US) -ˌfɔːr.məˈbɪl.ə.t̬i
conformab|le kənˈfɔː.mə.b|əl, (US) -ˈfɔːr- -ly -li
conformation ˌkɒn.fɔːˈmeɪ.ʃən, -fəˈ-, (US) ˌkɑːn.fəˈ-, -fɔːrˈ- -s -z
conformist kənˈfɔː.mɪst, (US) -ˈfɔːr- -s -s
conformit|y kənˈfɔː.mə.t|i, -ɪ.t|i, (US) -ˈfɔːr.mə.t̬|i -ies -iz
confound kənˈfaʊnd, kɒn-, (US) kən-, ˌkɑːn- -s -z -ing -ɪŋ -ed/ly -ɪd/li
confraternit|y ˌkɒn.frəˈtɜː.nə.t|i, -nɪ-, (US) ˌkɑːn.frəˈtɝː.nə.t̬|i -ies -iz
confrère ˈkɒn.freəʳ, (US) kɑːnˈfrer -s -z
con|front kən|ˈfrʌnt -fronts -ˈfrʌnts -fronting -ˈfrʌn.tɪŋ, (US) -ˈfrʌn.t̬ɪŋ -fronted -ˈfrʌn.tɪd, (US) -ˈfrʌn.t̬ɪd
confrontation ˌkɒn.frʌnˈteɪ.ʃən, -frənˈ-, (US) ˌkɑːn.frənˈ- -s -z
confrontational ˌkɒn.frʌnˈteɪ.ʃən.əl, -frənˈ-, -ˈteɪʃ.nəl, (US) ˌkɑːn.frənˈ- -ly -i
Confucian kənˈfjuː.ʃən -s -z
Confucian|ism kənˈfjuː.ʃən|ɪ.zəm -ist/s -ɪst/s
confus|e kənˈfjuːz -es -ɪz -ing/ly -ɪŋ/li -ed -d -edly -ɪd.li, -d.li -edness -ɪd.nəs, -d.nəs, -nɪs
confusing kənˈfjuː.zɪŋ -ly -li
confusion kənˈfjuː.ʒən -s -z
confutable kənˈfjuː.tə.bəl, (US) -t̬ə-
confutation ˌkɒn.fjʊˈteɪ.ʃən, (US) ˌkɑːn.fjuːˈ- -s -z
con|fute kən|ˈfjuːt -futes -ˈfjuːts -futing -ˈfjuː.tɪŋ, (US) -ˈfjuː.t̬ɪŋ -futed -ˈfjuː.tɪd, (US) -ˈfjuː.t̬ɪd
conga ˈkɒŋ.gə, (US) ˈkɑːŋ-, ˈkɔːŋ- -s -z
congé ˈkɔ̃ːn.ʒeɪ, ˈkɔːn-, ˈkɒn-, (US) koʊnˈʒeɪ, kɑːn-, ˈ-- -s -z
congeal kənˈdʒiːl -s -z -ing -ɪŋ -ed -d -able -ə.bəl
congee ˈkɒn.dʒiː, (US) ˈkɑːn- -s -z
congelation ˌkɒn.dʒɪˈleɪ.ʃən, -dʒəˈ-, (US) ˌkɑːn.dʒəˈ-
congener kənˈdʒiː.nəʳ; ˈkɒn.dʒɪ-, -dʒə-, (US) ˈkɑːn.dʒən.ə; (US) kənˈdʒiː.nə -s -z
congenial kənˈdʒiː.ni.əl, (US) ˈ-njəl, ˈ-ni.əl -ly -i
congeniality kənˌdʒiː.niˈæl.ə.ti, -ɪ.ti, (US) -ə.t̬i
congenital kənˈdʒen.ɪ.təl, (US) -ə.t̬əl -ly -i
conger ˈkɒŋ.gəʳ, (US) ˈkɑːŋ.gə, ˈkɔːŋ- -s -z **ˌconger ˈeel; ˈconger ˌeel**
congeries kənˈdʒɪə.ri.iːz, -riz, (US) ˈkɑːn.dʒə.riːz
congest kənˈdʒest -s -s -ing -ɪŋ -ed -ɪd -ive -ɪv
congestion kənˈdʒes.tʃən, -ˈdʒeʃ- -s -z
Congleton ˈkɒŋ.gəl.tən, (US) ˈkɑːŋ-, ˈkɔːŋ-
conglo|bate ˈkɒŋ.gləʊ|.beɪt, ˈkɒn-, (US) kənˈgloʊ|.beɪt; (US) ˈkɑːŋ.gloʊ-, ˈkɔːŋ- -bates -beɪts -bating -beɪ.tɪŋ, (US) -beɪ.t̬ɪŋ -bated -beɪ.tɪd, (US) -beɪ.t̬ɪd
conglobation ˌkɒn.gləʊˈbeɪ.ʃən, ˌkɒŋ-, (US) ˌkɑːn.gloʊˈ-, kɑːŋ-, ˌkɔːŋ-
conglomerate n, adj kənˈglɒm.ər.ət, kəŋ-, kɒn-, -eɪt, -ɪt, (US) kənˈglɑː.mə- -s -s
conglomer|ate v kənˈglɒm.ər|.eɪt, kəŋ-, kɒn-, (US) kənˈglɑː.mə.r|eɪt -ates -eɪts -ating -eɪ.tɪŋ, (US) -eɪ.t̬ɪŋ -ated -eɪ.tɪd, (US) -eɪ.t̬ɪd
conglomeration kənˌglɒm.əˈreɪ.ʃən, kəŋ-, kɒn-, ˌkɒn.glɒm-, ˌkɒŋ.glɒm-, (US) kənˌglɑː.məˈ- -s -z

Congo ˈkɒŋ.ɡəʊ, (US) ˈkɑːŋ.ɡoʊ, ˈkɔːŋ-

Congolese ˌkɒŋ.ɡəʊˈliːz, (US) ˌkɑːŋ.ɡəˈ-, ˌ-ɡoʊ-, ˌkɔːŋ-, -ˈliːs

congratu|late kənˈɡrætʃ.ə|.leɪt, kəŋ-, -ˈɡræt.jʊ-, -jə-, (US) -ˈɡrætʃ.ə-, -ˈɡrædʒ-, ˈ-ʊ- **-lates** -leɪts **-lating** -leɪ.tɪŋ, (US) -leɪ.t̬ɪŋ **-lated** -leɪ.tɪd, (US) -leɪ.t̬ɪd **-lator/s** -leɪ.təʳ/z, (US) -leɪ.t̬ɚ/z

congratulation kənˌɡrætʃ.əˈleɪ.ʃən, kəŋ-, -ˌɡræt.jʊˈ-, -jəˈ-, (US) -ˌɡrætʃ.əˈ-, -ˌɡrædʒ-, -ʊˈ- **-s** -z

congratulatory kənˌɡrætʃ.əˈleɪ.tər.i, kəŋ-, -ˌɡræt.jʊˈ-, -jəˈ-, -tri; kənˈɡrætʃ.əl.ə-, (US) kənˈɡrætʃ.əl.ə.tɔːr.i, -ˈɡrædʒ-

congre|gate ˈkɒŋ.ɡrɪ|.ɡeɪt, -ɡrə-, (US) ˈkɑːŋ-, ˈkɔːŋ- **-gates** -ɡeɪts **-gating** -ɡeɪ.tɪŋ, (US) -ɡeɪ.t̬ɪŋ **-gated** -ɡeɪ.tɪd, (US) -ɡeɪ.t̬ɪd

congregation ˌkɒŋ.ɡrɪˈɡeɪ.ʃən, -ɡrəˈ-, (US) ˌkɑːŋ-, ˌkɔːŋ- **-s** -z

congregational, C~ ˌkɒŋ.ɡrɪˈɡeɪ.ʃən.əl, -ɡrəˈ-, -ˈɡeɪʃ.nəl, (US) ˌkɑːŋ-, ˌkɔːŋ- **-ism** -ɪ.zəm **-ist/s** -ɪst/s

Congresbury ˈkɒŋz.bri, ˈkuːmz.bər.i, (US) ˈkɑːŋz.ber.i, ˈkɔːŋz-, ˈkuːmz-, -bɚ-

congress, C~ ˈkɒŋ.ɡres, (US) ˈkɑːŋ-, ˈkɔːŋ-, -ɡrəs **-es** -ɪz

congressional, C~ kənˈɡreʃ.ən.əl, kəŋ-, kɒŋ-, ˈ-nəl, (US) kəŋ-

congress|man ˈkɒŋ.ɡres|.mən, (US) ˈkɑːŋ-, ˈkɔːŋ-, -ɡrəs- **-men** -mən, -men

congress|woman ˈkɒŋ.ɡres|ˌwʊm.ən, (US) ˈkɑːŋ-, ˈkɔːŋ-, -ɡrəs- **-women** -ˌwɪm.ɪn

Congreve ˈkɒŋ.ɡriːv, (US) ˈkɑːn-, ˈkɑːŋ-

congruenc|e ˈkɒŋ.ɡru.ənts, (US) ˈkɑːŋ-, ˈkɔːŋ-, kənˈɡruː- **-es** -ɪz **-y** -i **-ies** -iz

congruent ˈkɒŋ.ɡru.ənt, (US) ˈkɑːŋ-; (US) kənˈɡruː- **-ly** -li

congruit|y kɒŋˈɡruː.ə.t|i, kən-, kəŋ-, -ɪ.t|i, (US) kɑːnˈɡruː.ə.t̬|i, kən- **-ies** -iz

congruous ˈkɒŋ.ɡru.əs, (US) ˈkɑːŋ-, ˈkɔːŋ- **-ly** -li **-ness** -nəs, -nɪs

conic ˈkɒn.ɪk, (US) ˈkɑː.nɪk **-s** -s

conical ˈkɒn.ɪ.kəl, (US) ˈkɑː.nɪ- **-ly** -i **-ness** -nəs, -nɪs

conifer ˈkɒn.ɪ.fəʳ, ˈkəʊ.nɪ-, -nə-, (US) ˈkɑː.nə.fɚ, ˈkoʊ- **-s** -z

coniferous kəʊˈnɪf.ər.əs, kɒnˈɪf-, (US) koʊˈnɪf-, kə-

coniform ˈkəʊ.nɪ.fɔːm, (US) ˈkoʊ.nɪ.fɔːrm

Coningham ˈkʌn.ɪŋ.əm, (US) -hæm

Coningsby ˈkɒn.ɪŋz.bi, ˈkʌn-, (US) ˈkʌn-

Conisbrough ˈkɒn.ɪs.brə, ˈkʌn-, (US) ˈkɑː.nɪs.bɚ.oʊ

Coniston ˈkɒn.ɪ.stən, (US) ˈkɑː.nɪ-

conjecturable kənˈdʒek.tʃər.ə.bəl

conjectural kənˈdʒek.tʃər.əl **-ly** -i

conject|ure kənˈdʒek.tʃ|əʳ, (US) -tʃ|ɚ **-ures** -əz, (US) -ɚz **-uring** -ər.ɪŋ **-ured** -əd, (US) -ɚd

conjoin kənˈdʒɔɪn, kɒn-, (US) kən- **-s** -z **-ing** -ɪŋ **-ed** -d

conjoint kənˈdʒɔɪnt, kɒn-, (US) kən- **-ly** -li

conjugal ˈkɒn.dʒʊ.ɡəl, -dʒə-, (US) ˈkɑːn.dʒə- **-ly** -i ˌ**conjugal** ˈ**rights**

conjugality ˌkɒn.dʒʊˈɡæl.ə.ti, -ɪ.ti, (US) ˌkɑːn.dʒəˈɡæl.ə.t̬i

conjugate n, adj ˈkɒn.dʒʊ.ɡət, -dʒə-, -ɡɪt, -ɡeɪt, (US) ˈkɑːn.dʒə- **-s** -s

conju|gate v ˈkɒn.dʒʊ|.ɡeɪt, -dʒə-, (US) ˈkɑːn.dʒə- **-gates** -ɡeɪts **-gating** -ɡeɪ.tɪŋ, (US) -ɡeɪ.t̬ɪŋ **-gated** -ɡeɪ.tɪd, (US) -ɡeɪ.t̬ɪd

conjugation ˌkɒn.dʒʊˈɡeɪ.ʃən, -dʒəˈ-, (US) ˌkɑːn.dʒəˈ- **-s** -z

conjunct n ˈkɒn.dʒʌŋkt, (US) ˈkɑːn- **-s** -s

conjunct adj kənˈdʒʌŋkt, kɒn-, (US) kən-; (US) ˈkɑːn.dʒʌŋkt **-ly** -li

conjunction kənˈdʒʌŋk.ʃən **-s** -z

conjunctiva ˌkɒn.dʒʌŋkˈtaɪ.və, (US) ˌkɑːn.dʒəŋkˈ-

conjunctive kənˈdʒʌŋk.tɪv **-ly** -li

conjunctivitis kənˌdʒʌŋk.tɪˈvaɪ.tɪs, -təˈ-, -təs, (US) -təˈvaɪ.t̬ɪs, -t̬əs

conjuncture kənˈdʒʌŋk.tʃəʳ, (US) -tʃɚ **-s** -z

conjuration ˌkɒn.dʒʊəˈreɪ.ʃən, (US) ˌkɑːn.dʒʊˈreɪ- **-s** -z

conjur|e *charge solemnly:* kənˈdʒʊəʳ, (US) -ˈdʒʊr **-es** -z **-ing** -ɪŋ **-ed** -d *summon by magic:* ˈkʌn.dʒ|əʳ, (US) -dʒ|ɚ **-ures** -əz, (US) -ɚz **-uring** -ər.ɪŋ **-ured** -əd, (US) -ɚd **-urer/s** -ər.əʳ/z, (US) -ɚ.ɚ/z **-uror/s** -ər.əʳ/z, (US) -ɚ.ɚ/z ˈ**conjuring** ˌ**trick**

conk kɒŋk, (US) kɑːŋk, kɔːŋk **-s** -s **-ing** -ɪŋ **-ed** -t

conker ˈkɒŋ.kəʳ, (US) ˈkɑːŋ.kɚ, ˈkɔːŋ- **-s** -z

Conleth ˈkɒn.ləθ, (US) ˈkɑːn-

Conley ˈkɒn.li, (US) ˈkɑːn-

Conlon ˈkɒn.lən, (US) ˈkɑːn-

con|man ˈkɒn|.mæn, (US) ˈkɑːn- **-men** -men

Conn. (abbrev. for **Connaught**) ˈkɒn.ɔːt, (US) ˈkɑː.nɑːt, -nɔːt

Conn. (abbrev. for **Connecticut**) kəˈnet.ɪ.kət, (US) -ˈnet̬-, -kɪt

Connah's Quay ˌkɒn.əzˈkiː, (US) ˌkɑː.nəzˈkiː, -ˈkeɪ, -ˈkweɪ

Connally ˈkɒn.əl.i, (US) ˈkɑː.nəl-

connate ˈkɒn.eɪt, -ˈ-, (US) ˈkɑː.neɪt, -ˈ-

Connaught ˈkɒn.ɔːt, (US) ˈkɑː.nɑːt, -nɔːt

connect kəˈnekt **-s** -s **-ing** -ɪŋ **-ed/ly** -ɪd/li **-able** -ə.bəl **-or/s** -əʳ/z, (US) -ɚ/z

connectible kəˈnek.tə.bəl, -tɪ-

Connecticut kəˈnet.ɪ.kət, (US) -ˈnet̬-, -kɪt

connection kəˈnek.ʃən **-s** -z

connective kəˈnek.tɪv **-s** -z **-ly** -li

connectivity ˌkɒn.ekˈtɪv.ɪ.ti; kəˌnekˈ-, ˈ-ə-, (US) ˌkɑː.nekˈtɪv.ə.t̬i

Connelly ˈkɒn.əl.i, (US) ˈkɑː.nəl-

Connemara ˌkɒn.ɪˈmɑː.rə, -əˈ-, (US) ˌkɑː.nəˈ-

Conner ˈkɒn.əʳ, (US) ˈkɑː.nɚ

Connery ˈkɒn.ər.i, (US) ˈkɑː.nɚ-

Connex® ˈkɒn.eks, (US) ˈkɑː.neks

connexion kəˈnek.ʃən **-s** -z

Connie ˈkɒn.i, (US) ˈkɑː.ni

conning tower ˈkɒn.ɪŋˌtaʊ.əʳ, -taʊəʳ, (US) ˈkɑː.nɪŋˌtaʊ.ɚ **-s** -z

conniption kəˈnɪp.ʃən

connivance kəˈnaɪ.vənts

conniv|e kəˈnaɪv **-es** -z **-ing** -ɪŋ **-ed** -d **-er/s** -əʳ/z, (US) -ɚ/z

connoisseur ˌkɒn.əˈsɜːʳ, -ɪˈ-, (US) ˌkɑː.nəˈsɝː **-s** -z

Connolly ˈkɒn.əl.i, (US) ˈkɑː.nəl-

Connor ˈkɒn.əʳ, (US) ˈkɑː.nɚ

conno|tate ˈkɒn.əʊ|.teɪt, (US) ˈkɑː.nə- **-tates** -teɪts **-tating** -teɪ.tɪŋ, (US) -teɪ.t̬ɪŋ **-tated** -teɪ.tɪd, (US) -teɪ.t̬ɪd

connotation ˌkɒn.əʊˈteɪ.ʃən, (US) ˌkɑː.nəˈ- **-s** -z

connotative ˈkɒn.əʊ.teɪ.tɪv; kəˈnəʊ.tə-, (US) kəˈnoʊ.t̬ə.t̬ɪv, ˈkɑː.nə.teɪ-

connot|e kəˈnəʊt, kɒnˈəʊt, (US) kəˈnoʊt **-es** -s **-ing** -ɪŋ, (US) kəˈnoʊ.t̬ɪŋ **-ed** -ɪd, (US) kəˈnoʊ.t̬ɪd

connubial kəˈnjuː.bi.əl, kɒnˈjuː-, (US) kəˈnuː-, -ˈnjuː- **-ly** -i

connubiality kəˌnjuː.biˈæl.ə.ti, kɒnˌjuː-, -ɪ.ti, (US) kəˌnuː.biˈæl.ə.t̬i, -ˌnjuː-

conoid ˈkəʊ.nɔɪd, (US) ˈkoʊ- **-s** -z

conoidal kəʊˈnɔɪ.dəl, (US) koʊ-

Conolly ˈkɒn.əl.i, (US) ˈkɑː.nəl-

Conor ˈkɒn.əʳ, (US) ˈkɑː.nɚ

conqu|er ˈkɒŋ.k|əʳ, (US) ˈkɑːŋ.k|ɚ, ˈkɔːŋ- **-ers** -əz, (US) -ɚz **-ering** -ər.ɪŋ **-ered** -əd, (US) -ɚd **-erable** -ər.ə.bəl

conqueror ˈkɒŋ.kər.əʳ, (US) ˈkɑːŋ.kɚ.ɚ, ˈkɔːŋ- **-s** -z

conquest, C~ ˈkɒŋ.kwest, (US) ˈkɑːn-, ˈkɑːŋ- **-s** -s

conquistador kɒnˈkɪs.tə.dɔːʳ, kɒŋ-, -ˈkwɪs-; ˌkɒn.kɪ.stəˈdɔːʳ, kɒŋ-, -kwɪ-, (US) kɑːŋˈkiː.stə.dɔːr, kɔːŋ-, kɑːn-, -ˈkwɪs.tə- **-s** -z

Conrad ˈkɒn.ræd, (US) ˈkɑːn-

Conran ˈkɒn.rən, -ræn, (US) ˈkɑːn-

Conroy ˈkɒn.rɔɪ, (US) ˈkɑːn-

consanguine kɒnˈsæŋ.ɡwɪn, (US) kɑːn-

consanguineous ˌkɒn.sæŋˈɡwɪn.i.əs, (US) ˌkɑːn.sæŋˈ-

consanguinity ˌkɒn.sæŋˈɡwɪn.ə.ti, -ɪ.ti, (US) ˌkɑːn.sæŋˈɡwɪn.ə.t̬i

conscienc|e ˈkɒn.tʃənts, (US) ˈkɑːn- **-es** -ɪz ˈ**conscience-**ˌ**stricken**

conscientious ˌkɒn.tʃiˈen.tʃəs, (US) ˌkɑːn.tʃiˈent.ʃəs **-ly** -li **-ness** -nəs, -nɪs **consci**ˌ**entious ob**ˈ**jector**

conscionab|le ˈkɒn.tʃən.ə.b|əl, (US) ˈkɑːn- **-ly** -li **-leness** -əl.nəs, -nɪs

conscious ˈkɒn.tʃəs, (US) ˈkɑːnt.ʃəs **-ly** -li **-ness** -nəs, -nɪs ˈ**consciousness** ˌ**raising**

conscrib|e kənˈskraɪb **-es** -z **-ing** -ɪŋ **-ed** -d

conscript n ˈkɒn.skrɪpt, (US) ˈkɑːn- **-s** -s

conscript v kənˈskrɪpt **-s** -s **-ing** -ɪŋ **-ed** -ɪd

conscription kənˈskrɪp.ʃən **-s** -z

conse|crate ˈkɒnt.sɪ|.kreɪt, -sə-, (US) ˈkɑːnt.sə- **-crates** -kreɪts **-crating** -kreɪ.tɪŋ, (US) -kreɪ.t̬ɪŋ **-crated** -kreɪ.tɪd, (US) -kreɪ.t̬ɪd **-crator/s** -kreɪ.təʳ/z, (US) -kreɪ.t̬ɚ/z

consecration ˌkɒnt.sɪˈkreɪ.ʃən, -səˈ-, (US) ˌkɑːnt.səˈ- **-s** -z

consecutive kənˈsek.jʊ.tɪv, -jə-, (US) -jə.t̬ɪv **-ly** -li **-ness** -nəs, -nɪs

consensual kənˈsent.sju.əl, kɒn-, -ˈsen.tʃu-, (US) kənˈsent.ʃu-, ˈ-ʃəl **-ly** -li

consensus kənˈsent.səs, kɒn-, (US) kən-

con|sent kən|ˈsent **-sents** -ˈsents **-senting** -ˈsen.tɪŋ, (US) -ˈsen.t̬ɪŋ **-sented** -ˈsen.tɪd, (US) -ˈsen.t̬ɪd

consequenc|e ˈkɒnt.sɪ.kwənts, -sə-, (US) ˈkɑːnt- **-es** -ɪz

consequent ˈkɒnt.sɪ.kwənt, -sə-, (US) ˈkɑːnt- **-ly** -li

consequential ˌkɒnt.sɪˈkwen.tʃəl, -səˈ-, (US) ˌkɑːnt- **-ly** -i

conservable kənˈsɜː.və.bəl, (US) -ˈsɝː-

conservanc|y kənˈsɜː.vənt.s|i, (US) -ˈsɝː- **-ies** -iz

conservation ˌkɒnt.səˈveɪ.ʃən, (US) ˌkɑːnt.sɚˈ-

conservationist ˌkɒnt.səˈveɪ.ʃən.ɪst, (US) ˌkɑːnt.sɚˈ- **-s** -s

conservatism kənˈsɜː.və.tɪ.zəm, (US) -ˈsɝː-

conservative, C~ kənˈsɜː.və.tɪv, (US) -ˈsɝː.və.t̬ɪv **-s** -z **-ly** -li **-ness** -nəs, -nɪs

conservatoire kənˈsɜː.və.twɑːʳ, kɒn-, (US) kənˈsɝː.və.twɑːr, -ˌsɝː.vəˈtwɑːr **-s** -z

conservator *preserver:* ˈkɒnt.sə.veɪ.təʳ, (US) ˈkɑːnt.sɚ.veɪ.t̬ɚ *official guardian:* kənˈsɜː.və.təʳ, (US) -ˈsɝː.və.t̬ɚ **-s** -z

conservator|y kənˈsɜː.və.tr|i, (US) -ˈsɝː.və.tɔːr|.i **-ies** -iz

conserve n kənˈsɜːv; ˈkɒn.sɜːv, (US) ˈkɑːn.sɝːv **-s** -z

conserv|e v kənˈsɜːv, (US) -ˈsɝːv **-es** -z **-ing** -ɪŋ **-ed** -d

Consett ˈkɒn.sɪt, -set, -sət, (US) ˈkɑːn-

consid|er kənˈsɪd|.əʳ, (US) -ɚ **-ers** -əz, (US) -ɚz **-ering** -ər.ɪŋ **-ered** -əd, (US) -ɚd

considerab|le kənˈsɪd.ər.ə.b|əl **-ly** -li **-leness** -əl.nəs, -nɪs

considerate kənˈsɪd.ər.ət, -ɪt **-ly** -li **-ness** -nəs, -nɪs

consideration kənˌsɪd.əˈreɪ.ʃən **-s** -z

consign kənˈsaɪn **-s** -z **-ing** -ɪŋ **-ed** -d **-er/s** -əʳ/z, (US) -ɚ/z **-able** -ə.bəl

consignation ˌkɒn.saɪˈneɪ.ʃən, (US) ˌkɑːn.sɪgˈ-, -sɪˈ-

consignee ˌkɒn.saɪˈniː, -sɪˈ-, (US) ˌkɑːn- **-s** -z

Consignia® kənˈsɪg.ni.ə

consignment kənˈsaɪn.mənt, -ˈsaɪm-, (US) -ˈsaɪn- **-s** -s

consist kənˈsɪst **-s** -s **-ing** -ɪŋ **-ed** -ɪd

consisten|ce kənˈsɪs.tənt|s **-cy** -si **-cies** -siz

consistent kənˈsɪs.tənt **-ly** -li

consistorial ˌkɒn.sɪˈstɔː.ri.əl, (US) ˌkɑːn.sɪˈstɔːr.i-

consistor|y kənˈsɪs.tər|.i, -tr|i, (US) -tɚ|.i **-ies** -iz

consolable kənˈsəʊ.lə.bəl, (US) -ˈsoʊ-

consolation ˌkɒn.səˈleɪ.ʃən, (US) ˌkɑːn- **-s** -z ˌ**consoˈlation** ˌ**prize**

consolatory kənˈsɒl.ə.tər.i, -ˈsəʊ.lə-, -tri, (US) -ˈsɑː.lə.tɔːr.i, -ˈsoʊ-

console n ˈkɒn.səʊl, (US) ˈkɑːn.soʊl **-s** -z

consol|e v kənˈsəʊl, (US) -ˈsoʊl **-es** -z **-ing** -ɪŋ **-ed** -d **-er/s** -əʳ/z, (US) -ɚ/z

consoli|date kənˈsɒl.ɪ|.deɪt, ˈ-ə-, (US) -ˈsɑː.lə- **-dates** -deɪts **-dating** -deɪ.tɪŋ, (US) -deɪ.t̬ɪŋ **-dated** -deɪ.tɪd, (US) -deɪ.t̬ɪd **-dator/s** -deɪ.təʳ/z, (US) -deɪ.t̬ɚ/z **-dative** -deɪ.tɪv, (US) -deɪ.t̬ɪv

consolidation kənˌsɒl.ɪˈdeɪ.ʃən, -əˈ-, (US) -ˌsɑː.ləˈ- **-s** -z

consols kənˈsɒlz; ˈkɒnt.səlz, (US) ˈkɑːn.sɑːlz; (US) kənˈsɑːlz

consommé kənˈsɒm.eɪ, kɒn-; ˈkɒnt.sə.meɪ, (US) ˌkɑːnt.səˈmeɪ, ˈ---

consonanc|e ˈkɒnt.sən.ənts, (US) ˈkɑːnt- **-es** -ɪz

consonant ˈkɒnt.sən.ənt, (US) ˈkɑːnt- **-s** -s **-ly** -li

consonantal ˌkɒnt.sənˈæn.təl, (US) ˌkɑːnt.səˈnæn.t̬əl **-ly** -i

consort n ˈkɒn.sɔːt, (US) ˈkɑːn.sɔːrt **-s** -s

con|sort v kən|ˈsɔːt, kɒn-, (US) kən|ˈsɔːrt **-sorts** -ˈsɔːts, (US) -ˈsɔːrts **-sorting** -ˈsɔː.tɪŋ, (US) -ˈsɔːr.t̬ɪŋ **-sorted** -ˈsɔː.tɪd, (US) -ˈsɔːr.t̬ɪd

consorti|um kənˈsɔː.ti|.əm, -ʃi-, ˈ-ʃ|əm, (US) -ˈsɔːr.t̬i|.əm, -ʃi-, ˈ-ʃ|əm **-ums** -əmz **-a** -ə

conspectus kənˈspek.təs **-es** -ɪz

conspicuous kənˈspɪk.ju.əs **-ly** -li **-ness** -nəs, -nɪs

conspirac|y kənˈspɪr.ə.s|i **-ies** -iz **conˈspiracy** ˌ**theory**

conspirator kənˈspɪr.ə.təʳ, -ɪ.təʳ, (US) -ə.t̬ɚ **-s** -z

conspiratorial kənˌspɪr.əˈtɔː.ri.əl, kɒn-, (US) kənˌspɪr.əˈtɔːr.i-

conspir|e kənˈspaɪ.əʳ, -ˈspaɪəʳ, (US) -ˈspaɪ.ɚ **-es** -z **-ing** -ɪŋ **-ed** -d **-er/s** -əʳ/z, (US) -ɚ/z

constable, C~ ˈkʌnt.stə.bəl, (US) ˈkɑːnt-, ˈkʌnt- **-s** -z

> Note: The pronunciation /ˈkɒnt-/ is increasingly widespread in British English, but cannot yet be recommended as representative of the accent being described here.

constabular|y kənˈstæb.jə.lər|.i, -jʊ-, (US) -jə.ler|.i **-ies** -iz

Constance ˈkɒnt.stənts, (US) ˈkɑːnt-

constancy ˈkɒnt.stənt.si, (US) ˈkɑːnt-

constant ˈkɒnt.stənt, (US) ˈkɑːnt- **-s** -s **-ly** -li **-ness** -nəs, -nɪs

Constanța kɒnˈstænt.sə

Constantine *Kings and Emperors:* ˈkɒnt.stən.taɪn, -tiːn, (US) ˈkɑːnt.stən.tiːn, -taɪn *city:* ˈkɒnt.stən.taɪn, -tiːn, (US) ˈkɑːnt-

Constantinople ˌkɒn.stæn.tɪˈnəʊ.pəl, (US) ˌkɑːn.stæn.tənˈoʊ-

constative kənˈstæt.ɪv, (US) -ˈstæt̬-

constellation ˌkɒnt.stəˈleɪ.ʃən, -stɪˈ-, (US) ˌkɑːnt- **-s** -z

conster|nate ˈkɒnt.stə|.neɪt, (US) ˈkɑːnt.stɚ- **-nates** -neɪts **-nating** -neɪ.tɪŋ, (US) -neɪ.t̬ɪŋ **-nated** -neɪ.tɪd, (US) -neɪ.t̬ɪd

consternation ˌkɒnt.stəˈneɪ.ʃən, (US) ˌkɑːnt.stɚˈ-

consti|pate ˈkɒnt.stɪ|.peɪt, -stə-, (US) ˈkɑːnt.stə- **-pates** -peɪts **-pating** -peɪ.tɪŋ, (US) -peɪ.t̬ɪŋ **-pated** -peɪ.tɪd, (US) -peɪ.t̬ɪd

constipation ˌkɒnt.stɪˈpeɪ.ʃən, -stəˈ-, (US) ˌkɑːnt.stəˈ-

constituen|cy kənˈstɪtʃ.u.ənt|.si, kɒn-, -ˈstɪt.ju-, (US) kənˈstɪtʃ.u- **-cies** -siz

constituent kənˈstɪtʃ.u.ənt, kɒn-, -ˈstɪt.ju-, (US) kənˈstɪtʃ.u- **-s** -s

consti|tute ˈkɒnt.stɪ|.tʃuːt, -stə-, -tjuːt, (US) ˈkɑːnt.stə|.tuːt, -tjuːt **-tutes** -tʃuːts, -tjuːts, (US) -tuːts, -tjuːts **-tuting** -tʃuː.tɪŋ, -tjuː.tɪŋ, (US) -tuː.t̬ɪŋ, -tjuː- **-tuted** -tʃuː.tɪd, -tjuː.tɪd, (US) -tuː.t̬ɪd, -tjuː-

constitution ˌkɒnt.stɪˈtʃuː.ʃən, -stəˈ-, -ˈtjuː-, (US) ˌkɑːnt.stəˈtuː-, -ˈtjuː- **-s** -z

constitutional ˌkɒnt.stɪˈtʃuː.ʃən.əl, -stəˈ-, -ˈtjuː-, -ˈtʃuːʃ.nəl, -ˈtjuːʃ-, (US) ˌkɑːnt.stəˈtuː-, -ˈtjuː-, -ˈtuːʃ.nəl, -ˈtjuːʃ- **-ly** -i

constitutional|ism ˌkɒnt.stɪˈtʃuː.ʃən.əl|.ɪ.zəm, -stəˈ-, -ˈtjuː-, (US) ˌkɑːnt.stəˈtuː-, -ˈtjuː- **-ist/s** -ɪst/s

constitutionality ˌkɒnt.stɪ.tʃuː.ʃənˈæl.ə.ti, -stə-, -tjuː-, ˈ-ɪ.ti, (US) ˌkɑːnt.stə.tuː.ʃənˈæl.ə.t̬i, -tjuː-

constitutionaliz|e, -is|e ˌkɒnt.stɪˈtʃuː.ʃən.əl.aɪz, -stəˈ-, -ˈtjuː-, (US) ˌkɑːnt.stəˈtuː.ʃən.ə.laɪz, -ˈtjuː- **-es** -ɪz **-ing** -ɪŋ **-ed** -d

constitutive kənˈstɪtʃ.ə.tɪv, kɒn-, -ˈstɪt.jʊ-, -ˈstɪt.jə-; ˈkɒnt.stɪ.tʃuː-,

-stə-, -tju:-, (US) ˈkɑ:nt.stə.tu:.t̬ɪv, -tju:-; (US) kənˈstɪtʃ.ə-
constrain kənˈstreɪn -s -z -ing -ɪŋ -ed -d -edly -ɪd.li, -d.li -able -ə.bəl
constraint kənˈstreɪnt -s -s
constrict kənˈstrɪkt -s -s -ing -ɪŋ -ed -ɪd -or/s -ər/z, (US) -ɚ/z -ive -ɪv
constriction kənˈstrɪk.ʃən -s -z
construct n ˈkɒn.strʌkt, (US) ˈkɑ:n- -s -s
construct v kənˈstrʌkt -s -s -ing -ɪŋ -ed -ɪd
construction kənˈstrʌk.ʃən -s -z
constructional kənˈstrʌk.ʃən.əl -ly -i
constructionist kənˈstrʌk.ʃən.ɪst -s -s
constructive kənˈstrʌk.tɪv -ly -li -ness -nəs, -nɪs
constructor kənˈstrʌk.tər, (US) -tɚ -s -z
constru|e kənˈstru:, kɒn-, (US) kən- -es -z -ing -ɪŋ -ed -d
consubstantial ˌkɒn.səbˈstæn.tʃəl, -ˈstɑ:n-, (US) ˌkɑ:n.səbˈstænt.ʃəl -ly -i
consubstanti|ate ˌkɒn.səbˈstæn.tʃi|.eɪt, -ˈstɑ:n-, -ˈstænt.si-, -ˈstɑ:nt.si-, (US) ˌkɑ:n.səbˈstænt.ʃi- -ates -eɪts -ating -eɪ.tɪŋ, (US) -eɪ.t̬ɪŋ -ated -eɪ.tɪd, (US) -eɪ.t̬ɪd
consubstantiation ˌkɒn.səbˌstæn.tʃiˈeɪ.ʃən, -ˌstɑ:n-, -ˌstænt.siˈ-, -ˌstɑ:nt.siˈ-, (US) ˌkɑ:n.səbˌstænt.ʃiˈ-
consuetude ˈkɒnt.swɪ.tʃu:d, -tju:d, (US) ˈkɑ:nt.swɪ.tu:d, -tju:d
consuetudinary ˌkɒnt.swɪˈtʃu:.dɪ.nər.i, -ˈtju:-, (US) ˌkɑ:nt.swɪˈtu:.dɪ.ner-, -ˈtju:-
consul ˈkɒnt.səl, (US) ˈkɑ:nt- -s -z -ship/s -ʃɪp/s
consular ˈkɒnt.sjʊ.lər, -sjə-, (US) ˈkɑ:nt-
consulate ˈkɒnt.sjʊ.lət, -sjə-, -lɪt, (US) ˈkɑ:nt- -s -s
con|sult kən|ˈsʌlt -sults -ˈsʌlts -sulting -ˈsʌl.tɪŋ, (US) -ˈsʌl.t̬ɪŋ -sulted -ˈsʌl.tɪd, (US) -ˈsʌl.t̬ɪd
consultanc|y kənˈsʌl.tənt.s|i -ies -iz
consultant kənˈsʌl.tənt -s -s
consultation ˌkɒn.səlˈteɪ.ʃən, -sʌlˈ-, (US) ˌkɑ:n- -s -z
consultative kənˈsʌl.tə.tɪv, (US) -tə.t̬ɪv; (US) ˈkɑ:nt.səl.teɪ-
consultatory kənˈsʌl.tə.tər.i, -tri; ˌkɒnt.səlˈteɪ-, (US) kənˈsʌl.tə.tɔ:r.i
consumable kənˈsju:.mə.bəl, -ˈsu:-, (US) -ˈsu:- -s -z
consum|e kənˈsju:m, -ˈsu:m, (US) -ˈsu:m -es -z -ing -ɪŋ -ed -d
consumer kənˈsju:.mər, -ˈsu:-, (US) -ˈsu:.mɚ -s -z **conˈsumer ˌgoods; conˈsumer soˌciety**
consumer|ism kənˈsju:.mə.r|ɪ.zəm, -ˈsu:-, (US) -ˈsu:.mɚ|.ɪ- -ist -ɪst
consummate adj kənˈsʌm.ət, -ɪt; ˈkɒnt.sə.mət, -sjʊ-, -mɪt, (US) ˈkɑ:nt.sə.mɪt; (US) kənˈsʌm.ɪt -ly -li
consum|mate v ˈkɒnt.sə|.meɪt, -sjʊ-, (US) ˈkɑ:nt.sə- -mates -meɪts -mating -meɪ.tɪŋ, (US) -meɪ.t̬ɪŋ -mated -meɪ.tɪd, (US) -meɪ.t̬ɪd -mator/s -meɪ.tər/z, (US) -meɪ.t̬ɚ/z
consummation ˌkɒnt.səˈmeɪ.ʃən, -sjʊˈ-, (US) ˌkɑ:nt.səˈ- -s -z
consummative ˈkɒnt.sə.meɪ.tɪv, -sʌm.eɪ-, -sjʊ.meɪ-; kənˈsʌm.ə-, (US) ˈkɑ:nt.sə.meɪ.t̬ɪv; (US) kənˈsʌm.ə-
consumption kənˈsʌmp.ʃən
consumptive kənˈsʌmp.tɪv -s -z -ly -li -ness -nəs, -nɪs
contact n, adj ˈkɒn.tækt, (US) ˈkɑ:n- -s -s **ˈcontact ˌlens**
contact v ˈkɒn.tækt; -ˈ-, kən-, (US) ˈkɑ:n.tækt -s -s -ing -ɪŋ -ed -ɪd
contactable kənˈtæk.tə.bəl; ˈkɒn.tæk-, (US) ˈkɑ:n.tækt-
contagion kənˈteɪ.dʒən -s -z
contagious kənˈteɪ.dʒəs -ly -li -ness -nəs, -nɪs
contain kənˈteɪn -s -z -ing -ɪŋ -ed -d -able -ə.bəl
container kənˈteɪ.nər, (US) -nɚ -s -z **conˈtainer ˌship**
containerization, -isa- kənˌteɪ.nər.aɪˈzeɪ.ʃən, -ɪˈ-, (US) -əˈ-
containeriz|e, -is|e kənˈteɪ.nər.aɪz, (US) -nə.raɪz -es -ɪz -ing -ɪŋ -ed -d
containment kənˈteɪn.mənt, -ˈteɪm-, (US) -ˈteɪn-
contaminant kənˈtæm.ɪ.nənt, ˈ-ə- -s -s
contami|nate kənˈtæm.ɪ|.neɪt, ˈ-ə- -nates -neɪts -nating -neɪ.tɪŋ, (US) -neɪ.t̬ɪŋ -nated -neɪ.tɪd, (US) -neɪ.t̬ɪd -nater/s -neɪ.tər/z, (US) -neɪ.t̬ɚ/z
contamination kənˌtæm.ɪˈneɪ.ʃən, -əˈ- -s -z
contaminative kənˈtæm.ɪ.nə.tɪv, ˈ-ə-, -neɪ-, (US) -t̬ɪv
contango kənˈtæŋ.gəʊ, kɒn-, (US) kənˈtæŋ.goʊ -s -z
contd (abbrev. for **continued**) kənˈtɪn.ju:d, -jud
contemn kənˈtem -s -z -ing -ɪŋ -ed -d -er/s -ər/z, -nər/z, (US) -ɚ/z, -nɚ/z
contem|plate ˈkɒn.təm|.pleɪt, -tem-, (US) ˈkɑ:n.t̬əm-, -tem- -plates -pleɪts -plating -pleɪ.tɪŋ, (US) -pleɪ.t̬ɪŋ -plated -pleɪ.tɪd, (US) -pleɪ.t̬ɪd -plator/s -pleɪ.tər/z, (US) -pleɪ.t̬ɚ/z
contemplation ˌkɒn.təmˈpleɪ.ʃən, -temˈ-, (US) ˌkɑ:n.t̬əmˈ-, -temˈ- -s -z
contemplative *pensive:* kənˈtem.plə.tɪv, ˈkɒn.tem.pleɪ.tɪv, -təm-, (US) kənˈtem.plə.t̬ɪv; (US) ˈkɑ:n.t̬əm.pleɪ- -ly -li -ness -nəs, -nɪs *of religious orders:* kənˈtem.plə.tɪv, (US) -t̬ɪv
contemporaneity kənˌtem.pər.əˈni:.ə.ti, kɒn-, -ˈneɪ-, -ɪ.ti; ˌkɒn.tem-, (US) kənˌtem.pɚ.əˈni:.ə.t̬i, -ˈneɪ-
contemporaneous kənˌtem.pərˈeɪ.ni.əs, kɒn-; ˌkɒn.tem-, (US) kən- -ly -li -ness -nəs, -nɪs
contemporar|y kənˈtem.pər.ər|.i, (US) -pə.rer- -ies -iz -ily -əl.i, -ɪ.li
contempt kənˈtempt
contemptibility kənˌtemp.təˈbɪl.ə.ti, -tɪˈ-, -ɪ.ti, (US) -təˈbɪl.ə.t̬i
contemptib|le kənˈtemp.tə.b|əl, -tɪ- -ly -li -leness -əl.nəs, -nɪs
contemptuous kənˈtemp.tʃu.əs, -tju- -ly -li -ness -nəs, -nɪs
contend kənˈtend -s -z -ing -ɪŋ -ed -ɪd -er/s -ər/z, (US) -ɚ/z
content n *what is contained:* ˈkɒn.tent, (US) ˈkɑ:n- *contentment:* kənˈtent
con|tent adj, v kən|ˈtent -tents -ˈtents -tenting -ˈten.tɪŋ, (US) -ˈten.t̬ɪŋ -tented/ly -ˈten.tɪd/li, (US) -ˈten.t̬ɪd/li -tentedness -ˈten.tɪd.nəs, -nɪs, (US) -ˈten.t̬ɪd-
contention kənˈten.tʃən -s -z
contentious kənˈten.tʃəs -ly -li -ness -nəs, -nɪs
contentment kənˈtent.mənt
contents n *what is contained:* ˈkɒn.tents, kənˈtents, (US) ˈkɑ:n.tents
contermin|al kɒnˈtɜ:.mɪ.n|əl, kən-, -mə-, (US) kənˈtɝ:- -ous -əs
contest n ˈkɒn.test, (US) ˈkɑ:n- -s -s
contest v kənˈtest -s -s -ing -ɪŋ -ed -ɪd -able -ə.bəl
contestant kənˈtes.tənt -s -s
contestation ˌkɒn.tesˈteɪ.ʃən, (US) ˌkɑ:n- -s -z
context ˈkɒn.tekst, (US) ˈkɑ:n- -s -s
contextual kənˈteks.tʃu.əl, kɒn-, -ˈtek.stju-, (US) kənˈteks.tʃu-, -ˈtek.stju-, kɑ:n-, -tʃəl -ly -i
contextualization, -isa- kənˌteks.tʃu.ə.laɪˈzeɪ.ʃən, -ˌtek.stju-, -lɪˈ-, (US) kənˌteks.tʃu.ə.ləˈ-, -ˌtek.stju-, kɑ:n-, -tʃəl.əˈ-
contextualiz|e, -is|e kənˈteks.tʃu.ə.laɪz, -tju-, (US) kənˈteks.tʃu-, -tju-, -tʃə.laɪz -es -ɪz -ing -ɪŋ -ed -d
Conti ˈkɒn.ti, (US) ˈkɑ:n.t̬i
contiguity ˌkɒn.tɪˈgju:.ə.ti, -təˈ-, -ɪ.ti, (US) ˌkɑ:n.t̬əˈgju:.ə.t̬i
contiguous kənˈtɪg.ju.əs -ly -li -ness -nəs, -nɪs
continen|ce ˈkɒn.tɪ.nənt|s, (US) ˈkɑ:n.tən.ənt|s -cy -si
continent, C~ ˈkɒn.tɪ.nənt, (US) ˈkɑ:n.tən.ənt -s -s -ly -li
continental ˌkɒn.tɪˈnen.təl, -təˈ-, (US) ˌkɑ:n.t̬ənˈen.t̬əl **ˌcontinental ˈbreakfast; ˌcontinental ˈquilt**
contingen|ce kənˈtɪn.dʒənt|s -cy -si -cies -siz
contingent kənˈtɪn.dʒənt -s -s -ly -li
continual kənˈtɪn.ju.əl -ly -i
continuan|ce kənˈtɪn.ju.ənt|s -t/s -t/s
continuation kənˌtɪn.juˈeɪ.ʃən -s -z
continuative kənˈtɪn.ju.ə.tɪv, -eɪ.tɪv, (US) kənˈtɪn.ju.eɪ.t̬ɪv, -ə-

C

continuator kən'tɪn.ju.eɪ.tər, ⓤⓢ -ţɚ **-s** -z
contin|ue kən'tɪn|.juː, -ju **-ues** -juːz, -juz **-uing** -ju.ɪŋ **-ued** -juːd, -jud **-uer/s** -ju.ər/z, ⓤⓢ -ju.ɚ/z
continuity ˌkɒn.tɪ'njuː.ə.ti, -tə'-, -ɪ.ti, ⓤⓢ ˌkɑːn.tən'uː.ə.ţi, -'juː-
continuo kən'tɪn.ju.əʊ, kɒn-, -u.əʊ, ⓤⓢ kən'tɪn.ju.oʊ
continuous kən'tɪn.ju.əs **-ly** -li **-ness** -nəs, -nɪs **conˌtinuous as'sessment**
continu|um kən'tɪn.ju|.əm **-ums** -əmz **-a** -ə
contoid 'kɒn.tɔɪd, ⓤⓢ 'kɑːn- **-s** -z
con|tort kən|'tɔːt, ⓤⓢ -'tɔːrt **-torts** -'tɔːts, ⓤⓢ -'tɔːrts **-torting** -'tɔː.tɪŋ, ⓤⓢ -'tɔːr.ţɪŋ **-torted** -'tɔː.tɪd, ⓤⓢ -'tɔːr.ţɪd
contortion kən'tɔː.ʃən, ⓤⓢ -'tɔːr- **-s** -z
contortionist kən'tɔː.ʃən.ɪst, kɒn-, ⓤⓢ kən'tɔːr- **-s** -s
contour 'kɒn.tʊər, -tɔːr, ⓤⓢ 'kɑːn.tʊr **-s** -z **-ing** -ɪŋ **-ed** -d
contra, C~ 'kɒn.trə, -trɑː, ⓤⓢ 'kɑːn.trə **-s** -z
contra- 'kɒn.trə, ⓤⓢ 'kɑːn.trə
contraband 'kɒn.trə.bænd, ⓤⓢ 'kɑːn- **-ist/s** -ɪst/s
contrabass ˌkɒn.trə'beɪs, '---, ⓤⓢ 'kɑːn.trə.beɪs **-es** -ɪz
contra bonos mores ˌkɒn.trɑːˌbəʊ.nəʊs'mɔː.reɪs, -ˌbɒn.əʊs-, ⓤⓢ ˌkɑːn.trɑːˌboʊ.noʊs'mɔːr.iːz
contraception ˌkɒn.trə'sep.ʃən, ⓤⓢ ˌkɑːn-
contraceptive ˌkɒn.trə'sep.tɪv, ⓤⓢ ˌkɑːn- **-s** -z
contract n 'kɒn.trækt, ⓤⓢ 'kɑːn- **-s** -s
contract v kən'trækt **-s** -s **-ing** -ɪŋ **-ed** -ɪd **-ive** -ɪv
contractibility kənˌtræk.tə'bɪl.ə.ti, -tɪ'-, -ɪ.ti, ⓤⓢ kənˌtræk.tə'bɪl.ə.ţi; ⓤⓢ ˌkɑːn.træk-
contractib|le kən'træk.tə.b|əl, -tɪ- **-ly** -li **-leness** -əl.nəs, -nɪs
contractile kən'træk.taɪl, ⓤⓢ -təl, -taɪl
contraction kən'træk.ʃən **-s** -z
contractionary kən'træk.ʃən.ər.i, -ʃən.ri, ⓤⓢ -ʃən.er.i
contractor *builder:* kən'træk.tər; 'kɒn.træk-, ⓤⓢ 'kɑːn.træk.tɚ *other senses:* kən'træk.tər, ⓤⓢ -tɚ **-s** -z
contractual kən'træk.tʃu.əl, -tju-, ⓤⓢ kən'træk.tʃu-, -tju-, kɑːn-, -*t*ʃəl **-ly** -i
contracture kən'træk.tʃər, -tjʊər, -ʃər, ⓤⓢ -tʃɚ **-s** -z
contradict ˌkɒn.trə'dɪkt, ⓤⓢ ˌkɑːn- **-s** -s **-ing** -ɪŋ **-ed** -ɪd
contradiction ˌkɒn.trə'dɪk.ʃən, ⓤⓢ ˌkɑːn- **-s** -z
contradictor|y ˌkɒn.trə'dɪk.tər|.i, -tr|i, ⓤⓢ ˌkɑːn- **-ily** -əl.i, -ɪ.li **-iness** -ɪ.nəs, -ɪ.nɪs
contradistinc|tion ˌkɒn.trə.dɪ'stɪŋ*k*|.ʃən, -də'-, ⓤⓢ ˌkɑːn.trə.dɪ'-, -də'- **-tive** -tɪv
contradistinguish ˌkɒn.trə.dɪ'stɪŋ.gwɪʃ, -də'-, ⓤⓢ ˌkɑːn.trə.dɪ'-, -də'- **-es** -ɪz **-ing** -ɪŋ **-ed** -t
contrafactive ˌkɒn.trə'fæk.tɪv, ⓤⓢ ˌkɑːn-
contraflow 'kɒn.trə.fləʊ, ⓤⓢ 'kɑːn.trə.floʊ **-s** -z
contraindi|cate ˌkɒn.trə'ɪn.dɪ|.keɪt, ⓤⓢ ˌkɑːn.trə- **-cates** -keɪts **-cating** -keɪ.tɪŋ, ⓤⓢ -keɪ.ţɪŋ **-cated** -keɪ.tɪd, ⓤⓢ -keɪ.ţɪd
contraindication ˌkɒn.trə.ɪn.dɪ'keɪ.ʃən, -də'-, ⓤⓢ ˌkɑːn.trə- **-s** -z
contraindicative ˌkɒn.trə.ɪn'dɪk.ə.tɪv, ⓤⓢ ˌkɑːn.trə.ɪn'dɪk.ə.ţɪv
contralti (plural of **contralto**) kən'træl.ti, -'trɑːl-, ⓤⓢ -'træl.ti
contralto kən'træl.təʊ, -'trɑːl-, ⓤⓢ -'træl.toʊ **-s** -z
contra pacem ˌkɒn.trɑː'pɑː.kem, -'pɑː.tʃem, ⓤⓢ ˌkɑːn.trɑː'pɑː.kem, -'peɪ.sem
contraposition ˌkɒn.trə.pə'zɪʃ.ən, ⓤⓢ ˌkɑːn-
contraption kən'træp.ʃən **-s** -z
contrapuntal ˌkɒn.trə'pʌn.təl, ⓤⓢ ˌkɑːn.trə'pʌn.ţəl **-ly** -i
contrapuntist ˌkɒn.trə'pʌn.tɪst, ⓤⓢ ˌkɑːn.trə'pʌn.ţɪst **-s** -s
contrariety ˌkɒn.trə'raɪ.ə.ti, -ɪ.ti, ⓤⓢ ˌkɑːn.trə'raɪ.ə.ţi
contrariwise kən'treə.ri.waɪz; 'kɒn.trə-, ⓤⓢ kən'trer.i-; ⓤⓢ 'kɑːn.trɚ-
contrar|y *opposed:* 'kɒn.trər|.i, ⓤⓢ 'kɑːn.trɚ|.i **-ies** -iz **-ily** -əl.i, -ɪ.li *perverse, obstinate:* kən'treə.r|i, ⓤⓢ -'trer|.i **-ies** -iz **-ily** -əl.i, -ɪ.li **-iness** -ɪ.nəs, -ɪ.nɪs
contrast n 'kɒn.trɑːst, ⓤⓢ 'kɑːn.træst **-s** -s
contrast v kən'trɑːst, ⓤⓢ -'træst **-s** -s **-ing/ly** -ɪŋ/li **-ed** -ɪd
contrastive kən'trɑː.stɪv, ⓤⓢ -'træs.tɪv
contraven|e ˌkɒn.trə'viːn, ⓤⓢ ˌkɑːn- **-es** -z **-ing** -ɪŋ **-ed** -d
contravention ˌkɒn.trə'ven.*t*ʃən, ⓤⓢ ˌkɑːn- **-s** -z
contretemps sing 'kɒn.trə.tɑ̃ː*ŋ*, 'kɔːn-, 'kɔ̃ː*n*-, ⓤⓢ 'kɑːn.trə.tɑ̃ː **plur** 'kɒn.trə.tɑ̃ː, -z, ⓤⓢ 'kɑːn.trə.tɑ̃ː, -z
contrib|ute kən'trɪb|.juːt; 'kɒn.trɪ.b|juːt, -b|jət, ⓤⓢ kən'trɪb|.juːt, -jət **-utes** -juːts, ⓤⓢ -juːts, -jəts **-uting** -jʊ.tɪŋ, ⓤⓢ -juː.ţɪŋ, -jə- **-uted** -jʊ.tɪd, ⓤⓢ -juː.ţɪd, -jə-
contribution ˌkɒn.trɪ'bjuː.ʃən, ⓤⓢ ˌkɑːn- **-s** -z
contributive kən'trɪb.jʊ.tɪv, -jə-, ⓤⓢ -jə.ţɪv
contributor kən'trɪb.jə.tər, -jʊ-; 'kɒn.trɪ.bjuː-, ⓤⓢ kən'trɪb.jə.ţɚ, -juː.ţɚ **-s** -z
contributory kən'trɪb.jʊ.tər.i, -jə-, -tri; ˌkɒn.trɪ'bjuː-, ⓤⓢ kən'trɪb.jə.tɔːr.i
contrite kən'traɪt, kɒn-, ⓤⓢ kən-, kɑːn- **-ly** -li **-ness** -nəs, -nɪs
contrition kən'trɪʃ.ən
contrivanc|e kən'traɪ.vənts **-es** -ɪz
contriv|e kən'traɪv **-es** -z **-ing** -ɪŋ **-ed** -d **-er/s** -ər/z, ⓤⓢ -ɚ/z
control n kən'trəʊl; *in machinery also:* 'kɒn.trəʊl, ⓤⓢ kən'troʊl **-s** -z
control v kən'trəʊl, ⓤⓢ -'troʊl **-s** -z **-ling** -ɪŋ **-led** -d **-lable** -ə.bəl
controller kən'trəʊ.lər, ⓤⓢ -'troʊ.lɚ **-s** -z
controversial ˌkɒn.trə'vɜː.ʃəl, '-si.əl, ⓤⓢ ˌkɑːn.trə'vɝː.ʃəl **-ly** -i
controversialist ˌkɒn.trə'vɜː.ʃəl.ɪst, '-si.əl-, ⓤⓢ ˌkɑːn.trə'vɝː.ʃəl- **-s** -s
controvers|y 'kɒn.trə.vɜː.s|i, -və.s|i; kən'trɒv.ə.s|i, ⓤⓢ 'kɑːn.trə.vɝː- **-ies** -iz

> Note: For some reason, this word seems to be the most often-quoted example of alternative English word stress patterns.

controver|t ˌkɒn.trə'vɜː|t, '---, ⓤⓢ 'kɑːn.trə.vɝː|t, ˌ--'- **-ts** -ts **-ting** -tɪŋ, ⓤⓢ -ţɪŋ **-ted** -tɪd, ⓤⓢ -ţɪd
controvertib|le ˌkɒn.trə'vɜː.tə.b|əl, -tɪ-, ⓤⓢ ˌkɑːn.trə'vɝː.ţə- **-ly** -li
contumacious ˌkɒn.tjʊ'meɪ.ʃəs, ⓤⓢ ˌkɑːn.tʊ'-, -tjʊ'-, -ţə'-, -tjə'- **-ly** -li **-ness** -nəs, -nəs
contumacy 'kɒn.tjʊ.mə.si, ⓤⓢ 'kɑːn.tʊ-; ⓤⓢ -tjʊ-; ⓤⓢ kən'tuː-
contumelious ˌkɒn.tjʊ'miː.li.əs, ⓤⓢ ˌkɑːn.tʊ'-, -tjuː'-, -tə'-, -tjə'- **-ly** -li **-ness** -nəs, -nɪs
contumel|y 'kɒn.tjuː.məl|.i, -tjʊ-, -mɪ.l|i; kən'tjʊm.ɪ.l|i, -əl|.i, -'tjuː.mɪ.l|i, -məl|.i, ⓤⓢ 'kɑːn.tuː.məl|.i, -tjuː-, '-ţəm.l|i; ⓤⓢ kən'tuː.mə.l|i, -'tjuː-, -'tʊm.ə- **-ies** -iz
contus|e kən'tʃuːz, -'tjuːz, ⓤⓢ -'tuːz, -'tjuːz **-es** -ɪz **-ing** -ɪŋ **-ed** -d
contusion kən'tʃuː.ʒən, -'tjuː-, ⓤⓢ -'tuː-, -'tjuː- **-s** -z
conundrum kə'nʌn.drəm **-s** -z
conurbation ˌkɒn.ɜː'beɪ.ʃən, -ə'-, ⓤⓢ ˌkɑː.nɝː'-, -nɚ'- **-s** -z
convalesc|e ˌkɒn.və'les, ⓤⓢ ˌkɑːn- **-es** -ɪz **-ing** -ɪŋ **-ed** -t
convalescence ˌkɒn.və'les.ənts, ⓤⓢ ˌkɑːn-
convalescent ˌkɒn.və'les.ənt, ⓤⓢ ˌkɑːn- **-s** -s
convection kən'vek.ʃən
convector kən'vek.tər, ⓤⓢ -tɚ **-s** -z
convenanc|e 'kɔ̃ː*n*.və.nɑ̃ː*n*s, 'kɒn-, -nɑːnts, ⓤⓢ 'kɑːn.və.nənts, -nænts **-es** -ɪz
conven|e kən'viːn **-es** -z **-ing** -ɪŋ **-ed** -d **-er/s** -ər/z, ⓤⓢ -ɚ/z **-or/s** -ər/z, ⓤⓢ -ɚ/z
convenienc|e kən'viː.ni.ənts, ⓤⓢ

-ˈviː.njənts -es -ɪz **conˈvenience ˌfood; conˈvenience ˌstore**
convenient kənˈviː.ni.ənt, ⓊⓈ -ˈviː.njənt -ly -li
convent ˈkɒn.vənt, -vent, ⓊⓈ ˈkɑːn- -s -s
conventicle kənˈven.tɪ.kəl, ⓊⓈ -t̬ə- -s -z
convention kənˈven.tʃən, ⓊⓈ -ˈvent.ʃən -s -z
conventional kənˈven.tʃən.əl, ⓊⓈ -ˈvent.ʃən- -ly -i
conventional|ism kənˈven.tʃən.əl|.ɪ.zəm, ⓊⓈ -ˈvent.ʃən- -ist/s -ɪst/s
conventionalit|y kənˌven.tʃəˈnæl.ə.t|i, -ɪ.t|i, ⓊⓈ -ˌvent.ʃəˈnæl.ə.t̬|i -ies -iz
conventionaliz|e, -is|e kənˈven.tʃən.əl.aɪz, ⓊⓈ -ˈvent.ʃən.ə.laɪz -es -ɪz -ing -ɪŋ -ed -d
conventual kənˈven.tʃu.əl, -tju-, -tʃəl, ⓊⓈ -tʃu.əl, -tju- -s -z
converg|e kənˈvɜːdʒ, kɒn-, ⓊⓈ kənˈvɝːdʒ -es -ɪz -ing -ɪŋ -ed -d
convergen|ce kənˈvɜː.dʒənt|s, kɒn-, ⓊⓈ kənˈvɝː- -ces -sɪz -cy -si
convergent kənˈvɜː.dʒənt, kɒn-, ⓊⓈ kənˈvɝː- -ly -li
conversable kənˈvɜː.sə.bəl, ⓊⓈ -ˈvɝː-
conversan|ce kənˈvɜː.sənt|s; ˈkɒn.və-, ⓊⓈ kənˈvɝː-; ⓊⓈ ˈkɑːn.vɚ- -cy -si
conversant kənˈvɜː.sənt; ˈkɒn.və-, ⓊⓈ kənˈvɝː-; ⓊⓈ ˈkɑːn.vɚ- -ly -li
conversation ˌkɒn.vəˈseɪ.ʃən, ⓊⓈ ˌkɑːn.vɚˈ- -s -z **converˈsation ˌpiece**
conversational ˌkɒn.vəˈseɪ.ʃən.əl, -ˈseɪʃ.nəl, ⓊⓈ ˌkɑːn.vɚˈ- -ly -i
conversationalist ˌkɒn.vəˈseɪ.ʃən.əl.ɪst, -ˈseɪʃ.nəl-, ⓊⓈ ˌkɑːn.vɚˈ- -s -s
conversazione ˌkɒn.və.sæt.siˈəʊ.neɪ, -ni, ⓊⓈ ˌkɑːn.vɚ.sɑːt.siˈoʊ.ni, ˌkoʊn- -s -z
convers|e n, adj ˈkɒn.vɜːs; kənˈvɜːs, ⓊⓈ ˈkɑːn.vɝːs; ⓊⓈ kənˈvɝːs -es -ɪz -ely -li
convers|e v kənˈvɜːs, ⓊⓈ -ˈvɝːs -es -ɪz -ing -ɪŋ -ed -t
conversion kənˈvɜː.ʃən, -ʒən, ⓊⓈ -ˈvɝː.ʒən, -ʃən -s -z **conˈversion ˌcourse**
convert n ˈkɒn.vɜːt, ⓊⓈ ˈkɑːn.vɝːt -s -s
con|vert v kən|ˈvɜːt, ⓊⓈ -ˈvɝːt -verts -ˈvɜːts, ⓊⓈ -ˈvɝːts -verting -ˈvɜː.tɪŋ, ⓊⓈ -ˈvɝː.t̬ɪŋ -verted -ˈvɜː.tɪd, ⓊⓈ -ˈvɝː.t̬ɪd -verter/s -ˈvɜː.təʳ/z, ⓊⓈ -ˈvɝː.t̬ɚ/z -vertor/s -ˈvɜː.təʳ/z, ⓊⓈ -ˈvɝː.t̬ɚ/z
convertibility kənˌvɜː.təˈbɪl.ə.ti, -tɪˈ-, -ɪ.ti, ⓊⓈ -ˌvɝː.t̬əˈbɪl.ə.t̬i
convertib|le kənˈvɜː.tə.b|əl, -tɪ-, ⓊⓈ -ˈvɝː.t̬ə- -les -əlz -ly -li
convex kɒnˈveks, ˈ--, ⓊⓈ ˈkɑːn.veks; ⓊⓈ kənˈveks -ly -li
convexit|y kɒnˈvek.sə.t|i, kən-, -ɪt|.i, ⓊⓈ kənˈvek.sə.t̬|i -ies -iz
convey kənˈveɪ -s -z -ing -ɪŋ -ed -d -er/s -əʳ/z, ⓊⓈ -ɚ/z -or/s -əʳ/z, ⓊⓈ -ɚ/z -able -ə.bəl **conˈveyor ˌbelt**
conveyanc|e kənˈveɪ.ənts -es -ɪz
conveyanc|er kənˈveɪ.ənt.s|əʳ, ⓊⓈ -s|ɚ -ers -əz, ⓊⓈ -ɚz -ing -ɪŋ
convict n ˈkɒn.vɪkt, ⓊⓈ ˈkɑːn- -s -s
convict v kənˈvɪkt -s -s -ing -ɪŋ -ed -ɪd
conviction kənˈvɪk.ʃən -s -z
convinc|e kənˈvɪnts -es -ɪz -ing -ɪŋ -ed -t
convincible kənˈvɪnt.sə.bəl
convincing kənˈvɪnt.sɪŋ -ly -li
convivial kənˈvɪv.i.əl -ly -i
conviviality kənˌvɪv.iˈæl.ə.ti, -ɪ.ti, ⓊⓈ -ɚ.t̬i
convocation ˌkɒn.vəʊˈkeɪ.ʃən, ⓊⓈ ˌkɑːn.vəˈ- -s -z
convok|e kənˈvəʊk, ⓊⓈ -ˈvoʊk -es -s -ing -ɪŋ -ed -t
convolu|te ˈkɒn.və.luː|t, -ljuː|t, ˌ--ˈ-, ⓊⓈ ˈkɑːn.və.luː|t -ted/ly -tɪd/li, ⓊⓈ -t̬ɪd/li
convolution ˌkɒn.vəˈluː.ʃən, -ˈljuː-, ⓊⓈ ˌkɑːn.vəˈluː- -s -z
convolv|e kənˈvɒlv, ⓊⓈ -ˈvɑːlv, -ˈvɔːlv -es -z -ing -ɪŋ -ed -d
convolvul|us kənˈvɒl.vjə.l|əs, -vjʊ-, ⓊⓈ -ˈvɑːl.vjə-, -vjʊ- -i -aɪ -uses -ə.sɪz
convoy ˈkɒn.vɔɪ, ⓊⓈ ˈkɑːn- -s -z -ing -ɪŋ -ed -d
convulsant kənˈvʌl.sənt -s -s
convuls|e kənˈvʌls -es -ɪz -ing -ɪŋ -ed -t
convulsion kənˈvʌl.ʃən -s -z
convulsive kənˈvʌl.sɪv -ly -li -ness -nəs, -nɪs
Conway ˈkɒn.weɪ, ⓊⓈ ˈkɑːn-
Conwy ˈkɒn.wi, ⓊⓈ ˈkɑːn-
con|y ˈkəʊ.n|i, ⓊⓈ ˈkoʊ- -ies -iz
Conybeare ˈkɒn.ɪ.bɪəʳ, ˈkʌn-, ⓊⓈ ˈkɑː.ni.bɪr, ˈkʌn.ɪ-
coo kuː -(e)s -z -ing -ɪŋ -ed -d
Coober Pedy ˌkuː.bəˈpiː.di, ⓊⓈ -bɚˈ-
Cooch kuːtʃ
cooee ˈkuː.i, -iː, ˌ-ˈ- -s -z -ing -ɪŋ -d -d
cook kʊk -s -s -ing -ɪŋ -ed -t
Cook(e) kʊk
cookbook ˈkʊk.bʊk -s -s
cook-chill ˌkʊkˈtʃɪl -s -z -ing -ɪŋ -ed -d
cooker ˈkʊk.əʳ, ⓊⓈ -ɚ -s -z
cookery ˈkʊk.ər.i **ˈcookery ˌbook**
Cookham ˈkʊk.əm, ⓊⓈ -əm, -hæm
cookhou|se ˈkʊk.haʊ|s -ses -zɪz
cookie ˈkʊk.i -s -z
cookout ˈkʊk.aʊt -s -s
Cookson ˈkʊk.sən
Cookstown ˈkʊks.taʊn
cookware ˈkʊk.weəʳ, ⓊⓈ -wer
cook|y ˈkʊk|.i -ies -iz
cool kuːl -er -əʳ, ⓊⓈ -ɚ -est -ɪst, -əst -ly -li, -i -ness -nəs, -nɪs -s -z -ing -ɪŋ -ed -d
coolant ˈkuː.lənt -s -s
coolbox ˈkuːl.bɒks, ⓊⓈ -bɑːks -es -ɪz
cooler ˈkuː.ləʳ, ⓊⓈ -lɚ -s -z
coolheaded ˌkuːlˈhed.ɪd -ness -nəs, -nɪs *stress shift:* **ˌcoolheaded ˈthinking**
coolibah ˈkuː.lɪ.bɑː, -lə- -s -z
Coolidge ˈkuː.lɪdʒ
coolie ˈkuː.li -s -z
Cooling ˈkuː.lɪŋ
cooling-off period ˌkuː.lɪŋˈɒfˌpɪə.ri.əd, ⓊⓈ -ˈɑːfˌpɪr.i- -s -z
coom kuːm -s -z
coomb kuːm -s -z
Coomb(e) kuːm
Coomber ˈkuːm.bəʳ, ⓊⓈ -bɚ
Coombes kuːmz
coon kuːn -s -z
coop kuːp -s -s -ing -ɪŋ -ed -t
co-op ˈkəʊ.ɒp, -ˈ-, ⓊⓈ ˈkoʊ.ɑːp -s -s
coop|er, C~ ˈkuː.p|əʳ, ⓊⓈ -p|ɚ -ers -əz, ⓊⓈ -ɚz -ering -ər.ɪŋ -ered -əd, ⓊⓈ -ɚd
cooperag|e ˈkuː.pər.ɪdʒ -es -ɪz
cooper|ate kəʊˈɒp.ər|.eɪt, ⓊⓈ koʊˈɑː.pə.r|eɪt -ates -eɪts -ating -eɪ.tɪŋ, ⓊⓈ -eɪ.t̬ɪŋ -ated -eɪ.tɪd, ⓊⓈ -eɪ.t̬ɪd -ator/s -eɪ.təʳ/z, ⓊⓈ -eɪ.t̬ɚ/z
cooperation kəʊˌɒp.əˈreɪ.ʃən, ˌkəʊ.ɒp-, ⓊⓈ koʊˌɑː.pəˈ- -s -z
cooperative kəʊˈɒp.ər.ə.tɪv, ⓊⓈ koʊˈɑː.pɚ.ə.t̬ɪv -s -z -ly -li
Cooperstown ˈkuː.pəz.taʊn, ⓊⓈ -pɚz-
coopery ˈkuː.pər.i
Coopman ˈkuːp.mən
co-opt kəʊˈɒpt, ⓊⓈ koʊˈɑːpt, ˈ-- -s -s -ing -ɪŋ -ed -ɪd
co-optation ˌkəʊ.ɒpˈteɪ.ʃən, ⓊⓈ ˌkoʊ.ɑːpˈ-
co-option kəʊˈɒp.ʃən, ⓊⓈ koʊˈɑːp- -s -z
coordinate n, adj kəʊˈɔː.dɪ.nət, -dən.ət, ⓊⓈ koʊˈɔːr.dən.ət, -eɪt -s -s -ly -li -ness -nəs, -nɪs
coordin|ate v kəʊˈɔː.dɪ.n|eɪt, -dən|.eɪt, ⓊⓈ koʊˈɔːr.dən.eɪt -ates -eɪts -ating -eɪ.tɪŋ, ⓊⓈ -eɪ.t̬ɪŋ -ated -eɪ.tɪd, ⓊⓈ -eɪ.t̬ɪd -ator/s -eɪ.təʳ/z, ⓊⓈ -eɪ.t̬ɚ/z
coordination kəʊˌɔː.dɪˈneɪ.ʃən, -dənˈeɪ-, ⓊⓈ koʊˌɔːr.dənˈeɪ-
coordinative kəʊˈɔː.dɪ.nə.tɪv, -dən.ə-, -eɪ-, ⓊⓈ koʊˈɔːr.dən.ə.t̬ɪv
Coors® kɔːz, kʊəz, ⓊⓈ kʊrz
coot kuːt -s -s
Coote kuːt
co-ownership ˌkəʊˈəʊ.nə.ʃɪp, ⓊⓈ ˌkoʊˈoʊ.nɚ-
cop kɒp, ⓊⓈ kɑːp -s -s -ping -ɪŋ -ped -t
Copacabana ˌkəʊ.pə.kəˈbæn.ə, ⓊⓈ ˌkoʊ-, -ˈbɑː.nə
copaiba kəʊˈpaɪ.bə, kɒpˈaɪ-, ⓊⓈ koʊˈpaɪ-
copal ˈkəʊ.pəl; kəʊˈpæl, ⓊⓈ ˈkoʊ.pəl, -pæl
coparcener ˌkəʊˈpɑː.sən.əʳ, -sɪ.nəʳ, ⓊⓈ ˌkoʊˈpɑːr.sən.ɚ -s -z
copartner ˌkəʊˈpɑːt.nəʳ, ⓊⓈ

C

ˈkoʊˌpɑːrt.nɚ, ˌ-ˈ-- -s -z -ship/s -ʃɪp/s

cop|e, C~ kəʊp, (US) koʊp -es -s -ing -ɪŋ -ed -t

copeck ˈkəʊ.pek, ˈkɒp.ek, (US) ˈkoʊ.pek -s -s

Copeland ˈkəʊp.lənd, (US) ˈkoʊp-

Copenhagen ˌkəʊ.pᵊnˈheɪ.gᵊn, -ˈhɑː-; ˈkəʊ.pᵊnˌheɪ-, -ˌhɑː-, (US) ˈkoʊ.pᵊnˌheɪ.gᵊn, -ˌhɑː-, ˌkoʊpᵊnˈheɪ-, -ˈhɑː-

coper ˈkəʊ.pəʳ, (US) ˈkoʊ.pɚ -s -z

Copernican kəʊˈpɜː.nɪ.kᵊn, (US) koʊˈpɝː-, kə-

Copernicus kəʊˈpɜː.nɪ.kəs, (US) koʊˈpɝː-, kə-

copestone ˈkəʊp.stəʊn, (US) ˈkoʊp.stoʊn -s -z

Cophetua kəʊˈfet.ju.ə, (US) koʊ-

copier ˈkɒp.i.əʳ, (US) ˈkɑː.pi.ɚ -s -z

co-pilot ˈkəʊˌpaɪ.lət, ˌ-ˈ--, (US) ˈkoʊˌpaɪ- -s -s

coping ˈkəʊ.pɪŋ, (US) ˈkoʊ- -s -z

copingstone ˈkəʊ.pɪŋ.stəʊn, (US) ˈkoʊ.pɪŋ.stoʊn -s -z

copious ˈkəʊ.pi.əs, (US) ˈkoʊ- -ly -li -ness -nəs, -nɪs

Copland ˈkɒp.lənd, ˈkəʊp-, (US) ˈkɑːp-, ˈkoʊp-

> Note: The name of the composer Aaron Copland is pronounced /ˈkəʊp.lənd/ (US) /ˈkoʊp-/.

Copleston ˈkɒp.ᵊl.stən, (US) ˈkɑː.pᵊl-

Copley ˈkɒp.li, (US) ˈkɑː.pli

cop-out ˈkɒp.aʊt, (US) ˈkɑːp- -s -s

Copp kɒp, (US) kɑːp

copp|er ˈkɒp|.əʳ, (US) ˈkɑː.p|ɚ -ers -əz, (US) -ɚz -ering -ᵊr.ɪŋ -ered -əd, (US) -ɚd **ˌcopper ˈbeech; ˌcopper ˈsulphate**

copperas ˈkɒp.ᵊr.əs, (US) ˈkɑː.pɚ-

copper-bottomed ˌkɒp.əˈbɒt.əmd, (US) ˌkɑː.pɚˈbɑː.t̬əmd *stress shift:* **ˌcopper-bottomed ˈprospect**

Copperfield ˈkɒp.ə.fiːld, (US) ˈkɑː.pɚ-

copperhead ˈkɒp.ə.hed, (US) ˈkɑː.pɚ- -s -z

copperplate ˈkɒp.ə.pleɪt, ˌ--ˈ-, (US) ˈkɑː.pɚ-

coppersmith, C~ ˈkɒp.ə.smɪθ, (US) ˈkɑː.pɚ- -s -s

coppery ˈkɒp.ᵊr.i, (US) ˈkɑː.pɚ-

coppic|e ˈkɒp.ɪs, (US) ˈkɑː.pɪs -es -ɪz -ing -ɪŋ -ed -t

Copping ˈkɒp.ɪŋ, (US) ˈkɑː.pɪŋ

Coppola ˈkɒp.ᵊl.ə, ˈkɑː.pᵊl.ə, (US) ˈkɑː.pᵊl.ə, ˈkoʊ.pᵊl.ə

Coppull ˈkɒp.ᵊl, (US) ˈkɑː.pᵊl

copra ˈkɒp.rə, (US) ˈkɑː.prə

copro- ˈkɒp.rəʊ, (US) ˈkɑː.proʊ, -prə

coproduc|e ˌkəʊ.prəˈdʒuːs, -ˈdjuːs, (US) ˌkoʊ.prəˈduːs, -ˈdjuːs -es -ɪz -ing -ɪŋ -ed -t -er/s -əʳ/z, (US) -ɚ/z

coproduction ˌkəʊ.prəˈdʌk.ʃᵊn, (US) ˌkoʊ- -s -z

cops|e kɒps, (US) kɑːps -es -ɪz

Copt kɒpt, (US) kɑːpt -s -s

copter ˈkɒp.təʳ, (US) ˈkɑːp- -s -z

Copthall ˈkɒp.tɔːl, ˈkɒpt.hɔːl, (US) ˈkɑːp.tɔːl, -tɑːl, ˈkɑːpt.hɔːl, -hɑːl

Coptic ˈkɒp.tɪk, (US) ˈkɑːp-

copul|a ˈkɒp.jə.l|ə, -jʊ-, (US) ˈkɑː.pjə- -ae -iː -as -əz

copu|late ˈkɒp.jə|.leɪt, -jʊ-, (US) ˈkɑː.pjə- -lates -leɪts -lating -leɪ.tɪŋ, (US) -leɪ.t̬ɪŋ -lated -leɪ.tɪd, (US) -leɪ.t̬ɪd

copulation ˌkɒp.jəˈleɪ.ʃᵊn, -jʊˈ-, (US) ˌkɑː.pjəˈ- -s -z

copula|tive ˈkɒp.jə.lə|.tɪv, -jʊ-, -leɪ-, (US) ˈkɑː.pjə.lə|.t̬ɪv -tory -tᵊr.i, -tri, (US) -tɔːr.i

cop|y ˈkɒp|.i, (US) ˈkɑː.p|i -ies -iz -ying -i.ɪŋ -ied -id

copybook ˈkɒp.i.bʊk, (US) ˈkɑː.pi- -s -s **ˌblot one's ˈcopybook**

copycat ˈkɒp.i.kæt, (US) ˈkɑː.pi- -s -s

Copydex® ˈkɒp.i.deks, (US) ˈkɑː.pi-

copy-ed|it ˈkɒp.iˌed|.ɪt, (US) ˈkɑː.pi- -its -ɪts -iting -ɪ.tɪŋ, (US) -ɪ.t̬ɪŋ -ited -ɪ.tɪd, (US) -ɪ.t̬ɪd -itor/s -ɪ.təʳ/z, (US) -ɪ.t̬ɚ/z

copyhold ˈkɒp.i.həʊld, (US) ˈkɑː.pi.hoʊld -s -z -er/s -əʳ/z, (US) -ɚ/z

copyist ˈkɒp.i.ɪst, (US) ˈkɑː.pi- -s -s

copy|right ˈkɒp.i|.raɪt, (US) ˈkɑː.pi- -rights -raɪts -righting -ˌraɪ.tɪŋ, (US) -ˌraɪ.t̬ɪŋ -righted -ˌraɪ.tɪd, (US) -ˌraɪ.t̬ɪd

copywrit|er ˈkɒp.iˌraɪ.t|əʳ, (US) ˈkɑː.piˌraɪ.t̬|ɚ -ers -əz, (US) -ɚz -ing -ɪŋ

coq au vin ˌkɒk.əʊˈvæ̃ŋ, -ˈvæn, (US) ˌkoʊk.oʊˈ-, ˌkɑːk-

Coquelles kɒkˈel, kəʊˈkel, (US) koʊˈkel

coqu|et kɒk|ˈet, kəʊˈk|et, (US) koʊˈk|et -ets -ets -etting -et.ɪŋ, (US) -et̬.ɪŋ -etted -et.ɪd, (US) -et̬.ɪd

Coquet ˈkəʊ.kɪt, (US) ˈkoʊ-

coquetr|y ˈkɒk.ə.tr|i, ˈkəʊ.kə-, -kɪ-, (US) ˈkoʊ.kə.tr|i, koʊˈket.r|i -ies -iz

coquette kɒkˈet, kəʊˈket, (US) koʊˈket -s -s

coquettish kɒkˈet.ɪʃ, kəʊˈket-, (US) koʊˈket̬- -ly -li -ness -nəs, -nɪs

cor kɔːʳ, (US) kɔːr -s -z

Cora ˈkɔː.rə, (US) ˈkɔːr.ə

coracle ˈkɒr.ə.kᵊl, (US) ˈkɔːr- -s -z

coral ˈkɒr.əl, (US) ˈkɔːr- -s -z **ˌcoral ˈreef**

corall|ine ˈkɒr.ᵊl|.aɪn, (US) ˈkɔːr.ə.l|aɪn -ite -aɪt

Coram ˈkɔː.rəm, (US) ˈkɔːr.əm

coram nobis ˌkɔː.rəmˈnəʊ.bɪs, -ræm-, (US) ˌkɔːr.æmˈnoʊ.bɪs

cor(s) anglais ˌkɔːˈrɒŋ.gleɪ, -ˈrɑːŋ-, (US) ˌkɔːr.ɑːŋˈgleɪ

corban ˈkɔː.bæn, -bᵊn, (US) ˈkɔːr-

corbel ˈkɔː.bᵊl, (US) ˈkɔːr- -s -z

Corbett ˈkɔː.bɪt, -bet, -bət, (US) ˈkɔːr-

Corbishley ˈkɔː.bɪʃ.li, (US) ˈkɔːr-

Corbridge ˈkɔː.brɪdʒ, (US) ˈkɔːr-

Corbusier kɔːˈbjuː.zi.eɪ, -ˈbuː-, (US) ˌkɔːr.buːˈzjeɪ

Corby ˈkɔː.bi, (US) ˈkɔːr-

Corbyn ˈkɔː.bɪn, (US) ˈkɔːr-

Corcoran ˈkɔː.kᵊr.ᵊn, (US) ˈkɔːr-

Corcyra ˌkɔːˈsaɪə.rə, (US) ˌkɔːrˈsaɪ-

cord kɔːd, (US) kɔːrd -s -z -ing -ɪŋ -ed -ɪd -age -ɪdʒ

Cordelia kɔːˈdiː.li.ə, (US) kɔːrˈdiːl.jə

cordelier, C~ ˌkɔː.dɪˈlɪəʳ, (US) ˌkɔːr.dɪˈlɪr -s -z

Cordero kɔːˈdeə.rəʊ, (US) kɔːrˈder.oʊ

cordial ˈkɔː.di.əl, (US) ˈkɔːr.dʒəl, -djəl -s -z -ly -i

cordialit|y ˌkɔː.diˈæl.ə.t|i, -ɪ.t|i, (US) ˌkɔːr.diˈæl.ə.t̬|i, -ˈdjæl.ə- -ies -iz

cordillera, C~ ˌkɔː.dɪˈljeə.rə, -dᵊlˈjeə-, -ˈeə-, (US) ˌkɔːr.dᵊlˈjer.ə; (US) kɔːrˈdɪl.ɚ-

cordite ˈkɔː.daɪt, (US) ˈkɔːr-

cordless ˈkɔːd.ləs, -lɪs, (US) ˈkɔːrd-

Cordoba, Córdoba ˈkɔː.də.bə, (US) ˈkɔːr-

cordon ˈkɔː.dᵊn, (US) ˈkɔːr- -s -z -ing -ɪŋ -ed -d

cordon bleu ˌkɔː.dɔ̃ː*m*ˈblɜː, -dɒnˈ-, (US) ˌkɔːr.dɔ̃ː*n*ˈbluː

cordon(s) sanitaire(s) ˌkɔː.dɔ̃ː*n*.sæn.ɪˈteəʳ, -dɒn-, -əˈ-, (US) kɔːrˌdɔ̃ː.sɑː.niˈter

Cordov|a ˈkɔː.də.v|ə, (US) ˈkɔːr- -an/s -ən/z

corduroy ˈkɔː.dʒə.rɔɪ, -djʊ-, -djə-, -dʒʊ-, ˌ--ˈ-, (US) ˈkɔːr.də- -s -z

cordwainer ˈkɔːdˌweɪ.nəʳ, (US) ˈkɔːrdˌweɪ.nɚ -s -z

cor|e kɔːʳ, (US) kɔːr -es -z -ing -ɪŋ -ed -d -er/s -əʳ/z, (US) -ɚ/z

CORE kɔːʳ, (US) kɔːr

co-referential ˌkəʊ.ref.əˈren.*t*ʃᵊl, (US) ˌkoʊ.ref.əˈrent.ʃᵊl

co-regent ˌkəʊˈriː.dʒᵊnt, (US) ˌkoʊ- -s -s

coreligionist ˌkəʊ.rɪˈlɪdʒ.ᵊn.ɪst, -rəˈ-, (US) ˌkoʊ.rəˈ-, -rɪˈ- -s -s

Corelli kəˈrel.i, kɒrˈel-, (US) koʊˈrel-, kəˈ-

co-representational ˌkəʊ.rep.rɪ.zenˈteɪ.ʃᵊn.ᵊl, -rə-, -ˈteɪʃ.nᵊl, (US) koʊ-

co-respondent ˌkəʊ.rɪˈspɒn.dənt, -rəˈ-, (US) ˌkoʊ.rɪˈspɑːn-, -rəˈ- -s -s

Corey ˈkɔː.ri, (US) ˈkɔːr.i

corf kɔːf, (US) kɔːrf -s -s

Corfe kɔːf, (US) kɔːrf

Corfu kɔːˈfuː, -ˈfjuː, (US) ˈkɔːr.fuː, -fjuː, -ˈ-

corgi, C~ ˈkɔː.gi, (US) ˈkɔːr- -s -z

coriander ˌkɒr.iˈæn.dəʳ, ˈkɒr.i.æn-, (US) ˈkɔːr.i.æn.dɚ, ˌkɔːr.iˈæn-

Corin ˈkɒr.ɪn, -ᵊn, (US) ˈkɔːr-

Corinne kəˈrɪn

Corinth ˈkɒr.ɪn*t*θ, (US) ˈkɔːr-

Corinthian kəˈrɪn*t*.θi.ən -s -z

Coriolanus ˌkɒr.i.əʊˈleɪ.nəs, -ˈlɑː-, (US) ˌkɔːr.i.əˈ-

Corioles kəˈraɪ.ə.liːz, kɒrˈaɪ.ə-, (US) kəˈraɪ.ə-

Coriolis kəˈraɪ.ə.lɪs, kɒrˈaɪ.ə-, (US) kəˈraɪ.ə-

cork, C~ kɔːk, (US) kɔːrk -s -s -ing -ɪŋ -ed -t

corkage ˈkɔː.kɪdʒ, (US) ˈkɔːr-

C

corker, C~ ˈkɔː.kəʳ, (US) ˈkɔːr.kɚ **-s** -z
Corkery ˈkɔː.kᵊr.i, (US) ˈkɔːr-
corkscrew ˈkɔːk.skruː, (US) ˈkɔːrk- **-s** -z **-ing** -ɪŋ **-ed** -d
corky ˈkɔː.ki, (US) ˈkɔːr-
Corleone ˌkɔː.liˈəʊ.ni, (US) ˌkɔːr.liˈoʊ-
corm kɔːm, (US) kɔːrm **-s** -z
Cormac ˈkɔː.mæk, ˈkɜː-, (US) ˈkɔːr-
Cormack ˈkɔː.mæk, (US) ˈkɔːr-
cormorant ˈkɔː.mᵊr.ənt, (US) ˈkɔːr- **-s** -s
corn kɔːn, (US) kɔːrn **-s** -z **-ing** -ɪŋ **-ed** -d **ˈCorn ˌBelt; ˈcorn ˌdolly; ˌcorned ˈbeef; ˈcorn ˌexchange**
cornball ˈkɔːn.bɔːl, ˈkɔːm-, (US) ˈkɔːrn-, -bɑːl **-s** -z
cornbread ˈkɔːn.bred, ˈkɔːm-, (US) ˈkɔːrn-
Cornbury ˈkɔːn.bᵊr.i, ˈkɔːm-, (US) ˈkɔːrn.ber-, -bɚ-
corncob ˈkɔːn.kɒb, (US) ˈkɔːrn.kɑːb **-s** -z
corncrake ˈkɔːn.kreɪk, ˈkɔːŋ-, (US) ˈkɔːrn- **-s** -s
corndog ˈkɔːn.dɒg, (US) ˈkɔːrn.dɑːg, -dɔːg **-s** -z
corne|a ˈkɔː.ni|.ə; kɔːˈniː|-, (US) ˈkɔːr.ni|- **-as** -əz **-al** -əl
Corneille kɔːˈneɪ, -ˈneɪl, (US) kɔːrˈneɪ
Cornelia kɔːˈniː.li.ə, (US) kɔːrˈniːl.jə
cornelian kɔːˈniː.li.ən, (US) kɔːrˈniːl.jən **-s** -z
Cornelius kɔːˈniː.li.əs, (US) kɔːrˈniːl.jəs
Cornell kɔːˈnel, (US) kɔːr-
corn|er ˈkɔː.n|əʳ, (US) ˈkɔːr.n|ɚ **-ers** -əz, (US) -ɚz **-ering** -ᵊr.ɪŋ **-ered** -əd, (US) -ɚd **ˌcorner ˈshop**
cornerback ˈkɔː.nə.bæk, (US) ˈkɔːr.nɚ- **-s** -s
-cornered ˈkɔː.nəd, (US) ˈkɔːr.nɚd
cornerstone ˈkɔː.nə.stəʊn, (US) ˈkɔːr.nɚ.stoʊn **-s** -z
cornet ˈkɔː.nɪt, (US) kɔːrˈnet **-s** -s
Cornetto® kɔːˈnet.əʊ, (US) kɔːrˈneţ.oʊ
cornfield ˈkɔːn.fiːld, (US) ˈkɔːrn- **-s** -z
cornflakes ˈkɔːn.fleɪks, (US) ˈkɔːrn-
cornflour ˈkɔːn.flaʊəʳ, -flaʊ.əʳ, (US) ˈkɔːrn.flaʊ.ɚ
cornflower ˈkɔːn.flaʊəʳ, -flaʊ.əʳ, (US) ˈkɔːrn.flaʊ.ɚ **-s** -z
Cornhill ˌkɔːnˈhɪl, (US) ˈkɔːrn.hɪl, ˌ-ˈ-
cornic|e ˈkɔː.nɪs, (US) ˈkɔːr- **-es** -ɪz
cornich|e, C~ kɔːˈniːʃ; ˈ--, -nɪʃ, (US) kɔːrˈniːʃ **-es** -ɪz
Cornish ˈkɔː.nɪʃ, (US) ˈkɔːr- **-man** -mən **-men** -mən, -men **-woman** -ˌwʊm.ən **-women** -ˌwɪm.ɪn **ˌCornish ˈpasty**
cornmeal ˈkɔːn.miːl, ˈkɔːm-, (US) ˈkɔːrn-
cornrow ˈkɔːn.rəʊ, (US) ˈkɔːrn.roʊ **-s** -z **-ing** -ɪŋ **-ed** -d
cornstarch ˈkɔːn.stɑːtʃ, (US) ˈkɔːrn.stɑːrtʃ
cornsyrup ˈkɔːnˌsɪr.əp, (US) ˈkɔːrnˌsɪr-, -ˌsɝː-
cornucopi|a ˌkɔː.njʊˈkəʊ.pi|.ə, (US) ˌkɔːr.nəˈkoʊ-, -njəˈ- **-as** -əz **-an** -ən
Cornwall ˈkɔːn.wɔːl, -wəl, (US) ˈkɔːrn.wɔːl, -wɑːl
Cornwallis kɔːnˈwɒl.ɪs, (US) kɔːrnˈwɑː.lɪs
Cornwell ˈkɔːn.wel, -wəl, (US) ˈkɔːrn-
corn|y ˈkɔː.n|i, (US) ˈkɔːr- **-ier** -i.əʳ, (US) -i.ɚ **-iest** -i.ɪst, -i.əst
corolla, C~® kəˈrɒl.ə, -ˈrəʊ.lə, (US) -ˈroʊ.lə, -ˈrɑː- **-s** -z

> Note: The suitable pronunciation for the car in American English is /kəˈroʊ-/.

corollar|y kəˈrɒl.ᵊr|.i, (US) ˈkɔːr.ə.ler- **-ies** -iz
Coromandel ˌkɒr.əʊˈmæn.dᵊl, (US) ˌkɔːr.oʊˈ-
coron|a kəˈrəʊ.n|ə, (US) -ˈroʊ- **-ae** -iː **-as** -əz
Corona *female name:* ˈkɒr.ə.nə, (US) ˈkɔːr-
coronach, C~ ˈkɒr.ə.nək, -nəx, -næk, (US) ˈkɔːr.ə.nək **-s** -s
coronal n ˈkɒr.ə.nᵊl, (US) ˈkɔːr- **-s** -z
coronal adj *pertaining to the sun's corona:* kəˈrəʊ.nᵊl, (US) -ˈroʊ- *medical, botanical and phonetic senses:* ˈkɒr.ə.nᵊl; kəˈrəʊ-, (US) ˈkɔːr.ə-; (US) kəˈroʊ-
coronar|y ˈkɒr.ə.nᵊr|.i, (US) ˈkɔːr.ə.ner- **-ies** -iz
coronation ˌkɒr.əˈneɪ.ʃᵊn, (US) ˌkɔːr- **-s** -z
Coronel ˈkɒr.ə.nel, (US) ˈkɔːr-
coroner ˈkɒr.ə.nəʳ, (US) ˈkɔːr.ᵊn.ɚ **-s** -z
coronet ˈkɒr.ə.nɪt, -net, -nət; ˌkɒr.əˈnet, (US) ˌkɔːr.əˈnet **-s** -s
corpora (plural of **corpus**) ˈkɔː.pᵊr.ə, -pə.rɑː, (US) ˈkɔːr.pɚ.ə
corporal ˈkɔː.pᵊr.ᵊl, ˈ-prᵊl, (US) ˈkɔːr- **-s** -z **-ly** -i **ˌcorporal ˈpunishment**
corporality ˌkɔː.pəˈræl.ə.ti, -ɪ.ti, (US) ˌkɔːr.pəˈræl.ə.ţi
corporate ˈkɔː.pᵊr.ət, -ɪt, ˈ-prət, ˈ-prɪt, (US) ˈkɔːr- **-ly** -li **-ness** -nəs, -nɪs
corporation ˌkɔː.pᵊrˈeɪ.ʃᵊn, (US) ˌkɔːr.pəˈreɪ- **-s** -z
corporative ˈkɔː.pᵊr.ə.tɪv, (US) ˈkɔːr.pɚ.ə.ţɪv
corporator ˈkɔː.pᵊr.eɪ.təʳ, (US) ˈkɔːr.pə.reɪ.ţɚ **-s** -z
corporeal kɔːˈpɔː.ri.əl, (US) kɔːrˈpɔːr- **-ly** -i
corps sing kɔːʳ, (US) kɔːr **plur** kɔːz, (US) kɔːrz
corps de ballet ˌkɔː.dəˈbæl.eɪ, -li, (US) ˌkɔːr.də.bælˈeɪ
corps|e kɔːps, (US) kɔːrps **-es** -ɪz **-ing** -ɪŋ **-ed** -t
corpulen|ce ˈkɔː.pjə.lənt|s, -pjʊ-, (US) ˈkɔːr.pjə- **-cy** -si
corpulent ˈkɔː.pjə.lənt, -pjʊ-, (US) ˈkɔːr.pjə-
corp|us ˈkɔː.p|əs, (US) ˈkɔːr- **-ora** -ə.rə, (US) -ɚ.ə **-uses** -ə.sɪz
Corpus Christi ˌkɔː.pəsˈkrɪs.ti, (US) ˌkɔːr-
corpuscle ˈkɔː.pʌs.ᵊl, -pə.sᵊl; kɔːˈpʌs-, (US) ˈkɔːr.pʌs.ᵊl, -pə.sᵊl **-s** -z
corpuscular kɔːˈpʌs.kjə.ləʳ, -kjʊ-, (US) kɔːrˈpʌs.kjə.lɚ
corpuscule kɔːˈpʌs.kjuːl, -kjʊl, (US) kɔːrˈpʌs.kjuːl **-s** -z
corpus delicti ˌkɔː.pʌs.dɪˈlɪk.taɪ, -pəs-, (US) ˌkɔːr-
corpus juris ˌkɔː.pʌsˈdʒʊə.rɪs, -pəs-, -ˈdʒɔː-, (US) ˌkɔːr.pʌsˈdʒʊr.ɪs
Corr kɔːʳ, (US) kɔːr **-s** -z
corral kəˈrɑːl, kɒrˈɑːl, (US) kəˈræl **-s** -z **-ling** -ɪŋ **-led** -d
correct kəˈrekt **-ly** -li **-ness** -nəs, -nɪs **-s** -s **-ing** -ɪŋ **-ed** -ɪd **-or/s** -əʳ/z, (US) -ɚ/z
correction kəˈrek.ʃᵊn **-s** -z
correctional kəˈrek.ʃᵊn.ᵊl
correctitude kəˈrek.tɪ.tʃuːd, -tjuːd, (US) -tə.tuːd, -tjuːd
corrective kəˈrek.tɪv **-s** -z
Correggio kəˈredʒ.i.əʊ, (US) ˈ-oʊ
correlate n ˈkɒr.ᵊl.ət, -ɪ.lət, -leɪt, (US) ˈkɔːr.ə.leɪt **-s** -s
corre|late v ˈkɒr.ə|.leɪt, ˈ-ɪ-, (US) ˈkɔːr.ə- **-lates** -leɪts **-lating** -leɪ.tɪŋ, (US) -leɪ.ţɪŋ **-lated** -leɪ.tɪd, (US) -leɪ.ţɪd **-latable** -leɪ.tə.bᵊl, (US) -leɪ.ţə.bᵊl
correlation ˌkɒr.əˈleɪ.ʃᵊn, -ɪˈ-, (US) ˌkɔːr.əˈ- **-s** -z
correlative kɒrˈel.ə.tɪv, kəˈrel-, (US) kəˈrel.ə.ţɪv **-ly** -li **-ness** -nəs, -nɪs
correspond ˌkɒr.ɪˈspɒnd, -əˈ-, (US) ˌkɔːr.əˈ- **-s** -z **-ing** -ɪŋ **-ed** -ɪd
correspondenc|e ˌkɒr.ɪˈspɒn.dənts, -əˈ-, (US) ˌkɔːr.əˈspɑːn- **-es** -ɪz **correˈspondence ˌcourse**
correspondent ˌkɒr.ɪˈspɒn.dᵊnt, -əˈ-, (US) ˌkɔːr.əˈspɑːn- **-s** -s
corresponding ˌkɒr.ɪˈspɒn.dɪŋ, -əˈ-, (US) ˌkɔːr.əˈspɑːn- **-ly** -li
corridor ˈkɒr.ɪ.dɔːʳ, ˈ-ə-, -dəʳ, (US) ˈkɔːr.ə.dɚ, ˈ-ɪ-, -dɔːr **-s** -z
corrie, C~ ˈkɒr.i, (US) ˈkɔːr-
Corrientes ˌkɒr.iˈen.tes, (US) ˌkɔːr-
Corrigan ˈkɒr.ɪ.gᵊn, ˈ-ə-, (US) ˈkɔːr.ə-, ˈ-ɪ-
corrigend|um ˌkɒr.ɪˈdʒen.d|əm, -əˈ-, -ˈgen-, (US) ˌkɔːr- **-a** -ə
corrigible ˈkɒr.ɪ.dʒə.bᵊl, -dʒɪ-, (US) ˈkɔːr-
Corringham ˈkɒr.ɪŋ.əm, (US) ˈkɔːr-, -hæm
corroborant kəˈrɒb.ᵊr.ᵊnt, (US) -ˈrɑː.bɚ- **-s** -s
corrobor|ate kəˈrɒb.ᵊr|.eɪt, (US) -ˈrɑː.bə.r|eɪt **-ates** -eɪts **-ating** -eɪ.tɪŋ, (US) -eɪ.ţɪŋ **-ated** -eɪ.tɪd, (US) -eɪ.ţɪd **-ator/s** -eɪ.təʳ/z, (US) -eɪ.ţɚ/z
corroboration kəˌrɒb.əˈreɪ.ʃᵊn, (US) -ˌrɑː.bəˈ- **-s** -z
corroborative kəˈrɒb.ᵊr.ə.tɪv, -eɪ-, (US) -ˈrɑː.bɚ.ə.ţɪv
corroboratory kəˈrɒb.ᵊr.ə.tᵊr.i, -tri; kəˌrɒb.əˈreɪ-, (US) -ˈrɑː.bɚ.ə.tɔːr.i
corroboree kəˈrɒb.ᵊr.i, kəˌrɒb.əˈriː, (US) -ˌrɑː.bəˈriː **-s** -z

C

corrod|e kəˈrəʊd, (US) -ˈroʊd **-es** -z **-ing** -ɪŋ **-ed** -ɪd
corrodible kəˈrəʊ.də.bəl, -dɪ-, (US) -ˈroʊ.də-
corrosion kəˈrəʊ.ʒən, (US) -ˈroʊ- **-s** -z
corrosive kəˈrəʊ.sɪv, -zɪv, (US) -ˈroʊ- **-s** -z **-ly** -li **-ness** -nəs, -nɪs
corru|gate ˈkɒr.ə|.geɪt, ˈ-ʊ-, (US) ˈkɔːr.ə- **-gates** -geɪts **-gating** -geɪ.tɪŋ, (US) -geɪ.t̬ɪŋ **-gated** -geɪ.tɪd, (US) -geɪ.t̬ɪd ˌ**corrugated** ˈ**iron**
corrugation ˌkɒr.əˈgeɪ.ʃən, -ʊˈ-, (US) ˌkɔːr.əˈ- **-s** -z
corrupt kəˈrʌpt **-est** -ɪst, -əst **-ly** -li **-ness** -nəs, -nɪs **-s** -s **-ing** -ɪŋ **-ed** -ɪd **-er/s** -əʳ/z, (US) -ɚ/z
corruptibility kəˌrʌp.təˈbɪl.ə.ti, -tɪˈ-, -ɪ.ti, (US) -təˈbɪl.ə.t̬i
corruptib|le kəˈrʌp.tə.b|əl, -tɪ-, (US) -tə- **-ly** -li **-leness** -əl.nəs, -nɪs
corruption kəˈrʌp.ʃən **-s** -z
corruptive kəˈrʌp.tɪv
Corry ˈkɒr.i, (US) ˈkɔːr-
Corsa® ˈkɔː.sə, (US) ˈkɔːr-
corsag|e kɔːˈsɑːʒ, ˈ--, (US) kɔːrˈsɑːʒ, -sɑːdʒ **-es** -ɪz
corsair ˈkɔː.seəʳ, -ˈ-, (US) ˈkɔːr.ser, -ˈ- **-s** -z
cors|e kɔːs, (US) kɔːrs **-es** -ɪz
corselet ˈkɔː.slət, -slɪt, (US) ˈkɔːr- **-s** -s
corset ˈkɔː.sɪt, -sət, (US) ˈkɔːr- **-s** -s
corsetry ˈkɔː.sə.tri, -sɪ-, (US) ˈkɔːr-
Corsham ˈkɔː.ʃəm, (US) ˈkɔːr-
Corsic|a ˈkɔː.sɪ.k|ə, (US) ˈkɔːr- **-an/s** -ən/z
corslet ˈkɔː.slət, -slɪt, (US) ˈkɔːr- **-s** -s
cortèg|e kɔːˈteɪʒ, -ˈteʒ, ˈ--, (US) kɔːrˈteʒ **-es** -ɪz
Cortes, Cortés ˈkɔː.tes, -tez, -ˈ-, (US) kɔːrˈtez
cort|ex ˈkɔː.t|eks, (US) ˈkɔːr- **-exes** -ek.sɪz **-ices** -ɪ.siːz
Corti ˈkɔː.ti, (US) ˈkɔːr.ti
cortical ˈkɔː.tɪ.kəl, (US) ˈkɔːr.t̬ɪ-
corticosteroid ˌkɔː.tɪ.kəʊˈstɪə.rɔɪd, -ˈster.ɔɪd, (US) ˌkɔːr.t̬ɪ.koʊˈster.ɔɪd, -ˈstɪr- **-s** -z
Cortina® kɔːˈtiː.nə, (US) kɔːr- **-s** -z
cortisone ˈkɔː.tɪ.zəʊn, -tə-, -səʊn, (US) ˈkɔːr.t̬ə.zoʊn, -soʊn
Cortney ˈkɔːt.ni, (US) ˈkɔːrt-
corundum kəˈrʌn.dəm
Corunna kɒrˈʌn.ə, kəˈrʌn-, (US) kəˈrʌn-
Corus® ˈkɔː.rəs, (US) ˈkɔːr.əs
corus|cate ˈkɒr.ə.s|keɪt, -ʌs|.keɪt, (US) ˈkɔːr.ə.s|keɪt **-cates** -keɪts **-cating** -keɪ.tɪŋ, (US) -keɪ.t̬ɪŋ **-cated** -keɪ.tɪd, (US) -keɪ.t̬ɪd
coruscation ˌkɒr.əˈskeɪ.ʃən, -ʌsˈkeɪ-, (US) ˌkɔːr.əˈskeɪ- **-s** -z
corvée ˈkɔː.veɪ, (US) kɔːrˈveɪ **-s** -z
corvette kɔːˈvet, (US) kɔːr- **-s** -s
Corwen ˈkɔː.wen, -wɪn, (US) ˈkɔːr-
Cory ˈkɔː.ri, (US) ˈkɔːr.i
Corybant ˈkɒr.i.bænt, (US) ˈkɔːr.ə- **-s** -s **Corybantes** ˌkɒr.iˈbæn.tiːz, (US) ˌkɔːr.ə-
Corydon ˈkɒr.i.dən, ˈ-ə-, -dɒn, (US) ˈkɔːr.ə.dən, -dɑːn
corymb ˈkɒr.ɪmb, -ɪm, (US) ˈkɔːr-
coryphae|us ˌkɒr.iˈfiː|.əs, (US) ˌkɔːr.əˈ- **-i** -aɪ
coryphée ˌkɒr.iˈfeɪ, (US) ˌkɔːr-
Coryton *in Devon:* ˈkɒr.ɪ.tən, ˈ-ə-, (US) ˈkɔːr- *in Essex:* ˈkɔː.rɪ.tən, ˈ-rə-, (US) ˈkɔːr-
Corzine ˈkɔː.zaɪn, ˈkɔːr-
cos conj *because:* kəz, kəs, kɒz, kɒs, (US) kəz, kəs, kɑːz, kɑːs
Note: Weak form word.
cos, C~ n *lettuce:* kɒs, kɒz, (US) kɑːs, koʊs
Cosa Nostra ˌkəʊ.zəˈnɒs.trə, (US) ˌkoʊ.səˈnoʊ.strə, -zəˈ-
Cosby ˈkɒz.bi, (US) ˈkɑːz-
cosec ˈkəʊ.sek, (US) ˈkoʊ-
cosecant ˌkəʊˈsiː.kənt, (US) ˌkoʊ- **-s** -s
co-set ˈkəʊ.set, (US) ˈkoʊ- **-s** -s
Cosgrave ˈkɒz.greɪv, (US) ˈkɑːz-
cosh kɒʃ, (US) kɑːʃ **-es** -ɪz **-ing** -ɪŋ **-ed** -t
Cosham ˈkɒs.əm, (US) ˈkɑː.səm
cosher adj *according to Jewish law:* ˈkəʊ.ʃəʳ, ˈkɒʃ.əʳ, (US) ˈkoʊ.ʃɚ
cosh|er v *feast, pamper:* ˈkɒʃ|.əʳ, (US) ˈkɑː.ʃ|ɚ **-ers** -əz, (US) -ɚz **-ering** -ər.ɪŋ **-ered** -əd, (US) -ɚd
Così Fan Tutte ˌkəʊ.si.fænˈtʊt.eɪ, -zi-, kəʊˌsiː-, -i, (US) koʊˌsiː.fɑːnˈtuː.teɪ
cosignator|y ˌkəʊˈsɪg.nə.tər|.i, -tr|i, (US) ˌkoʊˈsɪg.nə.tɔːr|.i **-ies** -iz
Cosima ˈkəʊ.sɪ.mə, (US) ˈkoʊ.zi-, -mɑː
cosine ˈkəʊ.saɪn, (US) ˈkoʊ- **-s** -z
CoSIRA kəʊˈsaɪə.rə, (US) koʊˈsaɪ-
cosmetic kɒzˈmet.ɪk, (US) kɑːzˈmet̬- **-s** -s **-al** -əl **-ally** -əl.i, -li
cosmic ˈkɒz.mɪk, (US) ˈkɑːz- **-al** -əl **-ally** -əl.i, -li
cosm|ism ˈkɒz.m|ɪ.zəm, (US) ˈkɑːz- **-ist/s** -ɪst/s
Cosmo ˈkɒz.məʊ, (US) ˈkɑːz.moʊ
cosmo- ˈkɒz.məʊ, kɒzˈmɒ, (US) ˈkɑːz.moʊ, -mə, kɑːzˈmɑː-
Note: Prefix. This may be stressed on the initial syllable (as in **cosmonaut** /ˈkɒz.mə.nɔːt/ (US) /ˈkɑːz.mə.nɑːt/) or on the second syllable (e.g. **cosmology** /kɒzˈmɒl.ə.dʒi/ (US) /kɑːzˈmɑː.lə.dʒi/).
cosmogonic ˌkɒz.məʊˈgɒn.ɪk, (US) ˌkɑːz.məˈgɑː.nɪk, ˌ-moʊ- **-al** -əl **-ally** -əl.i, -li
cosmogon|y kɒzˈmɒg.ən|.i, (US) kɑːzˈmɑː.gən- **-ist/s** -ɪst/s
cosmographic ˌkɒz.məʊˈgræf.ɪk, (US) ˌkɑːz.məˈ-, ˌ-moʊ- **-al** -əl **-ally** -əl.i, -li
cosmograph|y kɒzˈmɒg.rə.f|i, (US) kɑːzˈmɑː.grə- **-er/s** -əʳ/z, (US) -ɚ/z
cosmological ˌkɒz.məˈlɒdʒ.ɪ.kəl, (US) ˌkɑːz.məˈlɑː.dʒɪ-
cosmolog|y kɒzˈmɒl.ə.dʒ|i, (US) kɑːzˈmɑː.lə- **-ist/s** -ɪst/s
cosmonaut ˈkɒz.mə.nɔːt, (US) ˈkɑːz.mə.nɑːt, -nɔːt **-s** -s
cosmopolitan, C~® ˌkɒz.məˈpɒl.ɪ.tən, ˈ-ə-, (US) ˌkɑːz.məˈpɑː.lɪ- **-s** -z
cosmopolitanism ˌkɒz.məˈpɒl.ɪ.tən.ɪ.zəm, ˈ-ə-, -tɪ.nɪ-, (US) ˌkɑːz.məˈpɑː.lɪ.tən.ɪ-
cosmos, C~® ˈkɒz.mɒs, (US) ˈkɑːz.moʊs, -məs, -mɑːs
Cossack ˈkɒs.æk, (US) ˈkɑː.sæk **-s** -s
coss|et ˈkɒs|.ɪt, (US) ˈkɑː.s|ɪt **-ets** -ɪts **-e(t)ting** -ɪ.tɪŋ, (US) -ɪ.t̬ɪŋ **-e(t)ted** -ɪ.tɪd, (US) -ɪ.t̬ɪd
cost kɒst, (US) kɑːst **-s** -s **-ing** -ɪŋ **-ed** -ɪd ˌ**cost-efˈfective;** ˌ**cost of** ˈ**living**
Costa ˈkɒs.tə, (US) ˈkɑː.stə
Costa Blanca ˌkɒs.təˈblæŋ.kə, (US) ˌkɑː.stəˈblɑːŋ-, ˌkoʊ-
Costa Brava ˌkɒs.təˈbrɑː.və, (US) ˌkɑː.stə-, ˌkoʊ-
Costa del Sol ˌkɒs.tə.delˈsɒl, (US) ˌkɑː.stə.delˈsoʊl, ˌkoʊ-
Costain kɒsˈteɪn, ˈ--, (US) ˈkɑː.steɪn, -ˈ-
costal ˈkɒs.təl, (US) ˈkɑː.stəl
co-star n ˈkəʊ.stɑːʳ, (US) ˈkoʊ.stɑːr **-s** -z
co-star v kəʊˈstɑːʳ, (US) ˈkoʊ.stɑːr **-s** -z **-ring** -ɪŋ **-red** -d
costard ˈkʌs.təd, ˈkɒs-, (US) ˈkɑː.stɚd **-s** -z
Costard ˈkɒs.təd, -tɑːd, (US) ˈkɑː.stɚd, -stɑːrd
Costa Ric|a ˌkɒs.təˈriː.k|ə, (US) ˌkoʊ.stəˈ-, ˌkɑː- **-an/s** -ən/z
cost-cutting ˈkɒstˌkʌt.ɪŋ, (US) ˈkɑːstˌkʌt̬-
cost-effective ˌkɒst.ɪˈfek.tɪv, -əˈ-; ˈkɒst.ɪ.fek-, ˈ-ə-, (US) ˈkɑːst.ɪˌfek-, -əˌ-; (US) ˌkɑːst.ɪˈfekt-, -əˈ- **-ly** -li **-ness** -nəs, -nɪs
Costello kɒsˈtel.əʊ, kəˈstel-, ˈkɒs.təl.əʊ, (US) kɑːˈstel.oʊ, kə-; (US) ˈkɑː.stə.loʊ
coster ˈkɒs.təʳ, (US) ˈkɑː.stɚ **-s** -z
costermonger ˈkɒs.təˌmʌŋ.gəʳ, (US) ˈkɑː.stɚˌmʌŋ.gɚ, -ˌmɑːŋ- **-s** -z
costive ˈkɒs.tɪv, (US) ˈkɑː.stɪv **-ly** -li **-ness** -nəs, -nɪs
costl|y ˈkɒst.l|i, (US) ˈkɑːst- **-ier** -i.əʳ, (US) -i.ɚ **-iest** -i.ɪst, -i.əst **-iness** -ɪ.nəs, -ɪ.nɪs
costmary ˈkɒst.meə.ri, (US) ˈkɑːst.mer.i
Costner ˈkɒst.nəʳ, (US) ˈkɑːst.nɚ
cost-plus ˌkɒstˈplʌs, (US) ˌkɑːst-
costum|e ˈkɒs.tʃuːm, -tjuːm, (US) ˈkɑː.stuːm, -stjuːm **-es** -z **-ing** -ɪŋ **-ed** -d ˌ**costume** ˈ**jewellery**
costumier kɒsˈtʃuː.mi.əʳ, -ˈtjuː-, -eɪ, (US) kɑːˈstuː.mi.eɪ, -ˈstjuː-, -ɚ **-s** -z
Cosway ˈkɒz.weɪ, (US) ˈkɑːz- **-s** -z
cos|y ˈkəʊ.z|i, (US) ˈkoʊ- **-ies** -iz **-ier** -i.əʳ, (US) -i.ɚ **-iest** -i.ɪst, -i.əst **-ily** -əl.i, -ɪ.li **-iness** -ɪ.nəs, ɪ.nɪs
cot kɒt, (US) kɑːt **-s** -s ˈ**cot** ˌ**death**
cotangent ˌkəʊˈtæn.dʒənt, ˈ-ˌ--, (US) ˌkoʊˈtæn-, ˈ-ˌ-- **-s** -s
cot|e kəʊt, (US) koʊt **-es** -s **-ing** -ɪŋ, (US) ˈkoʊ.t̬ɪŋ **-ed** -ɪd, (US) ˈkoʊ.t̬ɪd
Côte d'Azur ˌkəʊt.dæˈzjʊəʳ, -dəˈ-, (US) ˌkoʊt.dəˈzʊr, -dɑːˈ-

C

Côte d'Ivoire ˌkəʊt.diːˈvwɑːʳ, ⓊⓈ ˌkoʊt.diːˈvwɑːr
Côte d'Or ˌkəʊtˈdɔːʳ, ⓊⓈ ˌkoʊtˈdɔːr
cotenancy ˌkəʊˈten.ənt.si, ⓊⓈ ˌkoʊ-
coterie ˈkəʊ.tᵊr.i, ⓊⓈ ˈkoʊ.ţɚ- **-s** -z
coterminous ˌkəʊˈtɜː.mɪ.nəs, ⓊⓈ ˌkoʊˈtɝː- **-ly** -li
Cotgrave ˈkɒt.greɪv, ⓊⓈ ˈkɑːt-
cotill(i)on kəˈtɪl.i.ən, kəʊ-, kɒtˈɪl-, ⓊⓈ koʊˈtɪl.jən, kə- **-s** -z
Coton ˈkəʊ.tᵊn, ⓊⓈ ˈkoʊ-
cotoneaster kəˌtəʊ.niˈæs.təʳ, ⓊⓈ -ˌtoʊ.niˈæs.tɚ **-s** -z
Cotonou ˌkəʊ.təˈnuː, ˌkɒt.ɒnˈuː, ⓊⓈ ˌkoʊ.toʊˈnuː, -tᵊnˈuː
Cotopaxi ˌkɒt.əʊˈpæk.si, ˌkəʊ.təʊˈ-, ⓊⓈ ˌkoʊ.ţəˈ-
Cotswold ˈkɒt.swəʊld, -swəld, ⓊⓈ ˈkɑːt.swoʊld **-s** -z
Cotsworth ˈkɒt.swəθ, -wɜːθ, ⓊⓈ ˈkɑːt.swɝːθ, -swɚθ
cottag|e ˈkɒt.ɪdʒ, ⓊⓈ ˈkɑː.ţɪdʒ **-es** -ɪz **-ing** -ɪŋ **-ey** -i ˌ**cottage** ˈ**cheese;** ˌ**cottage** ˈ**industry;** ˌ**cottage** ˈ**pie**
cottager ˈkɒt.ɪ.dʒəʳ, ⓊⓈ ˈkɑː.ţɪ.dʒɚ **-s** -z
Cottam ˈkɒt.əm, ⓊⓈ ˈkɑː.ţəm
Cottbus ˈkɒt.bəs, -bʊs, ⓊⓈ ˈkɑːt.bəs, -bʊs
Cottenham ˈkɒt.ᵊn.əm, ⓊⓈ ˈkɑː.tᵊn-, -hæm
cotter, C~ ˈkɒt.əʳ, ⓊⓈ ˈkɑː.ţɚ **-s** -z
Cotterell ˈkɒt.ᵊr.ᵊl, ⓊⓈ ˈkɑː.ţɚ-
Cotterill ˈkɒt.ᵊr.ᵊl, -ɪl, ⓊⓈ ˈkɑː.ţɚ-
Cottesloe ˈkɒt.sləʊ, -əz.ləʊ, ⓊⓈ ˈkɑːt.sloʊ, -əz.loʊ
Cottian ˈkɒt.i.ən, ⓊⓈ ˈkɑː.ţi-
Cottingham ˈkɒt.ɪŋ.əm, ⓊⓈ ˈkɑː.ţɪŋ-, -hæm
cotton, C~ ˈkɒt.ᵊn, ⓊⓈ ˈkɑː.tᵊn **-s** -z **-ing** -ɪŋ **-ed** -d ˈ**Cotton** ˌ**Belt;** ˌ**cotton** ˈ**candy;** ˌ**cotton** ˈ**wool**
cotton grass ˈkɒt.ᵊn.grɑːs, ⓊⓈ ˈkɑː.tᵊn.græs
cotton-picking ˈkɒt.ᵊnˌpɪk.ɪŋ, ⓊⓈ ˈkɑː.tᵊn-
cottonseed ˈkɒt.ᵊn.siːd, ⓊⓈ ˈkɑː.tᵊn-
cottontail ˈkɒt.ᵊn.teɪl, ⓊⓈ ˈkɑː.tᵊn- **-s** -z
cottonwood ˈkɒt.n̩.wʊd, ⓊⓈ ˈkɑː.tn̩- **-s** -z
cottony ˈkɒt.ᵊn.i, ⓊⓈ ˈkɑː.tᵊn-
Cottrell ˈkɒt.rᵊl; kəˈtrel, ⓊⓈ ˈkɑː.trᵊl; ⓊⓈ kəˈtrel
cotyledon ˌkɒt.ɪˈliː.dᵊn, -ᵊlˈiː-, ⓊⓈ ˌkɑː.ţəˈliː- **-s** -z
cotyledonous ˌkɒt.ɪˈliː.dᵊn.əs, -ᵊlˈiː-, ⓊⓈ ˌkɑː.ţəˈliː-
couch v, n *all verb senses, item of furniture:* kaʊtʃ **-es** -ɪz **-ing** -ɪŋ **-ed** -t ˈ**couch po**ˌ**tato;** ˌ**couch po**ˈ**tato**
couch n *grass:* kuːtʃ, kaʊtʃ
Couch kuːtʃ
couchant ˈkaʊ.tʃᵊnt, ˈkuː-
couchée ˈkuː.ʃeɪ, -ˈ-, ⓊⓈ kuːˈʃeɪ **-s** -z
couchette kuːˈʃet **-s** -s
Coué ˈkuː.eɪ **-ism** -ɪ.zᵊm
cougar ˈkuː.gəʳ, ⓊⓈ -gɚ **-s** -z
cough kɒf, ⓊⓈ kɑːf, kɔːf **-s** -s **-ing** -ɪŋ **-ed** -t **-er/s** -əʳ/z, ⓊⓈ -ɚ/z ˈ**cough** ˌ**drop;** ˈ**cough** ˌ**mixture;** ˈ**cough** ˌ**syrup**
Coughlan ˈkɒg.lən, ˈkɒf-, ˈkɒk-, ˈkɒx-, ˈkəʊ-, ⓊⓈ ˈkɑː.glən, ˈkoʊ.lən
Coughlin ˈkɒg.lɪn, ˈkɒf-, ˈkɒk-, ˈkɒx-, ⓊⓈ ˈkɑː.glɪn, ˈkɑːf-
.co.uk dɒtˌkəʊ.dɒt.juːˈkeɪ, ⓊⓈ dɑːtˌkoʊ.dɑːt-
could (from **can**) *strong form:* kʊd; *weak form:* kəd
Note: Weak-form word. The strong form is used for emphasis, e.g. 'You **could** be right', for contrast, e.g. 'whether she could or not', and in sentence-final position, e.g. 'as well as he could'.
couldn't (= **could not**) ˈkʊd.ᵊnt
couldn't've (= **could not have**) ˈkʊd.ᵊnt.ᵊv
couldst kʊdst
could've (= **could have**) ˈkʊd.ᵊv
coulee ˈkuː.li **-s** -z
coulis ˈkuː.li, ⓊⓈ ˌkuːˈli
coulisse kuːˈliːs, kʊ- **-s** -ɪz
couloir ˈkuːl.wɑːʳ, -wɔːʳ, ⓊⓈ kuːlˈwɑːr **-s** -z
coulomb, C~ ˈkuː.lɒm, ⓊⓈ -lɑːm, -loʊm **-s** -z
Coulsdon ˈkəʊlz.dᵊn, ˈkuːlz-, ⓊⓈ ˈkoʊlz-, ˈkuːlz-

Note: /ˈkəʊlz-/ ⓊⓈ /ˈkoʊlz-/ is the traditional local pronunciation. People unfamiliar with the place generally pronounce /ˈkuːlz-/, as do new residents in the district.

Coulson ˈkəʊl.sᵊn, ˈkuːl-, ⓊⓈ ˈkoʊl-, ˈkuːl-
coulter ˈkəʊl.təʳ, ˈkuː-, ⓊⓈ ˈkoʊl.tɚ **-s** -z
Coulthard ˈkuːl.tɑːd, ˈkəʊl-, ⓊⓈ -tɑːrd
Coulton ˈkəʊl.tᵊn, ⓊⓈ ˈkoʊl-
council ˈkaʊnt.sᵊl, -sɪl **-s** -z ˈ**council** ˌ**house;** ˈ**council** ˌ**tax**
council|man ˈkaʊnt.sᵊl|.mən, -sɪl-, -mæn **-men** -mən, -men **-woman** -ˌwʊm.ən **-women** -ˌwɪm.ɪn
counci(l)lor ˈkaʊnt.sᵊl.əʳ, -sɪ.ləʳ, ⓊⓈ -sᵊl.ɚ **-s** -z
counsel ˈkaʊnt.sᵊl **-s** -z **-(l)ing** -ɪŋ **-(l)ed** -d
counsel(l)or ˈkaʊnt.sᵊl.əʳ, ⓊⓈ -ɚ **-s** -z
count, C~ kaʊnt **-s** -s **-ing** -ɪŋ, ⓊⓈ ˈkaʊn.ţɪŋ **-ed** -ɪd, ⓊⓈ ˈkaʊn.ţɪd
countab|le ˈkaʊn.tə.b|ᵊl, ⓊⓈ -ţə- **-ly** -li
countdown ˈkaʊnt.daʊn
countenanc|e ˈkaʊn.tən.ənts, -tɪ.nənts, ⓊⓈ -ţən.ənts **-es** -ɪz **-ing** -ɪŋ **-ed** -t
count|er ˈkaʊn.t|əʳ, ⓊⓈ ˈkaʊn.ţ|ɚ **-ers** -əz, ⓊⓈ -ɚz **-ering** -ᵊr.ɪŋ **-ered** -əd, ⓊⓈ -ɚd ˌ**Counter-Refor**ˈ**mation**
counter- kaʊn.təʳ, ⓊⓈ kaʊn.ţɚ
Note: Prefix. Normally carries either primary stress on first syllable, as in **counterpart** /ˈkaʊn.tə.pɑːt/, ⓊⓈ /ˈkaʊn.ţɚ.pɑːrt/, or secondary, as in **counteract** /ˌkaʊn.tᵊrˈækt/, / ⓊⓈ ˌkaʊn.ţɚˈækt/.
counteract ˌkaʊn.tᵊrˈækt, ˈ---, ⓊⓈ ˌkaʊn.ţɚˈækt **-s** -s **-ing** -ɪŋ **-ed** -ɪd
counteraction *counteracting:* ˌkaʊn.təʳˈæk.ʃᵊn, ⓊⓈ -ţɚˈ- **-s** -z
counter-action *action by way of reply:* ˈkaʊn.təʳˌæk.ʃᵊn, ⓊⓈ -ţɚˌ- **-s** -z
counteractive ˌkaʊn.təʳˈæk.tɪv, ⓊⓈ -ţɚˈ- **-ly** -li
counterargument ˌkaʊn.təʳˈɑːg.jə.mənt, -jʊ-, ⓊⓈ ˈkaʊn.ţɚˌɑːrg.jə- **-s** -s
counterattack ˈkaʊn.təʳ.əˌtæk, ˌkaʊn.təʳ.əˈtæk, ⓊⓈ ˈkaʊn.ţɚ.əˌtæk, ˌkaʊn.ţɚ.əˈtæk **-s** -s **-ing** -ɪŋ **-ed** -t
counterattraction ˌkaʊn.təʳ.əˈtræk.ʃᵊn, ˈkaʊn.təʳ.ə.træk-, ⓊⓈ ˌkaʊn.ţɚ.əˈtræk-, ˈkaʊn.ţɚ.əˌtræk- **-s** -z
counterbalanc|e n ˈkaʊn.təˌbæl.ənts, ⓊⓈ -ţɚ- **-es** -ɪz
counterbalanc|e v ˌkaʊn.təˈbæl.ənts, ⓊⓈ -ţɚˈ- **-es** -ɪz **-ing** -ɪŋ **-ed** -t
counterbid ˈkaʊn.tə.bɪd, ⓊⓈ -ţɚ- **-s** -z **-ding** -ɪŋ
counterblast ˈkaʊn.tə.blɑːst, ⓊⓈ -ţɚ.blæst **-s** -s
counterblow ˈkaʊn.tə.bləʊ, ⓊⓈ -ţɚ.bloʊ **-s** -z
countercharg|e ˈkaʊn.tə.tʃɑːdʒ, ⓊⓈ -ţɚ.tʃɑːrdʒ **-es** -ɪz **-ing** -ɪŋ **-ed** -d
counterclaim ˈkaʊn.tə.kleɪm, ⓊⓈ -ţɚ- **-s** -z **-ing** -ɪŋ **-ed** -d
counterclockwise ˌkaʊn.təˈklɒk.waɪz, ⓊⓈ -ţɚˈklɑː.kwaɪz
counterespionage ˌkaʊn.təʳˈes.pi.ə.nɑːʒ, -nɑːdʒ, ⓊⓈ -ţɚˈ-
counter|feit ˈkaʊn.tə|.fɪt, -fiːt, ⓊⓈ -ţɚ|.fɪt **-feits** -fɪts, -fiːts, ⓊⓈ -fɪts **-feiting** -fɪ.tɪŋ, -fiː-, ⓊⓈ -fɪ.ţɪŋ **-feited** -fɪ.tɪd, -fiː-, ⓊⓈ -fɪ.ţɪd **-feiter/s** -fɪ.təʳ/z, -fiː-, ⓊⓈ -fɪ.ţɚ/z
counterfoil ˈkaʊn.tə.fɔɪl, ⓊⓈ -ţɚ- **-s** -z
counterinsurgen|cy ˌkaʊn.təʳ.ɪnˈsɜː.dʒən|t.si, ⓊⓈ -ţɚ.ɪnˈsɝː- **-t** -t
counterintelligence ˌkaʊn.təʳ.ɪnˈtel.ɪ.dʒənts, ˈkaʊn.təʳ.ɪn.tel-, ⓊⓈ ˌkaʊn.ţɚ.ɪnˈtel-, ˈkaʊn.ţɚ.ɪnˌtel-
counterintuitive ˌkaʊn.təʳ.ɪnˈtʃuː.ə.tɪv, -ˈtjuː-, -ɪ.tɪv, ⓊⓈ -ţɚ.ɪnˈtuː.ə.ţɪv, -ˈtjuː- **-ly** -li
countermand ˌkaʊn.təˈmɑːnd, ˈ---, ⓊⓈ ˌkaʊn.ţɚˈmænd, ˈ--- **-s** -z **-ing** -ɪŋ **-ed** -ɪd
countermeasure ˈkaʊn.təˌmeʒ.əʳ, ⓊⓈ -ţɚˌmeʒ.ɚ **-s** -z
countermove ˈkaʊn.tə.muːv, ⓊⓈ -ţɚ- **-s** -z
counteroffensive ˌkaʊn.təʳ.əˈfent.sɪv,

ˈkaʊn.təʳ.əˌfent-, (US) ˈkaʊn.t̬ɚ.əˌfent- -s -z

counterpane ˈkaʊn.tə.peɪn, -pɪn, (US) -t̬ɚ- -s -z

counterpart ˈkaʊn.tə.pɑːt, (US) -t̬ɚ.pɑːrt -s -s

counterplot ˈkaʊn.tə.plɒt, (US) -tɚ.plɑːt -s -s

counterpoint ˈkaʊn.tə.pɔɪnt, (US) -t̬ɚ-

counterpois|e ˈkaʊn.tə.pɔɪz, (US) -t̬ɚ- -es -ɪz -ing -ɪŋ -ed -d

counterproductive ˌkaʊn.tə.prəˈdʌk.tɪv, (US) -t̬ɚ- -ly -li -ness -nəs, -nɪs

counterrevolution ˌkaʊn.tə.rev.əˈluː.ʃən, -ˈljuː-, ˈkaʊn.tə.rev.əˌluː-, -ˌljuː-, (US) ˌkaʊn.t̬ɚ.rev.əˈluː-, ˈkaʊn.t̬ɚ.rev.əˌluː- -s -z

counterrevolutionar|y ˌkaʊn.tə.rev.əˈluː.ʃən.ər|.i, -ˈljuː-, ˈkaʊn.tə.rev.əˌluː-, -ˌljuː-, (US) ˌkaʊn.t̬ɚ.rev.əˈluː.ʃən.er-, ˈkaʊn.t̬ɚ.rev.əˌluː- -ies -iz

counterscarp ˈkaʊn.tə.skɑːp, (US) -t̬ɚ.skɑːrp -s -s

countersign n ˈkaʊn.tə.saɪn, (US) -t̬ɚ- -s -z -ed -d

countersign v ˈkaʊn.tə.saɪn, ˌ--ˈ-, (US) -t̬ɚ- -s -z -ing -ɪŋ -ed -d

counter|sink ˈkaʊn.tə|.sɪŋk, (US) -t̬ɚ- -sinks -sɪŋks -sinking -sɪŋ.kɪŋ -sunk -sʌŋk

countertenor ˌkaʊn.təˈten.əʳ, ˈkaʊn.təˌten-, (US) ˈkaʊn.t̬ɚˌten.ɚ -s -z

counterterror|ism ˌkaʊn.təˈter.ə.r|ɪ.zəm, (US) -t̬ɚˈter.ɚ|.ɪ- -ist/s -ɪst/s

countervail ˌkaʊn.təˈveɪl, ˈ---, (US) ˈkaʊn.t̬ɚ.veɪl, ˌ--ˈ- -s -z -ing -ɪŋ -ed -d

counterweight ˈkaʊn.tə.weɪt, (US) -t̬ɚ- -s -s

countess, C~ ˈkaʊn.tɪs, -tes, -təs; ˌkaʊnˈtes, (US) ˈkaʊn.t̬ɪs, -təs -es -ɪz

Countesthorpe ˈkaʊn.tɪs.θɔːp, (US) -θɔːrp

countinghou|se ˈkaʊn.tɪŋ.haʊ|s -ses -zɪz

countless ˈkaʊnt.ləs, -lɪs

countrified ˈkʌn.trɪ.faɪd

countr|y ˈkʌn.tr|i -ies -iz ˌ**country and ˈwestern**; ˌ**country ˈbumpkin**; ˌ**country ˈdancing** (US) ˈ**country ˌdancing**; ˌ**country ˈhouse**; ˌ**country ˈseat**

country-danc|e ˌkʌn.triˈdɑːnts, (US) -ˈdænts -es -ɪz -ing -ɪŋ

country|man ˈkʌn.trɪ|.mən -men -mən

countryside ˈkʌn.trɪ.saɪd

countrywide ˌkʌn.triˈwaɪd, (US) ˈ--- *stress shift, British only:* ˌ**countrywide ˈvoting**

country|woman ˈkʌn.trɪ|ˌwʊm.ən -women -ˌwɪm.ɪn

count|y ˈkaʊn.t|i, (US) -t̬|i -ies -iz ˌ**county ˈcourt**; ˌ**county ˈfair**; ˌ**county ˈhall**; ˌ**county ˈtown**

countywide ˌkaʊn.tiˈwaɪd, (US) -t̬i-

coup kuː -s -z

coup(s) de foudre ˌkuː.dəˈfuː.drə

coup(s) de grâce ˌkuː.dəˈgrɑːs

coup(s) de main ˌkuː.dəˈmæ̃ŋ, -ˈmæn

coup(s) d'état ˌkuː.deɪˈtɑː, -detˈɑː

coup(s) de théâtre ˌkuː.də.teɪˈɑː.trə

coupé, coupe ˈkuː.peɪ, -ˈ-, (US) kuːˈpeɪ, koʊp -s -z

Couper ˈkuː.pəʳ, (US) -pɚ

Couperin ˈkuː.pə.ræ̃ŋ, -ræn

Coupland ˈkuːp.lənd, ˈkəʊp-, (US) ˈkuːp-, ˈkoʊp-

coupl|e ˈkʌp.əl -es -z -ing -ɪŋ, ˈ-lɪŋ -ed -d

coupler ˈkʌp.ləʳ, (US) -lɚ -s -z

couplet ˈkʌp.lət, -lɪt -s -s

coupling ˈkʌp.lɪŋ -s -z

coupon ˈkuː.pɒn, (US) ˈkuː.pɑːn, ˈkjuː- -s -z

courage, C~ ˈkʌr.ɪdʒ

courageous kəˈreɪ.dʒəs -ly -li -ness -nəs, -nɪs

courante kuˈrɑ̃ːnt, -ˈrɑːnt, -ˈrænt, (US) -ˈrɑːnt -s -s

courgette kɔːˈʒet, kʊə-, (US) kʊr- -s -s

Couric ˈkʊə.rɪk, (US) ˈkʊrɪk

courier, C~ ˈkʊr.i.əʳ, ˈkʌr-, (US) ˈkʊr.i.ɚ, ˈkɝː- -s -z

Courland ˈkʊə.lənd, -lænd, (US) ˈkʊr-

cours|e, C~ kɔːs, (US) kɔːrs -es -ɪz -ing -ɪŋ -ed -t

coursebook ˈkɔːs.bʊk, (US) ˈkɔːrs- -s -s

courser ˈkɔː.səʳ, (US) ˈkɔːr.sɚ -s -s

coursework ˈkɔːs.wɜːk, (US) ˈkɔːrs.wɝːk

court, C~ kɔːt, (US) kɔːrt -s -s -ing -ɪŋ, (US) ˈkɔːr.t̬ɪŋ -ed -ɪd, (US) ˈkɔːr.t̬ɪd ˈ**court ˌcard**; ˌ**court of apˈpeal**; ˈ**court ˌorder**, ˌ**court ˈorder**; ˈ**court ˌshoe**

Courtauld ˈkɔː.təʊld, ˈkɔː.təʊ, (US) ˈkɔːr.toʊld, -toʊ -s -z

court-bouillon ˌkɔːt.buːˈjɒn, ˌkʊət-, ˌkʊə-, (US) ˌkɔːr.buːˈjɑːn

Courtelle® kɔːˈtel, kʊə-, (US) kɔːr-

Courtenay ˈkɔːt.ni, (US) ˈkɔːrt-

courteous ˈkɜː.ti.əs, (US) ˈkɝː.t̬i- -ly -li -ness -nəs, -nɪs

courtesan ˈkɔː.tɪ.zæn, ˈkʊə-, -tə-, –ˈ-, (US) ˈkɔːr.t̬ə.zən, -zæn -s -z

courtes|y ˈkɜː.tə.s|i, -tɪ-, (US) ˈkɝː.t̬ə- -ies -iz

Courthope ˈkɔː.təp, ˈkɔːt.həʊp, (US) ˈkɔːr.təp, ˈkɔːrt.hoʊp

courthou|se ˈkɔːt.haʊ|s, (US) ˈkɔːrt- -ses -zɪz

courtier ˈkɔː.ti.əʳ, (US) ˈkɔːr.t̬i.ɚ -s -z

courtl|y ˈkɔːt.l|i, (US) ˈkɔːrt- -ier -i.əʳ, (US) -i.ɚ -iest -i.ɪst, -i.əst -iness -ɪ.nəs, -ɪ.nɪs

court-martial ˌkɔːtˈmɑː.ʃəl, (US) ˈkɔːrtˌmɑːr- -s -z -(l)ing -ɪŋ -(l)ed -d **courts-martial** ˌkɔːts-, (US) ˈkɔːrts-

Courtneidge ˈkɔːt.nɪdʒ, (US) ˈkɔːrt-

Courtney ˈkɔːt.ni, (US) ˈkɔːrt-

courtroom ˈkɔːt.rʊm, -ruːm, (US) ˈkɔːrt.ruːm, -rʊm -s -z

courtship ˈkɔːt.ʃɪp, (US) ˈkɔːrt- -s -s

courtyard ˈkɔːt.jɑːd, (US) ˈkɔːrt.jɑːrd -s -z

Courvoisier® kʊəˈvwæz.i.eɪ, kɔː-, -ˈvwɑː.zi-, (US) ˌkɔːr.vwɑː.ziˈeɪ

couscous ˈkuːs.kuːs

cousin ˈkʌz.ən -s -z

Cousins ˈkʌz.ənz

Cousteau kuːˈstəʊ, ˈ--, (US) kuːˈstoʊ

couth kuːθ -ly -li -ness -nəs, -nɪs

Coutts kuːts

couture kuːˈtjʊəʳ, -tʊəʳ, (US) kuːˈtʊr

couturier kuːˈtjʊə.ri.eɪ, -ˈtʊə-, -əʳ, (US) -ˈtʊr.i.eɪ, -ɚ -s -z

Couzens ˈkʌz.ənz

covalenc|y ˌkəʊˈveɪ.lənt.s|i, ˈkəʊ.veɪ-, (US) ˌkoʊˈveɪ.lənt- -ies -iz

covalent ˌkəʊˈveɪ.lənt, ˈ---, (US) ˌkoʊˈveɪ-

covariance ˌkəʊˈveə.ri.ənts, ˈkəʊ.veə-, (US) ˌkoʊˈver.i-, -ˈvær-

cove, C~ kəʊv, (US) koʊv -s -z

coven ˈkʌv.ən -s -z

coven|ant ˈkʌv.ən|.ənt, (US) -ænt -ants -ənts, (US) -ænts -anting -ən.tɪŋ, (US) -ən.t̬ɪŋ, -æn- -anted -ən.tɪd, (US) -ən.t̬ɪd, -æn- -anter/s -ən.təʳ/z, (US) -ən.t̬ɚ/z, -æn-

covenantee ˌkʌv.ən.ənˈtiː, (US) -ænˈtiː, -ənˈ- -s -z

covenantor ˈkʌv.ən.ən.təʳ, (US) ˈkʌv.ən.æn.t̬ɚ; (US) ˌkʌv.ən.ænˈtɔːr -s -z

Covent ˈkɒv.ənt, ˈkʌv-, (US) ˈkʌv-, ˈkɑː.vənt ˌ**Covent ˈGarden**

Coventry ˈkɒv.ən.tri, ˈkʌv-, (US) ˈkʌv-, ˈkɑː.vən-

cov|er ˈkʌv|.əʳ, (US) -ɚ -ers -əz, (US) -ɚz -ering/s -ər.ɪŋ/z -ered -əd, (US) -ɚd ˈ**cover ˌcharge**; ˈ**cover ˌgirl**; ˌ**covered ˈwagon**

Coverack ˈkɒv.ər.æk, ˈkʌv-, -ək, (US) ˈkʌv.ə.ræk, ˈkɑː.və-

coverage ˈkʌv.ər.ɪdʒ

coverall ˈkʌv.ər.ɔːl, (US) -ɔːl, -ɑːl -s -z

Coverdale ˈkʌv.ə.deɪl, (US) ˈ-ɚ-

coverlet ˈkʌv.ə.lət, -lɪt, (US) ˈ-ɚ- -s -s

Coverley ˈkʌv.ə.li, (US) ˈ-ɚ-

cover-point ˌkʌv.əˈpɔɪnt, (US) -ɚˈ- -s -s

covert n *shelter, cloth:* ˈkʌv.ət, -ə, (US) ˈkʌv.ɚt, ˈkoʊ.vɚt -s -z

covert adj ˈkəʊ.vɜːt, ˈkʌv.ət, kəʊˈvɜːt, (US) ˈkoʊ.vɝːt, ˈkʌv.ɚt; (US) koʊˈvɝːt -ly -li

> Note: In British English, the pronunciation /ˈkʌv.ət/ used to be the most widespread, but has been overtaken by /ˈkəʊ.vɜːt/.

coverture ˈkʌv.ə.tʃəʳ, -tjəʳ, -tʃʊəʳ, -tjʊəʳ, (US) -ɚ.tʃɚ

cover-up ˈkʌv.əʳ.ʌp, (US) ˈ-ɚ- -s -s

cov|et ˈkʌv|.ɪt, -ət -ets -ɪts, -əts -eting/ly -ɪ.tɪŋ/li, -ə.tɪŋ/li, (US) -ə.t̬ɪŋ/li -eted -ɪ.tɪd, -ə.tɪd, (US)

Pronouncing the letters **CQU**

The letter combination **cqu** has two possible pronunciations: /kw/ and /k/. Generally speaking, /kw/ is used where the combination begins a stressed syllable, e.g.:

acquire əˈkwaɪəʳ (US) -ˈkwaɪ.ɚ

acquiesce ˌæk.wiˈes

The realization /k/ tends to appear before unstressed syllables, e.g.:

racquet ˈræk.ɪt

-ə.t̬ɪd **-etable** -ɪ.tə.bᵊl, -ə.tə.bᵊl, (US) -ə.t̬ə.bᵊl
covetous ˈkʌv.ɪ.təs, -ə.təs, (US) -ə.t̬əs **-ly** -li **-ness** -nəs, -nɪs
covey ˈkʌv.i **-s** -z
Covington ˈkʌv.ɪŋ.tən
cow kaʊ **-s** -z **-ing** -ɪŋ **-ed** -d ˈ**cow ˌparsley**, ˌ**cow** ˈ**parsley**; **till the** ˈ**cows come** ˌ**home**
Cowan kaʊ.ən
coward, C~ ˈkaʊ.əd, (US) ˈkaʊ.ɚd **-s** -z
cowardice ˈkaʊ.ə.dɪs, (US) ˈkaʊ.ɚ-
cowardl|y ˈkaʊ.əd.l|i, (US) ˈkaʊ.ɚd- **-iness** -ɪ.nəs, -ɪ.nɪs
cowbane ˈkaʊ.beɪn
cowbell ˈkaʊ.bel **-s** -z
cowboy ˈkaʊ.bɔɪ **-s** -z ˈ**cowboy** ˌ**boots**; ˈ**cowboy** ˌ**hat**
cowcatcher ˈkaʊˌkætʃ.əʳ, (US) -ɚ **-s** -z
Cowden ˈkaʊ.den, -dᵊn; kaʊˈden
Cowdenbeath ˌkaʊ.dᵊnˈbiːθ
Cowdray ˈkaʊ.dreɪ, -dri
Cowdrey ˈkaʊ.dri
Cowell ˈkaʊ.əl, kaʊəl, ˈkəʊ.əl, (US) ˈkaʊ.əl, kaʊl, ˈkoʊ.əl
Cowen ˈkaʊ.ən, ˈkaʊ.ɪn, ˈkəʊ.ən, ˈkəʊ.ɪn, (US) ˈkaʊ.ən, ˈkaʊ.ɪn, ˈkoʊ.ən, ˈkoʊ.ɪn
cower ˈkaʊ.əʳ, kaʊəʳ, (US) ˈkaʊ.ɚ **-s** -z **-ing** -ɪŋ **-ed** -d
Cowes kaʊz
cowgirl ˈkaʊ.gɜːl, (US) -gɝːl **-s** -z
cowhand ˈkaʊ.hænd **-s** -z
cowherd ˈkaʊ.hɜːd, (US) -hɝːd **-s** -z
cowhide ˈkaʊ.haɪd
Cowie ˈkaʊ.i
cowl kaʊl **-s** -z **-ing** -ɪŋ **-ed** -d
Cowley ˈkaʊ.li
cowlick ˈkaʊ.lɪk **-s** -s
cowlike ˈkaʊ.laɪk
Cowling ˈkaʊ.lɪŋ
cow|man ˈkaʊ|.mæn, -mən **-men** -mən
co-worker ˈkəʊˌwɜː.kəʳ, (US) ˈkoʊˌwɝː.kɚ, ˌ-ˈ-- **-s** -z
cowpat ˈkaʊ.pæt **-s** -s
Cowper ˈkaʊ.pəʳ, ˈkuː-, (US) ˈkaʊ.pɚ, ˈkuː-

> Note: The poet called himself /ˈkuː.pəʳ/ (US) /-pɚ/. /ˈkuː.pəʳ/ (US) /-pɚ/ is also the pronunciation in **Cowper Powys** /ˌkuː.pəˈpəʊ.ɪs/ (US) /-pɚˈpoʊ-/ and **Cowper-Black** /ˌkuː.pəˈblæk/ (US) /-pɚˈ-/.

cowpoke ˈkaʊ.pəʊk, (US) -poʊk **-s** -s
cowpox ˈkaʊ.pɒks, (US) -pɑːks
cowpuncher ˈkaʊˌpʌn.tʃəʳ, (US) -ˌpʌnt.ʃɚ **-s** -z
cowr|ie, cowr|y ˈkaʊ.r|i **-ies** -iz
co-writer ˈkəʊˌraɪ.təʳ, (US) ˈkoʊˌraɪ.t̬ɚ, ˌ-ˈ-- **-s** -z
cowshed ˈkaʊ.ʃed **-s** -z
cowslip ˈkaʊ.slɪp **-s** -s
cox, C~ kɒks, (US) kɑːks **-es** -ɪz **-ing** -ɪŋ **-ed** -t **-less** -ləs, -lɪs
Coxall ˈkɒk.sᵊl, -sɑːl, (US) ˈkɑːk-
coxcomb ˈkɒk.skəʊm, (US) ˈkɑːk.skoʊm **-s** -z
coxswain ˈkɒk.sᵊn, -sweɪn, (US) ˈkɑːk- **-s** -z
coy kɔɪ **-er** -əʳ, (US) -ɚ **-est** -ɪst, -əst **-ly** -li **-ness** -nəs, -nɪs
coyish ˈkɔɪ.ɪʃ **-ly** -li **-ness** -nəs, -nɪs
Coyle kɔɪl
coyote kɔɪˈəʊ.ti, kaɪ-; ˈkɔɪ.əʊt, ˈkaɪ-, (US) kaɪˈoʊ.t̬i; (US) ˈkaɪ.oʊt **-s** -z
coypu ˈkɔɪ.puː, -pjuː, -ˈ- **-s** -z
coz kʌz
cozen ˈkʌz.ᵊn **-s** -z **-ing** -ɪŋ **-ed** -d **-er/s** -əʳ/z, (US) -ɚ/z
Cozens, Cozzens ˈkʌz.ᵊnz
cozily ˈkəʊ.zᵊl.i, -zɪ.li, (US) ˈkoʊ-
coz|y ˈkəʊ.z|i, (US) koʊ- **-ier** -i.əʳ, (US) -i.ɚ **-iest** -i.ɪst, -i.əst
cozzie ˈkɒz.i, (US) ˈkɑː.zi **-s** -z
CPU ˌsiː.piːˈjuː
crab kræb **-s** -z **-bing** -ɪŋ **-bed** -d ˈ**crab** ˌ**apple**
Crabbe kræb
crabbed kræbd, ˈkræb.ɪd **-ly** -li **-ness** -nəs, -nɪs
crabb|y ˈkræb|.i **-ier** -i.əʳ, (US) -i.ɚ **-iest** -i.ɪst, -i.əst **-ily** -ᵊl.i, -ɪ.li **-iness** -ɪ.nəs, -ɪ.nɪs
crabgrass ˈkræb.grɑːs, (US) -græs
crabtree, C~ ˈkræb.triː **-s** -z
crabwise ˈkræb.waɪz
Crace kreɪs
crack kræk **-s** -s **-ing** -ɪŋ **-ed** -t ˌ**crack of** ˈ**dawn**
crackdown ˈkræk.daʊn **-s** -z
Crackenthorpe ˈkræk.ᵊn.θɔːp, (US) -θɔːrp
cracker ˈkræk.əʳ, (US) -ɚ **-s** -z
cracker-barrel ˈkræk.əˌbær.ᵊl, (US) -ɚˌber.ᵊl, -ˌbær-
Cracker Jack® ˈkræk.ə.dʒæk, (US) ˈ-ɚ-
crackerjack adj ˈkræk.ə.dʒæk, (US) ˈ-ɚ-
crackhead ˈkræk.hed **-s** -z
crackhou|se ˈkræk.haʊ|s **-ses** -zɪz
crackl|e ˈkræk.ᵊl **-es** -z **-ing** -ɪŋ, ˈ-lɪŋ **-ed** -d
crackling ˈkræk.lɪŋ
crackly ˈkræk.ᵊl.i, ˈkræk.li
cracknel ˈkræk.nᵊl **-s** -z
Cracknell ˈkræk.nᵊl
crackpot ˈkræk.pɒt, (US) -pɑːt **-s** -s
cracks|man ˈkræks|.mən **-men** -mən
Cracow ˈkræk.ɒf, -ɒv, -aʊ, -əʊ, (US) ˈkrɑː.kaʊ, ˈkræk.aʊ; (US) ˈkrɑː.kʊf
-cracy krə.si
Craddock ˈkræd.ək
cradl|e ˈkreɪ.dᵊl **-es** -z **-ing** -ɪŋ, ˈkreɪd.lɪŋ **-ed** -d
cradlesnatch ˈkreɪ.dᵊl.snætʃ **-ing** -ɪŋ **-er/s** -əʳ/z, (US) -ɚ/z
Cradley ˈkreɪd.li, ˈkræd-
craft krɑːft, (US) kræft **-s** -s **-ing** -ɪŋ **-ed** -ɪd
-craft krɑːft, (US) kræft
crafts|man ˈkrɑːfts|.mən, (US) ˈkræfts- **-men** -mən **-manship** -mən.ʃɪp
crafts|woman ˈkrɑːfts|ˌwʊm.ən, (US) ˈkræfts- **-women** -ˌwɪm.ɪn
craft|y ˈkrɑːf.t|i, (US) ˈkræf- **-ier** -i.əʳ, (US) -i.ɚ **-iest** -i.ɪst, -i.əst **-ily** -ᵊl.i, -ɪ.li **-iness** -ɪ.nəs, -ɪ.nɪs
crag kræg **-s** -z
Cragg kræg
cragg|y ˈkræg|.i **-ier** -i.əʳ, (US) -i.ɚ **-iest** -i.ɪst, -i.əst **-ily** -ᵊl.i, -ɪ.li **-iness** -ɪ.nəs, -ɪ.nɪs
crags|man ˈkrægz|.mən **-men** -mən, -men
craic kræk
Craig kreɪg
Craigavon ˌkreɪˈgæv.ᵊn
Craigie ˈkreɪ.gi
Craik kreɪk
Craiova krɑːˈjəʊ.və, krə-, (US) krɑːˈjoʊ-
crak|e kreɪk **-es** -s **-ing** -ɪŋ **-ed** -t
cram, C~ kræm **-s** -z **-ming** -ɪŋ **-med** -d
crambo ˈkræm.bəʊ, (US) -boʊ
Cramer ˈkrɑː.məʳ, ˈkreɪ-, (US) ˈkreɪ.mɚ
cram-full ˌkræmˈfʊl
Cramlington ˈkræm.lɪŋ.tən
crammer ˈkræm.əʳ, (US) -ɚ **-s** -z
cramp, C~ kræmp **-s** -s **-ing** -ɪŋ **-ed** -t
cramp-iron ˈkræmp.aɪən, -aɪ.ən, (US) -aɪ.ɚn **-s** -z
crampon ˈkræm.pɒn, -pən, (US) -pɑːn **-s** -z
Crampton ˈkræm*p*.tən
cran kræn **-s** -z
cranage ˈkreɪ.nɪdʒ
Cranage ˈkræn.ɪdʒ
cranberr|y ˈkræn.bᵊr|.i, ˈkræm-, (US) -ˌber- **-ies** -iz
Cranborne ˈkræn.bɔːn, ˈkræm-, (US) ˈkræn.bɔːrn
Cranbourn(e) ˈkræn.bɔːn, ˈkræm-, (US) ˈkræn.bɔːrn

Cranbrook ˈkræn.brʊk, ˈkræm-, US ˈkræn-
cran|e, C~ kreɪn **-es** -z **-ing** -ɪŋ **-ed** -d ˈ**crane ˌfly**
cranesbill ˈkreɪnz.bɪl **-s** -z
Cranfield ˈkræn.fiːld
Cranford ˈkræn.fəd, US -fɚd
cranial ˈkreɪ.ni.əl
cranio- ˈkreɪ.ni.əʊ, US ˈkreɪ.ni.oʊ, -ə
craniolog|y ˌkreɪ.niˈɒl.ə.dʒ|i, US -ˈɑː.lə- **-ist/s** -ɪst/s
crani|um ˈkreɪ.ni|.əm **-ums** -əmz **-a** -ə
crank kræŋk **-s** -s **-ing** -ɪŋ **-ed** -t
crankshaft ˈkræŋk.ʃɑːft, US -ʃæft **-s** -s
Crankshaw ˈkræŋk.ʃɔː, US -ʃɑː, -ʃɔː
crank|y ˈkræŋ.k|i **-ier** -i.əʳ, US -i.ɚ **-iest** -i.ɪst, -i.əst **-ily** -əl.i, -ɪ.li **-iness** -ɪ.nəs, -ɪ.nɪs
Cranleigh, Cranley ˈkræn.li
Cranmer ˈkræn.məʳ, ˈkræm-, US ˈkræn.mɚ
crann|y ˈkræn|.i **-ies** -iz **-ied** -id
Cranston ˈkræn.stən
Cranwell ˈkræn.wəl, -wel
Cranworth ˈkræn.wəθ, -wɜːθ, US -wɚθ, -wɜːθ
crap kræp **-s** -s **-ping** -ɪŋ **-ped** -t
crape kreɪp **-s** -s
crapper ˈkræp.əʳ, US -ɚ **-s** -z
crapp|y ˈkræp|.i **-ier** -i.əʳ, US -i.ɚ **-iest** -i.ɪst, -i.əst
craps kræps
crapshooter ˈkræpˌʃuː.təʳ, US -t̬ɚ **-s** -z
crapulen|ce ˈkræp.jə.lən|*t*s, -jʊ- **-t/ly** -t/li
crapulous ˈkræp.jə.ləs, -jʊ- **-ly** -li
crash kræʃ **-es** -ɪz **-ing** -ɪŋ **-ed** -t ˈ**crash ˌbarrier;** ˈ**crash ˌhelmet,** ˌ**crash** ˈ**helmet**
Crashaw ˈkræʃ.ɔː, US -ɑː, -ɔː
crash-div|e ˈkræʃ.daɪv, ˌ-ˈ- **-es** -z **-ing** -ɪŋ **-ed** -d **crash-dove** ˈkræʃ.dəʊv, US -doʊv
crash-land ˌkræʃˈlænd, US ˈkræʃ.lænd, ˌ-ˈ- **-s** -z **-ing/s** -ɪŋ/z **-ed** -ɪd *stress shift, British only:* ˌ**crash-land** ˈ**heavily**
cra|sis ˈkreɪ|.sɪs **-ses** -siːz
crass kræs **-er** -əʳ, US -ɚ **-est** -ɪst, -əst **-ly** -li **-ness** -nəs, -nɪs
-crat -kræt
cratch krætʃ **-es** -ɪz
Cratchit ˈkrætʃ.ɪt
crat|e kreɪt **-es** -s **-ing** -ɪŋ **-ed** -ɪd
crater ˈkreɪ.təʳ, US -t̬ɚ **-s** -z
Crathie ˈkræθ.i
-cratic -ˈkræt.ɪk, US -ˈkræt̬.ɪk
cra|vat krə|ˈvæt **-vats** -væts **-vatted** -væt.ɪd, US -væt̬.ɪd
crav|e kreɪv **-es** -z **-ing** -ɪŋ **-ed** -d **-er/s** -əʳ/z, US -ɚ/z
craven, C~ ˈkreɪ.vən **-s** -z **-ly** -li
craving ˈkreɪ.vɪŋ **-s** -z
craw krɔː, US krɑː, krɔː **-s** -z
crawfish ˈkrɔː.fɪʃ, US ˈkrɑː-, ˈkrɔː- **-es** -ɪz
Crawford ˈkrɔː.fəd, US ˈkrɑː.fɚd, ˈkrɔː-
crawl krɔːl, US krɑːl, krɔːl **-s** -z **-ing** -ɪŋ **-ed** -d **-er/s** -əʳ/z, US -ɚ/z
Crawley ˈkrɔː.li, US ˈkrɑː-, ˈkrɔː-
crawl|y ˈkrɔː.l|i, US ˈkrɑː-, ˈkrɔː- **-ier** -i.əʳ, US -i.ɚ **-iest** -i.ɪst, -i.əst **-iness** -ɪ.nəs, -ɪ.nɪs
Craxi ˈkræk.si
Cray kreɪ
crayfish ˈkreɪ.fɪʃ **-es** -ɪz
Crayford ˈkreɪ.fəd, US -fɚd
Crayola® kreɪˈəʊ.lə, US -ˈoʊ-
crayon ˈkreɪ.ɒn, -ən, US -ɑːn, -ən **-s** -z **-ing** -ɪŋ **-ed** -d
craz|e kreɪz **-es** -ɪz **-ed** -d
craz|y ˈkreɪ.z|i **-ier** -i.əʳ, US -i.ɚ **-iest** -i.ɪst, -i.əst **-ily** -əl.i, -ɪ.li **-iness** -ɪ.nəs, -ɪ.nɪs ˈ**Crazy ˌHorse;** ˌ**crazy** ˈ**paving**
CRE ˌsiː.ɑːʳˈiː, US -ɑːrˈ-
Creagh kreɪ
creak kriːk **-s** -s **-ing** -ɪŋ **-ed** -t
creak|y ˈkriː.k|i **-ier** -i.əʳ, US -i.ɚ **-iest** -i.ɪst, -i.əst **-ily** -əl.i, -ɪ.li **-iness** -ɪ.nəs, -ɪ.nɪs
cream kriːm **-s** -z **-ing** -ɪŋ **-ed** -d **-er/s** -əʳ/z, US -ɚ/z ˌ**cream** ˈ**cheese;** ˌ**cream** ˈ**cracker;** ˌ**cream** ˈ**soda;** ˌ**cream** ˈ**tea**
creamer|y ˈkriː.mər|.i **-ies** -iz
cream|y ˈkriː.m|i **-ier** -i.əʳ, US -i.ɚ **-iest** -i.ɪst, -i.əst **-ily** -əl.i, -ɪ.li **-iness** -ɪ.nəs, -ɪ.nɪs
creas|e kriːs **-es** -ɪz **-ing** -ɪŋ **-ed** -t
creasy ˈkriː.si
Creas(e)y ˈkriː.si
cre|ate kri|ˈeɪt **-ates** -eɪts **-ating** -eɪ.tɪŋ, US -eɪ.t̬ɪŋ **-ated** -eɪ.tɪd, US -eɪ.t̬ɪd
creation, C~ kriˈeɪ.ʃən **-s** -z
creation|ism kriˈeɪ.ʃən|.ɪ.zəm **-ist/s** -ɪst/s
creative kriˈeɪ.tɪv, US -t̬ɪv **-ly** -li **-ness** -nəs, -nɪs
creativity ˌkriː.eɪˈtɪv.ə.ti, -ɪ.ti, US -ə.t̬i
creator, C~ kriˈeɪ.təʳ, US -t̬ɚ **-s** -z
creature ˈkriː.tʃəʳ, US -tʃɚ **-s** -z ˌ**creature** ˈ**comfort** US ˈ**creature** ˌ**comfort**
crèch|e kreʃ, kreɪʃ **-es** -ɪz
Crécy ˈkres.i, US kreɪˈsiː
cred kred
Creda® ˈkriː.də
credence ˈkriː.dən*t*s
credential krɪˈden.*t*ʃəl, krə-, US -ˈdent.ʃəl **-s** -z
credibility ˌkred.əˈbɪl.ə.ti, -ɪˈ-, -ɪ.ti, US -əˈbɪl.ə.t̬i
credib|le ˈkred.ə.b|əl, ˈ-ɪ- **-ly** -li **-leness** -əl.nəs, -nɪs
cred|it ˈkred|.ɪt **-its** -ɪts **-iting** -ɪ.tɪŋ, US -ɪ.t̬ɪŋ **-ited** -ɪ.tɪd, US -ɪ.t̬ɪd ˈ**credit ˌcard**
creditab|le ˈkred.ɪ.tə.b|əl, US -t̬ə- **-ly** -li **-leness** -əl.nəs, -nɪs
Crediton ˈkred.ɪ.tən
creditor ˈkred.ɪ.təʳ, US -t̬ɚ **-s** -z
creditworth|y ˈkred.ɪtˌwɜː.ð|i, US -ˌwɜː- **-iness** -ɪ.nəs, -ɪ.nɪs
credo ˈkreɪ.dəʊ, ˈkriː-, US ˈkriː.doʊ, ˈkreɪ- **-s** -z
credulity krəˈdʒuː.lə.ti, -ˈdjuː-, krɪ-, kredʒˈuː-, kredˈjuː-, -lɪ-, US krəˈduː.lə-, -ˈdjuː-
credulous ˈkredʒ.ə.ləs, ˈkred.jə-, ˈkredʒ.ʊ-, ˈkred.jʊ- **-ly** -li **-ness** -nəs, -nɪs
Cree kriː
creed, C~ kriːd **-s** -z
creek, C~ kriːk **-s** -s
creel kriːl **-s** -z
creep kriːp **-s** -s **-ing** -ɪŋ **crept** krept
creeper ˈkriː.pəʳ, US -pɚ **-s** -z
creep|y ˈkriː.p|i **-ier** -i.əʳ, US -i.ɚ **-iest** -i.ɪst, -i.əst **-ily** -əl.i, -ɪ.li **-iness** -ɪ.nəs, -ɪ.nɪs
creepy-crawl|y ˌkriː.piˈkrɔː.l|i, ˈkriː.piˌkrɔː-, US ˌkriː.piˈkrɑː-, -ˈkrɔː-; US ˈkriː.piˌkrɑː-, -ˌkrɔː- **-ies** -iz
Crees kriːs, kriːz
Creevey ˈkriː.vi
Creighton ˈkraɪ.tən, ˈkreɪ-, US ˈkreɪ-, ˈkraɪ-
crema|te krɪˈmeɪ|t, krə-, US ˈkriː.meɪ|t; US krɪˈmeɪ|t **-tes** -ts **-ting** -tɪŋ, US -t̬ɪŋ **-ted** -tɪd, US -t̬ɪd **-tor/s** -təʳ/z, US -t̬ɚ/z
cremation krɪˈmeɪ.ʃən, krə-, US krɪ-, kriː- **-s** -z
crematori|um ˌkrem.əˈtɔː.ri|.əm, US ˌkriː.məˈtɔːr.i-, ˌkrem.əˈ- **-ums** -əmz **-a** -ə
cremator|y ˈkrem.ə.tər|.i, -tr|i, US ˈkriː.mə.tɔːr|.i, ˈkrem.ə- **-ies** -iz
creme krem, kriːm
crème brulée ˌkrem.bruːˈleɪ, ˌkreɪm-, ˌ-ˈ--
crème caramel ˌkrem.kær.əˈmel, ˌkreɪm-, -ˈkær.ə.mel, US -ker.əˈmel, -kær-; US -ˈker.ə.mel, -ˈkær-
crème de la crème ˌkrem.də.lɑːˈkrem, ˌkreɪm-, -ˈkreɪm
crème de menthe ˌkrem.dəˈmɑ̃ː*n*θ, ˌkreɪm-, -ˈmɑːn*t*θ, -ˈmɒn*t*θ, -ˈmɒnt, US -ˈmɑːnt, -ˈmen*t*θ
crème fraîche ˌkremˈfreɪʃ, ˌkreɪm-, US -ˈfreɪʃ, -ˈfreʃ
Cremona krɪˈməʊ.nə, krə-, US -ˈmoʊ-
Cremora® krɪˈmɔː.rə, krə-
crenate ˈkriː.neɪt
crenel(l)|ate ˈkren.əl|.eɪt, -ɪ.l|eɪt, US -ə.l|eɪt **-ates** -eɪts **-ating** -eɪ.tɪŋ, US -eɪ.t̬ɪŋ **-ated** -eɪ.tɪd, US -eɪ.t̬ɪd
crenel(l)ation ˌkren.əlˈeɪ.ʃən, -ɪˈleɪ-, US -əˈleɪ- **-s** -z
creole, C~ ˈkriː.əʊl, ˈkreɪ-, -ˈ-, US ˈkriː.oʊl, -ˈ- **-s** -z
Creolian kriːˈəʊ.li.ən, kreɪ-, US -ˈoʊ-
Creon ˈkriː.ən, -ɒn, US -ɑːn
creo|sote ˈkriː.ə|.səʊt, US -soʊt **-sotes** -səʊts, US -soʊts **-soting** -səʊ.tɪŋ, US -soʊ.t̬ɪŋ **-soted** -səʊ.tɪd, US -soʊ.t̬ɪd

crepe kreɪp -s -s ˌ**crepe** ˈ**paper** US ˈ**crepe** ˌ**paper**
crêpe krep, kreɪp
crêpe de chine ˌkrep.dəˈʃiːn, ˌkreɪp-
crêpe(s) suzette ˌkrep.suːˈzet, ˌkreɪp-
crepi|tate ˈkrep.ɪ|.teɪt -tates -teɪts -tating -teɪ.tɪŋ, US -teɪ.t̬ɪŋ -tated -teɪ.tɪd, US -teɪ.t̬ɪd
crepitation ˌkrep.ɪˈteɪ.ʃən -s -z
crépon ˈkrep.ɔ̃ːŋ, ˈkreɪ.pɔ̃ːŋ, -pɒn, US ˈkreɪ.pɑːn
crept (from **creep**) krept
crepuscular krɪˈpʌs.kjə.ləʳ, krə-, krepˈʌs-, -kjʊ-, US -kjə.lɚ
crepuscule ˈkrep.ə.skjuːl, US krɪˈpʌs.kjuːl
crescendo krɪˈʃen.dəʊ, krə-, US -doʊ -s -z
crescent n, adj *moon, shape:* ˈkres.ənt, ˈkrez-, US ˈkres- -s -s
crescent adj *growing, when applied to objects other than the moon:* ˈkres.ənt
Crespigny *surname:* ˈkrep.ɪ.ni, ˈkrep.ni, ˈkres.pɪ.ni; *in London streets:* kresˈpɪn.i
cress kres -es -ɪz
Cressida ˈkres.ɪ.də
Cresson ˈkres.ɔ̃ːŋ, -ɒn, US -ɑːn, -oʊn, -õ
Cresswell ˈkrez.wəl, -wel, ˈkres-, US ˈkres.wel, ˈkrez-, -wəl
Cressy ˈkres.i
crest krest -s -s -ing -ɪŋ -ed -ɪd
Cresta ˈkres.tə ˌ**Cresta** ˈ**Run**
crestfallen ˈkrestˌfɔː.lən, US -ˌfɔː-, -ˌfɑː- -ness -nəs, -nɪs
Creswell ˈkres.wəl, -wel, ˈkrez-
Creswick ˈkrez.ɪk, US ˈkres.wɪk; US ˈkrez.ɪk
cretaceous, C~ krɪˈteɪ.ʃəs, krə-, kretˈeɪ-, -ʃi.əs
Cretan ˈkriː.tən -s -z
Crete kriːt
Cretic ˈkriː.tɪk, US -t̬ɪk -s -s
cretin ˈkret.ɪn, US ˈkriː.tən -s -z
cretinism ˈkret.ɪ.nɪ.zəm, -ən.ɪ-, US ˈkriː.tən.ɪ-
cretinous ˈkret.ɪ.nəs, -ən.əs, US ˈkriː.tən.əs -ly -li
cretonne kretˈɒn, krɪˈtɒn, krə-; ˈkret.ɒn, US ˈkriː.tɑːn, krɪˈtɑːn -s -z
Creusa kriˈuː.zə, US -sə
Creuse krɜːz
Creutzfeldt-Jacob ˌkrɔɪts.feltˈjæk.ɒb, US -ˈjɑː.koʊb, -kɑːb ˌ**Creutzfeldt-**ˈ**Jacob di**ˌ**sease**
crevass|e krɪˈvæs, krə-, US krə- -es -ɪz -ed -t
Crèvecoeur krevˈkɜːʳ, US -ˈkʊr
crevic|e ˈkrev.ɪs -es -ɪz
crew kruː -s -z -ing -ɪŋ -ed -d ˈ**crew** ˌ**cut**; ˌ**crew** ˈ**neck**, ˈ**crew** ˌ**neck**
Crewe kruː
crewel ˈkruː.əl, -ɪl -s -z
Crewkerne ˈkruː.kɜːn, ˈkrʊk.ən, kruːˈkɜːn, US ˈkruː.kɝːn
Crianlarich ˌkriː.ənˈlær.ɪk, -ɪx, US -ˈler.ɪk, -ˈlær-
crib krɪb -s -z -bing -ɪŋ -bed -d -ber/s -əʳ/z, US -ɚ/z ˈ**crib** ˌ**death**
cribbage ˈkrɪb.ɪdʒ
Cribbins ˈkrɪb.ɪnz
Criccieth ˈkrɪk.i.eθ, -əθ
Crich kraɪtʃ
Crichel ˈkrɪtʃ.əl
Crichton ˈkraɪ.tən
crick, C~ krɪk -s -s -ing -ɪŋ -ed -t
crick|et ˈkrɪk|.ɪt -ets -ɪts -eter/s -ɪ.təʳ/z, US -ɪ.t̬ɚ/z -eting -ɪ.tɪŋ, US -ɪ.t̬ɪŋ
Crickhowell krɪkˈhaʊ.əl, -ˈhaʊl
cricoid ˈkraɪ.kɔɪd
cri(s) de coeur ˌkriː.deˈkɜːʳ, US -ˈkɝː
cried (from **cry**) kraɪd
Crieff kriːf
crier ˈkraɪ.əʳ, US -ɚ -s -z
cries (from **cry**) kraɪz
crikey ˈkraɪ.ki
crime kraɪm -s -z ˌ**crime of** ˈ**passion**
Crime|a kraɪˈmiː|.ə -an -ən
crimen falsi ˌkriː.m.enˈfæl.si, -ˈfɔːl-
crime(s) passionel(s) ˌkriːm.pæs.i.əˈnel, -pæʃ.əˈ-
Crimewatch ˈkraɪm.wɒtʃ, US -wɑːtʃ, -wɔːtʃ
criminal ˈkrɪm.ɪ.nəl, ˈ-ə- -s -z -ly -li ˌ**criminal** ˈ**damage**; ˌ**criminal** ˈ**law** US ˈ**criminal** ˌ**law**
criminality ˌkrɪm.ɪˈnæl.ə.ti, -əˈ-, -ɪ.ti, US -əˈnæl.ə.t̬i
criminalization, -isa- ˌkrɪm.ɪ.nəl.aɪˈzeɪ.ʃən, -ɪˈ-, US -əˈ-
criminaliz|e, -is|e ˈkrɪm.ɪ.nəl.aɪz, US -nə.laɪz -es -ɪz -ing -ɪŋ -ed -d
crimi|nate ˈkrɪm.ɪ|.neɪt, ˈ-ə- -nates -neɪts -nating -neɪ.tɪŋ, US -neɪ.t̬ɪŋ -nated -neɪ.tɪd, US -neɪ.t̬ɪd
crimination ˌkrɪm.ɪˈneɪ.ʃən, -əˈ- -s -z
criminolog|y ˌkrɪm.ɪˈnɒl.ə.dʒ|i, -əˈ-, US -ˈnɑː.lə- -ist/s -ɪst/s
crimp krɪmp -s -s -ing -ɪŋ -ed -t
Crimplene® ˈkrɪm.pliːn
crimson ˈkrɪm.zən -s -z -ing -ɪŋ -ed -d
cring|e krɪndʒ -es -ɪz -ing -ɪŋ -ed -d -er/s -əʳ/z, US -ɚ/z
cringe-making ˈkrɪndʒˌmeɪ.kɪŋ
crinkl|e ˈkrɪŋ.kəl -es -z -ing -ɪŋ, ˈ-klɪŋ -ed -d
crinkly ˈkrɪŋ.kli
crinoid ˈkraɪ.nɔɪd, ˈkrɪn.ɔɪd -s -z
crinoline ˈkrɪn.əl.ɪn -s -z
cripes kraɪps
Crippen ˈkrɪp.ɪn, -ən
crippl|e ˈkrɪp.əl -es -z -ing -ɪŋ, ˈ-lɪŋ -ed -d
Cripplegate ˈkrɪp.əl.geɪt
Cripps krɪps
Crisco® ˈkrɪs.kəʊ, US -koʊ
Criseyde krɪˈseɪ.də
cris|is ˈkraɪ.s|ɪs -es -iːz ˈ**crisis** ˌ**management**
crisp, C~ krɪsp -er -əʳ, US -ɚ -est -ɪst, -əst -s -s -ly -li -ness -nəs, -nɪs
crispbread ˈkrɪsp.bred -s -z
Crispian ˈkrɪs.pi.ən
Crispin ˈkrɪs.pɪn
crisp|y ˈkrɪs.p|i -ier -i.əʳ, US -i.ɚ -iest -i.ɪst, -i.əst -ily -əl.i, -ɪ.li -iness -ɪ.nəs, -ɪ.nɪs
crisscross ˈkrɪs.krɒs, US -krɑːs -es -ɪz -ing -ɪŋ -ed -t
Crist krɪst
Cristina krɪˈstiː.nə
crit krɪt -s -s
Critchley ˈkrɪtʃ.li
criteri|on, C~ kraɪˈtɪə.ri|.ən, US -ˈtɪr.i- -ons -ənz -a -ə
critic ˈkrɪt.ɪk, US ˈkrɪt̬- -s -s
critic|al ˈkrɪt.ɪ.k|əl, US ˈkrɪt̬- -ally -əl.i, -li -alness -əl.nəs, -nɪs
criticism ˈkrɪt.ɪ.sɪ.zəm, ˈ-ə-, US ˈkrɪt̬- -s -z
criticizable, -isa- ˈkrɪt.ɪ.saɪ.zə.bəl, ˈ-ə-; ˌkrɪt.ɪˈsaɪ-, -əˈ-, US ˈkrɪt̬.ɪ.saɪ-
criticiz|e, -is|e ˈkrɪt.ɪ.saɪz, ˈ-ə-, US ˈkrɪt̬- -es -ɪz -ing -ɪŋ -ed -d
critique krɪˈtiːk, krə- -s -s
Crittenden ˈkrɪt.ən.dən
critter ˈkrɪt.əʳ, US ˈkrɪt̬.ɚ -s -z
crittur ˈkrɪt.əʳ, US ˈkrɪt̬.ɚ -s -z
croak krəʊk, US kroʊk -s -s -ing/s -ɪŋ/z -ed -t -er/s -əʳ/z, US -ɚ/z
croak|y ˈkrəʊ.k|i, US ˈkroʊ- -ier -i.əʳ, US -i.ɚ -iest -i.ɪst, -i.əst -ily -əl.i, -ɪ.li -iness -ɪ.nəs, -ɪ.nɪs
Croat ˈkrəʊ.æt, -ət, US ˈkroʊ- -s -s
Croatia krəʊˈeɪ.ʃə, US kroʊ-
Croatian krəʊˈeɪ.ʃən, US kroʊ- -s -z
croc krɒk, US krɑːk -s -s
crochet ˈkrəʊ.ʃeɪ, -ʃi, US kroʊˈʃeɪ -s -z -ing -ɪŋ -ed -d ˈ**crochet** ˌ**hook** US **cro**ˈ**chet** ˌ**hook**
crock krɒk, US krɑːk -s -s
Crocker ˈkrɒk.əʳ, US ˈkrɑː.kɚ
crockery ˈkrɒk.ər.i, US ˈkrɑː.kɚ-
crocket ˈkrɒk.ɪt, US ˈkrɑː.kɪt -s -s
Crockett ˈkrɒk.ɪt, US ˈkrɑː.kɪt
Crockford ˈkrɒk.fəd, US ˈkrɑːk.fɚd
Crockpot® ˈkrɒk.pɒt, US ˈkrɑːk.pɑːt
crocodile ˈkrɒk.ə.daɪl, US ˈkrɑː.kə- -s -z ˌ**crocodile** ˈ**tears** US ˈ**crocodile** ˌ**tears**
crocodilian ˌkrɒk.əˈdɪl.i.ən, US ˌkrɑː.kəˈdɪl.jən -s -z
crocus ˈkrəʊ.kəs, US ˈkroʊ- -es -ɪz
Croesus ˈkriː.səs
croft, C~ krɒft, US krɑːft -s -s
crofter ˈkrɒf.təʳ, US ˈkrɑːf.tɚ -s -z
Crofton ˈkrɒf.tən, US ˈkrɑːf-
Crohn krəʊn, US kroʊn ˈ**Crohn's di**ˌ**sease**
croissant ˈkwæs.ɑ̃ːŋ, ˈkrwæs-, -ɒnt, US kwɑːˈsɑ̃ː, krə-, krwɑː-, -ˈsɑːnt -s -z
Croker ˈkrəʊ.kəʳ, US ˈkroʊ.kɚ
Cro-Magnon ˌkrəʊˈmæn.jɔ̃ːŋ, -jən, -ˈmæg.nən, -nɒn, US kroʊˈmæg.nən, -nɑːn, -ˈmæn.jən, -jɑːn
Cromarty ˈkrɒm.ə.ti, US ˈkrɑː.mɚ.t̬i
Crombie ˈkrɒm.bi, ˈkrʌm-, US ˈkrɑːm-, ˈkrʌm-
Crome krəʊm, US kroʊm
Cromer ˈkrəʊ.məʳ, US ˈkroʊ.mɚ

C

C

cromlech ˈkrɒm.lek, (US) ˈkrɑːm- **-s** -s
Crommelin ˈkrʌm.lɪn, ˈkrɒm-, (US) ˈkrɑːm-, ˈkrʌm-
Crompton ˈkrʌmp.tən, ˈkrɒmp-, (US) ˈkrɑːmp-
Cromwell ˈkrɒm.wəl, ˈkrʌm-, -wel, (US) ˈkrɑːm-
Cromwellian krɒmˈwel.i.ən, krʌm-, (US) krɑːm-
crone krəʊn, (US) kroʊn **-s** -z
Cronin ˈkrəʊ.nɪn, (US) ˈkroʊ-
Cronkite ˈkrɒŋ.kaɪt, (US) ˈkrɑːŋ.kaɪt
Cronos ˈkrəʊ.nɒs, (US) ˈkroʊ.nɑːs
cron|y ˈkrəʊ.n|i, (US) ˈkroʊ- **-ies** -iz
cronyism ˈkrəʊ.ni.ɪ.zᵊm, (US) ˈkroʊ-
crook, C~ krʊk **-s** -s **-ing** -ɪŋ **-ed** -t **by ˌhook or by ˈcrook**
Crookback ˈkrʊk.bæk
crookbacked ˈkrʊk.bækt
Crooke krʊk **-s** -s
crooked *not straight:* ˈkrʊk.ɪd **-er** -əʳ, (US) -ɚ **-est** -ɪst, -əst **-ly** -li **-ness** -nəs, -nɪs *having a crook:* krʊkt
Croome kruːm
croon kruːn **-s** -z **-ing** -ɪŋ **-ed** -d **-er/s** -əʳ/z, (US) -ɚ/z
crop krɒp, (US) krɑːp **-s** -s **-ping** -ɪŋ **-ped** -t
cropper ˈkrɒp.əʳ, (US) ˈkrɑː.pɚ **-s** -z
croquet ˈkrəʊ.keɪ, -ki, (US) kroʊˈkeɪ **-s** -z **-ing** -ɪŋ **-ed** -d
croquette krɒkˈet, krəʊˈket, (US) kroʊˈket **-s** -s
crore krɔːʳ, (US) krɔːr **-s** -z
Crosby ˈkrɒz.bi, ˈkrɒs-, (US) ˈkrɑːz-
Crosfield ˈkrɒs.fiːld, (US) ˈkrɑːs-
Croshaw ˈkrəʊ.ʃɔː, (US) ˈkroʊ.ʃɑː, -ʃɔː
crosier, C~ ˈkrəʊ.zi.əʳ, -ʒəʳ, (US) ˈkroʊ.ʒɚ **-s** -z
cross, C~ krɒs, (US) krɑːs **-es** -ɪz **-er** -əʳ, (US) -ɚ **-est** -ɪst, -əst **-ly** -li **-ness** -nəs, -nɪs **-ing** -ɪŋ **-ed** -t **ˈcross ˌaction; ˈcross ˌbench**
cross- krɒs, (US) krɑːs
crossbar ˈkrɒs.bɑːʳ, (US) ˈkrɑːs.bɑːr **-s** -z
crossbeam ˈkrɒs.biːm, (US) ˈkrɑːs- **-s** -z
crossbencher ˈkrɒsˌben.tʃəʳ, ˌ-ˈ--, (US) ˈkrɑːsˌbent.ʃɚ **-s** -z
crossbill ˈkrɒs.bɪl, (US) ˈkrɑːs- **-s** -z
crossbones ˈkrɒs.bəʊnz, (US) ˈkrɑːs.boʊnz
cross-border ˌkrɒsˈbɔː.dəʳ, (US) ˌkrɑːsˈbɔːr.dɚ *stress shift:* **ˌcross-border ˈtalks**
crossbow ˈkrɒs.bəʊ, (US) ˈkrɑːs.boʊ **-s** -z
crossbred ˈkrɒs.bred, (US) ˈkrɑːs-
crossbreed ˈkrɒs.briːd, (US) ˈkrɑːs- **-s** -z **-ing** -ɪŋ
cross-Channel ˌkrɒsˈtʃæn.ᵊl, (US) ˌkrɑːs- *stress shift:* **ˌcross-Channel ˈferry**
crosscheck n ˈkrɒs.tʃek, (US) ˈkrɑːs-
crosscheck v ˌkrɒsˈtʃek, ˈ--, (US) ˈkrɑːs.tʃek **-s** -s **-ing** -ɪŋ **-ed** -t
cross-claim ˈkrɒs.kleɪm, (US) ˈkrɑːs- **-s** -z
cross-contamination ˌkrɒs.kənˌtæm.ɪˈneɪ.ʃᵊn, -əˈ-; (US) ˌkrɑːs.kən.tæm.ɪˈneɪ-, -əˈ-
cross-country ˌkrɒsˈkʌn.tri, (US) ˌkrɑːs- *stress shift:* **ˌcross-country ˈrunner**
crosscourt ˈkrɒs.kɔːt, (US) ˈkrɑːs.kɔːrt
cross-cultural ˌkrɒsˈkʌl.tʃə.rᵊl, (US) ˌkrɑːsˈkʌl.tʃɚ.ᵊl **-ly** -li
crosscut ˈkrɒs.kʌt, ˌ-ˈ-, (US) ˈkrɑːs.kʌt **-s** -s
cross-dress|ing ˌkrɒsˈdres|.ɪŋ, (US) ˌkrɑːs- **-er/s** -əʳ/z, (US) -ɚ/z
Crosse krɒs, (US) krɑːs
cross-examination ˌkrɒs.ɪɡˌzæm.ɪˈneɪ.ʃᵊn, -eɡˌ-, -ɪkˌsæm-, -ekˌ-, -əˈ-, (US) ˌkrɑːs.ɪɡˌzæm-, -eɡˌ- **-s** -z
cross-examin|e ˌkrɒs.ɪɡˈzæm.ɪn, -eɡˈ-, -ɪkˈsæm-, -ekˈ-, (US) ˌkrɑːs.ɪɡˈzæm-, -eɡˈ- **-es** -z **-ing** -ɪŋ **-ed** -d **-er/s** -əʳ/z, (US) -ɚ/z
cross-eyed ˌkrɒsˈaɪd, ˈ--, (US) ˈkrɑːsˌaɪd *stress shift, British only:* **ˌcross-eyed ˈstare**
cross-fertilization, -isa- ˌkrɒsˌfɜː.tɪ.laɪˈzeɪ.ʃᵊn, -tə-, -lɪˈ-, -ləˈ-, (US) ˌkrɑːsˌfɝː.t̬ᵊl.əˈ-
cross-fertiliz|e, -is|e ˌkrɒsˈfɜː.tɪ.laɪz, -tə-, (US) ˌkrɑːsˈfɝː.t̬ə- **-es** -ɪz **-ing** -ɪŋ **-ed** -d
cross-fire ˈkrɒs.faɪəʳ, -faɪ.əʳ, (US) ˈkrɑːs.faɪ.ɚ
cross-grained ˌkrɒsˈɡreɪnd, (US) ˌkrɑːs-, ˈ-ˌ- *stress shift:* **ˌcross-grained ˈcutting**
crosshatch ˈkrɒs.hætʃ, (US) ˈkrɑːs- **-es** -ɪz **-ing** -ɪŋ **-ed** -t
crossing ˈkrɒs.ɪŋ, (US) ˈkrɑː.sɪŋ **-s** -z
cross-legged ˌkrɒsˈleɡd, ˈ--; ˌkrɒsˈleɡ.ɪd, -əd, (US) ˌkrɑːsˈleɡ.əd, -ˈleɡd
Crossley ˈkrɒs.li, (US) ˈkrɑː.sli
Crossman ˈkrɒs.mən, (US) ˈkrɑːs-
crossover ˈkrɒs.əʊ.vəʳ, (US) ˈkrɑːs.oʊ.vɚ **-s** -z
cross-party ˌkrɒsˈpɑː.ti, (US) ˌkrɑːsˈpɑːr.t̬i *stress shift:* **ˌcross-party ˈquestions**
crosspatch ˈkrɒs.pætʃ, (US) ˈkrɑːs- **-es** -ɪz
cross-purpos|e ˌkrɒsˈpɜː.pəs, (US) ˌkrɑːsˈpɝː-, ˈ-ˌ-- **-es** -ɪz
cross-question ˌkrɒsˈkwes.tʃᵊn, -ˈkweʃ-, (US) ˌkrɑːs-, ˈ-ˌ-- **-s** -z **-ing** -ɪŋ **-ed** -d
cross-refer ˌkrɒs.rɪˈfɜːʳ, -rəˈ-, (US) ˌkrɑːs.rəˈfɝː **-s** -z **-ring** -ɪŋ **-red** -d
cross-referenc|e ˌkrɒsˈref.ᵊr.ənts, ˈ-rᵊnts, (US) ˌkrɑːs-, ˈkrɑːsˌref.ɚ.ᵊnts, ˌ-rᵊnts **-es** -ɪz
crossroad ˈkrɒs.rəʊd, (US) ˈkrɑːs.roʊd **-s** -z
cross-section ˈkrɒs.sek.ʃᵊn, ˌ-ˈ--, (US) ˈkrɑːs.sek- **-s** -z
cross-stitch ˈkrɒs.stɪtʃ, (US) ˈkrɑːs-
cross-trainer ˈkrɒsˌtreɪ.nəʳ, (US) ˈkrɑːsˌtreɪ.nɚ **-s** -z
cross-training ˈkrɒsˌtreɪ.nɪŋ, (US) ˈkrɑːs-
crosswalk ˈkrɒs.wɔːk, (US) ˈkrɑːs.wɑːk, -wɔːk **-s** -s
crossway ˈkrɒs.weɪ, (US) ˈkrɑːs- **-s** -z
crosswind ˈkrɒs.wɪnd, (US) ˈkrɑːs- **-s** -z
crosswise ˈkrɒs.waɪz, (US) ˈkrɑːs-
crossword ˈkrɒs.wɜːd, (US) ˈkrɑːs.wɝːd **-s** -z **ˈcrossword ˌpuzzle**
Crosthwaite ˈkrɒs.θweɪt, (US) ˈkrɑːs-
crotch, C~ krɒtʃ, (US) krɑːtʃ **-es** -ɪz
crotch|et, C~ ˈkrɒtʃ|.ɪt, -ət, (US) ˈkrɑː.tʃ|ət **-ets** -ɪts, -əts, (US) -əts
crotchet|y ˈkrɒtʃ.ɪ.t|i, -ə.t|i, (US) ˈkrɑː.tʃə.t̬|i **-iness** -ɪ.nəs, -ɪ.nɪs
crotchless ˈkrɒtʃ.ləs, -lɪs, (US) ˈkrɑːtʃ-
Crothers ˈkrʌð.əz, (US) -ɚz
croton, C~ ˈkrəʊ.tᵊn, (US) ˈkroʊ-
crouch, C~ v kraʊtʃ **-es** -ɪz **-ing** -ɪŋ **-ed** -t
Crouch *village in Kent:* kruːtʃ
Crouchback ˈkraʊtʃ.bæk
croup kruːp **-s** -s
croupier ˈkruː.pi.eɪ, -pi.əʳ, (US) -eɪ, -ɚ **-s** -z
croustade kruːˈstɑːd **-s** -z
crouton ˈkruː.tɒn, -tɔ̃ːŋ, (US) ˈkruː.tɑːn, -ˈ- **-s** -z
crow, C~ krəʊ, (US) kroʊ **-s** -z **-ing** -ɪŋ **-ed** -d **crew** kruː **ˈcrow's ˌnest, ˌcrow's ˈnest; as the ˌcrow ˈflies**
crowbar ˈkrəʊ.bɑːʳ, (US) ˈkroʊ.bɑːr **-s** -z
Crowborough ˈkrəʊ.bᵊr.ə, (US) ˈkroʊ.bɚ.oʊ
crowd kraʊd **-s** -z **-ing** -ɪŋ **-ed** -ɪd
crowdsourc|e ˈkraʊdˌsɔːs, (US) -sɔːrs **-es** -ɪz **-ing** -ɪŋ **-ed** -t
Crowe krəʊ, (US) kroʊ
crow|foot ˈkrəʊ|.fʊt, (US) ˈkroʊ- **-foots** -fʊts **-feet** -fiːt
Crowhurst ˈkrəʊ.hɜːst, (US) ˈkroʊ.hɝːst
Crowland ˈkrəʊ.lənd, (US) ˈkroʊ-
Crowley ˈkrəʊ.li, ˈkraʊ-, (US) ˈkroʊ-, ˈkraʊ-
crown kraʊn **-s** -z **-ing** -ɪŋ **-ed** -d **ˌCrown ˈCourt; ˌcrown ˈglass; ˌcrown ˈjewels; ˌcrown ˈland; ˌcrown ˈprince**
Crowndale ˈkraʊn.deɪl
crow's|-foot ˈkrəʊz|.fʊt, (US) ˈkroʊz- **-feet** -fiːt
Crowther ˈkraʊ.ðəʳ, (US) -ðɚ
Crowthorne ˈkrəʊ.θɔːn, (US) ˈkroʊ.θɔːrn
Croxteth ˈkrɒk.stəθ, (US) ˈkrɑːk-
Croyden, Croydon ˈkrɔɪ.dᵊn
crozier, C~ ˈkrəʊ.zi.əʳ, -ʒəʳ, (US) ˈkroʊ.ʒɚ **-s** -z
CRT ˌsiː.ɑːˈtiː, (US) -ɑːrˈ-
cru kruː
crucial ˈkruː.ʃᵊl **-ly** -i
crucible ˈkruː.sɪ.bᵊl, -sə- **-s** -z
crucifer ˈkruː.sɪ.fəʳ, -sə-, (US) -fɚ **-s** -z
cruciferous kruːˈsɪ.fᵊr.əs
crucifix ˈkruː.sɪ.fɪks, -sə- **-es** -ɪz
crucifixion, C~ ˌkruː.səˈfɪk.ʃᵊn, -sɪˈ- **-s** -z

cruciform ˈkruː.sɪ.fɔːm, -sə-, US -fɔːrm
cruci|fy ˈkruː.sɪ|.faɪ, -sə- -fies -faɪz -fying -faɪ.ɪŋ -fied -faɪd -fier/s -faɪ.əʳ/z, US -faɪ.ɚ/z
crud krʌd -s -z -ding -ɪŋ -ded -ɪd
crudd|y ˈkrʌd|.i -ier -i.əʳ, US -i.ɚ -iest -i.ɪst, -i.əst
crud|e kruːd -er -əʳ, US -ɚ -est -ɪst, -əst -ely -li -eness -nəs, -nɪs
Cruden ˈkruː.dᵊn
crudité(s) ˈkruː.dɪ.teɪ, -də-, US ˌkruː.dɪˈteɪ
crudit|y ˈkruː.də.t|i, -dɪ.t|i, US -də.ţ|i -ies -iz
cruel ˈkruː.əl, kruəl, US ˈkruː.əl -(l)er -əʳ, US -ɚ -(l)est -ɪst, -əst -(l)y -li -ness -nəs, -nɪs
cruelt|y ˈkruː.əl.t|i, ˈkruəl-, US ˈkruː.əl.t|i -ies -iz
cruet ˈkruː.ɪt -s -s
Cruft krʌft -s -s
Crui(c)kshank ˈkrʊk.ʃæŋk
cruis|e, C~ kruːz -es -ɪz -ing -ɪŋ -ed -d -er/s -əʳ/z, US -ɚ/z ˈ**cruise conˌtrol**; ˌ**cruise ˈmissile** US ˈ**cruise ˌmissile**
cruiserweight ˈkruː.zə.weɪt, US -zɚ- -s -s
cruller ˈkrʌl.əʳ, US -ɚ -s -z
crumb krʌm -s -z -ing -ɪŋ -ed -d
crumbl|e ˈkrʌm.bᵊl -es -z -ing -ɪŋ, ˈ-blɪŋ -ed -d
crumbl|y ˈkrʌm.bl|i, -bᵊl|.i -ier -i.əʳ, US -i.ɚ -iest -i.ɪst, -i.əst
crumby ˈkrʌm.i
crumhorn ˈkrʌm.hɔːn, US -hɔːrn -s -z
Crumlin ˈkrʌm.lɪn
Crummock ˈkrʌm.ək
crumm|y ˈkrʌm|.i -ier -i.əʳ, US -i.ɚ -iest -i.ɪst
crump, C~ krʌmp -s -s -ing -ɪŋ -ed -t
crumpet ˈkrʌm.pɪt -s -s
crumpl|e ˈkrʌm.pᵊl -es -z -ing -ɪŋ, ˈ-plɪŋ -ed -d
crunch krʌntʃ -es -ɪz -ing -ɪŋ -ed -t
Crunchie® ˈkrʌn.tʃi
crunch|y ˈkrʌn.tʃ|i -ier -i.əʳ, US -i.ɚ -iest -i.ɪst, -i.əst -iness -ɪ.nəs, -ɪ.nɪs
crupper ˈkrʌp.əʳ, US -ɚ -s -z
crusad|e, C~ kruːˈseɪd -es -z -ing -ɪŋ -ed -ɪd
crusader kruːˈseɪ.dəʳ, US -dɚ -s -z
crus|e kruːz -es -ɪz
crush krʌʃ -es -ɪz -ing -ɪŋ -ed -t -er/s -əʳ/z, US -ɚ/z -able -ə.bᵊl
Crusoe ˈkruː.səʊ, US -soʊ
crust krʌst -s -s
crustace|an krʌsˈteɪ.ʃ|ᵊn, -ʃi|.ən -a -ə -ans -ənz
crustaceous krʌsˈteɪ.ʃəs, -ʃi.əs
crustate ˈkrʌs.teɪt
crustated krʌsˈteɪ.tɪd, US -ţɪd
crustation krʌsˈteɪ.ʃᵊn -s -z
crusted ˈkrʌs.tɪd
crust|y ˈkrʌs.t|i -ier -i.əʳ, US -i.ɚ -iest -i.ɪst, -i.əst -ily -ᵊl.i, -ɪ.li -iness -ɪ.nəs, -ɪ.nɪs
crutch krʌtʃ -es -ɪz -ed -t
Crutched Friars ˌkrʌtʃtˈfraɪ.əz, ˌkrʌtʃ.ɪdˈ-, US -ˈfraɪ.ɚz
Cruttwell ˈkrʌt.wəl, -wel
crux krʌks -es -ɪz
Cruyff kraɪf, krɔɪf, US krɔɪf
Cruz kruːz
cruzado kruˈzɑː.dəʊ, US -doʊ, -ˈzeɪ- -(e)s -z
cruzeiro kruˈzeə.rəʊ, US -ˈzer.oʊ -s -z
cr|y kr|aɪ -ies -aɪz -ying -aɪ.ɪŋ -ied -aɪd
cry-bab|y ˈkraɪˌbeɪ.b|i -ies -iz
cryo- ˌkraɪ.əʊ, US ˌkraɪ.oʊ, -ə
cryogenic ˌkraɪ.əʊˈdʒen.ɪk, US -əˈ- -s -s
cryonic kraɪˈɒn.ɪk, US -ˈɑː.nɪk -s -s
crypt krɪpt -s -s
crypt- krɪpt
cryptic ˈkrɪp.tɪk -al -ᵊl -ally -ᵊl.i, -li
crypto ˈkrɪp.təʊ, US -toʊ -s -z
cryptogam ˈkrɪp.təʊ.gæm, US -tə- -s -z
cryptogram ˈkrɪp.təʊ.græm, US -tə- -s -z -ic -ɪk
cryptograph ˈkrɪp.təʊ.grɑːf, -græf, US -tə.græf -s -s
cryptographer krɪpˈtɒg.rə.fəʳ, US -ˈtɑː.grə.fɚ -s -z
cryptography krɪpˈtɒg.rə.fi, US -ˈtɑː.grə-
cryptolog|y krɪpˈtɒl.ə.dʒ|i, US -ˈtɑː.lə- -ist/s -ɪst/s
crystal, C~ ˈkrɪs.tᵊl -s -z ˌ**crystal ˈball**; ˈ**crystal ˌgazing**
crystalizable, -isa- ˈkrɪs.tᵊl.aɪ.zə.bᵊl, US -tə.laɪ-
crystalline ˈkrɪs.tᵊl.aɪn, US -tə.laɪn
crystallization, -isa- ˌkrɪs.tᵊl.aɪˈzeɪ.ʃᵊn, -ɪˈ-, US -əˈ- -s -z
crystalliz|e, -is|e ˈkrɪs.tᵊl.aɪz, US -tə.laɪz -es -ɪz -ing -ɪŋ -ed -d
crystallographer ˌkrɪs.tᵊlˈɒg.rə.fəʳ, US -təˈlɑː.grə.fɚ -s -z
crystallography krɪs.tᵊlˈɒg.rə.fi, US -təˈlɑː.grə-
crystalloid ˈkrɪs.tᵊl.ɔɪd, US -tə.lɔɪd -s -z
CSE ˌsiː.esˈiː
C-section ˈsiːˌsek.ʃᵊn -s -z
ct (abbrev. for **carat**) ˈkær.ət, US ˈker-, ˈkær-
cub kʌb -s -z -bing -ɪŋ -bed -d
Cub|a ˈkjuː.b|ə -an/s -ən/z ˌ**Cuban ˈheel**
cubage ˈkjuː.bɪdʒ
cubb|y ˈkʌb|.i -ies -iz
cubbyhole ˈkʌb.i.həʊl, US -hoʊl -s -z
cub|e kjuːb -es -z -ing -ɪŋ -ed -d
cubic ˈkjuː.bɪk -al -ᵊl -ally -ᵊl.i, -li
cubicle ˈkjuː.bɪ.kᵊl -s -z
cub|ism ˈkjuː.b|ɪ.zᵊm -ist/s -ɪst/s
cubistic kjuːˈbɪs.tɪk
cu|bit ˈkjuː|.bɪt -bits -bɪts -bital -bɪ.tᵊl, -bɪ.ţᵊl
Cubitt ˈkjuː.bɪt
cuboid ˈkjuː.bɔɪd -s -z
cuchul(l)inn, cuchulain, C~ kuːˈkʊl.ɪn, -ˈxʊl-, US -ˈkʊl-
Cuckfield ˈkʊk.fiːld
Cuckmere ˈkʊk.mɪəʳ, US -mɪr
cuckold ˈkʌk.əʊld, -ᵊld, US -oʊld, -ᵊld -s -z -ing -ɪŋ -ed -ɪd -er/s -əʳ/z, US -ɚ/z -ry -ri
cuckoo ˈkʊk.uː, US ˈkuː.kuː, ˈkʊk.uː -s -z -ing -ɪŋ -ed -d ˈ**cuckoo ˌclock**; ˈ**cuckoo ˌspit**
cuckooflower ˈkʊk.uː.flaʊəʳ, -flaʊ.əʳ, US ˈkuː.kuː.flaʊ.ɚ, ˈkʊk.uːˌ- -s -z
cuckoopint ˈkʊk.uː.paɪnt, US ˈkuː.kuː-, ˈkʊk.uː -s -s
cucumber ˈkjuː.kʌm.bəʳ, US -bɚ -s -z
cud kʌd -s -z
cuddl|e ˈkʌd.ᵊl -es -z -ing -ɪŋ, ˈ-lɪŋ -ed -d -y -i
cudd|y ˈkʌd|.i -ies -iz
cudgel ˈkʌdʒ.ᵊl -s -z -(l)ing -ɪŋ -(l)ed -d
Cudworth ˈkʌd.wəθ, -wɜːθ, US -wɚθ, -wɝːθ
cu|e kjuː -es -z -ing -ɪŋ -ed -d
Cuenca ˈkweŋ.kɑː, -kə
Cuernavaca ˌkweə.nəˈvæk.ə, US ˌkwer.nəˈvɑː.kə, -nɑːˈvɑː.kɑː
cuff kʌf -s -s -ing -ɪŋ -ed -t
Cuffley ˈkʌf.li
cufflink ˈkʌf.lɪŋk -s -s
cui bono ˌkuː.iˈbəʊn.əʊ, ˌkwiː-, -ˈbɒn.əʊ, US ˌkwiːˈboʊ.noʊ
cuirass kwɪˈræs, kjuᵊ-, US kwɪˈræs -es -ɪz
cuirassier ˌkwɪ.rəˈsiː.əʳ, ˌkjuᵊ.rəˈ-, US ˌkwiː.rəˈsɪr, ˈkwɪr.ə.sɪr -s -z
cuisenaire ˌkwiː.zᵊnˈeəʳ, US -ˈer
Cuisinart® ˈkwiː.zᵊn.ɑːt, US -ɑːrt
cuisine kwɪzˈiːn, kwəˈziːn
cuisine minceur kwɪˌziːn.mæ̃nˈsɜːʳ, kwə-, US -ˈsɝː
cuiss|e kwɪs -es -ɪz
cuke kjuːk -s -s
Culcheth ˈkʌl.tʃəθ, -tʃɪθ
cul-de-sac ˈkʌl.də.sæk, ˈkʊl-, ˌ--ˈ- -s -s
Culham ˈkʌl.əm
culinary ˈkʌl.ɪ.nᵊr.i, ˈ-ə-, ˈkjuː.lɪ-, US ˈkʌl.ə.ner-
Culkin ˈkʌl.kɪn
cull kʌl -s -z -ing -ɪŋ -ed -d
Cullen ˈkʌl.ən, -ɪn
cullender ˈkʌl.ən.dəʳ, -ɪn-, US -dɚ -s -z
Culley ˈkʌl.i
Cullinan ˈkʌl.ɪ.nən, ˈ-ə-, -næn
Culloden kəˈlɒd.ᵊn, kʌlˈɒd-; kəˈləʊ.dᵊn, US kəˈlɑː.dᵊn, -ˈloʊ-
Cullompton kəˈlʌmp.tᵊn, ˈkʌl.əmp-
Cullum ˈkʌl.əm
culm, C~ kʌlm -s -z
Culme kʌlm
culmi|nate ˈkʌl.mɪ|.neɪt -nates -neɪts -nating -neɪ.tɪŋ, US -neɪ.ţɪŋ -nated -neɪ.tɪd, US -neɪ.ţɪd
culmination ˌkʌl.mɪˈneɪ.ʃᵊn, -məˈ- -s -z
culottes kjuːˈlɒts, kuː-, US ˈkuː.lɑːts, ˈkjuː-, -ˈ-

C

culpability ˌkʌl.pəˈbɪl.ə.ti, -ɪ.ti, US -ə.t̬i
culpab|le ˈkʌl.pə.b|əl **-ly** -li **-leness** -əl.nəs, -nɪs
culprit ˈkʌl.prɪt **-s** -s
Culross *Scottish surname & place:* ˈkuː.rɒs, -rəs, US -rɑːs *English surname and London street:* ˈkʌl.rɒs, -ˈ-, US ˈkʌl.rɑːs, -ˈ-
cult kʌlt **-s** -s
Culter ˈkuː.təʳ, US -t̬ɚ
cultivable ˈkʌl.tɪ.və.bəl, -tə-, US -tə-
culti|vate ˈkʌl.tɪ|.veɪt, -tə-, US -tə- **-vates** -veɪts **-vating** -veɪ.tɪŋ, US -veɪ.t̬ɪŋ **-vated** -veɪ.tɪd, US -veɪ.t̬ɪd **-vatable** -veɪ.tə.bəl, US -veɪ.t̬ə-
cultivation ˌkʌl.tɪˈveɪ.ʃən, -təˈ-, US -təˈ-
cultivator ˈkʌl.tɪ.veɪ.təʳ, -tə-, US -tə.veɪ.t̬ɚ **-s** -z
Cults kʌlts
cultural ˈkʌl.tʃər.əl **-ly** -i
culturality ˌkʌl.tʃəˈræl.ɪ.ti, -ə.ti, US -tʃəˈræl.ə.t̬i
culture ˈkʌl.tʃəʳ, US -tʃɚ **-s** -z **-d** -d ˈ**culture** ˌ**shock**
culver, C~ ˈkʌl.vəʳ, US -vɚ **-s** -z
culverin ˈkʌl.vər.ɪn **-s** -z
culvert ˈkʌl.vət, US -vɚt **-s** -s **-age** -ɪdʒ, US ˈkʌl.vɚ.t̬ɪdʒ
Culzean kəˈleɪn
cum kʌm, kʊm
Cumaean kjuːˈmiː.ən
cumbent ˈkʌm.bənt
cumb|er ˈkʌm.b|əʳ, US -b|ɚ **-ers** -əz, US -ɚz **-ering** -ər.ɪŋ **-ered** -əd, US -ɚd **-erer/s** -ər.əʳ/z, US -ɚ.ɚ/z
Cumberland ˈkʌm.bəl.ənd, US -bɚ.lənd
Cumbernauld ˌkʌm.bəˈnɔːld, ˈ---, US ˌkʌm.bɚˈnɑːld, -ˈnɔːld
cumbersome ˈkʌm.bə.səm, US -bɚ- **-ly** -li **-ness** -nəs, -nɪs
Cumbri|a ˈkʌm.bri|.ə **-an/s** -ən/z
cumbrous ˈkʌmb.rəs **-ly** -li **-ness** -nəs, -nɪs
cumin ˈkjuː.mɪn, ˈkʌm.ɪn, US ˈkuː-, ˈkjuː-
cum laude ˌkʌmˈlaʊ.deɪ, ˌkʊm-, -ˈlɔː.di, US ˌkʊmˈlaʊ.deɪ, -ˈlɑː-, -ˈlɔː-, -di, -də
cummerbund ˈkʌm.ə.bʌnd, US ˈ-ɚ- **-s** -z
cummin ˈkʌm.ɪn
Cumming ˈkʌm.ɪŋ **-s** -z
cummings, C~ ˈkʌm.ɪŋz
Cumnock ˈkʌm.nək
Cumnor ˈkʌm.nəʳ, US -nɚ
cumquat ˈkʌm.kwɒt, US -kwɑːt **-s** -s
cumulate adj ˈkjuː.mjə.lət, -mjʊ-, -lɪt, -leɪt, US -mjə-
cumu|late v ˈkjuː.mjə|.leɪt, -mjʊ-, US -mjə- **-lates** -leɪts **-lating** -leɪ.tɪŋ, US -leɪ.t̬ɪŋ **-lated** -leɪ.tɪd, US -leɪ.t̬ɪd
cumulation ˌkjuː.mjəˈleɪ.ʃən, -mjʊˈ-, US -mjəˈ- **-s** -z
cumulative ˈkjuː.mjə.lə.tɪv, -mjʊ-, -leɪ-, US -mjə.lə.t̬ɪv **-ly** -li **-ness** -nəs, -nɪs
cumulonimbus ˌkjuː.mjə.ləʊˈnɪm.bəs, -mjʊ-, US -mjə.loʊˈ- **-es** -ɪz
cumul|us ˈkjuː.mjə.l|əs, -mjʊ-, US -mjə- **-i** -aɪ, -iː, US -aɪ
Cunard ˌkjuːˈnɑːd, US ˌkjuːˈnɑːrd **-er/s** -əʳ/z, US -ɚ/z
cunctation kʌŋkˈteɪ.ʃən **-s** -z
cunctator kʌŋkˈteɪ.təʳ, US -t̬ɚ **-s** -z
cuneiform ˈkjuː.nɪ.fɔːm, -ni.ɪ-, -ə.fɔːm, US ˈkjuː.nə.fɔːrm, -ni.ə-
Cunliffe ˈkʌn.lɪf
cunnilingus ˌkʌn.ɪˈlɪŋ.gəs, US -əˈ-
cunning ˈkʌn.ɪŋ **-est** -ɪst, -əst **-ly** -li **-ness** -nəs, -nɪs
Cunningham ˈkʌn.ɪŋ.əm, US -hæm
cunt kʌnt **-s** -s
Cuomo ˈkwəʊ.məʊ, US ˈkwoʊ.moʊ
cup kʌp **-s** -s **-ping** -ɪŋ **-ped** -t ˈ**Cup** ˌ**Final**, ˌ**Cup** ˈ**Final**
Cupar ˈkuː.pəʳ, US -pɚ
cupbearer ˈkʌpˌbeə.rəʳ, US -ˌber.ɚ **-s** -z
cupboard ˈkʌb.əd, US -ɚd **-s** -z ˈ**cupboard** ˌ**love**
cupcake ˈkʌp.keɪk **-s** -s
cupful ˈkʌp.fʊl **-s** -z
cupid, C~ ˈkjuː.pɪd **-s** -z
cupidity kjuˈpɪd.ə.ti, -ɪ.ti, US -ə.t̬i
cupola ˈkjuː.pəl.ə **-s** -z
cuppa ˈkʌp.ə **-s** -z
cupreous ˈkjuː.pri.əs
cupric ˈkjuː.prɪk
Cuprinol® ˈkjuː.prɪ.nɒl, -prə-, US -nɑːl
cuprous kjuː.prəs
cur kɜːʳ, US kɝː **-s** -z
curability ˌkjʊə.rəˈbɪl.ə.ti, ˌkjɔː-, -ɪ.ti, US ˌkjʊr.əˈbɪl.ə.t̬i
curable ˈkjʊə.rə.bəl, ˈkjɔː-, US ˈkjʊr-
curaç|ao, C~ ˈkjʊə.rə.s|aʊ, ˈkjɔː-, -s|əʊ, ˌ--ˈ-, US ˈkjʊr.ə.s|oʊ, ˈkʊr-, -s|aʊ, ˌ--ˈ- **-oa** -əʊə, US -oʊə
curac|y ˈkjʊə.rə.s|i, ˈkjɔː-, US ˈkjʊr.ə- **-ies** -iz
Curan ˈkʌr.ən
curare kjʊəˈrɑː.ri, US kjʊˈrɑːr.i
curate n ˈkjʊə.rət, ˈkjɔː-, -rɪt, US ˈkjʊr.ət, -eɪt **-s** -s ˌ**curate's** ˈ**egg**
cura|te v ˈkjʊə.r|eɪt, ˈkjɔː-; -ˈ-, kjə-, US ˈkjʊr.|eɪt; US -ˈ-, kjɚ- **-tes** -ts **-ting** -tɪŋ, US -t̬ɪŋ **-ted** -tɪd, US -t̬ɪd
curative ˈkjʊə.rə.tɪv, ˈkjɔː-, US ˈkjʊr.ə.t̬ɪv **-ly** -li
curator kjʊəˈreɪ.təʳ, kjɔː-, US ˈkjʊr.eɪ.t̬ɚ, ˈkjɝː- **-s** -z **-ship/s** -ʃɪp/s
curb kɜːb, US kɝːb **-s** -z **-ing** -ɪŋ **-ed** -d
curbside ˈkɜːb.saɪd, US ˈkɝːb-
curbstone ˈkɜːb.stəʊn, US ˈkɝːb.stoʊn **-s** -z
curd kɜːd, US kɝːd **-s** -z
curdl|e ˈkɜː.dəl, US ˈkɝː- **-es** -z **-ing** -ɪŋ, ˈkɜːd.lɪŋ, US ˈkɝː.dəl.ɪŋ, ˈkɝːd.lɪŋ **-ed** -d
curd|y ˈkɜː.d|i, US ˈkɝː- **-ier** -i.əʳ, US -i.ɚ **-iest** -i.ɪst, -i.əst **-iness** -ɪ.nəs, -ɪ.nɪs
cur|e kjʊəʳ, kjɔːʳ, US kjʊr **-es** -z **-ing** -ɪŋ **-ed** -d **-er/s** -əʳ/z, US -ɚ/z
cure-all ˈkjʊəʳ.ɔːl, ˈkjɔːʳ-, US ˈkjʊr.ɑːl, ˈkjɝː-, -ɔːl **-s** -z
cu|ret kjʊə|ˈret, US kjʊ|ˈret **-rets** -ˈrets **-retting** -ˈret.ɪŋ, US -ˈret̬.ɪŋ **-retted** -ˈret.ɪd, US -ˈret̬.ɪd
curettage ˌkjʊə.rɪˈtɑːʒ, kjʊəˈret.ɪdʒ, US kjʊˈret̬.ɪdʒ, ˌkjʊr.əˈtɑːʒ
cu|rette kjʊə|ˈret, US kjʊ- **-rettes** -ˈrets **-retting** -ˈret.ɪŋ, US -ˈret̬.ɪŋ **-retted** -ˈret.ɪd, US -ˈret̬.ɪd
curettment kjʊəˈret.mənt, US kjʊ-
curfew ˈkɜː.fjuː, US ˈkɝː- **-s** -z
cur|ia ˈkjʊə.r|i.ə, ˈkjɔː-, ˈkʊə-, US ˈkjʊr|.i- **-iae** -i.iː, -i.aɪ
curie, C~ ˈkjʊə.ri, -iː, US ˈkjʊr.i, -iː **-s** -z
curio ˈkjʊə.ri.əʊ, ˈkjɔː-, US ˈkjʊr.i.oʊ **-s** -z
curiosit|y ˌkjʊə.riˈɒs.ə.t|i, ˌkjɔː-, -ɪ.t|i, US ˌkjʊr.iˈɑː.sə.t̬|i **-ies** -iz
curious ˈkjʊə.ri.əs, ˈkjɔː-, US ˈkjʊr.i- **-ly** -li **-ness** -nəs, -nɪs
curium ˈkjʊə.ri.əm, ˈkjɔː-, US ˈkjʊr.i-
curl kɜːl, US kɝːl **-s** -z **-ing** -ɪŋ **-ed** -d ˈ**curling** ˌ**tongs**
curler ˈkɜː.ləʳ, US ˈkɝː.lɚ **-s** -z
curlew ˈkɜː.ljuː, US ˈkɝː.luː, ˈkɝːl.juː **-s** -z
curlicue ˈkɜː.lɪ.kjuː, US ˈkɝː- **-s** -z
curling ˈkɜː.lɪŋ, US ˈkɝː-
curl|y ˈkɜː.l|i, US ˈkɝː- **-ier** -i.əʳ, US -i.ɚ **-iest** -i.ɪst, -i.əst **-iness** -ɪ.nəs, -ɪ.nɪs
curmudgeon kɜːˈmʌdʒ.ən, kə-, US kɚ- **-s** -z **-ly** -li
curragh, currach, C~ ˈkʌr.ə, US ˈkɝː- **-s** -z
Curran ˈkʌr.ən, US ˈkɝː-
currant ˈkʌr.ənt, US ˈkɝː- **-s** -s
currawong ˈkʌr.ə.wɒŋ, US -wɑːŋ, -wɔːŋ **-s** -z
currenc|y ˈkʌr.ənt.s|i, US ˈkɝː- **-ies** -iz
current ˈkʌr.ənt, US ˈkɝː- **-s** -s **-ly** -li **-ness** -nəs, -nɪs ˌ**current** **ac**ˈ**count**; ˌ**current** **af**ˈ**fairs**
Currer ˈkʌr.əʳ, US ˈkɝː.ɚ
curricle ˈkʌr.ɪ.kəl, US ˈkɝː- **-s** -z
curricul|um kəˈrɪk.jə.l|əm, -jʊ-, US -jə- **-a** -ə **-ums** -əmz **-ar** -əʳ, US -ɚ
curriculum vitae kəˌrɪk.jə.ləmˈviː.taɪ, -jʊ-, -teɪ, US -jə.ləmˈviː.taɪ, -tiː, -ˈvaɪ.t̬i **-s** -s
curricula vitae kəˌrɪk.jə.ləˈviː.taɪ, -jʊ-, -teɪ, US -jə.ləˈviː.taɪ, -tiː, -ˈvaɪ.t̬i
Currie ˈkʌr.i, US ˈkɝː.i
Currier ˈkʌr.i.əʳ, US ˈkɝː.i.ɚ
currish ˈkɜː.rɪʃ, US ˈkɝː.ɪʃ **-ly** -li **-ness** -nəs, -nɪs
curr|y, C~ ˈkʌr|.i, US ˈkɝː- **-ies** -iz **-ying** -i.ɪŋ **-ied** -id **-ier/s** -i.əʳ/z, US -i.ɚ/z ˈ**curry** ˌ**powder**
curs|e kɜːs, US kɝːs **-es** -ɪz **-ing** -ɪŋ **-ed** -t
cursed adj ˈkɜː.sɪd, US ˈkɝː- **-ly** -li **-ness** -nəs, -nɪs

cursive ˈkɜː.sɪv, US ˈkɝː- **-ly** -li **-ness** -nəs, -nɪs
cursor ˈkɜː.səʳ, US ˈkɝː.sɚ **-s** -z
Cursor Mundi ˌkɜː.sɔːˈmʊn.diː, -ˈmʌn.daɪ, US ˌkɝː.sɔːrˈmʊn.di, -sɚˈ-
cursor|y ˈkɜː.sᵊr|.i, US ˈkɝː- **-ily** -ᵊl.i, -ɪ.li **-iness** -ɪ.nəs, -ɪ.nɪs
curst kɜːst, US kɝːst
cursus ˈkɜː.səs, US ˈkɝː-
curt kɜːt, US kɝːt **-er** -əʳ, US ˈkɝː.t̬ɚ **-est** -ɪst, -əst, US ˈkɝː.t̬ɪst, -t̬əst **-ly** -li **-ness** -nəs, -nɪs
curtail kɜːˈteɪl, US kɚ- **-s** -z **-ing** -ɪŋ **-ed** -d **-ment/s** -mənt/s
curtain ˈkɜː.tᵊn, -tɪn, US ˈkɝː.tᵊn **-s** -z **-ed** -d ˈ**curtain** ˌ**call**; ˈ**curtain** ˌ**raiser**
curtes|y ˈkɜː.tə.s|i, -tɪ.s|i, US ˈkɝː.t̬ə- **-ies** -iz
Curtice ˈkɜː.tɪs, US ˈkɝː.t̬ɪs
curtilage ˈkɜː.tᵊl.ɪdʒ, -tɪ.lɪdʒ, US ˈkɝː.t̬ᵊl-
Curtis(s) ˈkɜː.tɪs, US ˈkɝː.t̬ɪs
curtsey ˈkɜːt.si, US ˈkɝːt- **-s** -z **-ing** -ɪŋ **-ed** -d
curts|y ˈkɜːt.s|i, US ˈkɝːt- **-ies** -iz **-ying** -i.ɪŋ **-ied** -id
curvaceous kɜːˈveɪ.ʃəs, US kɝː- **-ly** -li **-ness** -nəs, -nɪs
curvation kɜːˈveɪ.ʃᵊn, US kɝː- **-s** -z
curvature ˈkɜː.və.tʃəʳ, -tjəʳ, -tjʊəʳ, US ˈkɝː.və.tʃɚ **-s** -z
curv|e kɜːv, US kɝːv **-es** -z **-ing** -ɪŋ **-ed** -d ˈ**curve** ˌ**ball**
curveball ˈkɜːv.bɔːl, US ˈkɝːv-, -bɑːl **-s** -z
cur|vet kɜː|ˈvet, US kɝː- **-vets** -ˈvets **-vet(t)ing** -ˈvet.ɪŋ, US -ˈvet̬.ɪŋ **-vet(t)ed** -ˈvet.ɪd, US -ˈvet̬.ɪd
curviline|al ˌkɜː.vɪˈlɪn.i|.əl, -vəˈ-, US ˌkɝː.vəˈ- **-ar** -əʳ, US -ɚ
curv|y ˈkɜː.v|i, US ˈkɝː- **-ier** -i.əʳ, US -i.ɚ **-iest** -i.ɪst, -i.əst
Curwen ˈkɜː.wɪn, -wən, US ˈkɝː-
Curzon ˈkɜː.zᵊn, US ˈkɝː-
Cusack ˈkjuː.sæk, -zæk, -zək, US ˈkuː-, ˈkjuː-
Cush kʊʃ, kʌʃ **-ite/s** -aɪt/s
Cushing ˈkʊʃ.ɪŋ
cushion ˈkʊʃ.ᵊn **-s** -z **-ing** -ɪŋ **-ed** -d
cush|y ˈkʊʃ|.i **-ier** -i.əʳ, US -i.ɚ **-iest** -i.əst, -i.ɪst **-ily** -ᵊl.i, -ɪ.li **-iness** -ɪ.nəs, -ɪ.nɪs
cusp kʌsp **-s** -s
cuspid ˈkʌs.pɪd
cuspidor ˈkʌs.pɪ.dɔːʳ, US -pə.dɔːr **-s** -z
cuss kʌs **-es** -ɪz **-ing** -ɪŋ **-ed** -t
cussed **adj** ˈkʌs.ɪd, -əd **-ly** -li **-ness** -nəs, -nɪs
custard ˈkʌs.təd, US -tɚd **-s** -z ˈ**custard** ˌ**apple**; ˌ**custard** ˈ**pie**
Custer ˈkʌs.təʳ, US -tɚ
custodial kʌsˈtəʊ.di.əl, US -ˈtoʊ-
custodian kʌsˈtəʊ.di.ən, US -ˈtoʊ- **-s** -z
custody ˈkʌs.tə.di
custom ˈkʌs.təm **-s** -z
customarily ˈkʌs.tə.mᵊr.ᵊl.i, -ɪ.li; ˌkʌs.təˈmer-, US ˌkʌs.təˈmer-
customar|y ˈkʌs.tə.mᵊr|.i, US -mer- **-iness** -ɪ.nəs, -ɪ.nɪs
customer ˈkʌs.tə.məʳ, US -mɚ **-s** -z
customhou|se ˈkʌs.təm.haʊ|s **-ses** -zɪz
customization ˌkʌs.tə.maɪˈzeɪ.ʃᵊn, -mɪˈ-, US -məˈ-
customiz|e, -is|e ˈkʌs.tə.maɪz **-es** -ɪz **-ing** -ɪŋ **-ed** -d **-er/s** -əʳ/z, US -ɚ/z
custom-made ˌkʌs.təmˈmeɪd *stress shift, British only:* ˌ**custom-made** ˈ**suit**
custos **sing** ˈkʌs.tɒs, -təʊs, US -tɑːs; US ˈkʊs.toʊs **custodes** **plur** kʌsˈtəʊ.diːz, US -ˈtoʊ-
cut kʌt **-s** -s **-ting** -ɪŋ, US ˈkʌt̬.ɪŋ **-ter/s** -əʳ/z, US ˈkʌt̬.ɚ/z
cut-and-|dried ˌkʌt.ᵊn|ˈdraɪd **-dry** -ˈdraɪ
cut-and-paste ˌkʌt.ᵊndˈpeɪst, -ᵊmˈ-, US -ᵊndˈ-
cutaneous kjuːˈteɪ.ni.əs **-ly** -li
cutaway ˈkʌt.ə.weɪ, US ˈkʌt̬-
cutback ˈkʌt.bæk **-s** -s
Cutch kʌtʃ
cut|e kjuːt **-er** -əʳ, US ˈkjuː.t̬ɚ **-est** -ɪst, -əst, US ˈkjuː.t̬ɪst, -t̬əst **-ely** -li **-eness** -nəs, -nɪs
cutesy ˈkjuːt.si
cutey ˈkjuː.ti, US -t̬i **-s** -z
Cutforth ˈkʌt.fɔːθ, US -fɔːrθ
Cuthbert ˈkʌθ.bət, US -bɚt
Cuthbertson ˈkʌθ.bət.sᵊn, US -bɚt-
cuticle ˈkjuː.tɪ.kᵊl, US -t̬ə- **-s** -z
cuticular kjuːˈtɪk.jə.ləʳ, -jʊ-, US -lɚ
Cuticura® ˌkjuː.tɪˈkjʊə.rə, -ˈkjɔː-, US -t̬əˈkjʊr.ə
cutie ˈkjuː.ti, US -t̬i **-s** -z
cutie-pie ˈkjuː.ti.paɪ, US -t̬i-
cutis ˈkjuː.tɪs, US -t̬ɪs
cutlass ˈkʌt.ləs **-es** -ɪz
cutler, C~ ˈkʌt.ləʳ, US -lɚ **-s** -z
cutlery ˈkʌt.lᵊr.i
cutlet ˈkʌt.lət, -lɪt **-s** -s
cutoff ˈkʌt.ɒf, US ˈkʌt̬.ɑːf, -ɔːf **-s** -s
cutout ˈkʌt.aʊt, US ˈkʌt̬- **-s** -s
cut-price ˌkʌtˈpraɪs *stress shift:* ˌ**cut-price** ˈ**goods**
cut-rate ˌkʌtˈreɪt *stress shift:* ˌ**cut-rate** ˈ**tickets**
Cuttell kəˈtel
cutter ˈkʌt.əʳ, US ˈkʌt̬.ɚ **-s** -z
cutthroat ˈkʌt.θrəʊt, US -θroʊt **-s** -s
cutting ˈkʌt.ɪŋ, US ˈkʌt̬- **-s** -z ˌ**cutting** ˈ**edge**
cuttle, C~ ˈkʌt.ᵊl, US ˈkʌt̬- **-s** -z **-bone** -bəʊn, US -boʊn
cuttlefish ˈkʌt.ᵊl.fɪʃ, US ˈkʌt̬- **-es** -ɪz
cutt|y ˈkʌt|.i, US ˈkʌt̬- **-ies** -iz ˌ**Cutty** ˈ**Sark**
cutwater ˈkʌtˌwɔː.təʳ, US -ˌwɑː.t̬ɚ, -ˌwɔː- **-s** -z
cutworm ˈkʌt.wɜːm, US -wɝːm **-s** -z
cuvette kjuːˈvet, US kjuː-, kuː- **-s** -s
Cuvier ˈkjuː.vi.eɪ, ˈkuː-, US ˈkjuː.vi.eɪ; US ˌkuːˈvjeɪ
Cuxhaven ˈkʊksˌhɑː.vᵊn
Cuyahoga ˌkaɪ.əˈhəʊ.gə, US -ˈhoʊ-, -ˈhɑː-, -ˈhɔː-
Cuyp kaɪp, kɔɪp, US kɔɪp **-s** -s
Cuzco ˈkʊs.kəʊ, ˈkuː.skəʊ, US ˈkuː.skoʊ
CV ˌsiːˈviː **-s** -z
cwm kʊm, kuːm **-s** -z
Cwm Avon kʊmˈæv.ᵊn, kuːm-
Cwmbach kʊmˈbɑːx, kuːm-, US -ˈbɑːk
Cwmbran kʊmˈbrɑːn, kuːm-
cwt (abbrev. for **hundredweight**) ˈhʌn.drəd.weɪt, -drɪd- **-s** -s
cyan ˈsaɪ.æn, -ən
cyanate ˈsaɪ.ə.neɪt
cyanic saɪˈæn.ɪk
cyanide ˈsaɪ.ə.naɪd **-s** -z
cyanogen saɪˈæn.ə.dʒᵊn, -dʒɪn, -dʒen
cyanosis ˌsaɪ.əˈnəʊ.sɪs, US -ˈnoʊ-
cyber- saɪ.bəʳ, US -bɚ
cyberbull|y ˈsaɪ.bəˌbʊl|.i, US -bɚ- **-ies** -iz **-ying** -i.ɪŋ **-ied** -id
cybercafe ˈsaɪ.bəˌkæf.eɪ, US ˌsaɪ.bɚ.kæfˈeɪ, -kəˈfeɪ **-s** -z
cybercrime ˈsaɪ.bə.kraɪm, US -bɚ-
cyberfraud ˈsaɪ.bə.frɔːd, US -bɚ.frɑːd, -frɔːd
cybernetic ˌsaɪ.bəˈnet.ɪk, US -bɚˈnet̬- **-s** -s
cyberpet ˈsaɪ.bə.pet, US -bɚ- **-s** -s
cyberpunk ˈsaɪ.bə.pʌŋk, US -bɚ- **-s** -s
cybersex ˈsaɪ.bə.seks, US -bɚ-
cyberspace ˈsaɪ.bə.speɪs, US -bɚ-
cybersquatting ˈsaɪ.bəˌskwɒt.ɪŋ, US -bɚˌskwɑː.t̬ɪŋ
cyberterror|ism ˌsaɪ.bəˈter.ᵊr|.ɪ.zᵊm, ˈsaɪ.bəˌter.ər.ɪ.zəm, US -bɚˈ- **-ist/s** -ɪst/s
cybrarian saɪˈbreə.ri.ən, US -ˈbrer.i- **-s** -z
cybrar|y ˈsaɪ.brᵊr|.i, -br|i, US -brer|.i, -brær|.i **-ies** -iz
cycad ˈsaɪ.kæd, -kəd **-s** -z
Cyclades ˈsaɪ.klə.diːz, ˈsɪk.lə-
cyclamate ˈsaɪ.klə.meɪt, ˈsɪk.lə-, US ˈsaɪ.klə- **-s** -s
cyclamen ˈsɪk.lə.mən, ˈsaɪ.klə-, -men, US ˈsaɪ.klə- **-s** -z
cycl|e ˈsaɪ.kᵊl **-es** -z **-ing** -ɪŋ, ˈ-klɪŋ **-ed** -d
cyclic ˈsaɪ.klɪk, ˈsɪk.lɪk **-al** -ᵊl **-ally** -ᵊl.i, -li
cyclist ˈsaɪ.klɪst **-s** -s
cyclo- ˈsaɪ.kləʊ, saɪˈklɒ, US ˈsaɪ.kloʊ, saɪˈklɑː
Note: Prefix. This may be stressed on the initial syllable, e.g. **cyclostyle** /ˈsaɪ.kləʊ.staɪl/ US /ˈsaɪ.kloʊ-/ or on the second syllable, e.g. **cyclometer** /saɪˈklɒm.ɪ.tə/ US /saɪˈklɑː.mə.tɚ/.
cyclograph ˈsaɪ.kləʊ.grɑːf, -græf, US -klə.græf **-s** -s
cycloid ˈsaɪ.klɔɪd **-s** -z
cycloidal saɪˈklɔɪ.dᵊl
cyclometer saɪˈklɒm.ɪ.təʳ, ˈ-ə-, US -ˈklɑː.mə.t̬ɚ **-s** -z
cyclone ˈsaɪ.kləʊn, US -kloʊn **-s** -z

C

cyclonic saɪˈklɒn.ɪk, (US) -ˈklɑː.nɪk
cyclopaed|ia ˌsaɪ.kləʊˈpiː.d|i.ə, (US) -kloʊˈ-, -kləˈ- **-ias** -i.əz **-ic** -ɪk
cyclopean ˌsaɪ.kləʊˈpiː.ən; saɪˈkləʊ.pi-, (US) ˌsaɪ.kloʊˈpiː-, -kləˈ-; (US) saɪˈkloʊ.pi-
cycloped|ia ˌsaɪ.kləʊˈpiː.d|i.ə, (US) -kloʊˈ-, -kləˈ- **-ias** -i.əz **-ic** -ɪk
cyclops **sing** ˈsaɪ.klɒps, (US) -klɑːps **cyclopes** saɪˈkləʊ.piːz, (US) -ˈkloʊ-
cyclorama ˌsaɪ.kləˈrɑː.mə, (US) -kloʊˈræm.ə, -kləˈ-, -ˈrɑː.mə **-s** -z
cyclostyl|e ˈsaɪ.kləʊ.staɪl, (US) -klə- **-es** -z **-ing** -ɪŋ **-ed** -d
cyclothymia ˌsaɪ.kləʊˈθaɪ.mi.ə, (US) ˌsaɪ.kloʊˈ-, -kləˈ-
cyclotron ˈsaɪ.kləʊ.trɒn, (US) -klə.trɑːn **-s** -z
cyder ˈsaɪ.dəʳ, (US) -dɚ **-s** -z
cygnet ˈsɪg.nət, -nɪt **-s** -s
Cygnus ˈsɪg.nəs
cylinder ˈsɪl.ɪn.dəʳ, -ən-, (US) -dɚ **-s** -z
cylindric səˈlɪn.drɪk, sɪ- **-al** -əl **-ally** -əl.i, -li
cylindriform səˈlɪn.drɪ.fɔːm, sɪ-, (US) -drɪ.fɔːrm, -drə-
cylindroid ˈsɪl.ɪn.drɔɪd, səˈlɪn-, sɪ- **-s** -z
cyli|x ˈsaɪ.lɪ|ks, ˈsɪl.ɪ|ks **-ces** -siːz
cy|ma ˈsaɪ|.mə **-mae** -miː
cymbal ˈsɪm.bəl **-s** -z
cymbal|o ˈsɪm.bə.l|əʊ, (US) -l|oʊ **-o(e)s** -əʊz, (US) -oʊz
Cymbeline ˈsɪm.bə.liːn, -bɪ-
cyme saɪm **-s** -z
Cymric ˈkɪm.rɪk, ˈkʌm-, (US) ˈkɪm-
Cymru ˈkɪm.ri, ˈkʌm-
Cymry ˈkɪm.ri, ˈkʌm-, (US) ˈkɪm-
Cynewulf ˈkɪn.ɪ.wʊlf, ˈ-ə-
cynic ˈsɪn.ɪk **-s** -s
cynical ˈsɪn.ɪ.kəl **-ly** -i
cynicism ˈsɪn.ɪ.sɪ.zəm, ˈ-ə- **-s** -z
cynocephalic ˌsaɪ.nəʊ.sefˈæl.ɪk, -kefˈ-, (US) -noʊ-
cynocephalous ˌsaɪ.nəʊˈsef.ə.ləs, -ˈkef-, (US) -noʊˈ-
Cynon ˈkɪn.ən, ˈkʌn-
cynosure ˈsaɪ.nə.ʃʊəʳ, ˈsɪn.ə-, -sjʊəʳ, (US) -ʃʊr **-s** -z
Cynthi|a ˈsɪnt.θi|.ə **-us** -əs
cyph|er ˈsaɪ.f|əʳ, (US) -f|ɚ **-ers** -əz, (US) -ɚz **-ering** -ər.ɪŋ **-ered** -əd, (US) -ɚd
cy près ˌsiːˈpreɪ, ˌsaɪ-
cypress ˈsaɪ.prəs, -prɪs **-es** -ɪz
Cyprian ˈsɪp.ri.ən **-s** -z
Cypriot ˈsɪp.ri.ət **-s** -s
Cypriote ˈsɪp.ri.əʊt, (US) -oʊt **-s** -s
Cyprus ˈsaɪ.prəs
Cyrano ˈsɪər.ə.nəʊ; sɪˈrɑː-, sə-, (US) ˈsɪr.ə.noʊ ˌ**Cyrano de** ˈ**Bergerac**
Cyrenaica ˌsaɪə.rəˈneɪ.ɪ.kə, ˌsɪr.əˈ-, -ɪˈ-, -ˈnaɪ-, (US) ˌsaɪ.rəˈ-
Cyrene saɪəˈriː.ni, (US) saɪ-
Cyrenian saɪəˈriː.ni.ən, (US) saɪ-
Cyrenius saɪəˈriː.ni.əs, (US) saɪ-
Cyril ˈsɪr.əl, -ɪl
Cyrillic səˈrɪl.ɪk, sɪ-, (US) sə-
Cyrus ˈsaɪə.rəs, (US) ˈsaɪ-
cyst sɪst **-s** -s
cystic ˈsɪs.tɪk ˌ**cystic fib**ˈ**rosis**
cystitis sɪˈstaɪ.tɪs, -təs, (US) -t̬ɪs, -t̬əs
cystoid ˈsɪs.tɔɪd
Cythera sɪˈθɪə.rə, sə-, (US) -ˈθɪr.ə
cyto- ˈsaɪ.təʊ, saɪˈtɒ, (US) ˈsaɪ.t̬oʊ, -t̬ə, saɪˈtɑː
Note: Prefix. This may carry primary or secondary stress on the initial syllable, e.g. **cytoplasm** /ˈsaɪ.təʊ.plæz.əm/ (US) /ˈsaɪ.t̬ə-/ or on the second syllable, e.g. **cytology** /saɪˈtɒl.ə.dʒi/ (US) /saɪˈtɑːl-/.
cytogenetics ˌsaɪ.təʊ.dʒəˈnet.ɪks, -dʒenˈet-, -dʒɪˈnet-, (US) ˌsaɪ.t̬oʊ.dʒəˈnet̬-
cytology saɪˈtɒl.ə.dʒi, (US) -ˈtɑː.lə-
cytoplasm ˈsaɪ.təʊ.plæz.əm, (US) -t̬ə- **-s** -z
cytoplasmic ˌsaɪ.təʊˈplæz.mɪk, (US) -t̬əˈ-
czar, C~ zɑːʳ, tsɑːʳ, (US) zɑːr, tsɑːr **-s** -z
czardas ˈtʃɑː.dæʃ, ˈzɑː.dæs, -dəs, (US) ˈtʃɑːr.dɑːʃ, -dæʃ **-es** -ɪz
czarevitch, C~ ˈzɑː.rə.vɪtʃ, -rɪ-, (US) ˈzɑːr.ə-, ˈtsɑːr- **-es** -ɪz
czarevna, C~ zɑːˈrev.nə, tsɑː- **-s** -z
czarina zɑːˈriː.nə, tsɑː- **-s** -z
czarist ˈzɑː.rɪst, ˈtsɑː-, (US) ˈzɑːr.ɪst, ˈtsɑːr- **-s** -s
Czech tʃek **-s** -s
Czechoslovak ˌtʃek.əʊˈsləʊ.væk, (US) -oʊˈsloʊ.vɑːk, -væk **-s** -s
Czechoslovaki|a ˌtʃek.əʊ.sləʊˈvæk.i|.ə, -ˈvɑː.ki-, (US) -oʊ.sloʊˈvɑː.ki-, -ˈvæk.i- **-an** -ən
Czerny ˈtʃɜː.ni, ˈzɜː-, ˈtʃeə-, (US) ˈtʃer-

D

Pronouncing the letter D

When not used in the grammatical inflection *-ed*, the consonant letter **d** is most often realized as /d/, e.g.:

duck dʌk

However, in consonant clusters /d/ may be elided, e.g.:

grandson ˈgrænd.sʌn

In addition

d is sometimes realized as /dʒ/, e.g.:

procedure prəʊˈsiː.dʒəʳ (US) prəˈsiː.dʒɚ

soldier ˈsəʊl.dʒəʳ (US) ˈsoʊl.dʒɚ

Due to COALESCENCE between /d/ and /j/ in British English and omission of /j/ in American English, syllables beginning with **du** may have different pronunciations, e.g.:

due dʒuː (US) duː

The grammatical inflection –*ed*

There are three possible ways of pronouncing the grammatical inflection *-ed*.

Following /t/ and /d/ the inflection is realized as /ɪd/, e.g.:

started ˈstɑː.tɪd (US) ˈstɑːr.t̬ɪd

Following all other voiceless consonant sounds the inflection is realized as /t/, e.g.:

shaped ʃeɪpt

Following all other voiced consonant sounds and after vowel sounds, the inflection is realized as /d/, e.g.:

played pleɪd

d, D diː -'s -z
d' (from **do**) də, d
Note: See also **d'you**.
'd (from **had, would**) d
DA ˌdiːˈeɪ -s -z
dab dæb -s -z -bing -ɪŋ -bed -d -ber/s -əʳ/z, (US) -ɚ/z ˌ**dab** ˈ**hand**
dabbl|e ˈdæb.əl -es -z -ing -ɪŋ, ˈdæb.lɪŋ -ed -d -er/s -əʳ/z, ˈdæb.ləʳ/z, (US) -ɚ/z
dabchick ˈdæb.tʃɪk -s -s
da capo dɑːˈkɑː.pəʊ, də-, (US) -poʊ
Dacca ˈdæk.ə, (US) ˈdæk.ə, ˈdɑː.kə
dace deɪs
dacha ˈdætʃ.ə, (US) ˈdɑː.tʃə -s -z
Dachau *as if German:* ˈdæx.aʊ; ˈdæk-, (US) ˈdɑː.kaʊ
dachshund ˈdæk.sənd, ˈdæʃ.ənd, -hʊnd, -hʊnt, (US) ˈdɑːks.hʊnd, ˈdɑːk.sənd -s -z
Daci|a ˈdeɪ.si|.ə, -ʃi|-, ˈ-ʃ|ə, (US) ˈ-ʃ|ə -an/s -ən/z
dacoit dəˈkɔɪt -s -s
Dacre ˈdeɪ.kəʳ, (US) -kɚ -s -z
Dacron® ˈdæk.rɒn, ˈdeɪ.krɒn, (US) ˈdeɪ.krɑːn, ˈdæk.rɑːn
dactyl ˈdæk.tɪl, -təl -s -z
dactylic dækˈtɪl.ɪk
dactylogram dækˈtɪl.əʊ.græm; ˈdæk.tɪ.ləʊ-, -təl.əʊ-, (US) dækˈtɪl.ə- -s -z
dactylography ˌdæk.tɪˈlɒg.rə.fi, (US) -təˈlɑː.grə-
dad, D~ dæd -s -z
Dada ˈdɑː.dɑː, -də -ism -ɪ.zəm -ist/s -ɪst/s
dadaistic, D~ ˌdɑː.dɑːˈɪs.tɪk
Daddies® ˈdæd.iz
dadd|y ˈdæd|.i -ies -iz
daddy longlegs ˌdæd.iˈlɒŋ.legz, (US) -ˈlɑːŋ-, -ˈlɔːŋ-
dado ˈdeɪ.dəʊ, (US) -doʊ -s -z
Daedalus ˈdiː.dəl.əs, (US) ˈded.əl-
daemon ˈdiː.mən, ˈdaɪ-, ˈdeɪ- -s -z
daemonic diːˈmɒn.ɪk, dɪ-, də-, (US) -ˈmɑː.nɪk
D'Aeth deɪθ, deθ, diːθ
Daewoo® ˈdeɪ.uː, (US) ˌdeɪˈwuː
DAF® dæf
daffodil ˈdæf.ə.dɪl -s -z
daff|y ˈdæf|.i -ier -i.əʳ, (US) -i.ɚ -iest -i.ɪst, -i.əst -iness -ɪ.nəs, -ɪ.nɪs
Daffyd ap Gwilym ˌdæv.ɪð.ɑːpˈgwɪl.ɪm, -ɪd-, (US) ˌdɑː.vɪð-
daft dɑːft, (US) dæft -er -əʳ, (US) -ɚ -est -ɪst, -əst -ly -li -ness -nəs, -nɪs
Dafydd ˈdæv.ɪð, ˈdæf-
dag dæg -s -z -ging -ɪŋ -ged -d
da Gama dəˈgɑː.mə, (US) -ˈgɑː-, -ˈgæm.ə
Dagenham ˈdæg.ən.əm
Dagestan ˌdɑː.gɪˈstɑːn, -gəˈ-
dagga ˈdæx.ə, ˈdʌx-, ˈdɑː.xə, (US) ˈdæg.ə, ˈdɑː.gə
dagger ˈdæg.əʳ, (US) -ɚ -s -z **at** ˌ**daggers** ˈ**drawn**; **look** ˈ**daggers at someone**
Daggett ˈdæg.ɪt
dagg|y ˈdæg|.i -ier -i.əʳ, (US) -i.ɚ -iest -i.ɪst, -i.əst
Dagmar ˈdæg.mɑːʳ, (US) -mɑːr
dago ˈdeɪ.gəʊ, (US) -goʊ -(e)s -z
Dagobert ˈdæg.əʊ.bɜːt, (US) -ə.bɝːt
Dagon ˈdeɪ.gɒn, -gən, (US) -gɑːn
Dagonet ˈdæg.ə.nət, -nɪt
daguerreotype dəˈger.əʊ.taɪp, (US) ˈ-ə- -s -s
Dagwood ˈdæg.wʊd
dahl, D~ dɑːl
dahlia, D~ ˈdeɪ.li.ə, ˈ-ljə, (US) ˈdæl.jə, ˈdɑːl-, ˈdeɪl- -s -z
Dahomey dəˈhəʊ.mi, (US) -ˈhoʊ-
Dahrendorf ˈdɑː.rən.dɔːf, ˈdær.ən-, (US) -dɔːrf
Dai daɪ
Daiches ˈdeɪ.*t*ʃɪz, -*t*ʃəz, -*t*ʃɪs, -*t*ʃəs
Daihatsu® ˌdaɪˈhæt.suː, (US) -ˈhɑːt-
daikon ˈdaɪ.kɒn, -kən, (US) -kən, -kɑːn -s -z
Dail, Dáil dɔɪl
Dáil Eireann ˌdɔɪlˈeə.rən, (US) -ˈer.ən, -ˈeɪ.rən
daill|y ˈdeɪ.l|i -ies -iz
Daimler® ˈdeɪm.ləʳ, (US) -lɚ, ˈdaɪm- -s -z
Daintree ˈdeɪn.triː, -tri
daint|y ˈdeɪn.t|i, (US) -t̬|i -ies -iz -ier -i.əʳ, (US) -i.ɚ -iest -i.ɪst, -i.əst -ily -əl.i, -ɪ.li -iness -ɪ.nəs, -ɪ.nɪs
daiquiri, D~ ˈdaɪ.kɪ.ri, ˈdæk.ɪ-, -ər.i; daɪˈkɪə.ri, də-, (US) ˈdæk.ɚ.i, ˈdaɪ.kɚ-
dair|y ˈdeə.r|i, (US) ˈder|.i -ies -iz -ying -i.ɪŋ ˈ**dairy** ˌ**farm**; ˈ**dairy** ˌ**products**
Dairylea® ˌdeə.riˈliː, ˈ---, (US) ˌder.iˈliː, ˈ---
dairymaid ˈdeə.riˌmeɪd, (US) ˈder.i- -s -z
dairy|man ˈdeə.ri|.mən, -mæn, (US) ˈder.i- -men -mən, -men
dais ˈdeɪ.ɪs, deɪs, (US) ˈdeɪ.ɪs, ˈdaɪ- -es -ɪz
dais|y, D~ ˈdeɪ.z|i -ies -iz ˈ**daisy** ˌ**chain**; ˈ**daisy** ˌ**wheel**
daisywheel ˈdeɪ.zi.*h*wiːl -s -z
Dakar ˈdæk.ɑːʳ, -əʳ, (US) dəˈkɑːr; (US) ˈdæk.ɑːr
Dakota dəˈkəʊ.tə, (US) -ˈkoʊ.t̬ə -s -z
dal n *food:* dɑːl
dal *in Italian phrases:* dæl, dɑːl, (US) dɑːl
Dalai Lama ˌdæl.aɪˈlɑː.mə, ˌdɑː.laɪˈ-, (US) ˌdɑː.laɪˈ- -s -z
dalasi dəˈlɑː.si -s -z
Dalbeattie dælˈbiː.ti, dəl-, (US) -t̬i
Dalby ˈdɔːl.bi, ˈdɒl-, ˈdæl-, (US) ˈdɑːl-, ˈdɔːl-, ˈdæl-

Daldy ˈdæl.di, US ˈdɑːl.di

dale, D~ deɪl **-s** -z

Dalek ˈdɑː.lek, -lɪk **-s** -s

dales|man ˈdeɪlz|.mən, -mæn **-men** -mən, -men **-woman** -ˌwʊm.ən **-women** -ˌwɪm.ɪn

Daley ˈdeɪ.li

Dalgety dælˈget.i, dəl-, US -ˈget̬- *stress shift, see compound:* ˌ**Dalgety** ˈ**Bay**

Dalgleish, Dalglish dælˈgliːʃ, dəl-

Dalhousie dælˈhaʊ.zi, -ˈhuː-

Dali ˈdɑː.li

Dalkeith dælˈkiːθ

Dalkey ˈdɔː.ki, ˈdɔːl-

Dallas ˈdæl.əs

dallianc|e ˈdæl.i.ənts **-es** -ɪz

Dalloway ˈdæl.ə.weɪ

dall|y ˈdæl|.i **-ies** -iz **-ying** -i.ɪŋ **-ied** -id **-ier/s** -i.əʳ/z, US -i.ɚ/z

Dalmatia dælˈmeɪ.ʃə, -ʃi.ə

dalmatian, D~ dælˈmeɪ.ʃən, -ʃi.ən **-s** -z

Dalmeny dælˈmen.i, dəl-

Dalny ˈdæl.ni

Dalry dælˈraɪ, dəl-

Dalrymple dælˈrɪm.pəl, dəl-; ˈdæl.rɪm-

dal segno dælˈsen.jəʊ, dɑːl-, US dɑːlˈseɪ.njoʊ, -ˈsen.joʊ

Dalston ˈdɔːl.stən, ˈdɒl-, US ˈdɔːl-, ˈdɑːl-

Dalton ˈdɔːl.tən, ˈdɒl-, US ˈdɔːl-, ˈdɑːl-

Dalton-in-Furness ˌdɔːl.tən.ɪnˈfɜː.nɪs, ˌdɒl-, US ˌdɔːl.tən.ɪnˈfɝː-, ˌdɑːl-

Daltonism ˈdɔːl.tən.ɪ.zəm, ˈdɒl-, US ˈdɔːl-, ˈdɑːl-

Daltr(e)y ˈdɔːl.tri, ˈdɒl-, US ˈdɔːl-, ˈdɑːl-

Dalwhinnie dælˈ*h*wɪn.i, dəl-

Daly ˈdeɪ.li

Dalyell diːˈel

Dalzell diːˈel; ˈdæl.zel

Dalziel diːˈel; ˈdæl.ziːl, -zi.əl

> Note: The form /diːˈel/ is chiefly used in Scotland.

dam dæm **-s** -z **-ming** -ɪŋ **-med** -d

damag|e ˈdæm.ɪdʒ **-es** -ɪz **-ing/ly** -ɪŋ/li **-ed** -d

damaging ˈdæm.ɪ.dʒɪŋ **-ly** -li

Damaraland dəˈmɑː.rə.lænd; ˈdæm.ə.rə-, US dəˈmɑːr.ə-

Damart® ˈdæm.ɑːt, ˈdeɪ.mɑːt, US ˈdæm.ɑːrt, ˈdeɪ.mɑːrt

damascene ˈdæm.ə.siːn **-s** -z

Damascus dəˈmæs.kəs, -ˈmɑː.skəs, US -ˈmæs.kəs

damask ˈdæm.əsk **-s** -s

dame, D~ deɪm **-s** -z

Damian, Damien ˈdeɪ.mi.ən

Damman ˈdæm.æn, US dæmˈæn

dammit ˈdæm.ɪt

damn dæm **-s** -z **-ing** -ɪŋ **-ed** -d

damnab|le ˈdæm.nə.b|əl **-ly** -li **-leness** -əl.nəs, -əl.nɪs

damnation dæmˈneɪ.ʃən **-s** -z

damnatory ˈdæm.nə.tər.i, -tri, US -tɔːr.i

damnedest ˈdæm.dɪst, -dəst

damni|fy ˈdæm.nɪ|.faɪ **-fies** -faɪz **-fying** -faɪ.ɪŋ **-fied** -faɪd

damnum sine injuria ˌdæm.nəmˌsɪn.eɪ.ɪnˈdʒʊə.ri.ə, US -ˈdʒʊr.i.ə

Damoclean ˌdæm.əˈkliː.ən

Damocles ˈdæm.ə.kliːz

Damon ˈdeɪ.mən

damosel, damozel ˌdæm.əʊˈzel, US -əˈ-, -oʊˈ- **-s** -z

damp dæmp **-er** -əʳ, US -ɚ **-est** -ɪst, -əst **-ly** -li **-ness** -nəs, -nɪs **-ish** -ɪʃ **-s** -s **-ing** -ɪŋ **-ed** -t ˈ**damp** ˌ**course;** ˌ**damp** ˈ**squib**

dampen ˈdæm.pən **-s** -z **-ing** -ɪŋ, ˈdæmp.nɪŋ **-ed** -d

damper ˈdæm.pəʳ, US -pɚ **-s** -z

Dampier ˈdæm.pi.əʳ, -pɪəʳ, US -pi.ɚ

damp-proof ˈdæmp.pruːf **-s** -s **-ing** -ɪŋ **-ed** -d

damsel ˈdæm.zəl **-s** -z

damson ˈdæm.zən **-s** -z

dan, D~ dæn **-s** -z

Dana *forename in UK:* ˈdɑː.nə *in US:* ˈdeɪ.nə, US ˈdæn.ə

Danaan ˈdæn.i.ən **-s** -z

Danaë ˈdæn.eɪ.iː, ˈ-i-

Danaides, Danaïdes dəˈneɪ.ɪ.diːz, dænˈeɪ-, ˈ-ə-

Dan-Air® ˌdænˈeəʳ, US -ˈer

Danakil ˈdæn.ə.kiːl, -kɪl; dəˈnɑː.kiːl, -kɪl

Da Nang ˌdɑːˈnæŋ, US dəˈnæŋ, dɑːˈnɑːŋ

Danbury ˈdæn.bər.i, ˈdæm-, US ˈdæn.ber-, -bɚ-

Danby ˈdæn.bi, ˈdæm-, US ˈdæn-

danc|e dɑːnts, US dænts **-es** -ɪz **-ing** -ɪŋ **-ed** -t **-er/s** -əʳ/z, US -ɚ/z

Dance dɑːnts, dænts, US dænts

Dancer ˈdɑːnt.səʳ, US ˈdænt.sɚ

dandelion ˈdæn.dɪ.laɪ.ən, -laɪən, US -də-, -dɪ- **-s** -z

dandi|fy ˈdæn.dɪ|.faɪ, US -də- **-fies** -faɪz **-fying** -faɪ.ɪŋ **-fied** -faɪd

dandl|e ˈdæn.dəl **-es** -z **-ing** -ɪŋ, ˈdænd.lɪŋ **-ed** -d

Dando ˈdæn.dəʊ, US -doʊ

dandruff ˈdæn.drʌf, US -drəf

dand|y ˈdæn.d|i **-ies** -iz **-yish** -i.ɪʃ **-yism** -i.ɪ.zəm

Dane deɪn **-s** -z

Danebury ˈdeɪn.bər.i, ˈdeɪm-, US ˈdeɪn.ber-, -bɚ-

danegeld ˈdeɪn.geld, ˈdeɪŋ-, US ˈdeɪn-

Danelaw ˈdeɪn.lɔː, US -lɑː, -lɔː

danger ˈdeɪn.dʒəʳ, US -dʒɚ **-s** -z

Dangerfield ˈdeɪn.dʒə.fiːld, US -dʒɚ-

dangerous ˈdeɪn.dʒər.əs **-ly** -li **-ness** -nəs, -nɪs

dangerously ˈdeɪn.dʒər.ə.sli

dangl|e, D~ ˈdæŋ.gəl **-es** -z **-ing** -ɪŋ, ˈdæŋ.glɪŋ **-ed** -d **-er/s** -əʳ/z, ˈ-gləʳ/z, US ˈ-gəl.ɚ/z, ˈ-glɚ/z

dangly ˈdæŋ.gəl.i, ˈ-gli

Daniel ˈdæn.jəl **-s** -z

Danielle dænˈjel, ˌdæn.i.ˈel

Danish ˈdeɪ.nɪʃ ˌ**Danish** ˈ**blue;** ˌ**Danish** ˈ**pastry**

dank dæŋk **-er** -əʳ, US -ɚ **-est** -ɪst, -əst **-ly** -li **-ness** -nəs, -nɪs

Danks dæŋks

Dankworth ˈdæŋk.wəθ, -wɜːθ, US -wɚθ, -wɝːθ

Dann dæn

d'Annunzio dænˈʊnt.si.əʊ, US dɑːˈnʊnt.si.oʊ

Danny ˈdæn.i

Danone dænˈəʊn, dænˈɒn, US -ˈoʊn, -ɑːn

danse(s) macabre(s) ˌdɑ̃ːns.məˈkɑː.brə, -mækˈɑː-, US ˌdɑːnts.məˈkɑː.brə

danseuse(s) ˌdɑ̃ːnˈsɜːz, US ˌdɑːntˈsuːz, -ˈsʊz

Dansville ˈdænz.vɪl

Dante ˈdæn.ti, ˈdɑːn-, -teɪ, US ˈdɑːn.teɪ

Dantesque dænˈtesk, US dɑːn-

Danton ˈdæn.tɒn, -tən; *as if French:* dɑ̃ːnˈtɔ̃ːŋ; US dɑːnˈtɑːn, -toʊn; US ˈ--, -tən

Danube ˈdæn.juːb

Danubian dænˈjuː.bi.ən, dəˈnjuː-

Danuta dəˈnuː.tə, dænˈuː-, US dəˈnuː.t̬ə

Danvers ˈdæn.vəz, US -vɚz

Danville ˈdæn.vɪl

Danzig ˈdænt.sɪg, -sɪk

Dao|ism ˈdaʊ|.ɪ.zəm **-its/s** -ɪst/s

daphne, D~ ˈdæf.ni

Daphnis ˈdæf.nɪs

dapp|er, D~ ˈdæp|.əʳ, US -ɚ **-erest** -ər.ɪst, -ər.əst

dappl|e ˈdæp.əl **-es** -z **-ing** -ɪŋ, ˈ-lɪŋ **-ed** -d

dapple-grey ˌdæp.əlˈgreɪ

DAR ˌdiː.eɪˈɑːʳ, US -ˈɑːr

Darbishire ˈdɑː.bɪ.ʃəʳ, -ʃɪəʳ, US ˈdɑːr.bɪ.ʃɚ, -ʃɪr

Darby ˈdɑː.bi, US ˈdɑːr- ˌ**Darby and** ˈ**Joan**

d'Arc dɑːk, US dɑːrk

D'Arcy, Darcy ˈdɑː.si, US ˈdɑːr-

Dardanelles ˌdɑː.dənˈelz, US ˌdɑːr-

Dardanus ˈdɑː.dən.əs, US ˈdɑːr-

dar|e, D~ deəʳ, US der **-es** -z **-ing** -ɪŋ **-ed** -d **durst** dɜːst, US dɝːst

daredevil ˈdeəˌdev.əl, US ˈder- **-s** -z

daren't deənt, US dernt

Darent ˈdær.ənt, US ˈder-, ˈdær-

Darenth ˈdær.ənθ, US ˈder-, ˈdær-

Dares ˈdeə.riːz, US ˈder.iːz

daresay, dare say ˌdeəˈseɪ, US ˌder-

Daresbury ˈdɑːz.bər.i, US ˈdɑːrz.ber-, -bɚ-

Dar es Salaam ˌdɑː.res.səˈlɑːm, -rɪs-, -rez-, -rɪz-, US ˌdɑːr.es-

Darfield ˈdɑː.fiːld, US ˈdɑːr-

Darfur ˌdɑːˈfʊəʳ, US ˌdɑːrˈfʊr

Darien ˈdeə.ri.ən, ˈdær.i.ən, US ˈder.i-, ˈdær-; US ˌder.iˈen, ˌdær-

Darin ˈdær.ɪn, US ˈder-, ˈdær-

daring ˈdeə.rɪŋ, US ˈder.ɪŋ **-ly** -li

Dario ˈdær.i.əʊ, US ˈdɑː.ri.oʊ, ˈder.i-, ˈdær.i-

dariole ˈdær.i.əʊl, (US) ˈder.i.oʊl, ˈdær- **-s** -z
Darius dəˈraɪ.əs, ˈdeə.ri-, ˈdær.i-, ˈdɑː.ri-, (US) dəˈraɪ-; (US) ˈder.i-, ˈdær-
Darjeeling dɑːˈdʒiː.lɪŋ, (US) dɑːr-
dark dɑːk, (US) dɑːrk **-er** -əʳ, (US) -ɚ **-est** -ɪst, -əst **-ly** -li **-ness** -nəs, -nɪs **ˈDark ˌAges; ˌdark ˈglasses; ˌdark ˈhorse**
darken ˈdɑː.kᵊn, (US) ˈdɑːr- **-s** -z **-ing** -ɪŋ, ˈdɑːk.nɪŋ, (US) ˈdɑːr.kᵊn.ɪŋ, ˈdɑːrk.nɪŋ **-ed** -d
dark|ie ˈdɑː.k|.i, (US) ˈdɑːr.ki **-ies** -iz
darkish ˈdɑː.kɪʃ, (US) ˈdɑːr-
darkling ˈdɑː.klɪŋ, (US) ˈdɑːr-
darkroom ˈdɑːk.rʊm, -ruːm, (US) ˈdɑːrk.ruːm, -rʊm **-s** -z
darksome ˈdɑːk.səm, (US) ˈdɑːrk-
dark|y ˈdɑː.k|i, (US) ˈdɑːr- **-ies** -iz
Darlaston ˈdɑː.lə.stən, (US) ˈdɑːr-
Darleen, Darlene ˈdɑː.liːn, (US) dɑːrˈliːn
Darley ˈdɑː.li, (US) ˈdɑːr-
darling, D~ ˈdɑː.lɪŋ, (US) ˈdɑːr- **-s** -z
Darlington ˈdɑː.lɪŋ.tən, (US) ˈdɑːr-
Darlow ˈdɑː.ləʊ, (US) ˈdɑːr.loʊ
Darmstadt ˈdɑːm.stæt; *as if German:* -ʃtæt; (US) ˈdɑːrm-
darn dɑːn, (US) dɑːrn **-s** -z **-ing** -ɪŋ **-ed** -d **-er/s** -əʳ/z, (US) -ɚ/z **ˈdarning ˌneedle**
darnation dɑːˈneɪ.ʃᵊn, (US) dɑːr-
darnel ˈdɑː.nᵊl, (US) ˈdɑːr-
Darnell dɑːˈnel, (US) dɑːr-, ˈ--
Darney ˈdɑː.ni, (US) ˈdɑːr-
Darnley ˈdɑːn.li, (US) ˈdɑːrn-
Darracq dærˈæk, (US) der-, dær-
Darragh ˈdær.ə, -əx, (US) ˈder.ə, ˈdær-
Darrell ˈdær.ᵊl, (US) ˈder-, ˈdær-
Darren, Darron ˈdær.ᵊn, (US) ˈder-, ˈdær-
Darrow ˈdær.əʊ, (US) ˈder.oʊ, ˈdær-
Darryl ˈdær.ᵊl, -ɪl, (US) ˈder-, ˈdær-
dart, D~ dɑːt, (US) dɑːrt **-s** -s **-ing** -ɪŋ, (US) ˈdɑːr.t̬ɪŋ **-ed** -ɪd, (US) ˈdɑːr.t̬ɪd
D'Artagnan dɑːˈtæn.jən, -jɑ̃ːŋ, (US) dɑːrˈtæn.jən; (US) ˌdɑːr.tᵊnˈjɑːn
dartboard ˈdɑːt.bɔːd, (US) ˈdɑːrt.bɔːrd **-s** -z
darter ˈdɑː.təʳ, (US) ˈdɑːr.t̬ɚ **-s** -z
Dartford ˈdɑːt.fəd, (US) ˈdɑːrt.fɚd
Darth Vader ˌdɑːθˈveɪ.dəʳ, (US) ˌdɑːrθˈveɪ.dɚ
Dartington ˈdɑː.tɪŋ.tən, (US) ˈdɑːr.t̬ɪŋ-
Dartle ˈdɑː.tᵊl, (US) ˈdɑːr.t̬ᵊl
Dartmoor ˈdɑːt.mɔːʳ, -mʊəʳ, (US) ˈdɑːrt.mʊr, -mɔːr
Dartmouth ˈdɑːt.məθ, (US) ˈdɑːrt-
Darton ˈdɑː.tᵊn, (US) ˈdɑːr-
darts dɑːts, (US) dɑːrts
Darwen ˈdɑː.wɪn, (US) ˈdɑːr-
Darwin ˈdɑː.wɪn, (US) ˈdɑːr- **-ism** -ɪ.zᵊm
Darwinian dɑːˈwɪn.i.ən, (US) dɑːr-
Daryl(l) ˈdær.ᵊl, -ɪl, (US) ˈder-, ˈdær-
Daschle ˈdæʃ.ᵊl
Dasent ˈdeɪ.sᵊnt
dash, D~ dæʃ **-es** -ɪz **-ing** -ɪŋ **-ed** -t **-er/s** -əʳ/z, (US) -ɚ/z
dashboard ˈdæʃ.bɔːd, (US) -bɔːrd **-s** -z
dashing ˈdæʃ.ɪŋ **-ly** -li
Dashwood ˈdæʃ.wʊd
dastard ˈdæs.təd, ˈdɑː.stəd, (US) ˈdæs.tɚd **-s** -z **-ly** -li **-liness** -lɪ.nəs, -nɪs
DAT dæt; ˌdiː.eɪˈtiː
data ˈdeɪ.tə, ˈdɑː-, (US) ˈdeɪ.t̬ə, ˈdæt̬.ə, ˈdɑː.t̬ə
databank ˈdeɪ.tə.bæŋk, ˈdɑː-, (US) ˈdeɪ.t̬ə-, ˈdæt̬.ə-, ˈdɑː.t̬ə- **-s** -s
databas|e ˈdeɪ.tə.beɪs, ˈdɑː-, (US) ˈdeɪ.t̬ə-, ˈdæt̬.ə-, ˈdɑː.t̬ə- **-es** -ɪz
databus ˈdeɪ.tə.bʌs, ˈdɑː-, (US) ˈdeɪ.t̬ə-, ˈdæt̬.ə-, ˈdɑː.t̬ə- **-es** -ɪz
datafile ˈdeɪ.tə.faɪl, ˈdɑː-, (US) ˈdeɪ.t̬ə-, ˈdæt̬.ə-, ˈdɑː.t̬ə- **-s** -z
dataflow ˈdeɪ.tə.fləʊ, ˈdɑː-, (US) ˈdeɪ.t̬ə.floʊ, ˈdæt̬.ə-, ˈdɑː.t̬ə-
Dataglove® ˈdeɪ.tə.glʌv, ˈdɑː-, (US) ˈdeɪ.t̬ə-, ˈdæt̬.ə-, ˈdɑː.t̬ə- **-s** -z
Datapost® ˈdeɪ.tə.pəʊst, ˈdɑː-, (US) -t̬ə.poʊst
Datchery ˈdætʃ.ᵊr.i
Datchet ˈdætʃ.ɪt
dat|e deɪt **-es** -s **-ing** -ɪŋ, (US) ˈdeɪ.t̬ɪŋ **-ed** -ɪd, (US) ˈdeɪ.t̬ɪd **ˈdating ˌagency**
dated ˈdeɪ.tɪd, (US) -t̬ɪd
Datel® ˈdeɪ.tel
Dateline® ˈdeɪt.laɪn **-s** -z
date-stamp ˈdeɪt.stæmp **-s** -s **-ing** -ɪŋ **-ed** -t
datival dəˈtaɪ.vᵊl, deɪ-
dative ˈdeɪ.tɪv, (US) -t̬ɪv **-s** -z
Datsun® ˈdæt.sᵊn, (US) ˈdɑːt-, ˈdæt-
dat|um ˈdeɪ.t|əm, ˈdɑː-, (US) ˈdeɪ.t̬|əm, ˈdæt̬|.əm, ˈdɑː.t̬|əm **-a** -ə
daub dɔːb, (US) dɑːb, dɔːb **-s** -z **-ing** -ɪŋ **-ed** -d **-er/s** -əʳ/z, (US) -ɚ/z
daube dəʊb, (US) doʊb **-s** -z
Daubeney ˈdɔː.bᵊn.i, (US) ˈdɑː-, ˈdɔː-
Daudet ˈdəʊ.deɪ, (US) doʊˈdeɪ
Daugavpils ˈdaʊ.gæf.pɪls, (US) ˈdoʊ.gʌv-, ˈdaʊ-, -gʌf-, -gɑːf-, -pɪlz, -piːlz
daughter ˈdɔː.təʳ, (US) ˈdɑː.t̬ɚ, ˈdɔː- **-s** -z
daughter-in-law ˈdɔː.təʳ.ɪn.lɔː, (US) ˈdɑː.t̬ɚ.ɪn.lɑː, ˈdɔː-, -lɔː **daughters-in-law** ˈdɔː.təz.ɪn.lɔː, (US) ˈdɑː.t̬ɚz.ɪn.lɑː, ˈdɔː-, -lɔː
daughterl|y ˈdɔː.tə.l|i, (US) ˈdɑː.t̬ɚ-, ˈdɔː- **-iness** -ɪ.nəs, -ɪ.nɪs
Daun dɔːn, (US) dɑːn, dɔːn
daunt, D~ dɔːnt, (US) dɑːnt, dɔːnt **-s** -s **-ing** -ɪŋ, (US) ˈdɑːn.t̬ɪŋ, ˈdɔːn- **-ed** -ɪd, (US) ˈdɑːn.t̬ɪd, ˈdɔːn-
dauntless ˈdɔːnt.ləs, -lɪs, (US) ˈdɑːnt-, ˈdɔːnt **-ly** -li **-ness** -nəs, -nɪs
dauphin, D~ ˈdəʊ.fæ̃ŋ, ˈdɔː-, -ɪn, (US) ˈdɑː.fən, ˈdɔː-, ˈ-fɪn; (US) doʊˈfæn **-s** -z
dauphine, D~ ˈdəʊ.fiːn, ˈdɔː-, (US) dɑːˈfiːn, dɔː-, doʊ- **-s** -z
Dauphiné ˈdəʊ.fi.neɪ, ˈdɔː-, –ˈ-, (US) ˌdoʊ.fiːˈneɪ
Davao dævˈɑː.əʊ, dəˈvɑː-, (US) dɑːˈvaʊ
Dave deɪv
Davenant, D'Avenant ˈdæv.ᵊn.ənt, -ɪ.nənt
davenport, D~ ˈdæv.ᵊn.pɔːt, -ᵊm-, (US) -ᵊn.pɔːrt **-s** -s
Daventry ˈdæv.ᵊn.tri; *old-fashioned local pronunciation:* ˈdeɪn.tri
Davey ˈdeɪ.vi
David ˈdeɪ.vɪd **-s** -z
Davidge ˈdæv.ɪdʒ
Davidson ˈdeɪ.vɪd.sᵊn
Davie ˈdeɪ.vi
Davies ˈdeɪ.vɪs, (US) -viːz
Davina dəˈviː.nə
da Vinci dəˈvɪn.tʃi
Davis ˈdeɪ.vɪs
Davison ˈdeɪ.vɪ.sᵊn
davit ˈdæv.ɪt, ˈdeɪ.vɪt **-s** -s
Davos dævˈəʊs, dɑːˈvəʊs, -ˈvɒs; ˈdɑː.vɒs, -vəʊs, (US) dɑːˈvoʊs
dav|y, D~ ˈdeɪ.v|i **-ies** -iz **ˈdavy ˌlamp; ˌDavy ˌJones's ˈlocker**
daw, D~ dɔː, (US) dɑː, dɔː **-s** -z
dawdl|e ˈdɔː.dᵊl, (US) ˈdɑː-, ˈdɔː- **-es** -z **-ing** -ɪŋ, ˈdɔːd.lɪŋ, (US) ˈdɑːd-, ˈdɔːd- **-ed** -d **-er/s** -əʳ/z, ˈdɔːd.ləʳ/z, (US) ˈdɑː.dᵊl.ɚ/z, ˈdɔː-, ˈdɑːd.lɚ/z, ˈdɔːd-
Dawe dɔː, (US) dɑː, dɔː **-s** -z
Dawkes dɔːks, (US) dɑːks, dɔːks
Dawkins ˈdɔː.kɪnz, (US) ˈdɑː-, ˈdɔː-
Dawley ˈdɔː.li, (US) ˈdɑː-, ˈdɔː-
Dawlish ˈdɔː.lɪʃ, (US) ˈdɑː-, ˈdɔː-
dawn, D~ dɔːn, (US) dɑːn, dɔːn **-s** -z **-ing** -ɪŋ **-ed** -d
Dawson ˈdɔː.sᵊn, (US) ˈdɑː-, ˈdɔː-
day, D~ deɪ **-s** -z **ˈday ˌboy; ˈday ˌcamp; ˈday ˌgirl; ˈday ˌjob; ˈday ˌlily; ˈday ˌnursery; ˌday ˈout; ˈday ˌroom; ˈday ˌschool; at the ˌend of the ˈday; ˌcall it a ˈday**
daybreak ˈdeɪ.breɪk **-s** -s
daycare ˈdeɪ.keəʳ, (US) -ker
day|dream ˈdeɪ|.driːm **-dreams** -driːmz **-dreaming** -ˌdriː.mɪŋ **-dreamed** -drempt, -driːmd **-dreamt** -drempt **-dreamer/s** -ˌdriː.məʳ/z, (US) -ˌdriː.mɚ/z
Day-Glo®, dayglo ˈdeɪ.gləʊ, (US) -gloʊ
Daylesford ˈdeɪlz.fəd, ˈdeɪls-, (US) -fɚd
Day-Lewis ˌdeɪˈluː.ɪs
daylight ˈdeɪ.laɪt **-s** -s **ˌdaylight ˈrobbery; ˌdaylight ˈsaving; ˈdaylight ˌtime; ˌbeat the living ˈdaylights out of sb**
dayspring ˈdeɪ.sprɪŋ
daystar ˈdeɪ.stɑːʳ, (US) -stɑːr **-s** -z
daytime ˈdeɪ.taɪm
day-to-day ˌdeɪ.təˈdeɪ, (US) -t̬əˈ-
Dayton ˈdeɪ.tᵊn
Daytona deɪˈtəʊ.nə, (US) -ˈtoʊ- **DayˌtonaˈBeach**
day-tripper ˈdeɪˌtrɪp.əʳ, ˌ-ˈ--, (US) -ɚ **-s** -z
daywork ˈdeɪ.wɜːk, (US) -wɜːk
Daz® dæz
daz|e deɪz **-es** -ɪz **-ing** -ɪŋ **-ed** -d **-edly** -əd.li, -ɪd.li
dazzl|e ˈdæz.ᵊl **-es** -z **-ing/ly** -ɪŋ/li,

D

ˈdæz.lɪŋ/li **-ed** -d **-er/s** -ə^{r}/z, ˈ-lə^{r}/z, (US) ˈ-^{ə}l.ɚ/z, ˈ-lɚ/z
DBMS ˌdiː.biː.emˈes
DC ˌdiːˈsiː
D-Day ˈdiː.deɪ
DDT ˌdiː.diːˈtiː
de *in French names:* də, dɪ, di
de- ˌdiː, di, dɪ, də
Note: Prefix. In verbs containing **de-** where the stem is free, usually a noun, it is normally pronounced /ˌdiː-/, e.g. **debag** /ˌdiːˈbæg/, **declutch** /ˌdiːˈklʌtʃ/. Attached to bound stems the pronunciation is normally /dɪ-/ or /də-/ before a consonant, e.g. **debilitate** /dɪˈbɪl.ɪ.teɪt/, **demand** /dɪˈmɑːnd/ (US) /-mænd/; before a vowel the pronunciation is usually /di/, e.g. **deactivate** /diˈæk.tɪ.veɪt/. There are exceptions; see individual entries.
deacon, D~ ˈdiː.kən **-s** -z
deaconess ˌdiː.kəˈnes; ˈ---, -nɪs, (US) ˈdiː.k^{ə}n.əs **-es** -ɪz
deacon|hood ˈdiː.kən|.hʊd **-ship/s** -ʃɪp/s
deaconr|y ˈdiː.kən.r|i **-ies** -iz
deacti|vate diˈæk.tɪ|.veɪt, -tə- **-vates** -veɪts **-vating** -veɪ.tɪŋ, (US) -veɪ.t̬ɪŋ **-vated** -veɪ.tɪd, (US) -veɪ.t̬ɪd
deactivation diˌæk.tɪˈveɪ.ʃ^{ə}n, ˌdiː.æk-, -təˈ-, (US) diˌæk-
dead ded **-ness** -nəs, -nɪs **ˌdead ˈend; ˌdead ˈheat; ˌdead ˈletter; ˌdead or ˈalive; ˌdead ˈreckoning; ˌdead ˈringer; ˌDead ˈSea; ˌdead ˈset; as ˌdead as a ˈdoor-nail**
dead-and-alive ˌded.^{ə}nd.əˈlaɪv
deadbeat n ˈded.biːt, ˈdeb-, (US) ˈded- **-s** -s
dead beat adj ˌdedˈbiːt, ˌdeb-, (US) ˌded-
deadbolt ˈded.bəʊlt, ˈdeb-, (US) ˈded.boʊlt **-s** -s
deaden ˈded.^{ə}n **-s** -z **-ing** -ɪŋ **-ed** -d
dead-end ˌdedˈend *stress shift:* **ˌdead-end ˈstreet**
deadeye, D~ ˈded.aɪ **-s** -z
deadhead ˈded.hed, -ˈ- **-s** -z
deadline ˈded.laɪn **-s** -z
deadlock ˈded.lɒk, (US) -lɑːk **-s** -s **-ed** -t
deadl|y ˈded.l|i **-ier** -i.ə^{r}, (US) -i.ɚ **-iest** -i.ɪst, -i.əst **-iness** -ɪ.nəs, -ɪ.nɪs **ˌdeadly ˈnightshade**
deadnettle ˈded.net.^{ə}l, ˌ-ˈ--, (US) ˌdedˈnet̬-, ˈ-ˌ-- **-s** -z
deadpan ˈded.pæn, ˈdeb-, ˌ-ˈ-, (US) ˈded.pæn
deadweight ˌdedˈweɪt, ˈ-- **-s** -s
deadwood ˈded.wʊd, ˌ-ˈ-
deaf def **-er** -ə^{r}, (US) -ɚ **-est** -ɪst, -əst **-ly** -li **-ness** -nəs, -nɪs **ˌfall on ˌdeaf ˈears**
deaf-aid ˈdef.eɪd **-s** -z
deaf-and-dumb ˌdef.^{ə}ndˈdʌm
deafen ˈdef.^{ə}n **-s** -z **-ing/ly** -ɪŋ/li, ˈ-nɪŋ/li **-ed** -d
deaf-mute ˌdefˈmjuːt, ˈ-- **-s** -s
Deakin ˈdiː.kɪn
deal, D~ diːl **-s** -z **-ing** -ɪŋ **dealt** delt
dealer ˈdiː.lə^{r}, (US) -lɚ **-s** -z
dealership ˈdiː.lə.ʃɪp, (US) -lɚ- **-s** -s
dealing ˈdiː.lɪŋ **-s** -z
dealt (from **deal**) delt
Dealtry *surname:* ˈdɔːl.tri, ˈdɪəl-, (US) ˈdɑːl-, ˈdɔːl-, ˈdiːl- *road in London:* ˈdel.tri
deami|nate diˈæm.ɪ.neɪt, ˌdiː-, ˈ-ə-, (US) ˈ-ə- **-nates** -neɪts **-nating** -neɪ.tɪŋ, (US) -neɪ.t̬ɪŋ **-nated** -neɪ.tɪd, (US) -neɪ.t̬ɪd
deamination diˌæm.ɪˈneɪ.ʃ^{ə}n, ˌdiː-, -əˈ-, (US) -əˈ-
dean diːn **-s** -z **-ship/s** -ʃɪp/s
Dean(e) diːn
deaner|y ˈdiː.n^{ə}r|.i **-ies** -iz
Deanna diˈæn.ə; ˈdiː.nə, (US) diˈæn.ə
Deans diːnz
dear, D~ dɪə^{r}, (US) dɪr **-s** -z **-er** -ə^{r}, (US) -ɚ **-est** -ɪst, -əst **-ly** -li **-ness** -nəs, -nɪs
dear|ie ˈdɪə.r|i, (US) ˈdɪr|.i **-ies** -iz
Dearing ˈdɪə.rɪŋ, (US) ˈdɪr.ɪŋ
Dearne dɜːn, (US) dɝːn
dearth, D~ dɜːθ, (US) dɝːθ **-s** -s
dear|y ˈdɪə.r|i, (US) ˈdɪr|.i **-ies** -iz
death deθ **-s** -s **ˈdeath ˌduty; ˈdeath ˌmask; ˈdeath ˌpenalty; ˈdeath ˌrate; ˈdeath ˌrattle; ˌdeath ˈrow; ˈdeath ˌtoll; ˈdeath ˌtrap; ˌDeath ˈValley; ˈdeath ˌwarrant; ˈdeath ˌwish; like ˌdeath warmed ˈup; like ˌgrim ˈdeath**
Death *surname:* deɪθ, deθ, diːθ; diːˈæθ, deɪ-, -ˈɑːθ
deathbed ˈdeθ.bed **-s** -z
deathblow ˈdeθ.bləʊ, (US) -bloʊ **-s** -z
death-defying ˈdeθ.dɪˌfaɪ.ɪŋ, (US) -dɪˌ-, -diˌ-
deathless ˈdeθ.ləs, -lɪs
deathlike ˈdeθ.laɪk
deathl|y ˈdeθ.l|i **-ier** -i.ə^{r}, (US) -i.ɚ **-iest** -i.ɪst, -i.əst **-iness** -ɪ.nəs, -ɪ.nɪs
death's-head ˈdeθs.hed **-s** -z
deathwatch ˈdeθ.wɒtʃ, (US) -wɑːtʃ, -wɔːtʃ **ˌdeathwatch ˈbeetle**
Deauville ˈdəʊ.vɪl, -viːl, (US) ˈdoʊ-
Deayton ˈdiː.t^{ə}n
deb deb **-s** -z
débâcle deɪˈbɑː.k^{ə}l, də-, debˈɑː-, dɪˈbɑː-; ˈdeɪ.bɑː-, (US) dɪˈbɑː-, də-, deɪ-, -ˈbæk.^{ə}l **-s** -z
debag ˌdiːˈbæg **-s** -z **-ging** -ɪŋ **-ged** -d
debar ˌdiːˈbɑː^{r}, dɪ-, (US) -ˈbɑːr **-s** -z **-ring** -ɪŋ **-red** -d
debark ˌdiːˈbɑːk, dɪ-, (US) -ˈbɑːrk **-s** -s **-ing** -ɪŋ **-ed** -t
debarkation ˌdiː.bɑːˈkeɪ.ʃ^{ə}n, (US) -bɑːrˈ- **-s** -z
debas|e dɪˈbeɪs **-es** -ɪz **-ing/ly** -ɪŋ/li **-ed** -t **-ement** -mənt
debatab|le dɪˈbeɪ.tə.b|^{ə}l, də-, (US) dɪˈbeɪ.t̬ə- **-ly** -li
de|bate dɪ|ˈbeɪt, də-, (US) dɪ- **-bates** -ˈbeɪts **-bating** -ˈbeɪ.tɪŋ, (US) -ˈbeɪ.t̬ɪŋ **-bated** -ˈbeɪ.tɪd, (US) -ˈbeɪ.t̬ɪd **-bater/s** -ˈbeɪ.tə^{r}/z, (US) -ˈbeɪ.t̬ɚ/z
debauch dɪˈbɔːtʃ, (US) -ˈbɑːtʃ, -ˈbɔːtʃ **-es** -ɪz **-ing** -ɪŋ **-ed** -t **-er/s** -ə^{r}/z, (US) -ɚ/z
debauchee ˌdeb.ɔːˈtʃiː, -ˈʃiː, ˌdɪb-; dɪˌbɔː-, də-, (US) ˌdeb.ɑːˈʃiː, -ɔːˈ-; (US) dɪˌbɑːˈtʃiː, -ˌbɔːˈ- **-s** -z
debaucher|y dɪˈbɔː.tʃ^{ə}r|.i, dəˈ-, (US) dɪˈbɑː-, -ˈbɔː- **-ies** -iz
Debbie ˈdeb.i
de Beauvoir dəˈbəʊ.vwɑː^{r}, (US) -ˌboʊˈvwɑːr
Deben ˈdiː.b^{ə}n
de bene esse ˌdeɪˌben.iˈes.i, dəˌbiː.niːˈes.iː
Debenham ˈdeb.^{ə}n.əm, (US) -hæm **-'s** -z
debenture dɪˈben.tʃə^{r}, də-, (US) dɪˈbent.ʃɚ **-s** -z
debili|tate dɪˈbɪl.ɪ|.teɪt, də-, ˈ-ə-, (US) dɪ- **-tates** -teɪts **-tating** -teɪ.tɪŋ, (US) -teɪ.t̬ɪŋ **-tated** -teɪ.tɪd, (US) -teɪ.t̬ɪd
debilitation dɪˌbɪl.ɪˈteɪ.ʃ^{ə}n, də-, -əˈ-, (US) dɪ-
debility dɪˈbɪl.ə.ti, də-, -ɪ.ti, (US) dɪˈbɪl.ə.t̬i
deb|it ˈdeb|.ɪt **-its** -ɪts **-iting** -ɪ.tɪŋ, (US) -ɪ.t̬ɪŋ **-ited** -ɪ.tɪd, (US) -ɪ.t̬ɪd
Debnam ˈdeb.nəm
debonair ˌdeb.əˈneə^{r}, (US) -ˈner **-ly** -li **-ness** -nəs, -nɪs
de Bono dəˈbəʊ.nəʊ, (US) -ˈboʊ.noʊ
Deborah ˈdeb.^{ə}r.ə, ˈ-rə
debouch dɪˈbaʊtʃ, ˌdiː-, -buːʃ **-es** -ɪz **-ing** -ɪŋ **-ed** -t **-ment** -mənt
Debra ˈdeb.rə
Debrecen ˈdeb.rət.s^{ə}n, (US) ˌdeb.rətˈsen, ˈ---
Debrett dəˈbret, dɪ- **-'s** -s
debridement, débridement dɪˈbriːd.mənt, ˌdiː-, deɪ-; *as if French:* -ˌbriːdˈmɑ̃ːŋ; (US) dɪˈbriːd.mənt, deɪ-, -ˈbriːd.mɑ̃ːŋ
debrief ˌdiːˈbriːf **-s** -s **-ing** -ɪŋ **-ed** -t
debris ˈdeɪ.briː, ˈdeb.riː, (US) dəˈbriː; (US) ˈdeɪ.briː
debt det **-s** -s
debtor ˈdet.ə^{r}, (US) ˈdet̬.ɚ **-s** -z
debug ˌdiːˈbʌg **-s** -z **-ging** -ɪŋ **-ged** -d
debunk ˌdiːˈbʌŋk **-s** -s **-ing** -ɪŋ **-ed** -t
De Burgh dəˈbɜːg, (US) -ˈbɝːg
Debussy dəˈbuː.siː, -ˈbjuː-, (US) ˈdeɪ.bjuː.si; ˌdeɪ.bjuːˈsiː; dəˈbjuː.si

> Note: US street names are always /də-/.

début ˈdeɪ.bjuː, -buː; ˈdeb.juː, (US) deɪˈbjuː, ˈ-- **-s** -z **-ing** -ɪŋ **-ed** -d
débutant ˈdeb.jʊ.tɑ̃ːŋ, ˈdeɪ.bjʊ-, (US) ˈdeb.juː.tɑːnt, ˌ--ˈ- **-s** -z
débutante ˈdeb.juː.tɑ̃ːŋt, ˈdeɪ.bjuː-, (US) ˈdeb.juː.tɑːnt, ˌ--ˈ- **-s** -s
Dec. (abbrev. for **December**) dɪˈsem.bə^{r}, də-, (US) dɪˈsem.bɚ
deca- ˈdek.ə
Note: Prefix. Normally carries primary or secondary stress on the

first syllable, e.g. **decagon** /ˈdek.ə.gən/ (US) /-gɑːn/, **decahedron** /ˌdek.əˈhiː.drən/.

decachord ˈdek.ə.kɔːd, (US) -kɔːrd -s -z

decade *ten years:* ˈdek.eɪd; dekˈeɪd, dɪˈkeɪd *division of the rosary:* ˈdek.əd -s -z

decaden|ce ˈdek.ə.dᵊnt|s, (US) ˈdek.ə-; (US) dɪˈkeɪ- -cy -si

decadent ˈdek.ə.dᵊnt, (US) ˈdek.ə-; (US) dɪˈkeɪ- -ly -li

decaf, decaff ˈdiː.kæf

decaffei|nate dɪˈkæf.ɪ|.neɪt, ˌdiː-, ˈ-ə- -nates -neɪts -nating -neɪ.tɪŋ, (US) -neɪ.t̬ɪŋ -nated -neɪ.tɪd, (US) -neɪ.t̬ɪd

decagon ˈdek.ə.gən, (US) -gɑːn -s -z

decagram, decagramme ˈdek.ə.græm -s -z

decahedr|on ˌdek.əˈhiː.dr|ən, -ˈhed.r|ən, (US) -ˈhiː.dr|ən -ons -ənz -a -ə -al -ᵊl

decal ˈdiː.kæl; dɪˈkæl -s -z

decalcification ˌdiːˌkæl.sɪ.fɪˈkeɪ.ʃᵊn, -sə-, -fəˈ-

decalci|fy ˌdiːˈkæl.sɪ|.faɪ, -sə- -fies -faɪz -fying -faɪ.ɪŋ -fied -faɪd

decalitre, decaliter ˈdek.əˌliː.təʳ, (US) -t̬ɚ -s -z

Decalogue ˈdek.ə.lɒg, (US) -lɑːg, -lɔːg -s -z

Decameron dɪˈkæm.ᵊr.ᵊn, dekˈæm-, dəˈkæm-

decametre, decameter ˈdek.əˌmiː.təʳ, (US) -t̬ɚ -s -z

decamp ˌdiːˈkæmp, dɪ- -s -s -ing -ɪŋ -ed -t

decanal dɪˈkeɪ.nᵊl, dekˈeɪ-, dəˈkeɪ-; ˈdek.ᵊn.ᵊl

decani dɪˈkeɪ.naɪ, dekˈeɪ-

de|cant dɪ|ˈkænt, ˌdiː- -cants -ˈkænts -canting -ˈkæn.tɪŋ, (US) -ˈkæn.t̬ɪŋ -canted -ˈkæn.tɪd, (US) -ˈkæn.t̬ɪd

decantation ˌdiː.kænˈteɪ.ʃᵊn -s -z

decanter dɪˈkæn.təʳ, də-, (US) dɪˈkæn.t̬ɚ -s -z

decapi|tate dɪˈkæp.ɪ|.teɪt, ˌdiː-, ˈ-ə- -tates -teɪts -tating -teɪ.tɪŋ, (US) -teɪ.t̬ɪŋ -tated -teɪ.tɪd, (US) -teɪ.t̬ɪd

decapitation dɪˌkæp.ɪˈteɪ.ʃᵊn, ˌdiː-, -əˈ- -s -z

decapod ˈdek.ə.pɒd, (US) -pɑːd -s -z

Decapolis dekˈæp.ə.lɪs, dɪˈkæp-

decarbo|nate ˌdiːˈkɑː.bə|.neɪt, (US) -ˈkɑːr- -nates -neɪts -nating -neɪ.tɪŋ, (US) -neɪ.t̬ɪŋ -nated -neɪ.tɪd, (US) -neɪ.t̬ɪd

decarbonization, -isa- ˌdiːˌkɑː.bᵊn.aɪˈzeɪ.ʃᵊn, -ɪˈ-, (US) ˌdiːˌkɑːr.bə.nəˈ-

decarboniz|e, -is|e ˌdiːˈkɑː.bə.naɪz, (US) -ˈkɑːr- -es -ɪz -ing -ɪŋ -ed -d

decarburiz|e, -is|e ˌdiːˈkɑː.bjʊ.raɪz, -bjᵊr.aɪz, (US) -ˈkɑːr.bə.raɪz, -bjə-, -bjʊ- -es -ɪz -ing -ɪŋ -ed -d

decasyllabic ˌdek.ə.sɪˈlæb.ɪk, -səˈ-

decasyllable ˈdek.əˌsɪl.ə.bᵊl, ˌdek.əˈsɪl.ə- -s -z

decathlete dɪˈkæθ.liːt, dekˈæθ-, dəˈkæθ- -s -s

decathlon dɪˈkæθ.lɒn, dekˈæθ-, dəˈkæθ-, -lən, (US) dɪˈkæθ.lɑːn, -lən, də- -s -z

Decatur dɪˈkeɪ.təʳ, (US) -t̬ɚ

decay dɪˈkeɪ, də- -s -z -ing -ɪŋ -ed -d

Decca ˈdek.ə

Deccan ˈdek.ən, -æn

deceas|e dɪˈsiːs, də-, (US) dɪ- -es -ɪz -ing -ɪŋ -ed -t

decedent dɪˈsiː.dᵊnt, də-, (US) dɪ- -s -s

deceit dɪˈsiːt, də-, (US) dɪ- -s -s

deceitful dɪˈsiːt.fᵊl, də-, -fʊl, (US) dɪ- -ly -i -ness -nəs, -nɪs

deceivable dɪˈsiː.və.bᵊl, də-, (US) dɪ-

deceiv|e dɪˈsiːv, də-, (US) dɪ- -es -z -ing -ɪŋ -ed -d -er/s -əʳ/z, (US) -ɚ/z

deceler|ate dɪˈsel.ᵊr|.eɪt, ˌdiː-, (US) -ə.r|eɪt -ates -eɪts -ating -eɪ.tɪŋ, (US) -eɪ.t̬ɪŋ -ated -eɪ.tɪd, (US) -eɪ.t̬ɪd

deceleration dɪˌsel.əˈreɪ.ʃᵊn, ˌdiː.sel- -s -z

December dɪˈsem.bəʳ, də-, (US) dɪˈsem.bɚ -s -z

decemvir dɪˈsem.vəʳ, də-, -vɜːʳ, (US) diːˈsem.vɪr -s -z

decemvirate dɪˈsem.vɪ.rət, də-, -vᵊr.ət, -ɪt, -eɪt, (US) diːˈsem.vɚ.ɪt, -və.reɪt -s -s

decenc|y ˈdiː.sᵊnt.s|i -ies -iz

decennial dɪˈsen.i.əl, desˈen-, dəˈsen-, diː-, (US) dɪˈsen-, diː-

decent ˈdiː.sᵊnt -ly -li

decentralization, -isa- ˌdiːˌsen.trᵊl.aɪˈzeɪ.ʃᵊn, dɪ.sen-, -ɪˈ-, (US) -əˈ-

decentraliz|e, -is|e diːˈsen.trə.laɪz, ˌdɪ- -es -ɪz -ing -ɪŋ -ed -d

deception dɪˈsep.ʃᵊn, də-, (US) dɪ- -s -z

deceptive dɪˈsep.tɪv, də-, (US) dɪ- -ly -li -ness -nəs, -nɪs

de Chastelain dəˈtʃæs.tə.leɪn, (US) -t̬ə.lən

deci- ˈdes.ɪ

Note: Prefix. Normally carries primary or secondary stress on the first syllable, e.g. **decimal** /ˈdes.ɪ.mᵊl/, **decimalization** /ˌdes.ɪ.mᵊl.aɪˈzeɪ.ʃᵊn/ (US) /-ɪˈ-/. There are exceptions; see individual entries.

decibel ˈdes.ɪ.bel, -bəl, -bᵊl -s -z

decid|e dɪˈsaɪd, də-, (US) dɪ- -es -z -ing -ɪŋ -ed/ly -ɪd/li -er/s -əʳ/z, (US) -ɚ/z

deciduous dɪˈsɪd.ju.əs, də-, (US) dɪˈsɪdʒ.u- -ly -li -ness -nəs, -nɪs

decigram, decigramme ˈdes.ɪ.græm -s -z

decilitre, deciliter ˈdes.ɪˌliː.təʳ, (US) -t̬ɚ -s -z

decillion dɪˈsɪl.i.ən, ˈ-jən, (US) ˈ-jən -s -z

decimal ˈdes.ɪ.mᵊl, ˈ-ə- -s -z -ly -i **ˌdecimal ˈpoint** (US) **ˈdecimal ˌpoint**

decimalization, -isa- ˌdes.ɪ.mᵊl.aɪˈzeɪ.ʃᵊn, ˌ-ə-, -ɪˈ-, (US) -əˈ-

decimaliz|e, -is|e ˈdes.ɪ.mᵊl.aɪz, -ə-, (US) -mə.laɪz -es -ɪz -ing -ɪŋ -ed -d

deci|mate ˈdes.ɪ|.meɪt, ˈ-ə- -mates -meɪts -mating -meɪ.tɪŋ, (US) -meɪ.t̬ɪŋ -mated -meɪ.tɪd, (US) -meɪ.t̬ɪd -mator/s -meɪ.təʳ/z, (US) -meɪ.t̬ɚ/z

decimation ˌdes.ɪˈmeɪ.ʃᵊn, -əˈ-

decimetre, decimeter ˈdes.ɪˌmiː.təʳ, (US) -t̬ɚ -s -z

deciph|er dɪˈsaɪ.f|əʳ, ˌdiː-, (US) -f|ɚ -ers -əz, (US) -ɚz -ering -ᵊr.ɪŋ -ered -əd, (US) -ɚd

decipherable dɪˈsaɪ.fᵊr.ə.bᵊl, ˌdiː-

decision dɪˈsɪʒ.ᵊn, də-, (US) dɪ- -s -z

decision-mak|er dɪˈsɪʒ.ᵊnˌmeɪ.k|əʳ, də-, -ᵊm-, (US) dɪˈsɪʒ.ᵊnˌmeɪ.k|ɚ -ers -əz, (US) -ɚz -ing -ɪŋ

decisive dɪˈsaɪ.sɪv, də-, -zɪv, (US) dɪˈsaɪ.sɪv -ly -li -ness -nəs, -nɪs

Decius ˈdiː.ʃi.əs, ˈ-ʃəs, ˈ-si.əs; ˈdek.i.əs, ˈdes-, (US) ˈdiː.ʃi.əs, ˈ-ʃəs, ˈ-si.əs; (US) ˈdes.i.əs

deck dek -s -s -ing -ɪŋ -ed -t -er/s -əʳ/z, (US) -ɚ/z **ˌclear the ˈdecks; ˌhit the ˈdeck**

deckchair ˈdek.tʃeəʳ, (US) -tʃer -s -z

Decker ˈdek.əʳ, (US) -ɚ

deckhand ˈdek.hænd -s -z

deckhou|se ˈdek.haʊ|s -ses -zɪz

deckle ˈdek.ᵊl -s -z **ˌdeckle ˈedged**

declaim dɪˈkleɪm, də-, (US) dɪ- -s -z -ing -ɪŋ -ed -d -er/s -əʳ/z, (US) -ɚ/z -ant/s -ənt/s

declamation ˌdek.ləˈmeɪ.ʃᵊn -s -z

declamatory dɪˈklæm.ə.tᵊr.i, də-, -tri, (US) dɪˈklæm.ə.tɔːr.i

Declan ˈdek.lən

declarable dɪˈkleə.rə.bᵊl, də-, (US) dɪˈkler.ə-, -ˈklær-

declaration ˌdek.ləˈreɪ.ʃᵊn -s -z

declarative dɪˈklær.ə.tɪv, də-, -kleə.rə-, (US) dɪˈkler.ə.t̬ɪv, -ˈklær- -ly -li

declaratory dɪˈklær.ə.tᵊr.i, də-, -ˈkleə.rə-, -tri, (US) dɪˈkler.ə.tɔːr.i, -ˈklær-

declar|e dɪˈkleəʳ, də-, (US) dɪˈkler -es -z -ing -ɪŋ -ed -d -er/s -əʳ/z, (US) -ɚ/z

declaredly dɪˈkleə.rɪd.li, də-, -rəd-, (US) dɪˈkler-

declass ˌdiːˈklɑːs, (US) -ˈklæs -es -ɪz -ing -ɪŋ -ed -t

declassification ˌdiːˌklæs.ɪ.fɪˈkeɪ.ʃᵊn, ˌ-ə-, -fəˈ-

declassi|fy ˌdiːˈklæs.ɪ|.faɪ, ˈ-ə- -fies -faɪz -fying -faɪ.ɪŋ -fied -faɪd

declension dɪˈklen.*t*ʃᵊn, də-, (US) dɪˈklent.ʃᵊn -s -z

declination ˌdek.lɪˈneɪ.ʃᵊn, -ləˈ- -s -z

declin|e dɪˈklaɪn, də-, (US) dɪ- -es -z -ing -ɪŋ -ed -d -able -ə.bᵊl

declivit|y dɪˈklɪv.ə.t|i, də-, -ɪ.t|i, (US) dɪˈklɪv.ə.t̬|i -ies -iz

declutch ˌdiːˈklʌtʃ -es -ɪz -ing -ɪŋ -ed -t

decoct dɪˈkɒkt, ˌdiː-, (US) -ˈkɑːkt -s -s -ing -ɪŋ -ed -ɪd

D

decod|e ˌdiːˈkəʊd, (US) -ˈkoʊd **-es** -z **-ing** -ɪŋ **-ed** -ɪd
decoder ˌdiːˈkəʊ.dər, dɪ-, (US) -ˈkoʊ.dɚ **-s** -z
decok|e ˌdiːˈkəʊk, (US) -ˈkoʊk **-es** -s **-ing** -ɪŋ **-ed** -t
décolletage ˌdeɪ.kɒlˈtɑːʒ; -kɒl.ɪˈ-, -əˈ-, (US) -kɑː.ləˈ-, -kɑːlˈ-
décolleté(e) ˌdeɪ.kɒlˈteɪ; -kɒl.ɪˈ-, -əˈ-, (US) -kɑː.ləˈ-, -kɑːlˈ-
decolonization ˌdiːˌkɒl.ə.naɪˈzeɪ.ʃən, -nɪˈ-, (US) -ˌkɑː.lə.nəˈ-
decoloniz|e, -is|e ˌdiːˈkɒl.ə.naɪz, (US) -ˈkɑː.lə- **-es** -ɪz **-ing** -ɪŋ **-ed** -d
decolo(u)rization, -isa- ˌdiːˌkʌl.ə.raɪˈzeɪ.ʃən, dɪˌkʌl-, -ər.ɪˈ-, (US) dɪˌkʌl.ɚ.əˈ-
decolo(u)riz|e, -is|e ˌdiːˈkʌl.ər.aɪz, (US) -ə.raɪz **-es** -ɪz **-ing** -ɪŋ **-ed** -d
decommission ˌdiː.kəˈmɪʃ.ən **-s** -z **-ing** -ɪŋ **-ed** -d
decompos|e ˌdiː.kəmˈpəʊz, (US) -ˈpoʊz **-es** -ɪz **-ing** -ɪŋ **-ed** -d **-able** -ə.bəl
decomposition ˌdiː.kɒm.pəˈzɪʃ.ən, dɪˌkɒm-, (US) ˌdiː.kɑːm- **-s** -z
decompound ˌdiː.kəmˈpaʊnd **-s** -z **-ing** -ɪŋ **-ed** -ɪd
decompress ˌdiː.kəmˈpres **-es** -ɪz **-ing** -ɪŋ **-ed** -t **-er/s** -ər/z, (US) -ɚ/z
decompression ˌdiː.kəmˈpreʃ.ən
decongestant ˌdiː.kənˈdʒest.ənt **-s** -s
deconsecrat|e ˌdiːˈkɒnt.sɪ.kreɪt, -sə-, (US) -ˈkɑːnt- **-es** -s **-ing** -ɪŋ **-ed** -ɪd
deconsecration ˌdiː.kɒnt.sɪˈkreɪ.ʃən, dɪˌkɒnt-, -səˈ-, (US) ˌdiː.kɑːnt- **-s** -z
deconstruct ˌdiː.kənˈstrʌkt **-s** -s **-ing** -ɪŋ **-ed** -ɪd **-ive** -ɪv
deconstruction ˌdiː.kənˈstrʌk.ʃən **-ism** -ɪ.zəm **-ist/s** -ɪst/s
decontami|nate ˌdiː.kənˈtæm.ɪ|.neɪt, ˈ-ə- **-nates** -neɪts **-nating** -neɪ.tɪŋ, (US) -neɪ.t̬ɪŋ **-nated** -neɪ.tɪd, (US) -neɪ.t̬ɪd
decontamination ˌdiː.kənˌtæm.ɪˈneɪ.ʃən, -əˈ-
decontrol ˌdiː.kənˈtrəʊl, (US) -ˈtroʊl **-s** -z **-ling** -ɪŋ **-led** -d
decor, décor ˈdeɪ.kɔːr, ˈdek.ɔːr, ˈdɪk-, (US) deɪˈkɔːr, ˈ-- **-s** -z
decor|ate ˈdek.ər|.eɪt, (US) -ə.r|eɪt **-ates** -eɪts **-ating** -eɪ.tɪŋ, (US) -eɪ.t̬ɪŋ **-ated** -eɪ.tɪd, (US) -eɪ.t̬ɪd
decoration ˌdek.əˈreɪ.ʃən, (US) -əˈreɪ- **-s** -z
decorative ˈdek.ər.ə.tɪv, (US) -t̬ɪv **-ly** -li **-ness** -nəs, -nɪs
decorator ˈdek.ər.eɪ.tər, (US) -ə.reɪ.t̬ɚ **-s** -z
decorous ˈdek.ə.rəs; dɪˈkɔː-, (US) ˈdek.ɚ.əs **-ly** -li **-ness** -nəs, -nɪs
decorum dɪˈkɔː.rəm, də-, (US) dɪˈkɔːr-
De Courcy dəˈkʊə.si, -ˈkɔː-, -ˈkɜː-, (US) -ˈkʊr-, -ˈkɔːr-, -ˈkɝː-
decoy n ˈdiː.kɔɪ; dɪˈkɔɪ, də-, (US) ˈdiː.kɔɪ; (US) dɪˈkɔɪ **-s** -z
decoy v dɪˈkɔɪ, də-, (US) dɪ- **-s** -z **-ing** -ɪŋ **-ed** -d
decreas|e n ˈdiː.kriːs; dɪˈ-, diː-, də-, (US) ˈdiː.kriːs **-es** -ɪz
decreas|e v dɪˈkriːs, diː-, də-; ˈdiː.kriːs, (US) dɪˈkriːs; (US) ˈdiː.kriːs **-es** -ɪz **-ing/ly** -ɪŋ/li **-ed** -t
decree dɪˈkriː, də-, (US) dɪ- **-s** -z **-ing** -ɪŋ **-d** -d
decree nisi dɪˌkriːˈnaɪ.saɪ, -si
decrement ˈdek.rɪ.mənt, -rə- **-s** -s
decrepit dɪˈkrep.ɪt, də-, (US) dɪ- **-est** -ɪst, -əst
decrepitation dɪˌkrep.ɪˈteɪ.ʃən, də-, -əˈ-, (US) dɪ- **-s** -z
decrepitude dɪˈkrep.ɪ.tʃuːd, də-, ˈ-ə-, -tjuːd, (US) dɪˈkrep.ɪ.tuːd, ˈ-ə-, -tjuːd
decrescendo ˌdiː.krɪˈʃen.dəʊ, ˌdeɪ-, -krəˈ-, (US) -doʊ **-s** -z
De Crespigny dəˈkrep.ɪ.ni, -ˈkres.pɪ-
decrial dɪˈkraɪ.əl **-s** -z
decriminalization, -isa- ˌdiːˌkrɪm.ɪ.nəl.aɪˈzeɪ.ʃən, dɪ.krɪ.mɪ-, -mən.əl-, -ɪˈ-, (US) ˌdiː.krɪ.mɪ.nəl.əˈ-
decriminaliz|e, -is|e ˌdiːˈkrɪm.ɪ.nəl.aɪz, dɪ-, -ən.əl-, (US) -ɪ.nəl- **-es** -ɪz **-ing** -ɪŋ **-ed** -d
decr|y dɪˈkr|aɪ, də-, (US) dɪ- **-ies** -aɪz **-ying** -aɪ.ɪŋ **-ied** -aɪd **-ier/s** -aɪ.ər/z, (US) -aɪ.ɚ/z
decrypt ˌdiːˈkrɪpt, dɪ- **-s** -s **-ing** -ɪŋ **-ed** -ɪd
decumben|ce dɪˈkʌm.bənt|s, ˌdiː- **-cy** -si
decumbent dɪˈkʌm.bənt, ˌdiː- **-ly** -li
decuple ˈdek.jʊ.pəl, ˈ-jə-; dekˈjuː- **-es** -z **-ing** -ɪŋ, ˈdek.jʊ.plɪŋ, -juː- **-ed** -d
Dedalus ˈdiː.dəl.əs, (US) ˈded.əl.əs, ˈdiː.dəl-
Deddington ˈded.ɪŋ.tən
Dedham ˈded.əm
dedi|cate ˈded.ɪ|.keɪt **-cates** -keɪts **-cating** -keɪ.tɪŋ, (US) -keɪ.t̬ɪŋ **-cated/ly** -keɪ.tɪd/li, (US) -keɪ.t̬ɪd/li **-cator/s** -keɪ.tər/z, (US) -keɪ.t̬ɚ/z
dedicatee ˌded.ɪ.kəˈtiː **-s** -z
dedication ˌded.ɪˈkeɪ.ʃən, -əˈ- **-s** -z
dedicatory ˈded.ɪ.kə.tər.i, -keɪ-, -tri; ˌded.ɪˈkeɪ-, (US) ˈded.ɪ.kə.tɔːr-
de Dion dəˈdiː.ən, -ɒn; *as if French:* -ɔ̃ːŋ; (US) dəˈdiː.ɑːn; *as if French:* (US) -ɔ̃ːŋ **-s** -z
Dedlock ˈded.lɒk, (US) -lɑːk
Dedman ˈded.mən, ˈdeb-, -mæn, (US) ˈded-
deduc|e dɪˈdʒuːs, də-, -ˈdjuːs, (US) dɪˈduːs, -ˈdjuːs **-es** -ɪz **-ing** -ɪŋ **-ed** -t
deducibility dɪˌdʒuː.səˈbɪl.ə.ti, -ˌdjuː-, də-, -sɪˈ-, -ɪ.ti, (US) dɪˌduː.səˈbɪl.ə.t̬i, -ˌdjuː-
deducible dɪˈdʒuː.sə.bəl, -ˈdjuː-, də-, -sɪ-, (US) dɪˈduː-, -ˈdjuː-
deduct dɪˈdʌkt, də-, (US) dɪ- **-s** -s **-ing** -ɪŋ **-ed** -ɪd **-ible** -ə.bəl
deduction dɪˈdʌk.ʃən, də-, (US) dɪ- **-s** -z
deductive dɪˈdʌk.tɪv, də-, (US) dɪ- **-ly** -li
Dee diː
deed diːd **-s** -z ˈ**deed** ˌ**poll**
Deedes diːdz
deejay ˈdiː.dʒeɪ **-s** -z
Deek(e)s diːks
Deeley ˈdiː.li
deem diːm **-s** -z **-ing** -ɪŋ **-ed** -d
Deems diːmz
deemster ˈdiːm.stər, (US) -stɚ **-s** -z
deep diːp **-s** -s **-er** -ər, (US) -ɚ **-est** -ɪst, -əst **-ly** -li **-ness** -nəs, -nɪs ˌ**deep** ˈ**freeze** (US) ˈ**deep** ˌ**freeze**; ˌ**Deep** ˈ**South**; **go off the** ˈ**deep** ˌ**end**; ˌ**throw (someone) in at the** ˈ**deep** ˌ**end**
Deepcut ˈdiːp.kʌt
deepen ˈdiː.pən **-s** -z **-ing** -ɪŋ **-ed** -d
deep-fr|y ˌdiːpˈfr|aɪ, ˈ-- **-ies** -aɪz **-ying** -aɪ.ɪŋ **-ied** -aɪd *stress shift:* ˌ**deep-fried** ˈ**chicken**
deep-laid ˌdiːpˈleɪd *stress shift:* ˌ**deep-laid** ˈ**plans**
deep-rooted ˌdiːpˈruː.tɪd, (US) -t̬ɪd *stress shift:* ˌ**deep-rooted** ˈ**fears**
deep-sea ˌdiːpˈsiː *stress shift:* ˌ**deep-sea** ˈ**diving**
deep-seated ˌdiːpˈsiː.tɪd, (US) -t̬ɪd *stress shift:* ˌ**deep-seated** ˈ**sorrow**
deep-set ˌdiːpˈset *stress shift:* ˌ**deepset** ˈ**eyes**
deep-six ˌdiːpˈsɪks **-es** -ɪz **-ing** -ɪŋ **-ed** -t
deer dɪər, (US) dɪr ˈ**deer** ˌ**forest**; ˈ**deer** ˌ**park**; ˈ**Deer** ˌ**Park**
Deerfield ˈdɪə.fiːld, (US) ˈdɪr-
deerhound ˈdɪə.haʊnd, (US) ˈdɪr- **-s** -z
deerskin ˈdɪə.skɪn, (US) ˈdɪr-
Deerslayer ˈdɪəˌsleɪ.ər, (US) ˈdɪrˌsleɪ.ɚ
deerstalk|ing ˈdɪəˌstɔː.k|ɪŋ, (US) ˈdɪr-, -ˌstɑː-, -ˌstɔː- **-er/s** -ər/z, (US) -ɚ/z
Deery ˈdɪə.ri, (US) ˈdɪr.i
de-escal|ate ˌdiːˈes.kəl|.eɪt, (US) -kə.l|eɪt **-ates** -eɪts **-ating** -eɪ.tɪŋ, (US) -eɪ.t̬ɪŋ **-ated** -eɪ.tɪd, (US) -eɪ.t̬ɪd
de-escalation ˌdiː.es.kəˈleɪ.ʃən, diːˌes-, (US) diːˌes-
Deeside ˈdiː.saɪd
defac|e dɪˈfeɪs **-es** -ɪz **-ing** -ɪŋ **-ed** -t **-er/s** -ər/z, (US) -ɚ/z **-ement/s** -mənt/s
de facto ˌdeɪˈfæk.təʊ, ˌdiː-, (US) -toʊ
defae|cate ˈdef.ə|.keɪt, ˈdiː.fə-, -fɪ-, (US) ˈdef.ə-, ˈ-ɪ- **-cates** -keɪts **-cating** -keɪ.tɪŋ, (US) -keɪ.t̬ɪŋ **-cated** -keɪ.tɪd, (US) -keɪ.t̬ɪd
defaecation ˌdef.əˈkeɪ.ʃən, ˌdiː.fəˈ-, -fɪˈ-, (US) ˌdef.əˈ-, -ɪˈ-
defal|cate ˈdiː.fæl|.keɪt, diːˈfæl-; ˈdiː.fɔːl-, (US) diːˈfæl-, -ˈfɔːl- **-cates** -keɪts **-cating** -keɪ.tɪŋ, (US) -keɪ.t̬ɪŋ **-cated** -keɪ.tɪd, (US) -keɪ.t̬ɪd
defalcation ˌdiː.fælˈkeɪ.ʃən, -fɔːlˈ- **-s** -z
defamation ˌdef.əˈmeɪ.ʃən, ˌdiː.fəˈ-, (US) ˌdef.əˈ- **-s** -z

defamatory dɪˈfæm.ə.tᵊr.i, də-, -tri, (US) dɪˈfæm.ə.tɔːr.i
defam|e dɪˈfeɪm, də-, (US) dɪ- **-es** -z **-ing** -ɪŋ **-ed** -d **-er/s** -əʳ/z, (US) -ɚ/z
Defarge dəˈfɑːʒ, (US) -ˈfɑːrʒ
default n dɪˈfɔːlt, də-, -ˈfɒlt; ˈdiː.fɔːlt, -fɒlt, (US) dɪˈfɑːlt, -ˈfɔːlt
defaul|t v dɪˈfɔːl|t, də-, -ˈfɒl|t, (US) dɪˈfɑːl|t, -ˈfɔːl|t **-ts** -ts **-ting** -tɪŋ, (US) -t̬ɪŋ **-ted** -tɪd, (US) -t̬ɪd **-ter/s** -təʳ/z, (US) -t̬ɚ/z
defeasance dɪˈfiː.zᵊnts, də-, (US) dɪ-
defeasib|le dɪˈfiː.zə.b|ᵊl, də-, -zɪ-, (US) dɪ- **-ly** -li **-leness** -ᵊl.nəs, -nɪs
de|feat dɪ|ˈfiːt, də-, (US) dɪ- **-feats** -ˈfiːts **-feating** -ˈfiː.tɪŋ, (US) -ˈfiː.t̬ɪŋ **-feated** -ˈfiː.tɪd, (US) -ˈfiː.t̬ɪd
defeat|ism dɪˈfiː.t|ɪ.zᵊm, də-, (US) dɪˈfiː.t̬|ɪ- **-ist/s** -ɪst/s
defe|cate ˈdef.ə|.keɪt, ˈdiː.fə-, -fɪ-, (US) ˈdef.ə-, ˈ-ɪ- **-cates** -keɪts **-cating** -keɪ.tɪŋ, (US) -keɪ.t̬ɪŋ **-cated** -keɪ.tɪd, (US) -keɪ.t̬ɪd
defecation ˌdef.əˈkeɪ.ʃᵊn, ˌdiː.fəˈ-, -fɪˈ-, (US) ˌdef.əˈ-, -ɪˈ- **-s** -z
defect[1] n ˈdiː.fekt; dɪˈfekt, də-, (US) ˈdiː.fekt; (US) dɪˈfekt **-s** -s
defect[2] v dɪˈfekt, də-, (US) dɪ- **-s** -s **-ing** -ɪŋ **-ed** -ɪd
defection dɪˈfek.ʃᵊn, də-, (US) dɪ- **-s** -z
defective dɪˈfek.tɪv, də-, (US) dɪ- **-ly** -li **-ness** -nəs, -nɪs
defector dɪˈfek.təʳ, də-, (US) dɪˈfek.tɚ **-s** -z
defenc|e dɪˈfents, də-, (US) dɪ- **-es** -ɪz
defenceless dɪˈfent.sləs, də-, -slɪs, (US) dɪ- **-ly** -li **-ness** -nəs, -nɪs
defend dɪˈfend, də-, (US) dɪ- **-s** -z **-ing** -ɪŋ **-ed** -ɪd **-able** -ə.bᵊl
defendant dɪˈfen.dənt, də-, (US) dɪ- **-s** -s
defender dɪˈfen.dəʳ, də-, (US) dɪˈfen.dɚ **-s** -z
defens|e dɪˈfents, də-, (US) dɪ-; *esp. in sports:* (US) ˈdiː.fents **-es** -ɪz
defenseless dɪˈfent.sləs, də-, -slɪs, (US) dɪ- **-ly** -li **-ness** -nəs, -nɪs
defense|man dɪˈfents|.mən, də-, (US) dɪ-, -mæn **-men** -mən
defensibility dɪˌfent.səˈbɪl.ə.ti, də-, -sɪˈ-, -ɪ.ti, (US) dɪˌfent.səˈbɪl.ə.t̬i
defensib|le dɪˈfent.sə.b|ᵊl, də-, -sɪ-, (US) dɪ- **-ly** -li
defensive dɪˈfent.sɪv, də-, (US) dɪ- **-ly** -li **-ness** -nəs, -nɪs
defer dɪˈfɜːʳ, də-, (US) dɪˈfɝː **-s** -z **-ring** -ɪŋ **-red** -d **-rer/s** -əʳ/z, (US) -ɚ/z
deferen|ce ˈdef.ᵊr.ᵊn|ts **-t** -t
deferential ˌdef.ᵊˈren.tʃᵊl, (US) -ˈrent.ʃᵊl **-ly** -i
deferment dɪˈfɜː.mənt, də-, (US) dɪˈfɝː- **-s** -s
deferral dɪˈfɜː.rᵊl, də-, (US) dɪˈfɝː.ᵊl **-s** -z
defiance dɪˈfaɪ.ənts, də-, (US) dɪ-
defiant dɪˈfaɪ.ənt, də-, (US) dɪ- **-ly** -li **-ness** -nəs, -nɪs
defibrill|ate ˌdiːˈfɪb.rɪ.l|eɪt, -ˈfaɪ.brɪ-, -brᵊl|.eɪt, (US) -rɪ.l|eɪt, -rə- **-ates** -eɪts **-ating** -eɪ.tɪŋ, (US) -eɪ.t̬ɪŋ **-ated** -eɪ.tɪd, (US) -eɪ.t̬ɪd
defibrillation diː.fɪb.rɪˈleɪ.ʃᵊn, -ˌfaɪ.brɪˈ-, -brəˈ-; ˌdiː.fɪ.brɪˈ-
defibrillator ˌdiːˈfɪb.rɪ.leɪ.təʳ, -ˈfaɪ.brɪ-, -brə-, (US) -t̬ɚ **-s** -z
deficienc|y dɪˈfɪʃ.ᵊnt.s|i, də-, (US) dɪ- **-ies** -iz
deficient dɪˈfɪʃ.ᵊnt, də-, (US) dɪ- **-ly** -li
deficit ˈdef.ɪ.sɪt, ˈ-ə-; dəˈfɪs-, dɪ-, (US) ˈdef.ɪ.sɪt, ˈ-ə- **-s** -s
defilad|e ˌdef.ɪˈleɪd, -əˈ-, ˈ--- **-es** -z **-ing** -ɪŋ **-ed** -ɪd
defile n dɪˈfaɪl, ˌdiː-; ˈdiː.faɪl **-s** -z
defil|e v dɪˈfaɪl, də-, (US) dɪ- **-es** -z **-ing** -ɪŋ **-ed** -d **-er/s** -əʳ/z, (US) -ɚ/z **-ement** -mənt
definable dɪˈfaɪ.nə.bᵊl, də-, (US) dɪ-
defin|e dɪˈfaɪn, də-, (US) dɪ- **-es** -z **-ing** -ɪŋ **-ed** -d **-er/s** -əʳ/z, (US) -ɚ/z
definite ˈdef.ɪ.nət, -ᵊn.ət, -ɪt **-ly** -li **-ness** -nəs, -nɪs
definition ˌdef.ɪˈnɪʃ.ᵊn, -əˈ- **-s** -z
definitive dɪˈfɪn.ə.tɪv, də-, ˈ-ɪ-, (US) dɪˈfɪn.ə.t̬ɪv **-ly** -li **-ness** -nəs, -nɪs
defla|grate ˈdiː.flə|.greɪt, ˈdef.lə-, (US) ˈdef.lə- **-grates** -greɪts **-grating** -greɪ.tɪŋ, (US) -greɪ.t̬ɪŋ **-grated** -greɪ.tɪd, (US) -greɪ.t̬ɪd **-grator/s** -greɪ.təʳ/z, (US) -greɪ.t̬ɚ/z
deflagration ˌdiː.fləˈgreɪ.ʃᵊn, ˌdef.ləˈ-, (US) ˌdef.ləˈ- **-s** -z
de|flate dɪ|ˈfleɪt, ˌdiː- **-flates** -ˈfleɪts **-flating** -ˈfleɪ.tɪŋ, (US) -ˈfleɪ.t̬ɪŋ **-flated** -ˈfleɪ.tɪd, (US) -ˈfleɪ.t̬ɪd
deflation dɪˈfleɪ.ʃᵊn, ˌdiː- **-ary** -ᵊr.i, (US) -er.i
deflect dɪˈflekt, də-, (US) dɪ- **-s** -s **-ing** -ɪŋ **-ed** -ɪd **-or/s** -əʳ/z, (US) -ɚ/z
deflection, deflexion dɪˈflek.ʃᵊn, də-, (US) dɪ- **-s** -z
defloration ˌdiː.flɔːˈreɪ.ʃᵊn, ˌdef.lɔːˈ-, (US) ˌdef.ləˈ-, ˌdiː.fləˈ-, -flɔːˈ- **-s** -z
deflower dɪˈflaʊ.əʳ, ˌdiː-, (US) -ˈflaʊ.ɚ **-s** -z **-ing** -ɪŋ **-ed** -d
Defoe dɪˈfəʊ, də-, (US) -ˈfoʊ
defog ˌdiːˈfɒg, (US) -ˈfɑːg, -ˈfɔːg **-s** -z **-ging** -ɪŋ **-ged** -d **-ger/s** -əʳ/z, (US) -ɚ/z
defoliant ˌdiːˈfəʊ.li.ənt, dɪ-, (US) -ˈfoʊ- **-s** -s
defoli|ate ˌdiːˈfəʊ.li|.eɪt, dɪ-, (US) -ˈfoʊ- **-ates** -eɪts **-ating** -eɪ.tɪŋ, (US) -eɪ.t̬ɪŋ **-ated** -eɪ.tɪd, (US) -eɪ.t̬ɪd
defoliation ˌdiː.fəʊ.liˈeɪ.ʃᵊn; diːˌfəʊ-, dɪ-, (US) diːˌfoʊ-, dɪ-
deforest ˌdiːˈfɒr.ɪst, dɪ-, -əst, (US) -ˈfɔːr- **-s** -s **-ing** -ɪŋ **-ed** -ɪd
deforestation diːˌfɒr.ɪˈsteɪ.ʃᵊn, dɪ-; ˌdiː.fɔːr-, -əˈ-, (US) diːˌfɔːr-, dɪ-
deform dɪˈfɔːm, də-, ˌdiː-, (US) dɪˈfɔːrm, ˌdiː- **-s** -z **-ing** -ɪŋ **-ed** -d **-er/s** -əʳ/z, (US) -ɚ/z
deformation ˌdiː.fɔːˈmeɪ.ʃᵊn, ˌdef.əˈ-, (US) ˌdiː.fɔːrˈ-, ˌdef.ɚˈ- **-s** -z
deformit|y dɪˈfɔː.mə.t|i, də-, -mɪ-, (US) dɪˈfɔːr.mə.t̬|i **-ies** -iz
defraud dɪˈfrɔːd, ˌdiː-, də-, (US) dɪˈfrɑːd, ˌdiː-, -ˈfrɔːd **-s** -z **-ing** -ɪŋ **-ed** -ɪd **-er/s** -əʳ/z, (US) -ɚ/z
defray dɪˈfreɪ, də-, (US) dɪ- **-s** -z **-ing** -ɪŋ **-ed** -d **-er/s** -əʳ/z, (US) -ɚ/z **-ment** -mənt
defrayal dɪˈfreɪ.əl, də-, (US) dɪ- **-s** -z
De Freitas dəˈfreɪ.təs, (US) -t̬əs
defriend ˌdiːˈfrend **-s** -z **-ing** -ɪŋ **-ed** -ɪd
defrock ˌdiːˈfrɒk, (US) -ˈfrɑːk **-s** -s **-ing** -ɪŋ **-ed** -t
defrost ˌdiːˈfrɒst, dɪ-, (US) -ˈfrɑːst **-s** -s **-ing** -ɪŋ **-ed** -ɪd **-er/s** -əʳ/z, (US) -ɚ/z
deft deft **-er** -əʳ, (US) -ɚ **-est** -ɪst, -əst **-ly** -li **-ness** -nəs, -nɪs
defunct dɪˈfʌŋkt, də-; ˈdiː.fʌŋkt, (US) dɪˈfʌŋkt, ˌdiː- **-s** -s
defus|e ˌdiːˈfjuːz, dɪ-, də-, (US) ˌdiː-, dɪ- **-es** -ɪz **-ing** -ɪŋ **-ed** -d
def|y dɪˈf|aɪ, də-, (US) dɪ- **-ies** -aɪz **-ying** -aɪ.ɪŋ **-ied** -aɪd **-ier/s** -aɪ.əʳ/z, (US) -aɪ.ɚ/z
Deganwy dɪˈgæn.wi, də-
Degas dəˈgɑː, ˈdeɪ.gɑː
De Gaulle dəˈgəʊl, dɪ-, -ˈgɔːl, (US) -ˈgoʊl, -ˈgɔːl, -ˈgɑːl
degauss ˌdiːˈgaʊs, -ˈgɔːs, (US) -ˈgaʊs **-es** -ɪz **-ing** -ɪŋ **-ed** -t
degeneracy dɪˈdʒen.ᵊr.ə.si, də-, (US) dɪ-
degenerate adj dɪˈdʒen.ᵊr.ət, də-, -ɪt, (US) dɪ- **-ly** -li **-ness** -nəs, -nɪs
degener|ate v dɪˈdʒen.ᵊr|.eɪt, də-, (US) dɪˈdʒen.ə.r|eɪt **-ates** -eɪts **-ating** -eɪ.tɪŋ, (US) -eɪ.t̬ɪŋ **-ated** -eɪ.tɪd, (US) -eɪ.t̬ɪd
degeneration dɪˌdʒen.əˈreɪ.ʃᵊn, də-, (US) dɪ-
degenerative dɪˈdʒen.ᵊr.ə.tɪv, də-, -ə.reɪ-, (US) dɪˈdʒen.ɚ.ə.t̬ɪv, -ə.reɪ-
deglutin|ate ˌdiːˈgluː.tɪ.n|eɪt, dɪ-, (US) -tᵊn|.eɪt **-ates** -eɪts **-ating** -eɪ.tɪŋ, (US) -eɪ.t̬ɪŋ **-ated** -eɪ.tɪd, (US) -eɪ.t̬ɪd
deglutition ˌdiː.gluːˈtɪʃ.ᵊn
degradation ˌdeg.rəˈdeɪ.ʃᵊn **-s** -z
degrad|e dɪˈgreɪd, də-, (US) dɪ- **-es** -z **-ed** -ɪd **-able** -ə.bᵊl
degrading dɪˈgreɪ.dɪŋ, də-, (US) dɪ- **-ly** -li
degree dɪˈgriː, də-, (US) dɪ- **-s** -z
dehisc|e dɪˈhɪs, ˌdiː-, (US) ˌdiː-, dɪ- **-es** -ɪz **-ing** -ɪŋ **-ed** -t
dehiscen|ce dɪˈhɪs.ᵊn|ts, ˌdiː-, (US) ˌdiː-, dɪ- **-t** -t
Dehra Dun ˌdeə.rəˈduːn, ˌderᵊ-, (US) ˌder.əˈ-
dehumaniz|e, -is|e ˌdiːˈhjuː.mə.naɪz **-es** -ɪz **-ing** -ɪŋ **-ed** -d
dehumidifier ˌdiː.hjuːˈmɪd.ɪ.faɪ.əʳ, (US) -ə.faɪ.ɚ **-s** -z
dehy|drate ˌdiː.haɪ|ˈdreɪt, ˈ--- **-drates** -ˈdreɪts **-drating** -ˈdre.tɪŋ, (US) -ˈdreɪ.t̬ɪŋ **-drated** -ˈdreɪ.tɪd, (US) -ˈdreɪ.t̬ɪd
dehydration ˌdiː.haɪˈdreɪ.ʃᵊn
dehypnotiz|e, -is|e ˌdiːˈhɪp.nə.taɪz **-es** -ɪz **-ing** -ɪŋ **-ed** -d
de-ic|e ˌdiːˈaɪs **-es** -ɪz **-ing** -ɪŋ **-ed** -t **-er/s** -əʳ/z, (US) -ɚ/z

deicide ˈdeɪ.ɪ.saɪd, ˈdiː-, ˈ-ə-, (US) ˈdiː.ə- **-s** -z
dei|ctic ˈdaɪ|k.tɪk, ˈdeɪ|k- **-xis** -k.sɪs
deification ˌdeɪ.ɪ.fɪˈkeɪ.ʃən, ˌdiː-, ˌ-ə-, -fəˈ-, (US) ˌdiː.ə- **-s** -z
dei|fy ˈdeɪ.ɪ|.faɪ, ˈdiː-, ˈ-ə-, (US) ˈdiː.ɪ-, ˈdiː.ə- **-fies** -faɪz **-fying** -faɪ.ɪŋ **-fied** -faɪd
Deighton *surname:* ˈdeɪ.tən, ˈdaɪ- *place in North Yorkshire:* ˈdiː.tən
deign deɪn **-s** -z **-ing** -ɪŋ **-ed** -d
deindustrialization, -isa- ˌdiː.ɪnˌdʌs.tri.əl.aɪˈzeɪ.ʃən, -ɪˈ-, (US) -əˈ-
Deirdre ˈdɪə.dri, -dreɪ, (US) ˈdɪr.drə, -dri
de|ism ˈdeɪ|.ɪ.zəm, ˈdiː-, (US) ˈdiː- **-ist/s** -ɪst/s
deistic deɪˈɪs.tɪk, diː-, (US) diː- **-al** -əl
deit|y, D~ ˈdeɪ.ɪ.t|i, ˈdiː-, ˈ-ə-, (US) ˈdiː.ə.ţ|i **-ies** -iz
déjà vu ˌdeʒ.ɑːˈvuː, -ˈvjuː, (US) ˌdeɪ.ʒɑːˈvuː, -ˈvjuː
deject dɪˈdʒekt, də-, (US) dɪ- **-s** -s **-ing** -ɪŋ **-ed/ly** -ɪd/li **-edness** -ɪd.nəs, -nɪs
dejection dɪˈdʒek.ʃən, də-, (US) dɪ-
déjeuner ˈdeɪ.ʒə.neɪ, -ʒɜː-, (US) -ʒə- **-s** -z
de jure ˌdeɪˈdʒʊə.reɪ, di-, ˌdiː-, -ri, (US) diːˈdʒʊr.i, deɪ-
Dekker ˈdek.əʳ, (US) -ɚ
dekko ˈdek.əʊ, (US) -oʊ **-s** -z
de Klerk dəˈklɜːk, dəˈkleək, (US) -ˈklerk, -ˈklɝːk
de Kooning dəˈkəʊ.nɪŋ, -ˈkuː-, (US) -ˈkuː-
Del. (abbrev. for **Delaware**) ˈdel.ə.weəʳ, (US) -wer
de la Bère də.ləˈbɪəʳ, (US) də.ləˈbɪr
Delacroix ˈdel.ə.krwɑː, ˌ--ˈ-
Delafield ˈdel.ə.fiːld
Delagoa ˌdel.əˈgəʊ.ə, (US) -ˈgoʊ.ə
Delamain ˈdel.ə.meɪn
de la Mare də.lɑːˈmeəʳ, ˌdel.əˈ-, (US) də.ləˈmer, ˌdel.əˈ-
Delamere ˈdel.ə.mɪəʳ, (US) -mɪr
De Lancey dəˈlɑːnt.si, (US) -ˈlænt-
Delane dəˈleɪn, dɪ-
Delaney dəˈleɪ.ni, dɪ-
Delany dəˈleɪ.ni, dɪ-
De la Pole ˌdel.əˈpəʊl, də.lɑːˈ-, (US) də.ləˈpoʊl
de la Roche ˌdel.əˈrɒʃ, -ˈrəʊʃ; də.ləˈ-, (US) də.lɑːˈroʊʃ, -lə-, -ˈrɑːʃ
De la Rue ˌdel.əˈruː; də.lɑːˈ-; ˈdel.ə.ruː
de la Torre ˌdel.əˈtɔːʳ, də.lɑːˈ-, (US) -ˈtɔːr
Delaunay dəˈlɔː.neɪ, (US) -lɔːˈneɪ
Delaware ˈdel.ə.weəʳ, (US) -wer
De la Warr ˌdel.əˈweəʳ, də.lɑːˈ-, (US) -ˈwer
delay dɪˈleɪ, də-, (US) dɪ- **-s** -z **-ing** -ɪŋ **-ed** -d **-er/s** -əʳ/z, (US) -ɚ/z
delayering ˌdiːˈleɪ.ə.rɪŋ, dɪ-, -ˈleə-, (US) -ˈleɪ.ɚ-
Delbert ˈdel.bət, (US) -bɚt
del credere ˌdelˈkred.ər.eɪ, -ˈkreɪ.dər-, -i, (US) -ˈkreɪ.dɚ-
dele ˈdiː.liː, -li
delectab|le dɪˈlek.tə.b|əl, də-, (US) dɪ- **-ly** -li **-leness** -əl.nəs, -nɪs
delectation ˌdiː.lekˈteɪ.ʃən
delegac|y ˈdel.ɪ.gə.s|i, ˈ-ə- **-ies** -iz
delegate n ˈdel.ɪ.gət, ˈ-ə-, -geɪt, -gɪt, (US) -gət, -gɪt, -geɪt **-s** -s
dele|gate v ˈdel.ɪ|.geɪt, ˈ-ə- **-gates** -geɪts **-gating** -geɪ.tɪŋ, (US) -geɪ.ţɪŋ **-gated** -geɪ.tɪd, (US) -geɪ.ţɪd
delegation ˌdel.ɪˈgeɪ.ʃən, -əˈ- **-s** -z
delend|um dɪˈlen.d|əm, diː- **-a** -ə
de|lete dɪ|ˈliːt, də-, (US) dɪ- **-letes** -ˈliːts **-leting** -ˈliː.tɪŋ, (US) -ˈliː.ţɪŋ **-leted** -ˈliː.tɪd, (US) -ˈliː.ţɪd
deleterious ˌdel.ɪˈtɪə.ri.əs, ˌdɪl-, ˌdiː.lɪˈ-, -ləˈtɪə-, (US) ˌdel.əˈtɪr.i- **-ly** -li **-ness** -nəs, -nɪs
deletion dɪˈliː.ʃən, də-, (US) dɪ- **-s** -z
delf delf
Delft delft **-ware** -weəʳ, (US) -wer
Delham ˈdel.əm
Delhi ˈdel.i
deli ˈdel.i **-s** -z
Deli|a ˈdiː.li|.ə, (US) ˈdiː.l.j|ə, -li|.ə, -li- **-an/s** -ən/z
deliberate adj dɪˈlɪb.ər.ət, də-, -ɪt, (US) dɪ- **-ly** -li **-ness** -nəs, -nɪs
deliber|ate v dɪˈlɪb.ər|.eɪt, də-, (US) dɪˈlɪb.ə.r|eɪt **-ates** -eɪts **-ating** -eɪ.tɪŋ, (US) -eɪ.ţɪŋ **-ated** -eɪ.tɪd, (US) -eɪ.ţɪd **-ator/s** -eɪ.təʳ/z, (US) -eɪ.ţɚ/z
deliberation dɪˌlɪb.əˈreɪ.ʃən, də-, (US) dɪ- **-s** -z
deliberative dɪˈlɪb.ər.ə.tɪv, də-, (US) dɪˈlɪb.ɚ.ə.ţɪv, -rə.ţɪv **-ly** -li
Delibes dəˈliːb, dɪ-
delicac|y ˈdel.ɪ.kə.s|i, ˈ-ə- **-ies** -iz
delicate ˈdel.ɪ.kət, ˈ-ə-, -kɪt **-ly** -li **-ness** -nəs, -nɪs
delicatessen ˌdel.ɪ.kəˈtes.ən, ˌ-ə- **-s** -z
delicious dɪˈlɪʃ.əs, də-, (US) dɪ- **-ly** -li **-ness** -nəs, -nɪs
delict dɪˈlɪkt; ˈdiː.lɪkt, (US) dɪˈlɪkt **-s** -s
de|light dɪ|ˈlaɪt, də-, (US) dɪ- **-lights** -ˈlaɪts **-lighting** -ˈlaɪ.tɪŋ, (US) -ˈlaɪ.ţɪŋ **-lighted/ly** -ˈlaɪ.tɪd/li, (US) -ˈlaɪ.ţɪd/li
delightful dɪˈlaɪt.fəl, də-, -fʊl, (US) dɪ- **-ly** -i **-ness** -nəs, -nɪs
delightsome dɪˈlaɪt.səm, də-, (US) dɪ-
Delilah dɪˈlaɪ.lə, də-, (US) dɪ-
delim|it dɪˈlɪm|.ɪt, ˌdiː-, də-, (US) dɪ- **-its** -ɪts **-iting** -ɪ.tɪŋ, (US) -ɪ.ţɪŋ **-ited** -ɪ.tɪd, (US) -ɪ.ţɪd
delimitation dɪˌlɪm.ɪˈteɪ.ʃən, ˌdiː-, də-, (US) dɪ- **-s** -z
deline|ate dɪˈlɪn.i|.eɪt, də-, (US) dɪ- **-ates** -eɪts **-ating** -eɪ.tɪŋ, (US) -eɪ.ţɪŋ **-ated** -eɪ.tɪd, (US) -eɪ.ţɪd **-ator/s** -eɪ.təʳ/z, (US) -eɪ.ţɚ/z
delineation dɪˌlɪn.iˈeɪ.ʃən, də-, (US) dɪ- **-s** -z
delinquenc|y dɪˈlɪŋ.kwənt.s|i, də-, (US) dɪ- **-ies** -iz
delinquent dɪˈlɪŋ.kwənt, də-, (US) dɪ- **-s** -s
deliquesc|e ˌdel.ɪˈkwes, -əˈ- **-es** -ɪz **-ing** -ɪŋ **-ed** -t
deliquescen|ce ˌdel.ɪˈkwes.ən|ts **-t** -t
delirious dɪˈlɪr.i.əs, də-, -ˈlɪə.ri-, (US) dɪˈlɪr.i- **-ly** -li **-ness** -nəs, -nɪs
delirium dɪˈlɪr.i.əm, də-, -ˈlɪə.ri-, (US) dɪˈlɪr.i-
delirium tremens dɪˌlɪr.i.əmˈtriː.menz, -ˈtrem.enz, -ənz
Delisle *French name:* dəˈliːl
De l'Isle *English name:* dəˈlaɪl
Delius ˈdiː.li.əs
deliv|er dɪˈlɪv|.əʳ, də-, (US) dɪˈlɪv|.ɚ **-ers** -əz, (US) -ɚz **-ering** -ər.ɪŋ **-ered** -əd, (US) -ɚd **-erer/s** -ər.əʳ/z, (US) -ɚ.ɚ/z
deliverable dɪˈlɪv.ər.ə.bəl, də-, (US) dɪ- **-s** -z
deliveranc|e dɪˈlɪv.ər.ənts, də-, (US) dɪ- **-es** -ɪz
deliver|y dɪˈlɪv.ər|.i, də-, (US) dɪ- **-ies** -iz
delivery|man dɪˈlɪv.ər.ɪ|.mən, də-, -mæn, (US) dəˈlɪv.ri.mæn **-men** -mən, -men
dell, D~ del **-s** -z
Della ˈdel.ə
Dellar ˈdel.əʳ, (US) -ɚ
della Robbia ˌdel.əˈrɒb.i.ə, (US) ˌdel.əˈroʊ.biə, -ɑːˈ-, -ˈrɑː-, -bjə
Delma ˈdel.mə
Delmar delˈmɑːʳ, ˈ--, (US) ˈdel.mɑːr, -ˈ-
Delmarva delˈmɑː.və, (US) -ˈmɑːr- **Delˈmarva Peˌninsula**
Del Monte® delˈmɒn.teɪ, -ti, (US) -ˈmɑːn.ţi
Deloitte dəˈlɔɪt, dɪ-
Delores dəˈlɔː.rɪz, dɪ-, (US) dɪˈlɔːr.ɪs, də-
Deloria dəˈlɔː.ri.ə, (US) -ˈlɔːr.i-
Delors dəˈlɔːʳ, (US) -ˈlɔːr
Delos ˈdiː.lɒs, (US) -lɑːs, ˈdel.oʊs
delous|e ˌdiːˈlaʊs, (US) -ˈlaʊs, -ˈlaʊz **-es** -ɪz **-ing** -ɪŋ **-ed** -t, (US) -t, -d
Delph delf
Delphi *in Greece:* ˈdel.faɪ, -fi *city in US:* ˈdel.faɪ
Delph|ian ˈdel.f|i.ən **-ic** -ɪk ˌ**Delphic ˈoracle**
Delphine delˈfiːn
delphinium delˈfɪn.i.əm **-s** -z
Delroy ˈdel.rɔɪ
delta ˈdel.tə **-s** -z
deltoid ˈdel.tɔɪd
delud|e dɪˈluːd, də-, -ˈljuːd, (US) dɪˈluːd **-es** -z **-ing** -ɪŋ **-ed** -ɪd **-er/s** -əʳ/z, (US) -ɚ/z
delug|e ˈdel.juːdʒ **-es** -ɪz **-ing** -ɪŋ **-ed** -d
delusion dɪˈluː.ʒən, də-, -ˈljuː-, (US) dɪˈluː- **-s** -z
delusive dɪˈluː.sɪv, də-, -ˈljuː-, (US) dɪˈluː- **-ly** -li **-ness** -nəs, -nɪs
delusory dɪˈluː.sər.i, də-, -ˈljuː-, -zər-, (US) dɪˈluː-
de luxe, deluxe dɪˈlʌks, də-, -ˈluːks, -ˈlʊks, (US) dɪˈlʌks, də-, -ˈlʊks
delv|e delv **-es** -z **-ing** -ɪŋ **-ed** -d **-er/s** -əʳ/z, (US) -ɚ/z
Delyn ˈdel.ɪn

Dem (abbrev. for **Democrat**) ˈdem.ə.kræt (abbrev. for **Democratic**) ˌdem.əˈkræt.ɪk
demagnetization, -isa- ˌdiːˌmæg.nə.taɪˈzeɪ.ʃən, ˌdiː.mæg-, -nɪ-, -ɪˈ-, (US) diːˌmæg.nə.t̬əˈ- -s -z
demagnetiz|e, -is|e ˌdiːˈmæg.nə.taɪz, -nɪ- -es -ɪz -ing -ɪŋ -ed -d
demagog ˈdem.ə.gɒg, (US) -gɑːg, -gɔːg -s -z
demagogic ˌdem.əˈgɒg.ɪk, -ˈgɒdʒ-, (US) -ˈgɑː.dʒɪk, -gɪk; (US) -goʊ.dʒɪk -al -əl -ally -əl.i, -li
demagogue ˈdem.ə.gɒg, (US) -gɑːg, -gɔːg -s -z
demagoguery ˈdem.ə.gɒg.ər.i, (US) -gɑː.gɚ-
demagogy ˈdem.ə.gɒg.i, -gɒdʒ-, (US) -gɑː.dʒi, -gi; (US) -goʊ.dʒi
demand dɪˈmɑːnd, də-, (US) dɪˈmænd -s -z -ing -ɪŋ -ed -ɪd
demanding dɪˈmɑːn.dɪŋ, də-, (US) dɪˈmæn- -ly -li
demar|cate ˈdiː.mɑː|.keɪt, (US) diːˈmɑːr|.keɪt, ˈdiː.mɑːr- -cates -keɪts -cating -keɪ.tɪŋ, (US) -keɪ.t̬ɪŋ -cated -keɪ.tɪd, (US) -keɪ.t̬ɪd
demarcation ˌdiː.mɑːˈkeɪ.ʃən, (US) -mɑːrˈ-
demarcative ˌdiːˈmɑː.kə.tɪv, (US) -ˈmɑːr.kə.t̬ɪv
démarch|e ˈdeɪ.mɑːʃ, -ˈ-, (US) deɪˈmɑːrʃ, dɪ- -es -ɪz
demark dɪˈmɑːk, ˌdiː-, (US) -ˈmɑːrk -s -s -ing -ɪŋ -ed -t
demarkation ˌdiː.mɑːˈkeɪ.ʃən, (US) -mɑːrˈ-
Demas ˈdiː.mæs
dematerializ|e, -is|e ˌdiː.məˈtɪə.ri.ə.laɪz, (US) -ˈtɪr.i- -es -ɪz -ing -ɪŋ -ed -d
demean dɪˈmiːn, də-, (US) dɪ- -s -z -ing -ɪŋ -ed -d
demeano(u)r dɪˈmiː.nər, də-, (US) dɪˈmiː.nɚ -s -z
Demelza dɪˈmel.zə, də-, demˈel-
de Menezes dʒiː.menˈez.iːs
de|ment dɪ|ˈment, də-, (US) dɪ- -ments -ˈments -menting -ˈmen.tɪŋ, (US) -ˈmen.t̬ɪŋ -mented/ly -ˈmen.tɪd/li, (US) -ˈmen.t̬ɪd/li
dementia dɪˈmen.tʃə, də-, -tʃi.ə, (US) dɪˈment.ʃə
dementia praecox dɪˌmen.tʃəˈpriː.kɒks, -ˈpraɪ-, (US) -ment.ʃəˈpriː.kɑːks
demerara *sugar:* ˌdem.əˈreə.rə, -ˈrɑː-, (US) -ˈrɑːr.ə
Demerara *district in Guyana:* ˌdem.əˈrɑː.rə, (US) -ˈrɑːr.ə
demerg|e ˌdiːˈmɜːdʒ, (US) -ˈmɝːdʒ, də- -es -ɪz -ing -ɪŋ -ed -d
demerger ˌdiːˈmɜː.dʒər, (US) -ˈmɝː.dʒɚ -s -z
demerit ˌdiːˈmer.ɪt, ˈdiː.mer-, (US) dɪˈmer-, diː- -s -s
Demerol® ˈdem.ə.rɒl, (US) -rɑːl
demesne dɪˈmeɪn, də-, -ˈmiːn, (US) dɪ- -s -z
Demeter dɪˈmiː.tər, də-, (US) -t̬ɚ
Demetrius dɪˈmiː.tri.əs, də-
demi- ˈdem.i
Note: Prefix. Normally carries primary or secondary stress on the first syllable, e.g. **demigod** /ˈdem.i.gɒd/ (US) /-gɑːd/, **demisemiquaver** /ˌdem.iˈsem.iˌkweɪ.vər/ (US) /-vɚ/.
demigod ˈdem.i.gɒd, (US) -gɑːd -s -z
demigoddess ˈdem.iˌgɒd.es, (US) -ˌgɑː.des -es -ɪz
demijohn ˈdem.i.dʒɒn, (US) -dʒɑːn -s -z
demilitarization, -isa- diːˌmɪl.ɪ.tər.aɪˈzeɪ.ʃən, ˌdiː.mɪ.lɪ-, -lə-, -ɪˈ-, (US) diːˌmɪl.ɪ.t̬ɚ.əˈ-
demilitariz|e, -is|e ˌdiːˈmɪl.ɪ.tər.aɪz, ˈ-ə-, (US) -t̬ə.raɪz -es -ɪz -ing -ɪŋ -ed -d
de Mille dəˈmɪl, dɪ-
demimondaine ˌdem.i.mɒnˈdeɪn, (US) -mɑːnˈ- -s -z
demimonde ˌdem.iˈmɔ̃ːnd, -ˈmɔːnd, -ˈmɒnd, ˈ---, (US) ˈdem.i.mɑːnd
de minimis ˌdeɪˈmɪn.ɪ.miːs, ˈ-ə-
demis|e dɪˈmaɪz, də-, (US) dɪ- -es -ɪz -ing -ɪŋ -ed -d
demisemiquaver ˈdem.i.sem.iˌkweɪ.vər, ˌdem.iˈsem.i-, (US) ˌdem.iˈsem.iˌkweɪ.vɚ -s -z
demission dɪˈmɪʃ.ən -s -z
demist ˌdiːˈmɪst -s -s -ing -ɪŋ -ed -ɪd -er/s -ər/z, (US) -ɚ/z
demitass|e ˈdem.i.tæs, -tɑːs -es -ɪz
demiurg|e ˈdem.i.ɜːdʒ, ˈdiː.mi-, (US) -ɝːdʒ -es -ɪz
demo ˈdem.əʊ, (US) -oʊ -s -z
demob ˌdiːˈmɒb, (US) -ˈmɑːb -s -z -bing -ɪŋ -bed -d
demobilization, -isa- diːˌməʊ.bəl.aɪˈzeɪ.ʃən, dɪ-, -bɪ.laɪˈ-, -lɪˈ-, (US) -ˌmoʊ.bəl.əˈ-, -bɪ.ləˈ- -s -z
demobiliz|e, -is|e ˌdiːˈməʊ.bəl.aɪz, dɪ-, -bɪ.laɪz, (US) -ˈmoʊ.bə.laɪz, -bɪ- -es -ɪz -ing -ɪŋ -ed -d
democrac|y dɪˈmɒk.rə.s|i, də-, (US) dɪˈmɑːk- -ies -iz
democrat, D~ ˈdem.ə.kræt -s -s
democratic, D~ ˌdem.əˈkræt.ɪk, (US) -ˈkræt̬- -al -əl -ally -əl.i, -li
democratization, -isa- dɪˌmɒk.rə.taɪˈzeɪ.ʃən, də-, -tɪˈ-, (US) dɪˌmɑː.krə.t̬əˈ-
democratiz|e, -is|e dɪˈmɒk.rə.taɪz, də-, (US) dɪˈmɑː.krə- -es -ɪz -ing -ɪŋ -ed -d
Democritus dɪˈmɒk.rɪ.təs, də-, -rə-, (US) dɪˈmɑː.k.krə.t̬əs
démodé ˌdeɪˈməʊ.deɪ, (US) -moʊˈdeɪ
demodu|late ˌdiːˈmɒd.jə|.leɪt, dɪ-, -jʊ-; -ˈmɒdʒ.ə-, ˈ-ʊ-, (US) -ˈmɑː.dʒə-, -dʒʊ- -lates -leɪts -lating -leɪ.tɪŋ, (US) -leɪ.t̬ɪŋ -lated -leɪ.tɪd, (US) -leɪ.t̬ɪd
demodulation ˌdiːˌmɒd.jəˈleɪ.ʃən, dɪ-, -jʊˈ-; -mɒdʒ.əˈ-, -ʊˈ-, (US) -ˌmɑː.dʒəˈ-, -dʒʊ-
demodulator ˌdiːˈmɒd.jə.leɪ.tər, dɪ-, -jʊ-; -ˈmɒdʒ.ə-, ˈ-ʊ-, (US) -ˈmɑː.dʒə.leɪ.t̬ɚ, -dʒʊ- -s -z
demographer dɪˈmɒg.rə.fər, də-, ˌdiː-, (US) dɪˈmɑː.grə.fɚ, ˌdiː- -s -z
demographic ˌdem.əʊˈgræf.ɪk, ˌdiː.məʊˈ-, (US) ˌdem.əˈ-, ˌdiː.məˈ- -s -s
demography dɪˈmɒg.rə.fi, də-, ˌdiː-, (US) dɪˈmɑː.grə-, ˌdiː-
demoiselle ˌdem.wɑːˈzel, -wəˈ- -s -z
De Moivre dəˈmɔɪ.vər, dɪ-, (US) -vɚ
demolish dɪˈmɒl.ɪʃ, də-, (US) dɪˈmɑː.lɪʃ -es -ɪz -ing -ɪŋ -ed -t -er/s -ər/z, (US) -ɚ/z
demolition ˌdem.əˈlɪʃ.ən, ˌdiː.məˈ- -s -z
demon ˈdiː.mən -s -z
demonetization, -isa- ˌdiːˌmʌn.ɪ.taɪˈzeɪ.ʃən, -ˌmɒn-, -ə-, -tɪˈ-, (US) -ˌmɑː.nə.t̬əˈ-
demonetiz|e, -is|e ˌdiːˈmʌn.ɪ.taɪz, -ˈmɒn-, ˈ-ə-, (US) -ˈmɑː.nə- -es -ɪz -ing -ɪŋ -ed -d
demoniac dɪˈməʊ.ni.æk, də-, diː-, (US) dɪˈmoʊ-, diː- -s -s
demoniac|al ˌdiː.məʊˈnaɪ.ə.k|əl, (US) -məˈ- -ally -əl.i, -li
demonic dɪˈmɒn.ɪk, də-, diː-, (US) dɪˈmɑː.nɪk, diː- -al -əl -ally -əl.i, -li
demon|ism ˈdiː.mə.n|ɪ.zəm -ist/s -ɪst/s
demoniz|e, -is|e ˈdiː.mən.aɪz -es -ɪz -ing -ɪŋ -ed -d
demonology ˌdiː.məˈnɒl.ə.dʒi, (US) -ˈnɑː.lə-
demonstrability dɪˌmɒnt.strəˈbɪl.ə.ti, də-, -ɪ.ti; ˌdem.ən-, (US) dɪˌmɑːnt.strəˈbɪl.ə.t̬i; (US) ˌdem.ən-
demonstrab|le dɪˈmɒnt.strə.b|əl, də-; ˈdem.ən-, (US) dɪˈmɑːnt-, də-; (US) ˈdem.ən- -ly -li
demon|strate ˈdem.ən|.streɪt -strates -streɪts -strating -streɪ.tɪŋ, (US) -streɪ.t̬ɪŋ -strated -streɪ.tɪd, (US) -streɪ.t̬ɪd
demonstration ˌdem.ənˈstreɪ.ʃən -s -z
demonstrative dɪˈmɒnt.strə.tɪv, də-, (US) dɪˈmɑːnt.strə.t̬ɪv -s -z -ly -li -ness -nəs, -nɪs
demonstrator ˈdem.ən.streɪ.tər, (US) -t̬ɚ -s -z
de Montfort dəˈmɒnt.fət, -fɔːt, (US) -ˈmɑːnt.fɚt, -fɔːrt
demoralization, -isa- dɪˌmɒr.əl.aɪˈzeɪ.ʃən, ˌdiː.mɒr-, -ɪˈ-, (US) dɪˌmɔːr.əl.əˈ-
demoraliz|e, -is|e dɪˈmɒr.ə.laɪz, ˌdiː-, (US) -ˈmɔːr- -es -ɪz -ing -ɪŋ -ed -d
De Morgan dəˈmɔː.gən, (US) -ˈmɔːr-
Demos ˈdiː.mɒs, (US) -mɑːs
Demosthenes dɪˈmɒs.θə.niːz, də-, -θɪ-, (US) -ˈmɑːs-
de|mote dɪ|ˈməʊt, ˌdiː-, (US) -ˈmoʊt -motes -ˈməʊts, (US) -ˈmoʊts -moting -ˈməʊ.tɪŋ, (US) -ˈmoʊ.t̬ɪŋ -moted -ˈməʊ.tɪd, (US) -ˈmoʊ.t̬ɪd

demotic dɪˈmɒt.ɪk, də-, diː-, (US) dɪˈmɑː.t̬ɪk, diː-

demotion dɪˈməʊ.ʃᵊn, ˌdiː-, (US) -ˈmoʊ-

demoti|vate ˌdiːˈməʊ.tɪ|.veɪt, -tə-, (US) -ˈmoʊ.t̬ə- -vates -veɪts -vating -veɪ.tɪŋ, (US) -veɪ.t̬ɪŋ -vated -veɪ.tɪd, (US) -veɪ.t̬ɪd

Dempsey ˈdemp.si

Dempster ˈdemp.stəʳ, (US) -stɚ

demulcent dɪˈmʌl.sᵊnt, də-, ˌdiː-, (US) dɪ-, ˌdiː- -s -s

demur dɪˈmɜːʳ, də-, (US) dɪˈmɝː -s -z -ring -ɪŋ -red -d

demur|e dɪˈmjʊəʳ, də-, -mjɔːʳ, (US) dɪˈmjʊr -er -əʳ, (US) -ɚ -est -ɪst, -əst -ely -li -eness -nəs, -nɪs

demurrage dɪˈmʌr.ɪdʒ, də-, (US) dɪˈmɝː-

demurrer *person who demurs:* dɪˈmɜː.rəʳ, də-, (US) -ˈmɝː.ɚ *objection on grounds of irrelevance:* dɪˈmʌr.əʳ, də-, (US) dɪˈmɝː.ɚ -s -z

demutualization, -isa- ˌdiː.mjuː.tʃu.ə.laɪˈzeɪ.ʃᵊn, dɪˌmjuː-, -tju-, -ɪˈ-, (US) -tʃu.ə.ləˈ-, -tju-, -tʃə.laɪ-

demutualiz|e, -is|e ˌdiːˈmjuː.tʃu.ə.laɪz, dɪˈmjuː-, -tju-, (US) -tʃu-, -tʃə.laɪz -es -ɪz -ing -ɪŋ -ed -d

dem|y dɪˈm|aɪ, də-, (US) dɪ- -ies -aɪz

demystification ˌdiː.mɪ.stɪ.fɪˈkeɪ.ʃᵊn, -stə-, -fəˈ-; diːˌmɪs.tɪ-, -tə-, -fəˈ-, (US) diːˌmɪs-

demysti|fy ˌdiːˈmɪs.tɪ|.faɪ, -tə- -fies -faɪz -fying -faɪ.ɪŋ -fied -faɪd

demythologiz|e, -is|e ˌdiː.mɪˈθɒl.ə.dʒaɪz, -maɪˈ-, -məˈ-, (US) -mɪˈθɑː.lə- -es -ɪz -ing -ɪŋ -ed -d

den den -s -z

Denali dəˈnɑː.li

denari|us dɪˈneə.ri|.əs, də-, denˈeə-, -ˈɑː-, (US) dɪˈner.i-, -ˈnær- -i -aɪ, -iː

denary ˈdiː.nᵊr.i, ˈden.ᵊr-

denationalization, -isa- diːˌnæʃ.ᵊn.ᵊl.aɪˈzeɪ.ʃᵊn, ˌdiː.næʃ-, -nᵊl.aɪ-, -ɪˈ-, (US) diːˌnæʃ.ᵊn.ᵊl.əˈ-, -nᵊl.ə-

denationaliz|e, -is|e ˌdiːˈnæʃ.ᵊn.ᵊl.aɪz, ˈ-nᵊl- -es -ɪz -ing -ɪŋ -ed -d

denaturalization, -isa- diːˌnætʃ.ᵊr.ᵊl.aɪˈzeɪ.ʃᵊn, ˌdiː.nætʃ-, -ɪˈ-, (US) diːˌnætʃ.ɚ.ᵊl.əˈ-

denaturaliz|e, -is|e ˌdiːˈnætʃ.ᵊr.ᵊl.aɪz -es -ɪz -ing -ɪŋ -ed -d

denatur|e ˌdiːˈneɪ.tʃəʳ, (US) -tʃɚ -es -z -ing -ɪŋ -ed -d

Denbigh ˈden.bi, ˈdem-, (US) ˈden- -shire -ʃəʳ, -ʃɪəʳ, (US) -ʃɚ, -ʃɪr

Denby ˈden.bi, ˈdem-, (US) ˈden-

Dench dentʃ

dendrite ˈden.draɪt -s -s

dendritic denˈdrɪt.ɪk, (US) -ˈdrɪt̬- -al -ᵊl

dendroid ˈden.drɔɪd

dendrology denˈdrɒl.ə.dʒi, (US) -ˈdrɑː.lə-

dendron ˈden.drən, (US) -drən, -drɑːn -s -z

dene, D~ diːn -s -z

Deneb ˈden.eb

Denebola dɪˈneb.ə.lə, denˈeb-, dəˈneb-

Deneuve dəˈnɜːv

dengue ˈdeŋ.gi, -geɪ

Deng Xiaoping ˌdeŋ.ʃaʊˈpɪŋ, (US) ˌdʌŋ-, ˌdeŋ-

Denham ˈden.əm

Denholm *place in West Yorkshire:* ˈden.hɒlm, (US) -hoʊlm

Denholm(e) *name:* ˈden.əm

Denia ˈdiː.ni.ə -s -z

deniable dɪˈnaɪ.ə.bᵊl, də-, (US) dɪ-

denial dɪˈnaɪ.əl, də-, (US) dɪ- -s -z

denier *person who denies:* dɪˈnaɪ.əʳ, də-, (US) dɪˈnaɪ.ɚ *coin:* ˈden.i.əʳ, -eɪ; dəˈnɪəʳ, (US) dəˈnɪr *thickness of yarn:* ˈden.i.əʳ, -eɪ, (US) ˈden.jɚ -s -z

deni|grate ˈden.ɪ|.greɪt, ˈ-ə- -grates -greɪts -grating -greɪ.tɪŋ, (US) -greɪ.t̬ɪŋ -grated -greɪ.tɪd, (US) -greɪ.t̬ɪd

denigration ˌden.ɪˈgreɪ.ʃᵊn, -əˈ-

denim ˈden.ɪm, -əm -s -z

De Niro dəˈnɪə.rəʊ, (US) -ˈnɪr.oʊ

Denis ˈden.ɪs

Denise dəˈniːz, denˈiːz, dɪˈniːz, -ˈniːs, (US) dəˈniːs, denˈiːs, dɪˈniːs, -ˈniːz

Denison ˈden.ɪ.sᵊn

denizen ˈden.ɪ.zᵊn, ˈ-ə- -s -z

Denktash ˈdeŋk.tæʃ, (US) -tɑːʃ

Denman ˈden.mən, ˈdem-, (US) ˈden-

Denmark ˈden.mɑːk, ˈdem-, (US) ˈden.mɑːrk

Denning ˈden.ɪŋ

Dennis ˈden.ɪs

Dennison ˈden.ɪ.sᵊn

Denny ˈden.i -s -z

denomi|nate dɪˈnɒm.ɪ|.neɪt, dəˈ-, ˈ-ə-, (US) dɪˈnɑː.mə- -nates -neɪts -nating -neɪ.tɪŋ, (US) -neɪ.t̬ɪŋ -nated -neɪ.tɪd, (US) -neɪ.t̬ɪd

denomination dɪˌnɒm.ɪˈneɪ.ʃᵊn, də-, -əˈ-, (US) dɪˌnɑː.məˈ- -s -z

denominational dɪˌnɒm.ɪˈneɪ.ʃᵊn.ᵊl, də-, -əˈ-, (US) dɪˌnɑː.məˈ-

denominationalism dɪˌnɒm.ɪˈneɪ.ʃᵊn.ᵊl.ɪ.zᵊm, də-, -əˈ-, (US) dɪˌnɑː.məˈ-

denominative dɪˈnɒm.ɪ.nə.tɪv, də-, ˈ-ə-, (US) dɪˈnɑː.mə.nə.t̬ɪv

denominator dɪˈnɒm.ɪ.neɪ.təʳ, də-, ˈ-ə-, (US) dɪˈnɑː.mə.neɪ.t̬ɚ -s -z

denotation ˌdiː.nəʊˈteɪ.ʃᵊn, (US) -noʊˈ-, -nəˈ- -s -z

denotative dɪˈnəʊ.tə.tɪv, də-; ˈdiː.nəʊ.teɪ-, (US) ˈdiː.noʊ.teɪ.t̬ɪv; (US) dɪˈnoʊ.t̬ə-

de|note dɪ|ˈnəʊt, də-, (US) dɪ|ˈnoʊt -notes -ˈnəʊts, (US) -ˈnoʊts -noting -ˈnəʊ.tɪŋ, (US) -ˈnoʊ.t̬ɪŋ -noted -ˈnəʊ.tɪd, (US) -ˈnoʊ.t̬ɪd

dénouement deɪˈnuː.mɑ̃ːŋ, dɪ-, də-, (US) ˌdeɪ.nuːˈmɑ̃ːŋ

dénouements deɪˈnuː.mɑ̃ːŋ, dɪ-, də-, -mɑ̃ːŋz, (US) ˌdeɪ.nuːˈmɑ̃ːŋ, -ˈmɑ̃ːŋz

denounc|e dɪˈnaʊnts, də-, (US) dɪ- -es -ɪz -ing -ɪŋ -ed -t -er/s -əʳ/z, (US) -ɚ/z -ement/s -mənt/s

de novo deɪˈnəʊ.vəʊ, diː-, də-, (US) -ˈnoʊ.voʊ

dens|e dents -er -əʳ, (US) -ɚ -est -ɪst, -əst -ely -li -eness -nəs, -nɪs

densit|y ˈdent.sɪ.t|i, -sə-, (US) -sə.t̬|i -ies -iz

dent, D~ dent -s -s -ing -ɪŋ -ed -ɪd

dental ˈden.tᵊl -s -z ˈ**dental** ˌ**floss**; ˈ**dental** ˌ**surgeon**

dentaliz|e, -is|e ˈden.tᵊl.aɪz, (US) -t̬ə.laɪz -es -ɪz -ing -ɪŋ -ed -d

dentate ˈden.teɪt

dentated denˈteɪ.tɪd, ˈden.teɪ-, (US) -t̬ɪd

denticle ˈden.tɪ.kᵊl, (US) -t̬ɪ- -s -z

dentifric|e ˈden.tɪ.friːs, -tə-, -frɪs, (US) -t̬ə.frɪs -es -ɪz

dentil ˈden.tɪl, -tᵊl, (US) -tᵊl -s -z

dentilingual ˌden.tiˈlɪŋ.gwəl, (US) -t̬iˈ- -s -z

dentine ˈden.tiːn

dentist ˈden.tɪst, (US) -t̬ɪst -s -s

dentistry ˈden.tɪ.stri, -tə-, (US) -t̬ɪ-

dentition denˈtɪʃ.ᵊn

Denton ˈden.tən, (US) -tᵊn

denture ˈden.tʃəʳ, (US) ˈdent.ʃɚ -s -z

denudation ˌdiː.njuːˈdeɪ.ʃᵊn, ˌden.juːˈ-, (US) ˌdiː.nuːˈ-, -njuːˈ-; (US) ˌden.juːˈ- -s -z

denud|e dɪˈnjuːd, də-, ˌdiː-, (US) dɪˈnuːd, ˌdiː-, -ˈnjuːd -es -z -ing -ɪŋ -ed -ɪd

denunci|ate dɪˈnʌnt.si|.eɪt, də-, -ʃi-, (US) dɪˈnʌnt.si- -ates -eɪts -ating -eɪ.tɪŋ, (US) -eɪ.t̬ɪŋ -ated -eɪ.tɪd, (US) -eɪ.t̬ɪd -ator/s -eɪ.təʳ/z, (US) -eɪ.t̬ɚ/z

denunciation dɪˌnʌnt.siˈeɪ.ʃᵊn, də-, -ʃiˈ-, (US) dɪˌnʌnt.siˈ- -s -z

denunciatory dɪˈnʌnt.si.ə.tᵊr.i, də-, -ʃi-, -tri, (US) dɪˈnʌnt.si.ə.tɔːr.i

Denver ˈden.vəʳ, (US) -vɚ

den|y dɪˈn|aɪ, də-, (US) dɪ- -ies -aɪz -ying -aɪ.ɪŋ -ied -aɪd -ier/s -aɪ.əʳ/z, (US) -aɪ.ɚ/z

Denys ˈden.ɪs

Denzel ˈden.zᵊl, -zel, -zɪl, ˌdenˈzel

Denzil ˈden.zɪl, -zᵊl, (US) -zᵊl

deodand ˈdiː.əʊ.dænd, (US) ˈ-ə- -s -z

deodar ˈdiː.əʊ.dɑːʳ, (US) -ə.dɑːr -s -z

deodorant diˈəʊ.dᵊr.ᵊnt, (US) -ˈoʊ- -s -s

deodorization, -isa- diˌəʊ.dᵊr.aɪˈzeɪ.ʃᵊn, -ɪˈ-, (US) -oʊ.dɚ.əˈ- -s -z

deodoriz|e, -is|e diˈəʊ.dᵊr.aɪz, (US) -ˈoʊ.də.raɪz -es -ɪz -ing -ɪŋ -ed -d -er/s -əʳ/z, (US) -ɚ/z

deontic diˈɒn.tɪk, diː-, deɪ-, (US) -ˈɑːn.t̬ɪk

deoxidization, -isa- diˌɒk.sɪ.daɪˈzeɪ.ʃᵊn, ˌdiː-, -sə-, -dɪˈ-, (US) -ˌɑːk.sə.dəˈ- -s -z

deoxidiz|e, -is|e diˈɒk.sɪ.daɪz, ˌdiː-, -sə-, (US) -ˈɑːk.sə- -es -ɪz -ing -ɪŋ -ed -d -er/s -əʳ/z, (US) -ɚ/z

Depardieu ˌdep.ɑːˈdjɜː, də.pɑːˈ-; ˈdep.ɑː.djɜː, (US) ˌdep.ɑːrˈdjɜː, ˈ---
de|part dɪ|ˈpɑːt, də-, (US) dɪ|ˈpɑːrt **-parts** -ˈpɑːts, (US) -ˈpɑːrts **-parting** -ˈpɑː.tɪŋ, (US) -ˈpɑːr.t̬ɪŋ **-parted** -ˈpɑː.tɪd, (US) -ˈpɑːr.t̬ɪd
department dɪˈpɑːt.mənt, də-, (US) dɪˈpɑːrt- **-s** -s **deˈpartment ˌstore**
departmental ˌdiː.pɑːtˈmen.təl, (US) -pɑːrtˈmen.t̬əl **-ism** -ɪ.zəm
departure dɪˈpɑː.tʃər, də-, (US) dɪˈpɑːr.tʃɚ **-s** -z **deˈparture ˌlounge**
depast|ure ˌdiːˈpɑːs.tʃ|ər, (US) -ˈpæs.tʃ|ɚ **-ures** -əz, (US) -ɚz **-uring** -ər.ɪŋ **-ured** -əd, (US) -ɚd
depend dɪˈpend, də-, (US) dɪ- **-s** -z **-ing** -ɪŋ **-ed** -ɪd
dependability dɪˌpen.dəˈbɪl.ə.ti, də-, -ɪ.ti, (US) dɪˌpen.dəˈbɪl.ə.t̬i
dependab|le dɪˈpen.də.b|əl, də-, dɪ- **-ly** -li **-leness** -əl.nəs, -nɪs
dependant dɪˈpen.dənt, də-, (US) dɪ- **-s** -s
dependenc|e dɪˈpen.dənts, də-, (US) dɪ- **-y** -i **-ies** -iz
dependent dɪˈpen.dənt, də-, (US) dɪ- **-s** -s **-ly** -li
De Pere dɪˈpɪər, də-, (US) -ˈpɪr
depersonaliz|e, -is|e ˌdiːˈpɜː.sən.əl.aɪz, (US) -ˈpɝː- **-es** -ɪz **-ing** -ɪŋ **-ed** -d
Depew dɪˈpjuː, də-
depict dɪˈpɪkt, də-, (US) dɪ- **-s** -s **-ing** -ɪŋ **-ed** -ɪd
depiction dɪˈpɪk.ʃən, də-, (US) dɪ- **-s** -z
depi|late ˈdep.ɪ|.leɪt, ˈ-ə- **-lates** -leɪts **-lating** -leɪ.tɪŋ, (US) -leɪ.t̬ɪŋ **-lated** -leɪ.tɪd, (US) -leɪ.t̬ɪd
depilation ˌdep.ɪˈleɪ.ʃən, -əˈ-
depilator ˈdep.ɪ.leɪ.tər, ˈ-ə-, (US) -t̬ɚ **-s** -z
depilator|y dɪˈpɪl.ə.tər|.i, də-, -tr|i, (US) dɪˈpɪl.ə.tɔːr|.i **-ies** -iz
deplan|e ˌdiːˈpleɪn **-es** -z **-ing** -ɪŋ **-ed** -d
de|plete dɪ|ˈpliːt, də-, (US) dɪ- **-pletes** -ˈpliːts **-pleting** -ˈpliː.tɪŋ, (US) -ˈpliː.t̬ɪŋ **-pleted** -ˈpliː.tɪd, (US) -ˈpliː.t̬ɪd
depletion dɪˈpliː.ʃən, də-, (US) dɪ- **-s** -z
deplet|ive dɪˈpliː.t|ɪv, də-, (US) dɪˈpliː.t̬|ɪv **-ory** -ər.i
deplorab|le dɪˈplɔː.rə.b|əl, də-, (US) dɪˈplɔːr.ə- **-ly** -li **-leness** -əl.nəs, -nɪs
deplor|e dɪˈplɔːr, də-, (US) dɪˈplɔːr **-es** -z **-ing** -ɪŋ **-ed** -d
deploy dɪˈplɔɪ, də-, (US) dɪ- **-s** -z **-ing** -ɪŋ **-ed** -d
deployment dɪˈplɔɪ.mənt, də-, dɪ- **-s** -s
depolarization, -isa- diːˌpəʊ.lər.aɪˈzeɪ.ʃən, ˌdiː.pəʊ-, -ɪˈ-, (US) diːˌpoʊ.lɚ.əˈ-
depolariz|e, -is|e ˌdiːˈpəʊ.lər.aɪz, (US) -ˈpoʊ.lə.raɪz **-es** -ɪz **-ing** -ɪŋ **-ed** -d
depoliticization ˌdiː.pəˌlɪt.ɪ.saɪˈzeɪ.ʃən, ˌlɪt.ə-, -sɪˈ-, (US) -ˌlɪt̬.ɪ.səˈ-, ˌ-ə-
depoliticiz|e, -is|e ˌdiː.pəˈlɪt.ɪ.saɪz, ˈ-ə-, (US) -ˈlɪt̬- **-es** -ɪz **-ing** -ɪŋ **-ed** -d
de Pompadour dəˈpɒm.pə.dɔːr, -dʊər, (US) -ˈpɑːm.pə.dɔːr
deponent dɪˈpəʊ.nənt, də-, (US) dɪˈpoʊ- **-s** -s
Depo-Provera® ˌdep.əʊ.prəʊˈvɪə.rə, (US) -oʊ.proʊˈver.ə
depopu|late ˌdiːˈpɒp.jə|.leɪt, -jʊ-, (US) -ˈpɑː.pjə- **-lates** -leɪts **-lating** -leɪ.tɪŋ, (US) -leɪ.t̬ɪŋ **-lated** -leɪ.tɪd, (US) -leɪ.t̬ɪd **-lator/s** -leɪ.tər/z, (US) -leɪ.t̬ɚ/z
depopulation diːˌpɒp.jəˈleɪ.ʃən, ˌdiː.pɒp-, -jʊˈ-, (US) diːˌpɑː.pjəˈ-
de|port dɪ|ˈpɔːt, də-, (US) dɪ|ˈpɔːrt **-ports** -ˈpɔːts, (US) -ˈpɔːrts **-porting** -ˈpɔː.tɪŋ, (US) -ˈpɔːr.t̬ɪŋ **-ported** -ˈpɔː.tɪd, (US) -ˈpɔːr.t̬ɪd
deportation ˌdiː.pɔːˈteɪ.ʃən, (US) -pɔːrˈ- **-s** -z
deportee ˌdiː.pɔːˈtiː, (US) -pɔːrˈ- **-s** -z
deportment dɪˈpɔːt.mənt, də-, (US) dɪˈpɔːrt-
deposal dɪˈpəʊ.zəl, də-, (US) dɪˈpoʊ- **-s** -z
depos|e dɪˈpəʊz, də-, (US) dɪˈpoʊz **-es** -ɪz **-ing** -ɪŋ **-ed** -d
depos|it dɪˈpɒz|.ɪt, də-, (US) dɪˈpɑː.z|ɪt **-its** -ɪts **-iting** -ɪ.tɪŋ, (US) -ɪ.t̬ɪŋ **-ited** -ɪ.tɪd, (US) -ɪ.t̬ɪd **deˈposit acˌcount**
depositar|y dɪˈpɒz.ɪ.tər|.i, də-, ˈ-ə-, (US) dɪˈpɑː.zə.ter- **-ies** -iz
deposition ˌdep.əˈzɪʃ.ən, ˌdiː.pəˈ- **-s** -z
depositor dɪˈpɒz.ɪ.tər, də-, ˈ-ə-, (US) dɪˈpɑː.zə.t̬ɚ **-s** -z
depositor|y dɪˈpɒz.ɪ.tər|.i, də-, ˈ-ə-, -tr|i, (US) dɪˈpɑː.zə.tɔːr|.i **-ies** -iz
depot ˈdep.əʊ, (US) ˈdiː.poʊ, ˈdep.oʊ **-s** -z
Depp dep
depravation ˌdep.rəˈveɪ.ʃən
deprav|e dɪˈpreɪv, də-, (US) dɪ- **-es** -z **-ing** -ɪŋ **-ed** -d **-edly** -d.li, -ɪd.li **-edness** -d.nəs, -ɪd.nəs, -nɪs
depravity dɪˈpræv.ə.ti, də-, -ɪ.ti, (US) dɪˈpræv.ə.t̬i
depre|cate ˈdep.rə|.keɪt, -rɪ- **-cates** -keɪts **-cating/ly** -keɪ.tɪŋ/li, (US) -keɪ.t̬ɪŋ/li **-cated** -keɪ.tɪd, (US) -keɪ.t̬ɪd **-cator/s** -keɪ.tər/z, (US) -keɪ.t̬ɚ/z
deprecation ˌdep.rəˈkeɪ.ʃən, -prɪˈ- **-s** -z
deprecatory ˈdep.rə.kə.tər.i, -rɪ-, -tri; ˌdep.rəˈkeɪ-, (US) ˈdep.rə.kə.tɔːr.i
depreciable dɪˈpriː.ʃi.ə.bəl, də-, -si-, (US) dɪˈpriː.ʃi.ə.bəl, ˈ-ʃə.bəl
depreci|ate dɪˈpriː.ʃi|.eɪt, də-, -si-, (US) dɪˈpriː.ʃi- **-ates** -eɪts **-ating/ly** -eɪ.tɪŋ/li, (US) -eɪ.t̬ɪŋ/li **-ated** -eɪ.tɪd, (US) -eɪ.t̬ɪd **-ator/s** -eɪ.tər/z, (US) -eɪ.t̬ɚ/z
depreciation dɪˌpriː.ʃiˈeɪ.ʃən, də-, -siˈ-, (US) dɪˌpriː.ʃiˈ-
depreciatory dɪˈpriː.ʃi.ə.tər.i, də-, -si-, ˈ-ʃə.tər-, -tri, (US) dɪˈpriː.ʃi.ə.tɔːr.i, ˈ-ʃə.tɔːr-
depre|date ˈdep.rə|.deɪt, -rɪ- **-dates** -deɪts **-dating** -deɪ.tɪŋ, (US) -deɪ.t̬ɪŋ **-dated** -deɪ.tɪd, (US) -deɪ.t̬ɪd **-dator/s** -deɪ.tər/z, (US) -deɪ.t̬ɚ/z
depredation ˌdep.rəˈdeɪ.ʃən, -rɪˈ- **-s** -z
depredatory dɪˈpred.ə.tər.i, də-, -tri; ˌdep.rəˈdeɪ-, (US) ˈdep.rə.də.tɔːr.i, -deɪ.t̬ɚ-; (US) dɪˈpred.ə.tɔːr-
depress dɪˈpres, də-, (US) dɪ- **-es** -ɪz **-ing** -ɪŋ **-ed** -t **-or/s** -ər/z, (US) -ɚ/z **-ant/s** -ənt/s
depressing dɪˈpres.ɪŋ, də-, (US) dɪ- **-ly** -li
depression dɪˈpreʃ.ən, də-, (US) dɪ- **-s** -z
depressive dɪˈpres.ɪv, də-, (US) dɪ- **-s** -z
depressor dɪˈpres.ər, də-, (US) dɪˈpres.ɚ **-s** -z
depressurization, -isation diːˌpreʃ.ər.aɪˈzeɪ.ʃən, ˌdiː.preʃ-, -ɪˈ-, (US) diːˌpreʃ.ɚ.əˈ-
depressuriz|e, -is|e ˌdiːˈpreʃ.ər.aɪz, (US) -ə.raɪz **-es** -ɪz **-ing** -ɪŋ **-ed** -d
deprivation ˌdep.rɪˈveɪ.ʃən, -rəˈ-; ˌdiː.praɪˈ- **-s** -z
depriv|e dɪˈpraɪv, də-, (US) dɪ- **-es** -z **-ing** -ɪŋ **-ed** -d
de profundis ˌdeɪ.prɒfˈʊn.diːs, -prəˈfʊn-, (US) -proʊˈfʊn.dɪs
deprogram ˌdiːˈprəʊ.græm, (US) -ˈproʊ- **-s** -z **-(m)ing** -ɪŋ **-(m)ed** -d
deprogramm|e ˌdiːˈprəʊ.græm, (US) -ˈproʊ- **-s** -z **-ing** -ɪŋ **-er** -d
dept (abbrev. for **department**) dɪˈpɑːt.mənt, də-, (US) dɪˈpɑːrt-
Deptford ˈdet.fəd, ˈdep.fəd, (US) -fɚd
depth depθ **-s** -s **ˈdepth ˌcharge**
deputation ˌdep.jəˈteɪ.ʃən, -jʊˈ-, (US) -jəˈ- **-s** -z
de|pute dɪ|ˈpjuːt, də-, (US) dɪ- **-putes** -ˈpjuːts **-puting** -ˈpjuː.tɪŋ, (US) -ˈpjuː.t̬ɪŋ **-puted** -ˈpjuː.tɪd, (US) -ˈpjuː.t̬ɪd
deputiz|e, -is|e ˈdep.jə.taɪz, -jʊ- **-es** -ɪz **-ing** -ɪŋ **-ed** -d
deput|y ˈdep.jə.t|i, -jʊ-, (US) -t̬|i **-ies** -iz
De Quincey dəˈkwɪnt.si, dɪ-
deraci|nate dɪˈræs.ɪ|.neɪt, ˌdiː-, ˈ-ə- **-nates** -neɪts **-nating** -neɪ.tɪŋ, (US) -neɪ.t̬ɪŋ **-nated** -neɪ.tɪd, -neɪ.t̬ɪd
deracination diːˌræs.ɪˈneɪ.ʃən, ˌdiː.ræs-, -əˈ-, (US) diːˌræs-
derail dɪˈreɪl, ˌdiː- **-s** -z **-ing** -ɪŋ **-ed** -d
derailleur dɪˈreɪ.ljər, də-, -lər, (US) dɪˈreɪ.lɚ
derailment dɪˈreɪl.mənt, ˌdiː- **-s** -s
derang|e dɪˈreɪndʒ, də-, (US) dɪ- **-es** -ɪz **-ing** -ɪŋ **-ed** -d **-ement/s** -mənt/s
de|rate ˌdiː|ˈreɪt **-rates** -ˈreɪts **-rating** -ˈreɪ.tɪŋ, (US) -ˈreɪ.t̬ɪŋ **-rated** -ˈreɪ.tɪd, (US) -ˈreɪ.t̬ɪd

D

deration ˌdiːˈræʃ.ən **-s** -z **-ing** -ɪŋ **-ed** -d
derb|y ˈdɑː.b|i, (US) ˈdɜː- **-ies** -iz
Der|by ˈdɑː|.bi, (US) ˈdɑːr-, ˈdɜː- **-byshire** -bɪ.ʃəʳ, -ʃɪəʳ, (US) -ʃɚ, -ʃɪr

Note: American pronunciation sometimes uses (US) ˈdɑːr- for British references.

Derbys. (abbrev. for **Derbyshire**) ˈdɑː.bɪ.ʃəʳ, -ʃɪəʳ, (US) ˈdɑːr.bɪ.ʃɚ, ˈdɜː-, -ʃɪr

Note: American pronunciation sometimes uses (US) ˈdɑːr- for British references.

deregu|late ˌdiːˈreg.jə|.leɪt, -jʊ-, (US) -jə- **-lates** -leɪts **-lating** -leɪ.tɪŋ, (US) -leɪ.t̬ɪŋ **-lated** -leɪ.tɪd, (US) -leɪ.t̬ɪd
deregulation ˌdiː.reg.jəˈleɪ.ʃən, -jʊˈ-, (US) -jəˈ-
Dereham ˈdɪə.rəm, (US) ˈdɪr.əm
Derek ˈder.ɪk
derelict ˈder.ə.lɪkt, ˈ-ɪ- **-s** -s
dereliction ˌder.əˈlɪk.ʃən, -ɪˈ-
derequisition diːˌrek.wɪˈzɪʃ.ən, ˌdiː.rek-, -wəˈ-, (US) diːˌrek- **-s** -z **-ing** -ɪŋ **-ed** -d
De Reszke dəˈres.ki
Derg(h) dɜːg, (US) dɝːg
Derham ˈder.əm
derid|e dɪˈraɪd, də-, (US) dɪ- **-es** -z **-ing/ly** -ɪŋ/li **-ed** -ɪd **-er/s** -əʳ/z, (US) -ɚ/z
de rigueur də.rɪˈgɜːʳ, ˌdeɪ-, ˌdiː-, -riːˈ-, (US) -ˈgɝː
Dering ˈdɪə.rɪŋ, (US) ˈdɪr.ɪŋ
derision dɪˈrɪʒ.ən, də-, (US) dɪ-
derisive dɪˈraɪ.sɪv, dəˈraɪ-, -zɪv, -ˈrɪz.ɪv, (US) dɪˈraɪ.sɪv, -zɪv **-ly** -li **-ness** -nəs, -nɪs
derisory dɪˈraɪ.sər.i, də-, -zər-, (US) dɪˈraɪ-
derivation ˌder.ɪˈveɪ.ʃən, -əˈ- **-s** -z **-al** -əl
derivative dɪˈrɪv.ə.tɪv, də-, (US) dɪˈrɪv.ə.t̬ɪv **-s** -z **-ly** -li
deriv|e dɪˈraɪv, də-, (US) dɪ- **-es** -z **-ing** -ɪŋ **-ed** -d **-able** -ə.bəl
d'Erlanger ˌdeə.lɑ̃ːnˈʒeɪ, (US) ˌder.lɑːnˈ-
derm dɜːm, (US) dɝːm **-al** -əl
-derm dɜːm, (US) dɝːm
Note: Suffix. Does not normally carry stress, e.g. **pachyderm** /ˈpæk.ɪ.dɜːm/ (US) /-ə.dɝːm/.
dermabrasion ˌdɜː.məˈbreɪ.ʒən, (US) ˌdɝː-
-dermal dɜː.məl, (US) dɝː-
Note: Suffix. May or may not carry stress, e.g. **epidermal** /ˌep.ɪˈdɜː.məl/ (US) /-ˈdɝː-/; see individual entries.
dermatitis ˌdɜː.məˈtaɪ.tɪs, -təs, (US) ˌdɝː.məˈtaɪ.t̬ɪs, -t̬əs
dermatolog|y ˌdɜː.məˈtɒl.ə.dʒ|i, (US) ˌdɝː.məˈtɑː.lə- **-ist/s** -ɪst/s
dermatos|is ˌdɜː.məˈtəʊ.s|ɪs, (US) ˌdɝː.məˈtoʊ- **-es** -iːz
dermis ˈdɜː.mɪs, (US) ˈdɝː-

Dermot(t) ˈdɜː.mət, (US) ˈdɝː-
dernier cri ˌdɜː.ni.eɪˈkriː, ˌdeə-, (US) ˌder.njeɪˈ-, ˌdɝː-
dero|gate ˈder.əʊ|.geɪt, ˈdiː.rəʊ-, (US) ˈder.ə- **-gates** -geɪts **-gating** -geɪ.tɪŋ, (US) -geɪ.t̬ɪŋ **-gated** -geɪ.tɪd, (US) -geɪ.t̬ɪd
derogation ˌder.əʊˈgeɪ.ʃən, ˌdiː.rəʊˈ-, (US) ˌder.əˈ-
derogator|y dɪˈrɒg.ə.tər|.i, də-, -tr|i, (US) dɪˈrɑː.gə.tɔːr|.i **-ily** -əl.i, -ɪ.li **-iness** -ɪ.nəs, -ɪ.nɪs
Deronda dəˈrɒn.də, dɪ-, (US) dəˈrɑːn-
derrick, D~ ˈder.ɪk **-s** -s
Derrida dəˈriː.də, derˈiː-; ˈder.ɪ-, (US) ˈder.iː.dɑː
derrière ˈder.i.eəʳ, ˌ--ˈ-, (US) ˌder.iˈer, ˈ--- **-s** -z
derring-do ˌder.ɪŋˈduː, ˌdeə.rɪŋˈ-, (US) ˌder.ɪŋˈ-
derringer, D~ ˈder.ɪn.dʒəʳ, -ən-, (US) -dʒɚ **-s** -z
Derry ˈder.i
derv dɜːv, (US) dɝːv
dervish, D~ ˈdɜː.vɪʃ, (US) ˈdɝː- **-es** -ɪz
Dervla ˈdɜːv.lə, (US) ˈdɝːv-
Derwent ˈdɜː.wənt, ˈdɑː-, -went, -wɪnt, (US) ˈdɝː-, ˈdɑːr- ˈ**Derwent** ˌ**Water**

Note: /ˈdɑː-/ (US) /ˈdɑːr-/ is the normal pronunciation for the Baron.

Des dez, (US) des
DES ˌdiː.iːˈes
Desai desˈaɪ; ˈdeɪ.saɪ
desali|nate ˌdiːˈsæl.ɪ|.neɪt, ˈ-ə- **-nates** -neɪts **-nating** -neɪ.tɪŋ, (US) -neɪ.t̬ɪŋ **-nated** -neɪ.tɪd, (US) -neɪ.t̬ɪd
desalination diːˌsæl.ɪˈneɪ.ʃən, ˌdiː.sæl-, -əˈ-, (US) diːˌsæl- **-s** -z
desalinization, -isa- diːˌsæl.ɪ.naɪˈzeɪ.ʃən, ˌdiː.sæl-, ˌ-ə-, -nɪˈ-, (US) diːˌsæl.ə.nəˈ-
desaliniz|e, -is|e ˌdiːˈsæl.ɪ.naɪz, ˈ-ə- **-es** -ɪz **-ing** -ɪŋ **-ed** -d
Desart ˈdez.ət, (US) -ɚt
Desborough ˈdez.brə, (US) -bɚ.oʊ
descal|e ˌdiːˈskeɪl **-es** -z **-ing** -ɪŋ **-ed** -d
descant n ˈdes.kænt **-s** -s
descan|t v dɪˈskæn|t, desˈkæn|t, (US) ˈdes.kæn|t, -ˈ- **-ts** -ts **-ting** -tɪŋ, (US) -t̬ɪŋ **-ted** -tɪd, (US) -t̬ɪd
Descartes ˈdeɪ.kɑːt, deɪˈkɑːt, (US) deɪˈkɑːrt
descend dɪˈsend, də-, (US) dɪ- **-s** -z **-ing** -ɪŋ **-ed** -ɪd
descendant, descendent dɪˈsen.dənt, də-, (US) dɪ- **-s** -s
descender dɪˈsen.dəʳ, də-, (US) dɪˈsen.dɚ **-s** -z
descent dɪˈsent, də-, (US) dɪ- **-s** -s
describ|e dɪˈskraɪb, də-, (US) dɪ- **-es** -z **-ing** -ɪŋ **-ed** -d **-er/s** -əʳ/z, (US) -ɚ/z **-able** -ə.bəl
description dɪˈskrɪp.ʃən, də-, (US) dɪ- **-s** -z

descriptive dɪˈskrɪp.tɪv, də-, (US) dɪ- **-ly** -li **-ness** -nəs, -nɪs
descriptiv|ism dɪˈskrɪp.tɪ.v|ɪ.zəm, də-, (US) dɪ- **-ist** -ɪst
descr|y dɪˈskr|aɪ, də-, (US) dɪ- **-ies** -aɪz **-ying** -aɪ.ɪŋ **-ied** -aɪd
Desdemona ˌdez.dɪˈməʊ.nə, -dəˈ-, (US) -dəˈmoʊ-

Note: The Shakespearian character is pronounced with the stress on the third syllable. The character in Verdi's 'Otello' is pronounced with the stress on the second syllable.

dese|crate ˈdes.ɪ|.kreɪt, ˈ-ə- **-crates** -kreɪts **-crating** -kreɪ.tɪŋ, (US) -kreɪ.t̬ɪŋ **-crated** -kreɪ.tɪd, (US) -kreɪ.t̬ɪd **-crator/s** -kreɪ.təʳ/z, (US) -kreɪ.t̬ɚ/z
desecration ˌdes.ɪˈkreɪ.ʃən, -əˈ- **-s** -z
deseed ˌdiːˈsiːd **-s** -z **-ing** -ɪŋ **-ed** -d
desegre|gate ˌdiːˈseg.rɪ|.geɪt, -rə- **-gates** -geɪts **-gating** -geɪ.tɪŋ, (US) -geɪ.t̬ɪŋ **-gated** -geɪ.tɪd, (US) -geɪ.t̬ɪd
desegregation diːˌseg.rɪˈgeɪ.ʃən, ˌdiː.seg-, -rəˈ-, (US) diːˌseg-
deselect ˌdiː.səˈlekt, -sɪˈ- **-s** -s **-ing** -ɪŋ **-ed** -ɪd
deselection ˌdiː.səˈlek.ʃən, -sɪˈ-
de Selincourt dəˈsel.ɪŋ.kɔːt, -ɪn-, (US) -kɔːrt
desensitization diːˌsent.sɪ.taɪˈzeɪ.ʃən, ˌdiː.sent-, -sə-, -tɪˈ-, (US) diːˌsent.sɪ.t̬əˈ-, ˌ-sə-
desensitiz|e, -is|e ˌdiːˈsent.sɪ.taɪz, -sə- **-es** -ɪz **-ing** -ɪŋ **-ed** -d
de|sert v dɪ|ˈzɜːt, də-, (US) dɪ|ˈzɝːt **-serts** -ˈzɜːts, (US) -ˈzɝːts **-serting** -ˈzɜː.tɪŋ, (US) -ˈzɝː.t̬ɪŋ **-serted** -ˈzɜː.tɪd, (US) -ˈzɝː.t̬ɪd **-serter/s** -ˈzɜː.təʳ/z, (US) -ˈzɝː.t̬ɚ/z
desert n, adj *dry place:* ˈdez.ət, (US) -ɚt **-s** -s ˌ**desert** ˈ**island;** ˌ**desert** ˈ**rat**
desert n *what is deserved:* dɪˈzɜːt, də-, (US) dɪˈzɝːt **-s** -s **get one's** ˌ**just de**ˈ**serts**
desertification dɪˌzɜː.tɪ.fɪˈkeɪ.ʃən, də-, -tə-, -fəˈ-, (US) dɪˌzɝː.t̬ə-
desertion dɪˈzɜː.ʃən, də-, (US) dɪˈzɝː- **-s** -z
deserv|e dɪˈzɜːv, də-, (US) dɪˈzɝːv **-es** -z **-ing/ly** -ɪŋ/li **-ed** -d **-edly** -ɪd.li
desex ˌdiːˈseks **-es** -ɪz **-ing** -ɪŋ **-ed** -t
desexualiz|e, -is|e diːˈsek.ʃʊə.laɪz, -ʃu.əl.aɪz, -sjʊə.laɪz, -sju.əl.aɪz, (US) -ʃu.ə.laɪz **-es** -ɪz **-ing** -ɪŋ **-ed** -d
deshabille ˌdez.æbˈiːl, ˌdeɪ.zæbˈ-, ˌdes.æbˈ-, -əˈbiːl, ˈ---, (US) ˌdes.æbˈ-, ˌdez-; (US) ˈdɪs.ə.biːl
déshabillé ˌdeɪ.zæbˈiː.eɪ, ˌdez.æb-, ˌdes-, -əˈbiː-, -ˈbiːl
desiccant ˈdes.ɪ.kənt, ˈ-ə- **-s** -s
desic|cate ˈdes.ɪ|.keɪt, ˈ-ə- **-cates** -keɪts **-cating** -keɪ.tɪŋ, (US) -keɪ.t̬ɪŋ **-cated** -keɪ.tɪd, (US) -keɪ.t̬ɪd
desiccation ˌdes.ɪˈkeɪ.ʃən, -əˈ-
desiccative ˈdes.ɪ.kə.tɪv; desˈɪk.ə-,

dɪˈsɪk-, (US) ˈdes.ɪ.keɪ.t̬ɪv; (US) dəˈsɪk.ə-

desiccator ˈdes.ɪ.keɪ.təʳ, ˈ-ə-, (US) -t̬ɚ **-s** -z

desider|ate dɪˈzɪd.ᵊr|.eɪt, də-, -ˈsɪd-, (US) dɪˈsɪd.ə.r|eɪt, -ˈzɪd- **-ates** -eɪts **-ating** -eɪ.tɪŋ, (US) -eɪ.t̬ɪŋ **-ated** -eɪ.tɪd, (US) -eɪ.t̬ɪd

desideration dɪˌzɪd.əˈreɪ.ʃᵊn, də-, -ˌsɪd-, (US) dɪˌsɪd-, -ˌzɪd- **-s** -z

desiderative dɪˈzɪd.ᵊr.ə.tɪv, də-, -ˈsɪd-, (US) dɪˈsɪd.ɚ.ə.t̬ɪv, -ˈzɪd-

desiderat|um dɪˌzɪd.əˈrɑː.t|əm, də-, -ˌsɪd-, -ˈreɪ-, (US) dɪˌsɪd.əˈrɑː.t̬|əm, -ˌzɪd-, -ˈreɪ- **-a** -ə

design dɪˈzaɪn, də-, (US) dɪ- **-s** -z **-ing** -ɪŋ **-ed** -d **-edly** -ɪd.li **-able** -ə.bᵊl

designate adj ˈdez.ɪg.neɪt, -nɪt, -nət

desig|nate v ˈdez.ɪg|.neɪt **-nates** -neɪts **-nating** -neɪ.tɪŋ, (US) -neɪ.t̬ɪŋ **-nated** -neɪ.tɪd, (US) -neɪ.t̬ɪd **-nator/s** -neɪ.təʳ/z, (US) -neɪ.t̬ɚ/z

designation ˌdez.ɪgˈneɪ.ʃᵊn **-s** -z

designer dɪˈzaɪ.nəʳ, də-, (US) dɪˈzaɪ.nɚ **-s** -z

desinenc|e ˈdes.ɪ.nənts, ˈdez-, -ᵊn.ənts **-es** -ɪz

desirability dɪˌzaɪə.rəˈbɪl.ə.ti, də-, -ɪ.ti, (US) dɪˌzaɪ.rəˈbɪl.ə.t̬i

desirab|le dɪˈzaɪə.rə.b|ᵊl, də-, (US) dɪˈzaɪ- **-ly** -li **-leness** -ᵊl.nəs, -nɪs

desir|e dɪˈzaɪəʳ, -ˈzaɪ.əʳ, dəˈ-, (US) dɪˈzaɪ.ɚ **-es** -z **-ing** -ɪŋ **-ed** -d **-er/s** -əʳ/z, (US) -ɚ/z

Désirée deɪˈzɪə.reɪ, dezˈɪə-, (US) ˌdez.əˈreɪ

desirous dɪˈzaɪə.rəs, də-, (US) dɪˈzaɪ.rəs **-ly** -li

desist dɪˈsɪst, də-, dɪˈzɪst **-s** -s **-ing** -ɪŋ **-ed** -ɪd

desistance dɪˈsɪs.tᵊnts, dəˈ-, dɪˈzɪs-

desk desk **-s** -s **ˈdesk ˌjob**

de-skill ˌdiːˈskɪl **-s** -z **-ing** -ɪŋ **-ed** -d

desktop ˈdesk.tɒp, (US) -tɑːp **ˌdesktop ˈpublishing**

Des Moines dəˈmɔɪn, dɪ-, -ˈmɔɪnz, (US) -ˈmɔɪn

Desmond ˈdez.mənd

desolate adj ˈdes.ᵊl.ət, ˈdez-, -ɪt **-ly** -li **-ness** -nəs, -nɪs

desol|ate v ˈdes.ᵊl|.eɪt, ˈdez.ə.l|eɪt **-ates** -eɪts **-ating** -eɪ.tɪŋ, (US) -eɪ.t̬ɪŋ **-ated** -eɪ.tɪd, (US) -eɪ.t̬ɪd **-ator/s** -eɪ.təʳ/z, (US) -eɪ.t̬ɚ/z

desolation ˌdes.ᵊlˈeɪ.ʃᵊn, ˌdez- **-s** -z

de Soto dəˈsəʊ.təʊ, (US) -ˈsoʊ.toʊ

despair dɪˈspeəʳ, də-, (US) dɪˈsper **-s** -z **-ing/ly** -ɪŋ/li **-ed** -d

Despard ˈdes.pəd, -pɑːd, (US) -pɚd, -pɑːrd

despatch dɪˈspætʃ, də-, (US) dɪ- **-es** -ɪz **-ing** -ɪŋ **-ed** -t **-er/s** -əʳ/z, (US) -ɚ/z **desˈpatch ˌbox; desˈpatch ˌrider**

desperado ˌdes.pəˈrɑː.dəʊ, -ˈreɪ-, (US) -doʊ **-(e)s** -z

desperate ˈdes.pᵊr.ət, -ɪt **-ly** -li **-ness** -nəs, -nɪs

desperation ˌdes.pəˈreɪ.ʃᵊn

despicability dɪˌspɪk.əˈbɪl.ə.ti, də-, -ɪ.ti; ˌdes.pɪ.kəˈ-, (US) dɪˌspɪk.əˈbɪl.ə.t̬i; (US) ˌdes.pɪ.kəˈ-

despicab|le dɪˈspɪk.ə.b|ᵊl, də-; ˈdes.pɪ.kə-, (US) dɪˈspɪk.ə-; (US) ˈdes.pɪ.kə- **-ly** -li **-leness** -ᵊl.nəs, -nɪs

despis|e dɪˈspaɪz, də-, (US) dɪ- **-es** -ɪz **-ing** -ɪŋ **-ed** -d **-er/s** -əʳ/z, (US) -ɚ/z

despite dɪˈspaɪt, də-, (US) dɪ-

despiteful dɪˈspaɪt.fᵊl, də-, -fʊl, (US) dɪ- **-ly** -li

despoil dɪˈspɔɪl, də-, (US) dɪ- **-s** -z **-ing** -ɪŋ **-ed** -d **-er/s** -əʳ/z, (US) -ɚ/z

despoliation dɪˌspəʊ.liˈeɪ.ʃᵊn, də-, -ˌspɒl.iˈ-, (US) dɪˌspoʊ.liˈ-

despond, D~ dɪˈspɒnd, də-, (US) dɪˈspɑːnd **-s** -z **-ing/ly** -ɪŋ/li **-ed** -ɪd

desponden|ce dɪˈspɒn.dənt|s, də-, (US) dɪˈspɑːn- **-cy** -si

despondent dɪˈspɒn.dənt, də-, (US) dɪˈspɑːn- **-ly** -li

despot ˈdes.pɒt, -pət, (US) -pət **-s** -s

despotic dɪˈspɒt.ɪk, desˈpɒt-, dəˈspɒt-, (US) desˈpɑː.t̬ɪk **-al** -ᵊl **-ally** -ᵊl.i, -li **-alness** -ᵊl.nəs, -nɪs

despotism ˈdes.pə.tɪ.zᵊm **-s** -z

desqua|mate ˈdes.kwə|.meɪt **-mates** -meɪts **-mating** -meɪ.tɪŋ, (US) -meɪ.t̬ɪŋ **-mated** -meɪ.tɪd, (US) -meɪ.t̬ɪd

des res ˌdezˈrez

dessert dɪˈzɜːt, də-, (US) dɪˈzɝːt **-s** -s **desˈsert ˌwine, desˌsert ˈwine**

dessertspoon dɪˈzɜːt.spuːn, də-, (US) dɪˈzɝːt- **-s** -z

dessert|spoonful dɪˈzɜːt|ˌspuːn.fʊl, də-, (US) dɪˈzɝːt- **-spoonsful** -ˌspuːnz.fʊl **-spoonfuls** -ˌspuːn.fʊlz

destabilization, -isa- ˌdiːˌsteɪ.bᵊl.aɪˈzeɪ.ʃᵊn, dɪ-, -bɪ.laɪˈ-, -ɪˈ-, (US) -bᵊl.əˈ-, -bɪ.ləˈ-

destabiliz|e, -is|e ˌdiːˈsteɪ.bᵊl.aɪz, dɪ-, -bɪ.laɪz **-es** -ɪz **-ing** -ɪŋ **-ed** -d

destination ˌdes.tɪˈneɪ.ʃᵊn, -təˈ- **-s** -z

destin|e ˈdes.tɪn, -tᵊn **-es** -z **-ing** -ɪŋ **-ed** -d

destin|y ˈdes.tɪ.n|i, -tᵊn|.i **-ies** -iz

destitute ˈdes.tɪ.tʃuːt, -tjuːt, -tə-, (US) -tuːt, -tjuːt **-ly** -li **-ness** -nəs, -nɪs

destitution ˌdes.tɪˈtʃuː.ʃᵊn, -ˈtjuː-, -təˈ-, (US) -ˈtuː-, -ˈtjuː-

destroy dɪˈstrɔɪ, də-, (US) dɪ- **-s** -z **-ing** -ɪŋ **-ed** -d

destroyer dɪˈstrɔɪ.əʳ, də-, (US) dɪˈstrɔɪ.ɚ **-s** -z

destruct dɪˈstrʌkt, də-, (US) dɪ- **-s** -s **-ing** -ɪŋ **-ed** -ɪd

destructibility dɪˌstrʌk.təˈbɪl.ə.ti, də-, -tɪˈ-, -ɪ.ti, (US) dɪˌstrʌk.təˈbɪl.ə.t̬i, -tɪˈ-

destructible dɪˈstrʌk.tə.bᵊl, də-, -tɪ-, (US) dɪ-

destruction dɪˈstrʌk.ʃᵊn, də-, (US) dɪ- **-s** -z

destructive dɪˈstrʌk.tɪv, də-, (US) dɪ- **-ly** -li **-ness** -nəs, -nɪs

destructor dɪˈstrʌk.təʳ, də-, (US) dɪˈstrʌk.tɚ **-s** -z

desuetude dɪˈsjuː.ɪ.tʃuːd, -tjuːd; ˈdes.wɪ-, ˈdiː.swɪ-, (US) ˈdes.wɪ.tuːd, -tjuːd; (US) dɪˈsuː.ə-

desultor|y ˈdes.ᵊl.tᵊr|.i, ˈdez-, -tr|i, (US) -tɔːr|.i **-ily** -ᵊl.i, -ɪ.li **-iness** -ɪ.nəs, -ɪ.nɪs

Des Voeux deɪˈvɜː

detach dɪˈtætʃ, də-, (US) dɪ- **-es** -ɪz **-ing** -ɪŋ **-ed** -t **-edly** -t.li, -ɪd.li **-able** -ə.bᵊl

detachment dɪˈtætʃ.mənt, də-, (US) dɪ- **-s** -s

detail ˈdiː.teɪl; dɪˈteɪl, də-, (US) dɪˈteɪl; (US) ˈdiː.teɪl **-s** -z **-ing** -ɪŋ **-ed** -d

detain dɪˈteɪn, də-, (US) dɪ- **-s** -z **-ing** -ɪŋ **-ed** -d **-er/s** -əʳ/z, (US) -ɚ/z

detainee ˌdiː.teɪˈniː; dɪˌteɪˈ-, də-, (US) ˌdiː.teɪˈ- **-s** -z

detect dɪˈtekt, də-, (US) dɪ- **-s** -s **-ing** -ɪŋ **-ed** -ɪd

detectab|le dɪˈtek.tə.b|ᵊl, də-, (US) dɪ- **-ly** -li

detection dɪˈtek.ʃᵊn, də-, (US) dɪ- **-s** -z

detective dɪˈtek.tɪv, də-, (US) dɪ- **-s** -z

detector dɪˈtek.təʳ, də-, (US) dɪˈtek.tɚ **-s** -z

detent dɪˈtent, də-, (US) dɪ- **-s** -s

détente ˈdeɪ.tɑ̃ːnt, (US) deɪˈtɑːnt, ˈ--

detention dɪˈten.tʃᵊn, də-, (US) dɪ- **-s** -z **deˈtention ˌcentre**

deter dɪˈtɜːʳ, də-, (US) dɪˈtɝː **-s** -z **-ring** -ɪŋ **-red** -d

Deterding ˈdet.ə.dɪŋ, (US) ˈdet̬.ɚ-

detergent dɪˈtɜː.dʒᵊnt, də-, (US) dɪˈtɝː- **-s** -s

deterior|ate dɪˈtɪə.ri.ᵊr|.eɪt, də-, (US) dɪˈtɪr.i.ə.r|eɪt **-ates** -eɪts **-ating** -eɪ.tɪŋ, (US) -eɪ.t̬ɪŋ **-ated** -eɪ.tɪd, (US) -eɪ.t̬ɪd

deterioration dɪˌtɪə.ri.əˈreɪ.ʃᵊn, də-, (US) dɪˌtɪr.i-

determinable dɪˈtɜː.mɪ.nə.bᵊl, də-, -mᵊn.ə-, (US) dɪˈtɝː-

determinant dɪˈtɜː.mɪ.nənt, də-, (US) dɪˈtɝː- **-s** -s

determinate dɪˈtɜː.mɪ.nət, də-, -nɪt, (US) dɪˈtɝː- **-ly** -li **-ness** -nəs, -nɪs

determination dɪˌtɜː.mɪˈneɪ.ʃᵊn, də-, -məˈ-, (US) dɪˌtɝː- **-s** -z

determinative dɪˈtɜː.mɪ.nə.tɪv, də-, -mᵊn.ə-, (US) dɪˈtɝː.mɪ.neɪ.t̬ɪv, -nə-

determin|e dɪˈtɜː.mɪn, də-, -mən, (US) dɪˈtɝː- **-es** -z **-ing** -ɪŋ **-ed/ly** -d/li

determined dɪˈtɜː.mɪnd, də-, (US) dɪˈtɝː- **-ly** -li

determiner dɪˈtɜː.mɪ.nəʳ, də-, -mə-, (US) dɪˈtɝː.mɪ.nɚ **-s** -z

determin|ism dɪˈtɜː.mɪ.n|ɪ.zᵊm, də-, -mə-, (US) dɪˈtɝː- **-ist/s** -ɪst/s

deterrence dɪˈter.ᵊnts, də-, (US) dɪ-

deterrent dɪˈter.ᵊnt, də-, (US) dɪ- **-s** -s

detest dɪˈtest, də-, (US) dɪ- **-s** -s **-ing** -ɪŋ **-ed** -ɪd

detestab|le dɪˈtes.tə.b|ᵊl, də-, (US) dɪ- **-ly** -li **-leness** -ᵊl.nəs, -nɪs

detestation ˌdiː.tesˈteɪ.ʃᵊn, dɪˌtes-, (US) ˌdiː.tes-

dethron|e diːˈθrəʊn, ˌdɪ-, də-, US dɪˈθroʊn, ˌdiː- **-es** -z **-ing** -ɪŋ **-ed** -d **-ement** -mənt
detinue ˈdet.ɪ.njuː, US -ən.juː, -uː
Detlev ˈdet.lef, US -ləf, -lef
Detmold ˈdet.məʊld, US -moʊld
de Tocqueville dəˈtəʊk.vɪl, -ˈtɒk-, -viːl, US -ˈtoʊk.vɪl, -ˈtɑːk-
deton|ate ˈdet.ən|.eɪt **-ates** -eɪts **-ating** -eɪ.tɪŋ, US -eɪ.t̬ɪŋ **-ated** -eɪ.tɪd, US -eɪ.t̬ɪd
detonation ˌdet.ənˈeɪ.ʃən **-s** -z
detonator ˈdet.ən.eɪ.təʳ, US -t̬ɚ **-s** -z
detour ˈdiː.tʊəʳ, ˈdeɪ-, -tɔːʳ, US ˈdiː.tʊr; US -ˈ-, dɪ- **-s** -z
detox ˈdiː.tɒks, ˌdiːˈtɒks, dɪ-, US diːˈtɑːks, ˈ-- **-es** -ɪz **-ing** -ɪŋ **-ed** -t
detoxi|cate ˌdiːˈtɒk.sɪ|.keɪt, dɪ-, -sə-, US -ˈtɑːk- **-cates** -keɪts **-cating** -keɪ.tɪŋ, US -keɪ.t̬ɪŋ **-cated** -keɪ.tɪd, US -keɪ.t̬ɪd
detoxification diːˌtɒk.sɪ.fɪˈkeɪ.ʃən, dɪ-, -sə-, -fəˈ-; ˌdiː.tɒk-, US diːˌtɑːk-
detoxi|fy ˌdiːˈtɒk.sɪ|.faɪ, dɪ-, -sə-, US ˌdiːˈtɑːk- **-fies** -faɪz **-fying** -faɪ.ɪŋ **-fied** -faɪd
detract dɪˈtrækt, də-, US dɪ- **-s** -s **-ing/ly** -ɪŋ/li **-ed** -ɪd
detraction dɪˈtræk.ʃən, də-, US dɪ- **-s** -z
detract|ive dɪˈtræk.t|ɪv, də-, US dɪ- **-ory** -ər.i
detractor dɪˈtræk.təʳ, də-, US dɪˈtræk.tɚ **-s** -z
detrain ˌdiːˈtreɪn **-s** -z **-ing** -ɪŋ **-ed** -d
detriment ˈdet.rɪ.mənt, -rə- **-s** -s
detrimental ˌdet.rɪˈmen.təl, -rəˈ-, US -t̬əl
detrition dɪˈtrɪʃ.ən, də-, US dɪ-
detritus dɪˈtraɪ.təs, də-, US dɪˈtraɪ.t̬əs
Detroit dəˈtrɔɪt, dɪ-
de trop dəˈtrəʊ, US -troʊ
detrun|cate ˌdiːˈtrʌŋ|.keɪt, ˈ---, US ˌdiːˈtrʌŋ- **-cates** -keɪts **-cating** -keɪ.tɪŋ, US -keɪ.t̬ɪŋ **-cated** -keɪ.tɪd, US -keɪ.t̬ɪd
detruncation ˌdiː.trʌŋˈkeɪ.ʃən **-s** -z
Dettol® ˈdet.ɒl, -əl, US -tɑːl, -t̬əl
Dettori detˈɔː.ri, US -ˈɔːr.i
detumescen|ce ˌdiː.tʃuːˈmes.ən|ts, -tjuːˈ-, -tʃʊˈ-, -tjʊˈ-, US -tuːˈ-, -tjuːˈ- **-t** -t
Deucalion djuːˈkeɪ.li.ən, US duː-, djuː-
deuc|e dʒuːs, djuːs, US duːs, djuːs **-es** -ɪz
deuc|ed dʒuːs|t, djuːs|t; ˈdʒuː.s|ɪd, ˈdjuː-, US ˈduː.s|ɪd, ˈdjuː-; US duːs|t, djuːs|t **-edly** -ɪd.li
deus ex machina ˌdeɪ.əs.eksˈmɑː.k.ɪ.nə, -ˈmæk-, ˌdiː-, -ʊs-
deuterium dʒuːˈtɪə.ri.əm, djuː-, US duːˈtɪr.i-, djuː-
deuteronomic ˌdʒuː.tər.əˈnɒm.ɪk, ˌdjuː-, US ˌduː.t̬ɚ.əˈnɑː.mɪk, ˌdjuː-
Deuteronomy ˌdʒuː.təˈrɒn.ə.mi, ˌdjuː-, US ˌduː.t̬əˈrɑː.nə-, ˌdjuː-
Deutsche Mark ˌdɔɪ.tʃəˈmɑːk, US -ˈmɑːrk **-s** -s
deutschmark, D~ ˈdɔɪtʃ.mɑːk, US -mɑːrk **-s** -s
deutzia ˈdjuːt.si.ə, ˈdɔɪt-, US ˈduːt-, ˈdjuːt- **-s** -z
deux chevaux ˌdɜː.ʃəˈvəʊ, -ʃɪˈ-, US -ˈvoʊ
deva ˈdeɪ.və, ˈdiː.və **-s** -z
de Valera də.vəˈleə.rə, -ˈlɪə-; ˌdev.əˈ-, US -ˈler.ə, -ˈlɪr-
de Valois dəˈvæl.wɑː
devaluation ˌdiː.væl.juˈeɪ.ʃən; dɪˌvæl-, US ˌdiː.væl- **-s** -z
devalu|e ˌdiːˈvæl.juː, dɪ- **-es** -z **-ing** -ɪŋ **-ed** -d
Devanagari ˌdeɪ.vəˈnɑː.gər.i, ˌdev.əˈ-
Devant dəˈvænt, dɪ-
deva|state ˈdev.ə|.steɪt **-states** -steɪts **-stating/ly** -steɪ.tɪŋ/li, US -steɪ.t̬ɪŋ/li **-stated** -steɪ.tɪd, US -steɪ.t̬ɪd
devastation ˌdev.əˈsteɪ.ʃən **-s** -z
develop dɪˈvel.əp, də-, US dɪ- **-s** -s **-ing** -ɪŋ **-ed** -t **deˌveloping ˈcountry**
developer dɪˈvel.ə.pəʳ, də-, US -pɚ **-s** -z
development dɪˈvel.əp.mənt, də- **-s** -s
developmental dɪˌvel.əpˈmen.təl, də-, US -t̬əl **-ly** -li
Devenish ˈdev.ən.ɪʃ
Deventer ˈdev.ən.təʳ, US -tɚ
De Vere dəˈvɪəʳ, dɪ-, US -ˈvɪr
Devereux ˈdev.ə.ruː, -ruːks, -rɜː, -rəʊ, -reks, ˈ-ər.ə, US -ə.ruː, -rɜː, -rə, -uːks
Deveron ˈdev.ə.rən, US -ɚ.ən
Devers ˈdiː.vəz, ˈdev.əz, US ˈdiː.vɚz, ˈdev.ɚz
Devi ˈdeɪ.vi
devian|ce ˈdiː.vi.ənt|s **-cy** -si
deviant ˈdiː.vi.ənt **-s** -s
devi|ate ˈdiː.vi|.eɪt **-ates** -eɪts **-ating** -eɪ.tɪŋ, US -eɪ.t̬ɪŋ **-ated** -eɪ.tɪd, US -eɪ.t̬ɪd **-ator/s** -eɪ.təʳ/z, US -eɪ.t̬ɚ/z
deviation ˌdiː.viˈeɪ.ʃən **-s** -z
deviation|ism ˌdiː.viˈeɪ.ʃən|.ɪ.zəm **-ist/s** -ɪst/s
devic|e dɪˈvaɪs, də-, US dɪ- **-es** -ɪz **leave someone to their ˌown deˈvices**
devil ˈdev.əl **-s** -z **-(l)ing** -ɪŋ **-(l)ed** -d **ˌdevil's ˈadvocate; ˌdevil's ˈfood cake, ˈdevil's food ˌcake** US **ˈdevil's food ˌcake; between the ˌdevil and the ˌdeep blue ˈsea; give the ˌdevil his ˈdue; ˌtalk of the ˈdevil**
devilfish ˈdev.əl.fɪʃ **-es** -ɪz
devilish ˈdev.əl.ɪʃ **-ly** -li **-ness** -nəs, -nɪs
devil-may-care ˌdev.əl.meɪˈkeəʳ, US -ˈker *stress shift:* **ˌdevil-may-care ˈattitude**
devilment ˈdev.əl.mənt **-s** -s
devilr|y ˈdev.əl.r|i **-ies** -iz
Devine dəˈvaɪn, dɪ-
devious ˈdiː.vi.əs **-ly** -li **-ness** -nəs, -nɪs
devis|e dɪˈvaɪz, də-, US dɪ- **-es** -ɪz **-ing** -ɪŋ **-ed** -d **-er/s** -əʳ/z, US -ɚ/z **-able** -ə.bəl
devisee dɪˌvaɪˈziː, də-; ˌdev.ɪˈ-, US dɪˌvaɪˈ-; US ˌdev.əˈ- **-s** -z
devisor dɪˈvaɪ.zəʳ, də-; dəˌvaɪˈzɔːʳ, dɪ-; ˌdev.aɪˈ-, US dɪˈvaɪ.zɚ; US ˌdev.əˈzɔːr **-s** -z
devitalization, -isa- diːˌvaɪ.təl.aɪˈzeɪ.ʃən, ˌdiː.vaɪ-, -ɪˈ-, US diːˌvaɪ.t̬əl.əˈ-
devitaliz|e, -is|e ˌdiːˈvaɪ.təl.aɪz, US -t̬əl- **-es** -ɪz **-ing** -ɪŋ **-ed** -d
Devizes dɪˈvaɪ.zɪz, də-, -zəz
Devlin ˈdev.lɪn, -lən
devocalization, -isa- diːˌvəʊ.kəl.aɪˈzeɪ.ʃən, ˌdiː.vəʊ-, -ɪˈ-, US diːˌvoʊ.kəl.əˈ- **-s** -z
devocaliz|e, -is|e ˌdiːˈvəʊ.kəl.aɪz, US -ˈvoʊ- **-es** -ɪz **-ing** -ɪŋ **-ed** -d
devoic|e ˌdiːˈvɔɪs **-es** -ɪz **-ing** -ɪŋ **-ed** -t
devoid dɪˈvɔɪd, də-, US dɪ-
devolution ˌdiː.vəˈluː.ʃən, ˌdev.əˈ-, -ˈljuː-, US ˌdev.əˈluː-, ˌdiː.vəˈ- **-s** -z
devolv|e dɪˈvɒlv, də-, US dɪˈvɑːlv **-es** -z **-ing** -ɪŋ **-ed** -d
Devon ˈdev.ən **-shire** -ʃəʳ, -ʃɪəʳ, US -ʃɚ, -ʃɪr
Devonian devˈəʊ.ni.ən, dɪˈvəʊ-, də-, US dɪˈvoʊ- **-s** -z
Devonport ˈdev.ən.pɔːt, -əm-, US -ən.pɔːrt
de|vote dɪ|ˈvəʊt, də-, US dɪ|ˈvoʊt **-votes** -vəʊts, US -voʊts **-voting** -vəʊ.tɪŋ, US -voʊ.t̬ɪŋ **-voted** -vəʊ.tɪd, US -voʊ.t̬ɪd
devoted dɪˈvəʊ.tɪd, də-, US dɪˈvoʊ.t̬ɪd **-ly** -li **-ness** -nəs, -nɪs
devotee ˌdev.əʊˈtiː, US -əˈtiː, -ˈteɪ, -oʊ- **-s** -z
devotion dɪˈvəʊ.ʃən, də-, US dɪˈvoʊ- **-s** -z
devotional dɪˈvəʊ.ʃən.əl, də-, US dɪˈvoʊ- **-ly** -i
devour dɪˈvaʊ.əʳ, -ˈvaʊəʳ, də-, US dɪˈvaʊ.ɚ **-s** -z **-ing** -ɪŋ **-ed** -d **-er/s** -əʳ/z, US -ɚ/z
de|vout dɪ|ˈvaʊt, də-, US dɪ- **-vouter** -ˈvaʊ.təʳ, US -ˈvaʊ.t̬ɚ **-voutest** -ˈvaʊ.tɪst, -təst, US -ˈvaʊ.t̬ɪst, -t̬əst **-voutly** -ˈvaʊt.li **-voutness** -ˈvaʊt.nəs, -nɪs
dew dʒuː, djuː, US duː, djuː **-s** -z **ˈdew ˌpoint; ˈdew ˌpond**
Dewali dɪˈwɑː.li, US də-, dɪ-
Dewar ˈdjuː.əʳ, ˈdʒuː-; djʊəʳ, dʒʊəʳ, US ˈduː.ɚ, ˈdjuː-
dewberr|y ˈdʒuː.bər|.i, ˈdjuː-, -ber-, US ˈduː.ber-, ˈdjuː- **-ies** -iz
dewclaw ˈdʒuː.klɔː, ˈdjuː-, US ˈduː.klɑː, ˈdjuː-, -klɔː **-s** -z
dewdrop ˈdʒuː.drɒp, ˈdjuː-, US ˈduː.drɑːp, ˈdjuː- **-s** -s
D'Ewes djuːz, dʒuːz, US duːz, djuːz
De Wet dəˈvet, -ˈwet
Dewey ˈdjuː.i, ˈdʒuː-, US ˈduː-, ˈdjuː-
Dewhurst ˈdjuː.hɜːst, ˈdʒuː-, US ˈduː.hɝːst, ˈdjuː-

Dewi ˈde.wi, ˈdjuː.i

Note: This is a Welsh name. The anglicized pronunciation is /ˈdjuː.i/.

dewlap ˈdʒuː.læp, ˈdjuː-, (US) ˈduː-, ˈdjuː- **-s** -s
Dewsbury ˈdʒuːz.bᵊr.i, ˈdjuːz-, (US) ˈduːz.ber-, ˈdjuːz-, -bɚ-
dew|y ˈdʒuː|.i, ˈdjuː-, (US) ˈduː-, ˈdjuː- **-iness** -ɪ.nəs, -ɪ.nɪs
Dexedrine® ˈdek.sɪ.driːn, -sə-
dexter, D~ ˈdek.stəʳ, (US) -stɚ
dexterity dekˈster.ə.ti, -ɪ.ti, (US) -ə.t̬i
dexterous ˈdek.stᵊr.əs **-ly** -li **-ness** -nəs, -nɪs
dextrose ˈdek.strəʊs, -strəʊz, (US) -stroʊs
dextrous ˈdek.strəs **-ly** -li **-ness** -nəs, -nɪs
De Zoete dəˈzuːt
de Zoete Wedd dəˌzuːtˈwed
dg (abbrev. for **decigram**) ˈdes.ɪ.græm
Dhaka ˈdæk.ə, (US) ˈdæk.ə, ˈdɑː.kɑː
dhal dɑːl
dharma ˈdɑː.mə, (US) ˈdɑːr-
dhobi ˈdəʊ.bi, (US) ˈdoʊ- **-es** -z
dhoti ˈdəʊ.ti, (US) ˈdoʊ.t̬i **-es** -z
dhow daʊ **-s** -z
DHS ˌdiː.eɪtʃˈes
DHSS ˌdiː.eɪtʃ.esˈes
dhurrie ˈdʌr.i, (US) ˈdɜː- **-s** -z
Di daɪ
di- daɪ, dɪ

Note: Prefix. Where the meaning is **two**, it may carry either primary or secondary stress and is pronounced /daɪ-/, e.g. **digraph** /ˈdaɪ.grɑːf/ (US) /-græf/, **diglossia** /ˌdaɪˈglɒs.i.ə/ (US) /-ˈglɑː.si-/. In other instances, it may be pronounced /daɪ-/, /dɪ-/, or occasionally /də-/, and is not normally stressed in verbs and adjectives, e.g. **digest** /daɪˈdʒest/, **diverse** /daɪˈvɜːs/ (US) /dɪˈvɜːrs/. In nouns, however, it may carry stress, e.g. **digest** /ˈdaɪ.dʒest/. There are exceptions; see individual entries.

dia- ˈdaɪ.ə; daɪˈæ

Note: Prefix. Normally carries primary or secondary stress on the first syllable, e.g. **diadem** /ˈdaɪ.ə.dem/, **diabolic** /ˌdaɪ.əˈbɒl.ɪk/ (US) /-ˈbɑː.lɪk/, or primary stress on the second syllable, e.g. **diagonal** /daɪˈæg.ᵊn.ᵊl/.

diabetes ˌdaɪ.əˈbiː.tiːz, -tɪz, -tɪs, (US) -t̬əs, -t̬iːz
diabetic ˌdaɪ.əˈbet.ɪk, (US) -ˈbet̬- **-s** -s
diabolic ˌdaɪ.əˈbɒl.ɪk, (US) -ˈbɑː.lɪk **-al** -ᵊl **-ally** -ᵊl.i, -li
diabolism daɪˈæb.ᵊl.ɪ.zᵊm
diaboliz|e, -is|e daɪˈæb.ᵊl.aɪz, (US) -ə.laɪz **-es** -ɪz **-ing** -ɪŋ **-ed** -d
diabolo diˈæb.ᵊl.əʊ, daɪ-, -ɑː.bᵊl-, (US) daɪˈæb.ə.loʊ
diachronic ˌdaɪ.əˈkrɒn.ɪk, (US) -ˈkrɑː.nɪk **-ally** -ᵊl.i, -li
diacid daɪˈæs.ɪd **-s** -z
diaconal daɪˈæk.ə.nᵊl, di-
diaconate daɪˈæk.ə.neɪt, di-, -nɪt, -nət **-s** -s
diacritic ˌdaɪ.əˈkrɪt.ɪk, (US) -ˈkrɪt̬- **-s** -s **-al** -ᵊl
diadem ˈdaɪ.ə.dem, -dəm **-s** -z
diaeres|is daɪˈer.ə.s|ɪs, -ˈɪr.ə-, -ˈɪə.rə-, -rɪ-, (US) -ˈer.ə-, -ˈɪr- **-es** -iːz
Diaghilev diˈæg.ɪ.lef, ˈ-ə-, (US) -ˈɑː.gə.lef, -gɪ-
diagnos|e ˈdaɪ.əg.nəʊz, ˌ--ˈ-, (US) ˌdaɪ.əgˈnoʊs, -ˈnoʊz, ˈ--- **-es** -ɪz **-ing** -ɪŋ **-ed** -d
diagnos|is ˌdaɪ.əgˈnəʊ.s|ɪs, (US) -ˈnoʊ- **-es** -iːz
diagnostic ˌdaɪ.əgˈnɒs.tɪk, (US) -ˈnɑː.stɪk **-s** -s
diagnostician ˌdaɪ.əg.nɒsˈtɪʃ.ᵊn, (US) -nɑːˈstɪʃ- **-s** -z
diagonal daɪˈæg.ᵊn.ᵊl **-s** -z **-ly** -i
diagram ˈdaɪ.ə.græm **-s** -z
diagrammatic ˌdaɪ.ə.grəˈmæt.ɪk, (US) -ˈmæt̬- **-al** -ᵊl **-ally** -ᵊl.i, -li
dial daɪəl, ˈdaɪ.əl, (US) daɪəl **-s** -z **-(l)ing** -ɪŋ **-(l)ed** -d ˈ**dialling** ˌ**code**; ˈ**dialling** ˌ**tone**; ˈ**dial** ˌ**tone**
dialect ˈdaɪ.ə.lekt **-s** -s
dialectal ˌdaɪ.əˈlek.tᵊl
dialectic ˌdaɪ.əˈlek.tɪk **-s** -s **-al** -ᵊl **-ally** -ᵊl.i, -li
dialectician ˌdaɪ.ə.lekˈtɪʃ.ᵊn **-s** -z
dialectolog|y ˌdaɪ.ə.lekˈtɒl.ə.dʒ|i, (US) -ˈtɑː.lə- **-ist/s** -ɪst/s
diallage *figure of speech:* daɪˈæl.ə.gi, -dʒi *mineral:* ˈdaɪ.ə.lɪdʒ
dialog|ism daɪˈæl.ə.dʒ|ɪ.zᵊm **-ist/s** -ɪst/s
dialogue, dialog ˈdaɪ.ə.lɒg, (US) -lɑːg **-s** -z
dial-up ˈdaɪəl.ʌp
dialys|is daɪˈæl.ə.s|ɪs, ˈ-ɪ- **-es** -iːz
diamagnetic ˌdaɪ.ə.mægˈnet.ɪk, -məgˈ-, (US) -mægˈnet̬- **-s** -s **-ally** -ᵊl.i, -li
diamagnetism ˌdaɪ.əˈmæg.nə.tɪ.zᵊm, -nɪ-
diamanté ˌdiː.əˈmɑ̃ːn.teɪ, ˌdaɪ.əˈ-, -ˈmæn-, -ti, (US) ˌdiː.ə.mɑːnˈteɪ, -ˈmɑːn.teɪ
diameter daɪˈæm.ɪ.təʳ, ˈ-ə-, (US) -ə.t̬ɚ **-s** -z
diametral daɪˈæm.ɪ.trəl, ˈ-ə- **-ly** -i
diametric ˌdaɪ.əˈmet.rɪk **-al** -ᵊl **-ally** -ᵊl.i, -li
diamond, D~ ˈdaɪə.mənd, (US) ˈdaɪ.ə-, ˈdaɪ- **-s** -z
diamondback ˈdaɪə.mənd.bæk, (US) ˈdaɪ.ə-, ˈdaɪ- **-s** -s
diamorphine ˌdaɪ.əˈmɔː.fiːn, (US) -ˈmɔːr-
Diana daɪˈæn.ə
Diane daɪˈæn, di-
dianthus daɪˈænt.θəs **-es** -ɪz
diapason ˌdaɪ.əˈpeɪ.zᵊn, -sᵊn **-s** -z
diap|er ˈdaɪə.p|əʳ, ˈdaɪ.ə-, (US) -p|ɚ **-ers** -əz, (US) -ɚz **-ering** -ᵊr.ɪŋ **-ered** -əd, (US) -ɚd
diaphanous daɪˈæf.ᵊn.əs
diaphone ˈdaɪ.ə.fəʊn, (US) -foʊn **-s** -z
diaphragm ˈdaɪ.ə.fræm, -frəm, (US) -fræm **-s** -z
diaphragmatic ˌdaɪ.ə.frægˈmæt.ɪk, -frəgˈ-, (US) -ˈmæt̬-
diapositive ˌdaɪ.əˈpɒz.ɪ.tɪv, ˈ-ə-, (US) -ˈpɑː.zə.t̬ɪv **-s** -z
diarch|y ˈdaɪ.ɑː.k|i, (US) -ɑːr- **-ies** -iz
diarist ˈdaɪ.ə.rɪst **-s** -s
Diarmuid ˈdeə.mʊd, (US) ˈder-
diarrh(o)ea ˌdaɪ.əˈrɪə, ˌdaɪə-, (US) -ˈriː.ə
diar|y ˈdaɪə.r|i **-ies** -iz
diaspora, D~ daɪˈæs.pᵊr.ə
diastase ˈdaɪ.ə.steɪs, -steɪz
diastas|is daɪˈæs.tə.s|ɪs, ˌdaɪ.əˈsteɪ.s|ɪs **-es** -iːz
diastole daɪˈæs.tᵊl.i **-s** -z
diastolic ˌdaɪ.əˈstɒl.ɪk, (US) -ˈstɑː.lɪk
diasystem ˈdaɪ.əˌsɪs.təm
diatherm|ic ˌdaɪ.əˈθɜː.m|ɪk, (US) -ˈθɝː- **-ous** -əs
diatom ˈdaɪ.ə.təm, -tɒm, (US) -tɑːm **-s** -z
diatomaceous ˌdaɪ.ə.təˈmeɪ.ʃəs
diatomic ˌdaɪ.əˈtɒm.ɪk, (US) -ˈtɑː.mɪk
diatomite daɪˈæt.ə.maɪt, (US) -ˈæt̬-
diatonic ˌdaɪ.əˈtɒn.ɪk, (US) -ˈtɑː.nɪk **-ally** -ᵊl.i, -li
diatribe ˈdaɪ.ə.traɪb **-s** -z
diatype ˈdaɪ.ə.taɪp
Diaz ˈdiː.əs, -æs, -æθ, (US) -ɑːs, -ɑːz, -əs, -æz
diazepam daɪˈæz.ə.pæm, -ˈeɪ.zə-, -zɪ-, (US) -ˈæz.ə-
dib dɪb **-s** -z **-bing** -ɪŋ **-bed** -d **-ber/s** -əʳ/z, (US) -ɚ/z
dibasic daɪˈbeɪ.sɪk
dibasicity ˌdaɪ.beɪˈsɪs.ə.ti, -ɪ.ti, (US) -ə.t̬i
Dibb dɪb
dibbl|e ˈdɪb.ᵊl **-es** -z **-ing** -ɪŋ, ˈdɪb.lɪŋ **-ed** -d **-er/s** -əʳ/z, ˈ-ləʳ/z, (US) ˈ-ᵊl.ɚ/z, ˈ-lɚ/z
Dibdin ˈdɪb.dɪn
dibs dɪbz
DiCaprio dɪˈkæp.ri.əʊ, diːˈ-, (US) -oʊ
dicast ˈdɪk.æst, (US) ˈdɪk.æst, ˈdaɪ.kæst **-s** -s
dice (plural of **die**) daɪs
dic|e **v** daɪs **-es** -ɪz **-ing** -ɪŋ **-ed** -t
dicey, D~ ˈdaɪ.si
dichloride ˌdaɪˈklɔː.raɪd, (US) -ˈklɔːr.aɪd **-s** -z
dichotomous daɪˈkɒt.ə.məs, dɪ-, (US) -ˈkɑː.t̬ə-
dichotom|y daɪˈkɒt.ə.m|i, dɪ-, (US) -ˈkɑː.t̬ə- **-ies** -iz
dichromate ˌdaɪˈkrəʊ.meɪt, (US) -ˈkroʊ- **-s** -s
dick, D~ dɪk
dickens, D~ ˈdɪk.ɪnz
Dickensian dɪˈken.zi.ən, də-, -si-
dick|er, D~ ˈdɪk|.əʳ, (US) -ɚ **-ers** -əz, (US) -ɚz **-ering** -ᵊr.ɪŋ **-ered** -əd, (US) -ɚd
Dickerson ˈdɪk.ə.sᵊn, (US) ˈ-ɚ-
dickey, D~ ˈdɪk.i **-s** -z ˈ**dickey** ˌ**bow**
dickhead ˈdɪk.hed **-s** -z
Dickie ˈdɪk.i
Dickins ˈdɪk.ɪnz

Dickinson ˈdɪk.ɪn.sᵊn
Dickson ˈdɪk.sᵊn
dick|y, D~ ˈdɪk|.i **-ies** -iz
dickybird ˈdɪk.i.bɜːd, (US) -bɝːd **-s** -z
dicotyledon ˌdaɪ.kɒt.ɪˈliː.dᵊn, -ᵊlˈiː-, (US) -kɑː.t̬ᵊlˈiː- **-s** -z
Dictaphone® ˈdɪk.tə.fəʊn, (US) -foʊn **-s** -z
dictate n ˈdɪk.teɪt **-s** -s
dic|tate v dɪk|ˈteɪt, (US) ˈdɪk|.teɪt, -|ˈ- **-tates** -ˈteɪts, (US) -teɪts, -ˈteɪts **-tating** -ˈteɪ.tɪŋ, (US) -teɪ.t̬ɪŋ, -ˈteɪ- **-tated** -ˈteɪ.tɪd, (US) -teɪ.t̬ɪd, -ˈteɪ-
dictation dɪkˈteɪ.ʃᵊn **-s** -z
dictator dɪkˈteɪ.təʳ, (US) ˈdɪk.teɪ.t̬ɚ, -ˈ-- **-s** -z
dictatorial ˌdɪk.təˈtɔː.ri.əl, (US) -ˈtɔːr.i- **-ly** -i
dictatorship dɪkˈteɪ.tə.ʃɪp, (US) -t̬ɚ- **-s** -s
diction ˈdɪk.ʃᵊn
dictionar|y ˈdɪk.ʃᵊn.ᵊr|.i, -ʃᵊn.r|i, (US) -er|.i **-ies** -iz
dict|um ˈdɪk.t|əm **-a** -ə **-ums** -əmz
did (from **do**) dɪd
Didache ˈdɪd.ə.ki
didact ˈdaɪ.dækt **-s** -s
didactic dɪˈdæk.tɪk, daɪ-, də-, (US) daɪ-, dɪ- **-al** -ᵊl **-ally** -ᵊl.i, -li
didacticism dɪˈdæk.tɪ.sɪ.zᵊm, daɪ-, də-, (US) daɪ-, dɪ-, -tə-
Didcot ˈdɪd.kət, -kɒt, (US) -kɑːt
diddl|e ˈdɪd.ᵊl **-es** -z **-ing** -ɪŋ, ˈ-lɪŋ **-ed** -d **-er/s** -əʳ/z, ˈ-ləʳ/z, (US) ˈ-ᵊl.ɚ/z, ˈ-lɚ/z
diddly ˈdɪd.ᵊl.i, ˈ-li
diddlysquat ˌdɪd.ᵊl.iˈskwɒt, -liˈ-, (US) -ˈskwɑːt
diddums ˈdɪd.əmz
Diderot ˈdiː.də.rəʊ, (US) ˌdiː.dəˈroʊ
didgeridoo ˌdɪdʒ.ᵊr.iˈduː **-s** -z
Didier ˈdɪd.i.eɪ, ˈdiː.di-
didn't (= **did not**) ˈdɪd.ᵊnt
Dido ˈdaɪ.dəʊ, (US) -doʊ
didst dɪdst
Didymus ˈdɪd.ɪ.məs, ˈ-ə-
die n *stamp:* daɪ **-s** -z *cube:* daɪ **dice** daɪs
die v daɪ **-s** -z **dying** ˈdaɪ.ɪŋ **died** daɪd
die-casting ˈdaɪˌkɑː.stɪŋ, (US) -ˌkæs.tɪŋ
Diego diˈeɪ.gəʊ, (US) -goʊ
diehard ˈdaɪ.hɑːd, (US) -hɑːrd **-s** -z
dielectric ˌdaɪ.ɪˈlek.trɪk, -əˈ- **-s** -s
Dieppe diːˈep, di-
dieres|is daɪˈer.ə.s|ɪs, -ˈɪr-, -ˈɪə.rə-, -rɪ-, (US) -ˈer.ə- **-es** -iːz
dieretic ˌdaɪ.əˈret.ɪk, (US) -ˈret̬-
diesel ˈdiː.zᵊl, (US) -sᵊl, -zᵊl **-s** -z **ˈdiesel ˌengine**
dies irae ˌdiː.eɪzˈɪə.raɪ, -ezˈ-, -esˈ-, -reɪ, (US) -eɪzˈɪr.eɪ, -esˈ-
dies|is ˈdaɪ.ə.s|ɪs, ˈ-ɪ- **-es** -iːz
dies non ˌdaɪ.iːzˈnɒn, ˌdiː.eɪz-, (US) ˌdiː.eɪs.nɑːn, -es-; (US) ˌdiː.eɪzˈnɑːn, ˌdaɪ.iːzˈ- **-s** -z
diet daɪət, ˈdaɪ.ət, (US) ˈdaɪ.ət **-s** -s **-ing** -ɪŋ, (US) ˈdaɪ.ə.t̬ɪŋ **-ed** -ɪd, (US) ˈdaɪ.ə.t̬ɪd **-er/s** -əʳ/z, (US) -ɚ/z
dietar|y ˈdaɪ.ə.tᵊr|.i, ˈdaɪ.ɪ-, -tr|i, (US) ˈdaɪ.ə.ter|- **-ies** -iz ˌ**dietary ˈfibre**
dietetic ˌdaɪ.əˈtet.ɪk, ˌdaɪ.ɪˈ-, (US) -ˈtet̬- **-s** -s **-al** -ᵊl **-ally** -ᵊl.i, -li
dietician, dietitian ˌdaɪ.əˈtɪʃ.ᵊn, ˌdaɪ.ɪˈ-, (US) ˌdaɪ.əˈ- **-s** -z
Dietrich ˈdiː.trɪk, -trɪx, -trɪʃ
Dieu et mon droit ˌdjɜː.eɪ.mɔ̃ːnˈdrwɑː
diff|er ˈdɪf|.əʳ, (US) -ɚ **-ers** -əz, (US) -ɚz **-ering** -ᵊr.ɪŋ **-ered** -əd, (US) -ɚd
differenc|e ˈdɪf.ᵊr.ᵊnts, ˈ-rᵊnts **-es** -ɪz
different ˈdɪf.ᵊr.ᵊnt, ˈ-rᵊnt **-ly** -li
differenti|a ˌdɪf.ᵊˈren.tʃi|.ə, ˈ-tʃ|ə, (US) -ˈrent.ʃi|.ə, ˈ-ʃə **-ae** -iː
differentiable ˌdɪf.ᵊˈren.tʃi.ə.bᵊl, ˈ-tʃə-, (US) -ˈrent.ʃi.ə-, ˈ-ʃə-
differential ˌdɪf.ᵊˈren.tʃᵊl, (US) -ˈrent.ʃᵊl **-s** -z **-ly** -i
differenti|ate ˌdɪf.ᵊˈren.tʃi|.eɪt, (US) -ˈrent.ʃi- **-ates** -eɪts **-ating** -eɪ.tɪŋ, (US) -eɪ.t̬ɪŋ **-ated** -eɪ.tɪd, (US) -eɪ.t̬ɪd
differentiation ˌdɪf.ᵊr.en.tʃiˈeɪ.ʃᵊn, -ent.siˈ-, (US) -ə.rent.ʃiˈ-, -siˈ- **-s** -z
difficult ˈdɪf.ɪ.kᵊlt, ˈ-ə-
difficult|y ˈdɪf.ɪ.kᵊl.t|i, ˈ-ə- **-ies** -iz
diffidence ˈdɪf.ɪ.dᵊnts
diffident ˈdɪf.ɪ.dᵊnt **-ly** -li
diffract dɪˈfrækt **-s** -s **-ing** -ɪŋ **-ed** -ɪd
diffraction dɪˈfræk.ʃᵊn
diffuse adj dɪˈfjuːs **-ly** -li **-ness** -nəs, -nɪs
diffus|e v dɪˈfjuːz **-es** -ɪz **-ing** -ɪŋ **-ed** -d **-edly** -ɪd.li, -d.li **-edness** -ɪd.nəs, -d.nəs, -nɪs **-er/s** -əʳ/z, (US) -ɚ/z
diffusibility dɪˌfjuː.zəˈbɪl.ə.ti, -zɪˈ-, -ɪ.ti, (US) -zəˈbɪl.ə.t̬i
diffusible dɪˈfjuː.zə.bᵊl, -zɪ-
diffusion dɪˈfjuː.ʒᵊn
diffusive dɪˈfjuː.sɪv **-ly** -li **-ness** -nəs, -nɪs
dig n, v dɪg **-s** -z **-ging** -ɪŋ **-ged** -d **dug** dʌg
dig. (in phrase **infra dig.**) dɪg
digamma daɪˈgæm.ə, ˈ--- **-s** -z
Digby ˈdɪg.bi
digest n ˈdaɪ.dʒest **-s** -s
digest v daɪˈdʒest, dɪ-, də- **-s** -s **-ing** -ɪŋ **-ed** -ɪd
digestibility daɪˌdʒes.təˈbɪl.ə.ti, dɪ-, də-, -tɪˈ-, -ɪ.ti, (US) -ə.t̬i
digestible daɪˈdʒes.tə.bᵊl, dɪ-, də-, -tɪ-
digestif ˌdiː.ʒesˈtɪf **-s** -s
digestion daɪˈdʒes.tʃᵊn, dɪ-, də-, -ˈdʒeʃ- **-s** -z
digestive daɪˈdʒes.tɪv, dɪ-, də- **-s** -z **-ly** -li **-ness** -nəs, -nɪs **diˌgestive ˈbiscuit, diˈgestive ˌbiscuit**
digger ˈdɪg.əʳ, (US) -ɚ **-s** -z
Digges dɪgz
diggings ˈdɪg.ɪŋz
Diggle ˈdɪg.ᵊl **-s** -z
Diggory ˈdɪg.ᵊr.i
dight daɪt
Dighton ˈdaɪ.tᵊn
Digibox® ˈdɪdʒ.ɪ.bɒks, (US) -bɑːks **-es** -ɪz
digit ˈdɪdʒ.ɪt **-s** -s
digital ˈdɪdʒ.ɪ.tᵊl, ˈ-ə-, (US) -t̬ᵊl **-s** -z **-ly** -li
digitalin ˌdɪdʒ.ɪˈteɪ.lɪn, -əˈ-, -ˈtɑː-, (US) -ˈtæl.ɪn, -ˈteɪ.lɪn
digitalis ˌdɪdʒ.ɪˈteɪ.lɪs, -əˈ-, -ˈtɑː-, (US) -ˈtæl.is, -ˈteɪ.lɪs
digitalization, -isa- ˌdɪdʒ.ɪ.tᵊl.aɪˈzeɪ.ʃᵊn, ˌ-ə-, -ɪˈ-, (US) -t̬ᵊl.əˈ-
digitaliz|e, -is|e ˈdɪdʒ.ɪ.tᵊl.aɪz, ˈ-ə-, (US) -t̬ə.laɪz **-es** -ɪz **-ing** -ɪŋ **-ed** -d
digitization, -isa- ˌdɪdʒ.ɪ.taɪˈzeɪ.ʃᵊn, ˌ-ə-, -tɪˈ-, (US) -t̬əˈ-
digitiz|e, -is|e ˈdɪdʒ.ɪ.taɪz, ˈ-ə- **-es** -ɪz **-ing** -ɪŋ **-ed** -d
digloss|ia ˌdaɪˈglɒs|.i.ə, (US) -ˈglɑː.s|i- **-ic** -ɪk
digni|fy ˈdɪg.nɪ|.faɪ, -nə- **-fies** -faɪz **-fying** -faɪ.ɪŋ **-fied** -faɪd
dignitar|y ˈdɪg.nɪ.tᵊr|.i, -nə-, (US) -nə.ter- **-ies** -iz
dignit|y ˈdɪg.nə.t|i, -nɪ-, (US) -t̬|i **-ies** -iz
digraph ˈdaɪ.grɑːf, (US) -græf **-s** -s
digress daɪˈgres, dɪ- **-es** -ɪz **-ing** -ɪŋ **-ed** -t
digression daɪˈgreʃ.ᵊn, dɪ- **-s** -z
digressive daɪˈgres.ɪv, dɪ- **-ly** -li **-ness** -nəs, -nɪs
digs dɪgz
Dijon ˈdiː.ʒɔ̃ːŋ, (US) diːˈʒoʊn, -ˈʒɔːn
dik|e daɪk **-es** -s **-ing** -ɪŋ **-ed** -t
diktat ˈdɪk.tæt, -tɑːt, (US) dɪkˈtɑːt, ˈ-- **-s** -s
dilapi|date dɪˈlæp.ɪ|.deɪt, də-, ˈ-ə- **-dates** -deɪts **-dating** -deɪ.tɪŋ, (US) -deɪ.t̬ɪŋ **-dated** -deɪ.tɪd, (US) -deɪ.t̬ɪd
dilapidation dɪˌlæp.ɪˈdeɪ.ʃᵊn, də-, -əˈ- **-s** -z
dilatability daɪˌleɪ.təˈbɪl.ə.ti, dɪ-, də-, -ɪ.ti, (US) -t̬əˈbɪl.ə.t̬i
dilatation ˌdɪl.əˈteɪ.ʃᵊn, ˌdaɪ-, -leɪˈ-, (US) ˌdɪl.əˈteɪ.ʃᵊn; (US) ˈdaɪ.lə.teɪ- **-s** -z
dila|te daɪˈleɪ|t, dɪ-, də-, (US) ˈdaɪ.leɪ|t; (US) -ˈ-, də- **-tes** -ts **-ting** -tɪŋ, (US) -t̬ɪŋ **-ted** -tɪd, (US) -t̬ɪd **-ter/s** -təʳ/z, (US) -t̬ɚ/z **-table** -tə.bᵊl, (US) -t̬ə.bᵊl
dilation daɪˈleɪ.ʃᵊn, dɪ-, də- **-s** -z
dilator daɪˈleɪ.təʳ, dɪ-, də-, (US) -t̬ɚ **-s** -z
dilator|y ˈdɪl.ə.tᵊr|.i, -tr|i, (US) -tɔːr|.i **-ily** -ᵊl.i, -ɪ.li **-iness** -i.nəs, -i.nɪs
Dilbert ˈdɪl.bət, (US) -bɚt
dildo ˈdɪl.dəʊ, (US) -doʊ **-(e)s** -z
dilemma dɪˈlem.ə, daɪ-, də- **-s** -z
dilettante ˌdɪl.ɪˈtæn.ti, -əˈ-, -teɪ, (US) ˌdɪl.əˈtɑːnt, -ˈtænt, ˈ---; (US) ˌdɪl.əˈtæn.ti, -ˈtɑːn- **-s** -z
dilettanti (alternative plural of **dilettante**) ˌdɪl.ɪˈtæn.ti, -əˈ-, -teɪ, (US) ˌdɪl.əˈtɑːn.taɪ, -ˈtæn-, -ti
dilettantism ˌdɪl.ɪˈtæn.tɪ.zᵊm, -əˈ-, (US) -ˈtɑːn-, -ˈtæn-
Dili ˈdɪl.i
diligenc|e ˈdɪl.ɪ.dʒᵊnts, ˈ-ə-
diligent ˈdɪl.ɪ.dʒᵊnt, ˈ-ə- **-ly** -li
Dilke dɪlk **-s** -s
dill, D~ dɪl **-s** -z
Diller ˈdɪl.əʳ, (US) -ɚ
Dilley ˈdɪl.i

Dillinger ˈdɪl.ɪn.dʒəʳ, US -dʒɚ
Dillon ˈdɪl.ən
Dillwyn ˈdɪl.ɪn, ˈdɪl.wɪn
dill|y ˈdɪl|.i **-ies** -iz
dillydall|y ˈdɪl.iˌdæl|.i, ˌ--ˈ-- **-ies** -iz **-ying** -i.ɪŋ **-ied** -id
diluent ˈdɪl.ju.ənt **-s** -s
dilu|te daɪˈluː|t, dɪ-, -ˈljuː|t, US -ˈluː|t **-tes** -ts **-ting** -tɪŋ, US -t̬ɪŋ **-ted** -tɪd, US -t̬ɪd **-teness** -t.nəs, -t.nɪs
dilution daɪˈluː.ʃən, dɪ-, -ˈljuː-, US -ˈluː- **-s** -z
diluvi|al daɪˈluː.vi|.əl, dɪ-, -ˈljuː-, US dɪˈluː-, daɪ- **-an** -ən
diluvi|um daɪˈluː.vi|.əm, dɪ-, -ˈljuː-, US dɪˈluː-, daɪ- **-a** -ə
Dilwyn, Dilwen ˈdɪl.wɪn
Dilys ˈdɪl.ɪs
dim dɪm **-mer/s** -əʳ/z, US -ɚ/z **-mest** -ɪst, -əst **-ly** -li **-ness** -nəs, -nɪs **-s** -z **-ming** -ɪŋ **-med** -d
Di Maggio dɪˈmædʒ.i.əʊ, US -oʊ, dəˈmɑː.ʒi.oʊ
Dimbleby ˈdɪm.bəl.bi
dime daɪm **-s** -z
dimension ˌdaɪˈmen.tʃən, dɪ-, də-, US dɪˈment.ʃən, də-, ˌdaɪ- **-s** -z
dimensional ˌdaɪˈmen.tʃən.əl, dɪ-, də-, US dɪˈment.ʃən.əl, də-, ˌdaɪ-
dimeter ˈdɪm.ɪ.təʳ, ˈ-ə-, US -ə.t̬ɚ **-s** -z
diminish dɪˈmɪn.ɪʃ, də- **-es** -ɪz **-ing** -ɪŋ **-ed** -t **-able** -ə.bəl
diminuendo dɪˌmɪn.juˈen.dəʊ, də-, US -doʊ **-s** -z
diminution ˌdɪm.ɪˈnjuː.ʃən, US -əˈnuː-, -ˈnjuː- **-s** -z
diminutive dɪˈmɪn.jə.tɪv, də-, -jʊ-, US -jə.t̬ɪv **-ly** -li **-ness** -nəs, -nɪs
dimity ˈdɪm.ɪ.ti, -ə.ti, US -ə.t̬i, -ɪ.t̬i
dimmer ˈdɪm.əʳ, US -ɚ **-s** -z
Dimmesdale ˈdɪmz.deɪl
dimmish ˈdɪm.ɪʃ
Dimmock ˈdɪm.ək
dimorphism daɪˈmɔː.fɪ.zəm, US -ˈmɔːr-
dimorphous daɪˈmɔː.fəs, US -ˈmɔːr-
dimout ˈdɪm.aʊt **-s** -s
dimpl|e ˈdɪm.pəl **-es** -z **-ing** -ɪŋ, ˈdɪm.plɪŋ **-ed** -d
Dimplex® ˈdɪm.pleks
dimply ˈdɪm.pli
dim sum ˌdɪmˈsʊm, -ˈsʌm
dimwit ˈdɪm.wɪt **-s** -s
dim-witted ˌdɪmˈwɪt.ɪd, US ˈdɪmˌwɪt̬-, ˌ-ˈ-- **-ly** -li **-ness** -nəs, -nɪs *stress shift, British only:* **ˌdim-witted ˈidiot**
din dɪn **-s** -z **-ning** -ɪŋ **-ned** -d
Dina ˈdiː.nə, ˈdaɪ.nə
Dinah ˈdaɪ.nə
dinar ˈdiː.nɑːʳ, -ˈ-, US diːˈnɑːr, ˈ-- **-s** -z
Dinaric dɪˈnær.ɪk, də-, daɪ-, US -ˈner-, -ˈnær-
Dinas Powis ˌdiː.næsˈpaʊ.ɪs
din|e, D~ daɪn **-es** -z **-ing** -ɪŋ **-ed** -d **ˈdining ˌcar; ˈdining ˌroom; ˈdining ˌtable**
Dinefwr dɪˈnev.ʊəʳ, US -ʊr
diner ˈdaɪ.nəʳ, US -nɚ **-s** -z
Dinesen ˈdɪn.ɪ.sən, ˈ-ə-, US ˈdiː.nə-, ˈdɪn.ə-, ˈ-ɪ-, -sɪn
dinette daɪˈnet, dɪ-, US daɪ- **-s** -s
ding dɪŋ **-s** -z **-ing** -ɪŋ **-ed** -d
ding-a-ling ˈdɪŋ.ə.lɪŋ **-s** -z
dingbat ˈdɪŋ.bæt **-s** -s
ding-dong ˈdɪŋ.dɒŋ, US -dɑːŋ, -dɔːŋ
dingh|y ˈdɪŋ.g|i, -|i, US ˈdɪŋ|.i, -g|i **-ies** -iz
dingle, D~ ˈdɪŋ.gəl **-s** -z
Dingley ˈdɪŋ.li
dingo ˈdɪŋ.gəʊ, US -goʊ **-es** -z
Dingwall ˈdɪŋ.wɔːl, -wəl, US -wɑːl, -wɔːl, -wəl
ding|y ˈdɪn.dʒ|i **-ier** -i.əʳ, US -i.ɚ **-iest** -i.ɪst, -i.əst **-ily** -əl.i, -ɪ.li **-iness** -ɪ.nəs, -ɪ.nɪs
dink dɪŋk **-s** -s
Dinkins ˈdɪŋ.kɪnz, US ˈdɪŋ-, ˈdɪn-
dinkum ˈdɪŋ.kəm
dink|y ˈdɪŋ.k|i **-ier** -i.əʳ, US -i.ɚ **-iest** -i.ɪst, -i.əst **-iness** -ɪ.nəs, -ɪ.nɪs
Dinmont ˈdɪn.mɒnt, ˈdɪm-, -mənt, US ˈdɪn.mɑːnt, -mənt
Dinneford ˈdɪn.ɪ.fəd, US -fɚd
dinner ˈdɪn.əʳ, US -ɚ **-s** -z **ˈdinner ˌhour; ˈdinner ˌjacket; ˈdinner ˌlady; ˈdinner ˌparty; ˈdinner ˌservice; ˈdinner ˌplate; ˈdinner ˌset; ˈdinner ˌtable; ˈdinner ˌtime**
Dinnington ˈdɪn.ɪŋ.tən
Dinocrates daɪˈnɒk.rə.tiːz, dɪ-, US -ˈnɑː.krə-
Dinorah dɪˈnɔː.rə, US -ˈnɔːr.ə
dinosaur ˈdaɪ.nə.sɔːʳ, US -sɔːr **-s** -z
dinosaur|us ˌdaɪ.nəˈsɔː.r|əs, US -ˈsɔːr|.əs **-i** -aɪ
dinotheri|um ˌdaɪ.nəʊˈθɪə.ri|.əm, -əˈ-, US -noʊˈ-, -ˈθɪr.i- **-a** -ə
dint dɪnt
Dinwiddie dɪnˈwɪd.i, ˈ---
diocesan daɪˈɒs.ɪ.sən, ˈ-ə-, -zən, US -ˈɑː.sə-
dioces|e ˈdaɪ.ə.sɪs, -siːs, -siːz **-es** -ɪz
Diocles ˈdaɪ.ə.kliːz
Diocletian ˌdaɪ.əˈkliː.ʃən, -ʃi.ən
diode ˈdaɪ.əʊd, US -oʊd **-s** -z
Diodorus ˌdaɪ.əˈdɔː.rəs, US -ˈdɔːr.əs
Diogenes daɪˈɒdʒ.ɪ.niːz, ˈ-ə-, US -ˈɑː.dʒə-
Diomede ˈdaɪ.ə.miːd
Diomedes ˌdaɪəˈmiː.diːz; daɪˈɒm.ɪ-, US ˌdaɪəˈmiː-
Dion *Greek:* ˈdaɪ.ən, US -ɑːn *French:* ˈdiː.ən, -ɔ̃ːŋ, -ɒŋ, -ɒn, US diˈoʊn
Dionne diːˈɒn, di-; ˈdiː.ɒn, US -ˈɑːn
Dionysi|a ˌdaɪ.əˈnɪs.i|.ə, -ˈnɪz-, US -ˈnɪʃ.i|.ə, -ˈnɪs-, -ˈnɪz-, -ˈnɪʃ|.ə **-an** -ən
Dionysiac ˌdaɪ.əˈnɪs.i.æk, -ˈnɪz-
Dionysius ˌdaɪ.əˈnɪs.i.əs, -ˈnɪz-, US -ˈnɪʃ.əs, ˈ-i.əs, -ˈnɪs.i-, -ˈnaɪ.si-
Dionysus ˌdaɪ.əˈnaɪ.səs, US -ˈnaɪ.səs, -ˈniː-
dioptre, diopter daɪˈɒp.təʳ, US -ˈɑːp.tɚ **-s** -z
dioptric daɪˈɒp.trɪk, US -ˈɑːp-
Dior ˈdiː.ɔːʳ, diˈɔːʳ, US diˈɔːr
diorama ˌdaɪ.əˈrɑː.mə, US -ˈræm.ə, -ˈrɑː.mə **-s** -z
dioramic ˌdaɪ.əˈræm.ɪk
Dioscuri ˌdaɪ.əˈskjʊə.ri; ˌdaɪ.ɒsˈkjʊə-; daɪˈɒs.kjʊ.ri, -raɪ, US ˌdaɪ.ɑːˈskjʊr.aɪ
Diosy diˈəʊ.si, US -ˈoʊ-
dioxide daɪˈɒk.saɪd, US -ˈɑːk- **-s** -z
dioxin daɪˈɒk.sɪn, US -ˈɑːk- **-s** -z
dip dɪp **-s** -s **-ping** -ɪŋ **-ped** -t **-per/s** -əʳ/z, US -ɚ/z
diphenyl daɪˈfiː.naɪl, -ˈfen.aɪl, -əl, -ɪl, -ˈfen.ɪl, US -ˈfen.əl, -ˈfiː.nəl
diphtheria dɪfˈθɪə.ri.ə, dɪp-, US -ˈθɪr.i-
diphthong ˈdɪf.θɒŋ, ˈdɪp-, US -θɑːŋ, -θɔːŋ **-s** -z

> Note: the pronunciation /dɪp-/ was for a long time regarded as a mispronunciation, but it has now gained widespread acceptability.

diphthongal ˈdɪf.θɒŋ.əl, ˈdɪp-, -gəl, -ˈ--, US dɪfˈθɑːŋ.əl, dɪp-, -ˈθɔːŋ-, -gəl **-ly** -i
diphthongization, -isa- ˌdɪf.θɒŋ.aɪˈzeɪ.ʃən, -gaɪˈ-, -gɪˈ-, US -θɑːŋ.əˈ-, -θɔːŋ-, -gəˈ- **-s** -z
diphthongiz|e, -is|e ˈdɪf.θɒŋ.aɪz, ˈdɪp-, -gaɪz, US -θɑːŋ.aɪz, -θɔːŋ-, -gaɪz **-es** -ɪz **-ing** -ɪŋ **-ed** -d
Diplock ˈdɪp.lɒk, US -lɑːk
diplodoc|us dɪˈplɒd.ə.k|əs, ˌdɪp.ləʊˈdəʊ-, US dɪˈplɑː.də-, -ˈploʊ- **-uses** -ə.sɪz **-i** -aɪ
diploid ˈdɪp.lɔɪd **-s** -z
diploma dɪˈpləʊ.mə, US -ˈploʊ-, də- **-s** -z
diplomacy dɪˈpləʊ.mə.si, US -ˈploʊ-, də-
diplomat ˈdɪp.lə.mæt **-s** -s
diplomatic ˌdɪp.ləˈmæt.ɪk, US -ˈmæt̬- **-s** -s **-al** -əl **-ally** -əl.i, -li
diplomatist dɪˈpləʊ.mə.tɪst, US -ˈploʊ-, də- **-s** -s
diplomatiz|e, -is|e dɪˈpləʊ.mə.taɪz, US -ˈploʊ-, də- **-es** -ɪz **-ing** -ɪŋ **-ed** -d
diplosis dɪˈpləʊ.sɪs, US -ˈploʊ-
dipole ˈdaɪ.pəʊl, US -poʊl **-s** -z
dipper ˈdɪp.əʳ, US -ɚ **-s** -z
dipp|y ˈdɪp|.i **-ier** -i.əʳ, US -i.ɚ **-iest** -i.ɪst, -i.əst
dipsomania ˌdɪp.səʊˈmeɪ.ni.ə, US -səˈ-, -soʊˈ-, -njə
dipsomaniac ˌdɪp.səʊˈmeɪ.ni.æk, US -səˈ-, -soʊˈ- **-s** -s
dipstick ˈdɪp.stɪk **-s** -s
dipswitch ˈdɪp.swɪtʃ **-es** -ɪz
dipteran ˈdɪp.tə.rən, US -tɚ.ən **-s** -z
dipter|on ˈdɪp.tə.r|ən, US -r|ɑːn **-ons** -ənz, US -ɑːnz **-a** -ə **-ous** -əs
diptych ˈdɪp.tɪk **-s** -s
dir|e daɪəʳ, ˈdaɪ.əʳ, US ˈdaɪ.ɚ **-er** -əʳ, US -ɚ **-est** -ɪst, -əst **-ely** -li **-eness** -nəs, -nɪs
direct dɪˈrekt, daɪ-, də-, US dɪˈrekt, daɪ- **-s** -s **-ing** -ɪŋ **-ed** -ɪd **-est** -ɪst,

-əst -ness -nəs, -nɪs ˌ**direct ˈmail;** ˌ**direct ˈobject**
direction dɪˈrek.ʃən, daɪ-, də-, (US) dɪˈrek-, daɪ- **-s** -z **-less** -ləs, -lɪs
directional dɪˈrek.ʃən.əl, daɪ-, də-, (US) dɪˈrek-, daɪ-
directive dɪˈrek.tɪv, daɪ-, də-, (US) dɪˈrek-, daɪ- **-s** -z
directly dɪˈrekt.li, daɪ-, də-, (US) dɪ-, daɪ-
director dɪˈrek.təʳ, daɪ-, də-, (US) dɪˈrek.tɚ, daɪ- **-s** -z
directorate dɪˈrek.tər.ət, daɪ-, də-, -ɪt, (US) dɪˈrek-, daɪ- **-s** -s
directorial dɪˌrekˈtɔː.ri.əl, daɪ-, də-, (US) dɪˌrekˈtɔːr.i-, daɪ-
directorship dɪˈrek.tə.ʃɪp, daɪ-, də-, (US) dɪˈrek.tɚ-, daɪ- **-s** -s
director|y dɪˈrek.tər|.i, daɪ-, də-, (US) dɪˈrek-, daɪ- **-ies** -iz
direful ˈdaɪə.fəl, ˈdaɪ.ə-, -fʊl, (US) ˈdaɪ.ɚ- **-ly** -i **-ness** -nəs, -nɪs
dirg|e dɜːdʒ, (US) dɝːdʒ **-es** -ɪz
dirham ˈdɪ.ræm, ˈdɪər.æm, -əm, (US) dɪrˈhæm; (US) dəˈræm **-s** -z
dirigible ˈdɪr.ɪ.dʒə.bəl, -dʒɪ-; dɪˈrɪdʒ-, də-, (US) ˈdɪr.ə.dʒə-; (US) dɪˈrɪdʒ.ə-, də- **-s** -z
dirigisme ˌdɪr.ɪˈʒiː.zəm; ˈdɪr.ɪ.ʒɪ-, (US) ˌdɪr.ɪˈʒiː-
dirigiste ˌdɪr.ɪˈʒiːst; ˈdɪr.ɪ.ʒɪst, (US) ˈdɪr.ɪ.ʒɪst; (US) ˌdɪr.ɪˈʒiːst **-s** -s
dirk, D~ dɜːk, (US) dɝːk **-s** -s
dirndl ˈdɜːn.dəl, (US) ˈdɝːn- **-s** -z
dirt dɜːt, (US) dɝːt ˌ**dirt ˈcheap;** ˌ**dirt ˈpoor;** ˈ**dirt ˌtrack**
dirt|y ˈdɜː.t|i, (US) ˈdɝː.ţ|i **-ies** -iz **-ying** -i.ɪŋ **-ied** -id **-ier** -i.əʳ, (US) -i.ɚ **-iest** -i.ɪst, -i.əst **-ily** -əl.i, -ɪ.li **-iness** -ɪ.nəs, -ɪ.nɪs ˌ**dirty ˈtrick; do someone's ˈdirty ˌwork**
dis(s) dɪs **-es** -ɪz **-ing** -ɪŋ **-ed** -t
Dis dɪs
dis- dɪs, dɪz

Note: Prefix. In words containing **dis-**, the prefix will normally either not be stressed, e.g. **disable** /dɪˈseɪ.bəl/, or will take secondary stress if the stem is stressed on its second syllable, e.g. **ability** /əˈbɪl.ə.ti/ (US) /-ţi/, **disability** /ˌdɪs.əˈbɪl.ə.ti/ (US) /-ţi/. There is sometimes a difference in stress between nouns and verbs, e.g. **discharge**, noun /ˈdɪs.tʃɑːdʒ/ (US) /-tʃɑːrdʒ/, verb /dɪsˈtʃɑːdʒ/ (US) /-ˈtʃɑːrdʒ/. There are exceptions; see individual entries.

disabilit|y ˌdɪs.əˈbɪl.ə.t|i, -ɪ.t|i, (US) -ə.ţ|i **-ies** -iz
disabl|e dɪˈseɪ.bəl **-es** -z **-ing** -ɪŋ, -ˈeɪ.blɪŋ **-ed** -d **-ement** -mənt
disabus|e ˌdɪs.əˈbjuːz **-es** -ɪz **-ing** -ɪŋ **-ed** -d
disaccharide daɪˈsæk.ər.aɪd, -ɪd, (US) -ə.raɪd **-s** -z
disaccustom ˌdɪs.əˈkʌs.təm **-s** -z **-ing** -ɪŋ **-ed** -d
disadvantag|e ˌdɪs.ədˈvɑːn.tɪdʒ, (US) -ˈvæn.ţɪdʒ **-es** -ɪz **-ing** -ɪŋ **-ed** -d
disadvantageous ˌdɪsˌæd.vənˈteɪ.dʒəs, -əd-, -vɑːnˈ-, -vænˈ-; dɪˌsæd-, (US) ˌdɪsˌæd.vænˈ-, -vənˈ- **-ly** -li **-ness** -nəs, -nɪs
disaffect ˌdɪs.əˈfekt **-s** -s **-ing** -ɪŋ **-ed/ly** -ɪd/li **-edness** -ɪd.nəs, -nɪs
disaffection ˌdɪs.əˈfek.ʃən
disafforest ˌdɪs.əˈfɒr.ɪst, -əst, (US) -ˈfɔːr- **-s** -s **-ing** -ɪŋ **-ed** -ɪd
disafforestation ˌdɪs.əˌfɒr.ɪˈsteɪ.ʃən, -əˈ-, (US) -ˌfɔːr-
disagree ˌdɪs.əˈgriː **-s** -z **-ing** -ɪŋ **-d** -d
disagreeab|le ˌdɪs.əˈgriː.ə.b|əl **-ly** -li **-leness** -əl.nəs, -nɪs
disagreement ˌdɪs.əˈgriː.mənt **-s** -s
disallow ˌdɪs.əˈlaʊ **-s** -z **-ing** -ɪŋ **-ed** -d
disallowable ˌdɪs.əˈlaʊ.ə.bəl *stress shift:* ˌ**disallowable ˈgoals**
disallowance ˌdɪs.əˈlaʊ.ənts
disambigu|ate ˌdɪs.æmˈbɪg.ju|.eɪt **-ates** -eɪts **-ating** -eɪ.tɪŋ, (US) -eɪ.ţɪŋ **-ated** -eɪ.tɪd, (US) -eɪ.ţɪd
disambiguation ˌdɪs.æmˌbɪg.juˈeɪ.ʃən
disappear ˌdɪs.əˈpɪəʳ, (US) -ˈpɪr **-s** -z **-ing** -ɪŋ **-ed** -d
disappearanc|e ˌdɪs.əˈpɪə.rənts, (US) -ˈpɪr.ənts **-es** -ɪz
disap|point ˌdɪs.ə|ˈpɔɪnt **-points** -ˈpɔɪnts **-pointing/ly** -ˈpɔɪn.tɪŋ/li, (US) -ˈpɔɪn.ţɪŋ/li **-pointed** -ˈpɔɪn.tɪd, (US) -ˈpɔɪn.ţɪd
disappointment ˌdɪs.əˈpɔɪnt.mənt **-s** -s
disapprobation ˌdɪs.æp.rəʊˈbeɪ.ʃən, -rʊˈ-; dɪˌsæp-, (US) ˌdɪsˌæp.rəˈ-, -roʊˈ-
disapproval ˌdɪs.əˈpruː.vəl
disapprov|e ˌdɪs.əˈpruːv **-es** -z **-ing/ly** -ɪŋ/li **-ed** -d
disarm dɪˈsɑːm, -ˈzɑːm, (US) -ˈsɑːrm **-s** -z **-ing/ly** -ɪŋ/li **-ed** -d **-er/s** -əʳ/z, (US) -ɚ/z
disarmament dɪˈsɑː.mə.mənt, -ˈzɑː-, (US) -ˈsɑːr-
disarrang|e ˌdɪs.əˈreɪndʒ **-es** -ɪz **-ing** -ɪŋ **-ed** -d
disarrangement ˌdɪs.əˈreɪndʒ.mənt **-s** -s
disarray ˌdɪs.ərˈeɪ **-s** -z **-ing** -ɪŋ **-ed** -d
disarticu|late ˌdɪs.ɑːˈtɪk.jə|.leɪt, -jʊ-, (US) -ɑːrˈ- **-lates** -leɪts **-lating** -leɪ.tɪŋ, (US) -leɪ.ţɪŋ **-lated** -leɪ.tɪd, (US) -leɪ.ţɪd
disarticulation ˌdɪs.ɑːˌtɪk.jəˈleɪ.ʃən, -jʊˈ-, (US) -ɑːr-
disassoci|ate ˌdɪs.əˈsəʊ.si|.eɪt, -ʃi-, (US) -ˈsoʊ.ʃi-, -si- **-ates** -eɪts **-ating** -eɪ.tɪŋ, (US) -eɪ.ţɪŋ **-ated** -eɪ.tɪd, (US) -eɪ.ţɪd
disassociation ˌdɪs.ə.səʊ.siˈeɪ.ʃən, -ʃiˈ-, (US) -soʊ.ʃiˈ-, -siˈ-
disaster dɪˈzɑː.stəʳ, də-, (US) dɪˈzæs.tɚ **-s** -z
disastrous dɪˈzɑː.strəs, də-, (US) dɪˈzæs.trəs **-ly** -li **-ness** -nəs, -nɪs
disavow ˌdɪs.əˈvaʊ **-s** -z **-ing** -ɪŋ **-ed** -d **-al** -əl
disband dɪsˈbænd **-s** -z **-ing** -ɪŋ **-ed** -ɪd **-ment** -mənt
disbar dɪsˈbɑːʳ, (US) -ˈbɑːr **-s** -z **-ring** -ɪŋ **-red** -d
disbark dɪsˈbɑːk, (US) -ˈbɑːrk **-s** -s **-ing** -ɪŋ **-ed** -t
disbelief ˌdɪs.bɪˈliːf, -bəˈ-
disbeliev|e ˌdɪs.bɪˈliːv, -bəˈ- **-es** -z **-ing** -ɪŋ **-ed** -d **-er/s** -əʳ/z, (US) -ɚ/z
disburden dɪsˈbɜː.dən, (US) -ˈbɝː- **-s** -z **-ing** -ɪŋ **-ed** -d
disburdenment dɪsˈbɜː.dən.mənt, (US) -ˈbɝː-
disburs|e dɪsˈbɜːs, (US) -ˈbɝːs **-es** -ɪz **-ing** -ɪŋ **-ed** -t
disbursement dɪsˈbɜːs.mənt, (US) -ˈbɝːs- **-s** -s
disc dɪsk **-s** -s ˈ**disc ˌjockey**
discard n ˈdɪs.kɑːd, (US) -kɑːrd **-s** -z
discard v dɪˈskɑːd, (US) -ˈskɑːrd **-s** -z **-ing** -ɪŋ **-ed** -ɪd
discern dɪˈsɜːn, də-, (US) dɪˈsɝːn, -ˈzɝːn **-s** -z **-ing** -ɪŋ **-ed** -d **-er/s** -əʳ/z, (US) -ɚ/z
discernib|le dɪˈsɜː.nə.b|əl, də-, -nɪ-, (US) dɪˈsɝː-, -ˈzɝː- **-ly** -li **-leness** -əl.nəs, -nɪs
discerning dɪˈsɜː.nɪŋ, də-, (US) dɪˈsɝː-, -ˈzɝː- **-ly** -li
discernment dɪˈsɜːn.mənt, də-, (US) dɪˈsɝːn-, -ˈzɝːn-
discharg|e n ˈdɪs.tʃɑːdʒ, -ˈ-, (US) ˈdɪs.tʃɑːrdʒ, -ˈ- **-es** -ɪz
discharg|e v dɪsˈtʃɑːdʒ, (US) -ˈtʃɑːrdʒ **-es** -ɪz **-ing** -ɪŋ **-ed** -d **-er/s** -əʳ/z, (US) -ɚ/z
disciple dɪˈsaɪ.pəl, də-, (US) dɪ- **-s** -z **-ship** -ʃɪp
disciplinarian ˌdɪs.ə.plɪˈneə.ri.ən, ˌ-ɪ-, -pləˈ-, (US) -ˈner.i- **-s** -z
disciplinary ˌdɪs.əˈplɪ.nər.i, -ɪˈ-, ˈdɪs.ə.plɪ-, ˈ-ɪ-, (US) ˈdɪs.ə.plɪ.ner- ˌ**disciplinary ˈaction, disciˌplinary ˈaction** (US) ˈ**disciplinary ˌaction**
disciplin|e ˈdɪs.ə.plɪn, ˈ-ɪ- **-es** -z **-ing** -ɪŋ **-ed** -d
disclaim dɪsˈkleɪm **-s** -z **-ing** -ɪŋ **-ed** -d
disclaimer dɪsˈkleɪm.əʳ, (US) -mɚ **-s** -z
disclos|e dɪsˈkləʊz, (US) -ˈkloʊz **-es** -ɪz **-ing** -ɪŋ **-ed** -d
disclosure dɪsˈkləʊ.ʒəʳ, (US) -ˈkloʊ.ʒɚ **-s** -z
disco ˈdɪs.kəʊ, (US) -koʊ **-s** -z **-ing** -ɪŋ
discobol|us dɪˈskɒb.əl|.əs, (US) -ˈskɑː.bəl- **-i** -aɪ
discol|o(u)r dɪˈskʌl|.əʳ, (US) -ˈskʌl|.ɚ **-o(u)rs** -əz, (US) -ɚz **-o(u)ring** -ər.ɪŋ **-o(u)red** -əd, (US) -ɚd
discolo(u)ration dɪˌskʌl.əˈreɪ.ʃən; ˌdɪs.kʌl-, (US) dɪˌskʌl- **-s** -z
discombobu|late ˌdɪs.kəmˈbɒb.jə|.leɪt, -jʊ-, (US) -ˈbɑː.bjə-, -bjʊ- **-lates** -leɪts **-lating** -leɪ.tɪŋ, (US) -leɪ.ţɪŋ **-lated** -leɪ.tɪd, (US) -leɪ.ţɪd
discom|fit dɪˈskʌmp|.fɪt **-fits** -fɪts **-fiting** -fɪ.tɪŋ, (US) -fɪ.ţɪŋ **-fited** -fɪ.tɪd, (US) -fɪ.ţɪd

discomfiture dɪˈskʌmp.fɪ.tʃəʳ, -fə-, ⓊⓈ -tʃɚ
discom|fort dɪˈskʌmp|.fət, ⓊⓈ -fɚt **-forts** -fəts, ⓊⓈ -fɚts **-forting** -fə.tɪŋ, ⓊⓈ -fɚ.t̬ɪŋ **-forted** -fə.tɪd, ⓊⓈ -fɚ.t̬ɪd
discommod|e ˌdɪs.kəˈməʊd, ⓊⓈ -ˈmoʊd **-es** -z **-ing** -ɪŋ **-ed** -ɪd
discompos|e ˌdɪs.kəmˈpəʊz, ⓊⓈ -ˈpoʊz **-es** -ɪz **-ing** -ɪŋ **-ed** -d
discomposure ˌdɪs.kəmˈpəʊ.ʒəʳ, ⓊⓈ -ˈpoʊ.ʒɚ
discon|cert ˌdɪs.kən|ˈsɜːt, ⓊⓈ -ˈsɝːt **-certs** -ˈsɜːts, ⓊⓈ -ˈsɝːts **-certing/ly** -ˈsɜː.tɪŋ/li, ⓊⓈ -ˈsɝː.t̬ɪŋ/li **-certed** -ˈsɜː.tɪd, ⓊⓈ -ˈsɝː.t̬ɪd
disconnect ˌdɪs.kəˈnekt **-s** -s **-ing** -ɪŋ **-ed** -ɪd
disconnection ˌdɪs.kəˈnek.ʃən
disconsolate dɪˈskɒnt.səl.ət, -ɪt, ⓊⓈ -ˈskɑːnt- **-ly** -li **-ness** -nəs, -nɪs
discon|tent ˌdɪs.kən|ˈtent **-tented** -ˈten.tɪd, ⓊⓈ -ˈten.t̬ɪd **-tentedly** -ˈten.tɪd.li, ⓊⓈ -ˈten.t̬ɪd.li **-tentedness** -ˈten.tɪd.nəs, -nɪs, ⓊⓈ -ˈten.t̬ɪd.nəs, -nɪs **-tentment** -ˈtent.mənt
discontinuance ˌdɪs.kənˈtɪn.ju.ənts
discontinuation ˌdɪs.kənˌtɪn.juˈeɪ.ʃən
discontinu|e ˌdɪs.kənˈtɪn.juː **-es** -z **-ing** -ɪŋ **-ed** -d
discontinuit|y ˌdɪsˌkɒn.tɪˈnjuː.ə.t|i, -kɒn-, -ɪ.t|i; dɪˌskɒn-, ⓊⓈ ˌdɪs.kɑːn.tənˈuː.ə.t̬|i, -ˈjuː- **-ies** -iz
discontinuous ˌdɪs.kənˈtɪn.ju.əs **-ly** -li
discord n ˈdɪs.kɔːd, ⓊⓈ -kɔːrd **-s** -z
discord v dɪˈskɔːd, ⓊⓈ -ˈskɔːrd **-s** -z **-ing** -ɪŋ **-ed** -ɪd
discordan|ce dɪˈskɔː.dənt|s, ⓊⓈ -ˈskɔːr- **-cy** -si
discordant dɪˈskɔː.dənt, ⓊⓈ -ˈskɔːr- **-ly** -li
discotheque, discothèque ˈdɪs.kə.tek **-s** -s
discount n ˈdɪs.kaʊnt **-s** -s
dis|count v dɪˈs|kaʊnt **-counts** -kaʊnts **-counting** -kaʊn.tɪŋ, ⓊⓈ -kaʊn.t̬ɪŋ **-counted** -kaʊn.tɪd, ⓊⓈ -kaʊn.t̬ɪd **-counter/s** -kaʊn.təʳ/z, ⓊⓈ -kaʊn.t̬ɚ/z
discountenanc|e dɪˈskaʊn.tɪ.nənts, -tə-, ⓊⓈ -tən.ənts **-es** -ɪz **-ing** -ɪŋ **-ed** -t
discourag|e dɪˈskʌr.ɪdʒ, ⓊⓈ -ˈskɝː- **-es** -ɪz **-ing/ly** -ɪŋ/li **-ed** -d
discouragement dɪˈskʌr.ɪdʒ.mənt, ⓊⓈ -ˈskɝː- **-s** -s
discours|e n ˈdɪs.kɔːs, ⓊⓈ -kɔːrs **-es** -ɪz
discours|e v dɪˈskɔːs, ⓊⓈ -ˈskɔːrs **-es** -ɪz **-ing** -ɪŋ **-ed** -t **-er/s** -əʳ/z, ⓊⓈ -ɚ/z
discourteous dɪˈskɜː.ti.əs, ⓊⓈ -ˈskɝː.t̬i- **-ly** -li **-ness** -nəs, -nɪs
discourtesy dɪˈskɜː.tə.si, -tɪ-, ⓊⓈ -ˈskɝː.t̬ə-
discov|er dɪˈskʌv|.əʳ, ⓊⓈ -ɚ **-ers** -əz, ⓊⓈ -ɚz **-ering** -ər.ɪŋ **-ered** -əd, ⓊⓈ -ɚd **-erer/s** -ər.əʳ/z, ⓊⓈ -ɚ.ɚ/z
discoverable dɪˈskʌv.ər.ə.bəl
discovert dɪˈskʌv.ət, ⓊⓈ -ɚt
discover|y dɪˈskʌv.ər|.i **-ies** -iz
discred|it dɪˈskred|.ɪt **-its** -ɪts **-iting** -ɪ.tɪŋ, ⓊⓈ -ɪ.t̬ɪŋ **-ited** -ɪ.tɪd, ⓊⓈ -ɪ.t̬ɪd
discreditab|le dɪˈskred.ɪ.tə.b|əl, ⓊⓈ -t̬ə- **-ly** -li **-leness** -əl.nəs, -nɪs
dis|creet dɪˈs|kriːt **-creetest** -ˈkriː.tɪst, -təst, ⓊⓈ -ˈkriː.t̬ɪst, -t̬əst **-creetly** -ˈkriːt.li **-creetness** -ˈkriːt.nəs, -nɪs
discrepan|cy dɪˈskrep.ən|t.si **-cies** -t.siz **-t** -t
discrete dɪˈskriːt **-ly** -li **-ness** -nəs, -nɪs
discretion dɪˈskreʃ.ən **-s** -z
discretional dɪˈskreʃ.ən.əl **-ly** -i
discretionar|y dɪˈskreʃ.ən.ər|.i, -r|i, ⓊⓈ -er|.i **-ily** -əl.i, -ɪ.li
discriminate adj dɪˈskrɪm.ɪ.nət, ˈ-ə-, -nɪt **-ly** -li
discrimi|nate v dɪˈskrɪm.ɪ|.neɪt, ˈ-ə- **-nates** -neɪts **-nating/ly** -neɪ.tɪŋ/li, ⓊⓈ -neɪ.t̬ɪŋ/li **-nated** -neɪ.tɪd, ⓊⓈ -neɪ.t̬ɪd
discrimination dɪˌskrɪm.ɪˈneɪ.ʃən, -əˈ- **-s** -z
discriminative dɪˈskrɪm.ɪ.nə.tɪv, ˈ-ə-, -neɪ-, ⓊⓈ -neɪ.t̬ɪv, -nə- **-ly** -li
discriminatory dɪˈskrɪm.ɪ.nə.tər.i, ˈ-ə-, -tri; dɪˌskrɪm.ɪˈneɪ-, -əˈ-, ⓊⓈ dɪˈskrɪm.ɪ.nə.tɔːr.i
discursion dɪˈskɜː.ʃən, -ʒən, ⓊⓈ -ˈskɝː.ʒən, -ʃən **-s** -z
discursive dɪˈskɜː.sɪv, ⓊⓈ -skɝː- **-ly** -li **-ness** -nəs, -nɪs
discursory dɪˈskɜː.sər.i, ⓊⓈ -ˈskɝː-
disc|us ˈdɪs.k|əs **-i** -aɪ **-uses** -ə.sɪz
discuss dɪˈskʌs **-es** -ɪz **-ing** -ɪŋ **-ed** -t **-able** -ə.bəl
discussant dɪˈskʌs.ənt **-s** -s
discussion dɪˈskʌʃ.ən **-s** -z
disdain dɪsˈdeɪn, dɪz- **-s** -z **-ing** -ɪŋ **-ed** -d
disdainful dɪsˈdeɪn.fəl, dɪz-, -fʊl **-ly** -i **-ness** -nəs, -nɪs
diseas|e dɪˈziːz, də-, ⓊⓈ dɪ- **-es** -ɪz **-ed** -d
disembark ˌdɪs.ɪmˈbɑːk, -emˈ-, ⓊⓈ -ˈbɑːrk, ˈ--- **-s** -s **-ing** -ɪŋ **-ed** -t
disembarkation ˌdɪs.ɪm.bɑːˈkeɪ.ʃən, -em-, ⓊⓈ -bɑːrˈ- **-s** -z
disembarkment ˌdɪs.ɪmˈbɑːk.mənt, -emˈ-, ⓊⓈ -ˈbɑːrk- **-s** -s
disembarrass ˌdɪs.ɪmˈbær.əs, -emˈ-, ⓊⓈ -ˈber-, -ˈbær- **-es** -ɪz **-ing** -ɪŋ **-ed** -t
disembarrassment ˌdɪs.ɪmˈbær.əs.mənt, -emˈ-, ⓊⓈ -ˈber-, -ˈbær- **-s** -s
disembod|y ˌdɪs.ɪmˈbɒd|.i, -emˈ-, ⓊⓈ -ˈbɑː.d|i **-ies** -iz **-ying** -i.ɪŋ **-ied** -id
disembowel ˌdɪs.ɪmˈbaʊ.əl, -baʊəl, ⓊⓈ ˌdɪs.ɪmˈbaʊ.əl, -emˈ- **-s** -z **-(l)ing** -ɪŋ **-(l)ed** -d
disen|chant ˌdɪs.ɪn|ˈtʃɑːnt, -enˈ-, -ənˈ-, ⓊⓈ -ˈtʃænt **-chants** -ˈtʃɑːnts, ⓊⓈ -ˈtʃænts **-chanting** -ˈtʃɑːn.tɪŋ, ⓊⓈ -ˈtʃæn.t̬ɪŋ **-chanted** -ˈtʃɑːn.tɪd, ⓊⓈ -ˈtʃæn.t̬ɪd
disenchantment ˌdɪs.ɪnˈtʃɑːnt.mənt, -enˈ-, -ənˈ-, ⓊⓈ -ˈtʃænt- **-s** -s
disencumb|er ˌdɪs.ɪnˈkʌm.b|əʳ, -ɪŋˈ-, -enˈ-, -eŋˈ-, ⓊⓈ -b|ɚ **-ers** -əz, ⓊⓈ -ɚz **-ering** -ər.ɪŋ **-ered** -əd, ⓊⓈ -ɚd
disendow ˌdɪs.ɪnˈdaʊ, -enˈ- **-s** -z **-ing** -ɪŋ **-ed** -d
disendowment ˌdɪs.ɪnˈdaʊ.mənt, -enˈ-
disenfranchis|e ˌdɪs.ɪnˈfræn.tʃaɪz, -enˈ- **-es** -ɪz **-ing** -ɪŋ **-ed** -d
disenfranchisement ˌdɪs.ɪnˈfræn.tʃɪz.mənt, -enˈ-, -tʃaɪz-, ⓊⓈ -tʃaɪz-, -tʃɪz-
disengag|e ˌdɪs.ɪnˈgeɪdʒ, -ɪŋˈ-, -enˈ-, -eŋˈ-, ⓊⓈ -ɪnˈ-, -enˈ- **-es** -ɪz **-ing** -ɪŋ **-ed** -d
disengagement ˌdɪs.ɪnˈgeɪdʒ.mənt, -ɪŋˈ-, -enˈ-, -eŋˈ-, ⓊⓈ -ɪnˈ-, -enˈ-
disentail ˌdɪs.ɪnˈteɪl, -enˈ-, -ənˈ- **-s** -z **-ing** -ɪŋ **-ed** -d
disentangl|e ˌdɪs.ɪnˈtæŋ.gəl, -enˈ- **-es** -z **-ing** -ɪŋ, -ˈtæŋ.glɪŋ **-ed** -d
disentanglement ˌdɪs.ɪnˈtæŋ.gəl.mənt, -enˈ-
disequilibrium ˌdɪs.ek.wɪˈlɪb.ri.əm, -iː.kwɪˈ-, -kwəˈ-, ⓊⓈ ˌdɪs.iː.kwɪˈ-; ⓊⓈ dɪˌsek.wɪˈ-
disestablish ˌdɪs.ɪˈstæb.lɪʃ, -esˈtæb-, -əˈstæb-, ⓊⓈ -ɪˈstæb-, -esˈtæb-, ˈdɪs.ɪ.stæb-, -es.tæb- **-es** -ɪz **-ing** -ɪŋ **-ed** -t
disestablishment ˌdɪs.ɪˈstæb.lɪʃ.mənt, -esˈtæb-, -əˈstæb-, ⓊⓈ -ɪˈstæb-, -esˈtæb-
disestablishmentarian ˌdɪs.ɪˌstæb.lɪʃ.mənˈteə.ri.ən, -esˌtæb-, -əˌstæb-, ⓊⓈ -ɪˌstæb.lɪʃ.mənˈter.i-, -esˌtæb-
disfavo(u)r dɪsˈfeɪ.vəʳ, ⓊⓈ -vɚ
disfiguration dɪsˌfɪg.əˈreɪ.ʃən, ˌdɪs.fɪg-, -jʊˈ-, ⓊⓈ dɪsˌfɪg.jəˈ- **-s** -z
disfig|ure dɪsˈfɪg|.əʳ, ⓊⓈ -j|ɚ **-ures** -əz, ⓊⓈ -ɚz **-uring** -ər.ɪŋ **-ured** -əd, ⓊⓈ -ɚd **-urement/s** -ə.mənt/s, ⓊⓈ -ɚ.mənt/s
disforest dɪsˈfɒr.ɪst, -əst, ⓊⓈ -ˈfɔːr- **-s** -s **-ing** -ɪŋ **-ed** -ɪd
disfranchis|e dɪsˈfræn.tʃaɪz **-es** -ɪz **-ing** -ɪŋ **-ed** -d
disfranchisement dɪsˈfræn.tʃɪz.mənt, -tʃəz-, -tʃaɪz-, ⓊⓈ -tʃaɪz-, -tʃɪz-
disgorg|e dɪsˈgɔːdʒ, ⓊⓈ -ˈgɔːrdʒ **-es** -ɪz **-ing** -ɪŋ **-ed** -d
disgrac|e dɪsˈgreɪs, dɪz-, ⓊⓈ dɪs- **-es** -ɪz **-ing** -ɪŋ **-ed** -t
disgraceful dɪsˈgreɪs.fəl, dɪz-, -fʊl, ⓊⓈ dɪs- **-ly** -i **-ness** -nəs, -nɪs
disgruntled dɪsˈgrʌn.təld, ⓊⓈ -t̬əld
disgruntlement dɪsˈgrʌn.təl.mənt, ⓊⓈ -t̬əl-
disguis|e dɪsˈgaɪz, dɪz-, ⓊⓈ dɪs- **-es**

-ɪz -ing -ɪŋ -ed -d -er/s -əʳ/z, US -ɚ/z

disgust dɪsˈgʌst, dɪz-, US dɪs- -s -s -ing -ɪŋ -ed/ly -ɪd/li

disgusting dɪsˈgʌs.tɪŋ, dɪz-, US dɪs- -ly -li

dish dɪʃ -es -ɪz -ing -ɪŋ -ed -t

dishabille ˌdɪs.æbˈiːl, -əˈbiːl, US -əˈbiːl

disharmony dɪsˈhɑː.mᵊn.i, US -ˈhɑːr-

dish|cloth ˈdɪʃ|.klɒθ, US -klɑːθ -cloths -klɒθs, -klɒðz, US -klɑːθs, -klɑːðz

dishearten dɪsˈhɑː.tᵊn, US -ˈhɑːr- -s -z -ing/ly -ɪŋ/li -ed -d

dishevel dɪˈʃev.ᵊl -s -z -(l)ing -ɪŋ -(l)ed -d

dishful ˈdɪʃ.fʊl -s -z

dishonest dɪˈsɒn.ɪst, -ˈzɒn-, -əst, US -ˈsɑː.nɪst, -nəst -ly -li

dishonest|y dɪˈsɒn.ɪ.st|i, -ˈzɒn-, ˈ-ə-, US -ˈsɑː.nə- -ies -iz

dishono(u)r dɪˈsɒn.əʳ, -ˈzɒn-, US -ˈsɑː.nɚ -s -z -ing -ɪŋ -ed -d -er/s -əʳ/z, US -ɚ/z

dishono(u)rab|le dɪˈsɒn.ᵊr.ə.b|ᵊl, -ˈzɒn-, US -ˈsɑː.nɚ- -ly -li -leness -ᵊl.nəs, -nɪs

dishrag ˈdɪʃ.ræg -s -z

dishtowel ˈdɪʃ.taʊ.əl, -taʊəl, US ˈdɪʃ.taʊ.əl -s -z

dishwash|er ˈdɪʃˌwɒʃ|.əʳ, US -ˌwɑː.ʃ|ɚ, -ˌwɔː- -ers -əz, US -ɚz -ing -ɪŋ

dishwater ˈdɪʃˌwɔː.təʳ, US -ˌwɑː.t̬ɚ, -ˌwɔː-

dish|y ˈdɪʃ|.i -ier -i.əʳ, US -i.ɚ -iest -i.ɪst, -i.əst

disillusion ˌdɪs.ɪˈluː.ʒᵊn, -əˈ-, -ˈljuː-, US -ˈluː- -s -z -ing -ɪŋ -ed -d -ment/s -mənt/s

disincentive ˌdɪs.ɪnˈsen.tɪv, US -t̬ɪv -s -z

disinclination ˌdɪs.ɪn.klɪˈneɪ.ʃᵊn, -ɪŋ-, -kləˈ-, US -ɪn-

disinclin|e ˌdɪs.ɪnˈklaɪn, -ɪŋˈ-, US -ɪn- -es -z -ing -ɪŋ -ed -d

disinfect ˌdɪs.ɪnˈfekt -s -s -ing -ɪŋ -ed -ɪd

disinfectant ˌdɪs.ɪnˈfek.tənt -s -s

disinfection ˌdɪs.ɪnˈfek.ʃᵊn -s -z

disinfestation ˌdɪs.ɪn.fesˈteɪ.ʃᵊn

disinflation ˌdɪs.ɪnˈfleɪ.ʃᵊn

disinformation ˌdɪs.ɪn.fəˈmeɪ.ʃᵊn, -fɔːˈ-, US -fɚˈ-

disingenuous ˌdɪs.ɪnˈdʒen.ju.əs -ly -li -ness -nəs, -nɪs

disinher|it ˌdɪs.ɪnˈher|.ɪt -its -ɪts -iting -ɪ.tɪŋ, US -ɪ.t̬ɪŋ -ited -ɪ.tɪd, US -ɪ.t̬ɪd

disinheritance ˌdɪs.ɪnˈher.ɪ.tᵊn*t*s, US -t̬ᵊn*t*s

disintegrable dɪˈsɪn.tɪ.grə.bᵊl, -tə-, US -t̬ə-

disinte|grate dɪˈsɪn.tɪ|.greɪt, -tə-, US -t̬ə- -grates -greɪts -grating -greɪ.tɪŋ, US -greɪ.t̬ɪŋ -grated -greɪ.tɪd, US -greɪ.t̬ɪd -grator/s -greɪ.təʳ/z, US -greɪ.t̬ɚ/z

disintegration dɪˌsɪn.tɪˈgreɪ.ʃᵊn, -təˈ-; ˌdɪs.ɪn-, US ˌdɪs.ɪn.t̬əˈ- -s -z

disinter ˌdɪs.ɪnˈtɜːʳ, US -ˈtɝː -s -z -ring -ɪŋ -red -d

disinterest dɪˈsɪn.trəst, -trest, -trɪst; ˈ-tᵊr.əst, -est, -ɪst, US -ˈsɪn.trɪst, -trəst, -trest; US ˈ-t̬ɚ.ɪst, -əst, -est

disinterested dɪˈsɪn.trə.stɪd, -tres.tɪd, -trɪ.stɪd; ˈ-tᵊr.ə.stɪd, -es.tɪd, -ɪ.stɪd, US -ˈsɪn.trɪ.stɪd, -trə-, -tres.tɪd; US ˈ-t̬ɚ.ɪ.stɪd, -ə-, -es.tɪd -ly -li -ness -nəs, -nɪs

disinterment ˌdɪs.ɪnˈtɜː.mənt, US -ˈtɝː- -s -s

disinvest ˌdɪs.ɪnˈvest -s -s -ing -ɪŋ -ed -ɪd -ment -mənt

disjoin dɪsˈdʒɔɪn, dɪz-, US dɪs- -s -z -ing -ɪŋ -ed -d

disjoint dɪsˈdʒɔɪnt, dɪz-, US dɪs- -s -s -ing -ɪŋ -ed -ɪd

disjointed dɪsˈdʒɔɪn.tɪd, dɪz-, US dɪsˈdʒɔɪn.t̬ɪd -ly -li -ness -nəs, -nɪs

disjunct dɪsˈdʒʌŋ*k*t, ˈ--

disjunction dɪsˈdʒʌŋ*k*.ʃᵊn -s -z

disjunctive dɪsˈdʒʌŋ*k*.tɪv -ly -li

disk dɪsk -s -s ˈ**disk** ˌ**drive**

diskette dɪˈsket -s -s

dislik|e dɪˈslaɪk, dɪzˈlaɪk, US dɪˈslaɪk -es -s -ing -ɪŋ -ed -t -able -ə.bᵊl
Note: The stress /ˈ--/ is, however, used in the expression **likes and dislikes**.

dislo|cate ˈdɪs.ləʊ|.keɪt, US dɪˈsloʊ-; US ˈdɪs.loʊ- -cates -keɪts -cating -keɪ.tɪŋ, US -keɪ.t̬ɪŋ -cated -keɪ.tɪd, US -keɪ.t̬ɪd

dislocation ˌdɪs.ləʊˈkeɪ.ʃᵊn, US -loʊˈ- -s -z

dislodg|e dɪˈslɒdʒ, US -ˈslɑːdʒ -es -ɪz -ing -ɪŋ -ed -d -(e)ment -mənt

disloyal dɪˈslɔɪ.əl; ˌdɪsˈlɔɪəl -ly -i

disloyalt|y dɪˈslɔɪ.əl.t|i; ˌdɪsˈlɔɪəl- -ies -iz

dismal ˈdɪz.məl -ly -i -ness -nəs, -nɪs

dismantl|e dɪˈsmæn.tᵊl, dɪzˈmæn-, US dɪˈsmæn.t̬ᵊl -es -z -ing -ɪŋ, dɪˈsmænt.lɪŋ, dɪzˈmænt-, US dɪˈsmæn.tᵊl.ɪŋ, -ˈsmænt.lɪŋ -ed -d

dismast ˌdɪsˈmɑːst, US -ˈmæst -s -s -ing -ɪŋ -ed -ɪd

dismay dɪˈsmeɪ, dɪzˈmeɪ -s -z -ing -ɪŋ -ed -d

dismemb|er dɪˈsmem.b|əʳ, US -b|ɚ -ers -əz, US -ɚz -ering -ᵊr.ɪŋ -ered -əd, US -ɚd -erment -ə.mənt, US -ɚ.mənt

dismiss dɪˈsmɪs -es -ɪz -ing -ɪŋ -ed -t

dismissal dɪˈsmɪs.ᵊl -s -z

dismissive dɪˈsmɪs.ɪv -ly -li -ness -nəs, -nɪs

dis|mount dɪˈs|maʊnt -mounts -maʊnts -mounting -maʊn.tɪŋ, US -maʊn.t̬ɪŋ -mounted -maʊn.tɪd, US -maʊn.t̬ɪd

Disney ˈdɪz.ni ˈ**Disney** ˌ**World**®

Disneyland® ˈdɪz.ni.lænd

disobedience ˌdɪs.əʊˈbiː.di.ən*t*s, US -əˈ-, -oʊˈ-

disobedient ˌdɪs.əʊˈbiː.di.ənt, US -əˈ-, -oʊˈ- -ly -li

disobey ˌdɪs.əʊˈbeɪ, US -əˈ-, -oʊˈ- -s -z -ing -ɪŋ -ed -d

disoblig|e ˌdɪs.əˈblaɪdʒ -es -ɪz -ing/ly -ɪŋ/li -ingness -ɪŋ.nəs, -nɪs -ed -d

disord|er dɪˈsɔː.d|əʳ, -ˈzɔː-, US -ˈsɔːr.d|ɚ, -ˈzɔːr- -ers -əz, US -ɚz -ering -ᵊr.ɪŋ -ered -əd, US -ɚd

disorderl|y dɪˈsɔː.dᵊl|.i, -ˈzɔː-, US -ˈsɔːr.dɚ.l|i, -ˈzɔːr- -iness -ɪ.nəs, -ɪ.nɪs

disorganization, -isa- dɪˌsɔː.gə.naɪˈzeɪ.ʃᵊn, -ˌzɔː-, -nɪˈ-; ˌdɪs.ɔː-, ˌdɪz-, US dɪˌsɔːr.gə.nəˈ-, -ˌzɔːr-

disorganiz|e, -is|e dɪˈsɔː.gə.naɪz, -ˈzɔː-; ˌdɪsˈɔː-, ˌdɪzˈɔː-, US dɪˈsɔːr-, -ˈzɔːr- -es -ɪz -ing -ɪŋ -ed -d

disorien|t dɪˈsɔː.ri.ən|t, -en|t, US -ˈsɔːr.i.en|t -ts -ts -ting -tɪŋ, US -t̬ɪŋ -ted -tɪd, US -t̬ɪd

disorien|tate dɪˈsɔː.ri.ən|.teɪt, -en-; ˌdɪsˈɔːr-, US dɪˈsɔːr.i- -tates -teɪts -tating -teɪ.tɪŋ, US -teɪ.t̬ɪŋ -tated -teɪ.tɪd, US -teɪ.t̬ɪd

disorientation dɪˌsɔː.ri.ənˈteɪ.ʃᵊn, -enˈ-; ˌdɪsˌɔː-, US dɪˌsɔːr.i-

disown dɪˈsəʊn; ˌdɪsˈəʊn, US dɪˈsoʊn -s -z -ing -ɪŋ -ed -d

disparag|e dɪˈspær.ɪdʒ, US -ˈsper-, -ˈspær- -es -ɪz -ing/ly -ɪŋ/li -ed -d -er/s -əʳ/z, US -ɚ/z -ement -mənt

disparate ˈdɪs.pᵊr.ət, -ɪt, -eɪt, US -ət, -ɪt; US dɪˈsper-, -ˈspær- -s -s

disparit|y dɪˈspær.ə.t|i, -ɪ.t|i, US dɪsˈper.ə.t̬|i, -ˈspær- -ies -iz

dispassionate dɪˈspæʃ.ᵊn.ət, -ɪt -ly -li -ness -nəs, -nɪs

dispatch n dɪˈspætʃ, də-; ˈdɪs.pætʃ, US dɪˈspætʃ; US ˈdɪs.pætʃ -es -ɪz **disˈpatch ˌbox; disˈpatch ˌrider**

dispatch v dɪˈspætʃ, də-, US dɪ- -es -ɪz -ing -ɪŋ -ed -t -er/s -əʳ/z, US -ɚ/z

dispel dɪˈspel -s -z -(l)ing -ɪŋ -(l)ed -d

dispensable dɪˈspen*t*.sə.bᵊl

dispensar|y dɪˈspen*t*.sᵊr|.i -ies -iz

dispensation ˌdɪs.penˈseɪ.ʃᵊn, -pənˈ- -s -z

dispensator|y dɪˈspen.sə.tᵊr|.i, -tr|i, US -tɔːr|.i -ies -iz

dispens|e dɪˈspen*t*s -es -ɪz -ing -ɪŋ -ed -t -er/s -əʳ/z, US -ɚ/z

dispersal dɪˈspɜː.sᵊl, US -ˈspɝː- -s -z

dispers|e dɪˈspɜːs, US -ˈspɝːs -es -ɪz -ing -ɪŋ -ed -t -er/s -əʳ/z, US -ɚ/z -ant/s -ᵊnt/s

dispersion, D~ dɪˈspɜː.ʃᵊn, US -ˈspɝː.ʒᵊn, -ʃᵊn -s -z

dispersive dɪˈspɜː.sɪv, US -ˈspɝː.zɪv, -sɪv

dispir|it dɪˈspɪr|.ɪt -its -ɪts -iting -ɪ.tɪŋ, US -ɪ.t̬ɪŋ -ited/ly -ɪ.tɪd/li, US -ɪ.t̬ɪd/li -itedness -ɪ.tɪd.nəs, -nɪs, US -ɪ.t̬ɪd.nəs, -nɪs

displac|e dɪˈspleɪs -es -ɪz -ing -ɪŋ -ed -t

displacement dɪˈspleɪs.mənt

display dɪˈspleɪ **-s** -z **-ing** -ɪŋ **-ed** -d **-er/s** -əʳ/z, (US) -ɚ/z
displeas|e dɪˈspliːz **-es** -ɪz **-ing/ly** -ɪŋ/li **-ed** -d
displeasure dɪˈspleʒ.əʳ, (US) -ɚ
di|sport dɪ|ˈspɔːt, (US) -|ˈspɔːrt **-sports** -ˈspɔːts, (US) -ˈspɔːrts **-sporting** -ˈspɔː.tɪŋ, (US) -ˈspɔːr.t̬ɪŋ **-sported** -ˈspɔː.tɪd, (US) -ˈspɔːr.t̬ɪd
disposable dɪˈspəʊ.zə.bᵊl, də-, (US) dɪˈspoʊ-
disposal dɪˈspəʊ.zᵊl, də-, (US) dɪˈspoʊ- **-s** -z
Disposall® dɪˈspəʊ.zɔːl, də-, (US) dɪˈspoʊ.zɑːl, -zɔːl
dispos|e dɪˈspəʊz, də-, (US) -ˈspoʊz **-es** -ɪz **-ing** -ɪŋ **-ed** -d **-er/s** -əʳ/z, (US) -ɚ/z
disposition ˌdɪs.pəˈzɪʃ.ᵊn **-s** -z
dispossess ˌdɪs.pəˈzes **-es** -ɪz **-ing** -ɪŋ **-ed** -t
dispossession ˌdɪs.pəˈzeʃ.ᵊn
Disprin® ˈdɪs.prɪn **-s** -z
disproof dɪˈspruːf
disproportion ˌdɪs.prəˈpɔː.ʃᵊn, (US) -ˈpɔːr- **-ed** -d
disproportional ˌdɪs.prəˈpɔː.ʃᵊn.ᵊl, -ˈpɔːʃ.nᵊl, (US) -ˈpɔːr.ʃᵊn.ᵊl, -ˈpɔːrʃ.nᵊl **-ly** -i
disproportionate ˌdɪs.prəˈpɔː.ʃᵊn.ət, -ɪt, (US) -ˈpɔːr- **-ly** -li **-ness** -nəs, -nɪs
disproval dɪˈspruː.vᵊl; ˌdɪsˈpruː-
disprov|e dɪˈspruːv; ˌdɪsˈpruːv **-es** -z **-ing** -ɪŋ **-ed** -d
disputable dɪˈspjuː.tə.bᵊl, də-; ˈdɪs.pjʊ-, (US) dɪˈspjuː.t̬ə-; (US) ˈdɪs.pjʊ-, -pjə-
disputableness dɪˈspjuː.tə.bᵊl.nəs, də-, -nɪs, (US) dɪˈspjuː.t̬ə-
disputant dɪˈspjuː.tᵊnt; ˈdɪs.pjʊ-, (US) ˈdɪs.pjʊ.tᵊnt, -pjə-; (US) dɪˈspjuː- **-s** -s
disputation ˌdɪs.pjʊˈteɪ.ʃᵊn, (US) -pjuːˈ- **-s** -z
disputatious ˌdɪs.pjʊˈteɪ.ʃəs, (US) -pjuːˈ- **-ly** -li **-ness** -nəs, -nɪs
disputative dɪˈspjuː.tə.tɪv, (US) -t̬ə.t̬ɪv
dispute n dɪˈspjuːt; ˈdɪs.pjuːt, (US) dɪˈspjuːt **-s** -s
di|spute v dɪ|ˈspjuːt **-sputes** -ˈspjuːts **-sputing** -ˈspjuː.tɪŋ, (US) -ˈspjuː.t̬ɪŋ **-sputed** -ˈspjuː.tɪd, (US) -ˈspjuː.t̬ɪd **-sputer/s** -ˈspjuː.təʳ/z, (US) -ˈspjuː.t̬ɚ/z
disqualification dɪˌskwɒl.ɪ.fɪˈkeɪ.ʃᵊn, ˌ-ə-, -fəˈ-; ˌdɪsˌkwɒl-, (US) dɪˌskwɑː.lə- **-s** -z
disquali|fy dɪˈskwɒl.ɪ|.faɪ, ˈ-ə-; (US) dɪˈskwɑː.lɪ-, ˈ-lə-, ˌdɪsˈkwɒl.ɪ, ˈ-ə- **-fies** -faɪz **-fying** -faɪ.ɪŋ **-fied** -faɪd
di|squiet n, v dɪ|ˈskwaɪ.ət **-squiets** -ˈskwaɪ.əts **-squieting** -ˈskwaɪ.ə.tɪŋ, (US) -ˈskwaɪ.ə.t̬ɪŋ **-squieted** -ˈskwaɪ.ə.tɪd, (US) -ˈskwaɪ.ə.t̬ɪd
disquietude dɪˈskwaɪ.ə.tʃuːd, -tjuːd, -ˈskwaɪ.ɪ-, (US) -ˈskwaɪ.ə.tuːd, -tjuːd
disquisition ˌdɪs.kwɪˈzɪʃ.ᵊn, -kwəˈ- **-s** -z
disquisitional ˌdɪs.kwɪˈzɪʃ.ᵊn.ᵊl, -kwəˈ-, ˈ-nᵊl
disquisitive dɪˈskwɪz.ə.tɪv, -ɪ.tɪv, (US) -ə.t̬ɪv
d'Israeli dɪzˈreɪ.li, dɪs-
Disraeli dɪzˈreɪ.li, dɪs-
disregard ˌdɪs.rɪˈgɑːd, -rəˈ-, (US) -rɪˈgɑːrd **-s** -z **-ing** -ɪŋ **-ed** -ɪd
disregardful ˌdɪs.rɪˈgɑːd.fᵊl, -rəˈ-, -fʊl, (US) -rɪˈgɑːrd- **-ly** -i
disrepair ˌdɪs.rɪˈpeəʳ, -rəˈ-, (US) -rɪˈper
disreputability dɪsˌrep.jə.təˈbɪl.ə.ti, -jʊ-, -ɪ.ti, (US) -jə.t̬əˈ-
disreputab|le dɪsˈrep.jə.tə.b|ᵊl, -jʊ-, (US) -jə.t̬ə- **-ly** -li **-leness** -ᵊl.nəs, -nɪs
disrepute ˌdɪs.rɪˈpjuːt, -rəˈ-, (US) -rɪˈ-
disrespect ˌdɪs.rɪˈspekt, -rəˈ-, (US) -rɪˈ-
disrespectful ˌdɪs.rɪˈspekt.fᵊl, -rəˈ-, -fʊl, (US) -rɪˈ- **-ly** -i **-ness** -nəs, -nɪs
disrob|e dɪsˈrəʊb, (US) -ˈroʊb **-es** -z **-ing** -ɪŋ **-ed** -d
disrupt dɪsˈrʌpt **-s** -s **-ing** -ɪŋ **-ed** -ɪd
disruption dɪsˈrʌp.ʃᵊn **-s** -z
disruptive dɪsˈrʌp.tɪv **-ly** -li **-ness** -nəs, -nɪs
Diss dɪs
dissatisfaction dɪsˌsæt.ɪsˈfæk.ʃᵊn, ˌdɪs.sæt-, -əsˈ-, (US) ˌdɪs.sæt̬.əsˈ-
dissatisfactor|y dɪsˌsæt.ɪsˈfæk.tᵊr|.i, ˌdɪs.sæt-, -əsˈ-, (US) ˌdɪs.sæt̬.əsˈ- **-ily** -ᵊl.i, -ɪ.li **-iness** -i.nəs, -i.nɪs
dissatis|fy dɪsˈsæt.ɪs|.faɪ, ˌdɪs-, -əs-, (US) -ˈsæt̬.əs- **-fies** -faɪz **-fying** -faɪ.ɪŋ **-fied** -faɪd
dissect dɪˈsekt, də-, daɪ-, (US) dɪˈsekt, daɪ-; (US) ˈdaɪ.sekt **-s** -s **-ing** -ɪŋ **-ed** -ɪd **-or/s** -əʳ/z, (US) -ɚ/z **-ible** -ə.bᵊl, -ɪ.bᵊl

> Note: The pronunciation /daɪ-/ has become widespread, though all other words spelt 'diss-' have the /dɪs-/ pronunciation. This may be due to analogy with 'bisect' /baɪˈsekt/.

dissection dɪˈsek.ʃᵊn, də-, daɪ-, (US) dɪˈsek-, daɪ-; (US) ˈdaɪ.sek- **-s** -z
dissemblanc|e dɪˈsem.blənts **-es** -ɪz
dissembl|e dɪˈsem.bᵊl **-es** -z **-ing** -ɪŋ, ˈ-blɪŋ **-ed** -d **-er/s** -əʳ/z, ˈ-bləʳ/z, (US) -ɚ/z
dissemi|nate dɪˈsem.ɪ|.neɪt, ˈ-ə- **-nates** -neɪts **-nating** -neɪ.tɪŋ, (US) -neɪ.t̬ɪŋ **-nated** -neɪ.tɪd, (US) -neɪ.t̬ɪd **-nator/s** -neɪ.təʳ/z, (US) -neɪ.t̬ɚ/z
dissemination dɪˌsem.ɪˈneɪ.ʃᵊn, -əˈ-
dissension, dissention dɪˈsen.tʃᵊn **-s** -z
dis|sent dɪ|ˈsent **-sents** -ˈsents **-senting** -ˈsen.tɪŋ, (US) -ˈsen.t̬ɪŋ **-sented** -ˈsen.tɪd, (US) -ˈsen.t̬ɪd **-senter/s** -ˈsen.təʳ/z, (US) -ˈsen.t̬ɚ/z
dissentient dɪˈsen.tʃi.ənt, -tʃᵊnt, (US) -ˈsent.ʃᵊnt **-s** -s
dissertation ˌdɪs.əˈteɪ.ʃᵊn, -ɜːˈ-, (US) -ɚˈ- **-s** -z
disservic|e ˌdɪsˈsɜː.vɪs, dɪ-, (US) -ˈsɝː- **-es** -ɪz
dissev|er dɪsˈsev|.əʳ, (US) -ɚ **-ers** -əz, (US) -ɚz **-ering** -ᵊr.ɪŋ **-ered** -əd, (US) -ɚd **-erment** -ə.mənt, (US) -ɚ.mənt **-erance** -ᵊr.ᵊnts
dissidence ˈdɪs.ɪ.dᵊnts, ˈ-ə-
dissident ˈdɪs.ɪ.dᵊnt, ˈ-ə- **-s** -s
dissimilar ˌdɪsˈsɪm.ɪ.ləʳ, dɪ-, ˈ-ə-, (US) -lɚ **-ly** -li
dissimilarit|y ˌdɪsˌsɪm.ɪˈlær.ə.t|i, dɪ-, -əˈ-, -ɪ.t|i, (US) -ˈler.ə.t̬|i, -ˈlær- **-ies** -iz
dissimi|late dɪˈsɪm.ɪ|.leɪt, ˌdɪs-, ˈ-ə- **-lates** -leɪts **-lating** -leɪ.tɪŋ, (US) -leɪ.t̬ɪŋ **-lated** -leɪ.tɪd, (US) -leɪ.t̬ɪd
dissimilation ˌdɪsˌsɪm.ɪˈleɪ.ʃᵊn, dɪ-, -əˈ- **-s** -z
dissimilitude ˌdɪs.sɪˈmɪl.ɪ.tʃuːd, -tjuːd, -ɪˈ-, ˈ-ə-, (US) -tuːd, -tjuːd
dissimu|late dɪˈsɪm.jə|.leɪt, ˌdɪs-, -jʊ- **-lates** -leɪts **-lating** -leɪ.tɪŋ, (US) -leɪ.t̬ɪŋ **-lated** -leɪ.tɪd, (US) -leɪ.t̬ɪd **-lator/s** -leɪ.təʳ/z, (US) -leɪ.t̬ɚ/z
dissimulation ˌdɪsˌsɪm.jəˈleɪ.ʃᵊn, dɪ-, -jʊˈ- **-s** -z
dissi|pate ˈdɪs.ɪ|.peɪt, ˈ-ə- **-pates** -peɪts **-pating** -peɪ.tɪŋ, (US) -peɪ.t̬ɪŋ **-pated** -peɪ.tɪd, (US) -peɪ.t̬ɪd **-pative** -peɪ.tɪv, (US) -peɪ.t̬ɪv
dissipation ˌdɪs.ɪˈpeɪ.ʃᵊn, -əˈ- **-s** -z
dissociable *separable:* dɪˈsəʊ.ʃi.ə.bᵊl, ˌdɪs-, (US) -ˈsoʊ-, -ʃə.bᵊl *unsociable:* ˌdɪsˈsəʊ.ʃə.bᵊl, dɪ-, (US) -ˈsoʊ-
dissoci|ate dɪˈsəʊ.ʃi|.eɪt, -si-, (US) -ˈsoʊ- **-ates** -eɪts **-ating** -eɪ.tɪŋ, (US) -eɪ.t̬ɪŋ **-ated** -eɪ.tɪd, (US) -eɪ.t̬ɪd
dissociation dɪˌsəʊ.ʃiˈeɪ.ʃᵊn, ˌdɪs-, -siˈ-, (US) -ˌsoʊ-
dissolubility dɪˌsɒl.jəˈbɪl.ə.ti, -jʊˈ-, -ɪ.ti, (US) -ˌsɑːl.jəˈbɪl.ə.t̬i, -jʊˈ-
dissolub|le dɪˈsɒl.jə.b|ᵊl, -jʊ-, (US) -ˈsɑːl- **-ly** -li **-leness** -ᵊl.nəs, -nɪs
dissolute ˈdɪs.ə.luːt, -ljuːt, (US) -luːt **-s** -s **-ly** -li **-ness** -nəs, -nɪs
dissolution ˌdɪs.əˈluː.ʃᵊn, -ˈljuː-, (US) -ˈluː- **-s** -z
dissolvability dɪˌzɒl.vəˈbɪl.ə.ti, dəˌzɒl-, -ˌsɒl-, -ɪ.ti, (US) dɪˌzɑːl.vəˈbɪl.ə.t̬i, -ˌzɔːl-
dissolv|e dɪˈzɒlv, -ˈsɒlv, (US) -ˈzɑːlv, -ˈzɔːlv **-es** -z **-ing** -ɪŋ **-ed** -d **-able** -ə.bᵊl
dissolvent dɪˈzɒl.vənt, -ˈsɒl-, (US) -ˈzɑːl-, -ˈzɔːl- **-s** -s
dissonanc|e ˈdɪs.ᵊn.ənts **-es** -ɪz
dissonant ˈdɪs.ᵊn.ənt **-ly** -li
dissuad|e dɪˈsweɪd **-es** -z **-ing** -ɪŋ **-ed** -ɪd
dissuasion dɪˈsweɪ.ʒᵊn
dissuasive dɪˈsweɪ.sɪv, -zɪv, (US) -sɪv **-ly** -li **-ness** -nəs, -nɪs
dissymmetric ˌdɪs.ɪˈmet.rɪk, -sɪmˈ-
dissymmetry dɪˈsɪm.ə.tri, ˌdɪs-, ˈ-ɪ-

D

distaff ˈdɪs.tɑːf, (US) -tæf **-s** -s
distanc|e ˈdɪs.tᵊnts **-es** -ɪz **-ing** -ɪŋ **-ed** -t
distant ˈdɪs.tᵊnt **-ly** -li
distaste dɪˈsteɪst **-s** -s
distasteful dɪˈsteɪst.fᵊl, -fʊl **-ly** -i **-ness** -nəs, -nɪs
distemp|er dɪˈstem.p|əʳ, (US) -p|ɚ **-ers** -əz, (US) -ɚz **-ering** -ᵊr.ɪŋ **-ered** -əd, (US) -ɚd
distend dɪˈstend **-s** -z **-ing** -ɪŋ **-ed** -ɪd
distensible dɪˈstent.sə.bᵊl, -sɪ-
distension dɪˈsten.tʃᵊn, (US) -ˈstent.ʃᵊn
distich ˈdɪs.tɪk **-s** -s **-ous** -əs
distil(l) dɪˈstɪl, də-, (US) dɪ- **-s** -z **-ing** -ɪŋ **-ed** -d
distillate ˈdɪs.tɪ.lət, -tᵊl.ət, -eɪt, -ɪt, (US) -tə.leɪt, -tᵊl.ɪt; (US) dɪˈstɪl.ɪt **-s** -s
distillation ˌdɪs.tɪˈleɪ.ʃᵊn, -təˈ- **-s** -z
distillatory dɪˈstɪl.ə.tᵊr.i, də-, -tri, (US) dɪˈstɪl.ə.tɔːr.i
distiller dɪˈstɪl.əʳ, də-, (US) dɪˈstɪl.ɚ **-s** -z
distiller|y dɪˈstɪl.ᵊr|.i, də-, (US) dɪ- **-ies** -iz
distinct dɪˈstɪŋkt, də-, (US) dɪ- **-est** -ɪst, -əst **-ly** -li **-ness** -nəs, -nɪs
distinction dɪˈstɪŋk.ʃᵊn, də-, (US) dɪ- **-s** -z
distinctive dɪˈstɪŋk.tɪv, də-, (US) dɪ- **-ly** -li **-ness** -nəs, -nɪs
distinguish dɪˈstɪŋ.gwɪʃ, də-, (US) dɪ- **-es** -ɪz **-ing** -ɪŋ **-ed** -t
distinguishab|le dɪˈstɪŋ.gwɪ.ʃə.b|ᵊl, də-, (US) dɪ- **-ly** -li
di|stort dɪ|ˈstɔːt, (US) -ˈstɔːrt **-storts** -ˈstɔːts, (US) -ˈstɔːrts **-storting** -ˈstɔː.tɪŋ, (US) -ˈstɔːr.t̬ɪŋ **-storted** -ˈstɔː.tɪd, (US) -ˈstɔːr.t̬ɪd
distortion dɪˈstɔː.ʃᵊn, (US) -ˈstɔːr- **-s** -z
distract dɪˈstrækt, dəˈstrækt, (US) dɪ- **-s** -s **-ing** -ɪŋ **-ed/ly** -ɪd/li **-edness** -ɪd.nəs, -nɪs
distraction dɪˈstræk.ʃᵊn, də- **-s** -z
distrain dɪˈstreɪn, də-, (US) dɪ- **-s** -z **-ing** -ɪŋ **-ed** -d **-er/s** -əʳ/z, (US) -ɚ/z **-able** -ə.bᵊl
distrainee ˌdɪs.treɪˈniː **-s** -z
distrainor ˌdɪs.treɪˈnɔːʳ, (US) -ˈnɔːr, dɪˈstreɪ.nɚ **-s** -z
distraint dɪˈstreɪnt **-s** -s
distrait dɪˈstreɪ; ˈdɪs.treɪ, (US) dɪˈstreɪ
distraught dɪˈstrɔːt, (US) -ˈstrɑːt, -ˈstrɔːt
distress dɪˈstres **-es** -ɪz **-ing/ly** -ɪŋ/li **-ed** -t
distressful dɪˈstres.fᵊl, -fʊl **-ly** -i
distributable dɪˈstrɪb.jə.tə.bᵊl, -jʊ-, (US) -t̬ə-
distribu|te dɪˈstrɪb.juː|t; ˈdɪs.trɪ.bjuː|t, -trə-, (US) dɪˈstrɪb.juː|t, -jʊ|t, -jə|t **-tes** -ts **-ting** -tɪŋ, (US) -t̬ɪŋ **-ted** -tɪd, (US) -t̬ɪd
distribution ˌdɪs.trɪˈbjuː.ʃᵊn, -trəˈ- **-s** -z
distributive dɪˈstrɪb.jə.tɪv, -jʊ-, (US) -jə.t̬ɪv **-ly** -li
distributor dɪˈstrɪb.jə.təʳ, -jʊ-, (US) -t̬ɚ **-s** -z
district ˈdɪs.trɪkt **-s** -s ˌ**district atˈtorney;** ˌ**District of Coˈlumbia**
distrust dɪˈstrʌst; ˌdɪsˈtrʌst **-s** -s **-ing** -ɪŋ **-ed** -ɪd
distrustful dɪˈstrʌst.fᵊl, -fʊl; ˌdɪsˈtrʌst- **-ly** -i **-ness** -nəs, -nɪs
disturb dɪˈstɜːb, (US) -ˈstɝːb **-s** -z **-ing/ly** -ɪŋ/li **-ed** -d **-er/s** -əʳ/z, (US) -ɚ/z
disturbanc|e dɪˈstɜː.bᵊnts, (US) -ˈstɝː- **-es** -ɪz
distyle ˈdɪs.taɪl; ˈdaɪ.staɪl **-s** -z
disulphate daɪˈsʌl.feɪt, -fɪt **-s** -s
disulphide daɪˈsʌl.faɪd **-s** -z
disunion dɪˈsjuː.njən, -ni.ən, (US) -ˈ-njən **-s** -z
disu|nite ˌdɪs.juː|ˈnaɪt **-nites** -ˈnaɪts **-niting** -ˈnaɪ.tɪŋ, (US) -ˈnaɪ.t̬ɪŋ **-nited** -ˈnaɪ.tɪd, (US) -ˈnaɪ.t̬ɪd
disunity dɪˈsjuː.nɪ.ti, -nə-, (US) -t̬i
disuse n dɪˈsjuːs
disus|e v dɪˈsjuːz **-es** -ɪz **-ing** -ɪŋ **-ed** -d
disyllabic ˌdaɪ.sɪˈlæb.ɪk, ˌdɪs.ɪˈ-, -əˈ-
disyllable daɪˈsɪl.ə.bᵊl, dɪ- **-s** -z
ditch dɪtʃ **-es** -ɪz **-ing** -ɪŋ **-ed** -t **-er/s** -əʳ/z, (US) -ɚ/z
Ditchling ˈdɪtʃ.lɪŋ
ditchwater ˈdɪtʃˌwɔː.təʳ, (US) -ˌwɑː.t̬ɚ, -ˌwɔː- **as** ˌ**dull as** ˈ**ditch-water**
dith|er ˈdɪð|.əʳ, (US) -ɚ **-ers** -əz, (US) -ɚz **-ering** -ᵊr.ɪŋ **-ered** -əd, (US) -ɚd **-erer/s** -ᵊr.əʳ/z, (US) -ɚ.ɚ/z **-ery** -ᵊr.i
dithyramb ˈdɪθ.ɪ.ræmb, ˈ-ə- **-s** -z

> Note: The /b/ is rarely pronounced.

dithyramb|us ˌdɪθ.ɪˈræm.b|əs, -əˈ- **-i** -aɪ **-ic/s** -ɪk/s
ditransitive ˌdaɪˈtræn.sɪ.tɪv, -ˈtrɑːn-, -sə-, (US) -ˈtræn.sə.t̬ɪv **-s** -z **-ly** -li
dits|y ˈdɪt.s|i **-ier** -i.əʳ, (US) -i.ɚ **-iest** -i.ɪst, -i.əst
ditto ˈdɪt.əʊ, (US) ˈdɪt̬.oʊ **-s** -z
Ditton ˈdɪt.ᵊn
ditt|y ˈdɪt|.i, (US) ˈdɪt̬- **-ies** -iz
diures|is ˌdaɪ.jʊəˈriː.s|ɪs, -jəˈ-, (US) -jəˈ-, -əˈ-, -jʊrˈ- **-es** -iːz
diuretic ˌdaɪ.jʊəˈret.ɪk, -jəˈ-, (US) -jəˈret̬-, -əˈ- **-s** -s
diurnal daɪˈɜː.nᵊl, (US) -ˈɝː- **-s** -z **-ly** -i
div dɪv **-s** -z
diva ˈdiː.və **-s** -z
diva|gate ˈdaɪ.və|.geɪt; -veɪ-; ˈdɪv.ə-, (US) ˈdaɪ.və-, ˈdɪv.ə- **-gates** -geɪts **-gating** -geɪ.tɪŋ, (US) -geɪ.t̬ɪŋ **-gated** -geɪ.tɪd, (US) -geɪ.t̬ɪd
divagation ˌdaɪ.vəˈgeɪ.ʃᵊn, -veɪˈ-, (US) ˌdaɪ.vəˈ-, ˌdɪv.əˈ- **-s** -z
divalent ˌdaɪˈveɪ.lənt, ˈdaɪ.veɪ-
Divali dɪˈvɑː.li
divan dɪˈvæn, də-, daɪ-; ˈdaɪ.væn, (US) dɪˈvæn, daɪ-; (US) ˈdaɪ.væn **-s** -z
div|e daɪv **-es** -z **-ing** -ɪŋ **-ed** -d **dove** dəʊv, (US) doʊv ˈ**diving** ˌ**bell;** ˈ**diving** ˌ**board;** ˈ**diving** ˌ**suit**
dive-bomb ˈdaɪv.bɒm, (US) -bɑːm **-s** -z **-ing** -ɪŋ **-ed** -d **-er/s** -əʳ/z, (US) -ɚ/z
diver, D~ ˈdaɪ.vəʳ, (US) -vɚ **-s** -z
diverg|e daɪˈvɜːdʒ, dɪ-, (US) dɪˈvɝːdʒ, daɪ- **-es** -ɪz **-ing** -ɪŋ **-ed** -d
divergenc|e daɪˈvɜː.dʒənts, dɪ-, (US) dɪˈvɝː-, daɪ- **-es** -ɪz **-y** -i **-ies** -iz
divergent daɪˈvɜː.dʒənt, dɪ-, (US) dɪˈvɝː-, daɪ- **-ly** -li
divers ˈdaɪ.vəz, -vɜːz, -vɜːs; daɪˈvɜːs, (US) ˈdaɪ.vɚz
diverse daɪˈvɜːs, ˈ--, (US) dɪˈvɝːs, daɪ-; (US) ˈdaɪ.vɝːs **-ly** -li
diversification daɪˌvɜː.sɪ.fɪˈkeɪ.ʃᵊn, dɪ-, də-, -sə-, -fəˈ-, (US) dɪˌvɝː-, daɪ- **-s** -z
diversi|fy daɪˈvɜː.sɪ|.faɪ, dɪ-, ˈ-sə-, (US) dɪˈvɝː-, daɪ- **-fies** -faɪz **-fying** -faɪ.ɪŋ **-fied** -faɪd
diversion daɪˈvɜː.ʃᵊn, dɪ-, -ʒən, (US) dɪˈvɝː-, daɪ- **-s** -z
diversionary daɪˈvɜː.ʃᵊn.ᵊr.i, dɪ-, -ʒᵊn-, (US) dɪˈvɝː.ʒᵊn.er.i, daɪ-, -ʃᵊn-
diversionist daɪˈvɜː.ʃᵊn.ɪst, dɪ-, -ʒᵊn-, (US) dɪˈvɝː-, daɪ- **-s** -s
diversit|y daɪˈvɜː.sə.t|i, dɪ-, -ɪ.t|i, (US) dɪˈvɝː.sə.t̬|i, daɪ- **-ies** -iz
di|vert daɪ|ˈvɜːt, dɪ-, (US) dɪ|ˈvɝːt, daɪ- **-verts** -ˈvɜːts, (US) -ˈvɝːts **-verting/ly** -ˈvɜː.tɪŋ/li, (US) -ˈvɝː.t̬ɪŋ/li **-verted** -ˈvɜː.tɪd, (US) -ˈvɝː.t̬ɪd
diverticulitis ˌdaɪ.vəˌtɪk.jʊˈlaɪ.tɪs, -vɜːˌ-, -jəˈ-, -təs, (US) -vɚˌtɪk.jəˈlaɪ.t̬ɪs, -t̬əs, -jʊˈ-
diverticulosis ˌdaɪ.vəˌtɪk.jʊˈləʊ.sɪs, -vɜːˌ-, -jəˈ-, (US) -vɚˌtɪk.jəˈloʊ-, -jʊˈ-
diverticulum ˌdaɪ.vəˈtɪk.jʊ.ləm, -vɜːˈ-, -jə-, (US) -vɚˈtɪk.jə-, -jʊ-
divertimento dɪˌvɜː.tɪˈmen.təʊ, -ˌveə-, -təˈ-, (US) -ˌvɝː.t̬əˈmen.toʊ
divertissement ˌdiː.veəˈtiːs.mɑ̃ːŋ, -vəˈ-, -vɜːˈ-, dɪˈvɜː.tɪs.mənt, (US) ˌdɪv.erˈtiːs.mɑ̃ː
Dives *in Bible:* ˈdaɪ.viːz *surname:* daɪvz
divest daɪˈvest, dɪ-, (US) dɪ-, daɪ- **-s** -s **-ing** -ɪŋ **-ed** -ɪd
divestiture daɪˈves.tɪ.tʃəʳ, dɪ-, (US) dɪˈves.tɪ.tʃɚ, daɪ-
divestment daɪˈvest.mənt, dɪ-, (US) dɪ-, daɪ- **-s** -s
divid|e dɪˈvaɪd, də- **-es** -z **-ing** -ɪŋ **-ed/ly** -ɪd/li **-able** -ə.bᵊl
dividend ˈdɪv.ɪ.dend, ˈ-ə-, -dənd **-s** -z
divider dɪˈvaɪ.dəʳ, də-, (US) -dɚ **-s** -z
divination ˌdɪv.ɪˈneɪ.ʃᵊn, -əˈ- **-s** -z
divin|e n, adj dɪˈvaɪn, də- **-es** -z **-er** -əʳ, (US) -ɚ **-est** -ɪst, -əst **-ely** -li **-eness** -nəs, -nɪs **diˌvine** ˈ**right**
divin|e v dɪˈvaɪn, də- **-es** -z **-ing** -ɪŋ **-ed** -d **-er/s** -əʳ/z, (US) -ɚ/z **diˈvining** ˌ**rod**
divinit|y dɪˈvɪn.ə.t|i, də-, -ɪ.t|i, (US) -ə.t̬|i **-ies** -iz
divisibility dɪˌvɪz.əˈbɪl.ə.ti, də-, -ɪˈ-, -ɪ.ti, (US) -əˈbɪl.ə.t̬i
divisib|le dɪˈvɪz.ə.b|ᵊl, də-, ˈ-ɪ- **-ly** -li
division dɪˈvɪʒ.ᵊn, də- **-s** -z

divisional dɪˈvɪʒ.ən.əl, də-, ˈ-nəl
divisive dɪˈvaɪ.sɪv, də- **-ly** -li **-ness** -nəs, -nɪs
divisor dɪˈvaɪ.zəʳ, də-, (US) -zɚ **-s** -z
divorc|e dɪˈvɔːs, də-, (US) -ˈvɔːrs **-es** -ɪz **-ing** -ɪŋ **-ed** -t **-er/s** -əʳ/z, (US) -ɚ/z
divorcé(e), divorcee dɪˌvɔːˈsiː, də-, -ˈseɪ; ˌdɪv.ɔːˈ-, (US) dɪˌvɔːrˈseɪ, də-, -ˈsiː; (US) -ˈvɔːr.seɪ, -siː **-s** -z
divot ˈdɪv.ət **-s** -s
divulg|e daɪˈvʌldʒ, dɪ-, (US) dɪ-, daɪ- **-es** -ɪz **-ing** -ɪŋ **-ed** -d
divulsion daɪˈvʌl.ʃən, dɪ-, (US) dɪ-, daɪ- **-s** -z
divv|y ˈdɪv|.i **-ies** -iz **-ying** -i.ɪŋ **-ied** -id
divvy-up ˌdɪv.iˈʌp
Diwali dɪˈwɑː.li
Dix dɪks
Dixey, Dixie ˈdɪk.si
dixieland, D~ ˈdɪk.si.lænd
Dixon ˈdɪk.sən
Dixwell ˈdɪk.swəl, -swel
DIY ˌdiː.aɪˈwaɪ
dizz|y ˈdɪz|.i **-ier** -i.əʳ, (US) -i.ɚ **-iest** -i.ɪst, -i.əst **-ily** -əl.i, -ɪ.li **-iness** -ɪ.nəs, -ɪ.nɪs **-ies** -iz **-ying/ly** -i.ɪŋ **-ied** -id
DJ ˌdiːˈdʒeɪ, (US) ˈ-- **-s** -z *stress shift, British only:* ˌ**DJ** ˈ**culture**
Djakarta dʒəˈkɑː.tə, (US) -ˈkɑːr.t̬ə
Django ˈdʒæŋ.gəʊ, (US) -goʊ
djellaba(h) dʒəˈlɑː.bə **-s** -z
Djibouti dʒɪˈbuː.ti, dʒə-, (US) -t̬i
djinn dʒɪn **-s** -z
djinni dʒɪˈni, ˈdʒɪn.i
Djukanovic dʒʊˈkæn.ə.vɪtʃ, (US) -ˈkɑːn-, dʒuː-, -oʊ-
dl (abbrev. for **decilitre/s, deciliter/s**) *singular:* ˈdes.ɪˌliː.təʳ, (US) -t̬ɚ; *plural:* -z
DLit(t) ˌdiːˈlɪt
dm (abbrev. for **decimetre/s, decimeter/s**) *singular:* ˈdes.ɪˌmiː.təʳ, (US) -t̬ɚ; *plural:* -z
D-mark ˈdɔɪtʃ.mɑːk, (US) -mɑːrk **-s** -s
DNA ˌdiː.enˈeɪ
Dnepropetrovsk ˌdnjep.rɒp.jetˈrɒfsk, (US) ˌnep.roʊ.pəˈtrɔːfsk, ˌdnjep-, -pjəˈ-
Dnieper ˈdniː.pəʳ, (US) -pɚ
D-notic|e ˈdiːˌnəʊ.tɪs, (US) -ˌnoʊ.t̬ɪs **-es** -ɪz
do v *strong form:* duː; *weak forms:* də, du **dost** *strong form:* dʌst; *weak form:* dəst **doth** *strong form:* dʌθ; *weak form:* dəθ **doeth** ˈduː.ɪθ **does** *strong form:* dʌz; *weak form:* dəz **doing** ˈduː.ɪŋ **did** dɪd **done** dʌn **doer/s** ˈduː.əʳ/z, (US) -ɚ/z
Note: Weak-form word. The strong form /duː/ is normally used in final position (e.g. 'Yes, I do'), when it is used as a full verb rather than as an auxiliary (e.g. 'Do it yourself'), for emphasis (e.g. 'Why **do** you like him?') or for contrast (e.g. 'I do and I don't'). There are two weak forms: /də/ before consonants (e.g. 'How do they do it' /ˌhaʊ.də.ðeɪˈduː.ɪt/) and /du/ before vowels (e.g. 'Why do all the books disappear?' /ˌwaɪ.duˌɔːl.ðəˈbʊks.dɪs.ə.pɪəʳ/ (US) /-pɪɚ/).
do n *entertainment:* duː *musical note:* dəʊ, (US) doʊ **-s** -z
do. (abbrev. for **ditto**) ˈdɪt.əʊ, (US) ˈdɪt̬.oʊ
DOA ˌdiː.əʊˈeɪ, (US) -oʊˈ-
doable ˈduː.ə.bəl
Doane dəʊn, (US) doʊn
dob dɒb, (US) dɑːb **-s** -z **-bing** -ɪŋ **-bed** -d **-ber/s** -əʳ/z, (US) -ɚ/z
Dobb dɒb, (US) dɑːb **-s** -z
dobbin, D~ ˈdɒb.ɪn, (US) ˈdɑː.bɪn **-s** -z
Dobell dəʊˈbel, ˈdəʊ.bəl, (US) ˈdoʊ.bəl, -bel
doberman, D~ ˈdəʊ.bə.mən, (US) ˈdoʊ.bɚ- **-s** -z
Doberman pinscher ˌdəʊ.bə.mənˈpɪn.*t*ʃəʳ, (US) ˌdoʊ.bɚ.mənˈpɪnt.ʃɚ
Dobie ˈdəʊ.bi, (US) ˈdoʊ-
dobra ˈdəʊ.brə, (US) ˈdoʊ- **-s** -z
Dobrée ˈdəʊ.breɪ, (US) ˈdoʊ-
Dobson ˈdɒb.sən, (US) ˈdɑːb-
doc dɒk, (US) dɑːk **-s** -s
docent ˈdəʊ.sənt, dəʊˈsent, (US) ˈdoʊ.sənt, -sent; (US) doʊˈsent **-s** -s
Docet|ism dəʊˈsiː.t|ɪ.zəm; ˈdəʊ.sɪ-, (US) doʊˈsiː.t|ɪ-; (US) ˈdoʊ.sə.t̬|ɪ- **-ist/s** -ɪst/s
Docherty ˈdɒk.ə.ti, ˈdɒx-, (US) ˈdɑː.kɚ.t̬i
docile ˈdəʊ.saɪl, (US) ˈdɑː.səl, -saɪl **-ly** -li
docility dəʊˈsɪl.ə.ti, -ɪ.ti, (US) dɑːˈsɪl.ə.t̬i, doʊ-
dock dɒk, (US) dɑːk **-s** -s **-ing** -ɪŋ **-ed** -t
dockage ˈdɒk.ɪdʒ, (US) ˈdɑː.kɪdʒ
docker, D~ ˈdɒk.əʳ, (US) ˈdɑː.kɚ **-s** -z
Dockerill ˈdɒk.ər.əl, (US) ˈdɑː.kɚ-
dock|et ˈdɒk|.ɪt, (US) ˈdɑː.k|ɪt **-ets** -ɪts **-eting** -ɪ.tɪŋ, (US) -ɪ.t̬ɪŋ **-eted** -ɪ.tɪd, (US) -ɪ.t̬ɪd
dockland, D~ ˈdɒk.lænd, -lənd, (US) ˈdɑːk- **-s** -z
dockside ˈdɒk.saɪd, (US) ˈdɑːk-
dockworker ˈdɒkˌwɜː.kəʳ, (US) ˈdɑːkˌwɝː.kɚ **-s** -z
dockyard ˈdɒk.jɑːd, (US) ˈdɑːk.jɑːrd **-s** -z
Doc Martens® ˌdɒkˈmɑː.tɪnz, (US) ˌdɑːkˈmɑːr.tənz
doct|or ˈdɒk.t|əʳ, (US) ˈdɑːk.t|ɚ **-ors** -əz, (US) -ɚz **-oring** -ər.ɪŋ **-ored** -əd, (US) -ɚd
doctoral ˈdɒk.tər.əl, (US) ˈdɑːk-
doctorate ˈdɒk.tər.ət, -ɪt, (US) ˈdɑːk- **-s** -s
Doctorow ˈdɒk.tər.əʊ, (US) ˈdɑːk.tə.roʊ
doctrinaire ˌdɒk.trɪˈneəʳ, -trəˈ-, (US) ˌdɑːk.trəˈner **-s** -z
doctrinal dɒkˈtraɪ.nəl; ˈdɒk.trɪ-, (US) ˈdɑːk.trɪ- **-ly** -i
doctrinarian ˌdɒk.trɪˈneə.ri.ən, -trəˈ-, (US) ˌdɑːk.trɪˈner.i- **-s** -z
doctrine ˈdɒk.trɪn, (US) ˈdɑːk- **-s** -z
docudrama ˈdɒk.juˌdrɑː.mə, (US) ˈdɑː.kjuˌdrɑː.mə, -ˌdræm.ə **-s** -z
document n ˈdɒk.jə.mənt, -jʊ-, (US) ˈdɑː.kjə-, -jʊ- **-s** -s
docu|ment v ˈdɒk.jə|.ment, -jʊ-, (US) ˈdɑː.kjə-, -jʊ- **-ments** -ments **-menting** -men.tɪŋ, (US) -men.t̬ɪŋ **-mented** -men.tɪd, (US) -men.t̬ɪd
documental ˌdɒk.jəˈmen.təl, -jʊˈ-, (US) ˌdɑː.kjəˈmenˈt̬əl, -jʊ-
documentar|y n, adj ˌdɒk.jəˈmen.tər|.i, -jʊˈ-, ˈ-tr|i, (US) ˌdɑː.kjəˈmen.t̬ɚ|.i, -kjʊˈ- **-ies** -iz
documentation ˌdɒk.jə.menˈteɪ.ʃən, -jʊ-, -mənˈ-, (US) ˌdɑː.kjə-, -jʊ-
docusoap ˈdɒk.ju.səʊp, -jʊ-, (US) ˈdɑː.kjə.soʊp, -kjʊ- **-s** -s
Docwra ˈdɒk.rə, (US) ˈdɑːk-
Dod(d) dɒd, (US) dɑːd **-s** -z
dodd|er ˈdɒd|.əʳ, (US) ˈdɑː.d|ɚ **-ers** -əz, (US) -ɚz **-ering** -ər.ɪŋ **-ered** -əd, (US) -ɚd **-erer/s** -ər.əʳ/z, (US) -ɚ.ɚ/z
doddery ˈdɒd.ər.i, (US) ˈdɑː.dɚ-
Doddington ˈdɒd.ɪŋ.tən, (US) ˈdɑː.dɪŋ-
doddle ˈdɒd.əl, (US) ˈdɑː.dəl **-s** -z
Doddridge ˈdɒd.rɪdʒ, (US) ˈdɑː.drɪdʒ
dodecagon ˌdəʊˈdek.ə.gən, (US) ˌdoʊ- **-s** -z
dodecahedr|on ˌdəʊ.dek.əˈhiː.dr|ən, -dɪk-, -ˈhed.r|ən, (US) ˌdoʊ.dek.əˈhiː.dr|ən **-ons** -ənz **-a** -ə **-al** -əl
Dodecanese ˌdəʊ.dɪk.əˈniːz, -dek.əˈ-, (US) ˌdoʊ.dek-, -ˈniːs
dodg|e, D~ dɒdʒ, (US) dɑːdʒ **-es** -ɪz **-ing** -ɪŋ **-ed** -d **-er/s** -əʳ/z, (US) -ɚ/z ˌ**Dodge** ˈ**City**
dodgem ˈdɒdʒ.əm, (US) ˈdɑː.dʒəm **-s** -z
Dodgson ˈdɒdʒ.sən, (US) ˈdɑːdʒ-
dodg|y ˈdɒdʒ|.i, (US) ˈdɑː.dʒ|i **-ier** -i.əʳ, (US) -i.ɚ **-iest** -i.ɪst, -i.əst **-ily** -əl.i, -ɪ.li **-iness** -ɪ.nəs, -ɪ.nɪs
Dodington ˈdɒd.ɪŋ.tən, (US) ˈdɑː.dɪŋ-
dodo, D~ ˈdəʊ.dəʊ, (US) ˈdoʊ.doʊ **-(e)s** -z
Dodoma ˈdəʊ.də.mə, -mɑː, (US) ˈdoʊ.də.mɑː, -doʊ-, doʊˈ-
Dodona dəʊˈdəʊ.nə, (US) dəˈdoʊ-
Dodsley ˈdɒdz.li, (US) ˈdɑːdz-
Dodson ˈdɒd.sən, (US) ˈdɑːd-
Dodsworth ˈdɒdz.wəθ, -wɜːθ, (US) ˈdɑːdz.wəθ, -wɝːθ
Dodwell ˈdɒd.wəl, -wel, (US) ˈdɑːd-
doe, D~ dəʊ, (US) doʊ **-s** -z
doer ˈduː.əʳ, (US) -ɚ **-s** -z
-doer ˌduː.əʳ, (US) -ɚ
Note: Suffix. Normally carries secondary stress, e.g. **wrongdoer** /ˈrɒŋˌduː.əʳ/ (US) /ˈrɑːŋˌduː.ɚ/.
does (from **do**) *strong form:* dʌz; *weak form:* dəz
Note: Weak-form word. The strong form is used when **does** is used as a full verb (e.g. 'That's what he does for a living'), for emphasis (e.g. 'That **does** look nice') and for

contrast (e.g. 'It **does** cost a lot, but it **doesn't** need repairing'). The strong form also occurs in final position (e.g. 'I don't like it as much as she does'). When **does** occurs in other positions as an auxiliary, the weak form is normally used (e.g. 'Why does it stop?' /ˌwaɪ.dəz.ɪtˈstɒp/ (US) /-stɑːp/).

D

doeskin ˈdəʊ.skɪn, (US) ˈdoʊ- **-s** -z
doesn't ˈdʌz.ənt
doeth (from **do**) ˈduː.ɪθ
Note: Archaic.
doff, D~ dɒf, (US) dɑːf, dɔːf **-s** -s **-ing** -ɪŋ **-ed** -t **-er/s** -əʳ/z, (US) -ɚ/z
dog dɒg, (US) dɑːg, dɔːg **-s** -z **-ging** -ɪŋ **-ged** -d ˈ**dog** ˌ**biscuit**; ˈ**dog** ˌ**collar**; ˈ**dog** ˌ**days**; ˈ**dog** ˌ**paddle**; ˈ**dog** ˌ**rose**; ˌ**dog's** ˈ**breakfast**; ˈ**Dog** ˌ**Star**; **dressed up like a** ˌ**dog's** ˈ**dinner**; ˌ**go to the** ˈ**dogs**; **it's a** ˈ**dog's** ˌ**life**; **let** ˌ**sleeping dogs** ˈ**lie**
dogbane ˈdɒg.beɪn, (US) ˈdɑːg-, ˈdɔːg-
Dogberry ˈdɒg.ber.i, -bər-, (US) ˈdɑːg.ber-, ˈdɔːg-
dogcart ˈdɒg.kɑːt, (US) ˈdɑːg.kɑːrt, ˈdɔːg- **-s** -s
dogcatcher ˈdɒgˌkætʃ.əʳ, (US) ˈdɑːgˌkætʃ.ɚ, ˈdɔːg- **-s** -z
dog|e dəʊdʒ, dəʊʒ, (US) doʊdʒ **-es** -ɪz
dog-ear ˈdɒg.ɪəʳ, (US) ˈdɑːg.ɪr, ˈdɔːg- **-s** -z **-ing** -ɪŋ **-ed** -d
dog-eat-dog ˌdɒg.iːtˈdɒg, (US) ˌdɑːg.iːtˈdɑːg; (US) ˌdɔːg.iːtˈdɔːg
dog-end ˈdɒg.end, (US) ˈdɑːg-, ˈdɔːg- **-s** -z
dogfight ˈdɒg.faɪt, (US) ˈdɑːg-, ˈdɔːg- **-s** -s
dogfish ˈdɒg.fɪʃ, (US) ˈdɑːg-, ˈdɔːg- **-es** -ɪz
Doggart ˈdɒg.ət, (US) ˈdɑː.gɚt, ˈdɔː-
dogged ˈdɒg.ɪd, (US) ˈdɑː.gɪd, ˈdɔː- **-ly** -li **-ness** -nəs, -nɪs
dogger, D~ ˈdɒg.əʳ, (US) ˈdɑː.gɚ, ˈdɔː- **-s** -z ˌ**Dogger** ˈ**Bank** (US) ˈ**Dogger** ˌ**Bank**
doggerel ˈdɒg.ər.əl, -ɪl, (US) ˈdɑː.gɚ.əl, ˈdɔː-, ˈ-grəl
Doggert ˈdɒg.ət, (US) ˈdɑː.gɚt, ˈdɔː-
Doggett ˈdɒg.ɪt, (US) ˈdɑː.gɪt, ˈdɔː-
doggo ˈdɒg.əʊ, (US) ˈdɑː.goʊ, ˈdɔː-
doggone ˈdɒg.ɒn, (US) ˈdɑː.gɑːn; (US) ˈdɔː.gɔːn **-d** -d
dogg|y, dogg|ie ˈdɒg|.i, (US) ˈdɑː.g|i, ˈdɔː- **-ies** -iz ˈ**doggie** ˌ**bag**
doghou|se ˈdɒg.haʊ|s, (US) ˈdɑːg-, ˈdɔːg- **-ses** -zɪz
dogie ˈdəʊ.gi, (US) ˈdoʊ- **-s** -z
dogleg ˈdɒg.leg, (US) ˈdɑːg-, ˈdɔːg- **-s** -z **-ging** -ɪŋ **-ged** -ɪd, -legd
dogma ˈdɒg.mə, (US) ˈdɑːg-, ˈdɔːg- **-s** -z
dogmatic dɒgˈmæt.ɪk, (US) dɑːgˈmæṭ-, dɔːg- **-s** -s **-al** -əl **-ally** -əl.i, -li
dogmat|ism ˈdɒg.mə.t|ɪ.zəm, (US) ˈdɑːg.mə.t|ɪ-, ˈdɔːg- **-ist/s** -ɪst/s
dogmatiz|e, -is|e ˈdɒg.mə.taɪz, (US) ˈdɑːg-, ˈdɔːg- **-es** -ɪz **-ing** -ɪŋ **-ed** -d **-er/s** -əʳ/z, (US) -ɚ/z
do-good|er ˌduːˈgʊd|.əʳ, (US) ˈduːˌgʊd|.ɚ **-ers** -əz, (US) -ɚz **-ing** -ɪŋ
dogsbod|y ˈdɒgz.bɒd|.i, (US) ˈdɑːgz.bɑː.d|i, ˈdɔːgz- **-ies** -iz
dogsled ˈdɒg.sled, (US) ˈdɑːg-, ˈdɔːg- **-s** -z
dog-tired ˌdɒgˈtaɪəd, -taɪ.əd, (US) ˌdɑːgˈtaɪ.ɚd, ˌdɔːg- *stress shift:* ˌ**dog-tired** ˈ**worker**
dog|tooth ˈdɒg|.tuːθ, (US) ˈdɑːg-, ˈdɔːg- **-teeth** -tiːθ
dogwatch ˈdɒg.wɒtʃ, (US) ˈdɑːg.wɑːtʃ, ˈdɔːg- **-es** -ɪz
dogwood ˈdɒg.wʊd, (US) ˈdɑːg-, ˈdɔːg-
doh dəʊ, (US) doʊ **-s** -z
Doha ˈdəʊ.hɑː, -ə, (US) ˈdoʊ-
Doherty ˈdəʊ.ə.ti; ˈdɒ.hə-; ˈdɒx.ə-; dəʊˈhɜː-, (US) ˈdɔːr.ə.ṭi; (US) ˈdoʊ.ɚ-
Dohnanyi dɒkˈnɑːn.jiː, dɒx-, -ji, (US) ˈdoʊ.nɑː.nji; (US) dɑːkˈnɑːn.ji, dɑːx-
Doig dɔɪg, ˈdəʊ.ɪg, (US) dɔɪg, ˈdoʊ.ɪg
doil|y ˈdɔɪ.l|i **-ies** -iz
doing (from **do**) ˈduː.ɪŋ **-s** -z
Doister ˈdɔɪ.stəʳ, (US) -stɚ
doit dɔɪt **-s** -s
do-it-yourself ˌduː.ɪ.tʃəˈself, -ɪt.jɔːˈ-, -jəˈ-, (US) ˌduː.ɪt.jɚˈself, -ɪ.tʃɚˈ-
Dokic ˈdɒk.ɪtʃ, (US) ˈdɑː.kɪtʃ
Dolan ˈdəʊ.lən, (US) ˈdoʊ-
Dolby ˈdɒl.bi, (US) ˈdɑːl-, ˈdoʊl-
dolce ˈdɒl.tʃi, ˈdəʊl-, -tʃeɪ, (US) ˈdoʊl.tʃeɪ
dolce vita ˌdɒl.tʃiˈviː.tə, ˌdəʊ-, -tʃeɪˈ-, (US) ˌdoʊl.tʃeɪˈviː.tə
Dolcis® ˈdɒl.sɪs, -tʃɪs, (US) ˈdɑːl-
doldrum ˈdɒl.drəm, (US) ˈdoʊl-, ˈdɑːl- **-s** -z
dol|e, D~ dəʊl, (US) doʊl **-es** -z **-ing** -ɪŋ **-ed** -d
doleful ˈdəʊl.fəl, -fʊl, (US) ˈdoʊl- **-ly** -i **-ness** -nəs, -nɪs
dolerite ˈdɒl.ə.raɪt, (US) ˈdɑː.lə-
Dolgellau, Dolgelley dɒlˈgeθ.laɪ, -li, (US) dɑːl-
dolichocephalic ˌdɒl.ɪ.kəʊ.sefˈæl.ɪk, -sɪˈfæl-, -səˈ-, -kefˈæl-, -kɪˈfæl-, (US) ˌdɑː.lɪ.koʊ-
Dolittle ˈduː.lɪ.təl, (US) -ṭəl
doll dɒl, (US) dɑːl **-s** -z ˈ**doll's** ˌ**house**
dollar, D~ ˈdɒl.əʳ, (US) ˈdɑː.lɚ **-s** -z ˌ**bet one's** ˌ**bottom** ˈ**dollar**
Dollond ˈdɒl.ənd, (US) ˈdɑː.lənd
dollop ˈdɒl.əp, (US) ˈdɑː.ləp **-s** -s
doll|y, D~ ˈdɒl|.i, (US) ˈdɑː.l|i **-ies** -iz ˈ**dolly** ˌ**mixture**
dolman ˈdɒl.mən, (US) ˈdoʊl- **-s** -z
dolmen ˈdɒl.men, (US) ˈdoʊl- **-s** -z
dolomite, D~ ˈdɒl.ə.maɪt, (US) ˈdoʊ.lə-, ˈdɑː- **-s** -s
dolor ˈdɒl.əʳ, ˈdəʊ.ləʳ, (US) ˈdoʊ.lɚ, ˈdɑː-
Dolores dəˈlɔː.res, dɒlˈɔː-, -rɪs, -rəs, -rez, -rɪz, -rəz, (US) dəˈlɔːr.əs, -ɪs
dolorous ˈdɒl.ər.əs, (US) ˈdoʊ.lɚ-, ˈdɑː- **-ly** -li **-ness** -nəs, -nɪs
dolour ˈdɒl.əʳ, ˈdəʊ.ləʳ, (US) ˈdoʊ.lɚ, ˈdɑː-
dolphin ˈdɒl.fɪn, (US) ˈdɑːl- **-s** -z
dolt dəʊlt, (US) doʊlt **-s** -s
doltish ˈdəʊl.tɪʃ, (US) ˈdoʊl- **-ly** -li **-ness** -nəs, -nɪs
-dom dəm
Note: Suffix. Normally unstressed, e.g. **kingdom** /ˈkɪŋ.dəm/.
domain dəʊˈmeɪn, (US) doʊ-, də- **-s** -z
Dombey ˈdɒm.bi, (US) ˈdɑːm-
dome dəʊm, (US) doʊm **-s** -z **-d** -d
Domecq dəʊˈmek, dɒmˈek, (US) doʊ-
Domesday ˈduːmz.deɪ ˈ**Domesday** ˌ**book**
domestic dəˈmes.tɪk **-s** -s **-ally** -əl.i, -li **do**ˌ**mestic** ˈ**animal**; **do**ˌ**mestic** ˈ**violence**
domesti|cate dəˈmes.tɪ|.keɪt **-cates** -keɪts **-cating** -keɪ.tɪŋ, (US) -keɪ.ṭɪŋ **-cated** -keɪ.tɪd, (US) -keɪ.ṭɪd
domestication dəˌmes.tɪˈkeɪ.ʃən, -təˈ-
domesticity ˌdɒm.esˈtɪs.ə.ti, ˌdəʊ.mes-, -ɪ.ti, (US) ˌdoʊ.mesˈtɪs.ə.ṭi, dəˌmesˈ-
Domestos® dəˈmes.tɒs, dəʊ-, (US) dəˈmes.toʊs
domett dəʊˈmet, (US) də-, doʊ-; (US) ˈdɑː.mət
Domett ˈdɒm.ɪt, (US) ˈdɑː.mɪt
domicil|e ˈdɒm.ɪ.saɪl, ˈdəʊ.mɪ-, -sɪl, (US) ˈdɑː.mə-, ˈdoʊ.mə- **-es** -z **-ing** -ɪŋ **-ed** -d
domiciliary ˌdɒm.ɪˈsɪl.i.ər.i, -əˈ-, (US) ˌdɑː.məˈsɪl.i.er-, ˌdoʊ-
dominance ˈdɒm.ɪ.nənts, ˈ-ə-, (US) ˈdɑː.mə-
dominant ˈdɒm.ɪ.nənt, ˈ-ə-, (US) ˈdɑː.mə- **-s** -s **-ly** -li
domi|nate ˈdɒm.ɪ|.neɪt, ˈ-ə-, (US) ˈdɑː.mə- **-nates** -neɪts **-nating** -neɪ.tɪŋ, (US) -neɪ.ṭɪŋ **-nated** -neɪ.tɪd, (US) -neɪ.ṭɪd **-nator/s** -neɪ.təʳ/z, (US) -neɪ.ṭɚ/z
domination ˌdɒm.ɪˈneɪ.ʃən, -əˈ-, (US) ˌdɑː.məˈ- **-s** -z
dominatr|ix ˌdɒm.ɪˈneɪ.tr|ɪks, -əˈ-, (US) ˌdɑː.məˈ- **-ixes** -ɪk.sɪz **-ices** -ɪ.siːz
domineer ˌdɒm.ɪˈnɪəʳ, -əˈ-, (US) ˌdɑː.məˈnɪr **-s** -z **-ing/ly** -ɪŋ/li **-ed** -d
Domingo dəˈmɪŋ.gəʊ, dɒmˈɪŋ-, (US) dəˈmɪŋ.goʊ
Dominic ˈdɒm.ɪ.nɪk, ˈ-ə-, (US) ˈdɑː.mə-
Dominica dəˈmɪn.ɪ.kə; dɒm.ɪnˈiː-, (US) ˌdɑː.mɪˈniː-, dəˈmɪn.ɪ-
dominical dəˈmɪn.ɪ.kəl, dɒmˈɪn-, dəʊˈmɪn-, (US) doʊˈmɪn-, də-
Dominican *republic, religious order:* dəˈmɪn.ɪ.kən, dɒmˈɪn-, (US) doʊˈmɪn-, də- *of Dominica:* ˌdɒm.ɪˈniː.kən, (US) ˌdɑː.mɪˈniː- **-s** -z
dominie ˈdɒm.ɪ.ni, ˈ-ə-, (US) ˈdɑː.mɪ- **-s** -z
dominion, D~ dəˈmɪn.jən, -i.ən, (US) ˈ-jən **-s** -z

Dominique ˌdɒm.ɪˈniːk, -əˈ-, ˈ---, Ⓤ ˌdɑː.məˈ-, ˈ---
domino, D~ ˈdɒm.ɪ.nəʊ, ˈ-ə-, Ⓤ ˈdɑː.mə.noʊ **-(e)s** -z ˈ**domino efˌfect**
Domitian dəʊˈmɪʃ.i.ən, dɒmˈɪʃ-, -ˈɪʃ.ən, Ⓤ dəˈmɪʃ.ən, -i.ən
don, D~ dɒn, Ⓤ dɑːn **-s** -z **-ning** -ɪŋ **-ned** -d
dona(h) ˈdəʊ.nə, Ⓤ ˈdoʊ- **-s** -z
doña, dona ˈdɒn.jə, Ⓤ ˈdoʊ.njə, -nə
Donal ˈdəʊ.nəl, Ⓤ ˈdoʊ-
Donalbain ˈdɒn.əl.beɪn, Ⓤ ˈdɑː.nəl-
Donald ˈdɒn.əld, Ⓤ ˈdɑː.nəld
Donaldson ˈdɒn.əld.sən, Ⓤ ˈdɑː.nəld-
Donat ˈdəʊ.næt, Ⓤ ˈdoʊ-
do|nate dəʊ|ˈneɪt, Ⓤ ˈdoʊ|.neɪt, -|ˈ- **-nates** -ˈneɪts, Ⓤ -neɪts, -ˈneɪts **-nating** -ˈneɪ.tɪŋ, Ⓤ -neɪ.t̬ɪŋ, -ˈneɪ- **-nated** -ˈneɪ.tɪd, Ⓤ -neɪ.t̬ɪd, -ˈneɪ-
Donatello ˌdɒn.əˈtel.əʊ, Ⓤ ˌdɑː.nəˈtel.oʊ
donatio dəʊˈnɑː.ti.əʊ, Ⓤ doʊˈnɑː.ti.oʊ, -ˈneɪ-, -ʃi-
donation dəʊˈneɪ.ʃən, Ⓤ doʊˈneɪ- **-s** -z
Donatist ˈdəʊ.nə.tɪst, ˈdɒn.ə-, Ⓤ ˈdoʊ.nə-, ˈdɑː- **-s** -s
donative ˈdəʊ.nə.tɪv, ˈdɒn.ə-, Ⓤ ˈdoʊ.nə.t̬ɪv, ˈdɑː- **-s** -z
donator dəʊˈneɪ.təʳ, Ⓤ ˈdoʊ.neɪ.t̬ɚ, ˌdoʊˈneɪ- **-s** -z
donatory ˈdəʊ.nə.tər.i, ˈdɒn.ə-; -tri, dəʊˈneɪ-, Ⓤ ˈdoʊ.nə.tɔːr.i
Donatus dəʊˈneɪ.təs, -ˈnɑː-, Ⓤ doʊˈneɪ.t̬əs, -ˈnɑː-
Don Carlos ˌdɒnˈkɑː.lɒs, ˌdɒŋ-, Ⓤ ˌdɑːnˈkɑːr.loʊs
Doncaster ˈdɒŋ.kə.stəʳ, -ˌkɑː-, -ˌkæs.təʳ, Ⓤ ˈdɑːŋˌkæs.tɚ, -kə.stɚ, ˈdɑːn-
done (from **do**) dʌn
Done dəʊn, Ⓤ doʊn
donee dəʊˈniː, Ⓤ doʊ- **-s** -z
Donegal ˌdɒn.ɪˈgɔːl, ˌdʌn-, ˈ---, Ⓤ ˌdɑː.nɪˈgɔːl, -ˈgɑːl, ˈ---

> Note: /ˌdʌn.ɪˈgɔːl/ appears to be the most usual pronunciation in Ireland.

Donegall ˈdɒn.ɪ.gɔːl, Ⓤ ˈdɑː.nɪ.gɔːl, -gɑːl
Donelson ˈdɒn.əl.sən, Ⓤ ˈdɑː.nəl-
doner ˈdɒn.əʳ, Ⓤ ˈdoʊ.nɚ ˌ**doner keˈbab**
Donetsk dɒnˈjetsk, Ⓤ dəˈnjetsk, doʊ-
Donetz dɒnˈjets, Ⓤ dəˈnets, dɑːˈnjets
dong v dɒŋ, Ⓤ dɑːŋ, dɔːŋ **-s** -z **-ing** -ɪŋ **-ed** -d
dông *Vietnam currency:* dɒŋ, Ⓤ dɑːŋ, dɔːŋ
donga ˈdɒŋ.gə, Ⓤ ˈdɑːŋ.gə, ˈdɔːŋ- **-s** -z
Dönges ˈdɜːn.jes
Don Giovanni ˌdɒn.dʒəʊˈvɑː.ni, -dʒi.əʊˈ-, -ˈvæn.i, Ⓤ ˌdɑːn.dʒi.əˈvɑː.ni, -dʒoʊˈ-
dongle ˈdɒŋ.gəl, Ⓤ ˈdɑːŋ-, ˈdɔːŋ- **-s** -z
Dongola ˈdɒŋ.gə.lə, Ⓤ ˈdɑːŋ-
Donington ˈdɒn.ɪŋ.tən, ˈdʌn-, Ⓤ ˈdɑː.nɪŋ-
Donizetti ˌdɒn.ɪˈzet.i, -ɪdˈze-, -ɪtˈset-, Ⓤ ˌdɑː.nəˈzet̬.i, -nətˈset̬-
donjon ˈdɒn.dʒən, ˈdʌn-, Ⓤ ˈdɑːn- **-s** -z
Don Juan ˌdɒnˈdʒuː.ən, -ˈhwɑːn, Ⓤ ˌdɑːn-
donkey ˈdɒŋ.ki, Ⓤ ˈdɑːŋ-, ˈdɔːŋ-, ˈdʌŋ- **-s** -z ˈ**donkey ˌengine;** ˈ**donkey ˌjacket;** ˈ**donkey's ˌyears**
donkeywork ˈdɒŋ.ki.wɜːk, Ⓤ ˈdɑːŋ.ki.wɝːk, ˈdɔːŋ-, ˈdʌŋ-
Donleavy, Donlevy dɒnˈliː.vi, -ˈlev.i, Ⓤ ˈdɑːn.liː.vi, ˈdʌn-, -lev.i, -ˈ--
Donmar ˈdɒn.mɑːʳ, Ⓤ ˈdɑːn-
donna, D~ ˈdɒn.ə, Ⓤ ˈdɑː.nə
Donnan ˈdɒn.ən, Ⓤ ˈdɑː.nən
Donne dʌn, dɒn, Ⓤ dʌn, dɑːn
Donnell ˈdɒn.əl, Ⓤ ˈdɑː.nəl
Donnelly ˈdɒn.əl.i, Ⓤ ˈdɑː.nəl-
Donnington ˈdɒn.ɪŋ.tən, Ⓤ ˈdɑː.nɪŋ-
donnish ˈdɒn.ɪʃ, Ⓤ ˈdɑː.nɪʃ **-ly** -li **-ness** -nəs, -nɪs
Donny ˈdɒn.i, Ⓤ ˈdɑː.ni
Donnybrook ˈdɒn.i.brʊk, Ⓤ ˈdɑː.ni-
Donoghue ˈdʌn.ə.hjuː, ˈdɒn-, -hjuː, Ⓤ ˈdɑː.nə.huː, ˈdʌn.ə-, -huː
Donohoe ˈdʌn.ə.həʊ, ˈdɒn-, -huː, Ⓤ ˈdɑː.nə.hoʊ, ˈdʌn.ə-, -huː
Donohue ˈdʌn.ə.hjuː, ˈdɒn-, -huː, Ⓤ ˈdɑː.nə.hjuː, ˈdʌn.ə-, -huː
donor ˈdəʊ.nəʳ, -nɔːʳ, Ⓤ ˈdoʊ.nɚ **-s** -z
Donovan ˈdɒn.ə.vən, Ⓤ ˈdɑː.nə-, ˈdʌn.ə-
Don Pasquale ˌdɒn.pæsˈkwɑː.leɪ, ˈdɒm-, -li, Ⓤ ˌdɑːn.pəsˈ-
Don Quixote ˌdɒnˈkwɪk.sət, ˌdɒŋ-, -səʊt, -sɒt; *as if Spanish:* ˌdɒn.kiˈhəʊ.teɪ; ˌdɒŋ-, -ti, Ⓤ ˌdɑːn.kiːˈhoʊ.teɪ, -t̬i; Ⓤ -ˈkwɪk.sət
donship ˈdɒn.ʃɪp, Ⓤ ˈdɑːn- **-s** -s
don't dəʊnt, Ⓤ doʊnt
Note: Weak forms /dən, dn̩/ may sometimes be heard in the expression 'I don't know', and a weak form /dəm/ in the expression 'I don't mind'.
do|nut ˈdəʊ|.nʌt, Ⓤ ˈdoʊ- **-nuts** -nʌts **-nutting** -nʌt.ɪŋ, Ⓤ -nʌt̬.ɪŋ
Doo duː
Doobie ˈduː.bi
doodad ˈduː.dæd **-s** -z
doodah ˈduː.dɑː **-s** -z
doodl|e ˈduː.dəl **-es** -z **-ing** -ɪŋ, ˈduːd.lɪŋ **-ed** -d **-er/s** -əʳ/z, ˈduːd.ləʳ/z, Ⓤ ˈduː.dəl.ɚ/z, ˈduːd.lɚ/z
doodlebug ˈduː.dəl.bʌg **-s** -z
doofus ˈduː.fəs **-es** -ɪz
doohickey ˈduːˌhɪk.i **-s** -z
Doolittle ˈduː.lɪ.təl, Ⓤ -t̬əl
doom duːm **-s** -z **-ing** -ɪŋ **-ed** -d
doomsayer ˈduːmˌseɪ.əʳ, Ⓤ -ɚ **-s** -z
doomsday, D~ ˈduːmz.deɪ
Doon(e) duːn
Doona® ˈduː.nə **-s** -z
door dɔːʳ, Ⓤ dɔːr **-s** -z ˌ**show someone the ˈdoor;** ˌ**shut the ˌdoor in someone's ˈface**
doorbell ˈdɔː.bel, Ⓤ ˈdɔːr- **-s** -z
doorframe ˈdɔː.freɪm, Ⓤ ˈdɔːr- **-s** -z
doorjamb ˈdɔː.dʒæm, Ⓤ ˈdɔːr- **-s** -z
doorkeeper ˈdɔːˌkiː.pəʳ, Ⓤ ˈdɔːrˌkiː.pɚ **-s** -z
doorknob ˈdɔː.nɒb, Ⓤ ˈdɔːr.nɑːb **-s** -z
doorknocker ˈdɔːˌnɒk.əʳ, Ⓤ ˈdɔːrˌnɑː.kɚ **-s** -z
door|man ˈdɔː|.mən, -mæn, Ⓤ ˈdɔːr- **-men** -mən, -men
doormat ˈdɔː.mæt, Ⓤ ˈdɔːr- **-s** -s
doornail ˈdɔː.neɪl, Ⓤ ˈdɔːr- **-s** -z **as ˌdead as a ˈdoornail**
doorplate ˈdɔː.pleɪt, Ⓤ ˈdɔːr- **-s** -s
doorpost ˈdɔː.pəʊst, Ⓤ ˈdɔːr.poʊst **-s** -s
doorstep ˈdɔː.step, Ⓤ ˈdɔːr- **-s** -s **-ping** -ɪŋ **-ped** -t **-per/s** -əʳ/z, Ⓤ -ɚ/z
doorstop ˈdɔː.stɒp, Ⓤ ˈdɔːr.stɑːp **-s** -s
door-to-door ˌdɔː.təˈdɔːʳ, Ⓤ ˌdɔːr.t̬əˈdɔːr
doorway ˈdɔː.weɪ, Ⓤ ˈdɔːr- **-s** -z
doo-wop ˈduː.wɒp, Ⓤ -wɑːp
dopa ˈdəʊ.pə, Ⓤ ˈdoʊ-, -pɑː
dopamine ˈdəʊ.pə.miːn, -mɪn, Ⓤ ˈdoʊ-
dop|e dəʊp, Ⓤ doʊp **-es** -s **-ing** -ɪŋ **-ed** -t **-er/s** -əʳ/z, Ⓤ -ɚ/z
dop|ey ˈdəʊ.p|i, Ⓤ ˈdoʊ- **-ier** -i.əʳ, Ⓤ -i.ɚ **-iest** -i.ɪst, -i.əst **-ily** -əl.i, -ɪ.li **-iness** -ɪ.nəs, -ɪ.nɪs
doppelganger ˈdɒp.əlˌgæŋ.əʳ, Ⓤ ˈdɑː.pəlˌgæŋ.ɚ **-s** -z
doppelgänger ˈdɒp.əlˌgeŋ.əʳ, Ⓤ ˈdɑː.pəlˌgeŋ.ɚ **-s** -z
Doppler ˈdɒp.ləʳ, Ⓤ ˈdɑː.plɚ ˈ**Doppler efˌfect**
dop|y ˈdəʊ.p|i, Ⓤ ˈdoʊ- **-ier** -i.əʳ, Ⓤ -i.ɚ **-iest** -i.ɪst, -i.əst **-ily** -əl.i, -ɪ.li **-iness** -ɪ.nəs, -ɪ.nɪs
Dora ˈdɔː.rə, Ⓤ ˈdɔːr.ə
dorado, D~ dəˈrɑː.dəʊ, dɒrˈɑː-, Ⓤ doʊˈrɑː.doʊ, dəˈ- **-s** -z
Doran ˈdɔː.rən, Ⓤ ˈdɔːr.ən
Dorando dəˈræn.dəʊ, dɒrˈæn-, Ⓤ dɔːrˈæn.doʊ
Dorcas ˈdɔː.kəs, -kæs, Ⓤ ˈdɔːr-
Dorchester ˈdɔː.tʃɪ.stəʳ, Ⓤ ˈdɔːr.tʃes.tɚ
Dordogne dɔːˈdɔɪn, Ⓤ dɔːrˈdoʊn
Dordon ˈdɔː.dən, Ⓤ ˈdɔːr-
Dordrecht ˈdɔː.drext, -drekt, Ⓤ ˈdɔːr.drekt, -drext
Dore dɔːʳ, Ⓤ dɔːr
Doreen ˈdɔː.riːn; -ˈ-, də-, dɒrˈiːn, Ⓤ dɔːˈriːn
Dorian ˈdɔː.ri.ən, Ⓤ ˈdɔːr.i- **-s** -z
Doric ˈdɒr.ɪk, Ⓤ ˈdɔːr-

Doricism ˈdɒr.ɪ.sɪ.zəm, ˈ-ə-, (US) ˈdɔːr- **-s** -z

Dorigen ˈdɒr.ɪ.gən, (US) ˈdɔːr-

Doris *modern first name:* ˈdɒr.ɪs, (US) ˈdɔːr-, ˈdɑːr- *district and female name in Greek history:* ˈdɔː.rɪs, ˈdɒr.ɪs, (US) ˈdɔːr.ɪs, ˈdɑːr-

dork dɔːk, (US) dɔːrk **-s** -s

Dorking ˈdɔː.kɪŋ, (US) ˈdɔːr-

Dorling ˈdɔː.lɪŋ, (US) ˈdɔːr-

dorm dɔːm, (US) dɔːrm **-s** -z

dormancy ˈdɔː.mənt.si, (US) ˈdɔːr-

dormant ˈdɔː.mənt, (US) ˈdɔːr-

dormer, D~ ˈdɔː.məʳ, (US) ˈdɔːr.mɚ **-s** -z ˌ**dormer** ˈ**window**

dormie ˈdɔː.mi, (US) ˈdɔːr-

dormitor|y ˈdɔː.mɪ.tər|.i, -mə-, -tr|i, (US) ˈdɔːr.mə.tɔːr|.i **-ies** -iz

Dormobile® ˈdɔː.mə.biːl, (US) ˈdɔːr- **-s** -z

dor|mouse ˈdɔː|.maʊs, (US) ˈdɔːr- **-mice** -maɪs

dormy ˈdɔː.mi, (US) ˈdɔːr-

Dornoch ˈdɔː.nɒk, -nək, -nɒx, -nəx, (US) ˈdɔːr.nɑːk, -nək

Dornton ˈdɔːn.tən, (US) ˈdɔːrn-

Dorothea ˌdɒr.əˈθi.ə, (US) ˌdɔːr-, ˌdɑːr-

Dorothy ˈdɒr.ə.θi, (US) ˈdɔːr-, ˈdɑːr-

Dorr dɔːʳ, (US) dɔːr

Dorrit ˈdɒr.ɪt, (US) ˈdɔːr-

Dors dɔːz, (US) dɔːrz

dorsal ˈdɔː.səl, (US) ˈdɔːr- **-ly** -i

Dorset ˈdɔː.sɪt, -sət, (US) ˈdɔːr- **-shire** -ʃəʳ, -ʃɪəʳ, (US) -ʃɚ, -ʃɪr

Dorsey ˈdɔː.si, (US) ˈdɔːr-

dorsum ˈdɔː.səm, (US) ˈdɔːr-

Dortmund ˈdɔːt.mənd, -mʊnd, (US) ˈdɔːrt-

dor|y, D~ ˈdɔː.r|i, (US) ˈdɔːr|.i **-ies** -iz

DOS dɒs, (US) dɑːs

dosag|e ˈdəʊ.sɪdʒ, (US) ˈdoʊ- **-es** -ɪz

dos|e dəʊs, (US) doʊs **-es** -ɪz **-ing** -ɪŋ **-ed** -t **like a** ˌ**dose of** ˈ**salts**

dosh dɒʃ, (US) dɑːʃ

do-si-do ˌdəʊ.siˈdəʊ, -saɪˈ-, (US) ˌdoʊ.siˈdoʊ **-s** -z

Dos Passos ˌdɒsˈpæs.ɒs, (US) ˌdoʊsˈpæs.oʊs, dəs-, ˌdɑːs-

doss dɒs, (US) dɑːs **-es** -ɪz **-ing** -ɪŋ **-ed** -t **-er/s** -əʳ/z, (US) -ɚ/z

dossal ˈdɒs.əl, (US) ˈdɑː.səl **-s** -z

dosshou|se ˈdɒs.haʊ|s, (US) ˈdɑːs- **-ses** -zɪz

dossier ˈdɒs.i.eɪ, -əʳ, (US) ˈdɑː.si.eɪ, -ɚ **-s** -z

dost (from **do**) *strong form:* dʌst; *weak form:* dəst

Dostoievski, Dostoevsky ˌdɒs.tɔɪˈef.ski, (US) ˌdɔː.stəˈjef-, ˌdɑː-; (US) ˌdʌs.təˈ-, -tɔɪˈ-

dot, D~ dɒt, (US) dɑːt **-s** -s **-ting** -ɪŋ, (US) ˈdɑː.t̬ɪŋ **-ted** -ɪd, (US) ˈdɑː.t̬ɪd ˌ**dotted** ˈ**line**

dotage ˈdəʊ.tɪdʒ, (US) ˈdoʊ.t̬ɪdʒ

dotard ˈdəʊ.təd, -ɑːd, (US) ˈdoʊ.t̬ɚd **-s** -z

dot.com ˌdɒtˈkɒm, (US) ˈdɑːt.kɑːm, ˌ-ˈ- **-s** -z *stress shift:* ˌ**dot.com** ˈ**company**

dot|e dəʊt, (US) doʊt **-es** -s **-ing/ly** -ɪŋ/li, (US) ˈdoʊ.t̬ɪŋ/li **-ed** -ɪd, (US) ˈdoʊ.t̬ɪd **-er/s** -əʳ/z, (US) ˈdoʊ.t̬ɚ/z

doth (from **do**) *strong form:* dʌθ; *weak form:* dəθ

Dotheboys Hall ˌduː.ðə.bɔɪzˈhɔːl, (US) -ˈhɔːl, -ˈhɑːl

dot-matrix ˌdɒtˈmeɪ.trɪks, ˈ-ˌ--, (US) ˌdɑːtˈmeɪ- ˌ**dot-matrix** ˈ**printer, dot-**ˌ**matrix** ˈ**printer** (US) ˌ**dot-**ˈ**matrix printer**

dotterel ˈdɒt.rəl, (US) ˈdɑː.trəl **-s** -z

dottle ˈdɒt.əl, (US) ˈdɑː.t̬əl **-s** -z

dott|y ˈdɒt|.i, (US) ˈdɑː.t̬|i **-ier** -i.əʳ, (US) -i.ɚ **-iest** -i.ɪst, -i.əst **-ily** -əl.i, -ɪ.li **-iness** -ɪ.nəs, -ɪ.nɪs

Douai *French town:* ˈduː.eɪ, (US) -ˈ- *school near Reading:* ˈdaʊ.eɪ, ˈduː-, -i, (US) duːˈeɪ *version of Bible:* ˈdaʊ.eɪ, ˈduː-, -i, (US) duːˈeɪ, ˈ--

Douala duˈɑː.lə

doubl|e ˈdʌb.əl **-y** -i, ˈ-li **-eness** -nəs, -nɪs **-es** -z **-ing** -ɪŋ, ˈ-lɪŋ **-ed** -d ˌ**double** ˈ**agent;** ˌ**double** ˈ**bass;** ˌ**double** ˈ**chin;** ˌ**double** ˈ**dutch;** ˌ**double** ˈ**entry;** ˌ**double** ˈ**first;** ˌ**Double** ˈ**Gloucester;** ˌ**double in**ˈ**demnity;** ˌ**double** ˈ**jeopardy;** ˌ**double** ˈ**take** (US) ˈ**double** ˌ**take**

double-barrel(l)ed ˌdʌb.əlˈbær.əld, (US) -ˈber-, -ˈbær- *stress shift:* ˌ**double-barrel(l)ed** ˈ**name**

double-breasted ˌdʌb.əlˈbres.tɪd *stress shift:* ˌ**double-breasted** ˈ**jacket**

double-check ˌdʌb.əlˈtʃek, (US) ˈdʌb.əlˌtʃek, ˌ--ˈ- **-s** -s **-ing** -ɪŋ **-ed** -t

double-click ˌdʌb.əlˈklɪk **-s** -s **-ing** -ɪŋ **-ed** -t

double-cross ˌdʌb.əlˈkrɒs, (US) -ˈkrɑːs **-es** -ɪz **-ing** -ɪŋ **-ed** -t

Doubleday ˈdʌb.əl.deɪ

double-deal|er ˌdʌb.əlˈdiː.l|əʳ, (US) -l|ɚ **-ers** -əʳz, (US) -ɚz **-ing** -ɪŋ

double-decker ˌdʌb.əlˈdek.əʳ, (US) ˈdʌb.əlˌdek.ɚ, ˌdʌb.əlˈdek- **-s** -z *stress shift, British only:* ˌ**double-decker** ˈ**bus**

double-dip ˌdʌb.əlˈdɪp **-s** -s **-ping** -ɪŋ **-ped** -t

double-edged ˌdʌb.əlˈedʒd *stress shift:* ˌ**double-edged** ˈ**sword**

double entendre ˌduː.bəl.ɑ̃ːnˈtɑ̃ːn.drə, -ɑːnˈtɑːn-, (US) ˌdʌb.əl.ɑːnˈtɑːn.drə, ˌduː.blɑːnˈtrɑːn

double-glaz|e ˌdʌb.əlˈgleɪz **-es** -ɪz **-ing** -ɪŋ **-ed** -d *stress shift:* ˌ**double-glazed** ˈ**windows**

double-glazing ˌdʌb.əlˈgleɪ.zɪŋ

double-header ˌdʌb.əlˈhed.əʳ, (US) -ɚ **-s** -z

double-jointed ˌdʌb.əlˈdʒɔɪn.tɪd, (US) -t̬ɪd *stress shift:* ˌ**double-jointed** ˈ**gymnast**

double-park ˌdʌb.əlˈpɑːk, (US) -ˈpɑːrk **-s** -s **-ing** -ɪŋ **-ed** -t

double-quick ˌdʌb.əlˈkwɪk *stress shift:* ˌ**double-quick** ˈ**time**

double-spac|e ˌdʌb.əlˈspeɪs **-es** -ɪz **-ing** -ɪŋ **-ed** -d *stress shift:* ˌ**double-spaced** ˈ**typing**

doublespeak ˈdʌb.əl.spiːk

double-stop ˌdʌb.əlˈstɒp, (US) -ˈstɑːp **-s** -s **-ping** -ɪŋ **-ped** -t

doublet ˈdʌb.lɪt, -lət **-s** -s

doubletalk ˈdʌb.əl.tɔːk, (US) -tɔːk, -tɑːk

double-team ˈdʌb.əl.tiːm **-s** -z **-ing** -ɪŋ **-ed** -d

doublethink ˈdʌb.əl.θɪŋk

double-tongued ˌdʌb.əlˈtʌŋd, -tɒŋd, (US) -ˈtʌŋd

doubloon dʌbˈluːn **-s** -z

doubt daʊt **-s** -s **-ing/ly** -ɪŋ/li, (US) ˈdaʊ.t̬ɪŋ/li **-ed** -ɪd, (US) ˈdaʊ.t̬ɪd **-er/s** -əʳ/z, (US) ˈdaʊ.t̬ɚ/z ˌ**doubting** ˈ**Thomas**

doubtful ˈdaʊt.fəl, -fʊl **-lest** -ɪst, -əst **-ly** -i **-ness** -nəs, -nɪs

doubtless ˈdaʊt.ləs, -lɪs **-ly** -li

douch|e duːʃ **-es** -ɪz **-ing** -ɪŋ **-ed** -t

Doug dʌg

Dougal(l) ˈduː.gəl

Dougan ˈduː.gən

dough dəʊ, (US) doʊ

Dougherty ˈdɒx.ə.ti, ˈdəʊ-, ˈdaʊ-, (US) ˈdɔːr.ə.t̬i, ˈdɔːr.t̬i, ˈdoʊ.ɚ-, ˈdaʊ-, ˈdɑː.kɚ-

doughfaced ˈdəʊ.feɪst, (US) ˈdoʊ-

dough|nut ˈdəʊ|.nʌt, (US) ˈdoʊ- **-nuts** -nʌts **-nutting** -nʌt.ɪŋ, (US) -nʌt̬.ɪŋ

dought|y, D~ ˈdaʊ.t|i, (US) -t̬|i **-ier** -i.əʳ, (US) -i.ɚ **-iest** -i.ɪst, -i.əst **-ily** -əl.i, -ɪ.li **-iness** -ɪ.nəs, -ɪ.nɪs

dough|y ˈdəʊ|.i, (US) ˈdoʊ- **-ily** -əl.i, -ɪ.li **-iness** -ɪ.nəs, -ɪ.nɪs

Douglas(s) ˈdʌg.ləs

Douglas-Home ˌdʌg.ləsˈhjuːm

douloureux ˌduː.ləˈrɜː, -luːˈ-, -lʊˈ-

Doulton ˈdəʊl.tən, (US) ˈdoʊl-

Dounreay ˈduːn.reɪ, -ˈ-

dour dʊəʳ, ˈdaʊ.əʳ, (US) dʊr, ˈdaʊ.ɚ **-ly** -li **-ness** -nəs, -nɪs

Douro ˈdʊə.rəʊ, (US) ˈdɔːr.oʊ

dous|e daʊs **-es** -ɪz **-ing** -ɪŋ **-ed** -t

dove, D~ dʌv **-s** -z

dove (from **dive**) dəʊv, (US) doʊv

dovecot(e) ˈdʌv.kɒt, (US) -kɑːt **-s** -s

Dovedale ˈdʌv.deɪl

Dover ˈdəʊ.vəʳ, (US) ˈdoʊ.vɚ ˌ**Dover** ˈ**sole**

dovetail ˈdʌv.teɪl **-s** -z **-ing** -ɪŋ **-ed** -d

Dovey ˈdʌv.i

Dow daʊ ˌ**Dow** ˈ**Jones;** ˌ**Dow Jones** ˈ**index**

dowager ˈdaʊ.ə.dʒəʳ, ˈdaʊə-, ˈdaʊ.ɪ-, (US) -dʒɚ **-s** -z

Dowden ˈdaʊ.dən

Dowds daʊdz

dowd|y ˈdaʊ.d|i **-ies** -iz **-ier** -i.əʳ, (US) -i.ɚ **-iest** -i.ɪst, -i.əst **-ily** -əl.i, -ɪ.li **-iness** -ɪ.nəs, -ɪ.nɪs

dowel ˈdaʊ.əl **-s** -z **-(l)ing** -ɪŋ **-(l)ed** -d

Dowell ˈdaʊ.əl; ˈdaʊ.ɪl, -el

dower ˈdaʊ.əʳ, daʊəʳ, (US) ˈdaʊ.ɚ **-s** -z **-less** -ləs, -lɪs

Dowgate ˈdaʊ.gɪt, -geɪt

D

Dowie ˈdaʊ.i
Dowland ˈdaʊ.lənd
dowlas, D~ ˈdaʊ.ləs
Dowler ˈdaʊ.ləʳ, (US) -lɚ
Dowling ˈdaʊ.lɪŋ
down, D~ daʊn -s -z -ing -ɪŋ -ed -d **ˌdown ˈpayment; ˈDown's ˌsyndrome; ˌdown ˈunder**
Down *county:* daʊn -shire -ʃəʳ, -ʃɪəʳ, (US) -ʃɚ, -ʃɪr
down-and-out ˌdaʊn.əndˈaʊt -s -s *stress shift:* **ˌdown-and-out ˈperson**
down-at-heel ˌdaʊn.ətˈhiːl *stress shift:* **ˌdown-at-heel ˈperson**
downbeat ˈdaʊn.biːt, ˈdaʊm-, (US) ˈdaʊn- -s -s
downcast ˈdaʊn.kɑːst, ˈdaʊŋ-, ˌ-ˈ-, (US) ˈdaʊn.kæst
downdraught ˈdaʊn.drɑːft, (US) -dræft -s -s
downdrift ˈdaʊn.drɪft
Downe daʊn -s -z
downer ˈdaʊ.nəʳ, (US) -nɚ -s -z
Downey ˈdaʊ.ni
downfall ˈdaʊn.fɔːl, (US) -fɔːl, -fɑːl -s -z
downgrad|e ˌdaʊnˈɡreɪd, ˌdaʊŋ-, (US) ˈdaʊn.ɡreɪd -es -z -ing -ɪŋ -ed -ɪd *stress shift, British only:* **ˌdowngraded ˈworker**
Downham ˈdaʊ.nəm
downhearted ˌdaʊnˈhɑː.tɪd, (US) -ˈhɑːr.t̬ɪd -ly -li -ness -nəs, -nɪs *stress shift:* **ˌdownhearted ˈperson**
downhill ˌdaʊnˈhɪl *stress shift:* **ˌdownhill ˈslide**
down-home ˌdaʊnˈhəʊm, (US) -ˈhoʊm
Downie ˈdaʊ.ni
Downing ˈdaʊ.nɪŋ **ˈDowning ˌStreet**
downland, D~ ˈdaʊn.lænd, -lənd
download ˌdaʊnˈləʊd, ˈ--, (US) ˈdaʊn.loʊ|d -s -z -ing -ɪŋ -ed -ɪd -able -ə.bᵊl
downmarket ˌdaʊnˈmɑː.kɪt, ˌdaʊm-, (US) ˈdaʊnˌmɑːr- *stress shift, British only:* **ˌdownmarket ˈarea**
Downpatrick ˌdaʊnˈpæt.rɪk, ˌdaʊm-, (US) ˌdaʊn-
downpipe ˈdaʊn.paɪp, ˈdaʊm-, (US) ˈdaʊn- -s -s
downplay ˌdaʊnˈpleɪ, ˌdaʊm-, (US) ˈdaʊn.pleɪ -s -z -ing -ɪŋ -ed -d *stress shift, British only:* **ˌdownplayed ˈincident**
downpour ˈdaʊn.pɔːʳ, ˈdaʊm-, (US) ˈdaʊn.pɔːr -s -z
downright ˈdaʊn.raɪt -ness -nəs, -nɪs
downriver ˌdaʊnˈrɪv.əʳ, -ɚ *stress shift:* **ˌdownriver ˈsettlement**
downrush ˈdaʊn.rʌʃ -es -ɪz
Downs daʊnz
downscal|e ˌdaʊnˈskeɪl -es -s -ing -ɪŋ -ed -d *stress shift:* **ˌdownscaled ˈworkforce**
downshift ˈdaʊn.ʃɪft -s -s -ing -ɪŋ -ed -ɪd
downside, D~ ˈdaʊn.saɪd
downsiz|e ˌdaʊnˈsaɪz, (US) ˈ-- -es -ɪz -ing -ɪŋ -ed -d *stress shift, British only:* **ˌdownsized ˈpayments**
downspout ˈdaʊn.spaʊt -s -s
downstage ˌdaʊnˈsteɪdʒ, (US) ˈ-- *stress shift, British only:* **ˌdownstage ˈaction**
downstairs ˌdaʊnˈsteəz, (US) -ˈsterz *stress shift:* **ˌdownstairs ˈbathroom**
downstream ˌdaʊnˈstriːm *stress shift:* **ˌdownstream ˈsettlement**
downswing ˈdaʊn.swɪŋ -s -z
downtime ˈdaʊn.taɪm
down-to-earth ˌdaʊn.tuˈɜːθ, (US) -ˈɝːθ *stress shift:* **ˌdown-to-earth ˈperson**
Downton ˈdaʊn.tən, (US) -tᵊn
downtown ˌdaʊnˈtaʊn, (US) ˌdaʊnˈtaʊn, ˈ-- *stress shift, British only:* **ˌdowntown ˈarea**
downtrodden ˈdaʊnˌtrɒd.ᵊn, ˌ-ˈ--, (US) ˈdaʊnˌtrɑː.dᵊn
downturn ˈdaʊn.tɜːn, (US) -tɝːn -s -z
downward ˈdaʊn.wəd, (US) -wɚd -s -z
downwind ˌdaʊnˈwɪnd, (US) ˌdaʊnˈwɪnd, ˈ--
down|y ˈdaʊ.n|i -ier -i.əʳ, (US) -i.ɚ -iest -i.ɪst, -i.əst
dowr|y ˈdaʊ.r|i -ies -iz
dows|e daʊz, daʊs -es -ɪz -ing -ɪŋ -ed -d -er/s -əʳ/z, (US) -ɚ/z **ˈdowsing ˌrod**
Dowse daʊs
Dowson ˈdaʊ.sᵊn
Dowton ˈdaʊ.tᵊn
doxolog|y dɒkˈsɒl.ə.dʒ|i, (US) dɑːkˈsɑː.lə- -ies -iz
dox|y ˈdɒk.s|i, (US) ˈdɑːk- -ies -iz
doyen ˈdɔɪ.en, -ən; ˈdwaɪ.ɑ̃ːŋ; dɔɪˈen, (US) ˈdɔɪ.ən, -ən, dwɑːˈjen -s -z
doyenne dɔɪˈen; dwaˈjen -s -z
Doyle dɔɪl
doyl|(e)y ˈdɔɪ.li -l(e)ys -z -lies -z
D'Oyl(e)y ˈdɔɪ.li
d'Oyly Carte ˌdɔɪ.liˈkɑːt, (US) -ˈkɑːrt
doz|e dəʊz, (US) doʊz -es -ɪz -ing -ɪŋ -ed -d -er/s -əʳ/z, (US) -ɚ/z
dozen ˈdʌz.ᵊn -s -z -th -θ
doz|y ˈdəʊ.z|i, (US) ˈdoʊ- -ier -i.əʳ, (US) -i.ɚ -iest -i.ɪst, -i.əst -ily -ᵊl.i, -ɪ.li -iness -ɪ.nəs, -ɪ.nɪs
DPhil ˌdiːˈfɪl
dr (abbrev. for **dram**) dræm
Dr. (abbrev. for **Doctor**) ˈdɒk.təʳ, (US) ˈdɑːk.tɚ
drab dræb -s -z -ber -əʳ, (US) -ɚ -best -ɪst, -əst -ness -nəs, -nɪs
drabbl|e, D~ ˈdræb.ᵊl -es -z -ing -ɪŋ, ˈ-lɪŋ -ed -d
dracaena drəˈsiː.nə -s -z
drachm dræm -s -z
drachm|a ˈdræk.m|ə -as -əz -ae -iː, -eɪ
Draco *Greek legislator:* ˈdreɪ.kəʊ, (US) -koʊ *English surname:* ˈdrɑː.kəʊ, (US) -koʊ
draconian, D~ drəˈkəʊ.ni.ən, drækˈəʊ-, (US) drəˈkoʊ-, dreɪ-
Dracula ˈdræk.jə.lə, -jʊ-
draff dræf, drɑːf, (US) dræf
draft drɑːft, (US) dræft -s -s -ing -ɪŋ -ed -ɪd -er/s -əʳ/z, (US) -ɚ/z **ˈdraft ˌdodger**
draftee ˌdrɑːfˈtiː, (US) ˌdræf- -s -z
drafts|man ˈdrɑːfts|.mən, (US) ˈdræfts- -men -mən, -men -manship -mən.ʃɪp
drafts|woman ˈdrɑːfts|ˌwʊm.ən, (US) ˈdræfts- -women -ˌwɪm.ɪn
draft|y ˈdrɑːf.t|i, (US) ˈdræf- -ier -i.əʳ, (US) -i.ɚ -iest -i.ɪst, -i.əst -iness -ɪ.nəs, -ɪ.nɪs
drag dræɡ -s -z -ging -ɪŋ -ged -d **ˈdrag ˌqueen; ˈdrag ˌrace**
Drage dreɪdʒ
dragee, dragée dræʒˈeɪ, (US) dræʒˈeɪ, drɑːˈʒeɪ -s -z
draggl|e ˈdræɡ.ᵊl -es -z -ing -ɪŋ, ˈ-lɪŋ -ed -d
dragg|y ˈdræɡ|.i -ier -i.əʳ, (US) -i.ɚ -iest -i.ɪst, -i.əst
dragnet ˈdræɡ.net -s -s
drago|man ˈdræɡ.əʊ|.mən, -mæn, (US) -ə-, -oʊ- -mans -mənz, -mænz -men -mən, -men
dragon ˈdræɡ.ᵊn -s -z **ˈdragon's ˌblood, ˌdragon's ˈblood**
dragonet ˈdræɡ.ə.nɪt, -net -s -s
dragonfl|y ˈdræɡ.ᵊn.fl|aɪ -ies -aɪz
dragonnade ˌdræɡ.əˈneɪd -s -z
dragoon drəˈɡuːn -s -z
dragster ˈdræɡ.stəʳ, (US) -stɚ -s -z
drain dreɪn -s -z -ing -ɪŋ -ed -d -er/s -əʳ/z, (US) -ɚ/z **ˈdraining ˌboard**
drainage ˈdreɪ.nɪdʒ
drainpipe ˈdreɪn.paɪp, ˈdreɪm-, (US) ˈdreɪn- -s -s
drake, D~ dreɪk -s -s
Drakensberg ˈdræk.ənz.bɜːɡ, (US) ˈdrɑː.kənz.bɝːɡ
Dralon® ˈdreɪ.lɒn, (US) -lɑːn
dram dræm -s -z -ming -ɪŋ -med -d
drama ˈdrɑː.mə, (US) ˈdrɑːm.ə, ˈdræm.ə -s -z
Dramamine® ˈdræm.ə.miːn, -mɪn
dramatic drəˈmæt.ɪk, (US) -ˈmæt̬- -al -ᵊl -ally -ᵊl.i, -li -s -s
dramatis personae ˌdrɑː.mə.tɪs.pɜːˈsəʊ.naɪ, ˌdræm.ə-, -pəˈ-, (US) ˌdrɑː.mə.t̬ɪs.pɚˈsoʊ-, ˌdræm.ə-, -ni
dramatist ˈdræm.ə.tɪst, ˈdrɑː.mə-, (US) ˈdrɑː.mə.t̬ɪst, ˈdræm.ə- -s -s
dramatization, -isa- ˌdræm.ə.taɪˈzeɪ.ʃᵊn, ˌdrɑː.mə-, -tɪˈ-, (US) ˌdrɑː.mə.t̬əˈ-, ˌdræm.ə- -s -z
dramatiz|e, -is|e ˈdræm.ə.taɪz, ˈdrɑː.mə-, (US) ˈdrɑː.mə-, ˈdræm.ə- -es -ɪz -ing -ɪŋ -ed -d -able -ə.bᵊl
dramaturg|e ˈdræm.ə.tɜːdʒ, ˈdrɑː.mə-, (US) ˈdrɑː.mə.tɝːdʒ, ˈdræm.ə.- -es -ɪz
dramaturgic ˌdræm.əˈtɜː.dʒɪk, ˌdrɑː.mə-, (US) ˈdrɑː.mə.tɝː-; (US) ˌdræm.əˈtɝː- -al -ᵊl -ally -ᵊl.i, -li
dramaturgy ˈdræm.ə.tɜː.dʒi, ˈdrɑː.mə-, (US) ˈdrɑː.mə.tɝː-, ˈdræm.ə-
Drambuie® dræmˈbjuː.i, -ˈbuː-
Drane dreɪn
drank (from **drink**) dræŋk

drap|e dreɪp -es -s -ing -ɪŋ -ed -t
draper, D~ ˈdreɪ.pəʳ, US -pɚ -s -z
draper|y ˈdreɪ.pəʳr|.i -ies -iz
Drapier ˈdreɪ.pi.əʳ, US -ɚ
Draskovic ˈdræs.kə.vɪtʃ, US drɑːs-
drastic ˈdræs.tɪk, ˈdrɑː.stɪk, US ˈdræs.tɪk -ally -əl.i, -li

D

drat dræt
draught drɑːft, US dræft -s -s
draughtboard ˈdrɑːft.bɔːd, US ˈdræft.bɔːrd -s -z
draught-proof ˈdrɑːft.pruːf, US ˈdræft- -s -s -ing -ɪŋ -d -t
draughts|man ˈdrɑːfts|.mən, US ˈdræfts- -men -mən
draughts|woman ˈdrɑːfts|ˌwʊm.ən, US ˈdræfts- -women -ˌwɪm.ɪn
draught|y ˈdrɑːf.t|i, US ˈdræf- -ier -i.əʳ, US -i.ɚ -iest -i.ɪst, -i.əst -ily -əl.i, -ɪ.li -iness -ɪ.nəs, -ɪ.nɪs
Drava ˈdrɑː.və
Dravidian drəˈvɪd.i.ən -s -z
draw drɔː, US drɑː, drɔː -s -z -ing -ɪŋ drew druː drawn drɔːn, US drɑːn, drɔːn drawable ˈdrɔː.ə.bəl, US ˈdrɑː-, ˈdrɔː- **ˈdrawing ˌboard; ˈdrawing ˌpin; ˈdrawing ˌroom; ˈdrawing ˌtable; go ˌback to the ˈdrawing ˌboard**

> Note: The form 'drawing' (and the less common 'drawable') are sometimes heard with 'intrusive /r/': thus /ˈdrɔː.rɪŋ/ US /ˈdrɑː.rɪŋ/.

drawback ˈdrɔː.bæk, US ˈdrɑː-, ˈdrɔː- -s -s
drawbridg|e ˈdrɔː.brɪdʒ, US ˈdrɑː-, ˈdrɔː- -es -ɪz
drawdown ˈdrɔː.daʊn, US ˈdrɑː-, ˈdrɔː-
drawee ˌdrɔːˈiː, US ˌdrɑː-, ˌdrɔː- -s -z
drawer *sliding box:* drɔːʳ, US drɔːr *person who draws:* ˈdrɔː.əʳ, US ˈdrɑː.ɚ, ˈdrɔː- -s -z
drawers *garment:* drɔːz, US drɔːrz
drawl drɔːl, US drɑːl, drɔːl -s -z -ing -ɪŋ -ed -d -er/s -əʳ/z, US -ɚ/z
drawn (from **draw**) drɔːn, US drɑːn, drɔːn
drawstring ˈdrɔː.strɪŋ, US ˈdrɑː-, ˈdrɔː- -s -z
Drax dræks
dray dreɪ -s -z
dray|man ˈdreɪ|.mən, -mæn -men -mən, -men
Drayton ˈdreɪ.tən
dread dred -s -z -ing -ɪŋ -ed -ɪd
dreadful ˈdred.fəl, -fʊl -ly -i -ness -nəs, -nɪs
dreadlocks ˈdred.lɒks, US -lɑːks
dreadnought, dreadnaught, D~ ˈdred.nɔːt, US -nɑːt, -nɔːt -s -s
dream driːm -s -z -ing/ly -ɪŋ/li -ed drempt, driːmd, US driːmd, drempt -t drempt -er/s ˈdriː.məʳ/z, US -mɚ/z -like -laɪk **ˈdream ˌworld**
dreamboat ˈdriːm.bəʊt, US -boʊt -s -s
Dreamcast® ˈdriːm.kɑːst, US -kæst
dreamland ˈdriːm.lænd
dreamless ˈdriːm.ləs, -lɪs -ly -li
dreamtime ˈdriːm.taɪm
Dreamworks® ˈdriːm.wɜːks, US -wɝːks
dream|y ˈdriː.m|i -ier -i.əʳ, US -i.ɚ -iest -i.ɪst, -i.əst -ily -əl.i, -ɪ.li -iness -ɪ.nəs, -ɪ.nɪs
drear drɪəʳ, US drɪr
drear|y ˈdrɪə.r|i, US ˈdrɪr|.i -ier -i.əʳ, US -i.ɚ -iest -i.ɪst, -i.əst -ily -əl.i, -ɪ.li -iness -ɪ.nəs, -ɪ.nɪs
dredg|e dredʒ -es -ɪz -ing -ɪŋ -ed -d
dredger ˈdredʒ.əʳ, US -ɚ -s -z
Dre-fach Felindre drevˌɑːx.velˈɪn.drə
dregg|y ˈdreg|.i -ily -əl.i, -ɪ.li -iness -ɪ.nəs, -ɪ.nɪs
dregs dregz
Dreiser ˈdraɪ.zəʳ, -səʳ, US -zɚ, -sɚ
drench drentʃ -es -ɪz -ing -ɪŋ -ed -t -er/s -əʳ/z, US -ɚ/z
Dresden ˈdrez.dən
dress dres -es -ɪz -ing -ɪŋ -ed -t **ˌdress ˈcircle US ˈdress ˌcircle; ˌdress ˈcoat US ˈdress ˌcoat; ˈdress ˌcode; ˌdress reˈhearsal US ˈdress reˌhearsal; ˈdress ˌsense; ˌdress ˈsuit US ˈdress ˌsuit**
dressage ˈdres.ɑːʒ; -ɑːdʒ; -ɪdʒ; drəˈsɑːʒ, US drəˈsɑːʒ, dresˈɑːʒ
dresser ˈdres.əʳ, US -ɚ -s -z
dressing ˈdres.ɪŋ -s -z **ˈdressing ˌgown; ˈdressing ˌroom; ˈdressing ˌtable**
dressing-down ˌdres.ɪŋˈdaʊn -s -z
dressmak|er ˈdresˌmeɪ.k|əʳ, US -k|ɚ -ers -əz, US -ɚz -ing -ɪŋ
dress|y ˈdres|.i -ier -i.əʳ, US -i.ɚ -iest -i.ɪst, -i.əst -ily -əl.i, -ɪ.li -iness -ɪ.nəs, -ɪ.nɪs
drew (from **draw**) druː
Drew druː -s -z
Dreyfus(s) ˈdreɪ.fəs, ˈdraɪ-, -fʊs
dribbl|e ˈdrɪb.əl -es -z -ing -ɪŋ -ed -d, ˈ-lɪŋ -er/s -əʳ/z, ˈ-ləʳ/z, US ˈ-əl.ɚ/z, ˈ-lɚ/z
driblet ˈdrɪb.lət, -lɪt -s -s
dribs and drabs ˌdrɪbz.ənˈdræbz
dried (from **dry**) draɪd
drier ˈdraɪ.əʳ, US -ɚ -s -z
dries (from **dry**) draɪz
driest ˈdraɪ.ɪst, -əst
Driffield ˈdrɪf.iːld
drift drɪft -s -s -ing -ɪŋ -ed -ɪd
drifter ˈdrɪf.təʳ, US -tɚ -s -z
driftless ˈdrɪft.ləs, -lɪs
driftnet ˈdrɪft.net -s -s
driftwood ˈdrɪft.wʊd
drifty ˈdrɪf.ti
drill drɪl -s -z -ing -ɪŋ -ed -d **ˈdrill ˌsergeant**
drily ˈdraɪ.li
drink drɪŋk -s -s -ing -ɪŋ drank dræŋk drunk drʌŋk drinker/s ˈdrɪŋ.kəʳ/z, US -kɚ/z **ˈdrinking ˌfountain; ˈdrinking ˌhorn; ˈdrinking ˌwater**
drinkable ˈdrɪŋ.kə.bəl
drink-driv|ing ˌdrɪŋkˈdraɪ.v|ɪŋ -er/s -əʳ/z, US -ɚ/z
Drinkwater ˈdrɪŋkˌwɔː.təʳ, US -ˌwɑː.t̬ɚ, -ˌwɔː-
drip drɪp -s -s -ping -ɪŋ -ped -t
drip|-dry ˈdrɪp|.draɪ, ˌ-|ˈ- -dries -draɪz -drying -ˌdraɪ.ɪŋ -dried -draɪd
drip|-feed ˈdrɪp|.fiːd -feeds -fiːdz -feeding -ˌfiː.dɪŋ -fed -fed
dripping ˈdrɪp.ɪŋ -s -z
dripp|y ˈdrɪp|.i -ier -i.əʳ, US -i.ɚ -iest -i.ɪst, -i.əst
dripstone ˈdrɪp.stəʊn, US -stoʊn -s -z
Driscoll ˈdrɪs.kəl
driv|e draɪv -es -z -ing -ɪŋ drove drəʊv, US droʊv driven ˈdrɪv.ən **ˈdriving ˌiron; ˈdriving ˌlicence/license; ˈdriving ˌseat; ˈdriving ˌtest**
driveaway ˈdraɪv.əˌweɪ
drive-by ˈdraɪv.baɪ
drive-in ˈdraɪv.ɪn -s -z
drivel ˈdrɪv.əl -s -z -(l)ing -ɪŋ -(l)ed -d -(l)er/s -əʳ/z, US -ɚ/z
driven (from **drive**) ˈdrɪv.ən
driver, D~ ˈdraɪ.vəʳ, US -vɚ -s -z **ˈdriver's ˌlicense; in the ˈdriver's ˌseat**
drive-through ˈdraɪv.θruː -s -z
driveway ˈdraɪv.weɪ -s -z
Driza-bone® ˈdraɪ.zə.bəʊn, US -boʊn
drizzl|e ˈdrɪz.əl -es -z -ing -ɪŋ, ˈ-lɪŋ -ed -d
drizzly ˈdrɪz.əl.i, ˈ-li
Drogheda *place:* ˈdrɔɪ.ɪ.də, ˈdrɔː-, ˈ-ə-, ˈdrɒ.hə-, US ˈdrɔː.ɪ-, ˈdrɑː-, ˈ-ə- *Earl:* ˈdrɔɪ.ɪ.də
droid drɔɪd -s -z
droit drɔɪt, drwɑː -s -s
droit de seigneur ˌdrwɑː.də.seɪˈnjɜːʳ, -senˈjɜːʳ, -siːˈnjɜːʳ, US -seɪˈnjʊr, -senˈjʊr, -ˈjɝː
Droitwich ˈdrɔɪ.twɪtʃ
droll drəʊl, US droʊl -ness -nəs, -nɪs -er -əʳ, US -ɚ -est -ɪst, -əst -y -li, ˈdrəʊ.li, US ˈdroʊ.li
droller|y ˈdrəʊ.ləʳr|.i, US ˈdroʊ- -ies -iz
-drome drəʊm, US droʊm
Note: Suffix. Normally unstressed, e.g. **aerodrome** /ˈeə.rə.drəʊm/ US /ˈer.ə.droʊm/.
dromedar|y ˈdrɒm.ə.dəʳr|.i, ˈdrʌm-, ˈ-ɪ-, US ˈdrɑː.mə.der-, ˈdrʌm.ə- -ies -iz
Dromio ˈdrəʊ.mi.əʊ, US ˈdroʊ.mi.oʊ
Dromore ˈdrəʊ.mɔːʳ; drəˈmɔːʳ, US ˈdroʊ.mɔːr; US drəˈmɔːr
dron|e drəʊn, US droʊn -es -z -ing -ɪŋ -ed -d
Dronfield ˈdrɒn.fiːld, US ˈdrɑːn-
drongo ˈdrɒŋ.gəʊ, US ˈdrɑːŋ.goʊ -(e)s -z
Drood druːd

drool druːl **-s** -z **-ing** -ɪŋ **-ed** -d
droop druːp **-s** -s **-ing/ly** -ɪŋ/li **-ed** -t
droop|y ˈdruː.p|i **-ier** -i.əʳ, (US) -i.ɚ **-iest** -i.ɪst, -i.əst **-ily** -əl.i, -ɪ.li **-iness** -ɪ.nəs, -ɪ.nɪs
drop drɒp, (US) drɑːp **-s** -s **-ping** -ɪŋ **-ped** -t ˈ**drop** ˌ**scone**; ˈ**drop** ˌ**shot**; **a** ˌ**drop in the** ˈ**ocean**; **at the** ˌ**drop of a** ˈ**hat**
drop-in ˈdrɒp.ɪn, (US) ˈdrɑːp-
dropkick ˈdrɒp.kɪk, (US) ˈdrɑːp- **-s** -s
droplet ˈdrɒp.lət, -lɪt, (US) ˈdrɑːp- **-s** -s
dropout ˈdrɒp.aʊt, (US) ˈdrɑːp- **-s** -s
dropper ˈdrɒp.əʳ, (US) ˈdrɑː.pɚ **-s** -z
dropping ˈdrɒp.ɪŋ, (US) ˈdrɑː.pɪŋ **-s** -z
dropsic|al ˈdrɒp.sɪ.k|əl, (US) ˈdrɑːp- **-ally** -əl.i, -li **-alness** -əl.nəs, -nɪs
dropsy ˈdrɒp.si, (US) ˈdrɑːp-
droshk|y ˈdrɒʃ.k|i, (US) ˈdrɑːʃ- **-ies** -iz
drosophila drəˈsɒf.ɪ.lə, drɒsˈɒf-, -əl.ə, (US) droʊˈsɑː.fəl.ə, drə- **-s** -z
dross drɒs, (US) drɑːs **-y** -i
drought draʊt **-s** -s **-y** -i
drove drəʊv, (US) droʊv **-s** -z
drover ˈdrəʊ.vəʳ, (US) ˈdroʊ.vɚ **-s** -z
Drower ˈdraʊ.əʳ, (US) ˈdraʊ.ɚ
drown draʊn **-s** -z **-ing** -ɪŋ **-ed** -d
drows|e draʊz **-es** -ɪz **-ing** -ɪŋ **-ed** -d
drows|y ˈdraʊ.z|i **-ier** -i.əʳ, (US) -i.ɚ **-iest** -i.ɪst, -i.əst **-ily** -əl.i, -ɪ.li **-iness** -ɪ.nəs, -ɪ.nɪs
Droylsden ˈdrɔɪlz.dən
Drs. (abbrev. for **Doctors**) ˈdɒk.təz, (US) ˈdɑːk.tɚz
drub drʌb **-s** -z **-bing** -ɪŋ **-bed** -d
Druce druːs
Drucker ˈdrʊk.əʳ, (US) ˈdrʌk.ɚ, ˈdrʊk-
drudg|e drʌdʒ **-es** -ɪz **-ing/ly** -ɪŋ/li **-ed** -d
drudgery ˈdrʌdʒ.ər.i
drug drʌg **-s** -z **-ging** -ɪŋ **-ged** -d
drugget ˈdrʌg.ɪt **-s** -s
druggie ˈdrʌg.i **-s** -z
druggist ˈdrʌg.ɪst **-s** -s
drugg|y ˈdrʌg|.i **-ies** -iz
drugstore ˈdrʌg.stɔːʳ, (US) -stɔːr **-s** -z
druid ˈdruː.ɪd **-s** -z **-ess/es** -ɪs/ɪz, -es/ɪz **-ism** -ɪ.zəm
druidic druˈɪd.ɪk **-al** -əl
drum drʌm **-s** -z **-ming** -ɪŋ **-med** -d ˌ**drum** ˈ**major** (US) ˈ**drum** ˌ**major**; ˌ**drum major**ˈ**ette**
drumbeat ˈdrʌm.biːt **-s** -s
Drumcree drʌmˈkriː *stress shift:* ˌ**Drumcree** ˈ**residents**
drumfire ˈdrʌm.faɪəʳ, -faɪ.əʳ, (US) -faɪ.ɚ
drumhead ˈdrʌm.hed **-s** -z
drummer ˈdrʌm.əʳ, (US) -ɚ **-s** -z
Drummond ˈdrʌm.ənd
drumroll ˈdrʌm.rəʊl, (US) -roʊl **-s** -z
drumstick ˈdrʌm.stɪk **-s** -s
drunk (also from **drink**) **n, adj** drʌŋk **-s** -s **-er** -əʳ, (US) -ɚ
drunkard ˈdrʌŋ.kəd, (US) -kɚd **-s** -z
drunk-driv|ing ˌdrʌŋkˈdraɪ.v|ɪŋ **-er/s** -əʳ/z, (US) -ɚ/z
drunken ˈdrʌŋ.kən **-ly** -li **-ness** -nəs, -nɪs
drupe druːp **-s** -s
Drury ˈdrʊə.ri, (US) ˈdrʊr.i
drus|e *geological term:* druːz **-es** -ɪz
Druse *surname:* druːz, druːs
Drus|e, Druz|e *member of sect in Syria and Lebanon:* druːz **-es** -ɪz
Drusilla druːˈsɪl.ə, drʊ-
druthers ˈdrʌð.əz, (US) -ɚz
dr|y dr|aɪ **-ier** -aɪ.əʳ, (US) -aɪ.ɚ **-iest** -aɪ.ɪst, -əst **-yly** -aɪ.li **-yness** -aɪ.nəs, -nɪs **-ies** -aɪz **-ying** -aɪ.ɪŋ **-ied** -aɪd ˌ**dry** ˈ**goods** (US) ˈ**dry** ˌ**goods**; ˌ**dry** ˈ**ice**; ˌ**dry** ˈ**land**; ˌ**dry** ˈ**rot**
dryad ˈdraɪ.æd, -əd **-s** -z
Dryburgh ˈdraɪ.bər.ə, (US) -bɚ.ə
dry-clean ˌdraɪˈkliːn, (US) ˈ-- **-s** -z **-ing** -ɪŋ **-ed** -d **-er/s** -əʳ/z, (US) -ɚ/z
Dryden ˈdraɪ.dən
dry-dock ˌdraɪˈdɒk, ˈ--, (US) ˈdraɪ.dɑːk **-s** -s **-ing** -ɪŋ **-ed** -t
dryer ˈdraɪ.əʳ, (US) -ɚ **-s** -z
dry-eyed ˌdraɪˈaɪd
Dryfesdale ˈdraɪfs.deɪl
Dryhurst ˈdraɪ.hɜːst, (US) -hɝːst
drying (from **dry**) ˈdraɪ.ɪŋ
dryly ˈdraɪ.li
dryness ˈdraɪ.nəs, -nɪs
dry-nurs|e ˈdraɪ.nɜːs, (US) -nɝːs **-es** -ɪz **-ing** -ɪŋ **-ed** -t
drypoint ˈdraɪ.pɔɪnt
Drysdale ˈdraɪz.deɪl
dryshod ˈdraɪ.ʃɒd, (US) ʃɑːd
drywall ˈdraɪ.wɔːl, (US) -wɔːl, -wɑːl **-s** -z **-ing** -ɪŋ **-ed** -d
DTI ˌdiː.tiːˈaɪ
DTP ˌdiː.tiːˈpiː
DTs ˌdiːˈtiːz
dual ˈdʒuː.əl, ˈdjuː-; dʒʊəl, djʊəl, (US) ˈduː.əl, ˈdjuː- ˌ**dual** ˈ**carriage-way**
dual|ism ˈdʒuː.ə.l|ɪ.zəm, ˈdjuː-; ˈdʒʊə.l|ɪ-, ˈdlʊə-, (US) ˈduː.əl|.ɪ-, ˈdjuː- **-ist/s** -ɪst/s
dualistic ˌdʒuː.əˈlɪs.tɪk, ˌdjuː-; ˌdʒʊəˈlɪs-, ˌdjʊə-, (US) ˌduː.əlˈɪs-, ˌdjuː-
dualit|y dʒuˈæl.ə.t|i, dju-, -ɪ.t|i, (US) duˈæl.ə.ţ|i, dju- **-ies** -iz
dual-purpose ˌdʒuː.əlˈpɜː.pəs, ˌdjuː-; ˌdʒʊəl-, ˌdjʊəl-, (US) ˌduː.əlˈpɝː-, ˌdjuː- *stress shift:* ˌ**dual-purpose** ˈ**implement**
Duane dweɪn; duˈeɪn
dub dʌb **-s** -z **-bing** -ɪŋ **-bed** -d
Dubai duːˈbaɪ, dʊ-, djʊ-, (US) duː-, də-
Du Barry djuːˈbær.i, duː-, (US) duːˈber-, djuː-, -ˈbær-
dubbin ˈdʌb.ɪn
Dubcek ˈdʊb.tʃek, (US) ˈduːb-
dubiety dʒuːˈbaɪ.ə.ti, dʒʊ-, djuː-, djʊ-, -ɪ.ti, (US) duːˈbaɪ.ə.ţi, djuː-
dubious ˈdʒuː.bi.əs, ˈdjuː-, (US) ˈduː-, ˈdjuː- **-ly** -li **-ness** -nəs, -nɪs
dubi|tate ˈdʒuː.bɪ|.teɪt, ˈdjuː-, (US) ˈduː.bə-, ˈdjuː- **-tates** -teɪts **-tating** -teɪ.tɪŋ, (US) -teɪ.ţɪŋ **-tated** -teɪ.tɪd, (US) -teɪ.ţɪd
dubitation ˌdʒuː.bɪˈteɪ.ʃən, ˌdjuː-, (US) ˌduː.bəˈ-, ˌdjuː- **-s** -z
dubitative ˈdʒuː.bɪ.tə.tɪv, ˈdjuː-, -teɪ-, (US) ˈduː.bə-, ˈdjuː- **-ly** -li
Dublin ˈdʌb.lɪn
Dubliner ˈdʌb.lɪ.nəʳ, (US) -nɚ **-s** -z
DuBois, Du Bois duːˈbwɑː, djuː-
Dubonnet® djuːˈbɒn.eɪ, duː-, ˈ---, (US) ˌduː.bəˈneɪ, ˌdjuː-
Dubrovnik djʊˈbrɒv.nɪk, dʊ-, (US) duːˈbrɑːv-
Dubya ˈdʌb.jə
ducal ˈdʒuː.kəl, ˈdjuː-, (US) ˈduː-, ˈdjuː- **-ly** -i
Du Cane djuːˈkeɪn, duː-, (US) duː-, djuː-
ducat ˈdʌk.ət **-s** -s
duce, D~ ˈduː.tʃeɪ, -tʃi, (US) ˈduː.tʃeɪ
duces tecum ˌduː.kesˈteɪ.kʊm, (US) -siːzˈ-
Duchamp ˈdjuː.ʃɑ̃ːŋ, ˈduː-, ˌ-ˈ-, (US) ˌ-ˈ-, ˌduˈʃɑːmp
Duchesne djuːˈʃeɪn, duː-
duchess, D~ ˈdʌtʃ.ɪs, -es; dʌtʃˈes, (US) ˈdʌtʃ.ɪs **-es** -ɪz
duchesse duːˈʃes; ˈdʌtʃ.ɪs, -es, (US) ˈdʌtʃ.ɪs
Duchovny dʊˈkɒv.ni, duː-, (US) -ˈkɑːv-
duch|y ˈdʌtʃ|.i **-ies** -iz
Ducie ˈdjuː.si, ˈdʒuː-, (US) ˈduː-, ˈdjuː-
duck dʌk **-s** -s **-ing** -ɪŋ **-ed** -t ˈ**duck** ˌ**pond**; ˌ**ducks and** ˈ**drakes**; ˌ**take to something like a** ˌ**duck to** ˈ**water**
duckbill ˈdʌk.bɪl **-s** -z **-ed** -d ˌ**duckbilled** ˈ**platypus**
duckboard ˈdʌk.bɔːd, (US) -bɔːrd **-s** -z
duck-egg ˈdʌk.eg **-s** -z
duckling ˈdʌk.lɪŋ **-s** -z
duckweed ˈdʌk.wiːd
Duckworth ˈdʌk.wəθ, -wɜːθ, (US) -wɚθ, -wɝːθ
duck|y ˈdʌk|.i **-ies** -iz
duct dʌkt **-s** -s
ductile ˈdʌk.taɪl, (US) -tɪl, -taɪl
ductility dʌkˈtɪl.ə.ti, -ɪ.ti, (US) -ə.ţi
ductless ˈdʌkt.ləs, -lɪs ˌ**ductless** ˈ**gland**
dud dʌd **-s** -z
Duddeston ˈdʌd.ɪ.stən
Duddington ˈdʌd.ɪŋ.tən
Duddon ˈdʌd.ən
dude duːd, djuːd **-s** -z ˈ**dude** ˌ**ranch**
Dudeney ˈduːd.ni, ˈdjuːd-
dudgeon ˈdʌdʒ.ən **-s** -z
Dudley ˈdʌd.li
due dʒuː, djuː, (US) duː, djuː **-s** -z
duel ˈdʒuː.əl, ˈdjuː-, (US) ˈduː.əl, ˈdjuː- **-s** -z **-(l)ing** -ɪŋ **-(l)ed** -d **-(l)er/s** -əʳ/z, (US) -ɚ/z
duel(l)ist ˈdʒuː.əl.ɪst, ˈdjuː-, (US) ˈduː-, ˈdjuː- **-s** -s
duenna djuˈen.ə, du-, (US) du-, dju- **-s** -z
Duer ˈdʒuː.əʳ, ˈdjuː-, (US) ˈduː.ɚ, ˈdjuː-
Duessa dʒuˈes.ə, dju-, (US) du-, dju-
duet dʒuˈet, dju-, (US) du-, dju- **-s** -s

duettino ˌdjuː.etˈiː.nəʊ, ˌdʒuː-, (US) ˌduː.etˈiː.noʊ, ˌdjuː- **-s** -z
duettist djuˈet.ɪst, dʒu-, (US) duˈet̬-, dju- **-s** -s
duetto djuˈet.əʊ, dʒu-, (US) duˈet̬.oʊ, dju- **-s** -z
duff, D~ dʌf **-s** -s **-ing** -ɪŋ **-ed** -t
duffel ˈdʌf.əl ˈ**duffel** ˌ**bag**; ˈ**duffel** ˌ**coat**
duffer ˈdʌf.əʳ, (US) -ɚ **-s** -z
Dufferin ˈdʌf.ər.ɪn
Duffield ˈdʌf.iːld
Duffin ˈdʌf.ɪn
Duffy ˈdʌf.i
Dufy ˈduː.fi, (US) duːˈfiː
dug (also from **dig**) **n** dʌg **-s** -z
Dugald ˈduː.gəld
Dugan ˈduː.gən
Dugdale ˈdʌg.deɪl
Duggan ˈdʌg.ən
Dugmore ˈdʌg.mɔːʳ, (US) -mɔːr
dugong ˈdjuː-, ˈduː-, (US) ˈduː.gɑːŋ, -gɔːŋ **-s** -z
dugout ˈdʌg.aʊt **-s** -s
Duguid ˈdjuː.gɪd, ˈduː.gɪd, (US) ˈduː-, ˈdjuː-
DUI ˌdiː.juːˈaɪ
duiker ˈdaɪ.kəʳ, (US) -kɚ **-s** -z
Duisburg ˈdjuːz.bɜːg, ˈdjuːs-, (US) ˈduːs.bɝːg, ˈduːz-
Duisenberg ˈdaɪ.zən.bɜːg, ˈdɔɪ-, -zəm-, (US) ˈduː.zən.bɝːg, daɪ-
Dukakis dʊˈkɑː.kɪs, djʊ-, dʒʊ-, də-, (US) dʊˈkɑː.kəs, də-
Dukas ˈdjuː.kɑː, ˈduː-, -ˈ-, (US) duːˈkɑː, djuː-
duke, D~ dʒuːk, djuːk, (US) duːk, djuːk **-s** -s
dukedom ˈdʒuːk.dəm, ˈdjuːk-, (US) ˈduːk-, ˈdjuːk- **-s** -z
duker|y ˈdʒuː.kər|.i, ˈdjuː-, (US) ˈduː-, ˈdjuː- **-ies** -iz
Dukinfield ˈdʌk.ɪn.fiːld
Dulce ˈdʌl.si
dulcet ˈdʌl.sɪt, -sət
Dulcie ˈdʌl.si
dulci|fy ˈdʌl.sɪ|.faɪ, -sə- **-fies** -faɪz **-fying** -faɪ.ɪŋ **-fied** -faɪd
dulcimer ˈdʌl.sɪ.məʳ, -sə-, (US) -mɚ **-s** -z
Dulcinea ˌdʌl.sɪˈniː.ə, -ˈneɪ-; dʌlˈsɪn.i-, (US) ˌdʌl.səˈniː-; (US) dʌlˈsɪn.i-
dulia djʊˈlaɪ.ə, dʊ-, (US) duːˈlaɪ.ə, djuː-; (US) ˈduː.li.ə
dull dʌl **-er** -əʳ, (US) -ɚ **-est** -ɪst, -əst **-y** -li, -i **-ness** -nəs, -nɪs **-s** -z **-ing** -ɪŋ **-ed** -d **as** ˌ**dull as** ˈ**ditch-water**
dullard ˈdʌl.əd, -ɑːd, (US) -ɚd **-s** -z
Dulles ˈdʌl.ɪs, -əs
dullish ˈdʌl.ɪʃ
dullsville ˈdʌlz.vɪl
dulness ˈdʌl.nəs, -nɪs
Duluth dəˈluːθ, djʊ-, dʊ-, də-, (US) də-
Dulux® ˈdʒuː.lʌks, ˈdjuː-, (US) ˈduː-, ˈdjuː-
Dulwich ˈdʌl.ɪdʒ, -ɪtʃ
duly ˈdʒuː.li, ˈdjuː-, (US) ˈduː-, ˈdjuː-
Duma ˈduː.mə, ˈdjuː-, (US) ˈduː-
Dumain djʊˈmeɪn, dʒʊ-, (US) duː-, djuː-
Dumas ˈdjuː.mɑː, ˈduː-; dʊˈmɑː, (US) duːˈmɑː, djuː-
Du Maurier djuːˈmɔː.ri.eɪ, duː-, -ˈmɒr.i-, (US) duːˈmɔːr.i-, djuː-
dumb dʌm **-er** -əʳ, (US) -ɚ **-est** -ɪst, -əst **-ly** -li **-ness** -nəs, -nɪs **-s** -z **-ing** -ɪŋ **-ed** -d ˈ**dumb** ˌ**show**; ˌ**dumb** ˈ**waiter** (US) ˈ**dumb** ˌ**waiter**
Dumbarton dʌmˈbɑː.tən, dəm-, (US) -ˈbɑːr-

> Note: In **Dumbarton Oaks** (Washington DC), however, the pronunciation is /ˌdʌm.bɑː.tənˈəʊks/ (US) /-bɑːr.tənˈoʊks/.

dumbbell ˈdʌm.bel **-s** -z
dumbfound ˌdʌmˈfaʊnd, ˈ--, (US) ˈdʌm.faʊnd, ˌ-ˈ- **-s** -z **-ing** -ɪŋ **-ed** -ɪd
dumbo, D~ ˈdʌm.bəʊ, (US) -boʊ
dumbstricken ˈdʌmˌstrɪk.ən
dumbstruck ˈdʌm.strʌk
dum-dum ˈdʌm.dʌm **-s** -z
dumfound ˌdʌmˈfaʊnd, ˈ--, (US) ˈdʌm.faʊnd, ˌ-ˈ- **-s** -z **-ing** -ɪŋ **-ed** -ɪd
Dumfries dʌmˈfriːs, dəm- **-shire** -ʃəʳ, -ʃɪəʳ, dʌmˈfriːʃ.ʃəʳ, (US) dʌmˈfriːs.ʃɚ, -ʃɪr
dumm|y ˈdʌm|.i **-ies** -iz
dump dʌmp **-s** -s **-ing** -ɪŋ **-ed** -t ˈ**dump** ˌ**truck**
dumper ˈdʌm.pəʳ, (US) -pɚ **-s** -z
dumpish ˈdʌm.pɪʃ **-ly** -li **-ness** -nəs, -nɪs
dumpling ˈdʌm.plɪŋ **-s** -z
dumps dʌmps
Dumpster® ˈdʌmp.stəʳ, (US) -stɚ
dump|y ˈdʌm.p|i **-ier** -i.əʳ, (US) -i.ɚ **-iest** -i.ɪst, -i.əst **-iness** -ɪ.nəs, -ɪ.nɪs
dun dʌn **-s** -z **-ning** -ɪŋ **-ned** -d
Dunalley dʌnˈæl.i
Dunaway ˈdʌn.ə.weɪ
Dunbar dʌnˈbɑːʳ, dʌm-, ˈ--, (US) ˈdʌn.bɑːr, -ˈ-

> Note: In Scotland always -ˈ-.

Dunbarton dʌnˈbɑː.tən, dʌm-, (US) dʌnˈbɑːr- **-shire** -ʃəʳ, -ʃɪəʳ, (US) -ʃɚ, -ʃɪr
Dunblane dʌnˈbleɪn, dʌm-, (US) dʌn-
Duncan ˈdʌŋ.kən, ˈdʌn-
Duncannon dʌnˈkæn.ən, dʌŋ-, (US) dʌn-
Duncansby ˈdʌŋ.kənz.bi, ˈdʌn-
dunc|e dʌn*t*s **-es** -ɪz
Dunciad ˈdʌn*t*.si.æd
Duncombe ˈdʌn.kəm, ˈdʌŋ-
Dundalk dʌnˈdɔːk, -ˈdɔːlk, (US) -ˈdɔːk, -ˈdɑːk
Dundas dʌnˈdæs, ˈdʌn.dæs, ˈdʌn.dəs, (US) dʌnˈdæs, ˈdʌn.dəs
Dundee dʌnˈdiː, ˌdʌn- *stress shift:* ˌ**Dundee** ˈ**station**
dunderhead ˈdʌn.də.hed, (US) -dɚ- **-s** -z
Dundonald dʌnˈdɒn.əld, (US) -ˈdɑː.nəld
dundrear|y, D~ dʌnˈdrɪə.r|i, (US) -ˈdrɪr|.i **-ies** -iz
Dundrum dʌnˈdrʌm, ˈdʌn.drəm
dune dʒuːn, djuːn, (US) duːn, djuːn **-s** -z
Dunedin dʌnˈiː.dɪn, -dən
Dunell dʒʊˈnel, ˌdʒuː-, djʊ-, ˌdjuː-, (US) duː-, djuː-
Dunfermline dʌnˈfɜːm.lɪn, -lən, (US) -ˈfɝːm-
dung dʌŋ
Dungannon dʌnˈgæn.ən, dʌŋ-
dungaree ˌdʌŋ.gəˈriː, ˈ--- **-s** -z
Dungarvan dʌnˈgɑː.vən, dʌŋ-, (US) dʌnˈgɑːr-
Dungeness ˌdʌn.*d*ʒəˈnes, -*d*ʒɪˈ-
dungeon ˈdʌn.dʒən **-s** -z
dunghill ˈdʌŋ.hɪl **-s** -z
Dunglison ˈdʌŋ.glɪ.sən
dungy ˈdʌŋ.i
Dunham ˈdʌn.əm
Dunhill ˈdʌn.hɪl
Dunholme ˈdʌn.əm
dunk, D~ dʌŋk **-s** -s **-ing** -ɪŋ **-ed** -t
Dunkeld dʌnˈkeld, dʌŋ-, (US) dʌn-
Dunker ˈdʌŋ.kəʳ, (US) -kɚ **-s** -z
Dunkirk dʌnˈkɜːk, ˌdʌn-, dʌŋ-, ˌdʌŋ-, (US) ˈdʌn.kɝːk, dʌnˈkɝːk, ˌdʌn-
Dunkley ˈdʌŋ.kli
Dun Laoghaire dʌnˈlɪə.ri, duːn-, ˈleə-, -rə, (US) -ˈler.ə, -i
Dunlap ˈdʌn.læp, -læp, (US) -læp, -ləp
dunlin ˈdʌn.lɪn, -lən **-s** -z
Dunlop *surname:* ˈdʌn.lɒp, -ˈ-, (US) ˈdʌn.lɑːp, -ˈ-
Dunlop® ˈdʌn.lɒp, (US) -lɑːp **-s** -s
Dunmail dʌnˈmeɪl, dʌm-, (US) dʌn-
Dunmore dʌnˈmɔːʳ, dʌm-, (US) dʌnˈmɔːr
Dunmow ˈdʌn.məʊ, ˈdʌm-, (US) ˈdʌn.moʊ
Dunn(e) dʌn
dunnage ˈdʌn.ɪdʒ
Dunnet(t) ˈdʌn.ɪt
Dunning ˈdʌn.ɪŋ
dunno dəˈnəʊ, (US) -ˈnoʊ
dunnock ˈdʌn.ək **-s** -s
Dunnottar dʌnˈɒt.əʳ, dəˈnɒt-, (US) dʌnˈɑː.t̬ɚ, dəˈnɑː-
dunn|y ˈdʌn|.i **-ies** -ɪz
Dunoon dʌnˈuːn, dəˈnuːn
Dunraven dʌnˈreɪ.vən
Dunrobin dʌnˈrɒb.ɪn, (US) -ˈrɑː.bɪn
Dunsany dʌnˈseɪ.ni, -ˈsæn.i
Dunse dʌn*t*s
Dunsinane dʌnˈsɪn.ən, ˌdʌn*t*.sɪˈneɪn

> Note: This name has to be pronounced /ˌdʌn*t*.sɪˈneɪn/ in Shakespeare's 'Macbeth'.

Duns Scotus ˌdʌnzˈskɒt.əs, -ˈskəʊ.təs, (US) -ˈskoʊ.t̬əs
Dunstable ˈdʌn*t*.stə.bəl
Dunstaffnage dʌnˈstæf.nɪdʒ, -ˈstɑːf-, (US) -ˈstæf-

D

Dunstan ˈdʌnt.stᵊn
Dunster ˈdʌnt.stəʳ, (US) -stɚ
Dunston ˈdʌnt.stᵊn
Dunton ˈdʌn.tən, (US) -tᵊn
Dunwich ˈdʌn.ɪtʃ
Dunwoody dʌnˈwʊd.i
duo ˈdʒuː.əʊ, ˈdjuː-, (US) ˈduː.oʊ, ˈdjuː- **-s** -z
duo- ˈdʒuː.əʊ, ˈdjuː.əʊ; dʒuˈɒ, djuˈɒ, (US) ˈduː.oʊ, ˈdjuː-, ˈ-ə; (US) duˈɑː, djuˈɑː
Note: Prefix. Either carries primary or secondary stress on the first syllable, e.g. **duologue** /ˈdʒuː.ə.lɒɡ/ (US) /ˈduː.ə.lɑːɡ/, **duodecimal** /ˌdʒuː.əʊˈdes.ɪ.mᵊl/ (US) /ˌduː.oʊˈ-/, or primary stress on the second syllable, e.g. **duopoly** /dʒuˈɒp.ᵊl.i/ (US) /duˈɑː.pᵊl-/.
duodecennial ˌdʒuː.əʊ.dɪˈsen.i.əl, ˌdjuː-, -dəˈ-, (US) ˌduː.oʊ.dəˈ-, ˌdjuː-
duodecimal ˌdʒuː.əʊˈdes.ɪ.mᵊl, ˌdjuː-, ˈ-ə-, (US) ˌduː.oʊˈ-, ˌdjuː- **-s** -z
duodecimo ˌdʒuː.əʊˈdes.ɪ.məʊ, ˌdjuː-, (US) ˌduː.oʊˈdes.ə.moʊ, ˌdjuː- **-s** -z
duodenal ˌdʒuː.əʊˈdiː.nᵊl, ˌdjuː-, (US) ˌduː.əˈ-, ˌdjuː-; (US) duːˈɑː.dᵊn.ᵊl, djuː-
duodenary ˌdʒuː.əʊˈdiː.nᵊr.i, ˌdjuː-, (US) ˌduː.əˈ-, ˌdjuː-, -ˈdən.ɚ.i
duoden|um ˌdʒuː.əʊˈdiː.n|əm, ˌdjuː-, (US) ˌduː.əˈ-, ˌdjuː-; (US) duːˈɑː.dᵊn|.əm, djuː- **-ums** -əmz **-a** -ə
duologue ˈdʒuː.ə.lɒɡ, ˈdjuː-, (US) ˈduː.ə.lɑːɡ, ˈdjuː- **-s** -z
duopol|y dʒuˈɒp.ᵊl|.i, dju-, (US) duˈɑː.pᵊl-, dju- **-ies** -iz
dup|e dʒuːp, djuːp, (US) duːp, djuːp **-es** -s **-ing** -ɪŋ **-ed** -t
dupery ˈdʒuː.pᵊr.i, ˈdjuː-, (US) ˈduː-, ˈdjuː-
duple ˈdʒuː.pᵊl, ˈdjuː-, (US) ˈduː-, ˈdjuː-
Dupleix *governor in India:* djuːˈpleɪks, (US) duːˈpleɪks, djuː- *historian:* djuːˈpleɪ, (US) duːˈpleɪ, djuː-
duplex ˈdʒuː.pleks, ˈdjuː-, (US) ˈduː-, ˈdjuː- **-es** -ɪz
duplicate n, adj ˈdʒuː.plɪ.kət, ˈdjuː-, -plə-, -kɪt, (US) ˈduː-, ˈdjuː- **-s** -s
dupli|cate v ˈdʒuː.plɪ|.keɪt, ˈdjuː-, -plə-, (US) ˈduː-, ˈdjuː- **-cates** -keɪts **-cating** -keɪ.tɪŋ, (US) -keɪ.t̬ɪŋ **-cated** -keɪ.tɪd, (US) -keɪ.t̬ɪd **-cator/s** -keɪ.təʳ/z, (US) -keɪ.t̬ɚ/z
duplication ˌdʒuː.plɪˈkeɪ.ʃᵊn, ˌdjuː-, -pləˈ-, (US) ˌduː-, ˌdjuː- **-s** -z
duplicature ˈdʒuː.plɪ.keɪ.tʃəʳ, ˈdjuː-, -kə-, (US) ˈduː.plə.kə.tʃʊr, ˈdjuː-, -keɪ-, -tʃɚ **-s** -z
duplicitous dʒuˈplɪs.ɪ.təs, dju-, ˈ-ə-, (US) duːˈplɪs.ə.t̬əs, djuː- **-ly** -li **-ness** -nəs, -nɪs
duplicity dʒuˈplɪs.ə.ti, dju-, -ɪ.ti, (US) duːˈplɪs.ə.t̬i, djuː-
dupl|y dʒuˈpl|aɪ, dju-, (US) duː-, djuː- **-ies** -aɪz
Dupont djuˈpɒnt; ˈdjuː.pɒnt, (US) duːˈpɑːnt, djuː-, ˈ--
du Pré dʊˈpreɪ, djʊ-, (US) duː-, djuː-
Dupré(e) dʊˈpreɪ, djʊ-, -ˈpriː, (US) duː-, djuː-
Dupuytren dʊˈpwiː.trᵊn, djʊ-; ˈdjuː.pɪ.træ̃ŋ, ˌ--ˈ-, (US) ˈduː.pwiː.træn, ˈdjuː-
Duquesne *French naval commander:* djʊˈkeɪn, dʊ-, (US) duː-, djuː- *place in US:* djuːˈkeɪn, duː-, (US) duː-, dju-
durability ˌdʒʊə.rəˈbɪl.ə.ti, ˌdʒɔː-, ˌdjʊə-, ˌdjɔː-, -ɪ.ti, (US) ˌdʊr.əˈbɪl.ə.t̬i, ˌdjʊr-, ˌdɝː-
durab|le ˈdʒʊə.rə.b|ᵊl, ˈdʒɔː-, ˈdjʊə-, ˈdjɔː-, (US) ˈdʊr.ə-, ˈdjʊr-, ˈdɝː- **-ly** -li **-leness** -ᵊl.nəs, -nɪs
Duracell® ˈdʒʊə.rə.sel, ˈdjʊə-, ˈdʒɔː-, ˈdjɔː-, (US) ˈdʊr.ə-, ˈdjʊr-, ˈdɝː-
Duraglit® ˈdʒʊə.rə.ɡlɪt, ˈdjʊə-, (US) ˈdʊr.ə-, ˈdjʊr-
dural ˈdʒʊə.rᵊl, ˈdjʊə-, ˈdʒɔː-, ˈdjɔː-, (US) ˈdʊr.ᵊl, ˈdjʊr-
Duralumin® dʒʊəˈræl.jʊ.mɪn, dʒɔː-, djʊə-, djɔː-, -jə-, (US) duːˈræl.jə-, djuː-
Duran dʒʊəˈræn, dʊə-, djʊə-, (US) dʊˈræn, də- **Du,ran Du'ran**
durance ˈdʒʊə.rᵊnts, ˈdjʊə-, ˈdʒɔː-, ˈdjɔː-, (US) ˈdʊr.ᵊnts, ˈdjʊr-
Durand dʒʊəˈrænd, djʊə-, (US) dʊˈrænd, də-
Durango dəˈræŋ.ɡəʊ, dʊ-, (US) -ɡoʊ
Durant djʊˈrɑːnt, dʒʊ-, -ˈrænt, (US) ˈduː.rænt; (US) dəˈrænt
Durante djʊˈræn.ti, dʒʊ-, -teɪ, (US) dəˈræn.t̬i, dʊ-
duration dʒʊəˈreɪ.ʃᵊn, dʒɔː-, djʊə-, djɔː-, (US) dʊ-, djʊ-, də- **-s** -z
durative ˈdʒʊə.rə.tɪv, ˈdʒɔː-, ˈdjʊə-, ˈdjɔː-, (US) ˈdʊr.ə.t̬ɪv, ˈdjʊr-
Durban ˈdɜː.bən, (US) ˈdɝː-
durbar ˈdɜː.bɑːʳ, ˌ-ˈ-, (US) ˈdɝː.bɑːr **-s** -z
d'Urberville ˈdɜː.bə.vɪl, (US) ˈdɝː.bɚ- **-s** -z
Durbin ˈdɜː.bɪn, (US) ˈdɝː-
Durden ˈdɜː.dᵊn, (US) ˈdɝː-
durdle ˈdɜː.dᵊl, (US) ˈdɝː- **-s** -z
Durell djʊəˈrel, dʒʊə-, (US) duː-, djuː-
Dürer ˈdjʊə.rəʳ, (US) ˈdjuː.rɚ **-s** -z
duress dʒʊˈres, djʊ-, (US) dʊ-, djʊ-
durex, D~® ˈdʒʊə.reks, ˈdʒɔː-, ˈdjʊə-, ˈdjɔː-, (US) ˈdʊr.eks, ˈdjʊr- **-es** -ɪz
Durham ˈdʌr.ᵊm, (US) ˈdɝː-
durian, durion ˈdjʊə.ri.ən, ˈdʊr.i-, -æn, (US) ˈdʊr.i- **-s** -z
during ˈdʒʊə.rɪŋ, ˈdʒɔː-, ˈdjʊə-, ˈdjɔː-, (US) ˈdʊr.ɪŋ, ˈdjʊr-, ˈdɝː-
Durnford ˈdɜːn.fəd, (US) ˈdɝːn.fɚd
Durocher dəˈrəʊ.ʃəʳ, -tʃəʳ, (US) -ˈroʊ.ʃɚ, -tʃɚ
Durran dʌrˈæn, dəˈræn, (US) dəˈræn
Durrant ˈdʌr.ᵊnt, (US) ˈdɝː-; (US) dəˈrænt
Durrell ˈdʌr.ᵊl, (US) ˈdɝː-
Dürrenmat ˈdjʊə.rᵊn.mæt, ˈdʊə-, (US) ˈdʊr.ən.mɑːt
durrie ˈdʌr.i, (US) ˈdɝː- **-s** -z
Durrington ˈdʌr.ɪŋ.tən, (US) ˈdɝː-
Dursley ˈdɜːz.li, (US) ˈdɝːz-
durst (from **dare**) dɜːst, (US) dɝːst **-n't** ˈdɜː.sᵊnt, (US) ˈdɝː-
durum ˈdʒʊə.rəm, ˈdjʊə-, ˈdʒɔː-, ˈdjɔː-, (US) ˈdʊr.əm, ˈdɝː-
Durward ˈdɜː.wəd, (US) ˈdɝː.wɚd
Dury ˈdʒʊə.ri, ˈdjʊə-, (US) ˈdʊr.i, ˈdjʊr-
Duse ˈduː.zi
Dushanbe duːˈʃæn.bə, -ˈʃæm-, -ˈʃɑːn-, -ˈʃɑːm-, -bi, (US) duːˈʃɑːn.bi
dusk dʌsk **-s** -s **-ing** -ɪŋ **-ed** -t
dusk|y ˈdʌs.k|i **-ier** -i.əʳ, (US) -i.ɚ **-iest** -i.ɪst, -i.əst **-ily** -ᵊl.i, -ɪ.li **-iness** -ɪ.nəs, -ɪ.nɪs
Düsseldorf ˈdʊs.ᵊl.dɔːf, (US) ˈduː.sᵊl.dɔːrf, ˈdʊs.ᵊl-
dust dʌst **-s** -s **-ing** -ɪŋ **-ed** -ɪd ˈ**Dust ˌBowl**; ˈ**dust ˌcover**; ˈ**dust ˌjacket**; ˌ**bite the** ˈ**dust**
dustbin ˈdʌst.bɪn **-s** -z
dustcart ˈdʌst.kɑːt, (US) -kɑːrt **-s** -s
dustcoat ˈdʌst.kəʊt, (US) -koʊt **-s** -s
duster ˈdʌs.təʳ, (US) -tɚ **-s** -z
Dustin ˈdʌs.tɪn
dust|man ˈdʌst|.mən **-men** -mən
dustpan ˈdʌst.pæn **-s** -z
dustproof ˈdʌst.pruːf
dustsheet ˈdʌst.ʃiːt **-s** -s
dust-up ˈdʌst.ʌp **-s** -s
dust|y, D~ ˈdʌs.t|i **-ier** -i.əʳ, (US) -i.ɚ **-iest** -i.ɪst, -i.əst **-ily** -ᵊl.i, -ɪ.li **-iness** -ɪ.nəs, -ɪ.nɪs
Dutch dʌtʃ **-man** -mən **-men** -mən ˌ**Dutch** ˈ**cap**; ˌ**Dutch** ˈ**courage**; ˌ**Dutch** ˈ**elm diˌsease**; ˌ**Dutch** ˈ**oven**; ˌ**Dutch** ˈ**treat**
Dutch|woman ˈdʌtʃ|ˌwʊm.ən **-women** -ˌwɪm.ɪn
duteous ˈdʒuː.ti.əs, ˈdjuː-, (US) ˈduː.t̬i-, ˈdjuː- **-ly** -li **-ness** -nəs, -nɪs
Duthie ˈdʌθ.i
dutiable ˈdʒuː.ti.ə.bᵊl, ˈdjuː-, (US) ˈduː.t̬i-, ˈdjuː-
dutiful ˈdʒuː.tɪ.fᵊl, ˈdjuː-, -fʊl, (US) ˈduː.t̬ɪ-, ˈdjuː- **-ly** -i **-ness** -nəs, -nɪs
Dutton ˈdʌt.ᵊn
dut|y ˈdʒuː.t|i, ˈdjuː-, (US) ˈduː.t̬|i, ˈdjuː- **-ies** -iz
duty-free ˌdʒuː.tiˈfriː, ˌdjuː-, (US) ˌduː.t̬i-, ˌdjuː- ˌ**duty-**ˈ**free shop**
duumvir djuˈʌm.vəʳ, du-, -ˈʊm-; ˈdjuː.əm.vəʳ, ˈduː-, (US) duˈʌm.vɚ, dju- **-s** -z **-i** -aɪ, -iː
duumvirate djuˈʌm.vɪ.rət, du-, -vᵊr.ət, -ɪt, -eɪt, (US) duˈʌm.vɪ.rət, dju-, -vɚ.ət, -ɪt **-s** -s
Duvalier djʊˈvæl.i.eɪ, dʊ-, (US) duːˈvɑːl.jeɪ, djuː-
Duveen djʊˈviːn, (US) duː-, djuː-, də-
duvet ˈdʒuː.veɪ, ˈdjuː-, ˈduː-, (US) duːˈveɪ, djuː- **-s** -z
dux dʌks **-es** -ɪz
Duxbury ˈdʌks.bᵊr.i, (US) -ber-, -bɚ-
Duxford ˈdʌks.fəd, (US) -fɚd
DV ˌdiːˈviː
DVD ˌdiː.viːˈdiː **-s** -z
Dvorak *US family name:* ˈdvɔː.ræk, (US) ˈdvɔːr.æk

D

Dvořák *Czech composer:* ˈdvɔː.ʒɑːk, ˈvɔː-, -ʒæk, (US) ˈdvɔːr.ʒɑːk
dwale dweɪl
dwarf v dwɔːf, (US) dwɔːrf **-s** -s **-ing** -ɪŋ **-ed** -t
dwar|f n dwɔː|f, (US) dwɔːr|f **-s** -s **-ves** -vz
dwarfish ˈdwɔː.fɪʃ, (US) ˈdwɔːr- **-ly** -li **-ness** -nəs, -nɪs
Dwayne dweɪn
dweeb dwiːb **-s** -z
dwell dwel **-s** -z **-ing** -ɪŋ **-ed** -d, -t **dwelt** dwelt **dweller/s** ˈdwel.əʳ/z, (US) -ɚ/z
dwelling ˈdwel.ɪŋ **-s** -z
dwelt (from **dwell**) dwelt
DWI ˌdiːˌdʌb.əl.juːˈaɪ, (US) -juːˈ-, -jəˈ-
Dwight dwaɪt
dwindl|e ˈdwɪn.dəl **-es** -z **-ing** -ɪŋ **-ed** -d
Dworkin ˈdwɔː.kɪn, (US) ˈdwɔːr-
Dwyer ˈdwaɪ.əʳ, (US) ˈdwaɪ.ɚ
dyad ˈdaɪ.æd, -əd **-s** -z
Dyak ˈdaɪ.æk, -ək **-s** -s
dyarch|y ˈdaɪ.ɑː.k|i, (US) -ɑːr- **-ies** -iz
Dyce daɪs
dy|e, D~ daɪ **-es** -z **-eing** -ɪŋ **-ed** -d **-er/s** -əʳ/z, (US) -ɚ/z
dyed-in-the-wool ˌdaɪd.ɪn.ðəˈwʊl
Dyer daɪ.əʳ, (US) daɪ.ɚ
dyestuff ˈdaɪ.stʌf **-s** -s
dyewood ˈdaɪ.wʊd
dyeworks ˈdaɪ.wɜːks, (US) -wɝːks
Dyfed ˈdʌv.ɪd, -ed, -əd
Dyffryn ˈdʌf.rɪn, -rən
dying (from **die**) ˈdaɪ.ɪŋ
dyk|e, D~ daɪk **-es** -s **-ing** -ɪŋ **-ed** -t
Dylan ˈdɪl.ən, ˈdʌl-, (US) ˈdɪl-
Dymchurch ˈdɪm.tʃɜːtʃ, (US) -tʃɝːtʃ
Dymock, Dymoke ˈdɪm.ək
Dymond ˈdaɪ.mənd
Dymphna ˈdɪmp.nə
dynameter daɪˈnæm.ɪ.təʳ, dɪ-, ˈ-ə-, (US) -ə.t̬ɚ **-s** -z
dynamic daɪˈnæm.ɪk, dɪ- **-al** -əl **-ally** -əl.i, -li **-s** -s
dynamism ˈdaɪ.nə.mɪ.zəm
dyna|mite ˈdaɪ.nə|.maɪt **-mites** -maɪts **-miting** -maɪ.tɪŋ, (US) -maɪ.t̬ɪŋ **-mited** -maɪ.tɪd, (US) -maɪ.t̬ɪd **-miter/s** -maɪ.təʳ/z, (US) -maɪ.t̬ɚ/z
dynamo ˈdaɪ.nə.məʊ, (US) -moʊ **-s** -z
dynamometer ˌdaɪ.nəˈmɒm.ɪ.təʳ, ˈ-ə-, (US) -ˈmɑː.mə.t̬ɚ **-s** -z
dynamometric ˌdaɪ.nə.məʊˈmet.rɪk, (US) -moʊˈ- **-al** -əl
dynast ˈdɪn.əst, ˈdaɪ.nəst, -næst, (US) ˈdaɪ.næst, -nəst **-s** -s
dynastic dɪˈnæs.tɪk, daɪ-, də-, (US) daɪ-
dynast|y ˈdɪn.ə.st|i, ˈdaɪ.nə-, (US) ˈdaɪ.nə- **-ies** -iz
dynatron ˈdaɪ.nə.trɒn, (US) -trɑːn **-s** -z
dyne daɪn **-s** -s
Dynevor ˈdɪn.ɪ.vəʳ, ˈ-ə-, (US) -vɚ
d'you *strong forms:* dʒuː, djuː; *weak forms:* dʒə, djə, dʒu, dju
Note: Abbreviated form of 'do you': the spelling represents a pronunciation that is usually unstressed, and the pronunciation therefore parallels that of unstressed **you**, which has weak forms /jə/ before a consonant and /ju/ before vowels. When used contrastively, the strong form /dʒuː/ or /djuː/ may be used (e.g. 'I don't like it. **D'you** like it?').
Dysart ˈdaɪ.sət, -zət, -sɑːt, -zɑːt, (US) -sɑːrt, -zɑːrt, -sɚt
dysarthria dɪˈsɑː.θri.ə, (US) -ˈsɑːr-
dysenteric ˌdɪs.ənˈter.ɪk, -enˈ-, (US) -enˈ-
dysentery ˈdɪs.ən.tər.i, -tri, (US) -ter.i
dysfunction dɪsˈfʌŋk.ʃən **-s** -z **-ing** -ɪŋ **-ed** -d **-al** -əl
dysfunctional dɪsˈfʌŋk.ʃən.əl
dysgraphia dɪsˈgræf.i.ə
dysgraphic dɪsˈgræf.ɪk
dyslalia dɪˈsleɪ.li.ə, -ˈslæl.i-
dyslexia dɪˈslek.si.ə
dyslexic dɪˈslek.sɪk
dysmenorrh(o)ea ˌdɪs.men.əˈrɪə, (US) -ˈriː.ə
Dyson ˈdaɪ.sən
dyspepsia dɪˈspep.si.ə
dyspeptic dɪˈspep.tɪk **-s** -s
dysphagia dɪsˈfeɪ.dʒi.ə, (US) -dʒə, -dʒi.ə
dysphasia dɪsˈfeɪ.zi.ə, -ʒi-, ˈ-ʒə, (US) ˈ-ʒə, ˈ-ʒi.ə
dysphasic dɪsˈfeɪ.zɪk **-s** -s
dysphonia dɪsˈfəʊ.ni.ə, (US) -ˈfoʊ-
dysphonic dɪsˈfɒn.ɪk, (US) -ˈfɑː.nɪk
dyspn(o)ea dɪspˈniː.ə
dysprosium dɪˈsprəʊ.zi.əm, -si-, (US) -ˈsproʊ-
dystrophic dɪˈstrɒf.ɪk, (US) -ˈstrɑː.fɪk, -ˈstroʊ-
dystrophy ˈdɪs.trə.fi
dysuria dɪˈsjʊə.ri.ə, (US) -ˈsjʊr.i-
dziggetai ˈdʒɪg.ɪ.taɪ, ˈ-ə-, ˌ--ˈ-, (US) ˈdʒɪg.ɪ.taɪ **-s** -z

E

Pronouncing the letter E

→ *See also* **EA, EE, EI, EO, EOU, EU/EW, EY**

The vowel letter **e** has two main strong pronunciations linked to spelling: a 'short' pronunciation /e/ and a 'long' pronunciation /iː/. However, the situation is not clear cut and other pronunciations are available.

The 'short' pronunciation always occurs when the **e** is followed by a consonant which closes the syllable, or a double consonant before another vowel, e.g.:

bed	bed
bedding	ˈbed.ɪŋ

The 'long' pronunciation is usually found when the **e** is followed by a single consonant and then a vowel, e.g.:

Eve	iːv
credence	ˈkriː.dᵊnts

However, the 'short' pronunciation occurs in many cases where the **e** is followed by a single consonant and then a vowel, e.g.:

ever	ˈev.əʳ Ⓤⓢ -ɚ
prejudice	ˈpredʒ.ə.dɪs

The 'long' pronunciation may also occur where the **e** is followed by two consonants, e.g.:

negro	ˈniː.grəʊ Ⓤⓢ -roʊ
secret	ˈsiː.krət

When there is an **r** in the spelling, the strong pronunciation is one of four possibilities: /ɪə/ Ⓤⓢ /ɪr/, /eə/ Ⓤⓢ /er/, /ɜː/ Ⓤⓢ /ɝː/, or /e/, e.g.:

here	hɪəʳ Ⓤⓢ hɪr
there	ðeəʳ Ⓤⓢ ðer
were	wɜːʳ Ⓤⓢ wɝː
very	ˈver.i

It frequently happens that the letter **e** has no pronunciation at all, but is used as a spelling convention to show that a preceding vowel is realized with its 'long' pronunciation, e.g.:

brave	breɪv
mice	maɪs
hope	həʊp Ⓤⓢ hoʊp
use (v.)	juːz

In addition

There are other vowel sounds associated with the letter **e**, e.g.:

eɪ	ballet /ˈbæl.eɪ/ Ⓤⓢ /bælˈeɪ/

And, in rare cases:

ɑː Ⓤⓢ ɝː	clerk /klɑːk/ Ⓤⓢ /klɝːk/
ɪ	women /ˈwɪm.ɪn/

In weak syllables

The vowel letter **e** is realized with the vowels /ɪ/, /i/ and /ə/ in weak syllables, or may also not be pronounced at all due to syllabic consonant formation or compression, e.g.:

begin	bɪˈgɪn
react	riˈækt
arithmetic	əˈrɪθ.mə.tɪk
castle	ˈkɑː.sl̩ Ⓤⓢ ˈkæs.l̩

e, E iː **-'s** -z ˈ**E** ˌ**number**
E (abbrev. for **east**) iːst
E111 ˌiːˌwʌn.ɪˈlev.ən, -əˈ-
each iːtʃ ˌ**each** ˈ**other**
EACSO iːˈæk.səʊ, -ˈɑːk-, Ⓤⓢ -soʊ
Eadie, Eady ˈiː.di
eager ˈiː.gəʳ, Ⓤⓢ -gɚ **-ly** -li **-ness** -nəs, -nɪs ˌ**eager** ˈ**beaver**
eagle, E~ ˈiː.gᵊl **-s** -z ˈ**eagle** ˌ**owl**; ˌ**Eagle** ˈ**Scout** Ⓤⓢ ˈ**Eagle** ˌ**Scout**
eagle-eyed ˌiː.gᵊlˈaɪd, ˈiː.gᵊl.aɪd
Eaglefield ˈiː.gᵊl.fiːld
Eaglehawk ˈiː.gᵊl.hɔːk, Ⓤⓢ -hɑːk, -hɔːk
Eaglescliffe ˈiː.gᵊlz.klɪf
eaglet ˈiː.glɪt, -lət **-s** -s
eagre ˈeɪ.gəʳ, ˈiː-, Ⓤⓢ ˈiː.gɚ, ˈeɪ- **-s** -z
Eakin ˈeɪ.kɪn, ˈiː- **-s** -z
Ealing ˈiː.lɪŋ
Eames iːmz, eɪmz
Eamon(n) ˈeɪ.mən
-ean iː.ən, i.ən
Note: Suffix. **-ean** may take primary stress or alternatively words containing it may be stressed on the syllable before the prefix. An example where both possibilities occur is **Caribbean**, which is either /ˌkær.ɪˈbiː.ən/ Ⓤⓢ /ˌker-/, or /kəˈrɪb.i.ən/.
ear ɪəʳ, Ⓤⓢ ɪr **-s** -z ˈ**ear** ˌ**trumpet**; ˌ**give someone a** ˌ**thick** ˈ**ear**; ˌ**turn a** ˌ**deaf** ˈ**ear to**; ˌ**keep one's** ˌ**ear to the** ˈ**ground**; ˌ**prick up one's** ˈ**ears**
earache ˈɪə.reɪk, Ⓤⓢ ˈɪr-
earbashing ˈɪəˌbæʃ.ɪŋ, Ⓤⓢ ˈɪr- **-s** -z
Eardley ˈɜːd.li, Ⓤⓢ ˈɝːd-
eardrop ˈɪə.drɒp, Ⓤⓢ ˈɪr.drɑːp **-s** -s
eardrum ˈɪə.drʌm, Ⓤⓢ ˈɪr- **-s** -z
eared ɪəd, Ⓤⓢ ɪrd
earflaps ˈɪə.flæps, Ⓤⓢ ˈɪr-
earful ˈɪə.fʊl, Ⓤⓢ ˈɪr-
Earhart ˈeə.hɑːt, Ⓤⓢ ˈer.hɑːrt
earl, E~ ɜːl, Ⓤⓢ ɝːl **-s** -z **-dom/s** -dəm/z ˌ**Earl's** ˈ**Court**; ˌ**Earl** ˈ**Grey**; ˌ**earl** ˈ**marshal**
Earl(e) ɜːl, Ⓤⓢ ɝːl
earlobe ˈɪə.ləʊb, Ⓤⓢ ˈɪr.loʊb **-s** -z
earl|y ˈɜː.l|i, Ⓤⓢ ˈɝː- **-ier** -i.əʳ, Ⓤⓢ -i.ɚ **-iest** -i.ɪst, -i.əst **-iness** -ɪ.nəs, -ɪ.nɪs ˈ**early** ˌ**bird**; ˌ**early** ˈ**warning** ˌ**system**
earmark ˈɪə.mɑːk, Ⓤⓢ ˈɪr.mɑːrk **-s** -s **-ing** -ɪŋ **-ed** -t
earmuffs ˈɪə.mʌfs, Ⓤⓢ ˈɪr-
earn, E~ ɜːn, Ⓤⓢ ɝːn **-s** -z **-ing** -ɪŋ **-ed** -d, ɜːnt, Ⓤⓢ ɝːnt **-er/s** -əʳ/z, Ⓤⓢ -ɚ/z
earnest ˈɜː.nɪst, -nəst, Ⓤⓢ ˈɝː- **-s** -s **-ly** -li **-ness** -nəs, -nɪs
earnings ˈɜː.nɪŋz, Ⓤⓢ ˈɝː-
Earnshaw ˈɜːn.ʃɔː, Ⓤⓢ ˈɝːn.ʃɑː, -ʃɔː
Earp ɜːp, Ⓤⓢ ɝːp
earphone ˈɪə.fəʊn, Ⓤⓢ ˈɪr.foʊn **-s** -z
earpiec|e ˈɪə.piːs, Ⓤⓢ ˈɪr- **-es** -ɪz
earplug ˈɪə.plʌg, Ⓤⓢ ˈɪr- **-s** -z
earring ˈɪə.rɪŋ, Ⓤⓢ ˈɪr.ɪŋ, -rɪŋ **-s** -z
earshot ˈɪə.ʃɒt, Ⓤⓢ ˈɪr.ʃɑːt
earsplitting ˈɪəˌsplɪt.ɪŋ, Ⓤⓢ ˈɪrˌsplɪţ.ɪŋ **-ly** -li
earth, E~ n ɜːθ, Ⓤⓢ ɝːθ **-s** -s, ɜːðz, Ⓤⓢ ɝːðz ˈ**earth** ˌ**mother**
earth v ɜːθ, Ⓤⓢ ɝːθ **-s** -s **-ing** -ɪŋ **-ed** -t
earthborn ˈɜːθ.bɔːn, Ⓤⓢ ˈɝːθ.bɔːrn
earthbound ˈɜːθ.baʊnd, Ⓤⓢ ˈɝːθ-

Pronouncing the letters EA

The vowel digraph **ea** has two main strong pronunciations linked to spelling: a 'short' pronunciation /e/ and a 'long' pronunciation /iː/. However, it is not normally predictable which one will occur, e.g.:

bread	bred
bead	biːd
cleanse	klenz
clean	kliːn

When the digraph is followed by an **r** in the spelling, the strong pronunciation is one of four possibilities: /ɪə/ ⓤⓢ /ɪr/, /eə/ ⓤⓢ /er/, /ɜː/ ⓤⓢ /ɝː/, or /ɑː/ ⓤⓢ /ɑːr/, e.g:

fear (n.)	fɪəʳ ⓤⓢ fɪr
tear (v.)	teəʳ ⓤⓢ ter
pearl	pɜːl ⓤⓢ pɝːl
heart	hɑːt ⓤⓢ hɑːrt

In addition

There are other vowel sounds associated with the digraph **ea**, e.g.:

ɪə	idea /aɪˈdɪə/
i.ə	area /ˈeə.ri.ə/ ⓤⓢ /ˈer.i-/
eɪ	great /greɪt/
i.æ	theatrical /θiˈæt.rɪ.kəl/
i.eɪ	create /kriˈeɪt/

In addition, there are instances when the two letters **e** and **a** come together in closed compounds, e.g.:

whereas	*h*weəˈræz ⓤⓢ *h*werˈæz
hereafter	hɪərˈɑːf.təʳ ⓤⓢ hɪrˈæf.tɚ

In weak syllables

The vowel digraph **ea** is realized with the vowels /i/ and /ə/ in weak syllables and may result in a syllabic consonant, e.g.:

guinea	ˈgɪn.i
ocean	ˈəʊ.ʃən ⓤⓢ ˈoʊ-

earthen ˈɜː.θən, -ðən, ⓤⓢ ˈɝː-
earthenware ˈɜː.θən.weəʳ, -ðən-, ⓤⓢ ˈɝː.θən.wer, -ðən-
earthiness ˈɜː.θɪ.nəs, -nɪs, ⓤⓢ ˈɝː-
earthling ˈɜːθ.lɪŋ, ⓤⓢ ˈɝːθ- **-s** -z
earth|ly ˈɜːθ.l|i, ⓤⓢ ˈɝːθ- **-ier** -i.əʳ, ⓤⓢ -i.ɚ **-iest** -i.ɪst, -i.əst **-iness** -ɪ.nəs, -ɪ.nɪs
earthmover ˈɜːθˌmuː.vəʳ, ⓤⓢ ˈɝːθˌmuː.vɚ **-s** -z
earthquake ˈɜːθ.kweɪk, ⓤⓢ ˈɝːθ- **-s** -s
Earthsea ˈɜːθ.siː, ⓤⓢ ˈɝːθ-
earthshaking ˈɜːθˌʃeɪ.kɪŋ, ⓤⓢ ˈɝːθ-
earth-shattering ˈɜːθˌʃæt.ər.ɪŋ, ⓤⓢ ˈɝːθˌʃæţ- **-ly** -li
earthward ˈɜːθ.wəd, ⓤⓢ ˈɝːθ.wɚd **-s** -z
earthwork ˈɜːθ.wɜːk, ⓤⓢ ˈɝːθ.wɝːrk **-s** -s
earthworm ˈɜːθ.wɜːm, ⓤⓢ ˈɝːθ.wɝːrm **-s** -z
earth|y ˈɜː.θ|i, ⓤⓢ ˈɝː- **-ier** -i.əʳ, ⓤⓢ -i.ɚ **-iest** -i.əst, -i.ɪst **-ily** -əl.i, -ɪ.li **-iness** -ɪ.nəs, -ɪ.nɪs
earwax ˈɪə.wæks, ⓤⓢ ˈɪr-
earwig ˈɪə.wɪg, ⓤⓢ ˈɪr- **-s** -z **-ging** -ɪŋ **-ged** -d
Easdale ˈiːz.deɪl
Easdaq iˈæz.dæk
eas|e iːz **-es** -ɪz **-ing** -ɪŋ **-ed** -d
Easebourne ˈiːz.bɔːn, ⓤⓢ -bɔːrn
easeful ˈiːz.fəl, -fʊl **-ly** -li **-ness** -nəs, -nɪs
easel ˈiː.zəl **-s** -z
easement ˈiːz.mənt **-s** -s
Easey ˈiː.zi
easiness (from **easy**) ˈiː.zi.nəs, -nɪs
Easington ˈiː.zɪŋ.tən
Easley ˈiːz.li
east, E~ iːst ˌ**East ˈAnglia**; ˌ**East ˈEnd** *stress shift:* ˌ**East End ˈpub** ˌ**East ˈCoast** *stress shift:* ˌ**East Coast ˈaccent**
East Bergholt ˌiːstˈbɜːg.həʊlt, ⓤⓢ -ˈbɝːg.hoʊlt
eastbound ˈiː*st*.baʊnd
Eastbourne ˈiː*st*.bɔːn, ⓤⓢ -bɔːrn
Eastcheap ˈiː*st*.tʃiːp
Eastender ˌiːstˈen.dəʳ, ⓤⓢ -dɚ **-s** -z
Easter ˈiː.stəʳ, ⓤⓢ -stɚ **-s** -z ˌ**Easter ˈbonnet** ⓤⓢ ˈ**Easter ˌbonnet**; ˌ**Easter ˈBunny** ⓤⓢ ˈ**Easter ˌBunny**; ˌ**Easter ˈDay**; ˈ**Easter ˌegg**; ˈ**Easter ˌIsland**; ˌ**Easter ˈSunday**
Easterby ˈiː.stə.bi, ⓤⓢ -stɚ-
easter|ly ˈiː.stəl|.i, ⓤⓢ -stɚ.l|i **-ies** -iz
eastern, E~ ˈiː.stən, ⓤⓢ -stɚn **-most** -məʊst, -məst, ⓤⓢ -moʊst, -məst ˌ**Eastern ˈShore**; ˌ**Eastern ˈStandard ˌTime**
easterner, E~ ˈiː.s.tən.əʳ, ⓤⓢ -tɚ.nɚ **-s** -z
Eastertide ˈiː.stə.taɪd, ⓤⓢ -stɚ-
Eastfield ˈiːst.fiːld
Eastham ˈiːst.*h*əm
Easthampton ˌiːstˈhæm*p*.tən
easting ˈiː.stɪŋ **-s** -z
East Kilbride ˌiːst.kɪlˈbraɪd
Eastlake ˈiːst.leɪk
Eastleigh ˈiːst.liː, ˌiːstˈliː
Eastman ˈiː*st*.mən
east-northeast ˌiːst.nɔːθˈiːst, ⓤⓢ -nɔːrθˈ-; *in nautical usage also:* -nɔːˈriːst, ⓤⓢ -nɔːrˈiːst
Easton ˈiː.stən
Easton-in-Gordano ˌiː.stən.ɪn.gɔːˈdɑː.nəʊ, -ɪŋ-, ⓤⓢ -gɔːrˈdɑː.noʊ
Eastport ˈiː*st*.pɔːt, ⓤⓢ -pɔːrt
east-southeast ˌiːst.saʊθˈiːst; *in nautical usage also:* -saʊˈ-
eastward ˈiːst.wəd, ⓤⓢ -wɚd **-ly** -li **-s** -z
East-West ˌiːstˈwest *stress shift, see compound:* ˌ**East-West reˈlations**
Eastwood ˈiːst.wʊd
eas|y, E~ ˈiː.z|i **-ier** -i.əʳ, ⓤⓢ -i.ɚ **-iest** -i.ɪst, -i.əst **-ily** -əl.i, -ɪ.li **-iness** -ɪ.nəs, -ɪ.nɪs ˈ**easy ˌchair**; **as ˌeasy as ˈpie**; **on ˈeasy ˌstreet**; ˌ**take it ˈeasy**;
easygoing ˌiː.ziˈgəʊ.ɪŋ, ⓤⓢ -ˈgoʊ- *stress shift:* ˌ**easygoing ˈperson**
EasyJet® ˈiː.zi.dʒet
eat iːt **-s** -s **-ing** -ɪŋ, ⓤⓢ ˈiː.ţɪŋ **ate** et, eɪt, ⓤⓢ eɪt **eaten** ˈiː.tən, ⓤⓢ -ţən **eater/s** ˈiː.təʳ/z, ⓤⓢ -ţɚ/z ˈ**eating diˌsorder**; ˌ**eat one's ˈheart out**; ˌ**eat one's ˈwords**; ˌ**eat someone out of ˌhouse and ˈhome**
eatable ˈiː.tə.bəl, ⓤⓢ -ţə- **-s** -z
eaterie ˈiː.tər.i, ⓤⓢ -ţɚ- **-s** -z
eater|y ˈiː.tər|.i, ⓤⓢ -ţɚ- **-ies** -iz
Eaton ˈiː.tən
Eaton Socon ˌiː.tənˈsəʊ.kən, ⓤⓢ -ˈsoʊ-
eau de cologne ˌəʊ.də.kəˈləʊn, -dɪ-, ⓤⓢ ˌoʊ.də.kəˈloʊn *stress shift:* ˌ**eau de cologne ˈspray**
eau de nil ˌəʊ.dəˈniːl, ⓤⓢ ˌoʊ- *stress shift:* ˌ**eau de nil ˈpaint**
eau de parfum ˌəʊ.də.pɑːˈfʌm, ⓤⓢ ˌoʊ.də.pɑːrˈ-
eau de toilette ˌəʊ.də.twɑːˈlet, -twəˈ-, ⓤⓢ ˌoʊ-
eau-de-vie ˌəʊ.dəˈviː, ⓤⓢ ˌoʊ-
eave, E~ iːv **-s** -z
eavesdrop ˈiːvz.drɒp, ⓤⓢ -drɑːp **-s** -s **-ping** -ɪŋ **-ped** -t **-per/s** -əʳ/z, ⓤⓢ -ɚ/z
eBay® ˈiː.beɪ
ebb eb **-s** -z **-ing** -ɪŋ **-ed** -d ˌ**ebb ˈtide**
Ebbsfleet ˈebz.fliːt
Ebbw ˈeb.uː, -ə
Ebel ebˈel, ˈiː.bəl
Ebenezer ˌeb.əˈniː.zəʳ, -ɪˈ-, ⓤⓢ -zɚ *stress shift:* ˌ**Ebenezer ˈScrooge**

Eberhart ˈeɪ.bə.hɑːt, ⓤⓢ ˈeb.ɚ.hɑːrt, ˈeɪ.bɚ-
Ebionite ˈiː.bjə.naɪt, -bɪə- **-s** -s
Eblis ˈeb.lɪs
ebola, E~ iˈbəʊ.lə, ˈeb.əʊ.lə, ⓤⓢ ɪˈboʊ.lə
ebon ˈeb.ən
Ebonics ɪˈbɒn.ɪks, ⓤⓢ -ˈbɑː.nɪks
ebonite ˈeb.ə.naɪt
eboniz|e, -is|e ˈeb.ə.naɪz **-es** -ɪz **-ing** -ɪŋ **-ed** -d
ebony, E~ ˈeb.ən.i
e-book ˈiː.bʊk **-s** -s
Eboracum iːˈbɒr.ə.kəm, -ˈbɔː.rə-, ɪ-, ⓤⓢ ɪˈbɔːr-
Ebrington ˈeb.rɪŋ.tən
Ebro ˈiː.brəʊ, ˈeb.rəʊ, ⓤⓢ ˈeɪ.broʊ, ˈiː-, ˈeb.roʊ
ebullien|ce ɪˈbʌl.i.ən|ts, -ˈbʊl-, ⓤⓢ -ˈbʊl.jən|ts, -ˈbʌl- **-cy** -tsi
ebullient ɪˈbʌl.i.ənt, -ˈbʊl-, ⓤⓢ -ˈbʊl.jənt, -ˈbʌl- **-ly** -li
ebullition ˌeb.əˈlɪʃ.ən, -ʊˈ-, ⓤⓢ -əˈ-, -juːˈ- **-s** -z
Ebury ˈiː.bər.i, ⓤⓢ -ˌber-, -bɚ-
e-business ˈiːˌbɪz.nɪs, -nəs **-es** -ɪz
EC ˌiːˈsiː
écarté eɪˈkɑː.teɪ, ⓤⓢ ˌeɪ.kɑːrˈteɪ
e-cash ˈiː.kæʃ
Ecbatana ekˈbæt.ən.ə, ˌek.bəˈtɑː.nə, ⓤⓢ ekˈbæt.ən.ə
ecce homo ˌek.eɪˈhəʊ.məʊ, ˌetʃ-, -ˈhɒm.əʊ, ⓤⓢ -ˈhoʊ.moʊ
eccentric ɪkˈsen.trɪk, ek- **-s** -s **-al** -əl **-ally** -əl.i, -li
eccentricit|y ˌek.senˈtrɪs.ə.t|i, -sənˈ-, -ɪ.t|i, ⓤⓢ -ə.t̬|i **-ies** -iz
Ecclefechan ˌek.əlˈfek.ən, -ˈfex-
Eccles ˈek.əlz ˈEccles ˌcake
Ecclesfield ˈek.əlz.fiːld
ecclesi|a ɪˈkliː.zi|.ə, -ˈkleɪ-, ⓤⓢ ɪˈkliː-, ekˈliː-, -ˈleɪ- **-ast/s** -æst/s
Ecclesiastes ɪˌkliː.ziˈæs.tiːz, ⓤⓢ ɪˌkliː-, ekˌliː-
ecclesiastic ɪˌkliː.ziˈæs.tɪk, ⓤⓢ ɪˌkliː-, ekˌliː- **-s** -s **-al** -əl **-ally** -əl.i, -li
ecclesiasticism ɪˌkliː.ziˈæs.tɪ.sɪ.zəm, ⓤⓢ ɪˌkliː-, ekˌliː-
Ecclesiasticus ɪˌkliː.ziˈæs.tɪ.kəs, ⓤⓢ ɪˌkliː-, ekˌliː-
Eccleston ˈek.əl.stən
Ecclestone ˈek.əl.stən
eccrine ˈek.rɪn, -riːn, -rən, -raɪn
ECG ˌiː.siːˈdʒiː
echelon ˈeʃ.ə.lɒn, ˈeɪ.ʃə-, ⓤⓢ ˈeʃ.ə.lɑːn **-s** -z **-ned** -d
echidn|a ekˈɪd.n|ə, ɪˈkɪd-, ⓤⓢ iːˈkɪd- **-ae** -iː **-as** -əz
echinacea ˌek.ɪˈneɪ.ʃə, -əˈ-, -si.ə
echin|us ekˈaɪ.n|əs; ɪˈkaɪ-; ə-; ˈek.ɪn|.əs, ⓤⓢ ɪˈkaɪ.n|əs **-i** -aɪ
echo ˈek.əʊ, ⓤⓢ -oʊ **-es** -z **-ing** -ɪŋ **-ed** -d
echocardio|gram ˌek.əʊˈkɑː.di.əʊ|.græm, ⓤⓢ -oʊˈkɑːr.di.ə-, -oʊ- **-s** -z **-graph/s** -grɑːf/s, -græf/s, ⓤⓢ -græf/s
echoic ekˈəʊ.ɪk, ɪˈkəʊ-, əˈkəʊ-, ⓤⓢ ekˈoʊ-
echolalia ˌek.əʊˈleɪ.li.ə, ⓤⓢ -oʊˈ-
echolo|cate ˌek.əʊ.ləʊ|ˈkeɪt, ⓤⓢ -oʊ.loʊˈ- **-cates** -ˈkeɪts **-cating** -ˈkeɪ.tɪŋ, ⓤⓢ -ˈkeɪ.t̬ɪŋ **-cated** -ˈkeɪ.tɪd, ⓤⓢ -ˈkeɪ.t̬ɪd
echolocation ˌek.əʊ.ləʊˈkeɪ.ʃən, ⓤⓢ -oʊ.loʊˈ-
echt ext, ekt
Eckersl(e)y ˈek.əz.li, ⓤⓢ -ɚz-
Eckert ˈek.ət, ⓤⓢ -ɚt
Eckertford ˈek.ət.fəd, ⓤⓢ -ɚt.fɚd
Eckington ˈek.ɪŋ.tən
éclair ɪˈkleəʳ, eɪ-; ˈeɪ.kleəʳ, ⓤⓢ ɪˈkler, eɪ- **-s** -z
eclampsia ɪˈklæmp.si.ə, ekˈlæmp-, əˈklæmp-
éclat eɪˈklɑː, ˈ-- **-s** -z
eclectic ekˈlek.tɪk, ɪˈklek-, iː-, ⓤⓢ ekˈlek- **-s** -s **-al** -əl **-ally** -əl.i, -li
eclecticism ekˈlek.tɪ.sɪ.zəm, ɪˈklek-, iː-, -tə-, ⓤⓢ ekˈlek.tə-
eclips|e ɪˈklɪps, ə-, iː- **-es** -ɪz **-ing** -ɪŋ **-ed** -t
ecliptic ɪˈklɪp.tɪk, ə-, iː- **-s** -s
eclogue ˈek.lɒg, ⓤⓢ -lɑːg, -lɔːg **-s** -z
eco- ˈiː.kəʊ, ˈek.əʊ; iˈkɒ, ⓤⓢ ˈiː.koʊ, -kə, ˈek.oʊ, -ə; ⓤⓢ iˈkɑː
Note: Prefix. Either takes primary or secondary stress on the first syllable, e.g. **ecosphere** /ˈiː.kəʊ.sfɪəʳ/ ⓤⓢ /ˈiː.koʊ.sfɪr/, **economic** /ˌiː.kəˈnɒm.ɪk/ ⓤⓢ /ˌiː.kəˈnɑː.mɪk/, or primary or secondary stress on the second syllable, e.g. **ecology** /iˈkɒl.ə.dʒi/ ⓤⓢ /-ˈkɑː.lə-/, **econometric** /iˌkɒn.əˈmet.rɪk/ ⓤⓢ /-kɑː.nəˈ-/. The form /ˈek.əʊ-/ is not usually heard in British English in hyphenated compounds such as **eco-friendly**.
eco-friendly ˌiː.kəʊˈfrend.li, ⓤⓢ ˌiː.koʊˈ-, ˌek.oʊˈ-
eco-label ˈiː.kəʊˌleɪ.bəl, ⓤⓢ ˈiː.koʊˌ-, ˈek.oʊˌ- **-s** -z
E coli ˌiːˈkəʊ.laɪ, ⓤⓢ -ˈkoʊ-
ecologic|al ˌiː.kəˈlɒdʒ.ɪ.k|əl, ˌek.əˈ-, ⓤⓢ -ˈlɑː.dʒɪ- **-ally** -əl.i, -li ˌeco ˌlogically ˈsound
ecolog|y iˈkɒl.ə.dʒ|i, ɪ-, ekˈɒl-, ⓤⓢ iˈkɑː.lə-, ɪˈkɑː-, ekˈɑː- **-ist/s** -ɪst/s
e-commerce ˈiːˌkɒm.ɜːs, ⓤⓢ -ˌkɑː.mɝːs
econometric iˌkɒn.əˈmet.rɪk, ⓤⓢ -ˌkɑː.nəˈ- **-s** -s
econometrician iːˌkɒn.ə.metˈrɪʃ.ən, ɪ-, -məˈtrɪʃ-, ⓤⓢ -ˌkɑː.nə.məˈ- **-s** -z
econometrics iˌkɒn.əˈmet.rɪks, ⓤⓢ -ˌkɑː.nəˈ-
economic ˌiː.kəˈnɒm.ɪk, ˌek.əˈ-, ⓤⓢ -ˈnɑː.mɪk **-s** -s **-al** -əl **-ally** -əl.i, -li ˌeconomic ˈgrowth
economist iˈkɒn.ə.mɪst, ⓤⓢ -ˈkɑː.nə- **-s** -s
economiz|e, -is|e iˈkɒn.ə.maɪz, ⓤⓢ iˈkɑː.nə- **-es** -ɪz **-ing** -ɪŋ **-ed** -d **-er/s** -əʳ/z, ⓤⓢ -ɚ/z
econom|y iˈkɒn.ə.m|i, ⓤⓢ iˈkɑː.nə- **-ies** -iz eˈconomy ˌclass
ecosphere ˈiː.kəʊ.sfɪəʳ, ⓤⓢ ˈiː.koʊ.sfɪr, -ˈek.oʊ-
ecosystem ˈiː.kəʊˌsɪs.təm, ˈek.əʊ-, -tɪm, ⓤⓢ ˈek.oʊˌsɪs.təm, ˈiː.koʊ- **-s** -z
eco-tour|ism ˈiː.kəʊˌtʊə.r|ɪ.zəm, -ˌtɔː-, ⓤⓢ ˈiː.koʊˌtʊr.ɪ.zəm, ˈek.oʊ- **-ist/s** -ɪst/s
eco-warrior ˈiː.kəʊˌwɒr.i.əʳ, ⓤⓢ ˈiː.koʊˌwɔːr.jɚ, ˈek.oʊ-, -ˌwɑːr-, -i.ɚ **-s** -z
ecru ˈeɪ.kruː, ˈek.ruː
ecstas|y, E~ ˈek.stə.s|i **-ies** -iz
ecstatic ɪkˈstæt.ɪk, ek-, ək-, ⓤⓢ ekˈstæt̬-, ɪk- **-al** -əl **-ally** -əl.i, -li
ECT ˌiː.siːˈtiː
ecto- ˈek.təʊ, ⓤⓢ ˈek.toʊ, -tə
Note: Prefix. Normally takes primary or secondary stress on the first syllable, e.g. **ectomorph** /ˈek.təʊ.mɔːf/ ⓤⓢ /ˈek.toʊ.mɔːrf/, **ectomorphic** /ˌek.təʊˈmɔː.fɪk/ ⓤⓢ /ˌek.toʊˈmɔːr-/.
ectoderm ˈek.təʊ.dɜːm, ⓤⓢ -toʊ.dɝːm, -tə-
ectoderm|al ˌek.təʊˈdɜː.m|əl, ⓤⓢ -toʊˈdɝː-, -təˈ- **-ic** -ɪk
ectomorph ˈek.təʊ.mɔːf, ⓤⓢ -toʊ.mɔːrf, -tə- **-s** -s
ectomorph|ic ˌek.təʊˈmɔː.f|ɪk, ⓤⓢ -toʊˈmɔːr-, -təˈ- **-ism** -ɪ.zəm **-y** -i
-ectomy ˈek.tə.mi
Note: Suffix. Always carries primary stress, e.g. **appendix** /əˈpen.dɪks/, **appendectomy** /ˌæp.enˈdek.tə.mi/.
ectopic ekˈtɒp.ɪk, ˌek-, ɪk-, ⓤⓢ ekˈtɑː.pɪk ecˌtopic ˈpregnancy
ectoplasm ˈek.təʊ.plæz.əm, ⓤⓢ -toʊ-, -tə-
ecu, ECU (abbrev. for **European Currency Unit**) ˈek.juː, ˈeɪ.kjuː, ˈiː-; ˌiː.siːˈjuː, ⓤⓢ ˈeɪ.kuː; ⓤⓢ ˌiː.siːˈjuː **-s** -z
Ecuador ˈek.wə.dɔːʳ, ⓤⓢ -dɔːr
ecumenic ˌiː.kjʊˈmen.ɪk, ˌek.jʊˈ-, -jəˈ-, ⓤⓢ ˌek.jʊˈ-, -jəˈ- **-al** -əl
ecumenicism ˌiː.kjʊˈmen.ɪ.sɪ.zəm, ˌek.jʊˈ-, -jəˈ-, ⓤⓢ ˌek.jʊˈ-, -jəˈ-
ecumen|ism iːˈkjuː.mə.n|ɪ.zəm; ɪ-; ˈek.jʊ-, -jə-, ⓤⓢ ˈek.juː-, -jə-; ⓤⓢ ekˈjuː-, ɪˈkjuː- **-ist/s** -ɪst/s
eczema ˈek.sɪ.mə, -səm.ə, ⓤⓢ ˈek.sə.mə; ⓤⓢ ˈeg.zə-; ⓤⓢ ɪgˈziː.mə
eczematous ekˈsem.ə.təs, ɪk-; ɪgˈzem-, ⓤⓢ ɪgˈzem.ə.t̬əs, eg-; ⓤⓢ ɪkˈsem-
Ed ed
-ed t, d, ɪd
Note: Suffix. Unstressed. When preceded by /t/ or /d/, the pronunciation is /-ɪd/, e.g. **batted** /ˈbæt.ɪd/ ⓤⓢ /ˈbæt̬.ɪd/. When preceded by a voiceless consonant other than /t/, the pronunciation is /t/, e.g. **picked** /pɪkt/. When preceded by a voiced sound, including vowels and consonants, the pronunciation is /d/, e.g. **rigged** /rɪgd/. There are, however, exceptions, particularly in adjectival forms,

Pronouncing the letters EE

The most common pronunciation for the vowel digraph **ee** is iː, e.g.:

bee	biː

When followed by an **r** in the spelling, **ee** is pronounced as either /ɪə/ US /ɪr/ or /iː.ə/ US /iː.ɚ/, e.g.:

steer	stɪəʳ US stɪr
freer (comparative adj.)	ˈfriː.əʳ US -ɚ

In addition

There are other vowel sounds associated with the digraph **ee**, e.g.:

eɪ	fiancée /fiˈɑ̃ːn.seɪ/ US /ˌfiɑːnˈseɪ/
iː.ɪst	freest (superlative adj.) ˈfriː.ɪst

In weak syllables

The vowel digraph **ee** is realized with the vowel sound /i/ in weak syllables, e.g.:

coffee	ˈkɒf.i US ˈkɑː.fi

including **dogged** /ˈdɒg.ɪd/ US /ˈdɑː.gɪd/, and **learned** /ˈlɜː.nɪd/ US /ˈlɜːr-/; see individual entries.
edacious ɪˈdeɪ.ʃəs, iː-, edˈeɪ-, US ɪˈdeɪ-, iː-
Edam ˈiː.dæm, US ˈiː.dəm, -dæm
edamame ˌed.əˈmɑː.meɪ; ˈed.ə.mɑː.meɪ, US ˌed.əˈmɑː.meɪ
edaphic ɪˈdæf.ɪk, iː-
Edda ˈed.ə **-s** -z
Eddery ˈed.ᵊr.i
Eddie ˈed.i
Eddington ˈed.ɪŋ.tən
edd|y, E~ ˈed|.i **-ies** -iz **-ying** -i.ɪŋ **-ied** -id
Eddystone ˈed.ɪ.stᵊn, -stəʊn, US -stoʊn, -stən
Ede iːd
edelweiss ˈeɪ.dᵊl.vaɪs
edem|a ɪˈdiː.m|ə, iː- **-as** -əz **-ata** -ə.tə, US -ə.t̬ə
edematous ɪˈdiː.mə.təs, iː-, US -t̬əs
Eden ˈiː.dᵊn ˌ**Garden of ˈEden**
Edenbridge ˈiː.dᵊn.brɪdʒ
Edenfield ˈiː.dᵊn.fiːld
edentate iːˈden.teɪt, ɪ- **-s** -s
Edessa ɪˈdes.ə, iː-
Edgar ˈed.gəʳ, US -gɚ
Edgbaston ˈedʒ.bə.stᵊn, -bæs.tᵊn
edg|e, E~ edʒ **-es** -ɪz **-ing** -ɪŋ **-ed** -d
Edgecomb(e) ˈedʒ.kəm
Edgecote ˈedʒ.kəʊt, -kət, US -koʊt
Edgecumbe ˈedʒ.kəm, -kuːm
Edgehill *name of a hill:* ˌedʒˈhɪl *surname:* ˈedʒ.hɪl
edgeless ˈedʒ.ləs, -lɪs
Edgerton ˈedʒ.ə.tᵊn, US -ɚ.t̬ən
edge|ways ˈedʒ|.weɪz **-wise** -waɪz
edgewise ˈedʒ.waɪz
Edgeworth ˈedʒ.wəθ, -wɜːθ, US -wɚθ, -wɝːθ
edging ˈedʒ.ɪŋ **-s** -z
Edgington ˈedʒ.ɪŋ.tən
Edgley ˈedʒ.li
Edgware ˈedʒ.weəʳ, US -wer
edg|y ˈedʒ|.i **-ier** -i.əʳ, US -i.ɚ **-iest** -i.ɪst, -i.əst **-ily** ᵊl.i, ɪ.li
edibility ˌed.əˈbɪl.ə.ti, -ɪˈ-, -ɪ.ti, US -ə.t̬i
edible ˈed.ɪ.bᵊl, ˈ-ə- **-s** -z **-ness** -nəs, -nɪs
edict ˈiː.dɪkt **-s** -s
Edie ˈiː.di
edification ˌed.ɪ.fɪˈkeɪ.ʃᵊn, ˌ-ə-, -fəˈ-
edific|e ˈed.ɪ.fɪs, ˈ-ə- **-es** -ɪz
edi|fy ˈed.ɪ|.faɪ, ˈ-ə- **-fies** -faɪz **-fying** -faɪ.ɪŋ **-fied** -faɪd
Edina ɪˈdaɪ.nə, iː-, edˈaɪ-, -ˈiː-
Edinburgh ˈed.ɪn.bᵊr.ə, -ɪm-, -ᵊn-, -bʌr-, US -bɚ.ə
Edington ˈed.ɪŋ.tən
Edison ˈed.ɪ.sᵊn, ˈ-ə-
ed|it ˈed|.ɪt **-its** -ɪts **-iting** -ɪ.tɪŋ, US -ɪ.t̬ɪŋ **-ited** -ɪ.tɪd, US -ɪ.t̬ɪd
Edith ˈiː.dɪθ
edition ɪˈdɪʃ.ᵊn, ə-, US ɪ- **-s** -z
editor ˈed.ɪ.təʳ, US -tɚ **-s** -z
editorial ˌed.ɪˈtɔː.ri.əl, -əˈ-, US -əˈtɔːr.i- **-s** -z **-ly** -i
editorializ|e, -is|e ˌed.ɪˈtɔː.ri.ᵊl.aɪz, -əˈ-, US -əˈtɔːr.i.ə.laɪz **-es** -ɪz **-ing** -ɪŋ **-ed** -d
editor-in-chief ˌed.ɪ.təʳ.ɪnˈtʃiːf, US -t̬ɚ-
editorship ˈed.ɪ.tə.ʃɪp, US -t̬ɚ- **-s** -s
Edmond ˈed.mənd **-s** -z
Edmonton ˈed.mən.tən
Edmund ˈed.mənd **-s** -z
Edna ˈed.nə
Edom ˈiː.dəm **-ite/s** -aɪt/s
Edridge ˈed.rɪdʒ
Edsall ˈed.sᵊl
educability ˌedʒ.ʊ.kəˈbɪl.ə.ti, ˌed.jʊ-, ˌedʒ.ə-, ˌed.jə-, -ɪt.i, US ˌedʒ.ʊ.kəˈbɪl.ə.t̬i, ˌ-ə-
educable ˈedʒ.ʊ.kə.bᵊl, ˈed.jʊ-, ˈedʒ.ə-, ˈed.jə-, US ˈedʒ.ʊ-, ˈ-ə-
edu|cate ˈedʒ.ʊ|.keɪt, ˈed.jʊ-, ˈedʒ.ə-, ˈed.jə-, US ˈedʒ.ʊ|.keɪt, ˈ-ə- **-cates** -keɪts **-cating** -keɪ.tɪŋ, US -keɪ.t̬ɪŋ **-cated** -keɪ.tɪd, US -keɪ.t̬ɪd **-cator/s** -keɪ.təʳ/z, US -keɪ.t̬ɚ/z
education ˌedʒ.ʊˈkeɪ.ʃᵊn, ˌed.jʊˈ-, ˌedʒ.ə-, ed.jə-, US ˌedʒ.ʊˈkeɪ.ʃᵊn, -əˈ-
educational ˌedʒ.ʊˈkeɪ.ʃᵊn.ᵊl, ˌed.jʊˈ-, ˌedʒ.əˈ-, ˌed.jəˈ-, US ˌedʒ.ʊˈkeɪ.ʃᵊn.ᵊl, -əˈ- **-ly** -i
educationalist ˌedʒ.ʊˈkeɪ.ʃᵊn.ᵊl.ɪst, ˌed.jʊˈ-, ˌedʒ.ə, ˌed.jəˈ-, US ˌedʒ.ʊˈkeɪ.ʃᵊn.ᵊl.ɪst, -əˈ- **-s** -s
educationist ˌedʒ.ʊˈkeɪ.ʃᵊn.ɪst, ˌed.jʊˈ-, ˌedʒ.əˈ-, ˌed.jəˈ-, US ˌedʒ.ʊˈkeɪ.ʃᵊn.ɪst, -əˈ- **-s** -s
educative ˈedʒ.ʊ.kə.tɪv, ˈed.jʊ-, ˈedʒ.ə-, ˈed.jə-, -keɪ-, US ˈedʒ.ʊ.keɪ.t̬ɪv, ˈ-ə-
educ|e ɪˈdʒuːs, iː-, -ˈdjuːs, US -ˈduːs, -ˈdjuːs **-es** -ɪz **-ing** -ɪŋ **-ed** -t
eduction ɪˈdʌk.ʃᵊn, iː- **-s** -z
Edward ˈed.wəd, US -wɚd **-(e)s** -z
Edwardian edˈwɔː.di.ən, US -ˈwɔːr-, -ˈwɑːr- **-s** -z
Edwin ˈed.wɪn
Edwina edˈwiː.nə
Edwinstowe ˈed.wɪn.stəʊ, US -stoʊ
-ee iː, i
Note: Suffix. May be stressed or unstressed, e.g. **employee** /ˌem.plɔɪˈiː, ɪmˈplɔɪ.iː/, **committee** /kəˈmɪt.i/ US /-ˈmɪt̬-/.
-ée, -ee eɪ
Note: Suffix. May be stressed or unstressed in British English, e.g. **soirée** /ˈswɑː.reɪ, -ˈ-/, but normally stressed in American English, e.g. /swɑːˈreɪ/.
EEC ˌiː.iːˈsiː
EEG ˌiː.iːˈdʒiː
eejit ˈiː.dʒɪt **-s** -s
eek iːk
eel iːl **-s** -z
eelgrass ˈiːl.grɑːs, US -græs
eelworm ˈiːl.wɜːm, US -wɝːm **-s** -z
e'en iːn
eeny, meeny, miney, mo ˌiː.niˌmiː.niˌmaɪ.niˈməʊ, US -ˈmoʊ
e'er eəʳ, US er
-eer ˈɪəʳ, US ˈɪr
Note: Suffix. Normally carries stress, e.g., **musket** /ˈmʌskɪt/, **musketeer** /ˌmʌs.kɪˈtɪəʳ/ US /-kəˈtɪr/.
eer|ie ˈɪə.r|i, US ˈɪr|.i **-y** -i **-ily** -ᵊl.i, -ɪ.li **-iness** -ɪ.nəs, -ɪ.nɪs
Eeyore ˈiː.ɔːʳ, US -ɔːr
eff ef **-ing** -ɪŋ ˌ**eff ˈoff**; ˌ**effing and ˈblinding**
effac|e ɪˈfeɪs, efˈeɪs, US ɪˈfeɪs, ə- **-es** -ɪz **-ing** -ɪŋ **-ed** -t **-ement** -mənt **-eable** -ə.bᵊl
effect ɪˈfekt, US ɪˈfekt, ə-, iː- **-s** -s **-ing** -ɪŋ **-ed** -ɪd
effective ɪˈfek.tɪv, US ɪˈfek-, ə-, iː- **-s** -z **-ly** -li **-ness** -nəs, -nɪs
effectual ɪˈfek.tʃu.əl, -tju-, -tʃʊl, -tjʊl, US ɪˈfek.tʃuː.əl, ə-, iː- **-ly** -i
effectuality ɪˌfek.tʃuˈæl.ə.ti, -tjuˈ-, -ɪ.ti, US ɪˌfek.tʃuˈæl.ə.t̬i, -tjuˈ-, ə-, iː-
effectu|ate ɪˈfek.tʃu|.eɪt, -tju-, US ɪˈfek.tʃu-, -tju-, ə-, iː- **-ates** -eɪts **-ating** -eɪ.tɪŋ, US -eɪ.t̬ɪŋ **-ated** -eɪ.tɪd, US -eɪ.t̬ɪd
effeminacy ɪˈfem.ɪ.nə.si, efˈem-, əˈfem-, ˈ-ə-

Pronouncing the letters EI

There are several pronunciation possibilities for the vowel digraph **ei**. One is /iː/ when following a **c**; this is immortalized in the spelling rhyme 'I before E except after C, but only if the sound is /iː/', e.g.:

receive rɪˈsiːv

When followed by a silent **gh** in the spelling, it is usually pronounced as /eɪ/ but may be pronounced /aɪ/, e.g.:

eight eɪt
height haɪt

The pronunciation /aɪ/ also occurs in two words which do not include **gh**, but only in British English, e.g.:

either ˈaɪ.ðəʳ (US) ˈiː.ðɚ
neither ˈnaɪ.ðəʳ (US) ˈniː.ðɚ

When followed by an **r** in the spelling, **ei** is pronounced as /eə/ (US) /er/ and /ɪə/ (US) /ɪr/, e.g.:

their ðeəʳ (US) ðer
weir wɪəʳ (US) wɪr

In addition

Other vowel sounds are associated with the digraph **ei**, e.g.:

e Leicester /ˈles.təʳ/ (US) /-tɚ/
eɪ rein /reɪn/

In weak syllables

The vowel digraph **ei** is realized with the vowel /ɪ/ in weak syllables, e.g.:

foreign ˈfɒr.ɪn (US) ˈfɔːr-

effeminate adj ɪˈfem.ɪ.nət, efˈem-, əˈfem-, ˈ-ə-, -nɪt **-ly** -li **-ness** -nəs, -nɪs
effemi|nate v ɪˈfem.ɪ|.neɪt, efˈem-, ˈ-ə- **-nates** -neɪts **-nating** -neɪ.tɪŋ, (US) -neɪ.t̬ɪŋ **-nated** -neɪ.tɪd, (US) -neɪ.t̬ɪd
effendi efˈen.di, ɪˈfen-
efferent ˈef.ər.ənt, ˈiː.fər-, (US) ˈef.ər-
effervesc|e ˌef.əˈves, (US) -ɚˈ- **-es** -ɪz **-ing** -ɪŋ **-ed** -t
effervescen|t ˌef.əˈves.ən|t, (US) -ɚˈ- **-ce** -*ts* *stress shift:* ˌ**effervescent** ˈ**powder**
effete ɪˈfiːt, efˈiːt
efficacious ˌef.ɪˈkeɪ.ʃəs, -əˈ- **-ly** -li **-ness** -nəs, -nɪs
efficacity ˌef.ɪˈkæs.ə.ti, -əˈ-, -ɪ.ti, (US) -ə.t̬i
efficacy ˈef.ɪ.kə.si, ˈ-ə-
efficienc|y ɪˈfɪʃ.ənt.s|i, ə-, (US) ɪˈfɪʃ-, ə-, iː- **-ies** -iz
efficient ɪˈfɪʃ.ənt, ə-, (US) ɪˈfɪʃ-, ə-, iː- **-ly** -li
Effie ˈef.i
effig|y ˈef.ɪ.dʒ|i, ˈ-ə- **-ies** -iz
Effingham *in the UK:* ˈef.ɪŋ.əm, (US) ˈef.ɪŋ.əm, -hæm *in the US:* ˈef.ɪŋ.hæm
effloresc|e ˌef.lɔːˈres, -lɒrˈes, -ləˈres, (US) -ləˈres, -lɔːrˈ- **-es** -ɪz **-ing** -ɪŋ **-ed** -t
efflorescen|t ˌef.lɔːˈres.ən|t, (US) -ləˈ-, -lɔːrˈ- **-ce** -*ts*
effluence ˈef.lu.ən*t*s
effluent ˈef.lu.ənt **-s** -s
effluvi|um ɪˈfluː.vi|.əm, efˈluː- **-a** -ə **-al** -əl
efflux ˈef.lʌks **-es** -ɪz
effluxion efˈluk.ʃən, ɪˈflʌk- **-s** -z
effort ˈef.ət, (US) -ɚt **-s** -s
effortless ˈef.ət.ləs, -lɪs, (US) -ɚt- **-ly** -li **-ness** -nəs, -nɪs
effronter|y ɪˈfrʌn.tər|.i, efˈrʌn-, (US) efˈrʌn-, ɪˈfrʌn- **-ies** -iz
effulg|e ɪˈfʌldʒ, efˈʌldʒ **-es** -ɪz **-ing** -ɪŋ **-ed** -d
effulgen|ce ɪˈfʌl.dʒən|*t*s, efˈʌl- **-t/ly** -t/li
effuse adj ɪˈfjuːs, efˈjuːs
effus|e v ɪˈfjuːz, efˈjuːz **-es** -ɪz **-ing** -ɪŋ **-ed** -d
effusion ɪˈfjuː.ʒən, efˈjuː- **-s** -z
effusive ɪˈfjuː.sɪv, efˈjuː- **-ly** -li **-ness** -nəs, -nɪs
Efik ˈef.ɪk
E-fit ˈiː.fɪt **-s** -s
EFL ˌiː.efˈel
eft eft **-s** -s
EFTA ˈef.tə
e.g. ˌiːˈdʒiː; fər.ɪɡˈzɑːm.pəl, (US) ˌiːˈdʒiː; (US) fɚ.ɪɡˈzæm.pəl
egad iːˈɡæd, ɪ-
egalitarian ɪˌɡæl.ɪˈteə.ri.ən, iː-, -əˈ-; ˌiː.ɡæl-, (US) -ˈter.i- **-ism** -ɪ.zəm
Egan ˈiː.ɡən
Egbert ˈeɡ.bət, -bɜːt, (US) -bɚt, -bɝːt
Egdon ˈeɡ.dən
Egeria ɪˈdʒɪə.ri.ə, iː-, (US) -ˈdʒɪr.i-
Egerton ˈedʒ.ə.tən, (US) ˈ-ɚ-
Egeus ɪˈdʒiː.əs, iː-, (US) iːˈdʒiː.əs
egg eɡ **-s** -z **-ing** -ɪŋ **-ed** -d ˈ**egg** ˌ**timer; have** ˈ**egg on one's** ˌ**face; put** ˌ**all one's** ˌ**eggs in one** ˈ**basket**
eggcup ˈeɡ.kʌp **-s** -s
egghead ˈeɡ.hed **-s** -z
Eggleston ˈeɡ.əlz.tən, (US) -əl.stən
Eggleton ˈeɡ.əl.tən
eggnog ˌeɡˈnɒɡ, ˈ--, (US) ˈeɡ.nɑːɡ **-s** -z
eggplant ˈeɡ.plɑːnt, (US) -plænt **-s** -s
egg-shaped ˈeɡ.ʃeɪpt
eggshell ˈeɡ.ʃel **-s** -z
Egham ˈeɡ.əm
Eglamore, Eglamour ˈeɡ.lə.mɔːʳ, (US) -mɔːr
eglantine, E~ ˈeɡ.lən.taɪn, -tiːn
Eglingham ˈeɡ.lɪn.dʒəm
Eglinton ˈeɡ.lɪn.tən
Eglon ˈeɡ.lɒn, (US) -lɑːn
Egmont ˈeɡ.mɒnt, -mənt, (US) -mɑːnt
ego ˈiː.ɡəʊ, ˈeɡ.əʊ, (US) ˈiː.ɡoʊ, ˈeɡ.oʊ **-s** -z ˈ**ego** ˌ**trip**
egocentric ˌiː.ɡəʊˈsen.trɪk, ˌeɡ.əʊˈ-, (US) ˌiː.ɡoʊˈ-, ˌeɡ.oʊˈ- **-ally** -əl.i, -li
egocentricity ˌiː.ɡəʊ.senˈtrɪs.ɪ.ti, ˌeɡ.əʊ-, -ə.ti, (US) ˌiː.ɡoʊ.senˈtrɪs.ə.t̬i, ˌeɡ.oʊ-
egocentrism ˌiː.ɡəʊˈsen.trɪ.zəm, ˌeɡ.əʊˈ-, (US) ˌiː.ɡoʊˈ-, ˌeɡ.oʊˈ-
ego|ism ˈiː.ɡəʊ|.ɪ.zəm, ˈeɡ.əʊ-, (US) ˈiː.ɡoʊ-, ˈeɡ.oʊ- **-ist/s** -ɪst/s
egoistic ˌiː.ɡəʊˈɪs.tɪk, ˌeɡ.əʊˈ-, (US) ˌiː.ɡoʊˈ-, ˌeɡ.oʊˈ- **-al** -əl **-ally** -əl.i, -li
egomania ˌiː.ɡəʊˈmeɪ.ni.ə, ˌeɡ.əʊˈ-, (US) ˌiː.ɡoʊˈ-, ˌeɡ.oʊˈ-, -njə
egomaniac ˌiː.ɡəʊˈmeɪ.ni.æk, ˌeɡ.əʊˈ-, (US) ˌiː.ɡoʊˈ-, ˌeɡ.oʊˈ- **-s** -s
Egon ˈeɡ.ən, ˈiː.ɡən, -ɡɒn, (US) ˈeɪ.ɡɑːn, -ɡən

> Note: The restaurant critic Egon Ronay was popularly pronounced as /ˈiː.ɡɒn/ in the UK.

egot|ism ˈiː.ɡəʊ.t|ɪ.zəm, ˈeɡ.əʊ-, (US) ˈiː.ɡoʊ-, ˈeɡ.oʊ- **-ist/s** -ɪst/s
egotistic ˌiː.ɡəʊˈtɪs.tɪk, ˌeɡ.əʊˈ-, (US) ˌiː.ɡoʊˈ-, ˌeɡ.oʊˈ- **-al** -əl **-ally** -əl.i, -li
egregious ɪˈɡriː.dʒəs, əˈɡriː-, -dʒi.əs, (US) ɪ-, iː- **-ly** -li **-ness** -nəs, -nɪs
Egremont ˈeɡ.rə.mənt, -rɪ-, -mɒnt, (US) -mɑːnt
egress ˈiː.ɡres **-es** -ɪz
egression ɪˈɡreʃ.ən, iː- **-s** -z
egressive ɪˈɡres.ɪv, iː-
egret ˈiː.ɡrət, -ɡrɪt, -ɡret, (US) ˈiː.ɡret, ˈeɡ.ret, -rɪt **-s** -s
Egton ˈeɡ.tən
Egypt ˈiː.dʒɪpt
Egyptian iˈdʒɪp.ʃən, ə-, iː- **-s** -z
Egyptolog|y ˌiː.dʒɪpˈtɒl.ə.dʒ|i, (US) -ˈtɑː.lə- **-ist/s** -ɪst/s
eh eɪ
Ehrlich *European family name:* ˈeə.lɪk, -lɪx, (US) ˈer- *US family name:* ˈɜː.lɪk, (US) ˈɝː-, ˈer-
Eid iːd
eider ˈaɪ.dəʳ, (US) -dɚ **-s** -z ˈ**eider** ˌ**duck**
eiderdown ˈaɪ.də.daʊn, (US) -dɚ- **-s** -z
Eidos® ˈaɪ.dɒs, ˈeɪ-, (US) -dɑːs, -doʊs
Eifel ˈaɪ.fəl

Eiffel Tower ˌaɪ.fəlˈtaʊ.əʳ, -taʊəʳ, (US) -ˈtaʊ.ɚ **-s** -z
Eiger ˈaɪ.gəʳ, (US) -gɚ
Eigg eg
eight eɪt **-s** -s
eighteen ˌeɪˈtiːn **-s** -z **-th/s** -θ/s *stress shift:* **ˌeighteen ˈmonths**
eightfold ˈeɪt.fəʊld, (US) -foʊld
eighth eɪtθ **-s** -s
eightieth ˈeɪ.ti.əθ, -ti.ɪθ, (US) -t̬i.əθ **-s** -s
eightsome ˈeɪt.səm
eight|y ˈeɪ.t|i, (US) -t̬|i **-ies** -iz
eightyfold ˈeɪ.ti.fəʊld, (US) -t̬i.foʊld
eighty-six ˌeɪ.tiˈsɪks, (US) -t̬iˈ- **-es** -ɪz **-ing** -ɪŋ **-ed** -t
Eilat eɪˈlɑːt, -ˈlæt, (US) -ˈlɑːt
Eilean ˈel.ən, ˈiː.lən
Eileen ˈaɪ.liːn, (US) aɪˈliːn
Eiloart ˈaɪ.ləʊ.ɑːt, (US) -loʊ.ɑːrt
Eindhoven ˈaɪnd.həʊ.vən, (US) -hoʊ-
Einstein ˈaɪn.staɪn
einsteinium ˌaɪnˈstaɪ.ni.əm
Eire ˈeə.rə, (US) ˈer.ə, ˈeɪ.rə; (US) ˈaɪ.rə
eirenicon aɪəˈriː.nɪ.kɒn, -ˈren.ɪ-, (US) aɪˈriː.nɪ.kɑːn **-s** -z
Eisenhower ˈaɪ.zən.haʊəʳ, (US) -haʊɚ
Eisner ˈaɪz.nəʳ, (US) -nɚ
eisteddfod, E~ aɪˈsteð.vɒd, ɪ-, -ˈsted.fəd, (US) -ˈsteð.vɑːd, eɪ- **-s** -z
either ˈaɪ.ðəʳ, ˈiː-, (US) ˈiː.ðɚ, ˈaɪ-

> Note: in the UK, the /ˈiː-/ pronunciation seems to be gaining ground among younger speakers.

ejaculate n iˈdʒæk.jə.lət, iː-, -jʊ-, -lɪt, -leɪt, (US) -lət, -lɪt
ejacu|late v iˈdʒæk.jə|.leɪt, iː-, -jʊ- **-lates** -leɪts **-lating** -leɪ.tɪŋ, (US) -leɪ.t̬ɪŋ **-lated** -leɪ.tɪd, (US) -leɪ.t̬ɪd
ejaculation iˌdʒæk.jəˈleɪ.ʃən, iː-, -jʊˈ- **-s** -z
ejaculative iˈdʒæk.jə.lə.tɪv, -jʊ-, -leɪ.tɪv, (US) -jə.lə.t̬ɪv
ejaculatory iˈdʒæk.jə.lə.tər.i, iː-, -jʊ-, -leɪ-, -tri; iˌdʒæk.jəˈleɪ-, iː-, -jʊˈ-, (US) iˈdʒæk.jə.lə.tɔːr.i, iː-, -jʊ-
eject iˈdʒekt, iː- **-s** -s **-ing** -ɪŋ **-ed** -ɪd
ejection iˈdʒek.ʃən, iː- **-s** -z
ejective iˈdʒek.tɪv, iː- **-s** -z
ejectment iˈdʒekt.mənt, iː- **-s** -s
ejector iˈdʒek.təʳ, iː-, (US) -tɚ **-s** -z
ejusdem generis eɪˌʊs.demˈgen.ər.ɪs, (US) edʒˌuːs.demˈgen.ɚ.əs; (US) iː.dʒəs.demˈdʒen-
Ekaterinburg ɪˌkæt.ərˈiːn.bɜːg, (US) -bɝːg
ek|e iːk **-es** -s **-ing** -ɪŋ **-ed** -t
EKG ˌiː.keɪˈdʒiː
Ekron ˈek.rɒn, (US) -rɑːn
Ektachrome® ˈek.tə.krəʊm, (US) -kroʊm
el el
elaborate adj iˈlæb.ər.ət, -ɪt **-ly** -li **-ness** -nəs, -nɪs
elabor|ate v iˈlæb.ər.|eɪt **-ates** -eɪts **-ating** -eɪ.tɪŋ, (US) -eɪ.t̬ɪŋ **-ated** -eɪ.tɪd, (US) -eɪ.t̬ɪd **-ator/s** -eɪ.təʳ/z, (US) -eɪ.t̬ɚ/z
elaboration iˌlæb.əˈreɪ.ʃən **-s** -z
elaborative iˈlæb.ər.ə.tɪv, -eɪ-, (US) -ə.t̬ɪv
Elaine ɪˈleɪn, ə-, elˈeɪn
El Al® ˌelˈæl
El Alamein ˌelˈæl.ə.meɪn; elˌæl.əˈmeɪn, (US) ˌelˈæl.ə.meɪn, -ˈɑː.lə-; (US) elˌæl.əˈmeɪn, -ˌɑː.ləˈ-
Elam ˈiː.ləm **-ite/s** -aɪt/s
élan eɪˈlɑ̃ːn, ɪ-, -ˈlæn, (US) -ˈlɑːn, -ˈlɑ̃ːŋ, -ˈlæn *stress shift, see compound:* **ˌélan viˈtal**
eland, E~ ˈiː.lənd **-s** -z
elaps|e iˈlæps **-es** -ɪz **-ing** -ɪŋ **-ed** -t
elastic iˈlæs.tɪk, -ˈlɑː.stɪk, (US) -ˈlæs.tɪk **-s** -s **-ally** -əl.i, -li **eˌlastic ˈband**
elasti|cate iˈlæs.tɪ|.keɪt, -ˈlɑː.stɪ-, -stə-, (US) -ˈlæs.tɪ- **-cates** -keɪts **-cating** -keɪ.tɪŋ, (US) -keɪ.t̬ɪŋ **-cated** -keɪ.tɪd, (US) -keɪ.t̬ɪd
elasticity ˌɪl.æsˈtɪs.ə.ti, ˌel-, ˌiː.læs-, -ləˈstɪs-, -lɑːˈ-, -ɪ.ti; iˌlæsˈtɪs-, -ˌlɑːˈstɪs-, (US) iˌlæsˈtɪs.ə.t̬i; (US) ˌiː.læsˈ-
elasticiz|e, -is|e iˈlæs.tɪ.saɪz, -ˈlɑː.stɪ-, -stə-, -ˈlæs.tɪ- **-es** -ɪz **-ing** -ɪŋ **-ed** -d
elastin iˈlæs.tɪn, ə-, -ˈlɑː.stɪn, (US) iˈlæs.tɪn
Elastoplast® iˈlæs.təʊ.plɑːst, el-, iːˈlæs-, -plæst; -ˈlɑː.stəʊ.plɑːst, (US) iˈlæs.toʊ.plæst, iː-, -tə-
e|late i|ˈleɪt, iː- **-lates** -leɪts **-lating** -leɪ.tɪŋ, (US) -leɪ.t̬ɪŋ **-lated/ly** -leɪ.tɪd/li, (US) -leɪ.t̬ɪd/li
elation iˈleɪ.ʃən, iː-
Elba ˈel.bə
Elbe ˈel.bə, elb
elbow ˈel.bəʊ, (US) -boʊ **-s** -z **-ing** -ɪŋ **-ed** -d **ˈelbow ˌgrease; ˈelbow ˌroom**
El Cid ˌelˈsɪd
elder, E~ ˈel.dəʳ, (US) -dɚ **-s** -z **ˌelder ˈstatesman**
elderberr|y ˈel.dəˌber|.i, -bər-, (US) -dɚˌber- **-ies** -iz
elderflower ˈel.də.flaʊəʳ, -ˌflaʊ.əʳ, (US) -dɚˌflaʊ.ɚ **-s** -z
elderl|y ˈel.dəl|.i, (US) -dɚ.l|i **-iness** -ɪ.nəs, -ɪ.nɪs
eldest ˈel.dɪst, -dəst
Eldon ˈel.dən
El Dorado, Eldorado ˌel.dəˈrɑː.dəʊ, -dɒrˈɑː-, (US) -dəˈrɑː.doʊ, -ˈreɪ-
Eldred ˈel.drɪd, -dred, -drəd
Eldridge ˈel.drɪdʒ
Eleanor ˈel.ɪ.nəʳ, ˈ-ə-, (US) -nɚ, -nɔːr
Eleanora ˌel.i.əˈnɔː.rə, (US) -ˈnɔːr.ə
Eleazar ˌel.iˈeɪ.zəʳ, (US) -zɚ
elecampane ˌel.ɪ.kæmˈpeɪn, ˌ-ə- **-s** -z
elect iˈlekt **-s** -s **-ing** -ɪŋ **-ed** -ɪd **-able** -ə.bəl
election iˈlek.ʃən **-s** -z
electioneer iˌlek.ʃəˈnɪəʳ, (US) -ˈnɪr **-s** -z **-ing** -ɪŋ **-ed** -d **-er/s** -əʳ/z, (US) -ɚ/z
elective iˈlek.tɪv **-ly** -li
elector iˈlek.təʳ, (US) -tɚ **-s** -z
electoral iˈlek.tər.əl, ˈ-trəl
electorate iˈlek.tər.ət, -ɪt, ˈ-trət, ˈ-trɪt **-s** -s
Electra iˈlek.trə **Eˈlectra ˌcomplex**
electric iˈlek.trɪk **-al** -əl **-ally** -əl.i, -li **-s** -s **eˌlectric ˈblanket; eˌlectric ˈchair; eˌlectric guiˈtar; eˌlectric ˈshock; eˌlectric ˈshock ˌtherapy**
electrician ˌel.ɪkˈtrɪʃ.ən, ˌiː.lekˈ-; iˌlekˈ-, (US) iˌlekˈ-; (US) ˌiː.lekˈ- **-s** -z
electricity ˌel.ɪkˈtrɪs.ə.ti, ˌiː.lek-, -ɪ.ti; iˌlekˈ-, (US) iˌlekˈtrɪs.ə.t̬i; (US) ˌiː.lekˈ-
electrification iˌlek.trɪ.fɪˈkeɪ.ʃən, -trə-, -fəˈ- **-s** -z
electri|fy iˈlek.trɪ|.faɪ, -trə- **-fies** -faɪz **-fying** -faɪ.ɪŋ **-fied** -faɪd **-fiable** -faɪ.ə.bəl
electro- iˈlek.trəʊ; ˌel.ɪkˈtrɒ, ˌiː.lekˈ-; iˌlekˈ-, (US) iˈlek.troʊ, ˈ-trə-; (US) iˌlekˈtrɑː; (US) ˌiː.lekˈ-
Note: Prefix. Either takes primary or secondary stress on the second syllable, e.g. **electrocute** /iˈlek.trə.kjuːt/, **electrocution** /iˌlek.trəˈkjuː.ʃən/, or primary stress on the third syllable, with secondary stress on either the first or second syllable, e.g. **electrolysis** /ˌel.ɪkˈtrɒl.ə.sɪs, iˌlekˈ-/ (US) /iˌlekˈtrɑː.lə-, (US) ˌiː.lekˈ-/.
electrobiology iˌlek.trəʊ.baɪˈɒl.ə.dʒi, (US) -troʊ.baɪˈɑː.lə-
electrocardiogram iˌlek.trəʊˈkɑː.di.əʊ.græm, (US) -troʊˈkɑːr.di.ə- **-s** -z
electrocardiograph iˌlek.trəʊˈkɑː.di.əʊ.grɑːf, -græf, (US) -troʊˈkɑːr.di.ə.græf **-s** -s
electrochemistry iˌlek.trəʊˈkem.ɪ.stri, -ə.stri, (US) -troʊˈkem.ə-
electroconvulsive iˌlek.trəʊ.kənˈvʌl.sɪv, (US) -troʊ- **eˌlectroconˌvulsive ˈtherapy**
electro|cute iˈlek.trə|.kjuːt **-cutes** -kjuːts **-cuting** -kjuː.tɪŋ, (US) -kjuː.t̬ɪŋ **-cuted** -kjuː.tɪd, (US) -kjuː.t̬ɪd
electrocution iˌlek.trəˈkjuː.ʃən **-s** -z
electrode iˈlek.trəʊd, (US) -troʊd **-s** -z
electrodynamic ɪˌlek.trəʊ.daɪˈnæm.ɪk, -dɪˈ-, (US) -troʊ.daɪˈ- **-s** -s
electroencephalo|gram iˌlek.trəʊ.enˈsef.əl.əʊ|.græm, -ɪnˈ-, -ˈkef-, -eŋˈkef-, -ɪŋˈkef-, (US) -troʊ.enˈsef.ə.loʊ-, -lə- **-s** -z **-graph/s** -grɑːf/s, -græf/s, (US) -græf/s
electrokinetic iˌlek.trəʊ.kɪˈnet.ɪk, -kaɪˈ-, (US) -troʊ.kɪˈnet̬-, -trə- **-s** -s
electrolier iˌlek.trəʊˈlɪəʳ, (US) -trəˈlɪr **-s** -z
Electrolux® iˈlek.trəʊ.lʌks, (US) -trə-

electrolys|is ˌel.ɪkˈtrɒl.ə.s|ɪs, ˌiː.lek-, -ɪ.s|ɪs; iˌlekˈ-, ə-, US iˌlekˈtrɑː.lə-; US ˌiː.lek- **-es** -iːz
electrolyte iˈlek.trə.laɪt **-s** -s
electrolytic iˌlek.trəˈlɪt.ɪk, US -ˈlɪţ-
electrolyz|e, -ys|e iˈlek.trəl.aɪz, US -trə.laɪz **-es** -ɪz **-ing** -ɪŋ **-ed** -d
electromagnet iˌlek.trəʊˈmæg.nɪt, -nət, US -troʊˈ-, -trəˈ- **-s** -s **-ism** -ɪ.zəm
electromagnetic iˌlek.trəʊ.mægˈnet.ɪk, -məgˈ-, US -troʊ.mægˈneţ-, -trə-
electrometer ˌel.ɪkˈtrɒm.ɪ.təʳ, ˌiː.lek-, -mə.təʳ; iˌlekˈ-, US i.lekˈtrɑː.mə.ţɚ; US ˌiː.lekˈ- **-s** -z
electromotive iˌlek.trəʊˈməʊ.tɪv, US -troʊˈmoʊ.ţɪv, -trəˈ-
electromotor iˌlek.trəʊˈməʊ.təʳ, US -troʊˈmoʊ.ţɚ, -trəˈ- **-s** -z
electron iˈlek.trɒn, US -trɑːn **-s** -z
electronic ˌel.ekˈtrɒn.ɪk, -ɪkˈ-, ˌiː.lekˈ-; iˌlekˈ-, US iˌlekˈtrɑː.nɪk; US ˌiː.lekˈ- **-s** -s **-ally** -əl.i, -li *stress shift, see compound:* **ˌelectronic ˈmail**
electropalatogram iˌlek.trəʊˈpæl.ə.təʊ.græm, US -troʊˈpæl.ə.ţə- **-s** -z
electropalatography iˌlek.trəʊˌpæl.əˈtɒg.rə.fi, US -troʊˌpæl.əˈtɑː.grə-
electrophone iˈlek.trə.fəʊn, US -foʊn **-s** -z
electrophorus ˌel.ɪkˈtrɒf.ər.əs, ˌiː.lekˈ-, US iˌlekˈtrɑː.fɚ-; US ˌiː.lekˈ- **-es** -ɪz
electropla|te iˈlek.trəʊ.pleɪ|t, iˌlek.trəʊˈpleɪ|t, US iˈlek.troʊ.pleɪ|t, iː-, -trə- **-tes** -ts **-ting** -tɪŋ, US -ţɪŋ **-ted** -tɪd, US -ţɪd **-ter/s** -təʳ/z, US -ţɚ/z
electropolar iˌlek.trəʊˈpəʊ.ləʳ, US -troʊˈpoʊ.lɚ
electropositive iˌlek.trəʊˈpɒz.ə.tɪv, -ɪ.tɪv, US -troʊˈpɑː.zə.ţɪv
electroscope iˈlek.trəʊ.skəʊp, US -troʊ.skoʊp, -trə- **-s** -s
electrostatic iˌlek.trəʊˈstæt.ɪk, US -troʊˈstæţ- **-s** -s
electrotherapeutic iˌlek.trəʊˌθer.əˈpjuː.tɪk, US -troʊˌθer.əˈpjuː.ţɪk **-s** -s
electrotherapy iˌlek.trəʊˈθer.ə.pi, US -troʊˈ-
electrothermal iˌlek.trəʊˈθɜː.məl, US -troʊˈθɝː-
electrotype iˈlek.trəʊ.taɪp, US -troʊ- **-s** -s
electrovalency iˌlek.trəʊˈveɪ.lənt.si, US -troʊˈ-
electrum iˈlek.trəm
electuar|y iˈlek.tʃu.ər|i, -tju-, US -tʃu.er|.i, -tju- **-ies** -iz
eleemosynary ˌel.i.iːˈmɒs.ɪ.nər.i, ˌel.iːˈ-, ˌel.ɪˈ-, -ˈmɒz-, -ˈməʊ.zɪ-, -zən.ər-, US ˌel.ɪˈmɑː.sə.ner.i, ˌel.iː.əˈ-
elegance ˈel.ɪ.gənts, US ˈ-ə-
elegant ˈel.ɪ.gənt, US ˈ-ə- **-ly** -li
elegiac ˌel.ɪˈdʒaɪ.ək, -əˈ-, -æk, US ˌel.ɪˈdʒaɪ.ək, -əˈ-, -æk; US ɪˈliː.dʒiː.æk **-s** -s **-al** -əl
elegist ˈel.ɪ.dʒɪst, ˈ-ə- **-s** -s
elegit ɪˈliː.dʒɪt, elˈiː-
elegiz|e, -is|e ˈel.ɪ.dʒaɪz, ˈ-ə- **-es** -ɪz **-ing** -ɪŋ **-ed** -d
eleg|y ˈel.ɪ.dʒ|i, ˈ-ə- **-ies** -iz
Elektra iˈlek.trə
element ˈel.ɪ.mənt, ˈ-ə-, US ˈ-ə- **-s** -s
elemental ˌel.ɪˈmen.təl, -əˈ-, US -əˈmen.ţəl **-s** -z **-ly** -i
elementar|y ˌel.ɪˈmen.tər|.i, -əˈ-, ˈ-tr|i, US -əˈmen.ţɚ|.i, ˈ-tr|i **-ily** -əl.i, -ɪ.li **-iness** -ɪ.nəs, -ɪ.nɪs
eleˈmentary ˌschool
elemi ˈel.ɪ.mi
elenchus ɪˈleŋ.kəs, ə-
Eleonora ˌel.i.əˈnɔː.rə, US -ˈnɔːr.ə
Eleonore ˈel.i.ə.nɔːʳ, US -nɔːr
elephant ˈel.ɪ.fənt, ˈ-ə- **-s** -s
elephantiasis ˌel.ɪ.fənˈtaɪ.ə.sɪs, ˌ-ə-, -fænˈ-
elephantine ˌel.ɪˈfæn.taɪn, -əˈ-, US -taɪn, -tiːn, ˈel.ə.fən-
Eleusinian ˌel.juːˈsɪn.i.ən, -uːˈ-
Eleusis elˈjuː.sɪs, ɪˈljuː-, ə-, -ˈluː-, US ɪˈluː.sɪs
Eleuthera iˈluː.θər.ə, elˈuː-, -ˈjuː-, US iˈluː-
ele|vate ˈel.ɪ|.veɪt, ˈ-ə- **-vates** -veɪts **-vating** -veɪ.tɪŋ, US -veɪ.ţɪŋ **-vated** -veɪ.tɪd, US -veɪ.ţɪd
elevation ˌel.ɪˈveɪ.ʃən, -əˈ- **-s** -z
elevator ˈel.ɪ.veɪ.təʳ, ˈ-ə-, US -ţɚ **-s** -z
elevatory ˌel.ɪˈveɪ.tər.i, -əˈ-, ˈ-tri, US -ţɚ.i
eleven ɪˈlev.ən, ə- **-s** -z **-th/s** -θ/s
eleven-plus iˌlev.ənˈplʌs, ə-, -əmˈ-, US -ənˈ- **-es** -ɪz
elevenses iˈlev.ən.zɪz, ə-
el|f el|f **-ves** -vz
elfin ˈel.fɪn **-s** -z
elfish ˈel.fɪʃ **-ly** -li
Elfrida elˈfriː.də
Elgar *composer:* ˈel.gɑːʳ, US -gɑːr *surname:* ˈel.gɑːʳ, -gəʳ, US -gɑːr, -gɚ
Elgin ˈel.gɪn, -dʒɪn, US -gɪn, -dʒɪn
ˌElgin ˈMarbles

> Note: in Scotland, the pronunciation is always /ˈel.gɪn/.

El Greco ˌelˈgrek.əʊ, US -oʊ
Elham ˈiː.ləm
Eli ˈiː.laɪ
Elia ˈiː.li.ə
Elias iˈlaɪ.əs, elˈaɪ-, əˈlaɪ-, -ˈlaɪ.æs
Elibank ˈel.ɪ.bæŋk
elic|it iˈlɪs|.ɪt, ə-, iː- **-its** -ɪts **-iting** -ɪ.tɪŋ, US -ɪ.ţɪŋ **-ited** -ɪ.tɪd, US -ɪ.ţɪd
elicitation iˌlɪs.ɪˈteɪ.ʃən, ə-, iː-, -əˈ-
elid|e iˈlaɪd, iː- **-es** -z **-ing** -ɪŋ **-ed** -ɪd **-able** -ə.bəl
Elie ˈiː.li
eligibility ˌel.ɪ.dʒəˈbɪl.ə.ti, ˌ-ə-, -dʒɪˈ-, -ɪ.ti, US -dʒəˈbɪl.ə.ţi
eligib|le ˈel.ɪ.dʒə.b|əl, ˈ-ə-, -dʒɪ-, US -dʒə- **-ly** -li **-leness** -əl.nəs, -nɪs
Elihu iˈlaɪ.hjuː, elˈaɪ-, US ˈel.ɪ-; US iːˈlaɪ-, i-
Elijah iˈlaɪ.dʒə
elimi|nate iˈlɪm.ɪ|.neɪt, ə-, ˈ-ə- **-nates** -neɪts **-nating** -neɪ.tɪŋ, US -neɪ.ţɪŋ **-nated** -neɪ.tɪd, US -neɪ.ţɪd **-nator/s** -neɪ.təʳ/z, US -neɪ.ţɚ/z
elimination iˌlɪm.ɪˈneɪ.ʃən, ə-, -əˈ- **-s** -z
Elinor ˈel.ɪ.nəʳ, ˈ-ə-, US -nɚ, -nɔːr
Eliot ˈel.i.ət
Eliotson ˈel.i.ət.sən
Eliott ˈel.i.ət
Eliphaz ˈel.ɪ.fæz
Elis ˈiː.lɪs
Elisabeth iˈlɪz.ə.bəθ, ə-
Elise iˈliːz, US iˈliːz, -ˈliːs
Elisha *prophet:* iˈlaɪ.ʃə *place in Northumberland:* elˈɪʃ.ə
elision ɪˈlɪʒ.ən **-s** -z
elite, élite iˈliːt, eɪ- **-s** -s
elitism, élitism iˈliː.tɪ.zəm, eɪˈliː-
elitist, élitist iˈliː.tɪst, eɪˈliː- **-s** -s
elixir iˈlɪk.səʳ, elˈɪk-, əˈlɪk-, iː-, -sɪəʳ, US -sɚ **-s** -z
Eliza iˈlaɪ.zə
Elizabeth iˈlɪz.ə.bəθ, ə-
Elizabethan iˌlɪz.əˈbiː.θən, ə- **-s** -z *stress shift:* **EˌlizabethanˈLpoet**
Elizabethian iˌlɪz.əˈbiː.θi.ən, ə- **-s** -z *stress shift:* **Eˌlizabethian ˈpoet**
elk elk **-s** -s
Elkhart ˈelk.hɑːt, US -hɑːrt
Elkin ˈel.kɪn
Elkington ˈel.kɪŋ.tən
Elkins ˈel.kɪnz
ell el **-s** -z
Ella ˈel.ə
Elland ˈel.ənd
Ellangowan ˌel.ənˈgaʊ.ən, -əŋˈ-
Elle el
Ellen ˈel.ən, -ɪn
Ellenborough ˈel.ən.bər.ə, -ɪn-, US -bɚ.oʊ
Ellery ˈel.ər.i
Ellesmere ˈelz.mɪəʳ, US -mɪr
Ellice ˈel.ɪs
Ellicott ˈel.ɪ.kət, -kɒt, US -kət, -kɑːt
Elliman ˈel.ɪ.mən
Ellingham *in Northumberland:* ˈel.ɪn.dʒəm *surname:* ˈel.ɪŋ.əm
Ellington ˈel.ɪŋ.tən
Elliot ˈel.i.ət
Elliotson ˈel.i.ət.sən
Elliott ˈel.i.ət
ellipse iˈlɪps **-s** -ɪz
ellips|is iˈlɪp.s|ɪs **-es** -iːz
ellipsoid iˈlɪp.sɔɪd **-s** -z
ellipsoidal ˌel.ɪpˈsɔɪ.dəl; iˌlɪpˈ-; elˌɪp-, US iˌlɪpˈ-; US ˌel.ɪpˈ-
elliptic iˈlɪp.tɪk **-al** -əl **-ally** -əl.i, -li
ellipticity ˌel.ɪpˈtɪs.ə.ti, ˌɪl-, -ɪ.ti, US iˌlɪpˈtɪs.ə.ţi; US ˌel.ɪpˈ-
Ellis ˈel.ɪs
Ellison ˈel.ɪ.sən
Elliston ˈel.ɪ.stən
Ellon ˈel.ən
Ellsworth ˈelz.wəθ, -wɜːθ, US -wɚθ, -wɝːθ
Ellwood ˈel.wʊd
elm, E~ elm **-s** -z
Elmer ˈel.məʳ, US -mɚ

E

Elmer Gantry ˌel.məˈgæn.tri, (US) -mɚˈ-
Elmes elmz
Elmhurst ˈelm.hɜːst, (US) -hɝːst
Elmina elˈmiː.nə
Elmo ˈel.məʊ, (US) -moʊ
Elmore ˈel.mɔːʳ, (US) -mɔːr
Elmsley ˈelmz.li
Elmwood ˈelm.wʊd
elocution ˌel.əˈkjuː.ʃᵊn
elocutionary ˌel.əˈkjuː.ʃᵊn.ᵊr.i, -ri, (US) -er.i
elocutionist ˌel.əˈkjuː.ʃᵊn.ɪst **-s** -s
Elohim elˈəʊ.hɪm, ɪˈləʊ-, əˈləʊ-, -hiːm; ˌel.əʊˈhiːm, (US) elˈoʊ.hɪm, ɪˈloʊ-, əˈloʊ-, -hiːm; (US) ˌel.oʊˈhɪm, -ˈoʊ-
Eloi iˈləʊ.aɪ; ˈiː.ləʊ.aɪ, -lɔɪ, (US) ˈiː.lɔɪ, ˈeɪ-
Eloisa ˌel.əʊˈiː.zə, -sə, (US) -oʊˈ-
Éloise, Eloise ˌel.əʊˈiːz, (US) -oʊˈ-
elon|gate ˈiː.lɒŋ|.geɪt, (US) iˈlɑːŋ-, -ˈlɔːŋ- **-gates** -geɪts **-gating** -geɪ.tɪŋ, (US) -geɪ.t̬ɪŋ **-gated** -geɪ.tɪd, (US) -geɪ.t̬ɪd
elongation ˌiː.lɒŋˈgeɪ.ʃᵊn, (US) ˌiː.lɑːŋˈ-, -lɔːŋˈ-; (US) ɪˌlɑːŋˈ-, -ˌlɔːŋˈ- **-s** -z
elop|e iˈləʊp, (US) -ˈloʊp **-es** -s **-ing** -ɪŋ **-ed** -t **-ement/s** -mənt/s
eloquence ˈel.ə.kwənts
eloquent ˈel.ə.kwənt **-ly** -li
El Paso ˌelˈpæs.əʊ, (US) -oʊ
Elphick ˈel.fɪk
Elphin ˈel.fɪn
Elphinstone ˈel.fɪn.stən
Els els
Elsa *English name:* ˈel.sə *German name:* ˈel.zə
El Salvador ˌelˈsæl.və.dɔːʳ, (US) -dɔːr
Elsan® ˈel.sæn
else els **-'s** -ɪz
elsewhere ˌelsˈhweəʳ, ˈ--, (US) ˈels.hwer
Elsie ˈel.si
Elsinore ˈel.sɪ.nɔːʳ, ˌ--ˈ-, (US) ˈel.sə.nɔːr, ˌ--ˈ-

> Note: The stressing /ˌ--ˈ-/ has to be used in Shakespeare's 'Hamlet'.

Elsmere ˈelz.mɪəʳ, (US) -mɪr
Elson ˈel.sᵊn
Elspeth ˈel.spəθ, -speθ
Elstree ˈel.striː, ˈelz.triː, -tri
Elswick ˈel.sɪk, ˈel.zɪk, ˈelz.wɪk

> Note: **Elswick** in Tyne and Wear is locally /ˈel.sɪk/ or /ˈel.zɪk/.

Elsworthy ˈelz.wɜː.ði, (US) -wɝː-
ELT ˌiː.elˈtiː
Eltham ˈel.təm
Elton ˈel.tᵊn
eluci|date iˈluː.sɪ|.deɪt, əˈluː-, -ˈljuː-, -sə-, (US) iˈluː.sɪ-, -sə- **-dates** -deɪts **-dating** -deɪ.tɪŋ, (US) -deɪ.t̬ɪŋ **-dated** -deɪ.tɪd, (US) -deɪ.t̬ɪd **-dator/s** -deɪ.təʳ/z, (US) -deɪ.t̬ɚ/z
elucidation iˌluː.sɪˈdeɪ.ʃᵊn, əˌluː-, -ˌljuː-, -səˈ-, (US) iˌluː.sɪˈdeɪ-, -səˈ- **-s** -z
elucidative iˈluː.sɪ.deɪ.tɪv, əˈluː-, -ˈljuː-, -sə-, -də-, (US) iˈluː.sɪ.deɪ.t̬ɪv, -sə-
elucidatory iˈluː.sɪ.deɪ.tᵊr.i, əˈluː-, -ˈljuː-, -sə-, -tri; iˌluː.sɪˈdeɪ-, ə-, -ˌljuː-, -səˈ-, (US) iˈluː.sɪ.deɪ.tɔːr.i, -sə-; (US) iˌluː.sɪˈdeɪ.t̬ɚ-, -səˈ-
elud|e iˈluːd, əˈluːd, -ˈljuːd, (US) iˈluːd **-es** -z **-ing** -ɪŋ **-ed** -ɪd
elusion iˈluː.ʒᵊn, əˈluː-, -ˈljuː-, (US) iˈluː- **-s** -z
elusive iˈluː.sɪv, əˈluː-, -ˈljuː-, (US) iˈluː- **-ly** -li **-ness** -nəs, -nɪs
elusory iˈluː.sᵊr.i, əˈluː-, -ˈljuː-, (US) iˈluː-
elvan ˈel.vən
Elvedon ˈelv.dən, ˈel.dən
elver ˈel.vəʳ, (US) -vɚ **-s** -z
elves (plural of **elf**) elvz
Elvey ˈel.vi
Elvin ˈel.vɪn
Elvira elˈvɪə.rə, -ˈvaɪə-, (US) -ˈvaɪ.rə, -ˈvɪr.ə
Elvis ˈel.vɪs
Elwell ˈel.wel, -wəl
Elwes ˈel.wɪz, -wɪs, -wez
Ely *cities:* ˈiː.li *first name in US:* ˈiː.laɪ
Elyot ˈel.i.ət
Elyse elˈiːz, (US) iˈliːs
Elysée eɪˈliː.zeɪ, ɪ-, ə-, (US) ˌeɪ.liːˈzeɪ
Elysi|an iˈlɪz.i|.ən, iː-, (US) iˈlɪʒ|.ən **-um** -əm **EˌIysian ˈfields**
elzevir, E~ ˈel.zɪ.vɪəʳ, -sɪ-, -zə-, -sə-, (US) -vɪr
em em **-s** -z
em- em, ɪm
Note: Prefix. Either takes primary or secondary stress and is pronounced /em-/, e.g. **emblem** /ˈem.bləm/, **emblematic** /ˌem.bləˈmæt.ɪk/ (US) /-ˈmæt̬-/, or is unstressed and may be pronounced either /ɪm-/ or /em-/, e.g. **embed** /ɪmˈbed, em-/ (US) /em-, ɪm-/.
'em (weak form of **them**) əm, m̩
emaci|ate iˈmeɪ.ʃi|.eɪt, iː-, -si- **-ates** -eɪts **-ating** -eɪ.tɪŋ, (US) -eɪ.t̬ɪŋ **-ated** -eɪ.tɪd, (US) -eɪ.t̬ɪd
emaciation iˌmeɪ.ʃiˈeɪ.ʃᵊn, iː-, -siˈ-
e-mail, E-mail ˈiː.meɪl **-s** -z **-ing** -ɪŋ **-ed** -d
emalangeni (plural of **lilangeni**) ˈem.ə.lɑːŋˌgen.i, (US) ˌem.ə.lənˈgen-
ema|nate ˈem.ə|.neɪt **-nates** -neɪts **-nating** -neɪ.tɪŋ, (US) -neɪ.t̬ɪŋ **-nated** -neɪ.tɪd, (US) -neɪ.t̬ɪd **-native** -neɪ.tɪv, (US) -neɪ.t̬ɪv
emanation ˌem.əˈneɪ.ʃᵊn **-s** -z
emanci|pate iˈmænt.sɪ|.peɪt, -sə- **-pates** -peɪts **-pating** -peɪ.tɪŋ, (US) -peɪ.t̬ɪŋ **-pated** -peɪ.tɪd, (US) -peɪ.t̬ɪd **-pator/s** -peɪ.təʳ/z, (US) -peɪ.t̬ɚ/z
emancipation iˌmænt.sɪˈpeɪ.ʃᵊn, -səˈ- **-s** -z
Emanuel iˈmæn.ju.əl, -el
emasculate **adj** iˈmæs.kjʊ.lɪt, iː-, -kjə-, -lət
emascu|late **v** iˈmæs.kjʊ|.leɪt, iː-, -kjə- **-lates** -leɪts **-lating** -leɪ.tɪŋ, (US) -leɪ.t̬ɪŋ **-lated** -leɪ.tɪd, (US) -leɪ.t̬ɪd **-lator/s** -leɪ.təʳ/z, (US) -leɪ.t̬ɚ/z
emasculation ɪˌmæs.kjʊˈleɪ.ʃᵊn, iː-, -kjəˈ- **-s** -z
embalm ɪmˈbɑːm, em-, (US) em-, ɪm- **-s** -z **-ing** -ɪŋ **-ed** -d **-er/s** -əʳ/z, (US) -ɚ/z **-ment/s** -mənt/s
embank ɪmˈbæŋk, em-, (US) em-, ɪm- **-s** -s **-ing** -ɪŋ **-ed** -t
embankment, E~ ɪmˈbæŋk.mənt, em-, (US) em-, ɪm- **-s** -s
embarcation ˌem.bɑːˈkeɪ.ʃᵊn, (US) -bɑːrˈ- **-s** -z
embargo ɪmˈbɑː.gəʊ, em-, (US) emˈbɑːr.goʊ, ɪm- **-es** -z **-ing** -ɪŋ **-ed** -d
embark ɪmˈbɑːk, em-, (US) emˈbɑːrk, ɪm- **-s** -s **-ing** -ɪŋ **-ed** -t
embarkation ˌem.bɑːˈkeɪ.ʃᵊn, (US) -bɑːrˈ- **-s** -z
embarras de richesses ˌɑːm.bærˌɑː.də.riːˈʃes, ɑ̃ːm-, (US) ˌɑːm.bɑː.rɑː-
embarrass ɪmˈbær.əs, em-, (US) emˈber-, ɪm-, -ˈbær- **-es** -ɪz **-ing/ly** -ɪŋ/li **-ed** -t
embarrassment ɪmˈbær.əs.mənt, em-, (US) emˈber-, ɪm-, -ˈbær- **-s** -s
embass|y ˈem.bə.s|i **-ies** -iz
embattl|e ɪmˈbæt.ᵊl, em-, (US) emˈbæt̬-, ɪm- **-es** -z **-ing** -ɪŋ, -ˈbæt.lɪŋ **-ed** -d
embay ɪmˈbeɪ, em-, (US) em-, ɪm- **-s** -z **-ing** -ɪŋ **-ed** -d
embed ɪmˈbed, em-, (US) em-, ɪm- **-s** -z **-ding** -ɪŋ **-ded** -ɪd **-ment** -mənt
embellish ɪmˈbel.ɪʃ, em-, (US) em-, ɪm- **-es** -ɪz **-ing** -ɪŋ **-ed** -t **-er/s** -əʳ/z, (US) -ɚ/z
embellishment ɪmˈbel.ɪʃ.mənt, em-, (US) em-, ɪm- **-s** -s
ember, E~ ˈem.bəʳ, (US) -bɚ **-s** -z **ˈEmber ˌday**
embezzl|e ɪmˈbez.ᵊl, em-, (US) em-, ɪm- **-es** -z **-ing** -ɪŋ, ˈ-lɪŋ **-ed** -d **-er/s** -əʳ/z, ˈ-ləʳ/z, (US) -ɚ/z, ˈ-lɚ/z
embezzlement ɪmˈbez.ᵊl.mənt, em-, (US) em-, ɪm-
embitt|er ɪmˈbɪt|.əʳ, em-, (US) emˈbɪt̬|.ɚ, ɪm- **-ers** -əz, (US) -ɚz **-ering** -ᵊr.ɪŋ **-ered** -əd, (US) -ɚd **-erment** -ə.mənt, (US) -ɚ.mənt
emblazon ɪmˈbleɪ.zᵊn, em-, (US) em-, ɪm- **-s** -z **-ing** -ɪŋ **-ed** -d **-ment/s** -mənt/s **-ry** -ri
emblem ˈem.bləm, -blem, -blɪm, (US) -bləm **-s** -z
emblematic ˌem.bləˈmæt.ɪk, -blɪˈ-, (US) -bləˈmæt̬- **-al** -ᵊl **-ally** -ᵊl.i, -li
emblematiz|e, -is|e emˈblem.ə.taɪz, ˈ-ɪ-; ˈem.blem.ə-, (US) emˈblem.ə- **-es** -ɪz **-ing** -ɪŋ **-ed** -d
emblements ˈem.blə.mənts, -bᵊl-, (US) -blə-
embodiment ɪmˈbɒd.ɪ.mənt, em-, (US) emˈbɑː.di-, ɪm- **-s** -s
embod|y ɪmˈbɒd|.i, em-, (US)

emˈbɑː.d|i, ɪm- -ies -iz -ying -i.ɪŋ -ied -id
embolden ɪmˈbəʊl.dən, em-, (US) emˈboʊl-, ɪm- -s -z -ing -ɪŋ -ed -d
embolism ˈem.bə.lɪ.zəm -s -z
embonpoint ˌɑ̃ːm.bɔ̃ːmˈpwɑ̃ːŋ, (US) ˌɑ̃ːm.bõʊnˈpwæ̃n, -ˈpwɑ̃ːn
embosom ɪmˈbʊz.əm, em-, (US) em-, ɪm- -s -z -ing -ɪŋ -ed -d
emboss ɪmˈbɒs, em-, (US) emˈbɑːs, ɪm- -es -ɪz -ing -ɪŋ -ed -t -er/s -əʳ/z, (US) -ɚ/z -ment/s -mənt/s
embouchure ˌɑ̃ːm.buːˈʃʊəʳ, ˈ---, (US) ˌɑːm.buːˈʃʊr, ˈ--- -s -z
embowel ɪmˈbaʊ.əl, em-, (US) emˈbaʊəl, ɪm- -s -z -(l)ing -ɪŋ -(l)ed -d
embower ɪmˈbaʊ.əʳ, em-, (US) emˈbaʊ.ɚ, ɪm- -s -z -ing -ɪŋ -ed -d
embrac|e ɪmˈbreɪs, em-, (US) em-, ɪm- -es -ɪz -ing -ɪŋ -ed -t
embracery ɪmˈbreɪ.sər.i, em-, (US) em-, ɪm-
embranchment ɪmˈbrɑːntʃ.mənt, em-, (US) emˈbræntʃ-, ɪm- -s -s
embrasure ɪmˈbreɪ.ʒəʳ, em-, -ʒʊəʳ, (US) emˈbreɪ.ʒɚ, ɪm- -s -z
embro|cate ˈem.brəʊ|.keɪt, (US) -broʊ-, -brə- -cates -keɪts -cating -keɪ.tɪŋ, (US) -keɪ.t̬ɪŋ -cated -keɪ.tɪd, (US) -keɪ.t̬ɪd
embrocation ˌem.brəʊˈkeɪ.ʃən, (US) -broʊˈ-, -brəˈ- -s -z
embroglio ɪmˈbrəʊ.li.əʊ, em-, (US) emˈbroʊ.ljoʊ, ɪm- -s -z
embroid|er ɪmˈbrɔɪ.d|əʳ, em-, (US) emˈbrɔɪ.d|ɚ, ɪm- -ers -əz, (US) -ɚz -ering -ər.ɪŋ -ered -əd, (US) -ɚd -erer/s -ər.əʳ/z, (US) -ɚ.ɚ/z
embroider|y ɪmˈbrɔɪ.dər|.i, em-, (US) em-, ɪm- -ies -iz
embroil ɪmˈbrɔɪl, em-, (US) em-, ɪm- -s -z -ing -ɪŋ -ed -d -ment/s -mənt/s
embryo ˈem.bri.əʊ, (US) -oʊ -s -z
embryolog|y ˌem.briˈɒl.ə.dʒ|i, (US) -ˈɑː.lə- -ist/s -ɪst/s
embryonic ˌem.briˈɒn.ɪk, (US) -ˈɑː.nɪk
Embury, Emburey ˈem.bər.i, -bjʊ.ri, -bjə.ri, (US) -bɚ.i
emcee ˌemˈsiː -s -z -ing -ɪŋ -d -d
-eme iːm
Note: Suffix. Unstressed, e.g. **lexeme** /ˈlek.siːm/.
Emeline ˈem.ɪ.liːn, ˈ-ə-, (US) -ə.laɪn, -liːn
emend iˈmend, iː- -s -z -ing -ɪŋ -ed -ɪd -able -ə.bəl
emen|date ˈiː.men|.deɪt, ˈem.en-, (US) ˈiː.men-, -mən-; (US) ɪˈmen- -dates -deɪts -dating -deɪ.tɪŋ, (US) -deɪ.t̬ɪŋ -dated -deɪ.tɪd, (US) -deɪ.t̬ɪd -dator/s -deɪ.təʳ/z, (US) -deɪ.t̬ɚ/z
emendation ˌiː.menˈdeɪ.ʃən, ˌem.enˈ-, -ənˈ- -s -z
emendatory iˈmen.də.tər.i, iː-, -tri, (US) -tɔːr.i
emerald ˈem.ər.əld, ˈ-rəld -s -z ˈ**Emerald** ˌ**Isle**
emerg|e ɪˈmɜːdʒ, iː-, (US) -ˈmɝːdʒ -es -ɪz -ing -ɪŋ -ed -d
emergen|ce ɪˈmɜː.dʒən|ts, iː-, (US) -ˈmɝː- -t -t
emergenc|y ɪˈmɜː.dʒənt.s|i, iː-, (US) -ˈmɝː- -ies -iz eˈ**mergency** ˌ**room**
emeritus ɪˈmer.ɪ.təs, iː-, -ə.təs, (US) -ə.t̬əs
emersion iˈmɜː.ʃən, iː-, -ʒən, (US) -ˈmɝː.ʒən, -ʃən -s -z
Emerson ˈem.ə.sən, (US) ˈ-ɚ-
emery, E~ ˈem.ər.i ˈ**emery** ˌ**board**; ˈ**emery** ˌ**paper**
emetic iˈmet.ɪk, iː-, (US) -ˈmet̬- -s -s -al -əl -ally -əl.i, -li
émeute eɪˈmɜːt -s -s
EMF ˌiː.emˈef
EMI® ˌiː.emˈaɪ
emigrant ˈem.ɪ.grənt, (US) ˈ-ɪ-, ˈ-ə- -s -s
emi|grate ˈem.ɪ|.greɪt, (US) ˈ-ɪ-, ˈ-ə- -grates -greɪts -grating -greɪ.tɪŋ, (US) -greɪ.t̬ɪŋ -grated -greɪ.tɪd, (US) -greɪ.t̬ɪd -grator/s -greɪ.təʳ/z, (US) -greɪ.t̬ɚ/z
emigration ˌem.ɪˈgreɪ.ʃən, (US) -ɪˈ-, -əˈ- -s -z
emigratory ˈem.ɪ.grə.tər.i, -greɪ-, -tri; ˌem.ɪˈgreɪ-, (US) ˈem.ɪ.grə.tɔːr.i, ˈ-ə-
émigré ˈem.ɪ.greɪ -s -z
Emil emˈiːl, eɪˈmiːl, (US) ˈiː.məl, ˈeɪ-
Emile, Émile emˈiːl, eɪˈmiːl, (US) əˈmiːl; (US) eɪˈmiːl
Emilia ɪˈmɪl.i.ə, -ˈjə, emˈiː.li.ə, (US) ɪˈmɪl.jə, emˈiː.ljə
Emily ˈem.ɪ.li, ˈ-ə-
Emin ˈem.ɪn
Eminem ˌem.ɪˈnem
eminen|ce ˈem.ɪ.nənt|s, ˈ-ə- -ces -sɪz -cy -si
éminence grise ˌem.ɪ.nɑːntsˈgriːz; *as if French:* ˌeɪ.mɪ.nɑ̃ːntsˈgriːz; (US) ˌeɪ.miː.nɑːntsˈ-
eminent ˈem.ɪ.nənt, ˈ-ə- -ly -li
emir, E~ emˈɪəʳ, ɪˈmɪr, ə-, eɪ-; ˈem.ɪəʳ, (US) emˈɪr, əˈmɪr; (US) ˌeɪˈmɪr -s -z
emirate ˈem.ɪ.rət, -ər.ət, -ɪt, -eɪt; emˈɪə.rət, ɪˈmɪə-, ə-, eɪ-, -rɪt, -reɪt, (US) emˈɪr.eɪt, əˈmɪr-, -ət -s -s
emissar|y ˈem.ɪ.sər|.i, (US) -ser- -ies -iz
emission iˈmɪʃ.ən, iː- -s -z
emissive iˈmɪs.ɪv, iː-
e|mit i|ˈmɪt, iː- -mits -ˈmɪts -mitting -ˈmɪt.ɪŋ, (US) -ˈmɪt̬ɪŋ -mitted -ˈmɪt.ɪd, (US) -ˈmɪt̬ɪd -mitter/s -ˈmɪt.əʳ/z, (US) -ˈmɪt̬.ɚ/z
Emley ˈem.li
Emlyn ˈem.lɪn
Emma ˈem.ə
Emmanuel ɪˈmæn.ju.əl, -el
Emmanuelle ɪˌmæn.juˈel, emˌæn-
Emmaus emˈeɪ.əs, ɪˈmeɪ-
Emmeline ˈem.ɪ.liːn, ˈ-ə-, (US) -ə.laɪn, -liːn
Emmental, Emmenthal ˈem.ən.tɑːl
Emmerdale ˈem.ə.deɪl, (US) ˈ-ɚ-
emmet, E~ ˈem.ɪt -s -s
Emmie ˈem.i
Emmy ˈem.i -s -z ˈ**Emmy A**ˌ**ward**
emo ˈiː.məʊ, (US) -moʊ -s -z
emollient ɪˈmɒl.i.ənt, iː-, (US) -ˈmɑːl.jənt -s -s
emolument ɪˈmɒl.jʊ.mənt, -jə-, (US) -ˈmɑːl- -s -s
Emory ˈem.ər.i
e|mote ɪ|ˈməʊt, iː-, (US) -ˈmoʊt -motes -ˈməʊts, (US) -ˈmoʊts -moting -ˈməʊ.tɪŋ, (US) -ˈmoʊ.t̬ɪŋ -moted -ˈməʊ.tɪd, (US) -ˈmoʊ.t̬ɪd
emoticon ɪˈməʊ.tɪ.kɒn, (US) -ˈmoʊ.t̬ɪ.kɑːn -s -z
emotion ɪˈməʊ.ʃən, (US) -ˈmoʊ- -s -z -less -ləs, -lɪs
emotional ɪˈməʊ.ʃən.əl, (US) -ˈmoʊ- -ly -i
emotionalism ɪˈməʊ.ʃən.əl.ɪ.zəm, (US) -ˈmoʊ-
emotionaliz|e, -is|e ɪˈməʊ.ʃən.əl.aɪz, (US) -ˈmoʊ.ʃən.ə.laɪz -es -ɪz -ing -ɪŋ -ed -d
emotive ɪˈməʊ.tɪv, (US) -ˈmoʊ.t̬ɪv -ly -li
empanel ɪmˈpæn.əl, em-, (US) em-, ɪm- -s -z -(l)ing -ɪŋ -(l)ed -d -ment/s -mənt/s
empathetic ˌem.pəˈθet.ɪk, (US) -ˈθet̬-
empathic emˈpæθ.ɪk, ɪm-
empathiz|e, -is|e ˈem.pə.θaɪz -es -ɪz -ing -ɪŋ -ed -d
empathy ˈem.pə.θi
Empedocles emˈped.ə.kliːz, ɪm-
emperor, E~ ˈem.pər.əʳ, (US) -pɚ.ɚ -s -z
emphas|is ˈemp.fə.s|ɪs -es -iːz
emphasiz|e, -is|e ˈemp.fə.saɪz -es -ɪz -ing -ɪŋ -ed -d
emphatic ɪmˈfæt.ɪk, em-, (US) emˈfæt̬-, ɪm- -al -əl -ally -əl.i, -li
emphysema ˌemp.fɪˈsiː.mə, (US) -fəˈsiː-, -ˈziː- -s -z
empire, E~ ˈem.paɪəʳ, -paɪ.əʳ, (US) -paɪ.ɚ -s -z ˌ**Empire** ˈ**State** ˌ**Building**
empiric ɪmˈpɪr.ɪk, em-, (US) em-, ɪm- -s -s -al -əl -ally -əl.i, -li
empiric|ism ɪmˈpɪr.ɪ.s|ɪ.zəm, em-, ˈ-ə-, (US) em-, ɪm- -ist/s -ɪst/s
emplacement ɪmˈpleɪs.mənt, em-, (US) em-, ɪm- -s -s
employ ɪmˈplɔɪ, em-, (US) em-, ɪm- -s -z -ing -ɪŋ -ed -d -able -ə.bəl
employé ɑ̃ːm.plɔɪˈeɪ, ɔ̃ːm- -s -z
employee ɪmˈplɔɪ.iː, em-, əm-; ˌem.plɔɪˈiː, (US) emˈplɔɪ.iː, ɪm- -s -z
employer ɪmˈplɔɪ.əʳ, em-, (US) emˈplɔɪ.ɚ, ɪm- -s -z
employment ɪmˈplɔɪ.mənt, em-, (US) em-, ɪm- -s -s emˈ**ployment** ˌ**agency**
empori|um emˈpɔː.ri|.əm, ɪm-, (US) -ˈpɔːr.i- -ums -əmz -a -ə
empower ɪmˈpaʊ.əʳ, -ˈpaʊəʳ, em-, (US) emˈpaʊ.ɚ, ɪm- -s -z -ing -ɪŋ -ed -d
empowerment ɪmˈpaʊ.ə.mənt, -ˈpaʊə-, em-, (US) emˈpaʊ.ɚ-, ɪm-
empress, E~ ˈem.prəs, -prɪs, -pres -es -ɪz

E

Empson ˈemp.sᵊn
emption ˈem*p*.ʃᵊn
empt|y ˈem*p*.t|i **-ier** -i.əʳ, (US) -i.ɚ **-iest** -i.ɪst, -i.əst **-ily** -ᵊl.i, -ɪ.li **-iness** -ɪ.nəs, -ɪ.nɪs **-ies** -iz **-ying** -i.ɪŋ **-ied** -id
empty-handed ˌem*p*.tiˈhæn.dɪd *stress shift:* **ˌempty-handed ˈbeggar**
empty-headed ˌem*p*.tiˈhed.ɪd **-ness** -nəs, -nɪs *stress shift:* **ˌempty-headed ˈnonsense**
empyema ˌem.paɪˈiː.mə, (US) -paɪˈ-, -piˈ-
empyre|al ˌem.paɪəˈriː|.əl, -pɪˈ-, (US) emˈpɪr.i-, -ˈpaɪ.ri-; (US) ˌem.paɪˈriː-, -pəˈ- **-an** -ən
EMS ˌiː.emˈes
Emsworth ˈemz.wəθ, -wɜːθ, (US) -wɚθ, -wɝːθ
emu ˈiː.mjuː, (US) -mjuː, -muː **-s** -z
EMU ˌiː.emˈjuː, ˈiː.mjuː
emu|late ˈem.jə|.leɪt, -jʊ- **-lates** -leɪts **-lating** -leɪ.tɪŋ, (US) -leɪ.t̬ɪŋ **-lated** -leɪ.tɪd, (US) -leɪ.t̬ɪd **-lator/s** -leɪ.təʳ/z, (US) -leɪ.t̬ɚ/z
emulation ˌem.jəˈleɪ.ʃᵊn, -jʊˈ-
emulative ˈem.jə.lə.tɪv, -jʊ-, -leɪ-, (US) -leɪ.t̬ɪv
emulous ˈem.jə.ləs, -jʊ- **-ly** -li
emulsifier ɪˈmʌl.sɪ.faɪ.əʳ, -sə-, (US) -ɚ **-s** -z
emulsi|fy ɪˈmʌl.sɪ|.faɪ, -sə- **-fies** -faɪz **-fying** -faɪ.ɪŋ **-fied** -faɪd
emulsion ɪˈmʌl.ʃᵊn **-s** -z
en *in French phrases:* ɑ̃ː*ŋ*, ɒn, ɑːn
en- ɪn, en

Note: Prefix. It is usually unstressed and may be pronounced either /ɪn-/ or /en-/, e.g. **endear** /ɪnˈdɪəʳ, en-/ (US) /-ˈdɪr/. NB When followed by a /k/ or /g/, assimilation may take place, e.g. **encage** may also be /ɪŋˈkeɪdʒ, eŋ-/.

enabl|e ɪˈneɪ.bᵊl, enˈeɪ- **-es** -z **-ing** -ɪŋ, ˈ-blɪŋ **-ed** -d
enabler ɪˈneɪ.bləʳ, enˈeɪ-, -bᵊl.əʳ, (US) ˈ-blɚ, ˈ-bᵊl.ɚ **-s** -z
enact ɪˈnækt, enˈækt **-s** -s **-ing** -ɪŋ **-ed** -ɪd **-or/s** -əʳ/z, (US) -ɚ/z **-ment/s** -mənt/s **-ive** -ɪv
enaction ɪˈnæk.ʃᵊn, enˈæk- **-s** -z
enamel ɪˈnæm.ᵊl **-s** -z **-(l)ing** -ɪŋ **-(l)ed** -d **-(l)er/s** -əʳ/z, (US) -ɚ/z **-(l)ist/s** -ɪst/s
enamelware ɪˈnæm.ᵊl.weəʳ, (US) -wer
enamo(u)r ɪˈnæm.əʳ, enˈæm-, (US) -ɚ **-s** -z **-ing** -ɪŋ **-ed** -d
en banc ɑ̃ː*m*ˈbɑ̃ː*ŋ*k, (US) ɑ̃ːnˈbɑ̃ːŋ
en bloc ˌɑ̃ː*m*ˈblɒk, (US) ɑ̃ːnˈblɑːk, en-
Encaenia enˈsiː.ni.ə
encag|e ɪnˈkeɪdʒ, ɪŋ-, en-, eŋ-, (US) ɪn-, en- **-es** -ɪz **-ing** -ɪŋ **-ed** -d
encamp ɪnˈkæmp, ɪŋ-, en-, eŋ-, (US) ɪn-, en- **-s** -s **-ing** -ɪŋ **-ed** -t, -kæmt **-ment/s** -mənt/s
encapsu|late ɪnˈkæp.sjə|.leɪt, ɪŋ-, en-, eŋ-, -sjʊ-, (US) en-, ɪn- **-lates** -leɪts **-lating** -leɪ.tɪŋ, (US) -leɪ.t̬ɪŋ **-lated** -leɪ.tɪd, (US) -leɪ.t̬ɪd
encapsulation ɪnˌkæp.sjəˈleɪ.ʃᵊn, ɪŋ-, en-, eŋ-, -sjʊˈ-, (US) en-, ɪn-
Encarta® enˈkɑː.tə, eŋ-, ɪn-, ɪŋ-, (US) -ˈkɑːr.t̬ə
encas|e ɪnˈkeɪs, ɪŋ-, en-, eŋ-, (US) en-, ɪn- **-es** -ɪz **-ing** -ɪŋ **-ed** -t **-ement/s** -mənt/s
encaustic ɪnˈkɔː.stɪk, ɪŋ-, en-, eŋ-, enˈkɒs.tɪk, (US) enˈkɑː.stɪk, -ˈkɔː-, ɪn- **-s** -s **-ally** -ᵊl.i, -li
-ence ᵊn*t*s

Note: Suffix. Normally, **-ence** does not affect the stress pattern of the word it is attached to, e.g. **depend** /dɪˈpend/, **dependence** /dɪˈpen.dən*t*s/. In other cases, the stress may be on the penultimate or antepenultimate syllable, e.g. **excellence** /ˈek.sᵊl.ᵊn*t*s/. See individual entries.

enceinte ˌɑ̃ː*n*ˈsæ̃nt, (US) ˌɑ̃ː*n*-; (US) enˈseɪnt **-s** -s
Enceladus enˈsel.ə.dəs
encephalic ˌen.kəˈfæl.ɪk, ˌeŋ-, ˌɪn-, ˌɪŋ-, -kɪˈ-; ˌen.səˈ-, ˌɪn-, -sefˈæl-, -sɪˈfæl-, (US) ˌen.səˈfæl.ɪk, -sɪˈ-
encephalitis ˌen.kef.əˈlaɪ.tɪs, ˌeŋ-, ˌɪn-, ˌɪŋ-, -kɪ.fəˈ-; ˌen.sə.fəˈ-, ˌɪn-, -sef.əˈ-; enˌkef-, eŋ-, ɪn-, ɪŋ-; enˌsef-, ɪn-, -təs, (US) enˌsef.əˈlaɪ.t̬ɪs, -t̬əs
encephalogram enˈkef.ə.lə.græm, eŋ-, ɪn-, ɪŋ-; enˈsef-, ɪn-, (US) enˈsef.ə.loʊ- **-s** -z
encephalograph enˈkef.ə.lə.grɑːf, eŋ-, ɪn-, ɪŋ-; enˈsef-, ɪn-, -græf, (US) enˈsef.ə.loʊ.græf **-s** -s
encephalomyelitis enˌkef.ə.ləʊ.maɪ.əˈlaɪ.tɪs, eŋ-, ɪn-, ɪŋ-; enˌsef-, ɪnˌsef-; ˌen.kef-, ˌeŋ-, ˌɪn-, ˌɪŋ-; ˌen.sef-, ˌɪn.sef-, -təs, (US) enˌsef.ə.loʊ.maɪ.əˈlaɪ.t̬ɪs, -t̬əs
encephalopathic enˌkef.ə.ləʊˈpæθ.ɪk, eŋ-, ɪn-, ɪŋ-, enˌsef-, ɪnˌsef-, (US) enˌsef.ə.loʊˈ-
encephalopathy enˌkef.əˈlɒp.ə.θi, eŋ-, ɪn-, ɪŋ-; enˌsef-, ɪnˌsef-; ˌen.kef-, ˌeŋ-, ˌɪn-, ˌɪŋ-; ˌen.sef-, ˌɪn.sef-, (US) enˌsef.əˈlɑː.pə-
enchain ɪnˈtʃeɪn, en-, (US) en-, ɪn- **-s** -z **-ing** -ɪŋ **-ed** -d **-ment** -mənt
enchan|t ɪnˈtʃɑːn|t, en-, (US) enˈtʃæn|t, ɪn- **-ts** -ts **-ting/ly** -tɪŋ/li, (US) -t̬ɪŋ/li **-ted** -tɪd, (US) -t̬ɪd **-ter/s** -təʳ/z, (US) -t̬ɚ/z **-tress/es** -trɪs/ɪz **-tment/s** -t.mənt/s
enchilada ˌen.tʃɪˈlɑː.də **-s** -z
enchiridion ˌen.kaɪˈrɪd.i.ən, ˌeŋ-, -kɪˈ-, -ɒn, (US) ˌen.kaɪˈrɪd.i.ən, -kɪˈ- **-s** -z
enciph|er ɪnˈsaɪ.f|əʳ, en-, (US) enˈsaɪ.f|ɚ, ɪn- **-ers** -əz, (US) -ɚz **-ering** -ᵊr.ɪŋ **-ered** -əd, (US) -ɚd
encircl|e ɪnˈsɜː.kᵊl, en-, (US) enˈsɝː-, ɪn- **-es** -z **-ing** -ɪŋ, ˈ-klɪŋ **-ed** -d **-ement/s** -mənt/s
Encke ˈeŋ.kə
enclasp ɪnˈklɑːsp, ɪŋ-, en-, eŋ-, (US) enˈklæsp, ɪn- **-s** -s **-ing** -ɪŋ **-ed** -t
enclave ˈen.kleɪv, ˈeŋ-, (US) ˈen-, ˈɑːn- **-s** -z
enclitic ɪnˈklɪt.ɪk, ɪŋ-, en-, eŋ-, (US) enˈklɪt̬-, ɪn- **-s** -s **-ally** -ᵊl.i, -li
enclos|e ɪnˈkləʊz, ɪŋ-, en-, eŋ-, (US) enˈkloʊz, ɪn- **-es** -ɪz **-ing** -ɪŋ **-ed** -d
enclosure ɪnˈkləʊ.ʒəʳ, ɪŋ-, en-, eŋ-, (US) enˈkloʊ.ʒɚ, ɪn- **-s** -z
encod|e ɪnˈkəʊd, en-, eŋ-, ɪŋ-, (US) enˈkoʊd, ɪn- **-es** -z **-ing** -ɪŋ **-ed** -ɪd **-er/s** -əʳ/z, (US) -ɚ/z
encomi|ast ɪnˈkəʊ.mi|.æst, ɪŋ-, en-, eŋ-, (US) enˈkoʊ-, ɪn- **-asts** -æsts **-um/s** -əm/z **-a** -ə
encompass ɪnˈkʌm.pəs, ɪŋ-, en-, eŋ-, (US) en-, ɪn- **-es** -ɪz **-ing** -ɪŋ **-ed** -t
encore ˈɒŋ.kɔːʳ, ˈɑː*ŋ*-, -ˈ-, (US) ˈɑːn.kɔːr, -ˈ- **-es** -z **-ing** -ɪŋ **-ed** -d
encoun|ter ɪnˈkaʊn|.təʳ, ɪŋ-, en-, eŋ-, (US) enˈkaʊn|.t̬ɚ, ɪn- **-ters** -təz, (US) -t̬ɚz **-tering** -tᵊr.ɪŋ, (US) -t̬ɚ.ɪŋ **-tered** -təd, (US) -t̬ɚd
encourag|e ɪnˈkʌr.ɪdʒ, ɪŋ-, en-, eŋ-, (US) en.kɝː-, ɪn- **-es** -ɪz **-ing/ly** -ɪŋ/li **-ed** -d
encouragement ɪnˈkʌr.ɪdʒ.mənt, ɪŋ-, en-, eŋ-, (US) en.kɝː-, ɪn- **-s** -s
encroach ɪnˈkrəʊtʃ, ɪŋ-, en-, eŋ-, (US) enˈkroʊtʃ, ɪn- **-es** -ɪz **-ing** -ɪŋ **-ed** -t **-ment/s** -mənt/s
en croûte ˌɑ̃ː*ŋ*ˈkruːt, (US) ˌɑːnˈkruːt
encrust ɪnˈkrʌst, ɪŋ-, en-, eŋ-, (US) en-, ɪn- **-s** -s **-ing** -ɪŋ **-ed** -ɪd
encrustation ˌen.krʌsˈteɪ.ʃᵊn, ˌeŋ-, (US) ˌen- **-s** -z
encrypt ɪnˈkrɪpt, ɪŋ-, en-, eŋ-, (US) en-, ɪn- **-s** -s **-ing** -ɪŋ **-ed** -ɪd
encryption ɪnˈkrɪp.ʃᵊn, ɪŋ-, en-, eŋ-, (US) en-, ɪn-
encumb|er ɪnˈkʌm.b|əʳ, ɪŋ-, en-, eŋ-, (US) enˈkʌm.b|ɚ, ɪn- **-ers** -əz, (US) -ɚz **-ering** -ᵊr.ɪŋ **-ered** -əd, (US) -ɚd
encumbranc|e ɪnˈkʌm.brən*t*s, ɪŋ-, en-, eŋ-, (US) en-, ɪn- **-es** -ɪz
-ency ᵊn*t*.si

Note: Suffix. Words containing **-ency** are stressed in a similar way to those containing **-ence**; see above.

encyclic ɪnˈsɪk.lɪk, en-, -ˈsaɪ.klɪk, (US) en-, ɪn- **-s** -s **-al/s** -ᵊl/z
encyclop(a)edia ɪnˌsaɪ.kləˈpiː.di.ə, enˌsaɪ-, ˌɪn.saɪ-, ˌen-, (US) enˌsaɪ-, ɪn-, ˌen.saɪ-, ˌɪn- **-s** -z
encyclop(a)edic ɪnˌsaɪ.kləˈpiː.dɪk, enˌsaɪ-, ˌɪn.saɪ-, ˌen-, (US) enˌsaɪ-, ɪn-, ˌen.saɪ-, ˌɪn- **-ally** -ᵊl.i, -li
encyclop(a)ed|ism ɪnˌsaɪ.kləˈpiː.d|ɪ.zᵊm, enˌsaɪ-, ˌɪn.saɪ-, ˌen-, (US) enˌsaɪ-, ɪn-, ˌen.saɪ-, ˌɪn- **-ist/s** -ɪst/s
end end **-s** -z **-ing** -ɪŋ **-ed** -ɪd **ˌend ˈproduct; ˈend ˌuser; be at a ˌloose ˈend; be at ˌloose ˈends; ˌmake ends ˈmeet** (US) **ˌmake ˈends ˌmeet; go off the ˈdeep ˌend; ˌthrown in at the ˈdeep ˌend; at the ˌend of the ˈday**
endang|er ɪnˈdeɪn.dʒ|əʳ, en-, (US) enˈdeɪn.dʒ|ɚ, ɪn- **-ers** -əz, (US) -ɚz

-ering -ᵊr.ɪŋ **-ered** -əd, (US) -ɚd **-erment** -ə.mənt, (US) -ɚ.mənt
endear ɪnˈdɪəʳ, en-, (US) ɪnˈdɪr, en- **-s** -z **-ing/ly** -ɪŋ/li **-ed** -d **-ment** -mənt
endeav|o(u)r ɪnˈdev|.əʳ, en-, (US) enˈdev|.ɚ, ɪn- **-o(u)rs** -əz, (US) -ɚz **-o(u)ring** -ᵊr.ɪŋ **-o(u)red** -əd, (US) -ɚd
Endell ˈen.dᵊl
endemic enˈdem.ɪk **-s** -s **-al** -ᵊl **-ally** -ᵊl.i, -li
Enderby ˈen.də.bi, (US) -dɚ-
endermic enˈdɜː.mɪk, (US) -ˈdɝː- **-al** -ᵊl **-ally** -ᵊl.i, -li
endgame ˈend.geɪm, ˈeŋ-, (US) ˈend- **-s** -z
Endicott ˈen.dɪ.kət, -də-, -kɒt, (US) -kɑːt, -kət
ending ˈen.dɪŋ **-s** -z
endive ˈen.daɪv, -dɪv, (US) ˈen.daɪv, ˈɑːn.diːv **-s** -z
endless ˈend.ləs, -lɪs **-ly** -li **-ness** -nəs, -nɪs
endlong ˈend.lɒŋ, (US) -lɑːŋ, -lɔːŋ
endmost ˈend.məʊst, (US) -moʊst
endnote ˈend.nəʊt, (US) -noʊt **-s** -s
endo- ˈen.dəʊ; enˈdɒ, ɪnˈ-, (US) ˈen.doʊ, ˈ-də; (US) enˈdɑː, ɪnˈ-
Note: Prefix. Either carries primary or secondary stress on the first syllable, e.g. **endomorph** /ˈen.dəʊ.mɔːf/ (US) /-doʊ.mɔːrf/, **endomorphic** /ˌen.dəʊˈmɔː.fɪk/ (US) /-doʊˈmɔːr-/, or primary stress on the second syllable, e.g. **endogenous** /ɪnˈdɒdʒ.ɪ.nəs/ (US) /enˈdɑː.dʒə-/.
endocentric ˌen.dəʊˈsen.trɪk, (US) -doʊˈ-
endocrine ˈen.dəʊ.kraɪn, -krɪn, -kriːn, (US) -də.krɪn, -doʊ-, -kriːn, -kraɪn ˈ**endocrine** ˌ**gland**
endocrinolog|y ˌen.dəʊ.kraɪˈnɒl.ə.dʒ|i, -krɪˈ-, (US) -də.krɪˈnɑː.lə-, -doʊ- **-ist/s** -ɪst/s
endoderm ˈen.dəʊ.dɜːm, (US) -doʊ.dɝːm
endoderm|al ˌen.dəʊˈdɜː.m|ᵊl, (US) -doʊˈdɝː- **-ic** -ɪk
endogamy enˈdɒg.ə.mi, ɪn-, (US) enˈdɑː.gə-, ɪn-
endogenous enˈdɒdʒ.ɪ.nəs, ɪn-, ˈ-ə-, (US) enˈdɑː.dʒɪ-, ˈ-dʒə-, ɪn-
endometrial ˌen.dəʊˈmiː.tri.əl, (US) -doʊˈ-, -dəˈ-
endometriosis ˌen.dəʊˌmiː.triˈəʊ.sɪs, (US) -doʊˌmiː.triˈoʊ-, -dəˌ-
endometri|um ˌen.dəʊˈmiː.tri|.əm, (US) -doʊˈ-, -dəˈ- **-a** -ə
endomorph ˈen.dəʊ.mɔːf, (US) -doʊ.mɔːrf, ˈ-də- **-s** -s **-y** -i
endomorph|ic ˌen.dəʊˈmɔː.f|ɪk, (US) -doʊˈmɔːr-, ˌ-də- **-ism** -ɪ.zᵊm
endophoric ˌen.dəʊˈfɒr.ɪk, (US) -doʊˈfɔːr-, -dəˈ-
endoplasm ˈen.dəʊ.plæz.ᵊm, (US) -doʊ-, -də-
endoplasmic ˌen.dəʊˈplæz.mɪk, (US) -doʊˈ-, -dəˈ-
Endor ˈen.dɔːʳ, (US) -dɔːr
endorphin enˈdɔː.fɪn, ɪnˈ-, (US) -ˈdɔːr-, ɪn- **-s** -z
endors|e ɪnˈdɔːs, en-, (US) enˈdɔːrs, ɪn- **-es** -ɪz **-ing** -ɪŋ **-ed** -t **-er/s** -əʳ/z, (US) -ɚ/z **-ement/s** -mənt/s **-able** -ə.bᵊl
endorsee ˌen.dɔːˈsiː, (US) -dɔːrˈ- **-s** -z
endoscope ˈen.dəʊ.skəʊp, (US) -doʊ.skoʊp, -də- **-s** -s
endoscop|y enˈdɒs.kə.p|i, ɪnˈ-, (US) -ˈdɑː.skə- **-ies** -iz
endoskeleton ˌen.dəʊˈskel.ɪ.tᵊn, (US) -doʊˈ- **-s** -z
endosperm ˈen.dəʊ.spɜːm, (US) -doʊ.spɝːm **-s** -z
endow ɪnˈdaʊ, en-, (US) en-, ɪn- **-s** -z **-ing** -ɪŋ **-ed** -d **-ment/s** -mənt/s
endpaper ˈendˌpeɪ.pəʳ, (US) -pɚ **-s** -z
endpoint ˈend.pɔɪnt **-s** -s
end-stopped ˈend.stɒpt, (US) -stɑːpt
endu|e ɪnˈdʒuː, -ˈdjuː, en-, (US) enˈduː, ɪn-, -ˈdjuː **-es** -z **-ing** -ɪŋ **-ed** -d
endurab|le ɪnˈdʒʊə.rə.b|ᵊl, -ˈdjʊə-, en-, -ˈdʒɔː-, -ˈdjɔː-, (US) enˈdʊr.ə-, ɪn-, -ˈdjʊr- **-ly** -li
endurance ɪnˈdʒʊə.rᵊnts, -ˈdjʊə-, en-, -ˈdʒɔː-, -djɔː-, (US) enˈdʊr.ᵊnts, ɪn-, -ˈdjʊr-
endur|e ɪnˈdʒʊəʳ, -ˈdjʊəʳ, en-, -ˈdjɔːʳ, -ˈdʒɔːʳ, (US) enˈdʊr, ɪn-, -ˈdjʊr **-es** -z **-ing/ly** -ɪŋ/li **-ed** -d
end|ways ˈend|.weɪz **-wise** -waɪz
Endymion enˈdɪm.i.ən, ɪn-
ENE ˌiːst.nɔːθˈiːst, (US) -nɔːrθ-; *in nautical usage also:* -nɔːˈriːst, (US) -nɔːrˈiːst
-ene iːn
Note: Suffix. **-ene** is not stressed, e.g. **ethylene** /ˈeθ.ɪ.liːn/.
Eneas iːˈniː.əs, ɪ-, -æs
Eneid ˈiː.ni.ɪd, ɪˈniː-
enema ˈen.ə.mə, ˈ-ɪ-, (US) ˈ-ə- **-s** -z
enem|y ˈen.ə.m|i, ˈ-ɪ- **-ies** -iz
energetic ˌen.əˈdʒet.ɪk, (US) -ɚˈdʒet̬- **-s** -s **-ally** -ᵊl.i, -li
energiz|e, -is|e ˈen.ə.dʒaɪz, (US) ˈ-ɚ- **-es** -ɪz **-ing** -ɪŋ **-ed** -d **-er/s** -əʳ/z, (US) -ɚ/z
energumen ˌen.əˈgjuː.men, (US) -ɚˈ- **-s** -z
energ|y ˈen.ə.dʒ|i, (US) ˈ-ɚ- **-ies** -iz
ener|vate ˈen.ə|.veɪt, -ɜː-, (US) ˈ-ɚ- **-vates** -veɪts **-vating** -veɪ.tɪŋ, (US) -veɪ.t̬ɪŋ **-vated** -veɪ.tɪd, (US) -veɪ.t̬ɪd
enervation ˌen.əˈveɪ.ʃᵊn, -ɜːˈ-, (US) -ɚˈ-
en famille ˌɑ̃ːn.fæmˈiː
enfant(s) terrible(s) ˌɑ̃ːn.fɑ̃ːn.terˈiː.blə, ˌɒn.fɒn-, -təˈriː-, (US) ˌɑːn.fɑːn.terˈiː-, ˌɑ̃ːn.fɑ̃ːn-
enfeebl|e ɪnˈfiː.bᵊl, en-, (US) en-, ɪn- **-es** -z **-ing** -ɪŋ, ˈ-blɪŋ **-ed** -d **-ement** -mənt
enfeoff ɪnˈfiːf, en-, -ˈfef, (US) en-, ɪn- **-s** -s **-ing** -ɪŋ **-ed** -t **-ment/s** -mənt/s
Enfield ˈen.fiːld
enfilad|e ˌen.fɪˈleɪd, ˈ---, (US) ˈen.fə.leɪd **-es** -z **-ing** -ɪŋ **-ed** -ɪd
enfold ɪnˈfəʊld, en-, (US) enˈfoʊld, ɪn- **-s** -z **-ing** -ɪŋ **-ed** -ɪd **-ment** -mənt
enforc|e ɪnˈfɔːs, en-, (US) enˈfɔːrs, ɪn- **-es** -ɪz **-ing** -ɪŋ **-ed** -t **-edly** -ɪd.li **-eable** -ə.bᵊl
enforcement ɪnˈfɔːs.mənt, en-, (US) enˈfɔːrs-, ɪn-
enforcer ɪnˈfɔː.səʳ, (US) -ˈfɔːr.sɚ **-s** -z
enfranchis|e ɪnˈfræn.tʃaɪz, en-, (US) en-, ɪn- **-es** -ɪz **-ing** -ɪŋ **-ed** -d
enfranchisement ɪnˈfræn.tʃɪz.mənt, en-, -tʃəz-, (US) enˈfræn.tʃaɪz-, ɪn-, -tʃəz- **-s** -s
Engadine ˈeŋ.gə.diːn, ˌ--ˈ-
engag|e ɪnˈgeɪdʒ, ɪŋ-, en-, eŋ-, (US) en-, ɪn- **-es** -ɪz **-ing/ly** -ɪŋ/li **-ed** -d
engagement ɪnˈgeɪdʒ.mənt, ɪŋ-, en-, eŋ-, (US) en-, ɪn- **-s** -s **en**ˈ**gagement** ˌ**ring**
en garde ɑ̃ːŋˈgɑːd, (US) ˌɑːnˈgɑːrd, ɑ̃ːn-
Engels ˈeŋ.gᵊlz
engend|er ɪnˈdʒen.d|əʳ, en-, (US) enˈdʒen.d|ɚ, ɪn- **-ers** -əz, (US) -ɚz **-ering** -ᵊr.ɪŋ **-ered** -əd, (US) -ɚd
engine ˈen.dʒɪn **-s** -z ˈ**engine** ˌ**driver**
engineer ˌen.dʒɪˈnɪəʳ, -dʒəˈ-, (US) -ˈnɪr **-s** -z **-ing** -ɪŋ **-ed** -d
engird ɪnˈgɜːd, ɪŋ-, en-, eŋ-, (US) enˈgɝːd, ɪn- **-s** -z **-ing** -ɪŋ **-ed** -ɪd
England ˈɪŋ.glənd **-er/s** -əʳ/z, (US) -ɚ/z
Englefield ˈeŋ.gᵊl.fiːld
Englewood ˈeŋ.gᵊl.wʊd
English ˈɪŋ.glɪʃ ˌ**English** ˈ**Channel**; ˌ**English** ˈ**horn** (US) ˈ**English** ˌ**horn**
English|man ˈɪŋ.glɪʃ|.mən **-men** -mən, -men
English|woman ˈɪŋ.glɪʃ|ˌwʊm.ən **-women** -ˌwɪm.ɪn
engorg|e ɪnˈgɔːdʒ, ɪŋ-, en-, eŋ-, (US) -ˈgɔːrdʒ **-es** -ɪz **-ing** -ɪŋ **-ed** -d
engraft ɪnˈgrɑːft, ɪŋ-, en-, eŋ-, (US) enˈgræft, ɪn- **-s** -s **-ing** -ɪŋ **-ed** -ɪd **-ment** -mənt
engrailed ɪnˈgreɪld, ɪŋ-, en-, eŋ-, (US) en-, ɪn-
engrain ɪnˈgreɪn, ɪŋ-, en-, eŋ-, (US) en-, ɪn- **-s** -z **-ing** -ɪŋ **-ed** -d
engrav|e ɪnˈgreɪv, ɪŋ-, en-, eŋ-, (US) en-, ɪn- **-es** -z **-ing/s** -ɪŋ/z **-ed** -d **-er/s** -əʳ/z, (US) -ɚ/z **-ery** -ᵊr.i
en gros ˌɑ̃ːŋˈgrəʊ, (US) ˌɑːnˈgroʊ
engross ɪnˈgrəʊs, ɪŋ-, en-, eŋ-, (US) enˈgroʊs, ɪn- **-es** -ɪz **-ing** -ɪŋ **-ed** -t **-ment** -mənt
engulf ɪnˈgʌlf, ɪŋ-, en-, eŋ-, (US) en-, ɪn- **-s** -s **-ing** -ɪŋ **-ed** -t **-ment** -mənt
enhanc|e ɪnˈhɑːnts, en-, (US) -ˈhænts **-es** -ɪz **-ing** -ɪŋ **-ed** -t **-ement/s** -mənt/s **-er/s** -əʳ/z, (US) -ɚ/z
enharmonic ˌen.hɑːˈmɒn.ɪk, (US) -hɑːrˈmɑː.nɪk **-al** -ᵊl **-ally** -ᵊl.i, -li
Enid ˈiː.nɪd
enigma ɪˈnɪg.mə, enˈɪg-, əˈnɪg-, (US) ɪˈnɪg.mə, ə-, enˈɪg- **-s** -z
enigmatic ˌen.ɪgˈmæt.ɪk, (US) -ˈmæt̬-

-al -ᵊl -ally -ᵊl.i, -li *stress shift:* ˌenigmatic ˈsmile
enigmatist ɪˈnɪg.mə.tɪst, enˈɪg-, əˈnɪg-, (US) ɪˈnɪg-, ə-, enˈɪg- -s -s
enigmatiz|e, -is|e ɪˈnɪg.mə.taɪz, enˈɪg-, əˈnɪg-, (US) ɪˈnɪg-, ə-, enˈɪg- -es -ɪz -ing -ɪŋ -ed -d
enjamb(e)ment ɪnˈdʒæmb.mənt, en-, (US) en-, ɪn- -s -s
enjoin ɪnˈdʒɔɪn, en-, (US) en-, ɪn- -s -z -ing -ɪŋ -ed -d
enjoy ɪnˈdʒɔɪ, en-, (US) en-, ɪn- -s -z -ing -ɪŋ -ed -d
enjoyab|le ɪnˈdʒɔɪ.ə.b|ᵊl, en-, (US) en-, ɪn- -ly -li -leness -ᵊl.nəs, -nɪs
enjoyment ɪnˈdʒɔɪ.mənt, en-, (US) en-, ɪn- -s -s
enkindl|e ɪnˈkɪn.dᵊl, en-, ɪŋ-, eŋ-, (US) en-, ɪn- -es -z -ing -ɪŋ, ˈ-lɪŋ -ed -d
enlac|e ɪnˈleɪs, en-, (US) en-, ɪn- -es -ɪz -ing -ɪŋ -ed -t -ement/s -mənt/s
Enlai ˌenˈlaɪ
enlarg|e ɪnˈlɑːdʒ, en-, (US) enˈlɑːrdʒ, ɪn- -es -ɪz -ing -ɪŋ -ed -d -er/s -əʳ/z, (US) -ɚ/z -ement/s -mənt/s
enlighten ɪnˈlaɪ.tᵊn, en-, (US) en-, ɪn- -s -z -ing -ɪŋ -ed -d
enlightenment, E~ ɪnˈlaɪ.tᵊn.mənt, en-, (US) en-, ɪn-
enlist ɪnˈlɪst, en-, (US) en-, ɪn- -s -s -ing -ɪŋ -ed -ɪd -ment/s -mənt/s
enliven ɪnˈlaɪ.vᵊn, en-, (US) en-, ɪn- -s -z -ing -ɪŋ -ed -d
en masse ɑ̃ːmˈmæs, ɒn-, (US) ɑːn-, ɑ̃ːn-
enmesh ɪnˈmeʃ, en-, (US) en-, ɪn- -es -ɪz -ing -ɪŋ -ed -t
enmit|y ˈen.mə.t|i, -mɪ- -ies -iz
Ennis ˈen.ɪs
Enniscorthy ˌen.ɪˈskɔː.θi, (US) -ˈskɔːr-
Enniskillen ˌen.ɪˈskɪl.ən, -əˈ-, -ɪn
Ennius ˈen.i.əs
ennobl|e ɪˈnəʊ.bᵊl, enˈəʊ-, (US) enˈoʊ-, ɪˈnoʊ- -es -z -ing -ɪŋ, ˈ-blɪŋ -ed -d -ement -mənt
ennui ˌɑ̃ːnˈwiː, ˈɒn-, -ˈ-, (US) ˌɑːnˈwiː, ˈ--
Eno® ˈiː.nəʊ, (US) -noʊ -'s -z
Enoch ˈiː.nɒk, (US) -nɑːk, -nək
enormit|y ɪˈnɔː.mə.t|i, ə-, -mɪ-, (US) -ˈnɔːr.mə.ţ|i -ies -iz
enormous ɪˈnɔː.məs, ə-, (US) -ˈnɔːr- -ly -li -ness -nəs, -nɪs
Enos ˈiː.nɒs, (US) -nɑːs, -nəs
enough ɪˈnʌf, ə-
enounc|e iˈnaʊnts -es -ɪz -ing -ɪŋ -ed -t
enow ɪˈnaʊ
en passant ˌɑ̃ːmˈpæs.ɑ̃ːŋ, ˌ--ˈ-, (US) ˌɑ̃ː.pɑːˈsɑ̃ːn, -pəˈ-
enquir|e ɪnˈkwaɪəʳ, -ˈkwaɪ.əʳ, ɪŋ-, en-, eŋ-, (US) enˈkwaɪ.ɚ, ɪn- -es -z -ing/ly -ɪŋ/li -ed -d -er/s -əʳ/z, (US) -ɚ/z
enquir|y ɪnˈkwaɪə.r|i, ɪŋ-, en-, eŋ-, (US) enˈkwaɪ-, ɪn-; (US) ˈɪn.kwɚ.i -ies -iz
enrag|e ɪnˈreɪdʒ, en-, (US) en-, ɪn- -es -ɪz -ing -ɪŋ -ed -d
enrapt ɪnˈræpt, en-, (US) en-, ɪn-
enrapt|ure ɪnˈræp.tʃ|əʳ, en-, (US) enˈræp.tʃ|ɚ, ɪn- -ures -əz, (US) -ɚz -uring -ᵊr.ɪŋ -ured -əd, (US) -ɚd
enregist|er ɪnˈredʒ.ɪ.st|əʳ, en-, ˈ-ə-, (US) enˈredʒ.ɪ.st|ɚ, ɪn-, ˈ-ə- -ers -əz, (US) -ɚz -ering -ᵊr.ɪŋ -ered -əd, (US) -ɚd
enrich ɪnˈrɪtʃ, en-, (US) en-, ɪn- -es -ɪz -ing -ɪŋ -ed -t -ment -mənt
Enright ˈen.raɪt
enrob|e ɪnˈrəʊb, en-, (US) enˈroʊb, ɪn- -es -z -ing -ɪŋ -ed -d
enrol ɪnˈrəʊl, en-, (US) enˈroʊl, ɪn- -s -z -ling -ɪŋ -led -d
enroll ɪnˈrəʊl, en-, (US) enˈroʊl, ɪn- -s -z -ing -ɪŋ -ed -d
enrol(l)ment ɪnˈrəʊl.mənt, en-, (US) enˈroʊl-, ɪn- -s -s
Enron® ˈen.rɒn, (US) -rɑːn
en route ˌɑ̃ːnˈruːt, ˌɒn-, (US) ˌɑ̃ːnˈruːt
en|s en|z -tia -ʃi.ə, -ʃə, -ti.ə
ENSA ˈent.sə
ensample enˈsɑːm.pᵊl, ɪn-, (US) -ˈsæm- -s -z
ensanguined ɪnˈsæŋ.gwɪnd, en-, (US) en-, ɪn-
ensconc|e ɪnˈskɒnts, en-, (US) enˈskɑːnts, ɪn- -es -ɪz -ing -ɪŋ -ed -t
ensemble ɑ̃ːnˈsɑ̃ːm.bᵊl, ɒnˈsɒm-, (US) ˌɑːnˈsɑːm- -s -z
enshrin|e ɪnˈʃraɪn, en-, (US) en-, ɪn- -es -z -ing -ɪŋ -ed -d -ement -mənt
enshroud ɪnˈʃraʊd, en-, (US) en-, ɪn- -s -z -ing -ɪŋ -ed -ɪd
ensign n *flag:* ˈen.saɪn; *in the navy:* ˈent.sᵊn *officer:* ˈen.saɪn, (US) ˈen.sɪn -s -z
ensign v enˈsaɪn, ɪn- -s -z -ing -ɪŋ -ed -d
ensilag|e ˈent.sɪ.lɪdʒ, -sə; ɪnˈsaɪ-, en-, (US) ˈent.sə- -es -ɪz
ensil|e enˈsaɪl, ˈent.saɪl -es -z -ing -ɪŋ -ed -d
enslav|e ɪnˈsleɪv, en-, (US) en-, ɪn- -es -z -ing -ɪŋ -ed -d -er/s -əʳ/z, (US) -ɚ/z -ement -mənt
ensnar|e ɪnˈsneəʳ, en-, (US) enˈsner, ɪn- -es -z -ing -ɪŋ -ed -d -er/s -əʳ/z, (US) -ɚ/z
ensoul ɪnˈsəʊl, en-, (US) enˈsoʊl, ɪn- -s -z -ing -ɪŋ -ed -d
ensu|e ɪnˈsjuː, en-, -ˈsuː, (US) enˈsuː, ɪn-, -ˈsjuː -es -z -ing -ɪŋ -ed -d
en suite ˌɑ̃ːnˈswiːt, ˌɒn-, (US) ˌɑːn- *stress shift:* ˌ**en suite** ˈ**bathroom**
ensur|e ɪnˈʃɔːʳ, en-, -ˈʃʊəʳ, -ˈsjʊəʳ, (US) enˈʃʊr, ɪn- -es -z -ing -ɪŋ -ed -d
-ent ᵊnt
Note: Suffix. Words containing **-ent** are stressed in a similar way to those containing **-ence**; see above.
entablature enˈtæb.lə.tʃəʳ, ɪn-, -lɪ-, -tʃʊəʳ, -tjʊəʳ, (US) -lə.tʃɚ -s -z
entail ɪnˈteɪl, en-, (US) en-, ɪn- -s -z -ing -ɪŋ -ed -d -er/s -əʳ/z, (US) -ɚ/z -ment -mənt
entangl|e ɪnˈtæŋ.gᵊl, en-, (US) en-, ɪn- -es -z -ing -ɪŋ, ˈ-glɪŋ -ed -d -ement/s -mənt/s
Entebbe enˈteb.i, ɪn-, (US) -ə
entendre ɑ̃ːnˈtɑ̃ːn.drə, (US) ɑːnˈtɑːn.drə
entente ɑ̃ːnˈtɑ̃ːnt, (US) ɑːnˈtɑːnt -s -s
entente cordiale ˌɑ̃ːn.tɑ̃ːnt.kɔː.diˈɑːl, (US) -kɔːr.diˈ-
ent|er ˈen.t|əʳ, (US) -ţ|ɚ -ers -əz, (US) -ɚz -ering -ᵊr.ɪŋ -ered -əd, (US) -ɚd
enteric enˈter.ɪk
enteritis ˌen.təˈraɪ.tɪs, -təs, (US) ˌen.ţə- -ţɪs, -ţəs
enterokinas|e ˌen.tᵊr.əʊˈkaɪ.neɪz, (US) -ţə.roʊˈkaɪ.neɪs, -ˈkɪn.eɪs, -eɪz -es -ɪz
enterology ˌen.təˈrɒl.ə.dʒi, (US) -ţəˈrɑː.lə-
enterotomy ˌen.təˈrɒt.ə.mi, (US) -ţəˈrɑː.ţə-
enterovirus ˌen.tᵊr.əʊˈvaɪə.rəs, (US) -ţə.roʊˈvaɪ.rəs -es -ɪz
enterpris|e ˈen.tə.praɪz, (US) -ţɚ- -es -ɪz -ing/ly -ɪŋ/li
entertain ˌen.təˈteɪn, (US) -ţɚˈ- -s -z -ing/ly -ɪŋ/li -ed -d -er/s -əʳ/z, (US) -ɚ/z
entertainment ˌen.təˈteɪn.mənt, (US) -ţɚˈ- -s -s
enthral ɪnˈθrɔːl, en-, (US) enˈθrɔːl, ɪn-, -ˈθrɑːl -s -z -ling -ɪŋ -led -d -ment -mənt
enthrall ɪnˈθrɔːl, en-, (US) enˈθrɔːl, ɪn-, -ˈθrɑːl -s -z -ing -ɪŋ -ed -d -ment -mənt
enthron|e ɪnˈθrəʊn, en-, (US) enˈθroʊn, ɪn- -es -z -ing -ɪŋ -ed -d -ement/s -mənt/s
enthus|e ɪnˈθjuːz, en-, (US) enˈθuːz, ɪn-, -ˈθjuːz -es -ɪz -ing -ɪŋ -ed -d
enthusi|asm ɪnˈθjuː.zi|.æz.ᵊm, en-, -ˈθuː-, (US) enˈθuː-, ɪn-, -ˈθjuː- -asms -æzmz -ast/s -æst/s
enthusiastic ɪnˌθjuː.ziˈæs.tɪk, en-, -ˌθuː-, (US) enˌθuː-, ɪn-, -ˌθjuː- -ally -ᵊl.i, -li
entia (plural of **ens**) ˈen.ʃi.ə, -ʃə, -ti.ə
entic|e ɪnˈtaɪs, en-, (US) en-, ɪn- -es -ɪz -ing/ly -ɪŋ/li -ed -t -ement/s -mənt/s
entire ɪnˈtaɪəʳ, -ˈtaɪ.əʳ, en-, (US) enˈtaɪ.ɚ, ɪn- -ly -li -ness -nəs, -nɪs
entiret|y ɪnˈtaɪə.rə.t|i, en-, (US) enˈtaɪ.rə.ţ|i, -ˈtaɪr.ţ|i, ɪn- -ies -iz
entitl|e ɪnˈtaɪ.tᵊl, en-, (US) enˈtaɪ.ţᵊl, ɪn- -es -z -ing -ɪŋ, -ˈtaɪt.lɪŋ -ed -d
entitlement ɪnˈtaɪ.tᵊl.mənt, en-, (US) enˈtaɪ.ţᵊl-, ɪn- -s -s
entit|y ˈen.tɪ.t|i, -tə-, (US) -ţə.ţ|i -ies -iz
entomb ɪnˈtuːm, en-, (US) en-, ɪn- -s -z -ing -ɪŋ -ed -d -ment/s -mənt/s
entomological ˌen.tə.məˈlɒdʒ.ɪ.kᵊl, (US) -ţə.məˈlɑː.dʒɪ- -ly -i
entomologiz|e, -is|e ˌen.təˈmɒl.ə.dʒaɪz, (US) -ţəˈmɑː.lə- -es -ɪz -ing -ɪŋ -ed -d
entomolog|y ˌen.təˈmɒl.ə.dʒ|i, (US) -ţəˈmɑː.lə- -ist/s -ɪst/s

Pronouncing the letters EO

There are several pronunciation possibilities for the vowel digraph **eo**, e.g.:

iː	people /ˈpiː.pəl/
e	leopard /ˈlep.əd/ (US) /-ɚd/
i.ə	chameleon /kəˈmiː.li.ən/

When followed by an **r** in the spelling, **eo** is pronounced as /ɔː/ (US) /ɔːr/ and /ɪə/ (US) /ɪr/, e.g.:

George	dʒɔːdʒ (US) dʒɔːrdʒ
theory	ˈθɪə.ri (US) ˈθɪr.i

Where **geo-** is a prefix, there are several possible realizations, e.g.:

i.ɒ (US) i.ɑː	geography /dʒiˈɒg.rə.fi/ (US) /-ˈɑː.grə-/
iː.əʊ (US) iː.oʊ	geothermal /ˌdʒiː.əʊˈθɜː.məl/ (US) /-oʊˈθɝː-/

(In *geography*, the prefix may also be pronounced as /ˈdʒɒg-/ in British English.)

In addition

There are instances when the two letters **e** and **o** come together in closed compounds, e.g.:

thereof	ðeəˈrɒv (US) ðerˈɑːv
whereon	*h*weəˈrɒn (US) *h*werˈɑːn

In weak syllables

The vowel digraph **eo** is realized with the vowel /ə/ in weak syllables, e.g.:

pigeon	ˈpɪdʒ.ən
luncheon	ˈlʌntʃ.ən

entourag|e ˈɒn.tu.rɑːʒ, ˈɑ̃ːn-, -tʊə-, ˌ--ˈ-, (US) ˌɑːn.tuˈrɑːʒ **-es** -ɪz
entr'acte ˈɒn.trækt, ˈɑ̃ːn-, ˌ-ˈ-, (US) ˈɑːnˌtrækt, ɑ̃ːn-, ˌ-ˈ- **-s** -s
entrails ˈen.treɪlz
entrain ɪnˈtreɪn, en-, (US) en-, ɪn- **-s** -z **-ing** -ɪŋ **-ed** -d
entrammel ɪnˈtræm.əl, en-, (US) en-, ɪn- **-s** -z **-(l)ing** -ɪŋ **-(l)ed** -d
entranc|e n *entry, place of entry, etc.:* ˈen.trənts **-es** -ɪz
entranc|e v *put in state of trance, delight:* ɪnˈtrɑːnts, en-, (US) enˈtrænts, ɪn- **-es** -ɪz **-ing** -ɪŋ **-ed** -t **-ement/s** -mənt/s
entrant ˈen.trənt **-s** -s
entrap ɪnˈtræp, en-, (US) en-, ɪn- **-s** -s **-ping** -ɪŋ **-ped** -t **-ment** -mənt
en|treat ɪn|ˈtriːt, en-, (US) en-, ɪn- **-treats** -ˈtriːts **-treating/ly** -ˈtriː.tɪŋ/li, (US) -ˈtriː.t̬ɪŋ/li **-treated** -ˈtriː.tɪd, (US) -ˈtriː.t̬ɪd **-treatment** -ˈtriːt.mənt
entreat|y ɪnˈtriː.t|i, en-, (US) enˈtriː.t̬|i, ɪn- **-ies** -iz
entrechat ˈɑ̃ː*n*.trə.ʃɑː, ˈɒn-, (US) ˌɑːn.trəˈʃɑː, ˈ--- **-s** -z
entrecôte ˈɑ̃ː*n*.trə.kəʊt, ˈɒn-, (US) ˈɑːn.trə.koʊt, ˈɑ̃ːn-, ˌ--ˈ- **-s** -s
entrée ˈɑ̃ː*n*.treɪ, ˈɒn-, (US) ˈɑːn-, ˌ-ˈ- **-s** -z
entremets sing ˈɑ̃ː*n*.trə.meɪ, ˈɒnt-, (US) ˈɑːn.trə-, ˌ--ˈ- **plur** -z
entrench ɪnˈtrent*ʃ*, en-, (US) en-, ɪn- **-es** -ɪz **-ing** -ɪŋ **-ed** -t **-ment/s** -mənt/s
entre nous ˌɑ̃ː*n*.trəˈnuː, ˌɒn-, (US) ˌɑːn-
entrepôt ˈɑ̃ː*n*.trə.pəʊ, ˈɒn-, (US) ˈɑːn.trə.poʊ; (US) ˌ--ˈ- **-s** -z
entrepreneur ˌɒn.trə.prəˈnɜːʳ, ˌɑ̃ː*n*-, -prenˈɜːʳ, (US) ˌɑːn.trə.prəˈnɝː, -ˈnʊr, -ˈnjʊr **-s** -z **-ship** -ʃɪp
entrepreneurial ˌɒn.trə.prəˈnɜː.ri.əl, ˌɑ̃ː*n*-, (US) ˌɑːn.trə.prəˈnʊr.i-, -ˈnɝː-, -ˈnjʊr-
entresol ˈɑ̃ː*n*.trə.sɒl, ˈɒn-, (US) ˈɑːn.trə.sɑːl, ˌ--ˈ- **-s** -z
entropy ˈen.trə.pi
entrust ɪnˈtrʌst, en-, (US) en-, ɪn- **-s** -s **-ing** -ɪŋ **-ed** -ɪd
entr|y ˈen.tr|i **-ies** -iz
entry|ism ˈen.tri|.ɪ.zəm **-ist/s** -ɪst/s
entryphone ˈen.tri.fəʊn, (US) -foʊn **-s** -z
entryway ˈen.tri.weɪ **-s** -z
entwin|e ɪnˈtwaɪn, en-, (US) en-, ɪn- **-es** -z **-ing** -ɪŋ **-ed** -d
entwist ɪnˈtwɪst, en-, (US) en-, ɪn- **-s** -s **-ing** -ɪŋ **-ed** -ɪd
enumerable ɪˈnjuː.mər.ə.bəl, (US) -ˈnuː-, -ˈnjuː-
enumer|ate ɪˈnjuː.mər|.eɪt, (US) -ˈnuː.mə.r|eɪt, -ˈnjuː- **-ates** -eɪts **-ating** -eɪ.tɪŋ, (US) -eɪ.t̬ɪŋ **-ated** -eɪ.tɪd, (US) -eɪ.t̬ɪd **-ator/s** -eɪ.təʳ/z, (US) -eɪ.t̬ɚ/z
enumeration ɪˌnjuː.mərˈeɪ.ʃən, (US) -ˌnuː.məˈreɪ-, -ˌnjuː- **-s** -z
enumerative ɪˈnjuː.mər.ə.tɪv, -eɪ.tɪv, (US) -ˈnuː.mɚ.ə.t̬ɪv, -ˈnjuː-
enunciable ɪˈnʌnt.si.ə.bəl, -ʃi.ə-
enunci|ate ɪˈnʌnt.si|.eɪt, -ʃi- **-ates** -eɪts **-ating** -eɪ.tɪŋ, (US) -eɪ.t̬ɪŋ **-ated** -eɪ.tɪd, (US) -eɪ.t̬ɪd **-ator/s** -eɪ.təʳ/z, (US) -eɪ.t̬ɚ/z
enunciation ɪˌnʌnt.siˈeɪ.ʃən **-s** -z
enunciative ɪˈnʌnt.si.ə.tɪv, -ʃi.ə-, -eɪ.tɪv, (US) -ə.t̬ɪv
enur|e ɪˈnjʊəʳ, (US) -ˈnjʊr **-es** -z **-ing** -ɪŋ **-ed** -d
enuresis ˌen.jʊəˈriː.sɪs, (US) -juːˈ-
envelop ɪnˈvel.əp, en-, (US) en-, ɪn- **-s** -s **-ing** -ɪŋ **-ed** -t **-ment/s** -mənt/s
envelope ˈen.və.ləʊp, ˈɒn-, (US) ˈen.və.loʊp, ˈɑːn- **-s** -s
envenom ɪnˈven.əm, en-, (US) en-, ɪn- **-s** -z **-ing** -ɪŋ **-ed** -d
enviab|le ˈen.vi.ə.b|əl **-ly** -li **-leness** -əl.nəs, -nɪs
envious ˈen.vi.əs **-ly** -li **-ness** -nəs, -nɪs
environ v ɪnˈvaɪə.rən, en-, (US) enˈvaɪ-, ɪn-, -ɚn **-s** -z **-ing** -ɪŋ **-ed** -d
environment ɪnˈvaɪə.rən.mənt, en-, (US) enˈvaɪ-, ɪn-, -ɚn- **-s** -s
environmental ɪnˌvaɪə.rənˈmen.təl, en-, -rəmˈ-, (US) enˌvaɪ.rənˈmen.t̬əl, ɪn-, -ɚnˈ- **-ly** -i
environmental|ism ɪnˌvaɪə.rənˈmen.təl|.ɪ.zəm, en-, -rəmˈ-, (US) enˌvaɪ.rənˈmen.t̬əl-, ɪn-, -ɚnˈ- **-ist/s** -ɪst/s
environmentally-friendly ɪnˌvaɪə.rənˌmen.təl.iˈfrend.li, en-, -rəmˌ-, (US) enˌvaɪ.rənˌmen.t̬əl-, ɪn-, ˌ-ɚn-
environs n ɪnˈvaɪə.rənz, en-; ˈen.vɪ-, -vər.ənz, (US) enˈvaɪ.rənz, ɪn-, -ɚnz
envisag|e ɪnˈvɪz.ɪdʒ, en-, (US) en-, ɪn- **-es** -ɪz **-ing** -ɪŋ **-ed** -d
envision ɪnˈvɪʒ.ən, en-, (US) en-, ɪn- **-s** -z **-ing** -ɪŋ **-ed** -d
envoy ˈen.vɔɪ, (US) ˈɑːn-, ˈen- **-s** -z
env|y ˈen.v|i **-ies** -iz **-ying** -i.ɪŋ **-ied** -id
enwrap ɪnˈræp, en-, (US) en-, ɪn- **-s** -s **-ping** -ɪŋ **-ped** -t
enwreath|e ɪnˈriːð, en-, (US) en-, ɪn- **-es** -z **-ing** -ɪŋ **-ed** -d
enzyme ˈen.zaɪm **-s** -z
enzymolog|y ˌen.zaɪˈmɒl.ə.dʒ|i, (US) -zɪˈ-, -ˈmɑː.lə- **-ist/s** -ɪst/s
Eocene ˈiː.əʊ.siːn, (US) -oʊ-, -ə-
eolian, E~ iˈəʊ.li.ən, (US) -ˈoʊ-
eolith ˈiː.əʊ.lɪθ, (US) -oʊ-, -ə- **-s** -s
eolithic ˌiː.əʊˈlɪθ.ɪk, (US) -oʊˈ-, -əˈ-
eon ˈiː.ɒn, (US) -ɑːn **-s** -z
-eous i.əs, əs
Note: Suffix. Words containing **-eous** are normally stressed on the syllable preceding the suffix, e.g. **aqueous** /ˈeɪ.kwi.əs/.
EP ˌiːˈpiː
EPA ˌiː.piːˈeɪ
epact ˈiː.pækt, ˈep.ækt **-s** -s
Epaminondas epˌæm.ɪˈnɒn.dæs, ɪˌpæm-, -əˈ-, (US) ɪˌpæm.əˈnɑːn-
eparch ˈep.ɑːk, (US) -ɑːrk **-s** -s **-y** -i **-ies** -iz
epaulette, epaulet ˌep.əˈlet, -ɔːˈ-, ˈ---, (US) ˌep.əˈlet, ˈ--- **-s** -s
Epcot® ˈep.kɒt, (US) -kɑːt ˈ**Epcot** ˌ**Center**
epee, épée ˈep.eɪ, ˈeɪ.peɪ, -ˈ-, (US) epˈeɪ; (US) ˈeɪ.peɪ **-s** -z **-ist/s** -ɪst/s

Pronouncing the letters EOU

The vowel letter combination **eou** has two possible pronunciations. After **c** or **g** the pronunciation is /ə/, e.g.:

cretaceous krɪˈteɪ.ʃəs

gorgeous ˈɡɔː.dʒəs ⓤⓢ ˈɡɔːr-

After other letters, the pronunciation is /i.ə/, e.g.:

spontaneous spɒnˈteɪ.ni.əs ⓤⓢ spɑːn-

epenthes|is epˈent.θə.s|ɪs, ɪˈpent-, -θɪ-, ⓤⓢ ɪˈpent.θə- **-es** -iːz
epenthetic ˌep.enˈθet.ɪk, -ənˈ-, ⓤⓢ -enˈθeţ-
epergne iˈpɜːn, epˈɜːn, -ˈeən, ⓤⓢ iˈpɝːn, eɪ- **-s** -z
epexegesis epˌek.sɪˈdʒiː.sɪs, ɪˌpek-, -səˈ-, ⓤⓢ -səˈ-
epexegetic epˌek.sɪˈdʒet.ɪk, ɪˌpek-, -səˈ-, ⓤⓢ -səˈdʒeţ- **-al** -əl **-ally** -əl.i, -li
ephah ˈiː.fə **-s** -z
ephedrine ˈef.ə.drɪn, ˈ-ɪ-, -driːn, ɪˈfed.rɪn, -riːn, ⓤⓢ ɪˈfed.rin; ⓤⓢ ˈef.ə.driːn, -drɪn
ephemer|a ɪˈfem.ər|.ə, efˈem-, əˈfem-, -ˈfiː.mər|-, ⓤⓢ ɪˈfem.ɚ|-, efˈem-, ˈ-r|ə **-as** -əz **-al** -əl
ephemeralit|y ɪˌfem.əˈræl.ə.t|i, efˌem-, əˌfem-, -ˌfiː.məˈ-, -ɪ.t|i, ⓤⓢ ɪˌfem.əˈræl.ə.ţ|i, efˌem- **-ies** -iz
ephemeris ɪˈfem.ər.ɪs, efˈem-, əˈfem-, -ˈfiː.mər-, ⓤⓢ ɪˈfem-, efˈem-
ephemerides ˌef.ɪˈmer.ɪ.diːz, ⓤⓢ -əˈmer.ə-
ephemeron ɪˈfem.ər.ɒn, efˈem-, əˈfem-, -ˈfiː.mər-, -ən, ⓤⓢ ɪˈfem.ə.rɑːn, efˈem-, -rən **-s** -z
ephemerous ɪˈfem.ər.əs, efˈem-, əˈfem-, -ˈfiː.mər-, ⓤⓢ ɪˈfem.ɚ-, efˈem-
Ephesian ɪˈfiː.ʒən, efˈiː-, -ʒi.ən, -zi- **-s** -z
Ephesus ˈef.ə.səs, ˈ-ɪ-
ephod ˈiː.fɒd, ˈef.ɒd, ⓤⓢ -fɑːd, ˈef.ɑːd **-s** -z
Ephraim ˈiː.freɪ.ɪm, -fri-, -əm, -frəm, ⓤⓢ ˈiː.fri.əm, -frəm
Ephron ˈef.rɒn, ˈiː.frɒn, ⓤⓢ -rɑːn
epi- ˈep.ɪ, ⓤⓢ ˈep.ə, ˈ-ɪ; epˈɪ
Note: Prefix. Normally takes either primary or secondary stress on the first syllable, e.g. **epicycle** /ˈep.ɪ.saɪ.kəl/, **epicyclic** /ˌep.ɪˈsɪk.lɪk/, but may also be stressed on the second syllable, e.g. **epigraphy** /eˈpɪɡ.rə.fi/.
epiblast ˈep.ɪ.blæst, ⓤⓢ ˈ-ə-, ˈ-ɪ- **-s** -s
epic ˈep.ɪk **-s** -s
epicanth|ic ˌep.ɪˈkænt.θ|ɪk, ⓤⓢ -əˈ-, -ɪˈ- **-us/es** -əs/ɪz **-i** -aɪ
epicene ˈep.ɪ.siːn, ⓤⓢ ˈ-ə-, ˈ-ɪ- **-s** -z
epicenter ˈep.ɪ.sen.tər, ⓤⓢ ˈ-ə.sen.ţɚ, ˈ-ɪ- **-s** -z
epicentral ˌep.ɪˈsen.trəl, ⓤⓢ -əˈ-, -ɪˈ-
epicentre ˈep.ɪ.sen.tər, ⓤⓢ ˈ-ə.sen.ţɚ, ˈ-ɪ- **-s** -z
epicentr|um ˌep.ɪˈsen.tr|əm, ⓤⓢ -əˈ-, -ɪˈ- **-ums** -əmz **-a** -ə
Epicharmus ˌep.ɪˈkɑː.məs, ⓤⓢ -ˈkɑːr-
epic|ism ˈep.ɪ.s|ɪ.zəm, ⓤⓢ ˈ-ə-, ˈ-ɪ- **-ist/s** -ɪst/s
Epicoene ˈep.ɪ.siː.ni
epicotyl ˌep.ɪˈkɒt.ɪl, ⓤⓢ -əˈkɑː.ţəl, -ɪˈ- **-s** -z
Epictetus ˌep.ɪkˈtiː.təs, ⓤⓢ -ţəs
epicure ˈep.ɪ.kjʊər, ˈ-kjɔːr, ⓤⓢ ˈ-ə.kjʊr, ˈ-ɪ- **-s** -z
epicurean, E~ ˌep.ɪ.kjʊəˈriː.ən, -kjɔːˈ-, ⓤⓢ ˌ-ə.kjʊrˈiː-, ˌ-ɪ- **-s** -z
epicurism ˈep.ɪ.kjʊə.rɪ.zəm, -kjɔː-, ⓤⓢ ˈ-ə.kjʊr.ɪ-, ˈ-ɪ-
Epicurus ˌep.ɪˈkjʊə.rəs, -ˈkjɔː-, ⓤⓢ -ˈkjʊr.əs
epicycle ˈep.ɪ.saɪ.kəl, ⓤⓢ ˈ-ə-, ˈ-ɪ- **-s** -z
epicyclic ˌep.ɪˈsaɪ.klɪk, -ˈsɪk.lɪk, ⓤⓢ ˌ-ə-, ˌ-ɪ-
epicycloid ˌep.ɪˈsaɪ.klɔɪd, ⓤⓢ ˌ-ə-, ˌ-ɪ- **-s** -z
Epidaurus ˌep.ɪˈdɔː.rəs, ⓤⓢ -əˈdɔːr.əs
epideictic ˌep.ɪˈdaɪk.tɪk, ⓤⓢ -əˈ-, -ɪˈ-
epidemic ˌep.ɪˈdem.ɪk, ⓤⓢ -əˈ-, -ɪˈ- **-s** -s **-al** -əl **-ally** -əl.i, -li
epidemiological ˌep.ɪˌdiː.mi.əˈlɒdʒ.ɪ.kəl, ⓤⓢ -əˌdiː.mi.əˈlɑː.dʒɪ-, -ɪˌ-, -ˌdem.i- **-ly** -i
epidemiolog|y ˌep.ɪˌdiː.miˈɒl.ə.dʒ|i, ⓤⓢ -əˌdiː.miˈɑː.lə-, -ɪˌ-, -ˌdem.iˈ- **-ist/s** -ɪst/s
epiderm|al ˌep.ɪˈdɜː.m|əl, ⓤⓢ -əˈdɝː-, -ɪˈ- **-ic** -ɪk **-oid** -ɔɪd
epidermis ˌep.ɪˈdɜː.mɪs, ⓤⓢ -əˈdɝː-, -ɪˈ-
epidiascope ˌep.ɪˈdaɪ.ə.skəʊp, ⓤⓢ -əˈdaɪ.ə.skoʊp, -ɪˈ- **-s** -s
epididymis ˌep.ɪˈdɪd.ə.mɪs, ˈ-ɪ-, ⓤⓢ -əˈ-, -ɪˈ- **epididymides** ˌep.ɪ.dɪˈdɪm.ɪ.diːz, ⓤⓢ ˌ-ə-, ˌ-ɪ-
epidural ˌep.ɪˈdʒʊə.rəl, -ˈdjʊə-, -ˈdʒɔː-, -ˈdjɔː-, ⓤⓢ -əˈdʊr.əl, -ɪˈ-, -ˈdjʊr- **-s** -z
epige|al ˌep.ɪˈdʒiː|.əl, ⓤⓢ -əˈ-, -ɪˈ- **-an** -ən
epigene ˈep.ɪ.dʒiːn, ⓤⓢ ˈ-ə-, ˈ-ɪ-
epigenesis ˌep.ɪˈdʒen.ə.sɪs, ⓤⓢ -əˈ-, -ɪˈ-
epiglott|al ˌep.ɪˈɡlɒt|.əl, ˈep.ɪ.ɡlɒt-, ⓤⓢ ˌep.əˈɡlɑː.ţ|əl, -ɪˈ- **-ic** -ɪk
epiglottis ˌep.ɪˈɡlɒt.ɪs, ˈep.ɪ.ɡlɒt-, ⓤⓢ -əˈɡlɑː.ţɪs, -ɪˈ- **-es** -ɪz
epigone ˈep.ɪ.ɡəʊn, ⓤⓢ -ə.ɡoʊn, -ɪ- **-s** -z
Epigoni epˈɪ.ɡə.naɪ, ɪˈpɪɡ-, -niː
epigram ˈep.ɪ.ɡræm, ⓤⓢ ˈ-ə-, ˈ-ɪ- **-s** -z
epigrammatic ˌep.ɪ.ɡrəˈmæt.ɪk, ⓤⓢ -ə.ɡrəˈmæţ-, ˌ-ɪ- **-al** -əl **-ally** -əl.i, -li
epigrammatist ˌep.ɪˈɡræm.ə.tɪst, ⓤⓢ -əˈɡræm.ə.ţɪst, -ɪˈ- **-s** -s
epigrammatiz|e, -is|e ˌep.ɪˈɡræm.ə.taɪz, ⓤⓢ -əˈ-, -ɪˈ- **-es** -ɪz **-ing** -ɪŋ **-ed** -d
epigraph ˈep.ɪ.ɡrɑːf, -ɡræf, ⓤⓢ -ə.ɡræf, ˈ-ɪ- **-s** -s
epigrapher epˈɪɡ.rə.fər, ɪˈpɪɡ-, ⓤⓢ -fɚ **-s** -z
epigraphic ˌep.ɪˈɡræf.ɪk, ⓤⓢ -əˈ-, -ɪˈ-
epigraph|y epˈɪɡ.rə.f|i, ɪˈpɪɡ- **-ist/s** -ɪst/s
epilepsy ˈep.ɪ.lep.si, ⓤⓢ ˈ-ə-, ˈ-ɪ-
epileptic ˌep.ɪˈlep.tɪk, ⓤⓢ -əˈ-, -ɪˈ- **-s** -s **-al** -əl
epilog ˈep.ɪ.lɒɡ, ⓤⓢ -ə.lɑːɡ, ˈ-ɪ-, -lɔːɡ **-s** -z
epilogic ˌep.ɪˈlɒdʒ.ɪk, -əˈ-, ⓤⓢ -ɪˈ-, -əˈlɑː.dʒɪk
epilogiz|e, -is|e epˈɪl.ə.dʒaɪz, ɪˈpɪl- **-es** -ɪz **-ing** -ɪŋ **-ed** -d
epilogue ˈep.ɪ.lɒɡ, ⓤⓢ -ə.lɑːɡ, ˈ-ɪ-, -lɔːɡ **-s** -z
Epimenides ˌep.ɪˈmen.ɪ.diːz, -ə.diːz, ⓤⓢ -əˈ-, -ɪˈ-
Epinal ˈep.i.næl, ⓤⓢ ˌeɪ.piːˈnɑːl
epiphan|y, E~ ɪˈpɪf.ən|.i, epˈɪf-, əˈpɪf-, ⓤⓢ ɪˈpɪf.ə.n|i **-ies** -iz
epiphyte ˈep.ɪ.faɪt, ⓤⓢ ˈ-ə-, ˈ-ɪ- **-s** -s
Epirus epˈaɪə.rəs, ɪˈpaɪə-, ⓤⓢ ɪˈpaɪ-
episcopac|y ɪˈpɪs.kə.pə.s|i, epˈɪs- **-ies** -iz
episcopal ɪˈpɪs.kə.pəl, epˈɪs- **-ly** -i
episcopalian, E~ ɪˌpɪs.kəˈpeɪ.li.ən, epˌɪs-, ⓤⓢ -ˈpeɪ.li.ən, -ˈpeɪl.jən **-s** -z **-ism** -ɪ.zəm
episcopate ɪˈpɪs.kə.pət, epˈɪs-, -pɪt, -peɪt **-s** -s
episcope ˈep.ɪ.skəʊp, ⓤⓢ -ə.skoʊp, ˈ-ɪ- **-s** -s
episcopiz|e, -is|e ɪˈpɪs.kə.paɪz, epˈɪs- **-es** -ɪz **-ing** -ɪŋ **-ed** -d
episiotom|y ɪˌpɪs.iˈɒt.ə.m|i, epˌɪs-, ɪˌpɪz-, epˌɪz-, -ˌiː.siˈ-; ˌep.ɪ.ziˈ-, ⓤⓢ ɪˌpiː.siˈɑː.ţə-; ⓤⓢ ˌep.i.saɪˈ- **-ies** -iz
episode ˈep.ɪ.səʊd, ⓤⓢ -ə.soʊd, ˈ-ɪ- **-s** -z
episodic ˌep.ɪˈsɒd.ɪk, ⓤⓢ -əˈsɑː.dɪk, -ɪˈ- **-al** -əl **-ally** -əl.i, -li
epistemic ˌep.ɪˈstiː.mɪk, -ˈstem.ɪk, ⓤⓢ -əˈ-, -ɪˈ-
epistemological ɪˌpɪs.tɪ.məˈlɒdʒ.ɪ.kəl, epˌɪs-, ˌ-tə-, ⓤⓢ -ˈlɑː.dʒɪ- **-ly** -li
epistemology ɪˌpɪs.təˈmɒl.ə.dʒi, epˌɪs-, -tɪˈ-, ⓤⓢ -təˈmɑː.lə-
epistle, E~ ɪˈpɪs.əl, epˈɪs-, ⓤⓢ ɪˈpɪs- **-s** -z
epistolary ɪˈpɪs.təl.ər.i, epˈɪs-, ⓤⓢ ɪˈpɪs.təl.er-
epistoliz|e, -is|e ɪˈpɪs.təl.aɪz, epˈɪs-, ⓤⓢ ɪˈpɪs.tə.laɪz **-es** -ɪz **-ing** -ɪŋ **-ed** -d
epistyle ˈep.ɪ.staɪl, ⓤⓢ ˈ-ə-, ˈ-ɪ- **-s** -z
epitaph ˈep.ɪ.tɑːf, -tæf, ⓤⓢ -ə.tæf, ˈ-ɪ- **-s** -s

Epithalamion ˌep.ɪ.θəˈleɪ.mi.ən
epithalami|um ˌep.ɪ.θəˈleɪ.mi|.əm -a -ə -ums -əmz
epitheli|um ˌep.ɪˈθiː.li|.əm, ⓤⓢ -əˈ-, -ɪˈ- -ums -əmz -a -ə
epithet ˈep.ɪ.θet, ⓤⓢ ˈ-ə-, ˈ-ɪ-, -θet, -θət -s -s
epithetic ˌep.ɪˈθet.ɪk, ⓤⓢ -əˈθeţ-, ˌ-ɪ-
epitome ɪˈpɪt.ə.mi, epˈɪt-, əˈpɪt-, ⓤⓢ ɪˈpɪţ- -s -z
epitomic ˌep.ɪˈtɒm.ɪk, ⓤⓢ -ˈtɑː.mɪk -al -əl
epitomist ɪˈpɪt.ə.mɪst, epˈɪt-, ⓤⓢ ɪˈpɪţ- -s -s
epitomiz|e, -is|e ɪˈpɪt.ə.maɪz, epˈɪt-, ⓤⓢ ɪˈpɪţ- -es -ɪz -ing -ɪŋ -ed -d
epoch ˈiː.pɒk, ˈep.ək, ⓤⓢ ˈep.ək, -ɑːk, ˌiːˈpɑːk -s -s
epochal ˈiː.pɒk.əl, ˈep.ɒk-, -ə.kəl; iːˈpɒk.əl, ⓤⓢ ˈep.ə.kəl; ⓤⓢ -ɑː.kəl
epoch-making ˈiː.pɒkˌmeɪ.kɪŋ, ⓤⓢ ˈep.əkˌ-, -ɑːkˌ-
epode ˈep.əʊd, ⓤⓢ -oʊd -s -z
eponym ˈep.ə.nɪm -s -z
eponymous ɪˈpɒn.ɪ.məs, epˈɒn-, ˈ-ə-, ⓤⓢ ɪˈpɑː.nə-
eponymy ɪˈpɒn.ɪ.mi, epˈɒn-, ˈ-ə-, ⓤⓢ ɪˈpɑː.nə-
epos ˈep.ɒs, ˈiː.pɒs, ⓤⓢ ˈep.ɑːs -es -ɪz
Epos, EPOS ˈiː.pɒs, ⓤⓢ -pɑːs
epox|y ɪˈpɒk.si, epˈɒk-, ⓤⓢ ɪˈpɑːk- -ies -ɪz -ing -ɪŋ -ied -ɪd **eˌpoxy ˈresin**
Epping ˈep.ɪŋ
Epps eps
EPROM ˈiː.prɒm, ⓤⓢ -prɑːm -s -z
epsilon epˈsaɪ.lən, -lɒn; ˈep.sɪ.lən, -sə-, -lɒn, ⓤⓢ ˈep.sə.lɑːn, -lən -s -z
Epsom ˈep.səm **ˈEpsom ˌsalts; ˌEpsom ˈsalts**
Epstein ˈep.staɪn
Epstein-Barr ˌep.staɪnˈbɑːʳ, -staɪmˈ-, ⓤⓢ -staɪn.ˈbɑːr
Epworth ˈep.wəθ, -wɜːθ, ⓤⓢ -wɚθ, -wɝːθ
epylli|on epˈɪl.i|.ɒn, ɪˈpɪl-, -ən, ⓤⓢ -ɑːn, -ən -a -ə
equability ˌek.wəˈbɪl.ə.ti, ˌiː.kwəˈ-, -ɪ.ti, ⓤⓢ -ə.ţi
equab|le ˈek.wə.b|əl, ˈiː.kwə- -ly -li -leness -əl.nəs, -nɪs
equal ˈiː.kwəl -ly -i -ness -nəs, -nɪs -s -z -(l)ing -ɪŋ -(l)ed -d **ˌEqual Opporˈtunities Comˌmission; ˌEqual ˈRights Aˌmendment; ˌequal ˈrights; ˈequals ˌsign**
equalit|y iˈkwɒl.ə.t|i, iː-, -ɪ.t|i, ⓤⓢ -ˈkwɑː.lə.ţ|i, -ˈkwɔː- -ies -iz
equalization, -isa- ˌiː.kwəl.aɪˈzeɪ.ʃən, -ɪˈ-, ⓤⓢ -əˈ- -s -z
equaliz|e, -is|e ˈiː.kwəl.aɪz, ⓤⓢ -kwə.laɪz -es -ɪz -ing -ɪŋ -ed -d
equalizer, -iser ˈiː.kwə.laɪ.zəʳ, ⓤⓢ -zɚ -s -z
equanimity ˌek.wəˈnɪm.ə.ti, ˌiː.kwəˈ-, -ɪ.ti, ⓤⓢ -ə.ţi
equanimous ɪˈkwæn.ɪ.məs, iː-, ekˈwæn-, -ˈwɒn-, -ə.məs, ⓤⓢ ɪˈkwæn-, iː-, ekˈwæn- -ly -li -ness -nəs, -nɪs
e|quate ɪˈkweɪt, iː- -quates -kweɪts -quating -kweɪ.tɪŋ, ⓤⓢ -kweɪ.ţɪŋ -quated -kweɪ.tɪd, ⓤⓢ -kweɪ.ţɪd -quatable -kweɪ.tə.bəl, ⓤⓢ -kweɪ.ţə.bəl
equation ɪˈkweɪ.ʒən, ⓤⓢ ɪˈ-, iːˈ- -s -z
equational ɪˈkweɪ.ʒən.əl, iː-
equative ɪˈkweɪ.tɪv, ⓤⓢ -ţɪv
equator ɪˈkweɪ.təʳ, ⓤⓢ -ţɚ -s -z
equatorial ˌek.wəˈtɔː.ri.əl, ˌiː.kwəˈ-, ⓤⓢ -ˈtɔːr.i- -ly -i
equerr|y ˈek.wə.r|i; ɪˈkwer|.i, ⓤⓢ ˈek.wɚ|.i; ⓤⓢ ɪˈkwer- -ies -iz

> Note: The pronunciation at court is /ɪˈkwer.i/.

equestrian ɪˈkwes.tri.ən, ekˈwes-, ⓤⓢ ɪˈkwes- -s -z -ism -ɪ.zəm
equestrienne ɪˌkwes.triˈen, ekˌwes-, ⓤⓢ ɪˌkwes- -s -z
equi- ˈiː.kwɪ, ˈek.wɪ, -wi, -wə; ɪˈkwɪ
Note: Prefix. Either takes primary or secondary stress on the first syllable, e.g. **equinox** /ˈiː.kwɪ.nɒks/ ⓤⓢ /-nɑːks/, **equinoctial** /ˌiː.kwɪnˈɒk.ʃəl/ ⓤⓢ /-ˈnɑːk-/, or primary or secondary stress on the second syllable, e.g. **equivocate** /ɪˈkwɪv.ə.keɪt/, **equivocation** /ɪˌkwɪv.əˈkeɪ.ʃən/.
equiangular ˌiː.kwiˈæŋ.gjʊ.ləʳ, ˌek.wiˈ-, -gjə-, ⓤⓢ -lɚ
equidistant ˌiː.kwɪˈdɪs.tənt, ˌek.wɪˈ-, -wəˈ- -ly -li
equilateral ˌiː.kwɪˈlæt.ər.əl, ˌek.wɪˈ-, -wəˈ-, ⓤⓢ -ˈlæţ-, ˌek.wəˈ-
equilib|rate ˌiː.kwɪˈlaɪ.b|reɪt, ˌek.wɪˈ-, -wəˈ-, -ˈlɪb|.reɪt; iːˈkwɪl.ɪ.b|reɪt, ɪ-, ⓤⓢ ɪˈkwɪl-, iː- -rates -reɪts -rating -reɪ.tɪŋ, ⓤⓢ -reɪ.ţɪŋ -rated -reɪ.tɪd, ⓤⓢ -reɪ.ţɪd
equilibration ˌiː.kwɪ.laɪˈbreɪ.ʃən, ˌek.wɪ-, -wə-, -lɪˈbreɪ-; iːˌkwɪl.ɪˈ-, ɪ-, ⓤⓢ ɪˌkwɪl.ɪˈ-, iːˌ-
equilibrist iːˈkwɪl.ɪ.brɪst, ɪ-; ˌiː.kwɪˈlɪb.rɪst, ˌek.wɪˈ-, -wəˈ-, ⓤⓢ ɪˈkwɪl.ə.brɪst, iː-; ⓤⓢ ˌiː.kwəˈlɪb.rɪst -s -s
equilibrium ˌiː.kwɪˈlɪb.ri.əm, ˌek.wɪˈ-, -wəˈ-
equimultiple ˌiː.kwɪˈmʌl.tɪ.pəl, ˌek.wɪˈ-, -wəˈ-, -tə-, ⓤⓢ -tə- -s -z
equine ˈek.waɪn, ˈiː.kwaɪn, ⓤⓢ ˈiː.kwaɪn, ˈek.waɪn
equinoctial ˌiː.kwɪˈnɒk.ʃəl, ˌek.wɪˈ-, -wəˈ-, ⓤⓢ -ˈnɑːk- -s -z
equinox ˈiː.kwɪ.nɒks, ˈek.wɪ-, -wə-, ⓤⓢ -nɑːks -es -ɪz
equip ɪˈkwɪp -s -s -ping -ɪŋ -ped -t
equipag|e ˈek.wɪ.pɪdʒ, -wə- -es -ɪz
equipment ɪˈkwɪp.mənt
equipois|e ˈiː.kwɪ.pɔɪz, ˈek.wɪ-, -wə- -es -ɪz -ing -ɪŋ -ed -d
equipollent ˌiː.kwɪˈpɒl.ənt, ˌek.wɪˈ-, -wəˈ-, ⓤⓢ -ˈpɑː.lənt
equitab|le ˈek.wɪ.tə.b|əl, -wə-, ⓤⓢ -ţə- -ly -li -leness -əl.nəs, -nɪs
equitation ˌek.wɪˈteɪ.ʃən, -wəˈ-
equit|y, E~ ˈek.wɪ.t|i, -wə-, ⓤⓢ -ţ|i -ies -iz
equivalen|ce ɪˈkwɪv.əl.ənt|s -cy -si
equivalent ɪˈkwɪv.əl.ənt -s -s -ly -li
equivocal ɪˈkwɪv.ə.kəl, ˈ-ɪ- -ly -i -ness -nəs, -nɪs
equivo|cate ɪˈkwɪv.ə|.keɪt -cates -keɪts -cating -keɪ.tɪŋ, ⓤⓢ -keɪ.ţɪŋ -cated -keɪ.tɪd, ⓤⓢ -keɪ.ţɪd -cator/s -keɪ.təʳ/z, ⓤⓢ -keɪ.ţɚ/z
equivocation ɪˌkwɪv.əˈkeɪ.ʃən -s -z
equivoque, equivoke ˈek.wɪ.vəʊk, -wə-, ⓤⓢ -voʊk -s -s
Equuleus ekˈwʊl.i.əs
er ɜːʳ, ⓤⓢ ɝː
ER ˌiːˈɑːʳ, ⓤⓢ -ˈɑːr
-er əʳ, ⓤⓢ ɚ
Note: Suffix. Normally unstressed, e.g. **paint** /peɪnt/, **painter** /ˈpeɪn.təʳ/ ⓤⓢ /-tɚ/, **soon** /suːn/, **sooner** /ˈsuː.nəʳ/ ⓤⓢ /-nɚ/.
era ˈɪə.rə, ⓤⓢ ˈɪr.ə, ˈer- -s -z
ERA ˌiː.ɑːʳˈeɪ, ⓤⓢ -ɑːrˈ-
eradi|ate ɪˈreɪ.di|.eɪt, iː- -ates -eɪts -ating -eɪ.tɪŋ, ⓤⓢ -eɪ.ţɪŋ -ated -eɪ.tɪd, ⓤⓢ -eɪ.ţɪd
eradiation ɪˌreɪ.diˈeɪ.ʃən, iː-
eradicable ɪˈræd.ɪ.kə.bəl
eradi|cate ɪˈræd.ɪ|.keɪt -cates -keɪts -cating -keɪ.tɪŋ, ⓤⓢ -keɪ.ţɪŋ -cated -keɪ.tɪd, ⓤⓢ -keɪ.ţɪd
eradication ɪˌræd.ɪˈkeɪ.ʃən, -əˈ-
eradicative ɪˈræd.ɪ.kə.tɪv, -keɪ-, ⓤⓢ -kə.ţɪv
Érard ˈer.ɑːd, ⓤⓢ eɪˈrɑːrd, ˈer.ɑːrd -s -z
eras|e ɪˈreɪz, ⓤⓢ -ˈreɪs -es -ɪz -ing -ɪŋ -ed -d -er/s -əʳ/z, ⓤⓢ -ɚ/z -able -ə.bəl
erasion ɪˈreɪ.ʒən -s -z
Erasmian ɪˈræz.mi.ən, iˈræz- -s -z -ism -ɪ.zəm
Erasmus ɪˈræz.məs, iˈræz-
Erastian ɪˈræs.ti.ən, iˈræs- -s -z -ism -ɪ.zəm
Erastus ɪˈræs.təs, iˈræs-
erasure ɪˈreɪ.ʒəʳ, ⓤⓢ -ʃɚ -s -z
erbium ˈɜː.bi.əm, ⓤⓢ ˈɝː-
Erdington ˈɜː.dɪŋ.tən, ⓤⓢ ˈɝː-
ere eəʳ, ⓤⓢ er
Erebus ˈer.ɪ.bəs, ˈ-ə-
Erec ˈɪə.rek, ⓤⓢ ˈiː.rek, ˈer.ek
Erechtheum ˌer.ekˈθiː.əm, -ɪkˈ-, -əkˈ-
Erechtheus ɪˈrek.θjuːs, erˈek-, -θi.əs
erect ɪˈrekt -ly -li -ness -nəs, -nɪs -s -s -ing -ɪŋ -ed -ɪd
erectile ɪˈrek.taɪl, ⓤⓢ -təl, -taɪl
erection ɪˈrek.ʃən -s -z
erector ɪˈrek.təʳ, ⓤⓢ -tɚ -s -z
eremite ˈer.ɪ.maɪt, ˈ-ə- -s -s
eremitic ˌer.ɪˈmɪt.ɪk, -əˈ-, ⓤⓢ -əˈmɪţ- -al -əl
erepsin ɪˈrep.sɪn
Eretri|a ɪˈret.ri|.ə, erˈet- -an/s -ən/z
Erewash ˈer.ɪ.wɒʃ, ⓤⓢ -wɑːʃ, -wɔːʃ
erewhile eəˈ*h*waɪl, ⓤⓢ erˈ-
Erewhon ˈer.ɪ.*h*wɒn, ⓤⓢ -*h*wɑːn, -*h*wʌn
Erfurt ˈeə.fɜːt; *as if German:* -fʊət; ⓤⓢ ˈer.fʊrt, -fɝːt
erg ɜːg, ⓤⓢ ɝːg -s -z
ergative ˈɜː.gə.tɪv, ⓤⓢ ˈɝː.gə.ţɪv

ergativity ˌɜː.gəˈtɪv.ə.ti, -ɪ.ti, (US) ˌɝː.gəˈtɪv.ə.t̬i
ergo ˈɜː.gəʊ, ˈeə-, (US) ˈer.goʊ, ˈɝː-
ergon ˈɜː.gɒn, (US) ˈɝː.gɑːn -s -z
ergonic ɜːˈgɒn.ɪk, (US) ɝːˈgɑː.nɪk -s -s -ally -əl.i, -li
ergonomic ˌɜː.gəˈnɒm.ɪk, (US) ˌɝː.gəˈnɑː.mɪk -s -s
ergonomical ˌɜː.gəˈnɒm.ɪ.kəl, (US) ˌɝː.gəˈnɑː.mɪ- -ly -i
ergonomist ɜːˈgɒn.ə.mɪst, (US) ɝːˈgɑː.nə- -s -s
ergosterol ɜːˈgɒs.tə.rɒl, -trə-, (US) ɝːˈgɑː.stə.rɑːl, -rɔːl, -roʊl
ergot ˈɜː.gət, -gɒt, (US) ˈɝː.gət, -gɑːt -ism -ɪ.zəm
Eric ˈer.ɪk
Erica, erica ˈer.ɪ.kə
ericaceous ˌer.ɪˈkeɪ.ʃəs
Ericht ˈer.ɪxt
Eric(k)son ˈer.ɪk.sən
Ericsson® ˈer.ɪ.ksən
Erie ˈɪə.ri, (US) ˈɪr.i
Erik ˈer.ɪk
Erika ˈer.ɪ.kə
Eriksson ˈer.ɪk.sən
Erin ˈɪə.rɪn, ˈer.ɪn, ˈeə.rɪn, (US) ˈer.ɪn, ˈɪr-
Eris ˈer.ɪs, (US) ˈɪr-, ˈer-
eristic erˈɪs.tɪk, (US) ɪˈrɪs-, erˈɪs- -s -s
Erith ˈɪə.rɪθ, (US) ˈɪr.ɪθ
Eritre|a ˌer.ɪˈtreɪ|.ə, -əˈtreɪ-, -ˈtriː-, (US) -ˈtriː- -an/s -ən/z
Erle ɜːl, (US) ɝːl
erl-king ˈɜːl.kɪŋ, ˌ-ˈ-, (US) ˈɝːl.kɪŋ, ˈerl- -s -z
ERM ˌiː.ɑːrˈem, (US) -ɑːrˈ-
ermine ˈɜː.mɪn, (US) ˈɝː- -s -z -d -d
erne, E~ ɜːn, (US) ɝːn -s -z
Ernest ˈɜː.nɪst, -nəst, (US) ˈɝː-
Ernie ˈɜː.ni, (US) ˈɝː-
Ernle ˈɜːn.li, (US) ˈɝːn-
Ernst ɜːntst; *as if German:* eəntst; (US) ɝːntst; *as if German:* (US) ernst
erod|e ɪˈrəʊd, (US) -ˈroʊd -es -z -ing -ɪŋ -ed -ɪd
erogenous ɪˈrɒdʒ.ɪ.nəs, erˈɒdʒ-, əˈrɒdʒ-, ˈ-ə-, (US) ɪˈrɑː.dʒɪ-, -dʒə-
Eroica erˈəʊ.ɪ.kə, ɪˈrəʊ-, əˈrəʊ-, (US) ɪˈroʊ-, erˈoʊ-
Eros ˈɪə.rɒs, ˈer.ɒs, (US) ˈer.ɑːs, ˈɪr-, ˈer.oʊs
erosion ɪˈrəʊ.ʒən, (US) -ˈroʊ- -s -z
erosive ɪˈrəʊ.sɪv, -zɪv, (US) -ˈroʊ-
erotic ɪˈrɒt.ɪk, (US) -ˈrɑː.t̬ɪk -s -s -a -ə -ally -əl.i, -li
eroticism ɪˈrɒt.ɪ.sɪ.zəm, ˈ-ə-, (US) -ˈrɑː.t̬ə-
eroticization, -isa- ɪˌrɒt.ɪ.saɪˈzeɪ.ʃən, ˌ-ə-, -sɪˈ-, (US) -ˌrɑː.t̬ə.səˈ-
eroticiz|e, -is|e ɪˈrɒt.ɪ.saɪz, ˈ-ə-, (US) -ˈrɑː.t̬ə- -es -ɪs -ing -ɪŋ -ed -d
erotogenic ɪˌrɒt.əˈdʒen.ɪk, -ˌrəʊ.təˈ-, (US) ɪˌrɑː.t̬əˈdʒen-, -ˌroʊ- -ally -əl.i, -li
erotomani|a ɪˌrɒt.əʊˈmeɪ.ni|.ə, -ˌrəʊ.təʊˈ-, (US) ɪˌrɑː.t̬əˈmeɪ.ni|.ə, -ˌroʊ-, -njə -ac/s -æk/s
err ɜːr, (US) ɝː, er -s -z -ing -ɪŋ -ed -d
errand ˈer.ənd -s -z
errant ˈer.ənt -ly -li -ry -ri
errata (plural of **erratum**) erˈɑː.tə, ɪˈrɑː-, -ˈreɪ-, (US) -t̬ə
erratic ɪˈræt.ɪk, erˈæt-, (US) ɪˈræt̬- -ally -əl.i, -li
errat|um erˈɑː.t|əm, ɪˈrɑː-, -ˈreɪ-, (US) -t̬|əm -a -ə
Errol(l) ˈer.əl
erroneous ɪˈrəʊ.ni.əs, erˈəʊ-, (US) əˈroʊ-, erˈoʊ-, ɪˈroʊ- -ly -li -ness -nəs, -nɪs
error ˈer.əʳ, (US) -ɚ -s -z
ersatz ˈeə.sæts; *as if German:* ˈeə.zɑːts; (US) ˈer.zɑːts, -ˈ-
Erse ɜːs, (US) ɝːs
Erskine ˈɜː.skɪn, (US) ˈɝː-
erst ɜːst, (US) ɝːst
erstwhile ˈɜːst.*h*waɪl, (US) ˈɝːst-
erubescen|ce ˌer.ʊˈbes.ən|*t*s, -uːˈ- -cy -*t*si -t -t
eruct ɪˈrʌkt, iː- -s -s -ing -ɪŋ -ed -ɪd
eruc|tate ɪˈrʌk|.teɪt, iː- -tates -teɪts -tating -teɪ.tɪŋ, (US) -teɪ.t̬ɪŋ -tated -teɪ.tɪd, (US) -teɪ.t̬ɪd
eructation ˌiː.rʌkˈteɪ.ʃən, ˌer.ʌk-, -əkˈ-; ɪˌrʌkˈ-, (US) ˌiː.rʌkˈ-, ɪˌrʌkˈ- -s -z
erudite ˈer.ʊ.daɪt, -jʊ-, (US) -jə-, -ə-, -juː-, -uː- -ly -li -ness -nəs, -nɪs
erudition ˌer.ʊˈdɪʃ.ən, -jʊˈ-, (US) -juˈ-, -uˈ-, -jəˈ-, -əˈ-
erupt ɪˈrʌpt -s -s -ing -ɪŋ -ed -ɪd
eruption ɪˈrʌp.ʃən -s -z
eruptive ɪˈrʌp.tɪv -ly -li -ness -nəs, -nɪs
Ervine ˈɜː.vɪn, (US) ˈɝː-
Erving ˈɜː.vɪŋ, (US) ˈɝː-
erysipelas ˌer.ɪˈsɪp.əl.əs, -əˈ-, -ɪ.ləs, -lɪs
erythema ˌer.ɪˈθiː.mə, -əˈ-
erythrocyte ɪˈrɪθ.rəʊ.saɪt, (US) erˈɪθ.roʊ- -s -s
erythrocytic ɪˌrɪθ.rəʊˈsɪt.ɪk, (US) erˌɪθ.roʊˈsɪt̬-
erythromycin ɪˌrɪθ.rəʊˈmaɪ.sɪn, əˌrɪθ-, (US) ɪ.rɪθ.roʊˈ-, -rəˈ-
Erzerum ˈeə.zə.ruːm, (US) ˈer-
Esau ˈiː.sɔː, (US) -sɑː, -sɔː
Esbjerg ˈes.bjɜːg, (US) -bjerg
escalad|e ˌes.kəˈleɪd, ˈ--- -es -z -ing -ɪŋ -ed -ɪd
esca|late ˈes.kə|.leɪt -lates -leɪts -lating -leɪ.tɪŋ, (US) -leɪ.t̬ɪŋ -lated -leɪ.tɪd, (US) -leɪ.t̬ɪd
escalation ˌes.kəˈleɪ.ʃən
escalator ˈes.kə.leɪ.təʳ, (US) -t̬ɚ -s -z
escal(l)op ɪˈskɒl.əp, esˈkɒl-, -ˈkæl-, -ɒp; ˈes.kə.lɒp, (US) esˈkɑː.ləp, ɪˈskɑː-, -ˈskæl- -ed -t
escalope ˈes.kə.lɒp, ˈɪs-, -ləp; esˈkæl.əp, -ɒp, (US) ˌes.kəˈloʊp -s -s
escapade ˌes.kəˈpeɪd, ˈ--- -s -z
escap|e ɪˈskeɪp, esˈkeɪp, əˈskeɪp -es -s -ing -ɪŋ -ed -t -ement/s -mənt/s
escapee ɪˌskeɪˈpiː, ˌes.keɪˈ- -s -z
escap|ism ɪˈskeɪ.p|ɪ.zəm, esˈkeɪ- -ist/s -ɪst/s
escapolog|y ˌes.kəˈpɒl.ə.dʒ|i, -keɪˈ-, (US) -keɪˈpɑː.lə- -ist/s -ɪst/s
escargot ɪˈskɑː.gəʊ, esˈkɑː-; *as if French:* ˌes.kɑːˈgəʊ; (US) ˌes.kɑːrˈgoʊ -s -z
escarole ˈes.kə.rəʊl, (US) -kə.roʊl
escarp ɪˈskɑːp, esˈkɑːp, (US) esˈkɑːrp -s -s -ing -ɪŋ -ed -t
escarpment ɪˈskɑːp.mənt, esˈkɑːp-, (US) esˈkɑːrp- -s -s
-esce ˈes
Note: Suffix. Always carries primary stress, e.g. **convalesce** /ˌkɒn.vəˈles/ (US) /ˌkɑːn-/.
-escen|ce ˈes.ən|*t*s -t -t
Note: Suffix. Always carries primary stress, e.g. **convalescence** /ˌkɒn.vəˈles.ən*t*s/ (US) /ˌkɑːn-/.
eschar ˈes.kɑːʳ, (US) -kɑːr, -kɚ -s -z
eschatological ˌes.kə.təˈlɒdʒ.ɪ.kəl, -kæt.əˈ-, (US) -kə.t̬əˈlɑː.dʒɪ-; (US) esˌkæt̬.əlˈɑː-
eschatolog|y ˌes.kəˈtɒl.ə.dʒ|i, (US) -ˈtɑː.lə- -ist/s -ɪst/s
es|cheat ɪs|ˈtʃiːt, es- -cheats -ˈtʃiːts -cheating -ˈtʃiː.tɪŋ, (US) -ˈtʃiː.t̬ɪŋ -cheated -ˈtʃiː.tɪd, (US) -ˈtʃiː.t̬ɪd
Escher ˈeʃ.əʳ, (US) -ɚ
eschew ɪsˈtʃuː, es-, (US) es-, ɪs- -s -z -ing -ɪŋ -ed -d
eschscholtzia ɪˈskɒl.ʃə, esˈkɒl-, -tʃə; ɪʃˈɒlt.si.ə, eʃ-, əˈʃɒlt-, -ˈskɒlt-, (US) eʃˈoʊlt.si.ə -s -z
Escoffier ɪˈskɒf.i.eɪ, esˈkɒf-, (US) ˌes.kɑːˈfjeɪ
Escom ˈes.kɒm, -kɑːm, (US) -kɑːm
Escombe ˈes.kəm
Escondido ˌes.kənˈdiː.dəʊ, (US) -doʊ
Escorial ˌes.kɒr.iˈɑːl, -ˈæl; esˈkɔː.ri.æl, -ɑːl, (US) ˌes.kɔːr.iˈæl; (US) esˌkɔːr-, -ˌɑːl
escort, E~® **n** ˈes.kɔːt, (US) -kɔːrt -s -s
escor|t v ɪˈskɔː|t, esˈkɔː|t; ˈes.kɔː|t, (US) esˈkɔːr|t, ɪˈskɔːr|t; (US) ˈes.kɔːr|t -ts -ts -ting -tɪŋ, (US) -t̬ɪŋ -ted -tɪd, (US) -t̬ɪd
Escott ˈes.kɒt, (US) -kɑːt
Escow ˈes.kəʊ, (US) -koʊ
escritoire ˌes.kriːˈtwɑːʳ, ˈ---, (US) ˌes.kriːˈtwɑːr -s -z
escrow ˈes.krəʊ, -ˈ-, (US) ˈes.kroʊ, -ˈ-
escudo esˈkjuː.dəʊ, ɪˈskjuː-, -ˈskuː-; ɪʃˈkuː-, eʃ-, (US) esˈkuː.doʊ, ɪˈskuː- -s -z
esculent ˈes.kjə.lənt, -kjʊ- -s -s
Escurial esˈkjʊə.ri.əl, (US) -ˈkjʊr.i-
escutcheon ɪˈskʌtʃ.ən, esˈkʌtʃ- -s -z
Esda ˈes.də, ˈez- ˈ**Esda** ˌ**test**
Esdaile ˈez.deɪl
Esdras ˈez.dræs, -drəs
ESE ˌiːst.saʊθˈiːst; *in nautical usage also:* -saʊˈ-
-ese ˈiːz, (US) ˈiːz, ˈiːs
Note: Suffix. Always carries primary stress, e.g. **Japan** /dʒəˈpæn/, **Japanese** /ˌdʒæp.əˈniːz/.
Esfahan ˈeʃ.fə.hɑːn, ˈes-, (US) ˌes.fəˈhɑːn
Esher ˈiː.ʃəʳ, (US) -ʃɚ
Esias ɪˈzaɪ.əs, ezˈaɪ-, -æs
Esk esk
Eskimo ˈes.kɪ.məʊ, (US) -kə.moʊ -s -z
ESL ˌiː.esˈel
Esmé ˈez.mi, -meɪ

Esmeralda ˌez.məˈræl.də, -mɪˈ-
Esmond(e) ˈez.mənd
ESN ˌiː.esˈen
ESOL ˈiː.sɒl, (US) -sɑːl
ESOP ˈiː.sɒp, (US) -sɑːp
esophageal iˌsɒf.əˈdʒiː.əl, iː-, ə-; ˌiː.sɒf-, (US) iˌsɑː.fəˈ-; (US) ˌiː.sɑː-
esopha|gus iˈsɒf.ə|.gəs, iːˈ-, əˈ-, (US) iˈsɑː.fə-, iːˈ- **-gi** -gaɪ, -dʒaɪ **-guses** -gə.sɪz
esoteric ˌes.əʊˈter.ɪk, ˌiː.səʊˈ-, (US) ˌes.əˈ- **-al** -əl **-ally** -əl.i, -li
ESP ˌiː.esˈpiː
Espace® esˈpæs
espadrille ˌes.pəˈdrɪl, ˈ---, (US) ˈes.pə.drɪl **-s** -z
espalier ɪˈspæl.i.eɪ, esˈpæl-, -i.əʳ, (US) -ˈspæl.jɚ, -jeɪ **-s** -z **-ing** -ɪŋ **-ed** -d
esparto esˈpɑː.təʊ, ɪˈspɑː-, (US) esˈpɑːr.t̬oʊ **-s** -z
especial ɪˈspeʃ.əl, esˈpeʃ-, əˈspeʃ- **-ly** -i
Esperant|o ˌes.pərˈræn.t|əʊ, (US) -pəˈræn.t|oʊ, -ˈrɑːn- **-ist/s** -ɪst/s
espial ɪˈspaɪ.əl, esˈpaɪ-
espionage ˈes.pi.ə.nɑːʒ, -nɑːdʒ, -nɪdʒ; ˌes.pi.əˈnɑːʒ, -ˈnɑːdʒ
esplanade ˌes.pləˈneɪd, -ˈnɑːd, ˈ---, (US) ˈes.plə.nɑːd, -neɪd **-s** -z
Esplanade *in Western Australia:* ˈes.plə.nɑːd
ESPN ˌiː.es.piːˈen
Espoo ˈes.pəʊ, (US) -poʊ
espous|e ɪˈspaʊz, esˈpaʊz **-es** -ɪz **-ing** -ɪŋ **-ed** -d **-er/s** -əʳ/z, (US) -ɚ/z **-al/s** -əl/z
espressivo ˌes.presˈiː.vəʊ, (US) -voʊ
espresso esˈpres.əʊ, ɪˈspres-, (US) -oʊ **-s** -z

> Note: A common mispronunciation is /ɪkˈspres.əʊ/, (US) /-oʊ/.

esprit esˈpriː, ɪˈspriː, əˈspriː; ˈes.priː, (US) esˈpriː, ɪˈspriː
esprit de corps esˌpriː.dəˈkɔːʳ, ɪˌspriː-, əˌspriː-; ˌes.priː-, (US) esˌpriː.dəˈkɔːr, ɪˌspriː-
esp|y ɪˈsp|aɪ, esˈp|aɪ **-ies** -aɪz **-ying** -aɪ.ɪŋ **-ied** -aɪd
Espy ˈes.pi
Esq. (abbrev. for **Esquire**) ɪˈskwaɪəʳ, -ˈskwaɪ.əʳ, esˈkwaɪəʳ, -ˈkwaɪ.əʳ, (US) ˈes.kwaɪ.ɚ; (US) ɪˈskwaɪ.ɚ, esˈkwaɪ.ɚ
-esque ˈesk
Note: Suffix. Always carries primary stress, e.g. **picturesque** /ˌpɪk.tʃərˈesk/.
Esquiline ˈes.kwɪ.laɪn, -kwəl.aɪn, (US) -kwə.laɪn
Esquimalt esˈkwaɪ.mɔːlt, ɪˈskwaɪ-, -mɒlt, (US) -mɑːlt, -mɔːlt
esquire ɪˈskwaɪəʳ, -ˈskwaɪ.əʳ, esˈkwaɪəʳ, -ˈkwaɪ.əʳ, (US) ˈes.kwaɪ.ɚ; (US) ɪˈskwaɪ.ɚ, esˈkwaɪ.ɚ **-s** -z
ess es **-es** -ɪz
essay n *piece of writing:* ˈes.eɪ **-s** -z **-ist/s** -ɪst/s
essay n, v *attempt:* esˈeɪ, ˈ-- **-s** -z **-ing** -ɪŋ **-ed** -d **-er/s** -əʳ/z, (US) -ɚ/z
esse ˈes.i
Essen ˈes.ən
essenc|e ˈes.ənts **-es** -ɪz
Essene ˈes.iːn, -ˈ- **-s** -z
essential ɪˈsen.tʃəl, (US) ɪˈsent.ʃəl, esˈent- **-s** -z **-ly** -i **-ness** -nəs, -nɪs
esˌsential ˈoil
essentiality ɪˌsen.tʃiˈæl.ə.ti, esˌen-, -ɪ.ti, (US) -ə.t̬i
Essex ˈes.ɪks
essive ˈes.ɪv **-s** -z
Esso® ˈes.əʊ, (US) -oʊ
EST ˌiː.esˈtiː
-est ɪst, əst
Note: Suffix. Does not affect the stress pattern of the word, e.g. **happy** /ˈhæp.i/, **happiest** /ˈhæp.i.ɪst/.
establish ɪˈstæb.lɪʃ, esˈtæb- **-es** -ɪz **-ing** -ɪŋ **-ed** -t **-er/s** -əʳ/z, (US) -ɚ/z **-ment/s** -mənt/s
estate ɪˈsteɪt, esˈteɪt **-s** -s **esˈtate ˌagent; esˈtate ˌcar**
Estcourt ˈest.kɔːt, (US) -kɔːrt
Este ˈes.ti, (US) -teɪ
Estée ˈes.teɪ, -tiː, (US) -teɪ
esteem ɪˈstiːm, esˈtiːm **-s** -z **-ing** -ɪŋ **-ed** -d
Estelle ɪˈstel, esˈtel
ester ˈes.təʳ, (US) -tɚ **-s** -z
Esterhazy ˈes.tə.hɑː.zi, (US) -tɚ.hɑː.zi
Esther ˈes.təʳ, -θəʳ, (US) -tɚ
esthete ˈiːs.θiːt, (US) ˈes- **-s** -s
esthetic esˈθet.ɪk, ɪs-, iːs-, (US) esˈθet̬- **-al** -əl **-ally** -əl.i, -li **-s** -s
esthetic|ism esˈθet.ɪ.s|ɪ.zəm, ɪs-, iːs-, (US) esˈθet̬- **-ist/s** -ɪst/s
estimab|le ˈes.tɪ.mə.b|əl, -tə- **-ly** -li **-leness** -əl.nəs, -nɪs
estimate n ˈes.tɪ.mət, -tə-, -mɪt, -meɪt, (US) -mɪt, -mət **-s** -s
esti|mate v ˈes.tɪ|.meɪt, -tə-, -mət, (US) -meɪt **-mates** -meɪts, -məts, (US) -meɪts **-mating** -meɪ.tɪŋ, -mə-, (US) -meɪ.t̬ɪŋ **-mated** -meɪ.tɪd, -mə-, (US) -meɪ.t̬ɪd **-mator/s** -meɪ.təʳ/z, -mə-, (US) -meɪ.t̬ɚ/z
estimation ˌes.tɪˈmeɪ.ʃən, -təˈ-
estival iːˈstaɪ.vəl, esˈtaɪ-, (US) ˈes.tə-, esˈtaɪ-
Eston ˈes.tən
Estoni|a esˈtəʊ.ni|.ə, ɪˈstəʊ-, (US) esˈtoʊ- **-an/s** -ən/z
estop ɪˈstɒp, esˈtɒp, (US) esˈtɑːp **-s** -s **-ping** -ɪŋ **-ped** -t **-page** -ɪdʒ **-pel/s** -əl/z
Estoril ˌes.tərˈɪl, (US) ˌiː.stəˈrɪl
estovers ɪˈstəʊ.vəz, esˈtəʊ-, (US) esˈtoʊ.vɚz
estrade esˈtrɑːd, ɪˈstrɑːd, (US) esˈtrɑːd **-s** -z
Estragon ˈes.trə.gɒn, (US) -gɑːn
estrang|e ɪˈstreɪndʒ, esˈtreɪndʒ **-es** -ɪz **-ing** -ɪŋ **-ed** -d
estrangement ɪˈstreɪndʒ.mənt, esˈtreɪndʒ- **-s** -s
estrea|t ɪˈstriː|t, esˈtriː|t, (US) esˈtriː|t **-ts** -ts **-ting** -tɪŋ, (US) -t̬ɪŋ **-ted** -tɪd, (US) -t̬ɪd
Estremadura ˌes.trə.məˈdʊə.rə, -ˈdɔː-, (US) -ˈdʊr.ə
estrogen ˈiː.strə.dʒən, ˈes.trə-, (US) ˈes.trə.dʒən, -dʒen
estr(o)us ˈiː.strəs, ˈes.trəs, (US) ˈes.trəs **-es** -ɪz
estuarine ˈes.tʃu.ə.raɪn, -tju-, -riːn, -rɪn, (US) ˈes.tʃu.ə.raɪn, -tju-, -ɚ.ɪn
estuar|y ˈes.tʃu.ər|.i, -tju-, -tʃʊr|.i, -tjʊr|.i, (US) ˈes.tʃu.er|.i, -tju- **-ies** -iz
esurien|ce iˈsjʊə.ri.ən|ts, (US) iːˈsʊr.i-, -ˈsjʊr- **-cy** -*t*.si **-t** -t
eta *Greek alphabet:* ˈiː.tə, (US) ˈeɪ.t̬ə, ˈiː-
ETA *estimated time of arrival:* ˌiː.tiːˈeɪ
ETA *Basque separatist group:* ˈet.ə, (US) ˈet̬-
étagère, etagere ˌeɪ.təˈʒeəʳ, ˌet.ə-, -tæʒˈeəʳ, -tɑːˈʒeəʳ, (US) -tɑːˈʒer **-s** -z
Etah ˈiː.tə, (US) -t̬ə
e-tail ˈiː.teɪl **-er/s** -əʳ/z, (US) -ɚz
Etain ˈet.eɪn
et al etˈæl, (US) etˈɑːl, -ˈæl, -ˈɔːl
Etam® ˈiː.tæm
etc. ɪtˈset.ər.ə, et-, ət-, (US) -ˈset̬.ɚ-
etcetera ɪtˈset.ər.ə, et-, ət-, (US) -ˈset̬.ɚ- **-s** -z

> Note: A common mispronunciation is /ɪk-/.

etch etʃ **-es** -ɪz **-ing/s** -ɪŋ/z **-ed** -t **-er/s** -əʳ/z, (US) -ɚ/z
eternal ɪˈtɜː.nəl, (US) -ˈtɝː- **-ly** -i
eternaliz|e, -is|e ɪˈtɜː.nəl.aɪz, (US) -ˈtɝː.nə.laɪz **-es** -ɪz **-ing** -ɪŋ **-ed** -d
eternit|y ɪˈtɜː.nə.t|i, -nɪ.t|i, (US) -ˈtɝː.nə.t̬|i **-ies** -iz
eterniz|e, -is|e ɪˈtɜː.naɪz, (US) -ˈtɝː- **-es** -ɪz **-ing** -ɪŋ **-ed** -d
Etesian ɪˈtiː.ʒi.ən, -zi-, -ʒən
Ethan ˈiː.θən
ethane ˈiː.θeɪn, ˈeθ.eɪn, (US) ˈeθ.eɪn
ethanoic ˌeθ.əˈnəʊ.ɪk, ˈiː.θəˈ-, (US) ˌeθ.əˈnoʊ-
ethanol ˈeθ.ə.nɒl, ˈiː.θə-, (US) ˈeθ.ə.nɑːl, -noʊl
Ethel ˈeθ.əl
Ethelbert ˈeθ.əl.bɜːt, -bət, (US) -bɝːt, -bɚt
Ethelberta ˌeθ.əlˈbɜː.tə, ˈeθ.əlˌbɜː-, (US) ˌeθ.əlˈbɝː.t̬ə
Ethelburga ˌeθ.əlˈbɜː.gə, ˈeθ.əlˌbɜː-, (US) ˌeθ.əlˈbɝː-
Ethelred ˈeθ.əl.red
Ethelwulf ˈeθ.əl.wʊlf
ethene ˈeθ.iːn
ether ˈiː.θəʳ, (US) -θɚ **-s** -z
ethereal iˈθɪə.ri.əl, iː-, ə-, (US) -ˈθɪr.i- **-ly** -i
etherealiz|e, -is|e iˈθɪə.ri.əl.aɪz, iː-, ə-, (US) -ˈθɪr.i.ə.laɪz **-es** -ɪz **-ing** -ɪŋ **-ed** -d
Etherege ˈeθ.ər.ɪdʒ
etheric iːˈθer.ɪk, i- **-s** -s **-ally** -əl.i, -li
Etherington ˈeð.ər.ɪŋ.tən
etheriz|e, -is|e ˈiː.θər.aɪz, (US) -θə.raɪz **-es** -ɪz **-ing** -ɪŋ **-ed** -d
ethic ˈeθ.ɪk **-s** -s **-al** -əl **-ally** -əl.i, -li
Ethiop ˈiː.θi.ɒp, (US) -ɑːp **-s** -s

Pronouncing the letters EU, EW

The vowel digraphs **eu** and **ew** are similar in that their most common pronunciation is one of /juː/ or /uː/, e.g.:

feud fjuːd
flew fluː

Many words which have /juː/ in British English are pronounced without the /j/ in American English, e.g.:

news njuːz ⓤⓢ nuːz

When the digraph **eu** is followed by an **r** in the spelling, the strong pronunciation is usually /jʊə/ ⓤⓢ /jʊr/, although words borrowed from French may have /ɜː/ ⓤⓢ /ɝː/ in stressed syllables, and /əʳ/ ⓤⓢ /ɚ/ in unstressed syllables, e.g.:

European ˌjʊə.rəˈpiː.ən ⓤⓢ ˌjʊr.ə-
connoisseur ˌkɒn.əˈsɜːʳ ⓤⓢ ˌkɑː.nəˈsɝː
amateur ˈæm.ə.təʳ ⓤⓢ -tʃɚ

In addition

Other sounds associated with the digraphs **eu** and **ew** are as follows:

əʊ ⓤⓢ oʊ sew /səʊ/ ⓤⓢ /soʊ/
i.ə museum /mjuːˈzi.əm/
ɜː ⓤⓢ ɜː, uː masseuse /mæsˈɜːz/ ⓤⓢ /məˈsɜːz, -suːz/

In words borrowed from German, **eu** is pronounced /ɔɪ/, e.g.:

ɔɪ schadenfreude ˈʃɑː.dᵊnˌfrɔɪ.də

Ethiopi|a ˌiː.θiˈəʊ.pi|.ə, ⓤⓢ -ˈoʊ- **-an/s** -ən/z
Ethiopic ˌiː.θiˈɒp.ɪk, -ˈəʊ.pɪk, ⓤⓢ -ˈɑː.pɪk, -ˈoʊ.pɪk
ethnic ˈeθ.nɪk **-al** -ᵊl **-ally** -ᵊl.i, -li
ethnicity eθˈnɪs.ə.ti, -ɪ.ti, ⓤⓢ -ə.t̬i
ethno- ˈeθ.nəʊ; eθˈnɒ, ⓤⓢ ˈeθ.noʊ, ˈ-nə; ⓤⓢ eθˈnɑː
Note: Prefix. Either takes primary or secondary stress on the first syllable, e.g. **ethnographic** /ˌeθ.nəʊˈgræf.ɪk/ ⓤⓢ /-noʊˈ-/, or primary stress on the second syllable, e.g. **ethnographer** /eθˈnɒg.rə.fəʳ/ ⓤⓢ /-ˈnɑː.grə.fɚ/.
ethnocentr|ic ˌeθ.nəʊˈsen.tr|ɪk, ⓤⓢ -noʊˈ-, -nəˈ- **-ism** -ɪ.zᵊm **-ically** -ɪ.kᵊl.i, -ɪ.kli
ethnocentricity ˌeθ.nəʊ.senˈtrɪs.ə.ti, -ɪ.ti, ⓤⓢ -noʊ.senˈtrɪs.ə.t̬i
ethnographer eθˈnɒg.rə.fəʳ, ⓤⓢ -ˈnɑː.grə.fɚ **-s** -z
ethnographic ˌeθ.nəʊˈgræf.ɪk, ⓤⓢ -noʊˈ-, -nəˈ- **-al** -ᵊl
ethnography eθˈnɒg.rə.fi, ⓤⓢ -ˈnɑː.grə-
ethnologic ˌeθ.nəʊˈlɒdʒ.ɪk, ⓤⓢ -noʊˈlɑː.dʒɪk, -nəˈ- **-al** -ᵊl **-ally** -ᵊl.i, -li
ethnolog|y eθˈnɒl.ə.dʒ|i, ⓤⓢ -ˈnɑː.lə- **-ist/s** -ɪst/s
ethologic ˌiː.θəˈlɒdʒ.ɪk, ⓤⓢ -ˈlɑː.dʒɪk **-al** -ᵊl
etholog|y iːˈθɒl.ə.dʒ|i, ɪ-, ⓤⓢ iːˈθɑː.lə-, ɪˈ- **-ist/s** -ɪst/s
ethos ˈiː.θɒs, ⓤⓢ -θɑːs, ˈeθ.ɑːs, -oʊs
ethyl *commercial and general pronunciation:* ˈeθ.ɪl, -ᵊl, ⓤⓢ -ᵊl *chemists' pronunciation:* ˈiː.θaɪl
ethylene ˈeθ.ɪ.liːn, -ᵊl.iːn, ⓤⓢ -ə.liːn
etio|late ˈiː.ti.əʊ|.leɪt, ⓤⓢ -ə- **-lates** -leɪts **-lating** -leɪ.tɪŋ, ⓤⓢ -leɪ.t̬ɪŋ **-lated** -leɪ.tɪd, ⓤⓢ -leɪ.t̬ɪd
etiolog|y ˌiː.tiˈɒl.ə.dʒ|i, ⓤⓢ -ˈɑː.lə- **-ist/s** -ɪst/s
etiquette ˈet.ɪ.ket, -kət, ⓤⓢ ˈet̬.ɪ.kɪt, -ket
Etna ˈet.nə
Eton ˈiː.tᵊn
Etonian iˈtəʊ.ni.ən, iːˈ-, ⓤⓢ -ˈtoʊ- **-s** -z
Etruri|a ɪˈtrʊə.ri|.ə, ⓤⓢ -ˈtrʊr.i- **-an/s** -ən/z
Etruscan ɪˈtrʌs.kən **-s** -z
-ette et
Note: Suffix. Normally takes primary stress, e.g. **majorette** /ˌmeɪ.dʒᵊrˈet/.
Ettrick ˈet.rɪk
Etty ˈet.i, ⓤⓢ ˈet̬-
étude ˈeɪ.tjuːd, -ˈ-, ⓤⓢ ˈeɪ.tuːd, -tjuːd **-s** -z
etui etˈwiː, ⓤⓢ eɪˈtwiː **-s** -z
etymologic ˌet.ɪ.məˈlɒdʒ.ɪk, ˌ-ə-, ⓤⓢ ˌet̬.ɪ.məˈlɑː.dʒɪk **-al** -ᵊl **-ally** -ᵊl.i, -li
etymologist ˌet.ɪˈmɒl.ə.dʒɪst, -əˈ-, ⓤⓢ ˌet̬.ɪˈmɑː.lə- **-s** -s
etymologiz|e, -is|e ˌet.ɪˈmɒl.ə.dʒaɪz, -əˈ-, ⓤⓢ ˌet̬.ɪˈmɑː.lə- **-es** -ɪz **-ing** -ɪŋ **-ed** -d
etymolog|y ˌet.ɪˈmɒl.ə.dʒ|i, -əˈ-, ⓤⓢ ˌet̬.ɪˈmɑː.lə- **-ies** -iz
etymon ˈet.ɪ.mɒn, ˈ-ə-, ⓤⓢ ˈet̬.ə.mɑːn **-s** -z
EU ˌiːˈjuː
Euan ˈjuː.ən
Eubank ˈjuː.bæŋk
Euboea juːˈbiː.ə
eucalyptus ˌjuː.kᵊlˈɪp.təs **-es** -ɪz
Eucharist ˈjuː.kᵊr.ɪst **-s** -s
eucharistic ˌjuː.kᵊrˈɪs.tɪk **-al** -ᵊl **-ally** -ᵊl.i, -li
euchre ˈjuː.kəʳ, ⓤⓢ -kɚ **-s** -z **-ing** -ɪŋ **-d** -d
Euclid ˈjuː.klɪd **-s** -z
Euclidean juːˈklɪd.i.ən
eud(a)emon|ism juːˈdiː.mə.n|ɪ.zᵊm **-ist/s** -ɪst/s
eudiometer ˌjuː.diˈɒm.ɪ.təʳ, ˈ-ə-, ⓤⓢ -ˈɑː.mə.t̬ɚ **-s** -z
Eudocia juːˈdəʊ.ʃi.ə, -ʃə, -si.ə, ⓤⓢ -ˈdoʊ-
Eudora juːˈdɔː.rə, ⓤⓢ -ˈdɔːr.ə
Eudoxia juːˈdɒk.si.ə, ⓤⓢ -ˈdɑːk-
Eudoxus juːˈdɒk.səs, ⓤⓢ -ˈdɑːk-
Eugen *English name:* ˈjuː.dʒen, -dʒɪn, -dʒən *German name:* ˈɔɪ.gən
Eugene juːˈdʒiːn, -ˈdʒeɪn; ˈjuː.dʒiːn, ⓤⓢ juːˈdʒiːn, ˈ--
Eugene Onegin ˌjuː.dʒiːn.ɒnˈjeɪ.gɪn, ⓤⓢ -ɑːnˈ-, -oʊnˈ-
Eugénia juːˈdʒiː.ni.ə, -ˈʒiː-, -ˈdʒeɪ-, -ˈʒeɪ-
eugenic juːˈdʒen.ɪk **-s** -s
eugenicist juːˈdʒen.ɪ.sɪst, ˈ-ə- **-s** -s
Eugénie juːˈʒeɪ.ni, -ˈʒiː-, -ˈdʒiː-
Eugenius juːˈdʒiː.ni.əs, -ˈʒiː-, -ˈdʒeɪ-, ⓤⓢ -ˈʒeɪ-
Eulalia juːˈleɪ.li.ə
Eulenspiegel ˈɔɪ.lᵊnˌʃpiː.gᵊl
Euler *English name:* ˈjuː.ləʳ, ⓤⓢ -lɚ *German name:* ˈɔɪ.ləʳ, ⓤⓢ -lɚ
eulogist ˈjuː.lə.dʒɪst **-s** -s
eulogistic ˌjuː.ləˈdʒɪs.tɪk **-al** -ᵊl **-ally** -ᵊl.i, -li
eulogi|um juːˈləʊ.dʒi|.əm, ⓤⓢ -ˈloʊ- **-ums** -z **-a** -ə
eulogiz|e, -is|e ˈjuː.lə.dʒaɪz **-es** -ɪz **-ing** -ɪŋ **-ed** -d
eulog|y ˈjuː.lə.dʒ|i **-ies** -iz
Eumenides juːˈmen.ɪ.diːz, ˈ-ə-
Eunice *modern Christian name:* ˈjuː.nɪs *biblical name:* juːˈnaɪ.si
eunuch ˈjuː.nək **-s** -s **-ism** -ɪ.zᵊm
euonymus juːˈɒn.ɪ.məs, ˈ-ə-, ⓤⓢ -ˈɑː.nə- **-es** -ɪz
eupepsia juːˈpep.si.ə
eupeptic juːˈpep.tɪk
Euphemia juːˈfiː.mi.ə
euphemism ˈjuː.fə.mɪ.zᵊm, -fɪ- **-s** -z
euphemistic ˌjuː.fəˈmɪs.tɪk, -fɪˈ- **-al** -ᵊl **-ally** -ᵊl.i, -li
euphemiz|e, -is|e ˈjuː.fə.maɪz, -fɪ- **-es** -ɪz **-ing** -ɪŋ **-ed** -d
euphonic juːˈfɒn.ɪk, ⓤⓢ -ˈfɑː.nɪk **-al** -ᵊl **-ally** -ᵊl.i, -li
euphonious juːˈfəʊ.ni.əs, ⓤⓢ -ˈfoʊ- **-ly** -li
euphonium juːˈfəʊ.ni.əm, ⓤⓢ -ˈfoʊ- **-s** -z
euphoniz|e, -is|e ˈjuː.fə.naɪz **-es** -ɪz **-ing** -ɪŋ **-ed** -d
euphony ˈjuː.fə.ni
euphorbia juːˈfɔː.bi.ə, ⓤⓢ -ˈfɔːr-
euphoria juːˈfɔː.ri.ə, ⓤⓢ -ˈfɔːr.i-
euphoric juːˈfɒr.ɪk, ⓤⓢ -ˈfɔːr.ɪk **-ally** -ᵊl.i, -li
euphrasy ˈjuː.frə.si

Euphrates juːˈfreɪ.tiːz, (US) -t̬iːz
Euphrosyne juːˈfrɒz.ɪ.niː, ˈ-ə-, (US) -ˈfrɑː.zə-
Euphues ˈjuː.fju.iːz
euphu|ism ˈjuː.fju.|ɪ.zᵊm **-isms** -ɪ.zᵊmz **-ist/s** -ɪst/s
euphuistic ˌjuː.fjuˈɪs.tɪk
eupnoea juːpˈniː.ə
Eurasia jʊəˈreɪ.ʒə, jɔːˈ-, ˈ-ʒi.ə, ˈ-ʃə, (US) jʊˈreɪ.ʒə
Eurasian jʊəˈreɪ.ʒᵊn, jɔː-, (US) jʊrˈeɪ- **-s** -z
Euratom jʊəˈræt.əm, jɔːˈ-, (US) jʊˈræt̬-
eureka, E~ jʊəˈriː.kə, jɔːˈ-, (US) jʊ-
eurhythm|ic jʊəˈrɪð.m|ɪk, jɔːˈ-, -ˈrɪθ-, (US) jʊˈrɪð- **-ics** -ɪks **-y** -i
Euripides jʊəˈrɪp.ɪ.diːz, jɔːˈ-, ˈ-ə-, (US) jʊ-
Euripus jʊəˈraɪ.pəs, jɔːˈ-, (US) jʊ-
euro ˈjʊə.rəʊ, ˈjɔː-, (US) ˈjʊr.oʊ **-s** -z
Euro- ˈjʊə.rəʊ, jɔː-; jʊəˈrəʊ, (US) ˈjʊr.oʊ, -ə; (US) jʊˈroʊ
Note: Prefix. Usually takes primary or secondary stress on the first syllable, e.g. **Eurocrat** /ˈjʊə.rəʊ.kræt/ (US) /ˈjʊr.ə-/; **eurocentric** /ˌjʊə.rəʊˈsen.trɪk/(US) /ˈjʊr.ə-/. May also have stress on the second syllable, e.g. **europium** /jʊəˈrəʊ.pi.əm/ (US) /jʊˈroʊ-/.
Eurobond ˈjʊə.rəʊ.bɒnd, ˈjɔː-, (US) ˈjʊr.oʊ.bɑːnd **-s** -z
eurocentric ˌjʊə.rəʊˈsen.trɪk, ˌjɔː-, (US) ˌjʊr.oʊˈ-
Eurocheque® ˈjʊə.rəʊ.tʃek, ˈjɔː-, (US) ˈjʊr.oʊ- **-s** -s
Eurocommun|ism ˌjʊə.rəʊˈkɒm.jə.n|ɪ.zᵊm, ˌjɔː-, -jʊ-; ˈjʊə.rəʊˌkɒm-, ˈjɔː-, (US) ˌjʊr.oʊˈkɑːm.jə-, -əˈ- **-ist/s** -ɪst/s
Eurocrat ˈjʊə.rəʊ.kræt, ˈjɔː-, (US) ˈjʊr.ə- **-s** -s
Eurodisney® ˈjʊə.rəʊˌdɪz.ni, ˈjɔː-, (US) ˈjʊr.oʊ-
Eurodollar® ˈjʊə.rəʊˌdɒl.əʳ, ˈjɔː-, (US) ˈjʊr.oʊˌdɑː.lɚ **-s** -z
Euroland ˈjʊə.rəʊ.lænd, ˈjɔː-, (US) ˈjʊr.oʊ.lænd, ˈjɝ-
Europa jʊəˈrəʊ.pə, jɔːˈ-, (US) jʊˈroʊ-
Europe ˈjʊə.rəp, ˈjɔː-, (US) ˈjʊr.əp
European ˌjʊə.rəˈpiː.ən, ˌjɔː-, (US) ˌjʊr.əˈ- **-s** -z *stress shift:* **ˌEuropean Comˈmunity ˌEuropean Ecoˈnomic Comˈmunity; ˌEuropean ˈMonetary System**
europeaniz|e, -is|e ˌjʊə.rəˈpiː.ə.naɪz, ˌjɔː-, (US) ˌjʊr.əˈ- **-es** -ɪz **-ing** -ɪŋ **-ed** -d
europium jʊəˈrəʊ.pi.əm, jɔːˈ-, (US) jʊˈroʊ-
Eurosceptic ˈjʊə.rəʊˌskep.tɪk, ˈjɔː-, (US) ˈjʊr.oʊ-, ˈ-ə- **-s** -s
Eurostar® ˈjʊə.rəʊ.stɑːʳ, ˈjɔː-, (US) ˈjʊr.oʊ.stɑːr, -ə-
Eurotunnel® ˈjʊə.rəʊˌtʌn.ᵊl, ˈjɔː-, (US) ˈjʊr.oʊ-, ˈ-ə-
Eurovision® ˈjʊə.rəʊ.vɪ.ʒᵊn, ˈjɔː-, (US) ˈjʊr.ə-, -oʊ- **ˌEurovision ˈSong ˌContest**
Eurozone ˈjʊə.rəʊ.zəʊn, ˈjɔː-, (US) ˈjʊr.oʊ.zoʊn, ˈjɝ-
Eurus ˈjʊə.rəs, ˈjɔː-, (US) ˈjʊr.əs
Eurydice jʊəˈrɪd.ɪ.si, jɔːˈ-, ˈ-ə-, (US) jʊ-
eurythm|ic jʊəˈrɪð.m|ɪk, jɔːˈ-, -ˈrɪθ-, (US) jʊˈrɪð- **-ics** -ɪks **-y** -i
Eusden ˈjuːz.dən
Eusebius juːˈsiː.bi.əs
Eustace ˈjuː.stəs, -stɪs
eustachian juːˈsteɪ.ʃᵊn, -ʃi.ən, -ki.ən **euˌstachian ˈtube** (US) **euˈstachian ˌtube**
Eustachius juːˈsteɪ.ki.əs
Eustacia juːˈsteɪ.si.ə, -ʃə
Euston ˈjuː.stən
Euterpe juːˈtɜː.pi, (US) -ˈtɝː-
euthanasia ˌjuː.θəˈneɪ.zi.ə, ˈ-ʒə, (US) ˈ-ʒə, ˈ-zi.ə
Eutropius juːˈtrəʊ.pi.əs, (US) -ˈtroʊ-
Euxine ˈjuːk.saɪn
Euxton ˈek.stən
Eva ˈiː.və, (US) ˈiː.və, ˈeɪ-
evacu|ate ɪˈvæk.ju|.eɪt **-ates** -eɪts **-ating** -eɪ.tɪŋ, (US) -eɪ.t̬ɪŋ **-ated** -eɪ.tɪd, (US) -eɪ.t̬ɪd **-ator/s** -eɪ.təʳ/z, (US) -eɪ.t̬ɚ/z
evacuation ɪˌvæk.juˈeɪ.ʃᵊn **-s** -z
evacuee ɪˌvæk.juˈiː **-s** -z
evad|e ɪˈveɪd **-es** -z **-ing** -ɪŋ **-ed** -ɪd **-er/s** -əʳ/z, (US) -ɚ/z
Evadne ɪˈvæd.ni
evalu|ate ɪˈvæl.ju|.eɪt **-ates** -eɪts **-ating** -eɪ.tɪŋ, (US) -eɪ.t̬ɪŋ **-ated** -eɪ.tɪd, (US) -eɪ.t̬ɪd
evaluation ɪˌvæl.juˈeɪ.ʃᵊn **-s** -z
evaluative ɪˈvæl.ju.ə.tɪv, (US) -eɪ.t̬ɪv **-ly** -li
Evan ˈev.ᵊn
Evander ɪˈvæn.dəʳ, (US) -dɚ
evanesc|e ˌiː.vəˈnes, ˌev.əˈ-, (US) ˌev.əˈ- **-es** -ɪz **-ing** -ɪŋ **-ed** -t
evanescen|ce ˌiː.vəˈnes.ᵊn|*t*s, ˌev.əˈ-, (US) ˌev.əˈ- **-t/ly** -t/li
evangel ɪˈvæn.dʒəl, -dʒel **-s** -z
evangelic ˌiː.vænˈdʒel.ɪk, ˌev.ænˈ-, -ənˈ- **-s** -s
evangelic|al ˌiː.vænˈdʒel.ɪ.k|ᵊl, ˌev.ænˈ-, -ənˈ- **-als** -ᵊlz **-ally** -ᵊl.i, -li **-alism** -ᵊl.ɪ.zᵊm
Evangeline ɪˈvæn.dʒɪ.liːn, -dʒᵊl.iːn, -aɪn, (US) -dʒə.lɪn, -dʒɪ-, -liːn, -laɪn
evangel|ism ɪˈvæn.dʒə.l|ɪ.zᵊm, -dʒɪ- **-ist/s** -ɪst/s
evangelistic ɪˌvæn.dʒəˈlɪs.tɪk, -dʒɪˈ-
evangelization, -isa- ɪˌvæn.dʒᵊl.aɪˈzeɪ.ʃᵊn, -dʒɪ.laɪˈ-, -lɪˈ-, (US) -dʒᵊl.əˈ-
evangeliz|e, -is|e ɪˈvæn.dʒᵊl.aɪz, -dʒɪ-, (US) -dʒə.laɪz, -dʒɪ- **-es** -ɪz **-ing** -ɪŋ **-ed** -d
Evans ˈev.ᵊnz
Evanson ˈev.ᵊn.sᵊn
Evanston ˈev.ᵊn.stən
Evansville ˈev.ᵊnz.vɪl
evaporable ɪˈvæp.ᵊr.ə.bᵊl
evapor|ate ɪˈvæp.ᵊr|.eɪt, (US) -ə.r|eɪt **-ates** -eɪts **-ating** -eɪ.tɪŋ, (US) -eɪ.t̬ɪŋ **-ated** -eɪ.tɪd, (US) -eɪ.t̬ɪd **-ator/s** -eɪ.təʳ/z, (US) -eɪ.t̬ɚ/z **eˌvaporated ˈmilk**
evaporation ɪˌvæp.əˈreɪ.ʃᵊn **-s** -z
evasion ɪˈveɪ.ʒᵊn **-s** -z
evasive ɪˈveɪ.sɪv **-ly** -li **-ness** -nəs, -nɪs
eve, E~ iːv **-s** -z
Evele(i)gh ˈiː.v.li
Evelina ˌev.ɪˈliː.nə, -əˈ-
Eveline ˈiː.v.lɪn, ˈev.lɪn, ˈev.ɪ.liːn
Evelyn ˈiː.v.lɪn, ˈev.lɪn, ˈev.ə-, (US) ˈev.ə-, ˈev.lɪn, ˈiː.v-

> Note: The pronunciation /ˈiː.v.lɪn/ is used in the US only for British people of that name.

even ˈiː.vᵊn **-ly** -li **-ness** -nəs, -nɪs **-s** -z **-ing** -ɪŋ **-ed** -d
Evenden ˈev.ᵊn.dən
evenhanded ˌiː.vᵊnˈhæn.dɪd **-ly** -li **-ness** -nəs, -nɪs *stress shift:* **ˌevenhanded adˈministrator**
evening n ˈiː.v.nɪŋ **-s** -z **ˈevening ˌdress, ˌevening ˈdress; ˈevening ˌgown; ˌevening ˈprimrose; ˌevening ˈprimrose ˌoil**
Evens ˈev.ᵊnz
evensong ˈiː.vᵊn.sɒŋ, (US) -sɑːŋ, -sɔːŋ **-s** -z
even-steven ˌiː.vᵊnˈstiː.vᵊn **-s** -z
e|vent ɪ|ˈvent **-vents** -ˈvents **-venting** -ˈven.tɪŋ, (US) -ˈven.t̬ɪŋ **-vented** -ˈven.tɪd, (US) -ˈven.t̬ɪd **-venter/s** -ˈven.təʳ/z, (US) -ˈven.t̬ɚ/z
even-tempered ˌiː.vᵊnˈtem.pəd, (US) -pɚd *stress shift:* **ˌeven-tempered deˈbate**
eventful ɪˈvent.fᵊl, -fʊl **-ly** -i
eventide ˈiː.vᵊn.taɪd **-s** -z
eventive ɪˈven.tɪv, (US) -t̬ɪv
eventual ɪˈven.tʃu.əl, -tju-, -tʃʊl, -tjʊl, (US) -tʃu.əl, -tju- **-ly** -i
eventualit|y ɪˌven.tʃuˈæl.ə.t|i, -tjuˈ-, -ɪ.t|i, (US) -tʃuˈæl.ə.t̬|i, -tjuˈ- **-ies** -iz
eventu|ate ɪˈven.tʃu|.eɪt, -tju-, (US) -tʃu-, -tju- **-ates** -eɪts **-ating** -eɪ.tɪŋ, (US) -eɪ.t̬ɪŋ **-ated** -eɪ.tɪd, (US) -eɪ.t̬ɪd
ever ˈev.əʳ, (US) -ɚ
Everard ˈev.ᵊr.ɑːd, (US) -ə.rɑːrd
Everest ˈev.ᵊr.est, (US) -ə.rest, -ɚ.ɪst, ˈ-rɪst

> Note: Sir George Everest's surname is pronounced /ˈiːv.rɪst/, but the mountain named after him has the pronunciations shown above.

Everett ˈev.ᵊr.et, (US) -ə.ret, ˈev.rɪt
Everglades ˈev.ə.gleɪdz, (US) ˈ-ɚ-
evergreen ˈev.ə.griːn, (US) ˈ-ɚ- **-s** -z
Everitt ˈev.ᵊr.ɪt
everlasting ˌev.əˈlɑː.stɪŋ, (US) -ɚˈlæs.tɪŋ **-ly** -li **-ness** -nəs, -nɪs
Everl(e)y ˈev.ə.li, (US) ˈ-ɚ-
evermore ˌev.əˈmɔːʳ, (US) -ɚˈmɔːr
EverReady® ˈev.əˌred.i, (US) -ɚˌ-
Evers ˈev.əz, (US) -ɚz

Evershed ˈev.ə.ʃed, ⓤⓢ ˈ-ɚ-
eversion ɪˈvɜː.ʃən, iː-, ⓤⓢ -ˈvɝː.ʒən, -ʃən
Eversley ˈev.əz.li, ⓤⓢ -ɚz-
e|vert ɪ|ˈvɜːt, iː-, ⓤⓢ -ˈvɝːt **-verts** -ˈvɜːts, ⓤⓢ -ˈvɝːts **-verting** -ˈvɜː.tɪŋ, ⓤⓢ -ˈvɝː.t̬ɪŋ **-verted** -ˈvɜː.tɪd, ⓤⓢ -ˈvɝː.t̬ɪd
Evert ˈev.ət, ⓤⓢ -ɚt
Everton ˈev.ə.tən, ⓤⓢ ˈ-ɚ-
every ˈev.ri ˌ**every** ˌ**which** ˈ**way** ⓤⓢ ˌ**every** ˈ**which** ˌ**way**, ˈ**every** ˌ**which** ˌ**way**

Note: The meaning is slightly different in American English depending on the stress pattern. ˌ**Every** ˈ**which** ˌ**way** means 'akimbo'. ˈ**Every** ˌ**which** ˌ**way** means 'in all possible ways'.

everybody ˈev.riˌbɒd.i, ⓤⓢ -ˌbɑː.di
everyday ˈev.ri.deɪ, ˌ-ˈ-
Everyman ˈev.ri.mæn
everyone ˈev.ri.wʌn
everyplace ˈev.ri.pleɪs
everything ˈev.ri.θɪŋ
everywhere ˈev.ri.*h*weəʳ, ⓤⓢ -*h*wer
Evesham ˈiːv.ʃəm; *locally also:* ˈiː.vɪ-
Evett ˈev.ɪt
Evian® ˈev.i.ɒ̃ːŋ, ⓤⓢ ˌev.iˈɑːn, ˈev.i.ən
evict ɪˈvɪkt **-s** -s **-ing** -ɪŋ **-ed** -ɪd
eviction ɪˈvɪk.ʃən **-s** -z
evidenc|e ˈev.ɪ.dənts, ˈ-ə- **-es** -ɪz **-ing** -ɪŋ **-ed** -t
evident ˈev.ɪ.dənt, ˈ-ə- **-ly** -li
evidential ˌev.ɪˈden.tʃəl, -əˈ-, ⓤⓢ -ʃəl **-ly** -i
evidentiary ˌev.ɪˈden.tʃər.i, -əˈ-, ⓤⓢ -ˈdent.ʃɚ.i
evil ˈiː.vəl, -vɪl, ⓤⓢ -vəl **-s** -z **-ly** -i ˌ**evil** ˈ**eye** ⓤⓢ ˈ**evil** ˌ**eye**
evildoer ˈiː.vəlˌduː.əʳ, -vɪlˌ-; ˌiː.vəlˈduː-, -vɪlˈ-, ⓤⓢ ˈiː.vəlˌduː.ɚ, ˌiː.vəlˈduː- **-s** -z
evil-minded ˌiː.vəlˈmaɪn.dɪd, -vɪlˈ-, ˈiː.vəlˌmaɪn-; -vɪlˌ-, ⓤⓢ ˌiː.vəlˈmaɪn-, ˈiː.vəlˌmaɪn- **-ness** -nəs, -nɪs
evinc|e ɪˈvɪnts **-es** -ɪz **-ing** -ɪŋ **-ed** -t **-ive** -ɪv
evincib|le ɪˈvɪnt.sə.b|əl, -sɪ- **-ly** -li
evi|rate ˈiː.vɪ|.reɪt, ˈev.ɪ- **-rates** -reɪts **-rating** -reɪ.tɪŋ, ⓤⓢ -reɪ.t̬ɪŋ **-rated** -reɪ.tɪd, ⓤⓢ -reɪ.t̬ɪd
evisce|rate ɪˈvɪs.ə|.reɪt, iː- **-rates** -reɪts **-rating** -reɪ.tɪŋ, ⓤⓢ -reɪ.t̬ɪŋ **-rated** -reɪ.tɪd, ⓤⓢ -reɪ.t̬ɪd
evisceration ɪˌvɪs.əˈreɪ.ʃən, iːˌvɪs-
Evita evˈiː.tə, ɪˈviː-, ⓤⓢ -tə, -t̬ə
evo|cate ˈev.əʊ|.keɪt, ˈiː.vəʊ-, ⓤⓢ ˈev.ə-, ˈiː.voʊ- **-cates** -keɪts **-cating** -keɪ.tɪŋ, ⓤⓢ -keɪ.t̬ɪŋ **-cated** -keɪ.tɪd, ⓤⓢ -keɪ.t̬ɪd
evocation ˌev.əʊˈkeɪ.ʃən, ˌiː.vəʊˈ-, ⓤⓢ ˌev.əˈ-, ˌiː.voʊˈ- **-s** -z
evocative ɪˈvɒk.ə.tɪv, ⓤⓢ -ˈvɑː.kə.t̬ɪv **-ly** -li
evok|e ɪˈvəʊk, ⓤⓢ -ˈvoʊk **-es** -s **-ing** -ɪŋ **-ed** -t
evolute ˌiː.vəˈluːt, ˌev.əˈ-, -ˈljuːt, ⓤⓢ ˌev.əˈluːt, ˌiː.vəˈ- **-s** -s
evolution ˌiː.vəˈluː.ʃən, ˌev.əˈ-, -ˈljuː-, ⓤⓢ ˌev.əˈluː.ʃən, ˌiː.vəˈ- **-s** -z
evolutional ˌiː.vəˈluː.ʃən.əl, ˌev.əˈ-, -ˈljuː-, ⓤⓢ ˌev.əˈluː-, ˌiː.vəˈ-
evolutionary ˌiː.vəˈluː.ʃən.ər.i, ˌev.əˈ-, -ˈljuː-, -ri, ⓤⓢ ˌev.əˈluː.ʃən.er-, ˌiː.vəˈ-
evolution|ism ˌiː.vəˈluː.ʃən|.ɪ.zəm, ˌev.əˈ-, -ˈljuː-, ⓤⓢ ˌev.əˈluː-, ˌiː.vəˈ- **-ist/s** -ɪst/s
evolutive ɪˈvɒl.jə.tɪv, iː-, -jʊ-, ⓤⓢ ˌev.əˈluː.t̬ɪv, ˌiː.vəˈ-; ⓤⓢ iːˈvɑːl.jə-
evolv|e ɪˈvɒlv, ⓤⓢ -ˈvɑːlv **-es** -z **-ing** -ɪŋ **-ed** -d **-able** -ə.bəl
Évora ˈev.ə.rə, ⓤⓢ evˈʊr.ə
Evo-stik® ˈiː.vəʊ.stɪk, ⓤⓢ -voʊ-
evulsion ɪˈvʌl.ʃən, iː- **-s** -z
Ewan ˈjuː.ən
Ewart ˈjuː.ət, jʊət, ⓤⓢ ˈjuː.ɚt
Ewbank ˈjuː.bæŋk
ewe juː **-s** -z
Ewell ˈjuː.əl, jʊəl, ⓤⓢ ˈjuː.əl
Ewen ˈjuː.ən, -ɪn; jʊən, ⓤⓢ ˈjuː.ən
ewer ˈjuː.əʳ, jʊəʳ, ⓤⓢ ˈjuː.ɚ **-s** -z
Ewing ˈjuː.ɪŋ
ex eks
ex- eks, ɪks, egz, ɪgz
Note: Prefix. Takes either primary or secondary stress, e.g. **excellent** /ˈek.səl.ənt/, **excitation** /ˌek.sɪˈteɪ.ʃən/ ⓤⓢ /-saɪˈ-/ or may be unstressed, e.g. **excel** /ɪkˈsel/.
exacer|bate ɪgˈzæs.ə|.beɪt, eg-; ɪkˈsæs-, ek-, ⓤⓢ ɪgˈzæs.ɚ-, egˈ- **-bates** -beɪts **-bating** -beɪ.tɪŋ, ⓤⓢ -beɪ.t̬ɪŋ **-bated** -beɪ.tɪd, ⓤⓢ -beɪ.t̬ɪd
exacerbation ɪgˌzæs.əˈbeɪ.ʃən, egˌ-; ɪkˌsæs-, ekˌ-, ⓤⓢ ɪgˌzæs.ɚˈ-, egˈ- **-s** -z
exact ɪgˈzækt, egˈ-; ɪkˈsækt, ekˈ-, ⓤⓢ ɪgˈzækt, egˈ- **-ly** -li, -ˈzæk.li, -ˈsæk.li, ⓤⓢ -ˈzæk.li **-ness** -nəs, -nɪs **-s** -s **-ing/ly** -ɪŋ/li **-ed** -ɪd **-er/s** -əʳ/z, ⓤⓢ -ɚ/z **-or/s** -əʳ/z, ⓤⓢ -ɚ/z
exaction ɪgˈzæk.ʃən, egˈ-; ɪkˈsæk-, ekˈ-, ⓤⓢ ɪgˈzæk-, egˈ- **-s** -z
exactitude ɪgˈzæk.tɪ.tʃuːd, -tjuːd, egˈ-, -tə-; ɪkˈsæk-, ekˈ-, ⓤⓢ ɪgˈzæk.tə.tuːd, egˈ-, -tjuːd
exactly ɪgˈzækt.li, egˈ-; ɪkˈsækt-, ekˈ-, ⓤⓢ ɪgˈzækt-, egˈ-
exagger|ate ɪgˈzædʒ.ər|.eɪt, egˈ-; ɪkˈsædʒ-, ekˈ-, ⓤⓢ ɪgˈzædʒ.ə.r|eɪt, egˈ- **-ates** -eɪts **-ating** -eɪ.tɪŋ, ⓤⓢ -eɪ.t̬ɪŋ **-ated/ly** -eɪ.tɪd/li, ⓤⓢ -eɪ.t̬ɪd/li **-ator/s** -eɪ.təʳ/z, ⓤⓢ -eɪ.t̬ɚ/z
exaggeration ɪgˌzædʒ.ərˈeɪ.ʃən, egˌ-; ɪkˌsædʒ-, ekˌ-, ⓤⓢ ɪgˌzædʒ-, egˌ- **-s** ⓤⓢ -z
exaggerative ɪgˈzædʒ.ər.ə.tɪv, egˈ-; ɪkˈsædʒ-, ekˈ-, ⓤⓢ ɪgˈzædʒ.ɚ.ə.t̬ɪv, egˈ-
exal|t ɪgˈzɔːl|t, egˈ-, -ˈzɒl|t; ɪkˈsɔːl|t, ekˈ-, -ˈsɒl|t, ⓤⓢ ɪgˈzɔːl|t, eg-, -ˈzɑːl|t **-ts** -ts **-ting** -tɪŋ, ⓤⓢ -t̬ɪŋ **-ted/ly** -tɪd/li, ⓤⓢ -t̬ɪd/li **-tedness** -tɪd.nəs, ⓤⓢ -t̬ɪd.nəs, -nɪs
exaltation ˌeg.zɔːlˈteɪ.ʃən, ˌek.sɔːlˈ-, -sɒlˈ-, ⓤⓢ ˌeg.zɔːlˈ-, -zɑːlˈ-; ⓤⓢ ˌek.sɔːlˈ-, -sɑːlˈ- **-s** -z
exam ɪgˈzæm, egˈ-; ɪkˈsæm, ekˈ-, ⓤⓢ ɪgˈzæm, egˈ- **-s** -z
examen egˈzeɪ.men, ɪgˈ- **-s** -z
examination ɪgˌzæm.ɪˈneɪ.ʃən, egˌ-; ɪkˌsæm-, ekˌ-, -əˈ-, ⓤⓢ ɪgˌzæm-, egˌ- **-s** -z **exˌamiˈnation** ˌ**paper**
examin|e ɪgˈzæm.ɪn, egˈ-; ɪkˈsæm-, ekˈ-, ⓤⓢ ɪgˈzæm-, egˈ- **-es** -z **-ing** -ɪŋ **-ed** -d **-er/s** -əʳ/z, ⓤⓢ -ɚ/z
examinee ɪgˌzæm.ɪˈniː, egˌ-; ɪkˌsæm-, ekˌ-, -əˈ-, ⓤⓢ ɪgˌzæm-, egˌ- **-s** -z
exampl|e ɪgˈzɑːm.pəl, egˈ-; ɪkˈsɑːm-, ekˈ-, ⓤⓢ ɪgˈzæm-, egˈ- **-es** -z **-ing** -ɪŋ, ˈ-plɪŋ **-ed** -d
exarch ˈek.sɑːk, ⓤⓢ -sɑːrk **-s** -s **-ate/s** -eɪt/s
exasper|ate ɪgˈzæs.pər|.eɪt, egˈ-; ɪkˈsæs-, ekˈ-, -ˈzɑː.spər-, ⓤⓢ ɪgˈzæs.pə.r|eɪt, egˈ- **-ates** -eɪts **-ating/ly** -eɪ.tɪŋ/li, ⓤⓢ -eɪ.t̬ɪŋ/li **-ated/ly** -eɪ.tɪd/li, ⓤⓢ -eɪ.t̬ɪd/li
exasperation ɪgˌzæs.pəˈreɪ.ʃən, egˌ-; ɪkˌsæs-, ekˌ-, -ˌzɑː.spəˈ-, ⓤⓢ ɪgˈzæs.pəˈ-, eg-
Excalibur ekˈskæl.ɪ.bəʳ, ɪkˈ-, ˈ-ə-, ⓤⓢ -bɚ
ex cathedra ˌeks.kəˈθiː.drə, -ˈθed.rə, -rɑː, ⓤⓢ -kəˈθiː.drə; ⓤⓢ -ˈkæθ.ɪ-
exca|vate ˈek.skə|.veɪt **-vates** -veɪts **-vating** -veɪ.tɪŋ, ⓤⓢ -veɪ.t̬ɪŋ **-vated** -veɪ.tɪd, ⓤⓢ -veɪ.t̬ɪd **-vator/s** -veɪ.təʳ/z, ⓤⓢ -veɪ.t̬ɚ/z
excavation ˌeks.kəˈveɪ.ʃən **-s** -z
exceed ɪkˈsiːd, ek- **-s** -z **-ing/ly** -ɪŋ/li **-ed** -ɪd
exceeding ɪkˈsiː.dɪŋ, ek- **-ly** -li
excel ɪkˈsel, ek- **-s** -z **-ling** -ɪŋ **-led** -d
excellenc|e ˈek.səl.ənts **-es** -ɪz
excellenc|y, E~ ˈek.səl.ənt.s|i **-ies** -iz
excellent ˈek.səl.ənt **-ly** -li
excelsior ekˈsel.si.ɔːʳ, ɪk-, -əʳ, ⓤⓢ -ɔːr, -ɚ
except ɪkˈsept, ek- **-s** -s **-ing** -ɪŋ **-ed** -ɪd
exception ɪkˈsep.ʃən, ek- **-s** -z
exceptionab|le ɪkˈsep.ʃən.ə.b|əl, ek- **-ly** -li **-leness** -əl.nəs, -nɪs
exceptional ɪkˈsep.ʃən.əl, ek- **-ly** -i
excerpt n ˈek.sɜːpt, ˈeg.zɜːpt, ⓤⓢ ˈek.sɝːpt, ˈeg.zɝːpt **-s** -s
excerpt v ekˈsɜːpt, ɪkˈ-, ⓤⓢ ekˈsɝːpt, egˈzɝːpt **-s** -s **-ing** -ɪŋ **-ed** -ɪd
excerption ekˈsɜːp.ʃən, ɪk-, ⓤⓢ ekˈsɝːp-, egˈzɝːp- **-s** -z
excess ɪkˈses, ekˈ- **-es** -ɪz **-ing** -ɪŋ **-ed** -t *stress shift:* ˌ**excess** ˈ**baggage**
excessive ɪkˈses.ɪv, ekˈ- **-ly** -li **-ness** -nəs, -nɪs
exchang|e ɪksˈtʃeɪndʒ, eksˈ- **-es** -ɪz **-ing** -ɪŋ **-ed** -d **-er/s** -əʳ/z, ⓤⓢ -ɚ/z **-eable** -ə.bəl **exˈchange** ˌ**rate**; **Exˈchange** ˌ**Rate** ˌ**Mechanism**
exchangeability ɪksˌtʃeɪn.dʒəˈbɪl.ə.ti, eksˌ-, -ɪ.ti, ⓤⓢ -ə.t̬i
exchangee ˌeks.tʃeɪnˈdʒiː; ɪksˌtʃeɪnˈ- **-s** -z

exchequer, E~ ɪksˈtʃek.əʳ, eksˈ-, (US) -ɚ -s -z ˌ**Chancellor of the Exˈchequer**
excisable ekˈsaɪ.zə.bəl, ɪkˈ-, (US) ekˈsaɪ-, ˈek.saɪ-
excise n *tax:* ˈek.saɪz; ekˈsaɪz, ɪkˈ-, (US) ˈek.saɪz, -saɪs **-man** -mæn **-men** -men
excis|e v *cut out:* ekˈsaɪz, ɪk- **-es** -ɪz **-ing** -ɪŋ **-ed** -d
excision ekˈsɪʒ.ən, ɪkˈ- **-s** -z
excitability ɪkˌsaɪ.təˈbɪl.ə.ti, ekˌ-, -ɪ.ti, (US) -t̬əˈbɪl.ə.t̬i
excitab|le ɪkˈsaɪ.tə.b|əl, ekˈ-, (US) -t̬ə- **-ly** -li **-leness** -əl.nəs, -nɪs
excitant ˈek.sɪ.tənt; ɪkˈsaɪ-, ekˈ-, (US) ɪkˈsaɪ.tənt **-s** -s
excitation ˌek.sɪˈteɪ.ʃən, -səˈ-, -saɪˈ-, (US) ˌek.saɪˈ- **-s** -z
excita|tive ekˈsaɪ.tə|.tɪv, ɪkˈ-, (US) -t̬ə|.t̬ɪv **-tory** -tər.i, -tri, (US) -tɔːr.i
ex|cite ɪk|ˈsaɪt, ek|ˈ- **-cites** -ˈsaɪts **-citing/ly** -ˈsaɪ.tɪŋ/li, (US) -ˈsaɪ.t̬ɪŋ/li **-cited** -ˈsaɪ.tɪd, (US) -ˈsaɪ.t̬ɪd **-citer/s** -ˈsaɪ.təʳ/z, (US) -ˈsaɪ.t̬ɚ/z
excitement ɪkˈsaɪt.mənt, ekˈ- **-s** -s
exclaim ɪksˈkleɪm, eksˈ- **-s** -z **-ing** -ɪŋ **-ed** -d
exclamation ˌeks.kləˈmeɪ.ʃən **-s** -z **exclaˈmation ˌmark; exclaˈmation ˌpoint**
exclamatory eksˈklæm.ə.tər.i, ɪksˈ-, -tri, (US) -tɔːr.i
exclave ˈeks.kleɪv **-s** -z
exclud|e ɪksˈkluːd, eksˈ- **-es** -z **-ing** -ɪŋ **-ed** -ɪd
exclusion ɪksˈkluː.ʒən, eksˈ- **-s** -z
exclusionary ɪksˈkluː.ʒən.ər.i, eksˈ-, (US) -er-
exclusionist ɪksˈkluː.ʒən.ɪst, eksˈ- **-s** -s
exclusive ɪksˈkluː.sɪv, eksˈ- **-ly** -li **-ness** -nəs, -nɪs
exclusiv|ism ɪksˈkluː.sɪ.v|ɪ.zəm, eksˈ-, -sə- **-ist/s** -ɪst/s
exclusivistic ɪksˌkluː.sɪˈvɪs.tɪk, eksˌ-, -səˈ-
exclusivity ˌeks.kluːˈsɪv.ə.ti, -ɪ.ti, (US) -ə.t̬i
excogi|tate ekˈskɒdʒ.ɪ|.teɪt, ɪkˈ-, (US) -ˈskɑː.dʒɪ- **-tates** -teɪts **-tating** -teɪ.tɪŋ, (US) -teɪ.t̬ɪŋ **-tated** -teɪ.tɪd, (US) -teɪ.t̬ɪd
excogitation ˌek.skɒdʒ.ɪˈteɪ.ʃən; ɪkˌskɒdʒ.ɪˈ-, ekˌ-, (US) ɪkˌskɑː.dʒɪˈ-, ekˌ- **-s** -z
excommuni|cate ˌek.skəˈmjuː.nɪ|.keɪt, -nə- **-cates** -keɪts **-cating** -keɪ.tɪŋ, (US) -keɪ.t̬ɪŋ **-cated** -keɪ.tɪd, (US) -keɪ.t̬ɪd
excommunication ˌek.skəˌmjuː.nɪˈkeɪ.ʃən, -nəˈ- **-s** -z
excori|ate ekˈskɔː.ri|.eɪt, ɪkˈ-, -ˈskɒr.i-, (US) -ˈskɔːr.i- **-ates** -eɪts **-ating** -eɪ.tɪŋ, (US) -eɪ.t̬ɪŋ **-ated** -eɪ.tɪd, (US) -eɪ.t̬ɪd
excoriation ekˌskɔː.riˈeɪ.ʃən, ɪkˌ-, -ˌskɒr.iˈ-, (US) -ˌskɔːr.iˈ- **-s** -z
excrement ˈek.skrə.mənt, -skrɪ- **-s** -s
excremental ˌek.skrəˈmen.təl, -skrɪˈ-, (US) -t̬əl
excrescen|ce ɪkˈskres.ən|ts, ekˈ- **-ces** -t.sɪz **-t** -t
excreta ɪkˈskriː.tə, ekˈ-, (US) -t̬ə
ex|crete ɪkˈs|kriːt, ekˈ- **-cretes** -kriːts **-creting** -kriː.tɪŋ, (US) -kriː.t̬ɪŋ **-creted** -kriː.tɪd, (US) -kriː.t̬ɪd **-cretive** -kriː.tɪv, (US) -kriː.t̬ɪv **-cretory** -kriː.tər.i, (US) -kriː.t̬ɚ.i
excretion ɪkˈskriː.ʃən, ekˈ- **-s** -z
excret|um ɪkˈskriː.t|əm, ekˈ-, (US) -t̬|əm **-a** -ə
excruci|ate ɪkˈskruː.ʃi|.eɪt, ekˈ-, -si-, (US) -ʃi- **-ates** -eɪts **-ating/ly** -eɪ.tɪŋ/li, (US) -eɪ.t̬ɪŋ/li **-ated** -eɪ.tɪd, (US) -eɪ.t̬ɪd
excruciation ɪkˌskruː.ʃiˈeɪ.ʃən, ekˌ-, -siˈ-, (US) -ʃiˈ-
excul|pate ˈek.skʌl|.peɪt; ɪkˈskʌl-, ekˈ- **-pates** -peɪts **-pating** -peɪ.tɪŋ, (US) -peɪ.t̬ɪŋ **-pated** -peɪ.tɪd, (US) -peɪ.t̬ɪd
exculpation ˌek.skʌlˈpeɪ.ʃən
exculpatory ekˈskʌl.pə.tər.i, -tri, (US) -tɔːr.i
excurs|e ɪkˈskɜːs, ekˈ-, (US) -ˈskɝːs **-es** -ɪz **-ing** -ɪŋ **-ed** -t
excursion ɪkˈskɜː.ʃən, ekˈ-, -ʒən, (US) -ˈskɝː.ʒən **-s** -z
excursionist ɪkˈskɜː.ʃən.ɪst, ekˈ-, -ʒən-, (US) -ˈskɝː.ʒən- **-s** -s
excursioniz|e, -is|e ɪkˈskɜː.ʃən.aɪz, ekˈ-, -ʒən-, (US) -ˈskɝː.ʒən- **-es** -ɪz **-ing** -ɪŋ **-ed** -d
excursive ɪkˈskɜː.sɪv, ekˈ-, (US) -ˈskɝː- **-ly** -li **-ness** -nəs, -nɪs
excursus ekˈskɜː.səs, ɪkˈ-, (US) -ˈskɝː- **-es** -ɪz
excusab|le ɪkˈskjuː.zə.b|əl, ekˈ- **-ly** -li **-leness** -əl.nəs, -nɪs
excusatory ɪkˈskjuː.zə.tər.i, ekˈ-, -tri, (US) -tɔːr.i
excus|e n ɪkˈskjuːs, ekˈ- **-es** -ɪz
excus|e v ɪkˈskjuːz, ekˈ- **-es** -ɪz **-ing** -ɪŋ **-ed** -d
ex delicto ˌeks.delˈɪk.təʊ, (US) -diːˈlɪk.toʊ, -dɪˈ-
ex-directory ˌeks.dəˈrek.tər.i, -dɪˈ-, -daɪˈ-, ˈ-tri
Exe eks
exeat ˈek.si.æt, -seɪ- **-s** -s
exec ɪgˈzek, eg-, ɪkˈsek, ek-, (US) ɪgˈzek, əg- **-s** -s
execrab|le ˈek.sɪ.krə.b|əl, -sə- **-ly** -li **-leness** -əl.nəs, -nɪs
exe|crate ˈek.sɪ|.kreɪt, -sə- **-crates** -kreɪts **-crating** -kreɪ.tɪŋ, (US) -kreɪ.t̬ɪŋ **-crated** -kreɪ.tɪd, (US) -kreɪ.t̬ɪd
execration ˌek.sɪˈkreɪ.ʃən, -səˈ- **-s** -z
execra|tive ˈek.sɪ.kreɪ|.tɪv, -sə-, (US) -t̬ɪv **-tively** -tɪv.li, (US) -t̬ɪv.li **-tory** -tər.i, -tri, (US) -tɔːr.i
executant ɪgˈzek.jə.tənt, eg-, -jʊ-; ɪkˈsek-, ek-, (US) ɪgˈzek.jə-, eg- **-s** -s
exe|cute ˈek.sɪ|.kjuːt, -sə- **-cutes** -kjuːts **-cuting** -kjuː.tɪŋ, (US) -kjuː.t̬ɪŋ **-cuted** -kjuː.tɪd, (US) -kjuː.t̬ɪd **-cuter/s** -kjuː.təʳ/z, (US) -kjuː.t̬ɚ/z **-cutable** -kjuː.tə.bəl, (US) -kjuː.t̬ə.bəl
execution ˌek.sɪˈkjuː.ʃən, -səˈ- **-s** -z
executioner ˌek.sɪˈkjuː.ʃən.əʳ, -səˈ-, (US) -ɚ **-s** -z
executive ɪgˈzek.jə.tɪv, eg-, -jʊ-; ɪkˈsek-, ek-, (US) ɪgˈzek.jə.t̬ɪv, eg- **-s** (US) -z **-ly** (US) -li **exˌecutive ˈprivilege**
executor ɪgˈzek.jə.təʳ, eg-, -jʊ-; ɪkˈsek-, ek-, (US) ɪgˈzek.jə.t̬ɚ, eg- **-s** -z **-ship/s** -ʃɪp/s
executory ɪgˈzek.jə.tər.i, eg-, -jʊ-, -tri, ɪkˈsek-, ek-, (US) ɪgˈzek.jə.tɔːr.i, eg-
executr|ix ɪgˈzek.jə.tr|ɪks, eg-, -jʊ-; ɪkˈsek-, ek-, (US) ɪgˈzek.jə-, eg- **-ixes** -ɪk.sɪz **executrices** ɪgˌzek.jəˈtraɪ.siːz, eg-, -jʊ-; ɪkˌsek-, ek-, (US) ɪgˌzek.jəˈ-, eg-
exeges|is ˌek.sɪˈdʒiː.s|ɪs, -səˈ- **-es** -iːz
exegetic ˌek.sɪˈdʒet.ɪk, -səˈ-, -ˈdʒiː.tɪk, (US) -ˈdʒet̬- **-al** -əl **-ally** -əl.i, -li **-s** -s
exemplar ɪgˈzem.plɑːʳ, eg-; ɪkˈsem-, ek-, -pləʳ, (US) ɪgˈzem.plɑːr, eg-, -plɚ **-s** -z
exemplarity ˌeg.zemˈplær.ə.ti, -ɪ.ti, (US) -ˈpler.ə.t̬i, -ˈplær-
exemplar|y ɪgˈzem.plər|.i, eg-; ɪkˈsem-, ek-, (US) ɪgˈzem-, eg- **-ily** -əl.i, -ɪ.li **-iness** -ɪ.nəs, -ɪ.nɪs
exemplification ɪgˌzem.plɪ.fɪˈkeɪ.ʃən, eg-, -plə-, -fəˈ-; ɪkˌsem-, ek-, (US) ɪgˌzem.plə-, eg- **-s** -z
exempli|fy ɪgˈzem.plɪ|.faɪ, eg-, -plə-; ɪkˈsem-, ek-, (US) ɪgˈzem-, eg- **-fies** -faɪz **-fying** -faɪ.ɪŋ **-fied** -faɪd
exemplum ɪgˈzem.pləm, egˈ-; ɪkˈsem-, ekˈ-
exempt ɪgˈzempt, egˈ-; ɪkˈsempt, ekˈ-, (US) ɪgˈzempt, egˈ- **-s** -s **-ing** -ɪŋ **-ed** -ɪd
exemption ɪgˈzemp.ʃən, egˈ-; ɪkˈsemp-, ekˈ-, (US) ɪgˈzemp-, egˈ **-s** -z
exequatur ˌek.sɪˈkweɪ.təʳ, -səˈ-, (US) -t̬ɚ **-s** -z
exequies ˈek.sɪ.kwɪz, -sə-, (US) -kwiːz
exercis|e ˈek.sə.saɪz, (US) -sɚ- **-es** -ɪz **-ing** -ɪŋ **-ed** -d **-er/s** -əʳ/z, (US) -ɚ/z ˈ**exercise ˌbook**
exercitation egˌzɜː.sɪˈteɪ.ʃən, ɪgˌ-, (US) -ˌzɝː-
exergue ekˈsɜːg, ˈ--, (US) ˈek.sɝːg, ˈeg.zɝːg **-s** -z
exer|t ɪgˈzɜː|t, eg-; ɪkˈsɜː|t, ek-, (US) ɪgˈzɝː|t, eg- **-ts** -ts **-ting** -tɪŋ, (US) -t̬ɪŋ **-ted** -tɪd, (US) -t̬ɪd **-tive** -tɪv, (US) -t̬ɪv
exertion ɪgˈzɜː.ʃən, eg-; ɪkˈsɜː-, ek-, (US) ɪgˈzɝː-, eg- **-s** -z
Exeter ˈek.sɪ.təʳ, -sə-, (US) -t̬ɚ
exeunt ˈek.si.ʌnt, -seɪ-, -ʊnt, -si.ənt, (US) -si.ʌnt, -ənt
exfoliant eksˈfəʊ.li.ənt, (US) -ˈfoʊ- **-s** -s
exfoli|ate eksˈfəʊ.li|.eɪt, (US) -ˈfoʊ-

-ates -eɪts -ating -eɪ.tɪŋ, ⓤⓢ -eɪ.t̬ɪŋ -ated -eɪ.tɪd, ⓤⓢ -eɪ.t̬ɪd -ator -eɪ.təʳ, ⓤⓢ -eɪ.t̬ɚ
exfoliation eksˌfəʊ.liˈeɪ.ʃən, ˌeks.fəʊ-, ⓤⓢ eksˌfoʊ- **-s** -z
ex gratia eksˈgreɪ.ʃə, -ʃi.ə
exhalant, exhalent eksˈheɪ.lənt, ɪks-; egˈzeɪ-, ⓤⓢ eksˈheɪ-
exhalation ˌeks.*h*əˈleɪ.ʃən **-s** -z
exhal|e eksˈheɪl, ɪks-; egˈzeɪl, ⓤⓢ eksˈheɪl, ˈ-- **-es** -z **-ing** -ɪŋ **-ed** -d
exhaust ɪgˈzɔːst, egˈ-; ɪkˈsɔːst, ekˈ-, ⓤⓢ ɪgˈzɑːst, egˈ-, -ˈzɔːst **-s** -s **-ing** -ɪŋ **-ed** -ɪd **-er/s** -əʳ/z, ⓤⓢ -ɚ/z **-ible** -ə.bəl, -ɪ.bəl **-less** -ləs, -lɪs **exˈhaust ˌpipe**
exhaustion ɪgˈzɔːs.tʃən, eg-; ɪkˈsɔː-, ek-, ⓤⓢ ɪgˈzɑː-, eg-, -ˈzɔː-
exhaustive ɪgˈzɔː.stɪv, eg-; ɪkˈsɔː-, ek-, ⓤⓢ ɪgˈzɑː-, eg-, -ˈzɔː- **-ly** -li **-ness** -nəs, -nɪs
exhibit n ɪgˈzɪb.ɪt, eg-; ɪkˈsɪb-, ek-; ˈeg.zɪb-, ˈek.sɪb-, ⓤⓢ ɪgˈzɪb-, eg- **-s** -s
exhib|it v ɪgˈzɪb|.ɪt, eg-; ɪkˈsɪb-, ek-, ⓤⓢ ɪgˈzɪb-, eg- **-its** -ɪts **-iting** -ɪ.tɪŋ, ⓤⓢ -ɪ.t̬ɪŋ **-ited** -ɪ.tɪd, ⓤⓢ -ɪ.t̬ɪd **-itor/s** -ɪ.təʳ/z, ⓤⓢ -ɪ.t̬ɚ/z **-itive** -ɪ.tɪv, ⓤⓢ -ɪ.t̬ɪv **-itory** -ɪ.tər.i, -ɪ.tri, ⓤⓢ -ɪ.tɔːr.i
exhibition ˌek.sɪˈbɪʃ.ən, -səˈ- **-s** -z
exhibitioner ˌek.sɪˈbɪʃ.ən.əʳ, -səˈ-, ⓤⓢ -ɚ **-s** -z
exhibitionism ˌek.sɪˈbɪʃ.ən.ɪ.zəm, -səˈ-
exhibitionist ˌek.sɪˈbɪʃ.ən.ɪst, -səˈ- **-s** -s
exhibitionistic ˌek.sɪ.bɪ.ʃənˈɪs.tɪk, -sə- **-ally** -əl.i, -li
exhilarant ɪgˈzɪl.ər.ənt, eg-; ɪkˈsɪl-, ek-, ⓤⓢ ɪgˈzɪl-, eg- **-s** -s
exhilar|ate ɪgˈzɪl.ər|.eɪt, eg-; ɪkˈsɪl-, ek-, ⓤⓢ ɪgˈzɪl-, eg- **-ates** -eɪts **-ating** -eɪ.tɪŋ, ⓤⓢ -eɪ.t̬ɪŋ **-ated** -eɪ.tɪd, ⓤⓢ -eɪ.t̬ɪd
exhilaration ɪgˌzɪl.ərˈeɪ.ʃən, eg-; ɪkˌsɪl-, ek-, ⓤⓢ ɪgˌzɪl-, eg-
exhilarative ɪgˈzɪl.ər.ə.tɪv, eg-, -eɪ-; ɪkˈsɪl-, ek-, ⓤⓢ ɪgˈzɪl.ə.reɪ.t̬ɪv, eg-
exhor|t ɪgˈzɔː|t, eg-; ɪkˈsɔː|t, ek-, ⓤⓢ ɪgˈzɔːr|t, eg- **-ts** -ts **-ting** -tɪŋ, ⓤⓢ -t̬ɪŋ **-ted** -tɪd, ⓤⓢ -t̬ɪd
exhortation ˌeg.zɔːˈteɪ.ʃən, ˌek.sɔːˈ-, ⓤⓢ ˌeg.zɔːrˈ-, -zɚˈ-; ⓤⓢ ˌek.sɔːrˈ-, -sɚˈ- **-s** -z
exhorta|tive ɪgˈzɔː.tə|.tɪv, eg-; ɪkˈsɔː-, ek-, ⓤⓢ ɪgˈzɔːr.t̬ə|.t̬ɪv, eg- **-tory** -tər.i, -tri, ⓤⓢ -tɔːr.i
exhumation ˌeks.*h*juːˈmeɪ.ʃən, ⓤⓢ ˌeks.*h*juːˈ-, ˌeg.zjuːˈ- **-s** -z
exhum|e eksˈ*h*juːm, ɪksˈ-; ɪgˈzjuːm, egˈ-, ⓤⓢ egˈzuːm, ɪgˈ-, -ˈzjuːm **-es** -z **-ing** -ɪŋ **-ed** -d **-er/s** -əʳ/z, ⓤⓢ -ɚ/z
exigen|ce ˈek.sɪ.dʒən*t*|s, -sə-; ˈeg.zɪ-, -zə- **-ces** -sɪz
exigenc|y ˈek.sɪ.dʒən*t*.s|i, -sə-; ˈeg.zɪ-, -zə-; ɪgˈzɪdʒ.ən*t*-, eg-; ɪkˈsɪdʒ-, ek- **-ies** -iz
exigent ˈek.sɪ.dʒənt, -sə-; ˈeg.zɪ-, -zə- **-ly** -li
exiguity ˌek.sɪˈgjuː.ə.ti, -ɪ.ti, ⓤⓢ ˌek.sɪˈgjuː.ə.t̬i, ˌeg.zɪˈ-
exiguous egˈzɪg.ju.əs, ɪg-; ekˈsɪg-, ɪk-, ⓤⓢ egˈzɪg-, ɪg- **-ness** -nəs, -nɪs
exil|e ˈek.saɪl, ˈeg.zaɪl **-es** -z **-ing** -ɪŋ **-ed** -d
exist ɪgˈzɪst, eg-; ɪkˈsɪst, ek-, ⓤⓢ ɪgˈzɪst, eg- **-s** -s **-ing** -ɪŋ **-ed** -ɪd
existen|ce ɪgˈzɪs.tən|*t*s, eg-; ɪkˈsɪs-, ek-, ⓤⓢ ɪgˈzɪs-, eg- **-ces** -*t*.sɪz
existent ɪgˈzɪs.tənt, eg-; ɪkˈsɪs-, ek-, ⓤⓢ ɪgˈzɪs-, eg-
existential ˌeg.zɪˈsten.*t*ʃəl, -zəˈ-; ˌek.sɪˈ-, -səˈ-
existential|ism ˌeg.zɪˈsten.*t*ʃəl|.ɪ.zəm, -zəˈ-; ˌek.sɪˈ-, -səˈ- **-ist/s** -ɪst/s
exit ˈek.sɪt, ˈeg.zɪt **-s** -s **-ing** -ɪŋ **-ed** -ɪd **ˈexit ˌpoll**
ex libris ˌeksˈlɪb.riːs, -rɪs, -ˈlaɪ.brɪs, ⓤⓢ -ˈliː.brɪs
Exmoor ˈek.smɔːʳ, -smʊəʳ, ⓤⓢ -smʊr
Exmouth *in Devon:* ˈek.sməθ *in Australia:* ˈek.smaʊθ
exo- ˈek.sə*ʊ*; ɪkˈsɒ, ek-, ⓤⓢ ˈek.soʊ, -sə; ⓤⓢ ɪkˈsɑː, ek-
Note: Prefix. Either carries primary or secondary stress on the first syllable, e.g. **exocrine** /ˈek.sə*ʊ*.kraɪn/ ⓤⓢ /-sə.krən/, **exocentric** /ˌek.sə*ʊ*ˈsen.trɪk/ ⓤⓢ /-soʊˈ-/, or primary stress on the second syllable, e.g. **exogamy** /ekˈsɒg.ə.mi/ ⓤⓢ /-ˈsɑː.gə-/.
exocentric ˌek.sə*ʊ*ˈsen.trɪk, ⓤⓢ -soʊˈ-, -səˈ- **-ally** -ə.li, -li
Exocet® ˈek.sə*ʊ*.set, ⓤⓢ -soʊ-, -sə- **-s** -s
exocrine ˈek.sə*ʊ*.kraɪn, -krɪn, ⓤⓢ ˈek.sə.krən, -soʊ-, -kraɪn, -kriːn
exode ˈek.səʊd, ⓤⓢ -soʊd **-s** -z
exodus, E~ ˈek.sə.dəs **-es** -ɪz
ex officio ˌeks.əˈfɪʃ.i.əʊ, -ɒfˈɪʃ-, -ˈɪs-, ⓤⓢ -əˈfɪʃ.i.oʊ, -ˈfɪs-
exogam|y ɪkˈsɒg.ə.m|i, ek-, ⓤⓢ -ˈsɑː.gə- **-ous** -əs
exogenous ɪkˈsɒdʒ.ɪ.nəs, ek-, -ə.nəs, ⓤⓢ -ˈsɑː.dʒɪ-, ˈ-dʒə-
exon ˈek.sɒn, ⓤⓢ -sɑːn **-s** -z
exoner|ate ɪgˈzɒn.ər|.eɪt, eg-; ɪkˈsɒn-, ek-, ⓤⓢ ɪgˈzɑː.nə.r|eɪt, eg- **-ates** -eɪts **-ating** -eɪ.tɪŋ, ⓤⓢ -eɪ.t̬ɪŋ **-ated** -eɪ.tɪd, ⓤⓢ -eɪ.t̬ɪd
exoneration ɪgˌzɒn.əˈreɪ.ʃən, eg-; ɪkˌsɒn-, ek-, ⓤⓢ ɪgˌzɑː.nəˈ-, eg-
exonerative ɪgˈzɒn.ər.ə.tɪv, eg-, -eɪ-; ɪkˈsɒn-, ek-, -eɪ.tɪv, ⓤⓢ ɪgˈzɑː.nə.reɪ.t̬ɪv, eg-
exophora ekˈsɒf.ər.ə, ⓤⓢ -ˈsɑː.fɚ-
exophoric ˌek.sə*ʊ*ˈfɒr.ɪk, ⓤⓢ -səˈfɔːr-
exorbitan|ce ɪgˈzɔː.bɪ.tən*t*|s, eg-, -bə-; ɪkˈsɔː-, ek-, ⓤⓢ ɪgˈzɔːr.bə.t̬ən*t*|s, eg- **-cy** -si
exorbitant ɪgˈzɔː.bɪ.tənt, eg-, -bə-; ɪkˈsɔː-, ek-, ⓤⓢ ɪgˈzɔːr.bə.t̬ənt, eg- **-ly** -li
exorc|ism ˈek.sɔː.s|ɪ.zəm, -sə-; ˈeg.zɔː-, -zə-, ⓤⓢ ˈek.sɔːr-, -sɚ- **-ist/s** -ɪst/s
exorciz|e, -is|e ˈek.sɔː.saɪz, -sə-; ˈeg.zɔː-, -zə-, ⓤⓢ ˈek.sɔːr-, -sɚ- **-es** -ɪz **-ing** -ɪŋ **-ed** -d
exordi|um ekˈsɔː.di|.əm; egˈzɔː-, ⓤⓢ egˈzɔːr.di-, ɪg-; ⓤⓢ ekˈsɔːr-, ɪk- **-ums** -əmz **-a** -ə
exoskelet|on ˌek.səʊˈskel.ɪ.t|ən, ˈ-ə-, ˈek.səʊˌskel-, ⓤⓢ ˌek.soʊˈskel.ə- **-ons** -ənz **-al** -əl
exoteric ˌek.sə*ʊ*ˈter.ɪk, ⓤⓢ -səˈ-, -soʊˈ- **-s** -s **-al** -əl **-ally** -əl.i, -li
exotic ɪgˈzɒt.ɪk, eg-; ɪkˈsɒt-, ek-, ⓤⓢ ɪgˈzɑː.t̬ɪk, eg- **-s** -s **-a** -ə **-ally** -əl.i, -li
exoticism ɪgˈzɒt.ɪ.sɪ.zəm, eg-, ˈ-ə-; ɪkˈsɒt-, ek-, ək-, ⓤⓢ ɪgˈzɑː.t̬ə-, eg-
expand ɪkˈspænd, ek- **-s** -z **-ing** -ɪŋ **-ed** -ɪd **-er/s** -əʳ/z, ⓤⓢ -ɚ/z **-able** -ə.bəl
expans|e ɪkˈspæn*t*s, ek- **-es** -ɪz
expansibility ɪkˌspæn*t*.səˈbɪl.ə.ti, ek-, -sɪˈ-, -ɪ.ti, ⓤⓢ -ə.t̬i
expansib|le ɪkˈspæn*t*.sə.b|əl, ek-, -sɪ- **-ly** -li **-leness** -əl.nəs, -nɪs
expansile ɪkˈspæn*t*.saɪl, ek-, ⓤⓢ -sɪl
expansion ɪkˈspæn.*t*ʃən, ek- **-s** -z
expansion|ism ɪkˈspæn.*t*ʃən|.ɪ.zəm, ek-, ək- **-ist/s** -ɪst/s
expansive ɪkˈspæn*t*.sɪv, ek- **-ly** -li **-ness** -nəs, -nɪs
ex parte ˌeksˈpɑː.teɪ, -ti, ⓤⓢ -ˈpɑːr.ti
expat ˌekˈspæt, ˈ-- **-s** -s *stress shift:* ˌ**expat comˈmunity**

> Note: Abbreviation for ‘expatriate’. The stress pattern ˈ-- appears to be becoming more common, along with the written form ‘ex-pat’ that is occasionally (and incorrectly) expanded to ‘ex-patriot’.

expati|ate ekˈspeɪ.ʃi|.eɪt, ɪk- **-ates** -eɪts **-ating** -eɪ.tɪŋ, ⓤⓢ -eɪ.t̬ɪŋ **-ated** -eɪ.tɪd, ⓤⓢ -eɪ.t̬ɪd
expatiation ekˌspeɪ.ʃiˈeɪ.ʃən, ɪk- **-s** -z
expatia|tive ekˈspeɪ.ʃi.ə|.tɪv, ɪk-, -tɪv, ⓤⓢ -eɪ|.t̬ɪv **-tory** -tər.i, -tri, ⓤⓢ -tɔːr.i
expatriate n, adj ɪkˈspæt.ri.ət, ekˈ-, -ˈspeɪ.tri-, -ɪt, -eɪt, ⓤⓢ ekˈspeɪt-, ɪkˈ- **-s** -s
expatri|ate v ɪkˈspæt.ri|.eɪt, ekˈ-, -ˈspeɪ.tri-, ⓤⓢ ekˈspeɪt-, ɪkˈ- **-ates** -eɪts **-ating** -eɪ.tɪŋ, ⓤⓢ -eɪ.t̬ɪŋ **-ated** -eɪ.tɪd, ⓤⓢ -eɪ.t̬ɪd
expatriation ekˌspæt.riˈeɪ.ʃən, ɪk-, -ˌspeɪ.triˈ-, ˌek.speɪ-, ˌek.spæt.riˈ-, ⓤⓢ ekˌspeɪ.triˈeɪ-, ɪk-
expect ɪkˈspekt, ek- **-s** -s **-ing** -ɪŋ **-ed** -ɪd
expectan|cy ɪkˈspek.tən*t*|si, ek- **-ce** -s **-cies** -siz
expectant ɪkˈspek.tənt, ek- **-ly** -li
expectation ˌek.spekˈteɪ.ʃən **-s** -z
expectorant ɪkˈspek.tər.ənt, ek- **-s** -s
expector|ate ɪkˈspek.tər|.eɪt, ek- **-ates** -eɪts **-ating** -eɪ.tɪŋ, ⓤⓢ -eɪ.t̬ɪŋ **-ated** -eɪ.tɪd, ⓤⓢ -eɪ.t̬ɪd

expectoration ɪkˌspek.təʳˈeɪ.ʃən, ek-
Expedia ɪkˈspiː.di.ə, ek-
expedien|cy ɪkˈspiː.di.ənt|si, ek- -ce -s
expedient ɪkˈspiː.di.ənt, ek- -s -s -ly -li
expe|dite ˈek.spɪ|.daɪt, -spə- -dites -daɪts -diting -daɪ.tɪŋ, Ⓤⓢ -daɪ.t̬ɪŋ -dited -daɪ.tɪd, Ⓤⓢ -daɪ.t̬ɪd
expediter ˈek.spɪ.daɪ.təʳ, -spə-, Ⓤⓢ -t̬ɚ -s -z
expedition ˌek.spɪˈdɪʃ.ən, -spəˈ- -s -z
expeditionary ˌek.spɪˈdɪʃ.ən.ər.i, -spɪˈ-, -ri, Ⓤⓢ -er-
expeditious ˌek.spɪˈdɪʃ.əs, -spəˈ- -ly -li -ness -nəs, -nɪs
expeditor ˈek.spɪ.daɪ.təʳ, -spə-, Ⓤⓢ -t̬ɚ -s -z
expel ɪkˈspel, ek- -s -z -ling -ɪŋ -led -d -lable -ə.bəl
expend ɪkˈspend, ek- -s -z -ing -ɪŋ -ed -ɪd
expendable ɪkˈspen.də.bəl, ek- -s -z
expenditure ɪkˈspen.dɪ.tʃəʳ, ek-, -də-, Ⓤⓢ -tʃɚ -s -z
expens|e ɪkˈspents, ek- -es -ɪz
exˈpense acˌcount
expensive ɪkˈspent.sɪv, ek- -ly -li -ness -nəs, -nɪs
experienc|e ɪkˈspɪə.ri.ənts, ek-, Ⓤⓢ -ˈspɪr.i- -es -ɪz -ing -ɪŋ -ed -t
experiential ɪkˌspɪə.riˈen.tʃəl, ek-, Ⓤⓢ -ˌspɪr.iˈ- -ly -li
experiment n ɪkˈsper.ɪ.mənt, ek-, ˈ-ə- -s -s
experiment v ɪkˈsper.ɪ.ment, ek-, ˈ-ə- -s -s -ing -ɪŋ -ed -ɪd -er/s -əʳ/z, Ⓤⓢ -ɚ/z
experimental ɪkˌsper.ɪˈmen.təl, ek-, -əˈ-; ˌek.sper-, Ⓤⓢ ekˌsper-, ɪk- -ly -i
experimental|ism ɪkˌsper.ɪˈmen.təl|.ɪ.zəm, ek-, -əˈ-; ˌek.sper-, -əˈmen-, Ⓤⓢ ekˌsperɪˈmen.t̬əl|.ɪ.zəm, ɪk- -ist/s -ɪst/s
experimentaliz|e, -is|e ɪkˌsper.ɪˈmen.təl.aɪz, ek-, -əˈ-; ˌek.sper-, Ⓤⓢ ekˌsper.ɪˈmen.t̬ə.laɪz, ɪk- -es -ɪz -ing -ɪŋ -ed -d
experimentation ɪkˌsper.ɪ.menˈteɪ.ʃən, ek-, ˌ-ə- -s -z
expert ˈek.spɜːt, Ⓤⓢ -spɝːt -s -s -ly -li -ness -nəs, -nɪs
expertise ˌek.spɜːˈtiːz, -spəˈtiːz, Ⓤⓢ -spɝːˈ-, -spɚˈ-
expiable ˈek.spi.ə.bəl
expi|ate ˈek.spi|.eɪt -ates -eɪts -ating -eɪ.tɪŋ, Ⓤⓢ -eɪ.t̬ɪŋ -ated -eɪ.tɪd, Ⓤⓢ -eɪ.t̬ɪd -ator/s -eɪ.təʳ/z, Ⓤⓢ -eɪ.t̬ɚ/z
expiation ˌek.spiˈeɪ.ʃən -s -z
expiatory ˈek.spi.ə.tər.i, -eɪ-, -tri; ˌek.spiˈeɪ-, Ⓤⓢ ˈek.spi.ə.tɔːr.i
expiration ˌek.spɪˈreɪ.ʃən, -spəˈ-, -spaɪəˈ-, Ⓤⓢ -spəˈ- -s -z
expiratory ɪkˈspɪr.ə.tər.i, ek-, -ˈspaɪə.rə-, -tri, Ⓤⓢ -ˈspaɪ.rə.tɔːr.i
expir|e ɪkˈspaɪəʳ, -ˈspaɪ.əʳ, ekˈ-, Ⓤⓢ -ˈspaɪ.ɚ -es -z -ing -ɪŋ -ed -d
expiry ɪkˈspaɪə.ri, ek-, Ⓤⓢ -ˈspaɪ-; Ⓤⓢ ˈek.spɚ.i **exˈpiry ˌdate**
explain ɪkˈspleɪn, ekˈ- -s -z -ing -ɪŋ -ed -d -er/s -əʳ/z, Ⓤⓢ -ɚ/z -able -ə.bəl
explanation ˌek.spləˈneɪ.ʃən -s -z
explanator|y ɪkˈsplæn.ə.tər|.i, ekˈ-, ˈ-ɪ-, -tr|i, Ⓤⓢ -ə.tɔːr|.i -ily -əl.i, -ɪ.li -iness -ɪ.nəs, -ɪ.nɪs
expletive ɪkˈspliː.tɪv, ekˈ-, Ⓤⓢ ˈek.splə.t̬ɪv -s -z
expletory ɪkˈspliː.tər.i, ekˈ-, ˈ-tri, Ⓤⓢ -t̬ɚ.i
explicab|le ɪkˈsplɪk.ə.b|əl, ek-; ˈek.splɪ.kə- -ly -li
expli|cate ˈek.splɪ|.keɪt -cates -keɪts -cating -keɪ.tɪŋ, Ⓤⓢ -keɪ.t̬ɪŋ -cated -keɪ.tɪd, Ⓤⓢ -keɪ.t̬ɪd
explication ˌek.splɪˈkeɪ.ʃən, -spləˈ- -s -z
explicative ekˈsplɪk.ə.tɪv, ɪk-; ˈek.splɪ.keɪ.tɪv, Ⓤⓢ ˈek.splɪ.keɪ.t̬ɪv
explicatory ekˈsplɪk.ə.tər.i, ɪk-, -tri; ˈek.splɪ.keɪ-, ˌek.splɪˈkeɪ-, Ⓤⓢ ˈek.splɪ.kə.tɔːr.i; Ⓤⓢ ɪkˈsplɪk.ə-, ek-
explicit ɪkˈsplɪs.ɪt, ek- -ly -li -ness -nəs, -nɪs
explod|e ɪkˈspləʊd, ek-, Ⓤⓢ -ˈsploʊd -es -z -ing -ɪŋ -ed -ɪd -er/s -əʳ/z, Ⓤⓢ -ɚ/z
exploit n ˈek.splɔɪt -s -s
exploi|t v ɪkˈsplɔɪ|t, ek- -ts -ts -ting -tɪŋ, Ⓤⓢ -t̬ɪŋ -ted -tɪd, Ⓤⓢ -t̬ɪd -ter/s -təʳ/z, Ⓤⓢ -t̬ɚ/z
exploitation ˌek.splɔɪˈteɪ.ʃən
exploitative ɪkˈsplɔɪ.tə.tɪv, ek-, Ⓤⓢ -t̬ə.t̬ɪv -ly -li
exploitive ɪkˈsplɔɪ.tɪv, ek-, Ⓤⓢ -t̬ɪv -ly -li
exploration ˌek.spləˈreɪ.ʃən, -splɔːˈ-, Ⓤⓢ -splɔːr- -s -z
explorative ɪkˈsplɒr.ə.tɪv, ek-, -ˈsplɔː.rə-, Ⓤⓢ -ˈsplɔːr.ə.t̬ɪv
exploratory ɪkˈsplɒr.ə.tər.i, ek-, -ˈsplɔː.rə-, -tri, Ⓤⓢ -ˈsplɔːr.ə.tɔːr.i
explor|e ɪkˈsplɔːʳ, ek-, Ⓤⓢ -ˈsplɔːr -es -z -ing -ɪŋ -ed -d -er/s -əʳ/z, Ⓤⓢ -ɚ/z
explosion ɪkˈspləʊ.ʒən, ek-, Ⓤⓢ -ˈsploʊ- -s -z
explosive ɪkˈspləʊ.sɪv, ek-, -zɪv, Ⓤⓢ -ˈsploʊ.sɪv -s -z -ly -li -ness -nəs, -nɪs
expo ˈek.spəʊ, Ⓤⓢ -spoʊ -s -z
exponent ɪkˈspəʊ.nənt, ek-, Ⓤⓢ -ˈspoʊ- -s -s
exponential ˌek.spəʊˈnen.tʃəl, Ⓤⓢ -spoʊˈnent.ʃəl -ly -li
export n ˈek.spɔːt, Ⓤⓢ -spɔːrt -s -s
expor|t v ɪkˈspɔː|t, ek-; ˈek.spɔː|t, Ⓤⓢ ɪkˈspɔːr|t, ek-; Ⓤⓢ ˈek.spɔːr|t -ts -ts -ting -tɪŋ, Ⓤⓢ -t̬ɪŋ -ted -tɪd, Ⓤⓢ -t̬ɪd -ter/s -təʳ/z, Ⓤⓢ -t̬ɚ/z
exportable ɪkˈspɔː.tə.bəl, ek-, Ⓤⓢ -ˈspɔːr.t̬ə-
exportation ˌek.spɔːˈteɪ.ʃən, Ⓤⓢ -spɔːrˈ-
expos|e ɪkˈspəʊz, ek-, Ⓤⓢ -ˈspoʊz -es -ɪz -ing -ɪŋ -ed -d -edness -d.nəs, -nɪs -er/s -əʳ/z, Ⓤⓢ -ɚ/z
exposé ekˈspəʊ.zeɪ, ɪk-, Ⓤⓢ ˌek.spoʊˈzeɪ, ˈ--- -s -z
exposition ˌek.spəʊˈzɪʃ.ən, Ⓤⓢ -pəˈ- -s -z
expositive ɪkˈspɒz.ɪ.tɪv, ek-, -ə.tɪv, Ⓤⓢ -ˈspɑː.zə.t̬ɪv
exposi|tor ɪkˈspɒz.ɪ|.təʳ, ek-, -ə|.təʳ, Ⓤⓢ -ˈspɑː.zə|.t̬ɚ -tors -təz, Ⓤⓢ -t̬ɚz -tory -tər.i, -tri, Ⓤⓢ -tɔːr.i
ex post facto ˌeks.pəʊstˈfæk.təʊ, Ⓤⓢ -poʊstˈfæk.toʊ
expostu|late ɪkˈspɒs.tʃə|.leɪt, ek-, -tʃʊ-, -tjə-, -tjʊ-, Ⓤⓢ -ˈspɑːs.tʃə- -lates -leɪts -lating -leɪ.tɪŋ, Ⓤⓢ -leɪ.t̬ɪŋ -lated -leɪ.tɪd, Ⓤⓢ -leɪ.t̬ɪd -lator/s -leɪ.təʳ/z, Ⓤⓢ -leɪ.t̬ɚ/z
expostulation ɪkˌspɒs.tʃəˈleɪ.ʃən, ek-, -tʃʊˈ-, -tjəˈ-, -tjʊˈ-, Ⓤⓢ -ˌpɑːs.tʃəˈ- -s -z
expostulative ɪkˈspɒs.tʃə.lə.tɪv, ek-, -tʃʊ-, -tjə-, -tjʊ-, -leɪ-, Ⓤⓢ -ˈpɑːs.tʃə.leɪ.t̬ɪv
expostulatory ɪkˈspɒs.tʃə.lə.tər.i, ek-, -tʃʊ-, -tjə-, -tjʊ-, -leɪ-, -tri, Ⓤⓢ -ˈspɑːs.tʃə.lə.tɔːr.i
exposure ɪkˈspəʊ.ʒəʳ, ek-, Ⓤⓢ -ˈspoʊ.ʒɚ -s -z
expound ɪkˈspaʊnd, ek- -s -z -ing -ɪŋ -ed -ɪd -er/s -əʳ/z, Ⓤⓢ -ɚ/z
express ɪkˈspres, ek- -es -ɪz -ly -li -ness -nəs, -nɪs -ing -ɪŋ -ed -t **ˌexpress deˈlivery, exˌpress deˈlivery** Ⓤⓢ **ˌexpress deˈlivery**
expressible ɪkˈspres.ə.bəl, ek-, -sɪ-
expression ɪkˈspreʃ.ən, ek- -s -z
expressional ɪkˈspreʃ.ən.əl, ek-
expression|ism ɪkˈspreʃ.ən|.ɪ.zəm, ek- -ist/s -ɪst/s
expressionistic ɪkˌspreʃ.əˈnɪs.tɪk, ek- -ally -əl.i, -li
expressionless ɪkˈspreʃ.ən.ləs, ek-, -lɪs -ly -li -ness -nəs, -nɪs
expressive ɪkˈspres.ɪv, ek- -ly -li -ness -nəs, -nɪs
expresso ɪkˈspres.əʊ, ek-, Ⓤⓢ -oʊ -s -z
expressway ɪkˈspres.weɪ, ek- -s -z
expropri|ate ɪkˈsprəʊ.pri|.eɪt, ek-, Ⓤⓢ -ˈsproʊ- -ates -eɪts -ating -eɪ.tɪŋ, Ⓤⓢ -eɪ.t̬ɪŋ -ated -eɪ.tɪd, Ⓤⓢ -eɪ.t̬ɪd -ator/s -eɪ.təʳ/z, Ⓤⓢ -eɪ.t̬ɚ/z
expropriation ɪkˌsprəʊ.priˈeɪ.ʃən, ek-; ˌek.sprəʊ-, Ⓤⓢ ɪkˌsproʊ-, ek- -s -z
expulsion ɪkˈspʌl.ʃən, ek- -s -z
expulsive ɪkˈspʌl.sɪv, ek-
expung|e ɪkˈspʌndʒ, ek- -es -ɪz -ing -ɪŋ -ed -d
expur|gate ˈek.spə|.geɪt, -spɜː-, Ⓤⓢ -spɚ- -gates -geɪts -gating -geɪ.tɪŋ, Ⓤⓢ -geɪ.t̬ɪŋ -gated -geɪ.tɪd, Ⓤⓢ -geɪ.t̬ɪd -gator/s -geɪ.təʳ/z, Ⓤⓢ -geɪ.t̬ɚ/z
expurgation ˌek.spəˈgeɪ.ʃən, -spɜːˈ-, Ⓤⓢ -spɚˈ- -s -z
expurgatory ekˈspɜː.gə.tər.i, ɪkˈ-, -tri, Ⓤⓢ -ˈspɝː.gə.tɔːr.i
exquisite ɪkˈskwɪz.ɪt, ek-;

ˈek.skwɪ.zɪt, -zət -s -s -ly -li -ness -nəs, -nɪs
exscind ekˈsɪnd, ɪk- -s -z -ing -ɪŋ -ed -ɪd
exsect ekˈsekt, ɪk- -s -s -ing -ɪŋ -ed -ɪd
exsection ekˈsek.ʃən, ɪk- -s -z
ex-service ˌeksˈsɜː.vɪs, (US) ˌeksˈsɝː-
exsic|cate ˈek.sɪ|.keɪt, ˈeks- -cates -keɪts -cating -keɪ.tɪŋ, (US) -keɪ.t̬ɪŋ -cated -keɪ.tɪd, (US) -keɪ.t̬ɪd -cator/s -keɪ.təʳ/z, (US) -keɪ.t̬ɚ/z
extant ekˈstænt, ɪk-; ˈek.stənt, (US) ˈek.stənt; (US) ˌekˈstænt
extemporaneous ɪkˌstem.pəˈreɪ.ni.əs, ek-; ˌek.stem-, (US) ɪkˌstem.pəˈ-, ek- -ly -li -ness -nəs, -nɪs
extemporary ɪkˈstem.pər.ə.ri, ek-, (US) -er.i
extempore ɪkˈstem.pər.i, ek-
extemporization, -isa- ɪkˌstem.pər.aɪˈzeɪ.ʃən, ek-, -ɪˈ-, (US) -əˈ- -s -z
extemporiz|e, -is|e ɪkˈstem.pər.aɪz, ek-, (US) -pə.raɪz -es -ɪz -ing -ɪŋ -ed -d -er/s -əʳ/z, (US) -ɚ/z
extend ɪkˈstend, ek- -s -z -ing -ɪŋ -ed -ɪd -able -ə.bəl **exˌtended ˈfamily**
extensibility ɪkˌstent.səˈbɪl.ə.ti, ek-, -sɪˈ-, -ɪ.ti, (US) -ə.t̬i
extensible ɪkˈstent.sə.bəl, ek-, -sɪ-
extensile ɪkˈstent.saɪl, ek-, (US) -sɪl
extension ɪkˈsten.tʃən, ek- -s -z **exˈtension ˌlead**
extensive ɪkˈstent.sɪv, ek- -ly -li -ness -nəs, -nɪs
extensor ɪkˈstent.səʳ, ek-, (US) -sɚ -s -z
extent ɪkˈstent, ek- -s -s
extenu|ate ɪkˈsten.ju|.eɪt, ek- -ates -eɪts -ating/ly -eɪ.tɪŋ/li, (US) -eɪ.t̬ɪŋ/li -ated -eɪ.tɪd, (US) -eɪ.t̬ɪd **exˌtenuating ˈcircumstances**
extenuation ɪkˌsten.juˈeɪ.ʃən, ek- -s -z
extenuative ɪkˈsten.ju.ə.tɪv, ek-, -eɪ-, (US) -eɪ.t̬ɪv
extenuatory ɪkˈsten.ju.ə.tər.i, ek-, -eɪ-, -tri, (US) -ə.tɔːr.i
exterior ɪkˈstɪə.ri.əʳ, ek-, (US) -ˈstɪr.i.ɚ -s -z -ly -li
exteriority ɪkˌstɪə.riˈɒr.ə.ti, ek-, -ɪ.ti; ˌek.stɪə-, (US) ɪkˌstɪr.iˈɔːr.ə.t̬i, ek-
exterioriz|e, -is|e ɪkˈstɪə.ri.ər.aɪz, ek-, (US) -ˈstɪr.i.ə.raɪz -es -ɪz -ing -ɪŋ -ed -d
exterminable ɪkˈstɜː.mɪ.nə.bəl, ek-, -mə-, (US) -ˈstɝː-
extermi|nate ɪkˈstɜː.mɪ|.neɪt, ek-, -mə-, (US) -ˈstɝː- -nates -neɪts -nating -neɪ.tɪŋ, (US) -neɪ.t̬ɪŋ -nated -neɪ.tɪd, (US) -neɪ.t̬ɪd -nator/s -neɪ.təʳ/z, (US) -neɪ.t̬ɚ/z
extermination ɪkˌstɜː.mɪˈneɪ.ʃən, ek-, -məˈ-, (US) -ˌstɝː- -s -z
exterminative ɪkˈstɜː.mɪ.nə.tɪv, ek-, -mə-, -neɪ-, (US) -ˈstɝː.mə.neɪ.t̬ɪv, -nə-
exterminatory ɪkˈstɜː.mɪ.nə.tər.i, ek-, -mə-, -neɪ-, -tri, (US) -ˈstɝː.mə.nə.tɔːr.i
extern ˈek.stɜːn; ɪkˈstɜːn, ek-, (US) ˈek.stɝːn -s -z
external ɪkˈstɜː.nəl, ek-; ˈek.stɜː-, (US) ɪkˈstɝː-, ek-; (US) ˈek.stɝː- -s -z -ly -i
external|ism ɪkˈstɜː.nəl|.ɪ.zəm, ek-, (US) -ˈstɝː- -ist/s -ɪst/s
externality ˌek.stɜːˈnæl.ə.ti, -ɪ.ti, (US) -stɝːˈnæl.ə.t̬i
externalization, -isa- ɪkˌstɜː.nəl.aɪˈzeɪ.ʃən, ek-, -ɪˈ-, (US) -ˌstɝː.nəl.əˈ-
externaliz|e, -is|e ɪkˈstɜː.nəl.aɪz, ek-, (US) -ˈstɝː.nə.laɪz -es -ɪz -ing -ɪŋ -ed -d
exterritorial ˌek.ster.ɪˈtɔː.ri.əl, (US) -ˈtɔːr.i-
extinct ɪkˈstɪŋkt, ek-
extinction ɪkˈstɪŋk.ʃən, ek- -s -z
extinctive ɪkˈstɪŋk.tɪv, ek-
extinguish ɪkˈstɪŋ.gwɪʃ, ek- -es -ɪz -ing -ɪŋ -ed -t -er/s -əʳ/z, (US) -ɚ/z -ment -mənt -able -ə.bəl
extir|pate ˈek.stɜː|.peɪt, -stə-, (US) -stɚ-; (US) ɪkˈstɝː-, ek- -pates -peɪts -pating -peɪ.tɪŋ, (US) -peɪ.t̬ɪŋ -pated -peɪ.tɪd, (US) -peɪ.t̬ɪd -pator/s -peɪ.təʳ/z, (US) -peɪ.t̬ɚ/z
extirpation ˌek.stɜːˈpeɪ.ʃən, -stəˈ-, (US) -stɚˈ- -s -z
extol ɪkˈstəʊl, ek-, -ˈstɒl, (US) -ˈstoʊl, -ˈstɑːl -s -z -ling -ɪŋ -led -d
extoll ɪkˈstəʊl, ek-, -stɒl, (US) -ˈstoʊl, -ˈstɑːl -s -z -ing -ɪŋ -ed -d
Exton ˈek.stən
extor|t ɪkˈstɔː|t, ek-, (US) -ˈstɔːr|t -ts -ts -ting -tɪŋ, (US) -t̬ɪŋ -ted -tɪd, (US) -t̬ɪd -ter/s -təʳ/z, (US) -t̬ɚ/z
extortion ɪkˈstɔː.ʃən, ek-, (US) -ˈstɔːr- -s -z
extortionate ɪkˈstɔː.ʃən.ət, ek-, -ɪt, (US) -ˈstɔːr- -ly -li
extortioner ɪkˈstɔː.ʃən.əʳ, ek-, (US) -ˈstɔːr.ʃən.ɚ -s -z
extortionist ɪkˈstɔː.ʃən.ɪst, ek-, (US) -ˈstɔːr- -s -s
extra ˈek.strə -s -z **ˌextra ˈtime**
extra- ˈek.strə; ɪkˈstræ, ek-
Note: Prefix. Normally takes either primary or secondary stress on the first syllable, e.g. **extradite** /ˈek.strə.daɪt/, **extramural** /ˌeks.trəˈmjʊə.rəl/ (US) /-ˈmjʊr.əl/, but may also take primary stress on the second syllable, e.g. **extrapolate** /ɪkˈstræp.ə.leɪt/. In some cases, the second syllable seems to disappear altogether, e.g. **extraordinary** /ekˈstrɔː.dən.ər.i/ (US) /-ˈstrɔːr.dən.er-/.
extract n ˈek.strækt -s -s
extract v ɪkˈstrækt, ek- -s -s -ing -ɪŋ -ed -ɪd -able -ə.bəl **exˈtractor ˌfan**
extraction ɪkˈstræk.ʃən, ek- -s -z
extractive ɪkˈstræk.tɪv, ek- -ly -li
extractor ɪkˈstræk.təʳ, ek-, (US) -tɚ -s -z **exˈtractor ˌfan**
extracurricular ˌek.strə.kəˈrɪk.jə.ləʳ, -jʊ-, (US) -kəˈrɪk.jə.lɚ **ˌextracurˌricular acˈtivities**
extra|dite ˈek.strə|.daɪt -dites -daɪts -diting -daɪ.tɪŋ, (US) -daɪ.t̬ɪŋ -dited -daɪ.tɪd, (US) -daɪ.t̬ɪd -ditable -daɪ.tə.bəl, (US) -daɪ.t̬ə.bəl
extradition ˌek.strəˈdɪʃ.ən -s -z
extrados ekˈstreɪ.dɒs, (US) -dɑːs, -doʊs -es -ɪz
extragalactic ˌek.strə.gəˈlæk.tɪk
extrajudicial ˌek.strə.dʒuːˈdɪʃ.əl -ly -i
extramarital ˌek.strəˈmær.ɪ.təl, (US) -ˈmer.ə.t̬əl, -ˈmær- **ˌextramarital ˈsex**
extramural ˌek.strəˈmjʊə.rəl, -ˈmjɔː-, (US) -ˈmjʊr.əl
extraneous ɪkˈstreɪ.ni.əs, ek- -ly -li
extranet ˈek.strə.net -s -s
extraordinaire ɪkˌstrɔː.dɪˈneəʳ, ek-, -dənˈeəʳ, (US) -ˌstrɔːr.dəˈner
extraordinar|y ɪkˈstrɔː.dən.ər|.i, ek-, -dɪ.nər-; ˌek.strəˈɔː-, (US) ɪkˈstrɔːr.dən.er-, ek-; (US) ˌek.strəˈɔːr- -ily -əl.i, -ɪ.li -iness -ɪ.nəs, -ɪ.nɪs
extrapo|late ɪkˈstræp.ə|.leɪt, ek- -lates -leɪts -lating -leɪ.tɪŋ, (US) -leɪ.t̬ɪŋ -lated -leɪ.tɪd, (US) -leɪ.t̬ɪd
extrapolation ɪkˌstræp.əˈleɪ.ʃən, ek- -s -z
extrasensory ˌek.strəˈsent.sər.i **ˌextraˌsensory perˈception**
extraterrestrial ˌeks.trə.təˈres.tri.əl, -terˈes-, -tɪˈres-, (US) -təˈ- -s -z
extraterritorial ˌeks.trəˌter.ɪˈtɔː.ri.əl, -əˈ-, (US) -ˈtɔːr.i-
extravagan|ce ɪkˈstræv.ə.gənt|s, ek-, ˈ-ɪ- -ces -sɪz
extravagant ɪkˈstræv.ə.gənt, ˈ-ɪ- -ly -li
extravaganza ɪkˌstræv.əˈgæn.zə, ek-; ˌek.stræv-, (US) ɪkˌstræv-, ek- -s -z
extrava|sate ekˈstræv.ə|.seɪt, ɪk- -sates -seɪts -sating -seɪ.tɪŋ, (US) -seɪ.t̬ɪŋ -sated -seɪ.tɪd, (US) -seɪ.t̬ɪd
extravasation ekˌstræv.əˈseɪ.ʃən, ɪk-; -ˈzeɪ-, ˌek.stræv-, (US) ɪkˌstræv-, ek- -s -z
extra|vert ˈek.strə|.vɜːt, (US) -vɝːt -verts -vɜːts, (US) -vɝːts -verted -vɜː.tɪd, (US) -vɝː.t̬ɪd
Extremadura ˌek.strə.məˈdjʊə.rə, (US) -ˈdʊr.ə, -ˈdjʊr.ə
extrem|e ɪkˈstriːm, ek- -es -z -est -ɪst, -əst -ely -li -eness -nəs, -nɪs
extrem|ism ɪkˈstriː.m|ɪ.zəm, ek- -ist/s -ɪst/s
extremit|y ɪkˈstrem.ə.t|i, ek-, -ɪ.t|i, (US) -ə.t̬|i -ies -iz
extricable ɪkˈstrɪk.ə.bəl, ek-; ˈek.strɪ.kə-
extri|cate ˈek.strɪ|.keɪt -cates -keɪts -cating -keɪ.tɪŋ, (US) -keɪ.t̬ɪŋ -cated -keɪ.tɪd, (US) -keɪ.t̬ɪd
extrication ˌek.strɪˈkeɪ.ʃən, -strəˈ-
extrinsic ekˈstrɪnt.sɪk, ɪk-, -ˈstrɪn.zɪk -al -əl -ally -əl.i, -li

Pronouncing the letters EY

The most common position for the vowel digraph **ey** is in word-final position in an unstressed syllable.

In weak syllables the vowel digraph **ey** is realized with the vowel /i/, e.g.:

donkey	ˈdɒŋ.ki (US) ˈdɑːŋ-
Surrey	ˈsʌr.i (US) ˈsɝː-

However, there are several pronunciation possibilities for the digraph in stressed syllables, e.g.:

eɪ	they /ðeɪ/
iː	key /kiː/
aɪ	geyser /ˈgiː.zəʳ, ˈgaɪ-/ (US) /-zɚ/

extroversion ˌek.strəˈvɜː.ʃən, -ʒən, (US) ˈek.strə.vɝ.ʒən, -stroʊ-
extro|vert ˈek.strə|.vɜːt, (US) -strə|.vɝːt, -stroʊ- **-verts** -vɜːts, (US) -vɝːts **-verted** -vɜː.tɪd, (US) -vɝː.t̬ɪd
extrud|e ɪkˈstruːd, ek- **-es** -z **-ing** -ɪŋ **-ed** -ɪd
extrusion ɪkˈstruː.ʒən, ek- **-s** -z
extrus|ive ɪkˈstruː.s|ɪv, ek- **-ory** -ər.i, (US) -ɔːr.i
exuberan|ce ɪgˈzjuː.bər.ənt|s, eg-, -ˈzuː-; ɪkˈsjuː-, ek-, -ˈsuː-, (US) ɪgˈzuː-, eg- **-cy** -si
exuberant ɪgˈzjuː.bər.ənt, eg-, -ˈzuː-; ɪkˈsjuː-, ek-, -ˈsuː-, (US) ɪgˈzuː-, eg- **-ly** -li
exudation ˌek.sjuːˈdeɪ.ʃən, ˌeg.zjuːˈ-, (US) ˌek.sjuːˈ-, -suːˈ-, -səˈ-, ˌeg.zjuːˈ-, -zuːˈ- **-s** -z
exud|e ɪgˈzjuːd, eg-, -ˈzuːd; ɪkˈsjuːd, ek-, -ˈsuːd, (US) ɪgˈzuːd, ɪkˈsuːd, ek- **-es** -z **-ing** -ɪŋ **-ed** -ɪd
exul|t ɪgˈzʌl|t, eg-; ɪkˈsʌl|t, ek-, (US) ɪgˈzʌl|t, eg- **-ts** -ts **-ting/ly** -tɪŋ/li, (US) -t̬ɪŋ/li **-ted** -tɪd, (US) -t̬ɪd
exultan|ce ɪgˈzʌl.tənt|s, eg-; ɪkˈsʌl-, ek-, (US) ɪgˈzʌl-, eg- **-cy** -si
exultant ɪgˈzʌl.tənt, eg-; ɪkˈsʌl-, ek-, (US) ɪgˈzʌl-, eg- **-ly** -li
exultation ˌeg.zʌlˈteɪ.ʃən, -zəlˈ-; ˌek.sʌlˈ-, -səlˈ-, (US) ˌek.sʌlˈ-, -səlˈ-; (US) ˌeg.zʌlˈ-, -zəlˈ- **-s** -z
exurb ˈek.sɜːb; ˈeg.zɜːb, (US) ˈek.sɝːb; (US) ˈeg.zɝːb
exur|ban ekˈsɜː|.bən; egˈzɜː-, (US) ekˈsɝː-; (US) egˈzɝː- **-banite** -bən.aɪt **-bia** -bi.ə
exuviae ɪgˈzjuː.vi.iː, eg-; -ˈzuː-; ɪkˈsjuː-, ek-, -ˈsuː-, -aɪ, (US) ɪgˈzuː.vi.iː, ekˈsuː-, egˈzuː-, -aɪ
exuvial ɪgˈzjuː.vi.əl, eg-, -ˈzuː-; ɪkˈsjuː-, ek-, -ˈsuː-, (US) ɪgˈzuː-, ekˈsuː-, egˈzuː-
exuvi|ate ɪgˈzjuː.vi|.eɪt, eg-, -ˈzuː-; ɪkˈsjuː-, ek-, -ˈsuː-, (US) ɪgˈzuː-, ekˈsuː-, egˈzuː- **-ates** -eɪts **-ating** -eɪ.tɪŋ, (US) -eɪ.t̬ɪŋ **-ated** -eɪ.tɪd, (US) -eɪ.t̬ɪd
exuviation ɪgˌzjuː.viˈeɪ.ʃən, eg-, -ˌzuː-; ɪkˌsjuː-, ek-, -ˌsuː-, (US) ɪgˈzuː-, ekˈsuː-, egˈzuː-
ex voto ˌeksˈvəʊ.təʊ, (US) -ˈvoʊ.t̬oʊ
Exxon® ˈek.sɒn, (US) -sɑːn
ExxonMobil® ek.sɒnˈməʊ.bɪl, (US) ek.sɑːnˈmoʊ.bəl
Eyam ˈiː.əm, iːm
eyas aɪ.əs **-es** -ɪz
Eyck aɪk
eye **n, v** aɪ **-s** -z **-ing** -ɪŋ **-d** -d ˌ**give one's** ˌ**eye** ˈ**teeth; have** ˌ**eyes in the** ˌ**back of one's** ˈ**head; in a** ˌ**pig's** ˈ**eye;** ˌ**one in the** ˈ**eye;** ˌ**up to one's** ˈ**eyes; see** ˌ**eye to** ˈ**eye**
Eye *place:* aɪ
eyeball ˈaɪ.bɔːl, (US) -bɔːl, -bɑːl **-s** -z **-ing** -ɪŋ **-ed** -d
eyebath ˈaɪ.bɑːθ, (US) -bæθ **-s** -s
eyebright ˈaɪ.braɪt
eyebrow ˈaɪ.braʊ **-s** -z ˈ**eyebrow** ˌ**pencil**
eye-catching ˈaɪˌkætʃ.ɪŋ **-ly** -li
eyeful ˈaɪ.fʊl **-s** -z
eyeglass ˈaɪ.glɑːs, (US) -glæs **-es** -ɪz
eyelash ˈaɪ.læʃ **-es** -ɪz
eyelet ˈaɪ.lət, -lɪt **-s** -s
eyelid ˈaɪ.lɪd **-s** -z
eyeliner ˈaɪˌlaɪ.nəʳ, (US) -nɚ **-s** -z
Eyemouth ˈaɪ.maʊθ
eye-open|er ˈaɪˌəʊ.pən|.əʳ, -ˌəʊp.n|əʳ, (US) -ˌoʊ.pən|.ɚ **-ers** -əz, -ɚz **-ing** -ɪŋ
eyepatch ˈaɪ.pætʃ **-es** -ɪz
eyepiec|e ˈaɪ.piːs **-es** -ɪz
eyeshade ˈaɪ.ʃeɪd **-s** -z
eyeshot ˈaɪ.ʃɒt, (US) -ʃɑːt
eyesight ˈaɪ.saɪt
eyesore ˈaɪ.sɔːʳ, (US) -sɔːr **-s** -z
eyestrain ˈaɪ.streɪn
Eyetie ˈaɪ.taɪ **-s** -z
eye|tooth ˈaɪ|.tuːθ **-teeth** -tiːθ
eyewash ˈaɪ.wɒʃ, (US) -wɑːʃ, -wɔːʃ
eyewitness ˈaɪ.wɪt.nɪs, -nəs, -ˈ-- **-es** -ɪz
Eynon ˈaɪ.nən, (US) -nɑːn
Eynsford ˈeɪnz.fəd, ˈeɪnts-, (US) -fɚd
Eynsham *in Oxfordshire:* ˈeɪn.ʃəm; *locally:* ˈen.ʃəm
eyot eɪt, ˈeɪ.ət, aɪt **-s** -s

> Note: Word for a small island. The local pronunciation in the Thames valley is /eɪt/.

Eyre, eyre eəʳ, (US) er
eyr|ie, eyr|y ˈaɪə.r|i, ˈɪə-, ˈeə-, (US) ˈer.|i, ˈɪr- **-ies** -iz
Eysenck ˈaɪ.zeŋk
Eyton *in Shropshire:* ˈaɪ.tən *in Hereford and Worcester:* ˈeɪ.tən *surname:* ˈaɪ.tən, ˈiː-
Ezekiel ɪˈziː.ki.əl, ezˈiː-
e-zine ˈiː.ziːn **-s** -z
Ezra ˈez.rə

F

Pronouncing the letter F

The consonant letter **f** is most often realized as /f/, and is given as a double consonant **ff** at the ends of many words, e.g.:

fit fɪt
cuff kʌf

However, in one of the most common words containing **f** it is pronounced /v/:

of ɒv, əv (US) ɑːv, əv

F

f, F ef -'s -s
fa fɑː *stress shift:* ˌ**FA** ˈ**cup**
FA ˌefˈeɪ ˌ**sweet** ˌ**F**ˈ**A**
FAA ˌef.eɪˈeɪ
fab fæb
Faber *English name:* ˈfeɪ.bəʳ, (US) -bɚ *German name:* ˈfɑː.bəʳ, (US) -bɚ
Fabergé ˈfæb.ə.ʒeɪ, -dʒeɪ, (US) ˌfæb.ɚˈʒeɪ
Fabian ˈfeɪ.bi.ən **-s** -z **-ism** -ɪ.zᵊm ˈ**Fabian So**ˌ**ciety**
Fabius ˈfeɪ.bi.əs
fable ˈfeɪ.bᵊl **-s** -z **-d** -d
fabliau ˈfæb.li.əʊ, (US) -oʊ **-x** -z
Fablon® ˈfæb.lɒn, (US) -lɑːn
fabric ˈfæb.rɪk **-s** -s ˈ**fabric** ˌ**softener**
fabri|cate ˈfæb.rɪ|.keɪt **-cates** -keɪts **-cating** -keɪ.tɪŋ, (US) -keɪ.t̬ɪŋ **-cated** -keɪ.tɪd, (US) -keɪ.t̬ɪd **-cator/s** -keɪ.təʳ/z, (US) -keɪ.t̬ɚ/z
fabrication ˌfæb.rɪˈkeɪ.ʃᵊn, -rəˈ- **-s** -z
Fabricius fəˈbrɪʃ.i.əs, -ʃəs
fabulist ˈfæb.jə.lɪst, -jʊ-, (US) -jə- **-s** -s
fabulous ˈfæb.jə.ləs, -jʊ- **-ly** -li **-ness** -nəs, -nɪs
Fabyan ˈfeɪ.bi.ən
facade, façade fəˈsɑːd, fæsˈɑːd, (US) fəˈsɑːd **-s** -z
fac|e n, v feɪs **-es** -ɪz **-ing** -ɪŋ **-ed** -t ˈ**face** ˌ**pack;** ˌ**face** ˈ**value;** ˌ**cut off one's** ˌ**nose to** ˌ**spite one's** ˈ**face;** ˌ**fly in the** ˈ**face of;** ˌ**laugh on the other** ˌ**side of one's** ˈ**face; put a** ˌ**brave** ˈ**face on**
Facebook® ˈfeɪs.bʊk
face|cloth ˈfeɪs|.klɒθ, (US) -klɑːθ **-cloths** -klɒθs, -klɒðz, (US) -klɑːθs, -klɑːðz
faceless ˈfeɪs.ləs, -lɪs **-ness** -nəs, -nɪs
face-lift ˈfeɪs.lɪft **-s** -s
facemask ˈfeɪs.mɑːsk, (US) -mæsk **-s** -s
face-off ˈfeɪs.ɒf, (US) -ɑːf **-s** -s
faceplate ˈfeɪs.pleɪt **-s** -s
facer ˈfeɪ.səʳ, (US) -sɚ **-s** -z
face-sav|er ˈfeɪsˌseɪ|.vəʳ, (US) -vɚ **-ers** -z **-ing** -ɪŋ
fac|et ˈfæs|.ɪt, -ət, -et, (US) -ɪt **-ets** -ɪts **-et(t)ed** -ɪ.tɪd, (US) -ɪ.t̬ɪd
facetiae fəˈsiː.ʃi.iː, -ʃiː, (US) -ʃi.iː
facetious fəˈsiː.ʃəs **-ly** -li **-ness** -nəs, -nɪs
face-to-face ˌfeɪs.təˈfeɪs, (US) -t̬ə- *stress shift:* ˌ**face-to-face** ˈ**talk**
facia ˈfeɪ.ʃə, (US) -ʃi.ə, -ʃə **-s** -z
facial ˈfeɪ.ʃᵊl **-ly** -i **-s** -z
facies ˈfeɪ.ʃi.iːz, -ʃiːz
facile ˈfæs.aɪl, (US) -ɪl, -əl **-ly** -li **-ness** -nəs, -nɪs
facili|tate fəˈsɪl.ɪ|.teɪt, ˈ-ə- **-tates** -teɪts **-tating** -teɪ.tɪŋ, (US) -teɪ.t̬ɪŋ **-tated** -teɪ.tɪd, (US) -teɪ.t̬ɪd **-tator/s** -teɪ.təʳ/z, (US) -teɪ.t̬ɚ/z
facilitation fəˌsɪl.ɪˈteɪ.ʃᵊn, -əˈ-
facilit|y fəˈsɪl.ə.t|i, -ɪ.t|i, (US) -ə.t̬|i **-ies** -iz
facing ˈfeɪ.sɪŋ **-s** -z
facsimile fækˈsɪm.ᵊl.i, -ɪ.li **-s** -z
fact fækt **-s** -s ˌ**fact of** ˈ**life**
fact-find|ing ˈfæktˌfaɪn.d|ɪŋ **-er/s** -əʳ/z, (US) -ɚ/z
faction ˈfæk.ʃᵊn **-s** -z
factional ˈfæk.ʃᵊn.ᵊl
factional|ism ˈfæk.ʃᵊn.ᵊl|.ɪ.zᵊm **-ist/s** -ɪst/s
factionalization, -isa- ˌfæk.ʃᵊn.ᵊl.aɪˈzeɪ.ʃᵊn, -ɪˈ-, (US) -əˈ-
factionaliz|e, -is|e ˈfæk.ʃᵊn.ᵊl.aɪz, (US) -ə.laɪz **-es** -ɪz **-ing** -ɪŋ **-ed** -d
factious ˈfæk.ʃəs **-ly** -li **-ness** -nəs, -nɪs
factitious fækˈtɪʃ.əs **-ly** -li **-ness** -nəs, -nɪs
factitive ˈfæk.tɪ.tɪv, -tə.tɪv, (US) -tə.t̬ɪv
factive ˈfæk.tɪv
factivity fækˈtɪv.ə.ti, -ɪ.ti, (US) -ə.t̬i
factoid ˈfæk.tɔɪd **-s** -z
fact|or ˈfæk.t|əʳ, (US) -t|ɚ **-ors** -əz, (US) -ɚz **-oring** -ᵊr.ɪŋ **-ored** -ᵊrd **-orage** -ᵊr.ɪdʒ ˌ**Factor** ˈ**5**
factorial fækˈtɔː.ri.əl, (US) -ˈtɔːr.i-
factorization, -isa- ˌfæk.tᵊr.aɪˈzeɪ.ʃᵊn, -ɪˈ-, (US) -əˈ-
factoriz|e, -is|e ˈfæk.tᵊr.aɪz, (US) -tə.raɪz **-es** -ɪz **-ing** -ɪŋ **-ed** -d
factor|y ˈfæk.tᵊr|.i, ˈ-tr|i **-ies** -iz ˌ**factory** ˈ**farming,** ˈ**factory** ˌ**farming;** ˌ**factory** ˈ**floor**
factory-farmed ˌfæk.tᵊr.iˈfɑːmd, (US) -fɑːrmd *stress shift:* ˌ**factory-farmed** ˈ**food**
factotum fækˈtəʊ.təm, (US) -ˈtoʊ.t̬əm **-s** -z
factsheet ˈfækt.ʃiːt **-s** -s
factual ˈfæk.tʃu.əl, -tju-, (US) -tʃu.əl **-ly** -li **-ness** -nəs, -nɪs
factum ˈfæk.təm
factum probandum ˌfæk.təm.prəʊˈbæn.dəm, (US) -proʊˈbɑːn-
facul|a ˈfæk.jə.l|ə, -jʊ-, (US) -jə-, -juː- **-ae** -iː
facultative ˈfæk.ᵊl.tə.tɪv, -teɪ-, (US) -teɪ.t̬ɪv **-ly** -li
facult|y ˈfæk.ᵊl.t|i **-ies** -iz
fad fæd **-s** -z
faddish ˈfæd.ɪʃ **-ly** -li **-ness** -nəs, -nɪs
fadd|ism ˈfæd|.ɪ.zᵊm **-ist/s** -ɪst/s
fadd|y ˈfæd|.i **-ier** -i.əʳ, (US) -i.ɚ **-iest** -i.ɪst, -i.əst **-ily** -ᵊl.i, -ɪ.li **-iness** -ɪ.nəs, -ɪ.nɪs
fad|e feɪd **-es** -z **-ing** -ɪŋ **-ed** -ɪd
fadeout ˈfeɪd.aʊt **-s** -s
fado ˈfɑː.du, (US) ˈfɑː.ðuː, -ðoʊ, -doʊ **-s** -z
faecal ˈfiː.kᵊl
faeces ˈfiː.siːz
Faed feɪd
faerie, faery, F~ ˈfeə.ri, ˈfeɪ.ᵊr.i, (US) ˈfer.i
Faeroe ˈfeə.rəʊ, (US) ˈfer.oʊ **-s** -z
Faeroese ˌfeə.rəʊˈiːz, (US) ˌfer.oʊˈ-
faff fæf **-s** -s **-ing** -ɪŋ **-ed** -t
Fafner ˈfɑːf.nəʳ, ˈfæf-, (US) -nɚ
Fafnir ˈfæf.nɪəʳ, ˈfæv-, (US) -nɪr
fag fæg **-s** -z **-ging** -ɪŋ **-ged** -d ˈ**fag** ˌ**end,** ˌ**fag** ˈ**end;** ˈ**fag** ˌ**hag**
Fagan ˈfeɪ.gən
faggot ˈfæg.ət **-s** -s
Fagin ˈfeɪ.gɪn
fagot ˈfæg.ət **-s** -s
fah fɑː
Fahd fɑːd, ˈfæ.hæd
Fahey, Fahie ˈfeɪ.i, ˈfɑː.hi; feɪ
Fahrenheit ˈfær.ᵊn.haɪt, ˈfɑː.rᵊn-, (US) ˈfer.ᵊn-, ˈfær-
Fahy ˈfɑː.i, -hi; feɪ, (US) ˈfeɪ.i; (US) feɪ
faience, faïence faɪˈɑ̃ːns, feɪ-, -ɑːnts, (US) faɪˈɑːnts, feɪˈ-; (US) ˈfaɪ.ənts
fail feɪl **-s** -z **-ing/s** -ɪŋ/z **-ed** -d
faille feɪəl, faɪ, (US) faɪl, feɪl
failsafe ˈfeɪl.seɪf, -ˈ-, (US) ˈ--
Failsworth ˈfeɪlz.wəθ, -wɜːθ, (US) -wɚθ, -wɜːθ
failure ˈfeɪ.ljəʳ, (US) ˈfeɪl.jɚ **-s** -z

fain feɪn
Fainall ˈfeɪ.nɔːl, ⓤⓢ -nɔːl, -nɑːl
faint feɪnt **-er** -əʳ, ⓤⓢ ˈfeɪn.t̬ɚ **-est** -ɪst, -əst, ⓤⓢ ˈfeɪn.t̬ɪst, ˈfeɪn.t̬əst **-ly** -li **-ness** -nəs, -nɪs **-s** -s **-ing** -ɪŋ, ⓤⓢ ˈfeɪn.t̬ɪŋ **-ed** -ɪd, ⓤⓢ ˈfeɪn.t̬ɪd
fainthearted ˌfeɪntˈhɑː.tɪd, ⓤⓢ -ˈhɑːr.t̬ɪd **-ly** -li **-ness** -nəs, -nɪs *stress shift:* **ˌfainthearted ˈhero**
fair, F~ feəʳ, ⓤⓢ fer **-s** -z **-er** -əʳ, ⓤⓢ -ɚ **-est** -ɪst, -əst **-ness** -nəs, -nɪs **ˌfair ˈdo's; ˌfair ˈdinkum; ˌfair ˈgame; ˈFair ˌIsle; ˌfair ˈplay; ˌfair's ˈfair; ˌfair and ˈsquare**
Fairbairn ˈfeə.beən, ⓤⓢ ˈfer.bern **-s** -z
Fairbank ˈfeə.bæŋk, ⓤⓢ ˈfer- **-s** -s
Fairbrother ˈfeəˌbrʌð.əʳ, ⓤⓢ ˈferˌbrʌð.ɚ
Fairburn ˈfeə.bɜːn, ⓤⓢ ˈfer.bɝːn
Fairbury ˈfeə.bᵊr.i, ⓤⓢ ˈferˌber-, -bɚ-
Fairchild ˈfeə.tʃaɪld, ⓤⓢ ˈfer-
Fairclough ˈfeə.klʌf, -kləʊ, ⓤⓢ ˈfer.klʌf
fairfaced ˌfeəˈfeɪst, ⓤⓢ ˌfer- *stress shift:* **ˌfairfaced ˈchild**
Fairfax ˈfeə.fæks, ⓤⓢ ˈfer-
Fairfield ˈfeə.fiːld, ⓤⓢ ˈfer-
Fairford ˈfeə.fəd, ⓤⓢ ˈfer.fɚd
Fairgrieve ˈfeə.griːv, ⓤⓢ ˈfer-
fairground ˈfeə.graʊnd, ⓤⓢ ˈfer- **-s** -z
fair-haired ˌfeəˈheəd, ⓤⓢ ˌferˈherd *stress shift:* **ˌfair-haired ˈchild**
Fairhaven ˈfeəˌheɪ.vᵊn, ⓤⓢ ˈfer-
Fairholme ˈfeə.həʊm, ⓤⓢ ˈfer.hoʊm, -hoʊlm
Fairholt ˈfeə.həʊlt, ⓤⓢ ˈfer.hoʊlt
fairish ˈfeə.rɪʃ, ⓤⓢ ˈfer.ɪʃ
fairisle ˈfeə.raɪl, ⓤⓢ ˈfer-
Fairleigh ˈfeə.li, -liː, ⓤⓢ ˈfer-
Fairlight ˈfeə.laɪt, ⓤⓢ ˈfer-
fairly ˈfeə.li, ⓤⓢ ˈfer-
Fairman ˈfeə.mən, ⓤⓢ ˈfer-
fair-minded ˌfeəˈmaɪn.dɪd, ⓤⓢ ˌfer- **-ly** -li **-ness** -nəs, -nɪs *stress shift:* **ˌfair-minded ˈjudge**
Fairmont ˈfeə.mɒnt, -mənt, ⓤⓢ ˈfer.mɑːnt
Fairmount ˈfeə.maʊnt, ⓤⓢ ˈfer-
Fairport ˈfeə.pɔːt, ⓤⓢ ˈfer.pɔːrt
Fairscribe ˈfeə.skraɪb, ⓤⓢ ˈfer-
Fairtrade ˌfeəˈtreɪd, ⓤⓢ ˌfer- *stress shift:* **ˌFairtrade ˈcoffee**
Fairview ˈfeə.vjuː, ⓤⓢ ˈfer-
fairway ˈfeə.weɪ, ⓤⓢ ˈfer- **-s** -z
fair-weather ˈfeəˌweð.əʳ, ⓤⓢ ˈferˌweð.ɚ
Fairweather ˈfeəˌweð.əʳ, ⓤⓢ ˈferˌweð.ɚ
fair|y ˈfeə.r|i, ⓤⓢ ˈfer|.i **-ies** -iz **ˌfairy ˈgodmother; ˈfairy ˌlight; ˌfairy ˈring** ⓤⓢ **ˈfairy ˌring; ˈfairy ˌstory; ˈfairy ˌtale**
fairyland ˈfeə.ri.lænd, ⓤⓢ ˈfer.i-
fairylike ˈfeə.ri.laɪk, ⓤⓢ ˈfer.i-
Faisal ˈfaɪ.sᵊl
Faisalabad ˈfaɪ.sᵊl.ə.bæd, -zᵊl-, ⓤⓢ ˌfaɪ.sɑː.ləˈbɑːd, -sæl.əˈbæd
fait accompli ˌfeɪt.əˈkɒm.pliː, ˌfet-, -ˈkʌm-; *as if French:* -kɔ̃ːmˈpliː; ⓤⓢ ˌfeɪt.ə.kɑːmˈpliː, ˌfet- **faits accomplis** ˌfeɪz-, ˌfeɪts-, ˌfeɪt-, ˌfez-, -pliːz, ⓤⓢ ˌfeɪt.ə.kɑːmˈpliː, ˌfet-, -ˈpliːz
faith, F~ feɪθ **-s** -s **ˈfaith ˌhealer**
faith-based ˈfeɪθ.beɪst
faithful, F~ ˈfeɪθ.fᵊl, -fʊl **-ly** -i **-ness** -nəs, -nɪs
Faithfull ˈfeɪθ.fᵊl, -fʊl
faithless ˈfeɪθ.ləs, -lɪs **-ly** -li **-ness** -nəs, -nɪs
Faithorne ˈfeɪ.θɔːn, ⓤⓢ -θɔːrn
fajita fæˈhiː.tə, ⓤⓢ fæ-, fə-, -t̬ə
fak|e feɪk **-es** -s **-ing** -ɪŋ **-ed** -t **-er/s** -əʳ/z, ⓤⓢ -ɚ/z
Fakenham ˈfeɪ.kᵊn.əm
fakir ˈfeɪ.kɪəʳ, ˈfɑː-, ˈfæk.ɪəʳ, fəˈkɪəʳ, fækˈɪəʳ, ⓤⓢ fɑːˈkɪr, fækˈɪr; ⓤⓢ ˈfeɪ.kɚ **-s** -z **-ism** -ɪ.zᵊm
Fal fæl
falafel fəˈlɑː.fᵊl, -ˈlæf.ᵊl, ⓤⓢ -ˈlɑː.fᵊl
Falange fəˈlændʒ; ˈfæl.ændʒ, ⓤⓢ fəˈlændʒ, -ˈlɑːndʒ
Falangist fəˈlæn.dʒɪst **-s** -s
Falasha fəˈlæʃ.ə, ⓤⓢ -ˈlɑː.ʃə, fɑːˈ- **-s** -z
fal|cate ˈfæl|.keɪt **-cated** -keɪ.tɪd, ⓤⓢ -keɪ.t̬ɪd
falchion ˈfɔːl.tʃᵊn, ⓤⓢ ˈfɔːl-, ˈfɑːl- **-s** -z
falcon, F~ ˈfɔːl.kᵊn, ˈfɔː-, ˈfɒl-, ˈfæl-, ⓤⓢ ˈfæl-, ˈfɔːl-, ˈfɑːl-, ˈfɔː- **-s** -z **-er/s** -əʳ/z, ⓤⓢ -ɚ/z

> Note: /ˈfɔː-/ is the usual British pronunciation among people who practise the sport of falconry, with /ˈfɔː-/ and /ˈfɔːl-/ most usual among them in the US. The pronunciation with /l/ may be considered a spelling pronunciation.

Falconbridge ˈfɔːl.kᵊn.brɪdʒ, ˈfɔː-, ˈfɒl-, ˈfæl-, -kᵊm-, ⓤⓢ ˈfɔː.kᵊn-, ˈfɔːl-, ˈfæl-, ˈfɑːl-
Falconer ˈfɔːl.kᵊn.əʳ, ˈfɔː-, ˈfɒl-, ˈfæl-, ⓤⓢ ˈfɔː.kᵊn.ɚ, ˈfɔːl-, ˈfæl-, ˈfɑːl-
falconry ˈfɔːl.kᵊn.ri, ˈfɔː-, ˈfɒl-, ˈfæl-, ⓤⓢ ˈfæl-, ˈfɔːl-, ˈfɑːl-, ˈfɔː-

> Note: See note at **falcon**.

Falder ˈfɔːl.dəʳ, ˈfɒl-, ⓤⓢ ˈfɑːl.dɚ, ˈfɔːl-
falderal ˈfæl.də.ræl, -dɪ-, ˌ--ˈ-, ⓤⓢ ˈfɑːl.də.rɑːl, ˈfæl.də.ræl **-s** -z
Faldo ˈfæl.dəʊ, ⓤⓢ -doʊ
faldstool ˈfɔːld.stuːl **-s** -z
Falerii fəˈlɪə.ri.aɪ, fælˈɪə-, -iː, ⓤⓢ fəˈlɪr.i-
Falernian fəˈlɜː.ni.ən, ⓤⓢ -ˈlɝː-
Falk fɔːk, fɔːlk, ⓤⓢ fɔːk, fɔːlk, fɑːlk
Falkenbridge ˈfɔː.kᵊn.brɪdʒ, ˈfɔːl-, ˈfɒl-, ˈfæl-, -kᵊm-, ⓤⓢ ˈfɔː.kᵊn-, ˈfɔːl-, ˈfæl-, ˈfɑːl-
Falkender ˈfɔːl.kən.dəʳ, ⓤⓢ -dɚ
Falkirk ˈfɔːl.kɜːk, ˈfɒl-, -kək, ⓤⓢ ˈfɔːl.kɝːk, -kɚk
Falkland *Viscount:* ˈfɔː.klənd, ˈfɒl-, ⓤⓢ ˈfɔː- *place in Scotland:* ˈfɔːl.klənd, ˈfɒl-, ⓤⓢ ˈfɔːl-
Falkland Islands ˈfɔː.kləndˌaɪ.ləndz, ˈfɔːl-, ˈfɒl-, ⓤⓢ ˈfɔː-, ˈfɔːl-
Falkner ˈfɔː.k.nəʳ, ˈfɔːlk-, ˈfɒlk-, ˈfælk-, ⓤⓢ ˈfɔːk.nɚ, ˈfɔːlk-, ˈfɑːlk-, ˈfælk-
fall fɔːl, ⓤⓢ fɔːl, fɑːl **-s** -z **-ing** -ɪŋ **fell** fel **fallen** ˈfɔː.lən, ⓤⓢ ˈfɔː-, ˈfɑː- **ˈfall ˌguy; ˌfalling ˈstar**
Falla ˈfaɪ.jə; ˈfɑː.ljə, ˈfæl.jə, -ə, ⓤⓢ ˈfaɪ.jə; ⓤⓢ ˈfɑː.l.jɑː
fallacious fəˈleɪ.ʃəs **-ly** -li **-ness** -nəs, -nɪs
fallac|y ˈfæl.ə.s|i **-ies** -iz
fallal fælˈæl, -ˈlæl, ⓤⓢ fælˈæl, fɑːˈlɑːl **-s** -z
fallback ˈfɔːl.bæk, ⓤⓢ ˈfɔːl-, ˈfɑːl- **-s** -s
Faller ˈfæl.əʳ, ⓤⓢ -ɚ
fallibility ˌfæl.əˈbɪl.ə.ti, -ɪˈ-, -ɪ.ti, ⓤⓢ -ə.t̬i
fallib|le ˈfæl.ə.b|ᵊl, ˈ-ɪ- **-ly** -li **-leness** -ᵊl.nəs, -nɪs
falling-off ˌfɔː.lɪŋˈɒf, ⓤⓢ ˌfɔː.lɪŋˈɑːf, ˌfɑː-
falling-out ˌfɔː.lɪŋˈaʊt, ⓤⓢ ˌfɔː-, ˌfɑː- **fallings-out** ˌfɔː.lɪŋzˈaʊt, ⓤⓢ ˌfɔː-, ˌfɑː- **falling-outs** ˌfɔː.lɪŋˈaʊts, ⓤⓢ ˌfɔː-, ˌfɑː-
fall-off ˈfɔːl.ɒf, ⓤⓢ -ɑːf, ˈfɑːl- **-s** -s
Fallon ˈfæl.ən
fallopian, F~ fəˈləʊ.pi.ən, fælˈəʊ-, ⓤⓢ fəˈloʊ- **faˌllopian ˈtube**
fallout ˈfɔːl.aʊt, ⓤⓢ ˈfɔːl-, ˈfɑːl-
fallow, F~ ˈfæl.əʊ, ⓤⓢ -oʊ **-s** -z **-ness** -nəs, -nɪs **-ing** -ɪŋ **-ed** -d **ˈfallow ˌdeer, ˌfallow ˈdeer**
Fallowfield ˈfæl.əʊ.fiːld, ⓤⓢ -oʊ-
Fallows ˈfæl.əʊz, ⓤⓢ -oʊz
Falls fɔːlz, ⓤⓢ fɔːlz, fɑːlz **ˌFalls ˈRoad**
Falluja, Fallujah fəˈluː.dʒə, fælˈuː-, ⓤⓢ fəˈluː.dʒə
Falmer ˈfæl.məʳ, ˈfɔːl-, ⓤⓢ ˈfɑːl.mɚ, ˈfɔːl-
Falmouth ˈfæl.məθ
fals|e fɔːls, fɒls, ⓤⓢ fɔːls, fɑːls **-er** -əʳ, ⓤⓢ -ɚ **-est** -ɪst, -əst **-eness** -nəs, -nɪs **ˌfalse aˈlarm; ˌfalse preˈtences; ˌfalse ˈstart; ˌfalse ˈteeth**
falsehood ˈfɔːls.hʊd, ˈfɒls-, ⓤⓢ ˈfɔːls.hʊd, ˈfɑːls- **-s** -z
falsely ˈfɔːl.sli, ˈfɒl-, ⓤⓢ ˈfɔːl-, ˈfɑːl-
falsetto fɒlˈset.əʊ, fɔːl-, ⓤⓢ fɔːlˈset̬.oʊ, fɑːl- **-s** -z
Falshaw ˈfɔːl.ʃɔː, ˈfɒl-, ⓤⓢ ˈfɔːl.ʃɑː, ˈfɑːl-, -ʃɔː
falsies ˈfɒl.siz, ⓤⓢ ˈfɔːl-, ˈfɑːl-
falsification ˌfɔːl.sɪ.fɪˈkeɪ.ʃᵊn, ˌfɒl-, -sə-, -fəˈ-, ⓤⓢ ˌfɔːl-, ˌfɑːl- **-s** -z
falsi|fy ˈfɔːl.sɪ|.faɪ, ˈfɒl-, -sə-, ⓤⓢ ˈfɔːl-, ˈfɑːl- **-fies** -faɪz **-fying** -faɪ.ɪŋ **-fied** -faɪd **-fier/s** -faɪ.əʳ/z, ⓤⓢ -faɪ.ɚ/z
falsit|y ˈfɔːl.sə.t|i, ˈfɒl-, -ɪ.t|i, ⓤⓢ ˈfɔːl.sə.t̬|i, ˈfɑːl- **-ies** -iz

Falstaff ˈfɔːl.stɑːf, ˈfɒl-, US ˈfɔːl.stæf, ˈfɑːl-
Falstaffian fɔːlˈstɑː.fi.ən, fɒl-, US fɔːlˈstæf.i-, fɑːl-
falt|er ˈfɔːl.t|əʳ, ˈfɒl-, US ˈfɔːl.t|ɚ, ˈfɑːl- **-ers** -əz, US -ɚz **-ering/ly** -ər.ɪŋ/li **-ered** -əd, US -ɚd **-erer/s** -ər.əʳ/z, US -ɚ.ɚ/z
Faludi fəˈluː.di, fælˈuː.di
Famagusta ˌfæm.əˈgʊs.tə, ˌfɑː.məˈ-, US ˌfɑː.məˈguː.stə
fame feɪm **-d** -d
familial fəˈmɪl.i.əl
familiar fəˈmɪl.i.əʳ, US ˈ-jɚ, -i.ɚ **-s** -z **-ly** -li
familiarit|y fəˌmɪl.iˈær.ə.t|i, -ɪ.t|i, US -ˈer.ə.ţ|i, -ˈær- **-ies** -iz
familiariz|e, -is|e fəˈmɪl.i.ər.aɪz, US ˈ-jə.raɪz, ˈ-i.ə- **-es** -ɪz **-ing** -ɪŋ **-ed** -d
famil|y ˈfæm.əl|.i, -ɪ.l|i **-ies** -iz ˌ**family alˈlowance**; ˌ**family ˈcredit**; ˈ**family ˌman**; ˌ**family ˈplanning**; ˈ**family ˌroom**; ˈ**family ˌstyle**; ˌ**family ˈtree**
famine ˈfæm.ɪn **-s** -z
famish ˈfæm.ɪʃ **-es** -ɪz **-ing** -ɪŋ **-ed** -t
famosus libellus fæmˌəʊ.səs.lɪˈbel.əs, US -ˌoʊ-
famous ˈfeɪ.məs **-ly** -li **-ness** -nəs, -nɪs
fan fæn **-s** -z **-ning** -ɪŋ **-ned** -d
Fan *Welsh mountains:* væn
fan-assisted ˌfæn.əˈsɪs.tɪd *stress shift:* ˌ**fan-assisted ˈoven**
fanatic fəˈnæt.ɪk, US -ˈnæţ- **-s** -s **-al** -əl **-ally** -əl.i, -li
fanaticism fəˈnæt.ɪ.sɪ.zəm, ˈ-ə-, US -ˈnæţ-
fanaticiz|e, -is|e fəˈnæt.ɪ.saɪz, US -ˈnæţ- **-es** -ɪz **-ing** -ɪŋ **-ed** -d
fanbelt ˈfæn.belt **-s** -s
fanciable ˈfænt.si.ə.bəl
fanciful ˈfænt.sɪ.fəl, -fʊl **-ly** -i **-ness** -nəs, -nɪs
Fancourt ˈfæn.kɔːt, ˈfæŋ-, US -kɔːrt
fanc|y ˈfænt.s|i **-ies** -iz **-ying** -i.ɪŋ **-ied** -id **-ier/s** -i.əʳ/z, US -i.ɚ/z ˌ**fancy ˈdress**
fancy-free ˌfænt.siˈfriː ˌ**footloose and ˌfancy-ˈfree** US ˈ**footloose and ˌfancy ˌfree**
fancywork ˈfænt.si.wɜːk, US -wɝːk
fandango fænˈdæŋ.gəʊ, US -goʊ **-s** -z
fane, F~ feɪn **-s** -z
Faneuil ˈfæn.əl, -jəl, -jʊəl, US -jə.wəl
fanfare ˈfæn.feəʳ, US -fer **-s** -z
fanfaronade ˌfæn.fær.əˈnɑːd, -fər-, -ˈneɪd, US -fər.əˈneɪd, -ˈnɑːd **-s** -z
fang, F~ fæŋ **-s** -z **-ed** -d
fanjet ˈfæn.dʒet **-s** -s
fanlight ˈfæn.laɪt **-s** -s
fanner ˈfæn.əʳ, US -ɚ **-s** -z
Fannie Mae ˌfæn.iˈmeɪ
Fanning ˈfæn.ɪŋ
fann|y, F~ ˈfæn|.i **-ies** -iz ˈ**fanny ˌpack**
Fanshawe ˈfæn.ʃɔː, US -ʃɑː, -ʃɔː
Fanta® ˈfæn.tə, US -ţə
fantabulous fænˈtæb.jə.ləs, -jʊ-
fantail ˈfæn.teɪl **-s** -z
fantasia fænˈteɪ.zi.ə, -ˈtɑː-, ˈ-ʒə; ˌfæn.təˈziː.ə, -ˈsiː-, US fænˈteɪ.ʒə, -ʒi.ə; US ˌfæn.ţəˈziː.ə **-s** -z
fantasist ˈfæn.tə.sɪst, US -ţə- **-s** -s
fantasiz|e, -is|e ˈfæn.tə.saɪz, US -ţə- **-es** -ɪz **-ing** -ɪŋ **-ed** -d
fantasm ˈfæn.tæz.əm **-s** -z
fantastic fænˈtæs.tɪk, fən-, US fæn- **-al** -əl **-ally** -əl.i, -li **-alness** -əl.nəs, -nɪs
fantas|y ˈfæn.tə.s|i, -z|i, US -ţə- **-ies** -iz
Fanti, Fante ˈfæn.ti, US ˈfæn.ti, ˈfɑːn- **-s** -z
fanzine ˈfæn.ziːn **-s** -z
FAQ ˌef.eɪˈkjuː **-s** -z
far fɑːʳ, US fɑːr ˌ**Far ˈEast**
farad ˈfær.əd, -æd, US ˈfer-, ˈfær- **-s** -z
faraday, F~ ˈfær.ə.deɪ, US ˈfer-, ˈfær- **-s** -z
faradic fəˈræd.ɪk
Farage ˈfær.ɑːʒ; fəˈrɑːʒ, US ˈfær.ɑːʒ, ˈfer-; US fɚˈɑːʒ
faraway ˌfɑː.rəˈweɪ, US ˌfɑːr.əˈ- *stress shift:* ˌ**faraway ˈlook**
farc|e fɑːs, US fɑːrs **-es** -ɪz
farceur ˌfɑːˈsɜːʳ, US ˌfɑːrˈsɝː **-s** -z
farci(e) ˌfɑːˈsiː, US ˌfɑːr-
farcical ˈfɑː.sɪ.kəl, US ˈfɑːr- **-ly** -i
farcy ˈfɑː.si, US ˈfɑːr-
far|e n, v feəʳ, US fer **-es** -z **-ing** -ɪŋ **-ed** -d
Far East ˌfɑːʳˈiːst, US ˌfɑːr-
Farebrother ˈfeəˌbrʌð.əʳ, US ˈferˌbrʌð.ɚ
Fareham ˈfeə.rəm, US ˈfer.əm
farewell ˌfeəˈwel, US ˌfer- **-s** -z *stress shift:* ˌ**farewell ˈkiss**
Farewell ˈfeə.wel, -wəl, US ˈfer-
farfalle fɑːˈfæl.eɪ, US fɑːr-
far-fetched ˌfɑːˈfetʃt, US ˌfɑːr- *stress shift:* ˌ**far-fetched ˈtale**
far-flung ˌfɑːˈflʌŋ, US ˌfɑːr- *stress shift:* ˌ**far-flung ˈplaces**
Fargo ˈfɑː.gəʊ, US ˈfɑːr.goʊ
far-gone ˌfɑːˈgɒn, US ˌfɑːrˈgɑːn
Farhi ˈfɑː.hi, US ˈfɑːr-
Faribault ˈfær.ɪ.bəʊ, US ˈfer.ɪ.boʊ, ˈfær-
farina fəˈriː.nə, -ˈraɪ-, US -ˈriː-
Farina fəˈriː.nə
farinaceous ˌfær.ɪˈneɪ.ʃəs, -əˈ-, US ˌfer-, ˌfær-
Faringdon ˈfær.ɪŋ.dən, US ˈfer-, ˈfær-
Faringford ˈfær.ɪŋ.fəd, US ˈfer.ɪŋ.fɚd, ˈfær-
Farington ˈfær.ɪŋ.tən, US ˈfer-, ˈfær-
Farjeon ˈfɑː.dʒən, US ˈfɑːr-
Farleigh, Farley ˈfɑː.li, US ˈfɑːr-
farm fɑːm, US fɑːrm **-s** -z **-ing** -ɪŋ **-ed** -d
Farman ˈfɑː.mən, US ˈfɑːr-
Farmaner ˈfɑː.mə.nəʳ, US ˈfɑːr.mə.nɚ
farmer, F~ ˈfɑː.məʳ, US ˈfɑːr.mɚ **-s** -z
farmhand ˈfɑːm.hænd, US ˈfɑːrm- **-s** -z
farmhou|se ˈfɑːm.haʊ|s, US ˈfɑːrm- **-ses** -zɪz
Farmington ˈfɑː.mɪŋ.tən, US ˈfɑːr-
farmland ˈfɑːm.lænd, -lənd, US ˈfɑːrm.lænd
farmstead ˈfɑːm.sted, US ˈfɑːrm- **-s** -z
farmyard ˈfɑːm.jɑːd, US ˈfɑːrm.jɑːrd **-s** -z
Farn(e) fɑːn, US fɑːrn
Farnaby ˈfɑː.nə.bi, US ˈfɑːr-
Farnborough ˈfɑːn.bər.ə, ˈfɑːm-, US ˈfɑːrn-, -bɚ.oʊ
Farnham ˈfɑː.nəm, US ˈfɑːr-
Farnhamworth ˈfɑː.nəm.wəθ, -wɜːθ, US ˈfɑːr.nəm.wɚθ, -wɝːθ
faro *gambling game:* ˈfeə.rəʊ, US ˈfer.oʊ, ˈfær-
Faro *in Portugal:* ˈfɑː.rəʊ, ˈfeə-, US ˈfɑːr.oʊ, ˈfer-
Faroe ˈfeə.rəʊ, US ˈfer.oʊ
Faroese ˌfeə.rəʊˈiːz, US ˌfer.oʊˈ-
far-off ˌfɑːʳˈɒf, US ˌfɑːrˈɑːf *stress shift:* ˌ**far-off ˈtown**
farouche fəˈruːʃ, fɑː-
Farouk fəˈruːk, færˈuːk, US fəˈruːk
far-out ˌfɑːʳˈaʊt, US ˌfɑːr- *stress shift:* ˌ**far-out ˈmusic**
Farquhar ˈfɑː.kwəʳ, -kəʳ, US ˈfɑːr.kwɚ, -kwɑːr, -kɚ
Farquharson ˈfɑː.kwə.sən, -kə-, US ˈfɑːr.kwɚ-, -kɚ-
Farr fɑːʳ, US fɑːr
farraginous fəˈreɪ.dʒɪ.nəs, -ˈrædʒ.ɪ-, -ən.əs, US fəˈrædʒ.ɪ.nəs, ˈ-ə-
farrago fəˈrɑː.gəʊ, -ˈreɪ-, US fəˈrɑː.goʊ, -ˈreɪ- **-(e)s** -z
Farragut ˈfær.ə.gət, US ˈfer-, ˈfær-
Farrah ˈfær.ə, US ˈfer-, ˈfær-
Farrakhan ˈfær.ə.kæn, US ˈfer-, ˈfær-, -kɑːn, ˈfer.kɑːn
Farrant ˈfær.ənt, US ˈfer-, ˈfær-
far-reaching ˌfɑːˈriː.tʃɪŋ, US ˌfɑːr- *stress shift:* ˌ**far-reaching ˈconsequences**
Farrell ˈfær.əl, US ˈfer-, ˈfær-
Farren ˈfær.ən, US ˈfer-, ˈfær-
farrier ˈfær.i.əʳ, US ˈfer.i.ɚ, ˈfær- **-s** -z **-y** -i **-ies** -iz
Farringdon ˈfær.ɪŋ.dən, US ˈfer-, ˈfær-
Farringford ˈfær.ɪŋ.fəd, US ˈfer.ɪŋ.fɚd, ˈfær-
Farrington ˈfær.ɪŋ.tən, US ˈfer-, ˈfær-
farrow, F~ ˈfær.əʊ, US ˈfer.oʊ, ˈfær- **-s** -z **-ing** -ɪŋ **-ed** -d
farseeing ˌfɑːˈsiː.ɪŋ, US ˌfɑːr- *stress shift:* ˌ**farseeing ˈleader**
Farsi ˈfɑː.siː, ˌ-ˈ-, US ˈfɑːr- **-s** -z
farsighted fɑːˈsaɪ.tɪd, US fɑːrˈsaɪ.ţɪd **-ly** -li **-ness** -nəs, -nɪs
Farsley ˈfɑːz.li, US ˈfɑːrz-
fart fɑːt, US fɑːrt **-s** -s **-ing** -ɪŋ, US ˈfɑːr.ţɪŋ **-ed** -ɪd, US ˈfɑːr.ţɪd
farth|er ˈfɑː.ð|əʳ, US ˈfɑːr.ð|ɚ **-est** -ɪst, -əst
farthing ˈfɑː.ðɪŋ, US ˈfɑːr- **-s** -z

farthingale ˈfɑː.ðɪŋ.geɪl, (US) ˈfɑːr- **-s** -z
fartlek ˈfɑːt.lek, (US) ˈfɑːrt- **-s** -s
Faruk fəˈruːk, færˈuːk, (US) fəˈruːk
Farwell ˈfɑː.wel, -wəl, (US) ˈfɑːr-
fasces ˈfæs.iːz
fasci|a *medical term:* ˈfæʃ.i|.ə, -ʃ|ə, (US) -i|.ə *other senses:* ˈfeɪ.ʃ|ə, ˈ-ʃi|.ə, (US) ˈfæʃ.i|.ə, ˈfæʃ|.ə; *also when referring to classical architecture:* ˈfeɪ.si|.ə, (US) -ʃi- **-as** -əz **-ae** -iː
fasciated ˈfæʃ.i.eɪ.tɪd, (US) -t̬ɪd
fascicle ˈfæs.ɪ.kəl, ˈ-ə- **-s** -z
fascicule ˈfæs.ɪ.kjuːl, ˈ-ə- **-s** -z
fascin|ate ˈfæs.ɪ.n|eɪt, -ən|.eɪt, (US) -ən|.eɪt **-ates** -eɪts **-ated** -eɪ.tɪd, (US) -eɪ.t̬ɪd **-ator/s** -eɪ.təʳ/z, (US) -eɪ.t̬ɚ/z
fascinating ˈfæs.ɪ.neɪ.tɪŋ, -ən.eɪ-, (US) -ən.eɪ.t̬ɪŋ **-ly** -li
fascination ˌfæs.ɪˈneɪ.ʃən, -ənˈeɪ-, (US) -ənˈeɪ- **-s** -z
fascine fæsˈiːn, fəˈsiːn **-s** -z
fascism, F~ ˈfæʃ.ɪ.zəm
fascist, F~ ˈfæʃ.ɪst **-s** -s
Fascisti fæʃˈɪs.tiː, fəˈʃɪs-
fascistic, F~ fæʃˈɪs.tɪk, fəˈʃɪs- **-ally** -əl.i, -li
fash fæʃ **-es** -ɪz **-ing** -ɪŋ **-ed** -t
fashion ˈfæʃ.ən **-s** -z **-ing** -ɪŋ **-ed** -d **-er/s** -əʳ/z, (US) -ɚ/z **ˈfashion ˌplate**
fashionab|le ˈfæʃ.ən.ə.b|əl, ˈfæʃ.nə- **-ly** -li **-leness** -əl.nəs, -nɪs
fashionista ˌfæʃ.ənˈiː.stə, -ˈɪs.tə, (US) -ˈiː.stə **-s** -z
Faslane fæzˈleɪn, fəˈsleɪn
Fassbinder ˈfæs.bɪn.dəʳ, (US) ˈfɑːs.bɪn.dɚ
fast, F~ fɑːst, (US) fæst **-s** -s **-est** -ɪst, -əst **-ness** -nəs, -nɪs **-ing** -ɪŋ **-ed** -ɪd **-er/s** -əʳ/z, (US) -ɚ/z **ˌfast and ˈloose; ˈfast ˌday; ˌfast ˈfood; ˈfast ˌlane; ˌfast reˈactor; ˈfast ˌtrack; ˌlife in the ˈfast ˌlane; ˌpull a ˈfast ˌone**
fastball ˈfɑːst.bɔːl, (US) ˈfæst-, -bɑːl **-s** -z
fasten ˈfɑː.sən, (US) ˈfæs.ən **-s** -z **-ing** -ɪŋ, ˈfɑːs.nɪŋ, (US) ˈfæs- **-ed** -d
fastener ˈfɑːs.ən.əʳ, (US) ˈfæs.ən.ɚ **-s** -z
fastening ˈfɑː.sən.ɪŋ; ˈfɑːs.nɪŋ, (US) ˈfæs.ən.ɪŋ; (US) ˈfæs.nɪŋ **-s** -z
fast-forward ˌfɑːstˈfɔː.wəd, (US) ˌfæstˈfɔːr.wɚd **-s** -z **-ing** -ɪŋ **-ed** -ɪd
fasti, F~ ˈfæs.tiː, -taɪ
fastidious fæsˈtɪd.i.əs, fəˈstɪd- **-ly** -li **-ness** -nəs, -nɪs
fastness ˈfɑːst.nəs, -nɪs, (US) ˈfæst- **-es** -ɪz
Fastnet ˈfɑːst.net, -nɪt, (US) ˈfæst-
fast-talk ˌfɑːstˈtɔːk, (US) ˌfæst-, -ˈtɑːk **-s** -s **-ing** -ɪŋ **-ed** -t **-er/s** -əʳ/z, (US) -ɚ/z
fast-track ˈfɑːst.træk, (US) ˈfæst- **-s** -s **-ing** -ɪŋ **-ed** -t
fat fæt **-ter** -əʳ, (US) ˈfæt̬.ɚ **-test** -ɪst, -əst, (US) ˈfæt̬.ɪst, -əst **-ness** -nəs, -nɪs **ˈfat ˌcat; ˌfat ˈcity**
Fatah ˈfæt.ə, ˈ-ɑː
fatal ˈfeɪ.təl, (US) -t̬əl **-ly** -i
fatal|ism ˈfeɪ.təl|.ɪ.zəm, (US) -t̬əl- **-ist/s** -ɪst/s
fatalistic ˌfeɪ.təlˈɪs.tɪk, (US) -t̬əlˈ- **-ally** -əl.i, -li
fatalit|y fəˈtæl.ə.t|i, feɪ-, -ɪ.t|i, (US) -ə.t̬|i **-ies** -iz
fat|e, F~ feɪt **-es** -s **-ed** -ɪd, (US) ˈfeɪ.t̬ɪd
fateful ˈfeɪt.fəl, -fʊl **-ly** -i
fat-free ˌfætˈfriː *stress shift:* **ˌfat-free ˈdiet**
fathead ˈfæt.hed **-s** -z
fath|er, F~ ˈfɑː.ð|əʳ, (US) -ð|ɚ **-ers** -əz, (US) -ɚz **-ering** -ər.ɪŋ **-ered** -əd, (US) -ɚd **ˌFather ˈChristmas; ˈfather ˌfigure**
fatherhood ˈfɑː.ðə.hʊd, (US) -ðɚ-
father-in-law ˈfɑː.ðər.ɪn.lɔː, (US) -ðɚ.ɪn.lɑː, -lɔː- **fathers-in-law** ˈfɑː.ðəz-, (US) -ðɚz-
fatherland ˈfɑː.ðə.lænd, (US) -ðɚ- **-s** -z
fatherless ˈfɑː.ðə.ləs, -lɪs, (US) -ðɚ-
fatherl|y ˈfɑː.ðəl|.i, (US) -ðɚ.l|i **-iness** -ɪ.nəs, -ɪ.nɪs
fathom ˈfæð.əm **-s** -z **-ing** -ɪŋ **-ed** -d **-able** -ə.bəl **-less** -ləs, -lɪs
fatigu|e fəˈtiːg **-es** -z **-ing/ly** -ɪŋ/li **-ed** -d **ˌchronic faˈtigue ˌsyndrome**
Fatima ˈfæt.ɪ.mə, (US) ˈfæt̬-, ˈfɑː.t̬ɪ-; (US) fəˈtiː-
fatling ˈfæt.lɪŋ **-s** -z
fatsia ˈfæt.si.ə **-s** -z
fatso ˈfæt.səʊ, (US) -soʊ **-es** -z
fatted ˈfæt.ɪd, (US) ˈfæt̬- **ˌfatted ˈcalf**
fatten ˈfæt.ən **-s** -z **-ing** -ɪŋ **-ed** -d **-er/s** -əʳ/z, (US) -ɚ/z
fattish ˈfæt.ɪʃ, (US) ˈfæt̬-
fatt|y ˈfæt|.i, (US) ˈfæt̬- **-ies** -iz **-ier** -i.əʳ, (US) -i.ɚ **-iest** -i.ɪst, -i.əst **-iness** -ɪ.nəs, -ɪ.nɪs **ˌfatty ˈacid**
fatuity fəˈtʃuː.ə.ti, -ˈtjuː-, fætʃˈuː-, fætˈjuː-, -ɪ.ti, (US) fəˈtuː.ə.t̬i, -ˈtjuː-
fatuous ˈfæt.ju.əs, (US) ˈfætʃ.u- **-ly** -li **-ness** -nəs, -nɪs
fatwa ˈfæt.wɑː, -wə, (US) ˈfæt.wɑː, ˈfʌt- **-s** -z
faubourg ˈfəʊ.bʊəg, -bɜːg, (US) ˈfoʊ.bʊr, -bʊrg **-s** -z
faucal ˈfɔː.kəl, (US) ˈfɑː-, ˈfɔː-
fauces ˈfɔː.siːz, (US) ˈfɑː-, ˈfɔː-
faucet ˈfɔː.sɪt, -sət, (US) ˈfɑː-, ˈfɔː- **-s** -s
Faucett, Faucit ˈfɔː.sɪt, -ət, (US) ˈfɑː-, ˈfɔː-
Faulconbridge ˈfɔː.kən.brɪdʒ, ˈfɔːl-, -kəm-, (US) ˈfɑː.kən-, ˈfɑːl-, ˈfɔː-, ˈfɔːl-
Fauldhouse ˈfɔːld.haʊs, (US) ˈfɑːld-, ˈfɔːld-
Faulds fəʊldz, fɔːldz, (US) foʊldz, fɑːldz, fɔːldz
Faulhorn ˈfaʊl.hɔːn, (US) -hɔːrn
Faulk fɔːk, (US) fɑːk, fɔːk, fɑːlk
Faulkes fɔːks, fɔːlks, (US) fɑːks, fɑːlks, fɔːks, fɔːlks
Faulkland ˈfɔː.klənd, ˈfɔːl-, (US) ˈfɑː-, ˈfɑːl-, ˈfɔː-, ˈfɔːl-
Faulkner ˈfɔːk.nəʳ, (US) ˈfɑːk.nɚ, ˈfɔːk-, ˈfɑːlk-
Faulks fəʊks, (US) foʊks
faul|t fɔːl|t, fɒl|t, (US) fɔːl|t, fɑːl|t **-ts** -ts **-ting** -tɪŋ, (US) -t̬ɪŋ **-ted** -tɪd, (US) -t̬ɪd
faultfind|er ˈfɔːltˌfaɪn.d|əʳ, ˈfɒlt-, (US) ˈfɔːltˌfaɪn.d|ɚ, ˈfɑːlt- **-ers** -əz, (US) -ɚz **-ing** -ɪŋ
faultless ˈfɔːlt.ləs, ˈfɒlt-, -lɪs, (US) ˈfɔːlt-, ˈfɑːlt- **-ly** -li **-ness** -nəs, -nɪs
fault|y ˈfɔːl.t|i, ˈfɒl-, (US) ˈfɔːl.t|i, ˈfɑːl- **-ier** -i.əʳ, (US) -i.ɚ **-iest** -i.ɪst, -i.əst **-ily** -əl.i, -ɪ.li **-iness** -ɪ.nəs, -ɪ.nɪs
faun fɔːn, (US) fɑːn, fɔːn **-s** -z
fauna ˈfɔː.nə, (US) ˈfɑː-, ˈfɔː-
Faunch fɔːntʃ, (US) fɑːntʃ, fɔːntʃ
Fauntleroy ˈfɔːnt.lə.rɔɪ, ˈfɒnt-, (US) ˈfɑːnt-, ˈfɔːnt-
Fauré ˈfɔː.reɪ, ˈfɒr.eɪ, (US) foʊˈreɪ, fɔː-
Faust faʊst
Faustian ˈfaʊ.sti.ən
Faustina fɔːˈstiː.nə, faʊ-, (US) faʊ-, fɔː-
Faustus ˈfɔː.stəs, ˈfaʊ-, (US) ˈfaʊ-, ˈfɔː-
fauteuil ˈfəʊ.tɜː.i, fəʊˈtɜː.i, -ˈtɜːl, (US) ˈfoʊ.tɪl; (US) foʊˈtɜː.jə **-s** -z
fauve fəʊv, (US) foʊv
fauv|ism, F~ ˈfəʊ.v|ɪ.zəm, (US) ˈfoʊ- **-ist/s** -ɪst/s
Faux fəʊ, fɔːks, (US) foʊ
faux ami ˌfəʊz.æmˈi, (US) ˌfoʊz- **-s** -z
faux-naïf ˌfəʊ.naɪˈiːf, (US) ˌfoʊ.nɑːˈ- **-s** -s
faux pas *singular:* ˌfəʊˈpɑː, (US) ˌfoʊ-
faux pas *plural:* ˌfəʊˈpɑː, -ˈpɑːz, (US) ˌfoʊ-
fave feɪv **-s** -z
Favel ˈfeɪ.vəl
Faversham ˈfæv.ə.ʃəm, (US) ˈ-ɚ-
Favoni|an fəˈvəʊ.ni|.ən, feɪ-, (US) -ˈvoʊ- **-us** -əs
fav|o(u)r ˈfeɪ.v|əʳ, (US) -v|ɚ **-o(u)rs** -əz, (US) -ɚz **-o(u)ring** -ər.ɪŋ **-o(u)red** -əd, (US) -ɚd **-o(u)rer/s** -ər.əʳ/z, (US) -ɚ.ɚ/z
favo(u)rab|le ˈfeɪ.vər.ə.b|əl **-ly** -li **-leness** -əl.nəs, -nɪs
Favorit® ˈfæv.ər.ɪt
favo(u)rit|e ˈfeɪ.vər.ɪt, -ət, ˈfeɪv.rɪt **-es** -s **-ism** -ɪ.zəm **ˌfavo(u)rite ˈson**
favo(u)rless ˈfeɪ.və.ləs, -lɪs, (US) -vɚ-
Fawcett ˈfɔː.sɪt, -sət, ˈfɒs.ɪt, -ət, (US) ˈfɑː.sɪt, ˈfɔː-, -sət
Fawkes fɔːks, (US) fɑːks, fɔːks
Fawkner ˈfɔːk.nəʳ, (US) ˈfɑːk.nɚ, ˈfɔːk-
Fawley ˈfɔː.li, (US) ˈfɑː-, ˈfɔː-
Fawlty ˈfɔːl.ti, (US) ˈfɑːl-, ˈfɔːl-
fawn fɔːn, (US) fɑːn, fɔːn **-s** -z **-ing/ly** -ɪŋ/li **-ed** -d **-er/s** -əʳ/z, (US) -ɚ/z
Fawssett ˈfɔː.sɪt, -sət, (US) ˈfɑː.sɪt, ˈfɔː-, -sət
fax fæks **-es** -ɪz **-ing** -ɪŋ **-ed** -t **ˈfax maˌchine**
fay, F~ feɪ **-s** -z
Faye feɪ
Fayette feɪˈet *stress shift, see compound:* **ˌFayette ˈCity**
Fayetteville ˈfeɪ.et.vɪl, -ɪt-, -ət-; *locally also:* (US) ˈfeɪt.vəl
Faygate ˈfeɪ.geɪt
Faza(c)kerley fəˈzæk.əl.i, (US) -ɚ.li
faz|e feɪz **-es** -ɪz **-ing** -ɪŋ **-ed** -d

FBI ˌef.biːˈaɪ
FC ˌefˈsiː
FCO ˌef.siːˈəʊ, ⓤⓢ -ˈoʊ
FDA ˌef.diːˈeɪ
fe *name of note in Tonic Sol-fa:* fiː *syllable used in Tonic Sol-fa for counting a short note off the beat:* fi
FE (abbrev. for **Further Education**) ˌefˈiː
fealty ˈfiːl.ti
fear fɪəʳ, ⓤⓢ fɪr **-s** -z **-ing** -ɪŋ **-ed** -d
fearful ˈfɪə.fəl, -fʊl, ⓤⓢ ˈfɪr- **-ly** -i **-ness** -nəs, -nɪs
Fearghal ˈfɜː.gəl, ⓤⓢ ˈfɝː-
Feargus ˈfɜː.gəs, ⓤⓢ ˈfɝː-
Fearing ˈfɪə.rɪŋ, ⓤⓢ ˈfɪr.ɪŋ
fearless ˈfɪə.ləs, -lɪs, ⓤⓢ ˈfɪr- **-ly** -li **-ness** -nəs, -nɪs
Fearn(e) fɜːn, ⓤⓢ fɝːn
Fearnside ˈfɜːn.saɪd, ⓤⓢ ˈfɝːn-
Fearon ˈfɪə.rən, ⓤⓢ ˈfɪr.ən
fearsome ˈfɪə.səm, ⓤⓢ ˈfɪr- **-ly** -li **-ness** -nəs, -nɪs
feasibility ˌfiː.zəˈbɪl.ə.ti, -zɪˈ-, -ɪ.ti, ⓤⓢ -ə.t̬i
feasib|le ˈfiː.zə.b|əl, -zɪ- **-ly** -li **-leness** -əl.nəs, -nɪs
feast, F~ fiːst **-s** -s **-ing** -ɪŋ **-ed** -ɪd **-er/s** -əʳ/z, ⓤⓢ -ɚ/z
feat fiːt **-s** -s
feath|er ˈfeð|.əʳ, ⓤⓢ -ɚ **-ers** -əz, ⓤⓢ -ɚz **-ering** -ər.ɪŋ **-ered** -əd, ⓤⓢ -ɚd ˌ**feather** ˈ**bed**
featherbed ˈfeð.ə.bed, ˌ--ˈ-, ⓤⓢ -ɚ- **-s** -z **-ding** -ɪŋ **-ded** -ɪd
featherbrain ˈfeð.ə.breɪn, ⓤⓢ ˈ-ɚ- **-s** -z **-ed** -d
featheredg|e ˈfeð.əʳ.edʒ, ˌ--ˈ-, ⓤⓢ -ɚ- **-es** -ɪz
featherhead ˈfeð.ə.hed, ⓤⓢ ˈ-ɚ- **-s** -z **-ed** -ɪd
featherstitch ˈfeð.ə.stɪtʃ, ⓤⓢ ˈ-ɚ- **-es** -ɪz **-ing** -ɪŋ **-ed** -t
Featherston ˈfeð.ə.stən, ⓤⓢ ˈ-ɚ-
Featherstone ˈfeð.ə.stən, -stəʊn, ⓤⓢ -ɚ.stən, -stoʊn
Featherstonehaugh ˈfeð.ə.stən.hɔː; ˈfæn.ʃɔː; ˈfes.tən.hɔː, ˈfɪə.stən-; ˈfiː.sən.heɪ, ⓤⓢ ˈfeð.ɚ.stən.hɑː, -hɔː; ˈfæn.ʃɑː, -ʃɔː; ˈfes.tən.hɑː, ˈfɪr.stən-, -hɔː; ˈfiː.sən.heɪ
featherweight ˈfeð.ə.weɪt, ⓤⓢ ˈ-ɚ- **-s** -s
feather|y ˈfeð.ər|.i **-iness** -ɪ.nəs, -ɪ.nɪs
Featley ˈfiːt.li
featly ˈfiːt.li
feat|ure ˈfiː.tʃ|əʳ, ⓤⓢ -tʃ|ɚ **-ures** -əz, ⓤⓢ -ɚz **-uring** -ər.ɪŋ **-ured** -əd, ⓤⓢ -ɚd **-ureless** -ə.ləs, -lɪs, ⓤⓢ -ɚ.ləs, -lɪs
feature-length ˈfiː.tʃə.leŋkθ, ⓤⓢ -tʃɚ-
Feaver ˈfiː.vəʳ, ⓤⓢ -vɚ
Feb. (abbrev. for **February**) ˈfeb.ru.ər.i, ˈ-jʊ.ər.i, ˈ-jʊ.ri, ˈ-jər.i, ⓤⓢ ˈfeb.ruː.er.i, ˈ-juː-, ˈ-jə.wer-
febrifug|e ˈfeb.rɪ.fjuːdʒ, -rə- **-es** -ɪz
febrile ˈfiː.braɪl, ⓤⓢ -brɪl, ˈfeb.rɪl
February ˈfeb.ru.ər.i, ˈ-ju.ər.i, ˈ-jʊ.ri, ˈ-jər.i, ⓤⓢ ˈfeb.ru.er.i, ˈ-ju-, ˈ-jə.wer-

> Note: Pronunciations with /j/ in place of /r/ were until recently stigmatized as incorrect, but are now widespread.

fecal ˈfiː.kəl
feces ˈfiː.siːz
fecit ˈfiː.sɪt, ˈfeɪ.kɪt
Feckenham ˈfek.ən.əm
feckless ˈfek.ləs, -lɪs **-ly** -li **-ness** -nəs, -nɪs
feculen|t ˈfek.jə.lən|t, -jʊ-, ⓤⓢ -jə-, -juː- **-ce** *-ts*
fecund ˈfek.ənd, ˈfiː.kənd, -kʌnd
fecun|date ˈfek.ən|.deɪt, ˈfiː.kən-, -kʌn- **-dates** -deɪts **-dating** -deɪ.tɪŋ, ⓤⓢ -deɪ.t̬ɪŋ **-dated** -deɪ.tɪd, ⓤⓢ -deɪ.t̬ɪd
fecundation ˌfek.ənˈdeɪ.ʃən, ˌfiː.kənˈ-, -kʌnˈ-
fecundity fɪˈkʌn.də.ti, fiːˈkʌn-, fekˈʌn-, -dɪ.ti, ⓤⓢ -də.t̬i
fed (from **feed**) fed ˌ**fed** ˈ**up**
Fed fed **-s** -z
federal, F~ ˈfed.ər.əl, ˈ-rəl **-ly** -i ˌ**Federal Re**ˈ**serve**
federal|ism ˈfed.ər.əl|.ɪ.zəm, ˈ-rəl- **-ist/s** -ɪst/s
federalization, -isa- ˌfed.ər.əl.aɪˈzeɪ.ʃən, ˌ-rəl-, -ɪˈ-, ⓤⓢ -əˈ-
federaliz|e, -is|e ˈfed.ər.əl.aɪz, ˈ-rəl-, ⓤⓢ ˈ-ɚ.ə.laɪz, ˈ-rə- **-es** -ɪz **-ing** -ɪŋ **-ed** -d
federate n, adj ˈfed.ər.ət, -ɪt, -eɪt **-s** -s
feder|ate v ˈfed.ər|.eɪt **-ates** -eɪts **-ating** -eɪ.tɪŋ, ⓤⓢ -eɪ.t̬ɪŋ **-ated** -eɪ.tɪd, ⓤⓢ -eɪ.t̬ɪd
federation ˌfed.ərˈeɪ.ʃən, ⓤⓢ -əˈreɪ- **-s** -z
federative ˈfed.ər.ə.tɪv, -eɪ-, ⓤⓢ -ɚ.ə.t̬ɪv, -ə.reɪ- **-ly** -li
Federer ˈfed.ər.əʳ, ⓤⓢ -ɚ
FedEx® ˈfed.eks
fedora, F~ fɪˈdɔː.rə, fə-, fedˈɔː-, ⓤⓢ fəˈdɔːr.ə **-s** -z
fed up ˌfedˈʌp
fee fiː **-s** -z **-ing** -ɪŋ **-d** -d ˌ**fee** ˈ**simple**; ˌ**fee** ˈ**tail**
feeb|le ˈfiː.b|əl **-ler** -ləʳ, ⓤⓢ -lɚ **-lest** -əl.ɪst, -əst, -lɪst, -ləst **-ly** -li **-leness** -əl.nəs, -nɪs
feebleminded ˌfiː.bəlˈmaɪn.dɪd, ⓤⓢ ˌfiː.bəlˈmaɪn.dɪd, ˈfiː.bəlˌmaɪn.dɪd **-ness** -nəs, -nɪs *stress shift, British only:* ˌ**feebleminded** ˈ**simpleton**
feed fiːd **-s** -z **-ing** -ɪŋ **fed** fed **feeder/s** ˈfiː.dəʳ/z, ⓤⓢ -dɚ/z ˈ**feeding** ˌ**bottle**; ˈ**feed** ˌ**pipe**; ˈ**feed** ˌ**tank**
feedback ˈfiːd.bæk
feedbag ˈfiːd.bæg **-s** -z
feel fiːl **-s** -z **-ing** -ɪŋ **felt** felt
feeler ˈfiː.ləʳ, ⓤⓢ -lɚ **-s** -z
feelgood ˈfiːl.gʊd ˈ**feelgood** ˌ**factor**
feeling ˈfiː.lɪŋ **-s** -z **-ly** -li
Feeney ˈfiː.ni
fee-paying ˈfiːˌpeɪ.ɪŋ
feet (plural of **foot**) fiːt ˌ**drag one's** ˈ**feet**; ˌ**fall on one's** ˈ**feet**; ˌ**find one's** ˈ**feet**; **have/keep** ˌ**both feet on the** ˈ**ground**; **be** ˌ**rushed off one's** ˈ**feet**; ˌ**sweep someone off their** ˈ**feet**
Fegan ˈfiː.gən
Feiffer ˈfaɪ.fəʳ, ⓤⓢ -fɚ
feign feɪn **-s** -z **-ing** -ɪŋ **-ed** -d **-edly** -ɪd.li **-edness** -ɪd.nəs, -nɪs
Feilden ˈfiːl.dən
Feilding ˈfiːl.dɪŋ
Feinstein ˈfaɪn.staɪn
feint feɪnt **-s** -s **-ing** -ɪŋ, ⓤⓢ ˈfeɪn.t̬ɪŋ **-ed** -ɪd, ⓤⓢ ˈfeɪn.t̬ɪd
Feisal ˈfaɪ.səl, ˈfeɪ-
Feist fiːst
feist|y ˈfaɪ.st|i **-ier** -i.əʳ, ⓤⓢ -i.ɚ **-iest** -i.ɪst, -i.əst **-ily** -əl.i, -ɪ.li
felafel fəˈlɑː.fəl, -ˈlæf.əl, ⓤⓢ -ˈlɑː.fəl **-s** -z
Feldman ˈfeld.mən
feldspar ˈfeld.spɑːʳ, ˈfel-, ⓤⓢ ˈfeld.spɑːr
Felicia fəˈlɪs.i.ə, felˈɪs-, fɪˈlɪs-, -ˈlɪʃ-, ⓤⓢ fəˈlɪʃ.ə, -i.ə, -ˈliː.ʃə, -ˈlɪs.i.ə
felicitat|e fɪˈlɪs.ɪ|.teɪt, fə-, felˈɪs-, ˈ-ə-, ⓤⓢ fəˈlɪs- **-es** -teɪts **-ing** -teɪ.tɪŋ, ⓤⓢ -teɪ.t̬ɪŋ **-ed** -teɪ.tɪd, ⓤⓢ -teɪ.t̬ɪd
felicitation fɪˌlɪs.ɪˈteɪ.ʃən, fə-, felˌɪs-, -əˈ-, ⓤⓢ fəˌlɪs- **-s** -z
felicitous fɪˈlɪs.ɪ.təs, fə-, felˈɪs-, ˈ-ə-, ⓤⓢ fəˈlɪs.ɪ.t̬əs, ˈ-ə- **-ly** -li **-ness** -nəs, -nɪs
felicity, F~ fɪˈlɪs.ə.ti, fə-, felˈɪs-, -ɪ.ti, ⓤⓢ fəˈlɪs.ə.t̬i
feline ˈfiː.laɪn **-s** -z
felinity fɪˈlɪn.ə.ti, fiː-, fə-, -ɪ.ti, ⓤⓢ -ə.t̬i, -ɪ.t̬i
Felix ˈfiː.lɪks
Felixstowe ˈfiː.lɪk.stəʊ, ⓤⓢ -stoʊ
Felkin ˈfel.kɪn
fell, F~ fel **-s** -z **-ing** -ɪŋ **-ed** -d
fella ˈfel.ə **-s** -z
fellah ˈfel.ə, ⓤⓢ ˈfel.ə; ⓤⓢ fəˈlɑː **-in** -hiːn, ˌfel.əˈhiːn, ⓤⓢ -hiːn **-een** -hiːn, ˌfel.əˈhiːn, ⓤⓢ -hiːn
fella|te felˈeɪ|t, fəˈleɪ|t, fɪ-, ⓤⓢ ˈfel.eɪ|t, -ˈ- **-tes** -ts **-ting** -tɪŋ, ⓤⓢ -t̬ɪŋ **-ted** -tɪd, ⓤⓢ -t̬ɪd **-tor/s** -təʳ/z, ⓤⓢ -t̬ɚ/z **-trix/es** -trɪks/ɪz **-trice/s** -trɪs/ɪz
fellatio fəˈleɪ.ʃi.əʊ, felˈeɪ-, fɪˈleɪ-, ⓤⓢ fəˈleɪ.ʃi.oʊ, -ʃoʊ; ⓤⓢ -ˈlɑː.ti.oʊ
fellation fəˈleɪ.ʃən, felˈeɪ-, fɪˈleɪ-, ⓤⓢ fə-
feller ˈfel.əʳ, ⓤⓢ -ɚ **-z** -z
Felling ˈfel.ɪŋ
Fellini felˈiː.ni, fəˈliː-, fɪ-, ⓤⓢ fəˈliː-
felloe ˈfel.əʊ, ⓤⓢ -oʊ **-s** -z
fellow ˈfel.əʊ, ⓤⓢ -oʊ **-s** -z ˌ**fellow** ˈ**citizen**; ˌ**fellow** ˈ**feeling**; ˌ**fellow** ˈ**traveller**
Fellow(e)s ˈfel.əʊz, ⓤⓢ -oʊz
fellowship ˈfel.əʊ.ʃɪp, ⓤⓢ -oʊ- **-s** -s
Felltham ˈfel.θəm
felo-de-se ˌfiː.ləʊ.diːˈsiː, ˌfel.əʊ-, -dɪˈ-, -ˈseɪ, ⓤⓢ ˌfiː.loʊ.dɪˈsiː, ˌfel.oʊ- **felos-de-se** ˌfiː.ləʊz-, ˌfel.əʊz-, ⓤⓢ ˌfiː.loʊz-, ˌfel.oʊz- **felones-de-se**

ˌfiː.ləʊ.niːz-, ˌfel.əʊ.niːz-, (US) ˌfel.oʊ.niː.dɪˈsiː, ˌfiː.loʊ-
felon ˈfel.ən **-s** -z
felonious fəˈləʊ.ni.əs, felˈəʊ-, fɪˈləʊ-, (US) fəˈloʊ- **-ly** -li **-ness** -nəs, -nɪs
felon|y ˈfel.ə.n|i **-ies** -iz
Felpham ˈfel.pəm
felspar ˈfel.spɑːʳ, (US) -spɑːr
Felste(a)d ˈfel.stɪd, -sted
felt felt **-s** -s
Feltham *place:* ˈfel.təm *personal name:* ˈfel.θəm
felting ˈfel.tɪŋ **-s** -z
Felton ˈfel.tən
felt-tip ˌfeltˈtɪp **-s** -s *stress shift, see compound:* **ˌfelt-tip ˈpen**
felucca felˈʌk.ə, fəˈlʌk-, fɪ-, (US) fəˈlʌk-, -ˈluː.kə **-s** -z
FEMA ˈfiː.mə
female ˈfiː.meɪl **-s** -z **-ness** -nəs, -nɪs
feme fiːm, fem, (US) fem **-s** -z
Femidom® ˈfem.ɪ.dɒm, (US) -dɑːm
feminine ˈfem.ɪ.nɪn, ˈ-ə- **-ly** -li **-ness** -nəs, -nɪs
femininit|y ˌfem.ɪˈnɪn.ə.t|i, -əˈ-, -ɪ.t|i, (US) -ə.ţ|i **-ies** -iz
femin|ism ˈfem.ɪ.n|ɪ.zᵊm, ˈ-ə- **-ist/s** -ɪst/s
feminiz|e, -is|e ˈfem.ɪ.naɪz, ˈ-ə- **-es** -ɪz **-ing** -ɪŋ **-ed** -d
femme(s) fatale(s) ˌfæm.fəˈtɑːl, (US) ˌfem.fəˈtæl
femora (alternative plural of **femur**) ˈfem.ᵊr.ə, ˈfiː.mᵊr-, (US) ˈfem.ᵊr-
femoral ˈfem.ᵊr.ᵊl, ˈfiː.mᵊr-, (US) ˈfem.ᵊr-
femur ˈfiː.məʳ, (US) -mɚ **-s** -z **femora** ˈfem.ᵊr.ə, ˈfiː.mᵊr-, (US) ˈfem.ᵊr-
fen, F~ fen **-s** -z
fenc|e fents **-es** -ɪz **-ing** -ɪŋ **-ed** -t **-er/s** -əʳ/z, (US) -ɚ/z **-eless** -ləs, -lɪs ˌ**sit on the ˈfence**
fencesitt|er ˈfentsˌsɪt|.əʳ, (US) -ˌsɪţ- **-ers** -əʳz, (US) -ɚz **-ing** -ɪŋ
Fenchurch ˈfen.tʃɜːtʃ, (US) -tʃɝːtʃ
fend fend **-s** -z **-ing** -ɪŋ **-ed** -ɪd
fender ˈfen.dəʳ, (US) -dɚ **-s** -z
fender-bender ˈfen.dəˌben.dəʳ, (US) -dɚˌben.dɚ **-s** -z
Fendi ˈfen.di
Fenella fɪˈnel.ə, fə-
fenestr|a fɪˈnes.tr|ə, fə- **-ae** -iː **-al** -ᵊl
fenes|trate fɪˈnes|.treɪt, fəˈnes-; ˈfen.ɪ.s|treɪt, ˈ-ə-, (US) ˈfen.ɪ.s|treɪt; (US) fəˈnes|.treɪt **-trates** -treɪts **-trating** -treɪ.tɪŋ, (US) -treɪ.ţɪŋ **-trated** -treɪ.tɪd, (US) -treɪ.ţɪd
fenestration ˌfen.ɪˈstreɪ.ʃᵊn, -əˈ- **-s** -z
feng shui ˌfeŋˈʃuː.i, ˌfʌŋˈʃweɪ, (US) ˌfʌŋˈʃweɪ
Fenham ˈfen.əm
Fenian ˈfiː.ni.ən **-s** -z **-ism** -ɪ.zᵊm
Fenimore ˈfen.ɪ.mɔːʳ, (US) -mɔːr
fenland, F~ ˈfen.lənd, -lænd
Fenn fen
fennec ˈfen.ek, -ɪk **-s** -s
fennel ˈfen.ᵊl
Fennell ˈfen.ᵊl
Fennessy ˈfen.ɪ.si, ˈ-ə-
Fennimore ˈfen.ɪ.mɔːʳ, (US) -mɔːr
fenny, F~ ˈfen.i
Fenrir ˈfen.rɪəʳ, (US) -rɪr
Fenton ˈfen.tən, (US) -tᵊn
Fenty ˈfen.ti
fenugreek ˈfen.jʊ.griːk, -ʊ-, (US) -juː-, -jə-
Fenwick *English surname:* ˈfen.ɪk, -wɪk *American surname:* ˈfen.wɪk *places in UK:* ˈfen.ɪk
Feodor ˈfiː.əʊ.dɔːʳ, (US) -ə.dɔːr
Feodora ˌfiː.əʊˈdɔː.rə, (US) -əˈdɔːr.ə
feoff fef, fiːf **-s** -s **-ing** -ɪŋ **-ed** -t **-er/s** -əʳ/z, (US) -ɚ/z **-ment/s** -mənt/s
feoffee fefˈiː, fiːˈfiː **-s** -z
feoffor fefˈɔːʳ, fiːˈfɔːʳ, (US) fefˈɔːr, fiːˈfɔːr **-s** -z
ferae naturae ˌfer.aɪˌnɑːˈtjʊə.raɪ, -ˈtjɔː-, (US) ˌfiː.riː.nəˈtuː.riː, -ˈtʊr.iː
feral ˈfer.ᵊl, ˈfɪə.rᵊl, (US) ˈfer.ᵊl, ˈfɪr-
Ferdinand ˈfɜː.dɪ.nænd, -də-, -dᵊn.ænd, -nənd, (US) ˈfɝː.dᵊn.ænd
Fergal ˈfɜː.gᵊl, (US) ˈfɝː-
Fergie ˈfɜː.gi, (US) ˈfɝː-
Fergus ˈfɜː.gəs, (US) ˈfɝː-
Fergus(s)on ˈfɜː.gə.sᵊn, (US) ˈfɝː-
feria ˈfer.i.ə, ˈfɪə.ri-, (US) ˈfɪr-, ˈfer- **-l** -l
Feringhee fəˈrɪŋ.gi **-s** -z
Fermanagh fəˈmæn.ə, fɜː-, (US) fɚ-, fɝː-
ferment n ˈfɜː.ment, (US) ˈfɝː- **-s** -s
fer|ment v fə|ˈment, fɜː-, (US) fɚ- **-ments** -ˈments **-menting** -ˈmen.tɪŋ, (US) -ˈmen.ţɪŋ **-mented** -ˈmen.tɪd, (US) -ˈmen.ţɪd **-mentable** -ˈmen.tə.bᵊl, (US) -ˈmen.ţə.bᵊl
fermentation ˌfɜː.menˈteɪ.ʃᵊn, -mənˈ-, (US) ˌfɝː- **-s** -z
fermentative fəˈmen.tə.tɪv, (US) -ţə.ţɪv **-ly** -li **-ness** -nəs, -nɪs
Fermi ˈfeə.mi, (US) ˈfer-
fermium ˈfɜː.mi.əm, (US) ˈfɝː-
Fermor ˈfɜː.mɔːʳ, (US) ˈfɝː.mɔːr
Fermoy *near Cork:* fəˈmɔɪ, fɜː-, (US) fɚ-, fɝː- *street in London:* ˈfɜː.mɔɪ, (US) ˈfɝː-
fern, F~ fɜːn, (US) fɝːn **-s** -z
Fernandez fɜːˈnæn.dez, fə-, (US) fɚ-
Fernando fəˈnæn.dəʊ, (US) fɚˈnæn.doʊ
Ferndale ˈfɜːn.deɪl, (US) ˈfɝːn-
Ferndown ˈfɜːn.daʊn, (US) ˈfɝːn-
fernery ˈfɜː.nᵊr|.i, (US) ˈfɝː- **-ies** -iz
Fernhough ˈfɜːn.həʊ, (US) ˈfɝːn.hoʊ
Fernihough, Fernyhough ˈfɜː.ni.hʌf, -həʊ, (US) ˈfɝː.ni.hʌf, -hoʊ
ferny ˈfɜː.ni, (US) ˈfɝː-
ferocious fəˈrəʊ.ʃəs, fɪ-, (US) fəˈroʊ- **-ly** -li **-ness** -nəs, -nɪs
ferocity fəˈrɒs.ə.ti, fɪ-, -ɪ.ti, (US) fəˈrɑː.sə.ţi
-ferous fᵊr.əs
Note: Suffix. Words containing **-ferous** are normally stressed on the preceding syllable, e.g. **conifer** /ˈkɒn.ɪ.fəʳ/ (US) /ˈkɑː.nə.fɚ/, **coniferous** /kəʊˈnɪf.ᵊr.əs/ (US) /koʊˈnɪf-/.
Ferrand ˈfer.ᵊnd
Ferranti fəˈræn.ti, fɪ-, ferˈæn-, (US) fəˈrɑːn.ţi
Ferrar ˈfer.əʳ; fəˈrɑːʳ, (US) ˈfer.ɚ; (US) fəˈrɑːr
Ferrara fəˈrɑː.rə, fɪˈ-, ferˈɑː-, (US) -ˈrɑːr.ə
Ferrari® fəˈrɑː.ri, fɪˈ-, ferˈɑː-, (US) fəˈrɑːr.i
Ferraro fəˈrɑː.rəʊ, fɪˈ-, ferˈɑː-, (US) fəˈrɑːr.oʊ
Ferraud fəˈrəʊ, ferˈəʊ, (US) fəˈroʊ
ferrel, F~ ˈfer.ᵊl **-s** -z
ferreous ˈfer.i.əs
Ferrer ˈfer.əʳ; fəˈreəʳ, (US) ˈfer.ɚ; (US) fəˈrer **-s** -z
ferre|t, F~ ˈfer.ɪ|t, -ə|t **-ts** -ts **-ting** -tɪŋ, (US) -ţɪŋ **-ted** -tɪd, (US) -ţɪd
ferri- ˈfer.i
ferric ˈfer.ɪk
Ferrier ˈfer.i.əʳ, (US) -ɚ
ferris, F~ ˈfer.ɪs ˈ**ferris** ˌ**wheel**
Ferrisburg ˈfer.ɪs.bɜːg, (US) -bɝːg
ferrite ˈfer.aɪt
ferritic ferˈɪt.ɪk, fəˈrɪt-, (US) fəˈrɪţ-, ferˈɪţ-
ferro- ˈfer.əʊ, (US) ˈfer.oʊ
Note: Prefix. Normally carries either primary or secondary stress on the first syllable, e.g. **ferrotype** /ˈfer.əʊ.taɪp/ (US) /-oʊ-/, **ferromagnetic** /ˌfer.əʊ.mægˈnet.ɪk/ (US) /-oʊ.mægˈneţ-/.
ferroconcrete ˌfer.əʊˈkɒŋ.kriːt, (US) -oʊˈkɑːn.kriːt
ferromagnetic ˌfer.əʊ.mægˈnet.ɪk, (US) -oʊ.mægˈneţ-
ferromagnetism ˌfer.əʊˈmæg.nə.tɪ.zᵊm, (US) -oʊˈ-
ferrotype ˈfer.əʊ.taɪp, (US) -oʊ- **-s** -s
ferrous ˈfer.əs
ferruginous ferˈuː.dʒɪ.nəs, fəˈruː-, fɪ-, -dʒᵊn-, (US) fəˈruː.dʒɪ.nəs, ferˈuː-
ferrule ˈfer.uːl, -ᵊl, -juːl, (US) -ᵊl, -uːl **-s** -z
ferr|y, F~ ˈfer|.i **-ies** -iz **-ying** -i.ɪŋ **-ied** -id
ferryboat ˈfer.i.bəʊt, (US) -boʊt **-s** -s
Ferryhill ˈfer.i.hɪl
ferry|man ˈfer.i|.mən, -mæn **-men** -mən, -men
fertile ˈfɜː.taɪl, (US) ˈfɝː.ţᵊl **-ly** -li
fertility fəˈtɪl.ə.ti, fɜː-, -ɪ.ti, (US) fɚˈtɪl.ə.ţi
fertilization, -isa- ˌfɜː.tɪ.laɪˈzeɪ.ʃᵊn, -tᵊl.aɪˈ-, -ɪˈ-, (US) ˌfɝː.ţᵊl.əˈ-
fertiliz|e, -is|e ˈfɜː.tɪ.laɪz, -tᵊl.aɪz, (US) ˈfɝː.ţə.laɪz **-es** -ɪz **-ing** -ɪŋ **-ed** -d
fertilizer, -ise- ˈfɜː.tɪ.laɪ.zəʳ, -tᵊl.aɪ-, (US) ˈfɝː.ţᵊl.aɪ.zɚ **-s** -z
ferule ˈfer.uːl, -ᵊl, -juːl, (US) -ᵊl, -uːl **-s** -z
fervency ˈfɜː.vᵊnt.si, (US) ˈfɝː-
fervent ˈfɜː.vᵊnt, (US) ˈfɝː- **-ly** -li **-ness** -nəs, -nɪs
fervid ˈfɜː.vɪd, (US) ˈfɝː- **-ly** -li **-ness** -nəs, -nɪs
fervo(u)r ˈfɜː.vəʳ, (US) ˈfɝː.vɚ
fescue ˈfes.kjuː **-s** -z
fess fes **-es** -ɪs **-ing** -ɪŋ **-ed** -t
fess|e fes **-es** -ɪz
Fessenden ˈfes.ᵊn.dən

fest fest -s -s
festal ˈfes.tᵊl -ly -i
Feste ˈfes.ti, ⓊⓈ -teɪ
fest|er ˈfes.t|əʳ, ⓊⓈ -t|ɚ -ers -əz, ⓊⓈ -ɚz -ering -ᵊr.ɪŋ -ered -əd, ⓊⓈ -ɚd
Festiniog fesˈtɪn.i.ɒg, ⓊⓈ -ɑːg, -ɔːg
festival ˈfes.tɪ.vᵊl, -tə- -s -z
festive ˈfes.tɪv -ly -li -ness -nəs, -nɪs
festivit|y fesˈtɪv.ə.t|i, -ɪ.t|i, ⓊⓈ -ə.ţ|i -ies -iz
festoon fesˈtuːn, ⓊⓈ fesˈtuːn, fəˈstuːn -s -z -ing -ɪŋ -ed -d
festschrift ˈfest.ʃrɪft, ˈfeʃ- -en -ən -s -s
Festus ˈfes.təs
feta ˈfet.ə, ⓊⓈ ˈfeţ- ˌ**feta** ˈ**cheese**
fetal ˈfiː.tᵊl, ⓊⓈ -ţᵊl ˈ**fetal po**ˌ**sition**
fetch fetʃ -es -ɪz -ing -ɪŋ -ed -t -er/s -əʳ/z, ⓊⓈ -ɚ/z
fetching ˈfetʃ.ɪŋ -ly -li
fet|e, fêt|e feɪt, ⓊⓈ feɪt, fet -es -s -ing -ɪŋ, ⓊⓈ ˈfeɪ.ţɪŋ, ˈfeţ.ɪŋ -ed -ɪd, ⓊⓈ ˈfeɪ.ţɪd, ˈfeţ.ɪd ˌ**garden** ˈ**fete** ⓊⓈ ˈ**garden** ˌ**fete**
fête(s) champêtre(s) ˌfet.ʃɑ̃ːmˈpet.rə, ⓊⓈ -ʃɑːmˈ-
fetich ˈfet.ɪʃ, ⓊⓈ ˈfeţ- -es -ɪz
fetich|ism ˈfet.ɪ.ʃ|ɪ.zᵊm, ⓊⓈ ˈfeţ- -ist/s -ɪst/s
fetichistic ˌfet.ɪˈʃɪs.tɪk, ⓊⓈ ˌfeţ- -ally -ᵊl.i, -li
fetid ˈfet.ɪd, ˈfiː.tɪd, ⓊⓈ ˈfeţ.ɪd, ˈfiː.ţɪd -ly -li -ness -nəs, -nɪs
fetish ˈfet.ɪʃ, ⓊⓈ ˈfeţ- -es -ɪz
fetish|ism ˈfet.ɪ.ʃ|ɪ.zᵊm, ⓊⓈ ˈfeţ- -ist/s -ɪst/s
fetishistic ˌfet.ɪˈʃɪs.tɪk, ⓊⓈ ˌfeţ- -ally -ᵊl.i, -li
fetlock ˈfet.lɒk, ⓊⓈ -lɑːk -s -s -ed -t
fetolog|y fiːˈtɒl.ə.dʒ|i, ⓊⓈ -ˈtɑː.lə- -ist/s -ɪst/s
fetta ˈfet.ə, ⓊⓈ ˈfeţ- ˌ**fetta** ˈ**cheese**
fett|er, F~ ˈfet|.əʳ, ⓊⓈ ˈfeţ|.ɚ -ers -əz, ⓊⓈ -ɚz -ering -ᵊr.ɪŋ -ered -əd, ⓊⓈ -ɚd
Fettes *place:* ˈfet.ɪs, ⓊⓈ ˈfeţ- *surname:* ˈfet.ɪs, -ɪz, ⓊⓈ ˈfeţ-
Fettesian fetˈiː.zi.ən, -ʒᵊn -s -z
fettl|e ˈfet.ᵊl, ⓊⓈ ˈfeţ- -es -z -ing -ɪŋ, ˈ-lɪŋ, ⓊⓈ ˈfeţ.ᵊl.ɪŋ, ˈfet.lɪŋ -ed -d
fettuccine ˌfet.ʊˈtʃiː.ni, ⓊⓈ ˌfeţ.əˈ-
fetus ˈfiː.təs, ⓊⓈ -ţəs -es -ɪz
feu fjuː -s -z -ing -ɪŋ -ed -d
feud fjuːd -s -z -ing -ɪŋ
feudal ˈfjuː.dᵊl -ly -i
feudal|ism ˈfjuː.dᵊl|.ɪ.zᵊm -ist/s -ɪst/s
feudality fjuːˈdæl.ə.ti, -ɪ.ti, ⓊⓈ -ə.ţi
feudalization, -isa- ˌfjuː.dᵊl.aɪˈzeɪ.ʃᵊn, -ɪˈ-, ⓊⓈ -əˈ-
feudaliz|e, -is|e ˈfjuː.dᵊl.aɪz, ⓊⓈ -də.laɪz -es -ɪz -ing -ɪŋ -ed -d
feudatory ˈfjuː.də.tᵊr.i, -tri, ⓊⓈ -tɔːr.i
feuilleton ˈfɜː.ɪ.tɔ̃ːŋ, ˈfɜːl.tɔ̃ːŋ, ⓊⓈ ˈfɜː.jə.tɑːn, ˈfɝː-, -tɔ̃ːn -s -z
fever ˈfiː.vəʳ, ⓊⓈ -vɚ -s -z -ed -d ˈ**fever** ˌ**blister**; ˈ**fever** ˌ**pitch**
feverfew ˈfiː.və.fjuː, ⓊⓈ -vɚ-
feverish ˈfiː.vᵊr.ɪʃ -ly -li -ness -nəs, -nɪs
Feversham ˈfev.ə.ʃᵊm, ⓊⓈ ˈ-ɚ-
few, F~ fjuː -er -əʳ, ⓊⓈ -ɚ -est -ɪst, -əst -ness -nəs, -nɪs
fey feɪ -ness -nəs, -nɪs
Feydeau ˈfeɪ.dəʊ, ⓊⓈ feɪˈdoʊ
Feynman ˈfaɪn.mən
fez, F~ fez -(z)es -ɪz
Fezzan fezˈɑːn, -ˈæn, ⓊⓈ -ˈæn
Ffestiniog fesˈtɪn.i.ɒg, ⓊⓈ -ɑːg, -ɔːg
Ffion ˈfiː.ɒn, ⓊⓈ -ɑːn
Ffitch fɪtʃ
Ffoulkes fəʊks, fəʊlks, faʊks, fuːks, ⓊⓈ foʊks, foʊlks, faʊks, fuːks
Ffrangcon ˈfræŋ.kᵊn
-fiable faɪ.ə.bᵊl
Note: Suffix. Normally unstressed, e.g. **rectifiable** /ˈrek.tɪ.faɪ.ə.bᵊl/ ⓊⓈ /-tə-/, although some words containing **-fiable** may also be stressed on the antepenultimate syllable, especially in British English (e.g. **justifiable** /ˌdʒʌs.tɪˈfaɪ.ə.bᵊl/); see also entry for **-fy**.
fiacre fiˈɑː.krə, ⓊⓈ -kɚ -s -z
fiancé(e) fiˈɑ̃ːn.seɪ, -ˈɒnt-, ⓊⓈ ˌfiː.ɑːnˈseɪ, –ˈ– -s -z
Fianna Fail, Fianna Fáil ˌfiː.ə.nəˈfɔɪl, ˌfiː.nəˈ-, -ˈfɔːl, ⓊⓈ -ˈfɔɪl, -ˈfiːl
fiasco fiˈæs.kəʊ, ⓊⓈ -koʊ -(e)s -z
fiat *decree:* ˈfaɪ.æt, ⓊⓈ ˈfiː.ət, -æt, -ɑːt -s -s
Fiat® fɪət, ˈfiː.æt, ⓊⓈ ˈfiː.ɑːt -s -s
fiat justitia ˌfiː.æt.jʊsˈtɪt.i.ə, -ˈtɪs-, ⓊⓈ ˌfiː.ɑːt.jʊsˈtɪt.i.ə, -ˈtɪs-
fib fɪb -s -z -bing -ɪŋ -bed -d -ber/s -əʳ/z, ⓊⓈ -ɚ/z
fiber ˈfaɪ.bəʳ, ⓊⓈ -bɚ -s -z
fiberglass ˈfaɪ.bə.glɑːs, ⓊⓈ -bɚ.glæs
fiberlike ˈfaɪ.bə.laɪk, ⓊⓈ -bɚ-
Fibonacci ˌfɪb.əˈnɑː.tʃi, ˌfiː.bəˈ-
fibre ˈfaɪ.bəʳ, ⓊⓈ -bɚ -s -z -d -d -less -ləs, -lɪs
fibreglass ˈfaɪ.bə.glɑːs, ⓊⓈ -bɚ.glæs
fibreoptic ˌfaɪ.bəʳˈɒp.tɪk, ⓊⓈ -bɚˈɑːp- -s -s
fibre optics ˌfaɪ.bəʳˈɒp.tɪks, ⓊⓈ -bɚˈɑːp-
fibriform ˈfaɪ.brɪ.fɔːm, ˈfɪb.rɪ-, ⓊⓈ -fɔːrm
fibril ˈfaɪ.brɪl, -brəl, ⓊⓈ ˈfaɪ.brɪl, ˈfɪb.rɪl -s -s -lar -əʳ, ⓊⓈ -ɚ -lose -əʊs, ⓊⓈ -oʊs
fibril|late ˈfaɪ.brɪ|.leɪt, ˈfɪb.rɪ-, -rə-, ⓊⓈ ˈfɪb.rɪ-, ˈfaɪ.brɪ- -lates -leɪts -lating -leɪ.tɪŋ, ⓊⓈ -leɪ.ţɪŋ -lated -leɪ.tɪd, ⓊⓈ -leɪ.ţɪd
fibrillation ˌfaɪ.brɪˈleɪ.ʃᵊn, ˌfɪb.rɪˈ-, -rəˈ-, ⓊⓈ ˌfɪb.rɪˈ-, ˌfaɪ.brɪˈ- -s -z
fibrilliform faɪˈbrɪl.ɪ.fɔːm, fɪ-, ⓊⓈ fɪˈbrɪl.ɪ.fɔːrm, faɪˈ-
fibrin ˈfɪb.rɪn, ˈfaɪ.brɪn, ⓊⓈ ˈfaɪ.brɪn -ous -əs
fibrinogen fɪˈbrɪn.əʊ.dʒᵊn, faɪ-, -dʒen, ⓊⓈ faɪˈbrɪn.ə-
fibro- ˈfaɪ.brəʊ; faɪˈbrəʊ, ⓊⓈ ˈfaɪ.broʊ, -brə; ⓊⓈ faɪˈbroʊ
Note: Prefix. Normally carries primary or secondary stress on the first syllable, e.g. **fibrositis** /ˌfaɪ.brəʊˈsaɪ.tɪs/ ⓊⓈ /-broʊˈsaɪ.ţɪs/, or primary stress on the second syllable, e.g. **fibrosis** /faɪˈbrəʊ.sɪs/ ⓊⓈ /-ˈbroʊ-/.
fibroid ˈfaɪ.brɔɪd -s -z
fibroma faɪˈbrəʊ.mə, ⓊⓈ -ˈbroʊ- -s -z -ta -tə, ⓊⓈ -ţə
fibrosis faɪˈbrəʊ.sɪs, ⓊⓈ -ˈbroʊ-
fibrositis ˌfaɪ.brəʊˈsaɪ.tɪs, -təs, ⓊⓈ -broʊˈsaɪ.ţɪs, -brəˈ-, -ţəs
fibrous ˈfaɪ.brəs -ly -li -ness -nəs, -nɪs
fibul|a ˈfɪb.jə.l|ə, -jʊ-, ⓊⓈ -jə- -as -əz -ae -iː
FICA ˈfiː.kə, ⓊⓈ ˈfaɪ-, ˈfiː-
fich|e fiːʃ -es -ɪz
fichu ˈfiː.ʃuː, ˈfɪʃ.uː, ⓊⓈ ˈfɪʃ.uː; ⓊⓈ fiːˈʃuː -s -z
fickl|e ˈfɪk.ᵊl -er -əʳ, ˈ-ləʳ, ⓊⓈ ˈ-lɚ, -ᵊl.ɚ -est -ɪst, -əst -eness -nəs, -nɪs
fiction ˈfɪk.ʃᵊn -s -z
fictional ˈfɪk.ʃᵊn.ᵊl -ly -i
fictionalization ˌfɪk.ʃᵊn.ᵊl.aɪˈzeɪ.ʃᵊn, -ɪˈ-, ⓊⓈ -əˈ-
fictionaliz|e, -is|e ˈfɪk.ʃᵊn.ᵊl.aɪz, ⓊⓈ -ə.laɪz -es -ɪz -ing -ɪŋ -ed -d
fictionist ˈfɪk.ʃᵊn.ɪst -s -s
fictitious fɪkˈtɪʃ.əs -ly -li -ness -nəs, -nɪs
fictive ˈfɪk.tɪv
fid fɪd -s -z
fiddl|e ˈfɪd.ᵊl -es -z -ing -ɪŋ, ˈ-lɪŋ -ed -d -er/s -əʳ/z, ˈ-ləʳ/z, ˈ-ᵊl.ɚ/z, ⓊⓈ ˈ-lɚ/z **as** ˌ**fit as a** ˈ**fiddle**
fiddlededee ˌfɪd.ᵊl.dɪˈdiː, ⓊⓈ -diːˈdiː
fiddle-faddl|e ˈfɪd.ᵊlˌfæd.ᵊl -es -z -ing -ɪŋ, ˌ-lɪŋ -ed -d
fiddlesticks ˈfɪd.ᵊl.stɪks
fiddl|y ˈfɪd.ᵊl|.i, ˈfɪd.l|i -ier -i.əʳ, ⓊⓈ -i.ɚ -iest -i.ɪst, -i.əst -iness -ɪ.nəs, -ɪ.nɪs
Fidel fɪˈdel, fiː-, ˈfɪd.el
Fidelia fɪˈdiː.li.ə, fə-, -ˈdeɪ-, ⓊⓈ -ˈdiː.li.ə, -ˈdiːl.jə
Fidelio fɪˈdeɪ.li.əʊ, ⓊⓈ -oʊ
fidelity fɪˈdel.ə.ti, fə-, -ɪ.ti, ⓊⓈ -ə.ţi
fidg|et ˈfɪdʒ|.ɪt -ets -ɪts -eting -ɪ.tɪŋ, ⓊⓈ -ɪ.ţɪŋ -eted -ɪ.tɪd, ⓊⓈ -ɪ.ţɪd
fidget|y ˈfɪdʒ.ɪ.t|i, ˈ-ə- -ier -i.əʳ, ⓊⓈ -i.ɚ -iest -i.ɪst, -i.əst -iness -ɪ.nəs, -ɪ.nɪs
Fido ˈfaɪ.dəʊ, ⓊⓈ -doʊ
fiducial fɪˈdʒuː.ʃi.əl, -ˈdjuː-, fə-, faɪ-, -si-, ⓊⓈ -ˈduː.ʃᵊl, -ˈdjuː- -ly -i
fiduciar|y fɪˈdʒuː.ʃi.ə.r|i, -ˈdjuː-, fə-, faɪ-, -si-, -ʃᵊr|.i, ⓊⓈ fɪˈduː.ʃi.er.i, -ʃᵊr-, -ˈdjuː- -ies -iz
fie faɪ
Fiedler ˈfiːd.ləʳ, ⓊⓈ -lɚ
fief fiːf -s -s
fiefdom ˈfiːf.dəm -s -z
field, F~ ˈfiːld -s -z -ing -ɪŋ -ed -ɪd -er/s -əʳ/z, ⓊⓈ -ɚ/z ˈ**field** ˌ**glass**; ˈ**field** ˌ**goal**; ˈ**field** ˌ**gun**; ˌ**field** ˈ**hospital** ⓊⓈ ˈ**field** ˌ**hospital**; ˌ**field** ˈ**marshal** ⓊⓈ ˈ**field** ˌ**marshal**; ˈ**field** ˌ**mouse**; ˈ**field** ˌ**officer**; ˌ**field of** ˈ**vision**; ˈ**field** ˌ**trip**; **have a** ˈ**field** ˌ**day**
Fielden ˈfiːl.dᵊn

fielder, F~ ˈfiːl.dəʳ, (US) -dɚ **-s** -z
fieldfare ˈfiːld.feəʳ, (US) -fer **-s** -z
Fielding ˈfiːl.dɪŋ
Fields fiːlds
fields|man ˈfiːldz|.mən **-men** -mən, -men
field-test ˈfiːld.test **-s** -s **-ing** -ɪŋ **-ed** -ɪd
fieldwork ˈfiːld.wɜːk, (US) -wɝːk **-s** -s **-er/s** -əʳ/z, (US) -ɚ/z
fiend, F~ fiːnd **-s** -z
fiendish ˈfiːn.dɪʃ **-ly** -li **-ness** -nəs, -nɪs
Fiennes faɪnz
fierc|e fɪəs, (US) fɪrs **-er** -əʳ, (US) -ɚ **-est** -ɪst, -əst **-ely** -li **-eness** -nəs, -nɪs
fier|y ˈfaɪə.r|i, (US) ˈfaɪ-, ˈfaɪɚ|.i **-ier** -i.əʳ, (US) -i.ɚ **-iest** -i.ɪst, -i.əst **-ily** -ᵊl.i, -ɪ.li **-iness** -ɪ.nəs, -ɪ.nɪs
fiesta, F~® fiˈes.tə **-s** -z
FIFA, Fifa ˈfiː.fə
fif|e, F~ faɪf **-es** -s **-ing** -ɪŋ **-ed** -t **-er/s** -əʳ/z, (US) -ɚ/z
Fife faɪf **-shire** -ʃəʳ, -ʃɪəʳ, (US) -ʃɚ, -ʃɪr
Fifi ˈfiː.fiː
Fifield ˈfaɪ.fiːld
fifteen ˌfɪfˈtiːn **-s** -z **-th/s** -θ/s *stress shift:* **ˌfifteen ˈyears**
fifth fɪfθ **-s** -s **-ly** -li **ˌFifth Aˈmendment; ˌFifth ˈAvenue**

> Note: It is not uncommon to hear the pronunciation simplified to /fɪθ/.

fifth-column ˌfɪfθˈkɒl.əm, (US) -ˈkɑː.ləm **-ist/s** -ɪst/s, -nɪst/s **-ism** -ɪ.zᵊm, -nɪ.zᵊm
fiftieth ˈfɪf.ti.əθ **-s** -s
fift|y ˈfɪf.t|i **-ies** -iz
fifty-fifty ˌfɪf.tiˈfɪf.ti
fiftyfold ˈfɪf.ti.fəʊld, (US) -foʊld
fig fɪg **-s** -z **ˈfig ˌleaf; ˈfig ˌtree**
Figaro ˈfɪg.ə.rəʊ, (US) -roʊ
Figes ˈfɪg.ɪs
Figg fɪg
Figgis ˈfɪg.ɪs
fight faɪt **-s** -s **-ing** -ɪŋ, (US) ˈfaɪ.t̬ɪŋ **fought** fɔːt, (US) fɑːt, fɔːt **ˈfighting ˌcock**
fightback ˈfaɪt.bæk **-s** -s
fighter ˈfaɪ.təʳ, (US) -t̬ɚ **-s** -z
figment ˈfɪg.mənt **-s** -s
Figo ˈfiː.gəʊ, (US) -goʊ
Figueroa ˌfɪg.əˈrəʊ.ə, (US) -ˈroʊ-
figurability ˌfɪg.jᵊr.əˈbɪl.ə.ti, -ᵊr-, -jʊ.rəˈ-, -ɪ.ti, (US) -jɚ.əˈbɪl.ə.t̬i, -jʊ.rəˈ-
figurable ˈfɪg.jᵊr.ə.bᵊl, -ᵊr-, -jʊ.rə-, (US) -jɚ.ə-, -jʊ.rə-
figurative ˈfɪg.jᵊr.ə.tɪv, -ᵊr-, -jʊ.rə-, (US) -jɚ.ə.t̬ɪv, -jʊ.rə- **-ly** -li **-ness** -nəs, -nɪs
figur|e ˈfɪg.əʳ, (US) -jɚ, -jʊr **-es** -z **-ing** -ɪŋ **-ed** -d **ˌfigure ˈeight; ˌfigure of ˈeight; ˌfigure of ˈspeech; ˈfigure ˌskating**
figurehead ˈfɪg.ə.hed, (US) -jɚ- **-s** -z
figurine ˈfɪg.jə.riːn, ˈ-ə-, -jʊ-, ˌ--ˈ-, (US) ˌfɪg.jʊˈriːn, -jəˈ- **-s** -z
Fiji ˈfiː.dʒiː, -ˈ-, (US) ˈ--
Fijian fɪˈdʒiː.ən, fiː-, (US) ˈfiː.dʒiː-, -ˈ-- **-s** -z
filament ˈfɪl.ə.mənt **-s** -s
filamentous ˌfɪl.əˈmen.təs
filari|a fɪˈleə.ri|.ə, (US) -ˈler.i- **-ae** -iː **-al** -əl
filarias|is ˌfɪl.əˈraɪ.ə.s|ɪs; fɪˌleə.riˈeɪ-, fə-, (US) ˌfɪl.əˈraɪ.ə.s|ɪs **-es** -iːz
filature ˈfɪl.ə.tʃəʳ, -tjəʳ, (US) -tʃɚ **-s** -z
filbert ˈfɪl.bət, (US) -bɚt **-s** -s
filch fɪltʃ **-es** -ɪz **-ing** -ɪŋ **-ed** -t
Fildes faɪldz
fil|e faɪl **-es** -z **-ing/s** -ɪŋ/z **-ed** -d **ˈfiling ˌclerk**
filename ˈfaɪl.neɪm **-s** -z
filet ˈfɪl.eɪ, ˈfiː.leɪ, (US) fɪˈleɪ, ˈfɪl.eɪ **-s** -z **-(t)ing** -ɪŋ **-(t)ed** -d
filet(s) mignon(s) ˌfɪl.eɪˈmiː.njɔ̃ːŋ, ˌfiː.leɪ-, -ˈmɪn.jɒn, (US) ˌfɪl.eɪ.miːˈnjɑːn, -ˈnjoʊn; (US) fɪˌleɪ-
Filey ˈfaɪ.li
filial ˈfɪl.i.əl **-ly** -i **-ness** -nəs, -nɪs
filiation ˌfɪl.iˈeɪ.ʃᵊn
filibeg ˈfɪl.ɪ.beg, ˈ-ə- **-s** -z
filibust|er ˈfɪl.ɪ.bʌs.t|əʳ, ˈ-ə-, (US) -t|ɚ **-ers** -əz, (US) -ɚz **-ering** -ᵊr.ɪŋ **-ered** -əd, (US) -ɚd
filigree ˈfɪl.ɪ.griː, ˈ-ə- **-s** -z **-ing** -ɪŋ **-d** -d
filing ˈfaɪ.lɪŋ **-s** -z **ˈfiling ˌcabinet**
Filioque ˌfiː.liˈəʊ.kwi, ˌfaɪ-, ˌfɪl.iˈ-, (US) -ˈoʊ-
Filipino ˌfɪl.ɪˈpiː.nəʊ, -əˈ-, (US) -noʊ **-s** -z
Filkin ˈfɪl.kɪn **-s** -z
fill fɪl **-s** -z **-ing/s** -ɪŋ/z **-ed** -d **ˈfilling ˌstation; ˌfill the ˈbill**
filler *thing or person that fills:* ˈfɪl.əʳ, (US) -ɚ **-s** -z
filler, fillér *Hungarian currency:* ˈfiː.leəʳ, (US) ˈfɪl.er, ˈfiː.ler **-s** -z
fill|et ˈfɪl|.ɪt **-ets** -ɪts **-eting** -ɪ.tɪŋ, (US) -ɪ.t̬ɪŋ **-eted** -ɪ.tɪd, (US) -ɪ.t̬ɪd
fillibeg ˈfɪl.ɪ.beg, ˈ-ə- **-s** -z
fillip ˈfɪl.ɪp **-s** -s **-ing** -ɪŋ **-ed** -t
Fillmore ˈfɪl.mɔːʳ, (US) -mɔːr
fill|y ˈfɪl|.i **-ies** -iz
film fɪlm **-s** -z **-ing** -ɪŋ **-ed** -d **ˈfilm ˌstar**
filmgoer ˈfɪlmˌgəʊ.əʳ, (US) -ˌgoʊ.ɚ **-s** -z
filmgoing ˈfɪlmˌgəʊ.ɪŋ, (US) -ˌgoʊ-
filmic ˈfɪl.mɪk
filmmaker ˈfɪlmˌmeɪ.kəʳ, (US) -kɚ **-s** -z
film(s) noir(s) ˌfɪlmˈnwɑːʳ, -ˈnwɑːr
film|set ˈfɪlm|.set **-sets** -sets **-setting** -ˌset.ɪŋ, (US) -ˌset̬.ɪŋ
filmstrip ˈfɪlm.strɪp **-s** -s
film|y ˈfɪl.m|i **-ier** -i.əʳ, (US) -i.ɚ **-iest** -i.ɪst, -i.əst **-ily** -ᵊl.i, -ɪ.li **-iness** -ɪ.nəs, -ɪ.nɪs
filo ˈfiː.ləʊ, ˈfɪl.əʊ, (US) ˈfiː.loʊ, ˈfaɪ- **ˌfilo ˈpastry** (US) **ˈfilo ˌpastry**
Filofax® ˈfaɪ.ləʊ.fæks, (US) -loʊ-, -lə- **-es** -ɪz
Filon ˈfaɪ.lən, -lɒn, (US) ˌfiːˈlɑːn
fils *son:* fiːs *monetary unit:* fɪls
filt|er **n, v** ˈfɪl.t|əʳ, (US) -t|ɚ **-ers** -əz, (US) -ɚz **-ering** -ᵊr.ɪŋ **-ered** -əd, (US) -ɚd **ˈfilter ˌcoffee; ˈfilter ˌpaper; ˈfilter ˌtip**
filth fɪlθ
filth|y ˈfɪl.θ|i **-ier** -i.əʳ, (US) -i.ɚ **-iest** -i.ɪst, -i.əst **-ily** -ᵊl.i, -ɪ.li **-iness** -ɪ.nəs, -ɪ.nəs
filtrate **n** ˈfɪl.treɪt **-s** -s
fil|trate **v** fɪl|ˈtreɪt, (US) ˈ-- **-trates** -ˈtreɪts, (US) -treɪts **-trating** -ˈtreɪ.tɪŋ, (US) -treɪ.t̬ɪŋ **-trated** -ˈtreɪ.tɪd, (US) -treɪ.t̬ɪd
filtration fɪlˈtreɪ.ʃᵊn **-s** -z
FIMBRA ˈfɪm.brə
fin fɪn **-s** -z
Fina® ˈfiː.nə, ˈfaɪ-
finable ˈfaɪ.nə.bᵊl
finagl|e fɪˈneɪ.gᵊl **-es** -z **-ing** -ɪŋ, ˈ-glɪŋ **-ed** -d **-er/s** -əʳ/z, ˈ-gləʳ/z, (US) ˈ-ɚ/z, ˈ-glɚ/z
final ˈfaɪ.nᵊl **-s** -z **-ly** -i
finale fɪˈnɑː.li, fə-, -leɪ, (US) -ˈnæl.i, -ˈnɑː.leɪ, -li **-s** -z
finalist ˈfaɪ.nᵊl.ɪst **-s** -s
finality faɪˈnæl.ə.ti, -ɪ.ti, (US) faɪˈnæl.ə.t̬i, fə-
finalization ˌfaɪ.nᵊl.aɪˈzeɪ.ʃᵊn, -ɪˈ-, (US) -əˈ-
finaliz|e, -is|e ˈfaɪ.nᵊl.aɪz, (US) -nə.laɪz **-es** -ɪz **-ing** -ɪŋ **-ed** -d
financ|e ˈfaɪ.nænts; faɪˈnænts, fɪ-, fə- **-es** -ɪz **-ing** -ɪŋ **-ed** -t
financial faɪˈnæn.tʃᵊl, fɪ-, fə-, (US) -ˈnænt.ʃᵊl **-ly** -i **Fiˌnancial ˈTimes**
financier faɪˈnænt.si.əʳ, fɪ-, fə-, (US) fɪˈnænt.si.ɚ, fə-; (US) ˌfɪn.ənˈsɪr, ˌfaɪ.nænˈ-, -nənˈ- **-s** -z
Finbar ˈfɪn.bɑːʳ, ˈfɪm-, (US) ˈfɪn.bɑːr
finch, F~ fɪntʃ **-es** -ɪz
Finchale ˈfɪŋ.kᵊl
Fincham ˈfɪn.tʃəm
Finchampsted ˈfɪn.tʃəm.sted, -tʃəmp-, -stɪd
Finchley ˈfɪntʃ.li
find faɪnd **-s** -z **-ing/s** -ɪŋ/z **found** faʊnd **finder/s** ˈfaɪn.dəʳ/z, (US) -dɚ/z
fin de siècle ˌfæ̃n.dəˈsjek.lə, ˌfæn-, -siˈek-, (US) ˌfæ̃n.də.siˈek.lə, -ˈsjek-, -ᵊl
Findlater ˈfɪnd.lə.təʳ, -leɪ.təʳ, (US) -t̬ɚ
Findlay ˈfɪnd.leɪ, -li
Findley ˈfɪnd.li
Findus ˈfɪn.dəs
fin|e faɪn **-es** -z **-er** -əʳ, (US) -ɚ **-est** -ɪst, -əst **-eness** -nəs, -nɪs **-ing** -ɪŋ **-ed** -d **ˌfine ˈart; ˈfine ˌprint, ˌfine ˈprint**
finely ˈfaɪn.li
finery ˈfaɪ.nᵊr.i
fines herbes ˌfiːnˈeəb, -ˈɜːb, (US) ˌfiːnˈzerb
finespun ˌfaɪnˈspʌn, (US) ˈ-- *stress shift, British only:* **ˌfinespun ˈyarn**
finess|e **n, v** fɪˈnes, fə- **-es** -ɪz **-ing** -ɪŋ **-ed** -t
fine-tooth ˌfaɪnˈtuːθ **-ed** -t **ˌfine-toothed ˈcomb**
fine-tun|e ˌfaɪnˈtʃuːn, -ˈtjuːn, (US) -ˈtuːn, -ˈtjuːn **-es** -z **-ing** -ɪŋ **-ed** -d *stress shift:* **ˌfine-tuned ˈinstrument**
Fingal ˈfɪŋ.gᵊl **ˌFingal's ˈCave**

F

Fingall ˈfɪŋ.gɔːl, US -gɔːl, -gɑːl
fing|er ˈfɪŋ.g|əʳ, US -g|ɚ **-ers** -əz, US -ɚz **-ering/s** -ər.ɪŋ/z **-ered** -əd, US -ɚd **ˈfinger ˌbowl; ˈFinger ˌLakes; ˌall ˌfingers and ˈthumbs; ˌburn one's ˈfingers; have a ˌfinger in every ˈpie; keep one's ˈfingers ˌcrossed; ˌtwist someone round one's ˌlittle ˈfinger; ˌwork one's ˌfingers to the ˈbone**
fingerboard ˈfɪŋ.gə.bɔːd, US -gɚ.bɔːrd **-s** -z
fingermark ˈfɪŋ.gə.mɑːk, US -gɚ.mɑːrk **-s** -s
fingernail ˈfɪŋ.gə.neɪl, US -gɚ- **-s** -z
fingerplate ˈfɪŋ.gə.pleɪt, US -gɚ- **-s** -s
fingerpost ˈfɪŋ.gə.pəʊst, US -gɚ.poʊst **-s** -s
fingerprint ˈfɪŋ.gə.prɪnt, US -gɚ- **-s** -s **-ing** -ɪŋ
fingerstall ˈfɪŋ.gə.stɔːl, US -gɚ.stɔːl, -stɑːl **-s** -z
fingertip ˈfɪŋ.gə.tɪp, US -gɚ- **-s** -s
Fingest ˈfɪn.dʒɪst, ˈfɪŋ.gɪst
finial ˈfɪn.i.əl, ˈfaɪ.ni-, US ˈfɪn.i- **-s** -z
finical ˈfɪn.ɪ.kəl **-ly** -i **-ness** -nəs, -nəs
finicking ˈfɪn.ɪ.kɪŋ
finick|y ˈfɪn.ɪ.k|i **-ier** -i.əʳ, US -i.ɚ **-iest** -i.ɪst, -i.əst **-ily** -əl.i, -ɪ.li **-iness** -ɪ.nəs, -ɪ.nɪs
finis ˈfɪn.ɪs, ˈfiː.nɪs, US ˈfɪn.ɪs; US fiːˈniː; US ˈfaɪ.nɪs
finish ˈfɪn.ɪʃ **-es** -ɪz **-ing** -ɪŋ **-ed** -t **-er/s** -əʳ/z, US -ɚ/z **ˈfinishing ˌschool**
Finisterre ˌfɪn.ɪˈsteəʳ, -əˈ-, ˈ---, US ˌfɪn.ɪˈster
finite ˈfaɪ.naɪt **-ly** -li **-ness** -nəs, -nɪs
finito fɪˈniː.təʊ, fə-, US -toʊ
finitude ˈfaɪ.nɪ.tʃuːd, ˈfɪn.ɪ-, -tjuːd, US ˈfɪn.ɪ.tuːd, -tjuːd
fink fɪŋk **-s** -s **-ing** -ɪŋ **-ed** -t
Finlaison ˈfɪn.lɪ.sən
Finland ˈfɪn.lənd **-er/s** -əʳ/z, US -ɚ/z
Finlandization, -isa- ˌfɪn.lən.daɪˈzeɪ.ʃən, -dɪˈ-, US -dəˈ-
Finlandiz|e, -is|e ˈfɪn.lən.daɪz **-es** -ɪz **-ing** -ɪŋ **-ed** -d
Finlay ˈfɪn.leɪ, -li
Finlayson ˈfɪn.lɪ.sən
Finley ˈfɪn.li
Finn fɪn **-s** -z
Finnan ˈfɪn.ən
Finnegan ˈfɪn.ɪ.gən, ˈ-ə-
Finney ˈfɪn.i
Finnic ˈfɪn.ɪk
Finnie ˈfɪn.i
Finnish ˈfɪn.ɪʃ
Finnon ˈfɪn.ən
Finno-Ugrian ˌfɪn.əʊˈjuː.gri.ən, US -oʊˈuː-, -ˈjuː-
Finno-Ugric ˌfɪn.əʊˈjuː.grɪk, US -oʊˈuː-, -ˈjuː-
fino ˈfiː.nəʊ, US -noʊ **-s** -z
Finsberg ˈfɪnz.bɜːg, US -bɝːg
Finsbury ˈfɪnz.bər.i, US -ˌber-, -bɚ- **ˌFinsbury ˈPark**
Finucane fɪˈnuː.kən, fə-, ˌfɪn.əˈkeɪn
Finzi ˈfɪn.zi
Fiona fiˈəʊ.nə, US -ˈoʊ-
fiord fjɔːd; fiˈɔːd; ˈfiː.ɔːd, US fjɔːrd; US fiˈɔːrd **-s** -z
fiorin ˈfaɪ.ə.rɪn, US ˈfaɪ.ɚ.ɪn
Fiorino® ˌfiː.ɔːˈriː.nəʊ, US -noʊ
fioritur|a ˌfjɔː.riˈtjʊə.r|ə, ˌfiː.ə.riˈ-, US ˌfjɔː.riˈtuː.r|ɑː **-e** -eɪ
fir fɜːʳ, US fɝː **-s** -z **ˈfir ˌtree**
Firbank ˈfɜː.bæŋk, US ˈfɝː-
fir|e faɪəʳ, ˈfaɪ.əʳ, US ˈfaɪ.ɚ **-es** -z **-ing** -ɪŋ **-ed** -d **-er/s** -əʳ/z, US -ɚ/z **ˈfire aˌlarm; ˈfire briˌgade; ˈfire conˌtrol; ˈfire deˌpartment; ˈfire drill; ˈfire ˌengine; ˈfire esˌcape; ˈfire exˌtinguisher; ˈfire ˌfighter; ˈfire ˌhydrant; ˈfire ˌiron; ˈfire ˌscreen; ˌout of the ˌfrying pan ˌinto the ˈfire**
firearm ˈfaɪəʳ.ɑːm, US ˈfaɪ.ɚ.ɑːrm **-s** -z
fireball ˈfaɪə.bɔːl, ˈfaɪ.ə-, US ˈfaɪ.ɚ.bɔːl, -bɑːl **-s** -z
firebomb ˈfaɪə.bɒm, ˈfaɪ.ə-, US ˈfaɪ.ɚ.bɑːm **-s** -z **-ing** -ɪŋ **-ed** -d
firebox ˈfaɪə.bɒks, US ˈfaɪɚ.bɑːks **-es** -ɪz
firebrand ˈfaɪə.brænd, ˈfaɪ.ə-, US ˈfaɪ.ɚ- **-s** -z
firebreak ˈfaɪə.breɪk, ˈfaɪ.ə-, US ˈfaɪ.ɚ- **-s** -s
firebrick ˈfaɪə.brɪk, ˈfaɪ.ə-, US ˈfaɪ.ɚ- **-s** -s
firebug ˈfaɪə.bʌg, ˈfaɪ.ə-, US ˈfaɪ.ɚ- **-s** -z
fireclay ˈfaɪə.kleɪ, ˈfaɪ.ə-, US ˈfaɪ.ɚ-
firecracker ˈfaɪəˌkræk.əʳ, ˈfaɪ.ə-, US ˈfaɪ.ɚˌkræk.ɚ **-s** -z
firecrest ˈfaɪə.krest, ˈfaɪ.ə-, US ˈfaɪ.ɚ- **-s** -s
firedamp ˈfaɪə.dæmp, ˈfaɪ.ə-, US ˈfaɪ.ɚ-
firedog ˈfaɪə.dɒg, ˈfaɪ.ə-, US ˈfaɪ.ɚ.dɑːg, -dɔːg **-s** -z
fire-eat|er ˈfaɪəʳˌiː.t|əʳ, US ˈfaɪ.ɚˌiː.ţ|ɚ **-ers** -əz, US -ɚz **-ing** -ɪŋ
firefigh|t ˈfaɪə.faɪ|t, ˈfaɪ.ə-, US ˈfaɪ.ɚ- **-s** -z **-ting** -tɪŋ, US -ţɪŋ **-ter/s** -təʳ/z, US -ţɚ/z
firefl|y ˈfaɪə.fl|aɪ, ˈfaɪ.ə-, US ˈfaɪ.ɚ- **-ies** -aɪz
Firefox® ˈfaɪə.fɒks, ˈfaɪ.ə-, US ˈfaɪ.ɚ.fɑːks
fireguard ˈfaɪə.gɑːd, ˈfaɪ.ə-, US ˈfaɪ.ɚ.gɑːrd **-s** -z
firehou|se ˈfaɪə.haʊ|s, ˈfaɪ.ə-, US ˈfaɪ.ɚ- **-ses** -zɪz
fire|light ˈfaɪə|.laɪt, ˈfaɪ.ə-, US ˈfaɪ.ɚ- **-lighter/s** -ˌlaɪ.təʳ/z, US -ˌlaɪ.ţɚ/z
firelock ˈfaɪə.lɒk, ˈfaɪ.ə-, US ˈfaɪ.ɚ.lɑːk **-s** -s
fire|man ˈfaɪə|.mən, ˈfaɪ.ə-, US ˈfaɪ.ɚ- **-men** -mən, -men
fireplac|e ˈfaɪə.pleɪs, ˈfaɪ.ə-, US ˈfaɪ.ɚ- **-es** -ɪz
fireplug ˈfaɪə.plʌg, ˈfaɪ.ə-, US ˈfaɪ.ɚ- **-s** -z
firepower ˈfaɪəˌpaʊəʳ, ˈfaɪ.ə-, -ˌpaʊ.əʳ, US ˈfaɪ.ɚˌpaʊ.ɚ
fireproof ˈfaɪə.pruːf, ˈfaɪ.ə-, US ˈfaɪ.ɚ-
fire-rais|ing ˈfaɪəˌreɪ.z|ɪŋ, ˈfaɪ.ə-, US ˈfaɪ.ɚ-
firescreen ˈfaɪə.skriːn, ˈfaɪ.ə-, US ˈfaɪ.ɚ- **-s** -z
fireship ˈfaɪə.ʃɪp, ˈfaɪ.ə-, US ˈfaɪ.ɚ- **-s** -s
fireside ˈfaɪə.saɪd, ˈfaɪ.ə-, US ˈfaɪ.ɚ- **-s** -z
firestone, F~ ˈfaɪə.stəʊn, ˈfaɪ.ə-, US ˈfaɪ.ɚ.stoʊn
firestorm ˈfaɪə.stɔːm, ˈfaɪ.ə-, US ˈfaɪ.ɚ.stɔːrm **-s** -z
firetrail ˈfaɪə.treɪl, ˈfaɪ.ə-, US ˈfaɪ.ɚ- **-s** -z
firetrap ˈfaɪə.træp, ˈfaɪ.ə-, US ˈfaɪ.ɚ- **-s** -s
firewall ˈfaɪə.wɔːl, ˈfaɪ.ə-, US ˈfaɪ.ɚ-, -wɑːl **-s** -z
firewarden ˈfaɪəˌwɔː.dən, ˈfaɪ.ə-, US ˈfaɪ.ɚˌwɔːr- **-s** -z
firewater ˈfaɪəˌwɔː.təʳ, ˈfaɪ.ə-, US ˈfaɪ.ɚˌwɑː.ţɚ, -ˌwɔː-
firewood ˈfaɪə.wʊd, ˈfaɪ.ə-, US ˈfaɪ.ɚ-
firework ˈfaɪə.wɜːk, ˈfaɪ.ə-, US ˈfaɪ.ɚ.wɝːk **-s** -s
firing ˈfaɪə.rɪŋ, US ˈfaɪ.ɚ.ɪŋ **ˈfiring ˌline; ˈfiring ˌparty; ˈfiring ˌsquad**
firkin ˈfɜː.kɪn, US ˈfɝː- **-s** -z
firm fɜːm, US fɝːm **-s** -z **-er** -əʳ, US -ɚ **-est** -ɪst, -əst **-ing** -ɪŋ **-ed** -d **-ly** -li **-ness** -nəs, -nɪs
firmament ˈfɜː.mə.mənt, US ˈfɝː- **-s** -s
firmware ˈfɜːm.weəʳ, US ˈfɝːm.wer
Firsby ˈfɜːz.bi, US ˈfɝːz-
first ˈfɜːst, US ˈfɝːst **-s** -s **-ly** -li **ˌfirst ˈaid; ˌfirst ˈbase; ˌfirst ˈclass; ˌfirst ˈfloor; ˌfirst ˈlady; ˌFirst ˌWorld ˈWar**
first base ˌfɜːstˈbeɪs, US ˌfɝːst-
firstborn ˈfɜːst.bɔːn, US ˈfɝːst.bɔːrn
first-degree ˌfɜːst.dɪˈgriː, -dəˈ-, US ˌfɝːst.dɪˈ- *stress shift, see compound:* **ˌfirst-degree ˈmurder**
firstfruits ˈfɜːst.fruːts, US ˈfɝːst-
firsthand ˌfɜːstˈhænd, US ˌfɝːst- *stress shift:* **ˌfirsthand acˈcount**
firstling ˈfɜːst.lɪŋ, US ˈfɝːst- **-s** -z
firstly ˈfɜːst.li, US ˈfɝːst-
first-past-the-post ˌfɜːstˌpɑːst.ðəˈpəʊst, US ˌfɝːstˌpæst.ðəˈpoʊst *stress shift:* **ˌfirst-past-the-post ˈsystem**
first-rate ˌfɜːstˈreɪt, US ˌfɝːst- *stress shift:* **ˌfirst-rate ˈgame**
first-time ˌfɜːstˈtaɪm, US ˌfɝːst- *stress shift, see compound:* **ˌfirst-time ˈbuyer**
firth, F~ fɜːθ, US fɝːθ **-s** -s
fisc fɪsk
fiscal ˈfɪs.kəl **-s** -z
Fischer ˈfɪʃ.əʳ, US -ɚ
Fischler ˈfɪʃ.ləʳ, US -lɚ
fish, F~ fɪʃ **-es** -ɪz **-ing** -ɪŋ **-ed** -t **ˌfish and ˈchips; ˌfish ˈfinger; ˈfishing ˌrod; ˈfishing ˌtackle; ˈfish ˌknife; ˈfish ˌslice; ˈfish ˌstick; have ˌother ˈfish to ˌfry; like a ˌfish out of ˈwater; a ˈpretty ˌkettle of ˌfish**
fishbone ˈfɪʃ.bəʊn, US -boʊn **-s** -z

fishbowl ˈfɪʃ.bəʊl, (US) -boʊl **-s** -z
fishcake ˈfɪʃ.keɪk **-s** -s
fisher, F~ ˈfɪʃ.əʳ, (US) -ɚ **-s** -z
fisher|man ˈfɪʃ.ə|.mən, (US) ˈ-ɚ- **-men** -mən, -men
fisher|y ˈfɪʃ.ᵊr|.i **-ies** -iz
fisheye ˈfɪʃ.aɪ ˌ**fisheye** ˈ**lens**
Fishguard ˈfɪʃ.ɡɑːd, (US) -ɡɑːrd
fishhook ˈfɪʃ.*h*ʊk, (US) -hʊk **-s** -s
Fishkill ˈfɪʃ.kɪl
fishmonger ˈfɪʃˌmʌŋ.ɡəʳ, (US) -ˌmʌŋ.ɡɚ, -ˌmɑːŋ- **-s** -z
fish 'n' chips ˌfɪʃ.ᵊnˈtʃɪps
fishnet ˈfɪʃ.net **-s** -s ˌ**fishnet** ˈ**stockings**
fishplate ˈfɪʃ.pleɪt **-s** -s
fishpond ˈfɪʃ.pɒnd, (US) -pɑːnd **-s** -z
fishtail ˈfɪʃ.teɪl **-s** -z **-ing** -ɪŋ **-ed** -d
fishtank ˈfɪʃ.tæŋk **-s** -s
Fishwick ˈfɪʃ.wɪk
fish|wife ˈfɪʃ|.waɪf **-wives** -waɪvz
fish|y ˈfɪʃ|.i **-ier** -i.əʳ, (US) -i.ɚ **-iest** -i.ɪst, -i.əst **-ily** -ᵊl.i, -ɪ.li **-iness** -ɪ.nəs, -ɪ.nɪs
Fisk(e) fɪsk
Fison ˈfaɪ.sᵊn
fissile ˈfɪs.aɪl, (US) -ɪl
fission ˈfɪʃ.ᵊn, (US) ˈfɪʃ-, ˈfɪʒ- **-s** -z **-al** -ᵊl
fissionable ˈfɪʃ.ᵊn.ə.bᵊl, (US) ˈfɪʃ-, ˈfɪʒ-
fissiparous fɪˈsɪp.ᵊr.əs, fə-
fiss|ure ˈfɪʃ|.əʳ, -ʊəʳ, (US) -ɚ **-ures** -əz, (US) -ɚz **-uring** -ᵊr.ɪŋ **-ured** -əd, (US) -ɚd
fist fɪst **-s** -s **-ing** -ɪŋ **-ed** -ɪd **-ic** -ɪk
fistfight ˈfɪst.faɪt **-s** -s
fistful ˈfɪst.fʊl **-s** -z
fisticuffs ˈfɪs.tɪ.kʌfs
fistul|a ˈfɪs.tʃə.l|ə, -tʃʊ-, -tjə-, -tjʊ-, (US) -tʃə-, -tʃu- **-as** -əz **-ae** -iː **-ous** -əs
fit fɪt **-s** -s **-ting/ly** -ɪŋ/li, (US) ˈfɪṭ.ɪŋ/li **-ted** -ɪd, (US) ˈfɪṭ.ɪd **-ter/s** -əʳ/z, (US) ˈfɪṭ.ɚ/z **-test** -ɪst, (US) ˈfɪṭ.ɪst, -əst **-ly** -li ˌ**fitted** ˈ**kitchen**; ˈ**fitting** ˌ**room**; **as** ˌ**fit as a** ˈ**fiddle**
fitch, F~ fɪtʃ **-es** -ɪz
Fitchburg ˈfɪtʃ.bɜːɡ, (US) -bɝːɡ
fitchew ˈfɪtʃ.uː **-s** -z
fitful ˈfɪt.fᵊl, -fʊl **-ly** -i **-ness** -nəs, -nɪs
fitment ˈfɪt.mənt **-s** -s
fitness ˈfɪt.nəs, -nɪs
fitt fɪt **-s** -s
Fitzalan fɪtsˈæl.ən
Fitzcharles fɪtsˈtʃɑːlz, (US) -ˈtʃɑːrlz
Fitzclarence fɪtsˈklær.ən*t*s, (US) -ˈkler-, -ˈklær-
Fitzgeorge fɪtsˈdʒɔːdʒ, (US) -ˈdʒɔːrdʒ
Fitzgerald, FitzGerald fɪtsˈdʒer.əld
Fitzgibbon fɪtsˈɡɪb.ən
Fitzhardinge fɪtsˈhɑː.dɪŋ, (US) -ˈhɑːr-
Fitzharris fɪtsˈhær.ɪs, (US) -ˈher-, -ˈhær-
Fitzherbert fɪtsˈhɜː.bət, (US) -ˈhɝː.bɚt
Fitzhugh fɪtsˈhjuː
Fitzjames fɪtsˈdʒeɪmz

Note: In **James Fitzjames** often /ˈfɪts.dʒeɪmz/.

Fitzjohn fɪtsˈdʒɒn, (US) -ˈdʒɑːn
Fitzmaurice fɪtsˈmɒr.ɪs, (US) -ˈmɑːr-, -ˈmɔːr-
Fitzpatrick fɪtsˈpæt.rɪk
Fitzroy *surname:* fɪtsˈrɔɪ, ˈ-- *square and street in London:* ˈfɪts.rɔɪ
Fitzsimmons fɪt*s*ˈsɪm.ənz
Fitzstephen fɪtsˈstiː.vᵊn
Fitzwalter fɪtsˈwɔːl.təʳ, -ˈwɒl-, (US) -ˈwɔːl.tɚ, -ˈwɑːl-
Fitzwilliam fɪtsˈwɪl.jəm, ˈ-i.əm, (US) ˈ-jəm
five faɪv **-s** -z **-fold** -fəʊld, (US) -foʊld
five-and-dime ˌfaɪv.ᵊn*d*ˈdaɪm **-s** -z
fivepen|ce ˈfaɪf.pən*t*|s, ˈfaɪv- **-ces** -sɪz
fivepenny ˈfaɪv.pᵊn.i
fiver ˈfaɪ.vəʳ, (US) -vɚ **-s** -z
fix fɪks **-es** -ɪz **-ing** -ɪŋ **-ed** -t **-edness** -ɪd.nəs, -nɪs **-er/s** -əʳ/z, (US) -ɚ/z
fixable ˈfɪk.sə.bᵊl
fixa|te fɪkˈseɪ|t, (US) ˈ-- **-tes** -ts **-ting** -tɪŋ, (US) -ṭɪŋ **-ted** -tɪd, (US) -ṭɪd
fixation fɪkˈseɪ.ʃᵊn **-s** -z
fixative ˈfɪk.sə.tɪv, (US) -ṭɪv **-s** -z
fixedly ˈfɪk.sɪd.li, -səd-
fixit|y ˈfɪk.sə.t|i, -ɪ.t|i, (US) -sə.ṭ|i **-ies** -iz
fixture ˈfɪks.tʃəʳ, (US) -tʃɚ **-s** -z
fizz fɪz **-es** -ɪz **-ing** -ɪŋ **-ed** -d **-er/s** -əʳ/z, (US) -ɚ/z
fizzl|e ˈfɪz.ᵊl **-es** -z **-ing** -ɪŋ, ˈ-lɪŋ **-ed** -d
fizz|y ˈfɪz|.i **-ier** -i.əʳ, (US) -i.ɚ **-iest** -i.ɪst, -i.əst **-iness** -ɪ.nəs, -ɪ.nɪs
fjord fjɔːd; fiˈɔːd; ˈfiː.ɔːd, (US) fjɔːrd **-s** -z
Fla. (abbrev. for **Florida**) ˈflɒr.ɪ.də, (US) ˈflɔːr-, ˈflɑːr-
flab flæb
flabbergast ˈflæb.ə.ɡɑːst, (US) -ɚ.ɡæst **-s** -s **-ing** -ɪŋ **-ed** -ɪd
flabb|y ˈflæb|.i **-ier** -i.əʳ, (US) -i.ɚ **-iest** -i.ɪst, -i.əst **-ily** -ᵊl.i, -ɪ.li **-iness** -ɪ.nəs, -ɪ.nɪs
flaccid ˈflæk.sɪd, ˈflæs.ɪd **-ly** -li **-ness** -nəs, -nɪs
Note: The pronunciation /ˈflæs.ɪd/ is quite common. No other English word has /s/ as the pronunciation corresponding to the letters 'cc'.
flaccidity flækˈsɪd.ə.ti, flæsˈɪd-, -ɪ.ti, (US) -ə.ṭi
flack, F~ flæk **-s** -s
Flackwell ˈflæk.wel, -wəl
flag flæɡ **-s** -z **-ging** -ɪŋ **-ged** -d ˈ**flag** ˌ**day**; ˈ**flag** ˌ**officer**
flagellant ˈflædʒ.ᵊl.ənt, -ɪ.lənt; fləˈdʒel.ənt, flædʒˈel-, (US) ˈflædʒ.ᵊl.ənt, -ɪ.lənt; (US) fləˈdʒel.ənt **-s** -s
flagellate **n, adj** ˈflædʒ.ᵊl.ət, -ɪ.lət, -ɪt, -eɪt, (US) ˈflædʒ.ᵊl.eɪt, -ɪt; (US) fləˈdʒel.ɪt **-s** -s
flagell|ate **v** ˈflædʒ.ᵊl|.eɪt, ˈ-ɪ-, (US) -ə.l|eɪt **-ates** -eɪts **-ating** -eɪ.tɪŋ, (US) -eɪ.ṭɪŋ **-ated** -eɪ.tɪd, (US) -eɪ.ṭɪd **-ator/s** -eɪ.təʳ/z, (US) -eɪ.ṭɚ/z
flagellation ˌflædʒ.əˈleɪ.ʃᵊn, -ɪˈ- **-s** -z
flagell|um fləˈdʒel|.əm, flædʒˈel-, (US) fləˈdʒel- **-ums** -əmz **-a** -ə
flageolet ˌflædʒ.əʊˈlet, -ˈleɪ, ˈ---, (US) ˌflædʒ.əˈlet, -ˈleɪ **-s** -s
Flagg flæɡ
flag|man ˈflæɡ|.mən, -mæn **-men** -mən, -men
flagon ˈflæɡ.ən **-s** -z
flagpole ˈflæɡ.pəʊl, (US) -poʊl **-s** -z
flagrancy ˈfleɪ.ɡrən*t*.si
flagrant ˈfleɪ.ɡrənt **-ly** -li
flagrante delicto fləˌɡræn.teɪ.dɪˈlɪk.təʊ, flæɡˌræn-, -ti-, -dəˈ-, -deɪˈ-, (US) fləˌɡræn.ti.diːˈlɪk.toʊ
flagship ˈflæɡ.ʃɪp **-s** -s
flagstaff ˈflæɡ.stɑːf, (US) -stæf **-s** -s
flagstone ˈflæɡ.stəʊn, (US) -stoʊn **-s** -z
flag-waving ˈflæɡˌweɪ.vɪŋ
Flaherty ˈfleə.ti, ˈflɑː.*h*ə.ti, ˈflæ.hə.ti, (US) ˈflæ.ɚ.ṭi, ˈflɑː-; (US) ˈfler.ə-
flail fleɪl **-s** -z **-ing** -ɪŋ **-ed** -d
flair fleəʳ, (US) fler **-s** -z
flak flæk
flak|e fleɪk **-es** -s **-ing** -ɪŋ **-ed** -t ˌ**flake** ˈ**white**
flak|y ˈfleɪ.k|i **-ily** -ᵊl.i, -ɪ.li **-iness** -ɪ.nəs, -ɪ.nɪs ˌ**flaky** ˈ**pastry**
flam flæm **-s** -z
Flambard ˈflæm.bɑːd, -bəd, (US) -bɑːrd, -bɚd
flambé, flambe ˈflɑ̃ː*m*.beɪ, (US) flɑːmˈbeɪ **-s** -z **-ing** -ɪŋ **-ed** -d
flambeau, F~ ˈflæm.bəʊ, (US) -boʊ **-s** -z
flambée, flambee ˈflɑ̃ː*m*.beɪ, (US) flɑːmˈbeɪ **-d** -d
Flamborough ˈflæm.bᵊr.ə, (US) -bɚ.oʊ
flamboyance flæmˈbɔɪ.ən*t*s
flamboyant flæmˈbɔɪ.ənt **-ly** -li
flam|e fleɪm **-es** -z **-ing** -ɪŋ **-ed** -d
flamen ˈfleɪ.men **-s** -z
flamenco fləˈmeŋ.kəʊ, (US) -koʊ **-s** -z
flameproof ˈfleɪm.pruːf **-s** -s **-ing** -ɪŋ **-ed** -t
flamethrower ˈfleɪmˌθrəʊ.əʳ, (US) -ˌθroʊ.ɚ **-s** -z
flamingo fləˈmɪŋ.ɡəʊ, flæmˈɪŋ-, (US) fləˈmɪŋ.ɡoʊ **-(e)s** -z
Flaminius fləˈmɪn.i.əs, flæmˈɪn-, (US) fləˈmɪn-
flammability ˌflæm.əˈbɪl.ə.ti, -ɪ.ti, (US) -ə.ṭi
flammable ˈflæm.ə.bᵊl
Flamstead ˈflæm.stiːd, -stɪd
Flamsteed ˈflæm.stiːd
flan flæn **-s** -z
Flanagan ˈflæn.ə.ɡᵊn
Flanders ˈflɑːn.dəz, (US) ˈflæn.dɚz
flang|e flændʒ **-es** -ɪz **-ing** -ɪŋ **-ed** -d
flank flæŋk **-s** -s **-ing** -ɪŋ **-ed** -t **-er/s** -əʳ/z, (US) -ɚ/z
Flann flæn

flannel ˈflæn.əl -s -z -(l)ing -ɪŋ -(l)ed -d
flannelette, flannelet ˌflæn.əlˈet, (US) ˌflæn.əlˈet, -əˈlet
flannelly ˈflæn.əl.i
flap flæp -s -s -ping -ɪŋ -ped -t
flapdoodle ˈflæpˌduː.dəl
flapjack ˈflæp.dʒæk -s -s
flapper ˈflæp.əʳ, (US) -ɚ -s -z
flar|e fleəʳ, (US) fler -es -z -ing/ly -ɪŋ/li -ed -d
flarepa|th ˈfleə.pɑː|θ, (US) ˈfler.pæ|θ -ths -ðz
flare-up ˈfleəʳ.ʌp, (US) ˈfler- -s -s
flash, F~ flæʃ -es -ɪz -ing -ɪŋ -ed -t ˈ**flash** ˌ**card;** ˈ**flash** ˌ**point;** ˌ**flash in the** ˈ**pan;** ˌ**quick as a** ˈ**flash**
flashback ˈflæʃ.bæk -s -s
flashbulb ˈflæʃ.bʌlb -s -z
flasher ˈflæʃ.əʳ, (US) -ɚ -s -z
flash-fr|y ˌflæʃˈfr|aɪ -ies -aɪz -ying -aɪ.ɪŋ -ied -aɪd *stress shift:* ˌ**flash-fried** ˈ**food**
flashgun ˈflæʃ.gʌn -s -z
flashlight ˈflæʃ.laɪt -s -s
Flashman ˈflæʃ.mən
flash-mob ˈflæʃ.mɒb, (US) -mɑːb -bing -ɪŋ -ber/s -əʳ/z, (US) -ɚ/z
flash|y ˈflæʃ|.i -ier -i.əʳ, (US) -i.ɚ -iest -i.ɪst, -i.əst -ily -əl.i, -ɪ.li -iness -ɪ.nəs, -ɪ.nɪs
flask flɑːsk, (US) flæsk -s -s
flat flæt -s -s -ter -əʳ, (US) ˈflæţ.ɚ -test -ɪst, -əst, (US) ˈflæţ.ɪst, -əst -ly -li -ness -nəs, -nɪs
Flatbush ˈflæt.bʊʃ
flat-chested ˌflætˈtʃes.tɪd -ness -nəs, -nɪs *stress shift:* ˌ**flat-chested** ˈ**waif**
flatfish ˈflæt.fɪʃ -es -ɪz
flatfoot ˈflæt.fʊt
flat-footed ˌflætˈfʊt.ɪd, (US) -ˈfʊţ-, ˈ--- -ly -li -ness -nəs, -nɪs *stress shift, British only:* ˌ**flat-footed** ˈ**person**
flathead, F~ ˈflæt.hed -s -z
flatiron ˈflætˌaɪən, (US) ˈflætˌaɪ.ɚn -s -z
Flatland ˈflæt.lænd
flatlet ˈflæt.lət, -lɪt -s -s
flatmate ˈflæt.meɪt -s -s
flat-out ˌflætˈaʊt *stress shift:* ˌ**flat-out** ˈ**dash**
flatpack ˈflæt.pæk -s -s
flatten ˈflæt.ən -s -z -ing -ɪŋ -ed -d
flatt|er ˈflæt|.əʳ, (US) ˈflæţ|.ɚ -ers -əz, -ɚz -ering/ly -əʳ.ɪŋ/li -ered -əd, -ɚd -erer/s -əʳ.əʳ/z, (US) -ɚ.ɚ/z
flatter|y ˈflæt.əʳ|.i, (US) ˈflæţ- -ies -iz
flatties ˈflæt.iz, (US) ˈflæţ-
flattish ˈflæt.ɪʃ, (US) ˈflæţ-
flattop ˈflæt.tɒp, (US) -tɑːp -s -s
flatulen|ce ˈflætʃ.ə.lənt|s, -ˈʊ-, ˈflæt.jə-, ˈflæt.jʊ-, (US) ˈflætʃ.ə- -cy -si
flatulent ˈflæt.jə.lənt, -jʊ-, ˈflætʃ.ə-, ˈ-ʊ-, (US) ˈflætʃ.ə- -ly -li
flatus ˈfleɪ.təs, (US) -ţəs -es -ɪz
flatware ˈflæt.weəʳ, (US) -wer
flat|ways ˈflæt|.weɪz -wise -waɪz
flatworm ˈflæt.wɜːm, (US) -wɝːm -s -z

Flaubert ˈfləʊ.beəʳ, (US) ˈfloʊ.ber, -ˈ-
flaun|t flɔːn|t, (US) flɑːn|t, flɔːn|t -ts -ts -ting/ly -tɪŋ/li, (US) -ţɪŋ/li -ted -tɪd, (US) -ţɪd
flautist ˈflɔː.tɪst, (US) ˈflɑː.ţɪst, ˈflɔː-, ˈflaʊ- -s -s
Flavel ˈflæv.əl, ˈfleɪ.vəl
Flavell fləˈvel, ˈfleɪ.vəl
Flavi|a ˈfleɪ.vi|.ə -an -ən
flavin ˈfleɪ.vɪn, ˈflæv.ɪn, (US) ˈfleɪ.vɪn -s -z
flavin(e) ˈfleɪ.viːn, ˈflæv.iːn, -ɪn, (US) ˈfleɪ.viːn
Flavius ˈfleɪ.vi.əs
flav|or ˈfleɪ.v|əʳ, (US) -v|ɚ -ors -əz, (US) -ɚz -oring/s -əʳ.ɪŋ/z -ored -əd, (US) -ɚd ˌ**flavor of the** ˈ**month**
flavorful ˈfleɪ.və.fəl, -fʊl, (US) -vɚ-
flavoring ˈfleɪ.vəʳ.ɪŋ
flavorless ˈfleɪ.və.ləs, -lɪs, (US) -vɚ- -ness -nəs, -nɪs
flavorous ˈfleɪ.vəʳ.əs
flavorsome ˈfleɪ.və.səm, (US) -vɚ-
flav|our n, v ˈfleɪ.v|əʳ, (US) -v|ɚ -ours -əz, (US) -ɚz -ouring/s -əʳ.ɪŋ/z -oured -əd, (US) -ɚd ˌ**flavour of the** ˈ**month**
flavourful ˈfleɪ.və.fəl, -fʊl, (US) -vɚ-
flavouring ˈfleɪ.vəʳ.ɪŋ -s -z
flavourless ˈfleɪ.və.ləs, -lɪs, (US) -vɚ- -ness -nəs, -nɪs
flavoursome ˈfleɪ.və.səm, (US) -vɚ-
flaw flɔː, (US) flɑː, flɔː -s -z -ing -ɪŋ -ed -d
flawless ˈflɔː.ləs, -lɪs, (US) ˈflɑː-, ˈflɔː- -ly -li -ness -nəs, -nɪs
flax flæks -en -ən
Flaxman ˈflæks.mən
flay fleɪ -s -z -ing -ɪŋ -ed -d -er/s -əʳ/z, (US) -ɚ/z
flea fliː -s -z ˈ**flea** ˌ**market**
fleabag ˈfliː.bæg -s -z
fleabane ˈfliː.beɪn
flea|bite ˈfliː|.baɪt -bites -baɪts -bitten -bɪt.ən, (US) -bɪţ-
fleadh flɑː
fleam fliːm -s -z
fleapit ˈfliː.pɪt -s -s
flèch|e, flech|e fleɪʃ, fleʃ -es -ɪz
fleck flek -s -s -ing -ɪŋ -ed -t
Flecker ˈflek.əʳ, (US) -ɚ
Flecknoe ˈflek.nəʊ, (US) -noʊ
flection ˈflek.ʃən -s -z
flectional ˈflek.ʃən.əl
fled (from **flee**) fled
fledg|e fledʒ -es -ɪz -ing -ɪŋ -ed -d
fledg(e)ling ˈfledʒ.lɪŋ -s -z
flee fliː -s -z -ing -ɪŋ **fled** fled
fleec|e fliːs -es -ɪz -ing -ɪŋ -ed -t
fleec|y ˈfliː.s|i -ier -i.əʳ, (US) -i.ɚ -iest -i.ɪst, -i.əst -iness -ɪ.nəs, -ɪ.nɪs
fleer flɪəʳ, (US) flɪr -s -z -ing -ɪŋ -ed -d
fleet, F~ fliːt -s -s -er -əʳ, (US) ˈfliː.ţɚ -est -ɪst, -əst, (US) ˈfliː.ţɪst, -ţəst -ly -li -ness -nəs, -nɪs -ing -ɪŋ, (US) ˈfliː.ţɪŋ -ed -ɪd, (US) ˈfliː.ţɪd ˈ**Fleet** ˌ**Street**
fleeting ˈfliː.tɪŋ, (US) -ţɪŋ -ly -li
Fleetwood ˈfliːt.wʊd
Fleming ˈflem.ɪŋ -s -z
Flemings ˈflem.ɪŋz

Flemington ˈflem.ɪŋ.tən
Flemish ˈflem.ɪʃ
Flemming ˈflem.ɪŋ
flens|e flenz, flents, (US) flents -es -ɪz -ing -ɪŋ -ed -d
flesh fleʃ -es -ɪz -ing/s -ɪŋ/z -ed -t ˌ**flesh and** ˈ**blood;** ˈ**flesh** ˌ**wound;** ˌ**make someone's** ˈ**flesh** ˌ**creep**
fleshless ˈfleʃ.ləs, -lɪs
freshl|y ˈfleʃ.l|i -iness -ɪ.nəs, -ɪ.nɪs
fleshpot ˈfleʃ.pɒt, (US) -pɑːt -s -s
flesh|y ˈfleʃ|.i -iness -ɪ.nəs, -ɪ.nɪs
fletcher, F~ ˈfletʃ.əʳ, (US) -ɚ -s -z
Flete fliːt
fletton, F~ ˈflet.ən, (US) ˈfleţ-
Fleur flɜːʳ, (US) flɝː
fleur-de-lis ˌflɜː.dəˈliː, -liːs, (US) ˌflɝː-, ˌflʊr-
fleuron ˈflʊə.rɒn, ˈflɜː-, -rən, (US) ˈflɝː.ɑːn, ˈflʊr- -s -z
flew (from **fly**) fluː
flex fleks -es -ɪz -ing -ɪŋ -ed -t
flexibility ˌflek.səˈbɪl.ə.ti, -sɪˈ-, -ɪ.ti, (US) -ə.ţi
flexib|le ˈflek.sɪ.b|əl, -sə- -ly -li -leness -əl.nəs, -nɪs
flexion ˈflek.ʃən -s -z
flexitime ˈflek.si.taɪm
flexor ˈflek.səʳ, (US) -sɚ, -sɔːr -s -z
flextime ˈfleks.taɪm
flexure ˈflek.ʃəʳ, (US) -ʃɚ -s -z
flibbertigibbet ˌflɪb.ə.tiˈdʒɪb.ɪt, -ət, (US) ˈflɪb.ɚ.ţiˌdʒɪb- -s -s
flick flɪk -s -s -ing -ɪŋ -ed -t
flick|er ˈflɪk|.əʳ, (US) -ɚ -ers -əz, (US) -ɚz -ering -əʳ.ɪŋ -ered -əd, (US) -ɚd
flick-kni|fe ˈflɪk.naɪ|f -ves -vz
flier ˈflaɪ.əʳ, (US) -ɚ -s -z
flight, F~ flaɪt -s -s -less -ləs, -lɪs ˈ**flight at**ˌ**tendant;** ˈ**flight** ˌ**deck;** ˈ**flight** ˌ**path**
flight|y ˈflaɪ.t|i, (US) -ţ|i -ier -i.əʳ, (US) -i.ɚ -iest -i.ɪst, -i.əst -ily -əl.i, -ɪ.li -iness -ɪ.nəs, -ɪ.nɪs
flimflam ˈflɪm.flæm -s -z -ming -ɪŋ -med -d
flims|y ˈflɪm.z|i -ier -i.əʳ, (US) -i.ɚ -iest -i.ɪst, -i.əst -ily -əl.i, -ɪ.li -iness -ɪ.nəs, -ɪ.nɪs
flinch flɪntʃ -es -ɪz -ing/ly -ɪŋ/li -ed -t -er/s -əʳ/z, (US) -ɚ/z
flinders, F~ ˈflɪn.dəz, (US) -dɚz
fling flɪŋ -s -z -ing -ɪŋ **flung** flʌŋ
flint flɪnt -s -s ˈ**flint** ˌ**glass**
Flint flɪnt -shire -ʃəʳ, -ʃɪəʳ, (US) -ʃɚ, -ʃɪr
flintlock ˈflɪnt.lɒk, (US) -lɑːk -s -s
Flintoff ˈflɪn.tɒf, (US) -tɑːf
Flintshire ˈflɪnt.ʃəʳ, -ʃɪəʳ, (US) -ʃɚ, -ʃɪr
flintstone, F~ ˈflɪnt.stəʊn, (US) -stoʊn -s -z
flint|y ˈflɪn.t|i, (US) -ţ|i -ier -i.əʳ, (US) -i.ɚ -iest -i.ɪst, -i.əst -ily -əl.i, -ɪ.li -iness -ɪ.nəs, -ɪ.nɪs
flip flɪp -s -s -ping -ɪŋ -ped -t ˈ**flip** ˌ**side**
flip-flap ˈflɪp.flæp -s -s -ping -ɪŋ -ped -t
flip-flop ˈflɪp.flɒp, (US) -flɑːp -s -s -ping -ɪŋ -ped -t
flippancy ˈflɪp.ənt.si

flippant ˈflɪp.ənt **-ly** -li **-ness** -nəs, -nɪs

flipper ˈflɪp.əʳ, US -ɚ **-s** -z

flipside ˈflɪp.saɪd **-s** -z

flirt flɜːt, US flɝːt **-s** -s **-ing/ly** -ɪŋ/li, US ˈflɝː.t̬ɪŋ/li **-ed** -ɪd, US ˈflɝː.t̬ɪd

flirtation flɜːˈteɪ.ʃən, US flɝː- **-s** -z

flirtatious flɜːˈteɪ.ʃəs, US flɝː- **-ly** -li **-ness** -nəs, -nɪs

flirty ˈflɜː.ti, US ˈflɝː.t̬i

flit flɪt **-s** -s **-ting** -ɪŋ, US ˈflɪt̬.ɪŋ **-ted** -ɪd, US ˈflɪt̬.ɪd

flitch, F~ flɪtʃ **-es** -ɪz

flitt|er ˈflɪt|.əʳ, US ˈflɪt̬|.ɚ **-ers** -əz, US -ɚz **-ering** -ər.ɪŋ **-ered** -əd, US -ɚd

Flitwick ˈflɪt.ɪk, US ˈflɪt̬-

flivver ˈflɪv.əʳ, US -ɚ **-s** -z

Flixton ˈflɪk.stən

float fləʊt, US floʊt **-s** -s **-ing** -ɪŋ, US ˈfloʊ.t̬ɪŋ **-ed** -ɪd, US ˈfloʊ.t̬ɪd **-er/s** -əʳ/z, US ˈfloʊ.t̬ɚ/z **-age** -ɪdʒ, US ˈfloʊ.t̬ɪdʒ **ˌfloating ˈbridge; ˌfloating ˈdock**

floatation fləʊˈteɪ.ʃən, US floʊ-

floatplane ˈfləʊt.pleɪn, US ˈfloʊt- **-s** -z

floaty ˈfləʊ.ti, US ˈfloʊ.t̬i

floccu|late ˈflɒk.jə|.leɪt, -jʊ-, US ˈflɑː.kjuː-, -kjə- **-lates** -leɪts **-lating** -leɪ.tɪŋ, US -leɪ.t̬ɪŋ **-lated** -leɪ.tɪd, US -leɪ.t̬ɪd

flocculent ˈflɒk.jə.lənt, -jʊ-, US ˈflɑː.kjuː-, -kjə-

flock flɒk, US flɑːk **-s** -s **-ing** -ɪŋ **-ed** -t

Flockhart ˈflɒk.hɑːt, US ˈflɑːk.hɑːrt

Flockton ˈflɒk.tən, US ˈflɑːk-

Flodden ˈflɒd.ən, US ˈflɑː.dən

floe fləʊ, US floʊ **-s** -z

Floella fləʊˈel.ə, US floʊ-

flog flɒg, US flɑːg, flɔːg **-s** -z **-ging/s** -ɪŋ/z **-ged** -d

Flo-Jo ˈfləʊ.dʒəʊ, US ˈfloʊ.dʒoʊ

flood, F~ flʌd **-s** -z **-ing** -ɪŋ **-ed** -ɪd **ˌflood ˈtide**

floodgate ˈflʌd.geɪt **-s** -s

flood|light ˈflʌd|.laɪt **-lights** -laɪts **-lighting** -laɪ.tɪŋ, US -laɪ.t̬ɪŋ **-lit** -lɪt

floodwater ˈflʌdˌwɔː.təʳ, US -ˌwɑː.t̬ɚ, -ˌwɔː- **-s** -z

Flook flʊk, fluːk

floor flɔːʳ, US flɔːr **-s** -z **-ing** -ɪŋ **-ed** -d **-er/s** -əʳ/z, US -ɚ/z **ˈfloor ˌcloth; ˈfloor ˌplan; ˈfloor ˌshow**

floorboard ˈflɔː.bɔːd, US ˈflɔːr.bɔːrd **-s** -z

floorwalker ˈflɔːˌwɔː.kəʳ, US ˈflɔːrˌwɔː.kɚ, -ˌwɑː- **-s** -z

floosie ˈfluː.zi **-s** -z

flooz|y, flooz|ie ˈfluː.z|i **-ys** -iz **-ies** -iz

flop flɒp, US flɑːp **-s** -s **-ping** -ɪŋ **-ped** -t

flophou|se ˈflɒp.haʊ|s, US ˈflɑːp- **-ses** -zɪz

flopp|y ˈflɒp|.i, US ˈflɑː.p|i **-ier** -i.əʳ, US -i.ɚ **-iest** -i.ɪst, -i.əst **-ily** -əl.i, -ɪ.li **-iness** -ɪ.nəs, -ɪ.nɪs **ˌfloppy ˈdisk**

Flopsy ˈflɒp.si, US ˈflɑːp-

floptical ˈflɒp.tɪ.kəl, US ˈflɑːp- **ˌfloptical ˈdisk**

flor|a, F~ ˈflɔː.r|ə, US ˈflɔːr|.ə, ˈfloʊ.r|ə **-as** -əz **-ae** -iː

floral ˈflɔː.rəl, ˈflɒr.əl, US ˈflɔː.rəl, ˈfloʊ.rəl

Florence ˈflɒr.ənts, US ˈflɔːr-

florentine, F~ ˈflɒr.ən.taɪn, -tiːn, US ˈflɔːr- **-s** -z

Flores ˈflɔː.rɪz, US ˈflɔːr.es, -ɪz

florescen|ce flɔːˈres.ən|ts, flɒrˈes-, fləˈres-, US flɔːˈres-, flə-, floʊ- **-t** -t

floret ˈflɒr.ɪt, ˈflɔː.rɪt, -ret, US ˈflɔːr.ɪt, ˈfloʊ.rɪt **-s** -s

Florian ˈflɔː.ri.ən, US ˈflɔːr.i-

flori|ate ˈflɔː.ri|.eɪt, US ˈflɔːr.i-, ˈfloʊ.ri- **-ates** -eɪts **-ating** -eɪ.tɪŋ, US -eɪ.t̬ɪŋ **-ated** -eɪ.tɪd, US -eɪ.t̬ɪd

floribunda ˌflɒr.ɪˈbʌn.də, ˌflɔː.rɪˈ-, US ˌflɔːr.ɪˈ-, ˌfloʊ.rɪˈ-

floricultur|al ˌflɔː.rɪˈkʌl.tʃər|.əl, ˌflɒr.ɪˈ-, -tʃʊ.r|əl, US ˌflɔːr.ɪˈkʌl.tʃɚ|.əl, ˌfloʊ.rɪˈ- **-ist/s** -ɪst/s

floriculture ˈflɔː.rɪ.kʌl.tʃəʳ, ˈflɒr.ɪ-, US ˈflɔːr.ɪ.kʌl.tʃɚ, ˈfloʊ.rɪ-

florid ˈflɒr.ɪd, US ˈflɔːr- **-est** -ɪst, -əst **-ly** -li **-ness** -nəs, -nɪs

Florida ˈflɒr.ɪ.də, US ˈflɔːr-, ˈflɑːr- **ˌFlorida ˈKeys**

Floridian flɒrˈɪd.i.ən, fləˈrɪd-, US flɔːˈrɪd-, flɑːˈ- **-s** -z

floridity flɒrˈɪd.ə.ti, fləˈrɪd-, flɔː-, -ɪ.ti, US flɔːˈrɪd.ə.t̬i

floriferous flɔːˈrɪf.ər.əs, flɒrˈɪf-, fləˈrɪf-, US flɔːˈrɪf-, floʊˈ-

florin ˈflɒr.ɪn, US ˈflɔːr- **-s** -z

Florinda flɔːˈrɪn.də, flɒrˈɪn-, fləˈrɪn-, US flɔːˈrɪn-, floʊ-

Florio ˈflɔː.ri.əʊ, US ˈflɔːr.i.oʊ

florist ˈflɒr.ɪst, ˈflɔː.rɪst, US ˈflɔːr.ɪst, ˈfloʊ.rɪst **-s** -s

floristry ˈflɒr.ɪ.stri, ˈflɔː.rɪ-, US ˈflɔːr.ɪ-, ˈfloʊ.rɪ-

Florrie ˈflɒr.i, US ˈflɔːr-

floruit ˈflɔː.ru.ɪt, ˈflɒr.u-, US ˈflɔːr.ju-, ˈfloʊr-

floss, F~ flɒs, US flɑːs **-y** -i **-es** -ɪz **-ing** -ɪŋ **-ed** -t

Flossie ˈflɒs.i, US ˈflɑː.si

flotation fləʊˈteɪ.ʃən, US floʊ- **-s** -z

flotilla fləʊˈtɪl.ə, US floʊ- **-s** -z

flotsam ˈflɒt.səm, US ˈflɑːt- **ˌflotsam and ˈjetsam**

Flotta ˈflɒt.ə, US ˈflɑː.t̬ə

flounc|e flaʊnts **-es** -ɪz **-ing** -ɪŋ **-ed** -t

flouncy ˈflaʊnt.si

flound|er ˈflaʊn.d|əʳ, US -d|ɚ **-ers** -əz, US -ɚz **-ering** -ər.ɪŋ **-ered** -əd, US -ɚd

flour flaʊəʳ, flaʊ.əʳ, US flaʊɚ **-s** -z **-ing** -ɪŋ **-ed** -d

flourish ˈflʌr.ɪʃ, US ˈflɝː.ɪʃ **-es** -ɪz **-ing/ly** -ɪŋ/li **-ed** -t

floury ˈflaʊə.ri, US ˈflaʊɚ.i

flout flaʊt **-s** -s **-ing** -ɪŋ, US ˈflaʊ.t̬ɪŋ **-ed** -ɪd, US ˈflaʊ.t̬ɪd

flow fləʊ, US floʊ **-s** -z **-ing/ly** -ɪŋ/li **-ingness** -ɪŋ.nəs, -nɪs **-ed** -d **ˈflow ˌchart; ˈflow ˌdiagram**

flower, F~ flaʊəʳ, ˈflaʊ.əʳ, US ˈflaʊ.ɚ **-s** -z **-ing** -ɪŋ **-ed** -d **-er/s** -əʳ/z, US -ɚ/z **ˈflower ˌchild; ˈflower ˌgarden; ˈflower ˌgirl; ˈflower ˌpower**

flowerbed ˈflaʊə.bed, ˈflaʊ.ə-, US ˈflaʊ.ɚ- **-s** -z

floweret ˈflaʊə.rɪt, ˈflaʊ.ə-, -ret, US ˈflaʊ.ɚ.ɪt, -et **-s** -s

flowerless ˈflaʊə.ləs, ˈflaʊ.ə-, -lɪs, US ˈflaʊ.ɚ-

flowerpot ˈflaʊə.pɒt, ˈflaʊ.ə-, US ˈflaʊ.ɚ.pɑːt **-s** -s

flowery ˈflaʊə.ri, ˈflaʊ.ə.ri, US ˈflaʊ.ɚ.i

flown (from **fly**) fləʊn, US floʊn

Floyd flɔɪd

fl oz (abbrev. for **fluid ounce**) *singular:* ˌfluː.ɪdˈaʊnts; *plural:* -ˈaʊnt.sɪz

flu, ˈflu fluː

flub flʌb **-s** -z **-bing** -ɪŋ **-bed** -d

fluctuant ˈflʌk.tʃu.ənt, -tju-

fluctu|ate ˈflʌk.tʃu|.eɪt, -tju- **-ates** -eɪts **-ating** -eɪ.tɪŋ, US -eɪ.t̬ɪŋ **-ated** -eɪ.tɪd, US -eɪ.t̬ɪd

fluctuation ˌflʌk.tʃuˈeɪ.ʃən, -tjuˈ- **-s** -z

Flud(d) flʌd

Fludyer ˈflʌd.jəʳ, -i.əʳ, US ˈflʌd.jɚ

flue fluː **-s** -z **ˈflue ˌpipe**

Fluellen fluˈel.ɪn, -ən

fluency ˈfluː.ənt.si

fluent ˈfluː.ənt **-ly** -li **-ness** -nəs, -nɪs

fluff flʌf **-s** -s **-ing** -ɪŋ **-ed** -t

fluff|y ˈflʌf|.i **-ier** -i.əʳ, US -i.ɚ **-iest** -i.ɪst, -i.əst **-iness** -ɪ.nəs, -ɪ.nɪs

flugelhorn, flügelhorn ˈfluː.gəl.hɔːn, US -hɔːrn **-s** -z

fluid ˈfluː.ɪd **-s** -z **ˌfluid ˈounce**

fluidity fluˈɪd.ə.ti, -ɪ.ti, US -ə.t̬i

fluidization, -isa- ˌfluː.ɪ.daɪˈzeɪ.ʃən, -dɪˈ-, US -dəˈ-

fluidiz|e, -is|e ˈfluː.ɪ.daɪz **-es** -ɪz **-ing** -ɪŋ **-ed** -d **-er/s** -əʳ/z, US -ɚ/z

fluk|e fluːk **-es** -s **-ing** -ɪŋ **-ed** -t **-er/s** -əʳ/z, US -ɚ/z **-ish** -ɪʃ

fluk|y, fluk|ey ˈfluː.k|i **-ier** -i.əʳ, US -i.ɚ **-iest** -i.ɪst, -i.əst **-iness** -ɪ.nəs, -ɪ.nɪs

flume fluːm **-s** -z

flummery ˈflʌm.ər.i

flummox ˈflʌm.əks **-es** -ɪz **-ing** -ɪŋ **-ed** -t

flung (from **fling**) flʌŋ

flunk flʌŋk **-s** -s **-ing** -ɪŋ **-ed** -t

flunkey ˈflʌŋ.ki **-s** -z **-ism** -ɪ.zəm

flunk|y ˈflʌŋ.k|i **-ys** -iz **-ies** -iz **-yism** -i.ɪ.zəm

fluor ˈfluː.ɔːʳ, -əʳ, US -ɔːr, -ɚ

fluorescence flɔːˈres.ənts, flʊə-, flə-, US flɔː-, flʊ-, fluː-, floʊ-

fluorescent flɔːˈres.ənt, flʊə-, flə-, US flɔː-, flʊ-, fluː-, floʊ-

fluoric fluˈɒr.ɪk, US -ˈɔːr-

fluori|date ˈflɔː.rɪ|.deɪt, ˈflʊə-, -rə-, US ˈflɔːr.ə-, ˈflʊr- **-dates** -deɪts **-dating** -deɪ.tɪŋ, US -deɪ.t̬ɪŋ **-dated** -deɪ.tɪd, US -deɪ.t̬ɪd

fluoridation ˌflɔː.rɪˈdeɪ.ʃᵊn, ˌflʊə-, -raɪˈ-, -rəˈ-, (US) ˌflɔːr.əˈ-, ˌflʊr.əˈ-
fluoride ˈflɔː.raɪd, ˈflʊə-, (US) ˈflɔːr.aɪd, ˈflʊr- **-s** -z
fluoridization, -isa- ˌflɔː.rɪ.daɪˈzeɪ.ʃᵊn, ˌflʊə-, -raɪ-, -dɪˈ-, (US) ˌflɔːr.ə.dəˈ-, ˌflʊr-
fluoridiz|e, -is|e ˈflɔː.rɪ.daɪz, ˈflʊə-, (US) ˈflɔːr.ə-, ˈflʊr- **-es** -ɪz **-ing** -ɪŋ **-ed** -d
fluori|nate ˈflɔː.rɪ|.neɪt, ˈflʊə-, ˈflɒr.ɪ|-, ˈ-ə-, (US) ˈflɔːr.ə-, ˈflʊr- **-nates** -neɪts **-nating** -neɪ.tɪŋ, (US) -neɪ.t̬ɪŋ **-nated** -neɪ.tɪd, (US) -neɪ.t̬ɪd
fluorination ˌflɔː.rɪˈneɪ.ʃᵊn, ˌflʊə-, ˌflɒr.ɪˈ-, -əˈ-, (US) ˌflɔːr.əˈ-, ˌflʊr-
fluorine ˈflɔː.riːn, ˈflʊə-, (US) ˈflɔːr.iːn, ˈflʊr-, -ɪn
fluorisis flɔːˈraɪ.sɪs, flʊə-, flə-, (US) flɔː-, flʊ-
fluorite ˈflɔː.raɪt, ˈflʊə-, (US) ˈflɔːr.aɪt, ˈflʊr-
fluoro- ˈflɔː.rəʊ, ˈflʊə-; flɔːˈrɒ, flʊə-, flə-, -ˈrəʊ, (US) ˈflɔːr.ə, ˈflʊr-, ˈ-oʊ; (US) flɔːˈrɑː, flʊ-, -ˈroʊ
Note: Prefix. Either takes primary or secondary stress on the first syllable, e.g. **fluoroscope**/ˈflɔː.rəʊ.skəʊp/(US) /ˈflɔːr.ə.skoʊp/, **fluoroscopic** /ˌflɔː.rəʊˈskɒp.ɪk/ (US) /ˌflɔːr.əˈskɑː.pɪk/, or primary stress on the second syllable, e.g. **fluoroscopy** /flɔːˈrɒs.kə.pi/ (US) /-ˈrɑː.skə-/.
fluorocarbon ˌflɔː.rəʊˈkɑː.bᵊn, ˌflʊə-, (US) ˌflɔːr.əˈkɑːr-, ˌflʊr-, -oʊˈ- **-s** -z *stress shift:* **ˌfluorocarbon ˈdating techˌnique**
fluoroscop|e ˈflɔː.rəʊ.skəʊp, ˈflʊə-, (US) ˈflɔːr.ə.skoʊp, ˈflʊr-, -oʊ- **-es** -s **-ing** -ɪŋ **-ed** -t
fluoroscopic ˌflɔː.rəʊˈskɒp.ɪk, ˌflʊə-, (US) ˌflɔːr.əˈskɑː.pɪk, ˌflʊr-, -oʊˈ- **-ally** -ᵊl.i, -li
fluoroscop|y flɔːˈrɒs.kə.p|i, flʊə-, flə-, (US) flɔːˈrɑː.skə-, flʊ- **-ies** -iz **-ist/s** -ɪst/s
fluorosis flɔːˈrəʊ.sɪs, flʊə-, flə-, (US) flɔːˈroʊ-, flʊ-
fluorspar ˈflɔː.spɑːʳ, ˈflʊə-, (US) ˈflɔːr.spɑːr, ˈfluː.ɔːr-
flurr|y ˈflʌr|.i, (US) ˈflɝː- **-ies** -iz **-ying** -i.ɪŋ **-ied** -id
flush flʌʃ **-es** -ɪz **-ing** -ɪŋ **-ed** -t
flushing, F~ ˈflʌʃ.ɪŋ **-s** -z
flust|er ˈflʌs.t|əʳ, (US) -t|ɚ **-ers** -əz, (US) -ɚz **-ering** -ᵊr.ɪŋ **-ered** -əd, (US) -ɚd
flut|e, F~ fluːt **-es** -s **-ing** -ɪŋ, (US) ˈfluː.t̬ɪŋ **-ed** -ɪd, (US) ˈfluː.t̬ɪd **-y** -i, (US) ˈfluː.t̬i **-ier** -i.əʳ, (US) ˈfluː.t̬i.ɚ **-iest** -i.ɪst, -i.əst, (US) ˈfluː.t̬i.ɪst, -əst **-iness** -ɪ.nəs, -ɪ.nɪs, (US) ˈfluː.t̬ɪ.nəs, -nɪs
flutist ˈfluː.tɪst, (US) -t̬ɪst **-s** -s
flutt|er, F~ ˈflʌt|.əʳ, (US) ˈflʌt̬|.ɚ **-ers** -əz, (US) -ɚz **-ering** -ᵊr.ɪŋ **-ered** -əd, (US) -ɚd **-erer/s** -ᵊr.əʳ/z, (US) -ɚ.ɚ/z
fluvial ˈfluː.vi.əl
flux flʌks **-es** -ɪz
fluxion ˈflʌk.ʃᵊn **-s** -z
fluxional ˈflʌk.ʃᵊn.ᵊl

fl|y, F~ fl|aɪ **-ies** -aɪz **-ying** -aɪ.ɪŋ **flew** fluː **flown** fləʊn, (US) floʊn **flier/s** ˈflaɪ.əʳ/z, (US) -ɚ/z **ˈfly ˌball; ˌflying ˈbuttress; ˈflying ˌfish; ˈflying ˌofficer; ˌflying ˈsaucer; ˈflying ˌsquad; ˌflying ˈstart; ˈfly ˌsheet; he/she ˌwouldn't ˌharm a ˈfly**
flyable ˈflaɪ.ə.bᵊl
flyaway ˈflaɪ.ə.weɪ
flyb|y ˈflaɪ.b|aɪ **-ies** -aɪz
fly-by-night ˈflaɪ.baɪ.naɪt **-s** -s **-er/s** -əʳ/z, (US) -ɚ/z
fly-by-wire ˌflaɪ.baɪˈwaɪəʳ, -ˈwaɪ.əʳ, (US) -ˈwaɪ.ɚ
flycatcher ˈflaɪˌkætʃ.əʳ, (US) -ɚ **-s** -z
fly-drive ˈflaɪ.draɪv, ˌ-ˈ- **-s** -z
flyer ˈflaɪ.əʳ, (US) -ɚ **-s** -z
fly-fishing ˈflaɪˌfɪʃ.ɪŋ
flyingsaucer ˌflaɪ.ɪŋˈsɔː.səʳ, (US) -ˈsɑː.sɚ, -ˈsɔː- **-s** -z
flying squad ˈflaɪ.ɪŋ.skwɒd, (US) -skwɑːd **-s** -z
flylea|f ˈflaɪ.liː|f **-ves** -vz
Flymo® ˈflaɪ.məʊ, (US) -moʊ
Flyn(n) flɪn
Flynt flɪnt
flyover ˈflaɪ.əʊ.vəʳ, (US) -oʊ.vɚ **-s** -z
flypaper ˈflaɪˌpeɪ.pəʳ, (US) -pɚ **-s** -z
flypast ˈflaɪ.pɑːst, (US) -pæst **-s** -s
flyposter ˈflaɪˌpəʊ.stəʳ, (US) -ˌpoʊ.stɚ **-s** -z
flyswatter ˈflaɪˌswɒt.əʳ, (US) -ˌswɑː.t̬ɚ **-s** -z
Flyte flaɪt
flyway ˈflaɪ.weɪ **-s** -z
flyweight ˈflaɪ.weɪt **-s** -s
flywheel ˈflaɪ.*h*wiːl **-s** -z
FM ˌefˈem
Fo fəʊ, (US) foʊ
foal fəʊl, (US) foʊl **-s** -z **-ing** -ɪŋ **-ed** -d
foam fəʊm, (US) foʊm **-s** -z **-ing** -ɪŋ **-ed** -d **-y** -i **-iness** -ɪ.nəs, -ɪ.nɪs
Foard fɔːd, (US) fɔːrd
fob fɒb, (US) fɑːb **-s** -z **-bing** -ɪŋ **-bed** -d
focal ˈfəʊ.kᵊl, (US) ˈfoʊ- **ˈfocal ˌpoint; ˌfocal ˈpoint**
Foch fɒʃ, (US) fɑːʃ, fɔːʃ
Fochabers ˈfɒk.ə.bəz, ˈfɒx-, (US) ˈfɑːk.ə.bɚz
Focke fɒk, (US) fɑːk
fo'c'sle ˈfəʊk.sᵊl, (US) ˈfoʊk- **-s** -z
focus v ˈfəʊ.kəs, (US) ˈfoʊ- **-(s)es** -ɪz **-(s)ing** -ɪŋ **-(s)ed** -t
fo|cus n ˈfəʊ|.kəs, (US) ˈfoʊ- **-cuses** -kə.sɪz **-ci** -saɪ, -kiː
fodder ˈfɒd.əʳ, (US) ˈfɑː.dɚ
foe fəʊ, (US) foʊ **-s** -z
FoE (abbrev. for **Friends of the Earth**) ˌef.əʊˈiː, (US) -oʊˈ-
foehn fɜːn, (US) feɪn, fɜːn
foe|man ˈfəʊ|.mən, -mæn, (US) ˈfoʊ- **-men** -mən, -men
foetal ˈfiː.tᵊl, (US) -t̬ᵊl **ˈfoetal poˌsition**
foetid ˈfiː.tɪd, ˈfet.ɪd, (US) ˈfet̬.ɪd, ˈfiː.t̬ɪd **-ly** -li **-ness** -nəs, -nɪs
foetus ˈfiː.təs, (US) -t̬əs **-es** -ɪz

fog fɒg, (US) fɑːg, fɔːg **-s** -z **-ging** -ɪŋ **-ged** -d **ˈfog ˌlamp**
fogbound ˈfɒg.baʊnd, (US) ˈfɑːg-, ˈfɔːg-
Fogerty ˈfəʊ.gə.ti, ˈfɒg.ə.ti, (US) ˈfoʊ.gɚ.t̬i
fogey ˈfəʊ.gi, (US) ˈfoʊ- **-s** -z **-ish** -ɪʃ **-ism** -ɪ.zᵊm
Fogg fɒg, (US) fɑːg, fɔːg
fogg|y ˈfɒg|.i, (US) ˈfɑː.g|i, ˈfɔː- **-ier** -i.əʳ, (US) -i.ɚ **-iest** -i.ɪst, -i.əst **-ily** -ᵊl.i, -ɪ.li **-iness** -ɪ.nəs, -ɪ.nɪs **ˌFoggy ˈBottom**
foghorn ˈfɒg.hɔːn, (US) ˈfɑːg.hɔːrn, ˈfɔːg- **-s** -z
fog|y ˈfəʊ.g|i, (US) ˈfoʊ- **-ies** -iz **-yish** -i.ɪʃ **-yism** -i.ɪ.zᵊm
fohn, föhn fɜːn, (US) feɪn, fɜːn
foible ˈfɔɪ.bᵊl **-s** -z
foie gras ˌfwɑːˈgrɑː
foil fɔɪl **-s** -z **-ing** -ɪŋ **-ed** -d
foist fɔɪst **-s** -s **-ing** -ɪŋ **-ed** -ɪd
Fokker® ˈfɒk.əʳ, (US) ˈfɑː.kɚ
fold fəʊld, (US) foʊld **-s** -z **-ing** -ɪŋ **-ed** -ɪd
foldaway ˈfəʊld.ə.weɪ, (US) ˈfoʊld-
folder ˈfəʊl.dəʳ, (US) ˈfoʊl.dɚ **-s** -z
folderol ˈfɒl.dɪ.rɒl, -də-, (US) ˈfɑːl.də.rɑːl **-s** -z
foldout ˈfəʊld.aʊt, (US) ˈfoʊld- **-s** -s
Foley ˈfəʊ.li, (US) ˈfoʊ-
Folgate ˈfɒl.gɪt, -geɪt, (US) ˈfɑːl.geɪt
Folger ˈfəʊl.dʒəʳ, ˈfɒl-, (US) ˈfoʊl.dʒɚ
foliage ˈfəʊ.li.ɪdʒ, (US) ˈfoʊ- **-d** -d
foliar ˈfəʊ.li.ə, (US) ˈfoʊ.li.ɚ
foliate adj ˈfəʊ.li.ət, -ɪt, -eɪt, (US) ˈfoʊ-
foli|ate v ˈfəʊ.li|.eɪt, (US) ˈfoʊ- **-ates** -eɪts **-ating** -eɪ.tɪŋ, (US) -eɪ.t̬ɪŋ **-ated** -eɪ.tɪd, (US) -eɪ.t̬ɪd
foliation ˌfəʊ.liˈeɪ.ʃᵊn, (US) ˌfoʊ- **-s** -z
folic ˈfɒl.ɪk, ˈfəʊ.lɪk, (US) ˈfoʊ.lɪk **ˌfolic ˈacid**
Folies Bergère ˌfɒl.i.bɜːˈʒeəʳ, -bəˈ-, -beəˈ-, (US) ˌfoʊ.li.berˈʒer
folio ˈfəʊ.li.əʊ, (US) ˈfoʊ.li.oʊ **-s** -z
Foliot ˈfɒl.i.ət, (US) ˈfɑː.li-
folk fəʊk, (US) foʊk **-s** -s **ˈfolk ˌdance; ˈfolk ˌsong**
Folkes fəʊlks, fuːks, (US) foʊlks
Folkestone ˈfəʊk.stən, (US) ˈfoʊk-
folklore ˈfəʊk.lɔːʳ, (US) ˈfoʊk.lɔːr
folklorist ˈfəʊkˌlɔː.rɪst, (US) ˈfoʊkˌlɔːr.ɪst **-s** -s
folksinger ˈfəʊkˌsɪŋ.əʳ, (US) ˈfoʊkˌsɪŋ.ɚ **-s** -z
folks|y ˈfəʊk.s|i, (US) ˈfoʊk- **-ier** -i.əʳ, (US) -i.ɚ **-iest** -i.ɪst, -i.əst **-ily** -ᵊl.i, -ɪ.li **-iness** -ɪ.nəs, -ɪ.nɪs
folktale ˈfəʊk.teɪl, (US) ˈfoʊk- **-s** -z
Follen ˈfɒl.ɪn, -ən, (US) ˈfɑː.lɪn, -lən
Follett ˈfɒl.ɪt, -ət, (US) ˈfɑː.lɪt, -lət
Follick ˈfɒl.ɪk, (US) ˈfɑː.lɪk
follicle ˈfɒl.ɪ.kᵊl, (US) ˈfɑː.lɪ- **-s** -z
follow ˈfɒl.əʊ, (US) ˈfɑː.loʊ **-s** -z **-ing/s** -ɪŋ/z **-ed** -d **-er/s** -əʳ/z, (US) -ɚ/z
follow-my-leader ˌfɒl.əʊ.məˈliː.dəʳ, -mɪˈ-, -maɪˈ-, (US) ˌfɑː.loʊ.maɪˈliː.dɚ

follow-on ˈfɒl.əʊ.ɒn, (US) ˈfɑː.loʊ.ɑːn -s -z
follow-the-leader ˌfɒl.əʊ.ðəˈliː.dəʳ, (US) ˌfɑː.loʊ.ðəˈliː.dɚ
follow-through ˌfɒl.əʊˈθruː, (US) ˈ---, ˈfɑː.loʊ.θruː -s -z
follow-up ˈfɒl.əʊ.ʌp, (US) ˈfɑː.loʊ- -s -s
foll|y, F~ ˈfɒl|.i, (US) ˈfɑː.l|i -ies -iz
Fomalhaut ˈfəʊ.mə.ləʊt, ˈfɒm-, -əl.hɔːt, (US) ˈfoʊ.məl.hɑːt, -hɔːt, -mə.loʊ
fo|ment fəʊ|ˈment, (US) foʊ- -ments -ˈments -menting -ˈmen.tɪŋ, (US) -ˈmen.t̬ɪŋ -mented -ˈmen.tɪd, (US) -ˈmen.t̬ɪd -menter/s -ˈmen.təʳ/z, (US) -ˈmen.t̬ɚ/z
fomentation ˌfəʊ.menˈteɪ.ʃən, -mənˈ-, (US) ˌfoʊ- -s -z
fond fɒnd, (US) fɑːnd -er -əʳ, (US) -ɚ -est -ɪst, -əst -ly -li -ness -nəs, -nɪs
Fonda ˈfɒn.də, (US) ˈfɑːn-
fondant ˈfɒn.dənt, (US) ˈfɑːn- -s -s
fondl|e ˈfɒn.d|əl, (US) ˈfɑːn- -es -z -ing -ɪŋ, ˈfɒnd.lɪŋ, (US) ˈfɑːnd- -ed -d
fondly ˈfɒnd.li, (US) ˈfɑːnd-
fondu(e) ˈfɒn.djuː, -duː, -ˈ-, (US) fɑːnˈduː, -ˈdjuː, ˈ-- -s -z
font fɒnt, (US) fɑːnt -s -s -al -əl, (US) ˈfɑːn.t̬əl
Fontainebleau ˈfɒn.tɪn.bləʊ, -tɪm-, -təm-, (US) ˈfɑːn.tən.bloʊ
Fontane ˈfɒn.teɪn; *as if German:* fɒnˈtɑː.nə; (US) ˈfɑːn-
fontanelle, fontanel ˌfɒn.təˈnel, (US) ˌfɑːn.tənˈel -s -z
Fontenoy ˈfɒn.tə.nɔɪ, -tɪ.nɔɪ, (US) ˈfɑːn.tən.ɔɪ
Fonteyn fɒnˈteɪn, ˈ--, (US) fɑːnˈteɪn, ˈ--
Fonthill ˈfɒnt.hɪl, (US) ˈfɑːnt-
Foochow ˌfuːˈtʃaʊ
food fuːd -s -z -less -ləs, -lɪs ˈ**food** ˌ**poisoning**; ˈ**food** ˌ**processor**
foodie ˈfuː.di -s -z
foodstuff ˈfuːd.stʌf -s -s
fool fuːl -s -z -ing -ɪŋ -ed -d ˌ**fool's** ˈ**gold**, ˈ**fool's gold**; ˌ**make a** ˈ**fool of one**ˌ**self**
fooler|y ˈfuː.lər|.i -ies -iz
foolhard|y ˈfuːlˌhɑː.d|i, (US) -ˌhɑːr- -iest -i.ɪst, -i.əst -ily -əl.i, -ɪ.li -iness -ɪ.nəs, -ɪ.nɪs
foolish ˈfuː.lɪʃ -ly -li -ness -nəs, -nɪs
foolproof ˈfuːl.pruːf
foolscap, fool's cap *hat:* ˈfuːlz.kæp -s -s
foolscap *paper size:* ˈfuːl.skæp, ˈfuːlz.kæp
foot, F~ n fʊt **feet** fiːt ˈ**foot** ˌ**fault**; ˈ**foot** ˌ**passenger**; ˈ**foot** ˌ**soldier**; ˌ**one foot in the** ˈ**grave**; **put one's** ˌ**best foot** ˈ**forward**; ˌ**put one's** ˈ**foot down**; ˌ**put one's** ˈ**foot in it**
foot v fʊt -s -s -ing -ɪŋ, (US) ˈfʊt̬.ɪŋ -ed -ɪd, (US) ˈfʊt̬.ɪd
footage ˈfʊt.ɪdʒ, (US) ˈfʊt̬-
foot-and-mouth ˌfʊt.əndˈmaʊθ, -əmˈ-, (US) -əndˈ- ˌ**foot-and-**ˈ**mouth di**ˌ**sease**

football ˈfʊt.bɔːl, (US) -bɔːl, -bɑːl -s -z -ing -ɪŋ -er/s -əʳ/z, (US) -ɚ/z ˈ**football** ˌ**match**; ˈ**football** ˌ**pools**
footba|th ˈfʊt.bɑː|θ, (US) -bæ|θ -ths -ðz
footboard ˈfʊt.bɔːd, (US) -bɔːrd -s -z
footbridg|e ˈfʊt.brɪdʒ -es -ɪz
Foote fʊt
footer ˈfʊt.əʳ, (US) ˈfʊt̬.ɚ
footfall ˈfʊt.fɔːl, (US) -fɔːl, -fɑːl -s -z
foothill ˈfʊt.hɪl -s -z
foothold ˈfʊt.həʊld, (US) -hoʊld -s -z
footie ˈfʊt.i, (US) ˈfʊt̬-
footing ˈfʊt.ɪŋ, (US) ˈfʊt̬- -s -z
footl|e ˈfuː.təl, (US) -t̬əl -es -z -ing -ɪŋ, ˈfuːt.lɪŋ -ed -d
footlight ˈfʊt.laɪt -s -s
footlocker ˈfʊtˌlɒk.əʳ, (US) -ˌlɑː.kɚ -s -z
footloose ˈfʊt.luːs ˌ**footloose and** ˌ**fancy-**ˈ**free**
foot|man ˈfʊt|.mən -men -mən
footmark ˈfʊt.mɑːk, (US) -mɑːrk -s -s
footnote ˈfʊt.nəʊt, (US) -noʊt -s -s
footpad ˈfʊt.pæd -s -z
footpa|th ˈfʊt.pɑː|θ, (US) -pæ|θ -ths -ðz
footplate ˈfʊt.pleɪt -s -s
foot-pound ˌfʊtˈpaʊnd -s -z
footprint ˈfʊt.prɪnt -s -s
footrac|e ˈfʊt.reɪs -es -ɪz
footrest ˈfʊt.rest -s -s
footrule ˈfʊt.ruːl -s -z
footsie, F~ ˈfʊt.si
footslog ˈfʊt.slɒg, (US) -slɑːg, -slɔːg -s -z -ging -ɪŋ -ged -d
footsore ˈfʊt.sɔːʳ, (US) -sɔːr
footstep ˈfʊt.step -s -s
footstool ˈfʊt.stuːl -s -z
footsure ˈfʊt.ʃʊəʳ, -ʃɔːʳ, (US) -ʃʊr, -ʃɝː -ness -nəs, -nɪs
footwear ˈfʊt.weəʳ, (US) -wer
footwork ˈfʊt.wɜːk, (US) -wɝːk
footy ˈfʊt.i, (US) ˈfʊt̬-
foozl|e, F~ ˈfuː.zəl -es -z -ing -ɪŋ, ˈfuːz.lɪŋ -ed -d -er/s -əʳ/z, ˈfuːz.ləʳ/z, (US) ˈfuː.zəl.ɚ/z, ˈfuːz.lɚ/z
fop fɒp, (US) fɑːp -s -s
fopper|y ˈfɒp.ər|.i, (US) ˈfɑː.pɚ- -ies -iz
foppish ˈfɒp.ɪʃ, (US) ˈfɑː.pɪʃ -ly -li -ness -nəs, -nɪs
for *strong form:* fɔːʳ, (US) fɔːr; *weak form:* fəʳ, (US) fɚ; *alternative weak form before vowels:* fr
Note: Weak-form word. The strong form /fɔːʳ/ (US) /fɔːr/ is used contrastively (e.g. '**for** and **against**') and in sentence-final position (e.g. 'That's what it's for'). The weak form is /fə/ (US) /fɚ/ before consonants (e.g. 'Thanks for coming' /ˌθæŋks.fəˈkʌm.ɪŋ/ (US) /-fɚˈ-/); before vowels it is /fər/ (US) /fɚ/ (e.g. 'One for all' /ˌwʌn.fərˈɔːl/ (US) /-fɚˈɑːl/) or, in rapid speech, /fr/ (e.g. 'Time for another' /ˌtaɪm.fr.əˈnʌð.əʳ/ (US) /-ɚ/).
forag|e ˈfɒr.ɪdʒ, (US) ˈfɔːr- -es -ɪz -ing -ɪŋ -ed -d -er/s -əʳ/z, (US) -ɚ/z

foramen fəˈreɪ.men, fɒrˈeɪ-, -mən, (US) fəˈreɪ.mən, fɔː-, foʊ- **foramina** fəˈræm.ɪ.nə, fɒrˈeɪ-, (US) fəˈræm.ə-, fɔː-, foʊ-
forasmuch fərˌəzˈmʌtʃ, ˌfɔː.rəz-, ˌfɒr.əz-, (US) ˌfɔːr.æzˈ-, ˌfɚ-, -əzˈ-
foray ˈfɒr.eɪ, (US) ˈfɔːr- -s -z -ing -ɪŋ -ed -d
forbad (from **forbid**) fəˈbæd, fɔː-, (US) fɚ-, fɔːr-
forbade (from **forbid**) fəˈbæd, fɔː-, -beɪd, (US) fɚˈbæd, fɔːr-

> Note: The pronunciation /-beɪd/ may be considered to be a spelling pronunciation.

forbear n ˈfɔː.beəʳ, (US) ˈfɔːr.ber -s -z
for|bear v fɔː|ˈbeəʳ, fə-, (US) fɔːr|ˈber -bears -ˈbeəz, (US) -ˈberz -bearing/ly -ˈbeə.rɪŋ/li, (US) -ˈber.ɪŋ/li -bore -ˈbɔːʳ, (US) -ˈbɔːr -borne -ˈbɔːn, (US) -ˈbɔːrn
forbearance fɔːˈbeə.rənts, fə-, (US) fɔːrˈber.ənts
Forbes fɔːbz, ˈfɔː.bɪs, (US) fɔːrbz
for|bid fə|ˈbɪd, fɔː-, (US) fɚ-, fɔːr- -bids -ˈbɪdz -bidding/ly -ˈbɪd.ɪŋ/li -bad -ˈbæd -bade -ˈbæd, -ˈbeɪd, (US) -ˈbæd -bidden -ˈbɪd.ən
forbore (from **forbear**) fɔːˈbɔːʳ, (US) fɔːrˈbɔːr
forc|e, F~ fɔːs, (US) fɔːrs -es -ɪz -ing -ɪŋ -ed -t -edly -ɪd.li -edness -ɪd.nəs, -nɪs ˈ**force** ˌ**pump**; ˌ**forced** ˈ**march**
forcefeed ˌfɔːsˈfiːd, ˈ--, (US) ˈfɔːrs.fiːd, ˌ-ˈ- -s -z -ing -ɪŋ **forcefed** ˌfɔːsˈfed, ˈ--, (US) ˈfɔːrs.fed, ˌ-ˈ-
forceful ˈfɔːs.fəl, -fʊl, (US) ˈfɔːrs- -ly -i -ness -nəs, -nɪs
force majeure ˌfɔːs.mæʒˈɜːʳ, -mædʒˈʊəʳ, (US) ˌfɔːrs.mɑːˈʒɝː
forcemeat ˈfɔːs.miːt, (US) ˈfɔːrs-
forceps ˈfɔː.seps, -sɪps, -səps, (US) ˈfɔːr-
forcer ˈfɔː.səʳ, (US) ˈfɔːr.sɚ -s -z
forcib|le ˈfɔː.sə.b|əl, -sɪ-, (US) ˈfɔːr- -ly -li -leness -əl.nəs, -nɪs
ford, F~ fɔːd, (US) fɔːrd -s -z -ing -ɪŋ -ed -ɪd -able -ə.bəl
Fordcombe ˈfɔːd.kəm, (US) ˈfɔːrd-
Forde fɔːd, (US) fɔːrd
Forder ˈfɔː.dəʳ, (US) ˈfɔːr.dɚ
Fordham ˈfɔː.dəm, (US) ˈfɔːr-
Fordingbridge ˈfɔː.dɪŋ.brɪdʒ, (US) ˈfɔːr-
Fordyce ˈfɔː.daɪs, (US) ˈfɔːr-
fore fɔːʳ, (US) fɔːr
forearm n ˈfɔːʳ.ɑːm, (US) ˈfɔːr.ɑːrm -s -z
forearm v fɔːrˈɑːm, (US) fɔːrˈɑːrm -s -z -ing -ɪŋ -ed -d
forebear ˈfɔː.beəʳ, (US) ˈfɔːr.ber -s -s
forebod|e fɔːˈbəʊd, fə-, (US) fɔːrˈboʊd, fɚ- -es -z -ing/ly -ɪŋ/li -ed -ɪd -er/s -əʳ/z, (US) -ɚ/z
foreboding fɔːˈbəʊ.dɪŋ, fə-, (US) fɔːrˈboʊ-, fɚ- -s -z
forecast n ˈfɔː.kɑːst, (US) ˈfɔːr.kæst -s -s

forecast v ˈfɔː.kɑːst, (US) ˈfɔːr.kæst **-s** -s **-ing** -ɪŋ **-ed** -ɪd **-er/s** -əʳ/z, (US) -ɚ/z

forecastle ˈfəʊk.səl, (US) ˈfoʊk- **-s** -z

foreclos|e fɔːˈkləʊz, (US) fɔːrˈkloʊz **-es** -ɪz **-ing** -ɪŋ **-ed** -d

foreclosure fɔːˈkləʊ.ʒəʳ, (US) fɔːrˈkloʊ.ʒɚ **-s** -z

forecourt ˈfɔː.kɔːt, (US) ˈfɔːr.kɔːrt **-s** -s

forefather ˈfɔːˌfɑː.ðəʳ, (US) ˈfɔːrˌfɑː.ðɚ **-s** -z

forefinger ˈfɔːˌfɪŋ.gəʳ, (US) ˈfɔːrˌfɪŋ.gɚ **-s** -z

fore|foot ˈfɔː|.fʊt, (US) ˈfɔːr- **-feet** -fiːt

forefront ˈfɔː.frʌnt, (US) ˈfɔːr-

fore|go fɔː|ˈgəʊ, (US) fɔːr|ˈgoʊ **-goes** -ˈgəʊz, (US) -ˈgoʊz **-going** -ˈgəʊ.ɪŋ, (US) -ˈgoʊ.ɪŋ **-went** -ˈwent **-gone** -ˈgɒn, (US) -ˈgɑːn **-goer/s** -ˈgəʊ.əʳ/z, (US) -ˈgoʊ.ɚ/z

foregone (from **forego**) fɔːˈgɒn, (US) fɔːrˈgɑːn

foregone adj ˈfɔː.gɒn, (US) ˈfɔːr.gɑːn **ˌforegone conˈclusion**

foreground ˈfɔː.graʊnd, (US) ˈfɔːr- **-s** -z

foregrounding ˈfɔːˌgraʊn.dɪŋ, (US) ˈfɔːr-

forehand ˈfɔː.hænd, (US) ˈfɔːr- **-s** -z

forehanded fɔːˈhæn.dɪd, (US) ˈfɔːrˌ-, -ˈ-- **-ly** -li **-ness** -nəs, -nɪs *stress shift, British only:* **ˌforehanded ˈvolley**

forehead ˈfɔː.hed, ˈfɒr.ɪd, -ed, (US) ˈfɔːr.ed, -hed **-s** -z

> Note: The traditional pronunciation of this word is /ˈfɒr.ɪd/, but the spelling pronunciations /ˈfɔː.hed/ (US) /ˈfɔːr.ed/ have supplanted it.

foreign ˈfɒr.ɪn, -ən, (US) ˈfɔːr- **ˌforeign afˈfairs; ˌforeign correˈspondent; ˌforeign exˈchange; ˌforeign ˈlegion; ˈForeign ˌOffice; ˌforeign ˈpolicy; ˌforeign ˈsecretary; ˌForeign ˈService**

foreigner ˈfɒr.ɪ.nəʳ, ˈ-ə-, (US) ˈfɔːr.ɪ.nɚ **-s** -z

forejudg|e fɔːˈdʒʌdʒ, (US) fɔːr- **-es** -ɪz **-ing** -ɪŋ **-ed** -d

fore|know fɔː|ˈnəʊ, (US) fɔːr|ˈnoʊ **-knows** -ˈnəʊz, (US) -ˈnoʊz **-knowing** -ˈnəʊ.ɪŋ, (US) -ˈnoʊ.ɪŋ **-knew** -ˈnjuː, (US) -ˈnuː, -ˈnjuː **-known** -ˈnəʊn, (US) -ˈnoʊn

foreknowledge fɔːˈnɒl.ɪdʒ, (US) fɔːrˈnɑː.lɪdʒ

foreland, F~ ˈfɔː.lənd, (US) ˈfɔːr- **-s** -z

foreleg ˈfɔː.leg, (US) ˈfɔːr- **-s** -z

forelock ˈfɔː.lɒk, (US) ˈfɔːr.lɑːk **-s** -s

fore|man, F~ ˈfɔː|.mən, (US) ˈfɔːr- **-men** -mən

foremast ˈfɔː.mɑːst, (US) ˈfɔːr.mæst; *nautical pronunciation:* -məst **-s** -s

foremost ˈfɔː.məʊst, -məst, (US) ˈfɔːr.moʊst

forename ˈfɔː.neɪm, (US) ˈfɔːr- **-s** -z

forenoon ˈfɔː.nuːn, (US) ˈfɔːr-, ˌ-ˈ- **-s** -z

forensic fəˈrent.sɪk, fɒrˈent-, -ˈen.zɪk, (US) fəˈrent.sɪk, -ˈren.zɪk **-s** -s

foreordain ˌfɔːʳ.ɔːˈdeɪn, (US) ˌfɔːr.ɔːrˈ- **-s** -z **-ing** -ɪŋ **-ed** -d

forepart ˈfɔː.pɑːt, (US) ˈfɔːr.pɑːrt **-s** -s

foreplay ˈfɔː.pleɪ, (US) ˈfɔːr-

fore|run fɔː|ˈrʌn, (US) fɔːr- **-runs** -ˈrʌnz **-running** -ˈrʌn.ɪŋ **-ran** -ˈræn

forerunner ˈfɔːˌrʌn.əʳ, ˌ-ˈ--, (US) ˈfɔːrˌrʌn.ɚ, ˌ-ˈ-- **-s** -z

foresail ˈfɔː.seɪl, (US) ˈfɔːr-; *nautical pronunciation:* -səl **-s** -z

fore|see fɔː|ˈsiː, fə-, (US) fɔːr-, fɚ- **-sees** -ˈsiːz **-seeing** -ˈsiː.ɪŋ **-saw** -ˈsɔː, (US) -ˈsɑː, -ˈsɔː **-seen** -ˈsiːn **-seeable** -ˈsiː.ə.bəl

foreseeability fɔːˌsiː.əˈbɪl.ə.ti, ˌfɔː.siː-; fəˌsiː-, (US) fɔːrˌsiː.əˈbɪl.ə.t̬i, fɚ-

foreshadow fɔːˈʃæd.əʊ, (US) fɔːrˈʃæd.oʊ **-s** -z **-ing** -ɪŋ **-ed** -d **-er/s** -əʳ/z, (US) -ɚ/z

foreshore ˈfɔː.ʃɔːʳ, (US) ˈfɔːr.ʃɔːr **-s** -z

foreshorten fɔːˈʃɔː.tən, (US) fɔːrˈʃɔːr- **-s** -z **-ing** -ɪŋ **-ed** -d

foreshow fɔːˈʃəʊ, (US) fɔːrˈʃoʊ **-s** -z **-ing** -ɪŋ **-ed** -d **-n** -n

foresight ˈfɔː.saɪt, (US) ˈfɔːr- **-s** -s

foreskin ˈfɔː.skɪn, (US) ˈfɔːr- **-s** -z

forest, F~ ˈfɒr.ɪst, (US) ˈfɔːr- **-s** -s **ˌForest ˈHills; ˌforest ˈranger** (US) **ˈforest ˌranger; not see the ˌforest for the ˈtrees**

forestall fɔːˈstɔːl, (US) fɔːrˈstɔːl, -ˈstɑːl **-s** -z **-ing** -ɪŋ **-ed** -d **-er/s** -əʳ/z, (US) -ɚ/z

forester, F~ ˈfɒr.ɪ.stəʳ, ˈ-ə-, (US) ˈfɔːr.ɪ.stɚ **-s** -z

forestry ˈfɒr.ɪ.stri, ˈ-ə-, (US) ˈfɔːr-

foretaste n ˈfɔː.teɪst, (US) ˈfɔːr- **-s** -s

foretast|e v fɔːˈteɪst, (US) fɔːr- **-es** -s **-ing** -ɪŋ **-ed** -ɪd

fore|tell fɔː|ˈtel, (US) fɔːr- **-tells** -ˈtelz **-telling** -ˈtel.ɪŋ **-told** -ˈtəʊld, (US) -ˈtoʊld **-teller/s** -ˈtel.əʳ/z, (US) -ˈtel.ɚ/z

forethought ˈfɔː.θɔːt, (US) ˈfɔːr.θɑːt, -θɔːt

foretop, fore-top ˈfɔː.tɒp, (US) ˈfɔːr.tɑːp; *nautical pronunciation:* (US) -təp **-s** -s

fore-topmast fɔːˈtɒp.mɑːst, (US) fɔːrˈtɑːp.mæst; *nautical pronunciation:* (US) -məst **-s** -s

fore-topsail fɔːˈtɒp.seɪl, (US) fɔːrˈtɑːp-; *nautical pronunciation:* (US) -səl **-s** -z

forever fəˈre.vəʳ, (US) fɔːrˈev.ɚ, fɚ-

forewarn fɔːˈwɔːn, (US) fɔːrˈwɔːrn **-s** -z **-ing** -ɪŋ **-ed** -d

forewent (from **forego**) fɔːˈwent, (US) fɔːr-

fore|woman ˈfɔː|ˌwʊm.ən, (US) ˈfɔːr- **-women** -ˌwɪm.ɪn

foreword ˈfɔː.wɜːd, (US) ˈfɔːr.wɝːd **-s** -z

Forfar ˈfɔː.fəʳ, -fɑːʳ, (US) ˈfɔːr.fɚ, -fɑːr

forfei|t ˈfɔː.fɪ|t, (US) ˈfɔːr-, -fə|t **-ts** -ts **-ting** -tɪŋ, (US) -t̬ɪŋ **-ted** -tɪd, (US) -t̬ɪd **-ter/s** -təʳ/z, (US) -t̬ɚ/z **-table** -tə.bəl, (US) -t̬ə.bəl

forfeiture ˈfɔː.fɪ.tʃəʳ, (US) ˈfɔːr.fə.tʃɚ **-s** -z

forfend fɔːˈfend, (US) fɔːr- **-s** -z **-ing** -ɪŋ **-ed** -ɪd

forgath|er fɔːˈgæð|.əʳ, (US) fɔːrˈgæð|.ɚ **-ers** -əz, (US) -ɚz **-ering** -ər.ɪŋ **-ered** -əd, (US) -ɚd

forgave (from **forgive**) fəˈgeɪv, (US) fɚ-, fɔːr-

forg|e fɔːdʒ, (US) fɔːrdʒ **-es** -ɪz **-ing** -ɪŋ **-ed** -d **-er/s** -əʳ/z, (US) -ɚ/z

forger|y ˈfɔː.dʒər|.i, (US) ˈfɔːr- **-ies** -iz

for|get fə|ˈget, (US) fɚ-, fɔːr- **-gets** -ˈgets **-getting** -ˈget.ɪŋ, (US) -ˈget̬.ɪŋ **-got** -ˈgɒt, (US) -ˈgɑːt **-gotten** -ˈgɒt.ən, (US) -ˈgɑː.tən

forgetful fəˈget.fəl, -fʊl, (US) fɚ-, fɔːr- **-ly** -i **-ness** -nəs, -nɪs

forget-me-not fəˈget.mi.nɒt, (US) fɚˈget.mi.nɑːt, fɔːr- **-s** -s

forgettab|le fəˈget.ə.b|əl, (US) fɚˈget̬-, fɔːr- **-ly** -li

for|give fə|ˈgɪv, (US) fɚ-, fɔːr- **-gives** -ˈgɪvz **-giving** -ˈgɪv.ɪŋ **-gave** -ˈgeɪv **-given** -ˈgɪv.ən **-givable** -ˈgɪv.ə.bəl **-giveness** -ˈgɪv.nəs, -nɪs

for|go fɔː|ˈgəʊ, (US) fɔːr|ˈgoʊ **-goes** -ˈgəʊz, (US) -ˈgoʊz **-going** -ˈgəʊ.ɪŋ, (US) -ˈgoʊ.ɪŋ **-went** -ˈwent **-gone** -ˈgɒn, (US) -ˈgɑːn

forgot (from **forget**) fəˈgɒt, (US) fɚˈgɑːt, fɔːr-

forgotten (from **forget**) fəˈgɒt.ən, (US) fɚˈgɑː.tən, fɔːr-

Forington ˈfɒr.ɪŋ.tən, (US) ˈfɔːr-

forint ˈfɒr.ɪnt, (US) ˈfɔːr- **-s** -s

fork fɔːk, (US) fɔːrk **-s** -s **-ing** -ɪŋ **-ed** -t **-ful/s** -fʊl/z, -fəl/z

forklift ˈfɔːk.lɪft, ˌ-ˈ-, (US) ˈfɔːrk.lɪft **-s** -s **-ing** -ɪŋ **-ed** -ɪd **ˌforklift ˈtruck**

forlorn fəˈlɔːn, fɔː-, (US) fɔːrˈlɔːrn, fɚ- **-ly** -li **-ness** -nəs, -nɪs

form fɔːm, (US) fɔːrm **-s** -z **-ing** -ɪŋ **-ed** -d

formal ˈfɔː.məl, (US) ˈfɔːr- **-ly** -i

formaldehyde fɔːˈmæl.dɪ.haɪd, -də-, (US) fɔːr-, fɚ-

formalin ˈfɔː.məl.ɪn, (US) ˈfɔːr.mə.lɪn

formal|ism ˈfɔː.məl|.ɪ.zəm, (US) ˈfɔːr- **-ist/s** -ɪst/s

formalit|y fɔːˈmæl.ə.t|i, -ɪ.t|i, (US) -ə.t̬|i **-ies** -iz

formalization, -isa- ˌfɔː.məl.aɪˈzeɪ.ʃən, -ɪˈ-, (US) ˌfɔːr.məl.əˈ- **-s** -z

formaliz|e, -is|e ˈfɔː.məl.aɪz, (US) ˈfɔːr.mə.laɪz **-es** -ɪz **-ing** -ɪŋ **-ed** -d

Forman ˈfɔː.mən, (US) ˈfɔːr-

formant ˈfɔː.mənt, (US) ˈfɔːr- **-s** -s

for|mat ˈfɔː|.mæt, (US) ˈfɔːr- **-mats** -mæts **-matting** -mæt.ɪŋ, (US) -mæt̬.ɪŋ **-matted** -mæt.ɪd, (US) -mæt̬.ɪd **-matter/s** -mæt.əʳ/z, (US) -mæt̬.ɚ/z

formation fɔːˈmeɪ.ʃən, (US) fɔːr- **-s** -z

formative ˈfɔː.mə.tɪv, (US) ˈfɔːr.mə.t̬ɪv **-ly** -li **-ness** -nəs, -nɪs

Formby ˈfɔːm.bi, (US) ˈfɔːrm-

forme fɔːm, (US) fɔːrm **-s** -z

former ˈfɔː.məʳ, US ˈfɔːr.mɚ -ly -li
formic ˈfɔː.mɪk, US ˈfɔːr- ˌformic ˈacid
Formica® fɔːˈmaɪ.kə, fəˈmaɪ-, US fɔːr-, fɚ-
formidab|le ˈfɔː.mɪ.də.b|əl; fɔːˈmɪd.ə-, fə-, US ˈfɔːr.mə.də.b|əl; US fɔːrˈmɪd.ə-, fɚ- -ly -li -leness -əl.nəs, -nɪs
Formidable *name of ship:* fɔːˈmɪd.ə.bəl; ˈfɔː.mɪ.də-, US ˈfɔːr.mə.də-; US fɔːrˈmɪd.ə-
formless ˈfɔːm.ləs, US ˈfɔːrm-, -lɪs -ness -nəs, -nɪs
Formos|a fɔːˈməʊ.s|ə, -z|ə, US fɔːrˈmoʊ- -an/s -ən/z
formul|a ˈfɔː.mjə.l|ə, -mjʊ-, US ˈfɔːr.mjʊ-, -mjə- -ae -iː -as -əz
formulaic ˌfɔː.mjəˈleɪ.ɪk, -mjʊˈ-, US ˌfɔːr.mjʊˈ-, -mjəˈ-
formular|y ˈfɔː.mjə.lə.r|i, -mjʊ-, US ˈfɔːr.mjʊ.ler|.i, -mjə- -ies -iz
formu|late ˈfɔː.mjə|.leɪt, -mjʊ-, US ˈfɔːr.mjʊ-, -mjə- -lates -leɪts -lating -leɪ.tɪŋ, US -leɪ.t̬ɪŋ -lated -leɪ.tɪd, US -leɪ.t̬ɪd
formulation ˌfɔː.mjəˈleɪ.ʃən, -mjʊˈ-, US ˌfɔːr.mjʊˈ-, -mjəˈ- -s -z
Fornax ˈfɔː.næks, US ˈfɔːr-
Forney ˈfɔː.ni, US ˈfɔːr-
forni|cate ˈfɔː.nɪ|.keɪt, -nə-, US ˈfɔːr- -cates -keɪts -cating -keɪ.tɪŋ, US -keɪ.t̬ɪŋ -cated -keɪ.tɪd, US -keɪ.t̬ɪd -cator/s -keɪ.təʳ/z, US -keɪ.t̬ɚ/z
fornication ˌfɔː.nɪˈkeɪ.ʃən, -nəˈ-, US ˌfɔːr-
Forres ˈfɒr.ɪs, US ˈfɔːr-
Forrest ˈfɒr.ɪst, US ˈfɔːr-
Forrester ˈfɒr.ɪ.stəʳ, US ˈfɔːr.ɪ.stɚ
for|sake fə|ˈseɪk, fɔː-, US fɔːr-, fɚ- -sakes -ˈseɪks -saking -ˈseɪ.kɪŋ -sook -ˈsʊk -saken -ˈseɪ.kən
Forshaw ˈfɔː.ʃɔː, US ˈfɔːr.ʃɑː, -ʃɔː
forsooth fəˈsuːθ, fɔː-, US fɔːr-, fɚ-
Forster ˈfɔː.stəʳ, US ˈfɔːr.stɚ
for|swear fɔː|ˈsweəʳ, US fɔːr|ˈswer -swears -ˈsweəz, US -ˈswerz -swearing -ˈsweə.rɪŋ, US -ˈswer.ɪŋ -swore -ˈswɔːʳ, US -ˈswɔːr -sworn -ˈswɔːn, US -ˈswɔːrn
Forsyte ˈfɔː.saɪt, US ˈfɔːr-
Forsyth ˈfɔː.saɪθ, -ˈ-, US ˈfɔːr-, -ˈ-
forsythia fɔːˈsaɪ.θi.ə, fə-, -ˈsɪθ.i-, US fɔːrˈsɪθ.i-, -ˈsaɪ.θi- -s -z
fort fɔːt, US fɔːrt -s -s ˌFort ˈKnox; ˌFort ˈLauderdale; ˌFort ˈWorth; ˌhold the ˈfort
Fortaleza ˌfɔː.təˈleɪ.zə, US ˌfɔːr.t̬əˈ-
forte n *strong point:* ˈfɔː.teɪ, -ti, US fɔːrt, ˈfɔːr.teɪ -s -z, US fɔːrts; US ˈfɔːr.teɪz
forte n, adv *in music:* ˈfɔː.teɪ, -ti, US ˈfɔːr- -s -z
Fortescue ˈfɔː.tɪ.skjuː, -tə-, US ˈfɔːr.t̬ə-
Forteviot fɔːˈtiː.vi.ət, US fɔːr-
forth, F~ fɔːθ, US fɔːrθ
forthcoming ˌfɔːθˈkʌm.ɪŋ, US ˌfɔːrθˈ-, ˈ-ˌ-- *stress shift, British only:* ˌforthcoming ˈbook
forthright ˈfɔːθ.raɪt, ˌ-ˈ-, US ˈfɔːrθ-, ˌ-ˈ- -ness -nəs, -nɪs
forthwith ˌfɔːθˈwɪθ, -ˈwɪð, US ˌfɔːrθˈ-
Forties ˈfɔː.tiz, -tɪz, US ˈfɔːr.t̬iz
fortieth ˈfɔː.ti.əθ, -ɪθ, US ˈfɔːr.t̬i- -s -s
fortification ˌfɔː.tɪ.fɪˈkeɪ.ʃən, -tə-, -fəˈ-, US ˌfɔːr.t̬ə- -s -z
forti|fy ˈfɔː.tɪ|.faɪ, -tə-, US ˈfɔːr.t̬ɪ-, ˈ-t̬ə- -fies -faɪz -fying -faɪ.ɪŋ -fied -faɪd -fier/s -faɪ.əʳ/z, US -faɪ.ɚ/z -fiable -faɪ.ə.bəl
Fortinbras ˈfɔː.tɪn.bræs, -tɪm-, US ˈfɔːr.tən-, -t̬ɪn-
fort|is ˈfɔː.t|ɪs, US ˈfɔːr.t̬|ɪs -es -iːz, -eɪz
fortissimo fɔːˈtɪs.ɪ.məʊ, -ə-, US fɔːrˈtɪs.ə.moʊ -s -z
fortition fɔːˈtɪʃ.ən, US fɔːr-
fortitude ˈfɔː.tɪ.tʃuːd, -tjuːd, US ˈfɔːr.t̬ə.tuːd, -tjuːd
fortnight ˈfɔːt.naɪt, US ˈfɔːrt- -s -s
fortnightl|y, F~ ˈfɔːt.naɪt.l|i, US ˈfɔːrt- -ies -iz
Fortnum ˈfɔːt.nəm, US ˈfɔːrt-
Fortran, FORTRAN ˈfɔː.træn, US ˈfɔːr-
fortress ˈfɔː.trəs, -trɪs, US ˈfɔːr- -es -ɪz
fortuitous fɔːˈtʃuː.ɪ.təs, -ˈtjuː-, ˈ-ə-, US fɔːrˈtuː.ə.t̬əs, -ˈtjuː- -ly -li -ness -nəs, -nɪs
fortuit|y fɔːˈtʃuː.ə.t|i, -ˈtjuː-, ˈ-ɪ-, US fɔːrˈtuː.ə.t̬|i, -ˈtjuː- -ies -iz
Fortuna fɔːˈtjuː.nə, US fɔːrˈtuː-, -ˈtjuː-
fortunate ˈfɔː.tʃən.ət, -ɪt, US ˈfɔːr- -ly -li -ness -nəs, -nɪs
Fortunatus ˌfɔː.tjuˈnɑː.təs, -ˈneɪ-, US ˌfɔːr.tuːˈnɑː.t̬əs, -ˈneɪ-
fortune, F~ ˈfɔː.tʃuːn, -tjuːn, -tʃən, US ˈfɔːr.tʃən -s -z -less -ləs, -lɪs ˈfortune ˌcookie
fortune-teller ˈfɔː.tʃuːnˌtel.əʳ, -tjuːnˌ-, -tʃənˌ-, US ˈfɔːr.tʃənˌtel.ɚ -s -z
fort|y ˈfɔː.t|i, US ˈfɔːr.t̬|i -ies -iz ˌforty ˈwinks
forty-five ˌfɔː.tiˈfaɪv, US ˌfɔːr.t̬ɪˈ- -s -z
fortyfold ˈfɔː.ti.fəʊld, US ˈfɔːr.t̬i.foʊld
forty-niner ˌfɔː.tiˈnaɪ.nəʳ, US ˌfɔːr.t̬iˈnaɪ.nɚ -s -z
forum ˈfɔː.rəm, US ˈfɔːr.əm -s -z
forward ˈfɔː.wəd, US ˈfɔːr.wɚd; *nautical pronunciation:* ˈfɒr.əd, US ˈfɔːr- -ly -li -ness -nəs, -nɪs -er -əʳ, US -ɚ -est -ɪst, -əst -s -z -ing -ɪŋ -ed -ɪd ˌbackwards and ˈforwards
forward-looking ˌfɔː.wədˈlʊk.ɪŋ, US ˌfɔːr.wɚd- *stress shift:* ˌforward-looking ˈmove
forwards ˈfɔː.wədz, US ˈfɔːr.wɚdz
forwent (from **forgo**) fɔːˈwent, US fɔːr-
Fosbery ˈfɒz.bər.i, US ˈfɑːzˌber-, -bɚ-
Fosbury ˈfɒz.bər.i, US ˈfɑːzˌber-, -bɚ-
Fosco ˈfɒs.kəʊ, US ˈfɑː.skoʊ
Foss fɒs, US fɑːs
foss|e fɒs, US fɑːs -es -ɪz
fossick ˈfɒs.ɪk, US ˈfɑː.sɪk -s -s -ing -ɪŋ -ed -t
fossil ˈfɒs.əl, -ɪl, US ˈfɑː.səl -s -z
fossilization, -isa- ˌfɒs.əl.aɪˈzeɪ.ʃən, -ɪ.laɪˈ-, -lɪˈ-, US ˌfɑː.səl.əˈ-
fossiliz|e, -is|e ˈfɒs.əl.aɪz, -ɪ.laɪz, US ˈfɑː.sə.laɪz -es -ɪz -ing -ɪŋ -ed -d
fost|er, F~ ˈfɒs.t|əʳ, US ˈfɑː.st|ɚ -ers -əz, US -ɚz -ering -ər.ɪŋ -ered -əd, US -ɚd -erer/s -ər.əʳ/z, US -ɚ.ɚ/z -erage -ər.ɪdʒ ˈfoster ˌbrother; ˈfoster ˌchild; ˈfoster ˌchildren; ˈfoster ˌfather; ˈfoster ˌhome; ˈfoster ˌmother; ˈfoster ˌparent; ˈfoster ˌsister
Fothergill ˈfɒð.ə.gɪl, US ˈfɑː.ðɚ-
Fotheringay ˈfɒð.ər.ɪŋ.heɪ, -geɪ, US ˈfɑː.ðɚ-
Fotheringham ˈfɒð.ər.ɪŋ.əm, US ˈfɑː.ðɚ-
Foucault ˈfuː.kəʊ, -ˈ-, US ˌfuːˈkoʊ
fouetté ˈfuː.ə.teɪ, US fwetˈeɪ -s -z
fought (from **fight**) fɔːt, US fɑːt, fɔːt
foul faʊl -er -əʳ, US -ɚ -est -ɪst, -əst -ly -li, ˈfaʊ.li -ness -nəs, -nɪs -s -z -ing -ɪŋ -ed -d ˌfoul ˈplay
foulard ˈfuː.lɑːʳ, -lɑːd, -ˈ-, US fuːˈlɑːrd
Foulden ˈfəʊl.dən, US ˈfoʊl-
Foulds fəʊldz, US foʊldz
Foulerton ˈfʊl.ə.tən, US ˈ-ɚ-
Foulger ˈfuːl.dʒəʳ, -gəʳ, US ˈfuːl.dʒɚ, ˈfoʊl-, -gɚ
Foulis faʊlz
Foulkes fəʊks, faʊks, US foʊks, faʊks
foulmouthed ˌfaʊlˈmaʊðd, -ˈmaʊθt, US ˌ-ˈ-, ˈ-ˌ- *stress shift, British only:* ˌfoulmouthed ˈlanguage
foulness ˈfaʊl.nəs, -nɪs
Foulness ˌfaʊlˈnes *stress shift:* ˌFoulness ˈBeach
Foulsham ˈfəʊl.ʃəm, US ˈfoʊl-
foul-up ˈfaʊl.ʌp -s -s
found faʊnd -s -z -ing -ɪŋ -ed -ɪd
found (from **find**) faʊnd
foundation faʊnˈdeɪ.ʃən -s -z founˈdation ˌcourse; founˈdation ˌstone
foundationer faʊnˈdeɪ.ʃən.əʳ, US -ɚ -s -z
found|er ˈfaʊn.d|əʳ, US -d|ɚ -ers -əz, US -ɚz -ering -ər.ɪŋ -ered -əd, US -ɚd ˌfounder ˈmember
foundling, F~ ˈfaʊnd.lɪŋ -s -z
foundr|y ˈfaʊn.dr|i -ies -iz
fount *fountain, source:* faʊnt *in printing:* fɒnt, faʊnt, US fɑːnt, faʊnt -s -s

> Note: Those connected with printing have generally pronounced this /fɒnt/ US /fɑːnt/. The spelling is more usually ‘font’ nowadays.

fountain, F~ ˈfaʊn.tɪn, -tən, US -tən -s -z ˈfountain ˌpen

fountainhead ˈfaʊn.tɪn.hed, -tən-, ˌ--ˈ-, (US) ˈfaʊn.tᵊn.hed **-s** -z
four fɔːʳ, (US) fɔːr **-s** -z **-th/s** -θ/s **-thly** -θ.li ˌ**Four** ˈ**Corners**
four-cornered ˌfɔːˈkɔː.nəd, (US) ˌfɔːrˈkɔːr.nɚd *stress shift:* ˌ**four-cornered** ˈ**hat**
four-dimensional ˌfɔː.dɪˈmen.tʃᵊn.ᵊl, -daɪˈ-, (US) ˌfɔːr.dəˈment.ʃᵊn- *stress shift:* ˌ**four-dimensional** ˈ**model**
fourfold ˈfɔː.fəʊld, (US) ˈfɔːr.foʊld
four-footed ˌfɔːˈfʊt.ɪd, (US) ˌfɔːrˈfʊt̬- *stress shift:* ˌ**four-footed** ˈ**beast**
Fourier ˈfʊə.ri.əʳ, ˈfʊr.i-, -eɪ, (US) ˈfʊr.i.eɪ
four-in-hand ˌfɔːʳ.ɪnˈhænd, (US) ˈfɔːr.ɪnˌhænd **-s** -z
four-legged ˌfɔːˈleg.ɪd, -ˈlegd, (US) ˌfɔːr-, ˈfɔːrˌ- *stress shift:* ˌ**four-legged** ˈ**friend**
four-letter ˌfɔːˈlet.əʳ, (US) ˌfɔːrˈlet̬.ɚ *stress shift, see compound:* ˌ**four-letter** ˈ**word**
fourpence ˈfɔː.pᵊnts, (US) ˈfɔːr-
fourpenny ˈfɔː.pᵊn.i, (US) ˈfɔːr-
four-ply ˈfɔː.plaɪ, ˌ-ˈ-, (US) ˈfɔːr.plaɪ, ˌ-ˈ-
four-poster ˌfɔːˈpəʊ.stəʳ, (US) ˌfɔːrˈpoʊ.stɚ **-s** -z *stress shift, see compound:* ˌ**four-poster** ˈ**bed**
fourscore ˌfɔːˈskɔːʳ, (US) ˌfɔːrˈskɔːr *stress shift:* ˌ**fourscore** ˈ**years**
foursome ˈfɔː.səm, (US) ˈfɔːr- **-s** -z
foursquare ˌfɔːˈskweəʳ, ˈ--, (US) ˌfɔːrˈskwer, ˈ--
fourteen ˌfɔːˈtiːn, (US) ˌfɔːr- **-s** -z **-th/s** -θ/s *stress shift:* ˌ**fourteen** ˈ**years**
fourteener fɔːˈtiː.nəʳ, (US) fɔːrˈtiː.nɚ **-s** -z
fourth fɔːθ, (US) fɔːrθ **-s** -s **-ly** -li ˌ**Fourth of Ju**ˈ**ly**
four-wheel drive ˌfɔː.*h*wiːlˈdraɪv, (US) ˌfɔːr- *stress shift, British only:* ˌ**four-wheel drive** ˈ**car**
four-wheeler ˌfɔːˈ*h*wiː.ləʳ, (US) ˌfɔːrˈ*h*wiː.lɚ **-s** -z
fov|ea ˈfɒv|.i.ə, ˈfəʊ.v|i-, (US) ˈfoʊ.v|i- **-eae** -i.iː
Fowey fɔɪ, ˈfəʊ.i, (US) fɔɪ, ˈfoʊ.i
Fowke faʊk, fəʊk, (US) faʊk, foʊk
Fowkes fəʊks, faʊks, (US) foʊks, faʊks
fowl faʊl **-s** -z **-ing** -ɪŋ **-ed** -d **-er/s** -əʳ/z, (US) -ɚ/z ˈ**fowling** ˌ**piece**
Fowler ˈfaʊ.ləʳ, (US) -lɚ
Fowles faʊlz
fox, F~ fɒks, (US) fɑːks **-es** -ɪz **-ing** -ɪŋ **-ed** -t ˌ**fox** ˈ**terrier**
Foxboro' ˈfɒks.bᵊr.ə, (US) ˈfɑːks.bɚ.oʊ
Foxcroft ˈfɒks.krɒft, (US) ˈfɑːks.krɑːft
Foxe fɒks, (US) fɑːks
Foxfield ˈfɒks.fiːld, (US) ˈfɑːks-
foxglove ˈfɒks.glʌv, (US) ˈfɑːks- **-s** -z
foxhole ˈfɒks.həʊl, (US) ˈfɑːks.hoʊl **-s** -z
foxhound ˈfɒks.haʊnd, (US) ˈfɑːks- **-s** -z
fox|hunt ˈfɒks|.hʌnt, (US) ˈfɑːks- **-hunts** -hʌnts **-hunting** -ˌhʌn.tɪŋ, (US) -ˌhʌn.t̬ɪŋ
foxtrot ˈfɒks.trɒt, (US) ˈfɑːks.trɑːt **-s** -s
Foxwell ˈfɒks.wəl, -wel, (US) ˈfɑːks-
fox|y ˈfɒk.s|i, (US) ˈfɑːk- **-ier** -i.əʳ, (US) -i.ɚ **-iest** -i.ɪst, -i.əst **-ily** -ᵊl.i, -ɪ.li **-iness** -ɪ.nəs, -ɪ.nɪs
Foy fɔɪ
foyer ˈfɔɪ.eɪ, -əʳ; ˈfwaɪ.eɪ, (US) ˈfɔɪ.ɚ, -eɪ; (US) fɔɪˈeɪ, fwɑːˈ- **-s** -z
Foyers ˈfɔɪ.əz, (US) -ɚz
Foyle fɔɪl
Fr. (abbrev. for **Father**) ˈfɑː.ðəʳ, (US) -ðɚ
frabjous ˈfræb.dʒəs
fracas *singular:* ˈfræk.ɑː, (US) ˈfreɪ.kəs, ˈfræk.əs; *plural:* ˈfræk.ɑːz, (US) ˈfreɪ.kəs, ˈfræk.əs **-es** *American usage only:* (US) -ɪz
fractal ˈfræk.tᵊl **-s** -z
fraction ˈfræk.ʃᵊn **-s** -z
fractional ˈfræk.ʃᵊn.ᵊl **-ly** -i
fraction|ate ˈfræk.ʃᵊn|.eɪt **-ates** -eɪts **-ating** -eɪ.tɪŋ, (US) -eɪ.t̬ɪŋ **-ated** -eɪ.tɪd, (US) -eɪ.t̬ɪd
fractious ˈfræk.ʃəs **-ly** -li **-ness** -nəs, -nɪs
fract|ure ˈfræk.tʃ|əʳ, (US) -tʃ|ɚ **-ures** -əz, (US) -ɚz **-uring** -ᵊr.ɪŋ **-ured** -əd, (US) -ɚd
fragile ˈfrædʒ.aɪl, (US) ˈfrædʒ.ᵊl **-ly** -li
fragility frəˈdʒɪl.ə.ti, frædʒˈɪl-, -ɪ.ti, (US) frəˈdʒɪl.ə.t̬i
fragment n ˈfræg.mənt **-s** -s
fragmen|t v frægˈmen|t, (US) ˈfræg.men|t, -ˈ- **-ts** -ts **-ting** -tɪŋ, (US) -t̬ɪŋ **-ted** -tɪd, (US) -t̬ɪd
fragmental frægˈmen.tᵊl, (US) -t̬ᵊl
fragmentar|y ˈfræg.mən.tᵊr|.i, -tr|i; frægˈmen-, (US) ˈfræg.mən.ter|.i **-ily** -ᵊl.i, -ɪ.li **-iness** -ɪ.nəs, -ɪ.nɪs
fragmentation ˌfræg.mənˈteɪ.ʃᵊn, -menˈ-
Fragonard ˈfræg.ɒn.ɑːʳ, -ən-, (US) ˌfræg.əˈnɑːr, ˌfrɑː.goʊˈ-
fragranc|e ˈfreɪ.grənts **-es** -ɪz **-ed** -t
fragrant ˈfreɪ.grənt **-ly** -li **-ness** -nəs, -nɪs
frail freɪl **-er** -əʳ, (US) -ɚ **-est** -ɪst, -əst **-ly** -li **-ness** -nəs, -nɪs
frailt|y ˈfreɪl.t|i **-ies** -iz
frambesia, framboesia fræmˈbiː.zi.ə, -ʒə, -ʒi.ə, (US) -ʒə, -ʒi.ə
fram|e, F~ freɪm **-es** -z **-ing** -ɪŋ **-ed** -d **-er/s** -əʳ/z, (US) -ɚ/z
frame-up ˈfreɪm.ʌp **-s** -s
framework ˈfreɪm.wɜːk, (US) -wɝːk **-s** -s
Framingham *in UK:* ˈfreɪ.mɪŋ.əm *in US:* ˈfræm.ɪŋ.hæm
Framley ˈfræm.li
Framlingham ˈfræm.lɪŋ.əm
Framlington ˈfræm.lɪŋ.tən
Frampton ˈfræm*p*.tən
Fran fræn
franc fræŋk **-s** -s
France frɑːnts, (US) frænts
Frances ˈfrɑːn*t*.sɪs, (US) ˈfrænt-
Francesca frænˈtʃes.kə, (US) fræn-, frɑːn-
Franche-Comté ˌfrɑ̃ːn*ʃ*.kɔ̃ː*n*ˈteɪ, (US) -kõʊnˈ-
franchis|e ˈfræn.*t*ʃaɪz **-es** -ɪz **-ing** -ɪŋ **-ed** -d **-er/s** -əʳ/z, (US) -ɚ/z
franchisee ˌfræn.*t*ʃaɪˈziː **-s** -z
Francie ˈfrɑːn*t*.si, (US) ˈfrænt-
Francine frænˈt*ˈ*siːn, ˈ--
Francis ˈfrɑːn*t*.sɪs, (US) ˈfrænt-
Franciscan frænˈsɪs.kən **-s** -z
Francisco frænˈsɪs.kəʊ, (US) -koʊ *in* **San Francisco***:* frənˈsɪs.kəʊ, fræn-, (US) -koʊ
francium ˈfræn*t*.si.əm
Franck frɑ̃ː*ŋ*k, frɑːŋk, fræŋk, (US) frɑ̃ːŋk
Franco ˈfræŋ.kəʊ, (US) -koʊ
Franco-, franco- ˈfræŋ.kə*ʊ*, (US) ˈfræŋ.koʊ, -kə
Note: Prefix. Normally either takes primary or secondary stress on the first syllable, e.g. **francophile** /ˈfræŋ.kə*ʊ*.faɪl/ (US) /-kə-/. Where the prefix is used to mean 'French and ...', it usually carries secondary stress, and the diphthong in the second syllable is only rarely reduced to /ə/, e.g. **Franco-German** /ˌfræŋ.kəʊˈdʒɜː.mən/ (US) /-koʊˈdʒɝː-/.
Franco-German ˌfræŋ.kəʊˈdʒɜː.mən, (US) -koʊˈdʒɝː-
Francois, François ˈfrɑ̃ː*n*.swɑː, -ˈ-, (US) frɑ̃ːn*t*ˈswɑː, frænt*ˈ*-, ˈ-ˌ-
Francoise, Françoise ˈfrɑːn*t*.swɑːz, ˈfrɒnt-, ˈfrænt-, ˌ-ˈ-, (US) ˌfrɑːn*t*ˈswɑːz
francolin ˈfræŋ.kəʊ.lɪn, (US) -koʊ- **-s** -z
Franconi|a fræŋˈkəʊ.ni|.ə, (US) fræŋˈkoʊ-, fræn- **-an** -ən
francophile ˈfræŋ.kə*ʊ*.faɪl, (US) -kə-, -koʊ- **-s** -z
francophobe ˈfræŋ.kə*ʊ*.fəʊb, (US) -kə.foʊb, ˈ-koʊ- **-s** -z
francophone, F~ ˈfræŋ.kə*ʊ*.fəʊn, (US) -kə.foʊn, ˈ-koʊ- **-s** -z
francophonic, F~ ˌfræŋ.kə*ʊ*ˈfɒn.ɪk, (US) -kəˈfɑː.nɪk, -koʊˈ-
frangibility ˌfræn.dʒəˈbɪl.ə.ti, -dʒɪˈ-, -ɪ.ti, (US) -ə.t̬i
frangible ˈfræn.dʒɪ.bᵊl, -dʒə- **-ness** -nəs, -nɪs
frangipani ˌfræn.dʒɪˈpɑː.ni, -ˈpæn.i **-s** -z
franglais ˈfrɑ̃ː*ŋ*.gleɪ, ˈfrɒŋ-, (US) frɑ̃ːnˈgleɪ
frank, F~ fræŋk **-er** -əʳ, (US) -ɚ **-est** -ɪst, -əst **-ly** -li **-ness** -nəs, -nɪs **-s** -s **-ing** -ɪŋ **-ed** -t
Frankau ˈfræŋ.kəʊ, -kaʊ, (US) -kaʊ
Frankenstein ˈfræŋ.kᵊn.staɪn, -kɪn-
Frankfort ˈfræŋk.fət, (US) -fɚt
Frankfurt ˈfræŋk.fɜːt, -fət, (US) -fɝːt, -fɚt
frankfurter, F~ ˈfræŋk.fɜː.təʳ, (US) -fɝː.t̬ɚ **-s** -z

Frankie 'fræŋ.ki

frankincense 'fræŋ.kɪn.sents, -kᵊn-

Frankish 'fræŋ.kɪʃ

Frankland 'fræŋk.lənd

franklin, F~ 'fræŋk.lɪn -s -z

Franklyn 'fræŋk.lɪn

Franks fræŋks

frantic 'fræn.tɪk, (US) -t̬ɪk -ally -ᵊl.i, -li -ness -nəs, -nɪs

Franz *German name:* frænts, frɑːnts *US name:* frænz

frap fræp -s -s -ping -ɪŋ -ped -t

frappé 'fræp.eɪ, (US) -'-

Frascati fræs'kɑː.ti

Fraser 'freɪ.zəʳ, (US) -zɚ

Fraserburgh 'freɪ.zə.bᵊr.ə, -bʌr-, (US) -zɚ.bɚ.ə

Frasier 'freɪ.ʒəʳ, 'freɪ.zi.ə, (US) -ʒɚ

frat fræt -s -s

fraternal frə'tɜː.nᵊl, (US) -'tɝː- -ly -i

fraternit|y frə'tɜː.nə.t|i, -ɪ.t|i, (US) -'tɝː.nə.t̬|i -ies -iz

fraternization, -isa- ˌfræt.ᵊn.aɪ'zeɪ.ʃᵊn, -ɪ'-, (US) -ɚ.nə'-

fraterniz|e, -is|e 'fræt.ə.naɪz, (US) '-ɚ- -es -ɪz -ing -ɪŋ -ed -d -er/s -əʳ/z, (US) -ɚ/z

fratricidal ˌfræt.rɪ'saɪ.dᵊl, ˌfreɪ.trɪ'-, -trə'-, (US) ˌfræt.rə'saɪ-

fratricide 'fræt.rɪ.saɪd, 'freɪ.trɪ-, -trə-, (US) 'fræt.rə- -s -z

Fratton 'fræt.ᵊn

Frau fraʊ

fraud frɔːd, (US) frɑːd, frɔːd -s -z

fraudster 'frɔːd.stəʳ, (US) 'frɑːd.stɚ, 'frɔːd- -s -z

fraudulence 'frɔː.dʒə.lənts, -dʒʊ-, -djə-, -djʊ-, (US) 'frɑː.dʒə-, 'frɔː-, -dju-, -djə-

fraudulent 'frɔː.dʒə.lənt, -dʒʊ-, -djə-, -djʊ-, (US) 'frɑː.dʒə-, 'frɔː-, -djuː-, -djə- -ly -li

fraught frɔːt, (US) frɑːt, frɔːt

fraülein 'frɔɪ.laɪn, 'fraʊ- -s -z

fray freɪ -s -z -ing -ɪŋ -ed -d

Fray Bentos® ˌfreɪ'ben.tɒs, (US) -toʊs

Frayn freɪn

Frazer 'freɪ.zəʳ, (US) -zɚ

Frazier 'freɪ.zi.əʳ, (US) -ʒɚ, -ʒi.ɚ

frazil 'freɪ.zɪl, 'fræz.ɪl, -ᵊl, (US) 'freɪ.zɪl; (US) 'fræz.ᵊl; (US) frə'zɪl, -'ziːl

frazzl|e 'fræz.ᵊl -es -z -ing -ɪŋ, '-lɪŋ -ed -d

freak friːk -s -s -ing -ɪŋ -ed -t

Freake friːk

freakish 'friː.kɪʃ -ly -li -ness -nəs, -nɪs

freak|y 'friː.k|i -ier -i.əʳ, (US) -i.ɚ -iest -i.ɪst, -i.əst -ily -ᵊl.i, -ɪ.li -iness -ɪ.nəs, -ɪ.nɪs

Frean friːn

Frears frɪəz, freəz, (US) frɪrz, frerz

freckl|e 'frek.ᵊl -es -z -ing -ɪŋ, '-lɪŋ -ed -d

Freckleton 'frek.ᵊl.tən

freckly 'frek.ᵊl.i, 'frek.li

Fred fred

Freda 'friː.də

Freddie, Freddy 'fred.i

Freddie Mac ˌfred.i'mæk

Frederic(k) 'fred.ᵊr.ɪk

Frederica ˌfred.ᵊr'iː.kə, (US) -ə'riː-

Fredericksburg 'fred.ᵊr.ɪks.bɜːg, (US) -bɝːg

free, F~ friː -r -əʳ, (US) -ɚ -st -ɪst, -əst -ly -li -s -z -ing -ɪŋ -d -d -r/s -əʳ/z, (US) -ɚ/z **ˌfree 'enterprise; ˌfree 'house; ˌfree 'kick; ˌfree 'market; ˌfree 'ride; ˌfree 'trade; ˌfree 'will; give someone a ˌfree 'hand**

freebas|e 'friː.beɪs -es -ɪz -ing -ɪŋ -ed -t

freebie, freebee 'friː.bi -s -z

freeboard 'friː.bɔːd, (US) -bɔːrd

freebooter 'friːˌbuː.təʳ, (US) -t̬ɚ -s -z

freeborn ˌfriː'bɔːn, (US) -'bɔːrn *stress shift:* **ˌfreeborn 'citizen**

Freeborn 'friː.bɔːn, (US) -bɔːrn

Freeburn 'friː.bɜːn, (US) -bɝːn

freed|man 'friːd|.mæn, -mən -men -men, -mən

freedom 'friː.dəm -s -z **'freedom ˌfighter**

free-fall **v** 'friː.fɔːl, ˌ-'-, (US) 'friː.fɔːl, -fɑːl -ing -ɪŋ -er/s -əʳ/z, (US) -ɚ/z

Freefone® 'friː.fəʊn, (US) -foʊn

free-for-all 'friː.fəʳˌɔːl, ˌ--'-, (US) 'friː.fɚ.ɔːl, -ɑːl

free-form 'friː.fɔːm, (US) -fɔːrm

freegan 'friː.gən -s -z -ism -ɪzᵊm

freehand 'friː.hænd

freehearted ˌfriː'hɑː.tɪd, (US) -'hɑːr.t̬ɪd, '-ˌ-- -ly -li -ness -nəs, -nɪs *stress shift, British only:* **ˌfreehearted 'friend**

freehold 'friː.həʊld, (US) -hoʊld -s -z -er/s -əʳ/z, (US) -ɚ/z

freelanc|e 'friː.lɑːnts, ˌ-'-, (US) 'friː.lænts -es -ɪz -ing -ɪŋ -ed -t -er/s -əʳ/z, (US) -ɚ/z

Freeling 'friː.lɪŋ

freeload 'friː.ləʊd, (US) -loʊd -s -z -ing -ɪŋ -ed -ɪd -er/s -əʳ/z, (US) -ɚ/z

free|man 'friː|.mən, -mæn -men -mən, -men

Freeman *surname:* 'friː.mən

free market **n** ˌfriː'mɑː.kɪt, (US) -'mɑːr-

free-market **adj** 'friːˌmɑː.kɪt, (US) -ˌmɑːr-

freemason 'friːˌmeɪ.sᵊn -s -z

freemasonry 'friːˌmeɪ.sᵊn.ri, ˌfriː'meɪ-

freephone 'friː.fəʊn, (US) -foʊn

Freeport 'friː.pɔːt, (US) -pɔːrt

Freepost® 'friː.pəʊst, (US) -poʊst

free-range ˌfriː'reɪndʒ *stress shift, see compounds:* **ˌfree-range 'chickens; ˌfree-range 'eggs**

Freeserve® 'friː.sɜːv, (US) -sɝːv

freesheet 'friː.ʃiːt -s -s

freesia 'friː.ʒə, -zi.ə, -ʒi.ə, (US) -ʒi.ə, -ʒə -s -z

free-spoken ˌfriː'spəʊ.kᵊn, (US) ˌfriː'spoʊ-, '-ˌ-- *stress shift, British only:* **ˌfree-spoken 'person**

free-standing ˌfriː'stæn.dɪŋ, (US) ˌfriː'stæn.dɪŋ, '-ˌ-- *stress shift, British only:* **ˌfree-standing 'column**

freestone, F~ 'friː.stəʊn, (US) -stoʊn

freestyle 'friː.staɪl

Freeth friːθ

freethinker ˌfriː'θɪŋ.kəʳ, (US) -kɚ, '-ˌ-- -s -z

Freetown 'friː.taʊn

freeware 'friː.weəʳ, (US) 'friː.wer

freeway 'friː.weɪ -s -z

freewheel ˌfriː'hwiːl, (US) 'friː.hwiːl -s -z -ing -ɪŋ -ed -d *stress shift, British only:* **ˌfreewheel 'mechanism**

freewill ˌfriː'wɪl, '--

freez|e friːz -es -ɪz -ing -ɪŋ **froze** frəʊz, (US) froʊz **frozen** 'frəʊ.zᵊn, (US) 'froʊ- **freezer/s** 'friː.zəʳ/z, (US) -zɚ/z **'freeze ˌframe, ˌfreeze 'frame**

freeze|-dry 'friːz|.draɪ -dries -draɪz -drying -ˌdraɪ.ɪŋ -dried -draɪd

Freiburg 'fraɪ.bɜːg, (US) -bɝːg

freight freɪt -s -s -ing -ɪŋ, (US) 'freɪ.t̬ɪŋ -ed -ɪd, (US) 'freɪ.t̬ɪd -age -ɪdʒ, (US) 'freɪ.t̬ɪdʒ **'freight ˌcar**

freighter 'freɪ.təʳ, (US) -t̬ɚ -s -z

freightliner 'freɪtˌlaɪ.nəʳ, (US) -nɚ -s -z

Fremantle 'friː.mæn.tᵊl, (US) -t̬ᵊl

fremitus 'frem.ɪ.təs, (US) -t̬əs

Fremont 'friː.mɒnt, frɪ'mɒnt, (US) 'friː.mɑːnt

French, french frentʃ **ˌFrench 'bean; ˌFrench 'bread; ˌFrench 'dressing; ˌfrench 'fry** (US) **'french ˌfry; ˌFrench 'loaf; ˌFrench Revo'lution; ˌFrench 'stick; ˌFrench 'windows**

frenchi|fy 'fren.tʃɪ|.faɪ, -tʃə- -fies -faɪz -fying -faɪ.ɪŋ -fied -faɪd

French|man 'frentʃ|.mən -men -mən

french-polish ˌfrentʃ'pɒl.ɪʃ, (US) -'pɑː.lɪʃ -es -ɪz -ing -ɪŋ -ed -t -er/s -əʳ/z, (US) -ɚ/z

French|woman 'frentʃ|ˌwʊm.ən -women -ˌwɪm.ɪn

frenetic frə'net.ɪk, frɪ-, fren'et-, (US) frə'net̬- -ally -ᵊl.i, -li

frenz|y 'fren.z|i -ies -iz -ied/ly -id/li

frequen|ce 'friː.kwənt|s -cy -si -cies -siz

frequent **adj** 'friː.kwənt -ly -li -ness -nəs, -nɪs

frequen|t **v** fri'kwen|t, friː-, frə-, (US) friː-; (US) 'friː.kwen|t, -kwən|t -ts -ts -ting -tɪŋ, (US) -t̬ɪŋ -ted -tɪd, (US) -t̬ɪd -ter/s -təʳ/z, (US) -t̬ɚ/z

frequentative fri'kwen.tə.tɪv, friː-, frə-, (US) fri'kwen.t̬ə.t̬ɪv -s -z

Frere frɪəʳ, (US) frer

fresco 'fres.kəʊ, (US) -koʊ -(e)s -z

fresh freʃ -er -əʳ, (US) -ɚ -est -ɪst, -əst -ly -li -ness -nəs, -nɪs

freshen 'freʃ.ᵊn -s -z -ing -ɪŋ -ed -d

fresher 'freʃ.əʳ, (US) -ɚ -s -z

freshet 'freʃ.ɪt, -ət -s -s

fresh|man 'freʃ|.mən -men -mən

freshwater, F~ 'freʃˌwɔː.təʳ, ˌ-'--, (US) 'freʃˌwɑː.t̬ɚ, -ˌwɔː-

Fresno 'frez.nəʊ, (US) -noʊ

fret fret -s -s -ting -ɪŋ, (US) 'fret̬.ɪŋ -ted -ɪd, (US) 'fret̬.ɪd

F

fretboard ˈfret.bɔːd, ˈfrep-, (US) ˈfret.bɔːrd **-s** -z
fretful ˈfret.fəl, -fʊl **-ly** -i **-ness** -nəs, -nɪs
fretsaw ˈfret.sɔː, (US) -sɑː, -sɔː **-s** -z
Fretwell ˈfret.wel, -wəl
fretwork ˈfret.wɜːk, (US) -wɝːk
Freud frɔɪd **-ian** -i.ən ˌ**Freudian** ˈ**slip**
Frew fruː
Frey freɪ
Freya freɪ.ə
Freyberg ˈfraɪ.bɜːg, (US) -bɝːg
Freyer frɪəʳ; ˈfraɪ.əʳ, (US) ˈfraɪ.ɚ, -ɚ; (US) frɪr
Freyja freɪ.ə
Fri. (abbrev. for **Friday**) ˈfraɪ.deɪ, -di
friability ˌfraɪ.əˈbɪl.ə.ti, -ɪ.ti, (US) -ə.t̬i
friable ˈfraɪ.ə.bəl **-ness** -nəs, -nɪs
friar fraɪ.əʳ, (US) fraɪ.ɚ **-s** -z
friar|y ˈfraɪ.ə.r|i **-ies** -iz
fribbl|e ˈfrɪb.əl **-es** -z **-ing** -ɪŋ, ˈ-lɪŋ **-ed** -d
fricandeau ˈfrɪk.ən.dəʊ, -ɑ̃ːn-, (US) ˌfrɪk.ənˈdoʊ, ˈ--- **-s** -z
fricandeaux (alternative plural of **fricandeau**) ˈfrɪk.ən.dəʊ, -ɑ̃ːn-, -dəʊz, (US) ˌfrɪk.ənˈdoʊ, -ˈdoʊz, ˈ---
fricassee ˌfrɪk.əˈsiː, -ˈseɪ, ˈ---, (US) ˌfrɪk.əˈsiː, ˈ--- **-s** -z **-ing** -ɪŋ **-d** -d
fricative ˈfrɪk.ə.tɪv, (US) -t̬ɪv **-s** -z
friction ˈfrɪk.ʃən **-s** -z **-less** -ləs, -les, -lɪs
frictional ˈfrɪk.ʃən.əl
Friday ˈfraɪ.deɪ, -di **-s** -z
fridg|e frɪdʒ **-es** -ɪz ˌ**fridge-**ˈ**freezer**
fried (from **fry**) fraɪd
Frieda ˈfriː.də
Friedan friːˈdæn, ˈ--
Friedland ˈfriːd.lənd, -lænd
Friedman ˈfriːd.mən
Friel friːl
friend, F~ frend **-s** -z
friendless ˈfrend.ləs, -lɪs **-ness** -nəs, -nɪs
friendl|y, F~ ˈfrend.l|i **-ies** -iz **-ier** -i.əʳ, (US) -i.ɚ **-iest** -i.ɪst, -i.əst **-iness** -ɪ.nəs, -ɪ.nɪs
Friendl|y ˈfrend.l|i **-ies** -iz
friendship ˈfrend.ʃɪp **-s** -s
Friern ˈfraɪ.ən, ˈfriː-, (US) -ɚn
fries (from **fry**) fraɪz
Fries friːs, friːz
Friesian ˈfriː.ʒən, ˈ-zi.ən, (US) ˈfriː.ʒən
Friesland ˈfriːz.lənd, -lænd **-er/s** -əʳ/z, (US) -ɚ/z
friez|e, F~ friːz **-es** -ɪz
frig frɪg **-s** -z **-ging** -ɪŋ **-ged** -d
frigate ˈfrɪg.ət, -ɪt **-s** -s
fright fraɪt **-s** -s **-ing** -ɪŋ, (US) ˈfraɪ.t̬ɪŋ **-ed** -ɪd, (US) ˈfraɪ.t̬ɪd
frighten ˈfraɪ.tən **-s** -z **-ing/ly** -ɪŋ/li **-ed** -d **-er/s** -əʳ/z, (US) -ɚ/z
frightful ˈfraɪt.fəl, -fʊl **-ly** -i **-ness** -nəs, -nɪs
frigid ˈfrɪdʒ.ɪd **-ly** -li **-ness** -nəs, -nɪs
Frigidaire® ˌfrɪdʒ.ɪˈdeəʳ, -əˈ-, (US) -ˈder, ˈ--ˌ-
frigidity frɪˈdʒɪd.ə.ti, -ɪ.ti, (US) -ə.t̬i
Friis friːs
frijole friˈhəʊ.leɪ, -i, (US) friːˈhoʊ.liː, -ˈhoʊ, -ˈhoʊl **-s** -z
frill frɪl **-s** -z **-ing** -ɪŋ **-ed** -d
frill|y ˈfrɪl|.i **-ier** -i.əʳ, (US) -i.ɚ **-iest** -i.ɪst, -i.əst **-iness** -ɪ.nəs, -ɪ.nɪs
Frimley ˈfrɪm.li
fring|e frɪndʒ **-es** -ɪz **-ing** -ɪŋ **-ed** -d **-eless** -ləs, -lɪs ˈ**fringe** ˌ**benefit,** ˌ**fringe** ˈ**benefit;** ˌ**fringe** ˈ**theatre/**ˈ**theater**
Frink frɪŋk
Frinton ˈfrɪn.tən
fripper|y ˈfrɪp.ər|.i **-ies** -iz
Frisbee® ˈfrɪz.bi **-s** -z
frisé(e) ˈfriː.zeɪ, (US) friːˈzeɪ, frɪ- **-s** -z
frisette frɪˈzet, friː- **-s** -s
Frisian ˈfrɪz.i.ən, ˈfriː.zi-, -ʒi-, -ʒən, (US) ˈfrɪʒ.ən, ˈfriː.ʒən **-s** -z
frisk frɪsk **-s** -s **-ing** -ɪŋ **-ed** -t **-er/s** -əʳ/z, (US) -ɚ/z
frisk|y ˈfrɪs.k|i **-ier** -i.əʳ, (US) -i.ɚ **-iest** -i.ɪst, -i.əst **-ily** -əl.i, -ɪ.li **-iness** -ɪ.nəs, -ɪ.nɪs
frisson ˈfriː.sɔ̃ːŋ, -ˈ-, (US) friːˈsõʊn **-s** -z
Friston ˈfrɪs.tən
Friswell ˈfrɪz.wəl, -wel
frit frɪt **-s** -s **-ting** -ɪŋ, (US) ˈfrɪt̬.ɪŋ **-ted** -ɪd, (US) ˈfrɪt̬.ɪd
frith, F~ frɪθ **-s** -s
Frithsden ˈfriːz.dən, ˈfrɪz-, ˈfrɪθs.dən
fritillar|y frɪˈtɪl.ər|.i, frə-, (US) ˈfrɪt̬.əl.er|.i **-ies** -iz
Fritos® ˈfriː.təʊz, (US) -t̬oʊz, -toʊz
fritt|er ˈfrɪt|.əʳ, (US) ˈfrɪt̬|.ɚ **-ers** -əz, (US) -ɚz **-ering** -ər.ɪŋ **-ered** -əd, (US) -ɚd
fritz, F~ frɪts
Friuli friˈuː.li
frivol ˈfrɪv.əl **-s** -z **-(l)ing** -ɪŋ **-(l)ed** -d
frivolit|y frɪˈvɒl.ə.t|i, frə-, -ɪ.t|i, (US) -ˈvɑː.lə.t̬|i **-ies** -iz
frivolous ˈfrɪv.əl.əs **-ly** -li **-ness** -nəs, -nɪs
friz(z) frɪz **-es** -ɪz **-ing** -ɪŋ **-ed** -d
Frizelle frɪˈzel
frizzl|e ˈfrɪz.əl **-es** -z **-ing** -ɪŋ, ˈ-lɪŋ **-ed** -d
frizzl|y ˈfrɪz.əl|.i, ˈfrɪz.l|i **-iness** -ɪ.nəs, -ɪ.nɪs
frizz|y ˈfrɪz|.i **-ier** -i.əʳ, (US) -i.ɚ **-iest** -i.ɪst, -i.əst **-iness** -ɪ.nəs, -ɪ.nɪs
fro frəʊ, (US) froʊ
Frobisher ˈfrəʊ.bɪ.ʃəʳ, (US) ˈfroʊ.bɪ.ʃɚ
frock frɒk, (US) frɑːk **-s** -s ˌ**frock** ˈ**coat**
Frodo ˈfrəʊ.dəʊ, (US) ˈfroʊ.doʊ
Frodsham ˈfrɒd.ʃəm, (US) ˈfrɑːd-
Froebel ˈfrəʊ.bəl, ˈfrɜː-, (US) ˈfrɜː-, ˈfroʊ-
frog frɒg, (US) frɑːg, frɔːg **-s** -z **have a** ˈ**frog in one's** ˌ**throat**
Froggatt ˈfrɒg.ɪt, -ət, (US) ˈfrɑː.gɪt, -gət
frogg|y ˈfrɒg|.i, (US) ˈfrɑː.g|i **-ies** -iz
frog|man ˈfrɒg|.mən, (US) ˈfrɑːg-, ˈfrɔːg- **-men** -mən
frogmarch ˈfrɒg.mɑːtʃ, (US) ˈfrɑːg.mɑːrtʃ, ˈfrɔːg- **-es** -ɪz **-ing** -ɪŋ **-ed** -t
Frogmore ˈfrɒg.mɔːʳ, (US) ˈfrɑːg.mɔːr, ˈfrɔːg-
frogspawn ˈfrɒg.spɔːn, (US) ˈfrɑːg.spɑːn, ˈfrɔːg-, -spɔːn
Froissart ˈfrɔɪ.sɑːt, ˈfrwæs.ɑː, (US) -sɑːrt; *as if French:* (US) ˌfrwɑːˈsɑːr
frolic ˈfrɒl.ɪk, (US) ˈfrɑː.lɪk **-s** -s **-king** -ɪŋ **-ked** -t
frolicsome ˈfrɒl.ɪk.səm, (US) ˈfrɑː.lɪk- **-ness** -nəs, -nɪs
from *strong form:* frɒm, (US) frɑːm; *weak forms:* frəm, frm
Note: Weak-form word. The strong **from** /frɒm/ (US) /frɑːm/ is used contrastively (e.g. 'Travelling **to** and **from** London') and in sentence-final position (e.g. 'Where is it from?'). The weak form is /frəm/ (e.g. 'back from abroad' /ˌbæk.frəm.əˈbrɔːd/ (US) /-ˈbrɑːd/). In rapid speech this may be further weakened to /frm/ (e.g. 'one from each' /ˌwʌn.frmˈiːtʃ/).
fromage frais ˌfrɒm.ɑːʒˈfreɪ, (US) frəˌmɑːʒˈ-; (US) ˌfrɑː.mɑːʒˈ-
Frome *in Somerset:* fruːm *lake in Australia:* frəʊm, (US) froʊm

> Note: /frəʊm/ (US) /froʊm/ is suitable in the Edith Wharton novel 'Ethan Frome'.

Fromm frɒm, (US) frɑːm
frond frɒnd, (US) frɑːnd **-s** -z
front frʌnt **-s** -s **-ing** -ɪŋ, (US) ˈfrʌn.t̬ɪŋ **-ed** -ɪd, (US) ˈfrʌn.t̬ɪd ˌ**front** ˈ**line;** ˈ**front** ˌ**matter;** ˈ**front** ˌ**money**
frontag|e ˈfrʌn.tɪdʒ, (US) -t̬ɪdʒ **-es** -ɪz
frontal ˈfrʌn.təl, (US) -t̬əl **-s** -z
frontbench ˌfrʌntˈbentʃ **-er/s** -əʳ/z, (US) -ɚ/z *stress shift:* ˌ**frontbench** ˈ**spokesman**
Frontera® frɒnˈteə.rə, frʌn-, (US) frʌnˈter.ə, frɑːn-
frontier frʌnˈtɪəʳ; ˈ--, ˈfrɒn-, (US) frʌnˈtɪr, frɑːn- **-s** -z
frontiers|man frʌnˈtɪəz|.mən, (US) -ˈtɪrz- **-men** -mən
frontispiec|e ˈfrʌn.tɪs.piːs, -təs-, (US) -t̬ɪs- **-es** -ɪz
frontless ˈfrʌnt.ləs, -lɪs, -les
frontlet ˈfrʌnt.lɪt, -lət **-s** -s
front-load ˌfrʌntˈləʊd, (US) -ˈloʊd, ˈ-- **-s** -z **-ing** -ɪŋ **-ed** -ɪd **-er/s** -əʳ/z, (US) -ɚ/z *stress shift, British only:* ˌ**front-loading** ˈ**drier**
front|man ˈfrʌnt|.mæn **-men** -men
front-of-house ˌfrʌnt.əvˈhaʊs *stress shift:* ˌ**front-of-house** ˈ**manager**
front-page ˌfrʌntˈpeɪdʒ *stress shift, see compound:* ˌ**front-page** ˈ**news**
front-runner ˌfrʌntˈrʌn.əʳ, ˈ-ˌ--, (US) ˌfrʌntˈrʌn.ɚ **-s** -z
frosh frɒʃ, (US) frɑːʃ **-es** -ɪz
frost, F~ frɒst, (US) frɑːst **-s** -s **-ing/s** -ɪŋ/z **-ed** -ɪd

frost|bite ˈfrɒst|.baɪt, ⓤⓢ ˈfrɑːst- **-bitten** -ˌbɪt.ᵊn, ⓤⓢ -ˌbɪt̬.ᵊn
Frosties® ˈfrɒs.tiz, ⓤⓢ ˈfrɑː.stiz
frostwork ˈfrɒst.wɜːk, ⓤⓢ ˈfrɑːst.wɝːk
frost|y ˈfrɒs.t|i, ⓤⓢ ˈfrɑː.st|i **-ier** -i.əʳ, ⓤⓢ -i.ɚ **-iest** -i.ɪst, -i.əst **-ily** -ᵊl.i, -ɪ.li **-iness** -ɪ.nəs, -ɪ.nɪs
froth n frɒθ, ⓤⓢ frɑːθ **-s** -s
fro|th v frɒ|θ, ⓤⓢ frɑː|θ, frɑː|ð **-ths** -θs, ⓤⓢ -θs, -ðz **-thing** -θɪŋ, ⓤⓢ -θɪŋ, -ðɪŋ **-thed** -θt, ⓤⓢ -θt, -ðd
Frothingham ˈfrɒð.ɪŋ.əm, ⓤⓢ ˈfrɑː.ðɪŋ-
froth|y ˈfrɒθ|.i, ⓤⓢ ˈfrɑː.θ|i, -ð|i **-ier** -i.əʳ, ⓤⓢ -i.ɚ **-iest** -i.ɪst, -i.əst **-ily** -ᵊl.i, -ɪ.li **-iness** -ɪ.nəs, -ɪ.nɪs
frottage ˈfrɒt.ɑːʒ, -ɪdʒ; frɒtˈɑːʒ, ⓤⓢ frəˈtɑːʒ, frɑː-
Froud fraʊd, fruːd
Froude fruːd
froufrou ˈfruː.fruː
froward ˈfrəʊ.əd, ⓤⓢ ˈfroʊ.ɚd **-ly** -li **-ness** -nəs, -nɪs
frown fraʊn **-s** -z **-ing/ly** -ɪŋ/li **-ed** -d
frowst fraʊst **-s** -s **-ing** -ɪŋ **-ed** -ɪd
frowst|y ˈfraʊ.st|i **-iness** -ɪ.nəs, -ɪ.nɪs
frows|y, frowz|y ˈfraʊ.z|i **-ier** -i.əʳ, ⓤⓢ -i.ɚ **-iest** -i.ɪst, -i.əst **-iness** -ɪ.nəs, -ɪ.nɪs
froz|e (from **freeze**) frəʊz, ⓤⓢ froʊz **-en** -ᵊn
fructiferous frʌkˈtɪf.ᵊr.əs, ⓤⓢ frʌk-, frʊk-
fructification ˌfrʌk.tɪ.fɪˈkeɪ.ʃᵊn, -fəˈ-, ⓤⓢ ˌfrʌk.tə-, ˌfrʊk-
fructi|fy ˈfrʌk.tɪ|.faɪ, ˈfrʌk.tə-, ˈfrʊk- **-fies** -faɪz **-fying** -faɪ.ɪŋ **-fied** -faɪd
fructose ˈfrʌk.təʊs, ˈfrʊk-, -təʊz, ⓤⓢ -toʊs
frugal ˈfruː.gᵊl **-ly** -i
frugality fruːˈgæl.ə.ti, -ɪ.ti, ⓤⓢ -ə.t̬i
fruit fruːt **-s** -s **-ing** -ɪŋ, ⓤⓢ ˈfruː.t̬ɪŋ **-ed** -ɪd, ⓤⓢ ˈfruː.t̬ɪd ˈ**fruit maˌchine**
fruitarian fruːˈteə.ri.ən, ⓤⓢ -ˈter.i- **-s** -z
fruitcake ˈfruːt.keɪk **-s** -s
fruiterer ˈfruː.tᵊr.əʳ, ⓤⓢ -t̬ɚ.ɚ **-s** -z
fruitful ˈfruːt.fᵊl, -fʊl **-ly** -i **-ness** -nəs, -nɪs
fruition fruˈɪʃ.ᵊn
fruitless ˈfruːt.ləs, -lɪs **-ly** -li **-ness** -nəs, -nɪs
fruit|y ˈfruː.t|i, ⓤⓢ -t̬|i **-ier** -i.əʳ, ⓤⓢ -i.ɚ **-iest** -i.ɪst, -i.əst **-iness** -ɪ.nəs, -ɪ.nɪs
frumenty ˈfruː.mən.ti, ⓤⓢ -t̬i
frump frʌmp **-s** -s **-ish** -ɪʃ
frump|y ˈfrʌm.p|i **-ier** -i.əʳ, ⓤⓢ -i.ɚ **-iest** -i.ɪst, -i.əst **-ily** -ᵊl.i, -ɪ.li **-iness** -ɪ.nəs, -ɪ.nɪs
frustra|te frʌsˈtreɪ|t, ˈ--, ⓤⓢ ˈfrʌs.treɪ|t **-tes** -ts **-ting/ly** -tɪŋ/li, ⓤⓢ -t̬ɪŋ/li **-ted** -tɪd, ⓤⓢ -t̬ɪd
frustration frʌsˈtreɪ.ʃᵊn **-s** -z
frust|um ˈfrʌs.t|əm **-a** -ə **-ums** -əmz
fr|y, F~ fr|aɪ **-ies** -aɪz **-ying** -aɪ.ɪŋ **-ied** -aɪd **-yer** -aɪ.əʳ, ⓤⓢ -aɪ.ɚ ˈ**frying ˌpan; ˌout of the ˌfrying pan ˌinto the ˈfire**
Frye fraɪ
fry-up ˈfraɪ.ʌp **-s** -s
ft (abbrev. for **foot** or **feet**) *singular:* fʊt; *plural:* fiːt
FT ˌefˈtiː
FTSE, FT-SE ˈfʊt.si ˈ**FT-SE ˌIndex**
FT-SE 100 ˌfʊt.si.wʌnˈhʌn.drəd, -drɪd
Fuad fuːˈɑːd, -ˈæd, ⓤⓢ ˈfuː.ɑːd
fuchsia ˈfjuː.ʃə **-s** -z
fuchsine ˈfuːk.siːn, -sɪn, ⓤⓢ ˈfuːk.sɪn, ˈfjuːk-, ˈfʊk-, -siːn
fuck fʌk **-s** -s **-ing** -ɪŋ **-ed** -t **-er/s** -əʳ/z, ⓤⓢ -ɚ/z
fuck-up ˈfʌk.ʌp **-s** -s
fuckwit ˈfʌk.wɪt **-s** -s
fu|cus ˈfjuː|.kəs **-ci** -saɪ **-cuses** -kə.sɪz
fuddl|e ˈfʌd.ᵊl **-es** -z **-ing** -ɪŋ, ˈ-lɪŋ **-ed** -d
fuddy-dudd|y ˈfʌd.iˌdʌd|.i **-ies** -iz
fudg|e fʌdʒ **-es** -ɪz **-ing** -ɪŋ **-ed** -d
Fudge fʌdʒ, fjuːdʒ
fuehrer ˈfjʊə.rə, ˈfjɔː-, ⓤⓢ ˈfjʊr.ɚ
fuel ˈfjuː.əl, fjʊəl, ⓤⓢ ˈfjuː.əl, fjuːl **-s** -z **-(l)ing** -ɪŋ **-(l)ed** -d **add ˌfuel to the ˈfire**
fuel-injected ˌfjuː.əl.ɪnˈdʒek.tɪd, ˌfjʊəl.ɪn-, ˈfjuː.əl.ɪnˌdʒek.tɪd, ˈfjʊəl.ɪn-; ˌfjuː.əl.ɪnˈdʒek-, ˌfjʊəl.ɪnˈ-, ⓤⓢ ˈfjuːəl.ɪnˌdʒek.tɪd
Fuentes ˈfwen.tes, -teɪz
fug fʌg **-s** -z
fugacious fjuːˈgeɪ.ʃəs **-ly** -li **-ness** -nəs, -nɪs
fugacity fjuːˈgæs.ə.ti, -ɪ.ti, ⓤⓢ -ə.t̬i
fugal ˈfjuː.gᵊl
Fugard ˈfjuː.gɑːd, ˈfuː-, ⓤⓢ -gɑːrd
fuggles ˈfʌg.ᵊlz
fugg|y ˈfʌg|.i **-ier** -i.əʳ, ⓤⓢ -i.ɚ **-iest** -i.ɪst, -i.əst **-iness** -ɪ.nəs, -ɪ.nɪs
fugitive ˈfjuː.dʒə.tɪv, -dʒɪ-, ⓤⓢ -t̬ɪv **-s** -z **-ly** -li **-ness** -nəs, -nɪs
fugle|man ˈfjuː.gᵊl|.mæn, -mən **-men** -men, -mən
fugly ˈfʌg.li
fugue fjuːg **-s** -z
führer, F~ ˈfjʊə.rəʳ, ˈfjɔː-, ⓤⓢ ˈfjʊr.ɚ **-s** -z
Fujairah fuːˈdʒaɪə.rə, ⓤⓢ -ˈdʒaɪ-
Fuji ˈfuː.dʒi
Fujian fuːˈdʒɑːn
Fujimori ˌfuː.dʒiˈmɔːr.i
Fuji-san ˈfuː.dʒi.sæn, ⓤⓢ -sɑːn
Fujitsu fuˈdʒɪt.suː, fuː-, ⓤⓢ fuːˈ-, fʊ-
Fujiyama ˌfuː.dʒiˈjɑː.mə
Fukuoka ˌfuː.kuˈəʊ.kə, ⓤⓢ ˌfuː.kuˈoʊ-, ˌfʊk.uːˈ-
-ful fᵊl, fʊl
Note: Two suffixes are covered by this entry, both of which are not stressed. The first forms an adjective, e.g. **beauty** /ˈbjuː.ti/ ⓤⓢ /-t̬i/, **beautiful** /ˈbjuː.tɪ.fᵊl/ ⓤⓢ /-t̬ɪ-/; in this the pronunciation /-fᵊl/ is preferred. The second forms a measuring noun, e.g. **bucket** /ˈbʌk.ɪt/, **bucketful** /ˈbʌk.ɪt.fʊl/, and is normally /-fʊl/.
Fulani fuːˈlɑː.ni, ˈ--- **-s** -z
Fulbright ˈfʊl.braɪt **-s** -s
Fulcher ˈfʊl.tʃəʳ, ⓤⓢ -tʃɚ
fulcr|um ˈfʊl.kr|əm, ˈfʌl- **-a** -ə **-ums** -əmz
fulfil fʊlˈfɪl **-s** -z **-ling** -ɪŋ **-led** -d **-ment** -mənt
fulfill fʊlˈfɪl **-s** -z **-ing** -ɪŋ **-ed** -d **-ment** -mənt
Fulford ˈfʊl.fəd, ⓤⓢ -fɚd
fulgent ˈfʌl.dʒənt **-ly** -li
Fulham ˈfʊl.əm
fuliginous fjuːˈlɪdʒ.ɪ.nəs **-ly** -li
Fulke fʊlk
full fʊl **-er** -əʳ, ⓤⓢ -ɚ **-est** -ɪst, -əst **-ness** -nəs, -nɪs **ˌfull ˈboard; ˌfull ˈface; ˌfull ˈmoon; ˌfull ˈstop**
fullback ˈfʊl.bæk, ˌ-ˈ-, ⓤⓢ ˈ-- **-s** -s
full-blooded ˌfʊlˈblʌd.ɪd *stress shift:* **ˌfull-blooded ˈmale**
full-blown ˌfʊlˈbləʊn, ⓤⓢ -ˈbloʊn *stress shift:* **ˌfull-blown ˈargument**
full-bodied ˌfʊlˈbɒd.id, ⓤⓢ -ˈbɑː.did *stress shift:* **ˌfull-bodied ˈwine**
fuller, F~ ˈfʊl.əʳ, ⓤⓢ -ɚ **-s** -z
Fullerton ˈfʊl.ə.tᵊn, ⓤⓢ -ɚ-
full-face ˌfʊlˈfeɪs *stress shift:* **ˌfull-face ˈphotograph**
full-fledged ˌfʊlˈfledʒd *stress shift:* **ˌfull-fledged ˈbird**
full-frontal ˌfʊlˈfrʌn.tᵊl, ⓤⓢ -t̬ᵊl
full-grown ˌfʊlˈgrəʊn, ⓤⓢ -ˈgroʊn *stress shift:* **ˌfull-grown ˈman**
full-length ˌfʊlˈleŋkθ *stress shift:* **ˌfull-length ˈcoat**
full-on ˌfʊlˈɒn, ⓤⓢ -ɑːn, -ɔːn *stress shift:* **ˌfull-on ˈtreatment**
full-scale ˌfʊlˈskeɪl *stress shift:* **ˌfull-scale ˈwar**
full-time ˌfʊlˈtaɪm *stress shift:* **ˌfull-time ˈmother**
fully ˈfʊl.i
-fully fᵊl.i, fʊl.i
Note: Suffix. Words containing **-fully** are stressed in a similar way to adjectives containing **-ful**; see above.
fully-fledged ˌfʊl.iˈfledʒd *stress shift:* **ˌfully-fledged ˈbird**
fulmar ˈfʊl.məʳ, -mɑːʳ, ⓤⓢ -mɚ, -mɑːr **-s** -z
Fulmer ˈfʊl.məʳ, ⓤⓢ -mɚ
fulmi|nate ˈfʊl.mɪ|.neɪt, ˈfʌl-, -mə- **-nates** -neɪts **-nating** -neɪ.tɪŋ, ⓤⓢ -neɪ.t̬ɪŋ **-nated** -neɪ.tɪd, ⓤⓢ -neɪ.t̬ɪd
fulmination ˌfʊl.mɪˈneɪ.ʃᵊn, ˌfʌl-, -məˈ- **-s** -z
fulness ˈfʊl.nəs, -nɪs
fulsome ˈfʊl.səm **-ly** -li **-ness** -nəs, -nɪs
Fulton ˈfʊl.tᵊn
Fulvia ˈfʊl.vi.ə, ˈfʌl-
fulvous ˈfʌl.vəs, ˈfʊl-
Fulwood ˈfʊl.wʊd
Fu Manchu ˌfuː.mænˈtʃuː
fumbl|e ˈfʌm.bᵊl **-es** -z **-ing** -ɪŋ, ˈ-blɪŋ **-ed** -d **-er/s** -əʳ/z, ˈ-bləʳ/z, ⓤⓢ ˈ-bᵊl.ɚ/z, ˈ-blɚ/z
fum|e fjuːm **-es** -z **-ing** -ɪŋ **-ed** -d
fumi|gate ˈfjuː.mɪ|.geɪt, -mə-

F

-gates -geɪts -gating -geɪ.tɪŋ, US -geɪ.t̬ɪŋ -gated -geɪ.tɪd, US -geɪ.t̬ɪd -gator/s -geɪ.təʳ/z, US -geɪ.t̬ɚ/z
fumigation ˌfjuː.mɪˈgeɪ.ʃᵊn, -məˈ- -s -z
Fumo ˈfuː.məʊ, US -moʊ
fun fʌn
Funafuti ˌfuː.nəˈfuː.ti
funambulist fjuːˈnæm.bjə.lɪst, fjʊ-, -bjʊ-, US fjuːˈnæm.bjə-, -bjuː- -s -s
Funchal fʊnˈʃɑːl, -ˈtʃɑːl
function ˈfʌŋk.ʃᵊn -s -z -ing -ɪŋ -ed -d
functional ˈfʌŋk.ʃᵊn.ᵊl -ly -i
functional|ism ˈfʌŋk.ʃᵊn.ᵊl|.ɪ.zᵊm -ist/s -ɪst/s
functionality ˌfʌŋk.ʃᵊnˈæl.ə.ti, -ɪ.ti, US -ə.t̬i
functionar|y ˈfʌŋk.ʃᵊn.ᵊr.|i, -r|i, US -er|.i -ies -iz
functor ˈfʌŋk.təʳ, -tɔːʳ, US -tɚ, -tɔːr -s -z
fund fʌnd -s -z -ing -ɪŋ -ed -ɪd
fundament ˈfʌn.də.mənt -s -s
fundamental ˌfʌn.dəˈmen.tᵊl, US -t̬ᵊl -s -z -ly -i
fundamental|ism, F~ ˌfʌn.dəˈmen.tᵊl|.ɪ.zᵊm, US -t̬ᵊl- -ist/s -ɪst/s
fundamentality ˌfʌn.də.menˈtæl.ə.ti, -ɪ.ti, US -ə.t̬i
fundless ˈfʌnd.ləs, -lɪs, -les
fundrais|er ˈfʌndˌreɪ.z|əʳ, US -z|ɚ -er/s -əz, US -ɚz -ing -ɪŋ
Fundy ˈfʌn.di
funeral ˈfjuː.nᵊr.əl -s -z ˈ**funeral** ˌ**home**; ˈ**funeral** ˌ**parlo(u)r**
funerary ˈfjuː.nᵊr.ə.ri, US -er.i
funereal fjuːˈnɪə.ri.əl, US -ˈnɪr.i- -ly -i
funfair ˈfʌn.feəʳ, US -fer -s -z
fungal ˈfʌŋ.gᵊl
fungible ˈfʌn.dʒɪ.bᵊl, -dʒə- -s -z
fungicidal ˌfʌŋ.gɪˈsaɪ.dᵊl, ˌfʌn.dʒɪˈ-, US ˌfʌn.dʒɪˈ-, ˌfʌŋ.gəˈ- -li -i
fungicide ˈfʌŋ.gɪ.saɪd, ˈfʌn.dʒɪ-, US ˈfʌn.dʒɪ-, ˈfʌŋ.gə- -s -z
fungo ˈfʌŋ.gəʊ, US -goʊ -es -z
fun|gus ˈfʌŋ.|gəs -gi -gaɪ, -giː, ˈfʌn.dʒiː, -dʒaɪ -guses -gə.sɪz -goid -gɔɪd -gous -gəs
funicle ˈfjuː.nɪ.kᵊl -s -z
funicular fjuːˈnɪk.jə.ləʳ, fə-, -jʊ-, US -juː.lɚ -s -z
funicul|us fjuːˈnɪk.jə.l|əs, fə-, -jʊ-, US -juː- -i -aɪ
funk, F~ fʌŋk -s -s -ing -ɪŋ -ed -t
funk|y ˈfʌŋ.k|i -ier -i.əʳ, US -i.ɚ -iest -i.ɪst, -i.əst -ily -ᵊl.i, -ɪ.li -iness -ɪ.nəs, -ɪ.nɪs
funnel ˈfʌn.ᵊl -s -z -(l)ing -ɪŋ -(l)ed -d
funnel-web ˈfʌn.ᵊl.web -s -z
funnies ˈfʌn.iz
funn|y ˈfʌn|.i -ier -i.əʳ, US -i.ɚ -iest -i.ɪst, -i.əst -ily -ᵊl.i, -ɪ.li -iness -ɪ.nəs, -ɪ.nɪs ˈ**funny** ˌ**bone**; ˈ**funny** ˌ**business**
funny|man ˈfʌn.i|.mæn -men -men
fur fɜːʳ, US fɝː -s -z -ring -ɪŋ -red -d
fur (abbrev. for **furlong**) ˈfɜː.lɒŋ, US ˈfɝː.lɑːŋ, -lɔːŋ
Furbear ˈfɜː.beəʳ, US ˈfɝː.ber
furbelow ˈfɜː.bɪ.ləʊ, -bə-, US ˈfɝː.bɪ.loʊ, -bə- -s -z
furbish ˈfɜː.bɪʃ, US ˈfɝː- -es -ɪz -ing -ɪŋ -ed -t
furcate adj ˈfɜː.keɪt, -kɪt, -kət, US ˈfɝː-
fur|cate v ˈfɜː|.keɪt, -|ˈ-, US ˈfɝː|.keɪt -cates -keɪts, -ˈkeɪts, US -keɪts -cating -keɪ.tɪŋ, -ˈkeɪ-, US -keɪ.t̬ɪŋ -cated -keɪ.tɪd, -ˈkeɪ-, US -keɪ.t̬ɪd
furcation fɜːˈkeɪ.ʃᵊn, US fɝː- -s -z
furibund ˈfjʊə.rɪ.bʌnd, ˈfjɔː-, -bənd, US ˈfjʊr.ɪ-
furioso ˌfjʊə.riˈəʊ.zəʊ, ˌfjɔː-, -səʊ, US ˌfjʊr.iˈoʊ.soʊ, ˌfjɝː-, -zoʊ
furious ˈfjʊə.ri.əs, ˈfjɔː-, US ˈfjʊr.i-, ˈfjɝː- -ly -li
furl fɜːl, US fɝːl -s -z -ing -ɪŋ -ed -d
furlong ˈfɜː.lɒŋ, US ˈfɝː.lɑːŋ, -lɔːŋ -s -z
furlough ˈfɜː.ləʊ, US ˈfɝː.loʊ -s -z
furnac|e ˈfɜː.nɪs, -nəs, US ˈfɝː- -es -ɪz
Furneaux ˈfɜː.nəʊ, US fɝːˈnoʊ
Furness ˈfɜː.nɪs, fɜːˈnes, US ˈfɝː.nɪs, fɝːˈnes
Furneux ˈfɜː.nɪks, -nəʊ, US ˈfɝː.nɪks, -nuː, -noʊ

> Note: /ˈfɜː.nɪks/ is the more usual local pronunciation.

furnish ˈfɜː.nɪʃ, US ˈfɝː- -es -ɪz -ing/s -ɪŋ/z -ed -t -er/s -əʳ/z, US -ɚ/z
furniture ˈfɜː.nɪ.tʃəʳ, US ˈfɝː.nɪ.tʃɚ
Furnival(l) ˈfɜː.nɪ.vᵊl, US ˈfɝː-
furor ˈfjʊər.ɔː, US ˈfjʊr.ɔːr, -ɚ
furore fjʊəˈrɔː.ri, -reɪ; ˈfjʊə.rɔːʳ, ˈfjɔː-, US ˈfjʊr.ɔːr, -ɚ -s -z
furph|y, F~ ˈfɜː.f|i, US ˈfɝː- -ies -iz
furrier ˈfʌr.i.əʳ, US ˈfɝː.i.ɚ -s -z
furrier|y ˈfʌr.i.ᵊr|.i, US ˈfɝː- -ies -iz
furrow ˈfʌr.əʊ, US ˈfɝː.oʊ -s -z -ing -ɪŋ -ed -d
furr|y ˈfɜː.r|i, US ˈfɝː|.i -ier -i.əʳ, US -i.ɚ -iest -i.ɪst, -i.əst -iness -ɪ.nəs, -ɪ.nɪs
furth|er ˈfɜː.ð|əʳ, US ˈfɝː.ð|ɚ -ers -əz, US -ɚz -ering -ᵊr.ɪŋ -ered -əd, US -ɚd -erer/s -ᵊr.əʳ/z, US -ɚ.ɚ/z ˌ**further eduˈcation**
furtherance ˈfɜː.ðᵊr.ᵊnts, US ˈfɝː-
furthermore ˌfɜː.ðəˈmɔːʳ, ˈ---, US ˈfɝː.ðɚ.mɔːr
furthermost ˈfɜː.ðə.məʊst, US ˈfɝː.ðɚ.moʊst
furthest ˈfɜː.ðɪst, -ðəst, US ˈfɝː-
furtive ˈfɜː.tɪv, US ˈfɝː.t̬ɪv -ly -li -ness -nəs, -nɪs
furuncle ˈfjʊə.rʌŋ.kᵊl, ˈfjɔː-, US ˈfjʊr.ʌŋ- -s -z
fur|y, F~ ˈfjʊə.r|i, ˈfjɔː-, US ˈfjʊr|.i -ies -iz
furze fɜːz, US fɝːz
fus|e fjuːz -es -ɪz -ing -ɪŋ -ed -d ˈ**fuse** ˌ**box**
fusee fjuːˈziː, US fjuːˈziː, ˈ-- -s -z
fusel ˈfjuː.zᵊl, US ˈfjuː.zᵊl, -sᵊl ˈ**fusel** ˌ**oil**; ˌ**fusel** ˈ**oil**
fuselag|e ˈfjuː.zᵊl.ɑːʒ, -zɪ.lɑːʒ, US -sə.lɑːʒ, -zə-, -lɑːdʒ -es -ɪz
fusibility ˌfjuː.zəˈbɪl.ə.ti, -zɪˈ-, -ɪ.ti, US -ə.t̬i
fusible ˈfjuː.zɪ.bᵊl, -zə-
fusil ˈfjuː.zɪl, US -zɪl, -sɪl -s -z
fusile ˈfjuː.saɪl, -zaɪl, US -zᵊl, -zaɪl, -sɪl
fusilier ˌfjuː.zᵊlˈɪəʳ, -zɪˈlɪəʳ, US -zɪˈlɪr -s -z
fusillade ˌfjuː.zəˈleɪd, -zɪˈ-, US ˌfjuː.səˈlɑːd, -zəˈ-, -ˈleɪd, ˈ--- -s -z
fusilli fʊˈsiː.li, fjʊˈzɪl.i, US ˈfjuː.siː.li, -zə-
fusion ˈfjuː.ʒᵊn -s -z
fuss fʌs -es -ɪz -ing -ɪŋ -ed -t -er/s -əʳ/z, US -ɚ/z
fussbudget ˈfʌsˌbʌdʒ.ɪt -s -s
fusspot ˈfʌs.pɒt, US -pɑːt -s -s
fuss|y ˈfʌs|.i -ier -i.əʳ, US -i.ɚ -iest -i.ɪst, -i.əst -ily -ᵊl.i, -ɪ.li -iness -ɪ.nəs, -ɪ.nɪs
fustian ˈfʌs.ti.ən, US -tʃᵊn
fustic ˈfʌs.tɪk
fusti|gate ˈfʌs.tɪ|.geɪt, -tə- -gates -geɪts -gating -geɪ.tɪŋ, US -geɪ.t̬ɪŋ -gated -geɪ.tɪd, US -geɪ.t̬ɪd
fustigation ˌfʌs.tɪˈgeɪ.ʃᵊn, -təˈ- -s -z
fust|y ˈfʌs.t|i -ier -i.əʳ, US -i.ɚ -iest -i.ɪst, -i.əst -ily -ᵊl.i, -ɪ.li -iness -ɪ.nəs, -ɪ.nɪs
futhark ˈfuː.θɑːk, US -θɑːrk
futile ˈfjuː.taɪl, US -t̬əl, -taɪl -ly -li -ness -nəs, -nɪs
futilit|y fjuːˈtɪl.ə.t|i, -ɪ.t|i, US -ə.t̬|i -ies -iz
futon ˈfuː.tɒn, ˈfjuː-, ˈfʊt.ɒn, -ᵊn; ˌfuːˈtɒn, US ˈfuː.tɑːn -s -z
futtock ˈfʌt.ək, US ˈfʌt̬- -s -s
future ˈfjuː.tʃəʳ, US -tʃɚ -s -z
futur|ism ˈfjuː.tʃᵊr|.ɪ.zᵊm -ist/s -ɪst/s
futuristic ˌfjuː.tʃəˈrɪs.tɪk -ally -ᵊl.i, -li
futurit|y fjuːˈtʃʊə.rə.t|i, -ˈtjɔː-, -ˈtjʊə-, -ˈtʃɔː-, -ˈtjɔː-, -ɪ.t|i, US fjuːˈtʊr.ə.t̬|i, -ˈtjʊr-, -ˈtʃɝː- -ies -iz
futurolog|ist ˌfjuː.tʃəˈrɒl.ə.dʒ|ɪst, US -ˈrɑː.lə- -ists -ɪsts -y -i
fuz|e fjuːz -es -ɪz -ing -ɪŋ -ed -d
fuzee fjuːˈziː, US fjuːˈziː, ˈ-- -s -z
Fuzhou ˌfuːˈdʒəʊ, US -ˈdʒoʊ
fuzz fʌz -es -ɪz -ing -ɪŋ -ed -d
fuzz|y ˈfʌz|.i -ier -i.əʳ, US -i.ɚ -iest -i.ɪst, -i.əst -ily -ᵊl.i, -ɪ.li -iness -ɪ.nəs, -ɪ.nɪs
fuzzy-wuzz|y ˈfʌz.iˌwʌz|.i, ˌ--ˈ-- -ies -iz
f-word ˈefˌwɜːd, US -ˌwɝːd
Fyf(f)e faɪf
Fyfield ˈfaɪ.fiːld
Fylingdales ˈfaɪ.lɪŋ.deɪlz
Fyne faɪn

G

Pronouncing the letter G

→ *See also* **GG, GH, GU, NG**

There are two main pronunciations for the consonant letter **g**: /dʒ/ and /g/, e.g.:

gem	dʒem
age	eɪdʒ
geese	giːs
gig	gɪg

A following vowel letter **e**, **i**, or **y** may lead to the pronunciation /dʒ/. However, as can be seen in the above examples, this is not reliable as an indicator of which pronunciation to use. More reliably, before vowel letters **a**, **o**, or **u** the pronunciation is highly likely to be /g/, although there are exceptions, e.g.:

gaol	dʒeɪl

In addition

g is often silent before a consonant letter **m** or **n** at the beginning and end of words, e.g.:

gnat	næt
paradigm	ˈpær.ə.daɪm

G

g, G dʒiː -ˈs -z
g (abbrev. for **gram/s**) *singular:* græm; *plural:* -z
Ga. (abbrev. for **Georgia**) ˈdʒɔː.dʒə, Ⓤⓢ ˈdʒɔːr-
gab gæb **-s** -z **-bing** -ɪŋ **-bed** -d
gabardine ˌgæb.əˈdiːn, ˈ---, Ⓤⓢ ˈgæb.ɚ.diːn, ˌ--ˈ- **-s** -z
Gabbatha ˈgæb.ə.θə
gabbl|e ˈgæb.əl **-es** -z **-ing** -ɪŋ, ˈ-lɪŋ **-ed** -d **-er/s** -əʳ/z, ˈ-ləʳ/z, Ⓤⓢ ˈ-əl.ɚ/z, ˈ-lɚ/z
gabbro ˈgæb.rəʊ, Ⓤⓢ -roʊ **-s** -z
gabb|y ˈgæb|.i **-ier** -i.əʳ, Ⓤⓢ -i.ɚ **-iest** -i.ɪst, -i.əst
gaberdine ˌgæb.əˈdiːn, ˈ---, Ⓤⓢ ˈgæb.ɚ.diːn, ˌ--ˈ- **-s** -z
gaberlunzie ˌgæb.əˈlʌn.zi, -ˈluː.nji, ˈgæb.ə.lʌn.zi, -luː.nji, Ⓤⓢ ˌgæb.ɚˈlʌn.zi **-s** -z
gabfest ˈgæbˌfest **-s** -s
Gabii ˈgæb.i.iː, -bi.aɪ, Ⓤⓢ ˈgæb.i.aɪ, ˈgeɪ.bi-
gabion ˈgeɪ.bi.ən **-s** -z
gable, G~ ˈgeɪ.bəl **-s** -z **-d** -d
gablet ˈgeɪ.blɪt, -blət, Ⓤⓢ -blət **-s** -s
Gabon gæbˈɒn, gəˈbɒn; ˈgæb.ɒn; *as if French:* gæbˈɔ̃ːŋ; Ⓤⓢ gæbˈoʊn, gəˈboʊn
Gabonese ˌgæb.ɒnˈiːz, -əˈniːz, Ⓤⓢ -əˈniːz
Gaboon gəˈbuːn
Gabor gəˈbɔːʳ; ˈgɑː.bɔːʳ, Ⓤⓢ gəˈbɔːr; Ⓤⓢ ˈgɑː.bɔːr
Gaborone ˌgæb.əˈrəʊ.ni, Ⓤⓢ ˌgɑː.bəˈroʊ.neɪ, -ni
Gabriel ˈgeɪ.bri.əl
Gabriella ˌgæb.riˈel.ə, ˌgeɪ.briˈ-
Gabrielle ˌgæb.riˈel, ˌgeɪ.briˈ-
gab|y ˈgeɪ.b|i **-ies** -iz
Gaby ˈgæb.i, ˈgɑː.bi
gad, G~ gæd **-s** -z **-ding** -ɪŋ **-ded** -ɪd
gadabout ˈgæd.ə.baʊt **-s** -s
Gadafy, Gadaffi gəˈdæf.i, -ˈdɑː.fi, Ⓤⓢ -ˈdɑː.fi
Gadara ˈgæd.ər.ə
Gadarene ˈgæd.ə.riːn **-s** -z
Gaddafi gəˈdæf.i, -ˈdɑː.fi, Ⓤⓢ -ˈdɑː.fi
Gaddesden ˈgædz.dən
Gaddis ˈgæd.ɪs
Gade *English river:* geɪd *Danish composer:* ˈgɑː.də
Gades ˈgeɪ.diːz
gadfl|y ˈgæd.fl|aɪ **-ies** -aɪz
gadget ˈgædʒ.ɪt, -ət **-s** -s
gadgetry ˈgædʒ.ə.tri, ˈ-ɪ-
Gadhafi gəˈdæf.i, -ˈdɑː.fi, Ⓤⓢ -ˈdɑː.fi
Gadhel ˈgæd.el, Ⓤⓢ -əl **-s** -z
Gadhelic gædˈel.ɪk, gəˈdel-
gadolinium ˌgæd.əʊˈlɪn.i.əm, -əlˈɪn-, Ⓤⓢ -oʊˈlɪn-, gædˈlɪn-
gadroon gəˈdruːn **-s** -z
Gadsby ˈgædz.bi
Gadsden ˈgædz.dən
Gadshill ˈgædz.hɪl
gadwall ˈgæd.wɔːl, Ⓤⓢ -wɔːl **-s** -z
gadzooks ˌgædˈzuːks, gæd-, Ⓤⓢ -ˈzuːks, -ˈzʊks
Gael geɪl **-s** -z
Gaelic ˈgeɪ.lɪk, ˈgæl.ɪk

> Note: The name of the Gaelic language of Ireland is usually pronounced /ˈgeɪ.lɪk/, while that of the corresponding language of Scotland is pronounced /ˈgæl.ɪk/. 'Gaelic football' is usually /ˈgeɪ.lɪk/.

Gaeltacht ˈgeɪl.tæxt, -təxt
gaff gæf **-s** -s **-ing** -ɪŋ **-ed** -t
gaffe gæf **-s** -s
gaffer ˈgæf.əʳ, Ⓤⓢ -ɚ **-s** -z
gag gæg **-s** -z **-ging** -ɪŋ **-ged** -d
gaga ˈgɑː.gɑː, ˈgæg.ɑː, Ⓤⓢ ˈgɑː.gɑː **-s** -z
Gagarin gəˈgɑː.rɪn, gægˈɑː-, Ⓤⓢ gəˈgɑːr.ɪn
gag|e, G~ geɪdʒ **-es** -ɪz **-ing** -ɪŋ **-ed** -d
gaggle ˈgæg.əl **-s** -z
Gaia ˈgaɪ.ə, ˈgeɪ-
gaiet|y, G~ ˈgeɪ.ə.t|i, -ɪ.t|i, Ⓤⓢ -ə.t̬|i **-ies** -iz
Gail ˈgeɪl
gaily (from **gay**) ˈgeɪ.li
gain geɪn **-s** -z **-ing/s** -ɪŋ/z **-ed** -d **-er/s** -əʳ/z, Ⓤⓢ -ɚ/z
Gaines geɪnz
Gainesville ˈgeɪnz.vɪl, Ⓤⓢ -vɪl, -vəl
gainful ˈgeɪn.fəl, -fʊl **-ly** -i **-ness** -nəs, -nɪs
gain|say ˌgeɪn|ˈseɪ **-says** -ˈseɪz, -ˈsez **-saying** -ˈseɪ.ɪŋ **-sayed** -ˈseɪd **-said** -ˈsed, -ˈseɪd **-sayer/s** -ˈseɪ.əʳ/z, Ⓤⓢ -ˈseɪ.ɚ/z
Gainsborough ˈgeɪnz.bər.ə, Ⓤⓢ -bɚ.oʊ, -ə **-s** -z
Gairdner ˈgeəd.nəʳ, ˈgɑːd-, Ⓤⓢ ˈgerd.nɚ, ˈgɑːrd-
Gairloch ˈgeə.lɒx, -lɒk, Ⓤⓢ ˈger.lɑːk
Gaisford ˈgeɪs.fəd, Ⓤⓢ -fɚd
gait geɪt **-s** -s
gaiter ˈgeɪ.təʳ, Ⓤⓢ -t̬ɚ **-s** -z
Gaitskell ˈgeɪt.skəl, -skɪl
Gaius ˈgaɪ.əs, Ⓤⓢ ˈgaɪ-, ˈgeɪ-
gal *girl:* gæl **-s** -z
gal (abbrev. for **gallon**) ˈgæl.ən
gala *special occasion:* ˈgɑː.lə, ˈgeɪ-, Ⓤⓢ ˈgeɪ-, ˈgæl.ə, ˈgɑː.lə **-s** -z
Gala *river:* ˈgɑː.lə, Ⓤⓢ ˈgɑː.lə, ˈgæl.ə
galactic gəˈlæk.tɪk **-ally** -əl.i, -li
galacto- gəˈlæk.təʊ, Ⓤⓢ ˈ-tə, ˈ-toʊ
galactose gəˈlæk.təʊs, -təʊz, Ⓤⓢ -toʊs
galah gəˈlɑː **-s** -z
Galahad ˈgæl.ə.hæd
galantine ˈgæl.ən.tiːn, ˌ--ˈ- **-s** -z
Galapagos gəˈlæp.ə.gəs, -gɒs, Ⓤⓢ gəˈlɑː.pə.goʊs, -gəz
Galashiels ˌgæl.əˈʃiːlz *stress shift:* ˌGalashiels ˈstreets
Galata ˈgæl.ə.tə, Ⓤⓢ -t̬ə
Galatasaray ˌgæl.əˈtæs.ə.raɪ
Galatea ˌgæl.əˈti.ə
Galatia gəˈleɪ.ʃə, -ʃi.ə, ˌgæl.əˈti.ə
Galatian gəˈleɪ.ʃən, -ʃi.ən, ˌgæl.əˈti.ən **-s** -z
galax|y ˈgæl.ək.s|i **-ies** -iz
Galba ˈgæl.bə
galbanum ˈgæl.bə.nəm
Galbraith gælˈbreɪθ, Ⓤⓢ ˈ--
gale, G~ geɪl **-s** -z
Galen ˈgeɪ.lən, -lɪn

galena, G~ gəˈliː.nə
Galenic gəˈlen.ɪk, geɪ-, -ˈliː.nɪk **-al** -əl
Galerius gəˈlɪə.ri.əs, (US) -ˈlɪr.i-
Galesburg ˈgeɪlz.bɜːg, (US) -bɝːg
Galic|ia gəˈlɪs|.i.ə, gælˈɪs-, -ˈɪʃ|.ə, -ˈɪʃ|.i.ə, (US) gəˈlɪʃ|.ə **-ian/s** -i.ən/z, (US) -ən/z, -i.ən/z
Galilean ˌgæl.ɪˈliː.ən, -əˈ-, (US) -əˈ- **-s** -z
Galilee ˈgæl.ɪ.liː, ˈ-ə-, (US) ˈ-ə-
Galileo ˌgæl.ɪˈleɪ.əʊ, -əˈ-, -ˈliː.əʊ, (US) -əˈleɪ.oʊ, -ˈliː-
galingale ˈgæl.ɪŋ.geɪl
Galion ˈgæl.i.ən, (US) ˈgæl.jən
galipot ˈgæl.ɪ.pɒt, (US) -pɑːt
gall gɔːl, (US) gɔːl, gɑːl **-s** -z **-ing** -ɪŋ **-ed** -d **ˈgall ˌbladder**
Gallacher ˈgæl.ə.həʳ, -xəʳ, (US) -hɚ
Gallagher ˈgæl.ə.həʳ, -xəʳ, (US) -gɚ, -hɚ
Gallaher ˈgæl.ə.həʳ, -xəʳ, (US) -hɚ
gallant n ˈgæl.ənt **-s** -s
gallant adj *brave:* ˈgæl.ənt *attentive to women:* ˈgæl.ənt; (US) gəˈlænt, -ˈlɑːnt **-ly** gəˈlænt, (US) ˈgæl.ənt **-ness** -nəs, -nɪs
Gallant gəˈlɑ̃ːŋ
gallantr|y ˈgæl.ən.tr|i **-ies** -iz
Gallatin ˈgæl.ə.tɪn
Gallaudet ˌgæl.əˈdet *stress shift:* **ˌGallaudet ˈCollege**
Galle *port in Sri Lanka:* gɑːl, (US) gɑːl, gæl *German astronomer:* ˈgæl.ə
galleon ˈgæl.i.ən, (US) -i.ən, ˈ-jən **-s** -z
galler|y ˈgæl.ər|.i **-ies** -iz **-ied** -id
galley ˈgæl.i **-s** -z **ˈgalley ˌproof; ˈgalley ˌslave**
gallfl|y ˈgɔːl.fl|aɪ, (US) ˈgɔːl-, ˈgɑːl- **-ies** -aɪz
Gallia ˈgæl.i.ə
galliambic ˌgæl.iˈæm.bɪk **-s** -s
galliard ˈgæl.i.ɑːd, -əd, (US) ˈ-jɚd **-s** -z
gallic, G~ ˈgæl.ɪk
Gallican ˈgæl.ɪ.kən **-s** -z
gallice ˈgæl.ɪ.siː, -si
gallicism ˈgæl.ɪ.sɪ.zəm, ˈ-ə-, (US) ˈ-ə- **-s** -z
gallic|ize, -is|e ˈgæl.ɪ.saɪz, ˈ-ə-, (US) ˈ-ə- **-es** -ɪz **-ing** -ɪŋ **-ed** -d
gallimaufr|y ˌgæl.ɪˈmɔː.fr|i, -əˈ-, (US) -əˈmɑː-, -ˈmɔː- **-ies** -iz
gallinaceous ˌgæl.ɪˈneɪ.ʃəs, -əˈ-, (US) -əˈ-
Gallio ˈgæl.i.əʊ, (US) -oʊ
galliot ˈgæl.i.ət **-s** -s
Gallipoli gəˈlɪp.əl.i, gæˈlɪp-
Gallipolis *in US:* ˌgæl.ɪ.pəˈliːs, (US) ˌ-ə-, -ˈlɪs
gallipot ˈgæl.ɪ.pɒt, (US) -ə.pɑːt **-s** -s
gallium ˈgæl.i.əm
gallivant ˈgæl.ɪ.vænt, ˈ-ə-, ˌ--ˈ-, (US) ˈgæl.ə.vænt, ˌ--ˈ- **-s** -s **-ing** -ɪŋ **-ed** -ɪd
gallnut ˈgɔːl.nʌt, (US) ˈgɔːl-, ˈgɑːl- **-s** -s
gallon ˈgæl.ən **-s** -z
galloon gəˈluːn
gallop ˈgæl.əp **-s** -s **-ing** -ɪŋ **-ed** -t **-er/s** -əʳ/z, (US) -ɚ/s
gallopade ˌgæl.əˈpeɪd, -ˈpɑːd, (US) -ˈpeɪd **-s** -z
galloway, G~ ˈgæl.ə.weɪ **-s** -z
gallows ˈgæl.əʊz, (US) -oʊz
gallstone ˈgɔːl.stəʊn, (US) -stoʊn, ˈgɑːl- **-s** -z
Gallup ˈgæl.əp **ˈGallup ˌpoll**
Gallus ˈgæl.əs
galoot gəˈluːt **-s** -s
galop ˈgæl.əp; gælˈɒp, (US) ˈgæl.əp **-s** -s
galore gəˈlɔːʳ, (US) -ˈlɔːr
galosh gəˈlɒʃ, (US) -ˈlɑːʃ **-es** -ɪz
Galpin ˈgæl.pɪn
Galsham ˈgɔːl.səm, ˈgɒl-, (US) ˈgɔːl-, ˈgɑːl-
Galston ˈgɔːl.stən, ˈgɒl-, (US) ˈgɔːl-, ˈgɑːl-
Galsworthy ˈgɔːlz.wɜː.ði, ˈgɒlz-, ˈgælz-, (US) ˈgɔːlz.wɝː-, ˈgɑːlz-, ˈgælz-

> Note: John Galsworthy, the author, is commonly called /ˈgɔːlz.wɜː.ði/ (US) /-wɜːr-/.

Galt gɔːlt, gɒlt, (US) gɑːlt, gɔːlt
Galton ˈgɔːl.tən, ˈgɒl-, (US) ˈgɔːl-, ˈgɑːl-
galumphing gəˈlʌmp.fɪŋ
Galvani gælˈvɑː.ni
galvanic gælˈvæn.ɪk
galvanism ˈgæl.və.nɪ.zəm
galvaniz|e, -is|e ˈgæl.və.naɪz **-es** -ɪz **-ing** -ɪŋ **-ed** -d **-er/s** -əʳ/z, (US) -ɚ/z
galvanometer ˌgæl.vəˈnɒm.ɪ.təʳ, -ə.təʳ, (US) -ˈnɑː.mə.t̬ɚ **-s** -z
Galveston, Galvestone ˈgæl.vɪ.stən, -və-
Galway ˈgɔːl.weɪ, (US) ˈgɔːl-, ˈgɑːl-
gam gæm **-s** -z
Gama ˈgɑː.mə
Gamage ˈgæm.ɪdʒ **-'s** -ɪz
Gamaliel gəˈmeɪ.li.əl; *in Jewish usage also:* -ˈmɑː-; ˌgæm.əˈliː.əl
Gamay ˈgæm.eɪ, -ˈ-, (US) gæmˈeɪ
gamba ˈgæm.bə, (US) ˈgɑːm-, ˈgæm- **-s** -z
gambado gæmˈbeɪ.dəʊ, -ˈbɑː-, (US) -ˈbeɪ.doʊ **-(e)s** -z
gambadoes gæmˈbeɪ.dəʊz, (US) -doʊz
Gambetta gæmˈbet.ə, (US) -ˈbet̬-
Gambia ˈgæm.bi.ə **-n/s** -n/z
gambier *substance used in dyeing:* ˈgæm.bɪəʳ, (US) ˈgæm.bɪr
Gambier *surname:* ˈgæm.bi.əʳ, -bɪəʳ, -bi.eɪ, (US) ˈgæm.bɪr
gambit ˈgæm.bɪt **-s** -s
gambl|e, G~ ˈgæm.bəl **-es** -z **-ing** -ɪŋ, ˈ-blɪŋ **-ed** -d **-er/s** -əʳ/z, ˈ-bləʳ/z, (US) ˈ-bəl.ɚ/z, ˈ-blɚ/z
gamboge gæmˈbəʊʒ, -ˈbəʊdʒ, -ˈbuːʒ, (US) -ˈboʊdʒ
gambol ˈgæm.bəl **-s** -z **-(l)ing** -ɪŋ **-(l)ed** -d
Gambon ˈgæm.bən
gambrel ˈgæm.brəl **-s** -z
gam|e geɪm **-es** -z **-er** -əʳ, (US) -ɚ **-est** -ɪst, -əst **-ely** -li **-eness** -nəs, -nɪs **-ing** -ɪŋ **-ed** -d **ˈgame ˌshow**
gamebag ˈgeɪm.bæg **-s** -z
Gameboy® ˈgeɪm.bɔɪ **-s** -z
gamecock ˈgeɪm.kɒk, (US) -ˈkɑːk **-s** -s
gamekeeper ˈgeɪmˌkiː.pəʳ, (US) -pɚ **-s** -z
gamelan ˈgæm.ə.læn, ˈ-ɪ- **-s** -z
gamepad ˈgeɪm.pæd **-s** -z
gameplay ˈgeɪm.pleɪ
gamesmanship ˈgeɪmz.mən.ʃɪp
games|-master ˈgeɪmz|ˌmɑː.stəʳ, (US) -ˌmæs.tɚ **-masters** -ˌmɑː.stəz, (US) -ˌmæs.tɚz **-mistress/es** -ˌmɪs.trəs/ɪz, -trɪs/ɪz
gamester ˈgeɪm.stəʳ, (US) -stɚ **-s** -z
gamete ˈgæm.iːt, gəˈmiːt **-s** -s
gametic gəˈmet.ɪk, gæmˈet-, (US) gəˈmet̬-
gamey ˈgeɪ.mi
gamin gæmˈæ̃ŋ, ˈgæm.ɪn **-s** -z
gamine gæmˈiːn, ˈ-- **-s** -z
gamma ˈgæm.ə **-s** -z **ˈgamma ˌray**
Gammell ˈgæm.əl
gammer ˈgæm.əʳ, (US) -ɚ **-s** -z
gammon ˈgæm.ən **-s** -z **-ing** -ɪŋ **-ed** -d
gamm|y ˈgæm|.i **-ier** -i.əʳ, (US) -i.ɚ **-iest** -i.ɪst, -i.əst
-gamous gə.məs
Note: Suffix. Usually unstressed, e.g. **monogamous** /məˈnɒg.ə.məs/ (US) /-ˈnɑː.gə-/.
gamp, G~ gæmp **-s** -s
gamut ˈgæm.ət, -ʌt **-s** -s
gam|y ˈgeɪ.m|i **-ier** -i.əʳ, (US) -i.ɚ **-iest** -i.ɪst, -i.əst **-iness** -ɪ.nəs, -ɪ.nɪs
-gamy gə.mi
Note: Suffix. Normally unstressed, e.g. **monogamy** /məˈnɒg.ə.mi/ (US) /-ˈnɑː.gə-/.
Gandalf ˈgæn.dælf, (US) -dælf, -dɑːlf
gander, G~ ˈgæn.dəʳ, (US) -dɚ **-s** -z
Gandh|i ˈgæn.d|i, ˈgɑːn-, (US) ˈgɑːn-, ˈgæn- **-ian** -i.ən
Ganes(h)a gænˈeɪ.ʃə
Ganesh gɑːˈneɪʃ, gænˈeɪʃ
gang gæŋ **-s** -z **-ing** -ɪŋ **-ed** -d
gang-bang ˈgæŋ.bæŋ **-s** -z **-ing** -ɪŋ **-ed** -d
Ganges ˈgæn.dʒiːz
gangland ˈgæŋ.lænd, -lənd
gangling ˈgæŋ.glɪŋ
gangli|on ˈgæŋ.gli|.ən, -ɒn, (US) -ən **-a** -ə **-ons** -ənz, -ɒnz, (US) -ənz
gangl|y ˈgæŋ.gl|i **-ier** -i.əʳ, (US) -i.ɚ **-iest** -i.ɪst, -i.əst
gangmaster ˈgæŋˌmɑː.stəʳ, (US) -ˌmæs.tɚ **-s** -z
gangplank ˈgæŋ.plæŋk **-s** -s
gangren|e ˈgæŋ.griːn, (US) ˈ--, ˌ-ˈ- **-es** -z **-ing** -ɪŋ **-ed** -d
gangrenous ˈgæŋ.grɪ.nəs, (US) -grə-
gangsta ˈgæŋk.stə
gangster ˈgæŋk.stəʳ, (US) -stɚ **-s** -z **-ism** -ɪ.zəm
gangway ˈgæŋ.weɪ **-s** -z
ganister ˈgæn.ɪ.stəʳ, (US) -stɚ
ganja ˈgæn.dʒə, ˈgɑːn-, (US) ˈgɑːn-
gannet ˈgæn.ɪt, -ət **-s** -s

Gannett ˈgæn.ɪt, -ət
gannister ˈgæn.ɪ.stəʳ, US -stɚ
Gannon ˈgæn.ən
gantr|y, G~ ˈgæn.tr|i **-ies** -iz
Gantt gænt ˈ**Gantt** ˌ**chart**
Ganymede ˈgæn.ɪ.miːd, US ˈ-ə-
gaol dʒeɪl **-s** -z **-ing** -ɪŋ **-ed** -d
gaolbird ˈdʒeɪl.bɜːd, US -bɝːd **-s** -z
gaolbreak ˈdʒeɪl.breɪk **-s** -s
gaoler ˈdʒeɪ.ləʳ, US -lɚ **-s** -z
gap gæp **-s** -s
gap|e geɪp **-es** -s **-ing** -ɪŋ **-ed** -t
garag|e ˈgær.ɑːʒ, -ɪdʒ, -ɑːdʒ; *occasionally:* gəˈrɑːdʒ, -ˈrɑːʒ, US gəˈrɑːʒ, -ˈrɑːdʒ **-es** -ɪz **-ing** -ɪŋ **-ed** -d ˈ**garage** ˌ**sale** US **gaˈrage** ˌ**sale**
garam masala ˌgɑː.rəm.məˈsɑː.lə, -mɑːˈsɑː-
Garamond ˈgær.ə.mɒnd, US ˈger-, ˈgær-, -mɑːnd
garb gɑːb, US gɑːrb **-s** -z **-ed** -d
garbage ˈgɑː.bɪdʒ, US ˈgɑːr- ˈ**garbage** ˌ**can;** ˈ**garbage dis**ˌ**posal;** ˈ**garbage** ˌ**man**
garbanzo gɑːˈbæn.zəʊ, US gɑːrˈbɑːn.zoʊ **-s** -z
garbl|e ˈgɑː.bᵊl, US ˈgɑːr- **-es** -z **-ing** -ɪŋ, ˈ-blɪŋ **-ed** -d
Garbo ˈgɑː.bəʊ, US ˈgɑːr.boʊ
Garcia *English surname:* ˈgɑː.si.ə, ˈgɑː.ʃi.ə, US gɑːrˈsiː.ə, ˈgɑːr.si-
García, Garcia *Spanish surname:* gɑːˈsiː.ə, US gɑːr-
García Lorca gɑːˌsiː.əˈlɔː.kə, US gɑːrˌsiː.əˈlɔːr.kə
García Márquez gɑːˌsiː.əˈmɑː.kez, -kes, US gɑːrˌsiː.ə.mɑːrˈkez, -ˈkes, -ˈkeθ
garçon, garcon ˈgɑː.sɔ̃ːŋ, -sɒn; gɑːˈsɔ̃ːŋ, US gɑːrˈsɔ̃ːŋ, -ˈsoʊn **-s** -z
garda *Irish police:* ˈgɑː.də, US ˈgɑːr-
gardai gɑːˈdiː, US gɑːr-
Garda *Italian lake:* ˈgɑː.də, US ˈgɑːr-
garden, G~ ˈgɑː.dᵊn, US ˈgɑːr- **-s** -z **-ing** -ɪŋ **-ed** -d ˈ**garden** ˌ**centre;** ˌ**garden** ˈ**city;** ˈ**garden** ˌ**party**
gardener ˈgɑː.dᵊn.əʳ; ˈgɑːd.nəʳ, US ˈgɑːr.dᵊn.ɚ; US ˈgɑːrd.nɚ **-s** -z
gardenia gɑːˈdiː.ni.ə, US gɑːr-, ˈ-njə **-s** -z
Gardiner ˈgɑː.dᵊn.əʳ; ˈgɑːd.nəʳ, US ˈgɑːr.dᵊn.ɚ; US ˈgɑːrd.nɚ
Gardner ˈgɑːd.nəʳ, US ˈgɑːrd.nɚ
Gare du Nord ˌgɑː.djuˈnɔːʳ, US ˌgɑːr.duˈnɔːr, -djuːˈ-
garefowl ˈgeə.faʊl, US ˈger- **-s** -z
Gareth ˈgær.əθ, -eθ, -ɪθ, US ˈger-, ˈgær-
Garfield ˈgɑː.fiːld, US ˈgɑːr-
garfish ˈgɑː.fɪʃ, US ˈgɑːr-
Garforth ˈgɑː.fəθ, -fɔːθ, US ˈgɑːr.fɚθ, -fɔːrθ
Garfunkel ˌgɑːˈfʌŋ.kᵊl, ˈ---, US ˈgɑːr.fʌŋ-
garganey ˈgɑː.gə.ni, US ˈgɑːr- **-s** -z
Gargantua gɑːˈgæn.tʃu.ə, -tju-, US gɑːrˈgæn.tʃu-, -tju-
gargantuan gɑːˈgæn.tʃu.ən, -tju-, US gɑːrˈgæn.tʃu-, -tju-
Gargery ˈgɑː.dʒᵊr.i, US ˈgɑːr-
gargl|e ˈgɑː.gᵊl, US ˈgɑːr- **-es** -z **-ing/s** -ɪŋ/z, ˈ-glɪŋ **-ed** -d
gargoyle ˈgɑː.gɔɪl, US ˈgɑːr- **-s** -z
garibaldi, G~ ˌgær.ɪˈbɔːl.di, -əˈ-, -ˈbæl-, -ˈbɒl-, US ˌger-, ˌgær-, -ˈbɑːl- **-s** -z
Garioch ˈgær.i.ɒk, -ɒx, US ˈger.i.ɑːk, ˈgær-
garish ˈgeə.rɪʃ, ˈgɑː-, US ˈger.ɪʃ, ˈgær- **-ly** -li **-ness** -nəs, -nɪs
garland, G~ ˈgɑː.lənd, US ˈgɑːr- **-s** -z **-ing** -ɪŋ **-ed** -ɪd
garlic ˈgɑː.lɪk, US ˈgɑːr- **-ky** -i
Garlick ˈgɑː.lɪk, US ˈgɑːr-
Garman ˈgɑː.mən, US ˈgɑːr-
gar|ment ˈgɑː|.mənt, US ˈgɑːr- **-ments** -mənts **-mented** -mən.tɪd, US -mən.t̬ɪd
garner, G~ ˈgɑː.nəʳ, US ˈgɑːr.nɚ **-s** -z **-ing** -ɪŋ **-ed** -d
garnet ˈgɑː.nɪt, -nət, US ˈgɑːr- **-s** -s
Garnet(t) ˈgɑː.nɪt, -nət, US ˈgɑːr-
Garnham ˈgɑː.nəm, US ˈgɑːr-
garnish ˈgɑː.nɪʃ, US ˈgɑːr- **-es** -ɪz **-ing** -ɪŋ **-ed** -t
garnishee ˌgɑː.nɪˈʃiː, US ˌgɑːr- **-s** -z **-ing** -ɪŋ **-d** -d
garnishment ˈgɑː.nɪʃ.mənt, US ˈgɑːr- **-s** -s
garniture ˈgɑː.nɪ.tʃʊəʳ, US ˈgɑːr.nɪ.tʃɚ
Garonne gærˈɒn, US -ˈɔːn, -ˈɑːn
Garrard ˈgær.əd, -ɑːd, US ˈger.ɚd, ˈgær-; US gəˈrɑːrd
Garratt ˈgær.ət, US ˈger-, ˈgær-
Garraway ˈgær.ə.weɪ, US ˈger-, ˈgær-
garret ˈgær.ət, -ɪt, US ˈger-, ˈgær- **-s** -s
Garret(t) ˈgær.ət, -ɪt, US ˈger-, ˈgær-
Garrick ˈgær.ɪk, US ˈger-, ˈgær-
Garrioch *district in Scotland:* ˈgɪə.ri, US ˈger.i *surname:* ˈgær.i.ək, -əx, US ˈger-, ˈgær-
garrison, G~ ˈgær.ɪ.sᵊn, ˈ-ə-, US ˈger.ə-, ˈgær- **-s** -z **-ing** -ɪŋ **-ed** -d
Garrod ˈgær.əd, US ˈger-, ˈgær-
Garrold ˈgær.ᵊld, US ˈger-, ˈgær-
garrot ˈgær.ət, US ˈger-, ˈgær- **-s** -s
garro|t(t)e gəˈrɒ|t, US -ˈrɑː|t, -ˈroʊ|t; US ˈger.ə|t **-t(t)es** -ts **-t(t)ing** -tɪŋ, US -t̬ɪŋ **-t(t)ed** -tɪd, US -t̬ɪd **-t(t)er/s** -təʳ/z, US -t̬ɚ/z
garrulity gærˈuː.lə.ti, gəˈruː-, -ˈrjuː-, -lɪ-, US gerˈuː.lə.t̬i, gær-
garrulous ˈgær.ᵊl.əs, -ʊ.ləs, ˈ-jʊ-, US ˈger.ᵊl-, ˈger.jᵊl-, ˈ-ʊ.ləs, ˈ-jʊ.ləs **-ly** -li **-ness** -nəs, -nɪs
Garston ˈgɑː.stᵊn, US ˈgɑːr-
gart|er ˈgɑː.t|əʳ, US ˈgɑːr.t̬|ɚ **-ers** -əz, US -ɚz **-ering** -ᵊr.ɪŋ **-ered** -əd, US -ɚd
garth, G~ gɑːθ, US gɑːrθ **-s** -s
Gartmore ˈgɑːt.mɔːʳ, US ˈgɑːrt.mɔːr
Gartward ˈgɑːt.wəd, -wɔːd, US ˈgɑːrt.wɚd
Garuda gærˈuː.də, US ger-, gær-
Garvagh ˈgɑː.və, US ˈgɑːr-
Garvaghy ˌgɑːˈvæ.hi, US ˈgɑːr-
Garwood ˈgɑː.wʊd, US ˈgɑːr-
Gary ˈgær.i, US ˈger-, ˈgær-
Garza ˈgɑː.zə, US ˈgɑːr-
gas n gæs **-(s)es** -ɪz ˈ**gas** ˌ**chamber;** ˈ**gas** ˌ**mask;** ˈ**gas** ˌ**station**
gas v gæs **-ses** -ɪz **-sing** -ɪŋ **-sed** -t
gasbag ˈgæs.bæg **-s** -z
Gascoigne ˈgæs.kɔɪn, US gæsˈkɔɪn, ˈ--
Gascon ˈgæs.kən **-s** -z
gasconad|e ˌgæs.kəˈneɪd **-es** -z **-ing** -ɪŋ **-ed** -ɪd
Gascony ˈgæs.kə.ni
Gascoyne ˈgæs.kɔɪn, US gæsˈkɔɪn, ˈ--
gaselier ˌgæs.əˈlɪəʳ, US -ˈlɪr **-s** -z
gaseous ˈgæs.i.əs, ˈgeɪ.si-, ˈ-ʃəs; ˈgæʃ.əs, US ˈgæs.i.əs, ˈgæʃ-; US ˈgæʃ.əs **-ness** -nəs, -nɪs
gas-guzzler ˈgæsˌgʌz.ləʳ, -ˌgʌz.ᵊl.əʳ, US ˌ-ᵊl.ɚ, ˌ-lɚ **-s** -z
gash gæʃ **-es** -ɪz **-ing** -ɪŋ **-ed** -t
gasholder ˈgæsˌhəʊl.dəʳ, US -ˌhoʊl.dɚ **-s** -z
gasi|fy ˈgæs.ɪ|.faɪ, ˈ-ə- **-fies** -faɪz **-fying** -faɪ.ɪŋ **-fied** -faɪd
Gaskell ˈgæs.kᵊl, -kel
gasket ˈgæs.kɪt **-s** -s
gaskin, G~ ˈgæs.kɪn **-s** -z
gaslight ˈgæs.laɪt **-s** -s
gas|man ˈgæs|.mæn **-men** -men
gasohol ˈgæs.ə.hɒl, US -hɔːl, -hɑːl
gasoline, gasolene ˈgæs.ᵊl.iːn, ˌ--ˈ-, US ˌ--ˈ-, ˈ---
gasometer gæsˈɒm.ɪ.təʳ, gəˈsɒm-, -ə.təʳ, US gæsˈɑː.mə.t̬ɚ **-s** -z
gasp gɑːsp, US gæsp **-s** -s **-ing** -ɪŋ **-ed** -t
Gaspé gæsˈpeɪ
gasper ˈgɑː.spəʳ, US ˈgæs.pɚ **-s** -z
gass|y ˈgæs|.i **-ier** -i.əʳ, US -i.ɚ **-iest** -i.ɪst, -i.əst **-iness** -ɪ.nəs, -ɪ.nɪs
gasteropod ˈgæs.tᵊr.əʊ.pɒd, US -ə.pɑːd **-s** -z
Gaston ˈgæs.tɒn, gæsˈtɔ̃ːŋ, US -tən, gæsˈtɑːn, -ɔ̃ːn
gastric ˈgæs.trɪk
gastrin ˈgæs.trɪn
gastritis gæsˈtraɪ.tɪs, -təs, US -t̬ɪs, -t̬əs
gastro- ˈgæs.trəʊ; gæsˈtrɒ, US ˈgæs.troʊ, -trə; US gæsˈtrɑː
Note: Prefix. Normally takes either primary or secondary stress on the first syllable, e.g. **gastronome** /ˈgæs.trə.nəʊm/ US /-noʊm/, **gastronomic** /ˌgæs.trəˈnɒm.ɪk/ US /-ˈnɑː.mɪk/, or primary stress on the second syllable, e.g. **gastronomy** /gæsˈtrɒn.ə.mi/ US /-ˈtrɑː.nə-/.
gastroenteritis ˌgæs.trəʊˌen.təˈraɪ.tɪs, -təs, US -troʊˌen.t̬əˈraɪ.t̬ɪs, -t̬əs
gastroenterolog|ist ˌgæs.trəʊˌen.təˈrɒl.ə.dʒ|ɪst, US -troʊˌen.t̬əˈrɑː.lə.dʒ|ɪst **-ists** -ɪsts **-y** -i
gastrointestinal ˌgæs.trəʊˌɪn.tesˈtaɪ.nᵊl, -ɪnˈtes.tɪ.nᵊl, -tᵊn.ᵊl, US -troʊ.ɪnˈtes.tᵊn.ᵊl

gastronome ˈgæs.trə.nəʊm, (US) -noʊm -s -z
gastronomic ˌgæs.trəˈnɒm.ɪk, (US) -ˈnɑː.mɪk -al -ᵊl
gastronom|y gæsˈtrɒn.ə.m|i, (US) -ˈtrɑː.nə- -ist/s -ɪst/s
gastropod ˈgæs.trəʊ.pɒd, (US) -trə.pɑːd -s -z
gastropub ˈgæs.trəʊ.pʌb, (US) -troʊ- -s -z
gasworks ˈgæs.wɜːks, (US) -wɝːks
gat|e geɪt -es -s -ing -ɪŋ, (US) ˈgeɪ.t̬ɪŋ -ed -ɪd, (US) ˈgeɪ.t̬əd
gâteau, gateau ˈgæt.əʊ, (US) gætˈoʊ -s -z
gâteaux, gateaux ˈgæt.əʊ, -əʊz, (US) gætˈoʊ, -oʊz
gatecrash ˈgeɪt.kræʃ -es -ɪz -ing -ɪŋ -ed -t -er/s -əʳ/z, (US) -ɚ/z
gatehou|se ˈgeɪt.haʊ|s -ses -zɪz
gatekeeper ˈgeɪtˌkiː.pəʳ, (US) -pɚ -s -z
gateleg ˈgeɪt.leg -s -z
gate-legged ˈgeɪtˌlegd
gateless ˈgeɪt.ləs, -lɪs
gatepost ˈgeɪt.pəʊst, (US) -poʊst -s -s
Gates geɪts
Gateshead ˈgeɪts.hed, ˌgeɪtsˈhed
gateway, G~ ˈgeɪt.weɪ -s -z
Gath gæθ
gath|er ˈgæð|.əʳ, (US) -ɚ -ers -əz, (US) -ɚz -ering/s -ᵊr.ɪŋ/z -ered -əd, (US) -ɚd -erer/s -ᵊr.əʳ/z, (US) -ɚ.ɚ/z
Gatley ˈgæt.li
Gatling ˈgæt.lɪŋ
gator ˈgeɪ.tə, (US) -t̬ɚ -s -z
Gatorade® ˌgeɪ.tᵊrˈeɪd, (US) ˈgeɪ.t̬əˌreɪd
Gatsby ˈgæts.bi
Gatt, GATT gæt
Gatting ˈgæt.ɪŋ, (US) ˈgæt̬-
Gatty ˈgæt.i, (US) ˈgæt̬-
Gatwick ˈgæt.wɪk ˌ**Gatwick** ˈ**Airport**
gauche gəʊʃ, (US) goʊʃ -ly -li -ness -nəs, -nɪs
gaucherie ˈgəʊ.ʃᵊr.i; ˌgəʊ.ʃᵊrˈiː, (US) ˌgoʊ.ʃəˈriː -s -z
gaucho ˈgaʊ.tʃəʊ, (US) -tʃoʊ -s -z
gaud gɔːd, (US) gɑːd, gɔːd -s -z
Gauden ˈgɔː.dᵊn, (US) ˈgɑː-, ˈgɔː-
Gaudí ˈgaʊ.di, -ˈ-
gaud|y ˈgɔː.d|i, (US) ˈgɑː-, ˈgɔː- -ier -i.əʳ, (US) -i.ɚ -iest -i.ɪst, -i.əst -ily -ᵊl.i, -ɪ.li -iness -ɪ.nəs, -ɪ.nɪs
gaug|e geɪdʒ -es -ɪz -ing -ɪŋ -ed -d -eable -ə.bᵊl
gauger ˈgeɪ.dʒəʳ, (US) -dʒɚ -s -z
Gauguin ˈgəʊ.gæ̃ŋ, -gæn, (US) goʊˈgæ̃ŋ, -ˈgæn
Gaul gɔːl -s -z -ish -ɪʃ
gauleiter ˈgaʊ.laɪ.təʳ, (US) -t̬ɚ -s -z
Gaull|ism ˈgəʊ.l|ɪ.zᵊm, (US) ˈgɑː-, ˈgoʊ- -ist/s -ɪst/s
Gauloise(s)® ˈgəʊl.wɑːz, ˌ-ˈ-, (US) goʊlˈwɑːz, gɑːl-
Gault gɔːlt, gɒlt, (US) gɔːlt, gɑːlt
Gaultier ˈgɔːl.ti.eɪ, (US) ˈgɔːl-, ˈgɑːl-
Gaumont® ˈgəʊ.mɒnt, -mənt, (US) ˈgoʊ.mɑːnt
gaun|t, G~ gɔːn|t, (US) gɑːn|t, gɔːn|t -ter -təʳ, (US) -t̬ɚ -test -tɪst, -təst, (US) -t̬ɪst, -t̬əst -tly -t.li -tness -t.nəs, -nɪs
gauntle|t, G~ ˈgɔːnt.lə|t, -lɪ|t, (US) ˈgɑːnt-, ˈgɔːnt- -ts -ts -ted -tɪd, (US) -t̬ɪd
Gauntlett ˈgɔːnt.lət, -lɪt, (US) ˈgɑːnt-, ˈgɔːnt
gauss, G~ gaʊs -es -ɪz
gauz|e gɔːz, (US) gɑːz, gɔːz -es -ɪz -y -i -iness -ɪ.nəs, -ɪ.nɪs
gave (from **give**) geɪv
gavel ˈgæv.ᵊl -s -z
gavelkind ˈgæv.ᵊl.kaɪnd, -kɪnd
gavel-to-gavel ˌgæv.ᵊl.təˈgæv.ᵊl
Gaveston ˈgæv.ɪ.stᵊn, ˈ-ə-
Gavey ˈgeɪ.vi
Gavin ˈgæv.ɪn
gavotte gəˈvɒt, gæ-, (US) -ˈvɑːt -s -s
Gawain ˈgɑː.weɪn, ˈgæw.eɪn, -ɪn; gəˈweɪn
gawd gɔːd, (US) gɔːd, gɑːd
Gawith ˈgeɪ.wɪθ, ˈgaʊ.ɪθ
gawk gɔːk, (US) gɑːk, gɔːk -s -s -ing -ɪŋ -ed -t
gawk|y ˈgɔː.k|i, (US) ˈgɑː-, ˈgɔː- -ier -i.əʳ, (US) -i.ɚ -iest -i.ɪst, -i.əst -iness -ɪ.nəs, -ɪ.nɪs
gawp gɔːp, (US) gɑːp, gɔːp -s -s -ing -ɪŋ -ed -t
Gawthrop ˈgɔː.θrɒp, -θrəp, (US) ˈgɑː.θrɑːp, ˈgɔː-, -θrəp
gay, G~ geɪ -er -əʳ, (US) -ɚ -est -ɪst, -əst -s -z **gaily** ˈgeɪ.li **gayness** ˈgeɪ.nəs, -nɪs
gaydar ˈgeɪ.dɑːʳ, (US) -dɑːr -s -z
Gaye geɪ
Gayle geɪl
Gaylord ˈgeɪ.lɔːd, (US) -lɔːrd
Gay-Lussac ˌgeɪˈluː.sæk, (US) -luˈsæk
Gaynham ˈgeɪ.nəm
Gaynor ˈgeɪ.nəʳ, (US) -nɚ
Gaza *in the Middle East:* ˈgɑː.zə; *in biblical use also:* ˈgeɪ.zə, (US) ˈgɑː.zə, ˈgæz.ə, ˈgeɪ.zə ˌ**Gaza** ˈ**Strip** *Greek scholar:* ˈgɑː.zə
gaz|e geɪz -es -ɪz -ing -ɪŋ -ed -d -er/s -əʳ/z, (US) -ɚ/z
gazebo gəˈziː.bəʊ, (US) -ˈziː.boʊ, -ˈzeɪ- -s -z
gazelle gəˈzel -s -z
ga|zette gə|ˈzet -zettes -ˈzets -zetting -ˈzet.ɪŋ, (US) -ˈzet̬.ɪŋ -zetted -ˈzet.ɪd, (US) -ˈzet̬.əd
gazetteer ˌgæz.əˈtɪəʳ, -ɪˈ-, (US) -ˈtɪr -s -z
Gaziantep ˌgɑː.zi.ɑːnˈtep
gazogene ˈgæz.əʊ.dʒiːn, (US) ˈ-ə-
gazpacho gæsˈpætʃ.əʊ, (US) gəˈspɑː.tʃoʊ, gəzˈpɑː-
Gazprom ˈgæz.prɒm, (US) -prɑːm
gazump gəˈzʌmp -s -s -ing -ɪŋ -ed -t, -ˈzʌmt
gazunder gəˈzʌn.dəʳ, (US) -dɚ -s -s -ing -ɪŋ -ed -d
Gazza ˈgæz.ə
GB ˌdʒiːˈbiː
GBH ˌdʒiː.biːˈeɪtʃ
GCE ˌdʒiː.siːˈiː -s -z
GCHQ ˌdʒiː.siː.eɪtʃˈkjuː
GCSE ˌdʒiː.siː.esˈiː -s -z
Gdansk gəˈdæntsk, -ˈdaɪntsk, (US) -ˈdɑːntsk, -ˈdæntsk
g'day gəˈdeɪ
GDP ˌdʒiː.diːˈpiː
GDR ˌdʒiː.diːˈɑːʳ, (US) -ˈɑːr
GE® ˌdʒiːˈiː
gear gɪəʳ, (US) gɪr -s -z -ing -ɪŋ -ed -d ˈ**gear** ˌ**lever**
gearbox ˈgɪə.bɒks, (US) ˈgɪr.bɑːks -es -ɪz
Geare gɪəʳ, (US) gɪr
gearshift ˈgɪə.ʃɪft, (US) ˈgɪr- -s -s
Geary ˈgɪə.ri, (US) ˈgɪr.i
Geat giːt -s -s
gecko ˈgek.əʊ, (US) -oʊ -(e)s -z
Ged ged, dʒed
GED ˌdʒiː.iːˈdiː
Geddes ˈged.ɪs, (US) -iːz
geddit ˈged.ɪt, (US) -ət
gee, G~ dʒiː -s -z -ing -ɪŋ -d -d ˌ**gee** ˈ**whiz**
geegaw ˈgiː.gɔː, (US) -gɑː, -gɔː -s -z
geegee ˈdʒiː.dʒiː -s -z
geek giːk -s -s
geek|y ˈgiː.k|i -ier -i.əʳ, (US) -i.ɚ -iest -i.ɪst, -i.əst
Geelong dʒɪˈlɒŋ, dʒə-, (US) -ˈlɑːŋ, -ˈlɔːŋ
Geering ˈgɪə.rɪŋ, (US) ˈgɪr.ɪŋ
geese (plural of **goose**) giːs
Geeson ˈdʒiː.sᵊn, ˈgiː-
gee-up ˌdʒiːˈʌp, ˈdʒiː.ʌp
geezer ˈgiː.zəʳ, (US) -zɚ -s -z
Geffen ˈgef.ᵊn
gefilte gəˈfɪl.tə, gɪ- **ge**ˈ**filte** ˌ**fish**, **ge**ˌ**filte** ˈ**fish**
Gehazi gɪˈheɪ.zaɪ, ge-, gə-, -ˈhɑː-, -zi
Gehenna gɪˈhen.ə, gə-
Gehrig ˈger.ɪg
Gehry ˈgeə.ri, (US) ˈger.i
Geierstein ˈgaɪ.ə.staɪn, (US) ˈgaɪ.ɚ-
Geiger ˈgaɪ.gəʳ, (US) -gɚ ˈ**Geiger** ˌ**counter**
Geikie ˈgiː.ki
geisha ˈgeɪ.ʃə, (US) ˈgeɪ-, ˈgiː- -s -z
gel n *girl:* gel -s -z
gel n, v *jelly:* dʒel -s -s -ling -ɪŋ -led -d
gelatin ˈdʒel.ə.tɪn
gelatine ˈdʒel.ə.tiːn, -tɪn, ˌ--ˈ-
gelatiniz|e, -is|e dʒəˈlæt.ɪ.naɪz, dʒelˈæt-, dʒɪˈlæt-, -ᵊn.aɪz, (US) dʒəˈlæt.ᵊn.aɪz -es -ɪz -ing -ɪŋ -ed -d
gelatinous dʒəˈlæt.ɪ.nəs, dʒelˈæt-, dʒɪˈlæt-, -ᵊn.əs, (US) dʒəˈlæt.ᵊn.əs -ly -li
geld geld -s -z -ing -ɪŋ -ed -ɪd
Gelderland ˈgel.də.lænd, (US) -dɚ-
gelding ˈgel.dɪŋ -s -z
Geldof ˈgel.dɒf, (US) -dɑːf
gelid ˈdʒel.ɪd -ly -li -ness -nəs, -nɪs
gelignite ˈdʒel.ɪg.naɪt, -əg-
Gell gel, dʒel
Gellan ˈgel.ən
Gellatl(e)y ˈgel.ət.li, gelˈæt-, gəˈlæt-, (US) gelˈæt-, gəˈlæt-
Geller ˈgel.əʳ, (US) -ɚ

Gelligaer ˌgeθ.liˈgeəʳ, -ˈgaɪ.əʳ, ⓤⓢ -ˈger, -ˈgaɪɚ
gem, G~ dʒem **-s** -z
Gemara gəˈmɑː.rə, gemˈɑː-, gɪˈmɑː-
gemfish ˈdʒem.fɪʃ **-es** -ɪz
geminate adj ˈdʒem.ɪ.nət
gemi|nate v ˈdʒem.ɪ|.neɪt, ˈ-ə- **-nates** -neɪts **-nating** -neɪ.tɪŋ, ⓤⓢ -neɪ.t̬ɪŋ **-nated** -neɪ.tɪd, ⓤⓢ -neɪ.t̬əd
gemination ˌdʒem.ɪˈneɪ.ʃən, -əˈ-
Gemini *constellation:* ˈdʒem.ɪ.naɪ, ˈ-ə-, -niː *aircraft:* ˈdʒem.ɪ.ni, ˈ-ə-
Geminian ˌdʒem.ɪˈnaɪ.ən, -əˈ-, -ˈniː- **-s** -z
gem|ma, G~ ˈdʒem|.ə **-mae** -iː
gemmiferous dʒəˈmɪf.ər.əs, dʒemˈɪf-
gemmology dʒemˈɒl.ə.dʒi, ⓤⓢ -ˈɑː.lə-
gemmule ˈdʒem.juːl **-s** -z
gemology dʒemˈɒl.ə.dʒi, ⓤⓢ -ˈɑː.lə-
gemsbok ˈgemz.bɒk, -bʌk, ⓤⓢ -bɑːk **-s** -s
gemshorn ˈgemz.hɔːn, ⓤⓢ -hɔːrn **-s** -z
gemstone ˈdʒem.stəʊn, ⓤⓢ -stoʊn **-s** -z
gen dʒen **-s** -z **-ning** -ɪŋ **-ed** -d
gendarme ˈʒɑ̃ːn.dɑːm, ˈʒɔ̃ːn-, ˈʒɑːn-, ⓤⓢ ˈʒɑːn.dɑːrm **-s** -z
gender ˈdʒen.dəʳ, ⓤⓢ -dɚ **-s** -z **-ing** -ɪŋ **-ed** -d
gender-bender ˈdʒen.dəˌben.dəʳ, ⓤⓢ -dɚˌben.dɚ **-s** -z
gene, G~ dʒiːn **-s** -z
genealogical ˌdʒiː.ni.əˈlɒdʒ.ɪ.kəl, ⓤⓢ ˌdʒiː.ni.əˈlɑː.dʒɪ-, ˌdʒen.i- **-ly** -i
genealogist ˌdʒiː.niˈæl.ə.dʒɪst, ⓤⓢ ˌdʒiː.niˈ-, ˌdʒen.iˈ- **-s** -s
genealog|y ˌdʒiː.niˈæl.ə.dʒ|i, ⓤⓢ ˌdʒiː.niˈ-, ˌdʒen.iˈ- **-ies** -iz
genera (plural of **genus**) ˈdʒen.ər.ə
general ˈdʒen.ər.əl **-s** -z ˌ**general asˈsembly;** ˌ**general eˈlection;** ˌ**general pracˈtitioner;** ˌ**general ˈstore**
generalissimo ˌdʒen.ər.əˈlɪs.ɪ.məʊ, ˈ-ə-, ⓤⓢ -ə.moʊ **-s** -z
generalist ˈdʒen.ər.əl.ɪst, ˈdʒen.rəl- **-s** -s
generalit|y ˌdʒen.əˈræl.ə.t|i, -ɪ.t|i, ⓤⓢ -ə.t̬|i **-ies** -iz
generalization, -isa- ˌdʒen.ər.əl.aɪˈzeɪ.ʃən, -ɪˈ-, ⓤⓢ -əˈ- **-s** -z
generaliz|e, -is|e ˈdʒen.ər.əl.aɪz, ⓤⓢ -ə.laɪz **-es** -ɪz **-ing** -ɪŋ **-ed** -d **-able** -ə.bəl
generally ˈdʒen.ər.əl.i, ˈdʒen.rəl.i
generalship ˈdʒen.ər.əl.ʃɪp **-s** -s
gener|ate ˈdʒen.ər|.eɪt, ⓤⓢ -ə.r|eɪt **-ates** -eɪts **-ating** -eɪ.tɪŋ, ⓤⓢ -eɪ.t̬ɪŋ **-ated** -eɪ.tɪd, ⓤⓢ -eɪ.t̬ɪd
generation ˌdʒen.əˈreɪ.ʃən **-al** -əl **-s** -z **geneˈration** ˌ**gap**
generative ˈdʒen.ər.ə.tɪv, ⓤⓢ -ə.t̬ɪv, ˈ-ə.reɪ.t̬ɪv
generator ˈdʒen.ə.reɪ.təʳ, ⓤⓢ -t̬ɚ **-s** -z
generatri|x ˈdʒen.ə.reɪ.trɪ|ks, ⓤⓢ ˌdʒen.əˈreɪ- **-ces** -siːz
generic dʒəˈner.ɪk, dʒɪ-, dʒenˈer- **-ally** -əl.i, -li
generosity ˌdʒen.əˈrɒs.ə.ti, -ɪ.ti, ⓤⓢ -ˈrɑː.sə.t̬i
generous ˈdʒen.ər.əs **-ly** -li **-ness** -nəs, -nɪs
gene|sis, G~ ˈdʒen.ə|.sɪs, ˈ-ɪ- **-ses** -siːz
Genesius dʒəˈniː.si.əs, dʒenˈiː-, dʒɪˈniː-, ⓤⓢ -si-, -ʃi-, -zi-
Genesta dʒəˈnes.tə, dʒenˈes-, dʒɪˈnes-
genet *animal:* ˈdʒen.ɪt, ⓤⓢ ˈdʒen.ɪt, dʒəˈnet **-s** -s
Genet *French writer:* ʒəˈneɪ
genetic dʒəˈnet.ɪk, dʒɪ-, ⓤⓢ -ˈnet̬.ɪk **-s** -s **-ally** -əl.i, -li **geˌnetic enˈgiˈneering;** **geˌnetic ˈfingerprint**
geneticist dʒəˈnet.ɪ.sɪst, dʒɪ-, ˈ-ə-, ⓤⓢ -ˈnet̬.ə- **-s** -s
Geneva dʒəˈniː.və, dʒɪ- **Geˌneva Conˈvention**
Genevieve *English name:* ˈdʒen.ə.viːv, ˈ-ɪ-, ˌ--ˈ-
Geneviève *French name:* ˌʒen.əˈvjev, ⓤⓢ ˌʒen.əˈvjev, ˈdʒen.ə.viːv
Genghis Khan ˌgeŋ.gɪsˈkɑːn, ˌdʒeŋ-, -gɪzˈ-
genial *amiable:* ˈdʒiː.ni.əl **-ly** -i **-ness** -nəs, -nɪs *of the chin:* dʒɪˈniː.əl, dʒə-, -ˈnaɪ-
geniality ˌdʒiː.niˈæl.ə.ti, -ɪ.ti, ⓤⓢ -ə.t̬i
-genic ˈdʒen.ɪk, ˈdʒiː.nɪk
Note: Suffix. Words ending **-genic** normally carry primary stress on the penultimate syllable, e.g. **photogenic** /ˌfəʊ.təʊˈdʒen.ɪk/ ⓤⓢ /ˌfoʊ.t̬oʊˈ-/.
genie, G~ ˈdʒiː.ni **-s** -z
genii (from **genius**) ˈdʒiː.ni.aɪ
genista dʒəˈnɪs.tə, dʒɪ-, dʒenˈɪs- **-s** -z
genital ˈdʒen.ɪ.təl, ˈ-ə-, ⓤⓢ -ət̬.əl **-s** -z **-ly** -li
genitalia ˌdʒen.ɪˈteɪ.li.ə, -əˈ-, ⓤⓢ -ˈteɪ.li.ə, -ˈteɪl.jə
genitival ˌdʒen.ɪˈtaɪ.vəl, -əˈ-
genitive ˈdʒen.ɪ.tɪv, ˈ-ə-, ⓤⓢ -ə.t̬ɪv **-s** -z
genito-urinary ˌdʒen.ɪ.təʊˈjʊə.rɪ.nər.i, ˌ-ə-, -ˈjɔː-, -rən.ər-, ⓤⓢ -ə.t̬oʊˈjʊr.ə.ner.i
geni|us ˈdʒiː.ni|.əs **-i** -aɪ **-uses** -ə.sɪz
genius loci ˌdʒiː.ni.əsˈləʊ.saɪ, ⓤⓢ -ˈloʊ- **genii loci** ˌdʒiː.ni.aɪˈ-
Gennadi dʒəˈnɑː.di, ge-
Gennesare|t gəˈnes.ər.ɪ|t, gɪ-, genˈez-, -e|t, -ə|t, ⓤⓢ gəˈnes-, dʒə- **-th** -θ
Genoa ˈdʒen.əʊ.ə, dʒəˈnəʊ-, dʒɪ-, dʒenˈəʊ-, ⓤⓢ ˈdʒen.oʊ.ə, dʒəˈnoʊ.ə
genocidal ˌdʒen.əˈsaɪ.dəl *stress shift:* ˌ**genocidal ˈpolicies**
genocide ˈdʒen.ə.saɪd
Genoese ˌdʒen.əʊˈiːz, ⓤⓢ -oʊˈiːz *stress shift:* ˌ**Genoese ˈsailor**
genome ˈdʒiː.nəʊm, ⓤⓢ -noʊm **-s** -z
genotype ˈdʒen.əʊ.taɪp, ⓤⓢ ˈ-oʊ-
-genous dʒɪ.nəs, dʒə.nəs
Note: Suffix. Words containing **-genous** are normally stressed on the antepenultimate syllable, e.g. **autogenous** /ɔːˈtɒdʒ.ɪ.nəs/ ⓤⓢ /ɑːˈtɑː.dʒɪ.nəs/. Exceptions exist: see individual entries.
genre ˈʒɑ̃ːn.rə, ⓤⓢ ˈʒɑːn.rə **-s** -z
gen|s dʒen|z **-tes** -tiːz
Genseric ˈgen.sər.ɪk, ˈdʒen-
Gensing ˈgen.zɪŋ, ˈgent.sɪŋ
gent *gentleman:* dʒent **-s** -s
Gent *surname:* gent *place in Belgium:* gent, xent
genteel dʒenˈtiːl, dʒən- **-ly** -li **-ness** -nəs, -nɪs
gentes (plural of **gens**) ˈdʒen.tiːz
gentian ˈdʒen.tʃən, -tʃi.ən **-s** -z
gentile, G~ ˈdʒen.taɪl **-s** -z
gentility ˌdʒenˈtɪl.ə.ti, ⓤⓢ -t̬i
gent|le, G~ ˈdʒen.t|əl **-ler** -əl.əʳ, ˈdʒent.ləʳ, ⓤⓢ ˈdʒen.t̬əl.ɚ, ˈdʒent.lɚ **-lest** -əl.əst, -ɪst, ˈdʒent.lɪst, -ləst **-ly** -li **-leness** -əl.nəs, -nɪs ˈ**gentle** ˌ**sex**
gentlefolk ˈdʒen.təl.fəʊk, ⓤⓢ ˈdʒen.t̬əlfoʊk **-s** -s
gentle|man ˈdʒen.təl|.mən, ⓤⓢ ˈdʒen.t̬əl- **-men** -mən, -men ˌ**genˈtleman's ˈgentleman**
gentle|man-at-arms ˌdʒen.təl|.mən.ətˈɑːmz, ⓤⓢ -t̬əl|.mən.ətˈɑːrmz **-men-at-arms** -mən.ətˈɑːmz, -men-, ⓤⓢ -ˈɑːrmz
gentlemanlike ˈdʒen.təl.mən.laɪk, ⓤⓢ ˈdʒen.t̬əl-
gentlemanl|y ˈdʒen.təl.mən.l|i, ⓤⓢ ˈdʒen.t̬əl- **-iness** -ɪ.nəs, -ɪ.nɪs
gentle|woman ˈdʒen.təl|ˌwʊm.ən, ⓤⓢ ˈdʒen.t̬əl- **-women** -ˌwɪm.ɪn
gentrification ˌdʒen.trɪ.fɪˈkeɪ.ʃən, -trə-, -fəˈ- **-s** -z
gentrifier ˈdʒen.trɪ.faɪ.əʳ, -trə-, ⓤⓢ -ɚ **-s** -z
gentrif|y ˈdʒen.trɪ.f|aɪ, -trə- **-ies** -aɪz **-ying** -aɪ.ɪŋ **-ied** -aɪd
gentry, G~ ˈdʒen.tri
genuflect ˈdʒen.jʊ.flekt, -jə- **-s** -s **-ing** -ɪŋ **-ed** -ɪd
genuflection, genuflexion ˌdʒen.jʊˈflek.ʃən, -jə- **-s** -z
genuine ˈdʒen.ju.ɪn **-ly** -li **-ness** -nəs, -nɪs

> Note: Many British people believe, wrongly, that the typical American pronunciation of this word is /ˈdʒen.ju.aɪn/; this is in fact a minority pronunciation.

genus ˈdʒiː.nəs, ˈdʒen.əs **genera** ˈdʒen.ər.ə
-geny dʒə.ni, dʒɪ.ni
Note: Suffix. Words containing **-geny** are stressed in a similar way

to those containing **-genous**; see above.

geo- ˈdʒiː.əʊ; dʒiˈɒ, ˈdʒɒ, (US) ˈdʒiː.oʊ, -ə; (US) dʒiˈɑː
Note: Prefix. Normally takes either primary or secondary stress on the first syllable, e.g. **geomancy** /ˈdʒiː.əʊ.mænt.si/ (US) /ˈ-oʊ-/, **geocentric** /ˌdʒiː.əʊˈsen.trɪk/ (US) /-oʊˈ-/, or primary stress on the second syllable, e.g. **geography** /dʒiˈɒg.rə.fi/ (US) /-ˈɑː.grə-/.

geocentric ˌdʒiː.əʊˈsen.trɪk, (US) -oʊˈ-, -əˈ- **-al** -əl **-ally** -əl.i, -li

geochemical ˌdʒiː.əʊˈkem.ɪ.kəl, (US) -oʊˈ-, -əˈ-

geochemist ˌdʒiː.əʊˈkem.ɪst, ˈdʒiː.əʊˌkem-, (US) ˌdʒiː.oʊˈkem-, -əˈ- **-s** -s

geochemistry ˌdʒiː.əʊˈkem.ɪ.stri, (US) -oʊˈ-, -əˈ-

geode ˈdʒiː.əʊd, (US) -oʊd **-s** -z

geodesic ˌdʒiː.əʊˈdes.ɪk, -ˈdiː.sɪk, (US) -oʊˈ-, -əˈ- **-al** -əl

geodesy dʒiˈɒd.ɪ.si, ˈ-ə-, (US) -ˈɑː.də-

geodic dʒiˈɒd.ɪk, (US) -ˈɑː.dɪk

Geoff dʒef

Geoffr(e)y ˈdʒef.ri

Geoghegan ˈgeɪ.gən, ˈgəʊ.gən, gɪˈheɪ.gən, (US) ˈgoʊ.gən

geographer dʒiˈɒg.rə.fər; ˈdʒɒg-, (US) dʒiˈɑː.grə.fɚ **-s** -z

geographic ˌdʒiː.əʊˈgræf.ɪk, (US) -əˈ-, -oʊˈ- **-al** -əl **-ally** -əl.i, -li

geograph|y dʒiˈɒg.rə.f|i; ˈdʒɒg-, (US) dʒiˈɑː.grə- **-ies** -iz

geologic ˌdʒi.əʊˈlɒdʒ.ɪk, (US) -oʊˈlɑː.dʒɪk, -əˈ- **-al** -əl **-ally** -əl.i, -li

geologist dʒiˈɒl.ə.dʒɪst, (US) -ˈɑː.lə- **-s** -s

geologiz|e, -is|e dʒiˈɒl.ə.dʒaɪz, (US) -ˈɑː.lə- **-es** -ɪz **-ing** -ɪŋ **-ed** -d

geology dʒiˈɒl.ə.dʒi, (US) -ˈɑː.lə-

geomagnetic ˌdʒiː.əʊ.mægˈnet.ɪk, -məgˈ-, (US) -oʊ.mægˈneṭ.ɪk, -ə.mægˈ-

geomagnetism ˌdʒiː.əʊˈmæg.nɪ.tɪ.zəm, -nə-, (US) -oʊˈmæg.nə-, -əˈ-

geomancy ˈdʒiː.əʊ.mænt.si, (US) ˈ-oʊ-, ˈ-ə-

geometer dʒiˈɒm.ɪ.tər, ˈ-ə-, (US) -ˈɑː.mə.ṭɚ **-s** -z

geometric ˌdʒiː.əʊˈmet.rɪk, (US) -əˈ- **-al** -əl **-ally** -əl.i, -li

geometrician ˌdʒiː.əʊ.məˈtrɪʃ.ən, dʒiˌɒm.əˈ-, -ɪˈ-, (US) ˌdʒiː.ə.məˈ-; (US) dʒiˌɑː- **-s** -z

geometr|y dʒiˈɒm.ə.tr|i, ˈ-ɪ-; ˈdʒɒm-, (US) dʒiˈɑː.mə- **-ies** -iz

geomorphologic ˌdʒiː.əʊˌmɔː.fəˈlɒdʒ.ɪk, (US) -oʊˌmɔːr.fəˈlɑː.dʒɪk, -əˌ- **-al** -əl **-ally** -əl.i, -li

geomorpholog|y ˌdʒiː.əʊ.mɔːˈfɒl.ə.dʒ|i, (US) -oʊ.mɔːrˈfɑː.lə-, -ə.mɔːrˈ- **-ist/s** -ɪst/s

geophysical ˌdʒiː.əʊˈfɪz.ɪ.kəl, (US) -oʊˈ-, -əˈ-

geophysicist ˌdʒi.əʊˈfɪz.ɪ.sɪst, (US) -oʊˈ-, -əˈ- **-s** -s

geophysics ˌdʒiː.əʊˈfɪz.ɪks, (US) -oʊˈ-, -əˈ-

geopolitical ˌdʒiː.əʊ.pəˈlɪt.ɪ.kəl, (US) -oʊ.pəˈlɪṭ-, -ə.pəˈ- **-ly** -i

geopolitics ˌdʒiː.əʊˈpɒl.ə.tɪks, ˈ-ɪ-, (US) -oʊˈpɑː.lə-, -əˈ-

Geordie ˈdʒɔː.di, (US) ˈdʒɔːr- **-s** -z

George dʒɔːdʒ, (US) dʒɔːrdʒ

Georgetown ˈdʒɔːdʒ.taʊn, (US) ˈdʒɔːrdʒ-

georgette dʒɔːˈdʒet, (US) dʒɔːr-

Georgi|a ˈdʒɔː.dʒ|ə, -dʒi|.ə, (US) ˈdʒɔːr- **-an/s** -ən/z

Georgiana ˌdʒɔː.dʒiˈɑː.nə, -ˈdʒeɪ.nə, (US) ˌdʒɔːrˈdʒæn.ə, -dʒiˈæn-

georgic, G~ ˈdʒɔː.dʒɪk, (US) ˈdʒɔːr- **-s** -s

Georgina dʒɔːˈdʒiː.nə, (US) dʒɔːrˈ-

geoscience ˌdʒiː.əʊˈsaɪ.ənts, (US) -oʊˈ-, -əˈ-

geostationary ˌdʒiː.əʊˈsteɪ.ʃən.ər.i, -ri, (US) -oʊˈsteɪ.ʃən.er-, -əˈ-

geothermal ˌdʒiː.əʊˈθɜː.məl, (US) -oʊˈθɝː-, -əˈ-

geotropic ˌdʒiː.əʊˈtrɒp.ɪk, (US) -oʊˈtrɑː.pɪk, -əˈ-

geotropism dʒiˈɒt.rə.pɪ.zəm, (US) -ˈɑː.trə- **-s** -z

Geraint ˈger.aɪnt, -ˈ-, (US) dʒəˈreɪnt

Gerald ˈdʒer.əld

Geraldine ˈdʒer.əl.diːn, -daɪn

> Note: /ˈdʒer.əl.daɪn/ in Coleridge's 'Christabel'.

Geraldton ˈdʒer.əld.tən

geranium dʒəˈreɪ.ni.əm, dʒɪ- **-s** -z

Gerard ˈdʒer.ɑːd, ˈdʒer.əd, dʒerˈɑːd, dʒəˈrɑːd, (US) dʒəˈrɑːrd

Gerbeau ʒeəˈbəʊ, ʒɜː-, ˈ--, (US) ʒerˈboʊ, ˈ--

gerbil ˈdʒɜː.bəl, -bɪl, (US) ˈdʒɝː.bəl **-s** -z

gerfalcon ˈdʒɜːˌfɔːl.kən, -ˌfɔː.kən, (US) ˈdʒɝːˌfɑːl-, -ˌfæl-, -ˌfɔː- **-s** -z

> Note: In British English, those who practise the sport of falconry pronounce /-ˌfɔː-/.

Gerhardt ˈgeə.hɑːt, (US) ˈger.hɑːrd, -hɑːrt

geriatric ˌdʒer.iˈæt.rɪk **-s** -s

geriatrician ˌdʒer.i.əˈtrɪʃ.ən **-s** -z

geriatry ˈdʒer.i.ə.tri, -æt.ri

Geritol® ˈdʒer.ɪ.tɒl, (US) -tɑːl

Gerizim gerˈaɪ.zɪm, gəˈraɪ-, -ˈriː-; ˈger.ɪ.zɪm

germ dʒɜːm, (US) dʒɝːm **-s** -z ˌ**germ** ˈ**warfare**

Germain ˈdʒɜː.meɪn, (US) ˈdʒɝː-

Germaine dʒəˈmeɪn, dʒɜː-, (US) dʒɚ-

German ˈdʒɜː.mən, (US) ˈdʒɝː- **-s** -z ˌ**German** ˈ**measles**

germander dʒəˈmæn.dər, dʒɜː-, (US) dʒɚˈmæn.dɚ

germane, G~ dʒəˈmeɪn, dʒɜː-; ˈdʒɜː.meɪn, (US) dʒɚˈmeɪn **-ly** -li **-ness** -nəs, -nɪs

Germanic dʒəˈmæn.ɪk, dʒɜː-, (US) dʒɚ-

German|ism ˈdʒɜː.mə.n|ɪ.zəm, (US) ˈdʒɝː- **-isms** -ɪ.zəmz **-ist/s** -ɪst/s

germanium dʒəˈmeɪ.ni.əm, dʒɜː-, (US) dʒɚ-

germanization, -isa- ˌdʒɜː.mə.naɪˈzeɪ.ʃən, -ɪˈ-, (US) ˌdʒɝː.mə.nəˈ-

germaniz|e, -is|e ˈdʒɜː.mə.naɪz, (US) ˈdʒɝː- **-es** -ɪz **-ing** -ɪŋ **-ed** -d

German|y ˈdʒɜː.mə.n|i, (US) ˈdʒɝː- **-ies** -iz

germicidal ˌdʒɜː.mɪˈsaɪ.dəl, -məˈ-, ˈdʒɜː.mɪ.saɪ-, -mə-, (US) ˌdʒɝː.məˈsaɪ-

germicide ˈdʒɜː.mɪ.saɪd, -mə-, (US) ˈdʒɝː.mə- **-s** -z

germinal ˈdʒɜː.mɪ.nəl, -mə-, (US) ˈdʒɝː.mə-

germi|nate ˈdʒɜː.mɪ|.neɪt, -mə-, (US) ˈdʒɝː.mə- **-nates** -neɪts **-nating** -neɪ.tɪŋ, (US) -neɪ.ṭɪŋ **-nated** -neɪ.tɪd, (US) -neɪ.ṭɪd

germination ˌdʒɜː.mɪˈneɪ.ʃən, -məˈ-, (US) ˌdʒɝː.məˈ- **-s** -z

Germiston ˈdʒɜː.mɪ.stən, (US) ˈdʒɝː.mɪ-, -mə-

Germolene® ˈdʒɜː.mə.liːn, (US) ˈdʒɝː-

Geronimo dʒəˈrɒn.ɪ.məʊ, dʒɪ-, dʒerˈɒn-, ˈ-ə-, (US) -ˈrɑː.nə.moʊ

Gerontius gəˈrɒn.ti.əs, gɪ-, dʒə-, dʒɪ-, gerˈɒn-, -ʃi.əs, -ʃəs, (US) dʒəˈrɑːn-

gerontocrac|y ˌdʒer.ɒnˈtɒk.rə.s|i, -ənˈ-, (US) -ənˈtɑː.krə- **-cies** -iz

gerontocratic dʒəˌrɒn.təˈkræt.ɪk, ˌdʒer.ɒn-, dʒəˌrən.təˈ-, (US) dʒəˌrɑːn.ṭəˈkræṭ.ɪk

gerontological ˌdʒer.ən.təˈlɒdʒ.ɪ.kəl, (US) -lɑː.dʒɪ-

gerontolog|y ˌdʒer.ɒnˈtɒl.ə.dʒ|i, ˌger-, -ənˈ-, (US) ˌdʒer.ənˈtɑː.lə- **-ist/s** -ɪst/s

Gerrard ˈdʒer.əd, -ɑːd; dʒerˈɑːd, dʒəˈrɑːd, (US) ˈdʒer.ɚd ˌ**Gerrard's** ˈ**Cross**

Gerry ˈdʒer.i

gerrymand|er ˈdʒer.i.mæn.d|ər, ˌdʒer.iˈmæn-, (US) -d|ɚ **-ers** -əz, (US) -ɚz **-ering** -ər.ɪŋ **-ered** -əd, (US) -ɚd

Gershwin ˈgɜːʃ.wɪn, (US) ˈgɝːʃ-, -wən

Gertie ˈgɜː.ti, (US) ˈgɝː.ṭi

Gertrude ˈgɜː.truːd, (US) ˈgɝː-

Gerty ˈgɜː.ti, (US) ˈgɝː.ṭi

gerund ˈdʒer.ənd, -ʌnd **-s** -z

gerundival ˌdʒer.ənˈdaɪ.vəl

gerundive dʒəˈrʌn.dɪv, dʒɪ-, dʒerˈʌn- **-s** -z

Gervais ʒɜːˈveɪs, -veɪz, (US) ʒɝː-

Gerva(i)se ˈdʒɜː.veɪz, -vɪz; dʒɜːˈveɪz, -ˈveɪs, (US) ˈdʒɝː-

Geryon ˈger.i.ən, (US) ˈdʒɪr-, ˈger-

gesso ˈdʒes.əʊ, (US) -oʊ **-es** -z

gest dʒest **-s** -s

gestalt gəˈʃtælt, -ʃtɑːlt; ˈgeʃ.tælt, (US) gəˈʃtɑːlt

Pronouncing the letters GG

The main pronunciation for the consonant digraph **gg** is /g/, e.g.:

rugged ˈrʌg.ɪd

In addition

gg may be pronounced as /dʒ/, e.g.:

exaggerate ɪgˈzædʒ.ər.eɪt ⓤⓢ -ə.reɪt

And in rare cases for American English as /gdʒ/:

suggest səˈdʒest ⓤⓢ səgˈdʒest

Gestapo gesˈtɑː.pəʊ, geʃ-, ⓤⓢ gəˈstɑː.poʊ, gəʃˈtɑː-
Gesta Romanorum ˌdʒes.təˌrəʊ.məˈnɔː.rəm, -mɑː-, ˌges-, ⓤⓢ -ˌroʊ.məˈnɔːr.əm, -mɑː-
ges|tate dʒes|ˈteɪt, ˈ--, ⓤⓢ ˈdʒes|.teɪt **-tates** -ˈteɪts, ⓤⓢ -teɪts **-tating** -ˈteɪ.tɪŋ, ⓤⓢ -teɪ.t̬ɪŋ **-tated** -ˈteɪ.tɪd, ⓤⓢ -teɪ.t̬ɪd
gestation dʒesˈteɪ.ʃən **-s** -z
gestatorial ˌdʒes.təˈtɔː.ri.əl
gestatory dʒesˈteɪ.tər.i; ˈdʒes.tə-, ⓤⓢ ˈdʒes.tə.tɔːr-
Gestetner® gesˈtet.nəʳ, gɪˈstet-, gə-, ⓤⓢ -nɚ
gesticu|late dʒesˈtɪk.jə|.leɪt, -jʊ-, ⓤⓢ -jə- **-lates** -leɪts **-lating** -leɪ.tɪŋ, ⓤⓢ -leɪ.t̬ɪŋ **-lated** -leɪ.tɪd, ⓤⓢ -leɪ.t̬ɪd **-lator/s** -leɪ.təʳ/z, ⓤⓢ -leɪ.t̬ɚ/z
gesticulation dʒesˌtɪk.jəˈleɪ.ʃən, -jʊˈ-, ⓤⓢ -jəˈ- **-s** -z
gesticulatory dʒesˈtɪk.jʊ.leɪ.tər.i, -lə-, -je-, ⓤⓢ -jə.lə.tɔːr-
gestur|e ˈdʒes.tʃəʳ, ⓤⓢ -tʃɚ **-es** -z **-ing** -ɪŋ **-ed** -d
Gesundheit gəˈzʊnd.haɪt
get get **-s** -s **-ting** -ɪŋ, ⓤⓢ ˈget̬.ɪŋ **got** gɒt, ⓤⓢ gɑːt **gotten** ˈgɒt.ən, ⓤⓢ ˈgɑː.tən **ˌgive as ˌgood as one ˈgets**
Getae ˈgeɪ.taɪ, ˈdʒiː.tiː
getatable getˈæt.ə.bəl, ⓤⓢ get̬ˈæt̬-
getaway ˈget.ə.weɪ, ⓤⓢ ˈget̬- **-s** -z
Gethin ˈgeθ.ɪn
Gethsemane geθˈsem.ə.ni
get-rich-quick ˌget.rɪtʃˈkwɪk
get-together ˈget.tə.geð.ə, ⓤⓢ -geð.ɚ **-s** -z
Getty ˈget.i, ⓤⓢ ˈget̬.i
Gettysburg ˈget.iz.bɜːg, ⓤⓢ ˈget̬.iz.bɝːg **ˌGettysburg Adˈdress**
getup ˈget.ʌp, ⓤⓢ ˈget̬- **-s** -s
get-up-and-go ˌget.ʌp.ənˈgəʊ, -əŋˈ-, ⓤⓢ ˌget̬.ʌp.ənˈgoʊ
geum ˈdʒiː.əm **-s** -z
gewgaw ˈgjuː.gɔː, ⓤⓢ ˈguː.gɑː, ˈgjuː-, -gɔː **-s** -z
Gewürztraminer gəˈvʊət.strəˌmiː.nə, -ˈvɜːt-, ⓤⓢ -ˈvɝːt.strəˌmiː.nɚ
geyser *hot spring:* ˈgiː.zəʳ, ˈgaɪ-, ⓤⓢ ˈgaɪ.zɚ *apparatus for heating water:* ˈgiː.zəʳ, ⓤⓢ -zɚ **-s** -z

Note: In New Zealand the pronunciation is /ˈgaɪ.zəʳ/.

Ghana ˈgɑː.nə
Ghanaian gɑːˈneɪ.ən, ⓤⓢ -ˈniː-, -ˈneɪ- **-s** -z
ghastl|y ˈgɑːst.l|i, ⓤⓢ ˈgæst.l|i **-ier** -i.əʳ, ⓤⓢ -i.ɚ **-iest** -i.ɪst, -i.əst **-iness** -ɪ.nəs, -ɪ.nɪs
Ghat gɑːt, gɔːt **-s** -s
ghee giː
Ghent gent
gherkin ˈgɜː.kɪn, ⓤⓢ ˈgɝː- **-s** -z
ghetto ˈget.əʊ, ⓤⓢ ˈget̬.oʊ **-(e)s** -z **ˈghetto ˌblaster**
ghettoiz|e, -i|se ˈget.əʊ.aɪz, ⓤⓢ ˈget̬.oʊ- **-es** -ɪz **-ing** -ɪŋ **-ed** -d
Ghia ˈgiː.ə
Ghibelline ˈgɪb.ɪ.laɪn, ˈ-ə-, -liːn **-s** -z
ghillie ˈgɪl.i **-s** -z
ghost gəʊst, ⓤⓢ goʊst **-s** -s **-ing** -ɪŋ **-ed** -ɪd **-like** -laɪk **ˈghost ˌtown; ˌgive up the ˈghost**
ghostl|y ˈgəʊst.l|i, ⓤⓢ ˈgoʊst- **-iness** -ɪ.nəs, -ɪ.nɪs
ghost|write ˈgəʊst|.raɪt, ⓤⓢ ˈgoʊst- **-writes** -raɪts **-writing** -ˌraɪ.tɪŋ, ⓤⓢ -ˌraɪ.t̬ɪŋ **-wrote** -rəʊt, ⓤⓢ -roʊt
ghostwriter ˈgəʊstˌraɪ.təʳ, ⓤⓢ ˈgoʊstˌraɪ.t̬ɚ **-s** -z
ghoul guːl **-s** -z **-ish/ly** -ɪʃ/li
ghyll gɪl **-s** -z
GI ˌdʒiːˈaɪ *stress shift:* **ˌGI ˈbride**
giant dʒaɪ.ənt **-s** -s **-like** -laɪk **ˌGiant's ˈCauseway**
giantess ˈdʒaɪ.ən.tes, -tɪs, -təs; ˌdʒaɪ.ənˈtes, ⓤⓢ ˈdʒaɪ.ən.t̬əs **-es** -ɪz
Giaour ˈdʒaʊ.əʳ, ⓤⓢ ˈdʒaʊ.ɚ
Gibb gɪb
gibb|er ˈdʒɪb|.əʳ, ⓤⓢ -ɚ **-ers** -əz, ⓤⓢ -ɚz **-ering** -ər.ɪŋ **-ered** -əd, ⓤⓢ -ɚd
gibberish ˈdʒɪb.ə.rɪʃ
gibbet ˈdʒɪb.ɪt, -ət **-s** -s **-ing** -ɪŋ, ⓤⓢ ˈdʒɪb.ɪ.t̬ɪŋ **-ed** -ɪd, ⓤⓢ ˈdʒɪb.ɪ.t̬ɪd
Gibbie ˈdʒɪb.i
Gibbins ˈgɪb.ɪnz
gibbon, G~ ˈgɪb.ən **-s** -z
gibbosity gɪˈbɒs.ə.ti, dʒɪ-, -ɪ.ti, ⓤⓢ gɪˈbɑː.sə.t̬i
gibbous ˈgɪb.əs, ˈdʒɪb-, ⓤⓢ ˈgɪb- **-ly** -li **-ness** -nəs, -nɪs
Gibbs gɪbz
gib|e dʒaɪb **-es** -z **-ing/ly** -ɪŋ/li **-ed** -d **-er/s** -əʳ/z, ⓤⓢ -ɚ/z
Gibeon ˈgɪb.i.ən
giblet ˈdʒɪb.lət, -lɪt **-s** -s
Gibraltar dʒɪˈbrɔːl.təʳ, dʒə-, -ˈbrɒl-, ⓤⓢ -ˈbrɑːl.tɚ, -ˈbrɔːl-
Gibraltarian ˌdʒɪb.rɔːlˈteə.ri.ən, -rɒlˈ-; dʒɪˌbrɔːlˈ-, dʒə-, -ˌbrɒlˈ-, ⓤⓢ ˌdʒɪb.rɑːlˈter.i-, -rɔːlˈ- **-s** -z
Gibson ˈgɪb.sən
Gidding ˈgɪd.ɪŋ **-s** -z
Giddis ˈgɪd.ɪs
gidd|y, G~ ˈgɪd|.i **-ier** -i.əʳ, ⓤⓢ -i.ɚ **-iest** -i.ɪst, -i.əst **-ily** -əl.i, -ɪ.li **-iness** -ɪ.nəs, -ɪ.nɪs
Gide ʒiːd
Gidea ˈgɪd.i.ə
Gideon ˈgɪd.i.ən
Gielgud ˈgiːl.gʊd
GIF gɪf, dʒɪf
Giffard ˈdʒɪf.əd, ˈgɪf-, ⓤⓢ -ɚd
Giffen ˈgɪf.ɪn, ˈdʒɪf.ɪn, -ən
Giffnock ˈgɪf.nək
Gifford *place near Haddington:* ˈgɪf.əd, ⓤⓢ -ɚd *surname:* ˈgɪf.əd, ˈdʒɪf.əd, ⓤⓢ -ɚd
gift gɪft **-s** -s **-ed** -ɪd **ˈgift cerˌtificate; ˈgift ˌtoken; ˌgift of the ˈgab; ˌlook a ˌgift horse in the ˈmouth**
gift-wrap ˈgɪft.ræp **-s** -s **-ping** -ɪŋ **-ped** -t
gig gɪg **-s** -z
giga- ˈgɪg.ə, ˈgaɪ.gə, ˈdʒɪg.ə
gigabyte ˈgɪg.ə.baɪt, ˈgaɪ.gə-, ˈdʒɪg.ə- **-s** -s
gigahertz ˈgɪg.ə.hɜːts, ˈgaɪ.gə-, ˈdʒɪg.ə-, ⓤⓢ -hɝːts
gigantesque ˌdʒaɪ.gænˈtesk, -gən-
gigantic dʒaɪˈgæn.tɪk, ˌdʒaɪ-, ⓤⓢ -t̬ɪk **-ally** -əl.i, -li
gigantism dʒaɪˈgæn.tɪ.zəm, ˈdʒaɪ.gæn-, ⓤⓢ -t̬ɪ-
giggl|e n, v ˈgɪg.əl **-es** -z **-ing** -ɪŋ, ˈ-lɪŋ **-ed** -d **-er/s** -əʳ/z, ˈ-ləʳ/z, ⓤⓢ ˈ-əl.ɚ/z, ˈ-lɚ/z
giggleswick, G~ ˈgɪg.əlz.wɪk
giggly ˈgɪg.əl.i, ˈgɪg.li
Giggs gɪgz
Gight gɪkt, gɪxt
Gigi ˈʒiː.ʒiː
Gigli ˈdʒiː.li, -lji, ⓤⓢ ˈdʒiː.li, ˈdʒiːl.ji
Giglio ˈdʒiː.li.əʊ, ˈ-ljəʊ, ⓤⓢ ˈ-li.oʊ
GIGO ˈgaɪ.gəʊ, ˈdʒaɪ-, ⓤⓢ ˈgiː.g.oʊ, ˈgaɪ.goʊ
gigolo ˈdʒɪg.ə.ləʊ, ˈʒɪg-, ⓤⓢ -loʊ **-s** -z
gigot ˈdʒiː.gəʊ, ˈdʒɪg.ət, ⓤⓢ ʒiːˈgoʊ **-s** -s
gigue ʒiːg, ʒɪg **-s** -z
Gihon ˈgaɪ.hɒn, ⓤⓢ -hɑːn; *in Jewish usage sometimes:* ˈgiː.həʊn
gila, G~ ˈhiː.lə, ˈgiː-, ⓤⓢ ˈhiː- **-s** -z
Gilbert ˈgɪl.bət, ⓤⓢ -bɚt
Gilbertian gɪlˈbɜː.ti.ən, -ʃən, ⓤⓢ -ˈbɝː.t̬i.ən
Gilbey ˈgɪl.bi
Gilboa gɪlˈbəʊ.ə, ⓤⓢ -ˈboʊ-
Gilchrist ˈgɪl.krɪst
gild gɪld **-s** -z **-ing** -ɪŋ **-ed** -ɪd **gilt** gɪlt
Gildas ˈgɪl.dæs
gilder, G~ ˈgɪl.dəʳ, ⓤⓢ -dɚ **-s** -z
Gildersleeve ˈgɪl.də.sliːv, ⓤⓢ -dɚ-
Gildersome ˈgɪl.də.səm, ⓤⓢ -dɚ-
Gilding ˈgɪl.dɪŋ
Gildredge ˈgɪl.drɪdʒ, -dredʒ

Pronouncing the letters GH

The consonant digraph **gh** can be pronounced as /g/, /f/, or may be silent.

In syllable-initial position, **gh** is always pronounced as /g/, e.g.:

ghost	gəʊst US goʊst
aghast	əˈgɑːst US -ˈgæst

Following a vowel letter, the pronunciation may be silent. This is always the case after **i** and **ei**, e.g.:

high	haɪ
height	haɪt
plough	plaʊ
caught	kɔːt US kɑːt

Alternatively, the pronunciation may be /f/, e.g.:

rough	rʌf
laugh	lɑːf US læf

In addition

A unique pronunciation of the consonant digraph **gh** is /p/, e.g.:

hiccough	ˈhɪk.ʌp

G

Gilead ˈgɪl.i.æd, US -əd
Giles dʒaɪlz
Gilfil ˈgɪl.fɪl
Gilfillan gɪlˈfɪl.ən
Gilford ˈgɪl.fəd, US -fɚd
Gilgal ˈgɪl.gæl, -gɔːl
Gilgamesh ˈgɪl.gə.meʃ
Gilham ˈgɪl.əm
Gilkes dʒɪlks
gill *respiratory organ, ravine:* gɪl *measure:* dʒɪl **-s** -z
Gill *family name or male first name:* gɪl; *female first name:* dʒɪl
Gillam ˈgɪl.əm
Gillard ˈgɪl.ɑːd, -əd; gɪˈlɑːd, US ˈgɪl.ɚd
Gillen ˈgɪl.ən
Gilleney ˈgɪl.ən.i
Gillespie gɪˈles.pi, gə-
Gillett ˈgɪl.ɪt, ˈgɪl.et, gɪˈlet, dʒɪˈlet, dʒəˈlet
Gillette® dʒɪˈlet, US dʒəˈlet, dʒɪ- **-s** -s
Gilley ˈgɪl.i
Gilliam ˈgɪl.i.əm
Gillian ˈdʒɪl.i.ən, ˈgɪl-
Gilliat ˈgɪl.i.ət, -æt
Gillick ˈgɪl.ɪk
gillie, G~ ˈgɪl.i **-s** -z
Gillies ˈgɪl.ɪs
Gilligan ˈgɪl.i.gən
Gilliland ˈgɪl.ɪ.lænd
Gilling ˈgɪl.ɪŋ **-s** -z
Gillingham *in Kent:* ˈdʒɪl.ɪŋ.əm *in Dorset & Norfolk:* ˈgɪl- *surname:* ˈgɪl-, ˈdʒɪl-
Gillison ˈgɪl.ɪ.sᵊn
Gillmore ˈgɪl.mɔːʳ, US -mɔːr
Gillon ˈgɪl.ən
Gillott ˈdʒɪl.ət, ˈgɪl.ət
Gillow ˈgɪl.əʊ, US -oʊ
Gillray ˈgɪl.reɪ
Gills gɪlz
Gillson ˈdʒɪl.sᵊn
gilly ˈgɪl.i **-s** -z
gillyflower ˈdʒɪl.ɪˌflaʊəʳ, -ˌflaʊ.əʳ, US -ˌflaʊ.ɚ **-s** -z
Gilman ˈgɪl.mən
Gilmer ˈgɪl.məʳ, US -mɚ
Gilmore ˈgɪl.mɔːʳ, -məʳ, US -mɔːr
Gilmour ˈgɪl.mɔːʳ, -məʳ, US -mɔːr
Gilpatrick gɪlˈpæt.rɪk
Gilpin ˈgɪl.pɪn
Gilroy ˈgɪl.rɔɪ
Gilson ˈdʒɪl.sᵊn, ˈgɪl.sᵊn
gilt gɪlt **-s** -s
gilt-edged ˌgɪltˈedʒd *stress shift:* ˌ**gilt-edged** ˈ**stocks**
gimbal ˈgɪm.bəl, ˈdʒɪm- **-s** -z
gimbl|e ˈgɪm.bᵊl **-es** -z **-ing** -ɪŋ, ˈ-blɪŋ **-ed** -d
Gimblett ˈgɪm.*b*lɪt, -ət
gimcrack ˈdʒɪm.kræk **-s** -s
gimlet ˈgɪm.lət, -lɪt **-s** -s
gimme ˈgɪm.i
gimmick ˈgɪm.ɪk **-s** -s **-ry** -ri **-y** -i
gimp gɪmp
Gimson ˈgɪm*p*.sᵊn, ˈdʒɪm*p*.sᵊn
gin dʒɪn **-s** -z ˈ**gin** ˌ**mill**; ˌ**gin** ˈ**rummy**; ˌ**gin** ˈ**sling**
Gina ˈdʒiː.nə
Gingell ˈgɪn.dʒᵊl
ginger *spice, colour:* ˈdʒɪn.dʒəʳ, US -dʒɚ; *person with ginger hair:* ˈgɪŋ.əʳ, US -ɚ **-s** -z ˌ**ginger** ˈ**ale**; ˌ**ginger** ˈ**beer**
gingerbread, G~ ˈdʒɪn.dʒə.bred, US -dʒɚ- **-s** -z ˈ**gingerbread** ˌ**man**
gingerly ˈdʒɪn.dʒᵊl.i, US -dʒɚ.li
ginger|y ˈdʒɪn.dʒᵊr|.i **-iness** -ɪ.nəs, -ɪ.nɪs
gingham ˈgɪŋ.əm **-s** -z
gingival dʒɪnˈdʒaɪ.vᵊl, ˈdʒɪn.dʒɪ.vᵊl
gingivitis ˌdʒɪn.dʒɪˈvaɪ.tɪs, -dʒəˈ-, -təs, US -dʒəˈvaɪ.t̬ɪs, -t̬əs
gingko ˈgɪŋ.kəʊ, US -koʊ **-s** -z
Gingold ˈgɪŋ.gəʊld, US -goʊld
Gingrich ˈgɪŋ.grɪtʃ
ginkgo ˈgɪŋ.kəʊ, ˈgɪŋk.gəʊ, US ˈgɪŋ.koʊ, ˈgɪŋk.goʊ **-es** -z
Ginn gɪn
ginnel ˈgɪn.ᵊl, ˈdʒɪn- **-s** -z
Ginny ˈdʒɪn.i
Ginola ˈdʒɪ.nəʊ.lə, ˈʒɪn-, US -nə-, -ˌnoʊ-
ginormous dʒaɪˈnɔː.məs, US -ˈnɔːr-
Ginsberg ˈgɪnz.bɜːg, US -bɝːg
ginseng ˈdʒɪn.seŋ
Gioconda ˌdʒɪəˈkɒn.də, US -ˈkɑːn-
Giotto ˈdʒɒt.əʊ, dʒiˈɒt-, US ˈdʒɑː.t̬oʊ
Giovanni ˌdʒiː.əʊˈvɑː.ni, dʒəʊˈ-, -ˈvæn.i, US dʒoʊˈvɑː-, dʒə-
gip gɪp **-s** -s **-ping** -ɪŋ **-ped** -t
Gipp gɪp
Gippsland ˈgɪps.lænd
gippy ˈdʒɪp.i
gips|y ˈdʒɪp.s|i **-ies** -iz
giraffe dʒɪˈrɑːf, dʒə-, -ˈræf, US dʒəˈræf **-s** -s
Giralda dʒɪˈræl.də, hɪ-
girandole ˈdʒɪr.ən.dəʊl, US -doʊl **-s** -z
gird gɜːd, US gɝːd **-s** -z **-ing** -ɪŋ **-ed** -ɪd **girt** gɜːt, US gɝːt
girder ˈgɜː.dəʳ, US ˈgɝː.dɚ **-s** -z
girdl|e ˈgɜː.dᵊl, US ˈgɝː- **-es** -z **-ing** -ɪŋ, ˈgɜːd.lɪŋ, US ˈgɝː.dᵊl.ɪŋ, ˈgɝːd.lɪŋ **-ed** -d
Girdlestone ˈgɜː.dᵊl.stᵊn, US ˈgɝː-
girl gɜːl, US gɝːl **-s** -z **-hood** -hʊd
girlfriend ˈgɜːl.frend, US ˈgɝːl- **-s** -z
girlie ˈgɜː.li, US ˈgɝː-
girlish ˈgɜː.lɪʃ, US ˈgɝː- **-ly** -li **-ness** -nəs, -nɪs
girly ˈgɜː.li, US ˈgɝː-
giro, G~ ˈdʒaɪə.rəʊ, US ˈdʒaɪ.roʊ **-s** -z
Girobank® ˈdʒaɪə.rəʊ.bæŋk, US ˈdʒaɪ.roʊ-
Gironde dʒɪˈrɒnd, ʒɪ-; -ˈrɔ̃ːnd, US dʒəˈrɑːnd
Girondist dʒɪˈrɒn.dɪst, ʒɪ-, US dʒəˈrɑːn- **-s** -s
girt n gɜːt, US gɝːt **-s** -s
girt (from **gird**) gɜːt, US gɝːt
girth gɜːθ, US gɝːθ **-s** -s
Girtin ˈgɜː.tɪn, US ˈgɝː.tɪn, -tᵊn
Girton ˈgɜː.tᵊn, US ˈgɝː-
Girtonian gɜːˈtəʊ.ni.ən, US gɚˈtoʊ- **-s** -z
Girvan ˈgɜː.vən, US ˈgɝː.vᵊn
Gisbourne ˈgɪz.bɔːn, -bən, US -bɔːrn
Giscard d'Estaing ˌ*d*ʒiːs.kɑː.des.ˈtæ̃ŋ, US ʒiːsˌkɑːr.desˈtæ̃ŋ
Giselle ʒɪˈzel, dʒɪ-
Gish gɪʃ
gismo ˈgɪz.məʊ, US -moʊ **-s** -z
Gissing ˈgɪs.ɪŋ
gist dʒɪst **-s** -s
git gɪt **-s** -s
Gita ˈgiː.tə, US -t̬ə
Gitane® ʒiˈtɑːn, US -ˈtɑːn, -ˈtæn **-s** -z
gîte, gite ʒiːt **-s** -s
gittern ˈgɪt.ɜːn, US -ɚn **-s** -z
Gitty ˈgɪt.i, US ˈgɪt̬.i
Giuliani ˌdʒuː.liˈɑː.ni
Giuseppe dʒuˈsep.i
giv|e gɪv **-es** -z **-ing** -ɪŋ **gave** geɪv

giv|en ˈgɪv|.ən **-er/s** -əʳ/z, (US) -ɚ/z **ˈgiven ˌname; ˌgive as ˌgood as one ˈgets**
give-and-take ˌgɪv.ənˈdteɪk
giveaway ˈgɪv.ə.weɪ **-s** -z
giveback ˈgɪv.bæk **-s** -s
Givenchy® dʒiˈvɑ̃ːn.ʃi, (US) ʒiˈvɑ̃ːn-, -ˈʃiː
Giza, Gîza ˈgiː.zə
Gizeh ˈgiː.zeɪ, -zə
gizmo ˈgɪz.məʊ, (US) -moʊ **-s** -z
gizzard ˈgɪz.əd, (US) -ɚd **-s** -z
glabrous ˈgleɪ.brəs
glacé, glace ˈglæs.eɪ, (US) glæsˈeɪ **-ed** -d
glacial ˈgleɪ.si.əl, -ʃəl; ˈglæs.i.əl, (US) ˈgleɪ.ʃəl **-ly** -i
glaciation ˌgleɪ.siˈeɪ.ʃən, ˌglæs-, (US) ˌgleɪ.ʃiˈ-
glacier ˈglæs.i.əʳ, ˈgleɪ.si-, (US) ˈgleɪ.ʃɚ **-s** -z
glacis ˈglæs.ɪs, -i, (US) ˈgleɪ.sɪs, ˈglæs.ɪs, glæsˈiː **plur** ˈglæs.ɪz, (US) ˈgleɪ.siːz, ˈglæs.iːz, -ˈ-
glacises (alternative plural of **glacis**) ˈglæs.ɪ.sɪz, (US) ˈgleɪ.sɪ.ziːz, ˈglæs.ɪ-
glad glæd **-der** -əʳ, (US) -ɚ **-dest** -ɪst, -əst **-ness** -nəs, -nɪs **ˈglad ˌrags**
gladden ˈglæd.ən **-s** -z **-ing** -ɪŋ **-ed** -d
glade gleɪd **-s** -z
glad-hand ˈglædˌhænd, ˌ-ˈ- **-s** -z **-ing** -ɪŋ **-ed** -ɪd **-er/s** -əʳ/z
gladiator ˈglæd.i.eɪ.təʳ, (US) -t̬ɚ **-s** -z
gladiatorial ˌglæd.i.əˈtɔː.ri.əl, (US) -tɔːr.i.əl
gladiole ˈglæd.i.əʊl, (US) -oʊl **-s** -z
gladiol|us ˌglæd.iˈəʊ.l|əs, (US) -ˈoʊ- **-i** -aɪ **-uses** -ə.sɪz
gladly ˈglæd.li
gladsome ˈglæd.səm **-ly** -li **-ness** -nəs, -nɪs
Gladstone ˈglæd.stən, (US) -stoʊn, -stən
Gladstonian glædˈstəʊ.ni.ən, (US) -ˈstoʊ-
Gladwin ˈglæd.wɪn
Gladys ˈglæd.ɪs
glagolitic, G~ ˌglæg.əʊˈlɪt.ɪk, (US) -əˈlɪt̬-
glair gleəʳ, (US) gler
Glaisdale ˈgleɪz.deɪl; *locally:* -dəl
Glaisher ˈgleɪ.ʃəʳ, (US) -ʃɚ
glam glæm
Glam. (abbrev. for **Glamorgan**) gləˈmɔː.gən, (US) -ˈmɔːr-
Glamis glɑːmz, ˈglæm.ɪs

> Note: In Shakespeare /ˈglæm.ɪs/.

Glamorgan gləˈmɔː.gən, (US) -ˈmɔːr- **-shire** -ʃə, -ʃɪəʳ, (US) -ʃɚ, -ʃɪr
glamoriz|e, -is|e ˈglæm.ər.aɪz, (US) -ə.raɪz **-es** -ɪz **-ing** -ɪŋ **-ed** -d
glamorous ˈglæm.ər.əs **-ly** -li **-ness** -nəs, -nɪs
glamour ˈglæm.əʳ, (US) -ɚ
glamourous ˈglæm.ər.əs **-ly** -li **-ness** -nəs, -nɪs
glamourpuss ˈglæm.ə.pʊs, (US) -ɚ- **-es** -ɪz
glanc|e glɑːnts, (US) glænts **-es** -ɪz **-ing/ly** -ɪŋ/li **-ed** -t
gland glænd **-s** -z
glander|s ˈglæn.də|z, ˈglɑːn-, (US) ˈglæn.dɚ|z **-ed** -d
glandes (plural of **glans**) ˈglæn.diːz
glandular ˈglæn.dʒə.ləʳ, ˈ-djə-, ˈ-dʒʊ-, ˈ-djʊ-, (US) -dʒə.lɚ **ˌglandular ˈfever**
glandule ˈglæn.dʒuːl, ˈ-djuːl, (US) -dʒuːl **-s** -z
glans glænz **glandes** ˈglæn.diːz
Glanvill(e) ˈglæn.vɪl
Glapthorne ˈglæp.θɔːn, (US) -θɔːrn
glar|e gleəʳ, (US) gler **-es** -z **-ing/ly** -ɪŋ/li **-ingness** -ɪŋ.nəs, -nɪs **-ed** -d
Glarus *place in US:* ˈglær.əs, (US) ˈgler-, ˈglær- *other senses:* ˈglɑː.rəs
Glasgow ˈglɑːz.gəʊ, ˈglɑːs-, ˈglɑːs.kəʊ, ˈglæz.gəʊ, ˈglæs-, ˈglæs.kəʊ, (US) ˈglæs.koʊ, ˈglæz.goʊ
glasier, G~ ˈgleɪ.zi.əʳ, -ʒəʳ, (US) -ʒɚ **-s** -z
glasnost ˈglæs.nɒst, ˈglæz-, (US) ˈglæs.nɑːst, -noʊst
glass, G~ glɑːs, (US) glæs **-es** -ɪz **ˌglass ˈceiling; ˈglass ˌcutter**
glassblow|er ˈglɑːsˌbləʊ|.əʳ, (US) ˈglæsˌbloʊ|.ɚ **-ers** -əz, (US) -ɚz **-ing** -ɪŋ
Glasscock ˈglɑːs.kɒk, -kəʊ, (US) ˈglæs.kɑːk, -koʊ
glassful ˈglɑːs.fʊl, (US) ˈglæs- **-s** -z
glasshou|se ˈglɑːs.haʊ|s, (US) ˈglæs- **-ses** -zɪz
glasspaper, glass-paper ˈglɑːsˌpeɪ.pəʳ, (US) ˈglæsˌpeɪ.pɚ
glassware ˈglɑːs.weəʳ, (US) ˈglæs.wer
glasswork ˈglɑːs.wɜːk, (US) ˈglæs.wɝːk **-s** -s
glasswort ˈglɑːs.wɜːt, (US) ˈglæs.wɝːt, -wɔːrt
glass|y ˈglɑː.s|i, (US) ˈglæs|.i **-ier** -i.əʳ, (US) -i.ɚ **-iest** -i.ɪst, -i.əst **-ily** -əl.i, -ɪ.li **-iness** -ɪ.nəs, -ɪ.nɪs
Glastonbury ˈglæs.tən.bər.i, ˈglɑː.stən-, (US) ˈglæs.tənˌber.i, -bər.i
Glaswegian glæzˈwiː.dʒən, glɑːz-, glæs-, glɑːs-, -dʒi.ən, (US) glæs-, glæz- **-s** -z
glaucoma glɔːˈkəʊ.mə, glaʊ-, (US) glɑːˈkoʊ-, glɔː- **-tous** -təs
glaucous ˈglɔː.kəs, (US) ˈglɑː-, ˈglɔː-
Glaxo® ˈglæk.səʊ, (US) -soʊ
glaz|e gleɪz **-es** -ɪz **-ing** -ɪŋ **-ed** -d **-er/s** -əʳ/z, (US) -ɚ/z
Glazebrook ˈgleɪz.brʊk
glazier ˈgleɪ.zi.əʳ, ˈ-ʒəʳ, (US) ˈ-ʒɚ **-s** -z
Glazunov ˈglæz.u.nɒf, (US) ˈglæz.ə.nɑːf, ˈglɑː.zə-, -noʊf
gleam gliːm **-s** -z **-ing** -ɪŋ **-ed** -d **-y** -i
glean gliːn **-s** -z **-ing/s** -ɪŋ/z **-ed** -d **-er/s** -əʳ/z, (US) -ɚ/z
Gleason ˈgliː.sən
glebe gliːb **-s** -z
glee gliː **ˈglee ˌclub**
gleeful ˈgliː.fəl, -fʊl **-ly** -i **-ness** -nəs, -nɪs
glee|man ˈgliː|.mən, -mæn **-men** -mən, -men
Glegg gleg
Gleichen ˈglaɪ.kən
Glemsford ˈglems.fəd, ˈglemz-, (US) -fɚd
glen, G~ glen **-s** -z
Glenallan glenˈæl.ən
Glenalmond glenˈɑː.mənd
Glenavon glenˈæv.ən
Glenavy glenˈeɪ.vi
Glencairn glenˈkeən, gleŋ-, (US) glenˈkern
Glencoe glenˈkəʊ, gleŋ-, (US) glenˈkoʊ
Glenda ˈglen.də
Glendale glenˈdeɪl, ˈglen.deɪl, (US) ˈglen-
Glendenning glenˈden.ɪŋ
Glendin(n)ing glenˈdɪn.ɪŋ
Glendower glenˈdaʊ.əʳ, (US) -ɚ
Gleneagles glenˈiː.gəlz
Glenelg glenˈelg
Glenfiddich glenˈfɪd.ɪk, -ɪx
Glenfinnan glenˈfɪn.ən
glengarr|y, G~ glenˈgær|.i, gleŋ-, (US) glenˈger-, -ˈgær-, ˈ--- **-ies** -iz
Glenlivet glenˈlɪv.ɪt, -ət
Glenmorangie ˌglen.məˈræn.dʒi, ˌglem-, glenˈmɒr.ən.dʒi, (US) ˌglen-
Glenmore glenˈmɔːʳ, glem-, (US) ˈglen.mɔːr, -ˈ-
Glenn glen
Glenrothes glenˈrɒθ.ɪs, (US) -ˈrɑː.θəs
Glen Trool ˌglenˈtruːl
Glenwood ˈglen.wʊd
Glenys ˈglen.ɪs
glib glɪb **-ber** -əʳ, (US) -ɚ **-best** -ɪst, -əst **-ly** -li **-ness** -nəs, -nɪs
glid|e glaɪd **-es** -z **-ing/ly** -ɪŋ/li **-ed** -ɪd
glider ˈglaɪ.dəʳ, (US) -dɚ **-s** -z
glimmer ˈglɪm.əʳ, (US) -ɚ **-s** -z **-ing/s** -ɪŋ/z **-ingly** -ɪŋ.li **-ed** -d
glimps|e glɪmps **-es** -ɪz **-ing** -ɪŋ **-ed** -t
glinch glɪntʃ **-es** -ɪz
Glinka ˈglɪŋ.kə
glint glɪnt **-s** -s **-ing** -ɪŋ **-ed** -ɪd
gliom|a glaɪˈəʊ.m|ə, (US) -ˈoʊ-, gli- **-as** -əz **-ata** -ə.tə, (US) -ə.t̬ə
glissad|e **n, v** glɪˈsɑːd, -ˈseɪd **-es** -z **-ing** -ɪŋ **-ed** -ɪd
glissand|o glɪˈsæn.d|əʊ, (US) -ˈsɑːn.d|oʊ **-i** -iː **-os** -əʊz, (US) -oʊz
Glisson ˈglɪs.ən
glisten ˈglɪs.ən **-s** -z **-ing** -ɪŋ **-ed** -d
glist|er ˈglɪs.t|əʳ, (US) -t|ɚ **-ers** -əz, (US) -ɚz **-ering** -ər.ɪŋ **-ered** -əd, (US) -ɚd
glitch glɪtʃ **-es** -ɪz
glitt|er ˈglɪt|.əʳ, (US) ˈglɪt̬|.ɚ **-ers** -əz, (US) -ɚz **-ering/ly** -ər.ɪŋ/li **-ered** -əd, (US) -ɚd **-ery** -ər.i
glitterati ˌglɪt.əˈrɑː.tiː, -ti, (US) ˌglɪt̬.əˈrɑː.t̬i
glitz glɪts
glitz|y ˈglɪt.s|i **-ier** -i.əʳ, (US) -i.ɚ **-iest** -i.ɪst, -i.əst **-iness** -ɪ.nəs, -ɪ.nɪs

Gloag gləʊg, ⓤⓢ gloʊg
gloaming ˈgləʊ.mɪŋ, ⓤⓢ ˈgloʊ-
gloat gləʊt, ⓤⓢ gloʊt -s -s -ing/ly -ɪŋ, ⓤⓢ ˈgloʊ.t̬ɪŋ -ed -ɪd, ⓤⓢ ˈgloʊ.t̬əd
glob glɒb, ⓤⓢ glɑːb -s -z
global ˈgləʊ.bᵊl, ⓤⓢ ˈgloʊ- -ly -i -ism -ɪ.zᵊm ˌ**global** ˈ**village**; ˌ**global** ˈ**warming**
globalization, -isa- ˌgləʊ.bᵊl.aɪˈzeɪ.ʃᵊn, -ɪˈ-, ⓤⓢ ˌgloʊ.bᵊl.əˈ-
globaliz|e, -is|e ˈgləʊ.bᵊl.aɪz, ⓤⓢ ˈgloʊ.bə.laɪz -es -ɪz -ing -ɪŋ -ed -d
globe gləʊb, ⓤⓢ gloʊb -s -z
globe-trott|er ˈgləʊbˌtrɒt|.əʳ, ⓤⓢ ˈgloʊbˌtrɑː.t̬|ɚ -ers -əz, ⓤⓢ -ɚz -ing -ɪŋ
globose ˈgləʊ.bəʊs, gləʊˈbəʊs, ⓤⓢ ˈgloʊ.boʊs, -ˈ-
globosity gləʊˈbɒs.ə.ti, -ɪ.ti, ⓤⓢ gloʊˈbɑː.sə.t̬i
globous ˈgləʊ.bəs, ⓤⓢ ˈgloʊ-
globular ˈglɒb.jʊ.ləʳ, -jə-, ⓤⓢ ˈglɑː.bjə.lɚ -ly -li
globule ˈglɒb.juːl, ⓤⓢ ˈglɑː.bjuːl -s -z
globulin ˈglɒb.jʊ.lɪn, -jə-, ⓤⓢ ˈglɑː.bjə- -s -z
glockenspiel ˈglɒk.ᵊn.ʃpiːl, -spiːl, ⓤⓢ ˈglɑː.kᵊn.spiːl, -ʃpiːl -s -z
glom glɒm, ⓤⓢ glɑːm -s -z -ming -ɪŋ -med -d
gloom gluːm -s -z -ing -ɪŋ -ed -d
gloom|y ˈgluː.m|i -ier -i.əʳ, ⓤⓢ -i.ɚ -iest -i.ɪst, -i.əst -ily -ᵊl.i, -ɪ.li -iness -ɪ.nəs, -ɪ.nɪs
gloop gluːp -y -i
glop glɒp, ⓤⓢ glɑːp -py -i
Gloria ˈglɔː.ri.ə, ⓤⓢ ˈglɔːr.i- -s -z
Gloriana ˌglɔː.riˈɑː.nə, ⓤⓢ ˌglɔːr.iˈæn.ə, -ˈeɪ.nə
glorification ˌglɔː.rɪ.fɪˈkeɪ.ʃᵊn, -rə-, -fəˈ-, ⓤⓢ ˌglɔːr.ə.fəˈ-
glori|fy ˈglɔː.rɪ|.faɪ, -rə- -fies -faɪz -fying -faɪ.ɪŋ -fied -faɪd -fier/s -faɪ.əʳ/z, ⓤⓢ -faɪ.ɚ/z
glorious ˈglɔː.ri.əs, ⓤⓢ ˈglɔːr.i- -ly -li -ness -nəs, -nɪs
glor|y ˈglɔː.r|i, ⓤⓢ ˈglɔːr|.i -ies -iz -ying -i.ɪŋ -ied -id ˈ**glory** ˌ**hole**
Glos. (abbrev. for **Gloucestershire**) ˈglɒs.tə.ʃəʳ, -ʃɪəʳ, ⓤⓢ ˈglɑː.stɚ.ʃɚ, -ʃɪr
gloss glɒs, ⓤⓢ glɑːs -es -ɪz -ing -ɪŋ -ed -t -er/s -əʳ/z, ⓤⓢ -ɚ/z
glossal ˈglɒs.ᵊl, ⓤⓢ ˈglɑː.sᵊl
glossarial glɒsˈeə.ri.əl, ⓤⓢ glɑːˈser.i-
glossar|y ˈglɒs.ᵊr|.i, ⓤⓢ ˈglɑː.sᵊr- -ies -iz
glossectomy glɒsˈek.tə.mi, ⓤⓢ glɑːˈsek-
glossematics ˌglɒs.ɪˈmæt.ɪks, -əˈ-, ⓤⓢ ˌglɑː.səˈmæt̬.ɪks
glosseme ˈglɒs.iːm, ⓤⓢ ˈglɑː.siːm -s -z
glossitis glɒsˈaɪ.tɪs, -təs, ⓤⓢ glɑːˈsaɪ.t̬ɪs, -t̬əs
glossolalia ˌglɒs.əʊˈleɪ.li.ə, ⓤⓢ ˌglɑː.səˈ-
Glossop ˈglɒs.əp, ⓤⓢ ˈglɑː.səp
glossopharyngeal ˌglɒs.əʊˌfær.ɪnˈdʒiː.əl, -fəˈrɪn.dʒi.əl, ⓤⓢ ˌglɑː.soʊˌfer.ᵊnˈdʒiː.əl, -ˌfær-
gloss|y ˈglɒs|.i, ⓤⓢ ˈglɑː.s|i -ies -iz -ier -i.əʳ, ⓤⓢ -i.ɚ -iest -i.ɪst, -i.əst -ily -ᵊl.i, -ɪ.li -iness -ɪ.nəs, -ɪ.nɪs
Gloster ˈglɒs.təʳ, ⓤⓢ ˈglɑː.stɚ
glottal ˈglɒt.ᵊl, ⓤⓢ ˈglɑː.t̬ᵊl ˌ**glottal** ˈ**stop**
glottalic glɒtˈæl.ɪk, gləˈtæl-, ⓤⓢ glɑːˈtæl-
glott|is ˈglɒt|.ɪs, ⓤⓢ ˈglɑː.t̬|əs -ises -ɪ.sɪz, -ə.sɪz -ides -ɪ.diːz
glottochronology ˌglɒt.əʊ.krəˈnɒl.ə.dʒi, ⓤⓢ ˌglɑː.t̬oʊ.krəˈnɑː.lə-
glottology glɒtˈɒl.ə.dʒi, ⓤⓢ glɑːˈtɑː.lə-
Gloucester *in the UK:* ˈglɒs.təʳ, ⓤⓢ ˈglɑː.stɚ -shire -ʃəʳ, -ʃɪəʳ, ⓤⓢ -ʃɚ, -ʃɪr *in the US:* ˈglaʊ.stəʳ, ⓤⓢ -stɚ
glove glʌv -s -z -d -d ˈ**glove** **com**ˌ**partment**; ˈ**glove** ˌ**puppet**
glover, G~ ˈglʌv.əʳ, ⓤⓢ -ɚ -s -z
glow gləʊ, ⓤⓢ gloʊ -s -z -ing/ly -ɪŋ/li -ed -d
glower ˈglaʊ.əʳ, glaʊəʳ, ⓤⓢ ˈglaʊ.ɚ -s -z -ing -ɪŋ -ed -d
glowworm ˈgləʊ.wɜːm, ⓤⓢ ˈgloʊ.wɝːm -s -z
gloxinia glɒkˈsɪn.i.ə, ⓤⓢ glɑːkˈ- -s -z
gloz|e gləʊz, ⓤⓢ gloʊz -es -ɪz -ing -ɪŋ -ed -d
Gluck glʊk, gluːk, glʌk
glucose ˈgluː.kəʊs, -kəʊz, ⓤⓢ -koʊs, -koʊz
glu|e gluː -es -z -(e)ing -ɪŋ -ed -d -er/s -əʳ/z, ⓤⓢ -ɚ/z
gluesniff|ing ˈgluːˌsnɪf|.ɪŋ -er/s -əʳ/z, ⓤⓢ -ɚz
gluey ˈgluː.i -ness -nəs, -nɪs
glühwein ˈgluː.vaɪn
glum glʌm -mer -əʳ, ⓤⓢ -ɚ -mest -ɪst, -əst -ly -li -ness -nəs, -nɪs
Glusburn ˈglʌz.bɜːn, ⓤⓢ -bɝːn
glut glʌt -s -s -ting -ɪŋ, ⓤⓢ ˈglʌt̬.ɪŋ -ted -ɪd, ⓤⓢ ˈglʌt̬.əd
glutamate ˈgluː.tə.meɪt, ⓤⓢ -t̬ə- -s -s
gluteal ˈgluː.ti.əl, ⓤⓢ -t̬i-
gluten ˈgluː.tᵊn, -tɪn
glute|us ˈgluː.ti|.əs, ⓤⓢ -t̬i- -i -aɪ
gluteus maximus ˌgluː.ti.əsˈmæk.sɪm.əs, ⓤⓢ -t̬i-
glutinous ˈgluː.tɪ.nəs, -tᵊn.əs, ⓤⓢ -tᵊn.əs -ly -li -ness -nəs, -nɪs
glutton ˈglʌt.ᵊn -s -z
gluttoniz|e, -is|e ˈglʌt.ᵊn.aɪz -es -ɪz -ing -ɪŋ -ed -d
gluttonous ˈglʌt.ᵊn.əs -ly -li
gluttony ˈglʌt.ᵊn.i
glycemic glaɪˈsiː.mɪk **gly**ˌ**cemic** ˈ**index**
glyceride ˈglɪs.ᵊ.raɪd -s -z
glycerin ˈglɪs.ᵊr.ɪn, -iːn; ˌglɪs.əˈriːn
glycerine ˈglɪs.ᵊr.iːn, -ɪn; ˌglɪs.əˈriːn
glycerol ˈglɪs.ᵊ.rɒl, ⓤⓢ -rɑːl, -roʊl
glycogen ˈglaɪ.kəʊ.dʒən, ˈglɪk.əʊ-, -dʒen, ⓤⓢ ˈglaɪ.koʊ-, -kə-
glycol ˈglaɪ.kɒl, ˈglɪk.ɒl, ⓤⓢ ˈglaɪ.kɑːl, -koʊl
Glyde glaɪd
Glyn glɪn
Glynde glaɪnd
Glyndebourne ˈglaɪnd.bɔːn, ˈglaɪm-, ⓤⓢ ˈglaɪnd.bɔːrn
Glyndwr glɪnˈdaʊ.əʳ, glen-, ⓤⓢ -ˈdaʊ.ɚ
Glynis ˈglɪn.ɪs
Glynne glɪn
Glyn-Neath ˌglɪnˈniːθ
glyph glɪf -s -s
glyptic ˈglɪp.tɪk
gm (abbrev. for **gram/s**) *singular:* græm; *plural:* -z
GM ˌdʒiːˈem *stress shift:* ˌ**GM** ˈ**food**
G|-man ˈdʒiː|ˌmæn -men -ˌmen
GMO ˌdʒiː.emˈəʊ, ⓤⓢ -ˈoʊ -s -z
GMT ˌdʒiː.emˈtiː
gnarl nɑːl, ⓤⓢ nɑːrl -s -z -ed -d
gnash næʃ -es -ɪz -ing -ɪŋ -ed -t
gnat næt -s -s
gnathic ˈnæθ.ɪk
gnaw nɔː, ⓤⓢ nɑː, nɔː -s -z -ing -ɪŋ -ed -d
gneiss naɪs, gəˈnaɪs
gnocchi ˈnjɒk.i, ⓤⓢ ˈnjɑː.ki
gnome *goblin:* nəʊm, ⓤⓢ noʊm *maxim:* ˈnəʊ.miː, ⓤⓢ noʊm -s -z
gnomic ˈnəʊ.mɪk, ⓤⓢ ˈnoʊ-
gnomish ˈnəʊ.mɪʃ, ⓤⓢ ˈnoʊ-
gnomon ˈnəʊ.mɒn, -mən, ⓤⓢ ˈnoʊ.mɑːn, -mən -s -z
gnomonic nəʊˈmɒn.ɪk, ⓤⓢ noʊˈmɑː.nɪk -al -ᵊl -ally -ᵊl.i, -li
Gnosall ˈnəʊ.səl, ⓤⓢ ˈnoʊ-
gnostic, G~ ˈnɒs.tɪk, ⓤⓢ ˈnɑː.stɪk -s -s
gnosticism, G~ ˈnɒs.tɪ.sɪ.zᵊm, ⓤⓢ ˈnɑː.stə-
gnu nuː, njuː -s -z
go gəʊ, ⓤⓢ goʊ -es -z -ing -ɪŋ **went** went **gone** gɒn, ⓤⓢ gɑːn, gɔːn **goer/s** ˈgəʊ.əʳ/z, ⓤⓢ ˈgoʊ.ɚ/z
Goa gəʊ.ə, ⓤⓢ goʊ.ə
goad gəʊd, ⓤⓢ goʊd -s -z -ing -ɪŋ -ed -ɪd
go-ahead **adj** ˈgəʊ.ə.hed, ˌ-ˈ-ˈ-, ⓤⓢ ˈgoʊ-
go-ahead **n** ˈgəʊ.ə.hed, ⓤⓢ ˈgoʊ-
goal gəʊl, ⓤⓢ goʊl -s -z
goalie ˈgəʊ.li, ⓤⓢ ˈgoʊ.li -s -z
goalkeeper ˈgəʊlˌkiː.pəʳ, ⓤⓢ ˈgoʊlˌkiː.pɚ -s -z
goalless ˈgəʊl.ləs, -lɪs, ⓤⓢ ˈgoʊl-
goalmouth ˈgəʊl.maʊθ, ⓤⓢ ˈgoʊl-
goalpost ˈgəʊl.pəʊst, ⓤⓢ ˈgoʊl.poʊst -s -s
goalscorer ˈgəʊlˌskɔː.rəʳ, ⓤⓢ ˈgoʊlˌskɔːr.ɚ -s -z
goaltender ˈgəʊlˌten.dəʳ, ⓤⓢ ˈgoʊlˌten.dɚ -s -z
Goan gəʊ.ən, ⓤⓢ goʊ.ən
Goanese ˌgəʊ.əˈniːz, ⓤⓢ ˌgoʊ.ə-
goanna gəʊˈæn.ə, ⓤⓢ goʊ- -s -z
goat gəʊt, ⓤⓢ goʊt -s -s ˌ**get** **someone's** ˈ**goat**
goatee gəʊˈtiː, ⓤⓢ goʊ- -s -z *stress*

shift, British only, see compounds: **ˌgoatee ˈbeard** Ⓤⓢ **goaˈtee ˌbeard**
goatherd ˈɡəʊt.hɜːd, Ⓤⓢ ˈɡoʊt.hɝːd **-s** -z
Goathland ˈɡəʊθ.lənd, Ⓤⓢ ˈɡoʊθ-
goatish ˈɡəʊ.tɪʃ, Ⓤⓢ ˈɡoʊ-
goatskin ˈɡəʊt.skɪn, Ⓤⓢ ˈɡoʊt- **-s** -z
goatsucker ˈɡəʊtˌsʌk.əʳ, Ⓤⓢ ˈɡoʊtˌsʌk.ɚ **-s** -z
gob ɡɒb, Ⓤⓢ ɡɑːb **-s** -z **-bing** -ɪŋ **-bed** -d
gobbet ˈɡɒb.ɪt, Ⓤⓢ ˈɡɑː.bɪt **-s** -s
Gobbi ˈɡɒb.i, Ⓤⓢ ˈɡɑː.bi
gobbl|e ˈɡɒb.ᵊl, Ⓤⓢ ˈɡɑː.bᵊl **-es** -z **-ing** -ɪŋ, ˈɡɒb.lɪŋ, Ⓤⓢ ˈɡɑː.bᵊl.ɪŋ, ˈ-blɪŋ **-ed** -d **-er/s** -əʳ/z, ˈɡɒb.ləʳ/z, Ⓤⓢ ˈɡɑː.bᵊl.ɚ/z, ˈ-blɚ/z
gobbledygook, gobbledegook ˈɡɒb.ᵊl.diˌɡuːk, -ˌɡʊk, Ⓤⓢ ˈɡɑː.bᵊl-
Gobbo ˈɡɒb.əʊ, Ⓤⓢ ˈɡɑː.boʊ
Gobelin ˈɡəʊ.bᵊl.ɪn, ˈɡɒb.ᵊl-, Ⓤⓢ ˈɡoʊ.bᵊl-
go-between ˈɡəʊ.bɪˌtwiːn, -bə-, Ⓤⓢ ˈɡoʊ.bə- **-s** -z
Gobi ˈɡəʊ.bi, Ⓤⓢ ˈɡoʊ-
goblet ˈɡɒb.lət, -lɪt, Ⓤⓢ ˈɡɑː.blət **-s** -s
goblin ˈɡɒb.lɪn, Ⓤⓢ ˈɡɑː.blɪn **-s** -z
gobsmack ˈɡɒb.smæk, Ⓤⓢ ˈɡɑːb- **-s** -s **-ing** -ɪŋ **-ed** -t
gobstopper ˈɡɒbˌstɒp.əʳ, Ⓤⓢ ˈɡɑːbˌstɑː.pɚ **-s** -z
go-by ˈɡəʊˌbaɪ, Ⓤⓢ ˈɡoʊ-
gob|y ˈɡəʊ.b|i, Ⓤⓢ ˈɡoʊ- **-ies** -iz
go-cart ˈɡəʊˌkɑːt, Ⓤⓢ ˈɡoʊˌkɑːrt **-s** -s
god, G~ ɡɒd, Ⓤⓢ ɡɑːd **-s** -z
Godalming ˈɡɒd.ᵊl.mɪŋ, Ⓤⓢ ˈɡɑː.dᵊl-
Godard ˈɡɒd.ɑː, Ⓤⓢ ɡoʊˈdɑːr
god-awful ˌɡɒdˈɔː.fᵊl, -fʊl, Ⓤⓢ ˌɡɑːdˈɑː-, -ˈɔː- *stress shift:* **ˌgod-awful ˈnoise**
god|child ˈɡɒd|.tʃaɪld, Ⓤⓢ ˈɡɑːd- **-children** -ˌtʃɪl.drᵊn
goddam(n) ˈɡɒd.æm, ˈɡɒd.dæm, Ⓤⓢ ˌɡɑːdˈdæm, ˈɡɑːd-
goddamned ˈɡɒd.æmd, ˈɡɒd.dæmd, Ⓤⓢ ˈɡɑːd.æmd
Goddard ˈɡɒd.ɑːd, -əd, Ⓤⓢ ˈɡɑː.dɚd, -dɑːrd
goddaughter ˈɡɒdˌdɔː.təʳ, Ⓤⓢ ˈɡɑːdˌdɑː.t̬ɚ, -ˌdɔː- **-s** -z
Godden ˈɡɒd.ᵊn, Ⓤⓢ ˈɡɑː.dᵊn
goddess ˈɡɒd.es, -ɪs, -əs, Ⓤⓢ ˈɡɑː.dɪs, -dəs **-es** -ɪz
Goderich ˈɡəʊ.drɪtʃ, Ⓤⓢ ˈɡoʊ-
godetia ɡəʊˈdiː.ʃə, -ʃi.ə, Ⓤⓢ ɡə- **-s** -z
godfather, G~ ˈɡɒd.fɑː.ðəʳ, Ⓤⓢ ˈɡɑːd.fɑː.ðɚ **-s** -z
god-fearing, G~ ˈɡɒdˌfɪə.rɪŋ, Ⓤⓢ ˈɡɑːd.fɪr.ɪŋ
godforsaken ˈɡɒd.fəˌseɪ.kᵊn, Ⓤⓢ ˈɡɑːd.fɚ-
Godfrey ˈɡɒd.fri, Ⓤⓢ ˈɡɑːd-
god-given ˈɡɒdˌɡɪv.ᵊn, Ⓤⓢ ˈɡɑːd-
godhead, G~ ˈɡɒd.hed, Ⓤⓢ ˈɡɑːd- **-s** -z
Godiva ɡəˈdaɪ.və
Godkin ˈɡɒd.kɪn, Ⓤⓢ ˈɡɑːd-
godless ˈɡɒd.ləs, -lɪs, Ⓤⓢ ˈɡɑːd- **-ly** -li **-ness** -nəs, -nɪs
godlike ˈɡɒd.laɪk, Ⓤⓢ ˈɡɑːd-
godl|y ˈɡɒd.l|i, Ⓤⓢ ˈɡɑːd- **-ier** -i.əʳ, Ⓤⓢ -i.ɚ **-iest** -i.ɪst, -i.əst **-iness** -ɪ.nəs, -ɪ.nɪs
Godman ˈɡɒd.mən, Ⓤⓢ ˈɡɑːd-
Godmanchester ˈɡɒd.mənˌtʃes.təʳ, Ⓤⓢ ˈɡɑːd.mənˌtʃes.tɚ
godmother ˈɡɒd.mʌð.əʳ, Ⓤⓢ ˈɡɑːd.mʌð.ɚ **-s** -z
Godolphin ɡəˈdɒl.fɪn, Ⓤⓢ -ˈdɑːl-
Godot ˈɡɒd.əʊ, Ⓤⓢ ɡəˈdoʊ, ɡɑː-
godown ˈɡəʊ.daʊn, Ⓤⓢ ˈɡoʊ- **-s** -z
godparent ˈɡɒd.peə.rᵊnt, Ⓤⓢ ˈɡɑːd.per.ᵊnt, -pær- **-s** -s
godsend ˈɡɒd.send, Ⓤⓢ ˈɡɑːd- **-s** -z
God-slot ˈɡɒdˌslɒt, Ⓤⓢ ˈɡɑːdˌslɑːt **-s** -s
godson ˈɡɒd.sʌn, Ⓤⓢ ˈɡɑːd- **-s** -z
Godspeed ˌɡɒdˈspiːd, Ⓤⓢ ˌɡɑːd-
godsquad ˈɡɒd.skwɒd, Ⓤⓢ ˈɡɑːd.skwɑːd
Godunov ˈɡɒd.ə.nɒf, ˈɡʊd-, -u-, Ⓤⓢ ˈɡʊd.ə.nɑːf
Godward ˈɡɒd.wəd, Ⓤⓢ ˈɡɑːd.wɚd
Godwin ˈɡɒd.wɪn, Ⓤⓢ ˈɡɑːd-
godwit ˈɡɒd.wɪt, Ⓤⓢ ˈɡɑːd- **-s** -s
Godzilla ɡɒdˈzɪl.ə, Ⓤⓢ ɡɑːd-
Goebbels ˈɡɜː.bᵊlz, -bᵊls
Goering ˈɡɜː.rɪŋ, Ⓤⓢ ˈɡɝː-
Goethe ˈɡɜː.tə
gofer ˈɡəʊ.fəʳ, Ⓤⓢ ˈɡoʊ.fɚ **-s** -z
Goff(e) ɡɒf, Ⓤⓢ ɡɑːf
goff|er ˈɡəʊ.f|əʳ, ˈɡɒf|.əʳ, Ⓤⓢ ˈɡɑː.f|ɚ **-ers** -əz, Ⓤⓢ -ɚz **-ering** -ᵊr.ɪŋ **-ered** -əd, Ⓤⓢ -ɚd
Gog ɡɒɡ, Ⓤⓢ ɡɑːɡ, ɡɔːɡ
Gogarty ˈɡəʊ.ɡə.ti, Ⓤⓢ ˈɡoʊ.ɡɚ.t̬i
go-getter ˈɡəʊˌɡet.əʳ, ˌ-ˈ--, Ⓤⓢ ˈɡoʊˌɡet̬.ɚ **-s** -z
go-getting ˈɡəʊˌɡet.ɪŋ, Ⓤⓢ ˈɡoʊˌɡet̬.ɪŋ
goggl|e ˈɡɒɡ.ᵊl, Ⓤⓢ ˈɡɑː.ɡᵊl **-es** -z **-ing** -ɪŋ, ˈ-lɪŋ, Ⓤⓢ ˈ-ɡᵊl.ɪŋ, ˈ-ɡlɪŋ **-ed** -d
goggle-box ˈɡɒɡ.ᵊl.bɒks, Ⓤⓢ ˈɡɑː.ɡᵊl.bɑːks **-es** -ɪz
goggle-eyed ˌɡɒɡ.ᵊlˈaɪd, Ⓤⓢ ˈɡɑː.ɡᵊlˌaɪd *stress shift, British only:* **ˌgoggle-eyed ˈcrowd**
Gogmagog ˈɡɒɡ.mə.ɡɒɡ, Ⓤⓢ ˈɡɑːɡ.mə.ɡɑːɡ, ˈɡɔːɡ-, -ɡɔːɡ
go-go ˈɡəʊ.ɡəʊ, Ⓤⓢ ˈɡoʊ.ɡoʊ **ˈgo-go ˌdancer**
Gogo ˈɡəʊ.ɡəʊ, Ⓤⓢ ˈɡoʊ.ɡoʊ
Gogol ˈɡəʊ.ɡɒl, Ⓤⓢ ˈɡoʊ.ɡɑːl, -ɡᵊl
Goiânia ɡɔɪˈɑː.ni.ə
Goidelic ɡɔɪˈdel.ɪk
going-over ˌɡəʊ.ɪŋˈəʊ.vəʳ, ˈ--ˌ--, Ⓤⓢ ˌɡoʊ.ɪŋˈoʊ.vɚ, ɡɔː-, ˈ--ˌ--
goings ˈɡəʊ.ɪŋz, Ⓤⓢ ˈɡoʊ- **ˌcomings and ˈgoings; ˌgoings-ˈon**
goiter ˈɡɔɪ.təʳ, Ⓤⓢ -t̬ɚ **-s** -z **-ed** -d
goitre ˈɡɔɪ.təʳ, Ⓤⓢ -t̬ɚ **-s** -z **-d** -d
goitrous ˈɡɔɪ.trəs
go-kart ˈɡəʊ.kɑːt, Ⓤⓢ ˈɡoʊ.kɑːrt **-s** -s
Golan ˈɡəʊ.læn, -lɑːn; ɡəʊ.lɑːn, Ⓤⓢ ˈɡoʊ.lɑːn **ˌGolan ˈHeights**
Golborne ˈɡəʊl.bɔːn, Ⓤⓢ ˈɡoʊl.bɔːrn
Golby ˈɡəʊl.bi, Ⓤⓢ ˈɡoʊl-
Golconda ɡɒlˈkɒn.də, Ⓤⓢ ɡɑːlˈkɑːn.də
gold, G~ ɡəʊld, Ⓤⓢ ɡoʊld **-s** -z **ˈGold ˌCoast; ˈgold ˌdust; ˌgold ˈleaf; ˌgold ˈmedal; ˈgold ˌmine; ˈgold ˌrush; as ˌgood as ˈgold**
Golda ˈɡəʊl.də, Ⓤⓢ ˈɡoʊl-
Goldberg ˈɡəʊl*d*.bɜːɡ, Ⓤⓢ ˈɡoʊl*d*.bɝːɡ
goldbrick ˈɡəʊl*d*.brɪk, Ⓤⓢ ˈɡoʊl*d*- **-s** -s **-ing** -ɪŋ **-ed** -d **-er/s** -əʳ/z, Ⓤⓢ -ɚ/z
goldcrest ˈɡəʊl*d*.krest, Ⓤⓢ ˈɡoʊl*d*- **-s** -s
gold-digger ˈɡəʊl*d*ˌdɪɡ.əʳ, Ⓤⓢ ˈɡoʊl*d*ˌdɪɡ.ɚ **-s** -z
golden, G~ ˈɡəʊl.dᵊn, Ⓤⓢ ˈɡoʊl- **ˌgolden ˈage** Ⓤⓢ **ˈgolden ˌage; ˌgolden ˈhandshake; ˌgolden ˈrule; ˌgolden ˈsyrup**
goldeneye ˈɡəʊl.dᵊn.aɪ, Ⓤⓢ ˈɡoʊl- **-s** -z
goldfield ˈɡəʊl*d*.fiːld, Ⓤⓢ ˈɡoʊl*d*- **-s** -z
goldfinch ˈɡəʊl*d*.fɪntʃ, Ⓤⓢ ˈɡoʊl*d*- **-es** -ɪz
goldfish ˈɡəʊl*d*.fɪʃ, Ⓤⓢ ˈɡoʊl*d*- **-es** -ɪz **ˈgoldfish ˌbowl**
Goldilocks ˈɡəʊl.dɪ.lɒks, Ⓤⓢ ˈɡoʊl.di.lɑːks
Golding ˈɡəʊl.dɪŋ, Ⓤⓢ ˈɡoʊl-
Goldman ˈɡəʊl*d*.mən, Ⓤⓢ ˈɡoʊl*d*-
Goldsborough ˈɡəʊldz.bᵊr.ə, Ⓤⓢ ˈɡoʊldz.bɚ.oʊ
Goldschmidt ˈɡəʊld.ʃmɪt, Ⓤⓢ ˈɡoʊld-
goldsmith, G~ ˈɡəʊld.smɪθ, Ⓤⓢ ˈɡoʊld- **-s** -s
Goldstein ˈɡəʊld.staɪn, -stiːn, Ⓤⓢ ˈɡoʊld-
Goldwyn ˈɡəʊl.dwɪn, Ⓤⓢ ˈɡoʊl-
golem ˈɡəʊ.lem, Ⓤⓢ ˈɡoʊ- **-s** -z
golf n, v ɡɒlf; *old-fashioned, sometimes used by players:* ɡɒf, Ⓤⓢ ɡɑːlf **-s** -s **-ing** -ɪŋ **-ed** -t **ˈgolf ˌclub; ˈgolf ˌcourse; ˈgolf ˌlinks**
golfer ˈɡɒl.fəʳ, ˈɡɒf.əʳ, Ⓤⓢ ˈɡɑːl.fɚ **-s** -z
Golgotha ˈɡɒl.ɡə.θə, Ⓤⓢ ˈɡɑːl-
Goliath ɡəʊˈlaɪ.əθ, Ⓤⓢ ɡə-
Golightly ɡəʊˈlaɪt.li, Ⓤⓢ ɡoʊ-
Gollancz ɡəˈlænts, -ˈlæŋ*k*s, ɡɒlˈænts, -ˈæŋ*k*s, ˈɡɒl.ənts, -æŋ*k*s, Ⓤⓢ ɡəˈlænts, ˈɡɑː.lənts, -lænts
golliwog ˈɡɒl.i.wɒɡ, Ⓤⓢ ˈɡɑː.li.wɔːɡ, -wɑːɡ **-s** -z
golly ˈɡɒl.i, Ⓤⓢ ˈɡɑː.li
gollywog ˈɡɒl.i.wɒɡ, Ⓤⓢ ˈɡɑː.li.wɔːɡ, -wɑːɡ **-s** -z
golosh ɡəˈlɒʃ, Ⓤⓢ ɡəˈlɑːʃ **-es** -ɪz
Gomar ˈɡəʊ.məʳ, Ⓤⓢ ˈɡoʊ.mɚ
Gomer ˈɡəʊ.məʳ, Ⓤⓢ ˈɡoʊ.mɚ
Gomersal ˈɡɒm.ə.sᵊl, Ⓤⓢ ˈɡɑː.mɚ.sᵊl
Gomes ˈɡəʊ.mez, Ⓤⓢ ˈɡoʊ-
Gomez, Gómez ˈɡəʊ.mez, Ⓤⓢ ˈɡoʊ-
Gomme ɡɒm, Ⓤⓢ ɡɑːm

Gomorrah gəˈmɒr.ə, (US) -ˈmɔːr.ə, -ˈmɑːr-
Gompers ˈgɒm.pəz, (US) ˈgɑːm.pɚz
Gomshall ˈgʌm.ʃəl, ˈgɒm-, (US) ˈgɑːm-
gonad ˈgəʊ.næd, (US) ˈgoʊ- **-s** -z
Goncourt ˌgɒnˈkʊəʳ, ˌgɒŋ-, ˌgɔ̃ːŋ-, (US) ˌgoʊnˈkʊr
gondola ˈgɒn.dəl.ə, (US) ˈgɑːn- **-s** -z
gondolier ˌgɒn.dəˈlɪəʳ, -dəlˈɪəʳ, (US) ˌgɑːn.dəˈlɪr **-s** -z
Gondwana gɒndˈwɑː.nə, (US) gɑːnd- **-land** -lænd
gone (from **go**) gɒn, (US) gɑːn
goner ˈgɒn.əʳ, (US) ˈgɑː.nɚ **-s** -z
Goneril ˈgɒn.ər.ɪl, -əl, (US) ˈgɑː.nər.əl
gonfalon ˈgɒn.fəl.ən, (US) ˈgɑːn- **-s** -z
gong gɒŋ, (US) gɑːŋ, gɔːŋ **-s** -z
goniometer ˌgəʊ.niˈɒm.ɪ.təʳ, ˈ-ə-, (US) ˌgoʊ.niˈɑː.mə.t̬ɚ **-s** -z
goniometric ˌgəʊ.ni.əˈmet.rɪk, (US) ˌgoʊ-
gonk gɒŋk, (US) gɑːŋk, gɔːŋk **-s** -s
gonna gən.ə, ˈgɒn.ə, (US) ˈgɑː.nə, ˈgɔː-
gonorrh(o)e|a ˌgɒn.əˈriː|.ə, (US) ˌgɑː.nəˈ- **-al** -əl
Gonville ˈgɒn.vɪl, (US) ˈgɑːn-
Gonzales gɒnˈzɑː.lɪs, gən-, -lez, (US) gənˈzɑː.ləs, gɑːn-, -ˈsɑː-, -leɪs
Gonzalez gɒnˈzɑː.lɪz, gən-, -lez, -ləz, (US) gɑːnˈzɑː.ləs, gən-, -les, -lɪs
gonzo ˈgɒn.zəʊ, (US) ˈgɑːn.zoʊ
goo guː
goober ˈguː.bəʳ, (US) -bɚ **-s** -z
Gooch guːtʃ
good, G~ n, adj, interj gʊd **-s** -z **-ness** -nəs, -nɪs **ˌgood ˈday; ˌGood ˈFriday; ˌgood ˈgrief!; ˌGood ˈHeavens!; ˈgoods ˌtrain; as ˌgood as ˈgold**
Goodale ˈgʊd.eɪl
Goodall ˈgʊd.ɔːl, (US) -ɔːl, -ɑːl
Goodbody ˈgʊd.bɒd.i, (US) -bɑː.di
goodbye n gʊdˈbaɪ **-s** -z
goodbye interj gʊdˈbaɪ
Goodchild ˈgʊd.tʃaɪld
Goode gʊd
Goodell gʊˈdel
Goodenough ˈgʊd.ɪ.nʌf, ˈ-ə-, -ən.ʌf
Goodfellow ˈgʊdˌfel.əʊ, (US) -oʊ
good-for-nothing ˈgʊd.fəˌnʌθ.ɪŋ, -ˌnɒθ-; ˌgʊd.fəˈnʌθ-, -ˈnɒθ-, (US) ˈgʊd.fɚˌnʌθ-, ˌgʊd.fɚˈnʌθ- **-s** -z
Goodge guːdʒ, gʊdʒ
Goodhart ˈgʊd.hɑːt, (US) -hɑːrt
good-hearted ˌgʊdˈhɑː.tɪd, (US) -ˈhɑːr.t̬əd **-ness** -nəs, -nɪs *stress shift:* **ˌgood-hearted ˈperson**
good-humo(u)red ˌgʊdˈhjuː.məd, (US) -ˈhjuː.mɚd, -ˈjuː- **-ly** -li **-ness** -nəs, -nɪs *stress shift:* **ˌgood-humo(u)red ˈfriend**
goodie ˈgʊd.i **-s** -z
goodish ˈgʊd.ɪʃ
Goodison ˈgʊd.ɪ.sən, -ə-
Goodliffe ˈgʊd.lɪf
good-looking ˌgʊdˈlʊk.ɪŋ *stress shift:* **ˌgood-looking ˈguy**
goodl|y ˈgʊd.l|i **-ier** -i.əʳ, (US) -i.ɚ **-iest** -i.ɪst, -i.əst **-iness** -ɪ.nəs, -ɪ.nɪs
good|man ˈgʊd|.mæn **-men** -men
Goodman ˈgʊd.mən
good morning gʊdˈmɔː.nɪŋ, (US) -ˈmɔːr-
good-natured ˌgʊdˈneɪ.tʃəd, (US) -tʃɚd **-ly** -li **-ness** -nəs, -nɪs *stress shift:* **ˌgood-natured ˈsmile**
goodness ˈgʊd.nəs, -nɪs
good night ˌgʊdˈnaɪt
Goodrich ˈgʊd.rɪtʃ
Goodson ˈgʊd.sən
goods-train ˈgʊdz.treɪn **-s** -z
good-tempered ˌgʊdˈtem.pəd, (US) -pɚd **-ly** -li **-ness** -nəs, -nɪs *stress shift:* **ˌgood-tempered ˈhorse**
goodwill gʊdˈwɪl **-s** -z
Goodwin ˈgʊd.wɪn
Goodwood ˈgʊd.wʊd
good|y, G~ ˈgʊd|.i **-ies** -iz **ˌgoody-ˈtwo-shoes**
Goodyear® ˈgʊd.jɪəʳ, -jəʳ, -jɜːʳ, (US) -jɪr, -jɚ, ˈgʊdʒ.ɪr
Goodyer ˈgʊd.jəʳ
goody-good|y ˈgʊd.iˌgʊd|.i **-ies** -iz
goo|ey ˈguː|.i **-ier** -i.əʳ, (US) -i.ɚ **-iest** -i.ɪst, -i.əst **-iness** -ɪ.nəs, -ɪ.nɪs
goof guːf **-s** -s **-ing** -ɪŋ **-ed** -t
goofball ˈguːf.bɔːl, (US) -bɔːl, -bɑːl **-s** -z
goof|y, G~ ˈguː.f|i **-ier** -i.əʳ, (US) -i.ɚ **-iest** -i.ɪst, -i.əst **-ily** -əl.i, -ɪ.li **-iness** -ɪ.nəs, -ɪ.nɪs
Googe guːdʒ, gʊdʒ
Googie ˈguː.gi
Googl|e® ˈguː.gəl **-es** -z **-ing** -ɪŋ, ˈguːg.lɪŋ **-ed** -d
googl|y ˈguː.gl|i **-ies** -iz
googol ˈguː.gɒl, -gəl, (US) -gɑːl, -gəl **-s** -z
googolplex ˈguː.gɒl.pleks, -gəl-, (US) -gɑːl-, -gəl-
Goole guːl
gool|ie, gool|y ˈguː.l|i **-ies** -iz
goon guːn **-s** -z
Goonhilly ˌguːnˈhɪl.i, ˌgʊn- *stress shift:* **ˌGoonhilly ˈDown**
goop guːp
goop|y ˈguː.p|i **-ier** -i.əʳ, (US) -i.ɚ **-iest** -i.ɪst, -i.əst **-ily** -əl.i, -ɪ.li **-iness** -ɪ.nəs, -ɪ.nɪs
goosander guːˈsæn.dəʳ, (US) -dɚ **-s** -z
goose *bird:* guːs **geese** giːs **ˈgoose ˌbumps; ˈgoose ˌgrass; ˈgoose ˌpimples; ˌcook someone's ˈgoose; (kill) the ˌgoose that ˌlays the ˌgolden ˈeggs; ˌcouldn't say boo to a ˈgoose** *tailor's iron:* guːs **-es** -ɪz
goos|e v guːs **-es** -ɪz **-ing** -ɪŋ **-ed** -t
gooseberr|y ˈgʊz.bər|.i, ˈguːz-, ˈ-br|i, (US) ˈguːsˌber|.i, ˈguːz-, -bɚ- **-ies** -iz **ˌgooseberry ˈfool**
gooseflesh ˈguːs.fleʃ
goose-step ˈguːsˌstep **-s** -s **-ping** -ɪŋ **-ped** -t
goosey ˈguː.si **-s** -z
GOP ˌdʒiː.əʊˈpiː, (US) -oʊˈ-
gopher ˈgəʊ.fəʳ, (US) ˈgoʊ.fɚ **-s** -z
Gorazde gɔːˈræʒ.deɪ, gəˈ-
Gorbachev ˈgɔː.bə.tʃɒf, ˌ--ˈ-, (US) ˈgɔːr.bə.tʃɑːf, ˌ--ˈ-
Gorbals ˈgɔː.bəlz, (US) ˈgɔːr-
gorblimey ˌgɔːˈblaɪ.mi, (US) ˌgɔːr-
Gorboduc ˈgɔː.bə.dʌk, (US) ˈgɔːr-
Gordale ˈgɔː.deɪl, (US) ˈgɔːr-
Gordano gɔːˈdɑː.nəʊ, -ˈdeɪ-, (US) gɔːrˈdɑː.n.oʊ
Gordian knot ˌgɔː.di.ənˈnɒt, (US) ˌgɔːr.di.ənˈnɑːt
Gordimer ˈgɔː.dɪ.məʳ, (US) ˈgɔːr-
Gordon ˈgɔː.dən, (US) ˈgɔːr-
Gordonstoun ˈgɔː.dən.stən, (US) ˈgɔːr-
gor|e, G~ gɔːʳ, (US) gɔːr **-es** -z **-ing** -ɪŋ **-ed** -d
Gorebridge ˈgɔː.brɪdʒ, (US) ˈgɔːr-
Gorell ˈgɒr.əl, (US) ˌgɔːˈrel, ˈgɑː.rəl
Gore-Tex® ˈgɔː.teks, (US) ˈgɔːr-
gorg|e gɔːdʒ, (US) gɔːrdʒ **-es** -ɪz **-ing** -ɪŋ **-ed** -d
gorgeous ˈgɔː.dʒəs, (US) ˈgɔːr- **-ly** -li **-ness** -nəs, -nɪs
Gorges ˈgɔː.dʒɪz, (US) ˈgɔːr-
gorget ˈgɔː.dʒɪt, -dʒət, (US) ˈgɔːr.dʒət **-s** -s
Gorgie ˈgɔː.gi, (US) ˈgɔːr-
gorgon, G~ ˈgɔː.gən, (US) ˈgɔːr- **-s** -z
Gorgonzola ˌgɔː.gənˈzəʊ.lə, (US) ˌgɔːr.gənˈzoʊ-
Gorham ˈgɔː.rəm, (US) ˈgɔːr.əm
gorilla gəˈrɪl.ə **-s** -z
Goring ˈgɔː.rɪŋ, (US) ˈgɔːr.ɪŋ ˈgɜː.rɪŋ, (US) ˈgɝː.ɪŋ, ˈgɔːr-
Gorki, Gorky ˈgɔː.ki, (US) ˈgɔːr-
Gorleston ˈgɔːl.stən, (US) ˈgɔːrl-
Gorman ˈgɔː.mən, (US) ˈgɔːr-
gormandiz|e, -is|e ˈgɔː.mən.daɪz, (US) ˈgɔːr- **-es** -ɪz **-ing** -ɪŋ **-ed** -d **-er/s** -əʳ/z, (US) -ɚ/z
Gormenghast ˈgɔː.mən.gɑːst, -məŋ-, (US) ˈgɔːr.mən.gæst, -məŋ-
gormless ˈgɔːm.ləs, -lɪs, (US) ˈgɔːrm- **-ly** -li **-ness** -nəs, -nɪs
Gormley ˈgɔːm.li, (US) ˈgɔːrm-
Goronwy gəˈrɒn.wi, (US) -ˈrɑːn-
gorp gɔːp, (US) gɔːrp
Gorringe ˈgɒr.ɪndʒ, -əndʒ, (US) ˈgɑː.rɪndʒ, ˈgɔː-
gorse gɔːs, (US) gɔːrs
Gorseinon gɔːˈsaɪ.nən, (US) gɔːr-
Gorst gɔːst, (US) gɔːrst
Gorton ˈgɔː.tən, (US) ˈgɔːr-
gor|y ˈgɔː.r|i, (US) ˈgɔːr|.i **-ier** -i.əʳ, (US) -i.ɚ **-iest** -i.ɪst, -i.əst **-ily** -əl.i, -ɪ.li **-iness** -ɪ.nəs, -ɪ.nɪs
Goschen ˈgəʊ.ʃən, ˈgɒʃ.ən, (US) ˈgoʊ-
gosh gɒʃ, (US) gɑːʃ
goshawk ˈgɒs.hɔːk, (US) ˈgɑːs.hɑːk, -hɔːk **-s** -s
Goshen ˈgəʊ.ʃən, ˈgɒʃ.ən, (US) ˈgoʊ-
gosling, G~ ˈgɒz.lɪŋ, (US) ˈgɑːz- **-s** -z
go-slow ˌgəʊˈsləʊ, ˈ--, (US) ˈgoʊ.sloʊ **-s** -z
gospel, G~ ˈgɒs.pəl, -pel, (US) ˈgɑːs- **-s** -z **ˈgospel ˌmusic**
gospel(l)er ˈgɒs.pəl.əʳ, (US) ˈgɑː.spəl.ɚ **-s** -z
Gosport ˈgɒs.pɔːt, (US) ˈgɑːs.pɔːrt
Goss(e) gɒs, (US) gɑːs

gossamer ˈgɒs.ə.məʳ, ⓤⓢ ˈgɑː.sə.mɚ
gossip n, v ˈgɒs.ɪp, ⓤⓢ ˈgɑː.səp **-s** -s **-ing** -ɪŋ **-ed** -t **-y** -i
got (from **get**) gɒt, ⓤⓢ gɑːt
gotcha ˈgɒtʃ.ə, ⓤⓢ ˈgɑː.tʃə
Göteborg ˈjɜː.tə.bɔː, ⓤⓢ -bɔːr
goth, G~ gɒθ, ⓤⓢ gɑːθ **-s** -s
Gotha *in Germany:* ˈgəʊ.θə, ˈgəʊ.tə, ⓤⓢ ˈgoʊ.t̬ə *old-fashioned English spelling of* **Göta** *in Sweden:* ˈgəʊ.tə, ⓤⓢ ˈgoʊ.t̬ə
Gotham *in Nottinghamshire:* ˈgəʊ.təm, ⓤⓢ ˈgoʊ.t̬əm *New York:* ˈgɒθ.əm, ⓤⓢ ˈgɑː.θəm
Gothenburg ˈgɒθ.ən.bɜːg, ˈgɒt-, -ᵊm-, ⓤⓢ ˈgɑː.θᵊn.bɝːg, -tᵊn-
gothic, G~ ˈgɒθ.ɪk, ⓤⓢ ˈgɑː.θɪk
Gothicism ˈgɒθ.ɪ.sɪ.zᵊm, ˈ-ə-, ⓤⓢ ˈgɑː.θə-
gothiciz|e, -is|e ˈgɒθ.ɪ.saɪz, ˈ-ə-, ⓤⓢ ˈgɑː.θə- **-es** -ɪz **-ing** -ɪŋ **-ed** -d
Gothland ˈgɒθ.lənd, ⓤⓢ ˈgɑːt-
Gotland ˈgɒt.lənd, ⓤⓢ ˈgɑːt-
gotta ˈgɒt.ə, ⓤⓢ ˈgɑː.t̬ə
gotten (from **get**) ˈgɒt.ᵊn, ⓤⓢ ˈgɑː.tᵊn
götterdämmerung, G~ ˌgɜː.təˈdem.ə.rʊŋ, -ˈdeɪ.mə-, ⓤⓢ ˌgɝː.t̬ɚˈdem-
Gotthard ˈgɒt.ɑːd, ⓤⓢ ˈgɑː.tɑːrd
Gotti ˈgɒt.i, ⓤⓢ ˈgɑː.t̬i
Göttingen ˈgɜː.tɪŋ.ən, ⓤⓢ ˈgɝː-
gouache guˈɑːʃ, -ˈæʃ, gwɑːʃ, gwæʃ
Gouda ˈgaʊ.də, ⓤⓢ ˈguː-
Goudie ˈgaʊ.di
goug|e gaʊdʒ, guːdʒ, ⓤⓢ gaʊdʒ **-es** -ɪz **-ing** -ɪŋ **-ed** -d
Gough gɒf, ⓤⓢ gɑːf
goujon ˈguː.dʒɒn, -ʒɒn, -ʒɔ̃ːŋ, ⓤⓢ guːˈʒoʊn **-s** -z
goulash ˈguː.læʃ, ⓤⓢ -lɑːʃ, -læʃ **-es** -ɪz
Goulburn *place-name:* ˈgəʊl.bɜːn, ⓤⓢ ˈgoʊl.bɝːn *surname:* ˈguːl.bɜːn, ˈgəʊl.bən, ⓤⓢ ˈguːl.bɝːn, ˈgoʊl.bɚn
Gould guːld
Goulden ˈguːl.dən
Goulding ˈguːl.dɪŋ
Gounod ˈguː.nəʊ, ⓤⓢ -noʊ
gourd gʊəd, gɔːd, ⓤⓢ gɔːrd, gʊrd **-s** -z
gourde gʊəd, gɔːd, ⓤⓢ gɔːrd, gʊrd **-s** -z
Gourl|ay ˈgʊə.l|eɪ, -l|i, ⓤⓢ ˈgʊr.l|i **-ey** -i
gourmand ˈgʊə.mənd, ˈgɔː-, -mɑ̃ːŋ, ⓤⓢ gʊrˈmɑːnd, -mənd **-s** -z
gourmet ˈgʊə.meɪ, ˈgɔː-, ⓤⓢ ˈgʊr.meɪ, -ˈ- **-s** -z
Gourock ˈgʊə.rək, ⓤⓢ ˈgʊr.ək
gout gaʊt **-y** -i, ⓤⓢ ˈgaʊ.t̬i **-ily** -ᵊl.i, -ɪ.li, ⓤⓢ -t̬ᵊl.i, ˈgaʊ.t̬ɪ.li **-iness** -ɪ.nəs, -ɪ.nɪs, ⓤⓢ ˈgaʊ.t̬ɪ.nəs, -t̬ɪ-
Govan ˈgʌv.ᵊn
Gover ˈgəʊ.vəʳ, ⓤⓢ ˈgoʊ.vɚ
govern ˈgʌv.ᵊn, ⓤⓢ -ɚn **-s** -z **-ing** -ɪŋ **-ed** -d **-able** -ə.bᵊl
governance ˈgʌv.ᵊn.ənts, ⓤⓢ -ɚ.nᵊnts
governess ˈgʌv.ᵊn.əs, -ɪs, -es, ⓤⓢ -ɚ.nəs **-es** -ɪz
government ˈgʌv.ᵊn.mənt, -ᵊm.mənt, -və.mənt, ⓤⓢ -ɚn- **-s** -s
governmental ˌgʌv.ᵊnˈmen.tᵊl, -ᵊmˈmen-, -əˈmen-, ⓤⓢ -ɚnˈmen.t̬ᵊl
governor ˈgʌv.ᵊn.əʳ, ⓤⓢ -ɚ.nɚ **-s** -z
governor-general ˌgʌv.ᵊn.əˈdʒen.ᵊr.ᵊl, ⓤⓢ -ɚ.nɚˈ- **-s** -z
governorship ˈgʌv.ᵊn.ə.ʃɪp, ⓤⓢ -ɚ.nɚ- **-s** -s
Govey ˈgəʊ.vi, ⓤⓢ ˈgoʊ-
Govier ˈgəʊ.vi.əʳ, ⓤⓢ ˈgoʊ.vi.ɚ
Gow gaʊ
Gowan ˈgaʊ.ən
Gowdy ˈgaʊ.di
Gowen ˈgaʊ.ən, ˈgaʊ.ɪn
Gower gaʊəʳ, ˈgaʊ.əʳ, gɔːʳ, ⓤⓢ ˈgaʊ.ɚ

> Note: /gaʊəʳ/ or /ˈgaʊ.əʳ/ is used in **Gower Street** and for the place in Wales. /gɔːʳ/ is the family name of the Duke of Sutherland; this pronunciation is also used in **Leveson-Gower**.

Gowing ˈgaʊ.ɪŋ
gowk gaʊk **-s** -s
Gowlett ˈgaʊ.lət, -lɪt
gown gaʊn **-s** -z **-ed** -d
gowns|man ˈgaʊnz|.mən **-men** -mən, -men
Gowrie ˈgaʊ.ri
Gowther ˈgaʊ.ðəʳ, ⓤⓢ -ðɚ
Gowy ˈgaʊ.i
goy gɔɪ **-s** -z **-im** -ɪm **-ish** -ɪʃ
Goya ˈgɔɪ.ə
Gozo ˈgəʊ.zəʊ, ⓤⓢ ˈgoʊ.zoʊ
GP ˌdʒiːˈpiː **-s** -z
GPA ˌdʒiː.piːˈeɪ
GPO ˌdʒiː.piːˈəʊ, ⓤⓢ -ˈoʊ
GPS ˌdʒiː.piːˈes
grab græb **-s** -z **-bing** -ɪŋ **-bed** -d **-ber/s** -əʳ/z, ⓤⓢ -ɚ/z **ˈgrab ˌbag; ˌup for ˈgrabs**
grabbl|e ˈgræb.ᵊl **-es** -z **-ing** -ɪŋ, ˈ-lɪŋ **-ed** -d
grabb|y ˈgræb|.i **-ier** -i.əʳ, ⓤⓢ -i.ɚ **-iest** -i.ɪst, -i.əst
Grabham ˈgræb.əm
Gracch|us ˈgræk|.əs **-i** -iː, -aɪ
grac|e, G~ greɪs **-es** -ɪz **-ing** -ɪŋ **-ed** -t **ˈgrace ˌnote; ˌfall from ˈgrace**
Gracechurch ˈgreɪs.tʃɜːtʃ, ⓤⓢ -tʃɝːtʃ
graceful ˈgreɪs.fᵊl, -fʊl **-ly** -i **-ness** -nəs, -nɪs
Graceland ˈgreɪs.lænd, -lənd
graceless ˈgreɪ.sləs, -slɪs **-ly** -li **-ness** -nəs, -nɪs
Gracie ˈgreɪ.si
gracious ˈgreɪ.ʃəs **-ly** -li **-ness** -nəs, -nɪs
grackle ˈgræk.ᵊl **-s** -z
grad græd **-s** -z **ˈgrad ˌschool**
gradability ˌgreɪ.dəˈbɪl.ə.ti, -ɪ.ti, ⓤⓢ -ə.t̬i
gradable ˈgreɪ.də.bᵊl
gra|date grə|ˈdeɪt, ⓤⓢ ˈgreɪ|.deɪt **-dates** -ˈdeɪts, ⓤⓢ -deɪts **-dating** -ˈdeɪ.tɪŋ, ⓤⓢ -deɪ.t̬ɪŋ **-dated** -ˈdeɪ.tɪd, ⓤⓢ -deɪ.t̬əd
gradation grəˈdeɪ.ʃᵊn, ⓤⓢ greɪ- **-s** -z
gradational grəˈdeɪ.ʃᵊn.ᵊl, ⓤⓢ greɪ-
grad|e greɪd **-es** -z **-ing** -ɪŋ **-ed** -ɪd **ˌgrade point ˈaverage** ⓤⓢ **ˈgrade point ˌaverage; ˈgrade ˌschool; ˌmake the ˈgrade**
gradeable ˈgreɪ.də.bᵊl
gradely ˈgreɪd.li
Gradgrind ˈgræd.graɪnd
gradient ˈgreɪ.di.ənt **-s** -s
gradin ˈgreɪ.dɪn **-s** -z
graditative ˈgreɪ.dɪ.tə.tɪv, -də-, ⓤⓢ -də-
gradual ˈgrædʒ.u.əl, ˈgræd.ju.əl, ⓤⓢ ˈgrædʒ.u.əl **-s** -z **-ly** -i
graduate n ˈgrædʒ.u.ət, ˈgræd.ju-, -ɪt, ⓤⓢ ˈgrædʒ.u.ət, -ɪt **-s** -s
gradu|ate v ˈgræd.ju|.eɪt, ˈgrædʒ.u-, ⓤⓢ ˈgrædʒ.u- **-ates** -eɪts **-ating** -eɪ.tɪŋ, ⓤⓢ -eɪ.t̬ɪŋ **-ated** -eɪ.tɪd, ⓤⓢ -eɪ.t̬ɪd
graduation ˌgrædʒ.uˈeɪ.ʃᵊn, ˌgræd.juˈ-, ⓤⓢ ˌgrædʒ.uˈ- **-s** -z
graduator ˈgrædʒ.u.eɪ.təʳ, ˈgræd.ju-, ⓤⓢ ˈgrædʒ.u.eɪ.t̬ɚ **-s** -z
gradus ˈgræd.əs, ˈgreɪ.dəs **-es** -ɪz
Grady ˈgreɪ.di
Graecism ˈgriː.sɪ.zᵊm
Graeco- ˈgriː.kəʊ, ˈgrek.əʊ, ⓤⓢ ˈgrek.oʊ, ˈgriː.koʊ
Graeme ˈgreɪ.əm, greɪm
Graf grɑːf, græf, ⓤⓢ græf
graffiti grəˈfiː.ti, græfˈiː-, ⓤⓢ grəˈfiː.t̬i
Graf(f)ham ˈgræf.əm
graft grɑːft, ⓤⓢ græft **-s** -s **-ing** -ɪŋ **-ed** -ɪd **-er/s** -əʳ/z, ⓤⓢ -ɚ/z
Grafton ˈgrɑːf.tᵊn, ⓤⓢ ˈgræf-
Graham(e) ˈgreɪ.əm
graham cracker ˈgreɪ.əmˌkræk.əʳ, ⓤⓢ -ɚ, ˈgræm- **-s** -z
graham flour ˈgreɪ.əmˌflaʊ.əʳ, -flaʊəʳ, ⓤⓢ -ˌflaʊ.ɚ
Grahamston ˈgreɪ.əm.stᵊn
Grahamstown ˈgreɪ.əmz.taʊn
grail, G~ greɪl **-s** -z
grain greɪn **-s** -z **-ing** -ɪŋ **-ed** -d **-er/s** -əʳ/z, ⓤⓢ -ɚ/z **ˌgo aˌgainst the ˈgrain**
Grainger ˈgreɪn.dʒəʳ, ⓤⓢ -dʒɚ
grain|y ˈgreɪ.n|i **-ier** -i.əʳ, ⓤⓢ -i.ɚ **-iest** -i.ɪst, -i.əst
gram græm **-s** -z
gramercy grəˈmɜː.si, ⓤⓢ -ˈmɝː-
graminaceous ˌgræm.ɪˈneɪ.ʃəs, ˌgreɪ.mɪˈ-, -məˈ-, ⓤⓢ ˌgræm.əˈ-
gramineous grəˈmɪn.i.əs, græmˈɪn-
graminivorous ˌgræm.ɪˈnɪv.ᵊr.əs, ˌgreɪ-
grammalogue ˈgræm.ə.lɒg, ⓤⓢ -lɑːg, -lɔːg **-s** -z
grammar ˈgræm.əʳ, ⓤⓢ -ɚ **-s** -z **ˈgrammar ˌschool**
grammarian grəˈmeə.ri.ən, ⓤⓢ -ˈmer.i- **-s** -z

grammatical grəˈmæt.ɪ.kəl, US -ˈmæţ.ɪ- **-ly** -i
grammaticality grəˌmæt.ɪˈkæl.ə.ti, -ɪ.ti, US -ˌmæţ.əˈkæl.ə.ţi
grammaticiz|e, -is|e grəˈmæt.ɪ.saɪz, ˈ-ə-, US -ˈmæţ.ə- **-es** -ɪz **-ing** -ɪŋ **-ed** -d
gramme græm **-s** -z
Grammer ˈgræm.əʳ, US -ɚ
Gramm|y ˈgræm|.i **-ys** -iz **-ies** -iz
gramophone ˈgræm.ə.fəʊn, US -foʊn **-s** -z
Grampian ˈgræm.pi.ən **-s** -z
gramps græmps
grampus ˈgræm.pəs **-es** -ɪz
gran græn **-s** -z
Granada grəˈnɑː.də
granar|y ˈgræn.ər|.i **-ies** -iz ˈ**granary** ˌ**bread**
Granbury ˈgræn.bər.i, ˈgræm-, US ˈgrænˌber-, -bɚ-
Granby ˈgræn.bi, ˈgræm-, US ˈgræn-
Gran Canaria ˌgræn.kəˈneə.ri.ə, ˌgræŋ-, US ˌgrɑːn.kəˈnɑː-, -ˈner-
Gran Chaco ˌgrænˈtʃɑː.kəʊ, -ˈtʃæk.əʊ, US ˌgrɑːnˈtʃɑː.koʊ
grand grænd **-er** -əʳ, US -ɚ **-est** -ɪst, -əst **-ly** -li **-ness** -nəs, -nɪs, ˈgræn.nəs, -nɪs ˌ**Grand Caˈnary;** ˌ**Grand** ˈ**Canyon;** ˌ**grand** ˈ**duchess;** ˌ**grand** ˈ**duke;** ˌ**Grand** ˈ**Forks;** ˌ**grand** ˈ**jury;** ˌ**Grand** ˈ**National;** ˌ**grand piˈano**
grandad, G~ ˈgræn.dæd **-s** -z
grandadd|y ˈgræn.dæd|.i **-ies** -iz
grandam ˈgræn.dæm, -dəm **-s** -z
grandaunt ˈgrændˌɑːnt, US -ˌænt, -ˌɑːnt **-s** -s
grand|child ˈgrænd|.tʃaɪld **-children** -ˌtʃɪl.drən
granddad, G~ ˈgrænd.dæd **-s** -z
granddadd|y ˈgrænd.dæd|.i **-ies** -iz
granddaughter ˈgrændˌdɔː.təʳ, US -ˌdɑː.ţɚ, -ˌdɔː- **-s** -z
grande dame ˌgrɑːndˈdɑːm, ˌgrɑ̃ːn-, -ˈdæm **-s** -z
grandee grænˈdiː **-s** -z
grandeur ˈgræn.dʒəʳ, -djəʳ, -djʊəʳ, US -dʒɚ, -dʒʊr
grandfather ˈgrændˌfɑː.ðəʳ, US -ðɚ **-s** -z ˈ**grandfather** ˌ**clause;** ˌ**grandfather** ˈ**clock** US ˈ**grandfather** ˌ**clock**
Grand Guignol ˌgrɑ̃ːŋ.giːˈnjɒl, US ˌgrɑ̃ː.giːˈnjoʊl, ˌgrɑːn-, -ˈnjɑːl
grandiloquen|ce grænˈdɪl.ə.kwən|ts **-t/ly** -t/li
grandiose ˈgræn.di.əʊs, -əʊz, US -oʊs, -oʊz, ˌ--ˈ- **-ly** -li
grandiosity ˌgræn.diˈɒs.ə.ti, -ɪ.ti, US -ˈɑː.sə.ţi
Grandison ˈgræn.dɪ.sən
Grandissimes ˈgrænd.ɪ.siːmz
grandma ˈgrænd.mɑː, ˈgræm- **-s** -z ˌ**Grandma** ˈ**Moses**
grand mal ˌgrɑ̃ːndˈmæl, US ˌgrɑːndˈmɑːl, ˌgrænd-, -ˈmæl
grandmamma ˈgrænd.məˌmɑː, ˈgræm- **-s** -z
Grand Marnier®
ˌgrɑ̃ːndˈmɑː.ni.eɪ, US ˌgrɑːn.mɑːrˈnjeɪ **-s** -z
grandmaster ˈgrændˌmɑː.stəʳ, ˈgræm-, US ˈgrændˌmæs.tɚ **-s** -z
grandmother ˈgrændˌmʌð.əʳ, ˈgræm-, US ˈgrændˌmʌð.ɚ **-s** -z
grandnephew ˈgrændˌnev.juː, -ˌnef-, ˌ-ˈ--, US ˈgrændˌnef.juː **-s** -z
grandniec|e ˈgrænd.niːs, ˌ-ˈ- **-es** -ɪz
grandpa ˈgrænd.pɑː, ˈgræm- **-s** -z
grandpapa ˈgrænd.pəˌpɑː, ˈgræm- **-s** -z
grandparent ˈgrændˌpeə.rənt, ˈgræm-, US ˈgrændˌper.ənt, -ˌpær- **-s** -s
grand prix ˌgrɑ̃ːnˈpriː, ˌgrɒn-, ˌgrɒm-, US ˌgrɑːn- **grands prix** ˌgrɑ̃ːˈpriː, ˌgrɒn-, ˌgrɒm-, US ˌgrɑːn-
grandsire ˈgrænd.saɪəʳ, -saɪ.əʳ, US -saɪ.ɚ **-s** -z
grandson ˈgrænd.sʌn **-s** -z
grands prix ˌgrɑ̃ːˈpriː, ˌgrɒn-, ˌgrɒm-, US ˌgrɑːnˈ-
grandstand ˈgrænd.stænd **-s** -z **-ing** -ɪŋ **-ed** -ɪd
granduncle ˈgrændˌʌŋ.kəl **-s** -z
grang|e, G~ ˈgreɪndʒ **-es** -ɪz
Grangemouth ˈgreɪndʒ.maʊθ, -məθ
Granger ˈgreɪn.dʒəʳ, US -dʒɚ
grangeriz|e, -is|e ˈgreɪn.dʒər.aɪz, US -dʒə.raɪz **-es** -ɪz **-ing** -ɪŋ **-ed** -d
Grangetown ˈgreɪndʒ.taʊn
Grangeville ˈgreɪndʒ.vɪl
granita grəˈniː.tə, US -ˈniː.ţə
granite, G~ ˈgræn.ɪt, -ət **-s** -s
granitic grænˈɪt.ɪk, grəˈnɪt-, US grəˈnɪţ-
grann|y ˈgræn|.i **-ies** -iz ˈ**granny flat;** ˈ**granny** ˌ**knot;** ˌ**Granny** ˈ**Smith**
granola grəˈnəʊ.lə, grænˈəʊ-, US grəˈnoʊ-
granolithic ˌgræn.əʊˈlɪθ.ɪk, US -əˈ-
grant, G~ grɑːnt, US grænt **-s** -s **-ing** -ɪŋ, US ˈgræn.ţɪŋ **-ed** -ɪd, US ˈgræn.ţɪd
Granta ˈgræn.tə, ˈgrɑːn-, US ˈgræn-
Grantchester ˈgrɑːn.tʃɪ.stəʳ, ˈgræn-, -tʃə, -tʃes.təʳ, US ˈgrænˌtʃes.tɚ
grantee ˌgrɑːnˈtiː, US ˌgræn- **-s** -z
Granth grʌnt
Grantham ˈgrænt.θəm
Granton ˈgrɑːn.tən, ˈgræn-, US ˈgræn-
grantor ˌgrɑːnˈtɔːʳ; ˈgrɑːn.təʳ, US ˈgræn.ţɚ; US ˌgrænˈtɔːr **-s** -z
Grantown ˈgræn.taʊn
granular ˈgræn.jə.ləʳ, -jʊ-, US -jə.lɚ **-ly** -li
granularity ˌgræn.jəˈlær.ə.ti, -jʊˈ-, -ɪ.ti, US -jəˈler.ə.ţi, -ˈlær-
granu|late ˈgræn.jə|.leɪt, -jʊ-, US -jə- **-lates** -leɪts **-lating** -leɪ.tɪŋ, US -leɪ.ţɪŋ **-lated** -leɪ.tɪd, US -leɪ.ţɪd
granulation ˌgræn.jəˈleɪ.ʃən, -jʊˈ-, US -jəˈ- **-s** -z
granule ˈgræn.juːl **-s** -z
granulite ˈgræn.jə.laɪt, -jʊ-, US -jə-
granulitic ˌgræn.jəˈlɪt.ɪk, -jʊˈ-, US -jəˈlɪţ-
Granville ˈgræn.vɪl
Granville-Barker ˌgræn.vɪlˈbɑː.kəʳ, US -ˈbɑːr.kɚ
grape, G~ greɪp **-s** -s ˈ**grape** ˌ**sugar**
grapefruit ˈgreɪp.fruːt **-s** -s
grapeshot ˈgreɪp.ʃɒt, US -ʃɑːt
grapevine ˈgreɪp.vaɪn **-s** -z
graph grɑːf, græf, US græf **-s** -s ˈ**graph** ˌ**paper**
grapheme ˈgræf.iːm **-s** -z
graphemic græfˈiː.mɪk, grəˈfiː- **-ally** -əl.i, -li
-grapher grə.fəʳ, US grə.fɚ
Note: Suffix. Words containing **-grapher** are normally stressed on the antepenultimate syllable, e.g. **photographer** /fəˈtɒg.rə.fəʳ/ US /-ˈtɑː.grə.fɚ/.
graphic, G~ ˈgræf.ɪk **-s** -s **-al** -əl **-ally** -əl.i, -li ˌ**graphic deˈsign**
-graphic ˈgræf.ɪk
Note: Suffix. Normally carries primary stress, e.g. **photographic** /ˌfəʊ.təˈgræf.ɪk/ US /ˌfoʊ.ţəˈ-/.
graphite ˈgræf.aɪt
graphitic græfˈɪt.ɪk, grəˈfɪt-, US grəˈfɪţ-
graphological ˌgræf.əˈlɒdʒ.ɪ.kəl, US -ˈlɑː.dʒɪ- **-ly** -i
grapholog|y græfˈɒl.ə.dʒ|i, grəˈfɒl-, US grəˈfɑː.lə- **-ist/s** -ɪst/s
graphometer græfˈɒm.ɪ.təʳ, grəˈfɒm-, ˈ-ə-, US grəˈfɑː.mə.ţɚ **-s** -z
-graphy grə.fi
Note: Suffix. Words containing **-graphy** are normally stressed on the antepenultimate syllable, e.g. **photography** /fəˈtɒg.rə.fi/ US /-ˈtɑː.grə-/.
grapnel ˈgræp.nəl **-s** -z
grappa ˈgræp.ə, US ˈgrɑː.pə **-s** -z
Grappelli græpˈel.i, grəpˈ-
grappl|e ˈgræp.əl **-es** -z **-ing** -ɪŋ, ˈ-lɪŋ **-ed** -d **-er/s** -əʳ/z, ˈ-ləʳ/z, US ˈ-əl.ɚ/z, ˈ-lɚ/z ˈ**grappling** ˌ**iron**
grapy ˈgreɪ.pi
Grasmere ˈgrɑːs.mɪəʳ, US ˈgræs.mɪr
grasp grɑːsp, US græsp **-s** -s **-ing** -ɪŋ **-ed** -t **-er/s** -əʳ/z, US -ɚ/z **-able** -ə.bəl
grass, G~ grɑːs, US græs **-es** -ɪz **-ing** -ɪŋ **-ed** -t ˌ**grass** ˈ**widow;** **let the** ˌ**grass** ˌ**grow under one's** ˈ**feet**
grasshopper ˈgrɑːsˌhɒp.əʳ, US ˈgræsˌhɑː.pɚ **-s** -z
grassland ˈgrɑːs.lænd, -lənd, US ˈgræs-
grass roots n ˌgrɑːsˈruːts, US ˌgræs-
grass-roots adj ˌgrɑːsˈruːts, US ˌgræs- *stress shift:* ˌ**grass-roots** ˈ**feeling**
grasstree ˈgrɑː.striː, US ˈgræs.triː **-s** -z

grass|y ˈgrɑː.s|i, (US) ˈgræs|.i **-ier** -i.əʳ, (US) -i.ɚ **-iest** -i.ɪst, -i.əst
grat|e n, v greɪt **-es** -s **-ing/ly** -ɪŋ/li, (US) ˈgreɪ.t̬ɪŋ/li **-ed** -ɪd, (US) ˈgreɪ.t̬ɪd **-er/s** -əʳ/z, (US) ˈgreɪ.t̬ɚ/z
grateful ˈgreɪt.fᵊl, -fʊl **-ly** -i **-ness** -nəs, -nɪs
Gratian ˈgreɪ.ʃᵊn, -ʃi.ən
graticule ˈgræt.ɪ.kjuːl, ˈ-ə-, (US) ˈ-ə- **-s** -z
gratification ˌgræt.ɪ.fɪˈkeɪ.ʃᵊn, ˌ-ə-, -fəˈ-, (US) ˌgræt̬.ə- **-s** -z
grati|fy ˈgræt.ɪ|.faɪ, ˈ-ə-, (US) ˈgræt̬.ɪ-, ˈ-ə- **-fies** -faɪz **-fying/ly** -faɪ.ɪŋ/li **-fied** -faɪd
gratin ˈgræ.tæ̃ŋ, -tæn, (US) ˈgrɑː.tᵊn
grating n ˈgreɪ.tɪŋ, (US) -t̬ɪŋ **-s** -z
Gratiot ˈgræʃ.i.ət, ˈgræʃ.ət, ˈgreɪ.ʃi.ət, -ʃət, (US) ˈgræʃ.ət
gratis ˈgrɑː.tɪs, ˈgreɪ-, ˈgræt.ɪs, -əs, (US) ˈgræt̬.əs, ˈgrɑː.t̬əs, ˈgreɪ-
gratitude ˈgræt.ɪ.tʃuːd, -tjuːd, ˈ-ə-, (US) ˈgræt̬.ə.tuːd, -tjuːd
Grattan ˈgræt.ᵊn
gratuitous grəˈtʃuː.ɪ.təs, -ˈtjuː-, (US) -ˈtuː.ə.t̬əs, -ˈtjuː- **-ly** -li **-ness** -nəs, -nɪs
gratuit|y grəˈtʃuː.ə.t|i, -ˈtjuː-, -ɪ.t|i, (US) -ˈtuː.ə.t̬|i, -ˈtjuː- **-ies** -iz
graupel ˈgraʊ.pᵊl
gravadlax ˈgræv.əd.læks, (US) ˈgrɑː.vəd.lɑːks
gravamen grəˈveɪ.men, -ˈvɑː-, -mən, (US) -mən **-s** -z **gravamina** grəˈveɪ.mɪn.ə, -ˈvɑː-, (US) -ˈvæm.ɪn-
grave n *accent above a letter:* grɑːv, (US) grɑːv, greɪv
grav|e n, adj *other senses:* greɪv **-es** -z **-er** -əʳ, (US) -ɚ **-est** -ɪst, -əst **-ely** -li **-eness** -nəs, -nɪs **-ing** -ɪŋ **-ed** -d **-er/s** -əʳ/z, (US) -ɚ/z ˌ**turn in one's** ˈ**grave**
graveclothes ˈgreɪv.kləʊðz, (US) -kloʊðz
gravedigger ˈgreɪvˌdɪg.əʳ, (US) -ɚ **-s** -z
gravel ˈgræv.ᵊl **-s** -z **-(l)ing** -ɪŋ **-(l)ed** -d **-ly** -i
graven ˈgreɪ.vᵊn ˌ**graven** ˈ**image**
Graves *surname:* greɪvz *wine:* grɑːv
Gravesend ˌgreɪvzˈend
graveside ˈgreɪv.saɪd
gravestone ˈgreɪv.stəʊn, (US) -stoʊn **-s** -z
graveyard ˈgreɪv.jɑːd, (US) -jɑːrd **-s** -z ˈ**graveyard** ˌ**shift**, ˌ**graveyard** ˈ**shift**
gravid ˈgræv.ɪd **-ly** -li **-ness** -nəs, -nɪs
gravid|a ˈgræv.ɪ.d|ə **-as** -əz **-ae** -iː
gravidity grævˈɪd.ə.ti, grəˈvɪd-, (US) grəˈvɪd.ə.t̬i
gravitas ˈgræv.ɪ.tæs, ˈ-ə-, -tɑːs
gravi|tate ˈgræv.ɪ|.teɪt, ˈ-ə- **-tates** -teɪts **-tating** -teɪ.tɪŋ, (US) -teɪ.t̬ɪŋ **-tated** -teɪ.tɪd, (US) -teɪ.t̬ɪd
gravitation ˌgræv.ɪˈteɪ.ʃᵊn, -əˈ- **-al** -ᵊl **-ally** -ᵊl.i
gravitative ˈgræv.ɪ.teɪ.tɪv, ˈ-ə-, -tə.tɪv, (US) -teɪ.t̬ɪv
gravity ˈgræv.ə.ti, -ɪ.ti, (US) -ə.t̬i
gravlax ˈgræv.læks, (US) ˈgrɑːv.lɑːks
gravure grəˈvjʊəʳ, -ˈvjɔːʳ, (US) -ˈvjʊr
grav|y ˈgreɪ.v|i **-ies** -iz ˈ**gravy** ˌ**train**
gray, G~ greɪ **-s** -z **-er** -əʳ, (US) -ɚ **-est** -ɪst, -əst **-ness** -nəs, -nɪs **-ing** -ɪŋ
grayish ˈgreɪ.ɪʃ
grayling ˈgreɪ.lɪŋ **-s** -z
Grayson ˈgreɪ.sᵊn
graystone, G~ ˈgreɪ.stəʊn, (US) -stoʊn
Graz grɑːts
graz|e greɪz **-es** -ɪz **-ing** -ɪŋ **-ed** -d
grazier ˈgreɪ.zi.əʳ, -ʒəʳ, (US) -ʒɚ **-s** -z
GRE ˌdʒiː.ɑːrˈiː **-s** -z
Greasby ˈgriːz.bi
greas|e griːs **-es** -ɪz **-ing** -ɪŋ **-ed** -t
greasepaint ˈgriːs.peɪnt
greaseproof ˈgriːs.pruːf ˌ**grease-proof** ˈ**paper**
greaser ˈgriː.səʳ, (US) -sɚ, -zɚ **-s** -z
Greasley ˈgriːz.li
greas|y ˈgriː.s|i **-ier** -i.əʳ, (US) -i.ɚ **-iest** -i.ɪst, -i.əst **-ily** -ᵊl.i, -ɪ.li **-iness** -ɪ.nəs, -ɪ.nɪs
great greɪt **-er** -əʳ, (US) ˈgreɪ.t̬ɚ **-est** -ɪst, -əst, (US) ˈgreɪ.t̬ɪst, -t̬əst **-s** -s **-ness** -nəs, -nɪs ˌ**Great** ˌ**Barrier** ˈ**Reef**; ˌ**Great** ˈ**Britain**; ˌ**Great** ˈ**Falls**; ˌ**Great** ˈ**Lakes**; ˌ**Great** ˈ**Plains**
great-aunt ˌgreɪtˈɑːnt, (US) ˌgreɪtˈænt, -ˈɑːnt **-s** -s *stress shift:* ˌ**great-aunt** ˈ**Maud**
greatcoat ˈgreɪt.kəʊt, (US) -koʊt **-s** -s
great-grand|child ˌgreɪtˈgrænd|.tʃaɪld **-children** -ˌtʃɪl.drᵊn
great-granddaughter ˌgreɪtˈgrændˌdɔː.təʳ, (US) -ˌdɑː.t̬ɚ, -ˌdɔː- **-s** -z
great-grandfather ˌgreɪtˈgrændˌfɑː.ðəʳ, (US) -ðɚ **-s** -z
great-grandmother ˌgreɪtˈgrændˌmʌð.əʳ, -ˈgræm-, (US) -ˈgrændˌmʌð.ɚ **-s** -z
great-grandparent ˌgreɪtˈgrændˌpeə.rᵊnt, (US) -ˌper.ᵊnt, -ˌpær- **-s** -s
great-grandson ˌgreɪtˈgrænd.sʌn **-s** -z
Greatham *in Durham:* ˈgriː.təm, (US) ˈgriː.t̬əm *in Northamptonshire, Hampshire, and West Sussex:* ˈgret.əm, (US) ˈgreɪ.t̬əm
Greathead ˈgreɪt.hed
Greatheart ˈgreɪt.hɑːt, (US) -hɑːrt
greathearted ˌgreɪtˈhɑː.tɪd, (US) -ˈhɑːr.t̬ɪd *stress shift:* ˌ**greathearted** ˈ**warrior**
greatly ˈgreɪt.li
Greatorex ˈgreɪ.tə.reks, (US) -t̬ə-
Greats greɪts
great-uncle ˌgreɪtˈʌŋ.kᵊl, ˈ-ˌ-- **-s** -z *stress shift:* ˌ**great-uncle** ˈ**John**
Great Yarmouth ˌgreɪtˈjɑː.məθ, (US) -ˈjɑːr-
greave griːv **-s** -z
Greaves griːvz, greɪvz
grebe griːb **-s** -z
Grecian ˈgriː.ʃᵊn **-s** -z
Grecism ˈgriː.sɪ.zᵊm
Greco- ˈgriː.kəʊ, ˈgrek.əʊ, (US) ˈgrek.oʊ, ˈgriː.koʊ
Greece griːs
greed griːd
greed|y ˈgriː.d|i **-ier** -i.əʳ, (US) -i.ɚ **-iest** -i.ɪst, -i.əst **-ily** -ᵊl.i, -ɪ.li **-iness** -ɪ.nəs, -ɪ.nɪs ˈ**greedy** ˌ**guts**
Greek griːk **-s** -s ˌ**Greek** ˌ**Orthodox** ˈ**Church**
Greel(e)y ˈgriː.li
green, G~ griːn **-s** -z **-er** -əʳ, (US) -ɚ **-est** -ɪst, -əst **-ly** -li **-ness** -nəs, -nɪs **-ing** -ɪŋ **-ed** -d ˌ**green** ˈ**bean** (US) ˈ**green** ˌ**bean**; ˌ**Green Be**ˈ**ret**; ˈ**green** ˌ**card**; ˌ**green cross** ˈ**code**; ˈ**Green** ˌ**Party**
Green(e) griːn
Greenall ˈgriː.nɔːl **-s** -z
Greenaway ˈgriː.nə.weɪ
greenback ˈgriːn.bæk, ˈgriːm-, (US) ˈgriːn- **-s** -s
greenbelt, G~ ˈgriːn.belt, ˈgriːm-, (US) ˈgriːn- **-s** -s
Greenburg ˈgriːn.bɜːg, ˈgriːm-, (US) -bɝːg
greenery ˈgriː.nᵊr.i
green-eyed ˌgriːnˈaɪd, (US) ˈgriːn.aɪd *stress shift, British only:* ˌ**green-eyed** ˈ**monster**
greenfield, G~ ˈgriːn.fiːld
greenfinch ˈgriːn.fɪntʃ **-es** -ɪz
green|fly ˈgriːn|.flaɪ **-flies** -flaɪz
Greenford ˈgriːn.fəd, (US) -fɚd
greengag|e ˈgriːn.geɪdʒ, ˈgriːŋ-, (US) ˈgriːn- **-es** -ɪz
greengrocer ˈgriːnˌgrəʊ.səʳ, ˈgriːŋ-, (US) ˈgriːnˌgroʊ.sɚ **-s** -z
Greenhalgh ˈgriːn.hælʃ, -hældʒ, -hɔː
Greenham ˈgriː.nəm ˌ**Greenham** ˈ**Common**
Greenhaulgh ˈgriːn.hɔː
Greenhill ˈgriːn.hɪl
Greenhithe ˈgriːn.haɪð
greenhorn ˈgriːn.hɔːn, (US) -hɔːrn **-s** -z
greenhou|se ˈgriːn.haʊ|s **-ses** -zɪz ˈ**greenhouse ef**ˌ**fect**; ˌ**greenhouse** ˈ**gas**
greenish, G~ ˈgriː.nɪʃ
Greenland ˈgriːn.lənd, -lænd **-er/s** -əʳ/z
Greenleaf ˈgriːn.liːf
greenmarket ˈgriːnˌmɑː.kɪt, ˈgriːm-, (US) ˈgriːnˌmɑːr.kɪt **-s** -s
Greenock ˈgriː.nək, ˈgrɪn.ək, ˈgren-
Greenore ˈgriː.nɔːʳ, (US) -nɔːr
Greenough ˈgriː.nəʊ, (US) -noʊ
Greenpeace ˈgriːn.piːs, ˈgriːm-, (US) ˈgriːn-
Greenpoint ˈgriːn.pɔɪnt, ˈgriːm-, (US) ˈgriːn-
Greenport ˈgriːn.pɔːt, ˈgriːm-, (US) ˈgriːn.pɔːrt
greenroom ˈgriːn.rʊm, -ruːm, (US) -ruːm, -rʊm **-s** -z
greensand ˈgriːn.sænd
Greensboro ˈgriːnz.bᵊr.ə, (US) -bɚ.oʊ
greenshank ˈgriːn.ʃæŋk **-s** -s
Greenslade ˈgriːn.sleɪd

G

Greensleeves ˈgriːn.sliːvz
Greenspan ˈgriːn.spæn
greenstick ˈgriːn.stɪk **-s** -z ˌ**green-stick** ˈ**fracture**
greenstone ˈgriːn.stəʊn, (US) -stoʊn
greensward ˈgriːn.swɔːd, (US) -swɔːrd
Greenville ˈgriːn.vɪl
greenwash ˈgriːn.wɒʃ, (US) -wɑːʃ, -wɔːʃ **-ing** -ɪŋ
Greenway ˈgriːn.weɪ
Greenwell ˈgriːn.wəl, -wel
Greenwich ˈgren.ɪdʒ, ˈgrɪn-, -ɪtʃ, (US) ˈgren.ɪdʒ, ˈgrɪn-, -nɪtʃ, -wɪtʃ ˌ**Greenwich** ˈ**Mean Time,** ˌ**Greenwich** ˌ**Mean** ˈ**Time**
greenwood, G~ ˈgriːn.wʊd **-s** -z
Greer grɪəʳ, (US) grɪr
greet, G~ griːt **-s** -s **-ing/s** -ɪŋ/z, (US) ˈgriː.t̬ɪŋ/z **-ed** -ɪd, (US) ˈgriː.t̬ɪd ˈ**greetings** ˌ**card** (US) ˈ**greeting** ˌ**card**
Greetland ˈgriːt.lənd
Greg(g) greg
gregarious grɪˈgeə.ri.əs, grə-, (US) -ˈger.i- **-ly** -li **-ness** -nəs, -nɪs
Gregor ˈgreg.əʳ, (US) -ɚ
Gregorian grɪˈgɔː.ri.ən, grə-, gregˈɔː- **-s** -z **Gre**ˌ**gorian** ˈ**chant**
Gregory ˈgreg.ər.i
Greig greg
greige greɪʒ
greisen ˈgraɪ.zən
gremlin ˈgrem.lɪn **-s** -z
grenache grenˈæʃ
Grenada grəˈneɪ.də, grɪ-, grenˈeɪ-
grenade grəˈneɪd, grɪ-, grenˈeɪd **-s** -z
grenadier, G~ ˌgren.əˈdɪəʳ, (US) -ˈdɪr **-s** -z
grenadine ˈgren.ə.diːn, ˌgren.əˈdiːn
Grenadines ˌgren.əˈdiːnz
Grendel ˈgren.dəl
Grenfell ˈgren.fel, -fəl
Grenoble grəˈnəʊ.bəl, grɪˈnəʊ-, (US) grəˈnoʊ-
Grenville ˈgren.vɪl, -vəl
Gresham ˈgreʃ.əm
Gresley ˈgrez.li
Greswell ˈgrez.wəl, -wel
Greta ˈgriː.tə, ˈgret.ə, ˈgreɪ.tə, (US) ˈgret̬.ə, ˈgriː.t̬ə, ˈgreɪ.t̬ə
Gretchen ˈgretʃ.ən
Gretel ˈgret.əl
Gretna ˈgret.nə ˌ**Gretna** ˈ**Green**
Greuz|e grɜːz **-es** -ɪz
Greville ˈgrev.ɪl, -əl
grew, G~ (from **grow**) gruː
grey, G~ greɪ **-s** -z **-er** -əʳ, (US) -ɚ **-est** -ɪst, -əst **-ness** -nəs, -nɪs **-ing** -ɪŋ
greybeard ˈgreɪ.bɪəd, (US) -bɪrd **-s** -z
greycoat, G~ ˈgreɪ.kəʊt, (US) -koʊt **-s** -s
grey-haired ˌgreɪˈheəd, (US) -ˈherd *stress-shift:* ˌ**grey-haired** ˈ**person**
greyhound ˈgreɪ.haʊnd **-s** -z ˌ**Greyhound** ˈ**bus**
greyish ˈgreɪ.ɪʃ
greylag ˈgreɪ.læg **-s** -z
Greylock ˈgreɪ.lɒk, (US) -lɑːk
Greyson ˈgreɪ.sən
Greystoke ˈgreɪ.stəʊk, (US) -stoʊk
Gribbin ˈgrɪb.ɪn
gribble, G~ ˈgrɪb.əl **-s** -z
Grice graɪs
grid grɪd **-s** -z
griddl|e ˈgrɪd.əl **-es** -z **-ing** -ɪŋ **-ed** -d
gridiron ˈgrɪd.aɪən, -aɪ.ən, (US) -aɪ.ɚn **-s** -z
Gridley ˈgrɪd.li
gridlock ˈgrɪd.lɒk, (US) -lɑːk **-s** -s **-ed** -t
grief griːf **-s** -z ˈ**grief-**ˌ**stricken**
Grieg griːg
Grierson ˈgrɪə.sən, (US) ˈgrɪr-
grievanc|e ˈgriː.vənts **-es** -ɪz
griev|e, G~ griːv **-es** -z **-ing** -ɪŋ **-ed** -d **-er/s** -əʳ/z, (US) -ɚ/z
grievous ˈgriː.vəs **-ly** -li **-ness** -nəs, -nɪs ˌ**grievous** ˌ**bodily** ˈ**harm**

> Note: The common pronunciation /ˈgriː.vi.əs/ is considered a mispronunciation.

griffin, G~ ˈgrɪf.ɪn **-s** -z
Griffith ˈgrɪf.ɪθ **-s** -s
griffon ˈgrɪf.ən **-s** -z
grift grɪft **-s** -s **-ing** -ɪŋ **-ed** -ɪd
grifter ˈgrɪf.təʳ, (US) -tɚ **-s** -z
grig grɪg **-s** -z
Grigg grɪg **-s** -z
Grigson ˈgrɪg.sən
grill grɪl **-s** -z **-ing** -ɪŋ **-ed** -d **-er/s** -əʳ/z, (US) -ɚ/z
grillag|e ˈgrɪl.ɪdʒ **-es** -ɪz
grille grɪl **-s** -z
grillroom ˈgrɪl.rʊm, -ruːm, (US) -ruːm, -rʊm **-s** -z
grilse grɪls
grim grɪm **-mer** -əʳ, (US) -ɚ **-mest** -ɪst, -əst **-ly** -li **-ness** -nəs, -nɪs ˌ**Grim** ˈ**Reaper**
grimac|e ˈgrɪm.əs, -ɪs, grɪˈmeɪs, (US) ˈgrɪm.əs; (US) grɪˈmeɪs **-es** -ɪz **-ing** -ɪŋ **-ed** -t
Grimald ˈgrɪm.əld
Grimaldi grɪˈmɔːl.di, grə-, -ˈmɒl-, -ˈmæl-, (US) -ˈmɑːl-, -ˈmɔːl-
grimalkin grɪˈmæl.kɪn, -ˈmɔːl- **-s** -z
grim|e graɪm **-es** -z **-ing** -ɪŋ **-ed** -d
Grimes graɪmz
Grimethorpe ˈgraɪm.θɔːp, (US) -θɔːrp
Grimké ˈgrɪm.ki
Grimm grɪm
Grimond ˈgrɪm.ənd
Grimsby ˈgrɪmz.bi
Grimshaw ˈgrɪm.ʃɔː, (US) -ʃɑː, -ʃɔː
Grimwood ˈgrɪm.wʊd
grim|y ˈgraɪ.m|i **-ier** -i.əʳ, (US) -i.ɚ **-iest** -i.ɪst, -i.əst **-ily** -əl.i, -ɪ.li **-iness** -ɪ.nəs, -ɪ.nɪs
grin grɪn **-s** -z **-ning** -ɪŋ **-ned** -d
Grinch grɪntʃ
grind graɪnd **-s** -z **-ing** -ɪŋ **ground** graʊnd **grinder/s** ˈgraɪn.dəʳ/z, (US) -dɚ/z
Grindal ˈgrɪnd.əl
Grindelwald ˈgrɪn.dəl.vɑːld, -væld, (US) -vɑːld, -væld, -wɔːld
Grindon ˈgrɪn.dən
grindstone ˈgraɪnd.stəʊn, (US) -stoʊn **-s** -z ˌ**keep one's** ˌ**nose to the** ˈ**grindstone**
gringo ˈgrɪŋ.gəʊ, (US) -goʊ **-s** -z
Grinnell grɪˈnel
Grinstead ˈgrɪn.stɪd, -sted, (US) -sted
grip grɪp **-s** -s **-ping** -ɪŋ **-ped** -t
grip|e graɪp **-es** -s **-ing** -ɪŋ **-ed** -t ˈ**gripe** ˌ**water**
gripes graɪps
grippe griːp, grɪp, (US) grɪp
grisaille grɪˈzeɪl, grə-, griː-, -ˈzaɪ, -ˈzaɪl, (US) -ˈzaɪ, -ˈzeɪl
Griselda grɪˈzel.də, grə-
grisette grɪˈzet **-s** -s
Grisewood ˈgraɪz.wʊd
Grisham ˈgrɪʃ.əm
griskin ˈgrɪs.kɪn
grisl|y ˈgrɪz.l|i **-ier** -i.əʳ, (US) -i.ɚ **-iest** -i.ɪst, -i.əst **-iness** -ɪ.nəs, -ɪ.nɪs
Grisons griːˈzɔ̃ːŋ, -ˈzɔːŋ, (US) griːˈzɔ̃ːŋ, -ˈzɔːŋ
Grissel ˈgrɪs.əl
grist grɪst
gristle ˈgrɪs.əl
gristly ˈgrɪs.əl.i, ˈgrɪs.li
Griswold ˈgrɪz.wəʊld, -wəld, (US) -wɔːld, -wəld
grit grɪt **-s** -s **-ting** -ɪŋ, (US) ˈgrɪt̬.ɪŋ **-ted** -ɪd, (US) ˈgrɪt̬.ɪd
gritter ˈgrɪt.əʳ, (US) ˈgrɪt̬.ɚ **-s** -z
Gritton ˈgrɪt.ən
gritt|y ˈgrɪt|.i, (US) ˈgrɪt̬|.i **-ier** -i.əʳ, (US) -i.ɚ **-iest** -i.ɪst, -i.əst **-ily** -əl.i, -ɪ.li **-iness** -ɪ.nəs, -ɪ.nɪs
Grizedale ˈgraɪz.deɪl
Grizel grɪˈzel
grizzl|e ˈgrɪz.əl **-es** -z **-ing** -ɪŋ, ˈ-lɪŋ **-ed** -d
grizzl|y ˈgrɪz.l|i **-ies** -iz **-ier** -i.əʳ, (US) -i.ɚ **-iest** -i.ɪst, -i.əst ˈ**grizzly** ˌ**bear**
Gro grəʊ, gruː, grɔː, (US) groʊ, grɔː
groan grəʊn, (US) groʊn **-s** -z **-ing/s** -ɪŋ/z **-ed** -d
groat grəʊt, (US) groʊt **-s** -s
grocer ˈgrəʊ.səʳ, (US) ˈgroʊ.sɚ **-s** -z
grocer|y ˈgrəʊ.sər|.i, (US) ˈgroʊ- **-ies** -iz
grockle ˈgrɒk.əl, (US) ˈgrɑː.kəl **-s** -z
Grocott ˈgrɒk.ət, ˈgrəʊ.kɒt, (US) ˈgrɑː.kət, ˈgroʊ-
Grocyn ˈgrəʊ.sɪn, (US) ˈgroʊ-
grog grɒg, (US) grɑːg, grɔːg
grogg|y ˈgrɒg|.i, (US) ˈgrɑː.g|i, ˈgrɔː- **-ier** -i.əʳ, (US) -i.ɚ **-iest** -i.ɪst, -i.əst **-ily** -əl.i, -ɪ.li **-iness** -ɪ.nəs, -ɪ.nɪs
grogram ˈgrɒg.rəm, (US) ˈgrɑː.grəm
groin grɔɪn **-s** -z
grommet ˈgrɒm.ɪt, ˈgrʌm-, (US) ˈgrɑː.mɪt **-s** -s
gromwell ˈgrɒm.wəl, -wel, (US) ˈgrɑːm-
Gromyko grəˈmiː.kəʊ, (US) -koʊ
Groningen ˈgrəʊ.nɪŋ.ən, ˈgrɒn.ɪŋ-, (US) ˈgroʊ-
groom, G~ gruːm, grʊm **-s** -z **-ing** -ɪŋ **-ed** -d

Pronouncing the letters GU

At the beginning of words, the consonant digraph **gu** is usually realized as /g/, e.g.:

guest gest

Word-finally, **gu** is usually followed by **e** in nouns and is pronounced /g/, e.g.:

fatigue fəˈtiːg

gu may also be pronounced as /gw/, e.g.:

language ˈlæŋ.gwɪdʒ

G

grooms|man ˈgruːmz|.mən, ˈgrʊmz- **-men** -mən, -men
groov|e gruːv **-es** -z **-ing** -ɪŋ **-ed** -d
groov|y ˈgruː.v|i **-ier** -i.əʳ, (US) -i.ɚ **-iest** -i.ɪst, -i.əst **-iness** -ɪ.nəs, -ɪ.nɪs
grop|e grəʊp, (US) groʊp **-es** -s **-ing/ly** -ɪŋ/li **-ed** -t **-er/s** -əʳ/z, (US) -ɚ/z
Gropius ˈgrəʊ.pi.əs, (US) ˈgroʊ-
Grosart ˈgrəʊ.zɑːt, (US) ˈgroʊ.zɑːrt
grosbeak ˈgrəʊs.biːk, ˈgrɒs-, ˈgrɒz-, (US) ˈgroʊs- **-s** -s
groschen ˈgrɒʃ.ən, ˈgrəʊʃ.ən, (US) ˈgroʊ.ʃən
Grose grəʊs, grəʊz, (US) groʊs, groʊz
grosgrain ˈgrəʊ.greɪn, (US) ˈgroʊ-
Grosmont *in North Yorkshire:* ˈgrəʊ.mənt, -mɒnt; *locally also:* ˈgrəʊs.mənt, (US) ˈgroʊ.mɑːnt, ˈgroʊs- *in Gwent:* ˈgrɒs.mənt, (US) ˈgrɑːs-
gros point ˌgrəʊˈpɔɪnt, (US) ˈgroʊ.pɔɪnt
gross grəʊs, (US) groʊs **-er** -əʳ, (US) -ɚ **-est** -ɪst, -əst **-ly** -li **-ness** -nəs, -nɪs **-es** -ɪz **-ing** -ɪŋ **-ed** -t ˌ**gross doˌmestic ˈproduct;** ˌ**gross ˌnational ˈproduct**
Gross *surname:* grɒs, grəʊs, (US) grɑːs, groʊs
Grosseteste ˈgrəʊs.test, (US) ˈgroʊs-
Grossmith ˈgrəʊ.smɪθ, (US) ˈgroʊ-
grosso modo ˌgrɒs.əʊˈmɒd.əʊ, -ˈməʊ.dəʊ, (US) ˌgroʊ.soʊˈmoʊ.doʊ
Grosvenor ˈgrəʊv.nəʳ, (US) ˈgroʊv.nɚ
grosz grɔːʃ, (US) grɑːʃ, grɔːʃ **groszy** ˈgrɔː.ʃi, (US) ˈgrɑː-, ˈgrɔː-
Grote grəʊt, (US) groʊt
grotesque grəʊˈtesk, (US) groʊ- **-ly** -li **-ness** -nəs, -nɪs
Grotius ˈgrəʊ.ti.əs, (US) ˈgroʊ.ʃəs, -ʃi.əs
grotto ˈgrɒt.əʊ, (US) ˈgrɑː.t̬oʊ **-(e)s** -z
grott|y ˈgrɒt|.i, (US) ˈgrɑː.t̬|i **-ier** -i.əʳ, (US) -i.ɚ **-iest** -i.ɪst, -i.əst **-ily** -əl.i, -ɪ.li **-iness** -ɪ.nəs, -ɪ.nɪs
grouch graʊtʃ **-es** -ɪz **-ing** -ɪŋ **-ed** -t
Groucho ˈgraʊ.tʃəʊ, (US) -tʃoʊ
grouch|y ˈgraʊ.tʃ|i **-ier** -i.əʳ, (US) -i.ɚ **-iest** -i.ɪst, -i.əst **-ily** -əl.i, -ɪ.li **-iness** -ɪ.nəs, -ɪ.nɪs
ground graʊnd **-s** -z **-ing** -ɪŋ **-ed** -ɪd **-er/s** -əʳ/z, (US) -ɚ/z ˈ**ground ˌplan;** ˈ**ground ˌrule;** ˈ**ground ˌstroke;** ˈ**ground ˌswell;** ˌ**suit someone ˌdown to the ˈground**
groundbreaking ˈgraʊndˌbreɪ.kɪŋ
ground|cloth ˈgraʊnd|.klɒθ, ˈgraʊŋ-, (US) ˈgraʊnd|.klɑːθ **-cloths** -klɒθs, -klɒðz, (US) -klɑːθs, -klɑːðz
groundcover ˈgraʊndˌkʌv.əʳ, ˈgraʊŋ-, (US) ˈgraʊndˌkʌv.ɚ
groundhog ˈgraʊnd.hɒg, (US) -hɑːg, -hɔːg **-s** -z ˈ**Groundhog ˌDay**
groundless ˈgraʊnd.ləs, -lɪs **-ly** -li **-ness** -nəs, -nɪs
groundling ˈgraʊnd.lɪŋ **-s** -z
groundnut ˈgraʊnd.nʌt **-s** -s
groundout ˈgraʊnd.aʊt **-s** -s
groundsel ˈgraʊnd.səl
groundsheet ˈgraʊnd.ʃiːt **-s** -s
grounds|man ˈgraʊndz|.mən **-men** -mən, -men
groundspeed ˈgraʊnd.spiːd **-s** -z
groundstroke ˈgraʊnd.strəʊk, (US) -stroʊk **-s** -s
groundswell ˈgraʊnd.swel
groundwater ˈgraʊndˌwɔː.təʳ, (US) -ˌwɑː.t̬ɚ, -ˌwɔː-
groundwork ˈgraʊnd.wɜːk, (US) -wɝːk
group gruːp **-s** -s **-ing/s** -ɪŋ/z **-ed** -t
grouper ˈgruː.pəʳ, (US) -pɚ **-s** -z
groupie ˈgruː.pi **-s** -z
grous|e, G~ graʊs **-es** -ɪz **-ing** -ɪŋ **-ed** -t **-er/s** -əʳ/z, (US) -ɚ/z
grout graʊt **-s** -s **-ing** -ɪŋ, (US) ˈgraʊ.t̬ɪŋ **-ed** -ɪd, (US) ˈgraʊ.t̬ɪd **-er/s** -əʳ/z, (US) ˈgraʊ.t̬ɚ/z
grove, G~ grəʊv, (US) groʊv **-s** -z
grovel ˈgrɒv.əl, (US) ˈgrɑː.vəl, ˈgrʌv.əl **-s** -z **-(l)ing** -ɪŋ **-(l)ed** -d **-(l)er/s** -əʳ/z, (US) -ɚ/z
Grover ˈgrəʊ.vəʳ, (US) ˈgroʊ.vɚ
grow grəʊ, (US) groʊ **-s** -z **-ing** -ɪŋ **grew** gruː **grown** grəʊn, (US) groʊn ˈ**grow ˌbag;** ˈ**growing ˌpains**
grow-bag ˈgrəʊ.bæg, (US) ˈgroʊ- **-s** -z
grower ˈgrəʊ.əʳ, (US) ˈgroʊ.ɚ **-s** -z
growl graʊl **-s** -z **-ing** -ɪŋ **-ed** -d **-er/s** -əʳ/z, (US) -ɚ/z
grown (from **grow**) grəʊn, (US) groʊn
grown-up n ˈgrəʊn.ʌp, (US) ˈgroʊn- **-s** -s *stress shift:* ˌ**grown-up ˈlanguage**
grown-up adj ˌgrəʊnˈʌp, (US) ˌgroʊnˈ-
growth grəʊθ, (US) groʊθ **-s** -s
groyne grɔɪn **-s** -z
Grozny ˈgrɒz.ni, (US) ˈgrɑːz-
grub grʌb **-s** -z **-bing** -ɪŋ **-bed** -d **-ber/s** -əʳ/z, (US) -ɚ/z
grubb|y ˈgrʌb|.i **-ier** -i.əʳ, (US) -i.ɚ **-iest** -i.ɪst, -i.əst **-iness** -ɪ.nəs, -ɪ.nɪs
grubstak|e ˈgrʌb.steɪk **-es** -s **-ing** -ɪŋ **-ed** -t
grudg|e grʌdʒ **-es** -ɪz **-ing/ly** -ɪŋ/li **-ed** -d
gruel ˈgruː.əl, grʊəl, (US) ˈgruː.əl
gruel(l)ing ˈgrʊə.lɪŋ, ˈgruː.əl.ɪŋ, (US) ˈgruː.lɪŋ, -əl.ɪŋ
Gruenther ˈgrʌn.θəʳ, (US) -θɚ
gruesome ˈgruː.səm **-ly** -li **-ness** -nəs, -nɪs
gruff grʌf **-er** -əʳ, (US) -ɚ **-est** -ɪst, -əst **-ly** -li **-ness** -nəs, -nɪs
grumbl|e ˈgrʌm.bəl **-es** -z **-ing** -ɪŋ, ˈ-blɪŋ **-ed** -d **-er/s** -əʳ/z, ˈ-bləʳ/z, (US) ˈ-bəl.ɚ/z, ˈ-blɚ/z
Grumman ˈgrʌm.ən
grummet ˈgrʌm.ɪt, -ət **-s** -s
grump grʌmp **-s** -s
grump|y ˈgrʌm.p|i **-ier** -i.əʳ, (US) -i.ɚ **-iest** -i.ɪst, -i.əst **-ily** -əl.i, -ɪ.li **-iness** -ɪ.nəs, -ɪ.nɪs
Grundig® ˈgrʌn.dɪg, ˈgrʊn-
Grundtvig ˈgrʊnt.vɪg
Grundy ˈgrʌn.di
grunge grʌndʒ
grung|y ˈgrʌn.dʒ|i **-ier** -i.əʳ, (US) -i.ɚ **-iest** -i.ɪst, -i.əst
grunt grʌnt **-s** -s **-ing** -ɪŋ, (US) ˈgrʌn.t̬ɪŋ **-ed** -ɪd, (US) ˈgrʌn.t̬ɪd **-er/s** -əʳ/z, (US) ˈgrʌn.t̬ɚz
Gruyère ˈgruː.jeəʳ, -jəʳ; gruˈjeəʳ, (US) gruˈjer
Gryll grɪl
gryphon ˈgrɪf.ən **-s** -z
G-seven ˌdʒiːˈsev.ən
g-spot ˈdʒiː.spɒt, (US) -spɑːt
Gstaad kʃtɑːd; gəˈʃtɑːd, (US) gəˈʃtɑːt, -ˈʃtɑːd
G-string ˈdʒiː.strɪŋ **-s** -z
GTech® ˈdʒiː.tek
GTI ˌdʒiː.tiːˈaɪ **-s** -z
guacamole ˌgwɑː.kəˈməʊ.li, ˌgwæk-, -leɪ, (US) ˌgwɑː.k.əˈmoʊ.li
Guadalajara ˌgwɑː.dəl.əˈhɑː.rə, ˌgwæd.əl-, (US) ˌgwɑː.dəl.əˈhɑːr.ə
Guadalquivir ˌgwɑː.dəl.kwɪˈvɪəʳ, ˌgwæd.əl-, -kɪˈ-, (US) ˌgwɑː.dəl.kɪˈvɪr, -ˈkwɪv.ər
Guadeloupe ˌgwɑː.dəˈluːp, -dəlˈuːp, ˈ---
Guam gwɑːm
Guangdong ˌgwæŋˈdɒŋ, ˌgwɒŋ-, -ˈdʊŋ, (US) ˌgwɑːŋˈdɑːŋ, -ˈdʊŋ
Guangzhou ˌgwæŋˈʒəʊ, ˌgwɒŋ-, (US) ˌgwɑːŋˈdʒoʊ
guano ˈgwɑː.nəʊ, (US) -noʊ **-s** -z
Guantánamo gwænˈtæn.ə.məʊ, gwɑːn-, (US) gwɑːnˈtɑː.nə.moʊ
Guarani, Guaraní ˌgwɑː.rəˈniː, ˈgwɑː.rən.i **-s** -z
guarantee ˌgær.ənˈtiː, (US) ˌger-, ˌgær-, ˈ--- **-s** -z **-ing** -ɪŋ **-d** -d
guarantor ˌgær.ənˈtɔːʳ, (US) ˈger.ən.tɔːr, ˈgær-, ˌ--ˈ- **-s** -z
guarant|y ˈgær.ən.t|i, (US) ˈger.ən.t̬|i, ˈgær- **-ies** -iz

guard, G~ gɑːd, (US) gɑːrd **-s** -z **-ing** -ɪŋ **-ed/ly** -ɪd/li **-edness** -ɪd.nəs, -nɪs ˈ**guard's** ˌ**van**
guardian, G~ ˈgɑː.di.ən, (US) ˈgɑːr- **-s** -z **-ship** -ʃɪp
guardrail ˈgɑːd.reɪl, (US) ˈgɑːrd- **-s** -z
guardroom ˈgɑːd.rʊm, -ruːm, (US) ˈgɑːrd.ruːm, -rʊm **-s** -z
guards|man ˈgɑːdz|.mən, -mæn, (US) ˈgɑːrdz- **-men** -mən, -men
Guarneri gwɑːˈneə.ri, (US) gwɑːrˈner.i
Guatemal|a ˌgwæ.təˈmɑː.l|ə, ˌgwɑː.tə-, -ɪmˈɑː-, (US) ˌgwɑː.t̬əˈ- **-an/s** -ən/z
guava ˈgwɑː.və **-s** -z
Guayaquil ˌgwaɪ.əˈkiːl, -ˈkɪl
Guayra ˈgwaɪ.rə
gubbins, G~ ˈgʌb.ɪnz
gubernatorial ˌguː.bən.əˈtɔː.ri.əl, ˌgjuː-, (US) ˌguː.bɚ.nəˈtɔːr.i-
Gucci® ˈguː.tʃi
gudgeon ˈgʌdʒ.ən **-s** -z
Gudrun ˈgʊd.ruːn, gʊˈdruːn
Gue gjuː
guelder-ros|e ˈgel.də.rəʊz, ˌ--ˈ-, (US) ˈgel.dɚ.roʊz, ˌ--ˈ- **-es** -ɪz
Guelph, Guelf gwelf **-s** -s
Guenevere ˈgwɪn.ɪ.vɪər, ˈgwen-, ˈ-ə-, (US) -vɪr
guerdon ˈgɜː.dən, (US) ˈgɝː- **-s** -z
guerilla gəˈrɪl.ə, gjə-, gɜː-, (US) gə- **-s** -z
Guernica ˈgɜː.nɪk.ə, ˈgwɜː-; gɔːˈniː.kə, (US) ˈgwer.nɪk.ə
guernsey, G~ ˈgɜːn.zi, (US) ˈgɝːn- **-s** -z
guerrilla gəˈrɪl.ə, gjə-, gɜː-, (US) gə- **-s** -z
guess ges **-es** -ɪz **-ing** -ɪŋ **-ed** -t **-er/s** -ər/z, (US) -ɚ/z **-able** -ə.bəl ˈ**guessing** ˌ**game**
guesstimate n ˈges.tɪ.mət, -tə-, -mɪt, -meɪt **-s** -s
guessti|mate v ˈges.tɪ|.meɪt, -tə-, (US) -tə- **-mates** -meɪts **-mating** -meɪ.tɪŋ, (US) -meɪ.t̬ɪŋ **-mated** -meɪ.tɪd, (US) -meɪ.t̬ɪd
guesswork ˈges.wɜːk, (US) -wɝːk
guest, G~ gest **-s** -s **-ing** -ɪŋ **-ed** -ɪd ˈ**guest** ˌ**night;** ˈ**guest** ˌ**room**
guesthou|se ˈgest.haʊ|s **-ses** -zɪz
Guevara gəˈvɑː.rə, gɪ-, gevˈɑː-
guff gʌf
guffaw gʌfˈɔː, gəˈfɔː, (US) gʌfˈɑː, -ˈɔː, gəˈfɑː, -ˈfɔː **-s** -z **-ing** -ɪŋ **-ed** -d
Guggenheim ˈgʊg.ən.haɪm, ˈguː.gən-
Guggisberg ˈgʌg.ɪs.bɜːg, (US) -bɝːg
GUI ˈguː.i, ˌdʒiː.juːˈaɪ
Guiana gaɪˈæn.ə, giˈɑː.nə, (US) giˈæn.ə, gaɪ-, -ˈɑː.nə **-s** -z
Guianese ˌgaɪ.əˈniːz, (US) ˌgiː.əˈniːz, ˌgaɪ-, -ˈniːs *stress shift:* ˌ**Guianese** ˈ**people**
guidance ˈgaɪ.dənts
guid|e gaɪd **-es** -z **-ing** -ɪŋ **-ed** -ɪd ˈ**guide** ˌ**dog**
guidebook ˈgaɪd.bʊk **-s** -s
guideline ˈgaɪd.laɪn **-s** -z
guidepost ˈgaɪd.pəʊst, (US) -poʊst **-s** -s
Guido ˈgwiː.dəʊ, ˈgiː-, (US) -doʊ
guidon ˈgaɪ.dən **-s** -z
guild gɪld **-s** -z
Guildenstern ˈgɪl.dən.stɜːn, (US) -stɝːn
guilder ˈgɪl.dər, (US) -dɚ **-s** -z
Guildford ˈgɪl.fəd, (US) -fɚd
guildhall, G~ ˈgɪldˌhɔːl, ˌ-ˈ-, (US) -hɔːl, -hɑːl **-s** -z
Guilding ˈgɪl.dɪŋ
guile gaɪl
guileful ˈgaɪl.fəl, -fʊl **-ly** -i **-ness** -nəs, -nɪs
guileless ˈgaɪl.ləs, -lɪs **-ly** -li **-ness** -nəs, -nɪs
Guilford ˈgɪl.fəd, (US) -fɚd
guillemot ˈgɪl.ɪ.mɒt, ˈ-ə-, (US) -ə.mɑːt **-s** -s
Guillim ˈgwɪl.ɪm
guillotin|e ˈgɪl.ə.tiːn, ˌ--ˈ- **-es** -z **-ing** -ɪŋ **-ed** -d

> Note: Some people use /ˈgɪl.ə.tiːn/ for the noun and /ˌgɪl.əˈtiːn/ for the verb. The pronunciations /ˈgiː.ə.tiːn/ or /ˌgiː.əˈtiːn/, which are aimed at being closer to the French original, may be considered too old-fashioned to recommend.

guilt gɪlt
guiltless ˈgɪlt.ləs, -lɪs **-ly** -li **-ness** -nəs, -nɪs
guilt-ridden ˈgɪltˌrɪd.ən
guilt-trip ˈgɪlt.trɪp **-s** -s
guilt|y ˈgɪl.t|i **-ier** -i.ər, (US) -i.ɚ **-iest** -i.ɪst, -i.əst **-ily** -əl.i, -ɪ.li **-iness** -ɪ.nəs, -ɪ.nɪs
guimpe gɪmp, gæmp **-s** -s
guinea, G~ ˈgɪn.i **-s** -z ˈ**guinea** ˌ**fowl;** ˈ**guinea** ˌ**pig**
Guinea-Bissau ˌgɪn.i.bɪˈsaʊ
Guiness ˈgɪn.ɪs
Guinevere ˈgwɪn.ɪ.vɪər, ˈgɪn-, ˈ-ə-, (US) ˈgwɪn.ɪ.vɪr, ˈ-ə-
Guinness ˈgɪn.ɪs, -əs
guipure gɪˈpjʊər, (US) -ˈpjʊr, -ˈpʊr
Guisborough ˈgɪz.bər.ə, (US) -bɚ.oʊ
guis|e gaɪz **-es** -ɪz
Guise giːz, gwiːz
Guiseley ˈgaɪz.li
guitar gɪˈtɑːr, (US) -ˈtɑːr **-s** -z
guitarist gɪˈtɑː.rɪst, gə-, (US) -ˈtɑːr.ɪst **-s** -s
Gujarat ˌgʊdʒ.əˈrɑːt, ˌguː.dʒəˈ-
Gujarati ˌgʊdʒ.əˈrɑː.ti, ˌguː.dʒəˈ-, (US) -t̬i
Gujranwala guːdʒˈrɑːn.wʌl.ə, (US) -rənˈwɑː.lə
gulag, G~ ˈguː.læg, -lɑːg, (US) -lɑːg **-s** -z
Gulbenkian gʊlˈbeŋ.ki.ən
gulch gʌltʃ **-es** -ɪz
gulden ˈgʊl.dən, ˈguːl- **-s** -z
gules gjuːlz, dʒuːlz
gulf gʌlf **-s** -s **-y** -i ˌ**Gulf** ˈ**States;** ˈ**Gulf** ˌ**Stream;** ˈ**Gulf** ˌ**War,** ˌ**Gulf** ˈ**War**
gull, G~ gʌl **-s** -z **-ing** -ɪŋ **-ed** -d
gullet ˈgʌl.ɪt, -ət **-s** -s
gulley ˈgʌl.i **-s** -z
gullibility ˌgʌl.əˈbɪl.ə.ti, -ɪˈ-, -ɪ.ti, (US) -əˈbɪl.ə.t̬i
gullible ˈgʌl.ɪ.bəl, ˈ-ə-, (US) ˈ-ə-
Gullit ˈhʊl.ɪt; *as if Dutch:* ˈxʊl.ɪt
Gulliver ˈgʌl.ɪ.vər, ˈ-ə-, (US) -ə.vɚ
gull|y, G~ ˈgʌl|.i **-ies** -iz
gulp gʌlp **-s** -s **-ing** -ɪŋ **-ed** -t
gum gʌm **-s** -z **-ming** -ɪŋ **-med** -d **-mer/s** -ər/z, (US) -ɚ/z
gumball ˈgʌm.bɔːl, (US) -bɔːl, -bɑːl **-s** -z
Gumbley ˈgʌm.bli
gumbo, G~ ˈgʌm.bəʊ, (US) -boʊ **-s** -z
gumboil ˈgʌm.bɔɪl **-s** -z
gumboot ˈgʌm.buːt **-s** -s
gumdrop ˈgʌm.drɒp, (US) -drɑːp **-s** -s
Gummidge ˈgʌm.ɪdʒ
gumm|y ˈgʌm|.i **-ier** -i.ər, (US) -i.ɚ **-iest** -i.ɪst, -i.əst **-iness** -ɪ.nəs, -ɪ.nɪs
gumption ˈgʌmp.ʃən
gumshield ˈgʌm.ʃiːld **-s** -z
gumshoe ˈgʌm.ʃuː **-s** -z **-ing** -ɪŋ **-d** -d
gumtree ˈgʌm.triː **-s** -z
gun gʌn **-s** -z **-ning** -ɪŋ **-ned** -d **-ner/s** -ər/z, (US) -ɚ/z ˈ**gun** ˌ**carriage;** ˈ**gun** ˌ**dog;** ˈ**gun** ˌ**room;** ˌ**jump the** ˈ**gun**
gunboat ˈgʌn.bəʊt, ˈgʌm-, (US) ˈgʌn.boʊt **-s** -s
Gunby Hadath ˌgʌn.biˈhæd.əθ, ˌgʌm-, (US) ˌgʌn-
guncatcher ˈgʌn.kætʃ.ər, ˈgʌŋ-, (US) ˈgʌn.kætʃ.ɚ
guncotton ˈgʌn.kɒt.ən, ˈgʌŋ-, (US) ˈgʌn.kɑː.tən
gunfight ˈgʌn.faɪt **-s** -s **-er/s** -ər/z, (US) -ɚ/z
gunfire ˈgʌn.faɪər, -faɪ.ər, (US) -faɪ.ɚ
Gunga Din ˌgʌŋ.gəˈdɪn
gung|e gʌndʒ **-y** -i
gung ho ˌgʌŋˈhəʊ, (US) -ˈhoʊ
gunk gʌŋk **-y** -i
gun|man ˈgʌn|.mən, ˈgʌm-, -mæn, (US) ˈgʌn- **-men** -mən, -men
gunmetal ˈgʌnˌmet.əl, ˈgʌm-, (US) ˈgʌnˌmet̬.əl
Gunn gʌn
Gunnar ˈgʊn.ɑːr, (US) -ɑːr
gunnel, G~ ˈgʌn.əl **-s** -z
Gunnell ˈgʌn.əl
Gunner ˈgʌn.ər, (US) -ɚ
Gunnersbury ˈgʌn.əz.bər.i, (US) -ɚzˌber-, -bər-
gunnery ˈgʌn.ər.i
Gunning ˈgʌn.ɪŋ
Gunnison ˈgʌn.ɪ.sən
gunny ˈgʌn.i
gunnysack ˈgʌn.i.sæk **-s** -s
gunpoint ˈgʌn.pɔɪnt, ˈgʌm-, (US) ˈgʌn-
gunpowder ˈgʌn.paʊ.dər, ˈgʌm-, (US) ˈgʌn.paʊ.dɚ ˌ**Gunpowder** ˈ**Plot** (US) ˈ**Gunpowder** ˌ**Plot**

gunrunn|er ˈgʌn.rʌn|.əʳ, (US) -ɚ **-ers** -əz, (US) -ɚz **-ing** -ɪŋ
gunship ˈgʌn.ʃɪp **-s** -s
gunshot ˈgʌn.ʃɒt, (US) -ʃɑːt **-s** -s
gunslinger ˈgʌn.slɪŋ.əʳ **-s** -z
gunsmith ˈgʌn.smɪθ **-s** -s
Gunter ˈgʌn.təʳ, (US) -tɚ
Guntram ˈgʌn.trəm
gunwale ˈgʌn.əl **-s** -z
gupp|y, G~ ˈgʌp|.i **-ies** -iz
Gupta ˈgʊp.tə, ˈgʌp.tə
gurgl|e ˈgɜː.gəl, (US) ˈgɝː- **-es** -z **-ing** -ɪŋ, ˈ-glɪŋ **-ed** -d
Gurkha ˈgɜː.kə, (US) ˈgɝː- **-s** -z
Gurkhali ˌgɜːˈkɑː.li, ˌgʊə-, (US) ˌgɝː-
Gurley ˈgɜː.li, (US) ˈgɝː-
Gurnall ˈgɜː.nəl, (US) ˈgɝː-
gurnard, G~ ˈgɜː.nəd, (US) ˈgɝː.nɚd **-s** -z
gurnet ˈgɜː.nɪt, -nət, (US) ˈgɝː- **-s** -s
gurney, G~ ˈgɜː.ni, (US) ˈgɝː-
Gurton ˈgɜː.tən, (US) ˈgɝː-
guru ˈgʊr.uː, ˈguː.ruː, ˈgʊə-, (US) ˈguː.ruː **-s** -z
Gus gʌs
gush gʌʃ **-es** -ɪz **-ing/ly** -ɪŋ/li **-ed** -t **-er/s** -əʳ/z, (US) -ɚ/z
Gushington ˈgʌʃ.ɪŋ.tən
gusset ˈgʌs.ɪt **-s** -s **-ing** -ɪŋ **-ed** -ɪd
Gussie, Gussy ˈgʌs.i
gust gʌst **-s** -s **-ing** -ɪŋ **-ed** -ɪd
Gustafson ˈgʊs.tæf.sən, (US) ˈgʌs.təf-, -tɑːf-
gustation gʌsˈteɪ.ʃən
gustatory ˈgʌs.tə.tər.i; gʌsˈteɪ-, (US) ˈgʌs.tə.tɔːr-
Gustav, Gustave ˈgʊs.tɑːv, ˈgʌs-, (US) ˈgʌs-
Gustavus gʊsˈtɑː.vəs, gʌs-, gəˈstɑː-, (US) gʌsˈteɪ.vəs, -ˈtɑː-
gusto ˈgʌs.təʊ, (US) -toʊ
gust|y ˈgʌs.t|i **-ier** -i.əʳ, (US) -i.ɚ **-iest** -i.ɪst, -i.əst **-ily** -əl.i, -ɪ.li **-iness** -ɪ.nəs, -ɪ.nɪs
gut gʌt **-s** -s **-ting** -ɪŋ, (US) ˈgʌţ.ɪŋ **-ted** -ɪd, (US) ˈgʌţ.ɪd
Gutenberg ˈguː.tən.bɜːg, (US) -bɝːg
Guthrie ˈgʌθ.ri
Gutierrez guːˈtjer.ez
gutless ˈgʌt.ləs, -lɪs **-ly** -li **-ness** -nəs, -nɪs
guts|y ˈgʌt.s|i **-ier** -i.əʳ, (US) -i.ɚ **-iest** -i.ɪst, -i.əst **-ily** -əl.i, -ɪ.li **-iness** -ɪ.nəs, -ɪ.nɪs
gutt|a ˈgʌt|.ə, (US) ˈgʌţ|.ə **-ae** -iː
gutta-percha ˌgʌt.əˈpɜː.tʃə, (US) ˌgʌţ.əˈpɝː-
gutt|er ˈgʌt|.əʳ, (US) ˈgʌţ|.ɚ **-ers** -əz, (US) -ɚz **-ering** -ər.ɪŋ **-ered** -əd, (US) -ɚd **ˌgutter ˈpress** (US) **ˈgutter ˌpress**
guttersnipe ˈgʌt.ə.snaɪp, (US) ˈgʌţ.ɚ- **-s** -s
guttural ˈgʌt.ər.əl, (US) ˈgʌţ- **-s** -z **-ly** -i
guv gʌv
guvnor ˈgʌv.nəʳ, (US) -nɚ **-s** -z
guy, G~ gaɪ **-s** -z
Guyana gaɪˈɑː.nə, giˈɑː.nə, -æn.ə, (US) giˈæn.ə, gaɪ-, -ˈɑː.nə
Guyanese ˌgaɪ.əˈniːz, (US) ˌgiː.əˈniːz, gaɪ-, -ˈniːs *stress shift:* **ˌGuyanese ˈpeople**
Guy Fawkes ˌgaɪˈfɔːks, ˈ--, (US) -ˈfɔːks, -ˈfɑːks *stress shift, see compound:* **ˈGuy Fawkes ˌnight**
Guylian ˈgiː.li.ən
Guysborough ˈgaɪz.bər.ə, (US) -bɚ.oʊ
guzzl|e ˈgʌz.əl **-es** -z **-ing** -ɪŋ, ˈ-lɪŋ **-ed** -d **-er/s** -əʳ/z, ˈ-ləʳ/z, (US) ˈ-əl.ɚ/z, ˈ-lɚ/z
Gwalia ˈgwɑː.li.ə
Gwalior ˈgwɑː.li.ɔːʳ, (US) -ɔːr
Gwatkin ˈgwɒt.kɪn, (US) ˈgwɑːt-
Gwaun-Cae-Gurwen ˌgwaɪn.kəˈgɜː.wən, ˌgwaɪŋ-, (US) -ˈgɝː-
Gwen gwen
Gwenda ˈgwen.də
Gwendol|en ˈgwen.də.l|ɪn, -dəl.|ɪn **-ine** -ɪn, -iːn **-yn** -ɪn
Gwent gwent
Gwersyllt ˌgweəˈsɪlt, (US) ˌgwer-
Gwinnett gwɪˈnet
Gwladys ˈglæd.ɪs
Gwrych gʊˈrɪk, -ˈrɪx
Gwydion ˈgwɪd.i.ən
Gwydyr ˈgwɪd.ɪəʳ, -əʳ; ˈgwaɪ.dəʳ, (US) ˈgwɪd.ɪr
Gwyn(ne) gwɪn
Gwynedd ˈgwɪn.əð, -ɪð, -eð
Gwyneth ˈgwɪn.əθ, -ɪθ, -eθ
gwyniad ˈgwɪn.i.æd **-s** -z
gyb|e dʒaɪb **-es** -z **-ing** -ɪŋ **-ed** -d
Gye dʒaɪ, gaɪ
Gyges ˈgaɪ.dʒiːz
Gyle gaɪl
Gyles gaɪlz
gym dʒɪm **-s** -z
gymkhana dʒɪmˈkɑː.nə **-s** -z
gymnas|ium dʒɪmˈneɪ.z|i.əm **-iums** -z **-ia** -i.ə
gymnast ˈdʒɪm.næst, (US) -næst, -nəst **-s** -s
gymnastic dʒɪmˈnæs.tɪk **-s** -s **-al** -əl **-ally** -əl.i, -li
gymnosophist dʒɪmˈnɒs.ə.fɪst, (US) -ˈnɑː.sə- **-s** -s
gymnosperm ˈdʒɪm.nəʊ.spɜːm, ˈgɪm-, (US) -nə.spɝːm **-s** -z
gymnospermous ˌdʒɪm.nəʊˈspɜː.məs, ˌgɪm-, (US) -nəˈspɝː-
Gympie ˈgɪm.pi
gymslip ˈdʒɪm.slɪp **-s** -s
gyneci|um ˌdʒaɪˈniː.si|əm, ˌgaɪ- **-a** -ə
gyn(a)ecological ˌgaɪ.nə.kəˈlɒdʒ.ɪ.kəl, -nɪ-, (US) -ˈlɑː.dʒɪ- **-li** -i
gyn(a)ecolog|y ˌgaɪ.nəˈkɒl.ə.dʒ|i, -ɪˈ-, (US) -ˈkɑː.lə- **-ist/s** -ɪst/s
Gyngell ˈgɪn.dʒəl
gynoeci|um ˌdʒaɪˈniː.si|.əm, ˌgaɪ- **-a** -ə
Györ djɜːʳ, (US) djɝː, djɔːr
gyp dʒɪp **-s** -s **-ping** -ɪŋ **-ped** -t
Gyp *nickname:* dʒɪp *French novelist:* ʒiːp
gypsophila dʒɪpˈsɒf.ɪ.lə, -əl.ə, (US) -ˈsɑː.fɪ- **-s** -z
gypsum ˈdʒɪp.səm
gyps|y ˈdʒɪp.s|i **-ies** -iz
gyrate adj ˈdʒaɪə.rət, -reɪt, -rɪt, (US) ˈdʒaɪ.reɪt
gy|rate v dʒaɪə|ˈreɪt, (US) ˈdʒaɪ|.reɪt **-rates** -ˈreɪts, (US) -reɪts **-rating** -ˈreɪ.tɪŋ, (US) -reɪ.ţɪŋ **-rated** -ˈreɪ.tɪd, (US) -reɪ.ţɪd
gyration dʒaɪəˈreɪ.ʃən, (US) dʒaɪ- **-s** -z
gyratory ˈdʒaɪə.rə.tər.i; dʒaɪəˈreɪ-, (US) ˈdʒaɪ.rə.tɔːr-
gyr|e dʒaɪəʳ, (US) dʒaɪɚ **-es** -z **-ing** -ɪŋ **-ed** -d
gyrfalcon ˈdʒɜːˌfɔːl.kən, ˈdʒɪə-, -ˌfɔː-, (US) ˈdʒɝː.fæl-, -fɔːl- **-s** -z
gyro ˈdʒaɪə.rəʊ, (US) ˈdʒaɪ.roʊ, ˈgɪr.oʊ **-s** -z
gyro- ˈdʒaɪə.rəʊ, (US) ˈdʒaɪ.roʊ, -rə
Note: Prefix. Normally takes either primary or secondary stress on the first syllable, e.g. **gyroscope** /ˈdʒaɪə.rə.skəʊp/ (US) /ˈdʒaɪ.rə.skoʊp/, **gyroscopic** /ˌdʒaɪə.rəˈskɒp.ɪk/ (US) /ˌdʒaɪ.rəˈskɑː.pɪk/.
gyrocompass ˈdʒaɪə.rəʊˌkʌm.pəs, (US) ˈdʒaɪ.roʊ- **-es** -ɪz
gyromagnetic ˌdʒaɪə.rəʊ.mægˈnet.ɪk, -məgˈ-, (US) ˌdʒaɪ.roʊ.mægˈneţ.ɪk
gyron ˈdʒaɪə.rən, -rɒn, (US) ˈdʒaɪ.rən, -rɑːn **-s** -z
gyroscope ˈdʒaɪə.rə.skəʊp, (US) ˈdʒaɪ.rə.skoʊp **-s** -s
gyroscopic ˌdʒaɪə.rəˈskɒp.ɪk, (US) ˌdʒaɪ.rəˈskɑː.pɪk **-ally** -əl.i, -li
gyrostat ˈdʒaɪə.rəʊ.stæt, (US) ˈdʒaɪ.rə-, -roʊ- **-s** -s
gyrostatic ˌdʒaɪə.rəʊˈstæt.ɪk, (US) ˌdʒaɪ.rəˈstæţ- **-s** -s
gyv|e dʒaɪv **-es** -z **-ing** -ɪŋ **-ed** -d

Pronouncing the letter **H**

There are two main pronunciations for the consonant letter **h**: /h/ and silent.

The usual pronunciation is /h/, e.g.:

head hed

h has a silent realization at the end of a word, e.g.:

oh əʊ Ⓤⓢ oʊ
loofah ˈluː.fə

There is a group of words in which it is also silent initially: *heir*, *honest*, *honour*, and *hour*, and their derivatives, and *herb* for American English.

Following an initial **r**, **h** is silent, e.g.:

rhythm ˈrɪð.əm

In weak forms, **h** is often not pronounced, e.g.:

him ɪm
have əv

h, H eɪtʃ **-'s** -ɪz
H²O ˌeɪtʃ.tuːˈəʊ, Ⓤⓢ -ˈoʊ
ha *exclamation:* hɑː
ha (abbrev. for **hectare**) ˈhek.teəʳ, -tɑːʳ, -təʳ, Ⓤⓢ -ter
Haagen Dazs® ˌhɑː.gənˈdɑːz, Ⓤⓢ ˈhɑː.gənˌdæs
Haakon ˈhɔː.kɒn, ˈhɑː-, -kən, Ⓤⓢ ˈhɔː.kʊn, ˈhɑː-, -kɑːn, -kən
Haarlem ˈhɑː.ləm, -lem, Ⓤⓢ ˈhɑːr-
Habacuc, Habakkuk ˈhæb.ə.kək, -kʌk; həˈbæk.ək
Habberton ˈhæb.ə.tən, Ⓤⓢ -ɚ.t̬ən
habeas corpus ˌheɪ.bi.əsˈkɔː.pəs, -æsˈ-, Ⓤⓢ -ˈkɔːr-
haberdasher ˈhæb.ə.dæʃ.əʳ, Ⓤⓢ -ɚ.dæʃ.ɚ **-s** -z
haberdasher|y ˌhæb.əˈdæʃ.ər|.i, ˈhæb.ə.dæʃ-, Ⓤⓢ ˈhæb.ɚ.dæʃ- **-ies** -iz
Habgood ˈhæb.gʊd
Habibie həˈbiː.bi, hæbˈiː-
habiliment həˈbɪl.ɪ.mənt, hæbˈɪl-, ˈ-ə-, Ⓤⓢ həˈbɪl.ə- **-s** -s
habili|tate həˈbɪl.ɪ|.teɪt, hæbˈɪl-, ˈ-ə|-, Ⓤⓢ həˈbɪl.ə|- **-tates** -teɪts **-tating** -teɪ.tɪŋ, Ⓤⓢ -teɪ.t̬ɪŋ **-tated** -teɪ.tɪd, Ⓤⓢ -teɪ.t̬ɪd
habilitation həˌbɪl.ɪˈteɪ.ʃən, hæbˌɪl-, -əˈ-, Ⓤⓢ həˌbɪl.əˈ-
Habington ˈhæb.ɪŋ.tən
habit ˈhæb.ɪt **-s** -s
habitab|le ˈhæb.ɪ.tə.b|əl, Ⓤⓢ -t̬ə- **-ly** -li **-leness** -əl.nəs, -nɪs
habitant *inhabitant:* ˈhæb.ɪ.tənt, Ⓤⓢ -t̬ənt **-s** -s *in Canada and Louisiana:* ˈhæb.ɪ.tɑ̃ːŋ, ˈæb-, -tɒŋ, Ⓤⓢ ˈhæb.ɪ.tɑːnt, -tənt; Ⓤⓢ ˌæb.iˈtɑːn **-s** -z
habitat, H~® ˈhæb.ɪ.tæt, ˈ-ə- **-s** -s
habitation ˌhæb.ɪˈteɪ.ʃən, -əˈ- **-s** -z
habit-forming ˈhæb.ɪtˌfɔː.mɪŋ, Ⓤⓢ -ˌfɔːr-
habit|ual həˈbɪtʃ|.u.əl, hæbˈɪtʃ-, -ˈbɪt.j|u-, Ⓤⓢ həˈbɪtʃ|.u.əl **-ually** -ʊ.li, -ə.li
habitu|ate həˈbɪtʃ.u|.eɪt, hæbˈɪtʃ-, -ˈbɪt.ju-, Ⓤⓢ həˈbɪtʃ.u- **-ates** -eɪts **-ating** -eɪ.tɪŋ, Ⓤⓢ -eɪ.t̬ɪŋ **-ated** -eɪ.tɪd, Ⓤⓢ -eɪ.t̬ɪd
habitude ˈhæb.ɪ.tʃuːd, -tjuːd, Ⓤⓢ -tuːd, -tjuːd **-s** -z
habitué həˈbɪt.ju.eɪ, hæbˈɪt-, -ˈbɪtʃ.u.eɪ, Ⓤⓢ həˌbɪtʃ.uˈeɪ, həˈbɪtʃ.u.eɪ **-s** -z

> Note: Also occasionally /əˈbɪt.ju.eɪ/ in British English, when not initial. The indefinite article preceding this is 'an' /ən/.

Habsburg ˈhæps.bɜːg, Ⓤⓢ -bɝːg
háček ˈhɑː.tʃek, ˈhætʃ.ek
hachure hæʃˈʊəʳ, Ⓤⓢ hæʃˈʊr, -ˈjʊr, ˈhæʃ.ʊr **-s** -z
hacienda ˌhæs.iˈen.də, Ⓤⓢ ˌhɑː.siˈ- **-s** -z
hack, H~ hæk **-s** -s **-ing** -ɪŋ **-ed** -t
hackamore ˈhæk.ə.mɔːʳ, Ⓤⓢ -mɔːr **-s** -z
hackberr|y ˈhækˌber|.i, -bər|.i, Ⓤⓢ -ˌber- **-ies** -iz
hacker, H~ ˈhæk.əʳ, Ⓤⓢ -ɚ **-s** -z
Hackett ˈhæk.ɪt
hackl|e ˈhæk.əl **-es** -z **-ing** -ɪŋ, ˈhæk.lɪŋ **-ed** -d
hackney, H~ ˈhæk.ni **-s** -z **-ed** -d
hacksaw ˈhæk.sɔː, Ⓤⓢ -sɑː, -sɔː **-s** -z
hacktiv|ism ˈhæk.tɪ.v|ɪ.zəm **-ist/s** -ɪst/s
hackwork ˈhæk.wɜːk, Ⓤⓢ -wɝːk
had (from **have**) *strong form:* hæd; *weak forms:* həd, əd, d
Note: The strong form is used when **had** is used as a full verb rather than an auxiliary, e.g. 'We had some tea' The auxiliary verb is a weak-form word: the strong form /hæd/ is used contrastively, e.g. 'I don't know if she had or she hadn't', in final position, e.g. 'I'd read as much as he had' and quite frequently in initial position, e.g. 'Had anyone seen it before?'. It is also used for emphasis, e.g. 'It had to break down when it was raining'. Elsewhere, the weak form is usually /həd/ or /əd/. The form /d/ is usually used only after vowels.
Hadar ˈheɪ.dɑːʳ, Ⓤⓢ -dɑːr
hadarim (plural of **heder**) ˌhæd.ɑːˈriːm, Ⓤⓢ ˌhɑː.dɑːˈ-; *as if Hebrew:* ˌxæd-; Ⓤⓢ ˌxɑː-
Hadden ˈhæd.ən
Haddington ˈhæd.ɪŋ.tən
haddock, H~ ˈhæd.ək **-s** -s
Haddon ˈhæd.ən
had|e heɪd **-es** -z **-ing** -ɪŋ **-ed** -ɪd
Haden ˈheɪ.dən
Hades ˈheɪ.diːz
Hadfield ˈhæd.fiːld
hadj hædʒ, hɑːdʒ, Ⓤⓢ hædʒ **-es** -ɪz
hadji ˈhædʒ.i, ˈhɑː.dʒi, -dʒiː, Ⓤⓢ ˈhædʒ.iː **-s** -z
Hadleigh, Hadley ˈhæd.li
Hadlow ˈhæd.ləʊ, Ⓤⓢ -loʊ
hadn't (= **had not**) ˈhæd.ənt
hadn't've (= had not have) ˈhæd.ənt.əv
Hadrian ˈheɪ.dri.ən ˌ**Hadrian's ˈWall**
hadst *strong form:* hædst; *weak form:* hədst
Note: Weak form word, rarely used. See the note for **had**.
had've (= had have) ˈhæd.əv
haecceity hekˈsiː.ə.ti, hiːk-, haɪk-, -ɪ.ti, Ⓤⓢ hekˈsiː.ə.t̬i, hiːk-
haem hiːm
haematite ˈhiː.mə.taɪt, ˈhem.ə-, Ⓤⓢ ˈhiː.mə-
haematologic ˌhiː.mə.təˈlɒdʒ.ɪk, Ⓤⓢ -t̬əˈlɑːdʒ- **-al** -əl
haematolog|y ˌhiː.məˈtɒl.ə.dʒ|i, Ⓤⓢ -ˈtɑː.lə- **-ist/s** -ɪst/s
haematoma ˌhiː.məˈtəʊ.mə, ˌhem.əˈ-, Ⓤⓢ ˌhiː.məˈtoʊ- **-s** -z **-ta** -tə
haemoglobin ˌhiː.məʊˈgləʊ.bɪn, ˌhem.əʊˈ-, Ⓤⓢ ˈhiː.mə.gloʊ-, -mə-
haemophili|a ˌhiː.məˈfɪl.i|.ə, ˌhem.əˈ-, Ⓤⓢ ˌhiː.moʊˈ-, -məˈ-, -ˈfiːl.j|ə **-ac/s** -æk/s
haemorrhag|e ˈhem.ər.ɪdʒ, Ⓤⓢ -ɚ.ɪdʒ, ˈ-rɪdʒ **-es** -ɪz **-ing** -ɪŋ **-ed** -d
haemorrhoid ˈhem.ər.ɔɪd, Ⓤⓢ -ə.rɔɪd, ˈ-rɔɪd **-s** -z
haemosta|sis ˌhiː.məˈsteɪ|.sɪs, ˌhem.əˈ-, Ⓤⓢ ˌhiː.məˈ- **-ses** -siːz

hafnium ˈhæf.ni.əm
haft hɑːft, (US) hæft -s -s
hag hæg -s -z
Hag® hɑːg
Hagan ˈheɪ.gᵊn, (US) ˈheɪ-, ˈhɑː-
Hagar *biblical name:* ˈheɪ.gɑːʳ, -gəʳ, (US) -gɑːr *modern personal name:* ˈheɪ.gəʳ, (US) -gɑːr, -gɚ
Hagarene ˈhæg.ᵊr.iːn, ˈheɪ.gᵊr-, ˌ--ˈ-, (US) ˈhæg.ə.riːn, ˈheɪ.gə- -s -z
Hagerstown ˈheɪ.gəz.taʊn, (US) -gɚz-
Haggada(h) hægˈʌd.ə, -ˈɒd-, (US) həˈgɑː.dɑː, -də; (US) ˌhɑː.gɑːˈdɑː
Haggai ˈhæg.eɪ.aɪ, -i.aɪ, ˈhæg.aɪ; hægˈeɪ.aɪ, (US) ˈhæg.i.aɪ, ˈhæg.aɪ
Haggar ˈhæg.ɑːʳ, -əʳ, (US) -ɑːr, -ɚ
haggard, H~ ˈhæg.əd, (US) -ɚd -ly -li -ness -nəs, -nɪs
Hagger ˈhæg.əʳ, (US) -ɚ
Haggerston ˈhæg.ə.stᵊn, (US) ˈ-ɚ-
haggis ˈhæg.ɪs -es -ɪz
haggl|e ˈhæg.ᵊl -es -z -ing -ɪŋ, ˈhæg.lɪŋ -ed -d -er/s -əʳ/z, (US) -ɚ/z, ˈhæg.ləʳ/z, -lɚ/z
hagiograph|y ˌhæg.iˈɒg.rə.f|i, ˌheɪ.dʒiˈ-, (US) -ˈɑː.grə- -er/s -əʳ/z, (US) -ɚ/z
hagiolatry ˌhæg.iˈɒl.ə.tri, ˌheɪ.dʒiˈ-, (US) -ˈɑː.lə-
hagiolog|y ˌhæg.iˈɒl.ə.dʒ|i, ˌheɪ.dʒiˈ-, (US) -ˈɑː.lə- -ist/s -ɪst/s
hagioscope ˈhæg.i.ə.skəʊp, ˈheɪ.dʒi-, (US) -skoʊp -s -s
Hagley ˈhæg.li
Hagman ˈhæg.mən
hagridden ˈhægˌrɪd.ᵊn
Hague heɪg
ha-ha interj hɑːˈhɑː, ˈ--
ha-ha n *sunken fence:* ˈhɑː.hɑː -s -z
Hahn hɑːn
hahnium ˈhɑː.ni.əm
Haider ˈhaɪ.dəʳ, (US) -dɚ
Haifa ˈhaɪ.fə
Haig heɪg
Haigh heɪg, heɪ
Haight-Ashbury ˌheɪtˈæʃ.bᵊr.i, (US) -ˌber-
haiku ˈhaɪ.kuː
hail heɪl -s -z -ing -ɪŋ -ed -d ˌ**Hail** ˈ**Mary**
Hailes heɪlz
Haile Selassie ˌhaɪ.li.səˈlæs.i, -sɪˈ-, (US) -ˈlæs.i, -ˈlɑː.si
Hailey ˈheɪ.li
Haileybury ˈheɪ.li.bᵊr.i, (US) -ˌber-
hail-fellow-well-met ˌheɪlˌfel.əʊˌwelˈmet, (US) ˌ-oʊˌ-
Hailsham ˈheɪl.ʃəm
hailstone ˈheɪl.stəʊn, (US) -stoʊn -s -z
hailstorm ˈheɪl.stɔːm, (US) -stɔːrm -s -z
Hain heɪn
Hainan ˌhaɪˈnæn
Hainault ˈheɪ.nɔːt, -nɔːlt, -nɒlt, (US) -nɑːlt, -nɔːlt
Haines heɪnz
Haiphong ˌhaɪˈfɒŋ, (US) -ˈfɑːŋ
hair heəʳ, (US) her -s -z ˈ**hair** ˌ**gel;** ˈ**hair** ˌ**piece;** ˈ**hair's** ˌ**breadth;** ˌ**hair** ˈ**shirt;** ˈ**hair** ˌ**slide;** ˌ**hair** ˈ**trigger;** **let one's** ˈ**hair** ˌ**down;** ˌ**make someone's** ˈ**hair stand on** ˌ**end**
hairball ˈheə.bɔːl, (US) ˈher-, -bɑːl -s -z
hairband ˈheə.bænd, (US) ˈher- -s -z
hairbreadth ˈheə.bretθ, -bredθ, (US) ˈher- -s -s
hairbrush ˈheə.brʌʃ, (US) ˈher- -es -ɪz
haircloth ˈheə.klɒθ, (US) ˈher.klɑːθ
haircut ˈheə.kʌt, (US) ˈher- -s -s
haircutt|er ˈheəˌkʌt|.əʳ, (US) ˈherˌkʌţ|.ɚ -ers -əz, (US) -ɚz -ing -ɪŋ
hairdo ˈheə.duː, (US) ˈher- -s -z
hairdress|er ˈheəˌdres|.əʳ, (US) ˈherˌdres|.ɚ -ers -ez, (US) -ɚz -ing -ɪŋ
hairdryer, hairdrier ˈheəˌdraɪ.əʳ, (US) ˈherˌdraɪ.ɚ -s -z
-haired ˈheəd, (US) herd
Note: Suffix. Compounds ending **-haired** normally carry primary stress on the suffix in British English, but there is a stress shift when such words are used attributively, e.g. ˌ**golden-haired** ˈ**child**. In American English, compounds ending **-haired** are normally stressed on the first element, e.g. **golden-haired** /ˈgoʊl.dᵊn.herd/.
hairgrass ˈheə.grɑːs, (US) ˈher.græs
hairgrip ˈheə.grɪp, (US) ˈher- -s -s
hairless ˈheə.ləs, -lɪs, (US) ˈher- -ness -nəs, -nɪs
hairline ˈheə.laɪn, (US) ˈher- -s -z
hairnet ˈheə.net, (US) ˈher- -s -s
hairpiec|e ˈheə.piːs, (US) ˈher- -es -ɪz
hairpin ˈheə.pɪn, (US) ˈher- -s -z ˌ**hairpin** ˈ**bend;** ˌ**hairpin** ˈ**turn**
hair-raising ˈheəˌreɪ.zɪŋ, (US) ˈher-
hairsplitting ˈheəˌsplɪt.ɪŋ, (US) ˈherˌsplɪţ-
hairspray ˈheə.spreɪ, (US) ˈher- -s -z
hairspring ˈheə.sprɪŋ, (US) ˈher- -s -z
hairstyle ˈheə.staɪl, (US) ˈher- -s -z
hairstylist ˈheəˌstaɪ.lɪst, (US) ˈher- -s -s
hair|y ˈheə.r|i, (US) ˈher|.i -ier -i.əʳ, (US) -i.ɚ -iest -i.ɪst, -i.əst -iness -ɪ.nəs, -ɪ.nɪs
Haiti ˈheɪ.ti, ˈhaɪ-; haɪˈiː.ti, hɑː-, (US) ˈheɪ.ţi, -ti
Haitian ˈheɪ.ʃᵊn, -ʃi.ən, -ti-; haɪˈiː.ʃᵊn, hɑː-, -ʃi.ən, (US) ˈheɪ.ʃᵊn, -ti.ən -s -z
Haitink ˈhaɪ.tɪŋk
hajj hædʒ, hɑːdʒ, (US) hædʒ
hajji ˈhædʒ.i, ˈhɑː.dʒi, -dʒiː, (US) ˈhædʒ.iː -s -z
haka ˈhɑː.kə -s -z
hake heɪk -s -s
hakim *doctor:* hɑːˈkiːm, hə-, hækˈiːm, (US) hɑːˈkiːm *ruler:* ˈhɑː.kiːm, -ˈ-, (US) ˈhɑː.kiːm, -kɪm -s -z
Hakkinen ˈhæk.ɪ.nən
Hakluyt ˈhæk.luːt
Hakodate ˌhæk.əʊˈdɑː.ti, (US) ˌhɑː.koʊˈdɑː.teɪ
Hal hæl
Halakah hælˈʌk.ə, (US) ˌhɑː.lɑːˈkɑː, -ˈxɑː; (US) həˈlɑː.kə, -xə
halal hælˈæl; həˈlɑːl
halala, halalah həˈlæl.ə, hælˈæl.ə, (US) həˈlɑː.lə -s -z
halation həˈleɪ.ʃᵊn, hælˈeɪ-, (US) həˈleɪ- -s -z
halberd ˈhæl.bəd, ˈhɔːl-, -bɜːd, (US) ˈhæl.bɚd, ˈhɑːl- -s -z
halberdier ˌhæl.bəˈdɪəʳ, (US) -bɚˈdɪr -s -z
halcyon ˈhæl.si.ən -s -z
Halcyone hælˈsaɪ.ə.ni
Haldane ˈhɔːl.deɪn, ˈhɒl-, (US) ˈhɔːl-, ˈhɑːl-
Haldon ˈhɔːl.dᵊn
hal|e, H~ adj, v heɪl -er -əʳ, (US) -ɚ -est -ɪst, -əst -es -z -ing -ɪŋ -ed -d
haler ˈhɑː.ləʳ, (US) -lɚ, -ler -s -z -u -uː
Hales heɪlz
Halesowen ˌheɪlzˈəʊ.ɪn, -ən, (US) -ˈoʊ-
Halesworth ˈheɪlz.wəθ, -wɜːθ, (US) -wɝːθ, -wɚθ
Halex® ˈheɪ.leks
Haley ˈheɪ.li
hal|f hɑː|f, (US) hæ|f -ves -vz ˌ**half a** ˈ**dozen;** ˌ**half an** ˈ**hour;** ˌ**half** ˈ**cock;** ˌ**half** ˈ**measures;** ˌ**half** ˈ**nelson;** ˌ**half** ˈ**pay;** ˌ**half** ˈ**term**
Note: Compound words beginning with **half-** usually have secondary stress on this syllable and primary stress later in the compound word (e.g. **half-baked** has the stress pattern ˌ-ˈ-); however, the word is liable to undergo stress shift when a strongly stressed syllable follows (e.g. **half-baked plan** often has the pattern ˌ--ˈ-). Since there are many such words, notes about this stress shift for individual words are not given.
half-a-crown ˌhɑːf.əˈkraʊn, (US) ˌhæf-
half-assed ˌhɑːfˈæst, -ˈɑːst, (US) ˌhæfˈæst
halfback ˈhɑːf.bæk, (US) ˈhæf- -s -s
half-baked ˌhɑːfˈbeɪkt, (US) ˌhæf-
half-blood ˈhɑːf.blʌd, (US) ˈhæf-
half-board ˌhɑːfˈbɔːd, (US) ˌhæfˈbɔːrd
half-bred ˈhɑːf.bred, (US) ˈhæf-
half-breed ˈhɑːf.briːd, (US) ˈhæf- -s -z
half-brother ˈhɑːfˌbrʌð.əʳ, (US) ˈhæfˌbrʌð.ɚ -s -z
half-caste ˈhɑːf.kɑːst, (US) ˈhæf.kæst -s -s
half-crown ˌhɑːfˈkraʊn, (US) ˌhæf- -s -z
half-cut ˌhɑːfˈkʌt, (US) ˌhæf- *stress shift:* ˌ**half-cut** ˌ**partygoers**
half-dozen ˌhɑːfˈdʌz.ᵊn, (US) ˌhæf- -s -z
half-hardy ˌhɑːfˈhɑː.di, (US) ˌhæfˈhɑːr-

H

half-hearted ˌhɑːfˈhɑː.tɪd, (US) ˌhæfˈhɑːr.t̬ɪd
half-hearted|ly ˌhɑːfˈhɑː.tɪd|.li, (US) ˌhæfˈhɑːr.t̬ɪd- **-ness** -nəs, -nɪs
half-holiday ˌhɑːfˈhɒl.ə.deɪ, ˈ-ɪ-, -di, (US) ˌhæfˈhɑː.lə.deɪ **-s** -z
half-hour ˌhɑːfˈaʊəʳ, -ˈaʊ.əʳ, (US) ˌhæfˈaʊr, -ˈaʊ.ɚ **-s** -z
half-hourly ˌhɑːfˈaʊə.li, -ˈaʊ.ə-, (US) ˌhæfˈaʊr-, -ˈaʊ.ɚ-
half-length ˌhɑːfˈleŋθ, -ˈleŋkθ, (US) ˌhæf- **-s** -s *stress shift:* ˌ**half-length ˈcoat**
half-li|fe ˈhɑːf.laɪ|f, (US) ˈhæf- **-ves** -vz
half-mast ˌhɑːfˈmɑːst, (US) ˌhæfˈmæst
half-moon ˌhɑːfˈmuːn, (US) ˌhæf- **-s** -z
Halford ˈhæl.fəd, ˈhɔːl-, ˈhɒl-, (US) ˈhæl.fɚd, ˈhɔːl-, ˈhɑːl-
halfpence ˈheɪ.pᵊnts
halfpenn|y ˈheɪp.n|i, ˈheɪ.pᵊn|.i **-ies** -iz
Halfpenny ˈhɑːf.pen.i, -pə.ni, (US) ˈhæf-
halfpennyworth ˈheɪp.ni.wəθ, ˈheɪ.pᵊn.i-, -wɜːθ; ˌhɑːfˈpen.əθ, (US) ˈheɪ.pᵊn.i.wɝːθ **-s** -s
half-pint ˌhɑːfˈpaɪnt, (US) ˌhæf- **-s** -s
half-price ˌhɑːfˈpraɪs, (US) ˌhæf-
half-sister ˈhɑːfˌsɪs.təʳ, (US) ˈhæfˌsɪs.tɚ **-s** -z
half-size ˌhɑːfˈsaɪz, (US) ˈhæf.saɪz
half-time ˌhɑːfˈtaɪm, (US) ˈhæf.taɪm
halftone ˌhɑːfˈtəʊn, (US) ˈhæf.toʊn **-s** -z
half-tru|th ˌhɑːfˈtruː|θ, (US) ˈhæf.truː|θ **-ths** -ðz
half-volley ˌhɑːfˈvɒl.i, (US) ˈhæfˌvɑː.li **-s** -z
halfway ˌhɑːfˈweɪ, (US) ˌhæf- ˌ**halfway ˈhouse** (US) ˈ**halfway ˌhouse**
half-wit ˈhɑːf.wɪt, (US) ˈhæf- **-s** -s
half-witted ˌhɑːfˈwɪt.ɪd, (US) ˌhæfˈwɪt̬-
half-year ˌhɑːfˈjɪəʳ, (US) ˌhæfˈjɪr **-s** -z **-ly** -li
Haliburton ˌhæl.ɪˈbɜː.tᵊn, (US) ˈhæl.ɪ.bɝː-
halibut ˈhæl.ɪ.bət, -bʌt **-s** -s
Halicarnassus ˌhæl.ɪ.kɑːˈnæs.əs, (US) -kɑːrˈ-
Halidon ˈhæl.ɪ.dᵊn
Halifax ˈhæl.ɪ.fæks
halitosis ˌhæl.ɪˈtəʊ.sɪs, (US) -ˈtoʊ-
Halkett ˈhɔːl.kɪt, ˈhæl.kɪt, ˈhæk.ɪt
hall, H~ hɔːl, (US) hɔːl, hɑːl **-s** -z ˌ**Hall of ˈFame**; ˌ**hall of ˈresidence**; ˈ**residence ˌhall**
hallal hælˈæl, həˈlɑːl
Hallam ˈhæl.əm
Halle ˈhæl.ə, (US) ˈhɑː.lə
Hallé ˈhæl.eɪ, -i, (US) ˈhæl.eɪ
hallelujah, H~ ˌhæl.ɪˈluː.jə, -əˈ- **-s** -z
Haller ˈhæl.əʳ, (US) -ɚ
Hallett ˈhæl.ɪt
Halley ˈhæl.i, ˈhɔː.li, (US) ˈhæl.i, ˈheɪ.li ˌ**Halley's ˈComet**

> Note: Halley's Comet is usually referred to as /ˈhæl.iz/. There is a popular variant /ˈheɪ.liz/, possibly due to confusion with the 1950s rock and roll band Bill Haley and his Comets.

halliard ˈhæl.jəd, -i.əd, (US) -jɚd **-s** -z
Halliday ˈhæl.ɪ.deɪ, ˈ-ə-
Halliwell ˈhæl.ɪ.wel
hallmark ˈhɔːl.mɑːk, (US) -mɑːrk, ˈhɑːl- **-s** -s **-ing** -ɪŋ **-ed** -t
hallo(a) həˈləʊ, hælˈəʊ, helˈ-, ˈhʌl.əʊ, (US) həˈloʊ
halloo həˈluː, hælˈuː, (US) həˈluː **-s** -z **-ing** -ɪŋ **-ed** -d
hallow ˈhæl.əʊ, (US) -oʊ **-s** -z **-ing** -ɪŋ **-ed** -d
Halloween, Hallowe'en ˌhæl.əʊˈiːn, (US) ˌhæl.oʊˈ-, ˌhɑː.loʊˈ-, -ləˈwiːn
Hallowmas ˈhæl.əʊ.mæs, -məs, (US) -oʊ- **-es** -ɪz
Hallows ˈhæl.əʊz, (US) -oʊz
hallstand ˈhɔːl.stænd, (US) ˈhɔːl-, ˈhɑːl- **-s** -z
halluci|nate həˈluː.sɪ|.neɪt, -ˈljuː-, -sə-, (US) -ˈluː- **-nates** -neɪts **-nating** -neɪ.tɪŋ, (US) -neɪ.t̬ɪŋ **-nated** -neɪ.tɪd, (US) -neɪ.t̬ɪd
hallucination həˌluː.sɪˈneɪ.ʃᵊn, -ˌljuː-, -səˈ-, (US) -ˌluː- **-s** -z
hallucinatory həˈluː.sɪ.nə.tᵊr.i, -ˈljuː-, -sᵊn.ə-, -tri; həˌluː.sɪˈneɪ-, -ˌljuː-, -sᵊnˈeɪ-, (US) həˈluː.sɪ.nə.tɔːr.i
hallucinogen həˈluː.sɪ.nə.dʒen, -dʒᵊn; -ˈljuː-, -sᵊn.ə-, ˌhæl.uːˈsɪn-, (US) həˈluː.sɪ.nə.dʒen; (US) ˌhæl.juːˈsɪn.ə-, -jəˈ- **-s** -z
hallucinogenic həˌluː.sɪ.nəʊˈdʒen.ɪk, -ˌljuː-, -sᵊn.əˈ-, (US) -ˌluː.sɪ.noʊˈ-
hallway ˈhɔːl.weɪ, (US) ˈhɔːl-, ˈhɑːl- **-s** -z
halma ˈhæl.mə
halo ˈheɪ.ləʊ, (US) -loʊ **-(e)s** -z **-ing** -ɪŋ **-ed** -d
halogen ˈhæl.ə.dʒen, ˈheɪ.lə-, -dʒən, (US) ˈhæl.oʊ-, ˈ-ə- **-s** -z
halogenous həˈlɒdʒ.ɪ.nəs, -ə.nəs, (US) -ˈlɑː.dʒɪ.nəs, ˈ-dʒə-
Halper ˈhæl.pəʳ, (US) -pɚ
Halpern ˈhæl.pən, (US) -pɚn
Hals hæls, hælz, (US) hɑːls, hɑːlz
Halsbury ˈhɔːlz.bᵊr.i, ˈhɒlz-, (US) ˈhɔːlzˌber-, ˈhɑːlz-
Halsey ˈhɔːl.si, ˈhæl-, -zi, (US) ˈhɔːl.zi, ˈhɑːl-
Halstead ˈhɔːl.sted, ˈhɒl-, ˈhæl-, -stɪd, (US) ˈhɔːl-, ˈhɑːl-, ˈhæl-
halt hɒlt, hɔːlt, (US) hɔːlt, hɑːlt **-s** -s **-ing/ly** -ɪŋ/li, (US) ˈhɔːl.tɪŋ/li, ˈhɑːl- **-ed** -ɪd, (US) ˈhɔːl.tɪd, ˈhɑːl-
halter ˈhɔːl.təʳ, ˈhɒl-, (US) ˈhɔːl.tɚ, ˈhɑːl- **-s** -z
halterneck ˈhɒl.tə.nek, ˈhɔːl-, (US) ˈhɔːl.tɚ-, ˈhɑːl- **-s** -s
halva(h) ˈhæl.və, -vɑː, (US) hɑːlˈvɑː; (US) ˈ--, -və
halv|e hɑːv, (US) hæv **-es** -z **-ing** -ɪŋ **-ed** -d
Halvergate ˈhæl.və.geɪt, (US) -vɚ-
halves (plural of **half**) hɑːvz, (US) hævz
halyard ˈhæl.jəd, (US) -jɚd **-s** -z
ham, H~ hæm **-s** -z **-ming** -ɪŋ **-med** -d
hamadryad ˌhæm.əˈdraɪ.əd, -ˈdraɪ.æd **-s** -z
Hamah ˈhæm.ə, (US) ˈhɑː.mɑː
Haman *biblical name:* ˈheɪ.mæn, -mən, (US) -mən *modern surname:* ˈheɪ.mən
Hamar ˈheɪ.mɑːʳ, (US) -mɑːr
hamartia ˌhɑː.mɑːˈtiː.ə, (US) -mɑːrˈ-
Hamas hæmˈæs, ˈ--
Hamble ˈhæm.bᵊl
Hambleden ˈhæm.bᵊl.dən
Hambledon ˈhæm.bᵊl.dən
Hambleton ˈhæm.bᵊl.tən
Hamblin ˈhæmb.lɪn
Hambro ˈhæm.brəʊ, -brə, (US) ˈhæm.brə, -broʊ
Hamburg ˈhæm.bɜːg, (US) -bɝːg, ˈhɑːm.bʊrg
hamburger ˈhæmˌbɜː.gəʳ, (US) -ˌbɝː.gɚ **-s** -z
Hamed ˈhæm.ed, (US) ˈhɑːməd
Hamelin ˈhæm.lɪn, -ᵊl.ɪn, -ɪ.lɪn
Hamer ˈheɪ.məʳ, (US) -mɚ
Hamerton ˈhæm.ə.tᵊn, (US) ˈ-ɚ-
ham-fisted ˌhæmˈfɪs.tɪd, (US) ˈ-ˌ-- **-ly** -li **-ness** -nəs, -nɪs *stress shift, British only:* ˌ**ham-fisted ˈeffort**
ham-handed ˌhæmˈhæn.dɪd, (US) ˈhæmˌhæn- **-ly** -li **-ness** -nəs, -nɪs *stress shift, British only:* ˌ**ham-handed ˈgesture**
Hamhung ˌhɑːmˈhʊŋ
Hamilcar hæmˈɪl.kɑːʳ, həˈmɪl-; ˈhæm.ɪl-, -ᵊl-, (US) -kɑːr
Hamill ˈhæm.ᵊl
Hamilton ˈhæm.ᵊl.tən, -ɪl-
Hamiltonian ˌhæm.ᵊlˈtəʊ.ni.ən, -ɪlˈ-, (US) -ˈtoʊ-
Hamish ˈheɪ.mɪʃ
Hamite ˈhæm.aɪt **-s** -s
Hamitic hæmˈɪt.ɪk, həˈmɪt-, (US) hæmˈɪt̬-, həˈmɪt̬-
hamlet, H~ ˈhæm.lət, -lɪt **-s** -s
Hamley ˈhæm.li
Hamlin, Hamlyn ˈhæm.lɪn
hammam ˈhæm.æm, -əm, ˈhʌm.ʌm; həˈmɑːm, (US) ˈhæm.əm **-s** -z
Hammarskjöld ˈhæm.ə.ʃəʊld, (US) -ɚ.ʃoʊld, ˈhɑː.mɚ-
hamm|er, H~ ˈhæm|.əʳ, (US) -ɚ **-ers** -əz, (US) -ɚz **-ering** -ᵊr.ɪŋ **-ered** -əd, (US) -ɚd ˌ**go at it ˌhammer and ˈtongs**
Hammerfest ˈhæm.ə.fest, (US) ˈ-ɚ-
hammerhead ˈhæm.ə.hed, (US) ˈ-ɚ- **-s** -z
hammerlock ˈhæm.ə.lɒk, (US) -ɚ.lɑːk **-s** -s

Hammersmith ˈhæm.ə.smɪθ, ⓊⓈ ˈ-ɚ-

Hammerstein ˈhæm.ə.staɪn, -stiːn, ⓊⓈ ˈ-ɚ-

Hammett ˈhæm.ɪt

hammock ˈhæm.ək **-s** -s

Hammurabi ˌhæm.ʊˈrɑː.bi, ⓊⓈ ˌhɑː.mʊˈ-, ˌhæm.əˈ-

hamm|y ˈhæm|.i **-ier** -i.əʳ, ⓊⓈ -i.ɚ **-iest** -i.ɪst, -i.əst **-ily** -əl.i, -ɪ.li **-iness** -ɪ.nəs, -ɪ.nɪs

Hamoaze ˈhæm.əʊz, ⓊⓈ -oʊz

Ham(m)ond ˈhæm.ənd

Hampden ˈhæmp.dən

hamp|er ˈhæm.p|əʳ, ⓊⓈ -p|ɚ **-ers** -əz, ⓊⓈ -ɚz **-ering** -ər.ɪŋ **-ered** -əd, ⓊⓈ -ɚd

Hampshire ˈhæmp.ʃəʳ, -ʃɪəʳ, ⓊⓈ -ʃɚ, -ʃɪr

Hampstead ˈhæm*p*.sted, -stɪd **ˌHampstead ˈHeath**

Hampton ˈhæm*p*.tən **-s** -z **ˌHampton ˈCourt**

Hamshaw ˈhæm.ʃɔː, ⓊⓈ -ʃɑː, -ʃɔː

hamster ˈhæm*p*.stəʳ, ⓊⓈ -stɚ **-s** -z

ham|string ˈhæm|.strɪŋ **-strings** -strɪŋz **-stringing** -strɪŋ.ɪŋ **-strung** -strʌŋ

hamza ˈhæm.zə **-s** -z

Han hæn, ⓊⓈ hɑːn

Hanan ˈhæn.ən

Hananiah ˌhæn.əˈnaɪ.ə

Hanbury ˈhæn.bər.i, ˈhæm-, ⓊⓈ ˈhænˌber-

Hancock ˈhæn.kɒk, ˈhæŋ-, ⓊⓈ ˈhæn.kɑːk

Hancox ˈhæn.kɒks, ˈhæŋ-, ⓊⓈ ˈhæn.kɑːks

hand, H~ hænd **-s** -z **-ing** -ɪŋ **-ed** -ɪd **-er/s** -əʳ/z, ⓊⓈ -ɚ/z **-edness** -ɪd.nəs, -nɪs **ˈhand ˌcream; ˈhand greˌnade; ˌbite the ˌhand that ˈfeeds ˌone; ˌforce someone's ˈhand; ˌhand in ˈglove (with); ˌknow somewhere like the ˌback of one's ˈhand; ˌwait on someone ˌhand and ˈfoot**

handbag ˈhæn*d*.bæg, ˈhæm-, ⓊⓈ ˈhænd- **-s** -z **-ging** -ɪŋ **-ged** -d

handball ˈhæn*d*.bɔːl, ˈhæm-, ⓊⓈ ˈhæn*d*.bɔːl, -bɑːl **-s** -z

handbarrow ˈhæn*d*ˌbær.əʊ, ˈhæm-, ⓊⓈ ˈhæn*d*ˌber.oʊ, -ˌbær- **-s** -z

handbasin ˈhæn*d*ˌbeɪ.sən, ˈhæm-, -sɪn, ⓊⓈ ˈhænd- **-s** -z

handbell ˈhæn*d*.bel, ˈhæm-, ⓊⓈ ˈhænd- **-s** -z

handbill ˈhæn*d*.bɪl, ˈhæm-, ⓊⓈ ˈhænd- **-s** -z

handbook ˈhæn*d*.bʊk, ˈhæm-, ⓊⓈ ˈhænd- **-s** -s

handbrake ˈhæn*d*.breɪk, ˈhæm-, ⓊⓈ ˈhænd- **-s** -s

handcart ˈhæn*d*.kɑːt, ˈhæŋ-, ⓊⓈ ˈhæn*d*.kɑːrt **-s** -s

handclap ˈhæn*d*.klæp, ˈhæŋ-, ⓊⓈ ˈhænd- **-s** -s

Handcock ˈhæn*d*.kɒk, ⓊⓈ -kɑːk

handcraft ˈhæn*d*.krɑːft, ˈhæŋ-, ⓊⓈ ˈhæn*d*.kræft **-s** -s

handcuff ˈhæn*d*.kʌf **-s** -s **-ing** -ɪŋ **-ed** -t

Handel ˈhæn.dəl

Handelian hænˈdiː.li.ən, ⓊⓈ -ˈdel.i-, -ˈdiː.li-

handful ˈhæn*d*.fʊl **-s** -z

handgrip ˈhæn*d*.grɪp, ˈhæŋ-, ⓊⓈ ˈhænd- **-s** -s

handgun ˈhæn*d*.gʌn, ˈhæŋ-, ⓊⓈ ˈhænd- **-s** -z

hand-held ˌhændˈheld, ⓊⓈ ˌ-ˈ-, ˈ-- *stress shift, British only:* **ˌhand-held ˈcamera**

handhold ˈhæn*d*.həʊld, ⓊⓈ -hoʊld **-s** -z

hand-holding ˈhændˌhəʊl.dɪŋ, ⓊⓈ -ˌhoʊl-

handicap ˈhæn.di.kæp **-s** -s **-ping** -ɪŋ **-ped** -t **-per/s** -əʳ/z, ⓊⓈ -ɚ/z

handicraft ˈhæn.di.krɑːft **-s** -s

handiwork ˈhæn.di.wɜːk

handkerchie|f ˈhæŋ.kə.tʃiː|f, -tʃɪ|f, ⓊⓈ -kɚ.tʃɪ|f, -tʃiː|f **-fs** -fs **-ves** -vz

handknit ˌhæn*d*|ˈnɪt **-s** -ˈnɪts **-ting** -ˈnɪt.ɪŋ, ⓊⓈ -ˈnɪt̬.ɪŋ **-ted** -ˈnɪt.ɪd, ⓊⓈ -ˈnɪt̬.ɪd *stress shift:* **ˌhandknit ˈsweater**

handl|e ˈhæn.dəl **-es** -z **-ing** -ɪŋ, -ˈhænd.lɪŋ **-ed** -d **-er/s** -əʳ/z, ⓊⓈ -ɚ/z, ˈhænd.ləʳ/z, -lɚ/z

handlebar ˈhæn.dəl.bɑːʳ, ⓊⓈ -bɑːr **-s** -z

Handley ˈhæn*d*.li

handmade ˌhæn*d*ˈmeɪd, ˌhæm-, ⓊⓈ ˌhænd- *stress shift:* **ˌhandmade ˈsweets**

handmaid ˈhæn*d*.meɪd, ˈhæm-, ⓊⓈ ˈhænd- **-s** -z

handmaiden ˈhæn*d*ˌmeɪ.dən, ˈhæm-, ⓊⓈ ˈhænd- **-s** -z

hand-me-down ˈhæn*d*.mi.daʊn, ˈhæm-, ⓊⓈ ˈhænd- **-s** -z

handout ˈhænd.aʊt **-s** -s

handover ˈhæn.dəʊ.vəʳ, ⓊⓈ -doʊ.vɚ **-s** -z

hand-pick ˌhæn*d*ˈpɪk, ˌhæm-, ⓊⓈ ˌhænd- **-s** -s **-ing** -ɪŋ **-ed** -t

handrail ˈhænd.reɪl **-s** -z

Hands hændz

handsaw ˈhæn*d*.sɔː, ⓊⓈ -sɑː, -sɔː **-s** -z

handsel ˈhæn*d*.səl **-s** -z **-ling** -ɪŋ **-led** -d

handset ˈhæn*d*.set **-s** -s

handsful (plural of **handful**) ˈhændz.fʊl

handshak|e ˈhæn*d*.ʃeɪk **-es** -s **-ing** -ɪŋ

hands-off ˌhændzˈɒf, ⓊⓈ -ˈɑːf, -ˈɔːf *stress shift:* **ˌhands-off ˈmanner**

handsom|e ˈhæn*d*.səm **-er** -əʳ, ⓊⓈ -ɚ **-est** -ɪst, -əst **-ely** -li **-eness** -nəs, -nɪs

hands-on ˌhændzˈɒn, ⓊⓈ -ˈɑːn *stress shift:* **ˌhands-on ˈpractice**

handspring ˈhæn*d*.sprɪŋ **-s** -z

handstand ˈhæn*d*.stænd **-s** -z

hand-to-hand ˌhæn*d*.təˈhænd *stress shift:* **ˌhand-to-hand ˈfighting**

hand-to-mouth ˌhæn*d*.təˈmaʊθ *stress shift:* **ˌhand-to-mouth ˈliving**

handwork ˈhænd.wɜːk, ⓊⓈ -wɝːk

handwriting ˈhændˌraɪ.tɪŋ, ⓊⓈ -t̬ɪŋ **-s** -z

handwritten ˌhændˈrɪt.ən *stress shift:* **ˌhandwritten ˈnote**

hand|y, H~ ˈhæn.d|i **-ier** -i.əʳ, ⓊⓈ -i.ɚ **-iest** -i.ɪst, -i.əst **-ily** -əl.i, -ɪ.li **-iness** -ɪ.nəs, -ɪ.nɪs

handy|man ˈhæn.di|.mæn, -mən **-men** -men

hang hæŋ **-s** -z **-ing/s** -ɪŋ/z **-ed** -d **hung** hʌŋ

hangar ˈhæŋ.gəʳ, -əʳ, ⓊⓈ -ɚ **-s** -z

hangdog ˈhæŋ.dɒg, ⓊⓈ -dɑːg, -dɔːg **-s** -z

hanger, H~ ˈhæŋ.əʳ, ⓊⓈ -ɚ **-s** -z

hanger-on ˌhæŋ.ərˈɒn, ⓊⓈ -ɚˈɑːn **hangers-on** ˌhæŋ.əzˈɒn, ⓊⓈ -ɚzˈ-

hang-glid|er ˈhæŋˌglaɪ.d|əʳ, ⓊⓈ -d|ɚ **-ers** -əz, ⓊⓈ -ɚz **-ing** -ɪŋ

hang|man ˈhæŋ|.mən, -mæn **-men** -mən

hangnail ˈhæŋ.neɪl **-s** -z

hangout ˈhæŋ.aʊt **-s** -s

hangover ˈhæŋ.əʊ.vəʳ, ⓊⓈ -oʊ.vɚ **-s** -z

hang-up ˈhæŋ.ʌp **-s** -s

hank, H~ hæŋk **-s** -s

hank|er ˈhæŋ.k|əʳ, ⓊⓈ -k|ɚ **-ers** -əz, ⓊⓈ -ɚz **-ering** -ər.ɪŋ **-ered** -əd, ⓊⓈ -ɚd

hankie ˈhæŋ.ki **-s** -z

Hankow ˌhænˈkaʊ, ˌhæŋ-, ⓊⓈ ˌhæn-, ˌhɑːn-, -ˈkoʊ

Hanks hæŋks

hank|y ˈhæŋ.k|i **-ies** -iz

hanky-panky ˌhæŋ.kiˈpæŋ.ki, ⓊⓈ ˌhæŋ.kiˈpæŋ-, ˈhæŋ.kiˌpæŋ-

Hanley ˈhæn.li

Hanna(h) ˈhæn.ə

Hannay ˈhæn.eɪ

Hannen ˈhæn.ən

Hannibal ˈhæn.ɪ.bəl, ˈ-ə-

Hannington ˈhæn.ɪŋ.tən

Hanoi hænˈɔɪ, həˈnɔɪ, ⓊⓈ hænˈɔɪ, hɑːˈnɔɪ, hə- *stress shift:* **ˌHanoi ˈRocks**

Hanover ˈhæn.əʊ.vəʳ, ⓊⓈ -oʊ.vɚ

Hanoverian ˌhæn.əʊˈvɪə.ri.ən, -ˈveə-, ⓊⓈ -əˈvɪr.i-, -ˈver **-s** -z

Hans hæn*t*s, ⓊⓈ hɑːnz, hænz

Hansa ˈhæn*t*.sə, ˈhæn.zə

Hansard ˈhæn*t*.sɑːd, -səd, ⓊⓈ -sɚd

Hansberry ˈhænz.bər.i, ⓊⓈ -ˌber-

Hans|e hæn*t*s **-es** -ɪz

Hanseatic ˌhæn*t*.siˈæt.ɪk, ˌhæn.ziˈ-, ⓊⓈ -ˈæt̬-

hansel, H~ ˈhæn*t*.səl **-s** -z **-(l)ing** -ɪŋ **-(l)ed** -d

Hänsel ˈhæn*t*.səl, ˈhen*t*-

Hansell ˈhæn*t*.səl

Hansen ˈhæn*t*.sen

hansom, H~ ˈhæn*t*.səm **-s** -z **ˈhansom ˌcab**

Hanson ˈhæn*t*.sən

Hants. (abbrev. for **Hampshire**) hænts

Hanuk(k)ah ˈhʌn.ʊ.kə, ˈhæn-, (US) ˈhɑː.nə.kə, ˈxɑː-, -nuː-, -kɑː
Hanuman ˌhʌn.ʊˈmɑːn, (US) ˌhɑː.nʊˈmɑːn, ˈ---
Hanway ˈhæn.weɪ
Hanwell ˈhæn.wəl, -wel
hào haʊ
hap hæp **-s** -s **-ping** -ɪŋ **-ped** -t
haphazard ˌhæpˈhæz.əd, (US) -ɚd **-ly** -li **-ness** -nəs, -nɪs
hapless ˈhæp.ləs, -lɪs **-ly** -li **-ness** -nəs, -nɪs
haploid ˈhæp.lɔɪd **-s** -z
haplology hæpˈlɒl.ə.dʒi, (US) -ˈlɑː.lə-
haply ˈhæp.li
hap'orth ˈheɪ.pəθ, (US) -pɚθ **-s** -s
happ|en ˈhæp|.ᵊn **-ens** -ᵊnz **-ening/s** -ᵊn.ɪŋ/z, ˈhæp.nɪŋ/z **-ened** -ᵊnd
happenstance ˈhæp.ᵊn.stænts, -ᵊm-, -stɑːnts, (US) -ᵊn.stænts
Happisburgh ˈheɪz.bᵊr.ə, (US) -bɚ.ə
happ|y ˈhæp|.i **-ier** -i.əʳ, (US) -i.ɚ **-iest** -i.ɪst, -i.əst **-ily** -ᵊl.i, -ɪ.li **-iness** -ɪ.nəs, -ɪ.nɪs ˈ**happy** ˌ**hour;** ˌ**happy** ˈ**medium**
happy-go-lucky ˌhæp.i.gəʊˈlʌk.i, (US) -goʊˈ- *stress shift:* ˌ**happy-go-lucky** ˈ**fellow**
Hapsburg ˈhæps.bɜːg, (US) -bɝːg
hara-kiri ˌhær.əˈkɪr.i, -ˈkɪə.ri, (US) ˌhɑːr.əˈkɪr.i, ˌhær-
harangu|e həˈræŋ **-es** -z **-ing** -ɪŋ **-ed** -d **-er/s** -əʳ/z, (US) -ɚ/z
Harare həˈrɑː.ri, -reɪ, (US) hɑːˈrɑːr.i, hə-, -eɪ
harass ˈhær.əs; həˈræs, (US) həˈræs; (US) ˈher.əs, ˈhær- **-es** -ɪz **-ing** -ɪŋ **-ed** -t **-er/s** -əʳ/z, (US) -ɚ/z **-ment** -mənt

> Note: The pronunciation /həˈræs/ has become much more widespread in British pronunciation recently, despite being strongly disliked by more conservative speakers.

Harben ˈhɑː.bᵊn, (US) ˈhɑːr-
Harberton ˈhɑː.bə.tᵊn, (US) ˈhɑːr.bɚ.t̬ᵊn
Harbin hɑːˈbiːn, -ˈbɪn, (US) ˈhɑːr.bɪn
harbinger ˈhɑː.bɪn.dʒəʳ, (US) ˈhɑːr.bɪn.dʒɚ **-s** -z
harb|or ˈhɑː.b|əʳ, (US) ˈhɑːr.b|ɚ **-ors** -əz, (US) -ɚz **-oring** -ᵊr.ɪŋ **-ored** -əd, (US) -ɚd **-orage** -ᵊr.ɪdʒ **-orless** -ə.ləs, -lɪs, (US) -ɚ.ləs, -lɪs ˈ**harbor** ˌ**master**
Harborough ˈhɑː.bᵊr.ə, (US) ˈhɑːr.bɚ.oʊ
harb|our ˈhɑː.b|əʳ, (US) ˈhɑːr.b|ɚ **-ours** -əz, (US) -ɚz **-ouring** -ᵊr.ɪŋ **-oured** -əd, (US) -ɚd **-ourage** -ᵊr.ɪdʒ **-ourless** -ə.ləs, -lɪs, (US) -ɚ.ləs, -lɪs ˈ**harbour** ˌ**master**
Harcourt ˈhɑː.kət, -kɔːt, (US) ˈhɑːr.kɔːrt, -kɚt
hard, H~ hɑːd, (US) hɑːrd **-er** -əʳ, (US) -ɚ **-est** -ɪst, -əst **-ness** -nəs, -nɪs ˌ**hard** ˈ**copy,** ˈ**hard** ˌ**copy;** ˌ**hard** ˈ**currency;** ˌ**hard** ˈ**disk;** ˌ**no** ˌ**hard** ˈ**feelings;** ˌ**hard** ˈ**labour;** ˌ**hard** ˈ**luck;** ˌ**hard** ˈ**luck** ˌ**story;** ˌ**hard of** ˈ**hearing;** ˌ**hard** ˈ**sell;** ˌ**hard** ˈ**shoulder**
hardback ˈhɑːd.bæk, (US) ˈhɑːrd- **-s** -s
hardbake ˈhɑːd.beɪk, (US) ˈhɑːrd-
hard-baked ˌhɑːdˈbeɪkt, (US) ˌhɑːrd- *stress shift:* ˌ**hard-baked** ˈ**character**
hardball ˈhɑːd.bɔːl, (US) ˈhɑːrdbɑːl, -bɔːl
hard-bitten ˌhɑːdˈbɪt.ᵊn, (US) ˌhɑːrd- *stress shift:* ˌ**hard-bitten** ˈ**cynic**
hardboard ˈhɑːd.bɔːd, (US) ˈhɑːrd.bɔːrd
hard-boiled ˌhɑːdˈbɔɪld, (US) ˌhɑːrd- *stress shift:* ˌ**hard-boiled** ˈ**egg**
Hardcastle ˈhɑːdˌkɑː.sᵊl, (US) ˈhɑːrdˌkæs.ᵊl
hardcore n *rubble:* ˈhɑːd.kɔːʳ, (US) ˈhɑːrd.kɔːr
hard core n *nucleus:* ˌhɑːdˈkɔː, (US) ˌhɑːrdˈkɔːr
hard-core adj ˌhɑːdˈkɔːʳ, ˈ--, (US) ˌhɑːrdˈkɔːr *stress shift:* ˌ**hard-core** ˈ**porn**
hardcover ˈhɑːdˌkʌv.əʳ, (US) ˈhɑːrdˌkʌv.ɚ **-s** -z
hard-earned ˌhɑːdˈɜːnd, (US) ˌhɑːrdˈɝːnd *stress shift:* ˌ**hard-earned** ˈ**cash**
harden, H~ ˈhɑː.dᵊn, (US) ˈhɑːr- **-s** -z **-ing** -ɪŋ, ˈhɑːd.nɪŋ, (US) ˈhɑːrd- **-ed** -d
Hardern ˈhɑː.dᵊn, (US) ˈhɑːr.dɚn
hard-fought ˌhɑːdˈfɔːt, (US) ˌhɑːrdˈfɑːt, -ˈfɔːt *stress shift:* ˌ**hard-fought** ˈ**battle**
hardheaded ˌhɑːdˈhed.ɪd, (US) ˌhɑːrd- **-ness** -nəs, -nɪs *stress shift:* ˌ**hardheaded** ˈ**bargaining**
hardhearted ˌhɑːdˈhɑː.tɪd, (US) ˌhɑːrdˈhɑːr.t̬ɪd **-ly** -li **-ness** -nəs, -nɪs *stress shift:* ˌ**hardhearted** ˈ**villain**
hard-hit ˌhɑːdˈhɪt, (US) ˌhɑːrd- **-ting** -ɪŋ *stress shift:* ˌ**hard-hit** ˈ**region**
Hardicanute ˈhɑː.dɪ.kəˌnjuːt, -də-; ˌhɑː.dɪ.kəˈnjuːt, (US) ˌhɑːr.dɪ.kəˈnuːt, -ˈnjuːt
Hardie ˈhɑː.di, (US) ˈhɑːr-
hardihood ˈhɑː.di.hʊd, (US) ˈhɑːr-
Harding ˈhɑː.dɪŋ, (US) ˈhɑːr-
Hardinge ˈhɑː.dɪŋ, -dɪndʒ, (US) ˈhɑːr-
hardline ˌhɑːdˈlaɪn, (US) ˌhɑːrd- *stress shift:* ˌ**hardline** ˈ**leader**
hardliner ˌhɑːdˈlaɪ.nəʳ, ˈ-ˌ--, (US) ˌhɑːrdˈlaɪ.nɚ, ˈ-ˌ-- **-s** -z
hardly ˈhɑːd.li, (US) ˈhɑːrd-
hard-nosed ˌhɑːdˈnəʊzd, (US) ˌhɑːrdˈnoʊzd *stress shift:* ˌ**hard-nosed** ˈ**policy**
hard-on ˈhɑːd.ɒn, (US) ˈhɑːrd.ɑːn
hard-pressed ˌhɑːdˈprest, (US) ˌhɑːrd- *stress shift:* ˌ**hard-pressed** ˈ**leader**
hardship ˈhɑːd.ʃɪp, (US) ˈhɑːrd- **-s** -s
hardtop ˈhɑːd.tɒp, (US) ˈhɑːrd.tɑːp **-s** -s
hard-up ˌhɑːdˈʌp, (US) ˌhɑːrd- *stress shift:* ˌ**hard-up** ˈ**pensioner**
hardware ˈhɑːd.weəʳ, (US) ˈhɑːrd.wer
hard-wearing ˌhɑːdˈweə.rɪŋ, (US) ˌhɑːrdˈwer.ɪŋ *stress shift:* ˌ**hard-wearing** ˈ**carpet**
Hardwick(e) ˈhɑːd.wɪk, (US) ˈhɑːrd-
hard-won ˌhɑːdˈwʌn, (US) ˌhɑːrd- *stress shift:* ˌ**hard-won** ˈ**profits**
hardwood ˈhɑːd.wʊd, (US) ˈhɑːrd- **-s** -z
hard-working ˌhɑːdˈwɜː.kɪŋ, (US) ˌhɑːrdˈwɝː- *stress shift:* ˌ**hard-working** ˈ**secretary**
hard|y, H~ ˈhɑː.d|i, (US) ˈhɑːr- **-ier** -i.əʳ, (US) -i.ɚ **-iest** -i.ɪst, -i.əst **-ily** -ᵊl.i, -ɪ.li **-iness** -ɪ.nəs, -ɪ.nɪs
har|e, H~ heəʳ, (US) her **-es** -z **-ing** -ɪŋ **-ed** -d
harebell ˈheə.bel, (US) ˈher- **-s** -z
harebrained ˈheə.breɪnd, (US) ˈher-
Harefield ˈheə.fiːld, (US) ˈher-
Hare Krishna ˌhær.iˈkrɪʃ.nə, ˌhɑː.riˈ-, (US) ˌhɑː.riˈ- **-s** -z
harelip ˌheəˈlɪp, (US) ˌher- **-s** -s **-ped** -t
harem ˈhɑː.riːm, ˈheə-, -rəm; həˈriːm, hɑː-, (US) ˈher.əm, ˈhær- **-s** -z
Harewood ˈhɑː.wʊd, ˈheə.wʊd, (US) ˈhɑːr-, ˈher-

> Note: The Earl of Harewood pronounces /ˈhɑː.wʊd/ (US) /ˈhɑːr-/, and his house is called /ˌhɑː.wʊdˈhaʊs/ (US) /ˌhɑːr-/. The village in West Yorkshire is now generally pronounced /ˈheə.wʊd/ (US) /ˈher-/, though /ˈhɑː.wʊd/ (US) /ˈhɑːr-/ may sometimes be heard from old people there. Other people with the surname **Harewood** pronounce /ˈheə.wʊd/ (US) /ˈher-/.

Harford ˈhɑː.fəd, (US) ˈhɑːr.fɚd
Hargraves ˈhɑː.greɪvz, (US) ˈhɑːr-
Hargreaves ˈhɑː.griːvz, -greɪvz, (US) ˈhɑːr-
haricot ˈhær.ɪ.kəʊ, (US) ˈher.ɪ.koʊ, ˈhær- **-s** -z ˌ**haricot** ˈ**bean,** ˈ**haricot** ˌ**bean**
Haringey ˈhær.ɪŋ.geɪ, (US) ˈher-, ˈhær-
Harington ˈhær.ɪŋ.tən, (US) ˈher-, ˈhær-
Hariot ˈhær.i.ət, (US) ˈher-, ˈhær-, -ɑːt
hark hɑːk, (US) hɑːrk **-s** -s **-ing** -ɪŋ **-ed** -t
Harker ˈhɑː.kəʳ, (US) ˈhɑːr.kɚ
Harkin ˈhɑː.kɪn, (US) ˈhɑːr-
Harkinson ˈhɑː.kɪnt.sᵊn, (US) ˈhɑːr-
Harkness ˈhɑːk.nəs, -nɪs, (US) ˈhɑːrk-
Harland ˈhɑː.lənd, (US) ˈhɑːr-
Harlech ˈhɑː.lek, -lex, -lək, -ləx, (US) ˈhɑːr.lek

Harleian hɑːˈliː.ən; ˈhɑː.li-, US ˈhɑːr.li-; US hɑːrˈliː-
Harlem ˈhɑː.ləm, -lem, US ˈhɑːr- ˌ**Harlem** ˈ**Globetrotters**
harlequin ˈhɑː.lɪ.kwɪn, -lə-, -kɪn, US ˈhɑːr.lɪ- **-s** -z
harlequinade ˌhɑː.lɪ.kwɪˈneɪd, -lə-, -kɪˈ-, US ˌhɑːr.lɪ- **-s** -z
Harlesden ˈhɑːlz.dən, US ˈhɑːrlz-
Harley ˈhɑː.li, US ˈhɑːr- ˈ**Harley** ˌ**Street**
Harley Davidson® ˌhɑː.liˈdeɪ.vɪd.sən, US ˌhɑːr-
Harlock ˈhɑː.lɒk, US ˈhɑːr.lɑːk
harlot ˈhɑː.lət, US ˈhɑːr- **-s** -s **-ry** -ri
Harlow(e) ˈhɑː.ləʊ, US ˈhɑːr.loʊ
harm hɑːm, US hɑːrm **-s** -z **-ing** -ɪŋ **-ed** -d ˌ**out of** ˌ**harm's** ˈ**way**
Harman ˈhɑː.mən, US ˈhɑːr-
Harmer ˈhɑː.məʳ, US ˈhɑːr.mɚ
harmful ˈhɑːm.fəl, -fʊl, US ˈhɑːrm- **-ly** -i **-ness** -nəs, -nɪs
harmless ˈhɑːm.ləs, -lɪs, US ˈhɑːrm- **-ly** -li **-ness** -nəs, -nɪs
Harmon ˈhɑː.mən, US ˈhɑːr-
Harmondsworth ˈhɑː.məndz.wəθ, -wɜːθ, US ˈhɑːr.məndz.wɝːθ
Harmonia hɑːˈməʊ.ni.ə, US hɑːrˈmoʊ-
harmonic hɑːˈmɒn.ɪk, US hɑːrˈmɑː.nɪk **-s** -s **-al** -əl **-ally** -əl.i, -li
harmonica hɑːˈmɒn.ɪ.kə, US hɑːrˈmɑː.nɪ- **-s** -z
harmonious hɑːˈməʊ.ni.əs, US hɑːrˈmoʊ- **-ly** -li **-ness** -nəs, -nɪs
harmonist ˈhɑː.mə.nɪst, US ˈhɑːr- **-s** -s
harmonium hɑːˈməʊ.ni.əm, US hɑːrˈmoʊ- **-s** -z
harmonization, -isa- ˌhɑː.mə.naɪˈzeɪ.ʃən, -nɪˈ-, US ˌhɑːr.mə.nəˈ- **-s** -z
harmoniz|e, -is|e ˈhɑː.mə.naɪz, US ˈhɑːr- **-es** -ɪz **-ing** -ɪŋ **-ed** -d **-er/s** -əʳ/z, US -ɚ/z
harmon|y ˈhɑː.mə.n|i, US ˈhɑːr- **-ies** -iz
Harmsworth ˈhɑːmz.wəθ, -wɜːθ, US ˈhɑːrmz.wɝːθ
Harnack ˈhɑː.næk, US ˈhɑːr-
harness, H~ ˈhɑː.nɪs, -nəs, US ˈhɑːr- **-es** -ɪz **-ing** -ɪŋ **-ed** -t **-er/s** -əʳ/z, US -ɚ/z
Harold ˈhær.əld, US ˈher-, ˈhær-
harp hɑːp, US hɑːrp **-s** -s **-ing** -ɪŋ **-ed** -t
Harpenden ˈhɑː.pən.dən, US ˈhɑːr-
Harper ˈhɑː.pəʳ, US ˈhɑːr.pɚ
Harpham ˈhɑː.pəm, US ˈhɑːr-
Harpic® ˈhɑː.pɪk, US ˈhɑːr-
harpist ˈhɑː.pɪst, US ˈhɑːr- **-s** -s
harpoon ˌhɑːˈpuːn, US ˌhɑːr- **-s** -z **-ing** -ɪŋ **-ed** -d **-er/s** -əʳ/z, US -ɚ/z
harpsichord ˈhɑːp.sɪ.kɔːd, US ˈhɑːrp.sɪ.kɔːrd **-s** -z
harp|y, H~ ˈhɑː.p|i, US ˈhɑːr- **-ies** -iz
harquebus ˈhɑː.kwɪ.bəs, -kwə-, US ˈhɑːr.kwə- **-es** -ɪz
Harraden ˈhær.ə.dən, -den, US ˈher-, ˈhær-
Harrap ˈhær.əp, US ˈher-, ˈhær-
Harrell ˈhær.əl, US ˈher-, ˈhær-
harridan ˈhær.ɪ.dən, ˈ-ə-, US ˈher-, ˈhær- **-s** -z
Harrie ˈhær.i, US ˈher-, ˈhær-
harrier ˈhær.i.əʳ, US ˈher.i.ɚ, ˈhær- **-s** -z
Harries ˈhær.ɪs, -iz, US ˈher-, ˈhær-
Harriet ˈhær.i.ət, US ˈher-, ˈhær-
Harriman ˈhær.ɪ.mən, US ˈher-, ˈhær-
Harrington ˈhær.ɪŋ.tən, US ˈher-, ˈhær-
Harriot ˈhær.i.ət, US ˈher-, ˈhær-
Harris ˈhær.ɪs, US ˈher-, ˈhær- ˌ**Harris** ˈ**Tweed**
Harrisburg ˈhær.ɪs.bɜːg, US ˈher.ɪs.bɝːg, ˈhær-
Harris(s)on ˈhær.ɪ.sən, US ˈher-, ˈhær-
Harrod ˈhær.əd, US ˈher-, ˈhær- **-s** -z
Harrogate ˈhær.ə.gət, -geɪt, -gɪt, US ˈher-, ˈhær-
Harrop ˈhær.əp, US ˈher-, ˈhær-
Harrovian hærˈəʊ.vi.ən, həˈrəʊ-, US həˈroʊ- **-s** -z
harrow, H~ ˈhær.əʊ, US ˈher.oʊ, ˈhær- **-s** -z **-ing/ly** -ɪŋ/li **-ed** -d
Harrowby ˈhær.əʊ.bi, US ˈher.oʊ-, ˈhær-
harrumph həˈrʌmpf **-s** -s **-ing** -ɪŋ **-ed** -t
harr|y, H~ ˈhær|.i, US ˈher-, ˈhær- **-ies** -iz **-ying** -i.ɪŋ **-ied** -id
harsh hɑːʃ, US hɑːrʃ **-er** -əʳ, US -ɚ **-est** -ɪst, -əst **-ly** -li **-ness** -nəs, -nɪs
hart, H~ hɑːt, US hɑːrt **-s** -s
Harte hɑːt, US hɑːrt
hartebeest ˈhɑː.ti.biːst, -tə-, US ˈhɑːr.t̬ə-, -tə- **-s** -s
Hartford ˈhɑːt.fəd, US ˈhɑːrt.fɚd
Harthan ˈhɑː.ðən, ˈhɑː.θən, US ˈhɑːr-
Hartington ˈhɑː.tɪŋ.tən, US ˈhɑːr.t̬ɪŋ-
Hartland ˈhɑːt.lənd, US ˈhɑːrt-
Hartlepool ˈhɑːt.lɪ.puːl, -lə-, US ˈhɑːrt-
Hartley ˈhɑːt.li, US ˈhɑːrt-
Hartman ˈhɑːt.mən, US ˈhɑːrt-
Hartnell ˈhɑːt.nəl, US ˈhɑːrt-
Hartshill ˈhɑːts.hɪl, US ˈhɑːrts-
hartshorn, H~ ˈhɑːts.hɔːn, US ˈhɑːrts.hɔːrn
hart's-tongue ˈhɑːts.tʌŋ, -tɒŋ, US ˈhɑːrts.tʌŋ **-s** -z
Hartz hɑːts, US hɑːrts
harum-scarum ˌheə.rəmˈskeə.rəm, US ˌher.əmˈsker.əm, ˌhær-, -ˈskær-
Harun-al-Rashid hærˌuːn.æl.ræʃˈiːd, hɑːˌruːn-; ˌhær.uːn.ælˈræʃ.iːd, ˌhɑː.ruːn-, -ɪd, US hɑːˌruːn.ɑːl.rɑːˈʃiːd
haruspex həˈrʌs.peks, hærˈʌs-; ˈhær.ə.speks **haruspices** həˈrʌs.pɪ.siːz, hærˈʌs-
Harvard ˈhɑː.vəd, US ˈhɑːr.vɚd
Harverson ˈhɑː.və.sən, US ˈhɑːr.vɚ-
harvest ˈhɑː.vɪst, -əst, US ˈhɑːr- **-s** -s **-ing** -ɪŋ **-ed** -ɪd **-er/s** -əʳ/z, US -ɚ/z ˌ**harvest** ˈ**festival**; ˈ**harvest** ˌ**mite**; ˌ**harvest** ˈ**moon**; ˈ**harvest** ˌ**mouse**
Harvey ˈhɑː.vi, US ˈhɑːr-
Harwich ˈhær.ɪtʃ, -ɪdʒ, US ˈhær-, ˈher-
Harwood ˈhɑː.wʊd, US ˈhɑːr-
Harworth ˈhɑː.wəθ, US ˈhɑːr.wɚθ
Haryana ˌhær.iˈɑː.nə, US ˌhɑːrˈjɑː-
Harz hɑːts, US hɑːrts
has (from **have**) *strong form:* hæz; *weak forms:* həz, əz, z, s
Note: The strong form is used when **has** is used as a full verb rather than as an auxiliary, e.g. 'He has some money'. The auxiliary verb is a weak-form word: the strong form /hæz/ is used contrastively, e.g. 'I don't know if she has or she hasn't', in final position, e.g. 'I've read as much as he has' and quite frequently in initial position, e.g. 'Has anyone seen my glasses?'. It is also used for emphasis, e.g. 'She **has** to have one'. Elsewhere, the weak form is usually /həz/ or /əz/. The shortest weak forms are /s/ and /z/: the form /s/ is used only after voiceless consonants other than /s, ʃ, tʃ/, while the form /z/ is used only after a vowel or a voiced consonant other than /z, ʒ, dʒ/. After /s, z, ʃ, ʒ, tʃ, dʒ/, the weak form is usually /əz/.
has-been ˈhæz.biːn, -bɪn, US -bɪn **-s** -z
Hasdrubal ˈhæz.drʊ.bəl, -druː-, -bæl
Haselden ˈhæz.əl.dən, ˈheɪz-
hash hæʃ **-es** -ɪz **-ing** -ɪŋ **-ed** -t ˌ**hash** ˈ**brown**
Hashemite ˈhæʃ.ɪ.maɪt, -ə-
Hashimoto ˌhæʃ.ɪˈməʊ.təʊ, US -ˈmoʊ.t̬oʊ, ˌhɑːʃ-, -toʊ
hashish ˈhæʃ.iʃ, -iːʃ; hæʃˈiːʃ
hashtag ˈhæʃ.tæg **-s** -z
Hasid hæsˈiːd, hɑːˈsiːd **-im** -ɪm
Hasidic hæsˈɪd.ɪk, hɑːˈsɪd-, US hæsˈɪd-, həˈsɪd-, hɑː-
Hasidism hæsˈɪd.ɪ.zəm, ˈhæs-, US ˈhæs.ɪ.dɪ-, ˈhɑː.sɪ-; US hæsˈɪd.ɪ-, həˈsɪd-, hɑː-
Haslam ˈhæz.ləm
Haslemere ˈheɪ.zəl.mɪəʳ, US -mɪr
haslet ˈhæz.lət, ˈheɪz-, -lɪt, US ˈhæs-, ˈheɪz-
Haslett ˈhæz.lət, ˈheɪz.lət, -lɪt
Haslingden ˈhæz.lɪŋ.dən
Hasluck ˈhæz.lʌk, -lək
hasn't ˈhæz.ənt
hasp hɑːsp, hæsp, US hæsp **-s** -s **-ing** -ɪŋ **-ed** -t
Hassall ˈhæs.əl
Hassan *district in India:* ˈhʌs.ən, ˈhæs- *Arabic name:* həˈsɑːn, hæsˈɑːn; ˈhæs.ən, ˈhʌs-, US ˈhɑː.sɑːn; US həˈsɑːn
Hasselhoff ˈhæs.əl.hɒf, US -hɑːf

hassl|e ˈhæs.əl **-es** -z **-ing** -ɪŋ, ˈhæs.lɪŋ **-ed** -d
hassock, H~ ˈhæs.ək **-s** -s
hast, H~ (from **have**) *strong form:* hæst; *weak forms:* həst, əst, st
Note: This weak form word is little used. See the note for **have** for guidance on when to use the strong form.
hast|e heɪst **-es** -s **-ing** -ɪŋ **-ed** -ɪd
hasten ˈheɪ.sən **-s** -z **-ing** -ɪŋ, ˈheɪs.nɪŋ **-ed** -d
Hastie ˈheɪ.sti
Hastings ˈheɪ.stɪŋz
hast|y ˈheɪ.st|i **-ier** -i.əʳ, (US) -i.ɚ **-iest** -i.ɪst, -i.əst **-ily** -əl.i, -ɪ.li **-iness** -ɪ.nəs, -ɪ.nɪs

H

hat hæt **-s** -s ˈ**hat** ˌ**rack**; ˈ**hat** ˌ**stand**; ˈ**hat** ˌ**trick**; **at the** ˌ**drop of a** ˈ**hat**; **I'll** ˌ**eat my** ˈ**hat** ˌ**keep something** ˌ**under one's** ˈ**hat**
hatband ˈhæt.bænd **-s** -z
hatbox ˈhæt.bɒks, (US) -bɑːks **-es** -ɪz
hatch, H~ n, v hætʃ **-es** -ɪz **-ing** -ɪŋ **-ed** -t
hatchback ˈhætʃ.bæk **-s** -s
hatcher|y ˈhætʃ.ər|.i **-ies** -iz
hatchet ˈhætʃ.ɪt **-s** -s ˈ**hatchet** ˌ**job**; ˌ**bury the** ˈ**hatchet**
hatchling ˈhætʃ.lɪŋ **-s** -z
hatchment ˈhætʃ.mənt **-s** -s
hatchway, H~ ˈhætʃ.weɪ **-s** -z
hat|e heɪt **-es** -s **-ing** -ɪŋ, (US) ˈheɪ.t̬ɪŋ **-ed** -ɪd, (US) ˈheɪ.t̬ɪd **-er/s** -əʳ/z, (US) ˈheɪ.t̬ɚ/z
hateful ˈheɪt.fəl, -fʊl **-ly** -i **-ness** -nəs, -nɪs
Hatfield ˈhæt.fiːld
hath (from **have**) *strong form:* hæθ; *weak forms:* həθ, əθ
Note: This weak form word is little used. See the note for **has** for guidance on when to use the strong form.
hatha ˈhæθ.ə, ˈhʌθ-
Hathaway ˈhæθ.ə.weɪ
Hatherell ˈhæð.ər.əl
Hatherleigh ˈhæð.ə.li, (US) ˈ-ɚ-
Hatherley ˈhæð.ə.li, (US) ˈ-ɚ-
Hathersage ˈhæð.ə.seɪdʒ, -sɪdʒ, -sedʒ, (US) ˈ-ɚ-
Hatherton ˈhæð.ə.tən, (US) -ɚ.t̬ən
Hathorn(e) ˈhɔː.θɔːn, (US) ˈhɑː.θɔːrn, ˈhɔː-
Hathway ˈhæθ.weɪ
hatless ˈhæt.ləs, -lɪs, -les
hatpin ˈhæt.pɪn **-s** -z
hatred ˈheɪ.trɪd, -trəd
hatstand ˈhæt.stænd **-s** -z
hatter ˈhæt.əʳ, (US) ˈhæt̬.ɚ **-s** -z **as** ˌ**mad as a** ˈ**hatter**
Hatteras ˈhæt.ər.əs, (US) ˈhæt̬.ɚ-
Hattersley ˈhæt.əz.li, (US) ˈhæt̬.ɚz-
Hattie ˈhæt.i, (US) ˈhæt̬-
Hatton ˈhæt.ən
hauberk ˈhɔː.bɜːk, (US) ˈhɑː.bɝːk, ˈhɔː- **-s** -s
haugh hɔː, (US) hɑː, hɔː **-s** -z
Haughey ˈhɔː.hi, ˈhɒ-, (US) ˈhɑː-, ˈhɔː-
Haughton ˈhɔː.tən, (US) ˈhɑː-, ˈhɔː-
haught|y ˈhɔː.t|i, (US) ˈhɑː.t̬|i, ˈhɔː- **-ier** -i.əʳ, (US) -i.ɚ **-iest** -i.ɪst, -i.əst **-ily** -əl.i, -ɪ.li **-iness** -ɪ.nəs, -ɪ.nɪs
haul hɔːl, (US) hɑːl, hɔːl **-s** -z **-ing** -ɪŋ **-ed** -d **-er/s** -əʳ/z, (US) -ɚ/z
haulage ˈhɔː.lɪdʒ, (US) ˈhɑː-, ˈhɔː-
haulier ˈhɔː.li.əʳ, (US) ˈhɑːl.jɚ, ˈhɔː- **-s** -z
haulm hɔːm, (US) hɔːm, hɑːm **-s** -z
haunch hɔːntʃ, (US) hɑːntʃ, hɔːntʃ **-es** -ɪz
haunt hɔːnt, (US) hɑːnt, hɔːnt **-s** -s **-ing/ly** -ɪŋ/li, (US) ˈhɑːn.t̬ɪŋ/li, ˈhɔːn- **-ed** -ɪd, (US) ˈhɑːn.t̬ɪd, ˈhɔːn-
Hausa ˈhaʊ.sə, -zə **-s** -z
hausfrau ˈhaʊs.fraʊ **-s** -z **-en** -ən
Haussmann ˈhaʊs.mæn, (US) -mæn, -mən
hautbois sing ˈəʊ.bɔɪ, ˈhəʊ-, ˈhɔːt-, (US) ˈhoʊ-, ˈoʊ- **plur** ˈəʊ.bɔɪz, ˈhəʊ-, ˈhɔːt-, (US) ˈhoʊ-, ˈoʊ-
hautboy ˈəʊ.bɔɪ, ˈhəʊ-, ˈhɔːt-, (US) ˈhoʊ-, ˈoʊ- **-s** -z
haute couture ˌəʊt.kuˈtjʊəʳ, -kuːˈ-, -ˈtʊəʳ, (US) ˌoʊt.kuːˈtʊr
haute cuisine ˌəʊt.kwɪˈziːn, -kwəˈ-, (US) ˌoʊt-
hauteur əʊˈtɜːʳ, ˈ--, (US) hoʊˈtɝː, oʊˈ-
Havana həˈvæn.ə, hævˈæn-, -ˈvɑː.nə, (US) -ˈvæn.ə **-s** -z
Havant ˈhæv.ənt
Havard ˈhæv.ɑːd, -əd, (US) -ɑːrd, -ɚd
Havarti həˈvɑː.ti, (US) -ˈvɑːr-
have n *one who has:* hæv **-s** -z

> Note: This word usually occurs as a noun only in conjunction with **have-not**, in expressions such as 'There's a conflict between the haves and have-nots'.

have v *strong form:* hæv; *weak forms:* həv, əv, v **hast** *strong form:* hæst; *weak forms:* həst, əst, st **has** *strong form:* hæz; *weak forms:* həz, əz, z, s **having** ˈhæv.ɪŋ **had** *strong form:* hæd; *weak forms:* həd, əd, d
Note: When **have** occurs as a full verb, e.g. 'to have and to hold', the strong form is used. As an auxiliary verb, it is a weak-form word: the strong form is used contrastively, e.g. 'I don't know if you have or haven't', for emphasis, e.g. 'You **have** to see it', and also in final position, e.g. 'I've got as much as you have'. It is also quite often used in initial position, e.g. 'Have you seen my book?'. Elsewhere the weak form is commonly used; the form /v/ is only found after vowels. For **hast**, **has**, **had** and **hadst**, see notes provided for those word entries.
Havel ˈhɑː.vəl
Havell ˈhæv.əl
Havelo(c)k ˈhæv.lɒk, -lək, (US) -lɑːk, -lək
haven ˈheɪ.vən **-s** -z
have-not ˈhæv.nɒt, ˌ-ˈ-, (US) ˈhæv.nɑːt, ˌ-ˈ- **-s** -s
haven't ˈhæv.ənt
hav|er ˈheɪ.v|əʳ, (US) -v|ɚ **-ers** -əz, (US) -ɚz **-ering** -ər.ɪŋ **-ered** -əd, (US) -ɚd
Haverford ˈhæv.ə.fəd, (US) -ɚ.fɚd
Haverfordwest ˌhæv.ə.fədˈwest, ˌhɑː.fədˈwest, (US) ˌhæv.ɚ.fɚdˈ-, ˌhɑː.fɚdˈ-
Havergal ˈhæv.ə.gəl, (US) ˈ-ɚ-
Haverhill ˈheɪ.vər.ɪl, -əl; ˈheɪ.və.hɪl, (US) -vɚ.hɪl
Havering ˈheɪ.vər.ɪŋ
Havers ˈheɪ.vəz, (US) -vɚz
haversack ˈhæv.ə.sæk, (US) ˈ-ɚ- **-s** -s
haversian canal, H~ həˌvɜː.ʃən.kəˈnæl, hævˌɜː-, -ʒən-, (US) həˌvɝː.ʒən-
Haverstock ˈhæv.ə.stɒk, (US) -ɚ.stɑːk
Havilah ˈhæv.ɪ.lə, (US) -lə, -lɑː
Haviland ˈhæv.ɪ.lænd, ˈ-ə-, -lənd
Havisham ˈhæv.ɪ.ʃəm
havoc ˈhæv.ək
Havre *place in France:* ˈhɑː.vrə, -vəʳ, (US) -vɚ, -vrə *place in Maryland:* ˈhɑː.vəʳ, (US) -vɚ, ˈhæv.ɚ *place in Montana:* ˈhæv.əʳ, (US) -ɚ
Havre de Grace ˌhɑː.və.dəˈgrɑːs, ˌhæv.ə-, -ˈgræs, -ˈgreɪs, (US) ˌhɑː.vɚ-, ˌhæv.ɚ-
haw hɔː, (US) hɑː, hɔː **-s** -z **-ing** -ɪŋ **-ed** -d
Hawaii həˈwaɪ.iː, hɑː-, -i
Hawaiian həˈwaɪ.ən, hɑː-, ˈ-i.ən **-s** -z
Haward ˈheɪ.wəd, ˈhɔː.əd, hɑːd, hɔːd, (US) ˈheɪ.wɚd, ˈhɔː.ɚd, hɑːrd, hɔːrd
Hawarden *in Clwyd:* ˈhɑː.dən, ˈhɔː-, (US) ˈhɑːr-, ˈhɔːr *Viscount:* ˈheɪˌwɔː.dən, (US) -ˌwɔːr- *town in US:* ˈheɪˌwɑː.dən, (US) -ˌwɑːr-
Haweis ˈhɔː.ɪs, (US) ˈhɔː.ɪs, hɔɪs
Hawes hɔːz, (US) hɑːz, hɔːz
hawfinch ˈhɔː.fɪntʃ, (US) ˈhɑː-, ˈhɔː- **-es** -ɪz
haw-haw ˈhɔː.hɔː, ˌ-ˈ-, (US) ˈhɑː.hɑː, ˈhɔː.hɔː, ˌ-ˈ- **-s** -z
Hawick ˈhɔː.ɪk, hɔɪk, (US) ˈhɑː.ɪk, ˈhɔː-, hɔɪk
hawk hɔːk, (US) hɑːk, hɔːk **-s** -s **-ing** -ɪŋ **-ed** -t **-er/s** -əʳ/z, (US) -ɚ/z
Hawke hɔːk, (US) hɑːk, hɔːk **-s** -s
Hawker-Siddeley® ˌhɔː.kəˈsɪd.əl.i, ˈ-li, (US) ˌhɑː.kɚˈ-, ˌhɔː-
Hawkeye ˈhɔːk.aɪ, (US) ˈhɑːk-, ˈhɔːk-
hawk-eyed ˈhɔːk.aɪd, (US) ˈhɑːk-, ˈhɔːk-
Hawking ˈhɔː.kɪŋ, (US) ˈhɑː-, ˈhɔː-
Hawkins ˈhɔː.kɪnz, (US) ˈhɑː-, ˈhɔː-
hawkish ˈhɔː.kɪʃ, (US) ˈhɑː-, ˈhɔː- **-ly** -li **-ness** -nes, -nɪs
hawkmoth ˈhɔːk.mɒθ, (US) ˈhɑːk.mɑːθ, ˈhɔːk- **-s** -s
Hawks hɔːks, (US) hɑːks, hɔːks
hawksbill ˈhɔːks.bɪl, (US) ˈhɑːks-, ˈhɔːks- **-s** -z
Hawkshaw ˈhɔːk.ʃɔː, (US) ˈhɑːk.ʃɑː, ˈhɔːk-, -ʃɔː

Hawksley ˈhɔːk.sli, (US) ˈhɑːk-, ˈhɔːk-
Hawksmoor ˈhɔːks.mɔːʳ, (US) ˈhɑːks.mɔːr, ˈhɔːks-, -mʊr
hawkweed ˈhɔːk.wiːd, (US) ˈhɑːk-, ˈhɔːk-
Hawkwood ˈhɔːk.wʊd, (US) ˈhɑːk-, ˈhɔːk-
Hawley ˈhɔː.li, (US) ˈhɑː-, ˈhɔː-
Hawn hɔːn, (US) hɑːn, hɔːn
Haworth *place in Yorkshire:* ˈhaʊ.əθ, ˈhɔː.əθ, (US) ˈhɔː.wɚθ *surname:* ˈhaʊ.əθ, (US) ˈheɪ.wɚθ, ˈhaʊ.ɚθ, ˈhoʊ-; (US) hɑːrθ *place in New Jersey:* ˈhɔː.wəθ, (US) -wɚθ
haws|e hɔːz, (US) hɑːz, hɔːz **-es** -ɪz
hawser ˈhɔː.zəʳ, (US) ˈhɑː.zɚ, ˈhɔː- **-s** -z
hawthorn ˈhɔː.θɔːn, (US) ˈhɑː.θɔːrn, ˈhɔː- **-s** -z
Hawthornden ˈhɔː.θɔːn.dən, (US) ˈhɑː.θɔːrn-, ˈhɔː-
Hawthorne ˈhɔː.θɔːn, (US) ˈhɑː.θɔːrn, ˈhɔː-
Haxby ˈhæks.bi
hay, H~ heɪ ˈ**hay** ˌ**fever**
haybox ˈheɪ.bɒks, (US) -bɑːks **-es** -ɪz
haycart ˈheɪ.kɑːt, (US) -kɑːrt **-s** -s
haycock, H~ ˈheɪ.kɒk, (US) -kɑːk **-s** -s
Hayden ˈheɪ.dᵊn
Haydn *English surname:* ˈheɪ.dᵊn *Austrian composer:* ˈhaɪ.dᵊn
Haydock ˈheɪ.dɒk, (US) -dɑːk
Haydon ˈheɪ.dᵊn
Hayes heɪz
Hayesford ˈheɪz.fəd, (US) -fɚd
Hayhurst ˈhaɪ.əst, ˈheɪ.hɜːst, (US) ˈhaɪ.ɚst, ˈheɪ.hɝːst
Hayle heɪl
Hayles heɪlz
Hayley ˈheɪ.li
Hayling Island ˌheɪ.lɪŋˈaɪ.lənd, ˈheɪ.lɪŋˌaɪ-
hayloft ˈheɪ.lɒft, (US) -lɑːft **-s** -s
haymak|er ˈheɪˌmeɪ.k|əʳ, (US) -k|ɚ **-ers** -əz, (US) -ɚz **-ing** -ɪŋ
Haymarket ˈheɪˌmɑː.kɪt, (US) -ˌmɑːr-
Haynes heɪnz
hayrick ˈheɪ.rɪk **-s** -s
Hays heɪz
hayseed ˈheɪ.siːd **-s** -z
haystack ˈheɪ.stæk **-s** -s
Hayter, Haytor ˈheɪ.təʳ, (US) -t̬ɚ
hayward, H~ ˈheɪ.wəd, (US) -wɚd **-s** -z
haywire ˈheɪ.waɪəʳ, -waɪ.əʳ, (US) -waɪ.ɚ
Haywood ˈheɪ.wʊd
Hazara həˈzɑː.rə, (US) -ˈzɑːr.ə
hazard, H~ ˈhæz.əd, (US) -ɚd **-s** -z **-ing** -ɪŋ **-ed** -ɪd
hazardous ˈhæz.ə.dəs, (US) ˈ-ɚ- **-ly** -li **-ness** -nəs, -nɪs
haz|e heɪz **-es** -ɪz **-ing** -ɪŋ **-ed** -d
hazel ˈheɪ.zᵊl **-s** -z
Hazelhurst ˈheɪ.zᵊl.hɜːst, (US) -hɝːst
hazelnut ˈheɪ.zᵊl.nʌt **-s** -s
Hazen ˈheɪ.zᵊn
Hazledean ˈheɪ.zᵊl.diːn
Hazlemere ˈheɪ.zᵊl.mɪəʳ, (US) -mɪr
Hazlett ˈheɪz.lɪt, ˈhæz-, -lət
Hazlitt ˈheɪz.lɪt, ˈhæz-

> Note: William Hazlitt, the essayist, called himself /ˈheɪz.lɪt/, and the present members of this family pronounce the name in this way. He is, however, commonly referred to as /ˈhæz.lɪt/.

Hazor ˈheɪ.zɔːʳ, (US) -zɔːr
haz|y ˈheɪ.z|i **-ier** -i.əʳ, (US) -i.ɚ **-iest** -i.ɪst, -i.əst **-ily** -ᵊl.i, -ɪ.li **-iness** -ɪ.nəs, -ɪ.nɪs
Hazzard ˈhæz.əd, (US) -ɚd
H-Block ˈeɪtʃ.blɒk, (US) -blɑːk
HBO ˌeɪtʃ.biːˈəʊ
H-bomb ˈeɪtʃ.bɒm, (US) -bɑːm **-s** -z
HBOS ˈeɪtʃ.bɒs, (US) -bɑːs
HDTV ˌeɪtʃ.diː.tiːˈviː
he *strong form:* hiː; *weak forms:* hi, i
Note: Weak-form word. The strong form /hiː/ is usually used contrastively, e.g. 'I'm not interested in what **he** says, it's **her** I'm listening to' or for emphasis, e.g. '**he**'s the one'. The weak form is /hi/ in careful speech, e.g. 'Does he live here?' /ˌdʌz.hi ˌlɪvˈhɪə/ (US) /-ˈhɪr/; in rapid speech it may be pronounced /i/ when following a consonant, e.g. 'What does he want?' /ˌwɒt.dəz.iˈwɒnt/ (US) /ˌwɑːt.dəz.iˈwɑːnt/.
head, H~ hed **-s** -z **-ing** -ɪŋ **-ed** -ɪd ˌ**head of** ˈ**state**; ˌ**head** ˈ**start**; ˌ**head** ˈ**teacher**; ˌ**bite someone's** ˈ**head off**; **have** ˌ**eyes in the** ˌ**back of one's** ˈ**head**; ˌ**bang one's** ˌ**head against a** ˌ**brick** ˈ**wall**; ˌ**bury one's** ˌ**head in the** ˈ**sand**; ˌ**have one's** ˈ**head screwed on**; ˌ**head over** ˈ**heels**; ˌ**hold one's** ˌ**head** ˈ**high**; **keep one's** ˌ**head above** ˈ**water**; **make** ˌ**head or** ˈ**tail of**;
head|ache ˈhed|.eɪk **-aches** -eɪks **-achy** -ˌeɪ.ki
headband ˈhed.bænd **-s** -z
headbang ˈhed.bæŋ **-s** -z **-ing** -ɪŋ **-ed** -d **-er/s** -əʳ/z, (US) -ɚ/z
headboard ˈhed.bɔːd, (US) -bɔːrd **-s** -z
headcas|e ˈhed.keɪs, ˈheg-, (US) ˈhed- **-es** -ɪz
headcheese ˈhed.tʃiːz
headdress ˈhed.dres **-es** -ɪz
header ˈhed.əʳ, (US) -ɚ **-s** -z
headfirst ˌhedˈfɜːst, (US) -ˈfɝːst *stress shift:* ˌ**headfirst** ˈ**leap**
headgear ˈhed.gɪəʳ, (US) -gɪr **-s** -z
headhun|t ˈhed.hʌn|t **-ts** -ts **-ting** -tɪŋ, (US) -t̬ɪŋ **-ted** -tɪd, (US) -t̬ɪd
headhunt|er ˈhedˌhʌn.t|əʳ, (US) -t̬|ɚ **-ers** -əz, (US) -ɚz **-ing** -ɪŋ
heading, H~ ˈhed.ɪŋ **-s** -z
Headingl(e)y ˈhed.ɪŋ.li
Headlam ˈhed.ləm
headlamp ˈhed.læmp **-s** -s
headland ˈhed.lənd, -lænd **-s** -z
headless ˈhed.ləs, -lɪs **-ness** -nəs, -nɪs
headlight ˈhed.laɪt **-s** -s
headlin|e ˈhed.laɪn **-es** -z **-ing** -ɪŋ **-ed** -d
headlock ˈhed.lɒk, (US) -lɑːk
headlong ˈhed.lɒŋ, (US) -lɑːŋ, -lɔːŋ
headman *of group of workers:* ˌhedˈmæn, ˈ-- **headmen** ˌhedˈmen, ˈ-- **head|man** *of tribe:* ˈhed|.mæn, -mən **-men** -men, -mən
headmaster ˌhedˈmɑː.stəʳ, ˈ-ˌ--, (US) ˈhedˌmæs.tɚ **-s** -z
headmistress ˌhedˈmɪs.trəs, -trɪs, ˈ-ˌ--, (US) ˈhedˌmɪs- **-es** -ɪz
headnote ˈhed.nəʊt, (US) -noʊt **-s** -s
head-on ˌhedˈɒn, (US) -ˈɑːn *stress shift:* ˌ**head-on** ˈ**impact**
headphones ˈhed.fəʊnz, (US) -foʊnz
headpiec|e ˈhed.piːs **-es** -ɪz
headquarters ˌhedˈkwɔː.təz, ˈ---, (US) ˈhedˌkwɔːr.t̬ɚz
headrest ˈhed.rest **-s** -s
headroom ˈhed.rʊm, -ruːm, (US) -ruːm, -rʊm
headscar|f ˈhed.skɑː|f, (US) -skɑːr|f **-ves** -vz
headset ˈhed.set **-s** -s
headship ˈhed.ʃɪp **-s** -s
heads|man ˈhedz|.mən **-men** -mən
headstand ˈhed.stænd **-s** -z
headstone, H~ ˈhed.stəʊn, (US) -stoʊn **-s** -z
headstrong ˈhed.strɒŋ, (US) -strɑːŋ
heads-up ˌhedzˈʌp
headteacher ˌhedˈtiː.tʃəʳ, (US) -tʃɚ **-s** -z
headwater ˈhedˌwɔː.təʳ, (US) -ˌwɑː.t̬ɚ, -ˌwɔː- **-s** -z
headway ˈhed.weɪ
headwind ˈhed.wɪnd **-s** -z
headword ˈhed.wɜːd, (US) -wɝːd **-s** -z
headwork ˈhed.wɜːk, (US) -wɝːk
head|y ˈhed|.i **-ier** -i.əʳ, (US) -i.ɚ **-iest** -i.ɪst, -i.əst **-ily** -ᵊl.i, -ɪ.li **-iness** -ɪ.nəs, -ɪ.nɪs
Heagerty ˈheg.ə.ti, (US) -ɚ.t̬i
heal, H~ hiːl **-s** -z **-ing** -ɪŋ **-ed** -d **-er/s** -əʳ/z, (US) -ɚ/z
Healey ˈhiː.li
health helθ ˌ**health and** ˈ**safety**; ˈ**health** ˌ**farm**; ˈ**health** ˌ**food**; ˈ**health** ˌ**service**; ˈ**health** ˌ**visitor**
healthcare ˈhelθ.keəʳ, (US) -ker
healthful ˈhelθ.fᵊl, -fʊl **-ly** -i **-ness** -nəs, -nɪs
health-giving ˈhelθˌgɪv.ɪŋ
health|y ˈhel.θ|i **-ier** -i.əʳ, (US) -i.ɚ **-iest** -i.ɪst, -i.əst **-ily** -ᵊl.i, -ɪ.li **-iness** -ɪ.nəs, -ɪ.nɪs
Healy ˈhiː.li
Heaney ˈhiː.ni
Heanor ˈhiː.nəʳ, (US) -nɚ
heap hiːp **-s** -s **-ing** -ɪŋ **-ed** -t
hear hɪəʳ, (US) hɪr **-s** -z **-ing/s** -ɪŋ/z **heard** hɜːd, (US) hɝːd **hearer/s** ˈhɪə.rəʳ/z, (US) ˈhɪr.ɚ/z ˈ**hearing** ˌ**aid**; ˌ**hard of** ˈ**hearing**
heard, H~ (from **hear**) hɜːd, (US) hɝːd

H

hearing-impaired ˈhɪə.rɪŋ.ɪmˌpeəd, (US) ˈhɪr.ɪŋ.ɪmˌperd
hearken ˈhɑː.kᵊn, (US) ˈhɑːr- **-s** -z **-ing** -ɪŋ, ˈhɑːk.nɪŋ, (US) ˈhɑːr.kᵊn.ɪŋ, ˈhɑːrk.nɪŋ **-ed** -d
Hearn(e) hɜːn, (US) hɝːn
hearsay ˈhɪə.seɪ, (US) ˈhɪr-
hears|e hɜːs, (US) hɝːs **-es** -ɪz
Hearsey ˈhɜː.si, (US) ˈhɝː-
Hearst hɜːst, (US) hɝːst
heart hɑːt, (US) hɑːrt **-s** -s ˈ**heart atˌtack**; ˈ**heart ˌfailure**; ˌ**eat one's ˈheart out**; **have one's ˌheart in the ˌright ˈplace**; **in one's ˌheart of ˈhearts**; ˌ**set one's ˈheart on something**; ˌ**wear one's ˌheart on one's ˈsleeve**
heartache ˈhɑː.t.eɪk, (US) ˈhɑːrt-
heartbeat ˈhɑːt.biːt, (US) ˈhɑːrt- **-s** -s
heartbreak ˈhɑːt.breɪk, (US) ˈhɑːrt-
heartbreaking ˈhɑːtˌbreɪ.kɪŋ, (US) ˈhɑːrt- **-ly** -li
heartbroken ˈhɑːtˌbrəʊ.kᵊn, (US) ˈhɑːrtˌbroʊ-
heartburn ˈhɑːt.bɜːn, (US) ˈhɑːrt.bɝːn **-ing** -ɪŋ
-hearted ˈhɑː.tɪd, (US) ˈhɑːr.t̬ɪd
Note: Suffix. Compounds containing **-hearted** are normally stressed on the suffix as shown, but a stress shift occurs when the word is used attributively, e.g. ˌ**broken-hearted ˈlover**.
hearten ˈhɑː.tᵊn, (US) ˈhɑːr- **-s** -z **-ing/ly** -ɪŋ/li, ˈhɑːt.nɪŋ/li, (US) ˈhɑːrt- **-ed** -d
heartfelt ˈhɑːt.felt, (US) ˈhɑːrt-
hear|th hɑː|θ, (US) hɑːr|θ **-ths** -θs, -ðz ˈ**hearth ˌrug**
hearthstone ˈhɑːθ.stəʊn, (US) ˈhɑːrθ.stoʊn **-s** -z
heartland ˈhɑːt.lænd, (US) ˈhɑːrt- **-s** -z
heartless ˈhɑːt.ləs, -lɪs, (US) ˈhɑːrt- **-ly** -li **-ness** -nəs, -nɪs
heart-rending ˈhɑːtˌren.dɪŋ, (US) ˈhɑːrt- **-ly** -li
heart-searching ˈhɑːtˌsɜː.tʃɪŋ, (US) ˈhɑːrtˌsɝː- **-s** -z
heart's-ease ˈhɑːts.iːz, (US) ˈhɑːrts-
heart-shaped ˈhɑːt.ʃeɪpt, (US) ˈhɑːrt-
heartsick ˈhɑːt.sɪk, (US) ˈhɑːrt- **-ness** -nəs, -nɪs
heartsore ˈhɑːt.sɔːʳ, (US) ˈhɑːrt.sɔːr
heartstrings ˈhɑːt.strɪŋz, (US) ˈhɑːrt-
heart-throb ˈhɑːt.θrɒb, (US) ˈhɑːrt.θrɑːb **-s** -z
heart-to-heart ˌhɑːt.təˈhɑːt, (US) ˌhɑːrt.təˈhɑːrt **-s** -s *stress shift:* ˌ**heart-to-heart ˈtalk**
heart-warming ˈhɑːtˌwɔː.mɪŋ, (US) ˈhɑːrtˌwɔːr- **-ly** -li
heartwood ˈhɑːt.wʊd, (US) ˈhɑːrt-
heart|y ˈhɑː.t|i, (US) ˈhɑːr.t̬|i **-ier** -i.əʳ, (US) -i.ɚ **-iest** -i.ɪst, -i.əst **-ily** -ᵊl.i, -ɪ.li **-iness** -ɪ.nəs, -ɪ.nɪs
heat hiːt **-s** -s **-ing** -ɪŋ, (US) ˈhiː.t̬ɪŋ **-ed/ly** -ɪd/li, (US) ˈhiː.t̬ɪd/li ˈ**heat ˌrash**; ˈ**heat ˌspot**; ˈ**heat ˌwave**
heater ˈhiː.təʳ, (US) -t̬ɚ **-s** -z
heath, H~ hiːθ **-s** -s ˌ**Heath ˈRobinson**
Heathcliff(e) ˈhiːθ.klɪf
Heathcoat ˈhiːθ.kəʊt, (US) -koʊt
Heathcote ˈheθ.kət, ˈhiːθ.kət, (US) ˈhiːθ.koʊt, -kət
heathen ˈhiː.ðᵊn **-s** -z **-ish** -ɪʃ **-dom** -dəm
heathenism ˈhiː.ðᵊn.ɪ.zᵊm
heatheniz|e, -is|e ˈhiː.ðᵊn.aɪz **-es** -ɪz **-ing** -ɪŋ **-ed** -d
heath|er, H~ *shrub, female name:* ˈheð|.əʳ, (US) -ɚ **-ers** -əz, (US) -ɚz **-ery** -ᵊr.i
Heather *place in Leicestershire:* ˈhiː.ðəʳ, (US) -ðɚ
Heathfield ˈhiːθ.fiːld
heathland ˈhiːθ.lənd, -lænd
Heathrow ˌhiːθˈrəʊ, ˈ--, (US) -ˈroʊ ˌ**Heathrow ˈAirport**
Heath-Stubbs ˌhiːθˈstʌbz
heath|y ˈhiː.θ|i **-ier** -i.əʳ, (US) -i.ɚ **-iest** -i.ɪst, -i.əst
Heaton ˈhiː.tᵊn
heat-seeking ˈhiːtˌsiː.kɪŋ
heatstroke ˈhiːt.strəʊk, (US) -stroʊk
heav|e hiːv **-es** -z **-ing** -ɪŋ **-ed** -d **hove** həʊv, (US) hoʊv **heaver/s** ˈhiː.vəʳ/z, (US) -vɚ/z
heave-ho ˌhiːvˈhəʊ, (US) -ˈhoʊ
heaven, H~ ˈhev.ᵊn **-s** -z **move ˌheaven and ˈearth**
heavenl|y ˈhev.ᵊn.l|i **-iness** -ɪ.nəs, -ɪ.nɪs
heaven-sent ˌhev.ᵊnˈsent, (US) ˈ--- *stress shift, British only:* ˌ**heaven-sent ˈchance**
heavenward ˈhev.ᵊn.wəd, (US) -wɚd **-s** -z
Heaviside ˈhev.ɪ.saɪd
heav|y ˈhev|.i **-ier** -i.əʳ, (US) -i.ɚ **-iest** -i.ɪst, -i.əst **-ily** -ᵊl.i, -ɪ.li **-iness** -ɪ.nəs, -ɪ.nɪs ˌ**heavy ˈbreather**; ˌ**heavy ˈcream**; ˌ**heavy ˈmetal**
heavy-duty ˌhev.iˈdʒuː.ti, -ˈdjuː-, (US) -ˈduː.t̬i, -ˈdjuː- *stress shift:* ˌ**heavy-duty ˈbattery**
heavy-handed ˌhev.iˈhæn.dɪd **-ly** -li **-ness** -nəs, -nɪs *stress shift:* ˌ**heavy-handed ˈcriticism**
heavy-hearted ˌhev.iˈhɑː.tɪd, (US) -ˈhɑːr.t̬ɪd **-ly** -li **-ness** -nəs, -nɪs *stress shift:* ˌ**heavy-hearted ˈlover**
heavyweight ˈhev.i.weɪt **-s** -s
Heazell ˈhiː.zᵊl
Hebburn ˈheb.ɜːn, -ən, (US) -ɝːn, -ɚn
Hebden ˈheb.dən
hebdomadal hebˈdɒm.ə.dᵊl, (US) -ˈdɑː.mə- **-ly** -li
Hebe ˈhiː.bi
Heber ˈhiː.bəʳ, (US) -bɚ
Heberden ˈheb.ə.dən, (US) ˈ-ɚ-
Hebraic hiːˈbreɪ.ɪk, hɪˈbreɪ-, hebˈreɪ-, (US) hiːˈbreɪ-, hɪ- **-al** -ᵊl **-ally** -ᵊl.i, -li
Hebra|ism ˈhiː.breɪ|.ɪ.zᵊm, -bri- **-isms** -ɪ.zᵊmz **-ist/s** -ɪst/s
Hebraistic ˌhiː.breɪˈɪst.ɪk, -briˈ-
hebraiz|e, -is|e ˈhiː.breɪ.aɪz, -bri- **-es** -ɪz **-ing** -ɪŋ **-ed** -d
Hebrew ˈhiː.bruː **-s** -z
Hebridean ˌheb.rɪˈdiː.ən, -rəˈ- **-s** -z *stress shift:* ˌ**Hebridean ˈcattle**
Hebrides ˈheb.rɪ.diːz, -rə-
Hebron *biblical place-name:* ˈheb.rɒn, ˈhiː.brɒn, -brən, (US) ˈhiː.brən, ˈheb- *modern surname:* ˈheb.rən, -rɒn, (US) -rən, -rɑːn
Hecate ˈhek.ə.ti; *in Shakespeare sometimes:* ˈhek.ət
hecatomb ˈhek.ə.tuːm, -təʊm, -təm, (US) -toʊm, -tuːm **-s** -z
Hecht hekt
heck hek
heckl|e ˈhek.ᵊl **-es** -z **-ing** -ɪŋ, ˈhek.lɪŋ **-ed** -d **-er/s** -əʳ/z, (US) -ɚ/z, ˈhek.ləʳ/z, -lɚ/z
Heckmondwike ˈhek.mənd.waɪk
Hecla ˈhek.lə
hectare ˈhek.teəʳ, -tɑːʳ, -təʳ, (US) -ter **-s** -z
hectic ˈhek.tɪk **-ally** -ᵊl.i, -li
hectogram, hectogramme ˈhek.təʊ.græm, (US) -toʊ-, -tə- **-s** -z
hectograph ˈhek.təʊ.grɑːf, -græf, (US) -toʊ.græf, -tə- **-s** -s **-ing** -ɪŋ **-ed** -t
hectographic ˌhek.təʊˈgræf.ɪk, (US) -toʊˈ-, -təˈ-
hectolitre, hectoliter ˈhek.təʊˌliː.təʳ, (US) -toʊˌliː.t̬ɚ, -təˌ- **-s** -z
hectometre, hectometer ˈhek.təʊˌmiː.təʳ, (US) -toʊˌmiː.t̬ɚ, -təˌ- **-s** -z
hector, H~ ˈhek.təʳ, (US) -tɚ **-s** -z **-ing** -ɪŋ **-ed** -d
Hecuba ˈhek.jə.bə, -jʊ-
he'd (= **he would** or **he had**) *strong form:* hiːd; *weak forms:* hid, id
Note: See note for **he**.
heder ˈheɪ.dəʳ, (US) ˈheɪ.dɚ; *as if Hebrew:* (US) ˈxeɪ- **-s** -z **hadarim** ˌhæd.ɑːˈriːm, (US) ˌhɑː-; *as if Hebrew:* ˌxæd-; (US) ˌxɑː-
Hedgcock ˈhedʒ.kɒk, (US) -kɑːk
hedg|e hedʒ **-es** -ɪz **-ing** -ɪŋ **-ed** -d **-er/s** -əʳ/z, (US) -ɚ/z ˈ**hedge ˌsparrow**; ˌ**hedge one's ˈbets**
hedgehog ˈhedʒ.hɒg, (US) -hɑːg, -hɔːg **-s** -z
hedgehop ˈhedʒ.hɒp, (US) -hɑːp **-s** -s **-ping** -ɪŋ **-ped** -t
Hedgeley ˈhedʒ.li
Hedger ˈhedʒ.əʳ, (US) -ɚ
Hedgerley ˈhedʒ.ə.li, (US) ˈ-ɚ-
hedgerow ˈhedʒ.rəʊ, (US) -roʊ **-s** -z
Hedges ˈhedʒ.ɪz
Hedley ˈhed.li
hedon|ism ˈhiː.dᵊn|.ɪ.zᵊm, ˈhed.ᵊn-, (US) ˈhiː.dᵊn- **-ist/s** -ɪst/s
hedonistic ˌhiː.dᵊnˈɪs.tɪk, ˌhed.ᵊnˈ-, (US) ˌhiː.dᵊnˈ- **-ally** -ᵊl.i, -li
he'd've (= **he would have**) *strong form:* ˈhiː.dᵊv; *weak forms:* hi.dᵊv, i.dᵊv
Note: See note for **he**.
heebie-jeebies ˌhiː.biˈdʒiː.biz
heed hiːd **-s** -z **-ing** -ɪŋ **-ed** -ɪd
heedful ˈhiːd.fᵊl, -fʊl **-ly** -i **-ness** -nəs, -nɪs

heedless ˈhiːd.ləs, -lɪs **-ly** -li **-ness** -nəs, -nɪs
heehaw ˈhiːˌhɔː, ˌ-ˈ-, (US) ˈhiː.hɑː, -hɔː, ˌ-ˈ- **-s** -z **-ing** -ɪŋ **-ed** -d
heel hiːl **-s** -z **-ing** -ɪŋ **-ed** -d **ˌcool one's ˈheels; ˌdig one's ˈheels in; ˌdrag one's ˈheels; ˌhard on the ˈheels of; ˌkick one's ˈheels**
heeler ˈhiː.ləʳ, (US) -lɚ **-s** -z
Heeley ˈhiː.li
Heenan ˈhiː.nən
Heep hiːp
Heffer ˈhef.əʳ, (US) -ɚ
Hefner ˈhef.nəʳ, (US) -nɚ
heft heft **-s** -s **-ing** -ɪŋ **-ed** -tɪd
heft|y ˈhef.t|i **-ier** -i.əʳ, (US) -i.ɚ **-iest** -i.ɪst, -i.əst **-ily** -əl.i, -ɪ.li **-iness** -ɪ.nəs, -ɪ.nɪs
Hegarty ˈheg.ə.ti, (US) -ɚ.t̬i
Hegel ˈheɪ.gəl
Hegelian hɪˈgeɪ.li.ən, hegˈeɪ-; heɪˈgiː-, hegˈiː- **-ism** -ɪ.zəm
hegemonic ˌheg.ɪˈmɒn.ɪk, ˌhiː.gɪˈ-, ˌhedʒ.ɪˈ-, -əˈ-, (US) ˌhedʒ.ɪˈmɑː.nɪk
hegemony hɪˈgem.ə.ni, hiːˈgem-, -ˈdʒem-; ˈheg.ɪ.mə-, ˈhedʒ-, (US) hɪˈdʒem.ə-; (US) ˈhedʒ.ə.moʊ-
hegira, H~ ˈhedʒ.ɪ.rə, -ər.ə, hɪˈdʒaɪə.rə, hedʒˈaɪə-, (US) ˈhedʒ.ɪ.rə, -ɚ.ə, hɪˈdʒaɪ-, hedʒˈaɪ- **-s** -z
Hegley ˈheg.li
Heidegger ˈhaɪ.deg.əʳ, -dɪ.gəʳ, (US) -dɪ.gɚ
Heidelberg ˈhaɪ.dəl.bɜːg, (US) -bɝːg
Heidi ˈhaɪ.di
heifer ˈhef.əʳ, (US) -ɚ **-s** -z
heigh heɪ
heigh-ho ˌheɪˈhəʊ, (US) -ˈhoʊ
Heighington ˈheɪ.ɪŋ.tən, ˈhiː-
height haɪt **-s** -s
heighten ˈhaɪ.tən **-s** -z **-ing** -ɪŋ, ˈhaɪt.nɪŋ **-ed** -d
Heighton ˈheɪ.tən
Heighway ˈhaɪ.weɪ, ˈheɪ-
Heimlich manoeuvre, Heimlich maneuver ˈhaɪm.lɪk.məˌnuː.vəʳ, -lɪx-, (US) -vɚ
Heineken® ˈhaɪ.nɪ.kən, -nə-
Heinemann ˈhaɪ.nə.mən, -mæn
Heinlein ˈhaɪn.laɪn
heinous ˈheɪ.nəs, ˈhiː-, (US) ˈheɪ- **-ly** -li **-ness** -nəs, -nɪs
Heinz haɪnts, haɪnz

> Note: The trademark is always pronounced /haɪnz/.

heir eəʳ, (US) er **-s** -z **-dom** -dəm **-less** -ləs, -lɪs, -les **ˌheir apˈparent; ˌheir preˈsumptive**
heiress ˈeə.res, -rɪs, -res; eəˈres, (US) ˈer.ɪs **-es** -ɪz
heirloom ˈeə.luːm, (US) ˈer- **-s** -z
heirship ˈeə.ʃɪp, (US) ˈer-
Heisman ˈhaɪz.mən
heist haɪst **-s** -s **-ing** -ɪŋ **-ed** -ɪd
heister ˈhaɪ.stəʳ, (US) -stɚ **-s** -z
hejira, H~ ˈhedʒ.ɪ.rə, -ər.ə; hɪˈdʒaɪə.rə, hə- **-s** -z
Hekla ˈhek.lə

Hel hel
held (from **hold**) held
Helen ˈhel.ən, -ɪn
Helena ˈhel.ɪ.nə, ˈ-ə-; helˈiː.nə, hɪˈliː-, hə-

> Note: /ˈhel.ɪ.nə, ˈhel.ə.nə/ are the more usual pronunciations, except in the name of the island **St. Helena**; the city in Montana is normally /ˈhel-/.

Helene helˈeɪn, hɪˈleɪn, hə-, -ˈliːn
Helensburgh ˈhel.ənzˌbər.ə, -ɪnzˌ-, -ˌbʌr-, (US) -ˌbɚ.ə
Helenus ˈhel.ɪ.nəs, ˈ-ə-
Helga ˈhel.gə
heliacal hɪˈlaɪ.ə.kəl, hiː-, helˈaɪ.ə- **-ly** -i
Heliades helˈaɪ.ə.diːz, hɪˈlaɪ.ə-
helianth|us ˌhiː.liˈænt.θ|əs, ˌhel.iˈ- **-i** -aɪ **-uses** -ə.sɪz
helical ˈhel.ɪ.kəl, ˈhiː.lɪ- **-ly** -i
helices (plural of **helix**) ˈhiː.lɪ.siːz, ˈhel.ɪ-, -lə-
Helicon ˈhel.ɪ.kən, ˈ-ə-, -ɪ.kɒn, (US) -kɑːn, -kən
helicopter ˈhel.ɪ.kɒp.təʳ, ˈ-əˌ-, (US) -kɑːp.tɚ **-s** -z
Heligoland ˈhel.ɪ.gəʊ.lænd, ˈ-ə-, (US) -goʊ-
heliocentric ˌhiː.li.əʊˈsen.trɪk, (US) -oʊˈ-, -əˈ- **-al** -əl **-ally** -əl.i, -li *stress shift:* **ˌheliocentric ˈforce**
Heliogabalus ˌhiː.li.əʊˈgæb.əl.əs, (US) -oʊˈ-, -əˈ-
heliogram ˈhiː.li.əʊ.græm, (US) -oʊ-, -ə- **-s** -z
heliograph ˈhiː.li.əʊ.grɑːf, -græf, (US) -oʊ.græf, -ə- **-s** -s
heliograph|er ˌhiː.liˈɒg.rə.f|əʳ, (US) -ˈɑː.grə.f|ɚ **-ers** -əz, (US) -ɚz **-y** -i
heliographic ˌhiː.li.əʊˈgræf.ɪk, (US) -oʊˈ-, -əˈ- **-al** -əl
heliometer ˌhiː.liˈɒm.ɪ.təʳ, ˈ-ə-, (US) -ˈɑː.mə.t̬ɚ **-s** -z
heliometric ˌhiː.li.əʊˈmet.rɪk, (US) -oʊˈ- **-ally** -əl.i, -li
Heliopolis ˌhiː.liˈɒp.əl.ɪs, (US) -ˈɑː.pəl-
Helios ˈhiː.li.ɒs, (US) -ɑːs
helioscope ˈhiː.li.əʊ.skəʊp, (US) -oʊ.skoʊp, -ə- **-s** -s
heliostat ˈhiː.li.əʊ.stæt, (US) -oʊ-, -ə- **-s** -s
heliotrope ˈhiː.li.ə.trəʊp, ˈhel.i-, (US) ˈhiː.li.ə.troʊp **-s** -s
heliotropic ˌhiː.li.əˈtrɒp.ɪk, (US) -ˈtrɑː.pɪk **-ally** -əl.i, -li
heliotropism ˌhiː.liˈɒt.rə.pɪ.zəm; ˈhiː.li.əˌtrəʊ-, ˌhiː.li.əˈtrəʊ-, (US) ˌhiː.liˈɑː.trə-
helipad ˈhel.ɪ.pæd **-s** -z
heliport ˈhel.ɪ.pɔːt, (US) -pɔːrt **-s** -s
helium ˈhiː.li.əm
helix ˈhiː.lɪks **-es** -ɪz **helices** ˈhiː.lɪ.siːz, ˈhel.ɪ-, -lə-
hell, H~ hel **-s** -z **ˌHell's ˈAngel; come ˌhell or ˌhigh ˈwater**

he'll (= **he will**) *strong form:* hiːl; *weak forms:* hil, il
Note: See note for **he**.
hellacious helˈeɪ.ʃəs
Hellas ˈhel.æs, (US) -æs, -əs
hellbent ˌhelˈbent, (US) ˈ-ˌ-
hellebore ˈhel.ɪ.bɔːʳ, ˈ-ə-, (US) -bɔːr
helleborine ˈhel.ɪ.bə.raɪn, ˈ-ə-, -riːn; ˌhel.ɪˈbɔː.riːn, -əˈ-, (US) ˌhel.əˈbɔːr.ɪn, -iːn
Hellene ˈhel.iːn **-s** -z
Hellenic helˈiː.nɪk, hɪˈliː-, hə-, -ˈlen-, (US) həˈlen.ɪk
Hellen|ism ˈhel.ɪ.n|ɪ.zəm, ˈ-ə- **-isms** -ɪ.zəmz **-ist/s** -ɪst/s
Hellenistic ˌhel.ɪˈnɪs.tɪk, -əˈ- **-al** -əl **-ally** -əl.i, -li
helleniz|e, -is|e ˈhel.ɪ.naɪz, ˈ-ə- **-es** -ɪz **-ing** -ɪŋ **-ed** -d
Heller ˈhel.əʳ, (US) -ɚ
Hellespont ˈhel.ɪ.spɒnt, ˈ-ə-, (US) -spɑːnt
hellfire ˌhelˈfaɪəʳ, -ˈfaɪ.əʳ, ˈ--, (US) ˈhel.faɪ.ɚ
hellhole ˈhel.həʊl, (US) -hoʊl **-s** -z
hellhound ˈhel.haʊnd **-s** -z
Hellingly ˌhel.ɪŋˈlaɪ
hellish ˈhel.ɪʃ **-ly** -li **-ness** -nəs, -nɪs
Hellman ˈhel.mən
hello helˈəʊ, həˈləʊ, (US) helˈoʊ, həˈloʊ, ˈhel.oʊ **-(e)s** -z **-ing** -ɪŋ **-ed** -d
helluva ˈhel.ə.və
helm helm **-s** -z
Helmand helˈmænd, ˈ--
helme|t ˈhel.mə|t, -mɪ|t **-ts** -ts **-ted** -tɪd, (US) -t̬ɪd
Helmholtz ˈhelm.həʊlts, (US) -hoʊlts
helminth ˈhel.mɪntθ **-s** -s
helminthiasis ˌhel.mɪntˈθaɪ.ə.sɪs
Helmsley ˈhelmz.li; *locally:* ˈhemz-
helms|man ˈhelmz|.mən **-men** -mən, -men
Helmut ˈhel.mʊt
Héloïse el.əʊˈiːz, (US) -oʊˈ-; (US) ˈel.ə.wiːz
hel|ot ˈhel|.ət **-ots** -əts **-otage** -ə.tɪdʒ, (US) -ə.t̬ɪdʒ **-otism** -ə.tɪ.zəm, (US) -ə.t̬ɪ.zəm **-otry** -ət.ri
help help **-s** -s **-ing/s** -ɪŋ/s **-ed** -t **-er/s** -əʳ/z, (US) -ɚ/z
helpful ˈhelp.fəl, -fʊl **-ly** -i **-ness** -nəs, -nɪs
helpless ˈhelp.ləs, -lɪs **-ly** -li **-ness** -nəs, -nɪs
helpline ˈhelp.laɪn **-s** -z
helpmate ˈhelp.meɪt **-s** -s
helpmeet ˈhelp.miːt **-s** -s
Helsingborg ˈhel.sɪŋ.bɔːg, (US) -bɔːrg
Helsinki helˈsɪŋ.ki, ˈ---, (US) helˈsiŋ.ki, ˈ---
Helston(e) ˈhel.stən
helter-skelter ˌhel.təˈskel.təʳ, (US) -tɚˈskel.tɚ **-s** -z
helve helv **-s** -z
Helvellyn helˈvel.ɪn
Helveti|a helˈviː.ʃ|ə, -ʃi|.ə **-an/s** -ən/z
Helvetic helˈvet.ɪk, (US) -ˈvet̬-

Helvétius helˈviː.ʃəs, ˈ-ʃi.əs, (US) -ˈviː-, -ˈveɪ-
Hely ˈhiː.li
hem n, v hem **-s** -z **-ming** -ɪŋ **-med** -d
hemal ˈhiː.məl
he|-man ˈhiː|.mæn **-men** -men
Hemans ˈhem.ənz
hematite ˈhiː.mə.taɪt, ˈhem.ə-, (US) ˈhiː.mə-
hematologic ˌhiː.mə.təˈlɒdʒ.ɪk, (US) -ˈlɑː.dʒɪk **-al** -əl
hematolog|y ˌhiː.məˈtɒl.ə.dʒ|i, (US) -ˈtɑː.lə- **-ist/s** -ɪst/s
hematoma ˌhiː.məˈtəʊ.mə, ˌhem.əˈ-, (US) ˌhiː.məˈtoʊ- **-s** -z **-ta** -tə
heme hiːm
Hemel Hempstead ˌhem.əlˈhemp.stɪd, -stəd, -sted
hemicycle ˈhem.iˌsaɪ.kəl **-s** -z
hemidemisemiquaver ˌhem.iˌdem.iˈsem.iˌkweɪ.vəʳ, (US) -vɚ **-s** -z
Heming ˈhem.ɪŋ
Hemingway ˈhem.ɪŋ.weɪ
hemipleg|ia ˌhem.iˈpliː.dʒ|i.ə, -dʒ|ə **-ic** -ɪk
hemisphere ˈhem.ɪ.sfɪəʳ, ˈ-ə-, (US) -sfɪr **-s** -z
hemispheric ˌhem.ɪˈsfer.ɪk, -əˈ-, (US) -ˈsfɪr-, -ˈsfer- **-al** -əl **-ally** -əl.i, -li
hemistich ˈhem.i.stɪk **-s** -s
hemline ˈhem.laɪn **-s** -z
hemlock ˈhem.lɒk, (US) -lɑːk **-s** -s
Hemming ˈhem.ɪŋ
Hemmings ˈhem.ɪŋz
hemoglobin ˌhiː.məʊˈgləʊ.bɪn, ˌhem.əʊˈ-, (US) ˈhiː.moʊ.gloʊ-, ˈ-ə-
hemophili|a ˌhiː.məˈfɪl.i|.ə, ˌhem.əˈ-, (US) ˌhiː.moʊˈ-, -məˈ- **-ac/s** -æk/s
hemorrhag|e ˈhem.ər.ɪdʒ, (US) -ɚ.ɪdʒ, ˈ-rɪdʒ **-es** -ɪz **-ing** -ɪŋ **-ed** -d
hemorrhoid ˈhem.ər.ɔɪd, (US) -ə.rɔɪd, ˈ-rɔɪd **-s** -z
hemosta|sis ˌhiː.məˈsteɪ|.sɪs, ˌhem.əˈ-, (US) ˌhiː.məˈ- **-ses** -siːz
hemp hemp **-en** -ən
Hemp(e)l ˈhem.pəl
hemstitch ˈhem.stɪtʃ **-es** -ɪz **-ing** -ɪŋ **-ed** -t
Hemy ˈhem.i
hen hen **-s** -z ˈ**hen** ˌ**party**
henbane ˈhen.beɪn, ˈhem-, (US) ˈhen-
hence hents
henceforth ˌhentsˈfɔːθ, (US) ˈhents.fɔːrθ
henceforward ˌhentsˈfɔː.wəd, (US) -ˈfɔːr.wɚd
Henchard ˈhen.tʃɑːd, -tʃəd, (US) -tʃɚd, -tʃɑːrd
hench|man ˈhentʃ|.mən **-men** -mən
hencoop ˈhen.kuːp **-s** -s
hendecagon henˈdek.ə.gən, (US) -gɑːn **-s** -z
hendecagonal ˌhen.dɪˈkæg.ən.əl, -dekˈæg-
hendecasyllabic henˌdek.ə.sɪˈlæb.ɪk, -səˈ- **-s** -s
hendecasyllable ˌhen.dek.əˈsɪl.ə.bəl **-s** -z
Henderson ˈhen.də.sən, (US) -dɚ-
hendiadys henˈdaɪ.ə.dɪs
Hendon ˈhen.dən
Hendricks ˈhen.drɪks
Hendrickson ˈhen.drɪk.sən
Hendrix ˈhen.drɪks
Hendry ˈhen.dri
Heneage ˈhen.ɪdʒ
heng|e hendʒ **-es** -ɪz
Hengist ˈheŋ.gɪst
Henley ˈhen.li
Henlow ˈhen.ləʊ, (US) -loʊ
Henman ˈhen.mən
henna ˈhen.ə **-s** -z **-ing** -ɪŋ **-ed** -d
henner|y ˈhen.ər|.i **-ies** -iz
Henness(e)y ˈhen.ə.si, ˈ-ɪ-
Henniker ˈhen.ɪ.kəʳ, (US) -kɚ
Henning ˈhen.ɪŋ
henpeck ˈhen.pek, ˈhem-, (US) ˈhen- **-s** -s **-ing** -ɪŋ **-ed** -t
Henri *French name:* ˈɑ̃ːn.riː, -ˈ-, (US) ɑ̃ːnˈriː *US surname:* ˈhen.ri
Henrietta ˌhen.riˈet.ə, (US) -ˈet̬-
Henriques henˈriː.kɪz
henr|y, H~ ˈhen.r|i **-ys** -iz **-ies** -iz
Henryson ˈhen.rɪ.sən
Hensen ˈhent.sən
Hensley ˈhenz.li
Henslow(e) ˈhenz.ləʊ, (US) -loʊ
Henson ˈhent.sən
Henty ˈhen.ti, (US) -t̬i
Hentzau ˈhent.zaʊ
hepatic hɪˈpæt.ɪk, hepˈæt-, (US) hɪˈpæt̬-
hepatica hɪˈpæt.ɪ.kə, hepˈæt-, (US) hɪˈpæt̬- **-s** -z
hepatite ˈhep.ə.taɪt
hepati|tis ˌhep.əˈtaɪ|.tɪs, -təs, (US) -t̬ɪs, -t̬əs **-tides** -tɪ.diːz
Hepburn ˈheb.ɜːn, -bən; ˈhep.bɜːn, (US) ˈhep.bɝːn, -bɚn

> Note: The names of Katharine and Audrey Hepburn are usually pronounced /ˈhep.bɜːn/ (US) /-bɝːrn/.

Hephaestus hɪˈfiː.stəs, hefˈiː-, həˈfiː-, (US) hɪˈfes.təs
Hephzibah ˈhef.sɪ.bɑː, ˈhep-, -sə-
Hepplewhite ˈhep.əl.*h*waɪt
hepta- ˈhep.tə; hepˈtæ
Note: Prefix. Normally takes either primary or secondary stress on the first syllable, e.g. **heptagon** /ˈhep.tə.gən/ (US) /-gɑːn/, **heptahedron** /ˌhep.təˈhiː.drən/, or primary stress on the second syllable, e.g. **heptathlete** /hepˈtæθ.liːt/.
heptagon ˈhep.tə.gən, -gɒn, (US) -gɑːn **-s** -z
heptagonal hepˈtæg.ən.əl
heptahedr|on ˌhep.təˈhiː.dr|ən, -ˈhed.r|ən, -r|ɒn; ˈhep.təˌhiː.dr|ən, -ˌhed.r|ən, -r|ɒn, (US) ˌhep.təˈhiː.dr|ən **-ons** -ənz **-a** -ə **-al** -əl
heptameter hepˈtæm.ɪ.təʳ, ˈ-ə-, (US) -ə.t̬ɚ **-s** -z
heptarch ˈhep.tɑːk, (US) -tɑːrk **-s** -s **-y** -i **-ies** -iz
Heptateuch ˈhep.tə.tjuːk, (US) -tuːk, -tjuːk
heptathlete hepˈtæθ.liːt **-s** -s
heptathlon hepˈtæθ.lɒn, -lən, (US) -lɑːn **-s** -z
Hepworth ˈhep.wəθ, -wɜːθ, (US) -wɝːθ, -wɚθ
her *strong form:* hɜːʳ, (US) hɝː; *weak forms:* həʳ, əʳ, (US) hɚ, ɚ **-s** -z
Note: Weak-form word. The strong form /hɜːʳ/ (US) /hɝːr/ is used for emphasis, e.g. 'it was **her** fault' or contrast, e.g. 'his or her bank'. There is a weak form /həʳ/ (US) /hɚ/ which is used at the beginning of sentences, e.g. 'Her train was late' /həˈtreɪn.wəzˌleɪt/ (US) /hɚ-/ and elsewhere in slow, careful speech, e.g. 'I admired her skill', /aɪ.ədˌmaɪəd.həˈskɪl/ (US) /-ˌmaɪrd.hɚˈ-/. In rapid speech the weak form is likely to be /əʳ/ (US) /ɚ/, e.g. 'Let her through', /ˌlet.əˈθruː/ (US) /ˌlet̬.ɚˈ-/.
Hera ˈhɪə.rə, (US) ˈhɪr.ə, ˈhiː.rə
Heraclean ˌher.əˈkliː.ən
Heracles ˈher.ə.kliːz, ˈhɪə.rə-, (US) ˈher.ə-
Heraclitus ˌher.əˈklaɪ.təs, (US) -t̬əs
Heraklion herˈæk.li.ən
herald ˈher.əld **-s** -z **-ing** -ɪŋ **-ed** -ɪd
heraldic hɪˈræl.dɪk, həˈræl-, herˈæl-, (US) həˈræl-, herˈæl- **-ally** -əl.i, -li
heraldr|y ˈher.əl.dr|i **-ies** -iz
Herat herˈæt, hɪˈræt, həˈræt, -ˈrɑːt, (US) herˈɑːt
herb, H~ hɜːb, (US) ɝːb, hɝːb **-s** -z **-age** -ɪdʒ **-y** -i

> Note: The US pronunciation for the name **Herb** is always /hɝːb/.

herbaceous hɜːˈbeɪ.ʃəs, hə-, (US) hɚˈ-, ɚˈ- **her**ˌ**baceous** ˈ**border**
herbal ˈhɜː.bəl, (US) ˈhɝː-, ˈɝː-
herbal|ism ˈhɜː.bəl|.ɪ.zəm, (US) ˈhɝː-, ˈɝː- **-ist/s** -ɪst/s
herbarium hɜːˈbeə.ri.əm, (US) hɝːˈber.i-, ɝː- **-s** -z
Herbert ˈhɜː.bət, (US) ˈhɝː.bɚt
herbicidal ˌhɜː.bɪˈsaɪ.dəl, (US) ˌhɝː-, ˌɝː-
herbicide ˈhɜː.bɪ.saɪd, (US) ˈhɝː-, ˈɝː- **-s** -z
Herbie ˈhɜː.bi, (US) ˈhɝː-
herbivore ˈhɜː.bɪ.vɔːʳ, (US) ˈhɝː.bə.vɔːr, ˈɝː- **-s** -z
herbivorous hɜːˈbɪv.ər.əs, hə-, (US) hɝː-, hɚ-, ɝː-, ɚ-
herboriz|e, -is|e ˈhɜː.bər.aɪz, (US) ˈhɝː-, ˈɝː- **-es** -ɪz **-ing** -ɪŋ **-ed** -d
Herbst hɜːbst, (US) hɝːpst

Herculaneum ˌhɜː.kjəˈleɪ.ni.əm, -kjʊˈ-, (US) ˌhɝː.kjəˈ-
Hercule ˈeə.kjuːl, ˈɜː-, ˌ-ˈ-, (US) erˈkjuːl, ɝː- ˌ**Hercule** ˈ**Poirot**, ˌ**Hercule Poi**ˈ**rot**
herculean, H~ ˌhɜː.kjəˈliː.ən, -kjʊˈ-; hɜːˈkjuː.li-, (US) ˌhɝː.kjuˈliː-; (US) hɚˈkjuː.li-
Hercules ˈhɜː.kjə.liːz, -kjʊ-, (US) ˈhɝː.kjə-
herd, H~ hɜːd, (US) hɝːd **-s** -z **-ing** -ɪŋ **-ed** -ɪd ˌ**herd** ˈ**instinct**
herds|man ˈhɜːdz|.mən, (US) ˈhɝːdz- **-men** -mən
here hɪəʳ, (US) hɪr ˌ**here,** ˌ**there, and** ˈ**everywhere;** ˌ**neither** ˌ**here nor** ˈ**there**
hereabouts ˌhɪər.əˈbaʊts, ˈ---, (US) ˌhɪr.əˈbaʊts, ˈ---
hereafter ˌhɪərˈɑːf.təʳ, (US) ˌhɪrˈæf.tɚ
hereby ˌhɪəˈbaɪ, ˈ--, (US) ˌhɪrˈbaɪ, ˈ-- *stress shift:* **I** ˌ**hereby de**ˈ**clare**
hereditable hɪˈred.ɪ.tə.bᵊl, hə-, herˈed-, ˈ-ə-, (US) həˈred.ɪ.t̬ə-
hereditament ˌher.ɪˈdɪt.ə.mənt, -əˈ-, ˈ-ɪ-, (US) -əˈdɪt̬.ə- **-s** -s
hereditar|y hɪˈred.ɪ.tᵊr|.i, hə-, herˈed-, ˈ-ə-, (US) həˈred.ɪ.ter- **-ily** -ᵊl.i, -ɪ.li **-iness** -ɪ.nəs, -ɪ.nɪs

> Note: Old-fashioned British pronunciation treats this as having 'silent h' after the indefinite article, thus 'an hereditary title' /ən.ɪˈred.ɪ.tᵊr|.i-/.

heredity hɪˈred.ə.ti, hə-, herˈed-, -ɪ.ti, (US) həˈred.ɪ-
Hereford *place in UK:* ˈher.ɪ.fəd, -ə.fəd, (US) -ə.fɚd **-shire** -ʃəʳ, -ʃɪəʳ, (US) -ʃɚ, -ʃɪr *in US:* ˈhɜː.fəd, (US) ˈhɝː.fɚd
herein ˌhɪəʳˈɪn, (US) ˌhɪr-
hereinabove ˌhɪəʳ.ɪn.əˈbʌv, (US) ˌhɪr-
hereinafter ˌhɪəʳ.ɪnˈɑːf.təʳ, (US) ˌhɪr.ɪnˈæf.tɚ
hereinbefore ˌhɪəʳ.ɪn.bɪˈfɔːʳ, -bəˈfɔːʳ, (US) ˌhɪr.ɪn.bɪˈfɔːr, -bəˈ-
hereinbelow ˌhɪəʳ.ɪn.bɪˈləʊ, -bəˈ-, (US) ˌhɪr.ɪn.bɪˈloʊ, -bəˈ-
hereof ˌhɪəʳˈɒv, (US) ˌhɪrˈɑːv
hereon ˌhɪəʳˈɒn, (US) ˌhɪrˈɑːn
Herero həˈreə.rəʊ, herˈeə-, -ˈɪə-; ˈhɪə.rə.rəʊ, ˈher.ə-, (US) həˈrer.oʊ; (US) ˈher.ə.roʊ **-s** -z
heresiarch həˈriː.zi.ɑːk, hɪ-, herˈiː-; -si-, ˈher.ə.si-, (US) həˈriː.zi.ɑːrk; (US) ˈher.ə.si- **-s** -s
heres|y ˈher.ə.s|i, ˈ-ɪ- **-ies** -iz
heretic ˈher.ə.tɪk, -ɪ.tɪk, (US) ˈ-ə- **-s** -s
heretic|al həˈret.ɪ.k|ᵊl, hɪˈ-, herˈet-, (US) həˈret̬- **-ally** -ᵊl.i, -li
hereto ˌhɪəˈtuː, (US) ˌhɪr-
heretofore ˌhɪə.tuːˈfɔːʳ, (US) ˌhɪr.tuːˈfɔːr, ˈ---
hereunder ˌhɪəʳˈʌn.dəʳ, (US) ˌhɪrˈʌn.dɚ, ˈ---
hereunto ˌhɪəʳ.ʌnˈtuː, -ˈʌn.tuː, (US) ˌhɪr-, ˈ---
hereupon ˌhɪəʳ.əˈpɒn, (US) ˌhɪr.əˈpɑːn, ˈ---
Hereward ˈher.ɪ.wəd, -ə-, (US) -wɚd
herewith ˌhɪəˈwɪð, -ˈwɪθ, (US) ˌhɪrˈwɪð, ˈ--
Herford ˈhɜː.fəd, ˈhɑː-, (US) ˈhɝː.fɚd
Hergé eəˈʒeɪ, (US) er-
heriot, H~ ˈher.i.ət, -ɒt, (US) -ət **-s** -s
Heriot-Watt ˌher.i.ətˈwɒt, (US) -ˈwɑːt
heritable ˈher.ɪ.tə.bᵊl, ˈ-ə-, (US) -ɪ.t̬ə-
heritag|e ˈher.ɪ.tɪdʒ, ˈ-ə-, (US) -ɪ.t̬ɪdʒ **-es** -ɪz
heritor ˈher.ɪ.təʳ, ˈ-ə-, (US) -ɪ.t̬ɚ **-s** -z
Herkomer ˈhɜː.kə.məʳ, (US) ˈhɝː.kə.mɚ **-s** -z
Herman ˈhɜː.mən, (US) ˈhɝː-
hermaphrodite hɜːˈmæf.rə.daɪt, hə-, (US) hɚˈmæf.roʊ-, -rə- **-s** -s
hermaphroditic hɜːˌmæf.rəˈdɪt.ɪk, hə-, (US) hɚˌmæf.roʊˈdɪt̬-, -rəˈ- **-ally** -ᵊl.i, -li
hermeneutic ˌhɜː.mɪˈnjuː.tɪk, -məˈ-, (US) ˌhɝː.məˈnuː.t̬ɪk, -ˈnjuː- **-s** -s **-al** -ᵊl **-ally** -ᵊl.i, -li
Hermes ˈhɜː.miːz, (US) ˈhɝː-
Hermès® eəˈmes, (US) er-
Hermesetas® ˌhɜː.mɪˈsiː.təz, -məˈ-, -təs, (US) ˌhɝː.məˈsiː.t̬əz, -təs
hermetic hɜːˈmet.ɪk, hə-, (US) hɚˈmet̬- **-al** -ᵊl **-ally** -ᵊl.i, -li
Hermia ˈhɜː.mi.ə, (US) ˈhɝː-
Hermione hɜːˈmaɪ.ə.ni, hə-, (US) hɚ-
Hermiston ˈhɜː.mɪ.stᵊn, (US) ˈhɝː-
hermit ˈhɜː.mɪt, (US) ˈhɝː- **-s** -s ˈ**hermit** ˌ**crab**
hermitag|e, H~ ˈhɜː.mɪ.tɪdʒ, -mə-; *as if French:* ˌeə.mɪˈtɑːʒ; (US) ˈhɝː.mɪ.t̬ɪdʒ **-es** -ɪz
hermitic hɜːˈmɪt.ɪk, hə-, (US) hɚˈmɪt̬-
Hermocrates hɜːˈmɒk.rə.tiːz, hə-, (US) hɚˈmɑː.krə-
Hermogenes hɜːˈmɒdʒ.ɪ.niːz, hə-, -ən.iːz, (US) hɚˈmɑː.dʒə.niːz
Hermon ˈhɜː.mən, (US) ˈhɝː-
hern hɜːn, (US) hɝːn **-s** -z
Hernandez hɜːˈnæn.dez, (US) hɚ-; (US) erˈnɑːn.des
Herne hɜːn, (US) hɝːn
herni|a ˈhɜː.ni|.ə, (US) ˈhɝː- **-as** -əz **-ae** -iː **-al** -əl
herni|ate ˈhɜː.ni|.eɪt, (US) ˈhɝː- **-ates** -eɪts **-ating** -eɪ.tɪŋ, (US) -t̬ɪŋ **-ated** -eɪ.tɪd, (US) -t̬ɪd
herniation ˌhɜː.niˈeɪ.ʃᵊn, (US) ˌhɝː- **-s** -z
hero, H~ ˈhɪə.rəʊ, (US) ˈhɪr.oʊ, ˈhiː.roʊ **-es** -z ˈ**hero** ˌ**worship**
Herod ˈher.əd ˌ**Herod** ˈ**Antipas**
Herodian herˈəʊ.di.ən, həˈrəʊ-, hɪ-, (US) həˈroʊ- **-s** -z
Herodias herˈəʊ.di.æs, həˈrəʊ-, hɪ-, -əs, (US) həˈroʊ-
Herodotus herˈɒd.ə.təs, həˈrɒd-, hɪ-, (US) həˈrɑː.də.t̬əs
heroic hɪˈrəʊ.ɪk, hə-, herˈəʊ-, (US) hɪˈroʊ-, hiː- **-s** -s **-al** -ᵊl **-ally** -ᵊl.i, -li **he**ˌ**roic** ˈ**verse**
heroin ˈher.əʊ.ɪn, (US) -oʊ-
heroine ˈher.əʊ.ɪn, (US) -oʊ- **-s** -z
heroism ˈher.əʊ.ɪ.zᵊm, (US) -oʊ-
heron, H~ ˈher.ᵊn **-s** -z **-ry** -ri **-ries** -riz
herpes ˈhɜː.piːz, (US) ˈhɝː-
herpetologic ˌhɜː.pɪ.təˈlɒdʒ.ɪk, -pə-, (US) ˌhɝː.pə.t̬əˈlɑː.dʒɪk **-al** -ᵊl **-ally** -ᵊl.i, -li
herpetolog|y ˌhɜː.pɪˈtɒl.ə.dʒ|i, -pəˈ-, (US) -pəˈtɑː.lə- **-ist/s** -ɪst/s
Herr heəʳ, (US) her
Herrick ˈher.ɪk
Herries ˈher.ɪs, -ɪz
herring, H~ ˈher.ɪŋ **-s** -z
herringbone ˈher.ɪŋ.bəʊn, (US) -boʊn **-s** -z
Herriot ˈher.i.ət
Herron ˈher.ən
hers hɜːz, (US) hɝːz
Herschel(l) ˈhɜː.ʃᵊl, (US) ˈhɝː-
herself həˈself, (US) hɚ-; *when not initial:* ə-, (US) ɚ-
Hershey ˈhɜː.ʃi, (US) ˈhɝː-
Herstmonceux ˌhɜːst.mənˈsjuː, -mɒn-, -ˈsuː, (US) ˌhɝːst.mənˈsuː, -mɑːnˈ-
Hertford *in England:* ˈhɑː.t.fəd, ˈhɑː-, (US) ˈhɑːrt.fɚd, ˈhɑːr- **-shire** -ʃəʳ, -ʃɪəʳ, (US) -ʃɚ, -ʃɪr *in US:* ˈhɜːt.fəd, (US) ˈhɝːt.fɚd
Herts. (abbrev. for **Hertfordshire**) hɑːts; ˈhɑːt.fəd.ʃəʳ, ˈhɑː-, -ʃɪəʳ, (US) hɑːrts; (US) ˈhɑːrt.fɚd.ʃɚ, ˈhɑːr-, -ʃɪr
Hertslet ˈhɜːt.slɪt, (US) ˈhɝːt-
hertz hɜːts, (US) hɝːts
Hertz hɜːts, heəts, (US) hɝːts, herts **-ian** -i.ən

> Note: The trademark is pronounced /hɜːts/ (US) /hɝːts/.

Hertzog ˈhɜːt.sɒg, (US) ˈhɝːt.sɑːg, -sɔːg
Hervey ˈhɑː.vi, ˈhɜː.vi, (US) ˈhɝː-
Herzegovina ˌhɜːt.sə.gəʊˈviː.nə, ˌheət-, -sɪ.gəʊˈ-; -sɪˈgɒv.ɪ.nə, (US) ˌhɝːt.sə.goʊˈviː.nə
Herzog ˈhɜːt.sɒg, (US) ˈhɝːt.sɑːg, -sɔːg
he's (= **he is** or **he has**) *strong form:* hiːz; *weak forms:* hiz, iz
Note: See note for **he**.
Heseltine ˈhes.ᵊl.taɪn, ˈhez-
Heshbon ˈheʃ.bɒn, (US) -bɑːn
Hesiod ˈhiː.si.əd, ˈhes.i-, -ɒd, (US) -əd
hesitan|ce ˈhez.ɪ.tᵊnt|s, ˈ-ə- **-cy** -si
hesitant ˈhez.ɪ.tᵊnt, ˈ-ə- **-ly** -li
hesi|tate ˈhez.ɪ|.teɪt, ˈ-ə- **-tates** -teɪts **-tating/ly** -teɪ.tɪŋ/li, (US) -teɪ.t̬ɪŋ/li **-tated** -teɪ.tɪd, (US) -teɪ.t̬ɪd
hesitation ˌhez.ɪˈteɪ.ʃᵊn, -əˈ- **-s** -z
Hesketh ˈhes.kəθ, -kɪθ
Heskey ˈhes.ki
Hesperian hesˈpɪə.ri.ən, (US) -ˈpɪr.i-
Hesperides hesˈper.ɪ.diːz, hɪˈsper-, hə-, ˈ-ə-, (US) hesˈper.ɪ-
Hesperus ˈhes.pᵊr.əs
Hess hes

Hessayon ˈhes.i.ən
Hesse ˈhes.ə, hes
hessian, H~ ˈhes.i.ən, (US) ˈheʃ.ən -s -z
Hester ˈhes.təʳ, (US) -tɚ
Heston ˈhes.tən
Heswall ˈhez.wəl, (US) ˈhes.wɔːl
Hesychius hesˈɪk.i.əs
hetero ˈhet.ər.əʊ, (US) ˈheţ.ə.roʊ -s -z
heteroclite ˈhet.ər.əʊ.klaɪt, (US) ˈhet.ɚ.ə- -s -s
heterodox ˈhet.ər.əʊ.dɒks, (US) ˈheţ.ɚ.ə.dɑːks -y -i
heterodyne ˈhet.ər.əʊ.daɪn, (US) ˈheţ.ɚ.ə-
heterogeneity ˌhet.ər.əʊ.dʒəˈniː.ə.ti, -dʒɪˈ-, -ɪ.ti, (US) ˌheţ.ə.roʊ.dʒəˈniː.ə.ţi, ˈ-ɚ.ə-
heterogeneous ˌhet.ər.əʊˈdʒiː.ni.əs, (US) ˌheţ.ə.roʊˈ-, -ɚ.əˈ- -ly -li -ness -nəs, -nɪs
heterogenesis ˌhet.ər.əʊˈdʒen.ə.sɪs, ˈ-ɪ-, (US) ˌheţ.ə.roʊˈdʒen.ə.sɪs, -ɚ.əˈ-
heteronym ˈhet.ər.əʊ.nɪm, (US) ˈheţ.ə.roʊ-, -ɚ.ə- -s -z
heteronym|ous ˌhet.əˈrɒn.ɪ.m|əs, ˈ-ə-, (US) ˌheţ.əˈrɑː.nɪ- -y -i
heterosex|ism ˌhet.ər.əʊˈsek.s|ɪ.zəm, (US) ˌheţ.ə.roʊˈ-, -ɚ.əˈ- -ist/s -ɪst/s
heterosexual ˌhet.ər.əʊˈsek.ʃu.əl, ˈ-sju-, -ʃəl, (US) ˌheţ.ə.roʊˈsek.ʃu.əl, -ɚ.əˈ- -s -z -ly -i
heterosexuality ˌhet.ər.əʊˌsek.ʃuˈæl.ə.ti, -sjuˈ-, (US) ˌheţ.ə.roʊˌsek.ʃuˈæl.ə.ţi, -ɚ.əˌ-
heterozygous ˌhet.ər.əʊˈzaɪ.gəs, (US) ˌheţ.ə.roʊˈ-, -ɚ.əˈ-
Hetherington ˈheð.ər.ɪŋ.tən
Hetton-le-Hole ˌhet.ən.ləˈhəʊl, -lɪˈ-, (US) ˌheţ.ən.ləˈhoʊl
Hetty ˈhet.i, (US) ˈheţ-
het up ˌhetˈʌp, (US) ˌheţ- *stress shift:* **ˌhet up ˈteenager**
Heugh *place:* hjuːf *surname:* hjuː
heuristic hjʊəˈrɪs.tɪk, (US) hjuːˈ- -s -s -ally -əl.i, -li
Hever ˈhiː.vəʳ, (US) -vɚ
hew hjuː -s -z -ing -ɪŋ -ed -d -n -n -er/s -əʳ/z, (US) -ɚ/z
Heward ˈhjuː.əd, (US) -ɚd
Hewart ˈhjuː.ət, (US) -ɚt
Hewetson ˈhjuː.ɪt.sən
Hewett, Hewitt ˈhjuː.ɪt
Hewke hjuːk
Hewlett ˈhjuː.lɪt, -lət
Hewlettson ˈhjuː.lɪt.sən, -lət-
hewn (from **hew**) hjuːn
hex heks -es -ɪz -ing -ɪŋ -ed -t
hexa- ˈhek.sə; hekˈsæ

Note: Prefix. Normally either takes primary or secondary stress on the first syllable, e.g. **hexagon** /ˈhek.sə.gən/ (US) /-gɑːn/, **hexahedron** /ˌhek.səˈhiː.drən/, or primary stress on the second syllable, e.g. **hexagonal** /hekˈsæg.ən.əl/.

hexachord ˈhek.sə.kɔːd, (US) -kɔːrd -s -z
hexagon ˈhek.sə.gən, (US) -gɑːn -s -z
hexagonal hekˈsæg.ən.əl -ly -i
hexagram ˈhek.sə.græm -s -z
hexahedr|on ˌhek.səˈhiː.dr|ən, -ˈhed.r|ən, (US) -ˈhiː.dr|ən -ons -ənz -a -ə -al -əl
Hexam ˈhek.səm
hexameter hekˈsæm.ɪ.təʳ, hɪkˈ-, ˈ-ə-, (US) -ə.ţɚ -s -z
Hexateuch ˈhek.sə.tjuːk, (US) -tuːk, -tjuːk
Hexham ˈhek.səm
Hextable ˈhek.stə.bəl
hey heɪ
Heycock ˈheɪ.kɒk, (US) -kɑːk
heyday ˈheɪ.deɪ
Heyer ˈheɪ.əʳ, (US) ˈheɪ.ɚ
Heyerdahl ˈheɪ.ə.dɑːl, (US) ˈheɪ.ɚ-, ˈhaɪ.ɚ-
hey presto ˌheɪˈpres.təʊ, (US) -toʊ
Heysham ˈhiː.ʃəm
Heyward ˈheɪ.wəd, (US) -wɚd
Heywood ˈheɪ.wʊd
Hezbollah ˌhɪz.bɒlˈɑː, ˈhez-, (US) ˌhez.bəˈlɑː
Hezekiah ˌhez.ɪˈkaɪ.ə, -əˈ-
HGV ˌeɪtʃ.dʒiːˈviː -s -z
hi haɪ
hiatus haɪˈeɪ.təs, hi-, (US) haɪˈeɪ.ţəs -es -ɪz
Hiawatha ˌhaɪ.əˈwɒθ.ə, (US) -ˈwɑː.θə
hibachi hɪˈbɑː.tʃi, hiː- -s -z
Hibbert ˈhɪb.ət, -ɜːt, (US) -ɚt, -ɝːt
hibernal haɪˈbɜː.nəl, (US) -ˈbɝː-
hiber|nate ˈhaɪ.bə|.neɪt, (US) -bɚ- -nates -neɪts -nating -neɪ.tɪŋ, (US) -neɪ.ţɪŋ -nated -neɪ.tɪd, (US) -neɪ.ţɪd
hibernation ˌhaɪ.bəˈneɪ.ʃən, (US) -bɚˈ- -s -z
Hibernia haɪˈbɜː.ni.ə, hɪ-, (US) -ˈbɝː-
Hibernian **n, adj** haɪˈbɜː.ni.ən, (US) -ˈbɝː- *in name of football club:* hɪˈbɜː.ni.ən, (US) -ˈbɝː- -s -z
Hibernicism haɪˈbɜː.nɪ.sɪ.zəm, -nə-, (US) -ˈbɝː- -s -z
hibiscus hɪˈbɪs.kəs, haɪ-, (US) haɪ-, hɪ-
Hibs hɪbz
hiccough ˈhɪk.ʌp, -əp -s -s -ing -ɪŋ -ed -t
hiccup ˈhɪk.ʌp, -əp -s -s -(p)ing -ɪŋ -(p)ed -t
hick hɪk -s -s
hickey ˈhɪk.i -s -z
Hickman ˈhɪk.mən
Hickok ˈhɪk.ɒk, (US) -ɑːk
hickory, H~ ˈhɪk.ər.i, (US) -ɚ.i, ˈ-ri
Hicks hɪks
Hickson ˈhɪk.sən
hicksville ˈhɪks.vɪl
hid (from **hide**) hɪd
hidalgo, H~ hɪˈdæl.gəʊ, (US) -goʊ -s -z
hid|e haɪd -es -z -ing/s -ɪŋ/z **hid** hɪd **hidden** ˈhɪd.ən **ˌhide-and-ˈseek; ˈhiding ˌplace**
hideaway ˈhaɪd.ə.weɪ -s -z
hidebound ˈhaɪd.baʊnd
hideous ˈhɪd.i.əs -ly -li -ness -nəs, -nɪs
hideout ˈhaɪd.aʊt -s -s
hid(e)y-hole ˈhaɪ.di.həʊl, (US) -hoʊl -s -z
hie haɪ -s -z -ing -ɪŋ -d -d
Hierapolis ˌhaɪəˈræp.əl.ɪs, (US) ˌhaɪ.əˈræp.ə.lɪs
hierarch ˈhaɪə.rɑːk, (US) ˈhaɪ.rɑːrk -s -s
hierarchal ˌhaɪəˈrɑː.kəl, (US) ˌhaɪˈrɑːr-
hierarchic ˌhaɪəˈrɑː.kɪk, (US) ˌhaɪˈrɑːr- -al -əl -ally -əl.i, -li
hierarch|y ˈhaɪə.rɑː.k|i, (US) ˈhaɪ.rɑːr- -ies -iz
hieratic ˌhaɪəˈræt.ɪk, (US) ˌhaɪˈræţ-
hieroglyph ˈhaɪə.rəʊ.glɪf, (US) ˈhaɪ.roʊ- -s -s
hieroglyphic ˌhaɪə.rəʊˈglɪf.ɪk, (US) ˌhaɪ.roʊˈ- -s -s -al -əl -ally -əl.i, -li
Hieronimo hɪəˈrɒn.ɪ.məʊ, (US) hɪˈrɑː.nɪ.moʊ
Hieronymus hɪəˈrɒn.ɪ.məs, haɪəˈ-, (US) haɪˈrɑː.nɪ-
hierophant ˈhɪə.rəʊ.fænt, ˈhaɪə-, (US) ˈhaɪ.roʊ- -s -s
hifalutin ˌhaɪ.fəˈluː.tɪn, -tən, (US) ˌhaɪ.fəˈluː.tən *stress shift:* **ˌhifalutin ˈattitude**
hi-fi ˈhaɪ.faɪ, ˌ-ˈ- -s -z
Higginbotham ˈhɪg.ɪnˌbɒt.əm, -ənˌ-, -əmˌ-, -ˌbɒθ.əm, (US) -ˌbɑː.ţəm, -θəm
Higginbottom ˈhɪg.ɪnˌbɒt.əm, -ənˌ-, -əmˌ-, (US) -ˌbɑː.ţəm
Higgins ˈhɪg.ɪnz
Higginson ˈhɪg.ɪn.sən
higgl|e ˈhɪg.əl -es -z -ing -ɪŋ, ˈhɪg.lɪŋ -ed -d -er/s ˈhɪg.ləʳ/z, (US) -lɚ/z
higgledy-piggledy ˌhɪg.əl.diˈpɪg.əl.di
Higgs hɪgz
high haɪ -er -əʳ, (US) -ɚ -est -ɪst, -əst -s -z -ly -li -ness -nəs, -nɪs **ˈhigh ˌchair; ˌhigh ˈchurch; ˌhigh ˈchurchman; ˌHigh ˈCourt** *stress shift, British only:* **ˌHigh Court ˈjudge; ˈhigh ˌday; ˌhigh ˈfrequency; ˌhigh ˈheels; ˌhigh ˈhorse; ˈhigh ˌjump; ˌhigh ˈroller; ˈhigh ˌschool; ˈhigh ˌstreet; ˌhigh ˈtide; ˌhigh ˈwater; ˌhigh ˈwater mark; ˌhigh and ˈdry; ˌhigh and ˈlow; ˌhigher eduˈcation**
Higham ˈhaɪ.əm -s -z
high-and-mighty ˌhaɪ.ənˈmaɪ.ti, -əmˈ-, (US) -ənˈmaɪ.ţi *stress shift:* **ˌhigh-and-mighty ˈmanners**
highball ˈhaɪ.bɔːl, (US) -bɔːl, -bɑːl -s -z -ing -ɪŋ -ed -d
highborn ˌhaɪˈbɔːn, (US) ˈhaɪ.bɔːrn *stress shift, British only:* **ˌhighborn ˈlady**
highboy ˈhaɪ.bɔɪ -s -z
Highbridge ˈhaɪ.brɪdʒ
highbrow ˈhaɪ.braʊ -s -z
Highbury ˈhaɪ.bər.i, (US) -ber.i, -bɚ-
highchair ˈhaɪ.tʃeəʳ, ˌ-ˈ-, (US) -tʃer -s -z

High Church ˌhaɪˈtʃɜːtʃ, (US) -ˈtʃɝːtʃ **-man** -mən **-men** -mən, -men *stress shift:* **ˌHigh Church ˈmannerism**
high-class ˌhaɪˈklɑːs, (US) -ˈklæs *stress shift:* **ˌhigh-class ˈbutcher**
Highclere ˈhaɪ.klɪəʳ, (US) -klɪr
high-end ˈhaɪ.end
highfalut|in ˌhaɪ.fəˈluː.t|ɪn, -t|ən, (US) -t|ən **-ing** -ɪŋ *stress shift:* **ˌhighfalutin ˈattitude**
Highfield ˈhaɪ.fiːld
highflier, highflyer ˌhaɪˈflaɪ.əʳ, (US) -ɚ **-s** -z
highflown ˌhaɪˈfləʊn, (US) -ˈfloʊn *stress shift:* **ˌhigh-flown ˈrhetoric**
Highgate ˈhaɪ.geɪt, -gɪt, -gət
Highgrove ˈhaɪ.grəʊv, (US) -groʊv
high-handed ˌhaɪˈhæn.dɪd **-ly** -li **-ness** -nəs, -nɪs *stress shift:* **ˌhigh-handed ˈruler**
high-heeled ˌhaɪˈhiːld *stress shift:* **ˌhigh-heeled ˈshoes**
highjack ˈhaɪ.dʒæk **-s** -s **-ing** -ɪŋ **-ed** -t **-er/s** -əʳ/z, (US) -ɚ/z
highjinks ˈhaɪ.dʒɪŋks
highland, H~ ˈhaɪ.lənd **-s** -z **-er/s** -əʳ/z, (US) -ɚ/z **ˌHighland ˈfling**
high-level ˌhaɪˈlev.əl *stress shift:* **ˌhigh-level ˈlanguage**
high|light ˈhaɪ|.laɪt **-lights** -laɪts **-lighting** -ˌlaɪ.tɪŋ, (US) -ˌlaɪ.t̬ɪŋ **-lighted** -ˌlaɪ.tɪd, (US) -ˌlaɪ.t̬ɪd
highlighter ˈhaɪˌlaɪ.təʳ, (US) -t̬ɚ **-s** -z
highly ˈhaɪ.li
high-minded ˌhaɪˈmaɪn.dɪd **-ness** -nəs, -nɪs *stress shift:* **ˌhigh-minded ˈthinker**
Highness ˈhaɪ.nəs, -nɪs **-es** -ɪz
high-octane ˌhaɪˈɒk.teɪn, (US) -ˈɑːk- *stress shift:* **ˌhigh-octane ˈfuel**
high-pitched ˌhaɪˈpɪtʃt *stress shift:* **ˌhigh-pitched ˈvoice**
high-powered ˌhaɪˈpaʊ.əd, -ˈpaʊəd, (US) -ˈpaʊ.ɚd *stress shift:* **ˌhigh-powered ˈengine**
high-pressure ˌhaɪˈpreʃ.əʳ, (US) -ɚ *stress shift:* **ˌhigh-pressure ˈsalesman**
high-priced ˌhaɪˈpraɪst *stress shift:* **ˌhigh-priced ˈgoods**
high-priest ˌhaɪˈpriːst **-s** -s **-hood/s** -hʊd/z
high-priestess ˌhaɪ.priːˈstes, ˌ-ˈ--, (US) ˌhaɪˈpriː- **-es** -ɪz
high-profile ˌhaɪˈprəʊ.faɪl, (US) -ˈproʊ- *stress shift:* **ˌhigh-profile ˈmission**
high-ranking ˌhaɪˈræŋ.kɪŋ, ˈ--- *stress shift:* **ˌhigh-ranking ˈofficer**
high-ris|e ˌhaɪˈraɪz, ˈ--, (US) ˈ-- **-s** -ɪz *stress shift:* **ˌhigh-rise ˈflats**
high-risk ˌhaɪˈrɪsk *stress shift:* **ˌhigh-risk ˈstrategy**
highroad ˈhaɪ.rəʊd, (US) -roʊd **-s** -z
high-speed ˌhaɪˈspiːd *stress shift:* **ˌhigh-speed ˈchase**
high-spirited ˌhaɪˈspɪr.ɪ.tɪd, (US) -t̬ɪd **-ly** -li **-ness** -nəs, -nɪs
highspot ˈhaɪ.spɒt, (US) -spɑːt **-s** -s
high-strung ˌhaɪˈstrʌŋ *stress shift:* **ˌhigh-strung ˈhorse**
hightail ˈhaɪ.teɪl **-s** -z **-ing** -ɪŋ **-ed** -d
high-tech ˌhaɪˈtek *stress shift:* **ˌhigh-tech ˈoffice**
Highton ˈhaɪ.tən
high-up ˌhaɪˈʌp **-s** -s *stress shift:* **ˌhigh-up ˈsource**
highway ˈhaɪ.weɪ **-s** -z **ˌHighway ˈCode, ˈHighway ˌCode; ˌhighway ˈrobbery**
highway|man ˈhaɪ.weɪ|.mən **-men** -mən
Highworth ˈhaɪ.wəθ, -wɜːθ, (US) -wɚθ
High Wycombe ˌhaɪˈwɪk.əm
hijab hɪˈdʒɑːb, hə-, -ˈdʒæb; ˈhɪdʒ.ɑːb **-s** -z
hijack ˈhaɪ.dʒæk **-s** -s **-ing** -ɪŋ **-ed** -t **-er/s** -əʳ/z, (US) -ɚ/z
hijinks ˈhaɪ.dʒɪŋks
hik|e haɪk **-es** -s **-ing** -ɪŋ **-ed** -t **-er/s** -əʳ/z, (US) -ɚ/z
Hilaire hɪˈleəʳ; ˈhɪl.eəʳ, (US) hɪˈler; (US) ˈhɪl.er
hilarious hɪˈleə.ri.əs, hə-, (US) hɪˈler.i-, -ˈlær- **-ly** -li **-ness** -nəs, -nɪs
hilarity hɪˈlær.ə.ti, hə-, -ɪ.ti, (US) hɪˈler.ə.t̬i, -ˈlær-
Hilary ˈhɪl.ər.i
Hilda ˈhɪl.də
Hildebrand ˈhɪl.də.brænd, -dɪ-
Hildegard(e) ˈhɪl.də.gɑːd, -dɪ-, (US) -gɑːrd
hill, H~ hɪl **-s** -z **as ˌold as the ˈhills; ˌover the ˈhill**
Hillary ˈhɪl.ər.i
hillbill|y ˈhɪlˌbɪl|.i **-ies** -iz
Hillel ˈhɪl.el, -əl; hɪˈlel
Hillhead hɪlˈhed, ˈ--

> Note: The pronunciation in Scotland is /-ˈ-/.

Hilliard ˈhɪl.i.əd, -ɑːd, (US) ˈ-jɚd
Hillingdon ˈhɪl.ɪŋ.dən
hill|man ˈhɪl|.mæn, -mən **-men** -men
Hillman ˈhɪl.mən **-s** -z
hillock ˈhɪl.ək **-s** -s
Hillsboro ˈhɪlz.bər.ə, (US) -bɚ.oʊ
Hillsborough ˈhɪlz.bər.ə, (US) -bɚ.oʊ
hillside, H~ ˈhɪl.saɪd, ˌ-ˈ- **-s** -z
hilltop ˈhɪl.tɒp, (US) -tɑːp **-s** -s
hill|y ˈhɪl|.i **-ier** -i.əʳ, (US) -i.ɚ **-iest** -i.ɪst, -i.əst **-iness** -ɪ.nəs, -ɪ.nɪs
Hillyard ˈhɪl.jəd, -jɑːd, (US) -jɚd
Hillyer ˈhɪl.i.əʳ, (US) ˈ-jɚ
hilt hɪlt **-s** -s **-ed** -ɪd, (US) ˈhɪl.t̬ɪd
Hilton ˈhɪl.tən
hil|um ˈhaɪ.l|əm **-ums** -əmz **-a** -ə **-i** -aɪ **-us** -əs
Hilversum ˈhɪl.və.sʊm, -səm, (US) -vɚ-
him *strong form:* hɪm; *weak form:* ɪm
Note: Weak-form word. The strong form is mainly used for contrastive purposes, e.g. 'The gift is for **him**, not **her**'.
Himachal Pradesh hɪˌmɑː.tʃəl.prɑːˈdeʃ, (US) -prəˈ-
Himalaya ˌhɪm.əˈleɪ.ə, hɪˈmɑː.li.ə, -lə.jə **-s** -z **-n** -n
Himes haɪmz
Himmler ˈhɪm.ləʳ, (US) -lɚ
himself hɪmˈself; *when not initial:* ɪm-
Himyaritic ˌhɪm.jəˈrɪt.ɪk, (US) -ˈrɪt̬-
Hinayana ˌhiː.nəˈjɑː.nə, ˌhɪn.əˈ-, (US) ˌhiː.nəˈ-
Hinchcliffe ˈhɪntʃ.klɪf
Hinchingbrooke ˈhɪn.tʃɪŋ.brʊk
Hinchliffe ˈhɪntʃ.lɪf
Hinckley ˈhɪŋ.kli
hind, H~ haɪnd **-s** -z
Hinde haɪnd
Hindemith ˈhɪnd.ə.mɪt, -mɪθ
Hindenburg ˈhɪn.dən.bɜːg, -dəm-, (US) -bɝːg
hinder adj ˈhaɪn.dəʳ, (US) -dɚ **-most** -məʊst, (US) -moʊst
hind|er v ˈhɪn.d|əʳ, (US) -d|ɚ **-ers** -əz, (US) -ɚz **-ering** -ər.ɪŋ **-ered** -əd, (US) -ɚd **-erer/s** -ər.əʳ/z, (US) -ɚ.ɚ/z
Hinderwell ˈhɪn.də.wel, -wəl, (US) -dɚ-
Hindhead ˈhaɪnd.hed
Hindi ˈhɪn.diː, -di
Hindle ˈhɪn.dəl
Hindley *surname:* ˈhɪnd.li, ˈhaɪnd- *town in Greater Manchester:* ˈhɪnd.li
Hindlip ˈhɪnd.lɪp
hindmost ˈhaɪnd.məʊst, (US) -moʊst
Hindolveston ˌhɪn.dəlˈves.tən, -ˈvɪs-; *locally also:* ˈhɪl.də.stən
hindquarters ˌhaɪndˈkwɔː.təz, ˌhaɪŋ-, ˈ---, (US) ˈhaɪndˌkwɔːr.t̬ɚz
hindranc|e ˈhɪn.drənts **-es** -ɪz
hindsight ˈhaɪnd.saɪt
Hindu ˈhɪn.duː, -ˈ-, (US) ˈhɪn.duː **-s** -z
Hinduism ˈhɪn.duː.ɪ.zəm, hɪnˈduː-, (US) ˈhɪn.duː-
Hinduja hɪnˈduː.dʒə
Hindu Kush ˌhɪn.duːˈkuːʃ, -ˈkʊʃ
Hindustan ˌhɪn.dʊˈstɑːn, -ˈstæn **-i** -i
Hines haɪnz
hing|e ˈhɪndʒ **-es** -ɪz **-ing** -ɪŋ **-ed** -d
Hingis ˈhɪŋ.gɪs
Hingston ˈhɪŋk.stən
Hinkley ˈhɪŋ.kli
Hinkson ˈhɪŋk.sən
hinn|y ˈhɪn|.i **-ies** -iz **-ying** -i.ɪŋ **-ied** -id
hint hɪnt **-s** -s **-ing** -ɪŋ, (US) ˈhɪn.t̬ɪŋ **-ed** -ɪd, (US) ˈhɪn.t̬ɪd
hinterland ˈhɪn.tə.lænd, -lənd, (US) -t̬ɚ-
Hinton ˈhɪn.tən
hip hɪp **-s** -s **-ped** -t **-per** -əʳ, (US) -ɚ **-pest** -ɪst, -əst **ˈhip ˌbath; ˈhip ˌjoint**
hipbone ˈhɪp.bəʊn, (US) -boʊn **-s** -z
hip-hop ˈhɪp.hɒp, (US) -hɑːp
Hipomenes haɪˈpɒm.ɪ.niːz, (US) -ˈpɑː.mɪ-
Hipparchus hɪˈpɑː.kəs, (US) -ˈpɑːr-
Hippias ˈhɪp.i.æs, (US) -æs, -əs
hippie ˈhɪp.i **-s** -z
hippo ˈhɪp.əʊ, (US) -oʊ **-s** -z

H

hippocamp|us ˌhɪp.əʊˈkæm.p|əs, (US) -oʊˈ- -i -aɪ
Hippocrates hɪˈpɒk.rə.tiːz, (US) -ˈpɑː.krə-
Hippocratic ˌhɪp.əʊˈkræt.ɪk, (US) -əˈkræţ- ˌ**Hippocratic** ˈ**oath**
Hippocrene ˌhɪp.əʊˈkriː.niː, -ni; *also in poetry:* ˈhɪp.əʊ.kriːn, (US) ˈhɪp.oʊ.kriːn, ˌhɪp.oʊˈkriː.ni
hippodrome, H~ ˈhɪp.ə.drəʊm, (US) -droʊm -s -z
Hippolyta hɪˈpɒl.ɪ.tə, ˈ-ə-, (US) -ˈpɑː.lɪ.tə
Hippolyte hɪˈpɒl.ɪ.tiː, ˈ-ə-, (US) -ˈpɑː.lɪ.tiː
Hippolytus hɪˈpɒl.ɪ.təs, ˈ-ə-, (US) -ˈpɑː.lɪ.təs
hippopotam|us ˌhɪp.əˈpɒt.ə.m|əs, (US) -ˈpɑː.ţə- -uses -ə.sɪz -i -aɪ
hipp|y ˈhɪp|.i -ies -iz
hipster ˈhɪp.stəʳ, (US) -stɚ -s -z
Hiram *biblical name:* ˈhaɪə.rəm, -ræm, (US) ˈhaɪ.rəm *modern names:* ˈhaɪə.rəm, (US) ˈhaɪ-
hircine ˈhɜː.saɪn, (US) ˈhɝː-, -sɪn
Hird hɜːd, (US) hɝːd
hir|e haɪəʳ, haɪ.əʳ, (US) haɪ.ɚ -es -z -ing -ɪŋ -ed -d -er/s -əʳ/z, (US) -ɚ/z -eling/s -lɪŋ/z ˌ**hired** ˈ**hand**; ˌ**hire** ˈ**purchase**
hireling ˈhaɪə.lɪŋ, ˈhaɪ.ə-, (US) ˈhaɪr-, ˈhaɪ.ɚ- -s -z
Hirohito ˌhɪr.əʊˈhiː.təʊ, (US) -oʊˈhiː.toʊ
Hiroshima hɪˈrɒʃ.ɪ.mə, hə-, ˈ-ə-; ˌhɪr.ɒʃˈiː-, -əˈʃiː-, (US) ˌhɪr.əˈʃiː-, hɪˈroʊ.ʃɪ-
Hirst hɜːst, (US) hɝːst
hirsute ˈhɜː.sjuːt, -suːt, -ˈ-, (US) ˈhɝː.suːt, ˈhɪr-; (US) hɚˈsuːt -ness -nəs, -nɪs
hirsutism ˈhɜː.sjuː.tɪ.zəm, -suː-; hɜːˈsjuː-, -ˈsuː-, (US) ˈhɝː.suː.ţɪ-, ˈhɪr-; (US) hɚˈsuː-
his *strong form:* hɪz; *weak form:* ɪz
Note: Weak-form word. The strong form /hɪz/ is always used when the word occurs contrastively, e.g. 'It's **his**, not **hers**' and when it is in final position, e.g. 'He said it was **his**'. When the word is unstressed the weak pronuciation is usually /ɪz/, e.g. 'on his back', /ɒn.ɪzˈbæk/ (US) /ɑːn-/, though /hɪz/ occurs when it is the first word in a sentence, e.g. 'His shoes were wet', /hɪzˈʃuːz.wəˌwet/ (US) /-wɚ-/, and when the style of speech is slow and careful.
Hislop ˈhɪz.lɒp, -ləp, (US) -lɑːp
his'n'hers ˌhɪz.ənˈhɜːz, (US) -ˈhɝːz
Hispanic hɪˈspæn.ɪk -s -s
Hispanic|ism hɪˈspæn.ɪ.s|ɪ.zəm, ˈ-ə- -ist/s -ɪst/s
Hispaniola ˌhɪs.pæn.iˈəʊ.lə; -pænˈjəʊ-; hɪˌspæn-, (US) ˌhɪs.pənˈjoʊ-
hiss, H~ hɪs -es -ɪz -ing -ɪŋ -ed -t -er/s -əʳ/z, (US) -ɚ/z
hist sːt, hɪst

> Note: This spelling is used to represent the hissing sound made to attract someone's attention; it has a connotation of secrecy.

histamine ˈhɪs.tə.miːn, -mɪn -s -z
histogram ˈhɪs.tə.græm, (US) -toʊ-, -tə- -s -z
histological ˌhɪs.təˈlɒdʒ.ɪ.kəl, (US) -toʊˈlɑː.dʒɪ-, -təˈ- -ly -li
histolog|y hɪˈstɒl.ə.dʒ|i, (US) -ˈstɑː.lə- -ist/s -ɪst/s
Histon ˈhɪs.tən
historian hɪˈstɔː.ri.ən, (US) -ˈstɔːr.i- -s -z
historic hɪˈstɒr.ɪk, (US) hɪˈstɔːr.ɪk -al -əl -ally -əl.i, -li

> Note: Old-fashioned British pronunciation treats this as having 'silent h' after the indefinite article, thus 'an historic occasion' /ən.ɪˈstɒr.ɪk-/

historicism hɪˈstɒr.ɪ.sɪ.zəm, ˈ-ə-, (US) -ˈstɔːr.ə-
historicity ˌhɪs.tɒrˈɪs.ə.ti, -təˈrɪs-, -ɪ.ti, (US) -təˈrɪs.ə.ţi
historiograph|y hɪˌstɒr.iˈɒg.rə.f|i, (US) -ˌstɔːr.iˈɑː.grə- -er/s -əʳ/z, (US) -ɚ/z
histor|y ˈhɪs.tər|.i -ies -iz
histrionic ˌhɪs.triˈɒn.ɪk, (US) -ˈɑː.nɪk -s -s -al -əl -ally -əl.i, -li
histrionism ˈhɪs.tri.ə.nɪ.zəm
hit hɪt -s -s -ting -ɪŋ, (US) ˈhɪţ.ɪŋ -ter/s -əʳ/z, (US) ˈhɪţ.ɚ/z ˈ**hit** ˌ**list**; ˈ**hit** **pa**ˌ**rade**
Hitachi® hɪˈtɑː.tʃi, -ˈtætʃ.i, (US) -ˈtɑː.tʃi
hit-and-miss ˌhɪt.ənˈmɪs, -əmˈ-, (US) -ənˈ-
hit-and-run ˌhɪt.ənˈrʌn, -əmˈ-, (US) -ənˈ- *stress shift, see compound:* ˌ**hit-and-run** ˈ**driver**
hitch hɪtʃ -es -ɪz -ing -ɪŋ -ed -t
Hitchcock ˈhɪtʃ.kɒk, (US) -kɑːk
Hitchens ˈhɪtʃ.ɪnz
hitchhik|e ˈhɪtʃ.haɪk -es -s -ing -ɪŋ -ed -t -er/s -əʳ/z, (US) -ɚ/z
Hitchin ˈhɪtʃ.ɪn -s -z
Hite haɪt
hi-tech ˌhaɪˈtek *stress shift:* ˌ**hi-tech** ˈ**product**
hither, H~ ˈhɪð.əʳ, (US) -ɚ
hithermost ˈhɪð.ə.məʊst, (US) -ɚ.moʊst
hitherto ˌhɪð.əˈtuː, (US) -ɚˈ- *stress shift:* ˌ**hitherto** ˈ**named**
hitherwards ˈhɪð.ə.wədz, (US) -ɚ.wɚdz
Hitler ˈhɪt.ləʳ, (US) -lɚ
Hitlerian hɪtˈlɪə.ri.ən, (US) -ˈlɪr.i-
Hitlerism ˈhɪt.lər.ɪ.zəm, (US) -lɚ-
Hitlerite ˈhɪt.lər.aɪt, (US) -lɚ.aɪt -s -s
hit|man ˈhɪt|.mæn -men -men
Hittite ˈhɪt.aɪt, (US) ˈhɪţ- -s -s
HIV ˌeɪtʃ.aɪˈviː *stress shift, see compound:* ˌ**HIV** ˈ**positive**
hiv|e **n, v** haɪv -es -z -ing -ɪŋ -ed -d
Hivite ˈhaɪ.vaɪt -s -s
Hizbollah ˌhɪz.bɒlˈɑː, (US) ˌhez.bəˈlɑː
Hizbullah ˌhɪz.bʊˈlɑː, -bəˈ-
HMO ˌeɪtʃ.emˈəʊ, (US) -ˈoʊ
HMS ˌeɪtʃ.emˈes
HNC ˌeɪtʃ.enˈsiː
HND ˌeɪtʃ.enˈdiː
ho həʊ, (US) hoʊ
Hoadl(e)y ˈhəʊd.li, (US) ˈhoʊd-
hoag|ie, hoag|y ˈhəʊ.g|i, (US) ˈhoʊ- -ies -iz
hoar, H~ hɔːʳ, (US) hɔːr
hoard hɔːd, (US) hɔːrd -s -z -ing -ɪŋ -ed -ɪd -er/s -əʳ/z, (US) -ɚ/z
hoarding ˈhɔː.dɪŋ, (US) ˈhɔːr- -s -z
Hoare hɔːʳ, (US) hɔːr
hoarfrost ˈhɔː.frɒst, ˌ-ˈ-, (US) ˈhɔːr.frɑːst -s -s
hoars|e hɔːs, (US) hɔːrs -er -əʳ, (US) -ɚ -est -ɪst, -əst -ely -li -eness -nəs, -nɪs
hoar|y ˈhɔː.r|i, (US) ˈhɔːr|.i -ier -i.əʳ, (US) -i.ɚ -iest -i.ɪst, -i.əst -ily -əl.i, -ɪ.li -iness -ɪ.nəs, -ɪ.nɪs
hoax həʊks, (US) hoʊks -es -ɪz -ing -ɪŋ -ed -t -er/s -əʳ/z, (US) -ɚ/z
hob hɒb, (US) hɑːb -s -z
Hoban ˈhəʊ.bən, (US) ˈhoʊ-
Hobart ˈhəʊ.bɑːt, -bət; ˈhʌb.ət, (US) ˈhoʊ.bɑːrt, -bɚt; (US) ˈhʌb.ɚt
Hobbema ˈhɒb.ɪ.mə, (US) ˈhɑː.bə.mɑː, -mə -s -z
Hobbes hɒbz, (US) hɑːbz
hobbit, H~ ˈhɒb.ɪt, (US) ˈhɑː.bɪt -s -s
hobbl|e ˈhɒb.əl, (US) ˈhɑː.b|əl -es -z -ing -ɪŋ, ˈhɒb.lɪŋ, (US) ˈhɑː.blɪŋ -ed -d -er/s -əʳ/z, (US) -ɚ/z, ˈhɒb.ləʳ/z, ˈhɑː.blɚ/z
hobbledehoy ˌhɒb.əl.diˈhɔɪ, ˈhɒb.əl.di.hɔɪ, (US) ˈhɑː.bəl.di.hɔɪ -s -z
Hobbs hɒbz, (US) hɑːbz
hobb|y ˈhɒb|.i, (US) ˈhɑː.b|i -ies -iz
hobbyhors|e ˈhɒb.i.hɔːs, (US) ˈhɑː.bi.hɔːrs -es -ɪz
hobbyist ˈhɒb.i.ɪst, (US) ˈhɑː.bi- -s -s
Hobday ˈhɒb.deɪ, (US) ˈhɑːb-
hobgoblin ˌhɒbˈgɒb.lɪn, ˈ-ˌ--, (US) ˈhɑːbˌgɑːb- -s -z
Hobhouse ˈhɒb.haʊs, (US) ˈhɑːb-
hobnail ˈhɒb.neɪl, (US) ˈhɑːb- -s -z -ed -d ˌ**hobnail** ˈ**boots**
hobnob ˈhɒb.nɒb, ˌ-ˈ-, (US) ˈhɑːb.nɑːb -s -z -bing -ɪŋ -bed -d
hobo ˈhəʊ.bəʊ, (US) ˈhoʊ.boʊ -(e)s -z
Hoboken ˈhəʊ.bəʊ.kən, (US) ˈhoʊ.boʊ-
Hobsbaum ˈhɒbz.baʊm, (US) ˈhɑːbz-
Hobsbawm ˈhɒbz.bɔːm, (US) ˈhɑːbz.bɑːm, -bɔːm
Hobson ˈhɒb.sən, (US) ˈhɑːb- ˌ**Hobson's** ˈ**choice**
Hobson-Jobson ˌhɒb.sənˈdʒɒb.sən, (US) ˌhɑːb.sənˈdʒɑːb-
Hoby ˈhəʊ.bi, (US) ˈhoʊ-

Hoccleve ˈhɒk.liːv, (US) ˈhɑːk-
Ho Chi Minh ˌhəʊ.tʃiːˈmɪn, (US) ˌhoʊ-
Ho Chi Minh City ˌhəʊ.tʃiː.mɪnˈsɪt.i, (US) ˌhoʊ.tʃiː.mɪnˈsɪţ-
hock hɒk, (US) hɑːk **-s** -s **-ing** -ɪŋ **-ed** -t
hockey ˈhɒk.i, (US) ˈhɑː.ki **ˈhockey ˌstick**
Hockin ˈhɒk.ɪn, (US) ˈhɑː.kɪn
Hocking ˈhɒk.ɪŋ, (US) ˈhɑː.kɪŋ
Hockley ˈhɒk.li, (US) ˈhɑːk-
Hockney ˈhɒk.ni, (US) ˈhɑːk-
hockshop ˈhɒk.ʃɒp, (US) ˈhɑːk.ʃɑːp **-s** -s
hocus ˈhəʊ.kəs, (US) ˈhoʊ- **-es** -ɪz **-(s)ing** -ɪŋ **-(s)ed** -t
hocus-pocus ˌhəʊ.kəsˈpəʊ.kəs, (US) ˌhoʊ.kəsˈpoʊ-
hod hɒd, (US) hɑːd **-s** -z
Hodder ˈhɒd.əʳ, (US) ˈhɑː.dɚ
Hoddesdon ˈhɒdz.dən, (US) ˈhɑːdz-
Hoddinott ˈhɒd.ɪ.nɒt, -ən.ɒt, (US) ˈhɑː.dən.ɑːt
Hoddle ˈhɒd.əl, (US) ˈhɑː.dəl
Hodge hɒdʒ, (US) hɑːdʒ
hodgepodge ˈhɒdʒ.pɒdʒ, (US) ˈhɑːdʒ.pɑːdʒ
Hodges ˈhɒdʒ.ɪz, (US) ˈhɑː.dʒɪz
Hodgetts ˈhɒdʒ.ɪts, (US) ˈhɑː.dʒɪts
Hodgins ˈhɒdʒ.ɪnz, (US) ˈhɑː.dʒɪnz
Hodgkin ˈhɒdʒ.kɪn, (US) ˈhɑːdʒ- **ˈHodgkin's diˌsease**
Hodgkins ˈhɒdʒ.kɪnz, (US) ˈhɑːdʒ-
Hodgkinson ˈhɒdʒ.kɪn.sən, (US) ˈhɑːdʒ-
Hodgkiss ˈhɒdʒ.kɪs, (US) ˈhɑːdʒ-
Hodgson ˈhɒdʒ.sən; *in the North of England also:* ˈhɒdʒ.ən, (US) ˈhɑːdʒ.sən
hodometer hɒdˈɒm.ɪ.təʳ, -ə.təʳ, (US) hɑːˈdɑː.mə.ţɚ **-s** -z
Hodson ˈhɒd.sən, (US) ˈhɑːd-
hoe, H~ həʊ, (US) hoʊ **-s** -z **-ing** -ɪŋ **-d** -d
hoedown ˈhəʊ.daʊn, (US) ˈhoʊ- **-s** -z
Hoey hɔɪ, ˈhəʊ.i, (US) ˈhoʊ.i
Hoffa ˈhɒf.ə, (US) ˈhɑː.fə
Hoffman(n) ˈhɒf.mən, (US) ˈhɑːf-
Hofmannsthal ˈhɒf.mən.stɑːl, (US) ˈhɑːf.mɑːn-, ˈhɔːf-
Hofmeister ˈhɒfˌmaɪ.stəʳ, (US) ˈhɑːfˌmaɪ.stɚ
hog hɒg, (US) hɑːg, hɔːg **-s** -z **-ging** -ɪŋ **-ged** -d
Hogan ˈhəʊ.gən, (US) ˈhoʊ-
Hogarth ˈhəʊ.gɑːθ, ˈhɒg.ət, (US) ˈhoʊ.gɑːrθ
Hogarthian həʊˈgɑː.θi.ən, (US) hoʊˈgɑːr-
Hogben ˈhɒg.bən, -ben, (US) ˈhɑːg-, ˈhɔːg
Hogg hɒg, (US) hɑːg, hɔːg
Hoggart ˈhɒg.ət, (US) ˈhɑː.gɚt, ˈhɔː-
hogget, H~ ˈhɒg.ɪt, (US) ˈhɑː.gɪt, ˈhɔː- **-s** -s
hoggish ˈhɒg.ɪʃ, (US) ˈhɑː.gɪʃ, ˈhɔː- **-ly** -li **-ness** -nəs, -nɪs
hogmanay, H~ ˈhɒg.mə.neɪ, ˌ--ˈ-, (US) ˈhɑːg.mə.neɪ, ˈhɔːg-
hogshead ˈhɒgz.hed, (US) ˈhɑːgz-, ˈhɔːgz- **-s** -z
Hogwarts ˈhɒg.wɔːts, (US) ˈhɑːg.wɔːrts
hogwash ˈhɒg.wɒʃ, (US) ˈhɑːg.wɑːʃ, ˈhɔːg-, -wɔːʃ
hogweed ˈhɒg.wiːd, (US) ˈhɑːg-, ˈhɔːg- **-s** -z
Hohenlinden ˌhəʊ.ənˈlɪn.dən, (US) ˌhoʊ.ənˈ-, ˈhoʊ.ənˌlɪn-
Hohenzollern ˌhəʊ.ənˈzɒl.ən, (US) ˈhoʊ.ənˌzɑː.lɚn **-s** -z
hoi(c)k hɔɪk **-s** -s **-ing** -ɪŋ **-ed** -t
hoi polloi ˌhɔɪ.pəˈlɔɪ, -pɒlˈɔɪ; -ˈpɒl.ɔɪ, (US) ˌhɔɪ.pəˈlɔɪ
hoisin ˈhɔɪ.sɪn, -ˈ- **ˌhoisin ˈsauce**
hoist hɔɪst **-s** -s **-ing** -ɪŋ **-ed** -ɪd
hoity-toity ˌhɔɪ.tiˈtɔɪ.ti, (US) ˌhɔɪ.ţiˈtɔɪ.ţi
hokey ˈhəʊ.ki, (US) ˈhoʊ- **ˌhokey ˈcokey**
hokey-pokey ˌhəʊ.kiˈpəʊ.ki, (US) ˌhoʊ.kiˈpoʊ-
Hokkaido hɒkˈaɪ.dəʊ, (US) hɑːˈkaɪ.doʊ
hokum ˈhəʊ.kəm, (US) ˈhoʊ-
Holbeach ˈhɒl.biːtʃ, ˈhəʊl-, (US) ˈhɑːl-, ˈhoʊl-
Holbech ˈhəʊl.biːtʃ, ˈhɒl-, (US) ˈhoʊl-
Holbeck ˈhɒl.bek, ˈhəʊl-, (US) ˈhoʊl-
Holbein ˈhɒl.baɪn, (US) ˈhoʊl- **-s** -z
Holborn ˈhəʊ.bən, ˈhəʊl-, ˈhɒl-, (US) ˈhoʊl.bɚn, ˈhoʊ-
Holbrook(e) ˈhəʊl.brʊk, ˈhɒl-, (US) ˈhoʊl-
Holburn ˈhɒl.bɜːn, ˈhəʊl-, (US) ˈhoʊl.bɝːn
Holcroft ˈhəʊl.krɒft, (US) ˈhoʊl.krɑːft
hold həʊld, (US) hoʊld **-s** -z **-ing/s** -ɪŋ/z **held** held **ˌno ˌholds ˈbarred; ˈholding ˌcompany; ˌhold one's ˈown**
holdall ˈhəʊld.ɔːl, (US) ˈhoʊld-, -ɑːl **-s** -z
Holden ˈhəʊl.dən, (US) ˈhoʊl-
holder, H~ ˈhəʊl.dəʳ, (US) ˈhoʊl.dɚ **-s** -z
Holderness ˈhəʊl.də.nəs, -nɪs, -nes, (US) ˈhoʊl.dɚ-
holdout ˈhəʊld.aʊt, (US) ˈhoʊld- **-s** -s
holdover ˈhəʊldˌəʊ.vəʳ, (US) ˈhoʊldˌoʊ.vɚ **-s** -z
Holdsworth ˈhəʊldz.wəθ, -wɜːθ, (US) ˈhoʊldz.wɚθ, -wɝːθ
holdup ˈhəʊld.ʌp, (US) ˈhoʊld- **-s** -s
hol|e, H~ həʊl, (US) hoʊl **-es** -z **-ing** -ɪŋ **-ed** -d **ˌhole in ˈone** (US) **ˈhole in ˌone; ˌneed something like a ˌhole in the ˈhead** (US) **ˌneed something like a ˈhole in the ˌhead**
hole-and-corner ˌhəʊl.əndˈkɔː.nəʳ, -əŋˈ-, (US) ˌhoʊl.əndˈkɔːr.nɚ
hole-in-the-wall ˌhəʊl.ɪn.ðəˈwɔːl, (US) ˌhoʊl.ɪn.ðəˈwɔːl, -wɑːl
Holford ˈhəʊl.fəd, ˈhɒl-, (US) ˈhoʊl.fɚd
holiday, H~ ˈhɒl.ə.deɪ, ˈ-ɪ-, -di, (US) ˈhɑː.lə.deɪ **-s** -z **-ing** -ɪŋ **-ed** -d **ˈholiday ˌcamp**
holidaymaker ˈhɒl.ə.diˌmeɪ.kəʳ, ˈ-ɪ-, -deɪˌ-, (US) ˈhɑː.lə.deɪˌmeɪ.kɚ **-s** -z
holier-than-thou ˌhəʊ.li.ə.ðənˈðaʊ, (US) ˌhoʊ.li.ɚ- *stress shift:* **ˌholier-than-thou ˈattitude**
Holies ˈhəʊ.lɪz, (US) ˈhoʊ-
Holifield ˈhɒl.ɪ.fiːld, (US) ˈhoʊ.lɪ-, ˈhɑː-
Holinshed ˈhɒl.ɪn.ʃed, (US) ˈhɑː.lɪn-
holism ˈhəʊ.lɪ.zəm, ˈhɒl.ɪ-, (US) ˈhoʊ.lɪ-
holistic həʊˈlɪs.tɪk, hɒlˈɪs-, (US) hoʊlˈɪs- **-ally** -əl.i, -li
Holland, holland ˈhɒl.ənd, (US) ˈhɑː.lənd **-s** -z
hollandaise ˌhɒl.ənˈdeɪz, (US) ˌhɑː.lənˈ- *stress shift, see compound:* **ˌhollandaise ˈsauce** (US) **ˈhollandaise ˌsauce**
Hollander ˈhɒl.ən.dəʳ, (US) ˈhɑː.lən.dɚ **-s** -z
holl|er ˈhɒl|.əʳ, (US) ˈhɑː.l|ɚ **-ers** -əz, (US) -ɚz **-ering** -ər.ɪŋ **-ered** -əd, (US) -ɚd
Holles ˈhɒl.ɪs, (US) ˈhɑː.lɪs
Hollick ˈhɒl.ɪk, (US) ˈhɑː.lɪk
Holliday ˈhɒl.ɪ.deɪ, ˈ-ə-, -di, (US) ˈhɑː.lə-
Hollings ˈhɒl.ɪŋz, (US) ˈhɑː.lɪŋz
Hollingsworth ˈhɒl.ɪŋz.wəθ, -wɜːθ, (US) ˈhɑː.lɪŋz.wɚθ, -wɝːθ
Hollingworth ˈhɒl.ɪŋ.wəθ, -wɜːθ, (US) ˈhɑː.lɪŋ.wɚθ, -wɝːθ
Hollins ˈhɒl.ɪnz, (US) ˈhɑː.lɪnz
Hollis ˈhɒl.ɪs, (US) ˈhɑː.lɪs
hollo ˈhɒl.əʊ, ˈ-ə, (US) ˈhɑː.loʊ, ˈ-ə; (US) həˈloʊ **-es** -z **-ing** -ɪŋ **-ed** -d
hollo(a) hɒlˈəʊ, (US) hɑːˈloʊ; (US) həˈloʊ **-s** -z **-ing** -ɪŋ **-ed** -d
hollow ˈhɒl.əʊ, (US) ˈhɑː.loʊ **-s** -z **-er** -əʳ, (US) -ɚ **-est** -ɪst, -əst **-ly** -li **-ness** -nəs, -nɪs **-ing** -ɪŋ **-ed** -d
Holloway ˈhɒl.ə.weɪ, (US) ˈhɑː.lə-
holl|y, H~ ˈhɒl|.i, (US) ˈhɑː.l|i **-ies** -iz
hollyhock ˈhɒl.i.hɒk, (US) ˈhɑː.li.hɑːk **-s** -s
Hollywood ˈhɒl.i.wʊd, (US) ˈhɑː.li-
holm, H~ həʊm, (US) hoʊlm **-s** -z **ˈholm ˌoak**
Holman ˈhəʊl.mən, ˈhɒl-, (US) ˈhoʊl-
Holmby ˈhəʊm.bi, (US) ˈhoʊlm-
Holmer ˈhəʊl.məʳ, ˈhəʊ-, (US) ˈhoʊl.mɚ
Holmes həʊmz, (US) hoʊlmz
Holmesdale ˈhəʊmz.deɪl, (US) ˈhoʊlmz-
Holmfirth ˈhəʊm.fəθ, -fɜːθ, (US) ˈhoʊlm.fɚθ, -fɝːθ
holmium ˈhəʊl.mi.əm, ˈhɒl-, (US) ˈhoʊl-
holo- ˈhɒl.ə; hɒlˈɒ, (US) ˈhɑː.lə, ˈhoʊ-; (US) hoʊˈlɑː
Note: Prefix. Normally either takes primary or secondary stress on the first syllable, e.g. **holograph** /ˈhɒl.ə.grɑːf/ (US) /ˈhɑː.lə.græf/,

holographic /ˌhɒl.əˈgræf.ɪk/ (US) /ˌhɑː.ləˈ-/, or primary stress on the second syllable, e.g. **holography** /hɒlˈɒg.rə.fi/ (US) /hoʊˈlɑː.grə-/.

holocaust, H~ ˈhɒl.ə.kɔːst, -kɒst, (US) ˈhɑː.lə.kɑːst, ˈhoʊ-, -kɔːst **-s** -s

Holofernes ˌhɒl.əʊˈfɜː.niːz, həˈlɒf.ə-, (US) ˌhɑː.ləˈfɝː-

hologram ˈhɒl.ə.græm, (US) ˈhɑː.lə-, ˈhoʊ- **-s** -z

holograph ˈhɒl.ə.grɑːf, -græf, (US) ˈhɑː.lə.græf, ˈhoʊ- **-s** -s

holographic ˌhɒl.əˈgræf.ɪk, (US) ˌhɑː.lə-, ˌhoʊ- **-ally** -ᵊl.i, -li

holography hɒlˈɒg.rə.fi, (US) hoʊˈlɑː.grə-

Holon hɒlˈɒn, (US) hɑːˈlɑːn; (US) ˈhoʊ.lɑːn

holophras|e ˈhɒl.ə.freɪz, (US) ˈhɑː.lə-, ˈhoʊ- **-es** -ɪz

holophrastic ˌhɒl.əˈfræs.tɪk, (US) ˌhɑː.ləˈ-, ˌhoʊ-

Holroyd ˈhɒl.rɔɪd, ˈhəʊl-, (US) ˈhɑːl-

Holst həʊlst, (US) hoʊlst

holstein, H~ ˈhɒl.staɪn, ˈhəʊl-, (US) ˈhoʊl.staɪn, -stiːn

holster ˈhəʊl.stəʳ, (US) ˈhoʊl.stɚ **-s** -z **-ed** -d

holt, H~ həʊlt, (US) hoʊlt **-s** -s

Holtby ˈhəʊlt.bi, (US) ˈhoʊlt-

Holtham ˈhəʊl.θəm, ˈhɒl-, ˈhəʊ-, (US) ˈhoʊl-

holus-bolus ˌhəʊ.ləsˈbəʊ.ləs, (US) ˌhoʊ.ləsˈboʊ-

hol|y, H~ ˈhəʊ.l|i, (US) ˈhoʊ- **-ier** -i.əʳ, (US) -i.ɚ **-iest** -i.ɪst, -i.əst **-iness** -ɪ.nəs, -ɪ.nɪs ˌ**Holy ˈBible;** ˌ**Holy Comˈmunion;** ˌ**Holy ˈGhost;** ˌ**Holy ˈGrail;** ˈ**Holy ˌLand;** ˌ**Holy ˌRoman ˈEmpire;** ˌ**Holy ˈSpirit;** ˈ**Holy ˌWeek**

Holycross ˈhəʊ.li.krɒs, (US) ˈhoʊl.i.krɑːs

Holyfield ˈhəʊl.i.fiːld, (US) ˈhɑː.lɪ-

Holyhead ˌhɒl.iˈhed, ˈ---, (US) ˈhɑː.li-

Holyoke *place in Massachusetts:* ˈhəʊl.jəʊk, (US) ˈhoʊl.joʊk *all other senses:* ˈhəʊ.li.əʊk, (US) ˈhoʊ.li.oʊk

Holyrood ˈhɒl.i.ruːd, (US) ˈhɑː.li-

holyston|e ˈhəʊl.i.stəʊn, (US) ˈhoʊl.i.stoʊn **-es** -z **-ing** -ɪŋ **-ed** -d

Holywell ˈhɒl.i.wəl, -wel, (US) ˈhɑː.li-

homage ˈhɒm.ɪdʒ, (US) ˈhɑː.mɪdʒ, ˈɑː-

hombre ˈɒm.breɪ, -bri, (US) ˈɑːm- **-s** -z

homburg, H~ ˈhɒm.bɜːg, (US) ˈhɑːm.bɝːg **-s** -z

home həʊm, (US) hoʊm **-s** -z ˌ**home ˈbrew;** ˌ**Home ˈCounties;** ˌ**home ecoˈnomics;** ˌ**home ˈfree;** ˌ**home ˈfront** (US) ˈ**home ˌfront;** ˌ**home ˈhelp;** ˈ**Home ˌOffice;** ˈ**home ˌpage;** ˌ**home ˈrule;** ˌ**Home ˈSecretary;** ˌ**home ˈtruth;** ˌ**close to ˈhome;** ˌ**home from ˈhome**

Home həʊm, hjuːm, (US) hoʊm, hjuːm

> Note: /hjuːm/ in **Milne-Home, Douglas-Home**, and **Baron Home of the Hirsel.**

Homebase® ˈhəʊm.beɪs, (US) ˈhoʊm-

homeboy ˈhəʊm.bɔɪ, (US) ˈhoʊm- **-s** -z

homebred ˌhəʊmˈbred, (US) ˌhoʊm- *stress shift:* ˌ**homebred ˈlivestock**

homecoming ˈhəʊmˌkʌm.ɪŋ, (US) ˈhoʊm- **-s** -z

homegrown ˌhəʊmˈgrəʊn, (US) ˌhoʊmˈgroʊn *stress shift:* ˌ**home-grown ˈfood**

homeland, H~ ˈhəʊm.lænd, -lənd, (US) ˈhoʊm- **-s** -z

homeless ˈhəʊm.ləs, -lɪs, (US) ˈhoʊm- **-ness** -nəs, -nɪs

homelike ˈhəʊm.laɪk, (US) ˈhoʊm-

homel|y ˈhəʊm.l|i, (US) ˈhoʊm- **-ier** -i.əʳ, (US) -i.ɚ **-iest** -i.ɪst, -i.əst **-iness** -ɪ.nəs, -ɪ.nɪs

homemade ˌhəʊmˈmeɪd, (US) ˌhoʊm- *stress shift:* ˌ**homemade ˈjam**

homemaker ˈhəʊmˌmeɪ.kəʳ, (US) ˈhoʊmˌmeɪ.kɚ **-s** -z

homeo- ˈhəʊ.mi.əʊ, ˈhɒm.i.əʊ; ˌhəʊ.miˈɒ, ˌhɒm.iˈɒ, (US) ˈhoʊ.mi.oʊ, -ə; (US) ˌhoʊ.miˈɑː

Note: Prefix. Normally either takes primary or secondary stress on the first syllable, e.g. **homeopath** /ˈhəʊ.mi.əʊ.pæθ/ (US) /ˈhoʊ.mi.oʊ-/, **homeopathic** /ˌhəʊ.mi.əʊˈpæθ.ɪk/ (US) /ˌhoʊ.mi.oʊˈ-/, or primary stress on the third syllable with secondary stress on the first, e.g. **homeopathy** /ˌhəʊ.miˈɒp.ə.θi/ (US) /ˌhoʊ.miˈɑː.pə-/.

homeopath ˈhəʊ.mi.əʊ.pæθ, ˈhɒm.i-, (US) ˈhoʊ.mi.oʊ-, -ə- **-s** -s

homeopathic ˌhəʊ.mi.əʊˈpæθ.ɪk, ˌhɒm.i-, (US) ˌhoʊ.mi.oʊˈ-, -ə- **-al** -ᵊl **-ally** -ᵊl.i, -li

homeopathy ˌhəʊ.miˈɒp.ə.θi, ˌhɒm.iˈ-, (US) ˌhoʊ.miˈɑː.pə-

homeostasis ˌhəʊ.mi.əʊˈsteɪ.sɪs, ˌhɒm.i-, ˌ--ˈɒs.tə-, (US) ˌhoʊ.mi.oʊˈ-, -ˈstæs.ɪs

homeostatic ˌhəʊ.mi.əʊˈstæt.ɪk, ˌhɒm.i-, (US) ˌhoʊ.mi.oʊˈstæt̬- **-ally** -ᵊl.i, -li

homeowner ˈhəʊmˌəʊ.nəʳ, (US) ˈhoʊmˌoʊ.nɚ **-s** -z

homepag|e ˈhəʊm.peɪdʒ, (US) ˈhoʊm- **-es** -ɪz

homer ˈhəʊ.məʳ, (US) ˈhoʊ.mɚ **-s** -z

Homer ˈhəʊ.məʳ, (US) ˈhoʊ.mɚ

Homeric *relating to Homer:* həʊˈmer.ɪk, (US) hoʊ- *name of ship:* ˈhəʊ.mᵊr.ɪk, (US) ˈhoʊ-

Homerton ˈhɒm.ə.tᵊn, (US) ˈhɑː.mɚ-

homesick ˈhəʊm.sɪk, (US) ˈhoʊm- **-ness** -nəs, -nɪs

homespun ˈhəʊm.spʌn, (US) ˈhoʊm- **-s** -z

homestead ˈhəʊm.sted, -stɪd, (US) ˈhoʊm- **-s** -z

homesteader ˈhəʊmˌsted.əʳ, (US) ˈhoʊmˌsted.ɚ **-s** -z

homestretch ˌhəʊmˈstretʃ, ˈ--, (US) ˌhoʊmˈstretʃ, ˈ-- **-es** -ɪz

homeward ˈhəʊm.wəd, (US) ˈhoʊm.wɚd **-s** -z

homework ˈhəʊm.wɜːk, (US) ˈhoʊm.wɝːk

homeworker ˈhəʊmˌwɜː.kəʳ, (US) ˈhoʊmˌwɝː.kɚ **-s** -z

homey ˈhəʊ.mi, (US) ˈhoʊ-

homicidal ˌhɒm.ɪˈsaɪ.dᵊl, -əˈ-, (US) ˌhɑː.məˈ-, ˌhoʊ- *stress shift:* ˌ**homicidal ˈmaniac**

homicide ˈhɒm.ɪ.saɪd, ˈ-ə-, (US) ˈhɑː.mə-, ˈhoʊ- **-s** -z

homil|y ˈhɒm.ɪ.l|i, ˈ-ə-, (US) ˈhɑː.mə- **-ies** -iz

homing ˈhəʊ.mɪŋ, (US) ˈhoʊ- ˈ**homing deˌvice;** ˈ**homing ˌpigeon**

hominid ˈhɒm.ɪ.nɪd, ˈ-ə-, (US) ˈhɑː.mɪ-, -mə- **-s** -z

hominoid ˈhɒm.ɪ.nɔɪd, -ə-, (US) ˈhɑː.mɪ-, -mə- **-s** -z

hominy ˈhɒm.ɪ.ni, ˈ-ə-, (US) ˈhɑː.mɪ-, -mə-

homo ˈhəʊ.məʊ, ˈhɒm.əʊ, (US) ˈhoʊ.moʊ **-s** -z

homo- ˈhəʊ.mə, ˈhɒm.ə; həˈmɒ, hɒmˈɒ, (US) ˈhoʊ.mə, ˈhɑː-; (US) həˈmɑː, hoʊ-

Note: Prefix. Normally either takes primary or secondary stress on the first syllable, e.g. **homonym** /ˈhɒm.ə.nɪm/ (US) /ˈhɑː.mə-/, **homophobia** /ˌhɒm.əˈfəʊ.bi.ə/ (US) /ˌhoʊ.məˈfoʊ-/, or primary stress on the second syllable, e.g. **homonymy** /həˈmɒn.ɪ.mi/ (US) /hoʊˈmɑː.nə-/.

homoeopath ˈhəʊ.mi.əʊ.pæθ, ˈhɒm.i-, (US) ˈhoʊ.mi.oʊ- **-s** -s

homoeopathic ˌhəʊ.mi.əʊˈpæθ.ɪk, ˌhɒm.i-, (US) ˌhoʊ.mi.oʊˈ- **-al** -ᵊl **-ally** -əl.i, -li

homoeopathy ˌhəʊ.miˈɒp.ə.θi, ˌhɒm.iˈ-, (US) ˌhoʊ.miˈɑː.pə-

homoeostasis ˌhəʊ.mi.əʊˈsteɪ.sɪs, ˌ--ˈɒs.tə-, (US) ˌhoʊ.mi.oʊˈ-, -ˈstæs.ɪs

homoeostatic ˌhəʊ.mi.əʊˈstæt.ɪk, (US) ˌhoʊ.mi.oʊˈstæt̬- **-ally** -ᵊl.i, -li

homoerotic ˌhəʊ.məʊ.ɪˈrɒt.ɪk, ˌhɒm.əʊ-, -əˈ-, (US) ˌhoʊ.moʊ.ɪˈrɑː.t̬ɪk, -əˈ-

homoeroticism ˌhəʊ.məʊ.ɪˈrɒt.ɪ.sɪ.z.ᵊm, ˌhɒm.əʊ-, -əˈ-, ˈ-ə-, (US) ˌhoʊ.moʊ.ɪˈrɑː.t̬ə-, -əˈ-

homogeneity ˌhəʊ.məʊ.dʒəˈneɪ.ə.ti, ˌhɒm.əʊ-, -dʒenˈeɪ-, -dʒɪˈneɪ-, -iː.ə.ti, -ɪ.ti, (US) ˌhoʊ.moʊ.dʒəˈniː.ə.t̬i, ˌhɑː-, -mə-, -ˈneɪ-

homogeneous ˌhɒm.əˈdʒiː.ni.əs, ˌhəʊ.mə-, (US) ˌhoʊ.moʊˈdʒiː-, ˌhɑː-, -məˈ- **-ly** -li **-ness** -nəs, -nɪs

Note: A common mispronunciation is /həˈmɒdʒ.ɪ.nəs/ (US) /-ˈmɑːdʒ-/.

homogeniz|e, -is|e həˈmɒdʒ.ə.naɪz, hɒmˈɒdʒ-, ˈ-ɪ-, (US) həˈmɑː.dʒə- **-es** -ɪz **-ing** -ɪŋ **-ed** -d
homograph ˈhɒm.ə.grɑːf, ˈhəʊ.mə-, -græf, (US) ˈhɑː.mə.græf, ˈhoʊ- **-s** -s
homographic ˌhɒm.əˈgræf.ɪk, ˌhəʊ.məˈ-, (US) ˌhɑː.məˈ-, ˌhoʊ-
homoiotherm həˈmɔɪ.ə.θɜːm, hɒmˈɔɪ-, (US) hoʊˈmɔɪ.oʊ.θɝːm, -ə.θɝːm **-s** -z
homoiothermic həˌmɔɪ.əˈθɜː.mɪk, hɒmˌɔɪ-, (US) hoʊˌmɔɪ.oʊˈθɝː-, -əˈθɝː-
homolog ˈhɒm.ə.lɒg, (US) ˈhɑː.mə.lɑːg, ˈhoʊ-, -lɔːg **-s** -z
homologous həˈmɒl.ə.gəs, hɒmˈɒl-, (US) hoʊˈmɑː.lə-, hə-
homologue ˈhɒm.ə.lɒg, (US) ˈhɑː.mə.lɑːg, ˈhoʊ-, -lɔːg **-s** -z
homolog|y həˈmɒl.ə.dʒ|i, hɒmˈɒl-, (US) hoʊˈmɑː.lə-, hə- **-ies** -iz
homonym ˈhɒm.ə.nɪm, (US) ˈhɑː.mə- **-s** -z
homonymous həˈmɒn.ɪ.məs, hɒmˈɒn-, -ə.məs, (US) hoʊˈmɑː.nə-, hə- **-ly** -li
homonymy həˈmɒn.ɪ.mi, hɒmˈɒn-, -ə.mi, (US) hoʊˈmɑː.nə-, hə-
homophobe ˈhəʊ.məʊ.fəʊb, ˈhɒm.ə-, (US) ˈhoʊ.mə.foʊb **-s** -z
homophobia ˌhəʊ.məˈfəʊ.bi.ə, ˌhɒm.ə-, (US) ˌhoʊ.məˈfoʊ-
homophobic ˌhəʊ.məˈfəʊ.bɪk, ˌhɒm.ə-, (US) ˌhoʊ.məˈfoʊ-
homophone ˈhɒm.ə.fəʊn, ˈhəʊ.mə-, (US) ˈhɑː.mə.foʊn, ˈhoʊ- **-s** -z
homophonic ˌhɒm.əˈfɒn.ɪk, ˌhəʊ.məˈ-, (US) ˌhɑː.məˈfɑː.nɪk, ˌhoʊ- **-ally** -əl.i, -li
homophon|ous həˈmɒf.ən|.əs, hɒmˈɒf-, (US) hoʊˈmɑː.fən-, hə- **-y** -i
homorganic ˌhɒm.ɔːˈgæn.ɪk, (US) ˌhoʊ.mɔːrˈ-, ˌhɑː-
homo sapiens ˌhəʊ.məʊˈsæp.i.enz, -ənz, (US) ˌhoʊ.moʊˈ-
homosexual ˌhəʊ.məʊˈsek.ʃu.əl, ˌhɒm.əʊˈ-, ˈ-sju-, -ʃəl, (US) ˌhoʊ.moʊˈsek.ʃu.əl, -məˈ- **-s** -z **-ist/s** -ɪst/s
homosexuality ˌhəʊ.məʊˌsek.ʃuˈæl.ə.ti, ˌhɒm.əʊ-, -sjuˈ-, -ɪ.ti, (US) ˌhoʊ.moʊ.sek.ʃuˈæl.ə.ţi, -mə-
homozygous ˌhɒm.əˈzaɪ.gəs, (US) ˌhoʊ.məˈ-, ˌhɑː-
Homs hɒmz, (US) hɔːmz
homuncul|us hɒmˈʌŋ.kjə.l|əs, həˈmʌŋ-, -kjʊ-, (US) hoʊˈmʌŋ.kjə-, hə- **-i** -aɪ

hon., H~ (abbrev. for **honourable**) ˈɒn.ər.ə.bəl, (US) ˈɑː.nɚ- (abbrev. for **honorary**) ˈɒn.ər.ə.ri, ˈ-ər.i, (US) ˈɑː.nɚ.er.i
honcho ˈhɒn.tʃəʊ, (US) ˈhɑːn.tʃoʊ **-s** -z **-ing** -ɪŋ **-ed** -d
Honda® ˈhɒn.də, (US) ˈhɑːn.də
Hondur|as hɒnˈdjʊə.r|əs, -ˈdʊə-, -ˈdjɔː-, -r|æs, (US) hɑːnˈdʊr|.əs, -ˈdjʊr- **-an/s** -ən/z
hon|e, H~ həʊn, (US) hoʊn **-es** -z **-ing** -ɪŋ **-ed** -d
Honecker ˈhɒn.ɪ.kəʳ, -ek.əʳ, (US) ˈhɑː.nɪ.kɚ
Honegger ˈhɒn.ɪ.gəʳ, -eg.əʳ, (US) ˈhɑː.nɪ.gɚ, ˈhoʊ-
honest ˈɒn.ɪst, -əst, (US) ˈɑː.nɪst **-ly** -li
honest-to-goodness ˌɒn.ɪst.təˈgʊd.nəs, -əst-, -nɪs, (US) ˌɑː.nɪst.təˈ-
honesty ˈɒn.ɪ.sti, ˈ-ə-, (US) ˈɑː.nɪ-
hon|ey ˈhʌn|.i **-eyed** -id **-ied** -id
honeybee ˈhʌn.i.biː **-s** -z
Honeybourne ˈhʌn.i.bɔːn, (US) -bɔːrn
honeybun ˈhʌn.i.bʌn **-s** -z
honeybunch ˈhʌn.i.bʌntʃ **-es** -ɪz
Honeychurch ˈhʌn.i.tʃɜːtʃ, (US) -tʃɝːtʃ
honeycomb, H~ ˈhʌn.i.kəʊm, (US) -koʊm **-s** -z **-ed** -d
honeydew ˈhʌn.i.dʒuː, -djuː, (US) -duː, -djuː ˌ**honeydew** ˈ**melon**
honeyeater ˈhʌn.iˌiː.təʳ, (US) -ţɚ **-s** -z
honeymoon ˈhʌn.i.muːn **-s** -z **-ing** -ɪŋ **-ed** -d **-er/s** -əʳ/z, (US) -ɚ/z
honeysucker ˈhʌn.iˌsʌk.əʳ, (US) -ɚ **-s** -z
honeysuckle ˈhʌn.iˌsʌk.əl **-s** -z
Honeywell ˈhʌn.i.wel
hong hɒŋ, (US) hɑːŋ **-s** -z
Hong Kong ˌhɒŋˈkɒŋ, (US) ˈhɑːŋˌkɑːŋ, ˈhɔːŋ-, -ˌkɔːŋ, ˌ-ˈ-
Honiara ˌhəʊ.niˈɑː.rə, (US) ˌhoʊ.niˈɑːr.ə
Honi soit qui mal y pense ˌɒn.iˌswɑː.kiːˌmæl.iˈpɑ̃ːnts, (US) ˌɔː.ni-
Honiton ˈhɒn.ɪ.tən; *locally:* ˈhʌn-, (US) ˈhɑː.nə.ţən
honk hɒŋk, (US) hɑːŋk, hɔːŋk **-s** -s **-ing** -ɪŋ **-ed** -t
honk|ie, honk|y ˈhɒŋ.k|i, (US) ˈhɑːŋ-, ˈhɔːŋ- **-ies** -iz
honky-tonk ˈhɒŋ.ki.tɒŋk, ˌ--ˈ-, (US) ˈhɑːŋ.ki.tɑːŋk, ˈhɔːŋ-, -tɔːŋk
Honolulu ˌhɒn.əlˈuː.luː, (US) ˌhɑː.nəˈluː-
hon|or, H~ ˈɒn|.əʳ, (US) ˈɑː.n|ɚ **-ors** -əz, (US) -ɚz **-oring** -ər.ɪŋ **-ored** -əd, (US) -ɚd
honorab|le ˈhɒn.ər.ə.b|əl, (US) ˈɑː.nɚ- **-ly** -li **-leness** -əl.nəs, -nɪs
honorarium ˌɒn.əˈreə.ri.əm, -ˈrɑː-, (US) ˌɑː.nəˈrer.i- **-s** -z
honorary ˈɒn.ər.ə.ri, ˈ-ər.i, (US) ˈɑː.nə.rer.i

honorific ˌɒn.əˈrɪf.ɪk, (US) ˌɑː.nəˈrɪf- **-s** -s
Honorius həˈnɔː.ri.əs, hɒnˈɔː-, (US) hoʊˈnɔːr.i-, hə-
hon|our ˈɒn|.əʳ, (US) ˈɑː.n|ɚ **-ours** -əz, (US) -ɚz **-ouring** -ər.ɪŋ **-oured** -əd, (US) -ɚd ˈ**honours** ˌ**list**
honourab|le, H~ ˈɒn.ər.ə.b|əl, (US) ˈɑː.nɚ- **-ly** -li **-leness** -əl.nəs, -nɪs
Honshu ˈhɒn.ʃuː, (US) ˈhɑːn-
Honyman ˈhʌn.i.mən
Hoo huː
hooch huːtʃ
hood, H~ hʊd **-s** -z **-ing** -ɪŋ **-ed** -ɪd **-less** -ləs, -lɪs
-hood hʊd

Note: Suffix. Normally unstressed, e.g. **womanhood** /ˈwʊm.ən.hʊd/.

hoodlum ˈhuːd.ləm, ˈhʊd- **-s** -z
hoodwink ˈhʊd.wɪŋk **-s** -s **-ing** -ɪŋ **-ed** -t
hood|y ˈhʊd|.i **-ies** -iz
hooey ˈhuː.i
hoo|f huː|f, (US) hʊ|f, huː|f **-fs** -fs **-ves** -vz **-fing** -fɪŋ **-fed** -ft **-fer/s** -fəʳ/z, (US) -fɚ/z
Hoog(h)ly ˈhuː.gli
hoo-ha ˈhuː.hɑː **-s** -z
hook, H~ hʊk **-s** -s **-ing** -ɪŋ **-ed** -t ˌ**hook and** ˈ**eye**; ˌ**Hook of** ˈ**Holland**; **by** ˌ**hook or by** ˈ**crook**; ˌ**hook,** ˌ**line, and** ˈ**sinker**
hookah ˈhʊk.ə, -ɑː, (US) ˈhʊk.ə, ˈhuː.kə, -kɑː **-s** -z
Hooke hʊk
hooker, H~ ˈhʊk.əʳ, (US) -ɚ **-s** -z
hookey ˈhʊk.i
hookshot ˈhʊk.ʃɒt, (US) -ʃɑːt **-s** -s
hookup ˈhʊk.ʌp **-s** -s
hookworm ˈhʊk.wɜːm, (US) -wɝːm **-s** -z
hooky ˈhʊk.i
Hooley ˈhuː.li
hooligan, H~ ˈhuː.lɪ.gən, -lə-, (US) -lɪ- **-s** -z **-ism** -ɪ.zəm
Hoon huːn
hoop huːp, (US) huːp, hʊp **-s** -s **-ing** -ɪŋ **-ed** -t
hooper, H~ ˈhuː.pəʳ, (US) -pɚ **-s** -z
hoopla ˈhuːp.lɑː, ˈhʊp-
hoopoe ˈhuː.puː **-s** -z
hoorah hʊˈrɑː, hə-, ˌhuː- **-s** -z
hooray hʊˈreɪ, hə-, ˌhuː-
hooray Henr|y ˌhuː.reɪˈhen.r|i **-ies** -iz
hoot huːt **-s** -s **-ing** -ɪŋ, (US) ˈhuː.ţɪŋ **-ed** -ɪd, (US) ˈhuː.ţɪd
hootch huːtʃ
hootenan|ny ˈhuː.tən.æn|.i **-nies** -iz
hooter ˈhuː.təʳ, (US) -ţɚ **-s** -z
hoov|er, H~® ˈhuː.v|əʳ, (US) -v|ɚ **-ers** -əz, (US) -ɚz **-ering** -ər.ɪŋ **-ered** -əd, (US) -ɚd
hooves (from **hoof**) huːvz, (US) hʊvz, huːvz
hop hɒp, (US) hɑːp **-s** -s **-ping** -ɪŋ **-ped** -t ˌ**hopping** ˈ**mad**

H

Hopcraft ˈhɒp.krɑːft, (US) ˈhɑːp.kræft
hop|e, H~ həʊp, (US) hoʊp **-es** -s **-ing** -ɪŋ **-ed** -t **ˈhope ˌchest**
hopeful, H~ ˈhəʊp.fəl, -fʊl, (US) ˈhoʊp- **-s** -z **-ly** -i **-ness** -nəs, -nɪs
hopeless ˈhəʊp.ləs, -lɪs, (US) ˈhoʊp- **-ly** -li **-ness** -nəs, -nɪs
Hopi ˈhəʊ.pi, (US) ˈhoʊ-
Hopkins ˈhɒp.kɪnz, (US) ˈhɑːp-
Hopkinson ˈhɒp.kɪn.sən, (US) ˈhɑːp-
hoplite ˈhɒp.laɪt, (US) ˈhɑː.plaɪt **-s** -s
hopper, H~ ˈhɒp.əʳ, (US) ˈhɑː.pɚ **-s** -z
hop-pick|er ˈhɒpˌpɪk|.əʳ, (US) ˈhɑːpˌpɪk|.ɚ **-ers** -əz, (US) -ɚz **-ing** -ɪŋ
Hoppner ˈhɒp.nəʳ, (US) ˈhɑːp.nɚ **-s** -z
hopscotch ˈhɒp.skɒtʃ, (US) ˈhɑːp.skɑːtʃ
Hopton ˈhɒp.tən, (US) ˈhɑːp-
Hor hɔːʳ, (US) hɔːr
Horace ˈhɒr.ɪs, -əs, (US) ˈhɔːr.ɪs
Horae ˈhɔː.riː, (US) ˈhoʊ.riː, ˈhɔːr.iː
Horatian həˈreɪ.ʃən, hɒrˈeɪ-, -ʃi.ən, (US) hɔːˈreɪ-, hə-
Horatio həˈreɪ.ʃi.əʊ, hɒrˈeɪ-, (US) hɔːˈreɪ.ʃi.oʊ, hə-
Horati|us həˈreɪ.ʃ|əs, hɒrˈeɪ-, -ʃi|.əs, (US) hɔːˈreɪ-, hə-
Horbury ˈhɔː.bər.i, (US) ˈhɔːrˌber-
horde hɔːd, (US) hɔːrd **-s** -z
Horeb ˈhɔː.reb, (US) ˈhɔːr.eb
horehound ˈhɔː.haʊnd, (US) ˈhɔːr- **-s** -z
horizon həˈraɪ.zən **-s** -z
horizontal ˌhɒr.ɪˈzɒn.təl, -əˈ-, (US) ˌhɔːr.ɪˈzɑːn- **-ly** -i
Horley ˈhɔː.li, (US) ˈhɔːr-
Horlick ˈhɔː.lɪk, (US) ˈhɔːr-
Horlicks® ˈhɔː.lɪks, (US) ˈhɔːr-
hormonal hɔːˈməʊ.nəl, (US) hɔːrˈmoʊ-
hormone ˈhɔː.məʊn, (US) ˈhɔːr.moʊn **-s** -z **ˌhormone reˈplacement ˌtherapy**
Hormuz ˌhɔːˈmuːz, ˈhɔː.məz, (US) ˈhɔːr.mʌz, -muːz
horn, H~ hɔːn, (US) hɔːrn **-s** -z **ˌHorn of ˈAfrica; ˌhorn of ˈplenty; take the ˌbull by the ˈhorns**
hornbeam ˈhɔːn.biːm, ˈhɔːm-, (US) ˈhɔːrn- **-s** -z
hornbill ˈhɔːn.bɪl, ˈhɔːm-, (US) ˈhɔːrn- **-s** -z
hornblende ˈhɔːn.blend, ˈhɔːm-, (US) ˈhɔːrn-
Hornblower ˈhɔːnˌbləʊ.əʳ, ˈhɔːm-, (US) ˈhɔːrnˌbloʊ.ɚ
hornbook ˈhɔːn.bʊk, ˈhɔːm-, (US) ˈhɔːrn- **-s** -s
Hornby ˈhɔːn.bi, ˈhɔːm-, (US) ˈhɔːrn-
Horncastle ˈhɔːnˌkɑː.səl, ˈhɔːŋ-, (US) ˈhɔːrnˌkæs.əl
Hornchurch ˈhɔːn.tʃɜːtʃ, (US) ˈhɔːrn.tʃɝːtʃ
Horne hɔːn, (US) hɔːrn
horned *of cattle, birds, etc.:* hɔːnd, (US) hɔːrnd *poetic:* ˈhɔː.nɪd, (US) ˈhɔːr-
Hornell hɔːˈnel, (US) hɔːr-
Horner ˈhɔː.nəʳ, (US) ˈhɔːr.nɚ
hornet ˈhɔː.nɪt, -nət, (US) ˈhɔːr- **-s** -s **ˈhornet's ˌnest, ˌhornet's ˈnest**
Horniman ˈhɔː.nɪ.mən, (US) ˈhɔːr-
hornpipe ˈhɔːn.paɪp, ˈhɔːm-, (US) ˈhɔːrn- **-s** -s
horn-rimmed ˌhɔːnˈrɪmd, (US) ˈhɔːrn.rɪmd *stress shift, British only:* **ˌhorn-rimmed ˈspectacles**
Hornsea ˈhɔːn.siː, (US) ˈhɔːrn-
Hornsey ˈhɔːn.zi, (US) ˈhɔːrn-
hornswoggl|e ˈhɔːnˌswɒg.əl, (US) ˈhɔːrnˌswɑː.gəl **-es** -z **-ing** -ɪŋ **-ed** -d
Hornung ˈhɔː.nʊŋ, (US) ˈhɔːr-
hornwork ˈhɔːn.wɜːk, (US) ˈhɔːrn.wɝːk **-s** -s
horn|y ˈhɔː.n|i, (US) ˈhɔːr- **-ier** -i.əʳ, (US) -i.ɚ **-iest** -i.ɪst, -i.əst **-iness** -ɪ.nəs, -ɪ.nɪs
horography hɒrˈɒg.rə.fi, hɔːˈrɒg-, hə-, (US) hɔːˈrɑːg-
horolog|e ˈhɒr.ə.lɒdʒ, ˈhɔː.rə-, -ləʊdʒ, (US) ˈhɔːr.ə.loʊdʒ **-es** -ɪz
horologic ˌhɒr.əˈlɒdʒ.ɪk, ˌhɔː.rəˈ-, (US) ˌhɔːr.əˈlɑː.dʒɪk **-al** -əl
horological ˌhɒr.əˈlɒdʒ.ɪ.kəl, ˌhɔː.rəˈ-, (US) ˌhɔːr.əˈlɑː.dʒɪ-
horolog|y hɒrˈɒl.ə.dʒ|i, hɔːˈrɒl-, hə-, (US) hɔːrˈɑː.lə- **-er/s** -əʳ/z, (US) -ɚ/z **-ist/s** -ɪst/s
horoscope ˈhɒr.ə.skəʊp, (US) ˈhɔːr.ə.skoʊp **-s** -s
horoscopic ˌhɒr.əˈskɒp.ɪk, (US) ˌhɔːr.əˈskɑː.pɪk
Horovitz ˈhɒr.ə.vɪts, (US) ˈhɔːr-
Horowitz ˈhɒr.ə.vɪts, -wɪts, (US) ˈhɔːr.ə.wɪts
horrendous hɒrˈen.dəs, həˈren-, (US) hɔːˈren-, hə- **-ly** -li **-ness** -nəs, -nɪs
horrib|le ˈhɒr.ə.b|əl, ˈ-ɪ-, (US) ˈhɔːr- **-ly** -li **-leness** -əl.nəs, -nɪs
horrid ˈhɒr.ɪd, (US) ˈhɔːr- **-er** -əʳ, (US) -ɚ **-est** -ɪst, -əst **-ly** -li **-ness** -nəs, -nɪs
horrific hɒrˈɪf.ɪk, həˈrɪf-, (US) hɔːˈrɪf-, hə- **-ally** -əl.i, -li
horri|fy ˈhɒr.ɪ|.faɪ, ˈ-ə-, (US) ˈhɔːr- **-fies** -faɪz **-fying/ly** -faɪ.ɪŋ/li **-fied** -faɪd
horripilation hɒrˌɪp.ɪˈleɪ.ʃən, -əˈ-; ˌhɒr.ɪ.pɪˈ-, ˌ-ə-, (US) ˌhɔːr.ɪ.pəˈleɪ-
Horrocks ˈhɒr.əks, (US) ˈhɔːr-
horror ˈhɒr.əʳ, (US) ˈhɔːr.ɚ **-s** -z
horror|-stricken ˈhɒr.ə|ˌstrɪk.ən, (US) ˈhɔːr.ɚ|ˌ- **-struck** -strʌk
Horsa ˈhɔː.sə, (US) ˈhɔːr-
hors de combat ˌhɔː.dəˈkɔ̃ːm.bɑː, -ˈkɔːm-, -ˈkɒm-, -bæt, (US) ˌɔːr.də.kɔ̃ːmˈbɑː
hors d'oeuvre ˌɔːˈdɜːv, -ˈdɜːv.rə, (US) ˌɔːrˈdɝːv, -ˈdɝːv.rə **-s** -z
hors|e hɔːs, (US) hɔːrs **-es** -ɪz **-ing** -ɪŋ **-ed** -t **ˌhorse ˈchestnut; ˈhorse ˌopera; ˈhorse ˌsense; ˈhorse ˌshow; ˈhorse ˌtrials; ˌflog a ˌdead ˈhorse; ˌhold your ˈhorses; (ˌstraight) from the ˌhorse's ˈmouth**
horse-and-buggy ˌhɔːs.əndˈbʌg.i, -əmˈ-, (US) ˌhɔːrs-
horseback ˈhɔːs.bæk, (US) ˈhɔːrs- **ˈhorseback ˌriding**
horsebox ˈhɔːs.bɒks, (US) ˈhɔːrs.bɑːks **-es** -ɪz
horse-drawn ˈhɔːs.drɔːn, (US) ˈhɔːrs.drɑːn, -ˈdrɔːn
horseflesh ˈhɔːs.fleʃ, (US) ˈhɔːrs-
horsefl|y ˈhɔːs.fl|aɪ, (US) ˈhɔːrs- **-ies** -aɪz
Horseguard ˈhɔːs.gɑːd, (US) ˈhɔːrs.gɑːrd **-s** -z
horsehair ˈhɔːs.heəʳ, (US) ˈhɔːrs.her **-s** -z
horselaugh ˈhɔːs.lɑːf, (US) ˈhɔːrs.læf **-s** -s
horse|man, H~ ˈhɔːs|.mən, (US) ˈhɔːrs- **-men** -mən, -men **-manship** -mən.ʃɪp
horseplay ˈhɔːs.pleɪ, (US) ˈhɔːrs-
horsepower ˈhɔːsˌpaʊəʳ, -ˌpaʊ.əʳ, (US) ˈhɔːrsˌpaʊ.ɚ
horseradish ˈhɔːsˌræd.ɪʃ, (US) ˈhɔːrs- **-es** -ɪz
horseshoe ˈhɔːs.ʃuː, ˈhɔːʃ-, (US) ˈhɔːrs-, ˈhɔːrʃ- **-s** -z
horsetail ˈhɔːs.teɪl, (US) ˈhɔːrs- **-s** -z
horsetrad|e ˈhɔːs.treɪd, (US) ˈhɔːrs- **-es** -z **-ing** -ɪŋ **-ed** -ɪd **-er/s** -əʳ/z, (US) -ɚ/z
horse-trading ˈhɔːsˌtreɪ.dɪŋ, (US) ˈhɔːrs-
horsewhip ˈhɔːs.*h*wɪp, (US) ˈhɔːrs- **-s** -s **-ping** -ɪŋ **-ped** -t
horse|woman ˈhɔːs|ˌwʊm.ən, (US) ˈhɔːrs- **-women** -ˌwɪm.ɪn
hors|ey ˈhɔː.s|i, (US) ˈhɔːr- **-ier** -i.əʳ, (US) -i.ɚ **-iest** -i.ɪst, -i.əst **-ily** -əl.i, -ɪ.li **-iness** -ɪ.nəs, -ɪ.nɪs
Horsfall ˈhɔːs.fɔːl, (US) ˈhɔːrs.fɔːl, -fɑːl
Horsforth ˈhɔːs.fəθ, (US) ˈhɔːrs.fɚθ
Horsham ˈhɔː.ʃəm, (US) ˈhɔːr-
Horsley ˈhɔːz.li, ˈhɔːs-, (US) ˈhɔːrz-, ˈhɔːrs-
Horsmonden *in Kent:* ˌhɔːz.mənˈden; *old-fashioned local pronunciation:* ˌhɔː.sənˈ-, (US) ˌhɔːrz.mənˈ-
hors|y ˈhɔː.s|i, (US) ˈhɔːr- **-ier** -i.əʳ, (US) -i.ɚ **-iest** -i.ɪst, -i.əst **-ily** -əl.i, -ɪ.li **-iness** -ɪ.nəs, -ɪ.nɪs
horta|tive ˈhɔː.tə|.tɪv, (US) ˈhɔːr.ţə|.ţɪv **-tory** -tər.i, (US) -tɔːr.i
Hortensi|a hɔːˈten*t*.si|.ə, -ˈten.*t*ʃi|.ə, -*t*ʃ|ə, (US) hɔːrˈten.*t*ʃi|- **-us** -əs
horticultural ˌhɔː.tɪˈkʌl.tʃər.əl, -təˈ-, -tʃʊ.rəl, (US) ˌhɔːr.ţəˈkʌl.tʃɚ.əl **-ist/s** -ɪst/s
horticulture ˈhɔː.tɪ.kʌl.tʃəʳ, -tə-, (US) ˈhɔːr.ţə.kʌl.tʃɚ
Horton ˈhɔː.tən, (US) ˈhɔːr-
Horus ˈhɔː.rəs, (US) ˈhɔːr.əs
Horwich ˈhɒr.ɪtʃ, (US) ˈhɔːr.ɪtʃ
Hosack ˈhɒs.ək, (US) ˈhɑː.sək
hosanna həʊˈzæn.ə, (US) hoʊ- **-s** -z
hos|e həʊz, (US) hoʊz **-es** -ɪz **-ing** -ɪŋ **-ed** -d
Hosea həʊˈziː.ə, (US) hoʊˈzeɪ.ə, -ˈziː-

hosepipe ˈhəʊz.paɪp, (US) ˈhoʊz- **-s** -s
hoser ˈhəʊ.zəʳ, (US) ˈhoʊ.zɚ **-s** -z
hosier, H~ ˈhəʊ.zi.əʳ, -ʒəʳ, (US) ˈhoʊ.ʒɚ **-s** -z
hosiery ˈhəʊ.zi.ə.ri, -ʒəʳ.i, (US) ˈhoʊ.ʒɚ.i
Hoskins ˈhɒs.kɪnz, (US) ˈhɑː.skɪnz
Hosmer ˈhɒz.məʳ, (US) ˈhɑːz.mɚ
hospic|e ˈhɒs.pɪs, (US) ˈhɑː.spɪs **-es** -ɪz
hospitab|le hɒsˈpɪt.ə.b|ᵊl, həˈspɪt-; ˈhɒs.pɪ.tə-, (US) ˈhɑː.spɪ.t̬ə-; (US) hɑːˈspɪt̬.ə- **-ly** -li **-leness** -ᵊl.nəs, -nɪs
hospital ˈhɒs.pɪ.tᵊl, (US) ˈhɑː.spɪ.t̬ᵊl **-s** -z
Hospitaler ˈhɒs.pɪ.tᵊl.əʳ, (US) ˈhɑː.spɪ.t̬ᵊl.ɚ **-s** -z
hospitalit|y ˌhɒs.pɪˈtæl.ə.t|i, -pəˈ-, -ɪ.t|i, (US) ˌhɑː.spɪˈtæl.ə.t̬|i **-ies** -iz
hospitalization, -isa- ˌhɒs.pɪ.tᵊl.aɪˈzeɪ.ʃᵊn, -pə-, -ɪˈ-, (US) ˌhɑː.spɪ.t̬ᵊl.əˈ-
hospitaliz|e, -is|e ˈhɒs.pɪ.tᵊl.aɪz, -pə-, (US) ˈhɑː.spɪ.t̬ᵊl- **-es** -ɪz **-ing** -ɪŋ **-ed** -d
Hospitaller ˈhɒs.pɪ.tᵊl.əʳ, (US) ˈhɑː.spɪ.t̬ᵊl.ɚ **-s** -z
host, H~ həʊst, (US) hoʊst **-s** -s **-ing** -ɪŋ **-ed** -ɪd
hosta ˈhɒs.tə, ˈhəʊ.stə, (US) ˈhɑː.stə, ˈhoʊ- **-s** -z
hostag|e ˈhɒs.tɪdʒ, (US) ˈhɑː.stɪdʒ **-es** -ɪz
hostel ˈhɒs.tᵊl, (US) ˈhɑː.stᵊl **-s** -z
hostel|ler ˈhɒs.tᵊl|.əʳ, (US) ˈhɑː.stᵊl|.ɚ **-ers** -əz, (US) -ɚz **-ing** -ɪŋ
hostelr|y ˈhɒs.tᵊl.r|i, (US) ˈhɑː.stᵊl- **-ies** -iz
hostess ˈhəʊ.stɪs, -stes, -stəs; ˌhəʊˈstes, (US) ˈhoʊ.stɪs, -stəs **-es** -ɪz
hostile ˈhɒs.taɪl, (US) ˈhɑː.stᵊl, -staɪl **-ly** -li
hostilit|y hɒsˈtɪl.ə.t|i, -ɪ.t|i, (US) hɑːˈstɪl.ə.t̬|i **-ies** -iz
hostler ˈɒs.ləʳ, ˈhɒs-, (US) ˈhɑː.slɚ, ˈɑː- **-s** -z
hot hɒt, (US) hɑːt **-ter** -əʳ, (US) ˈhɑː.t̬ɚ **-test** -ɪst, -əst, (US) ˈhɑː.t̬ɪst, -t̬əst **-ly** -li **-ness** -nəs, -nɪs **-s** -s **-ting** -ɪŋ, (US) ˈhɑː.t̬ɪŋ **-ted** -ɪd, (US) ˈhɑː.t̬ɪd **hot ˈair; ˌhot cross ˈbun; ˈhot ˌdog; ˌhot ˈdog; ˈhot ˌpants; ˌhot poˈtato; ˈhot ˌseat; ˌhot ˈseat; ˌhot ˈstuff; ˌhot ˈticket; ˌhot ˈwater; ˌblow ˌhot and ˈcold; ˌsell like ˌhot ˈcakes** (US) **ˌsell like ˈhot ˌcakes**
hotbed ˈhɒt.bed, (US) ˈhɑːt- **-s** -z
hot-blooded ˌhɒtˈblʌd.ɪd, (US) ˌhɑːt- *stress shift:* **ˌhot-blooded ˈyouth**
Hotchkiss ˈhɒtʃ.kɪs, (US) ˈhɑːtʃ-
hotchpot ˈhɒtʃ.pɒt, (US) ˈhɑːtʃ.pɑːt **-s** -s
hotchpotch ˈhɒtʃ.pɒtʃ, (US) ˈhɑːtʃ.pɑːtʃ **-es** -ɪz
hotdesk ˈhɒt.desk, (US) ˈhɑːt- **-ing** -ɪŋ
hotdog ˈhɒt.dɒg, (US) ˈhɑːt.dɑːg, -dɔːg **-s** -z **-ging** -ɪŋ **-ged** -d

hotel həʊˈtel, əʊ-, (US) hoʊ- **-s** -z

> Note: Old-fashioned British pronunciation treats this as having 'silent h' after the indefinite article, thus 'an hotel' /ən.əʊˈtel/.

hotelier həʊˈtel.i.eɪ, əʊ-, -əʳ, (US) ˌhoʊ.tᵊlˈjeɪ, ˌoʊ-; (US) hoʊˈtel.jɚ **-s** -z
hoteling həʊˈtel.ɪŋ, (US) hoʊ-
hotfoo|t ˌhɒtˈfʊ|t, ˈ--, (US) ˈhɑːt.fʊ|t **-ts** -ts **-ting** -tɪŋ, (US) -t̬ɪŋ **-ted** -tɪd, (US) -t̬ɪd
Hotham ˈhʌð.əm
hothead ˈhɒt.hed, (US) ˈhɑːt- **-s** -z
hotheaded ˌhɒtˈhed.ɪd, ˈ-ˌ--, (US) ˈhɑːtˌhed.ɪd, ˌ-ˈ-- **-ly** -li **-ness** -nəs, -nɪs
hothou|se ˈhɒt.haʊ|s, (US) ˈhɑːt- **-ses** -zɪz
hotline ˈhɒt.laɪn, (US) ˈhɑːt- **-s** -z
Hotol ˈhɒt.ɒl, ˈhoʊ.tɒl, (US) ˈhɑː.tɑːl, ˈhoʊ-
hotplate ˈhɒt.pleɪt, (US) ˈhɑːt- **-s** -s
Hotpoint® ˈhɒt.pɔɪnt, (US) ˈhɑːt-
hotpot ˈhɒt.pɒt, (US) ˈhɑːt.pɑːt **-s** -s
hotrod ˈhɒt.rɒd, (US) ˈhɑːt.rɑːd **-s** -z **-ding** -ɪŋ **-ded** -ɪd **-der/s** -əʳ/z, (US) -ɚ/z
hotshot ˈhɒt.ʃɒt, (US) ˈhɑːt.ʃɑːt **-s** -s
hotspot ˈhɒt.spɒt, (US) ˈhɑːt.spɑːt **-s** -s
hotspur, H~ ˈhɒt.spɜːʳ, -spəʳ, (US) ˈhɑːt.spɝː, -spɚ **-s** -z
hot-tempered ˌhɒtˈtem.pəd, (US) ˌhɑːtˈtem.pɚd *stress shift:* **ˌhot-tempered ˈfighter**
Hottentot ˈhɒt.ᵊn.tɒt, (US) ˈhɑː.tᵊn.tɑːt **-s** -s
hot-water bottle ˌhɒtˈwɔː.təˌbɒt.ᵊl, (US) ˌhɑːtˈwɑː.t̬əˌbɑː.t̬ᵊl, -ˈwɔː- **-s** -z
hot-wir|e ˈhɒt.waɪəʳ, -waɪ.əʳ, (US) ˈhɑːt.waɪ.ɚ **-es** -z **-ing** -ɪŋ **-ed** -d
Houdini huːˈdiː.ni
hough hɒk, (US) hɑːk **-s** -s **-ing** -ɪŋ **-ed** -t
Hough hʌf, hɒf, haʊ, (US) hʌf, hɔːf, hɑːf
Houghall ˈhɒf.ᵊl, (US) ˈhɑː.fᵊl
Hougham ˈhʌf.əm
Houghton ˈhɔː.tᵊn, ˈhaʊ-, ˈhəʊ-, (US) ˈhoʊ-, ˈhɔː-, ˈhɑː-, ˈhaʊ-

> Note: /ˈhɔː.tᵊn, ˈhaʊ.tᵊn/ are more usual in British English when the word is a surname. The city in Michigan is /ˈhəʊ-/ (US) /ˈhoʊ-/.

Houghton-le-Spring ˌhəʊ.tᵊn.ləˈsprɪŋ, ˌhaʊ-, -liˈ-, (US) ˌhoʊ-, ˌhaʊ-
Houllier ˈ*h*uː.li.eɪ
Houltby ˈhəʊlt.bi, (US) ˈhoʊlt-
houm(o)us ˈhuː.mʊs, ˈhʊm.ʊs, -əs, (US) ˈhʌm.əs, ˈhʊm-
hound haʊnd **-s** -z **-ing** -ɪŋ **-ed** -ɪd
Houndsditch ˈhaʊndz.dɪtʃ
houndstooth ˈhaʊndz.tuːθ, ˌ-ˈ-, (US) ˈ--

Hounslow ˈhaʊnz.ləʊ, (US) -loʊ
hour aʊəʳ, ˈaʊ.əʳ, (US) ˈaʊ.ɚ, aʊr **-s** -z **-ly** -li
hourglass ˈaʊə.glɑːs, ˈaʊ.ə-, (US) ˈaʊ.ɚ.glæs, ˈaʊr- **-es** -ɪz
houri ˈhʊə.ri, (US) ˈhʊr.i, ˈhuːr- **-s** -z
Housden ˈhaʊz.dən
hou|se, H~ n haʊ|s **-ses** -zɪz **ˌhouse arˈrest; ˈhouse ˌhusband; ˈhouse ˌmartin; ˈhouse ˌmusic; ˌHouse of ˈCommons; ˌHouse of ˈLords; ˌHouse of RepreˈSentatives; ˌHouses of ˈParliament; ˈhouse ˌparty; ˈhouse ˌsparrow; ˌbring the ˈhouse ˌdown; ˌeat someone out of ˌhouse and ˈhome; get ˌon like a ˈhouse on ˌfire; ˌset one's ˈhouse in ˌorder**
hous|e v haʊz **-es** -ɪz **-ing** -ɪŋ **-ed** -d
houseboat ˈhaʊs.bəʊt, (US) -boʊt **-s** -s
housebound ˈhaʊs.baʊnd
housebreak|er ˈhaʊsˌbreɪ.k|əʳ, (US) -k|ɚ **-ers** -əz, (US) -ɚz **-ing** -ɪŋ
house-broken ˈhaʊsˌbrəʊ.kᵊn, (US) -ˌbroʊ-
housebuy|er ˈhaʊsˌbaɪ|.əʳ, (US) -ɚ **-ers** -z **-ing** -ɪŋ
housecoat ˈhaʊs.kəʊt, (US) -koʊt **-s** -s
housefather ˈhaʊsˌfɑː.ðəʳ, (US) -ðɚ **-s** -z
housefl|y ˈhaʊs.fl|aɪ **-ies** -aɪz
houseful ˈhaʊs.fʊl **-s** -z
houseguest ˈhaʊs.gest **-s** -s
household, H~ ˈhaʊs.*h*əʊld, (US) -*h*oʊld **-s** -z **-er/s** -əʳ/z, (US) -ɚ/z
housekeeper ˈhaʊsˌkiː.pəʳ, (US) -pɚ **-s** -z
housekeeping ˈhaʊsˌkiː.pɪŋ
Housel ˈhaʊ.zᵊl
houseleek ˈhaʊs.liːk **-s** -s
housemaid ˈhaʊs.meɪd **-s** -z
house|man ˈhaʊs|.mən, -mæn **-men** -mən, -men
housemaster ˈhaʊsˌmɑː.stəʳ, (US) -ˌmæs.tɚ **-s** -z
housemate ˈhaʊs.meɪt **-s** -s
housemistress ˈhaʊsˌmɪs.trəs, -trɪs **-es** -ɪz
housemother ˈhaʊsˌmʌð.əʳ, (US) -ɚ **-s** -z
houseplant ˈhaʊs.plɑːnt, (US) -plænt **-s** -s
houseproud ˈhaʊs.praʊd
houseroom ˈhaʊs.rʊm, -ruːm, (US) -ruːm, -rʊm
house|sit ˈhaʊs|.sɪt **-sits** -sɪts **-sitting** -ˌsɪt.ɪŋ, (US) -ˌsɪt̬.ɪŋ **-sat** -sæt **-sitter/s** -ˌsɪt.əʳ/z, (US) -ˌsɪt̬.ɚ/z
Housesteads Fort ˌhaʊs.stedzˈfɔːt, (US) -ˈfɔːrt
house-to-house ˌhaʊs.təˈhaʊs *stress shift:* **house-to-house ˈsearch**
housetop ˈhaʊs.tɒp, (US) -tɑːp **-s** -s
house-trained ˈhaʊs.treɪnd
housewares ˈhaʊs.weəz, (US) -werz
housewarming ˈhaʊsˌwɔː.mɪŋ, (US) -ˌwɔːr- **-s** -z

housewife *woman:* ˈhaʊs.waɪf **housewives** ˈhaʊs.waɪvz

Note: An older pronunciation of this word, /ˈhʌz.ɪf/, recorded in earlier editions of this dictionary, seems now to have become extinct. It also referred to a type of needle-case.

housewifel|y ˈhaʊsˌwaɪf.l|i **-iness** -ɪ.nəs, -ɪ.nɪs
housewifery ˈhaʊsˌwɪf.ər.i; *old-fashioned:* ˈhʌz.ɪ.fri, (US) ˈhaʊsˌwaɪ.fɚ.i, ˌ-fri
housework ˈhaʊs.wɜːk, (US) -wɝːk
housey-housey, housie-housie ˌhaʊ.siˈhaʊ.si, -ziˈhaʊ.zi
housing ˈhaʊ.zɪŋ **ˈhousing asˌsociation; ˈhousing deˌvelopment; ˈhousing eˌstate; ˈhousing ˌlist**
Housman ˈhaʊs.mən
Houston *English surname:* ˈhuː.stən, ˈhaʊ- *Scottish surname:* ˈhuː.stən *in US:* ˈhjuː.stən
Houyhnhnm ˈhuː.ɪ.nəm, (US) ˈhwɪn.əm, huˈɪn- **-s** -z
hove, H~ (from **heave**) həʊv, (US) hoʊv
hovel ˈhɒv.əl, ˈhʌv-, (US) ˈhʌv-, ˈhɑː.vəl **-s** -z
Hovell ˈhəʊ.vəl, ˈhɒv.əl, həʊˈvel, (US) ˈhoʊ.vəl, ˈhɑː-, hoʊˈvel
Hovenden ˈhɒv.ən.dən, (US) ˈhoʊ.vən-
hov|er ˈhɒv|.ər, (US) ˈhʌv|.ɚ, ˈhɑː.v|ɚ **-ers** -əz, (US) -ɚz **-ering** -ər.ɪŋ **-ered** -əd, (US) -ɚd
hovercraft ˈhɒv.ə.krɑːft, (US) ˈhʌv.ɚ.kræft, ˈhɑː.vɚ- **-s** -s
hoverfl|y ˈhɒv.ə.fl|aɪ, (US) ˈhʌv.ɚ-, ˈhɑː.vɚ- **-ies** -aɪz
hoverport ˈhɒv.ə.pɔːt, (US) ˈhʌv.ɚ.pɔːrt, ˈhɑː.vɚ- **-s** -s
Hovis® ˈhəʊ.vɪs, (US) ˈhoʊ-
how, H~ haʊ
Howard ˈhaʊ.əd, (US) ˈhaʊ.ɚd
Howarth ˈhaʊ.əθ, (US) ˈhaʊ.ɚθ
howdah ˈhaʊ.də **-s** -z
Howden ˈhaʊ.dən
how-do-you-do ˌhaʊ.dʒəˈduː, -djəˈ-, -dʒuˈ-, -djuˈ-, ˈ---, (US) ˈhaʊ.də.ju.duː, ˈ-djə.duː
howdy ˈhaʊ.di
howdy-do ˌhaʊ.diˈduː **-s** -z
Howe haʊ
Howell ˈhaʊ.əl **-s** -z
Howerd ˈhaʊ.əd, (US) ˈhaʊ.ɚd
Howers ˈhaʊ.əz, (US) ˈhaʊ.ɚz
Howes haʊz
however haʊˈev.ər, (US) -ɚ
Howick ˈhaʊ.ɪk
Howie ˈhaʊ.i
Howitt ˈhaʊ.ɪt
howitzer ˈhaʊ.ɪt.sər, (US) -sɚ **-s** -z
howl haʊl **-s** -z **-ing** -ɪŋ **-ed** -d
howler ˈhaʊ.lər, (US) -lɚ **-s** -z
Howlett ˈhaʊ.lɪt
Howley ˈhaʊ.li
Howorth ˈhaʊ.əθ, (US) ˈhaʊ.ɚθ
Howse haʊz
howsoever ˌhaʊ.səʊˈev.ər, (US) -soʊˈev.ɚ
Howson ˈhaʊ.sən
Howth həʊθ, (US) hoʊθ
how-to ˈhaʊ.tuː **-s** -z
Hoxha ˈhɒdʒ.ə, (US) ˈhɔː.ʒdɑː
Hoxton ˈhɒk.stən, (US) ˈhɑːk-
hoy, H~ hɔɪ **-s** -z
hoyden, H~ ˈhɔɪ.dən **-s** -z
Hoylake ˈhɔɪ.leɪk
Hoyland Nether ˌhɔɪ.lənd̚ˈneð.ər, (US) -ɚ
HP ˌeɪtʃˈpiː
HQ ˌeɪtʃˈkjuː
HRH ˌeɪtʃ.ɑːrˈeɪtʃ, (US) -ɑːrˈ-
HRT ˌeɪtʃ.ɑːˈtiː, (US) -ɑːrˈ-
HSBC ˌeɪtʃ.esˌbiːˈsiː
HTML ˌeɪtʃ.tiː.emˈel
http ˌeɪtʃ.tiː.tiːˈpiː
Hu huː
Huang Ho ˌhwæŋˈhəʊ, (US) ˌhwɑːŋˈhoʊ, ˌhwæŋ-
hub hʌb **-s** -z
Hubbard ˈhʌb.əd, (US) -ɚd
Hubble ˈhʌb.əl
hubble-bubble ˈhʌb.əlˌbʌb.əl **-s** -z
hubbub ˈhʌb.ʌb, -əb, (US) -ʌb **-s** -z
hubb|y ˈhʌb|.i **-ies** -iz
hubcap ˈhʌb.kæp **-s** -s
Hubert ˈhjuː.bət, (US) -bɚt
hubris ˈhjuː.brɪs, ˈhuː-, (US) ˈhjuː-
hubristic hjuːˈbrɪs.tɪk, huː-, (US) hjuː-
huckaback ˈhʌk.ə.bæk **-s** -s
Huckabee ˈhʌk.ə.biː
Huckle ˈhʌk.əl
huckleberr|y, H~ ˈhʌk.əl.bər|.i, -ˌber|.i, (US) -ˈber- **-ies** -iz
Hucknall, Hucknell ˈhʌk.nəl
huckster ˈhʌk.stər, (US) -stɚ **-s** -z
HUD hʌd
Huddersfield ˈhʌd.əz.fiːld, (US) -ɚz-
huddl|e ˈhʌd.əl **-es** -z **-ing** -ɪŋ, ˈhʌd.lɪŋ **-ed** -d
Hudibras ˈhjuː.dɪ.bræs, -də-
Hud(d)leston(e) ˈhʌd.əl.stən
Hudnott ˈhʌd.nɒt, -nət, (US) -nɑːt
Hudson ˈhʌd.sən
hue hjuː **-s** -z **ˌhue and ˈcry**
Hueffer ˈhef.ər, (US) -ɚ
Huelva ˈwel.və, (US) -və, -vɑː
huevos rancheros ˌweɪ.vɒs.rænˈtʃeə.rɒs, (US) -voʊs.rænˈtʃer.oʊs
huff, H~ hʌf **-s** -s **-ing** -ɪŋ **-ed** -t
huffish ˈhʌf.ɪʃ **-ly** -li **-ness** -nəs, -nɪs
Huffman ˈhʌf.mən
huff|y ˈhʌf|.i **-ier** -i.ər, (US) -i.ɚ **-iest** -i.ɪst, -i.əst **-ily** -əl.i, -ɪ.li **-iness** -ɪ.nəs, -ɪ.nɪs
hug hʌg **-s** -z **-ging** -ɪŋ **-ged** -d
Hugall ˈhjuː.gəl
hug|e hjuːdʒ **-er** -ər, (US) -ɚ **-est** -ɪst, -əst **-ely** -li **-eness** -nəs, -nɪs
hugger-mugger ˈhʌg.əˌmʌg.ər, ˌhʌg.əˈmʌg-, (US) ˈhʌg.ɚˌmʌg.ɚ
Huggin ˈhʌg.ɪn **-s** -z
Hugh hjuː
Hughenden ˈhjuː.ən.dən
Hughes hjuːz
Hugo ˈhjuː.gəʊ, (US) -goʊ
Hugon ˈhjuː.gən, -gɒn, (US) -gɑːn
Huguenot ˈhjuː.gə.nəʊ, ˈhuː-, -nɒt, (US) ˈhjuː.gə.nɑːt **-s** -z
Huish ˈhjuː.ɪʃ
hula ˈhuː.lə **-s** -z
Hula-Hoop® ˈhuː.lə.huːp **-s** -s
Hulbert ˈhʌl.bət, (US) -bɚt
hulk hʌlk **-s** -s **-ing** -ɪŋ
hull, H~ hʌl **-s** -z **-ing** -ɪŋ **-ed** -d
hullabaloo ˌhʌl.ə.bəˈluː **-s** -z
Hullah ˈhʌl.ə
Hullbridge ˈhʌl.brɪdʒ
hullo həˈləʊ, hʌlˈəʊ, (US) həˈloʊ, hʌlˈoʊ **-s** -z
Hulme hjuːm, huːm
Hulse hʌls
Hulsean hʌlˈsiː.ən
hum n, v hʌm **-s** -z **-ming** -ɪŋ **-med** -d **ˈhumming ˌtop**
human, H~ ˈhjuː.mən **-s** -z **-ly** -li **ˌhuman ˈbeing; ˌhuman ˈnature; ˌhuman ˈrace; ˌhuman ˈrights**
human|e hjuːˈmeɪn **-er** -ər, (US) -ɚ **-est** -ɪst, -əst **-ely** -li **-eness** -nəs, -nɪs
human|ism ˈhjuː.mə.n|ɪ.zəm **-ist/s** -ɪst/s
humanistic ˌhjuː.məˈnɪs.tɪk
humanitarian hjuːˌmæn.ɪˈteə.ri.ən, -əˈ-; ˌhjuː.mæn-, (US) hjuːˌmæn.əˈter.i- **-s** -z **-ism** -ɪ.zəm
humanit|y hjuːˈmæn.ə.t|i, -ɪ.t|i, (US) -ə.ţ|i **-ies** -iz
humanization, -isa- ˌhjuː.mə.naɪˈzeɪ.ʃən, -nɪˈ-, (US) -nəˈ-
humaniz|e, -is|e ˈhjuː.mə.naɪz **-es** -ɪz **-ing** -ɪŋ **-ed** -d
humankind ˌhjuː.mənˈkaɪnd, -məŋˈ-, (US) -mənˈ-
humanoid ˈhjuː.mə.nɔɪd **-s** -z
Humber ˈhʌm.bər, (US) -bɚ **-s** -z **-side** -saɪd
Humberston ˈhʌm.bə.stən, (US) -bɚ-
Humbert ˈhʌm.bət, (US) -bɚt
humb|le ˈhʌm.b|əl **-ler** -lər, (US) -lɚ **-lest** -lɪst, -ləst **-ly** -li **-leness** -əl.nəs, -nɪs **-les** -əlz **-ling** -əl.ɪŋ, (US) -lɪŋ **-led** -əld **eat ˌhumble ˈpie**
Humblethwaite ˈhʌm.bəl.θweɪt
Humboldt ˈhʌm.bəʊlt, ˈhʊm-, (US) -boʊlt
Humbrol® ˈhʌm.brɒl, (US) -brɑːl
humbug ˈhʌm.bʌg **-s** -z **-ging** -ɪŋ **-ged** -d
humdinger ˌhʌmˈdɪŋ.ər, (US) -ɚ **-s** -z
humdrum ˈhʌm.drʌm
Hume hjuːm
humectant hjuːˈmek.tənt **-s** -s
humer|us ˈhjuː.mər|.əs **-i** -aɪ **-al** -əl
Humian ˈhjuː.mi.ən
humid ˈhjuː.mɪd **-ness** -nəs, -nɪs
humidification hjuːˌmɪd.ɪ.fɪˈkeɪ.ʃən, ˌ-ə-, -fəˈ-
humidifier hjuːˈmɪd.ɪ.faɪ.ər, ˈ-ə-, (US) -ɚ **-s** -z
humidif|y hjuːˈmɪd.ɪ.f|aɪ, ˈ-ə- **-ies** -aɪz **-ying** -aɪ.ɪŋ **-ied** -aɪd **-ier/s** -aɪ.ər/z, (US) -aɪ.ɚ/z

humidity hjuːˈmɪd.ə.ti, -ɪ.ti, (US) -ə.t̬i
humili|ate hjuːˈmɪl.i|.eɪt **-ates** -eɪts **-ating/ly** -eɪ.tɪŋ/li, (US) -eɪ.t̬ɪŋ/li **-ated** -eɪ.tɪd, (US) -eɪ.t̬ɪd
humiliation hjuːˌmɪl.iˈeɪ.ʃən, ˌhjuː.mɪ.liˈ-, (US) hjuːˌmɪl.iˈ- **-s** -z
humility hjuːˈmɪl.ə.ti, -ɪt.i, (US) -ə.t̬i
Hummer® ˈhʌm.əʳ, (US) -ɚ **-s** -z
hummingbird ˈhʌm.ɪŋ.bɜːd, (US) -bɝːd **-s** -z
hummock ˈhʌm.ək **-s** -s **-y** -i
hummus ˈhʊm.ʊs, ˈhʌm-, -əs, ˈhuː.məs, (US) ˈhʌm.əs, ˈhʊm-
humongous hjuːˈmʌŋ.gəs
hum|or ˈhjuː.m|əʳ, (US) -m|ɚ **-ors** -əz, (US) -ɚz **-oring** -ər.ɪŋ **-ored** -əd, (US) -ɚd **-orless/ly** -ə.ləs/li, -ɚ.lɪs/li
humoral ˈhjuː.mər.əl
humoresque ˌhjuː.mərˈesk, (US) -məˈresk **-s** -s
humorist ˈhjuː.mər.ɪst **-s** -s
humoristic ˌhjuː.mərˈɪs.tɪk
humorous ˈhjuː.mər.əs **-ly** -li **-ness** -nəs, -nɪs
hum|our ˈhjuː.m|əʳ, (US) -m|ɚ **-ours** -əz, (US) -ɚz **-ouring** -ər.ɪŋ **-oured** -əd, (US) -ɚd **-ourless/ly** -ə.ləs/li, -ɚ.lɪs/li
humoursome ˈhjuː.mə.səm, (US) -mɚ- **-ly** -li **-ness** -nəs, -nɪs
hump hʌmp **-s** -s **-ing** -ɪŋ **-ed** -t
humpback ˈhʌmp.bæk **-s** -s **-ed** -t ˌ**humpbacked** ˈ**bridge**
Humperdinck ˈhʌm.pə.dɪŋk, (US) -pɚ-
humph **interj** m̥m, hə̃h, hʌmf

> Note: Interjection indicating annoyance or disapproval, with rapid fall in pitch. The transcriptions reflect a wide range of possible pronunciations. The small circle under the /m/ symbol indicates a voiceless consonant.

Humphries ˈhʌmp.friz
Humphr(e)y ˈhʌmp.fri **-s** -z
Humpty Dumpty ˌhʌmp.tiˈdʌmp.ti
hump|y ˈhʌm.p|i **-ier** -i.əʳ, (US) -i.ɚ **-iest** -i.ɪst, -i.əst **-iness** -ɪ.nəs, -ɪ.nɪs
humungous hjuːˈmʌŋ.gəs
humus ˈhjuː.məs
humvee, H~ ˈhʌm.viː **-s** -z
Hun hʌn **-s** -z
hunch hʌntʃ **-es** -ɪz **-ing** -ɪŋ **-ed** -t
hunchback ˈhʌntʃ.bæk **-s** -s **-ed** -t
hundred ˈhʌn.drəd, -drɪd **-s** -z
hundredfold ˈhʌn.drəd.fəʊld, -drɪd-, (US) -foʊld
hundredth ˈhʌn.drədθ, -drɪdθ, -drətθ, -drɪtθ **-s** -s
hundredweight ˈhʌn.drəd.weɪt, -drɪd- **-s** -s
hung (from **hang**) hʌŋ ˌ**hung** ˈ**jury**; ˌ**hung** ˈ**parliament**
Hungarian hʌŋˈgeə.ri.ən, (US) -ˈger.i- **-s** -z
Hungary ˈhʌŋ.gər.i
hung|er ˈhʌŋ.g|əʳ, (US) -g|ɚ **-ers** -əz, (US) -ɚz **-ering** -ər.ɪŋ **-ered** -əd, (US) -ɚd ˈ**hunger** ˌ**strike**; ˈ**hunger** ˌ**striker**
Hungerford ˈhʌŋ.gə.fəd, (US) -gɚ.fɚd
hungerstrik|e ˈhʌŋ.gə.straɪk, (US) -gɚ- **-es** -s **-ing** -ɪŋ **hungerstruck** ˈhʌŋ.gə.strʌk, (US) -gɚ-
hungover ˌhʌŋˈəʊ.vəʳ, (US) -ˈoʊ.vɚ
hungr|y ˈhʌŋ.gr|i **-ier** -i.əʳ, (US) -i.ɚ **-iest** -i.ɪst, -i.əst **-ily** -əl.i, -ɪ.li **-iness** -ɪ.nəs, -ɪ.nɪs
hunk hʌŋk **-s** -s
hunk|y ˈhʌŋ.k|i **-ier** -i.əʳ, (US) -i.ɚ **-iest** -i.ɪst, -i.əst
hunky-dory ˌhʌŋ.kiˈdɔː.ri, (US) -ˈdɔːr.i
hunnish, H~ ˈhʌn.ɪʃ
Hunslet ˈhʌnz.lət, -lɪt, ˈhʌn.slɪt, -slət
Hunstanton hʌnˈstæn.tən; *locally:* ˈhʌn.stən-
Hunsworth ˈhʌnz.wəθ, (US) -wɚθ
hunt, H~ hʌnt **-s** -s **-er/s** -əʳ/z, (US) -ɚ/z **-ing** -ɪŋ, (US) ˈhʌn.t̬ɪŋ **-ed** -ɪd, (US) ˈhʌn.t̬ɪd ˈ**hunting** ˌ**ground**; ˈ**hunting** ˌ**horn**; ˈ**hunting** ˌ**knife**
hunter-gatherer ˌhʌn.təˈgæð.ər.əʳ, (US) -t̬ɚˈgæð.ɚ.ɚ **-s** -z
Hunterian hʌnˈtɪə.ri.ən, (US) -ˈtɪr.i-
Huntingdon ˈhʌn.tɪŋ.dən **-shire** -ʃəʳ, -ʃɪəʳ, (US) -ʃɚ, -ʃɪr
Huntingdonian ˌhʌn.tɪŋˈdəʊ.ni.ən, (US) -ˈdoʊ- **-s** -z
Huntingford ˈhʌn.tɪŋ.fəd, (US) -fɚd
Huntington ˈhʌn.tɪŋ.tən ˌ**Huntington's cho**ˈ**rea**
Huntl(e)y ˈhʌnt.li
Hunton ˈhʌn.tən, (US) -tən
huntress ˈhʌn.trəs, -trɪs **-es** -ɪz
Hunts. (abbrev. for **Huntingdonshire**) hʌnts; ˈhʌn.tɪŋ.dən.ʃəʳ, -ʃɪəʳ, (US) hʌnts; (US) ˈhʌn.tɪŋ.dən.ʃɚ, -ʃɪr
hunts|man ˈhʌnts|.mən **-men** -mən, -men **-manship** -mən.ʃɪp
Huntsville ˈhʌnts.vɪl
Hunyadi ˈhʊn.jɑː.di, ˈhʌn-, -ˈ--, (US) ˈhʊn.jɑː.di
Hurd hɜːd, (US) hɝːd
hurdl|e ˈhɜː.dəl **-es** -z **-ing** -ɪŋ, ˈhɜːd.lɪŋ, (US) ˈhɝːd- **-ed** -d **-er/s** -əʳ/z, (US) -ɚ/z
hurdy-gurd|y ˈhɜː.diˌgɜː.d|i, ˌhɜː.diˈgɜː-, (US) ˌhɝː.diˈgɝː.d|i, ˈhɝː.diˌgɝː- **-ies** -iz
Hurford ˈhɜː.fəd, (US) ˈhɝː.fɚd
hurl hɜːl, (US) hɝːl **-s** -z **-ing** -ɪŋ **-ed** -d **-er/s** -əʳ/z, (US) -ɚ/z
hurley, H~ ˈhɜː.li, (US) ˈhɝː- **-s** -z
hurling ˈhɜː.lɪŋ, (US) ˈhɝː-
Hurlingham ˈhɜː.lɪŋ.əm, (US) ˈhɝː-
Hurlstone ˈhɜːl.stən, (US) ˈhɝːl-
hurly-burly ˈhɜː.liˌbɜː.li, ˌhɜː.liˈbɜː-, (US) ˈhɝː.liˌbɝːr-, ˌhɝː.liˈbɝːr-
Huron ˈhjʊə.rən, -rɒn, (US) ˈhjʊr.ɑːn, -ən
hurrah həˈrɑː, hʊ-, (US) -ˈrɑː, -ˈrɔː **-s** -z **-ing** -ɪŋ **-ed** -d
hurray həˈreɪ, hʊ- **-s** -z
Hurrell ˈhʌr.əl, ˈhʊə.rəl, (US) ˈhɝː.əl
hurricane ˈhʌr.ɪ.kən, ˈ-ə-, -keɪn, (US) ˈhɝː.ɪ.keɪn, -kən **-s** -z ˈ**hurricane** ˌ**lamp**
hurried ˈhʌr.id, (US) ˈhɝː- **-ly** -li
hurr|y, H~ ˈhʌr|.i, (US) ˈhɝː- **-ies** -i.z **-ying** -i.ɪŋ
hurry-scurry ˌhʌr.iˈskʌr.i, (US) ˌhɝː.iˈskɝːr-
hurst, H~ hɜːst, (US) hɝːst **-s** -s
Hurstmonceux ˌhɜːst.mənˈzuː, -mɒnˈ-, -ˈsjuː, -ˈsuː, (US) ˈhɝːst.mən.suː, ˌ--ˈ-
Hurston ˈhɜː.stən, (US) ˈhɝː-
Hurstpierpoint ˌhɜːst.pɪəˈpɔɪnt, (US) ˌhɝːst.pɪrˈ-
hurt, H~ hɜːt, (US) hɝːt **-s** -s **-ing** -ɪŋ, (US) ˈhɝː.t̬ɪŋ
hurtful ˈhɜːt.fəl, -fʊl, (US) ˈhɝːt- **-ly** -i **-ness** -nəs, -nɪs
hurtl|e ˈhɜː.təl, (US) -t̬əl **-es** -z **-ing** -ɪŋ, ˈhɜːt.lɪŋ, (US) ˈhɝːt- **-ed** -d
husband ˈhʌz.bənd **-s** -z **-ing** -ɪŋ **-ed** -ɪd **-ly** -li
husband|man ˈhʌz.bənd|.mən **-men** -mən, -men
husbandry ˈhʌz.bən.dri
hush hʌʃ **-es** -ɪz **-ing** -ɪŋ **-ed** -t ˈ**hush** ˌ**money**
hushaby ˈhʌʃ.ə.baɪ
hush-hush ˌhʌʃˈhʌʃ *stress shift:* ˌ**hush-hush** ˈ**service**
Hush Puppies® ˈhʌʃˌpʌp.iz
husk, H~ hʌsk **-s** -s
Huskisson ˈhʌs.kɪ.sən, -kə-
husk|y ˈhʌs.k|i **-ier** -i.əʳ, (US) -i.ɚ **-iest** -i.ɪst, -i.əst **-ily** -əl.i, -ɪ.li **-iness** -ɪ.nəs, -ɪ.nɪs
Hussain hʊˈseɪn, (US) huː-
hussar hʊˈzɑːʳ, hə-, (US) -ˈzɑːr **-s** -z
Hussein hʊˈseɪn, (US) huː-
Hussey ˈhʌs.i
Hussite ˈhʌs.aɪt, ˈhʊs-, (US) ˈhʌs- **-s** -s
huss|y, H~ ˈhʌs|.i, ˈhʌz- **-ies** -iz
hustings ˈhʌs.tɪŋz
hustl|e ˈhʌs.əl **-es** -z **-ing** -ɪŋ, ˈhʌs.lɪŋ **-ed** -d **-er/s** -əʳ/z, (US) -ɚ/z, ˈhʌs.ləʳ/z, -lɚ/z
Huston ˈhjuː.stən
hut hʌt **-s** -s
hutch hʌtʃ **-es** -ɪz
Hutchence ˈhʌtʃ.ənts, -ents
Hutcheson ˈhʌtʃ.ɪ.sən, ˈ-ə-
Hutchings ˈhʌtʃ.ɪŋz
Hutchinson ˈhʌtʃ.ɪn.sən
Hutchinsonian ˌhʌtʃ.ɪnˈsəʊ.ni.ən, (US) -ˈsoʊ- **-s** -z
Hutchison ˈhʌtʃ.ɪ.sən
Huth huːθ
Huthwaite ˈhuːθ.weɪt
hutment ˈhʌt.mənt **-s** -s
Hutton ˈhʌt.ən
Hutu ˈhuː.tuː **-s** -z
hutzpah ˈhʊt.spɑː, ˈxʊt-, -spə
Huw hjuː
Huxley ˈhʌk.sli
Huxtable ˈhʌk.stə.bəl
Huygens ˈhaɪ.gənz
Huyton ˈhaɪ.tən
huzza(h) hʊˈzɑː, hʌzˈɑː-, həˈzɑː, (US) həˈzɑː, -ˈzɔː **-s** -z

Hwang-ho ˌhwæŋˈhəʊ, US ˌhwɑːŋˈhoʊ

hwyl ˈhuː.ɪl, -əl

hyacinth, H~ ˈhaɪ.ə.sɪntθ -s -s

hyacinthine ˌhaɪ.əˈsɪnt.θaɪn, US -θaɪn, -θɪn

Hyades ˈhaɪ.ə.diːz

hyaena haɪˈiː.nə -s -z

hyalin ˈhaɪ.ə.lɪn

hyaline ˈhaɪ.ə.lɪn, -liːn, -laɪn

hyalite ˈhaɪ.ə.laɪt

hyaloid ˈhaɪ.ə.lɔɪd

Hyam haɪ.əm

Hyamson ˈhaɪ.əm.sən

Hyannis haɪˈæn.ɪs

hybrid ˈhaɪ.brɪd -s -z -ism -ɪ.zᵊm

hybridity haɪˈbrɪd.ə.ti, -ɪ.ti, US -ə.t̬i

hybridization, -isa- ˌhaɪ.brɪ.daɪˈzeɪ.ʃᵊn, ˌ-brə-, -dɪˈ-, US -dəˈ-

hybridiz|e, -is|e ˈhaɪ.brɪ.daɪz, -brə- -es -ɪz -ing -ɪŋ -ed -d -er/s -əʳ/z, US -ɚ/z

Hyde haɪd ˌ**Hyde** ˈ**Park;** ˌ**Hyde** ˌ**Park** ˈ**Corner**

Hyder® ˈhaɪ.dəʳ, US -dɚ

Hyderabad ˈhaɪ.dᵊr.ə.bæd, -bɑːd, ˌhaɪ.dᵊr.əˈbæd, -ˈbɑːd, US ˈhaɪ.dɚ.ə.bæd, -bɑːd, ˈ-drə.bæd, -bɑːd

hydra, H~ ˈhaɪ.drə -s -z

hydrangea haɪˈdreɪn.dʒə, ˈ-dʒi.ə, US -ˈdreɪn-, -ˈdræn- -s -z

hydrant ˈhaɪ.drᵊnt -s -s

hydrate n ˈhaɪ.dreɪt, -drɪt -s -s

hydra|te v haɪˈdreɪ|t, ˈ--, US ˈ-- -tes -ts -ting -tɪŋ, US -t̬ɪŋ -ted -tɪd, US -t̬ɪd

hydration haɪˈdreɪ.ʃᵊn

hydraulic haɪˈdrɔː.lɪk, -ˈdrɒl.ɪk, US -ˈdrɑː-, -ˈdrɔː- -s -s

hydrazine ˈhaɪ.drə.ziːn, -zɪn

hydro ˈhaɪ.drəʊ, US -droʊ -s -z

hydro- ˈhaɪ.drəʊ; haɪˈdrɒ, US ˈhaɪ.droʊ, -drə; US haɪˈdrɑː
Note: Prefix. Normally either takes primary or secondary stress on the first syllable, e.g. **hydrofoil** /ˈhaɪ.drəʊ.fɔɪl/ US /-droʊ-/, **hydrochloric** /ˌhaɪ.drəʊˈklɒr.ɪk/ US /-droʊˈklɔːr-/, or primary stress on the second syllable, e.g. **hydrogenate** /haɪˈdrɒdʒ.ɪ.neɪt/ US /-ˈdrɑː.dʒə-/.

hydrocarbon ˌhaɪ.drəʊˈkɑː.bᵊn, US -droʊˈkɑːr-, -drəˈ- -s -z

hydrocephalus ˌhaɪ.drəʊˈsef.ᵊl.əs, -ˈkef-, US -droʊˈsef-, -drəˈ-

hydrochloric ˌhaɪ.drəʊˈklɒr.ɪk, -ˈklɔː.rɪk, US -droʊˈklɔːr.ɪk, -drəˈ- *stress shift, see compound:* ˌ**hydrochloric** ˈ**acid**

hydrodynamic ˌhaɪ.drəʊ.daɪˈnæm.ɪk, -dɪˈ-, US -droʊ.daɪˈ-, -drə- -al -ᵊl -ally -ᵊl.i, -li -s -s

hydroelectric ˌhaɪ.drəʊ.ɪˈlek.trɪk, -əˈ-, US -droʊ- -s -s *stress shift:* ˌ**hydroelectric** ˈ**power**

hydroelectricity ˌhaɪ.drəʊ.ɪ.lekˈtrɪs.ɪ.ti, -ə-, US -droʊ.ɪ.lekˈtrɪs.ɪ.t̬i, -ə.t̬i

hydrofoil ˈhaɪ.drəʊ.fɔɪl, US -droʊ-, -drə- -s -z

hydrogen ˈhaɪ.drə.dʒən, -drɪ-, -dʒɪn, US -drə.dʒən ˈ**hydrogen** ˌ**bomb;** ˌ**hydrogen** ˈ**chloride;** ˌ**hydrogen** ˈ**fluoride;** ˌ**hydrogen** **peˈroxide**

hydroge|nate haɪˈdrɒdʒ.ɪ|.neɪt, ˈ-ə-; ˈhaɪ.drə.dʒɪ-, -dʒə-, US haɪˈdrɑː.dʒə-; US ˈhaɪ.drə- -nates -neɪts -nating -neɪ.tɪŋ, US -neɪ.t̬ɪŋ -nated -neɪ.tɪd, US -neɪ.t̬ɪd

hydrogenation ˌhaɪ.drə.dʒəˈneɪ.ʃᵊn, -dʒɪˈ-, US haɪˌdrɑː.dʒəˈ-

hydrogenous haɪˈdrɒdʒ.ɪ.nəs, ˈ-ə-, US -ˈdrɑː.dʒɪ-, -dʒə-

hydrographic ˌhaɪ.drəʊˈgræf.ɪk, US -droʊˈgræf-, -drəˈ- -al -ᵊl -ally -ᵊl.i, -li

hydrograph|y haɪˈdrɒg.rə.f|i, US -ˈdrɑː.grə- -er/s -əʳ/z, US -ɚ/z

hydrology haɪˈdrɒl.ə.dʒi, US -ˈdrɑː.lə-

hydrolysis haɪˈdrɒl.ə.sɪs, ˈ-ɪ-, US -ˈdrɑː.lɪ-

hydrolytic ˌhaɪ.drəˈlɪt.ɪk, US -ˈlɪt̬- -ally -ᵊl.i, -li

hydrolyz|e, -ys|e ˈhaɪ.drə.laɪz -es -ɪz -ing -ɪŋ -ed -d

hydromechanics ˌhaɪ.drəʊ.mɪˈkæn.ɪks, -məˈ-, US -droʊ.məˈ-, -drə-

hydrometer haɪˈdrɒm.ɪ.təʳ, ˈ-ə-, US -ˈdrɑː.mə.t̬ɚ -s -z

hydrometric ˌhaɪ.drəʊˈmet.rɪk, US -droʊˈ-, -drəˈ- -al -ᵊl -ally -ᵊl.i, -li

hydrometry haɪˈdrɒm.ə.tri, ˈ-ɪ-, US -ˈdrɑː.mə-

hydropathic ˌhaɪ.drəʊˈpæθ.ɪk, US -droʊˈ-, -drəˈ- -s -s -al -ᵊl -ally -ᵊl.i, -li

hydropath|y haɪˈdrɒp.ə.θ|i, US -ˈdrɑː.pə- -ist/s -ɪst/s

hydrophilic ˌhaɪ.drəʊˈfɪl.ɪk, US -droʊˈ-, -drəˈ-

hydrophobia ˌhaɪ.drəʊˈfəʊ.bi.ə, US -droʊˈfoʊ-, -drəˈ-

hydrophobic ˌhaɪ.drəʊˈfəʊ.bɪk, US -droʊˈfoʊ-, -drəˈ-

hydrophyte ˈhaɪ.drəʊ.faɪt, US -droʊ-, -drə- -s -s

hydroplan|e ˈhaɪ.drəʊ.pleɪn, US -droʊ-, -drə- -es -z -ing -ɪŋ -ed -d

hydroponic ˌhaɪ.drəʊˈpɒn.ɪk, US -droʊˈpɑː.nɪk, -drəˈ- -s -s -ally -ᵊl.i, -li

hydropower ˈhaɪ.drəʊ.paʊəʳ, -paʊ.əʳ, US -droʊ.paʊ.ɚ, -paʊr, -drə-

hydroscope ˈhaɪ.drəʊ.skəʊp, US -droʊ.skoʊp, -drə- -s -s

hydrostat ˈhaɪ.drəʊ.stæt, US -droʊ-, -drə- -s -s

hydrostatic ˌhaɪ.drəʊˈstæt.ɪk, US -droʊˈstæt̬-, -drəˈ- -al -ᵊl -ally -ᵊl.i, -li -s -s

hydrotherapy ˌhaɪ.drəʊˈθer.ə.pi, US -droʊˈ-, -drəˈ-

hydrotropism haɪˈdrɒt.rə.pɪ.zᵊm, US -ˈdrɑː.trə-

hydrous ˈhaɪ.drəs

hydroxide haɪˈdrɒk.saɪd, US -ˈdrɑːk- -s -z

hydroxyl haɪˈdrɒk.sɪl, US -ˈdrɑːk-

hyena haɪˈiː.nə -s -z

Hygeia haɪˈdʒiː.ə

hygiene ˈhaɪ.dʒiːn

hygienic haɪˈdʒiː.nɪk, US ˌhaɪˈdʒen.ɪk; US -ˈdʒiː.nɪk -ally -ᵊl.i, -li

hygienist haɪˈdʒiː.nɪst, US ˈhaɪ.dʒiː.nɪst; US -ˈ--, -ˈdʒen.ɪst -s -s

hygrometric ˌhaɪ.grəʊˈmet.rɪk, US -groʊˈ-, -grəˈ- -al -ᵊl -ally -ᵊl.i, -li

hygrome|try haɪˈgrɒm.ə.|tri, ˈ-ɪ-, US -ˈgrɑː.mə- -ter/s -təʳ/z, US -t̬ɚ/z

hygroscope ˈhaɪ.grəʊ.skəʊp, US -groʊ.skoʊp, -grə- -s -s

hygroscopic ˌhaɪ.grəʊˈskɒp.ɪk, US -groʊˈskɑː.pɪk, -grəˈ- -ally -ᵊl.i, -li

Hyksos ˈhɪk.sɒs, US -sɑːs

Hylas ˈhaɪ.læs, -ləs

Hylton ˈhɪl.tən

Hyman ˈhaɪ.mən

hymen, H~ ˈhaɪ.men, -mən, US -mən -s -z

hymene|al ˌhaɪ.menˈiː|.əl, -məˈniː-, -mɪˈ-, US -məˈniː- -an -ən

Hymettus haɪˈmet.əs, US -ˈmet̬-

hymn hɪm -s -z -ing -ɪŋ -ed -d ˈ**hymn** ˌ**book**

hymnal ˈhɪm.nᵊl -s -z

hymnar|y ˈhɪm.nᵊr|.i -ies -iz

hymnic ˈhɪm.nɪk

hymnody ˈhɪm.nə.di

hymnolog|y hɪmˈnɒl.ə.dʒi, US -ˈnɑː.lə- -ist/s -ɪst/s

Hyndley ˈhaɪnd.li

Hyndman ˈhaɪnd.mən

Hynes haɪnz

hyoid ˈhaɪ.ɔɪd

hyoscine ˈhaɪ.əʊ.siːn, US -ə.siːn, -sɪn

hypallage haɪˈpæl.ə.gi, -dʒi, US haɪ-, hə-; US ˌhaɪ.pəˈlædʒ.i, ˌhɪp.əˈ-

Hypatia haɪˈpeɪ.ʃə, -ʃi.ə

hyp|e haɪp -es -s -ing -ɪŋ -ed -t ˌ**hyped** ˈ**up**

hyper ˈhaɪ.pəʳ, US -pɚ

hyper- ˈhaɪ.pə; haɪˈpɜː, US ˈhaɪ.pɚ; US haɪˈpɝː
Note: Prefix. Normally either takes primary or secondary stress on the first syllable, e.g. **hypermarket** /ˈhaɪ.pəˌmɑː.kɪt/ US /-pɚˌmɑːr-/, **hyperactive** /ˌhaɪ.pᵊrˈæk.tɪv/ US /-pɚˈ-/, or primary stress on the second syllable, e.g. **hyperbole** /haɪˈpɜː.bᵊl.i/ US /-ˈpɝː-/. Note also that, although /r/ is normally assigned to a following strong syllable in US transcriptions, in **hyper-** it is perceived to be morphemically linked to that morpheme and is retained in the prefix as /ɚ/.

hyperactive ˌhaɪ.pəʳˈæk.tɪv, US -pɚ- *stress shift:* ˌ**hyperactive** ˈ**child**
hyperactivity ˌhaɪ.pəʳ.ækˈtɪv.ə.ti, -ɪ.ti, US -pɚ.ækˈtɪv.ə.t̬i
hyperacute ˌhaɪ.pəʳ.əˈkjuːt, US -pɚ- **-ness** -nəs, -nɪs
hyperbol|a haɪˈpɜː.bəl|.ə, US -ˈpɝː- **-ae** -iː **-as** -əz
hyperbole haɪˈpɜː.bəl.i, US -ˈpɝː- **-s** -z
hyperbolic ˌhaɪ.pəˈbɒl.ɪk, US -pɚˈbɑː.lɪk **-al** -əl **-ally** -əl.i, -li
hyperbol|ism haɪˈpɜː.bəl|.ɪ.zəm, US -ˈpɝː- **-ist/s** -ɪst/s
hyperboliz|e, -is|e haɪˈpɜː.bəl.aɪz, US -ˈpɝː- **-es** -ɪz **-ing** -ɪŋ **-ed** -d
hyperboloid haɪˈpɜː.bəl.ɔɪd, US -ˈpɝː- **-s** -z
hyperborean ˌhaɪ.pəˈbɔː.ri.ən; -bɔːˈriː.ən, -bɒrˈiː.ən, US -pɚ.bɔːˈriː-, -bəˈ- **-s** -z
hypercorrect ˌhaɪ.pə.kəˈrekt, US -pɚ.kəˈrekt **-ly** -li **-ness** -nəs, -nɪs
hypercorrection ˌhaɪ.pə.kəˈrek.ʃən, US -pɚ.kəˈrek- **-s** -z
hypercritic|al ˌhaɪ.pəˈkrɪt.ɪ.k|əl, US -pɚˈkrɪt̬- **-ally** -əl.i, US -li
hypercriticism ˌhaɪ.pəˈkrɪt.ɪ.sɪ.zəm, US -pɚˈkrɪt̬.ɪ-
hypercriticiz|e, -is|e ˌhaɪ.pəˈkrɪt.ɪ.saɪz, US -pɚˈkrɪt̬- **-es** -ɪz **-ing** -ɪŋ **-ed** -d
hyperglycaem|ia ˌhaɪ.pə.glaɪˈsiː.m|i.ə, US -pɚ- **-ic** -ɪk
hypericum haɪˈper.ɪ.kəm **-s** -z
Hyperides haɪˈper.ɪ.diːz; ˌhaɪ.pəˈraɪ-, US haɪˈper.ɪ-, hɪ-
hyperinflation ˌhaɪ.pəʳ.ɪnˈfleɪ.ʃən, US -pɚ-
Hyperion haɪˈpɪə.ri.ən, -ˈper.i-, US -ˈpɪr-
hyperlink ˈhaɪ.pə.lɪŋk, US -pɚ- **-s** -s
hypermarket ˈhaɪ.pəˌmɑː.kɪt, US -pɚˌmɑːr- **-s** -s
hypernym ˈhaɪ.pə.nɪm, US -pɚ- **-s** -z
hypersensitive ˌhaɪ.pəˈsent.sə.tɪv, -sɪ-, US -pɚˈsent.sə.t̬ɪv
hypersensitivity ˌhaɪ.pəˌsent.səˈtɪv.ə.ti, -sɪˈ-, -ɪ.ti, US -pɚˌsent.səˈtɪv.ə.t̬i
hyperspace ˈhaɪ.pə.speɪs, US -pɚ-
hypertension ˌhaɪ.pəˈten.tʃən, ˈhaɪ.pəˌten-, US ˌhaɪ.pɚˈtent.ʃən
hypertext ˈhaɪ.pə.tekst, US -pɚ-
hyperthyroid ˌhaɪ.pəˈθaɪ.rɔɪd, US -pɚˈ- **-ism** -ɪ.zəm
hypertroph|y haɪˈpɜː.trə.f|i, US -ˈpɝː- **-ied** -id
hyperventi|late ˌhaɪ.pəˈven.tɪ|.leɪt, -tə-, US -pɚˈven.t̬ə- **-lates** -leɪts **-lating** -leɪ.tɪŋ, US -leɪ.t̬ɪŋ **-lated** -leɪ.tɪd, US -leɪ.t̬ɪd
hyperventilation ˌhaɪ.pəˌven.tɪˈleɪ.ʃən, -təˈ-, US -pɚˌven.t̬əˈ-
hyph|a ˈhaɪ.f|ə **-ae** -iː
hyphal ˈhaɪ.fəl
hyphen ˈhaɪ.fən **-s** -z **-ing** -ɪŋ **-ed** -d
hyphen|ate ˈhaɪ.fən|.eɪt, -fɪ.n|eɪt, US -fə.neɪt **-ates** -eɪts **-ating** -eɪ.tɪŋ, US -eɪ.t̬ɪŋ **-ated** -eɪ.tɪd, US -eɪ.t̬ɪd
hyphenation ˌhaɪ.fənˈeɪ.ʃən
hypno- ˈhɪp.nəʊ; hɪpˈnɒ, -ˈnəʊ, US ˈhɪp.noʊ, -nə; US hɪpˈnɑː, -ˈnoʊ
Note: Prefix. Normally either takes primary or secondary stress on the first syllable, e.g. **hypnotism** /ˈhɪp.nə.tɪ.zəm/, **hypnotherapy** /ˌhɪp.nəʊˈθer.ə.pi/ US /-noʊˈ-/, or primary stress on the second syllable, e.g. **hypnotic** /hɪpˈnɒt.ɪk/ US /-ˈnɑː.t̬ɪk/.
hypnosis hɪpˈnəʊ.sɪs, US -ˈnoʊ-
hypnotherapist ˌhɪp.nəʊˈθer.ə.pɪst, US -noʊˈ- **-s** -s
hypnotherapy ˌhɪp.nəʊˈθer.ə.pi, US -noʊˈ-
hypnotic hɪpˈnɒt.ɪk, US -ˈnɑː.t̬ɪk
hypnot|ism ˈhɪp.nə.t|ɪ.zəm **-ist/s** -ɪst/s
hypnotization, -isa- ˌhɪp.nə.taɪˈzeɪ.ʃən, -tɪˈ-, US -t̬əˈ-
hypnotiz|e, -is|e ˈhɪp.nə.taɪz **-es** -ɪz **-ing** -ɪŋ **-ed** -d **-er/s** -əʳ/z, US -ɚ/z
hypo ˈhaɪ.pəʊ, US -poʊ **-s** -z
hypo- ˈhaɪ.pəʊ; haɪˈpɒ, US ˈhaɪ.poʊ, -pə; US haɪˈpɑː, hɪ-
Note: Prefix. Normally either takes primary or secondary stress on the first syllable, e.g. **hypocaust** /ˈhaɪ.pəʊ.kɔːst/ US /-poʊ-/, **hypothetic** /ˌhaɪ.pəʊˈθet.ɪk/ US /-poʊˈθet̬-/, or primary stress on the second syllable, e.g. **hypotenuse** /haɪˈpɒt.ən.juːz/ US /-ˈpɑː.tən.uːs/.
hypoallergenic ˌhaɪ.pəʊˌæl.əˈdʒen.ɪk, -ɜːˈ-, US -poʊˌæl.ɚˈ-
hypocaust ˈhaɪ.pəʊ.kɔːst, -kɒst, US -poʊ.kɔːst, -pə-, -kɑːst **-s** -s
hypochondri|a ˌhaɪ.pəʊˈkɒn.dri|.ə, US -poʊˈkɑːn-, -pəˈ- **-ac/s** -æk/s
hypochondriacal ˌhaɪ.pəʊ.kɒnˈdraɪ.ə.kəl, -kənˈ-, US -poʊ.kɑːnˈ-, -pə-
hypochondriasis ˌhaɪ.pəʊ.kɒnˈdraɪ.ə.sɪs, -kənˈ-, US -poʊ.kɑːnˈ-, -pə-
hypocotyl ˌhaɪ.pəˈkɒt.ɪl, US -poʊˈkɑː.t̬əl
hypocris|y hɪˈpɒk.rə.s|i, -rɪ-, US -ˈpɑː.krə- **-ies** -iz
hypocrite ˈhɪp.ə.krɪt **-s** -s
hypocritic|al ˌhɪp.əʊˈkrɪt.ɪ.k|əl, US -əˈkrɪt̬- **-ally** -əl.i, -li
hypocycloid ˌhaɪ.pəʊˈsaɪ.klɔɪd, US -poʊˈ-, -pəˈ- **-s** -z
hypodermic ˌhaɪ.pəʊˈdɜː.mɪk, US -poʊˈdɝː-, -pəˈ- *stress shift, see compounds:* ˌ**hypodermic** ˈ**needle** ˌ**hypodermic syˈringe**
hypodermis ˌhaɪ.pəʊˈdɜː.mɪs, US -poʊˈdɝː-, -pəˈ-
hypogeal ˌhaɪ.pəʊˈdʒiː.əl, US -poʊˈ-
hypoglyc(a)em|ia ˌhaɪ.pəʊ.glaɪˈsiː.m|i.ə, US -poʊ- **-ic** -ɪk
hypophosphate ˌhaɪ.pəʊˈfɒs.feɪt, -fɪt, US -poʊˈfɑːs-, -pəˈ- **-s** -s
hyposta|sis haɪˈpɒs.tə|.sɪs, US -ˈpɑː.stə-, hɪ- **-ses** -siːz
hypostatiz|e, -is|e haɪˈpɒs.tə.taɪz, US -ˈpɑː.stə-, hɪ- **-es** -ɪz **-ing** -ɪŋ **-ed** -d
hypostyle ˈhaɪ.pəʊ.staɪl, US -poʊ-
hyposulphite ˌhaɪ.pəʊˈsʌl.faɪt, US -poʊˈ-, -pəˈ- **-s** -s
hypotactic ˌhaɪ.pəʊˈtæk.tɪk, US -poʊˈ-, -pəˈ-
hypotax|is ˌhaɪ.pəʊˈtæk.s|ɪs, ˈhaɪ.pəʊ.tæk-, US ˌhaɪ.poʊˈtæk-, -pəˈ- **-es** -iːz
hypotension ˌhaɪ.pəʊˈten.tʃən, US ˈhaɪ.poʊˌten-, -pəˌ-
hypotenus|e haɪˈpɒt.ən.juːz, -ɪ.njuːz, -juːs, US -ˈpɑː.tən.uːs, -tɪ.nuːs, -njuːs **-es** -ɪz
hypothalamus ˌhaɪ.pəʊˈθæl.ə.məs, US -poʊˈ-, -pəˈ-
hypothe|cate haɪˈpɒθ.ə|.keɪt, ˈ-ɪ-, US -ˈpɑː.θə-, hɪ- **-cates** -keɪts **-cating** -keɪ.tɪŋ, US -keɪ.t̬ɪŋ **-cated** -keɪ.tɪd, US -keɪ.t̬ɪd
hypothecation haɪˌpɒθ.əˈkeɪ.ʃən, -ɪˈ-, US -pɑː.θəˈ-, hɪ- **-s** -z
hypothermal ˌhaɪ.pəʊˈθɜː.məl, US -poʊˈθɝː-, -pəˈ-
hypothermia ˌhaɪ.pəʊˈθɜː.mi.ə, US -poʊˈθɝː-, -pəˈ-
hypothes|is haɪˈpɒθ.ə.s|ɪs, ˈ-ɪ-, US -ˈpɑː.θə-, hɪ- **-es** -iːz
hypothesiz|e, -is|e haɪˈpɒθ.ə.saɪz, US -ˈpɑː.θə-, hɪ- **-es** -ɪz **-ing** -ɪŋ **-ed** -d
hypothetic ˌhaɪ.pəʊˈθet.ɪk, US -poʊˈθet̬-, -pəˈ- **-al** -əl **-ally** -əl.i, -li
hypothyroid ˌhaɪ.pəʊˈθaɪ.rɔɪd, US -poʊˈ- **-ism** -ɪ.zəm
hypoxia haɪˈpɒk.si.ə, US -ˈpɑːk-, hɪ-
hypoxic haɪˈpɒk.sɪk, US -ˈpɑːk-, hɪ-
hypsome|try hɪpˈsɒm.ə|.tri, ˈ-ɪ-, US -ˈsɑː.mə- **-ter/s** -təʳ/z, US -t̬ɚ/z
hyrax ˈhaɪ.ræks **-es** -ɪz
Hyslop ˈhɪz.ləp, -lɒp, US -lɑːp, -ləp
hyson, H~ ˈhaɪ.sən
hyssop ˈhɪs.əp
hysterectom|y ˌhɪs.təʳˈek.tə.m|i, US -təˈrek- **-ies** -iz
hysteria hɪˈstɪə.ri.ə, US -ˈster.i-, -ˈstɪr-
hysteric hɪˈster.ɪk **-s** -s **-al** -əl **-ally** -əl.i, -li
hysteron proteron ˌhɪs.tə.rɒnˈprɒt.ə.rɒn, -rɒmˈ-, -ˈprəʊ.tə-, US -rɑːnˈprɑː.t̬ə.rɑːn
hythe, H~ haɪð **-s** -z
Hytner ˈhaɪt.nəʳ, US -nɚ
Hyundai® haɪˈʌn.daɪ, -ən-, ˈhjʊn-, ˈhjʊn.deɪ, US ˈhjʌn.deɪ, ˈhʌn-
Hywel ˈhaʊ.əl
Hz (abbrev. for **Hertz**) hɜːts, heəts, US hɝːts, herts

I

Pronouncing the letter I

→ *See also* **IE, IEU, IO**

The vowel letter **i** has two main strong pronunciations linked to spelling: a 'short' pronunciation /ɪ/ and a 'long' pronunciation /aɪ/. In the 'short' pronunciation, the **i** is generally followed by a consonant which closes the syllable, or a double consonant before another vowel, e.g.:

ship	ʃɪp
shipping	ˈʃɪp.ɪŋ

The 'long' pronunciation is usually found when the **i** is followed by a single consonant and then a vowel, although it should be noted that this spelling does not regularly predict a 'long' pronunciation, e.g.:

pipe	paɪp
piping	ˈpaɪ.pɪŋ

In many cases, the 'short' pronunciation results from the above kind of spelling, e.g.:

give	gɪv
living	ˈlɪv.ɪŋ

Also, the 'long' pronunciation appears in some words where the vowel is followed by two consonants, e.g.:

mind	maɪnd
wild	waɪld

Preceding the letters **gh**, **i** is pronounced /aɪ/, except in some names such as *Brigham* and *Brighouse*, e.g.:

high	haɪ
light	laɪt
Brigham	ˈbrɪg.əm

When **i** is followed by **r** and no vowel follows within the word, the strong pronunciation is one of two possibilities: /aɪə/ Ⓤⓢ /aɪɚ/ or /ɜː/ Ⓤⓢ /ɝː/, e.g.:

fire	faɪəʳ Ⓤⓢ faɪ.ɚ
fir	fɜːʳ Ⓤⓢ fɝː

Another vowel sound associated with the letter **i** is /iː/, e.g.:

iː	machine /məˈʃiːn/

In weak syllables

The vowel letter **i** is realized with the vowels /ɪ/ and /ə/ in weak syllables, and may also be elided in British English, e.g.:

divide	dɪˈvaɪd, də-
medicine	ˈmed.sᵊn Ⓤⓢ ˈ-ɪ.sən

i, I aɪ **-'s** -z

Ia. (abbrev. for **Iowa**) ˈaɪ.əʊ.ə; ˈaɪ.əʊə, Ⓤⓢ ˈaɪ.ə.wə; Ⓤⓢ ˈaɪ.oʊ-

-iac i.æk
Note: Suffix. Does not normally affect stress patterning, e.g. **mania** /ˈmeɪ.ni.ə/, **maniac** /ˈmeɪ.ni.æk/.

Iachimo iˈæk.ɪ.məʊ, aɪ-, Ⓤⓢ -moʊ

Iago iˈɑː.gəʊ, Ⓤⓢ -goʊ

Iain ˈiː.ən

-ial i.əl, əl
Note: Suffix. Normally stressed on the syllable before the prefix, e.g. **filial** /ˈfɪl.i.əl/.

iamb ˈaɪ.æmb **-s** -z

iamb|ic aɪˈæm.b|ɪk **-us/es** -əs/ɪz

Ian ˈiː.ən

-ian i.ən, ən
Note: Suffix. Words ending **-ian** are stressed in a similar way to those ending **-ial**; see above.

I'Anson aɪˈænt.sən

Ianthe aɪˈænt.θi

IATA aɪˈɑː.tə, iː-, Ⓤⓢ ˌaɪˌeɪˌtiːˈeɪ, aɪˈɑː.t̬ə

iatrogenic aɪˌæt.rəʊˈdʒen.ɪk, ˌaɪ.æt-, Ⓤⓢ aɪˌæt.roʊˈ-, iː-, -rəˈ- **-ally** -ᵊl.i, -li

Ibadan ɪˈbæd.ᵊn, Ⓤⓢ iːˈbɑː.dɑːn, -dᵊn

Ibbertson ˈɪb.ət.sᵊn, Ⓤⓢ -ɚt-

Ibbetson ˈɪb.ɪt.sᵊn, -ət-

I-beam ˈaɪ.biːm **-s** -z

Iberi|a aɪˈbɪə.ri|.ə, Ⓤⓢ -ˈbɪr.i- **-an/s** -ən/z

iberis aɪˈbɪə.rɪs, Ⓤⓢ -ˈbɪr.ɪs

Iberus aɪˈbɪə.rəs, Ⓤⓢ -ˈbɪr.əs

ibex ˈaɪ.beks **-es** -ɪz

ibid ˈɪb.ɪd, ɪˈbɪd

ibidem ˈɪb.ɪ.dem, ˈ-ə-; ɪˈbaɪ.dem, Ⓤⓢ ˈɪb.ɪ.dem, ˈ-ə-; Ⓤⓢ ɪˈbiː.dem, -ˈbaɪ-

-ibility əˈbɪl.ə.ti, ɪˈ-, -ɪ.ti, Ⓤⓢ -ə.t̬i
Note: Suffix. Words containing **-ibility** always exhibit primary stress as shown above, e.g. **eligibility** /ˌel.ɪ.dʒəˈbɪl.ə.ti/ Ⓤⓢ /-t̬i/.

ibis ˈaɪ.bɪs **-es** -ɪz

Ibiza ɪˈbiː.θə, iː-, Ⓤⓢ iːˈbiː.sə, -θə; Ⓤⓢ aɪˈbiː.θə, -θɑː

-ible ə.bᵊl, ɪ-
Note: Suffix. Words containing **-ible** are normally stressed either on the antepenultimate syllable, e.g. **susceptible** /səˈsep.tə.bᵊl/, or two syllables preceding the suffix, e.g. **eligible** /ˈel.ɪ.dʒə.bᵊl/.

IBM® ˌaɪ.biːˈem

Ibo ˈiː.bəʊ, Ⓤⓢ -boʊ **-s** -z

iBook® ˈaɪ.bʊk

Ibrahim ˈɪb.rə.hiːm, -hɪm, ˌ--ˈ-

Ibrox ˈaɪ.brɒks, Ⓤⓢ -brɑːks

Ibsen ˈɪb.sᵊn

Ibstock ˈɪb.stɒk, Ⓤⓢ -stɑːk

ibuprofen ˌaɪ.bjuːˈprəʊ.fen, -fᵊn; aɪˈbjuː.prəʊ-, Ⓤⓢ ˌaɪ.bjuːˈproʊ.fᵊn

IC ˌaɪˈsiː **-s** -z

-ic ɪk
Note: Suffix. Words containing **-ic** are normally stressed on the penultimate syllable, e.g. **cubic** /ˈkjuː.bɪk/.

-ic|al ɪ.k|ᵊl **-ally** -ᵊl.i, -li
Note: Suffix. Words containing **-ical** are normally stressed on the antepenultimate syllable, e.g. **musical** /ˈmjuː.zɪ.kᵊl/.

Icari|a ɪˈkeə.ri|.ə, aɪ-, Ⓤⓢ -ˈker.i- **-an** -ən

Icarus ˈɪk.ᵊr.əs, ˈaɪ.kᵊr-, Ⓤⓢ ˈɪk.ɚ-

ICBM ˌaɪ.siː.biːˈem

ic|e aɪs **-es** -ɪz **-ing** -ɪŋ **-ed** -t ˈ**ice ˌage**; ˈ**ice ˌaxe**; ˈ**ice ˌbucket**; ˈ**ice ˌcap**; ˈ**ice ˌfield**; ˈ**ice ˌfloe**; ˈ**ice ˌhockey**; ˌ**ice ˈhockey**; ˈ**ice ˌlolly**; ˌ**ice ˈlolly**; ˈ**ice ˌpack**; ˈ**ice ˌrink**; ˌ**break the ˈice**; ˌ**skate on ˌthin ˈice**

iceberg ˈaɪs.bɜːg, Ⓤⓢ -bɝːg **-s** -z ˌ**iceberg ˈlettuce**

icebound ˈaɪs.baʊnd

icebox ˈaɪs.bɒks, Ⓤⓢ -bɑːks **-es** -ɪz

icebreaker ˈaɪsˌbreɪ.kəʳ, Ⓤⓢ -kɚ **-s** -z

ice cream ˌaɪsˈkriːm, ˈ--, Ⓤⓢ ˈ-- **-s** -z ˌ**ice ˈcream ˌparlo(u)r**; ˌ**ice cream ˈsoda**

icefall ˈaɪs.fɔːl, Ⓤⓢ -fɔːl, -fɑːl **-s** -z

icehou|se ˈaɪs.haʊ|s **-ses** -zɪz

Iceland ˈaɪs.lənd
Icelander ˈaɪs.lən.dər, -læn-, (US) -dɚ -s -z
Icelandic aɪsˈlæn.dɪk
icemaker ˈaɪsˌmeɪ.kər, (US) -kɚ -s -z
ice|man ˈaɪs|.mæn, -mən -men -men, -mən
Iceni aɪˈsiː.naɪ, -ni
icepick ˈaɪs.pɪk -s -s
ice|skate ˈaɪs|.skeɪt -skates -skeɪts -skating -ˌskeɪ.tɪŋ, (US) -ˌskeɪ.t̬ɪŋ -skated -ˌskeɪ.tɪd, (US) -ˌskeɪ.t̬ɪd -skater/s -ˌskeɪ.tər/z, (US) -ˌskeɪ.t̬ɚ/z
Ichabod ˈɪk.ə.bɒd, ˈɪx-, (US) ˈɪk.ə.bɑːd
ich dien ˌɪxˈdiːn
I Ching ˌiːˈtʃɪŋ, ˌaɪ-, -ˈdʒɪŋ, (US) ˌiː-
ich-laut ˈɪx.laʊt, ˈɪk-
ichneumon ɪkˈnjuː.mən, (US) -ˈnuː-, -ˈnjuː- -s -z
ichnographic ˌɪk.nəʊˈɡræf.ɪk, (US) -noʊˈ- -al -əl -ally -əl.i, -li
ichnography ɪkˈnɒɡ.rə.fi, (US) -ˈnɑː.ɡrə-
ichnological ˌɪk.nəʊˈlɒdʒ.ɪ.kəl, (US) -noʊˈlɑː.dʒɪ-
ichnology ɪkˈnɒl.ə.dʒi, (US) -ˈnɑː.lə-
ichor ˈaɪ.kɔːr, (US) -kɔːr, -kɚ
ichthyologic|al ˌɪk.θi.əˈlɒdʒ.ɪ.k|əl, (US) -ˈlɑː.dʒɪ- -ally -əl.i, -li
ichthyolog|y ˌɪk.θiˈɒl.ə.dʒ|i, (US) -ˈɑː.lə- -ist/s -ɪst/s
ichthyosaur ˈɪk.θi.ə.sɔːr, (US) -sɔːr -s -z
ichthyosaur|us ˌɪk.θi.əʊˈsɔː.r|əs, (US) -oʊˈsɔːr|.əs, -əˈ- -i -aɪ -uses -ə.sɪz
ICI® ˌaɪ.siːˈaɪ
-ician ˈɪʃ.ən
Note: Suffix. Normally carries primary stress as shown above, e.g. **musician** /mjuːˈzɪʃ.ən/, **technician** /tekˈnɪʃ.ən/.
icicle ˈaɪ.sɪ.kəl, -sə- -s -z
icing ˈaɪ.sɪŋ ˈ**icing** ˌ**sugar**
ick ɪk
Icke aɪk, ɪk
Icknield ˈɪk.niːld
ick|y ˈɪk|.i -ier -i.ər, (US) -i.ɚ -iest -i.ɪst, -i.əst
icon ˈaɪ.kɒn, -kən, (US) -kɑːn, -kən -s -z
iconic aɪˈkɒn.ɪk, (US) -ˈkɑː.nɪk
Iconium aɪˈkəʊ.ni.əm, ɪ-, (US) aɪˈkoʊ-
iconoclasm aɪˈkɒn.əʊˌklæz.əm, (US) -ˈkɑː.nə-
iconoclast aɪˈkɒn.əʊ.klæst, -klɑːst, (US) -ˈkɑː.nə.klæst -s -s
iconoclastic aɪˌkɒn.əʊˈklæs.tɪk, ˌaɪ.kɒn-, (US) aɪˌkɑː.nəˈ- -ally -əl.i, -li
iconographic ˌaɪ.kə.nəʊˈɡræf.ɪk, (US) -noʊ-
iconograph|y ˌaɪ.kəˈnɒɡ.rə.f|i, -kɒnˈɒɡ-, (US) -kəˈnɑː.ɡrə- -er/s -ər/z, (US) -ɚ/z
iconoscope aɪˈkɒn.ə.skəʊp, (US) -ˈkɑː.nə.skoʊp -s -s
icosahedr|on ˌaɪ.kɒs.əˈhiː.dr|ən, -kə.səˈ-; aɪˌkɒs-, (US) ˌaɪ.koʊ.səˈ-; (US) aɪˌkɑː- -ons -ənz -a -ə -al -əl
ICT ˌaɪ.siːˈtiː
ictus ˈɪk.təs -es -ɪz
ICU ˌaɪ.siːˈjuː
ic|y ˈaɪ.s|i -ier -i.ər, (US) -i.ɚ -iest -i.ɪst, -i.əst -ily -əl.i, -ɪ.li -iness -ɪ.nəs, -ɪ.nɪs
id ɪd
'Id iːd, (US) iːd, eɪd
I'd (= **I would** or **I had**) aɪd
ID ˌaɪˈdiː ˌ**I'D** ˌ**card**
Ida ˈaɪ.də
Ida. (abbrev. for **Idaho**) ˈaɪ.də.həʊ, (US) -hoʊ
Idaho ˈaɪ.də.həʊ, (US) -hoʊ
Iddesleigh ˈɪdz.li
Ide iːd
-ide aɪd
Note: Suffix. Words containing **-ide** are normally stressed on the penultimate or antepenultimate syllable, e.g. **hydroxide** /haɪˈdrɒk.saɪd/ (US) /-ˈdrɑːk-/.
idea aɪˈdɪə, (US) -ˈdiː.ə -s -z

> Note: In British English, the pronunciation /ˈaɪ.dɪə/ is also sometimes heard, especially when a stress immediately follows, e.g. 'I thought of the ˌ**idea** ˈ**first**'.

ideal n aɪˈdɪəl; -ˈdiː.əl, (US) -ˈdiː- -s -z
ideal adj aɪˈdɪəl, -ˈdiː.əl, ˈ--, (US) -ˈdiː- *stress shift:* ˌ**ideal** ˈ**home**
ideal|ism aɪˈdɪə.l|ɪ.zəm; ˈaɪ.dɪə-, (US) aɪˈdiː.ə.l|ɪ- -ist/s -ɪst/s
idealistic aɪˌdɪəˈlɪs.tɪk; ˌaɪ.dɪə-, (US) ˌaɪ.di.əˈ- -ally -əl.i, -li
ideality ˌaɪ.diˈæl.ə.ti, -ɪ.ti, (US) -ə.t̬i
idealization, -isa- aɪˌdɪə.laɪˈzeɪ.ʃən, -lɪˈ-; ˌaɪ.dɪə-, (US) aɪˌdiː.ə.ləˈ- -s -z
idealiz|e, -is|e aɪˈdɪə.laɪz, (US) -ˈdiː.ə- -es -ɪz -ing -ɪŋ -ed -d -er/s -ər/z, (US) -ɚ/z
ideally aɪˈdɪə.li, (US) -ˈdiː.li, -ə.li
ide|ate ˈaɪ.di|.eɪt -ates -eɪts -ating -eɪ.tɪŋ, (US) -t̬ɪŋ -ated -eɪ.tɪd, (US) -t̬ɪd
ideational ˌaɪ.diˈeɪ.ʃən.əl, -ˈeɪʃ.nəl
idée fixe ˌiː.deɪˈfiːks **idées fixes** ˌiː.deɪˈfiːks, -deɪzˈ-
idée reçue ˌiː.deɪ.rəˈsuː **idées reçues** ˌiː.deɪ.rəˈsuː, -deɪz-
idem ˈɪd.em, ˈiː.dem, ˈaɪ-, (US) ˈaɪ.dem, ˈiː-, ˈɪd.em
idempotent ˌɪd.əmˈpəʊ.tənt, ˌiː.dəm-, ˌaɪ-, -demˈ-, (US) ˌaɪ.demˈpoʊ-, ˌiː-, ˌɪd.emˈ-
identic|al aɪˈden.tɪ.k|əl, ɪ-, (US) -t̬ə- -ally -əl.i, -li -alness -əl.nəs, -əl.nɪs
identifiable aɪˈden.tɪ.faɪ.ə.bəl, -tə-, aɪˌden.tɪˈfaɪ-, -təˈ-, (US) aɪˌden.t̬əˈ-
identification aɪˌden.tɪ.fɪˈkeɪ.ʃən, -tə-, -fəˈ-, (US) -t̬ə- -s -z
identi|fy aɪˈden.tɪ|.faɪ, -tə-, (US) -t̬ɪ-, -t̬ə- -fies -faɪz -fying -faɪ.ɪŋ -fied -faɪd -fier/s -faɪ.ər/z, (US) -faɪ.ɚ/z
identikit, I~ aɪˈden.tɪ.kɪt, (US) -t̬ə- -s -s
identit|y aɪˈden.tə.t|i, -ɪ.t|i, (US) -t̬ə.t̬|i -ies -iz iˈ**dentity** ˌ**card**; iˈ**dentity** ˌ**crisis**; iˈ**dentity** **pa**ˌ**rade**; iˈ**dentity** ˌ**lineup**
ideogram ˈɪd.i.əʊ.ɡræm, ˈaɪ.di-, (US) -oʊ-, -ə- -s -z
ideograph ˈɪd.i.əʊ.ɡrɑːf, ˈaɪ.di-, -ɡræf, (US) -oʊ.ɡræf, -ə- -s -s
ideographic ˌɪd.i.əʊˈɡræf.ɪk, ˌaɪ.di-, (US) -oʊˈ-, -əˈ- -al -əl -ally -əl.i, -li
ideography ˌɪd.iˈɒɡ.rə.fi, ˌaɪ.diˈ-, (US) -ˈɑː.ɡrə-
ideologic|al ˌaɪ.di.əˈlɒdʒ.ɪ.k|əl, ˌɪd.i-, (US) -ˈlɑː.dʒɪ- -ally -əl.i, -li
ideologue ˈaɪ.di.əʊ.lɒɡ, ˈɪd.i-, (US) -ə.lɑːɡ -s -z
ideolog|y ˌaɪ.diˈɒl.ə.dʒ|i, ˌɪd.iˈ-, (US) -ˈɑː.lə- -ies -iz -ist/s -ɪst/s
ides, I~ aɪdz ˌ**Ides of** ˈ**March**
Idi Amin ˌiː.diˌɑːˈmiːn
idio- ˈɪd.i.əʊ; ˌɪd.iˈɒ, (US) ˈɪd.i.oʊ, -ə; (US) ˌɪd.iˈɑː
Note: Prefix. Normally takes either primary or secondary stress on the first syllable, e.g. **idiolect** /ˈɪd.i.əʊ.lekt/ (US) /-oʊ-/, **idiomatic** /ˌɪd.i.əʊˈmæt.ɪk/ (US) /-əˈmæt̬-/, or secondary stress on the first syllable and primary stress on the third, e.g. **idiotic** /ˌɪd.iˈɒt.ɪk/ (US) /-ˈɑː.t̬ɪk/.
idioc|y ˈɪd.i.ə.s|i -ies -iz
idiolect ˈɪd.i.əʊ.lekt, (US) -oʊ-, -ə- -s -s -al -əl
idiom ˈɪd.i.əm -s -z
idiomatic ˌɪd.i.əʊˈmæt.ɪk, (US) -əˈmæt̬- -al -əl -ally -əl.i, -li
idiophone ˈɪd.i.əʊ.fəʊn, (US) -oʊ.foʊn, -ə- -s -z
idiosyncras|y ˌɪd.i.əʊˈsɪŋ.krə.s|i, (US) -oʊˈsɪn-, -əˈ-, -ˈsɪŋ- -ies -iz
idiosyncratic ˌɪd.i.əʊ.sɪŋˈkræt.ɪk, (US) -oʊ.sɪnˈkræt̬-, -ə-, -sɪŋˈ- -ally -əl.i, -li
idiot ˈɪd.i.ət -s -s ˈ**idiot** ˌ**box**
idiotic ˌɪd.iˈɒt.ɪk, (US) -ˈɑː.t̬ɪk -al -əl -ally -əl.i, -li
idiotism ˈɪd.i.ə.tɪ.zəm, (US) -t̬ɪ- -s -z
idiot-proof ˈɪd.i.ətˌpruːf
idiot(s) savant(s) ˌiː.di.əʊ.sævˈɑ̃ːŋ, ˌɪd.i.ətˈsæv.ənt, (US) ˌiː.diː.oʊ.sævˈɑːnt, -ˈænt
Idist ˈiː.dɪst -s -s
id|le, I~ ˈaɪ.d|əl -ly -li -lest -lɪst, -ləst -leness -əl.nəs, -nɪs -les -əlz -ling -lɪŋ -led -əld -ler/s -lər/z, (US) -lɚ/z
Ido ˈiː.dəʊ, (US) -doʊ
idol ˈaɪ.dəl -s -z
idolater aɪˈdɒl.ə.tər, (US) -ˈdɑː.lə.t̬ɚ -s -z
idolatrous aɪˈdɒl.ə.trəs, (US) -ˈdɑː.lə- -ly -li -ness -nəs, -nɪs
idolatr|y aɪˈdɒl.ə.tr|i, (US) -ˈdɑː.lə- -ies -iz
idolization, -isa- ˌaɪ.dəl.aɪˈzeɪ.ʃən, -ɪˈ-, (US) -əˈ-
idoliz|e, -is|e ˈaɪ.dəl.aɪz -es -ɪz -ing -ɪŋ -ed -d -er/s -ər/z, (US) -ɚ/z
Idomeneus aɪˈdɒm.ɪ.njuːs, ɪˈ-, -ə-;

Pronouncing the letters IE

There are several pronunciation possibilities for the vowel digraph **ie**. One of the most common is /iː/:

achieve	əˈtʃiːv
piece	piːs

Another common pronunciation is /aɪ/, e.g.:

pie	paɪ
magnifies	ˈmæg.nɪ.faɪz

When followed by an **r** in the spelling, **ie** is pronounced as /ɪə/ ⓤⓢ /ɪr/, e.g.:

pier	pɪəʳ ⓤⓢ pɪr
fierce	fɪəs ⓤⓢ fɪrs

In addition

Other vowel sounds are associated with the digraph **ie**, e.g.:

ɪ	handkerchief /ˈhæŋ.kə.tʃɪf/ ⓤⓢ /-kɚ-/
aɪə	diet /daɪət/ ⓤⓢ /ˈdaɪ.ət/
e	friend /frend/
i.e	conscientious /ˌkɒn.tʃiˈen.tʃəs/ ⓤⓢ /ˌkɑːn.tʃiˈent.ʃəs/
i.iː	medieval /ˌmed.iˈiː.vᵊl/ ⓤⓢ /ˌmiː.diˈ-/

In weak syllables

The vowel digraph **ie** is realized with the vowel /ə/ in weak syllables, or can cause the following consonant to be realized as syllabic, e.g.:

patient	ˈpeɪ.ʃᵊnt

ɪˌdɒm.ɪˈniː.əs, aɪˌ-, -əˈ-, ⓤⓢ -ˈdɑː.mə.nuːs, -njuːs
Idris ˈɪd.rɪs, ˈaɪ.drɪs
Idumea ˌaɪ.djʊˈmiː.ə, ˌɪd.jʊˈ-, ⓤⓢ ˌɪd.juːˈmiː.ə, ˌiː.djuːˈ-, ˌiː.dʒuːˈ-
I'd've (= **I would have**) ˈaɪ.dᵊv
idyll ˈɪd.ᵊl, ˈaɪ.dᵊl, -dɪl, ⓤⓢ ˈaɪ.dᵊl -s -z
idyllic ɪˈdɪl.ɪk, aɪ-, ⓤⓢ aɪ- **-ally** -ᵊl.i, -li
idyllist ˈɪd.ᵊl.ɪst, ˈaɪ.dᵊl-, -dɪl-, ⓤⓢ ˈaɪ.dᵊl- **-s** -s
i.e. ˌaɪˈiː
if ɪf
Ife *surname:* aɪf *town in Nigeria:* ˈiː.feɪ
Iffley ˈɪf.li
iffy ˈɪf.i
Ifor ˈaɪ.vəʳ, -fəʳ, ˈiː.vɔːʳ, ⓤⓢ ˈaɪ.vɚ, ˈiː-
-ify ɪ.faɪ, ə-
Note: Suffix. Words containing **-ify** normally carry stress on the antepenultimate syllable, e.g. **person** /ˈpɜː.sᵊn/ ⓤⓢ /ˈpɜːr-/, **personify** /pəˈsɒn.ɪ.faɪ/ ⓤⓢ /pɚˈsɑː.nɪ-/. Exceptions exist; see individual entries.
Igbo ˈiː.bəʊ, ⓤⓢ -boʊ **-s** -z
Ightham ˈaɪ.təm, ⓤⓢ -t̬əm
Iglesias ɪˈgleɪ.si.æs, -əs, -zi-, ⓤⓢ -əs
igloo ˈɪg.luː **-s** -z
Ignatieff ɪgˈnæt.i.ef, ⓤⓢ -ˈnæt̬-
Ignatius ɪgˈneɪ.ʃəs
igneous ˈɪg.ni.əs
ignis fatu|us ˌɪg.nɪsˈfæt.ju|.əs, ⓤⓢ -ˈfætʃ.uː- **-i** -iː
ig|nite ɪg|ˈnaɪt **-nites** -ˈnaɪts **-niting** -ˈnaɪ.tɪŋ, ⓤⓢ -ˈnaɪ.t̬ɪŋ **-nited** -ˈnaɪ.tɪd, ⓤⓢ -ˈnaɪ.t̬ɪd **-nitable** -ˈnaɪ.tə.bᵊl, ⓤⓢ -ˈnaɪ.t̬ə.bᵊl
ignition ɪgˈnɪʃ.ᵊn **-s** -z
ignobility ˌɪg.nəʊˈbɪl.ə.ti, -ɪ.ti, ⓤⓢ -noʊˈbɪl.ə.t̬i, -nəˈ-
ignob|le ɪgˈnəʊ.b|ᵊl, ⓤⓢ -ˈnoʊ- **-ly** -li **-leness** -ᵊl.nəs, -nɪs
ignominious ˌɪg.nəʊˈmɪn.i.əs, ⓤⓢ -nəˈ- **-ly** -li **-ness** -nəs, -nɪs
ignominy ˈɪg.nə.mɪ.ni, -mə.ni, ⓤⓢ -nə.mɪ-
ignoramus ˌɪg.nəˈreɪ.məs **-es** -ɪz
ignorance ˈɪg.nᵊr.ᵊnts
ignorant ˈɪg.nᵊr.ᵊnt **-ly** -li
ignor|e ɪgˈnɔːʳ, ⓤⓢ -ˈnɔːr **-es** -z **-ing** -ɪŋ **-ed** -d **-able** -ə.bᵊl
Igoe ˈaɪ.gəʊ, ⓤⓢ -goʊ
Igor ˈiː.gɔːʳ, ⓤⓢ -gɔːr
Igorot ˌiː.gəˈrəʊt, ˌɪg.əˈ-, ⓤⓢ ˌiː.goʊˈroʊt, ˌɪg.oʊˈ- **-s** -s
Igraine ɪˈgreɪn, iː-
Iguaçú ˌiː.gwɑːˈsuː
iguana ɪˈgwɑː.nə, ˌɪg.juˈɑː-, ⓤⓢ ɪˈgwɑː-, iː- **-s** -z
iguanodon ɪˈgwɑː.nə.dɒn, ˌɪg.juˈɑː-, -ˈæn.ə-, -dən, ⓤⓢ ɪˈgwɑː.nə.dɑːn, iː- **-s** -z
Iguazú ˌiː.gwɑːˈsuː
ikat ˈiː.kɑːt
IKBS ˌaɪ.keɪ.biːˈes
Ike aɪk
Ikea® aɪˈkiː.ə; *as if Swedish:* ɪˈkeɪ.ə
ikon ˈaɪ.kɒn, -kən, ⓤⓢ -kɑːn, -kən **-s** -z
Ilchester ˈɪl.tʃɪs.təʳ, ⓤⓢ -tɚ
ilea (plural of **ileum**) ˈɪl.i.ə
ILEA ˈɪl.i.ə, ˌaɪ.el.iːˈeɪ
ileostom|y ˌɪl.iˈɒs.tə.m|i, ⓤⓢ -ˈɑː.stə- **-ies** -iz
ile|um ˈɪl.i|.əm **-a** -ə **-al** -əl
ilex ˈaɪ.leks **-es** -ɪz
Ilford ˈɪl.fəd, ⓤⓢ -fɚd
Ilfracombe ˈɪl.frə.kuːm
ilia (plural of **ilium**) ˈɪl.i.ə
iliac ˈɪl.i.æk
Iliad ˈɪl.i.æd, -əd, ⓤⓢ -əd, -æd
Iliffe ˈaɪ.lɪf
ili|um ˈɪl.i|.əm **-a** -ə
Ilium ˈɪl.i.əm, ˈaɪ.li-
ilk ɪlk
Ilkeston(e) ˈɪl.kɪ.stᵊn, -kə-
Ilkley ˈɪl.kli
ill ɪl **-s** -z ˌ**ill at** ˈ**ease**; ˌ**ill** ˈ**will**
I'll (= **I will** or **I shall**) aɪl
Ill. (abbrev. for **Illinois**) ˌɪl.ɪˈnɔɪ, -əˈ-
ill-advised ˌɪl.ədˈvaɪzd *stress shift:* ˌ**ill-advised** ˈ**plan**
ill-advisedly ˌɪl.ədˈvaɪ.zɪd.li
ill-assorted ˌɪl.əˈsɔː.tɪd, ⓤⓢ -ˈsɔːr.t̬ɪd *stress shift:* ˌ**ill-assorted** ˈ**candidates**
illative ɪˈleɪ.tɪv, ˈɪl.ə.tɪv, ⓤⓢ -t̬ɪv **-ly** -li
ill-bred ˌɪlˈbred *stress shift:* ˌ**ill-bred** ˈ**lout**
ill-breeding ˌɪlˈbriː.dɪŋ
ill-conceived ˌɪl.kənˈsiːvd *stress shift:* ˌ**ill-conceived** ˈ**plan**
ill-conditioned ˌɪl.kənˈdɪʃ.ᵊnd *stress shift:* ˌ**ill-conditioned** ˈ**crew**
ill-considered ˌɪl.kənˈsɪd.əd, ⓤⓢ -ɚd *stress shift:* ˌ**ill-considered** ˈ**action**
ill-disposed ˌɪl.dɪˈspəʊzd, ⓤⓢ -ˈspoʊzd *stress shift:* ˌ**ill-disposed** ˈ**patient**
illegal ɪˈliː.gᵊl, ⓤⓢ ɪˈliː-, ˌɪl- **-ly** -i **il**ˌ**legal** ˈ**alien**; **il**ˌ**legal** ˈ**immigrant**
illegalit|y ˌɪl.iːˈgæl.ə.t|i, -ɪˈ-, -ɪ.t|i, ⓤⓢ -ə.t̬|i **-ies** -iz
illegibility ɪˌledʒ.əˈbɪl.ə.ti, ˌɪl.ledʒ-, -ɪˈ-, -ɪ.ti, ⓤⓢ -ə.t̬i
illegib|le ɪˈledʒ.ə.b|ᵊl, ˌɪlˈledʒ-, ˈ-ɪ- **-ly** -li **-leness** -ᵊl.nəs, -nɪs
illegitimacy ˌɪl.ɪˈdʒɪt.ə.mə.si, -əˈ-, ˈ-ɪ-, ⓤⓢ -ˈdʒɪt̬.ə-
illegitimate ˌɪl.ɪˈdʒɪt.ə.mət, -əˈ-, ˈ-ɪ-, -mɪt, ⓤⓢ -ˈdʒɪt̬.ə- **-ly** -li
ill-equipped ˌɪl.ɪˈkwɪpt *stress shift:* ˌ**ill-equipped** ˈ**project**
ill-fated ˌɪlˈfeɪ.tɪd, ⓤⓢ -t̬ɪd *stress shift:* ˌ**ill-fated** ˈ**lovers**
ill-favoured ˌɪlˈfeɪ.vəd, ⓤⓢ -vɚd **-ly** -li **-ness** -nəs, -nɪs *stress shift:* ˌ**ill-favoured** ˈ**couple**
ill-feeling ˌɪlˈfiː.lɪŋ
ill-fitting ˌɪlˈfɪt.ɪŋ, ⓤⓢ -ˈfɪt̬- *stress shift:* ˌ**ill-fitting** ˈ**suit**
ill-founded ˌɪlˈfaʊn.dɪd *stress shift:* ˌ**ill-founded** ˈ**rumo(u)r**
ill-gotten ˌɪlˈgɒt.ᵊn, ⓤⓢ -ˈgɑː.tᵊn *stress shift, see compound:* ˌ**ill-gotten** ˈ**gains**
illiberal ɪˈlɪb.ᵊr.ᵊl, ˌɪl- **-ly** -i **-ness** -nəs, -nɪs
illiberalism ɪˈlɪb.ᵊr.ᵊl.ɪ.zᵊm, ˌɪl-
illiberality ɪˌlɪb.əˈræl.ə.ti, ˌɪl-, -ɪ.ti, ⓤⓢ -ə.t̬i
illicit ɪˈlɪs.ɪt, ˌɪl- **-ly** -li **-ness** -nəs, -nɪs
illimitab|le ɪˈlɪm.ɪ.tə.b|ᵊl, ˌɪl-, ⓤⓢ -t̬ə- **-ly** -li **-leness** -ᵊl.nəs, -nɪs
Illingworth ˈɪl.ɪŋ.wəθ, -wɜːθ, ⓤⓢ -wɚθ, -wɜːθ
Illinois ˌɪl.ɪˈnɔɪ, -əˈ-
illiteracy ɪˈlɪt.ᵊr.ə.si, ˌɪl-, ⓤⓢ -ˈlɪt̬-

Pronouncing the letters IEU

The vowel-letter combination **ieu** has a number of possible pronunciations, but most are associated with particular words, e.g.:

lieutenant	lefˈten.ənt (US) luː-
lieu	ljuː, luː (US) luː

illiterate ɪˈlɪt.ər.ət, ˌɪl-, -ɪt, (US) -ˈlɪţ- **-s** -s **-ly** -li **-ness** -nəs, -nɪs
ill-judged ˌɪlˈdʒʌdʒd *stress shift:* ˌ**ill-judged** ˈ**move**
ill-mannered ˌɪlˈmæn.əd, (US) -ɚd *stress shift:* ˌ**ill-mannered** ˈ**man**
ill-natured ˌɪlˈneɪ.tʃəd, (US) -tʃɚd **-ly** -li *stress shift:* ˌ**ill-natured** ˈ**dog**
illness ˈɪl.nəs, -nɪs **-es** -ɪz
illocution ˌɪl.əˈkjuː.ʃən **-s** -z **-ary** -ər.i, (US) -er-
illogic|al ɪˈlɒdʒ.ɪ.k|əl, ˌɪl-, (US) -ˈlɑː.dʒɪ- **-ally** -əl.i, -li **-alness** -əl.nəs, -nɪs
illogicalit|y ɪˌlɒdʒ.ɪˈkæl.ə.t|i, ˌɪl-, -ɪ.t|i, (US) -ˌlɑː.dʒɪˈkæl.ə.ţ|i **-ies** -iz
ill-omened ˌɪlˈəʊ.mend, -mənd, -mɪnd, (US) -ˈoʊ- *stress shift:* ˌ**ill-omened** ˈ**voyage**
ill-starred ˌɪlˈstɑːd, (US) -ˈstɑːrd *stress shift:* ˌ**ill-starred** ˈ**love**
ill-tempered ˌɪlˈtem.pəd, (US) -pɚd *stress shift:* ˌ**ill-tempered** ˈ**customer**
ill-timed ˌɪlˈtaɪmd *stress shift:* ˌ**ill-timed** ˈ**entrance**
ill|-treat ˌɪl|ˈtriːt, ɪl- **-treats** -ˈtriːts **-treating** -ˈtriː.tɪŋ, (US) -ˈtriː.ţɪŋ **-treated** -ˈtriː.tɪd, (US) -ˈtriː.ţɪd **-treatment** -ˈtriːt.mənt
illum|e ɪˈljuːm, -ˈluːm, (US) -ˈluːm **-es** -z **-ing** -ɪŋ **-ed** -d
illuminant ɪˈluː.mɪ.nənt, -ˈljuː-, -mə-, (US) -ˈluː.mə- **-s** -s
illumi|nate ɪˈluː.mɪ|.neɪt, -ˈljuː-, -mə-, (US) -ˈluː.mə- **-nates** -neɪts **-nating** -neɪ.tɪŋ, (US) -neɪ.ţɪŋ **-nated** -neɪ.tɪd, (US) -neɪ.ţɪd **-nator/s** -neɪ.təʳ/z, (US) -neɪ.ţɚ/z
illuminati, I~ ɪˌluː.mɪˈnɑː.tiː, -məˈ-, (US) -ˈnɑː.ţi
illumination ɪˌluː.mɪˈneɪ.ʃən, -ˌljuː-, -məˈ-, (US) -ˌluː- **-s** -z
illuminative ɪˈluː.mɪ.nə.təv, -ˈljuː-, -mə-, -neɪ-, (US) -ˈluː.mɪ.neɪ.ţɪv, -mə-
illumin|e ɪˈljuː.mɪn, -ˈluː-, (US) -ˈluː- **-es** -z **-ing** -ɪŋ **-ed** -d
ill-usage ˌɪlˈjuː.zɪdʒ, -sɪdʒ, (US) -sɪdʒ, -zɪdʒ **-s** -ɪz
ill-used ˌɪlˈjuːzd *stress shift:* ˌ**ill-used** ˈ**servant**
illusion ɪˈluː.ʒən, -ˈljuː-, (US) -ˈluː- **-s** -z
illusion|ism ɪˈluː.ʒən|.ɪ.zəm, -ˈljuː-, (US) -ˈluː- **-ist/s** -ɪst/s
illusive ɪˈluː.sɪv, -ˈljuː-, (US) -ˈluː- **-ly** -li **-ness** -nəs, -nɪs
illusor|y ɪˈluː.sər|.i, -ˈljuː-, -zər-, (US) -ˈluː- **-ily** -əl.i, -ɪ.li **-iness** -ɪ.nəs, -ɪ.nɪs
illu|strate ˈɪl.ə|.streɪt **-strates** -streɪts **-strating** -streɪ.tɪŋ, (US) -streɪ.ţɪŋ **-strated** -streɪ.tɪd, (US) -streɪ.ţɪd **-strator/s** -streɪ.təʳ/z, (US) -streɪ.ţɚ/z
illustration ˌɪl.əˈstreɪ.ʃən **-s** -z
illustrative ˈɪl.ə.strə.tɪv, -streɪ-; ɪˈlʌs.trə.tɪv, (US) ɪˈlʌs.trə.ţɪv; (US) ˈɪl.ə.streɪ- **-ly** -li
illustrious ɪˈlʌs.tri.əs **-ly** -li **-ness** -nəs, -nɪs
illuvi|um ɪˈluː.vi|.əm **-ums** -əmz **-a** -ə **-al** -əl
Illyri|a ɪˈlɪr.i|.ə **-an/s** -ən/z
Illyricum ɪˈlɪr.ɪ.kəm
Ilminster ˈɪl.mɪn.stəʳ, (US) -stɚ
Ilorin ɪˈlɒr.ɪn, (US) -ˈlɔːr-
Ilyushin ɪˈljuː.ʃɪn, -ʃən, (US) ɪlˈjuː-, ɪˈluː-
im- ɪm
Note: Prefix. The form of **in-** where the stem begins with /p/, /b/, or /m/. When a negative prefix, **im-** does not affect the stress pattern of the stem, e.g. **balance** /ˈbæl.ənts/, **imbalance** /ɪmˈbæl.ənts/. In other cases, the prefix is normally stressed in nouns but not in verbs, e.g. **imprint**, noun /ˈɪm.prɪnt/, verb /ɪmˈprɪnt/.
I'm (= **I am**) aɪm
imag|e ˈɪm.ɪdʒ **-es** -ɪz **-ing** -ɪŋ **-ed** -d
imager|y ˈɪm.ɪ.dʒər|.i, ˈ-ə- **-ies** -iz
imaginab|le ɪˈmædʒ.ɪ.nə.b|əl, -ən.ə- **-ly** -li **-leness** -əl.nəs, -nɪs
imaginar|y ɪˈmædʒ.ɪ.nər|.i, -ən.ər-, -nər|.i, (US) -ə.ner- **-ily** -əl.i, -ɪ.li **-iness** -ɪ.nəs, -ɪ.nɪs
imagination ɪˌmædʒ.ɪˈneɪ.ʃən, -əˈ- **-s** -z
imaginative ɪˈmædʒ.ɪ.nə.tɪv, ˈ-ə-, (US) -nə.ţɪv, -neɪ- **-ly** -li **-ness** -nəs, -nɪs
imagin|e ɪˈmædʒ.ɪn, -ən **-es** -z **-ing/s** -ɪŋ/z **-ed** -d
imagines (plural of **imago**) ɪˈmeɪ.dʒɪ.niːz, ɪˈmɑː-, -neɪz, (US) -niːz
imagism ˈɪm.ɪ.dʒɪ.zəm
ima|go ɪˈmeɪ|.gəʊ, ɪˈmɑː-, (US) -goʊ **-goes** -gəʊz, (US) -goʊz **-gines** -dʒɪ.niːz, -neɪz, (US) -niːz
imam ˈɪ.mɑːm, ɪˈmɑːm, (US) ɪˈmɑːm **-s** -z
IMAX® ˈaɪ.mæks
imbalanc|e ˌɪmˈbæl.ənts **-es** -ɪz
imbecile ˈɪm.bə.siːl, -bɪ-, -saɪl, (US) -sɪl, -səl **-s** -z
imbecilic ˌɪm.bəˈsɪl.ɪk, -bɪˈ-
imbecilit|y ˌɪm.bəˈsɪl.ə.t|i, -bɪˈ-, -ɪ.t|i, (US) -ə.ţ|i **-ies** -iz
imbed ɪmˈbed **-s** -z **-ding** -ɪŋ **-ded** -ɪd
Imbert ˈɪm.bət, (US) -bɚt
imbib|e ɪmˈbaɪb **-es** -z **-ing** -ɪŋ **-ed** -d **-er/s** -əʳ/z, (US) -ɚ/z
imbroglio ɪmˈbrəʊ.li.əʊ, (US) -ˈbroʊ.li.oʊ **-s** -z
imbru|e ɪmˈbruː **-es** -z **-ing** -ɪŋ **-ed** -d
imbu|e ɪmˈbjuː **-es** -z **-ing** -ɪŋ **-ed** -d
Imelda ɪˈmel.də
Imeson ˈaɪ.mɪ.sən
IMF ˌaɪ.emˈef
imitability ˌɪm.ɪ.təˈbɪl.ə.ti, ˌ-ə-, -ɪ.ti, (US) -ə.ţi
imitable ˈɪm.ɪ.tə.bəl, ˈ-ə-, (US) -ə.ţə-
imi|tate ˈɪm.ɪ|.teɪt, ˈ-ə- **-tates** -teɪts **-tating** -teɪ.tɪŋ, (US) -teɪ.ţɪŋ **-tated** -teɪ.tɪd, (US) -teɪ.ţɪd **-tator/s** -teɪ.təʳ/z, (US) -teɪ.ţɚ/z
imitation ˌɪm.ɪˈteɪ.ʃən, -əˈ- **-s** -z **-al** -əl
imitative ˈɪm.ɪ.tə.tɪv, ˈ-ə-, -teɪ-, (US) -teɪ.ţɪv **-ly** -li **-ness** -nəs, -nɪs
Imlay ˈɪm.leɪ
immaculate ɪˈmæk.jə.lət, -jʊ-, -lɪt **-ly** -li **-ness** -nəs, -nɪs **Imˌmaculate Conˈception**
immanen|ce ˈɪm.ə.nən|ts **-t** -t
Immanuel ɪˈmæn.ju.əl, (US) -el, -əl
immaterial ˌɪm.əˈtɪə.ri.əl, (US) -ˈtɪr.i- **-ly** -i **-ness** -nəs, -nɪs
immaterial|ism ˌɪm.əˈtɪə.ri.əl|.ɪ.zəm, (US) -ˈtɪr.i- **-ist/s** -ɪst/s
immateriality ˌɪm.əˌtɪə.riˈæl.ə.ti, -ɪ.ti, (US) -ˌtɪr.iˈæl.ə.ţi
immaterializ|e, -is|e ˌɪm.əˈtɪə.ri.əl.aɪz, (US) -ˈtɪr.i- **-es** -ɪz **-ing** -ɪŋ **-ed** -d
immature ˌɪm.əˈtʃʊəʳ, -ˈtjʊəʳ, -ˈtʃɔːʳ, -ˈtjɔːʳ, (US) -ˈtʊr, -ˈtjʊr **-ly** -li **-ness** -nəs, -nɪs
immaturit|y ˌɪm.əˈtʃʊə.rə.t|i, -ˈtjʊə-, -ˈtʃɔː-, -ˈtjɔː-, -rɪ-, (US) -ˈtʊr.ə.ţ|i, -ˈtjʊr- **-ies** -iz
immeasurab|le ɪˈmeʒ.ər.ə.b|əl, ˌɪm- **-ly** -li **-leness** -əl.nəs, -nɪs
immediacy ɪˈmiː.di.ə.si
immediate ɪˈmiː.di.ət, -ɪt, -dʒət, (US) -di.ɪt **-ly** -li
immemorial ˌɪm.ɪˈmɔː.ri.əl, -əˈ-, (US) -ˈmɔːr.i- **-ly** -li
immense ɪˈments **-ly** -li **-ness** -nəs, -nɪs
immensit|y ɪˈment.sə.t|i, -sɪ-, (US) -sə.ţ|i **-ies** -iz
immers|e ɪˈmɜːs, (US) -ˈmɝːs **-es** -ɪz **-ing** -ɪŋ **-ed** -t
immersion ɪˈmɜː.ʃən, -ʒən, (US) -ˈmɝː- **-s** -z **imˈmersion ˌheater**
immigrant ˈɪm.ɪ.grənt, ˈ-ə- **-s** -s
immi|grate ˈɪm.ɪ|.greɪt, ˈ-ə- **-grates** -greɪts **-grating** -greɪ.tɪŋ, (US) -greɪ.ţɪŋ **-grated** -greɪ.tɪd, (US) -greɪ.ţɪd
immigration ˌɪm.ɪˈgreɪ.ʃən, -əˈ- **-s** -z
imminence ˈɪm.ɪ.nənts, ˈ-ə-
imminent ˈɪm.ɪ.nənt, ˈ-ə- **-ly** -li
Immingham ˈɪm.ɪŋ.əm, (US) -hæm, -həm, -əm
immiscibility ɪˌmɪs.əˈbɪl.ə.ti, ˌɪm-, -ɪˈ-, -ɪ.ti, (US) -ə.ţi

immiscib|le ɪˈmɪs.ə.b|əl, ˌɪm-, ˈ-ɪ- **-ly** -li
immobile ɪˈməʊ.baɪl, ɪm-, US -ˈmoʊ.bəl, -bɪl, -baɪl
immobility ˌɪm.əʊˈbɪl.ə.ti, -ɪ.ti, US -moʊˈbɪl.ə.ţi
immobilization, -isa- ɪˌməʊ.bəl.aɪˈzeɪ.ʃən, ˌɪm-, -bɪ.laɪˈ-, -ləˈ-, US -ˌmoʊ.bə.lɪˈ-
immobiliz|e, -is|e ɪˈməʊ.bəl.aɪz, ˌɪm-, -bɪ.laɪz, US -ˈmoʊ- **-es** -ɪz **-ing** -ɪŋ **-ed** -d
immobilizer, -ise- ɪˈməʊ.bəl.aɪ.zər, US -zɚ **-s** -z
immoderate ɪˈmɒd.ər.ət, ˌɪm-, -ɪt, US -ˈmɑː.dɚ- **-ly** -li **-ness** -nəs, -nɪs
immoderation ɪˌmɒd.əˈreɪ.ʃən, ˌɪm-, US -ˌmɑː.dəˈ-
immodest ɪˈmɒd.ɪst, ˌɪm-, US -ˈmɑː.dɪst **-ly** -li
immodesty ɪˈmɒd.ə.sti, ˌɪm-, ˈ-ɪ-, US -ˈmɑː.də-
immo|late ˈɪm.əʊ|.leɪt, US ˈ-ə- **-lates** -leɪts **-lating** -leɪ.tɪŋ, US -leɪ.ţɪŋ **-lated** -leɪ.tɪd, US -leɪ.ţɪd **-lator/s** -leɪ.tər/z, US -leɪ.ţɚ/z
immolation ˌɪm.əʊˈleɪ.ʃən, US -əˈ- **-s** -z
immoral ɪˈmɒr.əl, ˌɪm-, US -ˈmɔːr- **-ly** -i
immoralit|y ˌɪm.əˈræl.ə.t|i, -ɒrˈæl-, -ɪ.t|i, US ɪ.mɔːˈræl.ə.ţ|i, ɪm.əˈ- **-ies** -iz
immortal ɪˈmɔː.təl, ˌɪm-, US -ˈmɔːr.ţəl **-s** -z **-ly** -i
immortality ˌɪm.ɔːˈtæl.ə.ti, -ɪ.ti, US -ɔːrˈtæl.ə.ţi
immortaliz|e, -is|e ɪˈmɔː.təl.aɪz, ˌɪm-, US -ˈmɔːr.ţəl- **-es** -ɪz **-ing** -ɪŋ **-ed** -d
immortelle ˌɪm.ɔːˈtel, US -ɔːrˈ- **-s** -z
immovability ɪˌmuː.vəˈbɪl.ə.ti, ˌɪm-, -ɪ.ti, US -ə.ţi
immovab|le ɪˈmuː.və.b|əl, ˌɪm- **-ly** -li **-leness** -əl.nəs, -nɪs
immune ɪˈmjuːn **imˈmune ˌsystem**
immunit|y ɪˈmjuː.nə.t|i, -nɪ-, US -nə.ţ|i **-ies** -iz
immunization, -isa- ˌɪm.jə.naɪˈzeɪ.ʃən, -jʊ-, -nɪˈ-, US -nəˈ- **-s** -z
immuniz|e, -is|e ˈɪm.jə.naɪz, -jʊ- **-es** -ɪz **-ing** -ɪŋ **-ed** -d
immuno- ˌɪm.jə.nəʊ, -jʊ-; ɪˌmjuː.nəʊ, US -noʊ
immunodeficiency ˌɪm.jə.nəʊ.dɪˈfɪʃ.ənt.si, -jʊ-; ɪˌmjuː-, US -noʊ-
immunologic|al ˌɪm.jə.nəʊˈlɒdʒ.ɪ.k|əl, -jʊ-; ɪˌmjuː.nəʊˈ-, US ˌɪm.jə.noʊˈlɑː.dʒɪ-, -jʊ- **-ally** -əl.i, -li
immunolog|y ˌɪm.jəˈnɒl.ə.dʒ|i, -jʊˈ-, US -ˈnɑː.lə- **-ist/s** -ɪst/s
immunosuppress|ant ˌɪm.jə.nəʊ.səˈpres|.ənt, -jʊ-; ɪˌmjuː-, US -noʊ- **-ive** -ɪv
immunosuppression ˌɪm.jə.nəʊ.səˈpreʃ.ən, -jʊ-; ɪˌmjuː-, US -noʊ-
immur|e ɪˈmjʊər, -ˈmjɔːr, US -ˈmjʊr **-es** -z **-ing** -ɪŋ **-ed** -d **-ement** -mənt
immutability ɪˌmjuː.təˈbɪl.ə.ti, -ɪ.ti; ˌɪm.jə-, -jʊ-, US ɪˌmjuː.ţəˈbɪl.ə.ţi
immutab|le ɪˈmjuː.tə.b|əl, US -ţə- **-ly** -li **-leness** -əl.nəs, -nɪs
Imogen ˈɪm.ə.dʒən, -dʒen, -dʒɪn, US -dʒen, -dʒən
Imogene ˈɪm.ə.dʒiːn
Imola ˈɪm.əʊ.lə, US -ə-, -ˌoʊ-
imp ɪmp **-s** -s **-ing** -ɪŋ **-ed** -t
impact n ˈɪm.pækt **-s** -s
impact v ɪmˈpækt, ˈ-- **-s** -s **-ing** -ɪŋ **-ed** -ɪd
impair ɪmˈpeər, US -ˈper **-s** -z **-ing** -ɪŋ **-ed** -d
impairment ɪmˈpeə.mənt, US -ˈper- **-s** -s
impala ɪmˈpɑː.lə, US -ˈpɑː.lə, -ˈpæl.ə **-s** -z
impal|e ɪmˈpeɪl **-es** -z **-ing** -ɪŋ **-ed** -d **-ement** -mənt
impalpab|le ɪmˈpæl.pə.b|əl, ˌɪm- **-ly** -li
impanel ɪmˈpæn.əl **-s** -z **-(l)ing** -ɪŋ **-(l)ed** -d
imparisyllabic ɪmˌpær.ɪ.sɪˈlæb.ɪk, ˌɪm.pær-, ˌ-ə-, US ɪmˌper-, -ˌpær-
im|part ɪm|ˈpɑːt, US -ˈpɑːrt **-parts** -ˈpɑːts, US -ˈpɑːrts **-parting** -ˈpɑː.tɪŋ, US -ˈpɑːr.ţɪŋ **-parted** -ˈpɑː.tɪd, US -ˈpɑːr.ţɪd
impartation ˌɪm.pɑːˈteɪ.ʃən, US -pɑːrˈ-
impartial ɪmˈpɑː.ʃəl, ˌɪm-, US -ˈpɑːr- **-ly** -i **-ness** -nəs, -nɪs
impartiality ɪmˌpɑː.ʃiˈæl.ə.ti, ˌɪm.pɑː-, ˌɪmˌpɑː-, -ɪ.ti, US ɪmˌpɑːr-, ˌɪm-
impassability ɪmˌpɑː.səˈbɪl.ə.ti, ˌɪm.pɑː-, ˌɪmˌpɑː-, -ɪ.ti, US ɪmˌpæs.əˈbɪl.ə.ţi, ˌɪm-
impassable ɪmˈpɑː.sə.bəl, ˌɪm-, US -ˈpæs.ə- **-ness** -nəs, -nɪs
impasse ˈæ̃m.pɑːs, ˈæm-, ˈɪm-, -pæs, -ˈ-, US ˈɪm.pæs, -ˈ- **-es** -ɪz
impassibility ɪmˌpæs.əˈbɪl.ə.ti, ˌɪm.pæs-, -sɪˈ-, -ɪ.ti, US ɪmˌpæs.əˈbɪl.ə.ţi
impassible ɪmˈpæs.ə.bəl, ˈ-ɪ-
impassioned ɪmˈpæʃ.ənd
impassive ɪmˈpæs.ɪv **-ly** -li **-ness** -nəs, -nɪs
impassivity ˌɪm.pæsˈɪv.ə.ti, -ɪ.ti, US -ə.ţi
impasto ɪmˈpæs.təʊ, US -toʊ, -ˈpɑː.stoʊ **-ed** -d
impatience ɪmˈpeɪ.ʃənts
impatiens ɪmˈpeɪ.ʃi.enz, -ˈpæt.i-
impatient ɪmˈpeɪ.ʃənt **-ly** -li
impeach ɪmˈpiːtʃ **-es** -ɪz **-ing** -ɪŋ **-ed** -t **-er/s** -ər/z, US -ɚ/z **-ment/s** -mənt/s **-able** -ə.bəl
impeccability ɪmˌpek.əˈbɪl.ə.ti, ˌɪm.pek-, -ɪ.ti, US ɪmˌpek.əˈbɪl.ə.ţi
impeccab|le ɪmˈpek.ə.b|əl **-ly** -li
impecunious ˌɪm.pɪˈkjuː.ni.əs, -pəˈ- **-ly** -li **-ness** -nəs, -nɪs
impedanc|e ɪmˈpiː.dənts **-es** -ɪz
imped|e ɪmˈpiːd **-es** -z **-ing** -ɪŋ **-ed** -ɪd
impediment ɪmˈped.ɪ.mənt, ˈ-ə- **-s** -s
impedimenta ɪmˌped.ɪˈmen.tə, ˌɪm.ped-
impel ɪmˈpel **-s** -z **-ling** -ɪŋ **-led** -d **-ler/s** -ər/z, US -ɚ/z **-lent** -ənt
impend ɪmˈpend **-s** -z **-ing** -ɪŋ **-ed** -ɪd
impenetrability ɪmˌpen.ɪ.trəˈbɪl.ə.ti, ˌɪm.pen-, ˌ-ə-, -ɪ.ti, US ɪmˌpen.ɪ.trəˈbɪl.ə.ţi, ˌ-ə-
impenetrab|le ɪmˈpen.ɪ.trə.b|əl, ˌɪm-, ˈ-ə- **-ly** -li **-leness** -əl.nəs, -nɪs
impenitence ɪmˈpen.ɪ.tənts, ˌɪm-, US ˈ-ə-
impenitent ɪmˈpen.ɪ.tənt, ˌɪm-, US ˈ-ə- **-ly** -li
imperative ɪmˈper.ə.tɪv, US -ţɪv **-s** -z **-ly** -li **-ness** -nəs, -nɪs
imperator ˌɪm.pəˈrɑː.tɔːr, -ˈreɪ-, -tər, US -ˈreɪ.tɔːr, -ˈrɑː-, -ţɚ **-s** -z
imperatorial ɪmˌper.əˈtɔː.ri.əl; ˌɪm.per-, -pər-, US ˌɪm.pɚ.əˈtɔːr.i.əl
imperceptibility ˌɪm.pəˌsep.təˈbɪl.ə.ti, -tɪˈ-, -ɪ.ti, US -pɚˌsep.təˈbɪl.ə.ţi
imperceptib|le ˌɪm.pəˈsep.tə.b|əl, -tɪ-, US -pɚˈsep.tə- **-ly** -li **-leness** -əl.nəs, -nɪs
imperceptive ˌɪm.pəˈsep.tɪv, US -pɚˈ- **-ness** -nəs, -nɪs
imperfect ɪmˈpɜː.fɪkt, ˌɪm-, -fekt, US -ˈpɝː- **-s** -s **-ly** -li **-ness** -nəs, -nɪs
imperfection ˌɪm.pəˈfek.ʃən, US -pɚˈ- **-s** -z
imperfective ˌɪm.pəˈfek.tɪv, US -pɚˈ-
imperforat|e ɪmˈpɜː.fər.ət, ˌɪm-, -ɪt, US -ˈpɝː- **-ed** -ɪd **-s** -s
imperial ɪmˈpɪə.ri.əl, US -ˈpɪr.i- **-s** -z **-ly** -i
imperial|ism ɪmˈpɪə.ri.ə.l|ɪ.zəm, US -ˈpɪr.i- **-ist/s** -ɪst/s
imperialist ɪmˈpɪə.ri.ə.lɪst, US -ˈpɪr.i-
imperialistic ɪmˌpɪə.ri.əˈlɪs.tɪk, US -ˌpɪr.i-
imperil ɪmˈper.əl, -ɪl, US -əl **-s** -z **-(l)ing** -ɪŋ **-(l)ed** -d
imperious ɪmˈpɪə.ri.əs, US -ˈpɪr.i- **-ly** -li **-ness** -nəs, -nɪs
imperishab|le ɪmˈper.ɪ.ʃə.b|əl, ˌɪm- **-ly** -li **-leness** -əl.nəs, -nɪs
impermanence ɪmˈpɜː.mə.nənts, ˌɪm-, US -ˈpɝː-
impermanent ɪmˈpɜː.mə.nənt, ˌɪm-, US -ˈpɝː- **-ly** -li
impermeability ɪmˌpɜː.mi.əˈbɪl.ə.ti, ˌɪm-, -ɪ.ti, US -ˌpɝː.mi.əˈbɪl.ə.ţi
impermeable ɪmˈpɜː.mi.ə.b|əl, ˌɪm-, US -ˈpɝː- **-ly** -li **-leness** -əl.nəs, -nɪs
impermissibility ˌɪm.pəˌmɪs.əˈbɪl.ə.ti, -ɪˈ-, -ɪ.ti, US -pɚˌmɪs.əˈbɪl.ə.ţi, -ɪˈ-
impermissib|le ˌɪm.pəˈmɪs.ə.b|əl, ˈ-ɪ-, US -pɚˈ- **-ly** -li

impers|onal ɪmˈpɜː.s|ən.əl, ˌɪm-, (US) -ˈpɝː- **-onally** -nə.li, -ən.əl.i
impersonality ɪmˌpɜː.sənˈæl.ə.ti, ˌɪm-, -ɪ.ti, (US) -ˌpɝː.sənˈæl.ə.t̬i
imperson|ate ɪmˈpɜː.sən|.eɪt, (US) -ˈpɝː- **-ates** -eɪts **-ating** -eɪ.tɪŋ, (US) -eɪ.t̬ɪŋ **-ated** -eɪ.tɪd, (US) -eɪ.t̬ɪd **-ator/s** -eɪ.təʳ/z, (US) -eɪ.t̬ɚ/z
impersonation ɪmˌpɜː.sənˈeɪ.ʃən, (US) -ˌpɝː- **-s** -z
impertinence ɪmˈpɜː.tɪ.nənts, ˌɪm-, -tən.ənts, (US) -ˈpɝː.t̬ən.ənts
impertinent ɪmˈpɜː.tɪ.nənt, ˌɪm-, -tən.ənt, (US) -ˈpɝː.t̬ən- **-ly** -li
imperturbability ˌɪm.pəˌtɜː.bəˈbɪl.ə.ti, -ɪ.ti, (US) -pɚˌtɝː.bəˈbɪl.ə.t̬i
imperturbab|le ˌɪm.pəˈtɜː.bə.b|əl, (US) -pɚˈtɝː- **-ly** -li **-leness** -əl.nəs, -nɪs
impervious ɪmˈpɜː.vi.əs, ˌɪm-, (US) -ˈpɝː- **-ly** -li **-ness** -nəs, -nɪs
impetigo ˌɪm.pɪˈtaɪ.gəʊ, -pəˈ-, -petˈaɪ-, (US) -pəˈtaɪ.goʊ
impetuosity ɪmˌpet.juˈɒs.ə.ti, (US) ˌɪm-, -ˌpetʃ.uˈɑː.sə-, -ɪ.ti, ɪmˌpetʃ.uˈɑː.sə.t̬i
impetuous ɪmˈpetʃ.u.əs, ˌɪm-, -ˈpet.ju-, (US) -ˈpetʃ.u- **-ly** -li **-ness** -nəs, -nɪs
impetus ˈɪm.pɪ.təs, -pə-, (US) -təs
Impey ˈɪm.pi
impiet|y ɪmˈpaɪ.ə.t|i, ˌɪm-, -ɪ.t|i, (US) -ə.t̬|i **-ies** -iz
imping|e ɪmˈpɪndʒ **-es** -ɪz **-ing** -ɪŋ **-ed** -d **-ement/s** -mənt/s
impious ˈɪm.pi.əs; ɪmˈpaɪ-, ˌɪm-, (US) ˈɪm.pi-; (US) ɪmˈpaɪ- **-ly** -li **-ness** -nəs, -nɪs
impish ˈɪm.pɪʃ **-ly** -li **-ness** -nəs, -nɪs
implacability ɪmˌplæk.əˈbɪl.ə.ti, ˌɪm-, -ɪ.ti, (US) -ə.t̬i
implacab|le ɪmˈplæk.ə.b|əl **-ly** -li **-leness** -əl.nəs, -nɪs
implant n ˈɪm.plɑːnt, (US) -plænt **-s** -s
implan|t v ɪmˈplɑːn|t, (US) -ˈplæn|t **-ts** -ts **-ting** -tɪŋ, (US) -t̬ɪŋ **-ted** -tɪd, (US) -t̬ɪd **-ter/s** -təʳ/z, (US) -t̬ɚ/z
implantation ˌɪm.plɑːnˈteɪ.ʃən, -plænˈ-, (US) -plænˈ-
implausibilit|y ɪmˌplɔː.zəˈbɪl.ə.t|i, ˌɪm.plɔː-, ˌɪmˌplɔː-, -zɪˈ-, -ɪ.t|i, (US) ɪmˌplɑː.zəˈbɪl.ə.t̬|i, ˌɪm-, -ˌplɔː- **-ies** -iz
implausib|le ɪmˈplɔː.zə.b|əl, ˌɪm-, -zɪ-, (US) -ˈplɑː-, -ˈplɔː- **-ly** -li **-leness** -əl.nəs, -nɪs
impleader ɪmˈpliː.dəʳ, (US) -dɚ **-s** -z
implement n ˈɪm.plɪ.mənt, -plə- **-s** -s
implemen|t v ˈɪm.plɪ.men|t, -plə-, -mən|t, (US) -men|t **-ts** -ts **-ting** -tɪŋ, (US) -t̬ɪŋ **-ted** -tɪd, (US) -t̬ɪd
implementation ˌɪm.plɪ.menˈteɪ.ʃən, -plə-, -mənˈ- **-s** -z
impli|cate ˈɪm.plɪ|.keɪt, -plə- **-cates** -keɪts **-cating** -keɪ.tɪŋ, (US) -keɪ.t̬ɪŋ **-cated** -keɪ.tɪd, (US) -keɪ.t̬ɪd
implication ˌɪm.plɪˈkeɪ.ʃən, -pləˈ- **-s** -z
implicative ɪmˈplɪk.ə.tɪv; ˈɪm.plɪ.keɪ.tɪv, -plə-, (US) ˈɪm.plɪ.keɪ.t̬ɪv; (US) ɪmˈplɪk.ə- **-ly** -li
implicature ɪmˈplɪk.ə.tʃəʳ, -tjʊəʳ, (US) -tʃɚ **-s** -z
implicit ɪmˈplɪs.ɪt **-ly** -li **-ness** -nəs, -nɪs
implod|e ɪmˈpləʊd, (US) -ˈploʊd **-es** -z **-ing** -ɪŋ **-ed** -ɪd
implor|e ɪmˈplɔːʳ, (US) -ˈplɔːr **-es** -z **-ing/ly** -ɪŋ/li **-ed** -d **-er/s** -əʳ/z, (US) -ɚ/z
implosion ɪmˈpləʊ.ʒən, (US) -ˈploʊ- **-s** -z
implosive ɪmˈpləʊ.sɪv, ˌɪm-, -zɪv, (US) -ˈploʊ.sɪv **-s** -z
impl|y ɪmˈpl|aɪ **-ies** -aɪz **-ying** -aɪ.ɪŋ **-ied** -aɪd
impolic|y ɪmˈpɒl.ə.s|i, ˌɪm-, ˈ-ɪ-, (US) -ˈpɑː.lə- **-ies** -iz
impolite ˌɪm.pəlˈaɪt, (US) -pəˈlaɪt **-ly** -li **-ness** -nəs, -nɪs
impolitic ɪmˈpɒl.ə.tɪk, ˌɪm-, ˈ-ɪ-, (US) -ˈpɑː.lə-
imponderab|le ɪmˈpɒn.dər.ə.b|əl, ˌɪm-, (US) -ˈpɑːn- **-les** -əlz **-ly** -li **-leness** -əl.nəs, -nɪs
import n ˈɪm.pɔːt, (US) -pɔːrt **-s** -s
impor|t v ɪmˈpɔː|t, ˌɪm-, ˈ--, (US) ɪmˈpɔːr|t, ˈ-- **-ts** -ts **-ting** -tɪŋ, (US) -t̬ɪŋ **-ted** -tɪd, (US) -t̬ɪd **-ter/s** -təʳ/z, (US) -t̬ɚ/z
importable ɪmˈpɔː.tə.bəl, ˌɪm-, (US) -ˈpɔːr.t̬ə-
importance ɪmˈpɔː.tənts, (US) -ˈpɔːr-
important ɪmˈpɔː.tənt, (US) -ˈpɔːr- **-ly** -li
importation ˌɪm.pɔːˈteɪ.ʃən, (US) -pɔːrˈ- **-s** -z
importunate ɪmˈpɔː.tʃə.nət, -tʃʊ-, -tjʊ-, -nɪt, (US) -ˈpɔːr.tʃə.nɪt, -nət **-ly** -li **-ness** -nəs, -nɪs
importun|e ˌɪm.pəˈtʃuːn, -ˈtjuːn; ɪmˈpɔː.tʃuːn, -tjuːn, (US) ˌɪm.pɔːrˈtuːn, -ˈtjuːn, ɪmˈpɔːr.tʃən **-es** -z **-ing** -ɪŋ **-ed** -d
importunit|y ˌɪm.pɔːˈtʃuː.nə.t|i, -ˈtjuː-, -pəˈ-, -nɪ-, (US) -pɔːrˈtuː.nə.t̬|i, -ˈtjuː- **-ies** -iz
impos|e ɪmˈpəʊz, (US) -ˈpoʊz **-es** -ɪz **-ing** -ɪŋ **-ed** -d **-er/s** -əʳ/z, (US) -ɚ/z **-able** -ə.bəl
imposing ɪmˈpəʊ.zɪŋ, (US) -ˈpoʊ- **-ly** -li **-ness** -nəs, -nɪs
imposition ˌɪm.pəˈzɪʃ.ən **-s** -z
impossibilit|y ɪmˌpɒs.əˈbɪl.ə.t|i, ˌɪm.pɒs-, ˌɪmˌpɒs-, -ɪˈ-, -ɪ.t|i, (US) ɪmˌpɑː.səˈbɪl.ə.t̬|i, ˌɪm- **-ies** -iz
impossib|le ɪmˈpɒs.ə.b|əl, ˌɪm-, ˈ-ɪ-, (US) -ˈpɑː.sə- **-ly** -li
impost ˈɪm.pəʊst, -pɒst, (US) -poʊst **-s** -s
impostor, imposter ɪmˈpɒs.təʳ, (US) -ˈpɑː.stɚ **-s** -z
imposture ɪmˈpɒs.tʃəʳ, -tjəʳ, (US) -ˈpɑːs.tʃɚ **-s** -z
impoten|ce ˈɪm.pə.tənt|s, (US) -t̬ənt|s **-cy** -si
impotent ˈɪm.pə.tənt, (US) -t̬ənt **-ly** -li
impound ɪmˈpaʊnd **-s** -z **-ing** -ɪŋ **-ed** -ɪd
impoverish ɪmˈpɒv.ər.ɪʃ, (US) -ˈpɑː.vɚ-, -ˈpɑːv.rɪʃ **-es** -ɪz **-ing** -ɪŋ **-ed** -t **-ment** -mənt
impracticabilit|y ɪmˌpræk.tɪ.kəˈbɪl.ə.t|i, ˌɪm-, -ɪ.t|i, (US) -ə.t̬|i **-ies** -iz
impracticab|le ɪmˈpræk.tɪ.kə.b|əl, ˌɪm- **-ly** -li **-leness** -əl.nəs, -nɪs
impractic|al ɪmˈpræk.tɪ.k|əl, ˌɪm- **-ally** -əl.i, (US) -li **-alness** -əl.nəs, -əl.nɪs
impracticalit|y ɪmˌpræk.tɪˈkæl.ə.t|i, ˌɪm.præk-, ˌɪmˌpræk-, -ɪ.t|i, (US) ɪmˌpræk.tɪˈkæl.ə.t̬|i, ˌɪm- **-ies** -iz
impre|cate ˈɪm.prɪ|.keɪt, -prə- **-cates** -keɪts **-cating** -keɪ.tɪŋ, (US) -keɪ.t̬ɪŋ **-cated** -keɪ.tɪd, (US) -keɪ.t̬ɪd **-cator/s** -keɪ.təʳ/z, (US) -keɪ.t̬ɚ/z
imprecation ˌɪm.prɪˈkeɪ.ʃən, -prəˈ-, -prekˈeɪ-, (US) -prɪˈkeɪ- **-s** -z
imprecatory ˈɪm.prɪ.keɪ.tər.i, ˌɪm.prɪˈkeɪ-; ɪmˈprek.ə-, (US) ˈɪm.prɪ.kə.tɔːr.i
imprecise ˌɪm.prɪˈsaɪs, -prəˈ- **-ly** -li **-ness** -nəs, -nɪs
imprecision ˌɪm.prɪˈsɪʒ.ən, -prəˈ-
impregnability ɪmˌpreg.nəˈbɪl.ə.ti, ˌɪm-, -ɪ.ti, (US) -ə.t̬i
impregnab|le ɪmˈpreg.nə.b|əl **-ly** -li
impregnate adj ɪmˈpreg.nɪt, -nət, -neɪt
impregna|te v ˈɪm.preg.neɪ|t, -ˈ--, (US) ɪmˈpreg.neɪ|t **-tes** -ts **-ting** -tɪŋ, (US) -t̬ɪŋ **-ted** -tɪd, (US) -t̬ɪd
impregnation ˌɪm.pregˈneɪ.ʃən, -prɪgˈ-, (US) -pregˈ- **-s** -z
impresario ˌɪm.prɪˈsɑː.ri.əʊ, -prəˈ-, -presˈɑː-, (US) ˌɪm.prəˈsɑːr.i.oʊ, -ˈser- **-s** -z
imprescriptible ˌɪm.prɪˈskrɪp.tə.bəl
impress n ˈɪm.pres **-es** -ɪz
impress v ɪmˈpres **-es** -ɪz **-ing** -ɪŋ **-ed** -t
impressibility ɪmˌpres.əˈbɪl.ə.ti, -ɪˈ-, -ɪ.ti, (US) -ə.t̬i
impressib|le ɪmˈpres.ə.b|əl, ˈ-ɪ- **-ly** -li **-leness** -əl.nəs, -nɪs
impression ɪmˈpreʃ.ən **-s** -z
impressionability ɪmˌpreʃ.ən.əˈbɪl.ə.ti, -ˌpreʃ.nəˈ-, -ɪ.ti, (US) -ə.t̬i
impressionab|le ɪmˈpreʃ.ən.ə.b|əl, -ˈpreʃ.nə- **-ly** -li
impression|ism, I~ ɪmˈpreʃ.ən|.ɪ.zəm **-ist/s** -ɪst/s
impressionistic ɪmˌpreʃ.ənˈɪs.tɪk **-ally** -əl.i, -li
impressive ɪmˈpres.ɪv **-ly** -li **-ness** -nəs, -nɪs
impressment ɪmˈpres.mənt **-s** -s
imprest ˈɪm.prest, -ˈ- **-s** -s
imprimatur ˌɪm.prɪˈmeɪ.təʳ, -praɪˈ-,

-ˈmɑː-, -tʊəʳ, -tɜːʳ, US -prɪˈmɑː.tɚ, -ˈmeɪ-, -tʊr **-s** -z

imprint n ˈɪm.prɪnt **-s** -s

im|print v ɪm|ˈprɪnt, ˌɪm- **-prints** -ˈprɪnts **-printing** -ˈprɪn.tɪŋ, US -ˈprɪn.t̬ɪŋ **-printed** -ˈprɪn.tɪd, US -ˈprɪn.t̬ɪd

imprison ɪmˈprɪz.ᵊn, ˌɪm- **-s** -z **-ing** -ɪŋ, -ˈprɪz.nɪŋ **-ed** -d

imprisonment ɪmˈprɪz.ᵊn.mənt, -ᵊm-, US -ᵊn-

improbabilit|y ɪmˌprɒb.əˈbɪl.ə.t|i, ˌɪm.prɒb-, ˌɪmˌprɒb-, -ɪ.t|i, US ˌɪm.prɑː.bəˈbɪl.ə.t̬|i **-ies** -iz

improbab|le ɪmˈprɒb.ə.b|ᵊl, ˌɪm-, US -ˈprɑː.bə- **-ly** -li

improbity ɪmˈprəʊ.bə.ti, ˌɪm-, -bɪ-, US -ˈproʊ.bə.t̬i

impromptu ɪmˈprɒmp.tjuː, -tʃuː, US -ˈprɑːmp.tuː, -tjuː **-s** -z

improper ɪmˈprɒp.əʳ, ˌɪm-, US -ˈprɑː.pɚ **-ly** -li ˌ**improper** ˈ**fraction**; **im**ˌ**proper** ˈ**fraction**

impropri|ate ɪmˈprəʊ.pri|.eɪt, US -ˈproʊ- **-ates** -eɪts **-ating** -eɪ.tɪŋ, US -eɪ.t̬ɪŋ **-ated** -eɪ.tɪd, US -eɪ.t̬ɪd **-ator/s** -eɪ.təʳ/z, US -eɪ.t̬ɚ/z

impropriation ɪmˌprəʊ.priˈeɪ.ʃᵊn, ˌɪm.prəʊ-, ˌɪmˌprəʊ-, US ɪmˌproʊ-, ˌɪm- **-s** -z

impropriet|y ˌɪm.prəˈpraɪ.ə.t|i, US -t̬|i **-ies** -iz

improvability ɪmˌpruː.vəˈbɪl.ə.ti, -ɪ.ti, US -ə.t̬i

improvab|le ɪmˈpruː.və.b|ᵊl **-ly** -li **-leness** -ᵊl.nəs, -nɪs

improv|e ɪmˈpruːv **-es** -z **-ing** -ɪŋ **-ed** -d **-er/s** -əʳ/z, US -ɚ/z

improvement ɪmˈpruːv.mənt **-s** -s

improvidence ɪmˈprɒv.ɪ.dᵊnts, ˌɪm-, ˈ-ə-, US -ˈprɑː.və-

improvident ɪmˈprɒv.ɪ.dᵊnt, ˌɪm-, US -ˈprɑː.və- **-ly** -li

improvisation ˌɪm.prə.vaɪˈzeɪ.ʃᵊn, US ɪmˌprɑː.vɪˈ-; US ˌɪm.prə- **-s** -z

improvisatory ˌɪm.prə.vaɪˈzeɪ.tᵊr.i; -ˈvaɪ.zə-, US ɪmˈprɑː.və.zə.tɔːr-; US ˌɪm.prəˈvaɪ-

improvis|e ˈɪm.prə.vaɪz **-es** -ɪz **-ing** -ɪŋ **-ed** -d **-er/s** -əʳ/z, US -ɚ/z **-or/s** -əʳ/z, US -ɚ/z

imprudence ɪmˈpruː.dᵊnts, ˌɪm-

imprudent ɪmˈpruː.dᵊnt, ˌɪm- **-ly** -li

impudence ˈɪm.pjə.dᵊnts, -pjʊ-

impudent ˈɪm.pjə.dᵊnt, -pjʊ- **-ly** -li

impugn ɪmˈpjuːn **-s** -z **-ing** -ɪŋ **-ed** -d **-er/s** -ə/ʳz, US -ɚ/z **-able** -ə.bᵊl **-ment** -mənt

impuissan|ce ɪmˈpjuː.ɪ.sᵊn|ts, US -ˈpjuː.ɪ-, -ˈpwɪs.ᵊn|ts; US ˌɪm.pjuːˈɪs.ᵊn|ts **-t** -t

impuls|e ˈɪm.pʌls **-es** -ɪz ˈ**impulse** ˌ**buying**

impulsion ɪmˈpʌl.ʃᵊn **-s** -z

impulsive ɪmˈpʌl.sɪv **-ly** -li **-ness** -nəs, -nɪs

impunit|y ɪmˈpjuː.nə.t|i, -nɪ-, US -t̬|i **-ies** -iz

impure ɪmˈpjʊəʳ, ˌɪm-, -ˈpjɔːʳ, US -ˈpjʊr **-ly** -li **-ness** -nəs, -nɪs

impurit|y ɪmˈpjʊə.rə.t|i, ˌɪm-, -ˈpjɔː-, -rɪ-, US -ˈpjʊr.ə.t̬|i **-ies** -iz

imputability ɪmˌpjuː.təˈbɪl.ə.ti, ˌɪm.pjuː-, ˌɪmˌpjuː-, -ɪ.ti, US ɪmˌpjuː.t̬əˈbɪl.ə.t̬i, ˌɪm-

imputation ˌɪm.pjʊˈteɪ.ʃᵊn **-s** -z

im|pute ɪm|ˈpjuːt **-putes** -ˈpjuːts **-puting** -ˈpjuː.tɪŋ, US -ˈpjuː.t̬ɪŋ **-puted** -ˈpjuː.tɪd, US -ˈpjuː.t̬ɪd **-putable** -ˈpjuː.tə.bᵊl, US -ˈpjuː.t̬ə.bᵊl

Imray ˈɪm.reɪ

Imrie ˈɪm.ri

IMRO ˈɪm.rəʊ, US -roʊ

in ɪn ˌ**ins and** ˈ**outs**

in- ɪn

Note: Prefix. When the meaning of the prefix is 'in', it often carries secondary stress, e.g. **inbuilt** /ˌɪnˈbɪlt/. The resulting compounds may undergo stress shift (see entry for **inbuilt**). As a negative prefix, **in-** does not normally affect the stress pattern of the stem to which it is added, e.g. **active** /ˈæk.tɪv/, **inactive** /ɪnˈæk.tɪv/. In other cases, the prefix is normally stressed in nouns but not in verbs, e.g. **increase** noun /ˈɪn.kriːs/, verb /ɪnˈkriːs/.

in. (abbrev. for **inch/es**) *singular:* ɪntʃ; *plural:* -ɪz

Ina ˈiː.nə, ˈaɪ-, US ˈaɪ-

inabilit|y ˌɪn.əˈbɪl.ə.t|i, -ɪ.t|i, US -ə.t̬|i **-ies** -iz

in absentia ˌɪn.æbˈsen.ti.ə, -tʃi-, -ɑː, US -ˈsen.tʃi.ə, -tʃə

inaccessibility ˌɪn.əkˌses.əˈbɪl.ə.ti, -ækˌ-, -ɪˈ-, -ɪ.ti, US -ə.t̬i

inaccessib|le ˌɪn.əkˈses.ə.b|ᵊl, -ækˈ-, ˈ-ɪ- **-ly** -li **-leness** -ᵊl.nəs, -nɪs

inaccurac|y ɪnˈæk.jə.rə.s|i, ˌɪn-, -jʊ-, -rɪ.s|i, US -jɚ.ə- **-ies** -iz

inaccurate ɪnˈæk.jə.rət, ˌɪn-, -jʊ-, -rɪt, US -jɚ.ət **-ly** -li

inaction ɪnˈæk.ʃᵊn, ˌɪn-

inacti|vate ɪnˈæk.tɪ|.veɪt, ˌɪn-, -tə- **-vates** -veɪts **-vating** -veɪ.tɪŋ, US -veɪ.t̬ɪŋ **-vated** -veɪ.tɪd, US -veɪ.t̬ɪd

inactive ɪnˈæk.tɪv, ˌɪn- **-ly** -li

inactivity ˌɪn.ækˈtɪv.ə.ti, -ɪ.ti, US -ə.t̬i

inadequac|y ɪˈnæd.ɪ.kwə.s|i, ˌɪnˈæd-, ˈ-ə- **-ies** -iz

inadequate ɪˈnæd.ɪ.kwət, ˌɪnˈæd-, -kwɪt **-ly** -li **-ness** -nəs, -nɪs

inadmissibility ˌɪn.ədˌmɪs.əˈbɪl.ə.ti, -ɪˈ-, -ɪ.ti, US -ə.t̬i

inadmissib|le ˌɪn.ədˈmɪs.ə.b|ᵊl, ˈ-ɪ- **-ly** -li

inadverten|ce ˌɪn.ədˈvɜː.tᵊnt|s, US -ˈvɝː- **-cy** -si

inadvertent ˌɪn.ədˈvɜː.tᵊnt, US -ˈvɝː- **-ly** -li

inadvisability ˌɪn.ədˌvaɪ.zəˈbɪl.ə.ti, -ɪ.ti, US -ə.t̬i

inadvisable ˌɪn.ədˈvaɪ.zə.bᵊl

inalienability ɪˌneɪ.li.ə.nəˈbɪl.ə.ti, ˌɪnˌeɪ-, -ɪ.ti, US -ə.t̬i

inalienab|le ɪˈneɪ.li.ə.nə.b|ᵊl, ˌɪnˈeɪ- **-ly** -li **-leness** -ᵊl.nəs, -nɪs

inamora|ta ɪˌnæm.əˈrɑː|.tə, ˌɪn.æm-, US -ˈrɑː|.t̬ə, -ˌnæm- **-as** -təz, US -t̬əz **-o/s** -təʊ/z, US -toʊ/z

inane ɪˈneɪn **-ly** -li **-ness** -nəs, -nɪs

inanimate ɪˈnæn.ɪ.mət, ˌɪnˈæn-, -mɪt **-ly** -li **-ness** -nəs, -nɪs

inanition ˌɪn.əˈnɪʃ.ᵊn, -ænˈɪʃ-

inanit|y ɪˈnæn.ə.t|i, -ɪ.t|i, US -ə.t̬|i **-ies** -iz

inappeasable ˌɪn.əˈpiː.zə.bᵊl

inapplicability ˌɪn.əˌplɪk.əˈbɪl.ə.ti, -ˌæp.lɪ.kəˈ-, -ɪ.ti; ˌɪn.əˌplɪk.əˈ-, US ˌɪn.əˌplɪk.əˈbɪl.ə.t̬i, -ˌæp.lɪ.kəˈ-

inapplicable ˌɪn.əˈplɪk.ə.bᵊl; ɪˈnæp.lɪ.kə-, ˌɪnˈæp-, US ɪˈnæp-, ˌɪnˈæp-; US ˌɪn.əˈplɪk.ə- **-ness** -nəs, -nɪs

inapposite ɪˈnæp.ə.zɪt, ˌɪnˈæp- **-ly** -li **-ness** -nəs, -nɪs

inappreciab|le ˌɪn.əˈpriː.ʃi.ə.b|ᵊl, -ʃə- **-ly** -li

inapprehensible ɪnˌæp.rɪˈhent.sə.bᵊl, ˈ-sɪ-

inapproachab|le ˌɪn.əˈprəʊ.tʃə.b|ᵊl, US -ˈproʊ- **-ly** -li

inappropriate ˌɪn.əˈprəʊ.pri.ət, -ɪt, US -ˈproʊ- **-ly** -li **-ness** -nəs, -nɪs

inapt ɪˈnæpt, ˌɪnˈæpt **-ly** -li **-ness** -nəs, -nɪs

inaptitude ɪˈnæp.tɪ.tʃuːd, -tjuːd, ˈ-tə-, ˌɪnˈæp-, US -tə.tuːd, -tjuːd

inarguab|le ɪˈnɑː.gju.ə.b|ᵊl, ˌɪnˈɑː-, US ˌɪnˈɑːr- **-ly** -li

inarticulate ˌɪn.ɑːˈtɪk.jə.lət, -jʊ-, -lɪt, US -ɑːrˈ- **-ly** -li **-ness** -nəs, -nɪs

inartistic ˌɪn.ɑːˈtɪs.tɪk, US -ɑːrˈ- **-al** -ᵊl **-ally** -ᵊl.i, -li

inasmuch ˌɪn.əzˈmʌtʃ

inattention ˌɪn.əˈten.tʃᵊn

inattentive ˌɪn.əˈten.tɪv, US -t̬ɪv **-ly** -li **-ness** -nəs, -nɪs

inaudibility ɪˌnɔː.dəˈbɪl.ə.ti, ˌɪn.ɔː-, -dɪˈ-, -ɪ.ti, US ɪˌnɑː.dɪˈbɪl.ə.t̬i, ˌɪnˌɑː-, ɪˌnɔː-, ˌɪnˌɔː-

inaudib|le ɪˈnɔː.də.b|ᵊl, ˌɪn.ɔː-, -dɪ-, US ɪˈnɑː-, ˌɪnˈɑː-, ɪˈnɔː-, ˌɪnˈɔː- **-ly** -li **-leness** -ᵊl.nəs, -nɪs

inaugural ɪˈnɔː.gjə.rᵊl, -jʊ-, US ɪˈnɑː.gjʊr.ᵊl, -ˈnɔːg-, -jɚ-, ˈ-ɚ-

inaugu|rate ɪˈnɔː.gjə|.reɪt, -jʊ-, US ɪˈnɑː.gjʊ|.reɪt, ɪˈnɔːg-, -jə-, ˈ-ə- **-rates** -reɪts **-rating** -reɪ.tɪŋ, US -reɪ.t̬ɪŋ **-rated** -reɪ.tɪd, US -reɪ.t̬ɪd **-rator/s** -reɪ.təʳ/z, US -reɪ.t̬ɚ/z

inauguration ɪˌnɔː.gjəˈreɪ.ʃᵊn, -jʊˈ-, US ɪˌnɑː.gjʊˈ-, -ˌnɔːg-, -jəˈ-, -əˈ- **-s** -z

inauspicious ˌɪn.ɔːˈspɪʃ.əs, -ɒsˈpɪʃ-, US -ɑːˈspɪʃ-, -ɔːˈ- **-ly** -li **-ness** -nəs, -nɪs

inboard ˌɪnˈbɔːd, ˌɪm-, US ˈɪn.bɔːrd *stress shift, British only:* ˌ**inboard** ˈ**motor**

inborn ˌɪnˈbɔːn, ˌɪm-, US ˈɪn.bɔːrn *stress shift, British only:* ˌ**inborn** ˈ**talent**

inbound ˈɪn.baʊnd

inbox ˈɪn.bɒks, ˈɪm-, US ˈɪn.bɑːks **-es** -ɪz

inbreath|e ˌɪnˈbriːð, ˌɪm-, US ˌɪn- **-es** -z **-ing** -ɪŋ **-ed** -d
inbreed ˌɪnˈbriːd, ˌɪm-, US ˈɪn.briːd **-s** -z **-ing** -ɪŋ **inbred** ˌɪnˈbred, ˌɪm-, US ˈɪn.bred *stress shift, British only:* **ˌinbred ˈtrait**
inbuilt ˌɪnˈbɪlt, ˌɪm-, ˈ--, US ˈɪn.bɪlt *stress shift, British only:* **ˌinbuilt ˈhazard**
inc. (abbrev. for **incorporated**) ɪŋˈkɔː.pᵊr.eɪ.tɪd, ɪŋk, US ɪŋˈkɔːr.pɚ.eɪ.t̬ɪd, ɪŋk
Inca ˈɪŋ.kə **-s** -z
incalculability ɪnˌkæl.kjə.ləˈbɪl.ə.ti, ˌɪn-, ɪŋ-, ˌɪŋ-, -kjʊ-, -ɪ.ti, US ɪnˌkæl.kjə.ləˈbɪl.ə.t̬i, ˌɪn-, -kjʊ-
incalculab|le ɪnˈkæl.kjə.lə.b|ᵊl, ˌɪn-, ɪŋ-, ˌɪŋ-, -kjʊ-, US ɪnˈkæl-, ˌɪn- **-ly** -li **-leness** -ᵊl.nəs, -nɪs
in camera ˌɪnˈkæm.ᵊr.ə, ˌɪŋ-, ˈ-rə, US ˌɪn-
incandescence ˌɪn.kænˈdes.ᵊnts, ˌɪŋ-, -kənˈ-, US ˌɪn.kənˈ-
incandescent ˌɪn.kænˈdes.ᵊnt, ˌɪŋ-, -kənˈ-, US ˌɪn.kənˈ- **-ly** -li
incantation ˌɪn.kænˈteɪ.ʃᵊn, ˌɪŋ-, US ˌɪn- **-s** -z
incapabilit|y ɪnˌkeɪ.pəˈbɪl.ə.t|i, ˌɪn-, ɪŋ-, ˌɪŋ-, -ɪ.t|i, US ɪnˌkeɪ.pəˈbɪl.ə.t̬|i, ˌɪn- **-ies** -iz
incapab|le ɪnˈkeɪ.pə.b|ᵊl, ˌɪn-, ɪŋ-, ˌɪŋ-, US ɪnˈkeɪ-, ˌɪn- **-ly** -li **-leness** -ᵊl.nəs, -nɪs
incapaci|tate ˌɪn.kəˈpæs.ɪ|.teɪt, ˌɪŋ-, ˈ-ə-, US ˌɪn- **-tates** -teɪts **-tating** -teɪ.tɪŋ, US -teɪ.t̬ɪŋ **-tated** -teɪ.tɪd, US -teɪ.t̬ɪd
incapacitation ˌɪn.kəˌpæs.ɪˈteɪ.ʃᵊn, ˌɪŋ-, -əˈ-, US ˌɪn- **-s** -z
incapacit|y ˌɪn.kəˈpæs.ə.t|i, ˌɪŋ-, -ɪ.t|i, US ˌɪn.kəˈpæs.ə.t̬|i **-ies** -iz
in capite ˌɪnˈkæp.ɪ.teɪ, US -teɪ, -ti
incarcer|ate ɪnˈkɑː.sᵊr|.eɪt, ɪŋ-, US ɪnˈkɑːr.sə.r|eɪt **-ates** -eɪts **-ating** -eɪ.tɪŋ, US -eɪ.t̬ɪŋ **-ated** -eɪ.tɪd, US -eɪ.t̬ɪd
incarceration ɪnˌkɑː.sᵊrˈeɪ.ʃᵊn, ˌɪn.kɑː-, ˌɪnˌkɑː-, ɪŋˌkɑː-, ˌɪŋ.kɑː-, US ɪnˌkɑːr.səˈreɪ-, ˌɪn- **-s** -z
incarnadine ɪnˈkɑː.nə.daɪn, ɪŋ-, US ɪnˈkɑːr-, -diːn, -dɪn
incarnate **adj** ɪnˈkɑː.nət, ɪŋ-, -neɪt, -nɪt, US ɪnˈkɑːr-
incar|nate **v** ˈɪn.kɑː|.neɪt, ˈɪŋ-, -ˈ--, US ɪnˈkɑːr- **-nates** -neɪts **-nating** -neɪ.tɪŋ, US -neɪ.t̬ɪŋ **-nated** -neɪ.tɪd, US -neɪ.t̬ɪd
incarnation, I~ ˌɪn.kɑːˈneɪ.ʃᵊn, ˌɪŋ-, US ˌɪn.kɑːrˈ- **-s** -z
incautious ɪnˈkɔː.ʃəs, ˌɪn-, ɪŋ-, ˌɪŋ-, US ɪnˈkɑː-, ˌɪn-, -ˈkɔː- **-ly** -li **-ness** -nəs, -nɪs
Ince ɪnts
Ince-in-Makerfield ˌɪnts.ɪnˈmeɪ.kə.fiːld, US -kɚ-
incendiar|y ɪnˈsen.di.ᵊr|.i, -dʒᵊr-, -djᵊr-, US -di.er|.i, -ɚ|.i **-ies** -iz **-ism** -ɪ.zᵊm
incense **n** ˈɪn.sents
incens|e **v** *enrage:* ɪnˈsents *burn incense:* ˈɪn.sents **-es** -ɪz **-ing** -ɪŋ **-ed** -t
incentive ɪnˈsen.tɪv, US -t̬ɪv **-s** -z
incentiviz|e ɪnˈsen.tɪ.vaɪz, US -t̬ə- **-es** -ɪz **-ing** -ɪŋ **-ed** -d
incept ɪnˈsept **-s** -s **-ing** -ɪŋ **-ed** -ɪd **-or/s** -əʳ/z, US -ɚ/z **-ive** -ɪv
inception ɪnˈsep.ʃᵊn **-s** -z
incertitude ɪnˈsɜː.tɪ.tʃuːd, -tjuːd, ˈ-tə-, US -ˈsɝː.t̬ɪ.tuːd, -tjuːd **-s** -z
incessant ɪnˈses.ᵊnt **-ly** -li
incest ˈɪn.sest
incestuous ɪnˈses.tʃu.əs, -tju-, US -tʃu-, -tju- **-ly** -li **-ness** -nəs, -nɪs
inch, I~ ɪntʃ **-es** -ɪz **-ing** -ɪŋ **-ed** -t **ˌgive him an ˌinch and he'll ˌtake a ˈmile; not ˌbudge an ˈinch**
Inchcape ˈɪntʃ.keɪp, ˌ-ˈ-
Inchinnan ɪnˈʃɪn.ən
inchoate **adj** ɪnˈkəʊ.eɪt, ɪŋ-, -ɪt, ˈ---, US ɪnˈkoʊ- **-ly** -li
incho|ate **v** ˈɪn.kəʊ|.eɪt, ˈɪŋ-, US ˈɪn.koʊ- **-ates** -eɪts **-ating** -eɪ.tɪŋ, US -eɪ.t̬ɪŋ **-ated** -eɪ.tɪd, US -eɪ.t̬ɪd
inchoation ˌɪn.kəʊˈeɪ.ʃᵊn, ˌɪŋ-, US ˌɪn.koʊˈ-
inchoative ˈɪn.kəʊ.eɪ.tɪv, ˈɪŋ-; ɪnˈkəʊ.ə.tɪv, ɪŋ-, US ɪnˈkoʊ.ə.t̬ɪv
Inchon ˌɪnˈtʃɒn, US ˈɪn.tʃɑːn
inchworm ˈɪntʃ.wɜːm, US -wɝːm **-s** -z
incidence ˈɪnt.sɪ.dᵊnts
incident ˈɪnt.sɪ.dᵊnt **-s** -s
incident|al ˌɪnt.sɪˈden.t|ᵊl, US -t̬|ᵊl **-ly** -ᵊl.i, -li **-ness** -nəs, -nɪs **-s** -z *stress shift:* **ˌincidental ˈmusic**
inciner|ate ɪnˈsɪn.ᵊr|.eɪt, US -ə.r|eɪt **-ates** -eɪts **-ating** -eɪ.tɪŋ, US -eɪ.t̬ɪŋ **-ated** -eɪ.tɪd, US -eɪ.t̬ɪd
incineration ɪnˌsɪn.ᵊrˈeɪ.ʃᵊn, US -əˈreɪ-
incinerator ɪnˈsɪn.ᵊr.eɪ.təʳ, US -ə.reɪ.t̬ɚ **-s** -z
incipien|ce ɪnˈsɪp.i.ənt|s **-cy** -si
incipient ɪnˈsɪp.i.ənt **-ly** -li
incis|e ɪnˈsaɪz **-es** -ɪz **-ing** -ɪŋ **-ed** -d
incision ɪnˈsɪʒ.ᵊn **-s** -z
incisive ɪnˈsaɪ.sɪv **-ly** -li **-ness** -nəs, -nɪs
incisor ɪnˈsaɪ.zəʳ, US -zɚ **-s** -z
incitation ˌɪnt.saɪˈteɪ.ʃᵊn, -sɪˈ-, US -səˈ- **-s** -z
in|cite ɪn|ˈsaɪt **-cites** -ˈsaɪts **-citing** -ˈsaɪ.tɪŋ, US -ˈsaɪ.t̬ɪŋ **-cited** -ˈsaɪ.tɪd, US -ˈsaɪ.t̬ɪd
incitement ɪnˈsaɪt.mənt **-s** -s
incivilit|y ˌɪn.sɪˈvɪl.ə.t|i, -səˈ-, -ɪ.t|i, US -ə.t̬|i **-ies** -iz
incl. (abbrev. for **including**) ɪnˈkluː.dɪŋ, ɪŋ-, US ɪn-(abbrev. for **inclusive**) ɪnˈkluː.sɪv, ɪŋ-, US ɪn-
Incledon ˈɪŋ.kᵊl.dən
inclemency ɪnˈklem.ənt.si, ˌɪn-, ɪŋ-, ˌɪŋ-, US ɪnˈklem-, ˌɪn-
inclement ɪnˈklem.ənt, ˌɪn-, ɪŋ-, ˌɪŋ-, US ɪnˈklem-, ˌɪn- **-ly** -li
inclination ˌɪn.klɪˈneɪ.ʃᵊn, ˌɪŋ-, -kləˈ-, US ˌɪn- **-s** -z
incline **n** ˈɪn.klaɪn, ˈɪŋ-, ˌ-ˈ-, US ˈɪn.klaɪn, ˌ-ˈ- **-s** -z
inclin|e **v** ɪnˈklaɪn, ɪŋ-, US ɪn- **-es** -z **-ing** -ɪŋ **-ed** -d **-able** -ə.bᵊl
inclos|e ɪnˈkləʊz, ɪŋ-, US ɪnˈkloʊz **-es** -ɪz **-ing** -ɪŋ **-ed** -d
inclosure ɪnˈkləʊ.ʒəʳ, ɪŋ-, US ɪnˈkloʊ.ʒɚ **-s** -z
includ|e ɪnˈkluːd, ɪŋ-, US ɪn- **-es** -z **-ing** -ɪŋ **-ed** -ɪd
inclusion ɪnˈkluː.ʒᵊn, ɪŋ-, US ɪn- **-s** -z
inclusive ɪnˈkluː.sɪv, ɪŋ-, US ɪn- **-ly** -li **-ness** -nəs, -nɪs
incognito ˌɪn.kɒɡˈniː.təʊ, ˌɪŋ-; ɪnˈkɒɡ.nɪ.təʊ, ɪŋ-, -nə-, US ˌɪn.kɑːɡˈniː.toʊ; US ɪnˈkɑːɡ.nɪ-, -t̬oʊ **-s** -z
incognizan|ce ɪnˈkɒɡ.nɪ.zᵊn|ts, ɪŋ-, US ɪnˈkɑːɡ- **-t** -t
incoherence ˌɪn.kəʊˈhɪə.rᵊnts, ˌɪŋ-, US ˌɪn.koʊˈhɪr.ᵊnts, -ˈher-
incoherent ˌɪn.kəʊˈhɪə.rᵊnt, ˌɪŋ-, US ˌɪn.koʊˈhɪr.ᵊnt, -ˈher- **-ly** -li
incombustibility ˌɪn.kəmˌbʌs.təˈbɪl.ə.ti, ˌɪŋ-, -tɪˈ-, -ɪ.ti, US ˌɪn.kəmˌbʌs.təˈbɪl.ə.t̬i, -tɪˈ-
incombustible ˌɪn.kəmˈbʌs.tə.bᵊl, ˌɪŋ-, -tɪ-, US ˌɪn- **-ness** -nəs, -nɪs
income ˈɪŋ.kʌm, ˈɪn-, -kəm, US ˈɪn- **-s** -z **ˌincome supˈport; ˈincome supˌport; ˈincome ˌtax**
incomer ˈɪnˌkʌm.əʳ, ˈɪŋ-, US ˈɪnˌkʌm.ɚ **-s** -z
incoming ˈɪnˌkʌm.ɪŋ, ˈɪŋ-, US ˈɪnˌkʌm- **-s** -z
incommensurability ˌɪn.kəˌmen.tʃᵊr.əˈbɪl.ə.ti, ˌɪŋ-, -tʃʊr-, -ɪ.ti, US ˌɪn.kəˌment.sɚ.əˈbɪl.ə.t̬i, -ʃɚ-
incommensurab|le ˌɪn.kəˈmen.tʃᵊr.ə.b|ᵊl, ˌɪŋ-, -tʃʊr-, US ˌɪn.kəˈment.sɚ-, -ʃɚ- **-les** -ᵊlz **-ly** -li **-leness** -ᵊl.nəs, -nɪs
incommensurate ˌɪn.kəˈmen.tʃᵊr.ət, ˌɪŋ-, -tʃʊr-, -ɪt, US ˌɪn.kəˈment.sɚ-, -ʃɚ- **-ly** -li **-ness** -nəs, -nɪs
incommod|e ˌɪn.kəˈməʊd, ˌɪŋ-, US ˌɪn.kəˈmoʊd **-es** -z **-ing** -ɪŋ **-ed** -ɪd
incommodious ˌɪn.kəˈməʊ.di.əs, ˌɪŋ-, US ˌɪn.kəˈmoʊ- **-ly** -li **-ness** -nəs, -nɪs
incommunicab|le ˌɪn.kəˈmjuː.nɪ.kə.b|ᵊl, ˌɪŋ-, US ˌɪn- **-ly** -li **-leness** -ᵊl.nəs, -nɪs
incommunicado ˌɪn.kəˌmjuː.nɪˈkɑː.dəʊ, ˌɪŋ-, -nəˈ-, US ˌɪn.kəˌmjuː.nɪˈkɑː.doʊ, -nəˈ-
incommutab|le ˌɪn.kəˈmjuː.tə.b|ᵊl, ˌɪŋ-, US ˌɪn.kəˈmjuː.t̬ə.b|ᵊl **-ly** -li **-leness** -ᵊl.nəs, -nɪs
incomparability ɪnˌkɒm.pᵊr.əˈbɪl.ə.ti, ɪŋ-, -ɪ.ti, US ɪnˌkɑːm.pɚ.əˈbɪl.ə.t̬i
incomparab|le ɪnˈkɒm.pᵊr.ə.b|ᵊl, ɪŋ-, US ɪnˈkɑːm- **-ly** -li **-leness** -ᵊl.nəs, -nɪs
incompatibilit|y ˌɪn.kəmˌpæt.əˈbɪl.ə.t|i, ˌɪŋ-, -ɪˈ-, -ɪ.t|i, US ˌɪn.kəmˌpæt̬.əˈbɪl.ə.t̬|i **-ies** -iz
incompatib|le ˌɪn.kəmˈpæt.ə.b|ᵊl,

I

ˌɪŋ-, ˈ-ɪ-, US ˌɪn.kəmˈpæt̬- -ly -li -leness -ᵊl.nəs, -nɪs

incompeten|ce ɪnˈkɒm.pɪ.tᵊn*t*|s, ˌɪn-, ɪŋ-, ˌɪŋ-, -pə-, US ɪnˈkɑːm.pə.t̬ən*t*|s, ˌɪn- -cy -si

incompetent ɪnˈkɒm.pɪ.tᵊnt, ˌɪn-, ɪŋ-, ˌɪŋ-, -pə-, US ɪnˈkɑːm.pə.t̬ənt, ˌɪn- -ly -li

incomplete ˌɪn.kəmˈpliːt, ˌɪŋ-, US ˌɪn- -ly -li -ness -nəs, -nɪs

incompletion ˌɪn.kəmˈpliː.ʃᵊn, ˌɪŋ-, US ˌɪn-

incomprehensibility ɪnˌkɒm.prɪˌhen*t*.səˈbɪl.ə.ti, ˌɪn-, ɪŋ-, ˌɪŋ-, -prəˌ-, -sɪˈ-, -ɪ.ti, US ˌɪn.kɑːm.prɪ.hen*t*.səˈbɪl.ə.t̬i

incomprehensib|le ɪnˌkɒm.prɪˈhen*t*.sə.b|ᵊl, ˌɪn-, ɪŋ-, ˌɪŋ-, -sɪ-, US ˌɪn.kɑːm- -ly -li -leness -ᵊl.nəs, -nɪs

incomprehension ɪnˌkɒm.prɪˈhen.*t*ʃᵊn, ˌɪn-, ɪŋ-, ˌɪŋ-, -prəˈ-, US ˌɪn.kɑːm-

incompressibility ˌɪn.kəmˌpres.əˈbɪl.ə.ti, ˌɪŋ-, -ɪˈ-, -ɪ.ti, US ˌɪn.kəmˌpres.əˈbɪl.ə.t̬i

incompressible ˌɪn.kəmˈpres.ə.bᵊl, ˌɪŋ-, ˈ-ɪ-, US ˌɪn- -ness -nəs, -nɪs

incomputab|le ˌɪn.kəmˈpjuː.tə.b|ᵊl, ˌɪŋ-; ɪnˈkɒm.pjə.tə.b|ᵊl, ˌɪn-, ɪŋ-, ˌɪŋ-, -pjʊ-, US ˌɪn.kəmˈpjuː.t̬ə- -ly -li

inconceivability ˌɪn.kənˌsiː.vəˈbɪl.ə.ti, ˌɪŋ-, -ɪ.ti, US ˌɪn.kənˌsiː.vəˈbɪl.ə.t̬i

inconceivab|le ˌɪn.kənˈsiː.və.b|ᵊl, ˌɪŋ-, US ˌɪn- -ly -li -leness -ᵊl.nəs, -nɪs

inconclusive ˌɪn.kənˈkluː.sɪv, ˌɪŋ-, -kəŋˈ-, US ˌɪn.kənˈ- -ly -li -ness -nəs, -nɪs

incondite ɪnˈkɒn.dɪt, ɪŋ-, -daɪt, US ɪnˈkɑːn-

incongruent ɪnˈkɒŋ.gru.ənt, ɪŋ-, US ɪnˈkɑːŋ-; US ˌɪn.kənˈgruː- -ly -li

incongruit|y ˌɪn.kɒŋˈgruː.ə.t|i, ˌɪŋ-, -ɪ.t|i, US ˌɪn.kənˈgruː.ə.t̬|i -ies -iz

incongruous ɪnˈkɒŋ.gru.əs, ɪŋ-, US ɪnˈkɑːŋ- -ly -li -ness -nəs, -nɪs

inconsequenc|e ɪnˈkɒn*t*.sɪ.kwən*t*s, ɪŋ-, -sə-, US ɪnˈkɑːn*t*- -es -ɪz

inconsequent ɪnˈkɒn*t*.sɪ.kwənt, ɪŋ-, -sə-, US ɪnˈkɑːn*t*- -ly -li

inconsequential ɪnˌkɒn*t*.sɪˈkwen.*t*ʃᵊl, ˌɪn-, ɪŋ-, ˌɪŋ-, -səˈ-, US ɪnˌkɑːn*t*- -ly -i

inconsiderab|le ˌɪn.kənˈsɪd.ᵊr.ə.b|ᵊl, ˌɪŋ-, US ˌɪn- -ly -li -leness -ᵊl.nəs, -nɪs

inconsiderate ˌɪn.kənˈsɪd.ᵊr.ət, ˌɪŋ-, -ɪt, US ˌɪn- -ly -li -ness -nəs, -nɪs

inconsideration ˌɪn.kənˌsɪd.əˈreɪ.ʃᵊn, ˌɪŋ-, US ˌɪn-

inconsistenc|y ˌɪn.kənˈsɪs.tᵊn*t*.s|i, ˌɪŋ-, US ˌɪn- -ies -iz

inconsistent ˌɪn.kənˈsɪs.tənt, ˌɪŋ-, US ˌɪn- -ly -li

inconsolab|le ˌɪn.kənˈsəʊ.lə.b|ᵊl, ˌɪŋ-, US ˌɪn.kənˈsoʊ- -ly -li -leness -ᵊl.nəs, -nɪs

inconsonant ɪnˈkɒn*t*.sə.nənt, ɪŋ-, US ɪnˈkɑːn*t*-

inconspicuous ˌɪn.kənˈspɪk.ju.əs, ˌɪŋ-, US ˌɪn- -ly -li -ness -nəs, -nɪs

inconstanc|y ɪnˈkɒn*t*.stᵊn*t*.s|i, ˌɪn-, ɪŋ-, ˌɪŋ-, US ɪnˈkɑːn*t*-, ˌɪn- -ies -iz

inconstant ɪnˈkɒn*t*.stənt, ˌɪn-, ɪŋ-, ˌɪŋ-, US ɪnˈkɑːn*t*-, ˌɪn- -ly -li

incontestability ˌɪn.kənˌtes.təˈbɪl.ə.ti, ˌɪŋ-, -ɪ.ti, US ˌɪn.kənˌtes.təˈbɪl.ə.t̬i

incontestab|le ˌɪn.kənˈtes.tə.b|ᵊl, ˌɪŋ-, US ˌɪn- -ly -li

incontinence ɪnˈkɒn.tɪ.nən*t*s, ˌɪn-, ɪŋ-, ˌɪŋ-, -tə-, US ɪnˈkɑːn.tᵊn.ᵊn*t*s, ˌɪn-

incontinent ɪnˈkɒn.tɪ.nənt, ˌɪn-, ɪŋ-, ˌɪŋ-, -tə-, US ɪnˈkɑːn.tᵊn.ᵊnt, ˌɪn- -ly -li

incontrollab|le ˌɪn.kənˈtrəʊ.lə.b|ᵊl, ˌɪŋ-, US ˌɪn.kənˈtroʊ- -ly -li

incontrovertibility ˌɪnˌkɒn.trəˌvɜː.təˈbɪl.ə.ti, ˌɪŋ-, -tɪˈ-, -ɪ.ti, US ˌɪn.kɑːn.trəˌvɝː.t̬əˈbɪl.ə.t̬i

incontrovertib|le ˌɪnˌkɒn.trəˈvɜː.tə.b|ᵊl, ˌɪŋ-, -tɪ-, US ˌɪnˌkɑːn.trəˈvɝː.t̬ə- -ly -li

inconvenienc|e ˌɪn.kənˈviː.ni.ən*t*s, ˌɪŋ-, US ˌɪn-, ˈ-njən*t*s -es -ɪz -ing -ɪŋ -ed -t

inconvenient ˌɪn.kənˈviː.ni.ənt, ˌɪŋ-, US ˌɪn-, ˈ-njənt -ly -li

inconvertibility ˌɪn.kənˌvɜː.təˈbɪl.ə.ti, ˌɪŋ-, -tɪˈ-, -ɪ.ti, US ˌɪn.kənˌvɝː.t̬əˈbɪl.ə.t̬i

inconvertib|le ˌɪn.kənˈvɜː.tə.b|ᵊl, ˌɪŋ-, -tɪ-, US ˌɪn.kənˈvɝː.t̬ə- -ly -li

incorporate adj ɪnˈkɔː.pᵊr.ət, ˌɪn-, ɪŋ-, ˌɪŋ-, -ɪt, US ɪnˈkɔːr-, ˌɪn-

incorpor|ate v ɪnˈkɔː.pᵊr|.eɪt, ɪŋ-, US ɪnˈkɔːr.pə.r|eɪt -ates -eɪts -ating -eɪ.tɪŋ, US -eɪ.t̬ɪŋ -ated -eɪ.tɪd, US -eɪ.t̬ɪd

incorporation ɪnˌkɔː.pᵊrˈeɪ.ʃᵊn, ɪŋ-, US ɪnˌkɔːr.pəˈreɪ- -s -z

incorporeal ˌɪn.kɔːˈpɔː.ri.əl, ˌɪŋ-, US ˌɪn.kɔːrˈpɔːr.i- -ly -i

incorrect ˌɪn.kᵊrˈekt, ˌɪŋ-, US ˌɪn.kəˈrekt -ly -li -ness -nəs, -nɪs

incorrigibility ɪnˌkɒr.ɪ.dʒəˈbɪl.ə.ti, ɪŋ-, -dʒɪˈ-, -ɪ.ti, US ɪnˌkɔːr.ə.dʒəˈbɪl.ə.t̬i

incorrigib|le ɪnˈkɒr.ɪ.dʒə.b|ᵊl, ɪŋ-, -dʒɪ-, US ɪnˈkɔːr.ə.dʒə- -ly -li -leness -ᵊl.nəs, -nɪs

incorruptibility ˌɪn.kəˌrʌp.təˈbɪl.ə.ti, ˌɪŋ-, -tɪˈ-, -ɪ.ti, US ˌɪn.kəˌrʌp.təˈbɪl.ə.t̬i

incorruptib|le ˌɪn.kəˈrʌp.tə.b|ᵊl, ˌɪŋ-, -tɪ-, US ˌɪn- -ly -li -leness -ᵊl.nəs, -nɪs

incorruption ˌɪn.kəˈrʌp.ʃᵊn, ˌɪŋ-, US ˌɪn-

increas|e n ˈɪn.kriːs, ˈɪŋ-, -ˈ-, US ˈɪn.kriːs, -ˈ- -es -ɪz

increas|e v ɪnˈkriːs, ɪŋ-, ˈ--, US ɪnˈkriːs, ˈ-- -es -ɪz -ing/ly -ɪŋ/li -ed -t

incredibility ɪnˌkred.əˈbɪl.ə.ti, ɪŋ-, -ɪˈ-, -ɪ.ti, US ɪnˌkred.ɪˈbɪl.ə.t̬i, -əˈ-

incredib|le ɪnˈkred.ə.b|ᵊl, ɪŋ-, ˈ-ɪ-, US ˌɪn- -ly -li -leness -ᵊl.nəs, -nɪs

incredulity ˌɪn.krəˈdʒuː.lə.ti, -ˈdjuː-, ˌɪŋ-, -krɪˈ-, -kredʒˈuː-, -kredˈjuː-, -ɪ.ti, US ˌɪn.krəˈduː.lə.t̬i, -ˈdjuː-

incredulous ɪnˈkredʒ.ə.ləs, ɪŋ-, ˈ-kred.jə-, -ˈkredʒ.ʊ-, -ˈkred.jʊ-, US ɪnˈkredʒ.ə-, -ˈkred.jə-, -ˈkredʒ.ʊ-, -ˈkred.jʊ- -ly -li -ness -nəs, -nɪs

increment ˈɪn.krə.mənt, ˈɪŋ-, -krɪ-, US ˈɪn- -s -s

incremental ˌɪn.krəˈmen.tᵊl, ˌɪŋ-, -krɪˈ-, US ˌɪn.krəˈmen.t̬ᵊl -ly -i

incrimi|nate ɪnˈkrɪm.ɪ|.neɪt, ɪŋ-, ˈ-ə-, US ɪn- -nates -neɪts -nating -neɪ.tɪŋ, US -neɪ.t̬ɪŋ -nated -neɪ.tɪd, US -neɪ.t̬ɪd

incrimination ɪnˌkrɪm.ɪˈneɪ.ʃᵊn, ɪŋ-, -əˈ-, US ɪn-

incriminatory ɪnˈkrɪm.ɪ.nə.tᵊr.i, ɪŋ-, -ᵊn.ə-, -neɪ.tᵊr-; ɪnˌkrɪm.ɪˈneɪ-, ˌɪn-, ɪŋ-, ˌɪŋ-, US ɪnˈkrɪm.ɪ.nə.tɔːr.i

incrust ɪnˈkrʌst, ɪŋ-, US ɪn- -s -s -ing -ɪŋ -ed -ɪd

incrustation ˌɪn.krʌsˈteɪ.ʃᵊn, ˌɪŋ-, US ˌɪn- -s -z

incu|bate ˈɪŋ.kjʊ|.beɪt, ˈɪn-, -kjə- -bates -beɪts -bating -beɪ.tɪŋ, US -beɪ.t̬ɪŋ -bated -beɪ.tɪd, US -beɪ.t̬ɪd -bative -beɪ.tɪv, US -beɪ.t̬ɪv

incubation ˌɪŋ.kjʊˈbeɪ.ʃᵊn, ˌɪn-, -kjəˈ- -s -z

incubator ˈɪŋ.kjʊ.beɪ.təʳ, ˈɪn-, -kjə-, US -t̬ɚ -s -z

incubatory ˈɪŋ.kjʊ.beɪ.tᵊr.i, ˈɪn-, -kjə-, US -bə.tɔːr-, ˌɪŋ.kjʊˈbeɪ.tɚ-, ˌɪn-, -kjəˈ-

incub|us ˈɪŋ.kjʊ.b|əs, ˈɪn-, -kjə- -uses -ə.sɪz -i -aɪ

incul|cate ˈɪn.kʌl|.keɪt, ˈɪŋ-, -kəl-; ɪnˈkʌl-, ɪŋ-, US ˈɪn.kʌl-, -kəl-; US ɪnˈkʌl- -cates -keɪts -cating -keɪ.tɪŋ, US -keɪ.t̬ɪŋ -cated -keɪ.tɪd, US -keɪ.t̬ɪd -cator/s -keɪ.təʳ/z, US -keɪ.t̬ɚ/z

inculcation ˌɪn.kʌlˈkeɪ.ʃᵊn, ˌɪŋ-, -kəlˈ-, US ˌɪn-

incul|pate ˈɪn.kʌl|.peɪt, ˈɪŋ-, -kəl-; ɪnˈkʌl-, ɪŋ-, US ˈɪn.kʌl-, -kəl-; US ɪnˈkʌl- -pates -peɪts -pating -peɪ.tɪŋ, US -peɪ.t̬ɪŋ -pated -peɪ.tɪd, US -peɪ.t̬ɪd

inculpation ˌɪn.kʌlˈpeɪ.ʃᵊn, ˌɪŋ-, -kəlˈ-, US ˌɪn-

inculpatory ɪnˈkʌl.pə.tᵊr.i, ɪŋ-; ˈɪn.kʌl.peɪ-, ˈɪŋ-, -kəl-, ˌɪn.kʌlˈpeɪ-, ˌɪŋ-, -kəlˈ-, US ɪnˈkʌl.pə.tɔːr.i

incumbenc|y ɪnˈkʌm.bən*t*.s|i, ɪŋ-, US ɪn- -ies -iz

incumbent ɪnˈkʌm.bənt, ɪŋ-, US ɪn- -s -s -ly -li

incumbranc|e ɪnˈkʌm.brən*t*s, ɪŋ-, US ɪn- -es -ɪz

incunabul|um ˌɪn.kjuːˈnæb.jə.l|əm, ˌɪŋ-, -jʊ-, US -kjəˈ-, -kjʊˈ- -a -ə

incur ɪnˈkɜːʳ, ɪŋ-, (US) ɪnˈkɝː **-s** -z **-ring** -ɪŋ **-red** -d **-rable** -ə.bəl
incurability ɪnˌkjʊə.rəˈbɪl.ə.ti, ˌɪn-, ɪŋ-, ˌɪŋ-, -ˌkjɔː-, -ɪ.ti, (US) ɪnˌkjʊr.əˈbɪl.ə.t̬i
incurab|le ɪnˈkjʊə.rə.b|əl, ˌɪn-, ɪŋ-, ˌɪŋ-, -ˈkjɔː-, (US) ɪnˈkjʊr.ə- **-ly** -li **-leness** -əl.nəs, -nɪs
incurious ɪnˈkjʊə.ri.əs, ˌɪn-, ɪŋ-, ˌɪŋ-, -ˈkjɔː-, (US) ɪnˈkjʊr.i- **-ly** -li **-ness** -nəs, -nɪs
incursion ɪnˈkɜː.ʃən, ɪŋ-, -ʒən, (US) ɪnˈkɝː- **-s** -z
incursive ɪnˈkɜː.sɪv, ɪŋ-, (US) ɪnˈkɝː-
incurvate adj ɪnˈkɜː.veɪt, ɪŋ-, -vət, -vɪt, (US) ɪnˈkɝː-
incur|vate v ˈɪn.kɜː|.veɪt, ˈɪŋ-, (US) ɪnˈkɝː-, ˈɪn.kɝː- **-vates** -veɪts **-vating** -veɪ.tɪŋ, (US) -veɪ.t̬ɪŋ **-vated** -veɪ.tɪd, (US) -veɪ.t̬ɪd
incurvation ˌɪn.kɜːˈveɪ.ʃən, ˌɪŋ-, (US) ˌɪn.kɝː-
incurv|e ˌɪnˈkɜːv, ˌɪŋ-, (US) ˌɪnˈkɝːv **-es** -z **-ing** -ɪŋ **-ed** -d *stress shift:* **ˌincurved ˈsurface**
incus|e ɪnˈkjuːz, ɪŋ-, (US) ɪnˈkjuːz, -ˈkjuːs **-es** -ɪz **-ing** -ɪŋ **-ed** -d
Ind *surname:* ɪnd *India:* ɪnd, aɪnd
Ind. (abbrev. for **Indiana**) ˌɪn.diˈæn.ə, -ˈɑː.nə, (US) -ˈæn.ə
ind. (abbrev. for **independent**) ˌɪn.dɪˈpen.dənt, -dəˈ-(abbrev. for **indicative**) ɪnˈdɪk.ə.tɪv, (US) -t̬ɪv (abbrev. for **industrial**) ɪnˈdʌs.tri.əl
Ind Coope® ˌɪndˈkuːp
indebted ɪnˈdet.ɪd, (US) -ˈdet̬- **-ness** -nəs, -nɪs
indecenc|y ɪnˈdiː.sənt.s|i, ˌɪn- **-ies** -iz
indecent ɪnˈdiː.sənt, ˌɪn- **-ly** -li **inˌdecent asˈsault; inˌdecent exˈposure**
indecipherable ˌɪn.dɪˈsaɪ.fər.ə.bəl, -dəˈ-
indecision ˌɪn.dɪˈsɪʒ.ən, -dəˈ-
indecisive ˌɪn.dɪˈsaɪ.sɪv, -dəˈ- **-ly** -li **-ness** -nəs, -nɪs
indeclinable ˌɪn.dɪˈklaɪ.nə.bəl, -dəˈ- **-s** -z
indecomposable ɪnˌdiː.kəmˈpəʊ.zə.bəl, ˌɪn-, (US) -ˈpoʊ-
indecorous ɪnˈdek.ər.əs, ˌɪn- **-ly** -li **-ness** -nəs, -nəs
indecorum ˌɪn.dɪˈkɔː.rəm, -dəˈ-, (US) -ˈkɔːr.əm
indeed adv ɪnˈdiːd **interj** ɪnˈdiːd, ˌɪn.diːd
indefatigab|le ˌɪn.dɪˈfæt.ɪ.gə.b|əl, -dəˈ-, (US) -ˈfæt̬- **-ly** -li **-leness** -əl.nəs, -nɪs
indefeasibility ˌɪn.dɪˌfiː.zəˈbɪl.ə.ti, -dəˌ-, -zɪˈ-, -ɪ.ti, (US) -ə.t̬i
indefeasib|le ˌɪn.dɪˈfiː.zə.b|əl, -dəˈ-, -zɪ- **-ly** -li
indefensibility ˌɪn.dɪˌfent.səˈbɪl.ə.ti, -dəˌ-, -sɪˈ-, -ɪ.ti, (US) -ə.t̬i
indefensib|le ˌɪn.dɪˈfent.sə.b|əl, -dəˈ-, -sɪ- **-ly** -li
indefinab|le ˌɪn.dɪˈfaɪ.nə.b|əl, -dəˈ- **-ly** -li
indefinite ɪnˈdef.ɪ.nət, ˌɪn-, -ən.ət, ˈ-nət, -nɪt, (US) -ə.nət, ˈ-nət **-ly** -li **-ness** -nəs, -nɪs **inˌdefinite ˈarticle**
indelibility ɪnˌdel.əˈbɪl.ə.ti, ˌɪn-, -ɪˈ-, -ɪ.ti, (US) -ə.t̬i
indelib|le ɪnˈdel.ə.b|əl, ˌɪn-, ˈ-ɪ- **-ly** -li
indelicac|y ɪnˈdel.ɪ.kə.s|i, ˌɪn-, ˈ-ə- **-ies** -iz
indelicate ɪnˈdel.ɪ.kət, ˌɪn-, ˈ-ə-, -kɪt **-ly** -li
in delicto ˌɪn.delˈɪk.təʊ, -dɪˈlɪk-, (US) -dəˈlɪk.toʊ
indemnification ɪnˌdem.nɪ.fɪˈkeɪ.ʃən, -nə-, -fəˈ- **-s** -z
indemni|fy ɪnˈdem.nɪ|.faɪ, -nə- **-fies** -faɪz **-fying** -faɪ.ɪŋ **-fied** -faɪd
indemnit|y ɪnˈdem.nə.t|i, -nɪ-, (US) -t̬|i **-ies** -iz
indemonstrab|le ɪnˈdem.ənt.strə.b|əl, ˌɪn-; ˌɪn.dɪˈmɒnt.strə-, -dəˈ-, (US) ˌɪn.dɪˈmɑːnt.strə-; (US) ɪnˈdem.ənt-, ˌɪn- **-ly** -li
indent n ˈɪn.dent, -ˈ- **-s** -s
in|dent v ɪn|ˈdent, ˌɪn- **-dents** -ˈdents **-denting** -ˈden.tɪŋ, (US) -ˈden.t̬ɪŋ **-dented** -ˈden.tɪd, (US) -ˈden.t̬ɪd
indentation ˌɪn.denˈteɪ.ʃən **-s** -z
indenture ɪnˈden.tʃəʳ, (US) -tʃɚ **-s** -z **-d** -d
independen|ce ˌɪn.dɪˈpen.dənt|s, -dəˈ- **-cy** -si **Indeˈpendence ˌDay**
independent, I~ ˌɪn.dɪˈpen.dənt, -dəˈ- **-s** -s **-ly** -li
in-depth ˌɪnˈdepθ *stress shift:* **ˌin-depth ˈtreatment**
indescribab|le ˌɪn.dɪˈskraɪ.bə.b|əl, -dəˈ- **-ly** -li
indestructibility ˌɪn.dɪˌstrʌk.təˈbɪl.ə.ti, -tɪˈ-, -ɪ.ti, (US) -ə.t̬i
indestructib|le ˌɪn.dɪˈstrʌk.tə.b|əl, -tɪ- **-ly** -li **-leness** -əl.nəs, -əl.nɪs
indetectab|le, -ib|le ˌɪn.dɪˈtek.tə.b|əl, -dəˈ- **-ly** -li
indeterminab|le ˌɪn.dɪˈtɜː.mɪ.nə.b|əl, -dəˈ-, (US) -ˈtɝː- **-ly** -li **-leness** -əl.nəs, -əl.nɪs
indeterminacy ˌɪn.dɪˈtɜː.mɪ.nə.si, -dəˈ-, -mən.ə-, (US) -ˈtɝː-
indeterminate ˌɪn.dɪˈtɜː.mɪ.nət, -dəˈ-, -nɪt, (US) -ˈtɝː- **-ly** -li **-ness** -nəs, -nɪs
indetermination ˌɪn.dɪˌtɜː.mɪˈneɪ.ʃən, -dəˌ-, -məˈ-, (US) -ˌtɝː-
ind|ex ˈɪn.d|eks **-exes** -ek.sɪz **-exing** -eks.ɪŋ **-exed** -ekst **-ices** -ɪ.siːz, -ə- **ˈindex ˌcard; ˌindex ˈfinger; ˈindex ˌfinger; ˈindex ˌnumber**
indexation ˌɪn.dekˈseɪ.ʃən
indexer ˈɪn.dek.səʳ, (US) -sɚ **-s** -z
index-linked ˌɪn.deksˈlɪŋkt
Indi|a ˈɪn.di|.ə **-an/s** -ən/z **ˌIndian ˈOcean; ˌIndia ˈrubber; ˌIndian ˈsummer**
Indiana ˌɪn.diˈæn.ə, -ˈɑː.nə, (US) -ˈæn.ə
Indianapolis ˌɪn.di.əˈnæp.əl.ɪs, (US) -ə.lɪs
Indic ˈɪn.dɪk
indi|cate ˈɪn.dɪ|.keɪt, -də- **-cates** -keɪts **-cating** -keɪ.tɪŋ, (US) -keɪ.t̬ɪŋ **-cated** -keɪ.tɪd, (US) -keɪ.t̬ɪd
indication ˌɪn.dɪˈkeɪ.ʃən, -dəˈ- **-s** -z
indicative n, adj *in grammar:* ɪnˈdɪk.ə.tɪv, (US) -t̬ɪv **-s** -z **-ly** -li
indicative adj *indicating:* ɪnˈdɪk.ə.tɪv; ˈɪn.dɪ.keɪ-, (US) ɪnˈdɪk.ə.t̬ɪv **-ly** -li
indicator ˈɪn.dɪ.keɪ.təʳ, -də-, (US) -t̬ɚ **-s** -z
indicatory ɪnˈdɪk.ə.tər.i; ˈɪn.dɪ.keɪ-, ˌɪn.dɪˈkeɪ-, (US) ˈɪn.dɪ.kə.tɔːr-; (US) ɪnˈdɪk.ə-
indices (plural of **index**) ˈɪn.dɪ.siːz, -də-
indicia ɪnˈdɪʃ.i.ə, (US) -ˈdɪʃ.ə, -i.ə
in|dict ɪn|ˈdaɪt **-dicts** -ˈdaɪts **-dicting** -ˈdaɪ.tɪŋ, (US) -ˈdaɪ.t̬ɪŋ **-dicted** -ˈdaɪ.tɪd, (US) -ˈdaɪ.t̬ɪd **-dicter/s** -ˈdaɪ.təʳ/z, (US) -ˈdaɪ.t̬ɚ/z **-dictable** -ˈdaɪ.tə.bəl, (US) -ˈdaɪ.t̬ə.bəl
indiction ɪnˈdɪk.ʃən **-s** -z
indictment ɪnˈdaɪt.mənt **-s** -s
indie ˈɪn.di **-s** -z
Indies ˈɪn.diz
indifference ɪnˈdɪf.ər.ənts, ˈ-rənts
indifferent ɪnˈdɪf.ər.ənt, ˈ-rənt **-ly** -li
indigen ˈɪn.dɪ.dʒən, -də- **-s** -z
indigence ˈɪn.dɪ.dʒənts
indigene ˈɪn.dɪ.dʒiːn **-s** -z
indigenous ɪnˈdɪdʒ.ɪ.nəs, -ə.nəs **-ly** -li **-ness** -nəs, -nɪs
indigent ˈɪn.dɪ.dʒənt **-s** -s **-ly** -li
indigestibility ˌɪn.dɪˌdʒes.təˈbɪl.ə.ti, -tɪˈ-, -ɪ.ti, (US) -dɪˌdʒes.təˈbɪl.ə.t̬i, -daɪˌ-
indigestib|le ˌɪn.dɪˈdʒes.tə.b|əl, -dəˈ-, -tɪ-, (US) -dɪˈ-, -daɪˈ- **-leness** -əl.nəs, -nɪs **-ly** -li
indigestion ˌɪn.dɪˈdʒes.tʃən, -dəˈ-, -ˈdʒeʃ-, (US) -dɪˈdʒes-, -daɪˈ-
indignant ɪnˈdɪg.nənt **-ly** -li
indignation ˌɪn.dɪgˈneɪ.ʃən
indignit|y ɪnˈdɪg.nə.t|i, -nɪ-, (US) -nə.t̬|i **-ies** -iz
indigo ˈɪn.dɪ.gəʊ, (US) -goʊ **-(e)s** -z
Indira ˈɪn.dɪ.rə, -dər.ə; ɪnˈdɪə.rə, (US) ɪnˈdɪr.ə
indirect ˌɪn.dɪˈrekt, -daɪˈ-, -dəˈ- **-ly** -li **-ness** -nəs, -nɪs **ˌindirect ˈobject; ˌindirect ˈspeech**
indiscernib|le ˌɪn.dɪˈsɜː.nə.b|əl, -ˈzɜː-, -nɪ-, (US) -ˈsɝː-, -ˈzɝː- **-ly** -li
indisciplin|e ɪnˈdɪs.ə.plɪn, ˌɪn-, ˈ-ɪ- **-ed** -d **-able** -ə.bəl
indiscreet ˌɪn.dɪˈskriːt, -dəˈ- **-ly** -li **-ness** -nəs, -nɪs
indiscrete ˌɪn.dɪˈskriːt, -dəˈ-
indiscretion ˌɪn.dɪˈskreʃ.ən, -dəˈ- **-s** -z
indiscriminate ˌɪn.dɪˈskrɪm.ɪ.nət, -dəˈ-, ˈ-ə-, -nɪt **-ly** -li **-ness** -nəs, -nɪs
indiscrimination ˌɪn.dɪˌskrɪm.ɪˈneɪ.ʃən, -dəˌ-, -əˈ-

indispensability ˌɪn.dɪˌspent.səˈbɪl.ə.ti, -dəˌ-, -ɪ.ti, (US) -ə.t̬i

indispensab|le, -ib|le ˌɪn.dɪˈspent.sə.b|ᵊl, -dəˈ- **-ly** -li **-leness** -nəs, -nɪs

indispos|e ˌɪn.dɪˈspəʊz, -dəˈ-, (US) -ˈspoʊz **-es** -ɪz **-ing** -ɪŋ **-ed** -d

indisposition ˌɪn.dɪ.spəˈzɪʃ.ᵊn; ɪnˌdɪs.pəˈ-, (US) ˌɪn.dɪ.spəˈ- **-s** -z

indisputability ˌɪn.dɪˌspjuː.təˈbɪl.ə.ti; ɪnˌdɪs.pjuː-, -ɪ.ti, (US) ˌɪn.dɪˌspjuː.t̬əˈbɪl.ə.t̬i

indisputab|le ˌɪn.dɪˈspjuː.tə.b|ᵊl; ɪnˈdɪs.pjuː-, (US) ˌɪn.dɪˈspjuː.t̬ə-; ɪnˈdɪs.pjuː-, -pjə- **-ly** -li **-leness** -ᵊl.nəs, -nɪs

indissociable ˌɪn.dɪˈsəʊ.ʃi.ə.bᵊl, -ʃə.bᵊl, (US) -ˈsoʊ-

indissolubility ˌɪn.dɪˌsɒl.jəˈbɪl.ə.ti, -dəˌ-, -jʊˈ-, -ɪ.ti, (US) -ˌsɑːl.jəˈbɪl.ə.t̬i

indissolub|le ˌɪn.dɪˈsɒl.jə.b|ᵊl, -dəˈ-, -jʊ-, (US) -ˈsɑːl- **-ly** -li **-leness** -ᵊl.nəs, -nɪs

indistinct ˌɪn.dɪˈstɪŋ*k*t, -dəˈ- **-ly** -li **-ness** -nəs, -nɪs

indistinctive ˌɪn.dɪˈstɪŋ*k*.tɪv, -dəˈ- **-ly** -li **-ness** -nəs, -nɪs

indistinguishab|le ˌɪn.dɪˈstɪŋ.gwɪ.ʃə.b|ᵊl, -dəˈ- **-ly** -li **-leness** -ᵊl.nəs, -nɪs

in|dite ɪn|ˈdaɪt **-dites** -ˈdaɪts **-diting** -ˈdaɪ.tɪŋ, (US) -ˈdaɪ.t̬ɪŋ **-dited** -ˈdaɪ.tɪd, (US) -ˈdaɪ.t̬ɪd **-diter/s** -ˈdaɪ.təʳ/z, (US) -ˈdaɪ.t̬ɚ/z

indium ˈɪn.di.əm

individual ˌɪn.dɪˈvɪdʒ.u.əl, -dəˈ-, -ˈvɪd.ju-, (US) -ˈvɪdʒ.u-, -ˈvɪdʒ.ᵊl **-s** -z **-ly** -i

individual|ism ˌɪn.dɪˈvɪdʒ.u.ə.l|ɪ.zᵊm, -dəˈ-, -ˈvɪd.ju.ə.l|ɪz-, (US) -ˈvɪdʒ.u-, -ˈvɪdʒ.ᵊl|.ɪ- **-ist/s** -ɪst/s

individualistic ˌɪn.dɪˌvɪdʒ.u.əˈlɪs.tɪk, -dəˌ-, -ˌvɪd.ju-, (US) -ˌvɪdʒ.u-, -ˌvɪdʒ.ᵊlˈɪs- **-ally** -ᵊl.i, -li

individualit|y ˌɪn.dɪˌvɪdʒ.uˈæl.ə.t|i, -dəˌ-, -ˌvɪd.juˈ-, -ɪ.t|i, (US) -ˌvɪdʒ.uˈæl.ə.t̬|i **-ies** -iz

individualization, -isa- ˌɪn.dɪˌvɪdʒ.u.ᵊl.aɪˈzeɪ.ʃᵊn, -dəˌ-, -ˌvɪd.ju-, -ɪˈ-, (US) -ˌvɪdʒ.u.ᵊl.əˈ-, -ˌvɪdʒ.ᵊl-

individualiz|e, -is|e ˌɪn.dɪˈvɪdʒ.u.ə.laɪz, -dəˈ-, -ˈvɪd.ju-, (US) -ˈvɪdʒ.u-, -ˈvɪdʒ.ᵊl.aɪz **-es** -ɪz **-ing** -ɪŋ **-ed** -d

individu|ate ˌɪn.dɪˈvɪdʒ.u|.eɪt, -dəˈ-, -ˈvɪd.ju-, (US) -ˈvɪdʒ.u- **-ates** -eɪts **-ating** -eɪ.tɪŋ, (US) -eɪ.t̬ɪŋ **-ated** -eɪ.tɪd, (US) -eɪ.t̬ɪd

individuation ˌɪn.dɪˌvɪdʒ.uˈeɪ.ʃᵊn, -dəˌ-, -ˌvɪd.juˈ-, (US) -ˌvɪdʒ.uˈ- **-s** -s

indivisibility ˌɪn.dɪˌvɪz.əˈbɪl.ə.ti, -ɪˈ-, -ɪ.ti, (US) -ə.t̬i

indivisib|le ˌɪn.dɪˈvɪz.ə.b|ᵊl, ˈ-ɪ- **-ly** -li **-leness** -ᵊl.nəs, -nɪs

Indo-China ˌɪn.dəʊˈtʃaɪ.nə, (US) -doʊˈ-

Indo-Chinese ˌɪn.dəʊ.tʃaɪˈniːz, (US) -doʊ-

indocile ɪnˈdəʊ.saɪl, ˌɪn-, (US) -ˈdɑː.səl

indocility ˌɪn.dəʊˈsɪl.ə.ti, -ɪ.ti, (US) -dɑːˈsɪl.ə.t̬i, -doʊˈ-

indoctri|nate ɪnˈdɒk.trɪ|.neɪt, -trə-, (US) -ˈdɑːk- **-nates** -neɪts **-nating** -neɪ.tɪŋ, (US) -neɪ.t̬ɪŋ **-nated** -neɪ.tɪd, (US) -neɪ.t̬ɪd **-nator/s** -neɪ.təʳ/z, (US) -neɪ.t̬ɚ/z

indoctrination ɪnˌdɒk.trɪˈneɪ.ʃᵊn, ˌɪn-, -trəˈ-, (US) -ˌdɑːk- **-s** -z

Indo-European ˌɪn.dəʊ.jʊə.rəˈpiː.ən, -ˌjɔː-, (US) -doʊ.jʊr.əˈ- **-s** -z

Indo-Germanic ˌɪn.dəʊ.dʒɜːˈmæn.ɪk, -dʒəˈ-, (US) -doʊ.dʒɝːˈ-

indolence ˈɪn.dᵊl.ən*ts*

indolent ˈɪn.dᵊl.ənt **-ly** -li

indomitab|le ɪnˈdɒm.ɪ.tə.b|ᵊl, ˈ-ə-, (US) -ˈdɑː.mə.t̬ə- **-ly** -li **-leness** -ᵊl.nəs, -nɪs

Indonesi|a ˌɪn.dəʊˈniː.ʒ|ə, -zi|.ə, -si|.ə, -ˈniː.ʃ|ə, (US) -dəˈniː.ʒ|ə, -ʃ|ə **-an/s** -ən/z

indoor ˌɪnˈdɔːʳ, (US) -ˈdɔːr *stress shift:* **ˌindoor ˈgames**

indoors ˌɪnˈdɔːz, (US) -ˈdɔːrz

Indore ˌɪnˈdɔːʳ, (US) -ˈdɔːr

indors|e ɪnˈdɔːs, (US) -ˈdɔːrs **-es** -ɪz **-ing** -ɪŋ **-ed** -t

indorsement ɪnˈdɔːs.mənt, (US) -ˈdɔːrs- **-s** -s

Indra ˈɪn.drə

indrawn ˌɪnˈdrɔːn, (US) ˈɪn.drɑːn, -drɔːn *stress shift, British only:* **ˌindrawn ˈbreath**

indubitab|le ɪnˈdʒuː.bɪ.tə.b|ᵊl, -ˈdjuː-, ˌɪn-, (US) -ˈduː.bɪ.t̬ə-, -ˈdjuː- **-ly** -li **-leness** -ᵊl.nəs, -nɪs

induc|e ɪnˈdʒuːs, -ˈdjuːs, (US) -ˈduːs, -ˈdjuːs **-es** -ɪz **-ing** -ɪŋ **-ed** -t **-er/s** -əʳ/z, (US) -ɚ/z

inducement ɪnˈdʒuːs.mənt, -ˈdjuːs-, (US) -ˈduːs-, -ˈdjuːs- **-s** -s

induct ɪnˈdʌkt **-s** -s **-ing** -ɪŋ **-ed** -ɪd **-or/s** -əʳ/z, (US) -ɚ/z

inductanc|e ɪnˈdʌk.tᵊn*ts* **-es** -ɪz

inductee ˌɪn.dʌkˈtiː **-s** -z

inductile ɪnˈdʌk.taɪl, ˌɪn-, (US) -tɪl

inductility ˌɪn.dʌkˈtɪl.ə.ti, -ɪ.ti, (US) -ə.t̬i

induction ɪnˈdʌk.ʃᵊn **-s** -z **inˈduction ˌcoil**

inductive ɪnˈdʌk.tɪv **-ly** -li

indulg|e ɪnˈdʌldʒ **-es** -ɪz **-ing** -ɪŋ **-ed** -d **-er/s** -əʳ/z, (US) -ɚ/z

indulgenc|e ɪnˈdʌl.dʒən*ts* **-es** -ɪz

indulgent ɪnˈdʌl.dʒənt **-ly** -li

indur|ate ˈɪn.dʒʊə.r|eɪt, ˈ-djʊə-, -dʒʊr|.eɪt, -djʊr|.eɪt, (US) -dʊ.r|eɪt, -djʊ-, -də-, -djə- **-ates** -eɪts **-ating** -eɪ.tɪŋ, (US) -eɪ.t̬ɪŋ **-ated** -eɪ.tɪd, (US) -eɪ.t̬ɪd **-ative** -ə.tɪv, (US) -t̬ɪv

induration ˌɪn.dʒʊəˈreɪ.ʃᵊn, -djʊəˈ-, -dʒʊˈ-, -djʊˈ-, (US) -dʊˈ-, -djʊˈ-, -dəˈ-, -djəˈ-

Indus ˈɪn.dəs

industrial ɪnˈdʌs.tri.əl **-ly** -i **inˌdustrial ˈaction; inˌdustrial disˈpute; inˌdustrial ˈdispute; inˌdustrial ˈespionage; inˌdustrial esˈtate; inˈdustrial ˌpark; inˌdustrial reˈlations; Inˌdustrial Revoˈlution; inˌdustrial triˈbunal**

industrial|ism ɪnˈdʌs.tri.əl|.ɪ.zᵊm **-ist/s** -ɪst/z

industrialization, -isa- ɪnˌdʌs.tri.ə.laɪˈzeɪ.ʃᵊn, -lɪˈ-, (US) -ləˈ-

industrializ|e, -is|e ɪnˈdʌs.tri.ə.laɪz **-es** -ɪz **-ing** -ɪŋ **-ed** -d

industrious ɪnˈdʌs.tri.əs **-ly** -li **-ness** -nəs, -nɪs

industr|y ˈɪn.də.str|i **-ies** -iz

industrywide ˌɪn.də.striˈwaɪd *stress shift:* **ˌindustrywide ˈslump**

indwel|l ˌɪnˈdwel, ˈ-- **-ls** -z **-ling** -ɪŋ **-t** -t

indweller ˈɪnˌdwel.əʳ, (US) -ɚ **-s** -z

-ine aɪn, iːn, ɪn

inebriate n, adj ɪˈniː.bri.ət, -ɪt, -eɪt **-s** -s

inebri|ate v ɪˈniː.bri|.eɪt **-ates** -eɪts **-ating** -eɪ.tɪŋ, (US) -eɪ.t̬ɪŋ **-ated** -eɪ.tɪd, (US) -eɪ.t̬ɪd

inebriation ɪˌniː.briˈeɪ.ʃᵊn

inebriety ˌɪn.iːˈbraɪ.ə.ti, -ɪˈ-, -ɪ.ti, (US) -ə.t̬i

inedible ɪˈned.ə.bᵊl, ˌɪnˈed-, ˈ-ɪ-, (US) ˌɪnˈed-, ɪˈned-

inedited ɪˈned.ɪ.tɪd, ˌɪnˈed-, ˈ-ə-, (US) ˌɪnˈed.ɪ.t̬ɪd, ɪˈned-, ˈ-ə-

ineducable ɪˈned.jə.kə.bᵊl, ˌɪnˈed-, -ˈedʒ.ə-, ˈ-ʊ-, (US) ˌɪnˈedʒ.ʊ-, ɪˈnedʒ-, ˈ-ə-

ineffab|le ɪˈnef.ə.b|ᵊl, ˌɪnˈef-, (US) ˌɪnˈef-, ɪˈnef- **-ly** -li **-leness** -ᵊl.nəs, -nɪs

ineffaceab|le ˌɪn.ɪˈfeɪ.sə.b|ᵊl, -efˈeɪ-, -əˈfeɪ- **-ly** -li

ineffective ˌɪn.ɪˈfek.tɪv, -əˈ- **-ly** -li **-ness** -nəs, -nɪs

ineffectual ˌɪn.ɪˈfek.tʃu.ᵊl, -əˈ-, -tju-, (US) -tʃu-, -tju- **-ly** -i **-ness** -nəs, -nɪs

inefficacious ˌɪn.ef.ɪˈkeɪ.ʃəs, ɪˌnef- **-ly** -li

inefficacy ɪˈnef.ɪ.kə.si, ˌɪnˈef-, (US) ˌɪnˈef-, ɪˈnef-

inefficiency ˌɪn.ɪˈfɪʃ.ᵊn*t*.si, -əˈ-

inefficient ˌɪn.ɪˈfɪʃ.ᵊnt, -əˈ- **-ly** -li

inelastic ˌɪn.ɪˈlæs.tɪk, -əˈ-, -ˈlɑː.stɪk, (US) -iːˈlæs-, -ɪˈ-

inelasticity ˌɪn.ɪ.læsˈtɪs.ə.ti, ˌ-ə-, -ˌiː.læsˈ-, -lɑːˈstɪs-, -ɪ.ti, (US) -iː.læsˈtɪs.ə.t̬i, ˌ-ɪ-

inelegance ɪˈnel.ɪ.gən*ts*, ˌɪnˈel-, ˈ-ə-, (US) ˌɪnˈel-, ɪˈnel-

inelegant ɪˈnel.ɪ.gənt, ˌɪnˈel-, ˈ-ə-, (US) ˌɪnˈel-, ɪˈnel- **-ly** -li

ineligibility ɪˌnel.ɪ.dʒəˈbɪl.ə.ti, ˌɪn.el-, -dʒɪˈ-, -ɪ.ti, (US) ˌɪn.el.ɪ.dʒəˈbɪl.ə.t̬i, ɪˈnel-, -dʒɪˈ-

ineligib|le ɪˈnel.ɪ.dʒə.b|ᵊl, ˌɪnˈel-, -dʒɪ-, (US) ˌɪnˈel-, ɪˈnel- **-ly** -li

ineluctab|le ˌɪn.ɪˈlʌk.tə.b|ᵊl, -əˈ- **-ly** -li

inept ɪˈnept, ˌɪnˈept, (US) ˌɪnˈept, ɪˈnept **-ly** -li **-ness** -nəs, -nɪs

ineptitude ɪˈnep.tɪ.tʃuːd, -tjuːd,

ˌɪnˈep-, -tə-, (US) ɪˈnep.tɪ.tuːd, -tə-, -tjuːd
inequab|le ɪˈnek.wə.b|əl, ˌɪnˈek-, (US) ˌɪnˈek-, ɪˈnek- **-ly** -li
inequalit|y ˌɪn.ɪˈkwɒl.ə.t|i, -iːˈ-, -əˈ-, -ɪ.t|i, (US) -ˈkwɑː.lə.ţ|i **-ies** -iz
inequitab|le ɪˈnek.wɪ.tə.b|əl, ˌɪnˈek-, (US) ˌɪnˈek.wə.ţə-, ɪˈnek- **-ly** -li
inequit|y ɪˈnek.wə.t|i, ˌɪnˈek-, -wɪ-, (US) ˌɪnˈek.wə.ţ|i, ɪˈnek- **-ies** -iz
ineradicab|le ˌɪn.ɪˈræd.ɪ.kə.b|əl, -əˈ- **-ly** -li
inert ɪˈnɜːt, (US) ˌɪnˈɝːt, ɪˈnɝːt **-ly** -li **-ness** -nəs, -nɪs
inertia ɪˈnɜː.ʃə, -ʃi.ə, (US) ˌɪnˈɝː-, ɪˈnɝː-
inescapab|le ˌɪn.ɪˈskeɪ.pə.b|əl, -əˈ- **-ly** -li
inessential ˌɪn.ɪˈsen.tʃəl, -əˈ-
inessive ɪˈnes.ɪv, ˌɪnˈes-, (US) ˌɪnˈes-, ɪˈnes-
inestimab|le ɪˈnes.tɪ.mə.b|əl, ˌɪnˈes-, -tə-, (US) ˌɪnˈes-, ɪˈnes- **-ly** -li
inevitability ɪˌnev.ɪ.təˈbɪl.ə.ti, ˌɪnˌev-, ˌ-ə-, -ɪ.ti, (US) ˌɪnˌev.ɪ.ţəˈbɪl.ə.ţi, ɪˌnev-, ˌ-ə-
inevitab|le ɪˈnev.ɪ.tə.b|əl, ˌɪnˈev-, ˈ-ə-, (US) ˌɪnˈev.ɪ.ţə-, ɪˈnev-, ˈ-ə- **-ly** -li **-leness** -əl.nəs, -nɪs
inexact ˌɪn.ɪgˈzækt, -egˈ-; -ɪkˈsækt, -ekˈ-, (US) -ɪgˈzækt, -egˈ- **-ly** -li **-ness** -nəs, -nɪs
inexactitude ˌɪn.ɪgˈzæk.tɪ.tʃuːd, -tjuːd, -egˈ-, -tə-; -ɪkˈsæk-, -ekˈ-, (US) -ɪgˈzæk.tə.tuːd, -egˈ-, -tjuːd **-s** -z
inexcusab|le ˌɪn.ɪkˈskjuː.zə.b|əl, -ekˈ- **-ly** -li **-leness** -əl.nəs, -nɪs
inexhaustibility ˌɪn.ɪgˌzɔː.stəˈbɪl.ə.ti, -egˌ-, -stɪˈ-, -ɪ.ti; -ɪkˌsɔː-, -ekˌ-, (US) -ɪgˌzɑː.stəˈbɪl.ə.ţi, -egˌ-, -ˌzɔː-
inexhaustib|le ˌɪn.ɪgˈzɔː.stə.b|əl, -egˈ-, -stɪ-; -ɪkˈsɔː-, -ekˈ-, (US) -ɪgˈzɑː.stə-, -egˈ-, -ˈzɔː- **-ly** -li **-leness** -əl.nəs, -nɪs
inexisten|t ˌɪn.ɪgˈzɪs.tən|t, -ekˈ-; -ɪkˈsɪs-, -ekˈ-, (US) -ɪgˈzɪs-, -egˈ- **-ce** -ts
inexorability ɪˌnek.sər.əˈbɪl.ə.ti, ˌɪnˌek-, -ɪ.ti, (US) ˌɪnˌek.sɚ.əˈbɪl.ə.ţi, ɪˌnek-
inexorab|le ɪˈnek.sər.ə.b|əl, ˌɪnˈek-, (US) ˌɪnˈek-, ɪˈnek- **-ly** -li **-leness** -əl.nəs, -nɪs
inexpedien|ce ˌɪn.ɪkˈspiː.di.ən|ts, -ekˈ- **-cy** -si
inexpedient ˌɪn.ɪkˈspiː.di.ənt, -ekˈ- **-ly** -li
inexpensive ˌɪn.ɪkˈspent.sɪv, -ekˈ- **-ly** -li **-ness** -nəs, -nɪs
inexperience ˌɪn.ɪkˈspɪə.ri.ənts, -ekˈ-, (US) -ˈspɪr.i- **-d** -t
inexpert ɪˈnek.spɜːt, ˌɪnˈek-, (US) ˌɪnˈek.spɝːt, ɪˈnek-; (US) ˌɪn.ɪkˈspɝːt, -ekˈ- **-ly** -li **-ness** -nəs, -nɪs
inexpiab|le ɪˈnek.spi.ə.b|əl, ˌɪnˈek-, (US) ˌɪnˈek-, ɪˈnek- **-ly** -li **-leness** -əl.nəs, -nɪs
inexplicability ˌɪn.ɪkˌsplɪk.əˈbɪl.ə.ti, -ekˌ-, -ɪ.ti; ˌɪnˌek.splɪk.əˈ-, ˌɪn-, (US) ɪˌnek.splɪ.kəˈbɪl.ə.ţi, ˌɪn.ek-
inexplicab|le ˌɪn.ɪkˈsplɪk.ə.b|əl, -ekˈ-; ɪˈnek.splɪ.kə-, ˌɪnˈek-, -splə-, (US) ˌɪnˈek.splɪ.kə-, ɪˈnek-, -splə-; ˌɪn.ɪkˈsplɪk.ə- **-ly** -li **-leness** -əl.nəs, -nɪs
inexplicit ˌɪn.ɪkˈsplɪs.ɪt, -ekˈ- **-ly** -li **-ness** -nəs, -nɪs
inexplorable ˌɪn.ɪkˈsplɔː.rə.bəl, -ekˈ-, (US) -ˈsplɔːr.ə-
inexpressib|le ˌɪn.ɪkˈspres.ə.b|əl, -ekˈ-, ˈ-ɪ- **-ly** -li
inexpressive ˌɪn.ɪkˈspres.ɪv, -ekˈ- **-ly** -li **-ness** -nəs, -nɪs
inexpugnab|le ˌɪn.ɪkˈspʌg.nə.b|əl, -ekˈ-, (US) -ˈspʌg-, -ˈspjuː- **-ly** -li **-leness** -əl.nəs, -nɪs
inextensible ˌɪn.ɪkˈstent.sə.bəl, -ekˈ-, -sɪ-
inextinguishab|le ˌɪn.ɪkˈstɪŋ.gwɪ.ʃə.b|əl, -ekˈ-, -wɪ- **-ly** -li
in extremis ˌɪn.ɪkˈstriː.mɪs, (US) -ɪkˈ-, -ekˈ-
inextricab|le ˌɪn.ɪkˈstrɪk.ə.b|əl, -ekˈ-; ɪˈnek.strɪ.kə-, ˌɪnˈek- **-ly** -li **-leness** -əl.nəs, -nɪs
Inez ˈiː.nez, ˈaɪ-, (US) iːˈnez, ɪ-, aɪ-, ˈiː.nez, ˈaɪ-, -nes
infallibility ɪnˌfæl.əˈbɪl.ə.ti, ˌɪn-, -ɪˈ-, -ɪ.ti, (US) -ə.ţi
infallib|le ɪnˈfæl.ə.b|əl, ˈ-ɪ- **-ly** -li
infamous ˈɪn.fə.məs **-ly** -li **-ness** -nəs, -nɪs
infam|y ˈɪn.fə.m|i **-ies** -iz
infanc|y ˈɪn.fənt.s|i **-ies** -iz
infant ˈɪn.fənt **-s** -s **ˈinfant ˌschool; ˌinfant morˈtality ˌrate**
infanta ɪnˈfæn.tə, (US) -ţə, -ˈfɑːn- **-s** -z
infante ɪnˈfæn.ti, (US) -teɪ, -ˈfɑːn- **-s** -z
infanticide ɪnˈfæn.tɪ.saɪd, -tə-, (US) -ţə- **-s** -z
infant|ile ˈɪn.fən.t|aɪl, (US) -t|aɪl, -t|ɪl **-ine** -aɪn **ˌinfantile paˈralysis**
infantilism ɪnˈfæn.tɪ.lɪ.zəm, -tə-, (US) ˈɪn.fən.ţə-, -taɪ-; (US) ɪnˈfæn.ţə-
infantry ˈɪn.fən.tri **-man** -mən, -mæn **-men** -mən, -men
infarct ˈɪn.fɑːkt, ˌ-ˈ-, (US) ˈɪn.fɑːrkt, ˌ-ˈ- **-s** -s
infarction ɪnˈfɑːk.ʃən, (US) -ˈfɑːrk- **-s** -z
infatu|ate ɪnˈfæt.ju|.eɪt, -ˈfætʃ.u-, (US) -ˈfætʃ.u- **-ates** -eɪts **-ating** -eɪ.tɪŋ, (US) -eɪ.ţɪŋ **-ated** -eɪ.tɪd, (US) -eɪ.ţɪd
infatuation ɪnˌfæt.juˈeɪ.ʃən, -ˌfætʃ.uˈ-, (US) -ˌfætʃ.uˈ- **-s** -z
infect ɪnˈfekt **-s** -s **-ing** -ɪŋ **-ed** -ɪd
infection ɪnˈfek.ʃən **-s** -z
infectious ɪnˈfek.ʃəs **-ly** -li **-ness** -nəs, -nɪs
infecundity ˌɪn.fɪˈkʌn.də.ti, -fiːˈ-, -fekˈʌn-, -dɪ-, (US) -fiːˈkʌn.də.ţi, -fɪˈ-
infelicitous ˌɪn.fəˈlɪs.ɪ.təs, -fɪˈ-, -felˈɪs-, ˈ-ə-, (US) -fəˈlɪs.ə.ţəs **-ly** -li
infelicit|y ˌɪn.fəˈlɪs.ə.t|i, -fɪˈ-, -felˈɪs-, -ɪ-, (US) -ə.ţ|i **-ies** -iz
infer ɪnˈfɜːr, (US) -ˈfɝː **-s** -z **-ring** -ɪŋ **-red** -d **-able** -ə.bəl
inferenc|e ˈɪn.fər.ənts, ˈ-frənts **-es** -ɪz
inferential ˌɪn.fərˈen.tʃəl, (US) -fəˈren- **-ly** -i
inferior ɪnˈfɪə.ri.ər, ˌɪn-, (US) -ˈfɪr.i.ɚ **-s** -z
inferiority ɪnˌfɪə.riˈɒr.ə.ti, ˌɪn-, -ɪ.ti, (US) -ˌfɪr.iˈɔːr.ə.ţi **inferiˈority ˌcomplex**
infernal ɪnˈfɜː.nəl, (US) -ˈfɝː- **-ly** -i
inferno, I~ ɪnˈfɜː.nəʊ, (US) -ˈfɝː.noʊ **-s** -z
infertile ɪnˈfɜː.taɪl, ˌɪn-, (US) -ˈfɝː.ţəl
infertility ˌɪn.fəˈtɪl.ə.ti, -fɜːˈ-, -ɪ.ti, (US) -fɚˈtɪl.ə.ţi
infest ɪnˈfest **-s** -s **-ing** -ɪŋ **-ed** -ɪd
infestation ˌɪn.fesˈteɪ.ʃən **-s** -z
infibu|late ɪnˈfɪb.jə|.leɪt, -jʊ- **-lates** -leɪts **-lating** -leɪ.tɪŋ, (US) -leɪ.ţɪŋ **-lated** -leɪ.tɪd, (US) -leɪ.ţɪd
infibulation ɪnˌfɪb.jəˈleɪ.ʃən, -jʊˈ-
infidel ˈɪn.fɪ.dəl, -fə-, -del, (US) -fə.del, -dəl **-s** -z
infidelit|y ˌɪn.fɪˈdel.ə.t|i, -fəˈ-, -ɪ.t|i, (US) -fəˈdel.ə.ţ|i **-ies** -iz
infield ˈɪn.fiːld **-s** -z
infielder ˈɪnˌfiːl.dər, (US) -dɚ **-s** -z
infighting ˈɪnˌfaɪ.tɪŋ
infill ˈɪn.fɪl **-s** -z **-ing** -ɪŋ **-ed** -d
infilling ˈɪnˌfɪl.ɪŋ
infil|trate ˈɪn.fɪl|.treɪt, -fəl-, (US) ɪnˈfɪl|.treɪt, ˈɪn.fɪl- **-trates** -treɪts **-trating** -treɪ.tɪŋ, (US) -treɪ.ţɪŋ **-trated** -treɪ.tɪd, (US) -treɪ.ţɪd **-trator/s** -treɪ.tər/z, (US) -treɪ.ţɚ/z
infiltration ˌɪn.fɪlˈtreɪ.ʃən, -fəlˈ- **-s** -z
in fine ˌɪnˈfaɪ.ni, -ˈfiː-, -neɪ
infinite *in non-technical sense:* ˈɪn.fɪ.nət, -fən.ət, -ɪt; *in church music:* ˈɪn.fɪ.naɪt, -faɪ-, (US) ˈɪn.fə.nɪt **-ly** -li **-ness** -nəs, -nɪs *in grammar:* ˌɪnˈfaɪ.naɪt *in mathematics:* ˈɪn.fɪ.nət, -fən.ət, -ɪt, -ˌfaɪ.naɪt
infinitesimal ˌɪn.fɪ.nɪˈtes.ɪ.məl, -fən.ɪˈ-, -əˈ-, -əm.əl, (US) -ˈtes-, -ˈtez- **-ly** -i
infinitival ɪnˌfɪn.ɪˈtaɪ.vəl, -əˈ-; ˌɪn.fɪ.nɪˈ-, -nəˈ-, (US) ɪnˌfɪn.ɪˈtaɪ-
infinitive ɪnˈfɪn.ə.tɪv, ˈ-ɪ-, (US) -ţɪv **-s** -z **-ly** -li
infinitude ɪnˈfɪn.ɪ.tʃuːd, ˌɪnˈ-, -tjuːd, ˈ-ə-, (US) -tuːd, -tjuːd **-s** -z
infinit|y ɪnˈfɪn.ə.t|i, -ɪ.t|i, (US) -ə.ţ|i **-ies** -iz
infirm ɪnˈfɜːm, ˌɪn-, (US) -ˈfɝːm **-ly** -li
infirmar|y ɪnˈfɜː.mər|.i, (US) -ˈfɝː- **-ies** -iz
infirmit|y ɪnˈfɜː.mə.t|i, -mɪ-, (US) -ˈfɝː.mə.ţ|i **-ies** -iz
infix n ˈɪn.fɪks **-es** -ɪz
infix v ˈɪn.fɪks, ˌ-ˈ- **-es** -ɪz **-ing** -ɪŋ **-ed** -t
in flagrante delicto ɪn.fləˌgræn.teɪ.dɪˈlɪk.təʊ, -ti-, -dəˈ-, -diːˈ-, -deɪˈ-, (US) -ˌgrɑːn.teɪ.dɪˈlɪk.toʊ, -ˌgræn-, -ti-, -dəˈ-, -diːˈ-, -deɪˈ-
inflam|e ɪnˈfleɪm **-es** -z **-ing** -ɪŋ **-ed** -d

I

inflammability ɪnˌflæm.əˈbɪl.ə.ti, -ɪ.ti, (US) -ə.t̬i

inflammable ɪnˈflæm.ə.bəl **-ness** -nəs, -nɪs

inflammation ˌɪn.fləˈmeɪ.ʃən **-s** -z

inflammatory ɪnˈflæm.ə.tər.i, (US) -tɔːr-

inflatable ɪnˈfleɪ.tə.bəl, (US) -t̬ə- **-s** -z

in|flate ɪn|ˈfleɪt **-flates** -ˈfleɪts **-flating** -ˈfleɪ.tɪŋ, (US) -ˈfleɪ.t̬ɪŋ **-flated** -ˈfleɪ.tɪd, (US) -ˈfleɪ.t̬ɪd **-flator/s** -ˈfleɪ.tər/z, (US) -ˈfleɪ.t̬ɚ/z

inflation ɪnˈfleɪ.ʃən **-s** -z **-ary** -ər.i

inflationism ɪnˈfleɪ.ʃən.ɪ.zəm

inflect ɪnˈflekt **-s** -s **-ing** -ɪŋ **-ed** -ɪd

inflection ɪnˈflek.ʃən **-s** -z

inflectional ɪnˈflek.ʃən.əl

inflective ɪnˈflek.tɪv

inflexibility ɪnˌflek.səˈbɪl.ə.ti, ˌɪn-, -sɪˈ-, -ɪ.ti, (US) -ə.t̬i

inflexib|le ɪnˈflek.sə.b|əl, -sɪ- **-ly** -li **-leness** -əl.nəs, -nɪs

inflexion ɪnˈflek.ʃən **-s** -z

inflexional ɪnˈflek.ʃən.əl

inflict ɪnˈflɪkt **-s** -s **-ing** -ɪŋ **-ed** -ɪd

infliction ɪnˈflɪk.ʃən **-s** -z

in-flight ˌɪnˈflaɪt, (US) ˈ-ˌ-, ˌ-ˈ- *stress shift, British only:* **ˌin-flight ˈservice**

inflorescence ˌɪn.flɔːˈres.ənts, -flɒrˈes-, -fləˈres-, (US) -fləˈres-, -flɔː-, -floʊ-

inflow ˈɪn.fləʊ, (US) -floʊ **-s** -z

influenc|e ˈɪn.flu.ənts, -fluənts, (US) -flu.ənts **-es** -ɪz **-ing** -ɪŋ **-ed** -t

influent ˈɪn.flu.ənt, -fluənt, (US) -flu.ənt **-s** -s

influential ˌɪn.fluˈen.tʃəl **-ly** -i

influenza ˌɪn.fluˈen.zə

influx ˈɪn.flʌks **-es** -ɪz

influxion ɪnˈflʌk.ʃən

info ˈɪn.fəʊ, (US) -foʊ

infomercial ˌɪn.fəʊˈmɜː.ʃəl, (US) ˈɪn.foʊ.mɝː- **-s** -z

inform ɪnˈfɔːm, (US) -ˈfɔːrm **-s** -z **-ing** -ɪŋ **-ed** -d **inˌformed oˈpinion**

informal ɪnˈfɔː.məl, ˌɪn-, (US) -ˈfɔːr- **-ly** -i

informalit|y ˌɪn.fɔːˈmæl.ə.t|i, -ɪ.t|i, (US) -fɔːrˈmæl.ə.t̬|i **-ies** -iz

informant ɪnˈfɔː.mənt, (US) -ˈfɔːr- **-s** -s

in forma pauperis ɪnˌfɔː.məˈpaʊ.pər.ɪs, (US) ɪnˌfɔːr.məˈpɑː.pɚ-, -ˈpɔː-

informatics ˌɪn.fəˈmæt.ɪks, -fɔːˈ-, (US) -fɚˈmæt̬-

information ˌɪn.fəˈmeɪ.ʃən, -fɔːˈ-, (US) -fɚˈ- **-s** -z **inforˌmation techˈnology** (US) **inforˌmation techˈnology inforˈmation techˌnology**

informa|tive ɪnˈfɔː.mə|.tɪv, (US) -ˈfɔːr.mə|.t̬ɪv **-tory** -tər.i, (US) -tɔːr.i

informer ɪnˈfɔː.mər, (US) -ˈfɔːr.mɚ **-s** -z

infotainment ˌɪn.fəʊˈteɪn.mənt, (US) ˈɪn.foʊ.teɪn-, ˌɪn.foʊˈteɪn-

infra ˈɪn.frə **ˌinfra ˈdig**

infract ɪnˈfrækt **-s** -s **-ing** -ɪŋ **-ed** -ɪd

infraction ɪnˈfræk.ʃən **-s** -z

infralapsarian ˌɪn.frə.læpˈseə.ri.ən, (US) -ˈser.i- **-s** -z

infrangibility ɪnˌfræn.dʒəˈbɪl.ə.ti, ˌɪn-, -dʒɪˈ-, -ɪ.ti, (US) -ə.t̬i

infrangib|le ɪnˈfræn.dʒɪ.b|əl, ˌɪn-, -dʒə- **-ly** -li **-leness** -əl.nəs, -nɪs

infrared ˌɪn.frəˈred *stress shift:* **ˌinfrared ˈcamera**

infrastructure ˈɪn.frəˌstrʌk.tʃər, (US) -tʃɚ **-s** -z

infrequency ɪnˈfriː.kwənt.si, ˌɪn-

infrequent ɪnˈfriː.kwənt, ˌɪn- **-ly** -li

infring|e ɪnˈfrɪndʒ **-es** -ɪz **-ing** -ɪŋ **-ed** -d **-er/s** -ər/z, (US) -ɚ/z

infringement ɪnˈfrɪndʒ.mənt **-s** -s

infuri|ate ɪnˈfjʊə.ri|.eɪt, -ˈfjɔː-, (US) -ˈfjʊr.i- **-ates** -eɪts **-ating/ly** -eɪ.tɪŋ/li, (US) -eɪ.t̬ɪŋ/li **-ated** -eɪ.tɪd, (US) -eɪ.t̬ɪd

infus|e ɪnˈfjuːz **-es** -ɪz **-ing** -ɪŋ **-ed** -d **-er/s** -ər/z, (US) -ɚ/z

infusible *capable of being infused:* ɪnˈfjuː.zə.bəl, -zɪ- *not fusible:* ɪnˈfjuː.zə.bəl, ˌɪn-, -zɪ-

infusion ɪnˈfjuː.ʒən **-s** -z

infusori|an ˌɪn.fjʊˈzɔː.ri|.ən, -ˈsɔː-, (US) -ˈsɔːr.i- **-al** -əl

infusory ɪnˈfjuː.zər.i, -sər-, (US) -sɚ-, -zɚ-

in futuro ˌɪn.fjuːˈtjʊə.rəʊ, (US) -ˈtʊr.oʊ, -ˈtjʊr-

-ing ɪŋ

Note: Suffix. Normally unstressed, e.g. **shopping** /ˈʃɒp.ɪŋ/ (US) /ˈʃɑː.pɪŋ/.

Inga ˈɪŋ.ə, -gə, (US) -gə

Ingall ˈɪŋ.gɔːl, (US) -gəl

Ingalls ˈɪŋ.gɔːlz, (US) -gəlz

Ingatestone ˈɪn.gət.stəʊn, ˈɪŋ-, (US) -stoʊn

ingathering ˈɪnˌgæð.ər.ɪŋ **-s** -z

Inge *surname:* ɪŋ, ɪndʒ *girl's name:* ˈɪŋ.ə, -gə, (US) -gə

Note: The American playwright is pronounced /ɪndʒ/.

Ingelow ˈɪn.dʒɪ.ləʊ, (US) -loʊ

in genere ˌɪnˈdʒen.ər.eɪ, (US) -ɚ.i

ingenious ɪnˈdʒiː.ni.əs, ˌɪn-, (US) ˈ-njəs, -ni.əs **-ly** -li **-ness** -nəs, -nɪs

ingénue, ingenue ˈæ̃n.ʒeɪ.njuː, ˈæn-, -ʒə-, -ʒen.juː, ˌ--ˈ-, (US) ˈæn.ʒə.nuː, ˈɑːn-, -dʒə-, -njuː **-s** -z

ingenuit|y ˌɪn.dʒɪˈnjuː.ə.t|i, -dʒəˈ-, -ɪ.t|i, (US) -ə.t̬|i **-ies** -iz

ingenuous ɪnˈdʒen.ju.əs **-ly** -li **-ness** -nəs, -nɪs

Ingersoll® ˈɪŋ.gə.sɒl, (US) -gɚ.sɑːl, -sɔːl **-s** -z

ingest ɪnˈdʒest **-s** -s **-ing** -ɪŋ **-ed** -ɪd **-ible** -ə.bəl, -ɪ-

inges|tion ɪnˈdʒes|.tʃən **-tive** -tɪv

Ingham ˈɪŋ.əm

ingle, I~ ˈɪŋ.gəl **-s** -z

Ingleborough ˈɪŋ.gəl.bər.ə, (US) -bɚ.oʊ

Ingleby ˈɪŋ.gəl.bi

inglenook ˈɪŋ.gəl.nʊk **-s** -s

Inglewood ˈɪŋ.gəl.wʊd

Inglis ˈɪŋ.gəlz, -glɪs

inglorious ɪnˈglɔː.ri.əs, ˌɪn-, ɪŋ-, ˌɪŋ-, (US) -ˈglɔːr.i- **-ly** -li **-ness** -nəs, -nɪs

Ingmar ˈɪŋ.mɑːr, (US) -mɑːr

ingoing ˈɪnˌgəʊ.ɪŋ, ˈɪŋ-, (US) ˈɪnˌgoʊ-

Ingold ˈɪŋ.gəʊld, (US) -goʊld

Ingoldsby ˈɪŋ.gəldz.bi

ingot ˈɪŋ.gət, -gɒt, (US) -gət **-s** -s

Ingraham ˈɪŋ.grə.həm, -grɪəm, (US) ˈɪŋ.grəm

ingrain ɪnˈgreɪn, ˌɪn-, ɪŋ-, ˌɪŋ-, (US) ɪn-, ˌɪn- **-s** -z **-ing** -ɪŋ **-ed** -d *stress shift:* **ˌingrained ˈhabits**

Ingram ˈɪŋ.grəm

Ingrams ˈɪŋ.grəmz

ingrate ˈɪn.greɪt, ˈɪŋ-, -ˈ-, (US) ˈɪn.greɪt, -ˈ- **-s** -s **-ly** -li

ingrati|ate ɪnˈgreɪ.ʃi|.eɪt, ɪŋ-, (US) ɪn- **-ates** -eɪts **-ating** -eɪ.tɪŋ, (US) -eɪ.t̬ɪŋ **-ated** -eɪ.tɪd, (US) -eɪ.t̬ɪd

ingratitude ɪnˈgræt.ɪ.tʃuːd, ˌɪnˈ-, -tjuːd, ɪŋ-, ˌɪŋ-, ˈ-ə-, (US) ɪnˈgræt̬.ə.tuːd, -tjuːd

Ingrebourne ˈɪŋ.grɪ.bɔːn, (US) -bɔːrn

ingredient ɪnˈgriː.di.ənt, ɪŋ-, (US) ɪn- **-s** -s

Ingres ˈæ̃ŋ.grə

ingress ˈɪn.gres, ˈɪŋ-, (US) ˈɪn-

ingressive ɪnˈgres.ɪv, ɪŋ-, (US) ɪn-

Ingrey ˈɪŋ.gri

Ingrid ˈɪŋ.grɪd

in-group ˈɪn.gruːp, ˈɪŋ-, (US) ˈɪn- **-s** -s

ingrow|ing ɪnˈgrəʊ|.ɪŋ, ˌɪn-, ɪŋ-, ˌɪŋ-, ˈ-ˌ--, (US) ˈɪn.groʊ- **ˌingrowing ˈtoenail**

ingrown ɪnˈgrəʊn, ˌɪn-, ɪŋ-, ˌɪŋ-, (US) ˈɪn.groʊn *stress shift, British only:* **ˌingrown ˈtoenail**

ingrowth ˈɪn.grəʊθ, ˈɪŋ-, (US) -groʊθ **-s** -s

inguinal ˈɪŋ.gwɪ.nəl, -gwə-

Ingushetia ˌɪŋ.gʊˈʃet.i.ə

inhab|it ɪnˈhæb|.ɪt **-its** -ɪts **-iting** -ɪ.tɪŋ, (US) -ɪ.t̬ɪŋ **-ited** -ɪ.tɪd, (US) -ɪ.t̬ɪd **-iter/s** -ɪ.tər/z, (US) -ɪ.t̬ɚ/z **-itable** -ɪ.tə.bəl, (US) -ɪ.t̬ə.bəl

inhabitant ɪnˈhæb.ɪ.tənt **-s** -s

inhabitation ɪnˌhæb.ɪˈteɪ.ʃən

inhalation ˌɪn.həˈleɪ.ʃən **-s** -z

inhal|e ɪnˈheɪl **-es** -z **-ing** -ɪŋ **-ed** -d **-ant/s** -ənt/s **-er/s** -ər/z, (US) -ɚ/z

inharmonious ˌɪn.hɑːˈməʊ.ni.əs, (US) -hɑːrˈmoʊ- **-ly** -li **-ness** -nəs, -nɪs

inher|e ɪnˈhɪər, (US) -ˈhɪr **-es** -z **-ing** -ɪŋ **-ed** -d

inheren|ce ɪnˈher.ənt|s, -ˈhɪə.rənt|s, (US) -ˈhɪr.ənt|s, -ˈher- **-cy** -si

inherent ɪnˈher.ənt, -ˈhɪə.rənt, (US) -ˈhɪr.ənt, -ˈher- **-ly** -li

inher|it ɪnˈher|.ɪt **-its** -ɪts **-iting** -ɪ.tɪŋ, (US) -ɪ.t̬ɪŋ **-ited** -ɪ.tɪd, (US) -ɪ.t̬ɪd **-itor/s** -ɪ.tər/z, (US) -ɪ.t̬ɚ/z **-itable** -ɪ.tə.bəl, (US) -ɪ.t̬ə.bəl

inheritanc|e ɪnˈher.ɪ.tənts **-es** -ɪz

inhib|it ɪnˈhɪb|.ɪt **-its** -ɪts **-iting** -ɪ.tɪŋ, (US) -ɪ.t̬ɪŋ **-ited** -ɪ.tɪd, (US) -ɪ.t̬ɪd **-itor/s** -ɪ.tər/z, (US) -ɪ.t̬ɚ/z **-itory** -ɪ.tər.i, (US) -ɪ.tɔːr.i

inhibition ˌɪn.hɪˈbɪʃ.ən -s -z
inhospitab|le ˌɪn.hɒsˈpɪt.ə.b|əl; ɪnˈhɒs.pɪ.tə-, ˌɪn-, -pə-, (US) ɪnˈhɑː.spɪ.t̬ə-, ˌɪn-; (US) ˌɪn.hɑːˈspɪt̬.ə- -ly -li -leness -əl.nəs, -nɪs
inhospitality ɪnˌhɒs.pɪˈtæl.ə.ti, ˌɪn-, -ɪ.ti, (US) -ˌhɑː.spəˈtæl.ə.t̬i
in-house ˌɪnˈhaʊs *stress shift:* ˌ**in-house proˈduction**
inhuman ɪnˈhjuː.mən, ˌɪn- -ly -li
inhumane ˌɪn.hjuːˈmeɪn, -hjʊˈ- -ly -li
inhumanit|y ˌɪn.hjuːˈmæn.ə.t|i, -hjʊˈ-, -ɪ.t|i, (US) -ə.t̬|i -ies -iz
inhumation ˌɪn.hjuːˈmeɪ.ʃən, -hjʊˈ- -s -z
inhum|e ɪnˈhjuːm -es -z -ing -ɪŋ -ed -d
Inigo ˈɪn.ɪ.gəʊ, (US) -goʊ
inimic|al ɪˈnɪm.ɪ.k|əl -ally -əl.i, -li
inimitability ɪˌnɪm.ɪ.təˈbɪl.ə.ti, ˌ-ə-, -ɪ.ti, (US) -t̬əˈbɪl.ə.t̬i
inimitab|le ɪˈnɪm.ɪ.tə.b|əl, ˈ-ə-, (US) -t̬ə- -ly -li -leness -əl.nəs, -nɪs
iniquitous ɪˈnɪk.wɪ.təs, -wə-, (US) -t̬əs -ly -li
iniquit|y ɪˈnɪk.wə.t|i, -wɪ-, (US) -t̬|i -ies -iz
initial ɪˈnɪʃ|.əl -s -əlz -ly -əl.i, -li -(l)ing -əl.ɪŋ, -lɪŋ -(l)ed -əld
initialization, -isa- ɪˌnɪʃ.əl.aɪˈzeɪ.ʃən, -ɪˈ-, (US) -əˈ-
initializ|e, -is|e ɪˈnɪʃ.əl.aɪz -es -ɪz -ing -ɪŋ -ed -d
initiate n ɪˈnɪʃ.i.ət, -eɪt, -ɪt -s -s
initi|ate v ɪˈnɪʃ.i|.eɪt -ates -eɪts -ating -eɪ.tɪŋ, (US) -eɪ.t̬ɪŋ -ated -eɪ.tɪd, (US) -eɪ.t̬ɪd -ator/s -eɪ.təʳ/z, (US) -eɪ.t̬ɚ/z
initiation ɪˌnɪʃ.iˈeɪ.ʃən -s -z
initiative ɪˈnɪʃ.ə.tɪv, -i.ə-, (US) -t̬ɪv -s -z
initiatory ɪˈnɪʃ.ə.tər.i, -i.ə-, -eɪ-, (US) -ə.tɔːr.i
initio ɪˈnɪʃ.i.əʊ, -ˈnɪt-, -ˈnɪs-, (US) -oʊ
inject ɪnˈdʒekt -s -s -ing -ɪŋ -ed -ɪd -or/s -əʳ/z, (US) -ɚ/z -able -ə.bəl
injection ɪnˈdʒek.ʃən -s -z
injudicious ˌɪn.dʒuːˈdɪʃ.əs -ly -li -ness -nəs, -nɪs
Injun ˈɪn.dʒən -s -z
injunction ɪnˈdʒʌŋk.ʃən -s -z
injurant ˈɪn.dʒʊ.rənt, -dʒə.rənt -s -s
inj|ure ˈɪn.dʒ|əʳ, (US) -dʒ|ɚ -ures -əz, (US) -ɚz -uring -ər.ɪŋ -ured -əd, (US) -ɚd -urer/s -ər.əʳ/z, (US) -ɚ.ɚ/z
injuria absque damno ɪnˌdʒʊə.ri.əˌæb.skweɪˈdæm.nəʊ, (US) -ˌdʒʊr.i.əˌæb.skweɪˈdæm.noʊ
injurious ɪnˈdʒʊə.ri.əs, -ˈdʒɔː-, (US) -ˈdʒʊr.i- -ly -li -ness -nəs, -nɪs
injur|y ˈɪn.dʒər|.i -ies -iz ˈ**injury ˌtime**
injustic|e ɪnˈdʒʌs.tɪs, ˌɪn- -es -ɪz
ink ɪŋk -s -s -ing -ɪŋ -ed -t -er/s -əʳ/z, (US) -ɚ/z
Inkatha ɪnˈkɑː.tə, ɪŋˈ-
inkblot ˈɪŋk.blɒt, (US) -blɑːt -s -s
Inkerman ˈɪŋ.kə.mən, (US) -kɚ-
inkhorn ˈɪŋk.hɔːn, (US) -hɔːrn -s -z
inkjet ˈɪŋk.dʒet -s -s
inkling ˈɪŋk.lɪŋ -s -z
Inkpen ˈɪŋk.pen
inkpot ˈɪŋk.pɒt, (US) -pɑːt -s -s
ink-stain ˈɪŋk.steɪn -s -z
inkstand ˈɪŋk.stænd -s -z
inkwell ˈɪŋk.wel -s -z
ink|y ˈɪŋ.k|i -ier -i.əʳ, (US) -i.ɚ -iest -i.ɪst, -i.əst -iness -ɪ.nəs, -ɪ.nɪs
INLA ˌaɪ.en.elˈeɪ
inlaid (from **inlay**) ɪnˈleɪd, (US) ˈ-- *stress shift, British only:* ˌ**inlaid ˈgold**
inland n, adj ˈɪn.lənd, -lænd -s -z ˌ**Inland ˈRevenue**
inland adv ˈɪn.lænd, -ˈ-
inlander ˈɪn.lən.dəʳ, (US) -dɚ, -læn- -s -z
in-law ˈɪn.lɔː, (US) -lɑː, -lɔː -s -z
inlay n ˈɪn.leɪ
in|lay v ɪn|ˈleɪ, ˌɪn-, (US) ɪn|ˈleɪ, ˌɪn-, ˈɪn|.leɪ -lays -ˈleɪz, (US) -ˈleɪz, -leɪz -laying -ˈleɪ.ɪŋ, (US) -ˈleɪ-, -ˌleɪ-
inlet ˈɪn.let, -lət, -lɪt -s -s
in loco parentis ɪnˌləʊ.kəʊ.pəˈren.tɪs, -ˌlɒk.əʊ-, (US) -ˌloʊ.koʊ.pəˈren.t̬ɪs
inly ˈɪn.li
Inman ˈɪn.mən, ˈɪm-, (US) ˈɪn-
inmate ˈɪn.meɪt, ˈɪm-, (US) ˈɪn- -s -s
in medias res ɪnˌmiː.di.æsˈreɪs, ɪm-, -ˌmeɪ-, -ˌmed.i-, -ɑːsˈ-, -əsˈ-, -ˈreɪz, (US) ɪnˌmiː.di.əsˈreɪs, -ˌmed.i-, -ˈreɪz
in memoriam ˌɪn.mɪˈmɔː.ri.əm, ˌɪm-, -məˈ-, -æm, (US) ˌɪn.mɪˈmɔːr.i-, -məˈ-
inmost ˈɪn.məʊst, ˈɪm-, (US) ˈɪn.moʊst
inn ɪn -s -z
innards ˈɪn.ədz, (US) -ɚdz
innate ɪˈneɪt, ˌɪnˈeɪt -ly -li -ness -nəs, -nɪs
innavigable *ɪn*ˈnæv.ɪ.gə.bəl, ˌɪnˈ*n*æv-, ˈ-ə-
inner ˈɪn.əʳ, (US) -ɚ ˌ**inner ˈcity;** ˈ**inner ˌtube**
inner-city ˈɪn.əˌsɪt.i, (US) -ɚˌsɪt̬-
innermost ˈɪn.ə.məʊst, (US) -ɚ.moʊst
inner|vate ˈɪn.ə|.veɪt; ɪˈnɜː-, ˌɪnˈɜː-, (US) ɪˈnɝː-, ˌɪnˈɝː-; ˈɪn.ɚ- -vates -veɪts -vating -veɪ.tɪŋ, (US) -veɪ.t̬ɪŋ -vated -veɪ.tɪd, (US) -veɪ.t̬ɪd
innervation ˌɪn.əˈveɪ.ʃən, (US) -ɚˈ-
Innes(s) ˈɪn.ɪs
inning ˈɪn.ɪŋ -s -z -ses -zɪz
innings ˈɪn.ɪŋz -es -ɪz
Innisfail ˌɪn.ɪsˈfeɪl, -əsˈ-
Innisfree ˌɪn.ɪsˈfriː, -əsˈ-
innit ˈɪn.ɪt
innkeeper ˈɪnˌkiː.pəʳ, ˈɪŋ-, (US) -pɚ -s -z
innocen|ce ˈɪn.ə.sənt|s -cy -si
innocent, I~ ˈɪn.ə.sənt -s -s -ly -li
innocuous ɪˈnɒk.ju.əs, (US) -ˈnɑːk- -ly -li -ness -nəs, -nɪs
innominate ɪˈnɒm.ɪ.nət, ˈ-ə-, -nɪt, -neɪt, (US) -ˈnɑː.mə-
inno|vate ˈɪn.əʊ|.veɪt, (US) ˈ-ə- -vates -veɪts -vating -veɪ.tɪŋ, (US) -veɪ.t̬ɪŋ -vated -veɪ.tɪd, (US) -veɪ.t̬ɪd -vator/s -veɪ.təʳ/z, (US) -veɪ.t̬ɚ/z
innovation ˌɪn.əʊˈveɪ.ʃən, (US) -əˈ- -s -z
innovative ˈɪn.ə.və.tɪv, -veɪ-; ɪˈnəʊ.və.tɪv, (US) ˈɪn.ə.veɪ.t̬ɪv
innovatory ˈɪn.əʊ.veɪ.tər.i, -və-, (US) ˈɪn.ə.və.tɔːr.i
innoxious ɪˈnɒk.ʃəs, (US) -ˈnɑːk- -ly -li -ness -nəs, -nɪs
Innsbruck ˈɪnz.brʊk
Innsworth ˈɪnz.wəθ, -wɜːθ, (US) -wɚθ, -wɝːθ
innuendo ˌɪn.juˈen.dəʊ, (US) -doʊ -(e)s -z
Innuit ˈɪn.u.ɪt, -ju-, (US) ˈ-u- -s -s
innumerability ɪˌnjuː.mər.əˈbɪl.ə.ti, ˌɪnˌjuː-, -ɪ.ti, (US) ɪˌnuː.mɚ.əˈbɪl.ə.t̬i, ˌɪnˌuː-, -ˌjuː-
innumerab|le ɪˈnjuː.mər.ə.b|əl, ˌɪnˈjuː-, (US) ɪˈnuː-, ˌɪnˈuː-, -ˈjuː- -ly -li -leness -əl.nəs, -nɪs
innumeracy ɪˈnjuː.mər.ə.si, ˌɪnˈjuː-, (US) ɪˈnuː-, ˌɪnˈuː-, -ˈjuː-
innumerate ɪˈnjuː.mər.ət, ˌɪnˈjuː-, (US) ɪˈnuː.mɚ-, ˌɪnˈuː-, -ˈjuː- -s -s
innutriti|on ˌɪn.*n*juːˈtrɪʃ|.ən, (US) -*n*uːˈ-, -*n*juːˈ- -ous -əs
inobservan|ce ˌɪn.əbˈzɜː.vən|*t*s, (US) -ˈzɝː- -t -t
inoccupation ɪˌnɒk.jʊˈpeɪ.ʃən, ˌɪnˌɒk-, (US) ɪˌnɑː.kjəˈ-, ˌɪnˌɑː-
inocu|late ɪˈnɒk.jə|.leɪt, -jʊ-, (US) -ˈnɑː.kjə- -lates -leɪts -lating -leɪ.tɪŋ, (US) -leɪ.t̬ɪŋ -lated -leɪ.tɪd, (US) -leɪ.t̬ɪd -lator/s -leɪ.təʳ/z, (US) -leɪ.t̬ɚ/z
inoculation ɪˌnɒk.jəˈleɪ.ʃən, -jʊˈ-, (US) -ˌnɑː.kjəˈ- -s -z
inodorous ɪˈnəʊ.dər.əs, ˌɪnˈəʊ-, (US) ˌɪnˈoʊ-, ɪˈnoʊ-
inoffensive ˌɪn.əˈfent.sɪv -ly -li -ness -nəs, -nɪs
inofficious ˌɪn.əˈfɪʃ.əs
in omnibus ˌɪnˈɒm.nɪ.bəs, -bʊs, (US) -ˈɑːm.nɪ-, -niː-
inoperable ɪˈnɒp.ər.ə.bəl, ˌɪnˈɒp-, (US) ˌɪnˈɑː.pɚ-, ɪˈnɑː-
inoperative ɪˈnɒp.ər.ə.tɪv, ˌɪnˈɒp-, (US) ˌɪnˈɑː.pɚ.ə.t̬ɪv, ɪˈnɑː-
inopportune ɪˈnɒp.ə.tʃuːn, ˌɪnˈɒp-, -tjuːn; ˌɪn.ɒp.əˈtʃuːn, -ˈtjuːn, (US) ˌɪnˌɑː.pɚˈtuːn, ɪˌnɑː-, -ˈtjuːn -ly -li -ness -nəs, -nɪs
inordinate ɪˈnɔː.dɪ.nət, ˌɪnˈɔː-, -dən.ət, -ɪt, (US) ˌɪnˈɔːr.dən.ɪt, ɪˈnɔːr- -ly -li -ness -nəs, -nɪs
inorganic ˌɪn.ɔːˈgæn.ɪk, (US) -ɔːrˈ- -ally -əl.i, -li
inoscu|late ɪˈnɒs.kjə|.leɪt, -kjʊ-, (US) -ˈnɑː.skjuː-, ˌɪnˈɑː- -lates -leɪts -lating -leɪ.tɪŋ, (US) -leɪ.t̬ɪŋ -lated -leɪ.tɪd, (US) -leɪ.t̬ɪd
inosculation ɪˌnɒs.kjəˈleɪ.ʃən, (US) -ˌnɑː.skjuːˈ-, ˌɪnˌɑː-
in pais ˌɪnˈpeɪs, (US) ˌɪnˈpeɪ
in pari delicto ɪnˌpær.i.dɪˈlɪk.təʊ, (US) -dəˈlɪk.toʊ, -ˌpɑːr-
in pari materia ɪnˌpær.i.məˈtɪə.ri.ə, (US) -ˈtɪr.i.ə, -ˌpɑːr-

inpatient ˈɪnˌpeɪ.ʃᵊnt **-s** -s
in personam ˌɪn.pɜːˈsəʊ.næm, ˌɪm-, -pəˈ-, -nəm, (US) ˌɪn.pɚˈsoʊ.næm
in praesenti ˌɪn.praɪˈsen.tiː, (US) -prɪˈzen.tiː
in|put ˈɪn|.pʊt, ˈɪm- **-puts** -pʊts **-putting** -ˌpʊt.ɪŋ, (US) -ˌpʊt̬.ɪŋ **-putted** -ˌpʊt.ɪd, (US) -ˌpʊt̬.ɪd **-putter/s** -ˌpʊt.əʳ/z, (US) -ˌpʊt̬.ɚ/z
input-output ˌɪn.pʊtˈaʊt.pʊt, ˌɪm-
inquest ˈɪŋ.kwest, ˈɪn-, (US) ˈɪn- **-s** -s
inquietude ɪnˈkwaɪə.tʃuːd, -tjuːd, ɪŋ-, -ˈkwaɪ.ɪ-, (US) ɪnˈkwaɪ.ə.tuːd, -ˈkwaɪ.ɪ-, -tjuːd
inquiline ˈɪŋ.kwɪ.laɪn, ˈɪn-, (US) ˈɪn.kwɪ.laɪn, -lɪn **-s** -z
inquir|e ɪnˈkwaɪəʳ, -ˈkwaɪ.əʳ, ɪŋ-, (US) ɪnˈkwaɪ.ɚ **-es** -z **-ing/ly** -ɪŋ/li **-ed** -d **-er/s** -əʳ/z, (US) -ɚ/z
inquir|y ɪnˈkwaɪə.r|i, ɪŋ-, (US) ɪnˈkwaɪ-; (US) ˈɪn.kwɚ|.i **-ies** -iz
inquisition, I~ ˌɪŋ.kwɪˈzɪʃ.ᵊn, ˌɪn-, (US) ˌɪn- **-s** -z
inquisitional ˌɪŋ.kwɪˈzɪʃ.ᵊn.ᵊl, ˌɪn-, (US) ˌɪn-
inquisitive ɪnˈkwɪz.ə.tɪv, ɪŋ-, ˈ-ɪ-, (US) ɪnˈkwɪz.ə.t̬ɪv, ˈ-ɪ- **-ly** -li **-ness** -nəs, -nɪs
inquisitor ɪnˈkwɪz.ɪ.təʳ, ɪŋ-, (US) ɪnˈkwɪz.ɪ.t̬ɚ **-s** -z
inquisitorial ɪnˌkwɪz.ɪˈtɔː.ri.əl, ɪŋ-; ˌɪn.kwɪ.zɪˈ-, ˌɪŋ-, (US) ɪnˌkwɪz.ɪˈtɔːr.i- **-ly** -i
inquorate ˌɪnˈkwɔː.reɪt, ˌɪŋ-, -rət, -rɪt, (US) ɪnˈkwɔːr.eɪt, -ət, -ɪt
in re ˌɪnˈreɪ
in rem ˌɪnˈrem
inroad ˈɪn.rəʊd, (US) -roʊd **-s** -z
inrush ˈɪn.rʌʃ **-es** -ɪz
INS ˌaɪ.enˈes
insalubr|ious ˌɪn.səˈluː.br|i.əs, -ˈljuː-, (US) -ˈluː- **-ity** -ə.ti, -ɪ.ti, (US) -ə.t̬i
insane ɪnˈseɪn, ˌɪn- **-ly** -li **-ness** -nəs, -nɪs
insanitar|y ɪnˈsæn.ɪ.tᵊr|.i, ˌɪn-, ˈ-ə-, -tr|i, (US) -ter|.i **-iness** -ɪ.nəs, -nɪs
insanity ɪnˈsæn.ə.ti, ˌɪn-, -ɪ.ti, (US) -ə.t̬i
insatiability ɪnˌseɪ.ʃəˈbɪl.ə.ti, -ʃi.əˈ-, -ɪ.ti, (US) -ə.t̬i
insatiab|le ɪnˈseɪ.ʃə.b|ᵊl, -ʃi.ə- **-ly** -li **-leness** -ᵊl.nəs, -nɪs
insatiate ɪnˈseɪ.ʃi.ət, -ɪt, -eɪt
inscape ˈɪn.skeɪp
inscrib|e ɪnˈskraɪb **-es** -z **-ing** -ɪŋ **-ed** -d **-er/s** -əʳ/z, (US) -ɚ/z
inscription ɪnˈskrɪp.ʃᵊn **-s** -z
inscrutability ɪnˌskruː.təˈbɪl.ə.ti, ˌɪn-, -ɪ.ti, (US) -ˌskruː.t̬əˈbɪl.ə.t̬i
inscrutab|le ɪnˈskruː.tə.b|ᵊl, ˌɪn-, (US) -t̬ə- **-ly** -li **-leness** -ᵊl.nəs, -nɪs
inseam ˈɪn.siːm
insect ˈɪn.sekt **-s** -s
insectari|um ˌɪn.sekˈteə.ri|.əm, (US) -ˈter.i- **-ums** -əmz **-a** -ə
insecticidal ɪnˌsek.tɪˈsaɪ.dᵊl, -təˈ- **-ly** -i
insecticide ɪnˈsek.tɪ.saɪd, -tə- **-s** -z
insectivore ɪnˈsek.tɪ.vɔːʳ, -tə-, (US) -vɔːr **-s** -z
insectivorous ˌɪn.sekˈtɪv.ᵊr.əs
insecure ˌɪn.sɪˈkjʊəʳ, -səˈ-, -ˈkjɔːʳ, (US) -ˈkjʊr **-ly** -li
insecurit|y ˌɪn.sɪˈkjʊə.rə.t|i, -səˈ-, -ˈkjɔː-, -rɪ-, (US) -ˈkjʊr.ə.t̬|i **-ies** -iz
insemi|nate ɪnˈsem.ɪ|.neɪt, ˈ-ə- **-nates** -neɪts **-nating** -neɪ.tɪŋ, (US) -neɪ.t̬ɪŋ **-nated** -neɪ.tɪd, (US) -neɪ.t̬ɪd **-nator/s** -neɪ.təʳ/z, (US) -neɪ.t̬ɚ/z
insemination ɪnˌsem.ɪˈneɪ.ʃᵊn, ˌɪn-, -əˈ-
insensate ɪnˈsent.seɪt, ˌɪn-, -sət, -sɪt **-ly** -li **-ness** -nəs, -nɪs
insensibility ɪnˌsent.səˈbɪl.ə.ti, ˌɪn-, -sɪˈ-, -ɪ.ti, (US) -ə.t̬i
insensib|le ɪnˈsent.sə.b|ᵊl, ˌɪn-, -sɪ- **-ly** -li **-leness** -ᵊl.nəs, -nɪs
insensitive ɪnˈsent.sə.tɪv, ˌɪn-, -sɪ-, (US) -t̬ɪv **-ness** -nəs, -nɪs
insensitivity ɪnˌsent.səˈtɪv.ə.ti, ˌɪn-, -sɪˈ-, -ɪ.ti, (US) -ə.t̬i
insentien|t ˌɪnˈsen.tʃᵊn|t, -tʃi.ən|t **-ce** -ts
inseparability ɪnˌsep.ᵊr.əˈbɪl.ə.ti, ˌɪn-, ˌ-rəˈ-, -ɪ.ti, (US) -ə.t̬i
inseparab|le ɪnˈsep.ᵊr.ə.b|ᵊl, ˌɪn-, ˈ-rə- **-ly** -li **-leness** -ᵊl.nəs, -nɪs
insert n ˈɪn.sɜːt, (US) -sɝːt **-s** -s
in|sert v ɪn|ˈsɜːt, (US) -ˈsɝːt **-serts** -ˈsɜːts, (US) -ˈsɝːts **-serting** -ˈsɜː.tɪŋ, (US) -ˈsɝː.t̬ɪŋ **-serted** -ˈsɜː.tɪd, (US) -ˈsɝː.t̬ɪd
insertion ɪnˈsɜː.ʃᵊn, (US) -ˈsɝː- **-s** -z
in-service ˌɪnˈsɜː.vɪs, (US) ˈɪnˌsɝː- *stress shift, British only:* ˌ**in-service** ˈ**training**
inset n ˈɪn.set **-s** -s
inse|t v ˌɪnˈse|t, (US) ɪnˈse|t, ˈ-- **-ts** -ts **-tting** -tɪŋ, (US) -t̬ɪŋ
inseverable ɪnˈsev.ᵊr.ə.bᵊl, ˌɪn-
inshore ˌɪnˈʃɔːʳ, (US) -ˈʃɔːr *stress shift:* ˌ**inshore** ˈ**rescue**
inside ˌɪnˈsaɪd, ˈ-- **-s** -z ˌ**inside** ˈ**job** (US) ˈ**inside** ˌ**job**; ˌ**inside** ˈ**out**
insider ɪnˈsaɪ.dəʳ, ˌɪn-, (US) ˈɪnˌsaɪ.dɚ, -ˈ-- **-s** -z **in**ˌ**sider** ˈ**dealing** (US) ˈ**insider** ˌ**dealing**; **in**ˌ**sider** ˈ**trading** (US) ˈ**insider** ˌ**trading**
insidious ɪnˈsɪd.i.əs **-ly** -li **-ness** -nəs, -nɪs
insight ˈɪn.saɪt **-s** -s
insightful ˈɪn.saɪt.fᵊl, -fʊl, (US) ˈɪn.saɪt.fᵊl, -ˈ-- **-ly** -li
insignia ɪnˈsɪg.ni.ə **-s** -z
insignifican|ce ˌɪn.sɪgˈnɪf.ɪ.kᵊnt|s **-cy** -si
insignificant ˌɪn.sɪgˈnɪf.ɪ.kᵊnt **-ly** -li
insincere ˌɪn.sɪnˈsɪəʳ, -sᵊnˈ-, (US) -ˈsɪr **-ly** -li
insincerit|y ˌɪn.sɪnˈser.ə.t|i, -sᵊnˈ-, -ɪ.t|i, (US) -ə.t̬|i **-ies** -iz
insinu|ate ɪnˈsɪn.ju|.eɪt **-ates** -eɪts **-ating/ly** -eɪ.tɪŋ/li, (US) -eɪ.t̬ɪŋ/li **-ated** -eɪ.tɪd, (US) -eɪ.t̬ɪd **-ator/s** -eɪ.təʳ/z, (US) -eɪ.t̬ɚ/z
insinuation ɪnˌsɪn.juˈeɪ.ʃᵊn, ˌɪn- **-s** -z
insipid ɪnˈsɪp.ɪd **-ly** -li **-ness** -nəs, -nɪs
insipidity ˌɪn.sɪˈpɪd.ə.ti, -ɪ.ti, (US) -ɪ.t̬i
insipien|ce ɪnˈsɪp.i.ən|ts **-t** -t
insist ɪnˈsɪst **-s** -s **-ing** -ɪŋ **-ed** -ɪd
insisten|ce ɪnˈsɪs.tᵊnt|s **-cy** -si
insistent ɪnˈsɪs.tᵊnt **-ly** -li
in situ ˌɪnˈsɪt.juː, -ˈsɪtʃ.uː, -tʃuː, (US) -ˈsaɪ.tuː, -ˈsiː-, -ˈsɪt.uː, -juː
Inskip ˈɪn.skɪp
insobriety ˌɪn.səʊˈbraɪ.ə.ti, -ˈbraɪ.ɪ-, (US) -soʊˈbraɪ.ə.t̬i
insofar ˌɪn.səʊˈfɑːʳ, (US) -soʊˈfɑːr
insolation ˌɪn.səʊˈleɪ.ʃᵊn, (US) -soʊˈ-
insole ˈɪn.səʊl, (US) -soʊl **-s** -z
insolence ˈɪnt.sᵊl.ənts
insolent ˈɪnt.sᵊl.ənt **-ly** -li
insolubility ɪnˌsɒl.jəˈbɪl.ə.ti, ˌɪn-, -jʊˈ-, -ɪ.ti, (US) -ˌsɑːl.jəˈbɪl.ə.t̬i
insolub|le ɪnˈsɒl.jə.b|ᵊl, ˌɪn-, -jʊ-, (US) -ˈsɑːl.jə- **-ly** -li **-leness** -ᵊl.nəs, -nɪs
insolvable ɪnˈsɒl.və.bᵊl, ˌɪn-, (US) -ˈsɑːl-
insolven|cy ɪnˈsɒl.vᵊn|t.si, ˌɪn-, (US) -ˈsɑːl- **-t** -t
insomnia ɪnˈsɒm.ni.ə, (US) -ˈsɑːm-
insomniac ɪnˈsɒm.ni.æk, (US) -ˈsɑːm- **-s** -s
insomuch ˌɪn.səʊˈmʌtʃ, (US) -soʊˈ-
insouciance ɪnˈsuː.si.ənts, (US) -si.ənts, -ʃənts
insouciant ɪnˈsuː.si.ənt, (US) -si.ənt, -ʃənt **-ly** -li
in specie ˌɪnˈspes.i.eɪ, (US) ˌɪnˈspiː.ʃi, -si
inspect ɪnˈspekt **-s** -s **-ing** -ɪŋ **-ed** -ɪd
inspection ɪnˈspek.ʃᵊn **-s** -z
inspector ɪnˈspek.təʳ, (US) -tɚ **-s** -z
inspectorate ɪnˈspek.tᵊr.ət, -ɪt **-s** -s
inspectorship ɪnˈspek.tə.ʃɪp, (US) -tɚ- **-s** -s
inspiration ˌɪnt.spᵊrˈeɪ.ʃᵊn, -spɪˈreɪ-, (US) -spəˈreɪ- **-s** -z
inspirational ˌɪnt.spᵊrˈeɪ.ʃᵊn.əl, -spɪˈreɪ-, (US) -spəˈreɪ- **-ly** -i
inspirator ˈɪnt.spᵊr.eɪ.təʳ, -spɪ.reɪ-, (US) -spə.reɪ.t̬ɚ **-s** -z
inspiratory ɪnˈspaɪə.rə.tᵊr.i, -ˈspɪr.ə-, (US) -ˈspaɪ.rə.tɔːr-
inspir|e ɪnˈspaɪəʳ, -ˈspaɪ.əʳ, (US) -ˈspaɪ.ɚ **-es** -z **-ing/ly** -ɪŋ/li **-ed** -d **-er/s** -əʳ/z, (US) -ɚ/z
inspir|it ɪnˈspɪr|.ɪt **-its** -ɪts **-iting** -ɪ.tɪŋ, (US) -ɪ.t̬ɪŋ **-ited** -ɪ.tɪd, (US) -ɪ.t̬ɪd
inspiss|ate ɪnˈspɪs|.eɪt; ˈɪn.spɪ.s|eɪt, (US) ɪnˈspɪs|.eɪt **-ates** -eɪts **-ating** -eɪ.tɪŋ, (US) -eɪ.t̬ɪŋ **-ated** -eɪ.tɪd, (US) -eɪ.t̬ɪd
inst. (abbrev. for **instant**) ɪntst, ˈɪnt.stᵊnt
inst., I~ (abbrev. for **institute**) ɪntst, ˈɪnt.stɪ.tʃuːt, -stə-, -tjuːt, (US) -tuːt, -tjuːt
instabilit|y ˌɪn.stəˈbɪl.ə.t|i, -ɪ.t|i, (US) -ə.t̬|i **-ies** -iz
instal ɪnˈstɔːl, (US) -ˈstɔːl, -ˈstɑːl **-s** -z **-ling** -ɪŋ **-led** -d
install ɪnˈstɔːl, (US) -ˈstɔːl, -ˈstɑːl **-s** -z **-ing** -ɪŋ **-ed** -d **-able** -ə.bᵊl
installation ˌɪn.stəˈleɪ.ʃᵊn **-s** -z

installer ɪnˈstɔː.ləʳ, US -ˈstɔː.lɚ, -ˈstɑː- **-s** -z
instal(l)ment ɪnˈstɔːl.mənt, US -ˈstɔːl-, -ˈstɑːl- **-s** -s **inˈstallment ˌplan**
instanc|e ˈɪnt.stənts **-es** -ɪz **-ing** -ɪŋ **-ed** -t
instant ˈɪnt.stənt **-s** -s **-ly** -li
instantaneous ˌɪnt.stənˈteɪ.ni.əs **-ly** -li **-ness** -nəs, -nɪs
instanter ɪnˈstæn.təʳ, US -t̬ɚ
in statu quo ɪnˌstæt.juːˈkwəʊ, US -ˌsteɪ.tuːˈkwoʊ, -ˌstɑː-
instead ɪnˈsted
instep ˈɪn.step **-s** -s
insti|gate ˈɪnt.stɪ|.geɪt, -stə- **-gates** -geɪts **-gating** -geɪ.tɪŋ, US -geɪ.t̬ɪŋ **-gated** -geɪ.tɪd, US -geɪ.t̬ɪd **-gator/s** -geɪ.təʳ/z, US -geɪ.t̬ɚ/z
instigation ˌɪnt.stɪˈgeɪ.ʃən, -stəˈ- **-s** -z
instil ɪnˈstɪl **-s** -z **-ling** -ɪŋ **-led** -d **-ment** -mənt
instill ɪnˈstɪl **-s** -z **-ing** -ɪŋ **-ed** -d **-ment** -mənt
instillation ˌɪnt.stɪˈleɪ.ʃən, -stəˈ-
instinct ˈɪnt.stɪŋkt **-s** -s
instinctive ɪnˈstɪŋk.tɪv **-ly** -li
institu|te ˈɪnt.stɪ.tʃuː|t, -stə-, -tjuː|t, US -tuː|t, -tjuː|t **-tes** -ts **-ting** -tɪŋ, US -t̬ɪŋ **-ted** -tɪd, US -t̬ɪd **-tor/s** -təʳ/z, US -t̬ɚ/z
institution ˌɪnt.stɪˈtʃuː.ʃən, -stəˈ-, -ˈtjuː-, US -ˈtuː-, -ˈtjuː- **-s** -z
institutional ˌɪnt.stɪˈtʃuː.ʃən.əl, -stəˈ-, -ˈtjuː-, US -ˈtuː-, -ˈtjuː- **-ly** -li
institutionalization, -isa- ˌɪnt.stɪˌtʃuː.ʃən.əl.aɪˈzeɪ.ʃən, -stəˌ-, -ˌtjuː-, -ɪˈ-, US -ˌtuː.ʃən.əl.əˈ-, -ˌtjuː-
institutionaliz|e, -is|e ˌɪnt.stɪˈtʃuː.ʃən.ə.laɪz, -stəˈ-, -ˈtjuː-, US -ˈtuː-, -ˈtjuː- **-es** -ɪz **-ing** -ɪŋ **-ed** -d
in-store ˌɪnˈstɔːʳ, US -ˈstɔːr *stress shift:* ˌ**in-store ˈrestaurant**
instruct ɪnˈstrʌkt **-s** -s **-ing** -ɪŋ **-ed** -ɪd
instruction ɪnˈstrʌk.ʃən **-s** -z
instructional ɪnˈstrʌk.ʃən.əl **-ly** -i
instructive ɪnˈstrʌk.tɪv **-ly** -li **-ness** -nəs, -nɪs
instructor ɪnˈstrʌk.təʳ, US -tɚ **-s** -z
instrument ˈɪnt.strə.mənt, -strʊ-, US -strə- **-s** -s
instrumental ˌɪnt.strəˈmen.təl, -strʊˈ-, US -strəˈmen.t̬əl **-s** -z **-ly** -i **-ist/s** -ɪst/s
instrumentality ˌɪnt.strə.menˈtæl.ə.ti, -strʊ-, -mənˈ-, -ɪ.ti, US -strə.menˈtæl.ə.t̬i, -mənˈ-
instrumentation ˌɪnt.strə.menˈteɪ.ʃən, -strʊ-, -mənˈ-, US -strə-
insubordinate ˌɪn.səˈbɔː.dən.ət, -dɪ.nət, -nɪt, US -ˈbɔːr.dən.ɪt **-s** -s
insubordination ˌɪn.səˌbɔː.dɪˈneɪ.ʃən, -dəˈ-, US -ˌbɔːr-
insubstantial ˌɪn.səbˈstæn.tʃəl, -ˈstɑːn-, US -ˈstæn- **-ly** -i
insufferab|le ɪnˈsʌf.ər.ə.b|əl **-ly** -li
insufficien|ce ˌɪn.səˈfɪʃ.ənt|s **-cy** -si
insufficient ˌɪn.səˈfɪʃ.ənt **-ly** -li
insular ˈɪnt.sjə.ləʳ, -sjʊ-, US -sə.lɚ, -sjə- **-ly** -li **-ism** -ɪ.zəm
insularity ˌɪnt.sjəˈlær.ə.ti, -sjʊˈ-, -ɪ.ti, US -səˈler.ə.t̬i, -sjəˈ-, -ˈlær-
insu|late ˈɪnt.sjə|.leɪt, -sjʊ-, US -sə-, -sjə- **-lates** -leɪts **-lating** -leɪ.tɪŋ, US -leɪ.t̬ɪŋ **-lated** -leɪ.tɪd, US -leɪ.t̬ɪd **-lator/s** -leɪ.təʳ/z, US -leɪ.t̬ɚ/z ˈ**insulating ˌtape**
insulation ˌɪnt.sjəˈleɪ.ʃən, -sjʊˈ-, US -səˈ-, -sjəˈ-
insulin ˈɪnt.sjə.lɪn, -sjʊ-, US -sə-
insult n ˈɪn.sʌlt **-s** -s **add ˌinsult to ˈinjury**
in|sult v ɪn|ˈsʌlt **-sults** -ˈsʌlts **-sulting/ly** -ˈsʌl.tɪŋ/li, US -ˈsʌl.t̬ɪŋ/li **-sulted** -ˈsʌl.tɪd, US -ˈsʌl.t̬ɪd **-sulter/s** -ˈsʌl.təʳ/z, US -ˈsʌl.t̬ɚ/z
insuperability ɪnˌsuː.pər.əˈbɪl.ə.ti, ˌɪn-, -ˌsjuː-, -ɪ.ti, US -ˌsuː.pɚ.əˈbɪl.ə.t̬i
insuperab|le ɪnˈsuː.pər.ə.b|əl, ˌɪn-, -ˈsjuː-, US -ˈsuː- **-ly** -li
insupportab|le ˌɪn.səˈpɔː.tə.b|əl, US -ˈpɔːr.t̬ə- **-ly** -li **-leness** -əl.nəs, -nɪs
insuppressib|le ˌɪn.səˈpres.ə.b|əl, ˈ-ɪ- **-ly** -li
insuranc|e ɪnˈʃʊə.rənts, -ˈʃɔː-, US -ˈʃʊr.ənts **-es** -ɪz **inˈsurance ˌbroker; inˈsurance ˌpolicy**
insur|e ɪnˈʃʊəʳ, -ˈʃɔːʳ, US -ˈʃʊr **-es** -z **-ing** -ɪŋ **-ed** -d **-er/s** -əʳ/z, US -ɚ/z **-able** -ə.bəl
insurgen|ce ɪnˈsɜː.dʒənt|s, US -ˈsɝː- **-cy** -si
insurgent ɪnˈsɜː.dʒənt, US -ˈsɝː- **-s** -s
insurmountability ˌɪn.səˌmaʊn.təˈbɪl.ə.ti, -ɪ.ti, US -sɚˌmaʊn.t̬əˈbɪl.ə.t̬i
insurmountab|le ˌɪn.səˈmaʊn.tə.b|əl, US -sɚˈmaʊn.t̬ə- **-ly** -li
insurrection ˌɪn.sərˈek.ʃən, US -səˈrek- **-s** -z
insurrectional ˌɪn.sərˈek.ʃən.əl, US -səˈrek-
insurrectionar|y ˌɪn.sərˈek.ʃən.ər|.i, US -səˈrek.ʃən.er- **-ies** -iz
insurrection|ism ˌɪn.sərˈek.ʃən|.ɪ.zəm, US -səˈrek- **-ist/s** -ɪst/s
insusceptibility ˌɪn.səˌsep.təˈbɪl.ə.ti, -tɪˈ-, -ɪ.ti, US -ə.t̬i
insusceptib|le ˌɪn.səˈsep.tə.b|əl, -tɪ- **-ly** -li
intact ɪnˈtækt, ˌɪn- **-ness** -nəs, -nɪs
intaglio ɪnˈtɑː.li.əʊ, -ˈtæl.i-, US -ˈtæl.joʊ, -ˈtɑːl- **-s** -z
intake ˈɪn.teɪk **-s** -s
intangibility ɪnˌtæn.dʒəˈbɪl.ə.ti, ˌɪn-, -dʒɪˈ-, -ɪ.ti, US -ə.t̬i
intangib|le ɪnˈtæn.dʒə.b|əl, ˌɪn-, -dʒɪ- **-ly** -li **-leness** -əl.nəs, -nɪs
integer ˈɪn.tɪ.dʒəʳ, -tə-, US -dʒɚ, -t̬ə- **-s** -z
integral n ˈɪn.tɪ.grəl, -tə-, US -t̬ə- **-s** -z
integral adj ˈɪn.tɪ.grəl, -tə-; ɪnˈteg.rəl, US ˈɪn.t̬ə.grəl; ɪnˈteg.rəl **-ly** -i

> Note: As a mathematical term always /ˈɪn.tɪ.grəl/ US /-t̬ə-/.

inte|grate ˈɪn.tɪ|.greɪt, -tə-, US -t̬ə- **-grates** -greɪts **-grating** -greɪ.tɪŋ, US -greɪ.t̬ɪŋ **-grated** -greɪ.tɪd, US -greɪ.t̬ɪd **-grator/s** -greɪ.təʳ/z, US -greɪ.t̬ɚ/z ˌ**integrated ˈcircuit**
integration ˌɪn.tɪˈgreɪ.ʃən, -təˈ-, US -t̬əˈ- **-s** -z
integrity ɪnˈteg.rə.ti, -rɪ-, US -t̬i
integument ɪnˈteg.jə.mənt, -jʊ- **-s** -s
Intel® ˈɪn.tel
intellect ˈɪn.təl.ekt, -tɪ.lekt, US -t̬ə.lekt **-s** -s
intellection ˌɪn.təlˈek.ʃən, -tɪˈlek-, US -t̬əˈlek-
intellective ˌɪn.təlˈek.tɪv, -tɪˈlek-, US -t̬əˈlek-
intellectual ˌɪn.təlˈek.tʃu.əl, -tju.əl, -tɪˈlek-, -tʃu-, US -t̬əlˈek.tʃu-, ˈ-tju- **-s** -z **-ly** -i
intellectual|ism ˌɪn.təlˈek.tʃu.ə.l|ɪ.zəm, ˈ-tju-, -tɪˈlek-, US ˈ-tʃu-, -t̬əlˈek.tʃu- **-ist/s** -ɪst/s
intellectuality ˌɪn.təlˌek.tʃuˈæl.ə.ti, -tɪˌlek-, -tjuˈ-, -ɪ.ti, US -tʃuˈæl.ə.t̬i, -tjuˈ-
intellectualiz|e, -is|e ˌɪn.təlˈek.tʃu.ə.laɪz, -tɪˈlek-, -tju-, US -t̬əlˈek.tʃu-, ˈ-tju- **-es** -ɪz **-ing** -ɪŋ **-ed** -d
intelligence ɪnˈtel.ɪ.dʒənts, ˈ-ə- **-es** -ɪz **-er/s** -əʳ/z, US -ɚ/z **inˈtelligence ˌtest**
intelligent ɪnˈtel.ɪ.dʒənt, ˈ-ə- **-ly** -li
intelligentsia ɪnˌtel.ɪˈdʒent.si.ə, ˌɪn-, US -ˈdʒent-, -ˈgent-
intelligibility ɪnˌtel.ɪ.dʒəˈbɪl.ə.ti, ˌ-ə-, -dʒɪˈ-, -ɪ.ti, US -ə.t̬i
intelligib|le ɪnˈtel.ɪ.dʒə.b|əl, ˈ-ə-, -dʒɪ- **-ly** -li **-leness** -əl.nəs, -nɪs
intemperance ɪnˈtem.pər.ənts, ˌɪn-, ˈ-prənts
intemperate ɪnˈtem.pər.ət, ˌɪn-, -ɪt, ˈ-prət, US -prɪt **-ly** -li **-ness** -nəs, -nɪs
intend ɪnˈtend **-s** -z **-ing** -ɪŋ **-ed** -ɪd
intendan|ce ɪnˈten.dən|ts **-cy** -tsi **-t/s** -t/s
intens|e ɪnˈtents **-er** -əʳ **-est** -ɪst, -əst **-ely** -li **-eness** -nəs, -nɪs
intensification ɪnˌtent.sɪ.fɪˈkeɪ.ʃən, -sə-, -fəˈ- **-s** -z
intensi|fy ɪnˈtent.sɪ|.faɪ, -sə- **-fies** -faɪz **-fying** -faɪ.ɪŋ **-fied** -faɪd **-fier/s** -faɪ.əʳ/z, US -faɪ.ɚ/z
intension ɪnˈten.tʃən
intensit|y ɪnˈtent.sə.t|i, -sɪ-, US -sə.t̬|i **-ies** -iz

intensive ɪnˈtent.sɪv -ly -li -ness -nəs, -nɪs inˌtensive ˈ**care**

in|tent ɪn|ˈtent -tents -ˈtents -tenter -ˈten.təʳ, US -ˈten.t̬ɚ -tentest -ˈten.tɪst, -ˈten.təst, US -ˈten.t̬ɪst, -ˈten.t̬əst -tently -ˈtent.li -tentness -ˈtent.nəs, -ˈtent.nɪs

intention ɪnˈten.tʃᵊn -s -z -ed -d

intentional ɪnˈten.tʃᵊn.ᵊl -ly -i

inter v ɪnˈtɜːʳ, US -ˈtɜː -s -z -ring -ɪŋ -red -d

inter (Latin prep., in such phrases as **inter alia, inter se**) ˈɪn.təʳ, US -t̬ɚ

inter- ˈɪn.təʳ, US ˈɪn.t̬ɚ

Note: Prefix. Normally takes either primary stress or secondary stress on the first syllable, with nouns often receiving front stress, e.g. **intercom** (noun) /ˈɪn.tə.kɒm/ US /-t̬ɚ.kɑːm/, **interact** (verb) /ˌɪn.təʳˈækt/ US /-t̬ɚˈækt/. Exceptions exist; see individual entries. Note also that, although /r/ is normally assigned to a following strong syllable in US transcriptions, in **inter-** it is perceived to be morphemically linked to that morpheme and is retained in the prefix as /ɚ/.

interact n ˈɪn.tᵊr.ækt, US -t̬ɚˈækt -s -s

interact v ˌɪn.tᵊrˈækt, US -t̬ɚˈækt -s -s -ing -ɪŋ -ed -ɪd

interaction ˌɪn.tᵊrˈæk.ʃᵊn, US -t̬ɚˈæk- -s -z

interactive ˌɪn.tᵊrˈæk.tɪv, US -t̬ɚˈæk- -ly -li

interactivity ˌɪn.tᵊr.ækˈtɪv.ə.ti, -ɪ.ti, US -t̬ɚ.ækˈtɪv.ə.t̬i

Interahamwe ˌɪn.tᵊr.əˈhæm.weɪ, US -t̬ɚ-

inter alia ˌɪn.təʳˈeɪ.li.ə, -ˈæl.i-, US -t̬ɚˈɑː-, -ˈeɪ-, -ɑː

interblend ˌɪn.təˈblend, US -t̬ɚˈ- -s -z -ing -ɪŋ -ed -ɪd

inter|breed ˌɪn.tə|ˈbriːd, US -t̬ɚˈ- -breeds -ˈbriːdz -breeding -ˈbriː.dɪŋ -bred -ˈbred

intercalary ɪnˈtɜː.kᵊl.ᵊr.i; ˌɪn.təˈkæl-, US ɪnˈtɜː.kə.ler-, ˌɪn.t̬ɚˈkæl.ɚ.i

interca|late ɪnˈtɜː.kə|.leɪt, ˈɪn.tə.kə-, US -ˈtɜː- -lates -leɪts -lating -leɪ.tɪŋ, US -leɪ.t̬ɪŋ -lated -leɪ.tɪd, US -leɪ.t̬ɪd

intercalation ɪnˌtɜː.kəˈleɪ.ʃᵊn, US -ˌtɜː- -s -z

interced|e ˌɪn.təˈsiːd, US -t̬ɚˈ- -es -z -ing -ɪŋ -ed -ɪd -er/s -əʳ/z, US -ɚ/z

intercept n ˈɪn.tə.sept, US -t̬ɚ- -s -s

intercept v ˌɪn.təˈsept, US -t̬ɚˈ- -s -s -ing -ɪŋ -ed -ɪd -er/s -əʳ/z, US -ɚ/z -or/s -əʳ/z, US -ɚ/z

interception ˌɪn.təˈsep.ʃᵊn, US -t̬ɚˈ- -s -z

interceptive ˌɪn.təˈsep.tɪv, US -t̬ɚˈ-

intercession ˌɪn.təˈseʃ.ᵊn, US -t̬ɚˈ- -s -z

intercessional ˌɪn.təˈseʃ.ᵊn.ᵊl, US -t̬ɚˈ-

intercessor ˌɪn.təˈses.əʳ, ˈɪn.tə.ses-, US ˌɪn.t̬ɚˈses.ɚ, ˈɪn.t̬ɚ.ses- -s -z

intercessory ˌɪn.təˈses.ᵊr.i, US -t̬ɚˈ-

interchang|e n ˈɪn.tə.tʃeɪndʒ, US -t̬ɚ- -es -ɪz

interchang|e v ˌɪn.təˈtʃeɪndʒ, US -t̬ɚˈ- -es -ɪz -ing -ɪŋ -ed -d

interchangeability ˌɪn.təˌtʃeɪn.dʒəˈbɪl.ə.ti, -ɪ.ti, US -t̬ɚˌtʃeɪn.dʒəˈbɪl.ə.t̬i

interchangeab|le ˌɪn.təˈtʃeɪn.dʒə.b|ᵊl, US -t̬ɚˈ- -ly -li -leness -ᵊl.nəs, -nɪs

intercity, I~ ˌɪn.təˈsɪt.i, US -t̬ɚˈsɪt̬- *stress shift:* ˌ**intercity** ˈ**train**

intercollegiate ˌɪn.tə.kəˈliː.dʒət, -kɒlˈiː-, -dʒi.ət, -ɪt, US -t̬ɚ.kəˈliː.dʒɪt

intercolonial ˌɪn.tə.kəˈləʊ.ni.əl, US -t̬ɚ.kəˈloʊ-

intercom ˈɪn.tə.kɒm, US -t̬ɚ.kɑːm -s -z

intercommuni|cate ˌɪn.tə.kəˈmjuː.nɪ|.keɪt, -nə-, US -t̬ɚ- -cates -keɪts -cating -keɪ.tɪŋ, US -keɪ.t̬ɪŋ -cated -keɪ.tɪd, US -keɪ.t̬ɪd -cator/s -keɪ.təʳ/z, US -keɪ.t̬ɚ/z

intercommunication ˌɪn.tə.kəˌmjuː.nɪˈkeɪ.ʃᵊn, -nəˈ-, -fəˈ-, US -t̬ɚ-

intercommunion ˌɪn.tə.kəˈmjuː.ni.ən, US -t̬ɚ.kəˈmjuː.njən

intercommunity ˌɪn.tə.kəˈmjuː.nə.ti, -nɪ-, US -t̬ɚ.kəˈmjuː.nə.t̬i

interconnect ˌɪn.tə.kəˈnekt, US -t̬ɚ- -s -s -ing -ɪŋ -ed -ɪd

interconnection ˌɪn.tə.kəˈnek.ʃᵊn, US -t̬ɚ- -s -z

intercontinental ˌɪn.təˌkɒn.tɪˈnen.tᵊl, -təˈ-, US -t̬ɚˌkɑːn.təˈnen.t̬ᵊl

intercostal ˌɪn.təˈkɒs.tᵊl, US -t̬ɚˈkɑː.stᵊl

intercourse ˈɪn.tə.kɔːs, US -t̬ɚ.kɔːrs

intercurrent ˌɪn.təˈkʌr.ᵊnt, US -t̬ɚˈkɝː- -ly -li

interdenominational ˌɪn.tə.dɪˌnɒm.ɪˈneɪ.ʃᵊn.ᵊl, -dəˌ-, -əˈ-, US -t̬ɚ.dɪˌnɑː.məˈ-, -dɪˌ- -ism -ɪ.zᵊm -ly -i

interdental ˌɪn.təˈden.tᵊl, US -t̬ɚˈden.t̬ᵊl

interdepartmental ˌɪn.tə.diː.pɑːtˈmen.tᵊl; ˌɪn.tə.dɪˌpɑːtˈ-, -dəˌ-, US -t̬ɚˌdiː.pɑːrtˈmen.t̬ᵊl, -dɪ-

interdependence ˌɪn.tə.dɪˈpen.dənts, -dəˈ-, US -t̬ɚ.diːˈ-, -dɪˈ-

interdependent ˌɪn.tə.dɪˈpen.dᵊnt, -dəˈ-, US -t̬ɚ.diːˈ-, -dɪˈ- -ly -li

interdict n ˈɪn.tə.dɪkt, -daɪt, US -t̬ɚ.dɪkt -s -s

interdict v ˌɪn.təˈdɪkt, -ˈdaɪt, US -t̬ɚˈdɪkt -s -s -ing -ɪŋ -ed -ɪd

interdiction ˌɪn.təˈdɪk.ʃᵊn, US -t̬ɚˈ- -s -z

interdigi|tate ˌɪn.təˈdɪdʒ.ɪ|.teɪt, ˈ-ə-, US -t̬ɚˈ- -tates -teɪts -tating -teɪ.tɪŋ, US -teɪ.t̬ɪŋ -tated -teɪ.tɪd, US -teɪ.t̬ɪd

interdisciplinary ˌɪn.təˈdɪs.ɪ.plɪ.nᵊr.i, ˈ-ə-; ˌɪn.tə.dɪs.ɪˈplɪn.ᵊr-, -əˈ-, US -t̬ɚˈdɪs.ə.plɪ.ner-

interest ˈɪn.trəst, -trest, -trɪst; -tᵊr.əst, -est, -ɪst, US ˈɪn.trɪst, -trəst, -trest; US -t̬ɚ.ɪst, -əst, -est -s -s -ing -ɪŋ -ed/ly -ɪd/li ˈ**interest** ˌ**rate**

interesting ˈɪn.trə.stɪŋ, -tres.tɪŋ, -trɪ.stɪŋ, -tᵊr.ə-, -es.tɪŋ, -ɪ.stɪŋ, US ˈɪn.trɪ.stɪŋ, -trə-, -tres.tɪŋ, -t̬ɚ.ɪ.stɪŋ, -es.tɪŋ -ly -li

interfac|e n ˈɪn.tə.feɪs, US -t̬ɚ- -es -ɪz

interfac|e v ˌɪn.təˈfeɪs, ˈ---, US ˈɪn.t̬ɚ.feɪs -es -ɪz -ing -ɪŋ -ed -t

> Note: The computer world uses first-syllable stress for both noun and verb.

interfaith ˌɪn.təˈfeɪθ, US ˈɪn.t̬ɚ.feɪθ *stress shift, British only:* ˌ**interfaith** ˈ**service**

interfer|e ˌɪn.təˈfɪəʳ, US -t̬ɚˈfɪr -es -z -ing -ɪŋ -ed -d -er/s -əʳ/z, US -ɚ/z

interferenc|e ˌɪn.təˈfɪə.rᵊnts, US -t̬ɚˈfɪr.ᵊnts -es -ɪz

interferon ˌɪn.təˈfɪə.rɒn, US -t̬ɚˈfɪr.ɑːn -s -z

Interflora® ˌɪn.təˈflɔː.rə, US -t̬ɚˈflɔːr.ə

interfus|e ˌɪn.təˈfjuːz, US -t̬ɚˈ- -es -ɪz -ing -ɪŋ -ed -d

interfusion ˌɪn.təˈfjuː.ʒᵊn, US -t̬ɚˈ-

intergalactic ˌɪn.tə.gəˈlæk.tɪk, US -t̬ɚ-

interglacial ˌɪn.təˈgleɪ.si.əl, -ʃi-, -ʃᵊl, US -t̬ɚˈgleɪ.ʃᵊl

intergovernmental ˌɪn.tə.gʌv.ᵊnˈmen.tᵊl, -ᵊmˈ-, US -t̬ɚˌgʌv.ɚnˈmen.t̬ᵊl

interim ˈɪn.tᵊr.ɪm, US -t̬ɚ-

interior ɪnˈtɪə.ri.əʳ, US -ˈtɪr.i.ɚ -s -z inˌ**terior** ˈ**decorator;** inˌ**terior de**ˈ**signer**

interioriz|e, -is|e ɪnˈtɪə.ri.ə.raɪz, US -ˈtɪr.i- -es -ɪz -ing -ɪŋ -ed -d

interject ˌɪn.təˈdʒekt, US -t̬ɚˈ- -s -s -ing -ɪŋ -ed -ɪd -or/s -əʳ/z, US -ɚ/z

interjection ˌɪn.təˈdʒek.ʃᵊn, US -t̬ɚˈ- -s -z -al/ly -əl/i

inter|knit ˌɪn.tə|ˈnɪt, US -t̬ɚˈ- -knits -ˈnɪts -knitting -ˈnɪt.ɪŋ, US -ˈnɪt̬.ɪŋ -knitted -ˈnɪt.ɪd, US -ˈnɪt̬.ɪd

interlac|e ˌɪn.təˈleɪs, US -t̬ɚˈ- -es -ɪz -ing -ɪŋ -ed -t -ement -mənt

Interlaken ˈɪn.tə.lɑː.kᵊn, ˌɪn.təˈlɑː-, US ˈɪn.t̬ɚ.lɑː-, ˌɪn.t̬ɚˈlɑː, -t̬ɚ-

interlanguage ˈɪn.təˌlæŋ.gwɪdʒ, US -t̬ɚ-

interlard ˌɪn.təˈlɑːd, US -t̬ɚˈlɑːrd -s -z -ing -ɪŋ -ed -ɪd

interlea|f ˈɪn.tə.liː|f, US -t̬ɚ- -ves -vz

interleav|e ˌɪn.təˈliːv, US -t̬ɚˈ- -es -z -ing -ɪŋ -ed -d

interlin|e ˌɪn.təˈlaɪn, US -t̬ɚˈ- -es -z -ing -ɪŋ -ed -d

interlinear ˌɪn.təˈlɪn.i.əʳ, (US) -t̬ɚˈlɪn.i.ɚ
interlineation ˌɪn.təˌlɪn.iˈeɪ.ʃən, (US) -t̬ɚ- **-s** -z
interlink ˌɪn.təˈlɪŋk, (US) -t̬ɚˈ- **-s** -s **-ing** -ɪŋ **-ed** -t
interlock ˌɪn.təˈlɒk, (US) -t̬ɚˈlɑːk **-s** -s **-ing** -ɪŋ **-ed** -t
interlocution ˌɪn.tə.ləˈkjuː.ʃən, -lɒkˈjuː-, (US) -t̬ɚ.loʊˈkjuː- **-s** -z
interlocutor ˌɪn.təˈlɒk.jə.təʳ, -jʊ-, (US) -t̬ɚˈlɑː.kjə.t̬ɚ, -kjʊ- **-s** -z **-y** -i
interlocu|tress ˌɪn.təˈlɒk.jə|.trəs, -jʊ-, -trɪs, (US) -t̬ɚˈlɑː.kjʊ|.trɪs, -kjə- **-trice** -trɪs **-trix** -trɪks
interlop|e ˌɪn.təˈləʊp, (US) ˈɪn.t̬ɚ.loʊp **-es** -s **-ing** -ɪŋ **-ed** -t
interloper ˈɪn.təˌləʊ.pəʳ, ˌɪn.təˈləʊ.pəʳ, (US) ˈɪn.t̬ɚˌloʊ.pɚ **-s** -z
interlude ˈɪn.tə.luːd, -ljuːd, (US) -t̬ɚ.luːd **-s** -z
intermarriag|e ˌɪn.təˈmær.ɪdʒ, (US) -t̬ɚˈmer-, -ˈmær- **-es** -ɪz
intermarr|y ˌɪn.təˈmær|.i, (US) ˈɪn.t̬ɚˌmer-, -ˈmær- **-ies** -iz **-ying** -i.ɪŋ **-ied** -id
intermeddl|e ˌɪn.təˈmed.əl, (US) -t̬ɚˈ- **-es** -z **-ing** -ɪŋ, -ˈmed.lɪŋ **-ed** -d **-er/s** -əʳ/z, -ˈmed.ləʳ/z, (US) -lɚ/z
intermediar|y ˌɪn.təˈmiː.di.ə.r|i, (US) -t̬ɚˈmiː.di.er.i, -ɚ- **-ies** -iz
intermediate ˌɪn.təˈmiː.di.ət, -ɪt, (US) -t̬ɚˈ- **-s** -s **-ly** -li
interment ɪnˈtɜː.mənt, (US) -ˈtɝː- **-s** -s
intermezz|o ˌɪn.təˈmet.s|əʊ, -ˈmed.z|əʊ, (US) -t̬ɚˈmet.s|oʊ, -ˈmed.z|oʊ **-os** -əʊz, (US) -oʊz **-i** -i, -iː
interminab|le ɪnˈtɜː.mɪ.nə.b|əl, ɪn-, -mən.ə-, (US) -ˈtɝː- **-ly** -li **-leness** -əl.nəs, -nɪs
intermingl|e ˌɪn.təˈmɪŋ.gəl, (US) -t̬ɚˈ- **-es** -z **-ing** -ɪŋ, -ˈmɪŋ.glɪŋ **-ed** -d
intermission ˌɪn.təˈmɪʃ.ən, (US) -t̬ɚˈ- **-s** -z
inter|mit ˌɪn.tə|ˈmɪt, (US) -t̬ɚˈ- **-mits** -ˈmɪts **-mitting/ly** -ˈmɪt.ɪŋ/li, (US) -ˈmɪt̬.ɪŋ/li **-mitted** -ˈmɪt.ɪd, (US) -ˈmɪt̬.ɪd
intermittent ˌɪn.təˈmɪt.ənt, (US) -t̬ɚˈmɪt- **-ly** -li
intermix ˌɪn.təˈmɪks, (US) -t̬ɚˈ- **-es** -ɪz **-ing** -ɪŋ **-ed** -t
intermixture ˌɪn.təˈmɪks.tʃəʳ, (US) -t̬ɚˈmɪks.tʃɚ **-s** -z
intermodal ˌɪn.təˈməʊ.dəl, (US) -t̬ɚˈmoʊ-
intern n ˈɪn.tɜːn, -ˈ-, (US) ˈɪn.tɝːn **-s** -z
intern v ɪnˈtɜːn, (US) ɪnˈtɝːn, ˈ-- **-s** -z **-ing** -ɪŋ **-ed** -d
internal ɪnˈtɜː.nəl, ˌɪn-, (US) -ˈtɝː- **-ly** -i **inˌternal comˈbustion; inˌternal comˈbustion ˌengine** (US) **inˌternal comˌbustion ˈengine; Inˌternal ˈRevenue ˌService**
internalization ɪnˌtɜː.nəl.aɪˈzeɪ.ʃən, ˌɪn-, -ɪˈ-, (US) -ˌtɝː.nəl.əˈ-
internaliz|e, -is|e ɪnˈtɜː.nəl.aɪz, (US) -ˈtɝː- **-es** -ɪz **-ing** -ɪŋ **-ed** -d
international ˌɪn.təˈnæʃ.ən.əl, -təˈnæʃ.nəl, (US) -t̬ɚˈ- **-s** -z **-ly** -i
Internationale ˌɪn.təˌnæʃ.əˈnɑːl, -ˌnæʃ.i.əˈnɑːl, (US) -t̬ɚˌnæʃ.əˈnæl, -ˈnɑːl
international|ism ˌɪn.təˈnæʃ.ən.əl|.ɪ.zəm, -ˈnæʃ.nəl-, (US) -t̬ɚˈ- **-ist/s** -ɪst/s
internationalization, -isa- ˌɪn.təˌnæʃ.ən.əl.aɪˈzeɪ.ʃən, -ˌnəl-, -ɪˈ-, (US) -t̬ɚˌnæʃ.ən.əl.əˈ-, -nəl-
internationaliz|e, -is|e ˌɪn.təˈnæʃ.ən.əl.aɪz, -ˈnæʃ.nəl-, (US) -t̬ɚˈ- **-es** -ɪz **-ing** -ɪŋ **-ed** -d
interne ˈɪn.tɜːn, (US) -tɝːn **-s** -z
internecine ˌɪn.təˈniː.saɪn, -tɜːˈ-, (US) -t̬ɚˈniː.sɪn, -siːn, -ˈnes.ɪn, -iːn
internee ˌɪn.tɜːˈniː, (US) -tɝːˈ- **-s** -z
Internet ˈɪn.tə.net, (US) -t̬ɚ-
internist ˈɪn.tɜː.nɪst, -ˈ--, (US) ˈɪn.tɝː-, -ˈ-- **-s** -s
internment ɪnˈtɜːn.mənt, -ˈtɜːm-, (US) -ˈtɝːn- **-s** -s
internodal ˌɪn.təˈnəʊ.dəl, (US) -t̬ɚˈnoʊ-
internode ˈɪn.tə.nəʊd, (US) -t̬ɚ.noʊd **-s** -z
internship ˈɪn.tɜːn.ʃɪp, -ˈ--, (US) ˈɪn.tɝːn-, -ˈ-- **-s** -s
interoceanic ˌɪn.tərˌəʊ.ʃiˈæn.ɪk, (US) -t̬ɚˌoʊ-
inter pares ˌɪn.təˈpɑː.riːz, -ˈpeə-, -reɪs, (US) -t̬ɚˈpɑː.res
inter partes ˌɪn.təˈpɑː.tiːz, -teɪs, (US) ˌɪn.t̬ɚˈpɑːr.tes
interpellant ˌɪn.təˈpel.ənt, (US) -t̬ɚˈ- **-s** -s
interpell|ate ɪnˈtɜː.pə.l|eɪt, -pɪ-, -pel|.eɪt; ˌɪn.təˈpel|.eɪt, (US) ˌɪn.t̬ɚˈpel-; (US) ɪnˈtɜː.pə.l|eɪt **-ates** -eɪts **-ating** -eɪ.tɪŋ, (US) -eɪ.t̬ɪŋ **-ated** -eɪ.tɪd, (US) -eɪ.t̬ɪd
interpellation ɪnˌtɜː.pəˈleɪ.ʃən, -pɪˈ-, -pelˈeɪ-; ˌɪn.tə.pəˈleɪ-, (US) ˌɪn.t̬ɚ.pəˈleɪ-; (US) ɪnˌtɝː- **-s** -z
interpene|trate ˌɪn.təˈpen.ɪ|.treɪt, ˈ-ə-, (US) -t̬ɚˈ- **-trates** -treɪts **-trating** -treɪ.tɪŋ, (US) -treɪ.t̬ɪŋ **-trated** -treɪ.tɪd, (US) -treɪ.t̬ɪd
interpenetration ˌɪn.təˌpen.ɪˈtreɪ.ʃən, -əˈ-, (US) -t̬ɚˌ-
interpersonal ˌɪn.təˈpɜː.sən.əl, (US) -t̬ɚˈpɝː- **-ly** -i
interplanetary ˌɪn.təˈplæn.ɪ.tər.i, ˈ-ə-, (US) -t̬ɚˈplæn.ə.ter-
interplay ˈɪn.tə.pleɪ, (US) -t̬ɚ-
interpleader ˌɪn.təˈpliː.dəʳ, (US) -t̬ɚˈpliː.dɚ **-s** -z
Interpol ˈɪn.tə.pɒl, (US) -t̬ɚ.pɑːl, -poʊl
interpo|late ɪnˈtɜː.pə|.leɪt, (US) -ˈtɝː- **-lates** -leɪts **-lating** -leɪ.tɪŋ, (US) -leɪ.t̬ɪŋ **-lated** -leɪ.tɪd, (US) -leɪ.t̬ɪd **-lator/s** -leɪ.təʳ/z, (US) -leɪ.t̬ɚ/z
interpolation ɪnˌtɜː.pəˈleɪ.ʃən, (US) -ˌtɝː- **-s** -z
interposal ˌɪn.təˈpəʊ.zəl, (US) -t̬ɚˈpoʊ- **-s** -z
interpos|e ˌɪn.təˈpəʊz, (US) -t̬ɚˈpoʊz **-es** -ɪz **-ing** -ɪŋ **-ed** -d **-er/s** -əʳ/z, (US) -ɚ/z
interposition ˌɪn.tə.pəˈzɪʃ.ən; ɪnˌtɜː-, (US) ˌɪn.t̬ɚ.pəˈ- **-s** -z
interpre|t ɪnˈtɜː.prɪ|t, -prə|t, (US) -ˈtɝː.prə|t **-ts** -ts **-ting** -tɪŋ, (US) -t̬ɪŋ **-ted** -tɪd, (US) -t̬ɪd **-table** -tə.bəl, (US) -t̬ə.bəl
interpretation ɪnˌtɜː.prɪˈteɪ.ʃən, -prəˈ-, (US) -ˌtɝː.prəˈ- **-s** -z **-al** -əl
interpretative ɪnˈtɜː.prɪ.tə.tɪv, -prə-, -teɪ-, (US) -ˈtɝː.prə.teɪ.t̬ɪv, -t̬ə- **-ly** -li
interpreter ɪnˈtɜː.prɪ.təʳ, -prə-, (US) -ˈtɝː.prə.t̬ɚ **-s** -z
interpretive ɪnˈtɜː.prɪ.tɪv, -prə-, (US) -ˈtɝː.prə.t̬ɪv **-ly** -li
interquartile ˌɪn.təˈkwɔː.taɪl, (US) -t̬ɚˈkwɔːr-, -tɪl, -t̬əl
interracial ˌɪn.təˈreɪ.ʃəl, -ʃi.əl, (US) -t̬ɚˈreɪ.ʃəl
interregn|um ˌɪn.təˈreg.n|əm, (US) -t̬ɚˈ- **-ums** -əmz **-a** -ə
interre|late ˌɪn.tə.rɪ|ˈleɪt, -rəˈ-, (US) -t̬ɚ.riˈ-, -rɪˈ- **-lates** -ˈleɪts **-lating** -ˈleɪ.tɪŋ, (US) -ˈleɪ.t̬ɪŋ **-lated** -ˈleɪ.tɪd, (US) -ˈleɪ.t̬ɪd
interrelation ˌɪn.tə.rɪˈleɪ.ʃən, -rəˈ-, (US) -t̬ɚ.riˈ-, -rɪˈ- **-s** -z
interrelationship ˌɪn.tə.rɪˈleɪ.ʃən.ʃɪp, (US) ˌɪn.t̬ɚ.rɪˈ-
interro|gate ɪnˈter.ə|.geɪt **-gates** -geɪts **-gating** -geɪ.tɪŋ, (US) -geɪ.t̬ɪŋ **-gated** -geɪ.tɪd, (US) -geɪ.t̬ɪd **-gator/s** -geɪ.təʳ/z, (US) -geɪ.t̬ɚ/z
interrogation ɪnˌter.əˈgeɪ.ʃən **-s** -z
interrogative ˌɪn.təˈrɒg.ə.tɪv, (US) -t̬ɚˈrɑː.gə.t̬ɪv **-s** -z **-ly** -li
interrogator|y ˌɪn.təˈrɒg.ə.tər|.i, (US) -t̬ɚˈrɑː.gə.tɔːr- **-ies** -iz
interrupt v ˌɪn.təˈrʌpt, (US) -t̬ɚˈ- **-s** -s **-ing** -ɪŋ **-ed** -ɪd **-er/s** -əʳ/z, (US) -ɚ/z
interrupt n ˈɪn.tə.rʌpt, (US) -t̬ɚ-
interruption ˌɪn.təˈrʌp.ʃən, (US) -t̬ɚˈ- **-s** -z
interscholastic ˌɪn.tə.skəˈlæs.tɪk, (US) -t̬ɚ.skəˈ-
intersect ˌɪn.təˈsekt, (US) -t̬ɚˈ- **-s** -s **-ing** -ɪŋ **-ed** -ɪd **-or/s** -əʳ/z, (US) -ɚ/z
intersection ˌɪn.təˈsek.ʃən, ˈɪn.təˌsek-, (US) ˌɪn.t̬ɚˈsek-, ˈɪn.t̬ɚˌsek- **-s** -z

> Note: /ˈɪn.t̬ɚˌsek.ʃən/ is the common US pronunciation for a place where streets meet.

interspac|e n ˈɪn.tə.speɪs, ˌ-ˈ-, (US) ˈɪn.t̬ɚ.speɪs **-es** -ɪz
interspac|e v ˌɪn.təˈspeɪs, (US) -t̬ɚˈ-, ˈ--- **-es** -ɪz **-ing** -ɪŋ **-ed** -t
interspers|e ˌɪn.təˈspɜːs, (US) -t̬ɚˈspɝːs **-es** -ɪz **-ing** -ɪŋ **-ed** -t
interspersion ˌɪn.təˈspɜː.ʃən, -ʒən, (US) -t̬ɚˈspɝː-
interstate, I~ ˌɪn.təˈsteɪt, (US) ˈɪn.t̬ɚ.steɪt *stress shift, British only:* **ˌinterstate ˈhighway**
interstellar ˌɪn.təˈstel.əʳ, (US) -t̬ɚˈstel.ɚ *stress shift:* **ˌinterstellar ˈtravel**

Note **into**: In British English, the pronunciation /ˈɪn.tuː/ is sometimes used in final position (e.g. 'That's the wall he walked into'), though the /u/ vowel is more usual. Elsewhere, the pronunciation /ˈɪn.tə/ is used before consonants (e.g. 'into debt' /ˌɪn.təˈdet/) and /ˈɪn.tu/ before vowels (e.g. 'into each' /ˌɪn.tuˈiːtʃ/). In American English the schwa form is usual before consonants and also vowels (e.g. 'into each' /ˌɪn.təˈiːtʃ/).

interstic|e ɪnˈtɜː.stɪs, (US) -ˈtɝː- **-es** -ɪz, -iːz

interstitial ˌɪn.təˈstɪʃ.ᵊl, (US) -t̬ɚˈ-

intertribal ˌɪn.təˈtraɪ.bᵊl, (US) -t̬ɚˈ-

intertwin|e ˌɪn.təˈtwaɪn, (US) -t̬ɚˈ- **-es** -z **-ing** -ɪŋ **-ed** -d

intertwist ˌɪn.təˈtwɪst, (US) -t̬ɚˈ- **-s** -s **-ing** -ɪŋ **-ed** -ɪd

interurban ˌɪn.tᵊrˈɜː.bᵊn, (US) -t̬ɚˈɝː-

interval ˈɪn.tə.vᵊl, (US) -t̬ɚ- **-s** -z

interven|e ˌɪn.təˈviːn, (US) -t̬ɚˈ- **-es** -z **-ing** -ɪŋ **-ed** -d **-er/s** -əʳ/z, (US) -ɚ/z

intervention ˌɪn.təˈven.tʃᵊn, (US) -t̬ɚˈ- **-s** -z

intervention|ism ˌɪn.təˈven.tʃᵊn|.ɪ.zᵊm, (US) -t̬ɚˈ- **-ist/s** -ɪst/s

interventionist ˌɪn.təˈven.tʃᵊn.ɪst, (US) -t̬ɚˈ-

interview ˈɪn.tə.vjuː, (US) -t̬ɚ- **-s** -z **-ing** -ɪŋ **-ed** -d **-er/s** -əʳ/z, (US) -ɚ/z

interviewee ˌɪn.tə.vjuˈiː, (US) -t̬ɚ- **-s** -z

inter vivos ˌɪn.təˈviː.vəʊs, (US) -təˈviː.voʊs, -ˈvaɪ-

intervocalic ˌɪn.tə.vəʊˈkæl.ɪk, (US) -t̬ɚ.voʊˈ-

interweav|e ˌɪn.təˈwiːv, (US) -t̬ɚˈ-, ˈ--- **-es** -z **-ing** -ɪŋ **-ed** -d **interwove** ˌɪn.təˈwəʊv, (US) -t̬ɚˈwoʊv, ˈ--- **interwoven** ˌɪn.təˈwəʊ.vᵊn, (US) -t̬ɚˈwoʊ.vᵊn, ˈɪn.t̬ɚˌwoʊ-

intestac|y ɪnˈtes.tə.s|i **-ies** -iz

intestate ɪnˈtes.teɪt, -tɪt, -tət **-s** -s

intestinal ɪnˈtes.tɪ.nᵊl, -tᵊn.ᵊl, ˌɪn.tesˈtaɪ.nᵊl, (US) ɪnˈtes.tɪ-

intestine ɪnˈtes.tɪn, -tiːn, (US) -tɪn, -tən **-s** -z

inthral(l) ɪnˈθrɔːl, (US) -ˈθrɑːl, -ˈθrɔːl **-s** -z **-ing** -ɪŋ **-ed** -d

intifada ˌɪn.tɪˈfɑː.də **-s** -z

intimac|y ˈɪn.tɪ.mə.s|i, -tə-, (US) -t̬ə-, -t̬ɪ- **-ies** -iz

intimate n, adj ˈɪn.tɪ.mət, -tə-, -mɪt, (US) -t̬ə.mət, -t̬ɪ- **-s** -s **-ly** -li

inti|mate v ˈɪn.tɪ|.meɪt, -tə-, (US) -t̬ə-, -t̬ɪ- **-mates** -meɪts **-mating** -meɪ.tɪŋ, (US) -meɪ.t̬ɪŋ **-mated** -meɪ.tɪd, (US) -meɪ.t̬ɪd **-mater/s** -meɪ.təʳ/z, (US) -meɪ.t̬ɚ/z

intimation ˌɪn.tɪˈmeɪ.ʃᵊn, -təˈ-, (US) -t̬əˈ-, -t̬ɪˈ- **-s** -z

intimi|date ɪnˈtɪm.ɪ|.deɪt, ˈ-ə- **-dates** -deɪts **-dating** -deɪ.tɪŋ, (US) -deɪ.t̬ɪŋ **-dated** -deɪ.tɪd, (US) -deɪ.t̬ɪd **-dator/s** -deɪ.təʳ/z, (US) -deɪ.t̬ɚ/z

intimidation ɪnˌtɪm.ɪˈdeɪ.ʃᵊn, -əˈ-

intituled ɪnˈtɪt.juːld

into ˈɪn.tə, -tu, -tuː, (US) -tə, -tu

intolerab|le ɪnˈtɒl.ᵊr.ə.b|ᵊl, ˌɪn-, (US) -ˈtɑː.lɚ- **-ly** -li **-leness** -ᵊl.nəs, -nɪs

intolerance ɪnˈtɒl.ᵊr.ᵊnts, ˌɪn-, (US) -ˈtɑː.lɚ-

intolerant ɪnˈtɒl.ᵊr.ᵊnt, ˌɪn-, (US) -ˈtɑː.lɚ- **-ly** -li

into|nate ˈɪn.təʊ|.neɪt, (US) -toʊ-, -tə- **-nates** -neɪts **-nating** -neɪ.tɪŋ, (US) -neɪ.t̬ɪŋ **-nated** -neɪ.tɪd, (US) -neɪ.t̬ɪd

intonation ˌɪn.təʊˈneɪ.ʃᵊn, (US) -toʊˈ-, -təˈ- **-s** -z

intonational ˌɪn.təʊˈneɪ.ʃᵊn.ᵊl, (US) -toʊˈ-, -təˈ-

inton|e ɪnˈtəʊn, (US) -ˈtoʊn **-es** -z **-ing** -ɪŋ **-ed** -d **-er/s** -əʳ/z, (US) -ɚ/z

in toto ɪnˈtəʊ.təʊ, (US) -ˈtoʊ.toʊ

Intourist® ˈɪnˌtʊə.rɪst, -ˌtɔː-, (US) -ˌtʊr.ɪst

intoxicant ɪnˈtɒk.sɪ.kᵊnt, -sə-, (US) -ˈtɑːk.sɪ- **-s** -s

intoxi|cate ɪnˈtɒk.sɪ|.keɪt, -sə-, (US) -ˈtɑːk.sɪ- **-cates** -keɪts **-cating** -keɪ.tɪŋ, (US) -keɪ.t̬ɪŋ **-cated** -keɪ.tɪd, (US) -keɪ.t̬ɪd **-cator/s** -keɪ.təʳ/z, (US) -keɪ.t̬ɚ/z

intoxication ɪnˌtɒk.sɪˈkeɪ.ʃᵊn, -səˈ-, (US) -ˌtɑːk.sɪˈ-

intra- ˈɪn.trə

Note: Prefix. Normally takes primary or secondary stress on the first syllable, e.g. **intranet** /ˈɪn.trə.net/, **intravenous** /ˌɪn.trəˈviː.nəs/.

intractability ɪnˌtræk.təˈbɪl.ə.ti, ˌɪn-, -ɪ.ti, (US) -ə.t̬i

intractab|le ɪnˈtræk.tə.b|ᵊl, ˌɪn- **-ly** -li **-leness** -ᵊl.nəs, -nɪs

intradepartmental ˌɪn.trəˌdiː.pɑːtˈmen.tᵊl, (US) -pɑːrtˈmen.t̬ᵊl

intrados ɪnˈtreɪ.dɒs, (US) -dɑːs; (US) ˈɪn.trə.dɑːs, -doʊs **-es** -ɪz

intramural ˌɪn.trəˈmjʊə.rᵊl, -ˈmjɔː-, (US) -ˈmjʊr.ᵊl

intramuscular ˌɪn.trəˈmʌs.kjə.ləʳ, -kjʊ-, (US) -lɚ **-ly** -li

intranet ˈɪn.trə.net **-s** -s

intransigence ɪnˈtrænt.sɪ.dʒᵊnts, -ˈtrɑːnt-, -sə-; -ˈtræn.zɪ-, -ˈtrɑːn-, -zə-, (US) -ˈtrænt.sə-

intransigent ɪnˈtrænt.sɪ.dʒᵊnt, -ˈtrɑːnt-, -sə-; -ˈtræn.zɪ-, -ˈtrɑːn-, -zə-, (US) -ˈtrænt.sə- **-s** -s **-ly** -li

intransitive ɪnˈtrænt.sə.tɪv, ˌɪn-, -ˈtrɑːnt-, -sɪ-; -ˈtræn.zə-, -ˈtrɑːn-, -zɪ-, (US) -ˈtrænt.sə.t̬ɪv **-s** -z **-ly** -li

intransitivity ɪnˌtrænt.səˈtɪv.ə.ti, ˌɪn-, -ˌtrɑːnt-, -sɪˈ-; -ˌtræn.zəˈ-, -ˌtrɑːn-, -zɪˈ-, -ɪ.ti, (US) -ˌtrænt.səˈtɪv.ə.t̬i

intrapersonal ˌɪn.trəˈpɜː.sᵊn.ᵊl, (US) -ˈpɝː-

intrauterine ˌɪn.trəˈjuː.tᵊr.aɪn, (US) -t̬ɚ.ɪn, -t̬ə.raɪn **ˌintraˌuterine deˈvice**

intravenous ˌɪn.trəˈviː.nəs **-ly** -li

in-tray ˈɪn.treɪ **-s** -z

intrench ɪnˈtrentʃ **-es** -ɪz **-ing** -ɪŋ **-ed** -t **-ment/s** -mənt/s

intrepid ɪnˈtrep.ɪd **-ly** -li

intrepidity ˌɪn.trəˈpɪd.ə.ti, -trɪˈ-, -trepˈɪd-, -ɪ.ti, (US) ˌɪn.trəˈpɪd.ə.t̬i, -trɪˈ-

intricac|y ˈɪn.trɪ.kə.s|i, -trə- **-ies** -iz

intricate ˈɪn.trɪ.kət, -trə-, -kɪt **-ly** -li **-ness** -nəs, -nɪs

intrigue n ˈɪn.triːg, ˌ-ˈ-

intrigu|e v ɪnˈtriːg **-es** -z **-ing/ly** -ɪŋ/li **-ed** -d **-er/s** -əʳ/z, (US) -ɚ/z

intrinsic ɪnˈtrɪnt.sɪk; -ˈtrɪn.zɪk **-ally** -ᵊl.i, -li

intro ˈɪn.trəʊ, (US) -troʊ **-s** -z

intro- ˈɪn.trəʊ, (US) ˈɪn.troʊ, -trə

Note: Prefix. Normally takes either primary or secondary stress on the first syllable, e.g. **introvert** (noun), /ˈɪn.trəʊ.vɜːt/ (US) /-troʊ.vɝːt/, **introspect** /ˌɪn.trəʊˈspekt/ (US) /-troʊˈ-/.

introduc|e ˌɪn.trəˈdʒuːs, -ˈdjuːs, (US) -ˈduːs, -ˈdjuːs **-es** -ɪz **-ing** -ɪŋ **-ed** -t **-er/s** -əʳ/z, (US) -ɚ/z

introduction ˌɪn.trəˈdʌk.ʃᵊn **-s** -z

introductor|y ˌɪn.trəˈdʌk.tᵊr|.i **-ily** -ᵊl.i, -ɪ.li **-iness** -ɪ.nəs, -nɪs

introit ˈɪn.trɔɪt, -trəʊ.ɪt; ɪnˈtrəʊ.ɪt, (US) ɪnˈtroʊ.ɪt; (US) ˈɪn.trɔɪt **-s** -s

intromission ˌɪn.trəʊˈmɪʃ.ᵊn, (US) -troʊˈ-, -trəˈ- **-s** -z

intro|mit ˌɪn.trəʊ|ˈmɪt, (US) -troʊˈ-, -trəˈ- **-mits** -ˈmɪts **-mitting** -ˈmɪt.ɪŋ, (US) -ˈmɪt̬.ɪŋ **-mitted** -ˈmɪt.ɪd, (US) -ˈmɪt̬.ɪd

introspect ˌɪn.trəʊˈspekt, (US) -troʊˈ-, -trəˈ- **-s** -s **-ing** -ɪŋ **-ed** -ɪd

introspection ˌɪn.trəʊˈspek.ʃᵊn, (US) -troʊˈ-, -trəˈ- **-ist/s** -ɪsts/s **-al** -ᵊl

introspective ˌɪn.trəʊˈspek.tɪv, (US) -troʊˈ-, -trəˈ- **-ly** -li **-ness** -nəs, -nɪs

introversion ˌɪn.trəʊˈvɜː.ʃᵊn, -ʒᵊn, (US) -troʊˈvɝː-, -trəˈ-

introvert n ˈɪn.trəʊ.vɜːt, (US) -troʊ.vɝːt, -trə- **-s** -s

introver|t v ˌɪn.trəʊˈvɜː|t, (US) -troʊˈvɝː|t, -trəˈ-, ˈ--- **-ts** -ts **-ting** -tɪŋ, (US) -t̬ɪŋ **-ted** -tɪd, (US) -t̬ɪd

intrud|e ɪnˈtruːd **-es** -z **-ing** -ɪŋ **-ed** -ɪd **-er/s** -əʳ/z, (US) -ɚ/z

intrusion ɪnˈtruː.ʒᵊn **-s** -z

intrusive ɪnˈtruː.sɪv **-ly** -li **-ness** -nəs, -nɪs

intu|it ɪnˈtʃuː|.ɪt, -ˈtjuː-, (US) ɪnˈtuː-, -ˈtjuː-, ˈɪn.tu|.ɪt **-its** -ɪts **-iting** -ɪ.tɪŋ, (US) -ɪ.t̬ɪŋ **-ited** -ɪ.tɪd, (US) -ɪ.t̬ɪd **-itable** -ɪ.t̬ə.bᵊl

intuition ˌɪn.tʃuˈɪʃ.ᵊn, -tjuˈ, (US) -tuˈ-, -tjuˈ- **-s** -z **-al** -ᵊl

intuitive ɪnˈtʃuː.ɪ.tɪv, -ˈtjuː-, ˈ-ə-, (US) -ˈtuː.ɪ.t̬ɪv, -ˈtjuː- **-ly** -li **-ness** -nəs, -nɪs

intumescen|ce ˌɪn.tʃuːˈmes.ᵊn|ts, -tjuːˈ-, (US) -tuːˈ-, -tjuːˈ- **-t** -t

Inuit ˈɪn.u.ɪt, -ju-, (US) ˈ-u- **-s** -s

inun|date ˈɪn.ʌn|.deɪt, -ən-, (US) -ən- **-dates** -deɪts **-dating** -deɪ.tɪŋ, (US) -deɪ.t̬ɪŋ **-dated** -deɪ.tɪd, (US) -deɪ.t̬ɪd

inundation ˌɪn.ʌnˈdeɪ.ʃᵊn, -ənˈ-, ⓊⓈ -ənˈ- **-s** -z

inur|e ɪˈnjʊəʳ, -ˈnjɔːʳ, ⓊⓈ -ˈnjʊr, -ˈnʊr **-es** -z **-ing** -ɪŋ **-ed** -d **-ement** -mənt

in utero ɪnˈjuː.tᵊr.əʊ, ⓊⓈ -t̬ɚ.oʊ

inutility ˌɪn.juːˈtɪl.ə.ti, -ɪ.ti, ⓊⓈ -ə.t̬i

invad|e ɪnˈveɪd **-es** -z **-ing** -ɪŋ **-ed** -ɪd **-er/s** -əʳ/z, ⓊⓈ -ɚ/z

invalid n, v, adj *infirm through illness, etc.:* ˈɪn.və.lɪd, -liːd, ⓊⓈ -lɪd **-s** -z **-ing** -ɪŋ **-ed** -ɪd

invalid adj *not valid:* ɪnˈvæl.ɪd, ˌɪn-

invali|date ɪnˈvæl.ɪ|.deɪt, ˌɪn-, ˈ-ə- **-dates** -deɪts **-dating** -deɪ.tɪŋ, ⓊⓈ -deɪ.t̬ɪŋ **-dated** -deɪ.tɪd, ⓊⓈ -deɪ.t̬ɪd

invalidation ɪnˌvæl.ɪˈdeɪ.ʃᵊn, ˌɪn-, -əˈ-

invalidity ˌɪn.vəˈlɪd.ə.ti, -ɪ.ti, ⓊⓈ -ə.t̬i **invaˈlidity ˌbenefit**

invaluab|le ɪnˈvæl.ju.ə.b|ᵊl, -jə.b|ᵊl, -jʊ-, ⓊⓈ -ju.ə- **-ly** -li

Invar® ɪnˈvɑːʳ, ˈ--, ˈɪn.vəʳ, ⓊⓈ ˈɪn.vɑːr

invariability ɪnˌveə.ri.əˈbɪl.ə.ti, ˌɪn-, -ɪ.ti, ⓊⓈ -ˌver.i.əˈbɪl.ə.t̬i

invariab|le ɪnˈveə.ri.ə.b|ᵊl, ˌɪn-, ⓊⓈ -ˈver.i- **-ly** -li **-leness** -ᵊl.nəs, -nɪs

invariance ɪnˈveə.ri.ənts, ˌɪn-, ⓊⓈ -ˈver.i-

invasion ɪnˈveɪ.ʒᵊn **-s** -z

invasive ɪnˈveɪ.sɪv, -zɪv, ⓊⓈ -zɪv, -sɪv **-ly** -li **-ness** -nəs, -nɪs

invective ɪnˈvek.tɪv **-s** -z

inveigh ɪnˈveɪ **-s** -z **-ing** -ɪŋ **-ed** -d

inveigl|e ɪnˈveɪ.gᵊl, -ˈviː- **-es** -z **-ing** -ɪŋ, -ˈveɪ.glɪŋ, -ˈviː- **-ed** -əd **-ement/s** -mənt/s

in|vent ɪn|ˈvent **-vents** -ˈvents **-venting** -ˈven.tɪŋ, ⓊⓈ -ˈven.t̬ɪŋ **-vented** -ˈven.tɪd, ⓊⓈ -ˈven.t̬ɪd

invention ɪnˈven.tʃᵊn **-s** -z

inventive ɪnˈven.tɪv, ⓊⓈ -t̬ɪv **-ly** -li **-ness** -nəs, -nɪs

inventor ɪnˈven.təʳ, ⓊⓈ -t̬ɚ **-s** -z

inventor|y ˈɪn.vᵊn.tr|i, -tᵊr|.i, ɪnˈven.tᵊr|.i, ⓊⓈ -tɔːr.i **-ies** -iz

Inverary ˌɪn.vᵊrˈeə.ri, -rə, ⓊⓈ -vəˈrer.i

Invercargill *in Scotland:* ˌɪn.vəˈkɑː.gɪl, -gᵊl; -kɑːˈgɪl, ⓊⓈ -vɚˈkɑːr.gɪl *in New Zealand:* ˌɪn.vəˈkɑː.gɪl, ⓊⓈ -vɚˈkɑːr-

Invergordon ˌɪn.vəˈgɔː.dᵊn, ⓊⓈ -vɚˈgɔːr-

Inverkeithing ˌɪn.vəˈkiː.ðɪŋ, ⓊⓈ -vɚˈ-

Inverness, inverness ˌɪn.vəˈnes, ⓊⓈ -vɚˈ- **-es** -ɪz *stress shift:* ˌ**Inverness** ˈ**train**

Inverness-shire ˌɪn.vəˈnes.ʃəʳ, -ˈneʃ-, -ʃɪəʳ, ⓊⓈ -vɚˈnes.ʃɚ, -ʃɪr

inverse ɪnˈvɜːs, ˈ--, ⓊⓈ -ˈvɝːs, ˈ-- **-s** -ɪz **-ly** -li

inversion ɪnˈvɜː.ʃᵊn, -ʒᵊn, ⓊⓈ -ˈvɝː.ʒᵊn, -ʃᵊn **-s** -z

invert n, adj ˈɪn.vɜːt, ⓊⓈ -vɝːt **-s** -s

in|vert v ɪn|ˈvɜːt, ⓊⓈ -ˈvɝːt **-verts** -ˈvɜːts, ⓊⓈ -ˈvɝːts **-verting** -ˈvɜː.tɪŋ, ⓊⓈ -ˈvɝː.t̬ɪŋ **-verted** -ˈvɜː.tɪd, ⓊⓈ -ˈvɝː.t̬ɪd **inˌverted ˈcomma; inˌverted ˈsnob; inˌverted ˈsnobbery**

invertase ɪnˈvɜː.teɪz, ⓊⓈ -ˈvɝː.teɪs, -teɪz, ˈ---

invertebrate ɪnˈvɜː.tɪ.breɪt, ˌɪn-, ˈ-tə-, -brət, -brɪt, ⓊⓈ -ˈvɝː.t̬ə.brɪt, -breɪt **-s** -s

Inverurie ˌɪn.vᵊrˈʊə.ri, ⓊⓈ -vəˈrʊr.i

invest ɪnˈvest **-s** -s **-ing** -ɪŋ **-ed** -ɪd

investi|gate ɪnˈves.tɪ|.geɪt, -tə- **-gates** -geɪts **-gating** -geɪ.tɪŋ, ⓊⓈ -geɪ.t̬ɪŋ **-gated** -geɪ.tɪd, ⓊⓈ -geɪ.t̬ɪd **-gator/s** -geɪ.təʳ/z, ⓊⓈ -geɪ.t̬ɚ/z

investigation ɪnˌves.tɪˈgeɪ.ʃᵊn, -təˈ- **-s** -z

investigative ɪnˈves.tɪ.gə.tɪv, -tə-, -geɪ-, ⓊⓈ -geɪ.t̬ɪv

investigatory ɪnˈves.tɪ.gə.tᵊr.i, -tə-, -geɪ-; ɪnˌves.tɪˈgeɪ-, -təˈ-, ⓊⓈ ɪnˈves.tɪ.gə.tɔːr-, -tə-

investiture ɪnˈves.tɪ.tʃəʳ, -tə-, -tjʊəʳ, ⓊⓈ -tʃɚ **-s** -z

investment ɪnˈvest.mənt **-s** -s **inˈvestment ˌbond**

investor ɪnˈves.təʳ, ⓊⓈ -tɚ **-s** -z

inveteracy ɪnˈvet.ᵊr.ə.si, ⓊⓈ -ˈvet̬-

inveterate ɪnˈvet.ᵊr.ət, -ɪt, ⓊⓈ -ˈvet̬- **-ly** -li **-ness** -nəs, -nɪs

invidious ɪnˈvɪd.i.əs **-ly** -li **-ness** -nəs, -nɪs

invigi|late ɪnˈvɪdʒ.ə|.leɪt, ˈ-ɪ- **-lates** -leɪts **-lating** -leɪ.tɪŋ, ⓊⓈ -leɪ.t̬ɪŋ **-lated** -leɪ.tɪd, ⓊⓈ -leɪ.t̬ɪd **-lator/s** -leɪ.təʳ/z, ⓊⓈ -leɪ.t̬ɚ/z

invigilation ɪnˌvɪdʒ.əˈleɪ.ʃᵊn, -ɪˈ- **-s** -z

invigor|ate ɪnˈvɪg.ᵊr|.eɪt, ⓊⓈ -ə.r|eɪt **-ates** -eɪts **-ating** -eɪ.tɪŋ, ⓊⓈ -eɪ.t̬ɪŋ **-ated** -eɪ.tɪd, ⓊⓈ -eɪ.t̬ɪd **-ator/s** -eɪ.təʳ/z, ⓊⓈ -eɪ.t̬ɚ/z

invigoration ɪnˌvɪg.ᵊrˈeɪ.ʃᵊn, ⓊⓈ -əˈreɪ-

invincibility ɪnˌvɪnt.səˈbɪl.ə.ti, -sɪˈ-, -ɪ.ti, ⓊⓈ -ə.t̬i

invincib|le ɪnˈvɪnt.sə.b|ᵊl, -sɪ- **-ly** -li **-leness** -ᵊl.nəs, -nɪs

inviolability ɪnˌvaɪ.ə.ləˈbɪl.ə.ti, ˌɪn-, -ɪ.ti, ⓊⓈ -ə.t̬i

inviolab|le ɪnˈvaɪ.ə.lə.b|ᵊl **-ly** -li **-leness** -ᵊl.nəs, -nɪs

inviolate ɪnˈvaɪ.ə.lət, -lɪt, -leɪt **-ly** -li **-ness** -nəs, -nɪs

invisibility ɪnˌvɪz.əˈbɪl.ə.ti, ˌɪn-, -ɪˈ-, -ɪ.ti, ⓊⓈ -ə.t̬i

invisib|le ɪnˈvɪz.ə.b|ᵊl, ˌɪn-, ˈ-ɪ- **-ly** -li **-leness** -ᵊl.nəs, -nɪs

invitation ˌɪn.vɪˈteɪ.ʃᵊn, -vəˈ- **-s** -z **-al/s** -ᵊl/z

invite n ˈɪn.vaɪt **-s** -s

in|vite v ɪn|ˈvaɪt **-vites** -ˈvaɪts **-viting/ly** -ˈvaɪ.tɪŋ/li, ⓊⓈ -ˈvaɪ.t̬ɪŋ/li **-vited** -ˈvaɪ.tɪd, ⓊⓈ -ˈvaɪ.t̬ɪd **-viter/s** -ˈvaɪ.təʳ/z, ⓊⓈ -ˈvaɪ.t̬ɚ/z

invitee ˌɪn.vaɪˈtiː, -vɪˈ-, ⓊⓈ -vaɪˈ-, -vəˈ-

in vitro ˌɪnˈviː.trəʊ, -ˈvɪt.rəʊ, ⓊⓈ -ˈviː.troʊ, -ˈvɪt.roʊ **in ˌvitro fertiliˈzation**

in vivo ˌɪnˈviː.vəʊ, ⓊⓈ -voʊ

invo|cate ˈɪn.vəʊ|.keɪt, ⓊⓈ -və- **-cates** -keɪts **-cating** -keɪ.tɪŋ, ⓊⓈ -keɪ.t̬ɪŋ **-cated** -keɪ.tɪd, ⓊⓈ -keɪ.t̬ɪd

invocation ˌɪn.vəʊˈkeɪ.ʃᵊn, ⓊⓈ -vəˈ- **-s** -z **-al** -ᵊl

invoic|e ˈɪn.vɔɪs **-es** -ɪz **-ing** -ɪŋ **-ed** -t

invok|e ɪnˈvəʊk, ⓊⓈ -ˈvoʊk **-es** -s **-ing** -ɪŋ **-ed** -t

involucre ˈɪn.və.luː.kəʳ, -ljuː-, ˌɪn.vəˈluː.kəʳ, -ˈljuː-, ⓊⓈ ˌɪn.voʊˈluː.kɚ, -vəˈ- **-s** -z

involuntar|y ɪnˈvɒl.ən.tᵊr|.i, ˌɪn-, -ᵊn-, -tr|i, ⓊⓈ -ˈvɑː.lən.ter|.i **-ily** -ᵊl.i, -ɪ.li **-iness** -ɪ.nəs, -ɪ.nɪs

involu|te ˈɪn.və.luː|t, -ljuː|t, ˌ--ˈ-, ⓊⓈ ˈɪn.və.luː|t **-tes** -ts **-ting** -tɪŋ, ⓊⓈ -t̬ɪŋ **-ted** -tɪd, ⓊⓈ -t̬ɪd

involution ˌɪn.vəˈluː.ʃᵊn, -ˈljuː-, ⓊⓈ -ˈluː- **-s** -z

involv|e ɪnˈvɒlv, ⓊⓈ -ˈvɑːlv, -ˈvɔːlv **-es** -z **-ing** -ɪŋ **-ed** -d

involvement ɪnˈvɒlv.mənt, ⓊⓈ -ˈvɑːlv-, -ˈvɔːlv- **-s** -s

invulnerability ɪnˌvʌl.nᵊr.əˈbɪl.ə.ti, ˌɪn-, -ˌvʌn.ᵊr-, -ɪ.ti, ⓊⓈ -ˌvʌl.nɚ.əˈbɪl.ə.t̬i

invulnerab|le ɪnˈvʌl.nᵊr.ə.b|ᵊl, ˌɪn-, -ˈvʌn.ᵊr-, ⓊⓈ -ˈvʌl.nɚ- **-ly** -li **-leness** -ᵊl.nəs, -nɪs

inward ˈɪn.wəd, ⓊⓈ -wɚd **-s** -z **-ly** -li **-ness** -nəs, -nɪs

Inwards ˈɪn.wədz, ⓊⓈ -wɚdz

inweav|e ɪnˈwiːv **-es** -z **-ing** -ɪŋ **-ed** -d **inwove** ɪnˈwəʊv, ⓊⓈ -ˈwoʊv **inwoven** ɪnˈwəʊ.vᵊn, ⓊⓈ -ˈwoʊ-

Inwood ˈɪn.wʊd

inwov|e (from **inweave**) ɪnˈwəʊv, ⓊⓈ -ˈwoʊv **-en** -ᵊn

inwrought ɪnˈrɔːt, ⓊⓈ -ˈrɑːt, -ˈrɔːt

io, Io ˈaɪ.əʊ, ⓊⓈ -oʊ **-s** -z

io|date ˈaɪ.əʊ|.deɪt, ⓊⓈ ˈ-ə- **-dates** -deɪts **-dating** -deɪ.tɪŋ, ⓊⓈ -deɪ.t̬ɪŋ **-dated** -deɪ.tɪd, ⓊⓈ -deɪ.t̬ɪd

iodic aɪˈɒd.ɪk, ⓊⓈ -ˈɑː.dɪk

iodide ˈaɪ.əʊ.daɪd, ⓊⓈ ˈ-ə- **-s** -z

iodine ˈaɪ.ə.diːn, -daɪn, ⓊⓈ -daɪn, -dɪn, -diːn

iodiz|e, -is|e ˈaɪ.ə.daɪz **-es** -ɪz **-ing** -ɪŋ **-ed** -d

iodoform aɪˈɒd.ə.fɔːm, ⓊⓈ -ˈoʊ.də.fɔːrm, -ˈɑː-

Iolanthe ˌaɪ.əʊˈlænt.θi, ⓊⓈ ˌaɪəˈ-, ˌaɪ.oʊˈ-

iolite ˈaɪ.əʊ.laɪt, ⓊⓈ ˈ-oʊ-

Iolo ˈjəʊ.ləʊ, ⓊⓈ ˈjoʊ.loʊ

ion ˈaɪ.ən, -ɒn, ⓊⓈ -ən, -ɑːn **-s** -z

Iona aɪˈəʊ.nə, ⓊⓈ -ˈoʊ-

Ione aɪˈəʊ.ni, ⓊⓈ -ˈoʊ-

Ionesco jɒnˈes.kəʊ, ˌiː.ɒnˈ-, ˌiː.əˈnes-, -kuː, ⓊⓈ jəˈnes.koʊ, ˌiː.əˈ-

Ioni|a aɪˈəʊ.ni|.ə, ⓊⓈ -ˈoʊ- **-an/s** -ən/z

ionic, I~ aɪˈɒn.ɪk, ⓊⓈ -ˈɑː.nɪk **-s** -s

Ionica® aɪˈɒn.ɪ.kə, ⓊⓈ -ˈɑːn.ɪ-

ionization, -isa- ˌaɪ.ə.naɪˈzeɪ.ʃᵊn, -nɪˈ-, ⓊⓈ -nəˈ- **-s** -z

ioniz|e, -is|e ˈaɪ.ə.naɪz **-es** -ɪz **-ing** -ɪŋ **-ed** -d **-er/s** -əʳ/z, ⓊⓈ -ɚ/z **-able** -ə.bᵊl

ionosphere aɪˈɒn.ə.sfɪəʳ, ⓊⓈ -ˈɑː.nə.sfɪr **-s** -z

Pronouncing the letters IO

There are several pronunciation possibilities for the vowel digraph **io**, e.g.:

aɪ.ə	lion /laɪ.ən/
i.əʊ US i.oʊ	radio /ˈreɪ.di.əʊ/ US /-oʊ/
aɪ.ɒ US	priority /praɪˈɒr.ə.ti/ US /-ˈɔːr.ə.ţi/
aɪ.ɑː, aɪ.ɔː	
i.ɒ US i.ɑː	curiosity /ˌkjʊə.riˈɒs.ə.ti/ US /ˌkjʊr.iˈɑː.sə.ţi/

In weak syllables

In weak syllables where it is preceded by the letters **s** and **t**, the vowel digraph **io** is realized with the vowel /ə/, and may be reduced to a syllabic consonant, e.g.:

station	ˈsteɪ.ʃᵊn
invasion	ɪnˈveɪ.ʒᵊn

In other weak syllable contexts, **io** is realized with /i.ə/ or /jə/, e.g.:

million	ˈmɪl.jən, -i.ən US -jən
patriot	ˈpeɪ.tri.ət

iota aɪˈəʊ.tə, US -ˈoʊ.ţə **-s** -z
IOU ˌaɪ.əʊˈjuː, US -oʊˈ- **-s** -z
Iowa ˈaɪ.əʊ.ə, ˈaɪ.ə.wə, US ˈaɪ.ə.wə **ˌIowa ˈCity**
IPA ˌaɪ.piːˈeɪ
iPad® ˈaɪ.pæd
ipecac ˈɪp.ɪ.kæk, ˈ-ə-
ipecacuanha ˌɪp.ɪˌkæk.juˈæn.ə, -əˌ-, -ˈɑː.nə, US -juˈæn.ə
Iphicrates ɪˈfɪk.rə.tiːz
Iphigenia ˌɪf.ɪ.dʒɪˈnaɪ.ə, ˌaɪ.fɪ-, -dʒəˈ-; ɪˌfɪdʒ.ɪˈ-, -əˈ-, US ˌɪf.ə.dʒəˈ-
iPhone® ˈaɪ.fəʊn, US -foʊn **-s** -z
iPod® ˈaɪ.pɒd, US -pɑːd **-s** -z
Ipoh ˈiː.pəʊ, US -poʊ
ipse dixit ˌɪp.siˈdɪk.sɪt, -seɪˈ-, US -siˈ-
ipso facto ˌɪp.səʊˈfæk.təʊ, US -soʊˈfæk.toʊ
ipso jure ˌɪp.səʊˈjʊə.reɪ, -ri, US -soʊˈdʒʊr.i
Ipswich ˈɪp.swɪtʃ
IQ ˌaɪˈkjuː **IˈQ ˌtest**
Iqbal ˈɪk.bæl, ˈɪg-, -bɑːl, US ɪkˈbɑːl
Iquique ɪˈkiː.ki, -keɪ, US iːˈkiː.keɪ
Iquitos ɪˈkiː.tɒs, US iːˈkiː.toʊs, -tɔːs
Ira ˈaɪə.rə, US ˈaɪ-
IRA ˌaɪ.ɑːrˈeɪ, US -ɑːrˈ-
Irabu ɪˈrɑː.buː, ˈɪr.ə.buː
Irak ɪˈrɑːk, -ˈræk, US ɪ-, iː- **-i/s** -i/z
Iran ɪˈrɑːn, -ˈræn, US -ˈræn
Iranian ɪˈreɪ.ni.ən, -ˈrɑː-, US ɪ- **-s** -z
Iraq ɪˈrɑːk, -ˈræk, US ɪ- **-i/s** -i/z
irascibility ɪˌræs.əˈbɪl.ə.ti, -ɪˈ-, -ɪ.ti, US -ə.ţi
irascib|le ɪˈræs.ə.b|ᵊl, ˈ-ɪ- **-ly** -li **-leness** -ᵊl.nəs, -nɪs
irate aɪˈreɪt, ˌaɪ-, US aɪˈreɪt, ˈ-- **-ly** -li
Irbid ˈɪə.bɪd, US ˈɪr-
ire aɪəʳ, ˈaɪ.əʳ, US aɪr, ˈaɪ.ɚ
Iredell ˈaɪ.ə.del, US ˈaɪ.ɚ-
ireful ˈaɪə.fᵊl, ˈaɪ.ə-, -fʊl, US ˈaɪr-, ˈaɪ.ɚ- **-ly** -i **-ness** -nəs, -nɪs
Ireland ˈaɪə.lənd, US ˈaɪr-
Iremonger ˈaɪəˌmʌŋ.gəʳ, US ˈaɪrˌmʌŋ.gɚ, -ˌmɑːŋ-
Irene ˈaɪ.riːn, -ˈ-; -ˈriː.ni, US aɪˈriːn; US -ˈriː.ni
irenic aɪˈriː.nɪk, -ˈren.ɪk, US -ˈren-, -ˈriː.nɪk **-al** -ᵊl
Ireton ˈaɪə.tᵊn, US ˈaɪr-
Irian ˈɪr.i.ən, -ɑːn, US -ɑːn, -ən
Irian Jaya ˌɪr.i.ɑːnˈdʒɑː.jə, -ənˈ-, -jɑː
irides (plural of **iris**) ˈaɪə.rɪ.diːz, ˈɪr.ɪ-, US ˈaɪ.rɪ-, ˈɪr.ɪ-
iridescence ˌɪr.ɪˈdes.ᵊnts, -əˈ-
iridescent ˌɪr.ɪˈdes.ᵊnt, -əˈ- **-ly** -li
iridium ɪˈrɪd.i.əm, aɪ-
iridolog|y ˌɪr.ɪˈdɒl.ə.dʒ|i, US -ˈdɑː.lə- **-ist/s** -ɪst/s
Irion ˈɪr.i.ən, -ɒn, US -ɑːn, -ən
iris, I~ ˈaɪə.rɪs, US ˈaɪ- **irises** ˈaɪə.rɪ.sɪz, US ˈaɪ- **irides** ˈaɪə.rɪ.diːz, ˈɪr.ɪ-, US ˈaɪ.rɪ-, ˈɪr.ɪ-
Irish ˈaɪə.rɪʃ, US ˈaɪ- **-ism/s** -ɪ.zᵊm/z **ˌIrish ˈcoffee; ˌIrish ReˈpuЬlic; ˌIrish ReˌpuЬlican ˈArmy; ˌIrish ˈSea; ˌIrish ˈstew**
Irish|man ˈaɪə.rɪʃ|.mən, US ˈaɪ- **-men** -mən, -men
Irishry ˈaɪə.rɪʃ.ri, US ˈaɪ-
Irish|woman ˈaɪə.rɪʃ|ˌwʊm.ən, US ˈaɪ- **-women** -ˌwɪm.ɪn
irk ɜːk, US ɝːk **-s** -s **-ing** -ɪŋ **-ed** -t
irksome ˈɜːk.səm, US ˈɝːk- **-ly** -li **-ness** -nəs, -nɪs
Irkutsk ɜːˈkʊtsk, ɪə-, US ɪr-
Irlam ˈɜː.ləm, US ˈɝː-
Irma ˈɜː.mə, US ˈɝː-
iron, I~ aɪən, ˈaɪ.ən, US aɪrn, ˈaɪ.ɚn **-s** -z **-ing** -ɪŋ **-ed** -d **ˈIron ˌAge; ˈironing ˌboard; ˌIron ˈCurtain; ˌiron ˈlung; ˈiron ˌmould; ˌstrike while the ˌiron's ˈhot**
ironbark ˈaɪən.bɑːk, ˈaɪ.ən-, US ˈaɪrn.bɑːrk, ˈaɪ.ɚn- **-s** -s
ironbound ˈaɪən.baʊnd, ˈaɪ.ən-, US ˈaɪrn-, ˈaɪ.ɚn-
Ironbridge ˈaɪən.brɪdʒ, ˈaɪ.ən-, -ˈ-, US ˈaɪ.ɚn-, ˈaɪrn-
ironclad ˈaɪən.klæd, ˈaɪ.ən-, US ˈaɪ.ɚn-, ˈaɪrn- **-s** -z
irongray, irongrey ˌaɪənˈgreɪ, ˌaɪəŋ-, ˌaɪ.ən-, US ˌaɪ.ɚnˈ-, ˌaɪrn- *stress shift:* **ˌirongray ˈbattleship**
ironic aɪəˈrɒn.ɪk, US aɪˈrɑː.nɪk **-al** -ᵊl **-ally** -ᵊl.i, -li
ironmonger ˈaɪənˌmʌŋ.gəʳ, ˈaɪəm-, ˈaɪ.ən-, US ˈaɪ.ɚnˌmʌŋ.gɚ, ˈaɪrn-, -ˌmɑːŋ- **-s** -z
ironmongery ˈaɪənˌmʌŋ.gᵊr.i, ˈaɪəm-, ˈaɪ.ən-, US ˈaɪ.ɚnˌ-, ˈaɪrn-, -ˌmɑːŋ-
ironside, I~ ˈaɪən.saɪd, ˈaɪ.ən-, US ˈaɪ.ɚn-, ˈaɪrn- **-s** -z
ironstone ˈaɪən.stəʊn, ˈaɪ.ən-, US ˈaɪ.ɚn.stoʊn, ˈaɪrn-
Ironton ˈaɪən.tən, ˈaɪ.ən-, US ˈaɪ.ɚn-, ˈaɪrn-
ironware ˈaɪən.weəʳ, ˈaɪ.ən-, US ˈaɪ.ɚn.wer, ˈaɪrn-
ironwood, I~ ˈaɪən.wʊd, ˈaɪ.ən-, US ˈaɪ.ɚn-, ˈaɪrn-
ironwork ˈaɪən.wɜːk, ˈaɪ.ən-, US ˈaɪ.ɚn.wɝːk, ˈaɪrn- **-s** -s
irony adj *like iron:* ˈaɪə.ni, US ˈaɪ.ɚ-, ˈaɪr-
iron|y n *sarcasm, etc.:* ˈaɪə.rᵊn|.i, US ˈaɪ- **-ies** -iz
Iroquoian ˌɪr.əʊˈkwɔɪ.ən, US -əˈ-
Iroquois (sing.) ˈɪr.ə.kwɔɪ, -kwɔɪ (plural) ˈɪr.ə.kwɔɪz, -kwɔɪ
irradian|ce ɪˈreɪ.di.ənt|s, US ɪrˈ- **-cy** -si
irradi|ate ɪˈreɪ.di|.eɪt, US ɪrˈ- **-ates** -eɪts **-ating** -eɪ.tɪŋ, US -eɪ.ţɪŋ **-ated** -eɪ.tɪd, US -eɪ.ţɪd
irradiation ɪˌreɪ.diˈeɪ.ʃᵊn, ˌɪr.eɪ-, US ɪrˈ-, ɪˌreɪ- **-s** -z
irradicab|le ɪˈræd.ɪ.kə.b|ᵊl, US ɪrˈ- **-ly** -li
irrational ɪˈræʃ.ᵊn.ᵊl, ˌɪrˈæʃ-, -ˈræʃ.nᵊl **-ly** -i
irrationality ɪˌræʃ.ᵊnˈæl.ə.ti, ˌɪrˌæʃ-, -ɪ.ti, US -ə.ţi
Irrawaddy ˌɪr.əˈwɒd.i, US -ˈwɑː.di, -ˈwɔː-
irrebuttable ˌɪr.ɪˈbʌt.ə.bᵊl, US -ˈbʌţ-
irreceptive ˌɪr.ɪˈsep.tɪv
irreclaimab|le ˌɪr.ɪˈkleɪ.mə.b|ᵊl **-ly** -li
irrecognizable, -isa- ɪˌrek.əgˈnaɪ.zə.bᵊl, ˌɪrˌek-
irreconcilability ɪˌrek.ᵊnˌsaɪ.ləˈbɪl.ə.ti, ˌɪrˌek-, -ɪ.ti, US -ə.ţi
irreconcilab|le ˌɪr.ek.ᵊnˈsaɪ.lə.b|ᵊl, ɪˌrek- **-ly** -li **-leness** -ᵊl.nəs, -nɪs
irrecoverab|le ˌɪr.ɪˈkʌv.ᵊr.ə.b|ᵊl, -əˈ- **-ly** -li **-leness** -ᵊl.nəs, -nɪs
irredeemab|le ˌɪr.ɪˈdiː.mə.b|ᵊl, -əˈ- **-ly** -li **-leness** -ᵊl.nəs, -nɪs
irredent|ism ˌɪr.ɪˈden.t|ɪ.zᵊm, -əˈ- **-ist/s** -ɪst/s
irreducib|le ˌɪr.ɪˈdʒuː.sə.b|ᵊl, -ˈdjuː-, -əˈ-, -sɪ-, US -ˈduː-, -ˈdjuː- **-ly** -li **-leness** -ᵊl.nəs, -nɪs
irrefutability ɪˌref.jə.təˈbɪl.ə.ti, -jʊ-, -ɪ.ti; ˌɪr.ɪˌfjuː.təˈ-, -əˌ-, US -ţəˈbɪl.ə.ţi

irrefutab|le ˌɪr.ɪˈfjuː.tə.b|ᵊl, -əˈ-; ɪˈref.jə-, -jʊ-, (US) ɪˈref.jə.t̬ə-; (US) ˌɪr.ɪˈfjuː-, -əˈ- **-ly** -li **-leness** -ᵊl.nəs, -nɪs
irregardless ˌɪr.ɪˈɡɑːd.ləs, -əˈ-, -lɪs, (US) -iˈɡɑːrd-
irregular ɪˈreɡ.jə.ləʳ, -jʊ-, (US) -lɚ **-ly** -li
irregularit|y ɪˌreɡ.jəˈlær.ə.t|i, ˌɪrˌeɡ-, -jʊˈ-, -ɪ.t|i, (US) ɪˌreɡ.jəˈler.ə.t̬|i, -ˈlær- **-ies** -iz
irrelevan|ce ɪˈrel.ə.vᵊnt|s, ˈ-ɪ-, (US) ɪrˈ- **-cy** -si **-cies** -siz
irrelevant ɪˈrel.ə.vᵊnt, ˈ-ɪ-, (US) ɪrˈ- **-ly** -li
irreligion ˌɪr.ɪˈlɪdʒ.ᵊn, -əˈ-
irreligious ˌɪr.ɪˈlɪdʒ.əs, -əˈ- **-ly** -li **-ness** -nəs, -nɪs
irremediab|le ˌɪr.ɪˈmiː.di.ə.b|ᵊl **-ly** -li
irremovability ˌɪr.ɪˌmuː.vəˈbɪl.ə.ti, -əˌ-, -ɪ.ti, (US) -ə.t̬i
irremovab|le ˌɪr.ɪˈmuː.və.b|ᵊl, -əˈ- **-ly** -li
irreparability ɪˌrep.ᵊr.əˈbɪl.ə.ti, ˌɪrˌep-, -ɪ.ti, (US) -ə.t̬i
irreparab|le ɪˈrep.ᵊr.ə.b|ᵊl **-ly** -li **-leness** -ᵊl.nəs, -nɪs
irreplaceable ˌɪr.ɪˈpleɪ.sə.bᵊl
irrepressib|le ˌɪr.ɪˈpres.ə.b|ᵊl, -əˈ-, ˈ-ɪ- **-ly** -li **-leness** -ᵊl.nəs, -nɪs
irreproachability ˌɪr.ɪˌprəʊ.tʃəˈbɪl.ə.ti, -əˌ-, -ɪ.ti, (US) -ˌproʊ.tʃəˈbɪl.ə.t̬i
irreproachab|le ˌɪr.ɪˈprəʊ.tʃə.b|ᵊl, -əˈ-, (US) -ˈproʊ- **-ly** -li **-leness** -ᵊl.nəs, -nɪs
irresistibility ˌɪr.ɪˌzɪs.təˈbɪl.ə.ti, -əˌ-, -tɪˈ-, -ɪ.ti, (US) -ə.t̬i
irresistib|le ˌɪr.ɪˈzɪs.tə.b|ᵊl, -əˈ-, -tɪ- **-ly** -li **-leness** -ᵊl.nəs, -nɪs
irresoluble ɪˈrez.əl.jə.bᵊl, -jʊ-, (US) ˌɪr.ɪˈzɑːl.jə-
irresolute ɪˈrez.ᵊl.uːt, ɪrˈez-, -juːt, (US) -uːt **-ly** -li **-ness** -nəs, -nɪs
irresolution ɪˌrez.ᵊlˈuː.ʃᵊn, -ˈljuː-, (US) -ˈuː-
irresolvability ˌɪr.ɪˌzɒl.vəˈbɪl.ə.ti, -əˌ-, -ɪ.ti, (US) -ˌzɑːl.vəˈbɪl.ə.t̬i
irresolvab|le ˌɪr.ɪˈzɒl.və.b|ᵊl, (US) -ˈzɑːl.və- **-ly** -li **-leness** -ᵊl.nəs, -nɪs
irrespective ˌɪr.ɪˈspek.tɪv, -əˈ- **-ly** -li
irresponsibility ˌɪr.ɪˌspɒnt.səˈbɪl.ə.ti, -əˌ-, -sɪˈ-, -ɪ.ti, (US) -ˌspɑːnt.səˈbɪl.ə.t̬i
irresponsib|le ˌɪr.ɪˈspɒnt.sə.b|ᵊl, -əˈ-, -sɪ-, (US) -ˈspɑːnt- **-ly** -li **-leness** -ᵊl.nəs, -nɪs
irresponsive ˌɪr.ɪˈspɒnt.sɪv, -əˈ-, (US) -ˈspɑːnt- **-ly** -li **-ness** -nəs, -nɪs
irretentive ˌɪr.ɪˈten.tɪv, -əˈ-, (US) -t̬ɪv
irretrievability ˌɪr.ɪˌtriː.vəˈbɪl.ə.ti, -əˌ-, -ɪ.ti, (US) -ə.t̬i
irretrievab|le ˌɪr.ɪˈtriː.və.b|ᵊl, -əˈ- **-ly** -li **-leness** -ᵊl.nəs, -nɪs
irreverence ɪˈrev.ᵊr.ᵊnts, ˌɪrˈev-
irreverent ɪˈrev.ᵊr.ᵊnt, ˌɪrˈev- **-ly** -li
irreversibility ˌɪr.ɪˌvɜː.səˈbɪl.ə.ti, -əˌ-, -sɪˈ-, -ɪ.ti, (US) -ˌvɝː.səˈbɪl.ə.t̬i, -sɪˈ-
irreversib|le ˌɪr.ɪˈvɜː.sə.b|ᵊl, -əˈ-, -sɪ-, (US) -ˈvɝː- **-ly** -li **-leness** -ᵊl.nəs, -nɪs
irrevocability ɪˌrev.ə.kəˈbɪl.ə.ti, -ɪ.ti, (US) -ə.t̬i
irrevocab|le ɪˈrev.ə.kə.b|ᵊl **-ly** -li *when applied to letters of credit:* ˌɪr.ɪˈvəʊ.kə.bᵊl, -əˈ-, (US) ɪˈrev.ə.kə-; (US) ˌɪr.ɪˈvoʊ-
irrigable ˈɪr.ɪ.ɡə.bᵊl, ˈ-ə-
irri|gate ˈɪr.ɪ|.ɡeɪt, ˈ-ə- **-gates** -ɡeɪts **-gating** -ɡeɪ.tɪŋ, (US) -ɡeɪ.t̬ɪŋ **-gated** -ɡeɪ.tɪd, (US) -ɡeɪ.t̬ɪd **-gator/s** -ɡeɪ.təʳ/z, (US) -ɡeɪ.t̬ɚ/z
irrigation ˌɪr.ɪˈɡeɪ.ʃᵊn, -əˈ- **-s** -z
irritability ˌɪr.ɪ.təˈbɪl.ə.ti, ˈ-ə-, -ɪ.ti, (US) -t̬əˈbɪl.ə.t̬i
irritab|le ˈɪr.ɪ.tə.b|ᵊl, ˈ-ə-, (US) -t̬ə- **-ly** -li **-leness** -ᵊl.nəs, -nɪs ˌ**irritable** ˈ**bowel** ˌ**syndrome**
irritant ˈɪr.ɪ.tᵊnt, ˈ-ə-, (US) -t̬ənt **-s** -s
irri|tate ˈɪr.ɪ|.teɪt, ˈ-ə- **-tates** -teɪts **-tating/ly** -teɪ.tɪŋ/li, (US) -teɪ.t̬ɪŋ/li **-tated** -teɪ.tɪd, (US) -teɪ.t̬ɪd **-tative** -teɪ.tɪv, (US) -teɪ.t̬ɪv **-tator/s** -teɪ.təʳ/z, (US) -teɪ.t̬ɚ/z
irritation ˌɪr.ɪˈteɪ.ʃᵊn, -əˈ- **-s** -z
irrupt ɪˈrʌpt **-s** -s **-ing** -ɪŋ **-ed** -ɪd **-ive/ly** -ɪv/li
irruption ɪˈrʌp.ʃᵊn **-s** -z
IRS ˌaɪ.ɑːrˈes
Irvine *name:* ˈɜː.vɪn, -vaɪn, (US) ˈɝː- *US city:* ˈɜː.vaɪn, (US) ˈɝː-
Irvinestown ˈɜː.vɪnz.taʊn, (US) ˈɝː-
Irving ˈɜː.vɪŋ, (US) ˈɝː-
Irwin ˈɜː.wɪn, (US) ˈɝː-
is (from **be**) *strong form:* ɪz; *weak forms:* z, s

> Note: /z/ is used only when the preceding word ends in a vowel or a voiced consonant other than /z/ or /ʒ/. /s/ is used only when the preceding word ends in a voiceless consonant other than /s/ or /ʃ/.

ISA, Isa ˈaɪ.sə **-s** -z
Isaac ˈaɪ.zək **-s** -s
Isaacson ˈaɪ.zək.sᵊn
Isabel ˈɪz.ə.bel
Isabella ˌɪz.əˈbel.ə
Isabelle ˈɪz.ə.bel
Isaiah aɪˈzaɪ.ə, (US) aɪˈzeɪ.ə, -ˈzaɪ.ə
Isambard ˈɪz.ᵊm.bɑːd, (US) -bɑːrd
Isard ˈɪz.ɑːd, (US) -ɑːrd
-isation aɪˈzeɪ.ʃᵊn, ɪˈ-, (US) əˈ-
Note: Suffix. Words containing **-isation** alway carry primary stress as shown above, e.g. **decimalisation** /ˌdes.ɪ.mᵊl.aɪˈzeɪ.ʃᵊn/ (US) /-əˈ-/.
ISBN ˌaɪ.es.biːˈen
Iscariot ɪsˈkær.i.ət, (US) -ˈker-, -ˈkær-
Ischia ˈɪs.ki.ə
-ise aɪz, iːz
Note: Suffix. Where **-ise** forms a verb, the pronunciation is /-aɪz/. See note for **-ize**. Where **-ise** forms a noun, it usually carries primary stress (e.g. **experˈtise**) and is pronounced /-iːz/.
Iseult iˈzuːlt, -ˈsuːlt, (US) -ˈsuːlt
-ish ɪʃ
Note: Suffix. When forming an adjective, **-ish** does not affect the stress pattern of the word, e.g. **yellowish** /ˈjel.əʊ.ɪʃ/ (US) /-oʊ-/. When forming a verb, the penultimate syllable is stressed, e.g. **demolish** /dɪˈmɒl.ɪʃ/ (US) /-ˈmɑː.lɪʃ/.
Isham ˈaɪ.ʃᵊm
Isherwood ˈɪʃ.ə.wʊd, (US) ˈ-ɚ-
Ishiguro ˌɪʃ.ɪˈɡʊər.əʊ, (US) -ˈɡʊr.oʊ
Ishmael ˈɪʃ.meɪ.əl, -mi.əl
Ishmae|lite ˈɪʃ.mi.ə|.laɪt, -meɪ-, -mə|- **-lites** -laɪts **-litish** -laɪ.tɪʃ, (US) -laɪ.t̬ɪʃ
Ishtar ˈɪʃ.tɑːʳ, (US) -tɑːr
Isidore ˈɪz.ɪ.dɔːʳ, ˈ-ə-, (US) -ə.dɔːr
Isidorian ˌɪz.ɪˈdɔː.ri.ən, -əˈ-, (US) -ˈdɔːr.i-
isinglass ˈaɪ.zɪŋ.ɡlɑːs, (US) -zɪn.ɡlæs, -zɪŋ-
Isis ˈaɪ.sɪs
Isla ˈaɪ.lə
Islam ˈɪz.lɑːm, ˈɪs-, -læm, -ləm; ɪzˈlɑːm, ɪs-
Islamabad ɪzˈlɑː.mə.bæd, ɪs-, -ˈlæm.ə-, -bɑːd, (US) -ˈlɑː.mə.bɑːd
Islamic ɪzˈlæm.ɪk, ɪs-, -ˈlɑː.mɪk, (US) -ˈlɑːm.ɪk, -ˈlæm.ɪk **-s** -s
Islam|ism ˈɪz.lə.m|ɪ.zᵊm, ˈɪs- **-ist/s** -ɪst/s
island ˈaɪ.lənd **-s** -z **-er/s** -əʳ/z, (US) -ɚ/z
Islay ˈaɪ.leɪ; *locally:* ˈaɪ.lə
isle aɪl **-s** -z
Isle of Dogs ˌaɪl.əvˈdɒɡz, (US) -ˈdɑːɡz, -ˈdɔːɡz
Isle of Man ˌaɪl.əvˈmæn
Isle of Wight ˌaɪl.əvˈwaɪt
islet ˈaɪ.lət, -lɪt, -let, (US) -lɪt **-s** -s
Isleworth ˈaɪ.zᵊl.wəθ, -wɜːθ, (US) -wɝːθ, -wɚθ
Islington ˈɪz.lɪŋ.tən
Islip *archbishop:* ˈɪz.lɪp *in Oxfordshire:* ˈaɪ.slɪp
Islwyn ˈɪs.lu.ɪn; ɪzˈluː.ɪn, ɪs-
-ism ɪ.zᵊm **-s** -z
Note: Suffix. When added to a free stem, **-ism** does not normally affect the stress pattern of the word, e.g. **absentee** /ˌæb.sᵊnˈtiː/, **absenteeism** /ˌæb.sᵊnˈtiː.ɪ.zᵊm/. When added to a bound stem, the word is normally stressed two syllables before the suffix, e.g. **exorcism** /ˈek.sɔː.sɪ.zᵊm/ (US) /-sɔːr-/. Exceptions exist; see individual entries.
Ismail ˌɪz.mɑːˈiːl, ˌɪs-; ˈɪz.maɪl, -meɪl
Ismailiya ˌɪz.maɪˈliː.ə, ˌɪs-, (US) ˌɪs.meɪ.əˈ-, ˌɪz-
Ismay ˈɪz.meɪ
isn't ˈɪz.ᵊnt
ISO ˌaɪ.esˈəʊ, (US) -ˈoʊ
iso- ˈaɪ.səʊ; aɪˈsɒ, (US) ˈaɪ.soʊ, -sə; (US) aɪˈsɑː
Note: Prefix. Normally takes either primary or secondary stress on the

I

first syllable, e.g. **isotope** /ˈaɪ.sə.təʊp/ US /-toʊp/, **isotopic** /ˌaɪ.səˈtɒp.ɪk/ US /-ˈtɑː.pɪk/, or primary stress on the second syllable, e.g. **isotropy** /aɪˈsɒt.rə.pi/ US /-ˈsɑː.trə-/.

isobar ˈaɪ.səʊ.bɑːʳ, US -soʊ.bɑːr, -sə- **-s** -z

Isobel ˈɪz.ə.bel

isochromatic ˌaɪ.səʊ.krəʊˈmæt.ɪk, US -soʊ.kroʊˈmæt̬.ɪk, -sə-

isochronal aɪˈsɒk.rə.nəl, US -ˈsɑː.krə- **-ly** -i

isochronous aɪˈsɒk.rə.nəs, US -ˈsɑː.krə- **-ly** -li

Isocrates aɪˈsɒk.rə.tiːz, US -ˈsɑː.krə-

isogloss ˈaɪ.səʊ.glɒs, US -soʊ.glɑːs, -sə- **-es** -ɪz

isolate n ˈaɪ.səl.ət, -ɪt, -eɪt, US -sə.lɪt **-s** -s

iso|late v ˈaɪ.sə|.leɪt **-lates** -leɪts **-lating** -leɪ.tɪŋ, US -leɪ.t̬ɪŋ **-lated** -leɪ.tɪd, US -leɪ.t̬ɪd **-lator/s** -leɪ.təʳ/z, US -leɪ.t̬ɚ/z

isolation ˌaɪ.səlˈeɪ.ʃən

isolation|ism ˌaɪ.səlˈeɪ.ʃən|.ɪ.zəm **-ist/s** -ɪst/s

isolative ˈaɪ.səl.ə.tɪv, -eɪ.tɪv, US -sə.leɪ.t̬ɪv, -soʊ- **-ly** -li

Isolda ɪˈzɒl.də, US -ˈsoʊl-, -ˈzoʊl-

Isolde ɪˈzɒl.də, US -ˈsoʊl-, -ˈzoʊl-; US -ˈsoʊld, -ˈzoʊld

isomer ˈaɪ.sə.məʳ, US -soʊ.mɚ, -sə- **-s** -z

isomeric ˌaɪ.səʊˈmer.ɪk, US -soʊˈ-, -səˈ-

isomer|ism aɪˈsɒm.əʳ|.ɪ.zəm, US -ˈsɑː.mɚ- **-ous** -əs

isometric ˌaɪ.səʊˈmet.rɪk, US -soʊˈ-, -səˈ- **-al** -əl **-ally** -əl.i, -li

isomorph ˈaɪ.səʊ.mɔːf, US -soʊ.mɔːrf, -sə- **-s** -s

isomorph|ism ˌaɪ.səʊˈmɔː.f|ɪ.zəm, US -soʊˈmɔːr- **-ic** -ɪk **-ous** -əs

Ison ˈaɪ.sən

isophone ˈaɪ.səʊ.fəʊn, US -soʊ.foʊn, -sə- **-s** -z

isosceles aɪˈsɒs.əl.iːz, -ɪ.liːz, US -ˈsɑː.səl.iːz

isotherm ˈaɪ.səʊ.θɜːm, US -soʊ.θɝːm, -sə- **-s** -z

isothermal ˌaɪ.səˈθɜː.məl, US -ˈθɝː- **-ly** -i

isotonic ˌaɪ.səˈtɒn.ɪk, US -ˈtɑː.nɪk

isotope ˈaɪ.sə.təʊp, US -toʊp **-s** -s

isotopic ˌaɪ.səˈtɒp.ɪk, US -ˈtɑː.pɪk **-ally** -əl.i, -li

isotropic ˌaɪ.səˈtrɒp.ɪk, US -ˈtrɑː.pɪk **-ally** -əl.i, -li

isotropy aɪˈsɒt.rə.pi, US -ˈsɑː.trə-

ISP ˌaɪ.esˈpiː

I-spy ˌaɪˈspaɪ

Israel ˈɪz.reɪəl, -ri.əl, -reɪ.el, US -ri.əl, -reɪ-, -rəl

Israeli ɪzˈreɪ.li **-s** -z

Israelite ˈɪz.ri.ə.laɪt, -reɪ-, -rə.laɪt, -rɪ-, US -ri.ə-, -reɪ- **-s** -s

Issachar ˈɪs.ə.kəʳ, -kɑːʳ, US -kɑːr

iss|ue ˈɪʃ|.uː, ˈɪs.j|uː, US ˈɪʃ|.uː **-ues** -uːz **-uing** -uː.ɪŋ **-ued** -uːd **-uer/s** -uː.əʳ/z, US -uː.ɚ/z **-uable** -u.ə.bəl **-uance** -u.ənts

-ist ɪst
Note: Suffix. When attached to a free stem, **-ist** does not normally affect the stress pattern of the stem, e.g. **modern** /ˈmɒd.ən/ US /ˈmɑː.dɚn/, **modernist** /ˈmɒd.ən.ɪst/ US /ˈmɑː.dɚ.nɪst/. When attached to a bound stem, the word is normally stressed on the penultimate syllable, e.g. **Baptist** /ˈbæp.tɪst/. Exceptions exist; see individual entries.

Istanbul ˌɪs.tænˈbʊl, -tɑːnˈ-, -tæmˈ-, -tɑːmˈ-, US -tɑːnˈ-, -tænˈ-, -ˈbuːl

isthmi (plural of **isthmus**) ˈɪs.maɪ, ˈɪsθ-, ˈɪst-, US ˈɪs-

isthmian, I~ ˈɪsθ.mi.ən, ˈɪst-, ˈɪs-, US ˈɪs-

isthmus ˈɪs.məs, ˈɪsθ-, ˈɪst-, US ˈɪs- **-es** -ɪz

-istic ˈɪs.tɪk
Note: Suffix. Normally takes primary stress as shown, e.g. **impressionistic** /ɪmˌpreʃ.ənˈɪs.tɪk/.

istle ˈɪst.li

Istria ˈɪs.tri.ə

it ɪt

IT ˌaɪˈtiː

Italian ɪˈtæl.i.ən, US ˈ-jən **-s** -z

italianate ɪˈtæl.i.ə.neɪt, -nət, -nɪt, US ˈ-jə.nɪt

italianism ɪˈtæl.i.ə.nɪ.zəm, US ˈ-jə- **-s** -z

italianiz|e, -is|e ɪˈtæl.i.ə.naɪz, US ˈ-jə- **-es** -ɪz **-ing** -ɪŋ **-ed** -d

italic, I~ ɪˈtæl.ɪk **-s** -s

italicization, -isa- ɪˌtæl.ɪ.saɪˈzeɪ.ʃən, ˌ-ə-, -sɪˈ-, US -səˈ-

italiciz|e, -is|e ɪˈtæl.ɪ.saɪz, ˈ-ə- **-es** -ɪz **-ing** -ɪŋ **-ed** -d

Italy ˈɪt.əl.i, US ˈɪt̬-

itch ɪtʃ **-es** -ɪz **-ing** -ɪŋ **-ed** -t

Itchen ˈɪtʃ.ɪn, -ən

itch|y ˈɪtʃ|.i **-ier** -i.əʳ, US -i.ɚ **-iest** -i.ɪst, -i.əst **-iness** -ɪ.nəs, -ɪ.nɪs

it'd (= **it would** or **it had**) ɪt.əd, US ɪt̬-

item ˈaɪ.təm, -tɪm, -tem, US -t̬əm **-s** -z

itemiz|e, -is|e ˈaɪ.tə.maɪz, -tɪ-, US -t̬ə- **-es** -ɪz **-ing** -ɪŋ **-ed** -d

iter|ate ˈɪt.əʳ|.eɪt, US ˈɪt̬.ə.r|eɪt **-ates** -eɪts **-ating** -eɪ.tɪŋ, US -eɪ.t̬ɪŋ **-ated** -eɪ.tɪd, US -eɪ.t̬ɪd

iteration ˌɪt.əʳˈeɪ.ʃən, US ˌɪt̬.əˈreɪ- **-s** -z

iterative ˈɪt.əʳ.ə.tɪv, -eɪ-, US ˈɪt̬.ə.reɪ.t̬ɪv, -ɚ.ə- **-ly** -li **-ness** -nəs, -nɪs

Ithaca ˈɪθ.ə.kə

itinerancy aɪˈtɪn.əʳ.ənt.si, ɪ-

itinerant aɪˈtɪn.əʳ.ənt, ɪ- **-s** -s

itinerar|y aɪˈtɪn.əʳ.əʳ|.i, ɪ-, US -ə.rer- **-ies** -iz

itiner|ate aɪˈtɪn.əʳ|.eɪt, ɪ-, US -ə.r|eɪt **-ates** -eɪts **-ating** -eɪ.tɪŋ, US -eɪ.t̬ɪŋ **-ated** -eɪ.tɪd, US -eɪ.t̬ɪd

-ition ˈɪʃ.ən
Note: Suffix. Always stressed as shown, e.g. **edition** /ɪˈdɪʃ.ən/.

-itious ˈɪʃ.əs
Note: Suffix. Always stressed as shown, e.g. **surreptitious** /ˌsʌr.əpˈtɪʃ.əs/ US /ˌsɝː.əpˈ-/.

-itis ˈaɪ.tɪs, -təs, US ˈaɪ.t̬ɪs, -t̬əs
Note: Suffix. Always stressed as shown, e.g. **tonsilitis** /ˌtɒnt.səlˈaɪ.tɪs/ US /ˌtɑːnt.səˈlaɪ.t̬ɪs/.

-itive ɪ.tɪv, ə-, US ə.t̬ɪv, ɪ-
Note: Suffix. Words containing **-itive** are normally stressed on the antepenultimate syllable, e.g. **competitive** /kəmˈpet.ɪ.tɪv/ US /-ə.t̬ɪv/. Exceptions exist; see individual entries.

it'll (= **it will** or **it shall**) ɪt.əl, US ɪt̬-

ITN ˌaɪ.tiːˈen

-itory ə.təʳr.i, ɪ-, tri, US ə.tɔːr.i, ɪ-
Note: Suffix. Words containing **-itory** are normally stressed on the syllable preceding the prefix, e.g. **territory** /ˈter.ɪ.təʳr.i/ US /ˈter.ɪ.tɔːr.i/. Exceptions exist; see individual entries.

its ɪts

it's (= **it is** or **it has**) ɪts

itself ɪtˈself

itsy-bitsy ˌɪt.siˈbɪt.si

itty-bitty ˌɪt.iˈbɪt.i, US ˌɪt̬.iˈbɪt̬-

iTunes® ˈaɪ.tʃuːnz, -tjuːnz, US -tuːnz, -tjuːnz

ITV ˌaɪ.tiːˈviː

-ity ə.ti, ɪ.ti, US ə.t̬i
Note: Suffix. Words containing **-ity** are normally stressed on the antepenultimate syllable, e.g. **conformity** /kənˈfɔː.mə.ti/ US /-ˈfɔːr.mə.t̬i/.

IUD ˌaɪ.juːˈdiː

Ivan ˈaɪ.vən, US ˈaɪ.vən *foreign name:* iːˈvæn, ɪ-, -ˈvɑːn, US -ˈvɑːn

Ivanhoe ˈaɪ.vən.həʊ, US -hoʊ

Ivanoff ɪˈvɑː.nəf, iː-, -nɒf, US ˈiː.və.nɑːf; US iːˈvɑː-

Ivanov ˈaɪ.və.nɒf, ɪˈvɑː.nɒf, US iː.vəˈnɑːf, aɪ-

Ivatt ˈaɪ.vət, -væt **-s** -s

I've (= **I have**) aɪv

-ive ɪv
Note: Suffix. Words containing **-ive** are either stressed on the penultimate syllable, e.g. **expensive** /ɪkˈspent.sɪv/, or on the antepenultimate syllable, e.g. **executive** /ɪgˈzek.jə.tɪv/ US /-t̬ɪv/.

Iveagh ˈaɪ.və, -veɪ

Iveco® ɪˈveɪ.kəʊ, aɪˈ-, -ˈviː-, US -ˈveɪ.koʊ

Ivens ˈaɪ.vənz

Iver ˈaɪ.vəʳ, US -vɚ

Ives *surname, and towns* **St. Ives** *in Cornwall and Cambridgeshire:* aɪvz *in Stevenson's 'St. Ives':* iːvz

Ivey ˈaɪ.vi

IVF ˌaɪ.viːˈef

Ivor ˈaɪ.vəʳ, ⓊⓈ -vɚ, ˈiː-
ivor|y, I~ ˈaɪ.vᵊr|.i **-ies** -iz ˌ**Ivory** ˈ**Coast;** ˌ**ivory** ˈ**tower**
ivory-black ˌaɪ.vᵊr.iˈblæk
iv|y, I~ ˈaɪ.v|i **-ies** -iz **-ied** -id ˈ**Ivy** ˌ**League**
Ivybridge ˈaɪ.vi.brɪdʒ
ixia ˈɪk.si.ə **-s** -z
Ixion ɪkˈsaɪ.ən, ⓊⓈ -ˈsaɪ.ən, -ˈsaɪ.ɑːn
Iza ˈaɪ.zə
Izaby ˈɪz.ə.bi
Izal® ˈaɪ.zᵊl
izard ˈɪz.əd, ⓊⓈ -ɚd **-s** -z
Izard ˈaɪ.zɑːd, -zəd; ˈɪz.əd, ⓊⓈ ˈaɪ.zɑːrd, -zɚd; ⓊⓈ ˈɪz.ɚd
-ization aɪˈzeɪ.ʃᵊn, ɪˈ-, ⓊⓈ əˈ-
Note: Suffix. Words containing **-ization** always carry primary stress as shown above, e.g. **decimalization** /ˌdes.ɪ.mᵊl.aɪˈzeɪ.ʃᵊn/ ⓊⓈ /-əˈ-/.
-ize, -ise aɪz
Note: Suffix. When attached to a free stem, **-ize** does not normally affect the stress pattern of the stem, e.g. **decimal** /ˈdes.ɪ.mᵊl/, **decimalize** /ˈdes.ɪ.mᵊl.aɪz/ ⓊⓈ /-mə.laɪz/. When attached to a bound stem, the word is normally stressed on the antepenultimate syllable, e.g. **recognize** /ˈrek.əg.naɪz/. Exceptions exist; see individual entries.
Izmir ˈɪz.mɪəʳ, -ˈ-, ⓊⓈ ɪzˈmɪr
Izzard ˈɪz.əd, -ɑːd, ⓊⓈ -ɚd, -ɑːrd

J

Pronouncing the letter J

In general, the consonant letter **j** is pronounced /dʒ/, e.g.:

jam dʒæm
raj rɑːdʒ

(The latter can also be pronounced /rɑːʒ/ in British English.)

In some exceptional cases, **j** is pronounced /j/, e.g.:

hallelujah ˌhæl.ɪˈluː.jə

j, J dʒeɪ -'s -z
jab dʒæb -s -z -bing -ɪŋ -bed -d
jabb|er ˈdʒæb|.əʳ, ⓊⓈ -ɚ -ers -əz, ⓊⓈ -ɚz -ering -ərˌɪŋ -ered -əd, ⓊⓈ -ɚd -erer/s -ər.əʳ/z, ⓊⓈ -ɚ.ɚ/z
Jabberwock ˈdʒæb.ə.wɒk, ⓊⓈ -ɚ.wɑːk
jabberwocky, J~ ˈdʒæb.ə.wɒk.i, ⓊⓈ -ɚ.wɑː.ki, -wɔː.ki
Jabez ˈdʒeɪ.bez, -bɪz
jabiru ˌdʒæb.əˈruː, -ɪˈ-, ˈ---, ⓊⓈ ˈdʒæb.ə.ruː, ˌ--ˈ- -s -z
jaborandi ˌdʒæb.əˈræn.di, ˌʒæb-, -ɔːˈ-; -rænˈdiː, ⓊⓈ ˌdʒæb.əˈræn.di; ⓊⓈ -rænˈdiː
jabot ˈʒæb.əʊ, ⓊⓈ ʒæbˈoʊ -s -z
jacamar ˈdʒæk.ə.mɑːʳ, ˈʒæk-, ⓊⓈ ˈdʒæk.ə.mɑːr -s -z
jacaranda ˌdʒæk.əˈræn.də -s -z
Jacinta dʒəˈsɪn.tə, hə-
jacinth, J~ ˈdʒæs.ɪntθ, ˈdʒeɪ.sɪntθ -s -s
Jacintha dʒəˈsɪnt.θə, dʒæsˈɪnt-
jack, J~ dʒæk -s -s -ing -ɪŋ -ed -t **ˌJack ˈFrost; ˌJack ˈRobinson; ˌJack ˈRussell; ˌjack ˈtar; ˌJack the ˈlad**
jackal ˈdʒæk.ɔːl, -əl, ⓊⓈ -əl -s -z
jackanapes ˈdʒæk.ə.neɪps -es -ɪz
jackaroo ˌdʒæk.ərˈuː, ⓊⓈ -əˈruː -s -z
jackass ˈdʒæk.æs -es -ɪz
jackboot ˈdʒæk.buːt -s -s -ed -ɪd
jackdaw ˈdʒæk.dɔː, ⓊⓈ -dɑː, -dɔː -s -z
jackeroo ˌdʒæk.ərˈuː, ⓊⓈ -əˈruː -s -z
jack|et ˈdʒæk|.ɪt -ets -ɪts -eting -ɪ.tɪŋ, ⓊⓈ -ɪ.t̬ɪŋ -eted -ɪ.tɪd, ⓊⓈ -ɪ.t̬ɪd
jackhammer ˈdʒækˌhæm.əʳ, ⓊⓈ -ɚ -s -z
Jackie ˈdʒæk.i
jack-in-office ˈdʒæk.ɪnˌɒf.ɪs, ⓊⓈ -ˌɑː.fɪs jacks-in-office ˈdʒæks-
jack-in-the-box ˈdʒæk.ɪn.ðə.bɒks, ⓊⓈ -bɑːks -es -ɪz
jackknif|e v ˈdʒæk.naɪf -es -s -ing -ɪŋ -ed -t
jack-kni|fe n ˈdʒæk.naɪ|f -ves -vz
Jacklin ˈdʒæk.lɪn
Jacklyn ˈdʒæk.lɪn
Jackman ˈdʒæk.mən
jack-of-all-trades ˌdʒæk.əvˈɔːl.treɪdz, -ɔːlˈtreɪdz, ⓊⓈ -ˈɔːl-, -ˈɑːl- jacks-of-all-trades ˌdʒæks-
jack-o'-lantern ˌdʒæk.əʊˈlæn.tən, ˈdʒæk.əʊˌlæn.tən, ⓊⓈ ˈdʒæk.əˌlæn.tən -s -z
jackpot ˈdʒæk.pɒt, ⓊⓈ -pɑːt -s -s **ˌhit the ˈjackpot**
jackrabbit ˈdʒækˌræb.ɪt -s -s
Jackson ˈdʒæk.sən
Jacksonian ˌdʒækˈsəʊ.ni.ən, ⓊⓈ -ˈsoʊ-
Jacksonville ˈdʒæk.sən.vɪl
jack-tar ˌdʒækˈtɑːʳ, ˈ--, ⓊⓈ ˌdʒækˈtɑːr, ˈ-- -s -z
Jacob ˈdʒeɪ.kəb **ˌJacob's ˈladder**
jacobean, J~ ˌdʒæk.əʊˈbiː.ən, ⓊⓈ -əˈ-, -oʊˈ- -s -z
Jacobi ˈdʒæk.ə.bi; dʒəˈkəʊ-, ⓊⓈ -ˈkoʊ-
jacobian, J~ dʒəˈkəʊ.bi.ən, ⓊⓈ -ˈkoʊ- -s -z
Jacobin ˈdʒæk.əʊ.bɪn, ⓊⓈ ˈ-ə- -s -z -ism -ɪ.zəm
Jacobit|e ˈdʒæk.əʊ.baɪt, ⓊⓈ ˈ-ə- -es -s -ism -ɪ.zəm
Jacobs ˈdʒeɪ.kəbz
Jacobson ˈdʒæk.əb.sən, ˈjæk-, ⓊⓈ ˈdʒeɪ.kəb-
jacobus, J~ dʒəˈkəʊ.bəs, ⓊⓈ -ˈkoʊ- -es -ɪz
Jacoby dʒəˈkəʊ.bi; ˈdʒæk.ə-, ⓊⓈ dʒəˈkoʊ-; ⓊⓈ ˈdʒæk.ə-
Jacquard ˈdʒæk.ɑːd, dʒəˈkɑːd, ⓊⓈ dʒəˈkɑːrd
Jacqueline ˈdʒæk.ə.liːn, ˈʒæk-, -lɪn; ˈdʒæk.liːn, -lɪn, ⓊⓈ ˈdʒæk.ə.lɪn, -liːn; ⓊⓈ ˈ-wə.lɪn
Jacques *English surname:* dʒeɪks, dʒæks *French name:* ʒæk, ⓊⓈ ʒɑːk
Jacqui ˈdʒæk.i
jactitation ˌdʒæk.tɪˈteɪ.ʃən -s -z
jacuzzi, J~® dʒəˈkuː.zi, dʒækˈuː-, ⓊⓈ dʒəˈkuː- -s -z
jad|e, J~ dʒeɪd -es -z -ing -ɪŋ -ed -ɪd
jaeger, J~® ˈjeɪ.gəʳ, ˈdʒeɪ-, ⓊⓈ -gɚ -s -z
Jael ˈdʒeɪ.əl, dʒeɪl, ˈdʒeɪ.el, ⓊⓈ ˈdʒeɪ.əl
Jaffa ˈdʒæf.ə, ⓊⓈ ˈdʒæf-, ˈdʒɑː.fə, ˈjɑː- -s -z
Jaffna ˈdʒæf.nə
Jaffrey ˈdʒæf.ri
jag dʒæg -s -z -ging -ɪŋ -ged -d
Jaggard ˈdʒæg.əd, ⓊⓈ -ɚd
jagged ˈdʒæg.ɪd -ly -li -ness -nəs, -nɪs
jagger, J~ ˈdʒæg.əʳ, ⓊⓈ -ɚ -s -z
jagg|y ˈdʒæg|.i -ier -i.əʳ, ⓊⓈ -i.ɚ -iest -i.ɪst, -i.əst -iness -ɪ.nəs, -ɪ.nɪs
Jago ˈdʒeɪ.gəʊ, ⓊⓈ -goʊ
jaguar, J~ ˈdʒæg.ju.əʳ, ⓊⓈ ˈdʒæg.wɑːr, ˈ-ju.ɑːr -s -z
Jah dʒɑː, jɑː
Jahveh ˈjɑː.veɪ, ˌjɑːˈveɪ, ˈdʒɑː.veɪ, ˈjɑː.və, ⓊⓈ ˈjɑː.veɪ
jai alai ˌhaɪ.əˈlaɪ, ˈ---; ˌhaɪˈlaɪ, ˈ--, ⓊⓈ ˈhaɪˌlaɪ, -əˌlaɪ; ⓊⓈ ˌhaɪ.əˈlaɪ
jail dʒeɪl -s -z -ing -ɪŋ -ed -d
jailbait ˈdʒeɪl.beɪt
jailbird ˈdʒeɪl.bɜːd, ⓊⓈ -bɝːd -s -z
jailbreak ˈdʒeɪl.breɪk -s -s
jailer, jailor ˈdʒeɪ.ləʳ, ⓊⓈ -lɚ -s -z
jailhou|se ˈdʒeɪl.haʊ|s -ses -zɪz
Jaime *English name:* ˈdʒeɪ.mi *Spanish name:* ˈhaɪ.mi
Jain dʒaɪn, dʒeɪn, ⓊⓈ dʒaɪn -s -z -ism -ɪ.zəm
Jaipur ˌdʒaɪˈpʊəʳ, -ˈpɔːʳ, ⓊⓈ -ˈpʊr
Jairus ˈdʒaɪə.rəs, dʒeɪˈaɪə-, ⓊⓈ ˈdʒaɪ-, dʒeɪˈaɪ-
Jaish-e-Mohamed dʒɑːˌiːʃ.ɪ.məʊˈhæm.ɪd, ˌ-eɪ-, -əd, -ɪd, ⓊⓈ dʒaɪ.iːʃ.ə.moʊˈhɑː.mɪd, -ˈhæm-
Jakarta dʒəˈkɑː.tə, ⓊⓈ -ˈkɑːr.t̬ə
Jake dʒeɪk
Jakes dʒeɪks
Jalalabad dʒəˈlɑː.lə.bɑːd, -ˈlæl.ə-, -bæd; dʒəˌlɑː.ləˈbɑːd, -ˌlæl.əˈ-, -ˈbæd
jalap ˈdʒæl.əp
jalapeño ˌhæl.əˈpeɪ.njəʊ, ⓊⓈ ˌhɑː.ləˈpeɪ.njoʊ, ˌhæl.əˈ- -s -z
Jalisco hɑːˈles.kəʊ, ⓊⓈ -ˈliːs.koʊ
jalop|y dʒəˈlɒp|.i, ⓊⓈ -ˈlɑː.p|i -ies -iz
jalousie ˈʒæl.u.ziː, ˌ--ˈ-, dʒəˈluː.si, ⓊⓈ ˈdʒæl.ə.si -s -z
jam dʒæm -s -z -ming -ɪŋ -med -d **ˈjam ˌjar; ˌjam ˈtart; ˈjam ˌsession**
Jam *Indian title:* dʒɑːm -s -z
Jamaic|a dʒəˈmeɪ.k|ə -an/s -ən/z
Jamal dʒəˈmɑːl
jamb dʒæm*b* -s -z
jambalaya ˌdʒæm.bəˈlaɪ.ə, ˌdʒʌm- -s -z
jamboree ˌdʒæm.bərˈiː, ˈ---, ⓊⓈ ˌdʒæm.bəˈriː -s -z
James dʒeɪmz
Jameson ˈdʒeɪm.sən, ˈdʒɪm-, ˈdʒem-, ˈdʒæm-; ˈdʒeɪ.mɪ.sən, ˈdʒɪm.ɪ-, ˈdʒem-, ˈdʒæm-, ˈ-ə-, ⓊⓈ ˈdʒeɪm.sən; ⓊⓈ ˈdʒeɪ.mɪ-
James's ˈdʒeɪm.zɪz

Jamestown ˈdʒeɪmz.taʊn

Jamia ˈdʒʌm.i.ə, ˈdʒæm-

Jamie ˈdʒeɪ.mi

Jamieson ˈdʒeɪ.mɪ.sən, ˈdʒæm.ɪ-, ˈdʒem-, ˈdʒɪm-, ˈ-ə-, ⓤⓢ ˈdʒeɪ.mɪ-

jam-jar ˈdʒæm.dʒɑːʳ, ⓤⓢ -dʒɑːr

Jammu ˈdʒæm.uː, ˈdʒʌm-, ⓤⓢ ˈdʒʌm-

jamm|y ˈdʒæm|.i **-ier** -i.əʳ, ⓤⓢ -i.ɚ **-iest** -i.ɪst, -i.əst **-iness** -ɪ.nəs, -ɪ.nɪs

jam-packed ˌdʒæmˈpækt *stress shift:* **ˌjam-packed ˈtrain**

jam-pot ˈdʒæm.pɒt, ⓤⓢ -pɑːt **-s** -s

Jamy ˈdʒeɪ.mi

Jan *female first name:* dʒæn; *male first name:* jæn

Jan. (abbrev. for **January**) ˈdʒæn.ju.ər.i, -jʊə.ri, -jʊ-, ⓤⓢ -ju.er.i

Jana ˈdʒæn.ə, ˈdʒeɪ.nə; *as if Czech or Polish:* ˈjɑː.nə; ⓤⓢ ˈdʒæn.ə

Janáček ˈjæn.ə.tʃek, ˈ-ɑː-, ⓤⓢ ˈjɑː.nə-

Jane dʒeɪn **ˌJane ˈDoe**

Janeiro dʒəˈnɪə.rəʊ, -ˈneə-, ⓤⓢ ʒəˈner.oʊ, dʒə-, -ˈnɪr-

Janet ˈdʒæn.ɪt, -ət

Jan(n)ette dʒəˈnet, dʒænˈet

jangl|e ˈdʒæŋ.gəl **-es** -z **-ing** -ɪŋ, ˈdʒæŋ.glɪŋ **-ed** -d **-er/s** -əʳ/z, ⓤⓢ -ɚ/z, ˈdʒæŋ.gləʳ/z, -glɚ/z

Janice ˈdʒæn.ɪs

Janine dʒəˈniːn

janissar|y ˈdʒæn.ɪ.sər|.i, ⓤⓢ -ə.ser- **-ies** -iz

janitor ˈdʒæn.ɪ.təʳ, ⓤⓢ -ə.t̬ɚ **-s** -z

Janjaweed ˈdʒæn.dʒə.wiːd, ⓤⓢ ˈdʒɑːn-, -dʒɑː-

Jansen ˈdʒænt.sən

Jansen|ism ˈdʒænt.sən|.ɪ.zəm **-ist/s** -ɪst/s

Jantzen® ˈjænt.sən, ˈdʒænt-, ⓤⓢ ˈdʒænt-

Januarius ˌdʒæn.juˈeə.ri.əs, ⓤⓢ -ˈer.i-

Januar|y ˈdʒæn.ju.ər|.i, -jʊə.r|i, -jʊ-, ⓤⓢ -ju.er|.i **-ies** -iz

Janus ˈdʒeɪ.nəs

Jap dʒæp **-s** -s

Japan, japan dʒəˈpæn **-s** -z **-ning** -ɪŋ **-ned** -d **-ner/s** -əʳ/z, ⓤⓢ -ɚ/z

Japanese ˌdʒæp.ənˈiːz, ⓤⓢ -ˈiːz, -ˈiːs

jap|e dʒeɪp **-es** -s **-ing** -ɪŋ **-ed** -t

Japhet ˈdʒeɪ.fet, -fɪt

Japheth ˈdʒeɪ.feθ, -fɪθ

japhetic dʒeɪˈfet.ɪk, dʒə-, ⓤⓢ dʒəˈfet̬-

japonica dʒəˈpɒn.ɪ.kə, ⓤⓢ -ˈpɑː.nɪ- **-s** -z

Jaques *name:* dʒeɪks, dʒæks *Shakespearian character:* ˈdʒeɪ.kwɪz, ⓤⓢ -kwɪz, -kiːz; ⓤⓢ dʒeɪks, dʒæks

jar dʒɑːʳ, ⓤⓢ dʒɑːr **-s** -z **-ring/ly** -ɪŋ/li **-red** -d

Jardine ˈdʒɑː.diːn, -ˈ-, ⓤⓢ ˈdʒɑːr.diːn, -ˈ-

jardinière ˌʒɑː.dɪ.niˈeəʳ, ˌdʒɑː-, -dɪˈnjeəʳ, ⓤⓢ ˌdʒɑːr.dənˈɪr, ˌʒɑːr-, -ˈjer **-s** -z

Jared ˈdʒær.əd, ⓤⓢ ˈdʒer-, ˈdʒær-

jarful ˈdʒɑː.fʊl, ⓤⓢ ˈdʒɑːr- **-s** -z

jargon ˈdʒɑː.gən, ⓤⓢ ˈdʒɑːr- **-s** -z

jargonelle ˌdʒɑː.gəˈnel, ⓤⓢ ˌdʒɑːr- **-s** -z

Jarley ˈdʒɑː.li, ⓤⓢ ˈdʒɑːr-

Jarlsberg® ˈjɑːlz.bɜːg, ⓤⓢ ˈjɑːrlz.bɝːg

Jarlshof ˈjɑːlz.hɒf, ⓤⓢ ˈjɑːrlz.hɑːf

Jarmaine dʒɑːˈmeɪn, ⓤⓢ dʒɑːr-

Jarman ˈdʒɑː.mən, ⓤⓢ ˈdʒɑːr-

Jarndyce ˈdʒɑːn.daɪs, ⓤⓢ ˈdʒɑːrn-

Jarratt ˈdʒær.ət, ⓤⓢ ˈdʒer-, ˈdʒær-

Jarrell dʒəˈrel, ⓤⓢ dʒəˈrel; ⓤⓢ ˈdʒer.əl, ˈdʒær-

Jarrett ˈdʒær.ət, ⓤⓢ ˈdʒer-, ˈdʒær-

Jarrod ˈdʒær.əd, ⓤⓢ ˈdʒer-, ˈdʒær-

Jarrold ˈdʒær.əld, ⓤⓢ ˈdʒer-, ˈdʒær-

Jarrow ˈdʒær.əʊ, ⓤⓢ ˈdʒer.oʊ, ˈdʒær-

Jarry ˈʒær.i, ⓤⓢ ʒɑːˈriː

Jaruzelski ˌjær.uˈzel.ski, ⓤⓢ ˌjɑː.ruːˈ-

jarvey ˈdʒɑː.vi, ⓤⓢ ˈdʒɑːr- **-s** -z

Jarvie ˈdʒɑː.vi, ⓤⓢ ˈdʒɑːr-

Jarvis ˈdʒɑː.vɪs, ⓤⓢ ˈdʒɑːr-

Jas. (abbrev. for **James**) dʒeɪmz, dʒæs, ⓤⓢ dʒeɪmz

jasey ˈdʒeɪ.zi **-s** -z

Jasher ˈdʒæʃ.əʳ, ⓤⓢ -ɚ

jasmine, J~ ˈdʒæz.mɪn, ˈdʒæs-

Jason ˈdʒeɪ.sən

jasper, J~ ˈdʒæs.pəʳ, ⓤⓢ ˈdʒæs.pɚ **-s** -z

Jaspers ˈjæs.pəz, ⓤⓢ ˈjɑː.spɚz

Jassy ˈdʒæs.i

jaundice ˈdʒɔːn.dɪs, ⓤⓢ ˈdʒɑːn-, ˈdʒɔːn- **-d** -t

jaun|t dʒɔːn|t, ⓤⓢ dʒɑːn|t, dʒɔːn|t **-ts** -ts **-ting/ly** -tɪŋ/li, ⓤⓢ -t̬ɪŋ/li **-ted** -tɪd, ⓤⓢ -t̬ɪd

jaunt|y ˈdʒɔːn.t|i, ⓤⓢ ˈdʒɑːn.t̬|i, ˈdʒɔːn- **-ier** -i.əʳ, ⓤⓢ -i.ɚ **-iest** -i.ɪst, -i.əst **-ily** -əl.i, -ɪ.li **-iness** -ɪ.nəs, -ɪ.nɪs

Java ˈdʒɑː.və, ⓤⓢ ˈdʒɑː-, ˈdʒæv.ə

> Note: **Java coffee** is more likely to be /ˈdʒæv.ə/ in the US.

Javan *of Java:* ˈdʒɑː.vən, ⓤⓢ ˈdʒɑː-, ˈdʒæv.ən *biblical name:* ˈdʒeɪ.væn

Javanese ˌdʒɑː.vənˈiːz, ⓤⓢ -ˈiːz, -ˈiːs *stress shift:* **ˌJavanese ˈpeople**

javelin, J~ ˈdʒæv.əl.ɪn, -lɪn **-s** -z

jaw dʒɔː, ⓤⓢ dʒɑː, dʒɔː **-s** -z **-ing** -ɪŋ **-ed** -d

jawbone ˈdʒɔː.bəʊn, ⓤⓢ ˈdʒɑː.boʊn, ˈdʒɔː- **-s** -z

jawboning ˈdʒɔːˌbəʊ.nɪŋ, ⓤⓢ ˈdʒɑːˌboʊ-, ˈdʒɔː-

jawbreak|er ˈdʒɔːˌbreɪ.k|ə, ⓤⓢ ˈdʒɑːˌbreɪ.k|ɚ, ˈdʒɔː- **-ers** -əz, ⓤⓢ -ɚz **-ing** -ɪŋ

jay, J~ dʒeɪ **-s** -z

Jayne dʒeɪn

jaywalk ˈdʒeɪ.wɔːk, ⓤⓢ -wɑːk, -wɔːk **-s** -s **-ing** -ɪŋ **-ed** -t **-er/s** -əʳ/z, ⓤⓢ -ɚ/z

jazz dʒæz **ˈjazz ˌband**

jazz|y ˈdʒæz|.i **-ier** -i.əʳ, ⓤⓢ -i.ɚ **-iest** -i.ɪst, -i.əst **-ily** -əl.i, -ɪ.li **-iness** -ɪ.nəs, -ɪ.nɪs

JCB ˌdʒeɪ.siːˈbiː

J-cloth® ˈdʒeɪ.klɒθ, ⓤⓢ -klɑːθ **-s** -s

JD ˌdʒeɪˈdiː

Jeakes dʒeɪks

jealous ˈdʒel.əs **-ly** -li **-ness** -nəs, -nɪs

jealous|y ˈdʒel.ə.s|i **-ies** -iz

jean *cotton fabric:* dʒeɪn, ⓤⓢ dʒiːn

Jean *female name:* dʒiːn *French name:* ʒɑ̃ːn, ⓤⓢ ʒɑ̃ːn

Jeanette dʒəˈnet, dʒɪ-

Jeanne *English name:* dʒæn, dʒiːn *French name:* ʒæn, ⓤⓢ ʒɑ̃ːn

Jeannie ˈdʒiː.ni

jeans dʒiːnz

Jeavons ˈdʒev.ənz

Jebb dʒeb

Jebusite ˈdʒeb.ju.zaɪt, ⓤⓢ -jə.saɪt **-s** -s

Jed dʒed

Jedburgh ˈdʒed.bər.ə, ⓤⓢ -bɚ.ə

Jeddah ˈdʒed.ə

Jedediah ˌdʒed.ɪˈdaɪ.ə

Jeep® dʒiːp **-s** -s

jeepers ˈdʒiː.pəz, ⓤⓢ -pɚz

jeer dʒɪəʳ, ⓤⓢ dʒɪr **-s** -z **-ing/ly** -ɪŋ/li **-ed** -d **-er/s** -əʳ/z, ⓤⓢ -ɚ/z

Jeeves dʒiːvz

jeez dʒiːz

Jeff dʒef

Jefferies ˈdʒef.riz

Jeffers ˈdʒef.əz, ⓤⓢ -ɚz

Jefferson ˈdʒef.ə.sən, ⓤⓢ ˈ-ɚ-

Jeffersonian ˌdʒef.əˈsəʊ.ni.ən, ⓤⓢ -ɚˈsoʊ-

Jeffery ˈdʒef.ri **-s** -z

Jeffrey ˈdʒef.ri **-s** -z

Jeffries ˈdʒef.riz

Jehoiachin dʒɪˈhɔɪ.ə.kɪn, dʒə-

Jehoiakim dʒɪˈhɔɪ.ə.kɪm, dʒə-

Jehoram dʒɪˈhɔː.rəm, dʒə-, -ræm, ⓤⓢ -ˈhɔːr.əm, -æm

Jehoshaphat dʒɪˈhɒʃ.ə.fæt, dʒə-, -ˈhɒs-, ⓤⓢ -ˈhɑː.ʃə-, -sə-

Jehovah dʒɪˈhəʊ.və, dʒə-, ⓤⓢ -ˈhoʊ- **Jeˌhovah's ˈwitness**

jehu, J~ ˈdʒiː.hjuː, ⓤⓢ -hjuː, -huː **-s** -z

jejune dʒɪˈdʒuːn, dʒə- **-ly** -li **-ness** -nəs, -nɪs

jejunum dʒɪˈdʒuː.nəm, dʒə- **-s** -z

Jekyll ˈdʒek.əl, -ɪl, ˈdʒiː.kɪl

jell dʒel **-s** -z **-ing** -ɪŋ **-ed** -d

jellaba(h) ˈdʒel.ə.bə **-s** -z

Jellicoe ˈdʒel.ɪ.kəʊ, ⓤⓢ -koʊ

Jell-O® ˈdʒel.əʊ, ⓤⓢ -oʊ

jello ˈdʒel.əʊ, ⓤⓢ -oʊ **-s** -z

jell|y ˈdʒel|.i **-ies** -iz **-ying** -i.ɪŋ **-ied** -id **ˈjelly ˌbag; ˈjelly ˌbaby; ˌjelly ˈbaby; ˈjelly ˌbean**

jellyfish ˈdʒel.i.fɪʃ **-es** -ɪz

jellyroll ˈdʒel.i.rəʊl, ⓤⓢ -roʊl **-s** -z

Jemima dʒɪˈmaɪ.mə, dʒə-

Jemma ˈdʒem.ə

jemm|y ˈdʒem|.i **-ies** -iz **-ying** -i.ɪŋ **-ied** -id

Jena ˈjeɪ.nə, ⓤⓢ -nɑː

je ne sais quoi ˌʒə.nə.seɪˈkwɑː, ⓤⓢ -seɪˈ-, -seˈ-

J

Jenkin ˈdʒeŋ.kɪn -s -z
Jenkinson ˈdʒeŋ.kɪn.sᵊn
Jenna ˈdʒen.ə
Jenner ˈdʒen.əʳ, ⓊⓈ -ɚ
jennet ˈdʒen.ɪt -s -s
Jennifer ˈdʒen.ɪ.fəʳ, ˈ-ə-, ⓊⓈ -fɚ
Jennings ˈdʒen.ɪŋz
jenn|y *in machinery:* ˈdʒen|.i *in billiards:* ˈdʒɪn|.i, ˈdʒen- -ies -iz
Jenny *female name:* ˈdʒen.i, ˈdʒɪn-, ⓊⓈ ˈdʒen-
Jensen ˈdʒent.sᵊn -s -z
jeopardiz|e, -is|e ˈdʒep.ə.daɪz, ⓊⓈ ˈ-ɚ- -es -ɪz -ing -ɪŋ -ed -d
jeopardy ˈdʒep.ə.di, ⓊⓈ ˈ-ɚ-
Jephthah ˈdʒef.θə
jerboa dʒɜːˈbəʊ.ə, dʒə-, ⓊⓈ dʒɚˈboʊ- -s -z
jeremiad ˌdʒer.ɪˈmaɪ.əd, -əˈ-, -æd, ⓊⓈ -əˈ- -s -z
Jeremiah ˌdʒer.ɪˈmaɪ.ə, -əˈ-, ⓊⓈ -əˈ-
Jeremy ˈdʒer.ə.mi, ˈ-ɪ-
Jerez həˈrez; *as if Spanish:* herˈeθ; ⓊⓈ -ˈres, -ˈreθ
Jericho ˈdʒer.ɪ.kəʊ, ⓊⓈ -koʊ
jerk dʒɜːk, ⓊⓈ dʒɝːk -s -s -ing -ɪŋ -ed -t
jerkin ˈdʒɜː.kɪn, ⓊⓈ ˈdʒɝː- -s -z
jerkwater ˈdʒɜːkˌwɔː.təʳ, ⓊⓈ ˈdʒɝːkˌwɑː.t̬ɚ, -ˌwɔː- ˈ**jerkwater** ˌ**town**
jerk|y ˈdʒɜː.k|i, ⓊⓈ ˈdʒɝː- -ier -i.əʳ, ⓊⓈ -i.ɚ -iest -i.ɪst, -i.əst -ily -ᵊl.i, -ɪ.li -iness -ɪ.nəs, -ɪ.nɪs
Jermaine dʒɜːˈmeɪn, dʒə-, dʒɜːr-, ⓊⓈ dʒɚ-
Jermyn ˈdʒɜː.mɪn, ⓊⓈ ˈdʒɝː-
jeroboam, J~ ˌdʒer.əˈbəʊ.əm, ⓊⓈ -ˈboʊ- -s -z
Jerome *Saint:* dʒəˈrəʊm, dʒerˈəʊm, dʒɪˈrəʊm, ⓊⓈ dʒəˈroʊm, dʒerˈoʊm, dʒɪˈroʊm *surname:* dʒəˈrəʊm, dʒerˈəʊm, dʒɪˈrəʊm, ˈdʒer.əm, ⓊⓈ dʒəˈroʊm, dʒerˈoʊm, dʒɪˈroʊm, ˈdʒer.əm

> Note: Jerome K. Jerome, the author, is pronounced /dʒəˈrəʊm/ ⓊⓈ /-ˈroʊm/.

Jerram ˈdʒer.əm
Jerrold ˈdʒer.ᵊld
jerr|y, J~ ˈdʒer|.i -ies -iz ˈ**jerry** ˌ**can**
jerry-build ˈdʒer.i.bɪld -s -z -ing -ɪŋ **jerry-built** ˈdʒer.i.bɪlt **jerry-builder/s** ˈdʒer.iˌbɪl.dəʳ/z, ⓊⓈ -dɚ/z
jersey, J~ ˈdʒɜː.zi, ⓊⓈ ˈdʒɝː- -s -z
Jerusalem dʒəˈruː.sᵊl.əm, dʒɪ-, -lem **Je**ˌ**rusalem** ˈ**artichoke**
Jervaulx ˈdʒɜː.vəʊ, ˈdʒɑː-, -vɪs, -vəs, ⓊⓈ ˈdʒɝː.voʊ, -vɪs, -vəs
Jervis ˈdʒɑː.vɪs, ˈdʒɜː.vɪs, ⓊⓈ ˈdʒɝː-
Jervois ˈdʒɜː.vɪs, ⓊⓈ ˈdʒɝː-
Jespersen ˈjes.pə.sᵊn, ⓊⓈ -pɚ-
jess, J~ dʒes -es -ɪz -ing -ɪŋ -ed -t
jessamine, J~ ˈdʒes.ə.mɪn
Jesse ˈdʒes.i
Jessel ˈdʒes.ᵊl
Jessica ˈdʒes.ɪ.kə
Jessie ˈdʒes.i
Jessop ˈdʒes.əp
jest dʒest -s -s -ing/ly -ɪŋ/li -ed -ɪd
jester ˈdʒes.təʳ, ⓊⓈ -tɚ -s -z
Jesu ˈdʒiː.zjuː, ⓊⓈ ˈdʒiː.zjuː, ˈdʒeɪ-, ˈjeɪ-, -suː, -zuː
Jesu|it ˈdʒez.ju|.ɪt, ˈ-u-, ˈdʒeʒ.u|.ɪt -its -ɪts -itism -ɪ.tɪ.zᵊm, ⓊⓈ -ɪ.t̬ɪ-
jesuitic ˌdʒez.juˈɪt.ɪk, -uˈ-, ˌdʒeʒ.uˈɪt-, ⓊⓈ -ˈɪt̬- -al -ᵊl -ally -ᵊl.i, -li
Jesus ˈdʒiː.zəs ˌ**Jesus** ˈ**Christ**
jet dʒet -s -s -ting -ɪŋ, ⓊⓈ ˈdʒet̬.ɪŋ -ted -ɪd, ⓊⓈ ˈdʒet̬.ɪd ˌ**jet** ˈ**engine**; ˈ**jet** ˌ**lag**; ˈ**jet** ˌ**set**; ˈ**jet** ˌ**setter**; ˈ**jet** ˌ**stream**
jeté ʒəˈteɪ -s -z
jetfoil ˈdʒet.fɔɪl -s -z
Jethro ˈdʒeθ.rəʊ, ⓊⓈ -roʊ
jetliner ˈdʒetˌlaɪ.nəʳ, ⓊⓈ -nɚ -s -z
jetsam ˈdʒet.səm, -sæm, ⓊⓈ -səm
jettison ˈdʒet.ɪ.sᵊn, -zᵊn, ⓊⓈ ˈdʒet̬.ə- -s -z -ing -ɪŋ -ed -d
jett|y ˈdʒet|.i, ⓊⓈ ˈdʒet̬- -ies -iz
Jetway® ˈdʒet.weɪ
jeu ʒɜː -s -z
jeunesse dorée ˌʒɜː.nes.dɔːˈreɪ, ⓊⓈ ʒɜːˌnes.dɔːˈ-
Jevons ˈdʒev.ᵊnz
Jew dʒuː -s -z ˌ**Jew's** ˈ**harp** ⓊⓈ ˈ**Jew's** ˌ**harp**
jewel, J~ ˈdʒuː.əl, dʒʊəl, ⓊⓈ ˈdʒuː.əl -s -z -(l)ing -ɪŋ -(l)ed -d
jewel(l)er ˈdʒuː.ə.ləʳ, ˈdʒʊə.ləʳ, ⓊⓈ ˈdʒuː.ə.lɚ, ˈdʒuː.lɚ -s -z
Jewell ˈdʒuː.əl, dʒʊəl, ⓊⓈ ˈdʒuː.əl
jewellery, jewelry ˈdʒuː.əl.ri, ˈdʒʊəl-, ⓊⓈ ˈdʒuː.əl-
Jewess ˈdʒuː.es, -ɪs, -əs; dʒuːˈes, ⓊⓈ ˈdʒuː.ɪs -es -ɪz
Jewett ˈdʒuː.ɪt
jewfish ˈdʒuː.fɪʃ -es -ɪz
Jewish ˈdʒuː.ɪʃ -ness -nəs, -nɪs
Jewry ˈdʒʊə.ri, ˈdʒuː-, ⓊⓈ ˈdʒuː.ri
Jewsbury ˈdʒuːz.bᵊr.i, ⓊⓈ -ˌber-
Jeyes dʒeɪz
Jezebel ˈdʒez.ə.bel, ˈ-ɪ-, -bᵊl
Jezreel ˈdʒez.ri.əl, ˌdʒezˈriːl
JFK ˌdʒeɪ.efˈkeɪ
Jhabvala ˌdʒɑːbˈvɑː.lə
Jiang Qing ˌdʒæŋˈtʃɪŋ
jiao dʒaʊ
jib dʒɪb -s -z -bing -ɪŋ -bed -d
jib-boom dʒɪbˈbuːm, ˈ-- -s -z
jib|e dʒaɪb -es -z -ing -ɪŋ -ed -d -er/s -əʳ/z, ⓊⓈ -ɚ/z
Jif® dʒɪf
jiff dʒɪf
jiff|y ˈdʒɪf|.i -ies -iz ˈ**Jiffy** ˌ**bag**®
jig dʒɪg -s -z -ging -ɪŋ -ged -d
jigger ˈdʒɪg.əʳ, ⓊⓈ -ɚ -s -z -ing -ɪŋ -ed -d
jiggered ˈdʒɪg.əd, ⓊⓈ -ɚd
jiggery-pokery ˌdʒɪg.ᵊr.iˈpəʊ.kᵊr.i, ⓊⓈ -ˈpoʊ-
jiggl|e ˈdʒɪg.ᵊl -es -z -ing -ɪŋ, ˈdʒɪg.lɪŋ -ed -d
jigsaw ˈdʒɪg.sɔː, ⓊⓈ -sɑː, -sɔː -s -z ˈ**jigsaw** ˌ**puzzle**
jihad dʒɪˈhæd, dʒə-, -ˈhɑːd, ⓊⓈ dʒiːˈhɑːd, ʒiː-, ˈdʒiː.hɑːd -i -i
Jill dʒɪl
jillaroo ˌdʒɪl.əˈruː -s -z
Jillian ˈdʒɪl.i.ən
jilt dʒɪlt -s -s -ing -ɪŋ, ⓊⓈ ˈdʒɪl.tɪŋ -ed -ɪd, ⓊⓈ ˈdʒɪl.tɪd
Jim dʒɪm -my -i
jim-dandy ˌdʒɪmˈdæn.di
jimjams ˈdʒɪm.dʒæmz
jimm|y, J~ ˈdʒɪm.i -ies -iz -ying -i.ɪŋ -ied -id
jimsonweed ˈdʒɪmp.sᵊn.wiːd
Jindal ˈdʒɪn.dᵊl
jingl|e, J~ ˈdʒɪŋ.gᵊl -es -z -ing -ɪŋ, ˈdʒɪŋ.glɪŋ -ed -d -y -i -er/s -əʳ/z, ⓊⓈ -ɚ/z
jingo, J~ ˈdʒɪŋ.gəʊ, ⓊⓈ -goʊ -es -z
jingo|ism ˈdʒɪŋ.gəʊ|.ɪ.zᵊm, ⓊⓈ -goʊ- -ist/s -ɪst/s
jingoistic ˌdʒɪŋ.gəʊˈɪs.tɪk, ⓊⓈ -goʊˈ- -ally -ᵊl.i, -li
jink dʒɪŋk -s -s -ing -ɪŋ -ed -t
jinks, J~ dʒɪŋks
jinn dʒɪn -s -z
Jinnah ˈdʒɪn.ə
jinrick|sha ˌdʒɪnˈrɪk|.ʃə, ⓊⓈ -ʃɑː, -ʃɔː -shas -ʃəz, ⓊⓈ -ʃɑːz, -ʃɔːz -shaw/s -ʃɔː/z, ⓊⓈ -ʃɑː/z, -ʃɔː/z
jinx dʒɪŋks -es -ɪz -ing -ɪŋ -ed -t
jitney ˈdʒɪt.ni -s -z
jitter ˈdʒɪt.əʳ, ⓊⓈ ˈdʒɪt̬.ɚ -s -z -ing -ɪŋ -ed -d
jitterbug ˈdʒɪt.ə.bʌg, ⓊⓈ ˈdʒɪt̬.ɚ- -s -z -ging -ɪŋ -ged -d
jitters ˈdʒɪt.əz, ⓊⓈ ˈdʒɪt̬.ɚz
jitter|y ˈdʒɪt.ᵊr|.i, ⓊⓈ ˈdʒɪt̬- -iness -ɪ.nəs, -ɪ.nɪs
jiujitsu ˌdʒuːˈdʒɪt.suː
jiv|e dʒaɪv -es -z -ing -ɪŋ -ed -d
jnr, J~ (abbrev. for **junior**) ˈdʒuː.ni.əʳ, ⓊⓈ ˈ-njɚ
jo, Jo dʒəʊ, ⓊⓈ dʒoʊ -es -z
Joab ˈdʒəʊ.æb, ⓊⓈ ˈdʒoʊ-
Joachim ˈjəʊ.ə.kɪm, ⓊⓈ ˈjoʊ-
Joan dʒəʊn, ⓊⓈ dʒoʊn
Joanna dʒəʊˈæn.ə, ⓊⓈ dʒoʊ-
Joanne dʒəʊˈæn, ⓊⓈ dʒoʊ-
Joash ˈdʒəʊ.æʃ, ⓊⓈ ˈdʒoʊ-
job dʒɒb, ⓊⓈ dʒɑːb -s -z -bing -ɪŋ -bed -d ˈ**Job** ˌ**Centre**; ˈ**job** **des**ˌ**cription**; ˌ**job** **des**ˈ**cription**; ˌ**job** ˈ**lot** ⓊⓈ ˈ**job** ˌ**lot**; ˈ**job** ˌ**share**; **give something** ˌ**up as a** ˌ**bad** ˈ**job**
Job dʒəʊb, ⓊⓈ dʒoʊb
jobber ˈdʒɒb.əʳ, ⓊⓈ ˈdʒɑː.bɚ -s -z
jobbery ˈdʒɒb.ᵊr.i, ⓊⓈ ˈdʒɑː.bɚ-
job-hop ˈdʒɒb.hɒp, ⓊⓈ ˈdʒɑːb.hɑːp -s -s -ping -ɪŋ -ped -t -per/s -əʳ/z, ⓊⓈ -ɚ/z
jobhunting ˈdʒɒbˌhʌn.tɪŋ, ⓊⓈ ˈdʒɑːbˌhʌn.t̬ɪŋ
jobless ˈdʒɒb.ləs, -lɪs, ⓊⓈ ˈdʒɑːb- -ness -nəs, -nɪs
jobmaster ˈdʒɒbˌmɑː.stəʳ, ⓊⓈ ˈdʒɑːbˌmæs.tɚ -s -z
jobseeker ˈdʒɒbˌsiː.kəʳ, ⓊⓈ ˈdʒɑːbˌsiː.kɚ -s -z
jobshar|e ˈdʒɒb.ʃeəʳ, ⓊⓈ ˈdʒɑːb.ʃer -ing -ɪŋ
jobsharing ˈdʒɒbˌʃeə.rɪŋ, ⓊⓈ ˈdʒɑːbˌʃer.ɪŋ

Jobson ˈdʒɒb.sən, ˈdʒəʊb-, (US) ˈdʒɑːb-, ˈdʒoʊb-
Jocasta dʒəʊˈkæs.tə, (US) dʒoʊ-
Jocelyn ˈdʒɒs.lɪn, ˈ-əl.ɪn, (US) ˈdʒɑː.səl.ɪn, ˈ-slɪn
jock, J~ dʒɒk, (US) dʒɑːk
jockey ˈdʒɒk.i, (US) ˈdʒɑː.ki **-s** -z **-ing** -ɪŋ **-ed** -d **-ship** -ʃɪp ˈ**Jockey** ˌ**Club**
jockstrap ˈdʒɒk.stræp, (US) ˈdʒɑːk- **-s** -s
jocose dʒəʊˈkəʊs, (US) dʒoʊˈkoʊs, dʒə- **-ly** -li **-ness** -nəs, -nɪs
jocosity dʒəʊˈkɒs.ə.ti, -ɪ.ti, (US) dʒoʊˈkɑː.sə.t̬i
jocular ˈdʒɒk.jə.ləʳ, -jʊ-, (US) ˈdʒɑː.kjə.lɚ **-ly** -li
jocularity ˌdʒɒk.jəˈlær.ə.ti, -jʊˈ-, -ɪ.ti, (US) ˌdʒɑː.kjəˈler.ə.t̬i, -ˈlær-
jocund ˈdʒɒk.ənd, ˈdʒəʊ.kənd, -kʌnd, (US) ˈdʒɑː.kənd, ˈdʒoʊ- **-ly** -li **-ness** -nəs, -nɪs
jocundity dʒəʊˈkʌn.də.ti, dʒɒkˈʌn-, -dɪ-, (US) dʒoʊˈkʌn.də.t̬i
jod jɒd, (US) jɑːd; *as if Hebrew:* (US) jʊd **-s** -z
jodhpurs ˈdʒɒd.pəz, -pɜːz, (US) ˈdʒɑːd.pɚz
Jodi ˈdʒəʊ.di, (US) ˈdʒoʊ-
Jodie ˈdʒəʊ.di, (US) ˈdʒoʊ-
Jodrell ˈdʒɒd.rəl, (US) ˈdʒɑː.drəl ˌ**Jodrell** ˈ**Bank**
Jody ˈdʒəʊ.di, (US) ˈdʒoʊ-
Joe dʒəʊ, (US) dʒoʊ ˌ**Joe** ˈ**Bloggs**; ˌ**Joe** ˈ**Blow**; ˌ**Joe** ˈ**Public**
Joel ˈdʒəʊ.əl, -el, (US) ˈdʒoʊ-
Joely ˈdʒəʊ.li, ˈdʒəʊ.ə.li, (US) ˈdʒoʊ-
joey, J~ ˈdʒəʊ.i, (US) ˈdʒoʊ- **-s** -z
Joffe ˈdʒɒf.i, (US) ˈdʒɑː.fi
jog dʒɒg, (US) dʒɑːg **-s** -z **-ging** -ɪŋ **-ged** -d **-ger/s** -əʳ/z, (US) -ɚ/z ˈ**jog** ˌ**trot**
joggl|e ˈdʒɒg.əl, (US) ˈdʒɑː.gəl **-es** -z **-ing** -ɪŋ, ˈdʒɒg.lɪŋ, (US) ˈdʒɑː.glɪŋ **-ed** -d **-er/s** -əʳ/z, (US) -ɚ/z
johannes *coin:* dʒəʊˈæn.ɪs, (US) dʒoʊˈhæn.iːz **-es** -ɪz
Johannes *personal name:* jəʊˈhæn.ɪs, (US) joʊˈhɑː.nɪs
Johannesburg dʒəʊˈhæn.ɪs.bɜːg, -ɪz-, -əs-, -əz-, (US) dʒoʊˈhæn.ɪs.bɝːg, joʊˈhɑː.nɪs-

> Note: There exists also a local pronunciation /dʒəˈhɒn.ɪs.bɜːg/, which is used by many English-speaking South Africans.

Johannine dʒəʊˈhæn.aɪn, (US) dʒoʊˈhæn.ɪn, -aɪn
Johannisburger jəʊˈhæn.ɪsˌbɜː.gəʳ, -ɪz-, -əs-, -əz-, (US) dʒoʊˈhæn.ɪsˌbɝː.gɚ, joʊˈhɑː.nɪs-
Johansson jəʊˈhæn.sən, (US) joʊˈ-
john, J~ dʒɒn, (US) dʒɑːn **-s** -z ˌ**John** ˈ**Bull**; ˌ**John** ˈ**Doe**; ˌ**John** ˈ**Dory**
Johnes dʒəʊnz, dʒɒnz, (US) dʒoʊnz, dʒɑːnz
Johnian ˈdʒəʊ.ni.ən, (US) ˈdʒoʊ- **-s** -z
johnn|y, J~ ˈdʒɒn|.i, (US) ˈdʒɑː.n|i **-ies** -iz
Johnny-come-latel|y ˌdʒɒn.i.kʌmˈleɪt.l|i, (US) ˌdʒɑː.ni- **-ies** -z
John o' Groat's ˌdʒɒn.əˈgrəʊts, (US) ˌdʒɑːn.əˈgroʊts
Johns dʒɒnz, (US) dʒɑːnz
Johnson ˈdʒɒnt.sən, (US) ˈdʒɑːnt-
Johnsonese ˌdʒɒnt.sənˈiːz, (US) ˌdʒɑːnt-
Johnsonian dʒɒnˈsəʊ.ni.ən, (US) dʒɑːnˈsoʊ-
Johnston(e) ˈdʒɒnt.stən, -sən, (US) ˈdʒɑːnt-
Johor(e) Baharu ˌdʒəʊ.hɔːˈbɑː.ruː, (US) dʒəˌhɔːrˈbɑːr.uː
Johore dʒəʊˈhɔːʳ, (US) dʒəˈhɔːr
joie de vivre ˌʒwɑː.dəˈviː.vrə, -ˈviːv
join dʒɔɪn **-s** -z **-ing** -ɪŋ **-ed** -d
joinder ˈdʒɔɪn.dəʳ, (US) -dɚ
joined-up ˌdʒɔɪndˈʌp *stress shift:* ˌ**joined-up** ˈ**thinking**
joiner ˈdʒɔɪ.nəʳ, (US) -nɚ **-s** -z
joinery ˈdʒɔɪ.nər.i
joint dʒɔɪnt **-s** -s **-ly** -li **-ing** -ɪŋ, (US) ˈdʒɔɪn.t̬ɪŋ **-ed** -ɪd, (US) ˈdʒɔɪn.t̬ɪd **-er/s** -əʳ/z, (US) ˈdʒɔɪn.t̬ɚ/z
joint-stock ˌdʒɔɪntˈstɒk, (US) -ˈstɑːk *stress shift:* ˌ**joint-stock** ˈ**bank**
jointure ˈdʒɔɪn.tʃəʳ, (US) -tʃɚ **-s** -z
Joinville ˈʒwæ̃n.viːl, (US) -ˈ-
joist dʒɔɪst **-s** -s
jojoba həʊˈhəʊ.bə, (US) hoʊˈhoʊ-, hə-
jok|e dʒəʊk, (US) dʒoʊk **-es** -s **-ing/ly** -ɪŋ/li **-ed** -t **-(e)y** -i
joker ˈdʒəʊ.kəʳ, (US) ˈdʒoʊ.kɚ **-s** -z
Jolie ˈdʒəʊ.li; dʒəʊˈliː, ʒəʊ-, (US) ˈdʒoʊ.li
Jolley ˈdʒɒl.i, (US) ˈdʒɑː.li
Jolliffe ˈdʒɒl.ɪf, (US) ˈdʒɑː.lɪf
jollification ˌdʒɒl.ɪ.fɪˈkeɪ.ʃən, ˌ-ə-, (US) ˌdʒɑː.lə- **-s** -z
jolli|fy ˈdʒɒl.ɪ|.faɪ, ˈ-ə-, (US) ˈdʒɑː.lɪ-, ˈ-lə- **-fies** -faɪz **-fying** -faɪ.ɪŋ **-fied** -faɪd
jollit|y ˈdʒɒl.ə.t|i, -ɪ.t|i, (US) ˈdʒɑː.lə.t̬|i **-ies** -iz
joll|y, J~ ˈdʒɒl|.i, (US) ˈdʒɑː.l|i **-ier** -i.əʳ, (US) -i.ɚ **-iest** -i.ɪst, -i.əst **-ily** -əl.i, -ɪ.li **-iness** -ɪ.nəs, -ɪ.nɪs **-ies** -ɪz **-ying** -i.ɪŋ **-ied** -ɪd ˌ**Jolly** ˈ**Roger**
jollyboat ˈdʒɒl.i.bəʊt, (US) ˈdʒɑː.li.boʊt **-s** -s
Jolson ˈdʒɒl.sən, ˈdʒəʊl-, (US) ˈdʒoʊl-
jolt dʒəʊlt, (US) dʒoʊlt **-s** -s **-ing/ly** -ɪŋ/li, (US) ˈdʒoʊl.tɪŋ/li **-ed** -ɪd, (US) ˈdʒoʊl.tɪd
jolt|y ˈdʒəʊl.t|i, (US) ˈdʒoʊl.t|i **-ier** -i.əʳ, (US) -i.ɚ **-iest** -i.ɪst, -i.əst **-ily** -əl.i, -ɪ.li **-iness** -ɪ.nəs, -ɪ.nɪs
Jolyon ˈdʒəʊ.li.ən, ˈdʒɒl.i-, (US) ˈdʒoʊ.li-, ˈdʒɑː-
Jon dʒɒn, (US) dʒɑːn
Jonah ˈdʒəʊ.nə, (US) ˈdʒoʊ-
Jonas ˈdʒəʊ.nəs, -næs, (US) ˈdʒoʊ.nəs
Jonathan, Jonathon ˈdʒɒn.ə.θən, (US) ˈdʒɑː.nə-
jones dʒəʊnz, (US) dʒoʊnz **-es** -ɪz **-ing** -ɪŋ **-d** -d
Jones dʒəʊnz, (US) dʒoʊnz **-es** -ɪz
Jonesboro ˈdʒəʊnz.bər.ə, (US) ˈdʒoʊnz.bɚ.oʊ
jongleur ʒɔ̃ːŋˈglɜːʳ, ʒɔːŋ-, ʒɒŋ-, (US) ˈdʒɑːŋ.glɚ **-s** -z
jonquil ˈdʒɒŋ.kwɪl, -kwəl, (US) ˈdʒɑːŋ.kwɪl, ˈdʒɑːn- **-s** -z
Jonson ˈdʒɒnt.sən, (US) ˈdʒɑːnt-
Jonty ˈdʒɒn.ti, (US) ˈdʒɑːn-
Joplin ˈdʒɒp.lɪn, (US) ˈdʒɑːp-
Joppa ˈdʒɒp.ə, (US) ˈdʒɑː.pə
Jopson ˈdʒɒp.sən, (US) ˈdʒɑːp-
Joram ˈdʒɔː.rəm, -ræm, (US) ˈdʒɔːr.əm
Jordan ˈdʒɔː.dən, (US) ˈdʒɔːr- **-s** -z
Jordanian dʒɔːˈdeɪ.ni.ən, (US) dʒɔːr- **-s** -z
Jorge ˈhɔː.heɪ; *as if Spanish:* ˈxɔː.xeɪ; (US) ˈhɔːr.heɪ
jorum ˈdʒɔː.rəm, (US) ˈdʒɔːr.əm, ˈdʒoʊ.rəm **-s** -z
Josceline ˈdʒɒs.lɪn, ˈ-əl.ɪn, (US) ˈdʒɑː.səl.ɪn, ˈ-slɪn
José, Jose həʊˈzeɪ, -ˈseɪ, (US) hoʊ-
joseph, J~ ˈdʒəʊ.zɪf, -zəf, (US) ˈdʒoʊ- **-s** -s
Josephine ˈdʒəʊ.zə.fiːn, -zɪ-, (US) ˈdʒoʊ-
Josephus dʒəʊˈsiː.fəs, (US) dʒoʊ-
josh, J~ dʒɒʃ, (US) dʒɑːʃ **-es** -ɪz **-ing/ly** -ɪŋ/li **-ed** -t **-er/s** -əʳ/z, (US) -ɚ/z
Joshua ˈdʒɒʃ.ju.ə, ˈ-u-, (US) ˈdʒɑːʃ-
Josiah dʒəʊˈsaɪ.ə, -ˈzaɪ-, (US) dʒoʊ-
Josias dʒəʊˈsaɪ.əs, -ˈzaɪ-, (US) dʒoʊ-
Josie ˈdʒəʊ.zi, -si, (US) ˈdʒoʊ-
Jospin ˈʒɒs.pæ̃ŋ, -ˈ-, dʒɑːsˈpæ̃ŋ
joss, J~ dʒɒs, (US) dʒɑːs **-es** -ɪz ˈ**joss** **house**; ˈ**joss** ˌ**stick**
Jost jəʊst, (US) joʊst
jostl|e ˈdʒɒs.əl, (US) ˈdʒɑː.səl **-es** -z **-ing** -ɪŋ, ˈdʒɒs.lɪŋ, (US) ˈdʒɑː.slɪŋ **-ed** -d **-er/s** -əʳ/z, (US) -ɚ/z
jot dʒɒt, (US) dʒɑːt **-s** -s **-ting/s** -ɪŋ/z, (US) ˈdʒɑː.t̬ɪŋ/z **-ted** -ɪd, (US) ˈdʒɑː.t̬ɪd
jotter ˈdʒɒt.əʳ, (US) ˈdʒɑː.t̬ɚ **-s** -z
joule *unit of energy:* dʒuːl, dʒaʊl **-s** -z
Joule *English surname:* dʒuːl, dʒəʊl, dʒaʊl, (US) dʒuːl, dʒoʊl, dʒaʊl
jounc|e dʒaʊnts **-es** -ɪz **-ing** -ɪŋ **-ed** -t
journal ˈdʒɜː.nəl, (US) ˈdʒɝː- **-s** -z
journalese ˌdʒɜː.nəlˈiːz, (US) ˌdʒɝː-
journal|ism ˈdʒɜː.nəl|.ɪ.zəm, (US) ˈdʒɝː- **-ist/s** -ɪst/s
journalistic ˌdʒɜː.nəlˈɪs.tɪk, (US) ˌdʒɝː- **-ally** -əl.i, -li
journaliz|e, -is|e ˈdʒɜː.nəl.aɪz, (US) ˈdʒɝː- **-es** -ɪz **-ing** -ɪŋ **-ed** -d
journey ˈdʒɜː.ni, (US) ˈdʒɝː- **-s** -z **-ing/s** -ɪŋ/z **-ed** -d
journey|man ˈdʒɜː.ni|.mən, (US) ˈdʒɝː- **-men** -mən
journo ˈdʒɜː.nəʊ, (US) ˈdʒɝː.noʊ **-s** -z
joust dʒaʊst **-s** -s **-ing** -ɪŋ **-ed** -ɪd **-er/s** -əʳ/z, (US) -ɚ/z
Jove dʒəʊv, (US) dʒoʊv
jovial ˈdʒəʊ.vi.əl, (US) ˈdʒoʊ- **-ly** -i **-ness** -nəs, -nɪs

J

joviality ˌdʒəʊ.viˈæl.ə.ti, -ɪ.ti, (US) ˌdʒoʊ.viˈæl.ə.t̬i
Jowell ˈdʒaʊ.əl, ˈdʒəʊ.əl, (US) ˈdʒaʊ.əl, ˈdʒoʊ.əl
Jowett, Jowitt ˈdʒaʊ.ɪt, ˈdʒəʊ-, (US) ˈdʒaʊ-, ˈdʒoʊ-
jowl dʒaʊl **-s** -z
jowly ˈdʒaʊ.li
joy, J~ dʒɔɪ **-s** -z **-ing** -ɪŋ **-ed** -d
Joyce dʒɔɪs
joyful ˈdʒɔɪ.fəl, -fʊl **-lest** -ɪst, -əst **-ly** -i **-ness** -nəs, -nɪs
joyless ˈdʒɔɪ.ləs, -lɪs **-ly** -li **-ness** -nəs, -nɪs
joyous ˈdʒɔɪ.əs **-ly** -li **-ness** -nəs, -nɪs
joypad ˈdʒɔɪ.pæd **-s** -z
joy|ride ˈdʒɔɪ|.raɪd **-rides** -raɪdz **-riding** -ˌraɪ.dɪŋ **-rode** -rəʊd, (US) -roʊd **-ridden** -rɪd.ən **-rider/s** -ˌraɪ.dər/z, (US) -dɚ/z
joystick ˈdʒɔɪ.stɪk **-s** -s
JPEG ˈdʒeɪ.peg
jr, Jr (abbrev. for **junior**) ˈdʒuː.ni.ər, (US) ˈ-njɚ
Juan *h*wɑːn; ˈdʒuː.ən; *as if Spanish:* xwɑːn; xwæn, (US) *h*wɑːn

> Note: In Byron's Don Juan, the pronunciation is /ˈdʒuː.ən/ in both British and American English.

Juan Carlos ˌ*h*wɑːnˈkɑː.lɒs, ˌ*h*wɑːŋ-; *as if Spanish:* ˌxwɑːn-; ˌxwæn-, (US) ˌ*h*wɑːnˈkɑːr.loʊs
Juan Fernandez ˌ*h*wɑːn.fəˈnæn.dez, -des; *as if Spanish:* ˌxwɑːn.fəˈnæn.dez; ˌxwæn-, (US) ˌ*h*wɑːn.fɚˈnɑːn.des
Juanita ˌdʒuː.əˈniː.tə; hwɑːˈniː.tə, hwænˈiː, (US) *h*wɑːˈniː.t̬ə, *h*wə-
jubilant ˈdʒuː.bɪ.lənt, -bəl.ənt **-ly** -li
jubi|late v ˈdʒuː.bɪ|.leɪt, -bə- **-lates** -leɪts **-lating** -leɪ.tɪŋ, (US) -leɪ.t̬ɪŋ **-lated** -leɪ.tɪd, (US) -leɪ.t̬ɪd
Jubilate n ˌdʒuː.bɪˈlɑː.teɪ, ˌjuː-, -bəˈ-, -ti, (US) ˌjuː.biːˈlɑː.teɪ **-s** -z
jubilation ˌdʒuː.bɪˈleɪ.ʃən, -bəˈ- **-s** -z
jubilee ˈdʒuː.bɪ.liː, -bə-, ˌ--ˈ- **-s** -z
Juda(h) ˈdʒuː.də
Judae|a dʒuːˈdiː|.ə **-an/s** -ən/z
Judaic dʒuːˈdeɪ.ɪk **-al** -əl **-ally** -əl.i, -li
Juda|ism ˈdʒuː.deɪ|.ɪ.zəm, -di-, (US) -deɪ-, -di-, -də- **-ist/s** -ɪst/s
judaiz|e, -is|e ˈdʒuː.deɪ.aɪz, (US) -deɪ-, -di-, -də- **-es** -ɪz **-ing** -ɪŋ **-ed** -d **-er/s** -ər/z, (US) -ɚ/z
Judas ˈdʒuː.dəs **-es** -ɪz ˈ**Judas** ˌ**tree**
Judd dʒʌd
judder ˈdʒʌd.ər, (US) -ɚ **-s** -z **-ing** -ɪŋ **-ed** -d
Jude dʒuːd
Jude|a dʒuːˈdiː|.ə **-an/s** -ən/z
judg|e, J~ dʒʌdʒ **-es** -ɪz **-ing** -ɪŋ **-ed** -d
judgeship ˈdʒʌdʒ.ʃɪp, ˈdʒʌd- **-s** -s
judg(e)ment ˈdʒʌdʒ.mənt **-s** -s ˈ**Judgement** ˌ**Day**
judgmental dʒʌdʒˈmen.təl, (US) -t̬əl **-ly** -i
judicator|y ˈdʒuː.dɪ.kə.tər|.i, (US) -tɔːr- **-ies** -iz
judicature ˈdʒuː.dɪ.kə.tʃər, -tjʊər, (US) -tʃɚ
judicial dʒuːˈdɪʃ.əl **-ly** -i **ju**ˌ**dicial re**ˈ**view**
judiciar|y dʒuːˈdɪʃ.ər|.i, -i.ər-, (US) -i.er-, -ˈdɪʃ.ɚ-, -i.ɚ- **-ies** -iz
judicious dʒuːˈdɪʃ.əs **-ly** -li **-ness** -nəs, -nɪs
Judith ˈdʒuː.dɪθ
judo ˈdʒuː.dəʊ, (US) -doʊ
Judson ˈdʒʌd.sən
Judy ˈdʒuː.di
jug dʒʌg **-s** -z **-ging** -ɪŋ **-ged** -d
jugful ˈdʒʌg.fʊl **-s** -z
juggernaut, J~ ˈdʒʌg.ə.nɔːt, (US) -ɚ.nɑːt, -nɔːt **-s** -s
juggins, J~ ˈdʒʌg.ɪnz **-es** -ɪz
juggl|e ˈdʒʌg.əl **-es** -z **-ing** -ɪŋ, ˈdʒʌg.lɪŋ **-ed** -d **-er/s** -ər/z, ˈdʒʌg.lər/z, (US) -ɚ/z, ˈdʒʌg.lɚ/z
jugglery ˈdʒʌg.lər.i
Jugoslav ˈjuː.gəʊ.slɑːv, ˌ--ˈ-, (US) ˈjuː.goʊ.slɑːv **-s** -z
Jugoslavi|a ˌjuː.gəʊˈslɑː.vi|.ə, (US) -goʊˈ- **-an** -ən
jugular ˈdʒʌg.jə.lər, -jʊ-, (US) -lɚ ˌ**jugular** ˈ**vein**; ˈ**jugular** ˌ**vein** (US) ˈ**jugular** ˌ**vein**
Jugurtha dʒuˈgɜː.θə, ju-, (US) dʒuːˈgɝː-
juic|e dʒuːs **-es** -ɪz **-ing** -ɪŋ **-ed** -t **-er/s** -ər/z, (US) -ɚ/z
juic|y ˈdʒuː.s|i **-ier** -i.ər, (US) -i.ɚ **-iest** -i.ɪst, -i.əst **-ily** -əl.i, -ɪ.li **-iness** -ɪ.nəs, -ɪ.nɪs
Juilliard ˈdʒuː.li.ɑːd, (US) -ɑːrd
jujitsu dʒuːˈdʒɪt.suː
jujube ˈdʒuː.dʒuːb **-s** -z
jukebox ˈdʒuːk.bɒks, (US) -bɑːks **-es** -ɪz
Jukes dʒuːks
Jul. (abbrev. for **July**) dʒʊˈlaɪ, dʒə-, dʒuː-
julep ˈdʒuː.lɪp, -lep, -ləp, (US) -ləp **-s** -s
Julia ˈdʒuː.li.ə, (US) ˈdʒuːl.jə
Julian ˈdʒuː.li.ən, (US) ˈdʒuːl.jən
Juliana ˌdʒuː.liˈɑː.nə, (US) -ˈæn.ə, -ˈɑː.nə
Julie ˈdʒuː.li
julienne ˌdʒuː.liˈen, ʒuː-, (US) ˌdʒuː-
Juliet ˈdʒuː.li.ət; ˌdʒuː.liˈet, (US) ˈdʒuː.li.et, -ɪt; (US) ˌdʒuː.liˈet; (US) ˈdʒuːl.jɪt
Juliette ˌdʒuː.liˈet, ˈ---
Julius ˈdʒuː.li.əs, (US) ˈdʒuːl.jəs
Julius Caesar ˌdʒuː.li.əsˈsiː.zər, (US) ˌdʒuːl.jəsˈsiː.zɚ
Jul|y dʒʊˈl|aɪ, dʒə-, ˌdʒuː- **-ies** -aɪz
Julyan ˈdʒuː.li.ən, (US) ˈdʒuːl.jən
jumbl|e ˈdʒʌm.bəl **-es** -z **-ing** -ɪŋ, ˈdʒʌm.blɪŋ **-ed** -d ˈ**jumble** ˌ**sale**
Jumbl|y ˈdʒʌm.bl|i **-ies** -iz
jumbo, J~ ˈdʒʌm.bəʊ, (US) -boʊ **-s** -z ˌ**jumbo** ˈ**jet**; ˈ**jumbo** ˌ**jet**
Jumna ˈdʒʌm.nə
jump dʒʌmp **-s** -s **-ing** -ɪŋ **-ed** -t **-er/s** -ər/z, (US) -ɚ/z ˈ**jumper** ˌ**cables**; ˌ**jumping** ˈ**jack** (US) ˈ**jumping** ˌ**jack**; ˈ**jump** ˌ**leads**; ˈ**jump** ˌ**rope**; ˌ**jump the** ˈ**gun**
jumped-up ˌdʒʌmptˈʌp *stress shift:* ˌ**jumped-up** ˈ**tyrant**
jumper ˈdʒʌm.pər, (US) -pɚ **-s** -z
jump-jet ˈdʒʌmp.dʒet **-s** -s
jump-off ˈdʒʌmp.ɒf, (US) -ɑːf **-s** -s
jump|-start ˈdʒʌmp|.stɑːt, (US) -stɑːrt **-starts** -stɑːts, (US) -stɑːrts **-starting** -ˌstɑː.tɪŋ, (US) -ˌstɑːr.t̬ɪŋ **-started** -ˌstɑː.tɪd, (US) -ˌstɑːr.t̬ɪd
jumpsuit ˈdʒʌmp.suːt, -sjuːt, (US) -suːt **-s** -s
jump|y ˈdʒʌm.p|i **-ier** -i.ər, (US) -i.ɚ **-iest** -i.ɪst, -i.əst **-ily** -əl.i, -ɪ.li **-iness** -ɪ.nəs, -ɪ.nɪs
Jun. (abbrev. for **June**) dʒuːn
jun. (abbrev. for **junior**) ˈdʒuː.ni.ər, (US) ˈ-njɚ
junction ˈdʒʌŋ*k*.ʃən **-s** -z ˈ**junction** ˌ**box**
juncture ˈdʒʌŋ*k*.*t*ʃər, (US) -tʃɚ **-s** -z
June dʒuːn **-s** -z
Juneau ˈdʒuː.nəʊ, -ˈ-, (US) ˈdʒuː.noʊ
Jung jʊŋ
Jungfrau ˈjʊŋ.fraʊ
Jungian ˈjʊŋ.i.ən **-s** -z
jungl|e ˈdʒʌŋ.gəl **-es** -z **-y** -i ˈ**jungle** ˌ**fowl**; ˈ**jungle** ˌ**gym**; ˌ**jungle** ˈ**gym**
junior ˈdʒuː.ni.ər, (US) ˈ-njɚ **-s** -z
juniority ˌdʒuː.niˈɒr.ə.ti, -ɪ.ti, (US) -ˈɔːr.ə.t̬i
juniper ˈdʒuː.nɪ.pər, -nə-, (US) -pɚ **-s** -z
Junius ˈdʒuː.ni.əs, (US) -njəs
junk dʒʌŋk **-s** -s **-ing** -ɪŋ **-ed** -t ˈ**junk** ˌ**bond**; ˈ**junk** ˌ**food**; ˌ**junk** ˈ**food**; ˈ**junk** ˌ**mail**; ˌ**junk** ˈ**mail**; ˈ**junk** ˌ**shop**
junker, J~ ˈjʊŋ.kər, (US) -kɚ *old car:* ˈdʒʌŋ.kər, (US) -kɚ **-s** -z
jun|ket ˈdʒʌŋ|.kɪt **-kets** -kɪts **-keting** -kɪ.tɪŋ, (US) -kɪ.t̬ɪŋ **-keted** -kɪ.tɪd, (US) -t̬ɪd
junkie ˈdʒʌŋ.ki **-s** -z
junkyard ˈdʒʌŋk.jɑːd, (US) -jɑːrd **-s** -z
Juno ˈdʒuː.nəʊ, (US) -noʊ
Junoesque ˌdʒuː.nəʊˈesk, (US) -noʊˈ-
junta ˈdʒʌn.tə, ˈdʒʊn-, ˈhʊn-, (US) ˈhʊn-, ˈdʒʊn-, ˈdʒʌn-, ˈhʌn- **-s** -z
junto ˈdʒʌn.təʊ, ˈdʒʊn-, ˈhʊn-, (US) -toʊ **-s** -z
jupe ʒuːp, (US) dʒuːp **-s** -s
Jupiter ˈdʒuː.pɪ.tər, -pə-, (US) -t̬ɚ
jupon ˈʒuː.pɒn, ˈdʒuː-, -pɔ̃ːŋ, -pɒŋ, (US) ˈdʒuː.pɑːn, -ˈ- **-s** -z
Jura ˈdʒʊə.rə, (US) ˈdʒʊr.ə
Jurassic dʒʊəˈræs.ɪk, (US) dʒʊ-, dʒə-
jurat ˈdʒʊə.ræt, (US) ˈdʒʊr.æt **-s** -s
Jürgen ˈjɜː.gən, ˈjʊə-, (US) ˈjɝː-
juridic|al dʒʊəˈrɪd.ɪ.k|əl, (US) dʒʊ- **-ally** -əl.i, -li
jurisdiction ˌdʒʊə.rɪsˈdɪk.ʃən, -rəsˈ-, -rɪzˈ-, -rəzˈ-, (US) ˌdʒʊr.ɪsˈ- **-s** -z **-al** -əl
jurisprudence ˌdʒʊə.rɪsˈpruː.dən*t*s, -rəs-;

ˈdʒʊə.rɪsˌpruː-, -rəs-, US ˌdʒʊr.ɪsˈpruː-
jurist ˈdʒʊə.rɪst, US ˈdʒʊr.ɪst **-s** -s
juror ˈdʒʊə.rəʳ, US ˈdʒʊr.ɚ, -ɔːr **-s** -z
jur|y ˈdʒʊə.r|i, US ˈdʒʊr.|i **-ies** -iz **ˈjury ˌbox; ˈjury ˌservice**
jury|man ˈdʒʊə.ri|.mən, US ˈdʒʊr.i- **-men** -mən, -men
jury-mast ˈdʒʊə.ri.mɑːst, US ˈdʒʊr.i.mæst; *nautical pronunciation:* -məst **-s** -s
jus ʒuː, US ʒuː, dʒuːs
just, J~ adj dʒʌst **-er** -əʳ, US -ɚ **-est** -ɪst, -əst **-ly** -li **-ness** -nəs, -nɪs
just adv *strong form:* dʒʌst; *weak form:* dʒəst
jus tertii ˌjʊsˈtɜː.ti.iː, US ˌdʒʌsˈterti:, ˌjuːs-
justic|e ˈdʒʌs.tɪs **-es** -ɪz **ˌjustice of the ˈpeace**
justiciable dʒʌsˈtɪʃ.i.ə.bəl, -ˈtɪʃ.ə-, US -i.ə-
justiciar dʒʌsˈtɪʃ.i.ɑːʳ, -ˈtɪs-, US -ˈtɪʃ.i.ɚ **-s** -z
justiciar|y dʒʌsˈtɪʃ.i.ər|.i, -ˈtɪʃ.ər-, -ˈtɪs.i-, US -ˈtɪʃ.i.er- **-ies** -iz
justifiab|le ˈdʒʌs.tɪ.faɪ.ə.b|əl, -təˈ-; ˌdʒʌs.tɪˈfaɪ-, -təˈ-, US ˈdʒʌs.tə.faɪ-, -tɪ- **-ly** -li **-leness** -əl.nəs, -nɪs
justification ˌdʒʌs.tɪ.fɪˈkeɪ.ʃən, -tə-, -fəˈ-, US -tə-, -tɪ- **-s** -z
justificatory ˈdʒʌs.tɪ.fɪ.keɪ.tər.i, -tə-; ˌdʒʌs.tɪ.fɪˈkeɪ-; ˌdʒʌs.tɪˈfɪk.ə-, US dʒəˈstɪf.ɪ.kə.tɔːr-; US ˈdʒʌs.tə.fɪ.keɪ.tɚ-
justi|fy ˈdʒʌs.tɪ|.faɪ, -tə- **-fies** -faɪz **-fying** -faɪ.ɪŋ **-fied** -faɪd **-fier/s** -faɪ.əʳ/z, US -faɪ.ɚ/z
Justin ˈdʒʌs.tɪn
Justine dʒʌsˈtiːn, ˈ--
Justinian dʒʌsˈtɪn.i.ən
Justus ˈdʒʌs.təs
jut dʒʌt **-s** -s **-ting** -ɪŋ, US ˈdʒʌţ.ɪŋ **-ted** -ɪd, US ˈdʒʌţ.ɪd
Juta ˈdʒuː.tə
jute, J~ dʒuːt **-s** -s
Jutland ˈdʒʌt.lənd
Juvenal ˈdʒuː.vən.əl, -vɪ.nəl
juvenescen|ce ˌdʒuː.vənˈes.ən|ts, -vɪˈnes- **-t** -t
juvenile ˈdʒuː.vən.aɪl, -vɪ.naɪl, US -və.nəl, -naɪl **-s** -z **ˌjuvenile deˈlinquent**
juvenilia ˌdʒuː.vəˈnɪl.i.ə, -vɪˈ-, -ˈniː.li-, US -vəˈnɪl.i-, ˈ-jə
juvenility ˌdʒuː.vəˈnɪl.ə.ti, -vɪˈ-, -ɪ.ti, US -ə.ţi
Juventus juːˈven.təs
juxtapos|e ˌdʒʌk.stəˈpəʊz, ˈ---, US ˈdʒʌk.stə.poʊz, ˌ--ˈ- **-es** -ɪz **-ing** -ɪŋ **-ed** -d
juxtaposition ˌdʒʌk.stə.pəˈzɪʃ.ən **-s** -z **-al** -əl

J

K

Pronouncing the letter K

In general, the consonant letter **k** is pronounced /k/, e.g.:

Kate keɪt

This is also the case in the digraph **kh**, e.g.:

khaki ˈkɑː.ki (US) ˈkæk.i

In words beginning **kn**, **k** is usually silent, e.g.:

knack næk

However, where the **k** appears before an **n** at a morpheme boundary, it is pronounced, e.g.:

sickness ˈsɪk.nəs

k, K keɪ -'s -z
K2 ˌkeɪˈtuː
Kaaba ˈkɑː.bə, ˈkɑː.ə.bɑː, (US) -bə
kabaka, K~ kəˈbɑː.kə -s -z
Kab(b)ala kəˈbɑː.lə, kæbˈɑː-, (US) ˈkæb.ə-; (US) kəˈbɑː-
kabbadi kɑːˈbɑː.di
Kabila kəˈbiː.lə, kæbˈiː-, (US) kɑːˈbiːlə
kabob kəˈbɒb, (US) -ˈbɑːb
kabuki kəˈbuː.ki, kæbˈuː-, (US) kə-, kɑː-
Kabul ˈkɑː.bᵊl, ˈkɔː-, -bʊl; kəˈbʊl, (US) ˈkɑː.bʊl; (US) kəˈbʊl
Kabwe ˈkæb.weɪ, (US) ˈkɑːb-
Kabyle kəˈbaɪl, kæbˈaɪl, -iːl -s -z
kachina, K~ kəˈtʃiː.nə -s -z
Kaczynski kəˈtʃɪnt.ski
Kaddish ˈkæd.ɪʃ, (US) ˈkɑː.dɪʃ -im -ɪm, -iːm
kaf(f)ir, K~ ˈkæf.əʳ -s -z
Kafka ˈkæf.kə, (US) ˈkɑːf-
Kafkaesque ˌkæf.kəˈesk, (US) ˌkɑːf-
kaftan ˈkæf.tæn, (US) -tən, -tæn -s -z
kagoule kəˈguːl -s -z
Kahn kɑːn
kailyard ˈkeɪl.jɑːd, (US) -jɑːrd -s -z
Kaine keɪn
Kaiser ˈkaɪ.zəʳ, (US) -zɚ -s -z
Kaiserslautern ˌkaɪ.zəzˈlaʊ.tɜːn, -tən, (US) ˌkaɪ.zɚzˈlaʊ.tɚn
Kaitlin, Kaitlyn ˈkeɪt.lɪn
kaizen ˈkaɪ.zen
Kakadu ˈkæk.ə.duː, –ˈ-
kakemono ˌkæk.iˈməʊ.nəʊ, (US) ˌkɑː.kəˈmoʊ.noʊ -s -z
Kalahari ˌkæl.əˈhɑː.ri, (US) ˌkɑː.lɑːˈhɑːr.i, ˌkæl-
Kalamazoo ˌkæl.ə.məˈzuː
Kalashnikov® kəˈlæʃ.nɪ.kɒf, -nə-, (US) -ˈlɑːʃ.nɪ.kɑːf -s -s
Kalat kəˈlɑːt
kale keɪl
kaleidoscope kəˈlaɪ.də.skəʊp, (US) -skoʊp -s -s
kaleidoscopic kəˌlaɪ.dəˈskɒp.ɪk, (US) -ˈskɑː.pɪk
kalends ˈkæl.endz, -ɪndz, -əndz, (US) -əndz, ˈkeɪ.ləndz
Kalevala ˈkɑː.ləˌvɑː.lə, (US) -lə, -lɑː
Kalgoorlie kælˈgʊə.li, (US) -ˈgʊr-
Kali ˈkɑː.li
kalif ˈkeɪ.lɪf, ˈkæl.ɪf, ˈkɑː.lɪf; kəˈlɪf, (US) ˈkeɪ.lɪf, ˈkæl.ɪf -s -s
Kalimantan ˌkæl.iˈmæn.tən, (US) ˌkɑː.liˈmɑːn.tɑːn
Kam|a *Hindu god:* ˈkɑː.m|ə -ic -ɪk *Russian river:* ˈkɑː.mə
Kamasutra ˌkɑː.məˈsuː.trə
Kamchatka kæmˈtʃæt.kə, (US) kæmˈtʃæt-, kɑːmˈtʃɑːt-
kamikaze ˌkæm.ɪˈkɑː.zi, (US) ˌkɑː.məˈkɑː.zi -s -z
Kampala kæmˈpɑː.lə, (US) kɑːm-
kampong ˈkæm.pɒŋ, -ˈ-, (US) ˈkɑːm.pɔːŋ, -pɑːŋ
Kampuche|a ˌkæm.pʊˈtʃiː|.ə, (US) -puˈ- -an/s -ən/z
kana ˈkɑː.nə, (US) -nə, -nɑː
Kananga kəˈnæŋ.gə, (US) -ˈnɑːŋ-
Kanarese ˌkæn.ᵊrˈiːz, (US) ˌkɑː.nəˈriːz, -ˈriːs
Kanchenjunga ˌkæn.tʃənˈdʒʊŋ.gə, -ˈdʒʌŋ-, (US) ˌkɑːn.tʃənˈdʒʊŋ-
Kandahar ˌkæn.dəˈhɑːʳ, (US) ˌkɑːn.dəˈhɑːr
Kandinsky kænˈdɪnt.ski
Kandy ˈkæn.di, (US) ˈkæn-, ˈkɑːn-
Kane keɪn
Kanga ˈkæŋ.gə
kangaroo ˌkæŋ.gᵊrˈuː; *sometimes in Australia:* ˈ---, (US) ˌkæŋ.gəˈruː -s -z *stress shift, see compound:* **ˌkangaroo ˈcourt**
Kangchenjunga ˌkæn.tʃənˈdʒʊŋ.gə, -ˈdʒʌŋ-, (US) ˌkɑːn.tʃənˈdʒʊŋ-
kanji ˈkæn.dʒi, ˈkɑːn-, (US) ˈkɑːn.dʒi -s -z
Kano ˈkɑː.nəʊ, ˈkeɪ-, (US) ˈkɑː.noʊ
Kanpur kɑːnˈpʊəʳ, (US) ˈkɑːn.pʊr
Kans. (abbrev. for **Kansas**) ˈkæn.zəs
Kansas ˈkæn.zəs **ˌKansas ˈCity; ˌKansas ˌCity ˈsteak**
Kant kænt, (US) kænt, kɑːnt
Kantian ˈkæn.ti.ən, (US) ˈkæn.ţi-, ˈkɑːn-
Kant|ism ˈkæn.t|ɪ.zᵊm, (US) ˈkæn.t|ɪ-, ˈkɑːn- -ist/s -ɪst/s
Kaohsiung ˌkaʊ.ʃiˈʊŋ, (US) ˌkaʊˈʃʊŋ
Kaolak ˈkɑː.əʊ.læk, ˈkaʊ.læk, (US) ˈkɑː.oʊ-, ˈkaʊ.læk
kaolin ˈkeɪ.ə.lɪn
kapellmeister kəˈpel.maɪ.stəʳ, kæpˈel-, (US) kɑːˈpel.maɪ.stɚ, kə- -s -z
Kaplan ˈkæp.lən
kapok ˈkeɪ.pɒk, (US) -pɑːk
Kaposi kəˈpəʊ.zi, kæpˈəʊ-, -si; ˈkɑː.pə.ʃi, ˈkæp.ə-, (US) kəˈpoʊ.zi, -si; (US) ˈkæp.ə- **Kaˌposi's sarˈcoma**
kappa ˈkæp.ə
kaput(t) kəˈpʊt, kæpˈʊt, (US) kəˈpʊt, -ˈpuːt
Kara ˈkɑː.rə, (US) ˈkɑːr.ə
Karachi kəˈrɑː.tʃi
Karadzic ˈkær.ə.dʒɪtʃ, -dɪtʃ, (US) kəˈrɑː.dʒɪtʃ
Karaganda ˌkær.əˈgæn.də, (US) ˌkɑːr.əˈgɑːn-
Karajan ˈkær.ə.jɑːn, (US) ˈkɑːr-, -jən
karaoke ˌkær.iˈəʊ.ki, (US) ˌker.iˈoʊ.ki, ˌkær- -s -z
karat ˈkær.ət, (US) ˈker-, ˈkær- -s -z
karate kəˈrɑː.ti, kærˈɑː-, (US) kəˈrɑː.ţi
Kareli|a kəˈreɪ.li|.ə, -ˈriː-, (US) -li|.ə, -lj|ə -ans -ənz
Karen *female name:* ˈkær.ən, (US) ˈker-, ˈkær- *of Burma:* kəˈren -s -z
Karenina kəˈren.ɪ.nə
Karl kɑːl, (US) kɑːrl
Karla ˈkɑː.lə, (US) ˈkɑːr-
Karl-Marx-Stadt ˌkɑːlˈmɑːksˌʃtæt, (US) ˌkɑːrlˈmɑːrksˌʃtɑːt
Karloff ˈkɑː.lɒf, (US) ˈkɑːr.lɑːf
Karlsbad ˈkɑːlz.bæd, (US) ˈkɑːrlz-
Karlsruhe ˈkɑːlz.ruː.ə, (US) ˈkɑːrlz-
karm|a ˈkɑː.m|ə, ˈkɜː-, (US) ˈkɑːr-, ˈkɜː- -ik -ɪk
Karnak ˈkɑː.næk, (US) ˈkɑːr-
Karnataka kəˈnɑː.tə.kə, (US) kɑːrˈnɑː.ţə-
Karpov ˈkɑː.pɒf, (US) ˈkɑːr.pɑːf
karroo kəˈruː -s -z
Kars kɑːz, (US) kɑːrz
Karsh kɑːʃ, (US) kɑːrʃ
kart kɑːt, (US) kɑːrt -s -s -ing -ɪŋ, (US) ˈkɑːr.ţɪŋ
Karzai ˈkɑː.zaɪ, (US) ˈkɑːr-
kasbah, K~ ˈkæz.bɑː, -bə, (US) -bɑː, ˈkɑːz- -s -z
Kasey ˈkeɪ.si
kasha ˈkæʃ.ə, ˈkɑː.ʃə, (US) ˈkɑː.ʃə
Kashgar ˈkæʃ.gɑːʳ, (US) ˈkɑːʃ.gɑːr
Kashmir ˌkæʃˈmɪəʳ, (US) ˈkæʃ.mɪr, -ˈ- -i/s -i/z *stress shift, British only:* **ˌKashmir ˈborder**
Kaspar ˈkæs.pəʳ, -pɑːʳ, (US) -pɚ, -pɑːr
Kasparov kæsˈpɑː.rɒf; ˈkæs.pə-, (US) kæsˈpɑːr.ɔːf, kəˈspɑːr-; (US) ˈkæs.pə.rɔːf
Kassala kəˈsɑː.lə, (US) kə-, kɑː-

Kassel ˈkæs.əl, (US) ˈkɑː.səl, ˈkæs.əl
Kasur kʌsˈɔːʳ, (US) -ˈʊr
katakana ˌkæt.əˈkɑː.nə, (US) ˌkɑː.t̬ə-
Kate keɪt
Katelyn ˈkeɪt.lɪn
Kater ˈkeɪ.təʳ, (US) -t̬ɚ
Katerina ˌkæt.əˈriː.nə, (US) ˌkæt̬.əˈriː-
Kath kæθ
Katharina ˌkæθ.əˈriː.nə, (US) -əˈriː-
Katharine, Katherine ˈkæθ.rɪn, -ər.ɪn
Kathie ˈkæθ.i
Kathleen ˈkæθ.liːn, ˌ-ˈ-
Kathmandu ˌkæt.mænˈduː, ˌkɑːt-, -mənˈ-, -mɑːnˈ-, (US) ˌkɑːt.mænˈ-, ˌkæt-
Kathryn ˈkæθ.rɪn
Kathy ˈkæθ.i
Katie ˈkeɪ.ti, (US) -t̬i
Katin ˈkeɪ.tɪn, (US) -t̬ɪn
Katmandu ˌkæt.mænˈduː, ˌkɑːt-, -mənˈ-, -mɑːnˈ-, (US) ˌkɑːt.mænˈ-, ˌkæt-
Katowice ˌkæt.əʊˈvɪt.seɪ, -ˈviːt-, (US) -əˈviːt.sə, -ɔːˈviːt.seɪ
Katrina kəˈtriː.nə
Katrine ˈkæt.rɪn
Kattegat ˌkæt.ɪˈgæt, ˈ---, (US) ˈkæt̬-
Katty ˈkæt.i, (US) ˈkæt̬-
Katy ˈkeɪ.ti, (US) -t̬i
katydid ˈkeɪ.ti.dɪd, (US) -t̬i- **-s** -z
Katyn ˈkæt.iːn, -ɪn, kætˈiːn
Katz kæts, keɪts
katzenjammer ˈkæt.sənˌdʒæm.əʳ, (US) -ɚ
Kaufman ˈkɔːf.mən, ˈkaʊf-, (US) ˈkɑːf-, ˈkɔːf-
Kaunas ˈkaʊ.nəs, (US) -nɑːs
Kaunda kɑːˈʊn.də, -ˈuːn-
Kaur ˈkaʊ.əʳ, (US) ˈkaʊ.ɚ
Kavanagh ˈkæv.ən.ə; kəˈvæn.ə, (US) ˈkæv.ə.nɑː, -nɔː

> Note: In Ireland always /ˈkæv.ən.ə/.

Kawasaki® ˌkaʊ.əˈsɑː.ki, ˌkɑː.wəˈ-, -ˈsæk.i, (US) ˌkɑː.wəˈsɑː.ki
Kay keɪ
kayak ˈkaɪ.æk **-s** -s **-ing** -ɪŋ **-ed** -t
Kaye keɪ **-s** -z
Kayla ˈkeɪ.lə
Kayleigh ˈkeɪ.li
Kayseri ˈkeɪ.sər.i
Kazakh ˈkæ.zæk, -ˈzɑːk, (US) ˈkɑː.zɑːk, -ˈzæk **-s** -s
Kazakhstan, Kazakstan ˌkæz.ækˈstɑːn, ˌkɑː.zækˈ-, -zɑːkˈ-, -ˈstæn, (US) ˈkɑː.zɪk.stɑːn, -zək-, -zæk-, -stæn
Kazan kəˈzæn, -ˈzɑːn, (US) kəˈzæn, kɑː-, -ˈzɑːn
kazi ˈkɑː.zi **-s** -z
kazoo kəˈzuː **-s** -z
kcal (abbrev. for **kilocalorie**) ˈkɪl.əʊˌkæl.ər.i, (US) ˈ-oʊ-, ˈ-ə-
kea ˈkeɪ.ə, ˈkiː- **-s** -z
Keady ˈkiː.di, (US) ˈkeɪ-
Kean(e) kiːn
Kearn(e)y ˈkɜː.ni, ˈkɑː-, (US) ˈkɑːr-, ˈkɝː-
Kearsley ˈkɪəz.li; *locally:* ˈkɜːz-, (US) ˈkɪrz-
Kearsney ˈkɜːz.ni, (US) ˈkɝːz-
Kearton ˈkɪə.tən, ˈkɜː-, (US) ˈkɪr-, ˈkɝː-
Keary ˈkɪə.ri, (US) ˈkɪr.i
Keating(e) ˈkiː.tɪŋ, (US) -t̬ɪŋ
Keaton ˈkiː.tən
Keats kiːts
kebab kɪˈbæb, kə-, (US) -ˈbɑːb **-s** -z
Keble ˈkiː.bəl
kebob kəˈbɒb, (US) -ˈbɑːb **-s** -z
kedg|e kedʒ **-es** -ɪz **-ing** -ɪŋ **-ed** -d
kedgeree ˌkedʒ.əˈriː; ˈkedʒ.ər.i, (US) ˈkedʒ.ər-; (US) ˌkedʒ.əˈriː **-s** -z
Kedleston ˈked.əl.stən
Kedron ˈked.rɒn, ˈkiː.drɒn, (US) ˈkiː.drɑːn, -drən
Keeble ˈkiː.bəl
Keegan ˈkiː.gən
keel kiːl **-s** -z **-ing** -ɪŋ **-ed** -d **on an ˌeven ˈkeel**
Keele kiːl
Keeler ˈkiː.ləʳ, (US) -lɚ
keelhaul ˈkiːl.hɔːl, (US) -hɑːl, -hɔːl **-s** -z **-ing** -ɪŋ **-ed** -d
Keeling ˈkiː.lɪŋ
keelson ˈkel.sən, ˈkiːl- **-s** -z
keen kiːn **-er** -əʳ, (US) -ɚ **-est** -ɪst, -əst **-s** -z **-ing** -ɪŋ **-ed** -d **-ly** -li **-ness** -nəs, -nɪs **as ˌkeen as ˈmustard**
Keen(e) kiːn
Keenan ˈkiː.nən
keep kiːp **-s** -s **-ing** -ɪŋ **kept** kept **keeper/s** ˈkiː.pəʳ/z, (US) -pɚ/z
keepnet ˈkiːp.net **-s** -s
keepsake ˈkiːp.seɪk **-s** -s
Kefauver ˈkiːˌfɔː.vəʳ, -ˌfəʊ-, (US) -ˌfɑː.vɚ, -ˌfɔː-
Keflavik ˈkef.lə.vɪk
keg keg **-s** -z
Kegan ˈkiː.gən
Keig kiːg
Keighley *in West Yorkshire:* ˈkiːθ.li *surname:* ˈkiːθ.li, ˈkiː-, ˈkaɪ-
Keightley ˈkiːt.li, ˈkaɪt-
Keigwin ˈkeg.wɪn
Keiller, Keillor ˈkiː.ləʳ, (US) -lɚ
Keir kɪəʳ, (US) kɪr
Keisha ˈkiː.ʃə
Keitel ˌkaɪˈtel
Keith kiːθ
Kelland ˈkel.ənd
Kellas ˈkel.æs
Keller ˈkel.əʳ, (US) -ɚ
Kelley, Kellie ˈkel.i
Kellogg ˈkel.ɒg, (US) -ɑːg, -ɔːg
Kelly ˈkel.i
kelly-green ˌkel.iˈgriːn *stress shift:* **ˌkelly-green ˈfabric**
Kelman ˈkel.mən
kelp kelp
kelpie ˈkel.pi **-s** -z
Kelsey ˈkel.si, -zi
Kelso ˈkel.səʊ, (US) -soʊ
kelson ˈkel.sən **-s** -z
Kelt kelt **-s** -s **-ic** -ɪk
Kelty ˈkel.ti
kelvin, K~ ˈkel.vɪn
Kelway ˈkel.wi, -weɪ
Kemal kemˈɑːl, kəˈmɑːl, (US) kəˈmɑːl
Kemble ˈkem.bəl
kemp kemp **-y** -i
Kemp(e) kemp
Kempenfelt ˈkem.pən.felt
Kempis ˈkem.pɪs
Kempson ˈkemp.sən
Kempston ˈkemp.stən
kempt kempt
Kempton ˈkemp.tən
Kemsing ˈkem.zɪŋ
ken, K~ ken **-s** -z **-ning** -ɪŋ **-ned** -d
Ken. (abbrev. for **Kentucky**) kenˈtʌk.i, kən-, (US) kən-
Kendal(l) ˈken.dəl
kendo ˈken.dəʊ, (US) -doʊ
Kendra ˈken.drə
Kendrick ˈken.drɪk
Keneal(l)y kɪˈniː.li, kə-, kenˈiː-
Kenelm ˈken.elm
Kenilworth ˈken.əl.wəθ, -ɪl-, -wɜːθ, (US) -wɚθ, -wɝːθ
Kenite ˈkiː.naɪt **-s** -s
Kénitra ˈkeɪ.niː.trə; kenˈiː-
Kenmare kenˈmeəʳ, (US) -ˈmer
Kenmore ˈken.mɔːʳ, (US) -mɔːr
Kennaird kəˈneəd, kenˈeəd, (US) kenˈerd, kəˈnerd
Kennan ˈken.ən
Kennard ˈken.ɑːd; kɪˈnɑːd, (US) ˈken.ɑːrd, kɪˈnɑːrd
Kennedy ˈken.ə.di, ˈ-ɪ-
kennel, K~ ˈken.əl **-s** -z **-(l)ing** -ɪŋ **-(l)ed** -d
Kennerley ˈken.əl.i, (US) -ɚ.li
Kennet ˈken.ɪt, -ət
Kenneth ˈken.ɪθ, -əθ
Kenney ˈken.i
Kennicot ˈken.ɪ.kət, (US) -kət, -kɑːt
Kennington ˈken.ɪŋ.tən
Kennish ˈken.ɪʃ
Kennoway ˈken.ə.weɪ
Kenny ˈken.i
keno ˈkiː.nəʊ, (US) -noʊ
Kenosha kɪˈnəʊ.ʃə, kə-, (US) kəˈnoʊ-
Kenrick ˈken.rɪk
Kensal ˈken.səl
Kensington ˈken.zɪŋ.tən
Kensit ˈken.zɪt, -sɪt
Kent kent **-s** -s **-ish** -ɪʃ
Kentucky kenˈtʌk.i, kən-, (US) kən- **KenˌtuckyˈDerby**
Kenwood® ˈken.wʊd
Kenya ˈken.jə, ˈkiː.njə **-n/s** -n/z

> Note: Both pronunciations are heard locally. In the UK, the pronunciation /ˈkiː.njə/ is regarded as old-fashioned.

Kenyatta kenˈjæt.ə, (US) -ˈjɑː.t̬ə
Kenyon ˈken.jən
Keogh kjəʊ; ˈkiː.əʊ, (US) ˈkiː.oʊ
Keown kjəʊn; kiˈoʊn; ˈkiː.əʊn, (US) kjoʊn; (US) kiˈoʊn; (US) ˈkiː.oʊn
kepi ˈkeɪ.pi, (US) ˈkeɪ-, ˈkep.i **-s** -z
Kepler ˈkep.ləʳ, (US) -lɚ
Keppel ˈkep.əl
kept (from **keep**) kept
Ker kɑːʳ, keəʳ, kɜːʳ (US) kɝː; *in Scotland:* kɛr

Kerala ˈker.əl.ə, kəˈrɑː.lə, (US) ˈker.ə.lə
Kerans ˈker.ənz
keratin ˈker.ə.tɪn, (US) -t̬ɪn
keratitis ˌker.əˈtaɪ.tɪs, -təs, (US) -t̬ɪs, -t̬əs
kerb kɜːb, (US) kɝːb -s -z
kerbside ˈkɜːb.saɪd, (US) ˈkɝːb-
kerbstone ˈkɜːb.stəʊn, (US) ˈkɝːb.stoʊn -s -z
ker|chief ˈkɜː|.tʃɪf, -tʃiːf, -tʃəf, (US) ˈkɝː|.tʃɪf, -tʃiːf **-chiefs** -tʃɪfs, -tʃiːfs **-chieves** -tʃɪvz, -tʃiːvz **-chiefed** -tʃɪft **-chieft** -tʃiːft
Kerensky kəˈrent.ski
kerfuffl|e kəˈfʌf.əl, (US) kɚ- **-es** -z **-ing** -ɪŋ **-ed** -d
Kerguelen ˈkɜː.gɪ.lɪn, -gəl.ɪn, -ən, (US) ˈkɝː.gəl.ən
Keri ˈker.i
Kerith ˈkɪə.rɪθ, ˈker.ɪθ, (US) ˈkɪr.ɪθ, ˈker-
kermes ˈkɜː.mɪz, -miːz, (US) ˈkɝː.miːz
Kermit ˈkɜː.mɪt, (US) ˈkɝː-
Kermode ˈkɜː.məʊd, -ˈ-, (US) ˈkɝː.moʊd, -ˈ-
kern, K~ kɜːn, (US) kɝːn **-s** -z **-ing** -ɪŋ **-ed** -d
Kernahan ˈkɜː.nə.hən, -ni.ən, (US) ˈkɝː-, -nə.hæn
kernel ˈkɜː.nəl, (US) ˈkɝː- **-s** -z
Kernohan ˈkɜː.nə.hən, (US) ˈkɝː-, -hæn
kerosene ˈker.ə.siːn, ˌ--ˈ-
Kerouac ˈker.u.æk, (US) ˈker.u.æk, ˈ-ə-
Kerr kɜːʳ, keəʳ, kɑːʳ, (US) kɝː, kɑːr
Kerri ˈker.i
kerria ˈker.i.ə **-s** -z
Kerridge ˈker.ɪdʒ
Kerry ˈker.i
Kerse kɜːs, (US) kɝːs
kersey, K~ ˈkɜː.zi, (US) ˈkɝː- **-s** -z
kerseymere, K~ ˈkɜː.zi.mɪəʳ, (US) ˈkɝː.zi.mɪr
Kershaw ˈkɜː.ʃɔː, (US) ˈkɝː.ʃɑː, -ʃɔː
Kes kes, kez
Kesey ˈkes.i, ˈkiː.si, -zi, (US) ˈkiː.si, -zi
Kesteven kesˈtiː.vən, kəˈstiː-
Keston ˈkes.tən
kestrel ˈkes.trəl **-s** -z
Keswick ˈkez.ɪk
ketch, K~ ketʃ **-es** -ɪz
ketchup ˈketʃ.ʌp, -əp, (US) -əp **-s** -s
ketone ˈkiː.təʊn, (US) -toʊn **-s** -z
Ketteridge ˈket.ər.ɪdʒ, (US) ˈket̬-
Kettering ˈket.ər.ɪŋ, (US) ˈket̬-
kettle, K~ ˈket.əl, (US) ˈket̬- **-s** -z **a ˈpretty ˌkettle of ˌfish**
kettledrum ˈket.əl.drʌm, (US) ˈket̬- **-s** -z
Kevin ˈkev.ɪn
Kevlar® ˈkev.lɑːʳ, (US) -lɑːr
Kevorkian kəˈvɔː.ki.ən, kevˈ-, (US) -ˈvɔːr-
Kew kjuː **ˌKew ˈGardens**
kewpie ˈkjuː.pi **-s** -z
key, K~ kiː **-s** -z **-ing** -ɪŋ **-ed** -d **ˈkey ˌring; ˈkey ˌsignature; ˌKey ˈWest**
keyboard ˈkiː.bɔːd, (US) -bɔːrd **-s** -z **-ing** -ɪŋ **-ed** -ɪd **-er/s** -əʳ/z, (US) -ɚ/z **-ist/s** -ɪst/s
keycard ˈkiː.kɑːd, (US) -kɑːrd **-s** -z
Keyes kiːz, kaɪz
keyhole ˈkiː.həʊl, (US) -hoʊl **-s** -z **ˌkeyhole ˈsurgery**
Key Largo ˌkiːˈlɑː.gəʊ, (US) -ˈlɑːr.goʊ
Keymer ˈkiː.məʳ, ˈkaɪ-, (US) -mɚ
Keymour ˈkiː.məʳ, (US) -mɚ
Keyne kiːn
Keynes *in Milton Keynes:* kiːnz *surname, other places:* keɪnz
Keynesian ˈkeɪn.zi.ən **-ism** -ɪ.zəm
keynote ˈkiː.nəʊt, ˌ-ˈ-, (US) ˈkiː.noʊt **-s** -s
Keynsham ˈkeɪn.ʃəm
keypad ˈkiː.pæd **-s** -z
keypunch ˈkiː.pʌntʃ **-es** -ɪz
Keyser ˈkiː.zəʳ, ˈkaɪ.zəʳ, (US) ˈkaɪ.zɚ
keystone, K~ ˈkiː.stəʊn, (US) -stoʊn **-s** -z
keystroke ˈkiː.strəʊk, (US) -stroʊk **-s** -s
keyword ˈkiː.wɜːd, (US) -wɝːd **-s** -z
Keyworth ˈkiː.wəθ, -wɜːθ, (US) -wɚθ, -wɝːθ
kg (abbrev. for **kilogram/s**) *singular:* ˈkɪl.ə.græm; *plural:* ˈkɪl.ə.græmz
KGB ˌkeɪ.dʒiːˈbiː
Khabarovsk kəˈbɑː.rɒfsk, (US) -rɔːfsk
Khachaturian ˌkætʃ.əˈtʊə.ri.ən, ˌkɑː.tʃəˈ-, -ˈtjʊə-, (US) -ˈtʊr.i-
khaki ˈkɑː.ki, (US) ˈkæk.i, ˈkɑː.ki **-s** -z
khalif ˈkeɪ.lɪf, (US) ˈkɑː-, ˈkæl.ɪf, ˈkɑː.lɪf; (US) kælˈɪf, ˈkeɪ.lɪf, ˈkæl.ɪf **-s** -s
Khalifa kɑːˈliː.fə, kəˈliː- **-s** -z
khalifate ˈkæl.ɪ.feɪt, ˈkeɪ.lɪ-, -lə-, (US) ˈkæl.ɪ-, ˈ-ə- **-s** -s
Khan kɑːn, (US) kɑːn, kæn
Khanpur ˌkɑːnˈpʊəʳ, ˌkɑːmˈ-, ˈ--, (US) ˌkɑːnˈpʊr
Kharkov ˈkɑː.kɒf, (US) ˈkɑːr.kɔːf
Khartoum ˌkɑːˈtuːm, kɑː-, (US) kɑːr-
Kharzai kɑːˈzaɪ, ˈ--, (US) kɑːrˈ-
Khatami ˌhɑː.tɑːˈmi, kætˈɑːmi, (US) ˈkɑː.tɑː.mi, kəˈ-, ˌhɑː.tɑːˈmiː
Khayyam kaɪˈæm, -ˈɑːm, (US) -ˈjɑːm, -ˈjæm
khazi ˈkɑː.zi **-s** -z
khedival kɪˈdiː.vəl, kedˈiː-, kəˈdiː-, (US) kəˈdiː-
khedive kɪˈdiːv, kedˈiːv, kəˈdiːv, (US) kəˈdiːv **-s** -z
khedivial kɪˈdiː.vi.əl, kedˈiː-, kəˈdiː-, (US) kəˈdiː-
Khmer kmeəʳ, kəˈmeəʳ, (US) kəˈmer **Khˌmer ˈRouge**
Khomeini kɒmˈeɪ.ni, kəʊˈmeɪ-, (US) koʊˈmeɪ-, kə-
Khrus(h)chev ˈkrʊs.tʃɒf, ˈkrʊʃ-, ˌ-ˈ-, (US) ˈkruːs.tʃef, -tʃɔːf; (US) kruːʃˈtʃɔːf
Khyber ˈkaɪ.bəʳ, (US) -bɚ **ˌKhyber ˈPass**
kHz (abbrev. for **kilohertz**) ˈkɪl.əʊ.hɜːts, (US) -ə.hɝːts
Kia Ora® ˌkɪəˈɔː.rə, ˌkiː.əˈ-, (US) ˌkiː.əˈɔːr.ə
kibbl|e ˈkɪb.əl **-es** -z **-ing** -ɪŋ, ˈkɪb.lɪŋ **-ed** -d
kibbutz kɪˈbʊts, (US) -ˈbʊts, -ˈbuːts **-nik/s** -nɪk **-es** -ɪz **kibbutzim** ˌkɪb.ʊtˈsiːm; kɪˈbʊt.siːm, (US) ˌkiː.buːtˈsiːm
kibe kaɪb **-s** -z
kibitz ˈkɪb.ɪts **-es** -ɪz **-ing** -ɪŋ **-ed** -t **-er/s** -əʳ/z, (US) -ɚ/z
kibosh ˈkaɪ.bɒʃ, (US) ˈkaɪ.bɑːʃ; (US) kɪˈbɑːʃ **-es** -ɪz **-ing** -ɪŋ **-ed** -t
kick kɪk **-s** -s **-ing** -ɪŋ **-ed** -t **-er/s** -əʳ/z, (US) -ɚ/z
kickabout ˈkɪk.ə.baʊt **-s** -s
kickback ˈkɪk.bæk **-s** -s
kickbox|ing ˈkɪkˌbɒk|.sɪŋ, (US) -ˌbɑː- **-er/s** -əʳ/z, (US) -ɚ/z
Kickham ˈkɪk.əm
kick-off ˈkɪk.ɒf, (US) -ɑːf **-s** -s
kickshaw ˈkɪk.ʃɔː, (US) -ʃɑː, -ʃɔː **-s** -z
kick|-start ˈkɪk|.stɑːt, (US) -stɑːrt **-starts** -stɑːts, (US) -stɑːrts **-starting** -ˌstɑː.tɪŋ, (US) -ˌstɑːr.t̬ɪŋ **-started** -ˌstɑː.tɪd, (US) -ˌstɑːr.t̬ɪd **-starter/s** -ˌstɑː.təʳ/z, (US) -ˌstɑːr.t̬ɚ/z
kid kɪd **-s** -z **-ding** -ɪŋ **-ded** -ɪd **ˌkid ˈglove**
Kidd kɪd
Kidderminster ˈkɪd.ə.mɪnt.stəʳ, (US) -ɚ.mɪnt.stɚ
kiddie ˈkɪd.i **-s** -z
kiddle, K~ ˈkɪd.əl **-s** -z
kidd|y ˈkɪd|.i **-ies** -iz
Kidlington ˈkɪd.lɪŋ.tən
Kidman ˈkɪd.mən
kidnap ˈkɪd.næp **-s** -s **-(p)ing/s** -ɪŋ/z **-(p)ed** -t **-(p)er/s** -əʳ/z, (US) -ɚ/z
kidney ˈkɪd.ni **-s** -z **ˈkidney ˌbean; ˈkidney maˌchine**
Kidsgrove ˈkɪdz.grəʊv, (US) -groʊv
kidult ˈkɪd.ʌlt **-s** -s
Kiel kiːl
kielbas(s)a kiːlˈbæs.ə, (US) -ˈbɑː.sə, kɪl-
Kielder ˈkiːl.dəʳ, (US) -dɚ
kier, K~ kɪəʳ, (US) kɪr **-s** -z
Kieran ˈkɪə.rən, (US) ˈkɪr.ən
Kierkegaard ˈkɪə.kə.gɑːd, -gɔːd, (US) ˈkɪr.kə.gɑːrd, -gɔːrd
Kiev ˈkiː.ev, -ef, ˌ-ˈ-
Kigali kɪˈgɑː.li, (US) kə-
kike kaɪk **-s** -s
Kikuyu kɪˈkuː.juː, (US) ki-
Kilbirnie kɪlˈbɜː.ni, (US) -ˈbɝː-
Kilbride kɪlˈbraɪd, (US) ˈkɪl.braɪd, -ˈ-
Kilburn ˈkɪl.bən, -bɜːn, (US) -bɚn, -bɝːn
Kilby ˈkɪl.bi
Kildale ˈkɪl.deɪl
Kildare kɪlˈdeəʳ, (US) -ˈder
kilderkin ˈkɪl.də.kɪn, (US) -dɚ- **-s** -z
Kilen ˈkaɪ.lən
Kiley ˈkaɪ.li
Kilfoyle kɪlˈfɔɪl
Kilham ˈkɪl.əm
kilim, K~ kɪˈliːm **-s** -z
Kilimanjaro ˌkɪl.ɪ.mənˈdʒɑː.rəʊ, ˌ-ə-, -mænˈ-, (US) -ə.mənˈdʒɑːr.oʊ
Kilkeel kɪlˈkiːl

Kilkenny kɪlˈken.i
kill kɪl -s -z -ing/s -ɪŋ/z -ed -d ˌ**dressed to ˈkill**
Killaloe ˌkɪl.əˈluː, ⓤⓢ kɪˈlæl.oʊ
Killamarsh ˈkɪl.ə.mɑːʃ, ⓤⓢ -mɑːrʃ
Killarney kɪˈlɑː.ni, ⓤⓢ -ˈlɑːr-
Killearn kɪˈlɜːn, ⓤⓢ -ˈlɝːn
killer ˈkɪl.əʳ, ⓤⓢ -ɚ -s -z ˈ**killer** ˌ**instinct**; ˈ**killer** ˌ**whale**
Killick ˈkɪl.ɪk
Killiecrankie ˌkɪl.iˈkræŋ.ki
Killigrew ˈkɪl.ɪ.gruː
Killin ˈkɪl.ɪn
Killingworth ˈkɪl.ɪŋ.wəθ, -wɜːθ, ⓤⓢ -wɚθ, -wɝːθ
killjoy ˈkɪl.dʒɔɪ -s -z
Killwick ˈkɪl.wɪk
Kilmainham kɪlˈmeɪ.nəm
Kilmarnock kɪlˈmɑː.nək, -nɒk, ⓤⓢ -ˈmɑːr.nək, -nɑːk
kiln kɪln -s -z

> Note: There used to be a pronunciation /kɪl/ in the speech of people concerned with the working of kilns.

Kilnsey ˈkɪln.zi
kilo ˈkiː.ləʊ, ⓤⓢ -loʊ -s -z
kilo- ˈkɪl.əʊ; kɪˈlɒ, ⓤⓢ ˈkɪl.oʊ, -ə; ⓤⓢ kɪˈlɑː
Note: Prefix. Normally carries primary stress on the first syllable, e.g. **kilogram** /ˈkɪl.əʊ.græm/ ⓤⓢ /-oʊ-/.
kilobyte ˈkɪl.əʊ.baɪt, ⓤⓢ ˈ-oʊ-, ˈ-ə- -s -s
kilocalorie ˈkɪl.əʊˌkæl.ər.i, ⓤⓢ ˈ-oʊ-, ˈ-ə- -s -z
kilocycle ˈkɪl.əʊˌsaɪ.kəl, ⓤⓢ -oʊˌ-, -əˌ- -s -z
kilogram, kilogramme ˈkɪl.əʊ.græm, ⓤⓢ ˈ-oʊ-, ˈ-ə- -s -z
kilohertz ˈkɪl.əʊ.hɜːts, -heəts, ⓤⓢ -oʊ.herts, ˈ-ə-, -hɝːts
kilojoule ˈkɪl.əʊ.dʒuːl, ⓤⓢ ˈ-oʊ-, ˈ-ə- -s -z
kilolitre, kiloliter ˈkɪl.əʊˌliː.təʳ, ⓤⓢ -oʊˌliː.t̬ɚ, -əˌ- -s -z
kilometre, kilometer kɪˈlɒm.ɪ.təʳ, ˈ-ə-; ˈkɪl.əʊˌmiː-, ⓤⓢ kɪˈlɑː.mə.t̬ɚ; ⓤⓢ ˈkɪl.əˌmiː- -s -z

> Note: The British pronunciation of this word is controversial. In the past, /kɪˈlɒm.ɪ.təʳ/ was regarded as inappropriate and American-inspired, but it has now become the dominant pronunciation.

kiloton ˈkɪl.əʊ.tʌn, ⓤⓢ ˈ-oʊ-, ˈ-ə- -s -z
kilovolt ˈkɪl.əʊ.vəʊlt, ⓤⓢ -oʊ.voʊlt, ˈ-ə- -s -s
kilowatt ˈkɪl.əʊ.wɒt, ⓤⓢ -oʊ.wɑːt, ˈ-ə- -s -s
Kilpatrick kɪlˈpæt.rɪk
Kilroy ˈkɪl.rɔɪ
Kilrush kɪlˈrʌʃ
Kilsyth kɪlˈsaɪθ
kilt kɪlt -s -s -ing -ɪŋ, ⓤⓢ ˈkɪl.t̬ɪŋ -ed -ɪd, ⓤⓢ ˈkɪl.t̬ɪd
kilter ˈkɪl.təʳ, ⓤⓢ -t̬ɚ
Kilvert ˈkɪl.vət, ⓤⓢ -vɚt
Kilwarden kɪlˈwɔː.dən, ⓤⓢ -ˈwɔːr-
Kilwinning kɪlˈwɪn.ɪŋ
Kim kɪm
Kimball ˈkɪm.bəl
Kimberl(e)y ˈkɪm.bəl.i, ⓤⓢ -bɚ.li
Kimbolton kɪmˈbəʊl.tən, ⓤⓢ -ˈboʊl-
Kimmeridge ˈkɪm.ər.ɪdʒ
Kimmins ˈkɪm.ɪnz
kimono kɪˈməʊ.nəʊ, ⓤⓢ kəˈmoʊ.noʊ, kɪ-, kiː- -s -z
kin kɪn
kina ˈkiː.nə
kinaesthesia ˌkɪn.isˈθiː.zi.ə, -əsˈ-, -ʒə
kinaesthetic ˌkɪn.isˈθet.ɪk, ˌkaɪ.nisˈ-, ⓤⓢ ˌkɪn.esˈθet̬.ɪk
Kincardine kɪnˈkɑː.dɪn, kɪŋ-, -dən, ⓤⓢ kɪnˈkɑːr- -shire -ʃəʳ, -ʃɪəʳ, ⓤⓢ -ʃɚ, -ʃɪr
kind kaɪnd -s -z -er -əʳ, ⓤⓢ -ɚ -est -ɪst, -əst -ly -li -ness/es -nəs/ɪz, -nɪs/ɪz
kinda ˈkaɪn.də
kindergarten ˈkɪn.dəˌgɑː.tən, ⓤⓢ -dɚˌgɑːr- -s -z
Kinder Scout ˌkɪn.dəˈskaʊt, ⓤⓢ -dɚ-
Kindersley ˈkɪn.dəz.li, ⓤⓢ -dɚz-
kind-hearted ˌkaɪndˈhɑː.tɪd, ⓤⓢ -ˈhɑːr.t̬ɪd -ly -li -ness -nəs, -nɪs
stress shift: ˌ**kind-hearted** ˈ**person**
kindl|e ˈkɪn.dəl -es -z -ing -ɪŋ, ˈkɪnd.lɪŋ -ed -d -er/s -əʳ/z, ˈkɪnd.ləʳ/z, ⓤⓢ -ɚ/z, ˈkɪnd.lɚ/z
kindling ˈkɪnd.lɪŋ, ˈkɪn.dəl.ɪŋ
kindl|y ˈkaɪnd.l|i -ier -i.əʳ, ⓤⓢ -i.ɚ -iest -i.ɪst, -i.əst -iness -ɪ.nəs, -ɪ.nɪs
kindred ˈkɪn.drəd, -drɪd ˌ**kindred** ˈ**spirit**
kine kaɪn
kinema ˈkɪn.ɪ.mə, ˈ-ə- -s -z
kinematic ˌkɪn.ɪˈmæt.ɪk, ˌkaɪ.nɪˈ-, -nəˈ-, ⓤⓢ ˌkɪn.əˈmæt̬- -al -əl -ally -əl.i, -li -s -s
kinematograph ˌkɪn.ɪˈmæt.ə.grɑːf, ˌkaɪ.nɪˈ-, -nəˈ-, -græf, ⓤⓢ ˌkɪn.əˈmæt̬.ə.græf -s -s
kinesics kɪˈniː.sɪks, kaɪ-, ⓤⓢ -sɪks, -zɪks
kinesiology kɪˌniː.siˈɒl.ə.dʒi, kaɪ-, -ziˈ-, ⓤⓢ kɪˌniː.siˈɑː.lə--, -ziˈ-
kinesis kɪˈniː.sɪs, kaɪ-, ⓤⓢ -sɪs, -zɪs
kinesthetic ˌkɪn.isˈθet.ɪk, ˌkaɪ.nisˈ-, ⓤⓢ ˌkɪn.ɪsˈθet̬-
kinetic kɪˈnet.ɪk, kaɪ-, ⓤⓢ kɪˈnet̬- -ally -əl.i, -li -s -s
kinfolk ˈkɪn.fəʊk, ⓤⓢ -foʊk -s -s
king, K~ kɪŋ -s -z ˌ**King's** ˈ**Bench**; ˌ**King Charles** ˈ**spaniel**; ˌ**King's** ˈ**Counsel**; ˌ**King's** ˈ**English**; ˌ**king's** ˈ**evidence**; ˌ**King's** ˈ**Lynn**; ˌ**king** ˈ**prawn**
king-at-arms ˌkɪŋ.ətˈɑːmz, ⓤⓢ -ˈɑːrms **kings-at-arms** ˌkɪŋz-
kingcraft ˈkɪŋ.krɑːft, ⓤⓢ -kræft
kingcup ˈkɪŋ.kʌp -s -s
kingdom, K~ ˈkɪŋ.dəm -s -z ˌ**kingdom** ˈ**come**; ˌ**Kingdom** ˈ**Hall**
Kingdon ˈkɪŋ.dən
kingfisher ˈkɪŋˌfɪʃ.əʳ, ⓤⓢ -ɚ -s -z
Kinghorn ˈkɪŋ.hɔːn, ⓤⓢ -hɔːrn
Kinglake ˈkɪŋ.leɪk
kingless ˈkɪŋ.ləs, -lɪs
kinglet ˈkɪŋ.lət, -lɪt -s -s
kinglike ˈkɪŋ.laɪk
kingl|y ˈkɪŋ.l|i -ier -i.əʳ, ⓤⓢ -i.ɚ -iest -i.ɪst, -i.əst -iness -ɪ.nəs, -ɪ.nɪs
kingmaker, K~ ˈkɪŋˌmeɪ.kəʳ, ⓤⓢ -kɚ -s -z
kingpin ˈkɪŋ.pɪn, ˌ-ˈ-, ⓤⓢ ˈkɪŋ.pɪn -s -z
Kingsborough ˈkɪŋz.bər.ə, ⓤⓢ -bɚ.oʊ
Kingsbury ˈkɪŋz.bər.i, ⓤⓢ -ˌber-
Kingscote ˈkɪŋz.kəʊt, ⓤⓢ -kət, -koʊt
Kings Cross ˌkɪŋzˈkrɒs, ⓤⓢ -ˈkrɑːs
stress shift: ˌ**Kings Cross** ˈ**Station**
kingship ˈkɪŋ.ʃɪp
king-size ˈkɪŋ.saɪz -d -d
Kingsley ˈkɪŋz.li
Kings|man ˈkɪŋz|.mən, -mæn -men -mən, -men
Kingsteignton kɪŋˈsteɪn.tən, ⓤⓢ -tən
Kingston(e) ˈkɪŋ.stən, ˈkɪŋk-, ˈkɪŋz.tən
Kingstown ˈkɪŋz.taʊn, ˈkɪŋ.stən, ˈkɪŋk-
Kingsway ˈkɪŋz.weɪ
Kingswinford kɪŋˈswɪn.fəd, ⓤⓢ -fɚd
Kingswood ˈkɪŋz.wʊd
Kington ˈkɪŋ.tən, ˈkɪŋk-
Kingussie kɪŋˈjuː.si
kink kɪŋk -s -s -ing -ɪŋ -ed -t
kinkajou ˈkɪŋ.kə.dʒuː -s -z
Kinkel ˈkɪŋ.kəl
kink|y ˈkɪŋ.k|i -ier -i.əʳ, ⓤⓢ -i.ɚ -iest -i.ɪst, -i.əst -iness -ɪ.nəs, -ɪ.nɪs
kinless ˈkɪn.ləs, -lɪs
Kinnaird kɪˈneəd, ⓤⓢ -ˈnerd
Kinnear kɪˈnɪəʳ, -ˈneəʳ, ⓤⓢ -ˈnɪr, -ˈner
Kinnock ˈkɪn.ək
Kinnoull kɪˈnuːl
kino ˈkiː.nəʊ, ⓤⓢ -noʊ
Kinros|s kɪnˈrɒs, ⓤⓢ -ˈrɑːs -shire -ʃəʳ, -ʃɪəʳ, ⓤⓢ -ʃɚ, -ʃɪr
Kinsale kɪnˈseɪl
Kinsella kɪnˈsel.ə, ˈkɪnt.sel.ə
Kinsey ˈkɪn.zi
kinsfolk ˈkɪnz.fəʊk, ⓤⓢ -foʊk
Kinshasa kɪnˈʃɑː.sə, -ˈʃæs.ə, ⓤⓢ -ˈʃɑː.sə, -sɑː
kinship ˈkɪn.ʃɪp
Kinski ˈkɪnt.ski
kins|man ˈkɪnz|.mən -men -mən, -men
kins|woman ˈkɪnz|ˌwʊm.ən -women -ˌwɪm.ɪn
Kintore kɪnˈtɔːʳ, ⓤⓢ -ˈtɔːr
Kintyre kɪnˈtaɪ.əʳ, -taɪ.əʳ, ⓤⓢ -ˈtaɪ.ɚ
kiosk ˈkiː.ɒsk, ⓤⓢ -ɑːsk, kiˈɑːsk -s -s
kip kɪp -s -s -ping -ɪŋ -ped -t
Kipling ˈkɪp.lɪŋ
Kippax ˈkɪp.æks, -əks

K

kipp|er ˈkɪp|.əʳ, ⓊⓈ -ɚ **-ers** -əz, ⓊⓈ -ɚz **-ering** -ᵊr.ɪŋ **-ered** -əd, ⓊⓈ -ɚd

Kipps kɪps

kir kɪəʳ, ⓊⓈ kɪr **-s** -z

Kirby ˈkɜː.bi, ⓊⓈ ˈkɝː-

Kircaldie kɜːˈkɔːl.di, kə-, ⓊⓈ kɝː-, kɚ-

Kirchner ˈkɜːk.nəʳ, ⓊⓈ ˈkɪrk.nɚ *US family name:* ˈkɜː.tʃ.nəʳ, ˈkɜːʃ-, ⓊⓈ ˈkɝː.tʃ.nɚ, ˈkɝːʃ-

Kirghiz ˈkɜː.gɪz, ˈkɪə-, ⓊⓈ kɪrˈgiːz

Kirghizia kɜːˈgɪz.i.ə, kɪə-, ⓊⓈ kɪrˈgiː.ʒə, -ʒi.ə

Kiribati ˈkɪr.ɪˌbæs; ˌkɪr.iˈbɑː.ti, ⓊⓈ ˈkɪr.ə.bæs; ⓊⓈ ˌkɪr.iˈbɑː.ti

Kiri Te Kanawa ˌkɪr.i.tɪˈkæn.ə.wə, ˌkɪə.ri-, -ˈkɑː.nə-, -teɪ-, ⓊⓈ ˌkɪr.i.təˈkɑː.nə.wɑː

Kiriyenko ˌkɪr.iˈjeŋ.kəʊ, ⓊⓈ -koʊ

kirk kɜːk, ⓊⓈ kɝːk **-s** -s

Kirk(e) kɜːk, ⓊⓈ kɝːk

Kirkby *surname:* ˈkɜː.bi, ˈkɜːk.bi, ⓊⓈ ˈkɝː-, ˈkɝːk- *place:* ˈkɜː.bi, ⓊⓈ ˈkɝː-

Kirkcaldy *place:* kɜːˈkɔː.di, kəˈkɒd.i, -ˈkɔː.di, ⓊⓈ kɝː-, kɚ- *surname:* kɜːˈkɔː.di, kə-, ⓊⓈ kɝː-, kɚ-

Kirkcudbright kɜːˈkuː.bri, kə-, ⓊⓈ kɝː-, kɚ- **-shire** -ʃəʳ, -ʃɪəʳ, ⓊⓈ -ʃɚ, -ʃɪr

Kirkdale ˈkɜːk.deɪl, ⓊⓈ ˈkɝːk-

Kirkham ˈkɜː.kəm, ⓊⓈ ˈkɝː-

Kirkintilloch ˌkɜː.kɪnˈtɪl.ək; *as if Scots:* -əx; ⓊⓈ ˌkɝː.kɪnˈtɪl.ək

Kirkland ˈkɜːk.lənd, ⓊⓈ ˈkɝːk-

Kirklees ˌkɜːkˈliːz, ⓊⓈ ˌkɝːk-

Kirkman ˈkɜːk.mən, ⓊⓈ ˈkɝːk-

Kirkness ˌkɜːkˈnes, ⓊⓈ ˌkɝːk-

Kirkpatrick ˌkɜːkˈpæt.rɪk, ⓊⓈ ˌkɝːk-

Kirkstall ˈkɜːk.stɔːl; *locally also:* -stᵊl, ⓊⓈ ˈkɝːk-

Kirkuk kɜːˈkʊk, ˈ--, ⓊⓈ kɪrˈkuːk

Kirkwall ˈkɜːk.wɔːl, ⓊⓈ ˈkɝːk-

Kirkwood ˈkɜːk.wʊd, ⓊⓈ ˈkɝːk-

Kirov ˈkɪə.rɒf, -rɒv, ⓊⓈ ˈkiː.rɔːf

Kirovabad kɪəˈrɒv.ə.bæd, kɪ-, ⓊⓈ kiːˈroʊ.və-, kɪ-

Kirriemuir ˌkɪr.iˈmjʊəʳ, -ˈmjɔːʳ, ⓊⓈ -ˈmjʊɚ

kirsch kɪəʃ, kɜːʃ, ⓊⓈ kɪrʃ

kirschwasser ˈkɪəʃˌvæs.əʳ, -ˌvɑː.səʳ, ⓊⓈ ˈkɪrʃˌvɑː.sɚ

Kirsten ˈkɜː.stɪn, ˈkɪə-, -stᵊn, ⓊⓈ ˈkɝː-, ˈkɪr-

Kirstie, Kirsty ˈkɜː.sti, ⓊⓈ ˈkɝː-

kirtle ˈkɜː.tᵊl, ⓊⓈ ˈkɝː.t̬ᵊl **-s** -z

Kisangani ˌkɪs.æŋˈgɑː.ni, ⓊⓈ ˌkiː.sɑːnˈgɑː-

kish kɪʃ

Kishinev ˈkɪʃ.ɪ.nɒf, -nef, ⓊⓈ -nev, -nef, -nɔːf

Kishon ˈkaɪ.ʃɒn; *with some Jews:* ˈkiː.ʃɒn, ⓊⓈ ˈkaɪ.ʃɑːn, -ʃᵊn

kismet ˈkɪz.met, ˈkɪs-, -mɪt, -mət, ⓊⓈ -met, -mɪt

kiss kɪs **-es** -ɪz **-ing** -ɪŋ **-ed** -t **-er/s** -əʳ/z, ⓊⓈ -ɚ/z ˌ**kiss of** ˈ**death**; ˌ**kiss of** ˈ**life**

kissagram, kiss-a-gram, kissogram ˈkɪs.ə.græm **-s** -z

kiss-and-tell ˌkɪs.ᵊndˈtel

Kissinger ˈkɪs.ɪn.dʒəʳ, -ɪŋ.əʳ, ⓊⓈ -ən.dʒɚ, -ɪn-

kiss-off ˈkɪs.ɒf, ⓊⓈ -ɑːf

Kisumu kɪˈsuː.muː, ⓊⓈ kiː-

kit, K~ kɪt **-s** -s **-ting** -ɪŋ, ⓊⓈ ˈkɪt̬.ɪŋ **-ted** -ɪd, ⓊⓈ ˈkɪt̬.ɪd ˌ**kit and caboodle**; ˈ**kit** ˌ**bag**; ˈ**kit** ˌ**car**

kitbag ˈkɪt.bæg **-s** -z

kit-cat, K~ ˈkɪt.kæt **-s** -s

kitchen, K~ ˈkɪtʃ.ɪn, -ᵊn **-s** -z ˌ**kitchen** ˈ**cabinet**; ˌ**kitchen** ˈ**garden**; ˌ**kitchen** ˈ**sink**; ˌ**kitchen** ˈ**unit**

kitchener, K~ ˈkɪtʃ.ɪ.nəʳ, -ᵊn.əʳ, ⓊⓈ -ə.nɚ **-s** -z

kitchenette ˌkɪtʃ.ɪˈnet, -əˈ- **-s** -s

kitchenmaid ˈkɪtʃ.ɪn.meɪd, -ᵊn- **-s** -z

kitchenware ˈkɪtʃ.ɪn.weəʳ, -ᵊn-, ⓊⓈ -wer

Kitchin ˈkɪtʃ.ɪn

Kitching ˈkɪtʃ.ɪŋ

kit|e kaɪt **-es** -s **-ing** -ɪŋ **-ed** -əd

Kit-E-Kat® ˈkɪt.i.kæt, ⓊⓈ ˈkɪt̬-

kitemark ˈkaɪt.mɑːk, ⓊⓈ -mɑːrk

kith kɪθ

Kithnos ˈkɪθ.nɒs, ⓊⓈ -nɑːs

Kit-Kat® ˈkɪt.kæt

kitsch kɪtʃ **-y** -i

Kitson ˈkɪt.sᵊn

kitten ˈkɪt.ᵊn **-s** -z

kittenish ˈkɪt.ᵊn.ɪʃ **-ly** -li

kittiwake ˈkɪt.ɪ.weɪk, ⓊⓈ ˈkɪt̬- **-s** -s

Kitto ˈkɪt.əʊ, ⓊⓈ ˈkɪt̬.oʊ

Kittredge ˈkɪt.rɪdʒ

Kitts kɪts

Kittson ˈkɪt.sᵊn

kitt|y, K~ ˈkɪt|.i, ⓊⓈ ˈkɪt̬- **-ies** -iz ˈ**Kitty** ˌ**Hawk**

Kitwe ˈkɪt.weɪ

Kitzbuhel, Kitzbühel ˈkɪts.bjuː.əl, -buː-, -bjuːl, -buːl

kiwi, K~® ˈkiː.wiː, -wi **-s** -z ˈ**kiwi** ˌ**fruit**

kJ (abbrev. for **kilojoule**) ˈkɪl.əʊˌdʒuːl, ⓊⓈ ˈ-oʊ-, ˈ-ə-

KKK (abbrev. for **Ku Klux Klan**) ˌkeɪ.keɪˈkeɪ

kl (abbrev. for **kilolitre/s**) *singular:* ˈkɪl.əʊˌliː.təʳ, ⓊⓈ -oʊˌliː.t̬ɚ, ˈ-ə-; *plural:* ˈkɪl.əʊˌliː.təz, ⓊⓈ -oʊˌliː.t̬ɚz, ˈ-ə-

Klagenfurt ˈklɑː.gᵊn.fɜːt, ⓊⓈ -fɝːt

Klan klæn

Klans|man ˈklænz|.mən, -mæn **-men** -mən, -men

klatch klætʃ, ⓊⓈ klætʃ, klɑːtʃ **-es** -ɪz

klaxon ˈklæk.sᵊn **-s** -z

Klee kleɪ

Kleenex® ˈkliː.neks

Klein klaɪn

Kleinwort ˈklaɪn.wɔːt, ⓊⓈ -wɔːrt

Kleist klaɪst

Klemperer ˈklem.pᵊr.əʳ, ⓊⓈ -ɚ

kleptomani|a ˌklep.təʊˈmeɪ.ni|.ə, ⓊⓈ -təˈ-, -toʊˈ-, -njə **-ac/s** -æk/s

Kline klaɪn

Klondike ˈklɒn.daɪk, ⓊⓈ ˈklɑːn-

Kluge *English name:* kluːdʒ *German name:* ˈkluː.gə

klutz klʌts **-es** -ɪz

klutz|y ˈklʌt.s|i **-iness** -ɪ.nəs, -ɪ.nɪs

km (abbrev. for **kilometre/s**) *singular:* kɪˈlɒm.ɪ.təʳ, ˈ-ə-; ˈkɪl.əʊˌmiː-, ⓊⓈ kɪˈlɑː.mə.t̬ɚ; ⓊⓈ ˈkɪl.əˌmiː-; *plural:* kɪˈlɒm.ɪ.təz, ˈ-ə-; ˈkɪl.əʊˌmiː.təz, ⓊⓈ kɪˈlɑː.mɪ.t̬ɚz; ⓊⓈ ˈkɪl.əˌmiː.t̬ɚz

K Mart® ˈkeɪˌmɑːt, ⓊⓈ -ˌmɑːrt

knack næk **-s** -s

knack|er ˈnæk|.əʳ, ⓊⓈ -ɚ **-ers** -əz, ⓊⓈ -ɚz **-ering** -ᵊr.ɪŋ **-ered** -əd, ⓊⓈ -ɚd

knacker|y ˈnæk.ᵊr|.i **-ies** -iz

knag næg **-s** -z **-gy** -i

knap næp **-s** -s **-ping** -ɪŋ **-ped** -t

Knapp næp

knapsack ˈnæp.sæk **-s** -s

knar nɑːʳ, ⓊⓈ nɑːr **-s** -z

Knaresborough ˈneəz.bᵊr.ə, ˈ-brə, ⓊⓈ ˈnerz.bɚ.oʊ

knave neɪv **-s** -z

knaver|y ˈneɪ.vᵊr|.i **-ies** -iz

knavish ˈneɪ.vɪʃ **-ly** -li **-ness** -nəs, -nɪs

knead niːd **-s** -z **-ing** -ɪŋ **-ed** -ɪd

Knebworth ˈneb.wəθ, -wɜːθ, ⓊⓈ -wɚθ, -wɝːθ

knee niː **-s** -z **-ing** -ɪŋ **-d** -d ˌ**knee**-ˈ**deep**; ˌ**weak at the** ˈ**knees**

knee-breeches ˈniːˌbrɪtʃ.ɪz

kneecap ˈniː.kæp **-s** -s **-ping** -ɪŋ **-ped** -t

kneehigh **n** ˈniː.haɪ **-s** -z

knee-high **adj** ˌniːˈhaɪ *stress shift:* ˌ**knee-high** ˈ**socks**

knee-jerk ˈniː.dʒɜːk, ⓊⓈ -dʒɝːk

knee-joint ˈniː.dʒɔɪnt **-s** -s

kneel niːl **-s** -z **-ing** -ɪŋ **-ed** -d **knelt** nelt

knees-up ˈniːz.ʌp

knell nel **-s** -z **-ing** -ɪŋ **-ed** -d

Kneller ˈnel.əʳ, ⓊⓈ -ɚ **-s** -z

knelt (from **kneel**) nelt

Knesset ˈknes.et, kəˈnes-, -ɪt

knew (from **know**) njuː, nuː, ⓊⓈ nuː, njuː

knicker ˈnɪk.əʳ, ⓊⓈ -ɚ **-s** -z

knickerbocker, K~ ˈnɪk.əˌbɒk.əʳ, ⓊⓈ -ɚˌbɑː.kɚ **-s** -z ˌ**knickerbocker** ˈ**glory**

knick-knack ˈnɪk.næk **-s** -s **-ery** -ᵊr.i

Knicks nɪks

kni|fe **n** naɪ|f **-ves** -vz

knif|e **v** naɪf **-es** -s **-ing** -ɪŋ **-ed** -t

knight, K~ naɪt **-s** -s **-ing** -ɪŋ, ⓊⓈ ˈnaɪ.t̬ɪŋ **-ed** -ɪd, ⓊⓈ ˈnaɪ.t̬ɪd

knight-errant ˌnaɪtˈer.ᵊnt **knights-errant** ˌnaɪtsˈer.ᵊnt

knighthood ˈnaɪt.hʊd **-s** -z

Knightley ˈnaɪt.li

knightl|y ˈnaɪt.l|i **-ier** -i.əʳ, ⓊⓈ -i.ɚ **-iest** -i.ɪst, -i.əst **-iness** -ɪ.nəs, -ɪ.nɪs

Knighton ˈnaɪ.tᵊn

Knightsbridge ˈnaɪts.brɪdʒ

knish kəˈnɪʃ **-es** -ɪz

knit nɪt **-s** -s **-ting** -ɪŋ, ⓊⓈ ˈnɪt̬.ɪŋ **-ted** -ɪd, ⓊⓈ ˈnɪt̬.ɪd **-ter/s** -əʳ/z, ⓊⓈ ˈnɪt̬.ɚ/z ˈ**knitting ma**ˌ**chine**; ˈ**knitting** ˌ**needle**

knitwear ˈnɪt.weəʳ, ⓊⓈ -wer

knob nɒb, ⓊⓈ nɑːb **-s** -z

K

knobbly ˈnɒb.əl.i, ˈ-li, (US) ˈnɑː.bəl.i, ˈ-bli
knobb|y ˈnɒb|.i, (US) ˈnɑː.b|i **-ier** -i.əʳ, (US) -i.ɚ **-iest** -i.ɪst, -i.əst **-iness** -ɪ.nəs, -ɪ.nɪs
knock nɒk, (US) nɑːk **-s** -s **-ing/s** -ɪŋ/z **-ed** -t **-er/s** -əʳ/z, (US) -ɚ/z
knockabout ˈnɒk.ə.baʊt, (US) ˈnɑːk- **-s** -s
Knockbreda nɒkˈbriː.də, (US) nɑːk-
knock-down ˈnɒk.daʊn, (US) ˈnɑːk.daʊn
knock-down-drag-out ˌnɒk.daʊnˈdræg.aʊt, (US) ˌnɑːk- *stress shift:* ˌ**knock-down-ˌdrag-out ˈfight**
knock-kneed ˌnɒkˈniːd, (US) ˈnɑːk.niːd *stress shift:* ˌ**knock-kneed ˈchild**
knockoff ˈnɒk.ɒf, (US) ˈnɑːk.ɑːf **-s** -s
knock-on adj ˌnɒkˈɒn, (US) ˌnɑːkˈɑːn *stress shift, see compound:* ˈ**knock-on efˌfect**
knock-on n ˌnɒkˈɒn, ˈ--, (US) ˌnɑːkˈɑːn, ˈ--
knock-out ˈnɒk.aʊt, (US) ˈnɑːk- **-s** -s ˈ**knockout ˌdrops**
knock-up ˈnɒk.ʌp, (US) ˈnɑːk- **-s** -s
knockwurst ˈnɒk.wɜːst, (US) ˈnɑːk.wɝːst, -wʊrst
Knole nəʊl, (US) noʊl
knoll nəʊl, (US) noʊl **-s** -z
Knolles, Knollys nəʊlz, (US) noʊlz
knop nɒp, (US) nɑːp **-s** -s
Knopf nɒpf, (US) nɑːpf
Knopfler ˈnɒp.fləʳ, (US) ˈnɑːp.flɚ
Knossos ˈknɒs.ɒs, ˈknəʊ.sɒs, -səs, (US) ˈnɑː.səs
knot nɒt, (US) nɑːt **-s** -s **-ting** -ɪŋ, (US) ˈnɑː.t̬ɪŋ **-ted** -ɪd, (US) ˈnɑː.t̬ɪd **at a ˌrate of ˈknots**
knotgrass ˈnɒt.grɑːs, (US) ˈnɑːt.græs
knothole ˈnɒt.həʊl, (US) ˈnɑːt.hoʊl **-s** -z
Knott nɒt, (US) nɑːt
Knottingley ˈnɒt.ɪŋ.li, (US) ˈnɑː.t̬ɪŋ-
knott|y ˈnɒt|.i, (US) ˈnɑː.t̬|i **-ier** -i.əʳ, (US) -i.ɚ **-iest** -i.ɪst, -i.əst **-ily** -əl.i, -ɪ.li **-iness** -ɪ.nəs, -ɪ.nɪs
Knotty Ash ˌnɒt.iˈæʃ, (US) ˌnɑː.t̬i-
knout naʊt **-s** -s **-ing** -ɪŋ, (US) ˈnaʊ.t̬ɪŋ **-ed** -ɪd, (US) ˈnaʊ.t̬ɪd
know nəʊ, (US) noʊ **-s** -z **-ing** -ɪŋ **knew** njuː, (US) nuː **known** nəʊn, (US) noʊn **knower/s** ˈnəʊ.əʳ/z, (US) ˈnoʊ.ɚ/z **knowable** ˈnəʊ.ə.bəl, (US) ˈnoʊ-
know-all ˈnəʊ.ɔːl, (US) ˈnoʊ-, -ɑːl **-s** -z
know-how ˈnəʊ.haʊ, (US) ˈnoʊ-
knowing ˈnəʊ.ɪŋ, (US) ˈnoʊ- **-ly** -li **-ness** -nəs, -nɪs
know-it-all ˈnəʊ.ɪt.ɔːl, (US) ˈnoʊ.ɪt̬-, -ɑːl **-s** -z
Knowle nəʊl, (US) noʊl
knowledg|e ˈnɒl.ɪdʒ, (US) ˈnɑː.lɪdʒ **-es** -ɪz
knowledgeab|le ˈnɒl.ɪ.dʒə.b|əl, (US) ˈnɑː.lɪ- **-ly** -li
Knowles nəʊlz, (US) noʊlz
known (from **know**) nəʊn, (US) noʊn
know-nothing ˈnəʊˌnʌθ.ɪŋ, -ˌnɒθ-, (US) ˈnoʊˌnʌθ.ɪŋ **-s** -z
Knox nɒks, (US) nɑːks
Knoxville ˈnɒks.vɪl, (US) ˈnɑːks-, -vəl
knuckl|e ˈnʌk.əl **-es** -z **-ing** -ɪŋ, ˈ-lɪŋ **-ed** -d **-y** -i, ˈ-li ˌ**knuckle ˈsandwich**
knuckleball ˈnʌk.əl.bɔːl, (US) -bɔːl, -bɑːl
knucklebone ˈnʌk.əl.bəʊn, (US) -boʊn **-s** -z
knuckle-duster ˈnʌk.əlˌdʌs.təʳ, (US) -tɚ **-s** -z
knucklehead ˈnʌk.əl.hed **-ed** -ɪd
knurled nɜːld, (US) nɝːld
Knutsford ˈnʌts.fəd, (US) -fɚd
KO, k.o. ˌkeɪˈəʊ, (US) -ˈoʊ **-'s** -z **-'ing** -ɪŋ **-'d** -d
koala kəʊˈɑː.lə, (US) koʊ- **-s** -z
Kobe ˈkəʊ.beɪ, -bi, (US) ˌkoʊˈbeɪ, ˈkoʊ.bi
Koblenz kəʊˈblents, (US) ˈkoʊ.blents
kobo ˈkɒb.əʊ, (US) ˈkɑː.boʊ, ˈkoʊ-; (US) ˈkɔː.bɔː
kobold ˈkɒb.əʊld, ˈkəʊ.bəʊld, -bəld, (US) ˈkoʊ.bɔːld, -bɑːld **-s** -z
Koch kəʊk, kɒtʃ; *as if German:* kɒx; (US) koʊk, kɑːk, kɑːtʃ; *as if German:* (US) kɔːx; (US) koʊx
Köchel ˈkɜː.kəl; *as if German:* -xəl ˈ**Köchel ˌnumber**
Kodak® ˈkəʊ.dæk, (US) ˈkoʊ- **-s** -s
Kodály ˈkəʊ.daɪ, -dɑː.i, (US) ˈkoʊ-; (US) koʊˈdɑː.i
Kodiak ˈkəʊ.di.æk, (US) ˈkoʊ-
Koestler ˈkɜːst.ləʳ, (US) ˈkest.lɚ
Koh-i-noor ˌkəʊ.iˈnʊəʳ, -ˈnɔːəʳ, -ˈnɔːʳ, ˈ---, (US) ˈkoʊ.i.nʊr
kohl kəʊl, (US) koʊl
Kohl kəʊl, (US) koʊl
kohlrab|i ˌkəʊlˈrɑː.b|i, (US) ˌkoʊl-, ˈ--- **-ies** -iz
koine, K~ ˈkɔɪ.neɪ, -niː, -ni, (US) kɔɪˈneɪ; (US) ˈkɔɪ.neɪ, -niː
Kojak ˈkəʊ.dʒæk, (US) ˈkoʊ-
kola, K~ ˈkəʊ.lə, (US) ˈkoʊ-
Kolkata ˌkɒlˈkʌt.ə, -ˈkɑː.tə, ˈkɒl-, (US) ˌkɔːlˈkɑː.t̬ə
kolkhoz ˌkɒlˈkɒz, -ˈkɔːz, -ˈhɔːz, (US) ˌkɑːlˈkɔːz **-es** -ɪz
Kolnai ˈkɒl.naɪ, (US) ˈkɑːl-
Komodo kəˈməʊ.dəʊ, (US) -ˈmoʊ.doʊ
Kongo ˈkɒŋ.gəʊ, (US) ˈkɑːŋ.goʊ
Konica® ˈkɒn.ɪ.kə, ˈkəʊ.nɪ-, (US) ˈkɑː.nɪ-
Königsberg ˈkɜː.nɪgz.bɜːg, -beəg, (US) ˈkɝː.nɪgz.bɝːrg, -berg
Konrad ˈkɒn.ræd, (US) ˈkɑːn-
Konya ˈkɔː.njɑː
koodoo ˈkuː.duː **-s** -z
kook kuːk **-s** -s
kookaburra ˈkʊk.əˌbʌr.ə, (US) -ˌbɝː-, -ˌbʌr- **-s** -z
kook|y ˈkuː.k|i **-ier** -i.əʳ, (US) -i.ɚ **-iest** -i.ɪst, -i.əst **-iness** -ɪ.nəs, -ɪ.nɪs
Kool-Aide® ˈkuːl.eɪd
Koori(e) ˈkʊə.ri, ˈkɔː-, (US) ˈkʊr.i
Kop kɒp, (US) kɑːp
kope(c)k ˈkəʊ.pek, ˈkɒp.ek, (US) ˈkoʊ.pek **-s** -s
kopje ˈkɒp.i, (US) ˈkɑː.pi **-s** -z
Kops kɒps, (US) kɑːps
Korah ˈkɔː.rə, (US) ˈkɔːr.ə
Koran kɒrˈɑːn, kɔːˈrɑːn, kʊ-, kə-, (US) kəˈræn, -ˈrɑːn; (US) ˈkɔːr.æn, -ɑːn
Koranic kɒrˈæn.ɪk, kɔːˈræn-, kʊ-, kə-, (US) kəˈræn.ɪk, -ˈrɑː.nɪk; (US) ˈkɔːr.æn.ɪk, -ɑː.nɪk
Kore|a kəˈriː|.ə, kɒrˈiː-, (US) kəˈriː-, kɔː- **-an/s** -ən/z
korma ˈkɔː.mə, (US) ˈkɔːr-
koruna kɒrˈuː.nə, kəˈruː-, (US) ˈkɔːr.uː- **-s** -z
koruny (plural of **koruna**) kɒrˈuː.ni, kəˈruː-, (US) ˈkɔːr.uː-
kosher ˈkəʊ.ʃəʳ; *occasionally, by non-Jews:* ˈkɒʃ.əʳ, (US) ˈkoʊ.ʃɚ
Kosice ˈkɒʃ.ɪt.seɪ, (US) ˈkɔː.ʃiːt.seɪ, -ʃɪt-
Kosov|o ˈkɒs.ə.v|əʊ, (US) ˈkoʊ.sə.v|oʊ, ˈkɑː-, ˈkɔː- **-an** -ən **-ar/s** -ɑːʳ/z, (US) -ɑːr/z
Kostunica kɒʃˈtuː.nɪt.sə, (US) kɑːʃˈtuː.nɪt.sə
Kosygin kəˈsiː.gɪn, (US) kə-, koʊ-
Kotex® ˈkəʊ.teks, (US) ˈkoʊ-
kotow ˌkəʊˈtaʊ, (US) ˌkoʊ- **-s** -z **-ing** -ɪŋ **-ed** -d **-er/s** -əʳ/z, (US) -ɚ/z
Kough kjəʊ, kəʊ, (US) kjoʊ, koʊ
koumiss ˈkuː.mɪs, -məs
Kournikova ˌkɔː.nɪˈkəʊ.və, -nəˈ-, (US) ˌkɔːr.nɪˈkoʊ-, -nəˈ-
Kowasaki kəʊ.əˈsɑː.ki, -ˈsæk.i, (US) koʊ-
Kowloon ˌkaʊˈluːn
kowtow ˌkaʊˈtaʊ, (US) ˌkaʊˈtaʊ, ˈ-- **-s** -z **-ing** -ɪŋ **-ed** -d **-er/s** -əʳ/z, (US) -ɚ/z
kraal krɑːl, krɔːl **-s** -z
Note: Usually pronounced /krɑːl/ in England, but /krɔːl/ in South Africa.
Kraft® krɑːft, (US) kræft
Kragujevac krægˈuː.jə.væts, (US) ˈkrɑː.guː.jə.vɑːts
krait kraɪt **-s** -s
Krajicek ˈkraɪ.tʃek, ˈkrɑː.jɪ.tʃek, ˈkraɪ.ə.tʃek
Krakatoa ˌkræk.əˈtəʊ.ə, (US) -ˈtoʊ-
kraken ˈkrɑː.kən, ˈkreɪ-, (US) ˈkrɑː- **-s** -z
Krakow ˈkræk.ɒv, -ɒf, -aʊ, (US) ˈkrɑː.kaʊ, ˈkræk.aʊ, ˈkreɪ.kaʊ; (US) ˈkrɑː.kʊf
Kramer ˈkreɪ.məʳ, (US) -mɚ
krantz, K~ krænts
Krasnodar ˌkrɑːs.nəʊˈdɑːʳ, (US) -noʊˈdɑːr
Krasnoyarsk ˌkrɑːs.nəʊˈjɑːsk, (US) -noʊˈjɑːrsk
Kravchuk krævˈtʃʊk
Kray kreɪ
kremlin, K~ ˈkrem.lɪn **-s** -z
Kremlinolog|y ˌkrem.lɪˈnɒl.ə.dʒ|i, (US) -ˈnɑː.lə- **-ist/s** -ɪst/s
kreu(t)zer, K~ ˈkrɔɪt.səʳ, (US) -sɚ **-s** -z
krill krɪl
kris kriːs **-es** -ɪz
Krishna ˈkrɪʃ.nə
Kris Kringle, Kriss Kringle ˌkrɪsˈkrɪŋ.gəl

Krista ˈkrɪs.tə
Kristen ˈkrɪs.tᵊn, -tɪn
Kristi ˈkrɪs.ti
Kristiansand ˈkrɪs.tʃᵊn.sænd
Kristie ˈkrɪs.ti
Kristin ˈkrɪs.tɪn
Kristina krɪˈstiː.nə
Kristine krɪˈstiːn
Kristopher ˈkrɪs.tə.fəʳ, (US) -fɚ
kro|na ˈkrəʊ|.nə, (US) ˈkroʊ- **-nor** -nɔːʳ, (US) -nɔːr
kró|na ˈkrəʊ|.nə, (US) ˈkroʊ- **-nur** -nʊəʳ, (US) -nɚ
kro|ne ˈkrəʊ|.nə, (US) ˈkroʊ- **-nes** -nəz **-ner** -nəʳ **-nen** -nən
Kronin ˈkrəʊ.nɪn, (US) ˈkroʊ-
Krons(h)tadt ˈkrɒnt.ʃtæt, (US) ˈkrɔːnt.ʃtɑːt
kroon kruːn
Krug kruːg
Kruger ˈkruː.gəʳ, (US) -gɚ
krugerrand, K~ ˈkruː.gᵊr.ænd, (US) -gɚ- **-s** -z
Krupp krʊp, krʌp
Krushchev ˈkrʊs.tʃɒf, ˈkrʊʃ-, ˌ-ˈ-, (US) ˈkruːs.tʃef, -tʃɔːf, -tʃev, kruːʃˈtʃɔːf
krypton ˈkrɪp.tɒn, -tən, (US) -tɑːn
kryptonite ˈkrɪp.tᵊn.aɪt, (US) -tə.naɪt
Krystal ˈkrɪs.tᵊl
Krystle ˈkrɪs.tᵊl
Kuala Lumpur ˌkwɑː.ləˈlʊm.pʊəʳ, ˌkwɒl-, -ˈlʌm-, -pəʳ, (US) ˌkwɑː.ləˈlʊm.pʊr
Kubla Khan ˌkuː.bləˈkɑːn, ˌkʊb.ləˈ-, (US) ˌkuː.bləˈ-
Kubrick ˈkjuː.brɪk, ˈkuː-
kudos ˈkjuː.dɒs, (US) ˈkuː.doʊz, ˈkjuː-, -doʊs, -dɑːs
Kudrow ˈkʊd.rəʊ, (US) ˈkuːdroʊ
kudu ˈkuː.duː **-s** -z
Ku Klux Klan ˌkuː.klʌksˈklæn, ˌkjuː-
kulak ˈkuː.læk, (US) kuːˈlɑːk, ˈ-- **-s** -s
kultur, K~ kʊlˈtʊəʳ, (US) -ˈtʊr
Kumanovo ˌkuː.məˈnəʊ.vəʊ, (US) ˈkʊm.əˌnoʊ.voʊ
Kumar kuːˈmɑːʳ, ˈ--, (US) ˈkuː.mɑːr
Kumasi kʊˈmæs.i, -ˈmɑː.si, (US) -ˈmɑː.si
Kumin ˈkjuː.mɪn, ˈkuː-, (US) ˈkuː-
kümmel ˈkʊm.ᵊl, ˈkɪm-, (US) ˈkɪm-
kumquat ˈkʌm.kwɒt, (US) -kwɑːt **-s** -s
Kundera ˈkʊn.də.rə, (US) -dɚ.ə
kung fu ˌkʊŋˈfuː, ˌkʌŋ-, (US) ˌkʌŋ-, ˌkʊŋ-, ˌgʊn-
Kunitz ˈkjuː.nɪts, ˈkuː-, (US) ˈkuː-
Kuomintang ˌkwəʊ.mɪnˈtæŋ, ˌgwəʊ-, (US) ˌkwoʊ-
Kuoni® kuˈəʊ.ni, (US) -ˈoʊ-
Kurath ˈkjʊə.ræθ, (US) ˈkʊr.ɑːt, ˈkjʊr-, -ɑːθ
Kurd kɜːd, (US) kɝːd, kʊrd **-s** -z **-ish** -ɪʃ
Kurdistan ˌkɜː.dɪˈstɑːn, -dəˈ-, -ˈstæn, (US) ˌkɝː.dɪˈstæn, ˌkʊr-, -dəˈ-, -ˈstɑːn
Kureishi kʊˈreʃ.i, -ˈreɪ.ʃi, -ˈriː-
Kuril(e) kʊˈriːl, kjuː-, (US) ˈkuː.rɪl; (US) kuːˈriːl **-s** -z
Kurosawa ˌkʊə.rəʊˈsɑː.wə, (US) ˌkʊr.əˈ-
kursaal ˈkʊə.zɑːl, ˈkɜː-, -sɑːl, -sᵊl, (US) ˈkʊr-, ˈkɝː- **-s** -z
Kursk kɜːsk, kʊəsk, (US) kɝːsk
Kurt kɜːt, (US) kɝːt
Kurtis ˈkɜː.tɪs, (US) ˈkɝː.t̬ɪs
Kurtz kɜːts, (US) kɝːts
kurus kʊˈrʊʃ, -ˈruːʃ, (US) -ˈruːʃ
Kutaisi kʊˈtaɪ.si, (US) kʊˈtaɪ.si, ˌkuː.təˈjiː.si
Ku|wait kuː|ˈweɪt, kjuː-, kə-, (US) kuː|ˈweɪt, -ˈwaɪt **-waiti/s** -ˈweɪ.ti/z, (US) -ˈweɪ.t̬i/z, -ˈwaɪ.t̬i/z
Kuyper ˈkaɪ.pəʳ, (US) -pɚ
kvas(s) kvɑːs, kvæs, (US) kvɑːs, kəˈvɑːs
kvetch kvetʃ, kəˈvetʃ **-es** -ɪz **-ing** -ɪŋ **-ed** -t
kW (abbrev. for **kilowatt**) ˈkɪl.əʊ.wɒt, (US) -oʊ.wɑːt, ˈ-ə-
kwacha ˈkwɑː.tʃɑː
Kwangtung ˌkwænˈtʌŋ, ˌkwæŋ-, (US) ˌkwɑːŋˈtʊŋ, ˌgwɑːŋ-
Kwantung ˌkwænˈtʌŋ, (US) ˌkwɑːŋˈtʊŋ, ˌgwɑːŋ-
kwanza ˈkwæn.zə, (US) ˈkwɑːn.zɑː, -zə **-s** -z
Kwanzaa ˈkwɑːn.zə, ˈkwæn-, -zɑː, (US) ˈkwɑːn- **-s** -z
kwashiorcor ˌkwæʃ.iˈɔː.kɔːʳ, -kəʳ, (US) ˌkwɑː.ʃiːˈɔːr.kɔːr
KwaZulu kwɑːˈzuː.luː
KwaZulu-Natal kwɑːˌzuː.luː.nəˈtæl, -ˈtɑːl
kwela ˈkweɪ.lə
KWIC kwɪk
Ky. (abbrev. for **Kentucky**) kenˈtʌk.i, kən-, (US) kən-
kyat kiˈɑːt, (US) tʃɑːt, kjɑːt
Kyd kɪd
Kyla ˈkaɪ.lə
kyle, K~ kaɪl **-s** -z
Kylie ˈkaɪ.li
kylin ˈkaɪ.lɪn **-s** -z
Kyllachy ˈkaɪ.lə.ki, -xi, (US) -ki
kymogram ˈkaɪ.məʊ.græm, (US) -moʊ-, -mə-
kymograph ˈkaɪ.məʊ.grɑːf, -græf, (US) -moʊ.græf, -mə- **-s** -s
kymographic ˌkaɪ.məʊˈgræf.ɪk, (US) -moʊˈ-, -məˈ-
Kynance ˈkaɪ.nænts
Kynaston ˈkɪn.ə.stᵊn
Kyoto ˈkjəʊ.təʊ, kiˈəʊ.təʊ, (US) kiːˈoʊ.toʊ, ˈkjoʊ-
Kyrgyzstan ˌkɜː.gɪˈstɑːn, (US) ˈkɪr.gɪ.stɑːn, -stæn, ˌ--ˈ-
kyrie ˈkɪr.i.eɪ, ˈkɪə.ri-, -iː, (US) ˈkɪr.i.eɪ **-s** -z
Kyrle kɜːl, (US) kɝːl
Kythe ˈkaɪ.θi
Kyushu ˈkjuː.ʃuː, kiˈuː-
Kyzyl-Kum kəˌzɪlˈkuːm, -ˈkʊm

L

Pronouncing the letter L

→ *See also* **LL**

In general, the consonant letter **l** is pronounced /l/, e.g.:

like	laɪk
wool	wʊl

However, **l** is frequently silent, particularly when preceded by an **a**, e.g.:

calf	kɑːf (US) kæf
calm	kɑːm (US) kɑːlm

In the past-tense form of modal verbs spelt **ould**, **l** is also silent, e.g.:

could	kʊd
would	wʊd

l, L el -'s -z
l (abbrev. for **litre/s**) *singular:* ˈliː.təʳ, (US) -t̬ɚ; *plural:* ˈliː.təz, (US) -t̬ɚz
la lɑː -s -z
LA ˌelˈeɪ ˌLA ˈlaw
La. (abbrev. for **Louisiana**) luˌiː.ziˈæn.ə, -ˈɑː.nə; ˌluː.i.ziˈ-, (US) luˌiː.ziˈæn.ə; (US) ˌluː.ziˈ-
laager ˈlɑː.gəʳ, (US) -gɚ -s -z
laari ˈlɑː.ri, (US) ˈlɑːr.i -s -z
lab læb -s -z
Laban *biblical character:* ˈleɪ.bən, -bæn, (US) -bən *US family name:* ləˈbæn
label ˈleɪ.bəl -s -z -(l)ing -ɪŋ, ˈleɪ.blɪŋ -(l)ed -d
labia (from **labium**) ˈleɪ.bi.ə
labial ˈleɪ.bi.əl -s -z -ly -i
labialization, -isa- ˌleɪ.bi.əl.aɪˈzeɪ.ʃən, -ɪˈ-, (US) -əˈ-
labializ|e, -is|e ˈleɪ.bi.əl.aɪz -es -ɪz -ing -ɪŋ -ed -d
labia majora ˌleɪ.bi.ə.məˈdʒɔː.rə, -maɪˈɔː-, (US) -məˈdʒɔːr.ə
labia minora ˌleɪ.bi.ə.mɪˈnɔː.rə, (US) -ˈnɔːr.ə
labiate ˈleɪ.bi.eɪt, -ət, -ɪt -s -s
Labienus ˌlæb.iˈiː.nəs, -ˈeɪ-
labile ˈleɪ.baɪl, (US) -baɪl, -bəl
labiodental ˌleɪ.bi.əʊˈden.təl, (US) -oʊˈden.t̬əl -s -z
labiopalatal ˌleɪ.bi.əʊˈpæl.ə.təl, (US) -oʊˈpæl.ə.t̬əl -s -z -ly -li
labiovelar ˌleɪ.bi.əʊˈviː.ləʳ, (US) -oʊˈviː.lɚ -s -z
labiovelariz|e, -is|e ˌleɪ.bi.əʊˈviː.lər.aɪz, (US) -oʊˈviː.lə.raɪz -es -ɪz -ing -ɪŋ -ed -d
labi|um ˈleɪ.bi|.əm -a -ə
La Bohème ˌlɑː.bəʊˈem, ˌlæ-, -ˈeɪm, (US) ˌlɑː.boʊˈ-
lab|or, L~ ˈleɪ.b|əʳ, (US) -b|ɚ -ors -əz, (US) -ɚz -oring -ər.ɪŋ -ored -əd, (US) -ɚd -orer/s -ər.əʳ/z, (US) -ɚ.ɚ/z ˌ**labor of ˈlove;** ˈ**labor ˌunion**
laborator|y ləˈbɒr.ə.tər|.i, -tr|i, (US) ˈlæb.rə.tɔːr|.i, ˈlæb.ɚ.ə- -ies -iz
labor-intensive ˌleɪ.bər.ɪnˈtent.sɪv, (US) -bɚ- *stress shift:* ˌ**labor-intensive ˈwork**
laborious ləˈbɔː.ri.əs, (US) -ˈbɔːr.i- -ly -li -ness -nəs, -nɪs
laborite, L~ ˈleɪ.bər.aɪt, (US) -bə.raɪt -s -s
labor-saving ˈleɪ.bəˌseɪ.vɪŋ, (US) -bɚˌ- *stress shift:* ˌ**labor-saving ˈgadget**
Labouchere ˌlæb.uˈʃeəʳ, -ʊˈ-, ˈ---, (US) ˌlæb.uˈʃer
lab|our, L~ ˈleɪ.b|əʳ, (US) -b|ɚ -ours -əz, (US) -ɚz -ouring -ər.ɪŋ -oured -əd, (US) -ɚd -ourer/s -ər.əʳ/z ˈ**labour exˌchange;** ;ˌ**labour of ˈlove;** ˈ**Labour ˌParty**
labour-intensive ˌleɪ.bər.ɪnˈtent.sɪv, (US) -bɚ- *stress shift:* ˌ**labour-intensive ˈwork**
labourite, L~ ˈleɪ.bər.aɪt, (US) -bə.raɪt -s -s
labour-saving ˈleɪ.bəˌseɪ.vɪŋ, (US) -bɚˌ- *stress shift:* ˌ**labour-saving ˈgadget**
Labrador ˈlæb.rə.dɔːʳ, (US) -dɔːr -s -z
Labuan ləˈbuː.ən, (US) ˌlɑː.buːˈɑːn, ləˈbuː.ən
laburnum ləˈbɜː.nəm, (US) -ˈbɝː- -s -z
labyrinth ˈlæb.ər.ɪntθ, -ɪ.rɪntθ, (US) -ɚ.ɪntθ, ˈ-rəntθ -s -s
labyrinth|ian ˌlæb.əˈrɪnt.θ|i.ən, -ɪˈ-, (US) -əˈrɪnt- -ine -aɪn, (US) -ɪn, -iːn, -aɪn
lac læk -s -s
Laccadive ˈlæk.ə.dɪv, ˈlɑː.kə-, -diːv, -daɪv, (US) ˈlæk.ə.daɪv; (US) ˈlɑː.kə.diːv -s -z
laccolith ˈlæk.ə.lɪθ
lac|e leɪs -es -ɪz -ing -ɪŋ -ed -t -er/s -əʳ/z, (US) -ɚ/z
Lacedaemon ˌlæs.əˈdiː.mən, -ɪˈ-, (US) -əˈ-
Lacedaemonian ˌlæs.ə.dɪˈməʊ.ni.ən, ˌ-ɪ-, -dəˈ-, (US) -ə.dɪˈmoʊ.ni- -s -z
lacer|ate ˈlæs.ər|.eɪt, (US) -ə.r|eɪt -ates -eɪts -ating -eɪ.tɪŋ, (US) -eɪ.t̬ɪŋ -ated -eɪ.tɪd, (US) -eɪ.t̬ɪd
laceration ˌlæs.ərˈeɪ.ʃən, (US) -əˈreɪ- -s -z
Lacert|a ləˈsɜː.t|ə, (US) -ˈsɝː.t̬|ə -ae -iː
Lacey ˈleɪ.si
laches ˈlætʃ.ɪz, ˈleɪ.tʃɪz, -tʃəz, (US) ˈlætʃ.ɪz, ˈleɪ.tʃɪz
Lachesis ˈlæk.ə.sɪs, -ɪ-, (US) ˈlæk-, ˈlætʃ-
Lachish ˈleɪ.kɪʃ
Lachlan ˈlæk.lən, ˈlɒk.lən, (US) ˈlɑːk-
lachrymal ˈlæk.rɪ.məl
lachrymatory ˌlæk.rɪˈmeɪ.tər.i; ˈlæk.rɪ.mə-, -meɪ-, (US) ˈlæk.rɪ.mə.tɔːr-
lachrymose ˈlæk.rɪ.məʊs, -rə-, -məʊz, (US) -rɪ.moʊs -ly -li
lack læk -s -s -ing -ɪŋ -ed -t
lackadaisic|al ˌlæk.əˈdeɪ.zɪ.k|əl -ally -əl.i, -li -alness -nəs, -nɪs
lackaday ˈlæk.ə.deɪ, ˌ--ˈ-
lackey ˈlæk.i -s -z -ing -ɪŋ -ed -d
lacklustre, lackluster ˈlækˌlʌs.təʳ, ˌ-ˈ--, (US) ˈlækˌlʌs.tɚ
Lacon ˈleɪ.kən
Laconi|a ləˈkəʊ.ni|.ə, (US) -ˈkoʊ- -an/s -ən/z
laconic, L~ ləˈkɒn.ɪk, (US) -ˈkɑː.nɪk -al -əl -ally -əl.i, -li
lacqu|er ˈlæk|.əʳ, (US) -ɚ -ers -əz, (US) -ɚz -ering -ər.ɪŋ -ered -əd, (US) -ɚd -erer/s -ər.əʳ/z, (US) -ɚ.ɚ/z
lacquey ˈlæk.i -s -z -ing -ɪŋ -ed -d
Lacroix lækˈrwɑː, (US) ləˈkwɑː, -ˈkrɔɪ
lacrosse ləˈkrɒs, (US) -ˈkrɑːs
lactase ˈlæk.teɪs, -teɪz, (US) -teɪs
lactate n ˈlæk.teɪt
lacta|te v lækˈteɪ|t, (US) ˈ-- -tes -ts -ting -tɪŋ, (US) -t̬ɪŋ -ted -tɪd, (US) -t̬ɪd
lactation lækˈteɪ.ʃən
lacteal ˈlæk.ti.əl
lactic ˈlæk.tɪk ˌ**lactic ˈacid**
lactometer lækˈtɒm.ɪ.təʳ, -ə.təʳ, (US) -ˈtɑː.mə.t̬ɚ -s -z
lactose ˈlæk.təʊs, -təʊz, (US) -toʊs
lacun|a ləˈkjuː.n|ə, lækˈjuː-, (US) ləˈkjuː- -ae -iː -as -əz
lacy, L~ ˈleɪ.si
lad læd -s -z
Lada® ˈlɑː.də -s -z
Ladakh ləˈdɑːk, -ˈdɔːk, (US) -ˈdɑːk
Ladbroke ˈlæd.brʊk, -brəʊk, (US) -brʊk, -broʊk
Ladbrokes ˈlæd.brəʊks, -brʊks, (US) -broʊks, -brʊks
ladd|er ˈlæd|.əʳ, (US) -ɚ -ers -əz, (US) -ɚz -ering -ər.ɪŋ -ered -əd, (US) -ɚd
ladderback ˈlæd.ə.bæk, (US) ˈ-ɚ-
laddie ˈlæd.i -s -z

laddish ˈlæd.ɪʃ **-ly** -li **-ness** -nəs, -nɪs

lad|e leɪd **-es** -z **-ing** -ɪŋ **-ed** -ɪd **-en** -ən

Ladefoged ˈlæd.ɪ.fəʊ.gɪd, ˈ-ə-, -gəd, (US) -ə.foʊ.gəd

laden (from **lade**) ˈleɪ.dən

la-di-da, lah-di-dah ˌlɑː.dɪˈdɑː, (US) -diˈ- *stress shift:* **ˌla-di-da ˈvoice**

ladies ˈleɪ.diz **ˈladies' ˌman; ˈladies' ˌroom**

ladieswear ˈleɪ.diz.weəʳ, (US) -wer

Ladislaus ˈlæd.ɪ.slɔːs, (US) -slɔːs, -slɑːs

Ladislaw ˈlæd.ɪ.slɔː, (US) -slɔː, -slɑː

ladl|e ˈleɪ.dəl **-es** -z **-ing** -ɪŋ, ˈleɪd.lɪŋ **-ed** -d

ladleful ˈleɪ.dəl.fʊl **-s** -z

Ladoga ˈlæd.əʊ.gə, ˈlɑː.dəʊ-; ləˈdəʊ-, (US) ˈlɑː.dɔː.gɑː, -də.gə

la dolce vita lɑːˌdɒl.tʃeɪˈviː.tə, (US) -ˌdoʊl.tʃeɪˈ-, -tʃəˈ-, -t̬ə

Ladrone ləˈdrəʊn, (US) -ˈdroʊn

lad|y, L~ ˈleɪ.d|i **-ies** -iz **ˌLady ˈBountiful; ˈlady ˌchapel; ˈLady ˌDay; ˈlady ˌfriend**

L

ladybird, L~® ˈleɪ.di.bɜːd, (US) -bɝːd **-s** -z

ladybug ˈleɪ.di.bʌg **-s** -z

ladyfinger ˈleɪ.diˌfɪŋ.gəʳ, (US) -gɚ **-s** -z

lady-in-waiting ˌleɪ.di.ɪnˈweɪ.tɪŋ, (US) -t̬ɪŋ **ladies-in-waiting** ˌleɪ.diz-

lady-killer ˈleɪ.diˌkɪl.əʳ, (US) -ɚ **-s** -z

ladylike ˈleɪ.di.laɪk

ladylove ˈleɪ.di.lʌv **-s** -z

ladyship ˈleɪ.di.ʃɪp **-s** -s

Ladysmith ˈleɪ.di.smɪθ

Laertes leɪˈɜː.tiːz, (US) -ˈɝː-, -ˈer-

Laestrygones liːˈstraɪ.gə.niːz, (US) lesˈtrɪg.ə-

Laetitia lɪˈtɪʃ.i.ə, liː-, lə-, -ˈtiː.ʃi-, ˈ-ʃə, (US) ləˈtɪʃ.ə, -ˈtiː.ʃə

Lafarge ləˈfɑːʒ, (US) -ˈfɑːrʒ

Lafayette *French name:* ˌlɑː.faɪˈet, ˌlæf-, -feɪˈ-, (US) ˌlæf.iːˈ-, ˌlɑː.fiːˈ-, -faɪˈ- *in Louisiana:* ˌlɑːˈfeɪt, lə-

Lafcadio læfˈkɑː.di.əʊ, (US) lɑːfˈkɑː.di.oʊ

Laffan ˈlæf.ən; ləˈfæn

Laf(f)itte læfˈiːt, lɑːˈfiːt, lə-, (US) lɑːˈfiːt, lə-

Lafontaine ˌlæf.ɒnˈten, ˌlɑː.fɒn-, -ˈteɪn, (US) ˌlɑː.fɔːn-, -foʊnˈ-

lag læg **-s** -z **-ging** -ɪŋ **-ged** -d **-ger/s** -əʳ/z, (US) -ɚ/z

Lagan ˈlæg.ən

lager *beer:* ˈlɑː.gəʳ, (US) -gɚ **-s** -z **ˈlager ˌlout**

Lager *English surname:* ˈleɪ.gəʳ, (US) -gɚ

Lagerfeld ˈlɑː.gə.felt, (US) -gɚ-

laggard ˈlæg.əd, (US) -ɚd **-s** -z **-ly** -li

lagn(i)appe ˈlæn.jæp, ˌ-ˈ-

lagoon ləˈguːn **-s** -z

Lagos ˈleɪ.gɒs, (US) -gɑːs; (US) ˈlɑː.goʊs

Lagrange lægˈrɑ̃ːnʒ, ləˈ-, -ˈgreɪndʒ, (US) lɑːˈgrɑ̃ːndʒ, lə-

La Guardia ləˈgwɑː.di.ə, (US) -ˈgwɑːr-

Laguna Beach ləˌguː.nəˈbiːtʃ

lah lɑː **-s** -z

lah-di-dah ˌlɑː.diˈdɑː, (US) -diːˈ- *stress shift:* **ˌlah-di-dah ˈaccent**

Lahore ləˈhɔːʳ, lɑː-, (US) -ˈhɔːr

laic ˈleɪ.ɪk **-al** -əl

laid (from **lay**) leɪd

laid-back ˌleɪdˈbæk *stress shift:* **ˌlaid-back ˈattitude**

Laidlaw ˈleɪd.lɔː, (US) -lɑː, -lɔː

lain (from **lie**) leɪn

Laindon ˈleɪn.dən

Laing læŋ, leɪŋ

lair leəʳ, (US) ler **-s** -z

laird, L~ leəd, (US) lerd **-s** -z **-ship** -ʃɪp

lairy ˈleə.ri, (US) ˈler.i

laissez-faire, laisser-faire ˌleɪ.seɪˈfeəʳ, ˌles.eɪˈ-, (US) ˌles.eɪˈfer, ˌleɪ.seɪˈ- *stress shift:* **ˌlaissez-faire ˈattitude**

laity ˈleɪ.ə.ti, -ɪ.ti, (US) -ti, -t̬i

Laius ˈlaɪ.əs, ˈleɪ-, (US) ˈleɪ-, ˈlaɪ-

lake, L~ leɪk **-s** -s

Lakeland ˈleɪk.lənd, -lænd

Lakenheath ˈleɪ.kən.hiːθ

Lake Placid ˌleɪkˈplæs.ɪd

Laker ˈleɪ.kəʳ, (US) -kɚ **-s** -z

lakeside, L~ ˈleɪk.saɪd **-s** -z

lakh lɑːk, læk **-s** -s

Lakin ˈleɪ.kɪn

Lalage ˈlæl.ə.gi, -dʒi

Lalique® lælˈiːk, ləˈliːk, (US) lɑːˈliːk, lə-

lam læm **-s** -z **-ming** -ɪŋ **-med** -d

lama, L~ ˈlɑː.mə **-s** -z

Lamarr ləˈmɑːʳ, (US) -ˈmɑːr

lamaser|y ˈlɑː.mə.sər|.i, ˈlæm.ə-, (US) ˈlɑː.mə.ser- **-ies** -iz

Lamaze ləˈmɑːz **Laˈmaze ˌmethod**

lamb, L~ læm **-s** -z **-ing** -ɪŋ **-ed** -d **ˌlamb's ˈlettuce; ˈlamb's ˌwool; ˌmutton dressed as ˈlamb**

lambada læmˈbɑː.də, (US) lɑːm- **-s** -z **-ing** -ɪŋ **-ed** -d

lambast læmˈbæst, (US) -ˈbeɪst, -ˈbæst **-s** -s **-ing** -ɪŋ **-ed** -ɪd

lambast|e læmˈbeɪst, (US) -ˈbeɪst, -ˈbæst **-es** -s **-ing** -ɪŋ **-ed** -ɪd

lambda ˈlæm.də **-s** -z

lambdacism ˈlæm.də.sɪ.zəm **-s** -z

Lambe læm

lamben|cy ˈlæm.bən|*t*.si **-t** -t

Lambert ˈlæm.bət, (US) -bɚt

Lambeth ˈlæm.bəθ

lambkin ˈlæm.kɪn **-s** -z

lamblike ˈlæm.laɪk

Lamborghini® ˌlæm.bɔːˈgiː.ni, -bəˈ-, (US) ˌlɑːm.bɔːrˈ-, ˌlæm-, -bɚˈ-

Lambretta® læmˈbret.ə, (US) -ˈbret̬-

lambrusco, L~ læmˈbrʊs.kəʊ, (US) -ˈbruː.skoʊ, lɑːm-, -ˈbrʊs.koʊ

lambskin ˈlæm.skɪn **-s** -z

Lambton ˈlæm*p*.tən

lam|e leɪm **-er** -əʳ, (US) -ɚ **-est** -ɪst, -əst **-ely** -li **-eness** -nəs, -nɪs **-es** -z **-ing** -ɪŋ **-ed** -d **ˌlame ˈduck**

lamé ˈlɑː.meɪ, (US) læmˈeɪ, lɑːˈmeɪ

lamebrain ˈleɪm.breɪn **-s** -z

Lamech ˈleɪ.mek, ˈlɑː-, -mex, (US) ˈleɪ.mek

lamell|a ləˈmel|.ə **-ae** -iː **-as** -əz **-ar** -əʳ, (US) -ɚ

la|ment lə|ˈment **-ments** -ˈments **-menting** -ˈmen.tɪŋ, (US) -ˈmen.t̬ɪŋ **-mented** -ˈmen.tɪd, (US) -ˈmen.t̬ɪd

lamentab|le ˈlæm.ən.tə.b|əl, -ɪn-; ləˈmen-, (US) ləˈmen.t̬ə-; (US) ˈlæm.ən.t̬ə- **-ly** -li

lamentation, L~ ˌlæm.enˈteɪ.ʃən, -ənˈ-, -ɪnˈ-, (US) -ənˈ- **-s** -z

Lamia *Greek town:* læmˈiː.ə, (US) ləˈmiː- *literary title, Keats:* ˈlɑː.mi.ə, ˈleɪ-, (US) ˈleɪ-

lamin|a ˈlæm.ɪ.n|ə, ˈ-ə- **-al** -əl **-ae** -iː **-as** -əz **-ar** -əʳ, (US) -ɚ

laminate n ˈlæm.ɪ.nət, ˈ-ə-, -nɪt, -neɪt, (US) -nɪt

lami|nate v ˈlæm.ɪ|.neɪt, ˈ-ə- **-nates** -neɪts **-nating** -neɪ.tɪŋ, (US) -neɪ.t̬ɪŋ **-nated** -neɪ.tɪd, (US) -neɪ.t̬ɪd

lamination ˌlæm.ɪˈneɪ.ʃən, -əˈ-

lamington, L~ ˈlæm.ɪŋ.tən

Lammas ˈlæm.əs **-tide** -taɪd

lammergeier, lammergeyer ˈlæm.ə.gaɪ.əʳ, (US) -ɚ.gaɪ.ɚ **-s** -z

Lammermoor ˈlæm.ə.mʊəʳ, -mɔːʳ, ˌ--ˈ-, (US) ˈlæm.ɚ.mʊr, -mɔːr, ˌ--ˈ-

Lammermuir ˈlæm.ə.mjʊəʳ, -mjɔːʳ, (US) -ɚ.mjʊr, -mjʊɚ

Lamond ˈlæm.ənd

Lamont *surname:* ləˈmɒnt; ˈlæm.ənt, (US) ləˈmɑːnt *in US:* ləˈmɒnt, (US) -ˈmɑːnt

lamp læmp **-s** -s

Lampard ˈlæm.pɑːd, (US) -pɑːrd

lampas *silk material:* ˈlæm.pəs *swelling in horse's mouth:* ˈlæm.pəz

lampblack ˈlæmp.blæk

Lampedusa ˌlæm.pɪˈdjuː.zə, (US) -pəˈduː.sə, -zə

Lampet ˈlæm.pɪt

Lampeter ˈlæm.pɪ.təʳ, -pə-, (US) -t̬ɚ

lampion ˈlæm.pi.ən **-s** -z

lamp|light ˈlæmp|.laɪt **-lighter/s** -ˌlaɪ.təʳ/z, (US) -ˌlaɪ.t̬ɚ/s

Lamplough ˈlæm.pluː, -plʌf

Lamplugh ˈlæm.pluː, -plə

lampoon læmˈpuːn **-s** -z **-ing** -ɪŋ **-ed** -d **-er/s** -əʳ/z, (US) -ɚ/z

lamp post ˈlæmp.pəʊst, (US) -poʊst **-s** -s

lamprey ˈlæm.pri **-s** -z

lampshade ˈlæmp.ʃeɪd **-s** -z

Lampson ˈlæm*p*.sən

lampstand ˈlæmp.stænd **-s** -z

LAN læn **-s** -z

Lana ˈlɑː.nə, (US) ˈlæn.ə, ˈlɑː.nə

Lanagan ˈlæn.ə.gən

Lanark ˈlæn.ək, (US) -ɚk **-shire** -ʃəʳ, -ʃɪəʳ, (US) -ʃɚ, -ʃɪr

Lancashire ˈlæŋ.kə.ʃəʳ, -ʃɪəʳ, (US) -ʃɚ, -ʃɪr

Lancaster ˈlæŋ.kə.stəʳ, -kæs.təʳ, (US) ˈlæŋ.kə.stɚ, ˈlæn-, -kæs.tɚ

Lancasterian ˌlæŋ.kæsˈtɪə.ri.ən, -kəˈstɪə-, (US) ˌlæŋ.kæsˈtɪr.i-, ˌlæn-, -kəˈstɪr- **-s** -z

Lancastrian læŋˈkæs.tri.ən, (US) læŋ-, læn- **-s** -z

lanc|e, L~ lɑːnts, (US) lænts **-es** -ɪz **-ing** -ɪŋ **-ed** -t **ˌlance ˈcorporal**

Lancelot ˈlɑːnt.sə.lɒt, -sᵊl.ɒt, -lət, (US) ˈlænt.sə.lɑːt, ˈlɑːnt-, -lət
lancer ˈlɑːnt.səʳ, (US) ˈlænt.sɚ -s -z
lancet, L~ ˈlɑːnt.sɪt, (US) ˈlænt- -s -s
Lancia® ˈlɑːnt.si.ə, ˈlænt- -s -z
Lancing ˈlɑːnt.sɪŋ, (US) ˈlænt-
Lancôme®, Lancome ˈlɑ̃ːŋ.kəʊm, -ˈ-, (US) ˈlæn.koʊm, -kəm, ˌlænˈkoʊm
Lancs. (abbrev. for **Lancashire**) læŋks
land, L~ lænd -s -z -ing -ɪŋ -ed -ɪd
landau ˈlæn.dɔː, -daʊ -s -z
Lander ˈlæn.dəʳ, (US) -dɚ
landfall ˈlænd.fɔːl, (US) -fɔːl, -fɑːl -s -z
landfill ˈlænd.fɪl -s -z
landforc|e ˈlænd.fɔːs, (US) -fɔːrs -es -ɪz
landgrabb|er ˈlændˌgræb|.əʳ, ˈlæŋ-, (US) ˈlændˌgræb|.ɚ -ers -əz, (US) -ɚz -ing -ɪŋ
landgrave ˈlænd.greɪv, ˈlæŋ-, (US) ˈlænd- -s -z
landholder ˈlændˌhəʊl.dəʳ, (US) -ˌhoʊl.dɚ -s -z
landholding ˈlændˌhəʊl.dɪŋ, (US) -ˌhoʊl-
landing ˈlæn.dɪŋ -s -z **ˈlanding ˌgear; ˈlanding ˌnet; ˈlanding ˌstage; ˈlanding ˌstrip**
landlad|y ˈlændˌleɪ.d|i -ies -iz
landline ˈlænd.laɪn -s -z
landlocked ˈlænd.lɒkt, (US) -lɑːkt
landlord ˈlænd.lɔːd, (US) -lɔːrd -s -z -ism -ɪ.zᵊm
landlubber ˈlændˌlʌb.əʳ, (US) -ɚ -s -z
landmark ˈlænd.mɑːk, ˈlæm-, (US) ˈlænd.mɑːrk -s -s
landmass ˈlænd.mæs, ˈlæm-, (US) ˈlænd- -es -ɪz
landmine ˈlænd.maɪn, ˈlæm-, (US) ˈlænd- -s -z
Landon ˈlæn.dən
Landor ˈlæn.dɔːʳ, -dəʳ, (US) -dɚ, -dɔːr
land-own|er ˈlændˌəʊ.n|əʳ, (US) -ˌoʊ.n|ɚ -ers -əz, (US) -ɚz -ing -ɪŋ
landrail ˈlænd.reɪl -s -z
Landrieu ˈlæn.druː
Land Rover® ˈlændˌrəʊ.vəʳ, (US) -ˌroʊ.vɚ -s -z
landscap|e ˈlænd.skeɪp -es -s -ing -ɪŋ -ed -t -er/s -əʳ/z, (US) -ɚ/z **ˌlandscape ˈgardener** (US) **ˈland-scape ˌgardener; ˈlandscape ˌmode**
Landseer ˈlændˌsiː.əʳ, -sɪəʳ, (US) -ˌsiː.ɚ, -ˌsɪr
Land's End ˌlændzˈend
landslide ˈlænd.slaɪd -s -z
landslip ˈlænd.slɪp -s -s
lands|man ˈlændz|.mən -men -mən
landward ˈlænd.wəd, (US) -wɚd
landwehr ˈlænd.veəʳ, (US) -veɪr
landwind ˈlænd.wɪnd -s -z
lane, L~ leɪn -s -z **in the ˈfast ˌlane**
Lanfranc ˈlæn.fræŋk
Lang læŋ
Langbaine ˈlæŋ.beɪn
Langbourne ˈlæŋ.bɔːn, (US) -bɔːrn
Langdale ˈlæŋ.deɪl
Langer ˈlæŋ.əʳ, (US) -ɚ
Langerhans ˈlæŋ.ə.hænz, -hænts, (US) ˈlæŋ.ɚ.hænz, ˈlɑːŋ.ɚ.hɑːnz
Langford ˈlæŋ.fəd, (US) -fɚd
Langham, Langholm(e) ˈlæŋ.əm
Langhorne ˈlæŋ.hɔːn, (US) -hɔːrn
Langland ˈlæŋ.lənd
langlauf ˈlɑːŋ.laʊf -s -s
Langley ˈlæŋ.li
Langmere ˈlæŋ.mɪəʳ, (US) -mɪr
langoustine ˌlɑ̃ːŋ.guˈstiːn, ˌlæn-, (US) ˌlæŋ.gəˈ- -s -z
Langridge ˈlæŋ.grɪdʒ
Langside ˈlæŋ.saɪd, ˌ-ˈ-
lang syne ˌlæŋˈsaɪn, (US) -ˈzaɪn, -ˈsaɪn
Langton ˈlæŋk.tən
Langtry ˈlæŋk.tri
languag|e ˈlæŋ.gwɪdʒ -es -ɪz
langue lɑ̃ːŋg, (US) lɑ̃ːŋg, lɑːŋ
langue de chat ˌlɑ̃ːŋ.dəˈʃɑː, (US) ˌlɑ̃ːŋg-, ˌlɑːŋ-
Languedoc ˈlɑ̃ːŋ.gə.dɒk, ˌ--ˈ-, (US) lɑ̃ːŋ.gəˈdɔːk
languid ˈlæŋ.gwɪd -ly -li -ness -nəs, -nɪs
languish, L~ ˈlæŋ.gwɪʃ -es -ɪz -ing/ly -ɪŋ/li -ed -t -ment -mənt
languor ˈlæŋ.gəʳ, (US) -gɚ -ous/ly -əs/li
langur ˈlæŋ.gəʳ, ˈlʌŋ-, -gʊəʳ, (US) lɑːŋˈgʊr -s -z
Lanier ˈlæn.jəʳ; ləˈnɪəʳ, (US) ləˈnɪr
Lanigan ˈlæn.ɪ.gᵊn, ˈ-ə-
lank læŋk -er -əʳ, (US) -ɚ -est -ɪst, -əst -ly -li -ness -nəs, -nɪs
Lankester ˈlæŋ.kɪ.stəʳ, -kə-, (US) -stɚ
lank|y ˈlæŋ.k|i -ier -i.əʳ, (US) -i.ɚ -iest -i.ɪst, -i.əst -ily -ᵊl.i, -ɪ.li -iness -ɪ.nəs, -ɪ.nɪs
lanolin(e) ˈlæn.ᵊl.ɪn, -ə.liːn, (US) -ə.lɪn
Lansbury ˈlænz.bᵊr.i, (US) -ber.i
Lansdown(e) ˈlænz.daʊn
Lansing ˈlɑːnt.sɪŋ, ˈlænt-, (US) ˈlænt-
Lansley ˈlændz.li
Lantau ˈlæn.taʊ, ˌ-ˈ-
lantern ˈlæn.tən, (US) -ṭɚn -s -z
lanthanum ˈlænt.θə.nəm
lanyard ˈlæn.jəd, -jɑːd, (US) -jɚd, -jɑːrd -s -z
Lanzarote ˌlæn.zəˈrɒt.i, (US) ˌlɑːnt.səˈroʊ.ṭi, -teɪ
Laocoön leɪˈɒk.əʊ.ɒn, -ən, (US) -ˈɑː.koʊ.ɑːn
Laodamia ˌleɪ.əʊ.dəˈmiː.ə, (US) leɪˌɑː.dəˈmiː.ə
Laodice|a ˌleɪ.əʊ.dɪˈsiː|.ə, -dəˈ-, (US) leɪˌɑː.dɪˈ-; (US) ˌleɪ.ə.dəˈ- -an/s -ən/z
Laois liːʃ
Laomedon leɪˈɒm.ɪ.dən, ˈ-ə-, (US) -ˈɑː.mə.dɑːn
Laos ˈlɑː.ɒs; laʊs, laʊz, (US) laʊs; (US) ˈleɪ.ɑːs, -oʊs
Laotian ˈlaʊ.ʃi.ən, leɪˈəʊ-, -ʃᵊn; lɑːˈɒʃ.ᵊn, (US) leɪˈoʊ.ʃᵊn; ˈlaʊ.ʃᵊn
Lao-tsze ˌlɑː.əʊˈtseɪ, ˌlaʊˈtseɪ, -ˈtsiː, (US) ˌlaʊˈdzuː, -ˈtseɪ
lap læp -s -s -ping -ɪŋ -ped -t -per/s -əʳ/z, (US) -ɚ/z **in the ˌlap of ˈluxury**
laparoscop|y ˌlæp.ᵊrˈɒs.kə.p|i, (US) -ˈɑː.skə- -ies -iz
laparotom|y ˌlæp.ᵊrˈɒt.ə.m|i, (US) -əˈrɑː.ṭə- -ies -iz
La Paz lɑːˈpæz, læ-, (US) ləˈpɑːz, lɑː-, -ˈpɑːs
lapdog ˈlæp.dɒg, (US) -dɑːg, -dɔːg -s -z
lapel ləˈpel -s -z
lapful ˈlæp.fʊl -s -z
lapidar|y ˈlæp.ɪ.dᵊr|.i, ˈ-ə-, (US) -ə.der- -ies -iz
lapis lazuli ˌlæp.ɪsˈlæz.jʊ.li, -jə-, -laɪ, (US) -ˈlæz.ə.li, -ˈlæʒ-, -jʊ-
Lapland ˈlæp.lænd -er/s -əʳ/z, (US) -ɚ/z
La Porte ləˈpɔːt, (US) -ˈpɔːrt
Lapp læp -s -s -ish -ɪʃ
lapp|et ˈlæp|.ɪt -ets -ɪts -eted -ɪ.tɪd, (US) -ɪ.ṭɪd
Lappin ˈlæp.ɪn
Lapsang ˈlæp.sæŋ
Lapsang Souchong ˌlæp.sæŋ.suːˈʃɒŋ, -ˈtʃɒŋ, (US) -ˈtʃɔːŋ, -ˈʃɔːŋ
laps|e læps -es -ɪz -ing -ɪŋ -ed -t
lapsus linguae ˌlæp.səsˈlɪŋ.gwaɪ, -sʊsˈ-, -gweɪ, (US) -səsˈlɪŋ.gwiː, -gwaɪ
laptop ˈlæp.tɒp, (US) -tɑːp -s -s
Laput|a ləˈpjuː.t|ə, (US) -ṭ|ə -an/s -ᵊn/z
lapwing ˈlæp.wɪŋ -s -z
lar, L~ lɑːʳ, (US) lɑːr **lares** ˈleə.riːz, ˈlɑː.reɪz, (US) ˈler.iːz, ˈlɑːr.iːz
Lara ˈlɑː.rə, (US) ˈlɑːr.ə, ˈler.ə
Laramie ˈlær.ə.mi, (US) ˈler-, ˈlær-
Larbert ˈlɑː.bət, -bɜːt, (US) ˈlɑːr.bɚt, -bɝːt
larboard ˈlɑː.bəd, -bɔːd, (US) -bɚd, -bɔːrd
larcenous ˈlɑː.sᵊn.əs, -sɪ.nəs, (US) ˈlɑːr.sən- -ly -li
larcen|y ˈlɑː.sᵊn|.i, -sɪ.n|i, (US) ˈlɑːr.sən- -ies -iz
larch lɑːtʃ, (US) lɑːrtʃ -es -ɪz
lard lɑːd, (US) lɑːrd -s -z -ing -ɪŋ -ed -ɪd
larder ˈlɑː.dəʳ, (US) ˈlɑːr.dɚ -s -z
Lardner ˈlɑːd.nəʳ, (US) ˈlɑːrd.nɚ
lardon ˈlɑː.dᵊn, (US) ˈlɑːr- -s -z
Laredo ləˈreɪ.dəʊ, (US) -doʊ
lares (plural of **lar**) ˈleə.riːz, ˈlɑː.reɪz, (US) ˈler.iːz, ˈlɑːr.iːz
Largactil® lɑːˈgæk.tɪl, -tᵊl, (US) lɑːr-
larg|e lɑːdʒ, (US) lɑːrdʒ -er -əʳ, (US) -ɚ -est -ɪst, -əst -ely -li -eness -nəs, -nɪs **as ˌlarge as ˈlife**
large-hearted ˌlɑːdʒˈhɑː.tɪd, (US) ˌlɑːrʒˈhɑːr.ṭɪd -ness -nəs, -nɪs *stress shift:* **ˌlarge-hearted ˈperson**
large-scale ˌlɑːdʒˈskeɪl, (US) ˌlɑːrdʒ- *stress shift:* **ˌlarge-scale ˈchanges**
largess|(e) lɑːˈʒes, -ˈdʒes; ˈ--, (US) lɑːrˈdʒes, -ˈʒes; (US) ˈlɑːr.dʒəs -es -ɪz
larghetto lɑːˈget.əʊ, (US) lɑːrˈgeṭ.oʊ -s -z
largish ˈlɑː.dʒɪʃ, (US) ˈlɑːr-
largo ˈlɑː.gəʊ, (US) ˈlɑːr.goʊ -s -z

L

Largs lɑːgz, (US) lɑːrgz
Larham ˈlɑː.rəm, (US) ˈlɑː-
lari|at ˈlær.i|.ət, (US) ˈler-, ˈlær- **-ats** -əts **-ating** -ə.tɪŋ, (US) -ə.t̬ɪŋ **-ated** -ə.tɪd, (US) -ə.t̬ɪd
Larisa, Larissa ləˈrɪs.ə
lark lɑːk, (US) lɑːrk **-s** -s **-ing** -ɪŋ **-ed** -t
Larkhall ˈlɑːk.hɔːl, (US) ˈlɑːrk-, -hɑːl
Larkin ˈlɑː.kɪn, (US) ˈlɑːr-
larkspur ˈlɑːk.spɜːʳ, -spəʳ, (US) ˈlɑːrk.spɝː, -spɚ **-s** -z
lark|y ˈlɑː.k|i, (US) ˈlɑːr- **-ier** -i.əʳ, (US) -i.ɚ **-iest** -i.ɪst, -i.əst **-iness** -ɪ.nəs, -ɪ.nɪs
Larmor, Larmour ˈlɑː.məʳ, (US) ˈlɑːr.mɚ, -mɔːr
Larne lɑːn, (US) lɑːrn
Larousse lærˈuːs, (US) lɑːˈruːs
larrikin ˈlær.ɪ.kɪn, ˈ-ə-, (US) ˈler-, ˈlær- **-s** -z
larrup ˈlær.əp, (US) ˈler-, ˈlær- **-s** -s **-ping** -ɪŋ **-ped** -t
Larry ˈlær.i, (US) ˈler-, ˈlær-
Larsen, Larson ˈlɑː.sᵊn, (US) ˈlɑːr-
Lars Porsena ˌlɑːzˈpɔː.sɪ.nə, -sə-, (US) ˌlɑːrzˈpɔːr-
larum ˈlær.əm, (US) ˈler-, ˈlær-; (US) ˈlɑːr.ʊm **-s** -z
larv|a ˈlɑː.v|ə, (US) ˈlɑːr- **-ae** -iː **-al** -ᵊl
laryngal ləˈrɪŋ.gᵊl, lærˈɪŋ-, (US) ləˈrɪŋ-, lerˈɪŋ-, lær-
laryngeal ləˈrɪn.dʒi.əl, lærˈɪn-, -dʒᵊl; ˌlær.ɪnˈdʒiː.əl, -ənˈ-, (US) ləˈrɪn.dʒi.əl, -dʒᵊl
laryngectom|y ˌlær.ɪnˈdʒek.tə.m|i, -ənˈ-, (US) ˌler-, ˌlær- **-ies** -iz
larynges (plural of **larynx**) lærˈɪn.dʒiːz, ləˈrɪn-, (US) lə-, lerˈɪn-, lær-
laryngitis ˌlær.ɪnˈdʒaɪ.tɪs, -ənˈ-, -təs, (US) ˌler.ɪnˈdʒaɪ.t̬ɪs, ˌlær-, -t̬əs
laryngolog|y ˌlær.ɪŋˈgɒl.ə.dʒ|i, -əŋˈ-, (US) ˌler.ɪŋˈgɑː.lə-, ˌlær-, -ɪnˈdʒɑː- **-ist/s** -ɪst/s
laryngoscope ləˈrɪŋ.gə.skəʊp, lærˈɪŋ-; ˈlær.ɪŋ-, (US) ləˈrɪŋ.goʊ.skoʊp, -gə-, -ˈrɪn.dʒə- **-s** -s
laryngoscopic ləˌrɪŋ.gəˈskɒp.ɪk, lærˌɪŋ-; ˌlær.ɪŋ-, (US) ləˌrɪŋ.goʊˈskɑː.pɪk, -gəˈ-, -ˌrɪn.dʒəˈ-
laryngoscop|y ˌlær.ɪŋˈgɒs.kə.p|i, -əŋˈ-, (US) ˌler.ɪŋˈgɑː.skə-, ˌlær-, -ɪnˈdʒɑː- **-ist/s** -ɪst/s
larynx ˈlær.ɪŋks, (US) ˈler-, ˈlær- **-es** -ɪz **larynges** lærˈɪn.dʒiːz, ləˈrɪn-, (US) lə-, lerˈɪn-, lær-
lasagne, lasagna ləˈzæn.jə, -ˈsæn-, -ˈzɑː.njə, -ˈsɑː-, (US) -ˈzɑː.njə, -ˈsɑː-
Lascar ˈlæs.kəʳ, (US) -kɚ **-s** -z
Lascaux ˈlæs.kəʊ, -ˈ-, (US) læsˈkoʊ
Lascelles ˈlæs.ᵊlz, ləˈselz
lascivious ləˈsɪv.i.əs **-ly** -li **-ness** -nəs, -nɪs
laser ˈleɪ.zəʳ, (US) -zɚ **-s** -z **ˈlaser ˌdisk; ˈlaser ˌprinter**
laserjet ˈleɪ.zə.dʒet, (US) -zɚ- **-s** -s
lash læʃ **-es** -ɪz **-ing/s** -ɪŋ/z **-ed** -t **-er/s** -əʳ/z, (US) -ɚ/z
Lasham ˈlæʃ.əm; *locally also:* ˈlæs.əm
Las Palmas ˌlæsˈpæl.məs, -ˈpɑːl-, (US) ˌlɑːsˈpɑːl-, -mɑːs
lass læs **-es** -ɪz
Lassa ˈlæs.ə, ˈlɑː.sə, (US) ˈlɑː.sə, ˈlæs.ə **ˌLassa ˈfever**
Lassalle ləˈsæl
Lassell læsˈel, ləˈsel
lassi ˈlæs.i **-s** -z
lassie, L~ ˈlæs.i **-s** -z
lassitude ˈlæs.ɪ.tʃuːd, -tjuːd, ˈ-ə-, (US) -tuːd, -tjuːd
lasso n læsˈuː; ˈlæs.əʊ, (US) ˈlæs.oʊ, -uː **-(e)s** -z
lasso v læsˈuː, ləˈsuː, (US) ˈlæs.oʊ, -uː **-(e)s** -z **-ing** -ɪŋ **-ed** -d
last, L~ lɑːst, (US) læst **-s** -s **-ing/ly** -ɪŋ/li **-ed** -ɪd **-ly** ˈlɑːst.li, (US) ˈlæst.li **ˌLast ˈJudgment; ˌlast ˈstraw; ˌLast ˈSupper; ˌlast ˈword; at the ˌlast ˈminute**
last-ditch ˌlɑːstˈdɪtʃ, (US) ˌlæst- *stress shift, see compound:* **ˌlast-ditch atˈtempt**
last-minute ˌlɑːstˈmɪn.ɪt, (US) ˌlæst- *stress shift:* **ˌlast-minute ˈplans**
Las Vegas ˌlæsˈveɪ.gəs, ˌlɑːs-, (US) ˌlɑːs-
lat læt **-s** -s
Latakia ˌlæt.əˈkiː.ə, (US) ˌlɑː.t̬əˈ-, ˌlæt̬.əˈ-
latch lætʃ **-es** -ɪz **-ing** -ɪŋ **-ed** -t
latchet ˈlætʃ.ɪt, -ət **-s** -s
latchkey ˈlætʃ.kiː **-s** -z **ˈlatchkey ˌchild; ˌlatchkey ˈchild**
lat|e leɪt **-er** -əʳ, (US) ˈleɪ.t̬ɚ **-est** -ɪst, -əst, (US) ˈleɪ.t̬ɪst, -t̬əst **-ely** -li **-eness** -nəs, -nɪs
latecomer ˈleɪtˌkʌm.əʳ, (US) -ɚ **-s** -z
lateen ləˈtiːn, (US) lætˈiːn, ləˈtiːn **-s** -z
latency ˈleɪ.tᵊnt.si
late-night ˈleɪtˌnaɪt **ˌlate-ˌnight ˈshopping**
latent ˈleɪ.tᵊnt **-ly** -li
lateral ˈlæt.ᵊr.ᵊl, ˈ-rᵊl, (US) ˈlæt̬.ɚ.ᵊl **-s** -z **-ly** -i **ˌlateral ˈthinking**
Lateran ˈlæt.ᵊr.ᵊn, (US) ˈlæt̬-
laterite ˈlæt.ᵊr.aɪt, (US) ˈlæt̬.ə.raɪt
latex ˈleɪ.teks **-es** -ɪz **latices** ˈlæt.ɪ.siːz, ˈleɪ.tɪ-, (US) ˈlæt̬.ɪ-, ˈleɪ.t̬ɪ-
lath læθ, lɑːθ, (US) læθ **-s** -s, lɑːðz, (US) -s, læðz
Latham ˈleɪ.θəm, -ðəm

> Note: Generally /ˈleɪ.θəm/ in the south of England; always /ˈleɪ.ðəm/ in the north.

Lathbury ˈlæθ.bᵊr.i, (US) -ber-
lath|e leɪð **-es** -z **-ing** -ɪŋ **-ed** -d
lath|er ˈlɑː.ð|əʳ, ˈlæð|.əʳ, (US) ˈlæð|.ɚ **-ers** -əz, (US) -ɚz **-ering** -ᵊr.ɪŋ **-ered** -əd, (US) -ɚd
lathi ˈlɑː.ti **-s** -z
Lathom ˈleɪ.θəm, -ðəm
Lathrop ˈleɪ.θrəp
latices (plural of **latex**) ˈlæt.ɪ.siːz, ˈleɪ.tɪ-, (US) ˈlæt̬.ɪ-, ˈleɪ.t̬ɪ-
Latimer ˈlæt.ɪ.məʳ, ˈ-ə-, (US) ˈlæt̬.ə.mɚ
Latin ˈlæt.ɪn, (US) -ᵊn **-ate** -eɪt **ˌLatin Aˈmerica**
latin|ism ˈlæt.ɪ.n|ɪ.zᵊm, (US) -ᵊn|.ɪ- **-isms** -ɪ.zᵊmz **-ist/s** -ɪst/s
latinity ləˈtɪn.ə.ti, lætˈɪn-, -ɪ.ti, (US) lætˈɪn.ə.t̬i
latiniz|e, -is|e ˈlæt.ɪ.naɪz, (US) -ᵊn.aɪz **-es** -ɪz **-ing** -ɪŋ **-ed** -d
latin|o, L~ ləˈtiː.n|əʊ, lætˈiː-, (US) -n|oʊ **-os** -əʊz, (US) -oʊz **-a/s** -ə/z, (US) -ɑː/z
Latinus ləˈtaɪ.nəs
latish ˈleɪ.tɪʃ, (US) -t̬ɪʃ
latitude ˈlæt.ɪ.tʃuːd, ˈ-ə-, -tjuːd, (US) ˈlæt̬.ə.tuːd, -tjuːd **-s** -z
latitudinal ˌlæt.ɪˈtʃuː.dɪ.nᵊl, -əˈ-, -ˈtjuː-, -dᵊn.ᵊl, (US) ˌlæt̬.əˈtuː-, -ˈtjuː-
latitudinarian ˌlæt.ɪˌtʃuː.dɪˈneə.ri.ən, -əˌ-, -ˌtjuː-, (US) ˌlæt̬.əˌtuː.dɪˈner.i-, -ˌtjuː- **-s** -z **-ism** -ɪ.zᵊm
Latium ˈleɪ.ʃi.əm, ˈlæt.i-, (US) ˈleɪ.ʃᵊm, -ʃi.əm
latke ˈlɑːt.kə **-s** -z
Latoya ləˈtɔɪ.ə
latria ləˈtraɪ.ə
latrine ləˈtriːn **-s** -z
Lattakia ˌlæt.əˈkiː.ə, (US) ˌlɑː.t̬əˈ-, ˌlæt̬.əˈ-
latte ˈlæt.eɪ, (US) ˈlɑː.teɪ
latter ˈlæt.əʳ, (US) ˈlæt̬.ɚ **-ly** -li
latter-day ˈlæt.ə.deɪ, (US) ˈlæt̬.ɚ- **ˌLatter-Day ˈSaint**
lattic|e ˈlæt.ɪs, (US) ˈlæt̬- **-es** -ɪz **-ed** -t
latticework ˈlæt.ɪs.wɜːk, (US) ˈlæt̬.ɪs.wɝːk
Latvi|a ˈlæt.vi|.ə **-an/s** -ən/z
laud, L~ lɔːd, (US) lɑːd, lɔːd **-s** -z **-ing** -ɪŋ **-ed** -ɪd
Lauda ˈlaʊ.də
laudab|le ˈlɔː.də.b|ᵊl, (US) ˈlɑː-, ˈlɔː- **-ly** -li **-leness** -ᵊl.nəs, -nɪs
laudanum ˈlɔː.dᵊn.əm, (US) ˈlɑː-, ˈlɔː-
laudatory ˈlɔː.də.tᵊr.i, (US) ˈlɑː.də.tɔːr-, ˈlɔː-
Lauder ˈlɔː.dəʳ, (US) ˈlɑː.dɚ, ˈlɔː-
Lauderdale ˈlɔː.də.deɪl, (US) ˈlɑː.dɚ-, ˈlɔː-
laugh lɑːf, (US) læf **-s** -s **-ing/ly** -ɪŋ/li **-ed** -t **-er/s** -əʳ/z, (US) -ɚ/z **ˈlaughing ˌgas; ˌlaughing ˈjackass; no ˌlaughing ˈmatter; no ˈlaughing ˌmatter; have the ˌlast ˈlaugh**
laughab|le ˈlɑː.fə.b|ᵊl, (US) ˈlæf.ə- **-ly** -li **-leness** -ᵊl.nəs, -nɪs
Laugharne lɑːn, (US) lɑːrn
laughingstock ˈlɑː.fɪŋ.stɒk, (US) ˈlæf.ɪŋ.stɑːk **-s** -s
Laughland ˈlɒk.lənd, (US) ˈlɑːk-
Laughlin ˈlɒk.lɪn, ˈlɒx-, ˈlɒf-, ˈlɑː.flɪn, (US) ˈlɑː-, ˈlɔː-
laughter ˈlɑːf.təʳ, (US) ˈlæf.tɚ
Laughton ˈlɔː.tᵊn, (US) ˈlɑː-, ˈlɔː-
launc|e lɑːnts, (US) lænts, lɑːnts, lɔːnts **-es** -ɪz
Launce lɑːnts, lɔːnts, (US) lænts, lɑːnts, lɔːnts
Launcelot ˈlɑːnt.sᵊl.ɒt, ˈlɔːnt-, -ət, (US) ˈlænt.sə.lɑːt, ˈlɑːnt-, ˈlɔːnt-, -lət
Launceston *in Cornwall:* ˈlɔːnt.stən, -sᵊn; *locally:* ˈlɑːnt- *in Tasmania:* ˈlɔːnt.səs.tᵊn; *locally:* ˈlɒnt-, (US) ˈlɑːnt-, ˈlɔːnt-

launch lɔːntʃ, (US) lɑːntʃ, lɔːntʃ **-es** -ɪz **-ing** -ɪŋ **-ed** -t **-er/s** -əʳ/z, (US) -ɚ/z
launchpad ˈlɔːntʃ.pæd, (US) ˈlɑːntʃ-, ˈlɔːntʃ- **-s** -z
laund|er ˈlɔːn.d|əʳ, (US) ˈlɑːn.d|ɚ, ˈlɔːn- **-ers** -əz, (US) -ɚz **-ering** -ər.ɪŋ **-ered** -əd, (US) -ɚd
launderette ˌlɔːn.dərˈet, ˌ-ˈdret, (US) ˌlɑːn.dəˈret, ˌlɔːn-, ˌ-ˈdret **-s** -s
laundress ˈlɔːn.dres, -drəs, -drɪs, (US) ˈlɑːn.drɪs, ˈlɔːn- **-es** -ɪz
laundrette ˌlɔːnˈdret, (US) ˌlɑːn-, ˌlɔːn- **-s** -s
Laundromat® ˈlɔːn.drə.mæt, (US) ˈlɔːn.droʊ-, ˈlɑːn-, -drə- **-s** -s
laundr|y ˈlɔːn.dr|i, (US) ˈlɑːn-, ˈlɔːn- **-ies** -iz ˈ**laundry** ˌ**basket**; ˈ**laundry** ˌ**list**
laundry|man ˈlɔːn.dri|.mæn, -mən, (US) ˈlɑːn-, ˈlɔːn- **-men** -mən, -men **-woman** -ˌwʊm.ən **-women** -ˌwɪm.ɪn
Laura ˈlɔː.rə, (US) ˈlɔːr.ə
laureate n, adj ˈlɔː.ri.ət, ˈlɒr.i-, -ɪt, (US) ˈlɔːr.i.ɪt, ˈlɑːr- **-s** -s **-ship/s** -ʃɪp/s
laure|ate v ˈlɔː.ri|.eɪt, ˈlɒr.i-, (US) ˈlɔːr.i-, ˈlɑːr- **-ates** -eɪts **-ating** -eɪ.tɪŋ, (US) -eɪ.t̬ɪŋ **-ated** -eɪ.tɪd, (US) -eɪ.t̬ɪd
laurel, L~ ˈlɒr.əl, (US) ˈlɔːr-, ˈlɑːr- **-s** -z
Lauren ˈlɔː.rən, ˈlɒr.ən, (US) ˈlɔːr.ən, ˈlɑːr-
Laurence ˈlɒr.ənts, (US) ˈlɔːr-, ˈlɑːr-
Laurent lɔːˈrɑ̃ːŋ, lə-, (US) lɑːˈrɑːnt, lə-
Laurie ˈlɒr.i, ˈlɔː.ri, (US) ˈlɔːr.i, ˈlɑːr-
Laurier *English name:* ˈlɒr.i.əʳ, (US) ˈlɔːr.i.ɚ, ˈlɑːr- *Canadian name:* ˈlɒr.i.eɪ, (US) ˈlɔːr.i.eɪ
Lauriston ˈlɒr.ɪ.stən, ˈ-ə-, (US) ˈlɔːr-, ˈlɑːr-
laurustinus ˌlɒr.əˈstaɪ.nəs, ˌlɔː.rəˈ-, (US) ˌlɑːr-, ˌlɔːr- **-es** -ɪz
Lausanne ləʊˈzæn, (US) loʊ-, -ˈzɑːn
Lauterbrunnen ˈlaʊ.tə.brʊn.ən, (US) -t̬ɚ-
Lautrec ləʊˈtrek, (US) loʊ-, lə-
lav læv **-s** -z
lava ˈlɑː.və, (US) ˈlɑː-, ˈlæv.ə
lavabo *ritual:* ləˈvɑː.bəʊ, lævˈɑː-, -ˈeɪ-, (US) ləˈvɑː.boʊ, -ˈveɪ- *basin:* ləˈveɪ.bəʊ; ˈlæv.ə.bəʊ, (US) ləˈvɑː.boʊ, -ˈveɪ- **-s** -z
lavage lævˈɑːʒ, ləˈvɑːʒ, -ˈvɑːdʒ; ˈlæv.ɪdʒ, -ɑːʒ, (US) ləˈvɑːʒ; (US) ˈlæv.ɪdʒ
Lavater lɑːˈvɑː.təʳ, ˈ---, (US) -t̬ɚ
lavatorial ˌlæv.əˈtɔː.ri.əl, (US) -ˈtɔːr.i-
lavator|y ˈlæv.ə.tər|.i, -tr|i, (US) -tɔːr.i **-ies** -iz
lav|e leɪv **-es** -z **-ing** -ɪŋ **-ed** -d
lavender, L~ ˈlæv.ən.dəʳ, -ɪn-, (US) -dɚ ˈ**lavender** ˌ**water**
Lavengro ləˈveŋ.grəʊ, lævˈeŋ-, (US) -groʊ
Lavenham ˈlæv.ən.əm
laver *seaweed:* ˈlɑː.vəʳ, (US) ˈleɪ.vɚ, ˈlɑː- *all other senses:* ˈleɪ.vəʳ, (US) -vɚ **-s** -z
Laver *name:* ˈleɪ.vəʳ, (US) -vɚ
Laverty ˈlæv.ə.ti, (US) -ɚ.t̬i
Lavery ˈleɪ.vər.i, ˈlæv.ər-
Lavin ˈlæv.ɪn
Lavington ˈlæv.ɪŋ.tən
Lavini|a ləˈvɪn.i|.ə **-an** -ən
lavish ˈlæv.ɪʃ **-ly** -li **-ness** -nəs, -nɪs **-es** -ɪz **-ing** -ɪŋ **-ed** -t
Lavoisier ləˈvwɑː.zi.eɪ, lævˈwɑː-, -ˈwæz.i-, (US) ləˈvwɑː.zi-
law, L~ lɔː, (US) lɑː, lɔː **-s** -z ˈ**law** ˌ**lord**; **be a** ˌ**law unto one**ˈ**self**; **take the** ˌ**law into one's** ˌ**own** ˈ**hands**

> Note: It seems that British speakers are particularly sensitive about this word being pronounced with 'intrusive /r/', most often when the phrase 'law and order' is pronounced as /ˌlɔː.rənˈɔː.də/. Although many older speakers deplore this, it is undoubtedly heard frequently.

law-abiding ˈlɔː.əˌbaɪ.dɪŋ, (US) ˈlɑː-, ˈlɔː-
lawbreak|er ˈlɔːˌbreɪ.k|əʳ, (US) ˈlɑːˌbreɪ.k|ɚ, ˈlɔː- **-ers** -əz, (US) -ɚz **-ing** -ɪŋ
Lawes lɔːz, (US) lɑːz, lɔːz
Lawesford ˈlɔːz.fəd, (US) ˈlɑːz.fɚd, ˈlɔːz-
lawful ˈlɔː.fəl, -fʊl, (US) ˈlɑː-, ˈlɔː- **-ly** -i **-ness** -nəs, -nɪs
lawgiv|er ˈlɔːˌgɪv|.əʳ, (US) ˈlɑːˌgɪv|.ɚ, ˈlɔː- **-ers** -əz, (US) -ɚz **-ing** -ɪŋ
lawks lɔːks, (US) lɑːks, lɔːks
lawless, L~ ˈlɔː.ləs, -lɪs, (US) ˈlɑː-, ˈlɔː- **-ly** -li **-ness** -nəs, -nɪs
Lawley, Lawly ˈlɔː.li, (US) ˈlɑː-, ˈlɔː-
lawmak|er ˈlɔːˌmeɪ.k|əʳ, (US) ˈlɑːˌmeɪ.k|ɚ, ˈlɔː- **-ers** -əz, (US) -ɚz **-ing** -ɪŋ
lawn lɔːn, (US) lɑːn, lɔːn **-s** -z ˈ**lawn** ˌ**mower**; ˌ**lawn** ˈ**tennis** (US) ˈ**lawn** ˌ**tennis**
Lawrence, Lawrance ˈlɒr.ənts, (US) ˈlɔːr-, ˈlɑːr-
lawrencium ləˈrent.si.əm, lɔː-, lɒrˈent-, (US) lɔːˈrent-, lɑː-
Lawrenson ˈlɒr.ənt.sən, (US) ˈlɔːr.ənt-, ˈlɑːr-
Lawrentian ləˈren.ʃi.ən, lɒrˈen-, -ʃən, (US) ləˈrent-, lɔː-, lɑː-
Lawson ˈlɔː.sən, (US) ˈlɑː-, ˈlɔː-
lawsuit ˈlɔː.suːt, -sjuːt, (US) ˈlɑː.suːt, ˈlɔː- **-s** -s
Lawton ˈlɔː.tən, (US) ˈlɑː-, ˈlɔː-
lawyer ˈlɔɪ.əʳ, ˈlɔː.jəʳ, (US) ˈlɑː.jɚ, ˈlɔː-, ˈlɔɪ- **-s** -z
lax læks **-er** -əʳ, (US) -ɚ **-est** -ɪst, -əst **-ly** -li **-ness** -nəs, -nɪs
laxative ˈlæk.sə.tɪv, (US) -t̬ɪv **-s** -z
laxity ˈlæk.sə.ti, -sɪ-, (US) -sə.t̬i
lay, L~ leɪ **-s** -z **-ing** -ɪŋ **laid** leɪd ˌ**lay** ˈ**reader** (US) ˈ**lay** ˌ**reader**; ˌ**lay of the** ˈ**land**
layabout ˈleɪ.əˌbaʊt **-s** -s
Layamon ˈlaɪ.ə.mən, -mɒn, (US) ˈleɪ.ə.mən, ˈlaɪ-
Layard ˈleɪ.ɑːd, leəd, (US) ˈleɪ.ɑːrd, lerd
layaway ˈleɪ.ə.weɪ
lay-by ˈleɪ.baɪ **-s** -z
Laycock ˈleɪ.kɒk, (US) -kɑːk
layer ˈleɪ.əʳ, leəʳ, (US) ˈleɪ.ɚ **-s** -z **-ing** -ɪŋ **-ed** -d
layette leɪˈet **-s** -s
lay|man ˈleɪ|.mən **-men** -mən
layoff ˈleɪ.ɒf, (US) -ɑːf **-s** -s
layout ˈleɪ.aʊt **-s** -s
layover ˈleɪˌəʊ.vəʳ, (US) -ˌoʊ.vɚ
lay|person ˈleɪˌpɜː.sən, (US) -ˌpɝː- **-people** -ˌpiː.pəl
Layton ˈleɪ.tən
layup ˈleɪ.ʌp **-s** -s
lay|woman ˈleɪ|ˌwʊm.ən **-women** -ˌwɪm.ɪn
lazar ˈlæz.əʳ, (US) ˈleɪ.zɚ, ˈlæz.ɚ **-s** -z
lazaretto ˌlæz.əˈret.əʊ, -ərˈet-, (US) -ˈret̬.oʊ **-s** -z
Lazarus ˈlæz.ər.əs
laz|e leɪz **-es** -ɪz **-ing** -ɪŋ **-ed** -d
Lazenby ˈleɪ.zən.bi, -zəm-, (US) -zən-
Lazio ˈlæt.si.əʊ, (US) ˈlɑːt.si.oʊ
lazuli ˈlæz.jə.liː, -jʊ-, ˈlæʒ.ə-, ˈ-ʊ-, -laɪ, (US) ˈlæʒ.juː-, ˈlæz-, ˈ-ə-
lazulite ˈlæz.jə.laɪt, -jʊ-, ˈlæʒ.ə-, -ˈʊ-, (US) ˈlæʒ.juː-, ˈlæz-, ˈ-ə-
laz|y ˈleɪ.z|i **-ier** -i.əʳ, (US) -i.ɚ **-iest** -i.ɪst, -i.əst **-ily** -əl.i, -ɪ.li **-iness** -ɪ.nəs, -ɪ.nɪs
lazybones ˈleɪ.ziˌbəʊnz, (US) -ˌboʊnz
lb (abbrev. for **pound/s**) *singular:* paʊnd; *plural:* paʊndz
lbw ˌel.biːˈdʌb.əl.juː
LCD ˌel.siːˈdiː
L-dopa ˌelˈdəʊ.pə, (US) -ˈdoʊ-
lea, L~ liː **-s** -z
LEA ˌel.iːˈeɪ
leach, L~ liːtʃ **-es** -ɪz **-ing** -ɪŋ **-ed** -t
Leachman ˈliːtʃ.mən
Leacock ˈliː.kɒk, ˈleɪ-, (US) -kɑːk
lead n *metal:* led **-s** -z **-ing** -ɪŋ **-ed** -ɪd ˌ**lead** ˈ**pencil** (US) ˈ**lead** ˌ**pencil**; ˌ**lead** ˈ**poisoning** *cable, flex:* liːd **-s** -z
lead v *guide:* liːd **-s** -z **-ing** -ɪŋ **led** led ˌ**leading** ˈ**light**; ˈ**leading** ˌ**rein**; ˈ**lead** ˌ**time**
Lead *surname:* liːd
Leadbetter ˈledˌbet.əʳ, -ˈ--, (US) ˈledˌbet̬.ɚ, -ˈ--
leaden ˈled.ən **-ly** -li **-ness** -nəs, -nɪs
Leadenhall ˈled.ən.hɔːl, (US) -hɔːl, -hɑːl
leader, L~ ˈliː.dəʳ, (US) -dɚ **-s** -z ˌ**leader of the** ˌ**oppo**ˈ**sition**
leaderboard ˈliː.də.bɔːd, (US) -dɚ.bɔːrd **-s** -z
leaderette ˌliː.dərˈet **-s** -s
leadership ˈliː.də.ʃɪp, (US) -dɚ- **-s** -s
lead-in ˈliːd.ɪn **-s** -z
lead-off ˈliːd.ɒf, (US) -ɑːf **-s** -s
leads n *roofing:* ledz
leaf v liːf **-s** -s **-ing** -ɪŋ **-ed** -t
lea|f n liː|f **-ves** -vz ˈ**leaf** ˌ**mould**; **take a** ˌ**leaf out of** ˌ**someone's** ˈ**book**; ˌ**turn over a** ˌ**new** ˈ**leaf**
leafless ˈliːf.ləs, -lɪs
leafle|t ˈliː.flə|t, -flɪ|t **-ts** -ts **-(t)ting** -tɪŋ, (US) -t̬ɪŋ **-(t)ted** -tɪd, (US) -t̬ɪd

L

leaf|y ˈliː.f|i -ier -i.əʳ, (US) -i.ɚ -iest -i.ɪst, -i.əst -iness -ɪ.nəs, -ɪ.nɪs
leagu|e liːg -es -z -ing -ɪŋ -ed -d **ˈleague ˌtable**
leaguer, L~ ˈliː.gəʳ, (US) -gɚ -s -z
Leah ˈliː.ə; lɪə, (US) ˈliː.ə
Leahy ˈliː.hi, (US) ˈleɪ-
leak liːk -s -s -ing -ɪŋ -ed -t
leakag|e ˈliː.kɪdʒ -es -ɪz
Leake liːk
Leakey ˈliː.ki
leak|y ˈliː.k|i -ier -i.əʳ, (US) -i.ɚ -iest -i.ɪst, -i.əst -iness -ɪ.nəs, -ɪ.nɪs
Leamington ˈlem.ɪŋ.tən **ˌLeamington ˈSpa**
lean liːn -er -əʳ, (US) -ɚ -est -ɪst, -əst -ly -li -ness -nəs, -nəs -s -z -ing/s -ɪŋ/z leaned -d, lent leant lent
Leander liˈæn.dəʳ, (US) -dɚ
Leanne liˈæn
lean-to ˈliːn.tuː -s -z
leap liːp -s -s -ing -ɪŋ -ed lept, liːpt -t lept -er/s -əʳ/z, (US) -ɚ/z **ˈleap ˌyear; by ˌleaps and ˈbounds**
leapfrog ˈliːp.frɒg, (US) -frɑːg, -frɔːg -s -z -ging -ɪŋ -ged -d
Lear lɪəʳ, (US) lɪr
learn lɜːn, (US) lɝːn -s -z -ing -ɪŋ -ed -d, -t -t -t -er/s -əʳ/z, (US) -ɚ/z **ˈlearning ˌcurve; ˈlearning disaˌbility**
learned **adj** *scholarly:* ˈlɜː.nɪd, (US) ˈlɝː- -ly -li -ness -nəs, -nɪs
Learney ˈleə.ni, (US) ˈler-
leas|e liːs -es -ɪz -ing -ɪŋ -ed -t **a ˌnew ˌlease of ˈlife; a ˌnew ˌlease on ˈlife**
leaseback ˈliːs.bæk
leasehold ˈliːs.*h*əuld, (US) -hould -s -z -er/s -əʳ/z, (US) -ɚ/z
lease-|lend ˌliːsˈlend -lends -ˈlendz -lending -ˈlen.dɪŋ -lent -ˈlent
leash liːʃ -es -ɪz -ing -ɪŋ -ed -t
least liːst
leastways ˈliːst.weɪz
leastwise ˈliːst.waɪz
leat liːt -s -s
Leatham ˈliː.θəm, -ðəm
Leathart ˈliː.θɑːt, (US) -θɑːrt
leath|er ˈleð|.əʳ, (US) -ɚ -ers -əz, (US) -ɚz -ering -ər.ɪŋ -ered -əd, (US) -ɚd
leatherback ˈleð.ə.bæk, (US) ˈ-ɚ-
Leatherette® ˌleð.ərˈet
Leatherhead ˈleð.ə.hed, (US) ˈ-ɚ-
leatherjacket ˈleð.əˌdʒæk.ɪt, (US) -ɚˌ- -s -s
leathern ˈleð.ən, (US) -ɚn
leatherneck ˈleð.ə.nek, (US) ˈ-ɚ- -s -s
leather|y ˈleð.ər|.i -iness -ɪ.nəs, -ɪ.nɪs
Leathes liːðz
leave **n** liːv -s -z
leav|e **v** liːv -es -z -ing/s -ɪŋ/z left left -er/s -əʳ/z, (US) -ɚ/z
leaved liːvd
leaven ˈlev.ən -s -z -ing -ɪŋ, ˈlev.nɪŋ -ed -d
Leavenworth ˈlev.ən.wəθ, -wɜːθ, (US) -wɚθ, -wɝːθ
leaves (plural of **leaf**) liːvz
leave-taking ˈliːvˌteɪ.kɪŋ
Leavis ˈliː.vɪs
Leavisite ˈliː.vɪ.saɪt -s -s
Leavitt ˈlev.ɪt
Lebanese ˌleb.əˈniːz *stress shift:* **ˌLebanese ˈcapital**
Lebanon ˈleb.ə.nən, -nɒn, (US) -nɑːn, -nən
Le Beau ləˈbəu, (US) -ˈbou
Lebed ˈleb.jed, -ed, -ˈ-, (US) -ed
lebensraum, L~ ˈleɪ.bənz.raum, -bəmz-, (US) -bənz-
Le Bon ləˈbɒn, (US) -ˈbɔːn
Lebowa ləˈbəu.ə, (US) -ˈbou-
Lebrun ləˈbrɜ̃ːŋ, (US) -ˈbrɜ̃ːn
Leburn ˈliː.bɜːn, (US) -bɝːn
Lec® lek
Le Carré, le Carré ləˈkær.eɪ, (US) -ˈkær.eɪ; (US) -kɑːˈreɪ
lech letʃ -es -ɪz -ing -ɪŋ -ed -t
Lech lek; *as if Polish:* lex
lecher ˈletʃ.əʳ, (US) -ɚ -s -z
lecherous ˈletʃ.ər.əs -ly -li -ness -nəs, -nɪs
lechery ˈletʃ.ər.i
Lechlade ˈletʃ.leɪd
Lechmere ˈleʃ.mɪəʳ, ˈletʃ-, (US) -mɪr
lecithin ˈles.ɪ.θɪn, ˈ-ə-, -θən, (US) -ɪ.θɪn
Leckhampton ˈlekˌhæm*p*.tən
Leckie ˈlek.i
Lecky ˈlek.i
Leclanché ləˈklɑ̃ː*n*.ʃeɪ
Leconfield ˈlek.ən.fiːld
Leconte ləˈkɒnt, ləˈkɔ̃ːt, (US) -ˈkɑːnt
Le Corbusier ˌlə.kɔːˈbuː.zi.eɪ, -ˈbjuː-, (US) -kɔːr.buːˈzjeɪ, -ziˈeɪ
lect lekt -al -əl
lectern ˈlek.tən, -tɜːn, (US) -tɚn, -tɝːn -s -z
lection ˈlek.ʃən -s -z
lectionar|y ˈlek.ʃən.ər|.i, (US) -er- -ies -iz
lector ˈlek.tɔːʳ, (US) -tɚ, -tɔːr -s -z
lect|ure ˈlek.tʃ|əʳ, (US) -tʃ|ɚ -ures -əz, (US) -ɚz -uring -ər.ɪŋ -ured -əd, (US) -ɚd
lecturer ˈlek.tʃər.əʳ, (US) -ɚ -s -z
lectureship ˈlek.tʃə.ʃɪp, (US) -tʃɚ- -s -s
led (from **lead**) led
LED ˌel.iːˈdiː
Leda ˈliː.də
Ledbury ˈled.bər.i, (US) ˈled.ber-
lederhosen ˈleɪ.dəˌhəu.zən, (US) -dɚˌhou-
ledg|e ledʒ -es -ɪz
ledger ˈledʒ.əʳ, (US) -ɚ -s -z **ˈledger ˌline**
Ledi ˈled.i
Lediard ˈled.i.əd, -ɑːd, ˈ-jəd, (US) ˈled.jɚd, ˈ-i.ɚd, -ɑːrd
Ledward ˈled.wəd, (US) -wɚd
Ledyard ˈled.jəd, (US) -jɚd
lee, L~ liː -s -z
leech, L~ liːtʃ -es -ɪz
Leeds liːdz
Lee-Enfield ˌliːˈen.fiːld
leek, L~ liːk -s -s
leer lɪəʳ, (US) lɪr -s -z -ing/ly -ɪŋ/li -ed -d
leer|y ˈlɪə.r|i, (US) ˈlɪr|.i -ier -i.əʳ, (US) -i.ɚ -iest -i.ɪst, -i.əst -ily -əl.i, -ɪ.li -iness -ɪ.nəs, -ɪ.nɪs
lees, L~ liːz
leeson, L~ ˈliː.sən
leet liːt -s -s
leetspeak ˈliːt.spiːk
leeward ˈliː.wəd, (US) -wɚd; *nautical pronunciation:* ˈluː.əd, ˈljuː.əd, (US) ˈluː.ɚd
Leeward *islands:* ˈliː.wəd, (US) -wɚd
leeway ˈliː.weɪ
Lefanu, Le Fanu ˈlef.ə.njuː, -nuː; ləˈfɑː.nuː, (US) ˈlef.ə.nuː, ləˈfɑː-
Lefevre ləˈfiː.vəʳ, -ˈfeɪ-, -ˈfev.rə, (US) -ˈfiː.vɚ

> Note: /ləˈfiː.vəʳ/ (US) /-vɚ/ in Sterne's 'Sentimental Journey'.

Lefroy ləˈfrɔɪ
left left **ˌLeft ˈBank** *stress shift:* **ˌLeft Bank ˈartist**
left-hand ˌleftˈhænd, ˈ--
left-hand|ed ˌleftˈhæn.d|ɪd -edness -ɪd.nəs, -nɪs -er/s -əʳ/z, (US) -ɚ/z *stress shift:* **ˌleft-handed ˈscissors**
left|ie ˈlef.t|i -ies -iz
leftist ˈlef.tɪst -s -s
left-luggage office ˌleftˈlʌg.ɪdʒˌɒf.ɪs, (US) -ˌɑː.fɪs
leftover ˈleftˌəu.vəʳ, (US) -ˌou.vɚ -s -z
leftward ˈleft.wəd, (US) -wɚd -s -z
left-wing ˌleftˈwɪŋ -er/s -əʳ/z, (US) -ɚ/z *stress shift:* **ˌleft-wing ˈtendencies**
left|y ˈlef.t|i -ies -iz
leg leg -s -z -ging -ɪŋ -ged -d **ˌleg before ˈwicket; ˌleg ˈbye; on one's ˌlast ˈlegs; not have a ˌleg to ˈstand on**
legac|y ˈleg.ə.s|i -ies -iz
legal ˈliː.gəl -ly -i **ˌlegal ˈaid; ˌlegal ˈtender**
legalese ˌliː.gəlˈiːz
legal|ism ˈliː.gəl|.ɪ.zəm -ist/s -ɪst/s
legalistic ˌliː.gəlˈɪs.tɪk -ally -əl.i, -li
legalit|y liːˈgæl.ə.t|i, lɪ-, -ɪ.t|i, (US) -ə.ţ|i -ies -iz
legalization, -isa- ˌliː.gəl.aɪˈzeɪ.ʃən, -ɪˈ-, (US) -əˈ-
legaliz|e, -is|e ˈliː.gəl.aɪz -es -ɪz -ing -ɪŋ -ed -d
legal-size ˈliː.gəlˌsaɪz
legate ˈleg.ət, -ɪt, -eɪt, (US) -ɪt -s -s
legatee ˌleg.əˈtiː -s -z
legation lɪˈgeɪ.ʃən, lə-, legˈeɪ-, (US) lɪˈgeɪ- -s -z
legatissimo ˌleg.ɑːˈtɪs.ɪ.məu, -əˈ-, (US) -ɪ.mou
legato lɪˈgɑː.təu, lə-, legˈɑː-, (US) -tou -s -z
legend ˈledʒ.ənd -s -z
legendary ˈledʒ.ən.dər.i, -ɪn-, (US) -der-
Leger ˈledʒ.əʳ, (US) -ɚ
Léger leɪˈʒeɪ
legerdemain ˌledʒ.ə.dəˈmeɪn; *as if French:* ˌleʒ.ə.dəˈmæ̃ŋ; (US) ˌ-ɚ-
Leggatt ˈleg.ət
Legge leg

-legged ˈleg.ɪd, ˈlegd
Note: Suffix. Normally carries primary stress on the penultimate syllable, e.g. **three-legged** /ˌθriːˈleg.ɪd/, but when a strong stress follows closely it undergoes stress shift, e.g. ˌ**three-legged** ˈ**stool**. However, the phrase 'three-legged race' is usually ˌ**three-**ˈ**legged** ˌ**race**.
Leggett ˈleg.ɪt, -ət
legging ˈleg.ɪŋ **-s** -z
leggy ˈleg.i
Legh liː
leghorn *fowl:* legˈɔːn, lɪˈgɔːn; ˈleg.ɔːn, ˈlɪg-, (US) ˈleg.hɔːrn, -ɚn **-s** -z
leghorn *straw hat:* ˈleg.hɔːn; legˈɔːn, lɪˈgɔːn, lə-, (US) ˈleg.hɔːrn, -ɚn **-s** -z
Leghorn *place:* ˈleg.hɔːn, -ˈ-, (US) -hɔːrn, -ˈ-
legibility ˌledʒ.əˈbɪl.ə.ti, -ɪˈ-, -ɪ.ti, (US) -ə.t̬i
legib|le ˈledʒ.ə.b|əl, ˈ-ɪ- **-ly** -li **-leness** -əl.nəs, -nɪs
legion, L~ ˈliː.dʒən **-s** -z ˌ**Legion of** ˈ**Honour**
legionar|y ˈliː.dʒə.nər|.i, (US) -ner- **-ies** -iz
legionnaire, L~ ˌliː.dʒəˈneər, (US) -ˈner **-s** -z **Legion**ˈ**naire's di**ˌ**sease**
legi|slate ˈledʒ.ɪ|.sleɪt, ˈ-ə- **-slates** -sleɪts **-slating** -sleɪ.tɪŋ, (US) -sleɪ.t̬ɪŋ **-slated** -sleɪ.tɪd, (US) -sleɪ.t̬ɪd
legislation ˌledʒ.ɪˈsleɪ.ʃən, -əˈ-
legislative ˈledʒ.ɪ.slə.tɪv, ˈ-ə-, -sleɪ-, (US) -sleɪ.t̬ɪv
legislator ˈledʒ.ɪ.sleɪ.tər, ˈ-ə-, (US) -t̬ɚ **-s** -z
legislature ˈledʒ.ɪ.slə.tʃər, -sleɪ-, -tʃʊər, -tjʊər, (US) -sleɪ.tʃɚ **-s** -z
legit ləˈdʒɪt, lɪ-
legitimacy lɪˈdʒɪt.ə.mə.si, lə-, ˈ-ɪ-, (US) ləˈdʒɪt̬.ə-
legitimate adj lɪˈdʒɪt.ə.mət, lə-, ˈ-ɪ-, -mɪt, (US) ləˈdʒɪt̬.ə- **-ly** -li **-ness** -nəs, -nɪs
legiti|mate v lɪˈdʒɪt.ə|.meɪt, lə-, ˈ-ɪ-, (US) ləˈdʒɪt̬.ə- **-mates** -meɪts **-mating** -meɪ.tɪŋ, (US) -meɪ.t̬ɪŋ **-mated** -meɪ.tɪd, (US) -meɪ.t̬ɪd
legitimation lɪˌdʒɪt.əˈmeɪ.ʃən, lə-, -ɪˈ-, (US) ləˌdʒɪt̬.əˈ-
legitimatiz|e, -is|e lɪˈdʒɪt.ə.mə.taɪz, lə-, ˈ-ɪ-, (US) ləˈdʒɪt̬.ə- **-es** -ɪz **-ing** -ɪŋ **-ed** -d
legitimist lɪˈdʒɪt.ə.mɪst, lə-, ˈ-ɪ-, (US) ləˈdʒɪt̬.ə- **-s** -s
legitimiz|e, -is|e lɪˈdʒɪt.ə.maɪz, lə-, ˈ-ɪ-, (US) ləˈdʒɪt̬.ə- **-es** -ɪz **-ing** -ɪŋ **-ed** -d
legless ˈleg.ləs, -lɪs
Lego® ˈleg.əʊ, (US) -oʊ
Legoland® ˈleg.əʊ.lænd, (US) -oʊ-
leg-pull ˈleg.pʊl **-s** -z **-ing** -ɪŋ **-ed** -d
Legree lɪˈgriː, lə-
legroom ˈleg.rʊm, -ruːm, (US) -ruːm, -rʊm
Legros ləˈgrəʊ, (US) -ˈgroʊ
legume ˈleg.juːm; lɪˈgjuːm, lə- **-s** -z
leguminous lɪˈgjuː.mɪ.nəs, lə-, legˈjuː-, -mə-, (US) ləˈgjuː-
leg-warmer ˈlegˌwɔː.mər, (US) -ˌwɔːr.mɚ **-s** -z
legwork ˈleg.wɜːk, (US) -wɝːk
Lehar, Lehàr leɪˈhɑːr, lɪ-, lə-; ˈleɪ.hɑːr, (US) ˈleɪ.hɑːr
Le Havre ləˈhɑː.vrə, -vər, (US) -ˈhɑː.vrə, -vɚ
Lehigh ˈliː.haɪ
Lehman(n) ˈleɪ.mən, ˈliː-
lehr lɪər, leər, (US) lɪr, ler **-s** -z
lei ˈleɪ.iː **-s** -z
lei (plural of **leu**) leɪ
Leibni(t)z ˈlaɪb.nɪts, ˈliːb-
Leica® ˈlaɪ.kə
Leicester ˈles.tər, (US) -tɚ **-shire** -ʃər, -ʃɪər, (US) -ʃɚ, -ʃɪr
Leics. (abbrev. for **Leicestershire**) ˈles.tə.ʃər, -ʃɪər, (US) -tɚ.ʃɚ, -ʃɪr
Leiden ˈlaɪ.dən, ˈleɪ-, (US) ˈlaɪ-
Leigh *surname:* liː *place name:* liː, laɪ

Note: The places in Essex and Greater Manchester are /liː/; those in Surrey, Kent, and Dorset are /laɪ/.

Leighton ˈleɪ.tən
Leila ˈliː.lə, ˈleɪ-
Leinster *Irish province:* ˈlent.stər, (US) -stɚ *Duke of:* ˈlɪnt.stər, (US) -stɚ *square in London:* ˈlent.stər, ˈlɪnt-, (US) -stɚ
Leipzig ˈlaɪp.sɪg, -sɪk
Leishman ˈliːʃ.mən, ˈlɪʃ-
leishmania ˌliːʃˈmeɪ.ni.ə, (US) -ni.ə, -njə
leishmaniasis ˌliːʃ.məˈnaɪ.ə.sɪs
leishmaniosis ˌliːʃ.mæn.iˈəʊ.sɪs
leister ˈliː.stər, (US) -stɚ **-s** -z
Leister ˈles.tər, (US) -tɚ
Leiston ˈleɪ.stən
leisure ˈleʒ.ər, (US) ˈliː.ʒɚ, ˈleʒ.ɚ **-d** -d **-ly** -li **-liness** -lɪ.nəs, -nɪs
Leith liːθ
leitmotif, leitmotiv ˈlaɪt.məʊˌtiːf, -ˌməʊ.tɪv, (US) -moʊˌtiːf **-s** -s, -z, (US) -s
Leitrim ˈliː.trɪm
Leix liːʃ
lek lek **-s** -s **-king** -ɪŋ **-ked** -t
lekker ˈlek.ər, (US) -ɚ
Leland ˈliː.lənd
Lelean ləˈliːn
Lely ˈliː.li, ˈlɪl.i
leman ˈlem.ən, ˈliː.mən **-s** -z
Leman *lake:* ; ləˈmɑ̃ːŋ, leɪˈ-; ləˈmæn *surname:* ˈlem.ən, ˈliː.mən *street in London:* ˈlem.ən; *formerly:* ˈlɪm.æn
Le Mans ləˈmɑ̃ːŋ, (US) -ˈmɑːn, -ˈmɑ̃ːn
Le Marchant ləˈmɑː.tʃənt, (US) -ˈmɑːr-
Lemare ləˈmeər, (US) -ˈmer
Lemberg ˈlem.bɜːg, (US) -bɝːg
Lemesurier, Le Mesurier ləˈmeʒ.ər.ər; lə.məˈʒʊə.ri.eɪ, (US) ləˈmeʒ.ɚ.ɚ; (US) lə.məˈʒʊr.i.eɪ
lemma ˈlem.ə **-s** -z
lemmatization, -isa- ˌlem.ə.taɪˈzeɪ.ʃən, -tɪˈ-, (US) -t̬əˈ-
lemmatiz|e, -is|e ˈlem.ə.taɪz **-es** -ɪz **-ing** -ɪŋ **-ed** -d **-er/s** -ər/z, (US) -ɚ/z
lemme ˈlem.i
lemming ˈlem.ɪŋ **-s** -z
Lemmon ˈlem.ən
lemnis|cus lemˈnɪs|.kəs **-ci** -aɪ, -kaɪ, -iː, -kiː, (US) -aɪ, -kaɪ
Lemnos ˈlem.nɒs, (US) -nɑːs, -noʊs
Lemoine ləˈmɔɪn
lemon, L~ ˈlem.ən **-s** -z ˈ**lemon** ˌ**grass**; ˈ**lemon** ˌ**juice**; ˌ**lemon** ˈ**sole**; ˌ**lemon** ˈ**squash**; ˌ**lemon me**ˌ**ringue** ˈ**pie**
lemonade ˌlem.əˈneɪd **-s** -z
Le Morte D'Arthur ləˌmɔːtˈdɑː.θər, (US) -ˌmɔːrtˈdɑːr.θɚ
lempira lemˈpɪə.rə, (US) -ˈpɪr.ə **-s** -z
Lempriere ˈlem.pri.eər, (US) -er
Lemsip® ˈlem.sɪp
Lemuel ˈlem.jʊəl, -ju.əl, (US) -ju.əl, -jʊl
lemur ˈliː.mər, (US) -mɚ **-s** -z
Len len
Lena *first name:* ˈliː.nə *Siberian river:* ˈleɪ.nə
lend lend **-s** -z **-ing** -ɪŋ **lent** lent **lender/s** ˈlen.dər/z, (US) -dɚ/z ˈ**lending** ˌ**library**
lenes (plural of **lenis**) ˈliː.neɪz, ˈleɪ-, (US) ˈliː.niːz, ˈleɪ-
length leŋ*k*θ **-s** -s
lengthen ˈleŋ*k*.θən **-s** -z **-ing** -ɪŋ, ˈleŋ*k*θ.nɪŋ **-ed** -d
length|man ˈleŋ*k*θ|.mən **-men** -mən
lengthways ˈleŋ*k*θ.weɪz
lengthwise ˈleŋ*k*θ.waɪz
length|y ˈleŋ*k*.θ|i **-ier** -i.ər, (US) -i.ɚ **-iest** -i.ɪst, -i.əst **-ily** -əl.i, -ɪ.li **-iness** -ɪ.nəs, -ɪ.nɪs
lenien|ce ˈliː.ni.ən*t*|s **-cy** -si
lenient ˈliː.ni.ənt **-ly** -li
Lenin ˈlen.ɪn **-ism** -ɪ.zəm **-ist/s** -ɪst/s **-ite/s** -aɪt/s
Leningrad ˈlen.ɪn.græd, -ɪŋ-, -grɑːd, (US) -græd
lenis ˈliː.nɪs, ˈleɪ-, (US) ˈliː.nɪs, ˈleɪ- **lenes** ˈliː.niːz, ˈleɪ-, -neɪz
lenition lɪˈnɪʃ.ən, lə-
lenitive ˈlen.ɪ.tɪv, (US) -ə.t̬ɪv **-s** -z
lenity ˈlen.ə.ti, ˈliː.nə-, -nɪ-, (US) ˈlen.ə.t̬i
Lennie ˈlen.i
Lennon ˈlen.ən
Lennox ˈlen.əks
Lenny ˈlen.i
leno ˈliː.nəʊ, (US) -noʊ **Leno** ˈlen.əʊ, ˈliː.nəʊ, (US) ˈlen.oʊ, ˈliː.noʊ

Note: The US television personality Jay Leno pronounces /ˈlen.oʊ/.

Lenoir *surname:* ləˈnwɑːr, (US) -ˈnwɑːr *town in US:* ləˈnɔːr, (US) -ˈnɔːr
Lenor® lɪˈnɔːr, lə-, (US) -ˈnɔːr
Lenore lɪˈnɔːr, lə-, (US) -ˈnɔːr
Lenox ˈlen.əks
lens lenz **-es** -ɪz
lent (from **lend**) lent
Lent lent **-en** -ən

Lenthall *surname:* ˈlen.tɔːl *place in Yorkshire:* ˈlen.θɔːl, -θəl
Lenthéric®, Lentheric ˈlɒnt.θər.ɪk, ˈlɑ̃ːn-, (US) ˈlɑːnt-
lenticel ˈlen.tɪ.sel, (US) -t̬ɪ- **-s** -z
lenticular lenˈtɪk.jə.ləʳ, -jʊ-, (US) -jə.lɚ
lentil ˈlen.təl, -tɪl, (US) -t̬əl **-s** -z
lentivirus ˈlen.tɪ.vaɪə.rəs, (US) -t̬ɪ.vaɪ- **-es** -ɪz
lento ˈlen.təʊ, (US) -toʊ
Lenton ˈlen.tən
Lentulus ˈlen.tjə.ləs, -tjʊ-, (US) -tuː-, -tə-
Lenz lents
Leo ˈliː.əʊ, (US) -oʊ
Leofric ˈleɪ.əʊ.frɪk, ˈlef.rɪk, (US) leɪˈɑː.frɪk, -ˈoʊ-
Leominster *place in Britain:* ˈlemp.stəʳ, (US) -stɚ *place in US:* ˈlem.ɪnt.stəʳ, (US) -stɚ
Leon ˈliː.ɒn, ˈleɪ-, -ən, (US) -ɑːn
León leɪˈɒn, (US) -ˈoʊn
Leonard ˈlen.əd, (US) -ɚd **-s** -z
Leonardo ˌliː.əˈnɑː.dəʊ, ˌleɪ-, (US) ˌliː.əˈnɑːr.doʊ **-s** -z
leone, L~ liˈəʊ.ni, (US) -ˈoʊ- **-s** -z
Leonid ˈliː.əʊ.nɪd, ˈleɪ-, (US) ˈ-ə- **-s** -z
Leonidas liˈɒn.ɪ.dæs, ˈ-ə-, (US) -ˈɑː.nə.dəs
Leonie liˈəʊ.ni, (US) -ˈoʊ-
leonine ˈliː.əʊ.naɪn, (US) ˈ-ə-
Leonora ˌliː.əˈnɔː.rə, (US) -ˈnɔːr.ə
Leontes liˈɒn.tiːz, leɪ-, (US) liˈɑːn-
leopard ˈlep.əd, (US) -ɚd **-s** -z **-ess/es** -es/ɪz, -ɪs/ɪz, -əs/ɪz
Leopardstown ˈlep.ədz.taʊn, (US) -ɚdz-
Leopold ˈliː.ə.pəʊld, ˈlɪə.pəʊld, (US) ˈliː.ə.poʊld
leotard ˈliː.ə.tɑːd, (US) -tɑːrd **-s** -z
Lepanto lɪˈpæn.təʊ, lə-, (US) lɪˈpæn.toʊ, -ˈpɑːn-
leper ˈlep.əʳ, (US) -ɚ **-s** -z
lepidopter|an ˌlep.ɪˈdɒp.tər|.ən, (US) -ˈdɑːp- **-ans** -ənz **-a** -ə
lepidopterist ˌlep.ɪˈdɒp.tər.ɪst, (US) -ˈdɑːp- **-s** -s
lepidopterology ˌlep.ɪˌdɒp.tərˈɒl.ə.dʒi, (US) -ˌdɑːp.təˈrɑː.lə-
lepidopter|on ˌlep.ɪˈdɒp.tər|.ən, (US) -ˈdɑːp- **-ons** -ənz **-a** -ə
Lepidus ˈlep.ɪ.dəs
Le Play ləˈpleɪ
leprechaun ˈlep.rə.kɔːn, -rɪ-, -hɔːn, (US) -rə.kɑːn, -kɔːn **-s** -z
leprosy ˈlep.rə.si
leprous ˈlep.rəs **-ly** -li **-ness** -nəs, -nɪs
Lepsius ˈlep.si.əs
lept|on ˈlep.t|ɒn, -t|ən, (US) -t|ɑːn **-a** -ə
Lepus ˈliː.pəs, ˈlep.əs, (US) ˈliː.pəs
Lermontov ˈleə.mɒn.tɒf, -mən-, -təf, (US) ˈler.mɑːn.tɔːf
Lerner ˈlɜː.nəʳ, (US) ˈlɝː.nɚ
Leroy ˈliː.rɔɪ, ləˈrɔɪ
Lerwick ˈlɜː.wɪk, (US) ˈlɝː-
les *in French phrases:* leɪ, leɪz
Note: The form /leɪz/ only occurs when the following word begins with a vowel.
Les *first name:* lez, (US) les
Lesbi|a ˈlez.bi|.ə **-an** -ən
lesbian ˈlez.bi.ən **-s** -z **-ism** -ɪ.zəm
Lesbos ˈlez.bɒs, (US) -bɑːs, -boʊs
lèse-majesté, lese-majesty ˌleɪzˈmædʒ.ə.steɪ, ˌliːz-, ˈ-ɪ-, -sti, (US) ˌliːzˌmæʒ.esˈteɪ; (US) -ˈmædʒ.ɪ.sti
lesion ˈliː.ʒən **-s** -z
Leskovac ˈles.kəʊ.vɑːts, -væts, (US) -kɔː-
Leslie, Lesley ˈlez.li, (US) ˈles-, ˈlez-
Lesmahagow ˌles.məˈheɪ.gəʊ, (US) -goʊ
Lesotho ləˈsuː.tuː, lɪ-, leɪ-, -ˈsəʊ-, -təʊ, (US) ləˈsoʊ.toʊ, -ˈsuː.tuː
less les **-er** -əʳ, (US) -ɚ
lessee lesˈiː **-s** -z
lessen ˈles.ən **-s** -z **-ing** -ɪŋ, ˈles.nɪŋ **-ed** -d
Lesseps ˈles.əps, -eps; lesˈeps, (US) ˈles.əps
Lessing ˈles.ɪŋ
lesson ˈles.ən **-s** -z ˌ**learn one's** ˈ**lesson**
lessor lesˈɔːʳ, ˈ--, (US) ˈles.ɔːr, -ˈ- **-s** -z
lest lest
Lester ˈles.təʳ, (US) -tɚ
L'Estrange ləˈstreɪndʒ, lɪ-
Le Sueur ləˈsuː.əʳ, (US) -ˈsʊr
let let **-s** -s **-ting** -ɪŋ, (US) ˈlet̬.ɪŋ
letch letʃ **-es** -ɪz **-ing** -ɪŋ **-ed** -t
Letchworth ˈletʃ.wəθ, -wɜːθ, (US) -wɚθ, -wɝːθ
letdown ˈlet.daʊn **-s** -z
lethal ˈliː.θəl **-ly** -i
lethargic ləˈθɑː.dʒɪk, lɪ-, leθˈɑː-, (US) lɪˈθɑːr-, lə- **-ally** -əl.i, -li
lethargy ˈleθ.ə.dʒi, (US) ˈ-ɚ-
Lethe ˈliː.θi, -θiː
Letheby ˈleθ.ə.bi
Lethem ˈleθ.əm
Letitia lɪˈtɪʃ.i.ə, liː-, lə-, -ˈtiː.ʃi-, ˈ-ʃə, (US) ləˈtɪʃ.ə, -ˈtiː.ʃə
Letraset® ˈlet.rə.set
Lett let **-s** -s
lett|er ˈlet|.əʳ, (US) ˈlet̬|.ɚ **-ers** -əz, (US) -ɚz **-ering** -ər.ɪŋ **-ered** -əd, (US) -ɚd ˈ**letter** ˌ**bomb**; ˈ**letter** ˌ**box**; ˈ**letter** ˌ**carrier**; ˈ**letter** ˌ**opener**
letterhead ˈlet.ə.hed, (US) ˈlet̬.ɚ- **-s** -z
Letterman ˈlet.ə.mən, (US) ˈlet̬.ɚ-
letter-perfect ˌlet.əˈpɜː.fɪkt, -fekt, (US) ˌlet̬.ɚˈpɝː.fɪkt
letterpress ˈlet.ə.pres, (US) ˈlet̬.ɚ-
letter-quality ˈlet.əˌkwɒl.ə.ti, -ɪ.ti, (US) ˈlet̬.ɚˌkwɑː.lə.t̬i
letter-size ˈlet.ə.saɪz, (US) ˈlet̬.ɚ-
Lettice ˈlet.ɪs, (US) ˈlet̬-
Lettish ˈlet.ɪʃ, (US) ˈlet̬-
lettuc|e ˈlet.ɪs, -əs, (US) ˈlet̬- **-es** -ɪz
Letty ˈlet.i, (US) ˈlet̬-
letup ˈlet.ʌp, (US) ˈlet̬- **-s** -s
Letwin ˈlet.wɪn
leu ˈleɪ.uː **lei** leɪ
Leuchars *place in Scotland:* ˈluː.kəz, ˈljuː-, -xəz, (US) ˈluː.kɚz *surname:* ˈluː.kəs, ˈljuː-, (US) ˈluː.kɚs
leucine ˈljuː.siːn, ˈluː-, -saɪn, (US) ˈluː-
leucite ˈljuː.saɪt, ˈluː-, (US) ˈluː-
leucocyte ˈljuː.kəʊ.saɪt, ˈluː-, (US) ˈluː.koʊ-, -kə- **-s** -s
leucotom|y ljuːˈkɒt.ə.m|i, luː-, (US) luːˈkɑː.t̬ə- **-ies** -iz
Leuctra ˈljuːk.trə, (US) ˈluːk-
leuk(a)emia ljuːˈkiː.mi.ə, luː-, (US) luː-
lev lev, (US) lef **leva** ˈlev.ə
levant **adj** ˈlev.ənt
le|vant, L~ **n, v** lə|ˈvænt, lɪ-, (US) lə- **-vants** -ˈvænts **-vanting** -ˈvæn.tɪŋ, (US) -ˈvæn.t̬ɪŋ **-vanted** -ˈvæn.tɪd, (US) -ˈvæn.t̬ɪd
levanter, L~ ləˈvæn.təʳ, lɪ-, (US) ləˈvæn.t̬ɚ **-s** -z
Levantine ˈlev.ən.taɪn, -tiːn, (US) ˈlev.ən.tiːn, -taɪn; (US) lɪˈvæn-
levee *royal reception:* ˈlev.i, -eɪ, (US) ˈlev.i; (US) ləˈviː, -ˈveɪ *embankment:* ˈlev.i **-s** -z
level ˈlev.əl **-s** -z **-(l)ing** -ɪŋ, ˈlev.lɪŋ **-(l)ed** -d **-(l)er/s** -əʳ/z, (US) -ɚ/z **-ness** -nəs, -nɪs **-ly** -li ˌ**level** ˈ**crossing**
level-headed ˌlev.əlˈhed.ɪd, (US) ˈlev.əlˌhed.ɪd *stress shift, British only:* ˌ**level-headed** ˈ**person**
Leven *loch:* ˈliː.vən *surname:* ˈlev.ən, ˈliː.vən

> Note: The Earl pronounces /ˈliː.vən/.

lev|er **n, v** *on machine:* ˈliː.v|əʳ, (US) ˈlev.|ɚ, ˈliː.v|ɚ **-ers** -əz, (US) -ɚz **-ering** -ər.ɪŋ **-ered** -əd, (US) -ɚd
Lever *surname:* ˈliː.vəʳ, (US) -vɚ
leverag|e ˈliː.vər.ɪdʒ, (US) ˈlev.ɚ-, ˈliː.vɚ- **-ing** -ɪŋ **-ed** -d
leveret ˈlev.ər.ɪt, -ət **-s** -s
Leverett ˈlev.ər.ɪt
Leverhulme ˈliː.və.hjuːm, (US) -vɚ-
Levertov ˈlev.ə.tɒf, (US) -ɚ.tɑːf
Leveson ˈlev.ɪ.sən
Leveson-Gower ˌluː.sənˈgɔːʳ, ˌljuː-, -səŋˈ-, (US) ˌluː.sənˈgɔːr
Levett ˈlev.ɪt
Levey ˈliː.vi, ˈlev.i
Levi ˈliː.vaɪ, ˈlev.i, ˈliː.vi
leviable ˈlev.i.ə.bəl
leviathan, L~ lɪˈvaɪ.ə.θən, lə- **-s** -z
Levin ˈlev.ɪn
Levine ləˈviːn, -ˈvaɪn
levirate ˈliː.vɪ.rət, ˈlev.ɪ-, -rɪt, (US) ˈlev.ə.rɪt, ˈliː.və-, -reɪt
Levis® *jeans brand:* ˈliː.vaɪz
Levis *in Quebec:* ˈlev.i
Lévi-Strauss ˌlev.iˈstraʊs, (US) ˌleɪ.vi-, ˌlev.iˈ-
levi|tate ˈlev.ɪ|.teɪt, ˈ-ə- **-tates** -teɪts **-tating** -teɪ.tɪŋ, (US) -teɪ.t̬ɪŋ **-tated** -teɪ.tɪd, (US) -teɪ.t̬ɪd
levitation ˌlev.ɪˈteɪ.ʃən, -əˈ- **-s** -z
Levite ˈliː.vaɪt **-s** -s
levitic ləˈvɪt.ɪk, lɪ-, (US) ləˈvɪt̬- **-al** -əl **-ally** -əl.i, -li
Leviticus ləˈvɪt.ɪ.kəs, lɪ-, (US) ləˈvɪt̬-
Levitt ˈlev.ɪt
levit|y ˈlev.ə.t|i, -ɪ.t|i, (US) -ə.t̬|i **-ies** -iz

lev|y n, v ˈlev|.i **-ies** -iz **-ying** -i.ɪŋ **-ied** -id **-ier/s** -i.əʳ/z, ⓤⓢ -i.ɚ/z
Levy *surname:* ˈliː.vi, ˈlev.i
lewd ljuːd, luːd, ⓤⓢ luːd **-er** -əʳ, ⓤⓢ -ɚ **-est** -ɪst, -əst **-ly** -li **-ness** -nəs, -nɪs
Lewes ˈluː.ɪs
Lewin ˈluː.ɪn
Lewinsky ləˈwɪnt.ski, ⓤⓢ luˈwɪn.ski
lewis, L~ ˈluː.ɪs **-es** -ɪz
Lewisham ˈluː.ɪ.ʃəm
Lewison ˈluː.ɪ.sən
Lewsey ˈljuː.si, ⓤⓢ ˈluː-
lexeme ˈlek.siːm **-s** -z
lexic|al ˈlek.sɪ.k|əl **-ally** -əl.i, -li
lexicographic ˌlek.sɪ.kəʊˈgræf.ɪk, ⓤⓢ -koʊˈ-, -kəˈ- **-al** -əl **-ally** -əl.i, -li
lexicograph|y ˌlek.sɪˈkɒg.rə.f|i, ⓤⓢ -ˈkɑː.grə- **-er/s** -əʳ/z, ⓤⓢ -ɚ/z
lexicological ˌlek.sɪ.kəˈlɒdʒ.ɪ.kəl, ⓤⓢ -ˈlɑː.dʒɪ-
lexicolog|y ˌlek.sɪˈkɒl.ə.dʒ|i, ⓤⓢ -ˈkɑː.lə- **-ist/s** -ɪst/s
lexicon ˈlek.sɪ.kən, -kɒn, ⓤⓢ -kɑːn, -kən **-s** -z
Lexington ˈlek.sɪŋ.tən
lexis ˈlek.sɪs
lex loci contractus ˌleksˌləʊ.saɪ.kɒnˈtræk.təs, -ˌləʊ.kiː-, ⓤⓢ -ˌloʊ.saɪ.kɑːnˈ-, -kiː-, -siː-
lex loci delicti ˌleksˌləʊ.saɪ.delˈɪk.tiː, -ˌləʊ.kiː-, -taɪ, ⓤⓢ -ˌloʊ.saɪ.dəˈlɪk-, -kiː-, -siː-
ley, L~ leɪ, liː ˈ**ley** ˌ**line**
Leybourne ˈleɪ.bɔːn, ⓤⓢ -bɔːrn
Leyburn ˈleɪ.bɜːn, ⓤⓢ -bɝːn
Leyden jar ˈlaɪ.dənˌdʒɑːʳ, ⓤⓢ -ˌdʒɑːr **-s** -z
Leyland ˈleɪ.lənd
Leys liːz
Leyton ˈleɪ.tən
Lhasa ˈlɑː.sə, ˈlæs.ə
li liː **-s** -z
liabilit|y ˌlaɪ.əˈbɪl.ə.t|i, -ɪ.t|i, ⓤⓢ -ə.ţ|i **-ies** -iz
liable ˈlaɪ.ə.bəl
liais|e liˈeɪz **-es** -ɪz **-ing** -ɪŋ **-ed** -d
liaison liˈeɪ.zən, -zɒn; *as if French:* -zɔ̃ːŋ; ⓤⓢ ˈliː.ə.zɑːn; ⓤⓢ liˈeɪ-, -zən **-s** -z
Note: In military use always /liˈeɪ.zən/ ⓤⓢ /-zɑːn, ⓤⓢ -zən/.
Liam ˈliː.əm
liana liˈɑː.nə, -ˈæn.ə
liar ˈlaɪ.əʳ, ⓤⓢ -ɚ **-s** -z
Lias ˈlaɪ.əs
Liassic laɪˈæs.ɪk, li-
lib lɪb ˌ**women's** ˈ**lib**
Libanus ˈlɪb.ə.nəs
libation laɪˈbeɪ.ʃən, lɪ-, ⓤⓢ laɪ- **-s** -z
libber ˈlɪb.əʳ, ⓤⓢ -ɚ **-s** -z ˌ**women's** ˈ**libber**
Libby ˈlɪb.i
Libdem ˌlɪbˈdem **-s** -z *stress shift:* ˌ**Libdem** ˈ**vote**
libel ˈlaɪ.bəl **-s** -z **-(l)ing** -ɪŋ **-(l)ed** -d **-(l)er/s** -əʳ/z, ⓤⓢ -ɚ/z
libel(l)ous ˈlaɪ.bəl.əs **-ly** -li
Liber ˈlaɪ.bəʳ, ⓤⓢ -bɚ
Liberace ˌlɪb.əʳˈɑː.tʃi, ⓤⓢ -əˈrɑː-
liberal, L~ ˈlɪb.ər.əl, ˈ-rəl **-s** -z **-ly** -i
Liberal Democrat ˌlɪb.ər.əlˈdem.ə.kræt, -rəlˈ- **-s** -s
liberalism, L~ ˈlɪb.ər.əl.ɪ.zəm, ˈ-rəl-
liberality ˌlɪb.əˈræl.ə.ti, lɪˈbræl-, ⓤⓢ ˌlɪb.əˈræl-, -ɪ.ti, -ə.ţi
liberalization, -isa- ˌlɪb.ər.əl.aɪˈzeɪ.ʃən, ˌ-rəl-, -ɪˈ-, ⓤⓢ -əˈ-
liberaliz|e, -is|e ˈlɪb.ər.əl.aɪz, ˈ-rəl- **-es** -ɪz **-ing** -ɪŋ **-ed** -d
liber|ate ˈlɪb.ər|.eɪt, ⓤⓢ -ə.r|eɪt **-ates** -eɪts **-ating** -eɪ.tɪŋ, ⓤⓢ -eɪ.ţɪŋ **-ated** -eɪ.tɪd, ⓤⓢ -eɪ.ţɪd **-ator/s** -eɪ.təʳ/z, ⓤⓢ -eɪ.ţɚ/z
liberation ˌlɪb.əʳˈeɪ.ʃən, ⓤⓢ -əˈreɪ-
Liberi|a laɪˈbɪə.ri|.ə, ⓤⓢ -ˈbɪr.i- **-an/s** -ən/z
libertarian ˌlɪb.əˈteə.ri.ən, ⓤⓢ -ɚˈter.i- **-s** -z **-ism** -ɪ.zəm
libertine ˈlɪb.ə.tiːn, -taɪn, ⓤⓢ -ɚ.tiːn, -tɪn **-s** -z
Liberton ˈlɪb.ə.tən, ⓤⓢ ˈ-ɚ-
libert|y, L~ ˈlɪb.ə.t|i, ⓤⓢ -ɚ.ţ|i **-ies** -iz ˌ**Liberty** ˈ**Island**
libidinous lɪˈbɪd.ɪ.nəs, lə-, -ən.əs, ⓤⓢ ləˈbɪd.ən.əs **-ly** -li **-ness** -nəs, -nɪs
libido lɪˈbiː.dəʊ, lə-, ⓤⓢ -doʊ **-s** -z
libr|a *pound:* ˈliː.br|ə, ˈlaɪ-, ⓤⓢ ˈliː- **-ae** -iː, -eɪ, -aɪ
Libr|a *constellation:* ˈliː.br|ə, ˈlɪb.r|ə, ˈlaɪ.br|ə, ⓤⓢ ˈliː-, ˈlaɪ- **-an/s** -ən/z
librarian laɪˈbreə.ri.ən, ⓤⓢ -ˈbrer.i- **-s** -z **-ship** -ʃɪp
librar|y ˈlaɪ.brər|.i, -br|i, ⓤⓢ -brer|.i **-ies** -iz
libration laɪˈbreɪ.ʃən **-s** -z
librettist lɪˈbret.ɪst, lə-, ⓤⓢ lɪˈbreţ- **-s** -s
librett|o lɪˈbret|.əʊ, lə-, ⓤⓢ lɪˈbreţ|.oʊ **-os** -əʊz, ⓤⓢ -oʊz **-i** -iː
Libreville ˈliː.brə.vɪl, ⓤⓢ -viːl, -vɪl
Librium® ˈlɪb.ri.əm
Liby|a ˈlɪb.i|.ə **-an/s** -ən/z
lice (plural of **louse**) laɪs
licenc|e ˈlaɪ.sənts **-es** -ɪz **-ed** -t
licens|e ˈlaɪ.sənts **-es** -ɪz **-ing** -ɪŋ **-ed** -t **-er/s** -əʳ/z, ⓤⓢ -ɚ/z **-or/s** -əʳ/z, ⓤⓢ -ɚ/z ˈ**license** ˌ**plate**
licensee ˌlaɪ.səntˈsiː **-s** -z
licentiate laɪˈsen.tʃi.ət, lɪ-, -tʃət, -tʃi.ɪt, ⓤⓢ -ʃi.ɪt, -ʃi.eɪt, -ʃət **-s** -s
licentious laɪˈsen.tʃəs **-ly** -li **-ness** -nəs, -nɪs
lichee ˌlaɪˈtʃiː; ˈlaɪ.tʃiː, ˈliː-, ⓤⓢ ˈliː.tʃiː **-s** -z
lichen ˈlaɪ.kən, -kɪn, ˈlɪtʃ.ən, -ɪn, ⓤⓢ ˈlaɪ.kən **-s** -z **-ed** -d
lichenous ˈlaɪ.kə.nəs, -kɪ-, ˈlɪtʃ.ə-, ˈ-ɪ-, ⓤⓢ ˈlaɪ.kə-
Lichfield ˈlɪtʃ.fiːld
lichgate ˈlɪtʃ.geɪt **-s** -s
Lichtenstein ˈlɪk.tən.staɪn; *as if German:* ˈlɪx.tən.ʃtaɪn
Licini|an laɪˈsɪn.i|.ən, lɪ- **-us** -əs
licit ˈlɪs.ɪt **-ly** -li **-ness** -nəs, -nɪs
lick lɪk **-s** -s **-ing/s** -ɪŋ/z **-ed** -t
lickety-split ˌlɪk.ə.tiˈsplɪt, ˌ-ɪ-, ⓤⓢ -ə.ţiˈ-
licorice ˈlɪk.ər.ɪs, -ɪʃ, ˈlɪk.rɪs, -rɪʃ, ⓤⓢ ˈlɪk.ɚ.ɪʃ, ˈ-rɪʃ, ˈlɪk.ɚ.ɪs
lictor ˈlɪk.təʳ, -tɔːʳ, ⓤⓢ -tɚ **-s** -z
lid lɪd **-s** -z **-ded** -ɪd
Liddell ˈlɪd.əl, lɪˈdel
Liddesdale ˈlɪdz.deɪl
Liddiment ˈlɪd.ɪ.mənt
Liddle ˈlɪd.əl
Liddon ˈlɪd.ən
Lidell lɪˈdel
Lidgate ˈlɪd.geɪt, -gɪt
Lidl® ˈlɪd.əl, ˈliː.dəl
lido, L~ ˈliː.dəʊ, ˈlaɪ-, ⓤⓢ ˈliː.doʊ **-s** -z
lie n, v *falsehood:* laɪ **-s** -z **lying/ly** ˈlaɪ.ɪŋ/li **lied** laɪd ˌ**lie through one's** ˈ**teeth**
lie v *recline:* laɪ **-s** -z **lying** ˈlaɪ.ɪŋ **lay** leɪ **lain** leɪn
lie-abed ˈlaɪ.ə.bed **-s** -z
Lieberman ˈliː.bə.mən, ⓤⓢ -bɚ-
liebfraumilch, L~ ˈliːb.fraʊ.mɪltʃ; *as if German:* -mɪlx; ⓤⓢ -mɪlk, ˈliːp-
Liebig ˈliː.bɪg; *as if German:* -bɪx; ⓤⓢ -bɪg; *as if German:* ⓤⓢ -bɪx
Liebknecht ˈliːb.knekt; *as if German:* -knext
Liechtenstein ˈlɪk.tən.staɪn; *as if German:* ˈlɪx.tən.ʃtaɪn
lied *German song:* liːd; *as if German:* liːt **lieder** ˈliː.dəʳ, ⓤⓢ -dɚ
lief liːf **-er** -əʳ, ⓤⓢ -ɚ
lieg|e liːdʒ **-es** -ɪz
Liège liˈeɪʒ, -ˈeʒ
lie-in ˌlaɪˈɪn, ˈ-- **-s** -z
lien ˈliː.ən, liːn, ⓤⓢ liːn, ˈliː.ən **-s** -z
Liepaja ˈliː.epˌɑː.jə
lieu ljuː, luː, ⓤⓢ luː
lieutenanc|y lefˈten.ənt.s|i, ləf-, ⓤⓢ luː- **-ies** -iz
lieutenant lefˈten.ənt, ləf-, ⓤⓢ luː- **-s** -s **lieu**ˌ**tenant** ˈ**colonel**; **lieu**ˌ**tenant com**ˈ**mander**; **lieu**ˌ**tenant** ˈ**general**; **lieu**ˌ**tenant** ˈ**governor**
li|fe laɪ|f **-ves** -vz ˈ**life** ˌ**cycle**; ˈ**life ex**ˌ**pectancy**; ˈ**life in**ˌ**surance**; ˌ**life** ˈ**savings**; ˌ**life** ˈ**sentence**
life-and-death ˌlaɪf.ənˈdeθ *stress shift:* ˌ**life-and-death** ˈ**issue**
lifebelt ˈlaɪf.belt **-s** -s
lifeblood ˈlaɪf.blʌd
lifeboat ˈlaɪf.bəʊt, ⓤⓢ -boʊt **-s** -s
life-buoy ˈlaɪf.bɔɪ, ⓤⓢ -bɔɪ, -ˌbuː.i **-s** -z
life-giving ˈlaɪfˌgɪv.ɪŋ
lifeguard ˈlaɪf.gɑːd, ⓤⓢ -gɑːrd **-s** -z
lifejacket ˈlaɪfˌdʒæk.ɪt **-s** -s
lifeless ˈlaɪf.ləs, -lɪs **-ly** -li **-ness** -nəs, -nɪs
lifelike ˈlaɪf.laɪk
lifeline ˈlaɪf.laɪn **-s** -z
lifelong ˌlaɪfˈlɒŋ, ⓤⓢ ˌlaɪfˈlɑːŋ, -ˈlɔːŋ *stress shift:* ˌ**lifelong** ˈ**dream**
life of Riley ˌlaɪf.əvˈraɪ.li
life-or-death ˌlaɪf.ɔːˈdeθ, ⓤⓢ -ɔːrˈ- *stress shift:* ˌ**life-or-death** ˈ**issue**
life-preserver ˈlaɪf.prɪˌzɜː.vəʳ, -prəˌ-, ⓤⓢ -priːˌzɝː.vɚ, -prɪˌ- **-s** -z
lifer ˈlaɪ.fəʳ, ⓤⓢ -fɚ **-s** -z
lifesaver ˈlaɪfˌseɪ.vəʳ, ⓤⓢ -vɚ **-s** -z
life-saving ˈlaɪfˌseɪ.vɪŋ *stress shift:* ˌ**life-saving** ˈ**medicine**
life-size ˈlaɪf.saɪz, ˌ-ˈ-

lifespan ˈlaɪf.spæn -s -z
lifestyle ˈlaɪf.staɪl -s -z
life-support ˈlaɪf.səˌpɔːt, ˌ--ˈ-, (US) ˈlaɪf.səˌpɔːrt **ˌlife-supˈport ˌsystem**; **ˈlife-supˌport ˌsystem** (US) **ˈlife-supˌport ˌsystem**
life-threatening ˈlaɪfˌθret.ᵊn.ɪŋ
lifetime ˈlaɪf.taɪm -s -z
lifework ˌlaɪfˈwɜːk, ˈ--, (US) ˌlaɪfˈwɝːk, ˈ-- -s -s
Liffe laɪf
Liffey ˈlɪf.i
Lifford ˈlɪf.əd, (US) -ɚd
lift lɪft -s -s -ing -ɪŋ -ed -ɪd -er/s -əʳ/z, (US) -ɚ/z
lift-off ˈlɪft.ɒf, (US) -ɑːf
ligament ˈlɪg.ə.mənt -s -s
ligament|al ˌlɪg.əˈmen.t|ᵊl, (US) -t̬|ᵊl -ous -əs
ligature ˈlɪg.ə.tʃəʳ, -tʃʊəʳ, -tjʊəʳ, (US) -tʃɚ -s -z -d -d
liger ˈlaɪ.gəʳ, (US) -gɚ -s -z
Ligeti ˈlɪg.et.i
Liggett ˈlɪg.ɪt, -ət
light laɪt -s -s -er -əʳ, (US) ˈlaɪ.t̬ɚ -est -ɪst, -əst, (US) ˈlaɪ.t̬ɪst, -t̬əst -ly -li -ness -nəs, -nɪs -ing -ɪŋ, (US) ˈlaɪ.t̬ɪŋ -ed -ɪd, (US) ˈlaɪ.t̬ɪd **lit** lɪt **ˌlight ˈaircraft**; **ˈlight ˌbulb**; **ˈlight ˌmeter**
lighten ˈlaɪ.tᵊn -s -z -ing -ɪŋ, ˈlaɪt.nɪŋ -ed -d
lighter ˈlaɪ.təʳ, (US) -t̬ɚ -s -z
lighterage ˈlaɪ.tᵊr.ɪdʒ, (US) -t̬ɚ-
light-fingered ˌlaɪtˈfɪŋ.gəd, (US) -gɚd *stress shift:* **ˌlight-fingered ˈthief**
lightfoot, L~ ˈlaɪt.fʊt
light-headed ˌlaɪtˈhed.ɪd -ly -li -ness -nəs, -nɪs *stress shift:* **ˌlight-headed ˈdaze**
light-hearted ˌlaɪtˈhɑː.tɪd, (US) -ˈhɑːr.t̬ɪd -ly -li -ness -nəs, -nɪs *stress shift:* **ˌlight-hearted ˈcomment**
lighthou|se ˈlaɪt.haʊ|s -ses -zɪz
lighthousekeeper ˈlaɪt.haʊsˌkiː.pəʳ, (US) -pɚ -s -z
lighting-up time ˌlaɪ.tɪŋˈʌpˌtaɪm, (US) -t̬ɪŋˈ-
lightning ˈlaɪt.nɪŋ -s -z
lightning-conductor ˈlaɪt.nɪŋ.kənˌdʌk.təʳ, (US) -tɚ -s -z
lightship ˈlaɪt.ʃɪp -s -s
lightweight ˈlaɪt.weɪt -s -s
light-year ˈlaɪt.jɪəʳ, (US) -jɪr -s -z
ligneous ˈlɪg.ni.əs
lignite ˈlɪg.naɪt
lignum ˈlɪg.nəm
Liguri|a lɪgˈjʊə.ri|.ə, -ˈjɔː-, (US) -ˈjʊr.i- -an/s -ən/z
likable ˈlaɪ.kə.bᵊl -ness -nəs, -nɪs
lik|e laɪk -es -s -ing -ɪŋ -ed -t
likeable ˈlaɪ.kə.bᵊl -ness -nəs, -nɪs
likelihood ˈlaɪ.kli.hʊd
likel|y ˈlaɪ.kl|i -ier -i.əʳ, (US) -i.ɚ -iest -i.ɪst, -i.əst -iness -ɪ.nəs, -ɪ.nɪs
likeminded ˌlaɪkˈmaɪn.dɪd, (US) ˈ-ˌ--, ˌ-ˈ-- *stress shift, British only:* **ˌlike-minded ˈfriend**
liken ˈlaɪ.kᵊn -s -z -ing -ɪŋ -ed -d
likeness ˈlaɪk.nəs, -nɪs -es -ɪz
likewise ˈlaɪk.waɪz
liking ˈlaɪ.kɪŋ -s -z
Likud lɪˈkʊd, -ˈkuːd, (US) -ˈkuːd
likuta liˈkuː.tɑː
lilac ˈlaɪ.lək, (US) -lək, -læk, -lɑːk -s -s
liliaceous ˌlɪl.iˈeɪ.ʃəs
Lilian ˈlɪl.i.ən
Lilias ˈlɪl.i.əs
Liliburlero ˌlɪl.i.bəˈleə.rəʊ, (US) -bɚˈler.oʊ
Lilith ˈlɪl.ɪθ
Lilla ˈlɪl.ə
Lille liːl
Lillehammer ˈlɪl.ɪ.hæm.əʳ, -əˌ-, (US) -ə.hɑː.mɚ, -hæm.ɚ
Lil-lets® lɪˈlets
Lilley ˈlɪl.i
Lillian ˈlɪl.i.ən
Lilliput ˈlɪl.ɪ.pʌt, ˈ-ə-, -pʊt, -pət, (US) -ə.pʌt, -pət, -pʊt
lilliputian, L~ ˌlɪl.ɪˈpjuː.ʃᵊn, -əˈ-, -ʃi.ən, (US) -əˈpjuː.ʃᵊn -s -z
Lilly ˈlɪl.i
Lillywhite ˈlɪl.i.*h*waɪt
Lilo® ˈlaɪ.ləʊ, (US) -loʊ -s -z
Lilongwe lɪˈlɒŋ.weɪ, (US) -ˈlɔːŋ-, -ˈlɑːŋ-
lilt lɪlt -s -s -ing -ɪŋ, (US) ˈlɪl.tɪŋ -ed -ɪd, (US) ˈlɪl.tɪd
lil|y, L~ ˈlɪl|.i -ies -iz **ˌlily of the ˈvalley**
lily-livered ˌlɪl.iˈlɪv.əd, (US) -ɚd *stress shift:* **ˌlily-livered ˈscoundrel**
lily-white ˌlɪl.iˈ*h*waɪt *stress shift:* **ˌlily-white ˈhands**
lima *bean:* ˈliː.mə, (US) ˈlaɪ-
Lima *in Peru:* ˈliː.mə *in US:* ˈlaɪ.mə
Limavady ˌlɪm.əˈvæd.i
limb lɪm -s -z -ed -d **ˌout on a ˈlimb**
Limbaugh ˈlɪm.bɔː
limber **n, adj** ˈlɪm.bəʳ, (US) -bɚ -s -z
limbo, L~ ˈlɪm.bəʊ, (US) -boʊ -s -z -ing -ɪŋ -ed -d
Limburg ˈlɪm.bɜːg, (US) -bɝːg
lim|e **n, v** laɪm -es -z -ing -ɪŋ -ed -d **ˌlime ˈgreen**
limeade ˌlaɪˈmeɪd, (US) ˌ-ˈ-, ˈlaɪ.meɪd
Limehouse ˈlaɪm.haʊs
limekiln ˈlaɪm.kɪln, -kɪl -s -z
limelight ˈlaɪm.laɪt -s -s
limen ˈlaɪ.men, -mən, (US) -mən
limerick, L~ ˈlɪm.ᵊr.ɪk, (US) -ɚ.ɪk, ˈ-rɪk -s -s
limescale ˈlaɪm.skeɪl
limestone ˈlaɪm.stəʊn, (US) -stoʊn
limewash ˈlaɪm.wɒʃ, (US) -wɑːʃ, -wɔːʃ -es -ɪz -ing -ɪŋ -ed -t
limewater ˈlaɪmˌwɔː.təʳ, (US) -ˌwɑː.t̬ɚ, -ˌwɔː-
limey ˈlaɪ.mi -s -z
liminal ˈlɪm.ɪ.nᵊl
lim|it **n, v** ˈlɪm|.ɪt -its -ɪts -iting -ɪ.tɪŋ, (US) -ɪ.t̬ɪŋ -ited/ness -ɪ.tɪd/nəs, -nɪs, (US) -ɪ.t̬ɪd/nəs, -nɪs -itable -ɪ.tə.bᵊl, (US) -ɪ.t̬ə.bᵊl
limitation ˌlɪm.ɪˈteɪ.ʃᵊn, -əˈ- -s -z
limitless ˈlɪm.ɪt.ləs, -lɪs
limn lɪm -s -z -ing -ɪŋ, -nɪŋ -ed -d -er/s -nəʳ/z, (US) -ɚ/z, -nɚ/z
limo ˈlɪm.əʊ, (US) -oʊ -s -z
Limoges liˈməʊʒ, (US) liːˈmoʊʒ
Limousin ˌlɪm.uˈzæn; *as if French:* -ˈzæ̃ŋ; (US) ˌliː.muːˈzæn
limousine ˌlɪm.əˈziːn, -ʊˈ-, ˈ---, (US) ˈlɪm.ə.ziːn, ˌ--ˈ- -s -z
limp lɪmp -s -s -er -əʳ, (US) -ɚ -est -ɪst, -əst -ly -li -ness -nəs, -nɪs -ing/ly -ɪŋ/li -ed -t
limpet ˈlɪm.pɪt -s -s
limpid ˈlɪm.pɪd -ly -li -ness -nəs, -nɪs
limpidity lɪmˈpɪd.ə.ti, -ɪ.ti, (US) -ə.t̬i
Limpopo lɪmˈpəʊ.pəʊ, (US) -ˈpoʊ.poʊ
limp-wristed ˌlɪmpˈrɪs.tɪd, (US) ˌ-ˈ--, ˈlɪmpˌrɪs-
limy ˈlaɪ.mi
Linacre ˈlɪn.ə.kəʳ, ˈ-ɪ-, (US) -kɚ
linag|e ˈlaɪ.nɪdʒ -es -ɪz
Linares lɪˈnɑː.rɪs, (US) lɪˈner.ɪs
linchpin ˈlɪntʃ.pɪn -s -z
Lincoln ˈlɪŋ.kən -shire -ʃəʳ, -ʃɪəʳ, (US) -ʃɚ, -ʃɪr
Lincs. (abbrev. for **Lincolnshire**) lɪŋks, lɪŋ.kən.ʃəʳ, -ʃɪəʳ, (US) ˈlɪŋ.kən.ʃɚ, -ʃɪr
linctus ˈlɪŋk.təs -es -ɪz
Lind lɪnd
Linda ˈlɪn.də
Lindbergh ˈlɪn*d*.bɜːg, (US) -bɝːg
linden, L~ ˈlɪn.dən -s -z
Lindisfarne ˈlɪn.dɪs.fɑːn, -dəs-, (US) -fɑːrn
Lindley ˈlɪn*d*.li
Lindon ˈlɪn.dən
Lindsay, Lindsey ˈlɪn*d*.zi
lin|e, L~ laɪn -es -z -ing -ɪŋ -ed -d **ˈline ˌdrawing**; **ˌread beˌtween the ˈlines**
lineag|e *family:* ˈlɪn.i.ɪdʒ *alternative spelling of* **linage**: ˈlaɪ.nɪdʒ -es -ɪz
lineal ˈlɪn.i.əl -ly -i
lineament ˈlɪn.i.ə.mənt -s -s
linear ˈlɪn.i.əʳ, (US) -ɚ -ly -li
lineation ˌlɪn.iˈeɪ.ʃᵊn -s -z
linebacker ˈlaɪnˌbæk.əʳ, ˈlaɪm-, (US) ˈlaɪnˌbæk.ɚ -s -z
line-engraving ˈlaɪn.ɪnˌgreɪ.vɪŋ, -ɪŋˌ-, (US) -ɪnˌ- -s -z
Lineker ˈlɪn.ɪ.kəʳ, ˈ-ə-, (US) -kɚ
line|man ˈlaɪn|.mən, ˈlaɪm-, (US) ˈlaɪn- -men -mən, -men
linen ˈlɪn.ɪn, -ən -s -z
lineout ˈlaɪn.aʊt -s -s
liner ˈlaɪ.nəʳ, (US) -nɚ -s -z
lines|man ˈlaɪnz|.mən -men -mən, -men
lineup ˈlaɪn.ʌp -s -s
Linford ˈlɪn.fəd, (US) -fɚd
ling, L~ lɪŋ -s -z
lingam ˈlɪŋ.gəm, -æm
Lingay ˈlɪŋ.gi
Lingen ˈlɪŋ.ən
ling|er ˈlɪŋ.g|əʳ, (US) -g|ɚ -ers -əz, (US) -ɚz -ering/ly -ᵊr.ɪŋ/li -ered -əd, (US) -ɚd -erer/s -ᵊr.əʳ/z, (US) -ɚ.ɚ/z
lingerie ˈlæ̃n.ʒᵊr.i, ˈlɒn-, -dʒᵊr-, -ri,

-reɪ, (US) ˌlɑːn.ʒəˈreɪ; ˌlæn.ʒəˈriː, -dʒəˈ-
Lingfield ˈlɪŋ.fiːld
lingo ˈlɪŋ.gəʊ, (US) -goʊ **-s** -z
lingua franca ˌlɪŋ.gwəˈfræŋ.kə
lingual ˈlɪŋ.gwəl **-ly** -i
Linguaphone® ˈlɪŋ.gwə.fəʊn, (US) -foʊn
Linguarama® ˌlɪŋ.gwəˈrɑː.mə, (US) -ˈræm.ə, -ˈrɑː.mə
linguine, linguini lɪŋˈgwiː.ni
linguist ˈlɪŋ.gwɪst **-s** -s
linguistic lɪŋˈgwɪs.tɪk **-s** -s **-al** -əl **-ally** -əl.i, -li
linguistician ˌlɪŋ.gwɪˈstɪʃ.ən **-s** -z
liniment ˈlɪn.ɪ.mənt, ˈ-ə- **-s** -s
lining ˈlaɪ.nɪŋ **-s** -z
link n, v lɪŋk **-s** -s **-ing** -ɪŋ **-ed** -t
linkag|e ˈlɪŋ.kɪdʒ **-es** -ɪz
Linklater ˈlɪŋkˌleɪ.təʳ, (US) -t̬ɚ
links lɪŋks
linkup ˈlɪŋk.ʌp
Linley ˈlɪn.li
Linlithgow lɪnˈlɪθ.gəʊ, (US) -goʊ **-shire** -ʃəʳ, -ʃɪəʳ, (US) -ʃɚ, -ʃɪr
Linnaean lɪˈniː.ən, -ˈneɪ-
Linnaeus lɪˈniː.əs, -ˈneɪ-
Linnean lɪˈniː.ən, -ˈneɪ-
linnet, L~ ˈlɪn.ɪt **-s** -s
lino ˈlaɪ.nəʊ, (US) -noʊ **-s** -z
linocut ˈlaɪ.nəʊ.kʌt, (US) -noʊ-, -nə- **-s** -s
linoleum lɪˈnəʊ.li.əm, (US) -ˈnoʊ- **-s** -z
Linotype® ˈlaɪ.nəʊ.taɪp, (US) -nə- **-s** -s
linseed ˈlɪn.siːd ˈ**linseed** ˌ**oil**; ˌ**linseed** ˈ**oil**
linsey, L~ ˈlɪn.zi
linsey-woolsey, Linsey-Woolsey ˌlɪn.ziˈwʊl.zi
lint lɪnt
lintel ˈlɪn.təl, (US) -t̬əl **-s** -z
Linthwaite ˈlɪn.θweɪt
Linton ˈlɪn.tən
Lintot(t) ˈlɪn.tɒt, (US) -tɑːt
Linus ˈlaɪ.nəs
Linux ˈlɪn.əks, ˈlaɪ.nəks, -nʌks, (US) ˈlɪn.əks
Linz lɪnts
lion laɪ.ən **-s** -z ˈ**lion** ˌ**tamer**
Lionel ˈlaɪə.nəl, ˈlaɪ.ə-, (US) ˈlaɪ.ə-
lioness ˈlaɪ.ə.nes, -nɪs; ˌlaɪ.əˈnes, (US) ˈlaɪ.ə.nes, -nɪs **-es** -ɪz
Lionheart ˈlaɪ.ən.hɑːt, (US) -hɑːrt
lion-hearted ˌlaɪ.ənˈhɑː.tɪd, (US) ˈlaɪ.ənˌhɑːr.t̬ɪd *stress shift, British only:* ˌ**lion-hearted** ˈ**warrior**
lionization, -isa- ˌlaɪ.ə.naɪˈzeɪ.ʃən, -nɪˈ-, (US) -nəˈ-
lioniz|e, -is|e ˈlaɪ.ə.naɪz **-es** -ɪz **-ing** -ɪŋ **-ed** -d
lip lɪp **-s** -s **-ping** -ɪŋ **-ped** -t ˈ**lip** ˌ**service**
Lipari ˈlɪp.ər.i, ˈliː.pær-
lipas|e ˈlaɪ.peɪz, ˈlɪp.eɪz, -eɪs, (US) ˈlɪp.eɪs, ˈlaɪ.peɪs **-es** -ɪz
lipbrush ˈlɪp.brʌʃ **-es** -ɪz
lipid(e) ˈlɪp.ɪd, ˈlaɪ.pɪd, (US) ˈlɪp.ɪd **-s** -z
Lipman ˈlɪp.mən
lipoid ˈlɪp.ɔɪd, ˈlaɪ.pɔɪd
lipoprotein ˌlɪp.əʊˈprəʊ.tiːn, ˌlaɪ.pəʊˈ-, (US) ˌlɪp.oʊˈproʊ.tiːn, ˌlaɪ.poʊˈ-, -pəˈ-, -tiː.ɪn **-s** -z
liposome ˈlɪp.əʊ.səʊm, (US) -ə.soʊm, ˈlaɪ.pə- **-s** -z
liposuction ˈlɪp.əʊˌsʌk.ʃən, (US) ˈlɪp.oʊˌ-, ˈlaɪ.poʊˌ-, -pəˌ-
Lippi ˈlɪp.i
Lippincott ˈlɪp.ɪŋ.kət, -kɒt, (US) -ɪn.kɑːt, -kət
Lippizaner ˌlɪp.ɪtˈsɑː.nəʳ, -ətˈ-, (US) -nɚ **-s** -z
Lippmann ˈlɪp.mən
lipp|y ˈlɪp|.i **-ier** -i.əʳ, (US) -i.ɚ **-iest** -i.ɪst, -i.əst **-iness** -ɪ.nəs, -ɪ.nɪs
lip|-read ˈlɪp|.riːd **-reads** -riːdz **-reading** -ˌriː.dɪŋ **-read** *past tense:* -red **-reader/s** -ˌriː.dəʳ/z, (US) -ˌriː.dɚ/z
lip-salve ˈlɪp.sælv, -sɑːlv, (US) -sæv, -sɑːv **-s** -z
Lipscomb(e) ˈlɪp.skəm
Lipstadt ˈlɪp.stæt
lipstick ˈlɪp.stɪk **-s** -s
lip-synch ˈlɪp.sɪŋk **-s** -s **-ing** -ɪŋ **-ed** -t
Lipton ˈlɪp.tən
liquefaction ˌlɪk.wɪˈfæk.ʃən, -wəˈ-
lique|fy ˈlɪk.wɪ|.faɪ, -wə- **-fies** -faɪz **-fying** -faɪ.ɪŋ **-fied** -faɪd **-fier/s** -faɪ.əʳ/z, (US) -faɪ.ɚ/z **-fiable** -faɪ.ə.bəl
liqueur lɪˈkjʊəʳ, lə-, -ˈkjɔːʳ, -ˈkjɜːʳ, (US) lɪˈkɝː, -ˈkʊr, -ˈkjʊr **-s** -z
liquid ˈlɪk.wɪd **-s** -z **-ly** -li **-ness** -nəs, -nɪs
liqui|date ˈlɪk.wɪ|.deɪt, -wə- **-dates** -deɪts **-dating** -deɪ.tɪŋ, (US) -deɪ.t̬ɪŋ **-dated** -deɪ.tɪd, (US) -deɪ.t̬ɪd **-dator/s** -deɪ.təʳ/z, (US) -deɪ.t̬ɚ/z
liquidation ˌlɪk.wɪˈdeɪ.ʃən, -wəˈ- **-s** -z
liquidity lɪˈkwɪd.ə.ti, lə-, -ɪ.ti, (US) -ə.t̬i
liquidiz|e, -is|e ˈlɪk.wɪ.daɪz, -wə- **-es** -ɪz **-ing** -ɪŋ **-ed** -d
liquidizer, -iser ˈlɪk.wɪ.daɪ.zəʳ, -wə-, (US) -zɚ **-s** -z
liquif|y ˈlɪk.wɪ.f|aɪ, -wə- **-ies** aɪz **-ying** aɪ.ɪŋ **-ied** -aɪd
liqu|or ˈlɪk|.əʳ, (US) -ɚ **-ors** -əz, (US) -ɚz **-oring** -ər.ɪŋ **-ored** -əd, (US) -ɚd
liquorice ˈlɪk.ər.ɪs, -ɪʃ, ˈlɪk.rɪs, -rɪʃ, (US) ˈlɪk.ɚ.ɪʃ, ˈ-rɪʃ, ˈlɪk.ɚ.ɪs

> Note: The pronunciation with /-ɪʃ/ used to be considered a mispronunciation, characteristic of children's speech, but has now become as widespread as the /-ɪs/ form. It is still disapproved of by some people.

lir|a ˈlɪə.r|ə, (US) ˈlɪr|.ə **-as** -əz **-e** -i, -eɪ
Lisa ˈliː.sə, -zə
Lisbet ˈlɪz.bət, -bet, -bɪt
Lisbeth ˈlɪz.bəθ, -beθ, -bɪθ
Lisbon ˈlɪz.bən
Lisburn ˈlɪz.bɜːn, (US) -bɝːn
lisente lɪˈsen.teɪ, (US) -ti
Lisette liˈzet
Liskeard ˈlɪs.kɑːd, (US) -kɑːrd
lisle *thread:* laɪl
Lisle laɪl, liːl

> Note: Baron Lisle pronounces /laɪl/.

Lismore *in Scotland and Ireland:* lɪzˈmɔːʳ, (US) -ˈmɔːr *in Australia:* ˈlɪz.mɔːʳ, (US) -mɔːr
lisp, LISP lɪsp **-s** -s **-ing/ly** -ɪŋ/li **-ed** -t **-er/s** -əʳ/z, (US) -ɚ/z
lis pendens ˌlɪsˈpen.denz
Liss lɪs
lissom(e) ˈlɪs.əm **-ness** -nəs, -nɪs
Lisson ˈlɪs.ən
list lɪst **-s** -s **-ing/s** -ɪŋ/z **-ed** -ɪd
listen ˈlɪs.ən **-s** -z **-ing** -ɪŋ, ˈlɪs.nɪŋ **-ed** -d **-er/s** -əʳ/z, ˈlɪs.nəʳ/z, (US) -ɚ/z, ˈlɪs.nɚ/z
Lister ˈlɪs.təʳ, (US) -tɚ
listeria lɪˈstɪə.ri.ə, (US) -ˈstɪr.i-
Listerine® ˈlɪs.tər.iːn, (US) ˌlɪs.təˈriːn
listeriosis lɪˌstɪə.riˈəʊ.sɪs, ˌlɪs.tɪə-, (US) lɪˌstɪr.iˈoʊ-
listless ˈlɪst.ləs, -lɪs **-ly** -li **-ness** -nəs, -nɪs
Liston ˈlɪs.tən
Listowel lɪˈstəʊ.əl, (US) -ˈstoʊ.əl, -ˈstaʊl
Liszt lɪst
lit (from **light**) lɪt
litan|y ˈlɪt.ən|.i **-ies** -iz
Litchfield ˈlɪtʃ.fiːld
litchi laɪˈtʃiː; ˈlaɪ.tʃiː, ˈliː-, (US) ˈliː.tʃiː **-s** -z
lite laɪt
liter ˈliː.təʳ, (US) -t̬ɚ **-s** -z
literacy ˈlɪt.ər.ə.si, ˈ-rə.si, (US) ˈlɪt̬.ɚ.ə-
literal ˈlɪt.ər.əl, ˈ-rəl, (US) ˈlɪt̬.ɚ.əl **-ly** -i **-ness** -nəs, -nɪs
literal|ism ˈlɪt.ər.əl|.ɪ.zəm, ˈ-rəl-, (US) ˈlɪt̬.ɚ.əl- **-ist/s** -ɪst/s
literality ˌlɪt.ərˈæl.ə.ti, -ɪ.ti, (US) -əˈræl.ə.t̬i
literar|y ˈlɪt.ər.ər|.i, ˈ-ər|.i, (US) ˈlɪt̬.ə.rer- **-ily** -əl.i, -ɪ.li **-iness** -ɪ.nəs, -ɪ.nɪs
literate ˈlɪt.ər.ət, -ɪt, ˈ-rət, -rɪt, (US) ˈlɪt̬.ɚ.ət **-s** -s
literati ˌlɪt.ərˈɑː.tiː, (US) ˌlɪt̬.əˈrɑː.t̬iː
literatim ˌlɪt.ərˈɑː.tɪm, (US) ˌlɪt̬.əˈreɪ.t̬ɪm, -ˈrɑː-
literature ˈlɪt.rə.tʃəʳ, -rɪ-, ˈ-ər.ə-, -ɪ-, (US) ˈlɪt̬.ɚ.ə.tʃɚ, -tʃʊr **-s** -z
litharge ˈlɪθ.ɑːdʒ, (US) -ɑːrdʒ; (US) lɪˈθɑːrdʒ
lith|e laɪð **-er** -əʳ, (US) -ɚ **-est** -ɪst, -əst **-ely** -li **-eness** -nəs, -nɪs
Litheby ˈlɪð.ɪ.bi, ˈ-ə-
Litherland ˈlɪð.ə.lænd, (US) ˈ-ɚ-
lithesome ˈlaɪð.səm **-ness** -nəs, -nɪs
Lithgow ˈlɪθ.gəʊ, (US) -goʊ
lithia ˈlɪθ.i.ə
lithic ˈlɪθ.ɪk
lithium ˈlɪθ.i.əm
litho ˈlɪθ.əʊ, ˈlaɪ.θəʊ, (US) ˈlɪθ.oʊ **-s** -z

Pronouncing the letters LL

In general, the consonant digraph **ll** is pronounced /l/, e.g.:

fall	fɔːl (US) fɑːl
illustrate	ˈɪl.ə.streɪt

Where the **ll** is produced by adding the suffix *–ly* or *–less* to a word ending in a single **l**, the pronunciation reflects this, e.g.:

coolly	ˈkuːl.li
soulless	ˈsəʊl.ləs (US) ˈsoʊl-

In addition

In Welsh words, **ll** may be pronounced by English speakers in a variety of different ways. In this dictionary, we suggest /hl/, which stands both for the phonetic [ɬ] used in Welsh and for the English approximation of either a voiceless or voiced [l], and also the variant /θl/ for British English speakers, e.g.:

Llanberis	*h*lænˈber.ɪs, θlæn- (US) *h*læn-

lithograph ˈlɪθ.əʊ.grɑːf, -græf, (US) -ə.græf, ˈ-oʊ- **-s** -s **-ing** -ɪŋ **-ed** -t

> Note: In British printers' usage /ˈlaɪ.θəʊ-/. So also with derived words (**lithographer,** etc.).

lithographer lɪˈθɒg.rə.fəʳ, (US) -ˈθɑː.grə.fɚ **-s** -z

lithographic ˌlɪθ.əʊˈgræf.ɪk, (US) -oʊˈ-, -əˈ- **-al** -əl **-ally** -əl.i, -li

lithography lɪˈθɒg.rə.fi, (US) -ˈθɑː.grə-

lithosphere ˈlɪθ.əʊˌsfɪəʳ, (US) -oʊˌsfɪr, -əˌ- **-s** -z

Lithuani|a ˌlɪθ.juˈeɪ.ni|.ə, -uˈ-, (US) -uˈeɪ-, -əˈweɪ- **-an/s** -ən/z

litigant ˈlɪt.ɪ.gənt, ˈ-ə-, (US) ˈlɪt̬- **-s** -s

liti|gate ˈlɪt.ɪ|.geɪt, ˈ-ə-, (US) ˈlɪt̬- **-gates** -geɪts **-gating** -geɪ.tɪŋ, (US) -geɪ.t̬ɪŋ **-gated** -geɪ.tɪd, (US) -geɪ.t̬ɪd **-gator/s** -geɪ.təʳ/z, (US) -geɪ.t̬ɚ/z

litigation ˌlɪt.ɪˈgeɪ.ʃən, -əˈ-, (US) ˌlɪt̬- **-s** -z

litigious lɪˈtɪdʒ.əs, lə-, (US) lɪ- **-ly** -li **-ness** -nəs, -nɪs

litmus ˈlɪt.məs ˈ**litmus** ˌ**paper**; ˈ**litmus** ˌ**test**

litotes laɪˈtəʊ.tiːz; ˈlaɪ.təʊ-, (US) ˈlaɪ.tə.tiːz; (US) laɪˈtoʊ-; (US) ˈlɪt.oʊ-

litre ˈliː.təʳ, (US) -t̬ɚ **-s** -z

Littel lɪˈtel

litt|er ˈlɪt|.əʳ, (US) ˈlɪt̬|.ɚ **-ers** -əz, (US) -ɚz **-ering** -ər.ɪŋ **-ered** -əd, (US) -ɚd

litterbug ˈlɪt.ə.bʌg, (US) ˈlɪt̬.ɚ- **-s** -z

littl|e, L~ ˈlɪt.əl, (US) ˈlɪt̬.əl **-er** -əʳ, (US) -ɚ **-est** -ɪst, -əst **-eness** -nəs, -nɪs

Littleborough ˈlɪt.əl.bər.ə, -ˌbʌr.ə, (US) ˈlɪt̬.əl.bɚ.oʊ

Littlechild ˈlɪt.əl.tʃaɪld

little-englander ˌlɪt.əlˈɪŋ.glən.dəʳ, (US) ˌlɪt̬.əlˈɪŋ.glən.dɚ **-s** -z

little-go ˈlɪt.əl.gəʊ, (US) ˈlɪt̬.əl.goʊ **-es** -z

Littlehampton ˈlɪt.əlˌhæmp.tən, ˌlɪt.əlˈhæmp-, (US) ˌlɪt̬.əlˈ-, ˈlɪt̬.əlˌ-

Littlejohn ˈlɪt.əl.dʒɒn, (US) ˈlɪt̬.əl.dʒɑːn

littleneck ˈlɪt.əl.nek, (US) ˈlɪt̬- **-s** -s

Littler ˈlɪt.əl.əʳ, ˈ-ləʳ, (US) ˈlɪt.lɚ, ˈlɪt̬.əl.ɚ

Littleton ˈlɪt.əl.tən, (US) ˈlɪt̬-

Littlewoods ˈlɪt.əl.wʊdz

Litton ˈlɪt.ən

littoral ˈlɪt.ər.əl, (US) ˈlɪt̬- **-s** -z

liturgic lɪˈtɜː.dʒɪk, lə-, (US) lɪˈtɝː- **-s** -s **-al** -əl **-ally** -əl.i, -li

liturgist ˈlɪt.ə.dʒɪst, ˈ-ɜː-, (US) ˈlɪt̬.ɚ- **-s** -s

liturg|y ˈlɪt.ə.dʒ|i, ˈ-ɜː-, (US) ˈlɪt̬.ɚ- **-ies** -iz

Litvinenko ˌlɪt.vɪˈnjeŋ.kəʊ, (US) -koʊ

livable ˈlɪv.ə.bəl

live adj laɪv

liv|e v lɪv **-es** -z **-ing** -ɪŋ **-ed** -d **-er/s** -əʳ/z, (US) -ɚ/z ˌ**living** ˈ**will**

live-circuit ˌlaɪvˈsɜː.kɪt, (US) -ˈsɝː- **-s** -s

live-in ˌlɪvˈɪn, ˈ-- ˌ**live-in** ˈ**lover**

livelihood ˈlaɪv.li.hʊd **-s** -z

livelong ˈlɪv.lɒŋ, ˈlaɪv-, (US) ˈlɪv.lɑːŋ, -lɔːŋ

livel|y, L~ ˈlaɪv.l|i **-ier** -i.əʳ, (US) -i.ɚ **-iest** -i.ɪst, -i.əst **-iness** -ɪ.nəs, -ɪ.nɪs

liven ˈlaɪ.vən **-s** -z **-ing** -ɪŋ, ˈlaɪv.nɪŋ **-ed** -d

Livens ˈlɪv.ənz

liv|er ˈlɪv|.əʳ, (US) -ɚ **-ers** -əz, (US) -ɚz **-erish** -ər.ɪʃ

Livermore ˈlɪv.ə.mɔːʳ, (US) -ɚ.mɔːr

Liverpool ˈlɪv.ə.puːl, (US) ˈ-ɚ-

Liverpudlian ˌlɪv.əˈpʌd.li.ən, (US) -ɚˈ- **-s** -z

Liversedge ˈlɪv.ə.sedʒ, (US) ˈ-ɚ-

liverwort ˈlɪv.ə.wɜːt, (US) -ɚ.wɝːt, -wɔːrt **-s** -s

liverwurst ˈlɪv.ə.wɜːst, (US) -ɚ.wɝːst

liver|y ˈlɪv.ər|.i, ˈ-r|i **-ies** -iz **-ied** -id

livery|man ˈlɪv.ər.i|.mən, -mæn, (US) ˈlɪv.ri.mən **-men** -mən, -men

livery-stable ˈlɪv.ər.iˌsteɪ.bəl, (US) ˈlɪv.riˌ- **-s** -z

lives (plural of **life**) laɪvz (from **live** v.) lɪvz

Livesey ˈlɪv.si, -zi

livestock ˈlaɪv.stɒk, (US) -stɑːk

live wire ˌlaɪvˈwaɪəʳ, -ˈwaɪ.əʳ, (US) -ˈwaɪ.ɚ, ˈ-- **-s** -z

Livia ˈlɪv.i.ə

livid ˈlɪv.ɪd **-ly** -li **-ness** -nəs, -nɪs

lividity lɪˈvɪd.ə.ti, -ɪ.ti, (US) -ə.t̬i

living ˈlɪv.ɪŋ **-s** -z

living-room ˈlɪv.ɪŋ.rʊm, -ruːm, (US) -ruːm, -rʊm **-s** -z

Livingston(e) ˈlɪv.ɪŋ.stən

Livoni|a lɪˈvəʊ.ni|.ə, (US) -ˈvoʊ-, ˈ-nj|ə **-an/s** -ən/z

Livorno lɪˈvɔː.nəʊ, (US) ləˈvɔːr.noʊ

Livy ˈlɪv.i

lixivi|ate lɪkˈsɪv.i|.eɪt **-ates** -eɪts **-ating** -eɪ.tɪŋ, (US) -eɪ.t̬ɪŋ **-ated** -eɪ.tɪd, (US) -eɪ.t̬ɪd

Liz lɪz

Liza ˈlaɪ.zə, ˈliː-, (US) ˈlaɪ-

lizard, L~ ˈlɪz.əd, (US) -ɚd **-s** -z

Lizzie ˈlɪz.i

Ljubljana ˌlʊb.liˈɑː.nə; *as if Slovene:* ˌljuːbˈljɑː.nə; (US) ˌluː.bliˈɑː.nə

llama, L~ ˈlɑː.mə, (US) ˈlɑː-, ˈjɑː- **-s** -z

Llanberis *h*lænˈber.ɪs, θlæn-, (US) *h*læn-

Llandaff ˈ*h*læn.dəf, ˈθlæn-; lænˈdæf, θlæn-, (US) *h*lænˈdɑːf

Llandeilo *h*lænˈdaɪ.ləʊ, θlæn-, (US) *h*lænˈdaɪ.loʊ

Llandovery *h*lænˈdʌv.ər.i, θlæn-, (US) *h*læn-

Llandrindod Wells *h*lænˌdrɪn.dɒdˈwelz, θlæn-, (US) *h*lænˌdrɪn.dɑːdˈ-

Llandudno *h*lænˈdɪd.nəʊ, θlæn-, -ˈdʌd-, (US) *h*lænˈdɪd.noʊ, -ˈdʌd-

Llanelli *h*lænˈeθ.li, ləˈneθ-, θlænˈeθ-, θləˈneθ-, (US) *h*lænˈeθ.li

Llanfair *h*lænˈfeəʳ, θlæn-, -ˈvaɪ.əʳ, (US) *h*lænˈfer

Llanfairfechan ˌ*h*læn.feəˈfek.ən, ˌθlæn-, -vaɪ.əˈ-, -ˈvek-, -ˈvex-, (US) ˌ*h*læn.ferˈfek-

Llangattock *h*lænˈgæt.ək, θlæn-, læŋ-, θlæŋ-, (US) *h*lænˈgæt̬.ək

Llangollen *h*lænˈgɒθ.lən, θlæn-, læŋ-, θlæŋ-, -len, (US) *h*lænˈgɑːθ.lən

Llanharan *h*lænˈhær.ən, θlæn-, (US) *h*lænˈhɑːr.ən

Llanrwst *h*lænˈruːst, θlæn-, (US) *h*læn-

Llantrisant *h*lænˈtrɪs.ənt

Llantwit Major ˌ*h*læn.twɪtˈmeɪ.dʒəʳ, (US) -dʒɚ

Llanuwchllyn *h*lænˈjuː.klɪn, θlæn-, -ˈjuːx.lɪn, (US) *h*lænˈjuː.klɪn

Llanwern *h*lænˈweən, (US) -ˈwern

Llechwedd *h*lekˈwed

Llewel(l)yn *English name:* luːˈel.ɪn, ləˈwel- *Welsh name:* *h*luːˈel.ɪn, θluː-, (US) *h*luː-

Lleyn *h*liːn, θliːn, *h*leɪn, θleɪn, (US) *h*liːn, *h*leɪn

Lliw *h*luː

Lloyd lɔɪd **-'s** -z

Lloyd Webber ˌlɔɪdˈweb.əʳ, (US) -ɚ

Llyn Tegid ˌ*h*lɪnˈteg.ɪd, ˌθlɪn-, (US) ˌ*h*lɪn-

Llywelyn hlə'wel.ɪn, θlə-, (US) hlə-
lo ləʊ, (US) loʊ
Loach ləʊtʃ, (US) loʊtʃ
load ləʊd, (US) loʊd **-s** -z **-ing** -ɪŋ **-ed** -ɪd **-er/s** -əʳ/z, (US) -ɚ/z
loadstone 'ləʊd.stəʊn, (US) 'loʊd.stoʊn **-s** -z
loaf v ləʊf, (US) loʊf **-s** -s **-ing** -ɪŋ **-ed** -t
loa|f n ləʊ|f, (US) loʊ|f **-ves** -vz
loafer 'ləʊ.fəʳ, (US) 'loʊ.fɚ **-s** -z
loam ləʊm, (US) loʊm
loam|y 'ləʊ.m|i, (US) 'loʊ.m|i **-ier** -i.əʳ, (US) -i.ɚ **-iest** -i.ɪst, -i.əst **-iness** -ɪ.nəs, -ɪ.nɪs
loan ləʊn, (US) loʊn **-s** -z **-ing** -ɪŋ **-ed** -d **-er/s** -əʳ/z, (US) -ɚ/z **'loan ˌshark**
Loanhead ˌləʊn'hed, (US) ˌloʊn-
loanword 'ləʊn.wɜːd, (US) 'loʊn.wɜːd **-s** -z
loath ləʊθ, ləʊð, (US) loʊð **-ness** -nəs, -nɪs
loath|e ləʊð, (US) loʊð **-es** -z **-ing/ly** -ɪŋ/li **-ed** -d
loathsome 'ləʊð.səm, 'ləʊθ-, (US) 'loʊð-, 'loʊθ- **-ly** -li **-ness** -nəs, -nɪs
loaves (plural of **loaf**) ləʊvz, (US) loʊvz
lob, L~ lɒb, (US) lɑːb **-s** -z **-bing** -ɪŋ **-bed** -d **-ber/s** -əʳ/z, (US) -ɚ/z
lobb|y 'lɒb|.i, (US) 'lɑː.b|i **-ies** -iz **-ying** -i.ɪŋ **-ied** -id
lobbyist 'lɒb.i.ɪst, (US) 'lɑː.bi- **-s** -s
lobe ləʊb, (US) loʊb **-s** -z **-d** -d
lobelia ləʊ'biː.li.ə, (US) loʊ'biːl.jə, -'biː.li.ə **-s** -z
lobotomiz|e, -is|e ləʊ'bɒt.ə.maɪz, (US) loʊ'bɑː.t̬ə-, lə- **-es** -ɪz **-ing** -ɪŋ **-ed** -d
lobotom|y ləʊ'bɒt.ə.m|i, (US) loʊ'bɑː.t̬ə-, lə- **-ies** -iz
lobster 'lɒb.stəʳ, (US) 'lɑːb.stɚ **-s** -z
lobular 'lɒb.jə.ləʳ, -jʊ-, (US) 'lɑː.bjə.lɚ
lobule 'lɒb.juːl, (US) 'lɑː.bjuːl **-s** -z
local 'ləʊ.kəl, (US) 'loʊ- **-s** -z **-ly** -i **ˌlocal 'colo(u)r; 'local ˌtime; ˌlocal 'time**
locale ləʊ'kɑːl, (US) loʊ'kæl **-s** -z
localism 'ləʊ.kəl.ɪ.zəm, (US) 'loʊ-
localit|y ləʊ'kæl.ə.t|i, -ɪ.t|i, (US) loʊ'kæl.ə.t̬|i **-ies** -iz
localization, -isa- ˌləʊ.kəl.aɪ'zeɪ.ʃən, -ɪ'-, (US) ˌloʊ.kəl.ə'-
localiz|e, -is|e 'ləʊ.kəl.aɪz, (US) 'loʊ- **-es** -ɪz **-ing** -ɪŋ **-ed** -d **-er/s** -əʳ/z, (US) -ɚ/z
Locarno ləʊ'kɑː.nəʊ, lɒk'ɑː-, (US) loʊ'kɑːr.noʊ
loca|te ləʊ'keɪ|t, (US) 'loʊ.keɪ|t, -'- **-tes** -ts **-ting** -tɪŋ, (US) -t̬ɪŋ **-ted** -tɪd, (US) -t̬ɪd
location ləʊ'keɪ.ʃən, (US) loʊ- **-s** -z
locative 'lɒk.ə.tɪv, (US) 'lɑː.kə.t̬ɪv **-s** -z
loc. cit. ˌlɒk'sɪt, ˌlɒk.əʊ.sɪ'tɑː.təʊ; *old-fashioned:* ˌləʊ.kəʊ.sɪ'teɪ.təʊ, (US) ˌlɑːk'sɪt
loch, L~ lɒk; *as if Scots:* lɒx; (US) lɑːk; *as if Scots:* (US) lɑːx **-s** -s

> Note: The ability to pronounce /x/ in 'loch' is often considered to be a test of Scottishness by Scottish speakers.

Lochaber lɒk'ɑː.bəʳ, -'æb.əʳ; *as if Scots:* lɒx-; (US) lɑː'kɑː.bɚ; *as if Scots:* (US) -'xɑː-
Lochgelly lɒk'gel.i; *as if Scots:* lɒx-; (US) lɑːk-; *as if Scots:* (US) lɑːx-
Lochhead 'lɒk.hed; *as if Scots:* 'lɒx-; (US) 'lɑːk-; *as if Scots:* (US) 'lɑːx-
Lochiel lɒk'iːl; *as if Scots:* lɒx-; (US) lɑː'kiːl; *as if Scots:* (US) -'xiːl
Lochinvar ˌlɒk.ɪn'vɑːʳ; *as if Scots:* ˌlɒx-; (US) ˌlɑː.kɪn'vɑːr; *as if Scots:* (US) -xɪn'-
Lochleven lɒk'liː.vən; *as if Scots:* lɒx-; (US) lɑːk-; *as if Scots:* (US) lɑːx-
Lochnagar ˌlɒk.nə'gɑːʳ; *as if Scots:* ˌlɒx-; (US) ˌlɑːk.nə'gɑːr; *as if Scots:* (US) ˌlɑːx-
loci (plural of **locus**) 'ləʊ.saɪ, -kaɪ, -kiː; 'lɒk.aɪ, 'lɒs-, (US) 'loʊ.saɪ, -kaɪ, -ki
lock, L~ lɒk, (US) lɑːk **-s** -s **-ing** -ɪŋ **-ed** -t **ˌlock, ˌstock, and 'barrel; under ˌlock and 'key**
Locke lɒk, (US) lɑːk
locker, L~ 'lɒk.əʳ, (US) 'lɑː.kɚ **-s** -z **'locker ˌroom**
Lockerbie 'lɒk.ə.bi, (US) 'lɑː.kɚ-
locket 'lɒk.ɪt, (US) 'lɑː.kɪt **-s** -s
Lockhart 'lɒk.ət, -hɑːt, (US) 'lɑːk.hɑːrt, 'lɑː.kɚt

> Note: The Bruce-Lockhart family pronounce /'lɒk.ət/ (or as Scots /'lɒk.ərt/).

Lockheed 'lɒk.hiːd, (US) 'lɑːk-
Lockie 'lɒk.i, (US) 'lɑː.ki
lockjaw 'lɒk.dʒɔː, (US) 'lɑːk.dʒɑː, -dʒɔː
lock-keeper 'lɒkˌkiː.pəʳ, (US) 'lɑːkˌkiː.pɚ **-s** -z
locknut 'lɒk.nʌt, (US) 'lɑːk- **-s** -s
lockout 'lɒk.aʊt, (US) 'lɑːk- **-s** -s
Locksley 'lɒk.sli, (US) 'lɑːk-
locksmith 'lɒk.smɪθ, (US) 'lɑːk- **-s** -s
lockstep 'lɒk.step, (US) 'lɑːk-
lockstitch 'lɒk.stɪtʃ, (US) 'lɑːk- **-es** -ɪz
lockup 'lɒk.ʌp, (US) 'lɑːk- **-s** -s
Lockwood 'lɒk.wʊd, (US) 'lɑːk-
Lockyer 'lɒk.jəʳ, (US) 'lɑː.kjɚ
loco 'ləʊ.kəʊ, (US) 'loʊ.koʊ **-s** -z
locomotion ˌləʊ.kə'məʊ.ʃən, (US) ˌloʊ.kə'moʊ-
locomotive ˌləʊ.kə'məʊ.tɪv, 'ləʊ.kəˌməʊ-, (US) ˌloʊ.kə'moʊ.t̬ɪv **-s** -z
locomotor ˌləʊ.kə'məʊ.təʳ, 'ləʊ.kəˌməʊ-, (US) ˌloʊ.kə'moʊ.t̬ɚ *stress shift, see compound:* **ˌlocomotor a'taxia**
Locri|a 'ləʊ.kri|.ə, (US) 'loʊ- **-an/s** -ən/z
Locrine 'lɒk.raɪn, (US) 'lɑː.kraɪn
Locris 'ləʊ.krɪs, (US) 'loʊ-
Loctite® 'lɒk.taɪt, (US) 'lɑːk-
locum 'ləʊ.kəm, (US) 'loʊ- **-s** -z
locum-tenens ˌləʊ.kəm'ten.enz, -'tiː.nenz, (US) ˌloʊ.kəm'tiː.nenz, -'ten.enz
locus 'ləʊ.kəs, 'lɒk.əs, (US) 'loʊ.kəs **-es** -ɪz **loci** 'ləʊ.saɪ, -kaɪ, -kiː; 'lɒk.aɪ, 'lɒs-, (US) 'loʊ.saɪ
locus delicti ˌləʊ.kəs.del'ɪk.taɪ, (US) ˌloʊ.kəs.də'lɪk.ti, -taɪ
locus in quo ˌləʊ.kəs.ɪn'kwəʊ, -ɪŋ'-, (US) ˌloʊ.kəs.ɪn'kwoʊ
locust 'ləʊ.kəst, (US) 'loʊ- **-s** -s
locution ləʊ'kjuː.ʃən, lɒk'juː-, (US) loʊ'kjuː- **-s** -z
locutionary ləʊ'kjuː.ʃən.ər.i, lɒk'juː-, (US) loʊ'kjuː.ʃən.er.i
locutor|y 'lɒk.jə.tər|.i, -jʊ-, (US) 'lɑː.kjə.tɔːr- **-ies** -iz
lode ləʊd, (US) loʊd **-s** -z
loden 'ləʊ.dən, (US) 'loʊ-
lodestar 'ləʊd.stɑːʳ, (US) 'loʊd.stɑːr **-s** -z
lodestone 'ləʊd.stəʊn, (US) 'loʊd.stoʊn **-s** -z
lodg|e, L~ lɒdʒ, (US) lɑːdʒ **-es** -ɪz **-ing/s** -ɪŋ/z **-ed** -d
lodger 'lɒdʒ.əʳ, (US) 'lɑː.dʒɚ **-s** -z
lodging-hou|se 'lɒdʒ.ɪŋ.haʊ|s, (US) 'lɑː.dʒɪŋ- **-ses** -zɪz
lodg(e)ment 'lɒdʒ.mənt, (US) 'lɑːdʒ- **-s** -s
Lodore ləʊ'dɔːʳ, (US) loʊ'dɔːr
Łódź wʊdʒ, wuːdʒ, (US) wuːdʒ, lɑːdʒ, loʊdz, luːdʒ
Loe luː
Loeb lɜːb, ləʊb, (US) loʊb
loess 'ləʊ.es, -ɪs, -əs; lɜːs, (US) 'loʊ.es, less, lɜːs
Loewe 'ləʊ.i, (US) loʊ
Lofoten ləʊ'fəʊ.tən; 'ləʊ.fəʊ-, (US) 'loʊ.fʊ-, -foʊ-
loft lɒft, (US) lɑːft **-s** -s **-ing** -ɪŋ **-ed** -ɪd **-er/s** -əʳ/z, (US) -ɚ/z
Lofthouse 'lɒf.təs, 'lɒft.haʊs, (US) 'lɑːf.təs, 'lɑːft.haʊs
Lofting 'lɒf.tɪŋ, (US) 'lɑːf-
Loftus 'lɒf.təs, (US) 'lɑːf-
loft|y 'lɒf.t|i, (US) 'lɑːf- **-ier** -i.əʳ, (US) -i.ɚ **-iest** -i.ɪst, -i.əst **-ily** -əl.i, -ɪ.li **-iness** -ɪ.nəs, -ɪ.nɪs
log lɒg, (US) lɑːg, lɔːg **-s** -z **-ging** -ɪŋ **-ged** -d **-ger/s** -əʳ/z, (US) -ɚ/z **ˌlog 'cabin; ˌsleep like a 'log**
-log lɒg, (US) lɑːg, lɔːg
Logan 'ləʊ.gən, (US) 'loʊ-
loganberr|y 'ləʊ.gən.bər.|i, -gəm-, -ˌber-, (US) 'loʊ.gənˌber- **-ies** -iz
logarithm 'lɒg.ər.ɪ.ðəm, -θəm, (US) 'lɑː.gɚ.ɪ.ðəm, 'lɔː- **-s** -z
logarithmic ˌlɒg.ər'ɪð.mɪk, -'rɪθ-, (US) ˌlɑː.gə'rɪθ-, ˌlɔː- **-al** -əl **-ally** -əl.i, -li
logbook 'lɒg.bʊk, (US) 'lɑːg-, 'lɔːg- **-s** -s
logger 'lɒg.əʳ, (US) 'lɑː.gɚ, 'lɔː- **-s** -z
loggerhead 'lɒg.ə.hed, (US) 'lɑː.gɚ-, 'lɔː- **-s** -z
loggia 'ləʊ.dʒə, 'lɒdʒ.ə, -i.ə, (US) 'lɑː.dʒə, -dʒi.ə **-s** -z
Logia 'lɒg.i.ə, (US) 'loʊ.gi-, 'lɑː-

logic ˈlɒdʒ.ɪk, (US) ˈlɑː.dʒɪk **-al** -əl **-ally** -əl.i, -li
Logica® ˈlɒdʒ.ɪ.kə, (US) ˈlɑː.dʒɪ-
logician lɒdʒˈɪʃ.ən, (US) loʊˈdʒɪʃ- **-s** -z
Logie ˈləʊ.gi, (US) ˈloʊ-
login ˈlɒg.ɪn, (US) ˈlɑːg-, ˈlɔːg- **-s** -z
-logist lə.dʒɪst
Note: Suffix. Words containing **-logist** are normally stressed on the syllable preceding the suffix, e.g. **sociologist** /ˌsəʊ.ʃiˈɒl.ə.dʒɪst/ (US) /ˌsoʊ.siˈɑː.lə-/.
logistic ləˈdʒɪs.tɪk, lɒdʒˈɪs-, (US) loʊˈdʒɪs- **-s** -s **-al** -əl **-ally** -əl.i, -li
logjam ˈlɒg.dʒæm, (US) ˈlɑːg-, ˈlɔːg- **-s** -z
logo ˈləʊ.gəʊ, ˈlɒg.əʊ, (US) ˈloʊ.goʊ **-s** -z
logogram ˈlɒg.əʊ.græm, (US) ˈlɑː.goʊ-, ˈlɔː-, ˈloʊ-, -gə- **-s** -z
logograph ˈlɒg.əʊ.grɑːf, -græf, (US) ˈlɑː.goʊ.græf, ˈlɔː-, ˈloʊ-, -gə- **-s** -s
logographic ˌlɒg.əʊˈgræf.ɪk, (US) ˌlɑː.goʊ-, ˌlɔː-, ˌloʊ-, -gə- **-al** -əl **-ally** -əl.i, -li
Logos ˈlɒg.ɒs, ˈləʊ.gɒs, (US) ˈloʊ.goʊs, ˈlɔː-, ˈlɑː-, -gɔːs, -gɑːs
logotype ˈlɒg.əʊ.taɪp, (US) ˈlɑː.gə-, ˈlɔː- **-s** -s
logroll ˈlɒg.rəʊl, (US) ˈlɑːg.roʊl, ˈlɔːg- **-s** -z **-ing** -ɪŋ **-ed** -d **-er/s** -əʳ/z, (US) -ɚ/z
Logue ləʊg, (US) loʊg
-logue lɒg, (US) lɑːg, lɔːg
-logy lə.dʒi
Note: Suffix. Words containing **-logy** are normally stressed on the syllable preceding the suffix, e.g. **biology** /baɪˈɒl.ə.dʒi/ (US) /-ˈɑː.lə-/.
Lohan ˈləʊ.ən, ˈləʊ.hæn, lɔːn, (US) ˈloʊ.ən, -hæn
Lohengrin ˈləʊ.ən.grɪn, -ɪn-, -əŋ-, -ɪŋ-, (US) ˈloʊ.ən-
loin lɔɪn **-s** -z
loin|cloth ˈlɔɪn|.klɒθ, (US) -klɑːθ **-cloths** -klɒθs, (US) -klɑːθs
Loire lwɑːʳ, (US) lwɑːr
Lois ˈləʊ.ɪs, (US) ˈloʊ-
loit|er ˈlɔɪ.t|əʳ, (US) -ţ|ɚ **-ers** -əz, (US) -ɚz **-ering** -ər.ɪŋ **-ered** -əd, (US) -ɚd **-erer/s** -ər.əʳ/z, (US) -ɚ.ɚ/z
Loki ˈləʊ.ki, (US) ˈloʊ-
Lola ˈləʊ.lə, (US) ˈloʊ-
Lolita lɒlˈiː.tə, ləʊˈliː-, (US) loʊˈliː.ţə
loll lɒl, (US) lɑːl **-s** -z **-ing** -ɪŋ **-ed** -d
Lollard ˈlɒl.əd, -ɑːd, (US) ˈlɑː.lɚd **-s** -z
lollipop ˈlɒl.i.pɒp, (US) ˈlɑː.li.pɑːp **-s** -s
lollop ˈlɒl.əp, (US) ˈlɑː.ləp **-s** -s **-ing** -ɪŋ **-ed** -t
lollo rosso ˌlɒl.əʊˈrɒs.əʊ, (US) ˌlɑː.loʊˈrɑː.soʊ, ˌloʊ-, ˈ-roʊ-
loll|y ˈlɒl|.i, (US) ˈlɑː.l|i **-ies** -iz
lollypop ˈlɒl.i.pɒp, (US) ˈlɑː.li.pɑːp **-s** -s
Loman ˈləʊ.mən, (US) ˈloʊ-
Lomas ˈləʊ.mæs, -məs, (US) ˈloʊ.mæs
Lomax ˈləʊ.mæks, -məks, (US) ˈloʊ.mæks
Lombard ˈlɒm.bəd, -bɑːd, (US) ˈlɑːm.bɑːrd, -bɚd, ˈlʌm- **-s** -z
Lombardy ˈlɒm.bə.di, (US) ˈlɑːm.bɚ-, ˈlʌm-
Lombok ˈlɒm.bɒk, (US) ˈlɑːm.bɑːk
Lomé ˈləʊ.meɪ, (US) loʊˈmeɪ
Lomond ˈləʊ.mənd, (US) ˈloʊ-
Londesborough ˈlɒnz.bər.ə, (US) ˈlɑːndz.bɚ.oʊ
London ˈlʌn.dən **-er/s** -əʳ/z, (US) -ɚ/z ˌ**London** ˈ**Bridge**; ˌ**London** ˈ**pride**; ˌ**London** ˈ**weighting**
Londonderry *place:* ˈlʌn.dən.der.i, ˌlʌn.dənˈder-, (US) ˈlʌn.dən.der- *Lord:* ˈlʌn.dən.dər.i, (US) -der-
lone ləʊn, (US) loʊn
lonel|y ˈləʊn.l|i, (US) ˈloʊn- **-ier** -i.əʳ, (US) -i.ɚ **-iest** -i.ɪst, -i.əst **-iness** -ɪ.nəs, -ɪ.nɪs ˌ**lonely** ˈ**hearts**
loner ˈləʊ.nəʳ, (US) ˈloʊ.nɚ **-s** -z
lonesome ˈləʊn.səm, (US) ˈloʊn- **-ness** -nəs, -nɪs
long, L~ n, adj lɒŋ, (US) lɑːŋ, lɔːŋ **-er** -gəʳ, (US) -gɚ **-est** -gɪst, -gəst ˌ**Long** ˈ**Island**; ˈ**long** ˌ**jump**; ˈ**long** ˌ**shot**; ˈ**long** ˌ**wave**; ˌ**long** **week**ˈ**end** (US) ˌ**long** ˈ**weekend**; **the** ˌ**long and the** ˈ**short of it**; **in the** ˈ**long** ˌ**run**
long v lɒŋ, (US) lɑːŋ, lɔːŋ **-s** -z **-ing/ly** -ɪŋ/li **-ed** -d **-er/s** -əʳ/z, (US) -ɚ/z
Longannet lɒŋˈæn.ɪt, -ət, (US) lɑːŋ-, lɔːŋ-
long-awaited ˌlɒŋ.əˈweɪ.tɪd, (US) ˌlɑːŋ.əˈweɪ.ţɪd, ˌlɔːŋ- *stress shift:* ˌ**long-awaited** ˈ**moment**
longboat ˈlɒŋ.bəʊt, (US) ˈlɑːŋ.boʊt, ˈlɔːŋ- **-s** -s
longbow, L~ ˈlɒŋ.bəʊ, (US) ˈlɑːŋ.boʊ, ˈlɔːŋ- **-s** -z
Longbridge ˈlɒŋ.brɪdʒ, (US) ˈlɑːŋ-, ˈlɔːŋ-
Longdendale ˈlɒŋ.ən.deɪl, (US) ˈlɑːŋ-, ˈlɔːŋ-
long-distance ˌlɒŋˈdɪs.tənts, (US) ˌlɑːŋ-, ˌlɔːŋ- *stress shift:* ˌ**long-distance** ˈ**driver**
long-drawn-out ˌlɒŋ.drɔːnˈaʊt, (US) ˌlɑːŋ.drɑːnˈ-, ˌlɔːŋ-, -drɔːnˈ- *stress shift:* ˌ**long-drawn-out** ˈ**sigh**
longeron ˈlɒn.dʒər.ən, (US) ˈlɑːn.dʒə.rɑːn, -dʒɚ.ən **-s** -z
longevity lɒnˈdʒev.ə.ti, ˈlɒŋ-, -ɪ.ti, (US) lɑːnˈdʒev.ə.ţi, lɑːŋ-, lɔːŋ-
Longfellow ˈlɒŋˌfel.əʊ, (US) ˈlɑːŋˌfel.oʊ, ˈlɔːŋ-
Longfield ˈlɒŋ.fiːld, (US) ˈlɑːŋ-, ˈlɔːŋ-
Longford ˈlɒŋ.fəd, (US) ˈlɑːŋ.fɚd, ˈlɔːŋ-
longhand ˈlɒŋ.hænd, (US) ˈlɑːŋ-, ˈlɔːŋ-
long-haul ˌlɒŋˈhɔːl, ˈ--, (US) ˌlɑːŋˈhɑːl, ˌlɔːŋ-, -hɔːl, ˈ-- *stress shift:* ˌ**long-haul** ˈ**jet**
longheaded ˌlɒŋˈhed.ɪd, (US) ˌlɑːŋ-, ˌlɔːŋ- *stress shift:* ˌ**longheaded** ˈ**elder**
longhorn ˈlɒŋ.hɔːn, (US) ˈlɑːŋ.hɔːrn, ˈlɔːŋ- **-s** -z
Longines® ˈlɒn.dʒiːn, -ˈ-, (US) ˌlɑːnˈdʒiːn
longing ˈlɒŋ.ɪŋ, (US) ˈlɑːŋ-, ˈlɔːŋ- **-s** -z
Longinus lɒnˈdʒaɪ.nəs, lɒŋˈgiː-, (US) lɑːnˈdʒaɪ-
longish ˈlɒŋ.ɪʃ, (US) ˈlɑːŋ-, ˈlɔːŋ-
longitude ˈlɒn.dʒɪ.tʃuːd, ˈlɒŋ.gɪ-, -tjuːd, (US) ˈlɑːn.dʒə.tuːd, -tjuːd **-s** -z
longitudinal ˌlɒn.dʒɪˈtʃuː.dɪ.nəl, -dʒəˈ-, -ˈtjuː-, ˌlɒŋ.gɪˈ-, -gəˈ-, -də-, (US) ˌlɑːn.dʒəˈtuː-, -ˈtjuː- **-ly** -i
long johns ˈlɒŋ.dʒɒnz, ˌ-ˈ-, (US) ˈlɑːŋ.dʒɑːnz, ˈlɔːŋ-, ˌ-ˈ-
Longland ˈlɒŋ.lənd, (US) ˈlɑːŋ-, ˈlɔːŋ-
long-lasting ˌlɒŋˈlɑː.stɪŋ, (US) ˌlɑːŋˈlæs.tɪŋ, ˌlɔːŋ- *stress shift:* ˌ**long-lasting** ˈ**friendship**
Longleat ˈlɒŋ.liːt, (US) ˈlɑːŋ-, ˈlɔːŋ-
long-life ˈlɒŋ.laɪf, (US) ˈlɑːŋ-, ˌlɔːŋ-
long-lived ˌlɒŋˈlɪvd, (US) ˌlɑːŋ-, ˌlɔːŋ-, -laɪvd *stress shift:* ˌ**long-lived** ˈ**person**
long-lost ˌlɒŋˈlɒst, (US) ˌlɑːŋˈlɑːst, ˌlɔːŋ- *stress shift:* ˌ**long-lost** ˈ**son**
Longman ˈlɒŋ.mən, (US) ˈlɑːŋ-, ˈlɔːŋ-
long-range ˌlɒŋˈreɪndʒ, (US) ˌlɑːŋ-, ˌlɔːŋ- *stress shift:* ˌ**long-range** ˈ**missile**
Longridge ˈlɒŋ.rɪdʒ, (US) ˈlɑːŋ-, ˈlɔːŋ-
long-running ˌlɒŋˈrʌn.ɪŋ, (US) ˌlɑːŋ-, ˌlɔːŋ- *stress shift:* ˌ**long-running** ˈ**problems**
longshore|man ˈlɒŋ.ʃɔː|.mən, (US) ˈlɑːŋ.ʃɔːr-, ˈlɔːŋ- **-men** -mən, -men
long-sighted ˌlɒŋˈsaɪ.tɪd, (US) ˌlɑːŋˈsaɪ.ţɪd, ˌlɔːŋ-, ˈ-ˌ-- **-ness** -nəs, -nɪs *stress shift, British only:* ˌ**long-sighted** ˈ**person**
Longstaff ˈlɒŋ.stɑːf, (US) ˈlɑːŋ.stæf, ˈlɔːŋ-
long-standing ˌlɒŋˈstæn.dɪŋ, (US) ˌlɑːŋ-, ˌlɔːŋ- *stress shift:* ˌ**long-standing** ˈ**feud**
Longstreet ˈlɒŋ.striːt, (US) ˈlɑːŋ-, ˈlɔːŋ-
long-suffering ˌlɒŋˈsʌf.ər.ɪŋ, (US) ˌlɑːŋ-, ˌlɔːŋ- *stress shift:* ˌ**long-suffering** ˈ**family**
long-term ˌlɒŋˈtɜːm, (US) ˌlɑːŋˈtɝːm, ˌlɔːŋ- *stress shift:* ˌ**long-term** ˈ**goal**
long-time ˈlɒŋˌtaɪm, (US) ˈlɑːŋ-, ˈlɔːŋ-
Longton ˈlɒŋk.tən, (US) ˈlɑːŋ-, ˈlɔːŋ-
Longtown ˈlɒŋ.taʊn, (US) ˈlɑːŋ-, ˈlɔːŋ-
longueur lɔ̃ːŋˈgɜːʳ, lɔːŋ-, lɒŋ-, (US) lɔ̃ːŋˈgɝː **-s** -z
Longus ˈlɒŋ.gəs, (US) ˈlɑːŋ-, ˈlɔːŋ-
longways ˈlɒŋ.weɪz, (US) ˈlɑːŋ-, ˈlɔːŋ-
long-winded ˌlɒŋˈwɪn.dɪd, (US) ˌlɑːŋ-, ˌlɔːŋ- **-ness** -nəs, -nɪs *stress shift:* ˌ**long-winded** ˈ**story**
longwise ˈlɒŋ.waɪz, (US) ˈlɑːŋ-, ˈlɔːŋ-
lonicera lɒnˈɪs.ər.ə, ləˈnɪs-, (US) loʊˈnɪs-; (US) ˌlɑː.nɪˈsɪr.ə **-s** -z
Lonrho® ˈlɒn.rəʊ, ˈlʌn-, (US) ˈlɑːn.roʊ
Lonsdale ˈlɒnz.deɪl, (US) ˈlɑːnz-
loo luː **-s** -z

loob|y ˈluː.b|i -ies -iz

Looe luː

loofah ˈluː.fə -s -z

look lʊk -s -s -ing -ɪŋ -ed -t -er/s -əʳ/z, ⓊⓈ -ɚ/z

lookalike ˈlʊk.ə.laɪk -s -s

looker-on ˌlʊk.əʳˈɒn, ⓊⓈ -kɚˈɑːn **lookers-on** ˌlʊk.əzˈɒn, ⓊⓈ -kɚzˈɑːn

look-in ˈlʊk.ɪn

looking-glass ˈlʊk.ɪŋ.glɑːs, ⓊⓈ -glæs -es -ɪz

lookout ˈlʊk.aʊt -s -s

look-see ˈlʊk.siː

loom luːm -s -z -ing -ɪŋ -ed -d

loon luːn -s -z

loonie ˈluː.ni -s -z

loon|y ˈluː.n|i -ies -iz ˈ**loony** ˌ**bin**; ˌ**loony** ˈ**left**

loop luːp -s -s -ing -ɪŋ -ed -t

loophol|e ˈluːp.həʊl, ⓊⓈ -hoʊl -es -z -ing -ɪŋ -ed -d

loop|y ˈluː.p|i -ier -i.əʳ, ⓊⓈ -i.ɚ -iest -i.ɪst, -i.əst

Loos ləʊs, luːs, ⓊⓈ luːs

loos|e luːs -er -əʳ, ⓊⓈ -ɚ -est -ɪst, -əst -eness -nəs, -nɪs -es -ɪz -ing -ɪŋ -ed -t ˌ**let someone** ˈ**loose on**

looseleaf ˌluːsˈliːf *stress shift:* ˌ**loose-leaf** ˈ**folder**

loosely ˈluː.sli

loosen ˈluː.sᵊn -s -z -ing -ɪŋ, ˈluːs.nɪŋ -ed -d

loosestrife ˈluːs.straɪf

loot luːt -s -s -ing -ɪŋ, ⓊⓈ ˈluː.t̬ɪŋ -ed -ɪd, ⓊⓈ ˈluː.t̬ɪd -er/s -əʳ/z, ⓊⓈ ˈluː.t̬ɚ/z

lop lɒp, ⓊⓈ lɑːp -s -s -ping -ɪŋ -ped -t

lop|e ləʊp, ⓊⓈ loʊp -es -s -ing -ɪŋ -ed -t

lop-eared ˌlɒpˈɪəd, ⓊⓈ ˈlɑːp.ɪrd *stress shift, British only:* ˌ**lop-eared** ˈ**rabbit**

Lopez ˈləʊ.pez, ⓊⓈ ˈloʊ-

lopping ˈlɒp.ɪŋ, ⓊⓈ ˈlɑː.pɪŋ -s -z

lop-sided ˌlɒpˈsaɪ.dɪd, ⓊⓈ ˌlɑːp- -ness -nəs, -nɪs *stress shift:* ˌ**lop-sided** ˈ**smile**

loquacious ləʊˈkweɪ.ʃəs, lɒkˈweɪ-, ⓊⓈ loʊˈkweɪ- -ly -li -ness -nəs, -nɪs

loquacity ləʊˈkwæs.ə.ti, lɒkˈwæs-, -ɪ.ti, ⓊⓈ loʊˈkwæs.ə.t̬i

loquat ˈləʊ.kwɒt, ˈlɒk.wɒt, -wæt, ⓊⓈ ˈloʊ.kwɑːt, -kwæt -s -s

lor lɔːʳ, ⓊⓈ lɔːr

Loraine ləˈreɪn, lɒrˈeɪn, ⓊⓈ ləˈreɪn

Loral ˈlɔː.ræl, ˈlɒr.æl, ⓊⓈ ˈlɔːr.æl

Loram ˈlɔː.rəm, ⓊⓈ ˈlɔːr.əm

Lorca ˈlɔː.kə, ⓊⓈ ˈlɔːr-

lord, L~ lɔːd, ⓊⓈ lɔːrd -s -z -ing -ɪŋ -ed -ɪd ˌ**Lord's** ˈ**Prayer**

> Note: British lawyers addressing a judge in court sometimes pronounce **my lord** as /mɪˈlʌd/ instead of the normal /mɪˈlɔːd/.

lordling ˈlɔːd.lɪŋ, ⓊⓈ ˈlɔːrd- -s -z

lordl|y ˈlɔːd.l|i, ⓊⓈ ˈlɔːrd- -ier -i.əʳ, ⓊⓈ -i.ɚ -iest -i.ɪst, -i.əst -iness -ɪ.nəs, -ɪ.nɪs

lordship, L~ ˈlɔːd.ʃɪp, ⓊⓈ ˈlɔːrd- -s -s

lore lɔːʳ, ⓊⓈ lɔːr

L'Oréal® ˈlɒr.i.æl, ⓊⓈ ˌlɔːr.iˈæl

Lorelei ˈlɔː.rə.laɪ, ˈlɒr.ə-, ⓊⓈ ˈlɔː-

Loren ˈlɔː.ren, -rᵊn; lɔːˈren, ⓊⓈ ˈlɔːr.ən

Lorenzo ləˈren.zəʊ, lɒrˈen-, ⓊⓈ ləˈren.zoʊ, lɔː-

Loretto ləˈret.əʊ, lɔː-, ⓊⓈ ləˈret̬.oʊ, lɔː-

lorgnette lɔːˈnjet, ⓊⓈ lɔːr- -s -s

Lori(e) ˈlɒr.i, ⓊⓈ ˈlɔːr-

lorikeet ˈlɒr.ɪ.kiːt, ˈ-ə-, ˌ--ˈ-, ⓊⓈ ˈlɔːr.ɪ- -s -s

lorimer, L~ ˈlɒr.ɪ.məʳ, ⓊⓈ ˈlɔːr.ɪ.mɚ -s -z

loris ˈlɔː.rɪs, ⓊⓈ ˈlɔːr.ɪs -es -ɪz

lorn lɔːn, ⓊⓈ lɔːrn

Lorna ˈlɔː.nə, ⓊⓈ ˈlɔːr-

Lorne lɔːn, ⓊⓈ lɔːrn

Lorraine ləˈreɪn, lɒrˈeɪn, ⓊⓈ ləˈreɪn, lɔː-

lorr|y ˈlɒr|.i, ⓊⓈ ˈlɔːr- -ies -iz

lor|y ˈlɔː.r|i, ⓊⓈ ˈlɔːr|.i -ies -iz

losable ˈluː.zə.bᵊl

Los Alamos lɒsˈæl.ə.mɒs, -məʊs, ⓊⓈ ˌlɑːsˈæl.ə.moʊs, ˌlɔːs-

Los Angeles lɒsˈæn.dʒɪ.liːz, -dʒə-, -lɪz, -lɪs, ⓊⓈ lɑːsˈæn.dʒə.ləs, lɔːs-, -gə-, -liːz

los|e luːz -es -ɪz -ing -ɪŋ **lost** lɒst, ⓊⓈ lɑːst

loser ˈluː.zəʳ, ⓊⓈ -zɚ -s -z

Losey ˈləʊ.zi, ⓊⓈ ˈloʊ-

loss lɒs, ⓊⓈ lɑːs -es -ɪz ˈ**loss** ˌ**leader**

Lossiemouth ˈlɒs.i.maʊθ, ˌlɒs.iˈmaʊθ, ⓊⓈ ˈlɑː.si-

lost (from **lose**) lɒst, ⓊⓈ lɑːst ˌ**lost** ˈ**property**

Lostwithiel lɒstˈwɪθ.i.əl, -ˈwɪð-, ⓊⓈ lɑːst-

lot, L~ lɒt, ⓊⓈ lɑːt -s -s -ting -ɪŋ, ⓊⓈ ˈlɑː.t̬ɪŋ -ted -ɪd, ⓊⓈ ˈlɑː.t̬ɪd

loth ləʊθ, ⓊⓈ loʊθ, loʊð

Lothair ləʊˈθeəʳ, ⓊⓈ loʊˈθer

Lothario ləʊˈθɑː.ri.əʊ, lɒθˈɑː-, -ˈeə-, ⓊⓈ loʊˈθer.i.oʊ, -ˈθɑːr-

Lothbury ˈləʊθ.bᵊr.i, ˈlɒθ-, ⓊⓈ ˈloʊθ.ber-, ˈlɑːθ-, -bɚ-

Lothian ˈləʊ.ði.ən, ⓊⓈ ˈloʊ-

loti ˈləʊ.ti, ⓊⓈ ˈloʊ-

lotion ˈləʊ.ʃᵊn, ⓊⓈ ˈloʊ- -s -z

Lott lɒt, ⓊⓈ lɑːt

lotta ˈlɒt.ə, ⓊⓈ ˈlɑː.t̬ə

lotter|y ˈlɒt.ᵊr|.i, ⓊⓈ ˈlɑː.t̬ɚ- -ies -iz

Lottie ˈlɒt.i, ⓊⓈ ˈlɑː.t̬i

lotto, L~ ˈlɒt.əʊ, ⓊⓈ ˈlɑː.t̬oʊ

lotus ˈləʊ.təs, ⓊⓈ ˈloʊ.t̬əs -es -ɪz ˈ**lotus po**ˌ**sition**

Lou luː

Louboutin ˌluː.buːˈtæ̃ŋ, -tæ̃n

louche luːʃ -ly -li -ness -nəs, -nɪs

loud laʊd -er -əʳ, ⓊⓈ -ɚ -est -ɪst, -əst -ly -li -ness -nəs, -nɪs

loud-hailer ˌlaʊdˈheɪ.ləʳ, ⓊⓈ -lɚ -s -z

loud|mouth ˈlaʊd|.maʊθ -mouths -maʊðz -mouthed -maʊθt

Loudo(u)n ˈlaʊ.dᵊn

loudspeaker ˌlaʊdˈspiː.kəʳ, ⓊⓈ ˈlaʊdˌspiː.kɚ -s -z

Loudwater ˈlaʊdˌwɔː.təʳ, ⓊⓈ -ˌwɑː.t̬ɚ, -ˌwɔː-

lough *lake:* lɒk; *as if Irish:* lɒx; ⓊⓈ lɑːk; *as if Irish:* ⓊⓈ lɑːx -s -s

Lough *surname:* lʌf, ləʊ, ⓊⓈ lʌf, loʊ

Loughborough ˈlʌf.bᵊr.ə, ⓊⓈ -bɚ.oʊ

Loughlin ˈlɒk.lɪn, -lən; *as if Irish:* ˈlɒx-; ⓊⓈ ˈlɑːk-; *as if Irish:* ⓊⓈ ˈlɑːx- **loughlin** ˈlɑːf

Loughman ˈlʌf.mən

Loughran ˈlɒk.rən; *as if Irish:* ˈlɒx-; ⓊⓈ ˈlɑːk-; *as if Irish:* ⓊⓈ ˈlɑːx-

Loughrea lɒkˈreɪ; *as if Irish:* lɒx-; ⓊⓈ lɑːk-; *as if Irish:* ⓊⓈ lɑːx-

Loughrey *as if Irish:* ˈlɒx.ri; ⓊⓈ ˈlɑːk-, ˈlɑːf-; *as if Irish:* ⓊⓈ ˈlɑːx-

Loughton ˈlaʊ.tᵊn

Louie ˈluː.i

Louis *English name:* ˈluː.i, -ɪs *French name:* ˈluː.i, -iː, luˈi

Louisa luˈiː.zə

Louisburg ˈluː.ɪs.bɜːg, ⓊⓈ -bɝːg

louis-d'or ˌluː.iˈdɔːʳ, ⓊⓈ -ˈdɔːr -s -z

Louise luˈiːz

Louisiana luˌiː.ziˈæn.ə, -ˈɑː.nə; ˌluː.ɪ.ziˈ-, ⓊⓈ luˌiː.ziˈæn.ə; ⓊⓈ ˌluː.ziˈ-

Louis Quatorze ˌluː.i.kætˈɔːz, ⓊⓈ -ˈɔːrz

Louis Quinze ˌluː.iˈkæ̃nz

Louisville ˈluː.i.vɪl, ⓊⓈ -ɪ.vɪl; *locally:* ⓊⓈ ˈluː.ə.vəl

loung|e laʊndʒ -es -ɪz -ing -ɪŋ -ed -d -er/s -əʳ/z, ⓊⓈ -ɚ/z ˈ**lounge bar**; ˈ**lounge** ˌ**lizard**; ˈ**lounge** ˌ**suit**

Lounsbury ˈlaʊnz.bᵊr.i, ⓊⓈ -ber-, -bɚ-

lour ˈlaʊ.əʳ, ⓊⓈ ˈlaʊ.ɚ -s -z -ing -ɪŋ -ed -d

Lourdes lʊəd, lʊədz, lɔːdz, ⓊⓈ lʊrd, lʊrdz

Lourenço Marques ləˌrent.səʊˈmɑː.kez, -kes, ⓊⓈ -soʊˈmɑːr.kes

louse n laʊs **lice** laɪs

lous|e v laʊz, laʊs, ⓊⓈ laʊs, laʊz -es -ɪz -ing -ɪŋ -ed -d, laʊst

lous|y ˈlaʊ.z|i -ier -i.əʳ, ⓊⓈ -i.ɚ -iest -i.ɪst, -i.əst -ily -ᵊl.i, -ɪ.li -iness -ɪ.nəs, -ɪ.nɪs

lout laʊt -s -s

Louth *in Ireland:* laʊð *in Lincolnshire:* laʊθ

loutish ˈlaʊ.tɪʃ, ⓊⓈ -t̬ɪʃ -ly -li -ness -nəs, -nɪs

Louvain ˈluː.væ̃ŋ, -veɪn; luˈvæ̃ŋ, -ˈvæn, ⓊⓈ luːˈvæn, -ˈvæ̃n

louver, louvre ˈluː.vəʳ, ⓊⓈ -vɚ -s -z

Louvre ˈluː.vrə, ⓊⓈ -vrə, luːv

lovab|le ˈlʌv.ə.b|ᵊl -ly -li -leness -ᵊl.nəs, -nɪs

lovage ˈlʌv.ɪdʒ

Lovat ˈlʌv.ət

lov|e, L~ lʌv -es -z -ing/ly -ɪŋ/li -ed -d ˈ**love af**ˌ**fair**; ˈ**love** ˌ**letter**;

ˌmake ˈlove; ˈlove song; ˈlove ˌstory; not for ˌlove nor ˈmoney

Note: The lengthened pronunciation /lɜːv/ can often be heard in pop songs to accommodate a long sung syllable. This pronunciation is represented humorously in print in British English by 'lurve', especially in contexts where it refers to a romantic or over-sentimentalized concept of love.

loveab|le ˈlʌv.ə.b|ᵊl **-ly** -li **-leness** -ᵊl.nəs, -nɪs
lovebird ˈlʌv.bɜːd, (US) -bɝːd **-s** -z
lovebite ˈlʌv.baɪt **-s** -s
love|-child ˈlʌv|.tʃaɪld **-children** -ˌtʃɪl.drᵊn
Loveday ˈlʌv.deɪ
loved-up ˌlʌvdˈʌp *stress shift:* ˌ**loved-up** ˈ**kids**
Lovejoy ˈlʌv.dʒɔɪ
Lovel ˈlʌv.ᵊl
Lovelace ˈlʌv.leɪs
loveless ˈlʌv.ləs, -lɪs **-ly** -li **-ness** -nəs, -nɪs
Lovell ˈlʌv.ᵊl
lovelorn ˈlʌv.lɔːn, (US) -lɔːrn
lovel|y ˈlʌv.l|i **-ies** -i.z **-ier** -i.əʳ, (US) -i.ɚ **-iest** -i.ɪst, -i.əst **-iness** -ɪ.nəs, -ɪ.nɪs
lovemaking ˈlʌvˌmeɪ.kɪŋ
love-match ˈlʌv.mætʃ **-es** -ɪz
love-potion ˈlʌvˌpəʊ.ʃᵊn, (US) -ˌpoʊ- **-s** -z
lover ˈlʌv.əʳ, (US) -ɚ **-s** -z
Loveridge ˈlʌv.rɪdʒ, -ᵊr.ɪdʒ
lovesick ˈlʌv.sɪk **-ness** -nəs, -nɪs
love-stor|y ˈlʌvˌstɔː.r|i, (US) -ˌstɔːr|.i **-ies** -ɪz
Lovett ˈlʌv.ɪt
lovey-dovey ˌlʌv.iˈdʌv.i, ˈlʌv.iˌdʌv-
Loveys ˈlʌv.ɪs
Lovibond ˈlʌv.ɪ.bɒnd, (US) -bɑːnd
Lovick ˈlʌv.ɪk
loving-cup ˈlʌv.ɪŋ.kʌp **-s** -s
low, L~ ləʊ, (US) loʊ **-er** -əʳ, (US) -ɚ **-est** -ɪst, -əst **-ness** -nəs, -nɪs **-s** -z **-ing** -ɪŋ **-ed** -d ˌ**Low** ˈ**Church**; ˌ**low** ˈ**profile**; ˈ**low** ˌ**season**
lowborn ˌləʊˈbɔːn, (US) ˈloʊ.bɔːrn *stress shift, British only:* ˌ**lowborn** ˈ**person**
lowbred ˌləʊˈbred, (US) ˈloʊ.bred *stress shift, British only:* ˌ**lowbred** ˈ**person**
lowbrow ˈləʊ.braʊ, (US) ˈloʊ-
low-cost ˌləʊˈkɒst, (US) ˌloʊˈkɑːst *stress shift:* ˌ**low-cost** ˈ**airline**
lowdown n ˈləʊ.daʊn, (US) ˈloʊ- *stress shift:* ˌ**low-down** ˈ**scoundrel**
low-down adj ˌləʊˈdaʊn, (US) ˌloʊ-
Lowe ləʊ, (US) loʊ
Lowell ˈləʊ.əl, (US) ˈloʊ-
lower v *look threatening:* laʊ.əʳ, (US) laʊr, ˈlaʊ.ɚ **-s** -z **-ing/ly** -ɪŋ/li **-ed** -d
low|er v, adj *cause to descend:* ˈləʊ|.əʳ, (US) ˈloʊ|.ɚ **-ers** -əz, -ɚs **-ering** -ᵊr.ɪŋ **-ered** -əd, (US) -ɚd
lower-case ˌləʊ.əˈkeɪs, (US) ˌloʊ.ɚˈ- *stress shift:* ˌ**lower-case** ˈ**letter**
lowermost ˈləʊ.ə.məʊst, -məst, (US) ˈloʊ.ɚ.moʊst
Lowery ˈlaʊə.ri, ˈlaʊ.ə.ri, (US) ˈlaʊ.ri
Lowes ləʊz, (US) loʊz
Lowestoft ˈləʊ.stɒft, ˈləʊ.ɪ-, -stəft, (US) ˈloʊ.stɑːft, ˈloʊ.ɪ-; *locally:* ˈləʊ.stəf, (US) ˈloʊ-
low-fat ˌləʊˈfæt, (US) ˌloʊ- *stress shift:* ˌ**low-fat** ˈ**cheese**
Lowick ˈləʊ.ɪk, (US) ˈloʊ-
Lowis ˈlaʊ.ɪs
lowkey ˌləʊˈkiː, (US) ˌloʊ-
low-key ˌləʊˈkiː, (US) ˌloʊ- *stress shift:* ˌ**low-key** **e**ˈ**vent**
lowland, L~ ˈləʊ.lənd, (US) ˈloʊ- **-s** -z **-er/s** -əʳ/z, (US) -ɚ/z
low-life ˈləʊ.laɪf, ˌ-ˈ-, (US) ˈloʊ-, ˌ-ˈ- **-s** -s
low-loader ˌləʊˈləʊ.dəʳ, (US) ˈloʊˌloʊ.dɚ **-s** -z
lowl|y ˈləʊ.l|i, (US) ˈloʊ- **-ier** -i.əʳ, (US) -i.ɚ **-iest** -i.ɪst, -i.əst **-iness** -ɪ.nəs, -ɪ.nɪs
low-lying ˌləʊˈlaɪ.ɪŋ, (US) ˌloʊ- *stress shift:* ˌ**low-lying** ˈ**cloud**
Lowndes laʊndz
low-necked ˌləʊˈnekt, (US) ˌloʊ- *stress shift:* ˌ**low-necked** ˈ**sweater**
Lowood ˈləʊ.wʊd, (US) ˈloʊ-
Lowries ˈlaʊə.rɪz, (US) ˈlaʊ-
Lowry ˈlaʊə.ri, (US) ˈlaʊ-
Lowsley ˈləʊz.li, (US) ˈloʊz-
Lowson ˈləʊ.sᵊn, ˈlaʊ-, (US) ˈloʊ-, ˈlaʊ-
Lowth laʊθ
Lowther ˈlaʊ.ðəʳ, (US) -ðɚ
Lowton ˈləʊ.tᵊn, (US) ˈloʊ-
Lowville ˈlaʊ.vɪl
lox lɒks, (US) lɑːks
Loxley ˈlɒk.sli, (US) ˈlɑːk-
loyal ˈlɔɪ.əl, lɔɪəl, (US) ˈlɔɪ.əl **-ly** -i
loyalist ˈlɔɪ.ə.lɪst, ˈlɔɪə.lɪst, (US) ˈlɔɪ.ə.lɪst **-s** -s
loyalt|y ˈlɔɪ.əl.t|i, ˈlɔɪəl-, (US) ˈlɔɪ.əl.t|i **-ies** -iz
Loyd lɔɪd
Loyola ˈlɔɪ.əʊ.lə; lɔɪˈəʊ-, (US) lɔɪˈoʊ-
lozeng|e ˈlɒz.ɪndʒ, -ᵊndʒ, (US) ˈlɑː.zəndʒ **-es** -ɪz
LP ˌelˈpiː
L-plate ˈel.pleɪt **-s** -s
LPN ˌel.piːˈen
LSD ˌel.esˈdiː
LSE ˌel.esˈiː
Ltd. (abbrev. for **Limited**) ˈlɪm.ɪ.tɪd, ˈ-ə-, (US) -ə.t̬ɪd
Luanda luˈæn.də, (US) -ˈæn-, -ˈɑːn-
luau ˈluː.aʊ
Lubavitcher ˈluː.bə.vɪ.tʃəʳ, (US) -tʃɚ **-s** -z
lubber ˈlʌb.əʳ, (US) -ɚ **-s** -z
Lubbock ˈlʌb.ək
lube luːb **-s** -z
Lübeck ˈluː.bek, ˈljuː-, (US) ˈluː-
Lubin ˈluː.bɪn
Lublin ˈluː.blɪn
lubricant ˈluː.brɪ.kənt, ˈljuː-, -brə-, (US) ˈluː- **-s** -s
lubri|cate ˈluː.brɪ|.keɪt, ˈljuː-, -brə-, (US) ˈluː- **-cates** -keɪts **-cating** -keɪ.tɪŋ, (US) -keɪ.t̬ɪŋ **-cated** -keɪ.tɪd, (US) -keɪ.t̬ɪd **-cator/s** -keɪ.təʳ/z, (US) -keɪ.t̬ɚ/z
lubrication ˌluː.brɪˈkeɪ.ʃᵊn, ˌljuː-, -brəˈ-, (US) ˌluː- **-s** -z
lubricious luːˈbrɪʃ.əs, ljuː-, (US) luː- **-ly** -li **-ness** -nəs, -nɪs
lubricity luːˈbrɪs.ə.ti, ljuː-, -ɪ.ti, (US) luːˈbrɪs.ə.t̬i
Lubumbashi ˌluː.bʊmˈbæʃ.i, (US) -ˈbɑː.ʃi
Luca ˈluː.kə
Lucan ˈluː.kən, ˈljuː-, (US) ˈluː-
Lucania luːˈkeɪ.ni.ə, ljuː-, (US) luː-
lucarne luːˈkɑːn, ljuː-, (US) luːˈkɑːrn **-s** -z
Lucas ˈluː.kəs
Luce luːs
lucen|t ˈluː.sᵊn|t, ˈljuː-, (US) ˈluː- **-cy** -*t*.si
lucern(e) luːˈsɜːn, ljuː-, ˈ--, (US) luːˈsɝːn
Lucerne luːˈsɜːn, ljuː-, (US) luːˈsɝːn
luces (plural of **lux**) ˈluː.siːz
Lucia ˈluː.si.ə, ˈ-ʃə; luːˈtʃiː.ə
Lucian ˈluː.si.ən, ˈ-ʃᵊn, -ʃi.ən, (US) ˈluː.ʃᵊn
Luciana ˌluː.siˈɑː.nə, ˌljuː-, (US) ˌluː-, -ˈæn.ə
Lucianus ˌluː.siˈɑː.nəs, ˌljuː-, -ˈeɪ-, (US) ˌluː.siˈɑː-
lucid ˈluː.sɪd, ˈljuː-, (US) ˈluː- **-ly** -li **-ness** -nəs, -nɪs
lucidity luːˈsɪd.ə.ti, ljuː-, -ɪ.ti, (US) luːˈsɪd.ə.t̬i
Lucie ˈluː.si, ˈljuː-, (US) ˈluː-
Lucien ˈluː.si.ən, ˈljuː-, (US) ˈluː-
Lucie-Smith ˌluː.siˈsmɪθ, ˌljuː-, (US) ˌluː-
lucifer, L~ ˈluː.sɪ.fəʳ, ˈljuː-, -sə-, (US) ˈluː.sə.fɚ **-s** -z
Lucilius luːˈsɪl.i.əs, ljuː-, (US) luː-
Lucille luːˈsiːl
Lucina luːˈsiː.nə, ljuː-, -ˈsaɪ-, -ˈtʃiː-, (US) luːˈsaɪ-, -ˈsiː-
Lucinda luːˈsɪn.də, ljuː-, (US) luː-
Lucite® ˈluː.saɪt, ˈljuː-, (US) ˈluː-
Lucius ˈluː.si.əs, ˈljuː-, ˈ-ʃəs, -ʃi.əs, (US) ˈluː.ʃəs
luck, L~ lʌk **to be** ˌ**down on one's** ˈ**luck**
luckless ˈlʌk.ləs, -lɪs **-ly** -li **-ness** -nəs, -nɪs
Lucknow ˈlʌk.naʊ, ˌ-ˈ-, (US) ˈlʌk.naʊ
luck|y ˈlʌk|.i **-ier** -i.əʳ, (US) -i.ɚ **-iest** -i.ɪst, -i.əst **-ily** -ᵊl.i, -ɪ.li **-iness** -ɪ.nəs, -ɪ.nɪs
Lucock ˈluː.kɒk, ˈljuː-, (US) ˈluː.kɑːk
Lucozade® ˈluː.kə.zeɪd
lucrative ˈluː.krə.tɪv, ˈljuː-, (US) ˈluː.krə.t̬ɪv **-ly** -li **-ness** -nəs, -nɪs
lucre ˈluː.kəʳ, ˈljuː-, (US) ˈluː.kɚ
Lucrece luːˈkriːs, ljuː-, (US) luː-
Lucretia luːˈkriː.ʃə, ljuː-, -ʃi.ə, (US) luːˈkriː.ʃə
Lucretius luːˈkriː.ʃəs, ljuː-, -ʃi.əs, (US) luːˈkriː.ʃəs

lucu|brate ˈluː.kjə|.breɪt, -kjʊ-, ˈljuː-, US ˈluː- **-brates** -breɪts **-brating** -breɪ.tɪŋ, US -breɪ.t̬ɪŋ **-brated** -breɪ.tɪd, US -breɪ.t̬ɪd
lucubration ˌluː.kjəˈbreɪ.ʃən, -kjʊˈ-, ˌljuː-, US ˌluː- **-s** -z
Lucullus luːˈkʌl.əs, ljuː-, -ˈsʌl-, US luːˈkʌl-
Lucy ˈluː.si
Lud lʌd
Luddite ˈlʌd.aɪt **-s** -s
Ludgate ˈlʌd.gət, -gɪt, -geɪt
ludicrous ˈluː.dɪ.krəs, ˈljuː-, -də-, US ˈluː- **-ly** -li **-ness** -nəs, -nɪs
Ludlow ˈlʌd.ləʊ, US -loʊ
Ludmilla lʊdˈmɪl.ə, lʌd-
ludo ˈluː.dəʊ, US -doʊ
Ludovic ˈluː.də.vɪk
Ludwig ˈlʊd.vɪg, ˈluːd-, US ˈlʊd-, ˈluːd-, ˈlʌd-, -wɪg
luff, L~ lʌf **-s** -s **-ing** -ɪŋ **-ed** -t
Lufthansa® ˈlʊftˌhænt.sə, -ˌhæn.zə, US lʊfˈtɑːn.zə
Luftwaffe ˈlʊftˌvɑː.f.ə, -ˌwæf-, -ˌvæf-, US -ˌvɑː-, -ˌwɑː.fə
lug lʌg **-s** -z **-ging** -ɪŋ **-ged** -d
Lugano luːˈgɑː.nəʊ, lə-, US luːˈgɑː.noʊ
Lugard ˈluː.gɑːd, -ˈ-, US ˈluː.gɑːrd, -ˈ-
lug|e luːʒ, luːdʒ, US luːʒ **-es** -ɪz **-(e)ing** -ɪŋ **-ed** -d
Luger® ˈluː.gər, US -gɚ
luggable ˈlʌg.ə.bəl
luggage ˈlʌg.ɪdʒ **ˈluggage ˌlabel; ˈluggage ˌrack**
lugger ˈlʌg.ər, US -ɚ **-s** -z
lughole ˈlʌg.həʊl, -əʊl, US -hoʊl **-s** -z
Lugosi luːˈgəʊ.si, US -ˈgoʊ-
lugsail ˈlʌg.seɪl; *nautical pronunciation:* -səl **-s** -z
lugubrious luːˈguː.bri.əs, ljuː-, lə-, US ləˈguː-, luː- **-ly** -li **-ness** -nəs, -nɪs
lugworm ˈlʌg.wɜːm, US -wɝːm **-s** -z
Luis ˈluː.ɪs
Luka ˈluː.kə
Lukacs, Lukács ˈluː.kætʃ, US -kɑːtʃ
Luke luːk
lukewarm ˌluːkˈwɔːm, ˈ--, US ˈluːk.wɔːrm, ˌ-ˈ- **-ly** -li **-ness** -nəs, -nɪs
lull lʌl **-s** -z **-ing** -ɪŋ **-ed** -d
lullab|y ˈlʌl.ə.b|aɪ **-ies** -aɪz
Lully ˈlʊl.i; *as if French:* luːˈliː; US luːˈliː
lulu, L~ ˈluː.luː
lumbago lʌmˈbeɪ.gəʊ, US -goʊ
lumbar ˈlʌm.bər, -bɑːr, US -bɑːr, -bɚ
lumb|er ˈlʌm.b|ər, US -b|ɚ **-ers** -əz, US -ɚz **-ering** -ər.ɪŋ **-ered** -əd, US -ɚd **-erer/s** -ər.ər/z, US -ɚ.ɚ/z **-erman** -ə.mən, US -ɚ.mən **-ermen** -ə.mən, -ə.men, US -ɚ.mən, -ɚ.men
lumberjack ˈlʌm.bə.dʒæk, US -bɚ- **-s** -s
lumberyard ˈlʌm.bə.jɑːd, US -bɚ.jɑːrd **-s** -z
lumiere, lumière ˈluː.mi.eər, ˌ--ˈ-, US ˌluː.miˈer
luminar|y ˈluː.mɪ.nər|.i, ˈljuː-, -mə-, US ˈluː.mə.ner- **-ies** -iz
luminesc|e ˌluː.mɪˈnes, ˌljuː-, -məˈ-, US ˌluː.məˈ- **-es** -ɪz **-ing** -ɪŋ **-ed** -t
luminescen|ce ˌluː.mɪˈnes.ən|*t*s, ˌljuː-, -məˈ-, US ˌluː.məˈ- **-t** -t
luminiferous ˌluː.mɪˈnɪf.ər.əs, ˌljuː-, -məˈ-, US ˌluː.məˈ-
luminosity ˌluː.mɪˈnɒs.ə.ti, ˌljuː-, -məˈ-, -ɪ.ti, US ˌluː.məˈnɑː.sə.t̬i
luminous ˈluː.mɪ.nəs, ˈljuː-, -mə-, US ˈluː.mə- **-ly** -li **-ness** -nəs, -nɪs
Lumley ˈlʌm.li
lumme ˈlʌm.i
lummox ˈlʌm.əks **-es** -ɪz
lump lʌmp **-s** -s **-ing** -ɪŋ **-ed** -t
lumpectom|y lʌmˈpek.tə.m|i **-ies** -iz
lumpen ˈlʌm.pən, ˈlʊm-
lumpenproletariat ˌlʌm.pənˌprəʊ.ləˈteə.ri.ət, ˌlʊm-, -pəmˌ-, -lɪˈ-, -æt, US -pənˌproʊ.ləˈter.i.ət
lumpfish ˈlʌmp.fɪʃ **-es** -ɪz
lumpish ˈlʌm.pɪʃ **-ly** -li **-ness** -nəs, -nɪs
Lumpkin ˈlʌmp.kɪn
lump|y ˈlʌm.p|i **-ier** -i.ər, US -i.ɚ **-iest** -i.ɪst, -i.əst **-iness** -ɪ.nəs, -ɪ.nɪs
Lumsden ˈlʌmz.dən
Luna ˈluː.nə, ˈljuː-, US ˈluː-
lunacy ˈluː.nə.si, ˈljuː-, US ˈluː-
lunar ˈluː.nər, ˈljuː-, US ˈluː.nɚ
lunate ˈluː.neɪt, ˈljuː-, -nət, -nɪt, US ˈluː.neɪt, -nɪt
lunatic ˈluː.nə.tɪk, ˈljuː-, US ˈluː- **-s** -s **ˈlunatic aˌsylum; ˌlunatic ˈfringe**
lunation luːˈneɪ.ʃən, ljuː-, US luː- **-s** -z
lunch lʌntʃ **-es** -ɪz **-ing** -ɪŋ **-ed** -t
lunchbox ˈlʌntʃ.bɒks, US -bɑːks **-es** -ɪz
luncheon ˈlʌn.*t*ʃən **-s** -z **ˈluncheon ˌmeat; ˈluncheon ˌvoucher**
luncheonette ˌlʌn.*t*ʃəˈnet **-s** -s
lunchroom ˈlʌntʃ.ruːm, -rʊm, US -ruːm, -rʊm **-s** -z
lunchtime ˈlʌntʃ.taɪm **-s** -z
Lund *place in Sweden:* lʊnd, US lʊnd, lʌnd *family name:* lʌnd
Lundy ˈlʌn.di
lune, L~ luːn, ljuːn, US luːn **-s** -z
Lüneburg ˈluː.nə.bɜːg, US -bɝːg
lunette luːˈnet, ljuː-, US luː- **-s** -s
lung lʌŋ **-s** -z
lung|e lʌndʒ **-es** -ɪz **-ing** -ɪŋ **-ed** -d **-er/s** -ər/z, US -ɚ/z
lungfish ˈlʌŋ.fɪʃ **-es** -ɪz
lunkhead ˈlʌŋk.hed **-s** -z
Lunn lʌn
lunul|a ˈluː.njə.l|ə, ˈljuː-, US -njʊ-, ˈluː.njə- **-ae** -iː
lunule ˈluː.njuːl, ˈljuː-, US ˈluː- **-s** -z
Lupercal ˈluː.pə.kæl, ˈljuː-, -pɜː-, US ˈluː.pɚ.kæl
Lupercalia ˌluː.pəˈkeɪ.li.ə, ˌljuː-, -pɜːˈ-, US ˌluː.pɚˈkeɪl.jə
lupin(e) **n** *flower:* ˈluː.pɪn **-s** -z
lupine **adj** *wolfish:* ˈluː.paɪn, ˈljuː-, US ˈluː-
lupus, L~ ˈluː.pəs, ˈljuː-, US ˈluː-
lurch lɜːtʃ, US lɝːtʃ **-es** -ɪz **-ing** -ɪŋ **-ed** -t **-er/s** -ər/z, US -ɚ/z **ˌleave someone in the ˈlurch**
lur|e lʊər, ljʊər, ljɔːr, US lʊr **-es** -z **-ing** -ɪŋ **-ed** -d
Lurex® ˈljʊə.reks, ˈlʊə-, ˈljɔː-, US ˈlʊr.eks
Lurgan ˈlɜː.gən, US ˈlɝː-
lurg|y ˈlɜː.g|i, US ˈlɝː- **-ies** -iz
lurid ˈlʊə.rɪd, ˈljʊə-, ˈljɔː-, US ˈlʊr.ɪd **-ly** -li **-ness** -nəs, -nɪs
lurk lɜːk, US lɝːk **-s** -s **-ing** -ɪŋ **-ed** -t **-er/s** -ər/z, US -ɚ/z
Lurpak® ˈlɜː.pæk, US ˈlɝː-
lurve lɜːv, US lɝːv
Lusaka luːˈsɑː.kə, lʊ-, -ˈzɑː-, US luːˈsɑː.kɑː
Lusardi luːˈsɑː.di, US -ˈsɑːr-
Lusati|a luːˈseɪ.ʃ|ə, -ʃi|.ə **-an/s** -ən/z
luscious ˈlʌʃ.əs **-ly** -li **-ness** -nəs, -nɪs
lush, L~ lʌʃ **-es** -ɪz **-er** -ər, US -ɚ **-est** -ɪst, -əst **-ing** -ɪŋ **-ed** -t **-ness** -nəs, -nɪs
Lushington ˈlʌʃ.ɪŋ.tən
Lusiad ˈluː.si.æd, ˈljuː-, US ˈluː- **-s** -z
Lusitania ˌluː.sɪˈteɪ.ni.ə, ˌljuː-, -səˈ-, US ˌluː-
lust lʌst **-s** -s **-ing** -ɪŋ **-ed** -ɪd
luster ˈlʌs.tər, US -tɚ **-s** -z **-less** -ləs, -lɪs
lustful ˈlʌst.fəl, -fʊl **-ly** -i **-ness** -nəs, -nɪs
lustral ˈlʌs.trəl
lustration lʌsˈtreɪ.ʃən **-s** -z
lustre ˈlʌs.tər, US -tɚ **-s** -z **-less** -ləs, -lɪs
lustrous ˈlʌs.trəs **-ly** -li **-ness** -nəs, -nɪs
lustr|um ˈlʌs.tr|əm **-ums** -əmz **-a** -ə
lust|y ˈlʌs.t|i **-ier** -i.ər, US -i.ɚ **-iest** -i.ɪst, -i.əst **-ily** -əl.i, -ɪ.li **-iness** -ɪ.nəs, -ɪ.nɪs
lutanist ˈluː.tən.ɪst, ˈljuː-, US ˈluː-
lute luːt, ljuːt, US luːt **-s** -s
lutein ˈluː.ti.ɪn, ˈljuː-, -tiːn, ˈluː.ti.ɪn
luteiniz|e, -is|e ˈluː.ti.ɪ.naɪz, ˈljuː-, -ə-; -tɪ.naɪz, -tə-, -tiː-, -tən.aɪz, US ˈluː.ti.ə.naɪz, -ə- **-es** -ɪz **-ing** -ɪŋ **-ed** -d
lutenist ˈluː.tən.ɪst, ˈljuː-, US ˈluː- **-s** -s
lutetium luːˈtiː.ʃəm, ljuː-, -ʃi.əm, US luːˈtiː.ʃi.əm
Luth|er ˈluː.θ|ər, US ˈluː.θ|ɚ **-eran/s** -ər.ən/z **-eranism** -ər.ən.ɪ.zəm **-erism** -ər.ɪ.zəm
Lutine luːˈtiːn, ˈ--
lutist ˈluː.tɪst, ˈljuː-, US ˈluː.t̬ɪst **-s** -s
Luton ˈluː.tən
Lutterworth ˈlʌt.ə.wəθ, -wɜːθ, US ˈlʌt̬.ɚ.wɚθ, -wɝːθ
Lutton ˈlʌt.ən
Luttrell ˈlʌt.rəl
Lutyens ˈlʌt.jənz, ˈlʌtʃ.ənz
luv lʌv **-s** -z
luvv|ie, luvv|y ˈlʌv|.i **-ies** -iz
Lux® lʌks

lux lʌks **luxes** ˈlʌk.sɪz
luxe lʌks, luːks, lʊks
Luxemb(o)urg ˈlʌk.səm.bɜːg, US -bɝːg
Luxor ˈlʌk.sɔːr, US -sɔːr, ˈlʊk-
luxuriance lʌgˈʒʊə.ri.ənts, ləg-, -ˈʒɔː-, -ˈzjʊə-, -ˈzjɔː-; lʌkˈʃʊə-, lək-, -ˈʃɔː-, US lʌgˈʒʊr.i-, -ˈzjʊr-; US lʌkˈʃʊr-, -ˈsjʊr-
luxuriant lʌgˈʒʊə.ri.ənt, ləg-, -ˈʒɔː-, -ˈzjʊə-, -ˈzjɔː-; lʌkˈʃʊə-, lək-, -ˈʃɔː-, US lʌgˈʒʊr.i-, -ˈzjʊr-; US lʌkˈʃʊr-, -ˈsjʊr- **-ly** -li
luxuri|ate lʌgˈʒʊə.ri|.eɪt, ləg-, -ˈʒɔː-, -ˈzjʊə-, -ˈzjɔː-; lʌkˈʃʊə-, lək-, -ˈʃɔː-, US lʌgˈʒʊr.i-, -ˈʒjʊr-; US lʌkˈʃʊr-, -ˈsjʊr- **-ates** -eɪts **-ating** -eɪ.tɪŋ, US -eɪ.t̬ɪŋ **-ated** -eɪ.tɪd, US -eɪ.t̬ɪd
luxurious lʌgˈʒʊə.ri.əs, ləg-, -ˈʒɔː-, -ˈzjʊə-, -ˈzjɔː-; lʌkˈʃʊə-, lək-, -ˈʃɔː-, US lʌgˈʒʊr.i-, -ˈzjʊr-; US lʌkˈʃʊr-, -ˈsjʊr- **-ly** -li **-ness** -nəs, -nɪs
luxur|y ˈlʌk.ʃər|.i, US ˈlʌk.ʃɚ|.i, -ʃʊr-; US ˈlʌg.ʒɚ-, -ʒʊr- **-ies** -iz **in the ˌlap of ˈluxury**
Luzon luːˈzɒn, US -ˈzɑːn
Lvov ləˈvɒf, US -ˈvɑːf
lwei ləˈweɪ **-s** -z
-ly li
Note: Suffix. Does not alter the stress pattern of the stem to which it is added, e.g. **rapid** /ˈræp.ɪd/, **rapidly** /ˈræp.ɪd.li/.
Lyall ˈlaɪ.əl
lycanthrope ˈlaɪ.kən.θrəʊp; laɪˈkænt.θrəʊp, US laɪˈkænt.θroʊp **-s** -s
lycanthropic ˌlaɪ.kənˈθrɒp.ɪk, US -ˈθrɑː.pɪk
lycanthropy laɪˈkænt.θrə.pi
lycée ˈliː.seɪ, US liːˈseɪ **-s** -z
Lycett ˈlaɪ.sɪt, -set
lyceum, L~ laɪˈsiː.əm, ˈlaɪ- **-s** -z
lychee ˌlaɪˈtʃiː; ˈlaɪ.tʃiː, ˈliː-, US ˈliː.tʃiː **-s** -z
lychgate ˈlɪtʃ.geɪt **-s** -s
lychnis ˈlɪk.nɪs
Lyci|a ˈlɪs.i|.ə, ˈlɪʃ-, ˈlɪʃ|.ə, US ˈlɪʃ|.ə, -i|.ə **-an/s** -ən/z
Lycidas ˈlɪs.ɪ.dæs, US -dæs, -dəs
Lycoming laɪˈkɒm.ɪŋ, US -ˈkʌm-
lycopene ˈlaɪ.kəʊ.piːn, US -koʊ-
lycopodium ˌlaɪ.kəʊˈpəʊ.di.əm, US -koʊˈpoʊ- **-s** -z
Lycra® ˈlaɪ.krə
Lycurgus laɪˈkɜː.gəs, US -ˈkɝː-
Lydall ˈlaɪ.dəl
Lydd lɪd
lyddite ˈlɪd.aɪt
Lydekker laɪˈdek.ər, US -ɚ
Lydgate *fifteenth-century poet, place in Greater Manchester:* ˈlɪd.geɪt, -gɪt *place in Yorkshire:* ˈlɪd.gɪt, ˈlɪ.gɪt *lane in Sheffield:* ˈlɪdʒ.ɪt
Lydi|a ˈlɪd.i|.ə **-an/s** -ən/z
Lydiate ˈlɪd.i.ət
Lydney ˈlɪd.ni
Lydon ˈlaɪ.dən
lye, L~ laɪ
Lyell laɪ.əl
Lygon ˈlɪg.ən
lying (from **lie**) ˈlaɪ.ɪŋ **ˌtake something ˌlying ˈdown**
Lyle laɪl
Lyly ˈlɪl.i
Lyme laɪm **ˈLyme diˌsease**
Lyme Regis ˌlaɪmˈriː.dʒɪs
Lymeswold® ˈlaɪmz.wəʊld, US -woʊld
Lymington ˈlɪm.ɪŋ.tən
Lymm lɪm
Lympany ˈlɪm.pə.ni
lymph lɪmpf **-s** -s
lymphatic lɪmˈfæt.ɪk, US -ˈfæt̬- **-s** -s **-ally** -əl.i, -li
lymphocyte ˈlɪmp.fəʊ.saɪt, US -foʊ-, -fə- **-s** -s
lymphoid ˈlɪmp.fɔɪd
lymphoma lɪmˈfəʊ.mə, US -ˈfoʊ- **-s** -z
Lympne lɪm
Lyn lɪn
Lynam ˈlaɪ.nəm
Lynas ˈlaɪ.nəs
lynch, L~ lɪntʃ, US lɪntʃ **-es** -ɪz **-ing** -ɪŋ **-ed** -t
Lynchburg ˈlɪntʃ.bɜːg, US -bɝːg
lynchpin ˈlɪntʃ.pɪn **-s** -z
Lynda ˈlɪn.də
Lyndhurst ˈlɪnd.hɜːst, US -hɝːst
Lyndon ˈlɪn.dən
Lyndsay, Lyndsey ˈlɪnd.zi
Lyness ˈlaɪ.nɪs, -nəs, -nes
Lynette lɪˈnet
Lynmouth ˈlɪn.məθ
Lynn(e) lɪn
Lynton ˈlɪn.tən
lynx lɪŋks **-es** -ɪz
Lyon laɪ.ən
lyonnaise ˌlaɪ.əˈneɪz, ˌliː.əˈ-
Lyons laɪ.ənz *French city:* ˈliː.ɔ̃ːŋ, -ɒn; laɪ.ənz; *as if French:* liˈɔ̃ːŋ; US liˈõʊn
Lyr|a ˈlaɪə.r|ə, US ˈlaɪ- **-ae** -iː
lyrate ˈlaɪə.rɪt, -reɪt, -rət, US ˈlaɪ.reɪt
lyre laɪ.ər, US laɪ.ɚ **-s** -z
lyrebird ˈlaɪə.bɜːd, US ˈlaɪr.bɝːd **-s** -z
lyric, L~ ˈlɪr.ɪk **-s** -s **-al** -əl **-ally** -əl.i, -li
lyricism ˈlɪr.ɪ.sɪ.zəm, ˈ-ə-
lyricist ˈlɪr.ɪ.sɪst, ˈ-ə- **-s** -s
lyrist *player on the lyre:* ˈlaɪə.rɪst, ˈlɪr.ɪst, US ˈlaɪr.ɪst *lyric poet:* ˈlɪr.ɪst **-s** -s
Lysander laɪˈsæn.dər, US -dɚ
lysergic laɪˈsɜː.dʒɪk, lɪ-, US laɪˈsɝː-
Lysias ˈlɪs.i.æs
Lysicrates laɪˈsɪk.rə.tiːz
Lysippus laɪˈsɪp.əs
-lysis lə.sɪs, lɪ-
Note: Suffix. Words containing **-lysis** are normally stressed on the syllable preceding the suffix, e.g. **paralysis** /pəˈræl.ə.sɪs/.
Lysistrata laɪˈsɪs.trə.tə, US ˌlɪs.ɪˈstrɑː-; US laɪˈsɪs.trə-
Lysol® ˈlaɪ.sɒl, US -sɑːl
Lystra ˈlɪs.trə
Lyte laɪt
Lytham ˈlɪð.əm
Lythe laɪð
Lyttelton ˈlɪt.əl.tən, US ˈlɪt̬-
Lyttle ˈlɪt.əl, US ˈlɪt̬-
Lytton ˈlɪt.ən

M

Pronouncing the letter M

→ *See also* **MN**

The consonant letter **m** is always realized as m.

m, M em -'s -z
m (abbrev. for **metre/s**) *singular:* ˈmiː.təʳ, ⓤⓢ -t̬ɚ; *plural:* -z
ma mɑː -s -z
MA ˌemˈeɪ
ma'am (abbrev. for **madam**) mæm, mɑːm, məm, m, ⓤⓢ mæm

> Note: /mɑːm/, or alternatively /mæm/, is used in addressing members of the Royal Family.

Maas mɑːs
Maastricht ˈmɑː.strɪkt, -strɪxt; *as if Dutch:* mɑːˈstrɪxt; ⓤⓢ ˈmɑː.strɪkt, -strɪxt
Mab mæb
Mabel ˈmeɪ.bəl
Mabinogion ˌmæb.ɪˈnɒg.i.ɒn, -əˈ-, -ən, ⓤⓢ -ˈnɔː.gi.ɑːn, -ˈnɑː-, -ən
Mablethorpe ˈmeɪ.bəl.θɔːp, ⓤⓢ -θɔːrp
Mabley ˈmæb.li, ⓤⓢ ˈmæb-, ˈmeɪb-
Mabs mæbz
mac, mack mæk -s -s
Mac mæk
macabre məˈkɑː.brə, mækˈɑː-, -bəʳ, ⓤⓢ məˈkɑː.brə, -ˈkɑːb, -ˈkɑː.bɚ
macadam məˈkæd.əm
MacAdam məˈkæd.əm
macadamia ˌmæk.əˈdeɪ.mi.ə -s -z ˌ**macaˈdamia** ˌ**nut**
macadamization, -isa- məˌkæd.ə.maɪˈzeɪ.ʃən, -mɪˈ-, ⓤⓢ -məˈ-
macadamiz|e, -is|e məˈkæd.ə.maɪz -es -ɪz -ing -ɪŋ -ed -d
Macalister məˈkæl.ɪ.stəʳ, ⓤⓢ -stɚ
Macan məˈkæn
Macao məˈkaʊ, mækˈaʊ, ⓤⓢ məˈkaʊ
macaque məˈkɑːk, -ˈkæk; ˈmæk.æk, ⓤⓢ məˈkɑːk -s -s
macaroni ˌmæk.əʳˈəʊ.ni, ⓤⓢ -əˈroʊ- -(e)s -z *stress shift, see compound:* ˌ**macaroni** ˈ**cheese**
macaroon ˌmæk.əʳˈuːn, ⓤⓢ -əˈruːn -s -z
MacArthur məˈkɑː.θəʳ, ⓤⓢ -ˈkɑːr.θɚ
macassar, M~ məˈkæs.əʳ, ⓤⓢ -ɚ **maˈcassar** ˌ**oil**
Macau məˈkaʊ, mækˈaʊ, ⓤⓢ məˈkaʊ
Macaulay məˈkɔː.li, ⓤⓢ -ˈkɑː.li, -ˈkɔː-
Macavity məˈkæv.ə.ti, -ɪ.ti, ⓤⓢ -ə.t̬i
MacAvoy ˈmæk.ə.vɔɪ
macaw məˈkɔː, ⓤⓢ -ˈkɑː, -ˈkɔː -s -z
MacBain məkˈbeɪn
Macbeth məkˈbeθ, mæk-

> Note: In Scotland always /mək-/.

Maccabaeus ˌmæk.əˈbiː.əs, -ˈbeɪ-, ⓤⓢ -ˈbiː-
Maccabean ˌmæk.əˈbiː.ən, -ˈbeɪ-, ⓤⓢ -ˈbiː-
Maccabees ˈmæk.ə.biːz
Maccabeus ˌmæk.əˈbiː.əs, -ˈbeɪ-, ⓤⓢ -ˈbiː-
MacCaig məˈkeɪg
MacCall məˈkɔːl, ⓤⓢ -ˈkɔːl, -ˈkɑːl
MacCallum məˈkæl.əm
MacCarthy məˈkɑː.θi, ⓤⓢ -ˈkɑːr-
macchiato ˌmæk.iˈɑː.təʊ, ⓤⓢ mɑːk.i.ˈɑː.t̬oʊ -s -z
Macclesfield ˈmæk.əlz.fiːld, -əls-
MacCunn məˈkʌn
MacDaire məkˈdɑː.rə, ⓤⓢ məkˈder
MacDiarmid məkˈdɜː.mɪd, -ˈdeə-, ⓤⓢ -ˈdɝː-
Macdonald, MacDonald məkˈdɒn.əld, mæk-, ⓤⓢ -ˈdɑː.nəld
MacDonaugh məkˈdɒn.ə, ⓤⓢ -ˈdɑː.nə
MacDon(n)ell məkˈdɒn.əl, ⓤⓢ -ˈdɑː.nəl
MacDougal məkˈduː.gəl
MacDuff məkˈdʌf, mæk-

> Note: In Scotland always /mək-/.

mace meɪs -s -ɪz
macedoine, macédoine ˌmæs.ɪˈdwɑːn, -əˈ-, ˈ---, ⓤⓢ ˌmæs.ɪˈdwɑːn -s -z
Macedon ˈmæs.ɪ.dən, ˈ-ə-, ⓤⓢ -ə.dɑːn, -dən
Macedoni|a ˌmæs.ɪˈdəʊ.ni|.ə, ⓤⓢ -əˈdoʊ.ni-, ˈ-nj|ə -an/s -ən/z
MacElder(r)y ˌmæk.əlˈder.i, məˈkel.dər-, ⓤⓢ məˈkel.dɚ-
MacElwain ˈmæk.əl.weɪn, məˈkel.weɪn
MacElwin ˈmæk.əl.wɪn
macer|ate ˈmæs.əʳ|.eɪt, ⓤⓢ -ə.r|eɪt -ates -eɪts -ating -eɪ.tɪŋ, ⓤⓢ -eɪ.t̬ɪŋ -ated -eɪ.tɪd, ⓤⓢ -eɪ.t̬ɪd
maceration ˌmæs.əʳˈeɪ.ʃən, ⓤⓢ -əˈreɪ- -s -z
macerator ˈmæs.əʳ.eɪ.təʳ, ⓤⓢ -ə.reɪ.t̬ɚ -s -z
MacFarlane məkˈfɑː.lən, ⓤⓢ -ˈfɑːr-
Macfarren məkˈfær.ən, ⓤⓢ -ˈfer-, -ˈfær-
Macgillicuddy, MacGillicuddy məˈgɪl.i.kʌd.i; ˈmæg.li-, ˈmæk.ɪl-, ⓤⓢ məˈgɪl.i-

> Note: **Macgillicuddy's Reeks** is pronounced /məˌgɪl.i.kʌd.izˈriːks/.

Macgregor, MacGregor məˈgreg.əʳ, ⓤⓢ -ɚ
Mach mæk, mɑːk, ⓤⓢ mɑːk, mæk
Machakos məˈtʃɑː.kɒs, ⓤⓢ -kɑːs
Macheath məkˈhiːθ, mæk-, ⓤⓢ mæk-, mək-
Machen ˈmeɪ.tʃɪn, -tʃən; ˈmæk.ɪn; *as if Welsh:* ˈmæx-; ⓤⓢ ˈmæk.ɪn
machete məˈtʃet.i, mætʃˈet-, -ˈeɪ.ti, ⓤⓢ məˈtʃet̬.i -s -z
Machiavelli ˌmæk.i.əˈvel.i, ˌ-jəˈ-
Machiavellian ˌmæk.i.əˈvel.i.ən, ˌmæk.jə- -s -z -ism -ɪ.zəm
machico|late məˈtʃɪk.əʊ|.leɪt, mætʃˈɪk-, ⓤⓢ məˈtʃɪk.oʊ-, ˈ-ə- -lates -leɪts -lating -leɪ.tɪŋ, ⓤⓢ -leɪ.t̬ɪŋ -lated -leɪ.tɪd, ⓤⓢ -leɪ.t̬ɪd
machicolation məˌtʃɪk.əʊˈleɪ.ʃən, mætʃˌɪk-, ⓤⓢ məˌtʃɪk.oʊˈ-, -əˈ- -s -z
Machin ˈmeɪ.tʃɪn
machi|nate ˈmæk.ɪ|.neɪt, ˈmæʃ-, ˈ-ə-, ⓤⓢ ˈmæk.ə|.neɪt -nates -neɪts -nating -neɪ.tɪŋ, ⓤⓢ -neɪ.t̬ɪŋ -nated -neɪ.tɪd, ⓤⓢ -neɪ.t̬ɪd -nator/s -neɪ.təʳ/z, ⓤⓢ -neɪ.t̬ɚ/s
machination ˌmæk.ɪˈneɪ.ʃən, ˌmæʃ-, -əˈ-, ⓤⓢ -əˈ- -s -z
machin|e məˈʃiːn -es -z -ing -ɪŋ -ed -d **maˈchine** ˌ**code**; **maˈchine** ˌ**tool**
machine-gun məˈʃiːn.gʌn, -ˈʃiːŋˌ-, ⓤⓢ -ˈʃiːnˌ- -s -z -ning -ɪŋ -ned -d -ner/s -əʳ/z, ⓤⓢ -ɚ/z
machine-made məˈʃiːn.meɪd
machine-readable məˌʃiːnˈriː.də.bəl *stress shift:* **maˌchine-readable** ˈ**dictionary**
machiner|y məˈʃiː.nər.i -ies -ɪz
machine-washable məˌʃiːnˈwɒʃ.ə.bəl, ⓤⓢ -ˈwɑː.ʃə- *stress shift:* **maˌchine-washable** ˈ**wool**
machinist məˈʃiː.nɪst -s -s
machismo mætʃˈɪz.məʊ, məˈtʃɪz-, -ˈkɪz-, ⓤⓢ mɑːˈtʃiːz.moʊ, məˈkɪz-

> Note: This word is sometimes pronounced with /k/ instead of /tʃ/, possibly because it is mistakenly assumed to be of Italian, not Spanish, origin.

macho ˈmætʃ.əʊ, ⓤⓢ ˈmɑː.tʃoʊ -s -z
macho-|man ˈmætʃ.əʊ|ˌmæn, ⓤⓢ ˈmɑː.tʃoʊ- -men -men
Machu Picchu ˌmɑː.tʃuːˈpiːk.tʃuː
Machynlleth məˈkʌn.hləθ

M

MacIlwain ˈmæk.əl.weɪn, -ɪl-

MacIlwraith ˈmæk.ɪl.reɪθ

Macindoe, MacIndoe ˈmæk.ɪn.dəʊ, -ən-, US -doʊ

MacInnes, MacInnis məˈkɪn.ɪs

MacIntosh ˈmæk.ɪn.tɒʃ, US -tɑːʃ **-es** -ɪz

MacIntyre ˈmæk.ɪn.taɪəʳ, -ən-, US -taɪ.ɚ

MacIver məˈkaɪ.vəʳ, -ˈkɪv.əʳ, US -vɚ

MacIvor məˈkaɪ.vəʳ, US -vɚ

Mack mæk

Mackay(e), MacKay(e) məˈkaɪ, məˈkeɪ

> Note: /məˈkeɪ/ mainly in the US.

Mackenzie məˈken.zi

mackerel ˈmæk.rəl, ˈmæk.ər.əl **-s** -z

Mackerras məˈker.əs

Mackeson ˈmæk.ɪ.sən, ˈ-ə-

Mackie ˈmæk.i

Mackin ˈmæk.ɪn

mackinaw ˈmæk.ɪ.nɔː, US -nɑː, -nɔː **-s** -z

Mackinlay, Mackinley məˈkɪn.li

mackintosh, M~ ˈmæk.ɪn.tɒʃ, US -tɑːʃ **-es** -ɪz

M

Mackowie, MacKowie məˈkaʊ.i

MacLachlan məˈklɒk.lən, -ˈklɒx-, -ˈklæk-, -ˈklæx-, US -ˈklɑː.klən

MacLagan məˈklæg.ən, US məkˈlɑː.ken, -ˈglɑː.kən

MacLaglan məˈklæg.lən, US -ˈklæg-, -ˈklɑːg-

Maclaren məˈklær.ən, US -ˈkler-, -ˈklær-

MacLaverty məˈklæv.ə.ti, US -ɚ.t̬i

Maclean məˈkleɪn, -ˈkliːn, US -ˈkliːn

Macleans® məˈkliːnz

MacLeish məˈkliːʃ

MacLeod məˈklaʊd

Maclise məˈkliːs

MacManus məkˈmæn.əs, -meɪ.nəs

Macmillan məkˈmɪl.ən, mæk-

Macmorran məkˈmɒr.ən, mæk-, US -ˈmɔːr-

MacNab məkˈnæb

Macnamara ˌmæk.nəˈmɑː.rə, US ˈmæk.nə.mer.ə, -mær-

MacNaught məkˈnɔːt, US -ˈnɑːt, -ˈnɔːt

MacNeice məkˈniːs

Macon ˈmeɪ.kən

Mâcon ˈmɑː.kɔ̃ːŋ, ˈmæk.ɔ̃ːŋ, -ɒn, -ən, US mɑːˈkoʊn

Maconchy məˈkɒŋ.ki, US -ˈkɑːŋ-, -ˈkɔːŋ-

Maconochie məˈkɒn.ə.ki, -xi, US -ˈkɑː.nə-

MacPhee məkˈfiː

MacPherson, Macpherson məkˈfɜː.sən, mæk-, -ˈfɪə-, US -ˈfɝː-, -ˈfɪr-

Macquarie məˈkwɒr.i, US -ˈkwɑːr-, -ˈkwɔːr-

macrame, macramé məˈkrɑː.meɪ, -mi, US ˈmæk.rə.meɪ

Macready məˈkriː.di

macro ˈmæk.rəʊ, US -roʊ **-s** -z

macro- ˈmæk.rəʊ, US ˈmæk.roʊ, -rə

macrobiotic ˌmæk.rəʊ.baɪˈɒt.ɪk, US -roʊ.baɪˈɑː.t̬ɪk, -rə- **-s** -s

macroclimate ˈmæk.rəʊˌklaɪ.mɪt, -mət, US -roʊˌ-, -rəˌ- **-s** -s

macroclimatic ˌmæk.rəʊ.klaɪˈmæt.ɪk, US -roʊ.klaɪˈmæt̬-, -rə-

macrocosm ˈmæk.rəʊˌkɒz.əm, US -roʊˌkɑː.zəm, -rə- **-s** -z

macroeconomic ˌmæk.rəʊ.iː.kəˈnɒm.ɪk, -ek.əˈ-, US -roʊˌek.əˈnɑː.mɪk, -ˌiː.kəˈ- **-s** -s

macron ˈmæk.rɒn, US ˈmeɪ.krɑːn, ˈmæk.rɑːn, -rən **-s** -z

macrophag|e ˈmæk.rəʊ.feɪdʒ, US -roʊ-, -rə- **-es** -ɪz

macrophagic ˌmæk.rəʊˈfeɪ.dʒɪk, US -roʊˈfædʒ.ɪk, -rə-

macroscopic ˌmæk.rəʊˈskɒp.ɪk, US -roʊˈskɑː.pɪk, -rə- **-al** -əl

Macrow məˈkrəʊ, US -ˈkroʊ

MacSwiney məkˈswiː.ni, -ˈswɪn-

MacTavish məkˈtæv.ɪʃ

macul|a ˈmæk.jʊ.l|ə, -jə-, US -jə-, -juː- **-as** -əz **-ae** -iː

Macy ˈmeɪ.si **Macy's**® ˈmeɪ.siz

mad mæd **-der** -əʳ, US -ɚ **-dest** -ɪst, -əst **-ly** -li **-ness** -nəs, -nɪs **as ˌmad as a ˈhatter; ˌmad ˈcow diˌsease**

Madagasc|ar ˌmæd.əˈgæs.k|əʳ, US -k|ɚ, -k|ɑːr **-an/s** -ən/z

madam ˈmæd.əm **-s** -z

madame, M~ ˈmæd.əm, məˈdæm, -ˈdɑːm **-s** -z

Madan ˈmæd.ən, ˈmeɪ.dən

madcap ˈmæd.kæp **-s** -s

Maddalo ˈmæd.əl.əʊ, US -oʊ

madden, M~ ˈmæd.ən **-s** -z **-ing** -ɪŋ **-ed** -d

madder ˈmæd.əʳ, US -ɚ **-s** -z

Maddie ˈmæd.i

madding ˈmæd.ɪŋ

Maddison ˈmæd.ɪ.sən, ˈ-ə-

Maddox ˈmæd.əks

made (from **make**) meɪd

Madeira məˈdɪə.rə, US -ˈdɪr.ə **-s** -z **Maˈdeira ˌcake**

Madejski məˈdeɪ.ski, mædˈeɪ-

Madeleine ˈmæd.əl.ɪn, -eɪn

Madeley ˈmeɪd.li

Madeline ˈmæd.əl.ɪn, -eɪn

mademoiselle, M~ ˌmæd.ə.mwəˈzel, ˌmæm.*wə*ˈ-, ˌmæmˈzel, US ˌmæd.ə.məˈ-, ˌmæmˈ- **-s** -z

made-to-measure ˌmeɪd.təˈmeʒ.əʳ, US -ɚ *stress shift:* **ˌmade-to-measure ˈsuit**

made-to-order ˌmeɪd.tuˈɔː.dəʳ, US -ˈɔːr.dɚ *stress-shift:* **ˌmade-to-order ˈsuit**

Madge mædʒ

madhou|se ˈmæd.haʊ|s **-ses** -zɪz

Madhya Pradesh ˌmʌd.jə.prɑːˈdeʃ, ˌmɑːd-, US -ˈprɑː.deʃ

Madingley ˈmæd.ɪŋ.li

Madison ˈmæd.ɪ.sən, ˈ-ə- **ˌMadison ˈAvenue**

mad|man ˈmæd|.mən, US -mən, -mæn **-men** -mən, -men **-woman** -ˌwʊm.ən **-women** -ˌwɪm.ɪn

Madoc ˈmæd.ək

Madoff ˈmeɪ.dɒf, US -dɑːf

madonna, M~ məˈdɒn.ə, US -ˈdɑː.nə **-s** -z

madras *fabric:* ˈmæd.rəs, US ˈmæd.rəs, məˈdræs, -ˈdrɑːs

Madras *in India:* məˈdrɑːs, -dræs

madras(s)a(h) məˈdræs.ə, -ˈdrɑː.sə, US –ˈdræs.ə **-s** -z

madrepore ˌmæd.rɪˈpɔːʳ, -rəˈ-, ˈ---, US ˈmæd.rə.pɔːr **-s** -z

Madrid məˈdrɪd

madrigal ˈmæd.rɪ.gəl, -rə- **-s** -z

madrigalist ˈmæd.rɪ.gəl.ɪst, -rə- **-s** -s

Madura məˈdjʊə.rə, -ˈdʒʊə-, -ˈdʊə-, US mɑːˈdʊr.ə

madwort ˈmæd.wɜːt, US -wɝːt, -wɔːrt

Mae meɪ

Maecenas maɪˈsiː.næs, miːˈ-, -nəs, US miːˈ-, mɪ-

maelstrom, M~ ˈmeɪl.strɒm, -strəʊm, US -strəm **-s** -z

maenad ˈmiː.næd **-s** -z

Maerdy ˈmɑː.di, ˈmeə-, US ˈmɑːr-, ˈmer-

Maesteg ˌmaɪˈsteɪg

maestoso ˌmɑː.esˈtəʊ.zəʊ, maɪˈstəʊ-, -səʊ, US maɪˈstoʊ.zoʊ

maestr|o, M~® ˈmaɪ.str|əʊ, US -str|oʊ **-os** -əʊz, US -oʊz **-i** -i

Maeterlinck ˈmeɪ.tə.lɪŋk, US ˈmeɪ.tɚ-, ˈmet.ɚ-

Maev(e) meɪv

Mae West ˌmeɪˈwest **-s** -s

Mafeking ˈmæf.ɪ.kɪŋ, ˈ-ə-

MAFF, Maff mæf

maffick ˈmæf.ɪk **-s** -s **-ing** -ɪŋ **-ed** -t **-er/s** -əʳ/z, US -ɚ/z

mafia, M~ ˈmæf.i.ə, ˈmɑː.fi-, US ˈmɑː.fi-

Mafikeng ˈmæf.ɪ.keŋ, ˈ-ə-

mafios|o, M~ ˌmæf.iˈəʊ.s|əʊ, ˌmɑː.fiˈ-, -z|əʊ, US ˌmɑː.fiˈoʊ.s|oʊ **-os** -əʊz, US -oʊz **-i** -iː

mag, M~ mæg **-s** -z

magalog ˈmæg.ə.lɒg, US -lɑːg **-s** -z

Magan ˈmeɪ.gən, məˈgæn

magazine ˌmæg.əˈziːn, ˈ---, US ˈmæg.ə.ziːn, ˌ--ˈ- **-s** -z

> Note: The stressing /ˈ---/ is usual in the north of England, but uncommon in the south.

Magdala ˈmæg.dəl.ə, ˌmægˈdɑː.lə, US ˈmæg.dəl.ə

Magdalen *biblical name, modern first name, Canadian islands:* ˈmæg.dəl.ɪn, -ən, US -ən, -ɪn *Oxford college and bridge:* ˈmɔːd.lɪn, US ˈmɑːd-, ˈmɔːd- *Oxford street:* ˈmæg.dəl.ɪn, -ən, US -ən, -ɪn

Magdalene *biblical name:* ˈmæg.də.liːn; -ɪn, (US) ˈmæg.dəl.iːn, -ən, -ɪn; (US) ˌmæg.dəˈliː.nə *modern first name:* ˈmæg.dəl.iːn, -ɪn, (US) -iːn, -ən, -ɪn *Cambridge college and street:* ˈmɔːd.lɪn, (US) ˈmɑːd-, ˈmɔːd-
Magdalenian ˌmæg.dəlˈiː.ni.ən
Magdeburg ˈmæg.də.bɜːg, ˈ-dɪ-, (US) ˈmæg.də.bɝːg, ˈmɑːg.də.bʊrg
mag|e meɪdʒ **-es** -ɪz
Magee məˈgiː
Magellan məˈgel.ən, (US) -ˈdʒel-
magenta, M~ məˈdʒen.tə, (US) -t̬ə
Maggie ˈmæg.i
Maggiore ˌmædʒˈɔː.reɪ, -ri; ˌ-iˈ-, məˈdʒɔː-, (US) məˈdʒɔːr.i
magg|ot ˈmæg|.ət **-ots** -əts **-oty** -ə.ti, (US) -ə.t̬i
Maghera ˌmæk.əˈrɑː, ˌmæ.həˈ-
Magherafelt ˌmæk.ər.əˈfelt, ˌmæ.hər-
Maghreb, Maghrib ˈmɑː.greb, ˈmʌg.reb, ˈmæg.reb, -rɪb, -rəb; məˈgreb, mɑː-, (US) ˈmʌg.rəb
Maghull məˈgʌl
Magi (plural of **Magus**) ˈmeɪ.dʒaɪ, -gaɪ, (US) -dʒaɪ
magic ˈmædʒ.ɪk **-al** -əl **-ally** -əl.i, -li ˌ**magic** ˈ**carpet**; ˌ**magic** ˈ**eye**; ˌ**magic** ˈ**lantern**; ˌ**magic** ˈ**mushroom**; ˌ**magic** ˈ**wand**
magician məˈdʒɪʃ.ən **-s** -z
Maginot ˈmæʒ.ɪ.nəʊ, ˈmædʒ-, ˈ-ə-, (US) -ə.noʊ ˈ**Maginot** ˌ**Line**
magisterial ˌmædʒ.ɪˈstɪə.ri.əl, -əˈ-, (US) -ɪˈstɪr.i- **-ly** -i
magistrac|y ˈmædʒ.ɪ.strə.s|i, ˈ-ə-, (US) ˈ-ɪ- **-ies** -iz
magistral məˈdʒɪs.trəl, mædʒˈɪs-; ˈmædʒ.ɪ.strəl, ˈ-ə-, (US) ˈmædʒ.ɪ.strəl
magistrate ˈmædʒ.ɪ.streɪt, ˈ-ə-, -strɪt, -strət, (US) -ɪ.streɪt, -strɪt **-s** -s
magistrature ˈmædʒ.ɪ.strə.tʃər, ˈ-ə-, -ˌtʃʊər, -ˌtjʊər, (US) -ɪ.streɪ.tʃɚ, -strə.tʃʊr **-s** -z
magma ˈmæg.mə
magmatic mægˈmæt.ɪk, (US) -ˈmæt̬-
Magna Carta ˌmæg.nəˈkɑː.tə, (US) -ˈkɑːr.t̬ə
magna cum laude ˌmæg.nɑː.kʊmˈlaʊ.deɪ
magnanimity ˌmæg.nəˈnɪm.ə.ti, -nænˈɪm-, -ɪ.ti, (US) -nəˈnɪm.ə.t̬i
magnanimous mægˈnæn.ɪ.məs, məg-, (US) mægˈnæn.ə- **-ly** -li
magnate ˈmæg.neɪt, -nɪt **-s** -s
magnesia *substance:* mægˈniː.zi.ə, məg-, ˈ-si.ə, -ʒi.ə, -ʒə, (US) mægˈniː.ʒə, -ʃə
Magnesia *city:* mægˈniː.zi.ə, -ʒi.ə, -ʒə, (US) -zi.ə, -ʒi.ə, -ʒə, -ʃə
magnesium mægˈniː.zi.əm, məg-, -si-, -ʒi-, (US) mægˈniː.zi-, -ʒi-, ˈ-ʒəm
magnet ˈmæg.nət, -nɪt **-s** -s
magnetic mægˈnet.ɪk, məg-, (US) mægˈnet̬- **-al** -əl **-ally** -əl.i, -li **mag**ˌ**netic** ˈ**field**; **mag**ˌ**netic** ˈ**north**; **mag**ˌ**netic** ˈ**storm**; **mag**ˌ**netic** ˈ**tape**
magnetism ˈmæg.nə.tɪ.zəm, -nɪ-, (US) -t̬ɪ-
magnetiz|e, -is|e ˈmæg.nə.taɪz, -nɪ- **-es** -ɪz **-ing** -ɪŋ **-ed** -d **-er/s** -ər/z, (US) -ɚ/z
magneto mægˈniː.təʊ, məg-, (US) mægˈniː.t̬oʊ **-s** -z
magnetron ˈmæg.nə.trɒn, -nɪ-, (US) -trɑːn **-s** -z
Magnificat mægˈnɪf.ɪ.kæt, məg-, ˈ-ə-, (US) mægˈnɪf-; (US) mɑːˈnjɪ.fɪ.kɑːt **-s** -s
magnification ˌmæg.nɪ.fɪˈkeɪ.ʃən, -nə-, -fəˈ- **-s** -z
magnificence mægˈnɪf.ɪ.sənts, məg-, ˈ-ə-, (US) mæg-
magnificent mægˈnɪf.ɪ.sənt, məg-, ˈ-ə-, (US) mæg- **-ly** -li
magnifico mægˈnɪf.ɪ.kəʊ, ˈ-ə-, (US) -koʊ **-(e)s** -z
magni|fy ˈmæg.nɪ|.faɪ, -nə- **-fies** -faɪz **-fying** -faɪ.ɪŋ **-fied** -faɪd **-fier/s** -faɪ.ər/z, (US) -faɪ.ɚ/z **-fiable** -faɪ.ə.bəl ˈ**magnifying** ˌ**glass**
magniloquen|ce mægˈnɪl.ə.kwən|ts **-t** -t
magnitude ˈmæg.nɪ.tʃuːd, -nə-, -tjuːd, (US) -tuːd, -tjuːd **-s** -z
magnolia mægˈnəʊ.li.ə, məg-, (US) mægˈnoʊl.jə, -ˈnoʊ.li.ə **-s** -z
Magnox ˈmæg.nɒks, (US) -nɑːks
magnum ˈmæg.nəm **-s** -z
magnum bonum ˌmæg.nəmˈbəʊ.nəm, -ˈbɒn.əm, (US) -ˈboʊ.nəm **-s** -z
magnum opus ˌmæg.nəmˈəʊ.pəs, -ˈɒp.əs, (US) -ˈoʊ.pəs
Magnus ˈmæg.nəs
Magnyficence mægˈnɪf.ɪ.sənts, ˈ-ə-
Magog ˈmeɪ.gɒg, (US) -gɑːg, -gɔːg
magpie ˈmæg.paɪ **-s** -z
Magrath məˈgrɑː, -ˈgrɑːθ, -ˈgræθ, (US) -ˈgræθ
Magritte mægˈriːt, məˈgriːt, (US) mɑːˈgriːt
Magruder məˈgruː.dər, (US) -dɚ
Maguiness məˈgɪn.ɪs, -əs
Maguire məˈgwaɪ.ər, (US) -ˈgwaɪ.ɚ
ma|gus, M~ ˈmeɪ|.gəs **-gi** -dʒaɪ, -gaɪ, (US) -dʒaɪ
Magwitch ˈmæg.wɪtʃ
Magyar ˈmæg.jɑːr, (US) -jɑːr **-s** -z
Mahabharata məˌhɑːˈbɑː.rə.tə, ˌmɑː.həˈ-, (US) məˌhɑːˈbɑːr.ə-, ˌmɑː-, -ˈrɑː.tɑː
Mahaffy məˈhæf.i
Mahan məˈhæn; mɑːn, (US) məˈhæn
Mahany ˈmɑː.ni
maharaja(h) ˌmɑː.*h*əˈrɑː.dʒə, (US) -həˈ- **-s** -z
maharani, maharanee ˌmɑː.*h*əˈrɑː.ni, (US) -həˈ- **-s** -z
Maharashtra ˌmɑː.*h*əˈræʃ.trə, -ˈrɑːʃ-, (US) -hɑːˈrɑːʃ-
maharishi, M~ ˌmɑː.*h*əˈriː.ʃi, (US) -həˈ- **-s** -z
mahatma, M~ məˈhɑːt.mə, -ˈhæt- **-s** -z
Mahayana məˌhɑːˈjɑː.nə, ˌmɑː.həˈ-, (US) ˌmɑː.həˈ-
Mahdi ˈmɑː.diː, -di **-s** -z
Mahé ˈmɑː.*h*eɪ, (US) mɑːˈheɪ
mah-jong(g) ˌmɑːˈdʒɒŋ, (US) -ˈdʒɔːŋ, -ˈdʒɑːŋ, -ˈʒɔːŋ, -ˈʒɑːŋ
Mahler ˈmɑː.lər, (US) -lɚ
mahlstick ˈmɔːl.stɪk, (US) ˈmɑːl-, ˈmɔːl- **-s** -s
Mahmud mɑːˈmuːd
mahogany məˈhɒg.ən.i, (US) -ˈhɑː.gən-
Mahomet, Mahomed məˈhɒm.ɪt, -et, (US) məˈhɑː.mɪt
Mahometan məˈhɒm.ɪ.tən, ˈ-ə-, (US) -ˈhɑː.mə.t̬ən **-s** -z
Mahommed məˈhɒm.ɪd, -ed, (US) -ˈhɑː.mɪd
Mahommedan məˈhɒm.ɪ.dən, (US) -ˈhɑː.mə- **-s** -z
Mahon *family name:* mɑːn; ˈmæ.hən; məˈhuːn, -ˈhəʊn, (US) mæn; (US) məˈhoʊn, -ˈhuːn *Spanish place name:* mɑːˈɒn, (US) mɑːˈoʊn
mahonia məˈhəʊ.ni.ə, mɑː-, (US) məˈhoʊ- **-s** -z
Mahon(e)y ˈmɑː.ə.nɪ, ˈmɑː.ni, məˈhəʊ.ni, (US) məˈhoʊ.ni
mahout məˈhaʊt, mɑː-, -ˈhuːt, (US) məˈhoʊt **-s** -s
Mahratta məˈræt.ə, (US) -ˈrɑː.t̬ə **-s** -z
Maia ˈmaɪ.ə, ˈmeɪ-
maid meɪd **-s** -z
Maida ˈmeɪ.də
maidan, M~ maɪˈdɑːn, mædˈɑːn **-s** -z
maiden ˈmeɪ.dən **-s** -z **-ly** -li ˌ**maiden** ˈ**name**
maidenhair ˈmeɪ.dən.heər, (US) -her **-s** -z
maidenhead, M~ ˈmeɪ.dən.hed
maidenhood ˈmeɪ.dən.hʊd
Maidens ˈmeɪ.dənz
maid-servant ˈmeɪdˌsɜː.vənt, (US) -ˌsɝː- **-s** -s
Maidstone ˈmeɪd.stən, -stəʊn, (US) -stoʊn, -stən
maieutic meɪˈuː.tɪk, maɪ-, (US) -ˈjuː.t̬ɪk
Maigret ˈmeɪ.greɪ, (US) ˌ-ˈ-
mail meɪl **-s** -z **-ing** -ɪŋ **-ed** -d **-er/s** -ər/z, (US) -ɚ/z ˈ**mail** ˌ**drop**; ˈ**mailing** ˌ**list**
mailbag ˈmeɪl.bæg **-s** -z
mailbox ˈmeɪl.bɒks, (US) -bɑːks **-es** -ɪz
Mailer ˈmeɪ.lər, (US) -lɚ
Mailgram® ˈmeɪl.græm
Maillard ˈmeɪ.ləd, (US) -lɚd
mail|man ˈmeɪl|.mæn **-men** -men, -mən
mail-order ˌmeɪlˈɔː.dər, (US) ˈmeɪlˌɔːr.dɚ *stress shift, British English:* ˌ**mail-order** ˈ**catalogue**
mailroom ˈmeɪl.rʊm, -ruːm, (US) -ruːm, -rʊm **-s** -z
mailshot ˈmeɪl.ʃɒt, (US) -ʃɑːt **-s** -s
maim meɪm **-s** -z **-ing** -ɪŋ **-ed** -d
main meɪn **-s** -z ˌ**main** ˈ**drag**; ˌ**main** ˈ**line**; ˈ**Main** ˌ**Street**
Main *German river:* maɪn, meɪn
mainbrac|e ˈmeɪn.breɪs, ˈmeɪm-, (US) ˈmeɪn- **-es** -ɪz
Maine meɪn
mainframe ˈmeɪn.freɪm **-s** -z

M

mainland ˈmeɪn.lənd, -lænd
Mainland ˈmeɪn.lænd
mainlin|e ˈmeɪn.laɪn, ˌ-ˈ-, (US) ˈ-- **-es** -z **-ing** -ɪŋ **-ed** -d **-er/s** -əʳ/z, (US) -ɚ/z
mainly ˈmeɪn.li
mainmast ˈmeɪn.mɑːst, ˈmeɪm-, (US) ˈmeɪn.mæst; *nautical pronunciation:* -məst **-s** -s
mainsail ˈmeɪn.seɪl; *nautical pronunciation:* -sᵊl **-s** -z
mainspring ˈmeɪn.sprɪŋ **-s** -z
mainstay ˈmeɪn.steɪ **-s** -z
mainstream ˈmeɪn.striːm, ˌ-ˈ-, (US) ˈ--
mainstreaming ˈmeɪnˌstriː.mɪŋ
maintain meɪnˈteɪn, mən-, men-, (US) meɪn- **-s** -z **-ing** -ɪŋ **-ed** -d **-able** -ə.bᵊl **-er/s** -əʳ/z, (US) -ɚ/z
maintenance ˈmeɪn.tᵊn.ənts, -tɪ.nənts, (US) -tᵊn.ənts
Mainwaring *surname:* ˈmæn.ᵊr.ɪŋ *in Wales:* ˈmeɪn.wə.rɪŋ, -weə-; ˌmeɪnˈweə-, (US) ˈmeɪn.wɚ.ɪŋ, -wer-; (US) ˌmeɪnˈwer-
Mainz maɪnts
Maisie ˈmeɪ.zi
maisonette ˌmeɪ.zᵊnˈet, -sᵊnˈ- **-s** -s
Maitland ˈmeɪt.lənd
maître d', maitre d' ˌmeɪ.trəˈdiː, ˌmet.rəˈ-, (US) ˌmeɪ.trəˈ-, -t̬ɚˈ- **-s** -z
maître(s) d'hôtel ˌmeɪ.trə.dəʊˈtel, ˌmet.rə-, (US) ˌmeɪ.trə.doʊˈ-, -t̬ɚ-
maize meɪz
majestic, M~ məˈdʒes.tɪk **-al** -ᵊl **-ally** -ᵊl.i, -li
majest|y, M~ ˈmædʒ.ə.st|i, ˈ-ɪ- **-ies** -iz
majolica məˈjɒl.ɪ.kə, -ˈdʒɒl-, (US) -ˈdʒɑː.lɪ-
maj|or, M~ ˈmeɪ.dʒ|əʳ, (US) -dʒ|ɚ **-ors** -əz, (US) -ɚz **-oring** -ᵊr.ɪŋ **-ored** -əd, (US) -ɚd
Majorca məˈjɔː.kə, maɪˈɔː-, (US) mɑːˈjɔːr-, mə-
majordomo ˌmeɪ.dʒəˈdəʊ.məʊ, (US) -dʒɚˈdoʊ.moʊ **-s** -z
majorette ˌmeɪ.dʒᵊrˈet **-s** -s
major-general ˌmeɪ.dʒəˈdʒen.ᵊr.ᵊl, ˈ-rᵊl, (US) -dʒɚˈ- **-s** -z
majorit|y məˈdʒɒr.ə.t|i, -ɪ.t|i, (US) -ˈdʒɔːr.ə.t̬|i **-ies** -iz
major-league ˌmeɪ.dʒəˈliːg, (US) ˌmeɪ.dzɚˈliːg *stress shift:* ˌ**major-league** ˈ**player**
majuscule ˈmædʒ.ə.skjuːl, (US) məˈdʒʌs.kjuːl; (US) ˈmædʒ.ə.skjuːl **-s** -z
Makarios məˈkɑː.ri.ɒs, -ˈkær.i-, (US) məˈkɑːr.i.oʊs, -ˈkær.i-, -ɑːs, -əs
mak|e meɪk **-es** -s **-ing** -ɪŋ **made** meɪd **maker/s** ˈmeɪ.kəʳ/z, (US) -kɚ/z
Makeba məˈkeɪ.bə
make-believe ˈmeɪk.bɪˌliːv, -bəˌ-, ˌ--ˈ-
Makeham ˈmeɪ.kəm
make-or-break ˌmeɪk.ɔːˈbreɪk, (US) -ɔːrˈ-, -ɚˈ- *stress shift:* ˌ**make-or-break** ˈ**deal**
makeover ˈmeɪkˌəʊ.vəʳ, (US) -ˌoʊ.vɚ **-s** -z
Makepeace ˈmeɪk.piːs
Makerere məˈker.ᵊr.i
makeshift ˈmeɪk.ʃɪft
make-up ˈmeɪk.ʌp **-s** -s
makeweight ˈmeɪk.weɪt **-s** -s
makings ˈmeɪ.kɪŋz
Makins ˈmeɪ.kɪnz
Makower məˈkaʊ.əʳ, (US) -ˈkaʊ.ɚ
makuta (plural of **likuta**) mɑːˈkuː.tɑː
mal- mæl
Note: Prefix. In verbs or adjectives, **mal-** usually carries secondary stress, e.g. **malfunction** /ˌmælˈfʌnk.ʃᵊn/, **maladjusted** /ˌmæl.əˈdʒʌs.tɪd/. Nouns containing **mal-** normally carry stress on the first syllable, e.g. **malcontent** /ˈmæl.kən.tent/. Exceptions exist; see individual entries.
Malabar ˈmæl.ə.bɑːʳ, ˌ--ˈ-, (US) ˈmæl.ə.bɑːr
Malabo məˈlɑː.bəʊ, (US) -boʊ; (US) ˈmæl.ə-
malabsorption ˌmæl.əbˈzɔːp.ʃᵊn, -ˈsɔːp-, (US) -ˈzɔːrp-, -ˈsɔːrp-
Malacca məˈlæk.ə, (US) -ˈlæk-, -ˈlɑː.kə
Malachi ˈmæl.ə.kaɪ
malachite ˈmæl.ə.kaɪt
maladjusted ˌmæl.əˈdʒʌs.tɪd *stress shift:* ˌ**maladjusted** ˈ**person**
maladjustment ˌmæl.əˈdʒʌst.mənt **-s** -s
maladministration ˌmæl.ədˌmɪn.ɪˈstreɪ.ʃᵊn, (US) -əˈ-
maladroit ˌmæl.əˈdrɔɪt, ˈ--- **-ly** -li **-ness** -nəs, -nɪs *stress shift:* ˌ**maladroit** ˈ**tactics**
malad|y ˈmæl.ə.d|i **-ies** -iz
mala fide ˌmeɪ.ləˈfaɪ.di, ˌmæl.əˈfɪd.i, -eɪ, (US) ˌmeɪ.ləˈfiː.di, ˌmæl.əˈfiː.deɪ
Malaga, Málaga ˈmæl.ə.gə, (US) ˈmæl.ə.gə, ˈmɑː.lɑː.gɑː
Malagasy ˌmæl.əˈgæs.i, -ˈgɑː.zi, (US) -ˈgæs.i
Malahide ˈmæl.ə.haɪd
malaise məˈleɪz, mælˈeɪz
Malamud ˈmæl.ə.mʊd, (US) -məd, -mʊd
Malan *English surname:* ˈmæl.ən *South African name:* məˈlæn, -ˈlɑːn
malaprop, M~ ˈmæl.ə.prɒp, (US) -prɑːp **-s** -s
malapropism ˈmæl.ə.prɒp.ɪ.zᵊm, (US) -prɑː.pɪ- **-s** -z
malapropos ˌmælˌæp.rəˈpəʊ, ˌ-ˈ---, (US) ˌmæl.æp.rəˈpoʊ
malari|a məˈleə.ri|.ə, (US) -ˈler.i- **-al** -əl **-an** -ən
malark(e)y məˈlɑː.ki, (US) -ˈlɑːr-
Malawi məˈlɑː.wi, (US) mɑː-, mə- **-an/s** -ən/z
Malay məˈleɪ, (US) ˈmeɪ.leɪ, məˈleɪ **-s** -z
Malay|a məˈleɪ|.ə **-an/s** -ən/z
Malayalam ˌmæl.iˈɑː.ləm, -eɪˈ-; -əˈjɑː-, (US) ˌmæl.əˈjɑː.ləm
Malaysi|a məˈleɪ.zi|.ə, -ʒi-, ˈ-ʒ|ə, (US) -ʒ|ə, -ʃ|ə **-an/s** -ən/z
Malchus ˈmæl.kəs
Malcolm ˈmæl.kəm
malcontent ˈmæl.kənˌtent **-s** -s
Malden ˈmɔːl.dᵊn, ˈmɒl-, (US) ˈmɔːl-, ˈmɑːl-
Maldive ˈmɔːl.diːv, ˈmɒl-, -dɪv, -daɪv, (US) ˈmɔːl.diːv, ˈmɑːl-, ˈmæl-, -daɪv **-s** -z
Maldivian mɔːlˈdɪv.i.ən, mɒl-, mɑːl-, (US) mɔːlˈdɪv.i.ən, mæl-, mɑːl- **-s** -z
Maldon ˈmɔːl.dᵊn, ˈmɒl-, (US) ˈmɔːl-, ˈmɑːl-
male meɪl **-s** -z **-ness** -nəs, -nɪs ˌ**male** ˈ**chauvinist**; ˌ**male** ˌ**chauvinist** ˈ**pig**
Malé ˈmɑː.liː, -leɪ, (US) -liː
malediction ˌmæl.ɪˈdɪk.ʃᵊn, -əˈ-, (US) -əˈ- **-s** -z
maledictory ˌmæl.ɪˈdɪk.tᵊr.i, -əˈ-, (US) -əˈ-
malefaction ˌmæl.ɪˈfæk.ʃᵊn, -əˈ-, (US) -əˈ- **-s** -z
malefactor ˈmæl.ɪ.fæk.təʳ, ˈ-ə-, (US) -ə.fæk.tɚ **-s** -z
malefic məˈlef.ɪk
maleficen|ce məˈlef.ɪ.sᵊn|ts, mælˈef-, (US) məˈlef.ə- **-t** -t
Malet ˈmæl.ɪt
malevolence məˈlev.ᵊl.ənts, mælˈev-, (US) məˈlev-
malevolent məˈlev.ᵊl.ənt, mælˈev-, (US) məˈlev- **-ly** -li
malfeasance mælˈfiː.zᵊnts
Malfi ˈmæl.fi
malformation ˌmæl.fɔːˈmeɪ.ʃᵊn, -fəˈ-, (US) -fɔːrˈ- **-s** -z
malformed ˌmælˈfɔːmd, (US) -ˈfɔːrmd
malfunction ˌmælˈfʌŋk.ʃᵊn **-s** -z **-ing** -ɪŋ **-ed** -d
Malham ˈmæl.əm
Mali ˈmɑː.li
Malibu ˈmæl.ɪ.buː, ˈ-ə-
malic ˈmæl.ɪk, ˈmeɪ-
malice ˈmæl.ɪs
malicious məˈlɪʃ.əs **-ly** -li **-ness** -nəs, -nɪs
Malick ˈmæl.ɪk
malign məˈlaɪn **-ly** -li **-s** -z **-ing** -ɪŋ **-ed** -d **-er/s** -əʳ/z, (US) -ɚ/z
malignancy məˈlɪg.nənt.si
malignant məˈlɪg.nənt **-ly** -li
malignity məˈlɪg.nə.ti, -nɪ-, (US) -nə.t̬i
Malik ˈmæl.ɪk
Malin ˈmæl.ɪn, ˈmeɪ.lɪn
Malines mælˈiːn
maling|er məˈlɪŋ.g|əʳ, (US) -g|ɚ **-ers** -əz, (US) -ɚz **-ering** -ᵊr.ɪŋ **-ered** -əd, (US) -ɚd **-erer/s** -ᵊr.əʳ/z, (US) -ɚ.ɚ/z
Malins ˈmeɪ.lɪnz, ˈmæl.ɪnz
malkin ˈmɔː.kɪn, ˈmɔːl-, ˈmɒl-, (US) ˈmɔː-, ˈmɔːl- **-s** -z
Malkin ˈmæl.kɪn
Malkovich ˈmæl.kə.vɪtʃ

mall mɔːl, mæl, (US) mɔːl, mɑːl **-s** -z
Note: The pronunciation /mɔːl/ for 'mall' meaning 'shopping arcade' appears to have come into British English from American, despite some resistance from those who prefer /mæl/. The 'Oxford English Dictionary' cites a 17th-century verse couplet in which 'mall' rhymes with 'ball'.
Mall (in **The Mall, Chiswick Mall, Pall Mall**) mæl
mallard, M~ ˈmæl.ɑːd, -ləd, (US) -ɚd **-s** -z
Mallarmé ˈmæl.ɑː.meɪ, (US) ˌmæl.ɑːrˈmeɪ
Malle mæl, mɑːl, (US) mɑːl
malleability ˌmæl.i.əˈbɪl.ə.ti, ˌmæl.əˈbɪl-, -ɪ.ti, (US) ˌmæl.i.əˈbɪl.ə.ţi
malleable ˈmæl.i.ə.bəl, ˈ-ə.bəl, (US) ˈ-i.ə- **-ness** -nəs, -nɪs
mallee ˈmæl.i
malleolar məˈliː.ə.ləʳ, (US) -lɚ
malleo|lus məˈliː.ə|.ləs **-li** -laɪ
mallet, M~ ˈmæl.ɪt, -ət **-s** -s
Mallett ˈmæl.ɪt, -ət
malle|us ˈmæl.i|.əs **-i** -aɪ
Malling ˈmɔː.lɪŋ, (US) ˈmɔː-, ˈmɑː-
Mallon ˈmæl.ən
Mallorca məˈjɔː.kə, maɪˈɔː-, (US) mɑːˈjɔːr.kə, mə-
Mallory ˈmæl.ər.i
mallow, M~ ˈmæl.əʊ, (US) -oʊ **-s** -z
Malmaison ˌmælˈmeɪ.zɔ̃ːŋ, -zɒn, ˌ--ˈ-, (US) -ˈzɑːn, -ˈzɔ̃ːn **-s** -z
Malmesbury ˈmɑːmz.bər.i, (US) -ber-, -bɚ-
Malmö ˈmæl.məʊ, -mɜː, (US) -moʊ
malmsey, M~ ˈmɑːm.zi
malnourished ˌmælˈnʌr.ɪʃt, (US) -ˈnɜː-
malnutrition ˌmæl.njuːˈtrɪ.ʃən, (US) -nuːˈ-
malodor ˌmælˈəʊ.dəʳ, (US) -ˈoʊ.dɚ **-s** -z
malodorous ˌmælˈəʊ.dər.əs, (US) -ˈoʊ- **-ly** -li **-ness** -nəs, -nɪs
Malone məˈləʊn, (US) -ˈloʊn
Maloney məˈləʊ.ni, (US) -ˈloʊ-
Malory ˈmæl.ər.i
Malpas *near Truro:* ˈməʊ.pəs, (US) ˈmoʊ- *in Gwent:* ˈmæl.pəs *in Cheshire:* ˈmɔːl.pəs, ˈmɔː-, ˈmæl-
Malpighi mælˈpiː.gi, (US) mɑːl-, mæl-
Malpighian mælˈpɪg.i.ən, -ˈpiː.gi-, (US) mɑːlˈpɪg.i-, mæl- **Malˌpighian ˈlayer**
Malplaquet ˈmæl.plə.keɪ, ˌ--ˈ-, (US) ˌmæl.plækˈeɪ, -pləˈkeɪ
malpractic|e ˌmælˈpræk.tɪs **-es** -ɪz
Malraux ˈmæl.rəʊ, (US) ˈmæl.roʊ, mɑːlˈroʊ
mal|t mɔːl|t, mɒl|t, (US) mɔːl|t, mɑːl|t **-ts** -ts **-ting** -tɪŋ, (US) -tɪŋ **-ted** -tɪd, (US) -tɪd **ˌmalted ˈmilk**
Malta ˈmɔːl.tə, ˈmɒl-, (US) ˈmɔːl.tə, ˈmɑːl-
maltase ˈmɔːl.teɪz, ˈmɒl-, (US) ˈmɔːl.teɪs, ˈmɑːl-
Maltby ˈmɔːlt.bi, ˈmɒlt-, (US) ˈmɔːlt-, ˈmɑːlt-
Maltese ˌmɔːlˈtiːz, ˌmɒl-, (US) ˌmɔːlˈtiːz, ˌmɑːl-, -ˈtiːs *stress shift, see compounds:* **ˌMaltese ˈcross; ˌMaltese ˈfalcon**
Maltesers® mɔːlˈtiː.zəz, mɒl-, (US) mɔːlˈtiː.zɚz, mɑːl-
Malthus ˈmæl.θəs
Malthusian mælˈθjuː.zi.ən, mɔːl-, mɒl-, -ˈθuː-, (US) mælˈθuː.ʒən, -zi.ən **-s** -z **-ism** -ɪ.zəm
maltings ˈmɔːl.tɪŋz, ˈmɒl-, (US) ˈmɔːl.tɪŋz, ˈmɑːl-
Malton ˈmɔːl.tən, ˈmɒl-, (US) ˈmɔːl-, ˈmɑːl-
maltose ˈmɔːl.təʊz, ˈmɒl-, (US) ˈmɔːl.toʊz, ˈmɑːl-, -toʊs
Maltravers mælˈtræv.əz, (US) -ɚz
mal|treat ˌmæl|ˈtriːt **-treats** -ˈtriːts **-treating** -ˈtriː.tɪŋ, (US) -ˈtriː.ţɪŋ **-treated** -ˈtriː.tɪd, (US) -ˈtriː.ţɪd **-treatment** -ˈtriːt.mənt **-treater/s** -ˈtriː.təʳ/z, (US) -ˈtriː.ţɚ/z
maltster ˈmɔːlt.stəʳ, ˈmɒlt-, (US) ˈmɔːlt.stɚ, ˈmɑːlt- **-s** -z
Maltz mɔːlts, mɒlts, (US) mɔːlts, mɑːlts
malum in se ˌmɑː.lʊm.ɪnˈseɪ, (US) ˌmɑː.ləm.ɪnˈseɪ
malum prohibitum ˌmɑː.lʊm.prəʊˈhɪb.ɪ.tʊm, (US) ˌmɑː.ləm.proʊˈhɪb.ɪ.təm
Malvasia ˌmæl.vəˈsiː.ə
Malvern *in UK:* ˈmɔːl.vən, ˈmɒl-, -vɜːn; *locally also:* ˈmɔː.vən, (US) ˈmɔːl.vɚn *in US:* ˈmæl.vən, (US) -vɚn
malversation ˌmæl.vɜːˈseɪ.ʃən, -vəˈ-, (US) -vɚˈ-
Malvinas mælˈviː.nəs
Malvolio mælˈvəʊ.li.əʊ, (US) -ˈvoʊ.li.oʊ, -ˈvoʊl.joʊ
Malyon ˈmæl.jən
mam mæm **-s** -z
mama məˈmɑː; ˈmæm.ə, (US) ˈmɑː.mə; (US) məˈmɑː **-s** -z
mamba ˈmæm.bə, (US) ˈmɑːm- **-s** -z
mambo ˈmæm.bəʊ, (US) ˈmɑːm.boʊ **-es** -z **-ing** -ɪŋ **-ed** -d
Mameluke ˈmæm.ɪ.luːk, ˈ-ə-, -ljuːk, (US) -ə.luːk **-s** -s
Mamet ˈmæm.ɪt, (US) -ət
Mamie ˈmeɪ.mi
Mamilius məˈmɪl.i.əs, mæmˈɪl-
mamma *mother:* məˈmɑː, (US) ˈmɑː.mə, məˈmɑː **-s** -z *milk-secreting organ:* ˈmæm|.ə **-ae** -iː
mammal ˈmæm.əl **-s** -z
mammalian mæmˈeɪ.li.ən, məˈmeɪ-
mammary ˈmæm.ər.i **ˈmammary ˌgland**
mammogram ˈmæm.ə.græm **-s** -z
mammograph ˈmæm.əʊ.grɑːf, -græf, (US) -oʊ.græf, -ə-, -oʊ- **-s** -s
mammography mæmˈɒg.rə.fi, məˈmɒg-, (US) məˈmɑː.grə-, mæmˈɑːg-
mammon, M~ ˈmæm.ən
mammoth ˈmæm.əθ **-s** -s
mamm|y ˈmæm|.i **-ies** -iz
man, M~ n mæn **men** men **ˌman ˈFriday; ˌman of the ˈworld**
man v mæn **-s** -z **-ning** -ɪŋ **-ned** -d
man-about-town ˌmæn.ə.baʊtˈtaʊn
manacl|e ˈmæn.ə.kəl **-es** -z **-ing** -ɪŋ, ˈmæn.ə.klɪŋ **-ed** -d
manag|e ˈmæn.ɪdʒ, -ədʒ **-es** -ɪz **-ing** -ɪŋ **-ed** -d **ˌmanaging diˈrector**
manageability ˌmæn.ɪ.dʒəˈbɪl.ə.ti, ˌ-ə-, -ɪ.ti, (US) -ə.ţi
manageab|le ˈmæn.ɪ.dʒə.b|əl, ˈ-ə- **-ly** -li **-leness** -əl.nəs, -nɪs
management ˈmæn.ɪdʒ.mənt, -ədʒ- **-s** -s
manager ˈmæn.ɪ.dʒəʳ, ˈ-ə-, (US) -dʒɚ **-s** -z
manageress ˌmæn.ɪ.dʒərˈes, ˌ-ə-; ˈmæn.ɪ.dʒər.es, ˈ-ə- **-es** -ɪz
managerial ˌmæn.əˈdʒɪə.ri.əl, (US) -ˈdʒɪr.i- **-ly** -i
Managua məˈnæg.wə, mænˈæg-, -ˈɑː.gwə, (US) məˈnɑː.gwɑː, mɑː-, -gwə
Manama məˈnɑː.mə, (US) -ˈnæm.ə
mañana mænˈjɑː.nə, məˈnjɑː-, (US) məˈnjɑː-, mɑː-
Manassas məˈnæs.əs
Manasseh məˈnæs.i, -ə, (US) -ə
Manasses məˈnæs.ɪz, -iːz
manatee, M~ ˌmæn.əˈtiː, (US) ˈmæn.ə.ti, ˌmæn.əˈtiː **-s** -z
Manáus məˈnaʊs, (US) mə-, mɑː-
Manchester ˈmæn.tʃɪs.təʳ, -tʃes-, -tʃəs-, (US) -tʃes.tɚ, -tʃɪ.stɚ
Manchu ˌmænˈtʃuː **-s** -z *stress shift:* **ˌManchu ˈdynasty**
Manchukuo ˌmænˌtʃuːˈkwəʊ, (US) -ˈkwoʊ
Manchuri|a mænˈtʃʊə.ri|.ə, -ˈtʃɔː-, (US) -ˈtʃʊr.i- **-an/s** -ən/z
Mancini mænˈsiː.ni
manciple ˈmænt.sɪ.pəl, -sə- **-s** -z
Mancunian mæŋˈkjuː.ni.ən, mæn-, (US) mæn- **-s** -z
mandala ˈmæn.dəl.ə; mənˈdɑː.lə, (US) ˈmæn.dəl.ə **-s** -z
Mandalay ˌmæn.dəlˈeɪ, ˈ---
mandamus mænˈdeɪ.məs **-es** -ɪz
mandarin, M~ ˈmæn.dər.ɪn, ˌ--ˈ-, (US) ˈmæn.dɚ.ɪn **-s** -z
mandate n ˈmæn.deɪt, -dɪt, -dət, (US) -deɪt **-s** -s
manda|te v mænˈdeɪ|t, ˈ--, (US) ˈ-- **-tes** -ts **-ting** -tɪŋ, (US) -ţɪŋ **-ted** -tɪd, (US) -ţɪd **-tor/s** -təʳ/z, (US) -ţɚ/z
mandator|y ˈmæn.də.tər|.i, -tr|i; mænˈdeɪ-, (US) ˈmæn.də.tɔːr|.i **-ies** -iz
Mandela mænˈdel.ə, -ˈdeɪ.lə, (US) -ˈdel.ə
Mandelson ˈmæn.dəl.sən, (US) -sən, -soʊn
Mandelstam ˈmæn.dəl.stæm, -stəm
Mander ˈmɑːn.dəʳ, ˈmæn-, (US) -dɚ
Mandeville ˈmæn.də.vɪl, -dɪ-
mandible ˈmæn.dɪ.bəl, -də- **-s** -z
Mandingo mænˈdɪŋ.gəʊ, (US) -goʊ **-(e)s** -z

M

mandolin ˌmæn.dəlˈɪn, ˈ--- -s -z
mandoline ˌmæn.dəlˈiːn -s -z
mandragora mænˈdræg.ər.ə, mən-, (US) mæn-
mandrake ˈmæn.dreɪk -s -s
mandrax, M~® ˈmæn.dræks -es -ɪz
mandrill ˈmæn.drɪl, -drəl, (US) -drɪl -s -z
Mandy ˈmæn.di
mane meɪn -s -z -d -d
man-eater ˈmænˌiː.təʳ, (US) -t̬ɚ -s -z
man-eating ˈmænˌiː.tɪŋ, (US) -t̬ɪŋ
manège, manege mænˈeɪʒ, -ˈeʒ, ˈ--, (US) mænˈeʒ, məˈneʒ, -ˈneɪʒ -s -ɪz
manes, M~ ˈmɑː.neɪz, -neɪs, ˈmeɪ.niːz, (US) ˈmeɪ.niːz, ˈmɑː.neɪs
Manet ˈmæn.eɪ, (US) mænˈeɪ, məˈneɪ
Manette mænˈet
maneuv|er məˈnuː.v|əʳ, (US) -v|ɚ -ers -əz, (US) -ɚz -ering/s -ər.ɪŋ/z -ered -əd, (US) -ɚd -erer/s -ər.əʳ/z, (US) -ɚ.ɚ/z
maneuverability məˌnuː.vər.əˈbɪl.ə.ti, -ɪ.ti, (US) -ə.t̬i
maneuverable məˈnuː.vər.ə.bəl
Manfred ˈmæn.fred, -frɪd
manful ˈmæn.fəl, -fʊl -ly -i -ness -nəs, -nɪs
manga ˈmæŋ.gə -s -z
Mangan ˈmæŋ.gən
manganate ˈmæŋ.gə.neɪt -s -s
manganese ˈmæŋ.gə.niːz, ˌ--ˈ-, (US) ˈ---, -niːs
manganic mæŋˈgæn.ɪk, mæn-, (US) mæn-
mange meɪndʒ
mangel-wurzel ˈmæŋ.gəlˌwɜː.zəl, ˌmæŋ.gəlˈwɜː-, (US) ˈmæŋ.gəlˌwɝː-, -ˌwɝː.t.səl -s -z
manger ˈmeɪn.dʒəʳ, (US) -dʒɚ -s -z
mangetout ˌmɑ̃ːnʒˈtuː, (US) ˌmɑ̃ːndʒ- -s -z
mangl|e ˈmæŋ.gəl -es -z -ing -ɪŋ, ˈmæŋ.glɪŋ -ed -d -er/s -əʳ/z, (US) -ɚ/z
mango ˈmæŋ.gəʊ, (US) -goʊ -(e)s -z
mangold, M~ ˈmæŋ.gəʊld, (US) -goʊld -s -z
mangosteen ˈmæŋ.gəʊ.stiːn, (US) -gə- -s -z
Mangotsfield ˈmæŋ.gəts.fiːld
mangrove ˈmæŋ.grəʊv, (US) ˈmæn.groʊv, ˈmæŋ- -s -z
mang|y ˈmeɪn.dʒ|i -ier -i.əʳ, (US) -i.ɚ -iest -i.ɪst, -i.əst -ily -əl.i, -ɪ.li -iness -ɪ.nəs, -ɪ.nɪs
manhandl|e ˈmænˌhæn.dəl, ˌ-ˈ--, (US) ˈ--- -es -z -ing -ɪŋ, -ˌhænd.lɪŋ -ed -d
manhattan, M~ mænˈhæt.ən, (US) mæn-, mən-
manhole ˈmæn.həʊl, (US) -hoʊl -s -z
manhood, M~ ˈmæn.hʊd
manhour ˈmæn.aʊəʳ, -aʊ.əʳ, (US) -aʊr, -aʊ.ɚ -s -z
manhunt ˈmæn.hʌnt -s -s
mania ˈmeɪ.ni.ə, (US) -ni.ə, -njə -s -z
maniac ˈmeɪ.ni.æk -s -s
maniac|al məˈnaɪ.ə.k|əl -ally -əl.i, (US) -li
manic ˈmæn.ɪk -s -s ˌ**manic deˈpression**
manic-depressive ˌmæn.ɪk.dɪˈpres.ɪv, -dəˈ- -s -z
Manich(a)ean ˌmæn.ɪˈkiː.ən, -əˈ- -s -z
manicur|e ˈmæn.ɪ.kjʊəʳ, ˈ-ə-, -kjɔːʳ, (US) -kjʊr -es -z -ing -ɪŋ -ed -d -ist/s -ɪst/s
manifest ˈmæn.ɪ.fest, ˈ-ə- -ly -li -s -s -ing -ɪŋ -ed -ɪd -ness -nəs, -nɪs
manifestation ˌmæn.ɪ.fesˈteɪ.ʃən, ˌ-ə-, -fəˈsteɪ- -s -z
manifesto ˌmæn.ɪˈfes.təʊ, -əˈ-, (US) -toʊ -(e)s -z
manifold ˈmæn.ɪ.fəʊld, ˈ-ə-, (US) -foʊld -ness -nəs, -nɪs
manikin ˈmæn.ɪ.kɪn, ˈ-ə- -s -z
manila, M~ məˈnɪl.ə -s -z
manilla məˈnɪl.ə -s -z
Manilow ˈmæn.ɪ.ləʊ, ˈ-ə-, (US) -loʊ
manioc ˈmæn.i.ɒk, (US) -ɑːk
maniple ˈmæn.ɪ.pəl, ˈ-ə- -s -z
manipu|late məˈnɪp.jə|.leɪt, -jʊ-, (US) -jə-, -juː- -lates -leɪts -lating -leɪ.tɪŋ, (US) -leɪ.t̬ɪŋ -lated -leɪ.tɪd, (US) -leɪ.t̬ɪd -lator/s -leɪ.təʳ/z, (US) -leɪ.t̬ɚ/z
manipulation məˌnɪp.jəˈleɪ.ʃən, -jʊˈ-, (US) -jəˈ-, -juːˈ- -s -z
manipulative məˈnɪp.jə.lə.tɪv, -jʊ-, (US) -jə.leɪ.t̬ɪv, -juː-, -lə- -ly -li -ness -nəs, -nɪs
Manitoba ˌmæn.ɪˈtəʊ.bə, -əˈ-, (US) -əˈtoʊ-
manit(o)u ˈmæn.ɪ.tuː, (US) ˈ-ə- -s -z
mankind mænˈkaɪnd, mæŋ-, (US) mæn-
mank|y ˈmæŋ.k|i -ier -i.əʳ, (US) -i.ɚ -iest -i.ɪst, -i.əst
Manley ˈmæn.li
manlike ˈmæn.laɪk
Manlius ˈmæn.li.əs
manl|y, M~ ˈmæn.l|i -ier -i.əʳ, (US) -i.ɚ -iest -i.ɪst, -i.əst -iness -ɪ.nəs, -ɪ.nɪs
man-made ˌmænˈmeɪd, ˌmæm-, (US) ˌmæn- *stress shift:* ˌ**man-made ˈfibre**
Mann mæn
manna ˈmæn.ə
mannequin ˈmæn.ɪ.kɪn, ˈ-ə- -s -z
manner ˈmæn.əʳ, (US) -ɚ -s -z -ed -d
mannerism, M~ ˈmæn.ər.ɪ.zəm -s -z
mannerist, M~ ˈmæn.ər.ɪst
mannerl|y ˈmæn.əl|.i, (US) -ɚ.l|i -iness -ɪ.nəs, -ɪ.nɪs
Manners ˈmæn.əz, (US) -ɚz
Mannesmann ˈmæn.ə.smæn, -smən
Mannheim ˈmæn.haɪm
mannikin ˈmæn.ɪ.kɪn, ˈ-ə- -s -z
Manning ˈmæn.ɪŋ
mannish ˈmæn.ɪʃ -ly -li -ness -nəs, -nɪs
Manns mænz
Manny ˈmæn.i
Mannyng of Brunne ˌmæn.ɪŋ.əvˈbrʊn
manoeuvrability məˌnuː.vər.əˈbɪl.ə.tɪ, -ɪ.ti, (US) -ə.t̬i
manoeuvrable məˈnuː.vər.ə.bəl
manoeuv|re məˈnuː.v|əʳ, (US) -v|ɚ -res -əz, (US) -ɚz -ring/s -ər.ɪŋ/z -red -əd, (US) -ɚd -rer/s -ər.əʳ/z, (US) -ɚ.ɚ/z
man-of-war ˌmæn.əvˈwɔːʳ, (US) -ˈwɔːr **men-of-war** ˌmen-
Manolo məˈnəʊ.ləʊ, (US) -ˈnoʊ.loʊ
manometer məˈnɒm.ɪ.təʳ, mænˈɒm-, ˈ-ə-, (US) məˈnɑː.mə.t̬ɚ -s -z
manometric ˌmæn.əʊˈmet.rɪk, (US) -əˈ- -al -əl -ally -əl.i, -li
manor ˈmæn.əʳ, (US) -ɚ -s -z
manor-hou|se ˈmæn.ə.haʊ|s, (US) ˈ-ɚ- -ses -zɪz
manorial məˈnɔː.ri.əl, mænˈɔː-, (US) məˈnɔːr.i-
manpower ˈmænˌpaʊəʳ, -ˌpaʊ.əʳ, ˈmæm-, (US) ˈmænˌpaʊ.ɚ
manqué ˈmɑ̃ːŋ.keɪ, (US) mɑ̃ːŋˈkeɪ
Manresa mænˈreɪ.sə, -zə, (US) mɑːnˈreɪ.sə, mæn-
Mansa ˈmænt.sə
mansard ˈmænt.sɑːd, (US) -sɑːrd -s -z
mans|e mænts -es -ɪz
Mansel(l) ˈmænt.səl
Mansergh *surname:* ˈmæn.zəʳ, ˈmænt.səʳ, -sɜːdʒ, (US) ˈmæn.zɚ, ˈmænt.sɚ, -sɝːdʒ *place in Cumbria:* ˈmæn.zəʳ, (US) -zɚ
manservant ˈmænˌsɜː.vənt, (US) -ˌsɝː- **menservants** ˈmenˌsɜː.vənts, (US) -ˌsɝː-
Mansfield ˈmænts.fiːld, (US) ˈmænz-
-manship mən.ʃɪp
mansion, M~ ˈmæn.tʃən -s -z
mansion-hou|se, M~ ˈmæn.tʃən.haʊ|s -ses -zɪz
man-sized ˈmæn.saɪzd
manslaughter ˈmænˌslɔː.təʳ, (US) -ˌslɑː.t̬ɚ, -ˌslɔː-
Manson ˈmænt.sən
Manston ˈmænt.stən
mansuetude ˈmæn.swɪ.tʃuːd, -tjuːd, (US) -tuːd, -tjuːd
Manta ˈmæn.tə
Mantegna mænˈten.jə, (US) mɑːnˈten.jɑː, -jə
mantel ˈmæn.təl -s -z
mantelpiec|e ˈmæn.təl.piːs -es -ɪz
mantelshel|f ˈmæn.təl.ʃel|f -ves -vz
-mantic ˈmæn.tɪk
mantilla mænˈtɪl.ə, (US) -ˈtɪl-, -ˈtiː.jə -s -z
mantis ˈmæn.tɪs, (US) -t̬ɪs -es -ɪz
mantissa mænˈtɪs.ə -s -z
mantl|e ˈmæn.təl -es -z -ing -ɪŋ, ˈmænt.lɪŋ -ed -d
Mantovani ˌmæn.təˈvɑː.ni, (US) ˌmɑːn-
mantra ˈmæn.trə, ˈmʌn-, (US) ˈmæn-, ˈmɑːn-, ˈmʌn- -s -z
mantrap ˈmæn.træp -s -s
Mantu|a, M~ ˈmæn.tju|.ə, -tu-, -tʃu-, (US) -tʃu|.ə, -tu- -an/s -ənz
manual ˈmæn.ju.əl -s -z -ly -i

Manuel *surname:* ˈmæn.ju.el, -əl *first name:* mænˈwel; ˌmæn.uˈel, -juˈ-, (US) mænˈwel, mɑːn-
manufact|ure ˌmæn.jəˈfæk.tʃ|əʳ, -jʊˈ-, -əˈ-, (US) -jəˈfæk.tʃ|ɚ, -juːˈ- **-ures** -əz, (US) -ɚz **-uring** -ər.ɪŋ **-ured** -əd, (US) -ɚd **-urer/s** -ər.əʳ/z, (US) -ɚ.ɚ/z
manuka, M~ *honey:* məˈnuː.kə *place:* məˈnuː.kə; *locally also:* ˈmɑː.nə.kə
manumission ˌmæn.jəˈmɪʃ.ən, -jʊˈ-, (US) -jəˈ-, -juː- **-s** -z
manu|mit ˌmæn.jə|ˈmɪt, -jʊˈ-, (US) -jəˈ-, -juːˈ- **-mits** -ˈmɪts **-mitting** -ˈmɪt.ɪŋ, (US) -ˈmɪṭ.ɪŋ **-mitted** -ˈmɪt.ɪd, (US) -ˈmɪṭ.ɪd
manur|e məˈnjʊəʳ, -njɔːʳ, (US) -ˈnʊr, -ˈnjʊr **-es** -z **-ing** -ɪŋ **-ed** -d
manuscript ˈmæn.jə.skrɪpt, -jʊ- **-s** -s
Manwaring ˈmæn.ər.ɪŋ
Manx mæŋks ˌ**Manx** ˈ**cat**
Manx|man ˈmæŋks|.mæn, -mən **-men** -men, -mən **-woman** -ˌwʊm.ən **-women** -ˌwɪm.ɪn
many ˈmen.i
manyfold ˈmen.i.fəʊld, (US) -foʊld
many-sided ˌmen.iˈsaɪ.dɪd **-ness** -nəs, -nɪs *stress shift:* ˌ**many-sided** ˈ**shape**
manzanilla, M~ ˌmæn.zəˈnɪl.ə, -jə, (US) -ˈniːl.jə, -ˈniː-, -ˈnɪl.ə
Manzoni mænˈzəʊ.ni, (US) mɑːnˈzoʊ-
Mao maʊ
Mao|ism ˈmaʊ|.ɪ.zəm **-ist/s** -ɪst/s
Maori ˈmaʊə.ri, (US) ˈmaʊ.ri; (US) ˈmɑː.oʊ.ri **-s** -z
Mao Tse-tung, Mao Zedong ˌmaʊ.tseɪˈtʊŋ, ˌmaʊ.dzeɪˈdʊŋ, (US) -tsəˈdʊŋ
map mæp **-s** -s **-ping** -ɪŋ **-ped** -t
maple, M~ ˈmeɪ.pəl **-s** -z ˈ**Maple** ˌ**Leaf**; ˌ**maple** ˈ**syrup**
Maplin Sands ˌmæp.lɪnˈsændz, -lənˈ-
mapmak|er ˈmæp.meɪ.k|əʳ, (US) -k|ɚ **-ing** -ɪŋ **-ers** -əz, (US) -ɚz
Mappin ˈmæp.ɪn
Mapplethorpe ˈmeɪ.pəl.θɔːp, (US) -θɔːrp
Maputo məˈpuː.təʊ, (US) -toʊ
maquillage ˌmæk.iːˈɑːʒ, -ˈjɑːʒ, (US) ˌmɑː.kiˈɑːʒ
maquis mækˈiː, ˈ--, (US) mɑːˈkiː, mækˈiː
mar, M~ mɑːʳ, (US) mɑːr **-s** -z **-ring** -ɪŋ **-red** -d
Mar. (abbrev. for **March**) mɑːtʃ, (US) mɑːrtʃ
marabou ˈmær.ə.buː, (US) ˈmer-, ˈmær- **-s** -z
maraca məˈræk.ə, (US) -ˈrɑː.kə **-s** -z
Maracaibo ˌmær.əˈkaɪ.bəʊ, (US) ˌmer.əˈkaɪ.boʊ, ˌmær-
Maradona ˌmær.əˈdɒn.ə, (US) ˌmer.əˈdɑː.nə, ˌmær-
maraschino, M~ ˌmær.əˈʃiː.nəʊ, -ˈskiː-, (US) ˌmer.əˈʃiː.noʊ, ˌmær-, -ˈskiː- **-s** -z ˌ**maraˌschino** ˈ**cherry**
Marat ˈmær.ɑː, (US) mɑːˈrɑː, mə-
Marathi məˈrɑː.ti **-s** -z
marathon, M~ ˈmær.ə.θən, (US) ˈmer.ə.θɑːn, ˈmær- **-s** -z
maraud məˈrɔːd, (US) -ˈrɑːd, -ˈrɔːd **-s** -z **-ing** -ɪŋ **-ed** -ɪd **-er/s** -əʳ/z, (US) -ɚ/z
Marazion ˌmær.əˈzaɪ.ən, (US) ˌmer-, ˌmær-
Marbella mɑːˈbeɪ.ə, -jə, (US) mɑːr-
marbl|e ˈmɑː.bəl, (US) ˈmɑːr- **-es** -z **-ing** -ɪŋ, ˈmɑː.blɪŋ, (US) ˈmɑːr- **-ed** -d
Marburg ˈmɑː.bʊəg, -bɜːg, (US) ˈmɑːr.bɝːg, -bʊrg
Marc mɑːk, (US) mɑːrk
marcasite ˈmɑː.kə.saɪt, (US) ˈmɑːr-
Marceau ˌmɑːˈsəʊ, ˈ--, (US) mɑːrˈsoʊ
Marcel mɑːˈsel, (US) mɑːr-
Marcella mɑːˈsel.ə, (US) mɑːr-
Marcelle mɑːˈsel, (US) mɑːr-
Marcellus mɑːˈsel.əs, (US) mɑːr-
march, M~ mɑːtʃ, (US) mɑːrtʃ **-es** -ɪz **-ing** -ɪŋ **-ed** -t **-er/s** -əʳ/z, (US) -ɚ/z
Marchant ˈmɑː.tʃənt, (US) ˈmɑːr-
Marchbank ˈmɑːtʃ.bæŋk, (US) ˈmɑːrtʃ- **-s** -s
marchioness ˌmɑː.ʃənˈes, -ˈɪs; ˈmɑː.ʃən.əs, (US) ˈmɑːr.ʃən.ɪs; (US) ˌmɑːr.ʃənˈes **-es** -ɪz
Marchmain ˈmɑːtʃ.meɪn, (US) ˈmɑːrtʃ-
Marchmont ˈmɑːtʃ.mənt, (US) ˈmɑːrtʃ-
march-past ˈmɑːtʃ.pɑːst, (US) ˈmɑːrtʃ.pæst
Marcia ˈmɑː.si.ə, ˈ-ʃə, (US) ˈmɑːr.ʃə
Marciano ˌmɑː.siˈɑː.nəʊ, -ʃiˈ-, (US) ˌmɑːr.siˈæn.oʊ, -ʃiˈ-, -ˈɑː.noʊ
Marco ˈmɑː.kəʊ, (US) ˈmɑːr.koʊ
Marconi mɑːˈkəʊ.ni, (US) mɑːrˈkoʊ-
marconigram mɑːˈkəʊ.ni.græm, (US) mɑːrˈkoʊ- **-s** -z
Marcos ˈmɑː.kɒs, (US) ˈmɑːr.koʊs
Marcus ˈmɑː.kəs, (US) ˈmɑːr-
Marcuse mɑːˈkuː.zə; mɑːˈkjuːz, (US) mɑːrˈkuː.zə
Mar del Plata ˌmɑː.delˈplɑː.tə, (US) ˌmɑːr.delˈplɑː.tə
Marden *in Kent:* ˈmɑː.dən; mɑːˈden, (US) ˈmɑːr.dən; (US) mɑːrˈden *other places:* ˈmɑː.dən, (US) ˈmɑːr-
Mardi Gras ˌmɑː.diˈgrɑː, (US) ˈmɑːr.diˌgrɑː, ˌ--ˈ-
Marduk ˈmɑː.dʊk, (US) ˈmɑːr-
mare *female horse:* meəʳ, (US) mer **-s** -z *lunar plain:* ˈmɑː.reɪ, (US) ˈmɑːr.eɪ **maria** ˈmɑː.ri.ə, (US) ˈmɑːr.i-
Marengo məˈreŋ.gəʊ, (US) -goʊ
mare's-nest ˈmeəz.nest, ˌ-ˈ-, (US) ˈmerz.nest **-s** -s
mare's-tail ˈmeəz.teɪl, ˌ-ˈ-, (US) ˈmerz- **-s** -z
Margaret ˈmɑː.gər.ət, -ɪt, ˈ-grət, -grɪt, (US) ˈmɑːr.grət
margarine ˌmɑː.dʒəˈriːn, -gəˈ-, ˈ---, (US) ˈmɑːr.dʒɚ.ɪn
margarita, M~ ˌmɑː.gərˈiː.tə, (US) -gəˈriː.ṭə **-s** -z
Margate ˈmɑː.geɪt, -gɪt, (US) ˈmɑːr-
marge mɑːdʒ, (US) mɑːrdʒ
Margerison mɑːˈdʒer.ɪ.sən, ˈ-ə-; ˈmɑː.dʒər-, (US) mɑːrˈdʒer-; (US) ˈmɑːr.dʒə.rɪ-, -rə-
Margery ˈmɑː.dʒər.i, (US) ˈmɑːr-
Margetts ˈmɑː.gɪts, (US) ˈmɑːr-
margin ˈmɑː.dʒɪn, (US) ˈmɑːr- **-s** -z
marginal ˈmɑː.dʒɪ.nəl, -dʒən.əl, (US) ˈmɑːr- **-s** -z **-ly** -i
marginalia ˌmɑː.dʒɪˈneɪ.li.ə, -dʒəˈ-, (US) ˌmɑːr-, -ˈneɪl.jə
marginalization, -isa- ˌmɑː.dʒɪ.nəl.aɪˈzeɪ.ʃən, -dʒən.əl-, -ɪˈ-, (US) ˌmɑːr.dʒɪ.nəl.əˈ-, -dʒən.əl-
marginaliz|e, -is|e ˈmɑː.dʒɪ.nəl.aɪz, -dʒən.əl-, (US) ˈmɑːr- **-es** -ɪz **-ing** -ɪŋ **-ed** -d
Margolis mɑːˈgəʊ.lɪs, (US) mɑːrˈgoʊ-
Margot ˈmɑː.gəʊ, (US) ˈmɑːr.goʊ
margrave, M~ ˈmɑː.greɪv, (US) ˈmɑːr- **-s** -z
margravine ˈmɑː.grə.viːn, (US) ˈmɑːr- **-s** -z
marguerite, M~ ˌmɑː.gərˈiːt, (US) ˌmɑːr.gəˈriːt **-s** -s
Margulies ˈmɑː.gʊ.lɪs, (US) mɑːrˈguː.lɪz
Marham *in Norfolk:* ˈmær.əm, ˈmɑː.rəm, (US) ˈmær.əm, ˈmɑːr-

> Note: The pronunciation of the local residents is /ˈmær.əm/.

Marhamchurch ˈmær.əm.tʃɜːtʃ, (US) -tʃɝːtʃ
maria (plural of **mare**) ˈmɑː.ri.ə, (US) ˈmɑːr.i-
Maria *first name:* məˈriː.ə, məˈraɪ.ə
Marian *first name:* ˈmær.i.ən, (US) ˈmer-, ˈmær-
Marian n, adj *of Mary, or person devoted to Mary:* ˈmeə.ri.ən, (US) ˈmer.i-, ˈmær-
Mariana *English name:* ˌmær.iˈæn.ə, ˌmeə.riˈ-, -ˈɑː.nə, (US) ˌmer.iˈæn.ə, ˌmær- *Spanish historian:* ˌmɑː.riˈɑː.nə, (US) ˌmɑːr.iˈɑː-
Marianne ˌmær.iˈæn, (US) ˌmer.iˈæn, ˌmær-
Maribor ˈmær.i.bɔːʳ, (US) ˈmɑːr.i.bɔːr
Maricopa ˌmær.ɪˈkəʊ.pə, (US) ˌmer.ɪˈkoʊ-, ˌmær-
Marie məˈriː, ˈmɑː.ri, ˈmær.i, (US) məˈriː
Marie Antoinette ˌmær.iˌæn.twəˈnet, -ˌɑ̃ːn-, (US) məˌriː.æn-
Marienbad ˈmær.i.ən.bæd, -əm-; məˈriː-, (US) ˈmer.i.ən-, ˈmær-
marigold, M~ ˈmær.ɪ.gəʊld, (US) ˈmer.ɪ.goʊld, ˈmær- **-s** -z
marijuana, marihuana ˌmær.ɪˈwɑː.nə, -əˈ-, (US) ˌmer.əˈ-, -ɪˈ-, ˌmær-
Marilla məˈrɪl.ə
Marilyn ˈmær.ɪ.lɪn, ˈ-ə-, (US) ˈmer-, ˈmær-
marimba məˈrɪm.bə **-s** -z
Marin məˈrɪn
marina, M~ məˈriː.nə **-s** -z
marinad|e ˌmær.ɪˈneɪd, ˈ---, (US)

ˌmer.ɪˈneɪd, ˌmær-, ˈ--- -es -z -ing -ɪŋ -ed -ɪd
marinara ˌmær.ɪˈnɑː.rə, -əˈ-, (US) ˌmer.ɪˈner.ə, -nær.ə, -nɑː.rə
marinat|e ˈmær.ɪ.neɪt, ˈ-ə-, (US) ˈmer-, ˈmær- -es -s -ing -ɪŋ -ed -ɪd
marination ˌmær.ɪˈneɪ.ʃən, -əˈ-, (US) ˌmer-, ˌmær-
marine məˈriːn -s -z
mariner ˈmær.ɪ.nəʳ, ˈ-ə-, (US) ˈmer.ɪ.nɚ, ˈmær-, ˈ-ə- -s -z
Marino Faliero məˌriː.nəʊˌfæl.iˈeə.rəʊ, (US) məˌriː.noʊˌfæl.iˈe.roʊ
Mario ˈmær.i.əʊ, ˈmɑː.ri-, (US) ˈmɑːr.i.oʊ, ˈmer-, ˈmær-
Marion ˈmær.i.ən, ˈmeə.ri-, (US) ˈmer.i-, ˈmær-
marionette ˌmær.i.əˈnet, (US) ˌmer-, ˌmær- -s -s
Marisa məˈrɪs.ə
Marischal ˈmɑː.ʃəl, ˈmɑː.rɪ.ʃɑːl, (US) ˈmɑːr.ɪ.ʃɑːl, ˈ-ʃɑːl, ˈ-ʃəl
Marissa məˈrɪs.ə
marital ˈmær.ɪ.təl, ˈ-ə-, (US) ˈmer.ɪ.t̬əl, ˈmær- -ly -i
maritime, M~ ˈmær.ɪ.taɪm, ˈ-ə-, (US) ˈmer-, ˈmær-
Marius ˈmær.i.əs, ˈmeə.ri-, ˈmɑː-, (US) ˈmer.i-, ˈmær-
Marivaux ˈmær.i.vəʊ, –ˈ-, (US) mær.iˈvoʊ
marjoram ˈmɑː.dʒər.əm, (US) ˈmɑːr.dʒɚ.əm
Marjoribanks ˈmɑːtʃ.bæŋks, (US) ˈmɑːrtʃ-
Marjorie, Marjory ˈmɑː.dʒər.i, (US) ˈmɑːr-
mark, M~ mɑːk, (US) mɑːrk -s -s -ing/s -ɪŋ/z -ed -t -edly -ɪd.li -er/s -əʳ/z, (US) -ɚ/z **ˌMark ˈAntony**
Markby ˈmɑːk.bi, (US) ˈmɑːrk-
markdown ˈmɑːk.daʊn, (US) ˈmɑːrk-
mar|ket, M~ ˈmɑː|.kɪt, (US) ˈmɑːr- -kets -kɪts -keting -kɪ.tɪŋ, (US) -kɪ.t̬ɪŋ -keted -kɪ.tɪd -keter/s -kɪ.təʳ/z, (US) -kɪ.t̬ɚ/z -keted (US) -kɪ.t̬ɪd -ketable -kɪ.tə.bəl, (US) -kɪ.t̬ə.bəl **ˌmarket eˈconomy; ˌmarket ˈgardening; ˌmarket reˈsearch** (US) **ˈmarket ˌresearch ˈmarket reˌsearch; ˈmarket ˌtown; ˌmarket ˈtown**
marketability ˌmɑː.kɪ.təˈbɪl.ə.ti, -ɪ.ti, (US) ˌmɑːr.kɪ.t̬əˈbɪl.ə.t̬i
Market Deeping ˌmɑː.kɪtˈdiː.pɪŋ, (US) ˌmɑːr-
marketeer ˌmɑː.kɪˈtɪəʳ, -kəˈ-, (US) ˌmɑːr.kəˈtɪr -s -z
market-plac|e ˈmɑː.kɪt.pleɪs, (US) ˈmɑːr- -es -ɪz
Market Rasen ˌmɑː.kɪtˈreɪ.zən, (US) ˌmɑːr-
Markham ˈmɑː.kəm, (US) ˈmɑːr-
markk|a ˈmɑː.k|ɑː, -k|ə, (US) ˈmɑːr- -aa -ɑː
Markov ˈmɑː.kɒf, -kɒv, (US) ˈmɑːr.kɔːf
Markova mɑːˈkəʊ.və, (US) mɑːrˈkoʊ-
Marks mɑːks, (US) mɑːrks
Marks and Spencer® ˌmɑːks.ənˈspent.səʳ, (US) ˌmɑːrks.ənˈspent.sɚ
marks|man ˈmɑːks|.mən, (US) ˈmɑːrks- -men -mən, -men -woman -ˌwʊm.ən -women -ˌwɪm.ɪn
marksmanship ˈmɑːks.mən.ʃɪp, (US) ˈmɑːrks-
markup ˈmɑːk.ʌp, (US) ˈmɑːrk- -s -s
marl mɑːl, (US) mɑːrl
Marlboro® ˈmɑːl.bər.ə, ˈmɔːl-, (US) ˈmɑːrl-
Marlborough *town in Wiltshire, family name:* ˈmɔːl.bər.ə, (US) ˈmɑːrl.bɚ.oʊ *London streets, town in US, New Zealand district:* ˈmɑːl.bər.ə, (US) ˈmɑːrl.bɚ-
Marlene *English name:* ˈmɑː.liːn, -ˈ-, (US) mɑːrˈliːn *German name:* mɑːˈleɪ.nə, (US) mɑːr-
Marler ˈmɑː.ləʳ, (US) ˈmɑːr.lɚ
Marley ˈmɑː.li, (US) ˈmɑːr-
marlin ˈmɑː.lɪn, (US) ˈmɑːr- -s -z
Marling ˈmɑː.lɪŋ, (US) ˈmɑːr-
Marlovian mɑːˈləʊ.vi.ən, (US) mɑːrˈloʊ-
Marlow(e) ˈmɑː.ləʊ, (US) ˈmɑːr.loʊ
Marmaduke ˈmɑː.mə.djuːk, (US) ˈmɑːr.mə.duːk, -djuːk
marmalade ˈmɑː.məl.eɪd, (US) ˈmɑːr- -s -z
Marmion ˈmɑː.mi.ən, (US) ˈmɑːr-
marmite, M~® ˈmɑː.maɪt, (US) ˈmɑːr-
Marmora ˈmɑː.mər.ə, (US) ˈmɑːr-
marmoreal mɑːˈmɔː.ri.əl, (US) mɑːrˈmɔːr.i- -ly -i
marmoset ˈmɑː.mə.set, -zet, ˌ--ˈ-, (US) ˈmɑːr.mə- -s -s
marmot ˈmɑː.mət, (US) ˈmɑːr- -s -s
Marne mɑːn, (US) mɑːrn
Marner ˈmɑː.nəʳ, (US) ˈmɑːr.nɚ
marocain ˈmær.ə.keɪn, ˌ--ˈ-, (US) ˈmer-, ˈmær-
maroon məˈruːn -s -z -ing -ɪŋ -ed -d
Marple ˈmɑː.pəl, (US) ˈmɑːr-
Marprelate ˈmɑː.prel.ət, -ɪt, (US) ˈmɑːr-
Marquand ˈmɑː.kwənd, (US) ˈmɑːr-
marque mɑːk, (US) mɑːrk -s -s
marquee mɑːˈkiː, (US) mɑːr- -s -z
Marquesas mɑːˈkeɪ.səs, -zəs, -sæs, -zæs, (US) mɑːrˈkeɪ.zəs, -səs
marquess ˈmɑː.kwɪs, -kwəs, (US) ˈmɑːr- -es -ɪz
marquetr|y ˈmɑː.kə.tr|i, -kɪ-, (US) ˈmɑːr- -ies -iz
marquis, M~ ˈmɑː.kwɪs, -kwəs; mɑːˈkiː, (US) ˈmɑːr.kwɪs, -kwəs; (US) mɑːrˈkiː marquises ˈmɑː.kwɪ.sɪz, -kwə-, (US) ˈmɑːr.kwɪ- (alternative plural of **marquis**) mɑːˈkiːz, (US) mɑːr-
marquis|e mɑːˈkiːz, (US) mɑːr- -es -ɪz
Marr mɑːʳ, (US) mɑːr
Marrakesh, Marrakech ˌmær.əˈkeʃ, məˈræk.eʃ, (US) ˈmer.ə.keʃ, ˈmær-; (US) ˌməˈrɑː.keʃ
marram grass ˈmær.əmˌgrɑːs, (US) ˈmer.əmˌgræs, ˈmær-
marriag|e ˈmær.ɪdʒ, (US) ˈmer-, ˈmær- -es -ɪz -eable -ə.bəl
Marriner ˈmær.ɪ.nəʳ, (US) ˈmer.ɪ.nɚ, ˈmær-
Marriott ˈmær.i.ət, (US) ˈmer-, ˈmær-, -ɑːt
marron ˈmær.ən, -ɔ̃ːŋ, (US) ˈmer.ən, ˈmær-; (US) məˈroʊn -s -z
marrons glacés ˌmær.ənˈglæs.eɪ, -əŋˈ-, -ɔ̃ːŋˈ-, (US) məˌroʊn.glɑːˈseɪ
marrow ˈmær.əʊ, (US) ˈmer.oʊ, ˈmær- -s -z -y -i
marrowbone ˈmær.əʊ.bəʊn, (US) ˈmer.oʊ.boʊn, ˈmær- -s -z
marrowfat ˈmær.əʊ.fæt, (US) ˈmer.oʊ-, ˈmær- -s -s
marr|y ˈmær|.i, (US) ˈmer-, ˈmær- -ies -iz -ying -i.ɪŋ -ied -id -ier/s -i.əʳ/z, (US) -i.ɚ/z
Marryat ˈmær.i.ət, (US) ˈmer-, ˈmær-
Mars mɑːz, (US) mɑːrz **ˈMars ˌbar®**
Marsala mɑːˈsɑː.lə, (US) mɑːrˈsɑː.lɑː
Marsalis mɑːˈsɑː.lɪs, (US) mɑːrˈsæ-
Marsden ˈmɑːz.dən, (US) ˈmɑːrz-
Marseillaise ˌmɑː.seɪˈjeɪz, -ˈeɪz, -səlˈeɪz, (US) ˌmɑːr.səlˈeɪz, -seɪˈez
Marseilles, Marseille ˌmɑːˈseɪ, (US) ˌmɑːr-
marsh, M~ mɑːʃ, (US) mɑːrʃ -es -ɪz
Marsha ˈmɑː.ʃə, (US) ˈmɑːr-
marshal ˈmɑː.ʃəl, (US) ˈmɑːr- -s -z -(l)ing -ɪŋ -(l)ed -d -(l)er/s -əʳ/z, (US) -ɚ/z
Marshall ˈmɑː.ʃəl, (US) ˈmɑːr-
marshland ˈmɑːʃ.lænd, -lənd, (US) ˈmɑːrʃ-
marshmallow ˌmɑːʃˈmæl.əʊ, (US) ˈmɑːrʃ.mel.oʊ, -mæl- -s -z
marsh|y ˈmɑː.ʃ|i, (US) ˈmɑːr- -ier -i.əʳ, (US) -i.ɚ -iest -i.ɪst, -i.əst -iness -ɪ.nəs, -ɪ.nɪs
Marske mɑːsk, (US) mɑːrsk
Marsland ˈmɑːz.lənd, (US) ˈmɑːrz-
Marston ˈmɑː.stən, (US) ˈmɑːr-
marsupial mɑːˈsuː.pi.əl, -ˈsjuː-, (US) mɑːrˈsuː- -s -z
mart mɑːt, (US) mɑːrt -s -s
Martel(l) mɑːˈtel, (US) mɑːr-
Martello tower mɑːˌtel.əʊˈtaʊ.əʳ, -ˈtaʊəʳ, (US) mɑːrˌtel.oʊˈtaʊ.ɚ -s -z
marten ˈmɑː.tɪn, (US) ˈmɑːr.tən -s -z
Martens ˈmɑː.tɪnz; mɑːˈtenz, (US) ˈmɑːr.tənz; (US) mɑːrˈtenz
Martha ˈmɑː.θə, (US) ˈmɑːr- **ˌMartha's ˈVineyard**
martial, M~ ˈmɑː.ʃəl, (US) ˈmɑːr- -ly -i **ˌmartial ˈlaw**
Martian ˈmɑː.ʃən, (US) ˈmɑːr- -s -z
martin, M~ ˈmɑː.tɪn, (US) ˈmɑːr.tən -s -z
Martina mɑːˈtiː.nə, (US) mɑːr-
Martine mɑːˈtiːn, (US) mɑːr-
Martineau ˈmɑː.tɪ.nəʊ, -tə-, (US) ˈmɑːr.tə.noʊ
martinet, M~ ˌmɑː.tɪˈnet, -təˈ-, -ˈneɪ, (US) ˌmɑːr.tənˈet, -ˈeɪ, ˈ--- -s -s
Martinez mɑːˈtiː.nez, (US) mɑːr-, -nəs

martingale ˈmɑː.tɪŋ.geɪl, (US) ˈmɑːr.tən- **-s** -z
martini, M~® mɑːˈtiː.ni, (US) mɑːr- **-s** -z
Martinique ˌmɑː.tɪˈniːk, -təˈ-, (US) ˌmɑːr.tənˈiːk
Martinmas ˈmɑː.tɪn.məs, -tɪm-, -mæs, (US) ˈmɑːr.tən.məs
Martyn ˈmɑː.tɪn, (US) ˈmɑːr.tən
mart|yr, M~ ˈmɑː.t|əʳ, (US) ˈmɑːr.ţ|ɚ **-yrs** -əz, (US) -ɚz **-yring** -ər.ɪŋ **-yred** -əd, (US) -ɚd
martyrdom ˈmɑː.tə.dəm, (US) ˈmɑːr.ţɚ- **-s** -z
martyriz|e, -is|e ˈmɑː.tər.aɪz, -tɪ.raɪz, (US) ˈmɑːr.ţə.raɪz **-es** -ɪz **-ing** -ɪŋ **-ed** -d
marvel ˈmɑː.vəl, (US) ˈmɑːr- **-s** -z **-(l)ing** -ɪŋ, ˈmɑːv.lɪŋ **-(l)ed** -d
Marvell ˈmɑː.vəl, (US) ˈmɑːr-
marvel(l)ous ˈmɑː.vəl.əs; ˈmɑːv.ləs, (US) ˈmɑːr.vəl.əs; (US) ˈmɑːrv.ləs **-ly** -li **-ness** -nəs, -nɪs
Marvin ˈmɑː.vɪn, (US) ˈmɑːr-
Marx mɑːks, (US) mɑːrks ˈ**Marx** ˌ**Brothers**
Marxian ˈmɑːk.si.ən, (US) ˈmɑːrk-
Marx|ism ˈmɑːk.s|ɪ.zəm, (US) ˈmɑːrk- **-ist/s** -ɪst/s
Marxism-Leninism ˌmɑːk.sɪ.zəmˈlen.ɪ.nɪ.zəm, (US) ˌmɑːrk-
Marxist-Leninist ˌmɑːk.sɪstˈlen.ɪ.nɪst, (US) ˌmɑːrk- **-s** -s
Mary ˈmeə.ri, (US) ˈmer.i
Maryborough ˈmeə.ri.bər.ə, -ˌbʌr.ə, (US) ˈmer.i.bɚ.oʊ
Maryland ˈmeə.ri.lænd, ˈmer.ɪ-, -lənd, (US) ˈmer.ə.lənd
Marylebone *road, district:* ˈmær.əl.ə.bən, -bəʊn; ˈ-ə.bən, ˈ-ɪ-; ˈmɑː.lɪ-, (US) ˈmer.əl.ə.bən, -boʊn; (US) ˈ-ə.bən, ˈ-ɪ-; (US) ˈmɑːr.lɪ-
Mary-le-Bone *preceded by 'St.':* ˈmær.ɪ.lə.bən, -əl.ə-, (US) ˈmer-
Maryport ˈmeə.ri.pɔːt, (US) ˈmer.i.pɔːrt
marzipan ˈmɑː.zɪ.pæn, -zə-, ˌ--ˈ-, (US) ˈmɑːr.zɪ.pæn, ˈmɑːrt.sɪ-, -pɑːn
Masaccio məˈzɑː.tʃəʊ, -ˈzætʃ.əʊ, -tʃi.əʊ, (US) -ˈsɑː.tʃi.oʊ
Masada məˈsɑː.də, mæsˈɑː-, (US) məˈsɑː.də; (US) ˌmɑː.sɑːˈdɑː
Masai ˈmɑː.saɪ; -ˈ-, məˈ-, (US) mɑːˈsaɪ, məˈ-
masala məˈsɑː.lə, mɑː-
Masaryk ˈmæs.ə.rɪk, ˈmæz-, (US) ˈmæs.ɚ.ɪk
Mascagni mæsˈkɑː.nji, -ˈkæn.ji, (US) mɑːs-
mascara məˈskɑː.rə, mæsˈkɑː-, (US) mæsˈker.ə, -ˈkær- **-s** -z
mascarpone ˌmæs.kɑːˈpəʊ.neɪ, (US) ˌmɑːs.kɑːrˈpoʊ-, ˌmæs-
mascot ˈmæs.kɒt, -kət, (US) -kɑːt, -kət **-s** -s
masculine ˈmæs.kjə.lɪn, -kjʊ-, (US) ˈmæs.kjə-, -kjuː- **-s** -z
masculinity ˌmæs.kjəˈlɪn.ə.ti, -kjʊˈ-, -ɪ.ti, (US) ˌmæs.kjəˈlɪn.ə.ţi, -kjuːˈ-
Masefield ˈmeɪs.fiːld
Masekela ˌmæs.əˈkeɪ.lə
maser ˈmeɪ.zəʳ, (US) -zɚ **-s** -z
Maserati® ˌmæz.ərˈɑː.ti, (US) ˌmɑː.səˈrɑː.ţi, ˌmæz.əˈ- **-s** -z
Maseru ˈmæs.ə.ruː, ˈmæz-, (US) ˈmæz.ə.ruː, ˌmɑː.səˈruː
mash, M~ mæʃ **-es** -ɪz **-ing** -ɪŋ **-ed** -t
MASH mæʃ
Masham *in North Yorkshire:* ˈmæs.əm *surname:* ˈmæs.əm, ˈmæʃ-
masher ˈmæʃ.əʳ, (US) -ɚ **-s** -z
mashie ˈmæʃ.i **-s** -z
Mashona məˈʃɒn.ə, -ˈʃəʊ.nə, (US) -ˈʃɑː.nə, -ˈʃoʊ- **-s** -z **-land** -lænd
mash|y ˈmæʃ|.i **-ies** -iz
Masie ˈmeɪ.zi
mask mɑːsk, (US) mæsk **-s** -s **-ing** -ɪŋ **-ed** -t ˈ**masking** ˌ**tape**
Maskell ˈmæs.kəl
Maskelyne ˈmæs.kɪ.lɪn, -kəl.ɪn, (US) -ɪn, -aɪn
masoch|ism ˈmæs.ə.k|ɪ.zəm, ˈmæz- **-ist/s** -ɪst/s
masochistic ˌmæs.əˈkɪs.tɪk, ˌmæz- **-ally** -əl.i, -li
mason, M~ ˈmeɪ.sən **-s** -z ˈ**mason** ˌ**jar**
Mason-Dixon ˌmeɪ.sənˈdɪk.sən ˌ**Mason-**ˈ**Dixon** ˌ**line**
masonic, M~ məˈsɒn.ɪk, (US) -ˈsɑː.nɪk
Masonite® ˈmeɪ.sən.aɪt
masonr|y, M~ ˈmeɪ.sən.r|i **-ies** -iz
masque mɑːsk, mæsk, (US) mæsk **-s** -s
masquerad|e ˌmæs.kərˈeɪd, ˌmɑː.skərˈ-, (US) ˌmæs.kəˈreɪd **-es** -z **-ing** -ɪŋ **-ed** -ɪd **-er/s** -əʳ/z, (US) -ɚ/z
mass mæs **-es** -ɪz **-ing** -ɪŋ **-ed** -t ˌ**mass** ˈ**media;** ˌ**mass pro**ˈ**duction**
mass, M~ n *religious service:* mæs, mɑːs, (US) mæs **-es** -ɪz
Mass. (abbrev. for **Massachusetts**) mæs
Massachusetts ˌmæs.əˈtʃuː.sɪts, -səts, (US) -sɪts
massac|re ˈmæs.ə.k|əʳ, ˈ-ɪ-, (US) -k|ɚ **-res** -əz, (US) -ɚz **-ring** -ər.ɪŋ **-red** -əd, (US) -ɚd
massag|e ˈmæs.ɑːdʒ, (US) məˈsɑːdʒ **-es** -ɪz **-ing** -ɪŋ **-ed** -d **-er/s** -əʳ/z, (US) -ɚ/z **-ist/s** -ɪst/s ˈ**massage** ˌ**parlour** (US) **mas**ˈ**sage** ˌ**parlor**
Massawa məˈsɑː.wə, (US) mɑːˈsɑː.wɑː, məˈsɑː.wə
Massenet ˈmæs.ən.eɪ, (US) ˌ--ˈ-
masseur mæsˈɜːʳ, məˈsɜːʳ, (US) -ˈsɝː, -ˈsuːr, -ˈsʊr **-s** -z
masseus|e mæsˈɜːz, məˈsɜːz, (US) mæˈsɜːz, -ˈsuːz, -ˈsʊz **-es** -ɪz
Massey ˈmæs.i
massif mæsˈiːf, ˈ--, (US) mæsˈiːf **-s** -s
Massif Central ˌmæs.iːf.sɑ̃ːnˈtrɑːl
Massinger ˈmæs.ɪn.dʒəʳ, (US) -dʒɚ
massive ˈmæs.ɪv **-ly** -li **-ness** -nəs, -nɪs
mass-market ˌmæsˈmɑː.kɪt, (US) -ˈmɑːr- **-s** -s **-ing** -ɪŋ **-ed** -ɪd
mass-meeting ˌmæsˈmiː.tɪŋ, ˈ-ˌ--, (US) -ţɪŋ **-s** -z
Masson ˈmæs.ən, (US) ˈmæs.ɑːn, -ˈ-
Massow ˈmæs.əʊ, (US) -oʊ
mass-produc|e ˌmæs.prəˈdʒuːs, -ˈdjuːs, (US) ˌmæs.prəˈduːs, -ˈdjuːs **-es** -ɪz **-ing** -ɪŋ **-ed** -t **-er/s** -əʳ/z, (US) -ɚ/z *stress shift:* ˌ**mass-produced** ˈ**goods**
mass-production ˌmæs.prəˈdʌk.ʃən, ˈmæs.prəˌ-, (US) ˌmæs.prəˈdʌk-, -proʊˈ-
mass|y ˈmæs|.i **-iness** -ɪ.nəs, -ɪ.nɪs
mast mɑːst, (US) mæst **-s** -s
mastectom|y mæsˈtek.tə.m|i, (US) məˈstek-, mæsˈtek- **-ies** -iz
mast|er ˈmɑː.st|əʳ, (US) ˈmæs.t|ɚ **-ers** -əz, (US) -ɚz **-ering** -ər.ɪŋ **-ered** -əd, (US) -ɚd ˌ**master** ˈ**bedroom;** ˈ**master** ˌ**class;** ˌ**master of** ˈ**ceremonies;** ˈ**master** ˌ**key;** ˈ**master** ˌ**race**
master-at-arms ˌmɑː.stər.ətˈɑːms, (US) ˌmæs.tɚ.ətˈɑːrms **masters-at-arms** ˌmɑː.stəz-, (US) ˌmæs.tɚz-
Mastercard® ˈmɑː.stə.kɑːd, (US) ˈmæs.tɚ.kɑːrd
masterclass ˈmɑː.stə.klɑːs, (US) ˈmæs.tɚ.klæs **-es** -ɪz
masterful ˈmɑː.stə.fəl, -fʊl, (US) ˈmæs.tɚ- **-ly** -i **-ness** -nəs, -nɪs
masterl|y ˈmɑː.stə.l|i, (US) ˈmæs.tɚ- **-iness** -ɪ.nəs, -ɪ.nɪs
Masterman ˈmɑː.stə.mən, (US) ˈmæs.tɚ-
mastermind ˈmɑː.stə.maɪnd, (US) ˈmæs.tɚ- **-s** -z **-ing** -ɪŋ **-ed** -ɪd
masterpiec|e ˈmɑː.stə.piːs, (US) ˈmæs.tɚ- **-es** -ɪz
Masters ˈmɑː.stəz, (US) ˈmæs.tɚz
mastership ˈmɑː.stə.ʃɪp, (US) ˈmæs.tɚ-
master-stroke ˈmɑː.stə.strəʊk, (US) ˈmæs.tɚ.stroʊk **-s** -s
masterwork ˈmɑː.stə.wɜːk, (US) ˈmæs.tɚ.wɝːk **-s** -s
master|y ˈmɑː.stər|.i, (US) ˈmæs.tɚ- **-ies** -iz
masthead ˈmɑːst.hed, (US) ˈmæst- **-s** -z
mastic ˈmæs.tɪk
masti|cate ˈmæs.tɪ|.keɪt, -tə- **-cates** -keɪts **-cating** -keɪ.tɪŋ, (US) -keɪ.ţɪŋ **-cated** -keɪ.tɪd, (US) -keɪ.ţɪd **-cator/s** -keɪ.təʳ/z, (US) -keɪ.ţɚ/z
mastication ˌmæs.tɪˈkeɪ.ʃən, -təˈ-
masticatory ˈmæs.tɪ.kə.tər.i, -keɪ-; ˌmæs.tɪˈkeɪ-, -təˈ-, (US) ˈmæs.tɪ.kə.tɔːr-, -tə-
mastiff ˈmæs.tɪf, ˈmɑː.stɪf, (US) ˈmæs.tif **-s** -s
mastitis mæsˈtaɪ.tɪs, məˈstaɪ-, -təs, (US) mæsˈtaɪ.ţɪs, məˈstaɪ-, -ţəs **mastitides** mæsˈtɪt.ə.diːz, məˈstɪt-, (US) mæsˈtɪţ.ə-, məˈstɪţ-
mastodon ˈmæs.tə.dɒn, -dən, (US) -dɑːn **-s** -z
mastoid ˈmæs.tɔɪd **-s** -z

M

Mastroianni ˌmæs.trəʊˈjɑː.ni, ˌmɑːs.trəʊ-, -ˈjæn.i, US -troʊˈ-
mastur|bate ˈmæs.tə|.beɪt, US -tɚ- **-bates** -beɪts **-bating** -beɪ.tɪŋ, US -beɪ.t̬ɪŋ **-bated** -beɪ.tɪd, US -beɪ.t̬ɪd **-bator/s** -beɪ.təʳ/z, US -beɪ.t̬ɚ/z
masturbation ˌmæs.təˈbeɪ.ʃən, US -tɚˈ- **-s** -z
masturbatory ˌmæs.təˈbeɪ.tər.i, ˈmæs.tə.beɪ-, US ˈmæs.tɚ.bə.tɔːr-
Masur məˈzʊəʳ, US -ˈzʊr
mat mæt **-s** -s **-ting** -ɪŋ, US ˈmæt̬.ɪŋ **-ted** -ɪd, US ˈmæt̬.ɪd
Matabel|e ˌmæt.əˈbiː.li, US ˌmæt̬- **-ies** -iz **-ie** -i
Matabeleland ˌmæt.əˈbiː.li.lænd, US ˌmæt̬-
matador ˈmæt.ə.dɔːʳ, US ˈmæt̬.ə.dɔːr **-s** -z
Mata Hari ˌmɑː.təˈhɑː.ri, US ˌmɑː.t̬əˈhɑːr.i, ˌmæt̬.əˈher-, -ˈhær-
Matalan® ˈmæt.əl.æn, US ˈmæt̬-
match mætʃ **-es** -ɪz **-ing** -ɪŋ **-ed** -t **-er/s** -əʳ/z, US -ɚ/z ˌ**match ˈpoint**
matchboard ˈmætʃ.bɔːd, US -bɔːrd
matchbook ˈmætʃ.bʊk **-s** -s
matchbox ˈmætʃ.bɒks, US -bɑːks **-es** -ɪz
matchless ˈmætʃ.ləs, -lɪs **-ly** -li **-ness** -nəs, -nɪs
matchlock ˈmætʃ.lɒk, US -lɑːk **-s** -s
matchmaker ˈmætʃˌmeɪ.kəʳ, US -kɚ **-s** -z
matchmaking ˈmætʃˌmeɪ.kɪŋ
matchplay ˈmætʃ.pleɪ
matchstick ˈmætʃ.stɪk **-s** -s
matchwood ˈmætʃ.wʊd
mat|e meɪt **-es** -s **-ing** -ɪŋ, US ˈmeɪ.t̬ɪŋ **-ed** -ɪd, US ˈmeɪ.t̬ɪd
maté ˈmɑː.teɪ, ˈmæt.eɪ
matelot ˈmæt.ləʊ, ˈ-əl.əʊ, US -əl.oʊ **-s** -z
mater ˈmeɪ.təʳ, ˈmɑː-, US -t̬ɚ **-s** -z
materfamilias ˌmæt.ə.fəˈmɪl.i.æs, US ˌmeɪ.t̬ɚ.fəˈmɪl.i.əs, ˌmɑː-
material məˈtɪə.ri.əl, US -ˈtɪr.i- **-s** -z **-ly** -i
material|ism məˈtɪə.ri.ə.l|ɪ.zəm, US -ˈtɪr.i- **-ist/s** -ɪst/s
materialistic məˌtɪə.ri.əˈlɪs.tɪk, US -ˌtɪr.i-
materialization, -isa- məˌtɪə.ri.əl.aɪˈzeɪ.ʃən, -ɪˈ-, US -ˌtɪr.i.əl.əˈ- **-s** -z
materializ|e, -is|e məˈtɪə.ri.ə.laɪz, US -ˈtɪr.i- **-es** -ɪz **-ing** -ɪŋ **-ed** -d
matériel, materiel məˌtɪə.riˈel, mætˌɪə-; məˈtɪə.ri.əl, US məˌtɪr.iˈel; US məˈtɪr.i.əl
maternal məˈtɜː.nəl, US -ˈtɝː- **-ly** -i
maternit|y məˈtɜː.nə.t|i, -ɪ.t|i, US -ˈtɝː.nə.t̬|i **-ies** -iz **maˈternity leave; maˈternity ˌward**
matey ˈmeɪ.ti, US -t̬i **-ness** -ɪ.nəs, -ɪ.nɪs
math mæθ
mathematic ˌmæθ.əmˈæt.ɪk, -ɪˈmæt-, mæθˈmæt-, US ˌmæθ.əˈmæt̬-, mæθˈmæt̬-
mathematic|al ˌmæθ.əmˈæt.ɪ.k|əl, -ɪˈmæt-, mæθˈmæt-, US ˌmæθ.əˈmæt̬-, mæθˈmæt̬- **-ally** -əl.i, -li
mathematician ˌmæθ.əm.əˈtɪʃ.ən, -ɪ.məˈ-, ˌmæθ.məˈ-, US ˌmæθ.ə.məˈ-, ˌmæθ.məˈ- **-s** -z
mathematics mæθ.əmˈæt.ɪks, -ɪˈmæt-, mæθˈmæt-, US ˌmæθ.əˈmæt̬-, mæθˈmæt̬-
Mather ˈmeɪ.ðəʳ, -θəʳ; ˈmæð.əʳ, US ˈmæð.ɚ **-s** -z
Matheson ˈmæθ.ɪ.sən, ˈ-ə-
Mathew ˈmæθ.juː, ˈmeɪ.θjuː
Mathews ˈmæθ.juːz, ˈmeɪ.θjuːz
Mathias məˈθaɪ.əs
Mathilda məˈtɪl.də
Mathis ˈmæθ.ɪs
maths mæθs
Matilda məˈtɪl.də
matinée, matinee ˈmæt.ɪ.neɪ, -ən.eɪ, US ˌmæt.ənˈeɪ **-s** -z ˈ**matinée ˌidol; matinˈée ˌidol**
matins ˈmæt.ɪnz, US -ənz
Matisse məˈtiːs, US mə-, mɑː-
Matlock ˈmæt.lɒk, US -lɑːk
Mato Grosso ˌmæt.əʊˈgrəʊ.səʊ, ˌmɑː.təʊˈ-, US ˌmæt̬.əˈgroʊ.soʊ, ˌmɑː.tuːˈgroʊ.suː, -ˈgrɔː-
Maton ˈmeɪ.tən
Matravers məˈtræv.əz, US -ɚz
matriarch ˈmeɪ.tri.ɑːk, ˈmæt.ri-, US ˈmeɪ.tri.ɑːrk **-y** -i
matriarchal ˌmeɪ.triˈɑː.kəl, ˌmæt.riˈ-, US ˌmeɪ.triˈɑːr-
matric məˈtrɪk
matrices (plural of **matrix**) ˈmeɪ.trɪ.siːz, -trə, ˈmæt.rɪ-, -rə-, US ˈmeɪ.trɪ-
matricidal ˌmæt.rɪˈsaɪ.dəl, ˌmeɪ.trɪˈ-, -trəˈ-
matricide ˈmæt.rɪ.saɪd, ˈmeɪ.trɪ-, -trə- **-s** -z
matricu|late məˈtrɪk.jə|.leɪt, -jʊ-, US -jə-, -juː- **-lates** -leɪts **-lating** -leɪ.tɪŋ, US -leɪ.t̬ɪŋ **-lated** -leɪ.tɪd, US -leɪ.t̬ɪd **-lator/s** -leɪ.təʳ/z, US -leɪ.t̬ɚ/z
matriculation məˌtrɪk.jəˈleɪ.ʃən, -jʊˈ-, US -jəˈ-, -juːˈ- **-s** -z
matrilineal ˌmæt.rɪˈlɪn.i.əl, ˌmeɪ.trɪˈ-, -trəˈ-, US -trəˈ- **-ly** -i
matrimonial ˌmæt.rɪˈməʊ.ni.əl, -rəˈ-, US -rəˈmoʊ- **-ly** -i
matrimon|y ˈmæt.rɪ.mə.n|i, -rə-, US -rə.moʊ- **-ies** -iz
mat|rix ˈmeɪ.t|rɪks, ˈmæt|.rɪks, US ˈmeɪ.t|rɪks **-rixes** -rɪk.sɪz **-rices** -rɪ.siːz, -rə-

> Note: British doctors generally pronounce /ˈmeɪ.trɪks/ when talking about the cell type. The traditional pronunciation in the printing trade used to be /ˈmæt.rɪks/.

matron ˈmeɪ.trən **-s** -z **-ly** -li ˌ**matron of ˈhonour**
Matrûh mætˈruː
Matsui® mætˈsuː.i
Matsushita® ˌmæt.suˈʃiː.tə, US -t̬ə
matt(e) mæt
matt|er ˈmæt|.əʳ, US ˈmæt̬|.ɚ **-ers** -əz, US -ɚz **-ering** -ər.ɪŋ **-ered** -əd, US -ɚz **as a ˌmatter of ˈfact**
Matterhorn ˈmæt.ə.hɔːn, US ˈmæt̬.ɚ.hɔːrn
matter-of-fact ˌmæt.ər.əvˈfækt, US ˌmæt̬.ɚ-
Matthau ˈmæθ.aʊ, ˈmæt-
Matthes ˈmæθ.əs
Matthew ˈmæθ.juː
Matthews ˈmæθ.juːz
Matthias məˈθaɪ.əs
Matthiessen ˈmæθ.ɪ.sən
matting ˈmæt.ɪŋ, US ˈmæt̬-
mattins ˈmæt.ɪnz, US -ənz
mattock ˈmæt.ək, US ˈmæt̬- **-s** -s
mattress ˈmæt.rəs, -trɪs **-es** -ɪz
matur|ate ˈmæt.jər|.eɪt, -jʊ.r|eɪt; ˈmætʃ.ər|.eɪt, US ˈmætʃ.ə.r|eɪt, -ʊ- **-ates** -eɪts **-ating** -eɪ.tɪŋ, US -eɪ.t̬ɪŋ **-ated** -eɪ.tɪd, US -eɪ.t̬ɪd
maturation ˌmæt.jərˈeɪ.ʃən, -jʊˈreɪ-; ˌmætʃ.ərˈeɪ-, US ˌmætʃ.əˈreɪ-, -ʊˈ-
matur|e, M~ məˈtʃʊəʳ, -ˈtʃɔːʳ, -ˈtjʊəʳ, -ˈtjɔːʳ, US -ˈtʊr, -ˈtjʊr, -ˈtʃʊr **-ely** -li **-eness** -nəs, -nɪs **-es** -z **-ing** -ɪŋ **-ed** -d
Maturin *surname:* ˈmæt.jʊə.rɪn, -jəˈ-, US ˈmæt.ju.rɪn, -təˈ-
Maturín *in Venezuela:* ˌmæt.jʊəˈrɪn, -jəˈ-, US ˌmɑː.tuːˈriːn, -t̬əˈ-
maturity məˈtʃʊə.rə.ti, -ˈtʃɔː-, -ˈtjʊə-, -ˈtjɔː-, -rɪ-, US -ˈtʊr.ə.t̬i, -ˈtjʊr-, -ˈtʃʊr-
matutinal ˌmæt.jʊˈtaɪ.nəl; məˈtjuː.tɪ-, -tə-, US məˈtuː.tən.əl, -ˈtjuː-
matzo(h) ˈmɒt.sə, ˈmæt-, ˈmɑːt-, -səʊ, US ˈmɑːt.sə, -soʊ **-s** -z
matzoth ˈmɒt.sət, ˈmæt-, ˈmɑːt-, -səʊθ, US -soʊt
maud, M~ mɔːd, US mɑːd, mɔːd **-s** -z
Maude mɔːd, US mɑːd, mɔːd
maudlin ˈmɔːd.lɪn, US ˈmɑːd-, ˈmɔːd-
Maudsley ˈmɔːdz.li, US ˈmɑːdz-, ˈmɔːdz-
Mauger ˈmeɪ.dʒəʳ, ˈmɔː.gəʳ, US ˈmɑː.gɚ, ˈmɔː-, ˈmeɪ.dʒɚ
Maugham mɔːm; ˈmɒf.əm, US mɑːm, mɔːm

> Note: The author Somerset Maugham is pronounced /mɔːm/.

Maughan mɔːn, US mɑːn, mɔːn
maugre ˈmɔː.gəʳ, US ˈmɑː.gɚ, ˈmɔː-
Maui ˈmaʊ.i
maul mɔːl, US mɑːl, mɔːl **-s** -z **-ing** -ɪŋ **-ed** -d **-er/s** -əʳ/z, US -ɚ/z
Mauleverer mɔːˈlev.ər.əʳ, mə-, US mɑːˈlev.ɚ.ɚ, mɔː-, mə-
maulstick ˈmɔːl.stɪk, US ˈmɑːl-, ˈmɔːl- **-s** -s
Mau Mau ˈmaʊˌmaʊ, ˌ-ˈ-
Mauna Kea ˌmaʊ.nəˈkeɪ.ə, US ˌmaʊ-, ˌmɑː-, ˌmɔː-
Mauna Loa ˌmaʊ.nəˈləʊ.ə, US -ˈloʊ-, ˌmɑː-, ˌmɔː-

maunder ˈmɔːn.dəʳ, (US) ˈmɑːn.dɚ, ˈmɔːn- **-s** -z **-ing** -ɪŋ **-ed** -d
maundy, M~ ˈmɔːn.di, (US) ˈmɑːn-, ˈmɔːn- ˌ**Maundy** ˈ**Thursday**
Maunsell ˈmænt.səl
Maupassant ˈməʊ.pæs.ɑ̃ːŋ, (US) ˈmoʊ.pə.sɑːnt
Maupin ˈmɔː.pɪn, -pæ̃ŋ, (US) ˈmɑː-
Maureen ˈmɔː.riːn, -ˈ-, (US) mɔːˈriːn, mə-
Mauretani|a ˌmɒr.ɪˈteɪ.ni|.ə, ˌmɔː.rɪˈ-, (US) ˌmɔːr.ɪˈ-, ˌmɑːr-, ˈ-nj|ə **-an/s** -ən/z
Mauriac ˈmɒr.i.æk, ˈmɔː.ri-, (US) ˈmɔːr-, ˈmɑːr-
Maurice ˈmɒr.ɪs, mɒrˈiːs, (US) mɔːˈriːs, mɑː-, mə-; (US) ˈmɑːr.ɪs, ˈmɔːr-
Mauritani|a ˌmɒr.ɪˈteɪ.ni|.ə, ˌmɔː.rɪˈ-, (US) ˌmɔːr.ɪˈ-, ˌmɑːr-, -ˈnj|ə **-an/s** -ən/z
Maurit|ius məˈrɪʃ|.əs, mɔː-, mɒrˈɪʃ|-, (US) mɔːˈrɪʃ.i|.əs, mɑː-, ˈ-əs **-ian/s** -ən/z
Mauser ˈmaʊ.zəʳ, (US) -zɚ **-s** -z
mausoleum ˌmɔː.səˈliː.əm, ˌmaʊ-, -zəˈ-, -ˈleɪ-, (US) ˌmɑː.səˈliː-, ˌmɔː-, -zəˈ- **-s** -z
mauve məʊv, (US) moʊv, mɑːv, mɔːv **-s** -z
maven ˈmeɪ.vən **-s** -z
maverick ˈmæv.ər.ɪk, (US) ˈmæv.ɚ-, ˈ-rɪk **-s** -s
mavis, M~ ˈmeɪ.vɪs
maw, M~ mɔː, (US) mɑː, mɔː **-s** -z
Mawer ˈmɔː.əʳ, mɔːʳ, (US) ˈmɔː.ɚ
Mawhinney, Mawhinny məˈ*h*wɪn.i
mawkish ˈmɔː.kɪʃ, (US) ˈmɑː-, ˈmɔː- **-ly** -li **-ness** -nəs, -nɪs
max, M~ mæks
Maxey ˈmæk.si
Max Factor® ˌmæksˈfæk.təʳ, (US) -tɚ
maxi ˈmæk.si **-s** -z
maxill|a mækˈsɪl|.ə **-ae** -iː **-as** -əz **-ary** -ər.i
maxim, M~ ˈmæk.sɪm **-s** -z
maximal ˈmæk.sɪ.məl, -sə- **-ly** -i
maximalist ˈmæk.sɪ.məl.ɪst, -sə- **-s** -s
Maximilian ˌmæk.sɪˈmɪl.i.ən, -səˈ-, (US) ˈ-jən, ˈ-i.ən
maximization, -isa- ˌmæk.sɪ.maɪˈzeɪ.ʃən, -sə-, (US) -məˈ- **-s** -z
maximiz|e, -is|e ˈmæk.sɪ.maɪz, -sə- **-es** -ɪz **-ing** -ɪŋ **-ed** -d **-er/s** -əʳ/z, (US) -ɚ/z
maxim|um ˈmæk.sɪ.m|əm, -sə- **-ums** -əmz **-a** -ə
Maximus ˈmæk.sɪ.məs, -sə-
Maxine mækˈsiːn, ˈ--, (US) mækˈsiːn
Maxse ˈmæk.si
Maxwell ˈmæk.swəl, -swel
may **auxil. v** meɪ
May meɪ ˈ**May** ˌ**Day**
May|a ˈmaɪ|.ə, (US) ˈmɑː.j|ə, ˈmaɪ|.ə **-as** -əz **-an/s** -ən/z
Mayall ˈmeɪ.ɔːl, -əl, (US) -ɔːl, -ɑːl, -əl
mayapple ˈmeɪˌæp.əl **-s** -z
maybe ˈmeɪ.bi, -biː, ˌ-ˈ-
maybug ˈmeɪ.bʌg **-s** -z
mayday, M~ ˈmeɪ.deɪ **-s** -z
Mayer ˈmeɪ.əʳ, (US) -ɚ
mayest ˈmeɪ.ɪst, -əst; meɪst
Mayfair ˈmeɪ.feəʳ, (US) -fer
Mayfield ˈmeɪ.fiːld
mayflower, M~ ˈmeɪ.flaʊəʳ, -flaʊ.əʳ, (US) -flaʊ.ɚ **-s** -z
mayfl|y ˈmeɪ.fl|aɪ **-ies** -aɪz
mayhap ˈmeɪ.hæp
mayhem ˈmeɪ.hem
Mayhew ˈmeɪ.hjuː
maying ˈmeɪ.ɪŋ
Maynard ˈmeɪ.nɑːd, -nəd, (US) -nɚd
Maynooth məˈnuːθ, meɪ-
mayn't (= **may not**) meɪnt; ˈmeɪ.ənt
Maynwaring ˈmæn.ər.ɪŋ
mayo (abbrev. for **mayonnaise**) ˈmeɪ.əʊ, (US) -oʊ
Mayo *in Ireland, surname:* ˈmeɪ.əʊ, -ˈ-, (US) -oʊ, -ˈ- *Native American:* ˈmaɪ.əʊ, (US) -oʊ **-s** -z
mayonnaise ˌmeɪ.əˈneɪz, (US) ˈmeɪ.ə.neɪz, ˌ--ˈ-
mayor, M~ meəʳ, (US) meɪɚ, mer **-s** -z
mayoral ˈmeə.rəl, (US) ˈmeɪ.ɔːr.əl
mayoralt|y ˈmeə.rəl.t|i, (US) ˈmeɪ.ɚ.əl.t|i, ˈmer- **-ies** -iz
mayoress, M~ ˌmeəˈres; ˈmeə.res, -rɪs, -rəs, (US) ˈmeɪ.ɚ.ɪs, ˈmer-, -əs **-es** -ɪz
mayorship ˈmeə.ʃɪp, (US) ˈmeɪ.ɚ-, ˈmer- **-s** -s
Mayotte maɪˈjɒt, (US) mɑːˈjɑːt
Mayou ˈmeɪ.uː
maypole ˈmeɪ.pəʊl, (US) -poʊl **-s** -z
mayst meɪst
may've (= **may have**) ˈmeɪ.əv
Mazda® ˈmæz.də, (US) ˈmɑːz- **-s** -z
maz|e meɪz **-es** -ɪz
Mazeppa məˈzep.ə
Mazo de la Roche ˌmæz.əʊ.də.lɑːˈrɒʃ, ˌmeɪ.zəʊ-, (US) ˌmɑː.zoʊ.də.lɑːˈroʊʃ
mazuma məˈzuː.mə
mazurka məˈzɜː.kə, (US) -ˈzɜː-, -ˈzʊr- **-s** -z
mazuzah məˈzuː.zə
maz|y ˈmeɪ.z|i **-ier** -i.əʳ, (US) -i.ɚ **-iest** -i.ɪst, -i.əst **-ily** -əl.i, -ɪ.li **-iness** -ɪ.nəs, -ɪ.nɪs
MBA ˌem.biːˈeɪ
Mbabane əm.bɑːˈbɑː.neɪ, (US) ˌem-
MBE ˌem.biːˈiː
Mbeki əmˈbek.i
Mbuji-Mayi əmˈbuː.dʒi.maɪ.i, (US) emˌbuː.dʒiˈmaɪ.ji, -ˈmɑː-
Mc mək, mæk
MC ˌemˈsiː
McAdam məˈkæd.əm
McAfee məˈkæf.i; ˌmæk.əˈfiː, (US) ˈmæk.ə.fiː; (US) məˈkæf.i
McAiley məˈkeɪ.li
McAleer ˌmæk.əˈlɪəʳ, (US) -ˈlɪr
McAleese ˌmæk.əˈliːs
McAlinden ˌmæk.əˈlɪn.dən
McAlister məˈkæl.ɪ.stəʳ, (US) -stɚ
McAllister məˈkæl.ɪ.stəʳ, ˈ-ə-, (US) -stɚ
McAll məˈkɔːl, (US) -ˈkɔːl, -ˈkɑːl
McAlpine məˈkæl.pɪn, -paɪn
McAnally ˌmæk.əˈnæl.i, (US) ˈmæk.ən.æl.i
McArdle məˈkɑː.dəl, (US) -ˈkɑːr-
McArthur məˈkɑː.θəʳ, (US) -ˈkɑːr.θɚ
McAteer ˌmæk.əˈtɪəʳ, ˈ---, (US) ˌmæk.əˈtɪr, ˈ---
McAulay məˈkɔː.li, (US) -ˈkɔː-, -ˈkɑː-
McAvoy ˈmæk.ə.vɔɪ
McBain məkˈbeɪn
McBeal məkˈbiːl
McBean məkˈbeɪn, -ˈbiːn
McBeth məkˈbeθ
McBrain məkˈbreɪn
McBride məkˈbraɪd
MCC ˌem.siːˈsiː
McCabe məˈkeɪb
McCaffrey məˈkæf.ri
McCain məˈkeɪn
McCall məˈkɔːl, (US) -ˈkɔːl, -ˈkɑːl
McCallie məˈkɔː.li, (US) -ˈkɑː.li, -ˈkɔː-
McCallion məˈkæl.i.ən
McCallum məˈkæl.əm
McCann məˈkæn
McCartan, McCarten məˈkɑː.tən, (US) -ˈkɑːr-
McCarthy məˈkɑː.θi, (US) -ˈkɑːr- **-ism** -ɪ.zəm **-ite/s** -aɪt/s
McCartney məˈkɑːt.ni, (US) -ˈkɑːrt-
McCaughey məˈkæx.i, -ˈkæ.hi, -ˈkɒf.i, (US) -ˈkæ.hi, -ˈkɑː.fi
McCausland məˈkɔːz.lənd, (US) -ˈkɑːz-, -ˈkɔːz-
McClain məˈkleɪn
McClean məˈkleɪn, -ˈkliːn
McClear məˈklɪəʳ, (US) -ˈklɪr
McClellan məˈklel.ən
McClelland məˈklel.ənd
McClintock məˈklɪn.tək, -tɒk, (US) -ţək, -tɑːk
McCloskey məˈklɒs.ki, (US) -ˈklɑː.ski, -ˈklʌs.ki
McClure məˈklʊəʳ, -ˈklɔːʳ, (US) -ˈklʊr
McColl məˈkɒl, (US) -ˈkɑːl, -ˈkɔːl
McCollum məˈkɒl.əm, (US) -ˈkɑː.ləm
McComb məˈkəʊm, (US) -ˈkoʊm
McConnell məˈkɒn.əl, (US) -ˈkɑː.nəl
McConochie məˈkɒn.ə.ki, -xi, (US) -ˈkɑː.nə-
McConville məˈkɒn.vɪl, (US) -ˈkɑːn-
McCormack məˈkɔː.mək, (US) -ˈkɔːr-
McCormick məˈkɔː.mɪk, (US) -ˈkɔːr-
McCorquodale məˈkɔː.kə.deɪl, (US) -ˈkɔːr-
McCorry məˈkɒr.i, (US) -ˈkɔːr-
McCourt məˈkɔːt, (US) -ˈkɔːrt
McCoy məˈkɔɪ
McCrae, McCrea məˈkreɪ
McCready məˈkriː.di
McCrory məˈkrɔː.ri, (US) -ˈkrɔːr.i
McCullagh məˈkʌl.ə
McCullam məˈkʌl.əm
McCullers məˈkʌl.əz, (US) -ɚz
McCulloch məˈkʌl.ək, -əx
McCusker məˈkʌs.kəʳ, (US) -kɚ
McDade məkˈdeɪd

M

McDaniels mək'dæn.jəlz
McDermot(t) mək'dɜː.mət, ⓤⓢ -'dɝː-
McDiarmid mək'dɜː.mɪd, -'deə-, ⓤⓢ -'dɝː-
McDonald mək'dɒn.əld, mæk-, ⓤⓢ -'dɑː.nəld
McDonaugh mək'dɒn.ə, ⓤⓢ -'dɑː.nə
McDon(n)ell mək'dɒn.əl, ˌmæk.də'nel, ⓤⓢ -'dɑː.nəl
McDono(u)gh mək'dʌn.ə, -'dɒn-, ⓤⓢ -'dɑː.nə, -'dʌn-
McDougal mək'duː.gəl
McDougall mək'duː.gəl
McDougall's® mək'duː.gəlz, mæk-
McDowell, McDowall mək'daʊəl, -'daʊ.əl, -'dəʊ.əl, ⓤⓢ -'daʊ.əl, -'doʊ.əl
McDuff mək'dʌf, mæk-

> Note: In Scotland always /mək-/.

McElder(r)y 'mæk.əlˌder.i, ˌmæk.əl'der-
McEldowney ˌmæk.əl'daʊ.ni, 'mæk.əlˌdaʊ-
McElroy 'mæk.əl.rɔɪ
McElwain mə'kel.weɪn; 'mæk.əl.weɪn
McElwin mə'kel.wɪn
McEnroe 'mæk.ɪn.rəʊ, -ən-, ⓤⓢ -roʊ
McEwen, McEwan mə'kjuː.ən, -ɪn
McFadzean mək'fæd.i.ən
McFarland mək'fɑː.lənd, ⓤⓢ -'fɑːr-
McFarlane mək'fɑː.lɪn, -lən, ⓤⓢ -'fɑːr-
McGahey mə'gæx.i, -'gæ.hi, ⓤⓢ -'geɪ.hi
McGee mə'giː
McGillicuddy 'mæg.li.kʌd.i, 'mæk.ɪl-; mə'gɪl.i.kʌd.i, ⓤⓢ mə'gɪl.i-
McGillivray mə'gɪl.ɪ.vri, -'gɪl.vri, -'glɪv.ri, -reɪ
McGoldrick mə'gəʊl.drɪk, ⓤⓢ -'goʊl-
McGough mə'gɒf, ⓤⓢ -'gɑːf
McGovern mə'gʌv.ən, ⓤⓢ -ɚn
McGowan mə'gaʊ.ən
McGrath mə'grɑː, -'grɑːθ, -'græθ, ⓤⓢ -'græθ
McGraw mə'grɔː, ⓤⓢ -'grɑː, -'grɔː
McGregor mə'greg.ər, ⓤⓢ -ɚ
McGuane mə'gweɪn
McGuigan mə'gwɪg.ən
McGuinness mə'gɪn.ɪs, -əs
McGuire mə'gwaɪ.ər, ⓤⓢ -'gwaɪ.ɚ
McIlrath 'mæk.əl.rɑːθ, -ɪl-, ⓤⓢ -ræθ
McIlroy 'mæk.əl.rɔɪ, -ɪl-, ˌ--'-
McIlvanney ˌmæk.əl'væn.i, -ɪl'-
McIlwraith 'mæk.əl.reɪθ, -ɪl-
McInlay, McInley mə'kɪn.li, ⓤⓢ mək'ɪn.li
McInroy 'mæk.ɪn.rɔɪ, -ən-
McIntosh 'mæk.ɪn.tɒʃ, -ən-, ⓤⓢ -tɑːʃ
McIntyre 'mæk.ɪn.taɪər, -ən-, ⓤⓢ -taɪ.ɚ
McIver mə'kaɪ.vər, -'kɪv.ər, ⓤⓢ -vɚ
McIvor mə'kiː.vər, -'kaɪ.vər, ⓤⓢ -vɚ
McKay mə'kaɪ, -'keɪ
McKee mə'kiː
McKellen mə'kel.ən
McKenna mə'ken.ə
McKenzie mə'ken.zi
McKeown mə'kjəʊn, -'kjʊən, ⓤⓢ -'kjoʊn
McKerras mə'ker.əs
McKie mə'kaɪ, -'kiː
McKinlay mə'kɪn.li
McKinley mə'kɪn.li
McKinnon mə'kɪn.ən
McKinny mə'kɪn.i
McKnight mək'naɪt
McLachlan mə'klɒk.lən, -'klɒx-, -'klæk-, -'klæx-, ⓤⓢ -'klɑː.klən
McLagan mə'klæg.ən
McLaine mə'kleɪn
McLaren mə'klær.ən, ⓤⓢ -'kler-, -'klær-, -ən
McLaughlin mə'klɒk.lɪn, -'klɒx-, ⓤⓢ -'klɑː.klɪn, -'klɑːf-, -'klɔːf-
McLay mə'kleɪ
McLean mə'kleɪn, -'kliːn, ⓤⓢ -'kliːn
McLeish mə'kliːʃ
McLeod mə'klaʊd
McMahon mək'mɑːn, ⓤⓢ -'mæn, -'meɪ.ən, -'mɑːn
McManaman mək'mæn.ə.mən
McManus mək'mæn.əs, -'meɪ.nəs
McMaster mək'mɑː.stər, ⓤⓢ -'mæs.tɚ
McMenem(e)y mək'men.ə.mi
McMichael mək'maɪ.kəl
McMillan mək'mɪl.ən
McMullen mək'mʌl.ən
McMurdo mək'mɜː.dəʊ, ⓤⓢ -'mɝː.doʊ
McNab mək'næb
McNaghten, McNachton mək'nɔː.tən, ⓤⓢ -'nɑː-, -'nɔː-
McNally mək'næl.i
McNamara ˌmæk.nə'mɑː.rə, ⓤⓢ 'mæk.nə.mer.ə, -mær-
McNaught mək'nɔːt, ⓤⓢ -'nɑːt, -'nɔːt **-on** -ən **-en** -ən
McNeice mək'niːs
McNeil mək'niːl
McPhee mək'fiː
McPherson mək'fɜː.sən, ⓤⓢ -'fɝː.sən
McQuarie mə'kwɒr.i, -'kwɑːr-, -'kwɔːr-, ⓤⓢ mə'kwɑː.ri
McQueen mə'kwiːn
McRae mə'kreɪ
McReady mə'kriː.di
McShane mək'ʃeɪn
McShea mək'ʃeɪ
McSwiney mək'swiː.ni, -'swɪn-
McTaggart mək'tæg.ət, ⓤⓢ -ɚt
McTavish mək'tæv.ɪʃ
McTeague mək'tiːg
McVay mək'veɪ
McVeagh mək'veɪ
McVean mək'veɪn, -viːn
McVeigh mək'veɪ
McVey mək'veɪ
McVicar mək'vɪk.ər, ⓤⓢ -ɚ
McVit(t)ie mək'vɪt.i, ⓤⓢ -'vɪt̬-
McVitie's® mək'vɪt.iz, ⓤⓢ -'vɪt̬-
McWhirter mək'hwɜː.tər, ⓤⓢ -'hwɝː.t̬ɚ
McWilliams mək'wɪl.jəmz, -i.əmz, ⓤⓢ '-jəmz
MD ˌem'di
Md. (abbrev. for **Maryland**) 'meə.ri.lænd, 'mer.ɪ-, -lənd, ⓤⓢ 'mer.ɪ.lənd
me *note in Tonic Sol-fa:* miː **-s** -z
me pron *normal form:* miː; *freq. weak form:* mi
ME ˌem'iː
Me. (abbrev. for **Maine**) meɪn
Meacher 'miː.tʃər, ⓤⓢ -tʃɚ
mea culpa ˌmeɪ.ə'kʊl.pə, -ɑː'-, -'kʌl-, -pɑː, ⓤⓢ -ɑː'kʊl.pɑː, miː-, -ə'kʌl.pə
mead, M~ miːd **-s** -z
Meaden 'miː.dən
meadow 'med.əʊ, ⓤⓢ -oʊ **-s** -z **-y** -i
meadowlark 'med.əʊ.lɑːk, ⓤⓢ -oʊ.lɑːrk **-s** -s
Meadows 'med.əʊz, ⓤⓢ -oʊz
meadowsweet 'med.əʊ.swiːt, ⓤⓢ -oʊ-
Meagan 'miː.gən
meag|er 'miː.g|ər, ⓤⓢ -g|ɚ **-erer** -ər.ər, ⓤⓢ -ɚ.ɚ **-erest** -ər.ɪst, -əst **-erly** -əl.i, ⓤⓢ -ɚ.li **-erness** -ə.nəs, -nɪs, ⓤⓢ -ɚ-
Meagher mɑːr, ⓤⓢ mɑːr
meag|re 'miː.g|ər, ⓤⓢ -g|ɚ **-rer** -ər.ər, ⓤⓢ -ɚ.ɚ **-rest** -ər.ɪst, -əst **-rely** -əl.i, ⓤⓢ -ɚ.li **-reness** -ə.nəs, -nɪs, ⓤⓢ -ɚ-
Meaker 'miː.kər, ⓤⓢ -kɚ
meal miːl **-s** -z ˌ**meals on** '**wheels**; '**meal** ˌ**ticket**
mealie 'miː.li **-s** -z
mealtime 'miːl.taɪm **-s** -z
meal|y 'miː.l|i **-ier** -i.ər, ⓤⓢ -i.ɚ **-iest** -i.ɪst, -i.əst **-iness** -ɪ.nəs, -ɪ.nɪs
mealybug 'miː.li.bʌg
mealy-mouthed ˌmiː.li'maʊðd, ⓤⓢ 'miː.li.maʊðd, -maʊθt, ˌ--'- *stress shift, British only:* ˌ**mealy-mouthed** '**person**
mean miːn **-s** -z **-er** -ər, ⓤⓢ -ɚ **-est** -ɪst, -əst **-ly** -li **-ness** -nəs, -nɪs **-ing** -ɪŋ **meant** ment '**means** ˌ**test**
meand|er, M~ mi'æn.d|ər, ⓤⓢ -d|ɚ **-ers** -əz, ⓤⓢ -ɚz **-ering/s** -ər.ɪŋ **-ered** -əd, ⓤⓢ -ɚd
meanie 'miː.ni **-s** -z
meaning 'miː.nɪŋ **-s** -z **-ly** -li
meaningful 'miː.nɪŋ.fəl, -fʊl **-ly** -i **-ness** -nəs, -nɪs
meaningless 'miː.nɪŋ.ləs, -lɪs **-ly** -li **-ness** -nəs, -nɪs
means-test 'miːnz.test **-s** -s **-ing** -ɪŋ **-ed** -ɪd
meant (from **mean**) ment
meantime ˌmiːn'taɪm, '--, ⓤⓢ 'miːn-
meanwhile ˌmiːn'hwaɪl, '--, ⓤⓢ 'miːn-
mean|y 'miː.n|i **-ies** -iz
Meany 'miː.ni

Mearns mɜːnz, meənz, mɪənz, ⓊⓈ mɝːnz, mernz, mɪrnz
Mears mɪəz, ⓊⓈ mɪrz
measles ˈmiː.zəlz
measly ˈmiːz.li
measurab|le ˈmeʒ.ər.ə.b|əl **-ly** -li **-leness** -əl.nəs, -nɪs
meas|ure ˈmeʒ|.ər, ⓊⓈ -ɚ **-ures** -əz, ⓊⓈ -ɚz **-uring** -ər.ɪŋ **-ured** -əd, ⓊⓈ -ɚd **-urer/s** -ər.ər/z, ⓊⓈ -ɚ.ɚ/z
measureless ˈmeʒ.ə.ləs, -lɪs, ⓊⓈ ˈ-ɚ- **-ly** -li **-ness** -nəs, -nɪs
measurement ˈmeʒ.ə.mənt, ⓊⓈ ˈ-ɚ- **-s** -s
meat miːt **-s** -s
meat-and-potatoes ˌmiːt.ənd.pəˈteɪ.təʊz, -əm-, ⓊⓈ -ənd.pəˈteɪ.t̬oʊz
meatball ˈmiːt.bɔːl, ⓊⓈ -bɔːl, -bɑːl **-s** -z
Meates miːts
Meath *Irish county:* miːð

Note: Often pronounced /miːθ/ by English people.

meathead ˈmiːt.hed **-s** -z
meatless ˈmiːt.ləs, -lɪs
meatloa|f ˈmiːt.ləʊ|f, ⓊⓈ -loʊ|f **-ves** -vz
meatpacking ˈmiːtˌpæk.ɪŋ
meatus miˈeɪ.təs, ⓊⓈ -t̬əs **-es** -ɪz
meat|y ˈmiː.t|i, ⓊⓈ -t̬|i **-ier** -i.ər, ⓊⓈ -i.ɚ **-iest** -i.ɪst, -i.əst **-iness** -ɪ.nəs, -ɪ.nɪs
mecca, M~ ˈmek.ə
Meccano® mɪˈkɑː.nəʊ, mekˈɑː-, məˈkɑː-, ⓊⓈ -noʊ
mechanic mɪˈkæn.ɪk, mə- **-s** -s **-al** -əl **-ally** -əl.i, -li
mechanician ˌmek.əˈnɪʃ.ən **-s** -z
mechanism ˈmek.ə.nɪ.zəm **-s** -z
mechanistic ˌmek.əˈnɪs.tɪk **-ally** -əl.i, -li
mechanization, -isa- ˌmek.ə.naɪˈzeɪ.ʃən, -nɪˈ-, ⓊⓈ -nəˈ-
mechaniz|e, -is|e ˈmek.ə.naɪz **-es** -ɪz **-ing** -ɪŋ **-ed** -d
Mecklenburg ˈmek.lɪn.bɜːg, -lən-, -lɪm-, -ləm-, ⓊⓈ -lɪn.bɝːg, -lən-
Med med
MEd ˌemˈed
medal ˈmed.əl **-s** -z
medalist ˈmed.əl.ɪst **-s** -s
medallion mɪˈdæl.i.ən, medˈæl-, məˈdæl-, ⓊⓈ məˈdæl.jən **-s** -z
medallist ˈmed.əl.ɪst **-s** -s
Medan ˈmed.ɑːn, ˈmeɪ.dɑːn, -ˈ-, ⓊⓈ meɪˈdɑːn, ˈ--
Medawar ˈmed.ə.wər, ⓊⓈ -wɚ
meddl|e ˈmed.əl **-es** -z **-ing** -ɪŋ, ˈ-lɪŋ **-ed** -d **-er/s** -ər/z, ⓊⓈ -ɚ/z, ˈ-lər/z, ˈ-əl.ɚ/z, ˈ-lɚ/z
meddlesome ˈmed.əl.səm **-ness** -nəs, -nɪs
Mede miːd **-s** -z
Medea mɪˈdɪə, mə-, -ˈdiː.ə, ⓊⓈ mɪˈdiː.ə, mə-
Medellín ˌmed.əlˈɪn, -ˈiːn; *as if Spanish:* ˌmed.eɪˈjiːn; ⓊⓈ -ˈiːn
medfl|y ˈmed.fl|aɪ **-ies** -aɪz
media (plural of **medium**) ˈmiː.di.ə
mediaeval, M~ ˌmed.iˈiː.vəl, medˈiː-, ⓊⓈ ˌmiː.diˈ-, ˌmed.iˈ-; ⓊⓈ məˈdiː- **-ism** -ɪ.zəm **-ist/s** -ɪst/s
medial ˈmiː.di.əl
median ˈmiː.di.ən **-s** -z ˈ**median** ˌ**strip**
mediant ˈmiː.di.ənt **-s** -s
mediastin|um ˌmiː.di.əˈstaɪ.n|əm, ⓊⓈ -æsˈtaɪ- **-a** -ə
mediate adj ˈmiː.di.ət, -ɪt **-ly** -li **-ness** -nəs, -nɪs
medi|ate v ˈmiː.di|.eɪt **-ates** -eɪts **-ating** -eɪ.tɪŋ, ⓊⓈ -eɪ.t̬ɪŋ **-ated** -eɪ.tɪd, ⓊⓈ -eɪ.t̬ɪd
mediation ˌmiː.diˈeɪ.ʃən **-s** -z
mediative ˈmiː.di.ə.tɪv, ⓊⓈ -t̬ɪv
mediator ˈmiː.di.eɪ.tər, ⓊⓈ -t̬ɚ **-s** -z
mediatorial ˌmiː.di.əˈtɔː.ri.əl, ⓊⓈ -ˈtɔːr.i- **-ly** -i
mediatory ˈmiː.di.ə.tər.i, -tri, ⓊⓈ -tɔːr.i
medic ˈmed.ɪk **-s** -s
Medicaid ˈmed.ɪ.keɪd
medic|al ˈmed.ɪ.k|əl **-als** -əlz **-ally** -əl.i, -li
medicament məˈdɪk.ə.mənt, mɪ-, medˈɪk-; ˈmed.ɪ.kə-, ⓊⓈ məˈdɪk.ə-; ⓊⓈ ˈmed.ɪ.kə- **-s** -s
Medicare ˈmed.ɪ.keər, ⓊⓈ -ker
medi|cate ˈmed.ɪ|.keɪt **-cates** -keɪts **-cating** -keɪ.tɪŋ, ⓊⓈ -keɪ.t̬ɪŋ **-cated** -keɪ.tɪd, ⓊⓈ -keɪ.t̬ɪd
medication ˌmed.ɪˈkeɪ.ʃən, -dəˈ- **-s** -z
Medici ˈmed.ɪ.tʃiː, -tʃi; medˈiː.tʃi, məˈdiː-, mɪ-, ⓊⓈ ˈmed.ə.tʃiː
medicinal məˈdɪs.ɪ.nəl, mɪ-, medˈɪs-, -ən.əl, ⓊⓈ məˈdɪs- **-ly** -i
medicine ˈmed.sən, -sɪn, ˈ-ɪ.sən, ˈ-ə-, -sɪn, ⓊⓈ ˈmed.ɪ.sən **-s** -z ˈ**medicine** ˌ**ball**; ˈ**medicine** ˌ**chest**; ˌ**give someone a** ˌ**taste of their** ˌ**own** ˈ**medicine**

Note: This word shows how pronunciations may come and go: the British pronunciation with two syllables must have evolved from an earlier three-syllable pronunciation through elision of the middle vowel, but there is now some evidence of a return to a three-syllable pronunciation, resembling that of American English.

medico ˈmed.ɪ.kəʊ, ⓊⓈ -koʊ **-s** -z
medico- ˈmed.ɪ.kəʊ, ⓊⓈ -koʊ
medieval, M~ ˌmed.iˈiː.vəl, medˈiː-, ⓊⓈ ˌmiː.diˈ-, ˌmed.iˈ-; ⓊⓈ məˈdiː- **-ism** -ɪ.zəm **-ist/s** -ɪst/s
Medill məˈdɪl
Medina *in Saudi Arabia:* medˈiː.nə, mɪˈdiː-, məˈdiː-, ⓊⓈ məˈdiː- *in US:* medˈaɪ.nə, mɪˈdaɪ-, mə-, ⓊⓈ mə-
mediocre ˌmiː.diˈəʊ.kər, ˈmiː.di.əʊ-, ⓊⓈ ˌmiː.diˈoʊ.kɚ, ˈmiː.di.oʊ-
mediocrit|y ˌmiː.diˈɒk.rə.t|i, ˌmed.iˈ-, -ɪ.t|i, ⓊⓈ ˌmiː.diˈɑː.krə.t̬|i **-ies** -iz
medi|tate ˈmed.ɪ|.teɪt, ˈ-ə- **-tates** -teɪts **-tating** -teɪ.tɪŋ, ⓊⓈ -teɪ.t̬ɪŋ **-tated** -teɪ.tɪd, ⓊⓈ -teɪ.t̬ɪd **-tator/s** -teɪ.tər/z, ⓊⓈ -teɪ.t̬ɚ/z
meditation ˌmed.ɪˈteɪ.ʃən, -əˈ- **-s** -z
meditative ˈmed.ɪ.tə.tɪv, ˈ-ə-, -teɪ-, ⓊⓈ -teɪ.t̬ɪv **-ly** -li **-ness** -nəs, -nɪs
Mediterranean ˌmed.ɪ.tərˈeɪ.ni.ən, ˌ-ə-, ⓊⓈ -təˈreɪ-
medi|um ˈmiː.di|.əm **-a** -ə **-ums** -əmz ˈ**medium** ˌ**wave**
Medjugorje ˈmed.ʒu.gɔː.rjə, ⓊⓈ -gɔːr.jə
medlar ˈmed.lər, ⓊⓈ -lɚ **-s** -z
medley, M~ ˈmed.li **-s** -z
Medlock ˈmed.lɒk, ⓊⓈ -lɑːk
Médoc ˈmeɪ.dɒk, ˈmed.ɒk, -ˈ-, ⓊⓈ ˈmeɪ.dɑːk, -ˈ- **-s** -s
medulla medˈʌl.ə, mɪˈdʌl-, məˈdʌl-, ⓊⓈ mɪˈdʌl- **-s** -z
medus|a, M~ mɪˈdʒuː.z|ə, -ˈdjuː-, mə-, medʒˈuː-, medˈjuː-, -s|ə, ⓊⓈ məˈduː-, -ˈdjuː- **-as** -əz **-ae** -iː
Medvedev medˈvjeɪ.def, -ˈvjed.ef
Medway ˈmed.weɪ
Mee miː
meed miːd **-s** -z
meek, M~ miːk **-er** -ər, ⓊⓈ -ɚ **-est** -ɪst, -əst **-ly** -li **-ness** -nəs, -nɪs
meerkat ˈmɪə.kæt, ⓊⓈ ˈmɪr- **-s** -s
meerschaum ˈmɪə.ʃəm, -ʃaʊm, ⓊⓈ ˈmɪr-, -ʃɑːm, -ʃɔːm **-s** -z
Meerut ˈmɪə.rət, ⓊⓈ ˈmiː-
meet miːt **-s** -s **-ness** -nəs, -nɪs **-ing** -ɪŋ, ˈmiː.t̬ɪŋ **met** met
meeting ˈmiː.tɪŋ, ⓊⓈ -t̬ɪŋ **-s** -z
Meg meg
mega- ˈmeg.ə, ˌmeg.əˈ

Note: Prefix. May carry primary or secondary stress on the first syllable, e.g. **megalith** /ˈmeg.ə.lɪθ/, **megalithic** /ˌmeg.əˈlɪθ.ɪk/.

megabit ˈmeg.ə.bɪt **-s** -s
megabucks ˈmeg.ə.bʌks
megabyte ˈmeg.ə.baɪt **-s** -s
megacycle ˈmeg.əˌsaɪ.kəl **-s** -z
megadeath ˈmeg.ə.deθ **-s** -s
megahertz ˈmeg.ə.hɜːts, ⓊⓈ -hɝːts, -herts
megalith ˈmeg.ə.lɪθ **-s** -s
megalithic ˌmeg.əˈlɪθ.ɪk
megalomania ˌmeg.əl.əʊˈmeɪ.ni.ə, ⓊⓈ -əˈ-, -oʊˈ-, ˈ-njə
megalomaniac ˌmeg.əl.əʊˈmeɪ.ni.æk, ⓊⓈ -oʊˈ-, -əˈ- **-s** -s
megalomaniacal ˌmeg.əl.əʊ.məˈnaɪ.ə.kəl, ⓊⓈ -oʊ-
megalopolis ˌmeg.əlˈɒp.ə.lɪs, ⓊⓈ -ˈɑː.pə-
Megan ˈmeg.ən, ⓊⓈ ˈmeg-, ˈmiː.gən
megaphone ˈmeg.ə.fəʊn, ⓊⓈ -foʊn **-s** -z
megapixel ˈmeg.əˌpɪk.səl **-s** -z
megaplex ˈmeg.ə.pleks **-es** -ɪz
megastar ˈmeg.ə.stɑːr, ⓊⓈ -stɑːr **-s** -z
megastore ˈmeg.ə.stɔːr, ⓊⓈ -stɔːr **-s** -z

M

megatheri|um ˌmeg.əˈθɪə.ri|.əm, (US) -ˈθɪr.i- **-a** -ə
megaton ˈmeg.ə.tʌn **-s** -z
megavolt ˈmeg.ə.vəʊlt, -vɒlt, (US) -voʊlt **-s** -s
megawatt ˈmeg.ə.wɒt, (US) -wɑːt **-s** -s
Meghan ˈmeg.ən, (US) ˈmeg-, ˈmiː.gən
megilp məˈgɪlp, mɪ-, (US) mə-
megrim ˈmiː.grɪm, -grəm, (US) -grɪm **-s** -z
Mehta ˈmeɪ.tə
Meier ˈmaɪ.əʳ, (US) -ɚ
Meikle ˈmiː.kəl
Meiklejohn ˈmɪk.əl.dʒɒn, ˈmiː.kəl-, (US) -dʒɑːn
meios|is maɪˈəʊ.s|ɪs, (US) -ˈoʊ- **-es** -iːz
Meir *English surname:* mɪəʳ, (US) mɪr *Israeli surname:* meɪˈɪəʳ, (US) meɪˈɪr, maɪ.ɚ
Meirionnydd mer.iˈɒn.ɪð, (US) -ˈɑː.nɪθ
Meissen ˈmaɪ.sən
Meistersinger ˈmaɪ.stəˌsɪŋ.əʳ, -ˌzɪŋ-, (US) -stɚˌsɪŋ.ɚ, -ˌzɪŋ- **-s** -z
Mekka ˈmek.ə
Meknès mekˈnes
Mekong ˌmiːˈkɒŋ, ˌmeɪ-, (US) ˌmeɪˈkɑːŋ, -kɔːŋ *stress shift:* ˌ**Mekong** ˈ**River**
Mel mel
melamine ˈmel.ə.miːn, -mɪn, (US) -miːn
melancholia ˌmel.ənˈkəʊ.li.ə, -əŋˈ-, (US) -ənˈkoʊ-
melancholic ˌmel.ənˈkɒl.ɪk, -əŋˈ-, (US) -ənˈkɑː.lɪk *stress shift:* ˌ**melancholic** ˈ**mood**
melancholy ˈmel.ən.kəl.i, -əŋ-, -kɒl-, (US) -ən.kɑː.li
Melanchthon məˈlæŋk.θɒn, mɪ-, melˈæŋk-, -θən, (US) məˈlæŋk.θən
Melanesi|a ˌmel.əˈniː.zi|.ə, -ʒi-, ˈ-ʒ|ə, (US) -ʒ|ə, -ʃ|ə **-an/s** -ən/z
mélang|e meɪˈlɑ̃ːnʒ, ˈ--, (US) meɪˈlɑ̃ːʒ, -ˈlɔ̃ːʒ, -ˈlɑːndʒ, -ˈlɔːndʒ **-es** -ɪz
Melanie ˈmel.ə.ni
mela|nin ˈmel.ə|.nɪn **-nism** -nɪ.zəm
melanom|a ˌmel.əˈnəʊ.m|ə, (US) -ˈnoʊ- **-as** -əz **-ata** -ə.tə, (US) -t̬ə
Melanthius məˈlænt.θi.əs, mɪ-, melˈænt-, -ɒs, (US) məˈlænt.θi.əs
Melba ˈmel.bə ˌ**Melba** ˈ**toast**
Melbourne ˈmel.bən, -bɔːn, (US) -bɚn, -bɔːrn

> Note: In Australia always /ˈmel.bən/.

Melchett ˈmel.tʃɪt
Melchior ˈmel.ki.ɔːʳ, (US) -ɔːr
Melchizedek melˈkɪz.ə.dek
Melcombe ˈmel.kəm
meld meld **-s** -z **-ing** -ɪŋ **-ed** -ɪd
Meldrew ˈmel.druː
Meleager ˌmel.iˈeɪ.gəʳ, (US) -dʒɚ
mêlée, melee ˈmel.eɪ, ˈmeɪ.leɪ, -ˈ-, (US) ˈmeɪ.leɪ, -ˈ- **-s** -z
Melhuish ˈmel.ɪʃ, ˈmel.ju.ɪʃ, -hju-; melˈjuː.ɪʃ, -ˈhjuː-
Melibeus ˌmel.ɪˈbiː.əs, -əˈ-, (US) -əˈ-
Melincourt ˈmel.ɪn.kɔːt, -ɪŋ-, (US) -ɪn.kɔːrt
Melinda məˈlɪn.də, mɪ-, melˈɪn-, (US) məˈlɪn-
melinite ˈmel.ɪ.naɪt
meliorable ˈmiː.li.ər.ə.bəl, (US) ˈmiːl.jɚ.ə-
melior|ate ˈmiː.li.ər|.eɪt, (US) ˈmiːl.jə.r|eɪt, ˈmiː.li.ə- **-ates** -eɪts **-ating** -eɪ.tɪŋ, (US) -eɪ.t̬ɪŋ **-ated** -eɪ.tɪd, (US) -eɪ.t̬ɪd
melioration ˌmiː.li.ərˈeɪ.ʃən, (US) ˌmiːl.jəˈreɪ.ʃən, ˌmiː.li.əˈ- **-s** -z
meliorative ˈmiː.li.ər.ə.tɪv, (US) ˈmiːl.jɚ.ə.t̬ɪv
meliorator ˈmiː.li.ər.eɪ.təʳ, (US) ˈmiːl.jə.reɪ.t̬ɚ **-s** -z
Melissa məˈlɪs.ə, mɪ-, melˈɪs-, (US) məˈlɪs-
Melita məˈliː.tə; ˈmel.ɪ-, (US) ˈmel.ɪ.t̬ə; (US) məˈliː-, -ˈlɪt̬.ə
Melksham ˈmelk.ʃəm
mellifluen|t mɪˈlɪf.lu.ən|t, mə-, melˈɪf-, (US) məˈlɪf- **-ce** -*t*s
mellifluous mɪˈlɪf.lu.əs, mə-, melˈɪf-, (US) məˈlɪf- **-ly** -li **-ness** -nəs, -nɪs
Mellin ˈmel.ɪn
Mellor ˈmel.əʳ, -ɔːʳ, (US) -ɚ, -ɔːr
Mellors ˈmel.əz, -ɔːz, (US) -ɚz, -ɔːrz
mellow ˈmel.əʊ, (US) -oʊ **-er** -əʳ, (US) -ɚ **-est** -ɪst, -əst **-ness** -nəs, -nɪs **-s** -z **-ing** -ɪŋ **-ed** -d
Melmoth ˈmel.məθ
Melmotte ˈmel.mɒt, -ˈ-, (US) ˈmel.mɑːt
melodic məˈlɒd.ɪk, mɪ-, melˈɒd-, (US) məˈlɑː.dɪk **-ally** -əl.i, -li
melodious məˈləʊ.di.əs, mɪ-, melˈəʊ-, (US) məˈloʊ- **-ly** -li **-ness** -nəs, -nɪs
melodist ˈmel.ə.dɪst **-s** -s
melodrama ˈmel.əʊˌdrɑː.mə, (US) -oʊˌdrɑː.mə, -əˌ-, -ˌdræm.ə **-s** -z
melodramatic ˌmel.əʊ.drəˈmæt.ɪk, (US) -oʊ.drəˈmæt̬-, ˌ-ə- **-s** -s **-ally** -əl.i, -li
melodramatist ˌmel.əʊˈdræm.ə.tɪst, (US) -oʊˈdrɑː.mə.t̬ɪst, -əˈ-, -ˈdræm.ə- **-s** -s
melod|y, M~ ˈmel.ə.d|i **-ies** -iz
Meloids® ˈmel.ɔɪdz
melon ˈmel.ən **-s** -z
Melos ˈmiː.lɒs, ˈmel.ɒs, (US) ˈmiː.lɑːs
Melpomene melˈpɒm.ə.ni, ˈ-ɪ-, -niː, (US) -ˈpɑː.mə-
Melrose ˈmel.rəʊz, (US) -roʊz
melt melt **-s** -s **-ing/ly** -ɪŋ/li, (US) ˈmel.t̬ɪŋ/li **-ed** -ɪd, (US) ˈmel.t̬ɪd ˈ**melting** ˌ**pot**
meltdown ˈmelt.daʊn **-s** -z
Meltham ˈmel.θəm
Melton ˈmel.tən
Meltonian® melˈtəʊ.ni.ən, (US) -ˈtoʊ-
Melton Mowbray ˌmel.tənˈməʊ.breɪ, -təmˈ-, -bri, (US) -tənˈmoʊ-
meltwater ˈmeltˌwɔː.təʳ, (US) -ˌwɑː.t̬ɚ, -ˌwɔː- **-s** -z
Melville ˈmel.vɪl
Melvin, Melvyn ˈmel.vɪn
member ˈmem.bəʳ, (US) -bɚ **-s** -z **-ship/s** -ʃɪp/s ˌ**Member of** ˈ**Parliament**
membrane ˈmem.breɪn **-s** -z
membraneous memˈbreɪ.ni.əs
membranous ˈmem.brə.nəs
Memel ˈmeɪ.məl
memento mɪˈmen.təʊ, memˈen-, məˈmen-, (US) məˈmen.toʊ **-(e)s** -z
memento mori mɪˌmen.təʊˈmɒr.i, memˌen-, məˌmen-, -ˈmɔː.raɪ, (US) məˌmen.toʊˈmɔːr.iː, -aɪ
Memnon ˈmem.nɒn, -nən, (US) -nɑːn
memo ˈmem.əʊ, (US) -oʊ **-s** -z
memoir ˈmem.wɑːʳ, (US) -wɑːr, -wɔːr **-s** -z
memorabilia ˌmem.ər.əˈbɪl.i.ə, -ˈbiː.li-, (US) -ˈbɪl.i-, ˈ-jə, -ˈbiː.li-, -ˈbiːl.jə
memorab|le ˈmem.ər.ə.b|əl **-ly** -li
memorand|um ˌmem.ərˈæn.d|əm, (US) -əˈræn- **-a** -ə **-ums** -əmz
memorial məˈmɔː.ri.əl, mɪˈ-, memˈɔː-, (US) məˈmɔːr.i- **-s** -z
memorializ|e, -is|e məˈmɔː.ri.ə.laɪz, mɪˈ-, memˈɔː-, (US) məˈmɔːr.i- **-es** -ɪz **-ing** -ɪŋ **-ed** -d
memoriz|e, -is|e ˈmem.ər.aɪz, (US) -ə.raɪz **-es** -ɪz **-ing** -ɪŋ **-ed** -d
memor|y ˈmem.ər|.i, ˈ-r|i **-ies** -iz
Memphis ˈmem*p*.fɪs
memsahib ˈmemˌsɑː.*h*ɪb, ˈ-sɑːb, (US) ˈmemˌsɑː.*h*ɪb, ˈ-sɑːb; (US) ˌmem.sɑːˈhiːb, -ˈɪb **-s** -z
men (plural of **man**) men ˈ**men's** ˌ**room**
menac|e ˈmen.ɪs, -əs, (US) -əs **-es** -ɪz **-ing/ly** -ɪŋ/li **-ed** -t
ménag|e menˈɑːʒ, meɪˈnɑːʒ, mə-, mɪ-, -ˈnæʒ, ˈ--, (US) meɪˈnɑːʒ, mə- **-es** -ɪz
ménage à trois menˌɑːʒ.ɑːˈtrwɑː, meɪˌnɑːz-, mə-, mɪ-, -ˌnæʒ, ˌmen.ɑːz-, ˌmeɪ.nɑːʒ-, -ˌnæʒ, (US) meɪˌnɑːʒ-, mə-
menagerie məˈnædʒ.ər.i, mɪ-, menˈædʒ-, -ˈæʒ-, (US) məˈnædʒ-, -ˈnæʒ- **-s** -z
Menai ˈmen.aɪ
Menander menˈæn.dəʳ, mɪ-, (US) menˈæn.dɚ
menarche menˈɑː.ki, mɪˈnɑː-, mə-; ˈmen.ɑːk, (US) məˈnɑːr.ki, men-
Mencap ˈmen.kæp, ˈmeŋ-, (US) ˈmen-
Mencken ˈmeŋ.kən
mend mend **-s** -z **-ing** -ɪŋ **-ed** -ɪd **-er/s** -əʳ/z, (US) -ɚ/z
mendacious menˈdeɪ.ʃəs **-ly** -li **-ness** -nəs, -nɪs
mendacity menˈdæs.ə.ti, -ɪ.ti, (US) -ə.t̬i
Mendel ˈmen.dəl

Mendeleev ˌmen.dᵊlˈeɪ.ev, -dɪˈleɪ-, -ef, -əf, (US) -dəˈleɪ.əf
mendelevium ˌmen.dᵊlˈiː.vi.əm, -dɪˈliː-, (US) -dəˈliː-
Mendeleyev ˌmen.dᵊlˈeɪ.ev, -dɪˈleɪ-, -ef, -əf, (US) -dəˈleɪ.əf
Mendelian menˈdiː.li.ən
Mendelssohn *English surname:* ˈmen.dᵊl.sᵊn *German composer:* ˈmen.dᵊl.sᵊn, -səʊn, (US) -sᵊn, -soʊn, -zoʊn
Mendes ˈmen.dez, -des, (US) -ˈ-
mendican|cy ˈmen.dɪ.kən|t.si **-t/s** -t/s
mendicity menˈdɪs.ə.ti, -ɪ.ti, (US) -ə.ţi
Mendip ˈmen.dɪp **-s** -s
Mendoza menˈdəʊ.zə, (US) -ˈdoʊ-, -sɑː
mene ˈmiː.ni
Menelaus ˌmen.ɪˈleɪ.əs, -ᵊlˈeɪ-
Menem ˈmen.em, (US) ˈmeɪn-
menfolk ˈmen.fəʊk, (US) -foʊk **-s** -s
menhir ˈmen.hɪəʳ, (US) -hɪr **-s** -z
menial ˈmiː.ni.əl, ˈ-njəl **-s** -z **-ly** -i
Ménière ˈmen.i.eəʳ, ˈmeɪ.ni-, ˌ--ˈ-; ˈmeɪ.njeəʳ, -ˈ-, (US) meɪˈnjer
meningeal menˈɪn.dʒi.əl, məˈnɪn-, mɪ-; ˌmen.ɪnˈdʒiː.əl, -ənˈ-, (US) məˈnɪn.dʒi-
meninges (plural of **meninx**) məˈnɪn.dʒiːz, mɪ-, menˈɪn-, (US) məˈnɪn-
meningitis ˌmen.ɪnˈdʒaɪ.tɪs, -ənˈ-, -təs, (US) -ţɪs, -ţəs
meningococcal məˌnɪn.dʒəʊˈkɒk.ᵊl, -ˌnɪŋ.gəʊˈ-, (US) -ˌnɪŋ.goʊˈkɑː.kᵊl
meningo|coccus məˌnɪn.dʒəʊ|ˈkɒk.əs, -ˌnɪŋ.gəʊˈ-, (US) -ˌnɪŋ.goʊ|ˈkɑː.kəs **-cocci** -ˈkɒk.saɪ, -aɪ, -iː, (US) -ˈkɑːk.saɪ, -ˈkɑː.kaɪ, -kiː
meninx ˈmen.ɪnks, (US) ˈmiː.nɪŋks, ˈmen.ɪŋks **meninges** məˈnɪn.dʒiːz, mɪ-, menˈɪn-, (US) məˈnɪn-
menisc|us məˈnɪs.k|əs, mɪ-, menˈɪs-, (US) məˈnɪs- **-uses** -ə.sɪz **-i** -aɪ, -iː
Menlo Park ˌmen.ləʊˈpɑːk, (US) -loʊˈpɑːrk
Mennonite ˈmen.ə.naɪt **-s** -s
Meno ˈmiː.nəʊ, (US) -noʊ
men-of-war (plural of **man-of-war**) ˌmen.əvˈwɔːʳ, (US) -ˈwɔːr
menopausal ˌmen.əʊˈpɔː.zᵊl, ˌmiː.nəʊˈ-, (US) ˈmen.ə.pɑː.zᵊl, -pɔː-
menopause ˈmen.əʊ.pɔːz, ˈmiː.nəʊ-, (US) ˈmen.ə.pɑːz, -pɔːz
menorah mɪˈnɔː.rə, mə-, (US) -ˈnɔːr.ə **-s** -z
Menorca menˈɔː.kə, məˈnɔː-, mɪ-, (US) məˈnɔːr.kə
Mensa ˈment.sə
menservants (plural of **manservant**) ˈmenˌsɜː.vᵊnts, (US) -ˌsɝː-
menses ˈment.siːz
Menshevik ˈmen.ʃə.vɪk, -ʃɪ-, (US) -ʃə.vɪk **-s** -s
mens rea ˌmenzˈreɪ.ə, (US) -ˈriː.ə
menstrual ˈment.struəl, -stru.əl, (US) -strəl, -stru.əl
menstru|ate ˈment.stru|.eɪt, (US) -stru-, -str|eɪt **-ates** -eɪts **-ating** -eɪ.tɪŋ, (US) -eɪ.ţɪŋ **-ated** -eɪ.tɪd, (US) -eɪ.ţɪd
menstruation ˌment.struˈeɪ.ʃᵊn, (US) -struˈeɪ-, -ˈstreɪ-
mensual ˈment.sju.əl, -sjʊəl, (US) -ʃu.əl
mensurability ˌment.ʃᵊr.əˈbɪl.ə.ti, -ʃʊ.rəˈ-, -sjᵊr.əˈ-, -sjʊ.rəˈ-, -ɪ.ti, (US) -ʃɚ.əˈbɪl.ə.ţi, -sɚ-
mensurable ˈment.ʃᵊr.ə.bᵊl, -ʃʊ.rə-, -sjᵊr.ə-, -sjʊ.rə-, (US) -ʃɚ.ə-, -sɚ-
mensuration ˌment.ʃᵊrˈeɪ.ʃᵊn, -ʃʊˈreɪ-, -sjᵊrˈeɪ-, -sjʊˈreɪ-, (US) -ʃəˈreɪ-, -səˈ-
menswear ˈmenz.weəʳ, (US) -wer
-ment mənt
mental ˈmen.tᵊl, (US) -ţᵊl **-ly** -i ˌ**mental** ˈ**age**; ˈ**mental** ˌ**hospital**
mentalism ˈmen.tᵊl.ɪ.zᵊm, (US) -ţᵊl-
mentalistic ˌmen.tᵊlˈɪs.tɪk, (US) -ţᵊlˈ- **-ally** -ᵊl.i, -li
mentalit|y menˈtæl.ə.t|i, -ɪ.t|i, (US) -ə.ţ|i **-ies** -iz
Menteith menˈtiːθ, mən-
menthol ˈment.θɒl, -θᵊl, (US) -θɔːl, -θɑːl, -θᵊl, -θoʊl
mentholated ˈment.θᵊl.eɪ.tɪd, (US) -ţɪd
mention ˈmen.tʃᵊn **-s** -z **-ing** -ɪŋ **-ed** -d **-able** -ə.bᵊl, ˈmentʃ.nə-
Mentone menˈtəʊ.neɪ, -ni, (US) -ˈtoʊ.ni
mentor ˈmen.tɔːʳ, -təʳ, (US) -tɚ, -tɔːr **-s** -z **-ing** -ɪŋ
menu ˈmen.juː **-s** -z
menu-driven ˈmen.juːˌdrɪv.ᵊn, ˌmen.juːˈdrɪv-, (US) ˈmen.juːˌdrɪv-
Menuhin ˈmen.ju.ɪn, -hɪn, (US) -ɪn
Menzies ˈmen.zɪz, ˈmeŋ.ɪs, ˈmɪŋ-, (US) ˈmen.ziːz
Meopham ˈmep.əm
meow miːˈaʊ **-s** -z **-ing** -ɪŋ **-ed** -d
MEP ˌem.iːˈpiː **-s** -z
Mepham ˈmef.əm
Mephisto məˈfɪs.təʊ, mɪ-, mefˈɪs-, (US) məˈfɪs.toʊ
Mephistophelean, -lian ˌmef.ɪ.stəˈfiː.li.ən, ˌ-ə-, -stɒfˈɪl-; məˌfɪs.təˈ-, mɪ-, mefˌɪs-; ˌmef.ɪˌstɒf.əˈliː-, (US) ˌmef.ɪ.stəˈfiː.li-; (US) məˌfɪs.təˈ-; (US) ˌmef.əˌstɑː.fəˈliː-, -ˌstoʊ-
Mephistopheles ˌmef.ɪˈstɒf.ɪ.liːz, -ᵊl.iːz, (US) -əˈstɑː.fə.liːz
mephitic mɪˈfɪt.ɪk, mefˈɪt-, (US) məˈfɪţ-
mephitis mɪˈfaɪ.tɪs, mefˈaɪ-, -təs, (US) məˈfaɪ.ţɪs, -ţəs
Merc mɜːk, (US) mɝːk **-s** -s
mercantile ˈmɜː.kᵊn.taɪl, (US) ˈmɝː-, -tiːl, -taɪl, -tɪl
mercantilism ˈmɜː.kᵊn.tɪ.lɪ.zᵊm, -taɪ-, -tᵊl.ɪ-, (US) ˈmɝː.kən.tiː-, -tɪ-, -taɪ-
Mercator mɜːˈkeɪ.təʳ, -tɔːʳ, (US) mɚˈkeɪ.ţɚ
Mercedes *English female name:* ˈmɜː.sɪ.diːz, (US) ˈmɝː-; (US) mɚˈseɪ.diːz *trademark:* məˈseɪ.diːz, mɜː-, (US) mɚ-, mɝː-
Mercedes-Benz məˌseɪ.diːzˈbents, mɜː-, -ˈbenz, (US) mɚˌseɪ.diːzˈbenz, mɝː-, -ˈbents
mercenar|y ˈmɜː.sᵊn.ᵊr|.i, -sɪ.nᵊr-, -sᵊn.r|i, (US) ˈmɝː.sə.ner.i **-ies** -iz
mercer, M~ ˈmɜː.səʳ, (US) ˈmɝː.sɚ **-s** -z
merceriz|e, -is|e ˈmɜː.sᵊr.aɪz, (US) ˈmɝː- **-es** -ɪz **-ing** -ɪŋ **-ed** -d
merchandise **n** ˈmɜː.tʃᵊn.daɪs, -daɪs, (US) ˈmɝː-
merchandiz|e, -is|e **v** ˈmɜː.tʃᵊn.daɪz, (US) ˈmɝː- **-es** -ɪz **-ing** -ɪŋ **-ed** -d **-er/s** -əʳ/z, (US) -ɚ/z
merchant ˈmɜː.tʃᵊnt, (US) ˈmɝː- **-s** -s **-able** -ə.bᵊl ˌ**merchant** ˈ**bank**; ˌ**merchant** ˈ**navy**
merchant|man ˈmɜː.tʃᵊnt|.mən, (US) ˈmɝː- **-men** -mən, -men
Merchison ˈmɜː.kɪ.sᵊn, (US) ˈmɝː-
Merchiston ˈmɜː.tʃɪ.stᵊn, (US) ˈmɝː-
Merci|a ˈmɜː.si|.ə, -ʃi|.ə, (US) ˈmɝː.ʃ|ə, ˈ-ʃi|.ə, -si|- **-an** -ən
merciful ˈmɜː.sɪ.fᵊl, -fʊl, (US) ˈmɝː- **-ly** -i **-ness** -nəs, -nɪs
merciless ˈmɜː.sɪ.ləs, -lɪs, (US) ˈmɝː- **-ly** -li **-ness** -nəs, -nɪs
Merck® mɜːk, (US) mɝːk
mercurial mɜːˈkjʊə.ri.əl, -ˈkjɔː-, (US) mɝːˈkjʊr.i- **-s** -z **-ly** -i
mercuric mɜːˈkjʊə.rɪk, -ˈkjɔː-, (US) mɝːˈkjʊr.ɪk
Mercurochrome® mɜːˈkjʊə.rə.krəʊm, -ˈkjɔː-, (US) mɝːˈkjʊr.ə.kroʊm
mercurous ˈmɜː.kjᵊr.əs, -kjʊ.rəs, (US) ˈmɝː.kjʊr.əs, -kjɚ-
mercury, M~ ˈmɜː.kjᵊr.i, -kjʊ.ri, (US) ˈmɝː.kjə.ri, -kjɚ-
Mercutio mɜːˈkjuː.ʃi.əʊ, (US) mɝːˈkjuː.ʃi.oʊ
merc|y, M~ ˈmɜː.s|i, (US) ˈmɝː- **-ies** -iz ˈ**mercy** ˌ**killing**
mere mɪəʳ, (US) mɪr **-s** -z
Meredith ˈmer.ə.dɪθ, ˈ-ɪ-; *as if Welsh:* merˈed.ɪθ
merely ˈmɪə.li, (US) ˈmɪr-
merest ˈmɪə.rɪst, -rəst, (US) ˈmɪr.ɪst, -əst
meretricious ˌmer.ɪˈtrɪʃ.əs, -əˈ-, (US) -əˈ- **-ly** -li **-ness** -nəs, -nɪs
merganser mɜːˈgænt.səʳ, -ˈgæn.zəʳ, (US) mɝːˈgænt.sɚ **-s** -z
merg|e mɜːdʒ, (US) mɝːdʒ **-es** -ɪz **-ing** -ɪŋ **-ed** -d
merger ˈmɜː.dʒəʳ, (US) ˈmɝː.dʒɚ **-s** -z
Meribel ˈmer.i.bel
Mérida ˈmer.i.də, (US) -iː.dɑː
meridian məˈrɪd.i.ən, mɪ-, (US) məˈrɪd- **-s** -z
meridional məˈrɪd.i.ə.nᵊl, mɪ-, (US) məˈrɪd- **-ly** -i
Mérimée ˈmer.ɪ.meɪ, (US) ˌmeɪ.riˈmeɪ
meringue məˈræŋ **-s** -z
merino məˈriː.nəʊ, (US) -noʊ **-s** -z

M

Merioneth ˌmer.iˈɒn.ɪθ, -neθ, -nəθ, (US) -ˈɑː.nɪθ **-shire** -ʃəʳ, -ʃɪəʳ, (US) -ʃɚ, -ʃɪr
meristem ˈmer.i.stem, ˈ-ə-, (US) ˈ-ə- **-s** -z
meristematic ˌmer.i.stɪˈmæt.ɪk, ˌ-ə-, -stəˈ-, (US) -ə.stəˈmæţ- **-ally** -əl.i, -li
mer|it ˈmer|.ɪt **-its** -ɪts **-iting** -ɪ.tɪŋ, (US) -ɪ.ţɪŋ **-ited** -ɪ.tɪd, (US) -ɪ.ţɪd
meritocrac|y ˌmer.ɪˈtɒk.rə.s|i, -əˈ-, (US) -əˈtɑː.krə- **-ies** -iz
meritocratic ˌmer.ɪ.təˈkræt.ɪk, (US) ˈkræţ-
meritorious ˌmer.ɪˈtɔː.ri.əs, -əˈ-, (US) -əˈtɔːr.i- **-ly** -li **-ness** -nəs, -nɪs
Merivale ˈmer.ɪ.veɪl
Merkel ˈmɜː.kəl; *as if German:* ˈmeə-; (US) ˈmɝː-
merl mɜːl, (US) mɝːl **-s** -z
merle, M~ mɜːl, (US) mɝːl **-s** -z
merlin, M~ ˈmɜː.lɪn, (US) ˈmɝː- **-s** -z
merlot, M~ ˈmeə.ləʊ, -ˈ-, (US) mɝːˈloʊ, mer- **-s** -z
mermaid ˈmɜː.meɪd, (US) ˈmɝː- **-s** -z
mer|man, M~ ˈmɜː|.mæn, (US) ˈmɝː- **-men** -men
Meroe ˈmer.əʊ.i, (US) -oʊ-
Merope ˈmer.ə.pi
Merovingian ˌmer.əʊˈvɪn.dʒi.ən, ˈ-dʒən, (US) -oʊˈ-, -əˈ-
Merrick ˈmer.ɪk
Merrilies ˈmer.ɪ.liz, -əl.iz
Merrill ˈmer.əl, -ɪl
Merrimac ˈmer.ɪ.mæk, ˈ-ə-
Merriman ˈmer.i.mən
merriment ˈmer.i.mənt
Merritt ˈmer.ɪt
Merrivale ˈmer.i.veɪl
merr|y, M~ ˈmer|.i **-ier** -i.əʳ, (US) -i.ɚ **-iest** -i.ɪst, -i.əst **-ily** -əl.i, -ɪ.li **-iness** -ɪ.nəs, -ɪ.nɪs
merry-andrew ˌmer.iˈæn.druː **-s** -z
Merrydown® ˈmer.i.daʊn
merry-go-round ˈmer.i.gəʊˌraʊnd, (US) -goʊˌ- **-s** -z
merrymak|er ˈmer.iˌmeɪ.k|əʳ, (US) -k|ɚ **-ers** -əz, (US) -ɚz **-ing** -ɪŋ
Merryweather ˈmer.iˌweð.əʳ, (US) -ɚ
Mersey ˈmɜː.zi, (US) ˈmɝː- **-side** -saɪd **-sider/s** -ˌsaɪ.dəʳ/z
Merson ˈmɜː.sən, (US) ˈmɝː-
Merthyr ˈmɜː.θəʳ, (US) ˈmɝː.θɚ
Merthyr Tydfil ˌmɜː.θəˈtɪd.vɪl, (US) ˌmɝː.θɚˈ-
Merton ˈmɜː.tən, (US) ˈmɝː-
Mervyn ˈmɜː.vɪn, (US) ˈmɝː-
Meryl ˈmer.əl, -ɪl
mesa ˈmeɪ.sə **-s** -z
mésallianc|e mezˈæl.i.ənts, meɪˈzæl-, -ɑ̃ːns; *as if French:* ˌmez.æl.i.ˈɑ̃ːns; (US) meɪˈzæl.i.ənts; (US) ˌmeɪ.zəˈliː- **-es** -ɪz
mescal ˈmes.kæl, -ˈ-, (US) -ˈ- **-s** -z
mescalin(e) ˈmes.kəl.ɪn, -iːn
mesdames, M~ (plural of **madame**) meɪˈdæm, -dæmz, ˈ--, (US) -ˈdɑːm, -ˈdæm
mesdemoiselles, M~ (plural of **mademoiselle**) ˌmeɪ.dəm.wəˈzel, -ˈzelz, (US) ˌmeɪd.mwɑːˈzel
meseems mɪˈsiːmz
mesembryanthemum məˌzem.briˈænt.θɪ.məm, mɪ-, -θəm.əm, (US) mesˌem-, mez- **-s** -z
mesh meʃ **-es** -ɪz **-ing** -ɪŋ **-ed** -t
Meshach, Meschak ˈmiː.ʃæk
Meshed ˈmeʃ.ed
mesial ˈmiː.zi.əl, (US) ˈmiː-, ˈmez.i-, ˈmes-
Mesmer ˈmez.məʳ, (US) -mɚ
mesmeric mezˈmer.ɪk
mesmer|ism ˈmez.mər|.ɪ.zəm **-ist/s** -ɪst/s
mesmeriz|e, -is|e ˈmez.mər.aɪz **-es** -ɪz **-ing** -ɪŋ **-ed** -d **-er/s** -əʳ/z, (US) -ɚ/z
mesne miːn
meso- ˈmes.əʊ, ˈmez-, ˈmiː.səʊ, -zəʊ, (US) ˈmez.oʊ, ˈmes-, -ə, ˈmiː.soʊ, -sə
Note: Prefix. May carry either primary or secondary stress on the first syllable, e.g. **mesoderm** /ˈmes.əʊ.dɜːm/ (US) /ˈmez.oʊ.dɝːm/, **mesodermal** /ˌmes.əʊˈdɜː.məl/ (US) /ˌmez.oʊˈdɝː-/.
mesoderm ˈmes.əʊ.dɜːm, ˈmez-, ˈmiː.səʊ-, -zəʊ-, (US) ˈmez.oʊ.dɝːm, ˈmes-, ˈ-ə-
mesodermal ˌmes.əʊˈdɜː.məl, ˌmez-, ˌmiː.səʊˈ-, -zəʊˈ-, (US) ˌmez.oʊˈdɝː-, ˌmes-, -əˈ-
mesodermic ˌmes.əʊˈdɜː.mɪk, ˌmez-, ˌmiː.səʊˈ-, -zəʊˈ-, (US) ˌmez.oʊˈdɝː-, ˌmes-, -əˈ-
mesolect ˈmes.əʊ.lekt, ˈmez-, ˈmiː.səʊ-, -zəʊ-, (US) ˈmez.oʊ-, ˈmes-, -ə- **-s** -s
mesolectal ˌmes.əʊˈlek.təl, ˌmez-, ˌmiː.səʊˈ-, -zəʊˈ-, (US) ˌmez.oʊˈ-, ˌmes-, -ə-
mesomorph ˈmes.əʊ.mɔːf, ˈmez-, ˈmiː.səʊ-, -zəʊ-, (US) ˈmez.oʊ.mɔːrf, ˈmes-, ˈ-ə- **-s** -s
meson ˈmiː.zɒn, ˈmeɪ-, -sɒn, ˈmes.ɒn, ˈmez-, (US) ˈmez.ɑːn, ˈmes-, ˈmeɪ.sɑːn, ˈmiː-, -zɑːn **-s** -z
Mesopotami|a ˌmes.ə.pəˈteɪ.mi|.ə **-an/s** -ən/z
mesotron ˈmes.əʊ.trɒn, ˈmez-, ˈmiː.səʊ-, -zəʊ-, (US) ˈmez.oʊ.trɑːn, ˈmes-, ˈ-ə- **-s** -z
Mesozoic ˌmes.əʊˈzəʊ.ɪk, ˌmiː.səʊˈ-, (US) ˌmez.oʊˈzoʊ-, ˌmes-, -əˈ-
mesquite, M~ mesˈkiːt, məˈskiːt, mɪ-; ˈmes.kɪt, (US) məˈskiːt, mesˈkiːt
mess mes **-es** -ɪz **-ing** -ɪŋ **-ed** -t
messag|e ˈmes.ɪdʒ **-es** -ɪz **-ing** -ɪŋ **-ed** -d
messeigneurs (plural of **monseigneur**) ˌmes.eɪˈnjɜː
messenger ˈmes.ɪn.dʒəʳ, -ən-, (US) -dʒɚ **-s** -z
Messerschmitt® ˈmes.ə.ʃmɪt, (US) ˈ-ɚ-
Messiaen ˈmes.jɑ̃ːŋ, -i.ɑ̃ːŋ; *as if French:* mesˈjɑ̃ːŋ; (US) mesˈjɑ̃ːn
messiah, M~ məˈsaɪ.ə, mɪ-, mesˈaɪ-, (US) məˈsaɪ- **-s** -z
messianic ˌmes.iˈæn.ɪk
messieurs meɪˈsjɜː, mesˈjɜːz, ˈmes.əz; *as if French:* mesˈjɜː; (US) ˈmes.ɚz, mesˈjɝː
Messina mesˈiː.nə, məˈsiː-, mɪ-, (US) məˈsiː-, mesˈiː-
messmate ˈmes.meɪt **-s** -s
Messrs. (plural of **Mr**) ˈmes.əz, (US) -ɚz
messuag|e ˈmes.wɪdʒ, -ju.ɪdʒ, (US) ˈ-wɪdʒ **-es** -ɪz
mess-up ˈmes.ʌp **-s** -s
mess|y ˈmes|.i **-ier** -i.əʳ, (US) -i.ɚ **-iest** -i.ɪst, -i.əst **-ily** -əl.i, -ɪ.li **-iness** -ɪ.nəs, -ɪ.nɪs
mestiz|o mesˈtiː.z|əʊ, məˈstiː-, mɪ-, (US) mesˈtiː.z|oʊ **-a** -ə **-os** -əʊz, (US) -oʊz **-as** -əz
Mestre ˈmes.treɪ
met (from **meet**) met
meta- ˈmet.ə; məˈtæ, metˈæ, mɪˈtæ, (US) ˈmeţ.ə; (US) məˈtæ, metˈæ
Note: Prefix. Normally carries primary or secondary stress on the first syllable, e.g. **metaplasm** /ˈmet.əˌplæz.əm/ (US) /ˈmeţ-/, **metabolic** /ˌmet.əˈbɒl.ɪk/ (US) /ˌmeţ.əˈbɑː.lɪk/, or primary stress on the second syllable, e.g. **metabolism** /məˈtæb.əl.ɪ.zəm/.
metabolic ˌmet.əˈbɒl.ɪk, (US) ˌmeţ.əˈbɑː.lɪk **-ally** -əl.i, -li
metabolism məˈtæb.əl.ɪ.zəm, mɪ-, metˈæb-, (US) məˈtæb- **-s** -z
metaboliz|e, -is|e məˈtæb.əl.aɪz, mɪ-, metˈæb-, (US) məˈ- **-es** -ɪz **-ing** -ɪŋ **-ed** -d
metacarp|al ˌmet.əˈkɑː.p|əl, (US) ˌmeţ.əˈkɑːr- **-us** -əs
metacentre, -center ˈmet.əˌsen.təʳ, (US) ˈmeţ.əˌsen.ţɚ **-s** -z
metagalax|y ˈmet.əˌgæl.ək.s|i, (US) ˈmeţ- **-ies** -iz
metal ˈmet.əl, (US) ˈmeţ- **-s** -z **-ling** -ɪŋ **-led** -d ˈ**metal deˌtector**
metalanguage ˈmet.əlˌæŋ.gwɪdʒ, (US) ˈmeţ-
metallic məˈtæl.ɪk, mɪ-, metˈæl-, (US) məˈtæl- **-ally** -əl.i, -li
Metallica metˈæl.ɪ.kə, məˈtæl-, mɪ-, -lə-
metalliferous ˌmet.əlˈɪf.ər.əs, (US) ˌmeţ-
metallography ˌmet.əlˈɒg.rə.fi, (US) ˌmeţ.əlˈɑː.grə-
metalloid ˈmet.əl.ɔɪd, (US) ˈmeţ-
metallurgic|al ˌmet.əlˈɜː.dʒɪ.k|əl, (US) ˌmeţ.əlˈɝː- **-ally** -əl.i, -li
metallurgist metˈæl.ə.dʒɪst, məˈtæl-, mɪ-; ˈmet.əl.ɜː-, (US) ˈmeţ.əl.ɝː- **-s** -s
metallurgy metˈæl.ə.dʒi, məˈtæl, mɪ-; ˈmet.əl.ɜː-, (US) ˈmeţ.əl.ɝː-
metalwork ˈmet.əl.wɜːk, (US) ˈmeţ.əl.wɝːk **-er/s** -əʳ/z, (US) -ɚ/z
metamorphic ˌmet.əˈmɔː.fɪk, (US) ˌmeţ.əˈmɔːr-

metamorphism ˌmet.əˈmɔː.fɪ.zᵊm, ⓊⓈ ˌmeţ.əˈmɔːr- **-s** -z
metamorphos|e ˌmet.əˈmɔː.fəʊz, ⓊⓈ ˌmeţ.əˈmɔːr.foʊz **-es** -ɪz **-ing** -ɪŋ **-ed** -d
metamorphos|is ˌmet.əˈmɔː.fə.s|ɪs; -mɔːˈfəʊ-, ⓊⓈ ˌmeţ.əˈmɔːr.fə-; ⓊⓈ -mɔːrˈfoʊ- **-es** -iːz
metaphor ˈmet.ə.fəʳ, -fɔːʳ, ⓊⓈ ˈmeţ.ə.fɔːr, -fɚ **-s** -z
metaphoric ˌmet.əˈfɒr.ɪk, ⓊⓈ ˌmeţ.əˈfɔːr.ɪk **-al** -ᵊl **-ally** -ᵊl.i, -li
metaphysic|al ˌmet.əˈfɪz.ɪ.k|ᵊl, ⓊⓈ ˌmeţ- **-ally** -ᵊl.i, -li
metaphysician ˌmet.ə.fɪˈzɪʃ.ᵊn, ⓊⓈ ˌmeţ- **-s** -z
metaphysics ˌmet.əˈfɪz.ɪks, ⓊⓈ ˌmeţ-, ˈmeţ.əˌfɪz-
metaplasm ˈmet.əˌplæz.ᵊm, ⓊⓈ ˈmeţ-
metastas|is metˈæs.təs|ɪs, mɪˈtæs-, məˈtæs-, ⓊⓈ məˈtæs- **-es** -iːz
metatarsal ˌmet.əˈtɑː.sᵊl, ⓊⓈ ˌmeţ.əˈtɑːr- **-s** -z
metatars|us ˌmet.əˈtɑː.s|əs, ⓊⓈ ˌmeţ.əˈtɑːr- **-i** -aɪ
metathes|is metˈæθ.ə.s|ɪs, mɪˈtæθ-, mə-, ˈ-ɪ-, ⓊⓈ məˈtæθ.ə- **-es** -iːz
Metaxa® metˈæk.sə, mɪˈtæk-, mə-, ⓊⓈ məˈtæk-
Metayers mɪˈteɪ.əz, mə-, ⓊⓈ -ˈteɪ.ɚz
Metcalfe ˈmet.kɑːf, -kəf, ⓊⓈ -kæf
met|e miːt **-es** -s **-ing** -ɪŋ, ⓊⓈ ˈmiː.ţɪŋ **-ed** -ɪd, ⓊⓈ ˈmiː.ţɪd
Metellus mɪˈtel.əs, metˈel-, ⓊⓈ mɪˈtel-
metempsychosis ˌmet.emp.saɪˈkəʊ.sɪs, -əmp-, -sɪˈ-; metˌemp-, ⓊⓈ mɪˌtemp.sɪˈkoʊ-; ⓊⓈ ˌmet.əmp.saɪˈ-
meteor ˈmiː.ti.əʳ, -ɔːʳ, ⓊⓈ -ţi.ɚ, -ɔːr **-s** -z
meteoric ˌmiː.tiˈɒr.ɪk, ⓊⓈ -ţiˈɔːr- **-ally** -ᵊl.i, -li
meteorite ˈmiː.ti.ᵊr.aɪt, ⓊⓈ -ţi.ə.raɪt **-s** -s
meteorologic ˌmiː.ti.ᵊr.əˈlɒdʒ.ɪk, ⓊⓈ -ţi.ɚ.əˈlɑː.dʒɪk **-al** -ᵊl **-ally** -ᵊl.i, -li
meteorologist ˌmiː.ti.ᵊrˈɒl.ə.dʒɪst, ⓊⓈ -ţi.əˈrɑːl- **-s** -s
meteorology ˌmiː.ti.ᵊrˈɒl.ə.dʒi, ⓊⓈ -əˈrɑː.lə-
met|er ˈmiː.t|əʳ, ⓊⓈ -ţ|ɚ **-ers** -əz, ⓊⓈ -ɚz **-ering** -ᵊr.ɪŋ **-ered** -əd, ⓊⓈ -ɚd
meth meθ **-s** -s
methadone ˈmeθ.ə.dəʊn, ⓊⓈ -doʊn
methamphetamine ˌmeθ.æmˈfet.ə.miːn, -mɪn, ⓊⓈ -ˈfeţ-
methane ˈmiː.θeɪn, ⓊⓈ ˈmeθ.eɪn
methanol ˈmeθ.ə.nɒl, ˈmiː.θə-, ⓊⓈ ˈmeθ.ə.nɑːl, -noʊl
metheglin meθˈeg.lɪn, mɪˈθeg-, mə-, ⓊⓈ məˈθeg-
Metheny məˈθiː.ni
methinks mɪˈθɪŋks
method ˈmeθ.əd **-s** -z
méthode champenoise ˌmeɪ.tɒd.ʃɑ̃ːm.pᵊnˈwɑːz, ⓊⓈ -toʊd.ʃɑːm-
methodic məˈθɒd.ɪk, mɪ-, meθˈɒd-, ⓊⓈ məˈθɑː.dɪk **-al** -ᵊl **-ally** -ᵊl.i, -li
Method|ism ˈmeθ.ə.d|ɪ.zᵊm **-ist/s** -ɪst/s
methodologi|cal ˌmeθ.ə.dᵊlˈɒdʒ.ɪ|.kᵊl, ⓊⓈ -dᵊlˈɑːdʒ- **-ally** -kᵊl.i, -kli
methodolog|y ˌmeθ.əˈdɒl.ə.dʒ|i, ⓊⓈ -ˈdɑː.lə- **-ies** -iz
methought mɪˈθɔːt, ⓊⓈ -ˈθɑːt, -ˈθɔːt
Methuen *surname:* ˈmeθ.ju.ən, -ɪn, ⓊⓈ mɪˈθjuː.ɪn, mə-, -ˈθuː-, -ən; ⓊⓈ ˈmeθ.juː-, -uː- *US town:* mɪˈθjuː.ɪn, mə-, -ˈθuː-, -ən
Methuselah məˈθjuː.zᵊl.ə, mɪ-, -ˈθuː-, ⓊⓈ məˈθuː-, -ˈθjuː-
Methven ˈmeθ.vən, -ven
methyl *commercial and general pronunciation:* ˈmeθ.ᵊl, -ɪl, ⓊⓈ -aɪl *chemists' pronunciation:* ˈmiː.θaɪl, ⓊⓈ ˈmeθ.aɪl
methylated ˈmeθ.ᵊl.eɪ.tɪd, -ɪ.leɪ-, ⓊⓈ -ɪ.leɪ.ţɪd **ˌmethylated ˈspirits**
methylene ˈmeθ.ᵊl.iːn, -ɪ.liːn, ⓊⓈ ˈ-ɪ.liːn
meti|cal ˌmet.ɪ|ˈkæl, ⓊⓈ ˌmeţ- **-cais** -ˈkaɪʃ
meticulous məˈtɪk.jə.ləs, mɪ-, metˈɪk-, -jʊ-, ⓊⓈ məˈtɪk.jə-, -jʊ- **-ly** -li **-ness** -nəs, -nɪs
métier ˈmet.i.eɪ, ˈmeɪ.ti-, ⓊⓈ meɪˈtjeɪ **-s** -z
metonym ˈmet.ə.nɪm, ⓊⓈ ˈmet- **-s** -z
metonymy metˈɒn.ə.mi, mɪˈtɒn-, mə-, ˈ-ɪ-, ⓊⓈ məˈtɑː.nə-
me-too ˌmiːˈtuː **-ism** -ɪ.zᵊm
metope ˈmet.əʊp; -əʊ.pi, ⓊⓈ ˈmeţ.ə.pi; ⓊⓈ ˈ-oʊp **-s** -s
metre ˈmiː.təʳ, ⓊⓈ -ţɚ **-s** -z
metric ˈmet.rɪk **-al** -ᵊl **-ally** -ᵊl.i, -li
metrication ˌmet.rɪˈkeɪ.ʃᵊn, -rəˈ-
metrics ˈmet.rɪks
metro, M~ ˈmet.rəʊ, ⓊⓈ -roʊ **-s** -z
metro- ˈmet.rəʊ, metˈrɒ, məˈtrɒ, mɪˈtrɒ, ⓊⓈ ˈmet.roʊ, -rə; ⓊⓈ məˈtrɑː
Metro-Goldwyn-Mayer ˌmet.rəʊˌgəʊld.wɪnˈmeɪ.əʳ, ⓊⓈ -roʊˌgoʊld.wɪnˈmeɪ.ɚ
Metroland ˈmet.rəʊ.lænd, ⓊⓈ -roʊ-
metronome ˈmet.rə.nəʊm, ⓊⓈ -noʊm **-s** -z
metronomic ˌmet.rəˈnɒm.ɪk, ⓊⓈ -ˈnɑː.mɪk **-al** -ᵊl **-ally** -ᵊl.i, -li
Metropole ˈmet.rə.pəʊl, ⓊⓈ -poʊl
metropolis məˈtrɒp.ə.lɪs, mɪ-, metˈrɒp-, -ᵊl.ɪs, ⓊⓈ məˈtrɑː.pᵊl.ɪs **-es** -ɪz
metropolitan ˌmet.rəˈpɒl.ɪ.tᵊn, ˈ-ə-, ⓊⓈ -ˈpɑː.lə- **-s** -z
metrosexual ˌmet.rəʊˈsek.ʃu.əl, ˈ-sju-, ˈ-ʃᵊl, ⓊⓈ -roʊˈsek.ʃu.əl, -rəˈ- **-s** -z
-metry mə.tri, mɪ-
Mets mets
mettle ˈmet.ᵊl, ⓊⓈ ˈmeţ- **-some** -səm
Metz mets; *as if French:* mes
meunière, meuniere ˌmɜː.niˈeəʳ, -ˈnjeəʳ, məˈ-, ˈ---, ⓊⓈ məˈnjer
Meursault ˈmɜː.səʊ, ⓊⓈ mɚˈsoʊ
Meuse mɜːz, ⓊⓈ mjuːz, mɜːz
Meux mjuːz, mjuːks, mjuː
Mevagissey ˌmev.əˈgɪs.i
mew, M~ mjuː **-s** -z **-ing** -ɪŋ **-ed** -d
mewl mjuːl **-s** -z **-ing** -ɪŋ **-ed** -d
mews mjuːz
Mexborough ˈmeks.bᵊr.ə, ⓊⓈ -bɚ.oʊ
Mexicali ˌmek.sɪˈkɑː.li, -ˈkæl.i, ⓊⓈ -ˈkæl.i
Mexican ˈmek.sɪ.kᵊn **ˌMexican ˈwave**
Mexico ˈmek.sɪ.kəʊ, ⓊⓈ -koʊ **ˌMexico ˈCity**
Mey meɪ
Meyer ˈmaɪ.əʳ, ˈmeɪ-, meəʳ, ⓊⓈ ˈmaɪ.ɚ
Meyerbeer ˈmaɪ.ə.bɪəʳ, -beəʳ, ⓊⓈ -ɚ.bɪr, -ber
Meyers ˈmaɪ.əz, ˈmeɪ.əz, meəz, ⓊⓈ ˈmaɪ.ɚz
Meynell ˈmen.ᵊl, ˈmeɪ.nᵊl; meɪˈnel
Meyrick ˈmer.ɪk, ˈmeɪ.rɪk
mezzanine ˈmet.sə.niːn, ˈmez.ə-, ⓊⓈ ˈmez.ə-, ˌ--ˈ- **-s** -z
mezzo ˈmet.səʊ, ˈmed.zəʊ, ⓊⓈ ˈmet.soʊ, ˈmed.zoʊ, ˈmez.oʊ **-s** -z
mezzo-soprano ˌmet.səʊ.səˈprɑː.nəʊ, ˌmed.zəʊ-, ⓊⓈ ˌmet.soʊ.səˈpræn.oʊ, -ˈprɑː.noʊ, ˌmed.zoʊ-, ˌmez.oʊ- **-s** -z
mezzotint ˈmet.səʊ.tɪnt, ˈmed.zəʊ-, ⓊⓈ ˈmet.soʊ-, ˈmed.zoʊ-, ˈmez.oʊ- **-s** -s
mg (abbrev. for **milligram/s**) *singular:* ˈmɪl.ɪ.græm; *plural:* ˈmɪl.ɪ.græmz
MGM® ˌem.dʒiːˈem
Mgr. (abbrev. for **Monseigneur, Monsignor**) mɒnˈsiː.njəʳ, -njɔːʳ, ⓊⓈ mɑːnˈsiː.njɚ **-s.** -z
MHz (abbrev. for **megahertz**) ˈmeg.ə.hɜːts, ⓊⓈ -hɝːts
mi miː **-s** -z
MI5 ˌem.aɪˈfaɪv
MI6 ˌem.aɪˈsɪks
Mia ˈmiː.ə
MIA ˌem.aɪˈeɪ
Miami maɪˈæm.i
Miami-Dade maɪˌæm.iˈdeɪd
miaow ˌmiːˈaʊ, miˈaʊ, ⓊⓈ miˈaʊ, mjaʊ **-s** -z **-ing** -ɪŋ **-ed** -d
miasm|a miˈæz.m|ə, maɪ-, ⓊⓈ maɪ-, mi- **-as** -əz **-ata** -ə.tə, ⓊⓈ -ə.ţə **-al** -ᵊl
mic maɪk **-s** -s
mica ˈmaɪ.kə
micaceous maɪˈkeɪ.ʃəs
Micah ˈmaɪ.kə
Micawber mɪˈkɔː.bəʳ, mə-, ⓊⓈ -ˈkɑː.bɚ, -ˈkɔː-
mice (plural of **mouse**) maɪs
Mich. (abbrev. for **Michigan**) ˈmɪʃ.ɪ.gən, ˈ-ə-, ⓊⓈ ˈ-ɪ-
Michael ˈmaɪ.kᵊl

Michaela mɪˈkaɪ.lə
Michaelmas ˈmɪk.əl.məs
Michelangelo ˌmaɪ.kəlˈæn.dʒə.ləʊ, -dʒɪ-, (US) -loʊ, ˌmɪk.əl-
Micheldever ˈmɪtʃ.əl.dev.əʳ, (US) -ɚ
Michele, Michèle mɪˈʃel, miː-
Michelin® ˈmɪtʃ.əl.ɪn, ˈmɪʃ-; *as if French:* ˈmiːʃ.læ̃ŋ, miːʃˈlæ̃ŋ; (US) ˈmɪʃ.ə.lɪn, ˈmɪtʃ- -s -z

> Note: In the UK, /miːʃˈlæ̃ŋ/ or /ˈmiːʃ.læ̃ŋ/ is used for the Guides, but not the tyres.

Michelle mɪˈʃel, miː-
Michelmore ˈmɪtʃ.əl.mɔːʳ, (US) -mɔːr
Michelson ˈmɪtʃ.əl.sən, ˈmɪk.əl-, ˈmaɪ.kəl-, (US) ˈmaɪ.kəl-, ˈmɪk.əl-
Michie ˈmɪx.i, ˈmiː.xi, ˈmɪk.i, (US) ˈmɪk.i
Michigan ˈmɪʃ.ɪ.gən, ˈ-ə-, (US) ˈ-ɪ-
Michmash ˈmɪk.mæʃ
Michoacán ˌmɪtʃ.əʊ.əˈkæn, (US) -ə.wɑːˈkɑːn
mick, M~ mɪk
mickey, M~ ˈmɪk.i ˌ**Mickey** ˈ**Finn**; ˌ**Mickey** ˈ**Mouse** (US) ˈ**Mickey** ˌ**Mouse**
mickey-mouse adj ˌmɪk.iˈmaʊs, (US) ˈ-‚- *stress shift, British only:* ˌ**mickey-mouse** ˈ**job**
Micra® ˈmaɪ.krə
micra (plural of **micron**) ˈmaɪ.krə
micro ˈmaɪ.krəʊ, (US) -kroʊ -s -z
micro- ˈmaɪ.krəʊ, (US) ˈmaɪ.kroʊ, ˈmaɪ.krə
Note: Prefix. May carry primary or secondary stress, e.g. **microfiche** /ˈmaɪ.krəʊ.fiːʃ/ (US) /-kroʊ-/, **microbiology** /ˌmaɪ.krəʊ.baɪˈɒl.ə.dʒi/ (US) /-kroʊ.baɪˈɑː.lə-/.
microbe ˈmaɪ.krəʊb, (US) -kroʊb -s -z
microbiologic|al ˌmaɪ.krəʊˌbaɪ.əˈlɒdʒ.ɪ.k|əl, (US) -kroʊˌbaɪ.əˈlɑː.dʒɪ-, -krə- -ally -əl.i, (US) -li
microbiologist ˌmaɪ.krəʊ.baɪˈɒl.ə.dʒɪst, (US) -kroʊ.baɪˈɑː.lə-, -krə- -s -s
microbiolog|y ˌmaɪ.krəʊ.baɪˈɒl.ə.dʒ|i, (US) -kroʊ.baɪˈɑː.lə-, -krə- -ist/s -ɪst/s
microblog ˈmaɪ.krəʊˌblɒg, (US) -oʊˌblɑːg, -krə-, -blɔːg -s -z -ging -ɪŋ -ged -d -ger/s -əʳ/z, (US) -ɚ/z
microbrewer|y ˌmaɪ.krəʊˈbruː.əʳ|.i, (US) -kroʊ-, -krə-, ˈ-r|i -ies -iz
microcephalic ˌmaɪ.krəʊ.sefˈæl.ɪk, -sɪˈfæl-, -kefˈæl-, -kɪˈfæl-, (US) -kroʊ.səˈfæl-, -krə-
microcephalous ˌmaɪ.krəʊˈsef.əl.əs, -ˈkef-, (US) -kroʊˈsef-, -krəˈ-
microchip ˈmaɪ.krəʊ.tʃɪp, (US) -kroʊ-, -krə- -s -s
microcircuit ˈmaɪ.krəʊˌsɜː.kɪt, (US) -kroʊˌsɝː-, -krə- -s -s
microclimate ˈmaɪ.krəʊˌklaɪ.mɪt, -mət, (US) kroʊˌklaɪ.mɪt, -krəˌ- -s -s
microcomputer ˈmaɪ.krəʊ.kəmˌpjuː.təʳ, (US) -kroʊ.kəmˌpjuː.t̬ɚ, -krə- -s -z
microcop|y ˈmaɪ.krəʊˌkɒp|.i, (US) -kroʊˌkɑː.p|i, -krə- -ies -iz
microcosm ˈmaɪ.krəʊˌkɒz.əm, (US) -kroʊˌkɑː.zəm, -krəˌ- -s -z
microdot ˈmaɪ.krəʊ.dɒt, (US) -kroʊ.dɑːt, -krə- -s -s
microeconomic ˌmaɪ.krəʊˌiː.kəˈnɒm.ɪk, -ˌek.əˈ-, (US) -kroʊˌek.əˈnɑː.mɪk, -ˌiː.kəˈ- -s -s
microelectronics ˌmaɪ.krəʊ.ɪl.ekˈtrɒn.ɪks, -ˌel-, -ˌel.ɪkˈ-, -ˌiː.lekˈ-, (US) -kroʊ.ɪˌlekˈtrɑː.nɪks, -ˌiː.lekˈ-
microfich|e ˈmaɪ.krəʊ.fiːʃ, (US) -kroʊ-, -krə- -es -ɪz
microfilm ˈmaɪ.krəʊ.fɪlm, (US) -kroʊ-, -krə- -s -z -ing -ɪŋ -ed -d
microgram, microgramme ˈmaɪ.krəʊ.græm, (US) -kroʊ-, -krə- -s -z
microgroove ˈmaɪ.krəʊ.gruːv, (US) -kroʊ-, -krə- -s -z
microlight, microlite ˈmaɪ.krəʊ.laɪt, (US) -kroʊ-, -krə- -s -s
micromesh ˈmaɪ.krəʊ.meʃ, (US) -kroʊ-, -krə-
micrometer maɪˈkrɒm.ɪ.təʳ, ˈ-ə-, (US) -ˈkrɑː.mə.t̬ɚ
micrometre, micrometer ˈmaɪ.krəʊˌmiː.təʳ, (US) -kroʊˌmiː.t̬ɚ, -krə- -s -z
micr|on ˈmaɪ.kr|ɒn, -kr|ən, (US) -kr|ɑːn -ons -ɒnz, -ənz, (US) -ɑːnz -a -ə
Micronesi|a ˌmaɪ.krəʊˈniː.zi|.ə, -ʒi|.ə, -ʒ|ə, -si|.ə, -ʃi|.ə, -ʃ|ə, (US) -kroʊˈniː.ʒ|ə, -krə-, -ʃ|ə -an/s -ən/z
microorganism ˌmaɪ.krəʊˈɔː.gən.ɪ.zəm, ˌmaɪ.krəʊˌɔː-, (US) ˌmaɪ.kroʊˈɔːr- -s -z
microphone ˈmaɪ.krə.fəʊn, (US) -foʊn -s -z
microprocessor ˌmaɪ.krəʊˈprəʊ.ses.əʳ, ˌmaɪ.krəʊˌprəʊ-, (US) ˈmaɪ.kroʊˌprɑː.ses.ɚ, -krə- -s -z
micropyle ˈmaɪ.krəʊ.paɪl, (US) -kroʊ-, -krə-
microscope ˈmaɪ.krə.skəʊp, (US) -skoʊp, -krə- -s -s
microscopic ˌmaɪ.krəˈskɒp.ɪk, (US) -ˈskɑː.pɪk -al -əl -ally -əl.i, (US) -li
microscopy maɪˈkrɒs.kə.pi, (US) -ˈkrɑː.skə-
microsecond ˈmaɪ.krəʊˌsek.ənd, (US) -kroʊˌ-, -krəˌ- -s -z
Microsoft® ˈmaɪ.krəʊ.sɒft, (US) -kroʊ.sɑːft, -krə-
microsurgery ˌmaɪ.krəʊˈsɜː.dʒər.i, (US) -kroʊˈsɝː-, -krəˈ-, ˈmaɪ.kroʊˌsɝː-
microsurgical ˌmaɪ.krəʊˈsɜː.dʒɪ.kəl, (US) -kroʊˈsɝː-, -krə- *stress shift:* ˌ**microsurgical** ˈ**graft**
microwav|e ˈmaɪ.krəʊ.weɪv, (US) -kroʊ-, -krə- -es -z -ing -ɪŋ -ed -d -eable -ə.bəl ˌ**microwave** ˈ**oven**
mictur|ate ˈmɪk.tʃər|.eɪt, -tʃʊ.reɪt, -tjʊ.reɪt, (US) -tjʊ.reɪt, -tjə-, -tə- -ates -eɪts -ating -eɪ.tɪŋ, (US) -eɪ.t̬ɪŋ -ated -eɪ.tɪd, (US) -eɪ.t̬ɪd
micturation ˌmɪk.tʃərˈeɪ.ʃən, -tʃʊˈreɪ-, -tjʊˈ-, (US) -tjʊˈreɪ-, -tjəˈ-, -təˈ- -s -z
micturition ˌmɪk.tʃərˈɪʃ.ən, -tʃʊˈrɪʃ-, -tjʊˈrɪʃ-, (US) -tʃʊˈ-, -tʃəˈ-, -təˈ-
mid mɪd
midair ˌmɪdˈeəʳ, mɪˈdeəʳ, (US) ˌmɪdˈer *stress shift:* ˌ**midair** ˈ**crash**
Midas ˈmaɪ.dəs, -dæs, (US) -dəs
midday ˌmɪdˈdeɪ -s -z *stress shift:* ˌ**midday** ˈ**sun**
midden ˈmɪd.ən -s -z
middle ˈmɪd.əl -s -z ˌ**middle** ˈ**age**; ˌ**Middle** ˈ**Ages**; ˌ**middle** ˈ**class**; ˌ**Middle** ˈ**East**; ˌ**middle** ˈ**management**; ˌ**middle** ˈ**name**; ˌ**middle of** ˈ**nowhere**; ˈ**middle** ˌ**school**
middle-aged ˌmɪd.əlˈeɪdʒd *stress shift, see compound:* ˌ**middle-aged** ˈ**spread**
middlebrow ˈmɪd.əl.braʊ -s -z
middle-class ˌmɪd.əlˈklɑːs, (US) -ˈklæs *stress shift:* ˌ**middle-class** ˈ**values**
middle distance n ˌmɪd.əlˈdɪs.tənts
middle-distance adj ˈmɪd.əlˌdɪs.tənts
Middle-Earth ˌmɪd.əlˈɜːθ, (US) -ˈɝːθ
Middle East ˌmɪd.əlˈiːst -ern -ən *stress shift:* ˌ**Middle Eastern** ˈ**customs**
Middleham ˈmɪd.əl.əm
middle|man ˈmɪd.əl|.mæn -men -men
Middlemarch ˈmɪd.əl.mɑːtʃ, (US) -mɑːrtʃ
Middlemast ˈmɪd.əl.mɑːst, -mæst, (US) -mæst
middlemost ˈmɪd.əl.məʊst, (US) -moʊst
middle-of-the-road ˌmɪd.əl.əv.ðəˈrəʊd, (US) -ˈroʊd
Middlesbro(ugh) ˈmɪd.əlz.brə
Middlesex ˈmɪd.əl.seks
Middleton ˈmɪd.əl.tən
middleweight ˈmɪd.əl.weɪt -s -s
Middlewich ˈmɪd.əl.wɪtʃ
middling ˈmɪd.əl.ɪŋ, ˈmɪd.lɪŋ
Middx. (abbrev. for **Middlesex**) ˈmɪd.əl.seks
middl|y ˈmɪd|.i -ies -iz
Mideast ˌmɪdˈiːst *stress shift:* ˌ**Mideast** ˈ**town**
midfield ˈmɪd.fiːld, -ˈ-
midfielder ˈmɪdˌfiːl.dəʳ, ˌ-ˈ--, (US) ˈmɪdˌfiːl.dɚ, ˌ-ˈ-- -s -z
Midgard ˈmɪd.gɑːd, (US) -gɑːrd
midg|e mɪdʒ -es -ɪz
midget ˈmɪdʒ.ɪt -s -s
Midhurst ˈmɪd.hɜːst, (US) -hɝːst
midi *style of clothes:* ˈmɪd.i -s -z
Midi *in France:* miːˈdiː, mɪdˈiː, (US) miːˈdi
MIDI *computer interface:* ˈmɪd.i

Midian ˈmɪd.i.ən **-ite/s** -aɪt/s
midland, M~ ˈmɪd.lənd **-s** -z
Midler ˈmɪd.ləʳ, (US) -lɚ
mid-life ˌmɪdˈlaɪf *stress shift, see compound:* ˌ**mid-life** ˈ**crisis**
Midlothian ˌmɪdˈləʊ.ði.ən, (US) -ˈloʊ-
midmorning ˌmɪdˈmɔː.nɪŋ, (US) -ˈmɔːr-
midnight ˈmɪd.naɪt
mid-off ˌmɪdˈɒf, (US) -ˈɑːf **-s** -s
mid-on ˌmɪdˈɒn, (US) -ˈɑːn **-s** -z
midpoint ˈmɪd.pɔɪnt **-s** -s
midriff ˈmɪd.rɪf **-s** -s
midsection ˈmɪd.sek.ʃən
midship|man ˈmɪd.ʃɪp|.mən, (US) ˈmɪdˌ-, ˌmɪdˈʃɪp- **-men** -mən
midships ˈmɪd.ʃɪps
midsized ˌmɪdˈsaɪzd *stress shift:* ˌ**midsized** ˈ**city**
midst mɪdst, mɪtst
midstream ˌmɪdˈstriːm
midsummer, M~ ˌmɪdˈsʌm.əʳ, ˈ-ˌ--, (US) -ɚ **-'s** -z *stress shift, see compounds:* **Midsummer** ˈ**Day;** ˌ**midsummer** ˈ**madness;** ˌ**Midsummer** ˌ**Night's** ˈ**Dream**
midterm n ˈmɪd.tɜːm, (US) -tɝːm *stress shift:* ˌ**mid-term** ˈ**crisis**
mid-term adj ˌmɪdˈtɜːm, (US) -ˈtɝːm
midtown ˈmɪd.taʊn
midway ˌmɪdˈweɪ, ˈ--
Midway *island:* ˈmɪd.weɪ
midweek ˌmɪdˈwiːk *stress shift:* ˌ**midweek** ˈ**news**
Midwest ˌmɪdˈwest *stress shift:* ˌ**Midwest** ˈ**town**
Midwestern ˌmɪdˈwes.tən, (US) -tɚn
midwi|fe ˈmɪd.waɪ|f **-ves** -vz
midwifery ˌmɪdˈwɪf.ər.i, ˈmɪdˌwɪf.ər-, (US) ˌmɪdˈwɪf.ɚ-; (US) ˈmɪdˌwaɪf.ɚ-
midwinter ˌmɪdˈwɪn.təʳ, (US) -t̬ɚ *stress shift:* ˌ**midwinter** ˈ**holiday**
mien miːn **-s** -z
Miers maɪ.əz, (US) maɪ.ɚz
Mies van der Rohe ˌmiːz.væn.dəˈrəʊ.ə, ˌmiːs-, (US) -dəˈroʊ.ə
miff mɪf **-s** -s **-ing** -ɪŋ **-ed** -t
MiG, MIG mɪg **-s** -z
might maɪt
mightn't (= **might not**) ˈmaɪ.tənt
mightn't've (= **might not have**) ˈmaɪ.tənt.əv
might've (= **might have**) ˈmaɪ.təv, (US) -t̬əv
might|y ˈmaɪ.t|i, (US) -t̬|i **-ier** -i.əʳ, (US) -i.ɚ **-iest** -i.ɪst, -i.əst **-ily** -əl.i, -ɪ.li **-iness** -ɪ.nəs, -ɪ.nɪs
mignon ˈmiː.njɒn, ˌ-ˈ-; *as if French:* mɪˈnjɔ̃ːŋ; (US) ˌmiːˈnjɑːn, -ˈnjɔ̃ːn
mignonette, M~ ˌmɪn.jəˈnet, ˈ-ˌ--, (US) ˌ--ˈ- **-s** -s
mignonne ˈmiː.njɒn, ˌ-ˈ-; *as if French:* miˈnjɔːn; (US) ˌmiːˈnjɑːn, -ˈnjɔːn
migraine ˈmiː.greɪn, ˈmaɪ-, ˈmɪg.reɪn, (US) ˈmaɪ.greɪn **-s** -z
migrant ˈmaɪ.grənt **-s** -s
migra|te maɪˈgreɪ|t, ˈ--, (US) ˈmaɪ.greɪ|t **-tes** -ts **-ting** -tɪŋ, (US) -t̬ɪŋ **-ted** -tɪd, (US) -t̬ɪd **-tor/s** -təʳ/z, (US) -t̬ɚ/z
migration maɪˈgreɪ.ʃən **-s** -z
migratory ˈmaɪ.grə.tər.i; maɪˈgreɪ-, (US) ˈmaɪ.grə.tɔːr-
Miguel mɪˈgel, miː-
mikado, M~ mɪˈkɑː.dəʊ, mə-, (US) mɪˈkɑː.doʊ **-s** -z
Mikardo mɪˈkɑː.dəʊ, mə-, (US) mɪˈkɑːr.doʊ
mike, M~ maɪk **-s** -s
Mikonos ˈmɪk.ə.nɒs, -ɒn.ɒs, (US) ˈmiː.kə.nɑːs
mil mɪl **-s** -z
milady mɪˈleɪ.di, mə-
Milan *in Italy:* mɪˈlæn, mə-, -ˈlɑːn, ˈmɪl.ən, (US) mɪˈlæn, -ˈlɑːn *in US:* ˈmaɪ.lən *Serbian king:* ˈmiː.lən, -læn

> Note: /ˈmɪl.ən/ is used for rhythm in Shakespeare's 'The Tempest'.

Milanese *from Milan:* ˌmɪl.əˈniːz, -ˈneɪz, (US) -ˈniːz, -ˈniːs *cookery term, as if Italian:* ˌmɪl.əˈneɪ.zeɪ; -ænˈeɪ-, -zi, (US) -əˈneɪz
Milburn ˈmɪl.bɜːn, -bən, (US) -bɚn
milch mɪltʃ
mild maɪld **-er** -əʳ, (US) -ɚ **-est** -ɪst, -əst **-ly** -li **-ness** -nəs, -nɪs
Mildenhall ˈmɪl.dən.hɔːl, (US) ˈmɪl.dən.hɔːl, -hɑːl
mildew ˈmɪl.dʒuː, -djuː, (US) -duː, -djuː **-s** -z **-ing** -ɪŋ **-ed** -d
mild-mannered ˌmaɪldˈmæn.əd, (US) -ɚd *stress shift:* ˌ**mild-mannered** **reˈporter**
Mildmay ˈmaɪld.meɪ
Mildred ˈmɪl.drəd, -drɪd, -dred
mile maɪl **-s** -z
mileag|e ˈmaɪ.lɪdʒ **-es** -ɪz
mileometer maɪˈlɒm.ɪ.təʳ, ˈ-ə-, (US) -ˈlɑː.mə.t̬ɚ **-s** -z
Miles maɪlz
Milesian maɪˈliː.zi.ən, mɪ-, -ʒi.ən, -ʒən, (US) -ʒən, -ʃən **-s** -z
milestone ˈmaɪl.stəʊn, (US) -stoʊn **-s** -z
Miletus maɪˈliː.təs, mɪ-, (US) maɪ-
milfoil ˈmɪl.fɔɪl **-s** -z
Milford ˈmɪl.fəd, (US) -fɚd
Milhaud ˈmiː.jəʊ, -əʊ; *as if French:* miːˈjəʊ; (US) miːˈjoʊ
Miliband ˈmɪl.ɪ.bænd, -ə-
milieu ˈmiː.ljɜː, -ˈ-, (US) miːlˈjɜː, mɪl-, -ˈjuː, ˈ-- **-s** -z
milieux (alternative plural of **milieu**) ˈmiː.ljɜː, -ljɜːz, -ˈ-, (US) miːlˈjɜː, mɪl-, -ˈjuː, -ˈjɜːz, -ˈjuːz, ˈ--
militancy ˈmɪl.ɪ.tənt.si, ˈ-ə-, (US) -tənt-
militant ˈmɪl.ɪ.tənt, ˈ-ə-, (US) -tənt **-s** -s **-ly** -li
militarily ˈmɪl.ɪ.tər.əl.i, -ə-, -ɪ.li, ˌmɪl.ɪˈter-, ˌmɪl.ɪˈtær-, -əˈ-, (US) ˌmɪl.əˈter-
militar|ism ˈmɪl.ɪ.tər|.ɪ.zəm, ˈ-ə-, (US) -tɚ- **-ist/s** -ɪst/s
militaristic ˌmɪl.ɪ.tərˈɪs.tɪk, ˌ-ə-, (US) -təˈrɪs- **-ally** -əl.i, -li
militarization, -isa- ˌmɪl.ɪ.tər.aɪˈzeɪ.ʃən, ˌ-ə-, -ɪˈ-, (US) -tɚ.əˈ-
militariz|e, -is|e ˈmɪl.ɪ.tər.aɪz, ˈ-ə-, (US) -tə.raɪz **-es** -ɪz **-ing** -ɪŋ **-ed** -d
military ˈmɪl.ɪ.tri, ˈ-ə-, -tər.i, (US) -ter.i ˌ**military poˈlice**
mili|tate ˈmɪl.ɪ|.teɪt, ˈ-ə- **-tates** -teɪts **-tating** -teɪ.tɪŋ, (US) -teɪ.t̬ɪŋ **-tated** -teɪ.tɪd, (US) -teɪ.t̬ɪd
militia mɪˈlɪʃ.ə, mə- **-s** -z **-man** -mən **-men** -mən, -men
milk mɪlk **-s** -s **-ing** -ɪŋ **-ed** -t **-er/s** -əʳ/z, (US) -ɚ/z ˌ**milk** ˈ**chocolate** (US) ˈ**milk** ˌ**chocolate;** ˈ**milk** ˌ**float;** ˌ**milk of magˈnesia;** ˈ**milk** ˌ**round;** ˈ**milk** ˌ**run;** ˈ**milk** ˌ**shake;** ˈ**milk** ˌ**tooth;** ˈ**milking maˌchine;** **it's** ˌ**no good** ˌ**crying over** ˌ**spilt** ˈ**milk**
milkfish ˈmɪlk.fɪʃ **-es** -ɪz
milkmaid ˈmɪlk.meɪd **-s** -z
milk|man ˈmɪlk|.mən, (US) -mæn, -mən **-men** -mən, -men
milksop ˈmɪlk.sɒp, (US) -sɑːp **-s** -s
milkwort ˈmɪlk.wɜːt, (US) -wɝːt, -wɔːrt **-s** -s
milk|y ˈmɪl.k|i **-ier** -i.əʳ, (US) -i.ɚ **-iest** -i.ɪst, -i.əst **-ily** -əl.i, -ɪ.li **-iness** -ɪ.nəs, -ɪ.nɪs ˌ**Milky** ˈ**Way**
mill, M~ mɪl **-s** -z **-ing** -ɪŋ **-ed** -d
Millais ˈmɪl.eɪ, -ˈ-, (US) mɪˈleɪ
Millar ˈmɪl.əʳ, (US) -ɚ
Millard ˈmɪl.əd, -ɑːd, (US) -ɚd
Millay mɪˈleɪ
Millbank ˈmɪl.bæŋk
millboard ˈmɪl.bɔːd, (US) -bɔːrd
millefeuille(s) ˌmiːlˈfɜː.jə
millenarian ˌmɪl.əˈneə.ri.ən, -ɪˈ-, (US) -əˈner.i- **-s** -z
millenarianism ˌmɪl.əˈneə.ri.ə.nɪ.zəm, -ɪˈ-, (US) -əˈner.i-
millenary mɪˈlen.ər.i, mə-, (US) ˈmɪl.ə.ner-
millenni|um mɪˈlen.i|.əm, mə-, (US) mɪ- **-ums** -əmz **-a** -ə **-al** -əl
millepede ˈmɪl.ɪ.piːd, ˈ-ə- **-s** -z
miller, M~ ˈmɪl.əʳ, (US) -ɚ **-s** -z
millesimal mɪˈles.ɪ.məl, mə-, ˈ-ə-, (US) mɪˈles.ə- **-ly** -i
millet, M~ ˈmɪl.ɪt
milliard ˌmɪl.iˈɑːd; mɪlˈjɑːd, (US) ˈmɪl.jɚd, -jɑːrd **-s** -z
millibar ˈmɪl.ɪ.bɑːʳ, (US) -bɑːr **-s** -z
Millicent ˈmɪl.ɪ.sənt, ˈ-ə-
Milligan ˈmɪl.ɪ.gən
milligram(me) ˈmɪl.ɪ.græm **-s** -z
millilitre, milliliter ˈmɪl.ɪˌliː.təʳ, ˈ-ə-, (US) -t̬ɚ **-s** -z
millimetre, millimeter ˈmɪl.ɪˌmiː.təʳ, ˈ-ə-, (US) -t̬ɚ **-s** -z
milliner ˈmɪl.ɪ.nəʳ, ˈ-ə-, (US) -nɚ **-s** -z
millinery ˈmɪl.ɪ.nər.i, ˈ-ə-, (US) -ner-
Millington ˈmɪl.ɪŋ.tən
million ˈmɪl.jən, -i.ən, (US) ˈ-jən **-s** -z **a** ˌ**chance in a** ˈ**million**
millionaire ˌmɪl.jəˈneəʳ, -i.əˈ-, (US) ˌ-jəˈner, ˈmɪl.jə.ner **-s** -z

millionairess ˌmɪl.jə.neəˈres, ˌ-i.ə-; -ˈneə.rɪs, -res, US -jəˈner.ɪs **-es** -ɪz
millionfold ˈmɪl.jən.fəʊld, -i.ən-, US -jən.foʊld
millionth ˈmɪl.jəntθ, -i.əntθ, US ˈ-jəntθ **-s** -s
millipede ˈmɪl.ɪ.piːd, ˈ-ə- **-s** -z
millisecond ˈmɪl.ɪˌsek.ənd, ˈ-ə- **-s** -z
Millom ˈmɪl.əm
millpond ˈmɪl.pɒnd, US -pɑːnd **-s** -z
millrac|e ˈmɪl.reɪs **-es** -ɪz
Mills mɪlz
millstone ˈmɪl.stəʊn, US -stoʊn **-s** -z
Milltimber ˈmɪlˌtɪm.bəʳ, US -bɚ
Millwall ˈmɪl.wɔːl, -wəl; mɪlˈwɔːl
Millward ˈmɪl.wɔːd, -wəd, US -wɚd
Milman ˈmɪl.mən
Milne mɪln, mɪl
Milner ˈmɪl.nəʳ, US -nɚ
Milnes mɪlz, mɪlnz
Milngavie mɪlˈgaɪ, mʌl-
Milnrow ˈmɪln.rəʊ, US -roʊ
Milo ˈmaɪ.ləʊ, ˈmiː-, US ˈmaɪ.loʊ
milometer maɪˈlɒm.ɪ.təʳ, ˈ-ə-, US -ˈlɑː.mə.t̬ɚ **-s** -z
milord mɪˈlɔːd, mə-, US -ˈlɔːrd **-s** -z
Milos ˈmiː.lɒs, US -lɑːs
Milosevic mɪˈlɒʃ.ə.vɪtʃ, -ˈlɒs-, US -ˈlɑː.sə-
Milosz ˈmiː.lɒʃ, US -lɑːʃ
milquetoast ˈmɪlk.təʊst, US -toʊst **-s** -s
Milton ˈmɪl.tᵊn
Miltonic mɪlˈtɒn.ɪk, US -ˈtɑː.nɪk
Milton Keynes ˌmɪl.tᵊnˈkiːnz
Milwaukee mɪlˈwɔː.ki, -iː, US -ˈwɑː-, -ˈwɔː-
mim|e maɪm **-es** -z **-ing** -ɪŋ **-ed** -d **-er/s** -əʳ/z, US -ɚ/z
mimeo ˈmɪm.i.əʊ, US -oʊ **-s** -z **-ing** -ɪŋ **-ed** -d
mimeograph ˈmɪm.i.əʊ.grɑːf, -græf, US -ə.græf **-s** -s **-ing** -ɪŋ **-ed** -t
mimesis mɪˈmiː.sɪs, maɪ-
mimetic mɪˈmet.ɪk, maɪ-
mimic ˈmɪm.ɪk **-s** -s **-king** -ɪŋ **-ked** -t **-ker/s** -əʳ/z, US -ɚ/z
mimicry ˈmɪm.ɪ.kri
mimosa mɪˈməʊ.zə, -sə, US -ˈmoʊ.sə, -zə **-s** -z
mimulus ˈmɪm.jə.ləs, -jʊ-, US -jə-, -juː- **-es** -ɪz
mina ˈmaɪ.nə **-s** -z
minaret ˌmɪn.əˈret, ˈ--- **-s** -s
minatory ˈmɪn.ə.tᵊr.i, ˈmaɪ-, US ˈmɪn.ə.tɔːr-
minc|e mɪnts **-es** -ɪz **-ing/ly** -ɪŋ/li **-ed** -t **-er/s** -əʳ/z, US -ɚ/z ˌ**mince** ˈ**pie**
mincemeat ˈmɪnts.miːt **make** ˈ**mincemeat of** ˌ**someone**
Minch mɪntʃ **-es** -ɪz
mind maɪnd **-s** -z **-ing** -ɪŋ **-ed** -ɪd ˈ**mind** ˌ**reader;** ˌ**mind's** ˈ**eye; give someone a** ˌ**piece of one's** ˈ**mind**

Mindanao ˌmɪn.dəˈnaʊ, US -ˈnaʊ, -ˈnɑː.oʊ
mind-blowing ˈmaɪndˌbləʊ.ɪŋ, US -ˌbloʊ- **-ly** -li
mind-boggling ˈmaɪndˌbɒg.ᵊl.ɪŋ, ˈmaɪm-, -ˌbɒg.lɪŋ, US ˈmaɪndˌbɑː.glɪŋ, -ˌbɑː.gᵊl.ɪŋ **-ly** -li
minder ˈmaɪn.dəʳ, US -dɚ **-s** -z
mind-expanding ˈmaɪnd.ɪkˌspæn.dɪŋ, -ekˌ-, US -ekˌ-, -ɪkˌ-
mindful ˈmaɪnd.fᵊl, -fʊl **-ly** -i **-ness** -nəs, -nɪs
mindless ˈmaɪnd.ləs, -lɪs **-ly** -li **-ness** -nəs, -nɪs
mind-numbing ˈmaɪndˌnʌm.ɪŋ **-ly** -li
mind-set ˈmaɪnd.set
Mindy ˈmɪn.di
min|e maɪn **-es** -z **-ing** -ɪŋ **-ed** -d
minefield ˈmaɪn.fiːld **-s** -z
Minehead ˈmaɪn.hed, ˌ-ˈ-
Minelli mɪˈnel.i, mə-
miner ˈmaɪ.nəʳ, US -nɚ **-s** -z
mineral ˈmɪn.ᵊr.ᵊl **-s** -z ˈ**mineral** ˌ**water**
mineraliz|e, -is|e ˈmɪn.ᵊr.ᵊl.aɪz **-es** -ɪz **-ing** -ɪŋ **-ed** -d
mineralogical ˌmɪn.ᵊr.əˈlɒdʒ.ɪ.kᵊl, US -ˈlɑː.dʒɪ- **-ly** -i
mineralog|y ˌmɪn.ᵊrˈæl.ə.dʒ|i, US -əˈrɑː.lə-, -ˈræl.ə- **-ist/s** -ɪst/s
Minerva mɪˈnɜː.və, US məˈnɝː-
minestrone ˌmɪn.ɪˈstrəʊ.ni, -əˈ-, US -əˈstroʊ-
minesweep|er ˈmaɪnˌswiː.p|əʳ, US -p|ɚ **-ers** -əz, US -ɚz **-ing** -ɪŋ
Ming mɪŋ
minger ˈmɪŋ.əʳ, US -ɚ **-s** z
Minghella mɪŋˈgel.ə
minging ˈmɪŋ.ɪŋ
mingl|e ˈmɪŋ.gᵊl **-es** -z **-ing** -ɪŋ, ˈmɪŋ.glɪŋ **-ed** -d
mingogram ˈmɪŋ.gəʊ.græm, -əʊ-, US -gə- **-s** -z
mingograph® ˈmɪŋ.gəʊ.grɑːf, -əʊ-, -græf, US -gə.græf **-s** -s
Mingus ˈmɪŋ.gəs
ming|y ˈmɪn.dʒ|i **-ier** -i.əʳ, US -i.ɚ **-iest** -i.ɪst, -i.əst
mini, M~® ˈmɪn.i **-s** -z
miniature ˈmɪn.ə.tʃəʳ, ˈ-ɪ-, US ˈ-i.ə.tʃɚ, ˈ-ə.tʃɚ **-s** -z
miniaturist ˈmɪn.ə.tʃᵊr.ɪst, ˈ-ɪ-, -tʃʊə.rɪst, -tjʊə.rɪst, US ˈ-i.ə.tʃɚ.ɪst, ˈ-ə.tʃɚ- **-s** -s
miniaturization, -isa- ˌmɪn.ə.tʃᵊr.aɪˈzeɪ.ʃᵊn, ˌ-ɪ-, -ɪˈ-, US -i.ə.tʃɚ.əˈ-, -ə.tʃɚ- **-s** -z
miniaturiz|e, -is|e ˈmɪn.ə.tʃᵊr.aɪz, ˈ-ɪ-, US ˈ-i.ə.tʃɚ-, ˈ-ə.tʃɚ- **-es** -ɪz **-ing** -ɪŋ **-ed** -d
minibus ˈmɪn.i.bʌs **-es** -ɪz
minicab ˈmɪn.i.kæb **-s** -z
minicam ˈmɪn.i.kæm **-s** -z
minicomputer ˈmɪn.i.kəmˌpjuː.təʳ, US ˌmɪn.i.kəmˈpjuː.t̬ɚ **-s** -z
MiniDisc® ˈmɪn.i.dɪsk **-s** -s
minim, M~ ˈmɪn.ɪm **-s** -z

minimal ˈmɪn.ɪ.mᵊl, ˈ-ə- **-ly** -i
minimal|ism ˈmɪn.ɪ.mᵊl|.ɪ.zᵊm, ˈ-ə- **-ist/s** -ɪst/s
minimization ˌmɪn.ɪ.maɪˈzeɪ.ʃᵊn, ˌ-ə-, -mɪˈ-, US -məˈ-
minimiz|e, -is|e ˈmɪn.ɪ.maɪz, ˈ-ə- **-es** -ɪz **-ing** -ɪŋ **-ed** -d
minim|um ˈmɪn.ɪ.m|əm **-a** -ə **-ums** -əmz ˌ**minimum** ˈ**wage**
mining ˈmaɪ.nɪŋ
minion ˈmɪn.jən **-s** -z
minipill ˈmɪn.i.pɪl
miniseries ˈmɪn.iˌsɪə.rɪz, -riːz, US -ˌsɪr.iːz
minish ˈmɪn.ɪʃ **-es** -ɪz **-ing** -ɪŋ **-ed** -t
miniskirt ˈmɪn.i.skɜːt, US -skɝːt **-s** -s **-ed** -ɪd
minist|er ˈmɪn.ɪ.st|əʳ, ˈ-ə-, US -st|ɚ **-ers** -əz, US -ɚz **-ering** -ᵊr.ɪŋ **-ered** -əd, US -ɚd
ministerial ˌmɪn.ɪˈstɪə.ri.əl, -əˈ-, US -ˈstɪr.i- **-ly** -i
ministration ˌmɪn.ɪˈstreɪ.ʃᵊn, -əˈ- **-s** -z
ministr|y ˈmɪn.ɪ.str|i, ˈ-ə- **-ies** -iz
mini-system ˈmɪn.iˌsɪs.təm **-s** -z
minivan ˈmɪn.i.væn, US -i- **-s** -z
miniver, M~ ˈmɪn.ɪ.vəʳ, ˈ-ə-, US -vɚ
mink mɪŋk **-s** -s
minke ˈmɪŋ.ki, -kə, US -kə **-s** -z
Minn. (abbrev. for **Minnesota**) ˌmɪn.ɪˈsəʊ.tə, -əˈ-, US -ˈsoʊ.t̬ə
Minneapolis ˌmɪn.iˈæp.ᵊl.ɪs
Minnehaha ˌmɪn.iˈhɑː.hɑː
Minnelli mɪˈnel.i, mə-
minneola ˌmɪn.iˈəʊ.lə, US -ˈoʊ- **-s** -z
minnesinger ˈmɪn.ɪˌsɪŋ.əʳ, -əˌ-, -gəʳ, US -sɪŋ.ɚ **-s** -z
Minnesot|a ˌmɪn.ɪˈsəʊ.t|ə, -əˈ-, US -ˈsoʊ.t̬|ə **-an/s** -ən/z
Minnie ˈmɪn.i
minnow ˈmɪn.əʊ, US -oʊ **-s** -z
Minoan mɪˈnəʊ.ən, mə-, maɪ-, US mɪˈnoʊ-
Minogue mɪˈnəʊg, mə-, US -ˈnoʊg
Minolta® mɪˈnɒl.tə, mə-, -ˈnəʊl-, US -ˈnoʊl-, -ˈnɑːl-
minor ˈmaɪ.nəʳ, US -nɚ **-s** -z **-ing** -ɪŋ **-ed** -d
Minorca mɪˈnɔː.kə, mə-, US -ˈnɔːr-
Minories ˈmɪn.ᵊr.iz
minorit|y maɪˈnɒr.ə.t|i, mɪ-, mə-, -ɪ.t|i, US maɪˈnɔːr.ə.t̬|i, mɪ- **-ies** -iz
Minos ˈmaɪ.nɒs, US -nɑːs, -nəs
Minotaur ˈmaɪ.nə.tɔːʳ, US ˈmɪn.ə.tɔːr **-s** -z
Minsk mɪntsk
Minsmere ˈmɪnz.mɪəʳ, US -mɪr
minster, M~ ˈmɪn.stəʳ, US -stɚ **-s** -z
minstrel ˈmɪnt.strᵊl **-s** -z
minstrel|sy ˈmɪnt.strᵊl|.si **-sies** -siz
mint mɪnt **-s** -s **-ing** -ɪŋ, US ˈmɪn.t̬ɪŋ **-ed** -ɪd, US ˈmɪn.t̬ɪd **-age** -ɪdʒ, US ˈmɪn.t̬ɪdʒ ˌ**mint con**ˈ**dition;** ˌ**mint** ˈ**julep;** ˌ**mint** ˈ**sauce** US ˈ**mint** ˌ**sauce**
Mintel ˈmɪn.tel
Minto ˈmɪn.təʊ, US -toʊ
Mintoff ˈmɪn.tɒf, US -tɑːf

minuet ˌmɪn.juˈet **-s** -s
minus ˈmaɪ.nəs **-es** -ɪz
minuscule ˈmɪn.ə.skjuːl, ˈ-ɪ-, (US) ˈ-ɪ-; (US) mɪˈnʌs.kjuːl **-s** -z
minute n *division of time, angle, memorandum:* ˈmɪn.ɪt **-s** -s
min|ute v ˈmɪn|.ɪt **-utes** -ɪts **-uting** -ɪ.tɪŋ, (US) -ɪ.t̬ɪŋ **-uted** -ɪ.tɪd, (US) -ɪ.t̬ɪd
minu|te adj *very small:* maɪˈnjuː|t, (US) -ˈnuː|t, -ˈnjuː|t **-test** -tɪst, -təst, (US) -t̬ɪst, -t̬əst **-tely** -t.li **-teness** -t.nəs, -t.nɪs
minute-gun ˈmɪn.ɪt.ɡʌn **-s** -z
minute-hand ˈmɪn.ɪt.hænd **-s** -z
minute|man, M~ ˈmɪn.ɪt|.mæn **-men** -men
minuti|a maɪˈnjuː.ʃi|.ə, mɪ-, mə-, -ˈnuː-, -ti-, (US) mɪˈnuː.ʃi-, -ˈnjuː-, ˈ-ʃ|ə **-ae** -iː, -aɪ
minx mɪŋks **-es** -ɪz
Miocene ˈmaɪ.əʊ.siːn, (US) ˈ-oʊ-, ˈ-ə-
mios|is maɪˈəʊ.s|ɪs, (US) -ˈoʊ- **-es** -iːz
miotic maɪˈɒt.ɪk, (US) -ˈɑː.t̬ɪk **-s** -s
mips, MIPS mɪps
Mir mɪəʳ, (US) mɪr
Mira ˈmaɪə.rə, ˈmɪr.ə, (US) ˈmaɪ.rə
Mirabell ˈmɪr.ə.bel
miracle ˈmɪr.ə.kəl, ˈ-ɪ- **-s** -z
miraculous mɪˈræk.jə.ləs, mə-, -jʊ-, (US) məˈræk.jə.ləs, -jʊ- **-ly** -li **-ness** -nəs, -nɪs
mirag|e ˈmɪr.ɑːʒ; məˈrɑːʒ, mɪˈ-, (US) mɪˈrɑːʒ, mə- **-es** -ɪz
Miramax ˈmɪr.ə.mæks
Miranda mɪˈræn.də, (US) mə-, mɪ-
MIRAS ˈmaɪə.rəs, -ræs, (US) ˈmaɪ-
mir|e maɪəʳ, ˈmaɪ.əʳ, (US) maɪ.ɚ **-es** -z **-ing** -ɪŋ **-ed** -d
Mirfield ˈmɜː.fiːld, (US) ˈmɝː-
Miriam ˈmɪr.i.əm
mirk|y ˈmɜː.k|i, (US) ˈmɝː- **-ier** -i.əʳ, (US) -i.ɚ **-iest** -i.ɪst, -i.əst **-ily** -əl.i, -ɪ.li **-iness** -ɪ.nəs, -ɪ.nɪs
Miró mɪˈrəʊ, (US) miːˈroʊ
Mirren ˈmɪr.ən
mirr|or ˈmɪr|.əʳ, (US) -ɚ **-ors** -əz, (US) -ɚz **-oring** -ər.ɪŋ **-ored** -əd, (US) -ɚd
 ˌ**mirror** ˈ**image**
mirth mɜːθ, (US) mɝːθ
mirthful ˈmɜːθ.fəl, -fʊl, (US) ˈmɝːθ- **-ly** -i **-ness** -nəs, -nɪs
mirthless ˈmɜːθ.ləs, -lɪs, (US) ˈmɝːθ- **-ly** -li **-ness** -nəs, -nɪs
MIRV mɜːv, (US) mɝːv **-s** -z **-ing** -ɪŋ **-ed** -d
mir|y ˈmaɪə.r|i **-ier** -i.əʳ, (US) -i.ɚ **-iest** -i.ɪst, -i.əst **-iness** -ɪ.nəs, -ɪ.nɪs
mis- mɪs
 Note: Prefix. In words containing **mis-**, the prefix may either be unstressed, e.g. **misdeal** /mɪsˈdiːl/, or receive secondary stress, especially if the stem is stressed on its second syllable, e.g. **align** /əˈlaɪn/, **misalign** /ˌmɪs.əˈlaɪn/. There is sometimes a difference between nouns and verbs, e.g. **miscount**, noun /ˈmɪs.kaʊnt/, verb /mɪˈskaʊnt/. There are exceptions; see individual entries.
misadventure ˌmɪs.ədˈven.tʃəʳ, (US) -tʃɚ **-s** -z
misalign ˌmɪs.əˈlaɪn **-s** -z **-ing** -ɪŋ **-d** -d
misalignment ˌmɪs.əˈlaɪn.mənt, -ˈlaɪm-, (US) -ˈlaɪn- **-s** -s
misallianc|e ˌmɪs.əˈlaɪ.ənts **-es** -ɪz
misandry mɪˈsæn.dri; ˈmɪs.ən-, (US) ˈmɪs.æn-
misanthrope ˈmɪs.ən.θrəʊp, ˈmɪz-, -æn-, (US) -ən.θroʊp **-s** -s
misanthropic ˌmɪs.ənˈθrɒp.ɪk, ˌmɪz-, -ænˈ-, (US) -ənˈθrɑː.pɪk **-al** -əl **-ally** -əl.i, -li
misanthrop|y mɪˈsæn.θrə.p|i, -ˈzæn- **-ist/s** -ɪst/s
misapplication ˌmɪs.æp.lɪˈkeɪ.ʃən, -ləˈ- **-s** -z
misappl|y ˌmɪs.əˈpl|aɪ **-ies** -aɪz **-ying** -aɪ.ɪŋ **-ied** -aɪd
misapprehend ˌmɪs.æp.rɪˈhend, -rəˈ- **-s** -z **-ing** -ɪŋ **-ed** -ɪd
misapprehension ˌmɪs.æp.rɪˈhen.tʃən, -rəˈ- **-s** -z
misappropri|ate ˌmɪs.əˈprəʊ.pri|.eɪt, (US) -ˈproʊ- **-ates** -eɪts **-ating** -eɪ.tɪŋ, (US) -eɪ.t̬ɪŋ **-ated** -eɪ.tɪd, (US) -eɪ.t̬ɪd
misappropriation ˌmɪs.əˌprəʊ.priˈeɪ.ʃən, (US) -ˌproʊ- **-s** -z
misbecoming ˌmɪs.bɪˈkʌm.ɪŋ, -bəˈ-
misbegotten ˌmɪs.bɪˈɡɒt.ən, -bəˈ-, ˈmɪs.bɪˌɡɒt-, -bəˌ-, (US) ˌmɪs.bɪˈɡɑː.tən
misbehav|e ˌmɪs.bɪˈheɪv, -bəˈ- **-es** -z **-ing** -ɪŋ **-ed** -d
misbehavio(u)r ˌmɪs.bɪˈheɪ.vjəʳ, -bəˈ-, (US) -vjɚ **-s** -z
misbelief ˌmɪs.bɪˈliːf, -bəˈ-, ˈ---, (US) ˌ--ˈ-
misbeliev|e ˌmɪs.bɪˈliːv, -bəˈ-, ˈ---, (US) ˌ--ˈ- **-es** -z **-ing** -ɪŋ **-ed** -d **-er/s** -əʳ/z, (US) -ɚ/z
misc. (abbrev. for **miscellaneous**) ˌmɪs.əlˈeɪ.ni.əs
miscalcu|late mɪsˈkæl.kjə|.leɪt, -kjʊ-; ˌmɪsˈkæl-, (US) -kjə-, -kjuː- **-lates** -leɪts **-lating** -leɪ.tɪŋ, (US) -leɪ.t̬ɪŋ **-lated** -leɪ.tɪd, (US) -leɪ.t̬ɪd
miscalculation ˌmɪs.kæl.kjəˈleɪ.ʃən, -kjʊˈ-, (US) -kjəˈ-, -kjuːˈ- **-s** -z
miscall mɪˈskɔːl; ˌmɪsˈkɔːl, (US) mɪsˈkɔːl, -ˈkɑːl; (US) ˌmɪsˈkɔːl, -ˈkɑːl **-s** -z **-ing** -ɪŋ **-ed** -d
miscarriag|e ˈmɪsˌkær.ɪdʒ; -ˈ--, (US) ˈmɪsˌker-, -ˌkær-; (US) mɪˈsker-, -ˈskær-; (US) ˌmɪsˈker-, -ˈkær- **-es** -ɪz
miscarr|y mɪˈskær|.i; ˌmɪsˈkær-, (US) ˈmɪsˌker-, -ˌkær-; (US) mɪˈsker-, -ˈskær-; (US) ˌmɪsˈker-, -ˈkær- **-ies** -iz **-ying** -i.ɪŋ **-ied** -id
miscast mɪˈskɑːst; ˌmɪsˈkɑːst, (US) mɪˈskæst; (US) ˌmɪsˈkæst **-s** -s **-ing** -ɪŋ
miscegenation ˌmɪs.ɪ.dʒɪˈneɪ.ʃən, ˌ-ə-, ˌ-e-, -dʒəˈ-, (US) -edʒ.əˈ-; (US) -ɪ.dʒəˈ- **-al** -əl
miscellanea ˌmɪs.əlˈeɪ.ni.ə
miscellaneous ˌmɪs.əlˈeɪ.ni.əs, -ɪˈleɪ- **-ly** -li **-ness** -nəs, -nɪs
miscellan|y mɪˈsel.ə.n|i, (US) ˈmɪs.ə.leɪ- **-ies** -iz
mischanc|e mɪsˈtʃɑːnts, ˌmɪs-, ˈ--, (US) mɪsˈtʃænts, ˌmɪs-, ˈ-- **-es** -ɪz
mischief ˈmɪs.tʃɪf, -tʃiːf, (US) -tʃɪf **-s** -s
mischief-mak|er ˈmɪs.tʃɪfˌmeɪ.k|əʳ, (US) -k|ɚ **-ers** -əz, (US) -ɚz **-ing** -ɪŋ
mischievous ˈmɪs.tʃɪ.vəs, -tʃə-, (US) -tʃə- **-ly** -li **-ness** -nəs, -nɪs

> Note: The pronunciation /mɪsˈtʃiː.vəs/ has existed for a long time in northern accents of English, but is now becoming more widespread elsewhere; /mɪsˈtʃiː.vi.əs/ is also heard, but is usually considered a mispronunciation.

miscibility ˌmɪs.əˈbɪl.ə.ti, -ɪˈ-, ˈ-ɪ-, (US) -əˈbɪl.ə.t̬i
miscible ˈmɪs.ɪ.bəl, ˈ-ə-, (US) ˈ-ə-
misconceiv|e ˌmɪs.kənˈsiːv **-es** -z **-ing** -ɪŋ **-ed** -d
misconception ˌmɪs.kənˈsep.ʃən **-s** -z
misconduct n mɪˈskɒn.dʌkt; ˌmɪsˈkɒn-, -dəkt, (US) mɪˈskɑːn.dʌkt; (US) ˌmɪsˈkɑːn-
misconduct v ˌmɪs.kənˈdʌkt **-s** -s **-ing** -ɪŋ **-ed** -ɪd
misconstruction ˌmɪs.kənˈstrʌk.ʃən **-s** -z
misconstru|e ˌmɪs.kənˈstruː, -kɒnˈ-, (US) -kənˈ- **-es** -z **-ing** -ɪŋ **-ed** -d
miscount n ˈmɪs.kaʊnt **-s** -s
miscoun|t v mɪsˈkaʊn|t **-ts** -ts **-ting** -tɪŋ, (US) -t̬ɪŋ **-ted** -tɪd, (US) -t̬ɪd
miscreant ˈmɪs.kri.ənt **-s** -s
miscu|e mɪˈskjuː; ˌmɪsˈkjuː, (US) mɪˈskjuː; (US) ˌmɪsˈkjuː, ˈ-- **-es** -z **-ing** -ɪŋ **-ed** -d
misdeal mɪsˈdiːl, ˌ-ˈ-, (US) mɪsˈdiːl, ˌ-ˈ-, ˈ-- **-s** -z **-ing** -ɪŋ **misdealt** -ˈdelt, ˌ-ˈ-, (US) -ˈ-, ˌ-ˈ-, ˈ--
misdeed mɪsˈdiːd, ˌ-ˈ-, ˈ-- **-s** -z
misdemeano(u)r ˌmɪs.dɪˈmiː.nəʳ, -dəˈ-, (US) -nɚ, ˈ-ˌ--- **-s** -z
misdiagnos|e mɪsˈdaɪ.əɡ.nəʊz, ˌ-ˈ---, (US) ˌmɪs.daɪ.əɡˈnoʊs, -ˈnoʊz; (US) -ˈ---, ˌ-ˈ---, -noʊz **-es** -ɪz **-ing** -ɪŋ **-ed** -d
misdiagnos|is ˌmɪs.daɪ.əɡˈnəʊ.s|ɪs, (US) -ˈnoʊ-
misdirect ˌmɪs.dɪˈrekt, -dəˈ-, -daɪəˈ-, (US) -dəˈ-, -daɪˈ- **-s** -s **-ing** -ɪŋ **-ed** -ɪd
misdirection ˌmɪs.dɪˈrek.ʃən, -dəˈ-, -daɪəˈ-, (US) -dəˈ-, -daɪˈ-
misdoing mɪsˈduː.ɪŋ, ˌmɪs- **-s** -z
mise-en-scène ˌmiːz.ɑ̃ːnˈseɪn, -ˈsen, (US) -ɑ̃ːnˈsen **mise-en-scènes** ˌmiːz.ɑ̃ːnˈseɪn, -ˈsen, -z, (US) -ɑ̃ːnˈsen, -z
miser ˈmaɪ.zəʳ, (US) -zɚ **-s** -z
miserab|le ˈmɪz.ər.ə.b|əl, ˈmɪz.rə- **-ly** -li **-leness** -əl.nəs, -nɪs
miserere ˌmɪz.əˈreə.ri, -ˈɪə-, -reɪ, (US) -ˈrer.eɪ **-s** -z

misericord mɪˈzer.ɪ.kɔːd, mə-, ˈ-ə-; ˈmɪz.ər.ɪ-, (US) mɪˈzer.ɪ.kɔːrd **-s** -z
miserl|y ˈmaɪ.zəl|.i, (US) -zɚ.l|i **-iness** -ɪ.nəs, -ɪ.nɪs
miser|y ˈmɪz.ər|.i, (US) ˈ-r|i, ˈ-ɚ|.i **-ies** -iz
misfeasance mɪsˈfiː.zənts, (US) ˌmɪs-
misfire n mɪsˈfaɪər, -faɪ.ər, ˌmɪs-, ˈ-,-, (US) ˈmɪs.faɪ.ɚ
misfir|e v mɪsˈfaɪər, -ˈfaɪ.ər, ˌmɪs-, (US) -ˈfaɪ.ɚ **-es** -z **-ing** -ɪŋ **-ed** -d
misfit n ˈmɪs.fɪt **-s** -s
misfortune mɪsˈfɔː.tʃuːn, ˌmɪs-, -tʃən, -tjuːn, (US) -ˈfɔːr.tʃən **-s** -z
misgiving mɪsˈgɪv.ɪŋ, ˌmɪs- **-s** -z
misgovern mɪsˈgʌv.ən, ˌmɪs-, (US) -ɚn **-s** -z **-ing** -ɪŋ **-ed** -d **-ment** -mənt
misguided mɪsˈgaɪ.dɪd, ˌmɪs- **-ly** -li **-ness** -nəs, -nɪs
mishandl|e mɪsˈhæn.dəl, ˌmɪs- **-es** -z **-ing** -ɪŋ, -ˈhænd.lɪŋ **-ed** -d
mishap ˈmɪs.hæp, -ˈ-, ˌ-ˈ-, (US) ˈmɪs.hæp **-s** -s
mis|hear mɪs|ˈhɪər, ˌmɪs-, (US) -ˈhɪr **-hears** -ˈhɪəz, (US) -ˈhɪrz **-hearing** -ˈhɪə.rɪŋ, (US) -ˈhɪr.ɪŋ **-heard** -ˈhɜːd, (US) -ˈhɝːd
Mishima ˈmɪʃ.ɪ.mə; mɪˈʃiː-, (US) ˈmɪʃ.ɪ-, ˈmiː.ʃɪ-
mis|hit mɪs|ˈhɪt, ˌmɪs- **-hits** -ˈhɪts **-hitting** -ˈhɪt.ɪŋ, (US) -ˈhɪţ.ɪŋ
mishmash ˈmɪʃ.mæʃ
misinform ˌmɪs.ɪnˈfɔːm, (US) -ˈfɔːrm **-s** -z **-ing** -ɪŋ **-ed** -d **-ant/s** -ənt/s **-er/s** -ər/z, (US) -ɚ/z
misinformation ˌmɪs.ɪn.fəˈmeɪ.ʃən, (US) -fɚˈ-
misinter|pret ˌmɪs.ɪnˈtɜː|.prɪt, (US) -ˈtɝː- **-prets** -prɪts **-preting** -prɪ.tɪŋ, (US) -prɪ.ţɪŋ **-preted** -prɪ.tɪd, (US) -prɪ.ţɪd
misinterpretation ˌmɪs.ɪnˌtɜː.prɪˈteɪ.ʃən, -prəˈ-, (US) -ˌtɝː.prɪˈ- **-s** -z
misjoinder mɪsˈdʒɔɪn.dər, ˌmɪs-, (US) -dɚ
misjudg|e mɪsˈdʒʌdʒ, ˌmɪs- **-es** -ɪz **-ing** -ɪŋ **-ed** -d
misjudg(e)ment mɪsˈdʒʌdʒ.mənt, ˌmɪs- **-s** -s
Miskolc ˈmɪʃ.kəʊlts, (US) -koːlts
mislay mɪˈsleɪ, ˌmɪsˈleɪ **-s** -z **-ing** -ɪŋ **mislaid** mɪˈsleɪd, ˌmɪsˈleɪd
mislead mɪˈsliːd, ˌmɪsˈliːd **-s** -z **-ing/ly** -ɪŋ/li **misled** mɪˈsled, ˌmɪsˈled
mismanag|e ˌmɪsˈmæn.ɪdʒ **-es** -ɪz **-ing** -ɪŋ **-ed** -d **-ement** -mənt
mismatch n ˈmɪs.mætʃ; -ˈ-, ˌ-ˈ- **-es** -ɪz
mismatch v mɪˈsmætʃ; ˌmɪsˈmætʃ, ˈ-,-, (US) mɪˈsmætʃ; (US) ˌmɪsˈmætʃ **-es** -ɪs **-ing** -ɪŋ **-ed** -t
misnomer mɪˈsnəʊ.mər; ˌmɪsˈnəʊ-, (US) mɪˈsnoʊ.mɚ, ˌmɪsˈnoʊ- **-s** -z
miso ˈmiː.səʊ, (US) -soʊ
misogynist mɪˈsɒdʒ.ən.ɪst, maɪ-, mə-, (US) -ˈsɑːdʒ- **-s** -s
misogynistic mɪˌsɒdʒ.ənˈɪs.tɪk, maɪ-, mə-, -dʒɪˈnɪs-, (US) -ˌɑː.dʒɪˈnɪs-
misogyn|y mɪˈsɒdʒ.ɪ.n|i, maɪ-, mə-, (US) -sɑːdʒ-
misplac|e mɪˈspleɪs, ˌmɪsˈpleɪs **-es** -ɪz **-ing** -ɪŋ **-ed** -t **-ement** -mənt *stress shift:* **ˌmisplaced ˈtrust**
misprint n ˈmɪs.prɪnt **-s** -s
misprin|t v mɪˈsprɪn|t; ˌmɪsˈprɪn|t **-ts** -ts **-ting** -tɪŋ, (US) -ţɪŋ **-ted** -tɪd, (US) -ţɪd
misprision mɪˈsprɪʒ.ən
mispronounc|e ˌmɪs.prəˈnaʊnts, (US) -prəˈ-, -proʊˈ- **-es** -ɪz **-ing** -ɪŋ **-ed** -t
mispronunciation ˌmɪs.prəˌnʌnt.siˈeɪ.ʃən, (US) -prəˌ-, -proʊˌ- **-s** -z
misquotation ˌmɪs.kwəʊˈteɪ.ʃən, (US) -kwoʊˈ- **-s** -z
misquo|te mɪˈskwəʊ|t; ˌmɪsˈkwəʊ|t, (US) mɪˈskwoʊ|t; (US) ˌmɪsˈkwoʊ|t **-tes** -ts **-ting** -tɪŋ, (US) -ţɪŋ **-ted** -tɪd, (US) -ţɪd
Misratah ˈmɪs.ræt.ɑː
misread mɪsˈriːd, ˌmɪs-; *past tense:* mɪsˈred, ˌmɪs- **-s** -z **-ing** -ɪŋ
misrememb|er ˌmɪs.rɪˈmem.b|ər, -rəˈ-, (US) -b|ɚ **-ers** -əz, (US) -ɚz **-ering** -ər.ɪŋ **-ered** -əd, (US) -ɚd
misre|port ˌmɪs.rɪ|ˈpɔːt, (US) -ˈpɔːrt **-ports** -ˈpɔːts, (US) -ˈpɔːrts **-porting** -ˈpɔː.tɪŋ, (US) -ˈpɔːr.ţɪŋ **-ported** -ˈpɔː.tɪd, (US) -ˈpɔːr.ţɪd
misrepre|sent ˌmɪs.rep.rɪ|ˈzent **-sents** -ˈzents **-senting** -ˈzen.tɪŋ, (US) -ˈzen.ţɪŋ **-sented** -ˈzen.tɪd, (US) -ˈzen.ţɪd
misrepresentation ˌmɪs.rep.rɪ.zenˈteɪ.ʃən, -zənˈ-, (US) -zenˈ- **-s** -z
misrule mɪsˈruːl, ˌmɪs-
miss, M~ mɪs **-es** -ɪz **-ing** -ɪŋ **-ed** -t
Miss. (abbrev. for **Mississippi**) ˌmɪs.ɪˈsɪp.i, (US) -əˈ-, -ɪˈ-
missal ˈmɪs.əl **-s** -z
missel thrush ˈmɪz.əlˌθrʌʃ, ˈmɪs-
Missenden ˈmɪs.ən.dən
misshapen mɪsˈʃeɪ.pən, ˌmɪs-, mɪʃ-, ˌmɪʃ- **-ly** -li
missile ˈmɪs.aɪl, (US) -əl **-s** -z
missing ˈmɪs.ɪŋ
mission ˈmɪʃ.ən **-s** -z
missionar|y ˈmɪʃ.ən.ər|.i, ˈmɪʃ.nər-, (US) ˈ-ən.er- **-ies** -iz ˈ**missionary poˌsition**
missioner ˈmɪʃ.ən.ər, (US) -ɚ **-s** -z
missis ˈmɪs.ɪz
Mississippi ˌmɪs.ɪˈsɪp.i, (US) -əˈ-, -ɪˈ- **-an/s** -ən/z
missive ˈmɪs.ɪv **-s** -z
Missoula mɪˈzuː.lə
Missouri mɪˈzʊə.ri, -ˈsʊə-, (US) -ˈzʊr.i; *locally:* (US) -ə
misspell mɪsˈspel, ˌmɪs- **-s** -z **-ing/s** -ɪŋ/z **-ed** -t, -d **misspelt** mɪsˈspelt, (US) ˌmɪs-
misspend mɪsˈspend, ˌmɪs **-s** -z **-ing** -ɪŋ **misspent** mɪsˈspent, ˌmɪs- ˌ**misspent ˈyouth**
mis|state mɪs|ˈsteɪt, ˌmɪs- **-states** -ˈsteɪts **-stating** -ˈsteɪ.tɪŋ, (US) -ˈsteɪ.ţɪŋ **-stated** -ˈsteɪ.tɪd, (US) -ˈsteɪ.ţɪd **-statement/s** -ˈsteɪt.mənt/s
missus ˈmɪs.ɪz, -ɪs
miss|y ˈmɪs|.i **-ies** -iz
mist mɪst **-s** -s **-ing** -ɪŋ **-ed** -ɪd **-er/s** -ər/z, -ɚ/z
mistak(e)able mɪˈsteɪ.kə.bəl
mistak|e mɪˈsteɪk **-es** -s **-ing** -ɪŋ **mistook** mɪˈstʊk
mistaken mɪˈsteɪ.kən **-ly** -li
mister, M~ ˈmɪs.tər, (US) -tɚ
mistim|e mɪsˈtaɪm; ˌmɪs- **-es** -z **-ing** -ɪŋ **-ed** -d
mistle thrush ˈmɪs.əlˌθrʌʃ, ˈmɪz-, (US) ˈmɪs-
mistletoe ˈmɪs.əl.təʊ, ˈmɪz-, (US) ˈmɪs.əl.toʊ
mistook (from **mistake**) mɪˈstʊk
mistral, M~ ˈmiː.strɑːl, miˈstrɑːl **-s** -z
mistransla|te ˌmɪs.trænˈsleɪ|t, -trɑːn-, -trən-; -trænzˈleɪ|t, -trɑːnzˈ-, -trənzˈ-, (US) ˌmɪsˈtræn.sleɪ|t, -ˈtrænz.leɪ|t; (US) mɪs.trænˈsleɪ|t; (US) -trænzˈleɪ|t **-tes** -ts **-ting** -tɪŋ, (US) -ţɪŋ **-ted** -tɪd, (US) -ţɪd
mistranslation ˌmɪs.trænˈsleɪ.ʃən, -trɑːnˈ-, -trənˈ-; -trænzˈleɪ-, -trænzˈ-, -trənzˈ-, (US) -trænˈsleɪ-; (US) -trænzˈleɪ- **-s** -z
mistrea|t mɪsˈtriː|t; ˌmɪs- **-ts** -ts **-ting** -tɪŋ, (US) -ţɪŋ **-ted** -tɪd, (US) -ţɪd
mistreatment mɪsˈtriːt.mənt; ˌmɪs-
mistress ˈmɪs.trəs, -trɪs, (US) -trɪs **-es** -ɪz
mistrial mɪˈstraɪ.əl; ˌmɪsˈtraɪ-, (US) ˈmɪsˌtraɪ.əl; (US) mɪˈstraɪ.əl; (US) ˌmɪsˈtraɪ.əl **-s** -z
mistrust mɪˈstrʌst; ˌmɪsˈtrʌst, (US) ˌmɪsˈtrʌst; (US) mɪˈstrʌst; (US) ˈmɪs.trʌst **-s** -s **-ing** -ɪŋ **-ed** -ɪd
mistrustful mɪˈstrʌst.fəl, ˌmɪsˈtrʌst-, -fʊl **-ly** -li
mist|y, M~ ˈmɪs.t|i **-ier** -i.ər, (US) -i.ɚ **-iest** -i.ɪst, -i.əst **-ily** -əl.i, -ɪ.li **-iness** -ɪ.nəs, -ɪ.nɪs
misty-eyed ˌmɪs.tiˈaɪd *stress shift:* ˌ**misty-eyed ˈsentiment**
misunder|stand ˌmɪs.ʌn.də|ˈstænd, (US) -dɚˈ- **-stands** -ˈstændz **-standing/s** -ˈstæn.dɪŋ/z **-stood** -ˈstʊd
misuse n ˌmɪsˈjuːs
misus|e v ˌmɪsˈjuːz **-es** -ɪz **-ing** -ɪŋ **-ed** -d
MIT ˌem.aɪˈtiː *stress shift:* ˌ**MIT ˈgraduate**
Mitch mɪtʃ
Mitcham ˈmɪtʃ.əm
Mitchel(l) ˈmɪtʃ.əl
Mitchison ˈmɪtʃ.ɪ.sən
Mitchum ˈmɪtʃ.əm
mite maɪt **-s** -s
mit|er ˈmaɪ.t|ər, (US) -ţ|ɚ **-ers** -əz, (US) -ɚz **-ering** -ər.ɪŋ **-ered** -əd, (US) -ɚd ˈ**miter ˌbox;** ˈ**miter ˌjoint**
Mitford ˈmɪt.fəd, (US) -fɚd
Mithr|a ˈmɪθ.r|ə **-as** -æs, (US) -əs, -æs
Mithraic mɪˈθreɪ.ɪk
Mithra|ism ˈmɪθ.reɪ|.ɪ.zəm;

Pronouncing the letters MN

The consonant digraph **mn** is word- or morpheme-final and usually realized as /m/, that is, the **n** is silent, e.g.:

hymn hɪm

condemning kənˈdem.ɪŋ

However, in some cases the **n** is pronounced, particularly (as in the case of *condemnation*) where the vowel following the **n** is in a stressed syllable, e.g.:

hymnal ˈhɪm.nᵊl

condemnation ˌkɒn.demˈneɪ.ʃᵊn (US) ˌkɑːn-

mɪˈθreɪ-, (US) ˈmɪθ.reɪ-, -rə- **-ist/s** -ɪst/s
Mithridates ˌmɪθ.rɪˈdeɪ.tiːz, (US) -rəˈ-
mitigable ˈmɪt.ɪ.gə.bᵊl, (US) ˈmɪţ-
miti|gate ˈmɪt.ɪ|.geɪt, (US) ˈmɪţ- **-gates** -geɪts **-gating** -geɪ.tɪŋ, (US) -geɪ.ţɪŋ **-gated** -geɪ.tɪd, (US) -geɪ.ţɪd **-gator/s** -geɪ.təʳ/z, (US) -geɪ.ţɚ/z
mitigation ˌmɪt.ɪˈgeɪ.ʃᵊn, (US) ˌmɪţ-
mitigatory ˈmɪt.ɪ.geɪ.tᵊr.i, (US) ˈmɪţ.ɪ.gə.tɔːr-
mitochondrial ˌmaɪ.təʊˈkɒn.dri.əl, (US) -toʊˈkɑːn-, -ţəˈ-
mitochondri|on ˌmaɪ.təʊˈkɒn.dri|.ən, (US) -toʊˈkɑːn-, -ţəˈ- **-a** -ə
mitosis maɪˈtəʊ.sɪs, (US) -ˈtoʊ-
mitrailleus|e ˌmɪt.raɪˈɜːz, (US) ˌmiː.treɪˈjɜːz **-es** -ɪz
mitral ˈmaɪ.trᵊl
mit|re ˈmaɪ.t|əʳ, (US) -ţ|ɚ **-res** -əz, (US) -ɚz **-ring** -ᵊr.ɪŋ **-red** -əd, (US) -ɚd **ˈmitre ˌbox; ˈmitre ˌjoint**
Mitrovice ˌmɪt.rəʊˈvɪt.sə, ˈmɪt.rəʊ.vɪt.sə, (US) mɪt.rəˈviːt.sə, -roʊˈ-
Mitsubishi® ˌmɪt.sʊˈbɪʃ.i, -suːˈ-, (US) -suːˈ-
mitt mɪt **-s** -s
mitten ˈmɪt.ᵊn **-s** -z
Mitterand, Mitterrand ˈmiː.tə.rɑ̃ːŋ, (US) ˈmiː.t.ə.rɑːnd, ˈmɪt-
Mitylene ˌmɪt.ᵊlˈiː.ni, -ɪˈliː-, (US) ˌmɪţ.əˈliː-
mitz|vah ˈmɪts|.və, (US) ˈmɪts-; (US) mɪtsˈvɑː **-vahs** -əz, (US) ˈmɪts.vəs; (US) mɪtsˈvɑːz **-voth** -vɒt, (US) ˈmɪts.voʊt, -voʊs
Mivart ˈmaɪ.vət, -vɑːt, (US) -vɚt, -vɑːrt
mix n, v mɪks **-es** -ɪz **-ing** -ɪŋ **-ed** -t **ˌmixed ˈbag; ˌmixed ˈblessing; ˌmixed ˈdoubles; ˌmixed ˈfarming; ˌmixed ˈgrill; ˌmixed ˈmarriage; ˌmixed ˈmetaphor**
mix-and-match ˌmɪks.ᵊndˈmætʃ, -ᵊmˈ-, (US) -ᵊndˈ- *stress shift:* **ˌmix-and-match ˈclothes**
mixed-ability ˌmɪkst.əˈbɪl.ə.ti, -ɪ.ti, (US) -ə.ţi *stress shift:* **ˌmixed-ability ˈstudents**
mixed blessing ˌmɪkstˈbles.ɪŋ
mixed-up ˌmɪkstˈʌp *stress shift:* **ˌmixed-up ˈkid**
mixer ˈmɪk.səʳ, (US) -sɚ **-s** -z
mixture ˈmɪks.tʃəʳ, (US) -tʃɚ **-s** -z
mix-up ˈmɪks.ʌp **-s** -s
Mizpah ˈmɪz.pə
mizzen ˈmɪz.ᵊn **-s** -z
mizzen-mast ˈmɪz.ᵊnˌmɑːst, -ᵊmˌ-, -ᵊnˌmæst; *nautical pronunciation:* -məst, (US) -ᵊn.mæst **-s** -s
mizzl|e ˈmɪz.ᵊl **-es** -z **-ing** -ɪŋ, ˈmɪz.lɪŋ **-ed** -d **-y** -i
ml (abbrev. for **millilitre/s**) *singular:* ˈmɪl.ɪˌliː.təʳ, ˈ-ə-, (US) -ţɚ; *plural:* -z
Mladic ˈmlæd.ɪtʃ, (US) məˈlæd.ɪtʃ
mm (abbrev. for **millimetre/s**) *singular:* ˈmɪl.ɪˌmiː.təʳ, ˈ-ə-, (US) -ţɚ; *plural:* -z
MMR ˌem.emˈɑːʳ, (US) -ˈɑːr
mnemonic nɪˈmɒn.ɪk, nə-, niː-, mnɪ-, mnə-, mniː-, (US) nɪˈmɑː.nɪk, niː- **-s** -s **-ally** -ᵊl.i, -li
Mnemosyne nɪˈmɒz.ɪ.ni, nə-, niː-, mnɪ-, mnə-, mniː-, -ˈmɒs-, -ᵊn.i, (US) nɪˈmɑː.sɪ-, niː-, -zɪ-
mo, mo' məʊ, (US) moʊ
Mo məʊ, (US) moʊ
Mo. (abbrev. for **Missouri**) mɪˈzʊə.ri, -ˈsʊə-, (US) -ˈzʊr.i; *locally:* (US) -ə
moa ˈməʊ.ə, (US) ˈmoʊ.ə **-s** -z
Moab ˈməʊ.æb, (US) ˈmoʊ-
Moabite ˈməʊ.ə.baɪt, (US) ˈmoʊ- **-s** -s
moan məʊn, (US) moʊn **-s** -z **-ing/s** -ɪŋ/z **-ed** -d
moat, M~ məʊt, (US) moʊt **-s** -s **-ing** -ɪŋ, (US) ˈmoʊ.ţɪŋ **-ed** -ɪd, (US) ˈmoʊ.ţɪd
mob mɒb, (US) mɑːb **-s** -z **-bing** -ɪŋ **-bed** -d
mobcap ˈmɒb.kæp, (US) ˈmɑːb- **-s** -s
Moberly ˈməʊ.bᵊl.i, (US) ˈmoʊ.bɚ.li
Mobil® ˈməʊ.bɪl, -bᵊl, (US) ˈmoʊ.bᵊl, -bɪl
mobile adj ˈməʊ.baɪl, (US) ˈmoʊ.bᵊl, -bɪl, -baɪl **ˌmobile ˈphone; ˌmobile ˈhome**
mobile n ˈməʊ.baɪl, (US) ˈmoʊ.biːl **-s** -z
mobility məʊˈbɪl.ə.ti, -ɪ.ti, (US) moʊˈbɪl.ə.ţi
mobilization, -isa- ˌməʊ.bɪ.laɪˈzeɪ.ʃᵊn, -bᵊl.aɪˈ-, -ɪˈ-, (US) ˌmoʊ.bᵊl.əˈ- **-s** -z
mobiliz|e, -is|e ˈməʊ.bɪ.laɪz, -bᵊl.aɪz, (US) -bə.laɪz **-es** -ɪz **-ing** -ɪŋ **-ed** -d
mobius, möbius, M~ ˈməʊ.bi.əs; *as if German:* ˈmɜː-; (US) ˈmeɪ.bi.əs, ˈmoʊ-, ˈmiː-; *as if German:* (US) ˈmɜː- **ˌMobius ˈstrip**
mobster ˈmɒb.stəʳ, (US) ˈmɑːb.stɚ **-s** -z
Mobutu məˈbuː.tuː
Moby Dick ˌməʊ.biˈdɪk, (US) ˌmoʊ-
moccasin ˈmɒk.ə.sɪn, (US) ˈmɑː.kə.sən, -sɪn **-s** -z
mocha *coffee, leather, etc.:* ˈmɒk.ə, ˈməʊ.kə, (US) ˈmoʊ.kə
Mocha *Arabian seaport:* ˈməʊ.kə, ˈmɒk.ə, (US) ˈmoʊ.kə
mock mɒk, (US) mɑːk **-s** -s **-ing/ly** -ɪŋ/li **-ed** -t **-er/s** -əʳ/z, (US) -ɚ/z
mockers ˈmɒk.əz, (US) ˈmɑː.kɚz **put the ˈmockers on ˌsomething**
mocker|y ˈmɒk.ᵊr|.i, (US) ˈmɑː.kɚ- **-ies** -iz
Mockett ˈmɒk.ɪt, (US) ˈmɑː.kɪt
mockingbird ˈmɒk.ɪŋˌbɜːd, (US) ˈmɑː.kɪŋˌbɝːd **-s** -z
mockney ˈmɒk.ni, (US) ˈmɑːk.ni
mock-turtle ˌmɒkˈtɜː.tᵊl, (US) ˌmɑːkˈtɝː.ţᵊl *stress shift:* **ˌmock-turtle ˈsoup**
mock-up ˈmɒk.ʌp, (US) ˈmɑːk- **-s** -s
mod, M~ mɒd, (US) mɑːd **-s** -z
MoD ˌem.əʊˈdiː, (US) -oʊˈ- *stress shift:* **ˌMoD ˈcuts**
modal ˈməʊ.dᵊl, (US) ˈmoʊ- **-s** -z **-ly** -i **ˌmodal ˈverb**
modality məʊˈdæl.ə.ti, -ɪ.ti, (US) moʊˈdæl.ə.ţi
mod con ˌmɒdˈkɒn, (US) ˌmɑːdˈkɑːn, ˈ-- **-s** -z
mode məʊd, (US) moʊd **-s** -z
model ˈmɒd.ᵊl, (US) ˈmɑː.dᵊl **-s** -z **-(l)ing** -ɪŋ, ˈmɒd.lɪŋ, (US) ˈmɑːd- **-(l)ed** -d **-(l)er/s** -əʳ/z, (US) -ɚ/z, ˈmɒd.ləʳ/z, ˈmɑːd.lɚ/z
modem ˈməʊ.dem, -dəm, (US) ˈmoʊ.dəm, -dem **-s** -z
Modena ˈmɒd.ɪ.nə; mɒdˈeɪ.nə, məˈdeɪ-, (US) ˈmoʊ.dᵊn.ə, ˈmɔː-, -ɑː
moderate n, adj ˈmɒd.ᵊr.ət, -ɪt, (US) ˈmɑː.dɚ- **-s** -s **-ly** -li **-ness** -nəs, -nɪs
moder|ate v ˈmɒd.ᵊr|.eɪt, (US) ˈmɑː.də.r|eɪt **-ates** -eɪts **-ating** -eɪ.tɪŋ, (US) -eɪ.ţɪŋ **-ated** -eɪ.tɪd, (US) -eɪ.ţɪd **-ator/s** -eɪ.təʳ/z, (US) -eɪ.ţɚ/z
moderation ˌmɒd.ᵊrˈeɪ.ʃᵊn, (US) ˌmɑː.dəˈreɪ- **-s** -z
moderato ˌmɒd.ᵊrˈɑː.təʊ, (US) ˌmɑː.dəˈrɑː.toʊ **-s** -z
modern ˈmɒd.ᵊn, (US) ˈmɑː.dɚn **-s** -z **-ly** -li **-ness** -nəs, -nɪs **ˌmodern ˈlanguages**
modern|ism, M~ ˈmɒd.ᵊn|.ɪ.zᵊm, (US) ˈmɑːd.ɚ.n|ɪ- **-ist/s** -ɪst/s
modernistic ˌmɒd.ᵊnˈɪs.tɪk, (US) ˌmɑː.dɚˈnɪs- **-ally** -ᵊl.i, -li
modernity mɒdˈɜː.nə.ti, məˈdɜː-, -ɪ.ti, (US) mɑːˈdɝː.nə.ţi, mə-, moʊ-

modernization, -isa- ˌmɒd.ən.aɪˈzeɪ.ʃən, -ɪˈ-, (US) ˌmɑː.dɚ.nəˈ- **-s** -z
moderniz|e, -is|e ˈmɒd.ən.aɪz, (US) ˈmɑː.dɚ.naɪz **-es** -ɪz **-ing** -ɪŋ **-ed** -d **-er/s** -əʳ/z, (US) -ɚ/z
modest ˈmɒd.ɪst, (US) ˈmɑː.dɪst **-ly** -li **-y** -i
modicum ˈmɒd.ɪ.kəm, ˈ-ə-, (US) ˈmɑː.dɪ- **-s** -z
modification ˌmɒd.ɪ.fɪˈkeɪ.ʃən, ˌ-ə-, -fəˈ-, (US) ˌmɑː.dɪ- **-s** -z
modi|fy ˈmɒd.ɪ|.faɪ, ˈ-ə-, (US) ˈmɑː.dɪ-, ˈ-də- **-fies** -faɪz **-fying** -faɪ.ɪŋ **-fied** -faɪd **-fier/s** -faɪ.əʳ/z, (US) -faɪ.ɚ/z **-fiable** -faɪ.ə.bəl
Modigliani ˌmɒd.ɪlˈjɑː.ni, (US) ˌmoʊ.diːlˈjɑː-
modish ˈməʊ.dɪʃ, (US) ˈmoʊ- **-ly** -li **-ness** -nəs, -nɪs
modiste məʊˈdiːst, (US) moʊ- **-s** -s
Modred ˈməʊ.drɪd, (US) ˈmoʊ-
modular ˈmɒd.jə.ləʳ, ˈmɒdʒ-, -jʊ-, (US) ˈmɑː.dʒə.lɚ
modularity ˌmɒd.jəˈlær.ə.ti, ˌmɒdʒ-, -jʊˈ-, -ɪ.ti, (US) ˌmɑː.dʒəˈler.ə.t̬i, -ˈlær-
modu|late ˈmɒd.jə|.leɪt, ˈmɒdʒ-, -jʊ-, (US) ˈmɑː.dʒə- **-lates** -leɪts **-lating** -leɪ.tɪŋ, (US) -leɪ.t̬ɪŋ **-lated** -leɪ.tɪd, (US) -leɪ.t̬ɪd **-lator/s** -leɪ.təʳ/z, (US) -leɪ.t̬ɚ/z
modulation ˌmɒd.jəˈleɪ.ʃən, ˌmɒdʒ-, -jʊˈ-, (US) ˌmɑː.dʒəˈ- **-s** -z
module ˈmɒd.juːl, ˈmɒdʒ-, (US) ˈmɑː.dʒuːl **-s** -z
modul|us ˈmɒd.jə.l|əs, -jʊ-, (US) ˈmɑː.dʒə- **-uses** -ə.sɪz **-i** -aɪ
modus ˈməʊ.dəs, (US) ˈmoʊ-
modus operandi ˌməʊ.dəsˌɒp.əˈræn.diː, ˌmɒd.əs-, -daɪ, (US) ˌmoʊ.dəsˌoʊ.pəˈrɑːn.di, -ˌɑː-, -ˈræn-
modus vivendi ˌməʊ.dəs.vɪˈven.diː, ˌmɒd.əs-, -viːˈ-, -daɪ, (US) ˌmoʊ.dəs.vɪˈven.di
Moesia ˈmiː.si.ə, -ʃə, -zi.ə, -ʒə, (US) -ʃi.ə, -ʃə
Moffat ˈmɒf.ət, (US) ˈmɑː.fət
Moffett ˈmɒf.ət, -ɪt, (US) ˈmɑː.fət
Mogadishu ˌmɒg.əˈdɪʃ.uː, (US) ˌmoʊ.gəˈdiː.ʃuː, ˌmɑː-, -gəˈ-, -ˈdɪʃ.uː
Mogadon® ˈmɒg.ə.dɒn, (US) ˈmɑː.gə.dɑːn
Mogador ˌmɒg.əˈdɔːʳ, ˈ---, (US) ˈmɑː.gə.dɔːr, ˌ--ˈ-
Moggach ˈmɒg.ək, -əx, (US) ˈmɑː.gək
mogg|y, mogg|ie ˈmɒg|.i, (US) ˈmɑː.g|i **-ies** -z
mogul, M~ ˈməʊ.gəl, -gʊl, -gʌl, (US) ˈmoʊ.gʌl, -gəl; (US) moʊˈgʌl **-s** -z
mohair ˈməʊ.heəʳ, (US) ˈmoʊ.her
Moham(m)ed məʊˈhæm.ɪd, -əd, -ed, (US) moʊ-
Mohammedan məʊˈhæm.ɪ.dən, ˈ-ə-, (US) moʊ- **-s** -z **-ism** -ɪ.zəm
Mohave məʊˈhɑː.vi, (US) moʊ-
Mohawk ˈməʊ.hɔːk, (US) ˈmoʊ.hɑːk, -hɔːk **-s** -s
Mohegan məʊˈhiː.gən, mə-, (US) moʊ- **-s** -z
Mohican məʊˈhiː.kən; ˈməʊ.ɪ-, (US) moʊˈhiː- **-s** -z
Mohun ˈməʊ.ən; ˈməʊ.hən; muːn, (US) muːn, ˈmoʊ.hən
moi mwɑː
moidore ˌmɔɪˈdɔːʳ, ˌməʊ.ɪˈ-; ˈmɔɪ.dɔːʳ, (US) ˈmɔɪ.dɔːr **-s** -z

> Note: In John Masefield's poem 'Cargoes' the stress is on the last syllable.

moiet|y ˈmɔɪ.ə.t|i, ˈ-ɪ-, (US) -ə.t̬|i **-ies** -iz
moil mɔɪl **-s** -z **-ing** -ɪŋ **-ed** -d
Moir ˈmɔɪ.əʳ, mɔɪəʳ, (US) mɔɪ.ɚ
Moira ˈmɔɪə.rə, (US) ˈmɔɪ-
moire mwɑːʳ, mwɔːʳ, (US) mwɑːr, mɔːr **-s** -z
moiré ˈmwɑː.reɪ, ˈmwɔː-, (US) mwɑːˈreɪ, mɔː-; (US) ˈmɔː.reɪ
moist mɔɪst **-er** -əʳ, (US) -ɚ **-est** -ɪst, -əst **-ly** -li **-ness** -nəs, -nɪs
moisten ˈmɔɪ.sən **-s** -z **-ing** -ɪŋ, ˈmɔɪs.nɪŋ **-ed** -d
moisture ˈmɔɪs.tʃəʳ, (US) -tʃɚ
moisturiz|e, -is|e ˈmɔɪs.tʃər.aɪz, (US) -tʃə.raɪz **-es** -ɪz **-ing** -ɪŋ **-ed** -d **-er/s** -əʳ/z, (US) -ɚ/z
Moivre ˈmɔɪ.vəʳ, (US) -vɚ
Mojave məʊˈhɑː.vi, (US) moʊ-
moke məʊk, (US) moʊk **-s** -s
molar ˈməʊ.ləʳ, (US) ˈmoʊ.lɚ **-s** -z
molasses məʊˈlæs.ɪz, -əz, (US) mə-
mold məʊld, (US) moʊld **-s** -z **-ing/s** -ɪŋ **-ed** -ɪd
Mold məʊld, (US) moʊld
Moldavi|a mɒlˈdeɪ.vi|.ə, (US) mɑːl-, ˈ-vj|ə **-an/s** -ən/z
mold|er ˈməʊl.d|əʳ, (US) ˈmoʊl.d|ɚ **-ers** -əz, (US) -ɚz **-ering** -ər.ɪŋ **-ered** -əd, (US) -ɚd
Moldov|a mɒlˈdəʊ.v|ə, (US) mɑːlˈdoʊ- **-an/s** -ən/z
mold|y ˈməʊl.d|i, (US) ˈmoʊl- **-ier** -i.əʳ, (US) -i.ɚ **-iest** -i.ɪst, -i.əst **-iness** -ɪ.nəs, -ɪ.nɪs
mole, M~ məʊl, (US) moʊl **-s** -z
Molech ˈməʊ.lek, (US) ˈmoʊ-
molecular məʊˈlek.jə.ləʳ, mɒlˈek-, -jʊ-, (US) məˈlek.jə.lɚ, moʊ-, -juː-
molecule ˈmɒl.ɪ.kjuːl, ˈməʊ.lɪ-, -lə-, (US) ˈmɑː.lɪ.kjuːl **-s** -z
molehill ˈməʊl.hɪl, (US) ˈmoʊl- **-s** -z
make a ˌmountain out of a ˈmolehill
Molesey ˈməʊl.zi, (US) ˈmoʊl-
moleskin ˈməʊl.skɪn, (US) ˈmoʊl- **-s** -z
molest məʊˈlest, (US) mə-, moʊ- **-s** -s **-ing** -ɪŋ **-ed** -ɪd **-er/s** -əʳ/z, (US) -ɚ/z
molestation ˌmɒl.esˈteɪ.ʃən, ˌməʊ.lesˈ-, (US) ˌmoʊ.lesˈ-, ˌmɑː- **-s** -z
molester məʊˈles.təʳ, (US) məˈles.tɚ, moʊ- **-s** -z
Molesworth ˈməʊlz.wəθ, -wɜːθ, (US) ˈmoʊlz.wɚθ, -wɜːθ
Molière ˈmɒl.i.eəʳ, ˈməʊ.li-, (US) ˌmoʊlˈjer
Moline məʊˈliːn, (US) moʊ-
moll, M~ mɒl, (US) mɑːl
mollification ˌmɒl.ɪ.fɪˈkeɪ.ʃən, ˌ-ə-, -fəˈ-, (US) ˌmɑː.lə-
molli|fy ˈmɒl.ɪ|.faɪ, ˈ-ə-, (US) ˈmɑː.lɪ-, ˈ-ə- **-fies** -faɪz **-fying** -faɪ.ɪŋ **-fied** -faɪd
mollusc ˈmɒl.əsk, -ʌsk, (US) ˈmɑː.ləsk **-s** -s
molluscan mɒlˈʌs.kən, məˈlʌs-, (US) məˈlʌs-
molluscoid mɒlˈʌs.kɔɪd, məˈlʌs-, (US) məˈlʌs-
moll|y, M~ ˈmɒl|.i, (US) ˈmɑː.l|i **-ies** -iz
mollycoddl|e ˈmɒl.iˌkɒd.əl, (US) ˈmɑː.liˌkɑː.dəl **-es** -z **-ing** -ɪŋ, -ˌkɒd.lɪŋ, (US) -ˌkɑːd.lɪŋ **-ed** -d
Moloch ˈməʊ.lɒk, (US) ˈmoʊ.lɑːk, ˈmɑː.lək
Molony məˈləʊ.ni, (US) -ˈloʊ-
Molotov ˈmɒl.ə.tɒf, (US) ˈmɑː.lə.tɔːf, ˈmoʊ-, -tɔːv ˌ**Molotov ˈcocktail**
molt məʊlt, (US) moʊlt **-s** -s **-ing** -ɪŋ, (US) ˈmoʊl.tɪŋ **-ed** -ɪd, (US) ˈmoʊl.tɪd **-er/s** -əʳ/z, (US) ˈmoʊl.tɚ/z
molten ˈməʊl.tən, (US) ˈmoʊl-
molto ˈmɒl.təʊ, (US) ˈmoʊl.toʊ
Molton ˈməʊl.tən, (US) ˈmoʊl-
Moluccas məʊˈlʌk.əz, (US) moʊ-, mə-
moly ˈməʊ.li, (US) ˈmoʊ-
molybdenum məˈlɪb.də.nəm, -dɪ-, mɒlˈɪb-, məʊˈlɪb-; ˌmɒl.ɪbˈdiː.nəm, (US) məˈlɪb.də-
Molyneux ˈmɒl.ɪ.njuː, ˈmʌl-, ˈ-ə-, -njuː, (US) ˈmʌl.ɪ.nuː, -njuː, -nuː
mom, M~ mɒm, (US) mɑːm **-s** -z
Mombasa mɒmˈbæs.ə, -ˈbɑː.sə, (US) mɑːmˈbɑː.sə, -ˈbæs.ə
moment ˈməʊ.mənt, (US) ˈmoʊ- **-s** -s
ˌ**moment of ˈtruth**
momenta (plural of **momentum**) məʊˈmen.tə, (US) moʊˈmen.t̬ə, mə-
momentarily ˈməʊ.mən.tər.əl.i, -ɪ.li; ˌməʊ.mənˈter-, (US) ˌmoʊ.mənˈter-, ˈmoʊ.mən.ter-
momentar|y ˈməʊ.mən.tər|.i, (US) ˈmoʊ.mən.ter- **-iness** -ɪ.nəs, -ɪ.nɪs
momentous məʊˈmen.təs, (US) moʊˈmen.t̬əs, mə- **-ly** -li **-ness** -nəs, -nɪs
moment|um məʊˈmen.t|əm, (US) moʊˈmen.t̬|əm, mə- **-ums** -əmz **-a** -ə
momma, M~ ˈmɒm.ə, (US) ˈmɑː.mə **-s** -z
momm|y ˈmɒm|.i, (US) ˈmɑː.m|i **-ies** -iz
Mon *language:* məʊn, mɒn, (US) moʊn
Mon. (abbrev. for **Monday**) ˈmʌn.deɪ, -di
mona, M~ ˈməʊ.nə, (US) ˈmoʊ- **-s** -z
ˌ**Mona ˈLisa**
Monaco ˈmɒn.ə.kəʊ, məˈnɑː-, (US) ˈmɑː.nə.koʊ, məˈnɑː-
monad ˈmɒn.æd, ˈməʊ.næd, (US) ˈmoʊ.næd, ˈmɑː.næd **-s** -z
Monadhliath ˌməʊ.nəˈliː.ə, (US) ˌmoʊ-

monadic mɒnˈæd.ɪk, məʊˈnæd-, (US) məˈnæd-, moʊ-
Monaghan ˈmɒn.ə.hən, -kən; *as if Irish:* -xən; (US) ˈmɑː.nə.gən
monarch ˈmɒn.ək, (US) ˈmɑː.nɚk, -nɑːrk **-s** -s
monarch|al mɒnˈɑː.k|əl, məˈnɑː-, (US) məˈnɑːr-, moʊ- **-ic** -ɪk **-ical** -ɪ.kəl
monarch|ism ˈmɒn.ə.k|ɪ.zəm, (US) ˈmɑː.nɚ-, -nɑːr- **-ist/s** -ɪst/s
monarchiz|e, -is|e ˈmɒn.ə.kaɪz, (US) ˈmɑː.nɚ-, -nɑːr- **-es** -ɪz **-ing** -ɪŋ **-ed** -d
monarch|y ˈmɒn.ə.k|i, (US) ˈmɑː.nɚ-, -nɑːr- **-ies** -iz
Monash ˈmɒn.æʃ, (US) ˈmɑː.næʃ
monaster|y ˈmɒn.ə.stər|.i, -str|i, (US) ˈmɑː.nə.ster|.i **-ies** -iz
monastic məˈnæs.tɪk, mɒnˈæs-, (US) mə-, moʊ- **-al** -əl **-ally** -əl.i, -li
monasticism məˈnæs.tɪ.sɪ.zəm, mɒnˈæs-, (US) məˈnæs-, moʊ-
monatomic ˌmɒn.əˈtɒm.ɪk, (US) ˌmɑː.nəˈtɑː.mɪk
monaural mɒnˈɔː.rəl, (US) mɑːˈnɔːr.əl
Monbiot ˈmɒn.bi.əʊ, (US) -oʊ, ˈmɑːn.bi.oʊ
Mönchen-Gladbach ˌmɜːn.ʃənˈglæd.bæk, ˌmʊn-, -kəŋˈ-, (US) -kənˈglɑːt.bɑːk
Monck mʌŋk
Monckton ˈmʌŋk.tən
Moncrieff mənˈkriːf, məŋ-, mɒn-, mɒŋ-, (US) mɑːn-, mən-; (US) ˈmɑːn.kriːf
Mond mɒnd, (US) mɑːnd
Mondale ˈmɒn.deɪl, (US) ˈmɑːn-
Monday ˈmʌn.deɪ, -di **-s** -z
Mondeo® ˌmɒnˈdeɪ.əʊ, (US) ˌmɑːnˈdeɪ.oʊ
Mondrian ˈmɒn.dri.æn, -ən, (US) ˈmɑːn.dri.ɑːn, -ən
Monegasque ˌmɒn.ɪˈgæsk, -əˈ-, (US) ˌmɑː.neɪˈ-
Monet ˈmɒn.eɪ; *as if French:* -ˈ-; (US) moʊˈneɪ, mə-
monetar|ism ˈmʌn.ɪ.tər|.ɪ.zəm, ˈ-ə-, (US) ˈmɑː.nə-, ˈmʌn.ə- **-ist/s** -ɪst/s
monetary ˈmʌn.ɪ.tər.i, ˈ-ə-, -tri, (US) ˈmɑː.nə.ter.i, ˈmʌn.ə-
monetiz|e, -is|e ˈmʌn.ɪ.taɪz, ˈ-ə-, (US) ˈmɑː.nə-, ˈmʌn.ə- **-es** -ɪz **-ing** -ɪŋ **-ed** -d
mon|ey, M~ ˈmʌn|.i **-eys** -z **-ies** -iz **-eyed** -id **-ied** -id **ˈmoney ˌbox; ˈmoney ˌchanger; ˈmoney ˌmarket; ˈmoney ˌorder; ˈmoney ˌsupply; ˌthrow good ˌmoney after ˈbad**
moneybag ˈmʌn.i.bæg **-s** -z
moneygrabb|ing ˈmʌn.iˌgræb|.ɪŋ **-er/s** -ər/z, (US) -ɚ/z
money-grubb|er ˈmʌn.iˌgrʌb|.ər, (US) -ɚ **-ers** -əz, (US) -ɚz **-ing** -ɪŋ
moneylend|er ˈmʌn.iˌlen.d|ər, (US) -d|ɚ **-ers** -əz, (US) -ɚz **-ing** -ɪŋ
money-market ˈmʌn.iˌmɑː.kɪt, (US) -ˌmɑːr- **-s** -s
money-off ˌmʌn.iˈɒf, (US) -ˈɑːf
Moneypenny ˈmʌn.iˌpen.i
money-spinner ˈmʌn.iˌspɪn.ər, (US) -ɚ **-s** -z
monger ˈmʌŋ.gər, (US) -gɚ, ˈmɑːŋ- **-s** -z
mongo ˈmɒŋ.gəʊ, (US) ˈmɑːŋ.goʊ **-s** -z
mongol, M~ ˈmɒŋ.gəl, -gɒl, (US) ˈmɑːŋ-, ˈmɑːn-, -gəl, -goʊl **-s** -z **-oid** -ɔɪd
Mongoli|a mɒŋˈgəʊ.li|.ə, (US) mɑːŋˈgoʊ-, mɑːn-, -ˈgoʊl.j|ə **-an/s** -ən/z
mongolism, M~ ˈmɒŋ.gəl.ɪ.zəm, -gɒl-, (US) ˈmɑːŋ.gəl-, ˈmɑːn-
mongoos|e ˈmɒŋ.guːs, ˈmʌŋ-, (US) ˈmɑːŋ-, ˈmɑːn- **-es** -ɪz
mongrel ˈmʌŋ.grəl, (US) ˈmɑːŋ-, ˈmʌŋ- **-s** -z

> Note: The pronunciation /ˈmɒŋ-/ is increasingly widespread in British English but cannot yet be recommended as representative of the accent described here.

Monica ˈmɒn.ɪ.kə, (US) ˈmɑː.nɪ-
monicker ˈmɒn.ɪ.kər, (US) ˈmɑː.nɪ.kɚ **-s** -z
Monier ˈmʌn.i.ər, ˈmɒn-, (US) ˈmɑː.ni.ɚ, ˈmʌn.i-
moniker ˈmɒn.ɪ.kər, (US) ˈmɑː.nɪ.kɚ **-s** -z
Monique mɒnˈiːk, (US) moʊˈniːk, mə-
mon|ism ˈmɒn|.ɪ.zəm, ˈməʊ.n|ɪ-, (US) ˈmoʊ.n|ɪ-, ˈmɑː- **-ist/s** -ɪst/s
monistic mɒnˈɪs.tɪk, məˈnɪs-, (US) moʊˈnɪs-, mə- **-al** -əl
monition məʊˈnɪʃ.ən, mɒnˈɪʃ-, (US) moʊˈnɪʃ-, mə- **-s** -z
monit|or ˈmɒn.ɪ.t|ər, -ə-, (US) ˈmɑː.nə.ţ|ɚ **-ors** -əz, (US) -ɚz **-oring** -ər.ɪŋ **-ored** -əd, (US) -ɚd
monitorial ˌmɒn.ɪˈtɔː.ri.əl, -əˈ-, (US) ˌmɑː.nɪˈtɔːr.i-
monitory ˈmɒn.ɪ.tər.i, ˈ-ə-, (US) ˈmɑː.nɪ.tɔːr-
monk, M~ mʌŋk **-s** -s **-ish** -ɪʃ
monkey ˈmʌŋ.ki **-s** -z **-ing** -ɪŋ **-ed** -d **ˈmonkey ˌbars; ˈmonkey ˌbusiness; ˈmonkey ˌwrench**
monkey-puzzle ˈmʌŋ.kiˌpʌz.əl **-s** -z
monkfish ˈmʌŋk.fɪʃ **-es** -ɪz
Monkhouse ˈmʌŋk.haʊs
Monkton ˈmʌŋk.tən
Monmouth ˈmɒn.məθ, (US) ˈmɑːn- **-shire** -ʃər, -ʃɪər, (US) -ʃɚ, -ʃɪr
mono *monotype:* ˈməʊ.nəʊ, ˈmɒn.əʊ, (US) ˈmɑː.noʊ *in sound recording:* ˈmɒn.əʊ, (US) ˈmɑː.noʊ **-s** -z
mono- ˈmɒn.əʊ; məˈnɒ, (US) ˈmɑː.noʊ, -nə; (US) məˈnɑː
Note: Prefix. Normally either takes primary or secondary stress on the first syllable, e.g. **monorail** /ˈmɒn.əʊ.reɪl/ (US) /ˈmɑː.nə.reɪl/, **monotonic** /ˌmɒn.əˈtɒ.nɪk/ (US) /ˌmɑː.nəˈtɑː.nɪk/, or primary stress on the second syllable, e.g. **monotony** /məˈnɒt.ən.i/ (US) /-ˈnɑː.tən-/.
monobasic ˌmɒn.əʊˈbeɪ.sɪk, (US) ˌmɑː.nəˈ-, -noʊˈ-
monoceros məˈnɒs.ər.ɒs, mɒnˈɒs-, (US) məˈnɑː.sɚ.ɑːs
monochloride ˌmɒn.əʊˈklɔː.raɪd, (US) ˌmɑː.nəˈklɔːr.aɪd, -oʊˈ- **-s** -z
monochord ˈmɒn.ə.kɔːd, (US) ˈmɑː.nə.kɔːrd **-s** -z
monochromatic ˌmɒn.əʊ.krəʊˈmæt.ɪk, (US) ˌmɑː.nə.kroʊˈmæţ-, ˌ-noʊ-, -krə-
monochrome ˈmɒn.ə.krəʊm, (US) ˈmɑː.nə.kroʊm **-s** -z
monocle ˈmɒn.ə.kəl, (US) ˈmɑː.nə- **-s** -z
monoclonal ˌmɒn.əʊˈkləʊ.nəl, (US) ˌmɑː.nəˈkloʊ-, -noʊˈ-
monocotyledon ˌmɒn.əʊˌkɒt.ɪˈliː.dən, -əlˈiː-, (US) ˌmɑː.nəˌkɑː.təlˈiː-, -noʊˌ- **-s** -z
monoculture ˈmɒn.əʊˌkʌl.tʃər, (US) ˈmɑː.nəˌkʌl.tʃɚ, -noʊˌ-
monod|y ˈmɒn.ə.d|i, (US) ˈmɑː.nə- **-ies** -iz
monogamist məˈnɒg.ə.mɪst, mɒnˈɒg-, (US) məˈnɑː.gə- **-s** -s
monogamous məˈnɒg.ə.məs, mɒnˈɒg-, (US) məˈnɑː.gə-
monogamy məˈnɒg.ə.mi, mɒnˈɒg-, (US) məˈnɑː.gə-
monoglot ˈmɒn.ə.glɒt, (US) ˈmɑː.nə.glɑːt **-s** -s
monogram ˈmɒn.ə.græm, (US) ˈmɑː.nə- **-s** -z **-ming** -ɪŋ **-med** -d
monograph ˈmɒn.ə.grɑːf, -græf, (US) ˈmɑː.nə.græf **-s** -s
monographic ˌmɒn.əˈgræf.ɪk, (US) ˌmɑː.nəˈ-
monolingual ˌmɒn.əʊˈlɪŋ.gwəl, (US) ˌmɑː.nəˈ-, -noʊˈ- **-s** -z **-ly** -i
monolinguist ˌmɒn.əʊˈlɪŋ.gwɪst, (US) ˌmɑː.nəˈ-, -noʊˈ- **-s** -s
monolith ˈmɒn.əʊ.lɪθ, (US) ˈmɑː.nə- **-s** -s
monolithic ˌmɒn.əˈlɪθ.ɪk, (US) ˌmɑː.nəˈ-
monolog(u)ist ˈmɒn.ə.lɒg.ɪst, -ɒdʒ-; məˈnɒl.ə.gɪst, -dʒɪst, (US) ˈmɑː.nə.lɑːg.ɪst, -lɔːg.ɪst, məˈnɑː.lə.dʒɪst **-s** -s
monologue, monolog ˈmɒn.əl.ɒg, (US) ˈmɑː.nə.lɑːg, -lɔːg **-s** -z
monomani|a ˌmɒn.əʊˈmeɪ.ni|.ə, (US) ˌmɑː.noʊˈ-, -nəˈ- **-ac/s** -æk/s
monomaniacal ˌmɒn.əʊ.məˈnaɪ.ə.kəl, (US) ˌmɑː.nə-, ˌ-noʊ-
mononuclear ˌmɒn.əʊˈnjuː.kli.ər, (US) ˌmɑː.noʊˈnuː.kli.ɚ, -nəˈ-, -ˈnjuː-
mononucleosis ˌmɒn.əʊˌnjuː.kliˈəʊ.sɪs, (US) ˌmɑː.noʊˌnuː.kliˈoʊ-, -nəˌ-, -ˌnjuː-
monophonic ˌmɒn.əʊˈfɒn.ɪk, (US) ˌmɑː.nəˈfɑː.nɪk, -noʊˈ-
monophthong ˈmɒn.əf.θɒŋ, ˈ-ə-, (US) ˈmɑː.nəf.θɑːŋ, -θɔːŋ **-s** -z

monophthong|al ˌmɒn.əf'θɒŋ.g|ᵊl, -ə'-, US ˌmɑː.nəf'θɑːŋ|.ᵊl, -'θɔːŋ-, -g|ᵊl **-ic** -ɪk

monophthongiz|e, -is|e 'mɒn.əf.θɒŋ.gaɪz, '-ə-, -aɪz, US 'mɑː.nəf.θɑːŋ-, -θɔːŋ- **-es** -ɪz **-ing** -ɪŋ **-ed** -d

monoplane 'mɒn.ə.pleɪn, US 'mɑː.nə- **-s** -z

monopole 'mɒn.ə.pəʊl, US 'mɑː.nə.poʊl

monopolism mə'nɒp.ᵊl.ɪ.zᵊm, US mə'nɑː.pə.lɪ-

monopolist mə'nɒp.ᵊl.ɪst, US -'nɑː.pə.lɪst **-s** -s

monopolistic məˌnɒp.ᵊl'ɪs.tɪk, US -ˌnɑː.pə'lɪs- **-ally** -ᵊl.i, -li

monopoliz|e, -is|e mə'nɒp.ᵊl.aɪz, US -'nɑː.pə.laɪz **-es** -ɪz **-ing** -ɪŋ **-ed** -d **-er/s** -əʳ/z

monopol|y mə'nɒp.ᵊl|.i, US -'nɑː.pᵊl- **-ies** -iz

monorail 'mɒn.ə.reɪl, US 'mɑː.nə- **-s** -z

monosaccharide ˌmɒn.əʊ'sæk.ᵊr.aɪd, US ˌmɑː.noʊ'sæk.ə.raɪd, -nə'- **-s** -z

monosodium ˌmɒn.əʊ'səʊ.di.əm, US ˌmɑː.noʊ'soʊ-, -nə'- *stress shift, see compound:* **ˌmonosodium 'glutamate**

monosyllabic ˌmɒn.əʊ.sɪ'læb.ɪk, US ˌmɑː.nə-, -noʊ- **-ally** -ᵊl.i, -li *stress shift:* **ˌmonosyllabic 'word**

monosyllable 'mɒn.əʊˌsɪl.ə.bᵊl, US 'mɑː.nəˌ-, -noʊˌ- **-s** -z

monothe|ism 'mɒn.əʊ.θi|.ɪ.zᵊm, ˌmɒn.əʊ'θiː-, US 'mɑː.noʊˌθiː-, -nəˌ- **-ist/s** -ɪst/s

monotheistic ˌmɒn.əʊ.θi'ɪs.tɪk, US ˌmɑː.noʊ- *stress shift:* **ˌmonotheistic 'culture**

monoton|e 'mɒn.ə.təʊn, US 'mɑː.nə.toʊn **-es** -z **-ing** -ɪŋ **-ed** -d

monotonic ˌmɒn.ə'tɒn.ɪk, US ˌmɑː.nə'tɑː.nɪk *stress shift:* **ˌmonotonic 'function**

monotonous mə'nɒt.ᵊn.əs, US -'nɑː.tᵊn- **-ly** -li **-ness** -nəs, -nɪs

monotony mə'nɒt.ᵊn.i, US -'nɑː.tᵊn-

monotype, M~® 'mɒn.əʊ.taɪp, 'məʊ.nəʊ-, US 'mɑː.noʊ-, -nə- **-s** -s

monovalen|ce ˌmɒn.əʊ'veɪ.lən|ts, 'mɒn.əʊˌveɪ-, US ˌmɑː.noʊ'veɪ-, 'mɑː.noʊˌveɪ-, -nə'- **-t** -t

monoxide mə'nɒk.saɪd, mɒn'ɒk-, US mə'nɑːk- **-s** -z

Monro(e) mən'rəʊ, mʌn'rəʊ, 'mʌn.rəʊ, US mən'roʊ

Monrovia mɒn'rəʊ.vi.ə, mən-, US mən'roʊ-

Mons mɒnz; *as if French:* mɔ̃ːns; US mõʊns

Monsanto® mɒn'sæn.təʊ, US mɑːn'-

Monsarrat 'mɒnt.sᵊr.æt, ˌ--'-, US ˌmɑːnt.sə'rɑːt, -'ræt

monseigneur ˌmɒn.sen'jɜːʳ, US ˌmɑːn.sən'jɝː **-s** -z **messeigneurs** ˌmes.eɪ'njɜː, US -'jɝː

monsieur, M~ mə'sjɜːʳ, -'sjəʳ, US -'sjɝː, -'sjɜː

> Note: /mə'sjɜːʳ/ is the form of address in isolation. When attached to the surname there is usually a secondary stress on the first syllable, e.g. Monsieur Dupont /ˌməs.jə dju'pɔ̃ːŋ/.

monsignor, M~ mɒn'siː.njəʳ, US mɑːn'siː.njɚ

Monson 'mʌnt.sᵊn

monsoon mɒn'suːn, mən-, US mɑːn- **-s** -z

monster 'mɒnt.stəʳ, US 'mɑːnt.stɚ **-s** -z **-ing** -ɪŋ **-ed** -d

monstranc|e 'mɒnt.strənts, US 'mɑːnt- **-es** -ɪz

monstrosit|y mɒn'strɒs.ə.t|i, mən-, -ɪ.t|i, US mɑːn'strɑː.sə.ţ|i **-ies** -iz

monstrous 'mɒnt.strəs, US 'mɑːnt- **-ly** -li **-ness** -nəs, -nɪs

Mont. (abbrev. for **Montana**) mɒn'tæn.ə, -'tɑː.nə, US mɑːn'tæn.ə

montag|e mɒn'tɑːʒ; '--, US mɑːn'tɑːʒ; US moʊn'tɑːʒ **-es** -ɪz

Montagu(e) 'mɒn.tə.gjuː, -tɪ-, 'mʌn-, US 'mɑːn-

Montaigne mɒn'teɪn, US mɑːn-

Montana mɒn'tæn.ə, -'tɑː.nə, US mɑːn'tæn.ə

Mont Blanc *as if French:* ˌmɔ̃ːm'blɑ̃ːŋ, US mõʊm'blɑ̃ːŋ

montbretia mɒn'briː.ʃə, mɒm-, -ʃi.ə, US mɑːnt'- **-s** -z

Mont Cenis ˌmɔ̃ːn.sə'niː, US ˌmõʊn-

monte, M~ 'mɒn.teɪ, -ti, US 'mɑːn.ţi

Monte Carlo ˌmɒnt.i'kɑː.ləʊ, US ˌmɑːn.ţi'kɑːr.loʊ

Montefiore ˌmɒn.ti.fi'ɔː.reɪ, -ri, -tə-, -'fjɔː-, US ˌmɑːn.ţi.fi'ɔːr.i

Montego® mɒn'tiː.gəʊ, US mɑːn'tiː.goʊ

Montego Bay mɒnˌtiː.gəʊ'beɪ, US mɑːnˌtiː.goʊ'-

monteith mɒn'tiːθ, US mɑːn- **-s** -s

Monteith mən'tiːθ, mɒn-, US mɑːn-

Montenegr|o ˌmɒn.tɪ'niː.gr|əʊ, -tə'-, -'neɪ-, US ˌmɑːn.tə'niː.gr|oʊ, -'neg.r|oʊ **-an/s** -ən/z

Monterey ˌmɒn.tə'reɪ, US mɑːn.ţɚ.eɪ

Monte Rosa ˌmɒn.tɪ'rəʊ.zə, -tə'-, US ˌmɑːn.ţə'roʊ-

Monterrey ˌmɒn.tᵊr.eɪ, -tɪ'reɪ, US ˌmɑːn.ţə'reɪ

Montesquieu ˌmɒn.tes'kjuː, -'kjɜː, '---, US 'mɑːn.ţə.skjuː

Montessori ˌmɒn.tes'ɔː.ri, -tɪ'sɔː-, US ˌmɑːn.ţə'sɔːr.i

Monteverdi ˌmɒn.tɪ'vɜː.di, -tə'-, -'veə-, US ˌmɑːn.ţə'ver-

Montevideo ˌmɒn.tɪ.vɪ'deɪ.əʊ, -tə-, US ˌmɑːn.ţə.və'deɪ.oʊ, -'vɪd.i.oʊ

Montezuma ˌmɒn.tɪ'zuː.mə, -tə'-, -'zjuː-, US ˌmɑːn.ţə'zuː-

Montfort 'mɒnt.fət, -fɔːt, US 'mɑːnt.fɚt, -fɔːrt

Montgomerie mənt'gʌm.ᵊr.i, mɒnt-, -'gɒm-, -'ri, US mɑːnt'gʌm.ri, mənt-, '-ɚ.i

Montgomery mənt'gʌm.ᵊr.i, mɒnt-, -'gɒm-, -'ri, US mɑːnt'gʌm.ri, mənt-, '-ɚ.i **-shire** -ʃəʳ, -ʃɪəʳ, US -ʃɚ, -ʃɪr

month mʌntθ **-s** -s **-ly** -li **in a ˌmonth of 'Sundays**

Monticello ˌmɒn.tɪ'tʃel.əʊ, US ˌmɑːn.tɪ'tʃel.oʊ, -'sel-

Montmorency ˌmɒnt.mᵊr'ent.si, US ˌmɑːnt-

Montpelier *in US, London street:* mɒnt'piː.li.əʳ, US mɑːnt'piːl.jɚ

Montpellier *in France:* mɔ̃ːm'pel.i.eɪ, US ˌmõʊn.pəl'jeɪ *in names of streets, etc.:* mɒnt'pel.i.əʳ, mənt-, US mɑːnt'pel.i.ɚ

Montreal ˌmɒn.tri'ɔːl, US ˌmɑːn.tri'ɔːl, ˌmʌn-, -'ɑːl

Montreux mɒn'trɜː; *as if French:* mɔ̃ːn-; US mɑːn-

Montrose mɒn'trəʊz, mən-, US mɑːn'troʊz

Mont-Saint-Michel ˌmɒntˌsæn.mɪ'ʃel, -ˌsæm-; *as if French:* ˌmɔ̃ːn-, US ˌmõʊnˌsæn.miː'ʃel

Montserrat *island in West Indies:* ˌmɒnt.sə'ræt, -ser'æt, US ˌmɑːnt.sə'ræt *monastery in Spain:* ˌmɒnt.sə'rɑːt, -ser'ɑːt, US ˌmɑːnt.sə'rɑːt

Monty 'mɒn.ti, US 'mɑːn.ţi, -ti

monument 'mɒn.jə.mənt, -jʊ-, US 'mɑːn.jə-, -juː- **-s** -s

monumental ˌmɒn.jə'men.tᵊl, -jʊ'-, US ˌmɑːn.jə'men.ţᵊl, -juː'- **-ly** -i

Monza 'mɒn.zə, US 'mɔːnt.sɑː, 'moʊnt-, 'mɑː-

Monzie mə'niː, mɒn'iː, US mɔːn'ziː, mɑːn-, '--

moo muː **-s** -z **-ing** -ɪŋ **-ed** -d

mooch muːtʃ **-es** -ɪz **-ing** -ɪŋ **-ed** -t **-er/s** -əʳ/z, US -ɚ/z

moo-cow 'muː.kaʊ **-s** -z

mood muːd **-s** -z

mood|y, M~ 'muː.d|i **-ier** -i.əʳ, US -i.ɚ **-iest** -i.ɪst, -i.əst **-ily** -ᵊl.i, -ɪ.li **-iness** -ɪ.nəs, -ɪ.nɪs

Moog® məʊg, muːg, US moʊg, muːg

moola(h) 'muː.lə

mooli 'muː.li

moon, M~ muːn **-s** -z **-ing** -ɪŋ **-ed** -d **over the 'moon**

moonbeam 'muːn.biːm, 'muːm-, US 'muːn- **-s** -z

mooncal|f 'muːn.kɑː|f, 'muːŋ-, US 'muːn.kæ|f **-ves** -vz

Mooney 'muː.ni

moonie, M~ ˈmuː.ni **-s** -z
moon|light ˈmuːn|.laɪt **-lit** -lɪt **-lights** -laɪts **-lighting** -ˌlaɪ.tɪŋ, (US) -ˌlaɪ.t̬ɪŋ **-lighted** -ˌlaɪ.tɪd, (US) -ˌlaɪ.t̬ɪd
moonscape ˈmuːn.skeɪp **-s** -s
moonshine ˈmuːn.ʃaɪn
moonstone ˈmuːn.stəʊn, (US) -stoʊn **-s** -z
moonstruck ˈmuːn.strʌk
moony ˈmuː.ni
moor, M~ mɔːʳ, mʊəʳ, (US) mʊr **-s** -z **-ing/s** -ɪŋ/z **-ed** -d
Moorall ˈmɔː.rɔːl, (US) ˈmɔːr.ɔːl, -ᵊl
moorcock, M~ ˈmɔː.kɒk, ˈmʊə-, (US) ˈmʊr.kɑːk **-s** -z
Moorcroft ˈmɔː.krɒft, ˈmʊə-, (US) ˈmʊr.krɑːft
Moore mɔːʳ, mʊəʳ, (US) mʊr, mɔːr
Moorends ˈmɔː.rendz, ˈmʊə-, (US) ˈmʊr.endz
Moorfoot ˈmɔː.fʊt, ˈmʊə-, (US) ˈmʊr-
Moorgate ˈmɔː.geɪt, ˈmʊə-, -gɪt, (US) ˈmʊr-
Moorhead ˈmɔː.hed, ˈmʊə-, (US) ˈmʊr-, ˈmɔːr-
moorhen ˈmɔː.hen, ˈmʊə-, (US) ˈmʊr- **-s** -z
Moorhouse ˈmɔː.haʊs, ˈmʊə-, (US) ˈmʊr-, ˈmɔːr-
mooring ˈmɔː.rɪŋ, ˈmʊə-, (US) ˈmʊr.ɪŋ **-s** -z
Moorish ˈmʊə.rɪʃ, ˈmɔː-, (US) ˈmʊr.ɪʃ
moorland ˈmɔː.lənd, ˈmʊə-, -lænd, (US) ˈmʊr- **-s** -z
Note: The variant /-lænd/ is not used when the word is attributive.
moos|e muːs **-es** -ɪz
moot muːt **-s** -s **-ing** -ɪŋ, (US) ˈmuː.t̬ɪŋ **-ed** -ɪd, (US) ˈmuː.t̬ɪd
mop mɒp, (US) mɑːp **-s** -s **-ping** -ɪŋ **-ped** -t
mop|e məʊp, (US) moʊp **-es** -s **-ing/ly** -ɪŋ/li **-ed** -t
moped **n** ˈməʊ.ped, (US) ˈmoʊ- **-s** -z
mopoke ˈməʊ.pəʊk, (US) ˈmoʊ.poʊk **-s** -s
moppet, M~ ˈmɒp.ɪt, (US) ˈmɑː.pɪt **-s** -s
Mopsy ˈmɒp.si, (US) ˈmɑːp-
moquette mɒkˈet, məʊˈket, (US) moʊˈket
mor|a ˈmɔː.r|ə, (US) ˈmɔːr|.ə, ˈmoʊ.r|ə **-ae** -iː, -aɪ **-as** -əz
Morag ˈmɔː.ræg, (US) ˈmɔːr.æg
moraine mɒrˈeɪn, məˈreɪn, (US) məˈreɪn, mɔː- **-s** -z
moral ˈmɒr.ᵊl, (US) ˈmɔːr- **-s** -z **-ly** -i
morale məˈrɑːl, mɒrˈɑːl, (US) məˈræl, mɔː-
Morales mɒrˈɑː.lez, -les, (US) məˈræl.ɪs, mɔːˈrɑː.lɪs
moralist ˈmɒr.ᵊl.ɪst, (US) ˈmɔːr- **-s** -s
moralistic ˌmɒr.ᵊlˈɪs.tɪk, (US) ˌmɔːr- **-ally** -ᵊl.i, -li
morality məˈræl.ə.ti, mɒrˈæl-, -ɪ.ti, (US) məˈræl.ə.t̬i, mɔː- **moˈrality ˌplay**
moraliz|e, -is|e ˈmɒr.ᵊl.aɪz, (US) ˈmɔːr- **-es** -ɪz **-ing** -ɪŋ **-ed** -d **-er/s** -əʳ/z, (US) -ɚ/z
Moran ˈmɔː.rən, ˈmɒr.ən; məˈræn, mɒrˈæn, (US) mɔːˈræn, mə-; (US) ˈmɔːr.ən
Morant məˈrænt, mɒrˈænt, (US) mɔːˈrænt, mə-
Morar ˈmɔː.rəʳ, (US) ˈmɔːr.ɚ
morass məˈræs, mɒrˈæs, (US) məˈræs, mɔː- **-es** -ɪz
moratori|um ˌmɒr.əˈtɔː.ri|.əm, ˌmɔː.rəˈ-, (US) ˌmɔːr.əˈtɔːr.i- **-ums** -əmz **-a** -ə
Moravi|a məˈreɪ.vi|.ə, mɒrˈeɪ-, (US) mɔːˈreɪ-, mə- **-an/s** -ən/z
moray *eel:* ˈmɒr.eɪ, ˈmɔː.reɪ; məˈreɪ, (US) ˈmɔːr.eɪ; (US) mɔːˈreɪ, mə- **-s** -z
Moray ˈmʌr.i, (US) ˈmɝː-
morbid ˈmɔː.bɪd, (US) ˈmɔːr- **-ly** -li **-ness** -nəs, -nɪs
morbidity mɔːˈbɪd.ə.ti, -ɪ.ti, (US) mɔːrˈbɪd.ə.t̬i
mordant ˈmɔː.dᵊnt, (US) ˈmɔːr- **-s** -s **-ly** -li
Mordaunt ˈmɔː.dᵊnt, -daʊnt, (US) ˈmɔːr-
Mordecai ˈmɔː.dɪ.kaɪ, -də-, -kaɪ.iː; (US) ˈmɔːr.də.kaɪ
Morden ˈmɔː.dᵊn, (US) ˈmɔːr-
mordent ˈmɔː.dᵊnt, (US) ˈmɔːr- **-s** -s
Mordor ˈmɔː.dɔːʳ, (US) ˈmɔːr.dɔːr
Mordred ˈmɔː.drɪd, -drəd, -dred, (US) ˈmɔːr.dred, -drəd
more, M~ mɔːʳ, (US) mɔːr
Morea mɒrˈiː.ə, məˈriː.ə, mɔː-, (US) mɔːˈriː.ə
Moreau mɒrˈəʊ, məˈrəʊ, (US) mɑːˈroʊ, məˈ-
Morecambe ˈmɔː.kəm, (US) ˈmɔːr-
moreish ˈmɔː.rɪʃ, (US) ˈmɔːr.ɪʃ
morel, M~ mɒrˈel, məˈrel, (US) mɔːˈrel, mə- **-s** -z
morello məˈrel.əʊ, mɒrˈel-, (US) məˈrel.oʊ **-s** -z
Morelos məˈrel.ɒs, mɔː-, (US) mɔːˈrel.ɑːs
Moreno məˈriː.nəʊ, mɒrˈiː-, (US) məˈriː.noʊ, mɔː-, -ˈren.oʊ
moreover mɔːʳˈəʊ.vəʳ, məʳ-, (US) mɔːrˈoʊ.vɚ, ˈ-ˌ--
mores ˈmɔː.reɪz, -riːz, (US) ˈmɔːr.eɪz, -iːz
Moresby *surname:* ˈmɔːz.bi, (US) ˈmɔːrz- *in Cumbria:* ˈmɒr.ɪs.bi, (US) ˈmɔːr.ɪs-
Moreton ˈmɔː.tᵊn, (US) ˈmɔːr-
Morgan ˈmɔː.gᵊn, (US) ˈmɔːr-
morganatic ˌmɔː.gəˈnæt.ɪk, (US) ˌmɔːr.gəˈnæt̬- **-ally** -ᵊl.i, (US) -li
Morgan le Fay ˌmɔː.gᵊn.ləˈfeɪ, (US) ˌmɔːr-
morgue mɔːg, (US) mɔːrg **-s** -z
MORI ˈmɔː.ri, ˈmɒr.i, (US) ˈmɔːr.i
Moriah mɒrˈaɪ.ə, mɔːˈraɪ.ə, mə-, (US) mə-, mɔːˈraɪ-, moʊ-
Moriarty ˌmɒr.iˈɑː.ti, (US) ˌmɔːr.iˈɑːr.t̬i
moribund ˈmɒr.ɪ.bʌnd, ˈmɔː.rɪ-, -bənd, (US) ˈmɔːr.ɪ.bʌnd
Morison ˈmɒr.ɪ.sᵊn, ˈ-ə-, (US) ˈmɔːr.ɪ-
Morley ˈmɔː.li, (US) ˈmɔːr-
Morlock ˈmɔː.lɒk, (US) ˈmɔːr.lɑːk **-s** -s
Mormon ˈmɔː.mən, (US) ˈmɔːr- **-s** -z **-ism** -ɪ.zᵊm
morn mɔːn, (US) mɔːrn **-s** -z
mornay ˈmɔː.neɪ, (US) mɔːrˈneɪ
morning ˈmɔː.nɪŋ, (US) ˈmɔːr- **-s** -z **ˈmorning ˌcoat; ˈmorning ˌdress; ˌmorning ˈdress; ˈmorning ˌroom; ˈmorning ˌsickness; ˌmorning ˈstar**
morning-after ˌmɔː.nɪŋˈɑːf.təʳ, (US) ˌmɔːr.nɪŋˈæf.tɚ **ˌmorning-ˈafter ˌpill**
Mornington ˈmɔː.nɪŋ.tən, (US) ˈmɔːr-
Moroccan məˈrɒk.ən, (US) -ˈrɑː.kən **-s** -z
Morocco, morocco məˈrɒk.əʊ, (US) -ˈrɑː.koʊ **-s** -z
moron ˈmɔː.rɒn, (US) ˈmɔːr.ɑːn **-s** -z
Moroni məˈrəʊ.ni, -naɪ, (US) -ˈroʊ.naɪ, mɔː-
moronic mɔːˈrɒn.ɪk, mə-, mɒrˈɒn-, (US) mɔːˈrɑː.nɪk, mə- **-ally** -ᵊl.i, -li
morose məˈrəʊs, mɒrˈəʊs, (US) məˈroʊs, mɔː- **-ly** -li **-ness** -nəs, -nɪs
Morpeth ˈmɔː.pəθ, -peθ, (US) ˈmɔːr-
morph mɔːf, (US) mɔːrf **-s** -s **-ing** -ɪŋ **-ed** -t
-morph mɔːf, (US) mɔːrf
Note: Suffix. Normally not stressed, e.g. **ectomorph** /ˈek.təʊ.mɔːf/ (US) /-tə.mɔːrf/.
morpheme ˈmɔː.fiːm, (US) ˈmɔːr- **-s** -z
morphemic mɔːˈfiː.mɪk, (US) mɔːr- **-ally** -ᵊl.i, -li
morphemics mɔːˈfiː.mɪks, (US) mɔːr-
Morpheus ˈmɔː.fi.əs, ˈ-fjəs, (US) ˈmɔːr.fi.əs, ˈ-fjuːs
morphia ˈmɔː.fi.ə, (US) ˈmɔːr-
morphine ˈmɔː.fiːn, (US) ˈmɔːr-
morpho- ˈmɔː.fəʊ; mɔːˈfɒ, (US) ˈmɔːr.foʊ, ˈ-fə; (US) mɔːrˈfɑː
Note: Prefix. Normally takes secondary stress on the first syllable, e.g. **morphologic** /ˌmɔː.fəˈlɒdʒ.ɪk/ (US) /ˌmɔːr.fəˈlɑː.dʒɪk/, or primary stress on the second syllable, e.g **morphology** /mɔːˈfɒl.ə.dʒi/ (US) /mɔːrˈfɑː.lə-/.
morphologic ˌmɔː.fəˈlɒdʒ.ɪk, (US) ˌmɔːr.fəˈlɑː.dʒɪk **-al** -ᵊl **-ally** -ᵊl.i, -li
morpholog|y mɔːˈfɒl.ə.dʒ|i, (US) mɔːrˈfɑː.lə- **-ies** -iz **-ist/s** -ɪst/s
morphophoneme ˌmɔː.fəʊˈfəʊ.niːm, (US) ˌmɔːr.foʊˈfoʊ- **-s** -z
morphophonemic ˌmɔː.fəʊ.fəˈniː.mɪk, (US) ˌmɔːr.foʊ- **-s** -s
morphophonology ˌmɔː.fəʊ.fəˈnɒl.ə.dʒi, (US) ˌmɔːr.foʊ.fəˈnɑː.lə-
morphosyntactic ˌmɔː.fəʊ.sɪnˈtæk.tɪk, (US) ˌmɔːr.foʊ- **-ally** -ᵊl.i, -li
morphosyntax ˌmɔː.fəʊˈsɪn.tæks, (US) ˌmɔːr.foʊ-
Morphy ˈmɔː.fi, (US) ˈmɔːr-

Morrell ˈmʌr.əl, məˈrel
Morrill ˈmɒr.ɪl, -əl, ⓊⓈ ˈmɔːr-
morris, M~ ˈmɒr.ɪs, ⓊⓈ ˈmɔːr- **-es** -ɪz ˈ**morris ˌdancing;** ˈ**morris ˌman**
Morrison ˈmɒr.ɪ.sən, ˈ-ə-, ⓊⓈ ˈmɔːr-
Morrissey ˈmɒr.ɪ.si, -ə-, ⓊⓈ ˈmɔːr-, ˈmɑːr-
Morristown ˈmɒr.ɪs.taʊn, ⓊⓈ ˈmɔːr-
morrow, M~ ˈmɒr.əʊ, ⓊⓈ ˈmɑːr.oʊ, ˈmɔːr- **-s** -z
mors|e, M~ mɔːs, ⓊⓈ mɔːrs **-es** -ɪz ˌ**Morse ˈcode;** ˈ**Morse ˌcode**
morsel ˈmɔː.səl, ⓊⓈ ˈmɔːr- **-s** -z
Morshead ˈmɔːz.hed, ⓊⓈ ˈmɔːrz-
mort, M~ mɔːt, ⓊⓈ mɔːrt **-s** -s
mortadella ˌmɔː.təˈdel.ə, ⓊⓈ ˌmɔːr-
mortal ˈmɔː.təl, ⓊⓈ ˈmɔːr.t̬əl **-s** -z **-ly** -i ˌ**mortal ˈsin**
mortalit|y, M~ mɔːˈtæl.ə.t|i, -ɪ.t|i, ⓊⓈ mɔːrˈtæl.ə.t̬|i **-ies** -iz
mort|ar ˈmɔː.t|əʳ, ⓊⓈ ˈmɔːr.t|ɚ **-ars** -əz, ⓊⓈ -ɚz **-aring** -ər.ɪŋ **-ared** -əd, ⓊⓈ -ɚd
mortarboard ˈmɔː.tə.bɔːd, ⓊⓈ ˈmɔːr.t̬ɚ.bɔːrd **-s** -z
Morte d'Arthur(e) ˌmɔːtˈdɑː.θəʳ, ⓊⓈ ˌmɔːrtˈdɑːr.θɚ
mortgag|e ˈmɔː.gɪdʒ, ⓊⓈ ˈmɔːr- **-es** -ɪz **-ing** -ɪŋ **-ed** -d
mortgagee ˌmɔː.gɪˈdʒiː, -gəˈ-, ⓊⓈ ˌmɔːr- **-s** -z
mortgagor ˌmɔː.gɪˈdʒɔːʳ, -gəˈ-; ˈmɔː.gɪ.dʒəʳ, -gə-, ⓊⓈ ˈmɔːr.gɪ.dʒɚ **-s** -z
mortic|e ˈmɔː.tɪs, ⓊⓈ ˈmɔːr.t̬ɪs **-es** -ɪz **-ing** -ɪŋ **-ed** -t
mortician mɔːˈtɪʃ.ən, ⓊⓈ mɔːr- **-s** -z
mortification ˌmɔː.tɪ.fɪˈkeɪ.ʃən, -tə-, -fəˈ-, ⓊⓈ ˌmɔːr.t̬ə.fɪˈ-
morti|fy ˈmɔː.tɪ|.faɪ, ˈ-tə-, ⓊⓈ ˈmɔːr.t̬ɪ-, ˈ-t̬ə- **-fies** -faɪz **-fying** -faɪ.ɪŋ **-fied** -faɪd
Mortimer ˈmɔː.tɪ.məʳ, -tə-, ⓊⓈ ˈmɔːr.t̬ə.mɚ
mortis|e ˈmɔː.tɪs, ⓊⓈ ˈmɔːr.t̬ɪs **-es** -ɪz **-ing** -ɪŋ **-ed** -t ˈ**mortise ˌlock**
Mortlake ˈmɔːt.leɪk, ⓊⓈ ˈmɔːrt-
Mortlock ˈmɔːt.lɒk, ⓊⓈ ˈmɔːrt.lɑːk
mortmain ˈmɔːt.meɪn, ⓊⓈ ˈmɔːrt-
Morton ˈmɔː.tən, ⓊⓈ ˈmɔːr-
mortuar|y ˈmɔː.tʃu.ər|.i, -tjʊ-, -tjʊ.r|i, -tʃər|.i, ⓊⓈ ˈmɔːr.tʃu.er|.i **-ies** -iz
Morwenna mɔːˈwen.ə, ⓊⓈ mɔːr-
mosaic, M~ məʊˈzeɪ.ɪk, ⓊⓈ moʊ- **-s** -s
Mosborough ˈmɒz.brə, -bər.ə, ⓊⓈ ˈmɑːz.bɚ.oʊ
Mosby ˈmɒz.bi, ⓊⓈ ˈmoʊz-
Mosca ˈmɒs.kə, ⓊⓈ ˈmɑːs-
Moscow ˈmɒs.kəʊ, ⓊⓈ ˈmɑː.skaʊ, -skoʊ
Moseley ˈməʊz.li, ⓊⓈ ˈmoʊz-
moselle, M~ məʊˈzel, ⓊⓈ moʊ- **-s** -z
Moses ˈməʊ.zɪz, ⓊⓈ ˈmoʊ- ˈ**Moses ˌbasket**
mosey ˈməʊ.zi, ⓊⓈ ˈmoʊ- **-s** -z **-ing** -ɪŋ **-ed** -d
mosh mɒʃ, ⓊⓈ mɑːʃ **-es** -ɪz **-ing** -ɪŋ **-ed** -t **-er/s** -əʳ/z, ⓊⓈ -ɚ/z
Mosimann ˈmɒs.ɪ.mən, ⓊⓈ ˈmɑː.sɪ-
Moslem ˈmɒz.ləm, ˈmʊz-, -lem, -lɪm, ⓊⓈ ˈmɑːz.lem, ˈmɑːs- **-s** -z
Mosley ˈməʊz.li, ˈmɒz-, ⓊⓈ ˈmoʊz-
mosque mɒsk, ⓊⓈ mɑːsk **-s** -s
mosquito, M~ mɒsˈkiː.təʊ, məˈskiː-, ⓊⓈ məˈskiː.t̬oʊ **-(e)s** -z mosˈ**quito ˌnet**
moss, M~ mɒs, ⓊⓈ mɑːs **-es** -ɪz
Mossad ˈmɒs.æd, ⓊⓈ moʊˈsɑːd
moss-grown ˈmɒs.grəʊn, ⓊⓈ ˈmɑːs.groʊn
Mossley ˈmɒs.li, ⓊⓈ ˈmɑːs-
Mossman *area of Sydney:* ˈmɒz.mən, ⓊⓈ ˈmɑːz- *other senses:* ˈmɒs.mən, ⓊⓈ ˈmɑːs-
Mossmorran mɒsˈmɒr.ən, ⓊⓈ mɑːsˈmɔːr-
moss|y ˈmɒs|.i, ⓊⓈ ˈmɑː.s|i **-ier** -i.əʳ, ⓊⓈ -i.ɚ **-iest** -i.ɪst, -i.əst **-iness** -ɪ.nəs, -ɪ.nɪs
mos|t məʊs|t, ⓊⓈ moʊs|t **-tly** -tli
Mostar ˈmɒs.tɑːʳ, ⓊⓈ ˈmɑː.stɑːr
Mostyn ˈmɒs.tɪn, ⓊⓈ ˈmɑː.stɪn
Mosul ˈməʊ.səl, ⓊⓈ moʊˈsuːl; ⓊⓈ ˈmoʊ.səl
mot məʊ, ⓊⓈ moʊ **-s** -z
MOT ˌem.əʊˈtiː, ⓊⓈ -oʊˈ- **-s** -z **-'s** -z **-'d** -d **-'ing** -ɪŋ ˌ**MOT cerˈtificate;** ˌ**MOˈT cerˌtificate;** ˌ**MOT ˈtest;** ˌ**MOˈT ˌtest**
mote məʊt, ⓊⓈ moʊt **-s** -s
motel məʊˈtel, ⓊⓈ moʊ- **-s** -z
motet məʊˈtet, ⓊⓈ moʊ- **-s** -s
moth mɒθ, ⓊⓈ mɑːθ **-s** -s
Mothaks® ˈmɒθ.æks, ⓊⓈ ˈmɑː.θæks
mothball ˈmɒθ.bɔːl, ⓊⓈ ˈmɑːθ-, -bɑːl **-s** -z **-ing** -ɪŋ **-ed** -d
moth-eaten ˈmɒθˌiː.tən, ⓊⓈ ˈmɑːθˌiː-
moth|er, M~ ˈmʌð|.əʳ, ⓊⓈ -ɚ **-ers** -əz, ⓊⓈ -ɚz **-ering** -ər.ɪŋ **-ered** -əd, ⓊⓈ -ɚd **-erless** -ə.ləs, -les, -lɪs, ⓊⓈ -ɚ- ˈ**mother ˌcountry;** ˌ**mother ˈhen;** ˌ**mother ˈnature;** ˌ**mother suˈperior;** ˈ**Mother's ˌDay;** ˌ**mother ˈtongue**
motherboard ˈmʌð.ə.bɔːd, ⓊⓈ -ɚ.bɔːrd **-s** -z
Mothercare® ˈmʌð.ə.keəʳ, ⓊⓈ -ɚ.ker
motherfucker ˈmʌð.əˌfʌk.əʳ, ⓊⓈ -ɚˌfʌk.ɚ **-s** -z
mother-fucking ˈmʌð.əˌfʌk.ɪŋ, ⓊⓈ -ɚˌ-
motherhood ˈmʌð.ə.hʊd, ⓊⓈ ˈ-ɚ-
mother-in-law ˈmʌð.ər.ɪnˌlɔː, ⓊⓈ -ɚ.ɪnˌlɑː, -ˌlɔː **mothers-in-law** ˈmʌð.əz-, ⓊⓈ -ɚz-
motherland ˈmʌð.ə.lænd, ⓊⓈ ˈ-ɚ- **-s** -z
motherl|y ˈmʌð.əl|.i, ⓊⓈ -ɚ.l|i **-iness** -ɪ.nəs, -ɪ.nɪs
mother-of-pearl ˌmʌð.ər.əvˈpɜːl, ⓊⓈ -ɚ.əvˈpɝːl
mothersill ˈmʌð.ə.sɪl, ⓊⓈ ˈ-ɚ-
Motherwell ˈmʌð.ə.wel, ⓊⓈ ˈ-ɚ-
motif məʊˈtiːf, ⓊⓈ moʊ- **-s** -s
motile ˈməʊ.taɪl, ⓊⓈ ˈmoʊ.t̬əl, -taɪl
motion, M~ ˈməʊ.ʃən, ⓊⓈ ˈmoʊ- **-s** -z **-ing** -ɪŋ, ˈməʊʃ.nɪŋ, ⓊⓈ ˈmoʊʃ- **-ed** -d **-less** -ləs, -lɪs ˌ**motion ˈpicture;** ˈ**motion ˌsickness**
moti|vate ˈməʊ.tɪ|.veɪt, -tə-, ⓊⓈ ˈmoʊ.t̬ə- **-vates** -veɪts **-vating** -veɪ.tɪŋ, ⓊⓈ -veɪ.t̬ɪŋ **-vated** -veɪ.tɪd, ⓊⓈ -veɪ.t̬ɪd **-vator/s** -veɪ.təʳ/z, ⓊⓈ -veɪ.t̬ɚ/z
motivation ˌməʊ.tɪˈveɪ.ʃən, -təˈ-, ⓊⓈ ˌmoʊ.t̬əˈ- **-al** -əl
motive ˈməʊ.tɪv, ⓊⓈ ˈmoʊ.t̬ɪv **-s** -z **-less** -ləs, -lɪs
mot juste ˌməʊˈʒuːst, ⓊⓈ ˌmoʊ-
motley, M~ ˈmɒt.li, ⓊⓈ ˈmɑːt-
motocross ˈməʊ.təʊ.krɒs, ⓊⓈ ˈmoʊ.t̬oʊ.krɑːs
mot|or ˈməʊ.t|əʳ, ⓊⓈ ˈmoʊ.t̬|ɚ **-ors** -əz, ⓊⓈ -ɚz **-oring** -ər.ɪŋ **-ored** -əd, ⓊⓈ -ɚd ˈ**motor ˌcar;** ˈ**motor ˌhome;** ˈ**motor ˌlodge;** ˈ**motor ˌscooter;** ˈ**motor ˌvehicle**
Motorail® ˈməʊ.tər.eɪl, ⓊⓈ ˈmoʊ.t̬ə.reɪl
motorbike ˈməʊ.tə.baɪk, ⓊⓈ ˈmoʊ.t̬ɚ- **-s** -s
motorboat ˈməʊ.tə.bəʊt, ⓊⓈ ˈmoʊ.t̬ɚ.boʊt **-s** -s
motorcade ˈməʊ.tə.keɪd, ⓊⓈ ˈmoʊ.t̬ɚ- **-s** -z
motorcycle ˈməʊ.təˌsaɪ.kəl, ⓊⓈ ˈmoʊ.t̬ɚ- **-s** -z
motorcyclist ˈməʊ.təˌsaɪ.klɪst, -kəl.ɪst, ⓊⓈ ˈmoʊ.t̬ɚ- **-s** -s
motorhome ˈməʊ.tə.həʊm, ⓊⓈ ˈmoʊ.t̬ɚ.hoʊm **-s** -z
motorist ˈməʊ.tər.ɪst, ⓊⓈ ˈmoʊ.t̬ɚ- **-s** -s
motoriz|e, -is|e ˈməʊ.tər.aɪz, ⓊⓈ ˈmoʊ.t̬ə.raɪz **-es** -ɪz **-ing** -ɪŋ **-ed** -d
motor|man ˈməʊ.tə|.mæn, ⓊⓈ ˈmoʊ.t̬ɚ-, -mən **-men** -men
motormou|th ˈməʊ.tə.maʊ|θ, ⓊⓈ ˈmoʊ.t̬ɚ- **-ths** -ðz
Motorola ˌməʊ.təˈrəʊ.lə, ⓊⓈ ˌmoʊ.t̬əˈroʊ.lə
motor-scooter ˈməʊ.təˌskuː.təʳ, ⓊⓈ ˈmoʊ.t̬ɚˌskuː.t̬ɚ **-s** -z
motorway ˈməʊ.tə.weɪ, ⓊⓈ ˈmoʊ.t̬ɚ- **-s** -z
Motown® ˈməʊ.taʊn, ⓊⓈ ˈmoʊ-
Mott mɒt, ⓊⓈ mɑːt
motte mɒt, ⓊⓈ mɑːt **-s** -s
Mottistone ˈmɒt.ɪ.stən, -stəʊn, ⓊⓈ ˈmɑː.t̬ɪ.stən, -stoʊn
mottl|e ˈmɒt.əl, ⓊⓈ ˈmɑː.t̬əl **-es** -z **-ing** -ɪŋ **-ed** -d
motto ˈmɒt.əʊ, ⓊⓈ ˈmɑː.t̬oʊ **-(e)s** -z
Mottram ˈmɒt.rəm, ⓊⓈ ˈmɑː.trəm
moue muː **-s** -z
mouf(f)lon ˈmuː.flɒn, ⓊⓈ -flɑːn **-s** -z
Moughton ˈməʊ.tən, ⓊⓈ ˈmoʊ-
Mouland ˈmuː.lænd, muˈlænd
mould məʊld, ⓊⓈ moʊld **-s** -z **-ing/s** -ɪŋ/z **-ed** -ɪd
mould|er ˈməʊl.d|əʳ, ⓊⓈ ˈmoʊl.d|ɚ **-ers** -əz, ⓊⓈ -ɚz **-ering** -ər.ɪŋ **-ered** -əd, ⓊⓈ -ɚd
mould|y ˈməʊl.d|i, ⓊⓈ ˈmoʊl- **-ier**

-i.əʳ, US -i.ɚ -iest -i.ɪst, -i.əst -iness -ɪ.nəs, -ɪ.nɪs
Moule məʊl, muːl, US moʊl, muːl
Moulinex® ˈmuː.lɪ.neks, -lə-
Moulin Rouge ˌmuː.læ̃nˈruːʒ
Moulmein ˈmaʊl.meɪn, US mʊlˈmeɪn, moʊl-
Moulsford ˈməʊls.fəd, ˈməʊlz-, US ˈmoʊls.fɚd, ˈmoʊlz-
moult məʊlt, US moʊlt -s -s -ing -ɪŋ, US ˈmoʊl.tɪŋ -ed -ɪd, US ˈmoʊl.tɪd
Moulton ˈməʊl.tᵊn, US ˈmoʊl-
Moultrie ˈmɔːl.tri, ˈmuː-
mound, M~ maʊnd -s -z
Mounsey ˈmaʊn.zi
mount, M~ maʊnt -s -s -ing -ɪŋ, US ˈmaʊn.t̬ɪŋ -ed -ɪd, US ˈmaʊn.t̬ɪd
mountain ˈmaʊn.tɪn, -tən, US -tᵊn -s -z **ˈmountain ˌbike; ˈmountain ˌlion; make a ˌmountain out of a ˈmole-hill**
mountain-ash ˌmaʊn.tɪnˈæʃ, -tənˈ-, US -tᵊnˈ- -es -ɪz
mountaineer ˌmaʊn.tɪˈnɪəʳ, -təˈ-, US -tᵊnˈɪr -s -z -ing -ɪŋ
mountainous ˈmaʊn.tɪ.nəs, -tə-, US -tᵊn.əs
mountainside ˈmaʊn.tɪn.saɪd, -tən-, US -tᵊn- -s -z
mountaintop ˈmaʊn.tɪn.tɒp, -tən-, US -tᵊn.tɑːp -s -s
mountant ˈmaʊn.tənt -s -s
Mountbatten maʊntˈbæt.ᵊn
mountebank ˈmaʊn.tɪ.bæŋk, -tə-, US -t̬ə- -s -s
Mount Everest ˌmaʊntˈev.ᵊr.ɪst, -est
Mountford ˈmaʊnt.fəd, US -fɚd
Mountie ˈmaʊn.ti, US -t̬i -s -z
Mountjoy ˌmaʊntˈdʒɔɪ, ˈ--
Mountsorrel ˌmaʊntˈsɒr.əl, US -ˈsɔːr-
Mount Vernon ˌmaʊntˈvɜː.nən, US -ˈvɝː-
Mount|y ˈmaʊn.t|i, US -t̬|i -ies -iz
Moura ˈmʊə.rə, US ˈmʊr.ə
Mourinho mɔːˈriː.njəʊ, mə-, US -njoʊ
mourn mɔːn, US mɔːrn -s -z -ing -ɪŋ -ed -d -er/s -əʳ/z, US -ɚ/z
Mourne mɔːn, US mɔːrn
mournful ˈmɔːn.fᵊl, -fʊl, US ˈmɔːrn- -ly -i -ness -nəs, -nɪs
Mousa ˈmuː.zə
Mousavi ˌmuː.sævˈiː
mouse n maʊs **mice** maɪs
mous|e v maʊs, maʊz, US maʊz -es -ɪz -ing -ɪŋ -ed -d
Mousehole ˈmaʊ.zᵊl
mouser ˈmaʊ.səʳ, -zəʳ, US -zɚ -s -z
mouse-trap ˈmaʊs.træp -s -s
mous|ey ˈmaʊ.s|i -ier -i.əʳ, US -i.ɚ -iest -i.ɪst, -i.əst
moussaka muˈsɑː.kə, ˈmuː.sæk.ə, US muˈsɑː.kə; US ˌmuː.sɑːˈkɑː
mousse muːs
Moussec® ˌmuːˈsek
mousseline ˈmuː.slɪn, ˌmuːˈsliːn, US ˌmuːˈsliːn
Moussorgsky mʊˈsɔːg.ski, muː-, US muːˈsɔːrg-, mə-, -ˈzɔːrg-, -ˈsɔːrk-, -ˈzɔːrk-
moustach|e məˈstɑːʃ, mʊ-, US ˈmʌs.tæʃ; US məˈstæʃ -es -ɪz
mous|y ˈmaʊ.s|i -ier -i.əʳ, US -i.ɚ -iest -i.ɪst, -i.əst
mouth v maʊð -s -z -ing -ɪŋ -ed -d
mou|th n maʊ|θ -ths -ðz **ˈmouth ˌorgan; from the ˌhorse's ˈmouth; ˌdown in the ˈmouth**
mouthful ˈmaʊθ.fʊl -s -z
mouthpiec|e ˈmaʊθ.piːs -es -ɪz
mouth-to-mouth ˌmaʊθ.təˈmaʊθ *stress shift, see compound:* **ˌmouth-to-mouth reˌsusciˈtation**
mouthwash ˈmaʊθ.wɒʃ, US -wɑːʃ, -wɔːʃ -es -ɪz
mouthwatering ˈmaʊθˌwɔː.tᵊr.ɪŋ, US -ˌwɑː.t̬ɚ-, -ˌwɔː- -ly -li
mouth|y ˈmaʊ.ð|i, -θ|i -ier -i.əʳ, US -i.ɚ -iest -i.ɪst, -i.əst
movability ˌmuː.vəˈbɪl.ə.ti, -ɪ.ti, US -ə.t̬i
movable ˈmuː.və.bᵊl -s -z -ness -nəs, -nɪs
movant ˈmuː.vənt -s -s
mov|e muːv -es -z -ing/ly -ɪŋ/li -ed -d -er/s -əʳ/z, US -ɚ/z -eable -ə.bᵊl
movement ˈmuːv.mənt -s -s
movie ˈmuː.vi -s -z
moviegoer ˈmuː.viˌgəʊ.əʳ, US -ˌgoʊ.ɚ -s -z
moviegoing ˈmuː.viˌgəʊ.ɪŋ, US -ˌgoʊ-
moviemak|er ˈmuː.viˌmeɪ.k|əʳ, US -k|ɚ -ers -əz, US -ɚz -ing -ɪŋ
mow v *cut down and stack:* məʊ, US moʊ -s -z -ing -ɪŋ -ed -d -n -n -er/s -əʳ/z, US -ɚ/z
mow n *stack:* maʊ *grimace:* maʊ, US moʊ, maʊ -s -z
Mowat, Mowatt ˈmaʊ.ət, ˈməʊ.ət, US ˈmaʊ.ət, ˈmoʊ.ət
Mowbray ˈməʊ.breɪ, -bri, US ˈmoʊ-
Mowgli ˈmaʊ.gli
Mowlam ˈməʊ.ləm, US ˈmoʊ-
mown (from **mow** v.) məʊn, US moʊn
Moxon ˈmɒk.sᵊn, US ˈmɑːk-
moya, M~ ˈmɔɪ.ə -s -z
Moyes mɔɪz
Moygashel *place:* mɔɪˈgæʃ.ᵊl *linen:* ˈmɔɪ.gə.ʃᵊl
Moynahan ˈmɔɪ.nə.hæn, -hən, US ˈmɔɪ.nə.hæn
Moynihan ˈmɔɪ.ni.ən, -hæn; -nə.hæn, US ˈmɔɪ.nɪ.hæn, -nə-
Mozambique ˌməʊ.zæmˈbiːk, -zəmˈ-, US ˌmoʊ-
Mozart ˈməʊt.sɑːt, US ˈmoʊt.sɑːrt
Mozartian məʊtˈsɑː.ti.ən, US moʊtˈsɑːr.t̬i- -s -z
Mozilla mɒzˈɪl.ə, məʊˈzɪl-, US moʊˈzɪl-
mozzarella ˌmɒt.səˈrel.ə, US ˌmɑːt-, ˌmoʊt-
MP ˌemˈpiː
MP3® ˌem.piːˈθriː
mph ˌem.piːˈeɪtʃ
MPhil ˌemˈfɪl
Mr ˈmɪs.təʳ, US -tɚ
Mrs ˈmɪs.ɪz
MRSA ˌem.ɑːʳ.esˈeɪ, US -ɑːr-
ms, MS (abbrev. for **manuscript**) ˌemˈes, ˈmæn.jə.skrɪpt, -jʊ-
Ms mɪz, məz, US mɪz

> Note: Used to avoid indicating a woman's marital status. The pronunciation is unstable in the UK.

MS (abbrev. for **multiple sclerosis**) ˌemˈes
M&S ˌem.ənˈdes
MSc ˌem.esˈsiː
MS-DOS® ˌem.esˈdɒs, US -ˈdɑːs
MSS (abbrev. for **manuscripts**) ˌem.esˈes, ˈmæn.jə.skrɪpts, -jʊ-
MTV ˌem.tiːˈviː
mu mjuː, US mjuː, muː
Mubarak mʊˈbɑː.rək, -ˈbær.æk, -ək, US muːˈbɑːr.ək
much mʌtʃ -ly -li
Muchalls ˈmʌk.ᵊlz, ˈmʌx-
muchness ˈmʌtʃ.nəs, -nɪs
mucilag|e ˈmjuː.sɪ.lɪdʒ, -sᵊl.ɪdʒ, US -sə.lɪdʒ -es -ɪz
mucilaginous ˌmjuː.sɪˈlædʒ.ɪ.nəs, -sᵊlˈædʒ-, ˈ-ə-, US -sɪˈlædʒ.ə-
muck mʌk -s -s -ing -ɪŋ -ed -t
muck|er ˈmʌk|.əʳ, US -ɚ -ers -əz, US -ɚz -ering -ᵊr.ɪŋ -ered -əd, US -ɚd
Muckle Flugga ˌmʌk.ᵊlˈflʌg.ə
muckrak|e ˈmʌk.reɪk -es -s -ing -ɪŋ -ed -t -er/s -əʳ/z, US -ɚ/z
muck|y ˈmʌk|.i -ier -i.əʳ, US -i.ɚ -iest -i.ɪst, -i.əst -iness -ɪ.nəs, -ɪ.nɪs
muc(o)us ˈmjuː.kəs ˌ**mucous ˈmembrane**
mud mʌd -s -z
mudba|th ˈmʌd.bɑː|θ, US -bæ|θ -ths -ðz
muddl|e ˈmʌd.ᵊl -es -z -ing -ɪŋ, ˈmʌd.lɪŋ -ed -d -er/s -əʳ/z, US -ɚ/z, ˈmʌd.ləʳ/z, -lɚ/z
muddleheaded ˌmʌd.ᵊlˈhed.ɪd, ˈmʌd.ᵊlˌhed-, US ˈmʌd.ᵊlˌhed- -ness -nəs, -nɪs
mudd|y ˈmʌd|.i -ier -i.əʳ, US -i.ɚ -iest -i.ɪst, -i.əst -ily -ᵊl.i, -ɪ.li -iness -ɪ.nəs, -ɪ.nɪs -ies -iz -ying -i.ɪŋ -ied -id
Mud(d)eford ˈmʌd.ɪ.fəd, US -fɚd
mudflap ˈmʌd.flæp -s -s
mudflat ˈmʌd.flæt -s -s
mudguard ˈmʌd.gɑːd, US -gɑːrd -s -z
Mudie ˈmjuː.di
mudlark ˈmʌd.lɑːk, US -lɑːrk -s -s
mudpack ˈmʌd.pæk -s -s
mudslide ˈmʌd.slaɪd -s -z
Mueller ˈmjuː.ləʳ, ˈmʊl.əʳ, US -lɚ
muesli ˈmjuːz.li, ˈmuːz-, US ˈmjuːz-, ˈmjuːs- -s -z
muezzin muˈez.ɪn, mju-, US mju-, mu- -s -z
muff mʌf -s -s -ing -ɪŋ -ed -t
muffin ˈmʌf.ɪn -s -z
muffl|e ˈmʌf.ᵊl -es -z -ing -ɪŋ, ˈmʌf.lɪŋ -ed -d
muffler ˈmʌf.ləʳ, US -lɚ -s -z

mufti ˈmʌf.ti
mug mʌg **-s** -z **-ging/s** -ɪŋ/z **-ged** -d ˈ**mug** ˌ**shot**
Mugabe mʊˈgɑː.beɪ, -bi
mugger ˈmʌg.əʳ, (US) -ɚ **-s** -z
muggins, M~ ˈmʌg.ɪnz **-es** -ɪz
Muggins ˈmʌg.ɪnz, ˈmjuː.gɪnz
Muggleton ˈmʌg.ᵊl.tᵊn, (US) -tən
Muggletonian ˌmʌg.ᵊlˈtəʊ.ni.ən, (US) -ˈtoʊ- **-s** -z
muggly ˈmʌg|.i **-ier** -i.əʳ, (US) -i.ɚ **-iest** -i.ɪst, -i.əst **-iness** -ɪ.nəs, -ɪ.nɪs
mugwump ˈmʌg.wʌmp **-s** -s
Muhammad mʊˈhæm.əd, mə-, -ɪd, -ed
Muir mjʊəʳ, mjɔːʳ, (US) mjʊr
Muirhead ˈmjʊə.hed, ˈmjɔː-, (US) ˈmjʊr-
mujahideen, M~ ˌmuː.dʒə.hedˈiːn, ˈmʊdʒ.ə-, ˈmuː.ʒə-, -ʒɑː-, -həˈdiːn, (US) muːˌdʒɑː.həˈdiːn
Muji ˈmuː.dʒi
Mukasey mjʊˈkeɪ.si
Mukden ˈmʊk.dən
mukluk ˈmʌk.lʌk **-s** -s
mulatto mjuːˈlæt.əʊ, mjə-, mjʊ-, mə-, (US) məˈlæt̬.oʊ, mjuː-, -ˈlɑː.t̬oʊ **-(e)s** -z
mulberr|y ˈmʌl.bᵊr|.i, (US) -ˌber- **-ies** -iz
Mulcaster ˈmʌl.kæs.təʳ, (US) -tɚ
mulch mʌltʃ **-es** -ɪz **-ing** -ɪŋ **-ed** -t
mulct mʌlkt **-s** -s **-ing** -ɪŋ **-ed** -ɪd
mulder ˈmʌl.dəʳ, (US) -dɚ
Muldoon mʌlˈduːn
mule mjuːl **-s** -z
muleteer ˌmjuː.lɪˈtɪəʳ, -ləˈ-, (US) -ləˈtɪr **-s** -z
mulga ˈmʊl.gə **-s** -z
Mulgrave ˈmʌl.greɪv
Mulholland mʌlˈhɒl.ənd, (US) -ˈhɑː.lənd
mulish ˈmjuː.lɪʃ **-ly** -li **-ness** -nəs, -nɪs
mull, M~ mʌl **-s** -z **-ing** -ɪŋ **-ed** -d
mullah, M~ ˈmʊl.ə, ˈmʌl.ə **-s** -z
Mullan, Mullen ˈmʌl.ən
mullein ˈmʌl.ɪn, -eɪn, (US) -ɪn
mullered ˈmʌl.əd, (US) -ɚd
mullet, M~ ˈmʌl.ɪt, -ət **-s** -s
Mulligan ˈmʌl.ɪ.gən, ˈ-ə-
mulligatawny ˌmʌl.ɪ.gəˈtɔː.ni, ˌ-ə-, (US) -ˈtɑː.ni, -ˈtɔː-
Mullinar, Mulliner ˈmʌl.ɪ.nəʳ, (US) -nɚ
Mullinger ˈmʌl.ɪn.dʒəʳ, -ᵊn-, (US) -dʒɚ
Mullins ˈmʌl.ɪnz
mullion, M~ ˈmʌl.jən, ˈ-i.ən, (US) ˈ-jən **-s** -z **-ed** -d
mullock ˈmʌl.ək
Mulready mʌlˈred.i
Mulroney mʌlˈrəʊ.ni, (US) -ˈroʊ-
Multan ˌmʌlˈtɑːn, (US) ˌmʊl-
multi- ˈmʌl.ti, -tɪ, -tə, (US) ˈmʌl.ti, -tə, -taɪ
Note: Prefix. Normally carries primary or secondary stress on the first syllable, e.g. **multiform** /ˈmʌl.ti.fɔːm/ (US) /-ti.fɔːrm/, **multilingual** /ˌmʌl.tiˈlɪŋ.gwᵊl/.
multicolo(u)red ˌmʌl.tiˈkʌl.əd, ˈmʌl.tiˌkʌl-, (US) ˌmʌl.tiˈkʌl.ɚd, ˈmʌl.tiˌkʌl-, -taɪ-
multicultural ˌmʌl.tiˈkʌl.tʃᵊr.ᵊl, (US) -t̬iˈ-, -tiˈkʌl.tʃɚ- **-ly** -i **-ism** -ɪ.zᵊm *stress shift:* ˌ**multicultural** ˈ**festival**
multi-disciplinary ˌmʌl.ti.dɪs.əˈplɪn.ᵊr.i, -ɪˈ-, -ˈdɪs.ə.plɪ.nᵊr-, ˈ-ɪ-, (US) -ti.ˈdɪs.ə.plɪ.ner-, -taɪˈ-
multiethnic ˌmʌl.tiˈeθ.nɪk, (US) -tiˈ-, -taɪˈ- *stress shift:* ˌ**multiethnic** ˈ**background**
multi-faceted ˌmʌl.tiˈfæs.ɪ.tɪd, (US) -tiˈfæs.ɪ.t̬ɪd, -taɪˈ-
multifarious ˌmʌl.tɪˈfeə.ri.əs, (US) -təˈfer.i- **-ly** -li **-ness** -nəs, -nɪs *stress shift:* ˌ**multifarious** ˈ**influences**
multiform ˈmʌl.ti.fɔːm, (US) -ti.fɔːrm, ˈ-taɪ-
multigym ˈmʌl.ti.dʒɪm, (US) -ti-, ˈ-taɪ- **-s** -z
multilateral ˌmʌl.tiˈlæt.ᵊr.ᵊl, (US) -tiˈlæt̬-, -taɪˈ- **-ly** -i *stress shift:* ˌ**multilateral** ˈ**talks**
multilingual ˌmʌl.tiˈlɪŋ.gwəl, (US) -tiˈ-, -taɪˈ- **-ly** -i *stress shift:* ˌ**multilingual** ˈ**people**
multimedia ˌmʌl.tiˈmiː.di.ə, (US) -tiˈ-, -taɪˈ-
multimillionaire ˌmʌl.tiˌmɪl.jəˈneəʳ, -i.əˈ-, (US) -tiˌmɪl.jəˈner, -taɪˌ-, ˌmʌl.tiˈmɪl.jə.ner, -taɪˈ- **-s** -z
multinational ˌmʌl.tiˈnæʃ.ᵊn.ᵊl, -ˈnæʃ.nᵊl, (US) -tiˈ-, -taɪˈ- **-s** -z *stress shift:* ˌ**multinational** ˈ**company**
multipartite ˌmʌl.tiˈpɑː.taɪt, (US) -tiˈpɑːr-, -taɪˈ- *stress shift:* ˌ**multipartite** ˈ**treaty**
multiplayer ˈmʌl.tiˌpleɪ.əʳ, -tə-, (US) -tiˌpleɪ.ɚ, ˈ-taɪ- **-s** -z
multiple ˈmʌl.tɪ.pᵊl, -tə-, (US) -tə- **-s** -z ˌ**multiple scle**ˈ**rosis**
multiple-choice ˌmʌl.tɪ.pᵊlˈtʃɔɪs, -tə-, (US) -tə- *stress shift:* ˌ**multiple-choice** ˈ**paper**
multiplex ˈmʌl.tɪ.pleks, -tə-, (US) -tə- **-es** -ɪz
multiplicand ˌmʌl.tɪ.plɪˈkænd, -tə-, (US) -tə- **-s** -z
multiplication ˌmʌl.tɪ.plɪˈkeɪ.ʃᵊn, -tə-, (US) -tə- **-s** -z
multiplicative ˌmʌl.tɪˈplɪk.ə.tɪv, -təˈ-; ˈmʌl.tɪ.plɪ.keɪ.tɪv, (US) ˈmʌl.tə.plɪ.keɪ.t̬ɪv; (US) ˌmʌl.təˈplɪk.ə-
multiplicator ˈmʌl.tɪ.plɪ.keɪ.təʳ, (US) -tɚ **-s** -z
multiplicit|y ˌmʌl.tɪˈplɪs.ə.t|i, -təˈ-, -ɪ.t|i, (US) -təˈplɪs.ə.t̬|i **-ies** -iz
multipl|y ˈmʌl.tɪ.pl|aɪ, -tə-, (US) -tə- **-ies** -aɪz **-ying** -aɪ.ɪŋ **-ied** -aɪd **-ier/s** -aɪ.əʳ/z, (US) -aɪ.ɚ/z
multiprocessing ˌmʌl.tiˈprəʊ.ses.ɪŋ, (US) -tiˈprɑː-, -taɪˈ-
multiprocessor ˌmʌl.tiˈprəʊ.ses.əʳ, (US) -tiˈprɑː.ses.ɚ, -taɪˈ- **-s** -z
multipurpose ˌmʌl.tiˈpɜː.pəs, (US) -tiˈpɝː-, -taɪˈ- *stress shift:* ˌ**multipurpose** ˈ**tool**
multiracial ˌmʌl.tiˈreɪ.ʃᵊl, -ʃi.əl, (US) -tiˈreɪ.ʃᵊl, -taɪˈ- *stress shift:* ˌ**multiracial** ˈ**area**
multiscreen ˌmʌl.tiˈskriːn, (US) ˌmʌl.ti-, -taɪˈ- *stress shift:* ˌ**multiscreen** ˈ**cinema**
multi-storey ˌmʌl.tiˈstɔː.ri, (US) -tiˈstɔːr.i, -taɪˈ- *stress shift, see compound:* ˌ**multi-storey** ˈ**car park**
multi-tasking ˌmʌl.tiˈtɑː.skɪŋ, ˈmʌl.tiˌtɑː-, (US) ˈmʌl.tiˌtæs.kɪŋ, -taɪˌ-
multitude ˈmʌl.tɪ.tʃuːd, -tə-, -tjuːd, (US) -tə.tuːd, -tjuːd **-s** -z
multitudinous ˌmʌl.tɪˈtʃuː.dɪ.nəs, -təˈ-, -ˈtjuː-, -dᵊn.əs, (US) -təˈtuː.dᵊn-, -ˈtjuː- **-ly** -li **-ness** -nəs, -nɪs
multivalen|t ˌmʌl.tiˈveɪ.lən|t, (US) -tiˈ-, -taɪˈ- **-ce** -*t*s
multivitamin ˌmʌl.tiˈvɪt.ə.mɪn, -ˈvaɪ.tə-, (US) -ˈvaɪ.tə-, -taɪˈ- **-s** -z
multum in parvo ˌmʊl.təm.ɪnˈpɑː.vəʊ, ˌmʌl-, (US) -ˈpɑːr.voʊ
mum, M~ mʌm **-s** -z
Mum and the Sothsegger ˌmʌm.ənd.ðəˈsɒθ.seg.əʳ, -ˈsəʊθ-, (US) -ænd.ðəˈsɑːθ.seg.ɚ
Mumbai ˌmʌmˈbaɪ
mumbl|e ˈmʌm.bᵊl **-es** -z **-ing/ly** -ɪŋ/li, ˈ-blɪŋ/li **-ed** -d **-er/s** -əʳ/z, (US) ˈ-bləʳ/z, ˈ-bᵊl.ɚ/z, ˈ-blɚ/z
Mumbles ˈmʌm.bᵊlz
mumbo-jumbo ˌmʌm.bəʊˈdʒʌm.bəʊ, (US) -boʊˈdʒʌm.boʊ
Mumm mʌm; *as if French:* mʊm
mumm|er ˈmʌm|.əʳ, (US) -ɚ **-ers** -əz, -ɚz **-ery** -ᵊr.i
mummification ˌmʌm.ɪ.fɪˈkeɪ.ʃᵊn, ˌ-ə-, -fəˈ-
mummi|fy ˈmʌm.ɪ|.faɪ, ˈ-ə- **-fies** -faɪz **-fying** -faɪ.ɪŋ **-fied** -faɪd
mumm|y, M~ ˈmʌm|.i **-ies** -iz
mumpish ˈmʌm.pɪʃ **-ly** -li **-ness** -nəs, -nɪs
mumps mʌmps
mums|y ˈmʌm.z|i **-ily** -ᵊl.i, -ɪ.li **-iness** -ɪ.nəs, -ɪ.nɪs
Munby ˈmʌn.bi, ˈmʌm-, (US) ˈmʌn-
munch mʌntʃ **-es** -ɪz **-ing** -ɪŋ **-ed** -t **-er/s** -əʳ/z, (US) -ɚ/z
Munch mʊŋk **-s** -s
Munchausen, Münchausen, Münchhausen ˈmʌn.*t*ʃaʊ.zᵊn, ˈmʊntʃ-, -haʊ-; mʌnˈtʃɔː.zᵊn, (US) ˈmʌn.tʃaʊ.zᵊn, ˈmʊn-, -tʃɔː-
munchies, M~® ˈmʌn.*t*ʃiz
munchkin ˈmʌntʃ.kɪn **-s** -z
Muncie ˈmʌn.*t*si
mundane mʌnˈdeɪn, ˈ-- **-ly** -li
Munera Pulveris ˌmjuː.nᵊr.əˈpʊl.vᵊr.ɪs
mung mʌŋ ˈ**mung** ˌ**bean**
mungo, M~ ˈmʌŋ.gəʊ, (US) -goʊ **-s** -z

Munich ˈmjuː.nɪk
municipal mjuːˈnɪs.ɪ.pəl, ˈ-ə-, (US) ˈ-ə-
municipalit|y mjuːˌnɪs.ɪˈpæl.ə.t|i, -əˈ-, -ɪ.t|i; ˌmjuː.nɪ.sɪˈ-, -səˈ-, (US) mjuːˌnɪs.əˈpæl.ə.t̬|i **-ies** -iz
municipaliz|e, -is|e mjuːˈnɪs.ɪ.pəl.aɪz, ˈ-ə-, (US) ˈ-ə.pə.laɪz **-es** -ɪz **-ing** -ɪŋ **-ed** -d
munificen|ce mjuːˈnɪf.ɪ.sən|ts, ˈ-ə-, (US) ˈ-ə- **-t/ly** -t/li
muniment ˈmjuː.nɪ.mənt, -nə-, (US) -nə- **-s** -s
munition mjuːˈnɪʃ.ən **-s** -z
Munro mʌnˈrəʊ, mənˈ-; ˈmʌn.rəʊ, (US) mənˈroʊ
Munsey ˈmʌn.zi
Munster *in Ireland:* ˈmʌnt.stər, (US) -stɚ
Münster *in Germany:* ˈmʊnt.stər, (US) -stɚ, ˈmʌnt-
muntjak, muntjac ˈmʌnt.dʒæk, ˈmʌnt.ʃæk, (US) ˈmʌnt.dʒæk **-s** -s
Muppet ˈmʌp.ɪt **-s** -s
mural ˈmjʊə.rəl, ˈmjɔː-, (US) ˈmjʊr.əl **-s** -z
Murchie ˈmɜː.ki; *in S. England also:* -tʃi, (US) ˈmɝː.tʃi
Murchison ˈmɜː.tʃɪ.sən, -kɪ-, (US) ˈmɝː.tʃɪ-
Murcia ˈmɜː.ʃi.ə; *as if Spanish:* ˈmʊə.θi.ə; (US) ˈmɝː.ʃə, -ʃi.ə
Murcott ˈmɜː.kət, (US) ˈmɝː-
murd|er ˈmɜː.d|ər, (US) ˈmɝː.d|ɚ **-ers** -əz, (US) -ɚz **-ering** -ər.ɪŋ **-ered** -əd, (US) -ɚd
murderer ˈmɜː.dər.ər, (US) ˈmɝː.dɚ.ɚ **-s** -z
murderess ˈmɜː.dər.ɪs, -es, -əs; ˌmɜː.dəˈres, (US) ˈmɝː.dɚ.əs; (US) ˌmɝː.dɚˈes **-es** -ɪz
murderous ˈmɜː.dər.əs, (US) ˈmɝː- **-ly** -li
Murdo ˈmɜː.dəʊ, (US) ˈmɝː.doʊ
Murdoch, Murdock ˈmɜː.dɒk, (US) ˈmɝː.dɑːk
Murdstone ˈmɜːd.stən, (US) ˈmɝːd-
Mure mjʊər, mjɔːr, (US) mjʊr
muriate ˈmjʊə.ri.ət, ˈmjɔː-, -ɪt, -eɪt, (US) ˈmjʊr.i.eɪt, -ɪt
muriatic ˌmjʊə.riˈæt.ɪk, ˌmjɔː-, ˈmjʊə.ri.æt-, ˈmjɔː-, (US) ˌmjʊr.iˈæt̬-
Muriel ˈmjʊə.ri.əl, ˈmjɔː-, (US) ˈmjʊr.i-
Murillo mjʊˈrɪl.əʊ, mjʊə-, -jəʊ; *as if Spanish:* mʊˈriː.jəʊ; (US) mjʊˈrɪl.oʊ, mə- **-s** -z
Murison ˈmjʊə.rɪ.sən, ˈmjɔː-, (US) ˈmjʊr.ɪ-
murk mɜːk, (US) mɝːk
murk|y ˈmɜː.k|i, (US) ˈmɝː- **-ier** -i.ər, (US) -i.ɚ **-iest** -i.ɪst, -i.əst **-ily** -əl.i, -ɪ.li **-iness** -ɪ.nəs, -ɪ.nɪs
Murmansk mɜːˈmæntsk, mə-, (US) mʊrˈmɑːntsk; (US) ˈmɝː.mæntsk
murm|ur ˈmɜː.m|ər, (US) ˈmɝː.m|ɚ **-urs** -əz, (US) -ɚz **-uring/ly** -ər.ɪŋ/li **-ured** -əd, (US) -ɚd **-urer/s** -ər.ər/z, (US) -ɚ.ɚ/z
murph|y, M~ ˈmɜː.f|i, (US) ˈmɝː- **-ies** -iz ˈ**Murphy's** ˌ**law**
murrain ˈmʌr.ɪn, -eɪn, (US) ˈmɝː.ɪn
Murray ˈmʌr.i, (US) ˈmɝː-, ˈmʌr-
Murrayfield ˈmʌr.i.fiːld
Murree ˈmʌr.i, (US) ˈmɝː-
Murrell ˈmʌr.əl; mʌrˈel, məˈrel, (US) ˈmɝː.əl; (US) məˈrel
Murrie ˈmjʊə.ri, (US) ˈmjʊr.i
Murrumbidgee ˌmʌr.əmˈbɪdʒ.i, (US) ˌmɝː-
Murry ˈmʌr.i, (US) ˈmɝː-
Murtagh ˈmɜː.tə, (US) ˈmɝː.tɑː
Murtle ˈmɜː.təl, (US) ˈmɝː.t̬əl
Murton ˈmɜː.tən, (US) ˈmɝː-
Mururoa mʊ.rʊˈrəʊ.ə, (US) ˌmuː.ruːˈroʊ-
muscadet, M~ ˈmʌs.kə.deɪ, ˌ--ˈ-, (US) ˈmʌs.kə.deɪ **-s** -z
muscat, M~ *grape:* ˈmʌs.kət, -kæt, (US) ˈmʌs.kæt, -kɑːt; *city:* ˈmʌs.kæt, (US) ˈmʌs.kɑːt, -kæt **-s** -s
muscatel ˌmʌs.kəˈtel **-s** -z
muscl|e ˈmʌs.əl **-es** -z **-ing** -ɪŋ, ˈmʌs.lɪŋ **-ed** -d
muscle-bound ˈmʌs.əlˌbaʊnd
muscle|man ˈmʌs.əl|.mæn **-men** -men
muscl|y ˈmʌs.l|i, ˈmʌs.əl|.i **-ier** -i.ər, (US) -i.ɚ **-iest** -i.ɪst, -i.əst
muscovado ˌmʌs.kəˈvɑː.dəʊ, -ˈveɪ-, (US) -doʊ
Muscovite ˈmʌs.kə.vaɪt **-s** -s
Muscovy ˈmʌs.kə.vi
muscular ˈmʌs.kjə.lər, -kjʊ-, (US) -kjə.lɚ, -kjuː- **-ly** -li ˌ**muscular** ˈ**dystrophy**
muscularity ˌmʌs.kjəˈlær.ə.ti, -kjʊˈ-, -ɪ.ti, (US) -kjəˈler.ə.t̬i, -kjuːˈ-, -ˈlær-
musculature ˈmʌs.kjə.lə.tʃər, -kjʊ-, -tʃʊər, -tjʊər, (US) -kjə.lə.tʃɚ, -kjuː- **-s** -z
mus|e, M~ mjuːz **-es** -ɪz **-ing/s** -ɪŋ/z **-ingly** -ɪŋ.li **-ed** -d
musette mjuːˈzet **-s** -s
museum mjuːˈziː.əm, mjʊ- **-s** -z
Museveni muˈsev.en.i
Musgrave ˈmʌz.greɪv
mush mʌʃ **-es** -ɪz **-ing** -ɪŋ **-ed** -t
Musharraf mʊˈʃær.æf, (US) -ˈʃɑːr.əf
mushroom ˈmʌʃ.rʊm, -ruːm, (US) -ruːm, -rʊm **-s** -z **-ing** -ɪŋ **-ed** -d
mush|y ˈmʌʃ|.i **-ier** -i.ər, (US) -i.ɚ **-iest** -i.ɪst, -i.əst **-iness** -ɪ.nəs, -ɪ.nɪs
music ˈmjuː.zɪk ˈ**music** ˌ**centre;** ˈ**music** ˌ**hall;** ˈ**music** ˌ**stand;** ˈ**music** ˌ**stool;** ˈ**music** ˌ**video;** ˌ**face the** ˈ**music**
music|al ˈmjuː.zɪ.k|əl, -zə- **-als** -əlz **-ally** -əl.i, -li **-alness** -əl.nəs, -nɪs ˈ**musical** ˌ**box;** ˌ**musical** ˈ**chairs**
musicale ˌmjuː.zɪˈkɑːl, -ˈkæl, (US) -ˈkæl **-s** -z
musicality ˌmjuː.zɪˈkæl.ə.ti, -ɪ.ti, (US) -ə.t̬i
musician mjuːˈzɪʃ.ən **-s** -z **-ly** -li **-ship** -ʃɪp
musicolog|y ˌmjuː.zɪˈkɒl.ə.dʒ|i, (US) -ˈkɑː.lə- **-ist/s** -ɪst/s
Musil ˈmuː.zɪl, -sɪl
musk mʌsk **-y** -i ˈ**musk** ˌ**deer;** ˈ**musk** ˌ**rose**
musket ˈmʌs.kɪt **-s** -s **-ry** -ri
musketeer ˌmʌs.kɪˈtɪər, -kəˈ-, (US) -kəˈtɪr **-s** -z
Muskett ˈmʌs.kɪt
Muskie ˈmʌs.ki
musk-ox ˈmʌsk.ɒks, ˌ-ˈ-, (US) ˈmʌsk.ɑːks **-en** -ən
muskrat ˈmʌsk.ræt **-s** -s
Muslim ˈmʊz.lɪm, ˈmʊs-, -ləm, (US) ˈmʌz.ləm, ˈmʌs-, ˈmʊz-, ˈmʊs-, ˈmuːz-, ˈmuːz-, -lɪm **-s** -z
muslin ˈmʌz.lɪn **-s** -z
muso ˈmjuː.zəʊ, (US) -zoʊ **-s** -z
musquash ˈmʌs.kwɒʃ, (US) -kwɑːʃ
muss mʌs **-es** -ɪz **-ing** -ɪŋ **-ed** -t
mussel ˈmʌs.əl **-s** -z
Musselburgh ˈmʌs.l.bər.ə, -ˌbʌr.ə, (US) -bɚ.ə
Mussolini ˌmʊs.əˈliː.ni, ˌmʌs-, (US) ˌmuː.səˈ-
Mussorgsky mʊˈsɔːg.ski, mə-, -ˈzɔːg-, (US) məˈsɔːrg-, -ˈsɔːrk-, -ˈzɔːrg-, -ˈzɔːrk-
Mussulman ˈmʌs.əl.mən, -mæn **-s** -z
must n, adj mʌst
must v *strong form:* mʌst; *weak forms:* məst, məs
Note: Weak-form word. There are two senses of **must**: one is concerned with supposition, or making deductions, and in this sense it is usual for the strong form to be used (e.g. 'If he's late, he must be ill'). The other sense is related to obligation: the word may be stressed, in which case it has the strong form (e.g. 'You must try harder'), or unstressed, in which case the pronunciation is either /məs/ before a consonant, or /məst/ before a vowel (e.g. 'Each of us must buy some' /ˈiːtʃ.əv.əs.məsˌbaɪ.sʌm/; 'You must always look first' /jʊ.məstˌɔːl.wɪz.lʊkˈfɜːst/ (US) /-ɑːl.weɪz.lʊkˈfɝːrst/).
mustach|e məˈstɑːʃ, mʊ-, (US) ˈmʌs.tæʃ; (US) məˈstæʃ **-es** -ɪz **-ed** -t
mustachio məˈstɑː.ʃi.əʊ, -ˈstæʃ.i-, (US) -ˈstæʃ.i.oʊ, -ˈstɑː.ʃi- **-s** -z **-ed** -d
mustang ˈmʌs.tæŋ **-s** -z
Mustapha ˈmʊs.tə.fə, ˈmʌs-, -fɑː, mʊˈstɑː.fə, mə-, (US) muːˈstɑː.fɑː, mʊ- *Egyptian:* mʊˈstɑː.fə, mə-, (US) ˈmʊs.tɑː.fɑː
Mustapha Kemal ˌmʊs.tə.fə.kemˈɑːl, -kɪˈmɑːl, (US) ˌmʊs.tɑː.fɑː.kemˈɑːl
mustard, M~ ˈmʌs.təd, (US) -tɚd ˈ**mustard** ˌ**gas;** ˈ**mustard** ˌ**plaster;** ˌ**as** ˌ**keen as** ˈ**mustard**
Mustel ˈmʌs.təl
must|er ˈmʌs.t|ər, (US) -t|ɚ **-ers** -əz, (US) -ɚz **-ering** -ər.ɪŋ **-ered** -əd, (US) -ɚd
musth mʌst
Mustique muːˈstiːk
mustn't (= **must not**) ˈmʌs.ənt
mustn't've (= must not have) ˈmʌs.ənt.əv

M

must've (= **must have**) *strong form:* ˈmʌst.ᵊv; *weak form:* məst.ᵊv
must|y ˈmʌs.t|i **-ier** -i.əʳ, (US) -i.ɚ **-iest** -i.ɪst, -i.əst **-ily** -ᵊl.i, -ɪ.li **-iness** -ɪ.nəs, -ɪ.nɪs
Mut muːt
mutability ˌmjuː.təˈbɪl.ə.ti, -ɪ.ti, (US) -t̬əˈbɪl.ə.t̬i
mutable ˈmjuː.tə.bᵊl, (US) -t̬ə-
mutant ˈmjuː.tᵊnt **-s** -s
muta|te mjuːˈteɪ|t, (US) ˈ-- **-tes** -ts **-ting** -tɪŋ, (US) -t̬ɪŋ **-ted** -tɪd, (US) -t̬ɪd
mutation mjuːˈteɪ.ʃᵊn **-s** -z
mutatis mutandis muːˌtɑː.tiːs.muˈtæn.diːs, mjuːˌteɪ.tiːs.mjuˈ-, (US) muːˌtɑː.t̬ɪs.muːˈtɑːn.dɪs, mjuːˌteɪ.t̬ɪs.mjuːˈtæn.dɪs
mut|e mjuːt **-es** -s **-ely** -li **-eness** -nəs, -nɪs **-ing** -ɪŋ, (US) ˈmjuː.t̬ɪŋ **-ed** -ɪd, (US) ˈmjuː.t̬ɪd
mutil|ate ˈmjuː.tɪ.l|eɪt, -tᵊl|.eɪt, (US) -t̬ᵊl|.eɪt **-ates** -eɪts **-ating** -eɪ.tɪŋ, (US) -eɪ.t̬ɪŋ **-ated** -eɪ.tɪd, (US) -eɪ.t̬ɪd **-ator/s** -eɪ.təʳ/z, (US) -eɪ.t̬ɚ/z
mutilation ˌmjuː.tɪˈleɪ.ʃᵊn, -tᵊlˈeɪ-, (US) -t̬ᵊlˈeɪ- **-s** -z
mutineer ˌmjuː.tɪˈnɪəʳ, -tᵊn.ɪəʳ, (US) -tᵊnˈɪr **-s** -z
mutinous ˈmjuː.tɪ.nəs, -tᵊn.əs, (US) -tᵊn.əs **-ly** -li **-ness** -nəs, -nɪs
mutin|y ˈmjuː.tɪ.n|i, -tᵊ|n.i **-ies** -iz **-ying** -i.ɪŋ **-ied** -id
mutism ˈmjuː.tɪ.zᵊm
mutt mʌt **-s** -s
mutt|er ˈmʌt|.əʳ, (US) ˈmʌt̬|.ɚ **-ers** -əz, (US) -ɚz **-ering/ly** -ᵊr.ɪŋ/li **-ered** -əd, (US) -ɚd **-erer/s** -ᵊr.əʳ/z, (US) -ɚ.ɚ/z **-erings** -ᵊr.ɪŋz, (US) -ɚ.ɪŋz
mutton, M~ ˈmʌt.ᵊn ˌ**mutton** ˌ**dressed as** ˈ**lamb**
muttonchops ˈmʌt.ᵊn.tʃɒps, (US) -tʃɑːps
muttonhead ˈmʌt.ᵊn.hed **-s** -z
mutual ˈmjuː.tʃu.əl, -tʃəl, -tʃu.əl, (US) -tju.əl **-s** -z **-ly** -i ˈ**mutual** ˌ**fund**
mutuality ˌmjuː.tʃuˈæl.ə.ti, -tjuˈ-, -ɪ.ti, (US) -tʃuˈæl.ə.t̬i
Muzak® ˈmjuː.zæk
muzzl|e ˈmʌz.ᵊl **-es** -z **-ing** -ɪŋ, ˈmʌz.l.ɪŋ **-ed** -d
muzzle-load|er ˈmʌz.ᵊlˌləʊ.d|əʳ, (US) -ˌloʊ.d|ɚ **-ers** -əz, (US) -ɚz **-ing** -ɪŋ
muzz|y ˈmʌz|.i **-ier** -i.əʳ, (US) -i.ɚ **-iest** -i.ɪst, -i.əst **-iness** -ɪ.nəs, -ɪ.nɪs
MVP ˌem.viːˈpiː **-s** -z
Mwanza məˈwæn.zə, (US) ˈmwɑːn.zɑː
my *normal form:* maɪ; *occasional weak form:* mɪ
Note: Occasional weak-form word. The strong form is used contrastively (e.g. 'My friends and your friends') or for emphasis (e.g. 'It's my turn'). Many speakers do not have a special weak form, and simply produce a brief, weakened pronunciation of /maɪ/. However, some speakers do use a weak form of **my** in common phrases. British English speakers may have the pronunciation /mi/ before a vowel (e.g. 'On my own' /ˌɒn.miˈəʊn/) and /mə/ before a consonant (e.g. 'On my back' /ˌɒn.məˈbæk/). For American English, the variant /mə/ may be used before a consonant, but /mi/ is not acceptable. In British English, there is also a special form of **my** used by lawyers in court, in phrases such as 'my Lord' or 'my learned friend', pronounced /mɪ/ or /mə/.
myalg|ia maɪˈæl.dʒ|ə, ˈ-dʒ|i.ə **-ic** -ɪk
Myanmar ˈmjæn.mɑːʳ, (US) ˈmjɑːn.mɑːr
Myatt maɪ.ət
myceli|um maɪˈsiː.li|.əm **-a** -ə
Mycenae maɪˈsiː.ni, -niː
Mycenaean ˌmaɪ.sɪˈniː.ən, -sᵊnˈiː-, (US) -səˈniː-
mycolog|ist maɪˈkɒl.ə.dʒ|ɪst, (US) -ˈkɑː.lə- **-ists** -ɪsts **-y** -i
mycolog|y maɪˈkɒl.ə.dʒ|i, (US) -ˈkɑː.lə-
myelitis ˌmaɪ.əˈlaɪ.tɪs, ˌmaɪ.ɪˈ-, maɪˈ-, -təs, (US) ˌmaɪ.əˈlaɪ.t̬ɪs, -t̬əs
Myers maɪ.əz, (US) maɪ.ɚz
Myerscough ˈmaɪ.ə.skəʊ, (US) ˈmaɪ.ɚ.skoʊ
Myfanwy məˈvæn.wi, mɪ-, -ˈfæn-
Myingyan mjɪŋˈjɑːn
Mylar® ˈmaɪ.lɑːʳ, (US) -lɑːr
myna(h) ˈmaɪ.nə **-s** -z ˈ**myna(h)** ˌ**bird**
mynheer maɪnˈhɪəʳ, -ˈheəʳ, (US) mɪˈner, -ˈnɪr; (US) maɪnˈher, -hɪr **-s** -z
Mynheer *form of address in S Africa:* məˈnɪəʳ, (US) -ˈner, -ˈnɪr
Mynott ˈmaɪ.nət
myocardi|um ˌmaɪ.əʊˈkɑː.di|.əm, -oʊˈkɑːr- **-al** -əl
myoelastic ˌmaɪ.əʊ.ɪˈlæs.tɪk, -ˈlɑː.stɪk, (US) -oʊ.ɪˈlæs.tɪk
myope ˈmaɪ.əʊp, (US) -oʊp **-s** -s
myopia maɪˈəʊ.pi.ə, (US) -ˈoʊ-
myopic maɪˈɒp.ɪk, (US) -ˈɑː.pɪk
myosin ˈmaɪ.əʊ.sɪn, (US) -oʊ-
myosis maɪˈəʊ.sɪs, (US) -ˈoʊ-
myosotis ˌmaɪ.əʊˈsəʊ.tɪs, (US) -oʊˈsoʊ.t̬ɪs
Myra ˈmaɪə.rə, (US) ˈmaɪ-
myriad ˈmɪr.i.əd **-s** -z
myrmidon, M~ ˈmɜː.mɪ.dᵊn, -dɒn, (US) ˈmɝː.mə.dɑːn, -dᵊn **-s** -z
myrrh mɜːʳ, (US) mɝː
Myrrha ˈmɪr.ə
myrrhic ˈmɜː.rɪk, ˈmɪr.ɪk, (US) ˈmɝː-
myrrhine ˈmɜː.raɪn, ˈmɪr.aɪn, (US) ˈmɝː.iːn, -ɪn
myrtle, M~ ˈmɜː.tᵊl, (US) ˈmɝː.t̬ᵊl **-s** -z
myself maɪˈself, mɪ-, (US) maɪ-, mə-
Mysia ˈmɪs.i.ə, ˈmɪʃ.ə
Mysore ˈmaɪ.sɔːʳ, (US) -sɔːr
MySpace ˈmaɪ.speɪs
mysterious mɪˈstɪə.ri.əs, (US) -ˈstɪr.i- **-ly** -li **-ness** -nəs, -nɪs
myster|y ˈmɪs.tᵊr|.i, ˈ-tr|i **-ies** -iz ˈ**mystery** ˌ**play**
mystic ˈmɪs.tɪk **-s** -s
mystic|al ˈmɪs.tɪ.k|ᵊl **-ally** -ᵊl.i, -li **-alness** -ᵊl.nəs, -nɪs
mysticism ˈmɪs.tɪ.sɪ.zᵊm, -tə-
mystification ˌmɪs.tɪ.fɪˈkeɪ.ʃᵊn, -tə-, -fəˈ-
mysti|fy ˈmɪs.tɪ|.faɪ, ˈ-tə- **-fies** -faɪz **-fying/ly** -faɪ.ɪŋ/li **-fied** -faɪd
mystique mɪˈstiːk
myth mɪθ **-s** -s
mythic ˈmɪθ.ɪk **-al** -ᵊl **-ally** -ᵊl.i, -li
Mytholmroyd ˈmaɪ.ðᵊmˌrɔɪd
mythologic ˌmɪθ.ᵊlˈɒdʒ.ɪk, ˌmaɪ.θᵊlˈ-, (US) ˌmɪθ.əˈlɑː.dʒɪk **-al** -ᵊl **-ally** -ᵊl.i, -li
mythologist mɪˈθɒl.ə.dʒɪst, maɪ-, (US) mɪˈθɑː.lə- **-s** -s
mythologiz|e, -is|e mɪˈθɒl.ə.dʒaɪz, maɪ-, (US) mɪˈθɑː.lə- **-es** -ɪz **-ing** -ɪŋ **-ed** -d
mytholog|y mɪˈθɒl.ə.dʒ|i, maɪ-, (US) -ˈθɑː.lə- **-ies** -iz
Mytilene ˌmɪt.ɪˈliː.ni, ˌmaɪ.tɪˈ-, -tᵊlˈiː-, -niː, (US) ˌmɪt.ᵊlˈiː-
myxomatosis ˌmɪk.sə.məˈtəʊ.sɪs, (US) -ˈtoʊ-

N

Pronouncing the letter N

→ *See also* **NG**

The consonant letter **n** has two pronunciations: /n/ and /ŋ/.

In most contexts, it is realized as /n/, e.g.:

nail	neɪl
mine	maɪn

Preceding the letters **k**, **qu**, **x**, and **c** realized as /k/, **n** is pronounced /ŋ/, e.g.:

bank	bæŋk
anxious	ˈæŋ*k*.ʃəs

However, when **k** is silent, **n** is pronounced as /n/, e.g.:

unknown	ʌnˈnəʊn (US) -ˈnoʊn

n, N en **-'s** -z
'n', 'n ᵊn ˌ**fish 'n' ˈchips;** ˌ**rock 'n' ˈroll**
N (abbrev. for **North**) nɔːθ, (US) nɔːrθ (abbrev. for **Northerly**) ˈnɔː.ðᵊl.i, (US) ˈnɔːr.ðɚ.li (abbrev. for **Northern**) ˈnɔː.ðᵊn, (US) ˈnɔːr.ðɚn
NAACP ˌen.dʌb.ᵊlˌeɪ.siːˈpiː
NAAFI, Naafi ˈnæf.i
Naaman ˈneɪ.ə.mən, ˈneɪ.mən
naan nɑːn, næn, (US) nɑːn **-s** -z
Naas neɪs, (US) neɪs, nɑːs
nab næb **-s** -z **-bing** -ɪŋ **-bed** -d
nabe neɪb **-s** -z
Nabisco® nəˈbɪs.kəʊ, næbˈɪs-, (US) -koʊ
nablab ˈnæb.læb **-s** -z
Nablus ˈnɑː.bləs, ˈnæb.ləs, (US) ˈnɑː.bləs, ˈnæb.ləs, -lʊs
nabob ˈneɪ.bɒb, (US) -bɑːb **-s** -z
Nabokov ˈnæb.ə.kɒf; nəˈbəʊ-, (US) nəˈbɑː.kɑːf; (US) ˈnɑː.bə-, ˈnæb.ə-
Naboth ˈneɪ.bɒθ, (US) -bɑːθ
nacelle nəˈsel, næsˈel, (US) nəˈsel **-s** -z
nacho ˈnɑː.tʃəʊ, ˈnætʃ.əʊ, (US) ˈnɑː.tʃoʊ **-s** -z
NACNE ˈnæk.niː
NACODS ˈneɪ.kɒdz, (US) -kɑːdz
nacre ˈneɪ.kəʳ, (US) -kɚ
nacreous ˈneɪ.kri.əs
nacrite ˈneɪ.kraɪt
NACRO, Nacro ˈnæk.rəʊ, (US) -roʊ
Nadal nædˈɑːl, nəˈdɑːl
Nader ˈneɪ.dəʳ, (US) -dɚ
Nadia ˈnɑː.di.ə, ˈneɪ-, (US) ˈnɑː-, ˈ-djə
Nadine neɪˈdiːn, nə-; ˈneɪ.diːn, (US) nəˈdiːn, neɪ-
nadir ˈneɪ.dɪəʳ, -dəʳ; ˈnæd.ɪəʳ, (US) ˈneɪ.dɚ, -dɪr **-s** -z
Nadir nædˈɪəʳ, (US) -ɪr
nads nædz
nae neɪ
naev|us ˈniː.v|əs **-uses** -ə.sɪz **-i** -aɪ
naff næf
NAFTA, Nafta ˈnæf.tə
nag næg **-s** -z **-ging** -ɪŋ **-ged** -d **-ger/s** -əʳ/z, (US) -ɚ/z
Naga ˈnɑː.gə **-s** -z
Nagano ˈnæg.ə.nəʊ, ˈnɑː.gə-, (US) ˈnɑː.gə.noʊ
Nagasaki ˌnæg.əˈsɑː.ki, -ˈsæk.i, (US) ˌnɑː.gəˈsɑː.ki
Nagin ˈneɪ.gɪn
Nagorno-Karabakh nəˌgɔː.nəʊˌkær.əˈbæk, (US) -ˌgɔːr.noʊ.kɑː.rɑːˈbɑːk
Nagoya nəˈgɔɪ.ə, (US) nɑːˈgɔː.jɑː, -ˈgɔɪ.ə
Nagpur ˌnægˈpʊəʳ, (US) ˌnɑːgˈpʊr
nah næː, (US) næː, nɑː

> Note: This is an informal pronunciation of **no**; in the British accent described, its usage is often semi-comical.

Nahuatl ˈnɑː.wɑː.tᵊl, -ˈ--, (US) ˈnɑː.wɑː.t̬ᵊl **-s** -z
Nahuatlan ˈnɑː.wɑː.tlən, nɑːˈwɑː-, (US) ˈnɑː.wɑː.t̬lən **-s** -z
Nahum ˈneɪ.həm, -hʌm, (US) -həm, -əm
naiad ˈnaɪ.æd, (US) ˈneɪ-, ˈnaɪ-, -əd **-s** -z
naif, naïf naɪˈiːf, nɑː-, (US) nɑː- **-s** -s
nail neɪl **-s** -z **-ing** -ɪŋ **-ed** -d ˈ**nail file;** ˈ**nail** ˌ**polish;** ˈ**nail** ˌ**scissors;** ˈ**nail** ˌ**varnish;** ˌ**hit the** ˌ**nail on the** ˈ**head**
nailbiting ˈneɪlˌbaɪ.tɪŋ, (US) -t̬ɪŋ **-ly** -li
nailbrush ˈneɪl.brʌʃ **-es** -ɪz
nailclipper ˈneɪlˌklɪp.əʳ, (US) -ɚ **-s** -z
Nailsea ˈneɪl.siː
Nailsworth ˈneɪlz.wəθ, -wɜːθ, (US) -wɚθ, -wɜːθ
Nain ˈneɪ.ɪn; neɪn
Naipaul ˈnaɪ.pɔːl, (US) -pɑːl, -pɔːl
naira ˈnaɪ.rə **-s** -z
Nairn(e) neən, (US) nern
Nairnshire ˈneən.ʃəʳ, -ʃɪəʳ, (US) ˈnern.ʃɚ, -ʃɪr
Nairobi naɪˈrəʊ.bi, (US) -ˈroʊ-
Naish næʃ, neɪʃ
naiv|e, naïv|e naɪˈiːv, nɑː-, (US) nɑː-, naɪ- **-ely** -li **-eness** -nəs, -nɪs
naiveté, naïveté nɑːˈiː.və.teɪ, naɪ-, -ˈiːv.teɪ, (US) ˌnɑː.iːvˈteɪ, ˌnaɪ-, -ˈ--
naivety, naïvety naɪˈiː.və.ti, nɑː-, (US) nɑːˈiː.və.t̬i, naɪ-
Nakasone ˌnæk.əˈsəʊ.neɪ, -ni, (US) ˌnɑːk.əˈsoʊ-
naked ˈneɪ.kɪd **-ly** -li **-ness** -nəs, -nɪs **the** ˌ**naked** ˈ**eye**
naker ˈneɪ.kəʳ, ˈnæk.əʳ, (US) ˈneɪ.kɚ **-s** -z
Nakhon Ratchasima ˌnɑː.kɒn.rɑːˈtʃɑː.si.mɑː, (US) -kɑːn-
NALGO ˈnæl.gəʊ, (US) -goʊ
Nam, 'Nam (abbrev. for **Vietnam**) nɑːm, næm
Namangan ˌnæm.æŋˈgɑːn, (US) ˌnɑː.mən-, nə-
namby-pamby ˌnæm.biˈpæm.bi **-ism** -ɪ.zᵊm
nam|e neɪm **-es** -z **-ing** -ɪŋ **-ed** -d **-eless** -ləs, -lɪs
name-brand ˈneɪm.brænd **-s** -z
namedrop ˈneɪm.drɒp, (US) -drɑːp **-s** -s **-ping** -ɪŋ **-ped** -t **-per/s** -əʳ/z, (US) -ɚ/z
namely ˈneɪm.li
nameplate ˈneɪm.pleɪt **-s** -s
namesake ˈneɪm.seɪk **-s** -s
nametag ˈneɪm.tæg **-s** -z
Namibi|a nəˈmɪb.i|.ə, næmˈɪb-, (US) nəˈmɪb- **-an/s** -ən/z
Namier ˈneɪ.mɪəʳ, -mi.əʳ, (US) -mi.ɚ
Nampula næmˈpuː.lə
Namur næmˈʊəʳ, (US) -ˈʊr, nɑːˈmʊr
nan *bread:* nɑːn, næn, (US) næn, nɑːn **-s** -z
Nan *name:* næn
nana ˈnæn.ə, (US) ˈnæn.ə, ˈnɑː.nə, -nɑː **-s** -z
Nanaimo nəˈnaɪ.məʊ, nænˈaɪ-, (US) nəˈnaɪ.moʊ
Nanak ˈnɑː.nək
nance, N~ nænts
nancy, N~ *female name or effeminate man:* ˈnænt.si ˈ**nancy** ˌ**boy**
Nancy *in France:* ˈnɑ̃ːn.si; *as if French:* nɑ̃ːnˈsiː; (US) ˈnɑ̃ːn.si, ˈnænt-
NAND nænd
nandrolone ˈnæn.drə.ləʊn
Nanette nænˈet, nəˈnet
Nanjing nænˈdʒɪŋ
nankeen næŋˈkiːn, næn-, (US) næn-
Nank|in ˌnænˈk|ɪn, ˌnæŋ-, (US) ˌnæn-, ˌnɑːn- **-ing** -ɪŋ *stress shift:* ˌ**Nankin** ˈ**highway**
Nannie ˈnæn.i
nann|y, N~ ˈnæn|.i **-ies** -iz ˈ**nanny** ˌ**goat**

nanometre, nanometer ˈnæn.əʊˌmiː.təʳ; nænˈɒm.ɪ-, (US) ˈnæn.oʊˌmiː.t̬ɚ; (US) nænˈɑː.mɪ-
Nanook ˈnæn.uːk, (US) -ʊk
nanosecond ˈnæn.əʊˌsek.ənd, (US) -oʊˌ-, -əˌ- **-s** -z
nanotechnology ˌnæn.əʊ.tekˈnɒl.ə.dʒi, (US) -oʊ.tekˈnɑː.lə-
Nansen ˈnænt.sən
Nantes nɑ̃ːnt, (US) nɑ̃ːnt, nænts
Nantucket nænˈtʌk.ɪt
Nantwich ˈnænt.wɪtʃ; *locally also:* -waɪtʃ
Naoise ˈniː.ʃə, (US) -si, ˈneɪ-
Naomi ˈneɪ.ə.mi; neɪˈəʊ-, (US) -ˈoʊ-; (US) ˈneɪ.oʊ-
nap næp **-s** -s **-ping** -ɪŋ **-ped** -t
napalm ˈneɪ.pɑːm, ˈnæp.ɑːm, (US) ˈneɪ.pɑːm **-s** -z **-ing** -ɪŋ **-ed** -d
Napa Valley ˌnæp.əˈvæl.i
nape neɪp **-s** -s
napery ˈneɪ.pər.i
Naphtali ˈnæf.tə.laɪ
naphtha ˈnæf.θə, ˈnæp-
naphthalene ˈnæf.θə.liːn, ˈnæp-
naphthol ˈnæf.θɒl, ˈnæp-, (US) -θɑːl
Napier ˈneɪ.pi.əʳ, nəˈpɪəʳ, (US) ˈneɪ.pi.ɚ, nəˈpɪr
Napierian nəˈpɪə.ri.ən, neɪ-, (US) -ˈpɪr.i-
napkin ˈnæp.kɪn **-s** -z **ˈnapkin ˌring**
Naples ˈneɪ.pəlz
napoleon, N~ nəˈpəʊ.li.ən, (US) -ˈpoʊ- **-s** -z
Napoleonic nəˌpəʊ.liˈɒn.ɪk, (US) -ˌpoʊ.liˈɑː.nɪk
napp|y ˈnæp|.i **-ies** -iz **ˈnappy ˌrash**
Napster ˈnæp.stəʳ, (US) -stɚ
Narayan nəˈraɪ.ən, (US) nɑːˈrɑː.jən
Narbonne nɑːˈbɒn, (US) nɑːrˈbɑːn
Narborough ˈnɑː.bər.ə, (US) ˈnɑːr.bɚ.oʊ
narc nɑːk, (US) nɑːrk **-s** -s
narcissi (plural of **narcissus**) nɑːˈsɪs.aɪ, (US) nɑːr-
narcissism ˈnɑː.sɪ.sɪ.zəm; nɑːˈsɪs.ɪ-, (US) ˈnɑːr.sə.sɪ-
narcissist ˈnɑː.sɪ.sɪst; nɑːˈsɪs.ɪst, (US) ˈnɑːr.sɪ- **-s** -s
narcissistic ˌnɑː.sɪˈsɪs.tɪk, (US) ˌnɑːr-
narciss|us, N~ nɑːˈsɪs|.əs, (US) nɑːr- **-uses** -ə.sɪz **-i** -aɪ
narcolepsy ˈnɑː.kəʊ.lep.si, (US) ˈnɑːr.kə-, -koʊ-
narcoleptic ˌnɑː.kəʊˈlep.tɪk, (US) ˌnɑːr.kəˈ-, -koʊ- **-s** -s
narcos|is nɑːˈkəʊ.s|ɪs, (US) nɑːrˈkoʊ- **-es** -iːz
narcotic nɑːˈkɒt.ɪk, (US) nɑːrˈkɑːt̬- **-s** -s
nard nɑːd, (US) nɑːrd
nares ˈneə.riːz, (US) ˈner.iːz
Nares neəz, (US) nerz
narghile, nargileh ˈnɑː.gɪ.leɪ, -gə-, -li, (US) ˈnɑːr.gə- **-s** -z
nark nɑːk, (US) nɑːrk **-s** -s **-ing** -ɪŋ **-ed** -t
nark|y ˈnɑː.k|i, (US) ˈnɑːr- **-ier** -i.əʳ, (US) -i.ɚ **-iest** -i.ɪst, -i.əst
Narnia ˈnɑː.ni.ə, (US) ˈnɑːr-
Narragansett ˌnær.əˈgæn.sɪt, (US) ˌnær-, ˌner-
narra|te nəˈreɪ|t, nærˈeɪ|t, (US) ˈner.eɪ|t, ˈnær-; (US) nəˈreɪ|t, nærˈeɪ|t **-tes** -ts **-ting** -tɪŋ, (US) -t̬ɪŋ **-ted** -tɪd, (US) -t̬ɪd
narration nəˈreɪ.ʃən, nærˈeɪ-, (US) nerˈeɪ-, nær- **-s** -z
narrative ˈnær.ə.tɪv, (US) ˈner.ə.t̬ɪv, ˈnær- **-s** -z
narrator nəˈreɪ.təʳ, nærˈeɪ-, ˈnær.ə.tə, (US) ˈner.eɪ.t̬ɚ, ˈnær-; (US) nəˈreɪ-, nærˈeɪ- **-s** -z
narrow ˈnær.əʊ, (US) ˈner.oʊ, ˈnær- **-s** -z **-er** -əʳ, (US) -ɚ **-est** -ɪst, -əst **-ly** -li **-ness** -nəs, -nɪs **-ing** -ɪŋ **-ed** -d **ˈnarrow ˌboat; ˌnarrow ˈgauge** *stress shift:* **ˌnarrow gauge ˈrailway**
narrowcast ˈnær.əʊˌkɑːst, (US) ˈner.oʊˌkæst, ˈnær- **-s** -s **-ing** -ɪŋ **-ed** -ɪd **-er/s** -əʳ/z, (US) -ɚ/z
narrow-minded ˌnær.əʊˈmaɪn.dɪd, (US) ˌner.oʊˈ-, ˌnær- **-ly** -li **-ness** -nəs, -nɪs *stress shift:* **ˌnarrow-minded ˈperson**
narw(h)al ˈnɑː.wəl, (US) ˈnɑːr- **-s** -z
nary ˈneə.ri, (US) ˈner.i
NASA ˈnæs.ə
nasal ˈneɪ.zəl **-s** -z **-ly** -i
nasalism ˈneɪ.zəl.ɪ.zəm
nasality neɪˈzæl.ə.ti, nə-, -ɪ.ti, (US) neɪˈzæl.ə.t̬i
nasalization, -isa- ˌneɪ.zəl.aɪˈzeɪ.ʃən, -ɪˈ-, (US) -əˈ- **-s** -z
nasaliz|e, -is|e ˈneɪ.zəl.aɪz **-es** -ɪz **-ing** -ɪŋ **-ed** -d
Nasby ˈnæz.bi
NASCAR ˈnæs.kɑːʳ, (US) -kɑːr
nascen|t ˈnæs.ən|t, ˈneɪ.sən|t **-ce** -*t*s **-cy** -*t*.si
Nasdaq ˈnæz.dæk
Naseby ˈneɪz.bi
Nash(e) næʃ
Nashville ˈnæʃ.vɪl; *locally:* -vəl
nasi goreng ˌnɑː.si.gəˈreŋ, -zi-, ˌnæs.i-
Nasmyth *name:* ˈneɪz.mɪθ, ˈneɪ.smɪθ, ˈnæz.mɪθ, ˈnæs-; *in US:* ˈneɪ.smɪθ
nasopharyngeal ˌneɪ.zəʊ.fær.ɪnˈdʒiː.əl, -ənˈ-; -fərˈɪn.dʒi.əl, -færˈ-, (US) -zoʊ.fəˈrɪn- *stress shift:* **ˌnasopharyngeal ˈport**
nasopharynx ˌneɪ.zəʊˈfær.ɪŋks, (US) -zoʊˈfer-, -ˈfær-
Nassau *in Bahamas and US:* ˈnæs.ɔː, (US) -ɔː, -ɑː *German province:* ˈnæs.aʊ, (US) ˈnɑː.saʊ *princely family:* ˈnæs.ɔː, -aʊ, (US) ˈnɑː.saʊ
Nasser ˈnæs.əʳ, ˈnɑː.səʳ, (US) ˈnæs.ɚ, ˈnɑː.sɚ
Nastase næsˈtɑː.zi, nəˈstɑː-, -zeɪ
nasturtium nəˈstɜː.ʃəm, (US) -ˈstɝː-, næsˈtɝː- **-s** -z
nast|y ˈnɑː.st|i, (US) ˈnæs.t|i **-ies** -iz **-ier** -i.əʳ, (US) -i.ɚ **-iest** -i.ɪst, -i.əst **-ily** -əl.i, -ɪ.li **-iness** -ɪ.nəs, -ɪ.nɪs
natal **adj** ˈneɪ.təl, (US) -t̬əl
Natal nəˈtæl, -ˈtɑːl
Natalie ˈnæt.əl.i, (US) ˈnæt̬-
Natasha nəˈtæʃ.ə
natation nəˈteɪ.ʃən, neɪ-, (US) neɪ-, nætˈeɪ-
natch nætʃ
NATFHE, Natfhe ˈnæt.fiː
Nathan ˈneɪ.θən, -θæn, (US) -θən
Nathaniel nəˈθæn.jəl
nation ˈneɪ.ʃən **-s** -z
national ˈnæʃ.ən.əl, ˈnæʃ.nəl **-s** -z **-ly** -i **ˌnational ˈanthem; ˌnational curˈriculum; ˌnational ˈdebt; ˌNational ˈFront; ˌNational ˈGuard; ˌNational ˈHealth ˌService; ˌnational ˈpark; ˌnational seˈcurity; ˌnational ˈservice; ˌNational ˈTrust**
national|ism ˈnæʃ.ən.əl|.ɪ.zəm, ˈnæʃ.nəl- **-ist/s** -ɪst/s
nationalistic ˌnæʃ.ən.əlˈɪs.tɪk, ˌnæʃ.nəlˈ- **-ally** -əl.i, -li
nationalit|y ˌnæʃ.ənˈæl.ə.t|i, ˌnæʃˈnæl-, -ɪ.t|i **-ies** -iz
nationalization, -isa- ˌnæʃ.ən.əl.aɪˈzeɪ.ʃən, ˌnæʃ.nəl-, -ɪˈ-, (US) -əˈ-
nationaliz|e, -is|e ˈnæʃ.ən.əl.aɪz, ˈnæʃ.nəl- **-es** -ɪz **-ing** -ɪŋ **-ed** -d
nationhood ˈneɪ.ʃən.hʊd
nation-state ˌneɪ.ʃənˈsteɪt, (US) ˈ--- **-s** -s
nationwide, N~® ˌneɪ.ʃənˈwaɪd *stress shift:* **ˌnationwide ˈsearch**
native ˈneɪ.tɪv, (US) -t̬ɪv **-s** -z **-ly** -li **ˌNative AˈMerican; ˌnative ˈspeaker**
nativit|y, N~ nəˈtɪv.ə.t|i, -ɪ.t|i, (US) -ə.t̬|i **-ies** -iz **naˈtivity ˌplay**
NATO, Nato ˈneɪ.təʊ, (US) -t̬oʊ
natron ˈneɪ.trən, -trɒn, (US) -trɑːn
natt|er ˈnæt|.əʳ, (US) ˈnæt̬|.ɚ **-ers** -əz, (US) -ɚz **-ering** -ər.ɪŋ, (US) -ɚ.ɪŋ **-ered** -əd, (US) -ɚd **-erer/s** -ər.əʳ/z, -ɚ.ɚ/z
natterjack ˈnæt.ə.dʒæk, (US) ˈnæt̬.ɚ- **-s** -s
natt|y ˈnæt|.i, (US) ˈnæt̬|.i **-ier** -i.əʳ, (US) -i.ɚ **-iest** -i.ɪst, -i.əst **-ily** -əl.i, -ɪ.li **-iness** -ɪ.nəs, -ɪ.nɪs
natural ˈnætʃ.ər.əl, -ʊ.rəl, (US) -ɚ.əl, ˈ-rəl **-s** -z **-ly** -i **-ness** -nəs, -nɪs **ˌnatural ˈchildbirth; ˌnatural ˈgas; ˌnatural ˈhistory; ˌnatural reˈsources** (US) **ˌnatural ˈresources; ˌnatural seˈlection**
natural|ism ˈnætʃ.ər.əl|.ɪ.zəm, -ʊr-, (US) -ɚ.əl-, ˈ-rəl- **-ist/s** -ɪst/s
naturalistic ˌnætʃ.ər.əlˈɪs.tɪk, -ʊr-, (US) -ɚ.əlˈ-, ˌ-rəlˈ- **-ally** -əl.i, -li
naturalization, -isa- ˌnætʃ.ər.əl.aɪˈzeɪ.ʃən, -ʊr-, -ɪˈ-, (US) -ɚ.əl.əˈ-, ˌ-rəl-
naturaliz|e, -is|e ˈnætʃ.ər.əl.aɪz, -ʊr-, (US) -ɚ.əl-, ˈ-rəl- **-es** -ɪz **-ing** -ɪŋ **-ed** -d
nature ˈneɪ.tʃəʳ, (US) -tʃɚ **-s** -z **-d** -d **ˈnature reˌserve**
natur|ism ˈneɪ.tʃər|.ɪ.zəm **-ist/s** -ɪst/s

N

naturopath ˈneɪ.tʃər.əʊ.pæθ, -tʃʊr-, ˈnætʃ.ər-, -ʊr-, (US) ˈneɪ.tʃɚ.ə- **-s** -s
naturopathic ˌneɪ.tʃər.əʊˈpæθ.ɪk, -tʃʊr-, ˌnætʃ.ər-, (US) ˌneɪ.tʃɚ.əˈ- **-ally** -əl.i, -li
naturopathy ˌneɪ.tʃərˈɒp.ə.θi, -tʃʊr-, ˌnætʃ.ərˈ-, -ʊrˈ-, (US) ˌneɪ.tʃəˈrɑː.pə-
NatWest® ˌnætˈwest *stress shift:* ˌ**NatWest** ˈ**Bank**
Naugahyde® ˈnɔː.gə.haɪd, (US) ˈnɑː.gə-, ˈnɔː-
naught nɔːt, (US) nɑːt, nɔːt **-s** -s
Naughtie ˈnɒx.ti, (US) ˈnɑːk-, ˈnɑːx-
naught|y ˈnɔː.t|i, (US) ˈnɑː.t̬|i, ˈnɔː- **-ier** -i.əʳ, (US) -i.ɚ **-iest** -i.ɪst, -i.əst **-ily** -əl.i, -ɪ.li **-iness** -ɪ.nəs, -ɪ.nɪs
Nauru nɑːˈuː.ruː; naʊˈruː, nɑː-, ˈ--, (US) nɑːˈuː.ruː
Nauruan nɑːˈuː.ruː.ən; naʊˈruː-, nɑː-, (US) nɑːˈuː.ruː- **-s** -z
nausea ˈnɔː.si.ə, -zi-, ˈ-ʒə, (US) ˈnɑː.zi.ə, ˈnɔː-, ˈ-ʒə, ˈ-ʃə, ˈ-si.ə
nause|ate ˈnɔː.si|.eɪt, -zi-, ˈ-ʒ|eɪt, (US) ˈnɑː.zi-, ˈnɔː-, -ʒi-, -ʃi-, -si- **-ates** -eɪts **-ating** -eɪ.tɪŋ, (US) -eɪ.t̬ɪŋ **-ated** -eɪ.tɪd, (US) -eɪ.t̬ɪd
nauseating ˈnɔː.si.eɪ.tɪŋ, -zi-, (US) ˈnɑː.zi-, ˈnɔː-, -ʒi-, -ʃi-, -si- **-ly** -li
nauseous ˈnɔː.si.əs, -zi-, ˈ-ʃəs, ˈ-ʒəs, (US) ˈnɑː.ʃəs, ˈnɔː-, ˈ-zi.əs **-ly** -li **-ness** -nəs, -nɪs
Nausicaa, Nausicaä nɔːˈsɪk.i.ə, -eɪ.ə, (US) nɑː-, nɔː-
nautch nɔːtʃ, (US) nɑːtʃ, nɔːtʃ **-es** -ɪz
nautic|al ˈnɔː.tɪ.k|əl, (US) ˈnɑː.t̬ɪ-, ˈnɔː- **-ally** -əl.i, -li ˌ**nautical** ˈ**mile**
nautil|us ˈnɔː.tɪ.l|əs, ˈ-təl-, (US) ˈnɑː.t̬ɪ-, ˈnɔː- **-uses** -ə.sɪz **-i** -aɪ, -iː
Navajo, Navaho ˈnæv.ə.həʊ, (US) -hoʊ, ˈnɑː.və- **-s** -z
naval ˈneɪ.vəl
Navan ˈneɪ.vən
navarin ˈnæv.ər.ɪn **-s** -z
Navarino ˌnæv.ərˈiː.nəʊ, (US) -əˈriː.noʊ
Navarre nəˈvɑːʳ, (US) -ˈvɑːr
nave neɪv **-s** -z
navel ˈneɪ.vəl **-s** -z
navicular nəˈvɪk.jə.ləʳ, -jʊ-, (US) -lɚ
navigability ˌnæv.ɪ.gəˈbɪl.ə.ti, -ɪ.ti, (US) -ə.t̬i
navigable ˈnæv.ɪ.gə.bəl **-ness** -nəs, -nɪs
navi|gate ˈnæv.ɪ|.geɪt **-gates** -geɪts **-gating** -geɪ.tɪŋ, (US) -geɪ.t̬ɪŋ **-gated** -geɪ.tɪd, (US) -geɪ.t̬ɪd
navigation ˌnæv.ɪˈgeɪ.ʃən **-al** -əl
navigator ˈnæv.ɪ.geɪ.təʳ, (US) -t̬ɚ **-s** -z
Navratilova nævˌræt.ɪˈləʊ.və, ˌnæv.rə-, (US) ˌnæv.rə.tɪˈloʊ.və, ˌnɑːv-
navv|y ˈnæv|.i **-ies** -iz
nav|y ˈneɪ.v|i **-ies** -iz ˌ**navy** ˈ**blue**
nawab, N~ nəˈwɑːb, (US) -ˈwɑːb, -ˈwɔːb **-s** -z
Nawanagar nəˈwɑː.nə.gəʳ, (US) ˌnɑː.wəˈnʌg.ɚ; (US) nəˈwɑː.nə.gɚ
Naxos ˈnæk.sɒs, (US) -sɑːs, -soʊs
nay neɪ
Nayarit ˈnɑː.jɑː.rɪt
Naylor ˈneɪ.ləʳ, (US) -lɚ
naysayer ˈneɪˌseɪ.əʳ, (US) -ɚ **-s** -z
Nazarene ˌnæz.ərˈiːn, ˈ---, (US) ˌnæz.əˈriːn, ˈ--- **-s** -z
Nazareth ˈnæz.ər.əθ, -ɪθ
Nazarite ˈnæz.ər.aɪt, (US) -ə.raɪt **-s** -s
Naze neɪz
Nazeing ˈneɪ.zɪŋ
nazi, N~ ˈnɑːt.si, (US) ˈnɑːt-, ˈnæt- **-s** -z
nazism, N~ ˈnɑːt.sɪ.zəm, (US) ˈnɑːt-, ˈnæt-
NB ˌenˈbiː; ˌnəʊ.təˈbiː.ni, -tɑːˈben.eɪ, (US) ˌenˈbiː; (US) ˌnoʊ.t̬əˈben.eɪ, -tɑːˈ-, -ˈbiː.ni
NBA ˌen.biːˈeɪ, (US) ˌen-
NBC ˌen.biːˈsiː, ˌem-, (US) ˌen-
N.C. ˌenˈsiː
NCAA ˌen.siː.eɪˈeɪ
NCO ˌen.siːˈəʊ, (US) -ˈoʊ **-s** -z
NCT ˌen.siːˈtiː
N.D. ˌenˈdiː
Ndebele ən.dɪˈbel.i, -dəˈ-, -ˈbeɪ.li, -ˈbiː-, -leɪ, (US) ən.dəˈbel.eɪ, -ˈbiː.li **-s** -z
N'Djamena ən.dʒɑːˈmeɪ.nə, -dʒæmˈeɪ-, (US) -dʒɑːˈmeɪ.nɑː
Ndola ənˈdəʊ.lə, (US) -ˈdoʊ-
NE (abbrev. for **northeast**) ˌnɔːθˈiːst, (US) ˌnɔːrθˈiːst
Neagh neɪ
Neagle ˈniː.gəl
Neal(e) niːl
Neanderthal niˈæn.də.tɑːl, -θɔːl, -təl, (US) -dɚ.θɔːl, -tɑːl
neap niːp **-s** -s
Neapolis niˈæp.ə.lɪs
neapolitan, N~ ˌniː.əˈpɒl.ɪ.tən, nɪəˈ-, ˈ-ə-, (US) ˌniː.əˈpɑː.lə- **-s** -z
near nɪəʳ, (US) nɪr **-er** -əʳ, (US) -ɚ **-est** -ɪst, -əst **-ness** -nəs, -nɪs **-s** -z **-ing** -ɪŋ **-ed** -d ˌ**Near** ˈ**East**; ˌ**near** ˈ**miss**; ˌ**nearest and** ˈ**dearest**
nearby ˌnɪəˈbaɪ, (US) ˌnɪr- *stress shift:* ˌ**nearby** ˈ**town**
nearly ˈnɪə.li, (US) ˈnɪr-
nearside ˌnɪəˈsaɪd, (US) ˌnɪr- *stress shift:* ˌ**nearside** ˈ**lane**
nearsighted ˌnɪəˈsaɪ.tɪd, (US) ˌnɪrˈsaɪ.t̬ɪd **-ness** -nəs, -nɪs *stress shift:* ˌ**nearsighted** ˈ**vision**
Neasden ˈniːz.dən
neat niːt **-er** -əʳ, (US) ˈniː.t̬ɚ **-est** -ɪst, -əst, (US) ˈniː.t̬ɪst, -t̬əst **-ly** -li **-ness** -nəs, -nɪs
neaten ˈniː.tən **-s** -z **-ing** -ɪŋ **-ed** -d
'neath niːθ
Neath niːθ
Nebo ˈniː.bəʊ, (US) -boʊ
Nebr. (abbrev. for **Nebraska**) nɪˈbræs.kə, nebˈræs-, nəˈbræs-, (US) nəˈbræs-
Nebrask|a nɪˈbræs.k|ə, nebˈræs-, nəˈbræs-, (US) nəˈbræs- **-an** -ən
Nebuchadnezzar ˌneb.jə.kədˈnez.əʳ, -jʊ-, (US) -ə.kədˈnez.ɚ, ˌneb.jə-
nebul|a ˈneb.jə.l|ə, -jʊ-, (US) -jə- **-ae** -iː **-as** -əz **-ar** -əʳ, (US) -ɚ **-ous** -əs
nebuliz|e, -is|e ˈneb.jə.laɪz, -jʊ-, (US) -jə- **-es** -ɪz **-ing** -ɪŋ **-ed** -d **-er/s** -əʳ/z, (US) -ɚ/z
nebulosity ˌneb.jəˈlɒs.ə.ti, -jʊˈ-, -ɪ.ti, (US) -jəˈlɑː.sə.t̬i
nebulous ˈneb.jə.ləs, -jʊ- **-ly** -li **-ness** -nəs, -nɪs
NEC ˌen.iːˈsiː
necessarily ˌnes.əˈser.əl.i, ˈ-ɪ-, -ɪ.li; ˈnes.ə.sər-, -ɪˈ-, (US) ˌnes.əˈser-; (US) ˈnes.ə.ser-
necessar|y ˈnes.ə.sər|.i, ˈ-ɪ-, -ser-, (US) -ser- **-ies** -iz **-iness** -ɪ.nəs, -ɪ.nɪs
necessi|tate nəˈses.ɪ|.teɪt, nɪ-, ˈ-ə-, (US) nə- **-tates** -teɪts **-tating** -teɪ.tɪŋ, (US) -teɪ.t̬ɪŋ **-tated** -teɪ.tɪd, (US) -teɪ.t̬ɪd
necessitous nəˈses.ɪ.təs, nɪ-, ˈ-ə-, (US) nəˈses.ə.t̬əs **-ly** -li **-ness** -nəs, -nɪs
necessit|y nəˈses.ə.t|i, nɪ-, -ɪ.t|i, (US) nəˈses.ə.t̬|i **-ies** -iz
neck nek **-s** -s **-ing** -ɪŋ **-ed** -t ˌ**neck and** ˈ**neck**; ˌ**neck of the** ˈ**woods**; ˌ**pain in the** ˈ**neck**; ˌ**up to one's** ˈ**neck**
Neckar ˈnek.əʳ; *as if German:* -ɑːʳ; (US) -ɚ; *as if German:* (US) -ɑːr
neckband ˈnek.bænd **-s** -z
neck|cloth ˈnek|.klɒθ, (US) -klɑːθ **-cloths** -klɒθs, -klɒðz, (US) -klɑːθs, -klɑːðz
necker|chief ˈnek.ə|.tʃɪf, -tʃiːf, (US) ˈ-ɚ- **-chiefs** -tʃɪfs **-chieves** -tʃiːvz
necklac|e ˈnek.ləs, -lɪs **-es** -ɪz **-ing** -ɪŋ **-ed** -t
necklet ˈnek.lət, -lɪt **-s** -s
neckline ˈnek.laɪn **-s** -z
necktie ˈnek.taɪ **-s** -z
neckwear ˈnek.weəʳ, (US) -wer
necro- ˈnek.rəʊ; nekˈrɒ, (US) ˈnek.roʊ, -rə; (US) nekˈrɑː, nəˈkrɑː
Note: Prefix. Normally takes either primary or secondary stress on the first syllable, e.g. **necrophile** /ˈnek.rəʊ.faɪl/ (US) /-rə-/, **necrophilia** /ˌnek.rəʊˈfɪl.i.ə/ (US) /-əˈ-/, or primary stress on the second syllable, e.g. **necrology** /nekˈrɒl.ə.dʒi/ (US) /-ˈrɑː.lə-/.
necrolatry nekˈrɒl.ə.tri, (US) -ˈrɑː.lə-, nəˈkrɑː-
necrological ˌnek.rəˈlɒdʒ.ɪ.kəl, (US) -ˈlɑː.dʒɪ-
necrolog|y nekˈrɒl.ə.dʒ|i, (US) -ˈrɑː.lə-, nəˈkrɑː- **-ies** -iz **-ist/s** -ɪst/s
necromanc|er ˈnek.rəʊ.mænt.s|əʳ, (US) -rə.mænt.s|ɚ **-ers** -əz, (US) -ɚz **-y** -i
necromantic ˌnek.rəʊˈmæn.tɪk, (US) -rə- **-ally** -əl.i, -li
necrophile ˈnek.rəʊ.faɪl, (US) -rə-, -roʊ- **-s** -z
necrophili|a ˌnek.rəʊˈfɪl.i|.ə, (US) -rəˈ-, -roʊˈfɪl.i|.ə, -ˈfiːl.j|ə **-ac/s** -æk/s
necrophilism nekˈrɒf.ɪ.lɪ.zəm, nɪˈkrɒf-, ˈ-ə-, (US) nekˈrɑː.fə-, nəˈkrɑː-
necropol|is nekˈrɒp.əl|.ɪs, nɪˈkrɒp-,

N

Ⓤ nek'rɑː.pəl-, nə'krɑː- -ises -ɪ.sɪz -i -aɪ
necrops|y 'nek.rɒp.s|i, Ⓤ -rɑːp- -ies -iz
necrosis nek'rəʊ.sɪs, nɪ'krəʊ-, Ⓤ nek'roʊ-, nə'kroʊ-
necrotic nek'rɒt.ɪk, nə'krɒt-, Ⓤ nek'rɑː.t̬ɪk, nə'krɑː-
nectar 'nek.təʳ, Ⓤ -tɚ -ous -əs
nectarial nek'teə.ri.əl, Ⓤ -'ter.i-
nectarine 'nek.tər.iːn, -ɪn, Ⓤ ˌnek.tə'riːn, '--- -s -z
nectar|y 'nek.tər|.i -ies -iz
Ned ned
Nedd|y 'ned|.i -ies -iz
Neden 'niː.dən
née, nee neɪ
need niːd -s -z -ing -ɪŋ -ed -ɪd
needful 'niːd.fəl, -fʊl -ly -i -ness -nəs, -nɪs
Needham 'niː.dəm
needl|e, N~ 'niː.dəl -es -z -ing -ɪŋ, 'niːd.lɪŋ -ed -d
needlecord 'niː.dəl.kɔːd, Ⓤ -kɔːrd
needlecraft 'niː.dəl.krɑːft, Ⓤ -kræft -s -s
needlepoint 'niː.dəl.pɔɪnt
needless 'niːd.ləs, -lɪs -ly -li -ness -nəs, -nɪs
needle|woman 'niː.dəl|ˌwʊm.ən -women -ˌwɪm.ɪn
needlework 'niː.dəl.wɜːk, Ⓤ -wɝːk
needn't 'niː.dənt
needs, N~ niːdz
need|y 'niː.d|i -ier -i.əʳ, Ⓤ -i.ɚ -iest -i.ɪst, -i.əst -ily -əl.i, -ɪ.li -iness -ɪ.nəs, -ɪ.nɪs
neep niːp -s -s
ne'er neəʳ, Ⓤ ner
ne'er-do-well 'neə.duˌwel, Ⓤ 'ner- -s -z
Neeson 'niː.sən
nefarious nɪ'feə.ri.əs, nə-, nef'eə-, Ⓤ nə'fer.i- -ly -li -ness -nəs, -nɪs
Nefertiti ˌnef.ə'tiː.ti, Ⓤ -ɚ'-
Neff® nef
neg. (abbrev. for **negative**) neg, 'neg.ə.tɪv, Ⓤ neg, 'neg.ə.t̬ɪv
nega|te nɪ'geɪ|t, nə-, neg'eɪ|t, Ⓤ nɪ'geɪ|t -tes -ts -ting -tɪŋ, Ⓤ -t̬ɪŋ -ted -tɪd, Ⓤ -t̬ɪd
negation nɪ'geɪ.ʃən, nə-, neg'eɪ-, Ⓤ nɪ'geɪ- -s -z
negativ|e 'neg.ə.tɪv, Ⓤ -t̬ɪv -es -z -ely -li -eness -nəs, -nɪs -ing -ɪŋ -ed -d **ˌnegative 'feedback**
negativ|ism 'neg.ə.tɪ.v|ɪ.zəm, Ⓤ -t̬ɪ- -ist/s -ɪst/s
negativity ˌneg.ə'tɪv.ə.ti, -ɪ.ti, Ⓤ -ə.t̬i
Negeb 'neg.eb
Negev 'neg.ev
neglect nɪ'glekt, nə-, Ⓤ nɪ- -s -s -ing -ɪŋ -ed -ɪd
neglectful nɪ'glekt.fəl, nə-, -fʊl, Ⓤ nɪ- -ly -i -ness -nəs, -nɪs
negligé(s), negligee(s) 'neg.lɪ.ʒeɪ, -lə-, -liː-, ˌ--'-, Ⓤ ˌneg.lə'ʒeɪ, '---
negligenc|e 'neg.lɪ.dʒənts, -lə- -es -ɪz
negligent 'neg.lɪ.dʒənt, -lə- -ly -li
negligibility ˌneg.lɪ.dʒə'bɪl.ə.ti, -lə-, -ɪ.ti, Ⓤ -t̬i
negligi|ble 'neg.lɪ.dʒə|.bəl, -lə-, -dʒɪ-, Ⓤ -dʒə- -bly -bli
negotiability nɪˌgəʊ.ʃi.ə'bɪl.ə.ti, nə-, ˌ-ʃə'-, -ɪ.ti, Ⓤ nɪˌgoʊ.ʃi.ə'bɪl.ə.t̬i, ˌ-ʃə'-
negotiable nɪ'gəʊ.ʃi.ə.bəl, nə-, '-ʃə-, Ⓤ nɪ'goʊ.ʃi.ə-, '-ʃə-
negoti|ate nɪ'gəʊ.ʃi|.eɪt, nə-, -si-, Ⓤ nɪ'goʊ- -ates -eɪts -ating -eɪ.tɪŋ, Ⓤ -eɪ.t̬ɪŋ -ated -eɪ.tɪd, Ⓤ -eɪ.t̬ɪd **ne'gotiating ˌtable**
negotiation nɪˌgəʊ.ʃi'eɪ.ʃən, nə-, -si'-, Ⓤ nɪˌgoʊ- -s -z
negotiator nɪ'gəʊ.ʃi.eɪ.təʳ, nə-, -si-, Ⓤ nɪ'goʊ.ʃi.eɪ.t̬ɚ, -si- -s -z
negotiatory nɪ'gəʊ.ʃi.eɪ.tər.i, nə-, -si-, Ⓤ nɪ'goʊ.ʃi.eɪ.t̬ɚ-
negress, N~ 'niː.grəs, -grɪs, -gres, Ⓤ -grɪs -es -ɪz
Negrillo nɪ'grɪl.əʊ, nə-, neg'rɪl-, Ⓤ nə'grɪl.oʊ -(e)s -z
Negrito nɪ'griː.təʊ, nə-, neg'riː-, Ⓤ nə'griː.t̬oʊ -(e)s -z
negritude 'neg.rɪ.tʃuːd, 'niː.grɪ-, -tjuːd, -grə-, Ⓤ -tuːd, -tjuːd
negro, N~ *person:* 'niː.grəʊ, Ⓤ -groʊ -es -z
Negro *river:* 'neɪ.grəʊ, 'neg.rəʊ, Ⓤ 'neɪ.groʊ
negroid 'niː.grɔɪd
negus, N~ 'niː.gəs -es -ɪz
Nehemiah ˌniː.*h*ɪ'maɪ.ə, ˌneɪ-, -*h*ə'-, Ⓤ ˌniː.ə'-, -hɪ'-
Nehru 'neə.ruː, Ⓤ 'neɪ-
neigh neɪ -s -z -ing -ɪŋ -ed -d
neighb|o(u)r 'neɪ.b|əʳ, Ⓤ -b|ɚ -o(u)rs -əz, Ⓤ -ɚz -o(u)ring -ər.ɪŋ
neighbo(u)rhood 'neɪ.bə.hʊd, Ⓤ -bɚ- -s -z **ˌneighbourhood 'watch**
neighbo(u)ring 'neɪ.bər.ɪŋ
neighbo(u)rl|y 'neɪ.bəl|.i, Ⓤ -bɚ.l|i -iness -ɪ.nəs, -ɪ.nɪs
Neil(l) niːl
Neilson 'niːl.sən
Neisse 'naɪ.sə
neither 'naɪ.ðəʳ, 'niː-, Ⓤ 'niː.ðɚ, 'naɪ-
nekton 'nek.tən, Ⓤ -tɑːn, -tən
Nell nel
Nellie 'nel.i
nelly, N~ 'nel.i
Nelson 'nel.sən
Nelsonian nel'səʊ.ni.ən, Ⓤ -'soʊ-
nematode 'nem.ə.təʊd, Ⓤ -toʊd -s -z
Nembutal® 'nem.bjə.tæl, -bjʊ-, -tɑːl, Ⓤ -bjə.tɑːl, -bjʊ-, -tɔːl
nem. con. ˌnem'kɒn, Ⓤ -'kɑːn
Neme|a nɪ'miː|.ə, nə-, nem'iː|-; 'nem.i|-, 'niː.mi|-, Ⓤ 'niː.mi|- -an -ən
nemesis, N~ 'nem.ə.sɪs, '-ɪ-, Ⓤ '-ə- nemeses 'nem.ə.siːz
Nemo 'niː.məʊ, Ⓤ -moʊ
nemophila nə'mɒf.ɪ.lə, nɪ-, -əl.ə, Ⓤ niː'mɑː.fəl.ə, nə- -s -z
Nemtsov 'nempt.sɒf, Ⓤ -sɑːv, -sɑːf
Nen nen
Nene *river:* niːn, nen
Nennius 'nen.i.əs
neo-, Neo- 'niː.*əʊ*; ni'ɒ, Ⓤ 'ni.oʊ, -ə; Ⓤ ni'ɑː
Note: Prefix. Normally either takes primary or secondary stress on the first syllable, e.g. **neonate** /'niː.əʊ.neɪt/ Ⓤ /-oʊ-/, **neonatal** /ˌniː.əʊ'neɪ.təl/ Ⓤ /-oʊ'neɪ.t̬əl/, or primary stress on the second syllable, e.g. **neologize** /ni'ɒl.ə.dʒaɪz/ Ⓤ /-'ɑː.lə-/.
neoclassic ˌniː.əʊ'klæs.ɪk, Ⓤ -oʊ'- -al -əl
neoclassic|ism ˌniː.əʊ'klæs.ɪ.s|ɪ.zəm, Ⓤ -oʊ'- -ist/s -ɪst/s
neocolonial|ism ˌniː.əʊ.kə'ləʊ.ni.əl|.ɪ.zəm, '-njəl-, Ⓤ -oʊ.kə'loʊ- -ist/s -ɪst/s
neocon 'niː.əʊ.kɒn, Ⓤ -oʊ.kɑːn -s -z
neodymium ˌniː.*əʊ*'dɪm.i.əm, Ⓤ -oʊ'-
neoimpressionism ˌniː.əʊ.ɪm'preʃ.ən.ɪ.zəm, Ⓤ -oʊ-
neoimpressionist ˌniː.əʊ.ɪm'preʃ.ən.ɪst, Ⓤ -oʊ- -s -s
Neo-Latin ˌniː.əʊ'læt.ɪn, Ⓤ -oʊ'læt.ən
neolithic, N~ ˌniː.*əʊ*'lɪθ.ɪk, Ⓤ -oʊ'-, -ə'-
neolog|ism ni'ɒl.ə.dʒ|ɪ.zəm, Ⓤ -'ɑː.lə- -isms -ɪ.zəmz -y -i
neologiz|e, -is|e ni'ɒl.ə.dʒaɪz, Ⓤ -'ɑː.lə- -es -ɪz -ing -ɪŋ -ed -d
neon 'niː.ɒn, Ⓤ -ɑːn **ˌneon 'light**
neonatal ˌniː.*əʊ*'neɪ.təl, Ⓤ -oʊ'neɪ.t̬əl, -ə'- -ly -i
neonate 'niː.*əʊ*.neɪt, Ⓤ -oʊ-, '-ə- -s -s
neophyte 'niː.*əʊ*.faɪt, Ⓤ -oʊ-, '-ə- -s -s
neoprene 'niː.*əʊ*.priːn, Ⓤ -oʊ-, '-ə-
Nepal nɪ'pɔːl, nə-, nep'ɔːl, -ɑːl, Ⓤ nə'pɔːl, -'pɑːl
Nepalese ˌnep.əl'iːz, -ɔː'liːz, Ⓤ -ə'liːz, -'liːs
Nepali nɪ'pɔː.li, nə-, nep'ɔː-, -'ɑː-, Ⓤ nɪ'pɔː-, nep'ɔː-, -'ɑː- -s -z
nepenthe nɪ'pent.θi, nə-, nep'ent-, Ⓤ nɪ'pent-
nephew 'nef.juː, 'nev-, Ⓤ 'nef- -s -z
nephrite 'nef.raɪt
nephritic nɪ'frɪt.ɪk, nə-, nef'rɪt-, Ⓤ nɪ'frɪt̬-, nef'rɪt̬-
nephritis nɪ'fraɪ.tɪs, nə-, nef'raɪ-, -təs, Ⓤ nɪ'fraɪ.t̬ɪs, -t̬əs, nef'raɪ-
nephron 'nef.rɒn, Ⓤ -rɑːn -s -z
Nephthys 'nef.tɪs, Ⓤ -θɪs
ne plus ultra ˌneɪ.plʊs'ʊl.trɑː, ˌniː-, -plʌs'-, -'ʌl-, -trə, Ⓤ -plʌs'ʌl.trə, -plʊs'-, -'ʊl-
Nepos 'niː.pɒs, 'nep.ɒs, Ⓤ 'niː.pɑːs, 'nep.ɑːs
nepotism 'nep.ə.tɪ.zəm, -ɒt.ɪ-, Ⓤ -ə.tɪ- -ist/s -ɪst/s
nepotistic nep.ə'tis.tik

Neptune ˈnep.tʃuːn, -tjuːn, (US) -tuːn, -tjuːn
neptunian, N~ nepˈtʃuː.ni.ən, -ˈtjuː-, (US) -ˈtuː-, -ˈtjuː-
neptunium nepˈtʃuː.ni.əm, -ˈtjuː-, (US) -ˈtuː-, -ˈtjuː-
nerd nɜːd, (US) nɝːd **-s** -z **-y** -i
nereid, N~ ˈnɪə.ri.ɪd, (US) ˈnɪr.i- **-s** -z
Nereus ˈnɪə.ri.uːs, -əs, (US) ˈnɪr.i.əs, -juːs
Neri ˈnɪə.ri, (US) ˈnɪr.i, ˈner-, ˈneɪ.ri
Nero ˈnɪə.rəʊ, (US) ˈnɪr.oʊ, ˈniː.roʊ
Neruda nəˈruː.də, nerˈuː-
nerv|e nɜːv, (US) nɝːv **-es** -z **-ing** -ɪŋ **-ed** -d ˈ**nerve** ˌ**cell**; ˈ**nerve** ˌ**centre**; ˈ**nerve** ˌ**gas**; ˌ**get on** ˌ**someone's** ˈ**nerves**
nerveless ˈnɜːv.ləs, -lɪs, (US) ˈnɝːv- **-ly** -li **-ness** -nəs, -nɪs
nerve-racking, nerve-wracking ˈnɜːvˌræk.ɪŋ, (US) ˈnɝːv-
nerves nɜːvz, (US) nɝːvz
nervine ˈnɜː.viːn, (US) ˈnɝː-, -vaɪn
nervous ˈnɜː.vəs, (US) ˈnɝː- **-ly** -li **-ness** -nəs, -nɪs ˌ**nervous** ˈ**break-down**; ˈ**nervous** ˌ**system**
nerv|y ˈnɜː.v|i, (US) ˈnɝː- **-ier** -i.əʳ, (US) -i.ɚ **-iest** -i.ɪst, -i.əst **-ily** -əl.i, -ɪ.li **-iness** -ɪ.nəs, -ɪ.nɪs
Nesbit(t) ˈnez.bɪt
Nescafé® ˈnes.kə.feɪ, -kæf.eɪ, (US) ˈnes.kə.feɪ, -kæf.eɪ, ˌ--ˈ-
nescien|ce ˈnes.i.ən|*t*s, (US) ˈneʃ.ən|*t*s, ˈ-i.ən|*t*s **-t** -t
Nesfield ˈnes.fiːld
Nesquik® ˈnes.kwɪk
ness, N~ nes **-es** -ɪz
-ness *noun-forming suffix:* nəs, nɪs
Note: Suffix. When added to a stem to form a noun, **-ness** does not change the existing stress pattern, e.g. **happy** /ˈhæp.i/, **happiness** /ˈhæp.ɪ.nəs/.
-ness *in place names:* ˈnes
Note: In place names, the suffix **-ness** normally takes primary stress, e.g. **Inverness** /ˌɪn.vəˈnes/ (US) /-vɚˈ-/. However, place names containing **-ness** are subject to stress shift; see individual entries.
Nessie ˈnes.i
nest nest **-s** -s **-ing** -ɪŋ **-ed** -ɪd ˈ**nest** ˌ**egg**
Nesta ˈnes.tə
Nestlé® ˈnes.leɪ, -li, -əl, (US) ˈnes.li
nestl|e ˈnes.əl **-es** -z **-ing** -ɪŋ, ˈnes.lɪŋ **-ed** -d
nestling ˈnes*t*.lɪŋ **-s** -z
Neston ˈnes.tən
Nestor ˈnes.tɔːʳ, -təʳ, (US) -tɚ, -tɔːr
Nestorian nesˈtɔː.ri.ən, (US) -ˈtɔːr.i- **-s** -z
net, N~ net **-s** -s **-ting** -ɪŋ, (US) ˈneṭ.ɪŋ **-ted** -ɪd, (US) ˈneṭ.ɪd
Netanyahu ˌnet.ənˈjɑː.hu, -ænˈ-, (US) ˌnet.ɑːnˈjɑː.hu, -ənˈ-
netball ˈnet.bɔːl, (US) -bɔːl, -bɑːl
netbook ˈnet.bʊk **-s** -s
netcronym ˈnet.krəʊ.nɪm, ˈnek-, (US) ˈnet.krə- **-s** -z
nether ˈneð.əʳ, (US) -ɚ **-most** -məʊst, (US) -moʊst
Nether|land ˈneð.ə|lənd, -ə|l.ənd, (US) -ɚ|lənd **-lands** -ləndz **-lander/s** -lən.dəʳ/z, (US) -lən.dɚ/z
netherworld ˈneð.ə.wɜːld, (US) -ɚ.wɝːld **-s** -z
netiquette ˈnet.ɪ.ket, (US) ˈneṭ-
netizen ˈnet.ɪ.zən, -ə-, (US) ˈneṭ- **-s** -z
Netley ˈnet.li
Netscape® ˈnet.skeɪp
netsuke ˈnet.skeɪ, -ski, ˈ-sʊ.ki, -keɪ, (US) -sʊ.ki, -sə.keɪ **-s** -z
Nettie, Netty ˈnet.i, (US) ˈneṭ-
netting ˈnet.ɪŋ, (US) ˈneṭ-
nettl|e ˈnet.əl, (US) ˈneṭ- **-es** -z **-ing** -ɪŋ, ˈnet.lɪŋ **-ed** -d ˈ**nettle** ˌ**rash**; ˌ**grasp the** ˈ**nettle**
Nettlefold ˈnet.əl.fəʊld, (US) ˈneṭ.əl.foʊld
nettlerash ˈnet.əl.ræʃ, (US) ˈneṭ-
Nettleship ˈnet.əl.ʃɪp, (US) ˈneṭ-
nettlesome ˈnet.əl.səm, (US) ˈneṭ-
network ˈnet.wɜːk, (US) -wɝːk **-s** -s **-ing** -ɪŋ **-ed** -t
Neuchâtel ˌnɜː.ʃætˈel, -ʃəˈtel, (US) ˌnuː.ʃəˈtel, ˌnɜː-
Neufchâtel ˌnɜː.ʃætˈel, -ʃəˈtel, (US) ˌnuː.ʃəˈtel, ˌnɜː-
neum(e) njuːm, (US) nuːm, njuːm **-s** -z
neural ˈnjʊə.rəl, ˈnjɔː-, (US) ˈnʊr.əl, ˈnjʊr-, ˈnɝː- ˌ**neural** ˈ**network**
neuralg|ia njʊəˈræl.dʒ|ə, njɔː-, njəʳˈæl-, njʊˈræl-, (US) nʊˈræl-, njʊ-, nə- **-ic** -ɪk
neurasthenia ˌnjʊə.rəsˈθiː.ni.ə, ˌnjɔː-, (US) ˌnʊr.æsˈ-, ˌnjʊr-
neurasthenic ˌnjʊə.rəsˈθen.ɪk, ˌnjɔː-, (US) ˌnʊr.æsˈ-, ˌnjʊr- **-s** -s
neuritis njʊəˈraɪ.tɪs, njɔː-, njəʳˈaɪ-, njʊˈraɪ-, -təs, (US) nʊˈraɪ.ṭɪs, njʊ-, -ṭəs
neuro- ˈnjʊə.rəʊ, ˈnjɔː-, njʊəˈrɒ, njɔːˈ-, (US) ˈnʊr.oʊ, ˈnjʊr-, ˈ-ə
Note: Prefix. Normally either takes primary or secondary stress on the first syllable, e.g. **neurosurgeon** /ˈnjʊə.rəʊˌsɜː.dʒən/ (US) /ˌnʊr.oʊˈsɝː.dʒən/, **neurological** /ˌnjʊə.rəˈlɒdʒ.ɪ.kəl/ (US) /ˌnʊr.əˈlɑː.dʒɪ-/, or primary stress on the second syllable, e.g. **neurologist** /njʊəˈrɒl.ə.dʒɪst/ (US) /nʊˈrɑː.lə-/.
neurologi|cal ˌnjʊə.rəˈlɒdʒ.ɪ|.kəl, ˌnjɔː-, (US) ˌnʊr.əˈlɑː.dʒɪ-, ˌnjʊr- **-cally** -kəl.i, -kli
neurolog|ist njʊəˈrɒl.ə.dʒ|ɪst, njɔː-, njəʳˈɒl-, njʊˈrɒl-, (US) nʊˈrɑː.lə-, njʊ- **-ist/s** -ɪst/s **-y** -i
neuron ˈnjʊə.rɒn, ˈnjɔː-, (US) ˈnʊr.ɑːn, ˈnjʊr- **-s** -z
neurone ˈnjʊə.rəʊn, ˈnjɔː-, (US) ˈnʊr.oʊn, ˈnjʊr- **-s** -z
neuroscien|ce ˌnjʊə.rəʊˈsaɪ.ən|*t*s, ˌnjɔː-, ˈnjʊə.rəʊˌ-, ˈnjɔː-, (US) ˌnʊr.oʊˈsaɪ-, ˌnjʊr-, ˈnʊr.oʊˌsaɪ-, ˈnjʊr- **-ces** -*t*sɪz **-tist/s** -tɪst/s
neuros|is njʊəˈrəʊ.s|ɪs, njɔː-, njəʳˈəʊ-, njʊˈrəʊ-, (US) nʊˈroʊ-, njʊ-, nə- **-es** -iːz
neurosurgeon ˈnjʊə.rəʊˌsɜː.dʒən, ˌnjɔː-, ˌ-ˈ--, (US) ˌnʊr.oʊˈsɝː-, ˌnjʊr- **-s** -z
neurosurg|ery ˌnjʊə.rəʊˈsɜː.dʒ|əʳr.i, ˌnjɔː-, (US) ˌnʊr.oʊˈsɝː-, ˌnjʊr- **-ical** -ɪ.kəl
neurotic njʊəˈrɒt.ɪk, njɔː-, njəʳˈrɒt-, njʊˈrɒt-, (US) nʊˈrɑː.ṭɪk, njʊ-, nə- **-s** -s **-ally** -əl.i, -li
neurotransmitter ˌnjʊə.rəʊ.trænzˈmɪt.əʳ, ˈ---ˌ--, ˌnjɔː-, (US) ˌnʊr.oʊ.trænˈsmɪṭ.ɚ, ˌnjʊr-, -trænzˈmɪṭ- **-s** -z
neut|er ˈnjuː.t|əʳ, (US) ˈnuː.ṭ|ɚ, ˈnjuː- **-ers** -əz, (US) -ɚz **-ering** -əʳr.ɪŋ **-ered** -əd, (US) -ɚd
neutral ˈnjuː.trəl, (US) ˈnuː-, ˈnjuː- **-s** -z **-ly** -i **-ness** -nəs, -nɪs
neutralism ˈnjuː.trəl.ɪ.zəm, (US) ˈnuː-, ˈnjuː-
neutralist ˈnjuː.trəl.ɪst, (US) ˈnuː-, ˈnjuː- **-s** -s
neutrality njuːˈtræl.ə.ti, -ɪ.ti, (US) nuːˈtræl.ə.ṭi, njuː-
neutralization, -isa- ˌnjuː.trəl.aɪˈzeɪ.ʃən, -ɪˈ-, (US) ˌnuː.trəl.əˈ-, ˌnjuː-
neutraliz|e, -is|e ˈnjuː.trəl.aɪz, (US) ˈnuː-, ˈnjuː- **-es** -ɪŋ **-ing** -ɪz **-ed** -d
neutrino njuːˈtriː.nəʊ, (US) nuːˈtriː.noʊ, njuː- **-s** -z
neutron ˈnjuː.trɒn, (US) ˈnuː.trɑːn, ˈnjuː- **-s** -z ˈ**neutron** ˌ**bomb**
Nev. (abbrev. for **Nevada**) nəˈvɑː.də, nɪ-, nevˈɑː-, (US) nəˈvæd.ə, -ˈvɑː.də
Neva ˈneɪ.və, ˈniː-, (US) ˈniː-
Nevada nəˈvɑː.də, nɪ-, nevˈɑː-, (US) nəˈvæd.ə, -ˈvɑː.də
névé ˈnev.eɪ, (US) neɪˈveɪ, ˈ--
Neve niːv
never ˈnev.əʳ, (US) -ɚ
never-ending ˌnev.əʳˈen.dɪŋ, (US) ˈnev.ɚ.en-
Neverland ˈnev.ə.lænd, (US) -ɚ-
nevermore ˌnev.əˈmɔːʳ, (US) -ɚˈmɔːr
never-never ˌnev.əˈnev.əʳ, (US) ˌ-ɚˈnev.ɚ **on the** ˌ**never-**ˈ**never**; ˌ**never-**ˈ**never** ˌ**land**
nevertheless ˌnev.ə.ðəˈles, (US) ˌ-ɚ-
Nevey ˈnev.i
Nevil ˈnev.əl, -ɪl, (US) -əl
Nevill(e) ˈnev.əl, -ɪl, (US) -əl
Nevin ˈnev.ɪn
Nevinson ˈnev.ɪn.sən
Nevis *in Scotland:* ˈnev.ɪs *in West Indies:* ˈniː.vɪs
nev|us ˈniː.v|əs **-uses** -ə.sɪz **-i** -aɪ
new njuː, (US) nuː, njuː **-er** -əʳ, (US) -ɚ **-est** -ɪst, -əst **-ish** -ɪʃ **-ly** -li **-ness** -nəs, -nɪs ˌ**New** ˈ**Age** *stress shift:* ˌ**New Age** ˈ**traveller**; ˌ**new** ˈ**broom**; ˌ**New** ˈ**Brunswick**; ˌ**New Cale**ˈ**donia**; ˌ**New** ˈ**Deal**; ˌ**New** ˈ**Delhi**; ˌ**New** ˈ**England** *stress shift:* ˌ**New England** ˈ**coast**; ˌ**New** ˈ**Forest** *stress shift:* ˌ**New Forest** ˈ**ponies**; ˌ**New** ˈ**Hampshire** *stress shift:* ˌ**New Hampshire** ˈ**primary**; ˌ**New** ˈ**Jersey** *stress shift:* ˌ**New**

N

Pronouncing the letters NG

The main realization for the consonant digraph **ng** is /ŋ/, e.g.:

sing sɪŋ
ringing ˈrɪŋ.ɪŋ

Other pronunciations are found, one being /ŋg/, e.g.:

finger ˈfɪŋ.gəʳ ⓤⓢ -gɚ

In addition

In many words spelt **nge**, or where **ng** is followed by **i** or **y**, the pronunciation is /ndʒ/, e.g.:

change tʃeɪndʒ
engine ˈen.dʒɪn

Jersey ˈturnpike; ˌnew ˈman; ˌNew ˈMexico; ˌNew ˈQuay *stress shift:* **ˌNew Quay ˈharbour; ˌNew South ˈWales; ˌNew ˈTestament; ˌNew ˈWave** *stress shift:* **ˌNew Wave ˈband; ˌNew ˈWorld** *stress shift:* **ˌNew World ˈSymphony; ˌNew ˈYear** *stress shift:* **ˌNew Year ˈparty; ˌNew ˌYear's ˈDay; ˌNew ˌYear's ˈEve**

Newark ˈnjuː.ək, ⓤⓢ ˈnuː.ɚk, ˈnjuː-

Newbery ˈnjuː.bᵊr.i, ⓤⓢ ˈnuː.ber-, ˈnjuː-

newbie ˈnjuː.bi, ⓤⓢ ˈnuː-, ˈnjuː- **-s** -z

Newbiggin *place:* ˈnjuː.bɪ.gɪn, ⓤⓢ ˈnuː-, ˈnjuː- *surname:* ˈnjuː.bɪ.gɪn, -ˈbɪg.ɪn, ⓤⓢ ˈnuː-, ˈnjuː-, -ˈbɪg.ɪn

Newbold ˈnjuː.bəʊld, ⓤⓢ ˈnuː.boʊld, ˈnjuː-

Newbolt ˈnjuː.bəʊlt, ⓤⓢ ˈnuː.boʊlt, ˈnjuː-

newborn ˌnjuːˈbɔːn, ⓤⓢ ˈnuː.bɔːrn, ˈnjuː- *stress shift, British only:* **ˌnewborn ˈbaby**

Newbridge ˈnjuː.brɪdʒ, ⓤⓢ ˈnuː-, ˈnjuː-

Newburg(h) *in the UK:* ˈnjuː.bᵊr.ə, ⓤⓢ ˈnuː-, ˈnjuː- *in the US:* ˈnjuː.bɜːg, ⓤⓢ ˈnuː.bɝːg, ˈnjuː-

Newburn ˈnjuː.bɜːn, ⓤⓢ ˈnuː.bɝːn, ˈnjuː-

Newbury ˈnjuː.bᵊr.i, ⓤⓢ ˈnuː.ber-, ˈnjuː-, -bɚ-

Newby ˈnjuː.bi, ⓤⓢ ˈnuː-, ˈnjuː-

Newcastle ˈnjuːˌkɑː.sᵊl, ⓤⓢ ˈnuːˌkæs.ᵊl, ˈnjuː-

Newcastle-under-Lyme ˌnjuː.kɑː.sᵊlˌʌn.dəˈlaɪm, ⓤⓢ ˌnuː.kæs.ᵊlˌʌn.dɚˈ-, ˌnjuː-

Newcastle upon Tyne ˌnjuː.kɑː.sᵊl.ə.pɒnˈtaɪn, ⓤⓢ ˌnuː.kæs.ᵊl.ə.pɑːn-, ˌnjuː-

> Note: /njuːˈkæs.ᵊl/ is the local form.

Newcome ˈnjuː.kəm, ⓤⓢ ˈnuː-, ˈnjuː- **-s** -z

newcomer ˈnjuːˌkʌm.əʳ, ⓤⓢ ˈnuːˌkʌm.ɚ, ˈnjuː- **-s** -z

Newdigate ˈnjuː.dɪ.geɪt, -gɪt, -gət, ⓤⓢ ˈnuː.dɪ.geɪt, ˈnjuː-, -gət

Newe njuː, ⓤⓢ nuː, njuː

newel ˈnjuː.əl, ⓤⓢ ˈnuː.əl, ˈnjuː- **-s** -z **ˈnewel ˌpost**

Newell ˈnjuː.əl, ⓤⓢ ˈnuː.əl, ˈnjuː-

Newey ˈnjuː.i, ⓤⓢ ˈnuː-, ˈnjuː-

newfangled ˌnjuːˈfæŋ.gᵊld, ⓤⓢ ˌnuː-, ˌnjuː- *stress shift:* **ˌnewfangled ˈways**

new-fashioned ˌnjuːˈfæʃ.ᵊnd, ⓤⓢ ˈnuːˌfæʃ-, ˈnjuː-

new-found ˌnjuːˈfaʊnd, ⓤⓢ ˌnuː-, ˌnjuː- *stress shift:* **ˌnew-found ˈlove**

Newfoundland *place:* ˈnjuː.fᵊnd.lənd, -lænd; njuːˈfaʊnd-; ˌnjuː.fᵊndˈlænd, ⓤⓢ ˈnuː.fənd.lənd, ˈnjuː-, -lænd; ⓤⓢ ˌnuː.faʊndˈlænd, ˌnjuː-; ⓤⓢ nuːˈfaʊnd.lənd, njuː-, -lænd **-er/s** -əʳ/z, ⓤⓢ -ɚ/z *dog:* njuːˈfaʊnd.lənd, ⓤⓢ ˈnuː.fənd.lənd, ˈnjuː-, -lænd; ⓤⓢ nuːˈfaʊnd-, njuː- **-s** -z

> Note: /ˌnjuː.fᵊndˈlænd/ is the local form; it is also the nautical pronunciation in England.

Newgate ˈnjuː.geɪt, -gɪt, -gət, ⓤⓢ ˈnuː.geɪt, ˈnjuː-

Newham ˈnjuː.əm; njuːˈhæm, ⓤⓢ ˈnuː.əm, ˈnjuː-; ⓤⓢ nuːˈhæm, njuː-

Newhaven ˈnjuː.heɪ.vᵊn, -ˈ--, ⓤⓢ ˈnuː.heɪ-, ˈnjuː-, -ˈ--

Newington ˈnjuː.ɪŋ.tən, ⓤⓢ ˈnuː-, ˈnjuː-

new-laid ˌnjuːˈleɪd, ⓤⓢ ˌnuː-, ˌnjuː- *stress shift:* **ˌnew-laid ˈeggs**

Newlands ˈnjuː.ləndz, ⓤⓢ ˈnuː-, ˈnjuː-

newlywed ˈnjuː.li.wed, ⓤⓢ ˈnuː-, ˈnjuː- **-s** -z

Newman ˈnjuː.mən, ⓤⓢ ˈnuː-, ˈnjuː-

Newmarket ˈnjuː.mɑː.kɪt, ⓤⓢ ˈnuː.mɑːr-, ˈnjuː-

Newnes njuːnz, ⓤⓢ nuːnz, njuːnz

Newnham ˈnjuː.nəm, ⓤⓢ ˈnuː-, ˈnjuː-

New Orleans ˌnjuːˈɔː.li.ənz, ˈ-lɪənz, ˈ-lənz; -ɔːˈliːnz, ⓤⓢ ˌnuːˈɔːr.li.ənz, ˌnjuː-, ˈ-lənz; ⓤⓢ -ɔːrˈliːnz

Newport ˈnjuː.pɔːt, ⓤⓢ ˈnuː.pɔːrt, ˈnjuː-

Newport Pagnell ˌnjuː.pɔːtˈpæg.nᵊl, ⓤⓢ ˌnuː.pɔːrtˈ-, ˌnjuː-

Newquay ˈnjuː.ki, ⓤⓢ ˈnuː-, ˈnjuː-

New Rossington ˌnjuːˈrɒs.ɪŋ.tən, ⓤⓢ ˌnuːˈrɑː.sɪŋ-, ˌnjuː-

Newry ˈnjʊə.ri, ⓤⓢ ˈnʊr.i, ˈnjʊr-

news njuːz, ⓤⓢ nuːz, njuːz **ˈnews ˌagency; ˈnews ˌconference**

newsagent ˈnjuːzˌeɪ.dʒᵊnt, ⓤⓢ ˈnuːz-, ˈnjuːz- **-s** -s

newsboy ˈnjuːz.bɔɪ, ⓤⓢ ˈnuːz-, ˈnjuːz- **-s** -z

newsbreak ˈnjuːz.breɪk, ⓤⓢ ˈnuːz-, ˈnjuːz- **-s** -s

newscast ˈnjuːz.kɑːst, ⓤⓢ ˈnuːz.kæst, ˈnjuːz- **-s** -s **-ing** -ɪŋ **-er/s** -əʳ/z, ⓤⓢ -ɚ/z

newscopy ˈnjuːzˌkɒp.i, ⓤⓢ ˈnuːzˌkɑː.pi, ˈnjuːz-

newsdealer ˈnjuːzˌdiː.ləʳ, ⓤⓢ ˈnuːzˌdiː.lɚ, ˈnjuːz- **-s** -z

newsflash ˈnjuːz.flæʃ, ⓤⓢ ˈnuːz-, ˈnjuːz- **-es** -ɪz

newsgroup ˈnjuːz.gruːp, ⓤⓢ ˈnuːz-, ˈnjuːz- **-s** -s

newshound ˈnjuːz.haʊnd, ⓤⓢ ˈnuːz-, ˈnjuːz- **-s** -z

newsletter ˈnjuːzˌlet.əʳ, ⓤⓢ ˈnuːzˌleṭ.ɚ, ˈnjuːz- **-s** -z

news|man ˈnjuːz|.mən, -mæn, ⓤⓢ ˈnuːz-, ˈnjuːz- **-men** -men, -mən

newsmonger ˈnjuːzˌmʌŋ.gəʳ, ⓤⓢ ˈnuːzˌmʌŋ.gɚ, ˈnjuːz-, -ˌmɑːŋ- **-s** -z

newspaper ˈnjuːsˌpeɪ.pəʳ, ˈnjuːz-, ⓤⓢ ˈnuːzˌpeɪ.pɚ, ˈnjuːz- **-s** -z

newspeak, N~ ˈnjuː.spiːk, ⓤⓢ ˈnuː-, ˈnjuː-

news|person ˈnjuːz|ˌpɜː.sᵊn, ⓤⓢ ˈnuːz|ˌpɝː-, ˈnjuːz- **-people** -ˌpiː.pᵊl

newsprint ˈnjuːz.prɪnt, ⓤⓢ ˈnuːz-, ˈnjuːz-

newsreader ˈnjuːzˌriː.dəʳ, ⓤⓢ ˈnuːzˌriː.dɚ, ˈnjuːz- **-s** -z

newsreel ˈnjuːz.riːl, ⓤⓢ ˈnuːz-, ˈnjuːz- **-s** -z

newsroom ˈnjuːz.rʊm, -ruːm, ⓤⓢ ˈnuːz.ruːm, ˈnjuːz-, -rʊm **-s** -z

news-sheet ˈnjuːz.ʃiːt, ˈnjuːʒ-, ⓤⓢ ˈnuːz-, ˈnjuːz- **-s** -s

newsstand ˈnjuːz.stænd, ⓤⓢ ˈnuːz-, ˈnjuːz- **-s** -z

Newstead ˈnjuː.stɪd, -sted, ⓤⓢ ˈnuː-, ˈnjuː-

newsvendor ˈnjuːzˌven.dəʳ, ⓤⓢ ˈnuːzˌven.dɚ, ˈnjuːz- **-s** -z

Newsweek ˈnjuːz.wiːk, ⓤⓢ ˈnuːz-, ˈnjuːz-

news|woman ˈnjuːz|ˌwʊm.ən, ⓤⓢ ˈnuːz-, ˈnjuːz- **-women** -ˌwɪm.ɪn

newsworthy ˈnjuːzˌwɜː.ði, ⓤⓢ ˈnuːzˌwɝː-, ˈnjuːz-

news|y ˈnjuː.z|i, ⓤⓢ ˈnuː-, ˈnjuː- **-iness** -ɪ.nəs, -ɪ.nɪs

newt njuːt, ⓤⓢ nuːt, njuːt **-s** -s

New Testament ˌnjuːˈtes.tə.mənt, ⓤⓢ ˌnuː-, ˌnjuː-

newton, N~ ˈnjuː.tᵊn, ⓤⓢ ˈnuː-, ˈnjuː-

Newtonian njuːˈtəʊ.ni.ən, ⓤⓢ nuːˈtoʊ-, njuː-

Newton-le-Willows ˌnjuː.tᵊn.liˈwɪl.əʊz, ⓤⓢ ˌnuː.tᵊn.liˈwɪl.oʊz, ˌnjuː-

Newtown ˈnjuː.taʊn, ⓊⓈ ˈnuː-, ˈnjuː-
Newtownabbey ˌnjuː.tᵊnˈæb.i, ⓊⓈ ˌnuː-, ˌnjuː-
Newtownards ˌnjuː.tᵊnˈɑːdz, ⓊⓈ ˌnuː.tᵊnˈɑːrdz, ˌnjuː-
Newtown St Boswells ˌnjuː.tᵊn.sᵊntˈbɒz.welz, ⓊⓈ ˌnuː.tᵊn.sᵊntˈbɑːz-, ˌnjuː-
New York ˌnjuːˈjɔːk, ⓊⓈ ˌnuːˈjɔːrk, ˌnjuː- **-er/s** -əʳ/z, ⓊⓈ -ɚ/z *stress shift, see compound:* **ˌNew York ˈCity**
New Zealand ˌnjuːˈziː.lənd, ⓊⓈ ˌnuː-, ˌnjuː- **-er/s** -əʳ/z, ⓊⓈ -ɚ/z
next nekst **ˌnext ˈdoor** *stress shift:* **ˌnext door ˈneighbours; ˌnext of ˈkin**
nexus ˈnek.səs **-es** -ɪz
NFL ˌen.efˈel
Ng ɪŋ, əŋ, eŋ
Ngaio ˈnaɪ.əʊ; *as if Maori:* ˈŋaɪ-; ⓊⓈ -oʊ
Ngami ᵊŋˈgɑː.mi, ⓊⓈ ᵊn-, ᵊŋ-
ngultrum ᵊŋˈguːl.trəm, ⓊⓈ -ˈʊl.trʊm; ⓊⓈ ənˈgʌl.trəm, əŋ- **-s** -z
ngwee ᵊŋˈgweɪ, ⓊⓈ -ˈgwiː
N.H. ˌenˈeɪtʃ
NHL ˌen.eɪtʃˈel
NHS ˌen.eɪtʃˈes
NI ˌenˈaɪ
niacin ˈnaɪ.ə.sɪn
Niagara naɪˈæg.ᵊr.ə, ⓊⓈ ˈ-rə, ˈ-ɚ.ə **Niˌagara ˈFalls**
Niall ˈnaɪ.əl, naɪl, niːl
Niamey niˈɑː.meɪ; nɪəˈmeɪ, ⓊⓈ niˈɑː.meɪ; ⓊⓈ njɑːˈmeɪ
Niamh niːv, nɪəv
nib nɪb **-s** -z
nibbl|e ˈnɪb.ᵊl **-es** -z **-ing** -ɪŋ, ˈnɪb.lɪŋ **-ed** -d **-er/s** -əʳ/z, -ɚ/z
Nibelung ˈniː.bə.lʊŋ, -bɪ-, ⓊⓈ -bə- **-s** -z **-en** -ən
Nibelungenlied ˌniː.bəˈlʊŋ.ənˌliːt, -ˌliːd
niblick ˈnɪb.lɪk **-s** -s
NiCad® ˈnaɪ.kæd
Nicaea naɪˈsiː.ə
NICAM ˈnaɪ.kæm
Nicaragu|a ˌnɪk.ᵊrˈæg.ju|.ə, -ˈɑː.gju-; -ˈɑː.gw|ə, -ˈæg.w|ə, ⓊⓈ -əˈrɑː.gw|ə **-an/s** -ən/z
nic|e adj naɪs **-er** -əʳ, ⓊⓈ -ɚ **-est** -ɪst, -əst **-ely** -li **-eness** -nəs, -nɪs
Nice *in France:* niːs
nicely ˈnaɪs.li
Nicene ˈnaɪ.siːn, -ˈ- **ˌNicene ˈCreed**
nicet|y ˈnaɪ.sə.t|i, -sɪ-, ⓊⓈ -sə.ţ|i **-ies** -iz
nich|e niːʃ, ⓊⓈ nɪtʃ, niːʃ **-es** -ɪz **-ed** -t
Nichol(l) ˈnɪk.ᵊl **-s** -z
Nicholas ˈnɪk.ᵊl.əs
Nicholson ˈnɪk.ᵊl.sᵊn
nick, N~ nɪk **-s** -s **-ing** -ɪŋ **-ed** -t **in the ˌnick of ˈtime**
nickel ˈnɪk.ᵊl **-s** -z **-(l)ing** -ɪŋ **-(l)ed** -d
nickel-and-dime ˌnɪk.ᵊl.ᵊndˈdaɪm **-s** -z **-ing** -ɪŋ **-ed** -d
nickelodeon ˌnɪk.ᵊlˈəʊ.di.ən, ⓊⓈ -ˈoʊ- **-s** -z
nicker ˈnɪk.əʳ, ⓊⓈ -ɚ
Nicklaus ˈnɪk.laʊs, -ləs, ⓊⓈ -ləs
Nickleby ˈnɪk.ᵊl.bi
Nicklin ˈnɪk.lɪn
nicknack ˈnɪk.næk **-s** -s
nicknam|e ˈnɪk.neɪm **-es** -z **-ing** -ɪŋ **-ed** -d
Nicobar ˈnɪk.əʊ.bɑːʳ, ⓊⓈ -oʊ.bɑːr, ˌ--ˈ-
Nicodemus ˌnɪk.əʊˈdiː.məs, ⓊⓈ -əˈ-
niçoise niːˈswɑːz, nɪ-
Nicol(l) ˈnɪk.ᵊl **-s** -z
Nicola ˈnɪk.ᵊl.ə
Nicolas ˈnɪk.ᵊl.əs
Nicole nɪˈkəʊl, niː-, ⓊⓈ -ˈkoʊl
Nicolson ˈnɪk.ᵊl.sᵊn
Nicomachean ˌnaɪ.kɒm.əˈkiː.ən, naɪˌkɒm-, ⓊⓈ ˌnɪk.oʊ.məˈ-; ⓊⓈ ˌnaɪ.kɑː.məˈ-
Nicomachus naɪˈkɒm.ə.kəs, ⓊⓈ nɪˈkɑː.mə.kəs; ⓊⓈ ˌnaɪ.koʊˈmæk.əs
Nicosia ˌnɪk.əʊˈsiː.ə, ⓊⓈ -əˈ-, -oʊˈ-
nicotine ˈnɪk.ə.tiːn, ˌ--ˈ-
nic|tate ˈnɪk|.teɪt **-tates** -teɪts **-tating** -teɪ.tɪŋ, ⓊⓈ -teɪ.ţɪŋ **-tated** -teɪ.tɪd, ⓊⓈ -teɪ.ţɪd
nictation nɪkˈteɪ.ʃᵊn
nicti|tate ˈnɪk.tɪ|.teɪt, ⓊⓈ -tə- **-tates** -teɪts **-tating** -teɪ.tɪŋ, ⓊⓈ -teɪ.ţɪŋ **-tated** -teɪ.tɪd, ⓊⓈ -teɪ.ţɪd
nictitation ˌnɪk.tɪˈteɪ.ʃᵊn, ⓊⓈ -təˈ-
niec|e niːs **-es** -ɪz
Niedersachsen ˈniː.dəˌzæk.sᵊn; *as if German:* -ˌzæx-; ⓊⓈ -dɚˌzɑːk-
Nielsen ˈniːl.sᵊn
Niersteiner ˈnɪə.staɪ.nəʳ; *as if German:* -ʃtaɪ-; ⓊⓈ ˈnɪr.staɪ.nɚ; *as if German:* ⓊⓈ -ʃtaɪ-
Nietzsche ˈniː.tʃə, ⓊⓈ -tʃə, -tʃi
niff nɪf **-s** -s **-ing** -ɪŋ **-ed** -t **-y** -i
nift|y ˈnɪf.t|i **-ier** -i.əʳ, ⓊⓈ -i.ɚ **-iest** -i.ɪst, -i.əst **-ies** -iz **-ily** -ᵊl.i, -ɪ.li
Nige naɪdʒ
Nigel ˈnaɪ.dʒᵊl
Nigella naɪˈdʒel.ə
Niger *river:* ˈnaɪ.dʒəʳ, ⓊⓈ -dʒɚ *country:* nɪˈʒeəʳ, ⓊⓈ ˈnaɪ.dʒɚ **-ien/s** -i.ən/z
Nigeri|a naɪˈdʒɪə.ri|.ə, ⓊⓈ -ˈdʒɪr.i- **-an/s** -ən/z
niggard ˈnɪg.əd, ⓊⓈ -ɚd **-s** -z
niggardl|y ˈnɪg.əd.l|i, ⓊⓈ -ɚd- **-iness** -ɪ.nəs, -ɪ.nɪs
nigger ˈnɪg.əʳ, ⓊⓈ -ɚ **-s** -z
niggl|e ˈnɪg.ᵊl **-es** -z **-ing** -ɪŋ, ˈnɪg.lɪŋ **-ed** -d
niggl|y ˈnɪg.l|i, ˈnɪg.ᵊl|.i **-iness** -ɪ.nəs, -ɪ.nɪs
nigh naɪ
night naɪt **-s** -s **ˌnight ˈblindness** ⓊⓈ **ˈnight ˌblindness; ˈnight ˌowl; ˌnight ˈporter** ⓊⓈ **ˈnight ˌporter; ˈnight ˌschool; ˈnight ˌshift; ˌnight ˈwatchman**
nightcap ˈnaɪt.kæp **-s** -s
nightclothes ˈnaɪt.kləʊðz, ⓊⓈ -kloʊðz
nightclub ˈnaɪt.klʌb **-s** -z **-bing** -ɪŋ **-ber/s** -əʳ/z, ⓊⓈ -ɚ/z
nightdress ˈnaɪt.dres **-es** -ɪz
nightfall ˈnaɪt.fɔːl, ⓊⓈ -fɔːl, -fɑːl
nightgown ˈnaɪt.gaʊn **-s** -z
nighthawk ˈnaɪt.hɔːk, ⓊⓈ -hɑːk, -hɔːk **-s** -s
nightie ˈnaɪ.ti, ⓊⓈ -ţi **-s** -z
nightingale, N~ ˈnaɪ.tɪŋ.geɪl, ⓊⓈ -tᵊn-, -ţɪŋ- **-s** -z
nightjar ˈnaɪt.dʒɑːʳ, ⓊⓈ -dʒɑːr **-s** -z
nightlife ˈnaɪt.laɪf
night-light ˈnaɪt.laɪt **-s** -s
nightlong ˌnaɪtˈlɒŋ, ⓊⓈ -ˈlɑːŋ, -ˈlɔːŋ *stress shift:* **ˌnightlong ˈvigil**
nightly ˈnaɪt.li
nightmar|e ˈnaɪt.meəʳ, ⓊⓈ -mer **-es** -z **-ish** -ɪʃ **-ishly** -ɪʃ.li **-ishness** -ɪʃ.nəs, -ɪʃ.nɪs
nightshade ˈnaɪt.ʃeɪd
nightshirt ˈnaɪt.ʃɜːt, ⓊⓈ -ʃɝːt **-s** -s
nightspot ˈnaɪt.spɒt, ⓊⓈ -spɑːt **-s** -s
nightstand ˈnaɪt.stænd **-s** -z
nightstick ˈnaɪt.stɪk **-s** -s
nighttime ˈnaɪt.taɪm
nightwatch ˈnaɪt.wɒtʃ, ˌ-ˈ-, ⓊⓈ ˈnaɪt.wɑːtʃ, -wɔːtʃ **-es** -ɪz
nightwear ˈnaɪt.weəʳ, ⓊⓈ -wer
nihil ˈniː.hɪl, ˈnaɪ-, -hᵊl, ⓊⓈ ˈnaɪ.hɪl, ˈniː-
nihil|ism ˈniː.ɪ.l|ɪ.zᵊm, ˈnaɪ-, ˈ-hɪ-, ˈ-ᵊl|.ɪ-, ˈ-hᵊl|-, ⓊⓈ ˈnaɪ.ə.l|ɪ-, ˈniː- **-ist/s** -ɪst/s **-istic** ˌ--ˈɪs.tɪk
Nijinsky nɪˈdʒɪnt.ski, nə-, -ˈʒɪnt-, ⓊⓈ nəˈdʒɪnt-
Nijmegen ˈnaɪ.meɪ.gən, -ˈ--, ⓊⓈ ˈ---
Nike *goddess:* ˈnaɪ.kiː *trademark:* ˈnaɪ.ki; naɪk, ⓊⓈ ˈnaɪ.ki
Nikita nɪˈkiː.tə, ⓊⓈ -ţə
Nikkei nɪˈkeɪ, ⓊⓈ ˈniː.keɪ *stress shift, see compound:* **ˌNikkei ˈindex**
Nikki ˈnɪk.i
Nikon® ˈnɪk.ɒn, ⓊⓈ ˈnaɪ.kɑːn, ˈniː-
nil nɪl
nil desperandum ˌnɪl.des.pəˈræn.dəm, -pᵊrˈæn-, -dʊm, ⓊⓈ -pəˈræn.dəm; ⓊⓈ -ˈrɑːn.dʊm
Nile naɪl
Nilgiri ˈnɪl.gɪ.ri **-s** -z
nilometer naɪˈlɒm.ɪ.təʳ, -ə.təʳ, ⓊⓈ -ˈlɑː.mə.ţɚ **-s** -z
Nilotic naɪˈlɒt.ɪk, ⓊⓈ -ˈlɑː.ţɪk
Nilsen ˈniːl.sᵊn, ˈnɪl-
Nilsson ˈniːl.sᵊn, ˈnɪl-
nimbi (plural of **nimbus**) ˈnɪm.baɪ
nimbl|e ˈnɪm.b|ᵊl **-ler** -ləʳ, -ᵊl.əʳ, ⓊⓈ -lɚ, -ᵊl.ɚ **-lest** -lɪst, -ləst, -ᵊl.ɪst, -ᵊl.əst **-ly** -li **-leness** -ᵊl.nəs, -ᵊl.nɪs
nimb|us ˈnɪm.b|əs **-uses** -ə.sɪz **-i** -aɪ
nimb|y, NIMB|Y ˈnɪm.b|i **-ies** -iz
Nîmes niːm
nimiety nɪˈmaɪ.ə.ti, -ˈmaɪ.ɪ.ti, ⓊⓈ -ţi
nimini-piminy, niminy-piminy ˌnɪm.ɪ.niˈpɪm.ɪ.ni, ˌ-ə-, ˈ-ə-, ⓊⓈ -ə.niˈpɪm.ə-
Nimmo ˈnɪm.əʊ, ⓊⓈ -oʊ
Nimrod ˈnɪm.rɒd, ⓊⓈ -rɑːd
Nin nɪn, ⓊⓈ nɪn, niːn
Nina ˈniː.nə, ⓊⓈ ˈniː-, ˈnaɪ-
nincompoop ˈnɪŋ.kəm.puːp, ˈnɪn-, ⓊⓈ ˈnɪn-, ˈnɪŋ- **-s** -s
nine naɪn **-s** -z **-fold** -fəʊld, ⓊⓈ -foʊld **ˌdressed ˌup to the ˈnines;**

N

ˌ**nine-to-ˈfive**; ˌ**nine days' ˈwonder**

ninepenc|e ˈnaɪn.pənts, ˈnaɪm-, (US) ˈnaɪn- **-es** -ɪz
Note: See note under **penny**.

ninepenny ˈnaɪn.pən.i, ˈnaɪm-, (US) ˈnaɪn-

ninepin ˈnaɪn.pɪn, ˈnaɪm-, (US) ˈnaɪn- **-s** -z

nineteen ˌnaɪnˈtiːn **-s** -z **-th/s** -tθ/s *stress shift:* ˌ**nineteen ˈyears**; ˌ**nineteen to the ˈdozen**

ninetieth ˈnaɪn.ti.əθ, -ɪθ, (US) -t̬i- **-s** -s

Ninette nɪˈnet, niː-

ninet|y ˈnaɪn.t|i, (US) -t̬|i **-ies** -iz

ninetyfold ˈnaɪn.ti.fəʊld, (US) -t̬i.foʊld

ninety-nine ˌnaɪn.tiˈnaɪn, (US) -t̬iˈ- *stress shift:* ˌ**ninety-nine ˈdays**

Nineveh ˈnɪn.ɪ.və, ˈ-ə-, (US) ˈ-ə-

ninish ˈnaɪ.nɪʃ

ninja ˈnɪn.dʒə **-s** -z ˌ**Ninja ˈwarriors**

ninn|y ˈnɪn|.i **-ies** -iz

Nintendo® nɪnˈten.dəʊ, (US) -doʊ

ninth naɪntθ **-s** -s **-ly** -li

Ninus ˈnaɪ.nəs

Niobe ˈnaɪ.əʊ.bi, (US) -oʊ-, ˈ-ə-

niobium naɪˈəʊ.bi.əm, (US) -ˈoʊ-

nip, N~ nɪp **-s** -s **-ping** -ɪŋ **-ped** -t ˌ**nip and ˈtuck**

nipper ˈnɪp.əʳ, (US) -ɚ **-s** -z

nipple ˈnɪp.əl **-s** -z

Nippon ˈnɪp.ɒn, (US) -ɑːn; (US) nɪˈpɑːn **-ese** –ˈiːz

nipp|y ˈnɪp|.i **-ier** -i.əʳ, (US) -i.ɚ **-iest** -i.ɪst, -i.əst **-ily** -əl.i, -ɪ.li **-iness** -ɪ.nəs, -ɪ.nɪs

NIREX®, **Nirex** ˈnaɪə.reks, (US) ˈnaɪ-

nirvana, N~ nɪəˈvɑː.nə, nɜː-, (US) nɪr-, nɚ- **-s** -z

Niš, Nish *in Serbia:* niːʃ

Nisan ˈnaɪ.sæn; *Jewish pronunciation:* ˈnɪs.ɑːn, (US) niːˈsɑːn; (US) ˈnɪs.ən

Nisbet(t) ˈnɪz.bɪt, -bət

nisei niːˈseɪ, (US) niːˈseɪ, ˈ-- **-s** -z

Nish *surname:* nɪʃ

nisi ˈnaɪ.saɪ, ˈniː-, -si, (US) ˈnaɪ.saɪ

nisi prius ˌnaɪ.saɪˈpraɪ.əs, ˌniː-, -siˈ-, -ˈpriː-, (US) ˌnaɪ.saɪˈpraɪ-

Nissan® ˈnɪs.æn, (US) ˈniː.sɑːn

Nissen ˈnɪs.ən ˈ**Nissen** ˌ**hut**

nisus ˈnaɪ.səs

nit nɪt **-s** -s

niter ˈnaɪ.təʳ, (US) -t̬ɚ

Nith nɪθ

nit-pick ˈnɪt.pɪk **-s** -s **-ing** -ɪŋ **-ed** -t **-er/s** -əʳ/z, (US) -ɚ/z

nitrate ˈnaɪ.treɪt, -trɪt, (US) -treɪt **-s** -s

nitre ˈnaɪ.təʳ, (US) -t̬ɚ

nitric ˈnaɪ.trɪk ˌ**nitric ˈacid**

nitrite ˈnaɪ.traɪt

nitro- ˈnaɪ.trəʊ, (US) ˈnaɪ.troʊ, ˈ-trə

nitrochalk ˈnaɪ.trəʊ.tʃɔːk, ˌ--ˈ-, (US) ˈnaɪ.troʊ.tʃɔːk, -tʃɑːk

nitrogen ˈnaɪ.trə.dʒən, -trɪ-, (US) -trə-

nitrogenous naɪˈtrɒdʒ.ɪ.nəs, -ə.nəs, (US) -ˈtrɑː.dʒɪ.nəs, ˈ-dʒə-

nitroglycerine, nitroglycerin ˌnaɪ.trəʊˈglɪs.ər.iːn, -ɪn, (US) -troʊˈ-, -trəˈ-

nitrous ˈnaɪ.trəs

nitty-gritty ˌnɪt.iˈgrɪt.i, (US) ˌnɪt̬.iˈgrɪt̬-

nitwit ˈnɪt.wɪt **-s** -s

Niue ˈnjuː.eɪ, niˈuː-, (US) niˈuː- **-an/s** -ən/z

Nivea® ˈnɪv.i.ə

Niven ˈnɪv.ən

nix nɪks **-es** -ɪz **-ing** -ɪŋ **-ed** -t

Nixdorf® ˈnɪks.dɔːf, (US) -dɔːrf

nixie ˈnɪk.si **-s** -z

Nixon ˈnɪk.sən

nizam, N~ naɪˈzæm, nɪ-, -ˈzɑːm, (US) nɪˈzɑːm; (US) naɪˈzæm **-ate** -eɪt **-s** -z

Nizhni Novgorod ˌnɪʒ.niˈnɒv.gər.ɒd, (US) -ˈnɑːv.gə.rɑːd

N.J. ˌenˈdʒeɪ

Nkomo əŋˈkəʊ.məʊ, (US) -ˈkoʊ.moʊ, ən-

Nkrumah əŋˈkruː.mə, (US) əŋ-, ən-

N.M. (abbrev. for **New Mexico**) ˌenˈem

NME ˌen.emˈiː

N.Mex. (abbrev. for **New Mexico**) ˌnjuːˈmek.sɪ.kəʊ, (US) ˌnuːˈmek.sə.koʊ

NNE (abbrev. for **north-northeast**) ˌnɔːθ.nɔːθˈiːst, (US) ˌnɔːrθ.nɔːrθˈ-; *nautical pronunciation:* ˌnɔː.nɔːˈriːst, (US) ˌnɔːr.nɔːrˈiːst

NNW (abbrev. for **north-northwest**) ˌnɔːθ.nɔːθˈwest, (US) ˌnɔːrθ.nɔːrθˈ-; *nautical pronunciation:* ˌnɔː.nɔːˈ-, (US) ˌnɔːr.nɔːrˈ-

no n, interj nəʊ, (US) noʊ **-es** -z

no adj *normal form:* nəʊ, (US) noʊ; *weak form:* nə
Note: Occasional weak-form word. The pronunciation of **no** is nearly always /nəʊ/ (US) /noʊ/, but, particularly in British English, there is a weak form /nə/ in a few common expressions such as "no more do I" /nəˌmɔː.duːˈaɪ/ (US) /-ˌmɔːr-/.

no., N~ (abbrev. for **number**) ˈnʌm.bəʳ, (US) -bɚ **nos.** -z

no-account ˈnəʊ.əˌkaʊnt, (US) ˈnoʊ-

Noah ˈnəʊ.ə, (US) ˈnoʊ- ˌ**Noah's ˈark**

Noakes nəʊks, (US) noʊks

Noam ˈnəʊ.əm, nəʊm, (US) ˈnoʊ.əm, noʊm

nob nɒb, (US) nɑːb **-s** -z

no-ball ˌnəʊˈbɔːl, (US) ˈnoʊ-, -bɑːl **-s** -z **-ing** -ɪŋ **-ed** -d

nobbl|e ˈnɒb.əl, (US) ˈnɑː.bəl **-es** -z **-ing** -ɪŋ, ˈnɒb.lɪŋ, (US) ˈnɑː.blɪŋ **-ed** -d

nobb|y ˈnɒb|.i, (US) ˈnɑː.b|i **-ier** -i.əʳ, (US) -i.ɚ **-iest** -i.ɪst, -i.əst **-ily** -əl.i, -ɪ.li **-iness** -ɪ.nəs, -ɪ.nɪs

Nobel nəʊˈbel, (US) noʊ- *stress shift, see compound:* ˌ**Nobel ˈprize**

nobelium nəʊˈbiː.li.əm, (US) noʊˈbel.i-

nobilit|y nəʊˈbɪl.ə.t|i, -ɪ.t|i, (US) noʊˈbɪl.ə.t̬|i **-ies** -iz

nob|le, N~ ˈnəʊ.b|əl, (US) ˈnoʊ- **-les** -əlz **-ler** -ləʳ, -əl.əʳ **-lest** -lɪst, -ləst, -əl.ɪst, -əl.əst **-ly** -li **-leness** -əl.nəs, -əl.nɪs

noble|man ˈnəʊ.bəl|.mən, (US) ˈnoʊ- **-men** -mən

noble-minded ˌnəʊ.bəlˈmaɪn.dɪd, (US) ˌnoʊ- **-ness** -nəs, -nɪs *stress shift:* ˌ**noble-minded ˈperson**

noblesse nəʊˈbles, (US) noʊ-

noblesse oblige nəʊˌbles.əʊˈbliːʒ, ˌnəʊ.bles-, (US) noʊˌbles.oʊˈ-

noble|woman ˈnəʊ.bəl|ˌwʊm.ən, (US) ˈnoʊ- **-women** -ˌwɪm.ɪn

nobod|y ˈnəʊ.bə.d|i, -bɒd|.i, (US) ˈnoʊ.bɑː.d|i, -bʌd|.i, -bə.d|i **-ies** -iz

no-brainer ˌnəʊˈbreɪ.nəʳ, (US) ˌnoʊˈbreɪ.nɚ

nock, N~ nɒk, (US) nɑːk

no-claim bonus ˌnəʊˈkleɪmˌbəʊ.nəs, ˌnəʊˌkleɪmˈbəʊ-, (US) ˌnoʊˈkleɪmˌboʊ-, ˌnoʊˌkleɪmˈboʊ- **-es** -ɪz

no-claims bonus ˌnəʊˈkleɪmzˌbəʊ.nəs, ˌnəʊˌkleɪmzˈbəʊ-, (US) ˌnoʊˈkleɪmzˌboʊ-, ˌnoʊˌkleɪmzˈboʊ- **-es** -ɪz

no-confidence ˌnəʊˈkɒn.fɪ.dənts, (US) ˌnoʊˈkɑːn-

noctambul|ism nɒkˈtæm.bjə.l|ɪ.zəm, -bjʊ-, (US) nɑːkˈtæm.bjuː-, -bjə- **-ist/s** -ɪst/s

Noctes Ambrosianae ˌnɒk.teɪsˌæm.brəʊ.ziˈɑː.naɪ, -brɒs.iˈ-, (US) ˌnɑːk.tiːz.æm.broʊ.siˈeɪ.ni

nocturn(e) ˈnɒk.tɜːn, ˌ-ˈ-, (US) ˈnɑːk.tɝːn **-s** -z

nocturnal nɒkˈtɜː.nəl, (US) nɑːkˈtɝː- **-ly** -i

nocuous ˈnɒk.ju.əs, (US) ˈnɑːk- **-ly** -li

nod, N~ nɒd, (US) nɑːd **-s** -z **-ding** -ɪŋ **-ded** -ɪd

nodal ˈnəʊ.dəl, (US) ˈnoʊ- **-ly** -i

nodding ˈnɒd.ɪŋ, (US) ˈnɑː.dɪŋ

noddle ˈnɒd.əl, (US) ˈnɑː.dəl **-s** -z

nodd|y, N~ ˈnɒd|.i, (US) ˈnɑː.d|i **-ies** -iz

node nəʊd, (US) noʊd **-s** -z

nodul|ar ˈnɒdʒ.ə.l|əʳ, ˈnɒd.jə-, ˈnɒdʒ.ʊ-, ˈnɒd.jʊ-, (US) ˈnɑː.dju.l|ɚ, -djə- **-ous** -əs

nodule ˈnɒdʒ.uːl, ˈnɒd.juːl, (US) ˈnɑː.djuːl **-s** -z

Noel, Noël *personal name:* ˈnəʊ.əl, nəʊəl, (US) ˈnoʊ.əl *Christmas:* nəʊˈel, (US) noʊ-

no-fault ˈnəʊ.fɔːlt, -fɒlt, (US) ˈnoʊ.fɔːlt, -fɑːlt

no-fly ˌnəʊˈflaɪ, (US) ˌnoʊ- *stress shift:* ˌ**no-fly ˈzone**

no-frills ˌnəʊˈfrɪlz, (US) ˌnoʊ- *stress shift:* ˌ**no-frills ˈservice**

noggin ˈnɒg.ɪn, (US) ˈnɑː.gɪn **-s** -z

no-go ˌnəʊˈgəʊ, (US) ˌnoʊˈgoʊ *stress shift, see compound:* ˌ**no-go ˈarea**

no-good ˌnəʊˈgʊd, (US) ˌnoʊ- *stress shift:* ˌ**no-good ˈcheat**

Noh nəʊ, (US) noʊ

no-holds-barred ˌnəʊˌhəʊldzˈbɑːd, (US) ˌnoʊˌhoʊldzˈbɑːrd *stress shift:* ˌ**no-holds-barred** ˈ**contest**
no-hoper ˌnəʊˈhəʊ.pəʳ, (US) ˌnoʊˈhoʊ.pɚ **-s** -z
nohow ˈnəʊ.haʊ, (US) ˈnoʊ-
noir nwɑːʳ, (US) nwɑːr
nois|e nɔɪz **-es** -ɪz **-ing** -ɪŋ **-ed** -d
noiseless ˈnɔɪz.ləs, -lɪs **-ly** -li **-ness** -nəs, -nɪs
noisemaker ˈnɔɪzˌmeɪ.kəʳ, (US) -kɚ **-s** -z
noisette nwɑːˈzet **noisettes** nwɑːˈzet, nwɑːˈzets
noisome ˈnɔɪ.səm **-ly** -li **-ness** -nəs, -nɪs
nois|y ˈnɔɪ.z|i **-ier** -i.əʳ, (US) -i.ɚ **-iest** -i.ɪst, -i.əst **-ily** -ᵊl.i, -ɪ.li **-iness** -ɪ.nəs, -ɪ.nɪs
Nokes nəʊks, (US) noʊks
Nokia ˈnɒk.i.ə, (US) ˈnoʊ.ki-
Nokomis nəʊˈkəʊ.mɪs, (US) noʊˈkoʊ-
Nolan ˈnəʊ.lən, (US) ˈnoʊ-
noli me tangere ˌnəʊ.liˌmeɪˈtæŋ.gə.reɪ, ˈ-dʒə-, (US) ˌnoʊ-
Noll nɒl, (US) nɑːl
nolo contendere ˌnəʊ.ləʊ.kɒnˈten.dᵊr.i, -eɪ, (US) ˌnoʊ.loʊ.kənˈ-
Nolte ˈnɒl.ti, (US) ˈnoʊl.ti
nom nom, nɒm, (US) nɑːm **-s** -z **-ming** -ɪŋ **-med** -d
noma ˈnəʊ.mə, (US) ˈnoʊ- **-s** -z
nomad ˈnəʊ.mæd, (US) ˈnoʊ- **-s** -z **-ism** -ɪ.zᵊm
nomadic nəʊˈmæd.ɪk, (US) noʊ- **-ally** -ᵊl.i, -li
no-man's-land ˈnəʊ.mænz.lænd, (US) ˈnoʊ-
nom(s) de guerre ˌnɔ̃ːn.dəˈgeəʳ, ˌnɒm-, (US) ˌnɑːm.dəˈger
nom(s) de plume ˌnɔ̃ːn.dəˈpluːm, ˌnɒm-, (US) ˌnɑːm.dəˈ-
-nome nəʊm, noʊm
Note: Suffix. Normally unstressed, e.g. **metronome** /ˈmet.rə.nəʊm/ (US) /-noʊm/.
nomenclature nəʊˈmeŋ.klə.tʃəʳ; ˈnəʊ.men.kleɪ-, -mən-, (US) ˈnoʊ.men.kleɪ.tʃɚ, -mən-; (US) noʊˈmen.klə- **-s** -z
-nomic ˈnɒm.ɪk, ˈnəʊ.mɪk, (US) ˈnɑː.mɪk, ˈnoʊ-
Note: Suffix. Words containing **-nomic** normally carry primary stress on the penultimate syllable, e.g. **ergonomic** /ˌɜː.gəˈnɒm.ɪk/ (US) /ˌɝː.gəˈnɑː.mɪk/.
nominal ˈnɒm.ɪ.nᵊl, -ᵊn.ᵊl, (US) ˈnɑː.mə.nᵊl **-ly** -i
nomi|nate ˈnɒm.ɪ|.neɪt, ˈ-ə-, (US) ˈnɑː.mə- **-nates** -neɪts **-nating** -neɪ.tɪŋ, (US) -neɪ.t̬ɪŋ **-nated** -neɪ.tɪd, (US) -neɪ.t̬ɪd **-nator/s** -neɪ.təʳ/z, (US) -neɪ.t̬ɚ/z
nomination ˌnɒm.ɪˈneɪ.ʃᵊn, -əˈ-, (US) ˌnɑː.məˈ- **-s** -z
nominative ˈnɒm.ɪ.nə.tɪv, -ᵊn.ə-, (US) ˈnɑː.mə.nə.t̬ɪv **-s** -z
nominee ˌnɒm.ɪˈniː, -əˈ-, (US) ˌnɑː.məˈ- **-s** -z
Nomura nəʊˈmʊə.rə, -ˈmjʊə-, (US) noʊˈmuː.rə
-nomy nə.mi
Note: Suffix. Words containing **-nomy** normally carry stress on the syllable preceding the suffix, e.g. **astronomy** /əˈstrɒn.ə.mi/ (US) /-ˈstrɑː.nə-/.
non nɒn, (US) nɑːn
non- ˌnɒn, (US) ˌnɑːn
Note: Prefix. In words containing **non-**, the stress pattern of the stem to which it is added does not normally change, e.g. **verbal** /ˈvɜː.bᵊl/ (US) /ˈvɝː-/, **non-verbal** /ˌnɒnˈvɜː.bᵊl/ (US) /ˌnɑːnˈvɝː-/.
non-acceptance ˌnɒn.əkˈsep.tᵊnts, -ækˈ-, (US) ˌnɑː.nəkˈ-
nonage ˈnəʊ.nɪdʒ, ˈnɒn.ɪdʒ, (US) ˈnɑː.nɪdʒ, ˈnoʊ-, -neɪdʒ
nonagenarian ˌnəʊ.nə.dʒəˈneə.ri.ən, ˌnɒn.ə-, -dʒɪˈ-, (US) ˌnɑː.nə.dʒəˈner.i-, ˌnoʊ- **-s** -z
nonaggression ˌnɒn.əˈgreʃ.ᵊn, (US) ˌnɑː.nəˈ-
nonagon ˈnɒn.ə.gɒn, ˈnəʊ.nə-, (US) ˈnɑː.nə.gɑːn, ˈnoʊ- **-s** -z
nonalcoholic ˌnɒn.æl.kəˈhɒl.ɪk, (US) ˌnɑː.næl.kəˈhɑː.lɪk
nonalign|ed ˌnɒn.ᵊlˈaɪn|d, (US) ˌnɑː.nəˈlaɪn|d **-ment** -mənt
non-appearance ˌnɒn.əˈpɪə.rᵊnts, (US) ˌnɑː.nəˈpɪr.ᵊnts
nonary ˈnəʊ.nᵊr.i, ˈnɒn.ᵊr-, (US) ˈnoʊ.nɚ-, ˈnɑː-
non-attendance ˌnɒn.əˈten.dənts, (US) ˌnɑː.nəˈ-
nonbeliever ˌnɒn.bɪˈliː.vəʳ, ˌnɒm-, -bəˈ-, (US) ˌnɑːn.bɪˈliː.vɚ, -bəˈ- **-s** -z
non-biological ˌnɒnˌbaɪ.əˈlɒdʒ.ɪ.kᵊl, (US) ˌnɑːn.baɪ.əˈlɑː.dʒɪ-
nonc|e nɒnts, (US) nɑːnts **-es** -ɪz ˈ**nonce** ˌ**word**
non-certifiable ˌnɒnˌsɜː.tɪˈfaɪ.ə.bᵊl, -təˈ-, (US) ˌnɑːnˌsɝː.t̬əˈ-
nonchalance ˈnɒn.tʃᵊl.ənts, (US) ˌnɑːn.ʃəˈlɑːnts
nonchalant ˈnɒn.tʃᵊl.ənt, (US) ˌnɑːn.ʃəˈlɑːnt **-ly** -li
non-collegiate ˌnɒn.kᵊlˈiː.dʒi.ət, ˌnɒŋ-, -kɒlˈ-, ˈ-dʒət, (US) ˌnɑːn.kəˈliː.dʒɪt, -dʒi.ɪt **-s** -s
non-combatant ˌnɒnˈkɒm.bə.tᵊnt, ˌnɒŋ-, -ˈkʌm-; -kəmˈbæt.ᵊnt, (US) ˌnɑːn.kəmˈbæt.ᵊnt; (US) ˌnɑːnˈkɑːm.bə.tᵊnt **-s** -s
noncommercial ˌnɒn.kəˈmɜː.ʃᵊl, ˌnɒŋ-, (US) ˌnɑːn.kəˈmɝː-
non-commissioned ˌnɒn.kəˈmɪʃ.ᵊnd, ˌnɒŋ-, (US) ˌnɑːn- *stress shift, see compound:* ˌ**non-commissioned** ˈ**officer**
noncommitt|al ˌnɒn.kəˈmɪt|.ᵊl, ˌnɒŋ-, (US) ˌnɑːn.kəˈmɪt̬- **-ally** -ᵊl.i *stress shift:* ˌ**noncommittal** ˈ**answer**
noncompetitive ˌnɒn.kəmˈpet.ə.tɪv, ˌnɒŋ-, ˈ-ɪ-, (US) ˌnɑːn.kəmˈpet̬.ə.t̬ɪv **-ly** -li *stress shift:* ˌ**noncompetitive** ˈ**games**
non-compliance ˌnɒn.kəmˈplaɪ.ənts, ˌnɒŋ-, (US) ˌnɑːn-
non compos mentis ˌnɒnˌkɒm.pəsˈmen.tɪs, ˌnɒŋ-, -pɒsˈ-, (US) ˌnɑːnˌkɑːm.poʊsˈmen.tɪs, -pəsˈ-
non-conducting ˌnɒn.kənˈdʌk.tɪŋ, ˌnɒŋ-, (US) ˌnɑːn- *stress shift:* ˌ**non-conducting** ˈ**substance**
nonconductor ˌnɒn.kənˈdʌk.təʳ, ˌnɒŋ-, (US) ˌnɑːn.kənˈdʌk.tɚ **-s** -z
nonconform|ist ˌnɒn.kənˈfɔː.m|ɪst, ˌnɒŋ-, (US) ˌnɑːn.kənˈfɔːr- **-ists** -ɪsts **-ism** -ɪ.zᵊm *stress shift:* ˌ**nonconformist** ˈ**stance**
nonconformity ˌnɒn.kənˈfɔː.mə.ti, ˌnɒŋ-, -mɪ-, (US) ˌnɑːn.kənˈfɔːr.mə.t̬i
noncontiguous ˌnɒn.kənˈtɪg.ju.əs, ˌnɒŋ-, -kɒnˈ-, (US) ˌnɑːn.kənˈ- **-ly** -li *stress shift:* ˌ**noncontiguous** ˈ**boundaries**
noncontributory ˌnɒn.kənˈtrɪb.jə.tᵊr.i, ˌnɒŋ-, -jʊ-, (US) ˌnɑːn.kənˈtrɪb.juː.tɔːr-, -jə- *stress shift:* ˌ**noncontributory** ˈ**action**
noncooperation ˌnɒn.kəʊˌɒp.ᵊrˈeɪ.ʃᵊn, ˌnɒŋ-, (US) ˌnɑːn.koʊˌɑː.pəˈreɪ-
noncooperationist ˌnɒn.kəʊˌɒp.ᵊrˈeɪ.ʃᵊn.ɪst, ˌnɒŋ-, (US) ˌnɑːn.koʊˌɑː.pəˈreɪ- **-s** -s *stress shift:* ˌ**non-cooperationist** ˈ**stance**
noncorrosive ˌnɒn.kᵊrˈəʊ.sɪv, ˌnɒŋ-, -zɪv, (US) ˌnɑːn.kəˈroʊ- *stress shift:* ˌ**noncorrosive** ˈ**acid**
non-custodial ˌnɒn.kʌsˈtəʊ.di.əl, ˌnɒŋ-, (US) ˌnɑːn.kʌsˈtoʊ- *stress shift:* ˌ**non-custodial** ˈ**sentence**
non-dairy ˌnɒnˈdeə.ri, (US) ˌnɑːnˈder.i *stress shift:* ˌ**non-dairy** ˈ**product**
non-delivery ˌnɒn.dɪˈlɪv.ᵊr.i, -dəˈ-, (US) ˌnɑːn.dəˈ-, ˈ-ri
nondenominational ˌnɒn.dɪˌnɒm.ɪˈneɪ.ʃᵊn.ᵊl, -dəˌ-, -ˈneɪʃ.nᵊl, (US) ˌnɑːn.dəˌnɑː.məˈ- *stress shift:* ˌ**nondenominational** ˈ**policy**
nondescript ˈnɒn.dɪ.skrɪpt, -də-, (US) ˈnɑːn.dɪ-, ˌ--ˈ- **-s** -s
nondriver ˌnɒnˈdraɪ.vəʳ, (US) ˌnɑːnˈdraɪ.vɚ **-s** -z
none adj, pron, adv *not any:* nʌn

> Note: The pronunciation /nɒn/ is increasingly widespread in British English, but cannot yet be recommended as representative of the accent being described here.

none, N~ n *church service:* nəʊn, (US) noʊn **-s** -z
nonentit|y ˌnɒnˈen.tə.t|i, nəˈnen-, -ɪ.t|i, (US) ˌnɑːˈnen.t̬ə.t̬|i **-ies** -iz
nones, N~ nəʊnz, (US) noʊnz

non-essential ˌnɒn.ɪˈsen.tʃəl, (US) ˌnɑː.nɪˈ- **-s** -z *stress shift:* ˌ**non-essential** ˈ**item**
nonesuch ˈnʌn.sʌtʃ **-es** -ɪz
nonet nəʊˈnet, nɒnˈet, (US) noʊˈnet **-s** -s
nonetheless ˌnʌn.ðəˈles
non-event ˌnɒn.ɪˈvent, ˈ---, (US) ˌnɑː.nɪˈvent **-s** -s
non-existen|t ˌnɒn.ɪgˈzɪs.tən|t, -egˈ-, -ɪkˈsɪs-, -ekˈ-, (US) ˌnɑː.nɪgˈzɪs-, -negˈ- **-ce** -ts *stress shift:* ˌ**nonexistent** ˈ**means**
nonfat ˌnɒnˈfæt, (US) ˌnɑːn- *stress shift:* ˌ**nonfat** ˈ**substance**
non-feasance ˌnɒnˈfiː.zənts, (US) ˌnɑːn-
nonfiction ˌnɒnˈfɪk.ʃən, (US) ˌnɑːn-
nonflammab|le ˌnɒnˈflæm.ə.b|əl, (US) ˌnɑːn- *stress shift:* ˌ**nonflammable** ˈ**clothing**
nonillion nəʊˈnɪl.jən, nɒnˈɪl-, ˈ-i.ən, (US) noʊˈnɪl.jən **-s** -z
non-intervention ˌnɒn.ɪn.təˈven.tʃən, (US) ˌnɑː.nɪn.t̬ɚˈvent.ʃən
non-interventionist ˌnɒn.ɪn.təˈven.tʃən.ɪst, (US) ˌnɑː.nɪn.təˈvent.ʃən- **-s** -s *stress shift:* ˌ**non-interventionist** ˈ**policy**
nonjudgmental ˌnɒn.dʒʌdʒˈmen.təl, (US) ˌnɑːn.dʒʌdʒˈmen.t̬əl **-ly** -i *stress shift:* ˌ**nonjudgmental** ˈ**view**
nonjuror ˌnɒnˈdʒʊə.rər, (US) ˌnɑːnˈdʒʊr.ɚ, -ɔːr **-s** -z
nonlinear ˌnɒnˈlɪn.i.ər, (US) ˌnɑːnˈlɪn.i.ɚ *stress shift:* ˌ**nonlinear** ˈ**theory**
non-member ˌnɒnˈmem.bər, ˈ---, (US) ˌnɑːnˈmem.bɚ, ˈ--- **-s** -z
non-nuclear ˌnɒnˈnjuː.kli.ər, (US) ˌnɑːnˈnuː.kli.ɚ, -ˈnjuː- *stress shift:* ˌ**non-nuclear** ˈ**power**
no-no ˈnəʊ.nəʊ, (US) ˈnoʊ.noʊ **-s** -z
non-observance ˌnɒn.əbˈzɜː.vənts, (US) ˌnɑː.nəbˈzɝː-
non obstante ˌnɒn.ɒbˈstæn.teɪ, (US) ˌnɑːn.əbˈstæn.ti, -ˈstɑːn-
non obstante verdicto ˌnɒn.ɒbˌstæn.teɪ.vɜːˈdɪk.təʊ, -vəˈ-, (US) ˌnɑːn.əbˌstæn.ti.verˈdɪk.toʊ, -ˌstɑːn-
nonoccurrence ˌnɒn.əˈkʌr.ənts, (US) ˌnɑː.nəˈkɝː-
no-nonsense ˌnəʊˈnɒnt.sənts, (US) ˌnoʊˈnɑːnt.sents *stress shift:* ˌ**no-nonsense** ˈ**attitude**
nonoperational ˌnɒn.ɒp.əˈreɪ.ʃən.əl, -ˈreɪʃ.nəl, (US) ˌnɑː.nɑː.pəˈreɪ.ʃən.əl, -ˈreɪʃ.nəl *stress shift:* ˌ**nonoperational** ˈ**forces**
nonpareil ˌnɒn.pəˈreɪl, ˌnɒm-, -ˈeɪ, (US) ˌnɑːn.pəˈrel
nonpartisan ˌnɒnˌpɑː.tɪˈzæn, -təˈ-, -ˈ---, (US) ˌnɑːnˈpɑːr.t̬ɪ.zən, -zæn
non-payment ˌnɒnˈpeɪ.mənt, ˌnɒm-, (US) ˌnɑːn-
nonplaying ˌnɒnˈpleɪ.ɪŋ, ˌnɒm-, (US) ˌnɑːn- *stress shift:* ˌ**nonplaying** ˈ**team**
nonplus ˌnɒnˈplʌs, ˌnɒm-, (US) ˌnɑːn- **-ses** -ɪz **-sing** -ɪŋ **-sed** -t
nonprofit ˌnɒnˈprɒf.ɪt, (US) ˌnɑːnˈprɑː.f- **-s** -s *stress shift:* ˌ**nonprofit organiˈzation**
non-profit-making ˌnɒnˈprɒf.ɪtˌmeɪ.kɪŋ, ˌnɒm-, (US) ˌnɑːnˈprɑː.fɪt- *stress shift, see compound:* ˌ**non-profit-making** ˌ**organiˈsation**
nonproliferation ˌnɒn.prəˌlɪf.əˈreɪ.ʃən, ˌnɒm-, (US) ˌnɑːn-
nonrefundable ˌnɒn.rɪˈfʌnd.ə.bəl, -riːˈ-, (US) ˌnɑːn- *stress shift:* ˌ**nonrefundable** ˈ**money**
nonresident ˌnɒnˈrez.ɪ.dənt, ˈ-ə-, (US) ˌnɑːn- **-s** -s
nonrestrictive ˌnɒn.rɪˈstrɪk.tɪv, -rəˈ-, (US) ˌnɑːn- *stress shift:* ˌ**nonrestrictive** ˈ**clause**
nonreturnable ˌnɒn.rɪˈtɜː.nə.bəl, -rəˈ-, (US) ˌnɑːn.rɪˈtɝː- *stress shift:* ˌ**nonreturnable** ˈ**goods**
nonsectarian ˌnɒn.sekˈteə.ri.ən, (US) ˌnɑːn.sekˈter.i- *stress shift:* ˌ**nonsectarian** ˈ**violence**
nonsense ˈnɒn.sənts, (US) ˈnɑːn.sents, -sənts ˈ**nonsense** ˌ**verse**
nonsensical ˌnɒnˈsent.sɪ.kəl, (US) ˌnɑːn- **-ly** -i **-ness** -nəs, -nɪs
non sequitur ˌnɒnˈsek.wɪ.tər, ˌnəʊn-, -wə-, (US) ˌnɑːnˈsek.wɪ.t̬ɚ **-s** -z
nonskid ˌnɒnˈskɪd, (US) ˌnɑːn- *stress shift:* ˌ**nonskid** ˈ**surface**
nonslip ˌnɒnˈslɪp, (US) ˌnɑːn- *stress shift:* ˌ**nonslip** ˈ**surface**
nonsmok|er ˌnɒnˈsməʊ.k|ər, (US) ˌnɑːnˈsmoʊ.k|ɚ **-ers** -əz, (US) -ɚz **-ing** -ɪŋ
nonspecific ˌnɒn.spəˈsɪf.ɪk, -spɪˈ-, (US) ˌnɑːn- *stress shift:* ˌ**nonspecific** ˈ**order**
nonstandard ˌnɒnˈstæn.dəd, (US) ˌnɑːnˈstæn.dɚd *stress shift:* ˌ**nonstandard** ˈ**fitting**
nonstarter ˌnɒnˈstɑː.tər, (US) ˌnɑːnˈstɑːr.t̬ɚ **-s** -z
nonstick ˌnɒnˈstɪk, (US) ˌnɑːn- *stress shift:* ˌ**nonstick** ˈ**coating**
non-stop ˌnɒnˈstɒp, (US) ˌnɑːnˈstɑːp *stress shift:* ˌ**non-stop** ˈ**music**
nonsuch, N~ ˈnʌn.sʌtʃ
nonsui|t ˌnɒnˈsuː|t, -ˈsjuː|t, (US) ˌnɑːnˈsuː|t **-ts** -ts **-ting** -tɪŋ, (US) -t̬ɪŋ **-ted** -tɪd, (US) -t̬ɪd
nonswimmer ˌnɒnˈswɪm.ər, (US) ˌnɑːnˈswɪm.ɚ **-s** -z
nontrivial ˌnɒnˈtrɪv.i.əl, (US) ˌnɑːn- *stress shift:* ˌ**nontrivial** ˈ**problem**
non-U ˌnɒnˈjuː, (US) ˌnɑːn- *stress shift:* ˌ**non-U** ˈ**accent**
nonunion ˌnɒnˈjuː.njən, ˈ-ni.ən, (US) ˌnɑːnˈjuː.njən *stress shift:* ˌ**nonunion** ˈ**members**
non-user ˌnɒnˈjuː.zər, (US) ˌnɑːnˈjuː.zɚ *stress shift:* ˌ**non-user** ˈ**guide**
non-verbal ˌnɒnˈvɜː.bəl, (US) ˌnɑːnˈvɝː- *stress shift:* ˌ**non-verbal** ˈ**message**
non-violen|t ˌnɒnˈvaɪ.ə.lən|t, (US) ˌnɑːn- **-ly** -li **-ce** -ts *stress shift:* ˌ**non-violent** ˈ**policy**
nonvoter ˌnɒnˈvəʊ.tər, (US) ˌnɑːnˈvoʊ.t̬ɚ **-s** -z
nonwhite ˌnɒnˈwaɪt, (US) ˌnɑːn- *stress shift:* ˌ**nonwhite** ˈ**prejudice**
noob nuːb **-s** -z
noodle ˈnuː.dəl **-s** -z
nook nʊk **-s** -s ˌ**nook and** ˈ**cranny**
nooky, nookie ˈnʊk.i
noon nuːn **-s** -z
Noonan ˈnuː.nən
noonday ˈnuːn.deɪ
no one ˈnəʊ.wʌn, (US) ˈnoʊ-
noontide ˈnuːn.taɪd
noos|e nuːs **-es** -ɪz **-ing** -ɪŋ **-ed** -t
nope nəʊp, (US) noʊp
noplace ˈnəʊ.pleɪs, (US) ˈnoʊ-
nor *normal form:* nɔːr, (US) nɔːr; *weak form:* nər, (US) nɚ
Note: Occasional weak-form word. The pronunciation is normally /nɔːr/ (US) /nɔːr/, but, particularly in British English, there is a weak form /nər/ (US) /nɚ/, as in 'no use to man nor beast' /nəʊ juːs.təˌmæn.nəˈbiːst/ (US) /noʊ juːs.təˌmæn.nɚˈ-/.
Nora(h) ˈnɔː.rə, (US) ˈnɔːr.ə
NORAD ˈnɔː.ræd, (US) ˈnɔːr.æd
noradrenalin(e) ˌnɔː.rəˈdren.əl.ɪn, ˌnɒr.əˈ-, -iːn, (US) ˌnɔːr.əˈdren.ə.lɪn
Noraid ˈnɔː.reɪd, (US) ˈnɔːr.eɪd
Norden ˈnɔː.dən, (US) ˈnɔːr-
Nordenfelt ˈnɔː.dən.felt, (US) ˈnɔːr-
Nordic ˈnɔː.dɪk, (US) ˈnɔːr-
Nore nɔːr, (US) nɔːr
Norf. (abbrev. for **Norfolk**) ˈnɔː.fək, (US) ˈnɔːr-, -fɔːk, -foʊk
Norfolk ˈnɔː.fək, (US) ˈnɔːr-, -fɔːk, -foʊk ˌ**Norfolk** ˈ**Broads**
Norgate ˈnɔː.geɪt, -gɪt, (US) ˈnɔːr-
Norham ˈnɒr.əm, ˈnɔː.rəm, (US) ˈnɔːr.əm
nori ˈnɒr.i, ˈnɔː.ri, (US) ˈnɔːr.i
Noriega ˌnɒr.iˈeɪ.gə, (US) ˌnɔːr-
Norland ˈnɔː.lənd, (US) ˈnɔːr-
norm nɔːm, (US) nɔːrm **-s** -z
Norma ˈnɔː.mə, (US) ˈnɔːr-
normal ˈnɔː.məl, (US) ˈnɔːr- **-ly** -i
normalcy ˈnɔː.məl.si, (US) ˈnɔːr-
normality nɔːˈmæl.ə.ti, -ɪ.ti, (US) nɔːrˈmæl.ə.t̬i
normalization, -isa- ˌnɔː.məl.aɪˈzeɪ.ʃən, -ɪˈ-, (US) ˌnɔːr.məl.əˈ-
normaliz|e, -is|e ˈnɔː.məl.aɪz, (US) ˈnɔːr- **-es** -ɪz **-ing** -ɪŋ **-ed** -d
normally ˈnɔː.məl.i, (US) ˈnɔːr-
Norman ˈnɔː.mən, (US) ˈnɔːr- **-s** -z ˌ**Norman** ˈ**conquest**
Normanby ˈnɔː.mən.bi, -məm-, (US) ˈnɔːr-
Normandy *in France:* ˈnɔː.mən.di, (US) ˈnɔːr- *in Surrey:* ˈnɔː.mən.di, (US) ˈnɔːr-; *also locally:* nɔːˈmæn.di, (US) nɔːr-

Normanton ˈnɔː.mən.tən, US ˈnɔːr-
normative ˈnɔː.mə.tɪv, US ˈnɔːr.mə.t̬ɪv **-ly** -li
Norn nɔːn, US nɔːrn **-s** -z
Norodom Sihanouk ˌnɒr.ə.dɒmˈsiː.jæn.ʊk, US ˌnɔːr.ə.dɑːm-, -jɑː.nʊk
norovirus ˈnɔː.rəʊˌvaɪə.rəs, ˈnɒr.əʊ-, US ˈnɔː.rəˌvaɪ.rəs, -oʊ-
Norris ˈnɒr.ɪs, US ˈnɔːr-
Norrköping ˈnɔː.tʃɜː.pɪŋ, US ˈnɔːr-
Norroy ˈnɒr.ɔɪ, US ˈnɔːr- **-s** -z
Norse nɔːs, US nɔːrs **-man** -mən **-men** -mən, -men
north, N~ nɔːθ, US nɔːrθ **ˌNorth Aˈmerica; ˌNorth Atˈlantic; ˌNorth Caroˈlina; ˌNorth Daˈkota; ˈNorth ˌIsland; ˌNorth Koˈrea; ˌnorth ˈpole; ˌNorth ˈSea**
Northallerton ˌnɔːˈθæl.ə.tən, US ˌnɔːrθˈæl.ɚ.t̬ən
Northampton ˌnɔːˈθæmp.tən, ˌnɔːθˈhæmp-; *locally:* nəˈθæmp-, US ˌnɔːrˈθæmp-, ˌnɔːrθˈhæmp- **-shire** -ʃəʳ, -ʃɪəʳ, US -ʃɚ, -ʃɪr
Northanger nɔːˈθæŋ.gəʳ, -əʳ; ˈnɔː.θæŋ-, ˈnɔː.θ.hæŋ-, US nɔːrˈθæŋ.gɚ, -ɚ; US ˈnɔːr.θæŋ-, ˈnɔːrθ.hæŋ-
Northants. (abbrev. for **Northamptonshire**) ˈnɔː.θænts, -ˈ-, US ˈnɔːr.θænts, -ˈ-
North Baddesley ˌnɔːθˈbædz.li, US ˌnɔːrθ-
northbound ˈnɔːθ.baʊnd, US ˈnɔːrθ-
Northbrook ˈnɔːθ.brʊk, US ˈnɔːrθ-
Northcliffe ˈnɔːθ.klɪf, US ˈnɔːrθ-
Northcote ˈnɔːθ.kət, -kəʊt, US ˈnɔːrθ.kət, -koʊt
northeast, N~ ˌnɔːθˈiːst, US ˌnɔːrθ-; *nautical pronunciation:* ˌnɔːˈriːst, US ˌnɔːrˈiːst **-wards** -wədz, US -wɚdz *stress shift:* **ˌnortheast ˈwind**
northeaster ˌnɔːθˈiː.stəʳ, US ˌnɔːrθˈiː.stɚ; *in nautical usage also:* ˌnɔːˈriː-, US ˌnɔːrˈiː- **-s** -z
northeasterl|y ˌnɔːθˈiː.stəl.|i, US ˌnɔːrθˈiː.stɚ.l|i; *in nautical usage also:* ˌnɔːˈriː-, US ˌnɔːrˈiː- **-ies** -iz
northeastern, N~ ˌnɔːθˈiː.stən, US ˌnɔːrθˈiː.stɚn; *in nautical usage also:* ˌnɔːˈriː-, US ˌnɔːrˈiː- **-er/s** -əʳ/z, US -ɚ/z
northeastward ˌnɔːθˈiːst.wəd, US ˌnɔːrθˈiːst.wɚd; *in nautical usage also:* ˌnɔːˈriː-, US ˌnɔːrˈiː- **-s** -z
Northen ˈnɔː.ðən, US ˈnɔːr-
northerl|y ˈnɔː.ðəl.|i, US ˈnɔːr.ðɚ.l|i **-ies** -iz
northern, N~ ˈnɔː.ðən, US ˈnɔːr.θɚn **-most** -məʊst, -məst, US -moʊst, -məst **ˌNorthern ˈIreland; ˌnorthern ˈlights; ˌNorthern ˈTerritory**
northerner, N~ ˈnɔː.ðən.əʳ, US ˈnɔːr.θɚ.nɚ **-s** -z
Northfield ˈnɔːθ.fiːld, US ˈnɔːrθ-
Northfleet ˈnɔːθ.fliːt, US ˈnɔːrθ-
northing ˈnɔː.θɪŋ, US ˈnɔːr-
Northland ˈnɔːθ.lənd, US ˈnɔːrθ.lænd, -lənd
North|man ˈnɔːθ|.mən, US ˈnɔːrθ- **-men** -mən, -men
north-northeast ˌnɔːθ.nɔːθˈiːst, US ˌnɔːrθ.nɔːrθˈ-; *in nautical usage also:* ˌnɔː.nɔːˈriːst, US ˌnɔːr.nɔːrˈiːst
north-northwest ˌnɔːθ.nɔːθˈwest, US ˌnɔːrθ.nɔːrθˈ-; *in nautical usage also:* ˌnɔː.nɔːˈ-, US ˌnɔːr.nɔːrˈ-
Northolt ˈnɔː.θəʊlt, US ˈnɔːr.θoʊlt
North-South ˌnɔːθˈsaʊθ, US ˌnɔːrθ- **ˌNorth-ˌSouth diˈvide**
Northumberland nɔːˈθʌmb.əl.ənd, nə-, US nɔːrˈθʌm.bɚ.lənd
Northumbri|a nɔːˈθʌm.bri|.ə, US nɔːr- **-an/s** -ən/z
northward ˈnɔːθ.wəd, US ˈnɔːrθ.wɚd **-s** -z **-ly** -li
northwest, N~ ˌnɔːθˈwest, US ˌnɔːrθ-; *nautical pronunciation:* ˌnɔːˈwest, US ˌnɔːr- **-wards** -wədz, US -wɚdz *stress shift, see compound:* **ˌNorthwest ˈTerritories**
northwesterl|y ˌnɔːθˈwes.təl.|i, US ˌnɔːrθˈwes.tɚ.l|i; *in nautical usage also:* ˌnɔː-, US ˌnɔːr- **-ies** -iz
northwestern, N~ ˌnɔːθˈwes.tən, US ˌnɔːrθˈwes.tɚn; *in nautical usage also:* ˌnɔː-, US ˌnɔːr- **-er/s** -əʳ/z, US -ɚ/z
northwestward ˌnɔːθˈwest.wəd, US ˌnɔːrθˈwest.wɚd; *in nautical usage also:* ˌnɔː-, US ˌnɔːr-
Northwich ˈnɔːθ.wɪtʃ, US ˈnɔːrθ-
Northwood ˈnɔːθ.wʊd, US ˈnɔːrθ-
Norton ˈnɔː.tən, US ˈnɔːr-
Norton Radstock ˌnɔː.tənˈræd.stɒk, US ˌnɔːr.tənˈræd.stɑːk
Norway ˈnɔː.weɪ, US ˈnɔːr-
Norwegian nɔːˈwiː.dʒən, US nɔːr- **-s** -z
Norwich *in England:* ˈnɒr.ɪdʒ, -ɪtʃ, US ˈnɔːr.ɪtʃ, -wɪtʃ *in US:* ˈnɔː.wɪtʃ, US ˈnɔːr-
Norwood ˈnɔː.wʊd, US ˈnɔːr-
nos., N~ (abbrev. for **numbers**) ˈnʌm.bəz, US -bɚz
nos|e nəʊz, US noʊz **-es** -ɪz **-ing** -ɪŋ **-ed** -d **ˈnose ˌring; ˌcut off one's ˌnose to ˌspite one's ˈface; ˌkeep one's ˌnose to the ˈgrindstone; ˌlook down one's ˈnose at; ˌpay through the ˈnose (for); ˌpoke one's ˈnose (into)**
nosebag ˈnəʊz.bæg, US ˈnoʊz- **-s** -z
nosebleed ˈnəʊz.bliːd, US ˈnoʊz- **-s** -z
nosediv|e ˈnəʊz.daɪv, US ˈnoʊz- **-es** -z **-ing** -ɪŋ **-ed** -d
no-see-um nəʊˈsiː.əm, US ˌnoʊ- **-s** -z
nosegay ˈnəʊz.geɪ, US ˈnoʊz- **-s** -z
nos|ey ˈnəʊ.z|i, US ˈnoʊ- **-ier** -i.əʳ, US -i.ɚ **-iest** -i.ɪst, -i.əst **-ily** -əl.i, -ɪ.li **-iness** -ɪ.nəs, -ɪ.nɪs
Nosferatu ˌnɒs.fəˈrɑː.tuː, US ˌnɑːs-
nosh nɒʃ, US nɑːʃ **-es** -ɪz **-ing** -ɪŋ **-ed** -t
no-show ˌnəʊˈʃəʊ, US ˈnoʊˌʃoʊ *stress shift, British only:* **ˌno-show ˈpassenger**
nosh-up ˈnɒʃ.ʌp, US ˈnɑːʃ- **-s** -s
nostalg|ia nɒsˈtæl.dʒ|ə, -dʒ|i.ə, US nɑːˈstæl.dʒ|ə, nə-, nɔː-, -dʒ|i.ə **-ic** -ɪk **-ically** -ɪ.kəl.i, -ɪ.kli
Nostradamus ˌnɒs.trəˈdeɪ.məs, -ˈdɑː-, US ˌnoʊ.strəˈdɑː-, ˌnɑː.strəˈdeɪ-
nostril ˈnɒs.trəl, -trɪl, US ˈnɑː.strəl **-s** -z
Nostromo nɒsˈtrəʊ.məʊ, US nɑːˈstroʊ.moʊ
nostrum ˈnɒs.trəm, US ˈnɑː.strəm **-s** -z
nos|y ˈnəʊ.z|i, US ˈnoʊ- **-ier** -i.əʳ, US -i.ɚ **-iest** -i.ɪst, -i.əst **-ily** -əl.i, -ɪ.li **-iness** -ɪ.nəs, -ɪ.nɪs
nosy parker ˌnəʊ.ziˈpɑː.kəʳ, US ˌnoʊ.ziˈpɑːr.kɚ **-s** -z
not nɒt, US nɑːt
nota bene ˌnəʊ.tɑːˈben.eɪ, -təˈbiː.ni, US ˌnoʊ.t̬əˈben.eɪ, -tɑːˈ-, -ˈbiː.ni
notabilit|y ˌnəʊ.təˈbɪl.ə.t|i, -ɪ.t|i, US ˌnoʊ.t̬əˈbɪl.ə.t̬|i **-ies** -iz
notab|le ˈnəʊ.tə.b|əl, US ˈnoʊ.t̬ə- **-ly** -li **-leness** -əl.nəs, -nɪs
notarial nəʊˈteə.ri.əl, US noʊˈter.i- **-ly** -i
notariz|e, -is|e ˈnəʊ.tər.aɪz, US ˈnoʊ.t̬ə.raɪz **-es** -ɪz **-ing** -ɪŋ **-ed** -d
notar|y ˈnəʊ.tər|.i, US ˈnoʊ.t̬ɚ- **-ies** -iz
nota|te nəʊˈteɪ|t, US ˈnoʊ.teɪ|t **-tes** -ts **-ting** -tɪŋ, US -t̬ɪŋ **-ted** -tɪd, US -t̬ɪd
notation nəʊˈteɪ.ʃən, US noʊ- **-s** -z
notch nɒtʃ, US nɑːtʃ **-es** -ɪz **-ing** -ɪŋ **-ed** -t
not|e nəʊt, US noʊt **-es** -s **-ing** -ɪŋ, US ˈnoʊ.t̬ɪŋ **-ed** -ɪd, US ˈnoʊ.t̬ɪd
notebook ˈnəʊt.bʊk, US ˈnoʊt- **-s** -s
notelet ˈnəʊt.lət, -lɪt, US ˈnoʊt- **-s** -s
notepad ˈnəʊt.pæd, US ˈnoʊt- **-s** -z
notepaper ˈnəʊtˌpeɪ.pəʳ, US ˈnoʊtˌpeɪ.pɚ
noteworth|y ˈnəʊtˌwɜː.ð|i, US ˈnoʊtˌwɝː- **-ily** -əl.i, -ɪ.li **-iness** -ɪ.nəs, -ɪ.nɪs
not-for-profit ˌnɒt.fəˈprɒf.ɪt, US ˌnɑːt.fɚˈprɑː.fɪt
nothing ˈnʌθ.ɪŋ **-s** -z **-ness** -nəs, -nɪs

> Note: The pronunciation /ˈnɒθ-/ is increasingly widespread in British English, but cannot yet be recommended as representative of the accent being described here.

notic|e ˈnəʊ.tɪs, US ˈnoʊ.t̬ɪs **-es** -ɪz **-ing** -ɪŋ **-ed** -t
noticeab|le ˈnəʊ.tɪ.sə.b|əl, US ˈnoʊ.t̬ɪ- **-ly** -li
notice-board ˈnəʊ.tɪs.bɔːd, US ˈnoʊ.t̬ɪs.bɔːrd **-s** -z
notifiable ˈnəʊ.tɪ.faɪ.ə.bəl, -tə-, ˌnəʊ.tɪˈfaɪ-, -təˈ-, US ˈnoʊ.t̬ə.faɪ-

notification ˌnəʊ.tɪ.fɪˈkeɪ.ʃən, -tə-, -fəˈ-, (US) ˌnoʊ.t̬ə- **-s** -z
noti|fy ˈnəʊ.tɪ|.faɪ, -tə-, (US) ˈnoʊ.t̬ɪ-, -t̬ə- **-fies** -faɪz **-fying** -faɪ.ɪŋ **-fied** -faɪd
notion ˈnəʊ.ʃən, (US) ˈnoʊ- **-s** -z
notional ˈnəʊ.ʃən.əl, ˈnəʊʃ.nəl, (US) ˈnoʊ.ʃən.əl, ˈnoʊʃ.nəl **-ly** -i
notoriety ˌnəʊ.təˈraɪ.ə.ti, (US) ˌnoʊ.t̬əˈraɪ.ə.t̬i
notorious nəʊˈtɔː.ri.əs, (US) noʊˈtɔːr.i- **-ly** -li **-ness** -nəs, -nɪs
Notre Dame *in France:* ˌnəʊ.trəˈdɑːm, ˌnɒt.rəˈ-, (US) ˌnoʊ.trəˈ-, ˌnoʊ.t̬ɚˈ-, -ˈdeɪm *in the US:* ˌnəʊ.trəˈdeɪm, (US) ˌnoʊ.t̬ɚˈ-
Nottingham ˈnɒt.ɪŋ.əm, (US) ˈnɑː.t̬ɪŋ- **-shire** -ʃəʳ, -ʃɪəʳ, (US) -ʃɚ, -ʃɪr
Notting Hill ˌnɒt.ɪŋˈhɪl, (US) ˌnɑː.t̬ɪŋˈ- *stress shift, see compound:* ˌ**Notting Hill** ˈ**Gate**
Notts. (abbrev. for **Nottinghamshire**) nɒts, (US) nɑːts
notwithstanding ˌnɒt.wɪθˈstæn.dɪŋ, -wɪðˈ-, (US) ˌnɑːt-
Nouakchott nuˈɑːk.ʃɒt, (US) ˈnwɑːk.ʃɑːt, -ˈ-
nougat ˈnuː.gɑː, ˈnʌg.ət, (US) ˈnuː.gət **nougats** ˈnuː.gɑːz, ˈnʌg.əts, (US) ˈnuː.gəts
nought nɔːt, (US) nɑːt, nɔːt **-s** -s ˌ**noughts and** ˈ**crosses**
noughties ˈnɔː.t.iz, (US) ˈnɑː.t̬iz, ˈnɔː-
noumen|on ˈnuː.mə.n|ɒn, ˈnaʊ-, -mɪ-, -n|ən, (US) ˈnuː.mə.n|ɑːn **-a** -ə **-al** -əl
noun naʊn **-s** -z
nourish ˈnʌr.ɪʃ, (US) ˈnɜː- **-es** -ɪz **-ing** -ɪŋ **-ed** -t **-ment** -mənt
nourishing ˈnʌr.ɪ.ʃɪŋ, (US) ˈnɜː-
nous naʊs, (US) nuːs, naʊs
nouveau(x) ˈnuː.vəʊ, -ˈ-, (US) nuːˈvoʊ, ˈ--
nouveau(x) riche(s) ˌnuː.vəʊˈriːʃ, (US) -voʊˈ-
nouveau roman ˌnuː.vəʊ.rəʊˈmɑ̃ːŋ, (US) -voʊ.roʊˈmɑːn
nouvelle cuisine ˌnuː.vel.kwɪˈziːn, nuːˌvel-, -kwəˈ-, -kwiː-, (US) nuːˌvel-
nouvelle vague, N~ ˌnuː.velˈvɑːg
Nov. (abbrev. for **November**) nəʊˈvem.bəʳ, (US) noʊˈvem.bɚ
nov|a, N~ ˈnəʊ.v|ə, (US) ˈnoʊ- **-ae** -iː **-as** -əz
Nova Scotia ˌnəʊ.vəˈskəʊ.ʃə, (US) ˌnoʊ.vəˈskoʊ-
novation nəʊˈveɪ.ʃən, (US) noʊ-
Novaya Zemlya ˌnɒv.ə.jə.zemˈljɑː, ˌ-ɑː-, (US) ˌnɔː.vɑː.jɑː-, ˌnoʊ-
novel ˈnɒv.əl, (US) ˈnɑː.vəl **-istic** –ˈɪs.tɪk **-s** -z
novelette ˌnɒv.əlˈet, (US) ˌnɑː.vəlˈ- **-s** -s
novelist ˈnɒv.əl.ɪst, (US) ˈnɑː.vəl- **-s** -s
novelization, -isation ˌnɒv.əl.aɪˈzeɪ.ʃən, -ɪˈ-, (US) ˌnɑː.vəl.əˈ- **-s** -z
noveliz|e, -is|e ˈnɒv.əl.aɪz, (US) ˈnɑː.və.laɪz **-es** -ɪz **-ing** -ɪŋ **-ed** -d
novel|la nəʊˈvel|.ə, (US) noʊ- **-las** -z **-le** -eɪ
Novello nəˈvel.əʊ, (US) -oʊ
novelt|y ˈnɒv.əl.t|i, (US) ˈnɑː.vəl.t|i **-ies** -iz
November nəʊˈvem.bəʳ, (US) noʊˈvem.bɚ **-s** -z
novena nəʊˈviː.nə, (US) noʊ- **-s** -z
Novgorod ˈnɒv.gə.rɒd, (US) ˈnɔːv.gə.rɑːd, ˈnɑːv-, -rɑːt
Novial ˈnəʊ.vi.əl, (US) ˈnoʊ-
novic|e ˈnɒv.ɪs, (US) ˈnɑː.vɪs **-es** -ɪz
novitiate nəʊˈvɪʃ.i.ət, nɒvˈɪʃ-, -eɪt, -ɪt, (US) noʊˈvɪʃ.ɪt, ˈ-i.ɪt, -eɪt **-s** -s
Novocaine® ˈnəʊ.vəʊ.keɪn, ˈnɒv.əʊ-, (US) ˈnoʊ.və-
Novosibirsk ˌnəʊ.vəʊ.sɪˈbɪəsk, ˌnɒv.əʊ-, -səˈ-, (US) ˌnoʊ.və.sɪˈbɪrsk, -səˈ-
Novotna nəʊˈvɒt.nə, ˈnɒv.ɒt.nə, (US) nəˈvɑːt.nə
Novum Organum ˌnəʊ.vəmˈɔː.gə.nəm, -ɔːˈgɑː.nəm, (US) ˌnoʊ.vəmˈɔːr.gə.nəm; (US) -ɔːrˈgæn-
now naʊ
nowadays ˈnaʊ.ə.deɪz, ˈnaʊə-
Nowell *personal name:* ˈnəʊ.əl; ˈnəʊ.el, (US) ˈnoʊ.əl; (US) ˈnoʊ.el *Christmas:* nəʊˈel, (US) noʊ-
nowhere ˈnəʊ.*h*weəʳ, (US) ˈnoʊ.*h*wer
no-win ˌnəʊˈwɪn, (US) ˌnoʊ- *stress shift, see compound:* ˌ**no-win situ**ˈ**ation**
no-win-no-fee ˌnəʊ.wɪnˌnəʊˈfiː, (US) ˌnoʊ.wɪnˌnoʊ- *stress shift:* ˌ**no-win-**ˌ**no-fee** ˈ**claim**
nowise ˈnəʊ.waɪz, (US) ˈnoʊ-
nowt naʊt
noxious ˈnɒk.ʃəs, (US) ˈnɑːk- **-ly** -li **-ness** -nəs, -nɪs
Noye nɔɪ
Noyes nɔɪz
nozzle ˈnɒz.əl, (US) ˈnɑː.zəl **-s** -z
nr (abbrev. for **near**) nɪəʳ, (US) nɪr
NSPCC ˌen.esˌpiː.siːˈsiː
-n't ənt
Note: Weak-form suffix. This spelling represents a weak form of **not** which occurs after auxiliary verbs.
nth en*t*θ
nu njuː, (US) nuː, njuː
nuanc|e ˈnjuː.ɑːnts, -ɑ̃ːns, -ˈ-, (US) ˈnuː.ɑːnts, ˈnjuː-, -ˈ- **-es** -ɪz **-ed** -t
nub nʌb
nubble ˈnʌb.əl **-s** -z
nubbly ˈnʌb.li, -əl.i
Nubi|a ˈnjuː.bi|.ə, (US) ˈnuː-, ˈnjuː- **-an/s** -ən/z
nubile ˈnjuː.baɪl, (US) ˈnuː.bɪl, ˈnjuː-, -baɪl, -bəl
nubility njuːˈbɪl.ə.ti, -ɪ.ti, (US) nuːˈbɪl.ə.t̬i, njuː-
nuclear ˈnjuː.kli.əʳ, (US) ˈnuː.kli.ɚ, ˈnjuː- ˌ**nuclear dis**ˈ**armament**; ˌ**nuclear** ˈ**energy**; ˌ**nuclear** ˈ**family**; ˌ**nuclear** ˈ**fusion**; ˌ**nuclear** ˈ**industry**; ˌ**nuclear re**ˈ**actor**; ˌ**nuclear** ˈ**winter**

> Note: This word is sometimes mispronounced by British speakers as if it were spelt ‘nucular’, thus /ˈnjuː.kjə.ləʳ/; words ending /-kjə.ləʳ/ are much more common than those ending /-kli.əʳ/, which may explain this pronunciation. The equivalent American pronunciation /ˈnuː.kjə.lɚ/ is particularly associated with the speech of George W. Bush, and is often ridiculed by educated speakers.

nuclear-free ˌnjuː.kli.əˈfriː, (US) ˌnuː.kli.ɚˈ-, ˌnjuː- *stress shift, British only, see compound:* ˌ**nuclear-free** ˈ**zone** (US) ˌ**nuclear-**ˈ**free** ˌ**zone**
nucleic njuːˈkliː.ɪk, -ˈkleɪ-, (US) nuːˈkliː-, njuː-, -ˈkleɪ- **nu**ˌ**cleic** ˈ**acid**
nucleo- ˈnjuː.kli.əʊ, (US) ˈnuː.kli.oʊ, ˈnjuː-, -ə
nucleo|lus njuːˈkliː.əl|.əs; ˌnjuː.kliˈəʊ.l|əs, (US) nuːˈkliː.əl|.əs, njuː- **-i** -aɪ
nucleotide ˈnjuː.kli.əʊ.taɪd, (US) ˈnuː.kli.oʊ-, ˈnjuː- **-s** -z
nucle|us ˈnjuː.kli|.əs, (US) ˈnuː-, ˈnjuː- **-uses** -əs.ɪz **-i** -aɪ
nuclide ˈnjuː.klaɪd, (US) ˈnuː-, ˈnjuː- **-s** -z
nude njuːd, (US) nuːd, njuːd **-s** -z
nudg|e nʌdʒ **-es** -ɪz **-ing** -ɪŋ **-ed** -d
nud|ism ˈnjuː.dɪ|.zəm, (US) ˈnuː-, ˈnjuː- **-ist/s** -ɪst/s
nudit|y ˈnjuː.də.t|i, -ɪ.t|i, (US) ˈnuː.də.t̬|i, ˈnjuː-
Nuevo Leon nweɪ.vəʊ.leɪˈɒn, (US) nuːˈeɪ.voʊ.leɪˈɑːn
Nuffield ˈnʌf.iːld
nugatory ˈnjuː.gə.tər.i; njuːˈgeɪ-, (US) ˈnuː.gə.tɔːr-, ˈnjuː-
Nugent ˈnjuː.dʒənt, (US) ˈnuː-, ˈnjuː-
nugg|et ˈnʌg|.ɪt **-ets** -ɪts **-ety** -ɪ.ti, (US) -ɪ.t̬i
nuisanc|e ˈnjuː.sənts, (US) ˈnuː-, ˈnjuː- **-es** -ɪz
Nuit nʌt, (US) nʌt, nuːt
NUJ ˌen.juːˈdʒeɪ
nuk|e njuːk, (US) nuːk, njuːk **-es** -s **-ing** -ɪŋ **-ed** -t
Nuku'alofa ˌnuː.kuː.əˈlɔː.fə
null nʌl ˌ**null and** ˈ**void**
nullah ˈnʌl.ə **-s** -z
Nullarbor ˈnʌl.ə.bɔːʳ, (US) -ɚ.bɔːr ˌ**Nullarbor** ˈ**Plains**
nullification ˌnʌl.ɪ.fɪˈkeɪ.ʃən, ˌ-ə-, -fəˈ-
nulli|fy ˈnʌl.ɪ|.faɪ, ˈ-ə- **-fies** -faɪz **-fying** -faɪ.ɪŋ **-fied** -faɪd
nullipar|a nʌlˈɪp.ər|.ə, (US) nʌl-, nəˈlɪp- **-ae** -iː **-as** -əz **-ous** -əs
nullit|y ˈnʌl.ə.t|i, -ɪ.t|i, (US) -ə.t̬|i **-ies** -iz
NUM ˌen.juːˈem

Numa Pompilius ˌnjuː.mə.pɒmˈpɪl.i.əs, US ˌnuː.mə.pɑːmˈ-, ˌnjuː-
numb nʌm **-ly** -li **-ness** -nəs, -nɪs **-s** -z **-ing** -ɪŋ **-ed** -d
numbat ˈnʌm.bæt **-s** -s
numb|er ˈnʌm.b|əʳ, US -b|ɚ **-ers** -əz, US -ɚz **-ering** -ᵊr.ɪŋ **-ered** -əd, US -ɚd **-erless** -ᵊl.əs, -ɪs, US -ɚ.ləs, -lɪs ˌ**number** ˈ**one** *stress shift:* ˌ**number one** ˈ**fan**; ˌ**Number** ˈ**10/Ten** *stress shift:* ˌ**Number 10/Ten** ˈ**Downing Street**
number-crunch ˈnʌm.bə.krʌntʃ, US -bɚ- **-es** -ɪz **-ing** -ɪŋ **-ed** -t **-er/s** -əʳ/z, US -ɚ/z
numberplate ˈnʌm.bə.pleɪt, US -bɚ- **-s** -s
Numbers ˈnʌm.bəz, US -bɚz
numbing ˈnʌm.ɪŋ **-ly** -li
numbskull ˈnʌm.skʌl **-s** -z
numerable ˈnjuː.mᵊr.ə.bᵊl, US ˈnuː-, ˈnjuː-
numeracy ˈnjuː.mᵊr.ə.si, US ˈnuː-, ˈnjuː-
numeral ˈnjuː.mᵊr.ᵊl, US ˈnuː-, ˈnjuː- **-s** -z
numerate **adj** ˈnjuː.mᵊr.ət, -ɪt, US ˈnuː-, ˈnjuː-
numer|ate **v** ˈnjuː.mᵊr|.eɪt, US ˈnuː.mə.r|eɪt, ˈnjuː- **-ates** -eɪts **-ating** -eɪ.tɪŋ, US -eɪ.t̬ɪŋ **-ated** -eɪ.tɪd, US -eɪ.t̬ɪd
numeration ˌnjuː.mᵊrˈeɪ.ʃᵊn, US ˌnuː.məˈreɪ-, ˌnjuː-
numerative ˈnjuː.mᵊr.ə.tɪv, US ˈnuː.mɚ.ə.t̬ɪv, ˈnjuː- **-s** -z
numerator ˈnjuː.mᵊr.eɪ.təʳ, US ˈnuː.mə.reɪ.t̬ɚ, ˈnjuː- **-s** -z
numeric njuːˈmer.ɪk, US nuː-, njuː- **-s** -s
numerical njuːˈmer.ɪ.kᵊl, US nuː-, njuː- **-ly** -i
numerologic|al ˌnjuː.mᵊr.əˈlɒdʒ.ɪ.k|ᵊl, US ˌnuː.mɚ.əˈlɑː.dʒɪ-, ˌnjuː- **-ally** -ᵊl.i, -li
numerolog|y ˌnjuː.mᵊrˈɒl.ə.dʒ|i, US ˌnuː.məˈrɑː.lə-, ˌnjuː- **-ist/s** -ɪst/s
numero uno ˌnuː.mᵊr.əʊˈuː.nəʊ, US ˌnuː.mə.roʊˈuː.noʊ, ˌnjuː-
numerous ˈnjuː.mᵊr.əs, US ˈnuː-, ˈnjuː- **-ly** -li **-ness** -nəs, -nɪs
Numidi|a njuːˈmɪd.i|.ə, US nuː-, njuː- **-an/s** -ən/z
numinous ˈnjuː.mɪ.nəs, US ˈnuː-, ˈnjuː-
numismatic ˌnjuː.mɪzˈmæt.ɪk, US ˌnuː.mɪzˈmæt̬.ɪk, ˌnjuː- **-s** -s **-ally** -ᵊl.i, -li
numismatist njuːˈmɪz.mə.tɪst, US nuː-, njuː- **-s** -s
numnah ˈnʌm.nə **-s** -z
numskull ˈnʌm.skʌl **-s** -z
nun, N~ nʌn **-s** -z
Nunc Dimittis ˌnʊŋk.dɪˈmɪt.ɪs, ˌnʌŋk-, -daɪˈ-, -dəˈ-, US ˌnʊŋk.dɪˈmɪt̬- **-es** -ɪz
nunciature ˈnʌnt.si.ə.tʃʊəʳ, -tjʊəʳ, -tʃəʳ, US -tjʊr, -tʃɚ
nuncio ˈnʌn.ʃi.əʊ, -ʃəʊ, ˈnʌnt.si-, US ˈnʌnt.si.oʊ, ˈnʊnt- **-s** -z
Nuneaton nʌnˈiː.tᵊn
Nuneham ˈnjuː.nəm, US ˈnuː-, ˈnjuː-
Nunn nʌn
nunner|y ˈnʌn.ᵊr|.i **-ies** -iz
Nupe *language and people:* ˈnuː.peɪ **-s** -z
nuptial ˈnʌp.tʃᵊl, -ʃᵊl **-s** -z

> Note: This word is sometimes pronounced as if it were 'nuptual', thus /ˈnʌp.tʃu.əl/, perhaps through a confusion with words like 'conceptual'. It is considered a mispronunciation.

Nuremberg ˈnjʊə.rəm.bɜːg, ˈnjɔː-, US ˈnʊr.əm.bɝːg, ˈnjʊr-
Nureyev ˈnjʊə.ri.ef; -reɪ-, njʊəˈreɪ-, -ev, US ˈnʊr.i.ef, nʊˈreɪ.jef
Nurofen® ˈnjʊə.rəʊ.fen, ˈnjɔː-, US nuːˈroʊ.fən, njʊˈ-
nurs|e nɜːs, US nɝːs **-es** -ɪz **-ing** -ɪŋ **-ed** -t
nursemaid ˈnɜːs.meɪd, US ˈnɝːs- **-s** -z
nurser|y ˈnɜː.sᵊr|.i, US ˈnɝː- **-ies** -iz ˈ**nursery** ˌ**rhyme**; ˈ**nursery** ˌ**school**; ˈ**nursery** ˌ**slope**
nurserymaid ˈnɜː.sᵊr.i.meɪd, US ˈnɝː- **-s** -z
nursery|man ˈnɜː.sᵊr.i|.mən, US ˈnɝː- **-men** -mən
nursing ˈnɜː.sɪŋ, US ˈnɝː- ˈ**nursing** ˌ**home**; ˌ**nursing** ˈ**mother**
nurs(e)ling ˈnɜːs.lɪŋ, US ˈnɝːs- **-s** -z
nurt|ure ˈnɜː.tʃ|əʳ, US ˈnɝː.tʃ|ɚ **-ures** -əz, US -ɚz **-uring** -ᵊr.ɪŋ **-ured** -əd, US -ɚd
NUS ˌen.juːˈes
nut *food:* nʌt **-s** -s **-ting** -ɪŋ **-ted** -ɪd
Nut *Egyptian goddess:* nʌt, US nʌt, nuːt
NUT *trades union:* ˌen.juːˈtiː
nu|tate njuː|ˈteɪt, US nuː-, njuː- **-tates** -ˈteɪts **-tating** -ˈteɪ.tɪŋ, US -ˈteɪ.t̬ɪŋ **-tated** -ˈteɪ.tɪd, US -ˈteɪ.t̬ɪd
nutation njuːˈteɪ.ʃᵊn, US nuː-, njuː- **-al** -ᵊl **-s** -z
nut-brown ˌnʌtˈbraʊn *stress shift:* ˌ**nut-brown** ˈ**hair**
nutcas|e ˈnʌt.keɪs **-es** -ɪz
nutcracker ˈnʌtˌkræk.əʳ, US -ɚ **-s** -z
nuthatch ˈnʌt.hætʃ **-es** -ɪz
nuthou|se ˈnʌt.haʊ|s **-ses** -zɪz
Nutkin ˈnʌt.kɪn
nutmeg ˈnʌt.meg **-s** -z
nutraceutical ˌnjuː.trəˈsjuː.tɪ.kᵊl, -ˈsuː-, -ˈkjuː-, US ˌnuː.trəˈsuː.t̬ɪ-, ˌnjuː-, -ˈsjuː- **-s** -z
Nutrasweet® ˈnjuː.trəˌswiːt, US ˈnuː-, ˈnjuː
nutria ˈnjuː.tri.ə, US ˈnuː-, ˈnjuː-
nutrient ˈnjuː.tri.ənt, US ˈnuː-, ˈnjuː- **-s** -s
nutriment ˈnjuː.trə.mənt, -trɪ-, US ˈnuː-, ˈnjuː- **-s** -s
nutrition njuːˈtrɪʃ.ᵊn, US nuː-, njuː- **-al** -ᵊl **-ally** -ᵊl.i
nutritionist njuːˈtrɪʃ.ᵊn.ɪst, -ˈtrɪʃ.nɪst, US nuː-, njuː- **-s** -s
nutritious njuːˈtrɪʃ.əs, US nuː-, njuː- **-ly** -li **-ness** -nəs, -nɪs
nutritive ˈnjuː.trə.tɪv, -trɪ-, US ˈnuː.trə.t̬ɪv, ˈnjuː-
nuts nʌts ˌ**nuts and** ˈ**bolts**
nutshell ˈnʌt.ʃel **-s** -z
Nutt nʌt
Nuttall ˈnʌt.ɔːl
nutter, N~ ˈnʌt.əʳ, US ˈnʌt̬.ɚ
nutt|y ˈnʌt|.i, US ˈnʌt̬|.i **-ily** -ᵊ.li, -ɪ.li **-iness** -ɪ.nəs, -ɪ.nɪs
nux vomica ˌnʌksˈvɒm.ɪ.kə, US -ˈvɑː.mɪ-
nuzzl|e ˈnʌz.ᵊl **-es** -z **-ing** -ɪŋ, ˈnʌz.lɪŋ **-ed** -d
NVQ ˌen.viːˈkjuː
NW (abbrev. for **northwest**) ˌnɔːθˈwest; US ˌnɔːrθ-
NY (abbrev. for **New York**) ˌnjuːˈjɔːk, US ˌnuːˈjɔːrk, ˌnjuː-
Nyanja ˈnjæn.dʒə
Nyanza niˈæn.zə, naɪ-; ˈnjæn-, US ˈnjæn-, niˈæn-, naɪ-
Nyasa naɪˈæs.ə, ni-; ˈnjæs-, US naɪˈæs.ə; US ˈnjɑː.sɑː
Nyasaland naɪˈæs.ə.lænd, ni-; ˈnjæs-, US naɪˈæs-; US ˈnjɑː.sɑː.lænd
Nyerere njəˈreə.ri, nɪə-, -ˈrer.i, US njəˈrer-, ˌni.əˈ-
nylon ˈnaɪ.lɒn, US -lɑːn **-s** -z
Nyman ˈnaɪ.mən
Nymex ˈnaɪ.meks
nymph nɪmpf **-s** -s **-al** -ᵊl
nymphet, nymphette nɪmpˈfet; ˈnɪmp.fɪt, -fət, -fet, US ˈnɪmp.fət; US nɪmpˈfet
nympho ˈnɪmp.fəʊ, US -foʊ **-s** -z
nymphomani|a ˌnɪmp.fəʊˈmeɪ.ni|.ə, US -fəˈ-, -foʊˈ-, -ˈ-nj|ə **-ac/s** -æk
Nyree ˈnaɪə.riː, -ri, US ˈnaɪ-
nystagmus nɪˈstæg.məs
NZ (abbrev. for **New Zealand**) ˌenˈzed, US -ˈziː

N

Pronouncing the letter O

→ *See also* **OA, OEU, OI/OY, OO, OU, OW**

The vowel letter **o** has several pronunciations. The two most predictable strong pronunciations linked to spelling are: a monophthongal pronunciation, sometimes described as 'short' in British English /ɒ/ ⓤⓢ /ɑː ɔː/ and a diphthongal pronunciation, sometimes described as 'long' /əʊ/ ⓤⓢ /oʊ/.

In the monophthongal pronunciation, the **o** is generally followed by a consonant which closes the syllable, or a double consonant before another vowel, e.g.:

cod	kɒd ⓤⓢ kɑːd
robbing	ˈrɒb.ɪŋ ⓤⓢ ˈrɑː.bɪŋ

The diphthongal pronunciation usually means the **o** is followed by a single consonant and then a vowel, e.g.:

code	kəʊd ⓤⓢ koʊd
robing	ˈrəʊ.bɪŋ ⓤⓢ ˈroʊ.bɪŋ

In many cases, the monophthongal pronunciation results from the above kind of spelling, e.g.:

gone	gɒn ⓤⓢ gɑːn
copy	ˈkɒp.i ⓤⓢ ˈkɑː.pi

Also, the 'long' pronunciation occasionally appears in words where the vowel is followed by a single consonant and no vowel, e.g.:

control	kənˈtrəʊl ⓤⓢ -ˈtroʊl

When **o** is followed by **r**, the strong pronunciation is one of several possibilities: /ɒ/ ⓤⓢ /ɔːr/, /ɔː/ ⓤⓢ /ɔːr/, /ʌ/ ⓤⓢ /ɝː/, or /ɜː/ ⓤⓢ /ɝː/, e.g.:

forest	ˈfɒr.ɪst ⓤⓢ ˈfɔːr-
foremost	ˈfɔː.məʊst ⓤⓢ ˈfɔːr.moʊst
borough	ˈbʌr.ə ⓤⓢ ˈbɝː-
word	wɜːd ⓤⓢ wɝːd

And exceptionally, /ʊ/, e.g.:

Worcester	ˈwʊs.təʳ ⓤⓢ -tɚ

In addition

There are other vowel sounds associated with the letter **o**, e.g.:

ʌ	colour /ˈkʌl.əʳ/ ⓤⓢ /-ɚ/
uː	move /muːv/
ʊ	woman /ˈwʊm.ən/
wʌ	once /wʌnts/
ɜː ⓤⓢ ɝː	colonel /ˈkɜː.nəl/ ⓤⓢ /ˈkɝː-/

And, exceptionally:

ɪ	women /ˈwɪm.ɪn/

In weak syllables

The vowel letter **o** is realized with the vowel /ə/ in weak syllables, /ɚ/ in American English when followed by an **r**, and may also be elided in British English, due to compression or realization as a syllabic consonant, e.g.:

observe	əbˈzɜːv ⓤⓢ -ˈzɝːv
forget	fəˈget ⓤⓢ fɚ-
factory	ˈfæk.tər.i, -tri

o *the letter:* əʊ, ⓤⓢ oʊ **-'s** -z **-es** -z
O interj əʊ, ⓤⓢ oʊ
o' (abbrev. for **of**) *weak form only:* ə
Note: This spelling is used to represent a weak form of **of** in archaic and slang expressions and names, for example 'pint o' bitter' /ˌpaɪnt.əˈbɪt.əʳ/ ⓤⓢ /-ˈbɪţ.ɚ/, 'will-o'-the-wisp' /ˌwɪl.ə.ðəˈwɪsp/. In Irish surnames, O' may be pronounced as /ə/ or as /əʊ/ – see individual entries.
O. (abbrev. of **Ohio**) əʊ; əʊˈhaɪ.əʊ, ⓤⓢ oʊ; ⓤⓢ oʊˈhaɪ.oʊ, ə-
Oadby ˈəʊd.bi, ⓤⓢ ˈoʊd-
oaf əʊf, ⓤⓢ oʊf **-s** -s
oafish ˈəʊ.fɪʃ, ⓤⓢ ˈoʊ- **-ly** -li **-ness** -nəs, -nɪs
Oahu əʊˈɑː.huː, ⓤⓢ oʊ-
oak əʊk, ⓤⓢ oʊk **-s** -s **-en** -ən **-y** -i
oak-apple ˈəʊkˌæp.əl, ⓤⓢ ˈoʊk- **-s** -z
Oakdale ˈəʊk.deɪl, ⓤⓢ ˈoʊk-
Oakeley ˈəʊk.li, ⓤⓢ ˈoʊk-
Oakengates ˈəʊ.kən.geɪts, -kəŋ-, ˌ--ˈ-, ⓤⓢ ˈoʊk.ən.geɪts, ˌ--ˈ-
Oakes əʊks, ⓤⓢ oʊks
Oakey ˈəʊ.ki, ⓤⓢ ˈoʊ-
Oakham ˈəʊ.kəm, ⓤⓢ ˈoʊ-
Oakhampton ˌəʊkˈhæmp.tən, ⓤⓢ ˈoʊkˌhæmp- *stress shift, British only:* **ˌOakhampton ˈcentre**
Oakland ˈəʊk.lənd, ⓤⓢ ˈoʊk- **-s** -z
Oakleigh, Oakley ˈəʊk.li, ⓤⓢ ˈoʊk-
Oaks əʊks, ⓤⓢ oʊks
oakum ˈəʊ.kəm, ⓤⓢ ˈoʊ-
Oakworth ˈəʊk.wəθ, -wɜːθ, ⓤⓢ ˈoʊk.wɚθ, -wɝːθ
OAP ˌəʊ.eɪˈpiː, ⓤⓢ ˌoʊ- **-s** -z
OAPEC ˌəʊˈeɪ.pek, ⓤⓢ ˌoʊ-
oar ɔːʳ, ⓤⓢ ɔːr **-s** -z **-ing** -ɪŋ **-ed** -d
ˌstick one's ˈoar in
oarlock ˈɔː.lɒk, ⓤⓢ ˈɔːr.lɑːk **-s** -s
oars|man ˈɔːz|.mən, ⓤⓢ ˈɔːrz- **-men** -mən **-woman** -ˌwʊm.ən **-women** -ˌwɪm.ɪn
OAS ˌəʊ.eɪ.ˈes, ⓤⓢ ˌoʊ-
oas|is, O~ əʊˈeɪ.s|ɪs, ⓤⓢ oʊ- **-es** -iːz
oast əʊst, ⓤⓢ oʊst **-s** -s
oasthou|se ˈəʊst.haʊ|s, ⓤⓢ ˈoʊst- **-ses** -zɪz
oat əʊt, ⓤⓢ oʊt **-s** -s
oatcake ˈəʊt.keɪk, ⓤⓢ ˈoʊt- **-s** -s
oaten ˈəʊ.tən, ⓤⓢ ˈoʊ-
Oates əʊts, ⓤⓢ oʊts
oa|th əʊ|θ, ⓤⓢ oʊ|θ **-ths** -ðz, -θs
Oatlands ˈəʊt.ləndz, ⓤⓢ ˈoʊt-
oatmeal ˈəʊt.miːl, ⓤⓢ ˈoʊt-
oats əʊts, ⓤⓢ oʊts
Oaxaca wəˈhɑː.kə, wɑː-, ⓤⓢ wɑːˈhɑː.kɑː, wə-, -kə
Ob ɒb, ⓤⓢ ɑːb, ɑːp
Obadiah ˌəʊ.bəˈdaɪ.ə, ⓤⓢ ˌoʊ-
Obama əʊˈbɑː.mə, -ˈbæm.ə, əˈ-, ⓤⓢ oʊˈbæm.ə
Oban ˈəʊ.bən, ⓤⓢ ˈoʊ-
obbligat|o ˌɒb.lɪˈgɑː.t|əʊ, -ləˈ-, ⓤⓢ ˌɑː.blɪˈgɑː.ţ|oʊ **-os** -əʊz, ⓤⓢ -oʊz **-i** -iː
obduracy ˈɒb.dʒər.ə.si, -djər-, -dʒʊ.rə-, -djʊ.rə-, ⓤⓢ ˈɑːb.dʊr.ə-, -djʊr-
obdurate ˈɒb.dʒər.ət, ˈ-djər-, -dʒʊ.rət, -djʊ.rət, -rɪt, -reɪt, ⓤⓢ ˈɑːb.dʊr.ɪt, -djʊr- **-ly** -li **-ness** -nəs, -nɪs
obduration ˌɒb.dʒərˈeɪ.ʃən, -dʒərˈ-, -dʒʊˈreɪ-, -djʊˈreɪ-, ⓤⓢ ˌɑː.b.dʊrˈeɪ, -djʊrˈ-
OBE ˌəʊ.biːˈiː, ⓤⓢ ˌoʊ- **-s** -z
obeah, O~ ˈəʊ.bi.ə, ⓤⓢ ˈoʊ-
obedience əʊˈbiː.di.ənts, ⓤⓢ oʊ-, ə-, ˈ-djənts

Pronouncing the letters OA

The vowel digraph **oa** has two main strong pronunciations: /əʊ/ (US) /oʊ/ and /ɔː/ (US) /ɑː/, e.g.:

road rəʊd (US) roʊd
broad brɔːd (US) brɑːd

When the digraph is followed by an **r** in the spelling, the strong pronunciation is /ɔː/ (US) /ɔːr/, e.g.:

board bɔːd (US) bɔːrd
soar sɔːʳ (US) sɔːr

In addition

Another vowel sound associated with the digraph **oa** is /əʊə/ (US) /oʊə/, e.g.:

coalescence kəʊ.əˈles.ənts (US) koʊ.ə-

In weak syllables

The vowel digraph **oa** is realized with the vowel /ə/ in weak syllables and with /ɚ/ in American English when followed by an **r**, e.g.:

cupboard ˈkʌb.əd (US) -ɚd

obedient əʊˈbiː.di.ənt, (US) oʊ-, ə-, ˈ-djənt **-ly** -li
obeisanc|e əʊˈbeɪ.sᵊnts, (US) oʊ-, -ˈbiː- **-es** -ɪz
obelisk ˈɒb.ᵊl.ɪsk, -ɪ.lɪsk, (US) ˈɑː.bᵊl.ɪsk **-s** -s
obel|us ˈɒb.ᵊl|.əs, -ɪ.l|əs, (US) ˈɑː.bᵊl|.əs, ˈoʊ- **-i** -aɪ
Oberammergau ˌəʊ.bəˈræm.ə.gaʊ, (US) ˌoʊ.bɚˈɑː.mɚ-
Oberland ˈəʊ.bə.lænd, (US) ˈoʊ.bɚ-
Oberlin ˈəʊ.bə.lɪn, (US) ˈoʊ.bɚ-
Oberon ˈəʊ.bᵊr.ɒn, -ᵊn, (US) ˈoʊ.bə.rɑːn, -bɚ.ən
obese əʊˈbiːs, (US) oʊ- **-ness** -nəs, -nɪs
obesity əʊˈbiː.sə.ti, -sɪ-, (US) oʊˈbiː.sə.ţi
obey əʊˈbeɪ, (US) oʊ-, ə- **-s** -z **-ing** -ɪŋ **-ed** -d **-er/s** -əʳ/z, (US) -ɚ/z
obfus|cate ˈɒb.fʌs|.keɪt, -fə.s|keɪt, (US) ˈɑː.b.fəs-; (US) ɑːbˈfʌs|.keɪt **-cates** -keɪts **-cating** -keɪ.tɪŋ, (US) -keɪ.ţɪŋ **-cated** -keɪ.tɪd, (US) -keɪ.ţɪd
obfuscation ˌɒb.fʌsˈkeɪ.ʃᵊn, -fəˈskeɪ-, (US) ˌɑː.b.fəˈskeɪ- **-s** -z
obfuscatory ˌɒb.fʌsˈkeɪ.tᵊr.i, -fəˈskeɪ-, (US) ɑːbˈfʌs.kə.tɔːr-, əb-
ob-gyn ˌəʊ.biːˌdʒiː.waɪˈen; ˌɒbˈgaɪn, (US) ˌoʊ.bi.dʒi.waɪˈen
obi ˈəʊ.bi, (US) ˈoʊ- **-s** -z
Obi *river in Siberia:* ˈəʊ.bi, (US) ˈoʊ-
Obie ˈəʊ.bi, (US) ˈoʊ- **-s** -z
obit ˈɒb.ɪt; əʊˈbɪt, (US) ˈoʊ-, -ˈ- **-s** -s
obiter dict|um ˌɒb.ɪ.təˈdɪk.t|ʊm, ˌəʊ.bɪ-, -t|əm, (US) ˌoʊ.bɪ.ţɚˈdɪk-, ˌɑː- **-a** -ə
obituarist əʊˈbɪtʃ.ʊə.rɪst, ɒbˈɪtʃ-, -ˈɪt.jʊə-, -jə-, -jʊ-, (US) oʊˈbɪtʃ.u.ɚ.ɪst, ə- **-s** -s
obituar|y əʊˈbɪtʃ.ʊə.r|i, ɒbˈɪtʃ-, -ˈɪt.jʊə-, -jə-, -jʊ-, (US) oʊˈbɪtʃ.u.er|.i, ə- **-ies** -iz
object n ˈɒb.dʒɪkt, -dʒekt, (US) ˈɑːb- **-s** -s ˈ**object** ˌ**lesson**
object v əbˈdʒekt **-s** -s **-ing** -ɪŋ **-ed** -ɪd **-or/s** -əʳ/z, (US) -ɚ/z
objecti|fy əbˈdʒek.tɪ|.faɪ, ɒb-, ˈ-tə-, (US) əbˈdʒek.tɪ-, ˈ-tə- **-fies** -faɪz **-fying** -faɪ.ɪŋ **-fied** -faɪd
objection əbˈdʒek.ʃᵊn **-s** -z
objectionab|le əbˈdʒek.ʃᵊn.ə.b|ᵊl, -ˈdʒekʃ.nə- **-ly** -li
objective əbˈdʒek.tɪv, ɒb-, (US) əb- **-s** -z **-ly** -li **-ness** -nəs, -nɪs
objectivism əbˈdʒek.tɪ.vɪ.zᵊm, ɒb-, (US) əbˈdʒek.tə-
objectivity ˌɒb.dʒɪkˈtɪv.ə.ti, -dʒek-, -ɪ.ti, (US) ˌɑː.b.dʒekˈtɪv.ə.ţi
objectless ˈɒb.dʒɪkt.ləs, -dʒekt-, -lɪs, (US) ˈɑː.b.dʒɪkt-
object-oriented ˌɒb.dʒɪktˈɔː.ri.en.tɪd, -dʒektˈ-, -ˈɒr.i-, (US) ˌɑː.b.dʒɪktˈɔːr.i.en.ţɪd
objet(s) d'art ˌɒb.ʒeɪˈdɑːʳ, (US) ˌɑː.b.ʒeɪˈdɑːr
objet(s) trouvé(s) ˌɒb.ʒeɪ.truːˈveɪ, (US) ˌɑːb-
objur|gate ˈɒb.dʒə|.geɪt, -dʒɜː-, (US) ˈɑː.b.dʒɚ-, əbˈdʒɝː- **-gates** -geɪts **-gating** -geɪ.tɪŋ, (US) -geɪ.ţɪŋ **-gated** -geɪ.tɪd, (US) -geɪ.ţɪd
objurgation ˌɒb.dʒəˈgeɪ.ʃᵊn, -dʒɜːˈ-, (US) ˌɑː.b.dʒɚˈ- **-s** -z
objurgatory ɒbˈdʒɜː.gə.tᵊr.i, əb-; ˌɒb.dʒəˈgeɪ-, -dʒɜːˈ-, (US) əbˈdʒɝː.gə.tɔːr-
oblate adj ˈɒb.leɪt; -ˈ-, əʊˈbleɪt, (US) ˈɑː.bleɪt, -ˈ- **-ly** -li **-ness** -nəs, -nɪs
oblate n ˈɒb.leɪt, (US) ˈɑː.bleɪt **-s** -s
oblation əʊˈbleɪ.ʃᵊn, ɒbˈleɪ-, (US) əˈbleɪ-, oʊ-, ɑː- **-s** -z
obligat|e ˈɒb.lɪ.geɪt, (US) ˈɑː.blɪ- **-es** -s **-ing** -ɪŋ **-ed** -ɪd
obligation ˌɒb.lɪˈgeɪ.ʃᵊn, -ləˈ-, (US) ˌɑː.bləˈ- **-s** -z
obligat|o ˌɒb.lɪˈgɑː.t|əʊ, -ləˈ-, (US) ˌɑː.blɪˈgɑː.ţ|oʊ **-os** -əʊz, (US) -oʊz **-i** -iː
obligator|y əˈblɪg.ə.tᵊr|.i, ɒbˈlɪg-; ˌɒb.lɪˈgeɪ-, -ləˈ-, (US) əˈblɪg.ə.tɔːr-; (US) ˈɑː.blə.gə- **-ily** -ᵊl.i, -ɪ.li **-iness** -ɪ.nəs, -ɪ.nɪs
oblig|e əˈblaɪdʒ, (US) ə-, oʊ- **-es** -ɪz **-ing/ly** -ɪŋ/li **-ingness** -ɪŋ.nəs, -nɪs **-ed** -d
obliged əˈblaɪdʒd, (US) ə-, oʊ-
obligee ˌɒb.lɪˈdʒiː, -ləˈ-, (US) ˌɑː.bləˈ- **-s** -z
obliging əˈblaɪ.dʒɪŋ, (US) ə-, oʊ-
obligor ˌɒb.lɪˈgɔːʳ, -ləˈ-, (US) ˌɑː.bləˈgɔːr, ˈ--- **-s** -z
oblique əʊˈbliːk, (US) oʊ-, ə-, -ˈblaɪk **-ly** -li **-ness** -nəs, -nɪs
obliquit|y əʊˈblɪk.wə.t|i, -wɪ-, (US) əˈblɪk.wə.ţ|i **-ies** -iz
obliter|ate əˈblɪt.ᵊr|.eɪt, (US) -ˈblɪţ.ə.r|eɪt, oʊ- **-ates** -eɪts **-ating** -eɪ.tɪŋ, (US) -eɪ.ţɪŋ **-ated** -eɪ.tɪd, (US) -eɪ.ţɪd
obliteration əˌblɪt.ᵊrˈeɪ.ʃᵊn, (US) -ˌblɪţ.əˈreɪ-, oʊ- **-s** -z
oblivion əˈblɪv.i.ən
oblivious əˈblɪv.i.əs **-ly** -li **-ness** -nəs, -nɪs
oblong ˈɒb.lɒŋ, (US) ˈɑː.b.lɑːŋ, -lɔːŋ **-s** -z
obloquy ˈɒb.lə.kwi, (US) ˈɑːb-
obnoxious əbˈnɒk.ʃəs, ɒb-, (US) əbˈnɑːk-, ɑːb- **-ly** -li **-ness** -nəs, -nɪs
oboe ˈəʊ.bəʊ, (US) ˈoʊ.boʊ **-s** -z
oboe d'amore ˌəʊ.bəʊ.dæmˈɔː.reɪ, -dəˈmɔː-, -riː, (US) ˌoʊ.boʊ.dəˈmɔːr.eɪ
oboist ˈəʊ.bəʊ.ɪst, (US) ˈoʊ.boʊ- **-s** -s
obol ˈɒb.ɒl, ˈəʊ.bɒl, -bᵊl, (US) ˈɑː.bᵊl, ˈoʊ- **-s** -z
Obote əʊˈbəʊ.teɪ, ɒbˈəʊ-, -ti, (US) oʊˈboʊ-
O'Boyle əʊˈbɔɪl, (US) oʊ-
O'Brady əʊˈbreɪ.di, -ˈbrɔː-, (US) oʊˈbreɪ-
O'Brien, O'Bryan əʊˈbraɪən, (US) oʊ-
obscene əbˈsiːn, ɒb-, (US) əb-, ɑːb- **-ly** -li **-ness** -nəs, -nɪs
obscenit|y əbˈsen.ə.t|i, ɒb-, -ɪ.t|i, (US) əbˈsen.ə.ţ|i, ɑːb- **-ies** -iz
obscurant ɒbˈskjʊə.rᵊnt, əb-, (US) ɑːbˈskjʊr.ᵊnt, əb-
obscurant|ism ˌɒb.skjʊəˈræn.t|ɪ.zᵊm; ɒbˈskjʊə.rən-, əb-, (US) ɑːbˈskjʊr.ən-, əb- **-ist/s** -ɪst/s
obscuration ˌɒb.skjʊəˈreɪ.ʃᵊn, -skjəˈ-, (US) ˌɑː.b.skjʊˈ- **-s** -z
obscur|e əbˈskjʊəʳ, -ˈskjɔːʳ, (US) əbˈskjʊr, ɑːb- **-er** -əʳ, (US) -ɚ **-est** -ɪst, -əst **-ely** -li **-eness** -nəs, -nɪs **-es** -z **-ing** -ɪŋ **-ed** -d
obscurit|y əbˈskjʊə.rə.t|i, -ˈskjɔː-, -rɪ-, (US) əbˈskjʊr.ə.ţ|i, ɑːb- **-ies** -iz
obse|crate ˈɒb.sɪ|.kreɪt, -sə-, (US) ˈɑː.b.sɪ- **-crates** -kreɪts **-crating** -kreɪ.tɪŋ, (US) -kreɪ.ţɪŋ **-crated** -kreɪ.tɪd, (US) -kreɪ.ţɪd
obsecration ˌɒb.sɪˈkreɪ.ʃᵊn, -səˈ-, (US) ˌɑː.b.səˈ- **-s** -z
obsequies ˈɒb.sɪ.kwiz, -sə-; ɒbˈsiː-, (US) ˈɑː.b.sɪ-
obsequious əbˈsiː.kwi.əs, ɒb-, (US) əb-, ɑːb- **-ly** -li **-ness** -nəs, -nɪs
observab|le əbˈzɜː.və.b|ᵊl, (US) -ˈzɝː- **-ly** -li **-leness** -ᵊl.nəs, -nɪs
observanc|e əbˈzɜː.vᵊnts, (US) -ˈzɝː- **-es** -ɪz

observant əbˈzɜː.vənt, (US) -ˈzɝː- -ly -li
observation ˌɒb.zəˈveɪ.ʃən, (US) ˌɑːb.zɚˈ-, -sɚˈ- -s -z
observational ˌɒb.zəˈveɪ.ʃən.əl, -veɪʃ.nəl, (US) ˌɑːb.zɚˈ-, -sɚˈ- -ly -i
observator|y əbˈzɜː.və.tr|i, -tər|.i, (US) -ˈzɝː.və.tɔːr- -ies -iz
observ|e əbˈzɜːv, (US) -ˈzɝːv -es -z -ing/ly -ɪŋ/li -ed -d
observer, O~ əbˈzɜː.vəʳ, (US) -ˈzɝː.vɚ -s -z
obsess əbˈses, ɒb-, (US) əb- -es -ɪz -ing -ɪŋ -ed -t
obsession əbˈseʃ.ən, ɒb-, (US) əb- -s -s -al -əl
obsessive əbˈses.ɪv, ɒb-, (US) əb- -s -z -ly -li -ness -nəs, -nɪs
obsidian ɒbˈsɪd.i.ən, əb-, (US) əb-, ɑːb-
obsolescence ˌɒb.səˈles.ənts, -səlˈes-, (US) ˌɑːb-
obsolescent ˌɒb.səˈles.ənt, -səlˈes-, (US) ˌɑːb- -ly -li
obsolete ˈɒb.səl.iːt, (US) ˌɑːb.səlˈiːt -ly -li -ness -nəs, -nɪs
obstacle ˈɒb.stə.kəl, -stɪ-, (US) ˈɑːb.stə- -s -z **ˈobstacle ˌcourse**
obstetric ɒbˈstet.rɪk, əb-, (US) əb-, ɑːb- -al -əl -s -s
obstetrician ˌɒb.stəˈtrɪʃ.ən, -stɪˈ-, -stetˈrɪʃ-, (US) ˌɑːb.stəˈtrɪʃ- -s -z
obstinac|y ˈɒb.stɪ.nə.s|i, -stən.ə-, (US) ˈɑːb.stə.nə- -ies -iz
obstinate ˈɒb.stɪ.nət, -stən.ət, -ɪt, (US) ˈɑːb.stə.nət -ly -li -ness -nəs, -nɪs
obstreperous əbˈstrep.ər.əs, ɒb-, (US) əb-, ɑːb- -ly -li -ness -nəs, -nɪs
obstruct əbˈstrʌkt -s -s -ing -ɪŋ -ed -ɪd -or/s -əʳ/z, (US) -ɚ/z
obstruction əbˈstrʌk.ʃən -s -z
obstructionism əbˈstrʌk.ʃən.ɪ.zəm
obstructionist əbˈstrʌk.ʃən.ɪst -s -s
obstructive əbˈstrʌk.tɪv -ly -li -ness -nəs, -nɪs
obstruent ˈɒb.stru.ənt, (US) ˈɑːb- -s -s
obtain əbˈteɪn -s -z -ing -ɪŋ -ed -d -er/s -əʳ/z, (US) -ɚ/z -able -ə.bəl
obtrud|e əbˈtruːd, ɒb-, (US) əb-, ɑːb- -es -z -ing -ɪŋ -ed -ɪd -er/s -əʳ/z, (US) -ɚ/z
obtrusion əbˈtruː.ʒən, ɒb-, (US) əb-, ɑːb- -s -z
obtrusive əbˈtruː.sɪv, ɒb-, -zɪv, (US) əb-, ɑːb- -ly -li -ness -nəs, -nɪs
obtu|rate ˈɒb.tʃʊə|.reɪt, -tjʊə-, -tʃə-, (US) ˈɑːb.tə-, -tjə-, -tʊ-, -tjʊ- -rates -reɪts -rating -reɪ.tɪŋ, (US) -reɪ.t̬ɪŋ -rated -reɪ.tɪd, (US) -reɪ.t̬ɪd -rator/s -reɪ.təʳ/z, (US) -reɪ.t̬ɚ/z
obturation ˌɒb.tʃʊəˈreɪ.ʃən, -tjʊˈ-, -tʃəˈ-, (US) ˌɑːb.təˈ-, -tjəˈ-, -tʊˈ-, -tjʊˈ- -s -z
obtuse əbˈtʃuːs, -ˈtjuːs, ɒb-, (US) ɑːbˈtuːs, əb-, -ˈtjuːs -ly -li -ness -nəs, -nɪs
obvers|e adj ˈɒb.vɜːs, (US) ɑːbˈvɝːs, əb-; (US) ˈɑːb.vɝːs
obvers|e n ˈɒb.vɜːs, (US) ˈɑːb.vɝːs -es -ɪz
obversely ˈɒb.vɜː.sli, (US) ɑːbˈvɝː-
ob|vert ɒb|ˈvɜːt, əb-, (US) ɑːb|ˈvɝːt, əb- -verts -ˈvɜːts, (US) -ˈvɝːts -verting -ˈvɜː.tɪŋ, (US) -ˈvɝː.t̬ɪŋ -verted -ˈvɜː.tɪd, (US) -ˈvɝː.t̬ɪd
obvi|ate ˈɒb.vi|.eɪt, (US) ˈɑːb- -ates -eɪts -ating -eɪ.tɪŋ, (US) -eɪ.t̬ɪŋ -ated -eɪ.tɪd, (US) -eɪ.t̬ɪd
obviative ˈɒb.vi.ə.tɪv, (US) ˈɑːb.vi.eɪ.t̬ɪv
obvious ˈɒb.vi.əs, (US) ˈɑːb- -ly -li -ness -nəs, -nɪs
O'Byrne əʊˈbɜːn, (US) oʊˈbɝːn
O'Callaghan əʊˈkæl.ə.hən, -gən, -hæn, (US) oʊˈkæl.ə.hən, -hæn
ocarina ˌɒk.ərˈiː.nə, (US) ˌɑː.kəˈriː- -s -z
O'Casey əʊˈkeɪ.si, (US) oʊ-
occam, O~ ˈɒk.əm, (US) ˈɑː.kəm
occasion əˈkeɪ.ʒən -s -z -ing -ɪŋ -ed -d **ˌrise to the ocˈcasion**
occasional əˈkeɪ.ʒən.əl, -ˈkeɪʒ.nəl -ly -i
occasional|ism əˈkeɪ.ʒən.əl|.ɪ.zəm, -ˈkeɪʒ.nəl- -ist/s -ɪst/s
occident, O~ ˈɒk.sɪ.dənt, -sə-, (US) ˈɑːk.sə.dənt, -sɪ-, -dent
occidental, O~ ˌɒk.sɪˈden.təl, -səˈ-, (US) ˌɑːk.səˈden.t̬əl, -sɪˈ- -s -z
occidental|ism, O~ ˌɒk.sɪˈden.təl|.ɪ.zəm, -səˈ-, (US) ˌɑːk.səˈden.t̬əl-, -sɪˈ- -ist/s -ɪst/s
occidentaliz|e, -is|e ˌɒk.sɪˈden.təl.aɪz, -səˈ-, (US) ˌɑːk.səˈden.t̬əl-, -sɪˈ- -es -ɪz -ing -ɪŋ -ed -d
occipita (from **occiput**) ɒkˈsɪp.ɪ.tə, (US) ɑːkˈsɪp.ɪ.t̬ə
occipital ɒkˈsɪp.ɪ.təl, ˈ-ə-, (US) ɑːkˈsɪp.ɪ.t̬əl -ly -i
occiput ˈɒk.sɪ.pʌt, -pʊt, -pət, (US) ˈɑːk.sɪ.pʌt, -pət -s -s **occipita** ɒkˈsɪp.ɪ.tə, (US) ɑːkˈsɪp.ɪ.t̬ə
occlud|e əˈkluːd, ɒkˈluːd, (US) əˈkluːd, ɑː- -es -z -ing -ɪŋ -ed -ɪd
occlusal əˈkluː.zəl, ɒkˈluː-, (US) əˈkluː-, ɑː-
occlusion əˈkluː.ʒən, ɒkˈluː-, (US) əˈkluː-, ɑː- -s -z
occlusive əˈkluː.sɪv, ɒkˈluː-, (US) əˈkluː-, ɑː- -s -z
occult adj ˈɒk.ʌlt; əˈkʌlt, ɒkˈʌlt, (US) əˈkʌlt; (US) ˈɑː.kʌlt -ly -li -ness -nəs, -nɪs
occul|t v ɒkˈʌl|t, əˈkʌl|t, (US) ə- -ts -ts -ting -tɪŋ, (US) -t̬ɪŋ -ted -tɪd, (US) -t̬ɪd
occultation ˌɒk.əlˈteɪ.ʃən, -ʌlˈ-, (US) ˌɑː.kʌlˈ- -s -z
occult|ism ˈɒk.əl.t|ɪ.zəm, -ʌl-; ɒkˈʌl-, əˈkʌl-, (US) əˈkʌl-; (US) ˈɑː.kʌl- -ist/s -ɪst/s
occupancy ˈɒk.jə.pənt.si, -jʊ-, (US) ˈɑː.kjə-, -kjʊ-
occupant ˈɒk.jə.pənt, -jʊ-, (US) ˈɑː.kjə-, -kjʊ- -s -s
occupation ˌɒk.jəˈpeɪ.ʃən, -jʊˈ-, (US) ˌɑː.kjəˈ-, -kjʊˈ- -s -z
occupational ˌɒk.jəˈpeɪ.ʃən.əl, -jʊˈ-, -ˈpeɪʃ.nəl, (US) ˌɑː.kjəˈ-, -kjʊˈ- -ly -i *stress shift, see compound:* **ˌoccupational ˈtherapy**
occupier ˈɒk.jə.paɪ.əʳ, -jʊ-, (US) ˈɑː.kjə.paɪ.ɚ, -kjʊ- -s -z
occup|y ˈɒk.jə.p|aɪ, -jʊ-, (US) ˈɑː.kjuː-, -kjə- -ies -aɪz -ying -aɪ.ɪŋ -ied -aɪd
occur əˈkɜːʳ, (US) -ˈkɝː -s -z -ring -ɪŋ -red -d
occurrenc|e əˈkʌr.ənts, (US) -ˈkɝː- -es -ɪz
ocean ˈəʊ.ʃən, (US) ˈoʊ- -s -z **a ˌdrop in the ˈocean**
oceanfront ˈəʊ.ʃən.frʌnt, (US) ˈoʊ- -s -s
ocean-going ˈəʊ.ʃənˌgəʊ.ɪŋ, (US) ˈoʊ.ʃənˌgoʊ-
Oceani|a ˌəʊ.ʃiˈɑː.ni|.ə, -siˈ|-, -ˈeɪ-, (US) ˌoʊ.ʃiˈæn.i|-, -ˈɑː.ni|-, -ˈeɪ- -an/s -ən/z
oceanic, O~ ˌəʊ.ʃiˈæn.ɪk, -siˈ-, (US) ˌoʊ.ʃiˈ-
oceanographic ˌəʊ.ʃən.əʊˈgræf.ɪk, -ʃi.ən-, (US) ˌoʊ.ʃə.noʊˈ-, -ʃi.ə- -ally -əl.i, -li
oceanograph|y ˌəʊ.ʃənˈɒg.rə.f|i, -ʃi.ənˈ-, (US) ˌoʊ.ʃəˈnɑː.grə-, -ʃi.əˈ- -er/s -əʳ/z, (US) -ɚ/z
oceanolog|y ˌəʊ.ʃənˈɒl.ə.dʒ|i, -ʃi.ənˈ-, (US) ˌoʊ.ʃəˈnɑː.lə-, -ʃi.əˈ- -ist/s -ɪst/s
Oceanus əʊˈsiː.ə.nəs, -ˈʃiː-, (US) oʊˈsiː-
ocell|us əʊˈsel|.əs, (US) oʊ- -i -aɪ, -iː
ocelot ˈɒs.əl.ɒt, ˈəʊ.səl-, -sɪ.lɒt, (US) ˈɑː.sə.lɑːt, ˈoʊ-, -lət -s -s
och ɒx, (US) ɑːk; *as if Scots:* (US) ɑːx
oche ˈɒk.i, (US) ˈɑː.ki -s -z
ocher ˈəʊ.kəʳ, (US) ˈoʊ.kɚ -ous -əs
Ochil(l) ˈəʊ.kəl, -xəl, (US) ˈoʊ.tʃɪl, ˈɑː-, -kəl
Ochiltree *in Scott's 'Antiquary':* ˈəʊ.kɪl.triː, -xɪl-, ˈɒk.ɪl-, ˈɒx-, -əl-, (US) ˈoʊ.kɪl-, ˈɑː-, -tʃɪl- *in US:* ˈəʊ.kɪl.triː, (US) ˈoʊ-
och|re ˈəʊ.k|əʳ, (US) ˈoʊ.k|ɚ -res -əz, (US) -ɚz -reing -ər.ɪŋ -red -əd, (US) -ɚd
ochreous ˈəʊ.kri.əs, -kər-, (US) ˈoʊ-
ochry ˈəʊ.kər.i, (US) ˈoʊ-
Ochterlony ˌɒk.təˈləʊ.ni, ˌɒx-, (US) ˌɑːk.tɚˈloʊ-
ocker, okker ˈɒk.əʳ, (US) ˈɑː.kɚ -s -z
Ockham ˈɒk.əm, (US) ˈɑː.kəm
Ockley ˈɒk.li, (US) ˈɑːk-
O'Clery əʊˈklɪə.ri, (US) oʊˈklɪr.i
o'clock əˈklɒk, (US) -ˈklɑːk
O'Connell əʊˈkɒn.əl, (US) oʊˈkɑː.nəl
O'Connor əʊˈkɒn.əʳ, (US) oʊˈkɑː.nɚ
Ocracoke ˈəʊ.krə.kəʊk, (US) ˈoʊ.krə.koʊk
Oct. (abbrev. for **October**) ɒkˈtəʊ.bəʳ, (US) ɑːkˈtoʊ.bɚ
octa- ˈɒk.tə; ɒkˈtæ, (US) ˈɑːk-; (US) ɑːkˈtæ
Note: Prefix. Normally either takes primary or secondary stress on the

Pronouncing the letters OEU

The vowel letter combination **oeu** (a chiefly British spelling) has two possible pronunciations: /uː/ and /ɜː/, e.g.:

manoeuvre məˈnuː.vəʳ (US) -vɚ
oeuvre ˈɜː.vrə

It should be noted that more recent borrowings from French, like *oeuvre* above, usually have the latter pronunciation (see, for example, *cri de coeur, hors d'oeuvre*).

first syllable, e.g. **octagon** /ˈɒk.tə.gən/ (US) /ˈɑːk.tə.gɑːn/, **octahedron** /ˌɒk.təˈhiː.drən/ (US) /ˌɑːk.təˈhiː.drən/, or primary stress on the second syllable, e.g. **octagonal** /ɒkˈtæg.ən.əl/ (US) /ɑːk-/.
octagon ˈɒk.tə.gən, (US) ˈɑːk.tə.gɑːn -s -z
octagonal ɒkˈtæg.ən.əl, (US) ɑːk- -ly -i
octahedr|on ˌɒk.təˈhiː.dr|ən, -ˈhed.r|ən, (US) ˌɑːk.təˈhiː.dr|ən -ons -ənz -a -ə -al -əl
octal ˈɒk.təl, (US) ˈɑːk-
octane ˈɒk.teɪn, (US) ˈɑːk-
octant ˈɒk.tənt, (US) ˈɑːk- -s -s
Octateuch ˈɒk.tə.tjuːk, (US) ˈɑːk.tə.tuːk, -tjuːk
octave *musical term:* ˈɒk.tɪv, -teɪv, (US) ˈɑːk- *ecclesiastical term:* ˈɒk.teɪv, -tɪv, (US) ˈɑːk.tɪv, -teɪv -s -z
Octavi|a ɒkˈteɪ.vi|.ə, -ˈtɑː-, (US) ɑːkˈteɪ- -an -ən
Octavius ɒkˈteɪ.vi.əs, -ˈtɑː-, (US) ɑːkˈteɪ-
octavo ɒkˈtɑː.vəʊ, -ˈteɪ-, (US) ɑːkˈteɪ.voʊ, -ˈtɑː- -s -z
octennial ɒkˈten.i.əl, (US) ɑːk- -ly -i
octet(te) ɒkˈtet, (US) ɑːk- -s -s
octillion ɒkˈtɪl.jən, -i.ən, (US) ɑːkˈtɪl.jən -s -z
octo- ˈɒk.təʊ, (US) ˈɑːk.toʊ, -tə
Note: Prefix. Normally takes primary or secondary stress on the first syllable, e.g. **octosyllable** /ˈɒk.təʊˌsɪl.ə.bəl/ (US) /ˈɑːk.toʊ-/, **octosyllabic** /ˌɒk.təʊ.sɪˈlæb.ɪk/ (US) /ˌɑːk.toʊ-/.
October ɒkˈtəʊ.bəʳ, (US) ɑːkˈtoʊ.bɚ -s -z
octodecimo ˌɒk.təʊˈdes.ɪ.məʊ, (US) ˌɑːk.toʊˈdes.ɪ.moʊ -s -z
octogenarian ˌɒk.təʊ.dʒəˈneə.ri.ən, -dʒɪˈ-, (US) ˌɑːk.toʊ.dʒɪˈner.i.-, -tə- -s -z
octop|us ˈɒk.tə.p|əs, -p|ʊs, (US) ˈɑːk.tə.p|əs -uses -ə.sɪz, -ʊ.sɪz, (US) -ə.sɪz -i -aɪ
octoroon ˌɒk.təˈruːn, (US) ˌɑːk- -s -z
octosyllabic ˌɒk.təʊ.sɪˈlæb.ɪk, -səˈ-, (US) ˌɑːk.toʊ-, -tə- *stress shift:* **ˌoctosyllabic ˈmeter**
octosyllable ˈɒk.təʊˌsɪl.ə.bəl, (US) ˈɑːk.toʊˌ-, -təˌ- -s -z
octroi ˈɒk.trwɑː, -trɔɪ, (US) ˈɑːk.trɔɪ -s -z
octuple ˈɒk.tʃʊ.pəl, ˈ-tjʊ-, ˈ-tʃə-, ˈ-tjə-; ɒkˈtʃuː-, -ˈtjuː-, (US) ˈɑːk.tə-; (US) ɑːkˈtuː-, -ˈtjuː-
ocular ˈɒk.jə.ləʳ, -jʊ-, (US) ˈɑː.kjə.lɚ, -kjʊ- -ly -li
oculist ˈɒk.jə.lɪst, -jʊ-, (US) ˈɑː.kjə-, -kjʊ- -s -s
O'Curry əʊˈkʌr.i, (US) oʊˈkɝː-
od, Od ɒd, (US) ɑːd -s -z
OD ˌəʊˈdiː, (US) ˌoʊ- -'s -z -'ing -ɪŋ -'d -d
odalisque, odalisk ˈɒd.əl.ɪsk, ˈəʊ.dəl-, (US) ˈoʊ.dəl- -s -s
O'Daly əʊˈdeɪ.li, (US) oʊ-
Odam ˈəʊ.dəm, (US) ˈoʊ-
odd ɒd, (US) ɑːd -er -əʳ, (US) -ɚ -est -ɪst, -əst -ly -li -ness -nəs, -nɪs **ˌodd man ˈout**
oddball ˈɒd.bɔːl, (US) ˈɑːd-, -bɑːl -s -z
Oddbins® ˈɒd.bɪnz, (US) ˈɑːd-
odd bod ˈɒd.bɒd, (US) ˈɑːd.bɑːd -s -z
Oddfellow ˈɒdˌfel.əʊ, (US) ˈɑːdˌfel.oʊ -s -z
Oddie ˈɒd.i, (US) ˈɑː.di
oddish ˈɒd.ɪʃ, (US) ˈɑː.dɪʃ
oddit|y ˈɒd.ɪ.t|i, -ə.t|i, (US) ˈɑː.də.t̬|i -ies -iz
odd-job |man ˌɒdˈdʒɒb|.mæn, (US) ˈɑːd.dʒɑːb- men -men
oddment ˈɒd.mənt, (US) ˈɑːd- -s -s
odds ɒdz, (US) ɑːdz **ˌodds and ˈends**
odds-on ˌɒdzˈɒn, (US) ˌɑːdzˈɑːn *stress shift:* **ˌodds-on ˈfavourite**
ode əʊd, (US) oʊd -s -z
O'Dea əʊˈdeɪ, (US) oʊ-
Odell əʊˈdel; ˈəʊ.dəl, (US) oʊˈdel
Odense ˈəʊ.dənt.sə, (US) ˈoʊ.dənt-, -θənt-
Odeon® ˈəʊ.di.ən, (US) ˈoʊ-
Oder ˈəʊ.dəʳ, (US) ˈoʊ.dɚ
Oder-Neisse Line ˌəʊ.dəˈnaɪ.səˌlaɪn, (US) ˌoʊ.dɚˈ-
Odessa əʊˈdes.ə, (US) oʊ-
Odets əʊˈdets, (US) oʊ-
Odette əʊˈdet, (US) oʊ-
ode|um əʊˈdiː|.əm; ˈəʊ.di-, (US) oʊˈdiː-; (US) ˈoʊ.di- -a -ə -ums -əmz
Odgers ˈɒdʒ.əz, (US) ˈɑː.dʒɚz
Odham ˈɒd.əm, (US) ˈɑː.dəm
Odiham ˈəʊ.di.əm, -həm, (US) ˈoʊ-
Odile əʊˈdiːl, (US) oʊ-
Odin ˈəʊ.dɪn, (US) ˈoʊ-
odious ˈəʊ.di.əs, (US) ˈoʊ- -ly -li -ness -nəs, -nɪs
odium ˈəʊ.di.əm, (US) ˈoʊ-
Odling ˈɒd.lɪŋ, (US) ˈɑːd-
Odlum ˈɒd.ləm, (US) ˈɑːd-
Odo ˈəʊ.dəʊ, (US) ˈoʊ.doʊ
Odoacer ˌɒd.əʊˈeɪ.səʳ, ˌəʊ.dəʊˈ-, (US) ˌoʊ.doʊˈeɪ.sɚ
O'Doherty əʊˈdəʊ.ə.ti, -ˈdɒ.hə.ti, -ˈdɒx.ə-, (US) oʊˈdɔːr.t̬i, -ˈdɑː.hɚ-
odometer əʊˈdɒm.ɪ.təʳ, ɒdˈɒm-, -ə.təʳ, (US) oʊˈdɑː.mə.t̬ɚ -s -z
O'Donnell əʊˈdɒn.əl, (US) oʊˈdɑː.nəl
odontolog|y ˌɒd.ɒnˈtɒl.ə.dʒ|i, ˌəʊ.dɒnˈ-, (US) ˌoʊ.dɑːnˈtɑː.lə- -ist/s -ɪst/s
odor ˈəʊ.dəʳ, (US) ˈoʊ.dɚ -s -z -ed -d -less -ləs, -lɪs
odoriferous ˌəʊ.dərˈɪf.ər.əs, ˌɒd.ərˈ-, (US) ˌoʊ.dəˈrɪf.ɚ.əs -ly -li -ness -nəs, -nɪs
odorous ˈəʊ.dər.əs, (US) ˈoʊ- -ly -li -ness -nəs, -nɪs
odour ˈəʊ.dəʳ, (US) ˈoʊ.dɚ -s -z -ed -d -less -ləs, -lɪs
O'Dowd əʊˈdaʊd, (US) oʊ-
odsbodikins ˌɒdzˈbɒd.ɪ.kɪnz, (US) ˌɑːdzˈbɑːd-
O'Dwyer əʊˈdwaɪ.əʳ, (US) oʊˈdwaɪ.ɚ
Ody ˈəʊ.di, (US) ˈoʊ-
Odysseus əˈdɪs.juːs, ɒdˈɪs-, əʊˈdɪs-, ˈ-i.əs, (US) oʊˈdɪs.i.əs, ˈ-juːs
odyssey, O~ ˈɒd.ɪ.si, ˈ-ə-, (US) ˈɑː.dɪ-
OECD ˌəʊ.iː.siːˈdiː, (US) ˌoʊ-
oecumenic ˌiː.kjʊˈmen.ɪk, (US) ˌek.jəˈ-, -jʊˈ- -al -əl *stress shift:* **ˌoecumenic ˈservice**
oedema ɪˈdiː.mə, iː-, (US) ɪ- -ta -tə, (US) -t̬ə
oedematous ɪˈdiː.mə.təs, iː-, -ˈdem.ə-, (US) ɪˈdem.ə.t̬əs
oedipal, O~ ˈiː.dɪ.pəl, -də-, (US) ˈed.ɪ-, ˈiː.dɪ-
Oedipus ˈiː.dɪ.pəs, -də-, (US) ˈed.ɪ-, ˈiː.dɪ- **ˈOedipus ˌcomplex**
OEEC ˌəʊ.iː.iːˈsiː, (US) ˌoʊ-
Oenomaus ˌiː.nəʊˈmeɪ.əs, (US) -nəˈ-, -noʊˈ-
Oenone iːˈnəʊ.niː, ɪ-, -ni, (US) iːˈnoʊ-
oenophile ˈiː.nəʊ.faɪl, (US) -nə-, -noʊ- -s -z
o'er (contracted form of **over**) ˈɔː.əʳ, ɔːʳ, əʊəʳ, (US) ɔːr, ˈoʊ.ɚ
oes (plural of **O**) əʊz, (US) oʊz
oesophageal ɪˌsɒf.əˈdʒiː.əl, iː-, ə-; ˌiː.sɒf-, (US) ɪˌsɑː.fəˈ-; (US) ˌiː.sɑː-
oesopha|gus iˈsɒf.ə|.gəs, ɪ-, ə-, (US) ɪˈsɑː.fə-, iː- -guses -gə.sɪz -gi -gaɪ, -dʒaɪ
oestrogen ˈiː.strəʊ.dʒən, ˈes.trəʊ-, (US) ˈes.trə-, -dʒen
oestrus ˈiː.strəs, (US) ˈes.trəs -es -ɪz
oeuvre ˈɜː.vrə -s -z
of *strong form:* ɒv, (US) ɑːv; *weak form:* əv
Note: Weak-form word. The strong form is usually found only in final position (e.g. 'She's the one I'm fond of'), though it can occur initially in some forms such as 'Of the ten who set out, only three returned'. Elsewhere the weak form /əv/ is used.
O'Faolain, O'Faoláin əʊˈfeɪ.lən, -ˈfæl.ən, (US) oʊ-
Ofcom ˈɒf.kɒm, (US) ˈɑːf.kɑːm

O

off ɒf, (US) ɑːf

> Note: This is one of a small number of words that has in the past also been pronounced with the /ɔː/ vowel in British English. The pronunciation /ɔːf/ is particularly associated with the Royal Family and the aristocracy. It is considered pretentious or old-fashioned.

Offa ˈɒf.ə, (US) ˈɑː.fə ˌ**Offa's** ˈ**Dyke**
offal ˈɒf.əl, (US) ˈɑː.fəl
Offaly ˈɒf.əl.i, (US) ˈɑː.fəl.i
off-bail ˌɒfˈbeɪl, (US) ˌɑːf- **-s** -z

> Note: Also ˈ-- when in contrast with **leg-bail**.

offbeat adj ˌɒfˈbiːt, (US) ˌɑːfˈbiːt
offbeat n ˈɒf.biːt, (US) ˈɑːf- **-s** -s
off-bye ˌɒfˈbaɪ, (US) ˌɑːf- **-s** -z

> Note: Also ˈ-- when in contrast with **leg-bye**.

off-chance ˈɒf.tʃɑːnts, (US) ˈɑːf.tʃænts ˌ**on the** ˈ**off-**ˌ**chance**
off-colo(u)r ˌɒfˈkʌl.əʳ, (US) ˌɑːfˈkʌl.ɚ
offcut ˈɒf.kʌt, (US) ˈɑːf- **-s** -s
off-drive ˈɒf.draɪv, (US) ˈɑːf- **-s** -z
off-duty ˌɒfˈdʒuː.ti, -ˈdjuː-, (US) ˌɑːfˈduː.t̬i *stress shift:* ˌ**off-duty** ˈ**soldier**
Offenbach ˈɒf.ən.bɑːk, -əm-, (US) ˈɑː.fən.bɑːk, ˈɔː-
offenc|e əˈfents **-es** -ɪz **-eless** -ləs, -lɪs
offend əˈfend **-s** -z **-ing** -ɪŋ **-ed** -ɪd **-er/s** -əʳ/z, (US) -ɚ/z
offens|e əˈfents, (US) ə-; *especially in sport:* (US) ˈɑː.fents **-es** -ɪz **-eless** -ləs, -lɪs
offensive əˈfent.sɪv, (US) ə-; *especially in sport:* (US) ˈɑː-, ˈʌf.ent- **-s** -z **-ly** -li **-ness** -nəs, -nɪs
off|er ˈɒf|.əʳ, (US) ˈɑː.f|ɚ **-ers** -əz, (US) -ɚz **-ering/s** -ər.ɪŋ/z **-ered** -əd, (US) -ɚd **-erer/s** -ər.əʳ/z, (US) -ɚ.ɚ/z **-erable** -ər.ə.bəl
offertor|y ˈɒf.ə.tər|.i, (US) ˈɑː.fɚ.tɔːr-, ˈɔː- **-ies** -iz
off-hand ˌɒfˈhænd, (US) ˌɑːf-
off-handed ˌɒfˈhæn.dɪd, (US) ˌɑːf- **-ly** -li **-ness** -nəs, -nɪs
offic|e ˈɒf.ɪs, (US) ˈɑː.fɪs **-es** -ɪz ˈ**office** ˌ**block**; ˈ**office** ˌ**hours**; ˌ**office** ˈ**hours**
office-bearer ˈɒf.ɪsˌbeə.rəʳ, (US) ˈɑː.fɪsˌber.ɚ **-s** -z
office-boy ˈɒf.ɪsˌbɔɪ, (US) ˈɑː.fɪs- **-s** -z
officer ˈɒf.ɪ.səʳ, (US) ˈɑː.fɪ.sɚ **-s** -z
official əˈfɪʃ|.əl, (US) ə-, oʊ- **-s** -z **-ly** -i **-ism** -ɪ.zəm **of**ˌ**ficial re**ˈ**ceiver; Of**ˌ**ficial** ˈ**Secrets** ˌ**Act**
officialdom əˈfɪʃ.əl.dəm, (US) ə-
officialese əˌfɪʃ.əlˈiːz, əˈfɪʃ.əl.iːz, (US) əˌfɪʃ.əlˈiːz
officiant əˈfɪʃ.i.ənt, ɒfˈɪʃ-, (US) əˈfɪʃ.ənt, -i.ənt **-s** -s
offici|ate əˈfɪʃ.i|.eɪt **-ates** -eɪts **-ating** -eɪ.tɪŋ, (US) -eɪ.t̬ɪŋ **-ated** -eɪ.tɪd, (US) -eɪ.t̬ɪd
officinal ˌɒf.ɪˈsaɪ.nəl; ɒfˈɪs.ɪ.nəl, (US) əˈfɪs.ɪ-; (US) ˌɑː.fɪˈsaɪ-
officious əˈfɪʃ.əs **-ly** -li **-ness** -nəs, -nɪs
offie ˈɒf.i, (US) ˈɑː.fi **-s** -z
offing ˈɒf.ɪŋ, (US) ˈɑː.fɪŋ **-s** -z
offish ˈɒf.ɪʃ, (US) ˈɑː.fɪʃ
off-key ˌɒfˈkiː, (US) ˌɑːf- *stress shift:* ˌ**off-key** ˈ**singing**
off-licenc|e ˈɒfˌlaɪ.sənts, (US) ˌɑːfˈlaɪ- **-es** -ɪz
off-limits ˌɒfˈlɪm.ɪts, (US) ˌɑːf-
offline ˌɒfˈlaɪn, (US) ˌɑːf- *stress shift:* ˌ**off-line** ˈ**printer**
off-load ˌɒfˈləʊd, (US) ˈɑːf.loʊd **-s** -z **-ing** -ɪŋ **-ed** -ɪd
off-message ˌɒfˈmes.ɪdʒ, (US) ˌɑːf-
Offor ˈɒf.əʳ, (US) ˈɑː.fɚ
off-peak ˌɒfˈpiːk, (US) ˌɑːf- *stress shift:* ˌ**off-peak** ˈ**travel**
off-piste ˌɒfˈpiːst, (US) ˌɑːf- *stress shift:* ˌ**off-piste** ˈ**skiing**
off-print ˈɒf.prɪnt, (US) ˈɑːf- **-s** -s
off-putting ˌɒfˈpʊt.ɪŋ, (US) ˈɑːfˌpʊt̬- *stress shift, British only:* ˌ**off-putting** ˈ**habit**
offscreen ˌɒfˈskriːn, (US) ˌɑːf- *stress shift:* ˌ**offscreen** ˈ**life**
off-season ɒfˈsiː.zən, (US) ɑːf- *stress shift:* ˌ**off-season** ˈ**prices**
off|set v *compensate:* ˌɒf|ˈset, (US) ˌɑːf- **-sets** -ˈsets **-setting** -ˈset.ɪŋ, (US) -ˈset̬.ɪŋ
offse|t n, v ˈɒf.se|t, (US) ˈɑːf-, -ˈ- **-ts** -ts **-tting** -tɪŋ, (US) -t̬ɪŋ
offshoot ˈɒf.ʃuːt, (US) ˈɑːf- **-s** -s
offshore ˌɒfˈʃɔːʳ, (US) ˌɑːfˈʃɔːr *stress shift:* ˌ**offshore** ˈ**savings**
offshoring ˌɒfˈʃɔːr.ɪŋ, (US) ˌɑːfˈʃɔːr-
offside ˌɒfˈsaɪd, (US) ˌɑːf- *stress shift:* ˌ**offside** ˈ**rule**
offspring ˈɒf.sprɪŋ, (US) ˈɑːf- **-s** -z
offstage ˌɒfˈsteɪdʒ, (US) ˌɑːf- *stress shift:* ˌ**offstage** ˈ**whisper**
off-street ˌɒfˈstriːt, (US) ˌɑːf- *stress shift:* ˌ**off-street** ˈ**shops**
off-the-cuff ˌɒf.ðəˈkʌf, (US) ˌɑːf- *stress shift:* ˌ**off-the-cuff** ˈ**comment**
off-the-peg ˌɒf.ðəˈpeg, (US) ˌɑːf- *stress shift:* ˌ**off-the-peg** ˈ**suit**
off-the-rack ˌɒf.ðəˈræk, (US) ˌɑːf- *stress shift:* ˌ**off-the-rack** ˈ**suit**
off-the-record ˌɒf.ðəˈrek.ɔːd, (US) ˌɑːf.ðəˈrek.ɔːrd, -ˈrek.ɚd *stress shift:* ˌ**off-the-record** ˈ**quote**
off-the-shelf ˌɒf.ðəˈʃelf, (US) ˌɑːf- *stress shift:* ˌ**off-the-shelf** ˈ**goods**
off-the-wall ˌɒf.ðəˈwɔːl, (US) ˌɑːf.ðəˈwɔːl, -ˈwɔːl *stress shift:* ˌ**off-the-wall** ˈ**comedy**
off-white ˌɒfˈhwaɪt, (US) ˌɑːf- *stress shift:* ˌ**off-white** ˈ**drapes**
Ofgas, OFGAS ˈɒf.gæs, (US) ˈɑːf-
O'Flaherty əʊˈfleə.ti, -ˈflæ.hə-, -ˈflɑː.ə-, -ˈflɑː-, (US) oʊˈfler.t̬i, -ˈflæ.hɚ-
O'Flynn əʊˈflɪn, (US) oʊ-
Ofsted ˈɒf.sted, (US) ˈɑːf-
oft ɒft, (US) ɑːft
Oftel, OFTEL ˈɒf.tel, (US) ˈɑːf-
often ˈɒf.ən, -tən, (US) ˈɑː.fən, ˈɑːf.tən **-times** -taɪmz **as** ˌ**often as** ˈ**not**

> Note: The pronunciation with /t/ is sometimes cited as an example of spelling pronunciation, but there is no evidence that it is a recent introduction.

often|er ˈɒf.ən|.əʳ, -tən-, ˈɒf.n|əʳ, (US) ˈɑː.fən|.ɚ, ˈɑːf.tən-, ˈɑːf.n|ɚ **-est** -ɪst, -əst
ofttimes ˈɒft.taɪmz, (US) ˈɑːft-
Ofwat, OFWAT ˈɒf.wɒt, (US) ˈɑːf.wɑːt
Og ɒg, (US) ɑːg, ɔːg
ogam ˈɒg.əm, (US) ˈɑː.gəm
Ogbomosho ˌɒg.bəˈməʊ.ʃəʊ, (US) ˌɑːg.bəˈmoʊ.ʃoʊ
Ogden ˈɒg.dən, (US) ˈɑːg-, ˈɔːg-
ogee ˈəʊ.dʒiː, -ˈ-, (US) ˈoʊ.dʒiː, -ˈ- **-s** -z
ogham ˈɒg.əm, (US) ˈɑː.gəm, ˈɔː-
oghamic ɒgˈæm.ɪk, (US) ɑːˈgæm-, ɔː-, oʊ-
Ogilby ˈəʊ.gəl.bi, (US) ˈoʊ-
Ogilvie, Ogilvy ˈəʊ.gəl.vi, (US) ˈoʊ-
ogival əʊˈdʒaɪ.vəl, -ˈgaɪ-, (US) oʊˈdʒaɪ-
ogive ˈəʊ.dʒaɪv, -gaɪv, -ˈ-, (US) ˈoʊ.dʒaɪv, -gaɪv, -ˈ- **-s** -z
ogl|e, O~ ˈəʊ.gəl, (US) ˈoʊ-, ˈɑː- **-es** -z **-ing** -ɪŋ, ˈəʊ.glɪŋ, ˈoʊ-, (US) ˈɑː- **-ed** -d **-er/s** -əʳ/z, (US) -ɚ/z, ˈəʊ.gləʳ/z, ˈoʊ.glɚ/z, ˈɑː-

> Note: A recent alternative pronunciation in British English is /ˈɒg.əl/; it seems likely that this was started for comic effect on what is quite a comical word. (A British sports car named Ogle was not a commercial success.)

Ogleby ˈəʊ.gəl.bi, (US) ˈoʊ-
Oglethorpe ˈəʊ.gəl.θɔːp, (US) ˈoʊ.gəl.θɔːrp
Ogmore ˈɒg.mɔːʳ, (US) ˈɑːg.mɔːr, ˈɔːg-
Ogoni əˈgəʊ.ni, ɒgˈ-, (US) -ˈgoʊ- **-land** -lænd
OGPU ˈɒg.puː, (US) ˈɑːg-, ˈɔːg-
O'Grady əʊˈgreɪ.di, (US) oʊ-
og|re ˈəʊ.g|əʳ, (US) ˈoʊ.g|ɚ **-res** -əz, (US) -ɚz **-reish** -ər.ɪʃ
ogress ˈəʊ.grəs, -rɪs, (US) ˈoʊ- **-es** -ɪz
Ogwr ˈɒg.ʊəʳ, (US) ˈɑː.gʊr
oh əʊ, (US) oʊ
O'Hagan əʊˈheɪ.gən, (US) oʊ-
O'Halloran əʊˈhæl.ər.ən, (US) oʊ-
O'Hanlon əʊˈhæn.lən, (US) oʊ-
O'Hara əʊˈhɑː.rə, (US) oʊˈher.ə, -ˈhær-
O'Hare əʊˈheəʳ, (US) oʊˈher
O'Hea əʊˈheɪ, (US) oʊ-
Ohio əʊˈhaɪ.əʊ, (US) oʊˈhaɪ.oʊ, ə- **-an/s** -ən/z
ohm, O~ əʊm, (US) oʊm **-s** -z
OHMS ˌəʊ.eɪtʃ.emˈes, (US) ˌoʊ-
oho əʊˈhəʊ, (US) oʊˈhoʊ

Pronouncing the letters OI, OY

The vowel letter digraphs **oi** and **oy** are similar in that their most common pronunciation is /ɔɪ/, e.g.:

boy	bɔɪ
boil	bɔɪl

When followed by an **r** in the spelling, **oi** is pronounced as /waɪə/ Ⓤⓢ /waɪɚ/ or /wɑː/ Ⓤⓢ /wɑːr/, e.g.:

choir	kwaɪəʳ Ⓤⓢ kwaɪ.ɚ
reservoir	ˈrez.əv.wɑːʳ Ⓤⓢ -ɚv.wɑːr

In addition

There are other vowel sounds associated with the digraph **oi**.

In the following examples, the pronunciation is due to the addition of the inflection *-ing* to words ending in **o**, e.g.:

əʊ.ɪ Ⓤⓢ oʊ.ɪ	going /ˈgəʊ.ɪŋ/ Ⓤⓢ /ˈgoʊ-/
uː.ɪ	doing /ˈduː.ɪŋ/

In words borrowed from French, the pronunciation of **oi** may be /wɑː/, e.g.:

Bois	bɔɪs, bwɑː
foie gras	ˌfwɑːˈgrɑː

In weak syllables

The vowel digraph **oi** is realized with the vowel /ə/ in weak syllables, e.g.:

tortoise	ˈtɔː.təs Ⓤⓢ ˈtɔːr.təs
connoisseur	ˌkɒn.əˈsɜːʳ Ⓤⓢ ˌkɑː.nəˈsɝː

oick ɔɪk **-s** -s

-oid ɔɪd
Note: Suffix. Does not normally change the stress pattern of the stem, e.g. **human** /ˈhjuː.mən/, **humanoid** /ˈhjuː.mə.nɔɪd/.

oik ɔɪk **-s** -s

oil ɔɪl **-s** -z **-ing** -ɪŋ **-ed** -d **-er/s** -əʳ/z, Ⓤⓢ -ɚ/z ˈ**oil** ˌ**can**; ˈ**oil** ˌ**field**; ˈ**oil** ˌ**paint**; ˈ**oil** ˌ**painting**; ˈ**oil** ˌ**slick**; ˈ**oil** ˌ**well**; ˌ**pour** ˌ**oil on** ˌ**troubled** ˈ**waters**; ˌ**burn the** ˌ**midnight** ˈ**oil**

oil|cloth ˈɔɪl|.klɒθ, Ⓤⓢ -klɑːθ **-cloths** -klɒθs, -klɒðz, Ⓤⓢ -klɑːθs, -klɑːðz

oil|man ˈɔɪl|.mæn, Ⓤⓢ -mæn, -mən **-men** -men

oil-rig ˈɔɪl.rɪg **-s** -z

oilseed ˈɔɪl.siːd

oilskin ˈɔɪl.skɪn **-s** -z

oil|y ˈɔɪ.l|i **-ier** -i.əʳ, Ⓤⓢ -i.ɚ **-iest** -i.ɪst, -i.əst **-iness** -ɪ.nəs, -ɪ.nɪs

oink ɔɪŋk **-s** -s **-ing** -ɪŋ **-ed** -t

ointment ˈɔɪnt.mənt **-s** -s

Oisin əˈʃiːn, Ⓤⓢ ˈɑː.ʃən, ə.ˈʃiːn

Oistrakh ˈɔɪ.strɑːk; *as if Russian:* -strɑːx

Ojai ˈəʊ.haɪ, Ⓤⓢ ˈoʊ-

Ojibwa(y) əʊˈdʒɪb.weɪ, ɒdʒˈɪb-, -wə, Ⓤⓢ oʊˈdʒɪb.weɪ, -wə **-s** -z

OK əʊˈkeɪ, Ⓤⓢ oʊ-, ə- **-s** -z **-ing** -ɪŋ **-ed** -d *stress shift:* ˌ**OK** ˈ**person**

O'Kane əʊˈkeɪn, Ⓤⓢ oʊ-

okapi əʊˈkɑː.pi, Ⓤⓢ oʊ- **-s** -z

Okara ɒkˈɑː.rə, Ⓤⓢ əˈkɑːr.ə

Okavango, Okovango ˌɒk.əˈvæŋ.gəʊ, Ⓤⓢ ˌoʊ.kəˈvæŋ.goʊ

okay əʊˈkeɪ, Ⓤⓢ oʊ-, ə- **-s** -z **-ing** -ɪŋ **-ed** -d *stress shift:* ˌ**okay** ˈ**person**

Okeechobee ˌəʊ.kɪˈtʃəʊ.bi, -kiːˈ-, Ⓤⓢ ˌoʊ.kɪˈtʃoʊ-, -kiːˈ-

O'Keef(f)e əʊˈkiːf, Ⓤⓢ oʊ-

Okehampton ˌəʊkˈhæmp.tən, Ⓤⓢ ˈoʊkˌhæmp- *stress shift, British only:* ˌ**Okehampton** ˈ**centre**

O'Kelly əʊˈkel.i, Ⓤⓢ oʊ-

okeydoke ˌəʊ.kiˈdəʊk, Ⓤⓢ ˌoʊ.kiˈdoʊk **-y** -i

Okhotsk əʊˈkɒtsk, ɒkˈɒtsk, Ⓤⓢ oʊˈkɑːtsk

Okie ˈəʊ.ki, Ⓤⓢ ˈoʊ- **-s** -z

Okinawa ˌɒk.ɪˈnɑː.wə, ˌəʊ.kɪˈ-, Ⓤⓢ ˌoʊ.kəˈnɑː.wə, -kɪ-

okker, ocker ˈɒk.əʳ, Ⓤⓢ ˈɑː.kɚ **-s** -z

Okla. (abbrev. for **Oklahoma**) ˌəʊ.kləˈhəʊ.mə, Ⓤⓢ ˌoʊ.kləˈhoʊ-

Oklahom|a ˌəʊ.kləˈhəʊ.m|ə, Ⓤⓢ ˌoʊ.kləˈhoʊ- **-an/s** -ən/z

Okovango, Okavango ˌɒk.əˈvæŋ.gəʊ, Ⓤⓢ ˌoʊ.kəˈvæŋ.goʊ

okra ˈɒk.rə, ˈəʊ.krə, Ⓤⓢ ˈoʊ-

Okri ˈɒk.ri, Ⓤⓢ ˈɑː.kri

Olaf, Olav ˈəʊ.læf, -ləf, Ⓤⓢ ˈoʊ.ləf, -lɑːf

Olave ˈɒl.ɪv, -əv, -eɪv, Ⓤⓢ ˈoʊ.ləf, -lɑːf, -ləv

Olcott ˈɒl.kət, Ⓤⓢ ˈɑːl-

old əʊld, Ⓤⓢ oʊld **-er** -əʳ, Ⓤⓢ -ɚ **-est** -ɪst, -əst **-ness** -nəs, -nɪs ˌ**Old** ˈ**Bailey**; ˈ**old boy**; ˌ**Old** ˈ**English**; ˌ**Old** ˌ**English** ˈ**sheepdog**; ˌ**Old** ˈ**Faithful**; ˌ**Old** ˈ**Glory**; ˌ**old** ˈ**guard**; ˌ**old** ˈ**hand**; ˌ**old** ˈ**hat**; ˌ**old** ˈ**lady**; ˌ**old** ˈ**maid**; ˌ**old** ˈ**man**; ˌ**old** ˈ**master**; ˈ**old** ˌ**school**; ˌ**Old** ˈ**Testament**; **as** ˌ**old as the** ˈ**hills**

old-age adj ˈəʊldˌeɪdʒ, Ⓤⓢ ˈoʊld-
old age n ˌəʊldˈeɪdʒ, Ⓤⓢ ˌoʊld-

old-age pension ˌəʊld.eɪdʒˈpen.tʃən, Ⓤⓢ ˌoʊld- **-s** -z **-er/s** -əʳ/z, Ⓤⓢ -ɚ/z

Oldbuck ˈəʊld.bʌk, Ⓤⓢ ˈoʊld-

Oldbury ˈəʊld.bər.i, Ⓤⓢ ˈoʊldˌber-, -bɚ.i

Oldcastle ˈəʊldˌkɑː.səl, Ⓤⓢ ˈoʊldˌkæs.əl

olden ˈəʊl.dən, Ⓤⓢ ˈoʊl-

Oldenburg ˈəʊl.dən.bɜːg, -dəm-, Ⓤⓢ ˈoʊl.dən.bɝːg

olde worlde ˌəʊl.diˈwɜːl.di, Ⓤⓢ ˌoʊl.diˈwɝːl-

Note: Joking imitation of spelling.

old-fashioned ˌəʊldˈfæʃ.ənd, Ⓤⓢ ˌoʊld- *stress shift:* ˌ**old-fashioned** ˈ**ways**

Oldfield ˈəʊld.fiːld, Ⓤⓢ ˈoʊld-

old-fog(e)yish ˌəʊldˈfəʊ.gi.ɪʃ, Ⓤⓢ ˌoʊldˈfoʊ-

Oldham ˈəʊl.dəm, Ⓤⓢ ˈoʊl-

oldie ˈəʊl.di, Ⓤⓢ ˈoʊl- **-s** -z

oldish ˈəʊl.dɪʃ, Ⓤⓢ ˈoʊl-

Oldrey ˈəʊl.dri, Ⓤⓢ ˈoʊl-

Oldsmobile® ˈəʊldz.mə.biːl, Ⓤⓢ ˈoʊldz-

oldster ˈəʊld.stəʳ, Ⓤⓢ ˈoʊld.stɚ **-s** -z

old-style ˈəʊld.staɪl, Ⓤⓢ ˈoʊld-

old-time ˌəʊldˈtaɪm, Ⓤⓢ ˌoʊldˈ- *stress shift:* ˌ**old-time** ˈ**dancing**

old-timer ˌəʊldˈtaɪ.məʳ, Ⓤⓢ ˈoʊldˌtaɪ.mɚ **-s** -z

old wives' tale ˌəʊldˈwaɪvzˌteɪl, Ⓤⓢ ˌoʊld-

old-world ˌəʊldˈwɜːld, Ⓤⓢ ˌoʊldˈwɝːld *stress shift:* ˌ**old-world** ˈ**values**

olé əʊˈleɪ, Ⓤⓢ oʊ-

oleaginous ˌəʊ.liˈædʒ.ɪ.nəs, ˈ-ə-, Ⓤⓢ ˌoʊ- **-ly** -li **-ness** -nəs, -nɪs

oleander, O~ ˌəʊ.liˈæn.dəʳ, Ⓤⓢ ˌoʊ.liˈæn.dɚ, ˈoʊ.liˌæn- **-s** -z

O'Leary əʊˈlɪə.ri, Ⓤⓢ oʊˈlɪr.i

oleaster ˌəʊ.liˈæs.təʳ, Ⓤⓢ ˌoʊ.liˈæs.tɚ **-s** -z

oleograph ˈəʊ.li.əʊ.grɑːf, ˈɒl.i-, -græf, Ⓤⓢ ˈoʊ.li.oʊ.græf, -ə- **-s** -s

O level ˈəʊˌlev.əl, Ⓤⓢ ˈoʊ- **-s** -z

olfactory ɒlˈfæk.tər.i, Ⓤⓢ ɑːl-, oʊl-

Olga ˈɒl.gə, Ⓤⓢ ˈɑːl-, ˈɔːl-, ˈoʊl-

Oliffe ˈɒl.ɪf, Ⓤⓢ ˈɑː.lɪf

oligarch ˈɒl.ɪ.gɑːk, Ⓤⓢ ˈɑː.lɪ.gɑːrk, ˈoʊ- **-s** -s

oligarchal ˌɒl.ɪˈgɑː.kəl, Ⓤⓢ ˌɑː.lɪˈgɑːr-, ˌoʊ- *stress shift:* ˌ**oligarchal** ˈ**state**

oligarchic ˌɒl.ɪˈgɑː.kɪk, Ⓤⓢ ˌɑː.lɪˈgɑːr-, ˌoʊ- *stress shift:* ˌ**oligarchic** ˈ**state**

oligarch|y ˈɒl.ɪ.gɑː.k|i, Ⓤⓢ ˈɑː.lɪ.gɑːr-, ˈoʊ- **-ies** -iz

Oligocene ˈɒl.ɪ.gəʊ.siːn; ɒlˈɪg.əʊ-, Ⓤⓢ ˈɑː.lɪ.goʊ-, ˈoʊ-

oligopol|y ˌɒl.ɪˈgɒp.əl|.i, Ⓤⓢ ˌɑː.lɪˈgɑː.pəl-, ˌoʊ- **-ies** -iz

olio ˈəʊ.li.əʊ, Ⓤⓢ ˈoʊ.li.oʊ **-s** -z

Oliphant ˈɒl.ɪ.fənt, ˈ-ə-, Ⓤⓢ ˈɑː.lɪ-

olivaceous ˌɒl.ɪˈveɪ.ʃəs, Ⓤⓢ ˌɑː.lɪˈ-

olive, O~ ˈɒl.ɪv, Ⓤⓢ ˈɑː.lɪv **-s** -z ˈ**olive** ˌ**branch**; ˌ**olive** ˈ**green**; ˌ**olive** ˈ**oil**; ˈ**olive** ˌ**oil**

O

oliver, O~ ˈɒl.ɪ.vəʳ, ˈ-ə-, (US) ˈɑː.lɪ.vɚ -s -z
Oliverian ˌɒl.ɪˈvɪə.ri.ən, -əˈ-, (US) ˌɑː.lɪˈver.i-
Olivet ˈɒl.ɪ.vet, ˈ-ə-, -vɪt, -vət, (US) ˈɑː.lɪ.vet, -lə-
Olivetti® ˌɒl.ɪˈvet.i, -əˈ-, (US) ˌɑː.ləˈveţ.i
Olivia əˈlɪv.i.ə, ɒlˈɪv-, əʊ-, (US) oʊˈlɪv-, ə-
Olivier əˈlɪv.i.eɪ, ɒlˈɪv-, -ə, (US) oʊˈlɪv.i.eɪ
olivine ˈɒl.ɪ.viːn, ˈ-ə-, ˌ--ˈ-, (US) ˈɑː.lə.viːn -s -z
olla podrida ˌɒl.jə.pɒdˈriː.də, -pəˈdriː-, (US) ˌɑː.lə.poʊˈdriː-, -pəˈ- -s -z
Ollendorf ˈɒl.ən.dɔːf, -ɪn-, (US) ˈɑː.lən.dɔːrf
Ollerton ˈɒl.ə.tᵊn, (US) ˈɑː.lɚ-
Olley, Ollie ˈɒl.i, (US) ˈɑː.li
Olliffe ˈɒl.ɪf, (US) ˈɑː.lɪf
Ollivant ˈɒl.ɪ.vənt, -vænt, (US) ˈɑː.lɪ-
Olmert ˈɒl.meət, (US) ˈɑːl.mert
Olmstead ˈɒm.sted, (US) ˈoʊm-, ˈɑːm-, -stəd
Olney ˈəʊl.ni, ˈəʊ-, (US) ˈoʊl-, ˈoʊ-, ˈɑːl-
-olog|y ˈɒl.ə.dʒ|i, (US) ˈɑː.lə.dʒ|i -ies -iz
Note: Suffix. Normally takes primary stress as shown, e.g. **biology** /baɪˈɒl.ə.dʒi/ (US) /-ˈɑː.lə-/, **pharmacology** /ˌfɑː.məˈkɒl.ə.dʒi/ (US) /ˌfɑːr.məˈkɑː.lə-/.
oloroso ˌɒl.əˈrəʊ.səʊ, ˌəʊ.ləˈ-, -zəʊ, (US) ˌoʊ.loʊˈroʊ.soʊ, -ləˈ- -s -z
Olsen, Olson ˈəʊl.sᵊn, (US) ˈoʊl-
Olver ˈɒl.vəʳ, ˈəʊl-, (US) ˈɑː.lvɚ
Olwen ˈɒl.wen, -wɪn, (US) ˈɑːl-
Olympi|a əʊˈlɪm.pi|.ə, (US) oʊ-, ə- -an -ən
Olympiad əʊˈlɪm.pi.æd, (US) oʊ-, ə- -s -z
Olympic əʊˈlɪm.pɪk, (US) oʊ-, ə- -s -s **Oˌlympic ˈGames**
Olympus əʊˈlɪm.pəs, (US) oʊ-, ə-
Olynthus əʊˈlɪnt.θəs, (US) oʊ-, ə-
om, Om əʊm, ɒm, (US) oʊm
Omagh ˈəʊ.mə, -mɑː, əʊˈmɑː, (US) ˈoʊ-
Omaha ˈəʊ.mə.hɑː, (US) ˈoʊ-, -hɔː
O'Malley əʊˈmæl.i, -ˈmeɪ.li, (US) oʊ-
Oman əʊˈmɑːn, (US) oʊ-
Omar ˈəʊ.mɑːʳ, (US) ˈoʊ.mɑːr
Omar Khayyám ˌəʊ.mɑː.kaɪˈæm, -ˈɑːm, (US) ˌoʊ.mɑːr.kaɪˈjɑːm, -ˈæm
ombre ˈɒm.bəʳ, (US) ˈɑːm.bɚ
ombuds|man ˈɒm.bʊdz|.mən, -bʌdz-, -bədz-, -mæn, (US) ˈɑːm.bədz-, -bʌdz-; (US) ɑːmˈbʌdz- -men -mən, -men
Omdurman ˌɒm.dɜːˈmɑːn, -dəˈ-, -ˈmæn; ˈɒm.də.mən, (US) ˌɑːm.dʊrˈmɑːn
O'Meara əʊˈmɑː.rə, -ˈmɪə-, (US) oʊˈmɪr.ə, -ˈmɑːr-
omega, O~ ˈəʊ.mɪ.gə, -meg.ə, (US) oʊˈmeɪ.gə, -ˈmeg.ə, -ˈmiː.gə; (US) ˈoʊ.meg- -s -z
omelet, omelette ˈɒm.lət, -lɪt, -let, (US) ˈɑːm.lət, -lɪt; (US) ˈɑː.mə- -s -s
omen ˈəʊ.mən, -men, (US) ˈoʊ- -s -z -ed -d
Omeprazole əʊˈmep.rə.zəʊl, (US) oʊˈmep.rə.zoʊl
omer, O~ ˈəʊ.məʳ, (US) ˈoʊ.mɚ -s -z
omertà ˌəʊ.məˈtɑː, (US) ˌoʊ.merˈtɑː
omicron əʊˈmaɪ.krɒn, -krᵊn; ˈɒm.ɪ-, (US) ˈoʊ.mɪ.krɑːn, ˈɑː- -s -z
ominous ˈɒm.ɪ.nəs, ˈəʊ.mɪ-, -mə-, (US) ˈɑː.mə- -ly -li -ness -nəs, -nɪs
omissible əʊˈmɪs.ɪ.bᵊl, ˈ-ə-, (US) oʊ-
omission əʊˈmɪʃ.ᵊn, (US) oʊ- -s -z
o|mit əʊ|ˈmɪt, (US) oʊ- -mits -ˈmɪts -mitting -ˈmɪt.ɪŋ, (US) -ˈmɪţ.ɪŋ -mitted -ˈmɪt.ɪd, (US) -ˈmɪţ.ɪd
ommatidi|um ˌɒm.əˈtɪd.i|.əm, (US) ˌɑː.məˈ- -a -ə -al -əl
omni- ˈɒm.nɪ, -nə, -ni; ɒmˈnɪ, (US) ˈɑːm.nɪ, -nə, -ni; (US) ɑːmˈnɪ
Note: Prefix. Normally takes either primary or secondary stress on the first syllable, e.g. **omnibus** /ˈɒm.nɪ.bəs/ (US) /ˈɑːm-/, **omnipresent** /ˌɒm.nɪˈpres.ᵊnt/ (US) /ˌɑːm-/, or primary stress on the second syllable, e.g. **omnipotent** /ɒmˈnɪp.ə.tᵊnt/ (US) /ɑːmˈnɪ.pə.ţənt/.
omnibus ˈɒm.nɪ.bəs, -nə-, -bʌs, (US) ˈɑːm- -es -ɪz
omnifarious ˌɒm.nɪˈfeə.ri.əs, (US) ˌɑːm.nɪˈfer.i-
omnificent ɒmˈnɪf.ɪ.sᵊnt, (US) ɑːm-
omnipotence ɒmˈnɪp.ə.tᵊnts, (US) ɑːmˈnɪp.ə.ţənts
omnipotent ɒmˈnɪp.ə.tᵊnt, (US) ɑːmˈnɪp.ə.ţənt -ly -li
omnipresen|t ˌɒm.nɪˈprez.ᵊn|t, -nəˈ-, (US) ˌɑːm.nɪˈ- -ce -ts
omniscience ɒmˈnɪs.i.ənts, -ˈnɪʃ-, -ˈnɪʃ.ᵊnts, (US) ɑːmˈnɪʃ.ᵊnts
omniscient ɒmˈnɪs.i.ənt, -ˈnɪʃ-, -ˈnɪʃ.ᵊnt, (US) ɑːmˈnɪʃ.ᵊnt -ly -li
omnium, O~ ˈɒm.ni.əm, (US) ˈɑːm- -s -z
omnium gatherum ˌɒm.ni.əmˈgæð.ᵊr.əm, (US) ˌɑːm- -s -z
omnivore ˈɒm.nɪ.vɔːʳ, -nə-, (US) ˈɑːm.nɪ.vɔːr -s -z
omnivorous ɒmˈnɪv.ᵊr.əs, (US) ɑːm- -ly -li
Omond ˈəʊ.mənd, (US) ˈoʊ-
omphalos ˈɒmp.fᵊl.ɒs, (US) ˈɑːmp.fᵊl.əs, -ɑːs
Omri ˈɒm.raɪ, (US) ˈɑːm-
Omsk ɒmsk, (US) ɔːmsk, ɑːmsk
on n, adj, adv, prep ɒn, (US) ɑːn, ɔːn
onager ˈɒn.ə.gəʳ, (US) ˈɑː.nə.gɚ -s -z
Onan ˈəʊ.næn, -nən, (US) ˈoʊ-
onan|ism ˈəʊ.nə.n|ɪ.zᵊm, -næn|.ɪ-, (US) ˈoʊ- -ist/s -ɪst/s
onanistic ˌəʊ.nəˈnɪs.tɪk, -nænˈɪst-, (US) ˌoʊ-
Onassis əʊˈnæs.ɪs, (US) oʊ-, -ˈnɑː.sɪs
on-board adj ˈɒn.bɔːd, (US) ˈɑːn.bɔːrd
once wʌnts ˌ**once and for** ˈ**all**

> Note: The pronunciation /wɒnts/ is becoming increasingly widespread in British English, but cannot yet be recommended as representative of the accent being described here.

once-over ˈwʌntsˌəʊ.vəʳ, ˈwɒnts-, ˌ-ˈ--, (US) ˈwʌntsˌoʊ.vɚ
oncer ˈwʌnt.səʳ, ˈwɒnt-, (US) ˈwʌnt.sɚ -s -z
onco- ˈɒŋ.kəʊ; ɒŋˈkɒ, (US) ˈɑːŋ.koʊ-, -kə; (US) ɑːŋˈkɑː
Note: Prefix. Normally either takes primary or secondary stress on the first syllable, e.g. **oncogene** /ˈɒŋ.kəʊ.dʒiːn/ (US) /ˈɑːŋ.kə-/, **oncogenic** /ˌɒŋ.kəʊˈdʒen.ɪk/ (US) /ˌɑːŋ.kə-/, or primary stress on the second syllable, e.g. **oncology** /ɒŋˈkɒl.ə.dʒi/ (US) /ɑːŋˈkɑː.lə-/.
oncogene ˈɒŋ.kəʊ.dʒiːn, (US) ˈɑːn.kə-, ˈɑːŋ- -s -z
oncogenic ˌɒŋ.kəʊˈdʒen.ɪk, (US) ˌɑːn.kəˈ-, ˌɑːŋ-
oncologic ˌɒŋ.kəʊˈlɒdʒ.ɪk, (US) ˌɑːn.kəˈlɑː.dʒɪk, ˌɑːŋ-
oncological ˌɒŋ.kəʊˈlɒdʒ.ɪ.kᵊl, (US) ˌɑːn.kəˈlɑː.dʒɪ-, ˌɑːŋ-
oncologist ɒŋˈkɒl.ə.dʒɪst, (US) ɑːnˈkɑː.lə-, ɑːŋ- -s -s
oncology ɒŋˈkɒl.ə.dʒi, (US) ɑːnˈkɑː.lə-, ɑːŋ-
oncoming ˈɒnˌkʌm.ɪŋ, ˈɒŋ-, (US) ˈɑːn-, ˈɔːn-
Ondaatje ɒnˈdɑː.tʃə, (US) ɑːnˈdɑː.tʃe
on-drive ˈɒn.draɪv, (US) ˈɑːn-, ˈɔːn- -s -z
one wʌn -s -z

> Note: The pronunciation /wɒn/ is increasingly widespread in British English, but cannot yet be recommended as representative of the accent being described here.

O'Neal əʊˈniːl, (US) oʊ-
one-armed ˌwʌnˈɑːmd, ˌwɒn-, (US) ˌwʌnˈɑːrmd ˌ**one-armed** ˈ**bandit**
one-eyed ˌwʌnˈaɪd, ˌwɒn-, (US) ˌwʌn- *stress shift:* ˌ**one-eyed** ˈ**pirate**
Onega ɒnˈeɪ.gə, əʊˈneɪ-, -ˈnjeg.ə; *old fashioned:* ˈəʊ.nɪ.gə, (US) oʊnˈjeg.ə, -neɪ-
Onegin ɒnˈjeɪ.gɪn, (US) ɑːn-
one-horse ˌwʌnˈhɔːs, ˌwɒn-, (US) ˌwʌnˈhɔːrs *stress shift, see compound:* ˌ**one-horse** ˈ**town**
O'Neil(l) əʊˈniːl, (US) oʊ-
one-legged ˌwʌnˈleg.ɪd, ˌwɒn-, (US) ˌwʌnˈlegd *stress shift:* ˌ**one-legged** ˈ**table**
one-liner ˌwʌnˈlaɪ.nəʳ, ˌwɒn-, (US) ˌwʌnˈlaɪ.nɚ -s -z
one-man ˌwʌnˈmæn, ˌwʌm-, ˌwɒn-, (US) ˌwʌn- *stress shift, see compound:* ˌ**one-man** ˈ**band**

O

Pronouncing the letters OO

The most common pronunciation for the vowel digraph **oo** is /uː/, e.g.:

boom buːm

The realization /ʊ/ is also quite common, e.g.:

book bʊk
stood stʊd

When followed by an **r** in the spelling, **oo** is pronounced as either /ɔː/ (US) /ɔːr/ or /ʊə/ (US) /ʊr/, e.g.:

door dɔːʳ (US) dɔːr
moor mɔːʳ, mʊəʳ (US) mʊr

It should be noted that, for many speakers, the form /mʊəʳ/ has dropped out of use in favour of /mɔːʳ/.

In addition

There are other vowel sounds associated with the digraph **oo**, e.g.:

ʌ blood blʌd
əʊ (US) oʊ brooch brəʊtʃ (US) broʊtʃ

oneness ˈwʌn.nəs, -nɪs, ˈwɒn-, (US) ˈwʌn.nəs, -nɪs
one-night stand ˌwʌn.naɪtˈstænd, ˌwɒn-, (US) ˌwʌn-
one-off ˌwʌnˈɒf, ˌwɒn-, ˈ--, (US) ˈwʌn.ɑːf **-s** -s
one-on-one ˌwʌn.ɒnˈwʌn, (US) -ɑːnˈ- *stress-shift:* **ˌone-on-one ˈteaching**
one-parent family ˌwʌn.peə.rᵊntˈfæm.ᵊl.i, ˌwʌm-, ˌwɒn-, -ɪ.li, (US) ˌwʌn.per.ᵊntˈ-, -pær-
one-piece ˈwʌn.piːs, ˈwʌm-, ˌwɒn-, (US) ˈwʌn-
oner ˈwʌn.əʳ, ˈwɒn-, (US) ˈwʌn.ɚ **-s** -z
onerous ˈəʊ.nᵊr.əs, ˈɒn.ᵊr-, (US) ˈɑː.nɚ-, ˈoʊ- **-ly** -li **-ness** -nəs, -nɪs
oneself wʌnˈself, wɒn-, (US) wʌn- **ˌkeep oneˌself to oneˈself**
onesided ˌwʌnˈsaɪ.dɪd, ˌwɒn-, (US) ˌwʌn- **-ly** -li **-ness** -nəs, -nɪs *stress shift:* **ˌonesided ˈargument**
Onesimus əʊˈnes.ɪ.məs, -ˈniː.sɪ-, -sə-, (US) oʊ-
one-stop ˌwʌnˈstɒp, ˌwɒn-, (US) ˌwʌnˈstɑːp *stress shift:* **ˌone-stop ˈshop**
onetime ˈwʌn.taɪm, ˈwɒn-, (US) ˈwʌn-
one-to-one ˌwʌn.təˈwʌn, -tuˈ-, (US) ˌwʌn.t̬əˈ- *stress-shift:* **ˌone-to-one ˈdialogue**
one-track mind ˌwʌn.trækˈmaɪnd, ˌwɒn-, (US) ˌwʌn- **-s** -z
one-upmanship ˌwʌnˈʌp.mən.ʃɪp, ˌwɒn-, (US) ˌwʌn-
one-way ˌwʌnˈweɪ, ˌwɒn-, (US) ˌwʌn- *stress shift, see compound:* **ˌone-way ˈstreet**
ongoing ˈɒnˌgəʊ.ɪŋ, ˈɒŋ-, ˌ-ˈ--, (US) ˈɑːnˌgoʊ- **-s** -z
Onians əˈnaɪ.ənz, əʊ-, (US) oʊ-
Onich ˈəʊ.nɪk, -nɪx, (US) ˈoʊ-
onion ˈʌn.jən **-s** -z **-y** -i
Onions ˈʌn.jənz, əʊˈnaɪ.ənz, (US) ˈʌn.jənz
online ˌɒnˈlaɪn, (US) ˌɑːn-, ˌɔːn- *stress shift:* **ˌonline ˈchat**
onlook|er ˈɒnˌlʊk|.əʳ, (US) ˈɑːnˌlʊk|.ɚ, ˈɔːn- **-ers** -əz, (US) -ɚz **-ing** -ɪŋ
only ˈəʊn.li, (US) ˈoʊn-
on-message ˌɒnˈmes.ɪdʒ, (US) ˌɑːn-
Ono ˈəʊ.nəʊ, (US) ˈoʊ.noʊ
onomasiological ˌɒn.əʊˌmeɪ.si.əˈlɒdʒ.ɪ.kᵊl, -zi-, (US) ˌɑː.noʊˌmeɪ.si.əˈlɑː.dʒɪ-, -nəˌ-
onomasiology ˌɒn.əʊˌmeɪ.siˈɒl.ə.dʒi, -ziˈ-, (US) ˌɑː.noʊˌmeɪ.siˈɑː.lə-, -nəˌ-
onomastic ˌɒn.əʊˈmæs.tɪk, (US) ˌɑː.noʊˈ-, -nəˈ- **-s** -s
onomatopoe|ia ˌɒn.əʊˌmæt.əˈpiː|.ə, (US) ˌɑː.noʊˌmæt̬.oʊˈ-, -nəˌ- **-ias** -əz **-ic** -ɪk
onrush ˈɒn.rʌʃ, (US) ˈɑːn-, ˈɔːn- **-ing** -ɪŋ
onscreen ˌɒnˈskriːn, (US) ˌɑːn-, ˌɔːn- *stress shift:* **ˌonscreen ˈdaughter**
onset ˈɒn.set, (US) ˈɑːn-, ˈɔːn- **-s** -s
onshore ˌɒnˈʃɔːʳ, (US) ˈɑːn.ʃɔːr, ˈɔːn- *stress shift, British only:* **ˌonshore ˈwind**
onside ˌɒnˈsaɪd, (US) ˈɑːn.saɪd, ˈɔːn- *stress shift, British only:* **ˌonside ˈplayer**
onslaught ˈɒn.slɔːt, (US) ˈɑːn.slɑːt, ˈɔːn-, -slɔːt **-s** -s
Onslow ˈɒnz.ləʊ, (US) ˈɑːnz.loʊ
onstage ˌɒnˈsteɪdʒ, (US) ˌɑːn-, ˌɔːn- *stress shift:* **ˌonstage ˈson**
onstream ˌɒnˈstriːm, (US) ˌɑːn-, ˌɔːn- *stress shift:* **ˌonstream ˈoilfield**
Ontario ɒnˈteə.ri.əʊ, (US) ɑːnˈter.i.oʊ
onto ˈɒn.tuː, -tə, -tu, (US) ˈɑːn.tuː, ˈɔːn-, -tə, -tu
Note: The pronunciation /ˈɒn.tuː/ (US) /ˈɑːn-/ is only rarely heard except in citation. The usual pronunciation is /ˈɒn.tə/ (US) /ɑːn.tə/ before consonants, e.g. 'onto ships' /ˌɒn.təˈʃɪps/ (US) /ɑːn.təˈ-/, and /ˈɒn.tu/ (US) /ˈɑːn-/ before vowels, e.g. 'onto aircraft' /ˌɒn.tuˈeə.krɑːft/ (US) /ˌɑːn.tuˈer.kræft/.
ontogenesis ˌɒn.təʊˈdʒen.ə.sɪs, ˈ-ɪ-, (US) ˌɑːn.toʊˈdʒen.ə-
ontogenetic ˌɒn.təʊ.dʒəˈnet.ɪk, -dʒɪˈ-, (US) ˌɑːn.toʊ.dʒəˈnet̬- **-ally** -ᵊl.i, -li
ontogeny ɒnˈtɒdʒ.ə.ni, ˈ-ɪ-, (US) ɑːnˈtɑː.dʒə-
ontologic ˌɒn.təˈlɒdʒ.ɪk, (US) ˌɑːn.toʊˈlɑː.dʒɪk **-al** -ᵊl **-ally** -ᵊl.i, -li
ontolog|y ɒnˈtɒl.ə.dʒ|i, (US) ɑːnˈtɑː.lə- **-ist/s** -ɪst/s
onus ˈəʊ.nəs, (US) ˈoʊ-
onward ˈɒn.wəd, (US) ˈɑːn.wɚd, ˈɔːn- **-s** -z
onyx ˈɒn.ɪks, (US) ˈɑː.nɪks **-es** -ɪz
oodles ˈuː.dᵊlz
oof uːf
ooh uː
oolite ˈəʊ.əʊ.laɪt, (US) ˈoʊ.ə- **-s** -s
oolitic ˌəʊ.əʊˈlɪt.ɪk, (US) ˌoʊ.əˈlɪt̬-
oolog|y əʊˈɒl.ə.dʒ|i, (US) oʊˈɑː.lə- **-ist/s** -ɪst/s
Oolong ˈuː.lɒŋ, ˌ-ˈ-, (US) ˈuː.lɑːŋ, -lɔːŋ
oompah ˈʊm.pɑː, ˈuːm-
oomph ʊmpf, uːmpf
oops uːps, ʊps
oops-a-daisy ˌʊps.əˈdeɪ.zi, ˌuːps-, ˌwʊps-, ˈʊps.əˌdeɪ-, ˈuːps-, ˈwʊps-
ooz|e uːz **-es** -ɪz **-ing** -ɪŋ **-ed** -d
ooz|y ˈuː.z|i **-ier** -i.əʳ, (US) -i.ɚ **-iest** -i.ɪst, -i.əst **-ily** -ᵊl.i, -ɪ.li **-iness** -ɪ.nəs, -ɪ.nɪs
op ɒp, (US) ɑːp **-s** -s
opacity əʊˈpæs.ə.ti, -ɪ.ti, (US) oʊˈpæs.ə.t̬i
opal ˈəʊ.pᵊl, (US) ˈoʊ- **-s** -z
opalescen|t ˌəʊ.pᵊlˈes.ᵊn|t, (US) ˌoʊ- **-ce** -*t*s
opaline adj ˈəʊ.pᵊl.aɪn, (US) ˈoʊ.pᵊl.iːn, -aɪn, -ɪn
opaline n ˈəʊ.pᵊl.iːn, -aɪn, (US) ˈoʊ- **-s** -z
opaque əʊˈpeɪk, (US) oʊ- **-ly** -li **-ness** -nəs, -nɪs
op art ˈɒpˌɑːt, (US) ˈɑːpˌɑːrt
op. cit. ˌɒpˈsɪt, (US) ˌɑːp-
op|e əʊp, (US) oʊp **-es** -s **-ing** -ɪŋ **-ed** -t
OPEC, Opec ˈəʊ.pek, (US) ˈoʊ-
Opel® ˈəʊ.pᵊl, (US) ˈoʊ-
open ˈəʊ.pᵊn, (US) ˈoʊ- **-er** -əʳ, (US) -ɚ **-est** -ɪst, (US) -əst **-s** -z **-ing** -ɪŋ, ˈəʊp.nɪŋ, (US) ˈoʊp- **-ed** -d **ˌopen ˈbook; ˈopen ˌday; ˌopen ˈhouse; ˌopen ˈmarket; ˌopen ˈprison; ˌopen ˈsesame; ˌOpen Uniˈversity; ˌopen ˈverdict**
open air ˌəʊ.pᵊnˈeəʳ, (US) ˌoʊ.pᵊnˈer
open-air adj ˌəʊ.pᵊnˈeəʳ, (US) ˌoʊ.pᵊnˈer *stress shift:* **ˌopen-air ˈconcert**
open-and-shut ˌəʊ.pᵊn.əndˈʃʌt, (US) ˌoʊ- *stress shift:* **ˌopen-and-shut ˈcase**
opencast ˈəʊ.pᵊn.kɑːst, -pᵊŋ-, (US) ˈoʊ.pᵊn.kæst
open-ended ˌəʊ.pᵊnˈend.ɪd, (US)

O

ˌoʊ- *stress shift:* ˌ**open-ended** ˈ**verdict**

opener ˈəʊ.pᵊn.əʳ, (US) ˈoʊ.pᵊn.ɚ -s -z

open-eyed ˌəʊ.pᵊnˈaɪd, (US) ˌoʊ- *stress shift:* ˌ**open-eyed** ˈ**onlooker**

open-handed ˌəʊ.pᵊnˈhæn.dɪd, ˈəʊ.pᵊnˌhæn-, (US) ˈoʊ.pᵊnˌhæn-, ˌoʊ.pᵊnˈhæn- -ness -nəs, -nɪs *stress shift, British only:* ˌ**open-handed** ˈ**benefactor**

open-heart ˌəʊ.pᵊnˈhɑːt, (US) ˌoʊ.pᵊnˈhɑːrt *stress shift, see compound:* ˌ**open-heart** ˈ**surgery**

open-hearted ˌəʊ.pᵊnˈhɑː.tɪd, ˈəʊ.pᵊnˌhɑː-, (US) ˈoʊ.pᵊnˌhɑːr.t̬ɪd, ˌoʊ.pᵊnˈhɑːr- -ly -li -ness -nəs, -nɪs *stress shift, British only:* ˌ**open-hearted** ˈ**person**

opening ˈəʊ.pᵊn.ɪŋ, ˈəʊp.nɪŋ, (US) ˈoʊ.pᵊn.ɪŋ, ˈoʊp.nɪŋ -s -z

opening time ˈəʊ.pᵊn.ɪŋˌtaɪm, ˈəʊp.nɪŋˌ-, (US) ˈoʊ.pᵊn.ɪŋˌtaɪm, ˈoʊp.nɪŋˌ-

openly ˈəʊ.pᵊn.li, (US) ˈoʊ-

open-minded ˌəʊ.pᵊnˈmaɪn.dɪd, -pᵊmˈ-, ˈəʊ.pᵊnˌmaɪn-, -pᵊmˌ-, (US) ˌoʊ.pᵊnˈmaɪn-, ˈoʊ.pᵊnˌmaɪn- -ly -li -ness -nəs, -nɪs *stress shift, British only:* ˌ**open-minded** ˈ**person**

open-mouthed ˌəʊ.pᵊnˈmaʊðd, -pᵊmˈ-, ˈəʊ.pᵊnˌmaʊðd, (US) ˈoʊ.pᵊnˌmaʊðd, -ˌmaʊθt, ˌ--ˈ- *stress shift, British only:* ˌ**open-mouthed** ˈ**children**

openness ˈəʊ.pᵊn.nəs, -nɪs, (US) ˈoʊ-

open-plan ˌəʊ.pᵊnˈplæn, -pᵊmˈ-, (US) ˌoʊ.pᵊn- *stress shift:* ˌ**open-plan** ˈ**offices**

open sesame ˌəʊ.pᵊnˈses.ə.mi, (US) ˌoʊ-

Openshaw ˈəʊ.pᵊn.ʃɔː, (US) ˈoʊ.pᵊn.ʃɑː, -ʃɔː

open-source ˌəʊ.pənˈsɔːs, (US) ˌoʊ.pənˈsɔːrs

open-work ˈəʊ.pᵊn.wɜːk, (US) ˈoʊ.pᵊn.wɝːk

opera ˈɒp.ᵊr.ə, ˈɒp.rə, (US) ˈɑː.pᵊr.ə, ˈɑː.prə -s -z ˈ**opera** ˌ**house**

operability ˌɒp.ᵊr.əˈbɪl.ɪ.ti, -ə.ti, (US) ˌɑː.pᵊr.əˈbɪl.ə.t̬i, ˌɑː.prəˈ-

operab|le ˈɒp.ᵊr.ə.b|ᵊl, (US) ˈɑː.pᵊr.ə-, ˈɑː.prə- -ly -li

opéra bouffe ˌɒp.ᵊr.əˈbuːf, (US) ˌɑː.pᵊr-, ˌɑː.prəˈ-

opera buffa ˌɒp.ᵊr.əˈbuː.fə, (US) ˌɑː.pᵊr.əˈ-, ˌɑː.prəˈ-

opéra comique ˌɒp.ᵊr.ə.kɒmˈiːk, (US) ˌɑː.pᵊr.ə.kɑːˈmiːk, ˌɑː.prə-

operant ˈɒp.ᵊr.ᵊnt, (US) ˈɑː.pᵊr- -s -s

oper|ate ˈɒp.ᵊr|.eɪt, (US) ˈɑː.pᵊr- -ates -eɪts -ating -eɪ.tɪŋ, (US) -eɪ.t̬ɪŋ -ated -eɪ.tɪd, (US) -eɪ.t̬ɪd -ator/s -eɪ.təʳ/z, (US) -eɪ.t̬ɚ/z ˈ**operating** ˌ**system**; ˈ**operating** ˌ**table**

operatic ˌɒp.ᵊrˈæt.ɪk, (US) ˌɑː.pəˈræt̬- -s -s -ally -ᵊl.i, -li

operation ˌɒp.ᵊrˈeɪ.ʃᵊn, (US) ˌɑː.pəˈreɪ- -s -z

operational ˌɒp.ᵊrˈeɪ.ʃᵊn.ᵊl, -ˈeɪʃ.nᵊl, (US) ˌɑː.pəˈreɪ.ʃᵊn.ᵊl, -ˈreɪʃ.nᵊl -ly -i

operative ˈɒp.ᵊr.ə.tɪv, -eɪ-, (US) ˈɑː.pɚ.ə.t̬ɪv, -pə.reɪ- -s -z -ly -li -ness -nəs, -nɪs

operetta ˌɒp.ᵊrˈet.ə, (US) ˌɑː.pəˈret̬- -s -z

operettist ˌɒp.ᵊrˈet.ɪst, (US) ˌɑː.pəˈret̬- -s -s

Ophelia əʊˈfiː.li.ə, ɒfˈiː-, (US) oʊˈfiːl.jə

ophicleide ˈɒf.ɪ.klaɪd, -kleɪd, (US) ˈɑː.fɪ- -s -z

ophidian ɒfˈɪd.i.ən, əʊˈfɪd-, (US) oʊˈfɪd-

Ophir ˈəʊ.fəʳ, (US) ˈoʊ.fɚ

Ophiuchus ɒfˈjuː.kəs, ˌɒf.iˈuː-, (US) ˌɑː.fiˈjuː.kəs, ˌoʊ-

ophthalmia ɒfˈθæl.mi.ə, ɒp-, (US) ɑːf-, ɑːp-

ophthalmic ɒfˈθæl.mɪk, ɒp-, (US) ɑːf-, ɑːp-

ophthalmo- ɒfˈθæl.məʊ, ɒp-, (US) ɑːfˈθæl.moʊ, ɑːp-, -mə

ophthalmolog|y ˌɒf.θælˈmɒl.ə.dʒ|i, ɒp-, (US) ˌɑːf.θælˈmɑː.lə-, ˌɑːp- -ist/s -ɪst/s

ophthalmoscope ɒfˈθæl.mə.skəʊp, ɒp-, (US) ɑːfˈθæl.mə.skoʊp, ɑːp- -s -s

ophthalmoscopy ˌɒf.θælˈmɒs.kə.pi, ɒp-, (US) ˌɑːf.θælˈmɑː.skə-, ˌɑːp-

opiate ˈəʊ.pi.ət, -ɪt, -eɪt, (US) ˈoʊ.pi.ɪt, -eɪt -s -s

opiated ˈəʊ.pi.eɪ.tɪd, (US) ˈoʊ.pi.eɪ.t̬ɪd

Opie ˈəʊ.pi, (US) ˈoʊ-

opin|e əʊˈpaɪn, (US) oʊ- -es -z -ing -ɪŋ -ed -d

opinion əˈpɪn.jən, (US) ə-, oʊ- -s -z **oˈpinion** ˌ**poll**

opinionated əˈpɪn.jə.neɪ.tɪd, (US) -t̬ɪd, oʊ-

opium ˈəʊ.pi.əm, (US) ˈoʊ- ˈ**opium** ˌ**den**

Oporto əʊˈpɔː.təʊ, (US) oʊˈpɔːr.toʊ

opossum əˈpɒs.əm, (US) -ˈpɑː.səm -s -z

Oppenheim ˈɒp.ᵊn.haɪm, (US) ˈɑː.pᵊn- -er -əʳ, (US) -ɚ

oppidan ˈɒp.ɪ.dᵊn, (US) ˈɑː.pɪ- -s -z

opponent əˈpəʊ.nənt, (US) -ˈpoʊ- -s -s

opportune ˈɒp.ə.tʃuːn, -tjuːn, ˌ--ˈ-, (US) ˌɑː.pɚˈtuːn, -ˈtjuːn -ly -li -ness -nəs, -nɪs

opportun|ism ˌɒp.əˈtʃuː.n|ɪ.zᵊm, -ˈtjuː-, ˈɒp.ə.tʃuː-, -tjuː-, (US) ˌɑː.pɚˈtuː-, -ˈtjuː- -ist/s -ɪst/s

opportunistic ˌɒp.ə.tʃuːˈnɪs.tɪk, -tjuːˈ-, (US) ˌɑː.pɚ.tuːˈ-, -tjuːˈ- -ally -ᵊl.i, -li

opportunit|y ˌɒp.əˈtʃuː.nə.t|i, -ˈtjuː-, -nɪ-, (US) ˌɑː.pɚˈtuː.nə.t̬|i, -ˈtjuː- -ies -iz

oppos|e əˈpəʊz, (US) -ˈpoʊz -es -ɪz -ing -ɪŋ -ed -d -er/s -əʳ/z, (US) -ɚ/z -able -ə.bᵊl

opposite ˈɒp.ə.zɪt, -sɪt, (US) ˈɑː.pə- -s -s -ly -li -ness -nəs, -nɪs ˌ**opposite** ˈ**number**

opposition ˌɒp.əˈzɪʃ.ᵊn, (US) ˌɑː.pəˈ- -s -z

oppress əˈpres -es -ɪz -ing -ɪŋ -ed -t

oppression əˈpreʃ.ᵊn -s -z

oppressive əˈpres.ɪv -ly -li -ness -nəs, -nɪs

oppressor əˈpres.əʳ, (US) -ɚ -s -z

opprobrious əˈprəʊ.bri.əs, (US) -ˈproʊ- -ly -li -ness -nəs, -nɪs

opprobrium əˈprəʊ.bri.əm, (US) -ˈproʊ-

oppugn əˈpjuːn -s -z -ing -ɪŋ -ed -d -er/s -əʳ/z, (US) -ɚ/z

Oprah ˈəʊ.prə, (US) ˈoʊ-

Opren® ˈɒp.rᵊn, -ren, (US) ˈɑː.prᵊn, -pren

opt ɒpt, (US) ɑːpt -s -s -ing -ɪŋ -ed -ɪd

optative ˈɒp.tə.tɪv; ɒpˈteɪ-, (US) ˈɑːp.tə.t̬ɪv -s -z

optic ˈɒp.tɪk, (US) ˈɑːp- -s -s

optical ˈɒp.tɪ.kᵊl, (US) ˈɑːp- -ly -i ˌ**optical** ˈ**fibre**; ˌ**optical ilˈlusion**

optician ɒpˈtɪʃ.ᵊn, (US) ɑːp- -s -z

optimal ˈɒp.tɪ.mᵊl, (US) ˈɑːp- -ly -i

optime ˈɒp.tɪ.meɪ, (US) ˈɑːp- -s -z

optim|ism ˈɒp.tɪ.m|ɪ.zᵊm, -tə-, (US) ˈɑːp.tə- -ist/s -ɪst/s

optimistic ˌɒp.tɪˈmɪs.tɪk, -təˈ-, (US) ˌɑːp.təˈ- -al -ᵊl -ally -ᵊl.i, -li

optimization ˌɒp.tɪ.maɪˈzeɪ.ʃᵊn, -tə-, -mɪˈ-, (US) ˌɑːp.tə.məˈzeɪ- -s -z

optimiz|e, -is|e ˈɒp.tɪ.maɪz, -tə-, (US) ˈɑːp.tə- -es -ɪz -ing -ɪŋ -ed -d

optim|um ˈɒp.tɪ.m|əm, -tə-, (US) ˈɑːp.tə- -ums -əmz -a -ə

option ˈɒp.ʃᵊn, (US) ˈɑːp- -s -z -ing -ɪŋ -ed -d

optional ˈɒp.ʃᵊn.ᵊl, (US) ˈɑːp.ʃᵊn.ᵊl -ly -i

optometric ˌɒp.təʊˈmet.rɪk, (US) ˌɑːp.təˈmet- -s -s

optometrist ɒpˈtɒm.ə.trɪst, ˈ-ɪ-, (US) ɑːpˈtɑː.mə- -s -s

optometry ɒpˈtɒm.ə.tri, ˈ-ɪ-, (US) ɑːpˈtɑː.mə-

opt-out ˈɒpt.aʊt, (US) ˈɑːpt- -s -z

Optrex® ˈɒp.treks, (US) ˈɑːp-

opulence ˈɒp.jə.lənts, -jʊ-, (US) ˈɑːp-

opulent ˈɒp.jə.lənt, -jʊ-, (US) ˈɑːp- -ly -li

opus ˈəʊ.pəs, ˈɒp.əs, (US) ˈoʊ.pəs -es -ɪz **opera** ˈɒp.ᵊr.ə, (US) ˈoʊ.pɚ.ə, ˈɑː-, ˈ-prə

opuscule ɒpˈʌs.kjuːl, əʊˈpʌs-, (US) oʊˈpʌs.kjuːl -s -z

Opus Dei ˌəʊ.pəsˈdeɪ.i, (US) ˌoʊ-

or n ɔːʳ, (US) ɔːr

or conj *normal form:* ɔːʳ, (US) ɔːr; *weak form:* əʳ, (US) ɚ

Note: Occasional weak-form word. The weak form /əʳ/ (US) /ɚ/ is used in phrases such as 'two or three pounds' /ˌtuː.əˌθriːˈpaʊndz/ (US) /-ɚˌ-/.

orach|(e) ˈɒr.ɪtʃ, (US) ˈɔːr.ətʃ -es -ɪz

oracle ˈɒr.ə.kᵊl, ˈ-ɪ-, (US) ˈɔːr.ə- -s -z

oracular ɒrˈæk.jə.ləʳ, ɔːˈræk-, ə-, -jʊ-, (US) ɔːˈræk.juː.lɚ, ə-, -jə- -ly -li -ness -nəs, -nɪs

oracy ˈɔː.rə.si, (US) ˈɔːr.ə-

Oradea ɒrˈɑː.di.ə, (US) ɔːˈrɑː.djɑː

oral ˈɔː.rəl, Ⓤⓢ ˈɔːr.əl **-s** -z **-ly** -i ˌ**oral ˈsex**
Oran ɔːˈrɑːn, ə-, ɒrˈɑːn, -ˈæn, Ⓤⓢ oʊˈrɑːn, -ˈræn
orang|e, O~ ˈɒr.ɪndʒ, -əndʒ, Ⓤⓢ ˈɔːr.ɪndʒ **-es** -ɪz ˌ**Orange ˈFree ˌState; ˈorange ˌjuice**
orangeade ˌɒr.ɪndʒˈeɪd, -əndʒˈ-, Ⓤⓢ ˌɔːr.ɪndʒˈ-
orange-blossom ˈɒr.ɪndʒˌblɒs.əm, -əndʒˌ-, Ⓤⓢ ˈɔːr.ɪndʒˌblɑː.səm **-s** -z
Orange|man ˈɒr.ɪndʒ|.mən, -əndʒ-, -mæn, Ⓤⓢ ˈɔːr.ɪndʒ- **-men** -mən, -men
oranger|y ˈɒr.ɪn.dʒər|.i, -ən-, ˈ-ɪndʒ.r|i, Ⓤⓢ ˈɔːr.ɪndʒ.ri **-ies** -iz
orangoutan, orangutan, orangutang ɔːˌræŋ.uːˈtæn, ɒrˌæŋ-, əˌræŋ-, -əˈ-, -juːˈ-, -ˈtɑːn, -ˈtæŋ; ɔːˈræŋ.uː.tæn, ɒrˈæŋ-, əˈræŋ-, ˈ-ə-, ˈ-juː-, -tɑːn, -tæŋ, Ⓤⓢ ɔːˈræŋ.ə.tæn, ə-, oʊ-, -tæŋ **-s** -z
ora|te ɔːˈreɪ|t, ɒrˈeɪ|t, əˈreɪ|t, Ⓤⓢ ˈɔːr.eɪ|t; Ⓤⓢ ɔːˈreɪ|t **-tes** -ts **-ting** -tɪŋ, Ⓤⓢ -t̬ɪŋ **-ted** -tɪd, Ⓤⓢ -t̬ɪd
oration ərˈeɪ.ʃən, ɒr-, Ⓤⓢ ɔː- **-s** -z
orator ˈɒr.ə.tər, Ⓤⓢ ˈɔːr.ə.t̬ɚ **-s** -z
oratorical ˌɒr.əˈtɒr.ɪ.kəl, Ⓤⓢ ˌɔːr.əˈtɔːr- **-ly** -i
oratorio ˌɒr.əˈtɔː.ri.əʊ, Ⓤⓢ ˌɔːr.əˈtɔːr.i.oʊ **-s** -z
orator|y, O~ ˈɒr.ə.tər|.i, Ⓤⓢ ˈɔːr.ə.tɔːr- **-ies** -iz
orb ɔːb, Ⓤⓢ ɔːrb **-s** -z **-ing** -ɪŋ **-ed** -d
Orbach ˈɔː.bæk, Ⓤⓢ ˈɔːr-
orbed ɔːbd, Ⓤⓢ ɔːrbd; *in poetry generally:* ˈɔː.bɪd, Ⓤⓢ ˈɔːr.bɪd
orbicular ɔːˈbɪk.jə.lər, -jʊ-, Ⓤⓢ ɔːrˈbɪk.juː.lɚ, -jə- **-ly** -li
Orbison ˈɔː.bɪ.sən, -bə-, Ⓤⓢ ˈɔːr-
or|bit ˈɔː|.bɪt, Ⓤⓢ ˈɔːr- **-bits** -bɪts **-biting** -bɪ.tɪŋ, Ⓤⓢ -bɪ.t̬ɪŋ **-bited** -bɪ.tɪd, Ⓤⓢ -bɪ.t̬ɪd **-bital** -bɪ.təl, Ⓤⓢ -t̬əl
orc ɔːk, Ⓤⓢ ɔːrk **-s** -s
Orcadian ɔːˈkeɪ.di.ən, Ⓤⓢ ɔːr- **-s** -z
orchard, O~ ˈɔː.tʃəd, Ⓤⓢ ˈɔːr.tʃɚd **-s** -z
Orchardson ˈɔː.tʃəd.sən, Ⓤⓢ ˈɔːr.tʃɚd-
orchestra ˈɔː.kɪ.strə, -kə-, -kes.trə, Ⓤⓢ ˈɔːr.kɪ.strə, -kes.trə **-s** -z
orchestral ɔːˈkes.trəl, Ⓤⓢ ɔːr-
orchest|rate ˈɔː.kɪ.st|reɪt, -kə-, -kes.t|reɪt, Ⓤⓢ ˈɔːr.kɪ.st|reɪt, -kes.t|reɪt **-rates** -reɪts **-rating** -reɪ.tɪŋ, Ⓤⓢ -reɪ.t̬ɪŋ **-rated** -reɪ.tɪd, Ⓤⓢ -reɪ.t̬ɪd
orchestration ˌɔː.kɪˈstreɪ.ʃən, -kəˈ-, -kesˈtreɪ-, Ⓤⓢ ˌɔːr.kɪˈstreɪ-, -kesˈtreɪ- **-s** -z
orchestrion ɔːˈkes.tri.ən, Ⓤⓢ ɔːr- **-s** -z
orchid ˈɔː.kɪd, Ⓤⓢ ˈɔːr- **-s** -z
orchidaceous ˌɔː.kɪˈdeɪ.ʃəs, Ⓤⓢ ˌɔːr-
orchil ˈɔː.tʃɪl, -kɪl, Ⓤⓢ ˈɔːr-
orchis ˈɔː.kɪs, Ⓤⓢ ˈɔːr- **-es** -ɪz
Orczy ˈɔːk.si, ˈɔːt-, Ⓤⓢ ˈɔːrk-, ˈɔːrt-
Ord ɔːd, Ⓤⓢ ɔːrd
ordain ɔːˈdeɪn, Ⓤⓢ ɔːr- **-s** -z **-ing** -ɪŋ **-ed** -d **-er/s** -ər/z, Ⓤⓢ -ɚ/z
Orde ɔːd, Ⓤⓢ ɔːrd
ordeal ɔːˈdiːl, ˈ--, Ⓤⓢ ɔːrˈdiːl, ˈ-- **-s** -z
ord|er ˈɔː.d|ər, Ⓤⓢ ˈɔːr.d|ɚ **-ers** -əz, Ⓤⓢ -ɚz **-ering** -ər.ɪŋ **-ered** -əd, Ⓤⓢ -ɚd **-erless** -əl.əs, -ɪs, Ⓤⓢ -ɚ.ləs, -lɪs
orderl|y ˈɔː.dəl|.i, Ⓤⓢ ˈɔːr.dɚ.l|i **-ies** -iz **-iness** -ɪ.nəs, -ɪ.nɪs
ordinaire ˌɔː.dɪˈneər, -dənˈeər, ˈ---, Ⓤⓢ ˌɔːr.dɪˈner
ordinal ˈɔː.dɪ.nəl, -dən.əl, Ⓤⓢ ˈɔːr.dən.əl, ˈɔːrd.nəl **-s** -z ˌ**ordinal ˈnumber**
ordinanc|e ˈɔː.dɪ.nənts, -dən.ənts, Ⓤⓢ ˈɔːr.dən-, ˈɔːrd.nənts **-es** -ɪz
ordinand ˈɔː.dɪ.nænd, -dən.ænd, ˌ--ˈ-, Ⓤⓢ ˈɔːr.dən.ænd **-s** -z
ordinarily ˈɔː.dən.ər.əl.i, -dɪ.nər-, -ɪ.li; ˌɔː.dənˈer.ɪ-, Ⓤⓢ ˈɔːr.dən.er.əl.i, ˌɔːr.dənˈer-
ordinariness ˈɔː.dən.ər.ɪ.nəs, -dɪ.nər-, -nɪs, Ⓤⓢ ˌɔːr.dənˈer-
ordinar|y ˈɔː.dən.ər|.i, -dɪ.nər-, Ⓤⓢ ˈɔːr.dən.er- **-ies** -iz
ordinate ˈɔː.dən.ət, -dɪ.nət, -nɪt, Ⓤⓢ ˈɔːr.dən.ɪt, -eɪt **-s** -s
ordination ˌɔː.dɪˈneɪ.ʃən, -dənˈeɪ-, Ⓤⓢ ˌɔːr.dənˈeɪ- **-s** -z
ordnance ˈɔːd.nənts, Ⓤⓢ ˈɔːrd- ˌ**Ordnance ˈSurvey**
ordure ˈɔː.dʒʊər, ˈ-djʊər, -dʒər, -djər, Ⓤⓢ ˈɔːr.dʒɚ, -djʊr
ore, O~ ɔːr, Ⓤⓢ ɔːr **-s** -z
öre, ore ˈɜː.rə, Ⓤⓢ ˈɝː.ə
Ore. (abbrev. for **Oregon**) ˈɒr.ɪ.gən, ˈ-ə-, -gɒn, Ⓤⓢ ˈɔːr.ɪ.gən, -gɑːn
oread ˈɔː.ri.æd, Ⓤⓢ ˈɔːr.i- **-s** -z
Örebro ˈɜː.rə.bruː, Ⓤⓢ ˈɝː.ə-
O'Regan əʊˈriː.gən, Ⓤⓢ oʊ-
oregano ˌɒr.ɪˈgɑː.nəʊ, -əˈ-, Ⓤⓢ ɔːˈreg.ə.noʊ, ə-
Oregon ˈɒr.ɪ.gən, ˈ-ə-, -gɒn, Ⓤⓢ ˈɔːr.ɪ.gən, -gɑːn
O'Reilly əʊˈraɪ.li, Ⓤⓢ oʊ-
Oreo® ˈɔː.ri.əʊ, Ⓤⓢ ˈɔːr.i.oʊ **-s** -z
Oresteia ˌɒr.ɪˈstaɪ.ə, ˌɔː.rɪˈ-, -ˈsteɪ.ə, Ⓤⓢ ˌɔːr.esˈtiː.ə, -əˈstiː-
Orestes ɒrˈes.tiːz, ɔːˈres-, ə-, Ⓤⓢ ɔː-
orfe ɔːf, Ⓤⓢ ɔːrf
Orfeo ˈɔː.fi.əʊ; *as if Italian:* ɔːˈfeɪ.əʊ; Ⓤⓢ ˈɔːr.fi.oʊ, -feɪ-
Orff ɔːf, Ⓤⓢ ɔːrf
Orford ˈɔː.fəd, Ⓤⓢ ˈɔːr.fɚd
organ ˈɔː.gən, Ⓤⓢ ˈɔːr- **-s** -z
organd|y, -|ie ˈɔː.gən.d|i, ɔːˈgæn-, Ⓤⓢ ˈɔːr.gən- **-ies** -iz
organelle ˌɔː.gənˈel, Ⓤⓢ ˌɔːr- **-s** -z
organ-grinder ˈɔː.gənˌgraɪn.dər, -gəŋˌ-, Ⓤⓢ ˈɔːr.gənˌgraɪn.dɚ **-s** -z
organic ɔːˈgæn.ɪk, Ⓤⓢ ɔːr- **-s** -s **-al** -əl **-ally** -əl.i, -li
organism ˈɔː.gən.ɪ.zəm, Ⓤⓢ ˈɔːr- **-s** -z
organist ˈɔː.gən.ɪst, Ⓤⓢ ˈɔːr- **-s** -s
organizability, -isa- ˌɔː.gənˌaɪ.zəˈbɪl.ə.ti, -ɪ.ti, Ⓤⓢ ˌɔːr.gənˌaɪ.zəˈbɪl.ə.t̬i
organization, -isa- ˌɔː.gən.aɪˈzeɪ.ʃən, -ɪˈ-, Ⓤⓢ ˌɔːr.gən.əˈ- **-s** -z
organizational, -isa- ˌɔː.gən.aɪˈzeɪ.ʃən.əl, -ɪˈ-, Ⓤⓢ ˌɔːr.gən.ɪˈ- **-ly** -i
organiz|e, -is|e ˈɔː.gən.aɪz, Ⓤⓢ ˈɔːr- **-es** -ɪz **-ing** -ɪŋ **-ed** -d **-er/s** -ər/z, Ⓤⓢ -ɚ/z **-able** -ə.bəl
organ|on ˈɔː.gə.n|ɒn, Ⓤⓢ ˈɔːr.gə.n|ɑːn **-ons** -ɒnz, Ⓤⓢ -ɑːnz **-a** -ə
organophosphate ɔːˌgæn.əʊˈfɒs.feɪt, -fɪt, -fət; ˌɔːr.gən.əʊ-, Ⓤⓢ ɔːrˌgæn.oʊˈfɑːs.feɪt, -əˈ-; Ⓤⓢ ˌɔːr.gən.oʊ- **-s** -s
organum ˈɔː.gə.nəm, Ⓤⓢ ˈɔːr- **-s** -z
organza ɔːˈgæn.zə, Ⓤⓢ ɔːr-
orgasm ˈɔː.gæz.əm, Ⓤⓢ ˈɔːr- **-s** -z
orgasmic ɔːˈgæz.mɪk, Ⓤⓢ ɔːr- **-ally** -əl.i, -li
orgiastic ˌɔː.dʒiˈæs.tɪk, Ⓤⓢ ˌɔːr- **-ally** -əl.i, -li
org|y ˈɔː.dʒ|i, Ⓤⓢ ˈɔːr- **-ies** -iz
Oriana ˌɒr.iˈɑː.nə, ˌɔː.riˈ-, Ⓤⓢ ˌɔːr.iˈæn.ə
oriel, O~ ˈɔː.ri.əl, Ⓤⓢ ˈɔːr.i- **-s** -z
orient, O~ n, adj ˈɔː.ri.ənt, ˈɒr.i-, Ⓤⓢ ˈɔːr.i- ˌ**Orient Exˈpress**
ori|ent v ˈɔː.ri|.ent, ˈɒr.i-, Ⓤⓢ ˈɔːr.i- **-ents** -ents **-enting** -en.tɪŋ, Ⓤⓢ -en.t̬ɪŋ **-ented** -en.tɪd, Ⓤⓢ -en.t̬ɪd
oriental, O~ ˌɔː.riˈen.təl, ˌɒr.iˈ-, Ⓤⓢ ˌɔːr.iˈ- **-s** -z
oriental|ism ˌɔː.riˈen.təl|.ɪ.zəm, ˌɒr.iˈ-, Ⓤⓢ ˌɔːr.iˈen.t̬əl- **-ist/s** -ɪst/s
orientaliz|e, -is|e ˌɔː.riˈen.təl.aɪz, ˌɒr.iˈ-, Ⓤⓢ ˌɔːr.iˈen.t̬əl- **-es** -ɪz **-ing** -ɪŋ **-ed** -d
orien|tate ˈɔː.ri.ən|.teɪt, ˈɒr.i-, -en-, Ⓤⓢ ˈɔːr.i.en-, ˌɔːr.iˈen- **-tates** -teɪts **-tating** -teɪ.tɪŋ, Ⓤⓢ -teɪ.t̬ɪŋ **-tated** -teɪ.tɪd, Ⓤⓢ -teɪ.t̬ɪd
orientation ˌɔː.ri.ənˈteɪ.ʃən, ˌɒr.i-, -enˈ-, Ⓤⓢ ˌɔːr.i.enˈ- **-s** -z
orienteer ˌɔː.ri.ənˈtɪər, ˌɒr.i-, -enˈ-, Ⓤⓢ ˌɔːr.i.enˈtɪr **-s** -z
orienteering ˌɔː.ri.ənˈtɪə.rɪŋ, ˌɒr.i-, -enˈ-, Ⓤⓢ ˌɔːr.i.enˈtɪr.ɪŋ
orific|e ˈɒr.ɪ.fɪs, ˈ-ə-, Ⓤⓢ ˈɔːr.ə- **-es** -ɪz
oriflamme ˈɒr.ɪ.flæm, ˈ-ə-, Ⓤⓢ ˈɔːr.ɪ- **-s** -z
origami ˌɒr.ɪˈgɑː.mi, -ˈgæm.i, Ⓤⓢ ˌɔːr.ɪˈgɑː.mi
Origen ˈɒr.ɪ.dʒen, ˈ-ə-, Ⓤⓢ ˈɔːr.ɪ.dʒən, -dʒen
origin ˈɒr.ɪ.dʒɪn, ˈ-ə-, -dʒən, Ⓤⓢ ˈɔːr.ə.dʒɪn **-s** -z
original əˈrɪdʒ.ən.əl, ɒrˈɪdʒ-, -ɪ.nəl, Ⓤⓢ əˈrɪdʒ.ɪ- **-s** -z **-ness** -nəs, -nɪs **o**ˌ**riginal ˈsin**
originalit|y əˌrɪdʒ.ənˈæl.ə.t|i, ɒrˌɪdʒ-, -ɪˈnæl-, -ɪ.t|i, Ⓤⓢ əˌrɪdʒ.ɪˈnæl.ə.t̬|i **-ies** -iz
originally əˈrɪdʒ.ən.əl.i, ɒrˈɪdʒ-, -ɪ.nəl-, Ⓤⓢ əˈrɪdʒ.ɪ-
origi|nate əˈrɪdʒ.ən|.eɪt, ɒrˈɪdʒ-, -ɪ.n|eɪt, Ⓤⓢ əˈrɪdʒ.ɪ- **-nates** -neɪts **-nating** -neɪ.tɪŋ, Ⓤⓢ -neɪ.t̬ɪŋ **-nated** -neɪ.tɪd, Ⓤⓢ -neɪ.t̬ɪd **-nator/s** -neɪ.tər/z, Ⓤⓢ -neɪ.t̬ɚ/z **-native** -neɪ.tɪv, Ⓤⓢ -neɪ.t̬ɪv
origination əˌrɪdʒ.ənˈeɪ.ʃən, ɒrˌɪdʒ-, -ɪˈneɪ-, Ⓤⓢ ˌə.rɪdʒ.ɪˈneɪ-

O

Orinoco ˌɒr.ɪˈnəʊ.kəʊ, -əˈ-, ⓤⓢ ˌɔːr.əˈnoʊ.koʊ
oriole ˈɔː.ri.əʊl, ˈɒr.i-, ⓤⓢ ˈɔːr.i.oʊl -s -z
Orion əˈraɪ.ən, ɒrˈaɪ.ən-, ɔːˈraɪ.ən, ⓤⓢ oʊ-, ə-
O'Riordan əʊˈrɪə.dᵊn, -ˈraɪ.ə-, ⓤⓢ oʊˈrɪr-
orison ˈɒr.ɪ.zᵊn, -ə-, ⓤⓢ ˈɔːr.ɪ.zᵊn, -sᵊn -s -z
Orissa ɒrˈɪs.ə, ɔːˈrɪs-, ə-, ⓤⓢ oʊˈrɪs-, ɔː-
Oriya ɒrˈiː.ə, ⓤⓢ ɔːˈriː.ə
ork ɔːk, ⓤⓢ ɔːrk -s -s
Orkney ˈɔːk.ni, ⓤⓢ ˈɔːrk- -s -z
Orlan® ˈɔː.lᵊn, -læn, ⓤⓢ ˈɔːr.lɑːn
Orlando ɔːˈlæn.dəʊ, ⓤⓢ ɔːrˈlæn.doʊ
Orleans *in US:* ˈɔː.li.ənz, ˈ-lɪənz, ˈ-lənz; ɔːˈliːnz, ⓤⓢ ˈɔːr.li.ənz, ˈ-lənz; ⓤⓢ ɔːrˈliːnz
Orléans *in France:* ɔːˈlɪənz, ˈ--; *as if French:* ˌɔː.leɪˈɑ̃ːŋ; ⓤⓢ -ˈliː.ənz; *as if French:* ⓤⓢ ˌɔːr.leɪˈɑ̃ːn
Orlon® ˈɔː.lɒn, ⓤⓢ ˈɔːr.lɑːn
Orly ˈɔː.li, ⓤⓢ ˈɔːr-
Orm(e) ɔːm, ⓤⓢ ɔːrm
ormer ˈɔː.məʳ, ⓤⓢ ˈɔːr.mɚ -s -z
Ormes ɔːmz, ⓤⓢ ɔːrmz
Ormiston ˈɔː.mɪ.stᵊn, ⓤⓢ ˈɔːr-
ormolu ˈɔː.mə.luː, -ljuː, ˌ--ˈ-, ⓤⓢ ˈɔːr.mə.luː
Ormond(e) ˈɔː.mənd, ⓤⓢ ˈɔːr-
Ormsby ˈɔːmz.bi, ⓤⓢ ˈɔːrmz-
Ormulum ˈɔː.mjə.ləm, -mjʊ-, ⓤⓢ ˈɔːr.mjuː-, -mjə-
ornament **n** ˈɔː.nə.mənt, ⓤⓢ ˈɔːr- -s -s
orna|ment ˈɔː.nə|.ment, ⓤⓢ ˈɔːr- -ments -ments -menting -men.tɪŋ, ⓤⓢ -men.t̬ɪŋ -mented -men.tɪd, ⓤⓢ -men.t̬ɪd
ornamental ˌɔː.nəˈmen.tᵊl, ⓤⓢ ˌɔːr.nəˈmen.t̬ᵊl -ly -i
ornamentation ˌɔː.nə.menˈteɪ.ʃᵊn, ⓤⓢ ˌɔːr- -s -z
ornate ɔːˈneɪt, ⓤⓢ ɔːr- -ly -li -ness -nəs, -nɪs
ornery ˈɔː.nᵊr.i, ⓤⓢ ˈɔːr.nɚ-
ornithologic|al ˌɔː.nɪ.θəˈlɒdʒ.ɪ.k|ᵊl, -θᵊlˈɒdʒ-, -nə-, ⓤⓢ ˌɔːr.nə.θəˈlɑː.dʒɪ- -ally -ᵊl.i, -li
ornitholog|y ˌɔː.nɪˈθɒl.ə.dʒ|i, -nəˈ-, ⓤⓢ ˌɔːr.nəˈθɑː.lə- -ist/s -ɪst/s
orographic ˌɒr.əʊˈgræf.ɪk, ˌɔː.rəʊˈ-, ⓤⓢ ˌɔːr.oʊˈ- -al -ᵊl
orography ɒrˈɒg.rə.fi, ɔːˈrɒg-, ⓤⓢ ɔːˈrɑː.grə-
orological ˌɒr.əˈlɒdʒ.ɪ.kᵊl, ˌɔː.rəˈ-, ⓤⓢ ˌɔːr.əˈlɑː.dʒɪ-
orology ɒrˈɒl.ə.dʒi, ɔːˈrɒl-, ⓤⓢ ɔːˈrɑː.lə-
Oronsay ˈɒr.ᵊn.seɪ, -zeɪ, ⓤⓢ ˈɔːr-, -ɑːn-
Orontes ɒrˈɒn.tiːz, əˈrɒn-, ⓤⓢ oʊˈrɑːn-
Oroonoko ˌɒr.uˈnəʊ.kəʊ, ⓤⓢ ˌɔːr.uˈnoʊ.koʊ
Orosius əˈrəʊ.si.əs, ɒrˈəʊ-, ⓤⓢ ɔːˈroʊ.ʒi.əs
orotund ˈɒr.əʊ.tʌnd, ˈɔː.rəʊ-, ⓤⓢ ˈɔːr.ə-, -oʊ-, ˈ-ə-
O'Rourke əʊˈrɔːk, ⓤⓢ oʊˈrɔːrk
orphan ˈɔː.fᵊn, ⓤⓢ ˈɔːr- -s -z -ing -ɪŋ -ed -d
orphanag|e ˈɔː.fᵊn.ɪdʒ, ⓤⓢ ˈɔːr- -es -ɪz
Orphean ɔːˈfiː.ən; ˈɔː.fi-, ⓤⓢ ˈɔːr.fi.ən
Orpheus ˈɔː.fi.əs, -fjuːs, ⓤⓢ ˈɔːr.fi.əs, ˈ-fjuːs
orpiment ˈɔː.pɪ.mənt, ⓤⓢ ˈɔːr-
Orpington ˈɔː.pɪŋ.tən, ⓤⓢ ˈɔːr- -s -z
Orr ɔːʳ, ⓤⓢ ɔːr
Orrell ˈɒr.ᵊl, ⓤⓢ ˈɔːr-
orrer|y, O~ ˈɒr.ᵊr|.i, ⓤⓢ ˈɔːr- -ies -iz
orris ˈɒr.ɪs, ⓤⓢ ˈɔːr-
Orsino ɔːˈsiː.nəʊ, ⓤⓢ ɔːrˈsiː.noʊ
Orson ˈɔː.sᵊn, ⓤⓢ ˈɔːr-
Ortega ɔːˈteɪ.gə, ⓤⓢ ɔːr-, -ˈtiː-
ortho- ˈɔː.θəʊ; ɔːˈθɒ, ⓤⓢ ˈɔːr.θoʊ, -θə; ⓤⓢ ɔːrˈθɑː
Note: Prefix. Normally either takes primary or secondary stress on the first syllable, e.g. **orthodox** /ˈɔː.θə.dɒks/ ⓤⓢ /ˈɔːr.θə.dɑːks/, **orthogenic** /ˌɔː.θəʊˈdʒen.ɪk/ ⓤⓢ /ˌɔːr.θoʊ-/, or primary stress on the second syllable, e.g. **orthography** /ɔːˈθɒg.rə.fi/ ⓤⓢ /ɔːrˈθɑː.grə-/.
orthochromatic ˌɔː.θəʊ.krəʊˈmæt.ɪk, ⓤⓢ ˌɔːr.θoʊ.kroʊˈmæt̬-, -θə-
orthodontic ˌɔː.θəʊˈdɒn.tɪk, ⓤⓢ ˌɔːr.θoʊˈdɑːn.t̬ɪk, -θəˈ-
orthodontist ˌɔː.θəʊˈdɒn.tɪst, ⓤⓢ ˌɔːr.θoʊˈdɑːn.t̬ɪst, -θəˈ- -s -s
orthodox ˈɔː.θə.dɒks, ⓤⓢ ˈɔːr.θə.dɑːks
orthodox|y ˈɔː.θə.dɒk.s|i, ⓤⓢ ˈɔːr.θə.dɑːk- -ies -iz
orthoep|y ˈɔː.θəʊ.ep|.i; ɔːˈθəʊ.ɪ.p|i; ˌɔː.θəʊˈep|.i, ⓤⓢ ɔːrˈθoʊ.ə.p|i, ˈɔːr.θoʊ-, -ep|.i -ist/s -ɪst/s
orthogenic ˌɔː.θəʊˈdʒen.ɪk, ⓤⓢ ˌɔːr.θoʊˈ-, -θəˈ-
orthogonal ɔːˈθɒg.ᵊn.ᵊl, ⓤⓢ ɔːrˈθɑː.gᵊn-
orthographer ɔːˈθɒg.rə.fəʳ, ⓤⓢ ɔːrˈθɑː.grə.fɚ -s -z
orthographic ˌɔː.θəʊˈgræf.ɪk, ⓤⓢ ˌɔːr.θoʊˈ-, -θəˈ- -al -ᵊl -ally -ᵊl.i, -li
orthograph|y ɔːˈθɒg.rə.f|i, ⓤⓢ ɔːˈθɑː.grə- -ist/s -ɪst/s
orthop(a)edic ˌɔː.θəʊˈpiː.dɪk, ⓤⓢ ˌɔːr.θoʊˈ-, -θəˈ- -s -s -ally -ᵊl.i, -li
orthop(a)ed|y ˌɔː.θəʊˈpiː.d|i, ⓤⓢ ˌɔːr.θoʊˈ-, -θəˈ- -ist/s -ɪst/s
orthopterous ɔːˈθɒp.tᵊr.əs, ⓤⓢ ɔːrˈθɑːp-
orthoptic ɔːˈθɒp.tɪk, ⓤⓢ ɔːrˈθɑːp-
Ortiz ˈɔː.tɪz, ɔːˈtɪz, -ˈtiːz, -ˈtiːs, ⓤⓢ ɔːrˈtiːz, -ˈtiːs
Ortler ˈɔːt.ləʳ, ⓤⓢ ˈɔːrt.lɚ
ortolan ˈɔː.tᵊl.ən, -æn, ⓤⓢ ˈɔːr.t̬ə.lən -s -z
Orton ˈɔː.tᵊn, ⓤⓢ ˈɔːr-
Oruro ɒrˈʊə.rəʊ, ⓤⓢ ɔːˈrʊr.oʊ, -ˈruː.roʊ
Orville ˈɔː.vɪl, ⓤⓢ ˈɔːr-
Orwell ˈɔː.wel, -wəl, ⓤⓢ ˈɔːr-
Orwellian ɔːˈwel.i.ən, ⓤⓢ ɔːr-
-ory ᵊr.i, -ri, ⓤⓢ ɔːr.i, ᵊr.i
Note: Suffix. When added to a free stem, **-ory** does not change the stress pattern of the word, e.g. **promise** /ˈprɒ.mɪs/ ⓤⓢ /ˈprɑː.mɪs/, **promissory** /ˈprɒm.ɪs.ᵊr.i/ ⓤⓢ /ˈprɑː.mɪ.sɔːr.i/. When added to a bound stem, stress may be one or two syllables before the suffix, e.g. **olfactory** /ɒlˈfæk.tᵊr.i/ ⓤⓢ /ɑːl-/.
oryx ˈɒr.ɪks, ⓤⓢ ˈoʊ.rɪks, ˈɔːr.ɪks -es -ɪz
Osage ˌəʊˈseɪdʒ, ˈ--, ⓤⓢ ˌoʊˈseɪdʒ, ˈ--
Osaka əʊˈsɑː.kə, ˈɔː.sə.kə, ⓤⓢ ˈoʊ.sɑː.kɑː, oʊˈsɑː.kɑː
Osama əʊˈsɑː.mə, ɒsˈɑː-, ʊsˈɑː-, ⓤⓢ oʊˈ-
Osbaldiston(e) ˌɒz.bᵊlˈdɪs.tᵊn, ⓤⓢ ˌɑːz-
Osbert ˈɒz.bət, -bɜːt, ⓤⓢ ˈɑːz.bɚt, -bɝːt
Osborn(e), Osbourne ˈɒz.bɔːn, -bən, ⓤⓢ ˈɑːz.bɔːrn, -bɚn
Oscan ˈɒs.kən, ⓤⓢ ˈɑːs- -s -z
Oscar ˈɒs.kəʳ, ⓤⓢ ˈɑː.skɚ -s -z
oscill|ate ˈɒs.ɪ.l|eɪt, -ᵊl|.eɪt, ⓤⓢ ˈɑː.sᵊl- -ates -eɪts -ating -eɪ.tɪŋ, ⓤⓢ -eɪ.t̬ɪŋ -ated -eɪ.tɪd, ⓤⓢ -eɪ.t̬ɪd -ator/s -eɪ.təʳ/z, ⓤⓢ -eɪ.t̬ɚ/z
oscillation ˌɒs.ɪˈleɪ.ʃᵊn, -ᵊlˈeɪ-, ⓤⓢ ˌɑː.sᵊlˈ- -s -z
oscillatory ˈɒs.ɪ.lə.tᵊr.i, -ᵊl.eɪ-, -leɪ-; ˌɒs.ɪˈleɪ-, -ᵊlˈeɪ-, ⓤⓢ ˈɑː.sᵊl.ə.tɔːr-
oscillogram əˈsɪl.ə.græm, ɒsˈɪl-, ⓤⓢ əˈsɪl- -s -z
oscillograph əˈsɪl.ə.grɑːf, ɒsˈɪl-, -græf, ⓤⓢ əˈsɪl.ə.græf -s -s
oscilloscope əˈsɪl.ə.skəʊp, ɒsˈɪl-, ⓤⓢ əˈsɪl.ə.skoʊp -s -s
osculant ˈɒs.kjə.lənt, -kjʊ-, ⓤⓢ ˈɑː.skjuː-, -skjə-
oscular ˈɒs.kjə.ləʳ, -kjʊ-, ⓤⓢ ˈɑː.skjuː.lɚ, -skjə-
oscu|late ˈɒs.kjə|.leɪt, -kjʊ-, ⓤⓢ ˈɑː.skjuː-, -skjə- -lates -leɪts -lating -leɪ.tɪŋ, ⓤⓢ -leɪ.t̬ɪŋ -lated -leɪ.tɪd, ⓤⓢ -leɪ.t̬ɪd
osculation ˌɒs.kjəˈleɪ.ʃᵊn, -kjʊˈ-, ⓤⓢ ˌɑː.skjuːˈ-, -skjəˈ- -s -z
osculator|y ˈɒs.kjə.lə.tᵊr|.i, -kjʊ-; ˌɒs.kjəˈleɪ-, -kjʊˈ-, ⓤⓢ ˈɑː.skjuː.lə.tɔːr-, -skjə- -ies -iz
Osgood ˈɒz.gʊd, ⓤⓢ ˈɑːz-
O'Shaughnessy əʊˈʃɔː.nɪ.si, -nə-, ⓤⓢ oʊˈʃɑː.nə-, -ˈʃɔː-
O'Shea əʊˈʃeɪ, ⓤⓢ oʊ-
Oshkosh ˈɒʃ.kɒʃ, ⓤⓢ ˈɑːʃ.kɑːʃ
Oshogbo əˈʃɒg.bəʊ, ⓤⓢ oʊˈʃɑːg.boʊ
osier ˈəʊ.zi.əʳ, -ʒəʳ, ⓤⓢ ˈoʊ.ʒɚ -s -z
Osijek ˈɒs.i.ek, ⓤⓢ ɔːˈsiː.ek
Osirian əʊˈsaɪə.ri.ən, ɒsˈaɪə-, ⓤⓢ oʊˈsaɪ- -s -z
Osiris əʊˈsaɪə.rɪs, ɒsˈaɪə-, ⓤⓢ oʊˈsaɪ-
-osis ə.sɪs; ˈəʊ.sɪs, ⓤⓢ ə.sɪs; ⓤⓢ ˈoʊ.sɪs
Note: Suffix. Words containing **-osis** either carry primary stress on the syllable preceding the suffix, or on the suffix itself e.g. **metamorphosis** /ˌmet.əˈmɔː.fə.sɪs;

-mɔːˈfəʊ-/ (US) /ˌmet̬.əˈmɔːr.fə-; (US) -mɔːrˈfoʊ-/. See individual entries.

-osity ˈɒs.ə.ti, -ɪ.ti, (US) ˈɑː.sə.t̬i
Note: Suffix. Normally takes primary stress as shown, e.g. **curious** /ˈkjʊə.ri.əs/ (US) /ˈkjʊr.i-/, **curiosity** /ˌkjʊə.riˈɒs.ə.ti/ (US) /ˌkjʊr.iˈɑː.sə.t̬i/.

Osler ˈəʊz.ləʳ, ˈəʊ.sləʳ, (US) ˈoʊz.lɚ, ˈoʊ.slɚ

Oslo ˈɒz.ləʊ, ˈɒs-, (US) ˈɑː.sloʊ, ˈɑːz-

Osman ɒzˈmɑːn, ɒs-; ˈ--, -mən, (US) ˈɑːz.mən, ˈɑːs-

Osmanli ɒzˈmæn.li, ɒs-, -ˈmɑːn-, (US) ɑːsˈmæn-, ɑːz- **-s** -z

osmium ˈɒz.mi.əm, (US) ˈɑːz-

Osmond ˈɒz.mənd, (US) ˈɑːz-

osmosis ɒzˈməʊ.sɪs, (US) ɑːzˈmoʊ-, ɑːs-

osmotic ɒzˈmɒt.ɪk, (US) ɑːzˈmɑː.t̬ɪk, ɑːs- **-ally** -əl.i, -li

osmund, O~ ˈɒz.mənd, (US) ˈɑːz-, ˈɑːs- **-s** -z

osmunda ɒzˈmʌn.də, (US) ɑːz-, ɑːs- **-s** -z

Osnaburg(h) ˈɒz.nə.bɜːg, (US) ˈɑːz.nə.bɝːg

osprey ˈɒs.preɪ, -pri, (US) ˈɑː.spri, -spreɪ **-s** -z

Ossa ˈɒs.ə, (US) ˈɑː.sə

osseous ˈɒs.i.əs, (US) ˈɑː.si-

Ossetia ɒsˈet.i.ə; ɒsˈiː.ʃə; (US) oʊˈset̬.i.ə

Ossett ˈɒs.ɪt, (US) ˈɑː.sɪt

Ossian ˈɒs.i.ən, (US) ˈɑː.si-

ossicle ˈɒs.ɪ.kəl, (US) ˈɑː.sɪ- **-s** -z

ossification ˌɒs.ɪ.fɪˈkeɪ.ʃən, ˌ-ə-, -fəˈ-, (US) ˌɑː.sə.fɪˈ-

ossifrag|e ˈɒs.ɪ.frɪdʒ, ˈ-ə-, -freɪdʒ, (US) ˈɑː.sə- **-es** -ɪz

ossi|fy ˈɒs.ɪ|.faɪ, ˈ-ə-, (US) ˈɑː.sɪ-, ˈ-sə- **-fies** -faɪz **-fying** -faɪ.ɪŋ **-fied** -faɪd

Ossining ˈɒs.ɪn.ɪŋ, (US) ˈɑː.sɪn-

osso buco ˌɒs.əʊˈbuː.kəʊ, (US) ˌɑː.soʊˈbuː.koʊ, ˌoʊ-

Ossory ˈɒs.ər.i, (US) ˈɑː.sɚ-

ossuar|y ˈɒs.jʊə.r|i, (US) ˈɑː.sjuː.er|.i **-ies** -iz

osteitis ˌɒs.tiˈaɪ.tɪs, -təs, (US) ˌɑː.stiˈaɪ.t̬ɪs, -t̬əs

Ostend ɒsˈtend, (US) ɑːˈstend, ˈ--

ostensibility ɒsˌtent.səˈbɪl.ə.ti, -sɪˈ-, -ɪ.ti, (US) ɑːˌstent.səˈbɪl.ə.t̬i

ostensib|le ɒsˈtent.sə.b|əl, -sɪ-, (US) ɑːˈstent.sə- **-ly** -li

ostentation ˌɒs.tenˈteɪ.ʃən, -tənˈ-, (US) ˌɑː.stənˈ-

ostentatious ˌɒs.tenˈteɪ.ʃəs, -tənˈ-, (US) ˌɑː.stənˈ- **-ly** -li **-ness** -nəs, -nɪs

osteo- ˈɒs.ti.əʊ, (US) ˈɑː.sti.oʊ, -ə

osteoarthritis ˌɒs.ti.əʊ.ɑːˈθraɪ.tɪs, -təs, (US) ˌɑː.sti.oʊ.ɑːrˈθraɪ.t̬ɪs, -t̬əs

osteologic|al ˌɒs.ti.əˈlɒdʒ.ɪ.k|əl, (US) ˌɑː.sti.oʊˈlɑː.dʒɪ- **-ally** -əl.i, -li

osteolog|y ˌɒs.tiˈɒl.ə.dʒ|i, (US) ˌɑː.stiˈɑː.lə- **-ist/s** -ɪst/s

osteomyelitis ˌɒs.ti.əʊ.maɪ.əlˈaɪ.tɪs, -təs, (US) ˌɑː.sti.oʊ.maɪ.əˈlaɪ.t̬ɪs, -t̬əs

osteopath ˈɒs.ti.əʊ.pæθ, (US) ˈɑː.sti.oʊ-, -ə- **-s** -s

osteopathic ˌɒs.ti.əʊˈpæθ.ɪk, (US) ˌɑː.sti.oʊˈ-

osteopathy ˌɒs.tiˈɒp.ə.θi, (US) ˌɑː.stiˈɑː.pə-

osteoporosis ˌɒs.ti.əʊ.pəˈrəʊ.sɪs, -pɔːˈ-, (US) ˌɑː.sti.oʊ.pəˈroʊ-

Osterley ˈɒs.təl.i, (US) ˈɑː.stɚ.li

Ostia ˈɒs.ti.ə, (US) ˈɑː.sti-

ostiar|y ˈɒs.ti.ər|.i, (US) ˈɑː.sti.er- **-ies** -iz

osti|um, O~ ˈɒs.ti|.əm, (US) ˈɑː.sti- **-a** -ə

ostler ˈɒs.ləʳ, (US) ˈɑː.slɚ **-s** -z

ostracism ˈɒs.trə.sɪ.zəm, (US) ˈɑː.strə-

ostraciz|e, -is|e ˈɒs.trə.saɪz, (US) ˈɑː.strə- **-es** -ɪz **-ing** -ɪŋ **-ed** -d

Ostrava ˈɒs.trə.və, (US) ˈɔː.strɑː.vɑː, ˈɑː-

ostrich ˈɒs.trɪtʃ, (US) ˈɑː.strɪtʃ **-es** -ɪz

Ostrogoth ˈɒs.trəʊ.gɒθ, (US) ˈɑː.strə.gɑːθ **-s** -s

O'Sullivan əʊˈsʌl.ɪ.vən, ˈ-ə-, (US) oʊ-

Oswald ˈɒz.wəld, (US) ˈɑːz-, -wɔːld

Oswaldtwistle ˈɒz.wəldˌtwɪs.əl, (US) ˈɑːz.wɔːld-

Oswego ɒzˈwiː.gəʊ, ɒs-, (US) ɑːˈswiː.goʊ **-s** -z

Oswestry ˈɒz.wə.stri, -wɪ-, (US) ˈɑːz-

Otago əʊˈtɑː.gəʊ, ɒtˈɑː-, (US) əˈtɑː.goʊ, oʊ-

Otaheite ˌəʊ.tɑːˈheɪ.ti, -təˈ-, (US) ˌoʊ.t̬əˈhiː.t̬i, -ˈheɪ-

otar|y ˈəʊ.tər|.i, (US) ˈoʊ.t̬ɚ- **-ies** -iz

OTB ˌəʊ.tiːˈbiː, (US) ˌoʊ-

Otford ˈɒt.fəd, (US) ˈɑːt.fɚd

Otfried ˈɒt.friːd, (US) ˈɑːt-

Othello əʊˈθel.əʊ, ɒθˈel-, (US) oʊˈθel.oʊ, ə-

other ˈʌð.əʳ, (US) -ɚ **-s** -z **-ness** -nəs, -nɪs

otherwise ˈʌð.ə.waɪz, (US) ˈ-ɚ-

otherworld|ly ˌʌð.əˈwɜːld|.li, (US) -ɚˈwɝːld- **-liness** -lɪ.nəs, -nɪs

Othman ɒθˈmɑːn, ˈ--, (US) ˈɑːθ.mən, ʊθˈmɑːn

Othniel ˈɒθ.ni.əl, (US) ˈɑːθ-

Otho ˈəʊ.θəʊ, (US) ˈoʊ.θoʊ

-otic ˈɒt.ɪk, ˈəʊ.tɪk, (US) ˈɑː.t̬ɪk, ˈoʊ.t̬ɪk
Note: Suffix. Normally takes primary stress as shown, e.g. **idiot** /ˈɪd.i.ət/, **idiotic** /ˌɪd.iˈɒt.ɪk/ (US) /-ˈɑː.t̬ɪk/.

otiose ˈəʊ.ti.əʊz, -ʃi-, -əʊs, (US) ˈoʊ.ʃi.oʊs, -t̬i- **-ly** -li **-ness** -nəs, -nɪs

otiosity ˌəʊ.tiˈɒs.ə.ti, -ʃiˈ-, -ɪ.ti, (US) ˌoʊ.ʃiˈɑː.sə.t̬i, -t̬iˈ-

Otis ˈəʊ.tɪs, (US) ˈoʊ.t̬ɪs

otitis əʊˈtaɪ.tɪs, -təs, (US) oʊˈtaɪ.t̬ɪs, -t̬əs

Otley ˈɒt.li, (US) ˈɑːt-

otolaryngolog|y ˌəʊ.təʊˌlær.ɪŋˈgɒl.ə.dʒ|i, -ˌleə.rɪŋˈ-, (US) ˌoʊ.t̬oʊˌler.ɪŋˈgɑː.lə-, -ˌlær- **-ist/s** -ɪst/s

otological ˌəʊ.təˈlɒdʒ.ɪ.kəl, (US) ˌoʊ.t̬əˈlɑː.dʒɪ-

otolog|y əʊˈtɒl.ə.dʒ|i, (US) oʊˈtɑː.lə- **-ist/s** -ɪst/s

otoscope ˈəʊ.tə.skəʊp, (US) ˈoʊ.t̬oʊ.skoʊp, -t̬ə- **-s** -s

Otranto ɒtˈræn.təʊ, ˈɒt.rən-, (US) oʊˈtrɑːn.toʊ

OTT ˌəʊ.tiːˈtiː, (US) ˌoʊ- *stress shift:* ˌOTT ˈspeech
Note: The letters OTT stand for 'over-the-top'; see also that entry.

ottava rima ɒtˈɑː.vəˌriː.mə, (US) oʊˈtɑː-

Ottaw|a ˈɒt.ə.w|ə, (US) ˈɑː.t̬ə.w|ə, -w|ɑː, -w|ɔː **-as** -əz, (US) -əz, -ɑːz, -ɔːz **-an/s** -ən/z

Ottaway ˈɒt.ə.weɪ, (US) ˈɑː.t̬ə-

otter ˈɒt.əʳ, (US) ˈɑː.t̬ɚ **-s** -z

Otterburn ˈɒt.ə.bɜːn, (US) ˈɑː.t̬ɚ.bɝːn

Ottery ˈɒt.ər.i, (US) ˈɑː.t̬ɚ-

Ottley ˈɒt.li, (US) ˈɑːt-

otto, O~ ˈɒt.əʊ, (US) ˈɑː.t̬oʊ

ottoman, O~ ˈɒt.əʊ.mən, (US) ˈɑː.t̬ə.mən **-s** -z

Ottoway ˈɒt.ə.weɪ, (US) ˈɑː.t̬ə-

Otway ˈɒt.weɪ, (US) ˈɑːt-

Ouagadougou ˌwɑː.gəˈduː.guː, ˌwæg.əˈ-, (US) ˌwɑː.gəˈ-

oubliette ˌuː.bliˈet **-s** -s

ouch aʊtʃ

Oudenarde ˈuː.də.nɑːd, -dɪ-, (US) -dən.ɑːrd; (US) ˌuː.dəˈnɑːr.də

Oudh aʊd

Ougham ˈɔː.əm

ought ɔːt, (US) ɑːt, ɔːt

Oughtershaw ˈaʊ.tə.ʃɔː, (US) -t̬ɚ.ʃɑː, -ʃɔː

Oughterside ˈaʊ.tə.saɪd, (US) -t̬ɚ-

oughtn't (= **ought not**) ˈɔː.tənt, (US) ˈɑː.tənt, ˈɔː.tənt

Oughton ˈaʊ.tən, ˈɔː.tən

Oughtred ˈɔː.tred, -trɪd, (US) ˈɔː-, ˈɑː-

ouguiya uːˈgwiː.ə, -ˈgiː-

Ouida ˈwiː.də

Ouija® ˈwiː.dʒə, -dʒɑː, -dʒi, (US) -dʒə, -dʒi

Oujda uːdʒˈdɑː

Ould əʊld, (US) oʊld

ounc|e aʊnts **-es** -ɪz

Oundle ˈaʊn.dəl

our aʊəʳ, ˈaʊ.əʳ, ɑːʳ, (US) ˈaʊ.ɚ, aʊr, ɑːr **-s** -z

oursel|f ˌaʊəˈsel|f, ˌaʊ.ə-, ˌɑː-, (US) ˌaʊ.ɚ-, ˌaʊr-, ˌɑːr- **-ves** -vz

Ouse uːz

ousel ˈuː.zəl **-s** -z

Ouseley ˈuːz.li

Ousey ˈuː.zi

Ousley ˈaʊ.sli

oust aʊst **-s** -s **-ing** -ɪŋ **-ed** -ɪd **-er/s** -əʳ/z, (US) -ɚ/z

Ouston ˈaʊ.stən

out aʊt **-s** -s **-ing** -ɪŋ, (US) ˈaʊ.t̬ɪŋ **-ed** -ɪd, (US) ˈaʊ.t̬ɪd

out- aʊt
Note: Prefix. Many compounds beginning with **out-** have the stress pattern ˌ**out**ˈ-; these are likely to undergo stress shift when a stressed syllable follows closely, especially in adjectives derived from verbs.

outag|e ˈaʊ.tɪdʒ, (US) -t̬ɪdʒ **-es** -ɪz

O

Pronouncing the letters **OU**

There are several possibilities for the strong pronunciation of the vowel digraph **ou**, e.g.:

aʊ	cloud /klaʊd/
əʊ (US) oʊ	though /ðəʊ/ (US) /ðoʊ/
ʌ	country /ˈkʌn.tri/
ɔː (US) ɑː	bought /bɔːt/ (US) /bɑːt/
uː	soup /suːp/
ʊ	could /kʊd/

When followed by a **gh** in the spelling which is realized as /f/, it is usually pronounced /ɒ/ (US) /ɑː/ or /ʌ/, e.g.:

cough	kɒf (US) kɑːf
enough	ɪˈnʌf

When followed by an **r** in the spelling, **ou** is pronounced as /ɔː/ (US) /ɔːr/, /aʊə/ (US) /aʊɚ/, /ɜː/ (US) /ɝː/, /ʌ/ (US) /ɝː/, and /ʊə/ (US) /ʊr/, e.g.:

four	fɔːʳ (US) fɔːr
flour	flaʊ.əʳ (US) flaʊ.ɚ
journey	ˈdʒɜː.ni (US) ˈdʒɝː-
flourish	ˈflʌr.ɪʃ (US) ˈflɝː-
tour	tʊəʳ, tɔːʳ (US) tʊr

In weak syllables

The vowel digraph **ou** is realized with the vowel /ə/ in weak syllables, and may also not be pronounced at all in British English, due to compression, e.g.:

famous	ˈfeɪ.məs
favourite	ˈfeɪ.vᵊr.ɪt, ˈfeɪv.rɪt

out-and-out ˌaʊt.ᵊndˈaʊt *stress shift:* ˌ**out-and-out** ˈ**scoundrel**
outback ˈaʊt.bæk
outbalanc|e ˌaʊtˈbæl.ənts, aʊt- **-es** -ɪz **-ing** -ɪŋ **-ed** -t
outbid ˌaʊtˈbɪd, aʊt- **-s** -z **-ding** -ɪŋ
outboard ˈaʊt.bɔːd, (US) -bɔːrd
outbound ˈaʊt.baʊnd
outbox ˈaʊt.bɒks, (US) -bɑːks **-es** -ɪz
outbrav|e ˌaʊtˈbreɪv, aʊt- **-es** -z **-ing** -ɪŋ **-ed** -d
outbreak ˈaʊt.breɪk **-s** -s
outbuilding ˈaʊtˌbɪl.dɪŋ **-s** -z
outburst ˈaʊt.bɜːst, (US) -bɝːst **-s** -s
outcast ˈaʊt.kɑːst, (US) -kæst **-s** -s
outcast|e ˈaʊt.kɑːst, (US) -kæst **-es** -s **-ing** -ɪŋ **-ed** -ɪd
outclass ˌaʊtˈklɑːs, aʊt-, (US) -ˈklæs **-es** -ɪz **-ing** -ɪŋ **-ed** -t
outcome ˈaʊt.kʌm **-s** -z
outcrop ˈaʊt.krɒp, (US) -krɑːp **-s** -s **-ping** -ɪŋ **-ped** -t
outcr|y ˈaʊt.kr|aɪ **-ies** -aɪz
out|date ˌaʊt|ˈdeɪt, aʊt- **-dates** -ˈdeɪts **-dating** -ˈdeɪ.tɪŋ, (US) -ˈdeɪ.t̬ɪŋ **-dated** -ˈdeɪ.tɪd, (US) -ˈdeɪ.t̬ɪd
outdated ˌaʊtˈdeɪ.tɪd, aʊt-, (US) -t̬ɪd *stress shift:* ˌ**outdated** ˈ**clothes**
outdistanc|e ˌaʊtˈdɪs.tᵊnts, aʊt- **-es** -ɪz **-ing** -ɪŋ **-ed** -t
out|do ˌaʊt|ˈduː, aʊt- **-does** -ˈdʌz **-doing** -ˈduː.ɪŋ **-did** -ˈdɪd **-done** -ˈdʌn
outdoor ˌaʊtˈdɔːʳ, aʊt-, (US) -ˈdɔːr **-s** -z *stress shift:* ˌ**outdoor** ˈ**sports**
outer ˈaʊ.təʳ, (US) -t̬ɚ **-most** -məʊst, (US) -məst, -moʊst ˌ**outer** ˈ**space**
outerwear ˈaʊ.tə.weəʳ, (US) -t̬ɚ.wer
outfac|e ˌaʊtˈfeɪs, aʊt- **-s** -ɪz **-ing** -ɪŋ **-ed** -t
outfall ˈaʊt.fɔːl **-s** -z
outfield ˈaʊt.fiːld **-s** -z **-er/s** -əʳ/z, (US) -ɚ/z
out|fit ˈaʊt|.fɪt **-fits** -fɪts **-fitting** -ˌfɪt.ɪŋ, (US) -ˌfɪt̬.ɪŋ **-fitted** -ˌfɪt.ɪd, (US) -ˌfɪt̬.ɪd **-fitter/s** -ˌfɪt.əʳ/z, (US) -ˌfɪt̬.ɚ/z
outflank ˌaʊtˈflæŋk, aʊt- **-s** -s **-ing** -ɪŋ **-ed** -t
outflow n ˈaʊt.fləʊ, (US) -floʊ **-s** -z
outflow v ˌaʊtˈfləʊ, aʊt-, (US) -ˈfloʊ **-s** -z **-ing** -ɪŋ **-ed** -d
outfox ˌaʊtˈfɒks, aʊt-, (US) -ˈfɑːks **-es** -ɪz **-ing** -ɪŋ **-ed** -t
outgeneral ˌaʊtˈdʒen.ᵊr.ᵊl, aʊt- **-s** -z **-(l)ing** -ɪŋ **-(l)ed** -d
outgo n ˈaʊt.gəʊ, (US) -goʊ **-es** -z
out|go v ˌaʊt|ˈgəʊ, aʊt-, (US) -ˈgoʊ **-goes** -ˈgəʊz, (US) -ˈgoʊz **-going** -ˈgəʊ.ɪŋ, (US) -ˈgoʊ.ɪŋ **-went** -ˈwent **-gone** -ˈgɒn, (US) -ˈgɑːn
outgoer ˈaʊtˌgəʊ.əʳ, (US) -ˌgoʊ.ɚ **-s** -z
outgoing ˌaʊtˈgəʊ.ɪŋ, aʊt-, ˈ---, (US) ˈaʊt.goʊ- **-s** -z
out|grow v ˌaʊt|ˈgrəʊ, aʊt-, (US) -ˈgroʊ **-grows** -ˈgrəʊz, (US) -ˈgroʊz **-growing** -ˈgrəʊ.ɪŋ, (US) -ˈgroʊ.ɪŋ **-grew** -ˈgruː **-grown** -ˈgrəʊn, (US) -ˈgroʊn
outgrowth ˈaʊt.grəʊθ, (US) -groʊθ **-s** -s
outguess ˌaʊtˈges, aʊt- **-es** -ɪz **-ing** -ɪŋ **-ed** -t
outgun ˌaʊtˈgʌn, aʊt- **-s** -z **-ning** -ɪŋ **-ned** -d
out-Herod ˌaʊtˈher.əd, aʊt- **-s** -z **-ing** -ɪŋ **-ed** -ɪd
outhou|se ˈaʊt.haʊ|s **-ses** -zɪz
Outhwaite ˈuː.θweɪt, ˈəʊ-, ˈaʊ-, (US) ˈuː-, ˈoʊ-, ˈaʊ-
outing ˈaʊ.tɪŋ, (US) -t̬ɪŋ **-s** -z
Outlander ˈaʊtˌlæn.dəʳ, (US) -dɚ **-s** -z
outlandish ˌaʊtˈlæn.dɪʃ, aʊt- **-ly** -li **-ness** -nəs, -nɪs
outlast ˌaʊtˈlɑːst, aʊt-, (US) -ˈlæst **-s** -s **-ing** -ɪŋ **-ed** -ɪd
outlaw ˈaʊt.lɔː, (US) -lɑː, -lɔː **-s** -z **-ing** -ɪŋ **-ed** -d **-ry** -ri
outlay n ˈaʊt.leɪ **-s** -z
out|lay v ˌaʊt|ˈleɪ, aʊt- **-lays** -ˈleɪz **-laying** -ˈleɪ.ɪŋ **-laid** -ˈleɪd
outlet ˈaʊt.let, -lət, -lɪt, (US) -let, -lət **-s** -s
outlier ˈaʊtˌlaɪ.əʳ, (US) -ɚ **-s** -z
outline n ˈaʊt.laɪn **-s** -z
outlin|e v ˈaʊt.laɪn, ˌ-ˈ-, aʊt-, (US) ˈ-- **-es** -z **-ing** -ɪŋ **-ed** -d
outliv|e ˌaʊtˈlɪv, aʊt- **-es** -z **-ing** -ɪŋ **-ed** -d
outlook ˈaʊt.lʊk **-s** -s
outlying ˈaʊtˌlaɪ.ɪŋ, ˌ-ˈ--, aʊt-, (US) ˈ-ˌ--
outmaneuv|er ˌaʊt.məˈnuː.v|əʳ, (US) -v|ɚ **-ers** -əz, (US) -ɚz **-ering** -ᵊr.ɪŋ **-ered** -əd, (US) -ɚd
outmanoeuv|re ˌaʊt.məˈnuː.v|əʳ, (US) -v|ɚ **-res** -əz, (US) -ɚz **-ring** -ᵊr.ɪŋ **-red** -əd, (US) -ɚd
outmarch ˌaʊtˈmɑːtʃ, aʊt-, (US) -ˈmɑːrtʃ **-es** -ɪz **-ing** -ɪŋ **-ed** -t
outmatch ˌaʊtˈmætʃ, aʊt- **-es** -ɪz **-ing** -ɪŋ **-ed** -t
outmoded ˌaʊtˈməʊ.dɪd, aʊt-, (US) -ˈmoʊ- *stress shift:* ˌ**outmoded** ˈ**clothes**
outmost ˈaʊt.məʊst, (US) -moʊst
outnumb|er ˌaʊtˈnʌm.b|əʳ, aʊt-, (US) -b|ɚ **-ers** -əz, (US) -ɚz **-ering** -ᵊr.ɪŋ **-ered** -əd, (US) -ɚd
out-of-court ˌaʊt.əvˈkɔːt, (US) ˌaʊt̬.əvˈkɔːrt *stress shift:* ˌ**out-of-court** ˈ**settlement**
out-of-date ˌaʊt.əvˈdeɪt, (US) ˌaʊt̬- *stress shift:* ˌ**out-of-date** ˈ**foodstuffs**
out-of-door ˌaʊt.əvˈdɔːʳ, (US) ˌaʊt̬.əvˈdɔːr **-s** -z *stress shift:* ˌ**out-of-door** ˈ**sports**
out-of-pocket ˌaʊt.əvˈpɒk.ɪt, (US) ˌaʊt̬.əvˈpɑː.kɪt *stress shift:* ˌ**out-of-pocket** ˈ**payment**
out-of-state ˌaʊt.əvˈsteɪt, (US) ˌaʊt̬- *stress shift:* ˌ**out-of-state** ˈ**visitors**
out-of-the-way ˌaʊt.əv.ðəˈweɪ, (US) ˌaʊt̬.əv.ðə- *stress shift:* ˌ**out-of-the-way** ˈ**places**
out-of-town ˌaʊt.əvˈtaʊn, (US) ˌaʊt̬.əv- *stress shift:* ˌ**out-of-town** ˈ**shopping**
outpac|e ˌaʊtˈpeɪs, aʊt- **-es** -ɪz **-ing** -ɪŋ **-ed** -t
outpatient ˈaʊtˌpeɪ.ʃᵊnt **-s** -s
outperform ˌaʊt.pəˈfɔːm, (US) -pɚˈfɔːrm **-s** -z **-ing** -ɪŋ **-ed** -d
outplacement ˈaʊtˌpleɪs.mənt

outplay ˌaʊtˈpleɪ, aʊt- **-s** -z **-ing** -ɪŋ **-ed** -d

outport ˈaʊt.pɔːt, (US) -pɔːrt **-s** -s

outpost ˈaʊt.pəʊst, (US) -poʊst **-s** -s

outpour n ˈaʊt.pɔːʳ, (US) -pɔːr **-s** -z

outpour v ˌaʊtˈpɔːʳ, aʊt-, (US) -ˈpɔːr **-s** -z **-ing** -ɪŋ **-ed** -d

outpouring ˈaʊtˌpɔː.rɪŋ, ˌ-ˈ--, aʊt-, (US) ˈaʊtˌpɔːr.ɪŋ **-s** -z

out|put ˈaʊt|.pʊt **-puts** -pʊts **-putting** -ˌpʊt.ɪŋ, (US) -ˌpʊţ.ɪŋ **-putted** -ˌpʊt.ɪd, (US) -ˌpʊţ.ɪd

outrage, O~ n ˈaʊt.reɪdʒ

outrag|e v ˈaʊt.reɪdʒ, ˌ-ˈ-, aʊt-, (US) ˈ-- **-es** -ɪz **-ing** -ɪŋ **-ed** -d

outrageous ˌaʊtˈreɪ.dʒəs, aʊt- **-ly** -li **-ness** -nəs, -nɪs

Outram ˈuː.trəm

outrang|e ˌaʊtˈreɪndʒ, aʊt- **-es** -ɪz **-ing** -ɪŋ **-ed** -d

outrank ˌaʊtˈræŋk, aʊt- **-s** -s **-ing** -ɪŋ **-ed** -t

outré ˈuː.treɪ, (US) -ˈ-

outreach n ˈaʊt.riːtʃ **-es** -ɪz

outreach v ˌaʊtˈriːtʃ, aʊt- **-es** -ɪz **-ing** -ɪŋ **-ed** -t

out|ride ˌaʊt|ˈraɪd, aʊt- **-rides** -ˈraɪdz **-riding** -ˈraɪ.dɪŋ **-rode** -ˈrəʊd, (US) -ˈroʊd **-ridden** -ˈrɪd.ᵊn

outrider ˈaʊtˌraɪ.dəʳ, (US) -dɚ **-s** -z

outrigger ˈaʊtˌrɪg.əʳ, (US) -ɚ **-s** -z

outright adj ˈaʊt.raɪt **adv** ˌaʊtˈraɪt, aʊt-

outrival ˌaʊtˈraɪ.vᵊl, aʊt- **-s** -z **-ling** -ɪŋ **-led** -d

out|run ˌaʊt|ˈrʌn, aʊt- **-runs** -ˈrʌnz **-running** -ˈrʌn.ɪŋ **-ran** -ˈræn

outrush ˈaʊt.rʌʃ **-es** -ɪz

out|sell ˌaʊt|ˈsel, aʊt- **-sells** -ˈselz **-selling** -ˈsel.ɪŋ **-sold** -ˈsəʊld, (US) -ˈsoʊld

outset ˈaʊt.set **-s** -s

out|shine ˌaʊt|ˈʃaɪn, aʊt- **-shines** -ˈʃaɪnz **-shining** -ˈʃaɪ.nɪŋ **-shined** -ˈʃaɪnd **-shone** -ˈʃɒn, (US) -ˈʃoʊn

outside ˌaʊtˈsaɪd, aʊt- **-s** -z *stress shift:* ˌ**outside** ˈ**toilet**

outsider ˌaʊtˈsaɪ.dəʳ, aʊt-, (US) aʊtˈsaɪ.dɚ, ˈ--- **-s** -z *stress shift, British only:* ˌ**outsider** ˈ**dealing**

outsiz|e ˌaʊtˈsaɪz, aʊt- **-es** -ɪz **-ed** -d *stress shift:* ˌ**outsize** ˈ**clothes**

outskirts ˈaʊt.skɜːts, (US) -skɝːts

out|smart ˌaʊt|ˈsmɑːt, aʊt-, (US) -ˈsmɑːrt **-smarts** -ˈsmɑːts, (US) -ˈsmɑːrts **-smarting** -ˈsmɑː.tɪŋ, (US) -ˈsmɑːr.ţɪŋ **-smarted** -ˈsmɑː.tɪd, (US) -ˈsmɑːr.ţɪd

outsourc|e ˈaʊt.sɔːs, (US) -sɔːrs **-es** -ɪz **-ing** -ɪŋ **-ed** -t

Outspan® ˈaʊt.spæn **-s** -z

outspan ˌaʊtˈspæn, aʊt- **-s** -z **-ning** -ɪŋ **-ned** -d

outspend ˌaʊtˈspend, aʊt- **-s** -z **-ing** -ɪŋ **outspent** ˌaʊtˈspent, aʊt-

outspoken ˌaʊtˈspəʊ.kᵊn, aʊt-, (US) -ˈspoʊ- **-ly** -li **-ness** -nəs, -nɪs *stress shift:* ˌ**outspoken** ˈ**person**

outspread ˌaʊtˈspred, (US) aʊt- **-s** -z **-ing** -ɪŋ *stress shift:* ˌ**outspread** ˈ**arms**

outstanding *very good:* ˌaʊtˈstæn.dɪŋ, aʊt- **-ly** -li *sticking out:* ˈaʊtˌstæn.dɪŋ

outstar|e ˌaʊtˈsteəʳ, aʊt-, (US) -ˈster **-es** -z **-ing** -ɪŋ **-ed** -d

outstation ˈaʊt.steɪ.ʃᵊn **-s** -z **-ed** -d

outstay ˌaʊtˈsteɪ, aʊt- **-s** -z **-ing** -ɪŋ **-ed** -d

outstretch ˌaʊtˈstretʃ, aʊt- **-es** -ɪz **-ing** -ɪŋ **-ed** -t *stress shift:* ˌ**outstretched** ˈ**arms**

outstrip ˌaʊtˈstrɪp, aʊt- **-s** -s **-ping** -ɪŋ **-ped** -t

outta ˈaʊ.ţə

> Note: This is a form of **out of**, and is only used by British speakers when imitating American speakers.

outtake ˈaʊt.teɪk **-s** -s

out|vote ˌaʊt|ˈvəʊt, aʊt-, (US) -ˈvoʊt **-votes** -ˈvəʊts, (US) -ˈvoʊts **-voting** -ˈvəʊ.tɪŋ, (US) -ˈvoʊ.ţɪŋ **-voted** -ˈvəʊ.tɪd, (US) -ˈvoʊ.ţɪd

outward ˈaʊt.wəd, (US) -wɚd **-s** -z **-ly** -li **-ness** -nəs, -nɪs

outward-bound ˌaʊt.wədˈbaʊnd, (US) -wɚdˈ- ˌ**Outward** ˈ**Bound** ˌ**course**

out|wear ˌaʊt|ˈweəʳ, aʊt-, (US) -ˈwer **-wears** -ˈweəz, (US) -ˈwers **-wearing** -ˈweə.rɪŋ, (US) -ˈwer.ɪŋ **-worn** -ˈwɔːn, (US) -ˈwɔːrn

outweigh ˌaʊtˈweɪ, aʊt- **-s** -z **-ing** -ɪŋ **-ed** -d

outwent (from **outgo**) ˌaʊtˈwent, aʊt-

out|wit ˌaʊt|ˈwɪt, aʊt- **-wits** -ˈwɪts **-witting** -ˈwɪt.ɪŋ, (US) -ˈwɪţ.ɪŋ **-witted** -ˈwɪt.ɪd, (US) -ˈwɪţ.ɪd

outwith ˌaʊtˈwɪθ, aʊt-, -ˈwɪð

outwork n ˈaʊt.wɜːk, (US) -wɝːk **-s** -s

outwork v ˌaʊtˈwɜːk, aʊt-, (US) -ˈwɝːk **-s** -s **-ing** -ɪŋ **-ed** -t

out-worker ˈaʊtˌwɜː.kəʳ, (US) -ˌwɝː.kɚ **-s** -z

outworn ˌaʊtˈwɔːn, aʊt-, (US) -ˈwɔːrn *stress shift:* ˌ**outworn** ˈ**theories**

ouzel ˈuː.zᵊl **-s** -z

ouzo ˈuː.zəʊ, (US) -zoʊ

ova (plural of **ovum**) ˈəʊ.və, (US) ˈoʊ-

oval, O~ ˈəʊ.vᵊl, (US) ˈoʊ- **-s** -z **-ly** -i ˈ**Oval** ˌ**Office**; ˌ**Oval** ˈ**Office**

Ovaltine® ˈəʊ.vᵊl.tiːn, (US) ˈoʊ-

ovari|an əʊˈveə.ri|.ən, (US) oʊˈver.i- **-al** -əl

ovariectomy əʊˌveə.riˈek.tə.mi, (US) oʊˌver.iˈ-

ovariotomy əʊˌveə.riˈɒt.ə.mi, (US) oʊˌver.iˈɑː.ţə-

ovar|y ˈəʊ.vᵊr|.i, (US) ˈoʊ- **-ies** -iz

ovate n *Welsh title:* ˈɒv.ət, -ɪt; ˈəʊ.veɪt, (US) ˈoʊ.veɪt; (US) ˈɑː.vət **-s** -s

ovate adj *egg-shaped:* ˈəʊ.veɪt, -vɪt, -vət, (US) ˈoʊ.veɪt

ovation əʊˈveɪ.ʃᵊn, (US) oʊ- **-s** -z ˌ**standing** oˈ**vation**

oven ˈʌv.ᵊn **-s** -z ˈ**oven** ˌ**glove**

ovenable ˈʌv.ᵊn.ə.bᵊl

ovenbird ˈʌv.ᵊn.bɜːd, -ᵊm-, (US) -ᵊn.bɝːd **-s** -s

ovenproof ˈʌv.ᵊn.pruːf, -ᵊm-, (US) -ᵊn-

oven-ready ˌʌv.ᵊnˈred.i *stress shift:* ˌ**oven-ready** ˈ**chicken**

ovenware ˈʌv.ᵊn.weəʳ, (US) -wer

over ˈəʊ.vəʳ, (US) ˈoʊ.vɚ **-s** -z ˌ**over and** ˈ**done** ˌ**with**

over- ˈəʊ.vəʳ, ˈoʊ.vɚ

Note: Prefix. Many compounds with **over-** have the stress pattern ˌ**over**ˈ-; these are likely to undergo stress shift when a stressed syllable follows, especially in adjectives derived from verbs.

over-abundan|ce ˌəʊ.vᵊr.əˈbʌn.dən|ts, (US) ˌoʊ.vɚ- **-t** -t

over-achiever ˌəʊ.vᵊr.əˈtʃiː.vəʳ, (US) ˌoʊ.vɚ.əˈtʃiː.vɚ, ˈoʊ.vɚ.əˌtʃiː- **-s** -z

overact ˌəʊ.vᵊrˈækt, (US) ˌoʊ.vɚˈ- **-s** -s **-ing** -ɪŋ **-ed** -ɪd

overactive ˌəʊ.vᵊrˈæk.tɪv, (US) ˌoʊ.vɚˈ- *stress shift:* ˌ**overactive** ˈ**gland**

over-age ˌəʊ.vᵊrˈeɪdʒ, (US) ˌoʊ.vɚˈ- *stress shift:* ˌ**over-age** ˈ**applicant**

overall, O~ n, adj ˈəʊ.vᵊr.ɔːl, (US) ˈoʊ- **-s** -z

overall adv ˌəʊ.vᵊrˈɔːl, (US) ˌoʊ.vɚˈ-, -ˈɑːl

over-ambitious ˌəʊ.vᵊr.æmˈbɪʃ.əs, (US) ˌoʊ.vɚ- *stress shift:* ˌ**over-ambitious** ˈ**partner**

over-anxiety ˌəʊ.vᵊr.æŋˈzaɪ.ə.ti, (US) ˌoʊ.vɚ.æŋˈzaɪ.ə.ţi

over-anxious ˌəʊ.vᵊrˈæŋk.ʃəs, (US) ˌoʊ.vɚˈ- **-ly** -li *stress shift:* ˌ**over-anxious** ˈ**parent**

overarching ˌəʊ.vᵊrˈɑː.tʃɪŋ, (US) ˌoʊ.vɚˈɑːr-

overarm ˈəʊ.vᵊr.ɑːm, (US) ˈoʊ.vɚ.ɑːrm

overaw|e ˌəʊ.vᵊrˈɔː, (US) ˌoʊ.vɚˈɑː, -ˈɔː **-es** -z **-ing** -ɪŋ **-ed** -d

overbalanc|e ˌəʊ.vəˈbæl.ənts, (US) ˌoʊ.vɚˈ- **-es** -ɪz **-ing** -ɪŋ **-ed** -t

overbear ˌəʊ.vəˈbeəʳ, (US) ˌoʊ.vɚˈber **-s** -z **-ing** -ɪŋ **over|bore** ˌəʊ.və|ˈbɔːʳ, (US) ˌoʊ.vɚ|ˈbɔːr **-borne** -ˈbɔːn, (US) -ˈbɔːrn

overbearing ˌəʊ.vəˈbeə.rɪŋ, (US) ˌoʊ.vɚˈber.ɪŋ **-ly** -li **-ness** -nəs, -nɪs *stress shift:* ˌ**overbearing** ˈ**relatives**

overbid v ˌəʊ.vəˈbɪd, (US) ˌoʊ.vɚ- **-s** -z **-ding** -ɪŋ

overbid n ˈəʊ.və.bɪd, (US) ˈoʊ.vɚ- **-s** -z

overbite ˈəʊ.və.baɪt, (US) ˈoʊ.vɚ-

over|blow ˌəʊ.və|ˈbləʊ, (US) ˌoʊ.vɚ|ˈbloʊ, ˈ--|- **-blows** -ˈbləʊz, (US) -ˈbloʊz, -bloʊz **-blowing** -ˈbləʊ.ɪŋ, (US) -ˈbloʊ.ɪŋ, -ˌbloʊ.ɪŋ **-blew** -ˈbluː, (US) -ˈbluː, -bluː **-blown** -ˈbləʊn, (US) -ˈbloʊn, -bloʊn

overboard ˈəʊ.və.bɔːd, ˌ--ˈ-, (US) ˈoʊ.vɚ.bɔːrd

overbook ˌəʊ.vəˈbʊk, (US) ˌoʊ.vɚˈ- **-s** -s **-ing** -ɪŋ **-ed** -t

O

overbreadth ˌəʊ.vəˈbredθ, -ˈbretθ, (US) ˌoʊ.vɚˈ-
overbrim ˌəʊ.vəˈbrɪm, (US) ˌoʊ.vɚˈ- **-s** -z **-ming** -ɪŋ **-med** -d
overbuild ˌəʊ.vəˈbɪld, (US) ˌoʊ.vɚˈ-, ˈ--- **-s** -z **-ing** -ɪŋ **overbuilt** ˌəʊ.vəˈbɪlt, (US) ˌoʊ.vɚˈ-, ˈ---
overburden ˌəʊ.vəˈbɜː.dᵊn, (US) ˌoʊ.vɚˈbɝː- **-s** -z **-ing** -ɪŋ **-ed** -d
Overbury ˈəʊ.və.bᵊr.i, (US) ˈoʊ.vɚˌber-, -bɚ-
overcapacity ˌəʊ.və.kəˈpæs.ə.ti, -ɪ.ti, (US) ˌoʊ.vɚ.kəˈpæs.ə.t̬i
over-careful ˌəʊ.vəˈkeə.fᵊl, -fʊl, (US) ˌoʊ.vɚˈker- **-ly** -i **-ness** -nəs, -nɪs
overcast ˈəʊ.və.kɑːst, ˌ--ˈ-, (US) ˈoʊ.vɚ.kæst, ˌoʊ.vɚˈkæst
over-cautious ˌəʊ.vəˈkɔː.ʃəs, (US) ˌoʊ.vɚˈkɑː-, -ˈkɔː- *stress shift:* ˌ**over-cautious** ˈ**person**
overcharg|e **v** ˌəʊ.vəˈtʃɑːdʒ, (US) ˌoʊ.vɚˈtʃɑːrdʒ, ˈ--- **-es** -ɪz **-ing** -ɪŋ **-ed** -d
overcloud ˌəʊ.vəˈklaʊd, (US) ˌoʊ.vɚˈklaʊd **-s** -z **-ing** -ɪŋ **-ed** -ɪd
overcoat ˈəʊ.və.kəʊt, (US) ˈoʊ.vɚ.koʊt **-s** -s
over|come ˌəʊ.və|ˈkʌm, (US) ˌoʊ.vɚˈ- **-comes** -ˈkʌmz **-coming** -ˈkʌm.ɪŋ **-came** -ˈkeɪm
overcompen|sate ˌəʊ.vəˈkɒm.pən|.seɪt, -pen-, (US) ˌoʊ.vɚˈkɑːm.pən- **-sates** -seɪts **-sating** -seɪ.tɪŋ, (US) -seɪ.t̬ɪŋ **-sated** -seɪ.tɪd, (US) -seɪ.t̬ɪd
overcompensation ˌəʊ.vəˌkɒm.pənˈseɪ.ʃᵊn, -penˈ-, (US) ˌoʊ.vɚˌkɑːm.pənˈ-
over-confidence ˌəʊ.vəˈkɒn.fɪ.dᵊnts, -fə-, (US) ˌoʊ.vɚˈkɑːn.fə-
over-confident ˌəʊ.vəˈkɒn.fɪ.dᵊnt, -fə-, (US) ˌoʊ.vɚˈkɑːn.fə- **-ly** -li *stress shift:* ˌ**over-confident** ˈ**candidate**
over-cook ˌəʊ.vəˈkʊk, (US) ˌoʊ.vɚˈ- **-s** -s **-ing** -ɪŋ **-ed** -t
overcrowd ˌəʊ.vəˈkraʊd, (US) ˌoʊ.vɚˈ- **-s** -z **-ing** -ɪŋ **-ed** -ɪd *stress shift:* ˌ**overcrowded** ˈ**room**
over-develop ˌəʊ.və.dɪˈvel.əp, -dəˈ-, (US) ˌoʊ.vɚ.dɪˈ- **-s** -s **-ing** -ɪŋ **-ed** -t **-ment** -mənt *stress shift:* ˌ**overdeveloped** ˈ**muscles**
over|do ˌəʊ.və|ˈduː, (US) ˌoʊ.vɚˈ- **-does** -ˈdʌz **-doing** -ˈduː.ɪŋ **-did** -ˈdɪd **-done** -ˈdʌn
overdone *over-cooked:* ˌəʊ.vəˈdʌn, (US) ˌoʊ.vɚˈ- *stress shift:* ˌ**overdone** ˈ**chicken**
overdos|e **n** ˈəʊ.və.dəʊs, (US) ˈoʊ.vɚ.doʊs **-es** -ɪz
overdos|e **v** ˌəʊ.vəˈdəʊs, ˈ---, (US) ˌoʊ.vɚˈdoʊs, ˈ--- **-es** -ɪz **-ing** -ɪŋ **-ed** -t
overdraft ˈəʊ.və.drɑːft, (US) ˈoʊ.vɚ.dræft **-s** -s
overdraught ˈəʊ.və.drɑːft, (US) ˈoʊ.vɚ.dræft **-s** -s
overdraw ˌəʊ.vəˈdrɔː, (US) ˌoʊ.vɚˈdrɑː, -ˈdrɔː, ˈ--- **-s** -z **-ing** -ɪŋ **overdrew** ˌəʊ.vəˈdruː, (US) ˌoʊ.vɚ-, ˈ--- **overdrawn** ˌəʊ.vəˈdrɔːn, (US) ˌoʊ.vɚˈdrɑːn, -ˈdrɔːn, ˈ---
overdress **v** ˌəʊ.vəˈdres, (US) ˌoʊ.vɚˈ-, ˈ--- **-es** -ɪz **-ing** -ɪŋ **-ed** -t
overdress **n** ˈəʊ.və.dres, (US) ˈoʊ.vɚ- **-es** -ɪz
overdrive **n** ˈəʊ.və.draɪv, (US) ˈoʊ.vɚ-
over|drive **v** ˌəʊ.və|ˈdraɪv, (US) ˌoʊ.vɚˈ- **-drives** -ˈdraɪvz **-driving** -ˈdraɪ.vɪŋ **-drove** -ˈdrəʊv, (US) -ˈdroʊv **-driven** -ˈdrɪv.ᵊn
overdue ˌəʊ.vəˈdʒuː, -ˈdjuː, (US) ˌoʊ.vɚˈduː, -ˈdjuː *stress shift:* ˌ**overdue** ˈ**payment**
over|eat ˌəʊ.vᵊr|ˈiːt, (US) ˌoʊ.vɚˈ- **-eats** -ˈiːts **-eating** -ˈiː.tɪŋ, (US) -ˈiː.t̬ɪŋ **-eaten** -ˈiː.tᵊn **-ate** -ˈet, -ˈeɪt, (US) -ˈeɪt
over-emphasis ˌəʊ.vᵊrˈemp.fə.sɪs, (US) ˌoʊ.vɚˈ-
over-emphasiz|e, -is|e ˌəʊ.vᵊrˈemp.fə.saɪz, (US) ˌoʊ.vɚˈ- **-es** -ɪz **-ing** -ɪŋ **-ed** -d
overestimate **n** ˌəʊ.vᵊrˈes.tɪ.mət, -tə-, -mɪt, -meɪt, (US) ˌoʊ.vɚˈes.tɪ.mɪt **-s** -s
overesti|mate **v** ˌəʊ.vᵊrˈes.tɪ|.meɪt, -tə-, (US) ˌoʊ.vɚˈes.tə- **-mates** -meɪts **-mating** -meɪ.tɪŋ, (US) -meɪ.t̬ɪŋ **-mated** -meɪ.tɪd, (US) -meɪ.t̬ɪd
over-estimation ˌəʊ.vᵊrˌes.tɪˈmeɪ.ʃᵊn, -təˈ-, (US) ˌoʊ.vɚˌes.təˈ-
overex|cite ˌəʊ.vᵊr.ɪk|ˈsaɪt, -ekˈ-, (US) ˌoʊ.vɚ- **-cites** -ˈsaɪts **-citing** -ˈsaɪ.tɪŋ, (US) -ˈsaɪ.t̬ɪŋ **-cited** -ˈsaɪ.tɪd, (US) -ˈsaɪ.t̬ɪd **-citement** -ˈsaɪt.mənt
overexer|t ˌəʊ.vᵊr.ɪɡˈzɜː|t, -eɡˈ-, (US) ˌoʊ.vɚ.ɪɡˈzɝː|t, -eɡˈ- **-ts** -ts **-ting** -tɪŋ, (US) -t̬ɪŋ **-ted** -tɪd, (US) -t̬ɪd
overexertion ˌəʊ.vᵊr.ɪɡˈzɜː.ʃᵊn, -eɡˈ-, (US) ˌoʊ.vɚ.ɪɡˈzɝː-, -eɡˈ-
overexpos|e ˌəʊ.vᵊr.ɪkˈspəʊz, -ekˈ-, (US) ˌoʊ.vɚ.ɪkˈspoʊz, -ekˈ- **-es** -ɪz **-ing** -ɪŋ **-ed** -d
over-exposure ˌəʊ.vᵊr.ɪkˈspəʊ.ʒəʳ, -ekˈ-, (US) ˌoʊ.vɚ.ɪkˈspoʊ.ʒɚ, -ekˈ-
overfatigu|e ˌəʊ.və.fəˈtiːɡ, (US) ˌoʊ.vɚ- **-es** -z **-ing** -ɪŋ **-ed** -d
overfeed ˌəʊ.vəˈfiːd, (US) ˌoʊ.vɚˈ- **-s** -z **-ing** -ɪŋ **overfed** ˌəʊ.vəˈfed, (US) ˌoʊ.vɚˈ- *stress shift:* ˌ**overfed** ˈ**pets**
overfishing ˌəʊ.vəˈfɪʃ.ɪŋ, (US) ˌoʊ.vɚ-
overflow **n** ˈəʊ.və.fləʊ, (US) ˈoʊ.vɚ.floʊ **-s** -z
overflow **v** ˌəʊ.vəˈfləʊ, (US) ˌoʊ.vɚˈfloʊ **-s** -z **-ing** -ɪŋ **-ed** -d
over|fly ˌəʊ.və|ˈflaɪ, (US) ˌoʊ.vɚˈ-, ˈ--- **-flies** -ˈflaɪz, (US) -ˈflaɪz, -flaɪz **-flying** -ˈflaɪ.ɪŋ, (US) -ˈflaɪ.ɪŋ, -flaɪ.ɪŋ **-flew** -ˈfluː, (US) -ˈfluː, -fluː **-flown** -ˈfləʊn, (US) -ˈfloʊn, -floʊn
over-fond ˌəʊ.vəˈfɒnd, (US) ˌoʊ.vɚˈfɑːnd
over-generalization, -isa- ˌəʊ.vəˌdʒen.ᵊr.ᵊl.aɪˈzeɪ.ʃᵊn, -ɪˈ-, (US) ˌoʊ.vɚˌdʒen.ɚ.ᵊl.əˈ-
overground ˈəʊ.və.ɡraʊnd, ˌ--ˈ-, (US) ˈoʊ.vɚ.ɡraʊnd, ˌ--ˈ-
over|grow ˌəʊ.və|ˈɡrəʊ, (US) ˌoʊ.vɚˈɡroʊ **-grows** -ˈɡrəʊz, (US) -ˈɡroʊz **-growing** -ˈɡrəʊ.ɪŋ, (US) -ˈɡroʊ.ɪŋ **-grew** -ˈɡruː **-grown** -ˈɡrəʊn, (US) -ˈɡroʊn
overgrowth ˈəʊ.və.ɡrəʊθ, (US) ˈoʊ.vɚ.ɡroʊθ **-s** -s
overhand **n, adj** ˈəʊ.və.hænd, (US) ˈoʊ.vɚ- **-s** -z
overhang **n** ˈəʊ.və.hæŋ, (US) ˈoʊ.vɚ- **-s** -z
overhang **v** ˌəʊ.vəˈhæŋ, (US) ˌoʊ.vɚˈ-, ˈ--- **-s** -z **-ing** -ɪŋ **overhung** ˌəʊ.vəˈhʌŋ, (US) ˌoʊ.vɚˈ-, ˈ---
over-hasty ˌəʊ.vəˈheɪ.sti, (US) ˌoʊ.vɚˈ- *stress shift:* ˌ**over-hasty** ˈ**choice**
overhaul **n** ˈəʊ.və.hɔːl, (US) ˈoʊ.vɚ.hɑːl, -hɔːl **-s** -z
overhaul **v** ˌəʊ.vəˈhɔːl, (US) ˌoʊ.vɚˈhɑːl, -ˈhɔːl, ˈ--- **-s** -z **-ing** -ɪŋ **-ed** -d
overhead **n, adj** ˈəʊ.və.hed, (US) ˈoʊ.vɚ- **-s** -z ˌ**overhead pro**ˈ**jector**
overhead **adv** ˌəʊ.vəˈhed, (US) ˌoʊ.vɚˈ-
overhear ˌəʊ.vəˈhɪəʳ, (US) ˌoʊ.vɚˈhɪr **-s** -z **-ing** -ɪŋ **overheard** ˌəʊ.vəˈhɜːd, (US) ˌoʊ.vɚˈhɝːd
over|heat ˌəʊ.və|ˈhiːt, (US) ˌoʊ.vɚˈ- **-heats** -ˈhiːts **-heating** -ˈhiː.tɪŋ, (US) -ˈhiː.t̬ɪŋ **-heated** -ˈhiː.tɪd, (US) -ˈhiː.t̬ɪd
over-impress|ed ˌəʊ.vᵊr.ɪmˈpres|t, (US) ˌoʊ.vɚ- **-ive** -ɪv
over-indulg|e ˌəʊ.vᵊr.ɪnˈdʌldʒ, (US) ˌoʊ.vɚ- **-es** -ɪz **-ing** -ɪŋ **-ed** -d **-ence** -ᵊnts
overjoyed ˌəʊ.vəˈdʒɔɪd, (US) ˌoʊ.vɚˈ- *stress shift:* ˌ**overjoyed** ˈ**winner**
overkill ˈəʊ.və.kɪl, (US) ˈoʊ.vɚ-
overladen ˌəʊ.vəˈleɪ.dᵊn, (US) ˌoʊ.vɚˈ- *stress shift:* ˌ**overladen** ˈ**basket**
overlaid ˌəʊ.vəˈleɪd, (US) ˌoʊ.vɚˈ-
overland **adj** ˈəʊ.və.lænd, (US) ˈoʊ.vɚ-
overland **adv** ˌəʊ.vəˈlænd, ˈ---, (US) ˌoʊ.vɚˈlænd, ˈ---
overlap **n** ˈəʊ.və.læp, (US) ˈoʊ.vɚ- **-s** -s
overlap **v** ˌəʊ.vəˈlæp, (US) ˌoʊ.vɚˈ- **-s** -s **-ping** -ɪŋ **-ped** -t
overlay **n** ˈəʊ.vᵊl.eɪ, (US) ˈoʊ.vɚ.leɪ **-s** -z
overlay **v** ˌəʊ.vᵊlˈeɪ, (US) ˌoʊ.vɚˈleɪ **-s** -z **-ing** -ɪŋ **overlaid** ˌəʊ.vᵊlˈeɪd, (US) ˌoʊ.vɚˈleɪd
overleaf ˌəʊ.vᵊlˈiːf, (US) ˈoʊ.vɚ.liːf
overload **n** ˈəʊ.vᵊl.əʊd, (US) ˈoʊ.vɚ.loʊd **-s** -z
overload **v** ˌəʊ.vᵊlˈəʊd, (US) ˌoʊ.vɚˈloʊd, ˈ--- **-s** -z **-ing** -ɪŋ **-ed** -ɪd
overlock ˈəʊ.vᵊl.ɒk, (US) ˈoʊ.vɚ.lɑːk **-s** -s **-ing** -ɪŋ **-ed** -t
overlong ˌəʊ.vəˈlɒŋ, (US) ˌoʊ.vɚˈlɑːŋ, -ˈlɔːŋ

O

overlook v ˌəʊ.vəˈlʊk, (US) ˌoʊ.vɚˈ- -s -s -ing -ɪŋ -ed -t
overlook n ˈəʊ.və.lʊk, (US) ˈoʊ.vɚ- -s -s
overlord ˈəʊ.və.lɔːd, (US) ˈoʊ.vɚ.lɔːrd -s -z
overly ˈəʊ.vəl.i, (US) ˈoʊ.vɚ.li
overlying ˌəʊ.vəlˈaɪ.ɪŋ, (US) ˌoʊ.vɚˈlaɪ- *stress shift:* ˌ**overlying** ˈ**structure**
overman v ˌəʊ.vəˈmæn, (US) ˌoʊ.vɚˈ- -s -z -ning -ɪŋ -ned -d
over|man n ˈəʊ.və|.mæn, (US) ˈoʊ.vɚ- -men -men
overmantel ˈəʊ.vəˌmæn.təl, (US) ˈoʊ.vɚˌmæn.t̬əl -s -z
overmast|er ˌəʊ.vəˈmɑː.st|əʳ, (US) ˌoʊ.vɚˈmæs.tɚ -ers -əz, (US) -ɚz -ering -ər.ɪŋ -ered -əd, (US) -ɚd
overmatch ˌəʊ.vəˈmætʃ, (US) ˌoʊ.vɚ-, ˈ--- -es -ɪz -ing -ɪŋ -ed -t
overmuch ˌəʊ.vəˈmʌtʃ, ˈ---, (US) ˌoʊ.vɚˈ-, ˈ---
overnight ˌəʊ.vəˈnaɪt, (US) ˌoʊ.vɚˈ- *stress shift:* ˌ**overnight** ˈ**sleeper**
overoptimistic ˌəʊ.vərˌɒp.tɪˈmɪs.tɪk, -təˈ-, (US) ˌoʊ.vɚˌɑːp.təˈ- -ally -əl.i, -li *stress shift:* ˌ**overoptimistic** ˈ**outlook**
overpass n ˈəʊ.və.pɑːs, (US) ˈoʊ.vɚ.pæs -es -ɪz
over|pay ˌəʊ.və|ˈpeɪ, (US) ˌoʊ.vɚˈ-, ˈ--|- -pays -ˈpeɪz -paying -ˈpeɪ.ɪŋ -paid -ˈpeɪd -payment/s -ˈpeɪ.mənt/s
overplay ˌəʊ.vəˈpleɪ, (US) ˌoʊ.vɚ- -s -z -ing -ɪŋ -ed -d
overplus ˈəʊ.və.plʌs, (US) ˈoʊ.vɚ- -es -ɪz
overpopu|late ˌəʊ.vəˈpɒp.jə|.leɪt, -jʊ-, (US) ˌoʊ.vɚˈpɑː.pjə-, -pjʊ- -lates -leɪts -lating -leɪ.tɪŋ, (US) -leɪ.t̬ɪŋ -lated -leɪ.tɪd, (US) -leɪ.t̬ɪd
overpopulation ˌəʊ.vəˌpɒp.jəˈleɪ.ʃən, -jʊˈ-, (US) ˌoʊ.vɚˌpɑː.pjəˈ-, -pjʊˈ-
overpower ˌəʊ.vəˈpaʊ.əʳ, -ˈpaʊəʳ, (US) ˌoʊ.vɚˈpaʊ.ɚ -s -z -ing/ly -ɪŋ/li -ed -d
overpriced ˌəʊ.vəˈpraɪst, (US) ˌoʊ.vɚ- *stress shift:* ˌ**overpriced** ˈ**goods**
overprint n ˈəʊ.və.prɪnt, (US) ˈoʊ.vɚ- -s -s
overprin|t v ˌəʊ.vəˈprɪn|t, ˈ---, (US) ˌoʊ.vɚˈ-, ˈ--- -ts -ts -ting -tɪŋ, (US) -t̬ɪŋ -ted -tɪd, (US) -t̬ɪd
overproduc|e ˌəʊ.və.prəˈdʒuːs, -ˈdjuːs, (US) ˌoʊ.vɚ.prəˈduːs, -proʊˈ-, -ˈdjuːs, ˈəʊ.və.prəˌduːs, -ˌdjuːs -es -ɪz -ing -ɪŋ -ed -t
overproduction ˌəʊ.və.prəˈdʌk.ʃən, (US) ˌoʊ.vɚ-
overprotect ˌəʊ.və.prəˈtekt, (US) ˌoʊ.vɚ- -s -s -ing -ɪŋ -ed -ɪd
overprotective ˌəʊ.və.prəˈtek.tɪv, (US) ˌoʊ.vɚ- *stress shift:* ˌ**overprotective** ˈ**parent**
overqualified ˌəʊ.vəˈkwɒl.ɪ.faɪd, ˈ-ə-, (US) ˌoʊ.vɚˈkwɑː.lɪ-, ˈoʊ.vɚˌkwɑː.lɪ- *stress shift, British only:* ˌ**overqualified** ˈ**applicant**
overra|te ˌəʊ.vərˈeɪ|t, (US) ˌoʊ.vɚˈreɪ|t, ˈ--- -tes -ts -ting -tɪŋ, (US) -t̬ɪŋ -ted -tɪd, (US) -t̬ɪd
overreach n ˈəʊ.vər.iːtʃ, (US) ˈoʊ.vɚ.riːtʃ -es -ɪz
overreach v ˌəʊ.vərˈiːtʃ, (US) ˌoʊ.vɚˈriːtʃ, ˈ--- -es -ɪz -ing -ɪŋ -ed -t
overreact ˌəʊ.vər.iˈækt, (US) ˌoʊ.vɚ.riˈ- -s -s -ing -ɪŋ -ed -ɪd
overreaction ˌəʊ.vər.iˈæk.ʃən, (US) ˌoʊ.vɚ.riˈ-
overrid|e ˌəʊ.vərˈaɪd, (US) ˌoʊ.vɚˈraɪd -es -z -ing -ɪŋ **overrode** ˌəʊ.vərˈəʊd, (US) ˌoʊ.vɚˈroʊd **overridden** ˌəʊ.vərˈɪd.ən, (US) ˌoʊ.vɚˈrɪd-
overrider ˈəʊ.vərˌaɪ.dəʳ, (US) ˈoʊ.vɚˌraɪ.dɚ -s -z
overripe ˌəʊ.vərˈaɪp, (US) ˌoʊ.vɚˈraɪp -ness -nəs, -nɪs *stress shift:* ˌ**overripe** ˈ**fruit**
overripen ˌəʊ.vərˈaɪ.pən, (US) ˌoʊ.vɚˈraɪ- -s -z -ing -ɪŋ, -vərˈaɪp.nɪŋ, (US) -vɚˈraɪp- -ed -d
overrul|e ˌəʊ.vərˈuːl, (US) ˌoʊ.vɚˈruːl -es -z -ing -ɪŋ -ed -d
overrun v ˌəʊ.vərˈʌn, (US) ˌoʊ.vɚˈrʌn -s -z -ning -ɪŋ **overran** ˌəʊ.vərˈæn, (US) ˌoʊ.vɚˈræn
overrun n ˈəʊ.vər.ʌn, (US) ˈoʊ.vɚ- -s -z
over-scrupulous ˌəʊ.vəˈskruː.pjə.ləs, -pjʊ-, (US) ˌoʊ.vɚˈskruː- -ly -li -ness -nəs, -nɪs *stress shift:* ˌ**over-scrupulous** ˈ**person**
oversea ˌəʊ.vəˈsiː, (US) ˌoʊ.vɚˈ-, ˈoʊ.vɚ.siː -s -z *stress shift:* ˌ**overseas** ˈ**applicant**
over|see ˌəʊ.və|ˈsiː, (US) ˌoʊ.vɚˈ- -sees -ˈsiːz -seeing -ˈsiː.ɪŋ -saw -ˈsɔː, (US) -ˈsɑː, -ˈsɔː -seen -ˈsiːn
overseer ˈəʊ.vəˌsiː.əʳ, (US) ˈoʊ.vɚˌsiː.ɚ, -ˌsɪr -s -z
over|sell ˌəʊ.və|ˈsel, (US) ˌoʊ.vɚ- -sells -selz -selling -sel.ɪŋ -sold -səʊld, (US) -soʊld
oversensitive ˌəʊ.vəˈsent.sɪ.tɪv, -sə-, (US) ˌoʊ.vɚˈsent.sə.t̬ɪv *stress shift:* ˌ**oversensitive** ˈ**person**
oversensitivity ˌəʊ.vəˌsent.sɪˈtɪv.ə.ti, -səˈ-, -ɪ.ti, (US) ˌoʊ.vɚˌsent.səˈtɪv.ə.t̬i
oversew ˈəʊ.və.səʊ, ˌ--ˈ-, (US) ˈoʊ.vɚ.soʊ, ˌ--ˈ- -s -z -ing -ɪŋ -ed -d -n -n
oversexed ˌəʊ.vəˈsekst, (US) ˌoʊ.vɚˈ- *stress shift:* ˌ**oversexed** ˈ**person**
overshadow ˌəʊ.vəˈʃæd.əʊ, (US) ˌoʊ.vɚˈʃæd.oʊ -s -z -ing -ɪŋ -ed -d
overshoe ˈəʊ.və.ʃuː, (US) ˈoʊ.vɚ- -s -z
overshoot n ˈəʊ.və.ʃuːt, (US) ˈoʊ.vɚ-
overshoot v ˌəʊ.vəˈʃuːt, (US) ˌoʊ.vɚˈ- -s -s -ing -ɪŋ **overshot** ˌəʊ.vəˈʃɒt, (US) ˌoʊ.vɚˈʃɑːt
overside adv ˈəʊ.və.saɪd, (US) ˈoʊ.vɚ-
oversight ˈəʊ.və.saɪt, (US) ˈoʊ.vɚ- -s -s
oversimplification ˌəʊ.vəˌsɪm.plɪ.fɪˈkeɪ.ʃən, -pləˈ-, -fəˈ-, (US) ˌoʊ.vɚˌsɪm.plə- -s -z
oversimpli|fy ˌəʊ.vəˈsɪm.plɪ|.faɪ, -plə-, (US) ˌoʊ.vɚˈsɪm.plɪ-, ˈ-plə-, ˈoʊ.vɚˌsɪm- -fies -faɪz -fying -faɪ.ɪŋ -fied -faɪd
oversize ˌəʊ.vəˈsaɪz, (US) ˌoʊ.vɚˈ-, ˈ--- -d -d *stress shift:* ˌ**oversize** ˈ**clothes**
oversleep ˌəʊ.vəˈsliːp, (US) ˌoʊ.vɚˈ- -s -s -ing -ɪŋ **overslept** ˌəʊ.vəˈslept, (US) ˌoʊ.vɚˈ-
oversold (from **oversell**) ˌəʊ.vəˈsəʊld, (US) ˌoʊ.vɚˈsoʊld *stress shift:* ˌ**oversold** ˈ**concept**
overspend ˌəʊ.vəˈspend, (US) ˌoʊ.vɚˈ-, ˈ--- -s -z -ing -ɪŋ **overspent** ˌəʊ.vəˈspent, (US) ˌoʊ.vɚˈ-, ˈ---
overspill ˈəʊ.və.spɪl, (US) ˈoʊ.vɚ-
overspread ˌəʊ.vəˈspred, (US) ˌoʊ.vɚˈ-, ˈ--- -s -z -ing -ɪŋ
overstaff ˌəʊ.vəˈstɑːf, (US) ˌoʊ.vɚˈstæf -s -s -ing -ɪŋ -ed -t
over|state ˌəʊ.və|ˈsteɪt, (US) ˌoʊ.vɚˈ- -states -ˈsteɪts -stating -ˈsteɪ.tɪŋ, (US) -ˈsteɪ.t̬ɪŋ -stated -ˈsteɪ.tɪd, (US) -ˈsteɪ.t̬ɪd *stress shift:* ˌ**overstated** ˈ**argument**
overstatement ˌəʊ.vəˈsteɪt.mənt, ˈəʊ.vəˌsteɪt-, (US) ˌoʊ.vɚˈsteɪt-, ˈoʊ.vɚˌsteɪt -s -s
overstay ˌəʊ.vəˈsteɪ, (US) ˌoʊ.vɚˈ-, ˈ--- -s -z -ing -ɪŋ -ed -d
overstep ˌəʊ.vəˈstep, (US) ˌoʊ.vɚˈ- -s -s -ping -ɪŋ -ped -t
overstimu|late ˌəʊ.vəˈstɪm.jə|.leɪt, -jʊ-, (US) ˌoʊ.vɚˈstɪm.jə-, -jʊ- -lates -leɪts -lating -leɪ.tɪŋ, (US) -leɪ.t̬ɪŋ -lated -leɪ.tɪd, (US) -leɪ.t̬ɪd
overstock ˌəʊ.vəˈstɒk, (US) ˌoʊ.vɚˈstɑːk -s -s -ing -ɪŋ -ed -t
overstrain n ˈəʊ.və.streɪn, ˌ--ˈ-, (US) ˌoʊ.vɚˈ-, ˈ---
overstrain v ˌəʊ.vəˈstreɪn, (US) ˌoʊ.vɚˈ- -s -z -ing -ɪŋ -ed -d
Overstrand ˈəʊ.və.strænd, (US) ˈoʊ.vɚ-
overstretch ˌəʊ.vəˈstretʃ, (US) ˌoʊ.vɚˈ- -es -ɪz -ing -ɪŋ -ed -t
overstrung *in state of nervous tension:* ˌəʊ.vəˈstrʌŋ, (US) ˌoʊ.vɚˈ- *of piano:* ˈəʊ.və.strʌŋ, (US) ˈoʊ.vɚ-
oversubscrib|e ˌəʊ.və.səbˈskraɪb, (US) ˌoʊ.vɚ- -es -z -ing -ɪŋ -ed -d
oversubscription ˌəʊ.və.səbˈskrɪp.ʃən, (US) ˌoʊ.vɚ-
oversupp|ly ˌəʊ.və.səˈpl|aɪ, (US) ˌoʊ.vɚ- -ies -aɪz
overt əʊˈvɜːt; ˈəʊ.vɜːt, (US) oʊˈvɝːt, ˈ-- -ly -li -ness -nəs, -nɪs
over|take ˌəʊ.və|ˈteɪk, (US) ˌoʊ.vɚˈ- -takes -ˈteɪks -taking -ˈteɪ.kɪŋ -took -ˈtʊk -taken -ˈteɪ.kən, -kəŋ, (US) -kən
overtask ˌəʊ.vəˈtɑːsk, (US) ˌoʊ.vɚˈtæsk -s -s -ing -ɪŋ -ed -t

Pronouncing the letters **OW**

There are two common pronunciations of the vowel digraph **ow**: /əʊ/ (US) /oʊ/ and /aʊ/, e.g.:

blow	bləʊ (US) bloʊ
brown	braʊn

In addition

A less common realization is /ɒ/ (US) /ɑː/, e.g.:

knowledge	ˈnɒl.ɪdʒ (US) ˈnɑː.lɪdʒ

overtax ˌəʊ.vəˈtæks, (US) ˌoʊ.vɚˈ- **-es** -ɪz **-ing** -ɪŋ **-ed** -t

over-the-counter ˌəʊ.və.ðəˈkaʊn.təʳ, (US) ˌoʊ.vɚ.ðəˈkaʊn.t̬ɚ *stress shift:* **ˌover-the-counter ˈsales**

over-the-top ˌəʊ.və.ðəˈtɒp, (US) ˌoʊ.vɚ.ðəˈtɑːp *stress shift:* **ˌover-the-top ˈspeech**

Note: See also **OTT**.

overthrow n ˈəʊ.və.θrəʊ, (US) ˈoʊ.vɚ.θroʊ **-s** -z

overthrow v ˌəʊ.vəˈθrəʊ, (US) ˌoʊ.vɚˈθroʊ, ˈ--- **-s** -z **-ing** -ɪŋ **overthrew** ˌəʊ.vəˈθruː, (US) ˌoʊ.vɚˈ-, ˈ--- **overthrown** ˌəʊ.vəˈθrəʊn, (US) ˌoʊ.vɚˈθroʊn, ˈ---

overthrust ˈəʊ.və.θrʌst, (US) ˈoʊ.vɚ- **-s** -s

overtime ˈəʊ.və.taɪm, (US) ˈoʊ.vɚ-

overtir|e ˌəʊ.vəˈtaɪəʳ, -ˈtaɪ.əʳ, (US) ˌoʊ.vɚˈtaɪ.ɚ **-es** -z **-ing** -ɪŋ **-ed** -d

overtone ˈəʊ.və.təʊn, (US) ˈoʊ.vɚ.toʊn **-s** -z

overtop ˌəʊ.vəˈtɒp, (US) ˌoʊ.vɚˈtɑːp **-s** -s **-ping** -ɪŋ **-ped** -t

Overtoun ˈəʊ.və.tᵊn, (US) ˈoʊ.vɚ-

Overtown ˈəʊ.və.tᵊn, (US) ˈoʊ.vɚ-

over-trump ˌəʊ.vəˈtrʌmp, (US) ˌoʊ.vɚˈ- **-s** -s **-ing** -ɪŋ **-ed** -t

overture ˈəʊ.və.tʃʊəʳ, -tʃəʳ, -tjʊəʳ, -tjəʳ, (US) ˈoʊ.vɚ.tʃɚ, -tʃʊr **-s** -z

overturn n ˈəʊ.və.tɜːn, (US) ˈoʊ.vɚ.tɝːn **-s** -z

overturn v ˌəʊ.vəˈtɜːn, (US) ˌoʊ.vɚˈtɝːn **-s** -z **-ing** -ɪŋ **-ed** -d

overuse n ˌəʊ.vəˈjuːs, (US) ˌoʊ.vɚˈ-

overus|e v ˌəʊ.vəˈjuːz, (US) ˌoʊ.vɚˈ- **-es** -ɪz **-ing** -ɪŋ **-ed** -d

overval|ue ˌəʊ.vəˈvæl|.juː, (US) ˌoʊ.vɚˈ- **-ues** -juːz **-uing** -juː.ɪŋ **-ued** -juːd

overview ˈəʊ.və.vjuː, (US) ˈoʊ.vɚ- **-s** -z

overweening ˌəʊ.vəˈwiː.nɪŋ, (US) ˌoʊ.vɚˈ-, ˈoʊ.vɚˌwiː- **-ly** -li *stress shift:* **ˌoverweening ˈpride**

overweigh|t v ˌəʊ.vəˈweɪ|t, (US) ˌoʊ.vɚˈ-, ˈ--- **-ts** -ts **-ting** -tɪŋ, (US) -t̬ɪŋ **-ted** -tɪd, (US) -t̬ɪd

overweight n ˈəʊ.və.weɪt, (US) ˈoʊ.vɚ- **-s** -s

overweight adj ˌəʊ.vəˈweɪt, (US) ˌoʊ.vɚˈ-, ˈ--- *stress shift, British only:* **ˌoverweight ˈperson**

overwhelm ˌəʊ.vəˈhwelm, (US) ˌoʊ.vɚˈ- **-s** -z **-ing/ly** -ɪŋ/li **-ed** -d

overwind ˌəʊ.vəˈwaɪnd, (US) ˌoʊ.vɚˈ-, ˈ--- **-s** -z **-ing** -ɪŋ **overwound** ˌəʊ.vəˈwaʊnd, (US) ˌoʊ.vɚˈ-, ˈ---

overwint|er ˌəʊ.vəˈwɪn.t|əʳ, (US) ˌoʊ.vɚˈwɪn.t̬|ɚ **-ers** -əz, (US) -ɚz **-ering** -ᵊr.ɪŋ **-ered** -əd, (US) -ɚd

overwork n ˈəʊ.və.wɜːk, (US) ˈoʊ.vɚ.wɝːk

overwork v ˌəʊ.vəˈwɜːk, (US) ˌoʊ.vɚˈwɝːk, ˈ--- **-s** -s **-ing** -ɪŋ **-ed** -t **-er/s** -əʳ/z, (US) -ɚ/z *stress shift:* **ˌoverworked ˈeditor**

overwrit|e ˌəʊ.vᵊrˈaɪt, (US) ˌoʊ.vɚˈraɪt **-es** -s **-ing** -ɪŋ **overwrote** ˌəʊ.vᵊrˈəʊt, (US) ˌoʊ.vɚˈroʊt **overwritten** ˌəʊ.vᵊrˈɪt.ᵊn, (US) ˌoʊ.vɚˈrɪt-

overwrought ˌəʊ.vᵊrˈɔːt, (US) ˌoʊ.vɚˈrɑːt, -ˈrɔːt *stress shift:* **ˌoverwrought ˈperson**

overzealous ˌəʊ.vəˈzel.əs, (US) ˌoʊ.vɚˈ- *stress shift:* **ˌoverzealous ˈfollower**

Ovett ˈəʊ.vet, -ˈ-, (US) ˈoʊ.vet, -ˈ-

Ovid *Latin poet:* ˈɒv.ɪd, (US) ˈɑː.vɪd *US surname:* ˈəʊ.vɪd, (US) ˈoʊ-

Ovidian əʊˈvɪd.i.ən, ɒvˈɪd-, (US) oʊˈvɪd-

Oviedo ˌɒv.iˈeɪ.dəʊ, (US) oʊˈvjeɪ.doʊ, -ðoʊ

oviform ˈəʊ.vɪ.fɔːm, (US) ˈoʊ.vɪ.fɔːrm

ovine ˈəʊ.vaɪn, (US) ˈoʊ-

Ovingdean ˈɒv.ɪŋ.diːn, (US) ˈɑː.vɪŋ-

Ovingham ˈɒv.ɪn.dʒəm, (US) ˈɑː.vɪn-

Ovington *in North Yorkshire, street in London:* ˈɒv.ɪŋ.tən, (US) ˈɑː.vɪŋ- *in Norfolk, surname:* ˈəʊ.vɪŋ.tən, (US) ˈoʊ-

oviparous əʊˈvɪp.ᵊr.əs, (US) oʊ- **-ly** -li **-ness** -nəs, -nɪs

ovoid ˈəʊ.vɔɪd, (US) ˈoʊ- **-s** -z

ovular ˈɒv.jə.ləʳ, ˈəʊ.vjə-, -vjʊ-, (US) ˈɑː.vjuː.lɚ, ˈoʊ-, -vjə-

ovu|late ˈɒv.jə|.leɪt, ˈəʊ.vjə-, (US) ˈɑː.vjuː-, ˈoʊ-, -vjə- **-lates** -leɪts **-lating** -leɪ.tɪŋ, (US) -leɪ.t̬ɪŋ **-lated** -leɪ.tɪd, (US) -leɪ.t̬ɪd

ovulation ˌɒv.jəˈleɪ.ʃᵊn, ˌəʊ.vjəˈ-, -vjʊˈ-, (US) ˌɑː.vjuːˈ-, ˌoʊ-, -vjəˈ-

ovule ˈɒv.juːl, ˈəʊ.vjuːl, (US) ˈɑːv-, ˈoʊv- **-s** -z

ov|um ˈəʊ.v|əm, (US) ˈoʊ- **-a** -ə

Owbridge ˈəʊ.brɪdʒ, (US) ˈoʊ-

ow|e əʊ, (US) oʊ **-es** -z **-ing** -ɪŋ **-ed** -d

Owen ˈəʊ.ɪn, (US) ˈoʊ- **-s** -z

Ower ˈaʊ.əʳ, (US) ˈaʊ.ɚ

Owers ˈəʊ.əz, ˈaʊ.əz, (US) ˈoʊ.ɚz, ˈaʊ.ɚz

owing (from **owe**) ˈəʊ.ɪŋ, (US) ˈoʊ-

owl aʊl **-s** -z

owler|y ˈaʊ.lᵊr|.i **-ies** -iz

Owles əʊlz, aʊlz, uːlz, (US) oʊlz, aʊlz, uːlz

owlet ˈaʊ.lət, -lɪt, -let, (US) -lɪt **-s** -s

Owlett ˈaʊ.lɪt, -let, (US) -lɪt

owlish ˈaʊ.lɪʃ **-ly** -li **-ness** -nəs, -nɪs

own əʊn, (US) oʊn **-s** -z **-ing** -ɪŋ **-ed** -d **-er/s** -əʳ/z, (US) -ɚ/z **ˌown ˈgoal**

own-brand ˌəʊnˈbrænd, ˌəʊm-, ˈ--, (US) ˌoʊnˈ-, ˈ-- **-s** -z **-ing** -ɪŋ

owner-driver ˌəʊ.nəˈdraɪ.vəʳ, (US) ˌoʊ.nɚˈdraɪ.vɚ **-s** -z *stress shift:* **ˌowner-driver ˈtaxi**

owner-occup|ier ˌəʊ.nəʳˈɒk.jə.p|aɪ.əʳ, -jʊ-, (US) ˌoʊ.nɚˈɑː.kjuː.p|aɪ.ɚ, -kjə- **-iers** -aɪ.əz, (US) -aɪ.ɚz **-ied** -aɪd

ownership ˈəʊ.nə.ʃɪp, (US) ˈoʊ.nɚ-

own-label ˌəʊnˈleɪ.bᵊl, (US) ˌoʊn-

Owsley ˈaʊz.li

owt aʊt, əʊt, (US) aʊt, oʊt

ox ɒks, (US) ɑːks **-en** -ᵊn

oxalate ˈɒk.sə.leɪt, -lɪt, -lət, (US) ˈɑːk.sə.leɪt **-s** -s

oxalic ɒkˈsæl.ɪk, (US) ɑːkˈ-

oxalis ɒkˈsɑː.lɪs, -ˈsæl.ɪs, -ˈseɪ.lɪs; ˈɒk.sə.lɪs, (US) ˈɑːk.sə.lɪs; (US) ɑːkˈsæl.ɪs

oxbow ˈɒks.bəʊ, (US) ˈɑːks.boʊ **-s** -z

Oxbridge ˈɒks.brɪdʒ, (US) ˈɑːks-

Oxbrow ˈɒks.braʊ, (US) ˈɑːks-

oxen (plural of **ox**) ˈɒk.sᵊn, (US) ˈɑːk-

Oxenden ˈɒk.sᵊn.dən, (US) ˈɑːk-

Oxenford ˈɒk.sᵊn.fɔːd, -fəd, (US) ˈɑːk.sən.fɔːrd, -fɚd

Oxenham ˈɒk.sᵊn.əm, (US) ˈɑːk-

Oxenhope ˈɒk.sᵊn.həʊp, (US) ˈɑːk.sᵊn.hoʊp

oxer ˈɒk.səʳ, (US) ˈɑːk.sɚ **-s** -z

oxeye ˈɒks.aɪ, (US) ˈɑːk.saɪ **-s** -z **-d** -d

Oxfam ˈɒks.fæm, (US) ˈɑːks-

Oxford ˈɒks.fəd, (US) ˈɑːks.fɚd **-shire** -ʃəʳ, -ʃɪəʳ, (US) -ʃɚ, -ʃɪr

oxidant ˈɒk.sɪ.dᵊnt, -sə-, (US) ˈɑːk.sɪ- **-s** -s

oxi|date ˈɒk.sɪ|.deɪt, -sə-, (US) ˈɑːk.sɪ- **-dates** -deɪts **-dating** -deɪ.tɪŋ, (US) -deɪ.t̬ɪŋ **-dated** -deɪ.tɪd, (US) -deɪ.t̬ɪd

oxidation ˌɒk.sɪˈdeɪ.ʃᵊn, -səˈ-, (US) ˌɑːk.sɪˈ-

oxide ˈɒk.saɪd, (US) ˈɑːk- **-s** -z

oxidization, -isa- ˌɒk.sɪ.daɪˈzeɪ.ʃᵊn, -sə-, -dɪˈ-, (US) ˌɑːk.sɪ.dəˈ-

oxidiz|e, -is|e ˈɒk.sɪ.daɪz, -sə-, (US) ˈɑːk.sɪ- **-es** -ɪz **-ing** -ɪŋ **-ed** -d **-er/s** -əʳ/z, (US) -ɚ/z **-able** -ə.bᵊl

Oxley ˈɒk.sli, (US) ˈɑːk-

oxlip ˈɒk.slɪp, (US) ˈɑːk- **-s** -s

oxo, O~® ˈɒk.səʊ, (US) ˈɑːk.soʊ

Oxon. ˈɒk.sᵊn, -sɒn, (US) ˈɑːk.sᵊn, -sɑːn

Oxonian ɒkˈsəʊ.ni.ən, (US) ɑːkˈsoʊ- **-s** -z

Oxshott ˈɒk.ʃɒt, (US) ˈɑːk.ʃɑːt

oxtail ˈɒks.teɪl, (US) ˈɑːks- **-s** -z **ˌoxtail ˈsoup**

Oxted ˈɒk.stɪd, (US) ˈɑːk-

ox-tongue ˈɒks.tʌŋ, -tɒŋ, (US) ˈɑːks.tʌŋ **-s** -z

Oxus ˈɒk.səs, (US) ˈɑːk-

oxy- ˈɒk.sɪ, -si; ɒkˈsɪ, ⓤⓢ ˈɑːk.sɪ, -si; ⓤⓢ ɑːkˈsɪ
Note: Prefix. Normally either takes primary or secondary stress on the first syllable, e.g. **oxygen** /ˈɒk.sɪ.dʒən/ ⓤⓢ /ˈɑːk-/, **oxychloride** /ˌɒk.sɪˈklɔː.raɪd/ ⓤⓢ /ˌɑːk.sɪˈklɔːr.aɪd/, or primary stress on the second syllable, e.g. **oxygenous** /ɒkˈsɪdʒ.ən.əs/ ⓤⓢ /ɑːk-/.

oxyacetylene ˌɒk.si.əˈset.əl.iːn, -ɪ.liːn, -lɪn, ⓤⓢ ˌɑːk.si.əˈset̬.əl.iːn, -ɪn

oxychloride ˌɒk.sɪˈklɔː.raɪd, ⓤⓢ ˌɑːk.sɪˈklɔːr.aɪd **-s** -z

oxygen ˈɒk.sɪ.dʒən, -sə-, ⓤⓢ ˈɑːk.sɪ-

oxyge|nate ˈɒk.sɪ.dʒə|.neɪt, -sə-, -dʒɪ-, ⓤⓢ ˈɑːk.sɪ.dʒə- **-nates** -neɪts **-nating** -neɪ.tɪŋ, ⓤⓢ -neɪ.t̬ɪŋ **-nated** -neɪ.tɪd, ⓤⓢ -neɪ.t̬ɪd

oxygenation ˌɒk.sɪ.dʒəˈneɪ.ʃən, -sə-, -dʒɪˈ-, ⓤⓢ ˌɑːk.sɪ.dʒəˈ-

oxygeniz|e, -is|e ˈɒk.sɪ.dʒə.naɪz, -sə-, ⓤⓢ ˈɑːk.sɪ- **-es** -ɪz **-ing** -ɪŋ **-ed** -d

oxygenous ɒkˈsɪdʒ.ɪ.nəs, -ə.nəs, ⓤⓢ ɑːk-

oxyhaemoglobin ˌɒk.siˌhiː.məʊˈgləʊ.bɪn, ⓤⓢ ˌɑːk.siˌhiː.məˈgloʊ-, -moʊˈ-

oxyhydrogen ˌɒk.sɪˈhaɪ.drə.dʒən, -drɪ-, ⓤⓢ ˌɑːk.sɪˈhaɪ.drə-

oxymoron ˌɒk.sɪˈmɔː.rɒn, -rən, ⓤⓢ ˌɑːk.sɪˈmɔːr.ɑːn **-s** -z

oxytone ˈɒk.sɪ.təʊn, ⓤⓢ ˈɑːk.sɪ.toʊn **-s** -z

oyer ˈɔɪ.əʳ, ⓤⓢ -ɚ ˌ**oyer and** ˈ**terminer**

oyes, oyez əʊˈjes, -ˈjez, -ˈjeɪ, ˈ--, ⓤⓢ ˈoʊ.jes, -jez, -jeɪ

oyster, O~ ˈɔɪ.stəʳ, ⓤⓢ -stɚ **-s** -z

oyster-catcher ˈɔɪ.stəˌkætʃ.əʳ, ⓤⓢ -stɚˌkætʃ.ɚ **-s** -z

Oystermouth ˈɔɪ.stə.maʊθ, ⓤⓢ -stɚ-

Oz ɒz, ⓤⓢ ɑːz

oz. (abbrev. for **ounce/s**) *singular:* aʊnts; *plural:* ˈaʊnt.sɪz

Ozalid® ˈəʊ.zəl.ɪd, ˈɒz.əl-, ⓤⓢ ˈɑː.zəl- **-s** -z

Ozanne əʊˈzæn, ⓤⓢ oʊ-

Ozarks ˈəʊ.zɑːks, ⓤⓢ ˈoʊ.zɑːrks

ozokerite əʊˈzəʊ.kər.ɪt, ɒzˈəʊ-, əˈzəʊ-, ⓤⓢ oʊˈzoʊ.kə.raɪt; ⓤⓢ ˌoʊ.zoʊˈkɪr.aɪt

ozone ˈəʊ.zəʊn, ⓤⓢ ˈoʊ.zoʊn ˈ**ozone** ˌ**layer**

ozone-friendly ˌəʊ.zəʊnˈfrend.li, ⓤⓢ ˌoʊ.zoʊnˈ- *stress shift:* ˌ**ozone-friendly** ˈ**chemicals**

ozonic əʊˈzɒn.ɪk, ⓤⓢ oʊˈzɑː.nɪk

ozoniferous ˌəʊ.zəʊˈnɪf.ər.əs, ⓤⓢ ˌoʊ.zəˈ-

ozonosphere əʊˈzɒn.ə.sfɪəʳ, -ˈzəʊ.nə-, ⓤⓢ oʊˈzoʊ.nə.sfɪr

Ozymandias ˌɒz.iˈmæn.di.əs, -æs, ⓤⓢ ˌɑː.zi-

Ozzie ˈɒz.i, ⓤⓢ ˈɑː.zi

P

Pronouncing the letter P

→ *See also* **PH**

The consonant letter **p** is most often realized as /p/, e.g.:

pen pen

In addition

p can be silent. There are three combinations in which this can occur: **pn**, **ps** and **pt**.

p is silent in **pn** and **ps** when word initial, e.g.:

pneumatic	njuːˈmæt.ɪk Ⓤⓢ nuːˈmæṭ-
psalm	sɑːm

pt can be silent word initially and word finally, e.g.:

pterodactyl	ˌter.əʊˈdæk.tɪl Ⓤⓢ ˌter.əˈdæk.təl
receipt	rɪˈsiːt

In addition

p can be silent in other instances, e.g.:

corps	kɔːʳ Ⓤⓢ kɔːr
cupboard	ˈkʌb.əd Ⓤⓢ -ɚd
raspberry	ˈrɑːz.bᵊr.i Ⓤⓢ ˈræzˌber.i

p, P piː -ˈs -z ˌ**p's and** ˈ**q's**
pa pɑː -s -z
PA ˌpiːˈeɪ
Pa. (abbrev. for **Pennsylvania**) ˌpent.sɪlˈveɪ.ni.ə, -sᵊlˈ-, ˈ-njə, Ⓤⓢ -sᵊlˈveɪ.njə, ˈ-ni.ə
pa'anga pɑːˈæŋ.gə, -ə, Ⓤⓢ -ˈɑːŋ.gə, ˈpɑːŋ-
pabulum ˈpæb.jə.ləm, -jʊ-
pace prep ˈpeɪ.si, ˈpɑː.tʃeɪ, -keɪ
pac|e n, v peɪs -es -ɪz -ing -ɪŋ -ed -t -er/s -əʳ/z, Ⓤⓢ -ɚ/z ˌ**put someone** ˌ**through their** ˈ**paces**
pacemaker ˈpeɪsˌmeɪ.kəʳ, Ⓤⓢ -kɚ -s -z
pace|man ˈpeɪ.smæn, -smən -men -men
pace-setter ˈpeɪsˌset.əʳ, Ⓤⓢ -ˌseṭ.ɚ -s -z
Pachmann ˈpɑːk.mən, -mɑːn
pachyderm ˈpæk.i.dɜːm, Ⓤⓢ -ə.dɝːm -s -z
pachydermatous ˌpæk.iˈdɜː.mə.təs, Ⓤⓢ -əˈdɝː.mə.ṭəs
pacific, P~ pəˈsɪf.ɪk -ally -ᵊl.i, -li
pacification ˌpæs.ɪ.fɪˈkeɪ.ʃᵊn, ˌ-ə-, -fəˈ-, Ⓤⓢ ˌ-ə- -s -z
pacificatory pəˈsɪf.ɪ.kə.tᵊr.i, pæsˈɪf-, ˌpæs.ɪ.fɪˈkeɪ-, ˌ-ə-; ˈ-ə-, Ⓤⓢ pəˈsɪf.ɪ.kə.tɔːr-
pacificist pəˈsɪf.ɪ.sɪst, pæsˈɪf-, Ⓤⓢ pəˈsɪf- -s -s
pacifism ˈpæs.ɪ.fɪ.zᵊm, ˈ-ə-, Ⓤⓢ ˈ-ə-
pacifist ˈpæs.ɪ.fɪst, ˈ-ə-, Ⓤⓢ ˈ-ə- -s -s
paci|fy ˈpæs.ɪ|.faɪ, ˈ-ə- -fies -faɪz -fying -faɪ.ɪŋ -fied -faɪd -fier/s -faɪ.əʳ/z, Ⓤⓢ -faɪ.ɚ/z
Pacino pəˈtʃiː.nəʊ, Ⓤⓢ -noʊ
pack pæk -s -s -ing -ɪŋ -ed -t -er/s -əʳ/z, Ⓤⓢ -ɚ/z ˈ**pack** ˌ**ice**; ˈ**packing** ˌ**case**
packag|e ˈpæk.ɪdʒ -es -ɪz -ing -ɪŋ -ed -d ˌ**package** ˈ**holiday**; ˈ**package** ˌ**store**
Packard ˈpæk.ɑːd, Ⓤⓢ -ɚd
packed pækt
Packer ˈpæk.əʳ, Ⓤⓢ -ɚ
packet ˈpæk.ɪt -s -s
packhors|e ˈpæk.hɔːs, Ⓤⓢ -hɔːrs -es -ɪz
packing|house ˈpæk.ɪŋ|.haʊs -houses -haʊ.zɪz
pack|man ˈpæk|.mən, -mæn -men -mən, Ⓤⓢ -mən, -men
Pac-man® ˈpæk.mæn
pact pækt -s -s
pactum ˈpæk.təm
pac|y ˈpeɪ.s|i -ier -i.əʳ, Ⓤⓢ -i.ɚ -iest -i.ɪst
pad pæd -s -z -ding -ɪŋ -ded -ɪd ˌ**padded** ˈ**cell**
Padang ˈpɑː.dɑːŋ, Ⓤⓢ pɑːˈdɑːŋ
Paddington ˈpæd.ɪŋ.tən
paddl|e ˈpæd.ᵊl -es -z -ing -ɪŋ, ˈpæd.lɪŋ -ed -d -er/s -əʳ/z, ˈpæd.ləʳ/z, Ⓤⓢ ˈpæd.ᵊl.ɚ/z, ˈpæd.lɚ/z ˈ**paddle** ˌ**steamer**; ˈ**paddle** ˌ**wheel**
paddleboard ˈpæd.ᵊl.bɔːd, Ⓤⓢ -bɔːrd -s -z
paddling-pool ˈpæd.ᵊl.ɪŋ.puːl, ˈ-lɪŋ- -s -z
paddock, P~ ˈpæd.ək -s -s
padd|y, P~ ˈpæd|.i -ies -iz
paddyfield ˈpæd.i.fiːld -s -z
paddywagon ˈpæd.iˌwæg.ᵊn -s -z
Paderewski ˌpæd.ᵊrˈef.ski, -ᵊrˈev-, Ⓤⓢ ˌpæd.əˈref-, ˌpɑː.dəˈ-
Padiham ˈpæd.i.əm
Padilla pædˈiː.jə, pəˈdiː-; pəˈdɪl.ə, pædˈɪl-
padlock ˈpæd.lɒk, Ⓤⓢ -lɑːk -s -s -ing -ɪŋ -ed -t
Padraic ˈpɑː.drɪk, ˈpæt.rɪk, Ⓤⓢ ˈpɑː.drɪk, -drɪg
Padraic Colum ˌpɑː.drɪkˈkɒl.əm, ˌpæt.rɪk-, Ⓤⓢ ˌpɑː.drɪkˈkɑː.ləm, -drɪgˈ-
Padraig ˈpɑː.drɪg
padre ˈpɑː.dreɪ, -dri -s -z
padrone pædˈrəʊ.neɪ, pəˈdrəʊ-, -ni, Ⓤⓢ pəˈdroʊ- -s -z
Padstow ˈpæd.stəʊ, Ⓤⓢ -stoʊ
Padu|a ˈpæd.ju|.ə, Ⓤⓢ ˈpædʒ.uː|-, ˈpæd.juː|- -an/s -ən/z
Paducah pəˈduː.kə, -ˈdʒuː-
paean ˈpiː.ən -s -z
paederast ˈpe.dᵊr.æst, ˈpiː.d.ᵊr-, Ⓤⓢ ˈped.ə.ræst -s -s -y -i
paediatric ˌpiː.diˈæt.rɪk -s -s
paediatrician ˌpiː.di.əˈtrɪʃ.ᵊn -s -z
paedophile ˈpiː.dəʊ.faɪl, Ⓤⓢ ˈped.ə-, ˈpiː.də-, -doʊ- -s -z
paedophili|a ˌpiː.dəʊˈfɪl.i|.ə, Ⓤⓢ ˌped.oʊˈfiː.li-, ˌpiː.doʊˈ-, -dəˈ-, -ˈfiːl.j|ə -ac/s -æk/s
paella paɪˈel.ə, Ⓤⓢ pɑːˈjel-, -ˈeɪ.jɑː -s -z
paeon ˈpiː.ən -s -z
paeonic piːˈɒn.ɪk, Ⓤⓢ -ˈɑː.nɪk
paeon|y ˈpiː.ə.n|i -ies -iz
pagan ˈpeɪ.gᵊn -s -z
Pagani pəˈgɑː.ni, Ⓤⓢ pə-, pɑː-
Paganini ˌpæg.əˈniː.ni
paganism ˈpeɪ.gᵊn.ɪ.zᵊm
paganiz|e, -is|e ˈpeɪ.gᵊn.aɪz -es -ɪz -ing -ɪŋ -ed -d
pag|e, P~ peɪdʒ -es -ɪz -ing -ɪŋ -ed -d
pageant ˈpædʒ.ənt -s -s
pageantry ˈpædʒ.ən.tri
pageboy ˈpeɪdʒ.bɔɪ -s -z
pager ˈpeɪ.dʒəʳ, Ⓤⓢ -dʒɚ -s -z
Paget ˈpædʒ.ɪt
page-turner ˈpeɪdʒˌtɜː.nəʳ, Ⓤⓢ -ˌtɝː.nɚ -s -s
paginal ˈpædʒ.ɪ.nᵊl, ˈpeɪ.dʒɪ-, Ⓤⓢ ˈpædʒ.ə-
pagin|ate ˈpædʒ.ɪ.n|eɪt, ˈpeɪ.dʒɪ-, -dʒᵊn|.eɪt, Ⓤⓢ ˈpædʒ.ᵊn|.eɪt -ates -eɪts -ating -eɪ.tɪŋ, Ⓤⓢ -eɪ.ṭɪŋ -ated -eɪ.tɪd, Ⓤⓢ -eɪ.ṭɪd
pagination ˌpædʒ.ɪˈneɪ.ʃᵊn, ˌpeɪ.dʒɪ-, -dʒᵊnˈeɪ-, Ⓤⓢ ˌpædʒ.ᵊnˈeɪ- -s -z
Paglia pɑː.li.ə, Ⓤⓢ ˈpæg.li.ə, ˈpeɪg.li.ə
Pagliacci ˌpæl.iˈɑː.tʃi, -ˈætʃ.i, Ⓤⓢ pɑːlˈjɑː.tʃi
Pagnell ˈpæg.nəl
pagoda pəˈgəʊ.də, Ⓤⓢ -ˈgoʊ- -s -z
Pagones pəˈgəʊ.nez, Ⓤⓢ -ˈgoʊ-
pah pɑː

Pahang pəˈhʌŋ, -ˈhæŋ, US -ˈhɑːŋ, pɑː-

> Note: Usually pronounced /pəˈhʌŋ/ in Malaysia.

paid (from **pay**) peɪd
paid-up ˌpeɪdˈʌp
Paige peɪdʒ
Paignton ˈpeɪn.tən, US -tᵊn
pail peɪl **-s** -z **-ful/s** -fʊl/z
paillass|e ˈpæl.i.æs, ˌ--ˈ-, US pælˈjæs, ˈ-- **-es** -ɪz
paillette pælˈjet, ˌpæl.iˈet, US ˌpælˈjet, ˈpɑː.jet **-s** -s
pain peɪn **-s** -z **-ing** -ɪŋ **-ed** -d **ˌpain in the ˈneck; be at ˌpains to ˈdo something**
Pain(e) peɪn
painful ˈpeɪn.fᵊl, -fʊl **-ly** -i **-ness** -nəs, -nɪs
painkill|er ˈpeɪnˌkɪl|.əʳ, ˈpeɪŋ-, US ˈpeɪnˌkɪl|.ɚ **-ers** -əz, US -ɚz **-ing** -ɪŋ
painless ˈpeɪn.ləs, -lɪs **-ly** -li **-ness** -nəs, -nɪs
painstaking ˈpeɪnzˌteɪ.kɪŋ, ˈpeɪns-, US ˈpeɪnz- **-ly** -li
Painswick ˈpeɪnz.wɪk
paint peɪnt **-s** -s **-ing/s** -ɪŋ/z, US ˈpeɪn.t̬ɪŋ **-ed** -ɪd, US ˈpeɪn.t̬ɪd **-er/s** -əʳ/z, US ˈpeɪn.t̬ɚ/z **ˌpainted ˈlady**
paintball ˈpeɪnt.bɔːl, US -bɔːl, -bɑːl **-ing** -ɪŋ **-er/s** -əʳ/z, US -ɚ/z
paintbox ˈpeɪnt.bɒks, US -bɑːks **-es** -ɪz
paintbrush ˈpeɪnt.brʌʃ **-es** -ɪz
Painter ˈpeɪn.təʳ, US -t̬ɚ
painterly ˈpeɪn.tᵊl.i, US -t̬ɚ.li
paintwork ˈpeɪnt.wɜːk, US -wɜːk
paint|y ˈpeɪn.t|i, US -t̬|i **-ier** -i.əʳ, US -i.ɚ **-iest** -i.ɪst, -i.əst
pair peəʳ, US per **-s** -z **-ing** -ɪŋ **-ed** -d
pais|a ˈpaɪ.s|ɑː **-e** -eɪ **-as** -ɑːz
paisley, P~ ˈpeɪz.li
pajama pəˈdʒɑː.mə, US -ˈdʒɑː-, -ˈdʒæm.ə **-s** -z
pak-choi ˌpækˈtʃɔɪ, ˌbɒk-, ˌpɑːk-, US ˌbɑːkˈtʃɔɪ
Pakeman ˈpeɪk.mən
Pakenham ˈpæk.ᵊn.əm
Paki ˈpæk.i **-s** -z
Pakistan ˌpɑː.kɪˈstɑːn, ˌpæk.ɪˈ-, -ˈstæn, US ˈpæk.ɪ.stæn, ˈpɑː.kɪ.stɑːn; US ˌpæk.ɪˈstæn, ˌpɑː.kɪˈstɑːn
Pakistani ˌpɑː.kɪˈstɑː.ni, ˌpæk.ɪˈ- **-s** -z
pakora pəˈkɔː.rə, US -ˈkɔːr.ə
pal pæl **-s** -z
palac|e ˈpæl.ɪs, -əs, US -əs **-es** -ɪz
paladin ˈpæl.ə.dɪn **-s** -z
palaeo- ˈpæl.i.əʊ-, ˈpeɪ.li.əʊ, US ˈpeɪ.li.oʊ, -ə
palaeobotany ˌpæl.i.əʊˈbɒt.ᵊn.i, ˌpeɪ.li-, US ˌpeɪ.li.oʊˈbɑː.tᵊn-
Palaeocene ˈpæl.i.əʊ.siːn, ˈpeɪ.li-, US ˈpeɪ.li.oʊ-, -ə-
palaeographic ˌpæl.i.əʊˈgræf.ɪk, ˌpeɪ.li-, US ˌpeɪ.li.oʊˈ-, -əˈ-
palaeograph|y ˌpæl.iˈɒg.rə.f|i, ˌpeɪ.li-, US ˌpeɪ.liˈɑː.grə- **-er/s** -əʳ/z, US -ɚ/z
palaeolithic, P~ ˌpæl.i.əʊˈlɪθ.ɪk, ˌpeɪ.li-, US ˌpeɪ.li.oʊˈ-, -əˈ-
palaeontological ˌpæl.iˌɒn.təˈlɒdʒ.ɪ.kᵊl, ˌpeɪ.li-, US ˌpeɪ.liˌɑːn.təˈlɑː.dʒɪ-
palaeontolog|y ˌpæl.i.ɒnˈtɒl.ə.dʒ|i, ˌpeɪ.li-, US ˌpeɪ.li.ɑːnˈtɑː.lə- **-ist/s** -ɪsts
palaeotype ˈpæl.i.əʊ.taɪp, ˈpeɪ.li-, US ˈpeɪ.li.oʊ-, -ə-
Palaeozoic ˌpæl.i.əʊˈzəʊ.ɪk, ˌpeɪ.li-, US ˌpeɪ.li.oʊˈzoʊ-, -ə-
Palamedes ˌpæl.əˈmiː.diːz
palamino ˌpæl.əˈmiː.nəʊ, US -noʊ **-s** -z
Palamon ˈpæl.ə.mən, -mɒn, US -mən, -mɑːn
palanquin ˌpæl.əŋˈkiːn, US -ənˈ- **-s** -z
palatab|le ˈpæl.ə.tə.b|ᵊl, ˈ-ɪ-, US -ə.t̬ə- **-ly** -li **-leness** -ᵊl.nəs, -nɪs
palatal ˈpæl.ə.tᵊl, US -t̬ᵊl **-s** -z
palatalization, -isa- ˌpæl.ə.tᵊl.aɪˈzeɪ.ʃᵊn, pəˌlæt.ᵊl-, -ɪˈ-, US ˌpæl.ə.t̬ᵊl.əˈ- **-s** -z
palataliz|e, -is|e ˈpæl.ə.tᵊl.aɪz, pəˈlæt.ᵊl-, US ˈpæl.ə.t̬ə.laɪz **-es** -ɪz **-ing** -ɪŋ **-ed** -d
palate ˈpæl.ət, -ɪt, US -ət **-s** -s
palatial pəˈleɪ.ʃᵊl, US -ʃᵊl **-ly** -i
palatinate, P~ pəˈlæt.ɪ.nət, -ᵊn.ət, -ɪt, US -ᵊn.eɪt, -ɪt **-s** -s
palatine, P~ ˈpæl.ə.taɪn, US -taɪn, -tɪn **-s** -z
palatogram ˈpæl.ə.təʊ.græm, pəˈlæt.əʊ-, US ˈpæl.ə.toʊ-, -t̬ə- **-s** -z
palatography ˌpæl.əˈtɒg.rə.fi, US -ˈtɑː.grə-
palav|er pəˈlɑː.v|əʳ, US -ˈlæv|.ɚ, -ˈlɑː.v|ɚ **-ers** -əz, US -ɚz **-ering** -ᵊr.ɪŋ **-ered** -əd, US -ɚd
palazzo pəˈlæt.səʊ, -sə; -ˈlæd.zəʊ, -zə, US pəˈlɑːt.soʊ, pɑː- **paˌlazzo ˈpants**
pal|e peɪl **-er** -əʳ, US -ɚ **-est** -ɪst, -əst **-ely** -li **-eness** -nəs, -nɪs **-es** -z **-ing** -ɪŋ **-ed** -d **ˌpale ˈale; beˌyond the ˈpale**
palefac|e ˈpeɪl.feɪs **-es** -ɪz
paleo- ˈpæl.i.əʊ, ˈpeɪ.li.əʊ, US ˈpeɪ.li.oʊ, -ə
paleobotany ˌpæl.i.əʊˈbɒt.ᵊn.i, ˌpeɪ.li-, US ˌpeɪ.li.oʊˈbɑː.tᵊn-
Paleocene ˈpæl.i.əʊ.siːn, ˈpeɪ.li-, US ˈpeɪ.li.oʊ-, -ə-
paleographic ˌpæl.i.əʊˈgræf.ɪk, ˌpeɪ.li-, US ˌpeɪ.li.oʊˈ-, -əˈ-
paleograph|y ˌpæl.iˈɒg.rə.f|i, ˌpeɪ.li-, US ˌpeɪ.liˈɑː.grə- **-er/s** -əʳ/z, US -ɚ/z
paleolithic, P~ ˌpæl.i.əʊˈlɪθ.ɪk, ˌpeɪ.li-, US ˌpeɪ.li.oʊˈ-, -əˈ-
paleontological ˌpæl.iˌɒn.təˈlɒdʒ.ɪ.kᵊl, ˌpeɪ.li-, US ˌpeɪ.liˌɑːn.təˈlɑː.dʒɪ-
paleontolog|y ˌpæl.i.ɒnˈtɒl.ə.dʒ|i, ˌpeɪ.li-, US ˌpeɪ.li.ɑːnˈtɑː.lə- **-ist/s** -ɪst/s
paleotype ˈpæl.i.əʊ.taɪp, ˈpeɪ.li-, US ˈpeɪ.li.oʊ-, -ə-
Palermo pəˈlɜː.məʊ, -ˈleə-, US -ˈler.moʊ
Palestine ˈpæl.ə.staɪn, ˈ-ɪ-, US -ə.staɪn
Palestinian ˌpæl.əˈstɪn.i.ən, -ɪˈ-, US -əˈstɪn- **-s** -z
Palestrina ˌpæl.əˈstriː.nə, -ɪˈ-, US -əˈstriː-
palette ˈpæl.ət, -ɪt, -et, US -ɪt **-s** -s **ˈpalette ˌknife**
Paley ˈpeɪ.li
palfrey, P~ ˈpɔːl.fri, ˈpɒl-, US ˈpɔːl-, ˈpɑːl- **-s** -z
Palgrave ˈpɔːl.greɪv, ˈpæl-, US ˈpæl-, ˈpɔːl-
Pali ˈpɑː.li
palimony ˈpæl.ɪ.mə.ni, ˈ-ə-, US -ə.moʊ-
palimpsest ˈpæl.ɪmp.sest, -əmp-, US -ɪmp- **-s** -s
Palin ˈpeɪ.lɪn
palindrome ˈpæl.ɪn.drəʊm, -ən-, US -ɪn.droʊm **-s** -z
palindromic ˌpæl.ɪnˈdrɒm.ɪk, -ənˈ-, US -ɪnˈdrɑː.mɪk, -ˈdroʊ-
paling ˈpeɪ.lɪŋ **-s** -z
palingenesis ˌpæl.ɪnˈdʒen.ə.sɪs, ˈ-ɪ-, US ˈ-ə-
palinode ˈpæl.ɪ.nəʊd, ˈ-ə-, US -ə.noʊd **-s** -z
palisad|e, P~ ˌpæl.ɪˈseɪd, -əˈ-, US -əˈ-, ˈ--- **-es** -z **-ing** -ɪŋ **-ed** -ɪd
palish ˈpeɪ.lɪʃ
Palk pɔːlk, pɒlk, US pɔːlk, pɔːk
pall pɔːl **-s** -z **-ing** -ɪŋ **-ed** -d
palladi|an, P~ pəˈleɪ.di|.ən **-um/s** -əm/z
Pallas ˈpæl.əs, -æs
pall-bearer ˈpɔːlˌbeə.rəʳ, US -ˌber.ɚ, ˈpɑːl- **-s** -z
pallet ˈpæl.ɪt, -ət, US -ɪt **-s** -s
palliass|e ˈpæl.i.æs, ˌ--ˈ-, US pælˈjæs, ˈ-- **-es** -ɪz
palli|ate ˈpæl.i|.eɪt **-ates** -eɪts **-ating** -eɪ.tɪŋ, US -eɪ.t̬ɪŋ **-ated** -eɪ.tɪd, US -eɪ.t̬ɪd
palliation ˌpæl.iˈeɪ.ʃᵊn
palliative ˈpæl.i.ə.tɪv, US -t̬ɪv **-s** -z
pallid ˈpæl.ɪd **-est** -ɪst, -əst **-ly** -li **-ness** -nəs, -nɪs
Palliser ˈpæl.ɪ.səʳ, US -sɚ
palli|um ˈpæl.i|.əm **-ums** -əmz **-a** -ə
pall-mall ˌpælˈmæl, US ˌpælˈmæl, ˌpelˈmel, ˌpɑːlˈmɑːl
Pall Mall ˌpælˈmæl, ˌpelˈmel, US ˌpælˈmæl, ˌpelˈmel, ˌpɔːlˈmɔːl *stress shift:* **ˌPall Mall ˈClub**
pallor ˈpæl.əʳ, US -ɚ
pally ˈpæl.i
palm pɑːm **-s** -z **-ing** -ɪŋ **-ed** -d **ˌPalm ˈBeach; ˌPalm ˈSprings; ˌPalm ˈSunday; ˌgrease one's ˈpalm**
Palma ˈpæl.mə, ˈpɑː-, ˈpɑːl-, US ˈpɑːl.mɑː
palmar ˈpæl.məʳ, -mɑːʳ, US -mɚ, ˈpɑːl-
palma|te ˈpæl.meɪ|t, ˈpɑː-, -mɪ|t, US

ˈpæl.meɪ|t, ˈpɑːl-, ˈpɑː- **-ted** -tɪd, (US) -t̬ɪd
palmer, P~ ˈpɑː.məʳ, (US) -mɚ **-s** -z
Palmerston ˈpɑː.mə.stᵊn, (US) -mɚ-
palmist ˈpɑː.mɪst **-s** -s
palmistry ˈpɑː.mɪ.stri
palm-oil ˈpɑːm.ɔɪl, ˌ-ˈ-, (US) ˈpɑːm.ɔɪl
Palmolive® pɑːˈmɒl.ɪv, (US) -ˈmɑː.lɪv
palmtop ˈpɑːm.tɒp, (US) -tɑːp **-s** -s
palm|y ˈpɑː.m|i **-ier** -i.əʳ, (US) -i.ɚ **-iest** -i.ɪst, -i.əst
palmyra, P~ pælˈmaɪə.rə, -ˈmɪə.rə, (US) -ˈmaɪ- **-s** -z
Palo Alto ˌpæl.əʊˈæl.təʊ, (US) -oʊˈæl.toʊ
Palomar ˈpæl.əʊ.mɑːʳ, (US) -ə.mɑːr
palomino ˌpæl.əˈmiː.nəʊ, (US) -noʊ, -oʊˈ- **-s** -z
palooka pəˈluː.kə **-s** -z
palpability ˌpæl.pəˈbɪl.ə.ti, ˈ-ɪ-, (US) -ə.t̬i
palpab|le ˈpæl.pə.b|ᵊl **-ly** -li **-leness** -ᵊl.nəs, -nɪs
palpate **adj** ˈpæl.peɪt, (US) -peɪt, -pɪt
palpa|te **v** pælˈpeɪ|t, (US) ˈ-- **-tes** -ts **-ting** -tɪŋ, (US) -t̬ɪŋ **-ted** -tɪd, (US) -t̬ɪd
palpation pælˈpeɪ.ʃᵊn
palpi|tate ˈpæl.pɪ|.teɪt, (US) -pə- **-tates** -teɪts **-tating** -teɪ.tɪŋ, (US) -teɪ.t̬ɪŋ **-tated** -teɪ.tɪd, (US) -teɪ.t̬ɪd
palpitation ˌpæl.pɪˈteɪ.ʃᵊn, (US) -pəˈ- **-s** -z
palsgrave, P~ ˈpɔːlz.greɪv, (US) ˈpɔːlz-, ˈpælz- **-s** -z
pals|y ˈpɔːl.z|i, ˈpɒl-, (US) ˈpɔːl-, ˈpɑːl- **-ies** -iz **-ied** -id
palt|er ˈpɔːl.t|əʳ, ˈpɒl-, (US) ˈpɔːl.t|ɚ, ˈpɑːl- **-ers** -əz, (US) -ɚz **-ering** -ᵊr.ɪŋ **-ered** -əd, (US) -ɚd **-erer/s** -ᵊr.əʳ/z, (US) -ɚ.ɚ/z
Paltrow ˈpæl.trəʊ, ˈpɒl-, (US) ˈpæl.troʊ, ˈpɑːl-
paltr|y ˈpɔːl.tr|i, ˈpɒl-, (US) ˈpɔːl-, ˈpɑːl- **-ier** -i.əʳ, (US) -i.ɚ **-iest** -i.ɪst, -i.əst **-ily** -ᵊl.i, -ɪ.li **-iness** -ɪ.nəs, -ɪ.nɪs
Pam pæm
Pamela ˈpæm.ᵊl.ə, -ɪ.lə, (US) -ᵊl.ə
Pamir pəˈmɪəʳ, (US) pɑːˈmɪr **-s** -z
Pampa ˈpæm.pə **-s** -z
pampas ˈpæm.pəs, (US) ˈpæm.pəs, ˈpɑːm- ˈ**pampas** ˌ**grass**
pamp|er ˈpæm.p|əʳ, (US) -p|ɚ **-ers** -əz, (US) -ɚz **-ering** -ᵊr.ɪŋ **-ered** -əd, (US) -ɚd **-erer/s** -ᵊr.əʳ/z, (US) -ɚ.ɚ/z
Pampers® ˈpæm.pəz, (US) -pɚz
pamphlet ˈpæm.flɪt, -flət, (US) -flɪt **-s** -s
pamphleteer ˌpæm.fləˈtɪəʳ, -flɪˈ-, (US) -flɪˈtɪr **-s** -z **-ing** -ɪŋ
Pamphyli|a pæmˈfɪl.i|.ə **-an/s** -ən/z
Pamplona pæmˈpləʊ.nə, (US) pæmˈploʊ.nə, pɑːm-, -nɑː
pan, P~ pæn **-s** -z **-ning** -ɪŋ **-ned** -d
panacea ˌpæn.əˈsiː.ə **-s** -z
panach|e pəˈnæʃ, pænˈæʃ-, -ˈɑːʃ, (US) pəˈnæʃ, -ˈnɑːʃ **-es** -ɪz
Panadol® ˈpæn.ə.dɒl, (US) -dɑːl
panama, P~ ˌpæn.əˈmɑː, ˈ---, (US) ˈ---, -mɔː **-s** -z ˌ**Panama Ca**ˈ**nal**; ˌ**Panama** ˈ**City**; ˌ**panama** ˈ**hat**
Panamanian ˌpæn.əˈmeɪ.ni.ən **-s** -z
Pan-American ˌpæn.əˈmer.ɪ.kən **-ism** -ɪ.zᵊm
Panasonic ˌpæn.əˈsɒn.ɪk, (US) -ˈsɑː.nɪk
panatel(l)a ˌpæn.əˈtel.ə **-s** -z
pancake ˈpæn.keɪk, ˈpæŋ-, (US) ˈpæn- **-s** -s ˈ**Pancake** ˌ**Day**
pancetta pænˈtʃet.ə, (US) -ˈtʃet̬-
panchromatic ˌpæn.krəʊˈmæt.ɪk, ˌpæŋ-, (US) ˌpæn.kroʊˈmæt̬-
Pancras ˈpæŋ.krəs
pancreas ˈpæŋ.kri.əs, -æs, (US) ˈpæn.kri.əs, ˈpæŋ- **-es** -ɪz
pancreatic ˌpæŋ.kriˈæt.ɪk, (US) ˌpæn.kriˈæt̬-, ˌpæŋ-
panda ˈpæn.də **-s** -z ˈ**panda** ˌ**car**
pandanus pænˈdeɪ.nəs, -ˈdæn.əs **-es** -ɪz
pandect ˈpæn.dekt **-s** -s
pandemic pænˈdem.ɪk **-s** -s
pandemonium, P~ ˌpæn.dəˈməʊ.ni.əm, -dɪˈ-, (US) -dəˈmoʊ- **-s** -z
pand|er ˈpæn.d|əʳ, (US) -d|ɚ **-ers** -əz, (US) -ɚz **-ering** -ᵊr.ɪŋ **-ered** -əd, (US) -ɚd
pandialectal ˌpæn.daɪ.əˈlek.tᵊl
pandit, P~ ˈpæn.dɪt **-s** -s
pandora, P~ pænˈdɔː.rə, (US) -ˈdɔːr.ə **-s** -z **Pan**ˌ**dora's** ˈ**box**
pandowd|y pænˈdaʊ.d|i **-ies** -iz
pane peɪn **-s** -z
panegyric ˌpæn.əˈdʒɪr.ɪk, -ɪˈ-, (US) -əˈ-, -ˈdʒaɪ.rɪk **-s** -s **-al** -ᵊl
panegyrist ˌpæn.əˈdʒɪr.ɪst, -ɪˈ-, ˈpæn.ə.dʒɪr-, ˈ-ɪ-, (US) ˌpæn.əˈdʒɪr-, -ˈdʒaɪ.rɪst **-s** -s
panegyriz|e, -is|e ˈpæn.ə.dʒɪ.raɪz, ˈ-ɪ-, -dʒᵊr.aɪz, (US) -dʒə.raɪz **-es** -ɪz **-ing** -ɪŋ **-ed** -d
panel ˈpæn.ᵊl **-s** -z **-(l)ing/s** -ɪŋ/z **-(l)ed** -d ˈ**panel** ˌ**beater**
panel(l)ist ˈpæn.ᵊl.ɪst **-s** -s
Panesar ˌpæn.əˈsɑːʳ, (US) -ˈsɑːr
panettone ˌpæn.əˈtəʊ.neɪ, -ni, (US) -ɪˈtoʊ- **-s** -z
pan-|fry ˈpæn|.fraɪ **-fries** -fraɪz **-frying** -fraɪ.ɪŋ **-fried** -fraɪd
panful ˈpæn.fʊl **-s** -z
pang pæŋ **-s** -z
panga ˈpæŋ.gə **-s** -z
Pangbourne ˈpæŋ.bɔːn, -bən, (US) -bɔːrn
Pangloss ˈpæŋ.glɒs, ˈpæn-, (US) ˈpæn.glɑːs
panglossian, P~ pæŋˈglɒs.i.ən, pæn-, (US) pænˈglɑː.si-
pangolin ˈpæŋ.gəʊ.lɪn; pæŋˈgəʊ-, (US) ˈpæn.goʊ-, ˈpæŋ-, -gə-; (US) pænˈgoʊ-, pæŋ- **-s** -z
panhandl|e ˈpænˌhæn.dᵊl **-es** -z **-ing** -ɪŋ, -ˌhænd.lɪŋ **-ed** -d **-er/s** -əʳ/z, (US) -ɚ/z, -ˌhænd.ləʳ/z, -lɚ/z
panic ˈpæn.ɪk **-s** -s **-king** -ɪŋ **-ked** -t ˈ**panic** ˌ**button**; ˈ**panic** ˌ**stations**
panicky ˈpæn.ɪ.ki
panicle ˈpæn.ɪ.kᵊl **-s** -z
panic-stricken ˈpæn.ɪkˌstrɪk.ᵊn
Panini ˈpɑː.nɪ.niː, -ni, (US) pɑːˈniː.ni
panjandr|um pænˈdʒæn.dr|əm, pən-, (US) pæn- **-ums** -əmz **-a** -ə
Pankhurst ˈpæŋk.hɜːst, (US) -hɝːst
panlectal ˌpænˈlek.tᵊl
panne pæn
pannier ˈpæn.i.əʳ, (US) ˈ-jɚ, ˈ-i.ɚ **-s** -z
pannikin ˈpæn.ɪ.kɪn, ˈ-ə-, (US) ˈ-ɪ- **-s** -z
Pannill ˈpæn.ɪl
panopl|y ˈpæn.ə.pl|i **-ies** -iz **-ied** -id
panorama ˌpæn.ᵊrˈɑː.mə, (US) -əˈræm.ə, -ˈrɑː.mə **-s** -z
panoramic ˌpæn.ᵊrˈæm.ɪk, -ˈɑː.mɪk, (US) -əˈræm.ɪk, -ˈrɑː.mɪk **-ally** -ᵊl.i, (US) -li
panpipe ˈpæn.paɪp, ˈpæm-, (US) ˈpæn- **-s** -s
Pan-Slavism ˌpænˈslɑː.vɪ.zᵊm, -ˈslæv.ɪ-
pans|y ˈpæn.z|i **-ies** -iz
pant pænt **-s** -s **-ing/ly** -ɪŋ/li, (US) ˈpæn.t̬ɪŋ/li **-ed** -ɪd, (US) ˈpæn.t̬ɪd
Pantagruel ˌpæn.tə.gruˈel; ˈpæn.tə.gru.əl, pænˈtæg.ru.əl, (US) ˌpæn.t̬ə.gruˈel; (US) -ˈgruː.əl; (US) pænˈtæg.ru.el
pantaloon ˌpæn.tᵊlˈuːn, ˈ---, (US) ˌpæn.t̬ᵊlˈuːn, ˈ--- **-s** -z
pantechnicon pænˈtek.nɪ.kən **-s** -z
panthe|ism ˈpænt.θi|.ɪ.zᵊm **-ist/s** -ɪst/s
pantheistic ˌpænt.θiˈɪs.tɪk **-al** -ᵊl
pantheon, P~ ˈpænt.θi.ən, (US) -ɑːn, -ən **-s** -z
panther ˈpænt.θəʳ, (US) -θɚ **-s** -z
pantie girdle ˈpæn.tiˌgɜː.dᵊl, (US) -t̬iˌgɝː- **-s** -z
panties ˈpæn.tiz, (US) -t̬iz
pantihose ˈpæn.ti.həʊz, (US) -t̬i.hoʊz
pantile ˈpæn.taɪl **-s** -z
panto ˈpæn.təʊ, (US) -toʊ **-s** -z
pantograph ˈpæn.təʊ.grɑːf, -græf, (US) -t̬ə.græf **-s** -s
pantographic ˌpæn.təʊˈgræf.ɪk, (US) -t̬əˈ- **-al** -ᵊl
pantomim|e ˈpæn.tə.maɪm, (US) -t̬ə- **-es** -z **-ist/s** -ɪst/s
pantomimic ˌpæn.təʊˈmɪm.ɪk, (US) -t̬əˈ- **-al** -ᵊl **-ally** -ᵊl.i, -li
pantr|y ˈpæn.tr|i **-ies** -iz
pants pænts
pantsuit ˈpænt.suːt, -sjuːt, (US) -suːt **-s** -s
pantyhose ˈpæn.ti.həʊz, (US) -t̬i.hoʊz
pantyliner ˈpæn.tiˌlaɪ.nəʳ, (US) -t̬iˌlaɪ.nɚ **-s** -z
Panza ˈpæn.zə
panzer ˈpænt.səʳ, ˈpæn.zəʳ, (US) ˈpæn.zɚ, ˈpɑːnt.sɚ **-s** -z
pap pæp **-s** -s **-ping** -ɪŋ **-ped** -t
papa pəˈpɑː, (US) ˈpɑː.pə; (US) pəˈpɑː **-s** -z
papac|y, P~ ˈpeɪ.pə.s|i **-ies** -iz
papal ˈpeɪ.pᵊl
papal|ism ˈpeɪ.pᵊl|.ɪ.zᵊm **-ist/s** -ɪst/s
Papandreou ˌpæp.ænˈdreɪ.uː

paparazz|o ˌpæp.ər'æt.s|əʊ, ⓤⓢ ˌpɑː.pɑː'rɑːt.s|oʊ -i -i
papaw 'pɔː.pɔː, pə'pɔː, ⓤⓢ pɔː'pɑː, -'ɔː, 'pɑː-, 'pɔː- -s -z
papaya pə'paɪ.ə, ⓤⓢ -'paɪ.ə, -'pɑː.jə -s -z
Papeete ˌpɑː.pi'eɪ.ti, -'iː-; pə'piː.ti, ⓤⓢ ˌpɑː.pi'eɪ.teɪ; ⓤⓢ pə'piː.ti
pap|er 'peɪ.p|əʳ, ⓤⓢ -p|ɚ -ers -əz, ⓤⓢ -ɚz -ering -ər.ɪŋ -ered -əd, ⓤⓢ -ɚ -erer/s -ər.əʳ/z, ⓤⓢ -ɚ.ɚ/z -ery -ər.i **ˌpaper 'bag; 'paper ˌboy; 'paper ˌchase; 'paper ˌclip; 'paper ˌknife; ˌpaper 'money; 'paper ˌround; ˌpaper 'tiger; 'paper ˌtrail**
paperback 'peɪ.pə.bæk, ⓤⓢ -pɚ- -s -s
paperbark 'peɪ.pə.bɑːk, ⓤⓢ -pɚ.bɑːrk -s -s
paperhang|er 'peɪ.pəˌhæŋ|.əʳ, ⓤⓢ -pɚˌhæŋ|.ɚ -ers -əz, ⓤⓢ -ɚz -ing -ɪŋ
paperless 'peɪ.pə.ləs, -lɪs, ⓤⓢ -pɚ-
paperweight 'peɪ.pə.weɪt, ⓤⓢ -pɚ- -s -s
paperwork 'peɪ.pə.wɜːk, ⓤⓢ -pɚ.wɝːk
Paphlagoni|a ˌpæf.lə'gəʊ.ni|.ə, ⓤⓢ -'goʊ- -an/s -ən/z
Paphos 'pæf.ɒs, ⓤⓢ 'peɪ.fɑːs
papier-mâché ˌpæp.i.eɪ'mæʃ.eɪ, ˌpeɪ.pə'-, ⓤⓢ ˌpeɪ.pɚ.mə'ʃeɪ, ˌpæp.jeɪ-
papill|a pə'pɪl|.ə -ae -iː
papillary pə'pɪl.ər.i, ⓤⓢ 'pæp.ə.ler-; ⓤⓢ pə'pɪl.ɚ-
papillote 'pæp.ɪ.lɒt, -ləʊt, -jɒt, ⓤⓢ -ə.loʊt, 'pɑː.pə-, -joʊt -s -s
papist, P~ 'peɪ.pɪst -s -s
papistry 'peɪ.pɪ.stri
papoos|e pə'puːs, ⓤⓢ pæp'uːs, pə'puːs -es -ɪz
Papp pæp
papp|us, P~ 'pæp|.əs -i -aɪ
pappy 'pæp.i
paprika 'pæp.rɪ.kə; pə'priː-, ⓤⓢ pæp'riː-, pə'priː-
Papu|a 'pæp.u|.ə, 'pɑː.pu|-, -pju|-, ⓤⓢ 'pæp.ju|.ə, pɑː'puː|- -an/s -ən/z **ˌPapua New 'Guinea**
Papworth 'pæp.wəθ, -wɜːθ, ⓤⓢ -wɚθ, -wɝːθ
papyr|us pə'paɪə.r|əs, ⓤⓢ -'paɪ- -i -aɪ -uses -ə.sɪz
par, P~ pɑːʳ, ⓤⓢ pɑːr
para *paratrooper, paramilitary:* 'pær.ə, ⓤⓢ 'per.ə, 'pær- *Serbian monetary unit:* 'pɑː.rə, ⓤⓢ 'pɑː.rɑː, -'- -s -z
Pará *Brazilian river:* pə'rɑː
para- 'pær.ə; pə'ræ, ⓤⓢ 'per.ə, 'pær.ə; ⓤⓢ pə'ræ
Note: Prefix. Normally either carries primary or secondary stress on the first syllable, e.g. **parachute** /'pær.ə.ʃuːt/ ⓤⓢ /'per-/, **parabolic** /ˌpær.ə'bɒl.ɪk/ ⓤⓢ /ˌper.ə'bɑː.lɪk/, or primary stress on the second syllable, e.g. **paraboloid** /pə'ræb.əl.ɔɪd/ ⓤⓢ /-ə.lɔɪd/.
parable 'pær.ə.bəl, ⓤⓢ 'per-, 'pær- -s -z
parabola pə'ræb.əl.ə -s -z
parabolic ˌpær.ə'bɒl.ɪk, ⓤⓢ ˌper.ə'bɑː.lɪk, ˌpær- -al -əl -ally -əl.i, -li
paraboloid pə'ræb.əl.ɔɪd, ⓤⓢ -ə.lɔɪd -s -z
Paracelsus ˌpær.ə'sel.səs, ⓤⓢ ˌper-, ˌpær-
paracetamol ˌpær.ə'siː.tə.mɒl, -'set.ə-, ⓤⓢ ˌper.ə'siː.t̬ə.mɑːl, ˌpær-, -'set̬.ə-, -moʊl -s -z
para|chute 'pær.ə|.ʃuːt, ⓤⓢ 'per-, 'pær- -chutes -ʃuːts -chuting -ˌʃuː.tɪŋ, ⓤⓢ -ˌʃuː.t̬ɪŋ -chuted -ˌʃuː.tɪd, ⓤⓢ -ˌʃuː.t̬ɪd
parachutist 'pær.əˌʃuː.tɪst, ⓤⓢ 'per.əˌʃuː.t̬ɪst, 'pær- -s -s
Paraclete 'pær.ə.kliːt, ⓤⓢ 'per-, 'pær-
parad|e pə'reɪd -es -z -ing -ɪŋ -ed -ɪd **pa'rade ˌground**
paradigm 'pær.ə.daɪm, ⓤⓢ 'per-, 'pær-, -dɪm -s -z
paradigmatic ˌpær.ə.dɪg'mæt.ɪk, ⓤⓢ ˌper.ə.dɪg'mæt̬-, ˌpær- -al -əl -ally -əl.i, -li
paradisal ˌpær.ə'daɪ.səl, -zəl, ⓤⓢ ˌper.ə'daɪ-, ˌpær-
paradis|e, P~ 'pær.ə.daɪs, ⓤⓢ 'per-, 'pær-, -daɪz -es -ɪz
paradisiac ˌpær.ə'dɪs.i.æk, -'dɪz-, ⓤⓢ ˌper.ə'dɪs-, ˌpær-
paradisiacal ˌpær.ə.dɪ'saɪ.ə.kəl, -də'-, -'zaɪ-, ⓤⓢ ˌper.ə.dɪ'-, ˌpær-
Paradiso ˌpær.ə'diː.səʊ, ⓤⓢ ˌper.ə'diː.soʊ, ˌpær-
parador 'pær.ə.dɔːʳ, ⓤⓢ 'per.ə.dɔːr, 'pær- **paradores** ˌpær.ə'dɔː.reɪs, -rɪs, ⓤⓢ ˌper.ə'dɔːr.əs, ˌpær-, -'dɔːrz
parados 'pær.ə.dɒs, ⓤⓢ 'per.ə.dɑːs, 'pær- -es -ɪz
paradox 'pær.ə.dɒks, ⓤⓢ 'per.ə.dɑːks, 'pær- -es -ɪz
paradoxic|al ˌpær.ə'dɒk.sɪ.k|əl, ⓤⓢ ˌper.ə'dɑːk-, ˌpær- -ally -əl.i, -li -alness -əl.nəs, -nɪs
paraffin 'pær.ə.fɪn, -fiːn, ˌ--'-, ⓤⓢ 'per.ə.fɪn, 'pær-
paraffine ˌpær.ə'fiːn, ⓤⓢ 'per.ə.fɪn, 'pær-, -fiːn
paragliding 'pær.əˌglaɪ.dɪŋ, ⓤⓢ 'per.ə-, 'pær-
paragoge ˌpær.ə'gəʊ.dʒi, ⓤⓢ 'per.ə.goʊ-, 'pær- -s -z
paragogic ˌpær.ə'gɒdʒ.ɪk, ⓤⓢ ˌper.ə'gɑː.dʒɪk, ˌpær-
paragon 'pær.ə.gən, ⓤⓢ 'per.ə.gɑːn, 'pær-, -gən -s -z
paragraph 'pær.ə.grɑːf, -græf, ⓤⓢ 'per.ə.græf, 'pær- -s -s -ing -ɪŋ -ed -t
Paraguay 'pær.ə.gwaɪ, -gweɪ, ˌ--'-, ⓤⓢ 'per.ə.gweɪ, 'pær-, -gwaɪ
Paraguayan ˌpær.ə'gwaɪ.ən, -'gweɪ-, ⓤⓢ ˌper.ə'gweɪ-, ˌpær-, -'gwaɪ-
parakeet ˌpær.ə'kiːt, '---, ⓤⓢ 'per.ə.kiːt, 'pær- -s -s
paraldehyde pə'ræl.dɪ.haɪd, pær'æl-, -də-, ⓤⓢ pə'ræl.də-
paralexia ˌpær.ə'lek.si.ə, ⓤⓢ ˌper-, ˌpær-
paralinguistic ˌpær.ə.lɪŋ'gwɪs.tɪk, ⓤⓢ ˌper-, ˌpær- -s -s -ally -əl.i, -li
parallax 'pær.ə.læks, ⓤⓢ 'per-, 'pær- -es -ɪz
parallel 'pær.ə.lel, -əl.əl, ⓤⓢ 'per-, 'pær- -s -z -ing -ɪŋ -ed -d -ism -ɪ.zəm **ˌparallel 'bars**
parallelepiped ˌpær.ə.lel'ep.ɪ.ped, -əl.ə'lep-; ˌpær.əˌlel.ə'paɪ-, ⓤⓢ ˌper.əˌlel.ə'paɪ-, ˌpær-, -'pɪp.əd, -ed -s -z
parallelogram ˌpær.ə'lel.ə.græm, ⓤⓢ ˌper-, ˌpær- -s -z
paralympian ˌpær.ə'lɪm.pi.ən, ⓤⓢ ˌper- -s -z
Paralympics ˌpær.ə'lɪm.pɪks, ⓤⓢ ˌper-, ˌpær-
paralys|e, -lyz|e 'pær.əl.aɪz, ⓤⓢ 'per-, 'pær- -es -ɪz -ing -ɪŋ -ed -d -er/s -əʳ/z, ⓤⓢ -ɚ/z
paralys|is pə'ræl.ə.s|ɪs, pər'æl-, '-ɪ-, ⓤⓢ '-ə- -es -iːz
paralytic ˌpær.ə'lɪt.ɪk, ⓤⓢ ˌper.ə'lɪt̬-, ˌpær- -s -s
paralyzation ˌpær.əl.aɪ'zeɪ.ʃən, ⓤⓢ ˌper.ə.lɪ'-, ˌpær-
Paramaribo ˌpær.ə'mær.ɪ.bəʊ, ⓤⓢ ˌper.ə'mer.ɪ.boʊ, ˌpær-, -'mær-
paramatta, P~ ˌpær.ə'mæt.ə, ⓤⓢ ˌper.ə'mæt̬-, ˌpær-
paramecium ˌpær.ə'miː.si.əm, ⓤⓢ ˌper-, ˌpær-, -ʃi-
paramedic ˌpær.ə'med.ɪk, ⓤⓢ ˌper.ə'med-, ˌpær-, 'per.əˌmed-, 'pær- -s -s -al -əl
parameter pə'ræm.ɪ.təʳ, pər'æm-, '-ə-, ⓤⓢ -ə.t̬ɚ -s -z
parametric ˌpær.ə'met.rɪk, ⓤⓢ ˌper-, ˌpær- -ally -əl.i, -li
paramilitar|y ˌpær.ə'mɪl.ɪ.tər|.i, '-ə-, ⓤⓢ ˌper.ə'mɪl.ə.ter-, ˌpær- -ies -iz
paramount, P~ 'pær.ə.maʊnt, ⓤⓢ 'per-, 'pær- -ly -li
paramour 'pær.ə.mʊəʳ, -mɔːʳ, ⓤⓢ 'per.ə.mʊr, 'pær- -s -z
Paraná pær.æn'ɑː
paranoi|a ˌpær.ə'nɔɪ|.ə, ⓤⓢ ˌper-, ˌpær- -ac -æk
paranoid 'pær.ən.ɔɪd, ⓤⓢ 'per.ə.nɔɪd, 'pær-
paranormal ˌpær.ə'nɔː.məl, ⓤⓢ ˌper.ə'nɔːr-, ˌpær- -ly -i
parape|t 'pær.ə.pɪ|t, -pe|t, -pə|t, ⓤⓢ 'per.ə.pe|t, 'pær-, -pə|t -ts -ts -ted -tɪd, ⓤⓢ -t̬ɪd
paraphernalia ˌpær.ə.fə'neɪ.li.ə, ⓤⓢ ˌper.ə.fɚ'neɪl.jə, ˌpær-, -'neɪ.li.ə
paraphras|e 'pær.ə.freɪz, ⓤⓢ 'per-, 'pær- -es -ɪz -ing -ɪŋ -ed -d
paraphrastic ˌpær.ə'fræs.tɪk, ⓤⓢ ˌper-, ˌpær- -ally -əl.i, -li
parapleg|ia ˌpær.ə'pliː.dʒ|ə, -dʒi|.ə, ⓤⓢ ˌper-, ˌpær- -ic/s -ɪk
paraprax|is ˌpær.ə'præk.s|ɪs, ⓤⓢ ˌper-, ˌpær- -es -ɪz

parapsychologic ˌpær.əˌsaɪ.kəˈlɒdʒ.ɪk, -kəlˈɒdʒ-, ⓊⓈ ˌper.ə.saɪ.kəˈlɑː.dʒɪk, ˌpær- **-al** -əl **-ally** -əl.i, -li
parapsycholog|y ˌpær.ə.saɪˈkɒl.ə.dʒ|i, -psaɪˈ-, ⓊⓈ ˌper.ə.saɪˈkɑː.lə-, ˌpær- **-ist/s** -ɪst/s
Paraquat® ˈpær.ə.kwɒt, -kwæt, ⓊⓈ ˈper.ə.kwɑːt, ˈpær-
parasailing ˈpær.əˌseɪ.lɪŋ, ⓊⓈ ˈper-, ˈpær-
parasang ˈpær.ə.sæŋ, ⓊⓈ ˈper-, ˈpær- **-s** -z
parascend|ing ˈpær.əˌsen.d|ɪŋ, ⓊⓈ ˈper-, ˈpær- **-er/s** -əʳ/z, ⓊⓈ -ɚ/z
parasite ˈpær.ə.saɪt, ⓊⓈ ˈper-, ˈpær- **-s** -s
parasitic ˌpær.əˈsɪt.ɪk, ⓊⓈ ˌper.əˈsɪţ-, ˌpær- **-al** -əl **-ally** -əl.i, -li **-alness** -əl.nəs, -nɪs
parasitolog|y ˌpær.ə.saɪˈtɒl.ə.dʒ|i, -sɪˈ-, ⓊⓈ ˌper.ə.saɪˈtɑː.lə-, ˌpær-, -sɪˈ- **-ist/s** -ɪst/s
parasol ˈpær.ə.sɒl, ˌ--ˈ-, ⓊⓈ ˈper.ə.sɔːl, ˈpær-, -sɑːl **-s** -z
paratactic ˌpær.əˈtæk.tɪk, ⓊⓈ ˌper-, ˌpær-
parataxis ˌpær.əˈtæk.sɪs, ⓊⓈ ˌper-, ˌpær-
parathyroid ˌpær.əˈθaɪə.rɔɪd, ⓊⓈ ˌper.əˈθaɪ-, ˌpær-
paratone ˈpær.ə.təʊn, ⓊⓈ ˈper.ə.toʊn, ˈpær- **-s** -z
paratroop ˈpær.ə.truːp, ⓊⓈ ˈper-, ˈpær- **-s** -s **-er/s** -əʳ/z, ⓊⓈ -ɚ/z
paratyphoid ˌpær.əˈtaɪ.fɔɪd, ⓊⓈ ˌper-, ˌpær-
paravane ˈpær.ə.veɪn, ⓊⓈ ˈper-, ˈpær- **-s** -z
parboil ˈpɑː.bɔɪl, ⓊⓈ ˈpɑːr- **-s** -z **-ing** -ɪŋ **-ed** -d
parcel ˈpɑː.səl, ⓊⓈ ˈpɑːr- **-s** -z **-(l)ing** -ɪŋ **-(l)ed** -d **ˈparcel ˌpost**
parch pɑːtʃ, ⓊⓈ pɑːrtʃ **-es** -ɪz **-ing** -ɪŋ **-ed** -t **-edness** -t.nəs, -nɪs
Parcheesi® pɑːˈtʃiː.zi, ⓊⓈ pɑːr-
parchment, P~ ˈpɑːtʃ.mənt, ⓊⓈ ˈpɑːrtʃ- **-s** -s
pard pɑːd, ⓊⓈ pɑːrd **-s** -z
pardner ˈpɑːd.nəʳ, ⓊⓈ ˈpɑːrd.nɚ **-s** -z
Pardoe ˈpɑː.dəʊ, ⓊⓈ ˈpɑːr.doʊ
pardon ˈpɑː.dən, ⓊⓈ ˈpɑːr- **-s** -z **-ing** -ɪŋ **-ed** -d **-er/s** -əʳ/z, ⓊⓈ -ɚ/z
pardonab|le ˈpɑː.dən.ə.b|əl, ⓊⓈ ˈpɑːr- **-ly** -li **-leness** -əl.nəs, -nɪs
par|e peəʳ, ⓊⓈ per **-es** -z **-ing** -ɪŋ **-ed** -d
paregoric ˌpær.ɪˈgɒr.ɪk, -əˈ-, ⓊⓈ ˌper.əˈgɔːr.ɪk, ˌpær-
paren|t ˈpeə.rən|t, ⓊⓈ ˈper.ən|t, ˈpær- **-ts** -ts **-tage** -tɪdʒ, ⓊⓈ -ţɪdʒ
parental pəˈren.təl, ⓊⓈ -ţəl **-ly** -i
parenthes|is pəˈrent.θə.s|ɪs, -θɪ-, ⓊⓈ -θə- **-es** -iːz
parenthesiz|e, -is|e pəˈrent.θə.saɪz, -θɪ-, ⓊⓈ -θə- **-es** -ɪz **-ing** -ɪŋ **-ed** -d
parenthetic ˌpær.ənˈθet.ɪk, -enˈ-, ⓊⓈ ˌper.ənˈθeţ-, ˌpær- **-al** -əl **-ally** -əl.i, -li

parenthood ˈpeə.rənt.hʊd, ⓊⓈ ˈper.ənt-, ˈpær-
parenting ˈpeə.rən.tɪŋ, ⓊⓈ ˈper.ən.ţɪŋ, ˈpær-
parentless ˈpeə.rənt.ləs, -lɪs, ⓊⓈ ˈper.ənt-, ˈpær-
parent-teacher ˌpeə.rəntˈtiː.tʃəʳ, ⓊⓈ ˌper.əntˈtiː.tʃɚ, ˌpær- **ˌparent-ˈteacher associˌation**
pareo pɑːˈreɪ.əʊ, ⓊⓈ -oʊ **-s** -z
paresis pəˈriː.sɪs; ˈpær.ə-, ⓊⓈ pəˈriː-; ⓊⓈ ˈper.ə-, ˈpær-
paretic pəˈret.ɪk, ⓊⓈ -ˈreţ-, -ˈriː.ţɪk
pareu pɑːˈreɪ.uː **-s** -z
par excellence ˌpɑːʳˈek.səl.ɑ̃ːns, -sel-, -ɑːnts, ˌpɑːʳ.ek.sәlˈɑ̃ːns, -selˈ-, -ˈɑːnts, ⓊⓈ ˌpɑːrˌek.səˈlɑːnts
parfait ˌpɑːˈfeɪ, ˈ--, ⓊⓈ pɑːrˈfeɪ **-s** -z
Parfitt ˈpɑː.fɪt, ⓊⓈ ˈpɑːr-
parfum ˈpɑː.fʌm, ⓊⓈ pɑːrˈfʌm
par|get ˈpɑː|.dʒɪt, ⓊⓈ ˈpɑːr- **-gets** -dʒɪts **-get(t)ing** -dʒɪ.tɪŋ, ⓊⓈ -dʒɪ.ţɪŋ **-get(t)ed** -dʒɪ.tɪd, ⓊⓈ -dʒɪ.ţɪd
Pargiter ˈpɑː.dʒɪ.təʳ, ⓊⓈ ˈpɑːr.dʒɪ.ţɚ
parheli|on pɑːˈhiː.li|.ən, -ɒn, ⓊⓈ pɑːrˈhiː-, -ˈhiːl.j|ən **-a** -ə
pariah pəˈraɪ.ə, ˈpær.i.ə, ⓊⓈ pəˈraɪ.ə **-s** -z
Parian ˈpeə.ri.ən, ⓊⓈ ˈper.i-, ˈpær- **-s** -z
parietal pəˈraɪ.ə.təl, -ˈraɪ.ɪ-, ⓊⓈ -ˈraɪ.ə-
paring ˈpeə.rɪŋ, ⓊⓈ ˈper.ɪŋ, ˈpær- **-s** -z
Paris ˈpær.ɪs, ⓊⓈ ˈper-, ˈpær-
parish, P~ ˈpær.ɪʃ, ⓊⓈ ˈper-, ˈpær- **-es** -ɪz **ˌparish ˈpriest**
parishioner pəˈrɪʃ.ən.əʳ, ⓊⓈ -ɚ **-s** -z
Parisian pəˈrɪz.i.ən, -ˈrɪʒ.ən, ⓊⓈ -ˈrɪʒ-, -ˈriː.ʒən **-s** -z
parisyllabic ˌpær.ɪ.sɪˈlæb.ɪk, ˌ-ə-, -səlˈæb-, ⓊⓈ ˌper-, ˌpær-
parity ˈpær.ə.ti, -ɪ.ti, ⓊⓈ ˈper.ə.ţi, ˈpær-
park, P~ pɑːk, ⓊⓈ pɑːrk **-s** -s **-ing** -ɪŋ **-ed** -t **ˈparking ˌlot; ˈparking ˌmeter; ˈparking ˌspace; ˈparking ˌticket; ˌpark-and-ˈride**
parka ˈpɑː.kə, ⓊⓈ ˈpɑːr- **-s** -z
Parke pɑːk, ⓊⓈ pɑːrk **-s** -s
Parker ˈpɑː.kəʳ, ⓊⓈ ˈpɑːr.kɚ
Parkestone ˈpɑːk.stən, ⓊⓈ ˈpɑːrk-
Parkhurst ˈpɑːk.hɜːst, ⓊⓈ ˈpɑːrk.hɝːst
parkin, P~ ˈpɑː.kɪn, ⓊⓈ ˈpɑːr-
parking meter ˈpɑː.kɪŋˌmiː.təʳ, ⓊⓈ ˈpɑːr.kɪŋˌmiː.ţɚ **-s** -z
Parkinson ˈpɑː.kɪn.sən, ⓊⓈ ˈpɑːr- **-ism** -ɪ.zəm **ˈParkinson's diˌsease**
parkland ˈpɑːk.lænd, ⓊⓈ ˈpɑːrk-
Parkman ˈpɑːk.mən, ⓊⓈ ˈpɑːrk-
parkour pɑːˈkʊəʳ; ⓊⓈ ˈpɑːr.kʊr, pɑːrˈkɔːr
Parks pɑːks, ⓊⓈ pɑːrks
Parkstone ˈpɑːk.stən, ⓊⓈ ˈpɑːrk-
parkway ˈpɑːk.weɪ, ⓊⓈ ˈpɑːrk- **-s** -z
park|y ˈpɑː.k|i, ⓊⓈ ˈpɑːr- **-ier** -i.əʳ, ⓊⓈ -i.ɚ **-iest** -i.ɪst, -i.əst

parlance ˈpɑː.lənts, ⓊⓈ ˈpɑːr-
parlay v ˈpɑː.li, ⓊⓈ ˈpɑːr.leɪ, -li; ⓊⓈ pɑːrˈleɪ **-s** -z **-ing** -ɪŋ **-ed** -d
parlay n ˈpɑː.li, ⓊⓈ ˈpɑːr.leɪ, -li **-s** -z
Parlement of Foules ˌpɑː.lə.mənt.əvˈfuːlz, ⓊⓈ ˌpɑːr-
parley, P~ ˈpɑː.li, ⓊⓈ ˈpɑːr- **-s** -z **-ing** -ɪŋ **-ed** -d
parliament, P~ ˈpɑː.lə.mənt, -lɪ-, -li.ə-, ⓊⓈ ˈpɑːr.lə- **-s** -s
parliamentarian, P~ ˌpɑː.lə.menˈteə.ri.ən, -lɪ-, -li.ə-, -mənˈ-, ⓊⓈ ˌpɑːr.lə.menˈter.i- **-s** -z
parliamentary ˌpɑː.ləˈmen.tər.i, -lɪˈ-, -li.əˈ-, ⓊⓈ ˌpɑːr.ləˈmen.ţɚ-, ˈ-tri
parlo(u)r ˈpɑː.ləʳ, ⓊⓈ ˈpɑːr.lɚ **-s** -z **ˈparlo(u)r ˌcar; ˈparlo(u)r ˌgame; ˈparlo(u)r ˌmaid**
parlous ˈpɑː.ləs, ⓊⓈ ˈpɑːr- **-ly** -li
Parma ˈpɑː.mə, ⓊⓈ ˈpɑːr- **ˌParma ˈham**
Parmar ˈpɑː.məʳ, ⓊⓈ ˈpɑːr.mɚ
Parmenter ˈpɑː.mɪn.təʳ, -mən-, ⓊⓈ ˈpɑːr.mən.tɚ
Parmesan ˈpɑː.mɪ.zæn, -mə-, ˌ--ˈ-, ⓊⓈ ˈpɑːr.mə.zɑːn, -ʒɑːn
Parminter ˈpɑː.mɪn.təʳ, ⓊⓈ ˈpɑːr.mɪn.tɚ
Parmiter ˈpɑː.mɪ.təʳ, ⓊⓈ ˈpɑːr.mɪ.ţɚ
Parnassian pɑːˈnæs.i.ən, ⓊⓈ pɑːr-
Parnassus pɑːˈnæs.əs, ⓊⓈ pɑːr-
Parnell pɑːˈnel; ˈpɑː.nəl, ⓊⓈ pɑːrˈnel; ⓊⓈ ˈpɑːr.nəl
parochial pəˈrəʊ.ki.əl, ⓊⓈ -ˈroʊ- **-ly** -i **-ism** -ɪ.zəm
parodist ˈpær.ə.dɪst, ⓊⓈ ˈper-, ˈpær- **-s** -s
parod|y ˈpær.ə.d|i, ⓊⓈ ˈper-, ˈpær- **-ies** -iz **-ying** -i.ɪŋ **-ied** -id
parol ˈpær.əl; pəˈrəʊl, ⓊⓈ -ˈroʊl, ˈper.əl, ˈpær-
parol|e pəˈrəʊl, ⓊⓈ -ˈroʊl **-es** -z **-ing** -ɪŋ **-ed** -d
Parolles pəˈrɒl.ɪz, -ɪs, -iːz, -es, -ez, ⓊⓈ pəˈrɑː.ləs
paronomazia, -sia ˌpær.ə.nəˈmeɪ.zi.ə, -si.ə, ˈ-ʒə, ⓊⓈ ˌper.ə.noʊˈmeɪ.ʒə, ˌpær-, ˈ-ʒi.ə
paronym ˈpær.ə.nɪm, ⓊⓈ ˈper-, ˈpær- **-s** -z
paronymy pəˈrɒn.ɪ.mi, pærˈɒn-, ˈ-ə-, ⓊⓈ pəˈrɑːn-
Paros ˈpær.ɒs, ⓊⓈ ˈper.ɑːs, ˈpær-, ˈpɑːr-
parotid pəˈrɒt.ɪd, ⓊⓈ -ˈrɑː.ţɪd **-s** -z
paroxysm ˈpær.ək.sɪ.zəm, -ɒk-; pəˈrɒk-, ⓊⓈ ˈper.ək-, ˈpær- **-s** -z
paroxysmal ˌpær.əkˈsɪz.məl, -ɒkˈ-, ⓊⓈ ˌper.əkˈ-, ˌpær-
paroxytone pəˈrɒk.sɪ.təʊn, pærˈɒk-, ⓊⓈ perˈɑːk.sɪ.toʊn, pær- **-s** -z
parquet ˈpɑː.keɪ, -ki, ⓊⓈ pɑːrˈkeɪ **-s** -z
parquetry ˈpɑː.kə.tri, -kɪ-, ⓊⓈ ˈpɑːr.kə-
parr, P~ pɑːʳ, ⓊⓈ pɑːr
parrakeet ˌpær.əˈkiːt, ˈ---, ⓊⓈ ˈper.ə.kiːt, ˈpær- **-s** -s

Parramatta ˌpær.əˈmæt.ə, (US) ˌper.əˈmæţ-, ˌpær-
Parratt ˈpær.ət, (US) ˈper-, ˈpær-
Parret ˈpær.ɪt, (US) ˈper-, ˈpær-
parricidal ˌpær.ɪˈsaɪ.dəl, -əˈ-, (US) ˌper.əˈ-, ˌpær-
parricide ˈpær.ɪ.saɪd, ˈ-ə-, (US) ˈper.ə-, ˈpær- **-s** -z
Parrish ˈpær.ɪʃ, (US) ˈper-, ˈpær-
parrot, P~ ˈpær.ət, (US) ˈper-, ˈpær- **-s** -s **-ing** -ɪŋ **-ed** -ɪd
parrot-fashion ˈpær.ətˌfæʃ.ən, (US) ˈper-, ˈpær-
parr|y, P~ ˈpær|.i, (US) ˈper-, ˈpær- **-ies** -iz **-ying** -i.ɪŋ **-ied** -id
pars|e pɑːz, (US) pɑːrs **-es** -ɪz **-ing** -ɪŋ **-ed** -d **-er/s** -əʳ/z, (US) -ɚ/z
Parsi, Parsee ˌpɑːˈsiː, ˈ--, (US) ˈpɑːr.siː, -ˈ- **-s** -z
Parsifal ˈpɑː.sɪ.fəl, -sə-, -fɑːl, -fæl, (US) ˈpɑːr.sə.fəl, -fɑːl
parsimonious ˌpɑː.sɪˈməʊ.ni.əs, -səˈ-, (US) ˌpɑːr.səˈmoʊ- **-ly** -li **-ness** -nəs, -nɪs
parsimony ˈpɑː.sɪ.mə.ni, -sə-, (US) ˈpɑːr.sə.moʊ-
parsley ˈpɑː.sli, (US) ˈpɑːr-
parsnip ˈpɑː.snɪp, (US) ˈpɑːr- **-s** -s
parson ˈpɑː.sən, (US) ˈpɑːr- **-s** -z **ˌparson's ˈnose**
parsonag|e ˈpɑː.sən.ɪdʒ, (US) ˈpɑːr- **-es** -ɪz
Parsons ˈpɑː.sənz, (US) ˈpɑːr-
part pɑːt, (US) pɑːrt **-s** -s **-ing** -ɪŋ, (US) ˈpɑːr.ţɪŋ **-ed** -ɪd, (US) ˈpɑːr.ţɪd **ˌpart and ˈparcel; ˌpart exˈchange; ˌparting ˈshot** (US) **ˈparting ˌshot; ˌpart of ˈspeech**
partak|e pɑːˈteɪk, (US) pɑːr- **-es** -s **-ing** -ɪŋ **partook** pɑːˈtʊk, (US) pɑːr- **partak|en** pɑːˈteɪ.k|ən, (US) pɑːr- **-er/s** -əʳ/z, (US) -ɚ/z
parterre pɑːˈteəʳ, (US) pɑːrˈter **-s** -z
Parthenia pɑːˈθiː.ni.ə, (US) pɑːr-
parthenogenesis ˌpɑː.θə.nəʊˈdʒen.ɪ.sɪs, -θɪ-, ˈ-ə-, (US) ˌpɑːr.θə.noʊˈdʒen.ə-
Parthenon ˈpɑː.θən.ən, -θɪ.nən, -nɒn, (US) ˈpɑːr.θə.nɑːn, -nən **-s** -z
Parthenope pɑːˈθen.ə.pi, (US) pɑːr-
Parthi|a ˈpɑː.θi|.ə, (US) ˈpɑːr- **-an/s** -ən/z
partial ˈpɑː.ʃəl, (US) ˈpɑːr- **-ly** -i
partiality ˌpɑː.ʃiˈæl.ə.ti, -ɪ.ti, (US) ˌpɑːr.ʃiˈæl.ə.ţi
participant pɑːˈtɪs.ɪ.pənt, ˈ-ə-, (US) pɑːrˈtɪs.ə-, pɚ- **-s** -s
partici|pate pɑːˈtɪs.ɪ|.peɪt, ˈ-ə-, (US) pɑːrˈtɪs.ə-, pɚ- **-pates** -peɪts **-pating** -peɪ.tɪŋ, (US) -peɪ.ţɪŋ **-pated** -peɪ.tɪd, (US) -peɪ.ţɪd **-pator/s** -peɪ.təʳ/z, (US) -peɪ.ţɚ/z
participation pɑːˌtɪs.ɪˈpeɪ.ʃən, ˌpɑː.tɪ.sɪˈ-, -səˈ-, (US) pɑːrˌtɪs.əˈ-, pɚ- **-s** -z
participatory pɑːˈtɪs.ɪ.pə.tər.i, ˈ-ə-; ˌpɑː.tɪ.sɪˈpeɪ-, -səˈ-, (US) pɑːrˈtɪs.ə.pəˌtɔːr-, pɚ-
participial ˌpɑː.tɪˈsɪp.i.əl, -təˈ-, (US) ˌpɑːr.ţɪˈ- **-ly** -i
participle pɑːˈtɪs.ɪ.pəl, ˈ-ə-, (US) ˈpɑːr.tɪ.sɪ- **-s** -z
particle ˈpɑː.tɪ.kəl, -tə-, (US) ˈpɑːr.ţə- **-s** -z
particleboard ˈpɑː.tɪ.kəlˌbɔːd, (US) ˈpɑːr.ţɪ.kəlˌbɔːrd
particolo(u)red ˈpɑː.tiˌkʌl.əd, ˌpɑː.tiˈkʌl-, (US) ˈpɑːr.ţiˌkʌl.ɚd
particular pəˈtɪk.jə.ləʳ, -jʊ-, (US) pɚˈtɪk.jə.lɚ, -juː- **-s** -z **-ly** -li
particularit|y pəˌtɪk.jəˈlær.ə.t|i, -jʊˈ-, -ɪ.t|i, (US) pɚˌtɪk.jəˈler.ə.ţ|i, -juːˈ-, -ˈlær- **-ies** -iz
particulariz|e, -is|e pəˈtɪk.jə.lər.aɪz, -jʊ-, (US) pɚˈtɪk.jə.lə.raɪz, -juː- **-es** -ɪz **-ing** -ɪŋ **-ed** -d
particulate pɑːˈtɪk.jə.lət, -jʊ-, (US) pɑːr-
parting ˈpɑː.tɪŋ, (US) ˈpɑːr.ţɪŋ **-s** -z
Partington ˈpɑː.tɪŋ.tən, (US) ˈpɑːr.ţɪŋ-
partisan ˌpɑː.tɪˈzæn, -təˈ-, ˈ---, (US) ˈpɑːr.ţɪ.zən, -zæn **-s** -z **-ship/s** -ʃɪp/s
partita pɑːˈtiː.tə, (US) pɑːrˈtiː.ţə
partite ˈpɑː.taɪt, (US) ˈpɑːr-
partition pɑːˈtɪʃ.ən, pə-, (US) pɑːr- **-s** -z **-ing** -ɪŋ **-ed** -d
partitive ˈpɑː.tɪ.tɪv, -tə-, (US) ˈpɑːr.ţə.ţɪv **-ly** -li
partly ˈpɑːt.li, (US) ˈpɑːrt-
partn|er ˈpɑːt.n|əʳ, (US) ˈpɑːrt.n|ɚ **-ers** -əz, (US) -ɚz **-ering** -ər.ɪŋ **-ered** -əd, (US) -ɚd
partnership ˈpɑːt.nə.ʃɪp, (US) ˈpɑːrt.nɚ- **-s** -s
Parton ˈpɑː.tən, (US) ˈpɑːr-
partook (from **partake**) pɑːˈtʊk, (US) pɑːr-
partridg|e, P~ ˈpɑː.trɪdʒ, (US) ˈpɑːr- **-es** -ɪz
part-singing ˈpɑːtˌsɪŋ.ɪŋ, (US) ˈpɑːrt-
part-song ˈpɑːt.sɒŋ, (US) ˈpɑːrt.sɑːŋ, -sɔːŋ **-s** -z
part-tim|e ˌpɑːtˈtaɪm, (US) ˌpɑːrt-, ˈ-- **-er/s** -əʳ/z, (US) -ɚ/z *stress shift, British only:* **ˌpart-time ˈjob**
parturition ˌpɑː.tʃʊəˈrɪʃ.ən, -tjʊəˈ-, -tʃərˈɪʃ-, (US) ˌpɑːr.tuːˈrɪʃ-, -tjuːˈ-, -ţəˈ-, -tʃəˈ- **-s** -z
partway ˌpɑːtˈweɪ, (US) ˌpɑːrt- *stress shift:* **ˌpartway ˈthere**
part|y ˈpɑː.t|i, (US) ˈpɑːr.ţ|i **-ies** -iz **-ying** -i.ɪŋ **-ied** -id **ˈparty ˌpiece; ˌparty ˈwall**
partygoer ˈpɑː.tiˌgəʊ.əʳ, (US) ˈpɑːr.ţiˌgoʊ.ɚ **-s** -z
party line *in politics:* ˌpɑː.tiˈlaɪn, (US) ˌpɑːr.ţiˈ- *telephone:* ˈpɑː.ti.laɪn, (US) ˈpɑːr.ţi-
party poop|er ˈpɑː.tiˌpuː.p|əʳ, (US) ˈpɑːr.ţiˌpuː.p|ɚ **-ers** -əz, (US) -ɚz **-ing** -ɪŋ
party-spirit ˌpɑː.tiˈspɪr.ɪt, (US) ˌpɑːr.ţiˈ-
parvenu(e) ˈpɑː.və.njuː, -nuː, (US) ˈpɑːr.və.nuː, -njuː **-s** -z
Parzival ˈpɑː.t.sɪ.fɑːl, (US) ˈpɑːrt-
pas *singular:* pɑː *plural:* pɑːz, pɑː
Pasadena ˌpæs.əˈdiː.nə
Pascal, PASCAL pæsˈkæl, -ˈkɑːl, (US) pæsˈkæl, pɑːˈskæl, ˈ--
paschal ˈpæs.kəl, ˈpɑː.skəl, (US) ˈpæs.kəl
pas de deux ˌpɑː.dəˈdɜː
pasha, P~ ˈpɑː.ʃə, ˈpæʃ.ə; pəˈʃɑː **-s** -z
pashmina pæʃˈmiː.nə **-s** -z
Pashtun pæʃˈtuːn, ˈpɑːʃ-
Pasiphae pəˈsɪf.i.iː, -eɪ, (US) ˈ-ə.i
paso doble ˌpæs.əʊˈdəʊ.bleɪ, (US) ˌpɑː.soʊˈdoʊ-
Pasolini ˌpæs.əʊˈliː.ni, (US) -oʊˈ-
pasquinade ˌpæs.kwɪˈneɪd, -kwəˈ-, (US) -kwɪˈ- **-s** -z
pass pɑːs, (US) pæs **-es** -ɪz **-ing** -ɪŋ **-ed** -t **-er/s** -əʳ/z, (US) -ɚ/z **ˈpass deˌgree; ˈpass ˌlaw**
passab|le ˈpɑː.sə.b|əl, (US) ˈpæs.ə- **-ly** -li **-leness** -əl.nəs, -nɪs
passacaglia ˌpæs.əˈkɑː.li.ə, -ˈkæl.jə, (US) ˌpɑː.səˈkɑːl.jə, ˌpæs.əˈ-, -ˈkæl- **-s** -z
passag|e ˈpæs.ɪdʒ **-es** -ɪz **-ing** -ɪŋ **-ed** -d
passageway ˈpæs.ɪdʒ.weɪ **-s** -z
passant *in heraldry:* ˈpæs.ənt *in chess:* pæsˈɑ̃ːŋ, pɑːˈsɑːŋ, (US) ˈpæs.ənt
Passat® pæsˈæt, -ˈɑːt, (US) pəˈsɑːt, pæsˈɑːt
passbook ˈpɑːs.bʊk, (US) ˈpæs- **-s** -s
passé(e) pæsˈeɪ, pɑːˈseɪ, ˈ--, (US) pæsˈeɪ, ˈ--; (US) pɑːˈseɪ
Passe pæs
passenger ˈpæs.ən.dʒəʳ, -ɪn-, (US) -ən.dʒɚ **-s** -z
passe-partout ˌpæs.pəˈtuː, ˌpɑːs-, -pɑːˈ-, ˈ---, (US) ˌpæs.pɑːrˈ-, ˌpɑːs- **-s** -z
passer-by ˌpɑː.səˈbaɪ, (US) ˌpæs.ɚˈ- **passers-by** ˌpɑː.səzˈbaɪ, (US) ˌpæs.ɚzˈ-
passerine ˈpæs.ə.raɪn, -riːn, (US) -ə.raɪn, -ɚ.ɪn
Passfield ˈpæs.fiːld, ˈpɑːs-, (US) ˈpæs-
passibility ˌpæs.əˈbɪl.ə.ti, -ɪˈ-, -ɪ.ti, (US) -ɪˈbɪl.ə.ţi
passible ˈpæs.ɪ.bəl, ˈ-ə-, (US) ˈ-ɪ-
passim ˈpæs.ɪm
passing note ˈpɑː.sɪŋˌnəʊt, (US) ˈpæs.ɪŋˌnoʊt **-s** -s
passion, P~ ˈpæʃ.ən **-s** -z **ˈpassion ˌplay**
passionate ˈpæʃ.ən.ət, -ɪt, (US) -ə.nɪt **-ly** -li **-ness** -nəs, -nɪs
passionflower ˈpæʃ.ənˌflaʊəʳ, -ˌflaʊ.əʳ, (US) -ˌflaʊ.ɚ **-s** -z
passionfruit ˈpæʃ.ən.fruːt **-s** -s
Passiontide ˈpæʃ.ən.taɪd
passive ˈpæs.ɪv **-ly** -li **-ness** -nəs, -nɪs **ˌpassive ˈsmoking**
passivity pæsˈɪv.ə.ti, pəˈsɪv-, -ɪ.ti, (US) pæsˈɪv.ə.ţi
passivization, -isa- ˌpæs.ɪ.vaɪˈzeɪ.ʃən, ˌ-ə-, -vəˈ-, (US) -ɪ.vɪˈ-
passiviz|e, -is|e ˈpæs.ɪ.vaɪz, ˈ-ə-, (US) ˈ-ɪ- **-es** -ɪz **-ing** -ɪŋ **-ed** -d

P

pass-key ˈpɑːs.kiː, (US) ˈpæs- **-s** -z
Passmore ˈpɑːs.mɔːʳ, ˈpæs-, (US) ˈpæs.mɔːr
Passover ˈpɑːsˌəʊ.vəʳ, (US) ˈpæsˌoʊ.vɚ **-s** -z
passport ˈpɑːs.pɔːt, (US) ˈpæs.pɔːrt **-s** -s
password ˈpɑːs.wɜːd, (US) ˈpæs.wɝːd **-s** -z
past pɑːst, (US) pæst **ˌpast parˈticiple** (US) **ˌpast ˈparticiple; ˌpast ˈperfect; ˌpast ˈtense**
pasta ˈpæs.tə, ˈpɑː.stə, (US) ˈpɑː.stə
past|e peɪst **-es** -s **-ing** -ɪŋ **-ed** -ɪd
pasteboard ˈpeɪst.bɔːd, (US) -bɔːrd
pastel ˈpæs.tᵊl, -tel; pæsˈtel, (US) pæsˈtel **-s** -z
pastelist ˈpæs.tᵊl.ɪst, (US) pæsˈtel-; (US) ˈpæs.tᵊl- **-s** -s
pastern ˈpæs.tɜːn, -tən, (US) -tɚn **-s** -z
Pasternak ˈpæs.tə.næk, (US) -tɚ-
paste-up ˈpeɪst.ʌp **-s** -s
Pasteur pæsˈtɜːʳ, pɑːˈstɜːʳ, (US) pæsˈtɝː, pɑːˈstɝː
pasteurization, -isa- ˌpæs.tʃᵊr.aɪˈzeɪ.ʃᵊn, ˌpɑːs-, -tʃᵊr-, -tᵊr-, -ɪˈ-, (US) ˌpæs.tʃɚ.əˈ-, -tɚ-
pasteuriz|e, -is|e ˈpæs.tʃᵊr.aɪz, ˈpɑːs-, -tʃᵊr-, -tᵊr-, (US) ˈpæs.tʃə.raɪz, -tə- **-es** -ɪz **-ing** -ɪŋ **-ed** -d
pastich|e pæsˈtiːʃ, ˈ--, (US) pæsˈtiːʃ, pɑːˈstiːʃ **-es** -ɪz
pastille ˈpæs.tᵊl, -tɪl, -tiːl; pæsˈtiːl, (US) pæsˈtiːl **-s** -z
pastime ˈpɑːs.taɪm, (US) ˈpæs- **-s** -z
pastis pæsˈtiːs
past-master ˌpɑːstˈmɑː.stəʳ, ˈ-ˌ--, (US) ˈpæstˌmæs.tɚ, ˌ-ˈ-- **-s** -z
Paston ˈpæs.tᵊn
pastor ˈpɑː.stəʳ, (US) ˈpæs.tɚ **-s** -z
pastoral ˈpɑː.stᵊr.ᵊl, ˈpæs.tᵊr-, (US) ˈpæs.tᵊr- **-s** -z
pastorale ˌpæs.tᵊrˈɑːl, -ˈæl, -ˈɑː.leɪ, (US) -təˈrɑːl, -ˈræl, -ˈrɑː.leɪ **-s** -z
pastoralism ˈpɑː.stᵊr.ᵊl.ɪ.zᵊm, ˈpæs.tᵊr-, (US) ˈpæs.tᵊr-
pastorate ˈpɑː.stᵊr.ət, -ɪt, (US) ˈpæs.tɚ.ɪt **-s** -s
pastrami pæsˈtrɑː.mi, pəˈstrɑː-, (US) pəˈstrɑː-
pastr|y ˈpeɪ.str|i **-ies** -iz
pastrycook ˈpeɪ.stri.kʊk **-s** -s
pasturage ˈpɑːs.tʃʊ.rɪdʒ, ˈpɑː.stjʊ-, -tʃᵊr.ɪdʒ, -tjᵊr-, (US) ˈpæs.tʃɚ.ɪdʒ, -tjɚ-
past|ure ˈpɑːs.tʃ|əʳ, ˈpɑː.stj|əʳ, (US) ˈpæs.tʃ|ɚ, -tj|ɚ **-ures** -əz, (US) -ɚz **-uring** -ᵊr.ɪŋ **-ured** -əd, (US) -ɚd
pastureland ˈpɑːs.tʃə.lænd, ˈpɑː.stjə-, (US) ˈpæs.tʃɚ-, -tjɚ-
past|y n ˈpæs.t|i; *for the Cornish kind also:* ˈpɑː.st|i, (US) ˈpæs.t|i **-ies** -iz
past|y adj ˈpeɪ.st|i **-ier** -i.əʳ, (US) -i.ɚ **-iest** -i.ɪst, -i.əst **-ily** -ᵊl.i, -ɪ.li **-iness** -ɪ.nəs, -ɪ.nɪs
pat, P~ pæt **-s** -s **-ting** -ɪŋ, (US) ˈpæt̬.ɪŋ **-ted** -ɪd, (US) ˈpæt̬.ɪd

pat-a-cake ˈpæt.ə.keɪk, (US) ˈpæt̬- **-s** -s
Patagoni|a ˌpæt.əˈgəʊ.ni|.ə, (US) ˌpæt̬.əˈgoʊ-, ˈ-nj|ə **-an/s** -ən/z
Pataki pəˈtɑːk.i, -ˈtæk-
Patara ˈpæt.ᵊr.ə
patch pætʃ **-es** -ɪz **-ing** -ɪŋ **-ed** -t
patchouli, patchouly pəˈtʃuː.li; ˈpætʃ.ʊ.li, -ᵊl.i, (US) ˈpætʃ.uː.li; (US) pəˈtʃuː-
patchwork ˈpætʃ.wɜːk, (US) -wɝːk **-s** -s **ˌpatchwork ˈquilt**
patch|y ˈpætʃ|.i **-ier** -i.əʳ, (US) -i.ɚ **-iest** -i.ɪst, -i.əst **-ily** -ᵊl.i, -ɪ.li **-iness** -ɪ.nəs, -ɪ.nɪs
pate peɪt **-s** -s
pâté ˈpæt.eɪ, -ˈ-, (US) pɑːˈteɪ, pætˈeɪ
pâté de foie ˌpæt.eɪ.dəˈfwɑː, (US) pɑːˌteɪ-, pætˌeɪ-
pâté de foie gras ˌpæt.eɪ.dəˌfwɑːˈgrɑː, (US) pɑːˌteɪ-, pætˌeɪ-
Patel pəˈtel, -ˈteɪl
Pateley ˈpeɪt.li
patell|a pəˈtel|.ə **-as** -əz **-ae** -iː **-ar** -əʳ, (US) -ɚ
paten ˈpæt.ᵊn **-s** -z
paten|t ˈpeɪ.tᵊn|t, ˈpæt.ᵊn|t, (US) ˈpæt-, ˈpeɪ.tᵊn|t **-ts** -ts **-ting** -tɪŋ, (US) -t̬ɪŋ **-ted** -tɪd, (US) -t̬ɪd **-table** -tə.bᵊl, (US) -t̬ə.bᵊl **ˌpatent ˈleather**

> Note: For British English, /ˈpæt.ᵊnt/ in **letters patent**. This pronunciation is used for the noun referring to legal protection of inventions, but rarely for the adjective in, for example, **patent medicine**; otherwise /ˈpeɪ.tᵊnt/ is more usual. For American English, the usual pronunciation is /ˈpæt.ᵊnt/, except for the meaning **obvious**, where /ˈpeɪ.tᵊnt/ is the normal form.

patentee ˌpeɪ.tᵊnˈtiː, ˌpæt.ᵊnˈ-, (US) ˌpæt.ᵊnˈtiː **-s** -z
patently ˈpeɪ.tᵊnt.li, (US) ˈpeɪ-, ˈpæt.ᵊnt-
pater, P~ ˈpeɪ.təʳ, ˈpɑː-, (US) ˈpeɪ.t̬ɚ, ˈpɑː- **-s** -z
Note: This word is never used to mean **father** in the US.
paterfamilias ˌpeɪ.tə.fəˈmɪl.i.æs, ˌpæt.ə-, -əs, (US) ˌpeɪ.t̬ɚ.fəˈmɪl.i.əs, ˌpɑː.t̬ɚ-, ˌpæt̬.ɚ-
paternal pəˈtɜː.nᵊl, (US) -ˈtɝː- **-ly** -li
paternal|ism pəˈtɜː.nᵊl|.ɪ.zᵊm, (US) -ˈtɝː- **-ist/s** -ɪst/s
paternalistic pəˌtɜː.nᵊlˈɪs.tɪk, (US) -ˌtɝː- **-ally** -ᵊl.i, -li
paternity pəˈtɜː.nə.ti, -nɪ-, (US) -ˈtɝː.nə.t̬i **paˈternity ˌleave; paˈternity ˌsuit; paˈternity ˌtest**
Paternoster *Lord's prayer:* ˌpæt.əˈnɒs.təʳ, (US) ˌpɑː.t̬ɚˈnɔː.stɚ, -ˈnoʊ- **-s** -z *Square:* ˈpæt.əˌnɒs.təʳ, (US) ˌpɑː.t̬ɚˈnɔː.stɚ, ˌpæt.ɚˈ-, ˌpeɪ.tɚˈ-, -ˈnɑː-

Paterson ˈpæt.ə.sᵊn, (US) ˈpæt̬.ɚ-
Patey ˈpeɪ.ti, (US) -t̬i
pa|th pɑː|θ, (US) pæ|θ **-ths** -ðz, (US) -θs, -ðz **ˌlead someone ˌup/ˌdown the ˌgarden ˈpath**
path. pæθ
-path pæθ
Note: Suffix. Normally unstressed, e.g. **psychopath** /ˈsaɪ.kəʊ.pæθ/ (US) /-kə-/.
Pathan pəˈtɑːn, (US) pəˈtɑːn, pətˈhɑːn **-s** -z
Pathé ˈpæθ.eɪ
pathetic pəˈθet.ɪk, (US) -ˈθet̬- **-ally** -ᵊl.i, -li
pathfinder, P~ ˈpɑːθˌfaɪn.dəʳ, (US) ˈpæθˌfaɪn.dɚ **-s** -z
-pathic ˈpæθ.ɪk
Note: Suffix. Words containing **-pathic** normally carry primary stress on the penultimate syllable, e.g. **psychopathic** /ˌsaɪ.kəʊˈpæθ.ɪk/ (US) /-kəˈ-/.
pathless ˈpɑːθ.ləs, -lɪs, (US) ˈpæθ-
patho- ˈpæθ.əʊ; pəˈθɒ, pæθˈɒ, (US) ˈpæθ.ə; (US) pəˈθɑː, pæθˈɑː
Note: Prefix. Normally either carries primary or secondary stress on the first syllable, e.g. **pathogen** /ˈpæθ.əʊ.dʒen/ (US) /-ə.dʒən/, **pathogenic** /ˌpæθ.əʊˈdʒen.ɪk/ (US) /-əˈ-/, or primary stress on the second syllable, e.g. **pathology** /pəˈθɒl.ə.dʒi/ (US) /-ˈθɑː.lə-/.
pathogen ˈpæθ.əʊ.dʒən, -dʒen, (US) -ə.dʒən **-s** -z
pathogenesis ˌpæθ.əʊˈdʒen.ə.sɪs, ˈ-ɪ-, (US) ˈ-ə-
pathogenic ˌpæθ.əʊˈdʒen.ɪk, (US) -əˈ- **-ally** -ᵊl.i, -li
pathologic ˌpæθ.əˈlɒdʒ.ɪk, (US) -ˈlɑː.dʒɪk **-al** -ᵊl **-ally** -ᵊl.i, -li
patholog|y pəˈθɒl.ə.dʒ|i, pæθˈɒl-, (US) pəˈθɑː.lə- **-ist/s** -ɪst/s
pathos ˈpeɪ.θɒs, (US) -θɑːs
pathway ˈpɑːθ.weɪ, (US) ˈpæθ- **-s** -z
-pathy pə.θi
Note: Suffix. Normally unstressed, e.g. **telepathy** /təˈlep.ə.θi/.
patience, P~ ˈpeɪ.ʃᵊnts
patient ˈpeɪ.ʃᵊnt **-s** -s **-ly** -li
patina ˈpæt.ɪ.nə, -ᵊn.ə; pəˈtiː.nə, (US) ˈpæt.ᵊn.ə; (US) pəˈtiː.nə
patio ˈpæt.i.əʊ, (US) ˈpæt̬.i.oʊ, ˈpɑː.t̬i- **-s** -z
patisserie pəˈtiː.sᵊr.i, pætˈɪs- **-s** -z
Patman ˈpæt.mən
Patmore ˈpæt.mɔːʳ, (US) -mɔːr
Patmos ˈpæt.mɒs, (US) -məs, ˈpɑːt-, -mɑːs
Patna ˈpæt.nə, ˈpʌt-, (US) ˈpʌt-, ˈpæt-
patois *singular:* ˈpæt.wɑː *plural:* -z
Paton ˈpeɪ.tᵊn
Patou ˈpæt.uː; *as if French:* -ˈ-
Patras pəˈtræs; ˈpæt.rəs
patrial ˈpeɪ.tri.əl, ˈpæt.ri-, (US) ˈpeɪ.tri-
patriarch ˈpeɪ.tri.ɑːk, ˈpæt.ri-, (US) ˈpeɪ.tri.ɑːrk **-s** -s **-y** -i **-ies** -iz

patriarch|al ˌpeɪ.triˈɑː.k|əl, ˌpæt.riˈ-, (US) ˌpeɪ.triˈɑːr- **-ic** -ɪk
patriarchate ˈpeɪ.tri.ɑː.kɪt, ˈpæt.ri-, -keɪt, -kət, (US) ˈpeɪ.tri.ɑːr.kɪt, -keɪt **-s** -s
Patricia pəˈtrɪʃ.ə, (US) -ˈtrɪʃ-, -ˈtriː.ʃə
patrician pəˈtrɪʃ.ən **-s** -z
patriciate pəˈtrɪʃ.i.ət, -ˈtrɪʃ.ət, (US) -ˈtrɪs.i-, -ɪt, -eɪt, -trɪʃ.i.ɪt, -eɪt; (US) -ˈtrɪʃ.ɪt
patricide ˈpæt.rɪ.saɪd, ˈpeɪ.trɪ-, -trə-, (US) ˈpæt.rə- **-s** -z
Patrick ˈpæt.rɪk
patrilineal ˌpæt.rɪˈlɪn.i.əl, -rəˈ-, (US) ˌpæt.rəˈ-
patrimonial ˌpæt.rɪˈməʊ.ni.əl, -rəˈ-, (US) ˌpæt.rəˈmoʊ- **-ly** -i
patrimon|y ˈpæt.rɪ.mə.n|i, -rə-, (US) -rə.moʊ- **-ies** -iz
patriot ˈpeɪ.tri.ət, ˈpæt.ri-, (US) ˈpeɪ-, -ɑːt **-s** -s
patriotic ˌpæt.riˈɒt.ɪk, ˌpeɪ.triˈ-, (US) ˌpeɪ.triˈɑː.t̬ɪk **-ally** -əl.i, -li
patriotism ˈpeɪ.tri.ə.tɪ.zəm, ˈpæt.ri-, (US) ˈpeɪ.tri-
patristic pəˈtrɪs.tɪk **-s** -s **-al** -əl
Patroclus pəˈtrɒk.ləs, (US) -ˈtroʊ.kləs; (US) ˈpæt.roʊ-
patrol pəˈtrəʊl, (US) -ˈtroʊl **-s** -z **-ling** -ɪŋ **-led** -d
patrolcar pəˈtrəʊl.kɑːr, (US) -ˈtroʊl.kɑːr **-s** -z
patrol|man pəˈtrəʊl|.mən, -mæn, (US) -ˈtroʊl- **-men** -mən, -men
patron ˈpeɪ.trən, ˈpæt.rən, (US) ˈpeɪ.trən **-s** -z
patronage ˈpæt.rən.ɪdʒ, ˈpeɪ.trən-, (US) ˈpeɪ.trən-, ˈpæt.rən-
patronal pəˈtrəʊ.nəl, pætˈrəʊ-, (US) ˈpeɪ.trən.əl, ˈpæt.rən-; (US) pəˈtroʊ.nəl
patroness ˌpeɪ.trəˈnes, ˌpæt.rəˈ-; ˈpeɪ.trən.es, ˈpæt.rən-, -ɪs, -əs, (US) ˈpeɪ.trə.nɪs **-es** -ɪz
patroniz|e, -is|e ˈpæt.rən.aɪz, (US) ˈpeɪ.trən-, ˈpæt.rən- **-es** -ɪz **-ing/ly** -ɪŋ/li **-ed** -d
patronymic ˌpæt.rəˈnɪm.ɪk, (US) -rəˈ-, -roʊˈ- **-s** -s
patroon pəˈtruːn **-s** -z
pats|y, P~ ˈpæt.s|i **-ies** -iz
patten, P~ ˈpæt.ən **-s** -z
patt|er ˈpæt|.ər, (US) ˈpæt̬|.ɚ **-ers** -əz, (US) -ɚz **-ering** -ər.ɪŋ **-ered** -əd, (US) -ɚd
Patterdale ˈpæt.ə.deɪl, (US) ˈpæt̬.ɚ-
pattern ˈpæt.ən, (US) ˈpæt̬.ɚn **-s** -z **-ing** -ɪŋ **-ed** -d
Patterson ˈpæt.ə.sən, (US) ˈpæt̬.ɚ-
Patteson ˈpæt.ɪ.sən, ˈ-ə-, (US) ˈpæt̬-
Patti(e) ˈpæt.i, (US) ˈpæt̬-
Pattison ˈpæt.ɪ.sən, (US) ˈpæt̬-
Patton ˈpæt.ən
patt|y ˈpæt|.i, (US) ˈpæt̬- **-ies** -iz
paucity ˈpɔː.sə.ti, -sɪ-, (US) ˈpɑː.sə.t̬i, ˈpɔː-
Paul pɔːl, (US) pɔːl, pɑːl **-'s** -z ˌ**Paul** ˈ**Jones**
Paula ˈpɔː.lə, (US) ˈpɑː-, ˈpɔː-
Paulding ˈpɔːl.dɪŋ, (US) ˈpɑːl-, ˈpɔːl-
Paulette pɔːˈlet, (US) pɑː-, pɔː-
Pauley ˈpɔː.li, (US) ˈpɑː-, ˈpɔː-
Pauli ˈpɔː.li, ˈpaʊ-, (US) ˈpaʊ-, ˈpɔː-
Paulin ˈpɔː.lɪn, (US) ˈpɑː-, ˈpɔː-
Pauline n, adj *scholar of St Paul's school, relating to St Paul:* ˈpɔː.laɪn, (US) ˈpɑː.laɪn, ˈpɔː-, -liːn **-s** -z
Pauline *female name:* ˈpɔː.liːn, -ˈ-, (US) pɑːˈliːn, pɔː-
Pauling ˈpɔː.lɪŋ, (US) ˈpɑː-, ˈpɔː-
Paulinus pɔːˈlaɪ.nəs, (US) pɑː-, pɔː-
Paulson ˈpɔːl.sən, (US) ˈpɔːl-, ˈpɑːl-
Paulus ˈpɔː.ləs, (US) ˈpɑː-, ˈpɔː-
Pauncefote ˈpɔːnts.fʊt, -fət, (US) ˈpɑːnts-, ˈpɔːnts-
paunch pɔːntʃ, (US) pɑːntʃ, pɔːntʃ **-es** -ɪz **-y** -i **-iness** -ɪ.nəs, -ɪ.nɪs
pauper ˈpɔː.pər, (US) ˈpɑː.pɚ, ˈpɔː- **-s** -z
pauperism ˈpɔː.pər.ɪ.zəm, (US) ˈpɑː-, ˈpɔː-
pauperization, -isa- ˌpɔː.pər.aɪˈzeɪ.ʃən, -ɪˈ-, (US) ˌpɑː.pɚ.əˈ-, ˌpɔː-
pauperiz|e, -is|e ˈpɔː.pər.aɪz, (US) ˈpɑː-, ˈpɔː- **-es** -ɪz **-ing** -ɪŋ **-ed** -d
Pausanias pɔːˈseɪ.ni.æs, -əs, (US) pɑːˈseɪ.ni.əs, pɔː-
paus|e pɔːz, (US) pɑːz, pɔːz **-es** -ɪz **-ing** -ɪŋ **-ed** -d
pavan(e) pəˈvæn; ˈpæv.ən, -ˈvɑːn, (US) pəˈvɑːn, -ˈvæn **-s** -z
Pavarotti ˌpæv.əˈrɒt.i, (US) -ˈrɔː.t̬i, ˌpɑː.vəˈ-
pav|e peɪv **-es** -z **-ing** -ɪŋ **-ed** -d **-er/s** -ər/z, (US) -ɚ/z ˈ**paving** ˌ**stone**
pavé ˈpæv.eɪ, -ˈ-, (US) pævˈeɪ, ˈ-- **-s** -z
pavement ˈpeɪv.mənt **-s** -s
Pavia pəˈviː.ə, pɑː-, pɑːˈviː.ɑː
pavid ˈpæv.ɪd
pavilion pəˈvɪl.jən, ˈ-i.ən, (US) ˈ-jən **-s** -z **-ing** -ɪŋ **-ed** -d
pavio(u)r ˈpeɪ.vjər, (US) -vjɚ **-s** -s
Pavitt ˈpæv.ɪt
Pavlov ˈpæv.lɒf, -lɒv, (US) -lɔːv, -lɔːf
pavlova pævˈləʊ.və, (US) pɑːvˈloʊ-, pæv- **-s** -z
Pavlova ˈpæv.lə.və, ˈpɑːv-; pævˈləʊ-, (US) pɑːvˈloʊ-, pæv-
Pavlovian pævˈləʊ.vi.ən, (US) pɑːvˈloʊ-, pæv-
paw n, v pɔː, (US) pɑː, pɔː **-s** -z **-ing** -ɪŋ **-ed** -d
pawk|y ˈpɔː.k|i, (US) ˈpɑː-, ˈpɔː- **-ier** -i.ər, (US) -i.ɚ **-iest** -i.ɪst, -i.əst **-ily** -əl.i, -ɪ.li **-iness** -ɪ.nəs, -ɪ.nɪs
pawl pɔːl, (US) pɑːl, pɔːl **-s** -z
pawn pɔːn, (US) pɑːn, pɔːn **-s** -z **-ing** -ɪŋ **-ed** -d
pawnbrok|er ˈpɔːnˌbrəʊ.k|ər, ˈpɔːm-, (US) ˈpɑːnˌbroʊ.k|ɚ, ˈpɔːn- **-ers** -əz, (US) -ɚz **-ing** -ɪŋ
Pawnee ˌpɔːˈniː, (US) ˌpɑː-, ˌpɔː- **-s** -z
pawnshop ˈpɔːn.ʃɒp, (US) ˈpɑːn.ʃɑːp, ˈpɔːn- **-s** -s
pawpaw ˈpɔː.pɔː, (US) ˈpɑː.pɑː; (US) ˈpɔː.pɔː **-s** -z
Pawtucket pɔːˈtʌk.ɪt, (US) pɑː-, pɔː-
pax pæks
Paxman ˈpæk.smən
Paxo® ˈpæk.səʊ, (US) -soʊ
Paxos ˈpæk.sɒs, (US) -sɑːs
Paxton ˈpæk.stən
pay peɪ **-s** -z **-ing** -ɪŋ **paid** peɪd **payer/s** ˈpeɪ.ər/z, (US) -ɚ/z ˈ**pay** ˌ**packet**
payable ˈpeɪ.ə.bəl
pay-as-you-go ˌpeɪ.əz.jʊˈgəʊ, -jəˈ-, (US) -ˈgoʊ
payback ˈpeɪ.bæk
paybed ˈpeɪ.bed
paycheck, -cheque ˈpeɪ.tʃek
payday ˈpeɪ.deɪ **-s** -z
PAYE ˌpiː.eɪ.waɪˈiː
payee peɪˈiː **-s** -z
payload ˈpeɪ.ləʊd, (US) -loʊd **-s** -z
paymaster ˈpeɪˌmɑː.stər, (US) -ˌmæs.tɚ **-s** -z ˌ**paymaster** ˈ**general**
payment ˈpeɪ.mənt **-s** -s
Payne peɪn
paynim, P~ ˈpeɪ.nɪm
Paynter ˈpeɪn.tər, (US) -t̬ɚ
payoff ˈpeɪ.ɒf, (US) -ɑːf **-s** -s
payola peɪˈəʊ.lə, (US) -ˈoʊ-
payout ˈpeɪ.aʊt **-s** -s
pay-per-view ˌpeɪ.pəˈvjuː, (US) -pɚˈ-
payphone ˈpeɪ.fəʊn, (US) -foʊn
payroll ˈpeɪ.rəʊl, (US) -roʊl **-s** -z
payslip ˈpeɪ.slɪp
paytrain ˈpeɪ.treɪn **-s** -z
paywall ˈpeɪ.wɔːl, (US) -wɔːl, -wɑːl **-s** -z
Paz pæz, (US) pɑːz, pɑːs
pazazz pəˈzæz
PBS ˌpiː.biːˈes
PC ˌpiːˈsiː
PDA ˌpiː.diːˈeɪ **-s** -z
PE ˌpiːˈiː
pea piː **-s** -z
Peabody ˈpiːˌbɒd.i, (US) -ˌbɑː.di
peac|e, P~ piːs **-es** -ɪz ˈ**Peace** ˌ**Corps**; ˈ**peace** ˌ**offering**; ˈ**peace** ˌ**pipe**
peaceab|le ˈpiː.sə.b|əl **-ly** -li **-leness** -əl.nəs, -nɪs
peaceful ˈpiːs.fəl, -fʊl **-ly** -i **-ness** -nəs, -nɪs
Peacehaven ˈpiːsˌheɪ.vən
peacekeep|er ˈpiːsˌkiː.p|ər, (US) -p|ɚ **-ers** -əz, (US) -ɚz **-ing** -ɪŋ
peacekeeping ˈpiːsˌkiː.pɪŋ
peacemaker ˈpiːsˌmeɪ.kər, (US) -kɚ **-s** -z
peacenik ˈpiːs.nɪk **-s** -s
peacetime ˈpiːs.taɪm
Peacey ˈpiː.si
peach piːtʃ **-es** -ɪz **-ing** -ɪŋ **-ed** -t **-er/s** -ər/z, (US) -ɚ/z
Peachey ˈpiː.tʃi
Peachum ˈpiː.tʃəm
peach|y ˈpiː.tʃ|i **-ier** -i.ər, (US) -i.ɚ **-iest** -i.ɪst, -i.əst **-iness** -ɪ.nəs, -ɪ.nɪs
peacock, P~ ˈpiː.kɒk, (US) -kɑːk **-s** -s
pea-green ˌpiːˈgriːn *stress shift:* ˌ**pea-green** ˈ**boat**
peahen ˈpiː.hen, ˌ-ˈ-, (US) ˈ-- **-s** -z
pea-jacket ˈpiːˌdʒæk.ɪt **-s** -s
peak, P~ piːk **-s** -s **-ing** -ɪŋ **-ed** -t ˈ**Peak** ˌ**District**; ˌ**peak** ˈ**time** *stress shift:* ˌ**peak time** ˈ**traffic**

Peake piːk
peaky ˈpiː.ki
peal piːl **-s** -z **-ing** -ɪŋ **-ed** -d
Peall piːl
pean *alternative spelling of* **paean**: ˈpiː.ən **-s** -z *in heraldry:* piːn
peanut ˈpiː.nʌt **-s** -s ˌ**peanut** ˈ**butter** (US) ˈ**peanut** ˌ**butter**
pear peəʳ, (US) per **-s** -z
Pear *surname:* pɪəʳ, (US) pɪr **-s** -z
Pearce pɪəs, (US) pɪrs
Peard pɪəd, (US) pɪrd
pearl, P~ pɜːl, (US) pɝːl **-s** -z **-ing** -ɪŋ **-ed** -d ˌ**Pearl** ˈ**Harbor**
pearlite ˈpɜː.laɪt, (US) ˈpɝː-
pearly ˈpɜː.li, (US) ˈpɝː- ˌ**pearly** ˈ**gates**; ˌ**pearly** ˈ**king**; ˌ**pearly** ˈ**queen**
pearmain ˈpeə.meɪn, ˈpɜː-, (US) ˈper- **-s** -z
Pearman ˈpɪə.mən, (US) ˈpɪr-
Pears pɪəz, peəz, (US) pɪrs, perz

> Note: /peəz/ (US) /perz/ in **Pears' soap**; /pɪəz/ (US) /pɪrz/ for the singer.

Pearsall ˈpɪə.sɔːl, -səl, (US) ˈpɪr-, -sɑːl
Pearse pɪəs, (US) pɪrs
pear-shaped ˈpeə.ʃeɪpt, (US) ˈper-
Pearson ˈpɪə.sən, (US) ˈpɪr-
Peart pɪət, (US) pɪrt
Peary ˈpɪə.ri, (US) ˈpɪr.i
peasant ˈpez.ənt **-s** -s
peasantry ˈpez.ən.tri
Peascod ˈpes.kəd, (US) -kəd, -kɑːd
pease, P~ piːz
Peaseblossom ˈpiːzˌblɒs.əm, (US) -ˌblɑː.səm
peasecod ˈpiːz.kɒd, (US) -kɑːd **-s** -z
pease-pudding ˌpiːzˈpʊd.ɪŋ, ˌpiːs-
peashooter ˈpiːˌʃuː.təʳ, (US) -t̬ɚ **-s** -z
pea-souper ˌpiːˈsuː.pəʳ, (US) ˌpiːˈsuː.pɚ, ˈ-ˌ-- **-s** -z
peat piːt ˈ**peat** ˌ**bog**
peat|y ˈpiː.t|i, (US) -t̬|i **-ier** -i.əʳ, (US) -i.ɚ **-iest** -i.ɪst, -i.əst **-iness** -ɪ.nəs, -ɪ.nɪs
pebble ˈpeb.əl **-s** -z
pebbledash ˈpeb.əl.dæʃ **-es** -ɪz **-ing** -ɪŋ **-ed** -t
pebbly ˈpeb.əl.i, ˈpeb.li
pecan ˈpiː.kæn, -kən; pɪˈkæn, (US) pɪˈkɑːn, piː-, -ˈkæn; (US) ˈpiː.kɑːn, -kæn **-s** -z ˌ**pecan** ˈ**pie**
peccability ˌpek.əˈbɪl.ə.ti, -ɪ.ti, (US) -ə.t̬i
peccable ˈpek.ə.bəl
peccadillo ˌpek.əˈdɪl.əʊ, (US) -oʊ **-(e)s** -z
peccant ˈpek.ənt **-ly** -li
peccar|y ˈpek.ər|.i **-ies** -iz
peccavi pekˈɑː.viː; *old-fashioned:* -ˈkeɪ.vaɪ, (US) perˈkɑː.vi **-s** -z
Pechey ˈpiː.tʃi
peck, P~ pek **-s** -s **-ing** -ɪŋ **-ed** -t **-er/s** -əʳ/z, (US) -ɚ/z ˈ**pecking** ˌ**order**
Peckham ˈpek.əm
Peckinpah ˈpek.ɪn.pɑː
peckish ˈpek.ɪʃ **-ly** -li **-ness** -nəs, -nɪs
Peckitt ˈpek.ɪt
Pecksniff ˈpek.snɪf
Pecock ˈpek.ɒk, (US) -ɑːk
pecorino, P~ ˌpek.ərˈiː.nəʊ, (US) -əˈriː.noʊ
Pecos ˈpeɪ.kəs, -kɒs, (US) -kəs, -koʊs
Pécs petʃ, (US) peɪtʃ
pect|in ˈpek.t|ɪn **-ic** -ɪk **-inous** -ɪ.nəs
pectoral ˈpek.tər.əl **-s** -z ˈ**pectoral** ˌ**muscle**
pecu|late ˈpek.jə|.leɪt **-lates** -leɪts **-lating** -leɪ.tɪŋ, (US) -leɪ.t̬ɪŋ **-lated** -leɪ.tɪd, (US) -leɪ.t̬ɪd **-lator/s** -leɪ.təʳ/z, (US) -leɪ.t̬ɚ/z
peculation ˌpek.jəˈleɪ.ʃən, -jʊˈ- **-s** -z
peculiar pɪˈkjuː.li.əʳ, pə-, (US) pɪˈkjuːl.jɚ, piː- **-s** -z **-ly** -li
peculiarit|y pɪˌkjuː.liˈær.ə.t|i, pə-, -ɪ.t|i, (US) pɪˌkjuː.liˈer.ə.t̬|i, piː-, -ˈær- **-ies** -iz
pecuniar|y pɪˈkjuː.njər|.i, -ni.ə.r|i, (US) pɪˈkjuː.ni.er-, piː- **-ily** -əl.i, -ɪ.li
pedagogic ˌped.əˈgɒdʒ.ɪk, -ˈgɒg-, -ˈgəʊ.dʒɪk, (US) -ˈgɑː.dʒɪk, -ˈgoʊ- **-s** -s **-al** -əl **-ally** -əl.i, -li *stress shift:* ˌ**pedagogic** ˈ**function**
pedagogue ˈped.ə.gɒg, (US) -gɑːg, -gɔːg **-s** -z
pedagogy ˈped.ə.gɒdʒ.i, -gɒg-, -gəʊ.dʒi, (US) -gɑː.dʒi, -goʊ-
pedal n, v ˈped.əl **-s** -z **-(l)ing** -ɪŋ **-(l)ed** -d ˈ**pedal** ˌ**pushers**
pedal adj *of the foot:* ˈpiː.dəl, ˈped.əl *in geometry:* ˈped.əl
pedalo ˈped.əl.əʊ, (US) -oʊ **-(e)s** -z
pedant ˈped.ənt **-s** -s
pedantic pɪˈdæn.tɪk, pə-, pedˈæn-, pəˈdæn-, (US) pedˈæn- **-al** -əl **-ally** -əl.i, -li
pedantism ˈped.ən.tɪ.zəm, pɪˈdæn-, pedˈæn-
pedantr|y ˈped.ən.tr|i **-ies** -iz
peddl|e ˈped.əl **-es** -z **-ing** -ɪŋ, ˈped.lɪŋ **-ed** -d **-er/s** -əʳ/z, (US) -ɚ/z, ˈped.ləʳ/z
Peden ˈpiː.dən, (US) ˈpiː.dən, ˈpeɪ-
pederast ˈped.ər.æst, ˈpiː.dər-, (US) ˈped.ə.ræst **-s** -s **-y** -i
pedestal ˈped.ɪ.stəl, ˈ-ə- **-s** -z
pedestrian pɪˈdes.tri.ən, pə-, (US) pə- **-s** -z **-ism** -ɪ.zəm peˌ**destrian** ˈ**crossing**
pedestrianiz|e, -is|e pɪˈdes.tri.ə.naɪz, pə-, (US) pə- **-es** -ɪz **-ing** -ɪŋ **-ed** -d
pediatric ˌpiː.diˈæt.rɪk **-s** -s
pediatrician ˌpiː.di.əˈtrɪʃ.ən **-s** -z
pedicel ˈped.ɪ.sel, ˈ-ə- **-s** -z
pedicle ˈped.ɪ.kəl, ˈ-ə- **-s** -z
pedicure ˈped.ɪ.kjʊəʳ, ˈ-ə-, -kjɔːʳ, (US) -ɪ.kjʊr **-s** -z
pedigree ˈped.ɪ.griː, ˈ-ə- **-s** -z **-d** -d
pediment ˈped.ɪ.mənt, ˈ-ə- **-s** -s
pedimental ˌped.ɪˈmen.təl, -əˈ-, (US) -t̬əl
pedimented ˈped.ɪ.men.tɪd, ˈ-ə-, -mən-, (US) -men.t̬ɪd
pedlar ˈped.ləʳ, (US) -lɚ **-s** -z
pedometer pɪˈdɒm.ɪ.təʳ, pə-, pedˈɒm-, ˈ-ə-, (US) pɪˈdɑː.mə.t̬ɚ, pə- **-s** -z
pedophile ˈpiː.dəʊ.faɪl, (US) ˈped.ə-, ˈpiː.də-, -doʊ- **-s** -z
pedophili|a ˌpiː.dəʊˈfɪl.i|.ə, (US) ˌped.oʊˈfiː.li-, ˌpiː.doʊˈ-, -dəˈ-, -ˈfiːl.j|ə **-ac/s** -æk/s
Pedro ˈped.rəʊ, ˈpiː.drəʊ, (US) ˈpeɪ.droʊ, ˈped.roʊ

> Note: The pronunciation /ˈpiː.drəʊ/ is generally used in Shakespeare's 'Much Ado'.

peduncle pɪˈdʌŋ.kəl, pə-, pedˈʌŋ-, (US) pɪˈdʌŋ-; (US) ˈpiː.dʌŋ- **-s** -z
pee piː **-s** -z **-ing** -ɪŋ **-d** -d
Peeb|les ˈpiː.b|əlz **-les-shire** -əlz.ʃəʳ, -əlʒ.ʃəʳ, -əl.ʃəʳ, -ʃɪəʳ, (US) -ʃɚ, -ʃɪr
peek, P~ piːk **-s** -s **-ing** -ɪŋ **-ed** -t
peekaboo ˈpiː.kə.buː
peel, P~ piːl **-s** -z **-ing/s** -ɪŋ/z **-ed** -d
Peele piːl
peeler ˈpiː.ləʳ, (US) -lɚ **-s** -z
peep, P~ piːp **-s** -s **-ing** -ɪŋ **-ed** -t **-er/s** -əʳ/z, (US) -ɚ/z
peepal ˈpiː.pəl **-s** -z
peep-bo ˈpiːp.bəʊ, -əʊ, ˌ-ˈ-, (US) ˈpiːp.boʊ, -oʊ, ˌ-ˈ-
peep-hole ˈpiːp.həʊl, (US) -hoʊl **-s** -z
peeping Tom ˌpiː.pɪŋˈtɒm, (US) -ˈtɑːm **-s** -z
peepshow ˈpiːp.ʃəʊ, (US) -ʃoʊ **-s** -z
peep-toe ˈpiːp.təʊ, (US) -toʊ **-d** -d
peepul ˈpiː.pəl **-s** -z
peer pɪəʳ, (US) pɪr **-s** -z **-ing** -ɪŋ **-ed** -d
peerag|e ˈpɪə.rɪdʒ, (US) ˈpɪr.ɪdʒ **-es** -ɪz
peeress pɪəˈres; ˈpɪə.rəs, -rɪs, -res, (US) ˈpɪr.ɪs **-es** -ɪz
peergroup ˈpɪə.gruːp, (US) ˈpɪr- **-s** -s
peerless, P~ ˈpɪə.ləs, -lɪs, (US) ˈpɪr- **-ly** -li **-ness** -nəs, -nɪs
peev|e piːv **-es** -z **-ing** -ɪŋ **-ed** -d
peevish ˈpiː.vɪʃ **-ly** -li **-ness** -nəs, -nɪs
peewee ˈpiː.wiː **-s** -z
peewit ˈpiː.wɪt **-s** -s
peg, P~ peg **-s** -z **-ging** -ɪŋ **-ged** -d
Pegasus ˈpeg.ə.səs
Pegeen pegˈiːn
Pegge peg
Peggotty ˈpeg.ə.ti, (US) -t̬i
Peggy ˈpeg.i
Pegram, Pegrum ˈpiː.grəm
Pegu pegˈuː
Pei peɪ
peignoir ˈpeɪ.nwɑːʳ, -nwɔːʳ, (US) peɪnˈwɑːr, pen-, ˈ-- **-s** -z
Peile piːl
Peiping ˌpeɪˈpɪŋ
Peirce pɪəs, (US) pɪrs, pɝːs
pejoration ˌpiː.dʒərˈeɪ.ʃən, ˌpedʒ.ərˈ-, (US) ˌpedʒ.əˈreɪ-, ˌpiː.dʒəˈ-
pejorative pɪˈdʒɒr.ə.tɪv, pə-, ˈpiː.dʒər-, (US) pɪˈdʒɔːr.ə.t̬ɪv; (US) ˈpedʒ.ə.reɪ-, ˈpiː.dʒə- **-s** -z **-ly** -li
peke piːk **-s** -s
Pekin ˌpiːˈkɪn, (US) ˈ--
pekines|e, P~ ˌpiː.kɪˈniːz, -kənˈiːz, (US) ˌpiː.kəˈniːz, -ˈniːs **-es** -ɪz

Peking ˌpiːˈkɪŋ *stress shift, see compound:* **ˌPeking ˈduck**
pekinges|e, P~ ˌpiː.kɪŋˈiːz, -kɪˈniːz, -kᵊnˈiːz, (US) -kɪŋˈiːz, -ˈiːs **-es** -ɪz
pekoe ˈpiː.kəʊ, (US) -koʊ
pelagic pəˈlædʒ.ɪk, pɪ-, pelˈædʒ-, (US) pəˈlædʒ-, pɪ-
pelargonium ˌpel.əˈgəʊ.ni.əm, -ɑːˈ-, (US) -ɑːrˈgoʊ- **-s** -z
Pelasgian pelˈæz.gi.ən, pɪˈlæz-, pə-, -dʒi-, (US) pəˈlæz.dʒi- **-s** -z
Pelé ˈpel.eɪ, -ˈ-, (US) ˈpel.eɪ
pelerine ˈpel.ᵊr.iːn, (US) -ə.riːn **-s** -z
Peleus ˈpiː.ljuːs, ˈpel.juːs, -jəs, -i.əs, (US) ˈpiː.li.əs, ˈpiːl.juːs
pelf pelf
pelham, P~ ˈpel.əm
Pelias ˈpiː.li.æs, ˈpel.i-, -əs, (US) -əs
pelican ˈpel.ɪ.kᵊn, ˈ-ə- **-s** -z **ˌpelican ˈcrossing**
peliss|e pelˈiːs, pɪˈliːs, pə-, (US) pəˈliːs **-es** -ɪz
pellagr|a pəˈlæg.r|ə, pelˈæg-, (US) pəˈleɪ.gr|ə, -ˈlæg.r|ə **-ous** -əs
Pelleas, Pelléas ˈpel.eɪ.æs, ˈ-i-, (US) ˈ-i-
Pelles ˈpel.iːz
pellet ˈpel.ɪt, -ət **-s** -s
Pelley ˈpel.i
pellicle ˈpel.ɪ.kᵊl, ˈ-ə- **-s** -z
pellitory ˈpel.ɪ.tᵊr.i, ˈ-ə-, (US) -tɔːr-
pell-mell ˌpelˈmel
pellucid pɪˈluː.sɪd, pə-, pelˈuː-, -ˈjuː-, (US) pəˈluː.sɪd **-ly** -li **-ness** -nəs, -nɪs
Pelman ˈpel.mən **-ism** -ɪ.zᵊm
pelmet ˈpel.mɪt, -mət **-s** -s
Peloponnese ˈpel.ə.pə.niːz, -niːs, ˌpel.ə.pəˈniːs, -ˈniːz, (US) ˌpel.ə.pəˈniːz, -ˈniːs
Peloponnesian ˌpel.ə.pəˈniː.ʒᵊn, -ʒi.ən, ˈ-ʃᵊn, (US) -ʒən, -ʃən **-s** -z
Peloponnesus ˌpel.ə.pəˈniː.səs
Pelops ˈpiː.lɒps, (US) -lɑːps
Pelosi pəˈləʊ.si, pelˈəʊ-, (US) pəˈloʊ-, pelˈoʊ-
pelota pəˈləʊ.tə, pɪ-, pelˈɒt-, (US) pəˈloʊ.t̬ə
peloton ˈpel.ə.tɒn, (US) ˌpel.əˈtɑːn, ˈ---
Pelsall ˈpel.sɔːl
pelt pelt **-s** -s **-ing** -ɪŋ, (US) ˈpel.t̬ɪŋ **-ed** -ɪd, (US) ˈpel.t̬ɪd
Peltier effect ˈpel.ti.eɪ.ɪˌfekt, (US) ˈpel.tjeɪ.ɪˌ-, -əˌ-, -iːˌ-
pelv|is ˈpel.v|ɪs **-ises** -ɪ.sɪz **-es** -iːz **-ic** -ɪk
Pemba ˈpem.bə
Pemberton ˈpem.bə.tᵊn, (US) -bɚ-
Pembridge ˈpem.brɪdʒ
Pembroke ˈpem.brʊk, -brək, (US) -brʊk, -broʊk **-shire** -ʃəʳ, -ʃɪəʳ, (US) -ʃɚ, -ʃɪr
Pembury ˈpem.bᵊr.i
pemmican ˈpem.ɪ.kən
pen, P~ pen **-s** -z **-ning** -ɪŋ **-ned** -d **ˈpen ˌfriend**; **ˈpen ˌname**; **ˈpen ˌpal**; **ˈpen ˌpusher**
penal ˈpiː.nᵊl **-ly** -i **ˈpenal ˌcolony**
penaliz|e, -is|e ˈpiː.nᵊl.aɪz, (US) ˈpiː-, ˈpen.ᵊl- **-es** -ɪz **-ing** -ɪŋ **-ed** -d
penalt|y ˈpen.ᵊl.t|i **-ies** -iz **ˈpenalty ˌbox**
penanc|e ˈpen.ənts **-es** -ɪz
pen-and-ink ˌpen.əndˈɪŋk *stress shift:* **ˌpen-and-ink ˈdrawing**
Penang penˈæŋ, pɪˈnæŋ, pə-, (US) pɪˈnæŋ, penˈæŋ
Penarth penˈɑːθ, pəˈnɑːθ, (US) penˈɑːrθ
penates penˈɑː.teɪz, pɪˈnɑː-, pə-, -ˈneɪ-, -tiːz, (US) pəˈneɪ.t̬iːz, -ˈnɑː-
pence (plural of **penny**) pents
Note: See **penny**.
penchant ˈpɑ̃ːŋ.ʃɑ̃ːŋ, (US) ˈpen.tʃənt **-s** -z
pencil ˈpent.sᵊl **-s** -z **-(l)ing** -ɪŋ **-(l)ed** -d **ˈpencil ˌcase**; **ˈpencil ˌsharpener**
Pencoed penˈkɔɪd, peŋ-, (US) pen-
pendant ˈpen.dənt **-s** -s
penden|cy ˈpen.dən|t.si **-t** -t
Pendennis penˈden.ɪs
pendente lite penˌden.tiˈlaɪ.ti
Pender ˈpen.dəʳ, (US) -dɚ
Pendine penˈdaɪn
pending ˈpen.dɪŋ
Pendle ˈpen.dᵊl
Pendlebury ˈpen.dᵊl.bᵊr.i, (US) -ˌber-, -bɚ-
Pendleton ˈpen.dᵊl.tən
pendragon, P~ penˈdræg.ən **-s** -z
pendulous ˈpen.dʒə.ləs, -dʒʊ.ləs, -djə.ləs, -djʊ-, (US) -dʒə.ləs, -djə-, -də-, -dʒʊ-, -djʊ- **-ly** -li **-ness** -nəs, -nɪs
pendulum ˈpen.dʒᵊl.əm, ˈ-djᵊl-, -dʒʊ.ləm, -djʊ.ləm, (US) -dʒə.ləm, -djə-, -də-, -dʒʊ- **-s** -z
Penelope pəˈnel.ə.pi, pɪ-, (US) pə-
penetrability ˌpen.ɪ.trəˈbɪl.ə.ti, ˌ-ə-, -ɪ.ti, (US) -ə.t̬i
penetrab|le ˈpen.ɪ.trə.b|ᵊl, ˈ-ə- **-ly** -li **-leness** -ᵊl.nəs, -nɪs
penetralia ˌpen.ɪˈtreɪ.li.ə, -əˈ-
pene|trate ˈpen.ɪ|.treɪt, ˈ-ə- **-trates** -treɪts **-trating/ly** -treɪ.tɪŋ/li, (US) -treɪ.t̬ɪŋ/li **-trated** -treɪ.tɪd, (US) -treɪ.t̬ɪd
penetration ˌpen.ɪˈtreɪ.ʃᵊn, -əˈ- **-s** -z
penetrative ˈpen.ɪ.trə.tɪv, ˈ-ə-, -treɪ-, (US) -treɪ.t̬ɪv **-ly** -li **-ness** -nəs, -nɪs
Penfold ˈpen.fəʊld, (US) -foʊld
penful ˈpen.fʊl **-s** -z
Penge pendʒ
penguin ˈpeŋ.gwɪn, (US) ˈpeŋ-, ˈpen- **-s** -z
Penhaligon penˈhæl.ɪ.gᵊn
penholder ˈpenˌhəʊl.dəʳ, (US) -ˌhoʊl.dɚ **-s** -z
penicillin ˌpen.ɪˈsɪl.ɪn, -əˈ-
penicillium ˌpen.ɪˈsɪl.i.əm, -əˈ-
Penicuik ˈpen.ɪ.kʊk
penile ˈpiː.naɪl, (US) -naɪl, -nɪl
peninsul|a, P~ pəˈnɪnt.sjə.l|ə, pɪ-, penˈɪnt-, -sjʊ-, -ʃə-, -ʃʊ-, (US) pəˈnɪnt.sə-, -sjə-, -ˈnɪn.tʃə- **-as** -əz **-ar** -əʳ, (US) -ɚ
penis ˈpiː.nɪs **-es** -ɪz **ˈpenis ˌenvy**
Penistone ˈpen.ɪ.stᵊn
penitence ˈpen.ɪ.tᵊnts, ˈ-ə-
penitent ˈpen.ɪ.tᵊnt, ˈ-ə- **-s** -s **-ly** -li
penitential ˌpen.ɪˈten.tʃᵊl, -əˈ-, (US) -ʃᵊl **-ly** -i
penitentiar|y ˌpen.ɪˈten.tʃᵊr|.i, -əˈ-, (US) -tʃə.r|iː **-ies** -iz
pennkni|fe ˈpen.naɪ|f **-ves** -vz
Penkridge ˈpeŋ.krɪdʒ
penlight ˈpen.laɪt **-s** -s
Penmaenmawr ˌpen.mənˈmaʊ.əʳ, -ˈmɔːʳ, (US) -ˈmaʊ.ɚ, -ˈmɔːr
pen|man ˈpen|.mən, ˈpem-, (US) ˈpen- **-men** -mən
Penman ˈpen.mən, ˈpem-, (US) ˈpen-
penmanship ˈpen.mən.ʃɪp, ˈpem-, (US) ˈpen-
Penn pen
Penn. (abbrev. for **Pennsylvania**) pen, ˌpent.sɪlˈveɪ.ni.ə, -sᵊlˈ-, ˈ-njə, (US) ˌpent.sᵊlˈveɪ.njə, ˈ-ni.ə, pen

> Note: The form /pen/ is especially used when referring to university names.

pennant, P~ ˈpen.ənt **-s** -s
penne ˈpen.eɪ, -i, (US) -i, -eɪ
Penney ˈpen.i
penn|i ˈpen|.i **-is** -ɪs **-ia** -i.ə
penniless ˈpen.i.ləs, -lɪs
Pennine ˈpen.aɪn **-s** -z
Pennington ˈpen.ɪŋ.tən
pennon ˈpen.ən **-s** -z
Pennsylvani|a ˌpent.sɪlˈveɪ.ni|.ə, -sᵊlˈ-, ˈ-nj|ə, (US) -sᵊlˈveɪ.nj|ə, ˈ-ni|.ə **-an/s** -ən/z **ˌPennsylˌvania ˈDutch**
penn|y, P~ ˈpen|.i **-ies** -iz **pence** pents **ˌpenny arˈcade**; **ˌpenny ˈblack**; **ˌpenny ˈdreadful**; **ˌpenny ˈfarthing**

> Note (British English): After decimalization of the currency in the UK in 1971, the pronunciation of compounds with **penny**, **pence** (now abbreviated to **p**) changed. Formerly (when the abbreviation of this word was **d**), compounds from **1/2d** to **11d** invariably had /-pᵊn.i, -pᵊnts/, e.g. see entries under **half-penny**, **fourpence**, etc.. These reduced forms are now rarely heard. Instead, the full forms /ˈpen.i/ and /pents/, or more commonly /piː/, are used, e.g. where **4d** was pronounced /ˈfɔː.pᵊnts/), **4p** is /ˌfɔːˈpents/ or /-ˈpiː/; **12p** is /ˌtwelvˈpents/ or /-ˈpiː/.

penny-ante ˌpen.iˈæn.ti, (US) -t̬i
penny-pinch|ing ˈpen.iˌpɪn.tʃ|ɪŋ **-er/s** -əʳ/z, (US) -ɚ/z
pennyroyal ˌpen.iˈrɔɪ.əl, -ˈrɔɪəl, (US) ˈpen.iˌrɔɪ.əl, ˌpen.iˈrɔɪ-
pennyweight ˈpen.i.weɪt **-s** -s
pennywort ˈpen.i.wɜːt, (US) -wɜːt, -wɔːrt

P

pennyworth ˈpen.i.wəθ, -wɜːθ, ˈpen.əθ, (US) ˈpen.i.wɝθ, -wɝːθ **-s** -s
Penobscot penˈɒb.skɒt, pəˈnɒb-, (US) pəˈnɑːb.skɑːt, penˈɑːb-, -skət
penological ˌpiː.nəˈlɒdʒ.ɪ.kəl, (US) -ˈlɑː.dʒɪ-
penolog|y piːˈnɒl.ə.dʒ|i, pɪ-, (US) piːˈnɑː.lə- **-ist/s** -ɪst/s
Penrhyn penˈrɪn
Penrith *town in Cumbria:* penˈrɪθ, ˈ-- *surname:* ˈpen.rɪθ
Penrose *surname:* ˈpen.rəʊz, -ˈ-, (US) ˈpen.roʊz, -ˈ- *place in Cornwall:* penˈrəʊz, (US) -ˈroʊz
Penryn penˈrɪn
Pensacola ˌpent.səˈkəʊ.lə, (US) -ˈkoʊ-
Pensarn penˈsɑːn, (US) -ˈsɑːrn
penseroso ˌpent.səˈrəʊ.zəʊ, -səʊ, (US) -ˈroʊ.soʊ
Penshurst ˈpenz.hɜːst, (US) -hɝːst
pension **n, v** *monetary allowance, etc.:* ˈpen.tʃən **-s** -z **-ing** -ɪŋ **-ed** -d
pension **n** *boarding house, board:* ˈpɑ̃ːn.sjɔ̃ːŋ, -ˈ-, (US) pɑ̃ːnˈsjõʊŋ, ˌpɑːnˈsjoʊn **-s** -z
pensionable ˈpen.tʃən.ə.bəl, (US) -ʃən-
pensioner ˈpen.tʃən.əʳ, (US) -ʃən.ɚ **-s** -z
pensive ˈpent.sɪv **-ly** -li **-ness** -nəs, -nɪs
penta- ˈpen.tə; penˈtæ, (US) ˈpen.t̬ə; (US) penˈtæ
Note: Prefix. Normally either takes primary or secondary stress on the first syllable, e.g. **pentagon** /ˈpen.tə.gən/ (US) /-t̬ə.gɑːn/, **pentatonic** /ˌpen.təˈtɒn.ɪk/ (US) /-t̬əˈtɑː.nɪk/, or primary stress on the second syllable, e.g. **pentagonal** /penˈtæg.ən.əl/.
pentad ˈpen.tæd **-s** -z
pentagon, P~ ˈpen.tə.gən, -gɒn, (US) -t̬ə.gɑːn **-s** -z
pentagonal penˈtæg.ən.əl **-ly** -i
pentagram ˈpen.tə.græm, (US) -t̬ə- **-s** -z
pentahedr|on ˌpen.təˈhiː.dr|ən, -dr|ɒn, (US) -t̬əˈhiː.dr|ən **-ons** -ənz, -ɒnz, (US) -ənz **-a** -ə **-al** -əl
pentameter penˈtæm.ɪ.təʳ, ˈ-ə-, (US) -ə.t̬ɚ **-s** -z
pentangle ˈpen.tæŋ.gəl **-s** -z
Pentateuch ˈpen.tə.tjuːk, (US) -t̬ə.tuːk, -tjuːk
pentathlete penˈtæθ.liːt **-s** -s
pentathlon penˈtæθ.lɒn, -lən, (US) -lɑːn, -lən
pentatonic ˌpen.təˈtɒn.ɪk, (US) -t̬əˈtɑː.nɪk *stress shift:* ˌ**pentatonic** ˈ**scale**
Pentax® ˈpen.tæks
Pentecost ˈpen.tɪ.kɒst, -tə-, (US) -t̬ɪ.kɑːst **-s** -s
Pentecostal ˌpen.tɪˈkɒs.təl, -təˈ-, (US) -t̬ɪˈkɑː.stəl **-ism** -ɪ.zəm **-ist/s** -ɪst/s *stress shift:* ˌ**Pentecostal** ˈ**feast**
Pentel® ˈpen.tel
Penthesilea ˌpent.θes.ɪˈliː.ə, -θə.sɪˈ-, -səˈ-, -ˈleɪ-, (US) -θə.səˈliː-
penthou|se, P~ ˈpent.haʊ|s **-ses** -zɪz
pentiment|o ˌpen.tɪˈmen.t|əʊ, (US) -t̬ɪˈmen.t|oʊ **-i** -iː
Pentium® ˈpen.ti.əm, (US) -t̬i-
Pentland ˈpent.lənd **-s** -z
Pentonville ˈpen.tən.vɪl
Pentothal® ˈpen.tə.θæl, -θɔːl, (US) -t̬ə.θɔːl, -θɑːl
pentstemon pentˈstem.ən, pen-, -ˈstiː.mən; ˈpent.stɪ.mən, -stə-, (US) pentˈstiː-; (US) ˈpent.stə-
pent-up ˌpentˈʌp *stress shift:* ˌ**pent-up** ˈ**anger**
pentyl ˈpen.taɪl, -tɪl, (US) -tɪl, -t̬əl
penult pəˈnʌlt, pɪ-, penˈʌlt, (US) ˈpiː.nʌlt; (US) pɪˈnʌlt **-s** -s
penultimate pəˈnʌl.tɪ.mət, pɪ-, penˈʌl-, -tə-, -mɪt, (US) pɪˈnʌl.tə.mət **-s** -s **-ly** -li
penumbr|a pəˈnʌm.br|ə, pɪ-, penˈʌm-, (US) pɪˈnʌm- **-as** -əz **-ae** -iː **-al** -əl
penurious pəˈnjʊə.ri.əs, pɪ-, penˈjʊə-, -ˈjɔː-, (US) pəˈnʊr.i-, penˈʊr-, -ˈjʊr- **-ly** -li **-ness** -nəs, -nɪs
penury ˈpen.jə.ri, -jʊ-, (US) -jʊ.ri, -jɚ.i
Pen-y-Ghent ˌpen.iˈgent
Penzance penˈzænts, pən-; *locally:* pənˈzɑːnts, (US) penˈzænts
peon *Indian servant:* ˈpiː.ən; ˈpjuːn; peɪˈɒn, (US) ˈpiː.ɑːn, ˈpeɪ-, -ən *in US:* ˈpiː.ən, (US) -ɑːn, -ən **-s** -z
peon|y ˈpiː.ə.n|i **-ies** -iz
peopl|e ˈpiː.pəl **-es** -z **-ing** -ɪŋ, ˈpiːp.lɪŋ **-ed** -d
Peoria piːˈɔː.ri.ə, (US) -ˈɔːr.i-
Peover ˈpiː.vəʳ, (US) -vɚ
pep pep **-s** -s **-ping** -ɪŋ **-ped** -t ˈ**pep** ˌ**pill**; ˈ**pep** ˌ**talk**
PEP pep, ˌpiː.iːˈpiː
Pepin ˈpep.ɪn
peplum ˈpep.ləm **-s** -z
pepp|er, P~ ˈpep|.əʳ, (US) -ɚ **-ers** -əz, (US) -ɚz **-ering** -ər.ɪŋ **-ered** -əd, (US) -ɚd ˈ**pepper** ˌ**pot**
pepperbox ˈpep.ə.bɒks, (US) -ɚ.bɑːks **-es** -ɪz
peppercorn ˈpep.ə.kɔːn, (US) -ɚ.kɔːrn **-s** -z
peppermint ˈpep.ə.mɪnt, (US) -ɚ-, -mənt **-s** -s
pepperoni ˌpep.əˈrəʊ.ni, (US) -ˈroʊ-
pepper|y ˈpep.ər|.i **-iness** -ɪ.nəs, -ɪ.nɪs
pepp|y ˈpep|.i **-ier** -i.əʳ, (US) -i.ɚ **-iest** -i.ɪst, -i.əst **-iness** -ɪ.nəs, -ɪ.nɪs **-ily** -əl.i, -ɪ.li
Pepsi® ˈpep.si
Pepsi-Cola® ˌpep.siˈkəʊ.lə, (US) -ˈkoʊ-
pepsin ˈpep.sɪn
Pepsodent® ˈpep.səʊ.dent, -sə.dənt, (US) -soʊ.dent, -sə-
peptic ˈpep.tɪk
Pepto-Bismol® ˌpep.təʊˈbɪz.mɒl, (US) -toʊˈbɪz.mɑːl, -tə-
peptone ˈpep.təʊn, (US) -toʊn **-s** -z
Pepys piːps; ˈpep.ɪs

> Note: Samuel Pepys is generally referred to as /piːps/. The pronunciation in the family of the present Lord Cottenham is /ˈpep.ɪs/.

per *strong form:* pɜːʳ, (US) pɝː; *weak form:* pəʳ, (US) pɚ
Note: This word has a weak form /pəʳ/ (US) /pɚ/, which is almost always used in the phrases **per cent**, **per annum**. It is also used in phrases such as **per capita**, **per centimetre**, **per head**, but the strong form /pɜːʳ/ (US) /pɝː/ is more usual.
peradventure pə.rədˈven.tʃəʳ, ˌpɜː.rədˈ-, ˌper.ədˈ-, (US) ˌpɝː.ədˈven.tʃɚ, ˌper-
Perak ˈpeə.rə, ˈpɪə.rə; pəˈræk, pɪ-, perˈæk, (US) ˈpeɪ.ræk, -rɑːk; (US) ˈper.ə, ˈpɪr-

> Note: English speakers who have lived in Malaysia pronounce /ˈpeə.rə/ (US) /ˈper.ə/ or /ˈpɪə.rə/ (US) /ˈpɪr.ə/.

perambu|late pəˈræm.bjə|.leɪt, -bjʊ- **-lates** -leɪts **-lating** -leɪ.tɪŋ, (US) -leɪ.t̬ɪŋ **-lated** -leɪ.tɪd, (US) -leɪ.t̬ɪd
perambulation pəˌræm.bjəˈleɪ.ʃən, -bjʊˈ- **-s** -z
perambulator pəˈræm.bjə.leɪ.təʳ, -bjʊ-, (US) -t̬ɚ **-s** -z
per annum pəʳˈæn.əm, (US) pɚ-
percale pəˈkeɪl, -ˈkɑːl, (US) pɚˈkeɪl
per capita pəˈkæp.ɪ.tə, ˌpɜː-, (US) ˌpɝːˈkæp.ɪ.t̬ə
perceivab|le pəˈsiː.və.b|əl, pɜː-, (US) pɚ- **-ly** -li
perceiv|e pəˈsiːv, (US) pɚ- **-es** -z **-ing** -ɪŋ **-ed** -d
per cent, percent pəˈsent, (US) pɚ-
percentag|e pəˈsen.tɪdʒ, (US) pɚˈsen.t̬ɪdʒ **-es** -ɪz
percentile pəˈsen.taɪl, (US) pɚˈsen-, -t̬əl **-s** -z
percept ˈpɜː.sept, (US) ˈpɝː- **-s** -s
perceptibility pəˌsep.təˈbɪl.ə.ti, -tɪˈ-, -ɪ.ti, (US) pɚˌsep.təˈbɪl.ə.t̬i
perceptib|le pəˈsep.tə.b|əl, -tɪ-, (US) pɚˈsep.tə- **-ly** -li **-leness** -əl.nəs, -nɪs
perception pəˈsep.ʃən, (US) pɚ- **-s** -z
perceptive pəˈsep.tɪv, (US) pɚ- **-ly** -li **-ness** -nəs, -nɪs
perceptual pəˈsep.tʃu.əl, -tju-, (US) -tʃu-, pɚˈsep.tju- **-ly** -i
Perceval ˈpɜː.sɪ.vəl, -sə-, (US) ˈpɝː-
perch pɜːtʃ, (US) pɝːtʃ **-es** -ɪz **-ing** -ɪŋ **-ed** -t
perchance pəˈtʃɑːnts, ˌpɜː-, (US) pɚˈtʃænts
Percheron ˈpɜː.ʃə.rɒn, (US) ˈpɝː.tʃə.rɑːn **-s** -z
percipien|t pəˈsɪp.i.ən|t, (US) pɚ- **-ce** -ts
Percival(e) ˈpɜː.sɪ.vəl, -sə-, (US) ˈpɝː-

percol|ate ˈpɜː.kəl|.eɪt, (US) ˈpɝː- **-ates** -eɪts **-ating** -eɪ.tɪŋ, (US) -eɪ.t̬ɪŋ **-ated** -eɪ.tɪd, (US) -eɪ.t̬ɪd
percolation ˌpɜː.kəlˈeɪ.ʃən, (US) ˌpɝː- **-s** -z
percolator ˈpɜː.kəl.eɪ.təʳ, (US) ˈpɝː.kəl.eɪ.t̬ɚ **-s** -z
per contra ˌpɜːˈkɒn.trə, (US) ˌpɝːˈkɑːn-
per curiam ˌpɜːˈkjʊə.ri.æm, -ˈkjɔː-, (US) ˌpɝːˈkjʊr.i-
percuss pəˈkʌs, pɜː-, (US) pɚ- **-es** -ɪz **-ing** -ɪŋ **-ed** -t
percussion pəˈkʌʃ.ən, pɜː-, (US) pɚ- **-s** -z **-ist/s** -ɪst/s
percussive pəˈkʌs.ɪv, pɜː-, (US) pɚ-
percutaneous ˌpɜː.kjuːˈteɪ.ni.əs, -kjʊˈ-, (US) ˌpɝː.kjuːˈ- **-ly** -li
Percy ˈpɜː.si, (US) ˈpɝː-
per diem ˌpɜːˈdiː.em, -ˈdaɪ-, (US) ˌpɝː-
Perdita ˈpɜː.dɪ.tə, (US) ˈpɝː.dɪ.t̬ə; (US) pɚˈdiː-
perdition pəˈdɪʃ.ən, pɜː-, (US) pɚ-
perdu(e) ˈpɜː.djuː, -ˈ-, (US) pɚˈduː, -ˈdjuː
père, pere peəʳ, (US) per
peregrin ˈper.ɪ.grɪn, ˈ-ə- **-s** -z
peregri|nate ˈper.ɪ.grɪ|.neɪt, ˈ-ə-, -grə-, (US) -ə.grɪ- **-nates** -neɪts **-nating** -neɪ.tɪŋ, (US) -neɪ.t̬ɪŋ **-nated** -neɪ.tɪd, (US) -neɪ.t̬ɪd
peregrination ˌper.ɪ.grɪˈneɪ.ʃən, ˌ-ə-, -grəˈ-, (US) -ə.grɪˈ- **-s** -z
peregrine, P~ n, adj ˈper.ɪ.grɪn, ˈ-ə-, -griːn, (US) -grɪn, -griːn, -graɪn **-s** -z ˌ**peregrine** ˈ**falcon**
Perelman ˈper.əl.mən, ˈpɜːl-, (US) ˈpɝːl-
peremptor|y pəˈremp.tər|.i, pɪ-; ˈper.əmp-, (US) pəˈremp- **-ily** -əl.i, -ɪ.li **-iness** -ɪ.nəs, -ɪ.nɪs

> Note: /ˈper.əmp-/ is more usual in British English when the word is used as a legal term. Otherwise /pəˈremp-/ and /pɪ-/ are commoner.

perennial pərˈen.i.əl, pɪˈren-, (US) pəˈren- **-s** -z **-ly** -i
Peres ˈper.ez
perestroika ˌper.əˈstrɔɪ.kə, -ɪˈ-
Perez ˈper.es, (US) ˈper.ez, -es, -əz, -əs
Pérez de Cuéllar ˌper.es.dəˈkweɪ.jɑː, (US) ˌper.ez.deɪˈkweɪ.jɑːr, ˌ-əz-, ˌ-es-
perfect v pəˈfekt, pɜː-, (US) pɝː-, pɚ- **-s** -s **-ing** -ɪŋ **-ed** -ɪd
perfec|t n, adj ˈpɜː.fɪk|t, (US) ˈpɝː- **-ts** -ts **-tly** -t.li **-tness** -t.nəs, -nɪs ˌ**perfect** ˈ**pitch**; ˌ**perfect** ˈ**tense**
perfectibility pəˌfek.təˈbɪl.ə.ti, pɜː-, -tɪˈ-, -ɪ.ti, (US) pɚˌfek.təˈbɪl.ə.t̬i
perfectible pəˈfek.tə.bəl, pɜː-, -tɪ-, (US) pɚ-
perfection pəˈfek.ʃən, (US) pɚ- **-s** -z **-ist/s** -ɪst/s **-ism** -ɪ.zəm
perfective pəˈfek.tɪv, (US) pɚ- **-ly** -li **-ness** -nəs, -nɪs
perfervid pɜːˈfɜː.vɪd, pə-, (US) pɚˈfɝː-
perfidious pəˈfɪd.i.əs, pɜː-, (US) pɚ- **-ly** -li **-ness** -nəs, -nɪs
perfid|y ˈpɜː.fɪ.d|i, -fə-, (US) ˈpɝː.fə- **-ies** -iz
perforable ˈpɜː.fər.ə.bəl, (US) ˈpɝː-
perforate adj ˈpɜː.fər.ɪt, -ət, -eɪt, (US) ˈpɝː.fɚ.ɪt, -fə.reɪt
perfor|ate v ˈpɜː.fər|.eɪt, (US) ˈpɝː.fə.r|eɪt **-ates** -eɪts **-ating** -eɪ.tɪŋ, (US) -eɪ.t̬ɪŋ **-ated** -eɪ.tɪd, (US) -eɪ.t̬ɪd **-ator/s** -eɪ.təʳ/z, (US) -eɪ.t̬ɚ/z
perforation ˌpɜː.fərˈeɪ.ʃən, (US) ˌpɝː.fəˈreɪ- **-s** -z
perforce pəˈfɔːs, pɜː-, (US) pɚˈfɔːrs
perform pəˈfɔːm, (US) pɚˈfɔːrm **-s** -z **-ing** -ɪŋ **-ed** -d **-er/s** -əʳ/z, (US) -ɚ/z **-able** -ə.bəl
performanc|e pəˈfɔː.mənts, (US) pɚˈfɔːr- **-es** -ɪz **perˈformance ˌart; perˌformance ˈart; perˌformance reˈlated; perˌformance -reˌlated ˈpay**
performative pəˈfɔː.mə.tɪv, (US) pɚˈfɔːr.mə.t̬ɪv **-s** -z
perfume n ˈpɜː.fjuːm, (US) ˈpɝː-, -ˈ- **-s** -z
perfum|e v pəˈfjuːm, pɜː-; ˈpɜː.fjuːm, (US) pɚˈfjuːm **-es** -z **-ing** -ɪŋ **-ed** -d
perfumed ˈpɜː.fjuːmd, (US) pɚˈfjuːmd
perfum|er pəˈfjuː.m|əʳ, pɜː-, (US) pɚˈfjuː.m|ɚ **-ers** -əz, (US) -ɚz **-ery** -ər.i
perfunctor|y pəˈfʌŋk.tər|.i, pɜː-, (US) pɚ- **-ily** -əl.i, -ɪ.li **-iness** -ɪ.nəs, -ɪ.nɪs
Pergam|um ˈpɜː.gə.m|əm, (US) ˈpɝː- **-us** -əs
pergola ˈpɜː.gəl.ə, (US) ˈpɝː- **-s** -z
Pergolese ˌpɜː.gəʊˈleɪ.zi, ˌpeə-, -zeɪ, (US) ˌper.goʊˈleɪ.zi, -si
Perham ˈper.əm
perhaps pəˈhæps; præps, (US) pɚˈhæps, -ˈæps

> Note: In British English, /pəˈhæps/ is more usual in formal speech, and colloquially when the word is said in isolation or used parenthetically (as in 'you know, perhaps, ...'). /præps/ is common in other situations, especially initially (e.g. in 'perhaps we shall', 'perhaps it's a mistake').

peri ˈpɪə.ri, (US) ˈpiː-, ˈpɪr.i **-s** -z
peri- ˈper.ɪ, -i; pəˈrɪ, perˈɪ
Note: Prefix. Normally either takes primary or secondary stress on the first syllable, e.g. **periscope** /ˈper.ɪ.skəʊp/ (US) /-skoʊp/, **periscopic** /ˌper.ɪˈskɒp.ɪk/ (US) /-ˈskɑː.pɪk/, or primary stress on the second syllable, e.g. **peripheral** /pəˈrɪf.ər.əl/.
perianth ˈper.i.æntθ **-s** -s
pericarditis ˌper.ɪ.kɑːˈdaɪ.tɪs, -təs, (US) -kɑːrˈdaɪ.t̬ɪs, -t̬əs
pericardi|um ˌper.ɪˈkɑː.di|.əm, (US) -ˈkɑːr- **-a** -ə
pericarp ˈper.ɪ.kɑːp, ˈ-ə-, (US) -ɪ.kɑːrp **-s** -s
Pericles ˈper.ɪ.kliːz, ˈ-ə-, (US) -ɪ.kliːz
peridot ˈper.ɪ.dɒt, (US) -dɑːt **-s** -s
perigee ˈper.ɪ.dʒiː, ˈ-ə-, (US) ˈ-ɪ- **-s** -z
periheli|on ˌper.ɪˈhiː.li|.ən, (US) -ˈhiː.li|.ən, -ˈhiːl.j|ən **-a** -ə
peril ˈper.əl, -ɪl, (US) -əl **-s** -z
perilous ˈper.əl.əs, -ɪ.ləs, (US) -əl.əs **-ly** -li **-ness** -nəs, -nɪs
perilune ˈper.ɪ.luːn, -ljuːn, (US) -luːn **-s** -z
Perim ˈper.ɪm, (US) pəˈrɪm
perimeter pəˈrɪm.ɪ.təʳ, pɪ-, perˈɪm-, ˈ-ə-, (US) pəˈrɪm.ə.t̬ɚ **-s** -z
perinatal ˌper.ɪˈneɪ.təl, (US) -t̬əl
perine|um ˌper.ɪˈniː|.əm **-a** -ə **-al** -əl
period ˈpɪə.ri.əd, (US) ˈpɪr.i- **-s** -z ˈ**period** ˌ**piece**
periodic ˌpɪə.riˈɒd.ɪk, (US) ˌpɪr.iˈɑː.dɪk *stress shift, see compound:* ˌ**periodic** ˈ**table**
periodic|al ˌpɪə.riˈɒd.ɪ.k|əl, (US) ˌpɪr.iˈɑː.dɪ- **-als** -əlz **-ally** -əl.i, -li
periodicit|y ˌpɪə.ri.əˈdɪs.ə.t|i, -ɒdˈɪs-, -ɪ.t|i, (US) ˌpɪr.i.oʊˈdɪs.ə.t̬|i, -əˈ- **-ies** -iz
periodontal ˌper.i.əʊˈdɒn.təl, (US) -oʊˈdɑːn.t̬əl, -əˈ- **-ly** -i
periodont|ic ˌper.i.əʊˈdɒn.t|ɪk, (US) -oʊˈdɑːn.t̬|ɪk, -əˈ- **-ics** -ɪks **-ist/s** -ɪst/s
peripatetic ˌper.ɪ.pəˈtet.ɪk, ˌ-ə-, (US) -ˈtet̬- **-ally** -əl.i, -li *stress shift:* ˌ**peripatetic** ˈ**teacher**
peripheral pəˈrɪf.ər.əl, pɪ-, perˈɪf-, (US) pəˈrɪf- **-s** -z **-ly** -i
peripher|y pəˈrɪf.ər|.i, pɪ-, perˈɪf-, (US) pəˈrɪf- **-ies** -iz
periphras|is pəˈrɪf.rə.s|ɪs, pɪ-, perˈɪf-, (US) pəˈrɪf- **-es** -iːz
periphrastic ˌper.ɪˈfræs.tɪk, -əˈ- **-ally** -əl.i, -li
periscope ˈper.ɪ.skəʊp, ˈ-ə-, (US) -ɪ.skoʊp **-s** -s
periscopic ˌper.ɪˈskɒp.ɪk, -əˈ-, (US) -ɪˈskɑː.pɪk
perish ˈper.ɪʃ **-es** -ɪz **-ing/ly** -ɪŋ/li **-ed** -t **-er/s** -əʳ/z, (US) -ɚ/z
perishability ˌper.ɪ.ʃəˈbɪl.ə.ti, -ɪ.ti, (US) -ə.t̬i
perishab|le ˈper.ɪ.ʃə.b|əl **-ly** -li **-leness** -əl.nəs, -nɪs
perispomenon ˌper.ɪˈspəʊ.mɪ.nən, -mə-, -nɒn, (US) -ˈspoʊ.mɪ.nɑːn
peristalsis ˌper.ɪˈstæl.sɪs, -əˈ-, (US) -ɪˈstɑːl-, -ˈstæl-
peristaltic ˌper.ɪˈstæl.tɪk, -əˈ-, (US) -ɪˈstɑːl.tɪk, -ˈstæl-
peristyle ˈper.ɪ.staɪl, ˈ-ə-, (US) ˈ-ɪ- **-s** -z
peritone|um ˌper.ɪ.təʊˈniː|.əm, ˌ-ə-, (US) ˌper.ɪ.ˈtoʊ.ni.əm, -təˈ- **-ums** -əmz **-a** -ə
peritonitis ˌper.ɪ.təʊˈnaɪ.tɪs, ˌ-ə-, -təs, (US) -ɪ.toʊˈnaɪ.t̬ɪs, -t̬əs
Perivale ˈper.ɪ.veɪl, ˈ-ə-, (US) ˈ-ɪ-

P

periwig ˈper.ɪ.wɪɡ, ˈ-ə-, (US) ˈ-ɪ- **-s** -z

periwinkle ˈper.ɪˌwɪŋ.kəl, ˈ-ə-, (US) -ɪˌ- **-s** -z

perj|ure ˈpɜː.dʒ|əʳ, (US) ˈpɝː.dʒ|ɚ **-ures** -əz, (US) -ɚz **-uring** -ər.ɪŋ **-ured** -əd, (US) -ɚd **-urer/s** -ər.əʳ/z, (US) -ɚ.ɚ/z

perjur|y ˈpɜː.dʒər|.i, (US) ˈpɝː- **-ies** -iz

perk pɜːk, (US) pɝːk **-s** -s **-ing** -ɪŋ **-ed** -t

Perkin ˈpɜː.kɪn, (US) ˈpɝː- **-s** -z

Perks pɜːks, (US) pɝːks

perk|y ˈpɜː.k|i, (US) ˈpɝː- **-ier** -i.əʳ, (US) -i.ɚ **-iest** -i.ɪst, -i.əst **-ily** -əl.i, -ɪ.li **-iness** -ɪ.nəs, -ɪ.nɪs

Perlis ˈpɜː.lɪs, (US) ˈpɝː-

perlite ˈpɜː.laɪt, (US) ˈpɝː-

Perlman ˈpɜːl.mən, (US) ˈpɝːl-

perlocutionary ˌpɜː.ləˈkjuː.ʃən.ər.i, -lɒkˈjuː-, (US) ˌpɝː.loʊˈkjuː.ʃən.er.i

perm pɜːm, (US) pɝːm **-s** -z **-ing** -ɪŋ **-ed** -d

Perm *Russian city:* pɜːm, peəm, (US) perm

permafrost ˈpɜː.mə.frɒst, (US) ˈpɝː.mə.frɑːst

permanenc|e ˈpɜː.mən.ənts, (US) ˈpɝː- **-es** -ɪz **-y** -i **-ies** -iz

permanent ˈpɜː.mən.ənt, (US) ˈpɝː- **-ly** -li

permanganate pɜːˈmæŋ.ɡə.neɪt, pə-, -nɪt, -nət, (US) pɚˈmæŋ.ɡə.neɪt

permeability ˌpɜː.mi.əˈbɪl.ə.ti, -ɪ.ti, (US) ˌpɝː.mi.əˈbɪl.ə.t̬i

permeab|le ˈpɜː.mi.ə.b|əl, (US) ˈpɝː- **-ly** -li **-leness** -əl.nəs, -nɪs

perme|ate ˈpɜː.mi|.eɪt, (US) ˈpɝː- **-ates** -eɪts **-ating** -eɪ.tɪŋ, (US) -eɪ.t̬ɪŋ **-ated** -eɪ.tɪd, (US) -eɪ.t̬ɪd

permeation ˌpɜː.miˈeɪ.ʃən, (US) ˌpɝː-

permissib|le pəˈmɪs.ə.b|əl, ˈ-ɪ-, (US) pɚˈmɪs.ə- **-ly** -li **-leness** -əl.nəs, -nɪs

permission pəˈmɪʃ.ən, (US) pɚ- **-s** -z

permissive pəˈmɪs.ɪv, (US) pɚ- **-ly** -li **-ness** -nəs, -nɪs **perˌmissive soˈciety**

permit n ˈpɜː.mɪt, (US) ˈpɝː-; (US) pɚˈmɪt **-s** -s

per|mit v pə|ˈmɪt, (US) pɚ- **-mits** -ˈmɪts **-mitting** -ˈmɪt.ɪŋ, (US) -ˈmɪt̬.ɪŋ **-mitted** -ˈmɪt.ɪd, (US) -ˈmɪt̬.ɪd

permutation ˌpɜː.mjʊˈteɪ.ʃən, -mjuːˈ-, -mjəˈ-, (US) ˌpɝː.mjuːˈ- **-s** -z

per|mute pə|ˈmjuːt, (US) pɚ- **-mutes** -ˈmjuːts **-muting** -ˈmjuː.tɪŋ, (US) -ˈmjuː.t̬ɪŋ **-muted** -ˈmjuː.tɪd, (US) -ˈmjuː.t̬ɪd **-mutable** -ˈmjuː.tə.bəl, (US) -ˈmjuː.t̬ə.bəl

Pernambuco ˌpɜː.næmˈbuː.kəʊ, -nəmˈ-, -ˈbjuː-, (US) ˌpɝː.nəmˈbuː.koʊ

pernicious pəˈnɪʃ.əs, pɜː-, (US) pɚ- **-ly** -li **-ness** -nəs, -nɪs

pernicket|y pəˈnɪk.ə.t|i, -ɪ.t|i, (US) pɚˈnɪk.ə.t̬|i **-iness** -ɪ.nəs, -ɪ.nɪs

Pernod® ˈpɜː.nəʊ, ˈpeə-, (US) perˈnoʊ

Perón, Peron pəˈrɒn, perˈɒn, pɪˈrɒn, (US) perˈoʊn, pəˈroʊn

peror|ate ˈper.ər|.eɪt, -ɒr-, (US) -ə.r|eɪt, -oʊ- **-ates** -eɪts **-ating** -eɪ.tɪŋ, (US) -eɪ.t̬ɪŋ **-ated** -eɪ.tɪd, (US) -eɪ.t̬ɪd

peroration ˌper.ərˈeɪ.ʃən, -ɒrˈ-, (US) ˌper.əˈreɪ-, -oʊˈ- **-s** -z

Perot pəˈrəʊ, perˈəʊ, (US) pəˈroʊ

Perowne pəˈrəʊn, pɪ-, perˈəʊn, (US) pəˈroʊn

peroxide pəˈrɒk.saɪd, (US) pəˈrɑːk- **-s** -z

perpend v pəˈpend, pɜː-, (US) pɚ- **-s** -z **-ing** -ɪŋ **-ed** -ɪd

perpend n ˈpɜː.pənd, (US) ˈpɝː- **-s** -z

perpendicular ˌpɜː.pənˈdɪk.jʊ.ləʳ, -kjə-, (US) ˌpɝː.pənˈdɪk.juː.lɚ, -jə- **-s** -z **-ly** -li

perpendicularity ˌpɜː.pənˌdɪk.jəˈlær.ə.ti, -jʊˈ-, -ɪ.ti, (US) ˌpɝː.pənˌdɪk.juːˈler.ə.t̬i, -jəˈ-, -ˈlær-

perpe|trate ˈpɜː.pɪ|.treɪt, -pə-, (US) ˈpɝː.pə|.treɪt **-trates** -treɪts **-trating** -treɪ.tɪŋ, (US) -treɪ.t̬ɪŋ **-trated** -treɪ.tɪd, (US) -treɪ.t̬ɪd **-trator/s** -treɪ.təʳ/z, (US) -treɪ.t̬ɚ/z

perpetration ˌpɜː.pɪˈtreɪ.ʃən, -pəˈ-, (US) ˌpɝː.pəˈ- **-s** -z

perpetual pəˈpetʃ.u.əl, -ˈpet.ju-, (US) pɚˈpetʃ.u- **-ly** -i

perpetu|ate pəˈpetʃ.u|.eɪt, pɜː-, -ˈpet.ju-, (US) pɚˈpetʃ.u- **-ates** -eɪts **-ating** -eɪ.tɪŋ, (US) -eɪ.t̬ɪŋ **-ated** -eɪ.tɪd, (US) -eɪ.t̬ɪd

perpetuation pəˌpetʃ.uˈeɪ.ʃən, pɜː-, -ˌpet.juˈ-, (US) ˌpɚ.petʃ.uˈ- **-s** -z

perpetuit|y ˌpɜː.pɪˈtʃuː.ə.t|i, -pəˈ-, -ˈtjuː-, -ɪ.t|i, (US) ˌpɝː.pəˈtuː.ə.t̬|i, -ˈtjuː- **-ies** -iz

perpetuum mobile pəˌpetʃ.u.ʊmˈməʊ.bɪ.leɪ, pɜː-, -ˌpet.ju-, -əmˈ-, (US) pɚˌpetʃ.u.əmˈmoʊ-

Perpignan ˈpɜː.piː.njɑ̃ːŋ, ˈpeə-, ˌ--ˈ-, (US) ˌper.piːˈnjɑ̃ːŋ

perplex pəˈpleks, (US) pɚ- **-es** -ɪz **-ing/ly** -ɪŋ/li **-ed** -t **-edly** -ɪd.li, -t.li **-edness** -ɪd.nəs, -t.nəs, -nɪs

perplexit|y pəˈplek.sə.t|i, -ɪ.t|i, (US) pɚˈplek.sə.t̬|i **-ies** -iz

perquisite ˈpɜː.kwɪ.zɪt, -kwə-, (US) ˈpɝː.kwɪ- **-s** -s

per quod ˌpɜːˈkwɒd, (US) ˌpɝːˈkwɑːd

Perrault ˈper.əʊ, -ˈ-, (US) perˈoʊ

Perrett ˈper.ɪt

Perrier® ˈper.i.eɪ, (US) -eɪ, ˌ--ˈ-

perrin, P~ ˈper.ɪn

perr|y, P~ ˈper|.i **-ies** -iz

per se ˌpɜːˈseɪ, (US) ˌpɝː-

Perse pɜːs, (US) pɝːs

perse|cute ˈpɜː.sɪ|.kjuːt, -sə-, (US) ˈpɝː.sɪ- **-cutes** -kjuːts **-cuting** -kjuː.tɪŋ, (US) -kjuː.t̬ɪŋ **-cuted** -kjuː.tɪd, (US) -kjuː.t̬ɪd **-cutor/s** -kjuː.təʳ/z, (US) -kjuː.t̬ɚ/z

persecution ˌpɜː.sɪˈkjuː.ʃən, -səˈ-, (US) ˌpɝː.sɪˈ- **-s** -z

Persephone pɜːˈsef.ən.i, pə-, (US) pɚ-

Persepolis pɜːˈsep.əl.ɪs, pə-, (US) pɚ-

Perseus ˈpɜː.si.əs, ˈ-sjuːs, (US) ˈpɝː-

persever|ate pəˈsev.ər|.eɪt, pɜː-, (US) pɚˈsev.ə.r|eɪt **-ates** -eɪts **-ating** -eɪ.tɪŋ, (US) -eɪ.t̬ɪŋ **-ated** -eɪ.tɪd, (US) -eɪ.t̬ɪd

perseveration pəˌsev.ərˈeɪ.ʃən, pɜː-, (US) pɚˌsev.əˈreɪ-

persever|e ˌpɜː.sɪˈvɪəʳ, -səˈ-, (US) ˌpɝː.səˈvɪr **-es** -z **-ing/ly** -ɪŋ/li **-ed** -d **-ance** -ənts

Pershing ˈpɜː.ʃɪŋ, (US) ˈpɝː-

Pershore ˈpɜː.ʃɔːʳ, (US) ˈpɝː.ʃɔːr

Persi|a ˈpɜː.ʒ|ə, -ʃ|ə, (US) ˈpɝː.ʒ|ə, -ʃ|ə **-an/s** -ən/z

persiflage ˈpɜː.sɪ.flɑːʒ, ˈpeə-, -sə-, ˌ--ˈ-, (US) ˈpɝː.sɪ-

Persil® ˈpɜː.sɪl, -səl, (US) ˈpɝː-

persimmon, P~ pəˈsɪm.ən, pɜː-, (US) pɚ- **-s** -z

persist pəˈsɪst, (US) pɚ- **-s** -s **-ing/ly** -ɪŋ/li **-ed** -ɪd

persisten|ce pəˈsɪs.tənt|s, (US) pɚ- **-cy** -si

persistent pəˈsɪs.tənt, (US) pɚ- **-ly** -li

persnickety pəˈsnɪk.ə.ti, -ɪ.ti, (US) pɚˈsnɪk.ə.t̬i

person ˈpɜː.sən, (US) ˈpɝː- **-s** -z

person|a pəˈsəʊ.n|ə, pɜː-, (US) pɚˈsoʊ- **-ae** -iː, -aɪ

personable ˈpɜː.sən.ə.bəl, (US) ˈpɝː-

personag|e ˈpɜː.sən.ɪdʒ, (US) ˈpɝː- **-es** -ɪz

personal ˈpɜː.sən.əl, ˈpɜːs.nəl, (US) ˈpɝː.sən.əl, ˈpɝːs.nəl **-ly** -i **ˌpersonal asˈsistant; ˈpersonal ˌcolumn; ˌpersonal comˈputer; ˌpersonal ˈhygiene; ˌpersonal ˈstereo**

personalit|y ˌpɜː.sənˈæl.ə.t|i, -ɪ.t|i, (US) ˌpɝː.sənˈæl.ə.t̬i **-ies** -iz

personalization, -isa- ˌpɜː.sən.əl.aɪˈzeɪ.ʃən, -ɪˈ-, (US) ˌpɝː.sən.əl.əˈ-

personaliz|e, -is|e ˈpɜː.sən.əl.aɪz, (US) ˈpɝː- **-es** -ɪz **-ing** -ɪŋ **-ed** -d

personalt|y ˈpɜː.sən.əl.t|i, (US) ˈpɝː.sən.əl.t̬|i **-ies** -iz

persona non grata pəˌsəʊ.nə.nɒnˈɡrɑː.tə, pɜː-, -nəʊnˈ-, (US) pɚˌsoʊ.nə.nɑːnˈɡrɑː.t̬ə, -ˈɡræt̬.ə

person|ate ˈpɜː.sən|.eɪt, (US) ˈpɝː- **-ates** -eɪts **-ating** -eɪ.tɪŋ, (US) -eɪ.t̬ɪŋ **-ated** -eɪ.tɪd, (US) -eɪ.t̬ɪd **-ator/s** -eɪ.təʳ/z, (US) -eɪ.t̬ɚ/z

personation ˌpɜː.sənˈeɪ.ʃən, (US) ˌpɝː- **-s** -s

personification pəˌsɒn.ɪ.fɪˈkeɪ.ʃən, pɜː-, ˌ-ə-, -fəˈ-, (US) pɚˌsɑː.nɪ- **-s** -z

personi|fy pəˈsɒn.ɪ|.faɪ, pɜː-, ˈ-ə-, (US) pɚˈsɑː.nɪ-, ˈ-nə- **-fies** -faɪz **-fying** -faɪ.ɪŋ **-fied** -faɪd

personnel ˌpɜː.sənˈel, (US) ˌpɝː- **-s** -z **personˈnel ˌmanager**

person-to-person ˌpɜː.sən.təˈpɜː.sən, (US) ˌpɝː.sən.təˈpɝːr.sən

perspective pəˈspek.tɪv, pɜː-, (US) pɚ- **-s** -z **-ly** -li

Perspex® ˈpɜː.speks, (US) ˈpɝː-

perspicacious ˌpɜː.spɪˈkeɪ.ʃəs,

-spəˈ-, (US) ˌpɝː.spɪˈ- **-ly** -li **-ness** -nəs, -nɪs
perspicacity ˌpɜː.spɪˈkæs.ə.ti, -spəˈ-, -ɪ.ti, (US) ˌpɝː.spɪˈkæs.ə.t̬i
perspicuity ˌpɜː.spɪˈkjuː.ə.ti, -ɪ.ti, (US) ˌpɝː.spɪˈkjuː.ə.t̬i
perspicuous pəˈspɪk.ju.əs, pɜː-, (US) pɚ- **-ly** -li **-ness** -nəs, -nɪs
perspiration ˌpɜː.spəʳˈreɪ.ʃən, (US) ˌpɝː.spəˈreɪ-
perspir|e pəˈspaɪəʳ, -ˈspaɪ.əʳ, (US) pɚˈspaɪ.ɚ **-es** -z **-ing** -ɪŋ **-ed** -d
per stirpes ˌpɜːˈstɜː.piːz, (US) ˌpɝːˈstɝː-
persuad|e pəˈsweɪd, (US) pɚ- **-es** -z **-ing** -ɪŋ **-ed** -ɪd **-er/s** -əʳ/z, (US) -ɚ/z
persuasion pəˈsweɪ.ʒən, (US) pɚ- **-s** -z
persuasive pəˈsweɪ.sɪv, -zɪv, (US) pɚˈsweɪ.sɪv **-ly** -li **-ness** -nəs, -nɪs
pert pɜːt, (US) pɝːt **-er** -əʳ, (US) ˈpɝː.t̬ɚ **-est** -ɪst, -əst, (US) ˈpɝː.t̬ɪst, -t̬əst **-ly** -li **-ness** -nəs, -nɪs
pertain pəˈteɪn, pɜː-, (US) pɚ- **-s** -z **-ing** -ɪŋ **-ed** -d
Perth pɜːθ, (US) pɝːθ **-shire** -ʃəʳ, -ʃɪəʳ, (US) -ʃɚ, -ʃɪr
pertinacious ˌpɜː.tɪˈneɪ.ʃəs, -təˈ-, (US) ˌpɝː.tənˈeɪ- **-ly** -li **-ness** -nəs, -nɪs
pertinacity ˌpɜː.tɪˈnæs.ə.ti, -təˈ-, -ɪ.ti, (US) ˌpɝː.tənˈæs.ə.t̬i
pertinen|ce ˈpɜː.tɪ.nənt|s, -tə-, (US) ˈpɝː.tən.ənt|s **-cy** -si
pertinent ˈpɜː.tɪ.nənt, -tə-, (US) ˈpɝː.tən.ənt **-ly** -li
perturb pəˈtɜːb, pɜː-, (US) pɚˈtɝːb **-s** -z **-ing** -ɪŋ **-ed** -d **-er/s** -əʳ/z **-able** -ə.bəl
perturbation ˌpɜː.təˈbeɪ.ʃən, -tɜːˈ-, (US) ˌpɝː.t̬ɚˈ- **-s** -z
pertussis pəˈtʌs.ɪs, pɜː-, (US) pɚ-
Pertwee ˈpɜː.twiː, (US) ˈpɝː-
Peru pəˈruː, pɪ-, (US) pə-
Perugia pəˈruː.dʒə, pɪ-, perˈuː-, -dʒi.ə, (US) perˈuː.dʒɑː, -dʒi.ə
Perugino ˌper.uˈdʒiː.nəʊ, (US) -noʊ
peruke pəˈruːk, pɪ-, perˈuːk, (US) pəˈruːk **-s** -s
perusal pəˈruː.zəl, pɪ-, (US) pəˈruː- **-s** -z
perus|e pəˈruːz, pɪ-, (US) pəˈruːz **-es** -ɪz **-ing** -ɪŋ **-ed** -d **-er/s** -əʳ/z, (US) -ɚ/z
Peruvian pəˈruː.vi.ən, pɪ-, perˈuː-, (US) pəˈruː- **-s** -z
pervad|e pəˈveɪd, pɜː-, (US) pɚ- **-es** -z **-ing** -ɪŋ **-ed** -ɪd
pervasion pəˈveɪ.ʒən, pɜː-, (US) pɚ-
pervasive pəˈveɪ.sɪv, pɜː-, -zɪv, (US) pɚˈveɪ.sɪv **-ly** -li **-ness** -nəs, -nɪs
perverse pəˈvɜːs, pɜː-, (US) pɚˈvɝːs **-ly** -li **-ness** -nəs, -nɪs
perversion pəˈvɜː.ʃən, pɜː-, -ʒən, (US) pɚˈvɝː.ʒən, -ʃən **-s** -z
perversit|y pəˈvɜː.sə.t|i, pɜː-, -ɪ.t|i, (US) pɚˈvɝː.sə.t̬|i **-ies** -iz
pervert n ˈpɜː.vɜːt, (US) ˈpɝː.vɝːt **-s** -s
per|vert v pə|ˈvɜːt, pɜː-, (US) pɚ|ˈvɝːt **-verts** -ˈvɜːts, (US) -ˈvɝːts **-verting** -ˈvɜː.tɪŋ, (US) -ˈvɝː.t̬ɪŋ **-verted** -ˈvɜː.tɪd, (US) -ˈvɝː.t̬ɪd **-verter/s** -ˈvɜː.təʳ/z, (US) -ˈvɝː.t̬ɚ/z
pervious ˈpɜː.vi.əs, (US) ˈpɝː- **-ly** -li **-ness** -nəs, -nɪs
pesante pezˈæn.teɪ, (US) pesˈɑːn-
Pescadores ˌpes.kəˈdɔː.rɪz, (US) -ˈdɔːr.iːz, -ɪs
peseta pəˈseɪ.tə, pɪ-, pesˈeɪ-, (US) pəˈseɪ.t̬ə **-s** -z
pesewa pɪˈseɪ.wɑː, (US) ˈpes.ə.wɑː; (US) peɪˈseɪ- **-s** -z
Peshawar pəˈʃɔː.əʳ, peʃˈɔː-, -ˈɑː-, -wə, (US) peʃˈɑː.wɚ, pəˈʃɑː-
peshwari peʃˈwɑː.ri
pesk|y ˈpes.k|i **-ier** -i.əʳ, (US) -i.ɚ **-iest** -i.ɪst, -i.əst **-ily** -əl.i, -ɪ.li **-iness** -ɪ.nəs, -ɪ.nɪs
peso ˈpeɪ.səʊ, (US) -soʊ **-s** -z
pessar|y ˈpes.ər|.i **-ies** -iz
pessim|ism ˈpes.ɪ.m|ɪ.zəm, ˈ-ə-, (US) ˈ-ə- **-ist/s** -ɪst/s
pessimistic ˌpes.ɪˈmɪs.tɪk, -əˈ-, (US) -əˈ- **-al** -əl **-ally** -əl.i, -li
pest, P~ pest **-s** -s
Pestalozzi ˌpes.təˈlɒt.si, (US) -ˈlɑːt-
pest|er ˈpes.t|əʳ, (US) -t|ɚ **-ers** -əz, (US) -ɚz **-ering/ly** -ər.ɪŋ/li **-ered** -əd, (US) -ɚd **-erer/s** -ər.əʳ/z, (US) -ɚ.ɚ/z
pesticide ˈpes.tɪ.saɪd, (US) -tə- **-s** -z
pestiferous pesˈtɪf.ər.əs **-ly** -li **-ness** -nəs, -nɪs
pestilenc|e ˈpes.tɪ.lənts, -təl.ənts, (US) -təl.ənts **-es** -ɪz
pestilent ˈpes.tɪ.lənt, -təl.ənt, (US) -təl.ənt **-ly** -li
pestilential ˌpes.tɪˈlen.tʃəl, -təˈ-, (US) -təˈlent.ʃəl **-ly** -i
pestl|e ˈpes.əl, -təl **-es** -z **-ing** -ɪŋ, ˈpes.lɪŋ, ˈpest.lɪŋ **-ed** -d
pesto ˈpes.təʊ, (US) -toʊ
pet pet **-s** -s **-ting** -ɪŋ, (US) ˈpet̬.ɪŋ **-ted** -ɪd, (US) ˈpet̬.ɪd
petal ˈpet.əl, (US) ˈpet̬- **-s** -z **-(l)ed** -d
pétanque peɪˈtɑ̃ːŋk
petard petˈɑːd, pɪˈtɑːd, pə-; ˈpet.ɑːd, (US) pɪˈtɑːrd **-s** -z ˌ**hoist by one's** ˌ**own pe**ˈ**tard**
Pete piːt
pet|er, P~ ˈpiː.t|əʳ, (US) -t̬|ɚ **-ers** -əz, (US) -ɚz **-ering** -ər.ɪŋ **-ered** -əd, (US) -ɚd ˌ**Peter** ˈ**Pan**
Peterborough, -boro' ˈpiː.tə.bər.ə, -ˌbʌr.ə, (US) -t̬ɚ.bɚ.oʊ
Peterhead ˌpiː.təˈhed, (US) -t̬ɚˈ- *stress shift:* ˌ**Peterhead** ˈ**resident**
Peterhouse ˈpiː.tə.haʊs, (US) -t̬ɚ-
Peterlee ˌpiː.təˈliː, ˈ---, (US) ˌpiː.t̬ɚˈliː, ˈ---
Peters ˈpiː.təz, (US) -t̬ɚz
Petersburg ˈpiː.təz.bɜːg, (US) -t̬ɚz.bɝːg
Petersfield ˈpiː.təz.fiːld, (US) -t̬ɚz-
petersham, P~ ˈpiː.tə.ʃəm, (US) -t̬ɚ- **-s** -z
Peterson, Petersen ˈpiː.tə.sən, (US) -t̬ɚ-
Pethick ˈpeθ.ɪk
petiole ˈpet.i.əʊl, ˈpiː.ti-, (US) ˈpet̬.i.oʊl **-s** -z
petit(s) bourgeois ˌpet.iˈbɔː.ʒwɑː, -ˈbʊə-, (US) pəˌtiː.bʊrˈʒwɑː; (US) ˌpet̬.i-
petite pəˈtiːt
petite bourgeoisie pəˌtiːtˌbɔː.ʒwɑːˈzi, -ˌbʊə-, (US) -ˌbʊr-
petit four ˌpet.iˈfɔːʳ, -fʊəʳ, (US) ˌpet̬.iˈfɔːr **-s** -z
petition pəˈtɪʃ.ən, pɪ-, (US) pə- **-s** -z **-ing** -ɪŋ **-ed** -d **-er/s** -əʳ/z
petit mal ˌpet.iˈmæl, (US) pəˌtiːˈmɑːl, -ˈmæl; (US) ˌpet̬.iˈ-
petit point ˌpet.iˈpɔɪnt, (US) ˈpet̬.iˌpɔɪnt
petit(s) pois ˌpet.iˈpwɑː, (US) pəˌtiːˈ-, ˌpet̬.iˈ-
Peto ˈpiː.təʊ, (US) -toʊ
Petra ˈpet.rə, (US) ˈpiː.trə, ˈpet.rə
Petraeus pəˈtreɪ.əs, petˈreɪ-
Petrarch ˈpet.rɑːk, (US) ˈpiː.trɑːrk, ˈpet.rɑːrk
Petrarchan petˈrɑː.kən, pəˈtrɑː-, pɪ-, (US) pɪˈtrɑːr-
Petre ˈpiː.təʳ, (US) -t̬ɚ
petrel ˈpet.rəl **-s** -z
petri dish ˈpet.riˌdɪʃ, (US) ˈpiː.tri- **-es** -ɪz
Petrie ˈpiː.tri
petrifaction ˌpet.rɪˈfæk.ʃən, -rəˈ-
petrification ˌpet.rɪ.fɪˈkeɪ.ʃən, -rə-, -fəˈ-
petri|fy ˈpet.rɪ|.faɪ, -rə- **-fies** -faɪz **-fying** -faɪ.ɪŋ **-fied** -faɪd
petrochem|ical ˌpet.rəʊˈkem|.ɪ.kəl **-istry** -ɪ.stri
petrodollar ˈpet.rəʊˌdɒl.əʳ, (US) -roʊˌdɑː.lɚ **-s** -z
Petrograd ˈpet.rəʊ.græd, -grɑːd, (US) -rə.græd
petrol ˈpet.rəl ˈ**petrol** ˌ**pump;** ˈ**petrol** ˌ**station**
petrolatum ˌpet.rəˈleɪ.təm, (US) -t̬əm
petrol-bomb ˈpet.rəl.bɒm, (US) -bɑːm **-s** -z **-ing** -ɪŋ **-ed** -d
petroleum pəˈtrəʊ.li.əm, pɪ-, (US) pəˈtroʊ- **pe**ˌ**troleum** ˈ**jelly**
petrolog|y petˈrɒl.ə.dʒ|i, pəˈtrɒl-, pɪ-, (US) pəˈtrɑː.lə- **-ist/s** -ɪst/s
Petruchio pɪˈtruː.ki.əʊ, pə-, petˈruː-, -tʃi-, (US) pɪˈtruː.ki.oʊ, pə-, -tʃi-
Petrushka pɪˈtruːʃ.kə, pə-, petˈruːʃ-
Pett pet
petticoat ˈpet.ɪ.kəʊt, (US) ˈpet̬.ɪ.koʊt **-s** -s
pettifogg|ing ˈpet.ɪˌfɒg|.ɪŋ, (US) ˈpet̬.ɪˌfɑː.g|ɪŋ, -ˌfɔː- **-er/s** -əʳ/z, (US) -ɚ/z
Pettigrew ˈpet.ɪ.gruː, (US) ˈpet̬-
pettish ˈpet.ɪʃ, (US) ˈpet̬- **-ly** -li **-ness** -nəs, -nɪs
Pettit ˈpet.ɪt, (US) ˈpet̬-
pettitoes ˈpet.ɪ.təʊz, (US) ˈpet̬.ɪ.toʊz
pett|y ˈpet|.i, (US) ˈpet̬- **-ier** -i.əʳ, (US) -i.ɚ **-iest** -i.ɪst, -i.əst **-ily** -əl.i, -ɪ.li **-iness/es** -ɪ.nəs/ɪz, -ɪ.nɪs/ɪz ˌ**petty** ˈ**cash;** ˌ**petty** ˈ**officer**
petty bourgeois ˌpet.iˈbɔː.ʒwɑː, -ˈbʊə-, (US) ˌpet̬.i.bʊrˈʒwɑː

Pronouncing the letters PH

The consonant digraph **ph** is usually pronounced as /f/, e.g.:

photo ˈfəʊ.təʊ (US) ˈfoʊ.t̬oʊ
alphabet ˈæl.fə.bet

However, the realization /v/ can occur in some words, e.g.:

nephew ˈnef.juː, ˈnev-
Stephen ˈstiː.vən

In addition

A much less common realization of the consonant digraph **ph** is /p/, e.g.:

shepherd ˈʃep.əd (US) -ɚd

petty bourgeoisie ˌpet.iˌbɔː.ʒwɑːˈzi, -ˌbʊə-, (US) ˌpet̬.iˌbʊr-
Petula pɪˈtʃuː.lə, pə-, -ˈtjuː-, petˈuː-, (US) petˈjuː-, pəˈtuː-, pəˈtjuː-
petulan|ce ˈpetʃ.ə.lənt|s, ˈpet.jʊ-, ˈpet.jə-, ˈpetʃ.ʊ-, (US) ˈpetʃ.ə- **-cy** -si
petulant ˈpetʃ.ə.lənt, ˈpet.jʊ-, ˈpet.jə-, ˈpetʃ.ʊ-, (US) ˈpetʃ.ə- **-ly** -li
petunia pɪˈtʃuː.ni.ə, pə-, -ˈtjuː-, ˈ-njə, (US) pəˈtuː.njə, -ˈtjuː-, ˈ-ni.ə **-s** -z
Petworth ˈpet.wəθ, -wɜːθ, (US) -wɚθ, -wɜːθ
Peugeot® ˈpɜː.ʒəʊ, (US) pɜːˈʒoʊ, puː-, pjuː- **-s** -z
Pevensey ˈpev.ən.zi
Peveril ˈpev.ər.ɪl
Pevsner ˈpevz.nər, (US) -nɚ
pew pjuː **-s** -z
pewit ˈpiː.wɪt, (US) ˈpiː-, ˈpjuː.ɪt **-s** -s
pewter ˈpjuː.tər, (US) -t̬ɚ
Peynell ˈpeɪ.nəl, -nel
peyote peɪˈəʊ.ti, (US) -ˈoʊ.t̬i **-s** -z
Peyton ˈpeɪ.tən
Pfeiffer ˈfaɪ.fər, ˈpfaɪ-, (US) -fɚ
pfennig ˈpfen.ɪg, (US) ˈfen- **-s** -z
Pfizer® ˈfaɪ.zər, (US) -zɚ-
pH ˌpiːˈeɪtʃ
Phaedo ˈfiː.dəʊ, ˈfaɪ-, (US) ˈfiː.doʊ
Phaedra ˈfiː.drə, ˈfaɪ-, (US) ˈfiː-, ˈfed.rə
Phaedrus ˈfiː.drəs, ˈfaɪ-, (US) ˈfiː-
Phaethon ˈfeɪ.ə.θən, ˈ-ɪ-, (US) -ə.θɑːn, -θən
phaeton *carriage:* ˈfeɪ.tən, -tɒn, (US) ˈfeɪ.ə.t̬ən, ˈfeɪ.tən **-s** -z
Phaeton *Greek mythology:* ˈfeɪ.ə.tən, ˈ-ɪ-, (US) -ə.tɑːn
phagocyte ˈfæg.əʊ.saɪt, (US) -oʊ-, -ə- **-s** -s
phagocytosis ˌfæg.əʊ.saɪˈtəʊ.sɪs, (US) -oʊ.saɪˈtoʊ-, ˌ-ə-
phalang|e ˈfæl.ændʒ; fəˈlændʒ, (US) feɪˈlændʒ, fə-; (US) ˈfæl.əndʒ **-es** -ɪz
phalanges (alternative plural of **phalanx**) fælˈæn.dʒiːz, fəˈlæn-, (US) fəˈlæn-, feɪˈlæn-
phalangist, P~ fælˈæn.dʒɪst, fəˈlæn-, (US) fəˈlæn-, feɪˈlæn- **-s** -s
phalanster|y ˈfæl.ən.stər|.i, (US) -ster- **-ies** -iz
phalanx ˈfæl.æŋks, (US) ˈfeɪ.læŋks, ˈfæl.æŋks **-es** -ɪz **phalanges** fælˈæn.dʒiːz, fəˈlæn-, (US) fə-, feɪ-
Phalaris ˈfæl.ə.rɪs
phalarope ˈfæl.ə.rəʊp, (US) -roʊp **-s** -s
phallic ˈfæl.ɪk
phallicism ˈfæl.ɪ.sɪ.zəm
phallocentric ˌfæl.əʊˈsen.trɪk, (US) -oʊ-, -ə- *stress shift:* ˌ**phallocentric** ˈ**culture**
phall|us ˈfæl|.əs **-uses** -ə.sɪz **-i** -aɪ
phanerogam ˈfæn.ər.əʊ.gæm, fəˈner-, (US) ˈfæn.ə.roʊ-, -ɚ.ə-; (US) fəˈner.oʊ-, ˈ-ə- **-s** -z
phanerogamic ˌfæn.ər.əʊˈgæm.ɪk, fəˌner-, (US) ˌfæn.ə.roʊˈ-, -ɚ.əˈ-, fəˌner.oʊˈ-, -əˈ-
phanerogamous ˌfæn.ərˈɒg.ə.məs, (US) -əˈrɑː.gə-
phantasm ˈfæn.tæz.əm **-s** -z
phantasmagoria ˌfæn.tæz.məˈgɔː.ri.ə, -təz-, -ˈgɒr.i-, (US) -ˈgɔːr.i-
phantasmagoric ˌfæn.tæz.məˈgɒr.ɪk, -təz-, (US) -ˈgɔːr.ɪk **-al** -əl
phantasm|al fænˈtæz.m|əl **-ally** -əl.i **-ic** -ɪk
phantas|y ˈfæn.tə.s|i, (US) -t̬ə- **-ies** -iz
phantom ˈfæn.təm, (US) -t̬əm **-s** -z
pharaoh, P~ ˈfeə.rəʊ, (US) ˈfer.oʊ, ˈfær-, ˈfeɪ.roʊ **-s** -z
pharaonic ˌfeə.reɪˈɒn.ɪk; færˈɒn.ɪk, (US) ˌfer.eɪˈɑː.nɪk, ˌfær-
pharisaic, P~ ˌfær.ɪˈseɪ.ɪk, -əˈ-, (US) ˌfer.ɪˈ-, ˌfær- **-al** -əl **-ally** -əl.i, -li **-alness** -əl.nəs, -nɪs
pharisaism, P~ ˈfær.ɪ.seɪ.ɪ.zəm, ˈ-ə-, (US) ˈfer.ɪ-, ˈfær-
pharisee, P~ ˈfær.ɪ.siː, ˈ-ə-, (US) ˈfer.ɪ-, ˈfær- **-s** -z
pharma ˈfɑː.mə, (US) ˈfɑːr-
pharmaceutic ˌfɑː.məˈsjuː.tɪk, -ˈsuː-, -ˈkjuː-, (US) ˌfɑːr.məˈsuː.t̬ɪk, -ˈsjuː- **-al/s** -əl/z **-ally** -əl.i, -li **-s** -s
pharmacist ˈfɑː.mə.sɪst, (US) ˈfɑːr- **-s** -s
pharmacolog|y ˌfɑː.məˈkɒl.ə.dʒ|i, (US) ˌfɑːr.məˈkɑː.lə- **-ist/s** -ɪst/s
pharmacop(o)ei|a ˌfɑː.mə.kəˈpiː|.ə, -kəʊˈ-, (US) ˌfɑːr.məˈkoʊ- **-as** -əz **-al** -əl
pharmac|y ˈfɑː.mə.s|i, (US) ˈfɑːr- **-ies** -iz
Pharos ˈfeə.rɒs, ˈfær.ɒs, (US) ˈfer.ɑːs
pharyngal fəˈrɪŋ.gəl, færˈɪŋ-, (US) fəˈrɪŋ-
pharyngeal ˌfær.ɪnˈdʒiː.əl; fəˈrɪn.dʒi.əl, færˈɪn-, (US) fəˈrɪn.dʒi-; (US) ˌfer.ɪnˈdʒiː-, ˌfær-
pharynges (plural of **pharynx**) færˈɪn.dʒiːz, fəˈrɪn-, (US) fəˈrɪn-
pharyngitis ˌfær.ɪnˈdʒaɪ.tɪs, -təs, (US) ˌfer.ɪnˈdʒaɪ.t̬ɪs, ˌfær-, -t̬əs
pharynx ˈfær.ɪŋks **-es** -ɪz **pharynges** færˈɪn.dʒiːz, fəˈrɪn-, (US) fə-
phas|e feɪz **-es** -ɪz **-ing** -ɪŋ **-ed** -d
phas|is ˈfeɪ.s|ɪs, (US) -s|ɪs, -z|ɪs **-es** -iːz
phatic ˈfæt.ɪk, (US) ˈfæt̬-
PhD ˌpiː.eɪtʃˈdiː **-s** -z
pheasant ˈfez.ənt **-s** -s
Phebe ˈfiː.bi
Phèdre ˈfed.rə
Phelps felps
phenacetin fɪˈnæs.ɪ.tɪn, fə-, fenˈæs-, ˈ-ə-, (US) fɪˈnæs.ə-, -tən
Phenic|ia fɪˈnɪʃ|.ə, fə-, fiː-, -ˈniː.ʃ|ə, -i|.ə, (US) fəˈnɪʃ|.ə, -ˈniː.ʃ|ə **-ian/s** -ən/z
pheno- ˈfiː.nəʊ, (US) ˈfiː.noʊ, ˈ-nə
phenobarbitone ˌfiː.nəʊˈbɑː.bɪ.təʊn, -bə-, (US) -noʊˈbɑːr.bɪ.toʊn, -nəˈ-
phenol ˈfiː.nɒl, (US) -noʊl, -nɔːl, -nɑːl
phenolphthalein ˌfiː.nɒlfˈθæl.iːn, -nɒlˈ-, -ˈθeɪ.li-, -i.ɪn, (US) -noʊlˈθæl.iːn, -noʊlfˈ-, -iː.ɪn
phenom fɪˈnɒm, fə-, (US) -ˈnɑːm **-s** -z
phenomenologic|al fɪˌnɒm.ɪ.nəˈlɒdʒ.ɪ.k|əl, fə-, ˌ-ə-, (US) fəˌnɑː.mə.nəˈlɑː.dʒɪ- **-ally** -əl.i, -li
phenomenology fɪˌnɒm.ɪˈnɒl.ə.dʒi, fə-, -əˈ-, (US) fəˌnɑː.məˈnɑː.lə-
phenomen|on fɪˈnɒm.ɪ.n|ən, fə-, ˈ-ə-, (US) fəˈnɑː.mə.n|ɑːn, -n|ən **-a** -ə **-al** -əl **-ally** -əl.i
phenotype ˈfiː.nəʊ.taɪp, (US) -noʊ-, -nə-
pheromonal ˈfer.ə.məʊ.nəl, (US) ˌfer.əˈmoʊ-
pheromon|e ˈfer.ə.məʊn, (US) -moʊn **-es** -s
phew fjuː, ɸː, pɸː

> Note: Expression of surprise, or exclamation indicating that the speaker is hot. It may have a spelling-based pronunciation /fjuː/ or be a non-verbal exclamation made by blowing air between the lips.

phi faɪ **-s** -z
phial ˈfaɪ.əl **-s** -z
Phi Beta Kappa ˌfaɪˌbiː.təˈkæp.ə, (US) -ˌbeɪ.t̬əˈ-, -ˌbiː-
Phidias ˈfaɪ.di.æs, ˈfɪd.i-, (US) ˈfɪd.i.əs
Phidippides faɪˈdɪp.ɪ.diːz
Phil fɪl
Philadelphi|a ˌfɪl.əˈdel.fi|.ə, (US) -fi|.ə, -fj|ə **-an/s** -ən/z
philand|er fɪˈlæn.d|ər, fə-, (US)

fɪˈlæn.d|ər -ers -əz, US -ɚz -ering -ər.ɪŋ -ered -əd, US -ɚd -erer/s -ər.ər/z, US -ɚ.ɚ/z

philanthrope ˈfɪl.ən.θrəʊp, -æn-, US -ən.θroʊp -s -s

philanthropic ˌfɪl.ənˈθrɒp.ɪk, US -ænˈ-, -ənˈθrɑː.pɪk -al -əl -ally -əl.i, -li

philanthrop|y fɪˈlænt.θrə.p|i, fə-, US fə-, fɪ-, -θroʊ- -ist/s -ɪst/s

Philaster fɪˈlæs.tər, US -tɚ

philatelic ˌfɪl.əˈtel.ɪk *stress shift:* ˌphilatelic ˈclub

philatel|y fɪˈlæt.əl|.i, fə-, US -ˈlæţ- -ist/s -ɪst/s

Philbrick ˈfɪl.brɪk

Philby ˈfɪl.bi

-phile, -phil faɪl, US faɪl, fɪl
Note: Suffix. Normally unstressed, e.g. **francophile** /ˈfræŋ.kəʊ.faɪl/ US /-koʊ-/.

Philemon fɪˈliː.mɒn, faɪ-, fə-, -mən, US fɪˈliː.mən, faɪ-

Philharmonia ˌfɪl.hɑːˈməʊ.ni.ə, -əˈ-, US -hɑːrˈmoʊ-, -ɚˈ-

philharmonic, P~ ˌfɪl.hɑːˈmɒn.ɪk, -əˈ-, US -hɑːrˈmɑː.nɪk, -ɚˈ- -s -s *stress shift:* ˌphilharmonic ˈorchestra

philhellene fɪlˈhel.iːn, ˈ---, US fɪlˈhel- -s -z

philhellenic ˌfɪl.helˈiː.nɪk, -həˈliː-, -ˈlen.ɪk, US -həˈlen.ɪk

philhellenism fɪlˈhel.ɪ.nɪ.zəm, ˈ-ə-, US ˈ-ə-

-philia ˈfɪl.i.ə, US ˈfɪl.i.ə, ˈ-jə
Note: Suffix. Words containing **-philia** are normally stressed on /-ˈfɪl-/, e.g. **haemophilia** /ˌhiː.məˈfɪl.i.ə/ US /-moʊˈ-/.

-philiac ˈfɪl.i.æk
Note: Suffix. Words containing **-philiac** are normally stressed on the antepenultimate syllable, e.g. **haemophiliac** /ˌhiː.məˈfɪl.i.æk/ US /-moʊˈ-/.

Philip ˈfɪl.ɪp -s -s

Philippa ˈfɪl.ɪ.pə, ˈ-ə-

Philippi fɪˈlɪp.aɪ, fə-; ˈfɪl.ɪ.paɪ, ˈ-ə-, US fɪˈlɪp.aɪ

Philippian fɪˈlɪp.i.ən, fə- -s -z

philippic fɪˈlɪp.ɪk, fə- -s -s

Philippine ˈfɪl.ɪ.piːn, ˈ-ə-, -paɪn, ˌ--ˈ-, US ˈfɪl.ə.piːn -s -z

Philippoussis ˌfɪl.ɪˈpuː.sɪs, -əˈ-

Philipps ˈfɪl.ɪps

Philistia fɪˈlɪs.ti.ə, fə-, US fə-

philistine, P~ ˈfɪl.ɪ.staɪn, ˈ-ə-, US ˈfɪl.ɪ.stiːn, -staɪn; US fɪˈlɪs.tɪn, -tiːn -s -z

philistinism ˈfɪl.ɪ.stɪ.nɪ.zəm, ˈ-ə-, US ˈfɪl.ɪ.stiː-, -staɪ-; US fɪˈlɪs.tɪ-

Phillies ˈfɪl.iz

Phillimore ˈfɪl.ɪ.mɔːr, US -mɔːr

Phillip(p)s ˈfɪl.ɪps

Phillpot ˈfɪl.pɒt, US -pɑːt -s -s

phillumenist fɪˈluː.mə.nɪst, fə-, -ˈljuː-, -mɪ-, US -ˈluː.mə- -s -s

philo- ˈfɪl.ə; fɪˈlɒ, fəˈ-, US ˈfɪl.oʊ, -ə; US fɪˈlɑː, fə-
Note: Prefix. Normally either takes primary or secondary stress on the first syllable, e.g. **philosophic** /ˌfɪl.əˈsɒf.ɪk/ US /-ˈsɑː.fɪk/, or primary stress on the second syllable, e.g. **philosophy** /fɪˈlɒs.ə.fi/ US /-ˈlɑː.sə-/.

Philoctetes ˌfɪl.əkˈtiː.tiːz, -ɒkˈ-, US -əkˈ-, -ɑːkˈ-

philodendron ˌfɪl.əˈden.drən -s -z

philologic ˌfɪl.əˈlɒdʒ.ɪk, US -ˈlɑː.dʒɪk -al -əl -ally -əl.i, -li

philolog|y fɪˈlɒl.ə.dʒ|i, fə-, US fɪˈlɑː.lə- -ist/s -ɪst/s

Philomel ˈfɪl.əʊ.mel, US -oʊ- -s -z

Philomela ˌfɪl.əʊˈmiː.lə, US -oʊˈ-

Philomena ˌfɪl.əʊˈmiː.nə, US -oʊˈ-

philosopher fɪˈlɒs.ə.fər, fə-, US -ˈlɑː.sə.fɚ -s -z

philosophic ˌfɪl.əˈsɒf.ɪk, US -əˈsɑː.fɪk, -oʊˈ- -al -əl -ally -əl.i, -li *stress shift:* ˌphilosophic ˈview

philosoph|ism fɪˈlɒs.ə.f|ɪ.zəm, fə-, US -ˈlɑː.sə- -ist/s -ɪst/s

philosophiz|e, -is|e fɪˈlɒs.ə.faɪz, fə-, US -ˈlɑː.sə- -es -ɪz -ing -ɪŋ -ed -d

philosoph|y fɪˈlɒs.ə.f|i, fə-, US -ˈlɑː.sə- -ies -iz

Philostratus fɪˈlɒs.trə.təs, fə-, US fɪˈlɑː.strə.ţəs

Philotas ˈfɪl.ə.tæs

Philpot ˈfɪl.pɒt, US -pɑːt

Philpotts ˈfɪl.pɒts, US -pɑːts

philtre, philter ˈfɪl.tər, US ˈ-tɚ -s -z

Phineas ˈfɪn.i.əs, -æs, US -əs

Phipps fɪps

phish|ing ˈfɪʃ|.ɪŋ -er/s -ər/z, US -ɚ/z

phiz, P~ fɪz

Phizackerley fɪˈzæk.əl.i, fə-, US -ɚ.li

phizog ˈfɪz.ɒg, US -ɑːg

phlebitic flɪˈbɪt.ɪk, flebˈɪt-, US fliːˈbɪţ.ɪk, flɪ-

phlebitis flɪˈbaɪ.tɪs, flebˈaɪ-, -təs, US fliːˈbaɪ.ţɪs, flɪ-, -ţəs

phlebotomy flɪˈbɒt.ə.mi, flebˈɒt-, US fliːˈbɑː.ţə-, flɪ-

Phlegethon ˈfleg.ɪ.θɒn, ˈ-ə-, -θən, US -ɪ.θɑːn, ˈfledʒ-

phlegm flem -s -z

phlegmatic flegˈmæt.ɪk, US -ˈmæţ- -al -əl -ally -əl.i, -li

phloem ˈfləʊ.em, -ɪm, US ˈfloʊ.em

phlogistic flɒdʒˈɪs.tɪk, flɒg-, fləˈdʒɪs-, fləˈgɪs-, US floʊˈdʒɪs-

phlogiston flɒdʒˈɪs.tən, flɒg-, fləˈdʒɪs-, fləˈgɪs-, -tɒn, US floʊˈdʒɪs.tɑːn, -tən

phlox flɒks, US flɑːks -es -ɪz

Phnom Penh ˌnɒmˈpen, pəˌnɒm-ˈ, US ˌnɑːmˈpen

-phobe fəʊb, US foʊb
Note: Suffix. Normally unstressed, e.g. **technophobe** /ˈtek.nəʊ.fəʊb/ US /-nə.foʊb/.

phob|ia ˈfəʊ.b|i.ə, US ˈfoʊ- -ias -i.əz -ic -ɪk

-phobia ˈfəʊ.bi.ə, US ˈfoʊ.bi.ə
Note: Suffix. Words containing **-phobia** are normally stressed on the antepenultimate syllable, e.g. **arachnophobia** /əˌræk.nəʊˈfəʊ.bi.ə/ US /-ˈfoʊ-/.

-phobic ˈfəʊ.bɪk, US ˈfoʊ.bɪk
Note: Suffix. Words containing **-phobic** are normally stressed on the penultimate syllable, e.g. **claustrophobic** /ˌklɔː.strəˈfəʊ.bɪk/ US /ˌklɑː.strəˈfoʊ-/.

Phocian ˈfəʊ.ʃi.ən, -si-, US ˈfoʊ.si- -s -z

Phocion ˈfəʊ.si.ən, -ɒn, US ˈfoʊ.si.ɑːn

Phocis ˈfəʊ.sɪs, US ˈfoʊ-

Phoebe ˈfiː.bi

Phoebus ˈfiː.bəs

Phoenic|ia fɪˈnɪʃ|.ə, fə-, fiː-, -ˈniː.ʃ|ə, -i|.ə, US fəˈnɪʃ|.ə, -ˈniː.ʃ|ə -ian/s -ən/z

phoenix, P~ ˈfiː.nɪks -es -ɪz

phon fɒn, US fɑːn -s -z

phonaesthesia ˌfəʊ.nɪsˈθiː.zi.ə, -niːsˈ-, -nəsˈ-, -ʒi.ə, -ʒə, US ˌfoʊ.nɪsˈθiː.ʒə, -niːsˈ-, -nəsˈ-

pho|nate fəʊ|ˈneɪt, US ˈfoʊ|.neɪt -nates -ˈneɪts, US -neɪt -nating -ˈneɪ.tɪŋ, US -neɪ.ţɪŋ -nated -ˈneɪ.tɪd, US -neɪ.ţɪd

phonation fəʊˈneɪ.ʃən, US foʊ-

phonatory ˈfəʊ.nə.tər.i, fəʊˈneɪ-, US ˈfoʊ.nə.tɔːr-

phon|e fəʊn, US foʊn -es -z -ing -ɪŋ -ed -d ˈphone ˌbook; ˈphone ˌbooth; ˈphone ˌbox; ˈphone ˌcall

phonecard ˈfəʊn.kɑːd, ˈfəʊŋ-, US ˈfoʊn.kɑːrd -s -z

phone-in ˈfəʊn.ɪn, US ˈfoʊn- -s -z

phonematic ˌfəʊ.nɪˈmæt.ɪk, -niːˈ-, US ˌfoʊ.nɪˈmæţ- -s -s -ally -əl.i, -li

phoneme ˈfəʊ.niːm, US ˈfoʊ- -s -z

phonemic fəʊˈniː.mɪk, US foʊ-, fə- -s -s -ally -əl.i, -li

phonemicist fəʊˈniː.mɪ.sɪst, -mə-, US foʊ-, fə- -s -s

phone-tapping ˈfəʊnˌtæp.ɪŋ, US ˈfoʊn-

phonetic fəʊˈnet.ɪk, US foʊˈneţ-, fə- -ally -əl.i, -li -s -s

phonetician ˌfəʊ.nɪˈtɪʃ.ən, ˌfɒn.ɪˈ-, -əˈ-, US ˌfoʊ.nəˈ- -s -z

phoneticiz|e, -is|e fəʊˈnet.ɪ.saɪz, ˈ-ə-, US foʊˈneţ-, fə- -es -ɪz -ing -ɪŋ -ed -d

phonetist ˈfəʊ.nɪ.tɪst, -nə-, -net.ɪst, US ˈfoʊ.nə.ţɪst -s -s

phon|ey ˈfəʊ.n|i, US ˈfoʊ- -ier -i.ər, US -i.ɚ -iest -i.ɪst, -i.əst -ily -əl.i, -ɪ.li -eys -iz -iness -ɪ.nəs, -ɪ.nɪs

phonic ˈfɒn.ɪk, US ˈfɑː.nɪk

phonics ˈfɒn.ɪks, US ˈfɑː.nɪks

phono- ˈfəʊ.nəʊ, ˈfɒn.əʊ; fəʊˈnɒ, US ˈfoʊ.nə, ˈfɑː-, -noʊ; US foʊˈnɑː, fə-
Note: Prefix. May take primary or secondary stress on the first syllable, e.g. **phonogram** /ˈfəʊ.nə.græm/ US /ˈfoʊ.nə-/, **phonographic** /ˌfəʊ.nəˈgræf.ɪk/ US /ˌfoʊ.nəˈ-/, or primary stress on the second syllable, e.g. **phonology** /fəʊˈnɒl.ə.dʒi/ US /fəˈnɑː.lə-/.

P

phonogram ˈfəʊ.nə.ɡræm, ⓊⓈ ˈfoʊ- **-s** -z
phonograph ˈfəʊ.nə.ɡrɑːf, -ɡræf, ⓊⓈ ˈfoʊ.nə.ɡræf **-s** -s
phonographer fəʊˈnɒɡ.rə.fəʳ, ⓊⓈ foʊˈnɑː.ɡrə.fɚ, fə- **-s** -z
phonographic ˌfəʊ.nəˈɡræf.ɪk, ⓊⓈ ˌfoʊ- **-al** -əl **-ally** -əl.i, -li *stress shift:* **ˌphonographic ˈsystem**
phonographist fəʊˈnɒɡ.rə.fɪst, ⓊⓈ foʊˈnɑː.ɡrə-, fə- **-s** -s
phonography fəʊˈnɒɡ.rə.fi, ⓊⓈ foʊˈnɑː.ɡrə-, fə-
phonological ˌfəʊ.nəˈlɒdʒ.ɪ.kəl, ˌfɒn.əˈ-, -əlˈɒdʒ-, ⓊⓈ ˌfoʊ.nəˈlɑː.dʒɪ-, -noʊˈ- **-ly** -i *stress shift:* **ˌphonological ˈtheory**
phonologist fəʊˈnɒl.ə.dʒɪst, ⓊⓈ fəˈnɑː.lə-, foʊ- **-s** -s
phonolog|y fəʊˈnɒl.ə.dʒ|i, ⓊⓈ fəˈnɑː.lə-, foʊ- **-ies** -iz
phonotactic ˌfəʊ.nəʊˈtæk.tɪk, ˌfɒn.əʊˈ-, ⓊⓈ ˌfoʊ.nəˈ-, -noʊˈ- **-s** -s **-ally** -əl.i, -li *stress shift:* **ˌphono-tactic ˈrules**
phonotype ˈfəʊ.nəʊ.taɪp, ⓊⓈ ˈfoʊ.nə-, -noʊ- **-s** -s
phon|y ˈfəʊ.n|i, ⓊⓈ ˈfoʊ- **-ier** -i.əʳ, ⓊⓈ -i.ɚ **-iest** -i.ɪst, -i.əst **-ily** -əl.i, -ɪ.li **-ies** -iz **-iness** -ɪ.nəs, -ɪ.nɪs
phooey ˈfuː.i
phosgene ˈfɒz.dʒiːn, ˈfɒs-, ⓊⓈ ˈfɑːs-, ˈfɑːz-
phosphate ˈfɒs.feɪt, -fɪt, -fət, ⓊⓈ ˈfɑːs.feɪt **-s** -s
phosphene ˈfɒs.fiːn, ⓊⓈ ˈfɑːs-, ˈfɑːz- **-s** -z
phosphide ˈfɒs.faɪd, ⓊⓈ ˈfɑːs- **-s** -z
phosphite ˈfɒs.faɪt, ⓊⓈ ˈfɑːs- **-s** -s
phospho- ˈfɒs.fəʊ, ⓊⓈ ˈfɑːs.foʊ, ˈ-fə
phosphor ˈfɒs.fəʳ, ⓊⓈ ˈfɑːs.fɚ, -fɔːr **-s** -z
phosphoresc|e ˌfɒs.fəʳˈes, ⓊⓈ ˌfɑːs.fəˈres **-es** -ɪz **-ing** -ɪŋ **-ed** -t
phosphorescence ˌfɒs.fəʳˈes.ənts, ⓊⓈ ˌfɑːs.fəˈres-
phosphorescent ˌfɒs.fəʳˈes.ənt, ⓊⓈ ˌfɑːs.fəˈres- *stress shift:* **ˌphosphor-escent ˈink**
phosphoric fɒsˈfɒr.ɪk, ⓊⓈ fɑːsˈfɔːr-
phosphorous ˈfɒs.fəʳr.əs, ⓊⓈ ˈfɑːs-; ⓊⓈ fɑːsˈfɔːr-
phosphorus ˈfɒs.fəʳr.əs, ⓊⓈ ˈfɑːs-
phossy ˈfɒs.i, ⓊⓈ ˈfɑː.si
photic ˈfəʊ.tɪk, ⓊⓈ ˈfoʊ.t̬ɪk
photo ˈfəʊ.təʊ, ⓊⓈ ˈfoʊ.t̬oʊ **-s** -z **ˌphoto ˈfinish**
photocall ˈfəʊ.təʊ.kɔːl, ⓊⓈ ˈfoʊ.t̬oʊ- **-s** -z
photocell ˈfəʊ.təʊ.sel, ⓊⓈ ˈfoʊ.t̬oʊ- **-s** -z
photochemical ˌfəʊ.təʊˈkem.ɪ.kəl, ⓊⓈ ˌfoʊ.t̬oʊ-
photochrome ˈfəʊ.təʊ.krəʊm, ⓊⓈ ˈfoʊ.t̬oʊ.kroʊm **-s** -z
photocompos|e ˌfəʊ.təʊ.kəmˈpəʊz, ⓊⓈ ˌfoʊ.t̬oʊ.kəmˈpoʊz **-es** -ɪz **-ing** -ɪŋ **-ed** -d
photocomposition ˌfəʊ.təʊˌkɒm.pəˈzɪʃ.ən, ⓊⓈ ˌfoʊ.t̬oʊˌkɑːm.pəˈ- **-s** -z
photocopiable ˌfəʊ.təʊˈkɒp.i.ə.bəl, ˈ-jə.bəl, ⓊⓈ ˌfoʊ.t̬oʊˈkɑː.pi.ə.bəl, -t̬əˈ-, ˈ-pjə.bəl
photocopier ˈfəʊ.təʊˌkɒp.i.əʳ, ˌfəʊ.təʊˈkɒp.i.əʳ, ⓊⓈ ˈfoʊ.t̬oʊˌkɑː.pi.ɚ, -t̬əˌ- **-s** -z
photocop|y ˈfəʊ.təʊˌkɒp|.i, ⓊⓈ ˈfoʊ.t̬oʊˌkɑː.p|i, -t̬əˌ- **-ies** -iz **-ying** -i.ɪŋ **-ied** -id
photoelectric ˌfəʊ.təʊ.ɪˈlek.trɪk, ⓊⓈ ˌfoʊ.t̬oʊ- *stress shift:* **ˌphoto-electric ˈcell**
photo-essay ˈfəʊ.təʊˌes.eɪ, ⓊⓈ ˌfoʊ.t̬oʊ- **-s** -z
Photofit® ˈfəʊ.təʊ.fɪt, ⓊⓈ ˈfoʊ.t̬oʊ-
photogenic ˌfəʊ.təʊˈdʒen.ɪk, -ˈdʒiː.nɪk, ⓊⓈ ˌfoʊ.t̬oʊˈdʒen.ɪk, -t̬əˈ- *stress shift:* **ˌphotogenic ˈperson**
photogrammetr|ist ˌfəʊ.təʊˈɡræm.ə.tr|ɪst, ˈ-ɪ-, ⓊⓈ ˌfoʊ.t̬oʊ- **-ists** -ɪsts **-y** -i
photograph ˈfəʊ.tə.ɡrɑːf, -ɡræf, ⓊⓈ ˈfoʊ.t̬oʊ.ɡræf, -t̬ə- **-s** -s **-ing** -ɪŋ **-ed** -t
photographer fəˈtɒɡ.rə.fəʳ, ⓊⓈ -ˈtɑː.ɡrə.fɚ **-s** -z
photographic ˌfəʊ.təˈɡræf.ɪk, ⓊⓈ ˌfoʊ.t̬əˈ- **-al** -əl **-ally** -əl.i, -li *stress shift:* **ˌphotographic ˈmodel**
photography fəˈtɒɡ.rə.fi, ⓊⓈ -ˈtɑː.ɡrə-
photogravure ˌfəʊ.təʊ.ɡrəˈvjʊəʳ, -ˈvjɔːʳ, ⓊⓈ ˌfoʊ.t̬oʊ.ɡrəˈvjʊr, -t̬ə- **-s** -z
photojournal|ism ˌfəʊ.təʊˈdʒɜː.nəl|.ɪ.zəm, ⓊⓈ ˌfoʊ.t̬oʊˈdʒɝː- **-ist/s** -ɪst/s
photomontag|e ˌfəʊ.təʊ.mɒnˈtɑːʒ, ⓊⓈ ˌfoʊ.t̬oʊ.mɑːnˈ- **-es** -ɪz
photon ˈfəʊ.tɒn, ⓊⓈ ˈfoʊ.tɑːn **-s** -z
photo-opportunit|y ˌfəʊ.təʊˌɒp.əˈtʃuː.nə.t|i, -ˈtjuː-, -nɪ-, ⓊⓈ ˌfoʊ.t̬oʊˌɑː.pɚˈtuː.nə.t̬|i, -ˈtjuː- **-ies** -iz
photosensitive ˌfəʊ.təʊˈsent.sɪ.tɪv, -sə-, ⓊⓈ ˌfoʊ.t̬oʊˈsent.sə-
photosensitivity ˌfəʊ.təʊˌsent.sɪˈtɪv.ə.ti, -səˈ-, -ə.ti, ⓊⓈ ˌfoʊ.t̬oʊˌsent.səˈt̬ɪv.ə.t̬i
photosensitiz|e, -is|e ˌfəʊ.təʊˈsent.sɪ.taɪz, ⓊⓈ ˌfoʊ.t̬oʊˈsent.sə- **-es** -ɪz **-ing** -ɪŋ **-ed** -d
Photoshop® ˈfəʊ.təʊˌʃɒp, ⓊⓈ ˈfoʊ.t̬oʊˌʃɑːp **-s** -s **-ping** -ɪŋ **-ped** -t
photosphere ˈfəʊ.təʊ.sfɪəʳ, ⓊⓈ ˈfoʊ.t̬oʊ.sfɪr **-s** -z
photo|stat® ˈfəʊ.təʊ|.stæt, ⓊⓈ ˈfoʊ.t̬oʊ-, -t̬ə- **-stats** -stæts **-statting** -stæt.ɪŋ, ⓊⓈ -stæt̬.ɪŋ **-statted** -stæt.ɪd, ⓊⓈ -stæt̬.ɪd
photostatic ˌfəʊ.təʊˈstæt.ɪk, ⓊⓈ ˌfoʊ.t̬oʊˈstæt̬.ɪk, -t̬əˈ- *stress shift:* **ˌphotostatic ˈcopy**
photosynthesis ˌfəʊ.təʊˈsɪnt.θə.sɪs, -θɪ-, ⓊⓈ ˌfoʊ.t̬oʊˈ-, -t̬əˈ-
photosynthesiz|e, -is|e ˌfəʊ.təʊˈsɪnt.θə.saɪz, -θɪ-, ⓊⓈ ˌfoʊ.t̬oʊˈ-, -t̬əˈ- **-es** -ɪz **-ing** -ɪŋ **-ed** -d
photosynthetic ˌfəʊ.təʊ.sɪnˈθet.ɪk, ⓊⓈ ˌfoʊ.t̬oʊ.sɪnˈθet̬-, -t̬ə- **-ally** -əl.i, -li
phototropic ˌfəʊ.təʊˈtrɒp.ɪk, ⓊⓈ ˌfoʊ.t̬oʊˈtrɑː.pɪk, -t̬əˈ-, -ˈtroʊ- **-ally** -əl.i, ⓊⓈ -li
phototropism fəʊˈtɒt.rə.pɪ.zəm; ˌfəʊ.təʊˈtrəʊ-, ⓊⓈ foʊˈtɑː.trə- **-s** -z
phrasal ˈfreɪ.zəl **-s** -z **ˌphrasal ˈverb**
phras|e freɪz **-es** -ɪz **-ing** -ɪŋ **-ed** -d **ˈphrase ˌbook**
phraseologic ˌfreɪ.zi.əˈlɒdʒ.ɪk, ⓊⓈ -ˈlɑː.dʒɪk **-al** -əl **-ally** -əl.i, -li
phraseolog|y ˌfreɪ.ziˈɒl.ə.dʒ|i, ⓊⓈ -ˈɑː.lə- **-ies** -iz
phrenetic frəˈnet.ɪk, frɪ-, frenˈet-, ⓊⓈ frɪˈnet̬-, frə- **-al** -əl **-ally** -əl.i, -li
phrenic ˈfren.ɪk
phrenologic|al ˌfren.əlˈɒdʒ.ɪ.k|əl, ⓊⓈ -əˈlɑː.dʒɪ- **-ally** -əl.i, -li
phrenolog|y frɪˈnɒl.ə.dʒ|i, frə-, frenˈɒl-, ⓊⓈ frɪˈnɑː.lə-, frə- **-ist/s** -ɪst/s
Phryg|ia ˈfrɪdʒ|.i.ə **-ian/s** -i.ən/z, ⓊⓈ -i.ən/z, -jən/z
Phryne ˈfraɪ.ni
phthalic ˈθæl.ɪk, ˈfθæl-, ˈθeɪ.lɪk, ⓊⓈ ˈθæl-, ˈfθæl-
phthisis ˈθaɪ.sɪs, ˈfθaɪ-, ⓊⓈ ˈθaɪ-, ˈtaɪ-, ˈfθaɪ-
Phuket ˌpuːˈket
phut fʌt
phylacter|y fɪˈlæk.təʳr|.i **-ies** -iz
Phyllis ˈfɪl.ɪs
phyllo ˈfaɪ.ləʊ, ˈfiː-, ˈfɪl.əʊ, ⓊⓈ ˈfiː.loʊ, ˈfaɪ- **ˌphyllo ˈpastry** ⓊⓈ **ˈphyllo ˌpastry**
phylloxer|a fɪˈlɒk.səʳr|.ə; ˌfɪl.ɒkˈsɪə.r|ə, ⓊⓈ fɪˈlɑːk.sɚ|.ə; ⓊⓈ ˌfɪl.ɑːkˈsɪr|- **-ae** -iː **-as** -əz
phyl|um ˈfaɪ.l|əm **-a** -ə
physiatric ˌfɪz.iˈæt.rɪk **-s** -s **-al** -əl
physiatricist ˌfɪz.iˈæt.rɪ.sɪst, -rə- **-s** -s
physic ˈfɪz.ɪk **-s** -s **-king** -ɪŋ **-ked** -t
physic|al ˈfɪz.ɪ.k|əl **-als** -əlz **-ally** -əl.i, -li **ˌphysical eduˈcation**; **ˌphysical ˈtherapy**
physicality ˌfɪz.ɪˈkæl.ə.ti, -ɪ.ti, ⓊⓈ -ə.t̬i
physician fɪˈzɪʃ.ən, fə-, ⓊⓈ fɪ- **-s** -z
physicist ˈfɪz.ɪ.sɪst, ˈ-ə-, ⓊⓈ ˈ-ɪ- **-s** -s
physio ˈfɪz.i.əʊ, ⓊⓈ -oʊ **-s** -z
physio- ˈfɪz.i.əʊ; ˌfɪz.iˈɒ, ⓊⓈ ˈfɪz.i.oʊ, -ə; ⓊⓈ ˌfɪz.iˈɑː
Note: Prefix. May have secondary stress on the first syllable, e.g. **physiologic** /ˌfɪz.i.əˈlɒdʒ.ɪk/ ⓊⓈ /-ˈlɑː.dʒɪk/, or secondary stress on the first syllable with primary stress on the third syllable, e.g. **physiology** /ˌfɪz.iˈɒl.ə.dʒi/ ⓊⓈ /-ˈɑː.lə-/.
physiognomic ˌfɪz.i.əʊˈnɒm.ɪk, ⓊⓈ -ɑːɡˈnɑː.mɪk, -əˈ- **-al** -əl **-ally** -əl.i, -li
physiognomist ˌfɪz.iˈɒn.ə.mɪst, ⓊⓈ -ˈɑːɡ.nə- **-s** -s

physiognom|y ˌfɪz.iˈɒn.ə.m|i, (US) -ˈɑːg.nə- **-ies** -iz
physiographic ˌfɪz.i.əʊˈgræf.ɪk, (US) -oʊˈ-, -əˈ- **-al** -əl
physiograph|y ˌfɪz.iˈɒg.rə.f|i, (US) -ˈɑː.grə- **-er/s** -əʳ/z, (US) -ɚ/z
physiologic ˌfɪz.i.əˈlɒdʒ.ɪk, (US) -ˈlɑː.dʒɪk **-al** -əl **-ally** -əl.i, -li
physiolog|y ˌfɪz.iˈɒl.ə.dʒ|i, (US) -ˈɑː.lə- **-ist/s** -ɪst/s
physiotherap|y ˌfɪz.i.əʊˈθer.ə.p|i, (US) -oʊˈ-, -əˈ- **-ist/s** -ɪst/s
physique fɪˈziːk, fə-, (US) fɪ-
phytoplankton ˌfaɪ.təʊˈplæŋk.tən, -tɒn, (US) -ţoʊˈplæŋk.tən
pi paɪ **-s** -z
Piaf ˈpiː.æf, -ˈ-, (US) ˈpiː.ɑːf, -ˈ-
piaff|e piˈæf, pjæf, (US) pjæf **-es** -s **-ing** -ɪŋ **-ed** -t
Piaget piˈæʒ.eɪ, -ˈɑː.ʒeɪ, (US) ˌpiː.əˈʒeɪ, pjɑːˈ-
pia mater ˌpaɪ.əˈmeɪ.təʳ, ˌpiː-, (US) -ˈmeɪ.ţɚ, -ˈmɑː-
pianissimo ˌpiː.əˈnɪs.ɪ.məʊ, -ænˈɪs-, pjɑːˈnɪs-, ˌpiː.ɑːˈ-, pjænˈɪs-, pjəˈnɪs-, (US) ˌpiː.əˈnɪs.ɪ.moʊ **-s** -z
pianist ˈpiː.ə.nɪst, piˈæn-, (US) ˈpiː.ən.ɪst; (US) piˈæn-, ˈpjæn- **-s** -s
piano n *instrument:* piˈæn.əʊ, ˈpjæn-, piˈɑː-, (US) piˈæn.oʊ, ˈpjæn- **-s** -z **piˌano acˈcordion; piˈano ˌbar; piˈano ˌstool**
piano adv, adj, n *softly:* ˈpjɑː.nəʊ, piˈɑː-, (US) -noʊ **-s** -z
pianoforte piˌæn.əʊˈfɔː.teɪ, ˌpjæn-, ˌpjɑː.nəʊˈ-, piˌɑː-, -ti, (US) piˌæn.oʊˈfɔːr.teɪ, -ti; (US) -ˈæn.oʊ.fɔːrt **-s** -z
Pianola® ˌpiː.əˈnəʊ.lə, pjænˈəʊ-, ˌpiː.ænˈ-, (US) ˌpiː.əˈnoʊ-, -ænˈoʊ- **-s** -z
piastre, piaster piˈæs.təʳ, -ˈɑː.stəʳ, (US) -ˈæs.tɚ **-s** -z
piazza piˈæt.sə, -ˈɑːt-, (US) -ˈɑːt.sə, -sɑː, -ˈɑː.zə, -ˈæt.sə, -ˈæz.ə **-s** -z
pibroch ˈpiː.brɒk, -brɒx, (US) -brɑːk **-s** -s
pica ˈpaɪ.kə
picador ˈpɪk.ə.dɔːʳ, (US) -dɔːr **-s** -z
picadores (alternative plural of **picador**) ˌpɪk.əˈdɔː.riːz, (US) -ˈdɔːr.iːz
picaninn|y ˌpɪk.əˈnɪn|.i, ˈpɪk.ə.nɪ.n|i, (US) ˈpɪk- **-ies** -iz
Picardy ˈpɪk.ə.di, -ɑː-, (US) ˈ-ɚ-, ˈ-ɑːr-
picaresque ˌpɪk.əˈresk, (US) -ɚˈ-
picaroon ˌpɪk.əˈruːn **-s** -z **-ing** -ɪŋ **-ed** -d
Picasso pɪˈkæs.əʊ, (US) -ˈkɑː.soʊ, -ˈkæs.oʊ
picayun|e ˌpɪk.əˈjuːn, -eɪˈ-, -iˈ-, (US) ˈpɪk.ə.juːn, ˌ--ˈ- **-es** -z **-ish** -ɪʃ
Piccadilly ˌpɪk.əˈdɪl.i *stress shift, see compound:* **ˌPiccadilly ˈCircus**
piccalilli ˌpɪk.əˈlɪl.i, (US) ˈpɪk.ə.lɪl-
piccaninn|y ˌpɪk.əˈnɪn|.i, ˈpɪk.ə.nɪ.n|i, (US) ˈpɪk- **-ies** -iz
piccolo ˈpɪk.ə.ləʊ, (US) -loʊ **-s** -z
pick pɪk **-s** -s **-ing** -ɪŋ **-ed** -t **-er/s** -əʳ/z, (US) -ɚ/z
pickaback ˈpɪk.ə.bæk
pickaninn|y ˌpɪk.əˈnɪn|.i, ˈpɪk.ə.nɪ.n|i, (US) ˈpɪk- **-ies** -iz
pickax|(e) ˈpɪk.æks **-es** -ɪz **-ing** -ɪŋ **-ed** -t
pickerel ˈpɪk.ər.əl **-s** -z
Pickering ˈpɪk.ər.ɪŋ
pick|et ˈpɪk|.ɪt **-ets** -ɪts **-eting** -ɪ.tɪŋ, (US) -ɪ.ţɪŋ **-eted** -ɪ.tɪd, (US) -ɪ.ţɪd **-er/s** -ɪ.təʳ/z, (US) -ɪ.ţɚ/z **ˈpicket ˌline**
Pickford ˈpɪk.fəd, (US) -fɚd
pickings ˈpɪk.ɪŋz
pickl|e ˈpɪk.əl **-es** -z **-ing** -ɪŋ, ˈpɪk.lɪŋ **-ed** -d
Pickles ˈpɪk.əlz
picklock ˈpɪk.lɒk, (US) -lɑːk **-s** -s
pick-me-up ˈpɪk.mi.ʌp **-s** -s
pickpocket ˈpɪkˌpɒk.ɪt, (US) -ˌpɑː.kɪt **-s** -s
pickup ˈpɪk.ʌp **-s** -s **ˈpick-up ˌtruck**
Pickwick ˈpɪk.wɪk **ˌPickwick ˈPapers** (US) **ˈPickwick ˌPapers**
Pickwickian pɪkˈwɪk.i.ən
pick|y ˈpɪk|.i **-ier** -i.əʳ, (US) -i.ɚ **-iest** -i.ɪst, -i.əst **-iness** -ɪ.nəs, -ɪ.nɪs
picnic ˈpɪk.nɪk **-s** -s **-king** -ɪŋ **-ked** -t **-ker/s** -əʳ/z, (US) -ɚ/z
picot ˈpiː.kəʊ; -ˈ-, pɪˈkəʊ, (US) ˈpiː.koʊ, -ˈ-
picotee ˌpɪk.əˈtiː, (US) ˌpɪk.əˈtiː, ˈ--- **-s** -z
picric ˈpɪk.rɪk
Pict pɪkt **-s** -s
Pictish ˈpɪk.tɪʃ
pictogram ˈpɪk.təʊ.græm, (US) -toʊ-, -tə- **-s** -z
pictograph ˈpɪk.təʊ.grɑːf, -græf, (US) -toʊ.græf, -tə- **-s** -s
Picton ˈpɪk.tən
pictorial pɪkˈtɔː.ri.əl, (US) -ˈtɔːr.i- **-ly** -i
pict|ure ˈpɪk.tʃ|əʳ, (US) -tʃ|ɚ **-ures** -əz, (US) -ɚz **-uring** -ər.ɪŋ **-ured** -əd, (US) -ɚd **ˈpicture ˌbook; ˌpicture ˈpostcard; ˌpicture ˈwindow**
picturesque ˌpɪk.tʃərˈesk **-ly** -li **-ness** -nəs, -nɪs
piddl|e ˈpɪd.əl **-es** -z **-ing** -ɪŋ, ˈpɪd.lɪŋ **-ed** -d **-er/s** -əʳ/z, (US) -ɚ/z, ˈpɪd.ləʳ/z, -lɚ/z
piddling adj ˈpɪd.əl.ɪŋ, ˈpɪd.lɪŋ
pidgin, P~ ˈpɪdʒ.ɪn **-s** -z
Pidsley ˈpɪdz.li
pie paɪ **-s** -z **ˈpie ˌchart; as ˌeasy as ˈpie; have a ˌfinger in ˌevery ˈpie; to ˌeat ˌhumble ˈpie; ˌpie in the ˈsky**
piebald ˈpaɪ.bɔːld, (US) -bɔːld, -bɑːld **-s** -z
piec|e piːs **-es** -ɪz **-ing** -ɪŋ **-ed** -t **ˈpiece ˌrate; ˌpiece of ˈcake**
pièce(s) de résistance piˌes.də.rez.ɪˈstɑ̃ːns, ˌpjes-, -rɪ.zɪˈ-, -rə-, (US) ˌpjes.də.reɪ.ziːˈstɑ̃ːns
piecemeal ˈpiːs.miːl
piecework ˈpiːs.wɜːk, (US) -wɝːk
piecrust ˈpaɪ.krʌst **-s** -s
pied paɪd **ˌpied ˈpiper**
pied(s)-à-terre ˌpjeɪd.ɑːˈteəʳ, ˌpjed-, (US) -ˈter
piedmont, P~ ˈpiːd.mənt, -mɒnt, (US) -mɑːnt
piedmontese, P~ ˌpiːd.mənˈtiːz, -mɒnˈ-, (US) -mɑːnˈ-
pie-eyed ˌpaɪˈaɪd *stress shift:* **ˌpie-eyed ˈreveller**
pier pɪəʳ, (US) pɪr **-s** -z
pierc|e, P~ pɪəs, (US) pɪrs **-es** -ɪz **-ing/ly** -ɪŋ/li **-ed** -t **-er/s** -əʳ/z, (US) -ɚ/z **-eable** -ə.bəl
Piercy ˈpɪə.si, (US) ˈpɪr-
pierglass ˈpɪə.glɑːs, (US) ˈpɪr.glæs **-es** -ɪz
pierhead ˈpɪə.hed, (US) ˈpɪr- **-s** -z
Pierian paɪˈer.i.ən, -ˈɪə.ri-, pi-, (US) paɪˈɪr.i-
Pierpoint ˈpɪə.pɔɪnt, (US) ˈpɪr-
Pierpont ˈpɪə.pɒnt, -pənt, (US) ˈpɪr.pɑːnt
Pierre *name:* piˈeəʳ, (US) piːˈer *place in US:* pɪəʳ, (US) pɪr
Pierrepont ˈpɪə.pɒnt, -pənt, (US) ˈpɪr.pɑːnt
pierrot, P~ ˈpɪə.rəʊ, ˈpjer.əʊ, (US) ˌpiː.əˈroʊ **-s** -z
Piers pɪəz, (US) pɪrz
Pierson ˈpɪə.sən, (US) ˈpɪr-
Piesporter ˈpiːz.pɔː.təʳ, (US) -pɔːr.ţɚ
pietà ˌpiː.etˈɑː, -eɪˈtɑː, ˈ---, (US) ˌpiː.eɪˈtɑː, ˌpjeɪˈ- **-s** -z
Pietermaritzburg ˌpiː.təˈmær.ɪts.bɜːg, (US) -ţɚˈmer.ɪts.bɝːg
Pieterson ˈpiː.tə.sən, (US) -ţɚ-
piet|ism ˈpaɪ.ə.t|ɪ.zəm, ˈpaɪ.ɪ-, (US) ˈpaɪ.ə- **-ist/s** -ɪst/s
pietistic ˌpaɪ.əˈtɪs.tɪk
piet|y ˈpaɪ.ə.t|i, ˈpaɪ.ɪ-, (US) ˈpaɪ.ə.ţ|i **-ies** -iz
piezoelectric piˌet.səʊ.ɪˈlek.trɪk; ˌpiː.zəʊ-; paɪˌiː.zəʊ-; ˌpaɪ.ɪ-, (US) piːˈeɪ.zoʊ-; (US) paɪˈiː-, ˈpiː- **-al** -əl
piezoelectricity piˌet.səʊˌel.ɪkˈtrɪs.ə.ti; ˌpiː.zəʊ-; paɪˌiː.zəʊ-; ˌpaɪ.ɪ-; -ˌiː.lekˈ-; -ɪ.lekˈ-; -ɪ.ti, (US) piːˌeɪ.zoʊˌiː.lekˈtrɪs.ə.ţi, paɪˌiː.zoʊ-, ˌpiː.zoʊ-, -iːˌlekˈ-
piffl|e ˈpɪf.əl **-es** -z **-ing** -ɪŋ, ˈpɪf.lɪŋ **-ed** -d
pig pɪg **-s** -z **-ging** -ɪŋ **-ged** -d **ˈpig ˌiron; ˌmake a ˌpig's ˈear of**
pigeon ˈpɪdʒ.ən, -ɪn, (US) -ən **-s** -z
pigeonhol|e n, v ˈpɪdʒ.ən.həʊl, -ɪn-, (US) -ən.hoʊl **-es** -z **-ing** -ɪŋ **-ed** -d
pigeon-toed ˌpɪdʒ.ənˈtəʊd, -ɪn-, (US) ˈpɪdʒ.ən.toʊd *stress shift, British only:* **ˌpigeon-toed ˈwalk**
pigger|y ˈpɪg.ər|.i **-ies** -iz
piggish ˈpɪg.ɪʃ **-ly** -li **-ness** -nəs, -nɪs
Piggott ˈpɪg.ət
pigg|y ˈpɪg|.i **-ies** -iz **-ier** -i.əʳ, (US) -i.ɚ **-iest** -i.ɪst, -i.əst
piggyback ˈpɪg.i.bæk
piggybank ˈpɪg.i.bæŋk **-s** -s
pigheaded ˌpɪgˈhed.ɪd **-ly** -li **-ness** -nəs, -nɪs *stress shift:* **ˌpigheaded ˈperson**
piglet ˈpɪg.lət, -lɪt, (US) -lɪt **-s** -s
pigment n ˈpɪg.mənt **-s** -s
pigmen|t v pɪgˈmen|t, ˈpɪg.mən|t, (US) ˈpɪg.mən|t **-ts** -ts **-ting** -tɪŋ, (US) -ţɪŋ **-ted** -tɪd, (US) -ţɪd

pigmentation ˌpɪg.mənˈteɪ.ʃən, -menˈ- -s -z
pigm|y ˈpɪg.m|i -ies -iz
pignut ˈpɪg.nʌt -s -s
Pigott ˈpɪg.ət
pigpen ˈpɪg.pen -s -z
pigskin ˈpɪg.skɪn -s -z
pig-sticking ˈpɪgˌstɪk.ɪŋ
pigst|y ˈpɪg.st|aɪ -ies -aɪz
pigswill ˈpɪg.swɪl
pigtail ˈpɪg.teɪl -s -z
Pikachu ˈpɪk.ə.tʃuː, (US) ˈpiː.kə-
pike, P~ paɪk -s -s ˌ**Pike's** ˈ**Peak**
pikelet ˈpaɪ.klət, -klɪt, (US) -klɪt -s -s
piker ˈpaɪ.kər, (US) -kɚ -s -z
pikestaff ˈpaɪk.stɑːf, (US) -stæf -s -s
pilaf(f) ˈpiː.læf, ˈpɪl.æf, -ˈ-, (US) piːˈlɑːf, ˈ-- -s -s
pilaster pɪˈlæs.tər, pə-, (US) pɪˈlæs.tɚ -s -z
Pilate ˈpaɪ.lət
Pilates pɪˈlɑː.tiːz, pə-
Pilatus pɪˈlɑː.təs, (US) pɪ-; (US) piːˈlɑː.tʊs
pilau ˈpiː.laʊ, ˈpɪl.aʊ, -ˈ-, (US) pɪˈlɔː, piː-, -ˈlaʊ, -ˈlɑː -s -z
pilchard ˈpɪl.tʃəd, (US) -tʃɚd -s -z
pil|e paɪl -es -z -ing -ɪŋ -ed -d
pile-driv|er ˈpaɪlˌdraɪ.v|ər, (US) -v|ɚ -ers -əz, (US) -ɚz -ing -ɪŋ
pile-up ˈpaɪl.ʌp -s -s
pilf|er ˈpɪl.f|ər, (US) -f|ɚ -ers -əz, (US) -ɚz -ering -ər.ɪŋ -ered -əd, (US) -ɚd -erer/s -ər.ər/z, (US) -ɚ.ɚ/z
pilferage ˈpɪl.fər.ɪdʒ
Pilger ˈpɪl.dʒər, (US) -dʒɚ
pilgrim ˈpɪl.grɪm -s -z ˌ**Pilgrim** ˈ**Father**
pilgrimag|e ˈpɪl.grɪ.mɪdʒ, -grə- -es -ɪz
piling ˈpaɪ.lɪŋ -s -z
Pilkington ˈpɪl.kɪŋ.tən
pill pɪl -s -z -ing -ɪŋ -ed -d
pillag|e ˈpɪl.ɪdʒ -es -ɪz -ing -ɪŋ -ed -d -er/s -ər/z, (US) -ɚ/z
pillar ˈpɪl.ər, (US) -ɚ -s -z -ed -d **from** ˌ**pillar to** ˈ**post**
pillar-box ˈpɪl.ə.bɒks, (US) -ɚ.bɑːks -es -ɪz
pillbox ˈpɪl.bɒks, (US) -bɑːks -es -ɪz
pillion ˈpɪl.i.ən, (US) ˈ-jən -s -z
pillock ˈpɪl.ək -s -s
pillor|y ˈpɪl.ər|.i -ies -iz -ying -i.ɪŋ -ied -id
pillow ˈpɪl.əʊ, (US) -oʊ -s -z -ing -ɪŋ -ed -d ˈ**pillow** ˌ**slip;** ˈ**pillow** ˌ**talk**
pillowcas|e ˈpɪl.əʊ.keɪs, (US) -oʊ- -es -ɪz
Pillsbury ˈpɪlz.bər.i, (US) -ˌber-
pilocarpine ˌpaɪ.ləʊˈkɑː.pɪn, -paɪn, (US) ˌpaɪ.loʊˈkɑːr.piːn, ˌpɪl.oʊˈ-, -pɪn
pi|lot ˈpaɪ|.lət -lots -ləts -loting -lə.tɪŋ, (US) -lə.t̬ɪŋ -loted -lə.tɪd, (US) -lə.t̬ɪd -lotage -lə.tɪdʒ, (US) -lə.t̬ɪdʒ ˈ**pilot** ˌ**light**
Pilsen ˈpɪl.zən, -sən
pilsener, P~ ˈpɪlz.nər, ˈpɪl.snər, -sən.ər, (US) ˈpɪlz.nɚ, ˈpɪl.snɚ
Pilsworth ˈpɪlz.wəθ, -wɜːθ, (US) -wɚθ, -wɜːθ
Piltdown ˈpɪlt.daʊn
pilule ˈpɪl.juːl -s -z
pimento pɪˈmen.təʊ, (US) -toʊ -s -z
pimiento pɪˈmjen.təʊ, -ˈmen-, (US) -toʊ -s -z
Pimlico ˈpɪm.lɪ.kəʊ, (US) -koʊ
Pimm pɪm -'s -z
pimp pɪmp -s -s -ing -ɪŋ -ed -t
pimpernel ˈpɪm.pə.nel, -nəl, (US) -pɚ- -s -z
pimple ˈpɪm.pəl -s -z -d -d
pimpl|y ˈpɪm.pəl|.i, ˈ-pl|i, (US) ˈ-pl|i -iness -ɪ.nəs, -ɪ.nɪs
pin pɪn -s -z -ning -ɪŋ -ned -d ˈ**pin** ˌ**money;** ˈ**pin** ˌ**tuck;** ˌ**pins and** ˈ**needles**
PIN pɪn ˈ**PIN** ˌ**number**
piña colada ˌpiː.nə.kəʊˈlɑː.də, -njə-, (US) -njə.koʊˈ- -s -z
pinafore, P~ ˈpɪn.ə.fɔːr, (US) -fɔːr -s -z ˈ**pinafore** ˌ**dress**
piñata pɪnˈjɑː.tə, (US) -t̬ə -s -z
pinball ˈpɪn.bɔːl, ˈpɪm-, (US) ˈpɪn-, -bɑːl -s -z ˈ**pinball ma**ˌ**chine**
pince-nez *singular:* ˌpæ̃nsˈneɪ, ˌpænts-, ˌpɪnts-, ˈ-ˌ- *plural:* -ˈneɪz
pincer ˈpɪnt.sər, (US) -sɚ -s -z
pinch pɪntʃ -es -ɪz -ing -ɪŋ -ed -t -er/s -ər/z, (US) -ɚ/z ˌ**take something with a** ˌ**pinch of** ˈ**salt**
pinchbeck ˈpɪntʃ.bek -s -s
Pinches ˈpɪn.tʃɪz
pinch-hit ˈpɪntʃ.hɪt -s -s -ting -ɪŋ, (US) -ˌhɪt̬.ɪŋ
Pinckney ˈpɪŋk.ni
pincushion ˈpɪnˌkʊʃ.ən, ˈpɪŋ-, (US) ˈpɪn- -s -z
Pindar ˈpɪn.dər, (US) -dɚ
Pindaric pɪnˈdær.ɪk, (US) -ˈdær-, -ˈder- -s -s
Pindus ˈpɪn.dəs
pin|e paɪn -es -z -ing -ɪŋ -ed -d ˈ**pine** ˌ**cone;** ˈ**pine** ˌ**kernel;** ˈ**pine** ˌ**marten;** ˈ**pine** ˌ**needle;** ˈ**pine** ˌ**nut**
pineal ˈpɪn.i.əl; paɪˈniː-, (US) ˈpɪn.i-
pineapple ˈpaɪ.næp.əl -s -z
Pinel pɪˈnel, (US) pɪ-, ˌpiː-
Pinero pɪˈnɪə.rəʊ, -ˈneə-, (US) -ˈnɪr.oʊ
piner|y ˈpaɪ.nər|.i -ies -iz
pinetum paɪˈniː.təm, (US) -t̬əm
pinewood, P~ ˈpaɪn.wʊd -s -z
ping pɪŋ -s -z -ing -ɪŋ -ed -d -er/s -ər/z, (US) -ɚ/z
ping-pong ˈpɪŋˌpɒŋ, (US) -ˌpɑːŋ, -ˌpɔːŋ
pinhead ˈpɪn.hed -s -z -ed -ɪd
pinhole ˈpɪn.həʊl, (US) -hoʊl -s -z ˌ**pinhole** ˈ**camera**
pinion ˈpɪn.jən -s -z -ing -ɪŋ -ed -d
pink, P~ pɪŋk -s -s -ing -ɪŋ -ed -t -er -ər, (US) -ɚ -est -ɪst, -əst ˌ**pink** ˈ**gin;** ˌ**pink** ˈ**slip;** ˈ**pinking** ˌ**shears**
pink-collar ˌpɪŋkˈkɒl.ər, (US) -ˈkɑː.lɚ *stress shift:* ˌ**pink-collar** ˈ**workers**
Pinker ˈpɪŋ.kər, (US) -kɚ
Pinkerton ˈpɪŋ.kə.tən, (US) -kɚ.t̬ən
pink-eye ˈpɪŋk.aɪ -d -d
pinkie ˈpɪŋ.ki -s -z
pinkish ˈpɪŋ.kɪʃ
pinko ˈpɪŋ.kəʊ, (US) -koʊ -(e)s -z
pink|y ˈpɪŋ.k|i -ies -iz
pinnac|e ˈpɪn.ɪs, -əs -es -ɪz
pinnacl|e ˈpɪn.ə.kəl, ˈ-ɪ- -es -z -ing -ɪŋ, ˈpɪn.ə.klɪŋ, ˈ-ɪ- -ed -d
pinnate ˈpɪn.eɪt, -ɪt, -ət, (US) -eɪt, -ɪt
pinner, P~ ˈpɪn.ər, (US) -ɚ -s -z
pinn|y ˈpɪn|.i -ies -iz
Pinocchio pɪˈnəʊ.ki.əʊ, -ˈnɒk.i-, (US) pəˈnoʊ.ki.oʊ, pɪ-
Pinochet ˈpɪn.əʊ.ʃeɪ, (US) ˈpiː.noʊ.ʃet, -ʃeɪ
pinoc(h)le ˈpiː.nʌk.əl, -nɒk-, (US) -nʌk-, -nɑː.kəl
pinot ˈpiː.nəʊ, -ˈ-, (US) piːˈnoʊ -s -z
Pinot Blanc ˌpiː.nəʊˈblɑ̃ːŋ, (US) -noʊˈ-
Pinot Noir ˌpiː.nəʊˈnwɑːr, (US) -noʊˈnwɑːr
pin|point ˈpɪn|.pɔɪnt, ˈpɪm-, (US) ˈpɪn- -points -pɔɪnts -pointing -ˌpɔɪn.tɪŋ, (US) -ˌpɔɪn.t̬ɪŋ -pointed -ˌpɔɪn.tɪd, (US) -ˌpɔɪn.t̬ɪd
pinprick ˈpɪn.prɪk, ˈpɪm-, (US) ˈpɪn- -s -s
Pinsent ˈpɪnt.sənt
pinstripe ˈpɪn.straɪp -s -s -d -t
pint paɪnt -s -s
pinta *pint of milk:* ˈpaɪn.tə, (US) -t̬ə -s -z
pinta, P~ *disease:* ˈpɪn.tə, ˈpiːn-, (US) ˈpɪn.t̬ə, -tɑː
pintado pɪnˈtɑː.dəʊ, (US) -doʊ -(e)s -z
pintail ˈpɪn.teɪl -s -z
Pinter ˈpɪn.tər, (US) -t̬ɚ
Pinteresque ˌpɪn.tərˈesk, (US) -t̬ɚˈ-
pinto ˈpɪn.təʊ, (US) -t̬oʊ -(e)s -z ˈ**pinto bean**
pint-pot ˈpaɪnt.pɒt, ˌ-ˈ-, (US) ˈpaɪnt.pɑːt -s -s
pint-size ˈpaɪnt.saɪz -d -d
pin-up ˈpɪn.ʌp -s -s
pinwheel ˈpɪn.hwiːl -s -z
pinxit ˈpɪŋk.sɪt
Pinxton ˈpɪŋk.stən
Pioline ˌpiː.əʊˈliːn, (US) ˌpiː.oʊˈliːn
pioneer, P~ ˌpaɪ.əˈnɪər, (US) -ˈnɪr -s -z -ing -ɪŋ -ed -d
pious ˈpaɪ.əs -ly -li -ness -nəs, -nɪs
pip, P~ pɪp -s -s -ping -ɪŋ -ped -t
pipal ˈpiː.pəl -s -z
pip|e, P~ paɪp -es -s -ing -ɪŋ -ed -t -er/s -ər/z, (US) -ɚ/z ˈ**pipe** ˌ**cleaner;** ˈ**pipe** ˌ**dream;** ˌ**pipe of** ˈ**peace**
pipeclay ˈpaɪp.kleɪ
pipeline ˈpaɪp.laɪn -s -z
Piper ˈpaɪ.pər, (US) -pɚ
pipette pɪˈpet, (US) paɪ-, pɪ- -s -s
piping ˈpaɪ.pɪŋ
pipistrel(le) ˌpɪp.ɪˈstrel, -əˈ-, ˈ---, (US) ˌpɪp.ɪˈstrel -s -z
pipit ˈpɪp.ɪt -s -s
pipkin ˈpɪp.kɪn -s -z
Pippa ˈpɪp.ə
pippin ˈpɪp.ɪn -s -z
pipsqueak ˈpɪp.skwiːk -s -s
piquancy ˈpiː.kənt.si
piquant ˈpiː.kənt, -kɑːnt -ly -li
piqu|e piːk -es -s -ing -ɪŋ -ed -t
piqué ˈpiː.keɪ, (US) -ˈ-
piquet *card game:* piːˈket, -ˈkeɪ;

ˈpɪk.et, -eɪ, (US) piːˈkeɪ, -ˈket *soldiers:* ˈpɪk.ɪt -s -s
Piquet *racing driver:* ˈpiː.keɪ
piracly ˈpaɪə.rə.s|i, (US) ˈpaɪ- -ies -iz
Piraeus paɪˈriː.əs, pɪˈreɪ-, pə-, (US) paɪˈriː-
Pirandello ˌpɪr.ənˈdel.əʊ, (US) -oʊ
piranha pɪˈrɑː.nə, pə-, -njə, (US) pəˈrɑː.njə, pɪ-, -nə -s -z
pira|te ˈpaɪə.rə|t, -rɪ|t, (US) ˈpaɪ.rə|t -tes -ts -ting -tɪŋ, (US) -t̬ɪŋ -ted -tɪd, (US) -t̬ɪd
piratical paɪəˈræt.ɪ.kəl, pə-, pɪ-, (US) paɪˈræt̬- -ly -i
Pirbright ˈpɜː.braɪt, (US) ˈpɝː-
Pirelli® pɪˈrel.i, pə-
Pirie ˈpɪr.i
pirogue pɪˈrəʊg, pə-, (US) -ˈroʊg -s -z
pirou|ette ˌpɪr.u|ˈet -ettes -ˈets -etting -ˈet.ɪŋ, (US) -ˈet̬.ɪŋ -etted -ˈet.ɪd, (US) -ˈet̬.ɪd *stress shift:* ˌ**pirouetting** ˈ**dancer**
Pisa ˈpiː.zə
pis aller ˌpiːzˈæl.eɪ, ˌ--ˈ-, (US) -ælˈeɪ -s -z
Piscator pɪˈskeɪ.təʳ, (US) -ˈskɑː.tɔːr
piscatorial ˌpɪs.kəˈtɔː.ri.əl, (US) -ˈtɔːr.i-
piscatory ˈpɪs.kə.tər.i, (US) -tɔːr-
Piscean ˈpaɪ.si.ən, ˈpɪs.i-, ˈpɪs.ki-; pɪˈsiː-, (US) ˈpaɪ.si-, ˈpɪs.i-
Pisces ˈpaɪ.siːz, ˈpɪs.iːz, ˈpɪs.kiːz, (US) ˈpaɪ.siːz, ˈpɪs.iːz
pisciculture ˈpɪs.ɪˌkʌl.tʃəʳ, (US) -tʃɚ
piscin|a pɪˈsiː.n|ə -as -əz -ae -iː
piscine ˈpɪs.aɪn, ˈpɪsk-, ˈpaɪ.saɪn, (US) ˈpaɪ.siːn, ˈpɪs.iːn-, -aɪn, -ɪn
Piscis| Austrinus ˌpɪs.ɪs|.ɒsˈtraɪ.nəs, ˌ-kɪs-, -ɔːˈstraɪ-, (US) ˌpaɪ.sɪs|.ɔːˈstraɪ-, ˌpɪs.ɪs-, -ɑːˈ- -Australis -ɒsˈtrɑː.lɪs, -ɔːˈstrɑː-, (US) -ɔːˈstreɪ-, -ɑːˈ-
Pisgah ˈpɪz.gə, -gɑː, (US) -gə
pish pɪʃ
Pisidia paɪˈsɪd.i.ə, (US) pɪ-
Pisistratus paɪˈsɪs.trə.təs, pɪ-
pismire ˈpɪs.maɪ.əʳ, (US) -maɪ.ɚ, ˈpɪz- -s -z
piss pɪs -es -ɪz -ing -ɪŋ -ed -t -er/s -əʳ/z, (US) -ɚ/z ˈ**piss** ˌ**artist**
pissant ˈpɪs.ənt, (US) -ænt -s -s
Pissarro pɪˈsɑː.rəʊ, (US) -ˈsɑːr.oʊ
pissed pɪst ˌ**pissed as a** ˈ**newt**; ˌ**pissed as a** ˈ**fart**
pisshead ˈpɪs.hed -s -z
pissoir ˈpɪs.wɑːʳ, ˈpiː.swɑːʳ, (US) piːˈswɑːr -s -z
piss-poor ˌpɪsˈpɔːʳ, -ˈpʊəʳ, (US) -ˈpʊr, ˈpɔːr *stress shift:* ˌ**piss-poor** ˈ**work**
pisspot ˈpɪs.pɒt, (US) -pɑːt -s -s
piss-take ˈpɪs.teɪk -s -s
piss-up ˈpɪs.ʌp -s -s
pistachio pɪˈstæʃ.i.əʊ, -ˈstɑː.ʃi-, (US) -ˈstæʃ.i.oʊ, -ˈstɑː.ʃi- -s -z
piste piːst -s -s
pistil ˈpɪs.tɪl, -təl -s -z
pistol ˈpɪs.təl -s -z
pistole pɪˈstəʊl; ˈpɪs.təʊl, (US) pɪˈstoʊl -s -z
pistol-whip ˈpɪs.təl.*h*wɪp -s -s -ping -ɪŋ -ped -t
piston ˈpɪs.tən -s -z ˈ**piston** ˌ**rod**
pit pɪt -s -s -ting -ɪŋ, (US) ˈpɪt̬.ɪŋ -ted -ɪd, (US) ˈpɪt̬.ɪd ˌ**pit bull** ˈ**terrier**; ˈ**pit** ˌ**pony**; ˈ**pit** ˌ**stop**
pita ˈpɪt.ə, (US) ˈpiː.t̬ə ˈ**pita** ˌ**bread**
pit-a-pat ˌpɪt.əˈpæt, ˈ---, (US) ˈpɪt̬.ə.pæt
Pitcairn *surname:* pɪtˈkeən, (US) -ˈkern *island:* ˈpɪt.keən, -ˈ-, (US) pɪtˈkern, ˈ--
pitch pɪtʃ -es -ɪz -ing -ɪŋ -ed -t ˈ**pitch** ˌ**pipe**
pitch-and-putt ˌpɪtʃ.ənˈdpʌt
pitch-and-toss ˌpɪtʃ.ən*d*ˈtɒs, (US) -ˈtɑːs
pitch-black ˌpɪtʃˈblæk *stress shift:* ˌ**pitch-black** ˈ**night**
pitchblende ˈpɪtʃ.blend
pitch-dark ˌpɪtʃˈdɑːk, (US) -ˈdɑːrk *stress shift:* ˌ**pitch-dark** ˈ**night**
pitcher, P~ ˈpɪtʃ.əʳ, (US) -ɚ -s -z ˈ**pitcher** ˌ**plant**
pitchfork ˈpɪtʃ.fɔːk, (US) -fɔːrk -s -s -ing -ɪŋ -ed -t
pitch|man ˈpɪtʃ|.mən, -mæn -men -mən, -men
pitchpine ˈpɪtʃ.paɪn -s -z
pitchy ˈpɪtʃ.i
piteous ˈpɪt.i.əs, (US) ˈpɪt̬- -ly -li -ness -nəs, -nɪs
pitfall ˈpɪt.fɔːl, (US) -fɔːl, -fɑːl -s -z
pith pɪθ -s -s -ing -ɪŋ -ed -t -less -ləs, -lɪs ˌ**pith** ˈ**helmet** (US) ˈ**pith** ˌ**helmet**
pithead ˈpɪt.hed -s -z
pithecanthrop|us ˌpɪθ.ɪ.kænˈθrəʊ.p|əs; -ˈkænt.θrə-, (US) -ˈkænt.θroʊ-, -θrə-; (US) -kænˈθroʊ- -i -aɪ
Pither ˈpaɪ.θəʳ, -ðəʳ, (US) -θɚ, -ðɚ
pith|y ˈpɪθ|.i -ier -i.əʳ, (US) -i.ɚ -iest -i.ɪst, -i.əst -ily -əl.i, -ɪ.li -iness -ɪ.nəs, -ɪ.nɪs
pitiab|le ˈpɪt.i.ə.b|əl, (US) ˈpɪt̬- -ly -li -leness -əl.nəs, -nɪs
pitiful ˈpɪt.ɪ.fəl, -fʊl, (US) ˈpɪt̬- -ly -i -ness -nəs, -nɪs
pitiless ˈpɪt.i.ləs, -lɪs, (US) ˈpɪt̬- -ly -li -ness -nəs, -nɪs
Pitlochry pɪtˈlɒk.ri, -ˈlɒx-, (US) -ˈlɑː.kri
pit|man, P~ ˈpɪt|.mən -men -mən, -men
piton ˈpiː.tɒn, -tɔ̃ːŋ, (US) -tɑːn -s -z
Pitsea ˈpɪt.siː, -si
Pitt pɪt
pitta ˈpɪt.ə, (US) ˈpɪt̬- ˈ**pitta** ˌ**bread**
pittanc|e ˈpɪt.ənts, (US) ˈpɪt- -es -ɪz
Pittaway ˈpɪt.ə.weɪ, (US) ˈpɪt̬-
pitted ˈpɪt.ɪd, (US) ˈpɪt̬-
pitter-patter ˈpɪt.əˌpæt.əʳ, ˌpɪt.əˈpæt-, (US) ˈpɪt̬.ɚˌpæt̬.ɚ
Pittman ˈpɪt.mən
Pitts pɪts
Pittsburgh ˈpɪts.bɜːg, (US) -bɝːg
pituitary pɪˈtʃuː.ɪ.tər.i, ˈ-ə-, -ˈtjuː-, (US) -ˈtuː.ə.ter-, pə-, -ˈtjuː- **pi**ˈ**tuitary** ˌ**gland**
pit|y ˈpɪt|.i, (US) ˈpɪt̬- -ies -iz -ying/ly -i.ɪŋ/li -ied -id
pityriasis ˌpɪt.ɪˈraɪ.ə.sɪs, -əˈ-, (US) ˌpɪt̬.ɪˈ-
Pius ˈpaɪ.əs
piv|ot ˈpɪv|.ət -ots -əts -oting -ə.tɪŋ, (US) -ə.t̬ɪŋ -oted -ə.tɪd, (US) -ə.t̬ɪd
pivotal ˈpɪv.ə.təl, (US) -t̬əl -ly -i
pix pɪks
pixel ˈpɪk.səl, -sel -s -z
pixellated ˈpɪk.səl.eɪ.tɪd, (US) -t̬ɪd
pix|ie, -|y ˈpɪk.s|i -ies -iz
pixilated ˈpɪk.sɪ.leɪ.tɪd, -sə-, (US) -t̬ɪd
Pizarro pɪˈzɑː.rəʊ, (US) -ˈzɑːr.oʊ
pizazz pɪˈzæz, pə-, (US) pɪ-
pizza ˈpiːt.sə, ˈpɪt-, (US) ˈpiːt- -s -z
pizzazz pɪˈzæz, pə-, (US) pɪ-
pizzeria ˌpiːt.səˈriː.ə, ˌpɪt-, (US) ˌpiːt- -s -z
Pizzey ˈpɪt.si; ˈpɪz.i
pizzicat|o ˌpɪt.sɪˈkɑː.t|əʊ, (US) -t|oʊ -os -əʊz, (US) -oʊz -i -iː
placability ˌplæk.əˈbɪl.ə.ti, -ə.ti, (US) -ə.t̬i, ˌpleɪ.kəˈ-
placab|le ˈplæk.ə.b|əl, (US) ˈplæk.ə-, ˈpleɪ.kə- -ly -li -leness -əl.nəs, -nɪs
placard n ˈplæk.ɑːd, (US) -ɑːrd, -ɚd
placard v ˈplæk.ɑːd, (US) -ɑːrd, -ɚd; (US) pləˈkɑːrd, plækˈɑːrd -s -z -ing -ɪŋ -ed -ɪd
placa|te pləˈkeɪ|t, pleɪ-, (US) ˈpleɪ.keɪ|t, ˈplæk.eɪ|t; (US) pleɪˈkeɪ|t -tes -ts -ting -tɪŋ, (US) -t̬ɪŋ -ted -tɪd, (US) -t̬ɪd
placatory pləˈkeɪ.tər.i, pleɪˈ-, (US) ˈpleɪ.kə.tɔːr-, ˈplæk.ə-
plac|e pleɪs -es -ɪz -ing -ɪŋ -ed -t -er/s -əʳ/z, (US) -ɚ/z ˈ**place** ˌ**setting**
placebo pləˈsiː.bəʊ, plæsˈiː-, (US) pləˈsiː.boʊ -s -z **pla**ˈ**cebo ef**ˌ**fect**
placekick ˈpleɪs.kɪk -s -s -ing -ɪŋ -ed -t
place|man ˈpleɪs|.mən -men -mən
placement ˈpleɪs.mənt -s -s
placent|a pləˈsen.t|ə, plæsˈen-, (US) pləˈsen.t̬|ə -as -əz -ae -iː
placet ˈpleɪ.set, -sɪt -s -s
placid, P~ ˈplæs.ɪd -ly -li -ness -nəs, -nɪs
placidity pləˈsɪd.ə.ti, plæsˈɪd-, -ɪ.ti, (US) pləˈsɪd.ə.t̬i
placket ˈplæk.ɪt -s -s
plagal ˈpleɪ.gəl
plag|e plɑːʒ -es -ɪz
plagiarism ˈpleɪ.dʒər.ɪ.zəm, -dʒi.ə.rɪ-, (US) -dʒɚ.ɪ-, -dʒi.ɚ- -s -z
plagiarist ˈpleɪ.dʒər.ɪst, -dʒi.ə.rɪst, (US) -dʒɚ.ɪst, -dʒi.ɚ- -s -s
plagiaristic ˌpleɪ.dʒərˈɪs.tɪk, -dʒi.əˈrɪs-, (US) -dʒəˈrɪs-, -dʒi.əˈ-
plagiariz|e, -is|e ˈpleɪ.dʒər.aɪz, -dʒi.ə.raɪz, (US) -dʒə.raɪz, -dʒi.ə- -es -ɪz -ing -ɪŋ -ed -d
plagiar|y ˈpleɪ.dʒər|.i, ˈ-dʒi.ə.r|i, (US) ˈ-dʒɚ|.i, ˈ-dʒi.ɚ|- -ies -iz
plagu|e pleɪg -es -z -ing -ɪŋ -ed -d -er/s -əʳ/z, (US) -ɚ/z
plagu|y ˈpleɪ.g|i -ily -əl.i, -ɪ.li -iness -ɪ.nəs, -ɪ.nɪs
plaice pleɪs
plaid plæd -s -z -ed -ɪd
Plaid Cymru ˌplaɪdˈkʌm.ri
plain pleɪn -s -z -er -əʳ, (US) -ɚ -est

-ɪst, -əst -ly -li -ness -nəs, -nɪs ˌ**plain 'clothes**; ˌ**plain 'sailing**
plainchant 'pleɪn.tʃɑːnt, US -tʃænt -s -s -ing -ɪŋ -ed -ɪd
plainsong 'pleɪn.sɒŋ, US -sɑːŋ, -sɔːŋ
plain-spoken ˌpleɪn'spəʊ.kən, US -'spoʊ-, '-ˌ-- -ness -nəs, -nɪs *stress shift:* ˌ**plain-spoken 'person**
plaint pleɪnt -s -s
plaintiff 'pleɪn.tɪf, US -t̬ɪf -s -s
plaintive 'pleɪn.tɪv, US -t̬ɪv -ly -li -ness -nəs, -nɪs
Plaistow 'plæs.təʊ, 'plɑː.stəʊ, US 'plæs.toʊ, 'plɑː.stoʊ

> Note: The local pronunciation is /'plɑː.stəʊ/.

plait plæt -s -s -ing -ɪŋ, US 'plæt̬.ɪŋ -ed -ɪd, US 'plæt̬.ɪd
plan plæn -s -z -ning -ɪŋ -ned -d -ner/s -əʳ/z, US -ɚ/z '**planning perˌmission**
planchet 'plɑːn.tʃɪt, US 'plæn-, -tʃet -s -s
planchette plɑ̃ːn'ʃet, plɑːn-, US plæn'ʃet -s -s
Planck plæŋk
plan|e pleɪn -es -z -ing -ɪŋ -ed -d '**plane ˌtree**
planer, P~ 'pleɪ.nəʳ, US -nɚ -s -z
planet 'plæn.ɪt -s -s
planetari|um ˌplæn.ɪ'teə.ri|.əm, -ə'-, US -ɪ'ter.i- -ums -əmz -a -ə
planetary 'plæn.ɪ.tᵊr.i, '-ə-, US -ɪ.ter-
plangent 'plæn.dʒᵊnt -ly -li
planimeter plæn'ɪm.ɪ.təʳ, plə'nɪm-, '-ə-, US plə'nɪm.ə.t̬ɚ, pleɪ- -s -z
planimetric ˌplæn.ɪ'met.rɪk, US ˌpleɪ.nɪ'-, ˌplæn.ɪ'-
planimetry plæn'ɪm.ə.tri, plə'nɪm-, '-ɪ-, US plə'nɪm-, pleɪ-
plank plæŋk -s -s -ing -ɪŋ -ed -t
plankton 'plæŋk.tən, -tɒn, US -tən
plant, P~ n, v plɑːnt, US plænt -s -s -ing -ɪŋ, US 'plæn.t̬ɪŋ -ed -ɪd, US 'plæn.t̬ɪd -er/s -əʳ/z, US 'plæn.t̬ɚ/z
Plantagenet plæn'tædʒ.ᵊn.ɪt, -ɪn-, -ət, -et, US -ə.nɪt -s -s
plantain 'plæn.teɪn, 'plɑːn-, -tɪn, US 'plæn.tɪn, -tᵊn -s -z
plantation plæn'teɪ.ʃᵊn, plɑːn-, US plæn- -s -z
Plantin 'plæn.tɪn, 'plɑːn-, US 'plɑːn.tæn, 'plæn-
plantocrac|y plɑːn'tɒk.rə.s|i, US plæn'tɑː.krə- -ies -iz
plaque plɑːk, plæk, US plæk -s -s
plash plæʃ -es -ɪz -ing -ɪŋ -ed -t -y -i
plasm 'plæz.ᵊm
plasm|a 'plæz.m|ə -ic -ɪk
plasmolysis plæz'mɒl.ə.sɪs, '-ɪ-, US -'mɑː.lɪ-
Plassey 'plæs.i
plast|er 'plɑː.st|əʳ, US 'plæs.t|ɚ -ers -əz, US -ɚz -ering -ᵊr.ɪŋ -ered -əd, US -ɚd -erer/s -ᵊr.əʳ/z, US -ɚ.ɚ/z ˌ**plaster 'cast**; ˌ**plaster of 'Paris**
plasterboard 'plɑː.stə.bɔːd, US 'plæs.tɚ.bɔːrd
plastic 'plæs.tɪk, 'plɑː.stɪk, US 'plæs.tɪk -s -s ˌ**plastic 'bullet**; ˌ**plastic 'money**; ˌ**plastic 'surgeon**; ˌ**plastic 'surgery**
Plasticine® 'plæs.tə.siːn, 'plɑː.stə-, -stɪ-, US 'plæs.tɪ-
plasticity plæs'tɪs.ə.ti, plɑː'stɪs-, -ɪ.ti, US plæs'tɪs.ə.t̬i
plasticiz|e, -is|e 'plæs.tɪ.saɪz, 'plɑː.stɪ-, -stə-, US 'plæs.tɪ- -es -ɪz -ing -ɪŋ -ed -d -er/s -əʳ/z, US -ɚ/z
plastid 'plæs.tɪd -s -z
Plata 'plɑː.tə, US -tɑː
Plataea plə'tiː.ə
platan 'plæt.ᵊn -s -z
plat(s) du jour ˌplɑː.djuː'ʒʊəʳ, -dʊ'-, -də'-, US -'ʒʊr
plat|e, P~ n, v pleɪt -es -s -ing -ɪŋ, US 'pleɪ.t̬ɪŋ -ed -ɪd, US 'pleɪ.t̬ɪd ˌ**plate tec'tonics**
plateau 'plæt.əʊ; -'-, plə'təʊ, US plæt'oʊ -s -z -x -z -ing -ɪŋ -ed -d
plateful 'pleɪt.fʊl -s -z
plate-glass ˌpleɪt'glɑːs, US -'glæs ˌ**plate-glass 'window**
platelayer 'pleɪtˌleɪ.əʳ, US -ɚ -s -z
platelet 'pleɪt.lət, -lɪt -s -s
platen 'plæt.ᵊn -s -z
platform 'plæt.fɔːm, US -fɔːrm -s -z -ing -ɪŋ -ed -d ˌ**platform 'shoes**
Plath plæθ
Platignum® plæt'ɪg.nəm, plə'tɪg-, US plə'tɪg-
platiniz|e, -is|e 'plæt.ɪ.naɪz, -ᵊn.aɪz, US -ᵊn.aɪz -es -ɪz -ing -ɪŋ -ed -d
platinum 'plæt.ɪ.nəm, -ᵊn.əm, US 'plæt.nəm ˌ**platinum 'blond(e)**
platitude 'plæt.ɪ.tʃuːd, '-ə-, -tuːd, US 'plæt̬.ə.tuːd, -tjuːd -s -z
platitudinarian ˌplæt.ɪˌtʃuː.dɪ'neə.ri.ən, -əˌ-, -ˌtjuː-, -də'-, US ˌplæt̬.əˌtuː.dɪ'ner.i-, -ˌtjuː- -s -z
platitudinous ˌplæt.ɪ'tʃuː.dɪ.nəs, -ə'-, -'tjuː-, -dᵊn.əs, US ˌplæt̬.ə'tuː.dᵊn.əs, -'tjuː- -ly -li
Plato 'pleɪ.təʊ, US -t̬oʊ
platonic plə'tɒn.ɪk, plæt'ɒn-, US plə'tɑː.nɪk, pleɪ- -al -ᵊl -ally -ᵊl.i, -li
Platon|ism 'pleɪ.tᵊn|.ɪ.zᵊm -ist/s -ɪst/s
platoon plə'tuːn -s -z
Platt plæt -s -s
platter 'plæt.əʳ, US 'plæt̬.ɚ -s -z
platyp|us 'plæt.ɪ.p|əs, '-ə-, US 'plæt̬.ɪ- -uses -ə.sɪz -i -aɪ
plaudit 'plɔː.dɪt, US 'plɑː-, 'plɔː- -s -s
plausibility ˌplɔː.zə'bɪl.ə.ti, -zɪ'-, -ɪ.ti, US ˌplɑː.zə'bɪl.ə.t̬i, ˌplɔː-
plausib|le 'plɔː.zɪ.b|ᵊl, -zə-, US 'plɑː.zə-, 'plɔː- -ly -li -leness -ᵊl.nəs, -nɪs
Plautus 'plɔː.təs, US 'plɑː.t̬əs, 'plɔː-
play pleɪ -s -z -ing -ɪŋ -ed -d -er/s -əʳ/z, US -ɚ/z ˌ**play on 'words**; **play the 'field**; '**playing ˌcard**; '**playing ˌfield**
playable 'pleɪ.ə.bᵊl
play-act 'pleɪ.ækt -s -z -ing -ɪŋ -ed -ɪd -or/s -əʳ/z, US -ɚ/z
playback 'pleɪ.bæk
playbill 'pleɪ.bɪl -s -z
playboy 'pleɪ.bɔɪ -s -z
Play-Doh® 'pleɪ.dəʊ, US -doʊ
player, P~ 'pleɪ.əʳ, US -ɚ -s -z
Playfair 'pleɪ.feəʳ, US -fer
playfellow 'pleɪˌfel.əʊ, US -oʊ -s -z
playful 'pleɪ.fᵊl, -fʊl -ly -i -ness -nəs, -nɪs
playgoer 'pleɪˌgəʊ.əʳ, US -ˌgoʊ.ɚ -s -z
playground 'pleɪ.graʊnd -s -z
playgroup 'pleɪ.gruːp -s -s
playhou|se 'pleɪ.haʊ|s -ses -zɪz
playlet 'pleɪ.lət, -lɪt -s -s
playlist 'pleɪ.lɪst -s -s
playmate 'pleɪ.meɪt -s -s
play-off 'pleɪ.ɒf, US -ɑːf -s -s
playpen 'pleɪ.pen -s -z
playroom 'pleɪ.rʊm, -ruːm, US -ruːm, -rʊm -s -z
playschool 'pleɪ.skuːl -s -z
PlayStation® 'pleɪˌsteɪ.ʃᵊn -s -z
playsuit 'pleɪ.suːt, -sjuːt, US -suːt -s -s
Playtex® 'pleɪ.teks
plaything 'pleɪ.θɪŋ -s -z
playtime 'pleɪ.taɪm -s -z
playwright 'pleɪ.raɪt -s -s
plaza, P~ 'plɑː.zə, US 'plɑː-, 'plæz.ə -s -z
plc ˌpiː.el'siː
plea pliː -s -z
plea-bargain 'pliːˌbɑː.gɪn, -gən, US -ˌbɑːr.gən -s -z -ing -ɪŋ -ed -d
plead pliːd -s -z -ing/ly -ɪŋ/li -ed -ɪd **pled** pled **pleader/s** 'pliː.dəʳ/z, US -dɚ/z
pleading 'pliː.dɪŋ -s -z
pleasance, P~ 'plez.ᵊnts
pleas|ant 'plez|.ᵊnt -anter -ᵊn.təʳ, US -ᵊn.t̬ɚ -antest -ᵊn.tɪst, -ᵊn.təst, US -ᵊn.t̬ɪst, -ᵊn.t̬əst -antly -ᵊnt.li -antness -ᵊnt.nəs, -ᵊnt.nɪs
pleasantr|y 'plez.ᵊn.tr|i -ies -iz
pleas|e pliːz -es -ɪz -ing/ly -ɪŋ/li -ed -d
pleasurab|le 'pleʒ.ᵊr.ə.b|ᵊl -ly -li -leness -ᵊl.nəs, -nɪs
pleasure 'pleʒ.əʳ, US -ɚ -s -z -ing -ɪŋ -ed -d '**pleasure ˌprinciple**
pleat pliːt -s -s -ing -ɪŋ, US 'pliː.t̬ɪŋ -ed -ɪd, US 'pliː.t̬ɪd
pleb pleb -s -z -by -i
plebe pliːb -s -z
plebeian plə'biː.ən, plɪ-, US plɪ-, plə- -s -z
plebiscite 'pleb.ɪ.sɪt, '-ə-, -saɪt, US -ə.saɪt, -sɪt -s -s
plectr|um 'plek.tr|əm -ums -əmz -a -ə
pled (past of **plead**) pled
pledg|e pledʒ -es -ɪz -ing -ɪŋ -ed -d -er/s -əʳ/z, US -ɚ/z
Pledger 'pledʒ.əʳ, US -ɚ
-plegia 'pliː.dʒi.ə, -dʒə
Note: Suffix. Words containing **-plegia** are always stressed on the

syllable **-ple-**, e.g. **paraplegia** /ˌpær.əˈpliː.dʒə/ (US) /ˌper-/.
-plegic ˈpliː.dʒɪk
Note: Suffix. Words containing **-plegic** are always stressed on the penultimate syllable, e.g. **paraplegic** /ˌpær.əˈpliː.dʒɪk/ (US) /ˌper-/.
Pleiad ˈplaɪ.æd, -əd, ˈpliː-, ˈpleɪ-, (US) ˈpliː.æd, ˈplaɪ-, -jæd, -əd **-s** -z **-es** -iːz
Pléiade ˈpleɪ.ɑːd, -æd, -ˈ- **-s** -z
Pleistocene ˈplaɪ.stəʊ.siːn, (US) -stoʊ-, -stə-
plenar|y ˈpliː.nər|.i, (US) ˈpliː-, ˈplen.ɚ- **-ily** -əl.i, -ɪ.li
plenipotentiar|y ˌplen.ɪ.pəʊˈtent.ʃər|.i, -ʃi.ər-, (US) ˌplen.ɪ.poʊˈtent.ʃi.er-, -pəˈ-, ˈ-ʃɚ- **-ies** -iz
plenitude ˈplen.ɪ.tʃuːd, -tjuːd, (US) -tuːd, -tjuːd
plenteous ˈplen.ti.əs, (US) -ṭi- **-ly** -li **-ness** -nəs, -nɪs
plentiful ˈplen.tɪ.fəl, -fʊl, (US) -ṭɪ- **-ly** -i **-ness** -nəs, -nɪs
plenty ˈplen.ti, (US) -ṭi
plen|um ˈpliː.n|əm, (US) ˈpliː-, ˈplen|.əm **-ums** -əmz **-a** -ə
pleonasm ˈpliː.əʊ.næz.əm, (US) -oʊ-, ˈ-ə- **-s** -z
pleonastic ˌpliː.əʊˈnæs.tɪk, (US) -oʊˈ-, -əˈ- **-al** -əl **-ally** -əl.i, -li
plesiosaur ˈpliː.si.əʊ.sɔːr, (US) -oʊ.sɔːr, -ə- **-s** -z
Plessey® ˈples.i
plethora ˈpleθ.ər.ə; pleθˈɔː.rə, pləˈθɔː-, plɪ-, (US) ˈpleθ.ɚ.ə
plethoric pleθˈɒr.ɪk, plə-, plɪ-, (US) pləˈθɔːr-
pleur|a ˈplʊə.r|ə, ˈplɔː-, (US) ˈplʊr|.ə **-ae** -iː **-as** -əz **-al** -əl
pleurisy ˈplʊə.rə.si, ˈplɔː-, -rɪ-, (US) ˈplʊr.ə-
pleuritic plʊəˈrɪt.ɪk, plɔː-, (US) plʊˈrɪṭ-
pleuro-pneumonia ˌplʊə.rəʊ.njuːˈməʊ.ni.ə, ˌplɔː-, (US) ˌplʊr.oʊ.nuːˈmoʊ.njə, -njuːˈ-
plexiglass, P~® ˈplek.si.glɑːs, (US) -sɪ.glæs
plexus ˈplek.səs **-es** -ɪz
Pleyel ˈpleɪ.el, ˈplaɪ-, (US) ˈplaɪ- **-s** -z
pliability ˌplaɪ.əˈbɪl.ə.ti, -ɪ.ti, (US) -ə.ṭi
pliab|le ˈplaɪ.ə.b|əl **-ly** -li **-leness** -əl.nəs, -nɪs
pliancy ˈplaɪ.ənt.si
pliant ˈplaɪ.ənt **-ly** -li **-ness** -nəs, -nɪs
plié ˈpliː.eɪ, -ˈ-, (US) -ˈ- **-s** -z
pliers ˈplaɪ.əz, (US) ˈplaɪ.ɚz
plight plaɪt **-s** -s **-ing** -ɪŋ, (US) ˈplaɪ.ṭɪŋ **-ed** -ɪd, (US) ˈplaɪ.ṭɪd
plimsoll, P~ ˈplɪmp.səl, -sɒl, (US) -səl, -sɑːl, -sɔːl **-s** -z **ˈPlimsoll ˌline**
Plinlimmon plɪnˈlɪm.ən
plinth plɪntθ **-s** -s
Pliny ˈplɪn.i
Pliocene ˈplaɪ.əʊ.siːn, (US) -oʊ-, ˈ-ə-
PLO ˌpiː.elˈəʊ, (US) -ˈoʊ
plod plɒd, (US) plɑːd **-s** -z **-ding** -ɪŋ **-ded** -ɪd **-der/s** -ər/z, (US) -ɚ/z
Ploesti, Ploiesti pləʊˈjeʃ.ti, (US) plɔː-, -ˈjeʃt.i
Plomer ˈpluː.mər, ˈplʌm.ər, (US) ˈpluː.mɚ
Plomley ˈplʌm.li
plonk n, v plɒŋk, (US) plʌŋk, plɑːŋk **-s** -s **-ing** -ɪŋ **-ed** -t
plonker ˈplɒŋ.kər, (US) ˈplʌŋ.kɚ **-s** -z
plop plɒp, (US) plɑːp **-s** -s **-ping** -ɪŋ **-ped** -t
plosion ˈpləʊ.ʒən, (US) ˈploʊ- **-s** -z
plosive ˈpləʊ.sɪv, -zɪv, (US) ˈploʊ.sɪv **-s** -z
plot plɒt, (US) plɑːt **-s** -s **-ting** -ɪŋ, (US) ˈplɑː.ṭɪŋ **-ted** -ɪd, (US) ˈplɑː.ṭɪd **-ter/s** -ər/z, (US) ˈplɑː.ṭɚ/z
plough, P~ plaʊ **-s** -z **-ing** -ɪŋ **-ed** -d **-er/s** -ər/z, (US) -ɚ/z **-able** -ə.bəl
ploughboy ˈplaʊ.bɔɪ **-s** -z
plough|man ˈplaʊ|.mən **-men** -mən, -men ˌ**Ploughman's ˈLunch**
ploughshare ˈplaʊ.ʃeər, (US) -ʃer **-s** -z
Plovdiv ˈplɒv.dɪv, -dɪf, (US) ˈplɔːv.dɪf
plover ˈplʌv.ər, (US) -ɚ **-s** -z
plow plaʊ **-s** -z **-ing** -ɪŋ **-ed** -d **-er/s** -ər/z, (US) -ɚ/z **-able** -ə.bəl
plowboy ˈplaʊ.bɔɪ **-s** -z
Plowden ˈplaʊ.dən
plow|man, P~ ˈplaʊ|.mən **-men** -mən, -men
Plowright ˈplaʊ.raɪt
plowshare ˈplaʊ.ʃeər, (US) -ʃer **-s** -z
ploy plɔɪ **-s** -z
pluck, P~ plʌk **-s** -s **-ing** -ɪŋ **-ed** -t
pluck|y ˈplʌk|.i **-ier** -i.ər, (US) -i.ɚ **-iest** -i.ɪst, -i.əst **-ily** -əl.i, -ɪ.li **-iness** -ɪ.nəs, -ɪ.nɪs
plug plʌg **-s** -z **-ging** -ɪŋ **-ged** -d
plughole ˈplʌg.həʊl, (US) -hoʊl **-s** -z
plug-in ˈplʌg.ɪn **-s** -z
plum plʌm **-s** -z ˌ**plum ˈpudding**
plumag|e ˈpluː.mɪdʒ **-es** -ɪz
plumb, P~ plʌm **-s** -z **-ing** -ɪŋ **-ed** -d
plumbago plʌmˈbeɪ.gəʊ, (US) -goʊ **-s** -z
Plumbe plʌm
plumber ˈplʌm.ər, (US) -ɚ **-s** -z
plumbic ˈplʌm.bɪk
plumbing ˈplʌm.ɪŋ
plumb-line ˈplʌm.laɪn **-s** -z
plumbous ˈplʌm.bəs
plum|e pluːm **-es** -z **-ing** -ɪŋ **-ed** -d
Plummer ˈplʌm.ər, (US) -ɚ
plumm|et ˈplʌm|.ɪt **-ets** -ɪts **-eting** -ɪ.tɪŋ, (US) -ɪ.ṭɪŋ **-eted** -ɪ.tɪd, (US) -ɪ.ṭɪd
plummy ˈplʌm.i
plump plʌmp **-er** -ər, (US) -ɚ **-est** -ɪst, -əst **-ly** -li **-ness** -nəs, -nɪs **-s** -z **-ing** -ɪŋ **-ed** -t
Plumpton ˈplʌmp.tən
Plumridge ˈplʌm.rɪdʒ
Plumstead ˈplʌmp.stɪd, -sted
Plum(p)tre ˈplʌmp.triː
plumule ˈpluː.mjuːl **-s** -z
plund|er ˈplʌn.d|ər, (US) -d|ɚ **-ers** -əz, (US) -ɚz **-ering** -ər.ɪŋ **-ered** -əd, (US) -ɚd **-erer/s** -ər.ər/z, (US) -ɚ.ɚ/z **-erous** -ər.əs
plung|e plʌndʒ **-es** -ɪz **-ing** -ɪŋ **-ed** -d
plunger ˈplʌn.dʒər, (US) -dʒɚ **-s** -z
plunk plʌŋk **-s** -s **-ing** -ɪŋ **-ed** -t
Plunket(t) ˈplʌŋ.kɪt
pluperfect ˌpluːˈpɜː.fɪkt, -fekt, (US) ˈpluːˌpɝː.fɪkt, ˌ-ˈ-- **-s** -s *stress shift, British only:* ˌ**pluperfect ˈtense**
plural ˈplʊə.rəl, ˈplɔː-, (US) ˈplʊr.əl **-s** -z **-ly** -i
plural|ism ˈplʊə.rəl|.ɪ.zəm, ˈplɔː-, (US) ˈplʊr.əl- **-ist/s** -ɪst/s
pluralistic ˌplʊə.rəlˈɪs.tɪk, (US) ˌplʊr.əlˈ- **-ally** -əl.i, -li *stress shift:* ˌ**pluralistic ˈsystem**
pluralit|y plʊəˈræl.ə.t|i, plɔː-, -ɪ.t|i, (US) plʊˈræl.ə.ṭ|i **-ies** -iz
pluraliz|e, -is|e ˈplʊə.rəl.aɪz, ˈplɔː-, (US) ˈplʊr.əl- **-es** -ɪz **-ing** -ɪŋ **-ed** -d
plurisegmental ˌplʊə.rɪ.segˈmen.təl, ˌplɔː-, (US) ˌplʊr.ɪ.segˈmen.ṭəl *stress shift:* ˌ**plurisegmental ˈitem**
plus plʌs **-(s)es** -ɪz
plus-fours ˌplʌsˈfɔːz, (US) -ˈfɔːrz
plush plʌʃ **-er** -ər, (US) -ɚ **-est** -ɪst, -əst **-es** -ɪz **-y** -i
Plutarch ˈpluː.tɑːk, (US) -tɑːrk
Pluto ˈpluː.təʊ, (US) -ṭoʊ
plutocracy pluːˈtɒk.rə.si, (US) -ˈtɑː.krə-
plutocrat ˈpluː.təʊ.kræt, (US) -ṭə-, -toʊ- **-s** -s
plutocratic ˌpluː.təʊˈkræt.ɪk, (US) -toʊˈkræṭ-, -ṭəˈ- **-ally** -əl.i, -li *stress shift:* ˌ**plutocratic ˈgovernment**
plutonian, P~ pluːˈtəʊ.ni.ən, (US) -ˈtoʊ-
plutonic, P~ pluːˈtɒn.ɪk, (US) -ˈtɑː.nɪk
plutonium pluːˈtəʊ.ni.əm, (US) -ˈtoʊ-
pluvi|al ˈpluː.vi|.əl **-ous** -əs
pluviometer ˌpluː.viˈɒm.ɪ.tər, ˈ-ə-, (US) -ˈɑː.mə.ṭɚ **-s** -z
pl|y pl|aɪ **-ies** -aɪz **-ying** -aɪ.ɪŋ **-ied** -aɪd
Plymouth ˈplɪm.əθ ˌ**Plymouth ˈBrethren;** ˌ**Plymouth ˈRock**
Plynlimon Fawr plɪnˌlɪm.ənˈvaʊ.ər, (US) -ˈvaʊ.ɚ
plywood ˈplaɪ.wʊd
PM ˌpiːˈem
p.m. ˌpiːˈem
PMS ˌpiː.emˈes
PMT ˌpiː.emˈtiː
pneumatic njuːˈmæt.ɪk, (US) nuːˈmæṭ-, njuː- **-s** -s **-al** -əl **-ally** -əl.i, -li **pneuˌmatic ˈdrill**
pneumatolog|y ˌnjuː.məˈtɒl.ə.dʒ|i, (US) ˌnuː.məˈtɑː.lə-, ˌnjuː- **-ist/s** -ɪst/s
pneumoconios|is ˌnjuː.məʊˌkəʊ.niˈəʊ.s|ɪs, -ˌkɒn.iˈ-, (US) ˌnuː.moʊˌkoʊ.niˈoʊ-, ˌnjuː-, -məˌ- **-es** -iːz
pneumonia njuːˈməʊ.ni.ə, (US) nuːˈmoʊ.njə, njuː-

P

pneumonic njuːˈmɒn.ɪk, ⓊⓈ nuːˈmɑː.nɪk, njuː-
Pnom Penh ˌnɒmˈpen, pəˌnɒm-ˈ, ⓊⓈ ˌnɑːm-
po, Po pəʊ, ⓊⓈ poʊ -es -z
PO ˌpiːˈəʊ, ⓊⓈ -ˈoʊ **ˈPO ˌbox**
poach pəʊtʃ, ⓊⓈ poʊtʃ -es -ɪz -ing -ɪŋ -ed -t -er/s -əʳ/z, ⓊⓈ -ɚ/z
Pocahontas ˌpɒk.əˈhɒn.təs, -tæs, ⓊⓈ ˌpoʊ.kəˈhɑːn.t̬əs
pochard ˈpəʊ.tʃəd, ˈpɒtʃ.əd, ⓊⓈ ˈpoʊ.tʃɚd, -kɚd -s -z
pochette pɒʃˈet, ⓊⓈ poʊˈʃet -s -s
pock pɒk, ⓊⓈ pɑːk -s -s -ed -t
pock|et ˈpɒk|.ɪt, ⓊⓈ ˈpɑː.k|ɪt -ets -ɪts -eting -ɪ.tɪŋ, ⓊⓈ -ɪ.t̬ɪŋ -eted -ɪ.tɪd, ⓊⓈ -ɪ.t̬ɪd -etable -ɪ.tə.bəl, ⓊⓈ -ɪ.t̬ə.bəl -etful/s -ɪt.fʊl/z **ˈpocket ˌmoney**
pocketbook ˈpɒk.ɪt.bʊk, ⓊⓈ ˈpɑː.kɪt- -s -s
pocket-handkerchie|f ˌpɒk.ɪtˈhæŋ.kə.tʃiː|f, -tʃɪ|f, ⓊⓈ ˌpɑː.kɪtˈhæŋ.kɚ- -fs -fs -ves -vz
pocketknif|e ˈpɒk.ɪt.naɪ|f, ⓊⓈ ˈpɑː.kɪt- -ves -vz
pocket-size ˈpɒk.ɪt.saɪz, ⓊⓈ ˈpɑː.kɪt- -d -d
Pocklington ˈpɒk.lɪŋ.tən, ⓊⓈ ˈpɑː.klɪŋ-
pockmark ˈpɒk.mɑːk, ⓊⓈ ˈpɑːk.mɑːrk -s -s -ing -ɪŋ -ed -t
poco ˈpəʊ.kəʊ, ⓊⓈ ˈpoʊ.koʊ
Pocock ˈpəʊ.kɒk, ⓊⓈ ˈpoʊ.kɑːk
pococurante ˌpəʊ.kəʊ.kjʊəˈræn.teɪ, -ti, ⓊⓈ ˌpoʊ.koʊ.kuːˈræn.t̬i, -kjuːˈ-, -ˈrɑːn- -s -z
pod pɒd, ⓊⓈ pɑːd -s -z -ding -ɪŋ -ded -ɪd
podagra pəʊˈdæg.rə, pɒdˈæg-, ˈpɒd.ə.grə, ⓊⓈ pəˈdæg.rə; ⓊⓈ ˈpɑː.də.grə
podcast ˈpɒd.kɑːst, ⓊⓈ ˈpɑːd.kæst -s -s -ing -ɪŋ
podg|y ˈpɒdʒ|.i, ⓊⓈ ˈpɑː.dʒ|i -ier -i.əʳ, ⓊⓈ -i.ɚ -iest -i.ɪst, -i.əst -ily -əl.i, -ɪ.li -iness -ɪ.nəs, -ɪ.nɪs
podiatric ˌpəʊ.diˈæt.rɪk, ˌpɒd.iˈ-, ⓊⓈ ˌpoʊ-
podiatr|y pəʊˈdaɪ.ə.tr|i, pɒdˈaɪ-, ⓊⓈ pəˈdaɪ-, poʊ- -ist/s -ɪst/s
podi|um ˈpəʊ.di|.əm, ⓊⓈ ˈpoʊ- -ums -əmz -a -ə
Podunk ˈpəʊ.dʌŋk, ⓊⓈ ˈpoʊ-
Poe pəʊ, ⓊⓈ poʊ
Poel ˈpəʊ.əl; ˈpəʊ.el, -ɪl, ⓊⓈ ˈpoʊ.əl; ⓊⓈ ˈpoʊ.el, -ɪl
poem ˈpəʊ.ɪm, -em; pəʊəm, ⓊⓈ ˈpoʊ.əm -s -z
Poema Morale pəʊˌeɪ.mə.mɒrˈɑː.leɪ, -mɔːˈrɑː-, ⓊⓈ poʊˌeɪ.mə.mɔːrˈɑː-
poesy ˈpəʊ.ɪ.zi, -ez.i; ˈpəʊə.zi, ⓊⓈ ˈpoʊ.ə.si, -zi
poet ˈpəʊ.ɪt, -et; pəʊət, ⓊⓈ poʊ.ət -s -s **ˌpoet ˈlaureate**
poetaster ˌpəʊ.ɪˈtæs.təʳ, ˌpəʊəˈ-, ⓊⓈ ˈpoʊ.ə.tæs.tɚ -s -z
poetess ˌpəʊ.ɪˈtes, ˌpəʊ.əˈ-, ˌpəʊə-; ˈpəʊ.ɪ.tɪs, ˈpəʊ.ə.tɪs, -tes, ⓊⓈ ˈpoʊ.ɪ.t̬ɪs -es -ɪz
poetic pəʊˈet.ɪk, ⓊⓈ poʊˈet̬- -al -əl -ally -əl.i, -li **poˌetic ˈjustice**
poeticism pəʊˈet.ɪ.sɪ.zəm, ˈ-ə-, ⓊⓈ poʊˈet̬.ə-
poeticiz|e, -is|e pəʊˈet.ɪ.saɪz, ˈ-ə-, ⓊⓈ poʊˈet̬.ə- -es -ɪz -ing -ɪŋ -ed -d -er/s -əʳ/z, ⓊⓈ -ɚ/z
poetiz|e, -is|e ˈpəʊ.ɪ.taɪz, ˈpəʊ.ə.taɪz, ⓊⓈ ˈpoʊ.ə.taɪz -es -ɪz -ing -ɪŋ -ed -d -er/s -əʳ/z, ⓊⓈ -ɚ/z
poetry ˈpəʊ.ə.tri, ˈpəʊ.ɪ.tri, ˈpəʊə-, ⓊⓈ ˈpoʊ.ə.tri
po-faced ˌpəʊˈfeɪst, ⓊⓈ ˌpoʊ- *stress shift:* **ˌpo-faced ˈperson**
Pogner ˈpəʊg.nəʳ, ⓊⓈ ˈpoʊg.nɚ
pogo ˈpəʊ.gəʊ, ⓊⓈ ˈpoʊ.goʊ -s -z -ing -ɪŋ -ed -d **ˈpogo ˌstick**
pogrom ˈpɒg.rəm, -rɒm, ⓊⓈ ˈpoʊ.grəm, -grɑːm; ⓊⓈ pəˈgrɑːm -s -z
poignancy ˈpɔɪ.njənt.si, -nənt-, ⓊⓈ -njənt.si
poignant ˈpɔɪ.njənt, -nənt, ⓊⓈ -njənt -ly -li
poikilotherm pɔɪˈkɪl.əʊ.θɜːm, ⓊⓈ -ə.θɝːm, ˈ-oʊ-
poikilotherm|ic ˌpɔɪ.kɪ.ləʊˈθɜː.m|ɪk, ⓊⓈ -ləˈθɝː-, -loʊˈ- -al -əl -ism -ɪ.zəm
Poindexter ˈpɔɪn.dek.stəʳ, ⓊⓈ -stɚ
poinsettia ˌpɔɪntˈset.i.ə, ⓊⓈ -ˈset̬-, ˈ-ə -s -z
point pɔɪnt -s -s -ing -ɪŋ, ⓊⓈ ˈpɔɪn.t̬ɪŋ -ed -ɪd, ⓊⓈ ˈpɔɪn.t̬ɪd -er/s -əʳ/z, ⓊⓈ ˈpɔɪn.t̬ɚ/z **ˌpoint of ˌno reˈturn; ˌpoint of ˈorder; ˌpoint of ˈview**
point-blank ˌpɔɪntˈblæŋk *stress shift:* **ˌpoint-blank ˈrange**
point-duty ˈpɔɪntˌdʒuː.ti, -ˌdjuː-, ⓊⓈ -ˌduː.t̬i, -ˌdjuː-
pointed ˈpɔɪn.tɪd, ⓊⓈ -t̬ɪd -ly -li -ness -nəs, -nɪs
Pointe-Noire ˌpwæ̃ntˈnwɑːʳ, ⓊⓈ -ˈnwɑːr
pointill|ism ˈpɔɪn.tɪ.l|ɪ.zəm, ˈpwæ̃n.tiː.|ɪ.zəm, ⓊⓈ ˈpwæn.tə.l|ɪ-, -tiː.|ɪ- -ist/s -ɪst/s
pointless ˈpɔɪnt.ləs, -lɪs -ly -li -ness -nəs, -nɪs
point-of-sale ˌpɔɪnt.əvˈseɪl
Pointon ˈpɔɪn.tən, ⓊⓈ -tən
points|man ˈpɔɪnts|.mən -men -mən, -men
point-to-point ˌpɔɪnt.təˈpɔɪnt *stress shift:* **ˌpoint-to-point ˈchampion**
point|y ˈpɔɪn.t|i, ⓊⓈ -t̬|i -ier -i.əʳ, ⓊⓈ -i.ɚ -iest -i.ɪst, -i.əst
Poirot ˈpwɑː.rəʊ, -ˈ-, ⓊⓈ pwɑːˈroʊ
pois|e pɔɪz -es -ɪz -ing -ɪŋ -ed -d
poison ˈpɔɪ.zən -s -z -ing -ɪŋ -ed -d -er/s -əʳ/z, ⓊⓈ -ɚ/z **ˌpoison ˈivy; ˌpoison ˈoak; ˈpoison ˌpill**
poisonous ˈpɔɪ.zən.əs -ly -li -ness -nəs, -nɪs
poison-pen letter ˌpɔɪ.zənˈpenˌlet.əʳ, ⓊⓈ -ˌlet̬.ɚ -s -z
Poitier ˈpwɒt.i.eɪ, ˈpwæt-, ˈpwɑː.ti-, ⓊⓈ ˈpwɑː.ti.eɪ, -tjeɪ
Poitiers ˈpwɑː.ti.eɪ, ˈpwɒt.i-, ˈpwæt.i-, ˌ--ˈ-, ⓊⓈ pwɑːˈtjeɪ, -tiˈeɪ
pok|e pəʊk, ⓊⓈ poʊk -es -s -ing -ɪŋ -ed -t
Pokémon® ˈpəʊ.kə.mɒn, -kɪ-, ˈpɒk-, ⓊⓈ ˈpoʊ.keɪ.mɑːn, -kiː-
poker ˈpəʊ.kəʳ, ⓊⓈ ˈpoʊ.kɚ -s -z **ˈpoker ˌface**
pok|ey ˈpəʊ.k|i, ⓊⓈ ˈpoʊ- -eys -iz -ies -iz
pokie ˈpəʊ.ki, ⓊⓈ ˈpoʊ- -s -z
pok|y ˈpəʊ.k|i, ⓊⓈ ˈpoʊ- -ier -i.əʳ, ⓊⓈ -i.ɚ -iest -i.ɪst, -i.əst -ily -əl.i, -ɪ.li -iness -ɪ.nəs, -ɪ.nɪs
Pola(c)k ˈpəʊ.læk, ⓊⓈ ˈpoʊ- -s -s
Poland ˈpəʊ.lənd, ⓊⓈ ˈpoʊ-
Polanski pəʊˈlænt.ski, pɒlˈænt-, ⓊⓈ pəˈlænt-, poʊ-
polar ˈpəʊ.ləʳ, ⓊⓈ ˈpoʊ.lɚ -s -z **ˌpolar ˈbear; ˈpolar ˌbear** ⓊⓈ **ˈpolar ˌbear**
Polaris pəʊˈlɑː.rɪs, -ˈlær.ɪs, -ˈleə.rɪs, ⓊⓈ pəˈler.ɪs, poʊ-, -ˈlær-
Note: In British English, the rocket and submarine are usually pronounced with /-ˈlɑː-/.
polariscope pəʊˈlær.ɪ.skəʊp, ˈ-ə-, ⓊⓈ poʊˈler.ɪ.skoʊp, -ˈlær- -s -s
polarity pəʊˈlær.ə.ti, -ɪ.ti, ⓊⓈ poʊˈler.ə.t̬i, -ˈlær-
polarization, -isa- ˌpəʊ.lər.aɪˈzeɪ.ʃən, -ɪˈ-, ⓊⓈ ˌpoʊ.lɚ.əˈ-
polariz|e, -is|e ˈpəʊ.lər.aɪz, ⓊⓈ ˈpoʊ.lə.raɪz -es -ɪz -ing -ɪŋ -ed -d -er/s -əʳ/z, ⓊⓈ -ɚ/z
Polaroid® ˈpəʊ.lər.ɔɪd, ⓊⓈ ˈpoʊ.lə.rɔɪd -s -z
polder ˈpɒl.dəʳ, ˈpəʊl-, ⓊⓈ ˈpoʊl.dɚ -s -z
pole pəʊl, ⓊⓈ poʊl -s -z **ˈPole ˌStar; ˈpole ˌvault**
Pole *inhabitant of Poland:* pəʊl, ⓊⓈ poʊl -s -z *surname:* pəʊl, puːl, ⓊⓈ poʊl, puːl
poleax|(e) ˈpəʊl.æks, ⓊⓈ ˈpoʊl- -es -ɪz -ing -ɪŋ -ed -t
polecat ˈpəʊl.kæt, ⓊⓈ ˈpoʊl- -s -s
polemic pəˈlem.ɪk, pɒlˈem-, ⓊⓈ pəˈlem- -s -s -al -əl -ally -əl.i, -li
polemicist pəˈlem.ɪ.sɪst, pɒlˈem-, ⓊⓈ pəˈlem- -s -s
polemiciz|e, -is|e pəˈlem.ɪ.saɪz, pɒlˈem-, ⓊⓈ pəˈlem.ɪ.saɪz -es -ɪz -ing -ɪŋ -ed -d
polenta pəʊˈlen.tə, ⓊⓈ poʊˈlen.t̬ə, pə-
polestar ˈpəʊl.stɑːʳ, ⓊⓈ ˈpoʊl.stɑːr -s -z
Polesworth ˈpəʊlz.wəθ, -wɜːθ, ⓊⓈ ˈpoʊlz.wɚθ, -wɝːθ
pole-vaul|t ˈpəʊl.vɔːl|t, -vɒl|t, ⓊⓈ ˈpoʊl.vɑːl|t, -vɔːl|t -ts -ts -ting -tɪŋ, ⓊⓈ -t̬ɪŋ -ted -tɪd, ⓊⓈ -t̬ɪd -ter/s -təʳ/z, ⓊⓈ -t̬ɚ/z
polic|e pəˈliːs, pliːs, ⓊⓈ pəˈliːs, poʊ-, pliːs -es -ɪz -ing -ɪŋ -ed -t **poˈlice car; poˌlice ˈconstable; poˈlice force; poˈlice ˌofficer; poˌlice ˈofficer; poˌlice ˈstate** ⓊⓈ **poˈlice ˌstate; poˈlice ˌstation**

P

police|man pəˈliːs|.mən, ˈpliːs-, ⓊⓈ pəˈliːs-, poʊ-, ˈpliːs- **-men** -mən

police|woman pəˈliːs|ˌwʊm.ən, ˈpliːs-, ⓊⓈ pəˈliːs-, poʊ-, ˈpliːs- **-women** -ˌwɪm.ɪn

polic|y ˈpɒl.ə.s|i, ˈ-ɪ-, ⓊⓈ ˈpɑː.lə- **-ies** -iz

policyholder ˈpɒl.ə.siˌhəʊl.dəʳ, ˈ-ɪ-, ⓊⓈ ˈpɑː.lə.siˌhoʊl.dɚ **-s** -z

policymaker ˈpɒl.ə.siˌmeɪ.kəʳ, -ɪ-, ⓊⓈ ˈpɑː.lə.siˌmeɪ.kɚ **-s** -z

polio ˈpəʊ.li.əʊ, ⓊⓈ ˈpoʊ.li.oʊ

poliomyelitis ˌpəʊl.i.əʊ.maɪ.əˈlaɪ.tɪs, -maɪ.ɪˈ-, -elˈaɪ-, -təs, ⓊⓈ ˌpoʊ.li.oʊˌmaɪ.əˈlaɪ.t̬ɪs, -t̬əs

polish **n, v** ˈpɒl.ɪʃ, ⓊⓈ ˈpɑː.lɪʃ **-es** -ɪz **-ing** -ɪŋ **-ed** -t **-er/s** -əʳ/z, ⓊⓈ -ɚ/z

Polish **adj** *of Poland:* ˈpəʊ.lɪʃ, ⓊⓈ ˈpoʊ-

politburo, P~ ˈpɒl.ɪtˌbjʊə.rəʊ, pɒlˈɪt-, -ˌbjɔː-; -bjəˌrəʊ, -bjʊˌ-, ⓊⓈ ˈpɑː.lɪtˌbjʊr.oʊ, ˈpoʊ-; ⓊⓈ poʊˈlɪt-, pə- **-s** -z

po|lite pə|ˈlaɪt, ⓊⓈ pə-, poʊ- **-litest** -ˈlaɪ.tɪst, -ˈlaɪ.təst, ⓊⓈ -ˈlaɪ.t̬ɪst, -ˈlaɪ.t̬əst **-litely** -ˈlaɪt.li **-liteness** -ˈlaɪt.nəs, -ˈlaɪt.nɪs

politic ˈpɒl.ə.tɪk, ˈ-ɪ-, ⓊⓈ ˈpɑː.lə- **-s** -s

politic|al pəˈlɪt.ɪ.k|əl, ⓊⓈ -ˈlɪt̬.-, poʊ- **-ally** -əl.i, -li **poˌlitical ˈprisoner; poˌlitical ˈscience**

politician ˌpɒl.ɪˈtɪʃ.ən, -əˈ-, ⓊⓈ ˌpɑː.ləˈ- **-s** -z

politiciz|e, -cis|e pəˈlɪt.ɪ.saɪz, ˈ-ə-, ⓊⓈ -ˈlɪt̬.ə-, poʊ- **-es** -ɪz **-ing** -ɪŋ **-ed** -d

politick ˈpɒl.ə.tɪk, ˈ-ɪ-, ⓊⓈ ˈpɑː.lə- **-s** -s **-ing** -ɪŋ **-ed** -t **-er/s** -əʳ/z, ⓊⓈ -ɚ/z

politico pəˈlɪt.ɪ.kəʊ, ⓊⓈ -ˈlɪt̬.ɪ.koʊ, poʊ- **-s** -z

politico- pəˈlɪt.ɪ.kəʊ, ⓊⓈ pəˈlɪt̬.ɪ.koʊ, poʊ-, -kə

polity ˈpɒl.ə.ti, -ɪ.ti, ⓊⓈ ˈpɑː.lə.t̬i

Polixenes pɒlˈɪk.sə.niːz, pəˈlɪk-, -sɪ-, ⓊⓈ pəˈlɪk.sə-

Polk pəʊk, ⓊⓈ poʊk

polka ˈpɒl.kə, ⓊⓈ ˈpoʊl- **-s** -z **ˈpolka ˌdot**

poll **n, v** pəʊl, ⓊⓈ poʊl **-s** -z **-ing** -ɪŋ **-ed** -d **ˈpoll ˌtax; ˈpolling ˌbooth; ˈpolling ˌstation**

pollard ˈpɒl.əd, -ɑːd, ⓊⓈ ˈpɑː.lɚd **-s** -z **-ing** -ɪŋ **-ed** -ɪd

Pollard ˈpɒl.ɑːd, ⓊⓈ ˈpɑː.lɚd

pollen, P~ ˈpɒl.ən, -ɪn, ⓊⓈ ˈpɑː.lən **-s** -z **ˈpollen ˌcount**

polli|nate ˈpɒl.ə|.neɪt, ˈ-ɪ-, ⓊⓈ ˈpɑː.lə- **-nates** -neɪts **-nating** -neɪ.tɪŋ, ⓊⓈ -neɪ.t̬ɪŋ **-nated** -neɪ.tɪd, ⓊⓈ -neɪ.t̬ɪd

pollination ˌpɒl.əˈneɪ.ʃən, -ɪˈ-, ⓊⓈ ˌpɑː.ləˈ-

Pollock ˈpɒl.ək, ⓊⓈ ˈpɑː.lək

pollster ˈpəʊl.stəʳ, ⓊⓈ ˈpoʊl.stɚ **-s** -z

pollutant pəˈluː.tənt, -ˈljuː-, ⓊⓈ -ˈluː- **-s** -s

pollu|te pəˈluː|t, -ˈljuː|t, ⓊⓈ -luː|t **-tes** -ts **-ting** -tɪŋ, ⓊⓈ -t̬ɪŋ **-ted** -tɪd, ⓊⓈ -t̬ɪd **-ter/s** -təʳ/z, ⓊⓈ -t̬ɚ/z

pollution pəˈluː.ʃən, -ˈljuː-, ⓊⓈ -ˈluː- **-s** -z

Pollux ˈpɒl.əks, ⓊⓈ ˈpɑː.ləks

Polly ˈpɒl.i, ⓊⓈ ˈpɑː.li

pollyanna, P~ ˌpɒl.iˈæn.ə, ⓊⓈ ˌpɑː.liˈ- **-s** -z

Polmont ˈpəʊl.mənt, ⓊⓈ ˈpoʊl.mɑːnt

polo, P~ ˈpəʊ.ləʊ, ⓊⓈ ˈpoʊ.loʊ **ˈpolo ˌneck**

polonais|e ˌpɒl.əˈneɪz, ⓊⓈ ˌpɑː.ləˈ-, ˌpoʊ- **-es** -ɪz

polonium pəˈləʊ.ni.əm, ⓊⓈ -ˈloʊ-

Polonius pəˈləʊ.ni.əs, pɒlˈəʊ-, ⓊⓈ pəˈloʊ-

polon|y pəˈləʊ.n|i, ⓊⓈ -ˈloʊ- **-ies** -iz

Pol Pot ˌpɒlˈpɒt, ⓊⓈ ˌpɑːlˈpɑːt

Polson ˈpəʊl.sən, ⓊⓈ ˈpoʊl-

poltergeist ˈpɒl.tə.gaɪst, ˈpəʊl-, ⓊⓈ ˈpoʊl.tɚ- **-s** -s

poltroon pɒlˈtruːn, ⓊⓈ pɑːl- **-s** -z **-ery** -ər.i

Polwarth *in Scotland:* ˈpəʊl.wəθ, ⓊⓈ ˈpoʊl.wɚθ *surname:* ˈpɒl.wəθ, ⓊⓈ ˈpɑːl.wɚθ

poly ˈpɒl.i, ⓊⓈ ˈpɑː.li **-s** -z

poly- ˈpɒl.i, -ɪ; pəˈlɪ, ⓊⓈ ˈpɑː.li, -lɪ, -lə; ⓊⓈ pəˈlɪ

Note: Prefix. Many compounds with **poly-** have the stress pattern **ˌpolyˈ-**; these are likely to undergo stress shift when a stressed syllable follows. The prefix may also be stressed on the second syllable, e.g. **polygonal** /pəˈlɪg.ən.əl/.

polyamide ˌpɒl.iˈæm.aɪd, -ˈeɪ.maɪd, ⓊⓈ ˌpɑː.liˈ- **-s** -z

polyandrous ˌpɒl.iˈæn.drəs, ⓊⓈ ˌpɑː.liˈ-

polyandry ˈpɒl.i.æn.dri, ˌpɒl.iˈæn-, ⓊⓈ ˈpɑː.liˌæn-, ˌpɑː.liˈæn-

polyanth|us ˌpɒl.iˈænt.θ|əs, ⓊⓈ ˌpɑː.liˈ- **-uses** -ə.sɪz **-i** -aɪ

polybag ˈpɒl.i.bæg, ˌ-ˈ-, ⓊⓈ ˈpɑː.li.bæg **-s** -z

Polybius pəˈlɪb.i.əs, pɒlˈɪb-, ⓊⓈ pəˈlɪb-, poʊ-

polycarbonate ˌpɒl.iˈkɑː.bə.neɪt, -nət, -nɪt, ⓊⓈ ˌpɑː.liˈkɑːr.bə.nɪt, -neɪt **-s** -s

Polycarp ˈpɒl.i.kɑːp, ⓊⓈ ˈpɑː.li.kɑːrp

Polycell® ˈpɒl.i.sel, ⓊⓈ ˈpɑː.li-

polyclinic ˌpɒl.iˈklɪn.ɪk, ⓊⓈ ˌpɑː.liˈ- **-s** -s

polycotton ˌpɒl.iˈkɒt.ən, ⓊⓈ ˌpɑː.liˈkɑː.tən

Polycrates pəˈlɪk.rə.tiːz, pɒlˈɪk-, ⓊⓈ pəˈlɪk-

Polydor® ˈpɒl.i.dɔːʳ, ⓊⓈ ˈpɑː.li.dɔːr

polyester ˌpɒl.iˈes.təʳ, ⓊⓈ ˌpɑː.liˈes.tɚ, ˈpɑː.li.es-

polyethylene ˌpɒl.iˈeθ.ɪ.liːn, ˈ-ə-, ⓊⓈ ˌpɑː.liˈeθ.ə-

Polyfilla® ˈpɒl.iˌfɪl.ə, ⓊⓈ ˈpɑː.liˌ-

polygam|y pəˈlɪg.ə.m|i, pɒlˈɪg-, ⓊⓈ pəˈlɪg-, -li- **-ist/s** -ɪst/s **-ous** -əs

polyglot ˈpɒl.i.glɒt, ⓊⓈ ˈpɑː.li.glɑːt **-s** -s

polygon ˈpɒl.i.gɒn, -gən, ⓊⓈ ˈpɑː.li.gɑːn **-s** -z

polygonal pəˈlɪg.ən.əl, pɒlˈɪg-, ⓊⓈ pəˈlɪg- **-ly** -i

polygonum pəˈlɪg.ən.əm, pɒlˈɪg-, ⓊⓈ pəˈlɪg-

Polygram® ˈpɒl.i.græm, ⓊⓈ ˈpɑː.li-

polygraph ˈpɒl.i.grɑːf, -græf, ⓊⓈ ˈpɑː.li.græf **-s** -s

polyhedr|on ˌpɒl.iˈhiː.dr|ən, -ˈhed.r|ən, ⓊⓈ ˌpɑː.liˈhiː- **-ons** -ənz **-a** -ə **-al** -əl

polylectal ˌpɒl.iˈlek.təl, ⓊⓈ ˌpɑː.liˈ-

polymath ˈpɒl.i.mæθ, ⓊⓈ ˈpɑː.li- **-s** -s

polymer ˈpɒl.ɪ.məʳ, ⓊⓈ ˈpɑː.lɪ.mɚ **-s** -z

polymeras|e ˈpɒl.ɪ.mər.eɪs, -eɪz, ⓊⓈ ˈpɑː.lɪ.mə.reɪz, -reɪs **-es** -ɪz

polymeric ˌpɒl.ɪˈmer.ɪk, ⓊⓈ ˌpɑː.lɪ- **-ally** -əl.i, -li

polymerism pəˈlɪm.ər.ɪ.zəm, pɒlˈɪm-; ˈpɒl.ɪ.mər-, ⓊⓈ pəˈlɪm.ɚ-; ⓊⓈ ˈpɑː.lɪ.mɚ-

polymerization, -isa- ˌpɒl.ɪ.mər.aɪˈzeɪ.ʃən, -lə-, -ɪˈ-, ⓊⓈ ˌpɑː.lɪ.mɚ.əˈ-

polymeriz|e, -is|e ˈpɒl.ɪ.mər.aɪz, ˈ-ə-, ⓊⓈ ˈpɑː.lɪ.mə.raɪz **-es** -ɪz **-ing** -ɪŋ **-ed** -d

polymerous pəˈlɪm.ər.əs, pɒlˈɪm-, ⓊⓈ pəˈlɪm-

polymorph|ic ˌpɒl.iˈmɔː.f|ɪk, ⓊⓈ ˌpɑː.liˈmɔːr- **-ism** -ɪ.zəm **-ous** -əs

Polynesi|a ˌpɒl.ɪˈniː.ʒ|ə, -zi|.ə, -ʒi|.ə, -si|.ə, -ʃi|.ə, -ʃ|ə, ⓊⓈ ˌpɑː.ləˈniː.ʒ|ə, -ʃ|ə **-an/s** -ən/z

polynomial ˌpɒl.iˈnəʊ.mi.əl, ⓊⓈ ˌpɑː.liˈnoʊ- **-s** -z

Poly-Olbion ˌpɒl.iˈɒl.bi.ən, ⓊⓈ ˌpɑː.liˈɑːl-

polyp ˈpɒl.ɪp, ⓊⓈ ˈpɑː.lɪp **-s** -s **-ous** -əs

polypeptide ˌpɒl.iˈpep.taɪd, ⓊⓈ ˌpɑː.liˈ- **-s** -z

Polyphemus ˌpɒl.ɪˈfiː.məs, -əˈ-, ⓊⓈ ˌpɑː.lɪˈ-

polyphon|ic ˌpɒl.iˈfɒn|.ɪk, ⓊⓈ ˌpɑː.liˈfɑː.n|ɪk **-ous** -əs

polyphony pəˈlɪf.ən.i, pɒlˈɪf-, ⓊⓈ pəˈlɪf-

polypody ˈpɒl.i.pəʊ.di, ⓊⓈ ˈpɑː.li.poʊ-

polyp|us ˈpɒl.ɪ.p|əs, ˈ-ə-, ⓊⓈ ˈpɑː.lɪ- **-i** -aɪ

polysaccharide ˌpɒl.iˈsæk.ər.aɪd, -ɪd, ⓊⓈ ˌpɑː.liˈsæk.ə.raɪd

polysemous pəˈlɪs.ɪ.məs, pɒlˈɪs-; ˌpɒl.ɪˈsiː-, ⓊⓈ ˌpɑː.lɪˈsiː-; ⓊⓈ pəˈlɪs.ə-

polysemy pəˈlɪs.ɪ.mi; ˌpɒl.ɪˈsiː.mi, ˈpɒl.ɪ.siː-, ⓊⓈ ˈpɑː.lɪ.siː-; ⓊⓈ pəˈlɪs.ə-

polystyrene ˌpɒl.iˈstaɪə.riːn, ⓊⓈ ˌpɑː.liˈstaɪ-

polysyllabic ˌpɒl.i.sɪˈlæb.ɪk, -səˈ-, ⓊⓈ ˌpɑː.li.sɪˈ- **-al** -əl **-ally** -əl.i, -li

polysyllable ˌpɒl.iˈsɪl.ə.bəl, ˈpɒl.iˌsɪl-, ⓊⓈ ˈpɑː.liˌsɪl- **-s** -z

polysyndeton ˌpɒl.iˈsɪn.də.tən, -dɪ-, ⓊⓈ ˌpɑː.liˈsɪn.də.tɑːn, -tən

polysynthesis ˌpɒl.iˈsɪnt.θə.sɪs, -θɪ-, (US) ˌpɑː.liˈ-
polysynthetic ˌpɒl.i.sɪnˈθet.ɪk, (US) ˌpɑː.li.sɪnˈθet̬.ɪk
polysystemic ˌpɒl.i.sɪˈstiː.mɪk, -səˈ-, (US) ˌpɑː.li-
polytechnic ˌpɒl.ɪˈtek.nɪk, (US) ˌpɑː.lɪˈ- **-s** -s
polythe|ism ˈpɒl.i.θiː|.ɪ.zᵊm, ˌpɒl.iˈθiː-, (US) ˈpɑː.li.θiː-, ˌpɑː.liˈθiː- **-ist/s** -ɪst/s
polytheistic ˌpɒl.i.θiˈɪs.tɪk; -θiːˈ-, (US) ˌpɑː.li.θiˈɪs.tɪk
polythene ˈpɒl.ɪ.θiːn, ˈ-ə-, (US) ˈpɑː.lɪ-
polytunnel ˈpɒl.iˌtʌn.ᵊl, (US) ˈpɑː.li- **-s** -z
polyunsaturate ˌpɒl.i.ʌnˈsætʃ.ᵊr.eɪt, -ˈsæt.jᵊr-, -ət, (US) ˌpɑː.li.ʌnˈsætʃ.ə.reɪt **-s** -s
polyunsaturated ˌpɒl.i.ʌnˈsætʃ.ᵊr.eɪ.tɪd, -ˈsæt.jᵊr-, (US) ˌpɑː.li.ʌnˈsætʃ.ə.reɪ.t̬ɪd
polyurethane ˌpɒl.ɪˈjʊə.rə.θeɪn, -ˈjɔː-, -iˈ-, -rɪ-, (US) ˌpɑː.lɪˈjʊr.ə-, -liˈ-
polyvalent ˌpɒl.iˈveɪ.lənt, (US) ˌpɑː.lɪˈ-, ˈpɑː.li.veɪ-
polyvinyl ˌpɒl.iˈvaɪ.nᵊl, -nɪl, (US) ˌpɑː.liˈvaɪ.nəl
Polyxen|a pəˈlɪk.sɪ.n|ə, pɒlˈɪk-, -sə-, (US) pəˈlɪk-; (US) ˌpoʊ.lɪkˈsiː- **-us** -əs
Polzeath pɒlˈzeθ, (US) pɑːl-
pom, P~ pɒm, (US) pɑːm **-s** -z
pomace ˈpʌm.ɪs, (US) ˈpʌm-, ˈpɑː.mɪs
pomade pəʊˈmeɪd, pɒmˈeɪd, -ˈɑːd, (US) pɑːˈmeɪd, poʊ-, ˈpɑː.meɪd, -mɑːd **-s** -z
Pomagne® pəˈmeɪn, pɒmˈeɪn, (US) pɑːˈmeɪn, pə-
pomander pəˈmæn.dəʳ, pɒmˈæn-, (US) ˈpoʊ.mæn.dɚ; (US) -ˈ--, pə- **-s** -z
pomatum pəˈmeɪ.təm, -ˈmɑː-, (US) -t̬əm, poʊ- **-s** -z
pome pəʊm, (US) poʊm **-s** -z
pomegranate ˈpɒm.ɪˌgræn.ɪt, -əˌ-, ˌpɒm.ɪˈgræn-, (US) ˈpɑːm.əˌgræn-, ˈpʌm.əˌ-, ˈpɑːmˌ-, ˈpʌmˌ- **-s** -s
pomelo ˈpɒm.ɪ.ləʊ, ˈ-ə-; pəˈmel.oʊ, (US) ˈpɑː.mə.loʊ **-s** -z
Pomerania ˌpɒm.əˈreɪ.ni.ə, (US) ˌpɑː.məˈ-
Pomeranian ˌpɒm.əˈreɪ.ni.ən, (US) ˌpɑː.məˈ- *stress shift:* ˌ**Pomeranian** ˈ**dog**
Pomeroy ˈpɒm.ə.rɔɪ, ˈpəʊm.rɔɪ, (US) ˈpɑː.mə.rɔɪ, ˈpɑːm.rɔɪ
pomfret *fish:* ˈpɒm.frɪt, (US) ˈpɑːm-, ˈpʌm- **-s** -s
Pomfret ˈpʌm.frɪt, ˈpɒm-, (US) ˈpʌm-, ˈpɑːm- ˈ**Pomfret** ˌ**cake**
pommel **n** ˈpɒm.ᵊl, (US) ˈpʌm.ᵊl, ˈpɑː.mᵊl **-s** -z
pommel **v** ˈpʌm.ᵊl, ˈpɒm-, (US) ˈpʌm-, ˈpɑː.mᵊl **-s** -z **-(l)ing** -ɪŋ **-(l)ed** -d
pomm|ie, pomm|y, P~ ˈpɒm|.i, (US) ˈpɑː.m|i **-ies** -iz
Pomona pəˈməʊ.nə, pɒmˈəʊ-, (US) pəˈmoʊ-
pomp pɒmp, (US) pɑːmp **-s** -s
pompadour, P~ ˈpɒm.pə.dʊəʳ, ˈpɔ̃ːm-, -dɔːʳ, (US) ˈpɑːm.pə.dɔːr, -dʊr **-s** -z
Pompeian pɒmˈpeɪ.ən, -ˈpiː-, (US) pɑːmˈpeɪ-
Pompeii pɒmˈpeɪ.i, -ˈpeɪ, (US) pɑːm-
Pompey ˈpɒm.pi, (US) ˈpɑːm-, -peɪ
Pompidou ˈpɒm.pɪ.duː, (US) ˈpɑːm- ˈ**Pompidou** ˌ**Centre**
pompom ˈpɒm.pɒm, (US) ˈpɑːm.pɑːm **-s** -z
pompon ˈpɒm.pɒn, -pɒŋ, ˈpɔ̃ːm.pɔ̃ːŋ, (US) ˈpɑːm.pɑːn **-s** -z
pomposity pɒmˈpɒs.ə.ti, -ɪ.ti, (US) pɑːmˈpɑː.sə.t̬i
pompous ˈpɒm.pəs, (US) ˈpɑːm- **-ly** -li **-ness** -nəs, -nɪs
ponc|e pɒnts, (US) pɑːnts **-es** -ɪz **-(e)y** -i
poncho ˈpɒn.tʃəʊ, (US) ˈpɑːn.tʃoʊ **-s** -z
pond, P~ pɒnd, (US) pɑːnd **-s** -z
pond|er ˈpɒn.d|əʳ, (US) ˈpɑːn.d|ɚ **-ers** -əz, (US) -ɚz **-ering/ly** -ᵊr.ɪŋ/li **-ered** -əd, (US) -ɚd
ponderable ˈpɒn.dᵊr.ə.bᵊl, (US) ˈpɑːn.dɚ- **-ness** -nəs, -nɪs
ponderous ˈpɒn.dᵊr.əs, (US) ˈpɑːn- **-ly** -li **-ness** -nəs, -nɪs
Ponders ˈpɒn.dəz, (US) ˈpɑːn.dɚz
Pondicherry ˌpɒn.dɪˈtʃer.i, -ˈʃer-, (US) ˌpɑːn.dɪˈtʃer-
pondweed ˈpɒnd.wiːd, (US) ˈpɑːnd-
pong pɒŋ, (US) pɑːŋ, pɔːŋ **-s** -z **-ing** -ɪŋ **-ed** -d
pongee ˌpɒnˈdʒiː, ˌpʌn-, (US) ˌpɑːnˈdʒiː; (US) ˈpɑːn.dʒi
poniard ˈpɒn.jəd, -jɑːd, (US) ˈpɑː.njɚd **-s** -z **-ing** -ɪŋ **-ed** -ɪd
pons asinorum ˌpɒnzˌæs.ɪˈnɔː.rəm, -rʊm, (US) ˌpɑːnzˌæs.ɪˈnɔːr.əm
Ponsonby ˈpʌnt.sᵊn.bi, ˈpɒnt-, -sᵊm-, (US) ˈpɑːnt.sᵊn-, ˈpʌnt-
Pontardawe ˌpɒn.təˈdaʊ.i, -eɪ, (US) ˌpɑːn.t̬ɚˈ-
Pontardulais ˌpɒn.təˈdɪl.əs, -ˈdʌl-, -aɪs, (US) ˌpɑːn.t̬ɚˈ-
Pontefract ˈpɒn.tɪ.frækt, (US) ˈpɑːn.t̬ɪ- ˈ**Pontefract** ˌ**cake**
Ponteland pɒnˈtiː.lənd, (US) pɑːn-
Pontiac ˈpɒn.ti.æk, (US) ˈpɑːn.t̬i- **-s** -s
pontifex, P~ ˈpɒn.tɪ.feks, (US) ˈpɑːn.t̬ɪ- **pontifices** pɒnˈtɪf.ɪ.siːz, (US) pɑːn-
pontiff ˈpɒn.tɪf, (US) ˈpɑːn.t̬ɪf **-s** -s
pontific pɒnˈtɪf.ɪk, (US) pɑːn- **-al/s** -ᵊl/z **-ally** -ᵊl.i, -li
pontificate **n** *pope:* pɒnˈtɪf.ɪ.kət, ˈ-ə-, -kɪt, -keɪt, (US) pɑːnˈtɪf.ɪ.kət, -keɪt **-s** -s
pontifi|cate **v** *give opinions:* pɒnˈtɪf.ɪ|.keɪt, ˈ-ə-, (US) pɑːn- **-cates** -keɪts **-cating** -keɪ.tɪŋ, -keɪ.t̬ɪŋ **-cated** -keɪ.tɪd, (US) -keɪ.t̬ɪd
pontification ˌpɒn.tɪ.fɪˈkeɪ.ʃᵊn, -tə-, -fəˈ-, (US) ˌpɑːn.tɪ-, -t̬ə- **-s** -z
Pontine ˈpɒn.taɪn, (US) ˈpɑːn.tiːn, -taɪn
Ponting ˈpɒn.tɪŋ, (US) ˈpɑːn.t̬ɪŋ
Pontins® ˈpɒn.tɪnz, (US) ˈpɑːn-
Pontius ˈpɒn.ti.əs, -tʃi.əs, ˈ-ʃəs, (US) ˈpɑːn.tʃəs, ˈ-t̬i.əs ˌ**Pontius** ˈ**Pilate**
Pont l'Évêque ˌpɔ̃ːn.leɪˈvek, (US) ˌpɑ̃ːnt.ləˈvek
Pontllanfraith ˌpɒnt.ɬlænˈvraɪθ, -θlænˈ-, (US) ˌpɑːnt.θlænˈ-
pontoon pɒnˈtuːn, (US) pɑːn- **-s** -z
Pont|us ˈpɒn.t|əs, (US) ˈpɑːn.t̬|əs **-ic** -ɪk
Pontyclun ˌpɒn.tɪˈklɪn, -təˈ-, (US) ˌpɑːn.t̬ɪˈ-
Pontypool ˌpɒn.tɪˈpuːl, -təˈ-, (US) ˌpɑːn.t̬ɪˈ-
Pontypridd ˌpɒn.tɪˈpriːð, -təˈ-, (US) ˌpɑːn.t̬ɪˈ-
pon|y ˈpəʊ.n|i, (US) ˈpoʊ- **-ies** -iz ˈ**pony** ˌ**trekking**
ponytail ˈpəʊ.ni.teɪl, (US) ˈpoʊ- **-s** -z
Ponzi ˈpɒn.zi, (US) ˈpɑːn- ˈ**Ponzi** ˌ**scheme**
poo(h), P~ *exclamation:* pɸuː, puː *other senses:* puː

> Note: /puː/ is the pronunciation for A. A. Milne's character Winnie the Pooh.

pooch puːtʃ **-es** -ɪz
pood puːd **-s** -z
poodle ˈpuː.dᵊl **-s** -z
poof pʊf, puːf, (US) puːf, pʊf **-s** -s
poofter ˈpʊf.təʳ, ˈpuːf-, (US) ˈpuːf.tɚ **-s** -z
poofy ˈpʊf.i, ˈpuː.fi, (US) ˈpuː.fi
Pooh-Bah ˌpuːˈbɑː, ˈ--, (US) ˈ--
pooh-pooh ˌpuːˈpuː **-s** -z **-ing** -ɪŋ **-ed** -d
Pook puːk, pʊk
pool puːl **-s** -z **-ing** -ɪŋ **-ed** -d
Poole puːl
Pooley ˈpuː.li
poolroom ˈpuːl.rʊm, -ruːm, (US) -ruːm, -rʊm **-s** -z
poon puːn **-s** -z
Poona ˈpuː.nə, -nɑː, (US) -nə
poontang ˈpuːn.tæŋ
poop puːp **-s** -s **-ing** -ɪŋ **-ed** -t ˈ**poop** ˌ**deck**
pooper ˈpuː.pəʳ, (US) -pɚ **-s** -z
pooper-scooper ˈpuː.pəˌskuː.pəʳ, (US) -pɚˌskuː.pɚ **-s** -z
poop-scoop ˈpuːp.skuːp **-s** -s
poor, P~ pɔːʳ, pʊəʳ, (US) pʊr **-er** -əʳ, (US) -ɚ **-est** -ɪst, -əst **-ly** -li **-ness** -nəs, -nɪs ˈ**poor** ˌ**box**; ˈ**poor** ˌ**law**; ˌ**poor re**ˈ**lation**; ˌ**poor** ˈ**white**
Poore pɔːʳ, pʊəʳ, (US) pʊr
poorhou|se ˈpɔː.haʊ|s, ˈpʊə-, (US) ˈpʊr- **-ses** -zɪz
poorly ˈpɔː.li, ˈpʊə-, (US) ˈpʊr-
Pooter ˈpuː.təʳ, (US) -t̬ɚ **-ish** -ɪʃ
poove puːv **-s** -z
pop pɒp, (US) pɑːp **-s** -s **-ping** -ɪŋ **-ped** -t **-per/s** -əʳ/z, (US) -ɚ/z ˈ**pop** ˌ**art**; ˈ**pop** ˌ**music** (US) ˌ**pop** ˈ**music**; ˈ**pop** ˌ**star**
popadom, -dum ˈpɒp.ə.dəm, (US) ˈpɑː.pə- **-s** -z
popcorn ˈpɒp.kɔːn, (US) ˈpɑːp.kɔːrn
pop-down ˈpɒp.daʊn, (US) ˈpɑːp-

P

pope, P~ pəʊp, (US) poʊp **-s** -s **-dom/s** -dəm/z
popery ˈpəʊ.pər.i, (US) ˈpoʊ-
Popeye ˈpɒp.aɪ, (US) ˈpɑː.paɪ
pop-eyed ˌpɒpˈaɪd, (US) ˈpɑːpˌaɪd *stress shift, British only:* ˌ**pop-eyed** ˈ**monster**
pop-gun ˈpɒp.gʌn, (US) ˈpɑːp- **-s** -z
Popham ˈpɒp.əm, (US) ˈpɑː.pəm
popinjay ˈpɒp.ɪn.dʒeɪ, (US) ˈpɑː.pɪn- **-s** -z
popish ˈpəʊ.pɪʃ, (US) ˈpoʊ- **-ly** -li **-ness** -nəs, -nɪs
poplar, P~ ˈpɒp.ləʳ, (US) ˈpɑː.plɚ **-s** -z
poplin ˈpɒp.lɪn, (US) ˈpɑː.plɪn **-s** -z
Popocatépetl ˌpɒp.əʊˌkæt.ɪˈpet.əl, ˌpəʊ.pəʊ-, -əˈ-, ˌpəʊ.pəʊˈkæt.ɪ.pet-, ˌpɒp.əʊˈ-, ˈ-ə-, (US) ˌpoʊ.pəˌkæt.əˈpeṭ.əl; (US) ˌpɑː.pɑː.kɑːˈteɪ-
popover ˈpɒpˌəʊ.vəʳ, (US) ˈpɑːˌpoʊ.vɚ **-s** -z
poppa ˈpɒp.ə, (US) ˈpɑː.pə **-s** -z
poppadom, -dum ˈpɒp.ə.dəm, (US) ˈpɑː.pə- **-s** -z
popper, P~ ˈpɒp.əʳ, (US) ˈpɑː.pɚ **-s** -z
Popperian pɒpˈɪə.ri.ən, (US) pɑːˈpɪr.i-
poppet ˈpɒp.ɪt, (US) ˈpɑː.pɪt **-s** -s
popping creas|e ˈpɒp.ɪŋˌkriːs, (US) ˈpɑː.pɪŋˌ- **-es** -ɪz
popp|le ˈpɒp.əl, (US) ˈpɑː.pəl **-es** -z **-ing** -ɪŋ, ˈpɒp.lɪŋ, (US) ˈpɑː.plɪŋ **-ed** -d
Popplewell ˈpɒp.əl.wel, (US) ˈpɑː.pəl-
popp|y, P~ ˈpɒp|.i, (US) ˈpɑː.p|i **-ies** -iz ˈ**Poppy** ˌ**Day**
poppycock ˈpɒp.ɪ.kɒk, (US) ˈpɑː.pɪ.kɑːk
popsicle, P~® ˈpɒp.sɪ.kəl, (US) ˈpɑːp- **-s** -z
pop|sy, pop|sie ˈpɒp|.si, (US) ˈpɑːp- **-sies** -siz
populace ˈpɒp.jə.ləs, -jʊ-, -lɪs, (US) ˈpɑː.pjə.lɪs, -pjʊ-, -ləs
popular ˈpɒp.jə.ləʳ, -jʊ-, (US) ˈpɑː.pjə.lɚ, -pjʊ- **-ly** -li
popularity ˌpɒp.jəˈlær.ə.ti, -jʊˈ-, -ɪ.ti, (US) ˌpɑː.pjəˈler.ə.ṭi, -pjʊˈ-, -ˈlær-
popularization, -isa- ˌpɒp.jə.lər.aɪˈzeɪ.ʃən, -jə-, -ɪˈ-, (US) ˌpɑː.pjə.lɚ.əˈ-, -pjʊ-
populariz|e, -is|e ˈpɒp.jə.lər.aɪz, -jʊ-, (US) ˈpɑː.pjə.lə.raɪz, -pjʊ- **-es** -ɪz **-ing** -ɪŋ **-ed** -d
popu|late ˈpɒp.jə|.leɪt, -jʊ-, (US) ˈpɑː.pjə-, -pjʊ- **-lates** -leɪts **-lating** -leɪ.tɪŋ, (US) -leɪ.ṭɪŋ **-lated** -leɪ.tɪd, (US) -leɪ.ṭɪd
population ˌpɒp.jəˈleɪ.ʃən, -jʊˈ-, (US) ˌpɑː.pjəˈ-, -pjʊˈ- **-s** -z **popuˈlation exˌplosion**
popu|lism ˈpɒp.jə.l|ɪ.zəm, -jʊ-, (US) ˈpɑː.pjə-, -pjʊ- **-ist/s** -ɪst/s
populous ˈpɒp.jə.ləs, -jʊ-, (US) ˈpɑː.pjə-, -pjʊ- **-ly** -li **-ness** -nəs, -nɪs
pop-up ˈpɒp.ʌp, (US) ˈpɑːp-
porcelain ˈpɔː.səl.ɪn, (US) ˈpɔːr-, ˈ-slɪn **-s** -z
porch pɔːtʃ, (US) pɔːrtʃ **-es** -ɪz
Porchester ˈpɔː.tʃɪ.stəʳ, -tʃə-, (US) ˈpɔːr.tʃɪ.stɚ, -tʃə-
porcine ˈpɔː.saɪn, (US) ˈpɔːr-, -sɪn
porcin|o pɔːˈtʃiː.n|əʊ, (US) pɔːrˈtʃiː.n|oʊ **-i** -iː
porcupine ˈpɔː.kjə.paɪn, -kjʊ-, (US) ˈpɔːr- **-s** -z
por|e pɔːʳ, (US) pɔːr **-es** -z **-ing** -ɪŋ **-ed** -d
porg|y *fish:* ˈpɔː.dʒ|i, (US) ˈpɔːr.g|i **-ies** -iz
Porgy *name:* ˈpɔː.gi, (US) ˈpɔːr-
pork pɔːk, (US) pɔːrk **-er/s** -əʳ/z, (US) -ɚ/z **-y** -i ˌ**pork** ˈ**pie**
pork-barrel ˈpɔːkˌbær.əl, (US) ˈpɔːrkˌber-, -ˌbær-
porkpie hat ˌpɔːk.paɪˈhæt, (US) ˌpɔːrk- **-s** -s
Porlock ˈpɔː.lɒk, (US) ˈpɔːr.lɑːk
porn pɔːn, (US) pɔːrn
porno ˈpɔː.nəʊ, (US) ˈpɔːr.noʊ
pornographic ˌpɔː.nəˈgræf.ɪk, (US) ˌpɔːr-
pornograph|y pɔːˈnɒg.rə.f|i, (US) pɔːrˈnɑː.grə- **-er/s** -əʳ/z, (US) -ɚ/z
porosity pɔːˈrɒs.ə.ti, -ɪ.ti, (US) pɔːˈrɑː.sə.ṭi, pə-
porous ˈpɔː.rəs, (US) ˈpɔːr.əs **-ly** -li **-ness** -nəs, -nɪs
porphyria pɔːˈfɪr.i.ə, -ˈfaɪ.ri-, (US) pɔːrˈfɪr.i-
porphyrin ˈpɔː.fər.ɪn, -fɪ.rɪn, (US) ˈpɔːr.fɚ.ɪn
porphyry, P~ ˈpɔː.fər.i, -fɪ.ri, (US) ˈpɔːr.fɚ.i
porpois|e ˈpɔː.pəs, (US) ˈpɔːr- **-es** -ɪz
porridge ˈpɒr.ɪdʒ, (US) ˈpɔːr-
porringer ˈpɒr.ɪn.dʒəʳ, (US) ˈpɔːr.ɪn.dʒɚ **-s** -z
Porritt ˈpɒr.ɪt, (US) ˈpɔːr-
Porsch|e® pɔːʃ, ˈpɔː.ʃ|ə, (US) pɔːrʃ, ˈpɔːr.ʃ|ə **-es** -ɪz, -əz
Porsena ˈpɔː.sɪ.nə, -sən.ə, (US) ˈpɔːr-
Porson ˈpɔː.sən, (US) ˈpɔːr-
port pɔːt, (US) pɔːrt **-s** -s **-ing** -ɪŋ, (US) ˈpɔːr.ṭɪŋ **-ed** -ɪd, (US) ˈpɔːr.ṭɪd ˌ**Port** ˈ**Moresby;** ˌ**port of** ˈ**call;** ˌ**port of** ˈ**entry;** ˌ**Port** ˈ**Stanley;** ˌ**Port** ˈ**Talbot**
portability ˌpɔː.təˈbɪl.ə.ti, -ɪ.ti, (US) ˌpɔːr.ṭəˈbɪl.ə.ṭi
portable ˈpɔː.tə.bəl, (US) ˈpɔːr.ṭə- **-ness** -nəs, -nɪs
Portadown ˌpɔː.təˈdaʊn, (US) ˌpɔːr.ṭəˈ-
portage ˈpɔː.tɪdʒ, (US) ˈpɔːr.ṭɪdʒ
Portakabin® ˈpɔː.təˌkæb.ɪn, (US) ˈpɔːr.ṭəˌ- **-s** -z
portal, P~ ˈpɔː.təl, (US) ˈpɔːr.ṭəl **-s** -z
portament|o ˌpɔː.təˈmen.t|əʊ, (US) ˌpɔːr.ṭəˈmen.t|oʊ **-i** -iː
Port-au-Prince ˌpɔː.təʊˈprɪnts, (US) ˌpɔːr.toʊˈ-
Portchester ˈpɔː.tʃɪ.stəʳ, -tʃə-, (US) ˈpɔːr.tʃə.stɚ, -tʃɪ-
portcullis ˌpɔːtˈkʌl.ɪs, (US) ˌpɔːrt- **-es** -ɪz
Porte pɔːt, (US) pɔːrt
portend pɔːˈtend, (US) pɔːr- **-s** -z **-ing** -ɪŋ **-ed** -ɪd
portent ˈpɔː.tent, -tənt, (US) ˈpɔːr.tent **-s** -s
portentous pɔːˈten.təs, (US) pɔːrˈten.ṭəs **-ly** -li **-ness** -nəs, -nɪs
Porteous ˈpɔː.ti.əs, (US) ˈpɔːr.ṭi-
porter, P~ ˈpɔː.təʳ, (US) ˈpɔːr.ṭɚ **-s** -z **-age** -ɪdʒ
porterhou|se ˈpɔː.tə.haʊ|s, (US) ˈpɔːr.ṭɚ- **-ses** -zɪz
Porteus ˈpɔː.ti.əs, (US) ˈpɔːr.ṭi-
portfolio ˌpɔːtˈfəʊ.li.əʊ, (US) ˌpɔːrtˈfoʊ.li.oʊ **-s** -z
Porthcawl ˌpɔːθˈkɔːl, -ˈkaʊl, (US) ˌpɔːrθˈkɑːl, -ˈkɔːl, -ˈkaʊl
porthole ˈpɔːt.həʊl, (US) ˈpɔːrt.hoʊl **-s** -z
Portia ˈpɔː.ʃə, -ʃi.ə, (US) ˈpɔːr.ʃə
portico ˈpɔː.tɪ.kəʊ, (US) ˈpɔːr.ṭɪ.koʊ **-(e)s** -z
portière ˌpɔː.tiˈeəʳ, (US) ˌpɔːrˈtjer, -tiˈer, ˌ-ˈtɪr **-s** -z
Portillo pɔːˈtɪl.əʊ, (US) pɔːrˈtɪl.oʊ
portion ˈpɔː.ʃən, (US) ˈpɔːr- **-s** -z **-ing** -ɪŋ **-ed** -d
Portishead ˈpɔː.tɪs.hed, (US) ˈpɔːr.ṭɪs-
Portland ˈpɔːt.lənd, (US) ˈpɔːrt- ˌ**Portland ceˈment;** ˌ**Portland** ˈ**stone**
portl|y ˈpɔːt.l|i, (US) ˈpɔːrt- **-ier** -i.əʳ, (US) -i.ɚ **-iest** -i.ɪst, -i.əst **-iness** -ɪ.nəs, -ɪ.nɪs
Portmadoc ˌpɔːtˈmæd.ək, (US) ˌpɔːrt-
Portman ˈpɔːt.mən, (US) ˈpɔːrt-
portmanteau pɔːtˈmæn.təʊ, (US) pɔːrtˈmæn.toʊ, ˌ--ˈ- **-s** -z **-x** -z
Portmeirion ˌpɔːtˈmer.i.ən, (US) ˌpɔːrt-
Porto Alegre ˌpɔː.təʊ.əˈleg.ri, (US) ˌpɔːr.tu.əˈleg.rə
Portobello ˌpɔː.təˈbel.əʊ, (US) ˌpɔːr.ṭəˈbel.oʊ, -ṭoʊˈ- *stress shift, see compound:* ˌ**Portobello** ˈ**Road**
Porto-Novo ˌpɔː.təʊˈnəʊ.vəʊ, (US) ˌpɔːr.ṭoʊˈnoʊ.voʊ
Porto Rico ˌpɔː.təʊˈriː.kəʊ, (US) ˌpɔːr.ṭoʊˈriː.koʊ, -ṭəˈ-
portrai|t ˈpɔː.trɪ|t, -trə|t, -treɪ|t, (US) ˈpɔːr.trɪ|t, -treɪ|t **-ts** -ts **-tist/s** -tɪst/s, (US) -ṭɪst/s
portraiture ˈpɔː.trɪ.tʃə, -trə-, -tjʊəʳ, (US) ˈpɔːr.trɪ.tʃɚ
portray pɔːˈtreɪ, pə-, (US) pɔːr- **-s** -z **-ing** -ɪŋ **-ed** -d **-er/s** -əʳ/z, (US) -ɚ/z
portrayal pɔːˈtreɪ.əl, pə-, (US) pɔːr- **-s** -z
Portrush ˌpɔːtˈrʌʃ, (US) ˌpɔːrt-
Port Said ˌpɔːtˈsaɪd, -sɑːˈiːd, (US) ˌpɔːrt.sɑːˈiːd, -ɪd
Port Salut ˌpɔː.səˈluː, -sælˈuː, (US) ˌpɔːr.sælˈuː
Portsea ˈpɔːt.si, -siː, (US) ˈpɔːrt-
Portslade ˌpɔːtˈsleɪd, (US) ˌpɔːrt-
Portsmouth ˈpɔːt.sməθ, (US) ˈpɔːrt-
Portstewart ˌpɔːtˈstʃuː.ət, -ˈstjuː-, (US) ˌpɔːrtˈstuː.ɚt, -ˈstjuː-
Portugal ˈpɔː.tʃə.gəl, -tʃʊ-, -tjə-, -tjʊ-, (US) ˈpɔːr.tʃə-

Portuguese ˌpɔː.tʃəˈgiːz, -tʃʊˈ-, -tjəˈ-, -tjʊˈ-, (US) ˌpɔːr.tʃəˈ-, -ˈgiːs, ˈ--- *stress shift, British only, see compound:* ˌ**Portuguese** ˌ**man-of-ˈwar**
pos|e pəʊz, (US) poʊz **-es** -ɪz **-ing** -ɪŋ **-ed** -d
Poseidon pəˈsaɪ.dᵊn, pɒsˈaɪ-, (US) poʊˈsaɪ-, pə-
poser ˈpəʊ.zəʳ, (US) ˈpoʊ.zɚ **-s** -z
poseur pəʊˈzɜːʳ, (US) poʊˈzɝː **-s** -z
posh pɒʃ, (US) pɑːʃ **-er** -əʳ, (US) -ɚ **-est** -ɪst, -əst
pos|it ˈpɒz|.ɪt, (US) ˈpɑː.z|ɪt **-its** -ɪts **-iting** -ɪ.tɪŋ, (US) -ɪ.t̬ɪŋ **-ited** -ɪ.tɪd, (US) -ɪ.t̬ɪd
position pəˈzɪʃ.ᵊn **-s** -z **-ing** -ɪŋ **-ed** -d
positional pəˈzɪʃ.ᵊn.ᵊl
positive ˈpɒz.ə.tɪv, ˈ-ɪ-, (US) ˈpɑː.zə.t̬ɪv **-s** -z **-ly** -li **-ness** -nəs, -nɪs ˌ**positive discrimiˈnation**
positiv|ism ˈpɒz.ɪ.tɪ.v|ɪ.zᵊm, ˈ-ə-, (US) ˈpɑː.zɪ.t̬ɪ- **-ist/s** -ɪst/s
positron ˈpɒz.ɪ.trɒn, -trən, (US) ˈpɑː.zɪ.trɑːn **-s** -z
posse ˈpɒs.i, (US) ˈpɑː.si **-s** -z
possess pəˈzes **-es** -ɪz **-ing** -ɪŋ **-ed** -t **-or/s** -əʳ/z, (US) -ɚ/z
possession pəˈzeʃ.ᵊn **-s** -z
possessive pəˈzes.ɪv **-s** -z **-ly** -li **-ness** -nəs, -nɪs **pos**ˌ**sessive** ˈ**adjective**; **pos**ˌ**sessive** ˈ**pronoun**
possessory pəˈzes.ᵊr.i
posset ˈpɒs.ɪt, (US) ˈpɑː.sɪt **-s** -s
possibilit|y ˌpɒs.əˈbɪl.ə.t|i, -ɪˈ-, -ɪ.t|i, (US) ˌpɑː.səˈbɪl.ə.t̬|i **-ies** -iz
possib|le ˈpɒs.ə.b|ᵊl, ˈ-ɪ-, (US) ˈpɑː.sə- **-ly** -li
possum ˈpɒs.əm, (US) ˈpɑː.səm **-s** -z
post pəʊst, (US) poʊst **-s** -s **-ing** -ɪŋ **-ed** -ɪd ˈ**post** ˌ**office**
postag|e ˈpəʊ.stɪdʒ, (US) ˈpoʊ- **-es** -ɪz ˈ**postage** ˌ**stamp**; ˌ**postage and** ˈ**packing**
postal ˈpəʊ.stᵊl, (US) ˈpoʊ- ˈ**postal** ˌ**order**
postbag ˈpəʊst.bæg, (US) ˈpoʊst- **-s** -z
postbellum ˌpəʊstˈbel.əm, (US) ˌpoʊst- *stress shift:* ˌ**postbellum** ˈ**building**
postbox ˈpəʊst.bɒks, (US) ˈpoʊst.bɑːks **-es** -ɪz
postcard ˈpəʊst.kɑːd, (US) ˈpoʊst.kɑːrd **-s** -z
post-chaise ˈpəʊst.ʃeɪz, ˌ-ˈ-, (US) ˈpoʊst.ʃeɪz, ˌ-ˈ- **-s** -ɪz
postcode ˈpəʊst.kəʊd, (US) ˈpoʊst.koʊd **-s** -z
postda|te ˌpəʊstˈdeɪ|t, ˈ--, (US) ˌpoʊstˈdeɪ|t, ˈ-- **-tes** -ts **-ting** -tɪŋ, (US) -t̬ɪŋ **-ted** -tɪd, (US) -t̬ɪd
post-diluvian ˌpəʊst.dɪˈluː.vi.ən, -daɪˈ-, -ˈljuː-, (US) ˌpoʊst.dɪˈluː-
postdoctoral ˌpəʊstˈdɒk.tᵊr.ᵊl, (US) ˌpoʊstˈdɑːk- *stress shift:* ˌ**postdoctoral** ˈ**contract**
poster ˈpəʊ.stəʳ, (US) ˈpoʊs.tɚ **-s** -z ˈ**poster** ˌ**paint**
poste restante ˌpəʊst.resˈtɑ̃ːnt, ˌ-ˈ--, (US) ˌpoʊst.resˈtɑːnt
posterior pɒsˈtɪə.ri.əʳ, (US) pɑːˈstɪr.i.ɚ, poʊ-, pə- **-ly** -li
posteriority pɒsˌtɪə.riˈɒr.ə.ti, ˌpɒs.tɪə-, -ɪ.ti, (US) pɑːˌstɪr.iˈɔːr.ə.t̬i, poʊ-
posterit|y pɒsˈter.ə.ti, -ɪ.t|i, (US) pɑːˈster.ə.t̬|i **-ies** -iz
postern ˈpɒs.tən, ˈpəʊ.stən, -stɜːn, (US) ˈpoʊ.stɚn, ˈpɑː- **-s** -z
post-free ˌpəʊstˈfriː, (US) ˌpoʊst- *stress shift:* ˌ**post-free** ˈ**system**
Postgate ˈpəʊst.geɪt, -gɪt, (US) ˈpoʊst.geɪt
postglacial ˌpəʊstˈgleɪ.si.əl, -ʃᵊl, -ˈglæs.i.əl, (US) ˌpoʊstˈgleɪ.ʃᵊl *stress shift:* ˌ**postglacial** ˈ**period**
postgrad ˈpəʊst.græd, (US) ˈpoʊst- **-s** -z
postgraduate ˌpəʊstˈgrædʒ.u.ət, -ˈgræd.ju-, -ɪt, (US) ˌpoʊstˈgrædʒ.u.ət, -ɪt; (US) ˈ-u.eɪt **-s** -s *stress shift:* ˌ**postgraduate** ˈ**student**
posthaste ˌpəʊstˈheɪst, (US) ˌpoʊst-
post hoc ˌpəʊstˈhɒk, (US) ˌpoʊstˈhɑːk, -ˈhoʊk
posthumous ˈpɒs.tʃə.məs, ˈ-tjə-, -tʃʊ-, -tjʊ-, (US) ˈpɑːs.tʃə.məs, -tʃʊ- **-ly** -li
Posthumus ˈpɒs.tʃʊ.məs, ˈ-tjʊ-, ˈpɒst.hjʊ-, (US) ˈpɑːs.tjuː-, -tʃuː-
postich|e pɒsˈtiːʃ, (US) pɑːˈstiːʃ, pɔː- **-es** -ɪz
postie ˈpəʊ.sti, (US) ˈpoʊ- **-s** -z
postil ˈpɒs.tɪl, (US) ˈpɑː.stɪl **-s** -z
postil(l)ion pəˈstɪl.i.ən, pɒsˈtɪl-, ˈ-jən, (US) poʊˈstɪl.jən, pɑː- **-s** -z
Post-impression|ism ˌpəʊst.ɪmˈpreʃ.ᵊn|.ɪ.zᵊm, (US) ˌpoʊst- **-ist/s** -ɪst/s
posting ˈpəʊ.stɪŋ, (US) ˈpoʊ- **-s** -z
Post-it® ˈpəʊst.ɪt, (US) ˈpoʊst-
Postlethwaite ˈpɒs.ᵊl.θweɪt, (US) ˈpɑː.sᵊl-
post|man ˈpəʊst|.mən, (US) ˈpoʊst- **-men** -mən **-woman** -ˌwʊm.ən **-women** -ˌwɪm.ɪn ˌ**postman's** ˈ**knock**
postmark ˈpəʊst.mɑːk, (US) ˈpoʊst.mɑːrk **-s** -s **-ing** -ɪŋ **-ed** -t
postmaster ˈpəʊst.mɑː.stəʳ, (US) ˈpoʊst.mæs.tɚ **-s** -z ˌ**Postmaster** ˈ**General**
post-meridian ˌpəʊst.məˈrɪd.i.ən, (US) ˌpoʊst-
postmistress ˈpəʊst.mɪs.trəs, -trɪs, (US) ˈpoʊst- **-es** -ɪz
postmodern ˌpəʊstˈmɒd.ən, (US) ˌpoʊstˈmɑː.dɚn **-ism** -ɪ.zᵊm **-ist/s** -ɪst/s *stress shift:* ˌ**postmodern** ˈ**artists**
postmortem ˌpəʊstˈmɔː.tem, -təm, (US) ˌpoʊstˈmɔːr.t̬əm **-s** -z
postnatal ˌpəʊstˈneɪ.tᵊl, (US) ˌpoʊstˈneɪ.t̬ᵊl *stress shift, see compound:* ˌ**postnatal deˈpression**
postnuptial ˌpəʊstˈnʌp.tʃᵊl, (US) ˌpoʊst-
postoperative ˌpəʊstˈɒp.ᵊr.ə.tɪv, (US) ˌpoʊstˈɑː.pɚ.ə.t̬ɪv
postpaid ˌpəʊstˈpeɪd, (US) ˌpoʊst- *stress shift:* ˌ**postpaid** ˈ**envelope**
post partum ˌpəʊstˈpɑː.təm, (US) ˌpoʊstˈpɑːr.t̬əm
postpon|e pəʊstˈpəʊn, pəs-, (US) poʊstˈpoʊn **-es** -z **-ing** -ɪŋ **-ed** -d **-ement/s** -mənt/s
postposition ˌpəʊst.pəˈzɪʃ.ᵊn, ˈpəʊst.pəˌzɪʃ-, (US) ˌpoʊst.pəˈzɪʃ- **-s** -z
postpositional ˌpəʊst.pəˈzɪʃ.ᵊn.ᵊl, (US) ˌpoʊst- *stress shift:* ˌ**postpositional** ˈ**particle**
postpositive ˌpəʊstˈpɒz.ə.tɪv, ˈ-ɪ-, (US) ˌpoʊstˈpɑː.zə.t̬ɪv *stress shift:* ˌ**postpositive** ˈ**adjective**
postscript ˈpəʊst.skrɪpt, (US) ˈpoʊst- **-s** -s
postseason ˌpəʊstˈsiː.zᵊn, (US) ˌpoʊst- *stress shift:* ˌ**postseason** ˈ**meeting**
post-structuralism ˌpəʊstˈstrʌk.tʃᵊr.ᵊl.ɪ.zᵊm, -tʃʊ.rᵊl-, (US) ˌpoʊstˈstrʌk.tʃɚ-
post-traumatic stress disorder ˌpəʊst.trɔːˌmæt.ɪkˈstres.dɪˌsɔː.dəʳ, -ˌzɔː-, (US) ˌpoʊst.trɑːˌmæt̬.ɪkˈstres.dɪˌsɔːr.dɚ, -trɔːˌ-
postulant ˈpɒs.tʃə.lənt, -tjə-, -tʃʊ-, -tjʊ-, (US) ˈpɑːs.tʃə-, ˈpɑː.stjə- **-s** -s
postulate n ˈpɒs.tʃə.lət, -tjə-, -tʃʊ-, -tjʊ-, -lɪt, (US) ˈpɑːs.tʃə.lɪt, -tʃʊ-, ˈpɑː.stjə-, -stjʊ- **-s** -s
postu|late v ˈpɒs.tʃə|.leɪt, -tjə-, -tʃʊ-, -tjʊ-, (US) ˈpɑːs.tʃə-, ˈpɑː.stjə- **-lates** -leɪts **-lating** -leɪ.tɪŋ, (US) -leɪ.t̬ɪŋ **-lated** -leɪ.tɪd, (US) -leɪ.t̬ɪd
postulation ˌpɒs.tʃəˈleɪ.ʃᵊn, -tjəˈ-, -tʃʊˈ-, -tjʊˈ-, (US) ˌpɑːs.tʃəˈ-, ˌpɑː.stjəˈ- **-s** -z
post|ure ˈpɒs.tʃ|əʳ, (US) ˈpɑːs.tʃ|ɚ **-ures** -əz, (US) -ɚz **-uring** -ᵊr.ɪŋ **-ured** -əd, (US) -ɚd
postviral ˌpəʊstˈvaɪə.rᵊl, (US) ˌpoʊstˈvaɪ- *stress shift, see compound:* ˌ**postviral faˈtigue** ˌ**syndrome**
post-war ˌpəʊstˈwɔːʳ, (US) ˌpoʊstˈwɔːr *stress shift:* ˌ**post-war** ˈ**politics**
pos|y ˈpəʊ.z|i, (US) ˈpoʊ- **-ies** -iz
pot pɒt, (US) pɑːt **-s** -s **-ting** -ɪŋ, (US) ˈpɑː.t̬ɪŋ **-ted** -ɪd, (US) ˈpɑː.t̬ɪd **-er/s** -əʳ/z, (US) ˈpɑː.t̬ɚ/z ˌ**pot** ˈ**luck**; ˈ**pot** ˌ**plant**; ˌ**potted** ˈ**plant**; ˈ**potting** ˌ**shed**
potable ˈpəʊ.tə.bᵊl, (US) ˈpoʊ.t̬ə- **-s** -z
potag|e pɒtˈɑːʒ, pəʊˈtɑːʒ, ˈ--, (US) poʊˈtɑːʒ **-es** -ɪz
potash ˈpɒt.æʃ, (US) ˈpɑːt-
potassium pəˈtæs.i.əm, (US) pə-, poʊ-
potation pəʊˈteɪ.ʃᵊn, (US) poʊ- **-s** -z
potato pəˈteɪ.təʊ, (US) -t̬oʊ **-es** -z **poˈtato** ˌ**chip**; **po**ˌ**tato** ˈ**crisp**
pot-au-feu ˌpɒt.əʊˈfɜː, (US) ˌpɑːt.oʊˈ-
pot-belll|y ˌpɒtˈbel|.i, ˈ-ˌ--, (US) ˈpɑːtˌbel- **-ied** -id
potboiler ˈpɒtˌbɔɪ.ləʳ, (US) ˈpɑːtˌbɔɪ.lɚ **-s** -z

P

potbound **adj** ˈpɒt.baʊnd, ⓤⓢ ˈpɑːt-
poteen pɒtˈiːn, pəʊˈtiːn, -ˈtʃiːn, ⓤⓢ poʊˈtiːn
Potemkin pəˈtemp.kɪn, pɒtˈemp-, pəˈtjɒm.kɪn, ⓤⓢ poʊˈtemp-, pə-
potency ˈpəʊ.tənt.si, ⓤⓢ ˈpoʊ-
potent ˈpəʊ.tənt, ⓤⓢ ˈpoʊ- **-ly** -li
potentate ˈpəʊ.tən.teɪt, ⓤⓢ ˈpoʊ- **-s** -s
potential pəʊˈten.tʃəl, ⓤⓢ poʊ-, pə- **-s** -z **-ly** -i
potentialit|y pəʊˌten.tʃiˈæl.ə.t|i, -ɪ.t|i, ⓤⓢ poʊˌten.tʃiˈæl.ə.ṭ|i, pə- **-ies** -iz
potentilla ˌpəʊ.tənˈtɪl.ə, ⓤⓢ ˌpoʊ- **-s** -z
potentiometer pəʊˌten.tʃiˈɒm.ɪ.təʳ, ˈ-ə-, ⓤⓢ poʊˌten.tʃiˈɑː.mə.ṭɚ, pə- **-s** -z
potheen pɒtˈiːn, pəʊˈtiːn, -tʃiːn, -θiːn, ˈpɒθ.iːn, ⓤⓢ poʊˈθiːn, -ˈtiːn
poth|er ˈpɒð|.əʳ, ⓤⓢ ˈpɑː.ð|ɚ **-ers** -əz, ⓤⓢ -ɚz **-ering** -ər.ɪŋ **-ered** -əd, ⓤⓢ -ɚd
pot-herb ˈpɒt.hɜːb, ⓤⓢ ˈpɑːt.hɝːb **-s** -z
pothole ˈpɒt.həʊl, ⓤⓢ ˈpɑːt.hoʊl **-s** -z
pothol|ing ˈpɒtˌhəʊ.l|ɪŋ, ⓤⓢ ˈpɑːtˌhoʊ- **-er/s** -əʳ/z, ⓤⓢ -ɚ/z
pothook ˈpɒt.hʊk, ⓤⓢ ˈpɑːt- **-s** -s
potthou|se ˈpɒt.haʊ|s, ⓤⓢ ˈpɑːt- **-ses** -zɪz
pot-hunter ˈpɒtˌhʌn.təʳ, ⓤⓢ ˈpɑːtˌhʌn.ṭɚ **-s** -z
potion ˈpəʊ.ʃən, ⓤⓢ ˈpoʊ- **-s** -z
Potiphar ˈpɒt.ɪ.fɑːʳ, ˈ-ə-, -fəʳ, ⓤⓢ ˈpɑː.ṭə.fɚ
Potomac pəˈtəʊ.mæk, -mək, ⓤⓢ -ˈtoʊ.mək
potometer pəʊˈtɒm.ɪ.təʳ, ˈ-ə-, ⓤⓢ pəˈtɑː.mə.tɚ
Potosi *in US:* pəˈtəʊ.si, ⓤⓢ -ˈtoʊ-
Potosí *in Bolivia:* ˌpɒt.əʊˈsiː, ⓤⓢ ˌpɔː.tɔːˈ-
potpourri ˌpəʊ.pəˈriː, -pʊˈ-, ⓤⓢ ˌpoʊ.pʊˈriː, -pəˈ-; ⓤⓢ ˈpoʊ.pʊr.i, -pɚ- **-s** -z
pot-roast ˈpɒt.rəʊst, ⓤⓢ ˈpɑːt.roʊst **-s** -s **-ing** -ɪŋ **-ed** -ɪd
Potsdam ˈpɒts.dæm, ⓤⓢ ˈpɑːts-
potsherd ˈpɒt.ʃɜːd, ⓤⓢ ˈpɑːt.ʃɝːd **-s** -z
potshot ˈpɒt.ʃɒt, ˌ-ˈ-, ⓤⓢ ˈpɑːt.ʃɑːt **-s** -s
Pott pɒt, ⓤⓢ pɑːt
pottage ˈpɒt.ɪdʒ, ⓤⓢ ˈpɑː.ṭɪdʒ
potted ˈpɒt.ɪd, ⓤⓢ ˈpɑː.ṭɪd
pott|er, P~ ˈpɒt|.əʳ, ⓤⓢ ˈpɑː.ṭ|ɚ **-ers** -əz, ⓤⓢ -ɚz **-ering** -ər.ɪŋ **-ered** -əd, ⓤⓢ -ɚd **-erer/s** -ər.əʳ/z, ⓤⓢ -ɚ.ɚ/z
potter|y, P~ ˈpɒt.ər|.i, ⓤⓢ ˈpɑː.ṭɚ- **-ies** -iz
pottle ˈpɒt.əl, ⓤⓢ ˈpɑː.ṭəl **-s** -z
Potts pɒts, ⓤⓢ pɑːts
pott|y ˈpɒt|.i, ⓤⓢ ˈpɑː.ṭ|i **-ier** -i.əʳ, ⓤⓢ -i.ɚ **-iest** -i.ɪst, -i.əst **-iness** -ɪ.nəs, -ɪ.nɪs
pouch paʊtʃ **-es** -ɪz **-ing** -ɪŋ **-ed** -t
pouf *derog. for homosexual:* pʊf, puːf, ⓤⓢ puːf **-s** -s
pouffe, pouf, pouff *seat, headdress:* puːf **-s** -s
Poughill ˈpɒf.ɪl, ˈpʌf-, ˈpaʊ-, ⓤⓢ ˈpɑː.fɪl, ˈpʌf.ɪl, ˈpaʊ-
Poughkeepsie pəˈkɪp.si, ⓤⓢ pə-, poʊ-
Poulenc ˈpuː.læ̃ŋk, ⓤⓢ puːˈlæ̃ŋk
Poulson ˈpəʊl.sən, ˈpuːl-, ⓤⓢ ˈpoʊl-, ˈpuːl-
poult *chicken:* pəʊlt, ⓤⓢ poʊlt **-s** -s *silk material:* puːlt, ⓤⓢ puːlt, puː
Poulter ˈpəʊl.təʳ, ⓤⓢ ˈpoʊl.tɚ
poulterer ˈpəʊl.tər.əʳ, ⓤⓢ ˈpoʊl.tɚ.ɚ **-s** -z
poultic|e ˈpəʊl.tɪs, ⓤⓢ ˈpoʊl.tɪs **-es** -ɪz **-ing** -ɪŋ **-ed** -t
Poultney ˈpəʊlt.ni, ⓤⓢ ˈpoʊlt-
Poulton ˈpəʊl.tən, ⓤⓢ ˈpoʊl-
Poulton-le-Fylde ˌpəʊl.tən.ləˈfaɪld, -lɪˈ-, ⓤⓢ ˌpoʊl-
poultry ˈpəʊl.tri, ⓤⓢ ˈpoʊl-
poultry|man ˈpəʊl.tri|.mən, -mæn, ⓤⓢ ˈpoʊl- **-men** -mən, -men
pounc|e paʊnts **-es** -ɪz **-ing** -ɪŋ **-ed** -t
Pouncefoot ˈpaʊnts.fʊt
pound, P~ paʊnd **-s** -z **-ing** -ɪŋ **-ed** -ɪd **-er/s** -əʳ/z, ⓤⓢ -ɚ/z ˌ**pound** ˈ**sterling**
poundag|e ˈpaʊn.dɪdʒ **-es** -ɪz
Pounds paʊndz
Pount(e)ney ˈpaʊnt.ni
Poupart ˈpuː.pɑːt, ⓤⓢ ˈpuː.pɑːrt
Pouparts ˈpuː.pɑːts, ⓤⓢ ˌpuːˈpɑːrts
pour pɔːʳ, ⓤⓢ pɔːr **-s** -z **-ing** -ɪŋ **-ed** -d **-er/s** -əʳ/z, ⓤⓢ -ɚ/z
pourboire ˈpʊə.bwɑːʳ, ˈpɔː-, ⓤⓢ pʊrˈbwɑːr **-s** -z
pourparler ˌpʊəˈpɑː.leɪ, ˌpɔː-, ⓤⓢ ˌpʊr.pɑːrˈleɪ **-s** -z
poussin, P~ ˈpuː.sæ̃ŋ, ⓤⓢ puːˈsæ̃ŋ **-s** -z
pout paʊt **-s** -s **-ing** -ɪŋ, ⓤⓢ ˈpaʊ.ṭɪŋ **-ed** -ɪd, ⓤⓢ ˈpaʊ.ṭɪd
poverty ˈpɒv.ə.ti, ⓤⓢ ˈpɑː.vɚ.ṭi ˈ**poverty** ˌ**trap**
poverty-stricken ˈpɒv.ə.tiˌstrɪk.ən, ⓤⓢ ˈpɑː.vɚ.ṭiˌ-
Povey ˈpəʊ.vi; pəˈveɪ, ⓤⓢ ˈpoʊ.vi; pəˈveɪ
Pow paʊ
POW ˌpiː.əʊˈdʌb.əl.juː, ⓤⓢ -oʊˈ- **-'s** -z
powd|er ˈpaʊ.d|əʳ, ⓤⓢ -d|ɚ **-ers** -əz, ⓤⓢ -ɚz **-ering** -ər.ɪŋ **-ered** -əd, ⓤⓢ -ɚd ˌ**powder** ˈ**blue**; ˈ**powder** ˌ**keg**; ˈ**powder** ˌ**puff**; ˈ**powder** ˌ**room**
powder|y ˈpaʊ.dər|.i **-iness** -ɪ.nəs, -ɪ.nɪs
Powell ˈpaʊ.əl, paʊəl, ˈpəʊ.əl, paʊəl; ˈpaʊ.ɪl, ˈpəʊ-, -el, ⓤⓢ ˈpaʊ.əl, ˈpoʊ.əl
power, P~ ˈpaʊ.əʳ, paʊəʳ, ⓤⓢ ˈpaʊ.ɚ **-s** -z **-ing** -ɪŋ **-ed** -d ˈ**power** ˌ**base**; ˈ**power** ˌ**cut**; ˌ**power of at**ˈ**torney**; ˌ**power** ˈ**politics**; ˈ**power** ˌ**station**; ˌ**power** ˈ**steering**
powerboat ˈpaʊ.ə.bəʊt, ˈpaʊə-, ⓤⓢ ˈpaʊ.ɚ.boʊt **-s** -s
powerful ˈpaʊ.ə.fəl, ˈpaʊə-, -fʊl, ⓤⓢ ˈpaʊ.ɚ- **-ly** -i **-ness** -nəs, -nɪs
Powergen ˈpaʊ.ə.dʒen, ˈpaʊə-, ⓤⓢ ˈpaʊ.ɚ-
powerhou|se ˈpaʊ.ə.haʊ|s, ˈpaʊə-, ⓤⓢ ˈpaʊ.ɚ- **-ses** -zɪz
powerless ˈpaʊ.ə.ləs, ˈpaʊə-, -lɪs, ⓤⓢ ˈpaʊ.ɚ- **-ly** -li **-ness** -nəs, -nɪs
powerpack ˈpaʊ.ə.pæk, ˈpaʊə-, ⓤⓢ ˈpaʊ.ɚ- **-s** -s
powerpoint ˈpaʊ.ə.pɔɪnt, ˈpaʊə-, ⓤⓢ ˈpaʊ.ɚ- **-s** -s
Powerscourt ˈpɔːz.kɔːt, ˈpaʊ.əz-, ⓤⓢ ˈpaʊ.ɚz.kɔːrt
power-sharing ˈpaʊ.əˌʃeə.rɪŋ, ˈpaʊə-, ⓤⓢ ˈpaʊ.ɚˌʃer.ɪŋ
Powicke ˈpəʊ.ɪk, ⓤⓢ ˈpoʊ-
Powis *place in Scotland, square in London:* ˈpaʊ.ɪs *surname:* ˈpəʊ.ɪs, ˈpaʊ-, ⓤⓢ ˈpoʊ-, ˈpaʊ-
Powles pəʊlz, ⓤⓢ poʊlz
Powlett ˈpɔː.lɪt, ⓤⓢ ˈpɑː-, ˈpɔː-
Pownall ˈpaʊ.nəl
powwow **n, v** ˈpaʊ.waʊ **-s** -z **-ing** -ɪŋ **-ed** -d
Powys ˈpəʊ.ɪs, ˈpaʊ.ɪs, ⓤⓢ ˈpoʊ-, ˈpaʊ-
pox pɒks, ⓤⓢ pɑːks
poxy ˈpɒk.si, ⓤⓢ ˈpɑːk-
Poyner ˈpɔɪ.nəʳ, ⓤⓢ -nɚ
Poynings ˈpɔɪ.nɪŋz
Poynter ˈpɔɪn.təʳ, ⓤⓢ -ṭɚ
Poynton ˈpɔɪn.tən
Poznan ˈpɒz.næn, ⓤⓢ ˈpoʊz-, -nɑːn
PR ˌpiːˈɑːʳ, ⓤⓢ -ˈɑːr
practicability ˌpræk.tɪ.kəˈbɪl.ə.ti, -ɪ.ti, ⓤⓢ -ə.ṭi
practicab|le ˈpræk.tɪ.kə.b|əl **-ly** -li **-leness** -əl.nəs, -nɪs
practical ˈpræk.tɪ.kəl **-ness** -nəs, -nɪs ˌ**practical** ˈ**joke**
practicalit|y ˌpræk.tɪˈkæl.ə.t|i, -ɪ.t|i, ⓤⓢ -ə.ṭ|i **-ies** -iz
practically ˈpræk.tɪ.kəl.i, ⓤⓢ -tɪ.kli
practic|e ˈpræk.tɪs **-es** -ɪz **-ing** -ɪŋ **-ed** -t
practician prækˈtɪʃ.ən **-s** -z
practis|e ˈpræk.tɪs **-es** -ɪz **-ing** -ɪŋ **-ed** -t ˌ**practise what one** ˈ**preaches**
practitioner prækˈtɪʃ.ən.əʳ, ⓤⓢ -ɚ **-s** -z
Prada® ˈprɑː.də
Prado ˈprɑː.dəʊ, ⓤⓢ -doʊ
praecox ˈpriː.kɒks, ˈpraɪ-, ⓤⓢ ˈpriː.kɑːks
Praed preɪd
prae|nomen ˌpriː|ˈnəʊ.men, ˌpraɪ-, ⓤⓢ ˌpriː|ˈnoʊ- **-nomens** -ˈnəʊ.mənz, ⓤⓢ -ˈnoʊ- **-nomina** -ˈnɒm.ɪ.nə, -ˈnəʊ.mɪ-, ⓤⓢ -ˈnɑː-, -ˈnoʊ-
praepostor ˌpriːˈpɒs.təʳ, ⓤⓢ -ˈpɑː.stɚ **-s** -z
praesidi|um prɪˈsɪd.i|.əm, prə-, praɪ- **-ums** -əmz **-a** -ə
Praeterita ˌpriːˈter.ɪ.tə, prɪ-, praɪ-, ⓤⓢ prɪˈter.ɪ.ṭə
praetor ˈpriː.təʳ, ˈpraɪ-, -tɔːʳ, ⓤⓢ ˈpriː.tɚ **-s** -z **-ship/s** -ʃɪp/s

praetori|al priː'tɔː.ri|.əl, praɪ'-, (US) -'tɔːr.i- **-an** -ən

pragmatic præg'mæt.ɪk, (US) -'mæţ- **-s** -s **-al** -ᵊl **-ally** -ᵊl.i, -li

pragmat|ism 'præg.mə.t|ɪ.zᵊm **-ist/s** -ɪst/s

Prague prɑːg

Praia 'praɪ.ə, (US) 'prɑː.jə

prairie, P~ 'preə.ri, (US) 'prer.i **-s** -z **ˈprairie ˌdog; ˌprairie ˈoyster**

prais|e preɪz **-es** -ɪz **-ing** -ɪŋ **-ed** -d **-er/s** -əʳ/z

praiseworth|y 'preɪzˌwɜː.ð|i, (US) -ˌwɝː- **-iness** -ɪ.nəs, -ɪ.nɪs

Prakrit 'prɑː.krɪt

praline 'prɑː.liːn, (US) 'prɑː-, 'preɪ- **-s** -z

Prall prɔːl, (US) prɔːl, prɑːl

pram *baby carriage:* præm *flat-bottomed boat:* prɑːm **-s** -z

pranc|e, P~ prɑːnts, (US) prænts **-es** -ɪz **-ing** -ɪŋ **-ed** -t **-er/s** -əʳ/z, (US) -ɚ/z

prandial 'præn.di.əl

prang præŋ **-s** -z **-ing** -ɪŋ **-ed** -d

prank præŋk **-s** -s **-ing** -ɪŋ **-ed** -t

prank|ish 'præŋ.k|ɪʃ **-some** -sᵊm

prankster 'præŋk.stəʳ, (US) -stɚ **-s** -z

praseodymium ˌpreɪ.zi.əʊ'dɪm.i.əm, ˌpraɪ.zəʊ'-, (US) ˌpreɪ.zi.oʊ'-, -si-

prat præt **-s** -s

Pratchett 'prætʃ.ɪt

prat|e preɪt **-es** -s **-ing** -ɪŋ **-ed** -ɪd **-er/s** -əʳ/z, (US) -ɚ/z

pratfall 'præt.fɔːl **-s** -z

pratincole 'præt.ɪŋ.kəʊl, 'preɪ.tɪŋ-, (US) 'præt.ɪn.koʊl, 'preɪ.tɪn-, -tᵊn-, -ɪŋ- **-s** -z

pratique 'præt.iːk, -ɪk, præt'iːk, (US) præt'iːk; 'præţ.ɪk **-s** -s

Pratt præt

prattl|e 'præt.ᵊl, (US) 'præţ- **-es** -z **-ing** -ɪŋ, 'præt.lɪŋ **-ed** -d **-er/s** -əʳ/z, 'præt.ləʳ/z, (US) 'præţ.ᵊl.ɚ/z, 'præt.lɚ/z

Pravda 'prɑːv.də

prawn prɔːn, (US) prɑːn, prɔːn **-s** -z **ˌprawn ˈcocktail; ˌprawn ˈcracker**

prax|is 'præk.s|ɪs **-es** -iːz

Praxiteles præk'sɪt.ᵊl.iːz, -tɪ.liːz, (US) -'sɪţ.ᵊl.iːz

pray, P~ preɪ **-s** -z **-ing** -ɪŋ **-ed** -d

prayer *person who prays:* 'preɪ.əʳ, (US) -ɚ *supplication:* preəʳ, (US) prer **ˈprayer ˌmat; ˈprayer ˌmeeting; ˈprayer ˌrug; ˈprayer ˌwheel** **-s** -z

prayer-book 'preə.bʊk, (US) 'prer- **-s** -s

prayerful 'preə.fᵊl, -fʊl, (US) 'prer- **-ly** -i **-ness** -nəs, -nɪs

prayerless 'preə.ləs, -lɪs, (US) 'prer- **-ly** -li **-ness** -nəs, -nɪs

praying mant|is ˌpreɪ.ɪŋ'mæn.t|ɪs, (US) -ţ|ɪs **-ises** -ɪ.sɪz **-es** -iːz

pre- priː, prɪ, pri, prə

Note: Prefix. In words containing **pre-** where the stem is free, and the meaning is **beforehand**, it generally takes secondary stress, e.g. **pre-eminence** /ˌpriː'em.ɪ.nənts/. Attached to bound stems the pronunciation is normally /prɪ-/ or /prə-/ for British English and /prɪ-/ or /priː-/ for American English, e.g. **prefer** /prɪ'fɜː/ (US) /priː'fɝː/. There are exceptions; see individual entries.

preach priːtʃ **-es** -ɪz **-ing** -ɪŋ **-ed** -t **-er/s** -əʳ/z, (US) -ɚ/z **ˌpreach to the conˈverted**

preachi|fy 'priː.tʃɪ|.faɪ, '-tʃə- **-fies** -faɪz **-fying** -faɪ.ɪŋ **-fied** -faɪd

preach|y 'priː.tʃ|i **-ily** -ᵊl.i, -ɪ.li **-iness** -ɪ.nəs, -ɪ.nɪs

Preager 'preɪ.gəʳ, (US) -gɚ

preamble 'priː.æm.bᵊl, pri'æm- **-s** -z

preamplifier pri'æm.plɪ.faɪ.əʳ, (US) -plə.faɪ.ɚ **-s** -z

prearrang|e ˌpriː.ə'reɪndʒ **-es** -ɪz **-ing** -ɪŋ **-ed** -d

Prebble 'preb.ᵊl

prebend 'preb.ənd **-s** -z

prebendar|y 'preb.ᵊn.dᵊr|.i, -ᵊm-, -ᵊn.der- **-ies** -ɪz

prebuilt ˌpriː'bɪlt *stress shift:* **ˌprebuilt ˈhousing**

Precambrian ˌpriː'kæm.bri.ən

precancerous ˌpriː'kænt.sᵊr.əs *stress shift:* **ˌprecancerous ˈtissue**

precarious prɪ'keə.ri.əs, prə-, (US) prɪ'ker.i-, priː- **-ly** -li **-ness** -nəs, -nɪs

precast ˌpriː'kɑːst, (US) 'priː.kæst, ˌ-'- *stress shift, British only:* **ˌprecast ˈconcrete**

preca|tory 'prek.ə|.tᵊr.i, (US) -tɔːr- **-tive** -tɪv, (US) -ţɪv

precaution prɪ'kɔː.ʃᵊn, prə-, (US) prɪ'kɑː-, priː-, -'kɔː- **-s** -z

precautionary prɪ'kɔː.ʃᵊn.ᵊr.i, prə-, (US) prɪ'kɑː.ʃᵊn.er-, priː-, -'kɔː-

preced|e priː'siːd, prɪ-, (US) prɪ-, priː- **-es** -z **-ing** -ɪŋ **-ed** -ɪd

precedenc|e 'pres.ɪ.dᵊnts, 'priː.sɪ-, (US) 'pres.ə.dents; (US) prɪ'siː.dᵊnts, priː- **-y** -i

precedent n 'pres.ɪ.dᵊnt, (US) '-ə- **-s** -s **-ed** -ɪd

precedent adj prɪ'siː.dᵊnt, 'pres.ɪ.dənt, (US) prɪ'siː.dᵊnt, priː-, 'pres.ə.dənt **-ly** -li

precentor priː'sen.təʳ, prɪ-, (US) priː'sen.ţɚ **-s** -z

precept 'priː.sept **-s** -s

preceptor prɪ'sep.təʳ, (US) priː'sep.tɚ, prɪ- **-s** -z

preceptor|y prɪ'sep.tᵊr|.i, (US) prɪ-, priː- **-ies** -iz

precession prɪ'seʃ.ᵊn, prə-, (US) prɪ-, priː- **-s** -z

precinct 'priː.sɪŋkt **-s** -s

preciosity ˌpres.i'ɒs.ə.ti, ˌpreʃ-, -ɪ.ti, (US) ˌpreʃ.i'ɑː.sə.ţi, ˌpres-

precious, P~ 'preʃ.əs **-ly** -li **-ness** -nəs, -nɪs **ˌprecious ˈmetal; ˌprecious ˈstone**

precipic|e 'pres.ɪ.pɪs, '-ə-, (US) '-ə- **-es** -ɪz

precipitanc|e prɪ'sɪp.ɪ.tᵊnts, prə-, '-ə-, (US) prɪ-, priː- **-y** -i

precipi|tate v prɪ'sɪp.ɪ|.teɪt, prə-, '-ə-, (US) prɪ'sɪp.ɪ-, priː- **-tates** -teɪts **-tating** -teɪ.tɪŋ, (US) -teɪ.ţɪŋ **-tated** -teɪ.tɪd, (US) -teɪ.ţɪd

precipitate n prɪ'sɪp.ɪ.teɪt, prə-, '-ə-, -tət, -tɪt, (US) prɪ'sɪp.ɪ.tɪt, priː-, -teɪt **-s** -s

precipitate adj prɪ'sɪp.ɪ.tət, prə-, '-ə-, -tɪt, (US) prɪ'sɪp.ɪ.tɪt, priː-, -teɪt **-ly** -li **-ness** -nəs, -nɪs

precipitation prɪˌsɪp.ɪ'teɪ.ʃᵊn, prə-, -ə'-, (US) prɪˌsɪp.ɪ'-, priː- **-s** -z

precipitous prɪ'sɪp.ɪ.təs, prə-, '-ə-, (US) prɪ'sɪp.ɪ.ţəs, priː- **-ly** -li **-ness** -nəs, -nɪs

précis *singular:* 'preɪ.siː, (US) 'preɪ.siː, -'- **-ing** -ɪŋ **-ed** -d *plural:* -z

precise prɪ'saɪs, prə-, (US) prɪ-, priː- **-ly** -li **-ness** -nəs, -nɪs

precision prɪ'sɪʒ.ᵊn, prə-, (US) prɪ-, priː-

preclassical ˌpriː'klæs.ɪ.kᵊl *stress shift:* **ˌpreclassical ˈmusic**

preclud|e prɪ'kluːd, (US) prɪ-, priː- **-es** -z **-ing** -ɪŋ **-ed** -ɪd

preclu|sion prɪ'kluː|.ʒᵊn, (US) prɪ-, priː- **-sive** -sɪv

precocious prɪ'kəʊ.ʃəs, prə-, (US) prɪ'koʊ-, priː- **-ly** -li **-ness** -nəs, -nɪs

precocity prɪ'kɒs.ə.ti, prə-, -ɪ.ti, (US) prɪ'kɑː.sə.ţi, priː-

precognition ˌpriː.kɒg'nɪʃ.ᵊn, (US) -kɑːg'-

preconceiv|e ˌpriː.kən'siːv **-es** -z **-ing** -ɪŋ **-ed** -d

preconception ˌpriː.kən'sep.ʃᵊn **-s** -z

precon|cert ˌpriː.kən|'sɜːt, (US) -'sɝːt **-certs** -'sɜːts, (US) -'sɝːts **-certing** -'sɜː.tɪŋ, (US) -'sɝː.ţɪŋ **-certed** -'sɜː.tɪd, (US) -'sɝː.ţɪd

precondition ˌpriː.kən'dɪʃ.ᵊn **-s** -z **-ing** -ɪŋ **-ed** -d

precook ˌpriː'kʊk **-s** -s **-ing** -ɪŋ **-ed** -t

precursor priː'kɜː.səʳ, prɪ-, (US) priː'kɝː.sɚ, prɪ- **-s** -z **-y** -i

preda|te ˌpriː'deɪ|t, (US) ˌpriː'deɪ|t, '-- **-tes** -ts **-ting** -tɪŋ, (US) -ţɪŋ **-ted** -tɪd, (US) -ţɪd *stress shift:* **ˌpredated ˈcheque**

predation prɪ'deɪ.ʃᵊn, prə-, (US) prɪ-, priː- **-s** -z

predator 'pred.ə.təʳ, '-ɪ-, (US) -ə.ţɚ **-s** -z

predator|y 'pred.ə.tᵊr|.i, (US) -tɔːr- **-ily** -ᵊl.i, -ɪ.li **-iness** -ɪ.nəs, -ɪ.nɪs

predeceas|e ˌpriː.dɪ'siːs, -də'-, (US) -də'-, -dɪ'- **-es** -ɪz **-ing** -ɪŋ **-ed** -t

predecessor 'priː.dɪˌses.əʳ, -də-, ˌpriː.dɪ'ses-, -də'-, (US) 'pred.ə.ses.ɚ, 'priː.də-; (US) ˌpred.ə'ses- **-s** -z

predestinate adj ˌpriː'des.tɪ.nət, prɪ-, -tə-, (US) ˌpriː'des.tə.nɪt

predesti|nate v ˌpriː'des.tɪ|.neɪt, prɪ-, -tə-, (US) ˌpriː'des.tə- **-nates** -neɪts **-nating** -neɪ.tɪŋ, (US) -neɪ.ţɪŋ **-nated** -neɪ.tɪd, (US) -neɪ.ţɪd

predestination ˌpriː.des.tɪ'neɪ.ʃᵊn, prɪˌdes-, (US) priː-, -tə'-, priːˌdes.tə'-

predestin|e ˌpriːˈdes.tɪn, prɪ-, (US) ˌpriː- -es -z -ing -ɪŋ -ed -d

predetermination ˌpriː.dɪˌtɜː.mɪˈneɪ.ʃən, -dəˌ-, -məˈ-, (US) -dɪˌtɝː.məˈ-

predetermin|e ˌpriː.dɪˈtɜː.mɪn, -dəˈ-, -mən, (US) -dɪˈtɝː.mən -es -z -ing -ɪŋ -ed -d *stress shift:* **ˌpredetermined ˈpath**

predeterminer ˌpriː.dɪˈtɜː.mɪ.nər, -dəˈ-, -mə-, (US) -dɪˈtɝː.mə.nɚ

predicability ˌpred.ɪ.kəˈbɪl.ə.ti, -ɪ.ti, (US) -ə.t̬i

predicable ˈpred.ɪ.kə.bəl

predicament prɪˈdɪk.ə.mənt, prə-, (US) prɪ-, priː- -s -s

predicate n ˈpred.ɪ.kət, ˈpriː.dɪ-, -də-, -kɪt, -keɪt, (US) ˈpred.ɪ.kɪt, ˈ-ə- -s -s

predi|cate v ˈpred.ɪ|.keɪt, ˈ-ə-, (US) ˈ-ɪ- -cates -keɪts -cating -keɪ.tɪŋ, (US) -keɪ.t̬ɪŋ -cated -keɪ.tɪd, (US) -keɪ.t̬ɪd

predication ˌpred.ɪˈkeɪ.ʃən, -əˈ-, (US) -ɪˈ- -s -z

predicative prɪˈdɪk.ə.tɪv, prə-, (US) prɪˈdɪk.ə.t̬ɪv, priː- -ly -li

predicatory ˈpred.ɪ.keɪ.tər.i, ˈ-ə-, ˌpred.ɪˈkeɪ-, -əˈ-, (US) ˈpred.ɪ.kə.tɔːr-

predict prɪˈdɪkt, prə-, (US) prɪ-, priː- -s -s -ing -ɪŋ -ed -ɪd -or/s -ər/z, (US) -ɚ/z

predictability prɪˌdɪk.təˈbɪl.ɪ.ti, prə-, (US) prɪˌdɪk.təˈbɪl.ə.t̬i, priː-

predictab|le prɪˈdɪk.tə.b|əl, prə-, (US) prɪ-, priː- -ly -li

prediction prɪˈdɪk.ʃən, prə-, (US) prɪ-, priː- -s -z

predictive prɪˈdɪk.tɪv -ly -li

predilection ˌpriː.dɪˈlek.ʃən, -dəˈ-, (US) ˌpred.əlˈek-, ˌpriː.dəlˈ- -s -z

predispos|e ˌpriː.dɪˈspəʊz, -dəˈ-, (US) -dɪˈspoʊz -es -ɪz -ing -ɪŋ -ed -d

predisposition ˌpriː.dɪ.spəˈzɪʃ.ən, priːˌdɪs.pəˈ- -s -z

predominance prɪˈdɒm.ɪ.nənts, prə-, ˈ-ə-, (US) prɪˈdɑː.mə-, priː-

predominant prɪˈdɒm.ɪ.nənt, prə-, ˈ-ə-, (US) prɪˈdɑː.mə-, priː- -ly -li

predomi|nate prɪˈdɒm.ɪ|.neɪt, prə-, ˈ-ə-, (US) prɪˈdɑː.mə-, priː- -nates -neɪts -nating -neɪ.tɪŋ, (US) -neɪ.t̬ɪŋ -nated -neɪ.tɪd, (US) -neɪ.t̬ɪd

predomination prɪˌdɒm.ɪˈneɪ.ʃən, prə-, -əˈ-, (US) prɪˌdɑː.məˈ-, priː-

Preece priːs

pre-eclampsia ˌpriː.ɪˈklæmp.si.ə

preemie ˈpriː.mi -s -z

pre-eminence ˌpriːˈem.ɪ.nənts, pri-, ˈ-ə-

pre-eminent ˌpriːˈem.ɪ.nənt, pri-, ˈ-ə- -ly -li

pre-empt ˌpriːˈempt, pri- -s -s -ing -ɪŋ -ed -ɪd

pre-emption ˌpriːˈemp.ʃən, pri-

pre-emptive ˌpriːˈemp.tɪv, pri- **pre-ˌemptive ˈstrike**

preen priːn -s -z -ing -ɪŋ -ed -d

pre-exist ˌpriː.ɪgˈzɪst, -egˈ-; -ɪkˈsɪst, -ekˈ-, (US) -ɪgˈzɪst, -egˈ- -s -s -ing -ɪŋ -ed -ɪd -ence -ənts -ent -ənt *stress shift:* **ˌpre-existing ˈrule**

prefab ˈpriː.fæb -s -z

prefabri|cate ˌpriːˈfæb.rɪ|.keɪt, -rə- -cates -keɪts -cating -keɪ.tɪŋ, (US) -keɪ.t̬ɪŋ -cated -keɪ.tɪd, (US) -keɪ.t̬ɪd

pre-fabrication ˌpriː.fæb.rɪˈkeɪ.ʃən, priːˌfæb-, -rəˈ-, (US) ˌpriː.fæb-

prefac|e ˈpref.ɪs, -əs, (US) -ɪs -es -ɪz -ing -ɪŋ -ed -t

prefatorial ˌpref.əˈtɔː.ri.əl, (US) -ˈtɔːr.i- -ly -i

prefatory ˈpref.ə.tər.i, (US) -tɔːr-

prefect ˈpriː.fekt -s -s

prefecture ˈpriː.fek.tʃər, -tʃʊər, -tjʊər, (US) -tʃɚ -s -z

prefer prɪˈfɜːr, prə-, (US) prəˈfɝː, prɪ- -s -z -ring -ɪŋ -red -d

preferability ˌpref.ər.əˈbɪl.ə.ti, -ɪ.ti, (US) -ə.t̬i

preferab|le ˈpref.ər.ə.b|əl -ly -li -leness -əl.nəs, -nɪs

preferenc|e ˈpref.ər.ənts -es -ɪz

preferential ˌpref.ərˈen.tʃəl -ly -i

preferment prɪˈfɜː.mənt, prə-, (US) prəˈfɝː-, prɪ- -s -s

prefigurative priːˈfɪg.ər.ə.tɪv, (US) -jɚ- -ly -li -ness -nəs, -nɪs

prefig|ure priːˈfɪg|.ər, (US) -j|ɚ -ures -əz, (US) -ɚz -uring -ər.ɪŋ -ured -əd, (US) -ɚd

prefigurement priːˈfɪg.ə.mənt, (US) -jɚ-, -jʊr- -s -s

prefix n ˈpriː.fɪks -es -ɪz

prefix v ˌpriːˈfɪks, ˈ--, (US) ˈpriː.fɪks, ˌ-ˈ- -es -ɪz -ing -ɪŋ -ed -t

preggers ˈpreg.əz, (US) -ɚz

pregnable ˈpreg.nə.bəl

pregnanc|y ˈpreg.nənt.s|i -ies -iz

pregnant ˈpreg.nənt -ly -li

pre|heat ˌpriː|ˈhiːt -heats -ˈhiːts -heating -ˈhiː.tɪŋ, (US) -ˈhiː.t̬ɪŋ -heated -ˈhiː.tɪd, (US) -ˈhiː.t̬ɪd *stress shift:* **ˌpreheated ˈmeal**

prehensible prɪˈhent.sə.bəl, -sɪ-, (US) priː-

prehensile prɪˈhent.saɪl, ˌpriː-, (US) priːˈhent.sɪl, -səl

prehistoric ˌpriː.hɪˈstɒr.ɪk, (US) -hɪˈstɔːr- -ally -əl.i, -li *stress shift:* **ˌprehistoric ˈmonster**

prehistory ˌpriːˈhɪs.tər.i

prejudg|e ˌpriːˈdʒʌdʒ -es -ɪz -ing -ɪŋ -ed -d -(e)ment -mənt

prejudic|e ˈpredʒ.ə.dɪs, ˈ-ʊ- -es -ɪz -ing -ɪŋ -ed -t

prejudicial ˌpredʒ.əˈdɪʃ.əl, -ʊˈ- -ly -i

prelac|y ˈprel.ə.s|i -ies -iz

prelate ˈprel.ɪt, -ət, (US) -ɪt -s -s

preliminar|y prɪˈlɪm.ɪ.nər|.i, prə-, -ən.ər-, (US) prɪˈlɪm.ə.ner-, priː- -ies -iz -ily -əl.i, -ɪ.li

prelims ˈpriː.lɪmz, ˌ-ˈ-; prɪ-, (US) ˈpriː.lɪms; (US) ˌpriːˈlɪmz, prɪ-

prelud|e ˈprel.juːd, (US) ˈprel-, -uːd; (US) ˈpreɪ.luːd, ˈpriː- -es -z -ing -ɪŋ -ed -ɪd

premarital ˌpriːˈmær.ɪ.təl, (US) -ˈmer.ə.t̬əl, -ˈmær- -ly -i *stress shift, see compound:* **ˌpremarital ˈsex**

premature ˈprem.ə.tʃər, ˈpriː.mə-, -tʃʊər, -tjʊər, -tʃɔːr, -tjɔːr; ˌ--ˈ-, (US) ˌpriː.məˈtʊr, -ˈtjʊr, -ˈtʃʊr -ly -li -ness -nəs, -nɪs *stress shift, British only:* **ˌpremature ˈaging**

premed ˌpriːˈmed -s -z *stress shift:* **ˌpremed ˈscience**

premedical ˌpriːˈmed.ɪ.kəl *stress shift:* **ˌpremedical ˈscience**

premedication ˌpriː.med.ɪˈkeɪ.ʃən, -əˈ-

premedi|tate priːˈmed.ɪ|.teɪt, ˈ-ə-, prɪ-, (US) priːˈmed.ɪ-, ˈ-ə- -tates -teɪts -tating -teɪ.tɪŋ, (US) -teɪ.t̬ɪŋ -tated/ly -teɪ.tɪd/li, (US) -teɪ.t̬ɪd/li

premeditation ˌpriː.med.ɪˈteɪ.ʃən, priˌmed-, -əˈ-, (US) ˌpriː-, -əˈ-

premenstrual ˌpriːˈment.stru.əl, (US) -strəl -ly -i *stress shift, see compounds:* **ˌpremenstrual ˈsyndrome; ˌpremenstrual ˈtension**

premier ˈprem.i.ər, ˈpriː.mi-, (US) prɪˈmɪr, -ˈmjɪr; (US) ˈpriː.miː.ɚ -s -z -ship/s -ʃɪp/s

premièr|e ˈprem.i.eər, ˌ--ˈ-, (US) prɪˈmɪr, premˈɪr, -ˈjer, -ˈjɪr -es -z -ing -ɪŋ -ed -d

Preminger ˈprem.ɪn.dʒər, ˈpreɪ.mɪŋ.ər, (US) ˈprem.ɪn.dʒɚ

premis|e n ˈprem.ɪs -s -ɪz

premis|e v prɪˈmaɪz, ˈprem.ɪs, (US) ˈprem.ɪs -es -ɪz -ing -ɪŋ -ed prɪˈmaɪzd, ˈprem.ɪst, (US) ˈprem.ɪst

premium ˈpriː.mi.əm -s -z **ˈpremium ˌbond**

premmie ˈprem.i -s -z

premodification ˌpriː.mɒd.ɪ.fɪˈkeɪ.ʃən, priːˌmɒd-, -ə-, -fəˈ-, (US) ˌpriː.mɑː.dɪ.fɪˈ-

premodif|y priːˈmɒd.ɪ.f|aɪ, ˈ-ə-, (US) -ˈmɑː.dɪ-, ˈ-də- -ies -aɪz -ying -aɪ.ɪŋ -ied -aɪd

premolar ˌpriːˈməʊ.lər, (US) -ˈmoʊ.lɚ -s -z *stress shift:* **ˌpremolar ˈteeth**

premonition ˌprem.əˈnɪʃ.ən, ˌpriː.məˈ- -s -z

premonitorily priːˈmɒn.ɪ.tər.əl.i, -ɪ.li, (US) ˌpriː.mɑː.nəˈtɔːr-, -ˈmɑː.nə.tɔːr-

premonitory priˈmɒn.ɪ.tər.i, (US) priːˈmɑː.nə.tɔːr-

prenatal ˌpriːˈneɪ.təl, (US) -t̬əl -ly -i *stress shift:* **ˌprenatal ˈcare**

Prendergast ˈpren.də.gɑːst, -gæst, (US) -dɚ.gæst

prentic|e, P~ ˈpren.tɪs, (US) -t̬ɪs -es -ɪz

Prentis(s) ˈpren.tɪs, (US) -t̬ɪs

prenuptial ˌpriːˈnʌp.tʃəl *stress shift, see compound:* **ˌprenuptial aˈgreement**

preoccupation priːˌɒk.jəˈpeɪ.ʃən, prɪ-, ˌpriː.ɒk-, -jʊˈ-, (US) priːˌɑː.kjuːˈ-, -kjəˈ- -s -z

preoccup|y priːˈɒk.jə.p|aɪ, pri-, (US) priːˈɑː.kjuː-, -kjə- -ies -aɪz -ying -aɪ.ɪŋ -ied -aɪd

preordain ˌpriː.ɔːˈdeɪn, (US) -ɔːrˈ- -s -z -ing -ɪŋ -ed -d *stress shift:* **ˌpreordained ˈdestiny**

pre-owned ˌpriːˈəʊnd, ⓤⓢ -ˈoʊnd *stress shift:* ˌ**pre-owned** ˈ**car**
prep prep -s -s -ping -ɪŋ -ped -t ˈ**prep** ˌ**school**
prepackag|e ˌpriːˈpæk.ɪdʒ -es -ɪz -ing -ɪŋ -ed -d *stress shift:* ˌ**prepackaged** ˈ**goods**
prepacked ˌpriːˈpækt *stress shift:* ˌ**prepacked** ˈ**goods**
prepaid (from **prepay**) ˌpriːˈpeɪd *stress shift:* ˌ**prepaid** ˈ**postage**
preparation ˌprep.ᵊrˈeɪ.ʃᵊn, ⓤⓢ -əˈreɪ- -s -z
preparative prɪˈpær.ə.tɪv, prə-, ⓤⓢ prɪˈper.ə.t̬ɪv, priː-, -ˈpær- -ly -li
preparator|y prɪˈpær.ə.tᵊr|.i, prə-, ⓤⓢ prɪˈper.ə.tɔːr-, priː-, -ˈpær-; ⓤⓢ ˈprep.ɚ.ə- -ily -ᵊl.i, -ɪ.li **pre**ˈ**paratory** ˌ**school**
prepar|e prɪˈpeəʳ, prə-, ⓤⓢ prɪˈper, priː- -es -z -ing -ɪŋ -ed -d -edly -d.li, -ɪd.li -edness -d.nəs, -nɪs, -ɪd.nəs, -nɪs -er/s -əʳ/z, ⓤⓢ -ɚ/z
prepay ˌpriːˈpeɪ -s -z -ing -ɪŋ
prepaid ˌpriːˈpeɪd *stress shift:* ˌ**prepaid** ˈ**postage**
prepayment ˌpriːˈpeɪ.mənt -s -s
prepense prɪˈpen*t*s -ly -li
preponderance prɪˈpɒn.dᵊr.ᵊn*t*s, prə-, ⓤⓢ prɪˈpɑːn-, priː-
preponderant prɪˈpɒn.dᵊr.ᵊnt, prə-, ⓤⓢ prɪˈpɑːn-, priː- -ly -li
preponder|ate prɪˈpɒn.dᵊr|.eɪt, prə-, ⓤⓢ prɪˈpɑːn.də.r|eɪt, priː- -ates -eɪts -ating/ly -eɪ.tɪŋ/li, ⓤⓢ -eɪ.t̬ɪŋ/li -ated -eɪ.tɪd, ⓤⓢ -eɪ.t̬ɪd
preponderation prɪˌpɒn.dᵊrˈeɪ.ʃᵊn, prə-, priː-, ⓤⓢ prɪˌpɑːn.dəˈreɪ-, priː-
preposition ˌprep.əˈzɪʃ.ᵊn -s -z
prepositional ˌprep.əˈzɪʃ.ᵊn.ᵊl, ˈ-nᵊl, ⓤⓢ -əˈ- -ly -i *stress shift, see compound:* ˌ**prepositional** ˈ**phrase**
prepositive prɪˈpɒz.ə.tɪv, priː-, ˈ-ɪ-, ⓤⓢ prɪˈpɑː.zə.t̬ɪv, priː- *stress shift:* ˌ**prepositive** ˈ**adjective**
prepossess ˌpriː.pəˈzes -es -ɪz -ing/ly -ɪŋ/li -ed -t
prepossession ˌpriː.pəˈzeʃ.ᵊn -s -z
preposterous prɪˈpɒs.tᵊr.əs, prə-, ⓤⓢ prɪˈpɑː.stɚ-, priː- -ly -li -ness -nəs, -nɪs
prepp|y, prepp|ie ˈprep|.i -ies -iz -ier -i.əʳ, ⓤⓢ -i.ɚ -iest -i.ɪst, -i.əst -iness -ɪ.nəs, -ɪ.nɪs
prepubescen|t ˌpriː.pjuːˈbes.ᵊn|t -ce -*t*s
prepuc|e ˈpriː.pjuːs -es -ɪz
prequel ˈpriː.kwəl -s -z
Pre-Raphaelite ˌpriːˈræf.i.ᵊl.aɪt, -eɪ-, -ˈræf.ᵊl-, -ɪ.laɪt, ⓤⓢ -ˈræf.i.ᵊl-, -ˈreɪ.fi- -s -s ˌ**Pre-**ˌ**Raphaelite** ˈ**Brotherhood**
prerecord ˌpriː.rɪˈkɔːd, -rəˈ-, ⓤⓢ -rɪˈkɔːrd -s -z -ing -ɪŋ -ed -ɪd
prerequisite ˌpriːˈrek.wɪ.zɪt, -wə- -s -s
prerogative prɪˈrɒg.ə.tɪv, prə-, ⓤⓢ -ˈrɑː.gə.t̬ɪv -s -z
presag|e **n** ˈpres.ɪdʒ -es -ɪz
presag|e **v** ˈpres.ɪdʒ; prɪˈseɪdʒ, prə-, ⓤⓢ prɪˈseɪdʒ; ˈpres.ɪdʒ -es -ɪz -ing -ɪŋ -ed -d
presbyopia ˌprez.biˈəʊ.pi.ə, ⓤⓢ -ˈoʊ-, ˌpres-
presbyter ˈprez.bɪ.təʳ, ⓤⓢ -t̬ɚ, ˈpres- -s -z
presbyterian, P~ ˌprez.bɪˈtɪə.ri.ən, -bəˈ-, ⓤⓢ -bɪˈtɪr.i-, ˌpres- -s -z -ism -ɪ.zᵊm
presbyter|y ˈprez.bɪ.tᵊr|.i, -bə-, ⓤⓢ -bɪ.ter-, ˈpres- -ies -iz
Prescel(l)y prɪˈsel.i, prə-, presˈel-
preschool ˈpriː.skuːl, ˌ-ˈ-, ⓤⓢ ˈ--
preschooler ˈpriːˌskuː.ləʳ, ⓤⓢ -lɚ -s -z
prescience ˈpres.i.ən*t*s, ˈpreʃ-, ⓤⓢ ˈpreʃ.ᵊn*t*s, ˈpriː.ʃᵊn*t*s, -ʃi.ən*t*s
prescient ˈpres.i.ənt, ˈpreʃ-, ⓤⓢ ˈpreʃ.ᵊnt, ˈpriː.ʃᵊnt, -ʃi.ənt -ly -li
prescind prɪˈsɪnd, prə-, priː-, ⓤⓢ prɪ-, priː- -s -z -ing -ɪŋ -ed -ɪd
Prescot(t) ˈpres.kət, -kɒt, ⓤⓢ -kət, -kɑːt
prescrib|e prɪˈskraɪb, prə-, ⓤⓢ prɪ-, priː- -es -z -ing -ɪŋ -ed -d -er/s -əʳ/z, ⓤⓢ -ɚ/z
prescript ˈpriː.skrɪpt -s -s
prescription prɪˈskrɪp.ʃᵊn, prə-, ⓤⓢ prɪ-, priː- -s -z
prescriptive prɪˈskrɪp.tɪv, prə-, priː-, ⓤⓢ prɪ-, priː- -ly -li
prescriptiv|ism prɪˈskrɪp.tɪ.v|ɪ.zᵊm, prə-, priː-, ⓤⓢ prɪ-, priː- -ist/s -ɪst/s
preseason ˌpriːˈsiː.zᵊn *stress shift:* ˌ**preseason** ˈ**meeting**
pre-season ˌpriːˈsiː.zᵊn *stress shift:* ˌ**pre-season** ˈ**sale**
Preseli prɪˈsel.i, prə-, priː-
presenc|e ˈprez.ᵊn*t*s -es -ɪz ˌ**presence of** ˈ**mind**
present **n** *ordinary senses:* ˈprez.ᵊnt *military term:* prɪˈzent, prə- -s -s
pre|sent **v** prɪ|ˈzent, prə-, ⓤⓢ prɪ-, priː- -sents -ˈzents -senting -ˈzen.tɪŋ, ⓤⓢ -ˈzen.t̬ɪŋ -sented -ˈzen.tɪd, ⓤⓢ -ˈzen.t̬ɪd
present **adj** ˈprez.ᵊnt -ly -li ˌ**present par**ˈ**ticiple** ⓤⓢ ˌ**present** ˈ**participle**; ˌ**present** ˈ**perfect**; ˌ**present** ˈ**tense**
presentab|le prɪˈzen.tə.b|ᵊl, prə-, ⓤⓢ prɪˈzen.t̬ə-, priː- -ly -li -leness -ᵊl.nəs, -nɪs
presentation ˌprez.ᵊnˈteɪ.ʃᵊn, -enˈ-, ⓤⓢ -ᵊnˈ-, ˌpriː.zᵊnˈ- -s -z -al -ᵊl
present-day ˌprez.ᵊntˈdeɪ *stress shift:* ˌ**present-day** ˈ**fashions**
presenter prɪˈzen.təʳ, prə-, ⓤⓢ prɪˈzen.t̬ɚ, priː- -s -z
presentient prɪˈsen*t*.ʃi.ənt, -ʃᵊnt, ⓤⓢ priː-, prɪ-
presentiment prɪˈzen.tɪ.mənt, ⓤⓢ prɪ-, priː- -s -s
presently ˈprez.ᵊnt.li
preservation ˌprez.əˈveɪ.ʃᵊn, ⓤⓢ -ɚˈ- -s -z -ist/s -ɪst/s **preser**ˈ**vation** ˌ**order**
preservative prɪˈzɜː.və.tɪv, prə-, ⓤⓢ prɪˈzɝː.və.t̬ɪv, priː- -s -z
preserv|e prɪˈzɜːv, prə-, ⓤⓢ prɪˈzɝːv, priː- -es -z -ing -ɪŋ -ed -d -er/s -əʳ/z, ⓤⓢ -ɚ/z -able -ə.bᵊl
pre|set priː|ˈset -sets -ˈsets -setting -ˈset.ɪŋ, ⓤⓢ -ˈset̬.ɪŋ *stress shift:* ˌ**preset** ˈ**channel**
pre|shrink ˌpriːˈʃrɪŋk -shrinks -ˈʃrɪŋks -shrinking -ˈʃrɪŋ.kɪŋ -shrank -ˈʃræŋk -shrunk -ˈʃrʌŋk -shrunken -ˈʃrʌŋ.kᵊn *stress shift:* ˌ**preshrunk** ˈ**jeans**
presid|e prɪˈzaɪd, prə-, ⓤⓢ prɪ-, priː- -es -z -ing -ɪŋ -ed -ɪd
presidenc|y ˈprez.ɪ.dᵊn*t*.s|i -ies -iz
president ˈprez.ɪ.dᵊnt -s -s
presidential ˌprez.ɪˈden.*t*ʃᵊl *stress shift:* ˌ**presidential** ˈ**suite**
presidi|um prɪˈsɪd.i|.əm, prə- -ums -əmz -a -ə
Presley ˈprez.li, ⓤⓢ ˈpres-, ˈprez-
pre|sort ˌpriː|ˈsɔːt, ⓤⓢ -ˈsɔːrt -sorts -ˈsɔːts, ⓤⓢ -ˈsɔːrts -sorting -ˈsɔː.tɪŋ, ⓤⓢ -ˈsɔːr.t̬ɪŋ -sorted -ˈsɔː.tɪd, ⓤⓢ -ˈsɔːr.t̬ɪd
press pres -es -ɪz -ing/ly -ɪŋ/li -ed -t -er/s -əʳ/z, ⓤⓢ -ɚ/z ˈ**press** ˌ**agent**; ˈ**press** ˌ**baron**; ˈ**press** ˌ**conference**; ˈ**press** ˌ**cutting**; ˈ**press** ˌ**office**; ˈ**press re**ˌ**lease**
pressgang ˈpres.gæŋ -s -z -ing -ɪŋ -ed -d
pressie ˈprez.i -s -z
pression ˈpreʃ.ᵊn
press|man ˈpres|.mæn, -mən -men -mən, -men
pressrun ˈpres.rʌn
press-stud ˈpres.stʌd -s -z
press-up ˈpres.ʌp -s -s
pressur|e ˈpreʃ.əʳ, ⓤⓢ -ɚ -es -z -ing -ɪŋ -ed -d ˈ**pressure** ˌ**cooker**; ˈ**pressure** ˌ**group**
pressurization ˌpreʃ.ᵊr.aɪˈzeɪ.ʃᵊn, -ɪˈ-, ⓤⓢ -əˈ-
pressuriz|e, -is|e ˈpreʃ.ᵊr.aɪz, ⓤⓢ -ə.raɪz -es -ɪz -ing -ɪŋ -ed -d
Prestage ˈpres.tɪdʒ
Prestatyn presˈtæt.ɪn, prɪˈstæt-
Presteign presˈtiːn
Prestel® ˈpres.tel
prestidigitation ˌpres.tɪˌdɪdʒ.ɪˈteɪ.ʃᵊn, ⓤⓢ -təˌ-
prestidigitator ˌpres.tɪˈdɪdʒ.ɪ.teɪ.təʳ, ⓤⓢ -təˈdɪdʒ.ə.teɪ.t̬ɚ -s -z
prestige presˈtiːʒ, ⓤⓢ -ˈtiː*d*ʒ
Prestige *surname:* ˈpres.tɪdʒ
prestigious presˈtɪdʒ.əs, prɪˈstɪdʒ-, prə-, -i.əs, ⓤⓢ presˈtɪdʒ.əs, -ˈtiː.dʒəs -ly -li -ness -nəs, -nɪs
prestissimo presˈtɪs.ɪ.məʊ, ˈ-ə-, ⓤⓢ -ə.moʊ
presto, P~ ˈpres.təʊ, ⓤⓢ -toʊ -s -z
Preston ˈpres.tᵊn
Prestonpans ˌpres.tᵊnˈpænz, -tᵊmˈ-, ⓤⓢ -tᵊnˈ-
prestressed ˌpriːˈstrest
Prestwich ˈpres.twɪtʃ
Prestwick ˈpres.twɪk
Prestwood ˈpres.twʊd
presumab|ly prɪˈzjuː.mə.b|li, prə-, -ˈzuː-, ⓤⓢ prɪˈzuː.mə-, priː- -le -ᵊl
presum|e prɪˈzjuːm, prə-, -ˈzuːm,

Ⓤⓢ prɪˈzuːm, priː- **-es** -z **-ing/ly** -ɪŋ/li **-ed** -d
presumption prɪˈzʌmp.ʃᵊn, prə-, Ⓤⓢ prɪ-, priː- **-s** -z
presumptive prɪˈzʌmp.tɪv, prə-, Ⓤⓢ prɪ-, priː- **-ly** -li
presumptuous prɪˈzʌmp.tʃu.əs, prə-, -tju-, -tʃəs, Ⓤⓢ prɪˈzʌmp.tʃuː.əs, priː-, -tʃə.wəs **-ly** -li **-ness** -nəs, -nɪs
presuppos|e ˌpriː.səˈpəʊz, Ⓤⓢ -ˈpoʊz **-es** -ɪz **-ing** -ɪŋ **-ed** -d
presupposition ˌpriː.sʌp.əˈzɪʃ.ᵊn **-s** -z
prêt-à-porter ˌpret.ɑːˈpɔː.teɪ, Ⓤⓢ -pɔːrˈteɪ
pre-tax ˌpriːˈtæks *stress shift:* **ˌpretax ˈprofit**
preteen ˌpriːˈtiːn **-s** -z *stress shift:* **ˌpreteen ˈyears**
pretenc|e prɪˈtents, prə-, Ⓤⓢ ˈpriː.tents; Ⓤⓢ prɪˈtents **-es** -ɪz
pretend prɪˈtend, prə-, Ⓤⓢ prɪ-, priː- **-s** -z **-ing** -ɪŋ **-ed** -ɪd **-er/s** -əʳ/z, Ⓤⓢ -ɚ/z
pretens|e prɪˈtents, prə-, Ⓤⓢ ˈpriː.tents; Ⓤⓢ prɪˈtents **-es** -ɪz
pretension prɪˈten.tʃᵊn, prə-, Ⓤⓢ prɪ-, priː- **-s** -z
pretentious prɪˈten.tʃəs, prə-, Ⓤⓢ prɪ-, priː- **-ly** -li **-ness** -nəs, -nɪs
preterit(e) ˈpret.ᵊr.ɪt, -ət, Ⓤⓢ ˈpreţ.ɚ.ɪt **-s** -s
pretermission ˌpriː.təˈmɪʃ.ᵊn, Ⓤⓢ -ţɚˈ-
preter|mit ˌpriː.tə|ˈmɪt, Ⓤⓢ -ţɚˈ- **-mits** -ˈmɪts **-mitting** -ˈmɪt.ɪŋ, Ⓤⓢ -ˈmɪţ.ɪŋ **-mitted** -ˈmɪt.ɪd, Ⓤⓢ -ˈmɪţ.ɪd
preternatural ˌpriː.təˈnætʃ.ᵊr.ᵊl, -ʊ.rᵊl, Ⓤⓢ -ţɚˈnætʃ.ɚ.ᵊl, ˈ-rᵊl **-ly** -i **-ness** -nəs, -nɪs *stress shift:* **ˌpreternatural ˈhappening**
pretext ˈpriː.tekst **-s** -s
pretor ˈpriː.təʳ, Ⓤⓢ -ţɚ **-s** -z **-ship/s** -ʃɪp/s
Pretori|a prɪˈtɔː.ri|.ə, prə-, Ⓤⓢ prɪˈtɔːr.i|-, priː- **-us** -əs
pretori|al prɪˈtɔː.ri|.əl, prə-, Ⓤⓢ prɪˈtɔːr.i-, priː- **-an** -ən
prettification ˌprɪt.ɪ.fɪˈkeɪ.ʃᵊn, ˌ-ə-, -fəˈ-, Ⓤⓢ ˌprɪţ-
prettif|y ˈprɪt.ɪ.f|aɪ, ˈ-ə-, Ⓤⓢ ˈprɪţ.ɪ-, ˈ-ə- **-ies** -aɪz **-ying** -aɪ.ɪŋ **-ied** -aɪd
prett|y **adj, adv** ˈprɪt|.i, Ⓤⓢ ˈprɪţ- **-ier** -i.əʳ, Ⓤⓢ -i.ɚ **-iest** -i.ɪst, -i.əst **-ily** -ᵊl.i, -ɪ.li **-iness** -ɪ.nəs, -ɪ.nɪs
Pretty *surname:* ˈprɪt.i, ˈpret-, Ⓤⓢ ˈprɪţ-, ˈpreţ-
pretty-pretty ˈprɪt.iˌprɪt.i, Ⓤⓢ ˈprɪţ.iˌprɪţ.i
Pret(t)yman ˈprɪt.ɪ.mən, Ⓤⓢ ˈprɪţ-
pretzel ˈpret.sᵊl **-s** -z
prevail prɪˈveɪl, prə-, Ⓤⓢ prɪ-, priː- **-s** -z **-ing** -ɪŋ **-ed** -d
Préval preɪˈvæl
prevalence ˈprev.ᵊl.ənts, Ⓤⓢ -ə.lənts
prevalent ˈprev.ᵊl.ənt, Ⓤⓢ -ə.lənt **-ly** -li
prevari|cate prɪˈvær.ɪ|.keɪt, prə-, ˈ-ə-, Ⓤⓢ prɪˈver.ɪ-, -ˈvær- **-cates** -keɪts **-cating** -keɪ.tɪŋ, Ⓤⓢ -keɪ.ţɪŋ **-cated** -keɪ.tɪd, Ⓤⓢ -keɪ.ţɪd **-cator/s** -keɪ.təʳ/z, Ⓤⓢ -keɪ.ţɚ/z
prevarication prɪˌvær.ɪˈkeɪ.ʃᵊn, prə-, -əˈ-, Ⓤⓢ prɪˌver-, -ˌvær- **-s** -z
pre|vent *hinder:* prɪ|ˈvent, prə-, Ⓤⓢ prɪ-, priː- *go before:* ˌpriː|ˈvent, prɪ-, Ⓤⓢ priː-, prɪ- **-vents** -ˈvents **-venting** -ˈven.tɪŋ, Ⓤⓢ -ˈven.ţɪŋ **-vented** -ˈven.tɪd, Ⓤⓢ -ˈven.ţɪd **-venter/s** -ˈven.təʳ/z, Ⓤⓢ -ˈven.ţɚ/z **-ventable** -ˈven.tə.bᵊl, Ⓤⓢ -ˈven.ţə.bᵊl
preventability prɪˌven.təˈbɪl.ə.ti, prə-, -ɪ.ti, Ⓤⓢ prɪˌven.ţəˈbɪl.ə.ţi, priː-
preventative prɪˈven.tə.tɪv, prə-, Ⓤⓢ prɪˈven.ţə.ţɪv, priː- **-s** -z
prevention prɪˈven.tʃᵊn, prə-, Ⓤⓢ prɪ-, priː-
preventive prɪˈven.tɪv, prə-, Ⓤⓢ prɪˈven.ţɪv, priː- **-ly** -li **-ness** -nəs, -nɪs
preverbal ˌpriːˈvɜː.bᵊl, Ⓤⓢ -ˈvɝː- *stress shift:* **ˌpreverbal ˈstate**
preview ˈpriː.vjuː **-s** -z **-ing** -ɪŋ **-ed** -d
Previn ˈprev.ɪn
previous ˈpriː.vi.əs, ˈ-vjəs, Ⓤⓢ -vi.əs **-ly** -li **-ness** -nəs, -nɪs
prevision ˌpriːˈvɪʒ.ᵊn, prɪ-, Ⓤⓢ priː-
prevocalic ˌpriː.vəʊˈkæl.ɪk, Ⓤⓢ -voʊˈ- **-ally** -ᵊl.i, -li *stress shift:* **ˌprevocalic ˈconsonant**
Prevost ˈprev.əʊ, ˈprev.əʊst, prevˈəʊ, Ⓤⓢ ˈpreɪ.voʊ, ˈprev.oʊ
pre-war ˌpriːˈwɔːʳ, Ⓤⓢ -ˈwɔːr *stress shift:* **ˌpre-war ˈpolitics**
Prewett ˈpruː.ɪt
prey preɪ **-s** -z **-ing** -ɪŋ **-ed** -d
prezzie ˈprez.i **-s** -z
Priam ˈpraɪ.əm, ˈpraɪ.æm
priapic praɪˈæp.ɪk, -ˈeɪ.pɪk
priapism ˈpraɪ.ə.pɪ.zᵊm
priapus, P~ praɪˈeɪ.pəs; ˈpraɪ.ə.pəs **-es** -ɪz
pric|e, P~ praɪs **-es** -ɪz **-ing** -ɪŋ **-ed** -t **ˈprice ˌtag; ˈprice ˌwar**
price-cutting ˈpraɪsˌkʌt.ɪŋ, Ⓤⓢ -ˌkʌţ-
priceless ˈpraɪ.sləs, -slɪs **-ness** -nəs, -nɪs
pric|ey ˈpraɪ.s|i **-ier** -i.əʳ, Ⓤⓢ -i.ɚ **-iest** -i.ɪst, -i.əst **-ily** -ᵊl.i, -ɪ.li **-iness** -ɪ.nəs, -ɪ.nɪs
prick prɪk **-s** -s **-ing/s** -ɪŋ/z **-ed** -t **-er/s** -əʳ/z, Ⓤⓢ -ɚ/z
prickl|e ˈprɪk.ᵊl **-es** -z **-ing** -ɪŋ, ˈprɪk.lɪŋ **-ed** -d
prickl|y ˈprɪk.l|i, -ᵊl|.i, Ⓤⓢ ˈ-l|i **-ier** -i.əʳ, Ⓤⓢ -i.ɚ **-iest** -ɪ.ɪst, -i.əst **-iness** -ɪ.nəs, -ɪ.nɪs **ˌprickly ˈpear**
prid|e, P~ praɪd **-es** -z **-ing** -ɪŋ **-ed** -ɪd **ˌpride of ˈplace**
Prideaux ˈprɪd.əʊ, ˈpriː.dəʊ, Ⓤⓢ ˈprɪd.oʊ
Pridham ˈprɪd.əm
prie-dieu ˌpriːˈdjɜː, ˈ--, Ⓤⓢ ˈpriː.djɜː **prie-dieus** ˌpriːˈdjɜːz, -ˈdjɜː, ˈ--, Ⓤⓢ ˈpriː.djɜːz
prie-dieux (alternative plural of **prie-dieu**) ˌpriːˈdjɜːz, -ˈdjɜː, ˈ--, Ⓤⓢ ˈpriː.djɜːz
priest, P~ priːst **-s** -s
priestess ˌpriːˈstes; ˈpriː.stəs, -stɪs, Ⓤⓢ ˈpriː.stɪs **-es** -ɪz
priesthood ˈpriːst.hʊd
Priestland ˈpriːst.lənd
Priestley ˈpriːst.li
priestl|y ˈpriːst.l|i **-iness** -ɪ.nəs, -ɪ.nɪs
prig prɪg **-s** -z **-gery** -ᵊr.i
priggish ˈprɪg.ɪʃ **-ly** -li **-ness** -nəs, -nɪs
prim, P~ prɪm **-mer** -əʳ, Ⓤⓢ -ɚ **-mest** -ɪst, -əst **-ly** -li **-ness** -nəs, -nɪs **-s** -z **-ming** -ɪŋ **-med** -d
prima ballerina ˌpriː.mə.bæl.ᵊrˈiː.nə, Ⓤⓢ -əˈriː- **-s** -z
primac|y ˈpraɪ.mə.s|i **-ies** -iz
prima donna ˌpriː.məˈdɒn.ə, Ⓤⓢ -ˈdɑː.nə, ˌprɪm.əˈ- **-s** -z
primaeval praɪˈmiː.vᵊl
prima facie ˌpraɪ.məˈfeɪ.ʃi, -ʃiː, ˈ-ʃi.iː, ˈ-si, -siː, ˈ-si.iː, Ⓤⓢ ˈ-ʃiː, ˈ-ʃiː, -ʃə
Primakov ˈpriː.mə.kɒf, ˌ--ˈ-, Ⓤⓢ ˈpriː.mə.kɔːf, -kɑːf
primal ˈpraɪ.mᵊl **ˌprimal ˈtherapy**
primarily praɪˈmer.ᵊl.i, -ˈmeə.rᵊl-, -ɪ.li; ˈpraɪ.mᵊr.ᵊl-, -ɪ.li, Ⓤⓢ praɪˈmer.ᵊl.i, ˈpraɪ.mer-
primar|y ˈpraɪ.mᵊr|.i, Ⓤⓢ -mer-, -mɚ- **-ies** -iz **-iness** -ɪ.nəs, -ɪ.nɪs **ˌprimary ˈcolour** Ⓤⓢ **ˈprimary ˌcolor; ˈprimary ˌschool; ˌprimary ˈstress**
primate *higher mammal:* ˈpraɪ.meɪt *archbishop:* ˈpraɪ.meɪt, -mɪt, -mət, Ⓤⓢ -mɪt **-s** -s
primateship ˈpraɪ.mət.ʃɪp, -mɪt-, -meɪt-, Ⓤⓢ -mɪt- **-s** -s
prim|e, P~ praɪm **-es** -z **-ing** -ɪŋ **-ed** -d **ˌprime ˈminister; ˌprime ˈmover; ˈprime ˌtime; ˌprime ˈtime**

> Note: 'Prime Minister' is often pronounced with a single /m/, thus /ˌpraɪˈmɪn.ɪ.stəʳ/

primer *thing that primes:* ˈpraɪ.məʳ, Ⓤⓢ -mɚ *elementary school book:* ˈpraɪ.məʳ, ˈprɪm.əʳ, Ⓤⓢ ˈprɪm.ɚ, ˈpraɪ.mɚ *printing type:* ˈprɪm.əʳ, Ⓤⓢ -ɚ **-s** -z
primetime ˈpraɪm.taɪm
primeval praɪˈmiː.vᵊl
primipar|a praɪˈmɪp.ᵊr|.ə **-as** -əz **-ae** -iː
primiparous praɪˈmɪp.ᵊr.əs
primitive ˈprɪm.ɪ.tɪv, ˈ-ə-, Ⓤⓢ -ɪ.ţɪv **-ly** -li **-ness** -nəs, -nɪs
primitiv|ism ˈprɪm.ɪ.tɪ.v|ɪ.zᵊm, ˈ-ə-, Ⓤⓢ -ɪ.ţɪ- **-ist/s** -ɪst/s
primo ˈpriː.məʊ, Ⓤⓢ -moʊ
primogenitor ˌpraɪ.məʊˈdʒen.ɪ.təʳ, ˌpriː-, ˈ-ə-, Ⓤⓢ ˌpraɪ.moʊˈdʒen.ɪ.ţɚ, -məˈ- **-s** -z
primogeniture

P

ˌpraɪ.məʊˈdʒen.ɪ.tʃəʳ, ˈ-ə-, -tjəʳ, -tʃʊəʳ, -tjʊəʳ, (US) ˌpraɪ.moʊˈdʒen.ɪ.tʃɚ, -məˈ-

primordial praɪˈmɔː.di.əl, (US) -ˈmɔːr- -s -z -ly -i

primp prɪmp -s -s -ing -ɪŋ -ed -t, prɪmt

primros|e, P~ ˈprɪm.rəʊz, (US) -roʊz -es -ɪz **ˌprimrose ˈpath**

primula ˈprɪm.jə.lə, -jʊ- -s -z

primum mobile ˌpraɪ.məmˈməʊ.bɪ.li, ˌpriː-, -mʊmˈ-, -bᵊl.i, -eɪ, (US) ˌpraɪ.məmˈmoʊ.bᵊl.i, ˌpriː-, -eɪ -s -z

primus, P~® ˈpraɪ.məs -es -ɪz

princ|e, P~ prɪn*t*s -es -ɪz **ˌprince ˈcharming; ˌprince ˈconsort; ˌPrince ˈEdward ˌIsland** (US) **ˌPrince ˌEdward ˈIsland; ˌPrince of ˈWales; ˌprince ˈregent**

princedom ˈprɪn*t*s.dəm -s -z

princeling ˈprɪn*t*s.lɪŋ -s -z

princel|y ˈprɪn*t*s.l|i -ier -i.əʳ, (US) -i.ɚ -iest -i.ɪst, -i.əst -iness -ɪ.nəs, -ɪ.nɪs

Princes Risborough ˌprɪn*t*.sɪzˈrɪz.bᵊr.ə, (US) -bɚ.oʊ

princess, P~ prɪnˈses, ˈprɪn*t*.ses, -ɪs, -əs, (US) ˈprɪn*t*.sɪs, -ses -es -ɪz **ˌprincess ˈroyal**

Princeton ˈprɪn*t*.stən

Princetown ˈprɪn*t*s.taʊn

princip|al, P~ ˈprɪn*t*.sə.p|ᵊl, -sɪ-, (US) -sə- -als -ᵊlz -ally -ᵊl.i, -li -alness -ᵊl.nəs, -nɪs **ˌprincipal ˈboy**

principalit|y ˌprɪn*t*.sɪˈpæl.ə.t|i, -səˈ-, -ɪ.t|i, (US) -səˈpæl.ə.t̬|i -ies -iz

principalship ˈprɪn*t*.sə.pᵊl.ʃɪp, -sɪ-, (US) -sə- -s -s

principate ˈprɪn*t*.sɪ.pət, -sə-, -pɪt, -peɪt, (US) -sə.peɪt, -pɪt -s -s

Principia prɪnˈsɪp.i.ə

principle ˈprɪn*t*.sə.pᵊl, -sɪ-, (US) -sə- -s -z -d -d

Pring prɪŋ

Pringle ˈprɪŋ.gᵊl

Prinknash ˈprɪn.ɪdʒ

Prinsep ˈprɪn*t*.sep

print prɪnt -s -s -ing/s -ɪn/z, (US) ˈprɪn.t̬ɪŋ/z -ed -ɪd, (US) ˈprɪn.t̬ɪd **ˈprint ˌrun; ˈprinting ˌpress**

printable ˈprɪn.tə.bᵊl, (US) -t̬ə-

printer ˈprɪn.təʳ, (US) -t̬ɚ -s -z

printmak|ing ˈprɪntˌmeɪ.k|ɪŋ -er/s -əʳ/z, (US) -ɚ/z

printout ˈprɪnt.aʊt -s -s

printwheel ˈprɪnt.*h*wiːl -s -z

prion ˈpraɪ.ɒn, (US) -ɑːn -s -z

prior, P~ praɪ.əʳ, (US) praɪ.ɚ -s -z

prioress ˈpraɪ.ə.rəs, -rɪs, -res; ˌpraɪ.əˈres, (US) ˈpraɪ.ɚ.ɪs -es -ɪz

prioritiz|e, -is|e praɪˈɒr.ɪ.taɪz, ˈ-ə-, (US) -ˈɔːr.ə- -es -ɪz -ing -ɪŋ -ed -d

priorit|y praɪˈɒr.ə.t|i, -ɪ.t|i, (US) -ˈɔːr.ə.t̬|i -ies -iz

prior|y ˈpraɪ.ə.r|i -ies -iz

Priscian ˈprɪʃ.i.ən, (US) ˈ-ən, -i.ən

Priscilla prɪˈsɪl.ə, prə-, (US) prɪ-

pris|e praɪz -es -ɪz -ing -ɪŋ -ed -d

prism ˈprɪz.ᵊm -s -z

prismatic prɪzˈmæt.ɪk, (US) -ˈmæt̬- -al -ᵊl -ally -ᵊl.i, -li

prison ˈprɪz.ᵊn -s -z **ˈprison ˌcamp; ˌprison ˈvisitor**

prisoner ˈprɪz.ᵊn.əʳ, ˈ-nəʳ, (US) ˈprɪz.ᵊn.ɚ, ˈ-nɚ -s -z **ˌprisoner of ˈconscience; ˌprisoner of ˈwar**

priss|y ˈprɪs|.i -ier -i.əʳ, (US) -i.ɚ -iest -i.ɪst, -i.əst -ily -ᵊl.i, -ɪ.li -iness -ɪ.nəs, -ɪ.nɪs

Pristina ˈprɪʃ.tɪ.nə

pristine ˈprɪs.tiːn, -taɪn, (US) -tiːn; prɪˈstiːn

Pritchard ˈprɪtʃ.əd, -ɑːd, (US) -ɚd

Pritchett ˈprɪtʃ.ɪt, -ət

prithee ˈprɪð.i, -iː

Prius® ˈpriː.əs, ˈpraɪ-, (US) ˈpriː-

privacy ˈprɪv.ə.si, ˈpraɪ.və-, (US) ˈpraɪ.və-

private ˈpraɪ.vɪt, -vət, (US) -vət -s -s -ly -li -ness -nəs, -nɪs **ˌprivate deˈtective; ˌprivate ˈenterprise; ˌprivate ˈeye; ˌprivate ˈmember's ˈbill; ˌprivate ˈsector** (US) **ˈprivate ˌsector; ˌprivate ˈschool**

privateer ˌpraɪ.vəˈtɪəʳ, -vɪˈ-, (US) -vəˈtɪr -s -z

privation praɪˈveɪ.ʃᵊn -s -z

privative ˈprɪv.ə.tɪv -ly -li

privatization, -isa- ˌpraɪ.vɪ.taɪˈzeɪ.ʃᵊn, -və-, -tɪˈ-, (US) -və.t̬əˈ- -s -z

privatiz|e, -is|e ˈpraɪ.vɪ.taɪz, -və-, (US) -və- -es -ɪz -ing -ɪŋ -ed -d

privet ˈprɪv.ɪt -s -s **ˈprivet ˌhedge; ˌprivet ˈhedge**

privileg|e ˈprɪv.ᵊl.ɪdʒ, -ɪ.lɪdʒ, (US) -ᵊl.ɪdʒ, ˈ-lɪdʒ -es -ɪz -ed -d

privity ˈprɪv.ə.ti, -ɪ.ti, (US) -ə.t̬i

priv|y ˈprɪv|.i -ies -iz -ily -ᵊl.i, -ɪ.li **ˌPrivy ˈCouncil; ˌPrivy ˈPurse; ˌPrivy ˈSeal**

priz|e praɪz -es -ɪz -ing -ɪŋ -ed -d **ˈprize ˌday**

prize|-fight ˈpraɪz|.faɪt -fights -faɪts -fighter/s -ˌfaɪ.təʳ/z, (US) -ˌfaɪ.t̬ɚ/z

prizewinn|er ˈpraɪzˌwɪn|.əʳ, (US) -ɚ -ers -əz, (US) -ɚz -ing -ɪŋ

Prizren ˈprɪz.rɪn, (US) ˈpriːz.rən

pro prəʊ, (US) proʊ -s -z **ˌpros and ˈcons**

PRO ˌpiː.ɑːˈrəʊ, (US) -ɑːrˈoʊ

pro- prəʊ, (US) proʊ, prə

Note: Prefix. In words containing **pro-** where the stem is free and the meaning is **in favour of**, it generally takes secondary stress, e.g. **pro-choice** /ˌprəʊˈtʃɔɪs/ (US) /ˌproʊ-/. Attached to bound stems, the pronunciation is normally /prəʊ-/ (US) /proʊ-, prə-/, e.g. **probation** /prəʊˈbeɪ.ʃᵊn/ (US) /proʊ-/. There are exceptions; see individual entries.

proactive ˌprəʊˈæk.tɪv, (US) ˌproʊ- -ly -li

pro-am ˌprəʊˈæm, (US) ˌproʊ-

probabilistic ˌprɒb.ə.bᵊlˈɪs.tɪk, -bɪˈlɪs-, (US) ˌprɑː.bə.bᵊlˈɪs-

probabilit|y ˌprɒb.əˈbɪl.ə.t|i, -ɪ.t|i, (US) ˌprɑː.bəˈbɪl.ə.t̬|i -ies -iz

probab|le ˈprɒb.ə.b|ᵊl, (US) ˈprɑː.bə- -ly -li

proba|te ˈprəʊ.beɪ|t, -bɪ|t, (US) ˈproʊ.beɪ|t -tes -ts -ting -tɪŋ, (US) -t̬ɪŋ -ted -tɪd, (US) -t̬ɪd

probation prəʊˈbeɪ.ʃᵊn, (US) proʊ- -s -z **proˈbation ˌofficer**

probationary prəʊˈbeɪ.ʃᵊn.ᵊr.i, -ˈbeɪʃ.nᵊr-, (US) proʊˈbeɪ.ʃᵊn.er-

probationer prəʊˈbeɪ.ʃᵊn.əʳ, -ˈbeɪʃ.nəʳ, (US) proʊˈbeɪ.ʃᵊn.ɚ, -ˈbeɪʃ.nɚ -s -z

probative ˈprəʊ.bə.tɪv, (US) ˈproʊ.bə.t̬ɪv

prob|e prəʊb, (US) proʊb -es -z -ing -ɪŋ -ed -d

Probert ˈprəʊ.bət, ˈprɒb.ət, (US) ˈproʊ.bɚt, ˈprɑː.bɚt

probiotic ˌprəʊ.baɪˈɒt.ɪk, (US) ˌproʊ.baɪˈɑː.t̬ɪk -s -s

probity ˈprəʊ.bə.ti, -ɪ.ti, (US) ˈproʊ.bə.t̬i

problem ˈprɒb.ləm, -lem, -lɪm, (US) ˈprɑː.bləm -s -z **ˈproblem ˌchild; ˈproblem ˌpage**

problematic ˌprɒb.ləˈmæt.ɪk, -lɪˈ-, -lemˈæt-, (US) ˌprɑː.bləˈmæt̬- -al -ᵊl -ally -ᵊl.i, -li *stress shift:* **ˌproblematic ˈstate**

pro bono ˌprəʊˈbəʊ.nəʊ, (US) ˌproʊˈboʊ.noʊ

proboscis prəʊˈbɒs.ɪs, (US) proʊˈbɑː.sɪs -es -iːz

Probus ˈprəʊ.bəs, (US) ˈproʊ-

Probyn ˈprəʊ.bɪn, (US) ˈproʊ-

procedural prəˈsiː.dʒᵊr.ᵊl, prəʊ-, -dʒʊ.rᵊl, -djʊ.rᵊl, -djᵊr.ᵊl, (US) prəˈsiː.dʒɚ.ᵊl, proʊ-

procedure prəʊˈsiː.dʒəʳ, -djəʳ, (US) prəˈsiː.dʒɚ, proʊ- -s -z

proceed v prəʊˈsiːd, (US) proʊ-, prə- -s -z -ing/s -ɪŋ/z -ed -ɪd

proceeds n ˈprəʊ.siːdz, (US) ˈproʊ-

pro-celebrity ˌprəʊ.səˈleb.rɪ.ti, -sɪˈ-, -rə-, (US) ˌproʊ.səˈleb.rə.t̬i *stress shift:* **ˌpro-celebrity ˈgolf**

process v *go in a procession:* prəʊˈses, (US) prə-, proʊ- *treat by a process:* ˈprəʊ.ses, -sɪs, (US) ˈprɑː.ses, -səs -es -ɪz -ing -ɪŋ -ed -t -or/s -əʳ/z, (US) -ɚ/z

proc|ess n ˈprəʊ.s|es, -s|ɪs, (US) ˈprɑː.s|es, -s|əs -esses -es.ɪz, -ɪ.sɪz, (US) -es.ɪz, -ə.sɪz

procession prəˈseʃ.ᵊn, (US) prə-, proʊ- -s -z

processional prəˈseʃ.ᵊn.ᵊl, (US) prə-, proʊ- -s -z

pro-choice ˌprəʊˈtʃɔɪs, (US) ˌproʊ-

proclaim prəʊˈkleɪm, (US) proʊ-, prə- -s -z -ing -ɪŋ -ed -d -er/s -əʳ/z, (US) -ɚ/z

proclamation ˌprɒk.ləˈmeɪ.ʃᵊn, (US) ˌprɑː.kləˈ- -s -z

proclitic prəʊˈklɪt.ɪk, (US) proʊˈklɪt̬- -s -s

proclivit|y prəʊˈklɪv.ə.t|i, -ɪ.t|i, (US) proʊˈklɪv.ə.t̬|i -ies -iz

proconsul prəʊˈkɒn*t*.sᵊl, (US) proʊˈkɑːn*t*- -s -z

proconsul|ar prəʊˈkɒn*t*.sjə.l|əʳ,

-sjʊ-, US proʊˈkɑːnt.sᵊl|.ɚ **-ate/s** -ət/s, -ɪt/s, -eɪt/s, US -ɪt/s
proconsulship prəʊˈkɒnt.sᵊl.ʃɪp, US proʊˈkɑːnt- **-s** -s
procrasti|nate prəʊˈkræs.tɪ|.neɪt, US proʊˈkræs.tə-, prə- **-nates** -neɪts **-nating** -neɪ.tɪŋ, US -neɪ.t̬ɪŋ **-nated** -neɪ.tɪd, US -neɪ.t̬ɪd **-nator/s** -neɪ.təʳ/z, US -neɪ.t̬ɚ/z
procrastination prəʊˌkræs.tɪˈneɪ.ʃᵊn, US proʊˌkræs.təˈ-, prə- **-s** -z
procreant ˈprəʊ.kri.ənt, US ˈproʊ-
procrea|te ˈprəʊ.kri.eɪ|t, ˌ--ˈ-, US ˈproʊ.kri.eɪ|t **-tes** -ts **-ting** -tɪŋ, US -t̬ɪŋ **-ted** -tɪd, US -t̬ɪd
procreation ˌprəʊ.kriˈeɪ.ʃᵊn, US ˌproʊ-
procreative ˈprəʊ.kri.eɪ.tɪv, -ə-, ˌprəʊ.kriˈeɪ-, US ˈproʊ.kri.eɪ.t̬ɪv
Procrust|es prəʊˈkrʌs.t|iːz, US proʊ- **-ean** -i.ən
Procter ˈprɒk.təʳ, US ˈprɑːk.tɚ
proctor, P~ ˈprɒk.təʳ, US ˈprɑːk.tɚ **-s** -z **-ing** -ɪŋ **-ed** -d
proctorial prɒkˈtɔː.ri.əl, US prɑːkˈtɔːr.i-
procumbent prəʊˈkʌm.bənt, US proʊ-
procuration ˌprɒk.jʊəˈreɪ.ʃᵊn, -jəˈ-, US ˌprɑːk.juːˈ-, -jəˈ- **-s** -z
procurator ˈprɒk.jʊə.reɪ.təʳ, -jə-, US ˈprɑː.kjə.reɪ.t̬ɚ, -kjʊ- **-s** -z
procurator fiscal ˌprɒk.jʊə.reɪ.təˈfɪs.kᵊl, -jə-, US ˌprɑː.kjə.reɪ.t̬ɚˈ-, -kjʊ-
procur|e prəˈkjʊəʳ, -kjɔːʳ, US proʊˈkjʊr, prə- **-es** -z **-ing** -ɪŋ **-ed** -d **-er/s** -əʳ/z, US -ɚ/z **-able** -ə.bᵊl
procurement prəˈkjʊə.mənt, -ˈkjɔː-, US proʊˈkjʊr-, prə-
procuress prəˈkjʊə.res, -ˈkjɔː-, -rɪs; ˈprɒk.jə-, -jʊ-, US proʊˈkjʊr.ɪs, prə- **-es** -ɪz
Procyon ˈprəʊ.si.ən, prəʊˈsaɪ.ən, US ˈproʊ.si.ɑːn
prod prɒd, US prɑːd **-s** -z **-ding** -ɪŋ **-ded** -ɪd
prodd|y ˈprɒd|.i, US ˈprɑː.d|i **-ies** -iz
Prodi ˈprəʊ.di, US ˈproʊ-
prodigal ˈprɒd.ɪ.gᵊl, US ˈprɑː.dɪ- **-s** -z **-ly** -i **-ness** -nəs, -nɪs ˌ**prodigal** ˈ**son**
prodigality ˌprɒd.ɪˈgæl.ə.ti, -ɪ.ti, US ˌprɑː.dɪˈgæl.ə.t̬i
prodigious prəˈdɪdʒ.əs, US prə-, proʊ- **-ly** -li **-ness** -nəs, -nɪs
prodig|y ˈprɒd.ɪ.dʒ|i, ˈ-ə-, US ˈprɑː.də- **-ies** -iz
produce n ˈprɒdʒ.uːs, ˈprɒd.juːs, US ˈprɑː.duːs, ˈproʊ-, -djuːs
produc|e v prəˈdʒuːs, -ˈdjuːs, US -ˈduːs, proʊ-, -ˈdjuːs **-es** -ɪz **-ing** -ɪŋ **-ed** -t **-er/s** -əʳ/z, US -ɚ/z
producible prəˈdʒuː.sə.bᵊl, -ˈdjuː-, -sɪ-, US -ˈduː.sə-, proʊ-, -ˈdjuː-
product ˈprɒd.ʌkt, -əkt, US ˈprɑː.dʌkt, -dəkt **-s** -s
production prəˈdʌk.ʃᵊn, US prə-, proʊ- **-s** -z **proˈduction** ˌ**line**
productional prəˈdʌk.ʃᵊn.ᵊl, US prə-, proʊ-
productive prəˈdʌk.tɪv, US prə-, proʊ- **-ly** -li **-ness** -nəs, -nɪs
productivity ˌprɒd.ʌkˈtɪv.ə.ti, -əkˈ-, -ɪ.ti, US ˌproʊ.dəkˈtɪv.ə.t̬i, ˌprɑː-; US proʊˌdʌkˈ-, prə-
proem ˈprəʊ.em, US ˈproʊ- **-s** -z
prof prɒf, US prɑːf **-s** -s
profanation ˌprɒf.əˈneɪ.ʃᵊn, US ˌprɑː.fəˈ- **-s** -z
profan|e prəˈfeɪn, US proʊ-, prə- **-est** -ɪst, -əst **-ely** -li **-eness** -nəs, -nɪs **-es** -z **-ing** -ɪŋ **-ed** -d **-er/s** -əʳ/z, US -ɚ/z
profanit|y prəˈfæn.ə.t|i, -ɪ.t|i, US proʊˈfæn.ə.t̬|i, prə- **-ies** -iz
profess prəˈfes, US prə-, proʊ- **-es** -ɪz **-ing** -ɪŋ **-ed** -t **-edly** -ɪd.li
profession prəˈfeʃ.ᵊn, US prə-, proʊ- **-s** -z
professional prəˈfeʃ.ᵊn.ᵊl, US prə-, proʊ- **-s** -z
professionalism prəˈfeʃ.ᵊn.ᵊl.ɪ.zᵊm, US prə-, proʊ-
professionally ˈ-nᵊl.i, US prə-, proʊ-
professor prəˈfes.əʳ, US -ɚ, proʊ- **-s** -z
professorate prəˈfes.ᵊr.ət, -eɪt, US -ɚ.ət, proʊ- **-s** -s
professorial ˌprɒf.ɪˈsɔː.ri.əl, -əˈ-, -esˈɔː-, US ˌproʊ.fəˈsɔːr.i-, ˌprɑː- **-ly** -i *stress shift:* ˌ**professorial** ˈ**duties**
professoriat(e) ˌprɒf.ɪˈsɔː.ri.ət, -əˈ-, -esˈɔː-, -ɪt, US ˌproʊ.fəˈsɔːr.i.ət, ˌprɑː- **-s** -s
professorship prəˈfes.ə.ʃɪp, US ˈ-ɚ-, proʊ- **-s** -s
proff|er ˈprɒf|.əʳ, US ˈprɑː.f|ɚ **-ers** -əz, US -ɚz **-ering** -ᵊr.ɪŋ **-ered** -əd, US -ɚd
proficiency prəˈfɪʃ.ᵊnt.si, US prə-, proʊ-
proficient prəˈfɪʃ.ᵊnt, US prə-, proʊ- **-ly** -li
profil|e ˈprəʊ.faɪl, US ˈproʊ- **-es** -z **-ing** -ɪŋ **-ed** -d
prof|it n, v ˈprɒf|.ɪt, US ˈprɑː.f|ɪt **-its** -ɪts **-iting** -ɪ.tɪŋ, US -ɪ.t̬ɪŋ **-ited** -ɪ.tɪd, US -ɪ.t̬ɪd ˌ**profit and** ˈ**loss**; ˈ**profit** ˌ**margin**
profitability ˌprɒf.ɪ.təˈbɪl.ɪ.ti, ˌ-ə-, -ə.ti, US ˌprɑː.fɪ.t̬əˈbɪl.ə.t̬i
profitab|le ˈprɒf.ɪ.tə.b|ᵊl, ˈ-ə-, US ˈprɑː.fɪ.t̬ə- **-ly** -li **-leness** -ᵊl.nəs, -nɪs
profiteer ˌprɒf.ɪˈtɪəʳ, -əˈ-, US ˌprɑː.fɪˈtɪr **-s** -z **-ing** -ɪŋ **-ed** -d
profiterole prəˈfɪt.ᵊr.əʊl, prəˈfɪt-; ˈprɒf.ɪ.tᵊr-, ˌprɒf.ɪ.tᵊrˈəʊl, US prəˈfɪt.ə.roʊl **-s** -z
profitless ˈprɒf.ɪt.ləs, -lɪs, US ˈprɑː.fɪt-
profitmaking ˈprɒf.ɪtˌmeɪ.kɪŋ, US ˈprɑː.fɪt-
profit-sharing ˈprɒf.ɪtˌʃeə.rɪŋ, US ˈprɑː.fɪtˌʃer.ɪŋ
profligacy ˈprɒf.lɪ.gə.si, US ˈprɑː.flɪ-
profligate ˈprɒf.lɪ.gət, -gɪt, US ˈprɑː.flɪ.gɪt **-s** -s **-ly** -li **-ness** -nəs, -nɪs
pro forma ˌprəʊˈfɔː.mə, US ˌproʊˈfɔːr-
profound prəˈfaʊnd, US prə-, proʊ- **-er** -əʳ, US -ɚ **-est** -ɪst, -əst **-ly** -li **-ness** -nəs, -nɪs
Profumo prəˈfjuː.məʊ, US -moʊ
profundit|y prəˈfʌn.də.t|i, -ɪ.t|i, US proʊ-, prə- **-ies** -iz
profus|e prəˈfjuːs, US prə-, proʊ- **-est** -ɪst, -əst **-ely** -li **-eness** -nəs, -nɪs
profusion prəˈfjuː.ʒᵊn, US prə-, proʊ- **-s** -z
prog prɒg, US prɑːg, prɔːg **-s** -z **-ging** -ɪŋ **-ged** -d
progenitor prəʊˈdʒen.ɪ.təʳ, ˈ-ə-, US proʊˈdʒen.ə.t̬ɚ, prə- **-s** -z
progeniture prəʊˈdʒen.ɪ.tʃəʳ, ˈ-ə-, -tʃʊəʳ, -tjʊəʳ, -tjəʳ, US proʊˈdʒen.ə.tʃɚ, prə-
progen|y ˈprɒdʒ.ə.n|i, ˈ-ɪ-, US ˈprɑː.dʒə- **-ies** -iz
progesterone prəʊˈdʒes.tᵊr.əʊn, US proʊˈdʒes.tə.roʊn
progestogen prəʊˈdʒes.tə.dʒɪn, -dʒən, US proʊˈdʒes.tə.dʒən, -dʒen **-s** -z
prognathic prɒgˈnæθ.ɪk, US prɑːg-, -ˈneɪ.θɪk
prognathism ˈprɒg.nə.θɪ.zᵊm; prɒgˈnæθ.ɪ-, US ˈprɑːg.nə.θɪ-; US prɑːgˈneɪ-
prognathous prɒgˈneɪ.θəs; ˈprɒg.nə.θəs, US ˈprɑːg.nə-; US prɑːgˈneɪ-
prognos|is prɒgˈnəʊ.s|ɪs, US prɑːgˈnoʊ- **-es** -iːz
prognostic prɒgˈnɒs.tɪk, prəg-, US prɑːgˈnɑː.stɪk
prognosti|cate prɒgˈnɒs.tɪ|.keɪt, prəg-, US prɑːgˈnɑː.stɪ- **-cates** -keɪts **-cating** -keɪ.tɪŋ, US -keɪ.t̬ɪŋ **-cated** -keɪ.tɪd, US -keɪ.t̬ɪd **-cator/s** -keɪ.təʳ/z, US -keɪ.t̬ɚ/z
prognostication prɒgˌnɒs.tɪˈkeɪ.ʃᵊn, prəg-, -təˈ-, US prɑːgˌnɑː.stɪˈ- **-s** -z
program ˈprəʊ.græm, US ˈproʊ-, -grəm **-s** -z **-ing** -ɪŋ **-ed** -d **-er/s** -əʳ/z, US -ɚ/z
programmable prəʊˈgræm.ə.bᵊl; ˈprəʊ.græm-, US ˈproʊ.græm.ə-, -grə.mə-
programmatic ˌprəʊ.grəˈmæt.ɪk, US ˌproʊ.grəˈmæt̬-
programm|e ˈprəʊ.græm, US ˈproʊ-, -grəm **-es** -z **-ing** -ɪŋ **-ed** -d **-er/s** -əʳ/z, US -ɚ/z
progress n ˈprəʊ.gres, US ˈprɑː- ˈ**progress re**ˌ**port**
progress v prəʊˈgres, US prə-, proʊ- **-es** -ɪz **-ing** -ɪŋ **-ed** -t
progression prəʊˈgreʃ.ᵊn, US prə-, proʊ- **-s** -z
progressional prəʊˈgreʃ.ᵊn.ᵊl, ˈ-nᵊl, US prə-, proʊ-
progressionist prəʊˈgreʃ.ᵊn.ɪst, US prə-, proʊ- **-s** -s

P

progressive prəʊˈgres.ɪv, (US) prə-, proʊ- **-s** -z **-ly** -li **-ness** -nəs, -nɪs
progressiv|ism prəʊˈgres.ɪ.v|ɪ.zəm, (US) prə-, proʊ- **-ist/s** -ɪst/s
prohib|it prəʊˈhɪb|.ɪt, (US) proʊ-, prə- **-its** -ɪts **-iting** -ɪ.tɪŋ, (US) -ɪ.ţɪŋ **-ited** -ɪ.tɪd, (US) -ɪ.ţɪd
prohibition, P~ ˌprəʊ.hɪˈbɪʃ.ən, (US) ˌproʊ- **-s** -z
prohibition|ism ˌprəʊ.hɪˈbɪʃ.ən|ɪ.zəm, (US) ˌproʊ- **-ist/s** -ɪst/s
prohibitive prəʊˈhɪb.ə.tɪv, (US) proʊˈhɪb.ə.ţɪv, prə- **-ly** -li
prohibitory prəʊˈhɪb.ɪ.tər.i, (US) proʊˈhɪb.ə.tɔːr-, prə-
project n ˈprɒdʒ.ekt, -ɪkt, (US) ˈprɑː.dʒekt, -dʒɪkt **-s** -s
project v prəʊˈdʒekt, (US) prə-, proʊ- **-s** -s **-ing** -ɪŋ **-ed** -ɪd
projectile prəʊˈdʒek.taɪl, (US) prəˈdʒek.təl, proʊ- **-s** -z
projection prəʊˈdʒek.ʃən, (US) prə-, proʊ- **-s** -z **-ist/s** -ɪst/s
projective prəʊˈdʒek.tɪv, (US) prə-, proʊ- **-ly** -li
projector prəʊˈdʒek.təʳ, (US) prəˈdʒek.tɚ, proʊ- **-s** -z
Prokofiev prəˈkɒf.i.ef, (US) proʊˈkɔː.fi.ef, prə-, -ˈkoʊ-
prolactin prəʊˈlæk.tɪn, (US) proʊ-
prolaps|e ˈprəʊ.læps, -ˈ-, (US) ˈproʊ- **-es** -ɪz **-ing** -ɪŋ **-ed** -t
prolate ˈprəʊ.leɪt, ˌ-ˈ-, (US) ˈproʊ.leɪt
prole prəʊl, (US) proʊl **-s** -z
prolegomen|on ˌprəʊ.lɪˈgɒm.ɪ.n|ən, -ləˈ-, -legˈɒm-, ˈ-ə-, -n|ɒn, (US) ˌproʊ.lɪˈgɑː.mə.n|ɑːn, -n|ən **-a** -ə
proleps|is prəʊˈlep.s|ɪs, -ˈliːp-, (US) proʊˈlep- **-es** -iːz
proleptic prəʊˈlep.tɪk, -ˈliːp-, (US) proʊˈlep- **-ally** -əl.i, -li
proletarian ˌprəʊ.lɪˈteə.ri.ən, -ləˈ-, -letˈeə-, (US) ˌproʊ.ləˈter.i-, -ˈtær- **-s** -z **-ism** -ɪ.zəm
proletariat ˌprəʊ.lɪˈteə.ri.ət, -ləˈ-, -letˈeə-, -æt, (US) ˌproʊ.ləˈter.i.ət, -ˈtær-
pro-life ˌprəʊˈlaɪf, (US) ˌproʊ-
prolifer|ate prəʊˈlɪf.ər|.eɪt, (US) proʊˈlɪf.ə.r|eɪt, prə- **-ates** -eɪts **-ating** -eɪ.tɪŋ, (US) -eɪ.ţɪŋ **-ated** -eɪ.tɪd, (US) -eɪ.ţɪd
proliferation prəʊˌlɪf.ərˈeɪ.ʃən, (US) proʊˌlɪf.əˈreɪ-, prə- **-s** -z
prolific prəʊˈlɪf.ɪk, (US) proʊ-, prə- **-ally** -əl.i, -li **-ness** -nəs, -nɪs
prolix ˈprəʊ.lɪks, (US) proʊˈlɪks, ˈ--
prolixity prəʊˈlɪk.sə-, -sɪ-, (US) proʊˈlɪk.sə.ţi, prə-
prolix|ly prəʊˈlɪk.s|li, ˈ---, (US) proʊˈlɪk.s|li, prə- **-ness** -nəs, -nɪs
prolocutor prəʊˈlɒk.jə.təʳ, -jʊ-, (US) proʊˈlɑː.kjə.ţɚ, -kjʊ- **-s** -z
prolog, PROLOG ˈprəʊ.lɒg, (US) ˈproʊ.lɑːg, -lɔːg **-s** -z
prologu|e ˈprəʊ.lɒg, (US) ˈproʊ.lɑːg, -lɔːg **-es** -z **-ing** -ɪŋ **-ed** -d
prolong prəʊˈlɒŋ, (US) proʊˈlɑːŋ, prə-, -ˈlɔːŋ **-s** -z **-ing** -ɪŋ **-ed** -d
prolongation ˌprəʊ.lɒŋˈgeɪ.ʃən, ˌprɒl.ɒŋˈ-, (US) ˌproʊ.lɑːŋˈ-, -lɔːŋˈ- **-s** -z
prom, P~ prɒm, (US) prɑːm **-s** -z
promenad|e ˌprɒm.əˈnɑːd, -ɪˈ-, (US) ˌprɑː.məˈneɪd, -ˈnɑːd **-es** -z **-ing** -ɪŋ **-ed** -ɪd **-er/s** -əʳ/z, (US) -ɚ/z *stress shift:* **ˌpromenade ˈconcert**

Note: A British pronunciation /ˌprɒm.əˈneɪd, -ɪ-/ also exists, used chiefly in square dancing.

Promethean prəʊˈmiː.θi.ən, (US) proʊ-, prə-
Prometheus prəʊˈmiː.θi.uːs, -əs, (US) proʊˈmiː.θi.əs, prə-, -uːs
promethium prəʊˈmiː.θi.əm, (US) proʊ-
prominenc|e ˈprɒm.ɪ.nənts, ˈ-ə-, (US) ˈprɑː.mə- **-es** -ɪz
prominent ˈprɒm.ɪ.nənt, ˈ-ə-, (US) ˈprɑː.mə- **-ly** -li
promiscuity ˌprɒm.ɪˈskjuː.ə.ti, -əˈ-, -ɪ.ti, (US) ˌprɑː.mɪˈskjuː.ə.ţi, ˌproʊ-
promiscuous prəˈmɪs.kju.əs, prɒmˈɪs-, (US) prəˈmɪs-, proʊ- **-ly** -li **-ness** -nəs, -nɪs
promis|e ˈprɒm.ɪs, (US) ˈprɑː.mɪs **-es** -ɪz **-ing/ly** -ɪŋ/li **-ed** -t ˌ**promised** ˈ**land** (US) ˈ**promised** ˌ**land**
promissory ˈprɒm.ɪ.sər.i; prəˈmɪs.ər-, (US) ˈprɑː.mɪ.sɔːr- ˌ**promissory** ˈ**note** (US) ˈ**promissory** ˌ**note**
promo ˈprəʊ.məʊ, (US) ˈproʊ.moʊ **-s** -z
promontor|y ˈprɒm.ən.tər|.i, (US) ˈprɑː.mən.tɔːr- **-ies** -iz
pro|mote prə|ˈməʊt, (US) -ˈmoʊt **-motes** -ˈməʊts, (US) -ˈmoʊts **-moting** -ˈməʊ.tɪŋ, (US) -ˈmoʊ.ţɪŋ **-moted** -ˈməʊ.tɪd, (US) -ˈmoʊ.ţɪd **-moter/s** -ˈməʊ.təʳ/z, (US) -ˈmoʊ.ţɚ/z
promotion prəˈməʊ.ʃən, (US) -ˈmoʊ-, proʊ- **-s** -z
promotional prəˈməʊ.ʃən.əl, (US) -ˈmoʊ-, proʊ- **-ly** -i
promotive prəˈməʊ.tɪv, (US) -ˈmoʊ.ţɪv, proʊ-
prompt prɒmpt, (US) prɑːmpt **-s** -s **-est** -ɪst, -əst **-ly** -li **-ness** -nəs, -nɪs **-ing/s** -ɪŋ/z **-ed** -ɪd **-er/s** -əʳ/z, (US) -ɚ/z
promptitude ˈprɒmp.tɪ.tʃuːd, ˈ-tə-, -tjuːd, (US) ˈprɑːmp.tɪ.tuːd, -tjuːd, ˈ-tə-
promul|gate ˈprɒm.əl|.geɪt, -ʌl-, (US) ˈprɑː.məl-; (US) proʊˈmʌl- **-gates** -geɪts **-gating** -geɪ.tɪŋ, (US) -geɪ.ţɪŋ **-gated** -geɪ.tɪd, (US) -geɪ.ţɪd **-gator/s** -geɪ.təʳ/z, (US) -geɪ.ţɚ/z
promulgation ˌprɒm.əlˈgeɪ.ʃən, -ʌlˈ-, (US) ˌprɑː.məlˈ- **-s** -z
prone prəʊn, (US) proʊn **-ly** -li **-ness** -nəs, -nɪs
prong prɒŋ, (US) prɑːŋ, prɔːŋ **-s** -z **-ing** -ɪŋ **-ed** -d
pronghorn ˈprɒŋ.hɔːn, (US) ˈprɑːŋ.hɔːrn, ˈprɔːŋ- **-s** -z
pronominal prəʊˈnɒm.ɪ.nəl, -ən.əl, (US) proʊˈnɑː.mə- **-ly** -i
pronominalization prəʊˌnɒm.ɪ.nəl.aɪˈzeɪ.ʃən, -ən.əl-, -ɪˈ-, (US) proʊˌnɑː.mɪ.nəl.əˈ- **-s** -z
pronominaliz|e, -is|e prəʊˈnɒm.ɪ.nəl.aɪz, -ən.əl-, (US) proʊˈnɑː.mɪ.nəl- **-es** -ɪz **-ing** -ɪŋ **-ed** -d
pronoun ˈprəʊ.naʊn, (US) ˈproʊ- **-s** -z
pronounc|e prəˈnaʊnts, (US) prə-, proʊ- **-es** -ɪz **-ing** -ɪŋ **-ed** -t **-edly** -t.li, -ɪd.li **-er/s** -əʳ/z, (US) -ɚ/z **-eable/ness** -ə.bəl/nəs, -nɪs
pronouncement prəʊˈnaʊnt.smənt, (US) prə-, proʊ- **-s** -s
pronto ˈprɒn.təʊ, (US) ˈprɑːn.ţoʊ
pronunciamento prəʊˌnʌnt.si.əˈmen.təʊ, -ʃi-, (US) proʊˌnʌnt.si.əˈmen.toʊ, prə- **-(e)s** -z
pronunciation prəˌnʌnt.siˈeɪ.ʃən, (US) prə-, proʊ- **-s** -z

Note: A common mispronunciation is /prəˌnaʊnt-/.

proof pruːf **-s** -s **-ing** -ɪŋ **-ed** -t
proofread ˈpruːf.riːd **-s** -z **-ing** -ɪŋ **-er/s** -əʳ/z, (US) -ɚ/z *past tense:* ˈpruːf.red
Proops pruːps
prop prɒp, (US) prɑːp **-s** -s **-ping** -ɪŋ **-ped** -t
propaedeutic ˌprəʊ.piːˈdʒuː.tɪk, -ˈdjuː-, (US) ˌproʊ.pɪˈduː.ţɪk, -ˈdjuː- **-al** -əl **-s** -s
propaganda ˌprɒp.əˈgæn.də, (US) ˌprɑː.pəˈ-
propagand|ism ˌprɒp.əˈgæn.d|ɪ.zəm, (US) ˌprɑː.pəˈ- **-ist/s** -ɪst/s
propagandiz|e, -is|e ˌprɒp.əˈgæn.daɪz, (US) ˌprɑː.pəˈ- **-es** -ɪz **-ing** -ɪŋ **-ed** -d
propa|gate ˈprɒp.ə|.geɪt, (US) ˈprɑː.pə- **-gates** -geɪts **-gating** -geɪ.tɪŋ, (US) -geɪ.ţɪŋ **-gated** -geɪ.tɪd, (US) -geɪ.ţɪd **-gator/s** -geɪ.təʳ/z, (US) -geɪ.ţɚ/z
propagation ˌprɒp.əˈgeɪ.ʃən, (US) ˌprɑː.pəˈ-
propane ˈprəʊ.peɪn, (US) ˈproʊ-
proparoxytone ˌprəʊ.pərˈɒk.sɪ.təʊn, -pærˈ-, ˈ-ə-, -tən, (US) ˌproʊ.pəˈrɑːk.sɪ.toʊn, -pærˈ- **-s** -z
propel prəˈpel **-s** -z **-ling** -ɪŋ **-led** -d **proˌpelling ˈpencil**
propellant, propellent prəˈpel.ənt **-s** -s
propeller, propellor prəˈpel.əʳ, (US) -ɚ **-s** -z
propene ˈprəʊ.piːn, (US) ˈproʊ-
propensit|y prəʊˈpent.sə.t|i, -ɪ.t|i, (US) prəˈpent.sə.ţ|i, proʊ- **-ies** -iz

proper ˈprɒp.əʳ, ⓊⓈ ˈprɑː.pɚ ˌ**proper** ˈ**noun**
properly ˈprɒp.əl.i, ˈ-li, ⓊⓈ ˈprɑː.pɚ.li
Propertius prəʊˈpɜː.ʃəs, -ʃi.əs, ⓊⓈ proʊˈpɝː-
propert|y ˈprɒp.ə.t|i, ⓊⓈ ˈprɑː.pɚ.ţ|i **-ies** -iz **-ied** -id
prophec|y n ˈprɒf.ə.s|i, ˈ-ɪ-, ⓊⓈ ˈprɑː.fə- **-ies** -iz
prophes|y v ˈprɒf.ə.s|aɪ, ˈ-ɪ-, ⓊⓈ ˈprɑː.fə- **-ies** -aɪz **-ying** -aɪ.ɪŋ **-ied** -aɪd **-ier/s** -aɪ.əʳ/z, ⓊⓈ -aɪ.ɚ/z
prophet ˈprɒf.ɪt, ⓊⓈ ˈprɑː.fɪt **-s** -s
prophetess ˌprɒf.ɪˈtes; ˈprɒf.ɪ.tɪs, -tes, ⓊⓈ ˈprɑː.fɪ.ţəs **-es** -ɪz
prophetic prəʊˈfet.ɪk, ⓊⓈ prə-, proʊ- **-al** -əl **-ally** -əl.i, -li
prophylactic ˌprɒf.ɪˈlæk.tɪk, -əˈ-, ⓊⓈ ˌproʊ.fəˈ-, ˌprɑː- **-s** -s **-ally** -əl.i, -li *stress shift:* ˌ**prophylactic** ˈ**medicine**
prophylax|is ˌprɒf.ɪˈlæk.s|ɪs, -əˈ-, ⓊⓈ ˌproʊ.fəˈ-, ˌprɑː- **-es** -iːz
propinquity prəʊˈpɪŋ.kwə.ti, prɒpˈɪŋ-, -kwɪ-, ⓊⓈ proʊˈpɪŋ.kwə.ţi, -ˈpɪn-
propiti|ate prəˈpɪʃ.i|.eɪt, ⓊⓈ proʊ-, prə- **-ates** -eɪts **-ating** -eɪ.tɪŋ, ⓊⓈ -eɪ.ţɪŋ **-ated** -eɪ.tɪd, ⓊⓈ -eɪ.ţɪd **-ator/s** -eɪ.təʳ/z, ⓊⓈ -eɪ.ţɚ/z
propitiation prəˌpɪʃ.iˈeɪ.ʃən, ⓊⓈ proʊ-, prə- **-s** -z
propitiatory prəˈpɪʃ.i.ə.tər.i, -ˈpɪʃ.ə-, -eɪ.tər-; prəʊˌpɪʃ.iˈeɪ-, ⓊⓈ proʊˈpɪʃ.i.ə.tɔːr-, prə-
propitious prəˈpɪʃ.əs, ⓊⓈ prə-, proʊ- **-ly** -li **-ness** -nəs, -nɪs
propjet ˈprɒp.dʒet, ⓊⓈ ˈprɑːp- **-s** -s
Pro-Plus® ˌprəʊˈplʌs, ⓊⓈ ˌproʊ-
proponent prəʊˈpəʊ.nənt, ⓊⓈ prəˈpoʊ-, proʊ- **-s** -s
proportion prəˈpɔː.ʃən, ⓊⓈ -ˈpɔːr- **-s** -z **-ing** -ɪŋ **-ed** -d
proportionab|le prəˈpɔː.ʃən.ə.b|əl, ⓊⓈ -ˈpɔːr- **-ly** -li **-leness** -əl.nəs, -nɪs
proportional prəˈpɔː.ʃən.əl, -ˈpɔːʃ.nəl, ⓊⓈ -ˈpɔːr.ʃən.əl, -ˈpɔːrʃ.nəl **-ly** -i **pro**ˌ**portional** ˌ**representation**
proportionality prəˌpɔː.ʃənˈæl.ə.ti, -ɪ.ti, ⓊⓈ -ˌpɔːr.ʃənˈæl.ə.ţi
proportionate prəˈpɔː.ʃən.ət, -ˈpɔːʃ.nət, -nɪt, ⓊⓈ -ˈpɔːr.ʃən.ɪt, -ˈpɔːrʃ.nɪt **-ly** -li **-ness** -nəs, -nɪs
proposal prəˈpəʊ.zəl, ⓊⓈ -ˈpoʊ- **-s** -z
propos|e prəˈpəʊz, ⓊⓈ -ˈpoʊz **-es** -ɪz **-ing** -ɪŋ **-ed** -d **-er/s** -əʳ/z, ⓊⓈ -ɚ/z
proposition ˌprɒp.əˈzɪʃ.ən, ⓊⓈ ˌprɑː.pəˈ- **-s** -z **-ing** -ɪŋ **-ed** -d
propound prəˈpaʊnd, ⓊⓈ prə-, proʊ- **-s** -z **-ing** -ɪŋ **-ed** -ɪd **-er/s** -əʳ/z, ⓊⓈ -ɚ/z
propranolol prəʊˈpræn.ə.lɒl, ⓊⓈ proʊˈpræn.oʊ.lɔːl, ˈ-ə-, -loʊl
proprietary prəˈpraɪ.ə.tər.i, ⓊⓈ -ter-
proprietor prəˈpraɪ.ə.təʳ, ⓊⓈ proʊˈpraɪ.ə.ţɚ, prə- **-s** -z **-ship/s** -ʃɪp/s
proprietorial prəˌpraɪ.əˈtɔː.ri.əl, ⓊⓈ -ˈtɔːr.i-, proʊ- **-ly** -i
proprietress prəˈpraɪ.ə.trɪs, -tres, ⓊⓈ proʊ-, -trɪs, -trəs **-es** -ɪz
propriet|y prəˈpraɪ.ə.t|i, ⓊⓈ -ţ|i, proʊ- **-ies** -iz
propriocep|tion ˌprəʊ.pri.əʊˈsep|.ʃən, ˌprɒp.ri-, ⓊⓈ ˌproʊ.pri.oʊˈ-, -əˈ- **-tive** -tɪv
propul|sion prəˈpʌl|.ʃən, ⓊⓈ prə-, proʊ- **-sive** -sɪv
propylae|um, P~ ˌprɒp.ɪˈliː|.əm, -əˈ-, ⓊⓈ ˌprɑː.pəˈ- **-a** -ə
propylene ˈprɒp.ɪ.liːn, ˈ-ə-, ⓊⓈ ˈproʊ.pə-
pro rata ˌprəʊˈrɑː.tə, -ˈreɪ-, ⓊⓈ ˌproʊˈræţ.ə, -ˈrɑː.ţə, -ˈreɪ-
prorogation ˌprəʊ.rəʊˈgeɪ.ʃən, ˌprɒr.əʊˈ-, ⓊⓈ ˌproʊ.roʊˈ- **-s** -z
prorogu|e prəʊˈrəʊg, ⓊⓈ proʊˈroʊg **-es** -z **-ing** -ɪŋ **-ed** -d
prosaic prəʊˈzeɪ.ɪk, ⓊⓈ proʊ- **-al** -əl **-ally** -əl.i, -li **-ness** -nəs, -nɪs
prosceni|um prəʊˈsiː.ni|.əm, ⓊⓈ proʊ- **-ums** -əmz **-a** -ə **pro**ˌ**scenium** ˈ**arch**
prosciutto prəʊˈʃuː.təʊ, ⓊⓈ proʊˈʃuː.ţoʊ
proscrib|e prəʊˈskraɪb, ⓊⓈ proʊ- **-es** -z **-ing** -ɪŋ **-ed** -d **-er/s** -əʳ/z, ⓊⓈ -ɚ/z
proscription prəʊˈskrɪp.ʃən, ⓊⓈ proʊ- **-s** -z
proscriptive prəʊˈskrɪp.tɪv, ⓊⓈ proʊ-
pros|e prəʊz, ⓊⓈ proʊz **-es** -ɪz **-ing** -ɪŋ **-ed** -d **-er/s** -əʳ/z, ⓊⓈ -ɚ/z
pro se ˌprəʊˈseɪ, ⓊⓈ ˌproʊ-
prose|cute ˈprɒs.ɪ|.kjuːt, ˈ-ə-, ⓊⓈ ˈprɑː.sɪ- **-cutes** -kjuːts **-cuting** -kjuː.tɪŋ, ⓊⓈ -kjuː.ţɪŋ **-cuted** -kjuː.tɪd, ⓊⓈ -kjuː.ţɪd ˌ**prosecuting** **at**ˈ**torney**
prosecution ˌprɒs.ɪˈkjuː.ʃən, -əˈ-, ⓊⓈ ˌprɑː.sɪˈ- **-s** -z *stress shift:* ˌ**prosecution** ˈ**witness**
prosecutor ˈprɒs.ɪ.kjuː.təʳ, ˈ-ə-, ⓊⓈ ˈprɑː.sɪ.kjuː.ţɚ **-s** -z
prosecutorial ˌprɒs.ɪ.kjuːˈtɔː.ri.əl, ⓊⓈ ˌprɑː.sɪ.kjuːˈtɔːr.i-
prosecutrix ˈprɒs.ɪ.kjuː.trɪks, ˈ-ə-; ˌprɒs.ɪˈkjuː-, -əˈ-, ⓊⓈ ˈprɑː.sɪ.kjuː-, ˌprɑː.sɪˈkjuː- **-es** -ɪz
proselyte ˈprɒs.ə.laɪt, ˈ-ɪ-, ⓊⓈ ˈprɑː.sə- **-s** -s
proselytism ˈprɒs.əl.ɪ.tɪ.zəm, -ɪ.lɪ-, -lə-, ⓊⓈ ˈprɑː.sə.lɪ-, -laɪ-
proselytiz|e, -is|e ˈprɒs.əl.ɪ.taɪz, -ɪ.lɪ-, -lə-, ⓊⓈ ˈprɑː.sə.lɪ- **-es** -ɪz **-ing** -ɪŋ **-ed** -d
Proserpina prəˈsɜː.pɪ.nə, prɒsˈɜː-, ⓊⓈ proʊˈsɝː-
Proserpine ˈprɒs.ə.paɪn, ⓊⓈ ˈprɑː.sɚ-; ⓊⓈ proʊˈsɝː.pɪ.niː
prosit ˈprəʊ.zɪt, -sɪt; prəʊst, ⓊⓈ ˈproʊ.sɪt, -zɪt; ⓊⓈ proʊst
prosodic prəˈsɒd.ɪk, ⓊⓈ proʊˈsɑː.dɪk, prə- **-al** -əl **-ally** -əl.i, -li
prosodist ˈprɒs.ə.dɪst, ˈprɒz-, ⓊⓈ ˈprɑː.sə-, -zə- **-s** -s
prosod|y ˈprɒs.ə.d|i, ˈprɒz-, ⓊⓈ ˈprɑː.sə-, -zə- **-ies** -iz
prospect, P~ n ˈprɒs.pekt, ⓊⓈ ˈprɑː.spekt **-s** -s
prospect v prəˈspekt, prɒsˈpekt; ˈprɒs.pekt, ⓊⓈ ˈprɑː.spekt **-s** -s **-ing** -ɪŋ **-ed** -ɪd
prospective prəˈspek.tɪv, prɒsˈpek-, ⓊⓈ prəˈspek-, proʊ-, prɑː- **-ly** -li **-ness** -nəs, -nɪs
prospector prəˈspek.təʳ, prɒsˈpek-, ⓊⓈ ˈprɑː.spek.tɚ **-s** -z
prospectus prəˈspek.təs, ⓊⓈ prə-, proʊ-, prɑː- **-es** -ɪz
prosp|er ˈprɒs.p|əʳ, ⓊⓈ ˈprɑː.sp|ɚ **-ers** -əz, ⓊⓈ -ɚz **-ering** -ər.ɪŋ **-ered** -əd, ⓊⓈ -ɚd
prosperity prɒsˈper.ə.ti, prəˈsper-, -ɪ.ti, ⓊⓈ prɑːˈsper.ə.ţi
Prospero ˈprɒs.pər.əʊ, ⓊⓈ ˈprɑː.spə.roʊ
prosperous ˈprɒs.pər.əs, ⓊⓈ ˈprɑː.spɚ- **-ly** -li **-ness** -nəs, -nɪs
Prosser ˈprɒs.əʳ, ⓊⓈ ˈprɑː.sɚ
Prost prɒst, ⓊⓈ proʊst
prostaglandin ˌprɒs.təˈglæn.dɪn, ⓊⓈ ˌprɑː.stəˈ- **-s** -z
prostate ˈprɒs.teɪt, ⓊⓈ ˈprɑː.steɪt **-s** -s ˈ**prostate** ˌ**gland**
prostatic prɒsˈtæt.ɪk, prəˈstæt-, ⓊⓈ proʊˈstæţ.ɪk, prɑː-
prosthes|is *grammatical term:* ˈprɒs.θɪ.s|ɪs, -θə-; ˈprɑːs.θə- *medical term:* ˈprɒs.θə.s|ɪs, -θɪ-; prɒsˈθiː-, ⓊⓈ ˈprɑːs.θə.s|ɪs; ⓊⓈ prɑːsˈθiː- **-es** ⓊⓈ -iːz
prosthetic prɒsˈθet.ɪk, ⓊⓈ prɑːsˈθeţ- **-s** -s
prosthetist prɒsˈθiː.tɪst, prəs-, ⓊⓈ ˈprɑːs.θɪ.tɪst **-s** -s
prostitu|te ˈprɒs.tɪ.tʃuː|t, -tə-, -tjuː|t, ⓊⓈ ˈprɑː.stə.tuː|t, -tjuː|t **-tes** -ts **-ting** -tɪŋ, ⓊⓈ -ţɪŋ **-ted** -tɪd, ⓊⓈ -ţɪd
prostitution ˌprɒs.tɪˈtʃuː.ʃən, -təˈ-, -ˈtjuː-, ⓊⓈ ˌprɑː.stəˈtuː-, -ˈtjuː- **-s** -z
prostrate adj ˈprɒs.treɪt, -ˈ-, ⓊⓈ ˈprɑː.streɪt
prostra|te v prɒsˈtreɪ|t, prəˈstreɪ|t, ⓊⓈ ˈprɑː.streɪ|t **-tes** -ts **-ting** -tɪŋ, ⓊⓈ -ţɪŋ **-ted** -tɪd, ⓊⓈ -ţɪd
prostration prɒsˈtreɪ.ʃən, prəˈstreɪ-, ⓊⓈ prɑːˈstreɪ- **-s** -z
pros|y ˈprəʊ.z|i, ⓊⓈ ˈproʊ- **-ier** -i.əʳ, ⓊⓈ -i.ɚ **-iest** -i.ɪst, -i.əst **-ily** -əl.i, -ɪ.li **-iness** -ɪ.nəs, -ɪ.nɪs
protactinium ˌprəʊ.tækˈtɪn.i.əm, ⓊⓈ ˌproʊ-
protagonist prəʊˈtæg.ən.ɪst, ⓊⓈ proʊ- **-s** -s
Protagoras prəʊˈtæg.ər.æs, -ɒr-, -əs, ⓊⓈ proʊˈtæg.ɚ.əs
pro tanto ˌprəʊˈtæn.təʊ, ⓊⓈ ˌproʊˈtæn.toʊ, -ˈtɑːn-
protas|is ˈprɒt.ə.s|ɪs, ⓊⓈ ˈprɑː.ţə- **-es** -iːz
protean prəʊˈtiː.ən; ˈprəʊ.ti-, ⓊⓈ ˈproʊ-; ⓊⓈ proʊˈtiː-

P

protease ˈprəʊ.ti.eɪz, -eɪs, (US) ˈproʊ.ţi- **-s** -z
protect prəˈtekt, (US) prə-, proʊ- **-s** -s **-ing/ly** -ɪŋ/li **-ed** -ɪd **-or/s** -əʳ/z, (US) -ɚ/z
protection prəˈtek.ʃən, (US) prə-, proʊ- **-s** -z
protection|ism prəˈtek.ʃən|.ɪ.zəm, (US) prə-, proʊ- **-ist/s** -ɪst/s
protective prəˈtek.tɪv, (US) prə-, proʊ- **-ly** -li **-ness** -nəs, -nɪs
protectorate prəˈtek.tər.ət, -ɪt, (US) -ɪt, proʊ- **-s** -s
protectress prəˈtek.trəs, -trɪs, (US) -trɪs, proʊ- **-es** -ɪz
protégé(e), protege(e) ˈprɒt.ɪ.ʒeɪ, ˈprəʊ.tɪ-, -tə-, -teʒ.eɪ, -teɪ.ʒeɪ, (US) ˈproʊ.ţə.ʒeɪ, ˌ--ˈ- **-s** -z
protein ˈprəʊ.tiːn, (US) ˈproʊ- **-s** -z
pro tem ˌprəʊˈtem, (US) ˌproʊˈtem
protest n ˈprəʊ.test, (US) ˈproʊ.test **-s** -s
protest v prəʊˈtest, (US) proʊˈtest, prə-; (US) ˈproʊ.test **-s** -s **-ing/ly** -ɪŋ/li **-ed** -ɪd **-er/s** -əʳ/z, (US) -ɚ/z **-or/s** -əʳ/z, (US) -ɚ/z
protestant, P~ ˈprɒt.ɪ.stənt, ˈ-ə-, (US) ˈprɑː.ţə- **-s** -s **-ism** -ɪ.zəm
protestantiz|e, -is|e ˈprɒt.ɪ.stən.taɪz, ˈ-ə-, (US) ˈprɑː.ţə- **-es** -ɪz **-ing** -ɪŋ **-ed** -d
protestation ˌprɒt.esˈteɪ.ʃən; ˌprəʊ.tesˈ-, -tɪˈsteɪ-, -təˈ-, (US) ˌprɑː.ţesˈteɪ-, ˌproʊ-, -ţəˈsteɪ- **-s** -z
Proteus ˈprəʊ.ti.uːs, -əs, (US) ˈproʊ.ţi.əs
prothalami|on ˌprəʊ.θəˈleɪ.mi|.ən, (US) ˌproʊ.θəˈleɪ-, -ɑːn **-um** -əm **-a** -ə
Protheroe ˈprɒð.ər.əʊ, (US) ˈprɑː.ðə.roʊ
prothes|is ˈprɒθ.ɪ.s|ɪs, ˈ-ə-, (US) ˈprɑː.θə- **-es** -iːz
protium ˈprəʊ.ti.əm, (US) ˈproʊ.ţi-
proto- ˈprəʊ.təʊ, (US) ˈproʊ.ţoʊ, -ţə
Note: Prefix. Normally takes primary or secondary stress on the first syllable, e.g. **prototype** /ˈprəʊ.təʊ.taɪp/ (US) /ˈproʊ.tə-/, **prototypic** /ˌprəʊ.təʊˈtɪp.ɪk/ (US) /ˌproʊ.ţəˈ-/.
protocol ˈprəʊ.tə.kɒl, (US) ˈproʊ.ţə.kɔːl, -ţoʊ-, -kɑːl **-s** -z
proton, P~® ˈprəʊ.tɒn, (US) ˈproʊ.tɑːn **-s** -z
protoplasm ˈprəʊ.təʊ.plæz.əm, (US) ˈproʊ.ţə-, -ţoʊ-
prototype ˈprəʊ.təʊ.taɪp, (US) ˈproʊ.ţə-, -ţoʊ- **-s** -s
prototypic ˌprəʊ.təʊˈtɪp.ɪk, (US) ˌproʊ.ţəˈ-, -ţoʊˈ- **-al** -əl
protozo|a ˌprəʊ.təʊˈzəʊ|.ə, (US) ˌproʊ.ţəˈzoʊ|-, -ţoʊˈ- **-an/s** -ən/z **-on** -ɒn, (US) -ɑːn **-ic** -ɪk
protract prəʊˈtrækt, (US) proʊ-, prə- **-s** -s **-ing** -ɪŋ **-ed/ly** -ɪd/li **-ile** -aɪl, (US) -əl
protraction prəʊˈtræk.ʃən, (US) proʊ-, prə- **-s** -z
protractor prəʊˈtræk.təʳ, (US) proʊˈtræk.ţɚ, prə- **-s** -z
protrud|e prəʊˈtruːd, (US) proʊ-, prə- **-es** -z **-ing** -ɪŋ **-ed** -ɪd
protrusion prəʊˈtruː.ʒən, (US) proʊ-, prə- **-s** -z
protrusive prəʊˈtruː.sɪv, (US) proʊ-, prə- **-ly** -li **-ness** -nəs, -nɪs
protuberanc|e prəʊˈtʃuː.bər.ənts, -ˈtjuː-, (US) proʊˈtuː-, prə-, -ˈtjuː- **-es** -ɪz
protuberant prəʊˈtʃuː.bər.ənt, -ˈtjuː-, (US) proʊˈtuː-, prə-, -ˈtjuː- **-ly** -li
proud praʊd **-er** -əʳ, (US) -ɚ **-est** -ɪst, -əst **-ly** -li **-ness** -nəs, -nɪs
Proudfoot ˈpraʊd.fʊt
Proudhon ˈpruː.dɒn, (US) -dɑːn, -doʊn
Proudie ˈpraʊ.di
Proulx pruː
Proust pruːst
Proustian ˈpruː.sti.ən
Prout praʊt
provab|le ˈpruː.və.b|əl **-ly** -li **-leness** -əl.nəs, -nɪs
prov|e pruːv **-es** -z **-ing** -ɪŋ **-ed** -d **-er/s** -əʳ/z, (US) -ɚ/z
proven ˈpruː.vən, ˈprəʊ-, (US) ˈpruː-
provenance ˈprɒv.ən.ənts, -ɪ.nənts, (US) ˈprɑː.vən.ənts
Provençal(e) ˌprɒv.ɑ̃ːnˈsɑːl, -ɔ̃ːn-, -vəntˈ-, (US) ˌproʊ.vɑːnˈ-, ˌprɑː-, -vənˈ-
Provence prɒvˈɑ̃ːns, prəˈvɑ̃ːns, -ˈvɔ̃ːns, -ˈvɑːnts, (US) prɑːˈvɑ̃ːnts, proʊ-
provender ˈprɒv.ɪn.dəʳ, -ən-, (US) ˈprɑː.vən.dɚ
proverb, P~ ˈprɒv.ɜːb, (US) ˈprɑː.vɝːb **-s** -z
proverbial prəʊˈvɜː.bi.əl, (US) prəˈvɝː-, proʊ- **-ly** -i
provid|e prəʊˈvaɪd, (US) prə-, proʊ- **-es** -z **-ing** -ɪŋ **-ed** -ɪd **-er/s** -əʳ/z, (US) -ɚ/z
providen|ce, P~ ˈprɒv.ɪ.dən|ts, (US) ˈprɑː.və- **-t/ly** -t/li
providential ˌprɒv.ɪˈden.tʃəl, (US) ˌprɑː.vəˈ- **-ly** -i
provinc|e ˈprɒv.ɪnts, (US) ˈprɑː.vɪnts **-es** -ɪz
provincial prəʊˈvɪn.tʃəl, (US) prəˈvɪnt.ʃəl, proʊ- **-s** -z **-ly** -i
provincialism prəʊˈvɪn.tʃəl.ɪ.zəm, (US) prəˈvɪnt.ʃəl-, proʊ- **-s** -z
provinciality prəʊˌvɪn.tʃiˈæl.ə.ti, -ɪ.ti, (US) prəˌvɪnt.ʃiˈæl.ə.ţi, proʊ-
provincializ|e, -is|e prəʊˈvɪn.tʃəl.aɪz, (US) prəˈvɪnt.ʃəl-, proʊ- **-es** -ɪz **-ing** -ɪŋ **-ed** -d
provision prəʊˈvɪʒ.ən, (US) prə-, proʊ- **-s** -z **-ing** -ɪŋ **-ed** -d
provisional prəʊˈvɪʒ.ən.əl, ˈ-nəl, (US) prə-, proʊ-, prəˈvɪʒ.ən.əl **-ly** -i
proviso prəʊˈvaɪ.zəʊ, (US) prəˈvaɪ.zoʊ, proʊ- **-(e)s** -z
provisor prəʊˈvaɪ.zəʳ, (US) prəˈvaɪ.zɚ, proʊ- **-s** -z
provisor|y prəʊˈvaɪ.zər|.i, (US) prə-, proʊ- **-ily** -əl.i, -ɪ.li
Provo ˈprəʊ.vəʊ, (US) ˈproʊ.voʊ **-s** -z
provocation ˌprɒv.əˈkeɪ.ʃən, (US) ˌprɑː.vəˈ- **-s** -z
provocative prəˈvɒk.ə.tɪv, (US) -ˈvɑː.kə.ţɪv, proʊ- **-ly** -li
provok|e prəˈvəʊk, (US) -ˈvoʊk, proʊ- **-es** -s **-ing/ly** -ɪŋ/li **-ed** -t
provost ˈprɒv.əst, (US) ˈproʊ.voʊst, -vəst; (US) ˈprɑː.vəst; *also in the US military:* (US) ˈproʊ.voʊ **-s** -s ˌ**provost** ˈ**marshal**
provostship ˈprɒv.əst.ʃɪp, (US) ˈproʊ.voʊst-, -vəst-; (US) ˈprɑː.vəst- **-s** -s
prow praʊ **-s** -z
prowess ˈpraʊ.ɪs, -es; praʊˈes, (US) ˈpraʊ.ɪs
prowl praʊl **-s** -z **-ing** -ɪŋ **-ed** -d **-er/s** -əʳ/z, (US) -ɚ/z
Prowse praʊs, praʊz
prox. prɒks; ˈprɒk.sɪ.məʊ, -sə-, (US) ˈprɑːk.sə.moʊ
proximal ˈprɒk.sɪ.məl, -sə-, (US) ˈprɑːk.sə- **-ly** -i
proximate ˈprɒk.sɪ.mət, -sə-, -mɪt, (US) ˈprɑːk.sə.mət **-ly** -li
proxime access|it ˌprɒk.sɪ.meɪ.ækˈses|.ɪt, -əkˈ-, -əˈkes-, (US) ˌprɑːk.sə.meɪ.ækˈses.ɪt, -sɪm- **-erunt** -ə.rʊnt
proximit|y prɒkˈsɪm.ə.t|i, -ɪ.t|i, (US) prɑːkˈsɪm.ə.ţ|i **-ies** -iz
proximo ˈprɒk.sɪ.məʊ, -sə-, (US) ˈprɑːk.sə.moʊ
prox|y ˈprɒk.s|i, (US) ˈprɑːk- **-ies** -iz
Prozac® ˈprəʊ.zæk, (US) ˈproʊ-
prud|e pruːd **-es** -z **-ery** -ər.i
prudence, P~ ˈpruː.dənts
prudent ˈpruː.dənt **-ly** -li
prudential pruːˈden.tʃəl, (US) -ˈdent.ʃəl **-ly** -i
Prudhoe ˈprʌd.həʊ, ˈpruː.dəʊ, ˈpruːd.həʊ, (US) ˈpruːd.hoʊ, ˈpruː.doʊ, ˈprʌd.hoʊ
prudish ˈpruː.dɪʃ **-ly** -li **-ness** -nəs, -nɪs
Prufrock ˈpruː.frɒk, (US) -frɑːk
prun|e pruːn **-es** -z **-ing** -ɪŋ **-ed** -d
prunella, P~ pruːˈnel.ə **-s** -z
prurience ˈprʊə.ri.ənts, (US) ˈprʊr.i-
prurient ˈprʊə.ri.ənt, (US) ˈprʊr.i- **-ly** -li
prurigo prʊəˈraɪ.gəʊ, (US) prʊˈraɪ.goʊ
pru|ritus prʊə|ˈraɪ.təs, (US) prʊ|ˈraɪ.ţəs **-ritic** -ˈrɪt.ɪk, (US) -ˈrɪţ-
Prussia ˈprʌʃ.ə
Prussian ˈprʌʃ.ən **-s** -z ˌ**Prussian** ˈ**blue**
prussiate ˈprʌʃ.i.ət, ˈprʌʃ.ət, -ɪt, (US) ˈprʌs.i.eɪt, ˈprʌʃ-, -ɪt **-s** -s
prussic acid ˌprʌs.ɪkˈæs.ɪd
Pruth pruːt
pr|y pr|aɪ **-ies** -aɪz **-ying/ly** -aɪ.ɪŋ/li **-ied** -aɪd **-yer/s** -aɪ.əʳ/z, (US) -aɪ.ɚ/z
Pryce praɪs
Pryde praɪd
Pryke praɪk
Prynne prɪn
Pryor ˈpraɪ.əʳ, (US) ˈpraɪ.ɚ
Przewalski pʃəˈvæl.ski, -ˈvɑːl-, (US) pʃəˈvɑːl- **Prze**ˌ**walski's** ˈ**horse**

PS ˌpiːˈes -ˈs -ɪz
psalm, P~ sɑːm -s -z -ist/s -ɪst/s
psalmodic sælˈmɒd.ɪk, ⓊⓈ sɑːˈmɑː.dɪk, sæl-
psalmod|y ˈsæl.mə.d|i, ˈsɑː.mə-, ⓊⓈ ˈsɑː-, ˈsæl- -ist/s -ɪst/s
psalter ˈsɔːl.təʳ, ˈsɒl-, ⓊⓈ ˈsɔːl.tɚ, ˈsɑːl- -s -z
psalt(e)r|y ˈsɔːl.tᵊr|.i, ˈsɒl-, ⓊⓈ ˈsɔːl.tɚ-, ˈsɑːl- -ies -iz

> Note: In the following words beginning with **ps-**, the form with /p/ is rare.

psepholog|y psɪˈfɒl.ə.dʒ|i, psə-, psefˈɒl-, ⓊⓈ siːˈfɑː.lə- -ist/s -ɪst/s
pseud sjuːd, suːd, ⓊⓈ suːd -s -z
pseudo ˈsjuː.dəʊ, ˈsuː-, ⓊⓈ ˈsuː.doʊ -s -z
pseudo- ˈsjuː.dəʊ, ˈsuː-, ⓊⓈ ˈsuː.doʊ, ˈ-də
pseudonym ˈsjuː.də.nɪm, ˈsuː-, ⓊⓈ ˈsuː.də.nɪm -s -z
pseudonymity ˌsjuː.dəˈnɪm.ə.ti, ˌsuː-, -ɪ.ti, ⓊⓈ ˌsuː.dᵊnˈɪm.ə.ţi
pseudonymous sjuːˈdɒn.ɪ.məs, suː-, ⓊⓈ suːˈdɑː.nɪ-
pseudopodi|um ˌsjuː.dəˈpəʊ.di|.əm, ˌsuː-, ⓊⓈ ˌsuː.doʊˈpoʊ- -a -ə
Pseudoxia Epidemica sjuːˌdɒk.si.ə.ep.ɪˈdem.ɪ.kə, suː-, ⓊⓈ suːˌdɑːk.si-
pshaw **interj** pʃɔː, *pɸː*, ⓊⓈ *pʃɔː*, *pʃɑː*

> Note: Sound of derision or protest: the spelling was probably originally intended to represent a voiceless bilabial affricate (a more polite version of the bilabial trill known as a 'raspberry' in British English and also as a 'Bronx Cheer' in American English), but it is usually now given a spelling-based pronunciation.

psi psaɪ, saɪ, ⓊⓈ saɪ, psiː
Psion ˈ*p*saɪ.ɒn, ⓊⓈ -ɑːn
psittacosis ˌ*p*sɪt.əˈkəʊ.sɪs, ⓊⓈ ˌsɪt.əˈkoʊ-
Psmith smɪθ
psoriasis *p*səˈraɪ.ə.sɪs, *p*sɒrˈaɪ.ə-, *p*sɔːˈraɪ.ə-, *p*sʊ-, ⓊⓈ səˈraɪ.ə-, soʊ-
psych saɪk -s -s -ing -ɪŋ -ed -t
psyche **n** ˈsaɪ.ki, -kiː -s -s
psych|e **v** saɪk -es -s -ing -ɪŋ -ed -t
psychedelia ˌsaɪ.kɪˈdiː.li.ə, -kəˈ-, ⓊⓈ -kəˈdiː.li.ə, -ˈdiːl.jə
psychedelic ˌsaɪ.kɪˈdel.ɪk, -kəˈ-, ⓊⓈ -kəˈ- -ally -ᵊl.i, -li *stress shift:* ˌ**psychedelic** ˈ**colours**
psychiatric ˌsaɪ.kiˈæt.rɪk -al -ᵊl -ally -ᵊl.i, -li *stress shift:* ˌ**psychiatric** ˈ**nurse**
psychiatr|y saɪˈkaɪ.ə.tr|i, sɪ-, sə-, ⓊⓈ saɪ-, sɪ- -ist/s -ɪst/s
psychic ˈsaɪ.kɪk -al -ᵊl -ally -ᵊl.i, -li
psycho ˈsaɪ.kəʊ, ⓊⓈ -koʊ -s -z
psycho- ˈsaɪ.kəʊ; saɪˈkɒ, ⓊⓈ ˈsaɪ.koʊ, -kə; ⓊⓈ saɪˈkɑː
Note: Prefix. Normally either takes primary or secondary stress on the first syllable, e.g. **psychodrama** /ˈsaɪ.kəʊˌdrɑː.mə/ ⓊⓈ /-koʊˌ-/, **psychodramatic** /ˌsaɪ.kəʊ.drəˈmæt.ɪk/ ⓊⓈ /-koʊ.drəˈmæţ.ɪk/, or primary stress on the second syllable, e.g. **psychotic** /saɪˈkɒt.ɪk/ ⓊⓈ /-ˈkɑː.ţɪk/.
psychoanalys|e ˌsaɪ.kəʊˈæn.ᵊl.aɪz, ⓊⓈ -koʊˈæn.ə.laɪz -es -ɪz -ing -ɪŋ -ed -d
psychoanalysis ˌsaɪ.kəʊ.əˈnæl.ə.sɪs, ˈ-ɪ-, ⓊⓈ -koʊ-
psychoanalyst ˌsaɪ.kəʊˈæn.ᵊl.ɪst, ⓊⓈ -koʊˈæn.ə.lɪst -s -s
psychoanalytic ˌsaɪ.kəʊˌæn.ᵊlˈɪt.ɪk, ⓊⓈ -koʊˌæn.əˈlɪţ.ɪk -al -ᵊl -ally -ᵊl.i, -li *stress shift:* ˌ**psychoanalytic** ˈ**counselling**
psychoanalyz|e ˌsaɪ.kəʊˈæn.ᵊl.aɪz, ⓊⓈ -koʊˈæn.ə.laɪz -es -ɪz -ing -ɪŋ -ed -d
psychobabble ˈsaɪ.kəʊˌbæb.ᵊl, ⓊⓈ -koʊˌ-
psychodrama ˈsaɪ.kəʊˌdrɑː.mə, ⓊⓈ -koʊˌ-, -ˌdræm.ə -s -z
psychodramatic ˌsaɪ.kəʊ.drəˈmæt.ɪk, ⓊⓈ -koʊ.drəˈmæţ-
psychokinesis ˌsaɪ.kəʊ.kaɪˈniː.sɪs, -kɪˈ-, ⓊⓈ -koʊ.kɪˈ-, -kaɪˈ-
psychokinetic ˌsaɪ.kəʊ.kɪˈnet.ɪk, -kaɪˈ-, ⓊⓈ -koʊ- *stress shift:* ˌ**psychokinetic** ˈ**powers**
psycholinguist ˌsaɪ.kəʊˈlɪŋ.gwɪst, ⓊⓈ -koʊˈ- -s -s
psycholinguistic ˌsaɪ.kəʊ.lɪŋˈgwɪs.tɪk, ⓊⓈ -koʊ- -s -s -ally -ᵊl.i, -li *stress shift:* ˌ**psycholinguistic** ˈ**process**
psychologic ˌsaɪ.kəˈlɒdʒ.ɪk, ⓊⓈ -ˈlɑː.dʒɪk *stress shift:* ˌ**psychologic** ˈ**warfare**
psychological ˌsaɪ.kᵊlˈɒdʒ.ɪ.kᵊl, ⓊⓈ -kəˈlɑː.dʒɪ- -ly -i *stress shift, see compound:* ˌ**psychological** ˈ**warfare**
psychologiz|e, -is|e saɪˈkɒl.ə.dʒaɪz, ⓊⓈ -ˈkɑː.lə- -es -ɪz -ing -ɪŋ -ed -d
psycholog|y saɪˈkɒl.ə.dʒ|i, ⓊⓈ -ˈkɑː.lə- -ist/s -ɪst/s
psychometric ˌsaɪ.kəʊˈmet.rɪk, ⓊⓈ -koʊˈ- -s -s *stress shift:* ˌ**psychometric** ˈ**measurement**
psychometr|y saɪˈkɒm.ə.tr|i, ˈ-ɪ-, ⓊⓈ -ˈkɑː.mə- -ist/s -ɪst/s
psychopath ˈsaɪ.kəʊ.pæθ, ⓊⓈ -kə-, -koʊ- -s -s
psychopathic ˌsaɪ.kəʊˈpæθ.ɪk, ⓊⓈ -kəˈ-, -koʊˈ- -ally -ᵊl.i, -li *stress shift:* ˌ**psychopathic** ˈ**tendencies**
psychopatholog|y ˌsaɪ.kəʊ.pæθˈɒl.ə.dʒ|i, ⓊⓈ -koʊ.pæθˈɑː.lə- -ist/s -ɪst/s
psychophysical ˌsaɪ.kəʊˈfɪz.ɪ.kᵊl, ⓊⓈ -koʊˈ- -ly -li *stress shift:* ˌ**psychophysical** ˈ**stimulus**
psychosexual ˌsaɪ.kəʊˈsek.ʃʊəl, -sjʊəl, ⓊⓈ -ʃu.əl -ly -i *stress shift:* ˌ**psychosexual** ˈ**aspects**
psychos|is saɪˈkəʊ.s|ɪs, ⓊⓈ -ˈkoʊ- -es -iːz
psychosocial ˌsaɪ.kəʊˈsəʊ.ʃᵊl, ⓊⓈ -koʊˈsoʊ- *stress shift:* ˌ**psychosocial** ˈ**problems**
psychosomatic ˌsaɪ.kəʊ.səʊˈmæt.ɪk, ⓊⓈ -koʊ.soʊˈmæţ- -ally -ᵊl.i, -li *stress shift:* ˌ**psychosomatic** ˈ**symptoms**
psychotherap|y ˌsaɪ.kəʊˈθer.ə.p|i, ⓊⓈ -koʊˈ- -ist/s -ɪst/s
psychotic saɪˈkɒt.ɪk, ⓊⓈ -ˈkɑː.ţɪk -ally -ᵊl.i, -li
pt (abbrev. for **pint**) paɪnt
PTA ˌpiː.tiːˈeɪ
Ptah tɑː, ptɑː, pəˈtɑː, ⓊⓈ pəˈtɑː
ptarmigan ˈtɑː.mɪ.gən, -mə-, ⓊⓈ ˈtɑːr-
pterodactyl ˌter.əʊˈdæk.tɪl, -təl, ⓊⓈ -əˈdæk.təl, -oʊˈ- -s -z
pterosaur ˈter.əʊ.sɔːʳ, ⓊⓈ -ə.sɔːr, -oʊ-, -sɑːr -s -z
PTO ˌpiː.tiːˈəʊ, ⓊⓈ -ˈoʊ
Ptolemaeus ˌtɒl.əˈmiː.əs, -ɪˈ-, -ˈmeɪ-, ⓊⓈ ˌtɑː.ləˈmeɪ-, -ˈmiː-
Ptolema|ic ˌtɒl.əˈmeɪ|.ɪk, -ɪˈ-, ⓊⓈ ˌtɑː.ləˈ- -ist -ɪst
Ptolemy ˈtɒl.ə.mi, ˈ-ɪ-, ⓊⓈ ˈtɑː.lə-
ptomaine ˈtəʊ.meɪn; təʊˈmeɪn, ⓊⓈ ˈtoʊ.meɪn
Pty (abbrev. for **Proprietary**) prəˈpraɪ.ə.tᵊr.i, ⓊⓈ proʊˈpraɪ.ə.ter.i, prə-
ptyalin ˈtaɪ.ə.lɪn
pub pʌb -s -z -by -i
pub-crawl ˈpʌb.krɔːl, ⓊⓈ -krɑːl, -krɔːl -s -z -ing -ɪŋ -ed -d -er/s -əʳ/z, ⓊⓈ -ɚ/z
puberty ˈpjuː.bə.ti, ⓊⓈ -bɚ.ţi
pubes *slang for pubic hair:* pjuːbz *plural of* **pubis***:* ˈpjuː.biːz
pubescen|ce pjuːˈbes.ᵊn|*t*s, pjʊ- -t -t
pubic ˈpjuː.bɪk ˌ**pubic** ˈ**hair** ⓊⓈ ˈ**pubic** ˌ**hair**
pub|is ˈpjuː.b|ɪs -es -iːz
public ˈpʌb.lɪk -ly -li ˌ**public con**ˈ**venience;** ˌ**public** ˈ**enemy;** ˌ**public** ˈ**house;** ˌ**public o**ˈ**pinion;** ˌ**public re**ˈ**lations;** ˌ**public** ˈ**school;** ˌ**public** ˈ**sector** ⓊⓈ ˈ**public** ˌ**sector** *stress shift, British only:* ˌ**public sector** ˈ**services** ˌ**public** ˈ**speaking;** ˌ**public** ˈ**transport**
public-address system ˌpʌb.lɪk.əˈdresˌsɪs.təm -s -z
publican ˈpʌb.lɪ.kən -s -z
publication ˌpʌb.lɪˈkeɪ.ʃᵊn, -ləˈ- -s -z
publicist ˈpʌb.lɪ.sɪst, -lə- -s -s
publicity pʌbˈlɪs.ə.ti, pəˈblɪs-, -ɪ.ti, ⓊⓈ -ə.ţi
publiciz|e, -is|e ˈpʌb.lɪ.saɪz, -lə- -es -ɪz -ing -ɪŋ -ed -d
public-spirited ˌpʌb.lɪkˈspɪr.ɪ.tɪd, ˈ-ə-, ⓊⓈ -ə.ţɪd -ness -nəs, -nɪs *stress shift:* ˌ**public-spirited** ˈ**policies**

publish ˈpʌb.lɪʃ -es -ɪz -ing -ɪŋ -ed -t -er/s -əʳ/z, (US) -ɚ/z
Publius ˈpʌb.li.əs
Puccini pʊˈtʃiː.ni, (US) puː-
puce pjuːs
puck, P~ pʌk -s -s
puck|er ˈpʌk|.əʳ, (US) -ɚ -ers -əz, (US) -ɚz -ering -ᵊr.ɪŋ -ered -d, (US) -ɚd
puckish ˈpʌk.ɪʃ -ly -li -ness -nəs, -nɪs
pud pʊd -s -z
pudding ˈpʊd.ɪŋ -s -z **the ˌproof of the ˌpudding is ˌin the ˈeating**
puddl|e ˈpʌd.ᵊl -es -z -ing -ɪŋ, ˈpʌd.lɪŋ -ed -d -er/s -əʳ/z, (US) -ɚ/z, ˈpʌd.ləʳ/z, (US) -lɚ/z
pudend|um pjuːˈden.d|əm, pjʊ-, (US) pjuː- -a -ə
pudg|y ˈpʌdʒ|.i -ier -i.əʳ, (US) -i.ɚ -iest -i.ɪst, -i.əst -iness -ɪ.nəs, -ɪ.nɪs
Pudsey ˈpʌd.zi; *locally:* ˈpʊt.si
Puebla ˈpweb.lə, puˈeb-, (US) ˈpweb.lɑː
pueblo, P~ ˈpweb.ləʊ, puˈeb-, (US) ˈpweb.loʊ -s -z
puerile ˈpjʊə.raɪl, ˈpjɔː-, (US) ˈpjuː.ɚ.ɪl, ˈpjʊr.ɪl, -aɪl -ly -li
puerilit|y pjʊəˈrɪl.ə.t|i, pjɔː-, -ɪ.t|i, (US) ˌpjuː.əˈrɪl.ə.ţ|i, pjʊˈ- -ies -iz
puerperal pjuˈɜː.pᵊr.ᵊl, (US) -ˈɝː-
Puerto Ric|o ˌpwɜː.təʊˈriː.k|əʊ, ˌpweə-, (US) ˌpwer.ţəˈriː.koʊ, -toʊˈ-, ˌpɔːr.ţəˈ- -an/s -ən/z
Puerto Vallarta ˌpwɜː.təʊ.vælˈɑː.tə; *as if Spanish:* ˌpweə.təʊ.vaɪˈ-; (US) ˌpwer.toʊ.vɑːˈjɑːr.ţə, -tɑː
puff pʌf -s -s -ing -ɪŋ -ed -t -er/s -əʳ/z, (US) -ɚ/z ˈ**puff ˌadder**; ˌ**puff ˈpastry**
puffball ˈpʌf.bɔːl, (US) -bɔːl, -bɑːl -s -z ˌ**puffball ˈskirt**
puffed sleeve ˌpʌftˈsliːv -s -z
puffery ˈpʌf.ᵊr.i, (US) -ɚ-
puffin, P~ ˈpʌf.ɪn -s -z
puff|y ˈpʌf|.i -ier -i.əʳ, (US) -i.ɚ -iest -i.ɪst, -i.əst -ily -ᵊl.i, -ɪ.li -iness -ɪ.nəs, -ɪ.nɪs
pug pʌg -s -z
Pugh pjuː
pugil|ism ˈpjuː.dʒɪ.l|ɪ.zᵊm, -dʒə- -ist/s -ɪst/s
pugilistic ˌpjuː.dʒɪˈlɪs.tɪk, -dʒəˈ- -ally -ᵊl.i, -li *stress shift:* ˌ**pugilistic ˈattitude**
Pugin ˈpjuː.dʒɪn
pugnacious pʌgˈneɪ.ʃəs -ly -li -ness -nəs, -nɪs
pugnacity pʌgˈnæs.ə.ti, -ɪ.ti, (US) -ə.ţi
pug-nos|e ˌpʌgˈnəʊz, (US) ˈpʌg.noʊz -es -ɪz -ed -d *stress shift, British only:* ˌ**pug-nose ˈface**
puisne ˈpjuː.ni
puissance *in show-jumping:* ˈpwiː.sɑ̃ːns, -sɑːnts, -sᵊnts
puissan|ce *power:* ˈpjuː.ɪ.sᵊn|ts, ˈpwɪs.ᵊn|ts; *sometimes in poetry:* pjuˈɪ.sᵊn|ts -t -t
puk|e pjuːk -es -s -ing -ɪŋ -ed -t
pukka ˈpʌk.ə
pul puːl -s -z -i -iː
pula ˈpjuː.lə, ˈpuː-, (US) ˈpuː.lɑː
Pulaski pəˈlæs.ki, pjuː-, (US) pə-, pʊˈlæs-
pulchritude ˈpʌl.krɪ.tʃuːd, -krə-, -tjuːd, (US) -tuːd, -tjuːd
pulchritudinous ˌpʌl.krɪˈtʃuː.dɪ.nəs, -krəˈ-, -ˈtjuː-, -dᵊn.əs, (US) -ˈtuː.dᵊn.əs, -ˈtjuː-
pul|e pjuːl -es -z -ing -ɪŋ -ed -d
Puleston ˈpʊl.ɪ.stᵊn; *locally also:* ˈpɪl.sᵊn
Pulham ˈpʊl.əm
Pulitzer *US publisher:* ˈpʊl.ɪt.səʳ, (US) ˈpʊl.ɪt.sɚ, ˈpjuː.lɪt- *prize at Columbia University:* ˈpjuː.lɪt.səʳ, (US) ˈpʊl.ɪt.sɚ, ˈpjuː.lɪt- ˈ**Pulitzer ˌprize**; ˌ**Pulitzer ˈprize**
pull pʊl -s -z -ing -ɪŋ -ed -d -er/s -əʳ/z, (US) -ɚ/z
pullback ˈpʊl.bæk -s -s
pull-down ˈpʊl.daʊn
pullet ˈpʊl.ɪt, -ət -s -s
pulley ˈpʊl.i -s -z
pull-in ˈpʊl.ɪn -s -z
pullman, P~ ˈpʊl.mən -s -z
pullout ˈpʊl.aʊt -s -s
pullover ˈpʊl.əʊ.vəʳ, (US) -oʊ.vɚ -s -z
pull-tab ˈpʊl.tæb -s -z
pullu|late ˈpʌl.jə|.leɪt, -jʊ- -lates -leɪts -lating -leɪ.tɪŋ, (US) -leɪ.ţɪŋ -lated -leɪ.tɪd, (US) -leɪ.ţɪd
pullulation ˌpʌl.jəˈleɪ.ʃᵊn, -jʊˈ-
pull-up ˈpʊl.ʌp -s -s
pulmonary ˈpʌl.mə.nᵊr.i, ˈpʊl-, (US) -ner-
pulmonic pʌlˈmɒn.ɪk, pʊl-, (US) -ˈmɑː.nɪk
pulp pʌlp -s -s -ing -ɪŋ -ed -t
pulpi|fy ˈpʌl.pɪ|.faɪ, ˈ-pə- -fies -faɪz -fying -faɪ.ɪŋ -fied -faɪd
pulpit ˈpʊl.pɪt, (US) ˈpʊl-, ˈpʌl- -s -s
pulp|y ˈpʌl.p|i -ier -i.əʳ, (US) -i.ɚ -iest -i.ɪst, -i.əst -iness -ɪ.nəs, -ɪ.nɪs
pulsar ˈpʌl.sɑːʳ, -səʳ, (US) -sɑːr, -sɚ -s -z
pul|sate pʌl|ˈseɪt, (US) ˈ-- -sates -ˈseɪts, (US) -seɪts -sating -ˈseɪ.tɪŋ, (US) -seɪ.ţɪŋ -sated -ˈseɪ.tɪd, (US) -seɪ.ţɪd
pulsatile ˈpʌl.sə.taɪl, (US) -tɪl, -taɪl
pulsation pʌlˈseɪ.ʃᵊn -s -z
pulsative ˈpʌl.sə.tɪv, (US) -ţɪv
pulsatory ˈpʌl.sə.tᵊr.i, pʌlˈseɪ-, (US) ˈpʌl.sə.tɔːr-
puls|e pʌls -es -ɪz -ing -ɪŋ -ed -t
Pulteney *surname:* ˈpʌlt.ni, ˈpəʊlt-, ˈpʊlt-, (US) ˈpʌlt-, ˈpoʊlt-, ˈpʊlt- *bridge in Bath:* ˈpʌlt.ni
pulverization, -isa- ˌpʌl.vᵊr.aɪˈzeɪ.ʃᵊn, -ɪˈ-, (US) -əˈ- -s -z
pulveriz|e, -is|e ˈpʌl.vᵊr.aɪz, (US) -və.raɪz -es -ɪz -ing -ɪŋ -ed -d
puma ˈpjuː.mə, (US) ˈpjuː-, ˈpuː- -s -z
Pumblechook ˈpʌm.bᵊl.tʃʊk
pumic|e ˈpʌm.ɪs -es -ɪz -ing -ɪŋ -ed -t ˈ**pumice ˌstone**
pummel ˈpʌm.ᵊl -s -z -(l)ing -ɪŋ -(l)ed -d
pump pʌmp -s -s -ing -ɪŋ -ed -t -er/s -əʳ/z, (US) -ɚ/z ˈ**pump ˌroom**
pump-action ˈpʌmpˌæk.ʃᵊn
pumpernickel ˈpʌm.pəˌnɪk.ᵊl, (US) -pɚˌ-
pumpkin ˈpʌmp.kɪn -s -z ˌ**pumpkin ˈpie**
pun pʌn -s -z -ning -ɪŋ -ned -d -ner/s -əʳ/z, (US) -ɚ/z
punch, P~ pʌntʃ, (US) pʌntʃ -es -ɪz -ing -ɪŋ -ed -t -er/s -əʳ/z, (US) -ɚ/z
Punch-and-Judy ˌpʌntʃ.ᵊndˈdʒuː.di, (US) ˌpʌntʃ- ˌ**Punch-and-ˈJudy ˌshow**
punchbag ˈpʌntʃ.bæg, (US) ˈpʌntʃ- -s -z
punchball ˈpʌntʃ.bɔːl, (US) ˈpʌntʃ.bɑːl, -bɔːl -s -z
punchbowl ˈpʌntʃ.bəʊl, (US) ˈpʌntʃ.boʊl -s -z
punch-drunk ˈpʌntʃ.drʌŋk, (US) ˈpʌntʃ-
puncheon ˈpʌn.tʃᵊn, (US) -tʃᵊn -s -z
punchinello, P~ ˌpʌn.tʃɪˈnel.əʊ, -tʃəˈ-, (US) -tʃəˈnel.oʊ
punchline ˈpʌntʃ.laɪn, (US) ˈpʌntʃ- -s -z
punch-up ˈpʌntʃ.ʌp, (US) ˈpʌntʃ- -s -s
punch|y ˈpʌn.tʃ|i, (US) -tʃ|i -ier -i.əʳ, (US) -i.ɚ -iest -i.ɪst, -i.əst -ily -ᵊl.i, -ɪ.li -iness -ɪ.nəs, -ɪ.nɪs
punctilio pʌŋkˈtɪl.i.əʊ, (US) -oʊ -s -z
punctilious pʌŋkˈtɪl.i.əs -ly -li -ness -nəs, -nɪs
punctual ˈpʌŋk.tʃu.əl, -tʃʊəl, -tju.əl, -tjʊəl, (US) ˈpʌŋk.tʃu.əl -ly -i
punctuality ˌpʌnk.tʃuˈæl.ə.ti, -tjuˈ-, -ɪ.ti, (US) -ə.ţi
punctu|ate ˈpʌŋk.tʃu|.eɪt, -tju-, (US) -tʃu- -ates -eɪts -ating -eɪ.tɪŋ, (US) -eɪ.ţɪŋ -ated -eɪ.tɪd, (US) -eɪ.ţɪd -ator/s -eɪ.təʳ/z, (US) -eɪ.ţɚ/z
punctuation ˌpʌŋk.tʃuˈeɪ.ʃᵊn, -tjuˈ-, (US) -tʃuˈ- -s -z
punct|ure ˈpʌŋk.tʃ|əʳ, (US) -tʃ|ɚ -ures -əz, (US) -ɚz -uring -ᵊr.ɪŋ -ured -əd, (US) -ɚd
pundit ˈpʌn.dɪt -s -s
Pune pjuːn
pungency ˈpʌn.dʒənt.si
pungent ˈpʌn.dʒᵊnt -ly -li
Punic ˈpjuː.nɪk
puniness ˈpjuː.nɪ.nəs, -nɪs, (US) -ni-
punish ˈpʌn.ɪʃ -es -ɪz -ing/ly -ɪŋ/li -ed -t -er/s -əʳ/z, (US) -ɚ/z -able/ness -ə.bᵊl/nəs, -nɪs
punishment ˈpʌn.ɪʃ.mənt -s -s
puni|tive ˈpjuː.nə|.tɪv, -nɪ-, (US) -nə|.ţɪv -tively -tɪv.li, (US) -ţɪv.li -tory -tᵊr.i, (US) -tɔːr.i
Punjab ˌpʌnˈdʒɑːb, pʊn-, ˈ--, (US) pʌnˈdʒɑːb; (US) ˈpʌn.dʒɑːb, -dʒæb -i -iː, -i
Punjabi pʌnˈdʒɑː.biː, pʊn-, -bi, (US) pʌn-
punk pʌŋk -s -s -y -i -ier -i.əʳ, (US) -i.ɚ -iest -i.ɪst, -i.əst ˌ**punk ˈrock**; ˌ**punk ˈrocker**
punkah ˈpʌŋ.kə -s -z
punnet ˈpʌn.ɪt -s -s
Punshon ˈpʌn.ʃᵊn
punster ˈpʌn.stəʳ, (US) -stɚ -s -z

punt n, v *boat:* pʌnt **-s** -s **-ing** -ɪŋ, US ˈpʌn.t̬ɪŋ **-ed** -ɪd, US ˈpʌn.t̬ɪd
punt n *currency:* pʊnt **-s** -s
punter ˈpʌn.təʳ, US -t̬ɚ **-s** -z
Punto® ˈpʊn.təʊ, ˈpʌn-, US -toʊ
pun|y ˈpjuː.n|i **-ier** -i.əʳ, US -i.ɚ **-iest** -i.ɪst, -i.əst **-iness** -ɪ.nəs, -ɪ.nɪs
pup pʌp **-s** -s **-ping** -ɪŋ **-ped** -t
pup|a ˈpjuː.p|ə **-ae** -iː **-as** -əz **-al** -ᵊl
pupil ˈpjuː.pᵊl, -pɪl, US -pᵊl **-s** -z
pupil(l)age ˈpjuː.pɪ.lɪdʒ, -pᵊl.ɪdʒ, US -pᵊl.ɪdʒ
pupillary ˈpjuː.pɪ.lᵊr.i, -pᵊl.ᵊr-, US -pᵊl.er-
puppet ˈpʌp.ɪt **-s** -s ˌ**puppet** ˈ**government**
puppeteer ˌpʌp.ɪˈtɪəʳ, -əˈ-, US -əˈtɪr **-s** -z
pupp|y ˈpʌp|.i **-ies** -iz ˈ**puppy** ˌ**dog;** ˈ**puppy** ˌ**fat;** ˈ**puppy** ˌ**love**
Purbeck ˈpɜː.bek, US ˈpɝː-
purblind ˈpɜː.blaɪnd, US ˈpɝː- **-ness** -nəs, -nɪs
Purcell ˈpɜː.sel, -sᵊl; pɜːˈsel, US ˈpɝː.sᵊl, -ˈ-
purchas|e ˈpɜː.tʃəs, -tʃɪs, US ˈpɝː.tʃəs **-es** -ɪz **-ing** -ɪŋ **-ed** -t **-er/s** -əʳ/z, US -ɚ/z **-able** -ə.bᵊl
purdah ˈpɜː.də, -dɑː, US ˈpɝː.də
Purdie, Purdy ˈpɜː.di, US ˈpɝː-
Purdue pɜːˈdjuː, US pɝːˈduː
pur|e pjʊəʳ, pjɔːʳ, US pjʊr **-er** -əʳ, US -ɚ **-est** -ɪst, -əst **-ely** -li **-eness** -nəs, -nɪs
purebred ˈpjʊə.bred, ˈpjɔː-, US ˈpjʊr- **-s** -z
purée, puree ˈpjʊə.reɪ, ˈpjɔː-, US pjʊˈreɪ; US ˈpjʊr.eɪ **-s** -z **-ing** -ɪŋ **-d** -d
purfl|e ˈpɜː.fᵊl, US ˈpɝː- **-es** -z **-ing** -ɪŋ, ˈ-flɪŋ **-ed** -d
purgation pɜːˈgeɪ.ʃᵊn, US pɝː- **-s** -z
purgative ˈpɜː.gə.tɪv, US ˈpɝː.gə.t̬ɪv **-s** -z
purgatorial ˌpɜː.gəˈtɔː.ri.əl, US ˌpɝː.gəˈtɔːr.i-
Purgatorio ˌpɜː.gəˈtɔː.ri.əʊ, US ˌpɝː.gəˈtɔːr.i.oʊ
purgator|y, P~ ˈpɜː.gə.tᵊr|.i, -tr|i, US ˈpɝː.gə.tɔːr|- **-ies** -iz
purg|e pɜːdʒ, US pɝːdʒ **-es** -ɪz **-ing** -ɪŋ **-ed** -d
purification ˌpjʊə.rɪ.fɪˈkeɪ.ʃᵊn, ˌpjɔː-, -rə-, -fəˈ-, US ˌpjʊr.ə- **-s** -z
purificatory ˌpjʊə.rɪ.fɪˈkeɪ.tᵊr.i, ˌpjɔː-, -rə-, US pjʊˈrɪf.ɪ.kə.tɔːr-
puri|fy ˈpjʊə.rɪ|.faɪ, ˈpjɔː-, -rə-, US ˈpjʊr.ɪ-, ˈ-ə- **-fies** -faɪz **-fying** -faɪ.ɪŋ **-fied** -faɪd **-fier/s** -faɪ.əʳ/z, US -faɪ.ɚ/z
Purim ˈpʊə.rɪm, ˈpjʊə-, US ˈpʊr.ɪm; US puːˈriːm
purism ˈpjʊə.rɪ.zᵊm, ˈpjɔː-, US ˈpjʊr.ɪ-
purist ˈpjʊə.rɪst, ˈpjɔː-, US ˈpjʊr.ɪst **-s** -s
puristic pjʊəˈrɪs.tɪk, pjɔː-, US pjʊ- **-al** -ᵊl
puritan, P~ ˈpjʊə.rɪ.tᵊn, ˈpjɔː-, US ˈpjʊr.ɪ- **-s** -z **-ism** -ɪ.zᵊm
puritanic ˌpjʊə.rɪˈtæn.ɪk, ˌpjɔː-, US ˌpjʊr.ɪˈ- **-al** -ᵊl **-ally** -ᵊl.i, -li
purity ˈpjʊə.rə.ti, ˈpjɔː-, -rɪ-, US ˈpjʊr.ɪ.t̬i, ˈ-ə-
Purkinje pɜːˈkɪn.ji, US pɝː-
Purkiss ˈpɜː.kɪs, US ˈpɝː-
purl pɜːl, US pɝːl **-s** -z **-ing** -ɪŋ **-ed** -d
Purley ˈpɜː.li, US ˈpɝː-
purlieu ˈpɜː.ljuː, US ˈpɝːl.juː, ˈpɝː.luː **-s** -z
purlin(e) ˈpɜː.lɪn, US ˈpɝː- **-s** -z
purloin pɜːˈlɔɪn, ˈ--, US pɚˈlɔɪn; US ˈpɝː.lɔɪn **-s** -z **-ing** -ɪŋ **-ed** -d
purloiner pɜːˈlɔɪ.nəʳ, US pɚˈlɔɪ.nɚ **-s** -z
Purnell pɜːˈnel, US pɝː-
purpl|e ˈpɜː.pᵊl, US ˈpɝː- **-er** -əʳ, ˈpɜː.pləʳ, US ˈpɝː.plɚ **-est** -ɪst, -əst, ˈpɜː.plɪst, -pləst, -pləst, US ˈpɝː- **-es** -z **-ing** -ɪŋ, ˈpɜː.plɪŋ, US ˈpɝː- **-ed** -d ˌ**Purple** ˈ**Heart**
purplish ˈpɜː.pᵊl.ɪʃ, -plɪʃ, US ˈpɝː-
purpor|t pəˈpɔː|t, pɜː-; ˈpɜː.pə|t, -pɔː|t, US pɝːˈpɔːr|t, ˈ-- **-ts** -ts **-ting** -tɪŋ, US -t̬ɪŋ **-ted/ly** -tɪd/li, US -t̬ɪd/li
purpos|e ˈpɜː.pəs, US ˈpɝː- **-es** -ɪz **-ing** -ɪŋ **-ed** -t
purpose-built ˌpɜː.pəsˈbɪlt, US ˌpɝː- *stress shift:* ˌ**purpose-built** ˈ**residence**
purposeful ˈpɜː.pəs|.fᵊl, -fʊl, US ˈpɝː- **-ly** -i **-ness** -nəs, -nɪs
purposeless ˈpɜː.pəs.ləs, -lɪs, US ˈpɝː- **-ly** -li **-ness** -nəs, -nɪs
purposely ˈpɜː.pə.sli, US ˈpɝː-
purposive ˈpɜː.pə.sɪv, US ˈpɝː- **-ly** -li **-ness** -nəs, -nɪs
purpura ˈpɜː.pjʊ.rə, -pjə-, US ˈpɝː.pɚ.ə, -pjɚ-, -pʊ.rə
purr pɜːʳ, US pɝː **-s** -z **-ing** -ɪŋ **-ed** -d
purs|e pɜːs, US pɝːs **-es** -ɪz **-ing** -ɪŋ **-ed** -t
purser ˈpɜː.səʳ, US ˈpɝː.sɚ **-s** -z
purse-string ˈpɜːs.strɪŋ, US ˈpɝːs- **-s** -z
purslane ˈpɜː.slɪn, -slən, -sleɪn, US ˈpɝː.slɪn, -sleɪn
pursuance pəˈsjuː.ənts, pɜː-, -ˈsuː-, US pɚˈsuː-
pursuant pəˈsjuː.ənt, pɜː-, -ˈsuː-, US pɚˈsuː- **-ly** -li
pursu|e pəˈsjuː, pɜː-, -ˈsuː, US pɚˈsuː **-es** -z **-ing** -ɪŋ **-ed** -d **-er/s** -əʳ/z, US -ɚ/z
pursuit pəˈsjuːt, pɜː-, -ˈsuːt, US pɚˈsuːt **-s** -s
pursuivant ˈpɜː.sɪ.vənt, -sə-, US ˈpɝː.sɪ-, -swɪ- **-s** -s
Purton ˈpɜː.tᵊn, US ˈpɝː-
purulency ˈpjʊə.rʊ.lənt.si, ˈpjɔː-, -rjʊ-, -rə-, US ˈpjʊr.ə-, -jə-
purulent ˈpjʊə.rʊ.lənt, -rjʊ-, -rə-, US ˈpjʊr.ə-, -rjə- **-ly** -li
Purver ˈpɜː.vəʳ, US ˈpɝː.vɚ
Purves ˈpɜː.vɪs, US ˈpɝː-
purvey pəˈveɪ, pɜː-, US pɚ- **-s** -z **-ing** -ɪŋ **-ed** -d
purvey|ance pəˈveɪ|.ənts, pɜː-, US pɚ- **-or/s** -əʳ/z, US -ɚ/z
purview ˈpɜː.vjuː, US ˈpɝː- **-s** -z
pus pʌs
Pusan ˌpuːˈsæn, US -ˈsɑːn
Pusey ˈpjuː.zi **-ism** -ɪ.zᵊm **-ite/s** -aɪt/s
push pʊʃ **-es** -ɪz **-ing/ly** -ɪŋ/li **-ed** -t **-er/s** -əʳ/z, US -ɚ/z
pushball ˈpʊʃ.bɔːl, US -bɔːl, -bɑːl
pushbike ˈpʊʃ.baɪk **-s** -s
push-button ˈpʊʃˌbʌt.ᵊn **-s** -z
push-cart ˈpʊʃ.kɑːt, US -kɑːrt **-s** -s
pushchair ˈpʊʃ.tʃeəʳ, US -tʃer **-s** -z
pushdown ˈpʊʃ.daʊn
pushful ˈpʊʃ.fᵊl, -fʊl **-ness** -nəs, -nɪs
Pushkin ˈpʊʃ.kɪn
pushover ˈpʊʃˌəʊ.vəʳ, US -ˌoʊ.vɚ **-s** -z
pushpin ˈpʊʃ.pɪn **-s** -z
push|-start ˈpʊʃ|.stɑːt, US -stɑːrt **-starts** -stɑːts, US -stɑːrts **-starting** -ˌstɑː.tɪŋ, US -ˌstɑːr.t̬ɪŋ **-started** -ˌstɑː.tɪd, US -ˌstɑːr.t̬ɪd
Pushtu ˈpʌʃ.tuː, ˌ-ˈ-, US ˈpʌʃ.tuː
pushup ˈpʊʃ.ʌp **-s** -s
push|y ˈpʊʃ|.i **-ier** -i.əʳ, US -i.ɚ **-iest** -i.ɪst, -i.ɪst **-iness** -ɪ.nəs, -ɪ.nɪs
pusillanimity ˌpjuː.sɪ.ləˈnɪm.ə.ti, -zɪ-, -lænˈɪm-, -ɪ.ti, US -sɪ.ləˈnɪm.ə.t̬i
pusillanimous ˌpjuː.sɪˈlæn.ɪ.məs, -zɪˈ-, ˈ-ə-, US -sɪˈlæn.ə- **-ly** -li **-ness** -nəs, -nɪs
puss pʊs **-es** -ɪz
puss|y ˈpʊs|.i **-ies** -iz ˌ**pussy** ˈ**willow**
pussycat ˈpʊs.i.kæt **-s** -s
pussy|foot ˈpʊs.i|.fʊt **-foots** -fʊts **-footing** -ˌfʊt.ɪŋ, US -ˌfʊt̬.ɪŋ **-footed** -ˌfʊt.ɪd, US -ˌfʊt̬.ɪd **-footer/s** -ˌfʊt.əʳ/z, US -ˌfʊt̬.ɚ/z
pustular ˈpʌs.tʃə.ləʳ, ˈ-tjə-, -tʃʊ-, -tjʊ-, US -tʃə.lɚ, -tjə-, -tjʊ-
pustu|late ˈpʌs.tʃə|.leɪt, ˈ-tjə-, -tʃʊ-, -tjʊ-, US -tjʊ-, -tjə-, -tʃə- **-lated** -leɪ.tɪd, US -leɪ.t̬ɪd
pustulation ˌpʌs.tʃəˈleɪ.ʃᵊn, -tjəˈ-, -tʃʊˈ-, -tjʊˈ-, US -tʃəˈ-, -tjəˈ-, -tjʊˈ- **-s** -z
pustule ˈpʌs.tʃuːl, -tjuːl, US -tʃuːl, -tjuːl **-s** -z
pustulous ˈpʌs.tʃə.ləs, -tjə-, -tʃʊ-, -tjʊ-, US -tʃə-, -tjə-, -tʃʊ-, -tjʊ-
put pʊt **-s** -s **-ting** -ɪŋ, US ˈpʊt̬.ɪŋ
putative ˈpjuː.tə.tɪv, US -t̬ə.t̬ɪv **-ly** -li
put-down ˈpʊt.daʊn **-s** -z
Putin ˈpuː.tɪn, ˈpjuː-, US ˈpuː.tɪn, ˈpuː.t.n̩
Putnam ˈpʌt.nəm
Putney ˈpʌt.ni
put-on ˈpʊt.ɒn, US -ɑːn **-s** -z
putrefaction ˌpjuː.trɪˈfæk.ʃᵊn, -trəˈ-, US -trəˈ-
putre|fy ˈpjuː.trɪ|.faɪ, -trə-, US -trə- **-fies** -faɪz **-fying** -faɪ.ɪŋ **-fied** -faɪd
putrescenc|e pjuːˈtres.ᵊn|ts **-t** -t
putrid ˈpjuː.trɪd **-ly** -li **-ness** -nəs, -nɪs
putridity pjuːˈtrɪd.ə.ti, -ɪ.ti, US -ə.t̬i
putsch pʊtʃ **-es** -ɪz
putt, P~ pʌt **-s** -s **-ing** -ɪŋ, US ˈpʌt̬.ɪŋ

P

-ed -ɪd, (US) ˈpʌt̬.ɪd -er/s -əʳ/z, (US) ˈpʌt̬.ɚ/z ˈ**putting ˌgreen**
puttee ˈpʌt.iː, -i; pʌtˈiː, (US) pʌtˈiː, ˈ-- -s -z
Puttenham ˈpʌt.ən.əm
putter (from **putt**) ˈpʌt.əʳ, (US) ˈpʌt̬.ɚ -s -z -ing -ɪŋ -ed -d
putter (from **put**) ˈpʊt.əʳ, (US) ˈpʊt̬.ɚ -s -z
putti (plural of **putto**) ˈpʊt.i, -iː, (US) ˈpuː.ti, -tiː
Puttick ˈpʌt.ɪk, (US) ˈpʌt̬-
Puttnam ˈpʌt.nəm
putt|o ˈpʊt|.əʊ, (US) ˈpuː.t|oʊ -i -i, -iː
putt|y ˈpʌt|.i, (US) ˈpʌt̬- -ies -iz -ying -i.ɪŋ -ied -id
put-upon ˈpʊt.ə.pɒn, (US) ˈpʊt̬.ə.pɑːn
putz pʌts -es -ɪz
puy pwiː
puzzl|e ˈpʌz.əl -es -z -ing/ly -ɪŋ/li, ˈ-lɪŋ/li -ed -d
puzzlement ˈpʌz.əl.mənt
puzzler ˈpʌz.ləʳ, -əl.əʳ, (US) ˈ-lɚ, -əl.ɚ -s -z
PVC ˌpiː.viːˈsiː
Pwllheli pʊθˈlel.i; *as if Welsh:* pʊˈɬlel.i
pwn pəʊn, pɔːn, puːn; əʊn, (US) poʊn, pɔːn, puːn; oʊn -s -z -ing -ɪŋ -ed -d -age -ɪdʒ

> Note: Internet slang, based on the common 'typo' caused by hitting the 'p' key while typing the word 'own', thus producing 'pwn'. To 'own', in Internet gaming, means to conquer or take possession of someone or something. Since the word is more often seen in print than pronounced, its pronunciation is extremely variable, and those given above may not be the only ones in use.

PWR ˌpiːˌdʌb.əl.juˈɑːʳ, (US) -ˈɑːr
pya pjɑː, piˈɑː, (US) pjɑː -s -z
pyaemia paɪˈiː.mi.ə
Pybus ˈpaɪ.bəs
Pye paɪ
pygmaean pɪɡˈmiː.ən
Pygmalion pɪɡˈmeɪ.li.ən, (US) -ˈmeɪl.jən, -ˈmeɪ.li.ən
pygm|y ˈpɪɡ.m|i -ies -iz
pyjama pɪˈdʒɑː.mə, pə-, (US) pəˈdʒɑː-, -ˈdʒæm.ə -s -z
Pyke paɪk
Pylades ˈpɪl.ə.diːz, ˈpaɪ.lə-
Pyle paɪl
pylon ˈpaɪ.lɒn, -lən, (US) -lɑːn, -lən -s -z
pylor|us paɪˈlɔː.r|əs, (US) -ˈlɔːr|.əs, pɪ- -i -aɪ -ic -ɪk
Pym pɪm
Pynchon ˈpɪn.tʃən, (US) ˈpɪn.tʃən
Pyongyang ˌpjɒŋˈjæŋ, (US) ˌpjʌŋˈjɑːŋ, ˌpjɑːŋ-, -ˈjæŋ
pyorrhoea ˌpaɪ.əˈrɪə, (US) -ˈriː.ə
pyracantha ˌpaɪə.rəˈkænt.θə, (US) ˌpaɪ-, ˌpɪr.əˈ- -s -z
pyramid ˈpɪr.ə.mɪd -s -z ˈ**pyramid ˌselling**; ˌ**pyramid ˈselling**
pyramidal pɪˈræm.ɪ.dəl, pə-, ˈ-ə-, (US) pɪˈræm.ɪ-, pə-, ˈ-ə-; (US) ˌpɪr.əˈmɪd.əl -ly -i
Pyramus ˈpɪr.ə.məs
pyre paɪəʳ, ˈpaɪ.əʳ, (US) ˈpaɪ.ɚ -s -z
Pyrene paɪəˈriː.ni, (US) paɪˈriːn
Pyren|ees ˌpɪr.əˈn|iːz, -ɪˈ-, (US) -əˈ- -ean -iː.ən
pyrethrin paɪəˈriː.θrɪn, (US) paɪ-, -ˈreθ.rɪn
pyrethrum paɪəˈriː.θrəm, (US) paɪ-, -ˈreθ.rəm -s -z
pyretic paɪəˈret.ɪk, pɪ-, (US) paɪˈret̬-
Pyrex® ˈpaɪə.reks, (US) ˈpaɪ-
pyriform ˈpɪr.ɪ.fɔːm, (US) -fɔːrm
pyrite ˈpaɪə.raɪt, (US) ˈpaɪ-
pyrites paɪəˈraɪ.tiːz, pɪ-, pə-, (US) paɪˈraɪ.tiːz, pɪ-; (US) ˈpaɪ.raɪts
pyritic paɪəˈrɪt.ɪk, (US) paɪˈrɪt̬-
pyro- ˈpaɪə.rəʊ; paɪəˈrɒ, (US) ˈpaɪ.roʊ, ˈ-rə; (US) paɪˈrɑː

Note: Prefix. Normally either takes primary or secondary stress on the first syllable, e.g. **pyromania** /ˌpaɪə.rəʊˈmeɪ.ni.ə/ (US) /ˌpaɪ.roʊˈ-/, or primary stress on the second syllable, e.g. **pyrolysis** /paɪəˈrɒl.ə.sɪs/ (US) /paɪˈrɑː.lə-/.

pyrocanthus ˌpaɪə.rəʊˈkæn.θəs, (US) ˌpaɪ.roʊ-
pyrogallic ˌpaɪə.rəʊˈɡæl.ɪk, (US) ˌpaɪ.roʊˈ-, -ˈɡɑː.lɪk
pyrolysis, P~ paɪəˈrɒl.ə.sɪs, ˈ-ə-, (US) paɪˈrɑː.lə-
pyromani|a ˌpaɪə.rəʊˈmeɪ.ni|.ə, (US) ˌpaɪ.rəˈ-, -roʊˈ-, ˈ-nj|ə -ac -æk
pyromet|er paɪəˈrɒm.ɪ.t|əʳ, ˈ-ə-, (US) paɪˈrɑː.mə.t̬|ɚ -ers -əz, (US) -ɚz -ry -ri
pyrometric ˌpaɪə.rəʊˈmet.rɪk, (US) ˌpaɪ.roʊˈ-, -rəˈ- -ally -əl.i, -li *stress shift:* ˌ**pyrometric ˈmeasurement**
pyrotechnic ˌpaɪə.rəʊˈtek.nɪk, (US) ˌpaɪ.roʊˈ-, -rəˈ- -al -əl -ally -əl.i, -li -s -s *stress shift:* ˌ**pyrotechnic ˈsubstance**
Pyrrh|a ˈpɪr|.ə -us -əs
pyrrhic, P~ ˈpɪr.ɪk -s -s ˌ**Pyrrhic ˈvictory**
Pytchley ˈpaɪtʃ.li
Pythagoras paɪˈθæɡ.ər.əs, -ɒr-, -æs, (US) pɪˈθæɡ.ɚ.əs **Pyˌthagorasʼ ˈtheorem**
Pythagorean paɪˌθæɡ.əˈriː.ən, ˌpaɪ.θæɡ-, -ɒrˈ-, (US) pɪˌθæɡ.əˈriː- -s -z
Pythian ˈpɪθ.i.ən
Pythias ˈpɪθ.i.æs, (US) -əs
python ˈpaɪ.θən, (US) -θɑːn, -θən -s -z
Pythonesque ˌpaɪ.θənˈesk
pythoness ˈpaɪ.θən.es, -ɪs, (US) ˈpaɪ-, ˈpɪθ.ən-, -ɪs -es -ɪz
pythonic paɪˈθɒn.ɪk, (US) -ˈθɑː.nɪk, pɪ-
pyx pɪks -es -ɪz
pzazz pəˈzæz, pɪ-

Q

Pronouncing the letter Q

In general, the consonant letter **q** is followed by **u** and pronounced /kw/ or /k/, e.g.:

queen	kwiːn
antiquated	ˈæn.tɪ.kweɪ.tɪd ⓤⓢ ˈæn.t̬ə.kweɪ.t̬ɪd
quay	kiː
antique	ænˈtiːk

In words borrowed from Arabic, **q** is not always followed by **u**, e.g.:

Qatar	ˈkʌt.ɑːʳ, kəˈtɑːʳ ⓤⓢ ˈkɑː.tɑːr, kəˈtɑːr

q, Q kjuː -'s -z
Qaddafi, Qadhafi gəˈdɑː.fi, -ˈdæf.i, ⓤⓢ kəˈdɑː-
Qantas® ˈkwɒn.təs, -tæs, ⓤⓢ ˈkwɑːn.təs
Qatar ˈkʌt.ɑːʳ, ˈkæt-, ˈgæt-; kəˈtɑːʳ, gætˈɑːʳ, kæt-, ⓤⓢ ˈkɑː.tɑːr; ⓤⓢ kəˈtɑːr
Qatari kætˈɑː.ri, gæt-, kəˈtɑː-, ⓤⓢ kæˈtɑːr-, gæt-, kəˈtɑːr-
QC ˌkjuːˈsiː -'s -z
q.e.d., QED ˌkjuː.iːˈdiː
qt ˌkjuːˈtiː
Q-Tip® ˈkjuː.tɪp -s -s
qua kweɪ, kwɑː
quack kwæk -s -s -ing -ɪŋ -ed -t -ery -ᵊr.i -ish -ɪʃ
quad kwɒd, ⓤⓢ kwɑːd -s -z
Quadragesim|a ˌkwɒd.rəˈdʒes.ɪ.m|ə, ˈ-ə-, ⓤⓢ ˌkwɑː.drəˈ-, ˈdʒeɪ.zɪ- -al -ᵊl
quadrangle ˈkwɒd.ræŋ.gᵊl, kwɒdˈræŋ-, ⓤⓢ ˈkwɑː.dræŋ- -s -z
quadrangular kwɒdˈræŋ.gjə.ləʳ, kwəˈdræŋ-, -gjʊ-, ⓤⓢ kwɑːˈdræŋ.gjə.lɚ, -gjʊ-
quadrant ˈkwɒd.rᵊnt, ⓤⓢ ˈkwɑː.drᵊnt -s -s
quadraphonic ˌkwɒd.rəˈfɒn.ɪk, ⓤⓢ ˌkwɑː.drəˈfɑː.nɪk -ally -ᵊl.i, -li -s -s *stress shift:* ˌ**quadraphonic** ˈ**sound**
quadraphony kwɒdˈrɒf.ᵊn.i, kwəˈdrɒf-, -ˈdræf-; ˈkwɒd.rə.fɒn-, ⓤⓢ kwɑːˈdræf.ᵊn-
quadrate n, adj ˈkwɒd.rət, -rɪt, -reɪt, ⓤⓢ ˈkwɑː.drɪt, -dreɪt -s -s
quadra|te v kwɒdˈreɪ|t, kwəˈdreɪ|t, ⓤⓢ kwɑːˈdreɪ|t -tes -ts -ting -tɪŋ, ⓤⓢ -t̬ɪŋ -ted -tɪd, ⓤⓢ -t̬ɪd
quadratic kwɒdˈræt.ɪk, kwəˈdræt-, ⓤⓢ kwɑːˈdræt̬- -s -s **quad**ˌ**ratic e**ˈ**quation**
quadrature ˈkwɒd.rə.tʃəʳ, -rɪ-, -tʃʊəʳ, -tjʊəʳ, ⓤⓢ ˈkwɑː.drə.tʃɚ
quadric ˈkwɒd.rɪk, ⓤⓢ ˈkwɑː.drɪk -s -s
quadri|ga kwɒdˈriː|.gə, kwəˈdriː-, -ˈdraɪ-, ⓤⓢ kwɑːˈdraɪ- -gae -dʒiː, ⓤⓢ -giː, -dʒiː -gas -gəz
quadrilateral ˌkwɒd.rɪˈlæt.ᵊr.ᵊl, -rəˈ-, ˈ-rᵊl, ⓤⓢ ˌkwɑː.drɪˈlæt̬- -s -z *stress shift:* ˌ**quadrilateral** ˈ**shape**
quadrilingual ˌkwɒd.rɪˈlɪŋ.gwəl, -rəˈ-, ⓤⓢ ˌkwɑː.drɪˈ- *stress shift:* ˌ**quadrilingual** ˈ**nation**
quadrille kwəˈdrɪl, kwɒdˈrɪl, ⓤⓢ kwəˈdrɪl, kwɑː- -s -z
quadrillion kwɒdˈrɪl.jən, kwəˈdrɪl-, ˈ-i.ən, ⓤⓢ kwɑːˈdrɪl.jən -s -z
quadriplegia ˌkwɒd.rɪˈpliː.dʒə, -rəˈ-, ˈ-dʒi.ə, ⓤⓢ ˌkwɑː.drɪˈpliː-
quadriplegic ˌkwɒd.rɪˈpliː.dʒɪk, -rəˈ-, ⓤⓢ ˌkwɑː.drɪˈ- -s -s *stress shift:* ˌ**quadriplegic** ˈ**state**
quadrisyllabic ˌkwɒd.rɪ.sɪˈlæb.ɪk, -rə-, -səˈ-, ⓤⓢ ˌkwɑː.drɪ- *stress shift:* ˌ**quadrisyllabic** ˈ**word**
quadrisyllable ˌkwɒd.rɪˈsɪl.ə.bᵊl, ⓤⓢ ˌkwɑː.drɪˈsɪl- -s -z
quadroon kwɒdˈruːn, kwəˈdruːn, ⓤⓢ kwɑːˈdruːn -s -z
quadrophonic ˌkwɒd.rəˈfɒn.ɪk, ⓤⓢ ˌkwɑː.drəˈfɑː.nɪk -ally -ᵊl.i, -li -s -s *stress shift:* ˌ**quadrophonic** ˈ**sound**
quadrophony kwɒdˈrɒf.ᵊn.i, kwəˈdrɒf-; ˈkwɒd.rə.fɒn-, ⓤⓢ kwɑːˈdrɑː.fᵊn-
quadrumana kwɒdˈruː.mə.nə, kwəˈdruː-, ⓤⓢ kwɑːˈdruː-
quadrumanous kwɒdˈruː.mə.nəs, kwəˈdruː-, ⓤⓢ kwɑːˈdruː-
quadruped ˈkwɒd.rə.ped, -rʊ-, ⓤⓢ ˈkwɑː.drʊ-, -drə- -s -z
quadrupl|e ˈkwɒd.rʊp.ᵊl, -rəp-; kwɒdˈruː.pᵊl, kwəˈdruː-, ⓤⓢ kwɑːˈdruː.pᵊl, kwə-, -ˈdrʊp.ᵊl; ⓤⓢ ˈkwɑː.druː.pᵊl, -drʊ-, -drə- -es -z -y -i -ing -ɪŋ -ed -d
quadruplet ˈkwɒd.rʊ.plət, -plɪt, -plet, ˈ-rə-; kwɒdˈruː-, ⓤⓢ kwɑːˈdruː.plɪt; ⓤⓢ ˈkwɑː.druː-, -drə-; ⓤⓢ kwɑːˈdrʌp.lɪt -s -s
quadruplicate n, adj kwɒdˈruː.plɪ.kət, kwəˈdruː-, -plə-, -kɪt, -keɪt, ⓤⓢ kwɑːˈdruː.plɪ.kɪt, -keɪt -s -s
quadrupli|cate v kwɒdˈruː.plɪ|.keɪt, kwəˈdruː-, ⓤⓢ kwɑːˈdruː- -cates -keɪts -cating -keɪ.tɪŋ, ⓤⓢ -keɪ.t̬ɪŋ -cated -keɪ.tɪd, ⓤⓢ -keɪ.t̬ɪd
quaestor ˈkwiː.stəʳ, ˈkwaɪ-, -stɔːʳ, ⓤⓢ ˈkwes.tɚ, ˈkwiː.stɚ -s -z
quaff kwɒf, kwɑːf, ⓤⓢ kwɑːf, kwæf, kwɔːf -s -s -ing -ɪŋ -ed -t -er/s -əʳ/z, ⓤⓢ -ɚ/z
quag kwɒg, kwæg, ⓤⓢ kwæg, kwɑːg -s -z
quagga ˈkwæg.ə, ˈkwɒg-, ⓤⓢ ˈkwæg-, ˈkwɑː.gə -s -z
Quaglino's® kwægˈliː.nəʊz, ⓤⓢ -noʊz
quagmire ˈkwɒg.maɪəʳ, -maɪ.əʳ, ˈkwæg-, ⓤⓢ ˈkwæg.maɪ.ɚ, ˈkwɑːg- -s -z
quail, Q~ kweɪl -s -z -ing -ɪŋ -ed -d
Quain kweɪn
quaint kweɪnt -er -əʳ, ⓤⓢ ˈkweɪn.t̬ɚ -est -ɪst, -əst, ⓤⓢ ˈkweɪn.t̬ɪst, -t̬əst -ly -li -ness -nəs, -nɪs
quak|e kweɪk -es -s -ing -ɪŋ -ed -t
Quaker ˈkweɪ.kəʳ, ⓤⓢ -kɚ -s -z
qualification ˌkwɒl.ɪ.fɪˈkeɪ.ʃᵊn, ˌ-ə-, -fəˈ-, ⓤⓢ ˌkwɑː.lɪ- -s -z
qualificative ˈkwɒl.ɪ.fɪ.kə.tɪv, ˈ-ə-, ⓤⓢ ˈkwɑː.lɪ.fɪ.keɪ.t̬ɪv -s -z
qualificatory ˌkwɒl.ɪ.fɪˈkeɪ.tᵊr.i, ˌ-ə-, ⓤⓢ ˈkwɑː.lɪ.fə.kə.tɔːr-
quali|fy ˈkwɒl.ɪ|.faɪ, ˈ-ə-, ⓤⓢ ˈkwɑː.lɪ-, ˈ-lə- -fies -faɪz -fying -faɪ.ɪŋ -fied -faɪd -fier/s -faɪ.əʳ/z, ⓤⓢ -faɪ.ɚ/z
qualitative ˈkwɒl.ɪ.tə.tɪv, -teɪ-, ⓤⓢ ˈkwɑː.lɪ.teɪ.t̬ɪv -ly -li
qualit|y ˈkwɒl.ə.t|i, -ɪ.t|i, ⓤⓢ ˈkwɑː.lə.t̬|i -ies -iz ˈ**quality con**ˌ**trol**; ˈ**quality** ˌ**time**
qualm kwɑːm, kwɔːm, ⓤⓢ kwɑːm -s -z
qualmish ˈkwɑː.mɪʃ, ˈkwɔː-, ⓤⓢ ˈkwɑː- -ly -li -ness -nəs, -nɪs
quandar|y, Q~ ˈkwɒn.dᵊr|.i, -dr|i, ⓤⓢ ˈkwɑːn- -ies -iz
quango ˈkwæŋ.gəʊ, ⓤⓢ -goʊ -s -z
Quant kwɒnt, ⓤⓢ kwɑːnt
quanta (plural of **quantum**) ˈkwɒn.tə, ⓤⓢ ˈkwɑːn.t̬ə
quantal ˈkwɒn.tᵊl, ⓤⓢ ˈkwɑːn.t̬ᵊl
quantic ˈkwɒn.tɪk, ⓤⓢ ˈkwɑːn.t̬ɪk -s -s
quantifiable ˈkwɒn.tɪ.faɪ.ə.bᵊl, -tə-, ˌkwɒn.tɪˈfaɪ-, -təˈ-, ⓤⓢ ˈkwɑːn.t̬ə.faɪ-, ˌkwɑːn.t̬əˈfaɪ-
quantification ˌkwɒn.tɪ.fɪˈkeɪ.ʃᵊn, -tə-, -fəˈ-, ⓤⓢ ˌkwɑːn.t̬ə-
quanti|fy ˈkwɒn.tɪ|.faɪ, -tə-, ⓤⓢ ˈkwɑːn.t̬ɪ-, ˈ-t̬ə- -fies -faɪz -fying -faɪ.ɪŋ -fied -faɪd -fier/s -faɪ.əʳ/z, ⓤⓢ -faɪ.ɚ/z
quantitative ˈkwɒn.tɪ.tə.tɪv, -teɪ-, ⓤⓢ ˈkwɑːn.t̬ə.teɪ.t̬ɪv -ly -li
quantit|y ˈkwɒn.tə.t|i, -tɪ-, ⓤⓢ

Q

ˈkwɑːn.t̬ə.t̬|i -ies -iz ˌ**quantity surˈveyor**, ˈ**quantity surˌveyor**
quantiz|e, -is|e ˈkwɒn.taɪz, (US) ˈkwɑːn- -es -ɪz -ing -ɪŋ -ed -d
Quantock ˈkwɒn.tək, -tɒk, (US) ˈkwɑːn.t̬ək, -tɑːk
quantum *in Latin phrases:* ˈkwæn.tʊm, ˈkwɒn-, -təm, (US) ˈkwɑːn.t̬əm, -tʊm
quant|um *amount:* ˈkwɒn.t|əm, (US) ˈkwɑːn.t̬|əm -a -ə ˌ**quantum** ˈ**jump**; ˌ**quantum** ˈ**leap**; ˌ**quantum meˈchanics**; ˈ**quantum** ˌ**theory**
quantum meruit ˌkwæn.tʊmˈmer.u.ɪt, ˌkwɒn-, -təmˈ-, (US) ˌkwɑːn.tʊmˈ-, -t̬əmˈ-
quarantin|e ˈkwɒr.ən.tiːn, -taɪn, (US) ˈkwɔːr.ən.tiːn, ˈkwɑːr- -es -z -ing -ɪŋ -ed -d
quare clausim fregit ˌkwɑː.reɪˌklaʊ.səmˈfreɪ.gɪt, (US) ˌkwɑːr.iˌklaʊ.səmˈfreɪ.gət, -gɪt
Quaritch ˈkwɒr.ɪtʃ, (US) ˈkwɑːr-
quark *in physics:* kwɑːk, kwɔːk, (US) kwɑːrk, kwɔːrk -s -s *soft cheese:* kwɑːk, (US) kwɑːrk, kwɔːrk
Quarles kwɔːlz, (US) kwɔːrlz, kwɑːrlz
Quarmby ˈkwɔːm.bi, (US) ˈkwɔːrm-
quarrel ˈkwɒr.əl, (US) ˈkwɔːr-, ˈkwɑːr- -s -z -(l)ing -ɪŋ -(l)ed -d -(l)er/s -ər/z, (US) -ɚ/z
quarrelsome ˈkwɒr.əl.səm, (US) ˈkwɔːr-, ˈkwɑːr- -ly -li -ness -nəs, -nɪs
quarr|y ˈkwɒr|.i, (US) ˈkwɔːr-, ˈkwɑːr- -ies -iz -ying -i.ɪŋ -ied -id ˈ**quarry** ˌ**tile**; ˌ**quarry** ˈ**tile**
quarry|man ˈkwɒr.i|.mən, -mæn, (US) ˈkwɔːr-, ˈkwɑːr- -men -mən, -men
quart n *measurement:* kwɔːt, kɔːt, (US) kwɔːrt -s -s
quart n, v *in card games, fencing:* kɑːt, (US) kɑːrt -s -s -ing -ɪŋ, (US) ˈkɑːr.t̬ɪŋ -ed -ɪd, (US) ˈkɑːr.t̬ɪd
quartan ˈkwɔː.tən, (US) ˈkwɔːr-
quarte n, v *in card games, fencing:* kɑːt, (US) kɑːrt -s -s -ing -ɪŋ, (US) ˈkɑːr.t̬ɪŋ -ed -ɪd, (US) ˈkɑːr.t̬ɪd
quart|er ˈkwɔː.t|ər, kɔː-, (US) ˈkwɔːr.t̬|ɚ -ers -əz, (US) -ɚz -ering/s -ər.ɪŋ/z -ered -əd, (US) -ɚd -erage -ər.ɪdʒ ˈ**quarter** ˌ**day**; ˈ**quarter** ˌ**note**; ˈ**Quarter** ˌ**Sessions**; ˈ**quarter** ˌ**tone**
quarterback ˈkwɔː.tə.bæk, (US) ˈkwɔːr.t̬ɚ- -s -s
quarterdeck ˈkwɔː.tə.dek, (US) ˈkwɔːr.t̬ɚ- -s -s
quarterfinal ˌkwɔː.təˈfaɪ.nəl, (US) ˌkwɔːr.t̬ɚˈ- -s -z
quarterfinalist ˌkwɔː.təˈfaɪ.nəl.ɪst, (US) ˌkwɔːr.t̬ɚˈ- -s -s
quarterl|y ˈkwɔː.təl|.i, (US) ˈkwɔːr.t̬ɚ.l|i -ies -iz
Quartermain(e) ˈkwɔː.tə.meɪn, (US) ˈkwɔːr.t̬ɚ-
quartermaster ˈkwɔː.təˌmɑː.stər, (US) ˈkwɔːr.t̬ɚˌmæs.tɚ -s -z
quartern ˈkwɔː.tən, (US) ˈkwɔːr.t̬ɚn -s -z
quarter|staff ˈkwɔː.tə|.stɑːf, (US) ˈkwɔːr.t̬ɚ|.stæf -aves -steɪvz
quartet(te) kwɔːˈtet, (US) kwɔːr- -s -s
quartic ˈkwɔː.tɪk, (US) ˈkwɔːr.t̬ɪk -s -s
quartile ˈkwɔː.taɪl, (US) ˈkwɔːr-, -t̬ɪl, -t̬əl -s -z
quarto ˈkwɔː.təʊ, (US) ˈkwɔːr.t̬oʊ -s -z
quartus, Q~ ˈkwɔː.təs, (US) ˈkwɔːr.t̬əs
quartz ˈkwɔːts, (US) ˈkwɔːrts
quasar ˈkweɪ.zɑːr, -sɑːr, (US) -zɑːr, -sɑːr -s -z
quash kwɒʃ, (US) kwɑːʃ, kwɔːʃ -es -ɪz -ing -ɪŋ -ed -t
quasi ˈkweɪ.zaɪ, ˈkwɑː-, -saɪ, -zi, (US) ˈkweɪ.saɪ, -zaɪ; (US) ˈkwɑː.zi, -si
quasi- ˈkweɪ.zaɪ, ˈkwɑː-, -saɪ, -zi, (US) ˈkweɪ.saɪ, -zaɪ; (US) ˈkwɑː.zi, -si
Note: Prefix. Words beginning with **quasi-** are normally hyphenated, with **quasi-** taking secondary stress on the first syllable, e.g. **quasi-stellar** /ˌkweɪ.zaɪˈstel.ər/ (US) /-saɪˈstel.ɚ/.
quasi in rem ˌkweɪ.zi.ɪnˈrem, (US) ˌkwɑː-, -ənˈ-
Quasimodo ˌkwɑː.ziˈməʊ.dəʊ, ˌkwɒz.iˈ-, ˌkwæz-, (US) ˌkwɑː.ziˈmoʊ.doʊ
quassia ˈkwɒʃ.ə, -i.ə, (US) ˈkwɑː.ʃə, ˈ-ʃi.ə
quatercentenar|y ˌkwæt.ə.senˈtiː.nər|.i, ˌkwɔː.tə-, ˌkwɒt.ə-, ˌkweɪ.tə-, -ˈten.ər-, (US) ˌkwɑː.t̬ɚ.senˈten.ɚ|.i; (US) -ˈsen.tən.er- -ies -iz
Quatermain ˈkwɔː.tə.meɪn, (US) ˈkwɑː.t̬ɚ-
quaternar|y, Q~ kwəˈtɜː.nər|.i, kwɒtˈɜː-, (US) ˈkwɑː.t̬ɚ.ner-; (US) kwəˈtɝː.nɚ- -ies -iz
quaternion kwəˈtɜː.ni.ən, kwɒtˈɜː-, (US) kwəˈtɝː-, kwɑː- -s -z
quatorzain kəˈtɔː.zeɪn, kætˈɔː-; ˈkæt.ə-, (US) kəˈtɔːr-, kætˈɔːr-; (US) ˈkæt̬.ɚ- -s -z
quatrain ˈkwɒt.reɪn, -rən, (US) ˈkwɑː.treɪn, -ˈ- -s -z
quatrefoil ˈkæt.rə.fɔɪl, ˈ-ə-, (US) ˈkæt̬.ɚ.fɔɪl, -rə- -s -z
quatrillion kwɒtˈrɪl.jən, kwəˈtrɪl-, ˈ-i.ən, (US) kwɑːˈtrɪl-, kwə- -s -z
quattrocento, Q~ ˌkwæt.rəʊˈtʃen.təʊ, ˌkwɒt-, (US) ˌkwɑː.troʊˈtʃen.toʊ
quav|er ˈkweɪ.v|ər, (US) -v|ɚ -ers -əz, (US) -ɚz -ering/ly -ər.ɪŋ/li -ered -əd, (US) -ɚd
quay kiː, (US) kiː, keɪ, kweɪ -s -z -age -ɪdʒ
Quay *place name:* kiː *surname:* kweɪ
Quayle kweɪl
quayside ˈkiː.saɪd
quean kwiːn -s -z
queas|y ˈkwiː.z|i -ier -i.ər, (US) -i.ɚ -iest -i.ɪst, -i.əst -ily -əl.i, -ɪ.li -iness -ɪ.nəs, -ɪ.nɪs
Quebec kwɪˈbek, kwə-, kɪ-, kə-; *as if French:* kebˈek; (US) kwəˈbek, kwɪ-, kɪ-; *as if French:* kebˈek
Quebecois, Québecois ˌkeɪ.bekˈwɑː, ˌkeb.ekˈ-, -ɪˈkwɑː, -əˈ-, (US) ˌkeɪ.bekˈwɑː
Quechu|a ˈketʃ.u|.ə, -w|ə, (US) -w|ɑː, -w|ə -an/s -ən/z
queen kwiːn -s -z -ing -ɪŋ -ed -d ˌ**Queen's** ˈ**Counsel**; ˌ**Queen's** ˈ**English**; ˌ**queen's** ˈ**evidence**; ˌ**Queen** ˈ**Mother**
Queenborough ˈkwiːn.bər.ə, ˈkwiːm-, (US) ˈkwiːn.bɚ.oʊ
Queenie ˈkwiː.ni
queenlike ˈkwiːn.laɪk
queenl|y ˈkwiːn.l|i -ier -i.ər, (US) -i.ɚ -iest -i.ɪst, -i.əst -iness -ɪ.nəs, -ɪ.nɪs
Queens kwiːnz
Queensberry ˈkwiːnz.bər.i, (US) -ˌber.i, -bɚ- ˌ**Queensberry** ˈ**rules**
Queensbury ˈkwiːnz.bər.i
Queensferry ˈkwiːnzˌfer.i
Queensland ˈkwiːnz.lənd, -lænd
Queenstown ˈkwiːnz.taʊn
Queensway ˈkwiːnz.weɪ
queer kwɪər, (US) kwɪr -s -z -ing -ɪŋ -ed -d -er -ər, (US) -ɚ -est -ɪst, (US) -əst -ly -li -ness -nəs, -nɪs -ish -ɪʃ ˈ**queer** ˌ**street**
quell kwel -s -z -ing -ɪŋ -ed -d
quench kwentʃ -es -ɪz -ing -ɪŋ -ed -t -er/s -ər/z, (US) -ɚ/z -able -ə.bəl
Quen(n)ell kwɪˈnel, kwə-, ˈkwen.əl, (US) kwəˈnel, ˈkwen.əl
quenelle kəˈnel, kɪ-, (US) kə- -s -z
Quentin ˈkwen.tɪn, (US) -tən
Querétaro kəˈreɪ.tər.əʊ, (US) -ˈret.ə.roʊ; (US) kɚ.əˈtɑːr.oʊ
quern kwɜːn, (US) kwɝːn -s -z
querulous ˈkwer.ə.ləs, -jʊ-, ˈ-ʊ-, (US) ˈkwer.jə.ləs, -jʊ-, ˈ-ə-, ˈ-ʊ- -ly -li -ness -nəs, -nɪs
quer|y ˈkwɪə.r|i, (US) ˈkwɪr|.i -ies -iz -ying -i.ɪŋ -ied -id
quesadilla ˌkeɪ.səˈdiː.jə, -ljə, (US) -jə -s -z
Quesnel ˈkeɪ.nəl
quest kwest -s -s -ing -ɪŋ -ed -ɪd
Quested ˈkwes.tɪd
question ˈkwes.tʃən, ˈkweʃ-, ˈ-tjən, (US) ˈkwes.tʃən, -tjən -s -z -ing/ly -ɪŋ/li -ed -d -er/s -ər/z, (US) -ɚ/z ˈ**question** ˌ**mark**; ˈ**question** ˌ**time**; ˌ**out of the** ˈ**question**
questionab|le ˈkwes.tʃə.nə.b|əl, ˈkweʃ-, ˈ-tjə-, (US) ˈkwes.tʃə-, -tjə- -ly -li -leness -əl.nəs, -nɪs
questionar|y ˈkwes.tʃə.nər|.i, ˈkweʃ-, ˈ-tjə-, (US) ˈkwes.tʃə.ner-, -tjə- -ies -iz
question-master ˈkwes.tʃənˌmɑː.stər, ˈkweʃ-, ˈ-tjən-, -tʃəmˌ-, (US) ˈkwes.tʃənˌmæs.tɚ, -tjənˌ- -s -z

questionnaire ˌkwes.tʃəˈneəʳ, -tjəˈ-, ˌkweʃ-, ˌkes-, ˈ---, US ˌkwes.tʃəˈner, -tjəˈ- -s -z

Note: The pronunciation /ˌkes-/, which is based on the word's French origin, should now be considered old-fashioned.

Quetta ˈkwet.ə, US ˈkweţ-
quetzal ˈkwet.səl, US ketˈsɑːl -s -z
quetzales kwetˈsɑː.les, US ket-
Quetzalcoatl ˌket.səl.kəʊˈæt.əl, US -sɑːl.koʊˈɑː.ţəl
queue kjuː -s -z -ing -ɪŋ -d -d
queue-jump ˈkjuː.dʒʌmp -s -s -ing -ɪŋ -ed -t -er/s -əʳ/z, US -ɚ/z
Quex kweks
Quezon City ˌkeɪ.zɒnˈsɪt.i, -sɒnˈ-, US ˌkeɪ.sɑːnˈsɪţ-
quibbl|e ˈkwɪb.əl -es -z -ing -ɪŋ, ˈkwɪb.lɪŋ -ed -d -er/s -əʳ/z, ˈkwɪb.ləʳ/z, US ˈkwɪb.əl.ɚ/z, ˈ-lɚ/z
Quibell ˈkwaɪ.bəl, ˈkwɪb.əl; kwɪˈbel, kwaɪˈbel
quich|e kiːʃ -es -ɪz
quick, Q~ kwɪk -er -əʳ, US -ɚ -est -ɪst, -əst -ly -li -ness -nəs, -nɪs **ˌquick ˈmarch; ˈquick ˌtime**
quick-change ˌkwɪkˈtʃeɪndʒ *stress shift:* **ˌquick-change ˈtyres**
Quicke kwɪk
quicken ˈkwɪk.ən -s -z -ing -ɪŋ -ed -d
quickfire ˈkwɪk.faɪəʳ, -faɪ.əʳ, -ˈ-, US -faɪ.ɚ
quick-freez|e ˌkwɪkˈfriːz, ˈ--, US ˈkwɪk.friːz -es -ɪz -ing -ɪŋ **quick-froze** ˌkwɪkˈfrəʊz, ˈ--, US ˈkwɪk.froʊz **quick frozen** -ən **quick-freezer/s** ˌkwɪkˈfriː.zəʳ/z, ˈ-ˌ--, US ˈkwɪkˌfriː.zɚ/z
quickie ˈkwɪk.i -s -z
quicklime ˈkwɪk.laɪm
Quickly ˈkwɪk.li
quicksand ˈkwɪk.sænd -s -z
quickset ˈkwɪk.set
quicksilver ˈkwɪkˌsɪl.vəʳ, US -vɚ
quickstep ˈkwɪk.step -s -s
quick-tempered ˌkwɪkˈtem.pəd, US -pɚd, ˈ-ˌ-- *stress shift, British only:* **ˌquick-tempered ˈperson**
quick-witted ˌkwɪkˈwɪt.ɪd, US -ˈwɪţ-, ˈ-ˌ-- -ly -li -ness -nəs, -nɪs *stress shift, British only:* **ˌquick-witted ˈperson**
quid kwɪd -s -z
Quidditch ˈkwɪd.ɪtʃ
quiddit|y ˈkwɪd.ɪ.t|i, -ə.t|i, US -ə.ţ|i -ies -iz
quid pro quo ˌkwɪd.prəʊˈkwəʊ, US -proʊˈkwoʊ -s -z
quiescence kwiˈes.ənts, US kwaɪ-, kwi-
quiescent kwiˈes.ənt, US kwaɪ-, kwi- -ly -li
quiet kwaɪət, ˈkwaɪ.ət, US ˈkwaɪ.ət -er -əʳ, US ˈkwaɪ.ə.ţɚ -est -ɪst, -əst, US ˈkwaɪ.ə.ţɪst, -ţəst -ly -li -ness -nəs, -nɪs -s -s -ing -ɪŋ, US ˈkwaɪə.ţɪŋ -ed -ɪd, US ˈkwaɪə.ţɪd
quieten ˈkwaɪə.tən, ˈkwaɪ.ə-, US ˈkwaɪ.ə- -s -z -ing -ɪŋ -ed -d
quiet|ism ˈkwaɪə.t|ɪ.zəm, ˈkwaɪ.ɪ-, US ˈkwaɪ.ə.t|ɪ- -ist/s -ɪst/s
quietude ˈkwaɪə.tʃuːd, ˈkwaɪ.ɪ-, -tjuːd, US ˈkwaɪ.ə.tuːd, -tjuːd
quietus kwaɪˈiː.təs, -ˈeɪ-, US -ˈiː.ţəs
quiff kwɪf -s -s
Quigg kwɪg
Quiggin ˈkwɪg.ɪn
Quigley ˈkwɪg.li
quill kwɪl -s -z -ing -ɪŋ -ed -d
Quiller-Couch ˌkwɪl.əˈkuːtʃ, US -ɚˈ-
Quilliam ˈkwɪl.i.əm
Quilp kwɪlp
quilt kwɪlt -s -s -ing -ɪŋ, US ˈkwɪl.ţɪŋ -ed -ɪd, US ˈkwɪl.ţɪd
Quilter ˈkwɪl.təʳ, US -ţɚ
quin, Q~ kwɪn -s -z
Quinault *North American people:* ˈkwɪn.əlt, -ɔːlt, US kwɪˈnɑːlt *French dramatist:* ˈkiː.nəʊ, US kɪˈnoʊ
quinc|e, Q~ kwɪnts -es -ɪz
quincentenar|y ˌkwɪn.senˈtiː.nər|.i, -ˈten.ər-, -ˈtɪn-, US kwɪnˈsen.tə.ner|.i; US ˌkwɪn.senˈten.ɚ- -ies -iz
Quincey ˈkwɪnt.si
quincunx ˈkwɪn.kʌŋks, ˈkwɪŋ-, US ˈkwɪn- -es -ɪz
Quincy ˈkwɪnt.si
quindecagon kwɪnˈdek.ə.gən, US -gɑːn -s -z
quinella kwɪˈnel.ə
quingentenar|y ˌkwɪn.dʒenˈtiː.nər|.i, -ˈten.ər-, -ˈtɪn- -ies -iz
quinine ˈkwɪn.iːn, -ˈ-; kwə-, US ˈkwaɪ.naɪn
Quink® kwɪŋk
Quinn kwɪn
Quinney ˈkwɪn.i
quinoa ˈkiːn.wɑː, kiˈnəʊ.ə, US ˈkiːn.wɑː, kiˈnoʊ.ə
quinquagenarian ˌkwɪŋ.kwə.dʒəˈneə.ri.ən, -kwɪ-, -dʒɪˈ-, US ˌkwɪn.kwə.dʒəˈner.i-, ˌkwɪŋ- -s -z
Quinquagesima ˌkwɪŋ.kwəˈdʒes.ɪ.mə, -kwɪˈ-, ˈ-ə-, US ˌkwɪn.kwəˈdʒeɪ.zɪ-, ˌkwɪŋ-, -ˈdʒes.ɪ-
quinquennial kwɪŋˈkwen.i.əl, US kwɪn-, kwɪŋ-
quinquennium kwɪŋˈkwen.i.əm, US kwɪn-, kwɪŋ- -s -z
quinsy ˈkwɪn.zi
quint *organ stop:* kwɪnt *in piquet:* kɪnt, kwɪnt; *old fashioned:* kent *US for quintuplet:* kwɪnt -s -s
quintain ˈkwɪn.tɪn -s -z
quintal ˈkwɪn.təl, US -ţəl -s -z
Quintana Roo kɪnˌtɑː.nəˈrəʊ.əʊ, US -ˈroʊ.oʊ
quintessence kwɪnˈtes.ənts
quintessential ˌkwɪn.tɪˈsen.tʃəl, -təˈ-, US -ţəˈsent.ʃəl -ly -i
quintet, quintette kwɪnˈtet -s -s
quintic ˈkwɪn.tɪk, US -ţɪk -s -s
Quintilian kwɪnˈtɪl.i.ən, US ˈ-jən, -i.ən
quintillion kwɪnˈtɪl.jən, ˈ-i.ən, US ˈ-jən -s -z
Quintin ˈkwɪn.tɪn, US -tɪn, -tən
Quinton ˈkwɪn.tən, US -tən
quintupl|e ˈkwɪn.tʃʊ.pəl, ˈ-tjʊ-, ˈ-tʃə-, ˈ-tjə-; kwɪnˈtʃuː-, -ˈtjuː-, US kwɪnˈtuː-, -ˈtjuː-; US ˈkwɪn.ţə- -es -z -ing -ɪŋ -ed -d
quintuplet ˈkwɪn.tʃʊ.plət, ˈ-tjʊ-, -plɪt, -plet, ˈ-tʃə-, ˈ-tjə-; kwɪnˈtʃuː-, -ˈtjuː-, US kwɪnˈtʌp.lɪt, -ˈtuː.plɪt, -ˈtjuː-; US ˈkwɪn.ţə.plet, -plɪt -s -s
quintus, Q~ ˈkwɪn.təs, US -ţəs
quip kwɪp -s -s -ping -ɪŋ -ped -t
quire ˈkwaɪ.əʳ, kwaɪəʳ, US ˈkwaɪ.ɚ -s -z
Quirinal ˈkwɪr.ɪ.nəl, -ən.əl, US ˈkwɪr.ɪ.nəl; US kwɪˈraɪ-
Quirinus kwɪˈraɪ.nəs
quirk, Q~ kwɜːk, US kwɝːk -s -s
quirk|y ˈkwɜː.k|i, US ˈkwɝː- -ier -i.əʳ, US -i.ɚ -iest -i.ɪst, -i.əst -ily -əl.i, -ɪ.li -iness -ɪ.nəs, -ɪ.nɪs
quisling ˈkwɪz.lɪŋ -s -z
quit kwɪt -s -s -ting -ɪŋ, US ˈkwɪţ.ɪŋ -ted -ɪd, US ˈkwɪţ.ɪd
quitclaim ˈkwɪt.kleɪm -s -s
quite kwaɪt
Quito ˈkiː.təʊ, US -ţoʊ, -toʊ
quit-rent ˈkwɪt.rent -s -s
quits kwɪts
quittanc|e ˈkwɪt.ənts -es -ɪz
quitter ˈkwɪt.əʳ, US ˈkwɪţ.ɚ -s -z
quiv|er ˈkwɪv|.əʳ, US -ɚ -ers -əz, US -ɚz -ering/ly -ər.ɪŋ/li -ered -əd, US -ɚd
Quiverful ˈkwɪv.ə.fʊl, US ˈ-ɚ-
qui vive ˌkiːˈviːv
Quixote ˈkwɪk.sət, -səʊt; kɪˈhəʊ.ti, -teɪ, US kiːˈhoʊ.ţi, kɪ-, -teɪ; US ˈkwɪk.sət
quixotic kwɪkˈsɒt.ɪk, US -ˈsɑː.ţɪk -ally -əl.i, -li
quiz kwɪz -zes -ɪz -zing -ɪŋ -zed -d
quiz-master ˈkwɪzˌmɑː.stəʳ, US -ˌmæs.tɚ -s -z
quizzic|al ˈkwɪz.ɪ.k|əl -ally -əl.i, -li
quod kwɒd, US kwɑːd -s -z -ding -ɪŋ -ded -ɪd
quod erat demonstrandum ˌkwɒdˌer.ætˌdem.ənˈstræn.dəm, US ˌkwɑːd-, -ˈstrɑːn-
quodlibet ˈkwɒd.lɪ.bet, US ˈkwɑːd.lə- -s -s
quoin kɔɪn, kwɔɪn -s -z -ing -ɪŋ -ed -d
quoit kɔɪt, kwɔɪt -s -s
quokka ˈkwɒk.ə, US ˈkwɑː.kə -s -z
quondam ˈkwɒn.dæm, -dəm, US ˈkwɑːn.dəm, -dæm
Quonset® ˈkwɒnt.sɪt, -sət, -set, US ˈkwɑːnt- **ˈQuonset ˌhut**
quorate ˈkwɔː.reɪt, -rət, -rɪt, US ˈkwɔːr.ɪt, -eɪt
Quorn® kwɔːn, US kwɔːrn

Q

quorum ˈkwɔː.rəm, ⓤⓢ ˈkwɔːr.əm -s -z

quota ˈkwəʊ.tə, ⓤⓢ ˈkwoʊ.t̬ə -s -z -ing -ɪŋ -ed -d

quotable ˈkwəʊ.tə.bəl, ⓤⓢ ˈkwoʊ.t̬ə-

quotation kwəʊˈteɪ.ʃən, ⓤⓢ kwoʊ- -s -z **quoˈtation ˌmark**

quot|e kwəʊt, ⓤⓢ kwoʊt -es -s -ing -ɪŋ, ⓤⓢ ˈkwoʊ.t̬ɪŋ -ed -ɪd, ⓤⓢ ˈkwoʊ.t̬ɪd

quoth kwəʊθ, ⓤⓢ kwoʊθ -a -ə

quotidian kwəʊˈtɪd.i.ən, kwɒtˈɪd-, ⓤⓢ kwoʊˈtɪd-

quotient ˈkwəʊ.ʃənt, ⓤⓢ ˈkwoʊ- -s -s

quo warranto ˌkwəʊ.wɒrˈæn.təʊ, ⓤⓢ ˌkwoʊ.wəˈræn.toʊ, -ˈrɑːn-, -wɔːˈ-

Qur'an, Quran kɒrˈɑːn, kɔːˈrɑːn, kʊ-, kə-, ⓤⓢ kəˈrɑːn, kɔː-, kʊ-, -ˈræn

qursh ˈkuː.əʃ; kʊəʃ, ⓤⓢ ˈkuː.ɚʃ; ⓤⓢ kʊrʃ

Quy kwaɪ

q.v. ˌkjuːˈviː, ˌwɪtʃˈsiː, ˌkwɒdˈvɪd.eɪ, ⓤⓢ ˌkjuːˈviː, ˌwɪtʃˈsiː, ˌkwɑːdˈvɪd.eɪ

qwerty, QWERTY ˈkwɜː.ti, ⓤⓢ ˈkwɝː.t̬i

Q

R

Pronouncing the letter R

→ *See also* **RRH**

In British English, **r** is pronounced only where it appears before a vowel. In American English, **r** is pronounced in all positions, e.g.:

red	red
bore	bɔːʳ (US) bɔːr
boring	ˈbɔː.rɪŋ ˈbɔːr.ɪŋ

See the discussion at LIAISON in the Glossary for comments concerning 'linking r' in British English.

In addition

In the word *iron*, **r** is not pronounced in British English but colours the vowel in the second syllable in US English, e.g.:

iron	aɪən (US) ˈaɪ.ɚn, aɪrn

r, R ɑːʳ, (US) ɑːr -ˈs -z
Ra rɑː
Rabat rəˈbɑːt, rɑː-, -ˈbæt, (US) rəˈbɑːt, rɑː-
rabbet ˈræb.ɪt **-s** -s **-ing** -ɪŋ **-ed** -ɪd
rabbi ˈræb.aɪ **-s** -z
rabbinate ˈræb.ɪ.nət, ˈ-ə-, -nɪt, -neɪt, (US) -ɪ.nɪt, -neɪt **-s** -s
rabbinic rəˈbɪn.ɪk, ræbˈɪn-, (US) rəˈbɪn- **-al** -ᵊl **-ally** -ᵊl.i, -li
rabb|it ˈræb|.ɪt **-its** -ɪts **-iting** -ɪ.tɪŋ, (US) -ɪ.t̬ɪŋ **-ited** -ɪ.tɪd, (US) -ɪ.t̬ɪd **ˈrabbit ˌhole; ˈrabbit ˌhutch; ˈrabbit ˌwarren**
rabble ˈræb.ᵊl **-s** -z
rabble-rous|er ˈræb.ᵊlˌraʊ.z|əʳ, (US) -z|ɚ **-ers** -əz, (US) -ɚz **-ing** -ɪŋ
Rabelais ˈræb.ᵊl.eɪ, (US) ˌræb.əˈleɪ, ˈ---
Rabelaisian ˌræb.ᵊlˈeɪ.zi.ən, -ʒᵊn, (US) -əˈleɪ.ʒᵊn, ˈ-zi.ən
rabid ˈræb.ɪd, ˈreɪ.bɪd, (US) ˈræb.ɪd **-ly** -li **-ness** -nəs, -nɪs
rabies ˈreɪ.biːz, -biz
Rabin ˈreɪ.bɪn *Israeli politician:* ræbˈiːn, (US) rɑːˈbiːn
Rabindranath Tagore rəˌbɪn.drə.nɑːt.təˈgɔːʳ, -nɑːθ-, (US) -ˌben.drə.nɑːt.təˈgɔːr, -nɑːθ-
Rabinowitz rəˈbɪn.ə.wɪts, ræbˈɪn-, -vɪts
Raby ˈreɪ.bi
RAC ˌɑːr.eɪˈsiː, (US) ˌɑːr-
Racal® ˈreɪ.kᵊl, -kɔːl
raccoon rəˈkuːn, rækˈuːn, (US) rækˈuːn, rəˈkuːn **-s** -z
rac|e reɪs **-es** -ɪz **-ing** -ɪŋ **-ed** -t **-er/s** -əʳ/z, (US) -ɚ/z **ˌrace reˈlations** (US) **ˈrace ˌrelations**
racecar ˈreɪs.kɑːʳ, (US) -kɑːr **-s** -z
racecours|e ˈreɪs.kɔːs, (US) -kɔːrs **-es** -ɪz
racegoer ˈreɪsˌgəʊ.əʳ, (US) -ˌgoʊ.ɚ **-s** -z
racehors|e ˈreɪs.hɔːs, (US) -ˌhɔːrs **-es** -ɪz
raceme ˈræs.iːm, ˈreɪ.siːm; rəˈsiːm, ræsˈiːm, (US) reɪˈsiːm, rə- **-s** -z
race-meeting ˈreɪsˌmiː.tɪŋ, (US) -t̬ɪŋ **-s** -z
racemic rəˈsiː.mɪk, ræsˈiː-, reɪˈsiː-, -ˈsem.ɪk, (US) reɪˈsiː-, rə-
racetrack ˈreɪs.træk **-s** -s
Rachael, Rachel ˈreɪ.tʃᵊl
Rachelle rəˈʃel; ˈreɪ.tʃᵊl
rachitic rəˈkɪt.ɪk, rækˈɪt-, (US) rəˈkɪt.ɪk
rachitis rəˈkaɪ.tɪs, rækˈaɪ-, -təs, (US) -t̬ɪs, -t̬əs
Rachman ˈræk.mən
Rachmaninoff, Rachmaninov rækˈmæn.ɪ.nɒf, ræxˈ-, (US) rɑːkˈmɑːn.ɪ.nɔːf
rachmanism, R~ ˈræk.mə.nɪ.zᵊm
racial ˈreɪ.ʃᵊl, -ʃi.əl, (US) ˈ-ʃᵊl **-ly** -i
racial|ism ˈreɪ.ʃᵊl|.ɪ.zᵊm, -ʃi.ᵊl|-, (US) ˈ-ʃᵊl|- **-ist/s** -ɪst/s
Racine *English personal name, city in US:* rəˈsiːn, (US) rə-, reɪ- *French author:* ræsˈiːn, rəˈsiːn, (US) rɑːˈsiːn, rə-
rac|ism ˈreɪ.s|ɪ.zᵊm **-ist/s** -ɪst/s
rack ræk **-s** -s **-ing** -ɪŋ **-ed** -t
rack|et ˈræk|.ɪt **-ets** -ɪts **-eting** -ɪ.tɪŋ, (US) -ɪ.t̬ɪŋ **-eted** -ɪ.tɪd, (US) -ɪ.t̬ɪd **-ety** -ə.ti, -ɪ.ti, (US) -ə.t̬i
racketball ˈræk.ɪt.bɔːl, (US) -bɔːl, -bɑːl
racketeer ˌræk.ɪˈtɪəʳ, -əˈ-, (US) -əˈtɪr **-s** -z **-ing** -ɪŋ **-ed** -d
Rackham ˈræk.əm
rack|-rent ˈræk|.rent **-rents** -rents **-renter/s** -ˌren.təʳ/z, (US) -ˌren.t̬ɚ/z
raclette rækˈlet
raconteur ˌræk.ɒnˈtɜːʳ, -ɔ̃ːnˈ-, (US) -ɑːnˈtɝː, -ənˈ- **-s** -z
racoon rəˈkuːn, rækˈuːn, (US) rækˈuːn, rəˈkuːn **-s** -z
racquet ˈræk.ɪt **-s** -s
racquetball ˈræk.ɪt.bɔːl, (US) -bɔːl, -bɑːl
rac|y ˈreɪ.s|i **-ier** -i.əʳ, (US) -i.ɚ **-iest** -i.ɪst, -i.əst **-ily** -ᵊl.i, -ɪ.li **-iness** -ɪ.nəs, -ɪ.nɪs
rad ræd **-s** -z
RADA ˈrɑː.də
radar ˈreɪ.dɑːʳ, (US) -dɑːr
Radcliffe ˈræd.klɪf
raddled ˈræd.ᵊld
Radetzky rəˈdet.ski, rædˈet-, (US) rɑːˈdet-, rə-
Radford ˈræd.fəd, (US) -fɚd
radial ˈreɪ.di.əl **-ly** -i
radian ˈreɪ.di.ən **-s** -z
radianc|e ˈreɪ.di.ənts **-es** -ɪz
radiant ˈreɪ.di.ənt **-s** -s **-ly** -li
radi|ate ˈreɪ.di|.eɪt **-ates** -eɪts **-ating** -eɪ.tɪŋ, (US) -eɪ.t̬ɪŋ **-ated** -eɪ.tɪd, (US) -eɪ.t̬ɪd
radiation ˌreɪ.diˈeɪ.ʃᵊn **-s** -z **radiˈation ˌsickness**
radiator ˈreɪ.di.eɪ.təʳ, (US) -t̬ɚ **-s** -z
radic|al ˈræd.ɪ.k|ᵊl **-als** -ᵊlz **-ally** -ᵊl.i, -li **-alness** -ᵊl.nəs, -ᵊl.nɪs **-alism** -ᵊl.ɪ.zᵊm **ˌradical ˈchic; ˌradical ˈsign**
radicaliz|e, -is|e ˈræd.ɪ.kᵊl.aɪz **-es** -ɪz **-ing** -ɪŋ **-ed** -d
radicchio rəˈdɪk.i.əʊ, rædˈɪk-, (US) rəˈdiː.ki.oʊ, rɑː-, ˈ-kjoʊ **-s** -z
Radice rəˈdiː.tʃi, -tʃeɪ
radicle ˈræd.ɪ.kᵊl **-s** -z
radii (plural of **radius**) ˈreɪ.di.aɪ
radio n, v ˈreɪ.di.əʊ, (US) -oʊ **-s** -z **-ing** -ɪŋ **-ed** -d **ˌradio aˈlarm; ˈradio ˌcar; ˌradio ˈtelescope; ˈradio ˌwave**
radioactive ˌreɪ.di.əʊˈæk.tɪv, (US) -oʊˈ- **-ly** -li *stress shift:* **ˌradioactive ˈwaste**
radioactivity ˌreɪ.di.əʊ.ækˈtɪv.ə.ti, -ɪ.ti, (US) -oʊ.ækˈtɪv.ə.t̬i
radiocarbon ˌreɪ.di.əʊˈkɑː.bᵊn, (US) -oʊˈkɑːr-
radiogenic ˌreɪ.di.əʊˈdʒen.ɪk, (US) -oʊˈ- *stress shift:* **ˌradiogenic ˈoutput**
radiogram ˈreɪ.di.əʊ.græm, (US) -oʊ- **-s** -z
radiograph ˈreɪ.di.əʊ.grɑːf, -græf, (US) -oʊ.græf **-s** -s
radiograph|y ˌreɪ.diˈɒg.rə.f|i, (US) -ˈɑː.grə- **-er/s** -əʳ/z, (US) -ɚ/z
Radiohead ˈreɪ.di.əʊ.hed, (US) -oʊ-
radioisotope ˌreɪ.di.əʊˈaɪ.sə.təʊp, (US) -oʊˈaɪ.sə.toʊp **-s** -s
radiolo|cate ˌreɪ.di.əʊ.ləʊ|ˈkeɪt, (US) -oʊ.loʊˈ- **-cates** -ˈkeɪts **-cating** -ˈkeɪ.tɪŋ, (US) -ˈkeɪ.t̬ɪŋ **-cated** -ˈkeɪ.tɪd, (US) -ˈkeɪ.t̬ɪd
radiolocation ˌreɪ.di.əʊ.ləʊˈkeɪ.ʃᵊn, (US) -oʊ.loʊˈ-

radiolog|y ˌreɪ.diˈɒl.ə.dʒ|i, (US) -ˈɑː.lə- **-ist/s** -ɪst/s
radiometer ˌreɪ.diˈɒm.ɪ.təʳ, ˈ-ə-, (US) -ˈɑː.mə.ţɚ **-s** -z
radionics ˌreɪ.diˈɒn.ɪks, (US) -ˈɑː.nɪks
radiopag|e ˌreɪ.di.əʊˈpeɪdʒ, ˈreɪ.di.əʊ.peɪdʒ, (US) ˈreɪ.di.oʊ- **-es** -ɪz **-ing** -ɪŋ **-ed** -d **-er/s** -əʳ/z, (US) -ɚ/z
radiophone ˈreɪ.di.əʊ.fəʊn, (US) -oʊ.foʊn **-s** -z
radiophonic ˌreɪ.di.əʊˈfɒn.ɪk, (US) -oʊˈfɑː.nɪk
radiotelegram ˌreɪ.di.əʊˈtel.ɪ.græm, ˈ-ə-, (US) -oʊˈtel.ə- **-s** -z
radiotelegraph ˌreɪ.di.əʊˈtel.ɪ.grɑːf, ˈ-ə-, -græf, (US) -oʊˈtel.ə.græf **-s** -s
radiotelephone ˌreɪ.di.əʊˈtel.ɪ.fəʊn, ˈ-ə-, (US) -oʊˈtel.ə.foʊn **-s** -z
radiotherap|y ˌreɪ.di.əʊˈθer.ə.p|i, (US) -oʊˈ- **-ist/s** -ɪst/s
radish ˈræd.ɪʃ **-es** -ɪz
radium ˈreɪ.di.əm
radi|us ˈreɪ.di|.əs **-i** -aɪ
rad|ix ˈreɪ.d|ɪks, ˈræd- **-ixes** -ɪk.sɪz **-ices** -ɪ.siːz, (US) ˈræd.ə.siːz, ˈreɪ.də-
Radlett ˈræd.lɪt, -lət
Radley ˈræd.li
Radnor ˈræd.nəʳ, -nɔːʳ, (US) -nɚ, -nɔːr **-shire** -ʃəʳ, -ʃɪəʳ, (US) -ʃɚ, -ʃɪr
radon ˈreɪ.dɒn, (US) -dɑːn
Radovan ˈræd.ə.væn
Radox® ˈreɪ.dɒks, (US) -dɑːks
Rae reɪ
Raeburn ˈreɪ.bɜːn, (US) -bɝːn **-s** -z
Raf ræf
RAF ˌɑːʳ.eɪˈef; ræf, (US) ˌɑːr-
Rafferty ˈræf.ə.ti, (US) -ɚ.ţi
raffia ˈræf.i.ə
raffish ˈræf.ɪʃ **-ly** -li **-ness** -nəs, -nɪs
raffl|e ˈræf.əl **-es** -z **-ing** -ɪŋ, ˈræf.lɪŋ **-ed** -d ˈ**raffle** ˌ**ticket**
Raffles ˈræf.əlz
Rafsanjani ˌræf.sɑːnˈdʒɑː.ni, -sænˈ-, -ˈdʒæn.i; -dʒɑːˈniː, (US) ˌrɑːf.sɑːnˈdʒɑː.ni; (US) ˌrʌf.sənˈdʒæn.i
raft rɑːft, (US) ræft **-s** -s **-ing** -ɪŋ **-ed** -ɪd
rafter ˈrɑːf.təʳ, (US) ˈræf.tɚ **-s** -z **-ed** -d
rag ræg **-s** -z **-ging** -ɪŋ **-ged** -d ˌ**rag** ˈ**doll**; ˈ**rag** ˌ**trade**
raga ˈrɑː.gə; rɑːg, (US) ˈrɑː.gə **-s** -z
ragamuffin ˈræg.əˌmʌf.ɪn **-s** -z
rag-and-bone|-man ˌræg.ənˈbəʊn|.mæn, -əmˈ-, (US) -ənˈboʊn- **-men** -men
ragbag ˈræg.bæg **-s** -z
rag|e reɪdʒ **-es** -ɪz **-ing/ly** -ɪŋ/li **-ed** -d
ragga ˈræg.ə
ragged ˈræg.ɪd **-er** -əʳ, (US) -ɚ **-est** -ɪst, -əst **-ly** -li **-ness** -nəs, -nɪs **-y** -i
raggle-taggle ˈræg.əlˌtæg.əl, ˌræg.əlˈtæg-
raglan, R~ ˈræg.lən ˌ**raglan** ˈ**sleeve**
ragout rægˈuː, ˈ--, (US) rægˈuː **-s** -z
rags-to-riches ˌrægz.təˈrɪtʃ.ɪz
ragtag ˈræg.tæg
ragtime ˈræg.taɪm
ragweed ˈræg.wiːd
ragwort ˈræg.wɜːt, (US) -wɝːt, -wɔːrt **-s** -s
Rahman ˈrɑː.mən
rah-rah ˈrɑː.rɑː
raid reɪd **-s** -z **-ing** -ɪŋ **-ed** -ɪd **-er/s** -əʳ/z, (US) -ɚ/z
Raikes reɪks
rail reɪl **-s** -z **-ing** -ɪŋ **-ed** -d
railcard ˈreɪl.kɑːd, (US) -kɑːrd **-s** -z
railhead ˈreɪl.hed **-s** -z
railing ˈreɪ.lɪŋ **-s** -z
railler|y ˈreɪ.lər|.i **-ies** -iz
railroad ˈreɪl.rəʊd, (US) -roʊd **-s** -z **-ing** -ɪŋ **-ed** -ɪd
Railtrack® ˈreɪl.træk
railway ˈreɪl.weɪ **-s** -z
railway|man ˈreɪl.weɪ|.mən, -mæn **-men** -mən, -men
raiment ˈreɪ.mənt
rain reɪn **-s** -z **-ing** -ɪŋ **-ed** -d **-less** -ləs, -lɪs ˈ**rain** ˌ**forest**; ˌ**take a** ˈ**rain** ˌ**check**; **come** ˌ**rain or** ˈ**shine**
rainbow ˈreɪn.bəʊ, ˈreɪm-, (US) ˈreɪn.boʊ **-s** -z ˌ**rainbow** ˈ**trout**
rainbow-colo(u)red ˈreɪn.bəʊˌkʌl.əd, ˈreɪm-, (US) ˈreɪn.boʊˌkʌl.ɚd
raincoat ˈreɪn.kəʊt, ˈreɪŋ-, (US) ˈreɪn.koʊt **-s** -s
raindrop ˈreɪn.drɒp, (US) -drɑːp **-s** -s
Raine reɪn
Rainey ˈreɪ.ni
rainfall ˈreɪn.fɔːl, (US) -fɔːl, -fɑːl
Rainford ˈreɪn.fəd, (US) -fɚd
rainforest ˈreɪnˌfɒr.ɪst, (US) -ˌfɔːr- **-s** -s
rain-gaug|e ˈreɪn.geɪdʒ, ˈreɪŋ-, (US) ˈreɪn- **-es** -ɪz
Rainier *prince of Monaco:* ˈreɪ.ni.eɪ, (US) reɪˈnɪr, rə-; (US) renˈjeɪ *Mount:* ˈreɪ.ni.əʳ; reɪˈnɪəʳ, rə-, (US) rəˈnɪr, reɪ-
rainmak|ing ˈreɪnˌmeɪ.k|ɪŋ, ˈreɪm-, (US) ˈreɪn- **-er/s** -əʳ/z, (US) -ɚ/z
rainproof ˈreɪn.pruːf, ˈreɪm-, (US) ˈreɪn-
rainstorm ˈreɪn.stɔːm, (US) -stɔːrm **-s** -z
rainwater ˈreɪnˌwɔː.təʳ, (US) -ˌwɑː.ţɚ, -ˌwɔː-
Rainworth ˈreɪn.wəθ, -wɜːθ, (US) -wɝːθ, -wɚθ
rain|y ˈreɪ.n|i **-ier** -i.əʳ, (US) -i.ɚ **-iest** -i.ɪst, -i.əst **-iness** -ɪ.nəs, -ɪ.nɪs ˌ**save something for a** ˌ**rainy** ˈ**day**
Raisa raɪˈiː.sə, rɑː-, (US) rɑː-
rais|e reɪz **-es** -ɪz **-ing** -ɪŋ **-ed** -d
raisin ˈreɪ.zən **-s** -z
raison d'être ˌreɪ.zɔ̃ːŋˈdet.rə, -zɒnˈ-, (US) ˌreɪ.zoʊnˈdet.rə, ˌrez.ɑːnˈ-, -ˈdet.rə
raj, R~ rɑːdʒ, rɑːʒ, (US) rɑːdʒ
raja(h), R~ ˈrɑː.dʒə, (US) -dʒə, -dʒɑː **-s** -z
Rajasthan ˌrɑː.dʒəˈstɑːn, (US) -dʒɑːˈ-
Rajasthani ˌrɑː.dʒəˈstɑː.ni, (US) -dʒɑːˈ-
Rajiv rɑːˈdʒiːv *stress shift:* ˌ**Rajiv** ˈ**Ghandi**
Rajput ˈrɑːdʒ.pʊt, (US) -puːt
Rajputana ˌrɑːdʒ.pʊˈtɑː.nə, (US) -puːˈ-
rak|e reɪk **-es** -s **-ing** -ɪŋ **-ed** -t
rakee ˈrɑː.ki, ˈræk.i; rɑːˈkiː
rake-off ˈreɪk.ɒf, (US) -ɑːf **-s** -s
raki ˈrɑː.ki, ˈræk.i; rɑːˈkiː
rakish ˈreɪ.kɪʃ **-ly** -li **-ness** -nəs, -nɪs
rale rɑːl, ræl, (US) rɑːl **-s** -z
Rale(i)gh ˈrɔː.li, ˈrɑː-, ˈræl.i, (US) ˈrɑː.li, ˈrɔː-

> Note: The family of the late Sir Walter Raleigh pronounced /ˈrɔː.li/ (US) /ˈrɑː-, rɔː-/. Raleigh bicycles are generally called /ˈræl.i/ in the UK and /ˈrɑː.li/ in the US. When used as the name of a ship, the British English pronunciation is /ˈræl.i/.

rallentand|o ˌræl.enˈtæn.d|əʊ, -ənˈ-, -ɪnˈ-, (US) ˌrɑː.lənˈtɑːn.d|oʊ **-os** -əʊz, (US) -oʊz **-i** -i
rall|y ˈræl|.i **-ies** -iz **-ying** -i.ɪŋ **-ied** -id ˈ**rally** ˌ**driver**
rallycross ˈræl.i.krɒs, (US) -krɑːs
Ralph rælf, reɪf
Ralph Cross ˌrɑːlfˈkrɒs, ˌrælf-, (US) ˌrælfˈkrɑːs
Ralston ˈrɔːl.stən
ram, R~ ræm **-s** -z **-ming** -ɪŋ **-med** -d **-mer/s** -əʳ/z, (US) -ɚ/z
RAM ræm
Rama(h) ˈrɑː.mə
Ramad(h)an ˌræm.əˈdæn, ˌrɑː.məˈ-, -ˈdɑːn, ˈ---, (US) ˌræm.əˈdɑːn, ˌrɑː.məˈ-
Ramage ˈræm.ɪdʒ
Ramallah rəˈmɑː.lə, -ˈmæl-
Ramaphosa ˌræm.əˈpəʊ.zə, (US) -ˈpoʊ-
Ramayana rɑːˈmaɪ.ə.nə, rə-, -ˈmɑː-, (US) rɑːˈmɑː.jə-
Rambert ˈrɑ̃ːm.beə, -ˈ-, (US) rɑːmˈber
rambl|e ˈræm.bəl **-es** -z **-ing** -ɪŋ, ˈræm.blɪŋ **-ed** -d
rambler, R~ ˈræm.bləʳ, (US) -blɚ **-s** -z
rambling ˈræm.blɪŋ, -bəl.ɪŋ **-s** -z **-ly** -li
Rambo ˈræm.bəʊ, (US) -boʊ
Ramboesque ˌræm.bəʊˈesk, (US) -boʊˈ-
Rambouillet ˌrɑ̃ːm.buːˈjeɪ, -ˈ--, (US) ˌræm.buːˈjeɪ
rambunctious ræmˈbʌŋk.ʃəs **-ly** -li **-ness** -nəs, -nɪs
rambutan ræmˈbuː.tən; ˌræm.bʊˈtæn, -ˈtɑːn, (US) ræmˈbuː.tən **-s** -z
ramekin, ramequin ˈræm.ɪ.kɪn, ˈ-ə-, ˈ-kɪn, (US) ˈ-ə.kɪn **-s** -z
Rameses ˈræm.ɪ.siːz, ˈ-ə-
ramification ˌræm.ɪ.fɪˈkeɪ.ʃən, ˌ-ə-, -fəˈ- **-s** -z
rami|fy ˈræm.ɪ|.faɪ, ˈ-ə- **-fies** -faɪz **-fying** -faɪ.ɪŋ **-fied** -faɪd

R

Ramillies ˈræm.ɪ.liz
Ramirez rəˈmɪə.rez, (US) -ˈmɪr.ez, -ˈmiː.reɪs, rɑːˈmɪr.ez, -ˈmiː.reθ
ramjet ˈræm.dʒet **-s** -s
Ramos ˈrɑː.mɒs, (US) ˈreɪ.moʊs, rɑːˈmoʊs
ramp ræmp **-s** -s **-ing** -ɪŋ **-ed** -t
rampag|e **n** ˈræm.peɪdʒ, -ˈ-, (US) ˈræm.peɪdʒ **-es** -ɪz **v** ræmˈpeɪdʒ, ˈ-- **-es** -ɪz **-ing** -ɪŋ **-ed** -d
rampageous ræmˈpeɪ.dʒəs **-ly** -li **-ness** -nəs, -nɪs
rampant ˈræm.pənt **-ly** -li
rampart ˈræm.pɑːt, -pət, (US) -pɑːrt, -pɚt **-s** -s
rampion ˈræm.pi.ən **-s** -z
Rampling ˈræm.plɪŋ
Ramprakash ˈræm.prə.kæʃ
Rampton ˈræm*p*.tən
ram-raid ˈræm.reɪd **-s** -z **-er/s** -əʳ/z, (US) -ɚ/z **-ing** -ɪŋ
ramrod ˈræm.rɒd, (US) -rɑːd **-s** -z
Ramsaran ˈrɑːm*p*.sᵊr.ən
Ramsay ˈræm.zi
Ramsbottom ˈræmzˌbɒt.əm, (US) -ˌbɑː.t̬əm
Ramsden ˈræmz.dən
Ramses ˈræm.siːz
Ramsey ˈræm.zi
Ramsgate ˈræmz.geɪt, -gɪt
ramshackle ˈræmˌʃæk.ᵊl
ran (from **run**) ræn
Ranariddh ˌræn.əˈrɪt
rance rænts
Rance *surname:* rɑːnts, (US) rænts
ranch rɑːntʃ, ræntʃ, (US) ræntʃ **-es** -ɪz **-ing** -ɪŋ **-ed** -t **-er/s** -əʳ/z, (US) -ɚ/z ˈ**ranch** ˌ**house**
ranchero rɑːnˈtʃeə.rəʊ, ræn-, (US) rænˈtʃer.oʊ **-s** -z
rancid ˈrænt.sɪd **-ness** -nəs, -nɪs
rancidity rænˈsɪd.ə.ti, -ɪ.ti, (US) -ə.t̬i
ranco(u)r ˈræŋ.kəʳ, (US) -kɚ
rancorous ˈræŋ.kᵊr.əs **-ly** -li
rand, R~ *South African money and region:* rænd, rɑːnd, rɑːnt, rɒnt, (US) rænd, rɑːnd, rɑːnt *strip, border:* rænd **-s** -z
Randall, Randell ˈræn.dᵊl
Randalstown ˈræn.dᵊlz.taʊn
R and B ˌɑːʳ.ᵊnˈdbiː, -ᵊmˈ-, (US) ˌɑːr-
R and D ˌɑːʳ.ᵊnˈdiː, (US) ˌɑːr-
Randi ˈræn.di
Randle ˈræn.dᵊl
Randolph ˈræn.dɒlf, -dᵊlf, (US) -dɑːlf, -dᵊlf
random ˈræn.dəm **-ly** -li **-ness** -nəs, -nɪs
random-access ˌræn.dəmˈæk.ses *stress shift:* ˌ**random-access** ˈ**memory**
randomization, -isa- ˌræn.dəm.aɪˈzeɪ.ʃᵊn, -ɪˈ-, (US) -əˈ-
randomiz|e, -is|e ˈræn.də.maɪz **-es** -ɪz **-ing** -ɪŋ **-ed** -d
R and R ˌɑːʳ.ᵊndˈɑːʳ, (US) ˌɑːr.ᵊndˈɑːr
rand|y, R~ ˈræn.d|i **-ier** -i.əʳ, (US) -i.ɚ **-iest** -i.ɪst, -i.əst **-ily** -ᵊl.i, -ɪ.li **-iness** -ɪ.nəs, -ɪ.nɪs
ranee, R~ ˈrɑː.niː, ˌ-ˈ-, (US) ˈrɑː.niː **-s** -z
Ranelagh ˈræn.ɪ.lə, -ᵊl.ə, -ɔː, (US) -ᵊl.ə
rang (from **ring**) ræŋ
rang|e reɪndʒ **-es** -ɪz **-ing** -ɪŋ **-ed** -d
range-finder ˈreɪndʒˌfaɪn.dəʳ, (US) -dɚ **-s** -z
ranger, R~ ˈreɪn.dʒəʳ, (US) -dʒɚ **-s** -z
Rangoon ˌræŋˈguːn, (US) ˌræn-, ˌræŋ- *stress shift:* ˌ**Rangoon** ˈ**streets**
rang|y ˈreɪn.dʒ|i **-ier** -i.əʳ, (US) -i.ɚ **-iest** -i.ɪst, -i.əst **-iness** -ɪ.nəs, -ɪ.nɪs
rani ˈrɑː.niː, ˌ-ˈ-, (US) ˈrɑː.niː **-s** -z
rank, R~ ræŋk **-s** -s **-ing** -ɪŋ **-ed** -t **-ly** -li **-ness** -nəs, -nɪs ˌ**rank and** ˈ**file**
Rankin(e) ˈræŋ.kɪn
rankl|e ˈræŋ.kᵊl **-es** -z **-ing** -ɪŋ, ˈræŋ.klɪŋ **-ed** -d
Rannoch ˈræn.ək, -əx, (US) -ək
ransack ˈræn.sæk **-s** -s **-ing** -ɪŋ **-ed** -t **-er/s** -əʳ/z, (US) -ɚ/z
ransom, R~ ˈrænt.sᵊm **-s** -z **-ing** -ɪŋ **-ed** -d **-er/s** -əʳ/z, (US) -ɚ/z
Ransome ˈrænt.səm
rant rænt **-s** -s **-ing/ly** -ɪŋ/li, (US) ˈræn.t̬ɪŋ/li **-ed** -ɪd, (US) ˈræn.t̬ɪd **-er/s** -əʳ/z, (US) ˈræn.t̬ɚ/z
Rantzen ˈrænt.sᵊn
Ranulph ˈræn.ʌlf, -ᵊlf
ranuncul|us rəˈnʌŋ.kjə.l|əs, rænˈʌŋ-, -kjʊ-, (US) rəˈnʌŋ- **-uses** -ə.sɪz **-i** -aɪ
Ranworth ˈræn.wəθ, -wɜːθ, (US) -wɚθ, -wɜːθ
rap ræp **-s** -s **-ping** -ɪŋ **-ped** -t **-per/s** -əʳ/z, (US) -ɚ/z
rapacious rəˈpeɪ.ʃəs **-ly** -li **-ness** -nəs, -nɪs
rapacity rəˈpæs.ə.ti, -ɪ.ti, (US) -ə.t̬i
rap|e reɪp **-es** -s **-ing** -ɪŋ **-ed** -t **-ist/s** -ɪst/s
Raphael *angel:* ˈræf.eɪ.əl; ˌræf.ɑːˈel; ˈræf.eɪl; ˈreɪ.fi.əl; *and in Jewish usage:* ˈreɪ.fᵊl, (US) ˈræf.i.əl; (US) ˌrɑː.fiˈel; (US) ˈreɪ.fi.el *modern name:* ˈreɪ.fᵊl, ˈræf.eɪl *Italian artist:* ˈræf.eɪ.əl, -fi.əl, -feɪl, (US) ˈræf.i.əl; (US) ˌrɑː.fiˈel; (US) ˈreɪ.fi.el
rapid ˈræp.ɪd **-est** -ɪst, -əst **-ly** -li **-ness** -nəs, -nɪs **-s** -z ˌ**rapid** ˈ**eye** ˌ**movement**; ˌ**rapid** ˈ**transit**
rapid-fire ˌræp.ɪdˈfaɪəʳ, -ˈfaɪ.əʳ, (US) -ˈfaɪ.ɚ *stress shift:* ˌ**rapid-fire** ˈ**shooting**
rapidity rəˈpɪd.ə.ti, ræpˈɪd-, -ɪ.ti, (US) rəˈpɪd.ə.t̬i
rapier ˈreɪ.pi.əʳ, (US) -pi.ɚ, ˈ-pjɚ **-s** -z
rapine ˈræp.aɪn, -ɪn, (US) -ɪn
rapparee ˌræp.ᵊrˈiː, (US) -əˈriː **-s** -z
rappel ræpˈel **-s** -z **-ling** -ɪŋ **-led** -d
rapport ræpˈɔːʳ, rəˈpɔːʳ; ˈræp.ɔːʳ, (US) ræpˈɔːr, rəˈpɔːr
rapporteur ˌræp.ɔːˈtɜːʳ, (US) -ɔːrˈtɜː **-s** -z
rapprochement ræpˈrɒʃ.mɑ̃ːŋ, -ˈrəʊʃ-, (US) ˌræp.rɔːʃˈmɑ̃ːŋ, -roʊʃˈ- **-s** -z
rapscallion ræpˈskæl.jən, ˈ-i.ən, (US) ˈ-jən **-s** -z
rapt ræpt
rapture ˈræp.tʃəʳ, (US) -tʃɚ **-s** -z **-d** -d
rapturous ˈræp.tʃᵊr.əs **-ly** -li
Rapunzel rəˈpʌn.zᵊl
Raquel rəˈkel, rækˈel
rara avis ˌrɑː.rəˈæv.ɪs, ˌreə-, -ˈeɪ.vɪs, (US) ˌrer.əˈeɪ.vɪs
rare reəʳ, (US) rer **-r** -əʳ, (US) -ɚ **-st** -ɪst, -əst **-ly** -li **-ness** -nəs, -nɪs ˌ**rare** ˈ**earth**
rarebit ˈreə.bɪt, (US) ˈrer- **-s** -s

> Note: The pronunciation /ˈræb.ɪt/ is sometimes used in British English in the phrase **Welsh rarebit**.

rarefaction ˌreə.rɪˈfæk.ʃᵊn, -rəˈ-, (US) ˌrer.əˈ-
rarefication ˌreə.rɪ.fɪˈkeɪ.ʃᵊn, -rə-, -fəˈ-, (US) ˌrer.ə-
rare|fy ˈreə.rɪ|.faɪ, -rə-, (US) ˈrer.ə- **-fies** -faɪz **-fying** -faɪ.ɪŋ **-fied** -faɪd
raring **adj** ˈreə.rɪŋ, (US) ˈrer.ɪŋ
rarit|y ˈreə.rə.t|i, -ɪ.t|i, (US) ˈrer.ə.t̬|i **-ies** -iz
Rarotonga ˌreə.rəʊˈtɒŋ.gə, ˌrær.əʊˈ-, (US) ˌrɑːr.oʊˈtɔːŋ.gə, ˌrer.əˈ-
Ras al Khaimah ˌrɑːs.ælˈkaɪ.mə
rascal ˈrɑː.skᵊl, (US) ˈræs.kᵊl **-s** -z
rascalit|y rɑːˈskæl.ə.t|i, -ɪ.t|i, (US) ræsˈkæl.ə.t̬|i **-ies** -iz
rascally ˈrɑː.skᵊl.i, (US) ˈræs.kᵊl-
ras|e reɪz **-es** -ɪz **-ing** -ɪŋ **-ed** -d
rash ræʃ **-es** -ɪz **-er** -əʳ, (US) -ɚ **-est** -ɪst, -əst **-ly** -li **-ness** -nəs, -nɪs
rasher ˈræʃ.əʳ, (US) -ɚ **-s** -z
Rashid ræʃˈiːd, (US) ræʃ-, rɑːˈʃiːd
rasp rɑːsp, (US) ræsp **-s** -s **-ing** -ɪŋ **-ed** -t
raspberr|y ˈrɑːz.bᵊr|.i, ˈrɑːs-, (US) ˈræzˌber|.i, -bɚ- **-ies** -iz
Rasputin ræsˈpjuː.tɪn, -ˈpuː-, (US) -ˈpjuː-
rasp|y ˈrɑː.sp|i, (US) ˈræsp|.i **-iness** -ɪ.nəs, -ɪ.nɪs
Rasselas ˈræs.ɪ.ləs, (US) ˈ-ə-, -læs
Rasta ˈræs.tə, (US) ˈrɑː.stə, ˈræs.tə **-s** -z
Rastafarian ˌræs.təˈfeə.ri.ən, (US) ˌrɑː.stəˈfer.i-, ˌræs.təˈ-, -ˈfɑːr- **-s** -z **-ism** -ɪ.zᵊm
Rasta|man ˈræs.tə|.mæn, (US) ˈrɑː.stə-, ˈræs.tə- **-men** -men
rat ræt **-s** -s **-ting** -ɪŋ, (US) ˈræt̬.ɪŋ **-ted** -ɪd, (US) ˈræt̬.ɪd ˈ**rat** ˌ**race**; ˈ**rat** ˌ**trap**
rata ˈreɪ.tə, (US) ˈrɑː.t̬ə **-s** -z
rata (in **pro rata**) ˈrɑː.tə, ˈreɪ-, (US) -t̬ə
ratability ˌreɪ.təˈbɪl.ə.ti, -ɪ.ti, (US) -t̬əˈbɪl.ə.t̬i
ratab|le ˈreɪ.tə.b|ᵊl, (US) -t̬ə- **-ly** -li
ratafia ˌræt.əˈfiː.ə **-s** -z
rataplan ˌræt.əˈplæn, (US) ˈræt̬.ə.plæn
rat-arsed ˈræt.ɑːst, (US) ˈræt̬.ɑːrst
rat-a-tat ˌræt.əˈtæt, ˈ---, (US) ˌræt̬-, ˈ---
ratatouille ˌræt.əˈtuː.i, -ˈtwiː, (US) -ˈtuː.i, ˌrɑː.tɑːˈ-
ratbag ˈræt.bæg **-s** -z
rat-catcher ˈrætˌkætʃ.əʳ, (US) -ɚ **-s** -z

R

ratchet ˈrætʃ.ɪt **-s** -s **-ing** -ɪŋ **-ed** -ɪd
Ratcliff(e) ˈræt.klɪf
rat|e reɪt **-es** -s **-ing** -ɪŋ, (US) ˈreɪ.t̬ɪŋ **-ed** -ɪd, (US) ˈreɪ.t̬ɪd ˌ**rate of exˈchange**
rateab|le ˈreɪ.tə.b|əl, (US) -t̬ə- **-ly** -li ˌ**rateable ˈvalue**
rate-cap ˈreɪt.kæp **-s** -s **-ping** -ɪŋ **-ped** -t
ratel ˈreɪ.təl, ˈrɑː-, -tel, (US) ˈreɪ.t̬əl, ˈrɑː- **-s** -z
ratepayer ˈreɪtˌpeɪ.əʳ, (US) -ɚ **-s** -z
Rath ræθ
Rathbone ˈræθ.bəʊn, -bən, (US) -boʊn, -bən
rather adv ˈrɑː.ðəʳ, (US) ˈræð.ɚ **interj** *British only, old-fashioned:* ˌrɑːˈðɜːʳ
Rather ˈræð.əʳ, (US) ˈræð.ɚ
Rathfarnham ræθˈfɑː.nəm, (US) -ˈfɑːr-
Rathlin ˈræθ.lɪn
ratification ˌræt.ɪ.fɪˈkeɪ.ʃən, ˌ-ə-, -fəˈ-, (US) ˌræt̬.ə- **-s** -z
rati|fy ˈræt.ɪ|.faɪ, ˈ-ə-, (US) ˈræt̬.ɪ-, ˈ-ə- **-fies** -faɪz **-fying** -faɪ.ɪŋ **-fied** -faɪd **-fier/s** -faɪ.əʳ/z, (US) -faɪ.ɚ/z
rating ˈreɪ.tɪŋ, (US) -t̬ɪŋ **-s** -z
ratio ˈreɪ.ʃi.əʊ, (US) -oʊ, ˈ-ʃoʊ **-s** -z
ratioci|nate ˌræt.iˈɒs.ɪ|.neɪt, ˌræʃ-, -ˈəʊ.sɪ-, -sə-, (US) ˌræʃ.iˈɑː.sə- **-nates** -neɪts **-nating** -neɪ.tɪŋ, (US) -neɪ.t̬ɪŋ **-nated** -neɪ.tɪd, (US) -neɪ.t̬ɪd
ratiocination ˌræt.i.ɒs.ɪˈneɪ.ʃən, ˌræʃ-, -əʊ.sɪˈ-, -səˈ-, (US) ˌræʃ.i.ɑː.səˈ- **-s** -z
ratio decidendi ˌræt.i.əʊˌdeɪ.sɪˈden.di, (US) ˌræt̬.i.oʊˌ-, ˌrɑː.t̬i-
ratio legis ˌræt.i.əʊˈleɪ.gɪs, (US) ˌræt̬.i.oʊˈleg.ɪs, ˌrɑː.t̬i-
ration ˈræʃ.ən, (US) ˈræʃ.ən, ˈreɪ- **-s** -z **-ing** -ɪŋ **-ed** -d
rational ˈræʃ.ən.əl, ˈ-nəl **-ly** -i
rationale ˌræʃ.əˈnɑːl, -ˈnæl, -ˈnɑː.leɪ, (US) -əˈnæl **-s** -z
rational|ism ˈræʃ.ən.əl|.ɪ.zəm, ˈ-nəl- **-ist/s** -ɪst/s
rationalistic ˌræʃ.ən.əlˈɪs.tɪk, ˌ-nəlˈ- **-ally** -əl.i, -li
rationality ˌræʃ.ənˈæl.ə.ti, -ɪ.ti, (US) -ə.t̬i
rationalization, -isa- ˌræʃ.ən.əl.aɪˈzeɪ.ʃən, ˌ-nəl-, -ɪˈ-, (US) -əˈ-
rationaliz|e, -is|e ˈræʃ.ən.əl.aɪz, ˈ-nəl-, (US) -ən.ə.laɪz, ˈ-nə- **-es** -ɪz **-ing** -ɪŋ **-ed** -d
Ratisbon ˈræt.ɪz.bɒn, -ɪs-, -əz-, -əs-, (US) -ɪz.bɑːn, -ɪs-
ratline ˈræt.lɪn **-s** -z
Ratner ˈræt.nəʳ, (US) -nɚ **-'s** -z
rat-race ˈræt.reɪs
rat-tail ˈræt.teɪl **-s** -z **-ed** -d
rattan rəˈtæn, rætˈæn **-s** -z
Rattigan ˈræt.ɪ.gən, ˈ-ə-, (US) ˈræt̬-
rattl|e, R~ ˈræt.əl, (US) ˈræt̬- **-es** -z **-ing** -ɪŋ, ˈræt.lɪŋ **-ed** -d **-er/s** -əʳ/z, (US) -ɚ/z, ˈræt.ləʳ/z, -lɚ/z
rattlesnake ˈræt.əl.sneɪk, (US) ˈræt̬- **-s** -s
rattling ˈræt.lɪŋ, -əl.ɪŋ, (US) ˈræt.lɪŋ, ˈræt̬.əl.ɪŋ
ratt|y, R~ ˈræt|.i, (US) ˈræt̬- **-ier** -i.əʳ, (US) -i.ɚ **-iest** -i.ɪst, -i.əst **-ily** -əl.i, -ɪ.li **-iness** -ɪ.nəs, -ɪ.nɪs
Ratzinger ˈræt.sɪŋ.əʳ, -zɪŋ-, -gəʳ, (US) -ɚ-, -gɚ
raucous ˈrɔː.kəs, (US) ˈrɑː-, ˈrɔː- **-ly** -li **-ness** -nəs, -nɪs
raunch|y ˈrɔːn.tʃ|i, (US) ˈrɑːn.tʃ|i, ˈrɔːn- **-ier** -i.əʳ, (US) -i.ɚ **-iest** -i.ɪst, -i.əst **-ily** -əl.i, -ɪ.li **-iness** -ɪ.nəs, -ɪ.nɪs
Raunds rɔːndz, (US) rɑːndz, rɔːndz
Rauschenberg ˈraʊ.ʃən.bɜːg, (US) -bɝːg
ravag|e ˈræv.ɪdʒ **-es** -ɪz **-ing** -ɪŋ **-ed** -d **-er/s** -əʳ/z, (US) -ɚ/z
Ravana rəˈvɑː.nə, (US) ˈrɑː.və-; (US) rəˈvɑː-
rav|e reɪv **-es** -z **-ing/s** -ɪŋ/z **-ed** -d
ravel ˈræv.əl **-s** -z **-(l)ing** -ɪŋ **-(l)ed** -d
Ravel *French composer:* rævˈel, (US) rəˈvel, rɑː-
ravelin ˈræv.əl.ɪn **-s** -z
raven, R~ n ˈreɪ.vən **-s** -z
raven v ˈræv.ən **-s** -z **-ing** -ɪŋ **-ed** -d
Ravening ˈreɪ.vən.ɪŋ, ˈræv.ən-
Ravenna rəˈven.ə, rævˈen-, (US) rə-, rɑː-
ravenous ˈræv.ən.əs, -ɪ.nəs, (US) -ən.əs **-ly** -li **-ness** -nəs, -nɪs
Ravensbourne ˈreɪ.vənz.bɔːn, (US) -bɔːrn
Ravenshead ˈreɪ.vənz.hed
Ravenshoe ˈreɪ.vənz.həʊ, (US) -hoʊ
raver ˈreɪ.vəʳ, (US) -vɚ **-s** -z
Raverat ˈrɑː.vər.ɑː, (US) -və.rɑː
rave-up ˈreɪv.ʌp **-s** -s
ravin ˈræv.ɪn
ravine rəˈviːn **-s** -z
raving ˈreɪ.vɪŋ **-s** -z
ravioli ˌræv.iˈəʊ.li, (US) -ˈoʊ-
ravish ˈræv.ɪʃ **-es** -ɪz **-ing/ly** -ɪŋ/li **-ed** -t **-er/s** -əʳ/z, (US) -ɚ/z **-ment** -mənt
raw rɔː, (US) rɑː, rɔː **-er** -əʳ, (US) -ɚ **-est** -ɪst, -əst **-ly** -li **-ness** -nəs, -nɪs ˌ**raw ˈdeal;** ˌ**raw maˈterial**
Rawalpindi ˌrɑː.wəlˈpɪn.di, ˌrɔːlˈpɪn-, (US) ˌrɑː.wəlˈ-
Rawdon ˈrɔː.dən, (US) ˈrɑː-, ˈrɔː-
rawhid|e ˈrɔː.haɪd, (US) ˈrɑː-, ˈrɔː- **-es** -z **-ing** -ɪŋ **-ed** -ɪd
Rawlings ˈrɔː.lɪŋz, (US) ˈrɑː-, ˈrɔː-
Rawlins ˈrɔː.lɪnz, (US) ˈrɑː-, ˈrɔː-
Rawlinson ˈrɔː.lɪn.sən, (US) ˈrɑː-, ˈrɔː-
Rawlplug® ˈrɔːl.plʌg, (US) ˈrɑːl-, ˈrɔːl-
Rawmarsh ˈrɔː.mɑːʃ, (US) ˈrɑː.mɑːrʃ, ˈrɔː-
Rawnsley ˈrɔːnz.li, (US) ˈrɑːnz-, ˈrɔː-
Rawtenstall ˈrɒt.ən.stɔːl, ˈrɔː.tən-, (US) ˈrɑː.tən-, ˈrɔː-
ray, R~ reɪ **-s** -z
Ray-Bans® ˈreɪ.bænz
Raybould ˈreɪ.bəʊld, (US) -boʊld
Rayburn ˈreɪ.bɜːn, (US) -bɝːn
Rayleigh ˈreɪ.li
Rayment ˈreɪ.mənt
Raymond ˈreɪ.mənd
Rayner ˈreɪ.nəʳ, (US) -nɚ
Raynes reɪnz
Raynsford ˈreɪnz.fəd, (US) -fɚd
rayon ˈreɪ.ɒn, -ən, (US) -ɑːn
raz|e reɪz **-es** -ɪz **-ing** -ɪŋ **-ed** -d
razoo rəˈzuː, (US) rə-, rɑː-
razor ˈreɪ.zəʳ, (US) -zɚ **-s** -z ˈ**razor** ˌ**blade**
razorback ˈreɪ.zə.bæk, (US) -zɚ- **-s** -s
razorbill ˈreɪ.zə.bɪl, (US) -zɚ- **-s** -z
razor-blade ˈreɪ.zə.bleɪd, (US) -zɚ- **-s** -z
razor-shell ˈreɪ.zə.ʃel, (US) -zɚ- **-s** -z
razzamat(t)azz ˌræz.ə.məˈtæz, ˈræz.ə.mə.tæz, (US) ˈræz.ə.mə.tæz
razzia ˈræz.i.ə **-s** -z
razzle ˈræz.əl ˌ**on the ˈrazzle**
razzle-dazzle ˌræz.əlˈdæz.əl, ˈræz.əlˌdæz-, (US) ˌræz.əlˈdæz-
razzmatazz ˌræz.məˈtæz, ˈ---, (US) ˈræz.mə.tæz
RC (abbrev. for **Roman Catholic**) ɑːˈsiː; ˌrəʊ.mənˈkæθ.əl.ɪk, -məŋˈ-, ˈ-lɪk, (US) ˌɑːr-; ˌroʊ.mənˈkæθ.əl.ɪk, ˈ-lɪk
Rd (abbrev. for **Road**) rəʊd, (US) roʊd
re *note in Tonic Sol-fa:* reɪ **-s** -z
re prep *with regard to:* riː
RE (abbrev. for **Religious Education**) ɑːʳˈiː, (US) ˌɑːr-
re- *prefix denoting repetition:* ˌriː, rɪ, ri, rə
Note: Prefix. In compounds containing **re-** where the stem is free and the meaning is 'again', it is normally pronounced /ˌriː-/, e.g. **re-read** /ˌriːˈriːd/. Many such compounds are likely to undergo stress shift, especially in adjectives derived from verbs, e.g. ˌ**re-arˈrange,** ˌ**rearranged ˈfurniture.** Attached to bound stems the pronunciation is normally /rɪ-, ri-/ or /rə-/, e.g. **refer** /rɪˈfɜːʳ/ (US) /-ˈfɝː/. There are exceptions; see individual entries.
Rea reɪ, rɪə, riː
reach riːtʃ **-es** -ɪz **-ing** -ɪŋ **-ed** -t
reach-me-down ˈriːtʃ.mi.daʊn **-s** -z
react riˈækt **-s** -s **-ing** -ɪŋ **-ed** -ɪd
reactant riˈæk.tənt, (US) -tənt **-s** -s
reaction riˈæk.ʃən **-s** -z
reactionar|y riˈæk.ʃən.ər|.i, (US) -er- **-ies** -iz
reacti|vate riˈæk.tɪ|.veɪt, ˌriː-, -tə-, (US) -tə- **-vates** -veɪts **-vating** -veɪ.tɪŋ, (US) -veɪ.t̬ɪŋ **-vated** -veɪ.tɪd, (US) -veɪ.t̬ɪd
reactivation ˌriː.æk.tɪˈveɪ.ʃən, riˌæk-, -təˈ-, (US) riˌæk-
reactive riˈæk.tɪv **-ly** -li
reactor riˈæk.təʳ, (US) -tɚ **-s** -z
read, R~ *present tense:* riːd **-s** -z **-ing** -ɪŋ *past tense:* red
readability ˌriː.dəˈbɪl.ə.ti, -ɪ.ti, (US) -ə.t̬i
readab|le ˈriː.də.b|əl **-ly** -li **-leness** -əl.nəs, -nɪs

R

re-address ˌriː.əˈdres -es -ɪz -ing -ɪŋ -ed -t
Reade riːd
reader, R~ ˈriː.dəʳ, Ⓤⓢ -dɚ -s -z
readership ˈriː.də.ʃɪp, Ⓤⓢ -dɚ- -s -s
readies ˈred.iz
reading n ˈriː.dɪŋ -s -z
Reading ˈred.ɪŋ
readjust ˌriː.əˈdʒʌst -s -s -ing -ɪŋ -ed -ɪd
readjustment ˌriː.əˈdʒʌst.mənt -s -s
readmission ˌriː.ədˈmɪʃ.ən -s -z
read|mit ˌriː.əd|ˈmɪt -mits -ˈmɪts -mitting -ˈmɪt.ɪŋ, Ⓤⓢ -ˈmɪţ.ɪŋ -mitted -ˈmɪt.ɪd, Ⓤⓢ -ˈmɪţ.ɪd -mittance -ˈmɪt.ənts
readout ˈriː.daʊt -s -s
read|y ˈred|.i -ier -i.əʳ, Ⓤⓢ -i.ɚ -iest -i.ɪst, -i.əst -ily -əl.i, -ɪ.li -iness -ɪ.nəs, -ɪ.nɪs -ies -iz -ying -i.ɪŋ -ied -id **ˌready ˈmoney**
ready-made ˌred.iˈmeɪd *stress shift:* **ˌready-made ˈmeal**
ready-to-wear ˌred.i.təˈweəʳ, Ⓤⓢ -ˈwer, ˈred.i.təˌwer *stress shift, British only:* **ˌready-to-wear ˈsuit**
reaffirm ˌriː.əˈfɜːm, Ⓤⓢ -ˈfɝːm -s -z -ing -ɪŋ -ed -d
reafforest ˌriː.əˈfɒr.ɪst, Ⓤⓢ -ˈfɔːr.ɪst -s -s -ing -ɪŋ -ed -ɪd
reafforestation ˌriː.əˌfɒr.ɪˈsteɪ.ʃən, -əˈ-, Ⓤⓢ -ˌfɔːr.ɪˈ-
Reagan ˈreɪ.gən, ˈriː-

> Note: The former US president is normally /ˈreɪ-/.

Reaganomics ˌreɪ.gənˈɒm.ɪks, Ⓤⓢ -ˈɑː.mɪks
reagent ˌriːˈeɪ.dʒənt -s -s
real adj rɪəl, Ⓤⓢ riːl, ˈriː.əl **ˈreal eˌstate; ˌreal ˈlife**
real *monetary unit:* reɪˈɑːl, Ⓤⓢ reɪˈɑːl; Ⓤⓢ ˈreɪ.əl -s -z
realia riˈeɪ.li.ə, -ˈɑː-, Ⓤⓢ riˈeɪ-; Ⓤⓢ reɪˈɑː-
realign ˌriː.əˈlaɪn -s -z -ing -ɪŋ -ed -d -ment/s -mənt/s
real|ism ˈrɪə.l|ɪ.zəm, Ⓤⓢ ˈriː-, ˈriː.ə- -ist/s -ɪst/s
realistic ˌrɪəˈlɪs.tɪk, Ⓤⓢ ˌriː.əˈ- -ally -əl.i, -li
realit|y riˈæl.ə.t|i, -ɪ.t|i, Ⓤⓢ -ə.ţ|i -ies -iz
realization, -isa- ˌrɪə.laɪˈzeɪ.ʃən, -lɪˈ-, Ⓤⓢ ˌriː.ə.ləˈ- -s -z
realiz|e, -is|e ˈrɪə.laɪz, Ⓤⓢ ˈriː.ə- -es -ɪz -ing -ɪŋ -ed -d -able -ə.bəl
real-life ˌrɪəlˈlaɪf, Ⓤⓢ ˌriː.əlˈ- *stress shift:* **ˌreal-life ˈdrama**
reallo|cate riˈæl.ə|.keɪt -cates -keɪts -cating -keɪ.tɪŋ, Ⓤⓢ -keɪ.ţɪŋ -cated -keɪ.tɪd, Ⓤⓢ -keɪ.ţɪd
reallocation ˌriː.æl.əˈkeɪ.ʃən, riˌæl-, Ⓤⓢ ˌriː.æl-
really ˈrɪə.li, Ⓤⓢ ˈriː.ə-, ˈriː.li
realm relm -s -z
realpolitik reɪˈɑːl.pɒl.ɪˌtiːk, -ə-, Ⓤⓢ -poʊ.lɪˌ- -s -s
real-time ˈrɪəl.taɪm, Ⓤⓢ ˈriː.əl-
realtor, R~® ˈriː.əl.təʳ, ˈrɪəl-, -tɔːʳ, Ⓤⓢ ˈriː.əl.tɚ, -tɔːr -s -z
realty ˈrɪəl.ti, Ⓤⓢ ˈriː.əl.ti
ream riːm -s -z -ing -ɪŋ -ed -d
reamer ˈriː.məʳ, Ⓤⓢ -mɚ -s -z
reap riːp -s -s -ing -ɪŋ -ed -t -er/s -əʳ/z, Ⓤⓢ -ɚ/z
reappear ˌriː.əˈpɪəʳ, Ⓤⓢ -ˈpɪr -s -z -ing -ɪŋ -ed -d
reappearanc|e ˌriː.əˈpɪə.rənts, Ⓤⓢ -ˈpɪr.ənts -es -ɪz
reapplication ˌriː.æp.lɪˈkeɪ.ʃən, riˌæp-, -ləˈ-, Ⓤⓢ ˌriː.æp- -s -z
reappl|y ˌriː.əˈpl|aɪ -ies -aɪz -ying -aɪ.ɪŋ -ied -aɪd
reap|point ˌriː.ə|ˈpɔɪnt -points -ˈpɔɪnts -pointing -ˈpɔɪn.tɪŋ, Ⓤⓢ -ˈpɔɪn.ţɪŋ -pointed -ˈpɔɪn.tɪd, Ⓤⓢ -ˈpɔɪn.ţɪd -pointment/s -ˈpɔɪnt.mənt/s
reappraisal ˌriː.əˈpreɪ.zəl -s -z
reapprais|e ˌriː.əˈpreɪz -es -ɪz -ing -ɪŋ -ed -d
rear rɪəʳ, Ⓤⓢ rɪr -s -z -ing -ɪŋ -ed -d **ˌbring up the ˈrear**
rear-admiral ˌrɪəʳˈæd.mər.əl, -mɪ.rəl, Ⓤⓢ ˌrɪr- -s -z
rear-end ˌrɪəʳˈend, Ⓤⓢ ˌrɪrˈend -s -z -ing -ɪŋ -ed -ɪd
rearguard ˈrɪə.gɑːd, Ⓤⓢ ˈrɪr.gɑːrd -s -z **ˌrearguard ˈaction**
rearm ˌriːˈɑːm, Ⓤⓢ -ˈɑːrm -s -z -ing -ɪŋ -ed -d
rearmament riˈɑː.mə.mənt, ˌriː-, Ⓤⓢ -ˈɑːr-
rearmost ˈrɪə.məʊst, Ⓤⓢ ˈrɪr.moʊst
rearrang|e ˌriː.əˈreɪndʒ -es -ɪz -ing -ɪŋ -ed -d -ement/s -mənt/s
rearview ˌrɪəˈvjuː, Ⓤⓢ ˌrɪr- *stress shift, see compound:* **ˌrearview ˈmirror**
rearward ˈrɪə.wəd, Ⓤⓢ ˈrɪr.wɚd -s -z
reason ˈriː.zən -s -z -ing/s -ɪŋ/z -ed -d -er/s -əʳ/z, Ⓤⓢ -ɚ/z
reasonab|le ˈriː.zən.ə.b|əl -ly -li -leness -əl.nəs, -nɪs
reassembl|e ˌriː.əˈsem.bəl -es -z -ing -ɪŋ, ˌriː.əˈsem.blɪŋ -ed -d
reas|sert ˌriː.ə|ˈsɜːt, Ⓤⓢ -ˈsɝːt -serts -ˈsɜːts, Ⓤⓢ -ˈsɝːts -serting -ˈsɜː.tɪŋ, Ⓤⓢ -ˈsɝː.ţɪŋ -serted -ˈsɜː.tɪd, Ⓤⓢ -ˈsɝː.ţɪd
reassess ˌriː.əˈses -es -ɪz -ing -ɪŋ -ed -t -ment/s -mənt/s
reassign ˌriː.əˈsaɪn -s -z -ing -ɪŋ -ed -d
reassuranc|e ˌriː.əˈʃʊə.rənts, -ˈʃɔː-, Ⓤⓢ -ˈʃʊr.ənts, -ˈʃɝː- -es -ɪz
reassur|e ˌriː.əˈʃʊəʳ, -ˈʃɔːʳ, Ⓤⓢ -ˈʃʊr, -ˈʃɝː -es -z -ing/ly -ɪŋ/li -ed -d
Réaumur ˈreɪ.əʊ.mjʊəʳ, -məʳ, Ⓤⓢ ˌreɪ.əˈmjʊr, -oʊˈ-
reawaken ˌriː.əˈweɪ.kən -s -z -ing -ɪŋ -ed -d
Reay reɪ
Reba ˈriː.bə
rebarbative rɪˈbɑː.bə.tɪv, rə-, Ⓤⓢ rɪˈbɑːr.bə.ţɪv -ly -li
rebate n *discount:* ˈriː.beɪt; rɪˈbeɪt, rə-, Ⓤⓢ ˈriː.beɪt -s -s
reba|te v *deduct:* rɪˈbeɪ|t, rə-; ˈriː.beɪ|t, Ⓤⓢ ˈriː.beɪ|t, rɪˈbeɪ|t *in masonry and woodworking:* ˈræb.ɪ|t, ˈriː.beɪ|t, Ⓤⓢ ˈriː.beɪ|t, ˈræb.ɪ|t -tes -ts -ting -tɪŋ, Ⓤⓢ -ţɪŋ -ted -tɪd, Ⓤⓢ -ţɪd
rebec(k) ˈriː.bek, ˈreb.ek -s -s
Rebecca rɪˈbek.ə, rə-
Rebekah rɪˈbek.ə, rə-
rebel n ˈreb.əl -s -z
rebel v rɪˈbel, rə- -s -z -ling -ɪŋ -led -d
rebellion rɪˈbel.i.ən, rə-, ˈ-jən, Ⓤⓢ ˈ-jən -s -z
rebellious rɪˈbel.i.əs, rə-, Ⓤⓢ rɪˈbel.jəs -ly -li -ness -nəs, -nɪs
rebirth ˌriːˈbɜːθ, Ⓤⓢ -ˈbɝːθ -s -s
rebirthing ˌriːˈbɜː.θɪŋ, Ⓤⓢ -ˈbɝː-
reboot ˌriːˈbuːt -s -s -ing -ɪŋ, Ⓤⓢ ˈbuː.ţɪŋ -ed -ɪd, Ⓤⓢ ˈbuː.ţɪd
reborn ˌriːˈbɔːn, Ⓤⓢ -ˈbɔːrn
rebound n ˈriː.baʊnd -s -z **ˌon the ˈrebound**
rebound adj *of books, etc.:* ˌriːˈbaʊnd
rebound v rɪˈbaʊnd, ˌriː-, Ⓤⓢ ˈriː.baʊnd-; Ⓤⓢ ˌriːˈbaʊnd, rɪ- -s -z -ing -ɪŋ -ed -ɪd
rebrand ˌriːˈbrænd -s -z -ing -ɪŋ -ed -ɪd
Rebuck ˈriː.bʌk
rebuff rɪˈbʌf, rə- -s -s -ing -ɪŋ -ed -t
rebuild ˌriːˈbɪld -s -z -ing -ɪŋ
rebuilt ˌriːˈbɪlt
rebuk|e rɪˈbjuːk, rə- -es -s -ing/ly -ɪŋ/li -ed -t
rebus ˈriː.bəs -es -ɪz
re|but rɪ|ˈbʌt -buts -ˈbʌts -butting -ˈbʌt.ɪŋ, Ⓤⓢ -ˈbʌţ.ɪŋ -butted -ˈbʌt.ɪd, Ⓤⓢ -ˈbʌţ.ɪd
rebuttable rɪˈbʌt|.ə.bəl, Ⓤⓢ -ˈbʌţ-
rebutt|al rɪˈbʌt|.əl, Ⓤⓢ -ˈbʌţ- -er/s -əʳ/z, Ⓤⓢ -ɚ/z
recalcitran|t rɪˈkæl.sɪ.trən|t, rə-, -sə-, Ⓤⓢ -sɪ- -ts -ts -ce -ts
recall v rɪˈkɔːl, rə-, Ⓤⓢ rɪ-, rə-; Ⓤⓢ ˈriː.kɔːl, -kɑːl -s -z -ing -ɪŋ -ed -d
recall n rɪˈkɔːl, rə-; ˈriː.kɔːl, Ⓤⓢ ˈriː.kɔːl, -kɑːl -s -z
re|cant rɪ|ˈkænt -cants -ˈkænts -canting -ˈkæn.tɪŋ, Ⓤⓢ -ˈkæn.ţɪŋ -canted -ˈkæn.tɪd, Ⓤⓢ -ˈkæn.ţɪd
recantation ˌriː.kænˈteɪ.ʃən -s -z
recap n *recapitulation:* ˈriː.kæp *a recapped tyre:* ˈriː.kæp -s -s
recap v *recapitulate:* ˈriː.kæp; ˌriːˈkæp, rɪ-, rə-, Ⓤⓢ ˈriː.kæp *retread a tyre:* ˌriːˈkæp, Ⓤⓢ ˌriːˈkæp, ˈ-- -s -s -ping -ɪŋ -ped -t
recapitu|late ˌriː.kəˈpɪtʃ.ə|.leɪt, -ˈpɪt.jə-, -ˈpɪtʃ.ʊ-, ˈpɪt.jʊ-, Ⓤⓢ -ˈpɪtʃ.ə- -lates -leɪts -lating -leɪ.tɪŋ, Ⓤⓢ -leɪ.ţɪŋ -lated -leɪ.tɪd, Ⓤⓢ -leɪ.ţɪd
recapitulation ˌriː.kəˌpɪtʃ.əˈleɪ.ʃən, -ˌpɪtʃ.ʊˈ-, -ˌpɪt.jʊˈ-, -ˌpɪt.jəˈ-, -ʊˈ-, Ⓤⓢ -ˌpɪtʃ.əˈ- -s -z
recapitulatory ˌriː.kəˈpɪtʃ.ə.lə.tər.i, ˈ-ʊ-, -ˈpɪt.jə-, -ˈpɪt.jʊ-, -leɪ-, Ⓤⓢ -ˈpɪtʃ.ə.lə.tɔːr-
recapt|ure ˌriːˈkæp.tʃ|əʳ, Ⓤⓢ -tʃ|ɚ

R

-ures -əz, (US) -ɚz -uring -ər.ɪŋ -ured -əd, (US) -ɚd
recast ˌriːˈkɑːst, (US) -ˈkæst -s -s -ing -ɪŋ
recce, R~ ˈrek.i -s -z -ing -ɪŋ -(e) d -d
reced|e rɪˈsiːd, rə-, ˌriː- -es -z -ing -ɪŋ -ed -ɪd
re|ceipt rɪ|ˈsiːt, rə- -ceipts -ˈsiːts -ceipting -ˈsiː.tɪŋ, (US) -ˈsiː.t̬ɪŋ -ceipted -ˈsiː.tɪd, (US) -ˈsiː.t̬ɪd
receiv|e rɪˈsiːv, rə- -es -z -ing -ɪŋ -ed -d -er/s -ər/z, (US) -ɚ/z -able -ə.bəl
Reˌceived Pronunciˈation; ˌon the reˈceiving ˌend (of)
receivership rɪˈsiː.və.ʃɪp, rə-, (US) -vɚ-
recency ˈriː.sənt.si
recension rɪˈsent.ʃən, rə- -s -z
recent ˈriː.sənt -ly -li -ness -nəs, -nɪs
receptacle rɪˈsep.tə.kəl, rə- -s -z
reception rɪˈsep.ʃən, rə- -s -z
receptionist rɪˈsep.ʃən.ɪst, rə- -s -s
receptive rɪˈsep.tɪv, rə- -ly -li -ness -nəs, -nɪs
receptivity ˌriː.sepˈtɪv.ə.ti, ˌrɪs.epˈ-, ˌres.epˈ-, -ɪ.ti, (US) ˌriː.sepˈtɪv.ə.t̬i, rɪˈsep-
receptor rɪˈsep.tər, rə-, (US) -tɚ -s -z
recess rɪˈses, rə-; ˈriː.ses, (US) ˈriː.ses; rɪˈses -es -ɪz
recession rɪˈseʃ.ən, rə- -s -z
recessional rɪˈseʃ.ən.əl, rə- -s -z
recessive rɪˈses.ɪv, rə- -ly -li -ness -nəs, -nɪs
Rechabite ˈrek.ə.baɪt
recharge **n** ˈriː.tʃɑːdʒ, (US) -tʃɑːrdʒ
recharg|e **v** ˌriːˈtʃɑːdʒ, rɪ-, (US) ˌriːˈtʃɑːrdʒ -es -ɪz -ing -ɪŋ -ed -d -able -ə.bəl -er/s -ər/z, (US) -ɚ/z
recherché rəˈʃeə.ʃeɪ, (US) -ˈʃer-, –ˈ-
rechristen ˌriːˈkrɪs.ən -s -z -ing -ɪŋ -ed -d
recidivism rɪˈsɪd.ɪ.vɪ.zəm, rə-, ˈ-ə-, (US) ˈ-ə-
recidivist rɪˈsɪd.ɪ.vɪst, rə-, ˈ-ə-, (US) ˈ-ə- -s -s
Recife resˈiː.fə, (US) rəˈsiː-, resˈiː
recipe ˈres.ɪ.pi, ˈ-ə-, -piː -s -z
recipient rɪˈsɪp.i.ənt, rə- -s -s
reciproc|al rɪˈsɪp.rə.k|əl, rə- -als -əlz -ally -əl.i, -li -alness -əl.nəs, -nɪs
recipro|cate rɪˈsɪp.rə|.keɪt, rə- -cates -keɪts -cating -keɪ.tɪŋ, (US) -keɪ.t̬ɪŋ -cated -keɪ.tɪd, (US) -keɪ.t̬ɪd
reciprocation rɪˌsɪp.rəˈkeɪ.ʃən, rə-
reciprocity ˌres.ɪˈprɒs.ə.ti, -ɪ.ti, (US) -ˈprɑː.sə.t̬i
recis(s)ion rɪˈsɪʒ.ən, rə-
recital rɪˈsaɪ.təl, rə-, (US) -t̬əl -s -z
recitation ˌres.ɪˈteɪ.ʃən -s -z
recitative **adj** *relating to* **recital***:* rɪˈsaɪ.tə.tɪv, (US) ˈres.ɪ.teɪ.t̬ɪv; (US) rɪˈsaɪ.t̬ə-
recitative **n, adj** *in music:* ˌres.ɪ.təˈtiːv, (US) -t̬əˈ- -s -z
re|cite rɪ|ˈsaɪt, rə- -cites -ˈsaɪts -citing -ˈsaɪ.tɪŋ, (US) -ˈsaɪ.t̬ɪŋ -cited -ˈsaɪ.tɪd, (US) -ˈsaɪ.t̬ɪd -citer/s -ˈsaɪ.tər/z, (US) -ˈsaɪ.t̬ɚ/z
reck rek -s -s -ing -ɪŋ -ed -t
reckless ˈrek.ləs, -lɪs -ly -li -ness -nəs, -nɪs
reckon ˈrek.ən -s -z -ing/s -ɪŋ/z -ed -d -er/s -ər/z, (US) -ɚ/z
reclaim rɪˈkleɪm, ˌriː- -s -z -ing -ɪŋ -ed -d
reclaimable rɪˈkleɪ.mə.bəl, ˌriː-
reclamation ˌrek.ləˈmeɪ.ʃən -s -z
reclin|e rɪˈklaɪn, rə- -es -z -ing -ɪŋ -ed -d
recliner rɪˈklaɪ.nər, rə-, (US) -nɚ -s -z
reclus|e rɪˈkluːs, rə-, (US) ˈrek.luːs; (US) rɪˈkluːs -es -ɪz -ive -ɪv
recognition ˌrek.əgˈnɪʃ.ən -s -z
recognizab|le, -isa- ˈrek.əg.naɪ.zə.b|əl, ˌrek.əgˈnaɪ-, (US) ˈrek.əg.naɪ- -ly -li
recognizanc|e, -isa- rɪˈkɒg.nɪ.zənts, rə-, -ˈkɒn.ɪ-, (US) -ˈkɑːg.nɪ-, -ˈkɑː- -es -ɪz
recogniz|e, -is|e ˈrek.əg.naɪz -es -ɪz -ing -ɪŋ -ed -d
recoil **n** ˈriː.kɔɪl; rɪˈkɔɪl, rə- -s -z
recoil **v** rɪˈkɔɪl, rə- -s -z -ing -ɪŋ -ed -d
recollect ˌrek.əlˈekt, ˈ---, (US) ˌrek.əˈlekt -s -s -ing -ɪŋ -ed -ɪd
recollection ˌrek.əlˈek.ʃən, (US) -əˈlek- -s -z
recombinant ˌriːˈkɒm.bɪ.nənt, rɪ-, rə-, -bə-, (US) -ˈkɑːm.bə-
recommenc|e ˌriː.kəˈments, ˌrek.əˈ- -es -ɪz -ing -ɪŋ -ed -t
recommend ˌrek.əˈmend -s -z -ing -ɪŋ -ed -ɪd -able -ə.bəl
recommendation ˌrek.ə.menˈdeɪ.ʃən, -mənˈ-, (US) -mənˈ- -s -z
recompens|e ˈrek.əm.pents -es -ɪz -ing -ɪŋ -ed -t
recompos|e ˌriː.kəmˈpəʊz, (US) -ˈpoʊz -es -ɪz -ing -ɪŋ -ed -d
recon ˈriː.kɒn, (US) -kɑːn
reconcilab|le ˈrek.ən.saɪ.lə.b|əl, ˌrek.ənˈsaɪ-, (US) ˌrek.ənˈsaɪ- -ly -li
reconcil|e ˈrek.ən.saɪl -es -z -ing -ɪŋ -ed -d -er/s -ər/z, (US) -ɚ/z
reconciliation ˌrek.ənˌsɪl.iˈeɪ.ʃən -s -z
recondite ˈrek.ən.daɪt; rɪˈkɒn-, rə-, (US) ˈrek.ən-; (US) rɪˈkɑːn-, rə-
recondition ˌriː.kənˈdɪʃ.ən -s -z -ing -ɪŋ -ed -d
reconduct ˌriː.kənˈdʌkt -s -s -ing -ɪŋ -ed -ɪd
reconnaissanc|e rɪˈkɒn.ɪ.sənts, rə-, ˈ-ə-, (US) -ˈkɑː.nə-, -zənts -es -ɪz
reconnoit|er ˌrek.əˈnɔɪ.t|ər, (US) ˌriː.kəˈnɔɪ.t̬|ɚ, ˌrek.əˈ- -ers -əz, (US) -ɚz -ering -ər.ɪŋ -ered -əd, (US) -ɚd
reconnoit|re ˌrek.əˈnɔɪ.t|ər, (US) ˌriː.kəˈnɔɪ.t̬|ɚ, ˌrek.əˈ- -res -əz, (US) -ɚz -ring -ər.ɪŋ -red -əd, (US) -ɚd
reconqu|er ˌriːˈkɒŋ.k|ər, (US) -ˈkɑːŋ.k|ɚ -ers -əz, (US) -ɚz -ering -ər.ɪŋ -ered -əd, (US) -ɚd
reconquest ˌriːˈkɒŋ.kwest, (US) -ˈkɑːŋ- -s -s
reconsid|er ˌriː.kənˈsɪd|.ər, (US) -ɚ -ers -əz, (US) -ɚz -ering -ər.ɪŋ -ered -əd, (US) -ɚz
reconsideration ˌriː.kənˌsɪd.ərˈeɪ.ʃən, (US) -əˈreɪ-
reconstitu|te ˌriːˈkɒn.stɪ.tʃuː|t, -stə-, -tjuː|t, (US) -ˈkɑːn.stə.tuː|t, -tjuː|t -tes -ts -ting -tɪŋ, (US) -t̬ɪŋ -ted -tɪd, (US) -t̬ɪd
reconstitution ˌriːˌkɒnt.stɪˈtʃuː.ʃən, -stəˈ-, -ˈtjuː-, (US) -ˌkɑːnt.stəˈtuː-, -ˈtjuː- -s -z
reconstruct ˌriː.kənˈstrʌkt -s -s -ing -ɪŋ -ed -ɪd -ive -ɪv
reconstruction ˌriː.kənˈstrʌk.ʃən -s -z
reconven|e ˌriː.kənˈviːn -es -z -ing -ɪŋ -ed -d
reconversion ˌriː.kənˈvɜː.ʃən, -ʒən, (US) -ˈvɝː.ʒən, -ʃən -s -z
recon|vert ˌriː.kən|ˈvɜːt, (US) -ˈvɝːt -verts -ˈvɜːts, (US) -ˈvɝːts -verting -ˈvɜː.tɪŋ, (US) -ˈvɝː.t̬ɪŋ -verted -ˈvɜː.tɪd, (US) -ˈvɝː.t̬ɪd
reconvey ˌriː.kənˈveɪ -s -z -ing -ɪŋ -ed -d
record **n** ˈrek.ɔːd, (US) -ɚd -s -z
ˈrecord ˌplayer
record **v** rɪˈkɔːd, rə-, (US) -ˈkɔːrd -s -z -ing/s -ɪŋ/z -ed -ɪd -able -ə.bəl **reˌcorded deˈlivery**
record-break|ing ˈrek.ɔːdˌbreɪ.k|ɪŋ, (US) -ɚdˌ- -er/s -ər/z, (US) -ɚ/z
recorder rɪˈkɔː.dər, rə-, (US) -ˈkɔːr.dɚ -s -z
recordist rɪˈkɔː.dɪst, rə-, (US) -ˈkɔːr- -s -s
recount **n** ˈriː.kaʊnt, ˌ-ˈ-, (US) ˈriː.kaʊnt -s -s
re|count **v** *count again:* ˌriː|ˈkaʊnt *narrate:* rɪ|ˈkaʊnt, rə- -counts -ˈkaʊnts -counting -ˈkaʊn.tɪŋ, (US) -ˈkaʊn.t̬ɪŋ -counted -ˈkaʊn.tɪd, (US) -ˈkaʊn.t̬ɪd
recoup rɪˈkuːp, rə-, ˌriː-, (US) rɪ-, rə- -s -s -ing -ɪŋ -ed -t -ment -mənt
recourse rɪˈkɔːs, rə-, (US) ˈriː.kɔːrs; (US) rɪˈkɔːrs
recov|er *get back, come back to health, etc.:* rɪˈkʌv|.ər, rə-, (US) -ɚ *cover again:* ˌriːˈkʌv|.ər, (US) -ɚ -ers -əz, (US) -ɚz -ering -ər.ɪŋ -ered -əd, (US) -ɚd -erable -ər.ə.bəl
recover|y rɪˈkʌv.ər|.i, rə-, (US) -ɚ|.i, ˈ-r|i -ies -iz
recreant ˈrek.ri.ənt -s -s -ly -li
recre|ate *create anew:* ˌriː.kri|ˈeɪt -ates -ˈeɪts -ating -ˈeɪ.tɪŋ, (US) -ˈeɪ.t̬ɪŋ -ated -ˈeɪ.tɪd, (US) -ˈeɪ.t̬ɪd *refresh:* ˈrek.ri.|eɪt -ates -eɪts -ating -eɪ.tɪŋ, (US) -eɪ.t̬ɪŋ -ated -eɪ.tɪd, (US) -eɪ.t̬ɪd -ative -eɪ.tɪv, (US) -eɪ.t̬ɪv
recreation *creating anew:* ˌriː.kriˈeɪ.ʃən -s -z *refreshment, amusement:* ˌrek.riˈeɪ.ʃən -s -z -al -əl
recrimi|nate rɪˈkrɪm.ɪ|.neɪt, rə-, ˈ-ə-, (US) ˈ-ə- -nates -neɪts -nating -neɪ.tɪŋ, (US) -neɪ.t̬ɪŋ -nated -neɪ.tɪd, (US) -neɪ.t̬ɪd -nator/s -neɪ.tər/z, (US) -neɪ.t̬ɚ/z

R

recrimination rɪˌkrɪm.ɪˈneɪ.ʃᵊn, rə-, -əˈ-, US -əˈ- -s -z

recriminatory rɪˈkrɪm.ɪ.nə.tᵊr.i, rə-, ˈ-ə-, US -ə.nə.tɔːr-

recross ˌriːˈkrɒs, US -ˈkrɑːs -es -ɪz -ing -ɪŋ -ed -t

recrudesc|e ˌriː.kruːˈdes, ˌrek.ruːˈ-, US ˌriː.kruːˈ- -es -ɪz -ing -ɪŋ -ed -t

recrudescen|ce ˌriː.kruːˈdes.ᵊn|*t*s, ˌrek.ruːˈ-, US ˌriː.kruːˈ- -t -t

re|cruit rɪ|ˈkruːt, rə- -cruits -ˈkruːts -cruiting -ˈkruː.tɪŋ, US -ˈkruː.t̬ɪŋ -cruited -ˈkruː.tɪd, US -ˈkruː.t̬ɪd -cruiter/s -ˈkruː.təʳ/z, US -ˈkruː.t̬ɚ/z -cruitment -ˈkruːt.mənt

rectal ˈrek.tᵊl -ly -i

rectangle ˈrek.tæŋ.gᵊl -s -z

rectangular rekˈtæŋ.gjə.ləʳ, -gjʊ-, US -gjə.lɚ -ly -li

rectification ˌrek.tɪ.fɪˈkeɪ.ʃᵊn, -tə-, -fəˈ-, US -tə- -s -z

recti|fy ˈrek.tɪ|.faɪ, -tə- -fies -faɪz -fying -faɪ.ɪŋ -fied -faɪd -fier/s -faɪ.əʳ/z, US -faɪ.ɚ/z -fiable -faɪ.ə.bᵊl

rectiline|al ˌrek.tɪˈlɪn.i|.əl, -təˈ-, US -təˈ- -ar -əʳ, US -ɚ

rectitude ˈrek.tɪ.tʃuːd, -tə-, -tjuːd, US -tə.tuːd, -tjuːd

recto ˈrek.təʊ, US -toʊ

rector ˈrek.təʳ, US -tɚ -s -z

rectorate ˈrek.tᵊr.ət, -ɪt, -eɪt, US -ɪt -s -s

rectorial rekˈtɔː.ri.əl, US -ˈtɔːr.i-

rectorship ˈrek.tə.ʃɪp, US -tɚ- -s -s

rector|y ˈrek.tᵊr|.i -ies -ɪz

rect|um ˈrek.t|əm -ums -əmz -a -ə

rect|us ˈrek.t|əs -i -aɪ

Reculver rɪˈkʌl.vəʳ, rə-, US -vɚ -s -z

recumben|ce rɪˈkʌm.bən|*t*s, rə- -cy -si

recumbent rɪˈkʌm.bənt, rə- -ly -li

recuper|ate rɪˈkjuː.pᵊr|.eɪt, rə-, -ˈkuː-, US -ˈkuː.pə.r|eɪt, -ˈkjuː- -ates -eɪts -ating -eɪ.tɪŋ, US -eɪ.t̬ɪŋ -ated -eɪ.tɪd, US -eɪ.t̬ɪd

recuperation rɪˌkjuː.pᵊrˈeɪ.ʃᵊn, rə-, -ˌkuː-, US -ˌkuː.pəˈreɪ-, -ˌkjuː-

recuperative rɪˈkjuː.pᵊr.ə.tɪv, rə-, -ˈkuː-, US -ˈkuː.pɚ.ə.t̬ɪv, -ˈkjuː-

recur rɪˈkɜːʳ, rə-, US -ˈkɝː -s -z -ring -ɪŋ -red -d

recurrenc|e rɪˈkʌr.ᵊn*t*s, rə-, US -ˈkɝː- -es -ɪz

recurrent rɪˈkʌr.ənt, rə-, US -ˈkɝː- -ly -li

recursive rɪˈkɜː.sɪv, ˌriː-, US -ˈkɝː- -s -z -ly -li

recurved ˌriːˈkɜːvd, rɪ-, rə-, US -ˈkɝːvd

recusan|cy ˈrek.jʊ.zᵊn*t*|.si, -jə-; rɪˈkjuː-, rə-, US ˈrek.jʊ-; US rɪˈkjuː-, rə- -ce -s

recusant ˈrek.jʊ.zᵊnt, -jə-; rɪˈkjuː-, rə-, US ˈrek.jʊ-; US rɪˈkjuː-, rə- -s -s

recycl|e ˌriːˈsaɪ.kᵊl -es -z -ing -ɪŋ, ˈ-klɪŋ -ed -d -able -ə.bᵊl, ˈ-klə.bᵊl

red, R~ red -s -z -der -əʳ, US -ɚ -dest -ɪst, -əst -ness -nəs, -nɪs **ˌred aˈlert; ˌred ˈcard; ˌred ˈcarpet; ˌRed ˈCrescent; ˌRed ˈCross; ˌred ˈherring; ˌRed ˈIndian; ˌRed ˈSea; ˌred ˈtape; in the ˈred; see ˈred; ˌnot worth a ˌred ˈcent; ˌreds under the ˈbed**

redact rɪˈdækt, rə- -s -s -ing -ɪŋ -ed -ɪd -or/s -əʳ/z, US -ɚ/z

redaction rɪˈdæk.ʃᵊn, rə- -s -z

red-blooded ˌredˈblʌd.ɪd -ness -nəs, -nɪs *stress shift:* **ˌred-blooded ˈmale**

Redbourn ˈred.bɔːn, US ˈred.bɔːrn

redbreast ˈred.brest -s -s

redbrick ˈred.brɪk, ˌ-ˈ-, US ˈred.brɪk **ˌredbrick uniˈversity**

Redbridge ˈred.brɪdʒ

redbud ˈred.bʌd -s -z

redcap ˈred.kæp -s -s

Redcar ˈred.kɑːʳ; *locally:* -kə, US ˈred.kɑːr

Redcliffe, Redclyffe ˈred.klɪf

redcoat ˈred.kəʊt, US -koʊt -s -s

redcurrant ˈredˌkʌr.ənt -s -s

Reddaway ˈred.ə.weɪ

redden ˈred.ᵊn -s -z -ing -ɪŋ -ed -d

Redding ˈred.ɪŋ

reddish ˈred.ɪʃ -ness -nəs, -nɪs

Redditch ˈred.ɪtʃ

redecor|ate ˌriːˈdek.ᵊr|.eɪt, US -ə.r|eɪt -ates -eɪts -ating -eɪ.tɪŋ, US -eɪ.t̬ɪŋ -ated -eɪ.tɪd, US -eɪ.t̬ɪd

redeem rɪˈdiːm, rə- -s -z -ing -ɪŋ -ed -d -able -ə.bᵊl

redeemer, R~ rɪˈdiː.məʳ, rə-, US -mɚ -s -z

redefin|e ˌriː.dɪˈfaɪn, -dəˈ- -es -z -ing -ɪŋ -ed -d

redeliv|er ˌriː.dɪˈlɪv|.əʳ, -dəˈ-, US -ɚ -ers -əz, US -ɚz -ering -ᵊr.ɪŋ -ered -əd, US -ɚd -ery -ᵊr.i

redemption, R~ rɪˈdem*p*.ʃᵊn, rə- -s -z

redemptive rɪˈdem*p*.tɪv, rə-

re-deploy ˌriː.dɪˈplɔɪ, -dəˈ- -s -z -ing -ɪŋ -ed -d -ment/s -mənt/s

redesign ˌriː.dɪˈzaɪn, -dəˈ- -s -z -ing -ɪŋ -ed -d

redevelop ˌriː.dɪˈvel.əp, -dəˈ- -s -s -ing -ɪŋ -ed -t -ment/s -mənt/s

red-eye ˈred.aɪ -s -z

Redfern ˈred.fɜːn, US -fɝːn

Redfield ˈred.fiːld

Redford ˈred.fəd, US -fɚd

Redgrave ˈred.greɪv, ˈreg-, US ˈred-

red-handed ˌredˈhæn.dɪd

redhead, R~ ˈred.hed -s -z

Redheugh ˈred.hjuːf, -juːf, -jəf

Redhill ˌredˈhɪl, ˈ--

red-hot ˌredˈhɒt, US -ˈhɑːt *stress shift:* **ˌred-hot ˈpoker**

re-dial ˌriːˈdaɪəl, -ˈdaɪ.əl, US -ˈdaɪəl -s -z -ling -ɪŋ -led -d

Rediffusion® ˌriː.dɪˈfjuː.ʒᵊn, -dəˈ-

redintegration rɪˌdɪn.tɪˈgreɪ.ʃᵊn, redˌɪn-, -təˈ-, US redˌɪn.t̬əˈ-, rɪˌdɪn-

redirect ˌriː.dɪˈrekt, -daɪ-, -də-, US -dɪˈ-, -daɪˈ- -s -s -ing -ɪŋ -ed -ɪd

rediscov|er ˌriː.dɪˈskʌv|.əʳ, US -ɚ -ers -əz, US -ɚz -ering -ᵊr.ɪŋ -ered -əd, US -ɚd -ery -ᵊr.i

redistribu|te ˌriː.dɪˈstrɪb.juː|t, -jʊ|t, -dəˈ-; -strɪˈbjuː|t, -stəˈ-, US ˌriː.dɪˈstrɪb.juː|t, -jʊ|t -tes -ts -ting -tɪŋ, US -t̬ɪŋ -ted -tɪd, US -t̬ɪd

redistribution ˌriː.dɪ.strɪˈbjuː.ʃᵊn, -strəˈ- -s -z

redivid|e ˌriː.dɪˈvaɪd, -dəˈ- -es -z -ing -ɪŋ -ed -ɪd

redivivus ˌred.ɪˈvaɪ.vəs, -əˈ-, -ˈviː-

Redknapp ˈred.næp

red-letter day ˌredˈlet.əˌdeɪ, US -ˈlet̬.ɚˌ- -s -z

red-light district ˌredˈlaɪtˌdɪs.trɪkt, US ˈred.laɪtˌ- -s -s

Redman ˈred.mən, ˈreb-, US ˈred.mæn

Redmond ˈred.mənd

redneck ˈred.nek -s -s

re|-do ˌriː|ˈduː -does -ˈdʌz -doing -ˈduː.ɪŋ -did -ˈdɪd -done -ˈdʌn

redolen|t ˈred.ᵊl.ən|t, -əʊ.lən|t, US -ᵊl.ən|t -ce -*t*s

redoubl|e ˌriːˈdʌb.ᵊl, rɪ- -es -z -ing -ɪŋ, ˌriːˈdʌb.lɪŋ, rɪˈdʌb- -ed -d

redoubt rɪˈdaʊt, rə- -s -s

redoubtab|le rɪˈdaʊ.tə.b|ᵊl, rə-, US -t̬ə- -ly -li

redound rɪˈdaʊnd, rə- -s -z -ing -ɪŋ -ed -ɪd

Redpath ˈred.pɑːθ, ˈreb-, US ˈred.pæθ

redraft ˌriːˈdrɑːft, US -ˈdræft -s -s -ing -ɪŋ -ed -ɪd

re-draw ˌriːˈdrɔː, US -ˈdrɑː, -ˈdrɔː -s -z -ing -ɪŋ **re-drew** ˌriːˈdruː **re-drawn** ˌriːˈdrɔːn, US -ˈdrɑːn, -ˈdrɔːn

redress v rɪˈdres, rə- -es -ɪz -ing -ɪŋ -ed -t

redress n rɪˈdres, rə-; ˈriː.dres, US ˈriː.dres

Redriff ˈred.rɪf

Redruth ˌredˈruːθ, ˈ--

redshank ˈred.ʃæŋk -s -s

redskin, R~ ˈred.skɪn -s -z

redstart ˈred.stɑːt, US -stɑːrt -s -s

reduc|e rɪˈdʒuːs, -ˈdjuːs, rə-, US -ˈduːs, -ˈdjuːs -es -ɪz -ing -ɪŋ -ed -t -er/s -əʳ/z, US -ɚ/z

reducibility rɪˌdʒuː.səˈbɪl.ə.ti, -ˌdjuː-, rə-, -sɪˈ-, -ɪ.ti, US -ˌduː.səˈbɪl.ə.t̬i, -ˌdjuː-

reducible rɪˈdʒuː.sə.bᵊl, -ˈdjuː-, rə-, -sɪ-, US -ˈduː.sə-, -ˈdjuː-

reductio ad absurdum rɪˌdʌk.ti.əʊ.æd.æbˈsɜː.dəm, rə-, -ʃi-, -əbˈ-, US -ti.oʊ.æd.æbˈsɝː-, ˈ-ʃi-

reduction rɪˈdʌk.ʃᵊn, rə- -s -z

reduction|ism rɪˈdʌk.ʃᵊn|.ɪ.zᵊm -ist/s -ɪst/s

reductionistic rɪˌdʌk.ʃᵊnˈɪs.tɪk, rə-

reductive rɪˈdʌk.tɪv, rə-

redundan|cy rɪˈdʌn.dən*t*|.si, rə- -cies -siz -ce -s

redundant rɪˈdʌn.dənt, rə- -ly -li

redupli|cate rɪˈdʒuː.plɪ|.keɪt, rə-, ˌriː-, -ˈdjuː-, -plə-, US -ˈduː.plə-, -ˈdjuː- -cates -keɪts -cating -keɪ.tɪŋ, US -keɪ.t̬ɪŋ -cated -keɪ.tɪd, US -keɪ.t̬ɪd

reduplication rɪˌdʒuː.plɪˈkeɪ.ʃᵊn,

rə-, ˌriː-, -ˌdjuː-, -plə'-, US -ˌduː.plə'-, -ˌdjuː- -s -z
reduplicative rɪ'dʒuː.plɪ.kə.tɪv, rə-, -'djuː-, -plə-, -keɪ-, US -'duː.plə.keɪ.t̬ɪv, -'dju-
redwing 'red.wɪŋ -s -z
redwood, R~ 'red.wʊd -s -z
Reebok® 'riː.bɒk, US -bɑːk -s -s
Reece riːs
re-echo ˌriː'ek.əʊ, ri-, US -oʊ -es -z -ing -ɪŋ -ed -d
reed, R~ riːd -s -z
re-ed|it ˌriː'ed|.ɪt -its -ɪts -iting -ɪ.tɪŋ, US -ɪ.t̬ɪŋ -ited -ɪ.tɪd, US -ɪ.t̬ɪd
re-edition ˌriː.ɪ'dɪʃ.ən, -ə'- -s -z
re-edu|cate ˌriː'edʒ.ʊ|.keɪt, '-ə-, -'ed.jʊ-, -jə-, US -'edʒ.ʊ-, '-ə- -cates -keɪts -cating -keɪ.tɪŋ, US -keɪ.t̬ɪŋ -cated -keɪ.tɪd, US -keɪ.t̬ɪd
re-education ˌriːˌedʒ.ʊ'keɪ.ʃən, -ə'-, -ˌed.jʊ'-, -jə'-, US -ˌedʒ.ʊ'-, -ə'-
reed-warbler 'riːdˌwɔː.bləʳ, ˌ-'--, US 'riːdˌwɔːr.blɚ -s -z
reed|y 'riː.d|i -ier -i.əʳ, US -i.ɚ -iest -i.ɪst, -i.əst -iness -ɪ.nəs, -ɪ.nɪs
reef riːf -s -s -ing -ɪŋ -ed -t 'reef ˌknot
reefer 'riː.fəʳ, US -fɚ -s -z
reek riːk -s -s -ing -ɪŋ -ed -t
Reekie 'riː.ki
reel riːl -s -z -ing -ɪŋ -ed -d
re-elect ˌriː.ɪ'lekt, -ə'- -s -s -ing -ɪŋ -ed -ɪd
re-election ˌriː.ɪ'lek.ʃən, -ə'- -s -z
reel-to-reel ˌriːl.tə'riːl, -tʊ'-
re-embark ˌriː.ɪm'bɑːk, -em'-, US -'bɑːrk -s -s -ing -ɪŋ -ed -t
re-embarkation ˌriː.ɪm.bɑː'keɪ.ʃən, -em-; riˌem-, US ˌriː.ɪm.bɑːr'-, -em- -s -z
re-enact ˌriː.ɪ'nækt, -ə'-, -en'ækt -s -s -ing -ɪŋ -ed -ɪd -ment/s -mənt/s
reenforc|e ˌriː.ɪn'fɔːs, -ən'-, US -'fɔːrs -es -ɪz -ing -ɪŋ -ed -t
re-engag|e ˌriː.ɪŋ'geɪdʒ, -eŋ'-, -ɪn'-, -en'-, US -ɪn'-, -en'- -es -ɪz -ing -ɪŋ -ed -d -ement/s -mənt/s
re-enlist ˌriː.ɪn'lɪst, -en'- -s -s -ing -ɪŋ -ed -ɪd
re-ent|er ˌriː'en.t|əʳ, ri-, US -t̬|ɚ -ers -əz, US -ɚz -ering -ər.ɪŋ -ered -əd, US -ɚd
re-entr|y ˌriː'en.tr|i, ri- -ies -iz
Rees(e) riːs
re-establish ˌriː.ɪ'stæb.lɪʃ, -es'tæb- -es -ɪz -ing -ɪŋ -ed -t -ment -mənt
reeve, R~ riːv -s -z
Reeves riːvz
re-examination ˌriː.ɪgˌzæm.ɪ'neɪ.ʃən, -egˌ-, -ə'- -s -z
re-examin|e ˌriː.ɪg'zæm.ɪn, -eg'- -es -z -ing -ɪŋ -ed -d
re-expor|t v ˌriː.ɪk'spɔː|t, -ek'-, US -'spɔːr|t; US -'ek.spɔːr|t -ts -ts -ting -tɪŋ, US -t̬ɪŋ -ted -tɪd, US -t̬ɪd
ref, R~ ref -s -s
refac|e ˌriː'feɪs -es -ɪz -ing -ɪŋ -ed -t
refashion ˌriː'fæʃ.ən -s -z -ing -ɪŋ -ed -d
refection rɪ'fek.ʃən, rə-
refector|y rɪ'fek.tər|.i, rə-, 'ref.ɪk-, US rɪ'fek-, rə- -ies -iz
refer rɪ'fɜːʳ, rə-, US -'fɝː -s -z -ring -ɪŋ -red -d
referable rɪ'fɜː.rə.bəl, rə-; 'ref.ər-, US rɪ'fɝː.ə-, rə-; US 'ref.ɚ-
referee ˌref.ər'iː, US -ə'riː -s -z -ing -ɪŋ -d -d
referenc|e 'ref.ər.ənts, '-rənts -es -ɪz 'reference ˌbook; 'reference ˌlibrary
referend|um ˌref.ər'en.d|əm, US -ə'ren- -ums -əmz -a -ə
referent 'ref.ər.ənt, '-rənt -s -s
referential ˌref.ər'en.tʃəl, US -ə'rent.ʃəl -ly -i
referral rɪ'fɜː.rəl, rə-, US -'fɝː.əl -s -z
refill n 'riː.fɪl -s -z
refill v ˌriː'fɪl -s -z -ing -ɪŋ -ed -d
refin|e rɪ'faɪn, rə- -es -z -ing -ɪŋ -ed -d -er/s -əʳ/z, US -ɚ/z -ement/s -mənt/s
refiner|y rɪ'faɪ.nər|.i, rə- -ies -iz
refit n 'riː.fɪt, ˌ-'-
re|fit v ˌriː|'fɪt -fits -'fɪts -fitting -'fɪt.ɪŋ, US -'fɪt̬.ɪŋ -fitted -'fɪt.ɪd, US -'fɪt̬.ɪd
re|flate ˌriː|'fleɪt -flates -'fleɪts -flating -'fleɪ.tɪŋ, US -'fleɪ.t̬ɪŋ -flated -'fleɪ.tɪd, US -'fleɪ.t̬ɪd
reflation ˌriː'fleɪ.ʃən
reflationary ˌriː'fleɪ.ʃən.ər.i, rɪ-, US -er-
reflect rɪ'flekt, rə- -s -s -ing -ɪŋ -ed -ɪd -or/s -əʳ/z, US -ɚ/z
reflection rɪ'flek.ʃən, rə- -s -z
reflective rɪ'flek.tɪv, rə- -ly -li -ness -nəs, -nɪs
reflex 'riː.fleks -es -ɪz
reflexed rɪ'flekst, ˌriː-; 'riː.flekst
reflexive rɪ'flek.sɪv, rə- -ly -li -ness -nəs, -nɪs
reflexolog|y ˌriː.flek'sɒl.ə.dʒ|i, US -'sɑː.lə- -ist/s -ɪst/s
re|float ˌriː|'fləʊt, US -'floʊt -floats -'fləʊts, US -'floʊts -floating -'fləʊ.tɪŋ, US -'floʊ.t̬ɪŋ -floated -'fləʊ.tɪd, US -'floʊ.t̬ɪd
refluent 'ref.lu.ənt
reflux 'riː.flʌks -es -ɪz
reforest ˌriː'fɒr.ɪst, US -'fɔːr.ɪst -s -s -ing -ɪŋ -ed -ɪd
reforestation ˌriː.fɒr.ɪ'steɪ.ʃən, -ə'-, US -fɔːr.ɪ'-
reform n, v *make better, become better, etc.:* rɪ'fɔːm, rə-, US -'fɔːrm -s -z -ing -ɪŋ -ed -d -er/s -əʳ/z, US -ɚ/z -able -ə.bəl re'form ˌschool
re-form v *form again:* ˌriː'fɔːm, US -'fɔːrm -s -z -ing -ɪŋ -ed -d
reformation, R~ ˌref.ə'meɪ.ʃən, -ɔː'-, US -ɚ'- -s -z
reformative rɪ'fɔː.mə.tɪv, rə-, US -'fɔːr.mə.t̬ɪv
reformator|y rɪ'fɔː.mə.tər|.i, rə-, US -'fɔːr.mə.tɔːr- -ies -iz
reformist rɪ'fɔː.mɪst, rə-, US -'fɔːr-
refract rɪ'frækt, rə- -s -s -ing -ɪŋ -ed -ɪd -or/s -əʳ/z, US -ɚ/z -ive -ɪv
refraction rɪ'fræk.ʃən, rə- -s -z
refractor|y rɪ'fræk.tər|.i, rə- -ily -əl.i, -ɪ.li -iness -ɪ.nəs, -ɪ.nɪs
refrain rɪ'freɪn, rə- -s -z -ing -ɪŋ -ed -d
refresh rɪ'freʃ, rə- -es -ɪz -ing/ly -ɪŋ/li -ed -t -er/s -əʳ/z, US -ɚ/z re'fresher ˌcourse
refreshment rɪ'freʃ.mənt, rə- -s -s
refried ˌriː'fraɪd *stress shift, see compound:* ˌrefried 'beans
refriger|ate rɪ'frɪdʒ.ər|.eɪt, rə-, US -ə.r|eɪt -ates -eɪts -ating -eɪ.tɪŋ, US -eɪ.t̬ɪŋ -ated -eɪ.tɪd, US -eɪ.t̬ɪd
refrigeration rɪˌfrɪdʒ.ər'eɪ.ʃən, rə-, US -ə'reɪ-
refrigerator rɪ'frɪdʒ.ər.eɪ.təʳ, rə-, US -ə.reɪ.t̬ɚ -s -z
reft reft
re-fuel ˌriː'fjuː.əl, -'fjʊəl, US -'fjuː.əl, -'fjuːl -s -z -(l)ing -ɪŋ -(l)ed -d
refug|e 'ref.juːdʒ -es -ɪz
refugee ˌref.jʊ'dʒiː, -jə'-, US ˌref.jʊ'dʒiː, -jə'-; US 'ref.jʊ.dʒi, -jə- -s -z
refulgen|ce rɪ'fʌl.dʒən|ts, rə-, US -'fʌl-, -'fʊl- -t/ly -t/li
refund n 'riː.fʌnd -s -z
refund v ˌriː'fʌnd, rɪ-, rə-; 'riː.fʌnd, US ˌriː'fʌnd, rɪ-, rə- -s -z -ing -ɪŋ -ed -ɪd
refurbish ˌriː'fɜː.bɪʃ, US -'fɝː- -es -ɪz -ing -ɪŋ -ed -t -ment/s -mənt/s
refurnish ˌriː'fɜː.nɪʃ, US -'fɝː- -es -ɪz -ing -ɪŋ -ed -t
refusal rɪ'fjuː.zəl, rə- -s -z
refuse n, adj 'ref.juːs
refus|e v rɪ'fjuːz, rə- -es -ɪz -ing -ɪŋ -ed -d -able -ə.bəl
refusenik rɪ'fjuːz.nɪk, rə- -s -s
refutability ˌref.jʊ.tə'bɪl.ə.ti, -jə-, -ɪ.ti; rɪˌfjuː-, rə-, US rɪˌfjuː.t̬ə'bɪl.ə.t̬i; US ˌref.jə.t̬ə'-
refutab|le 'ref.jʊ.tə.b|əl, -jə-; rɪ'fjuː-, rə-, US rɪ'fjuː.t̬ə-, rə-; US 'ref.jə- -ly -li
refutation ˌref.jʊ'teɪ.ʃən, -jə'- -s -z
re|fute rɪ|'fjuːt, rə- -futes -'fjuːts -futing -'fjuː.tɪŋ, US -'fjuː.t̬ɪŋ -futed -'fjuː.tɪd, US -'fjuː.t̬ɪd
Reg redʒ
-reg *car numberplate:* ˌredʒ

> Note: Used in the UK to refer to the year of registration of a car, which was indicated on the number plate until 2001 by a letter, e.g. **an F-reg,** and subsequently by a two-digit code, e.g. **54-reg.**

regain rɪ'geɪn, ˌriː- -s -z -ing -ɪŋ -ed -d
regal 'riː.gəl -ly -i
regal|e rɪ'geɪl, rə- -es -z -ing -ɪŋ -ed -d
regalia rɪ'geɪ.li.ə, rə-, US -'geɪl.jə, -'geɪ.li.ə
Regan 'riː.gən
regard rɪ'gɑːd, rə-, US -'gɑːrd -s -z -ing -ɪŋ -ed -ɪd -ant -ənt

regardful rɪˈgɑːd.fᵊl, rə-, -fʊl, ⓊⓈ -ˈgɑːrd- **-ly** -i **-ness** -nəs, -nɪs
regardless rɪˈgɑːd.ləs, rə-, -lɪs, ⓊⓈ -ˈgɑːrd- **-ly** -li **-ness** -nəs, -nɪs
regatta rɪˈgæt.ə, rə-, ⓊⓈ -ˈgɑː.t̬ə, -ˈgæt̬.ə **-s** -z
regenc|y, R~ ˈriː.dʒənt.s|i **-ies** -iz
regenerat|e adj rɪˈdʒen.ᵊr.ət, rə-, -ɪt, -eɪt, ⓊⓈ -ɪt **-ive** -ɪv
regener|ate v rɪˈdʒen.ᵊr|.eɪt, rə-, ˌriː-, ⓊⓈ -ə.r|eɪt **-ates** -eɪts **-ating** -eɪ.tɪŋ, ⓊⓈ -eɪ.t̬ɪŋ **-ated** -eɪ.tɪd, ⓊⓈ -eɪ.t̬ɪd
regeneration rɪˌdʒen.ᵊrˈeɪ.ʃᵊn, rə-, ˌriː.dʒen-, ⓊⓈ -əˈreɪ- **-s** -z
Regensburg ˈreɪ.gᵊnz.bɜːg, ⓊⓈ -bɝːg
regent, R~ ˈriː.dʒᵊnt **-s** -s
regentship ˈriː.dʒᵊnt.ʃɪp **-s** -s
reggae ˈreg.eɪ
Reggie ˈredʒ.i
Reggio ˈredʒ.i.əʊ, ⓊⓈ ˈ-oʊ
regicidal ˌredʒ.ɪˈsaɪ.dᵊl, -əˈ-
regicide ˈredʒ.ɪ.saɪd, ˈ-ə- **-s** -z
regime, régime reɪˈʒiːm, rɪ-, rə-, reʒˈiːm; ˈreɪ.ʒiːm, ⓊⓈ rəˈʒiːm, rɪ-, reɪ- **-s** -z
regimen ˈredʒ.ɪ.mən, ˈ-ə-, -men, ⓊⓈ ˈ-ə- **-s** -z
regiment n ˈredʒ.ɪ.mənt, ˈ-ə-, ⓊⓈ ˈ-ə- **-s** -s
regimen|t v ˈredʒ.ɪ.men|t, ˈ-ə-, ˌ--ˈ-, ⓊⓈ ˈredʒ.ə.men|t **-ts** -ts **-ting** -tɪŋ, ⓊⓈ -t̬ɪŋ **-ted** -tɪd, ⓊⓈ -t̬ɪd
regimental ˌredʒ.ɪˈmen.tᵊl, -əˈ-, ⓊⓈ -əˈmen.t̬ᵊl **-s** -z *stress shift:* **ˌregimental ˈcolours**
regimentation ˌredʒ.ɪ.menˈteɪ.ʃᵊn, -ə-, -mənˈ-, ⓊⓈ -ə.mənˈ-, -menˈ-
Regina rɪˈdʒaɪ.nə, rə-, ⓊⓈ -ˈdʒiː-, -ˈdʒaɪ-

> Note: In the US, /-ˈdʒiː-/ is especially suitable for the female name.

Reginald ˈredʒ.ɪ.nᵊld
region ˈriː.dʒᵊn **-s** -z
regional ˈriː.dʒᵊn.ᵊl **-ly** -i
regional|ism ˈriː.dʒᵊn.ᵊl|.ɪ.zᵊm **-ist/s** -ɪst/s
regionalistic ˌriː.dʒᵊn.ᵊlˈɪs.tɪk
Regis ˈriː.dʒɪs
regist|er ˈredʒ.ɪ.st|əʳ, ˈ-ə-, ⓊⓈ -st|ɚ **-ers** -əz, ⓊⓈ -ɚz **-ering** -ᵊr.ɪŋ **-ered** -əd, ⓊⓈ -ɚd **ˌregistered ˈmail**
registrant ˈredʒ.ɪ.strənt, ˈ-ə- **-s** -s
registrar ˌredʒ.ɪˈstrɑːʳ, -əˈ-, ˈ---, ⓊⓈ ˈredʒ.ɪ.strɑːr, ˌ--ˈ- **-s** -z
registrar|y ˈredʒ.ɪ.strᵊr|.i, ˈ-ə-, ⓊⓈ -ɪ.strer- **-ies** -iz
registration ˌredʒ.ɪˈstreɪ.ʃᵊn, -əˈ- **-s** -z **regiˈstration ˌnumber**
registr|y ˈredʒ.ɪ.str|i, ˈ-ə- **-ies** -iz **ˈregistry ˌoffice**
Regius ˈriː.dʒi.əs, -dʒəs
regn|al ˈreg.n|ᵊl **-ant** -ənt
regress n ˈriː.gres
regress v rɪˈgres, ˌriː-, rə- **-es** -ɪz **-ing** -ɪŋ **-ed** -t
regression rɪˈgreʃ.ᵊn, ˌriː-, rə- **-s** -z
regressive rɪˈgres.ɪv, ˌriː-, rə- **-ly** -li **-ness** -nəs, -nɪs
re|gret rɪ|ˈgret, rə- **-grets** -ˈgrets **-gretting** -ˈgret.ɪŋ, ⓊⓈ -ˈgret̬.ɪŋ **-gretted** -ˈgret.ɪd, ⓊⓈ -ˈgret̬.ɪd
regretful rɪˈgret.fᵊl, rə-, -fʊl **-ly** -i
regrettab|le rɪˈgret.ə.b|ᵊl, rə-, ⓊⓈ -ˈgret̬- **-ly** -li
regroup ˌriːˈgruːp **-s** -s **-ing** -ɪŋ **-ed** -t
regular ˈreg.jə.ləʳ, -jʊ-, ⓊⓈ -lɚ **-s** -z **-ly** -li
regularity ˌreg.jəˈlær.ə.ti, -jʊˈ-, -ɪ.ti, ⓊⓈ -ˈler.ə.t̬i, -ˈlær-
regularization, -isa- ˌreg.jə.lᵊr.aɪˈzeɪ.ʃᵊn, -jʊ-, -ɪˈ-, ⓊⓈ -əˈ-
regulariz|e, -is|e ˈreg.jə.lᵊr.aɪz, -jʊ-, ⓊⓈ -lə.raɪz **-es** -ɪz **-ing** -ɪŋ **-ed** -d
regu|late ˈreg.jə|.leɪt, -jʊ- **-lates** -leɪts **-lating** -leɪ.tɪŋ, ⓊⓈ -leɪ.t̬ɪŋ **-lated** -leɪ.tɪd, ⓊⓈ -leɪ.t̬ɪd **-lator/s** -leɪ.təʳ/z, ⓊⓈ -leɪ.t̬ɚ/z
regulation ˌreg.jəˈleɪ.ʃᵊn, -jʊˈ- **-s** -z
regulative ˈreg.jə.lə.tɪv, -jʊ-, -leɪ-, ⓊⓈ -leɪ.t̬ɪv, -lə-
regulatory ˈreg.jə.lə.tᵊr.i, -jʊ-; ˌreg.jəˈleɪ-, -jəˈ-, ⓊⓈ ˈreg.jə.lə.tɔːr-, -jʊ-
regul|us, R~ ˈreg.jə.l|əs, -jʊ- **-uses** -ə.sɪz **-i** -aɪ
regurgi|tate rɪˈgɜː.dʒɪ|.teɪt, rə-, ˌriː-, -dʒə-, ⓊⓈ -ˈgɝː.dʒə- **-tates** -teɪts **-tating** -teɪ.tɪŋ, ⓊⓈ -teɪ.t̬ɪŋ **-tated** -teɪ.tɪd, ⓊⓈ -teɪ.t̬ɪd
regurgitation rɪˌgɜː.dʒɪˈteɪ.ʃᵊn, rə-, ˌriː-, -dʒəˈ-, ⓊⓈ -ˌgɝː.dʒəˈ-
rehab ˈriː.hæb **-s** -z **-bing** -ɪŋ **-bed** -d
rehabili|tate ˌriː.həˈbɪl.ɪ|.teɪt, -əˈ-, ˈ-ə-, ⓊⓈ ˈ-ə- **-tates** -teɪts **-tating** -teɪ.tɪŋ, ⓊⓈ -teɪ.t̬ɪŋ **-tated** -teɪ.tɪd, ⓊⓈ -teɪ.t̬ɪd
rehabilitation ˌriː.həˌbɪl.ɪˈteɪ.ʃᵊn, -əˌ-, -əˈ-, ⓊⓈ -əˈ- **-s** -z
Rehan ˈriː.ən, ˈreɪ-, ⓊⓈ ˈriː-
rehash n ˈriː.hæʃ, ˌ-ˈ- **-es** -ɪz
rehash v ˌriːˈhæʃ **-es** -ɪz **-ing** -ɪŋ **-ed** -t
rehear ˌriːˈhɪəʳ, ⓊⓈ -ˈhɪr **-s** -z **-ing** -ɪŋ
reheard ˌriːˈhɜːd, ⓊⓈ -ˈhɝːd
rehearsal rɪˈhɜː.sᵊl, rə-, ⓊⓈ -ˈhɝː- **-s** -z
rehears|e rɪˈhɜːs, rə-, ⓊⓈ -ˈhɝːs **-es** -ɪz **-ing** -ɪŋ **-ed** -t
re|heat ˌriː|ˈhiːt **-heats** -ˈhiːts **-heating** -ˈhiː.tɪŋ, ⓊⓈ -ˈhiː.t̬ɪŋ **-heated** -ˈhiː.tɪd, ⓊⓈ -ˈhiː.t̬ɪd **-heater/s** -ˈhiː.təʳ/z, ⓊⓈ -ˈhiː.t̬ɚ/z
Rehnquist ˈren.kwɪst, ˈreŋ-
rehoboam, R~ ˌriː.əˈbəʊ.əm, -həˈ-, ⓊⓈ -həˈboʊ- **-s** -z
re-hous|e ˌriːˈhaʊz **-es** -ɪz **-ing** -ɪŋ **-ed** -d
rehy|drate ˌriː.haɪ|ˈdreɪt, ⓊⓈ -ˈhaɪ|.dreɪt **-drates** -ˈdreɪts, ⓊⓈ -dreɪts **-drating** -ˈdreɪ.tɪŋ, ⓊⓈ -dreɪ.t̬ɪŋ **-drated** -ˈdreɪ.tɪd, ⓊⓈ -dreɪ.t̬ɪd
rehydration ˌriː.haɪˈdreɪ.ʃᵊn
Reich raɪk; *as if German:* raɪx
Reichstag ˈraɪk.stɑːg; *as if German:* ˈraɪx-; -tɑːk, ⓊⓈ ˈraɪk.stɑːg; *as if German:* ⓊⓈ ˈraɪx-
Reid riːd
reification ˌreɪ.ɪ.fɪˈkeɪ.ʃᵊn, ˌriː-, ˌ-ə-, -fəˈ-, ⓊⓈ ˌ-ə-
rei|fy ˈreɪ.ɪ|.faɪ, ˈriː-, ˈ-ə-, ⓊⓈ ˈriː.ɪ-, ˈ-ə- **-fies** -faɪz **-fying** -faɪ.ɪŋ **-fied** -faɪd
Reigate ˈraɪ.geɪt, -gɪt
reign n, v reɪn **-s** -z **-ing** -ɪŋ **-ed** -d **ˌreign of ˈterror**
Reigny ˈreɪ.ni
reiki ˈreɪ.ki
Reill(e)y ˈraɪ.li
reimburs|e ˌriː.ɪmˈbɜːs, -əmˈ-, ⓊⓈ -ˈbɝːs **-es** -ɪz **-ing** -ɪŋ **-ed** -t **-ement/s** -mənt/s
re-im|port ˌriː.ɪm|ˈpɔːt, ⓊⓈ -ˈpɔːrt, -ˈ-- **-ports** -ˈpɔːts, ⓊⓈ -ˈpɔːrts **-porting** -ˈpɔː.tɪŋ, ⓊⓈ -ˈpɔːr.t̬ɪŋ **-ported** -ˈpɔː.tɪd, ⓊⓈ -ˈpɔːr.t̬ɪd
reimpos|e ˌriː.ɪmˈpəʊz, ⓊⓈ -ˈpoʊz **-es** -ɪz **-ing** -ɪŋ **-ed** -d
reimpression ˌriː.ɪmˈpreʃ.ᵊn **-s** -z
Reims riːmz
rein reɪn **-s** -z **-ing** -ɪŋ **-ed** -d
reincarnate adj ˌriː.ɪnˈkɑː.nət, -ɪŋˈ-, -nɪt, -neɪt, ⓊⓈ -ɪnˈkɑːr.nɪt, -neɪt
reincarna|te v ˌriː.ɪn.kɑːˈneɪ|t, -ɪŋ-; ˌriːˈɪn.kɑː.neɪ|t, -ˈɪŋ-, ⓊⓈ ˌriː.ɪnˈkɑːr.neɪ|t **-tes** -ts **-ting** -tɪŋ, ⓊⓈ -t̬ɪŋ **-ted** -tɪd, ⓊⓈ -t̬ɪd
reincarnation ˌriː.ɪn.kɑːˈneɪ.ʃᵊn, -ɪŋ-, ⓊⓈ -ɪn.kɑːrˈ- **-s** -z
reindeer ˈreɪn.dɪəʳ, ⓊⓈ -dɪr
reinforc|e ˌriː.ɪnˈfɔːs, ⓊⓈ -ˈfɔːrs **-es** -ɪz **-ing** -ɪŋ **-ed** -t **-ement/s** -mənt/s
Reinhard(t) ˈraɪn.hɑːt, ⓊⓈ -hɑːrt
reinstal|l ˌriː.ɪnˈstɔːl, ⓊⓈ -stɔːl, -stɑːl **-(l)s** -z **-(l)ing** -ɪŋ **-(l)ed** -d **-ment** -mənt
rein|state ˌriː.ɪn|ˈsteɪt **-states** -ˈsteɪts **-stating** -ˈsteɪ.tɪŋ, ⓊⓈ -ˈsteɪ.t̬ɪŋ **-stated** -ˈsteɪ.tɪd, ⓊⓈ -ˈsteɪ.t̬ɪd **-statement** -ˈsteɪt.mənt
reinsur|e ˌriː.ɪnˈʃʊəʳ, -ˈʃɔːʳ, ⓊⓈ -ˈʃʊr **-es** -z **-ing** -ɪŋ **-ed** -d **-ance/s** -ᵊnts/ɪz
reintroduc|e ˌriː.ɪn.trəˈdʒuːs, -ˈdjuːs, ⓊⓈ -ˈduːs, -ˈdjuːs **-es** -ɪz **-ing** -ɪŋ **-ed** -t
reintroduction ˌriː.ɪn.trəˈdʌk.ʃᵊn **-s** -z
rein|vent ˌriː.ɪn|ˈvent **-vents** -ˈvents **-venting** -ˈven.tɪŋ, ⓊⓈ -ˈven.t̬ɪŋ **-vented** -ˈven.tɪd, ⓊⓈ -ˈven.t̬ɪd
reinvention ˌriː.ɪnˈven.tʃᵊn, ⓊⓈ -ˈvent.ʃᵊn
reinvest ˌriː.ɪnˈvest **-s** -s **-ing** -ɪŋ **-ed** -ɪd
reinvigor|ate ˌriː.ɪnˈvɪg.ᵊr|.eɪt, ⓊⓈ -ə.r|eɪt **-ates** -eɪts **-ating** -eɪ.tɪŋ, ⓊⓈ -eɪ.t̬ɪŋ **-ated** -eɪ.tɪd, ⓊⓈ -eɪ.t̬ɪd
reinvigoration ˌriː.ɪn.vɪ.gᵊrˈeɪ.ʃᵊn, ⓊⓈ -gəˈreɪ-

R

reissu|e ˌriːˈɪʃ.uː, -ˈɪs.juː, (US) -ˈɪʃ.juː, -uː **-es** -z **-ing** -ɪŋ **-ed** -d
reiter|ate riˈɪt.ᵊr|.eɪt, (US) -ˈɪt̬.ə.r|eɪt **-ates** -eɪts **-ating** -eɪ.tɪŋ, (US) -eɪ.t̬ɪŋ **-ated** -eɪ.tɪd, (US) -eɪ.t̬ɪd
reiteration riˌɪt.ᵊrˈeɪ.ʃᵊn, (US) -ˌɪt̬.əˈreɪ- **-s** -z
reiterative riˈɪt.ᵊr.ə.tɪv, -eɪ-, (US) -ˈɪt̬.ə.reɪ.t̬ɪv, ˈ-ɚ.ə- **-ly** -li **-ness** -nəs, -nɪs
Reith riːθ
reject **n** ˈriː.dʒekt **-s** -s
reject **v** rɪˈdʒekt, rə- **-s** -s **-ing** -ɪŋ **-ed** -ɪd **-or/s** -əʳ/z, (US) -ɚ/z
rejection rɪˈdʒek.ʃᵊn, rə- **-s** -z
rejig ˌriːˈdʒɪg **-s** -z **-ging** -ɪŋ **-ged** -d
rejoic|e rɪˈdʒɔɪs, rə- **-es** -ɪz **-ing/ly** -ɪŋ/li **-ed** -t
rejoin *answer:* rɪˈdʒɔɪn, rə- *join again:* ˌriːˈdʒɔɪn, rɪ- **-s** -z **-ing** -ɪŋ **-ed** -d
rejoinder rɪˈdʒɔɪn.dəʳ, rə-, (US) -dɚ **-s** -z
rejuven|ate rɪˈdʒuː.vᵊn|.eɪt, -vɪ.n|eɪt, (US) -və- **-ates** -eɪts **-ating** -eɪ.tɪŋ, (US) -eɪ.t̬ɪŋ **-ated** -eɪ.tɪd, (US) -eɪ.t̬ɪd
rejuvenation rɪˌdʒuː.vᵊnˈeɪ.ʃᵊn, rə-, -vɪˈneɪ-, (US) -vəˈneɪ-
rejuvenescen|ce ˌriː.dʒuː.vᵊnˈes.ᵊn|*t*s, rɪˌdʒuː-, -vɪˈnes-, (US) rɪˌdʒuː.vəˈ- **-t** -t
rekindl|e ˌriːˈkɪn.dᵊl **-es** -z **-ing** -ɪŋ, ˌriːˈkɪnd.lɪŋ **-ed** -d
re-label ˌriːˈleɪ.bᵊl **-s** -z **-ling** -ɪŋ, -ˈleɪ.blɪŋ **-led** -d
relaid (past of **relay** = lay again) riːˈleɪd, rɪ-, rə-
relapse **n** rɪˈlæps, rə-; ˈriː.læps
relaps|e **v** rɪˈlæps, rə- **-es** -ɪz **-ing** -ɪŋ **-ed** -t
re|late, R~ rɪ|ˈleɪt, rə- **-lates** -ˈleɪts **-lating** -ˈleɪ.tɪŋ, (US) -ˈleɪ.t̬ɪŋ **-lated** -ˈleɪ.tɪd, (US) -ˈleɪ.t̬ɪd **-later/s** -ˈleɪ.təʳ/z, (US) -ˈleɪ.t̬ɚ/z
relation rɪˈleɪ.ʃᵊn, rə- **-s** -z
relational rɪˈleɪ.ʃᵊn.ᵊl, rə-
relationship rɪˈleɪ.ʃᵊn.ʃɪp, rə- **-s** -s
relatival ˌrel.əˈtaɪ.vᵊl
relative ˈrel.ə.tɪv, (US) -t̬ɪv **-s** -z **-ly** -li ˌ**relative** ˈ**clause**; ˌ**relative** ˈ**pronoun**
relativ|ism ˈrel.ə.tɪ.v|ɪ.zᵊm, (US) -t̬ɪ- **-ist/s** -ɪst/s
relativistic ˌrel.ə.tɪˈvɪs.tɪk, (US) -t̬ɪˈ-
relativity ˌrel.əˈtɪv.ə.ti, -ɪ.ti, (US) -ə.t̬i
relaunch **n** ˈriː.lɔːn*t*ʃ, (US) -lɑːn*t*ʃ **-es** -ɪz
relaunch **v** ˌriːˈlɔːn*t*ʃ, (US) -ˈlɑːn*t*ʃ, -ˈlɔːn*t*ʃ **-es** -ɪz **-ing** -ɪŋ **-ed** -t
relax rɪˈlæks, rə- **-es** -ɪz **-ing** -ɪŋ **-ed** -t **-ant/s** -ᵊnt/s
relaxation ˌriː.lækˈseɪ.ʃᵊn **-s** -z
relay **n** ˈriː.leɪ, rɪˈleɪ, rə-, (US) ˈriː.leɪ **-s** -z ˈ**relay** ˌ**race**
relay **v** *lay again:* ˌriːˈleɪ **-s** -z **-ing** -ɪŋ **relaid** ˌriːˈleɪd *send, broadcast:* rɪˈleɪ, ˈriː.leɪ, rə-, riː- **-s** -z **-ing** -ɪŋ **-ed** -d
releas|e rɪˈliːs, rə- **-es** -ɪz **-ing** -ɪŋ **-ed** -t
rele|gate ˈrel.ɪ|.geɪt, ˈ-ə-, (US) ˈ-ə- **-gates** -geɪts **-gating** -geɪ.tɪŋ, (US) -geɪ.t̬ɪŋ **-gated** -geɪ.tɪd, (US) -geɪ.t̬ɪd
relegation ˌrel.ɪˈgeɪ.ʃᵊn, -əˈ-, (US) -əˈ-
re|lent rɪ|ˈlent, rə- **-lents** -ˈlents **-lenting** -ˈlen.tɪŋ, (US) -ˈlen.t̬ɪŋ **-lented** -ˈlen.tɪd, (US) -ˈlen.t̬ɪd
relentless rɪˈlent.ləs, rə-, -lɪs **-ly** -li **-ness** -nəs, -nɪs
Relenza rɪˈlen.zə
re|-let ˌriː|ˈlet **-lets** -ˈlets **-letting** -ˈlet.ɪŋ, (US) -ˈlet̬.ɪŋ
relevan|ce ˈrel.ə.vᵊn*t*|s, ˈ-ɪ-, (US) ˈ-ə- **-cy** -si
relevant ˈrel.ə.vᵊnt, ˈ-ɪ-, (US) ˈ-ə- **-ly** -li
reliability rɪˌlaɪ.əˈbɪl.ə.ti, rə-, -ɪ.ti, (US) -ə.t̬i
reliab|le rɪˈlaɪ.ə.b|ᵊl, rə- **-ly** -li **-leness** -ᵊl.nəs, -nɪs
relian|ce rɪˈlaɪ.ən|*t*s, rə-
reliant rɪˈlaɪ.ənt, rə-
relic ˈrel.ɪk **-s** -s
relict ˈrel.ɪkt **-s** -s
relief rɪˈliːf, rə- **-s** -s **re**ˈ**lief** ˌ**map**
reliev|e rɪˈliːv, rə- **-es** -z **-ing** -ɪŋ **-ed** -d **-able** -ə.bᵊl
relievo rɪˈliː.vəʊ, (US) -voʊ
Religio Laici rɪˌlɪg.i.əʊˈlɑː.ɪ.siː, rə-, -kiː, (US) rɪˌlɪdʒ.i.oʊˈleɪ.ə-
religion rɪˈlɪdʒ.ᵊn, rə- **-s** -z
religion|ism rɪˈlɪdʒ.ᵊn|.ɪ.zᵊm, rə- **-ist/s** -ɪst/s
religiosity rɪˌlɪdʒ.iˈɒs.ə.ti, rə-, -ɪ.ti, (US) -ˈɑː.sə.t̬i
religious rɪˈlɪdʒ.əs, rə- **-ly** -li **-ness** -nəs, -nɪs
relin|e ˌriːˈlaɪn **-es** -z **-ing** -ɪŋ **-ed** -d
relinquish rɪˈlɪŋ.kwɪʃ, rə- **-es** -ɪz **-ing** -ɪŋ **-ed** -t **-ment** -mənt
reliquar|y ˈrel.ɪ.kwᵊr|.i, (US) -ə.kwer- **-ies** -ɪz
relish ˈrel.ɪʃ **-es** -ɪz **-ing** -ɪŋ **-ed** -t
reliv|e ˌriːˈlɪv **-es** -z **-ing** -ɪŋ **-ed** -d
reload ˌriːˈləʊd, (US) -ˈloʊd **-s** -z **-ing** -ɪŋ **-ed** -ɪd
relo|cate ˌriː.ləʊ|ˈkeɪt, (US) -ˈloʊ|.keɪt **-cates** -ˈkeɪts, (US) -keɪts **-cating** -ˈkeɪ.tɪŋ, (US) -keɪ.t̬ɪŋ **-cated** -ˈkeɪ.tɪd, (US) -keɪ.t̬ɪd
relocation ˌriː.ləʊˈkeɪ.ʃᵊn, (US) -loʊˈ-
reluctance rɪˈlʌk.tᵊn*t*s, rə-
reluctant rɪˈlʌk.tᵊnt, rə- **-ly** -li
reluctivity ˌrel.ʌkˈtɪv.ə.ti, ˌriː.lʌkˈ-; rɪˌlʌkˈ-, rə-, -ɪ.ti, (US) ˌrel.əkˈtɪv.ə.t̬i
re|ly rɪ|ˈlaɪ, rə- **-lies** -ˈlaɪz **-lying** -ˈlaɪ.ɪŋ **-lied** -ˈlaɪd
REM, rem ˌɑːʳ.iːˈem; rem, (US) ˌɑːr.iːˈem; rem
remain rɪˈmeɪn, rə- **-s** -z **-ing** -ɪŋ **-ed** -d
remainder rɪˈmeɪn.dəʳ, rə-, (US) -dɚ **-s** -z **-ing** -ɪŋ **-ed** -d
re-make **n** ˈriː.meɪk **-s** -s
remak|e **v** ˌriːˈmeɪk **-es** -s **-ing** -ɪŋ **remade** ˌriːˈmeɪd
remand rɪˈmɑːnd, rə-, (US) -ˈmænd **-s** -z **-ing** -ɪŋ **-ed** -ɪd **re**ˈ**mand** ˌ**home**
remanence ˈrem.ə.nən*t*s
remark rɪˈmɑːk, rə-, (US) -ˈmɑːrk **-s** -s **-ing** -ɪŋ **-ed** -t
remarkab|le rɪˈmɑː.kə.b|ᵊl, rə-, (US) -ˈmɑːr- **-ly** -li **-leness** -ᵊl.nəs, -nɪs
Remarque rɪˈmɑːk, rə-, (US) -ˈmɑːrk
remarriag|e ˌriːˈmær.ɪdʒ, (US) -ˈmer-, -ˈmær- **-es** -ɪz
remarr|y ˌriːˈmær|.i, (US) -ˈmer-, -ˈmær- **-ies** -iz **-ying** -i.ɪŋ **-ied** -id
remaster ˌriːˈmɑː.stəʳ, (US) -ˈmæs.tɚ **-s** -z **-ing** -ɪŋ **-ed** -d
rematch ˈriː.mætʃ **-es** -ɪz
Rembrandt ˈrem.brænt, -brənt, (US) -brænt, -brɑːnt **-s** -s
REME ˈriː.mi
remediable rɪˈmiː.di.ə.bᵊl, rə-
remedial rɪˈmiː.di.əl, rə- **-ly** -i
remediation rɪˌmiː.diˈeɪ.ʃᵊn, rə-
remed|y ˈrem.ə.d|i, ˈ-ɪ- **-ies** -iz **-ying** -i.ɪŋ **-ied** -id
rememb|er rɪˈmem.b|əʳ, rə-, (US) -b|ɚ **-ers** -əz, (US) -ɚz **-ering** -ᵊr.ɪŋ **-ered** -əd, (US) -ɚd
remembranc|e rɪˈmem.brᵊn*t*s, rə- **-es** -ɪz **-er/s** -əʳ/z, (US) -ɚ/z **Re**ˈ**membrance** ˌ**Day**
re-militariz|e, -is|e ˌriːˈmɪl.ɪ.tᵊr.aɪz, ˈ-ə-, (US) -t̬ə.raɪz **-es** -ɪz **-ing** -ɪŋ **-ed** -d
remind rɪˈmaɪnd, rə- **-s** -z **-ing** -ɪŋ **-ed** -ɪd **-er/s** -əʳ/z, (US) -ɚ/z
Remington ˈrem.ɪŋ.tən **-s** -z
reminisc|e ˌrem.ɪˈnɪs, -əˈ-, (US) -əˈ- **-es** -ɪz **-ing** -ɪŋ **-ed** -t
reminiscenc|e ˌrem.ɪˈnɪs.ᵊn*t*s, -əˈ-, (US) -əˈ- **-es** -ɪz
reminiscent ˌrem.ɪˈnɪs.ᵊnt, -əˈ-, (US) -əˈ-
remiss rɪˈmɪs, rə- **-ly** -li **-ness** -nəs, -nɪs
remission rɪˈmɪʃ.ᵊn, rə- **-s** -z
remit **n** ˈriː.mɪt; rɪˈmɪt, rə-, riː-, (US) rɪˈmɪt, rə- **-s** -s
re|mit **v** rɪ|ˈmɪt, rə- **-mits** -ˈmɪts **-mitting** -ˈmɪt.ɪŋ, (US) -ˈmɪt̬.ɪŋ **-mitted** -ˈmɪt.ɪd, (US) -ˈmɪt̬.ɪd **-mitter/s** -ˈmɪt.əʳ/z, (US) -ˈmɪt̬.ɚ/z
remittal rɪˈmɪt.ᵊl, rə-, (US) -ˈmɪt̬- **-s** -z
remittanc|e rɪˈmɪt.ᵊn*t*s, rə- **-es** -ɪz
remittitur rɪˈmɪt.ɪ.tʊəʳ, rə-, -tɜːʳ, (US) rəˈmɪt̬.ə.t̬ɚ
remix **n** ˈriː.mɪks **-es** -ɪz
remix **v** ˌriːˈmɪks **-es** -ɪz **-ing** -ɪŋ **-ed** -t
remnant ˈrem.nənt **-s** -s
remodel ˌriːˈmɒd.ᵊl, (US) -ˈmɑː.dᵊl **-s** -z **-(l)ing** -ɪŋ **-(l)ed** -d
remold **v** ˌriːˈməʊld, (US) -ˈmoʊld **-s** -z **-ing** -ɪŋ **-ed** -ɪd
remold **n** ˈriː.məʊld, (US) -moʊld **-s** -z
remonetiz|e, -is|e ˌriːˈmʌn.ɪ.taɪz, ˈ-ə-, (US) -ˈmɑː.nə-, -ˈmʌn.ə- **-es** -ɪz **-ing** -ɪŋ **-ed** -d
remonstranc|e rɪˈmɒn*t*.strᵊn*t*s, rə-, (US) -ˈmɑːn*t*- **-es** -ɪz
remonstrant rɪˈmɒn*t*.strᵊnt, rə-, (US) -ˈmɑːn*t*- **-ly** -li
remon|strate ˈrem.ən|.streɪt; rɪˈmɒn*t*-, rə-, (US) rɪˈmɑːn*t*-, rə-; (US) ˈrem.ən*t*- **-strates** -streɪts **-strating** -streɪ.tɪŋ, (US) -streɪ.t̬ɪŋ **-strated** -streɪ.tɪd, (US) -streɪ.t̬ɪd

remonstrative rɪˈmɒnt.strə.tɪv, rə-, ⓤⓢ -ˈmɑːnt.strə.t̬ɪv -ly -li
remorse rɪˈmɔːs, rə-, ⓤⓢ -ˈmɔːrs
remorseful rɪˈmɔːs.fᵊl, rə-, -fʊl, ⓤⓢ -ˈmɔːrs- -ly -i
remorseless rɪˈmɔː.sləs, rə-, -lɪs, ⓤⓢ -ˈmɔːrs.ləs -ly -li -ness -nəs, -nɪs
remortgag|e ˌriːˈmɔː.gɪdʒ, ⓤⓢ -ˈmɔːr- -es -ɪz -ing -ɪŋ -ed -d
remote rɪˈməʊt, rə-, ⓤⓢ -ˈmoʊt -ly -li -ness -nəs, -nɪs **reˌmote conˈtrol**
remould v ˌriːˈməʊld, ⓤⓢ -ˈmoʊld -s -z -ing -ɪŋ -ed -ɪd
remould n ˈriː.məʊld, ⓤⓢ -moʊld -s -z
remount n ˈriː.maʊnt, ˌ-ˈ-, ⓤⓢ ˈriː.maʊnt -s -s
re|mount v ˌriː|ˈmaʊnt -mounts -ˈmaʊnts -mounting -ˈmaʊn.tɪŋ, ⓤⓢ -ˈmaʊn.t̬ɪŋ -mounted -ˈmaʊn.tɪd, ⓤⓢ -ˈmaʊn.t̬ɪd
removability rɪˌmuː.vəˈbɪl.ə.ti, rə-, -ɪ.ti, ⓤⓢ -ə.t̬i
removal rɪˈmuː.vᵊl, rə- -s -z **reˈmoval ˌvan**
remov|e rɪˈmuːv, rə- -es -z -ing -ɪŋ -ed -d -er/s -əʳ/z, ⓤⓢ -ɚ/z -able -ə.bᵊl
Remploy® ˈrem.plɔɪ
remuner|ate rɪˈmjuː.nᵊr|.eɪt, rə-, ⓤⓢ -nə.r|eɪt -ates -eɪts -ating -eɪ.tɪŋ, ⓤⓢ -eɪ.t̬ɪŋ -ated -eɪ.tɪd, ⓤⓢ -eɪ.t̬ɪd
remuneration rɪˌmjuː.nᵊrˈeɪ.ʃᵊn, rə-, ⓤⓢ -nəˈreɪ- -s -z
remunerative rɪˈmjuː.nᵊr.ə.tɪv, rə-, ⓤⓢ -nə.reɪ.t̬ɪv, -nɚ.ə-
Remus ˈriː.məs
renaissance, R~ rəˈneɪ.sᵊnts, rɪ-, ˌren.eɪˈsɑ̃ːns, -ˈsɑːnts, ⓤⓢ ˈren.ə.sɑːnts, -zɑːnts, ˈ--- **ReˌnaisSance ˈman**
renal ˈriː.nᵊl
renam|e ˌriːˈneɪm -es -z -ing -ɪŋ -ed -d
renascen|t rɪˈneɪ.sᵊn|t, rə-, -ˈnæs.ᵊn|t, ⓤⓢ -ˈnæs.ᵊn|t, -ˈneɪ.sᵊn|t -ce -ts
Renault® ˈren.əʊ, ⓤⓢ rəˈnoʊ, -ˈnɔːlt -s -z
rend rend -s -z -ing -ɪŋ -ed -ɪd **rent** rent
Rendell ˈren.dᵊl
rend|er ˈren.d|əʳ, ⓤⓢ -d|ɚ -ers -əz, ⓤⓢ -ɚz -ering/s -ᵊr.ɪŋ/z -ered -əd, ⓤⓢ -ɚd
rendezvous *singular:* ˈrɒn.dɪ.vuː, -deɪ-, ⓤⓢ ˈrɑːn.deɪ-, -diː-, -dɪ- -ing -ɪŋ -ed -d *plural:* -z
rendition renˈdɪʃ.ᵊn -s -z
Renee, Renée ˈren.eɪ; rəˈneɪ; ˈriː.ni, ⓤⓢ rəˈneɪ
renegade ˈren.ɪ.geɪd, ˈ-ə-, ⓤⓢ ˈ-ə- -s -z
reneg(u)|e rɪˈniːg, rə-, -ˈneɪg, -ˈneg, ⓤⓢ -ˈneg, -ˈniːg -es -z -ing -ɪŋ -ed -d
renegoti|ate ˌriː.nɪˈgəʊ.ʃi|.eɪt, -nəˈ-, ⓤⓢ -nəˈgoʊ- -ates -eɪts -ating -eɪ.tɪŋ, ⓤⓢ -eɪ.t̬ɪŋ -ated -eɪ.tɪd, ⓤⓢ -eɪ.t̬ɪd
renegotiation ˌriː.nɪˌgəʊ.ʃiˈeɪ.ʃᵊn, -nəˌ-, ⓤⓢ -nəˌgoʊ- -s -z
renew rɪˈnjuː, rə-, ⓤⓢ rɪˈnuː, -ˈnjuː -s -z -ing -ɪŋ -ed -d -able/s -ə.bᵊl/z
renewal rɪˈnjuː.əl, rə-, -ˈnjʊəl, ⓤⓢ -ˈnuː.əl, -ˈnjuː- -s -z
Renfrew ˈren.fruː -shire -ʃəʳ, -ʃɪəʳ, ⓤⓢ -ʃɚ, -ʃɪr
renin ˈriː.nɪn, ⓤⓢ ˈriː.nɪn, ˈren.ən
renminbi renˈmɪn.bi, ⓤⓢ ˈren.mɪn-
Rennes ren
rennet ˈren.ɪt
Rennie ˈren.i
Rennies® ˈren.iz
rennin ˈren.ɪn
Reno ˈriː.nəʊ, ⓤⓢ -noʊ
Renoir ˈren.wɑːʳ; rənˈwɑːʳ, ˌ-ˈ-, ⓤⓢ rənˈwɑːr, ˈren.wɑːr
renounc|e rɪˈnaʊnts, rə- -es -ɪz -ing -ɪŋ -ed -t -ement -mənt
reno|vate ˈren.ə|.veɪt -vates -veɪts -vating -veɪ.tɪŋ, ⓤⓢ -veɪ.t̬ɪŋ -vated -veɪ.tɪd, ⓤⓢ -veɪ.t̬ɪd -vator/s -veɪ.təʳ/z, ⓤⓢ -veɪ.t̬ɚ/z
renovation ˌren.əˈveɪ.ʃᵊn -s -z
renown rɪˈnaʊn, rə- -ed -d
Renshaw ˈren.ʃɔː, ⓤⓢ -ʃɑː, -ʃɔː
rent rent -s -s -ing -ɪŋ, ⓤⓢ ˈren.t̬ɪŋ -ed -ɪd, ⓤⓢ ˈren.t̬ɪd -er/s -əʳ/z, ⓤⓢ ˈren.t̬ɚ/z
rent-a-crowd ˈrent.ə.kraʊd, ⓤⓢ ˈrent̬-
rental ˈren.tᵊl, ⓤⓢ -t̬ᵊl -s -z
rent-free ˌrentˈfriː *stress shift:* **ˌrent-free ˈflat**
rentier ˈrɑːn.ti.eɪ, ⓤⓢ -ˈtjeɪ -s -z
Rentokil® ˈren.təʊ.kɪl, ⓤⓢ -t̬ə-, -toʊ-
Renton ˈren.tən, ⓤⓢ -tᵊn
rent-roll ˈrent.rəʊl, ⓤⓢ -roʊl -s -z
renunciation rɪˌnʌnt.siˈeɪ.ʃᵊn, rə- -s -z
renvoi renˈvɔɪ
Renwick ˈren.ɪk, -wɪk
Note: For US names, /ˈren.wɪk/ is the likely pronunciation.
reoccupation riːˌɒk.jəˈpeɪ.ʃᵊn, ri-, -jʊˈ-, ⓤⓢ -ˌɑː.kjəˈ-, -kjʊˈ- -s -z
reoccup|y ˌriːˈɒk.jə.p|aɪ, ri-, -jʊ-, ⓤⓢ -ˈɑː.kjə-, -kjʊ- -ies -aɪz -ying -aɪ.ɪŋ -ied -aɪd
reoffend ˌriː.əˈfend -s -z -ing -ɪŋ -ed -ɪd -er/s -əʳ/z, ⓤⓢ -ɚ/z
reopen ˌriːˈəʊ.pᵊn, ri-, -pᵊm, ⓤⓢ -ˈoʊ.pᵊn -s -z -ing -ɪŋ -ed -d
reorganization, -isa- riːˌɔː.gᵊn.aɪˈzeɪ.ʃᵊn, ri-, -ɪˈ-, ⓤⓢ -ˌɔːr.gᵊn.əˈ-; ⓤⓢ ˌriː.ɔːr- -s -z
reorganiz|e, -is|e ˌriːˈɔː.gᵊn.aɪz, ri-, ⓤⓢ -ˈɔːr- -es -ɪz -ing -ɪŋ -ed -d
reori|ent ˌriːˈɔː.ri|.ənt, ri-, ⓤⓢ -ˈɔːr.i- -ents -ənts -enting -ən.tɪŋ, ⓤⓢ -ən.t̬ɪŋ -ented -ən.tɪd, ⓤⓢ -ən.t̬ɪd
reorien|tate ˌriːˈɔː.ri.ən|.teɪt, -ˈɒr.i-, -en-, ⓤⓢ ˌriːˈɔːr.i.en-, -ən- -tates -teɪts -tating -teɪ.tɪŋ, ⓤⓢ -teɪ.t̬ɪŋ -tated -teɪ.tɪd, ⓤⓢ -teɪ.t̬ɪd
reorientation riːˌɔː.ri.ənˈteɪ.ʃᵊn, -ˌɒr.i-, -enˈ-, ⓤⓢ -ˌɔːr.i.enˈ-, -ənˈ-
rep rep -s -s
repackag|e ˌriːˈpæk.ɪdʒ -s -ɪz -ing -ɪŋ -ed -d
repaid (from **repay,** pay back) rɪˈpeɪd, rə-, ˌriː- (from **repay,** pay a second time) ˌriːˈpeɪd
repair rɪˈpeəʳ, rə-, ⓤⓢ -ˈper -s -z -ing -ɪŋ -ed -d -er/s -əʳ/z, ⓤⓢ -ɚ/z
repairable rɪˈpeə.rə.bᵊl, rə-, ⓤⓢ -ˈper.ə-
reparability ˌrep.ᵊr.əˈbɪl.ə.ti, -ɪ.ti, ⓤⓢ -ə.t̬i
reparable ˈrep.ᵊr.ə.bᵊl
reparation ˌrep.ᵊrˈeɪ.ʃᵊn, ⓤⓢ -əˈreɪ- -s -z
repartee ˌrep.ɑːˈtiː, ⓤⓢ -ɑːrˈ-, -ɚˈ-, -ˈteɪ
repass ˌriːˈpɑːs, ⓤⓢ -ˈpæs -es -ɪz -ing -ɪŋ -ed -t
repast rɪˈpɑːst, rə-, ⓤⓢ -ˈpæst -s -s
repatri|ate ˌriːˈpæt.ri|.eɪt, rɪ-, ⓤⓢ -ˈpeɪ.tri- -ates -eɪts -ating -eɪ.tɪŋ, ⓤⓢ -eɪ.t̬ɪŋ -ated -eɪ.tɪd, ⓤⓢ -eɪ.t̬ɪd
repatriation ˌriː.pæt.riˈeɪ.ʃᵊn; rɪˌpæt-, ⓤⓢ rɪˌpeɪ.triˈ-
repay *pay back:* rɪˈpeɪ, rə-, ˌriː- *pay again:* ˌriːˈpeɪ -s -z -ing -ɪŋ **repaid** ˌriːˈpeɪd
repayable rɪˈpeɪ.ə.bᵊl, ˌriː-
repayment rɪˈpeɪ.mənt, ˌriː- -s -s
repeal rɪˈpiːl, rə- -s -z -ing -ɪŋ -ed -d
re|peat rɪ|ˈpiːt, rə- -peats -ˈpiːts -peating -ˈpiː.tɪŋ, ⓤⓢ -ˈpiː.t̬ɪŋ -peated/ly -ˈpiː.tɪd/li, ⓤⓢ -ˈpiː.t̬ɪd/li -peater/s -ˈpiː.təʳ/z, ⓤⓢ -ˈpiː.t̬ɚ/z
repeatability rɪˌpiː.təˈbɪl.ɪ.ti, rə-, -ə.ti, ⓤⓢ -t̬əˈbɪl.ə.t̬i
repêchage, repechage ˈrep.ə.ʃɑːʒ, ˈ-ɪ-, ˌ--ˈ-, ⓤⓢ ˌrep.əˈʃɑːʒ; ⓤⓢ rəˌpeʃˈ-
repel rɪˈpel, rə- -s -z -ling -ɪŋ -led -d
repellent, repellant rɪˈpel.ᵊnt, rə- -s -s
re|pent rɪ|ˈpent, rə- -pents -ˈpents -penting -ˈpen.tɪŋ, ⓤⓢ -ˈpen.t̬ɪŋ -pented -ˈpen.tɪd, ⓤⓢ -ˈpen.t̬ɪd
repentanc|e rɪˈpen.tənts, rə-, ⓤⓢ -tᵊnts -es -ɪz
repentant rɪˈpen.tənt, rə-, ⓤⓢ -tᵊnt -ly -li
repercussion ˌriː.pəˈkʌʃ.ᵊn, ⓤⓢ -pɚˈ-, ˌrep.ɚˈ- -s -z
repertoire ˈrep.ə.twɑːʳ, ⓤⓢ -ɚ.twɑːr, ˈ-ə- -s -z
repertor|y ˈrep.ə.tᵊr|.i, ⓤⓢ -ɚ.tɔːr-, ˈ-ə- -ies -iz
répétiteur rɪˌpet.ɪˈtɜːʳ, rə-, ⓤⓢ ˌrep.et̬.iˈtɝː -s -z
repetition ˌrep.ɪˈtɪʃ.ᵊn, -əˈ-, ⓤⓢ -əˈ- -s -z
repetitious ˌrep.ɪˈtɪʃ.əs, -əˈ-, ⓤⓢ -əˈ- -ly -li -ness -nəs, -nɪs
repetitive rɪˈpet.ə.tɪv, rə-, ˈ-ɪ-, ⓤⓢ -ˈpet̬.ə.t̬ɪv -ly -li -ness -nəs, -nɪs **reˌpetitive ˈstrain ˌinjury; reˌpetitive ˈmotion ˌinjury**
rephras|e ˌriːˈfreɪz -es -ɪz -ing -ɪŋ -ed -d
repin|e rɪˈpaɪn, rə- -es -z -ing -ɪŋ -ed -d

R

replac|e rɪˈpleɪs, rə-, ˌriː- -es -ɪz -ing -ɪŋ -ed -t

replaceable rɪˈpleɪ.sə.bəl, rə-, ˌriː-

replacement rɪˈpleɪs.mənt, rə-, ˌriː- -s -s

re|plant ˌriː|ˈplɑːnt, (US) -ˈplænt -plants -ˈplɑːnts, (US) -ˈplænts -planting -ˈplɑːn.tɪŋ, (US) -ˈplæn.t̬ɪŋ -planted -ˈplɑːn.tɪd, (US) -ˈplæn.t̬ɪd

replay n ˈriː.pleɪ -s -z

replay v ˌriːˈpleɪ -s -z -ing -ɪŋ -ed -d

replenish rɪˈplen.ɪʃ, rə- -es -ɪz -ing -ɪŋ -ed -t -ment -mənt

replete rɪˈpliːt -ness -nəs, -nɪs

repletion rɪˈpliː.ʃən

replevin rɪˈplev.ɪn, rə-

replevy rɪˈplev.i, rə-

replica ˈrep.lɪ.kə, -lə-, (US) -lɪ- -s -z

replicable ˈrep.lɪ.kə.bəl, -lə-, (US) -lɪ-

repli|cate ˈrep.lɪ|.keɪt, -lə-, (US) -lɪ- -cates -keɪts -cating -keɪ.tɪŋ, (US) -keɪ.t̬ɪŋ -cated -keɪ.tɪd, (US) -keɪ.t̬ɪd

replication ˌrep.lɪˈkeɪ.ʃən, -ləˈ-, (US) -ləˈ- -s -z

repl|y rɪˈpl|aɪ, rə- -ies -aɪz -ying -aɪ.ɪŋ -ied -aɪd

repo ˈriː.pəʊ, (US) -poʊ -s -z

re|point ˌriː|ˈpɔɪnt -points -ˈpɔɪnts -pointing -ˈpɔɪn.tɪŋ, (US) -ˈpɔɪn.t̬ɪŋ -pointed -ˈpɔɪn.tɪd, (US) -ˈpɔɪn.t̬ɪd

repolish ˌriːˈpɒl.ɪʃ, (US) -ˈpɑː.lɪʃ -es -ɪz -ing -ɪŋ -ed -t

repopu|late ˌriːˈpɒp.jə|.leɪt, rɪˈ-, -jʊ-, (US) -ˈpɑː.pjə-, -pjʊ- -lates -leɪts -lating -leɪ.tɪŋ, (US) -leɪ.t̬ɪŋ -lated -leɪ.tɪd, (US) -leɪ.t̬ɪd

re|port rɪ|ˈpɔːt, rə-, (US) -ˈpɔːrt -ports -ˈpɔːts, (US) -ˈpɔːrts -porting -ˈpɔː.tɪŋ, (US) -ˈpɔːr.t̬ɪŋ -ported/ly -ˈpɔː.tɪd/li, (US) -ˈpɔːr.t̬ɪd/li reˌported ˈspeech

reportage ˌrep.ɔːˈtɑːʒ; rɪˈpɔː.tɪdʒ, rə-, (US) rɪˈpɔːr.t̬ɪdʒ, rə-; (US) ˌrep.ɚˈtɑːʒ

reporter rɪˈpɔː.təʳ, rə-, (US) -ˈpɔːr.t̬ɚ -s -z

repos|e rɪˈpəʊz, rə-, (US) -ˈpoʊz -es -ɪz -ing -ɪŋ -ed -d

reposeful rɪˈpəʊz.fəl, rə-, -fʊl, (US) -ˈpoʊz- -ly -i

reposition ˌriː.pəˈzɪʃ.ən -s -z -ing -ɪŋ -ed -d

repositor|y rɪˈpɒz.ɪ.tər|.i, rə-, (US) -ˈpɑː.zɪ.tɔːr- -ies -iz

repossess ˌriː.pəˈzes -es -ɪz -ing -ɪŋ -ed -t

repossession ˌriː.pəˈzeʃ.ən -s -z

repoussé rəˈpuː.seɪ, rɪ-, (US) rəˌpuːˈseɪ

reprehend ˌrep.rɪˈhend, -rəˈ-, (US) -rɪˈ- -s -z -ing -ɪŋ -ed -ɪd

reprehensib|le ˌrep.rɪˈhent.sə.b|əl, -rəˈ-, -sɪ-, (US) -sə- -ly -li

reprehension ˌrep.rɪˈhen.tʃən, -rəˈ-

repre|sent ˌrep.rɪ|ˈzent, -rəˈ-, (US) -rɪˈ- -sents -ˈzents -senting -ˈzen.tɪŋ, (US) -ˈzen.t̬ɪŋ -sented -ˈzen.tɪd, (US) -ˈzen.t̬ɪd

representation ˌrep.rɪ.zenˈteɪ.ʃən, -rə-, -zənˈ-, (US) -rɪ.zenˈ- -s -z

representational ˌrep.rɪ.zenˈteɪ.ʃən.əl, -rə-, -zənˈ-, (US) -rɪ.zenˈ- -ly -i

representative ˌrep.rɪˈzen.tə.tɪv, -rəˈ-, (US) -rɪˈzen.t̬ə.t̬ɪv -s -z -ly -li

repress rɪˈpres, rə- -es -ɪz -ing -ɪŋ -ed -t -ible -ə.bəl, -ɪ.bəl

repression rɪˈpreʃ.ən, rə- -s -z

repressive rɪˈpres.ɪv, rə- -ly -li -ness -nəs, -nɪs

repriev|e rɪˈpriːv, rə- -es -z -ing -ɪŋ -ed -d

reprimand n ˈrep.rɪ.mɑːnd, -rə-, (US) -rə.mænd -s -z

reprimand v ˈrep.rɪ.mɑːnd, -rə-, ˌ--ˈ-, (US) ˈrep.rə.mænd, ˌ--ˈ- -s -z -ing -ɪŋ -ed -ɪd

reprint n ˈriː.prɪnt, ˌ-ˈ-, (US) ˈriː.prɪnt -s -s

re|print v ˌriː|ˈprɪnt -prints -ˈprɪnts -printing -ˈprɪn.tɪŋ, (US) -ˈprɪn.t̬ɪŋ -printed -ˈprɪn.tɪd, (US) -ˈprɪn.t̬ɪd

reprisal rɪˈpraɪ.zəl, rə- -s -z

repris|e n, v *in music:* rɪˈpriːz, rə- *legal term:* rɪˈpraɪz, rə-, -ˈpriːz, (US) -ˈpraɪz -es -ɪz -ing -ɪŋ -ed -d

repro ˈriː.prəʊ, (US) -proʊ -s -z

reproach rɪˈprəʊtʃ, rə-, (US) -ˈproʊtʃ -es -ɪz -ing -ɪŋ -ed -t -able -ə.bəl

reproachful rɪˈprəʊtʃ.fəl, rə-, -fʊl, (US) -ˈproʊtʃ- -ly -i -ness -nəs, -nɪs

reprobate n, adj ˈrep.rəʊ.beɪt, -bɪt, (US) -rə.beɪt, -bɪt -s -s

repro|bate v ˈrep.rəʊ|.beɪt, (US) -rə- -bates -beɪts -bating -beɪ.tɪŋ, (US) -beɪ.t̬ɪŋ -bated -beɪ.tɪd, (US) -beɪ.t̬ɪd

reprobation ˌrep.rəʊˈbeɪ.ʃən, (US) -rəˈ-

reprocess ˌriːˈprəʊ.ses, -sɪs, (US) -ˈprɑː.ses, -səs -es -ɪz -ing -ɪŋ -ed -t

reproduc|e ˌriː.prəˈdʒuːs, -ˈdjuːs, (US) -ˈduːs, -ˈdjuːs -es -ɪz -ing -ɪŋ -ed -t -er/s -əʳ/z, (US) -ɚ/z

reproduction ˌriː.prəˈdʌk.ʃən -s -z

reproductive ˌriː.prəˈdʌk.tɪv -ness -nəs, -nɪs

reprogram ˌriːˈprəʊ.græm, (US) -ˈproʊ- -s -z -(m)ing -ɪŋ -(m)ed -d

reprographic ˌriː.prəʊˈgræf.ɪk, ˌrep.rəʊˈ-, (US) ˌriː.proʊˈ-, -prəˈ- -s -s

reprograph|y rɪˈprɒg.rə.f|i, riː-, (US) -ˈprɑː.grə- -er/s -əʳ/z, (US) -ɚ/z

reproof rɪˈpruːf, rə- -s -s

re-proof v ˌriːˈpruːf -s -s -ing -ɪŋ -ed -t

reproval rɪˈpruː.vəl, rə- -s -z

reprov|e rɪˈpruːv, rə- -es -z -ing/ly -ɪŋ/li -ed -d -er/s -əʳ/z, (US) -ɚ/z

reptile ˈrep.taɪl, (US) -taɪl, -təl -s -z

reptilian repˈtɪl.i.ən, (US) -i.ən, ˈ-jən -s -z

Repton ˈrep.tən

republic, R~ rɪˈpʌb.lɪk, rə- -s -s

republican, R~ rɪˈpʌb.lɪ.kən, rə- -s -z -ism -ɪ.zəm

republication ˌriː.pʌb.lɪˈkeɪ.ʃən, -ləˈ-, (US) ˌriː.pʌb.lɪˈ- -s -z

republish ˌriːˈpʌb.lɪʃ -es -ɪz -ing -ɪŋ -ed -t

repudi|ate rɪˈpjuː.di|.eɪt, rə- -ates -eɪts -ating -eɪ.tɪŋ, (US) -eɪ.t̬ɪŋ -ated -eɪ.tɪd, (US) -eɪ.t̬ɪd -ater/s -eɪ.təʳ/z, (US) -eɪ.t̬ɚ/z

repudiation rɪˌpjuː.diˈeɪ.ʃən, rə-

repugnance rɪˈpʌg.nənts, rə-

repugnant rɪˈpʌg.nənt, rə- -ly -li

repuls|e rɪˈpʌls, rə- -es -ɪz -ing -ɪŋ -ed -t

repulsion rɪˈpʌl.ʃən, rə-

repulsive rɪˈpʌl.sɪv, rə- -ly -li -ness -nəs, -nɪs

repurpos|e ˌriːˈpɜː.pəs, (US) -ˈpɝː- -es -ɪz -ing -ɪŋ -ed -d

reputability ˌrep.jə.təˈbɪl.ə.ti, -jʊ-, -ɪ.ti, (US) -t̬əˈbɪl.ə.t̬i

reputab|le ˈrep.jə.tə.b|əl, -jʊ-, (US) -t̬ə- -ly -li

reputation ˌrep.jəˈteɪ.ʃən, -jʊˈ- -s -z

re|pute rɪ|ˈpjuːt, rə- -puted/ly -ˈpjuː.tɪd/li, (US) -ˈpjuː.t̬ɪd/li

request rɪˈkwest, rə- -s -s -ing -ɪŋ -ed -ɪd

requiem ˈrek.wi.əm, -em -s -z ˌrequiem ˈmass

requiescat ˌrek.wiˈes.kæt, (US) ˌreɪ.kwiˈ-, ˌrek.wiˈ-, -kɑːt

requir|e rɪˈkwaɪəʳ, -ˈkwaɪ.əʳ, rə-, (US) -ˈkwaɪ.ɚ -es -z -ing -ɪŋ -ed -d

requirement rɪˈkwaɪə.mənt, -ˈkwaɪ.ə-, rə-, (US) -ˈkwaɪ.ɚ- -s -s

requisite ˈrek.wɪ.zɪt, -wə- -s -s -ly -li -ness -nəs, -nɪs

requisition ˌrek.wɪˈzɪʃ.ən, -wəˈ- -s -z -ing -ɪŋ -ed -d

re|quite rɪ|ˈkwaɪt, rə- -quites -ˈkwaɪts -quiting -ˈkwaɪ.tɪŋ, (US) -ˈkwaɪ.t̬ɪŋ -quited -ˈkwaɪ.tɪd, (US) -ˈkwaɪ.t̬ɪd -quital -ˈkwaɪ.təl, (US) -ˈkwaɪ.t̬əl

re-read *present tense:* ˌriːˈriːd -s -z -ing -ɪŋ *past tense:* ˌriːˈred

reredos ˈrɪə.dɒs, (US) ˈrɪr.dɑːs -es -ɪz

releas|e v ˌriː.rɪˈliːs -es -ɪz -ing -ɪŋ -ed -t

rereleas|e n ˈriː.rɪ.liːs -s -ɪz

rerou|te ˌriːˈruː|t, (US) -ˈruː|t, -ˈraʊ|t -tes -ts -ting -tɪŋ, (US) -t̬ɪŋ -ted -tɪd, (US) -t̬ɪd

rerun v ˌriːˈrʌn -s -z -ning -ɪŋ reran ˌriːˈræn

rerun n ˈriː.rʌn -s -z

res reɪz, reɪs, riːz, (US) reɪs, riːz

resale ˈriː.seɪl, ˌ-ˈ-, (US) ˈriː.seɪl -s -z

reschedul|e ˌriːˈʃed.juːl, -ˈʃedʒ.uːl, (US) -ˈskedʒ.uːl, -əl -es -z -ing -ɪŋ -ed -d

rescind rɪˈsɪnd, rə- -s -z -ing -ɪŋ -ed -ɪd

rescission rɪˈsɪʒ.ən, rə-

rescript ˈriː.skrɪpt -s -s

rescu|e ˈres.kjuː -es -z -ing -ɪŋ -ed -d -er/s -əʳ/z, (US) -ɚ/z

research n rɪˈsɜːtʃ, rə-, ˈriː.sɜːtʃ, (US) ˈriː.sɝːtʃ; rɪˈsɝːtʃ, rə- -es -ɪz

> Note: The pronunciation with initial stress is relatively new to British English and is disliked by many people.

research v rɪˈsɜːtʃ, rə-, ˈriː.sɜːtʃ, (US)

-ˈsɜːtʃ; (US) ˈriː.sɜːtʃ -es -ɪz -ing -ɪŋ -ed -t -er/s -əʳ/z, (US) -ɚ/z

Note: The pronunciation with initial stress is relatively new to British English and is disliked by many people.

re|seat ˌriː|ˈsiːt **-seats** -ˈsiːts **-seating** -ˈsiː.tɪŋ, (US) -ˈsiː.t̬ɪŋ **-seated** -ˈsiː.tɪd, (US) -ˈsiː.t̬ɪd
resection ˌriːˈsek.ʃən, rɪ- **-s** -z
reseda ˈres.ɪ.də, ˈrez-, ˈ-ə-; rɪˈsiː.də, rə-, (US) rɪˈsiː.də, rə-, -ˈsed.ə **-s** -z
reselect ˌriː.sɪˈlekt, -səˈ- **-s** -s **-ing** -ɪŋ **-ed** -ɪd
reselection ˌriː.sɪˈlek.ʃən, -səˈ-
resell ˌriːˈsel **-s** -z **-ing** -ɪŋ **resold** ˌriːˈsəʊld, (US) -ˈsoʊld
resemblanc|e rɪˈzem.blənts, rə- **-es** -ɪz
resembl|e rɪˈzem.bəl, rə- **-es** -z **-ing** -ɪŋ, -ˈzem.blɪŋ **-ed** -d
re|send ˌriː|ˈsend **-sends** -ˈsendz **-sending** -ˈsend.ɪŋ **-sent** -sent
re|sent rɪ|ˈzent, rə- **-sents** -ˈzents **-senting** -ˈzen.tɪŋ, (US) -ˈzen.t̬ɪŋ **-sented** -ˈzen.tɪd, (US) -ˈzen.t̬ɪd
resentful rɪˈzent.fəl, rə-, -fʊl **-ly** -li
resentment rɪˈzent.mənt, rə-
reservation ˌrez.əˈveɪ.ʃən, (US) -ɚˈ- **-s** -z
reserv|e rɪˈzɜːv, rə-, (US) -ˈzɝːv **-es** -z **-ing** -ɪŋ **-ed** -d
reservedly rɪˈzɜː.vɪd.li, rə-, (US) -ˈzɝː-
reservist rɪˈzɜː.vɪst, rə-, (US) -ˈzɝː- **-s** -s
reservoir ˈrez.əv.wɑːʳ, (US) -ɚv.wɑːr, -wɔːr, ˈ-ɚ.vɔːr, ˈ-ə- **-s** -z
re|set ˌriː|ˈset **-sets** -ˈsets **-setting/s** -ˈset.ɪŋ/z, (US) -ˈset̬.ɪŋ/z
resettle ˌriːˈset.əl **-s** -z **-ing** -ɪŋ **-ed** -d **-ment** -mənt
res gestae ˌreɪsˈges.taɪ, ˌreɪz-, ˌriːz-, -ˈdʒes-, -tiː
reshap|e ˌriːˈʃeɪp **-es** -s **-ing** -ɪŋ **-ed** -t
reship ˌriːˈʃɪp **-s** -s **-ping** -ɪŋ **-ped** -t **-ment/s** -mənt/s
reshuffle n ˌriːˈʃʌf.əl, ˈ-ˌ--, (US) ˌriːˈʃʌf- **-s** -z
reshuffl|e v ˌriːˈʃʌf.əl **-es** -z **-ing** -ɪŋ, -ˈʃʌf.lɪŋ **-ed** -d
resid|e rɪˈzaɪd, rə- **-es** -z **-ing** -ɪŋ **-ed** -ɪd
residenc|e ˈrez.ɪ.dənts **-es** -ɪz
residenc|y ˈrez.ɪ.dənt.s|i **-ies** -iz
resident ˈrez.ɪ.dənt **-s** -s
residential ˌrez.ɪˈden.tʃəl
residual rɪˈzɪd.ju.əl, rə-, -ˈzɪdʒ.u-, (US) -ˈzɪdʒ- **-ly** -i
residuary rɪˈzɪd.ju.əri, rə-, -ˈzɪdʒ.ʊə-, (US) -ˈzɪdʒ.u.er-
residue ˈrez.ɪ.dʒuː, ˈ-ə-, -djuː, (US) -ə.duː, -djuː **-s** -z
residu|um rɪˈzɪd.ju|.əm, rə-, -ˈzɪdʒ.u-, (US) -ˈzɪdʒ- **-a** -ə
resign rɪˈzaɪn, rə- **-s** -z **-ing** -ɪŋ **-ed** -d **-edly** -ɪd.li
resignation ˌrez.ɪgˈneɪ.ʃən, -əgˈ-, (US) -ɪgˈ- **-s** -z
resilien|ce rɪˈzɪl.i.ənt|s, rə-, -ˈsɪl-, (US) -ˈzɪl.jənt|s, ˈ-i.ənt|s **-cy** -si
resilient rɪˈzɪl.i.ənt, rə-, -ˈsɪl-, (US) -ˈzɪl.jənt, ˈ-i.ənt **-ly** -li
resin ˈrez.ɪn **-s** -z **-ous** -əs
res ipsa loquitur ˌreɪs.ɪp.sɑːˈlɒk.wɪ.tʊəʳ, ˌreɪz-, ˌriːz-, -səˈ-, -təʳ, (US) ˌreɪs.ɪp.səˈlɑː.wɪ.tʊr
resist rɪˈzɪst, rə- **-s** -s **-ing** -ɪŋ **-ed** -ɪd **-or/s** -əʳ/z, (US) -ɚ/z
resistanc|e rɪˈzɪs.tənts, rə- **-es** -ɪz
resistant rɪˈzɪs.tənt, rə- **-ly** -li
resistivity ˌriː.zɪˈstɪv.ə.ti, ˌrez.ɪˈ-, -ɪ.ti, (US) ˌriː.zɪˈstɪv.ə.t̬i; (US) rɪˌzɪsˈtɪv-
resistless rɪˈzɪst.ləs, rə-, -lɪs
resistor rɪˈzɪs.təʳ, rə-, (US) -tɚ **-s** -z
resit n ˈriː.sɪt **-s** -s
re|sit v ˌriː|ˈsɪt **-sits** -ˈsɪts **-sitting** -ˈsɪt.ɪŋ, (US) -ˈsɪt̬.ɪŋ **resat** ˌriːˈsæt
res judicata ˌreɪs.dʒuː.dɪˈkɑː.tə, ˌreɪz-, ˌriːz-, -dəˈ-, (US) ˌreɪs-, ˌreɪz-, ˌriːz-, ˌriːs-
reskill ˌriːˈskɪl **-s** -z **-ing** -ɪŋ **-ed** -d
resol|e ˌriːˈsəʊl, (US) -ˈsoʊl **-es** -z **-ing** -ɪŋ **-ed** -d
resoluble rɪˈzɒl.jə.bəl, rə-, -jʊ-; ˈrez.əl-, (US) rɪˈzɑːl.jə-, rə-, -jʊ-; (US) ˈrez.əl-
resolute ˈrez.əl.uːt, -juːt, (US) -ə.luːt **-ly** -li **-ness** -nəs, -nɪs
resolution ˌrez.əlˈuː.ʃən, -ˈjuː-, (US) -əˈluː- **-s** -z
resolvability rɪˌzɒl.vəˈbɪl.ə.ti, rə-, -ɪ.ti, (US) -ˌzɑːl.vəˈbɪl.ə.t̬i
resolv|e rɪˈzɒlv, rə-, (US) -ˈzɑːlv **-es** -z **-ing** -ɪŋ **-ed** -d **-able** -ə.bəl
resonanc|e ˈrez.ən.ənts **-es** -ɪz
resonant ˈrez.ən.ənt **-ly** -li
reson|ate ˈrez.ən|.eɪt **-ates** -eɪts **-ating** -eɪ.tɪŋ, (US) -eɪ.t̬ɪŋ **-ated** -eɪ.tɪd, (US) -eɪ.t̬ɪd
resonator ˈrez.ən.eɪ.təʳ, (US) -t̬ɚ **-s** -z
resorb rɪˈzɔːb, rə-, -ˈsɔːb, (US) -ˈsɔːrb, -ˈzɔːrb **-s** -z **-ing** -ɪŋ **-ed** -d
resorp|tion rɪˈsɔːp|.ʃən, rə-, -ˈzɔːp-, (US) -ˈsɔːrp-, -ˈzɔːrp- **-tive** -tɪv
re|sort n, v rɪ|ˈzɔːt, rə-, (US) -ˈzɔːrt **-sorts** -ˈzɔːts, (US) -ˈzɔːrts **-sorting** -ˈzɔː.tɪŋ, (US) -ˈzɔːr.t̬ɪŋ **-sorted** -ˈzɔː.tɪd, (US) -ˈzɔːr.t̬ɪd
re|-sort v *sort again:* ˌriː|ˈsɔːt, (US) -ˈsɔːrt **-sorts** -ˈsɔːts, (US) -ˈsɔːrts **-sorting** -ˈsɔː.tɪŋ, (US) -ˈsɔːr.t̬ɪŋ **-sorted** -ˈsɔː.tɪd, (US) -ˈsɔːr.t̬ɪd
resound rɪˈzaʊnd, rə- **-s** -z **-ing** -ɪŋ **-ed** -ɪd
resourc|e rɪˈzɔːs, rə-, -ˈsɔːs; ˈriː.sɔːs, (US) ˈriː.sɔːrs, -zɔːrs; (US) rɪˈsɔːrs, rə-, -ˈzɔːrs **-es** -ɪz **-ing** -ɪŋ **-ed** -t
resourceful rɪˈzɔːs.fəl, rə-, -ˈsɔːs-, -fʊl, (US) -ˈsɔːrs-, -ˈzɔːrs- **-ly** -i **-ness** -nəs, -nɪs
respect rɪˈspekt, rə- **-s** -s **-ing** -ɪŋ **-ed** -ɪd **-er/s** -əʳ/z, (US) -ɚ/z
respectability rɪˌspek.təˈbɪl.ə.ti, rə-, -ɪ.ti, (US) -ə.t̬i
respectab|le rɪˈspek.tə.b|əl, rə- **-ly** -li **-leness** -əl.nəs, -nɪs
respectful rɪˈspekt.fəl, rə-, -fʊl **-ly** -i **-ness** -nəs, -nɪs
respective rɪˈspek.tɪv, rə- **-ly** -li
Respighi resˈpiː.gi, rɪˈspiː-, rə-
respirable ˈres.pɪ.rə.bəl, rɪˈspaɪə-, rə-, (US) ˈres.pɚ.ə.bəl; (US) rɪˈspaɪ.rə-, rə-
respiration ˌres.pərˈeɪ.ʃən, -pɪˈreɪ-, (US) -pəˈreɪ- **-s** -z
respirator ˈres.pər.eɪ.təʳ, -pɪ.reɪ-, (US) -pə.reɪ.t̬ɚ **-s** -z
respiratory rɪˈspɪr.ə.tər.i, -ˈspaɪə.rə-, rə-, resˈpaɪə-, ˈres.pɪ.rə-, -reɪ-, (US) ˈres.pɚ.ə.tɔːr-; (US) rɪˈspaɪ.rə-, rə-
respir|e rɪˈspaɪəʳ, -ˈspaɪ.əʳ, rə-, (US) -ˈspaɪ.ɚ **-es** -z **-ing** -ɪŋ **-ed** -d
respi|te ˈres.paɪ|t, -pɪ|t, (US) -pɪ|t **-tes** -ts **-ting** -tɪŋ, (US) -t̬ɪŋ **-ted** -tɪd, (US) -t̬ɪd
resplenden|ce rɪˈsplen.dənt|s, rə- **-cy** -si
resplendent rɪˈsplen.dənt, rə- **-ly** -li
respond rɪˈspɒnd, rə-, (US) -ˈspɑːnd **-s** -z **-ing** -ɪŋ **-ed** -ɪd **-er/s** -əʳ/z, (US) -ɚ/z
respondeat resˈpɒn.deɪ.æt, rɪs-, -di-, (US) resˈpɑːn.di.ət
respondent rɪˈspɒn.dənt, rə-, (US) -ˈspɑːn- **-s** -s
respons|e rɪˈspɒnts, rə-, (US) -ˈspɑːnts **-es** -ɪz
responsibilit|y rɪˌspɒnt.səˈbɪl.ə.t|i, rə-, -sɪˈ-, -ɪ.t|i, (US) -ˌspɑːnt.səˈbɪl.ə.t̬|i **-ies** -iz
responsib|le rɪˈspɒnt.sə.b|əl, rə-, -sɪ-, (US) -ˈspɑːnt.sə- **-ly** -li **-leness** -əl.nəs, -nɪs
responsive rɪˈspɒnt.sɪv, rə-, (US) -ˈspɑːnt- **-ly** -li **-ness** -nəs, -nɪs
respray n ˈriː.spreɪ **-s** -z
respray v ˌriːˈspreɪ **-s** -z **-ing** -ɪŋ **-ed** -d
rest rest **-s** -s **-ing** -ɪŋ **-ed** -ɪd ˈ**rest** ˌ**home**; ˈ**resting** ˌ**place**; ˈ**rest** ˌ**room**
re|start ˌriː|ˈstɑːt, (US) -ˈstɑːrt **-starts** -ˈstɑːts, (US) -ˈstɑːrts **-starting** -ˈstɑː.tɪŋ, (US) -ˈstɑːr.t̬ɪŋ **-started** -ˈstɑː.tɪd, (US) -ˈstɑːr.t̬ɪd
re|state ˌriː|ˈsteɪt **-states** -ˈsteɪts **-stating** -ˈsteɪ.tɪŋ, (US) -ˈsteɪ.t̬ɪŋ **-stated** -ˈsteɪ.tɪd, (US) -ˈsteɪ.t̬ɪd
re-statement ˌriːˈsteɪt.mənt **-s** -s
restaur|ant ˈres.tər|.ɔ̃ːŋ, -ɑ̃ːŋ, -ɑːŋ, -ɒnt, -ənt, ˈ-tr|ɔ̃ːŋ, -tr|ɑ̃ːŋ, -tr|ɑːŋ, -tr|ɒnt, -tr|ənt, (US) -tə.r|ɑːnt, -tɚ|.ənt, ˈ-tr|ɑːnt, -tr|ənt **-ants** -ɔ̃ːŋz, -ɑ̃ːŋz, -ɑːŋz, -ɒŋz, -ɒnts, -ənts, (US) -ɑːnts, -ənts ˈ**restaurant** ˌ**car**
restaurateur ˌres.tɒr.əˈtɜːʳ, -tər-, -tɔː.rəˈ-, (US) -tɚ.əˈtʊr, -ˈtɝː **-s** -z
restful ˈrest.fəl, -fʊl **-ly** -i **-ness** -nəs, -nɪs
restitution ˌres.tɪˈtʃuː.ʃən, -ˈtjuː-, (US) -ˈtuː-, -ˈtjuː-
restive ˈres.tɪv **-ly** -li **-ness** -nəs, -nɪs

R

restless ˈrest.ləs, -lɪs **-ly** -li **-ness** -nəs, -nɪs
restock ˌriːˈstɒk, (US) -ˈstɑːk **-s** -s **-ing** -ɪŋ **-ed** -t
restoration, R~ ˌres.tərˈeɪ.ʃən, (US) -təˈreɪ- **-s** -z
restorative rɪˈstɒr.ə.tɪv, rə-, resˈtɒr-, -ˈtɔː.rə-, (US) rɪˈstɔːr.ə.t̬ɪv, rə- **-s** -z
restor|e rɪˈstɔːr, rə-, (US) -ˈstɔːr **-es** -z **-ing** -ɪŋ **-ed** -d **-er/s** -ər/z, (US) -ɚ/z **-able** -ə.bəl
restrain rɪˈstreɪn, rə- **-s** -z **-ing** -ɪŋ **-ed** -d **-er/s** -ər/z, (US) -ɚ/z
restraint rɪˈstreɪnt, rə- **-s** -s
restrict rɪˈstrɪkt, rə- **-s** -s **-ing** -ɪŋ **-ed** -ɪd
restriction rɪˈstrɪk.ʃən, rə- **-s** -z
restrictionism rɪˈstrɪk.ʃən.ɪ.zəm, rə-
restrictive rɪˈstrɪk.tɪv, rə- **-ly** -li **-ness** -nəs, -nɪs **reˌstrictive ˈpractice**
restroom ˈrest.rʊm, -ruːm, (US) -ruːm, -rʊm **-s** -z
restruct|ure ˌriːˈstrʌk.tʃ|ər, (US) -tʃ|ɚ **-ures** -əz, (US) -ɚz **-uring** -ər.ɪŋ **-ured** -əd, (US) -ɚd
Restylane® ˈres.ti.leɪn
re|sult rɪ|ˈzʌlt, rə- **-sults** -ˈzʌlts **-sulting** -ˈzʌl.tɪŋ, (US) -ˈzʌl.t̬ɪŋ **-sulted** -ˈzʌl.tɪd, (US) -ˈzʌl.t̬ɪd **-sultant/s** -ˈzʌl.tənt/s
resultative rɪˈzʌl.tə.tɪv, rə-, (US) -tə.t̬ɪv
resum|e rɪˈzjuːm, rə-, -ˈzuːm, (US) -ˈzuːm **-es** -z **-ing** -ɪŋ **-ed** -d
résumé, resumé ˈrez.juː.meɪ, ˈreɪ.zuː-, -zjʊ-, -zʊ-; rɪˈzjuː-, rə-, (US) ˈrez.ʊ.meɪ, ˈ-ə-, ˌ--ˈ- **-s** -z
resumption rɪˈzʌmp.ʃən, rə- **-s** -z
resumptive rɪˈzʌmp.tɪv, rə-
resurfac|e ˌriːˈsɜː.fɪs, -fəs, (US) -ˈsɝː- **-es** -ɪz **-ing** -ɪŋ **-ed** -t
resurgenc|e rɪˈsɜː.dʒənts, rə-, (US) -ˈsɝː- **-es** -ɪz
resurgent rɪˈsɜː.dʒənt, rə-, (US) -ˈsɝː-
resurrect ˌrez.ərˈekt, (US) -əˈrekt **-s** -s **-ing** -ɪŋ **-ed** -ɪd
resurrection, R~ ˌrez.ərˈek.ʃən, (US) -əˈrek- **-s** -z
resusci|tate rɪˈsʌs.ɪ|.teɪt, rə-, ˈ-ə-, (US) ˈ-ə- **-tates** -teɪts **-tating** -teɪ.tɪŋ, (US) -teɪ.t̬ɪŋ **-tated** -teɪ.tɪd, (US) -teɪ.t̬ɪd **-tator/s** -teɪ.tər/z, (US) -teɪ.t̬ɚ/z
resuscitation rɪˌsʌs.ɪˈteɪ.ʃən, rə-, -əˈ-, (US) -əˈ- **-s** -z
retail n, adj ˈriː.teɪl, ˌ-ˈ-, (US) ˈriː.teɪl ˌ**retail ˈprice**
retail v *sell:* ˈriː.teɪl, ˌ-ˈ-, (US) ˈriː.teɪl; (US) rɪˈteɪl *tell:* rɪˈteɪl, rə-, ˌriː- **-s** -z **-ing** -ɪŋ **-ed** -d **-er/s** -ər/z, (US) -ɚ/z
retain rɪˈteɪn, rə- **-s** -z **-ing** -ɪŋ **-ed** -d **-er/s** -ər/z, (US) -ɚ/z
retake n ˈriː.teɪk **-s** -s
re|take v ˌriːˈteɪk **-takes** -ˈteɪks **-taking** -ˈteɪ.kɪŋ **-took** -ˈtʊk **-taken** -ˈteɪ.kən
retali|ate rɪˈtæl.i|.eɪt, rə- **-ates** -eɪts **-ating** -eɪ.tɪŋ, (US) -eɪ.t̬ɪŋ **-ated** -eɪ.tɪd, (US) -eɪ.t̬ɪd
retaliation rɪˌtæl.iˈeɪ.ʃən, rə-
retaliatory rɪˈtæl.i.ə.tər.i, rə-, -eɪ-; rɪˌtæl.iˈeɪ-, rə-, (US) rɪˈtæl.i.ə.tɔːr-, rə-, ˈ-jə-
retard v rɪˈtɑːd, rə-, (US) -ˈtɑːrd **-s** -z **-ing** -ɪŋ **-ed** -ɪd
retard n ˈriː.tɑːd, (US) -tɑːrd **-s** -z
retardant rɪˈtɑː.dənt, rə-, (US) -ˈtɑːr- **-s** -s
retardation ˌriː.tɑːˈdeɪ.ʃən, (US) -tɑːrˈ- **-s** -z
retch retʃ, riːtʃ, (US) retʃ **-es** -ɪz **-ing** -ɪŋ **-ed** -t
retell ˌriːˈtel **-s** -z **-ing** -ɪŋ **retold** ˌriːˈtəʊld, (US) -ˈtoʊld
retention rɪˈten.tʃən, rə-
retentive rɪˈten.tɪv, rə-, (US) -t̬ɪv **-ly** -li **-ness** -nəs, -nɪs
Retford ˈret.fəd, (US) -fɚd
rethink v ˌriːˈθɪŋk **-s** -s **-ing** -ɪŋ **rethought** ˌriːˈθɔːt, (US) -ˈθɑːt, -ˈθɔːt
rethink n ˈriː.θɪŋk **-s** -s
reticence ˈret.ɪ.sənts, ˈ-ə-, (US) ˈret̬.ə-
reticent ˈret.ɪ.sənt, ˈ-ə-, (US) ˈret̬.ə- **-ly** -li
reticle ˈret.ɪ.kəl, (US) ˈret̬.ɪ- **-s** -z
reticulate adj rɪˈtɪk.jə.lət, rə-, retˈɪk-, -jʊ-, -lɪt, -leɪt, (US) rɪˈtɪk.jə.lɪt, rə-, -jʊ-, -leɪt
reticu|late v rɪˈtɪk.jə|.leɪt, rə-, retˈɪk-, -jʊ-, (US) rɪˈtɪk-, rə- **-lates** -leɪts **-lating** -leɪ.tɪŋ, (US) -leɪ.t̬ɪŋ **-lated** -leɪ.tɪd, (US) -leɪ.t̬ɪd
reticulation rɪˌtɪk.jəˈleɪ.ʃən, rə-, retˌɪk-, -jʊˈ-, (US) rɪˌtɪk-, rə- **-s** -z
reticule ˈret.ɪ.kjuːl, ˈ-ə-, (US) ˈret̬.ə- **-s** -z
retin|a ˈret.ɪ.n|ə, (US) -ən|.ə **-as** -əz **-ae** -iː **-al** -əl
retinol ˈret.ɪ.nɒl, (US) ˈret̬.ə.nɑːl, -nɔːl
retinue ˈret.ɪ.njuː, (US) -ən.uː, -juː **-s** -z
retir|e rɪˈtaɪər, -ˈtaɪ.ər, rə-, (US) -ˈtaɪ.ɚ **-es** -z **-ing** -ɪŋ **-ed** -d **-ant/s** -ənts
retiree rɪˌtaɪəˈriː, rə-, (US) rɪˈtaɪ.riː, rə- **-s** -z
retirement rɪˈtaɪə.mənt, -ˈtaɪ.ə-, rə-, (US) -ˈtaɪ.ɚ- **reˈtirement ˌage; reˈtirement ˌhome**
retold (from **retell**) ˌriːˈtəʊld, (US) -ˈtoʊld
re|tort rɪ|ˈtɔːt, rə-, (US) -ˈtɔːrt **-torts** -ˈtɔːts, (US) -ˈtɔːrts **-torting** -ˈtɔː.tɪŋ, (US) -ˈtɔːr.t̬ɪŋ **-torted** -ˈtɔː.tɪd, (US) -ˈtɔːr.t̬ɪd
retouch ˌriːˈtʌtʃ **-es** -ɪz **-ing** -ɪŋ **-ed** -t
retrac|e rɪˈtreɪs, ˌriː- **-es** -ɪz **-ing** -ɪŋ **-ed** -t
retract rɪˈtrækt, rə- **-s** -s **-ing** -ɪŋ **-ed** -ɪd **-or/s** -ər/z, (US) -ɚ/z
retractable rɪˈtræk.tə.bəl, rə-
retractation ˌriː.trækˈteɪ.ʃən
retraction rɪˈtræk.ʃən, rə- **-s** -z
retrain ˌriːˈtreɪn **-s** -z **-ing** -ɪŋ **-ed** -d
retransla|te ˌriː.trænˈsleɪ|t, -trɑːnˈ-, -trænzˈleɪ|t, -trɑːnzˈ-, -trənˈsleɪ|t, -trənzˈleɪ|t, (US) ˌriːˈtræn.sleɪ|t, -ˈtrænz.leɪ|t, ˌ--ˈ- **-tes** -ts **-ting** -tɪŋ, (US) -t̬ɪŋ **-ted** -tɪd, (US) -t̬ɪd
retranslation ˌriː.trænˈsleɪ.ʃən, -trɑːnˈ-, -trænzˈleɪ-, -trɑːnzˈ-, -trənˈsleɪ-, -trənzˈleɪ-, (US) -trænˈsleɪ-, -trænzˈleɪ- **-s** -z
retread n ˈriː.tred **-s** -z
retread v ˌriːˈtred **-s** -z **-ing** -ɪŋ
retrod ˌriːˈtrɒd, (US) -ˈtrɑːd
re|treat rɪ|ˈtriːt, rə- **-treats** -ˈtriːts **-treating** -ˈtriː.tɪŋ, (US) -ˈtriː.t̬ɪŋ **-treated** -ˈtriː.tɪd, (US) -ˈtriː.t̬ɪd
retrench rɪˈtrentʃ, rə-, (US) -ˈtrentʃ **-es** -ɪz **-ing** -ɪŋ **-ed** -t **-ment/s** -mənt/s
retrial ˌriːˈtraɪ.əl, ˈ--, (US) ˈriː.traɪəl, ˌ-ˈ- **-s** -z
retribution ˌret.rɪˈbjuː.ʃən, -rəˈ-, (US) -rəˈ-
retribu|tive rɪˈtrɪb.jə|.tɪv, rə-, -jʊ-, -t̬ɪv **-tory** -tər.i, (US) -tɔːr-
retrievab|le rɪˈtriː.və.b|əl, rə- **-ly** -li **-leness** -əl.nəs, -nɪs
retrieval rɪˈtriː.vəl, rə-
retriev|e rɪˈtriːv, rə- **-es** -z **-ing** -ɪŋ **-ed** -d **-er/s** -ər/z, (US) -ɚ/z
retrim ˌriːˈtrɪm **-s** -z **-ming** -ɪŋ **-med** -d
retro ˈret.rəʊ, (US) -roʊ
retro- ˈret.rəʊ, (US) ˈret.roʊ, ˈ-rə
Note: Prefix. Normally takes primary or secondary stress on the first syllable, e.g. **retrograde** /ˈret.rəʊ.greɪd/ (US) /-rə-/, **retroact** /ˌret.rəʊˈækt/ (US) /-roʊˈ-/.
retroact ˌret.rəʊˈækt, (US) -roʊˈ- **-s** -s **-ing** -ɪŋ **-ed** -ɪd
retroaction ˌret.rəʊˈæk.ʃən, (US) -roʊˈ-
retroactive ˌret.rəʊˈæk.tɪv, (US) -roʊˈ- **-ly** -li *stress shift:* ˌ**retroactive ˈlaws**
retroced|e ˌret.rəʊˈsiːd, (US) -roʊˈ-, -rəˈ- **-es** -z **-ing** -ɪŋ **-ed** -ɪd
retrocession ˌret.rəʊˈseʃ.ən, (US) -roʊˈ-, -rəˈ- **-s** -z
retroflex ˈret.rəʊ.fleks, (US) -rə- **-ed** -t
retroflexion ˌret.rəʊˈflek.ʃən, (US) -rəˈ-
retrograde ˈret.rəʊ.greɪd, (US) -rə-, -roʊ-
retrogress ˌret.rəʊˈgres, (US) ˈret.rə.gres, -roʊ-, ˌ--ˈ- **-es** -ɪz **-ing** -ɪŋ **-ed** -t **-ive/ly** -ɪv/li
retrogression ˌret.rəʊˈgreʃ.ən, (US) -rəˈ-, -roʊˈ-
retro-rocket ˈret.rəʊˌrɒk.ɪt, (US) -roʊˌrɑː.kɪt **-s** -s
retrospect ˈret.rəʊ.spekt, (US) -rə- **-s** -s
retrospection ˌret.rəʊˈspek.ʃən, (US) -rəˈ- **-s** -z
retrospective ˌret.rəʊˈspek.tɪv, (US) -rəˈ- **-s** -z **-ly** -li *stress shift:* ˌ**retrospective ˈview**
retroussé rəˈtruː.seɪ, rɪ-, (US) rəˌtruːˈseɪ, retˌruː-
retroversion ˌret.rəʊˈvɜː.ʃən, -ʒən, (US) -roʊˈvɝː.ʒən, -rəˈ-, -ʃən **-s** -z

R

retrovert n ˈret.rəʊ.vɜːt, (US) -roʊ.vɝːt, -rə- -s -s

retro|vert v ˌret.rəʊˈvɜːt, (US) -roʊˈvɝːt, -rə- -verts -ˈvɜːts, (US) -ˈvɝːts -verting -ˈvɜː.tɪŋ, (US) -ˈvɝː.t̬ɪŋ -verted -ˈvɜː.tɪd, (US) -ˈvɝː.t̬ɪd

retrovirus ˈret.rəʊ.vaɪə.rəs, ˌret.rəʊˈvaɪə-, (US) ˈret.roʊˌvaɪ- -es -ɪz

retr|y ˌriːˈtr|aɪ -ies -aɪz -ying -aɪ.ɪŋ -ied -aɪd

retsina retˈsiː.nə, ˈret.sɪ.nə

returf ˌriːˈtɜːf, (US) -ˈtɝːf -s -s -ing -ɪŋ -ed -t

return rɪˈtɜːn, rə-, (US) -ˈtɝːn -s -z -ing -ɪŋ -ed -d -able -ə.bᵊl -er/s -əʳ/z, (US) -ɚ/z

returnee rɪˌtɜːˈniː, rə-, -ˈtɜː.niː, (US) rɪˌtɝːˈniː, rə- -s -z

Reuben ˈruː.bən, -bɪn, (US) -bən

reunification ˌriː.juː.nɪ.fɪˈkeɪ.ʃᵊn, riːˌjuː-, -nə-, -fəˈ-, (US) riːˌjuː.nə- -s -z

reuni|fy ˌriːˈjuː.nɪ|.faɪ, -nə- -fies -faɪz -fying -faɪ.ɪŋ -fied -faɪd

reunion ˌriːˈjuː.ni.ən, (US) ˈ-njən -s -z

Réunion ˌriːˈjuː.ni.ən; *as if French:* ˌreɪ.uːˈnjɔ̃ːŋ; (US) ˌriːˈjuːn.jən

reu|nite ˌriː.juː|ˈnaɪt -nites -ˈnaɪts -niting -ˈnaɪ.tɪŋ, (US) -ˈnaɪ.t̬ɪŋ -nited -ˈnaɪ.tɪd, (US) -ˈnaɪ.t̬ɪd

reusable ˌriːˈjuː.zə.bᵊl

re-use n ˌriːˈjuːs, ˈ--, (US) ˌriːˈjuːs

re-us|e v ˌriːˈjuːz -es -ɪz -ing -ɪŋ -ed -d

Reuter ˈrɔɪ.təʳ, (US) -t̬ɚ -s -z

rev n, v rev -s -z -ving -ɪŋ -ved -d **ˈrev ˌcounter**

Rev. (abbrev. for **Reverend**) ˈrev.ᵊr.ᵊnd, rev

revalu|e riːˈvæl.juː, ˌriː- -es -z -ing -ɪŋ -ed -d

revamp v ˌriːˈvæmp -s -s -ing -ɪŋ -ed -t

revamp n ˈriː.væmp -s -s

revanch|ist rɪˈvæntʃ|.ɪst -ists -ɪsts -ism -ɪ.zᵊm

Revd (abbrev. for **Reverend**) ˈrev.ᵊr.ᵊnd

reveal rɪˈviːl, rə- -s -z -ing -ɪŋ -ed -d -er/s -əʳ/z, (US) -ɚ/z -able -ə.bᵊl

revealing rɪˈviː.lɪŋ -ly -li

reveille rɪˈvæl.i, rə-, -ˈvel-, (US) ˈrev.ᵊl.i -s -z

revel ˈrev.ᵊl -s -z -(l)ing -ɪŋ -(l)ed -d -(l)er/s -əʳ/z, (US) -ɚ/z

revelation, R~ ˌrev.ᵊlˈeɪ.ʃᵊn -s -z

revelatory ˌrev.əˈleɪ.tᵊr.i, (US) ˈrev.ə.lə.tɔːr.i

Revell ˈrev.ᵊl

revelr|y ˈrev.ᵊl.r|i -ies -iz

Revelstoke ˈrev.ᵊl.stəʊk, (US) -stoʊk

revendication rɪˌven.dɪˈkeɪ.ʃᵊn, rə-, -dəˈ-, (US) -dəˈ- -s -z

reveng|e rɪˈvendʒ, rə- -es -ɪz -ing -ɪŋ -ed -d

revengeful rɪˈvendʒ.fᵊl, rə-, -fʊl -ly -i -ness -nəs, -nɪs

revenue ˈrev.ᵊn.juː, -ɪ.njuː, (US) ˈrev.ə.nuː, -njuː -s -z

reverber|ate rɪˈvɜː.bᵊr|.eɪt, rə-, (US) -ˈvɝː.bə.r|eɪt -ates -eɪts -ating -eɪ.tɪŋ, (US) -eɪ.t̬ɪŋ -ated -eɪ.tɪd, (US) -eɪ.t̬ɪd -ator/s -eɪ.təʳ/z, (US) -eɪ.t̬ɚ/z

reverberation rɪˌvɜː.bᵊrˈeɪ.ʃᵊn, rə-, (US) -ˌvɝː.bəˈreɪ- -s -z

reverberatory rɪˈvɜː.bᵊr.ə.tᵊr.i, rə-, -reɪ-, (US) -ˈvɝː.bɚ.ə.tɔːr-

rever|e, R~ rɪˈvɪəʳ, rə-, (US) -ˈvɪr -es -z -ing -ɪŋ -ed -d

reverenc|e ˈrev.ᵊr.ᵊnts, ˈ-rᵊnts -es -ɪz -ing -ɪŋ -ed -t

reverend, R~ ˈrev.ᵊr.ᵊnd, ˈ-rᵊnd -s -z

reverent ˈrev.ᵊr.ᵊnt, ˈ-rᵊnt -ly -li

reverential ˌrev.ᵊrˈen.tʃᵊl, (US) -əˈrent.ʃᵊl -ly -i

reverie ˈrev.ᵊr.i, (US) -ə.ri -s -z

revers *singular:* rɪˈvɪəʳ, rə-, -ˈveəʳ, (US) -ˈvɪr, -ˈver *plural:* -z

reversal rɪˈvɜː.sᵊl, rə-, (US) -ˈvɝː- -s -z

revers|e rɪˈvɜːs, rə-, (US) -ˈvɝːs -es -ɪz -ing -ɪŋ -ed -t

reversibility rɪˌvɜː.səˈbɪl.ə.ti, rə-, -sɪˈ-, -ɪ.ti, (US) -ˌvɝː.səˈbɪl.ə.t̬i

reversible rɪˈvɜː.sə.bᵊl, rə-, -sɪ-, (US) -ˈvɝː.sə-

reversion rɪˈvɜː.ʃᵊn, rə-, (US) -ˈvɝː.ʒᵊn, -ʃᵊn -s -z

reversionary rɪˈvɜː.ʃᵊn.ᵊr.i, rə-, -ʒᵊn-, (US) -ˈvɝː.ʒᵊn.er-, -ʃᵊn-

re|vert rɪ|ˈvɜːt, rə-, (US) -ˈvɝːt -verts -ˈvɜːts, (US) -ˈvɝːts -verting -ˈvɜː.tɪŋ, (US) -ˈvɝː.t̬ɪŋ -verted -ˈvɜː.tɪd, (US) -ˈvɝː.t̬ɪd

reverter rɪˈvɜː.təʳ, rə-, (US) -ˈvɝː.t̬ɚ

re|vet rɪ|ˈvet, rə- -vets -ˈvets -vetting -ˈvet.ɪŋ, (US) -ˈvet̬.ɪŋ -vetted -ˈvet.ɪd, (US) -ˈvet̬.ɪd -vetment/s -ˈvet.mənt/s

review rɪˈvjuː, rə- -s -z -ing -ɪŋ -ed -d -er/s -əʳ/z, (US) -ɚ/z

revil|e rɪˈvaɪl, rə- -es -z -ing -ɪŋ -ed -d -er/s -əʳ/z, (US) -ɚ/z

revis|e rɪˈvaɪz, rə- -es -ɪz -ing -ɪŋ -ed -d -er/s -əʳ/z, (US) -ɚ/z **Reˌvised ˈVersion; Reˈvised ˌVersion**

revision rɪˈvɪʒ.ᵊn, rə- -s -z

revision|ism rɪˈvɪʒ.ᵊn|.ɪ.zᵊm, rə- -ist/s -ɪst/s

revis|it ˌriːˈvɪz|.ɪt -its -ɪts -iting -ɪ.tɪŋ, (US) -ɪ.t̬ɪŋ -ited -ɪ.tɪd, (US) -ɪ.t̬ɪd

revisualiz|e, -is|e ˌriːˈvɪz.ju.ᵊl.aɪz, -ˈvɪʒ-, -u-, (US) -ˈvɪʒ.u- -es -ɪz -ing -ɪŋ -ed -d

revitaliz|e, -is|e ˌriːˈvaɪ.tᵊl.aɪz, (US) -t̬ᵊl- -es -ɪz -ing -ɪŋ -ed -d

revival rɪˈvaɪ.vᵊl, rə- -s -z

revival|ism rɪˈvaɪ.vᵊl|.ɪ.zᵊm, rə- -ist/s -ɪst/s

reviv|e rɪˈvaɪv, rə- -es -z -ing -ɪŋ -ed -d

revivi|fy ˌriːˈvɪv.ɪ|.faɪ, rɪ-, ˈ-ə- -fies -faɪz -fying -faɪ.ɪŋ -fied -faɪd

reviviscence ˌrev.ɪˈvɪs.ᵊnts, ˌriː.vaɪˈ-, (US) ˌrev.əˈ-

Revlon® ˈrev.lɒn, (US) -lɑːn

revocability ˌrev.ə.kəˈbɪl.ə.ti, -ɪ.ti, (US) -ə.t̬i

revocable ˈrev.ə.kə.bᵊl *when applied to letters of credit:* rɪˈvəʊ.kə.bᵊl, rə-, (US) -ˈvoʊ-

revocation ˌrev.əʊˈkeɪ.ʃᵊn, (US) -əˈ- -s -z

revok|e rɪˈvəʊk, rə-, (US) -ˈvoʊk -es -s -ing -ɪŋ -ed -t

re|volt rɪ|ˈvəʊlt, rə-, (US) -ˈvoʊlt -volts -ˈvəʊlts, (US) -ˈvoʊlts -volting -ˈvəʊl.tɪŋ, (US) -ˈvoʊl.tɪŋ -volted -ˈvəʊl.tɪd, (US) -ˈvoʊl.tɪd

revolution ˌrev.ᵊlˈuː.ʃᵊn, -ˈjuː-, (US) -əˈluː- -s -z

revolutionar|y ˌrev.ᵊlˈuː.ʃᵊn.ᵊr|.i, -ˈjuː-, (US) -əˈluː.ʃᵊn.er- -ies -iz

revolutionist ˌrev.ᵊlˈuː.ʃᵊn.ɪst, -ˈjuː-, (US) -əˈluː- -s -s

revolutioniz|e, -is|e ˌrev.ᵊlˈuː.ʃᵊn.aɪz, -ˈjuː-, (US) -əˈluː- -es -ɪz -ing -ɪŋ -ed -d

revolv|e rɪˈvɒlv, rə-, (US) -ˈvɑːlv -es -z -ing -ɪŋ -ed -d **reˌvolving ˈcredit; reˌvolving ˈdoor; reˌvolving ˈfund**

revolver rɪˈvɒl.vəʳ, rə-, (US) -ˈvɑːl.vɚ -s -z

revue rɪˈvjuː, rə- -s -z

revulsion rɪˈvʌl.ʃᵊn, rə- -s -z

reward rɪˈwɔːd, rə-, (US) -ˈwɔːrd -s -z -ing -ɪŋ -ed -ɪd

rewind ˌriːˈwaɪnd -s -z -ing -ɪŋ **rewound** ˌriːˈwaʊnd

rewir|e ˌriːˈwaɪəʳ, -ˈwaɪ.əʳ, (US) -ˈwaɪ.ɚ -es -z -ing -ɪŋ -ed -d

reword ˌriːˈwɜːd, (US) -ˈwɝːd -s -z -ing -ɪŋ -ed -ɪd

rework ˌriːˈwɜːk -s -s -ing -ɪŋ -ed -t

rewrite n ˈriː.raɪt -s -s

re|write v ˌriː|ˈraɪt -writes -ˈraɪts -writing -ˈraɪ.tɪŋ, (US) -ˈraɪ.t̬ɪŋ -wrote ˌriːˈrəʊt, (US) -ˈroʊt -written ˌriːˈrɪt.ᵊn

Rex reks

Reyes raɪz, reɪz

Reykjavik ˈreɪ.kjə.vɪk, ˈrek.jə-, -viːk, (US) ˈreɪ.kjə.viːk, -vɪk

reynard ˈren.ɑːd, ˈreɪ.nɑːd, -nəd, (US) ˈren.ɚd, ˈreɪ.nɚd, -nɑːrd -s -z

Reynard ˈren.əd, -ɑːd, ˈreɪ.nɑːd, (US) ˈren.ɑːrd, ˈreɪ.nɚd, ˈren.ɚd

Reynold ˈren.ᵊld -s -z

Rezco ˈrez.kəʊ, (US) -koʊ

rezon|e ˌriːˈzəʊn, (US) -ˈzoʊn -es -z -ing -ɪŋ -ed -d

Rh (abbrev. for **rhesus**) ˈriː.səs

Rhadamanthus ˌræd.əˈmænt.θəs

Rhaeti|a ˈriː.ʃi|.ə, ˈ-ʃ|ə, (US) -ʃ|ə, ˈ-ʃi|.ə -an -ən

Rhaetic ˈriː.tɪk, (US) -t̬ɪk

Rhaeto-Roman|ce ˌriː.təʊ.rəʊˈmæn|ts, (US) -t̬oʊ.roʊˈ- -ic -ɪk

rhapsodic ræpˈsɒd.ɪk, (US) -ˈsɑː.dɪk -al -ᵊl -ally -ᵊl.i, -li

rhapsodiz|e, -is|e ˈræp.sə.daɪz -es -ɪz -ing -ɪŋ -ed -d

rhapsod|y ˈræp.sə.d|i -ies -iz

rhea, R~ ˈriː.ə, rɪə, (US) ˈriː.ə -s -z

Rhea Silvia ˌriː.əˈsɪl.vi.ə, ˌrɪəˈ-, (US) ˌriː.əˈ-

R

Rheims riːmz
Rhenish ˈren.ɪʃ
rhenium ˈriː.ni.əm
rheostat ˈriː.əʊ.stæt, (US) -oʊ-, ˈ-ə- **-s** -s
rhesus ˈriː.səs **-es** -ɪz **ˈrhesus ˌfactor; ˌrhesus ˈmonkey; ˈrhesus ˌmonkey**
rhetoric ˈret.ᵊr.ɪk, (US) ˈreţ-
rhetoric|al rɪˈtɒr.ɪ.k|ᵊl, rə-, (US) -ˈtɔːr.ɪ- **-ally** -ᵊl.i, -li **rheˌtorical ˈquestion**
rhetorician ˌret.ᵊrˈɪʃ.ᵊn, -ɒrˈ-, (US) ˌreţ.əˈrɪʃ- **-s** -z
Rhett ret
rheum ruːm
rheumatic ruːˈmæt.ɪk, (US) -ˈmæţ- **-s** -s **-ky** -i
rheumatism ˈruː.mə.tɪ.zᵊm
rheumatoid ˈruː.mə.tɔɪd **ˌrheumatoid arthˈritis**
rheumatolog|y ˌruː.məˈtɒl.ə.dʒ|i, (US) -ˈtɑː.lə- **-ist/s** -ɪst/s
rheumy ˈruː.mi
Rhiannon riˈæn.ən
Rhine raɪn **-land** -lænd, -lənd
Rhineland-Palatinate ˌraɪn.lænd.pəˈlæt.ɪ.nət, -lənd-, -nɪt, -neɪt, (US) -lænd.pəˈlæt.ᵊn.eɪt, -lənd-, -ɪt
rhinestone ˈraɪn.stəʊn, (US) -stoʊn **-s** -z
rhinitis raɪˈnaɪ.tɪs, -təs, (US) -ţɪs, -ţəs
rhino ˈraɪ.nəʊ, (US) -noʊ **-s** -z
rhino- ˈraɪ.nəʊ; raɪˈnɒ, (US) ˈraɪ.noʊ, ˈ-nə; (US) raɪˈnɑː
Note: Prefix. Normally either takes primary or secondary stress on the first syllable, e.g. **rhinoplasty** /ˈraɪ.nəʊ.plæs.ti/ (US) /-noʊ-/, or primary stress on the second syllable, e.g. **rhinoceros** /raɪˈnɒs.ᵊr.əs/ (US) /-ˈnɑː.sɚ-/.
rhinoceri (alternative plural of **rhinoceros**) raɪˈnɒs.ᵊr.aɪ, (US) -ˈnɑː.sə.raɪ
rhinoceros raɪˈnɒs.ᵊr.əs, (US) -ˈnɑː.sɚ- **-es** -ɪz
rhinolog|y raɪˈnɒl.ə.dʒ|i, (US) -ˈnɑː.lə- **-ist/s** -ɪst/s
rhinoplasty ˈraɪ.nəʊ.plæs.ti, (US) -noʊ-, -nə-
rhinoscope ˈraɪ.nəʊ.skəʊp, (US) -nə.skoʊp **-s** -s
rhinoscopy raɪˈnɒs.kə.pi, (US) -ˈnɑː.skə-
rhizome ˈraɪ.zəʊm, (US) -zoʊm **-s** -z
rho rəʊ, (US) roʊ
Rhoads rəʊdz, (US) roʊdz
Rhoda ˈrəʊ.də, (US) ˈroʊ-
Rhode Island *state in US:* ˌrəʊdˈaɪ.lənd, (US) ˌroʊd- **-er/s** -ər/z, (US) -ɚ/z *stress shift, see compound:* **ˌRhode Island ˈRed**
Rhodes rəʊdz, (US) roʊdz **ˌRhodes ˈscholar**
Rhodesi|a rəʊˈdiː.ʒ|ə, -ʃ|ə, (US) roʊ-, ˈ-ʒi|.ə **-an** -ən
Rhodian ˈrəʊ.di.ən, (US) ˈroʊ- **-s** -z
rhodium ˈrəʊ.di.əm, (US) ˈroʊ-
rhododendron ˌrəʊ.dəˈden.drən, -drˈ-, (US) ˌroʊ.dəˈ- **-s** -z
rhomb rɒm, (US) rɑːmb **-s** -z
rhomboid ˈrɒm.bɔɪd, (US) ˈrɑːm- **-s** -z
rhomb|us ˈrɒm.b|əs, (US) ˈrɑːm- **-uses** -ə.sɪz **-i** -aɪ
Rhona ˈrəʊ.nə, (US) ˈroʊ-
Rhonda ˈrɒn.də, (US) ˈrɑːn-
Rhondda ˈrɒn.də, -ðə, (US) ˈrɑːn-
Rhone rəʊn, (US) roʊn
Rhosllanerchrugog ˌrəʊs.*h*læn.əˈkrɪg.ɒg, -θlæn-, (US) ˌroʊs.*h*læn.əˈkriː.gɑːg
rhotacism ˈrəʊ.tə.sɪ.zᵊm, (US) ˈroʊ.ţə-
rhotacization, -isa- ˌrəʊ.tə.saɪˈzeɪ.ʃᵊn, -tɪ-, -sɪˈ-, (US) ˌroʊ.ţə.səˈ- **-s** -z
rhotaciz|e, -is|e ˈrəʊ.tə.saɪz, (US) ˈroʊ.ţə- **-es** -ɪz **-ing** -ɪŋ **-ed** -d
rhotic ˈrəʊ.tɪk, (US) ˈroʊ.ţɪk **-s** -s
rhoticity rəʊˈtɪs.ɪ.ti, -ə.ti, (US) roʊˈtɪs.ə.ţi
rhubarb ˈruː.bɑːb, (US) -bɑːrb
Rhuddlan ˈrɪð.lən, -læn
rhumb rʌm, (US) rʌmb **-s** -z
Rhyl rɪl
rhym|e raɪm **-es** -z **-ing** -ɪŋ **-ed** -d **-er/s** -ər/z, (US) -ɚ/z
rhymester ˈraɪm.stər, (US) -stɚ **-s** -z
Rhymney ˈrʌm.ni
Rhys *Welsh name:* riːs *family name of Baron Dynevor:* raɪs
Rhys-Jones ˌriːsˈdʒəʊnz, (US) -ˈdʒoʊnz
rhythm ˈrɪð.ᵊm, ˈrɪθ-, (US) ˈrɪð- **-s** -z **ˌrhythm and ˈblues; ˈrhythm ˌmethod**
rhythmic ˈrɪð.mɪk, ˈrɪθ-, (US) ˈrɪð- **-al** -ᵊl **-ally** -ᵊl.i, (US) -li
RI ˌɑːrˈaɪ, (US) ˌɑːr-
ria ˈriː.ə, rɪə, (US) ˈriː.ə **-s** -z
rial riˈɑːl; ˈraɪ.əl, ˈraɪ.əl, (US) ˈriː.ɔːl, -ɑːl **-s** -z

> Note: The usual pronunciation for the Saudi Arabian currency is /riˈɑːl/ (US) /ˈriː.ɔːl/.

rialto, R~ riˈæl.təʊ, (US) -toʊ **-s** -z
rib rɪb **-s** -z **-bing** -ɪŋ **-bed** -d **ˈrib ˌcage**
ribald ˈrɪb.ᵊld, ˈraɪ.bᵊld, -bɔːld, (US) ˈrɪb.ᵊld, ˈraɪ.bɔːld **-s** -z **-ry** -ri
riband ˈrɪb.ənd **-s** -z
Ribbentrop ˈrɪb.ᵊn.trɒp, (US) -trɑːp
Ribble ˈrɪb.ᵊl
ribbon ˈrɪb.ᵊn **-s** -z
Ribena® raɪˈbiː.nə
riboflavin ˌraɪ.bəʊˈfleɪ.vɪn, ˈraɪ.bəʊ.fleɪ-, (US) ˈraɪ.bə.fleɪ.vɪn; (US) ˌraɪ.bəˈfleɪ-, -boʊˈ-
ribosomal ˌraɪ.bəʊˈsəʊ.mᵊl, (US) -bəˈsoʊ-
ribosome ˈraɪ.bəʊ.səʊm, (US) -bə.soʊm **-s** -z
Rica ˈriː.kə
Ricardo rɪˈkɑː.dəʊ, (US) -ˈkɑːr.doʊ
Ricci ˈriː.tʃi
Riccio ˈrɪtʃ.i.əʊ, ˈrɪt.si-, (US) ˈrɪt.ʃi.oʊ; (US) ˈriːt.ʃoʊ
ric|e, R~ raɪs **-es** -ɪz **-ing** -ɪŋ **-ed** -t **ˈrice ˌpaper; ˌrice ˈpudding**
Rice Krispies® ˌraɪsˈkrɪs.piz
rich, R~ rɪtʃ **-es** -ɪz **-er** -ər, (US) -ɚ **-est** -ɪst, -əst **-ly** -li **-ness** -nəs, -nɪs
Richard ˈrɪtʃ.əd, (US) -ɚd **-s** -z
Richardson ˈrɪtʃ.əd.sᵊn, (US) -ɚd-
Richelieu ˈriː.ʃᵊl.jɜː, ˈrɪʃ.ᵊl-, -juː, (US) ˈrɪʃ.ə.luː, ˈriː.ʃ-
Riches ˈrɪtʃ.ɪz
Richey, Richie ˈrɪtʃ.i
Richie ˈrɪtʃ.i
Richler ˈrɪtʃ.lər, (US) -lɚ
Richmond ˈrɪtʃ.mənd
Richter ˈrɪk.tə, ˈrɪx-, (US) ˈrɪk.tɚ **ˈRichter ˌscale**
Richthofen ˈrɪk.təʊ.fən, ˈrɪx-, (US) -toʊ-
ricin ˈraɪ.sɪn
rick rɪk **-s** -s **-ing** -ɪŋ **-ed** -d
Rickard ˈrɪk.ɑːd, (US) -ɑːrd **-s** -z
rickets ˈrɪk.ɪts
Rickett ˈrɪk.ɪt
Ricketts ˈrɪk.ɪts
rickettsi|a rɪˈket.si|.ə **-ae** -iː **-as** -əz
ricket|y ˈrɪk.ə.t|i, -ɪ.t|i, (US) -ə.ţ|i **-ier** -i.ər, (US) -i.ɚ **-iest** -i.ɪst, -i.əst **-ily** -ᵊl.i, -ɪ.li **-iness** -ɪ.nəs, -ɪ.nɪs
Rickmansworth ˈrɪk.mənz.wəθ, -wɜːθ, (US) -wɚθ, -wɜːθ
rickshaw ˈrɪk.ʃɔː, (US) -ʃɑː, -ʃɔː **-s** -z
Ricky ˈrɪk.i
Rico ˈriː.kəʊ, (US) -koʊ
ricoch|et ˈrɪk.ə.ʃ|eɪ, -ɒʃ|.eɪ, -et, ˌ--ˈ-, (US) ˈrɪk.ə.ʃ|eɪ, ˌ--ˈ- **-ets** -eɪz, -ets, (US) -eɪz **-eting** -eɪ.ɪŋ, -et.ɪŋ, (US) -eɪ.ɪŋ **-eted** -eɪd, -et.ɪd, (US) -eɪd
ricotta rɪˈkɒt.ə, rə-, (US) -ˈkɑː.ţə
rictus ˈrɪk.təs
rid rɪd **-s** -z **-ding** -ɪŋ
Ridd rɪd
riddance ˈrɪd.ᵊn*t*s
Riddell ˈrɪd.ᵊl; rɪˈdel
-ridden ˌrɪd.ᵊn
Ridding ˈrɪd.ɪŋ
riddl|e ˈrɪd.ᵊl **-es** -z **-ing** -ɪŋ, ˈrɪd.lɪŋ **-ed** -d
rid|e, R~ raɪd **-es** -z **-ing** -ɪŋ **rode** rəʊd, (US) roʊd **ridden** ˈrɪd.ᵊn
rid|er, R~ ˈraɪ.d|ər, (US) -d|ɚ **-ers** -əz, (US) -ɚz **-erless** -ᵊl.əs, -ɪs, -es, (US) -ɚ.ləs, -lɪs, -les
ridg|e, R~ rɪdʒ **-es** -ɪz **-ed** -d
ridgepole ˈrɪdʒ.pəʊl, (US) -poʊl **-s** -z
Ridg(e)way ˈrɪdʒ.weɪ
ridicul|e ˈrɪd.ɪ.kjuːl, ˈ-ə- **-es** -z **-ing** -ɪŋ **-ed** -d
ridiculous rɪˈdɪk.jə.ləs, rə-, -jʊ- **-ly** -li **-ness** -nəs, -nɪs
Riding ˈraɪ.dɪŋ **-s** -z
Ridley ˈrɪd.li
Ridout ˈrɪd.aʊt, ˈraɪ.daʊt
Ridpath ˈrɪd.pɑːθ, (US) -pæθ
riel ˈriː.əl, (US) riˈel
Rienzi riˈen.zi, -ˈent.si, (US) -ˈen.zi
Riesling ˈriː.slɪŋ, ˈriːz.lɪŋ, (US) ˈriːz-, ˈriː.slɪŋ

Rievaulx ˈriː.vəʊ, -vəʊz; ˈrɪv.əz, (US) ˈriː.voʊ, -voʊz

Note: /ˈriː.vəʊ/ (US) /-voʊ/ is the usual local pronunciation.

rife raɪf
riff rɪf **-s** -s
riffl|e ˈrɪf.ᵊl **-es** -z **-ing** -ɪŋ, ˈrɪf.lɪŋ **-ed** -d
riff-raff ˈrɪf.ræf
Rifkind ˈrɪf.kɪnd
rifl|e ˈraɪ.fᵊl **-es** -z **-ing** -ɪŋ, ˈraɪ.flɪŋ **-ed** -d ˈ**rifle** ˌ**range**
rift rɪft **-s** -s **-ing** -ɪŋ **-ed** -ɪd ˌ**rift** ˈ**valley**; ˈ**rift** ˌ**valley**
rig rɪɡ **-s** -z **-ging** -ɪŋ **-ged** -d
Riga ˈriː.ɡə
rigamarole ˈrɪɡ.ə.mə.rəʊl, (US) -roʊl **-s** -z
rigatoni ˌrɪɡ.əˈtəʊ.ni, (US) -ˈtoʊ-
Rigby ˈrɪɡ.bi
Rigel ˈraɪ.ɡᵊl, -dʒᵊl, (US) -dʒᵊl, -ɡᵊl
Rigg rɪɡ
rigger ˈrɪɡ.əʳ, (US) -ɚ **-s** -z
rigging n ˈrɪɡ.ɪŋ **-s** -z
right, R~ raɪt **-s** -s **-ly** -li **-ness** -nəs, -nɪs **-ing** -ɪŋ, (US) ˈraɪ.t̬ɪŋ **-ed** -ɪd, (US) ˈraɪ.t̬ɪd ˈ**right** ˌ**angle**; ˌ**right** ˈ**wing**
rightabout ˈraɪt.əˌbaʊt, (US) ˈraɪt̬-
right angle n ˈraɪtˌæŋ.ɡᵊl, (US) ˈraɪt̬- **-s** -z
right-angled adj ˈraɪtˌæŋ.ɡᵊl*d*, (US) ˈraɪt̬-, ˌ-ˈ--
righteous ˈraɪ.tʃəs, -ti.əs, (US) -tʃəs **-ly** -li **-ness** -nəs, -nɪs
rightful ˈraɪt.fᵊl, -fʊl **-ly** -i **-ness** -nəs, -nɪs
right-hand ˌraɪtˈhænd, (US) ˌraɪtˈhænd, ˈ-- *stress shift, British only, see compound:* ˌ**right-hand** ˈ**man**
right-handed ˌraɪtˈhæn.dɪd *stress shift:* ˌ**right-handed** ˈ**player**
right|ism, R~ ˈraɪ.t|ɪ.zᵊm, (US) -t̬|ɪ-
rightist ˈraɪ.tɪst **-s** -s
right-minded ˌraɪtˈmaɪn.dɪd **-ly** -li **-ness** -nəs, -nɪs *stress shift:* ˌ**right-minded** ˈ**person**
right(h)o ˌraɪtˈəʊ, (US) -ˈoʊ
right-of-way ˌraɪt.əvˈweɪ, (US) ˌraɪt.əvˈweɪ, ˈ--ˌ- **rights-of-way** ˌraɪts-, (US) ˌraɪts-, ˈ--ˌ-
right-on ˌraɪtˈɒn, (US) -ˈɑːn *stress shift:* ˌ**right-on** ˈ**speaker**
right-wing adj ˌraɪtˈwɪŋ **-er/s** -əʳ/s, (US) -ɚ/z *stress shift:* ˌ**right-wing** ˈ**policies**
righty-ho ˌraɪ.tiˈhəʊ, (US) -t̬iˈhoʊ
rigid ˈrɪdʒ.ɪd **-ly** -li **-ness** -nəs, -nɪs
rigidity rɪˈdʒɪd.ə.ti, -ɪ.ti, (US) -ə.t̬i
rigmarole ˈrɪɡ.mᵊr.əʊl, (US) -mə.roʊl **-s** -z
Rigoletto ˌrɪɡ.əʊˈlet.əʊ, (US) -əˈlet.oʊ
rigor ˈrɪɡ.əʳ, (US) -ɚ
rigor mortis ˌrɪɡ.əˈmɔː.tɪs, ˌraɪ.ɡɔːˈ-, (US) ˌrɪɡ.ɚˈmɔːr.t̬ɪs, ˌraɪ.ɡɔːrˈ-
rigorous ˈrɪɡ.ᵊr.əs **-ly** -li **-ness** -nəs, -nɪs
rigour ˈrɪɡ.əʳ, (US) -ɚ **-s** -z
rig-out ˈrɪɡ.aʊt
Rig-Veda ˌrɪɡˈveɪ.də, (US) -ˈveɪ-, -ˈviː-
Rijeka riˈek.ə, (US) -ˈjek-, -ˈek-
Rikki-Tiki-Tavi ˌrɪk.iˌtɪk.iˈtɑː.vi, -ˈteɪ-, (US) -ˈtɑː-, -ˈtæv.i
rill|e rɪl **-es** -z **-ing** -ɪŋ **-ed** -d
Riley ˈraɪ.li
rilievo ˌrɪl.iˈeɪ.vəʊ, (US) -voʊ, -ˈjeɪ-
Rilke ˈrɪl.kə
rill rɪl **-s** -z
rim rɪm **-s** -z **-ming** -ɪŋ **-med** -d **-less** -ləs, -lɪs
Rimbaud ˈræ̃m.bəʊ, (US) ræmˈboʊ
rime raɪm **-s** -z
Rimington ˈrɪm.ɪŋ.tən
Rimini ˈrɪm.ɪ.ni, ˈ-ə-, (US) ˈ-ə-
Rimsky-Korsakov ˌrɪm*p*.skiˈkɔː.sə.kɒf, -kɒv, (US) -ˈkɔːr.sə.kɔːf
Rinaldo rɪˈnæl.dəʊ, (US) rɪˈnɑːl.doʊ, -næl-
rind raɪnd **-s** -z
Rind rɪnd
rinderpest ˈrɪn.də.pest, (US) -dɚ-
ring n, v *encircle, put a ring on, etc.:* rɪŋ **-s** -z **-ing** -ɪŋ **-ed** -d ˈ**ring** ˌ**binder**; ˌ**ring** ˈ**binder**; ˈ**ring** ˌ**finger**; ˈ**ring** ˌ**road**; ˌ**run** ˈ**rings round** ˌ**someone**
ring n, v *sound, etc.:* rɪŋ **-s** -z **-ing** -ɪŋ **rang** ræŋ **rung** rʌŋ **-er/s** -əʳ/z, (US) -ɚ/z
ringgit ˈrɪŋ.ɡɪt **-s** -s
ringleader ˈrɪŋˌliː.dəʳ, (US) -dɚ **-s** -z
ring|let ˈrɪŋ|.lɪt, -lət, (US) -lɪt **-lets** -lɪts, -ləts, (US) -lɪts **-leted** -lɪ.tɪd, -lə.tɪd, (US) -lɪ.t̬ɪd
ringmaster ˈrɪŋˌmɑː.stəʳ, (US) -ˌmæs.tɚ **-s** -z
Ringo ˈrɪŋ.ɡəʊ, (US) -ɡoʊ
ringpull ˈrɪŋ.pʊl **-s** -z
Ringshall ˈrɪŋ.ʃᵊl
ringside ˈrɪŋ.saɪd ˌ**ringside** ˈ**seat**
ring-tailed ˈrɪŋ.teɪld
ringtone ˈrɪŋ.təʊn, (US) -toʊn **-s** -z
ringtoss ˈrɪŋ.tɒs, (US) -tɑːs
Ringwood ˈrɪŋ.wʊd
ringworm ˈrɪŋ.wɜːm, (US) -wɝːm
rink rɪŋk **-s** -s
rinky-dink ˈrɪŋ.ki.dɪŋk
rins|e rɪn*t*s **-es** -ɪz **-ing** -ɪŋ **-ed** -t
Rintoul ˈrɪn.tuːl, -ˈ-
Rio ˈriː.əʊ, (US) -oʊ
Rio de Janeiro ˌriː.əʊ.də.dʒəˈnɪə.rəʊ, -deɪ-, -dɪ-, -ʒəˈ-, -ˈneə-, (US) -oʊ.deɪ.ʒəˈner.oʊ, -diː-, -də-, -dʒəˈ-, -ˈnɪr-
Rio Grande ˌriː.əʊˈɡrænd, -ˈɡræn.di, -deɪ, (US) -oʊˈɡrænd, -ˈɡræn.di, -ˈɡrɑːn.deɪ
rioja, R~ riˈɒk.ə, -ˈɒx-, -ˈəʊ.kə, (US) -ˈɔː.hɑː, -ˈoʊ-
riot ˈraɪ.ət **-s** -s **-ing** -ɪŋ, (US) ˈraɪ.ə.t̬ɪŋ **-ed** -ɪd, (US) ˈraɪ.ə.t̬ɪd **-er/s** -əʳ/z, (US) ˈraɪ.ə.t̬ɚ/z ˈ**riot po**ˌ**lice**; ˌ**read someone the** ˈ**riot act**
riotous ˈraɪ.ə.təs, (US) -t̬əs **-ly** -li **-ness** -nəs, -nɪs
rip rɪp **-s** -s **-ping** -ɪŋ **-ped** -t
RIP ˌɑːʳ.aɪˈpiː, (US) ˌɑːr-
riparian raɪˈpeə.ri.ən, rɪ-, (US) rɪˈper.i-, raɪ-
ripcord ˈrɪp.kɔːd, (US) -kɔːrd **-s** -z
rip|e raɪp **-er** -əʳ, (US) -ɚ **-est** -ɪst, -əst **-ely** -li **-eness** -nəs, -nɪs
ripen ˈraɪ.pᵊn **-s** -z **-ing** -ɪŋ **-ed** -d
ripien|o ˌrɪp.iˈeɪ.n|əʊ, rɪˈpjeɪ-, (US) rɪˈpjeɪ.n|oʊ **-os** -əʊz, (US) -oʊz **-i** -iː
Ripken ˈrɪp.kɪn
Ripley ˈrɪp.li
Ripman ˈrɪp.mən
rip-off ˈrɪp.ɒf, (US) -ɑːf **-s** -s
Ripon ˈrɪp.ən
ripost|e, ripost rɪˈpɒst, -ˈpəʊst, (US) -ˈpoʊst **-(e)s** -s **-ing** -ɪŋ **-ed** -ɪd
ripper ˈrɪp.əʳ, (US) -ɚ **-s** -z
ripping ˈrɪp.ɪŋ **-ly** -li
rippl|e ˈrɪp.ᵊl **-es** -z **-ing** -ɪŋ, ˈrɪp.lɪŋ **-ed** -d
Rippon ˈrɪp.ᵊn
rip-roaring ˌrɪpˈrɔː.rɪŋ, (US) -ˈrɔːr.ɪŋ *stress shift:* ˌ**rip-roaring** ˈ**wave**
ripsnort|ing ˌrɪpˈsnɔː.t|ɪŋ, (US) -ˈsnɔːr.t̬|ɪŋ **-er/s** -əʳ/z, (US) -ɚ/z *stress shift:* ˌ**ripsnorting** ˈ**finish**
riptide ˈrɪp.taɪd **-s** -z
Ripuarian ˌrɪp.juˈeə.ri.ən, (US) -ˈer.i-
Rip van Winkle ˌrɪp.vænˈwɪŋ.kᵊl
Risca ˈrɪs.kə
ris|e raɪz **-es** -ɪz **-ing** -ɪŋ **rose** rəʊz, (US) roʊz **risen** ˈrɪz.ᵊn
riser ˈraɪ.zəʳ, (US) -zɚ **-s** -z
Rishton ˈrɪʃ.tᵊn
risibility ˌrɪz.əˈbɪl.ə.ti, ˌraɪ.zəˈ-, -zɪˈ-, -ɪ.ti, (US) ˌrɪz.əˈbɪl.ə.t̬i
risib|le ˈrɪz.ə.b|ᵊl, ˈraɪ.zə-, -zɪ-, (US) ˈrɪz.ə- **-ly** -li
rising ˈraɪ.zɪŋ **-s** -z
risk rɪsk **-s** -s **-ing** -ɪŋ **-ed** -t
risk|y ˈrɪs.k|i **-ier** -i.əʳ, (US) -i.ɚ **-iest** -i.ɪst, -i.əst **-iness** -ɪ.nəs, -ɪ.nɪs
Risley ˈrɪz.li
risotto rɪˈzɒt.əʊ, -ˈsɒt-, (US) -ˈzɑː.t̬oʊ, -ˈsɑː- **-s** -z
risqué ˈrɪs.keɪ, ˈriː.skeɪ, (US) rɪˈskeɪ
rissole ˈrɪs.əʊl, (US) -oʊl **-s** -z
Rita ˈriː.tə, (US) -t̬ə
Ritalin® ˈrɪt.ᵊl.ɪn, (US) ˈrɪt̬-, ˈrɪd.l̩n
ritardando ˌrɪt.ɑːˈdæn.dəʊ, (US) ˌriː.tɑːrˈdɑːn.doʊ **-s** -z
Ritchie ˈrɪtʃ.i
rite raɪt **-s** -s ˌ**rite of** ˈ**passage**
ritornell|o ˌrɪt.ɔːˈnel|.əʊ, -ᵊnˈel-, (US) -ɚˈnel|.oʊ, -ɔːrˈ- **-os** -əʊz, (US) -oʊz **-i** -iː
Ritson ˈrɪt.sᵊn
Ritter ˈrɪt.əʳ, (US) ˈrɪt̬.ɚ
ritual ˈrɪt.ju.əl, ˈrɪtʃ.u-, (US) ˈrɪtʃ- **-s** -z **-ly** -i
ritual|ism ˈrɪt.ju.ᵊl|.ɪ.zᵊm, ˈrɪtʃ.u-, (US) ˈrɪtʃ- **-ist/s** -ɪst/s
ritualistic ˌrɪt.ju.ᵊlˈɪs.tɪk, ˌrɪtʃ.u-, (US) ˌrɪtʃ- **-ally** -ᵊl.i, -li
ritualiz|e, -is|e ˈrɪt.ju.ᵊl.aɪz, ˈrɪtʃ.u-, (US) ˈrɪtʃ- **-es** -ɪz **-ing** -ɪŋ **-ed** -d
Ritz rɪts
ritz|y ˈrɪt.s|i **-ier** -i.əʳ, (US) -i.ɚ **-iest** -i.ɪst, -i.əst **-iness** -ɪ.nəs, -ɪ.nɪs
rival ˈraɪ.vᵊl **-s** -z **-(l)ing** -ɪŋ **-(l)ed** -d
rivalr|y ˈraɪ.vᵊl.r|i **-ies** -iz
riv|e raɪv **-es** -z **-ing** -ɪŋ **-ed** -d

riven ˈrɪv.ən
river, R~ ˈrɪv.əʳ, ⓊⓈ -ɚ **-s** -z ˈ**river** ˌ**bank**; ˌ**river** ˈ**bank**; ˈ**river** ˌ**bed**; ˌ**river** ˈ**bed**; ˌ**sell someone** ˌ**down the** ˈ**river**
Rivera rɪˈveə.rə, ⓊⓈ -ˈver.ə
riverboat ˈrɪv.ə.bəʊt, ⓊⓈ -ɚ.boʊt **-s** -s
Rivers ˈrɪv.əz, ⓊⓈ -ɚz
riverside, R~ ˈrɪv.ə.saɪd, ⓊⓈ ˈ-ɚ-
riv|et ˈrɪv|.ɪt, -ət, ⓊⓈ -ɪt **-ets** -ɪts, -əts, ⓊⓈ -ɪts **-eting** -ɪ.tɪŋ, -ə.tɪŋ, ⓊⓈ -ɪ.ţɪŋ **-eted** -ɪ.tɪd, -ə.tɪd, ⓊⓈ -ɪ.ţɪd **-eter/s** -ɪ.təʳ/z, -ə.təʳ/z, ⓊⓈ -ɪ.ţɚ/z
Riviera ˌrɪv.iˈeə.rə, ⓊⓈ -ˈer.ə
Rivington ˈrɪv.ɪŋ.tən **-s** -z
rivulet ˈrɪv.jə.lət, -jʊ-, -lɪt, -let, ⓊⓈ -lɪt **-s** -s
Rix rɪks
Riyadh ˈriː.æd; -ɑːd, -ˈ-, ⓊⓈ riːˈjɑːd
riyal riˈɑːl, -ˈæl; ˈriː.ɑːl, -æl, ⓊⓈ riːˈjɑːl, -ˈjɔːl, -ˈɑːl, -ˈɔːl **-s** -z
Rizla® ˈrɪz.lə
Rizzio ˈrɪt.si.əʊ, ⓊⓈ -oʊ
RN (abbrev. for **Royal Navy**) ˌɑːʳˈen; ˌrɔɪ.əlˈneɪ.vi, ˌrɔɪəl-, ⓊⓈ ˌɑːrˈen; ˌrɔɪ.əlˈneɪ.vi
roach, R~ rəʊtʃ, ⓊⓈ roʊtʃ **-es** -ɪz
road rəʊd, ⓊⓈ roʊd **-s** -z ˈ**road** ˌ**hog**; ˈ**road** ˌ**rage**; ˈ**road** ˌ**tax**
roadblock ˈrəʊd.blɒk, ⓊⓈ ˈroʊd.blɑːk **-s** -s
roadholding ˈrəʊdˌhəʊl.dɪŋ, ⓊⓈ ˈroʊdˌhoʊl-
roadhou|se ˈrəʊd.haʊ|s, ⓊⓈ ˈroʊd- **-ses** -zɪz
roadie ˈrəʊ.di, ⓊⓈ ˈroʊ- **-s** -z
roadrunner ˈrəʊdˌrʌn.əʳ, ⓊⓈ ˈroʊdˌrʌn.ɚ **-s** -z
roadshow ˈrəʊd.ʃəʊ, ⓊⓈ ˈroʊd.ʃoʊ **-s** -z
roadside ˈrəʊd.saɪd, ⓊⓈ ˈroʊd-
roadstead ˈrəʊd.sted, ⓊⓈ ˈroʊd- **-s** -z
roadster ˈrəʊd.stəʳ, ⓊⓈ ˈroʊd.stɚ **-s** -z
road-test ˈrəʊd.test, ⓊⓈ ˈroʊd- **-s** -s **-ing** -ɪŋ **-ed** -ɪd
roadway ˈrəʊd.weɪ, ⓊⓈ ˈroʊd- **-s** -z
roadworks ˈrəʊd.wɜːks, ⓊⓈ ˈroʊd.wɝːks
roadworth|y ˈrəʊdˌwɜː.ð|i, ⓊⓈ ˈroʊdˌwɝː- **-iness** -ɪ.nəs, -ɪ.nɪs
Roald ˈrəʊ.əld, ⓊⓈ ˈroʊ.əld
roam rəʊm, ⓊⓈ roʊm **-s** -z **-ing** -ɪŋ **-ed** -d
roan, R~ rəʊn, ⓊⓈ roʊn **-s** -z
Roanoke ˈrəʊ.ə.nəʊk, ˌrəʊ.əˈnəʊk, ⓊⓈ ˈroʊ.ə.noʊk
roar rɔːʳ, ⓊⓈ rɔːr **-s** -z **-ing** -ɪŋ **-ed** -d
roast rəʊst, ⓊⓈ roʊst **-s** -s **-ing** -ɪŋ **-ed** -ɪd **-er/s** -əʳ/z, ⓊⓈ -ɚ/z
rob, R~ rɒb, ⓊⓈ rɑːb **-s** -z **-bing** -ɪŋ **-bed** -d
Robards ˈrəʊ.bɑːdz, ⓊⓈ ˈroʊ.bɑːrdz
Robb rɒb, ⓊⓈ rɑːb
robber ˈrɒb.əʳ, ⓊⓈ ˈrɑː.bɚ **-s** -z
robber|y ˈrɒb.ər|.i, ⓊⓈ ˈrɑː.bɚ|.i, ˈ-br|i **-ies** -iz
Robbins ˈrɒb.ɪnz, ⓊⓈ ˈrɑː.bɪnz
rob|e rəʊb, ⓊⓈ roʊb **-es** -z **-ing** -ɪŋ **-ed** -d
Robens ˈrəʊ.bɪnz, ⓊⓈ ˈroʊ-
Roberson ˈrəʊ.bə.sən, ˈrɒb.ə-, ⓊⓈ ˈroʊ.bɚ-, ˈrɑː-

> Note: In **Roberson's medium** the usual pronunciation is /ˈrɒb.ə-/ ⓊⓈ /ˈrɑː.bɚ-/.

Robert ˈrɒb.ət, ⓊⓈ ˈrɑː.bɚt **-s** -s
Roberta rəʊˈbɜː.tə, rɒbˈɜː-, ⓊⓈ rəˈbɝː.ţə, roʊ-
Roberto rəʊˈbɜː.təʊ, rɒbˈɜː-, ⓊⓈ rəˈbɝː.ţoʊ, roʊ-, -toʊ
Robertson ˈrɒb.ət.sən, ⓊⓈ ˈrɑːb.ɚt-
Robeson ˈrəʊb.sən, ⓊⓈ ˈroʊb-
Robespierre ˈrəʊbz.pjeəʳ, -pɪəʳ, ˈrəʊb.spjeəʳ, -spɪəʳ, ⓊⓈ ˌroʊbzˈpjer, -ˈpɪr, -piˈer
robin, R~ ˈrɒb.ɪn, ⓊⓈ ˈrɑː.bɪn **-s** -z ˌ**Robin** ˈ**Hood** ⓊⓈ ˈ**Robin** ˌ**Hood**; ˌ**Robin Hood's** ˈ**Bay**
Robina rɒbˈiː.nə, rəʊˈbiː-, ⓊⓈ rəˈbiː-, roʊ-
Robins ˈrəʊ.bɪnz, ˈrɒb.ɪnz, ⓊⓈ ˈrɑː.bɪnz, ˈroʊ-
Robinson ˈrɒb.ɪn.sən, ⓊⓈ ˈrɑː.bɪn- ˌ**Robinson** ˈ**Crusoe**
robot ˈrəʊ.bɒt, ⓊⓈ ˈroʊ.bɑːt, -bət **-s** -s
Robotham ˈrəʊ.bɒθ.əm, -bɒt-, ⓊⓈ ˈroʊ.bɑː.θəm, -bɑː.ţəm
robotic rəʊˈbɒt.ɪk, ⓊⓈ roʊˈbɑː.ţɪk **-s** -s
Rob Roy ˌrɒbˈrɔɪ, ⓊⓈ ˌrɑːb-
Robsart ˈrɒb.sɑːt, ⓊⓈ ˈrɑːb.sɑːrt
Robson ˈrɒb.sən, ⓊⓈ ˈrɑːb-
robust rəʊˈbʌst, ⓊⓈ roʊ-, ˈ-- **-ly** -li **-ness** -nəs, -nɪs
Roby ˈrəʊ.bi, ⓊⓈ ˈroʊ-
Robyn ˈrɒb.ɪn, ⓊⓈ ˈrɑː.bɪn
Rocha ˈrɒʃ.ə, ⓊⓈ ˈrɑː.ʃə
Rochdale ˈrɒtʃ.deɪl, ⓊⓈ ˈrɑːtʃ-
Roche rəʊtʃ, rəʊʃ, rɒʃ, ⓊⓈ roʊtʃ, roʊʃ, rɑːʃ
Rochester ˈrɒtʃ.ɪ.stəʳ, ˈ-ə-, ⓊⓈ ˈrɑː.tʃə.stɚ, -tʃes.tɚ
rochet ˈrɒtʃ.ɪt, ⓊⓈ ˈrɑː.tʃɪt **-s** -s
Rochford ˈrɒtʃ.fəd, ⓊⓈ ˈrɑːtʃ.fɚd
rock, R~ rɒk, ⓊⓈ rɑːk **-s** -s **-ing** -ɪŋ **-ed** -t **-er/s** -əʳ/z, ⓊⓈ -ɚ/z ˈ**rock** ˌ**cake**; ˈ**rock** ˌ**climbing**; ˈ**rock** ˌ**garden**; ˈ**rock** ˌ**salmon**; ˈ**rock** ˌ**salt**; ˈ**rocking** ˌ**chair**; ˈ**rocking** ˌ**horse**
rockabilly ˈrɒk.əˌbɪl.i, ⓊⓈ ˈrɑː.kəˌ-
rock-and-roll ˌrɒk.ənd̆ˈrəʊl, ⓊⓈ ˌrɑːk.ənd̆ˈroʊl **-er/s** -əʳ/z, ⓊⓈ -ɚ/z *stress shift:* ˌ**rock-and-roll** ˈ**music**
rock-bottom ˌrɒkˈbɒt.əm, ⓊⓈ ˌrɑːkˈbɑː.ţəm *stress shift:* ˌ**rock-bottom** ˈ**level**
rockbound ˈrɒk.baʊnd, ⓊⓈ ˈrɑːk-
Rockefeller ˈrɒk.əˌfel.əʳ, -ɪˌ-, ⓊⓈ ˈrɑː.kəˌfel.ɚ ˈ**Rockefeller** ˌ**Center** ⓊⓈ ˌ**Rockefeller** ˈ**Center**
rocker|y ˈrɒk.ər|.i, ⓊⓈ ˈrɑː.kɚ- **-ies** -iz
rock|et ˈrɒk|.ɪt, ⓊⓈ ˈrɑː.k|ɪt **-ets** -ɪts **-eting** -ɪ.tɪŋ, ⓊⓈ -ɪ.ţɪŋ **-eted** -ɪ.tɪd, ⓊⓈ -ɪ.ţɪd ˈ**rocket** ˌ**base**; ˈ**rocket** ˌ**range**
rocketry ˈrɒk.ɪ.tri, ˈ-ə-, ⓊⓈ ˈrɑː.kɪ-, -kə-
rockfall ˈrɒk.fɔːl, ⓊⓈ ˈrɑːk-, -fɑːl **-s** -z
Rockhampton rɒkˈhæmp.tən, ⓊⓈ rɑːk-
Rockies ˈrɒk.iz, ⓊⓈ ˈrɑː.kiz
Rockingham ˈrɒk.ɪŋ.əm, ⓊⓈ ˈrɑː.kɪŋ-
rockmelon ˈrɒkˌmel.ən, ⓊⓈ ˈrɑːk- **-s** -z
Rockne ˈrɒk.ni, ⓊⓈ ˈrɑːk-
rock 'n' roll ˌrɒk.ənd̆ˈrəʊl, ⓊⓈ ˌrɑːk.ənd̆ˈroʊl **-er/s** -əʳ/z, ⓊⓈ -ɚ/z *stress shift:* ˌ**rock 'n' roll** ˈ**music**
rockros|e ˈrɒk.rəʊz, ⓊⓈ ˈrɑːk.roʊz **-es** -ɪz
Rockwell ˈrɒk.wel, -wəl, ⓊⓈ ˈrɑː.kwel, -kwəl
rock|y, R~ ˈrɒk|.i, ⓊⓈ ˈrɑː.k|i **-ier** -i.əʳ, ⓊⓈ -i.ɚ **-iest** -i.ɪst, -i.əst **-iness** -ɪ.nəs, -ɪ.nɪs ˌ**Rocky** ˈ**Mountains**
rococo rəʊˈkəʊ.kəʊ, ⓊⓈ rəˈkoʊ.koʊ; ⓊⓈ ˌroʊ.kəˈkoʊ
rod, R~ rɒd, ⓊⓈ rɑːd **-s** -z **make a** ˌ**rod for one's** ˌ**own** ˈ**back**; ˌ**rule someone with a** ˌ**rod of** ˈ**iron**
Roddick ˈrɒd.ɪk, ⓊⓈ ˈrɑː.dɪk
rode (from **ride**) rəʊd, ⓊⓈ roʊd
Roden ˈrəʊ.dən, ⓊⓈ ˈroʊ-
rodent ˈrəʊ.dənt, ⓊⓈ ˈroʊ- **-s** -s
rodeo rəʊˈdeɪ.əʊ; ˈrəʊ.di-, ⓊⓈ ˈroʊ.di.oʊ; ⓊⓈ roʊˈdeɪ.oʊ **-s** -z
Roderic(k) ˈrɒd.ər.ɪk, ⓊⓈ ˈrɑː.dɚ-
Rodger ˈrɒdʒ.əʳ, ⓊⓈ ˈrɑː.dʒɚ **-s** -z
Rodgers ˈrɒdʒ.əz, ⓊⓈ ˈrɑː.dʒɚz
Rodham ˈrɒd.əm, ⓊⓈ ˈrɑː.dəm
Rodin ˈrəʊ.dæ̃ŋ, ⓊⓈ roʊˈdæ̃n
Roding ˈrəʊ.dɪŋ; *locally sometimes:* ˈruː.dɪŋ, -ðɪŋ, ⓊⓈ ˈroʊ.dɪŋ, ˈruː-, -ðɪŋ
Rodman ˈrɒd.mən, ˈrɒb-, ⓊⓈ ˈrɑːd-
Rodmell ˈrɒd.məl, ⓊⓈ ˈrɑːd-
Rodney ˈrɒd.ni, ⓊⓈ ˈrɑːd-
rodomontad|e ˌrɒd.ə.mɒnˈteɪd, ˌrəʊ.də-, -ˈtɑːd, ⓊⓈ ˌrɑː.də.mənˈteɪd, ˌroʊ-, -ˈtɑːd **-es** -z **-ing** -ɪŋ **-ed** -ɪd
Rodriguez rɒdˈriː.gez, ⓊⓈ rɑːˈdriː.ges, -geɪs, -geɪz, -gəz
Rodway ˈrɒd.weɪ, ⓊⓈ ˈrɑːd-
roe, R~ rəʊ, ⓊⓈ roʊ **-s** -z
Roebling ˈrəʊ.blɪŋ, ⓊⓈ ˈroʊ-
roebuck, R~ ˈrəʊ.bʌk, ⓊⓈ ˈroʊ- **-s** -s
Roedean ˈrəʊ.diːn, ⓊⓈ ˈroʊ-
Roehampton rəʊˈhæmp.tən, ⓊⓈ roʊ- *stress shift:* ˌ**Roehampton** ˈ**College**
roentgen, R~ ˈrɒn.tjən, ˈrɜːn-, ˈrɒnt.gən, ˈrɜːnt-, ⓊⓈ ˈrent.gən, ˈrɝːnt-, ˈrʌnt-, ˈren.tʃən, ˈrɝːn-, ˈrʌn- **-s** -z
Roethke ˈret.kə, ⓊⓈ ˈret-, ˈreθ-, -ki
rogation, R~ rəʊˈgeɪ.ʃən, ⓊⓈ roʊ- **-s** -z
rogatory ˈrɒg.ə.tər.i, -tri, ⓊⓈ ˈrɑː.gə.tɔːr-
rog|er, R~ ˈrɒdʒ|.əʳ, ⓊⓈ ˈrɑː.dʒ|ɚ

-ers -əz, (US) -ɚz -ering -ᵊr.ɪŋ -ered -əd, (US) -ɚz
Roget ˈrɒʒ.eɪ, ˈrəʊ.ʒeɪ, (US) ˌroʊˈʒeɪ, ˈ-- ˌRoget's Theˈsaurus
rogue rəʊg, (US) roʊg -s -z ˌrogue's ˈgallery
roguer|y ˈrəʊ.gᵊr|.i, (US) ˈroʊ- -ies -iz
roguish ˈrəʊ.gɪʃ, (US) ˈroʊ- -ly -li -ness -nəs, -nɪs
roil rɔɪl -s -z -ing -ɪŋ -ed -d
roist|er ˈrɔɪ.st|əʳ, (US) -st|ɚ -ers -əz, (US) -ɚz -ering -ᵊr.ɪŋ -ered -əd, (US) -ɚd -erer/s -ᵊr.əʳ/z, (US) -ɚ.ɚ/z
Rokeby ˈrəʊk.bi, (US) ˈroʊk-
Roker ˈrəʊ.kəʳ, (US) ˈroʊ.kɚ
Roland ˈrəʊ.lənd, (US) ˈroʊ-
role, rôle rəʊl, (US) roʊl -s -z ˈrole ˌmodel
roleplay ˈrəʊl.pleɪ, (US) ˈroʊl- -s -z -ing -ɪŋ -ed -d
Rolex® ˈrəʊ.leks, (US) ˈroʊ-
Rolf(e) rɒlf, rəʊf, (US) rɑːlf
roll rəʊl, (US) roʊl -s -z -ing -ɪŋ -ed -d ˈroll ˌbar; ˈroll ˌcall; ˈrolling ˌpin; ˈrolling ˌstock; ˌrolling ˈstone; ˌRolling ˈStones
Rollason ˈrɒl.ə.sᵊn, (US) ˈrɑː.lə-
roller ˈrəʊ.ləʳ, (US) ˈroʊ.lɚ -s -z ˈroller ˌblind; ˈroller ˌcoaster; ˌroller ˈcoaster
Rollerblade® ˈrəʊ.lə.bleɪd, (US) ˈroʊ.lɚ- -s -z
rollerblading ˈrəʊ.ləˌbleɪ.dɪŋ, (US) -lɚ-
roller|-skate ˈrəʊ.lə|.skeɪt, (US) ˈroʊ.lɚ- -skates -skeɪts -skating -skeɪ.tɪŋ, (US) -skeɪ.t̬ɪŋ -skated -skeɪ.tɪd, (US) -skeɪ.t̬ɪd
Rolleston ˈrəʊl.stᵊn, (US) ˈroʊl-
rollicking ˈrɒl.ɪ.kɪŋ, (US) ˈrɑː.lɪ- -ly -li
Rollins ˈrɒl.ɪnz, (US) ˈrɑː.lɪnz
rollmop ˈrəʊl.mɒp, (US) ˈroʊl.mɑːp -s -s
rollneck ˈrəʊl.nek, (US) ˈroʊl- -s -s
Rollo ˈrɒl.əʊ, (US) ˈrɑː.loʊ
roll-on ˈrəʊl.ɒn, (US) ˈroʊl.ɑːn -s -z
roll-out ˈrəʊl.aʊt, (US) ˈroʊl- -s -s
rollover ˈrəʊˌləʊ.vəʳ, (US) ˈroʊˌloʊ.vɚ -s -z
Rolls rəʊlz, (US) roʊlz
Rolls-Royc|e® ˌrəʊlzˈrɔɪs, (US) ˌroʊlz- -es -ɪz *stress shift:* ˌRolls-Royce ˈengine
roll-top ˈrəʊl.tɒp, (US) ˈroʊl.tɑːp -s -s
roll-up ˈrəʊl.ʌp, (US) ˈroʊl- -s -s
Rolo® ˈrəʊ.ləʊ, (US) ˈroʊ.loʊ
Rolodex® ˈrəʊ.lə.deks, (US) ˈroʊ-
Rolph rɒlf, (US) rɑːlf
roly-pol|y ˌrəʊ.liˈpəʊ.l|i, (US) ˌroʊ.liˈpoʊ- -ies -iz *stress shift:* ˌroly-poly ˈpudding
ROM rɒm, (US) rɑːm
Roma ˈrəʊ.mə, (US) ˈroʊ-
Romagna rəʊˈmɑː.njə, (US) roʊˈ-
Romaic rəʊˈmeɪ.ɪk, (US) roʊ-
romaine rəʊˈmeɪn, (US) rə-, roʊ- roˌmaine ˈlettuce, ˌromaine ˈlettuce
Roman ˈrəʊ.mən, (US) ˈroʊ- -s -z ˌRoman ˈcandle; ˌRoman ˈCatholic; ˌRoman Caˈtholicism; ˌRoman ˈEmpire; ˌRoman ˈholiday; ˌRoman ˈnose; ˌRoman ˈnumeral
roman(s) à clef rəʊˌmɑ̃ːn.ɑːˈkleɪ, (US) roʊ-
roman(s) à thèse rəʊˌmɑ̃ːn.ɑːˈteɪz, (US) roʊ-
romanc|e, R~ rəʊˈmænts; ˈrəʊ.mænts, (US) roʊˈmænts, ˈ-- -es -ɪz -ing -ɪŋ -ed -t -er/s -əʳ/z, (US) -ɚ/z
Romanes *surname:* rəʊˈmɑː.nɪz, -nɪs, -nes, (US) roʊˈmɑː.nɪz *gypsy language:* ˈrɒm.ə.nes, -nɪs, (US) ˈrɑː.mə-
Romanesque ˌrəʊ.mᵊnˈesk, (US) ˌroʊ- *stress shift:* ˌRomanesque ˈchurch
roman(s) fleuve rəʊˌmɑ̃ːŋˈflɜːv, (US) roʊ-
Romani|a rʊˈmeɪ.ni|.ə, rəʊ-, ruː-, (US) roʊ-, ruː-, ˈ-nj|ə -an/s -ən/z
Romanic rəʊˈmæn.ɪk, (US) roʊ-
Roman|ism ˈrəʊ.mᵊn|.ɪ.zᵊm, (US) ˈroʊ- -ist/s -ɪst/s
romanization, -isa- ˌrəʊ.mᵊn.aɪˈzeɪ.ʃᵊn, -ɪˈ-, (US) ˌroʊ.mᵊn.əˈ- -s -z
romaniz|e, -is|e ˈrəʊ.mᵊn.aɪz, (US) ˈroʊ- -es -ɪz -ing -ɪŋ -ed -d
Romanov ˈrəʊ.mᵊn.ɒf, -nɒv, (US) ˈroʊ.mə.nɔːf; (US) roʊˈmɑː-
Romans(c)h rəʊˈmænʃ, rʊ-, (US) roʊˈmɑːnʃ, -ˈmænʃ
romantic, R~ rəʊˈmæn.tɪk, (US) roʊˈmæn.t̬ɪk -ally -ᵊl.i, -li
romantic|ism, R~ rəʊˈmæn.tɪ.s|ɪ.zᵊm, -tə-, (US) roʊˈmæn.t̬ə- -ist/s -ɪst/s
romanticization, -isa- rəʊˌmæn.tɪ.saɪˈzeɪ.ʃᵊn, -tə-, -sɪˈ-, (US) roʊˌmæn.t̬ə.səˈ-
romanticiz|e, -is|e rəʊˈmæn.tɪ.saɪz, -tə-, (US) roʊˈmæn.t̬ə- -es -ɪz -ing -ɪŋ -ed -d
Roman|y ˈrəʊ.mə.n|i, ˈrɒm.ə-, (US) ˈrɑː.mə-, ˈroʊ- -ies -iz
romaunt rəʊˈmɔːnt, (US) roʊˈmɑːnt, -ˈmɔːnt -s -s
Rombauer ˈrɒm.baʊ.əʳ, (US) ˈrɑːm.baʊ.ɚ
Rome rəʊm, (US) roʊm
Romeo ˈrəʊ.mi.əʊ; rəʊˈmeɪ-, (US) ˈroʊ.mi.oʊ -s -z
Romero rəʊˈmeə.rəʊ, (US) roʊˈmer.oʊ, rə-
Romford ˈrɒm.fəd, ˈrʌm-, (US) ˈrɑːm.fɚd
romic, R~ ˈrəʊ.mɪk, (US) ˈroʊ-
Romiley ˈrɒm.ᵊl.i, -ɪ.li, (US) ˈrɑː.mᵊl.i
Romilly ˈrɒm.ᵊl.i, -ɪ.li, (US) ˈrɑː.mᵊl.i
Romish ˈrəʊ.mɪʃ, (US) ˈroʊ-
Rommel ˈrɒm.ᵊl, (US) ˈrɑː.mᵊl
Romney ˈrɒm.ni, ˈrʌm-, (US) ˈrɑːm-, ˈrʌm- -s -z
Romola ˈrɒm.ᵊl.ə, (US) ˈrɑː.mᵊl-
romp rɒmp, (US) rɑːmp -s -s -ing -ɪŋ -ed -t
romper ˈrɒm.pəʳ, (US) ˈrɑːm.pɚ -s -z ˈromper ˌsuit
Romsey ˈrʌm.zi, ˈrɒm-, (US) ˈrɑːm-
Romulus ˈrɒm.jʊ.ləs, -jə-, (US) ˈrɑː.mjə-, -mjʊ-
Ron rɒn, (US) rɑːn
Ronald ˈrɒn.ᵊld, (US) ˈrɑː.nᵊld
Ronaldo rəˈnæl.dəʊ, rɒnˈæl-, (US) rəˈnɑːl.doʊ
Ronaldshay ˈrɒn.ᵊld.ʃeɪ, (US) ˈrɑː.nᵊld-
Ronaldsway ˈrɒn.ᵊldz.weɪ, (US) ˈrɑː.nᵊldz-
Ronan ˈrəʊ.nən, (US) ˈroʊ-
Ronay ˈrəʊ.neɪ, (US) ˈroʊ-
ron|deau ˈrɒn|.dəʊ, (US) ˈrɑːn|.doʊ -deaus -dəʊz, -dəʊ, (US) -doʊz -deaux -dəʊ, (US) -doʊ
rondel ˈrɒn.dᵊl, (US) ˈrɑːn-, -del -s -z
rondo ˈrɒn.dəʊ, (US) ˈrɑːn.doʊ -s -z
roneo, R~® ˈrəʊ.ni.əʊ, (US) ˈroʊ.ni.oʊ -s -z -ing -ɪŋ -ed -d
Ronnie ˈrɒn.i, (US) ˈrɑː.ni
Ronson ˈrɒnt.sᵊn, (US) ˈrɑːnt-
Ronstadt ˈrɒn.stæt, (US) ˈrɑːn-
röntgen, rontgen, R~ ˈrɒn.tjən, ˈrɜːn-, ˈrɒnt.gən, ˈrɜːnt-, (US) ˈrent.gən, ˈrɜːnt-, ˈrʌnt-, ˈren.tʃən, ˈrɜːn-, ˈrʌn- -s -z
Ronuk ˈrɒn.ək, (US) ˈrɑː.nək
roo ruː -s -z
rood ruːd -s -z ˈrood ˌscreen
roof v ruːf, (US) ruːf, rʊf -s -s -ing -ɪŋ -ed -t
roo|f n ruː|f, (US) ruː|f, rʊ|f -fs -fs -ves -vz ˈroof ˌgarden; ˈroof ˌrack
roofer ˈruː.fəʳ, (US) -fɚ, ˈrʊf.ɚ -s -z
rooftop ˈruːf.tɒp, (US) -tɑːp, ˈrʊf- -s -s
rooibos ˈrɔɪ.bɒs, (US) –bɔːs, -bɑːʃ
rook rʊk -s -s -ing -ɪŋ -ed -t
Rooke rʊk -s -s
rooker|y ˈrʊk.ᵊr|.i -ies -iz
rookie ˈrʊk.i -s -z
room, R~ ruːm, rʊm -s -z -ing -ɪŋ -ed -d -er/s -əʳ/z, (US) -ɚ/z ˈroom ˌservice; ˈrooming ˌhouse
roomful ˈruːm.fʊl, ˈrʊm- -s -z
roommate ˈruːm.meɪt, ˈrʊm- -s -s
Rooms ruːmz
room|y ˈruː.m|i, ˈrʊm|.i -ier -i.əʳ, (US) -i.ɚ -iest -i.ɪst, -i.əst -ily -ᵊl.i, -ɪ.li -iness -ɪ.nəs, -ɪ.nɪs
Rooney ˈruː.ni
Roosevelt ˈrəʊ.zə.velt, ˈruː-, -sə-; ˈruːs.velt, (US) ˈroʊ.zə.velt, ˈruː-, -vəlt; (US) ˈroʊz.velt
Note: /ˈrəʊ.zə.velt/ (US) /ˈroʊ-/ is the pronunciation used in the families of the late presidents of the US.
roost, R~ ruːst -s -s -ing -ɪŋ -ed -ɪd
rooster ˈruː.stəʳ, (US) -stɚ -s -z
root, R~ ruːt -s -s -ing -ɪŋ, (US) ˈruː.t̬ɪŋ -ed -ɪd, (US) ˈruː.t̬ɪd -less/ness -ləs/nəs, -lɪs/nɪs ˈroot ˌbeer; ˌroot ˈbeer; ˈroot caˌnal; ˈroot ˌvegetable; ˌroot ˈvegetable
Rootham ˈruː.təm, (US) -t̬əm
rootstock ˈruːt.stɒk, (US) -stɑːk -s -s
rop|e rəʊp, (US) roʊp -es -s -ing -ɪŋ -ed -t ˌrope ˈladder
Roper ˈrəʊ.pəʳ, (US) ˈroʊ.pɚ
rop|ey, rop|y ˈrəʊ.p|i, (US) ˈroʊ- -ier

-i.əʳ, US -i.ɚ -iest -i.ɪst, -i.əst -iness -ɪ.nəs, -ɪ.nɪs

Roquefort® ˈrɒk.fɔːʳ, US ˈroʊk.fɚt

roquet ˈrəʊ.ki, -keɪ, US roʊˈkeɪ -s -z -ing -ɪŋ -ed -d

Rorke rɔːk, US rɔːrk

Rorqual ˈrɔː.kwᵊl, -kᵊl, US ˈrɔːr.kwᵊl -s -z

Rorschach ˈrɔː.ʃɑːk, -ʃæk, US ˈrɔːr.ʃɑːk

rort rɔːt, US rɔːrt -s -s -ing -ɪŋ, ˈrɔːr.t̬ɪŋ -ed -ɪd, US ˈrɔːr.t̬ɪd

Rory ˈrɔː.ri, US ˈrɔːr.i

Ros (abbrev. for **Rosalind**) rɒz, US rɑːz

Ros *surname:* rɒs, US rɑːs

Rosa ˈrəʊ.zə, US ˈroʊ-

rosaceous rəʊˈzeɪ.ʃəs, US roʊ-

Rosalba rəʊˈzæl.bə, rɒzˈæl-, US roʊˈzɑːl-, -bɑː

Rosalie ˈrəʊ.zᵊl.i, ˈrɒz.ᵊl-, US ˈroʊ.zə.li, ˈrɑː-

Rosalind ˈrɒz.ᵊl.ɪnd, US ˈrɑː.zə.lɪnd

Rosaline ˈrɒz.ᵊl.aɪn, -iːn, US ˈrɑː.zə.lɪn, -laɪn

Rosalynde ˈrɒz.ᵊl.ɪnd, US ˈrɑː.zə.lɪnd

Rosamond ˈrɒz.ə.mənd, US ˈrɑː.zə-, ˈroʊ-

Rosario rəʊˈsɑː.ri.əʊ, US roʊˈzɑːr.i.oʊ, -sɑːr-

rosarium rəʊˈzeə.ri.əm, US roʊˈzer.i- -s -z

rosar|y ˈrəʊ.zᵊr|.i, US ˈroʊ- -ies -iz

Roscius ˈrɒʃ.i.əs, ˈrɒs-; ˈrɒs.ki.əs, US ˈrɑː.ʃi-, ˈ-ʃəs

Roscoe ˈrɒs.kəʊ, US ˈrɑː.skoʊ

Roscommon rɒsˈkɒm.ən, US rɑːˈskɑː.mən

rose (from **rise**) rəʊz, US roʊz

ros|e, R~ rəʊz, US roʊz -es -ɪz ˈ**rose** ˌ**bush**; ˈ**rose** ˌ**garden**; ˈ**rose** ˌ**water**; ˌ**rose** ˈ**window**

rosé ˈrəʊ.zeɪ, -ˈ-, US roʊˈzeɪ

Roseanne rəʊˈzæn, US roʊ-

roseate ˈrəʊ.zi.ət, -ɪt, -eɪt, US ˈroʊ.zi.ɪt, -eɪt

Roseau rəʊˈzəʊ, US roʊˈzoʊ

Rosebery ˈrəʊz.bᵊr.i, US ˈroʊzˌber-

rosebud ˈrəʊz.bʌd, US ˈroʊz- -s -z

rose-colo(u)red ˈrəʊzˌkʌl.əd, US ˈroʊzˌkʌl.ɚd

rosehip ˈrəʊz.hɪp, US ˈroʊz- -s -s

rosella rəʊˈzel.ə, US roʊ-, rə- -s -z

rosemary, R~ ˈrəʊz.mᵊr.i, US ˈroʊz.mer-

Rosenberg ˈrəʊ.zᵊn.bɜːg, -zᵊm-, US ˈroʊ.zᵊn.bɝːg

Rosencrantz ˈrəʊ.zᵊn.krænts, -zᵊŋ-, US ˈroʊ-

Rosenkavalier ˌrəʊ.zᵊn.kæv.əˈlɪəʳ, -zᵊŋ-, ˈrəʊ.zᵊnˌkæv.ə.lɪəʳ, US ˌroʊ.zᵊn.kæv.əˈlɪr

Rosenkranz ˈrəʊ.zᵊn.krænts, -zᵊŋ-, US ˈroʊ.zᵊn-

Rosenthal ˈrəʊ.zᵊn.tɑːl, -θɔːl, US ˈroʊ.zᵊn.θɑːl, -θɔːl, -tɑːl, -tɔːl

roseola rəʊˈziː.ᵊl.ə; ˌrəʊ.ziˈəʊ.lə, US roʊˈziː.ᵊl.ə; US ˌroʊ.ziˈoʊ.lə

Rosetta rəʊˈzet.ə, US roʊˈzet̬- **Ro**ˌ**setta** ˈ**Stone** US **Ro**ˈ**setta** ˌ**Stone**

rosette rəʊˈzet, US roʊ- -s -s

rosewood ˈrəʊz.wʊd, US ˈroʊz-

Rosh Hashana ˌrɒʃ.hæʃˈɑː.nə, -həˈʃɑː-, US ˌroʊʃ.həˈʃɔː.nə, ˌrɑːʃ-, -ˈʃɑː-

Rosicrucian ˌrəʊ.zɪˈkruː.ʃᵊn, ˌrɒz.ɪˈ-, -ʃi.ən, US ˌroʊ.zəˈkruː.ʃən, ˌrɑː- -s -z

Rosie ˈrəʊ.zi, US ˈroʊ-

Rosier ˈrəʊ.zɪəʳ, -zi.əʳ, US ˈroʊ.ʒɚ; US roʊˈzɪr

rosin ˈrɒz.ɪn, US ˈrɑː.zən

Rosina rəʊˈziː.nə, US roʊ-

Roslin ˈrɒz.lɪn, US ˈrɑːz-

Ross rɒs, US rɑːs

Rossall ˈrɒs.ᵊl, US ˈrɑː.sᵊl

Ross|e rɒs, US rɑːs -er -əʳ, US -ɚ

Rossellini ˌrɒs.əˈliː.ni, US ˌrɑː.səˈ-

Rossetti rəˈzet.i, rɒzˈet-, rəˈset-, rɒsˈet-, US roʊˈzet̬-, rə-, -ˈset̬-

Rossini rɒsˈiː.ni, rəˈsiː-, US roʊˈsiː-, rɑː-

Rossiter ˈrɒs.ɪ.təʳ, ˈ-ə-, US ˈrɑː.sə.t̬ɚ

Rosslare ˌrɒsˈleəʳ, US rɑːˈsler *stress shift:* ˌ**Rosslare** ˈ**streets**

Rosslyn ˈrɒs.lɪn, US ˈrɑː.slɪn

Ross-on-Wye ˌrɒs.ɒnˈwaɪ, US ˌrɑːs.ɑːnˈ- *stress shift:* ˌ**Ross-on-Wye** ˈ**streets**

rost|er ˈrɒs.t|əʳ, US ˈrɑː.st|ɚ -ers -əz, US -ɚz -ering -ᵊr.ɪŋ -ered -əd, US -ɚd

Rostock ˈrɒs.tɒk, US ˈrɑː.stɑːk

Rostov ˈrɒs.tɒv, US ˈrɑː.stɑːf; US rəˈstɔːf

Rostrevor rɒsˈtrev.əʳ, US rɑːˈstrev.ɚ

Rostropovich ˌrɒs.trəˈpəʊ.vɪtʃ, US ˌrɑː.strəˈpoʊ.viːtʃ, -strɑːˈpɔː-

rostr|um ˈrɒs.tr|əm, US ˈrɑː.str|əm -ums -əmz -a -ə

ros|y, R~ ˈrəʊ.z|i, US ˈroʊ- -ier -i.əʳ, US -i.ɚ -iest -i.ɪst, -i.əst -ily -ᵊl.i, -ɪ.li -iness -ɪ.nəs, -ɪ.nɪs

Rosyth rɒsˈaɪθ, rəˈsaɪθ, US rɑːˈsaɪθ, rə-

rot rɒt, US rɑːt -s -s -ting -ɪŋ, US ˈrɑː.t̬ɪŋ -ted -ɪd, US ˈrɑː.t̬ɪd

rota ˈrəʊ.tə, US ˈroʊ.t̬ə -s -z

Rotarian rəʊˈteə.ri.ən, US roʊˈter.i- -s -z

rotar|y ˈrəʊ.tᵊr|.i, US ˈroʊ.t̬ɚ- -ies -iz ˈ**Rotary** ˌ**Club**

rotatable rəʊˈteɪ.tə.bᵊl, US ˈroʊ.teɪ.t̬ə-

rota|te rəʊˈteɪ|t, US ˈroʊ.teɪ|t, -ˈ- -tes -ts -ting -tɪŋ, US -t̬ɪŋ -ted -tɪd, US -t̬ɪd -tor/s -təʳ/z, US -t̬ɚ/z

rotation rəʊˈteɪ.ʃᵊn, US roʊ- -s -z

rotatory ˈrəʊ.tə.tᵊr.i; rəʊˈteɪ-, US ˈroʊ.tə.tɔːr-

ROTC ˌɑːʳ.əʊˌtiːˈsiː; ˌrɒtˈsiː, US ˌɑːr.oʊ.tiːˈsiː; ˈrɑːt.si

rote rəʊt, US roʊt

rotgut ˈrɒt.gʌt, US ˈrɑːt-

Roth rɒθ, rəʊθ, US rɑːθ

Rothamsted ˈrɒθ.ᵊm.sted, US ˈrɑː.θəm-

Rothenstein ˈrəʊ.θᵊn.staɪn, -tᵊn-; ˈrɒθ.ᵊn-, US ˈrɑː.θən-, ˈroʊ-

Rother ˈrɒð.əʳ, US ˈrɑː.ðɚ

Rotherfield ˈrɒð.ə.fiːld, US ˈrɑː.ðɚ-

Rotherham ˈrɒð.ᵊr.əm, US ˈrɑː.ðɚ-

Rotherhithe ˈrɒð.ə.haɪð, US ˈrɑː.ðɚ-

Rothermere ˈrɒð.ə.mɪəʳ, US ˈrɑː.ðɚ.mɪr

Rotherston ˈrɒð.ə.stᵊn, US ˈrɑː.ðɚ-

Rotherwick ˈrɒð.ᵊr.ɪk, -ə.wɪk, US ˈrɑː.ðɚ.ɪk, -wɪk

Rothes ˈrɒθ.ɪs, US ˈrɑː.θɪs

Rothesay ˈrɒθ.si, -seɪ, US ˈrɑːθ-

Rothko ˈrɒθ.kəʊ, US ˈrɑːθ.koʊ

Rothman ˈrɒθ.mən, US ˈrɑːθ-

Rothschild ˈrɒθ.tʃaɪld, ˈrɒs-, ˈrɒθs-, US ˈrɑːθ-, ˈrɔːθ-, ˈrɑːθs-, ˈrɔːθs-

Rothwell ˈrɒθ.wel, -wəl, US ˈrɑːθ.wel, -wəl

roti ˈrəʊ.ti, US roʊˈtiː -s -z

rotisserie rəʊˈtɪs.ᵊr.i, -ˈtiː.sᵊr-, US roʊˈtɪs.ɚ- -s -z

rotogravure ˌrəʊ.təʊ.grəˈvjʊəʳ, US ˌroʊ.t̬ə.grəˈvjʊr; US ˈroʊ.t̬əˌgreɪ.vjɚ

rotor ˈrəʊ.təʳ, US ˈroʊ.t̬ɚ -s -z

Rotorua ˌrəʊ.təˈruː.ə, US ˌroʊ.t̬əˈ-

roto|vate ˈrəʊ.tə|.veɪt, US ˈroʊ.t̬ə- -vates -veɪts -vating -veɪ.tɪŋ, US -veɪ.t̬ɪŋ -vated -veɪ.tɪd, US -veɪ.t̬ɪd

rotovator, R~® ˈrəʊ.tə.veɪ.təʳ, US ˈroʊ.t̬ə.veɪ.t̬ɚ -s -z

rotten ˈrɒt.ᵊn, US ˈrɑː.tᵊn -est -ɪst, -əst -ly -li -ness -nəs, -nɪs ˌ**rotten** ˈ**borough**

rottenstone ˈrɒt.ᵊn.stəʊn, US ˈrɑː.tᵊn.stoʊn

rotter ˈrɒt.əʳ, US ˈrɑː.t̬ɚ -s -z

Rotterdam ˈrɒt.ə.dæm, ˌ--ˈ-, US ˈrɑː.t̬ɚ.dæm

Rottingdean ˈrɒt.ɪŋ.diːn, ˌ--ˈ-, US ˈrɑː.t̬ɪŋ.diːn

rottweiler, R~ ˈrɒt.waɪ.ləʳ, -vaɪ-, US ˈrɑːt.waɪ.lɚ, ˈrɔːt.vaɪ- -s -z

rotund rəʊˈtʌnd; ˈrəʊ.tʌnd, US roʊˈ- -ity -ə.ti, -ɪ.ti, US -ə.t̬i -ness -nəs, -nɪs

rotunda, R~ rəʊˈtʌn.də, US roʊ- -s -z

rouble ˈruː.bᵊl -s -z

Rouch raʊtʃ

roué ˈruː.eɪ, -ˈ-, US ruˈeɪ; US ˈruː.eɪ -s -z

Rouen ˈruː.ɑ̃ːŋ, -ɑːŋ, -ˈ-, US ruˈɑ̃ːŋ, -ˈɑːn

roug|e ruːʒ -es -ɪz -ing -ɪŋ -ed -d

rough rʌf -s -s -er -əʳ, US -ɚ -est -ɪst, -əst -ly -li -ness -nəs, -nɪs -ing -ɪŋ -ed -t ˌ**rough** ˈ**diamond**; ˈ**rough** ˌ**stuff**; ˌ**rough** ˈ**trade**; **take the** ˌ**rough with the** ˈ**smooth**

roughage ˈrʌf.ɪdʒ

rough-and-ready ˌrʌf.ᵊnᵈˈred.i *stress shift:* ˌ**rough-and-ready** ˈ**treatment**

rough-and-tumble ˌrʌf.ᵊnᵈˈtʌm.bᵊl *stress shift:* ˌ**rough-and-tumble** ˈ**games**

roughcast ˈrʌf.kɑːst, US -kæst

roughen ˈrʌf.ᵊn -s -z -ing -ɪŋ, ˈrʌf.nɪŋ -ed -d

rough-hew ˌrʌfˈhjuː -s -z -ing -ɪŋ

Pronouncing the letters RRH

The consonant letter combination **rrh** behaves like the letter **r**, e.g.:

myrrh mɜːʳ (US) mɜːr
diarrh(o)ea ˌdaɪ.əˈrɪə (US) -ˈriː.ə

-ed -d -n -n *stress shift:* ˌ**rough-hewn** ˈ**stone**
roughhous|e ˈrʌf.haʊs -es -ɪz -ing -ɪŋ -ed -t
roughish ˈrʌf.ɪʃ
roughneck ˈrʌf.nek -s -s
roughrider ˈrʌfˌraɪ.dəʳ, (US) -dɚ -s -z
roughshod ˈrʌf.ʃɒd, (US) -ʃɑːd ˌ**ride** ˈ**roughshod over**
rough-spoken ˌrʌfˈspəʊ.kən, (US) -ˈspoʊ- *stress shift:* ˌ**rough-spoken** ˈ**person**
Rough Tor ˌraʊˈtɔːʳ, (US) -ˈtɔːr
roulade ruːˈlɑːd -s -z
roulette ruːˈlet
Roulston ˈrəʊl.stən, (US) ˈroʊl-
Roumani|a rʊˈmeɪ.ni|.ə, rʊ-, rəʊ-, (US) ruː-, roʊ-, ˈ-nj|ə -an/s -ən/z
round, R~ raʊnd -s -z -er -əʳ, (US) -ɚ -est -ɪst, -əst -ly -li -ness -nəs, ˈraʊn.nəs, -nɪs -ish -ɪʃ -ing -ɪŋ -ed -ɪd ˌ**round** ˈ**robin;** ˌ**Round** ˈ**Table** (US) ˈ**Round** ˌ**Table;** ˌ**round** ˈ**trip**
roundabout ˈraʊnd.əˌbaʊt -s -s
roundel ˈraʊn.dəl -s -z
roundelay ˈraʊn.dɪ.leɪ, -dəl.eɪ, (US) -də.leɪ -s -z
rounders ˈraʊn.dəz, (US) -dɚz
roundhand ˈraʊnd.hænd
Roundhay ˈraʊnd.heɪ; *locally:* ˈraʊn.deɪ
Roundhead ˈraʊnd.hed -s -z
roundhou|se ˈraʊnd.haʊ|s -ses -zɪz
round-shouldered ˌraʊndˈʃəʊl.dəd, (US) -ˈʃoʊl.dɚd *stress shift:* ˌ**round-shouldered** ˈ**person**
rounds|man ˈraʊndz|.mən -men -mən
round-table ˌraʊndˈteɪ.bəl, (US) ˈ-ˌ-- *stress shift:* ˌ**round-table** ˈ**conference**
round-the-clock ˌraʊnd.ðəˈklɒk, (US) -ˈklɑːk *stress shift:* ˌ**round-the-clock** ˈ**vigil**
round-up ˈraʊnd.ʌp -s -s
roundworm ˈraʊnd.wɜːm, (US) -wɜːm -s -z
Rourke rɔːk, (US) rɔːrk
Rous raʊs
rous|e raʊz -es -ɪz -ing/ly -ɪŋ/li -ed -d
Rouse raʊs, ruːs
Rousseau ˈruː.səʊ, -ˈ-, (US) ruːˈsoʊ
Roussillon ˈruː.si.jɔ̃ːŋ, –ˈ-, (US) -ˈjõʊn
roustabout ˈraʊst.əˌbaʊt -s -s
rout raʊt -s -s -ing -ɪŋ, (US) ˈraʊ.t̬ɪŋ -ed -ɪd, (US) ˈraʊ.t̬ɪd
rout|e ruːt, (US) ruːt, raʊt -es -s -(e)ing/s -ɪŋ/z, (US) ˈruː.t̬ɪŋ, ˈraʊ- -ed -ɪd, (US) ˈruː.t̬ɪd, ˈraʊ- ˈ**route** ˌ**march**
router *thing that routes:* ˈruː.təʳ, (US) ˈruː.t̬ɚ, ˈraʊ.t̬ɚ; *tool:* ˈraʊ.təʳ, (US) -t̬ɚ
Routh raʊθ
routine ruːˈtiːn -s -z -ly -li
Routledge ˈraʊt.lɪdʒ, -ledʒ, ˈrʌt-
Routley ˈraʊt.li
roux, R~ ruː
rov|e rəʊv, (US) roʊv -es -z -ing -ɪŋ -ed -d -er/s -əʳ/z, (US) -ɚ/z
Rover® ˈrəʊ.vəʳ, (US) ˈroʊ.vɚ -s -z
row n, v *quarrel:* raʊ -s -z -ing -ɪŋ -ed -d
row n, v *all other senses:* rəʊ, (US) roʊ -s -z -ing -ɪŋ -ed -d ˈ**row** ˌ**house;** ˈ**rowing** ˌ**boat**
Rowallan rəʊˈæl.ən, (US) roʊ-
rowan *tree:* ˈrəʊ.ən, ˈraʊ.ən; ˈrəʊ.æn, (US) ˈroʊ.ən, ˈraʊ.ən -s -z

> Note: More commonly /ˈraʊ.ən/ in Scotland.

Rowan *name:* ˈrəʊ.ən, ˈraʊ.ən, (US) ˈroʊ.ən, ˈraʊ.ən
rowanberr|y ˈrəʊ.ənˌber|.i, ˈrəʊ.əm-, (US) ˈroʊ.ən- -ies -iz
Rowant ˈraʊ.ənt
row-boat ˈrəʊ.bəʊt, (US) ˈroʊ.boʊt -s -s
Rowbottom, Rowbotham ˈrəʊˌbɒt.əm, (US) ˈroʊˌbɑː.t̬əm
Rowden ˈraʊ.dən
rowd|y ˈraʊ.d|i -ies -iz -ier -i.əʳ, (US) -i.ɚ -iest -i.ɪst, -i.əst -ily -əl.i, -ɪ.li -iness -ɪ.nəs, -ɪ.nɪs -yism -i.ɪ.zəm
Rowe rəʊ, (US) roʊ
rowel ˈraʊ.əl -s -z
Rowell ˈraʊ.əl
Rowena rəʊˈiː.nə, (US) roʊ-, -ˈwiː-
Rowenta® rəʊˈen.tə, (US) roʊˈen.t̬ə
rower ˈrəʊ.əʳ, (US) ˈroʊ.ɚ -s -z
Rowland ˈrəʊ.lənd, (US) ˈroʊ- -s -z
Rowlandson ˈrəʊ.lənd.sən, (US) ˈroʊ-
Rowles rəʊlz, (US) roʊlz
Rowley ˈrəʊ.li, ˈraʊ-, (US) ˈroʊ-, ˈraʊ-
Rowling ˈrəʊ.lɪŋ, ˈraʊ-, (US) ˈroʊ-
Rowlinson ˈrəʊ.lɪn.sən, (US) ˈroʊ-
rowlock ˈrɒl.ək, ˈrəʊ.lɒk, ˈrʌl.ək, (US) ˈroʊ.lɑːk -s -s
Rowney ˈrəʊ.ni, ˈraʊ-, (US) ˈroʊ-, ˈraʊ-
Rowntree ˈraʊn.triː ˌ**Rowntree** ˈ**Mackintosh**®
Rowridge ˈraʊ.rɪdʒ
Rowse raʊs
Rowton ˈraʊ.tən, ˈrɔː-
Roxana rɒkˈsɑː.nə, -ˈsæn.ə, (US) rɑːkˈsæn.ə
Roxanne rɒkˈsæn, (US) rɑːk-
Roxburgh(e) ˈrɒks.bər.ə, (US) ˈrɑːks- -shire -ʃəʳ, -ʃɪəʳ, (US) -ʃɚ, -ʃɪr
Roxy ˈrɒk.si, (US) ˈrɑːk-
Roy rɔɪ
royal ˈrɔɪ.əl, rɔɪəl, (US) ˈrɔɪ.əl -s -z -ly -i ˌ**Royal** ˈ**Air** ˌ**Force;** ˌ**royal** ˈ**blue;** ˌ**royal** ˈ**family;** ˌ**Royal** ˈ**Highness;** ˌ**royal** ˈ**jelly;** ˌ**Royal** ˈ**Mail;** ˌ**Royal** ˈ**Navy**
royal|ism ˈrɔɪ.ə.l|ɪ.zəm, ˈrɔɪə.lɪz-, (US) ˈrɔɪ.ə.l|ɪ.zəm -ist/s -ɪst/s
royalt|y ˈrɔɪ.əl.t|i, ˈrɔɪəl-, (US) ˈrɔɪ.əl.t|i -ies -iz
Royce rɔɪs
Royle rɔɪl
Royston ˈrɔɪ.stən
Royton ˈrɔɪ.tən
RP ˌɑːˈpiː, (US) ˌɑːr-
rpm, R~ ˌɑː.piːˈem, (US) ˌɑːr-
RSA ˌɑːʳ.esˈeɪ, (US) ˌɑːr-
RSC ˌɑːʳ.esˈsiː, (US) ˌɑːr-
RSPB ˌɑːʳ.esˌpiːˈbiː, (US) ˌɑːr-
RSPCA ˌɑːʳ.esˌpiː.siːˈeɪ, (US) ˌɑːr-
RSVP ˌɑːʳ.es.viːˈpiː, (US) ˌɑːr-
Rt. Hon. (abbrev. for **Right Honourable**) ˌraɪtˈɒn.ər.ə.bəl, (US) -ˈɑː.nɚ.ə- *stress shift:* ˌ**Rt. Hon.** ˈ**member**
Ruabon ruˈæb.ən
Ruanda ruˈæn.də, (US) -ˈɑːn-
rub rʌb -s -z -bing -ɪŋ -bed -d
Rubáiyát ˈruː.baɪ.jæt, -beɪ-, (US) ˌruː.baɪˈjɑːt, -biːˈ-, ˈ---
rubato ruːˈbɑː.təʊ, rʊ-, (US) ruːˈbɑː.toʊ -s -z
rubb|er ˈrʌb|.əʳ, (US) -ɚ -ers -əz, (US) -ɚz -ery -ər.i ˌ**rubber** ˈ**band;** ˈ**rubber** ˌ**plant**
rubberiz|e, -is|e ˈrʌb.ər.aɪz, (US) -ə.raɪz -es -ɪz -ing -ɪŋ -ed -d
rubberneck ˈrʌb.ə.nek, (US) ˈ-ɚ- -s -s -ing -ɪŋ -ed -t -er/s -əʳ/z, (US) -ɚ/z
rubber-stamp ˌrʌb.əˈstæmp, (US) -ɚˈ- -s -s -ing -ɪŋ -ed -t *stress shift:* ˌ**rubber-stamped** ˈ**document**
rubbish ˈrʌb.ɪʃ -es -ɪz -ing -ɪŋ -ed -t -y -i
rubble ˈrʌb.əl
Rubbra ˈrʌb.rə
Rube Goldberg ˌruːbˈgəʊld.bɜːg, (US) -ˈgoʊld.bɝːg
rubella ruːˈbel.ə, rʊ-, (US) ruː-
Ruben ˈruː.bɪn, -bən, (US) -bən
Rubenesque ˌruː.bɪˈnesk, -bənˈesk, (US) -bəˈnesk
Rubens ˈruː.bənz, -bɪnz, (US) -bənz
rubeola ruːˈbiː.əʊ.lə, rʊ-; ˌruː.biˈəʊ.lə, (US) ruːˈbi.əl.ə; ˌruː.biˈoʊ.lə
Rubicon ˈruː.bɪ.kən, -kɒn, (US) -kɑːn
rubicund ˈruː.bɪ.kənd, -kʌnd, (US) -bə.kʌnd, -bɪ-, -kənd
rubidium ruːˈbɪd.i.əm, rʊ-, (US) ruː-
Rubik ˈruː.bɪk ˌ**Rubik's** ˈ**Cube**
Rubin ˈruː.bɪn
Rubinstein ˈruː.bɪn.staɪn, -bən-, (US) -bɪn-
ruble ˈruː.bəl -s -z
rubric ˈruː.brɪk -s -s
rub|y, R~ ˈruː.b|i -ies -iz
RUC ˌɑː.juːˈsiː, (US) ˌɑːr-
ruch|e ruːʃ -es -ɪz -ing -ɪŋ -ed -t
ruck rʌk -s -s -ing -ɪŋ -ed -t
rucksack ˈrʌk.sæk, ˈrʊk- -s -s
ruckus ˈrʌk.əs
ruction ˈrʌk.ʃən -s -z
rudd, R~ rʌd -s -z

rudd|er ˈrʌd|.əʳ, (US) -ɚ **-ers** -əz, (US) -ɚz **-erless** -əl.əs, -ɪs, (US) -ɚ.ləs, -lɪs
Rudderham ˈrʌd.ər.əm
Ruddigore ˈrʌd.ɪ.gɔːʳ, (US) -gɔːr
rudd|le ˈrʌd.əl **-es** -z **-ing** -ɪŋ, ˈrʌd.lɪŋ **-ed** -d
Ruddlington ˈrʌd.lɪŋ.tən
Ruddock ˈrʌd.ək
rudd|y ˈrʌd|.i **-ier** -i.əʳ, (US) -i.ɚ **-iest** -i.ɪst, -i.əst **-ily** -əl.i, -ɪ.li **-iness** -ɪ.nəs, -ɪ.nɪs
rud|e ruːd **-er** -əʳ, (US) -ɚ **-est** -ɪst, -əst **-ely** -li **-eness** -nəs, -nɪs
Rudge rʌdʒ
Rudi ˈruː.di
rudiment ˈruː.dɪ.mənt, -də-, (US) -də- **-s** -s
rudimentary ˌruː.dɪˈmen.tər.i, -dəˈ-, ˈ-tri, (US) -dəˈ- *stress shift:* ˌ**rudimentary** ˈ**knowledge**
Rudolf, Rudolph ˈruː.dɒlf, (US) -dɑːlf
Rudy ˈruː.di
Rudyard *first name:* ˈrʌd.jəd, -jɑːd, (US) -jɚd, -jɑːrd *in Staffordshire:* ˈrʌdʒ.əd, (US) -ɚd
rue ruː **-s** -z **-ing** -ɪŋ **-d** -d
rueful ˈruː.fəl, -fʊl **-ly** -i **-ness** -nəs, -nɪs
ruff rʌf **-s** -s **-ing** -ɪŋ **-ed** -t
ruffian ˈrʌf.i.ən **-s** -z **-ly** -li **-ism** -ɪ.zəm
ruffl|e ˈrʌf.əl **-es** -z **-ing** -ɪŋ, ˈrʌf.lɪŋ **-ed** -d
rufiyaa ˈruː.fi.jɑː
rufous ˈruː.fəs
Rufus ˈruː.fəs
rug rʌg **-s** -z
Rugbeian rʌgˈbiː.ən **-s** -z
rugby, R~ ˈrʌg.bi ˌ**Rugby** ˈ**League**; ˌ**Rugby** ˈ**Union**
Rugeley ˈruːdʒ.li, ˈruːʒ-
rugged ˈrʌg.ɪd **-ly** -li **-ness** -nəs, -nɪs
rugger ˈrʌg.əʳ, (US) -ɚ
rugrat, R~ ˈrʌg.ræt **-s** -s
Ruhr rʊəʳ, (US) rʊr
ruin ˈruː.ɪn **-s** -z **-ing** -ɪŋ **-ed** -d
ruination ˌruː.ɪˈneɪ.ʃən, rʊɪˈ-, (US) ˌruː.əˈ-
ruinous ˈruː.ɪ.nəs, (US) ˈruː.ə- **-ly** -li **-ness** -nəs, -nɪs
Ruislip ˈraɪ.slɪp, ˈraɪz.lɪp
Ruiz ruˈiːs, ruˈiːθ; (US) ruːˈiːs
rul|e, R~ ruːl **-es** -z **-ing** -ɪŋ **-ed** -d **-er/s** -əʳ/z, (US) -ɚ/z
rulebook ˈruːl.bʊk **-s** -s
ruling ˈruː.lɪŋ **-s** -z ˌ**ruling** ˈ**class** (US) ˈ**ruling** ˌ**class**
rum rʌm **-mer** -əʳ, (US) -ɚ **-mest** -ɪst, -əst
Rumani|a rʊˈmeɪ.ni|.ə, rəʊ-, ruː-, (US) roʊ-, ruː-, ˈ-nj|ə **-an/s** -ənz
rumba ˈrʌm.bə **-s** -z
Rumbelow ˈrʌm.bə.ləʊ, -bɪ-, (US) -loʊ
rumbl|e ˈrʌm.bəl **-es** -z **-ing/s** -ɪŋ/z, ˈrʌm.blɪŋ/z **-ed** -d
Rumbold ˈrʌm.bəʊld, (US) -boʊld
rumbustious rʌmˈbʌs.ti.əs, ˈ-tʃəs, (US) -tʃəs **-ness** -nəs, -nɪs

Rumelia ruːˈmiː.li.ə, (US) -li.ə, -ˈmiːl.jə
rumen ˈruː.men, -mɪn, -mən, (US) -mən **-s** -z **rumina** ˈruː.mɪ.nə, -mə-, (US) -mə-
Rumford ˈrʌm.fəd, (US) -fɚd
ruminant ˈruː.mɪ.nənt, -mə-, (US) -mə- **-s** -s
rumi|nate ˈruː.mɪ|.neɪt, -mə-, (US) -mə- **-nates** -neɪts **-nating** -neɪ.tɪŋ, (US) -neɪ.t̬ɪŋ **-nated** -neɪ.tɪd, (US) -neɪ.t̬ɪd
rumination ˌruː.mɪˈneɪ.ʃən, -məˈ-, (US) -məˈ- **-s** -z
ruminative ˈruː.mɪ.nə.tɪv, -mə-, -neɪ-, (US) -məˌneɪ.t̬ɪv
rummag|e ˈrʌm.ɪdʒ **-es** -ɪz **-ing** -ɪŋ **-ed** -d ˈ**rummage** ˌ**sale**
rumm|y ˈrʌm|.i **-ier** -i.əʳ, (US) -i.ɚ **-iest** -i.ɪst, -i.əst **-ily** -əl.i, -ɪ.li **-iness** -ɪ.nəs, -ɪ.nɪs
rumo(u)r ˈruː.məʳ, (US) -mɚ **-s** -z **-ed** -d
rumo(u)r-monger ˈruː.məˌmʌŋ.g|əʳ, (US) -mɚˌmʌŋ.g|ɚ, -ˌmɑːŋ- **-ers** -əz, (US) -ɚz **-ering** -ər.ɪŋ
rump rʌmp **-s** -s ˌ**rump** ˈ**steak**
Rumpelstiltskin ˌrʌm.pəlˈstɪlt.skɪn
rumpl|e ˈrʌm.pəl **-es** -z **-ing** -ɪŋ, ˈrʌm.plɪŋ **-ed** -d
Rumpole ˈrʌm.pəʊl, (US) -poʊl
rumpus ˈrʌm.pəs **-es** -ɪz
rum-runner ˈrʌmˌrʌn.əʳ, (US) -ɚ **-s** -z
Rumsfeld ˈrʌmz.felt, (US) -feld
run rʌn **-s** -z **-ning** -ɪŋ **ran** ræn ˌ**running** ˈ**water**; ˌ**take a** ˌ**running** ˈ**jump**; ˈ**running** ˌ**shoe**
runabout ˈrʌn.əˌbaʊt **-s** -s
runagate ˈrʌn.əˌgeɪt **-s** -s
runaround ˈrʌn.ərˌaʊnd
runaway ˈrʌn.əˌweɪ **-s** -z
runcible ˈrʌnt.sɪ.bəl, -sə-, (US) -sə-
Runcie ˈrʌnt.si
Runciman ˈrʌnt.sɪ.mən
Runcorn ˈrʌŋ.kɔːn, (US) -kɔːrn
rundown **n** ˈrʌn.daʊn **-s** -z
run-down **adj** ˌrʌnˈdaʊn *stress shift:* ˌ**run-down** ˈ**area**
rune, R~ ruːn **-s** -z
rung rʌŋ **-s** -z
rung (from **ring**) rʌŋ
Runham ˈrʌn.əm
runic, R~ ˈruː.nɪk
run-in ˈrʌn.ɪn **-s** -z
runnel ˈrʌn.əl **-s** -z
runner ˈrʌn.əʳ, (US) -ɚ **-s** -z ˌ**runner** ˈ**bean**; ˈ**runner** ˌ**bean**
runner-up ˌrʌn.əʳˈʌp, (US) -ɚˈ- **runners-up** ˌrʌn.əzˈ-, (US) -ɚzˈ- *stress shift:* ˌ**runner-up** ˈ**prizes**
running-board ˈrʌn.ɪŋ.bɔːd, (US) -bɔːrd **-s** -z
runn|y ˈrʌn|.i **-ier** -i.əʳ, (US) -i.ɚ **-iest** -i.ɪst, -i.əst **-iness** -ɪ.nəs, -ɪ.nɪs
Runnymede ˈrʌn.i.miːd
runoff ˈrʌn.ɒf, (US) -ɑːf **-s** -s
run-of-the-mill ˌrʌn.əv.ðəˈmɪl *stress shift:* ˌ**run-of-the-mill** ˈ**job**
runt rʌnt **-s** -s **-y** -i, (US) ˈrʌn.t̬i

run-through ˈrʌn.θruː **-s** -z
Runton ˈrʌn.tən, (US) -tən
run-up ˈrʌn.ʌp
runway ˈrʌn.weɪ **-s** -z
Runyon ˈrʌn.jən
rupee ruːˈpiː, (US) ˈruː.piː, -ˈ- **-s** -z
Rupert ˈruː.pət, (US) -pɚt
rupiah ruːˈpiː.ə **-s** -z
rupt|ure ˈrʌp.tʃ|əʳ, (US) -tʃ|ɚ **-ures** -əz, (US) -ɚz **-uring** -ər.ɪŋ **-ured** -əd, (US) -ɚd
rural ˈrʊə.rəl, (US) ˈrʊr.əl **-ly** -i
ruridecanal ˌrʊə.rɪ.dɪˈkeɪ.nəl, -rə-, (US) ˌrʊr.ɪ.dəˈ-; (US) -ˈdek.ə.næl
Ruritani|a ˌrʊə.rɪˈteɪ.ni|.ə, -rəˈ-, (US) ˌrʊr.ɪˈ- **-an** -ən
Rusbridger ˈrʌsˌbrɪdʒ.əʳ, (US) -ɚ
rus|e ruːz, (US) ruːz, ruːs **-es** -ɪz
rusé ˈruː.zeɪ, (US) ruːˈzeɪ
Rusedski rʊˈset.ski, -ˈsed-, -ˈzet-, -ˈzed-
rush, R~ rʌʃ **-es** -ɪz **-ing** -ɪŋ **-ed** -t **-er/s** -əʳ/z, (US) -ɚ/z ˈ**rush** ˌ**hour**
Rushall ˈrʌʃ.əl
Rushden ˈrʌʃ.dən
Rushdie ˈrʊʃ.di, ˈrʌʃ-
Rushforth ˈrʌʃ.fɔːθ, -fəθ, (US) -fɔːrθ, -fɚθ
rushlight ˈrʌʃ.laɪt **-s** -s
Rushmere ˈrʌʃ.mɪəʳ, (US) -mɪr
Rushmore ˈrʌʃ.mɔːʳ, (US) -mɔːr
Rusholme ˈrʌʃ.əm, -həʊm, (US) -əm, -hoʊm
Rushton ˈrʌʃ.tən
Rushworth ˈrʌʃ.wəθ, -wɜːθ, (US) -wɚθ, -wɝːθ
rushy ˈrʌʃ.i
rusk, R~ rʌsk **-s** -s
Ruskin ˈrʌs.kɪn
Rusper ˈrʌs.pəʳ, (US) -pɚ
Russell ˈrʌs.əl
russet ˈrʌs.ɪt **-s** -s
Russia ˈrʌʃ.ə
Russian ˈrʌʃ.ən **-s** -z ˌ**Russian rou**ˈ**lette**
russianism, R~ ˈrʌʃ.ən.ɪ.zəm **-s** -z
russianiz|e, -is|e, R~ ˈrʌʃ.ən.aɪz **-es** -ɪz **-ing** -ɪŋ **-ed** -d
Russo ˈrʌs.əʊ, (US) -oʊ
Russo- ˈrʌs.əʊ, (US) ˈrʌs.oʊ, ˈ-ə
rust, R~ rʌst **-s** -s **-ing** -ɪŋ **-ed** -ɪd
rustbelt ˈrʌst.belt
rustbucket ˈrʌstˌbʌk.ɪt **-s** -s
rustic ˈrʌs.tɪk **-s** -s **-ally** -əl.i, -li
rusti|cate ˈrʌs.tɪ|.keɪt, (US) -tə- **-cates** -keɪts **-cating** -keɪ.tɪŋ, (US) -keɪ.t̬ɪŋ **-cated** -keɪ.tɪd, (US) -keɪ.t̬ɪd
rustication ˌrʌs.tɪˈkeɪ.ʃən, -təˈ-, (US) -təˈ-
rusticity rʌsˈtɪs.ə.ti, -ɪ.ti, (US) -ə.t̬i
rustl|e ˈrʌs.əl **-es** -z **-ing** -ɪŋ, ˈrʌs.lɪŋ **-ed** -d **-er/s** -əʳ/z, (US) -ɚ/z, ˈrʌs.ləʳ/z, -lɚ/z
rustproof ˈrʌst.pruːf
Rustum ˈrʌs.təm
rust|y, R~ ˈrʌs.t|i **-ier** -i.əʳ, (US) -i.ɚ **-iest** -i.ɪst, -i.əst **-iness** -ɪ.nəs, -ɪ.nɪs
Ruswarp ˈrʌs.əp, ˈrʌz-, (US) -ɚp
rut rʌt **-s** -s **-ting** -ɪŋ, (US) ˈrʌt̬.ɪŋ **-ted** -ɪd, (US) ˈrʌt̬.ɪd
rutabaga ˌruː.təˈbeɪ.gə, ˌrʊt.əˈ-,

R

ˈruː.təˌbeɪ-, ˈrʊt.əˌ-, ⓊⓈ ˈruː.t̬əˌbeɪ- **-s** -z
Rutgers ˈrʌt.gəz, ⓊⓈ -gɚz
Ruth, ruth ruːθ
Ruthenia ruːˈθiː.ni.ə, ⓊⓈ -ni.ə, ˈ-njə
Ruthenian ruːˈθiː.ni.ən, ⓊⓈ -ni.ən, ˈ-njən **-s** -z
ruthenium ruːˈθiː.ni.əm
Rutherford ˈrʌð.ə.fəd, ⓊⓈ -ɚ.fɚd, ˈrʌθ-
rutherfordium ˌrʌð.əˈfɔː.di.əm, ⓊⓈ -ɚˈfɔːr-
Rutherglen ˈrʌð.ə.glen, ⓊⓈ ˈ-ɚ-
ruthful ˈruːθ.fəl, -fʊl **-ly** -li **-ness** -nəs, -nɪs
Ruthin ˈrɪθ.ɪn, ˈruː.θɪn
ruthless ˈruːθ.ləs, -lɪs **-ly** -li **-ness** -nəs, -nɪs
Ruthven *personal name:* ˈruːθ.vən, ˈrɪv.ən *Baron, place in Angus:* ˈrɪv.ən *place in Aberdeenshire, loch in Highland region:* ˈrʌθ.vən
Ruthwell ˈrʌθ.wəl; *locally:* ˈrɪð.əl
rutilant ˈruː.tɪ.lənt, ⓊⓈ -təl.ənt
rutile ˈruː.taɪl, ⓊⓈ -tiːl, -taɪl
rutin ˈruː.tɪn, -tən, ⓊⓈ -tən
Rutland ˈrʌt.lənd
Rutledge ˈrʌt.lɪdʒ
Rutskoi ˌrʊtˈskɔɪ, ˌruːt-
Rutter ˈrʌt.əʳ, ⓊⓈ ˈrʌt̬.ɚ
Rutterford ˈrʌt.ə.fəd, ⓊⓈ ˈrʌt̬.ɚ.fɚd
rutt|y ˈrʌt|.i, ⓊⓈ ˈrʌt̬- **-ier** -i.əʳ, ⓊⓈ -i.ɚ **-iest** -i.ɪst, -i.əst **-iness** -ɪ.nəs, -ɪ.nɪs
Ruysdael ˈraɪz.dɑːl, ˈriːz-, -deɪl, ⓊⓈ ˈraɪs.dɑːl, ˈraɪz-, ˈrɔɪs-
Ruyter ˈraɪ.təʳ, ⓊⓈ ˈrɔɪ.t̬ɚ, ˈraɪ-
RV ˌɑːˈviː, ⓊⓈ ˌɑːr-
Rwanda ruˈæn.də, ⓊⓈ -ˈɑːn- **-n/s** -n/z
Ryan raɪ.ən
Ryanair® ˌraɪ.ənˈeəʳ, ˈ---, ⓊⓈ -ˈer
Rydal ˈraɪ.dəl
Ryde raɪd
Ryder ˈraɪ.dəʳ, ⓊⓈ -dɚ **ˌRyder ˈCup**
rye, R~ raɪ **ˈrye ˌbread; ˈrye ˌgrass**
Ryecroft ˈraɪ.krɒft, ⓊⓈ -krɑːft
Ryle raɪl
Rylstone ˈrɪl.stən, -stəʊn, ⓊⓈ -stən, -stoʊn
Ryman ˈraɪ.mən
Rymer ˈraɪ.məʳ, ⓊⓈ -mɚ
ryot raɪ.ət **-s** -s
Ryswick ˈrɪz.wɪk
Ryton ˈraɪ.tən
Ryukyu riˈuː.kjuː, ⓊⓈ -ˈjuː-, -ˈuː-
Ryvita® raɪˈviː.tə, ⓊⓈ -t̬ə

R

S

Pronouncing the letter S

→ *See also* **SC, SCH, SH**

The consonant letter **s** has five realizations: /s/, /z, /ʃ/, /ʒ/, and silent. The most obvious of these is /s/, e.g.

sack	sæk
case	keɪs

/z/ is a very common realization of **s**, but it is not usually word-initial, e.g.:

rise	raɪz
losing	ˈluː.zɪŋ

It particularly occurs in the verb form of homographs, and in words ending **sm**.

close (v.)	kləʊz Ⓤⓢ kloʊz
use (v.)	juːz
spasm	ˈspæz.əm

In suffixes *-sion*, *-sure*, *-sia* and their derivatives, **s** is realized as /tʃ/ or /ʒ/, e.g.:

Asia	ˈeɪ.ʃə, -ʒə Ⓤⓢ ˈeɪ.ʒə
insure	ɪnˈʃʊəʳ Ⓤⓢ ɪnˈʃʊr
tension	ˈten.*t*ʃən Ⓤⓢ ˈten*t*.ʃən
treasure	ˈtreʒ.əʳ Ⓤⓢ -ɚ
persuasion	pəˈsweɪ.ʒən Ⓤⓢ pɚ-

In addition

s can be silent. This usually happens in word-final position, where the word is a borrowing from French, e.g.:

debris	ˈdeɪ.briː Ⓤⓢ dəˈbriː

The grammatical inflections *-(e)s*, *-'s*

There are three possible ways of pronouncing the grammatical inflections *-(e)s* and *-'s*. Following /s/, /z/, /ʃ/, /ʒ/, /tʃ/, and /dʒ/, the inflection is realized as /ɪz/, e.g.:

horses	ˈhɔː.sɪz Ⓤⓢ ˈhɔːr-
rises	ˈraɪ.zɪz

Following all other voiceless consonant sounds the inflection is realized as /s/, e.g.:

laughs	lɑːfs Ⓤⓢ læfs
shapes	ʃeɪps

Following all other voiced consonant sounds and after vowel sounds, the inflection is realized as /z/, e.g.:

John's	dʒɒnz Ⓤⓢ dʒɑːnz
plays	pleɪz

s, S es **-'s** -ɪz

S (abbrev. for **south**) saʊθ

Saab® sɑːb

Saarbrücken ˌsɑːˈbrʊk.ᵊn; *as if German:* ˌzɑː-; Ⓤⓢ ˈsɑːrˌbrʊk-; *as if German:* Ⓤⓢ ˈzɑːr-

Saarland ˈsɑː.lænd; *as if German:* ˈzɑː-; Ⓤⓢ ˈsɑːr-; *as if German:* Ⓤⓢ ˈzɑːr-

Saatchi ˈsɑː.tʃi

Saba *in Arabia:* ˈsɑː.bə, ˈseɪ-, Ⓤⓢ ˈseɪ.bə, ˈsɑː- *in West Indies:* ˈseɪ.bə, ˈsɑː-, Ⓤⓢ ˈsɑː.bə

Sabaean səˈbiː.ən, sæbˈiː-, Ⓤⓢ səˈbiː-

Sabah ˈsɑː.bɑː

Sabaoth sæbˈeɪ.ɒθ, səˈbeɪ-, ˈsæb.eɪ.ɒθ, -əθ, Ⓤⓢ ˈsæb.eɪ.ɑːθ, -ə.ɔːθ; Ⓤⓢ səˈbeɪ.ɔːθ

Sabatini ˌsæb.əˈtiː.ni

Sabbatarian ˌsæb.əˈteə.ri.ən, Ⓤⓢ -ˈter.i- **-s** -z **-ism** -ɪ.zᵊm

Sabbath ˈsæb.əθ **-s** -s

sabbatical səˈbæt.ɪ.kᵊl, Ⓤⓢ -ˈbæt̬-

Sabena® səˈbiː.nə, sæbˈiː-

sab|er ˈseɪ.b|əʳ, Ⓤⓢ -b|ɚ **-ers** -əz, Ⓤⓢ -ɚz **-ering** -ᵊr.ɪŋ **-ered** -əd, Ⓤⓢ -ɚd

Sabin ˈseɪ.bɪn, ˈsæb.ɪn, Ⓤⓢ ˈseɪ.bɪn

Sabine *Italian people:* ˈsæb.aɪn, ˈseɪ.baɪn, Ⓤⓢ ˈseɪ.baɪn **-s** -z *surname:* ˈsæb.aɪn, ˈseɪ.baɪn, -bɪn, Ⓤⓢ ˈseɪ- *river, lake, pass in US:* səˈbiːn, sæbˈiːn, Ⓤⓢ səˈbiːn

sable ˈseɪ.bᵊl **-s** -z

sabot ˈsæb.əʊ, -ˈ-, Ⓤⓢ sæbˈoʊ, ˈ-- **-s** -z

sabotag|e ˈsæb.ə.tɑː*d*ʒ, Ⓤⓢ -tɑːʒ, ˌ--ˈ- **-es** -ɪz **-ing** -ɪŋ **-ed** -d

saboteur ˌsæb.əˈtɜːʳ, ˈ---, Ⓤⓢ ˌsæb.əˈtʊr, -ˈtɝː **-s** -z

sabra, S~ ˈsɑː.brə

sab|re ˈseɪ.b|əʳ, Ⓤⓢ -b|ɚ **-res** -əz, Ⓤⓢ -ɚz **-ring** -ᵊr.ɪŋ **-red** -əd, Ⓤⓢ -ɚd **ˈsabre ˌrattling**

sabretach|e ˈsæb.ə.tæʃ, Ⓤⓢ ˈseɪ.bɚ-, ˈsæb.ɚ- **-es** -ɪz

sabre-toothed ˌseɪ.bəˈtuːθt, Ⓤⓢ ˈseɪ.bɚ.tuːθt *stress shift, British only, see compound:* **ˌsabre-toothed ˈtiger**

Sabrina səˈbriː.nə

sac sæk **-s** -s

saccade sækˈɑːd, səˈkɑːd, -ˈkeɪd, Ⓤⓢ sækˈɑːd, səˈkɑːd **-s** -z

> Note: In British psychology, /sækˈeɪd, səˈkeɪd/ is the usual pronunciation.

saccharide ˈsæk.ᵊr.aɪd, -ɪd, Ⓤⓢ -ə.raɪd **-s** -z

saccharin(e) n ˈsæk.ᵊr.ɪn, -iːn, Ⓤⓢ -ɪn, -ən

saccharine adj ˈsæk.ᵊr.ɪn, -aɪn, -iːn, Ⓤⓢ -ɚ.ɪn, -ə.raɪn

sacerdotal ˌsæs.əˈdəʊ.tᵊl, Ⓤⓢ -ɚˈdoʊ.t̬ᵊl, ˌsæk- **-ly** -i

sachem ˈseɪ.tʃəm, -tʃem, Ⓤⓢ -tʃəm **-s** -z

sachet ˈsæʃ.eɪ, Ⓤⓢ -ˈ- **-s** -z

Sacheverell səˈʃev.ᵊr.ᵊl, sæʃˈev-

Sachs sæks

sack sæk **-s** -s **-ing/s** -ɪŋ/z **-ed** -t

sackbut ˈsæk.bʌt, -bət, Ⓤⓢ -bʌt **-s** -s

sackcloth ˈsæk.klɒθ, Ⓤⓢ -klɑːθ **ˌsackcloth and ˈashes**

sackful ˈsæk.fʊl **-s** -z **sacksful** ˈsæks.fʊl

sacking ˈsæk.ɪŋ

sackload ˈsæk.ləʊd, Ⓤⓢ -loʊd **-s** -z

Sackville-West ˌsæk.vɪlˈwest

sacral ˈseɪ.krᵊl

sacrament, S~ ˈsæk.rə.mənt **-s** -s

sacramental ˌsæk.rəˈmen.tᵊl, Ⓤⓢ -t̬ᵊl **-ly** -i **-ism** -ɪ.zᵊm

Sacramento ˌsæk.rəˈmen.təʊ, Ⓤⓢ -t̬oʊ

sacred ˈseɪ.krɪd **-ly** -li **-ness** -nəs, -nɪs **ˌsacred ˈcow**

sacrific|e ˈsæk.rɪ.faɪs, -rə-, Ⓤⓢ -rə- **-es** -ɪz **-ing** -ɪŋ **-ed** -t

sacrificial ˌsæk.rɪˈfɪʃ.ᵊl, -rəˈ-, Ⓤⓢ -rəˈ- **-ly** -i

sacrilege ˈsæk.rɪ.lɪdʒ, -rə-, Ⓤⓢ -rə-

sacrilegious ˌsæk.rɪˈlɪdʒ.əs, -rəˈ-, Ⓤⓢ -rəˈ- **-ly** -li **-ness** -nəs, -nɪs

sacristan ˈsæk.rɪ.stᵊn, -rə-, Ⓤⓢ -rɪ- **-s** -z

Sacriston ˈsæk.rɪ.stᵊn, -rə-, Ⓤⓢ -rɪ-

sacrist|y ˈsæk.rɪ.st|i, -rə-, Ⓤⓢ -rɪ- **-ies** -iz

sacrosanct ˈsæk.rəʊ.sæŋ*k*t, Ⓤⓢ -roʊ- **-ity** -ə.ti, -ɪ.ti, Ⓤⓢ -ə.t̬i

sacr|um ˈseɪ.kr|əm, ˈsæk.r|əm **-a** -ə
sad sæd **-der** -əʳ, (US) -ɚ **-dest** -ɪst, -əst **-ly** -li **-ness** -nəs, -nɪs
SAD ˌes.eɪˈdiː
Sadat səˈdæt, sædˈæt, (US) səˈdɑːt, sɑː-, -ˈdæt
Saddam səˈdæm, sædˈæm; ˈsæd.əm, (US) sɑːˈdɑːm, sə-, sædˈæm, səˈdæm
sadden ˈsæd.ᵊn **-s** -z **-ing** -ɪŋ **-ed** -d
saddhu ˈsɑː.duː **-s** -z
saddl|e ˈsæd.ᵊl **-es** -z **-ing** -ɪŋ, ˈsæd.lɪŋ **-ed** -d ˈ**saddle** ˌ**horse**; ˈ**saddle** ˌ**sore**
saddleback ˈsæd.ᵊl.bæk
saddlebag ˈsæd.ᵊl.bæg **-s** -z
saddle|cloth ˈsæd.ᵊl|.klɒθ, (US) -klɑːθ **-cloths** -klɒθs, -klɒðz, (US) -klɑːθs, -klɑːðz
saddler ˈsæd.ləʳ, -ᵊl.əʳ, (US) ˈ-lɚ, -ᵊl.ɚ **-s** -z **-y** -i
saddle-sore ˈsæd.ᵊl.sɔːʳ, (US) -sɔːr
saddo ˈsæd.əʊ, (US) -oʊ **-s** -z
Sadducee ˈsæd.jʊ.siː, -jə-, (US) ˈsædʒ.ʊ-, ˈsæd.jʊ- **-s** -z
Sade sɑːd, (US) sɑːd, sæd
sadhu ˈsɑː.duː **-s** -z
Sadie ˈseɪ.di
sad|ism ˈseɪ.d|ɪ.zᵊm, (US) ˈsæd|.ɪ-, ˈseɪ.d|ɪ- **-ist/s** -ɪst/s
sadistic səˈdɪs.tɪk, sædˈɪs-, (US) səˈdɪs-, seɪ-, sædˈɪs- **-ally** -ᵊl.i, -li
Sadleir ˈsæd.ləʳ, (US) -lɚ
Sadler ˈsæd.ləʳ, (US) -lɚ
sadomasoch|ism ˌseɪ.dəʊˈmæs.ə.k|ɪ.zᵊm, -ˈmæz-, (US) ˌsæd.oʊˈ-, ˌseɪ.doʊˈ- **-ist/s** -ɪst/s
sadomasochistic ˌseɪ.dəʊˌmæs.əˈkɪs.tɪk, -ˌmæz-, (US) ˌsæd.oʊˌ-, ˌseɪ.doʊˌ-
Sadova ˈsɑː.dəʊ.ə, -və, (US) -dɔː.vɑː, sɑːˈdɔː-
Sadr ˈsæd.əʳ, (US) ˈsɑː.dɚ ˌ**Sadr** ˈ**City**
sad-sack ˈsæd.sæk
sae, SAE ˌes.eɪˈiː
safari səˈfɑː.ri, (US) -ˈfɑːr.i **-s** -z **saˈfari** ˌ**park**; **saˈfari** ˌ**suit**
saf|e seɪf **-es** -s **-er** -əʳ, (US) -ɚ **-est** -ɪst, -əst **-ely** -li **-eness** -nəs, -nɪs ˈ**safe** ˌ**house**; ˌ**safe** ˈ**house** (US) ˈ**safe** ˌ**house**; ˌ**safe** ˈ**sex**
safe-break|er ˈseɪfˌbreɪ.k|əʳ, (US) -k|ɚ **-s** -z **-ing** -ɪŋ
safe-conduct ˌseɪfˈkɒn.dʌkt, -dəkt, (US) -ˈkɑːn.dʌkt **-s** -s
safe-crack|er ˈseɪfˌkræk|.əʳ, (US) -ɚ **-s** -z **-ing** -ɪŋ
safe-deposit ˈseɪf.dɪˌpɒz.ɪt, -dəˌ-, (US) -dɪˈpɑː.zɪt **-s** -s ˈ**safe-deˌposit** ˌ**box**; ˌ**safe-deˈposit** ˌ**box** (US) ˈ**safe-deˌposit** ˌ**box**
safeguard ˈseɪf.gɑːd, (US) -gɑːrd **-s** -z **-ing** -ɪŋ **-ed** -ɪd
safekeeping ˌseɪfˈkiː.pɪŋ
safety ˈseɪf.ti ˈ**safety** ˌ**belt**; ˈ**safety** ˌ**curtain**; ˈ**safety** ˌ**lamp**; ˈ**safety** ˌ**match**; ˈ**safety** ˌ**net**; ˈ**safety** ˌ**pin**; ˈ**safety** ˌ**razor**; ˈ**safety** ˌ**valve**
Safeway® ˈseɪf.weɪ
Saffell səˈfel
safflower ˈsæf.laʊəʳ, -laʊ.əʳ, (US) -laʊ.ɚ **-s** -z
saffron, S~ ˈsæf.rən, -rɒn, (US) -rən
Safin ˈsɑː.fɪn
sag sæg **-s** -z **-ging** -ɪŋ **-ged** -d
saga ˈsɑː.gə **-s** -z
sagacious səˈgeɪ.ʃəs **-ly** -li **-ness** -nəs, -nɪs
sagacity səˈgæs.ə.ti, -ɪ.ti, (US) -ə.t̬i
Sagan *English name:* ˈseɪ.gən *French name:* səˈgɑ̃ːŋ, sægˈɑ̃ːŋ, (US) ˈseɪ.gᵊn; (US) sɑːˈgɑ̃ːn
sag|e, S~ seɪdʒ **-es** -ɪz **-ely** -li **-eness** -nəs, -nɪs
sagg|y ˈsæg|.i **-ier** -i.əʳ, (US) -i.ɚ **-iest** -i.ɪst, -i.əst **-iness** -i.nəs, -i.nɪs
sagitt|a, S~ səˈdʒɪt|.ə, -ˈgɪt-, (US) -ˈdʒɪt̬- **-ae** -iː, -aɪ
sagittal ˈsædʒ.ɪ.tᵊl, (US) -ə.t̬ᵊl **-ly** -i
Sagittarian ˌsædʒ.ɪˈteə.ri.ən, ˌsæg-, -əˈ-, -ˈtɑː-, (US) ˌsædʒ.əˈter.i- **-s** -z
Sagittarius ˌsædʒ.ɪˈteə.ri.əs, ˌsæg-, -əˈ-, -ˈtɑː-, (US) ˌsædʒ.əˈter.i-
sago ˈseɪ.gəʊ, (US) -goʊ
Sahara səˈhɑː.rə, (US) -ˈher.ə, -ˈhær-, -ˈhɑːr-
Sahel sɑːˈhel, sə-, (US) sɑː-
sahib, S~ sɑːb; ˈsɑː.*h*ɪb, (US) ˈsɑː.*h*ɪb, -*h*iːb, -ˈ- **-s** -z
said (from **say**) sed
Said (in **Port Said**) saɪd, seɪd, sɑːˈiːd, (US) sɑːˈiːd
Saigon saɪˈgɒn, (US) -ˈgɑːn, ˈ--
Saigonese ˌsaɪ.gɒnˈiːz, -gᵊnˈ-, (US) -gɑːˈniːz, -gəˈ- *stress shift:* ˌ**Saigonese** ˈ**exports**
sail seɪl **-s** -z **-ing/s** -ɪŋ/z **-ed** -d ˈ**sailing** ˌ**boat**; ˈ**sailing** ˌ**ship**
sailboard ˈseɪl.bɔːd, (US) -bɔːrd **-s** -z **-ing** -ɪŋ **-er/s** -əʳ/z, (US) -ɚ/z
sailboat ˈseɪl.bəʊt, (US) -boʊt **-s** -s
sailcloth ˈseɪl.klɒθ, (US) -klɑːθ
sailor ˈseɪ.ləʳ, (US) -lɚ **-s** -z ˈ**sailor** ˌ**suit**
sailplane ˈseɪl.pleɪn **-s** -z
sainfoin ˈsæn.fɔɪn, ˈseɪn-, (US) ˈseɪn-, ˈsæn-
Sainsbury ˈseɪnz.bᵊr.i, (US) -bɚ-, -ber- **-'s** -z
saint, S~ *strong form:* seɪnt **-s** -s **-ed** -ɪd **-hood** -hʊd *weak forms:* sᵊnt, sɪnt

Note: The weak forms are usual in British English for the names of saints (and places containing the word **Saint**), while the strong form is used when the word occurs on its own. For example, 'This would try the patience of a saint' would have the strong form, while **St. John**, **St. Cecilia** (saints' names), **St Alban's**, **St Helen's** (place names, usually printed without a full stop after **St**) have the weak forms. In American English, the strong form is usually used in all cases. When **Saint** occurs in British family names (e.g. **St. Clair**) the pronunciation is variable and individual names should be checked in their dictionary entries.

Saint-Etienne ˌsæ̃nt.eɪˈtjen
Saint Laurent ˌsæ̃n.lɔːˈrɑ̃ːŋ, -ləˈ-, (US) -lɑːˈrɑːnt, -ləˈ-
saintl|y ˈseɪnt.l|i **-ier** -i.əʳ, (US) -i.ɚ **-iest** -i.ɪst, -i.əst **-iness** -ɪ.nəs, -ɪ.nɪs
Saint-Saëns ˌsæ̃nˈsɑ̃ːŋ, -ˈsɑ̃ːns
Saintsbury ˈseɪnts.bᵊr.i
saith (from **say**) seθ, seɪθ
sake *cause, purpose:* seɪk **-s** -s *drink:* ˈsɑː.ki, ˈsæk.i, (US) ˈsɑː.ki
Sakhalin ˌsæk.əˈliːn, ˌsɑː.kə-, -ˈlɪn, ˈ---; *as if Russian:* ˌsæx.əˈljiːn; (US) ˌsæk.əˈliːn, ˈ---
Sakharov ˈsæk.ə.rɒf, -rɒv; *as if Russian:* ˈsæx-; (US) ˈsɑː.kə.rɔːf, ˈsæk.ə-, -rɑːf
saki, S~ ˈsɑː.ki
salaam səˈlɑːm, sælˈɑːm, (US) səˈlɑːm **-s** -z **-ing** -ɪŋ **-ed** -d
salability ˌseɪ.ləˈbɪl.ə.ti, -ɪ.ti, (US) -ə.t̬i
salable ˈseɪ.lə.bᵊl
salacious səˈleɪ.ʃəs **-ly** -li **-ness** -nəs, -nɪs
salacity səˈlæs.ə.ti, -ɪ.ti, (US) -ə.t̬i
salad ˈsæl.əd **-s** -z ˈ**salad** ˌ**bar**; ˈ**salad** ˌ**cream**; ˌ**salad** ˈ**cream** (US) ˈ**salad** ˌ**cream**; ˈ**salad** ˌ**days**; ˈ**salad** ˌ**dressing**; ˈ**salad** ˌ**onion**
Saladin ˈsæl.ə.dɪn
Salamanca ˌsæl.əˈmæŋ.kə
salamander ˈsæl.ə.mæn.dəʳ, (US) -dɚ **-s** -z
salami səˈlɑː.mi **-s** -z
Salamis ˈsæl.ə.mɪs
sal ammoniac ˌsæl.əˈməʊ.ni.æk, (US) -ˈmoʊ-
salariat səˈleə.ri.æt, (US) -ˈler.i-
salar|y ˈsæl.ᵊr|.i **-ies** -iz **-ied** -id
salary|man ˈsæl.ᵊr.i|.mæn, (US) -ɚ- **-men** -men
Salazar ˌsæl.əˈzɑːʳ, (US) -ˈzɑːr
Salcombe ˈsɔːl.kəm, ˈsɒl-, (US) ˈsɔːl-, ˈsɑːl-
sale, S~ seɪl **-s** -z ˌ**sale or reˈturn**; ˌ**sale of** ˈ**work**; ˈ**sales** ˌ**tax**
saleability ˌseɪ.ləˈbɪl.ə.ti, -ɪ.ti, (US) -ə.t̬i
saleable ˈseɪ.lə.bᵊl
Salem ˈseɪ.ləm, -lem, (US) -ləm
Salerno səˈlɜː.nəʊ, -ˈleə-, (US) -ˈlɝː.noʊ; (US) sɑːˈler-
Salesbury ˈseɪlz.bᵊr.i
salesclerk ˈseɪlz.klɑːk, (US) -klɝːk **-s** -s
salesgirl ˈseɪlz.gɜːl, (US) -gɝːl **-s** -z
sales|man ˈseɪlz|.mən **-men** -mən, -men
salesmanship ˈseɪlz.mən.ʃɪp
sales|person ˈseɪlz|ˌpɜː.sᵊn, (US) -ˌpɝː- **-people** -ˌpiː.pᵊl
salesroom ˈseɪlz.rʊm, -ruːm, (US) -ruːm, -rʊm **-s** -z
salestalk ˈseɪlz.tɔːk, (US) -tɑːk, -tɔːk
sales|woman ˈseɪlz|ˌwʊm.ən **-women** -ˌwɪm.ɪn
Salford ˈsɔːl.fəd, ˈsɒl-, (US) ˈsɔːl.fɚd, ˈsɑːl-
Salfords ˈsæl.fədz, (US) -fɚdz

S

Salian ˈseɪ.li.ən **-s** -z
Salic, Salique ˈsæl.ɪk, ˈseɪ.lɪk
salicylate səˈlɪs.ɪ.leɪt, sælˈɪs-, -əl.eɪt, (US) səˈlɪs.ə.leɪt; (US) ˌsæl.əˈsɪl.eɪt, -ɪt **-s** -s
salicylic ˌsæl.ɪˈsɪl.ɪk, -əˈ-; *stress shift, see compound:* (US) -əˈ- ˌ**salicylic ˈacid**
salienc|e ˈseɪ.li.ənts **-y** -i
salient ˈseɪ.li.ənt, (US) ˈseɪl.jənt, ˈseɪ.li.ənt **-s** -s **-ly** -li
Salieri ˌsæl.iˈeə.ri, (US) -ˈer.i
saline adj ˈseɪ.laɪn, ˈsæl.aɪn, (US) ˈseɪ.liːn, -laɪn
saline n ˈseɪ.laɪn, ˈsæl.aɪn, (US) ˈseɪ.liːn, -laɪn; (US) səˈliːn
Saline *in Fife:* ˈsæl.ɪn *in US:* səˈliːn
Salinger ˈsæl.ɪn.dʒəʳ, ˈseɪ.lɪn-, (US) ˈsæl.ɪn.dʒɚ
salinity səˈlɪn.ə.ti, -ɪ.ti, (US) -ə.t̬i
Salisbury ˈsɔːlz.bər.i, ˈsɒlz-, (US) ˈsɔːlz-, ˈsɑːlz-, -ber- ˌ**Salisbury ˈPlain**
saliva səˈlaɪ.və
salivary ˈsæl.ɪ.vər.i, ˈ-ə-; səˈlaɪ-, (US) ˈsæl.ə.ver- **saˈlivary ˌgland**; **ˈsalivary ˌgland**
sali|vate ˈsæl.ɪ|.veɪt, ˈ-ə|-, (US) ˈ-ə|- **-vates** -veɪts **-vating** -veɪ.tɪŋ, (US) -veɪ.t̬ɪŋ **-vated** -veɪ.tɪd, (US) -veɪ.t̬ɪd **-vation** ˌ--ˈveɪ.ʃən
Salk sɔːlk ˈ**Salk ˌvaccine**
sallet ˈsæl.ɪt, -ət, (US) -ɪt **-s** -s
Sallis ˈsæl.ɪs
sallow ˈsæl.əʊ, (US) -oʊ **-er** -əʳ, (US) -ɚ **-est** -ɪst, -əst **-s** -z **-y** -i **-ness** -nəs, -nɪs
Sallust ˈsæl.əst
sall|y, S~ ˈsæl|.i **-ies** -iz **-ying** -i.ɪŋ **-ied** -id ˌ**Sally ˈArmy**
Sally Lunn ˌsæl.iˈlʌn **-s** -z
salmagundi ˌsæl.məˈgʌn.di
Salman ˈsæl.mæn, -mən
salmi ˈsæl.mi **-s** -z
salmon ˈsæm.ən
Salmon *surname:* ˈsæm.ən, ˈsæl.mən, ˈsɑː- *river, etc. in Canada & US:* ˈsæm.ən *biblical name:* ˈsæl.mɒn, -mən, (US) -mən
salmonberr|y ˈsæm.ən.bər|.i, ˈ-əm-, (US) -ˌber- **-ies** -iz
Salmond ˈsæm.ənd
salmonella ˌsæl.məˈnel.ə
Salome səˈləʊ.mi, -meɪ, (US) -ˈloʊ-; (US) ˈsæl.ə.meɪ
Salomon ˈsæl.ə.mən, (US) ˈsɑːl-
salon ˈsæl.ɔ̃ːŋ, -lɒn, (US) səˈlɑːn; (US) ˈsæl.ɑːn **-s** -z
Salonika, Salonica səˈlɒn.ɪ.kə, ˌsæl.əˈniː-, (US) səˈlɑː.nə-; (US) ˌsæl.əˈnaɪ-, -ˈniː-
saloon səˈluːn **-s** -z **saˌloon ˈbar**; **saˈloon ˌcar**
Salop ˈsæl.əp
Salopian səˈləʊ.pi.ən, (US) -ˈloʊ- **-s** -z
Salpeter ˈsæl.piː.təʳ, (US) -t̬ɚ
salpingitis ˌsæl.pɪnˈdʒaɪ.tɪs, -təs, (US) -t̬ɪs, -t̬əs
salsa ˈsæl.sə, (US) ˈsɑːl-
salsify ˈsæl.sɪ.fi, -sə-, -faɪ, (US) -sə.fiː, -faɪ, sɔːl.sə.faɪ
salt, SALT, S~ sɔːlt, sɒlt, (US) sɔːlt, sɑːlt **-s** -s **-ing** -ɪŋ, (US) ˈsɔːl.t̬ɪŋ **-ed** -ɪd, (US) ˈsɔːl.t̬ɪd **-ness** -nəs, -nɪs ˈ**salt ˌcellar**; ˌ**Salt ˌLake ˈCity**; ˈ**salt ˌmarsh**; ˈ**salt ˌshaker**; **rub ˌsalt into someone's ˈwounds**; ˌ**salt of the ˈearth**; ˌ**take something with a ˌpinch/grain of ˈsalt**
Saltaire sɔːlˈteəʳ, sɒl-, (US) sɑːlˈter
saltant ˈsæl.tənt, ˈsɔːl-, ˈsɒl-, (US) ˈsæl.tənt
Saltash ˈsɔːl.tæʃ, ˈsɒl-, (US) ˈsɑːl-
saltation sælˈteɪ.ʃən **-s** -z
Saltburn ˈsɔːlt.bɜːn, ˈsɒlt-, (US) ˈsɔːlt.bɝːn, ˈsɑːlt-
Saltcoats ˈsɔːlt.kəʊts, ˈsɒlt-, (US) ˈsɔːlt.koʊts, ˈsɑːlt-
Saltdean ˈsɔːlt.diːn, ˈsɒlt-, (US) ˈsɔːlt-, ˈsɑːlt-
Salter ˈsɔːl.təʳ, ˈsɒl-, (US) ˈsɔːl.t̬ɚ, ˈsɑːl-
Salterton ˈsɔːl.tə.tən, ˈsɒl-, (US) ˈsɔːl.tɚ.tən, ˈsɑːl-
Saltfleetby ˈsɔːltˌfliːt.bi, ˈsɒlt-; *locally also:* ˈsɒl.ə.bi, (US) ˈsɔːltˌfliːt.bi, ˈsɑːlt-
Salting ˈsɔːl.tɪŋ, ˈsɒl-, (US) ˈsɔːl.tɪŋ, ˈsɑːl-
saltire ˈsɔːl.taɪəʳ, -taɪ.əʳ, ˈsɒl-, ˈsæl-, (US) ˈsɔːl.tɪr, ˈsɑːl-, ˈsæl-, -taɪ.ɚ **-s** -z
Saltmarsh ˈsɔːlt.mɑːʃ, ˈsɒlt-, (US) ˈsɔːlt.mɑːrʃ, ˈsɑːlt-
Salto ˈsæl.təʊ, (US) ˈsɑːl.toʊ
Saltoun ˈsɔːl.tən, ˈsɒlt-, (US) ˈsɔːl.tən, ˈsɑːl-
saltpan ˈsɔːlt.pæn, ˈsɒlt-, (US) ˈsɔːlt-, ˈsɑːlt- **-s** -z
saltpetre, saltpeter ˌsɔːltˈpiː.təʳ, ˌsɒlt-, ˈ---, (US) ˈsɔːltˌpiː.t̬ɚ, ˈsɑːlt-
saltwater ˈsɔːltˌwɔː.təʳ, ˈsɒlt-, (US) ˈsɔːltˌwɑː.t̬ɚ, ˈsɑːlt-, -ˌwɔː-
salt|y ˈsɔːl.t|i, ˈsɒl-, (US) ˈsɔːl.t|i, ˈsɑːl- **-ier** -i.əʳ, (US) -i.ɚ **-iest** -i.ɪst, -i.əst **-iness** -ɪ.nəs, -ɪ.nɪs
salubrious səˈluː.bri.əs, -ˈljuː-, (US) -ˈluː- **-ly** -li **-ness** -nəs, -nɪs
salubrity səˈluː.brə.ti, -ˈljuː-, -brɪ-, (US) -ˈluː.brə.t̬i
Salusbury ˈsɔːlz.bər.i
Salut (in **Port Salut**) səˈluː
salutar|y ˈsæl.jə.tər|.i, -jʊ-, (US) -ter- **-ily** -əl.i, -ɪ.li **-iness** -ɪ.nəs, -ɪ.nɪs
salutation ˌsæl.jəˈteɪ.ʃən, -jʊˈ- **-s** -z
salu|te səˈluː|t, -ˈljuː|t, (US) -ˈluː|t **-tes** -ts **-ting** -tɪŋ, (US) -t̬ɪŋ **-ted** -tɪd, (US) -t̬ɪd
salvable ˈsæl.və.bəl
Salvador ˈsæl.və.dɔːʳ, ˌ--ˈ-, (US) ˈsæl.və.dɔːr **-an/s** -ən/z
Salvadorean, Salvadorian ˌsæl.vəˈdɔː.ri.ən, (US) -ˈdɔːr.i- **-s** -z
salvag|e ˈsæl.vɪdʒ **-es** -ɪz **-ing** -ɪŋ **-ed** -d **-eable** -ə.bəl **-er/s** -əʳ/z, (US) -ɚ/z
Salvarsan® ˈsæl.və.sən, -sæn, (US) -vɚ-
salvation sælˈveɪ.ʃən **-s** -z **Salˌvation ˈArmy**
salvation|ism sælˈveɪ.ʃən|.ɪ.zəm **-ist/s** -ɪst/s
salv|e *anoint, soothe:* sælv, sɑːv, (US) sæv, sɑːv *save ship, cargo:* sælv **-es** -z **-ing** -ɪŋ **-ed** -d
Salve *Catholic antiphon:* ˈsæl.veɪ **-s** -z
salver ˈsæl.vəʳ, (US) -vɚ **-s** -z
salvia ˈsæl.vi.ə **-s** -z
salvo ˈsæl.vəʊ, (US) -voʊ **-(e)s** -z **-ing** -ɪŋ **-ed** -d
sal volatile ˌsæl.vəʊˈlæt.əl.i, -vɒlˈæt-, (US) -voʊˈlæt̬.əl-
Salyut səˈljuːt, sælˈjuːt, (US) ˈsæl.juːt
Salzburg ˈsælts.bɜːg, ˈsɑːlts-, (US) ˈsɔːlz.bɝːg, ˈsɑːlz-
Sam sæm ˌ**Sam ˌBrowne ˈbelt**
Samantha səˈmænt.θə
Samara səˈmɑː.rə, (US) -ˈmɑːr.ə, -ˈmær-
Samaria səˈmeə.ri.ə, (US) -ˈmer.i-, -ˈmær-
Samaritan səˈmær.ɪ.tən, (US) -ˈmer.ə-, -ˈmær- **-s** -z ˌ**good Saˈmaritan**
samarium səˈmeə.ri.əm, (US) -ˈmer.i-, -ˈmær-
Samarkand ˌsæm.ɑːˈkænd, -əˈ-, ˈ---, (US) ˈsæm.ɚ.kænd, ˌ--ˈ-
samarskite səˈmɑː.skaɪt, (US) -ˈmɑːr-; (US) ˈsæm.ɚ-
samba ˈsæm.bə, (US) ˈsɑːm-, ˈsæm- **-s** -z **-ing** -ɪŋ **-ed** -d
sambo, S~ ˈsæm.bəʊ, (US) -boʊ **-s** -z
same seɪm **-y** -i **-ness** -nəs, -nɪs
S. America (abbrev. for **South America**) ˌsaʊθ.əˈmer.ɪ.kə
same-sex ˌseɪmˈseks *stress shift:* ˌ**same-sex ˈcouples**
samite ˈseɪ.maɪt, ˈsæm.aɪt, (US) ˈsæm.aɪt, ˈseɪ.maɪt
samizdat ˌsæm.ɪzˈdæt, ˈ---, (US) ˈsɑː.mɪz.dɑːt, ˌ--ˈ-
Sammy ˈsæm.i
Samnite ˈsæm.naɪt **-s** -s
Samo|a səˈməʊ.|ə, sɑː-, (US) səˈmoʊ.|ə **-an/s** -ən/z
Samos ˈseɪ.mɒs, ˈsæm-, (US) -mɑːs; (US) ˈsæm.oʊs
samosa səˈməʊ.sə, sæmˈəʊ-, -zə, (US) səˈmoʊ.sə **-s** -z
Samothrace ˈsæm.əʊ.θreɪs, (US) ˈ-ə-, -oʊ-
samovar ˈsæm.ə.vɑːʳ, ˌ--ˈ-, (US) ˈsæm.ə.vɑːr; (US) ˌsɑː.məˈvɑːr **-s** -z
Samoyed *people:* ˌsæm.ɔɪˈed; -ˈ--, -ɪd, (US) ˈsæm.ə.jed; (US) səˈmɔɪ.ed *dog:* səˈmɔɪ.ed, -ɪd, (US) ˈsæm.ə.jed; (US) səˈmɔɪ.ed **-s** -z
sampan ˈsæm.pæn **-s** -z
Samper ˈsæm.pəʳ, (US) -pɚ
samphire ˈsæmp.faɪəʳ, (US) -faɪ.ɚ
sampl|e ˈsɑːm.pəl, (US) ˈsæm- **-es** -z **-ing** -ɪŋ, ˈsɑːm.plɪŋ, (US) ˈsæm- **-ed** -d
sampler ˈsɑːm.pləʳ, (US) ˈsæm.plɚ **-s** -z
Sampras ˈsæm.prəs, -præs
Sampson ˈsæmp.sən
Samson ˈsæmp.sən
Samsonite® ˈsæmp.sən.aɪt
Samsung® ˈsæm.sʌŋ, -sʊŋ
Samuel ˈsæm.juəl, -ju.əl, (US) -ju.əl, -jʊl **-s** -z

S

samurai, S~ ˈsæm.ʊ.raɪ, -jʊ-, (US) -ə.raɪ **-s** -z
San Antonio ˌsæn.ænˈtəʊ.ni.əʊ, (US) -ˈtoʊ.ni.oʊ
sanatari|um ˌsæn.əˈteə.ri|.əm, (US) -ˈter.i- **-ums** -əmz **-a** -ə
Sanatogen® səˈnæt.ə.dʒᵊn, -dʒen, (US) -ˈnæţ-
sanatori|um ˌsæn.əˈtɔː.ri|.əm, (US) -ˈtɔːr.i- **-ums** -əmz **-a** -ə
Sancerre sænˈseəʳ, sɑ̃ːnˑ-, (US) sɑːnˈser
Sanchez ˈsæn.tʃez
Sancho Panza ˌsæn.tʃəʊˈpæn.zə, (US) ˌsɑːn.tʃoʊˈpɑːn-
San Cristóbal ˌsæn.krɪˈstəʊ.bæl, ˌsæŋ-, (US) ˌsæn.krɪˈstoʊ.bəl, -bɑːl
sanctification ˌsæŋk.tɪ.fɪˈkeɪ.ʃᵊn, -tə-
sancti|fy ˈsæŋk.tɪ|.faɪ, -tə- **-fies** -faɪz **-fying** -faɪ.ɪŋ **-fied** -faɪd
sanctimonious ˌsæŋk.tɪˈməʊ.ni.əs, -təˈ-, (US) -ˈmoʊ- **-ly** -li **-ness** -nəs, -nɪs
sanction ˈsæŋk.ʃᵊn **-s** -z **-ing** -ɪŋ **-ed** -d
sanctity ˈsæŋk.tə.ti, -tɪ-, (US) -tə.ţi
sanctuar|y ˈsæŋk.tʃʊə.r|i, -tʃᵊ.r|i, -tjʊə.r|i, -tjᵊr|.i, (US) -tʃu.er|.i **-ies** -ɪz
sanct|um ˈsæŋk.t|əm **-ums** -əmz **-a** -ə ˌ**inner** ˈ**sanctum**
Sanctus ˈsæŋk.təs **-es** -ɪz
sand *on beach:* sænd **-s** -z **-ing** -ɪŋ **-ed** -ɪd **-er/s** -əʳ/z, (US) -ɚ/z ˈ**sand** ˌ**dollar;** ˈ**sand** ˌ**trap;** ˌ**bury one's** ˌ**head in the** ˈ**sand;** ˌ**bury one's** ˈ**head in the** ˌ**sand** (US) ˌ**bury one's** ˌ**head in the** ˈ**sand**
Sand *French novelist:* sɑ̃ːnd, (US) sænd, sɑ̃ːnd
sandal ˈsæn.dᵊl **-s** -z
sandalwood ˈsæn.dᵊl.wʊd
Sanday ˈsæn.deɪ, -di
Sandbach ˈsænd.bætʃ, ˈsæm-, (US) ˈsænd-
sandbag ˈsænd.bæg, ˈsæm-, (US) ˈsænd- **-s** -z **-ging** -ɪŋ **-ged** -d **-ger/s** -əʳ/z, (US) -ɚ/z
sandbank ˈsænd.bæŋk, ˈsæm-, (US) ˈsænd- **-s** -s
sandbar ˈsænd.bɑːʳ, ˈsæm-, (US) ˈsænd.bɑːr **-s** -z
sandblast ˈsænd.blɑːst, ˈsæm-, (US) ˈsænd.blæst **-s** -s **-ing** -ɪŋ **-ed** -ɪd **-er/s** -əʳ/z, (US) -ɚ/z
sandbox ˈsænd.bɒks, ˈsæm-, (US) -bɑːks **-es** -ɪz
sandboy ˈsænd.bɔɪ, ˈsæm-, (US) ˈsænd- **-s** -z ˌ**happy as a** ˈ**sandboy**
Sandburg ˈsænd.bɜːg, (US) -bɝːg
sandcastle ˈsændˌkɑː.sᵊl, ˈsæŋ-, (US) ˈsændˌkæs.ᵊl **-s** -z
sanderling ˈsæn.dᵊl.ɪŋ, (US) -dɚ.lɪŋ **-s** -z
Sanders ˈsɑːn.dəz, (US) ˈsæn.dɚz
Sanderson ˈsɑːn.də.sᵊn, (US) ˈsæn.dɚ-
Sanderstead ˈsɑːn.də.sted, -stɪd, (US) ˈsæn.dɚ-
sandfl|y ˈsænd.fl|aɪ **-ies** -aɪz
Sandford ˈsænd.fəd, -fɔːd; ˈsæn.əd, (US) ˈsænd.fɚd, -fɔːrd
Sandgate ˈsænd.geɪt, ˈsæŋ-, -gɪt, (US) ˈsænd-
sandhi ˈsæn.diː, ˈsʌn-; ˈsænd.hiː, ˈsʌnd-, (US) ˈsæn.di, ˈsɑːn-, ˈsʌn-
sandhopper ˈsændˌhɒp.əʳ, (US) -ˌhɑː.pɚ **-s** -z
Sandhurst ˈsænd.hɜːst, (US) -hɝːst
San Diego ˌsæn.diˈeɪ.gəʊ, (US) -goʊ
Sandinista ˌsæn.dəˈnɪs.tə, -dɪˈ-, (US) -ˈniː.stə **-s** -z
Sanditon ˈsæn.dɪ.tᵊn, (US) -ţən
Sandling ˈsænd.lɪŋ
sand|man ˈsænd|.mæn, ˈsæm-, (US) ˈsænd- **-men** -men
San Domingo ˌsæn.dəˈmɪŋ.gəʊ, -dəʊˈ-, -dɒmˈɪŋ-, (US) -dəˈmɪŋ.goʊ, -doʊˈ-
Sandown ˈsæn.daʊn
sandpail ˈsænd.peɪl, ˈsæm-, (US) ˈsænd- **-s** -z
sandpap|er ˈsændˌpeɪ.p|əʳ, ˈsæm-, (US) ˈsændˌpeɪ.p|ɚ **-ers** -əz, (US) -ɚz **-ering** -ᵊr.ɪŋ **-ered** -əd, (US) -ɚd
sandpiper ˈsændˌpaɪ.pəʳ, ˈsæm-, (US) ˈsændˌpaɪ.pɚ **-s** -z
sandpit ˈsænd.pɪt, ˈsæm-, (US) ˈsænd- **-s** -s
Sandra ˈsæn.drə, ˈsɑːn-, (US) ˈsæn-
Sandringham ˈsæn.drɪŋ.əm
Sands sændz
sandstone ˈsænd.stəʊn, (US) -stoʊn
sandstorm ˈsænd.stɔːm, (US) -stɔːrm **-s** -z
sand|wich ˈsæn|.wɪdʒ, ˈsæm-, -wɪtʃ, (US) ˈsænd|.wɪtʃ **-wiches** -wɪdʒ.ɪz, -wɪtʃ.ɪz, (US) -wɪtʃ.ɪz **-wiching** -wɪdʒ.ɪŋ, -wɪtʃ.ɪŋ, (US) -wɪtʃ.ɪŋ **-wiched** -wɪdʒd, -wɪtʃt, (US) -wɪtʃt ˈ**sandwich** ˌ**board;** ˈ**sandwich** ˌ**course**

> Note: Some British speakers use /-wɪtʃ/ in the uninflected form and /-wɪdʒ/ in the inflected forms of this word.

Sandwich *in Kent:* ˈsænd.wɪtʃ, ˈsæm-, -wɪdʒ, (US) ˈsænd.wɪtʃ
sandwich|man ˈsænd.wɪdʒ|.mæn, ˈsæm-, -wɪtʃ-, (US) ˈsænd.wɪtʃ- **-men** -men
Sandwick ˈsænd.wɪk
sand|y, S~ ˈsæn.d|i **-ier** -i.əʳ, (US) -i.ɚ **-iest** -i.ɪst, -i.əst **-iness** -ɪ.nəs, -ɪ.nɪs
Sandys sændz
san|e seɪn **-er** -əʳ, (US) -ɚ **-est** -ɪst, -əst **-ely** -li **-eness** -nəs, -nɪs
San Fernando ˌsæn.fəˈnæn.dəʊ, (US) -fɚˈnæn.doʊ
Sanford ˈsæn.fəd, (US) -fɚd
sanforiz|e, -is|e ˈsæn.fᵊr.aɪz, (US) -fə.raɪz **-es** -ɪz **-ing** -ɪŋ **-ed** -d
San Francisco ˌsæn.frənˈsɪs.kəʊ, -frænˈ-, (US) -koʊ
sang (from **sing**) sæŋ
Sanger ˈsæŋ.gəʳ, -əʳ, (US) -ɚ
sang-froid ˌsɑ̃ːŋˈfrwɑː, (US) ˌsɑ̃ːŋ-, ˌsɑ̃ːn-
Sangin sæŋˈgiːn
sangria sæŋˈgriː.ə
Sangster ˈsæŋk.stəʳ, (US) -stɚ
sanguinar|y ˈsæŋ.gwɪ.nᵊr|.i, -gwə-, (US) -gwɪ.ner- **-ily** -ᵊl.i, -ɪ.li **-iness** -ɪ.nəs, -ɪ.nɪs
sanguine ˈsæŋ.gwɪn **-ly** -li **-ness** -nəs, -nɪs
sanguineous sæŋˈgwɪn.i.əs
sanitari|um ˌsæn.ɪˈteə.ri|.əm, -əˈ-, (US) -ˈter.i- **-ums** -əmz **-a** -ə
sanitar|y ˈsæn.ɪ.tᵊr|.i, -tr|i, (US) -ter|.i **-ily** -ᵊl.i, -ɪ.li **-iness** -ɪ.nəs, -ɪ.nɪs ˈ**sanitary** ˌ**napkin;** ˈ**sanitary** ˌ**towel**
sanitation ˌsæn.ɪˈteɪ.ʃᵊn, -əˈ- **sani**ˈ**tation** ˌ**worker**
sanitization, -isa- ˌsæn.ɪ.taɪˈzeɪ.ʃᵊn, ˌ-ə-, (US) -ţəˈ-
sanitiz|e, -is|e ˈsæn.ɪ.taɪz, ˈ-ə- **-es** -ɪz **-ing** -ɪŋ **-ed** -d
sanitori|um ˌsæn.əˈtɔː.ri|.əm, -ɪˈ-, (US) -ˈtɔːr.i- **-ums** -əmz **-a** -ə
sanity ˈsæn.ə.ti, -ɪ.ti, (US) -ə.ţi
San José ˌsæn.həʊˈzeɪ, -əʊˈ-, (US) -hoʊˈ-, -əˈ-
San Juan ˌsænˈhwɑːn, (US) -ˈhwɑːn, -ˈwɔːn
sank (from **sink**) sæŋk
Sankey ˈsæŋ.ki
San Marino ˌsæn.məˈriː.nəʊ, ˌsæm-, (US) ˌsæn.məˈriː.noʊ
San Miguel ˌsæn.mɪˈgel, ˌsæm-, (US) ˌsæn-
San Pedro Sula sænˌped.rəʊˈsuː.lə, sæm-, (US) sænˌpeɪ.droʊˈ-, -ˌped.roʊˈ-, -ˌpiː.droʊˈ-
San Remo ˌsænˈreɪ.məʊ, -ˈriː-, (US) -ˈriː.moʊ, -ˈreɪ-
sans *English word:* sænz *in French phrases:* sɑ̃ːŋ, (US) sænz, sɑ̃ːn
San Salvador ˌsænˈsæl.və.dɔːʳ, -ˌsæl.vəˈdɔːʳ, (US) -ˈsæl.və.dɔːr
sans-culotte ˌsænz.kjʊˈlɒt, (US) -kuːˈlɑːt, -kjuːˈ- **-s** -s
San Sebastian ˌsæn.sɪˈbæs.ti.ən, -səˈ-, (US) -sɪˈbæs.tʃən
Sanskrit ˈsæn.skrɪt
sanskritic, S~ sænˈskrɪt.ɪk, (US) -ˈskrɪţ-
sans serif ˌsænˈser.ɪf
Santa ˈsæn.tə, (US) -ţə **-s** -z
Santa Ana ˌsæn.təˈæn.ə, (US) -ţəˈ-
Santa Claus ˌsæn.təˈklɔːz, ˈ--ˌ-, (US) ˈsæn.ţəˌklɑːz, -ˌklɔːz **-es** -ɪz
Santa Cruz ˌsæn.təˈkruːz, (US) ˈsæn.ţə.kruːz, ˌ--ˈ-
Santa Fe ˌsæn.təˈfeɪ, (US) ˈsæn.ţə.feɪ, ˌ--ˈ-
Santa Marta ˌsæn.təˈmɑː.tə, (US) -ţəˈmɑːr.ţə
Santander ˌsæn.tənˈdeəʳ, -tænˈ-, (US) ˌsɑːn.tɑːnˈder
Santayana ˌsæn.taɪˈɑː.nə, (US) -ţiˈæn-, -ˈɑː.nə
Santer ˈsæn.təʳ, sɑ̃ːˈteə, (US) sɑːn.ţɚ
Santiago ˌsæn.tiˈɑː.gəʊ, (US) -ţiˈɑː.goʊ, ˌsɑːn-
Santley ˈsænt.li
Santo Domingo ˌsæn.təʊ.dəʊ-

S

ˈmɪŋ.gəʊ, -dɒmˈɪŋ-, ⓊⓈ -toʊ.dəˈmɪŋ.goʊ, ˌsɑːn-, -doʊˈ-
Sanyo® ˈsæn.jəʊ, ⓊⓈ -joʊ
Saoirse ˈsɪə.ʃə, ˈseə-, ⓊⓈ ˈsɪr-, ˈser-
Saône səʊn, ⓊⓈ soʊn
São Paulo saʊˈpaʊ.ləʊ, saʊm-, ⓊⓈ sɑ̃ːʊˈpaʊ.lu, -loʊ
São Tomé ˌsaʊ.təˈmeɪ, ˌsaʊn-, ⓊⓈ ˌsɑ̃ːʊ.toʊˈ-, -təˈ-
sap sæp **-s** -s **-ping** -ɪŋ **-ped** -t
sapele, S~ sæpˈiː.li, səˈpiː-, ⓊⓈ səˈpiː.li **saˌpele maˈhogany**
sapien|ce ˈseɪ.pi.ən|ts, ˈsæp.i-, ⓊⓈ ˈseɪ.pi- **-t/ly** -t/li
sapiens ˈsæp.i.enz, -seɪ.pi-
Sapir səˈpɪəʳ, sæpˈɪəʳ; ˈseɪ.pɪəʳ, ⓊⓈ sæpˈɪr, səˈpɪr
sapless ˈsæp.ləs, -lɪs **-ness** -nəs, -nɪs
sapling ˈsæp.lɪŋ **-s** -z
saponaceous ˌsæp.əʊˈneɪ.ʃəs, ⓊⓈ -əˈ- **-ness** -nəs, -nɪs
saponification səˌpɒn.ɪ.fɪˈkeɪ.ʃən, sæpˌɒn-, ˌ-ə-, -fəˈ-, ⓊⓈ səˌpɑː.nə-
saponi|fy səˈpɒn.ɪ|.faɪ, sæpˈɒn-, ˈ-ə-, ⓊⓈ səˈpɑː.nɪ-, ˈ-nə- **-fies** -faɪz **-fying** -faɪ.ɪŋ **-fied** -faɪd
sapper ˈsæp.əʳ, ⓊⓈ -ɚ **-s** -z
sapphic, S~ ˈsæf.ɪk **-s** -s
Sapphira səˈfaɪə.rə, sæfˈaɪə-, ⓊⓈ səˈfaɪ-
sapphire ˈsæf.aɪəʳ, -aɪ.əʳ, ⓊⓈ -aɪ.ɚ **-s** -z
sapph|ism, S~ ˈsæf|.ɪ.zəm **-ist/s** -ɪst/s
Sappho ˈsæf.əʊ, ⓊⓈ -oʊ
Sapporo səˈpɔː.rəʊ, sæpˈɔː-, -ˈɒr.əʊ, ⓊⓈ səˈpɔːr.oʊ, sɑː-
sapp|y ˈsæp|.i **-iness** -ɪ.nəs, -ɪ.nɪs
saprophyte ˈsæp.rəʊ.faɪt, ⓊⓈ -rə- **-s** -s
sapwood ˈsæp.wʊd
Sara ˈsɑː.rə, ˈseə-, ⓊⓈ ˈser.ə, ˈsær-
saraband(e) ˈsær.ə.bænd, ˌ--ˈ-, ⓊⓈ ˈsær.ə.bænd, ˈser- **-s** -z
Saracen ˈsær.ə.sən, -sɪn, -sen, ⓊⓈ -sən, ˈser-, ˈsær- **-s** -z
Saracenic ˌsær.əˈsen.ɪk, ⓊⓈ ˌser-, ˌsær-
Saragossa ˌsær.əˈgɒs.ə, ⓊⓈ -ˈgɑː.sə, ˌser-, ˌsær-
Sarah ˈseə.rə, ⓊⓈ ˈser.ə, ˈsær-
Sarajevo ˌsær.əˈjeɪ.vəʊ, ⓊⓈ -voʊ, ˌser-, ˌsær-
Saran® səˈræn **Saˈran ˌwrap**
Sarandon ˈsær.ən.dən, ⓊⓈ səˈræn.dən
Sarasate ˌsær.əˈsɑː.teɪ, ⓊⓈ ˌsɑːr.ɑːˈsɑː.teɪ
Saratoga ˌsær.əˈtəʊ.gə, ⓊⓈ ˌser.əˈtoʊ-, ˌsær-
Sarawak səˈrɑː.wæk, -wək, -wə, ⓊⓈ -ˈrɑː.wɑːk
Sarawakian ˌsær.əˈwæk.i.ən, ⓊⓈ ˌser.əˈwɑː.ki-, ˌsær- **-s** -z
sarcasm ˈsɑː.kæz.əm, ⓊⓈ ˈsɑːr- **-s** -z
sarcastic sɑːˈkæs.tɪk, ⓊⓈ sɑːr- **-ally** -əl.i, -li
sarcenet ˈsɑːs.net, -nət, -nɪt, ⓊⓈ ˈsɑːr.snet
sarcoma sɑːˈkəʊ.mə, ⓊⓈ sɑːrˈkoʊ- **-s** -z **-ta** -tə **-tous** -təs
sarcopha|gus sɑːˈkɒf.ə|.gəs, ⓊⓈ sɑːrˈkɑː.fə- **-guses** -gə.sɪz **-gi** -gaɪ, -dʒaɪ
Sardanapalus ˌsɑː.dəˈnæp.əl.əs; -nəˈpɑː.ləs, ⓊⓈ ˌsɑːr.dəˈnæp.əl.əs; ⓊⓈ -nəˈpeɪ.ləs
sardine *fish:* sɑːˈdiːn, ⓊⓈ sɑːr- *stone:* ˈsɑː.daɪn, ⓊⓈ ˈsɑːr.dɪn, -daɪn **-s** -z
Sardini|a sɑːˈdɪn.i|.ə, ⓊⓈ sɑːr-, ˈ-j|ə **-an/s** -ən/z
Sardis ˈsɑː.dɪs, ⓊⓈ ˈsɑːr-
sardius ˈsɑː.di.əs, ⓊⓈ ˈsɑːr- **-es** -ɪz
sardonic sɑːˈdɒn.ɪk, ⓊⓈ sɑːrˈdɑː.nɪk **-ally** -əl.i, -li
sardonyx ˈsɑː.dən.ɪks; sɑːˈdɒn-, ⓊⓈ sɑːrˈdɑː.nɪks; ⓊⓈ ˈsɑːr.də- **-es** -ɪz
Sargant ˈsɑː.dʒənt, ⓊⓈ ˈsɑːr-
sargasso, S~ sɑːˈgæs.əʊ, ⓊⓈ sɑːrˈgæs.oʊ **-(e)s** -z **Sarˌgasso ˈSea**
sarge sɑːdʒ, ⓊⓈ sɑːrdʒ
Sargeant, Sargent ˈsɑː.dʒənt, ⓊⓈ ˈsɑːr-
Sargeson ˈsɑː.dʒɪ.sən, ⓊⓈ ˈsɑːr-
Sargon ˈsɑː.gɒn, ⓊⓈ ˈsɑːr.gɑːn
sari ˈsɑː.ri, ⓊⓈ ˈsɑːr.i **-s** -z
Sark sɑːk, ⓊⓈ sɑːrk
Sarkozy sɑːˈkəʊ.zi, ˌsɑː.kəʊˈziː, ⓊⓈ ˌsɑːr.koʊˈziː
sark|y ˈsɑː.k|i, ⓊⓈ ˈsɑːr- **-ier** -i.əʳ, ⓊⓈ -i.ɚ **-iest** -i.ɪst, -i.əst
Sarmati|a sɑːˈmeɪ.ʃi|.ə, ˈ-ʃ|ə, ⓊⓈ sɑːrˈmeɪ.ʃ|ə, -ʃi|.ə **-an/s** -ən/z
sarnie ˈsɑː.ni, ⓊⓈ ˈsɑːr- **-s** -z
sarong səˈrɒŋ, sɑː-, særˈɒŋ, ⓊⓈ səˈrɔːŋ, -ˈrɑːŋ **-s** -z
Saro-Wiwa ˌsær.əʊˈwiː.wə, -wɑː, ⓊⓈ ˌsær.oʊˈwiː.wɑː, ˌsɑːr-
Saroyan səˈrɔɪ.ən
SARS sɑːz, ⓊⓈ sɑːrz
sarsaparilla ˌsɑː.spəˈrɪl.ə, -sə.pəˈ-, ⓊⓈ ˌsɑːr.spəˈrɪl-; ⓊⓈ ˌsæs.pəˈ-
sarsenet ˈsɑːs.net, -nət, -nɪt, ⓊⓈ ˈsɑːr.snet
Sarton ˈsɑː.tən, ⓊⓈ ˈsɑːr-
Sartor ˈsɑː.tɔːʳ, -təʳ, ⓊⓈ ˈsɑːr.tɔːr, -t̬ɚ
sartorial sɑːˈtɔː.ri.əl, ⓊⓈ sɑːrˈtɔːr.i-
Sartre ˈsɑː.trə, ⓊⓈ ˈsɑːr-; ⓊⓈ sɑːrt
Sarum ˈseə.rəm, ⓊⓈ ˈser.əm
SAS ˌes.eɪˈes
SASE ˌes.eɪ.esˈiː
sash sæʃ **-es** -ɪz **-ed** -t ˌ**sash ˈwindow**
Sasha ˈsæʃ.ə, ⓊⓈ ˈsɑː.ʃə, ˈsæʃ.ə
sashay ˈsæʃ.eɪ, -ˈ-, ⓊⓈ sæʃˈeɪ **-s** -z **-ing** -ɪŋ **-ed** -d
sashimi sæʃˈiː.mi, səˈʃiː-, ⓊⓈ sɑːˈʃiː.mi
Saskatchewan səˈskætʃ.ɪ.wən, sæsˈkætʃ-, ˈ-ə-, -wɒn, ⓊⓈ sæsˈkætʃ.ə.wɑːn, -wən **-er/s** -əʳ/z, ⓊⓈ -ɚ/z
saskatoon, S~ ˌsæs.kəˈtuːn
Saskia ˈsæs.ki.ə
sasquatch, S~ ˈsæs.kwɒtʃ, -kwætʃ, ⓊⓈ -kwɑːtʃ, -kwætʃ **-es** -ɪz
sass sæs
sassafras ˈsæs.ə.fræs **-es** -ɪz
Sassenach ˈsæs.ə.næk, -næx, -nək, -nəx, ⓊⓈ -næk **-s** -s
Sassoon səˈsuːn, sæsˈuːn, ⓊⓈ sæsˈuːn, səˈsuːn
sass|y ˈsæs|.i **-ier** -i.əʳ, ⓊⓈ -i.ɚ **-iest** -i.ɪst, -i.əst
sat (from **sit**) sæt
SAT sæt, ⓊⓈ es.eɪˈtiː **-s** -z
Sat. (abbrev. for **Saturday**) ˈsæt.ə.deɪ, -di, ⓊⓈ ˈsæt̬.ɚ-
Satan ˈseɪ.tən **-ism** -ɪ.zəm **-ist/s** -ɪst/s
satang sætˈæŋ, ⓊⓈ sɑːˈtæŋ **-s** -z
satanic səˈtæn.ɪk, seɪˈtæn- **-ally** -əl.i, ⓊⓈ -li
satay, saté ˈsæt.eɪ, ˈsɑː.teɪ, ⓊⓈ sɑːˈteɪ **-s** -z ˌ**satay ˈsauce** ⓊⓈ ˈ**satay ˌsauce**
satchel ˈsætʃ.əl **-s** -z
Satchwell ˈsætʃ.wel
sate seɪt **-s** -s **-ing** -ɪŋ, ⓊⓈ seɪt̬ɪŋ **-ed** -ɪd, ⓊⓈ seɪt̬ɪd
sated ˈseɪ.tɪd, ⓊⓈ -t̬ɪd
sateen sætˈiːn, səˈtiːn **-s** -z
satellite ˈsæt.əl.aɪt, -ɪ.laɪt, ⓊⓈ ˈsæt̬.əl.aɪt **-s** -s ˈ**satellite ˌdish**; ˌ**satellite ˈtelevision** ⓊⓈ ˈ**satellite ˌtelevision**
sati ˈsɑː.tiː **-s** -z
satiable ˈseɪ.ʃi.ə.bəl, ˈ-ʃə.bəl, ⓊⓈ -ʃə-, -ʃi.ə-
satiate **adj** ˈseɪ.ʃi.ət, -ɪt, -eɪt, ⓊⓈ -ɪt
sati|ate **v** ˈseɪ.ʃi|.eɪt **-ates** -eɪts **-ating** -eɪ.tɪŋ, ⓊⓈ -eɪ.t̬ɪŋ **-ated** -eɪ.tɪd, ⓊⓈ -eɪ.t̬ɪd
satiation ˌseɪ.ʃiˈeɪ.ʃən
Satie ˈsæt.i, ˈsɑː.ti, -ˈ-, ⓊⓈ sɑːˈtiː
satiety səˈtaɪ.ə.ti, -ˈtaɪ.ɪ-; ˈseɪ.ʃə.ti, -ʃi.ə-, ⓊⓈ səˈtaɪ.ə.t̬i
satin ˈsæt.ɪn, ⓊⓈ -ən **-s** -z **-y** -i
satinette, satinet ˌsæt.ɪˈnet, ⓊⓈ -ənˈet
satinwood ˈsæt.ɪn.wʊd, ⓊⓈ -ən-
satire ˈsæt.aɪəʳ, -aɪ.əʳ, ⓊⓈ -aɪ.ɚ **-s** -z
satiric|al səˈtɪr.ɪ.k|əl **-ally** -əl.i, -li
satirist ˈsæt.ər.ɪst, -ɪ.rɪst, ⓊⓈ ˈsæt̬.ɚ.ɪst **-s** -s
satiriz|e, -is|e ˈsæt.ər.aɪz, -ɪ.raɪz, ⓊⓈ ˈsæt̬.ə.raɪz **-es** -ɪz **-ing** -ɪŋ **-ed** -d
satisfaction ˌsæt.ɪsˈfæk.ʃən, -əsˈ-, ⓊⓈ ˌsæt̬-
satisfactor|y ˌsæt.ɪsˈfæk.tər|.i, -əsˈ-, -tr|i, ⓊⓈ ˌsæt̬- **-ily** -əl.i, -ɪ.li **-iness** -ɪ.nəs, -ɪ.nɪs
satis|fy ˈsæt.ɪs|.faɪ, ⓊⓈ -əs-, ˈsæt̬- **-fies** -faɪz **-fying** -faɪ.ɪŋ **-fied** -faɪd
satnav ˈsæt.næv
satrap ˈsæt.ræp, -rəp, ⓊⓈ ˈseɪ.træp, ˈsæt.ræp **-s** -s **-y** -i **-ies** -iz
satsuma ˌsætˈsuː.mə; -sʊ-, ⓊⓈ ˈsæt.sə.mɑː; ⓊⓈ sɑːtˈsuː.mə **-s** -z
saturate **adj** ˈsætʃ.ər.eɪt, -ʊ.reɪt, ˈsæt.jər.eɪt, -jʊ.reɪt, ⓊⓈ ˈsætʃ.ɚ.ɪt
satur|ate **v** ˈsætʃ.ər|.eɪt, -ʊ.r|eɪt, -tjər|.eɪt, -tjʊ.r|eɪt, ⓊⓈ ˈsætʃ.ə.r|eɪt **-ates** -eɪts **-ating** -eɪ.tɪŋ, ⓊⓈ -eɪ.t̬ɪŋ **-ated** -eɪ.tɪd, ⓊⓈ -eɪ.t̬ɪd ˌ**saturated ˈfat**
saturation ˌsætʃ.ərˈeɪ.ʃən, -tʃʊˈreɪ-, -tjərˈeɪ-, -tjʊˈreɪ-, ⓊⓈ ˌsætʃ.əˈreɪ- **satuˈration ˌpoint**
Saturday ˈsæt.ə.deɪ, -di, ⓊⓈ ˈsæt̬.ɚ- **-s** -z
Saturn ˈsæt.ən, -ɜːn, ⓊⓈ ˈsæt̬.ɚn

S

Pronouncing the letters SC

The consonant digraph **sc** has two main pronunciations: /s/ and /sk/.

It is normally pronounced /s/ before the letters **e**, **i**, or **y**, e.g.:

scene	siːn
science	ˈsaɪ.ənts
scythe	saɪð
coalesce	ˌkəʊ.əˈles ⓊⓈ ˌkoʊ-

However, the realization /sk/ can occur before **e**, and /tʃ/ is possible before **i**, e.g.:

sceptic	ˈskep.tɪk
conscious	ˈkɒn.tʃəs ⓊⓈ ˈkɑːnt.ʃəs

In other cases, /sk/ is the usual pronunciation in word initial position, and /s/ in the combination *–scle*, e.g.:

scale	skeɪl
Scotland	ˈskɒt.lənd ⓊⓈ ˈskɑːt-
muscle	ˈmʌs.əl

saturnalia, S~ ˌsæt.əˈneɪ.li.ə, -ɜːˈ-, ⓊⓈ ˌsæţ.ɚˈ-, -ˈneɪl.jə **-n** -n **-s** -z
saturnian, S~ sætˈɜː.ni.ən, səˈtɜː-, ⓊⓈ səˈtɝː-
saturnine ˈsæt.ə.naɪn, ⓊⓈ ˈsæţ.ɚ-
satyr ˈsæt.əʳ, ⓊⓈ ˈseɪ.ţɚ, ˈsæţ.ɚ **-s** -z
satyriasis ˌsæt.ərˈaɪ.ə.sɪs, ⓊⓈ ˌseɪ.ţəˈraɪ.ə.sɪs, ˌsæţ-
satyric səˈtɪr.ɪk, ⓊⓈ seɪ-, sə-
sauc|e sɔːs, ⓊⓈ sɑːs, sɔːs **-es** -ɪz **-ing** -ɪŋ **-ed** -d **ˈsauce ˌboat**
saucepan ˈsɔːs.pən, ⓊⓈ ˈsɑːs-, ˈsɔːs- **-s** -z
saucer ˈsɔː.səʳ, ⓊⓈ ˈsɑː.sɚ, ˈsɔː- **-s** -z
Sauchiehall ˌsɔː.kɪˈhɔːl, ˌsɒk.ɪˈ-, ˈ---, ⓊⓈ ˌsɑː.kiˈ-, ˌsɔː-
sauc|y ˈsɔː.s|i, ⓊⓈ ˈsɑː-, ˈsɔː- **-ier** -i.əʳ, ⓊⓈ -i.ɚ **-iest** -i.ɪst, -i.əst **-ily** -əl.i, -ɪ.li **-iness** -ɪ.nəs, -ɪ.nɪs
Saudi ˈsaʊ.di, ˈsɔː-, ⓊⓈ ˈsaʊ-, ˈsɔː-, ˈsɑː- **-s** -z **ˌSaudi Aˈrabia**
sauerbraten ˈsaʊ.əˌbrɑː.tən, ⓊⓈ ˈsaʊ.ɚ-
sauerkraut ˈsaʊ.ə.kraʊt, ⓊⓈ ˈsaʊ.ɚ-
Saul sɔːl, ⓊⓈ sɔːl, sɑːl
Sault St. Marie ˌsuː.seɪnt.məˈriː
sauna ˈsɔː.nə, ˈsaʊ-, ⓊⓈ ˈsaʊ-, ˈsɔː-, ˈsɑː- **-s** -z
Saunders ˈsɔːn.dəz, ˈsɑːn-, ⓊⓈ ˈsɑːn.dɚz, ˈsɔːn-
Saunderson ˈsɔːn.də.sən, ˈsɑːn-, ⓊⓈ ˈsɑːn.dɚ-, ˈsɔːn-
saunt|er ˈsɔːn.t|əʳ, ⓊⓈ ˈsɑːn.ţ|ɚ, ˈsɔːn- **-ers** -əz, ⓊⓈ -ɚz **-ering** -ər.ɪŋ **-ered** -əd, ⓊⓈ -ɚd **-erer/s** -ə.rəʳ/z, ⓊⓈ -ɚ.ɚ/z
saurian ˈsɔː.ri.ən, ⓊⓈ ˈsɑːr.i-, ˈsɔːr- **-s** -z
sausag|e ˈsɒs.ɪdʒ, ⓊⓈ ˈsɑː.sɪdʒ, ˈsɔː- **-es** -ɪz **ˈsausage ˌdog; ˈsausage maˌchine; ˌsausage ˈroll** ⓊⓈ **ˈsausage ˌroll**
Saussure səʊˈsjʊəʳ, -ˈsʊəʳ, ⓊⓈ soʊˈsʊr
sauté ˈsəʊ.teɪ, ˈsɔː-, ⓊⓈ sɔːˈteɪ, soʊ-, sɑː- **-s** -z **-ing** -ɪŋ **-(e)d** -d
Sauternes, Sauterne səʊˈtɜːn, -ˈteən, ⓊⓈ soʊˈtɝːn, sɔː-, sɑː-
Sauvage ˈsæv.ɪdʒ; səʊˈvɑːʒ, ⓊⓈ ˈsæv.ɪdʒ; soʊˈvɑːʒ
Sauvignon ˈsəʊ.viː.njɔ̃ːŋ, -vɪ-, -njɒn, ˌ--ˈ-, ⓊⓈ ˌsoʊ.viːˈnjõʊn, ˈ--- **ˌSauvignon ˈBlanc**
savag|e, S~ ˈsæv.ɪdʒ **-es** -ɪz **-est** -ɪst, -əst **-ely** -li **-eness** -nəs, -nɪs **-ery** -ər.i, -ri **-ing** -ɪŋ **-ed** -d
savanna(h), S~ səˈvæn.ə **-s** -z
savant ˈsæv.ənt, ⓊⓈ sævˈɑːnt; ⓊⓈ səˈvænt; ⓊⓈ ˈsæv.ənt **-s** -s
sav|e seɪv **-es** -z **-ing/s** -ɪŋ/z **-ed** -d **-er/s** -əʳ/z, ⓊⓈ -ɚ/z **-(e)able** -ə.bəl
saveloy ˈsæv.ə.lɔɪ, ˈ-ɪ-, ˌ--ˈ-, ⓊⓈ ˈsæv.ə.lɔɪ **-s** -z
Savels ˈsæv.əlz
Savernake ˈsæv.ə.næk, ⓊⓈ ˈ-ɚ-
Savery ˈsæv.ər.i
Savile ˈsæv.ɪl, -əl **ˌSavile ˈRow**
Savill(e) ˈsæv.ɪl, -əl
saving ˈseɪ.vɪŋ **-s** -z **ˌsaving ˈgrace; ˈsavings acˌcount; ˈsavings ˌbank; ˈsavings ˌbond; ˈsavings cerˌtificate; ˈsavings ˌstamp**
savio(u)r, S~ ˈseɪ.vjəʳ, ⓊⓈ -vjɚ **-s** -z
Savlon® ˈsæv.lɒn, ⓊⓈ -lɑːn
savoir faire ˌsæv.wɑːˈfeəʳ, ⓊⓈ -wɑːrˈfer, -wɑːˈ-
savoir vivre ˌsæv.wɑːˈviː.vrə, ⓊⓈ -wɑːrˈ-, -wɑːˈ-
Savonarola ˌsæv.ən.əˈrəʊ.lə, ⓊⓈ -ˈroʊ-
sav|or ˈseɪ.v|əʳ, ⓊⓈ -v|ɚ **-ors** -əz, ⓊⓈ -ɚz **-oring** -ər.ɪŋ **-ored** -əd, ⓊⓈ -ɚd **-orless** -ə.ləs, -lɪs, ⓊⓈ -ɚ.ləs, -lɪs
savory, S~ ˈseɪ.vər.i **-ies** -iz **-iness** -ɪ.nəs, -ɪ.nɪs
sav|our ˈseɪ.v|əʳ, ⓊⓈ -v|ɚ **-ours** -əz, ⓊⓈ -ɚz **-ouring** -ər.ɪŋ **-oured** -əd, ⓊⓈ -ɚd **-ourless** -ə.ləs, -lɪs, ⓊⓈ -ɚ.ləs, -lɪs
savour|y ˈseɪ.vər|.i **-ies** -iz **-iness** -ɪ.nəs, -ɪ.nɪs
savoy, S~ səˈvɔɪ **-s** -z **saˌvoy ˈcabbage**
Savoyard səˈvɔɪ.ɑːd; ˌsæv.ɔɪˈɑːd, ⓊⓈ səˈvɔɪ.ɚd; ⓊⓈ ˌsæv.ɔɪˈɑːrd **-s** -z
savvy ˈsæv.i
saw sɔː, ⓊⓈ sɑː, sɔː **-s** -z **-ing** -ɪŋ **-ed** -d **-n** -n
saw (from **see**) sɔː, ⓊⓈ sɑː, sɔː
saw|bones *singular:* ˈsɔː|.bəʊnz, ⓊⓈ ˈsɑː|.boʊnz, ˈsɔː- *plural:* ˈsɔː|.bəʊnz, ⓊⓈ ˈsɑː|.boʊnz, ˈsɔː- **-boneses** -ˌbəʊn.zɪz, ⓊⓈ -ˌboʊn-
Sawbridgeworth ˈsɔː.brɪdʒ.wɜːθ; *old-fashioned:* ˈsæp.swəθ, ⓊⓈ ˈsɑː.brɪdʒ.wɝːθ, ˈsɔː-
sawbuck ˈsɔː.bʌk, ⓊⓈ ˈsɑː-, ˈsɔː- **-s** -s
sawd|er ˈsɔː.d|əʳ, ⓊⓈ ˈsɑː.d|ɚ, ˈsɔː- **-ers** -əz, ⓊⓈ -ɚz **-ering** -ər.ɪŋ **-ered** -əd, ⓊⓈ -ɚd
sawdust ˈsɔː.dʌst, ⓊⓈ ˈsɑː-, ˈsɔː-
sawfish ˈsɔː.fɪʃ, ⓊⓈ ˈsɑː-, ˈsɔː-
sawfl|y ˈsɔː.fl|aɪ, ⓊⓈ ˈsɑː-, ˈsɔː- **-ies** -aɪz
sawhors|e ˈsɔː.hɔːs, ⓊⓈ ˈsɑː.hɔːrs, ˈsɔː- **-es** -ɪz
sawmill ˈsɔː.mɪl, ⓊⓈ ˈsɑː-, ˈsɔː- **-s** -z
sawn (from **saw**) sɔːn, ⓊⓈ sɑːn, sɔːn
Sawney ˈsɔː.ni, ⓊⓈ ˈsɑː-, ˈsɔː- **-s** -z
sawn-off ˌsɔːnˈɒf, ⓊⓈ ˌsɑːnˈɑːf, ˌsɔːn- *stress shift, see compound:* **ˌsawn-off ˈshotgun**
Sawoniuk səˈvɒn.i.ʊk, ⓊⓈ -vɑːn-
Sawston ˈsɔːs.tən, ⓊⓈ ˈsɑːz-, ˈsɔːz-
sawtooth ˈsɔː.tuːθ, ⓊⓈ ˈsɑː-, ˈsɔː- **-ed** -t
Sawtry ˈsɔː.tri, ⓊⓈ ˈsɑː-, ˈsɔː-
sawyer, S~ ˈsɔː.jəʳ, ˈsɔɪ.əʳ, ⓊⓈ ˈsɑː.jɚ, ˈsɔː-, ˈsɔɪ.ɚ **-s** -z
sax sæks **-es** -ɪz
Saxe-Coburg-Gotha ˌsæksˌkəʊ.bɜːgˈgəʊ.θə, -tə, ⓊⓈ -ˌkoʊ.bɝːgˈgoʊ-
saxhorn ˈsæks.hɔːn, ⓊⓈ -hɔːrn **-s** -z
saxifrag|e ˈsæk.sɪ.frɪdʒ, -sə-, -freɪdʒ, ⓊⓈ -sə.frɪdʒ **-es** -ɪz
Saxmundham sæksˈmʌn.dəm
Saxon ˈsæk.sən **-s** -z
Saxone® ˈsæk.səʊn, -ˈ-, ⓊⓈ -soʊn
saxony, S~ ˈsæk.sən.i
saxophone ˈsæk.sə.fəʊn, ⓊⓈ -foʊn **-s** -z
saxophonist sækˈsɒf.ən.ɪst, ⓊⓈ ˈsæk.sə.foʊ.nɪst **-s** -s
say seɪ **says** sez **saying** ˈseɪ.ɪŋ **said** sed
Sayce seɪs
SAYE ˌes.eɪ.waɪˈiː
sayer, S~ ˈseɪ.əʳ, ⓊⓈ ˈseɪ.ɚ **-s** -z
saying ˈseɪ.ɪŋ **-s** -z
Sayle seɪl
say-so ˈseɪ.səʊ, ⓊⓈ -soʊ
SC (abbrev. for **South Carolina**) ˌsaʊθ.kær.əlˈaɪ.nə, ⓊⓈ -ker.əˈlaɪ-, -kær-
scab skæb **-s** -z **-by** -i **-biness** -ɪ.nəs, -ɪ.nɪs **-bing** -ɪŋ **-bed** -d
scabbard ˈskæb.əd, ⓊⓈ -ɚd **-s** -z
scabies ˈskeɪ.biːz, -biz
scabious ˈskeɪ.bi.əs **-es** -ɪz
scabrous ˈskeɪ.brəs, ⓊⓈ ˈskæb.rəs, ˈskeɪ.brəs **-ly** -li **-ness** -nəs, -nɪs
Scacchi ˈskæk.i

S

scad skæd **-s** -z
Scafell ˌskɔːˈfel *stress shift, see compound:* ˌ**Scafell** ˈ**Pike**
scaffold ˈskæf.əʊld, -ᵊld, (US) -ᵊld, -oʊld **-s** -z
scaffolding ˈskæf.ᵊl.dɪŋ **-s** -z
scag skæg
Scala ˈskɑː.lə
scalable ˈskeɪ.lə.bᵊl
scalar ˈskeɪ.ləʳ, -lɑːʳ, (US) -lɚ, -lɑːr
scalawag ˈskæl.ə.wæg, ˈ-ɪ-, (US) ˈ-ə- **-s** -z
Scalby ˈskæl.bi
scald skɔːld, (US) skɑːld, skɔːld **-s** -z **-ing** -ɪŋ **-ed** -ɪd
scal|e skeɪl **-es** -z **-ing** -ɪŋ **-ed** -d **-less** -ləs, -lɪs **-er/s** -əʳ/z, (US) -ɚ/z
scalene ˈskeɪ.liːn; -ˈ-, skælˈiːn, (US) ˈskeɪ.liːn, -ˈ-
scales, S~ skeɪlz ˌ**tip the** ˈ**scales**
Scaliger ˈskæl.ɪ.dʒəʳ, (US) -dʒɚ
scallion ˈskæl.i.ən, ˈ-jən, (US) ˈ-jən **-s** -z
scallop ˈskæl.əp, ˈskɒl-, (US) ˈskɑː.ləp, ˈskæl.əp **-s** -s **-ing** -ɪŋ **-ed** -t
scallywag ˈskæl.i.wæg **-s** -z
scalp skælp **-s** -s **-ing** -ɪŋ **-ed** -t **-er/s** -əʳ/z, (US) -ɚ/z
scalpel ˈskæl.pᵊl **-s** -z
scal|y ˈskeɪ.l|i **-ier** -i.əʳ, (US) -i.ɚ **-iest** -i.ɪst, -i.əst **-iness** -ɪ.nəs, -ɪ.nɪs
scam skæm **-s** -z
Scammell ˈskæm.ᵊl
scamp skæmp **-s** -s **-ing** -ɪŋ **-ed** -t **-ish** -ɪʃ
scamp|er ˈskæm.p|əʳ, (US) -p|ɚ **-ers** -əz, (US) -ɚz **-ering** -ᵊr.ɪŋ **-ered** -əd, (US) -ɚd
scampi ˈskæm.pi
scan skæn **-s** -z **-ning** -ɪŋ **-ned** -d
scandal ˈskæn.dᵊl **-s** -z
scandalization, -isa- ˌskæn.dᵊl.aɪˈzeɪ.ʃᵊn, -ɪˈ-, (US) -əˈ-
scandaliz|e, -is|e ˈskæn.dᵊl.aɪz, (US) -də.laɪz **-es** -ɪz **-ing** -ɪŋ **-ed** -d
scandalmong|er ˈskæn.dᵊlˌmʌŋ.g|əʳ, (US) -ˌmɑːŋ.g|ɚ, -ˌmʌŋ- **-ers** -əz, (US) -ɚz **-ering** -ᵊr.ɪŋ
scandalous ˈskæn.dᵊl.əs **-ly** -li **-ness** -nəs, -nɪs
scandent ˈskæn.dənt
Scandian ˈskæn.di.ən
Scandinavi|a ˌskæn.dɪˈneɪ.vi|.ə, -dəˈ-, (US) -vi|.ə, ˈ-vj|ə **-an/s** -ən/z
scandium ˈskæn.di.əm
Scania® ˈskæn.i.ə, ˈ-jə
Scanlan, Scanlon ˈskæn.lən
Scannell ˈskæn.ᵊl; skəˈnel
scanner ˈskæn.əʳ, (US) -ɚ **-s** -z
scansion ˈskæn.ʃᵊn **-s** -z
scant skænt **-ly** -li **-ness** -nəs, -nɪs
scant|y ˈskæn.t|i, (US) -t̬|i **-ier** -i.əʳ, (US) -i.ɚ **-iest** -i.ɪst, -i.əst **-ily** -ᵊl.i, -ɪ.li **-iness** -ɪ.nəs, -ɪ.nɪs
Scapa Flow ˌskɑː.pəˈfləʊ, ˌskæp.əˈ-, (US) -ˈfloʊ
scape skeɪp **-s** -s
-scape skeɪp
Note: Suffix. Normally unstressed, e.g. **landscape** /ˈlænd.skeɪp/.
scapegoat ˈskeɪp.gəʊt, (US) -goʊt **-s** -s **-ing** -ɪŋ **-ed** -ɪd
scapegrac|e ˈskeɪp.greɪs **-es** -ɪz
scapul|a ˈskæp.jə.l|ə, -jʊ- **-as** -əz **-ae** -iː **-ar/s** -əʳ/z
scar, S~ skɑːʳ, (US) skɑːr **-s** -z **-ring** -ɪŋ **-red** -d ˈ**scar** ˌ**tissue**
scarab ˈskær.əb, (US) ˈsker-, ˈskær- **-s** -z
scarabae|us ˌskær.əˈbiː|.əs, (US) ˌsker-, ˌskær- **-uses** -ə.sɪz **-i** -aɪ
scaramouch(e), S~ ˌskær.əˈmuːʃ, -muːtʃ, ˈ---, (US) ˌsker.əˈmuːʃ, ˌskær-, -muːtʃ **-(e)s** -ɪz
Scarborough, Scarboro' ˈskɑː.bᵊr.ə, (US) ˈskɑːr.bɚ.oʊ, -ə
Scarbrough ˈskɑː.brə, (US) ˈskɑːr-, -broʊ
scarc|e skeəs, (US) skers **-er** -əʳ, (US) -ɚ **-est** -ɪst, -əst **-ely** -li **-eness** -nəs, -nɪs
scarcity ˈskeə.sə.ti, -sɪ-, (US) ˈsker.sə.t̬i
Scardino skɑːˈdiː.nəʊ, (US) skɑːrˈdiː.noʊ
scar|e skeəʳ, (US) sker **-es** -z **-ing** -ɪŋ **-ed** -d **-er/s** -əʳ/z, (US) -ɚ/z ˈ**scare** ˌ**story**
scarecrow ˈskeə.krəʊ, (US) ˈsker.kroʊ **-s** -z
scaredy-cat ˈskeə.di.kæt, (US) ˈsker- **-s** -s
scaremong|er ˈskeəˌmʌŋ.g|əʳ, (US) ˈskerˌmɑːŋ.g|ɚ, -ˌmʌŋ- **-ers** -əz, (US) -ɚz **-ering** -ᵊr.ɪŋ
scar|ey ˈskeə.r|i, (US) ˈsker|.i **-ier** -i.əʳ, (US) -iɚ **-iest** -i.ɪst, -i.əst **-ily** -ᵊl.i, -ɪ.li **-iness** -ɪ.nəs, -ɪ.nɪs
scarf v skɑːf, (US) skɑːrf **-s** -s **-ing** -ɪŋ **-ed** -t
scar|f n skɑː|f, (US) skɑːr|f **-ves** -vz **-fs** -fs
Scarfe skɑːf, (US) skɑːrf
Scargill ˈskɑː.gɪl, (US) ˈskɑːr-
scarification ˌskær.ɪ.fɪˈkeɪ.ʃᵊn, ˌskeə.rɪ-, -rə-, -fəˈ-, (US) ˌsker.ə.fɪˈ-, ˌskær-
scari|fy ˈskær.ɪ|.faɪ, ˈskeə.rɪ-, -rə-, (US) ˈsker.ɪ-, ˈ-ə-, ˈskær- **-fies** -faɪz **-fying** -faɪ.ɪŋ **-fied** -faɪd
scarlatina ˌskɑː.ləˈtiː.nə, -lɪˈ-, (US) ˌskɑːr.ləˈ-
Scarlatti skɑːˈlæt.i, (US) skɑːrˈlɑː.t̬i
scarlet, S~ ˈskɑː.lət, -lɪt, (US) ˈskɑːr- ˌ**scarlet** ˈ**fever**; ˌ**scarlet** ˈ**pimpernel**; ˌ**scarlet** ˈ**woman**
Scarlett ˈskɑː.lət, -lɪt, (US) ˈskɑːr-
Scarman ˈskɑː.mən, (US) ˈskɑːr-
scarp skɑːp, (US) skɑːrp **-s** -s **-ing** -ɪŋ **-ed** -t
scarper ˈskɑː.pəʳ, (US) ˈskɑːr.pɚ **-s** -z **-ing** -ɪŋ **-ed** -d
scarves (plural of **scarf**) skɑːvz, (US) skɑːrvs
scar|y ˈskeə.r|i, (US) ˈsker|.i **-ier** -i.əʳ, (US) -i.ɚ **-iest** -i.ɪst, -i.əst **-ily** -ᵊl.i, -ɪ.li **-iness** -ɪ.nəs, -ɪ.nɪs
Scase skeɪs
scat skæt **-s** -s **-ting** -ɪŋ, (US) ˈskæt̬.ɪŋ **-ted** -ɪd, (US) ˈskæt̬.ɪd
scath|e skeɪð **-es** -z **-ing/ly** -ɪŋ/li **-ed** -d **-eless** -ləs, -lɪs
scathing ˈskeɪ.ðɪŋ **-ly** -li
scatological ˌskæt.əˈlɒdʒ.ɪ.kᵊl, (US) ˌskæt̬.əˈlɑː.dʒɪ-
scatolog|y skætˈɒl.ə.dʒ|i, (US) -ˈɑː.lə-, skəˈtɑː- **-ist/s** -ɪst/s
scatt|er ˈskæt|.əʳ, (US) ˈskæt̬|.ɚ **-ers** -əz, (US) -ɚz **-ering** -ᵊr.ɪŋ **-ered** -əd, (US) -ɚd
scatterbrain ˈskæt.ə.breɪn, (US) ˈskæt̬.ɚ- **-s** -z **-ed** -d
scatt|y ˈskæt|.i, (US) ˈskæt̬|.i **-ier** -i.əʳ, (US) -i.ɚ **-iest** -i.ɪst, -i.əst **-iness** -ɪ.nəs, -ɪ.nɪs
scaup skɔːp, (US) skɑːp, skɔːp **-s** -s
scaveng|e ˈskæv.ɪndʒ, -ᵊndʒ **-es** -ɪz **-ing** -ɪŋ **-ed** -d **-er/s** -əʳ/z, (US) -ɚ/z
Scawfell ˌskɔːˈfel, (US) ˌskɑː-, ˌskɔː- *stress shift, see compound:* ˌ**Scawfell** ˈ**Pike**
scena ˈʃeɪ.nə **-s** -z
scenario sɪˈnɑː.ri.əʊ, sə-, senˈɑː-, (US) səˈner.i.oʊ, -ˈnær-, -ˈnɑːr- **-s** -z
scenarist ˈsiː.nᵊr.ɪst, (US) səˈner-, -ˈnær-, -ˈnɑːr- **-s** -s
scene siːn **-s** -z
scenery ˈsiː.nᵊr.i
sceneshifter ˈsiːnˌʃɪf.təʳ, (US) -tɚ **-s** -z
scenic ˈsiː.nɪk, ˈsen.ɪk, (US) ˈsiː- **-ally** -ᵊl.i, -li ˌ**scenic** ˈ**railway**
scent sent **-s** -s **-ing** -ɪŋ, (US) ˈsen.t̬ɪŋ **-ed** -ɪd, (US) ˈsen.t̬ɪd
scepter ˈsep.təʳ, (US) -tɚ **-s** -z **-ed** -əd ˌ**scepter'd** ˈ**isle**
sceptic ˈskep.tɪk **-s** -s **-al** -ᵊl **-ally** -ᵊl.i, -li
scepticism ˈskep.tɪ.sɪ.zᵊm, -tə-
sceptre ˈsep.təʳ, (US) -tɚ **-s** -z **-d** -d
schadenfreude ˈʃɑː.dᵊnˌfrɔɪ.də
Schaefer ˈʃeɪ.fəʳ, (US) -fɚ
Schaffer ˈʃeɪ.fəʳ, ˈʃæf.əʳ, (US) ʃeɪ.fɚ, ˈʃæf.ɚ
Schama ˈʃɑː.mə
schedul|e ˈʃedʒ.uːl, ˈʃed.juːl, -ᵊl; ˈskedʒ.uːl, ˈsked.juːl, -ᵊl, (US) ˈskedʒ.uːl, -u.əl, -ᵊl **-es** -z **-ing** -ɪŋ **-ed** -d

> Note: The pronunciation with /ske-/ in British English has long been discussed, and until recently treated as less acceptable than /ʃe-/, but it is now clearly well established among younger speakers.

Scheherazade ʃɪˌher.əˈzɑː.də, ʃə-, -ˌhɪə.rəˈ-, -ˈzɑːd, (US) ʃəˌher.əˈzɑːd, -ˈzɑː.də
Scheldt skelt, ʃelt, (US) skelt
schema ˈskiː.mə **-s** -z **schemata** ˈskiː.mə.tə; skɪˈmɑː.tə, (US) skiːˈmɑː.t̬ə; (US) ˈskiː.mə.t̬ə
schematic skiːˈmæt.ɪk, skɪ-, (US) skiːˈmæt̬-, skə- **-ally** -ᵊl.i, -li
schematiz|e, -is|e ˈskiː.mə.taɪz **-es** -ɪz **-ing** -ɪŋ **-ed** -d

Pronouncing the letters SCH

The consonant letter combination **sch** has several possible pronunciations, the most common being /sk/, e.g.:

school sku:l

scheme ski:m

Other possible realizations are /ʃ/ and /s/.

schedule ˈʃed.ju:l (US) ˈsked-

schism ˈskɪz.ᵊm, ˈsɪz-

For words of German origin, the pronunciation is /ʃ/, e.g.:

schmalz ʃmɔ:lts

In addition

When the three letters come together due to the addition of a prefix, the pronunciation is /s.tʃ/, e.g.:

mischance ˈmɪs.tʃɑ:nts (US) -tʃænts

schem|e ski:m **-es** -z **-ing/ly** -ɪŋ/li **-ed** -d **-er/s** -əʳ/z, (US) -ɚ/z
Schenectady skɪˈnek.tə.di, skə-, (US) skə-
scherzand|o skeətˈsæn.d|əʊ, skɜ:t-, (US) skertˈsɑ:n.d|oʊ, -ˈsæn- **-os** -əʊz, (US) -oʊz **-i** -i
scherz|o ˈskeət.s|əʊ, ˈskɜ:t-, (US) ˈskert.s|oʊ **-os** -əʊz, (US) -oʊz **-i** -i
Schiaparelli ˌskjæp.əˈrel.i, ˌskæp-, ˌʃæp-, (US) ˌskjæp-, ˌʃæp-, ˌskjɑ:.pɑ:ˈ-
Schiedam skɪˈdæm, ˈskɪd.æm, (US) skɪˈdɑ:m
Schiffer ˈʃɪf.əʳ, (US) -ɚ
Schiller ˈʃɪl.əʳ, (US) -ɚ
schilling, S~ ˈʃɪl.ɪŋ **-s** -z
Schindler ˈʃɪnd.ləʳ, (US) -lɚ
schipperke, S~ ˈʃɪp.ə.ki, ˈskɪ-; ˈʃɪp.ək, (US) ˈskɪp.ɚ.ki **schipperkes** ˈʃɪp.ə.kiz, ˈskɪ-; ˈʃɪp.əks, (US) ˈskɪp.ɚ.kiz
schism ˈskɪz.əm, ˈsɪz-, (US) ˈskɪz-, ˈsɪz- **-s** -z
schismatic skɪzˈmæt.ɪk, sɪz-, (US) skɪzˈmæţ-, sɪz- **-al** -ᵊl **-ally** -ᵊl.i, -li
schist ʃɪst **-s** -s **-ose** -əʊs, (US) -oʊs
schizo ˈskɪt.səʊ, (US) -soʊ **-s** -z
schizoid ˈskɪt.sɔɪd
schizophrenia ˌskɪt.səʊˈfri:.ni.ə, ˌskɪd.zəʊˈ-, (US) ˌskɪt.səˈ-, -soʊˈ-, -ˈfren.i-
schizophrenic ˌskɪt.səʊˈfren.ɪk, ˌskɪd.zəʊˈ-, -ˈfri:.nɪk, (US) ˌskɪt.səˈ-, -soʊˈ- **-ally** -ᵊl.i, -li **-s** -s
Schlegel ˈʃleɪ.gᵊl
schlemiel ʃləˈmi:l **-s** -z
schlep(p) ʃlep **-s** -s **-ping** -ɪŋ **-ped** -t
Schlesinger ˈʃlez.ɪn.dʒəʳ, ˈʃles-, (US) ˈʃles.ɪŋ.ɚ; (US) ˈʃlez.ɪn.dʒɚ, ˈʃleɪ.zɪŋ-
Schleswig-Holstein ˌʃlez.vɪgˈhəʊl.staɪn, ˌʃles-, -wɪgˈ-, (US) -wɪgˈhoʊl-, ˌʃles.vɪgˈ-, -ˈhɔ:l.ʃtaɪn
schlock ʃlɒk, (US) ʃlɑ:k **-s** -s
schlockmeister ˈʃlɒkˌmaɪ.stəʳ, (US) ˈʃlɑ:kˌmaɪ.stɚ **-s** -z
schmal(t)z ʃmɔ:lts, ʃmɒlts, ʃmælts, (US) ʃmɑ:lts, ʃmɔ:lts **-y** -i **-ier** -i.əʳ, (US) -i.ɚ **-iest** -i.ɪst, -i.əst
Schmidt ʃmɪt
schmo ʃməʊ, (US) ʃmoʊ **-es** -z
schmooz|e ʃmu:z **-es** -ɪz **-ing** -ɪŋ **-ed** -d
schmuck ʃmʌk **-s** -s
Schnabel ʃnɑ:.bᵊl
schnap(p)s ʃnæps, (US) ʃnɑ:ps, ʃnæps
schnauzer ˈʃnaʊt.səʳ, (US) ˈʃnaʊ.zɚ **-s** -z
Schneider ˈʃnaɪ.dəʳ, (US) -dɚ
schnitzel ˈʃnɪt.sᵊl **-s** -z
Schnitzler ˈʃnɪt.sləʳ, (US) -slɚ
schnorkel ˈʃnɔ:.kᵊl, (US) ˈʃnɔ:r- **-s** -z
schnozzle ˈʃnɒz.ᵊl, (US) ˈʃnɑ:.zᵊl **-s** -z
Schoen ʃəʊn, ʃɜ:n, (US) ʃoʊn, ʃɜ:rn
Schoenberg ˈʃɜ:n.bɜ:g, -beəg, (US) ˈʃɜ:rn.bɚg, ˈʃoʊn-
Schofield ˈskəʊ.fi:ld, (US) ˈskoʊ-
scholar ˈskɒl.əʳ, (US) ˈskɑ:.lɚ **-s** -z **-ly** -li
scholarship ˈskɒl.ə.ʃɪp, (US) ˈskɑ:.lɚ- **-s** -s
scholastic skəˈlæs.tɪk, skɒlˈæs-, (US) skəˈlæs- **-ally** -ᵊl.i, -li
scholasticism skəˈlæs.tɪ.sɪ.zᵊm, skɒlˈæs-, (US) skəˈlæs.tə-
Scholes skəʊlz, (US) skoʊlz
scholiast ˈskəʊ.li.æst, (US) ˈskoʊ-, -əst **-s** -s
scholi|um ˈskəʊ.li|.əm, (US) ˈskoʊ- **-a** -ə
Scholl ʃɒl, ʃəʊl, skɒl, (US) ʃoʊl
Schönberg ˈʃɜ:n.bɜ:g, -beəg, (US) ˈʃɜ:rn.bɚg, ˈʃoʊn-
school sku:l **-s** -z **-ing** -ɪŋ **-ed** -d ˌ**school** ˈ**leaver**; ˌ**school** ˈ**tie**
schoolbag ˈsku:l.bæg **-s** -z
schoolbook ˈsku:l.bʊk **-s** -s
schoolboy ˈsku:l.bɔɪ **-s** -z **-ish** -ɪʃ
school|child ˈsku:l|.tʃaɪld **-children** -ˌtʃɪl.drᵊn
schooldays ˈsku:l.deɪz
schoolgirl ˈsku:l.gɜ:l, (US) -gɜ:l **-s** -z **-ish** -ɪʃ
schoolhou|se ˈsku:l.haʊ|s **-ses** -zɪz
schoolkid ˈsku:l.kɪd **-s** -z
schoolmarm ˈsku:l.mɑ:m, (US) -mɑ:rm **-s** -z **-ish** -ɪʃ
schoolmaster ˈsku:lˌmɑ:.stəʳ, (US) -ˌmæs.tɚ **-s** -z
schoolmate ˈsku:l.meɪt **-s** -s
schoolmistress ˈsku:lˌmɪs.trɪs, -trəs **-es** -ɪz
schoolroom ˈsku:l.rʊm, -ru:m, (US) -ru:m, -rʊm **-s** -z
schoolteacher ˈsku:lˌti:.tʃəʳ, (US) -tʃɚ **-s** -z
schooltime ˈsku:l.taɪm
schoolwork ˈsku:l.wɜ:k, (US) -wɜ:k
schoolyard ˈsku:l.jɑ:d, (US) -jɑ:rd
schooner ˈsku:.nəʳ, (US) -nɚ **-s** -z
Schopenhauer ˈʃəʊ.pᵊn.haʊ.əʳ, ˈʃɒp.ᵊn-, (US) ˈʃoʊ.pᵊn.haʊ.ɚ
schottisch|e ʃɒtˈi:ʃ, ʃəˈti:ʃ, (US) ˈʃɑ:.ţɪʃ **-es** -ɪz
Schreiner ˈʃraɪ.nəʳ, (US) -nɚ
Schrödinger ˈʃrɜ:.dɪŋ.əʳ, (US) ˈʃroʊ.dɪŋ.ɚ, ˈʃrɜ:r-
Schroeder ˈʃrɜ:.dəʳ, (US) ˈʃroʊ.dɚ, ˈʃreɪ-
schtuck ʃtʊk
Schubert ˈʃu:.bət, -bɜ:t, (US) -bɚt
Schultz ʃʊlts
Schumacher ˈʃu:ˌmæk.əʳ, (US) -mɑ:k.ɚ, -mæk-
Schuman ˈʃu:.mən
Schumann ˈʃu:.mən, -mæn, -mɑ:n, (US) -mɑ:n, -mən
schuss ʃʊs, ʃu:s **-es** -ɪz **-ing** -ɪŋ **-ed** -t
Schuster ˈʃʊs.tə, ˈʃu:.stəʳ, (US) -tɚ
schwa ʃwɑ: **-s** -z
Schwabe ʃwɑ:b, ˈʃwɑ:.bə
Schwann ʃwɒn; *as if German:* ʃvæn; (US) ʃvɑ:n, ʃwɑ:n
Schwartz ʃwɔ:ts; *as if German:* ʃvɑ:ts; (US) ʃwɔ:rts
Schwarzenegger ˈʃwɔ:ts.ᵊn.eg.əʳ, (US) ˈʃwɔ:rts.ᵊn.eg.ɚ
Schwarzkopf ˈʃvɑ:ts.kɒpf, ˈʃwɑ:ts-, ˈʃwɔ:ts-, (US) ˈʃwɔ:rts.kɑ:pf
Schwarzwald ˈʃvɑ:ts.væld, ˈʃwɑ:ts-, -wæld, (US) ˈʃvɑ:rts.vɑ:lt
Schweitzer ˈʃwaɪt.səʳ; *as if German:* ˈʃvaɪt-; (US) ˈʃwaɪt.sɚ; *as if German:* (US) ˈʃvaɪt-
Schweizer ˈʃwaɪt.səʳ; *as if German:* ˈʃvaɪt-; (US) ˈʃwaɪt.sɚ; *as if German:* (US) ˈʃvaɪt-
Schweppes® ʃweps
Schwerin ʃveəˈri:n, ʃweə-, (US) ʃverˈi:n, ʃveɪˈri:n
sciatic saɪˈæt.ɪk, (US) -ˈæţ-
sciatica saɪˈæt.ɪ.kə, (US) -ˈæţ-
scienc|e ˈsaɪ.ənts, saɪənᵗs, (US) ˈsaɪ.ənts **-es** -ɪz ˌ**science** ˈ**fiction**; ˈ**science** ˌ**park**
scientific ˌsaɪ.ənˈtɪf.ɪk **-ally** -ᵊl.i, -li
scientist ˈsaɪ.ən.tɪst, (US) -ţɪst **-s** -s
scientologist, S~ ˌsaɪ.ənˈtɒl.ə.dʒɪst, (US) -ˈtɑ:.lə- **-s** -s
Scientology® ˌsaɪ.ənˈtɒl.ə.dʒi, (US) -ˈtɑ:.lə-
sci-fi ˈsaɪˌfaɪ
scilicet ˈsaɪ.lɪ.set, ˈsɪl.ɪ-, (US) ˈsɪl.ɪ-
Scillonian sɪˈləʊ.ni.ən, (US) -ˈloʊ- **-s** -z
Scill|y ˈsɪl|.i **-ies** -ɪz ˈ**Scilly** ˌ**Isles**
scimitar ˈsɪm.ɪ.təʳ, ˈ-ə-, -tɑ:ʳ, (US) -ə.ţɚ, -tɑ:r **-s** -z
scintilla sɪnˈtɪl.ə
scintill|ate ˈsɪn.tɪ.l|eɪt, -tᵊl|.eɪt, (US)

S

-ţəl|.eɪt -ates -eɪts -ating -eɪ.tɪŋ, ⓤⓢ -eɪ.ţɪŋ -ated -eɪ.tɪd, ⓤⓢ -eɪ.ţɪd
scintillation ˌsɪn.tɪˈleɪ.ʃən, -təlˈeɪ-, ⓤⓢ -ţəlˈeɪ- -s -z
sciol|ism ˈsaɪ.əʊ.l|ɪ.zəm, ⓤⓢ ˈ-ə- -ist/s -ɪst/s
scion ˈsaɪ.ən -s -z
Scipio ˈskɪp.i.əʊ, ˈsɪp-, ⓤⓢ ˈsɪp.i.oʊ
scire facias ˌsaɪə.riˈfeɪ.ʃi.æs, -əs, ⓤⓢ ˌsaɪ.riːˈfeɪ.ʃi.æs
scirocco ʃɪˈrɒk.əʊ, sɪ-, sə-, ⓤⓢ ʃɪˈrɑː.koʊ, sə- -s -z
scission ˈsɪʒ.ən, ˈsɪʃ- -s -z
sciss|or ˈsɪz|.əʳ, ⓤⓢ -ɚ -ors -əz, ⓤⓢ -ɚz -oring -ər.ɪŋ -ored -əd, ⓤⓢ -ɚd
scissors ˈsɪz.əz, ⓤⓢ -ɚz
scissors-and-paste ˌsɪz.əz.əndˈpeɪst, ⓤⓢ -ɚz-
scler|a ˈsklɪə.r|ə, ⓤⓢ ˈsklɪr|.ə -as -əz -ae -iː
scleros|is skləˈrəʊ.s|ɪs, sklɪ-, sklerˈəʊ-, sklɪəˈrəʊ-, ⓤⓢ sklɪˈroʊ- -es -iːz
sclerotic skləˈrɒt.ɪk, sklɪ-, sklerˈɒt-, sklɪəˈrɒt-, ⓤⓢ sklɪˈrɑː.ţɪk
scoff skɒf, ⓤⓢ skɑːf -s -s -ing/ly -ɪŋ/li -ed -t -er/s -əʳ/z, ⓤⓢ -ɚ/z
scofflaw ˈskɒf.lɔː, ⓤⓢ ˈskɑːf.lɑː, -lɔː -s -z
Scofield ˈskəʊ.fiːld, ⓤⓢ ˈskoʊ-
Scoggin ˈskɒg.ɪn, ⓤⓢ ˈskɑː.gɪn -s -z
scold skəʊld, ⓤⓢ skoʊld -s -z -ing/s -ɪŋ/z -ed -ɪd
scoliosis ˌskɒl.iˈəʊ.sɪs, ⓤⓢ ˌskoʊ.liˈoʊ-, ˌskɑː-
scollop ˈskɒl.əp, ⓤⓢ ˈskɑː.ləp -s -s -ing -ɪŋ -ed -t
sconc|e skɒnts, ⓤⓢ skɑːnts -es -ɪz -ing -ɪŋ -ed -t
scone skɒn, skəʊn, ⓤⓢ skoʊn, skɑːn -s -z
Scone skuːn ˌStone of ˈScone
scoop skuːp -s -s -ing -ɪŋ -ed -t
scoot skuːt -s -s -ing -ɪŋ, ⓤⓢ ˈskuː.ţɪŋ -ed -ɪd, ⓤⓢ ˈskuː.ţɪd
scooter ˈskuː.təʳ, ⓤⓢ -ţɚ -s -z
scope skəʊp, ⓤⓢ skoʊp -s -s
-scope skəʊp, ⓤⓢ skoʊp
Note: Suffix. Normally unstressed, e.g. **microscope** /ˈmaɪ.krə.skəʊp/ ⓤⓢ /-skoʊp/.
-scopic ˈskɒp.ɪk, ⓤⓢ ˈskɑː.pɪk
Note: Suffix. Words containing **-scopic** normally carry primary stress on the penultimate syllable, e.g. **microscopic** /ˌmaɪ.krəˈskɒp.ɪk/ ⓤⓢ /-ˈskɑː.pɪk/.
scopolamine skəˈpɒl.ə.miːn, -mɪn; ˌskəʊ.pəˈlæm.ɪn, ⓤⓢ skəˈpɑː.lə.miːn, skoʊ-, -mɪn
-scopy skə.pi
Note: Suffix. Words containing **-scopy** normally carry primary stress on the antepenultimate syllable, e.g. **microscopy** /maɪˈkrɒs.kə.pi/ ⓤⓢ /-ˈkrɑː.skə-/.
scorbutic skɔːˈbjuː.tɪk, ⓤⓢ skɔːrˈbjuː.ţɪk
scorch skɔːtʃ, ⓤⓢ skɔːrtʃ -es -ɪz -ing/ly -ɪŋ/li -ed -t -er/s -əʳ/z, ⓤⓢ -ɚ/z ˌ**scorched** ˈ**earth**
scor|e skɔːʳ, ⓤⓢ skɔːr -es -z -ing -ɪŋ -ed -d -er/s -əʳ/z, ⓤⓢ -ɚ/z -less -ləs, -lɪs
scoreboard ˈskɔː.bɔːd, ⓤⓢ ˈskɔːr.bɔːrd -s -z
scorecard ˈskɔː.kɑːd, ⓤⓢ ˈskɔːr.kɑːrd -s -z
scorekeeper ˈskɔːˌkiː.pəʳ, ⓤⓢ ˈskɔːrˌkiː.pɚ -s -z
score-line ˈskɔː.laɪn, ⓤⓢ ˈskɔːr- -s -z
scoresheet ˈskɔː.ʃiːt, ⓤⓢ ˈskɔːr- -s -s
scoria ˈskɔː.ri.ə, ˈskɒr.i-, ⓤⓢ ˈskɔːr.i-
scoriaceous ˌskɔː.riˈeɪ.ʃəs, ˌskɒr.iˈ-, ⓤⓢ ˌskɔːr.iˈ-
scorn skɔːn, ⓤⓢ skɔːrn -s -z -ing -ɪŋ -ed -d
scornful ˈskɔːn.fəl, -fʊl, ⓤⓢ ˈskɔːrn- -ly -i -ness -nəs, -nɪs
Scorpi|o ˈskɔː.pi|.əʊ, ⓤⓢ ˈskɔːr.pi|.oʊ -os -əʊz, ⓤⓢ -oʊz -an/s -ən/z
scorpion ˈskɔː.pi.ən, ⓤⓢ ˈskɔːr- -s -z
Scorsese skɔːˈseɪ.zi, -zeɪ, ⓤⓢ skɔːrˈseɪ.zi
scot, S~ skɒt, ⓤⓢ skɑːt -s -s
scotch, S~ skɒtʃ, ⓤⓢ skɑːtʃ -es -ɪz -ing -ɪŋ -ed -t ˌ**Scotch** ˈ**broth**; ˌ**Scotch** ˈ**egg**; ˌ**Scotch** ˈ**mist**; ˌ**Scotch** ˈ**pine**; ˌ**Scotch** ˈ**tape**®
Scotch|man ˈskɒtʃ|.mən, ⓤⓢ ˈskɑːtʃ- -men -mən
Scotch|woman ˈskɒtʃ|ˌwʊm.ən, ⓤⓢ ˈskɑːtʃ- -women -ˌwɪm.ɪn
scoter ˈskəʊ.təʳ, ⓤⓢ ˈskoʊ.ţɚ -s -z
scot-free ˌskɒtˈfriː, ⓤⓢ ˌskɑːt-
scotia, S~ ˈskəʊ.ʃə, ⓤⓢ ˈskoʊ-
Scotland ˈskɒt.lənd, ⓤⓢ ˈskɑːt- ˌ**Scotland** ˈ**Yard**
Scots skɒts, ⓤⓢ skɑːts ˌ**Scots** ˈ**pine**
Scots|man ˈskɒts|.mən, ⓤⓢ ˈskɑːts- -men -mən
Scots|woman ˈskɒts|ˌwʊm.ən, ⓤⓢ ˈskɑːts- -women -ˌwɪm.ɪn
Scott skɒt, ⓤⓢ skɑːt
Scotticism ˈskɒt.ɪ.sɪ.zəm, ⓤⓢ ˈskɑː.ţɪ- -s -z
Scotticiz|e, -is|e ˈskɒt.ɪ.saɪz, ⓤⓢ ˈskɑː.ţɪ- -es -ɪz -ing -ɪŋ -ed -d
scottie, S~ ˈskɒt.i, ⓤⓢ ˈskɑː.ţi
Scottish ˈskɒt.ɪʃ, ⓤⓢ ˈskɑː.ţɪʃ -ness -nəs, -nɪs ˌ**Scottish** ˈ**terrier**
Scottsdale ˈskɒts.deɪl, ⓤⓢ ˈskɑːts-
scoundrel ˈskaʊn.drəl -s -z -ly -i
scour ˈskaʊ.əʳ, skaʊəʳ, ⓤⓢ ˈskaʊ.ɚ -s -z -ing -ɪŋ -ed -d -er/s -əʳ/z, ⓤⓢ -ɚ/z ˈ**scouring** ˌ**pad**
scourg|e skɜːdʒ, ⓤⓢ skɝːdʒ -es -ɪz -ing -ɪŋ -ed -d
Scous|e skaʊs -er/s -əʳ/z, ⓤⓢ -ɚ/z
scout skaʊt -s -s -ing -ɪŋ, ⓤⓢ ˈskaʊ.ţɪŋ -ed -ɪd, ⓤⓢ ˈskaʊ.ţɪd -er/s -əʳ/z, ⓤⓢ ˈskaʊ.ţɚ/z ˌ**scout's** ˈ**hono(u)r**
scoutmaster ˈskaʊtˌmɑː.stəʳ, ⓤⓢ -ˌmæs.tɚ -s -z
scow skaʊ -s -z
scowl skaʊl -s -z -ing/ly -ɪŋ/li -ed -d
scrabbl|e, S~® ˈskræb.əl -es -z -ing -ɪŋ, ˈskræb.lɪŋ -ed -d
scrag skræg -s -z -ging -ɪŋ -ged -d
scrag-end ˌskrægˈend -s -z
scraggly ˈskræg.əl.i -ier -i.əʳ, ⓤⓢ -i.ɚ -iest -i.ɪst -iness -ɪ.nəs, -ɪ.nɪs
scragg|y ˈskræg|.i -ier -i.əʳ, ⓤⓢ -i.ɚ -iest -i.ɪst, -i.əst -iness -ɪ.nəs, -ɪ.nɪs
scram skræm -s -z -ming -ɪŋ -med -d
scrambl|e ˈskræm.bəl -es -z -ing -ɪŋ, ˈskræm.blɪŋ -ed -d ˌ**scrambled** ˈ**eggs**
scrambler ˈskræm.bləʳ, ⓤⓢ -blɚ -s -z
scramjet ˈskræm.dʒet -s -s
scran skræn -s -z
Scranton ˈskræn.tən
scrap skræp -s -s -ping -ɪŋ -ped -t -per/s -əʳ/z, ⓤⓢ -ɚ/z ˈ**scrap** ˌ**heap**; ˈ**scrap** ˌ**merchant**; ˌ**scrap** ˈ**metal** ⓤⓢ ˈ**scrap** ˌ**metal**
scrapbook ˈskræp.bʊk -s -s
scrap|e skreɪp -es -s -ing/s -ɪŋ/z -ed -t -er/s -əʳ/z, ⓤⓢ -ɚ/z
scraperboard ˈskreɪ.pə.bɔːd, ⓤⓢ -pɚ.bɔːrd -s -z
scrapie ˈskreɪ.pi, ⓤⓢ ˈskreɪ-, ˈskræp.i
scrappage ˈskræp.ɪdʒ
scrapple ˈskræp.əl
scrapp|y ˈskræp|.i -ier -i.əʳ, ⓤⓢ -i.ɚ -iest -i.ɪst, -i.əst -ily -əl.i, -ɪ.li -iness -ɪ.nəs, -ɪ.nɪs
scrapyard ˈskræp.jɑːd, ⓤⓢ -jɑːrd -s -z
scratch skrætʃ -es -ɪz -ing -ɪŋ -ed -t -er/s -əʳ/z, ⓤⓢ -ɚ/z ˈ**scratch** ˌ**pad**; ˈ**scratch** ˌ**paper**
scratchcard ˈskrætʃ.kɑːd, ⓤⓢ -kɑːrd -s -z
scratchpad ˈskrætʃ.pæd -s -z
scratch|y ˈskrætʃ|.i -ier -i.əʳ, ⓤⓢ -i.ɚ -iest -i.ɪst, -i.əst -ily -əl.i, -ɪ.li -iness -ɪ.nəs, -ɪ.nɪs
scrawl skrɔːl, ⓤⓢ skrɑːl, skrɔːl -s -z -ing -ɪŋ -ed -d
scrawl|y ˈskrɔː.l|i, ⓤⓢ ˈskrɑː-, ˈskrɔː- -ier -i.əʳ, ⓤⓢ -i.ɚ -iest -i.ɪst, -i.əst -iness -ɪ.nəs, -ɪ.nɪs
scrawn|y ˈskrɔː.n|i, ⓤⓢ ˈskrɑː-, ˈskrɔː- -ier -i.əʳ, ⓤⓢ -i.ɚ -iest -i.ɪst, -i.əst -iness -ɪ.nəs, -ɪ.nɪs
scream skriːm -s -z -ing/ly -ɪŋ/li -ed -d -er/s -əʳ/z, ⓤⓢ -ɚ/z
scree skriː -s -z
screech skriːtʃ -es -ɪz -ing -ɪŋ -ed -t -er/s -əʳ/z, ⓤⓢ -ɚ/z ˈ**screech** ˌ**owl**
screed skriːd -s -z
screen skriːn -s -z -ing/s -ɪŋ -ed -d ˈ**screen** ˌ**printing**; ˈ**screen** ˌ**test**
screenplay ˈskriːn.pleɪ, ˈskriːm-, ⓤⓢ ˈskriːn- -s -z
screensaver ˈskriːnˌseɪ.vəʳ, ⓤⓢ -vɚ -s -z
screenwriter ˈskriːnˌraɪ.təʳ, ⓤⓢ -ţɚ -s -z
screw skruː -s -z -ing -ɪŋ -ed -d ˌ**screw** ˈ**cap** ⓤⓢ ˈ**screw** ˌ**cap**; ˌ**screw** ˈ**top** ⓤⓢ ˈ**screw** ˌ**top**; ˌ**screwed** ˈ**up**
screwball ˈskruː.bɔːl, ⓤⓢ -bɔːl, -bɑːl -s -z
screwdriver ˈskruːˌdraɪ.vəʳ, ⓤⓢ -vɚ -s -z

S

screw-top ˈskruː.tɒp, Ⓤⓢ -tɑːp -s -s
screw|y ˈskruː|.i -ier -i.əʳ, Ⓤⓢ -i.ɚ -iest -i.ɪst, -i.əst -iness -ɪ.nəs, -ɪ.nɪs
Scriabin ˈskrɪə.bɪn, skriˈæb.ɪn, Ⓤⓢ skriˈɑː.bɪn
scribal ˈskraɪ.bəl
scribbl|e ˈskrɪb.əl -es -z -ing -ɪŋ, ˈskrɪb.lɪŋ -ed -d -er/s -əʳ/z, ˈskrɪb.ləʳ/z, Ⓤⓢ ˈ-əl.ɚ/z, ˈ-lɚ/z
scribe skraɪb -s -z
Scriblerus skrɪˈblɪə.rəs, Ⓤⓢ -ˈbler.əs, -ˈblɪr-
Scribner ˈskrɪb.nəʳ, Ⓤⓢ -nɚ
scrim skrɪm
scrimmag|e ˈskrɪm.ɪdʒ -es -ɪz -ing -ɪŋ -ed -d
scrimp skrɪmp -s -s -ing -ɪŋ -ed -t -er/s -əʳ/z, Ⓤⓢ -ɚ/z
scrimshaw ˈskrɪm.ʃɔː, Ⓤⓢ -ʃɑː, -ʃɔː -s -z -ing -ɪŋ -ed -d
scrip skrɪp -s -s
script skrɪpt -s -s -ing -ɪŋ -ed -ɪd
scriptori|um skrɪpˈtɔː.ri|.əm, Ⓤⓢ -ˈtɔːr.i- -ums -əmz -a -ə
scriptural ˈskrɪp.tʃər.əl, -tʃʊ.rəl, Ⓤⓢ -tʃɚ.əl -ly -i
scripture, S~ ˈskrɪp.tʃəʳ, Ⓤⓢ -tʃɚ -s -z
scriptwriter ˈskrɪptˌraɪ.təʳ, Ⓤⓢ -t̬ɚ -s -z
Scriven ˈskrɪv.ən
scrivener, S~ ˈskrɪv.ən.əʳ, ˈ-nəʳ, Ⓤⓢ ˈ-ən.ɚ, ˈ-nɚ -s -z
scrofula ˈskrɒf.jʊ.lə, Ⓤⓢ ˈskrɑː.fjə-
scrofulous ˈskrɒf.jə.ləs, -jʊ-, Ⓤⓢ ˈskrɑː.fjə-, ˈ-fjʊ- -ly -li -ness -nəs, -nɪs
scroll skrəʊl, Ⓤⓢ skroʊl -s -z -ing -ɪŋ -ed -d
scrooge, S~ skruːdʒ -s -ɪz
Scroope skruːp
Scrope skruːp, skrəʊp, Ⓤⓢ skruːp, skroʊp
scrot|um ˈskrəʊ.t|əm, Ⓤⓢ ˈskroʊ.t̬|əm -ums -əmz -a -ə -al -əl
scroung|e skraʊndʒ -es -ɪz -ing -ɪŋ -ed -d -er/s -əʳ/z, Ⓤⓢ -ɚ/z
scrub skrʌb -s -z -bing -ɪŋ -bed -d ˈ**scrubbing** ˌ**brush**; ˈ**scrub** ˌ**brush**
scrubber ˈskrʌb.əʳ, Ⓤⓢ -ɚ -s -z
scrubb|y ˈskrʌb|.i -ier -i.əʳ, Ⓤⓢ -i.ɚ -iest -i.ɪst, -i.əst -iness -ɪ.nəs, -ɪ.nɪs
scrubland ˈskrʌb.lənd, -lænd, Ⓤⓢ -lænd -s -z
scruff skrʌf -s -s
scruff|y ˈskrʌf|.i -ier -i.əʳ, Ⓤⓢ -i.ɚ -iest -i.ɪst, -i.əst -iness -ɪ.nəs, -ɪ.nɪs -ily -əl.i, -ɪ.li
scrum skrʌm -s -z
scrum-|half ˌskrʌm|ˈhɑːf, Ⓤⓢ -ˈhæf -halfs -ˈhɑːfs, Ⓤⓢ -ˈhæfs -halves -ˈhɑːvz, Ⓤⓢ -ˈhævz
scrummag|e ˈskrʌm.ɪdʒ -es -ɪz -ing -ɪŋ -ed -d -er/s -əʳ/z, Ⓤⓢ -ɚ/z
scrummy ˈskrʌm.i -ier -i.əʳ, Ⓤⓢ -i.ɚ -iest -i.ɪst -iness -ɪ.nəs, -ɪ.nɪs
scrump skrʌmp -s -s -ing -ɪŋ -ed -t
scrumptious ˈskrʌmp.ʃəs, -tʃəs
scrumpy ˈskrʌm.pi
scrunch skrʌntʃ -es -ɪz -ing -ɪŋ -ed -t -y -i -ies -iz

scrupl|e ˈskruː.pəl -es -z -ing -ɪŋ, ˈskruː.plɪŋ -ed -d
scrupulosity ˌskruː.pjəˈlɒs.ə.ti, -pjʊˈ-, -ɪ.ti, Ⓤⓢ -ˈlɑː.sə.t̬i
scrupulous ˈskruː.pjə.ləs, -pjʊ- -ly -li -ness -nəs, -nɪs
scrutator skruːˈteɪ.təʳ, Ⓤⓢ -t̬ɚ -s -z
scrutineer ˌskruː.tɪˈnɪəʳ, -tənˈɪəʳ, Ⓤⓢ -tənˈɪr -s -z
scrutiniz|e, -is|e ˈskruː.tɪ.naɪz, -tən.aɪz, Ⓤⓢ -tən.aɪz -es -ɪz -ing -ɪŋ -ed -d
scrutin|y ˈskruː.tɪ.n|i, -tən|.i, Ⓤⓢ -tən|.i -ies -iz
Scruton ˈskruː.tən
scr|y skr|aɪ -ies -aɪz -ying -aɪ.ɪŋ -ied -aɪd
Scrymgeour ˈskrɪm.dʒəʳ, Ⓤⓢ -dʒɚ
scuba ˈskuː.bə, ˈskjuː-, Ⓤⓢ ˈskuː- ˈ**scuba** ˌ**diving**
scud, S~ skʌd -s -z -ding -ɪŋ -ded -ɪd
Scudamore ˈskjuː.də.mɔːʳ, Ⓤⓢ ˈskuː.də.mɔːr
scuff skʌf -s -s -ing -ɪŋ -ed -t
scuffl|e ˈskʌf.əl -es -z -ing -ɪŋ, ˈskʌf.lɪŋ -ed -d
scull skʌl -s -z -ing -ɪŋ -ed -d -er/s -əʳ/z, Ⓤⓢ -ɚ/z
sculler|y ˈskʌl.ər|.i -ies -iz ˈ**scullery** ˌ**maid**
scullion, S~ ˈskʌl.i.ən, Ⓤⓢ ˈ-jən -s -z
Scully ˈskʌl.i
sculpsit ˈskʌlp.sɪt
sculpt skʌlpt -s -s -ing -ɪŋ -ed -ɪd
sculptor ˈskʌlp.təʳ, Ⓤⓢ -tɚ -s -z
sculpt|ure ˈskʌlp.tʃ|əʳ, Ⓤⓢ -tʃ|ɚ -ures -əz, Ⓤⓢ -ɚz -uring -ər.ɪŋ -ured -əd, Ⓤⓢ -ɚd -ural -ər.əl
scum skʌm -s -z -ming -ɪŋ -med -d -my -i
scumbag ˈskʌm.bæg -s -z
Scunthorpe ˈskʌn.θɔːp, Ⓤⓢ -θɔːrp
scupper ˈskʌp.əʳ, Ⓤⓢ -ɚ -s -z -ing -ɪŋ -ed -d
scurf skɜːf, Ⓤⓢ skɝːf -y -i -iness -ɪ.nəs, -ɪ.nɪs
scurrility skʌrˈɪl.ə.ti, skəˈrɪl-, -ɪ.ti, Ⓤⓢ skəˈrɪl.ə.t̬i
scurrilous ˈskʌr.ə.ləs, ˈ-ɪ-, Ⓤⓢ ˈskɝː- -ly -li -ness -nəs, -nɪs
scurr|y ˈskʌr|.i, Ⓤⓢ ˈskɝː- -ies -iz -ying -i.ɪŋ -ied -id
scurv|y ˈskɜː.v|i, Ⓤⓢ ˈskɝː- -ier -i.əʳ, Ⓤⓢ -i.ɚ -iest -i.ɪst, -i.əst -ily -əl.i, -ɪ.li -iness -ɪ.nəs, -ɪ.nɪs
Scutari ˈskuː.tər.i; skuːˈtɑː.ri, skʊ-, Ⓤⓢ ˈskuː.t̬ɚ.i, -tɑː-
scutcheon ˈskʌtʃ.ən -s -z
scutt|er ˈskʌt|.əʳ, Ⓤⓢ ˈskʌt̬|.ɚ -ers -əz, Ⓤⓢ -ɚz -ering -ər.ɪŋ -ered -əd, Ⓤⓢ -ɚd
scuttl|e ˈskʌt.əl, Ⓤⓢ ˈskʌt̬- -es -z -ing -ɪŋ, ˈskʌt.lɪŋ -ed -d
scuttlebutt ˈskʌt.əl.bʌt -s -s
scut|um ˈskjuː.t|əm, Ⓤⓢ -t̬|əm -ums -əmz -a -ə
scuzz|y ˈskʌz|.i -ier -i.əʳ, Ⓤⓢ -i.ɚ -iest -i.ɪst, -i.əst -iness -ɪ.nəs, -ɪ.nɪs
Scylla ˈsɪl.ə
scyth|e saɪð -es -z -ing -ɪŋ -ed -d

Scythi|a ˈsɪð.i|.ə, ˈsɪθ-, Ⓤⓢ ˈsɪθ-, ˈsɪð- -an/s -ən/z
S.D. (abbrev. for **South Dakota**) ˌsaʊθ.dəˈkəʊ.tə, Ⓤⓢ -ˈkoʊ.t̬ə
S.D.I. ˌes.diːˈaɪ
SDP ˌes.diːˈpiː
SE (abbrev. for **southeast**) ˌsaʊθˈiːst
sea siː -s -z ˌ**sea** ˈ**breeze** Ⓤⓢ ˈ**sea** ˌ**breeze**; ˈ**sea** ˌ**captain**; ˈ**sea** ˌ**change**; ˈ**sea** ˌ**cow**; ˈ**sea** ˌ**elephant**; ˈ**sea** ˌ**fog**; ˌ**sea** ˈ**green**; ˈ**sea** ˌ**horse**; ˈ**sea** ˌ**legs**; ˈ**sea** ˌ**level**; ˈ**sea** ˌ**lion**; ˈ**sea** ˌ**power**; ˈ**sea** ˌ**serpent**; ˈ**sea** ˌ**slug**; ˈ**sea** ˌ**snail**; ˈ**sea** ˌ**urchin**; **between the** ˌ**devil and the** ˌ**deep** ˌ**blue** ˈ**sea**
seabed ˈsiː.bed, -ˈ-
seabird ˈsiː.bɜːd, Ⓤⓢ -bɝːd -s -z
seaboard ˈsiː.bɔːd, Ⓤⓢ -bɔːrd
seaborne ˈsiː.bɔːn, Ⓤⓢ -bɔːrn
Seabright ˈsiː.braɪt
seadog ˈsiː.dɒg, Ⓤⓢ -dɑːg, -dɔːg -s -z
seafar|er ˈsiːˌfeə.r|əʳ, Ⓤⓢ -ˌfer|.ɚ -ers -əz, Ⓤⓢ -ɚz -ing -ɪŋ
seafood ˈsiː.fuːd
Seaford ˈsiː.fəd, -fɔːd, Ⓤⓢ -fɚd, -fɔːrd
Seaforth ˈsiː.fɔːθ, Ⓤⓢ -fɔːrθ -s -s
seafront ˈsiː.frʌnt -s -s
Seager ˈsiː.gəʳ, Ⓤⓢ -gɚ
seagoing ˈsiːˌgəʊ.ɪŋ, Ⓤⓢ -ˌgoʊ-
Seagram® ˈsiː.grəm
seagull ˈsiː.gʌl -s -z
Seaham ˈsiː.əm
Seahawks ˈsiː.hɔːks, Ⓤⓢ -hɑːks, -hɔːks
seakale ˈsiː.keɪl, ˌ-ˈ-, Ⓤⓢ ˈsiː.keɪl
seal siːl -s -z -ing -ɪŋ -ed -d ˈ**sealing** ˌ**wax**
sealant ˈsiː.lənt -s -s
sealer ˈsiː.ləʳ, Ⓤⓢ -lɚ -s -z
sealskin ˈsiːl.skɪn -s -z
Sealyham ˈsiː.li.əm -s -z
seam siːm -s -z -ing -ɪŋ -ed -d -less/ly -ləs/li, -lɪs/li
sea|man, S~ ˈsiː|.mən -men -mən, -men -manship -mən.ʃɪp -manlike -mən.laɪk
Seamas ˈʃeɪ.məs
seamer ˈsiː.məʳ, Ⓤⓢ -mɚ -s -z
seamstress ˈsemp.strɪs, ˈsiːmp-, -strəs, Ⓤⓢ ˈsiːmp- -es -ɪz
Seamus ˈʃeɪ.məs
seamy ˈsiː.mi -ier -i.əʳ, Ⓤⓢ -i.ɚ -iest -i.ɪst, -i.əst -iness -ɪ.nəs, -ɪ.nɪs
Sean ʃɔːn, Ⓤⓢ ʃɑːn, ʃɔːn
seanc|e, séance ˈseɪ.ɑ̃ːnts, Ⓤⓢ ˈseɪ.ɑːnts -es -ɪz
sea-pink ˈsiː.pɪŋk
seaplane ˈsiː.pleɪn -s -z
seaport ˈsiː.pɔːt, Ⓤⓢ -pɔːrt -s -s
sear sɪəʳ, Ⓤⓢ sɪr -s -z -ing/ly -ɪŋ -ed -d
search sɜːtʃ, Ⓤⓢ sɝːtʃ -es -ɪz -ing/ly -ɪŋ/li -ed -t -er/s -əʳ/z, Ⓤⓢ -ɚ/z -able -ə.bəl ˈ**search** ˌ**party**; ˈ**search** ˌ**warrant**
searchlight ˈsɜːtʃ.laɪt, Ⓤⓢ ˈsɝːtʃ- -s -s
Searle sɜːl, Ⓤⓢ sɝːl

Sears sɪəz, (US) sɪrz
Seascale ˈsiː.skeɪl
seascape ˈsiː.skeɪp **-s** -s
seashell ˈsiː.ʃel **-s** -z
seashore ˈsiː.ʃɔːʳ, ˌ-ˈ-, (US) ˈsiː.ʃɔːr **-s** -z
seasick ˈsiː.sɪk **-ness** -nəs, -nɪs
seaside ˈsiː.saɪd
season ˈsiː.zᵊn **-s** -z **-ing** -ɪŋ **-ed** -d ˌ**Season's** ˈ**Greetings;** ˈ**season** ˌ**ticket** (US) ˌ**season** ˈ**ticket**
seasonab|le ˈsiː.zᵊn.ə.b|ᵊl, ˈsiːz.nə- **-ly** -li **-leness** -ᵊl.nəs, -nɪs
seasonal ˈsiː.zᵊn.ᵊl **-ly** -i
seasonality ˌsiː.zᵊnˈæl.ə.ti, -ɪ.ti, (US) -ə.t̬i
seasoning ˈsiː.zᵊn.ɪŋ **-s** -z
seat siːt **-s** -s **-ing** -ɪŋ, (US) ˈsiː.t̬ɪŋ **-ed** -ɪd, (US) ˈsiː.t̬ɪd **-er/s** -əʳ/z, (US) -ɚ/z ˈ**seat** ˌ**belt**
SEATO ˈsiː.təʊ, (US) -t̬oʊ
Seaton ˈsiː.tᵊn
Seaton Delavel ˌsiː.tᵊnˈdel.ə.vᵊl
Seattle siˈæt.ᵊl, (US) -ˈæt̬-
seawall ˌsiːˈwɔːl, ˈ--, (US) ˈsiː.wɔːl, -wɑːl **-s** -z
seaward ˈsiː.wəd, (US) -wɚd
seawater ˈsiːˌwɔː.təʳ, (US) -ˌwɑː.t̬ɚ, -ˌwɔː-
seaway ˈsiː.weɪ **-s** -z
seaweed ˈsiː.wiːd
seaworth|y ˈsiːˌwɜː.ð|i, (US) -ˌwɝː- **-iness** -ɪ.nəs, -ɪ.nɪs
sebaceous sɪˈbeɪ.ʃəs, sebˈeɪ-, (US) səˈbeɪ- **se**ˈ**baceous** ˌ**gland**
Sebald ˈzeɪ.bælt
Sebastian sɪˈbæs.ti.ən, səˈbæs-, sebˈæs-, (US) səˈbæs.tʃən
Sebastopol sɪˈbæs.tə.pɒl, sə-, sebˈæs-, -pᵊl, (US) sɪˈbæs.tə.poʊl
seborrhea ˌseb.əˈriː.ə, -ˈrɪə, (US) -ˈriː.ə
sebum ˈsiː.bəm
sec sek **-s** -s
secant ˈsiː.kᵊnt, ˈsek.ᵊnt, (US) ˈsiː.kᵊnt, -kænt **-s** -s
secateurs ˌsek.əˈtɜːz; ˈ---, -təz, (US) ˈsek.ə.tɚz
seced|e sɪˈsiːd, siː-, sə-, (US) sɪ- **-es** -z **-ing** -ɪŋ **-ed** -ɪd **-er/s** -əʳ/z, (US) -ɚ/z
secession sɪˈseʃ.ᵊn, sə- **-s** -z **-ist/s** -ɪst/s
seclud|e sɪˈkluːd, sə- **-es** -z **-ing** -ɪŋ **-ed** -ɪd
seclusion sɪˈkluː.ʒᵊn, sə-
Secombe ˈsiː.kəm
second n, adj, v *most senses:* ˈsek.ᵊnd **-s** -z **-ly** -li **-ing** -ɪŋ **-ed** -ɪd **-er/s** -əʳ/z, (US) -ɚ/z ˌ**second** ˈ**best;** ˌ**Second** ˈ**Coming;** ˌ**second** ˈ**cousin;** ˌ**second** ˈ**fiddle;** ˌ**second** ˈ**nature;** ˌ**second** ˈ**person** *stress shift:* ˌ**second person** ˈ**singular** ˌ**second** ˈ**reading;** ˌ**second** ˈ**sight;** ˌ**second** ˈ**thoughts;** ˌ**second** ˈ**wind;** ˌ**Second** ˌ**World** ˈ**War**
second v *to release for temporary service:* sɪˈkɒnd, sə-, (US) -ˈkɑːnd **-s** -z **-ing** -ɪŋ **-ed** -ɪd **-ment/s** -mənt/s
secondar|y ˈsek.ᵊn.dᵊr|.i, -dr|i, (US) -der|.i **-ies** -iz **-ily** -ᵊl.i, -ɪ.li ˌ**secondary** ˈ**modern;** ˈ**secondary** ˌ**school**
second-class ˌsek.ᵊndˈklɑːs, (US) -ˈklæs ˌ**second-class** ˈ**citizen**
second-generation ˌsek.ᵊnˌdʒen.ᵊrˈeɪ.ʃᵊn, (US) -əˈreɪ-
second-guess ˌsek.ᵊndˈges **-es** -ɪz **-ing** -ɪŋ **-ed** -t
secondhand ˌsek.ᵊndˈhænd *stress shift:* ˌ**secondhand** ˈ**books**
Secondi *town in Ghana:* ˌsek.ənˈdiː *surname:* sɪˈkɒn.di, sə-, (US) -ˈkɑːn-
secondment sɪˈkɒnd.mənt, sə-, (US) -ˈkɑːnd-
secondo sekˈɒn.dəʊ, sɪˈkɒn-, (US) sɪˈkɑːn.doʊ **-s** -z
second|-rate ˌsek.ᵊnd|ˈreɪt **-rater/s** -ˈreɪ.təʳ/z, (US) -ˈreɪ.t̬ɚ/z
secrecy ˈsiː.krə.si, -krɪ-
secret ˈsiː.krət, -krɪt **-s** -s **-ly** -li ˌ**secret** ˈ**agent;** ˌ**secret po**ˈ**lice;** ˌ**secret** ˈ**service**
secretarial ˌsek.rəˈteə.ri.əl, -rɪˈ-, (US) -rəˈter.i-
secretariat ˌsek.rəˈteə.ri.ət, -rɪˈ-, -æt, (US) -rəˈter.i.ət **-s** -s
secretar|y ˈsek.rə.tᵊr|.i, -rɪ-, -tr|i, (US) -rə.ter|.i **-ies** -iz **-yship/s** -i.ʃɪp/s ˌ**Secretary of** ˈ**State**
secretary-general, (S G) ˌsek.rə.tᵊr.iˈdʒen.ᵊr.ᵊl, -rɪ-, (US) -rə.ter.iˈ- **-s** -z **secretaries-general** ˌsek.rə.tᵊr.izˈ-, -rɪ-, (US) -rə.ter.izˈ-
se|crete sɪ|ˈkriːt, siː-, sə-, (US) sɪ- **-cretes** -ˈkriːts **-creting** -ˈkriː.tɪŋ, (US) -ˈkriː.t̬ɪŋ **-creted** -ˈkriː.tɪd, (US) -ˈkriː.t̬ɪd
secretion sɪˈkriː.ʃᵊn, siː-, sə-, (US) sɪ- **-s** -z
secretive *inclined to secrecy:* ˈsiː.krə.tɪv, -krɪ-, (US) -krə.t̬ɪv **-ly** -li **-ness** -nəs, -nɪs *of secretion:* sɪˈkriː.tɪv, sə-, (US) -t̬ɪv
sect sekt **-s** -s
sectarian sekˈteə.ri.ən, (US) -ˈter.i- **-s** -z **-ism** -ɪ.zᵊm
sectar|y ˈsek.tᵊr|.i **-ies** -iz
section ˈsek.ʃᵊn **-s** -z **-ing** -ɪŋ **-ed** -d
sectional ˈsek.ʃᵊn.ᵊl **-ly** -i
sectional|ism ˈsek.ʃᵊn.ᵊl|.ɪ.zᵊm **-ist/s** -ɪst/s
sectionaliz|e, -is|e ˈsek.ʃᵊn.ᵊl.aɪz, (US) -ə.laɪz **-es** -ɪz **-ing** -ɪŋ **-ed** -d
sector ˈsek.təʳ, (US) -tɚ **-s** -z
secular ˈsek.jə.ləʳ, -jʊ-, (US) -lɚ **-ly** -li
secular|ism ˈsek.jə.lᵊr|.ɪ.zᵊm, -jʊ- **-ist/s** -ɪst/s
secularity ˌsek.jəˈlær.ə.ti, -jʊˈ-, -ɪ.ti, (US) -ˈler.ə.t̬i, -ˈlær-
secularization, -isa- ˌsek.jə.lᵊr.aɪˈzeɪ.ʃᵊn, -jʊ-, -ɪˈ-, (US) -əˈ-
seculariz|e, -is|e ˈsek.jə.lᵊr.aɪz, -jʊ-, (US) -lə.raɪz **-es** -ɪz **-ing** -ɪŋ **-ed** -d
secur|e sɪˈkjʊəʳ, sə-, -ˈkjɔːʳ, (US) -ˈkjʊr **-er** -əʳ, (US) -ɚ **-est** -ɪst, -əst **-ely** -li **-es** -z **-ing** -ɪŋ **-ed** -d **-able** -rə.bᵊl
Securicor® sɪˈkjʊə.rɪ.kɔːʳ, sə-, -ˈkjɔː-, -rə-, (US) -ˈkjʊr.ə.kɔːr
securit|y sɪˈkjʊə.rə.t|i, sə-, -ˈkjɔː-, -ɪ.t|i, (US) -ˈkjʊr.ə.t̬|i **-ies** -iz **se**ˈ**curity** ˌ**guard;** **Se**ˈ**curity** ˌ**Council;** **se**ˈ**curity** ˌ**risk**
sedan, S~ sɪˈdæn, sə- **se**ˌ**dan** ˈ**chair** (US) **se**ˈ**dan** ˌ**chair**
sedate adj sɪˈdeɪt, sə- **-ly** -li **-ness** -nəs, -nɪs
se|date v sɪ|ˈdeɪt, sə- **-dates** -ˈdeɪts **-dating** -ˈdeɪ.tɪŋ, (US) -ˈdeɪ.t̬ɪŋ **-dated** -ˈdeɪ.tɪd, (US) -ˈdeɪ.t̬ɪd
sedation sɪˈdeɪ.ʃᵊn, sə-
sedative ˈsed.ə.tɪv, (US) -t̬ɪv **-s** -z
Sedbergh *name of town:* ˈsed.bəʳ, (US) -bɚ *public school:* ˈsed.bəʳ, -bɜːg, (US) -bɝːg, -bɚ
Sedding ˈsed.ɪŋ
Seddon ˈsed.ᵊn
sedentar|y ˈsed.ᵊn.tᵊr|.i, -tr|i, (US) -ter|.i **-ily** -ᵊl.i, -ɪ.li **-iness** -ɪ.nəs, -ɪ.nɪs
sedg|e sedʒ **-es** -ɪz ˈ**sedge** ˌ**warbler;** ˌ**sedge** ˈ**warbler** (US) ˈ**sedge** ˌ**warbler**
Sedgefield ˈsedʒ.fiːld
Sedgemoor ˈsedʒ.mɔːʳ, -mʊəʳ, (US) -mʊr, -mɔːr
Sedgley ˈsedʒ.li
Sedgwick ˈsedʒ.wɪk
sedilia sedˈiː.li.ə, sɪˈdiː-, sə-, -ˈdaɪ-, (US) sɪˈdɪl.i.ə, ˈ-jə
sediment ˈsed.ɪ.mənt, ˈ-ə-, (US) ˈ-ə- **-s** -s **-ation** ˌ--menˈteɪ.ʃᵊn
sedimentary ˌsed.ɪˈmen.tᵊr.i, -əˈ-, ˈ-tri
sedition sɪˈdɪʃ.ᵊn, sə- **-s** -z
seditious sɪˈdɪʃ.əs, sə- **-ly** -li **-ness** -nəs, -nɪs
Sedlescombe ˈsed.ᵊlz.kəm
Sedley ˈsed.li
seduc|e sɪˈdʒuːs, sə-, -ˈdjuːs, (US) -ˈduːs, -ˈdjuːs **-es** -ɪz **-ing** -ɪŋ **-ed** -t **-er/s** -əʳ/z, (US) -ɚ/z
seduction sɪˈdʌk.ʃᵊn, sə- **-s** -z
seductive sɪˈdʌk.tɪv, sə- **-ly** -li **-ness** -nəs, -nɪs
seductress sɪˈdʌk.trɪs, -trəs **-es** -ɪz
sedulous ˈsedʒ.ə.ləs, ˈ-ʊ-, ˈsed.jə-, ˈ-jʊ-, (US) ˈsedʒ.ə-, ˈ-ʊ- **-ly** -li **-ness** -nəs, -nɪs
sedum ˈsiː.dəm **-s** -z
see, S~ siː **-s** -z **-ing** -ɪŋ **saw** sɔː, (US) sɑː, sɔː **seen** siːn
Seebeck ˈsiː.bek
seed siːd **-s** -z **-ing** -ɪŋ **-ed** -ɪd ˌ**go to** ˈ**seed;** ˈ**seed po**ˌ**tato;** ˌ**seed po**ˈ**tato**
seedbed ˈsiːd.bed **-s** -z
seedcake ˈsiːd.keɪk **-s** -s
seedcas|e ˈsiːd.keɪs **-es** -ɪz
seedless ˈsiːd.ləs, -lɪs
seedling ˈsiːd.lɪŋ **-s** -z
seeds|man ˈsiːdz|.mən **-men** -mən, -men
seedtime ˈsiːd.taɪm **-s** -z
seed|y ˈsiː.d|i **-ier** -i.əʳ, (US) -i.ɚ **-iest** -i.ɪst, -i.əst **-ily** -ᵊl.i, -ɪ.li **-iness** -ɪ.nəs, -ɪ.nɪs
Seeger ˈsiː.gəʳ, (US) -gɚ
seek siːk **-s** -s **-ing** -ɪŋ **sought** sɔːt, (US) sɑːt, sɔːt **seeker/s** ˈsiː.kəʳ/z, (US) -kɚ/z

seel(e)y ˈsiː.li
seem siːm **-s** -z **-ing/ly** -ɪŋ/li **-ed** -d
seeml|y ˈsiːm.l|i **-ier** -i.əʳ, (US) -i.ɚ **-iest** -i.ɪst, -i.əst **-iness** -ɪ.nəs, -ɪ.nɪs
seen (from **see**) siːn
seep siːp **-s** -s **-ing** -ɪŋ **-ed** -t
seepage ˈsiː.pɪdʒ
seer *prophet:* ˈsiː.əʳ, sɪəʳ, (US) sɪr, ˈsiː.ɚ *Indian weight:* sɪəʳ, (US) siːr, sɪr **-s** -z
seersucker ˈsɪəˌsʌk.əʳ, (US) ˈsɪrˌsʌk.ɚ
seesaw ˈsiː.sɔː, (US) -sɑː, -sɔː **-s** -z **-ing** -ɪŋ **-ed** -d
seeth|e siːð **-es** -z **-ing** -ɪŋ **-ed** -d
see-through ˈsiː.θruː
Sefton ˈsef.tᵊn, (US) -tən
Sega® ˈseɪ.gə, ˈsiː-
Segal ˈsiː.gəl
segment n ˈseg.mənt **-s** -s
segmen|t v segˈmen|t, səg-, sɪg-, (US) ˈseg.men|t, -ˈ- **-ts** -ts **-ting** -tɪŋ, (US) -t̬ɪŋ **-ted** -tɪd, (US) -t̬ɪd
segmental segˈmen.tᵊl, səg-, sɪg-, (US) segˈmen.t̬ᵊl
segmentation ˌseg.menˈteɪ.ʃᵊn, -mənˈ-
segn|o ˈsen.j|əʊ, ˈseɪ.nj|əʊ, (US) ˈseɪ.nj|oʊ **-i** -i
Segovia sɪˈgəʊ.vi.ə, sə-, segˈəʊ-, (US) sɪˈgoʊ-, sə-
segregate n ˈseg.rɪ.gət, -rə-, -geɪt, -gɪt, (US) -rə.gɪt
segre|gate v ˈseg.rɪ|.geɪt, -rə-, (US) -rə- **-gates** -geɪts **-gating** -geɪ.tɪŋ, (US) -geɪ.t̬ɪŋ **-gated** -geɪ.tɪd, (US) -geɪ.t̬ɪd
segregation ˌseg.rɪˈgeɪ.ʃᵊn, -rəˈ-, (US) -rəˈ-
segu|e ˈseg.weɪ, ˈseɪ.gweɪ, -gwi **-es** -z **-ing** -ɪŋ **-d** -d
seguidilla ˌseg.ɪˈdiː.jə, -li.ə, (US) -əˈdiː.jə, ˌseɪ.gəˈ-, -ˈdiːl- **-s** -z
Segway® ˈseg.weɪ **-s** -z
seich|e seɪʃ, (US) seɪʃ, siːtʃ **-es** -ɪz
Seidlitz ˈsed.lɪts
seigneur senˈjɜːʳ, seɪˈnjɜːʳ; ˈseɪ.njəʳ, (US) seɪˈnjɝː, senˈjɝː **-s** -z **-ial** -i.əl
seignior *lord:* ˈseɪ.njəʳ, (US) ˈseɪ.njɚ; (US) seɪˈnjɔːr **-s** -z
Seignior *surname:* ˈsiː.njəʳ, (US) -njɚ
seignior|y ˈseɪ.njᵊr|.i, (US) ˈseɪ- **-ies** -iz
Seiko® ˈseɪ.kəʊ, (US) -koʊ
sein|e *net:* seɪn **-es** -z **-ing** -ɪŋ **-ed** -d
Seine *river in France:* seɪn, sen
Seinfeld ˈsaɪn.feld
Seir ˈsiː.əʳ, (US) -ɚ
seis|e siːz **-es** -ɪz **-ing** -ɪŋ **-ed** -d
seisin ˈsiː.zɪn **-s** -z
seismic ˈsaɪz.mɪk, (US) ˈsaɪz-, ˈsaɪs-
seismo- ˈsaɪz.məʊ; saɪzˈmɒ, (US) ˈsaɪz.moʊ, ˈsaɪs-, -mə; (US) saɪzˈmɑː, saɪsˈ-
Note: Prefix. Normally takes either primary or secondary stress on the first syllable, e.g. **seismograph** /ˈsaɪz.məʊ.grɑːf/ (US) /-mə.græf/, **seismographic** /ˌsaɪz.məʊˈgræf.ɪk/ (US) /-məˈ-/, or primary stress on the second syllable, e.g. **seismographer** /saɪzˈmɒg.rə.fəʳ/ (US) /-ˈmɑː.grə.fɚ/.
seismograph ˈsaɪz.məʊ.grɑːf, -græf, (US) -mə.græf, ˈsaɪs-, -moʊ- **-s** -s
seismograph|er saɪzˈmɒg.rə.f|əʳ, (US) -ˈmɑː.grə.f|ɚ, saɪs- **-ers** -əz, (US) -ɚz **-y** -i
seismographic ˌsaɪz.məʊˈgræf.ɪk, (US) -məˈ-, saɪs-, -moʊˈ-
seismologic|al ˌsaɪz.məˈlɒdʒ.ɪ.k|ᵊl, (US) -məˈlɑː.dʒɪ-, saɪs- **-ally** -ᵊl.i, (US) -li
seismolog|y saɪzˈmɒl.ə.dʒ|i, (US) -ˈmɑː.lə-, seɪs- **-ist/s** -ɪst/s
seismometer saɪzˈmɒm.ɪ.təʳ, ˈ-ə-, (US) -ˈmɑː.mə.t̬ɚ, saɪs- **-s** -z
seizable ˈsiː.zə.bᵊl
seiz|e siːz **-es** -ɪz **-ing** -ɪŋ **-ed** -d
seizin ˈsiː.zɪn **-s** -z
seizure ˈsiː.ʒəʳ, (US) -ʒɚ **-s** -z
sejant ˈsiː.dʒənt
Sejanus sɪˈdʒeɪ.nəs, sə-, sedʒˈeɪ-, (US) sɪˈdʒeɪ-
Sekhmet ˈsek.met
selah ˈsiː.lə, -lɑː, (US) ˈsiː.lə, ˈsel.ə, -ɑː **-s** -z
Selangor ˈsel.æŋ.ɔːʳ, sɪˈlæŋ.gɔːʳ, (US) selˈɑːŋ.gɔːr
Selassie səˈlæs.i, (US) -ˈlæs-, -ˈlɑː.si
Selborne ˈsel.bɔːn, -bən, (US) -bɔːrn, -bɚn
Selby ˈsel.bi
Selden ˈsel.dᵊn
seldom ˈsel.dəm
select sɪˈlekt, sə-, (US) sə- **-ness** -nəs, -nɪs **-s** -s **-ing** -ɪŋ **-ed** -ɪd **seˌlect comˈmittee**
selection sɪˈlek.ʃᵊn, sə-, (US) sə- **-s** -z
selective sɪˈlek.tɪv, sə-, (US) sə- **-ly** -li **-ness** -nəs, -nɪs
selectivity ˌsɪl.ekˈtɪv.ə.ti, ˌsel-, ˌsiː.lekˈ-, -ɪ.ti; səˌlekˈ-, sɪ-, (US) səˌlekˈtɪv.ə.t̬i, sɪ-; (US) ˌsiː.lekˈ-
selector sɪˈlek.təʳ, sə-, (US) səˈlek.tɚ **-s** -z
Selena sɪˈliː.nə, sə-
selenite *substance:* ˈsel.ɪ.naɪt, ˈ-ə-, (US) ˈ-ə-
Selenite *inhabitant of moon:* sɪˈliː.naɪt, sə-, (US) sɪˈliː-, sə-; (US) ˈsel.ə- **-s** -s
selenium sɪˈliː.ni.əm, sə-, (US) sə-
Seles ˈsel.ez, -əs
Seleuci|a sɪˈljuː.ʃi|.ə, sə-, -ˈluː-, -si-, (US) səˈluː.ʃi|-, ˈ-ʃ|ə **-an/s** -ən/z
Seleucid sɪˈljuː.sɪd, sə-, -ˈluː-, (US) səˈluː- **-s** -z
Seleucus sɪˈljuː.kəs, sə-, -ˈluː-, (US) səˈluː-
sel|f sel|f **-ves** -vz
self- self
Note: Many compounds beginning with **self-** have the stress pattern ˌ**self**ˈ-; these are likely to undergo stress shift when a stressed syllable follows closely, especially in adjectives or adjectives derived from verbs.
self-abuse ˌself.əˈbjuːs
self-addressed ˌself.əˈdrest
self-appointed ˌself.əˈpɔɪn.tɪd, (US) -t̬ɪd
self-assembly ˌself.əˈsem.bli
self-assurance ˌself.əˈʃʊə.rᵊnts, (US) -ˈʃʊr.ᵊnts
self-assured ˌself.əˈʃʊəd, (US) -ˈʃʊrd
self-catering ˌselfˈkeɪ.tᵊr.ɪŋ, (US) -t̬ɚ-
self-centred, self-centered ˌselfˈsen.təd, (US) -t̬ɚd **-ly** -li **-ness** -nəs, -nɪs
self-command ˌself.kəˈmɑːnd, (US) -ˈmænd
self-confessed ˌself.kənˈfest
self-conscious ˌselfˈkɒn.tʃəs, (US) -ˈkɑːnt.ʃəs **-ly** -li **-ness** -nəs, -nɪs
self-contained ˌself.kənˈteɪnd **-ly** -li **-ness** -nəs, -nɪs **-ment** -mənt
self-control ˌself.kənˈtrəʊl, (US) -ˈtroʊl **-led** -d
self-critic|al ˌselfˈkrɪt.ɪ.k|ᵊl, (US) -ˈkrɪt̬- **-ally** -ᵊl.i, -li
self-deception ˌself.dɪˈsep.ʃᵊn
self-defence, self-defense ˌself.dɪˈfents
self-denial ˌself.dɪˈnaɪ.əl
self-denying ˌself.dɪˈnaɪ.ɪŋ
self-destruct ˌself.dɪˈstrʌkt **-s** -s **-ing** -ɪŋ **-ed** -ɪd **-ive** -ɪv **-ion** -ʃᵊn
self-determination ˌself.dɪˌtɜː.mɪˈneɪ.ʃᵊn, (US) -ˌtɝː-
self-discipline ˌselfˈdɪs.ɪ.plɪn, ˈ-ə- **-d** -d
self-drive ˌselfˈdraɪv
self-effac|ing ˌself.ɪˈfeɪ.s|ɪŋ **-ingly** -ɪŋ.li **-ement** -mənt
self-employed ˌself.ɪmˈplɔɪd, -emˈ-
self-esteem ˌself.ɪˈstiːm, -əˈ-
self-evident ˌselfˈev.ɪ.dᵊnt
self-explanatory ˌself.ɪkˈsplæn.ə.tᵊr.i, -ekˈ-, ˈ-ɪ-, (US) -tɔːr-
self-fulfilling ˌself.fʊlˈfɪl.ɪŋ
self-governing ˌselfˈgʌv.ᵊn.ɪŋ, (US) -ɚ.nɪŋ
self-government ˌselfˈgʌv.ᵊn.mənt, -ᵊm-, -və.mənt, (US) -ɚn.mənt
self-heal ˌselfˈhiːl
self-help ˌselfˈhelp
self-image ˌselfˈɪm.ɪdʒ **-s** -ɪz
self-importan|ce ˌself.ɪmˈpɔː.tᵊn|ts, (US) -ˈpɔːr- **-t/ly** -t/li
self-imposed ˌself.ɪmˈpəʊzd, (US) -ˈpoʊzd
self-indulgen|ce ˌself.ɪnˈdʌl.dʒᵊn|ts **-t/ly** -t/li
self-inflicted ˌself.ɪnˈflɪk.tɪd
self-interest ˌselfˈɪn.trəst, -trəst; -tᵊr.əst, -est, -ɪst, (US) -ˈɪn.trɪst, -trəst, -trest; (US) -t̬ɚ.ɪst, -əst, -est
selfish ˈsel.fɪʃ **-ly** -li **-ness** -nəs, -nɪs
selfless ˈsel.fləs, -flɪs **-ly** -li **-ness** -nəs, -nɪs
self-made ˌselfˈmeɪd
self-pity ˌselfˈpɪt.i, (US) -ˈpɪt̬-
self-portrait ˌselfˈpɔː.trɪt, -trət, -treɪt, (US) -ˈpɔːr.trɪt, -treɪt **-s** -s
self-possessed ˌself.pəˈzest
self-possession ˌself.pəˈzeʃ.ᵊn
self-preservation ˌselfˌprez.əˈveɪ.ʃᵊn, (US) -ɚˈ-

S

self-proclaimed ˌself.prəʊˈkleɪmd, US -proʊˈ-, -prəˈ-
self-raising ˌselfˈreɪ.zɪŋ **ˌself-raising ˈflour; self-ˌraising ˈflour**
self-relian|ce ˌself.rɪˈlaɪ.ən|ts, -rəˈ- **-t** -t
self-respect ˌself.rɪˈspekt, -rəˈ-
self-respecting ˌself.rɪˈspek.tɪŋ, -rəˈ-
self-restraint ˌself.rɪˈstreɪnt, -rəˈ-
Selfridge ˈsel.frɪdʒ **-'s** -ɪz
Selfridges ˈsel.frɪdʒ.ɪz
self-righteous ˌselfˈraɪ.tʃəs, -tjəs, US -tʃəs **-ly** -li **-ness** -nəs, -nɪs
self-rising ˌselfˈraɪ.zɪŋ **ˌself-rising ˈflour; self-ˌrising ˈflour**
self-rul|e ˌselfˈruːl **-ing** -ɪŋ
self-sacrific|e ˌselfˈsæk.rɪ.faɪs, -rə- **-ing/ly** -ɪŋ/li
selfsame ˈself.seɪm
self-satisfaction ˌselfˌsæt.ɪsˈfæk.ʃᵊn, US -ˌsæt̬-
self-satisfied ˌselfˈsæt.ɪs.faɪd, US -ˈsæt̬-
self-service ˌselfˈsɜː.vɪs, US -ˈsɝː-
self-starter ˌselfˈstɑː.təʳ, US -ˈstɑːr.t̬ɚ **-s** -z
self-styled ˌselfˈstaɪld
self-sufficien|cy ˌself.səˈfɪʃ.ᵊn|*t*.si **-t** -t
self-taught ˌselfˈtɔːt, US -ˈtɑːt, -ˈtɔːt
self-will ˌselfˈwɪl **-ed** -d
self-winding ˌselfˈwaɪn.dɪŋ
Selhurst ˈsel.hɜːst, US -hɝːst
Selina səˈliː.nə
Selkirk ˈsel.kɜːk, US -kɝːk
sell, S~ sel **-s** -z **-ing** -ɪŋ **sold** səʊld, US soʊld **seller/s** ˈsel.əʳ/z, US -ɚ/z
Sellafield ˈsel.ə.fiːld
Sellar ˈsel.əʳ, US -ɚ
sell-by ˈsel.baɪ **ˈsell-by ˌdate**
Sellers ˈsel.əz, US -ɚz
sellotap|e® ˈsel.əʊ.teɪp, US -oʊ- **-es** -s **-ing** -ɪŋ **-ed** -t
sellout ˈsel.aʊt **-s** -s
Selma ˈsel.mə
Selous səˈluː
Selsey ˈsel.si
Selston ˈsel.stᵊn
seltzer, S~ ˈselt.səʳ, US -sɚ **-s** -z
selva ˈsel.və **-s** -z
selvag|e, selvedg|e ˈsel.vɪdʒ **-es** -ɪz
selves (plural of **self**) selvz
Selwyn ˈsel.wɪn
Selznick ˈselz.nɪk
semantic sɪˈmæn.tɪk, sə-, semˈæn-, siːˈmæn-, US səˈmæn.t̬ɪk, sɪ- **-s** -s **-ally** -ᵊl.i, -li
semanticism sɪˈmæn.tɪ.sɪ.zᵊm, sə-, semˈæn-, siːˈmæn-, US səˈmæn.t̬ə-, sɪ-
semanticist sɪˈmæn.tɪ.sɪst, sə-, semˈæn-, siːˈmæn-, -tə-, US səˈmæn.t̬ə-, sɪ- **-s** -s
semanticiz|e, -is|e sɪˈmæn.tɪ.saɪz, sə-, semˈæn-, siːˈmæn-, -tə-, US səˈmæn.t̬ə-, sɪ- **-es** -ɪz **-ing** -ɪŋ **-ed** -d
semaphore ˈsem.ə.fɔːʳ, US -fɔːr **-s** -z **-ing** -ɪŋ **-ed** -d
semaphoric ˌsem.əˈfɒr.ɪk, US -ˈfɔːr- **-ally** -ᵊl.i, -li
semasiology sɪˌmeɪ.siˈɒl.ə.dʒi, sə-, semˌeɪ-, -ziˈ-, US sɪˌmeɪ.siˈɑː.lə-
sematology ˌsem.əˈtɒl.ə.dʒi, ˌsiː.məˈ-, US -ˈtɑː.lə-
semblanc|e ˈsem.blən*t*s **-es** -ɪz
seme siːm **-s** -z
Semele ˈsem.ɪ.li, US ˈ-ə-
sememe ˈsiː.miːm, US ˈsem.iːm **-s** -z
sememic sɪˈmiː.mɪk, sə-, US sə-, sɪ- **-s** -s
semen ˈsiː.mən, -men, US -mən
semester sɪˈmes.təʳ, sə-, US səˈmes.tɚ **-s** -z
semi *house:* ˈsem.i **-s** -z
semi- sem.i, US sem.i, -aɪ, -ə
Note: Many compounds beginning with **semi-** have the stress pattern **ˌsemiˈ-**; these are likely to undergo stress shift when a stressed syllable follows closely, especially in adjectives and adjectives derived from verbs.
semiautomatic ˌsem.i.ɔː.təˈmæt.ɪk, US -ɑː.t̬əˈmæt̬.ɪk, ˌ-aɪ-, -ɔː- **-s** -s
semiautonomous ˌsem.i.ɔːˈtɒn.ə.məs, US -ɑːˈtɑː.nə-, ˌ-aɪ-, -ɔːˈ-
semibreve ˈsem.i.briːv **-s** -z
semicircle ˈsem.iˌsɜː.kᵊl, US -ˌsɝː-, -aɪˌ- **-s** -z
semicircular ˌsem.iˈsɜː.kjə.ləʳ, -kjʊ-, US -ˈsɝː.kjə.lɚ, -aɪˈ-
semicolon ˌsem.iˈkəʊ.lən, ˈsem.iˌkəʊ-, -lɒn, US ˈsem.iˌkoʊ.lən, ˈ-aɪ- **-s** -z
semiconductivity ˌsem.iˌkɒn.dʌkˈtɪv.ə.ti, -ɪ.ti, US -iˌkɑːn.dʌkˈtɪv.ə.t̬i, -aɪˌ-
semiconduc|tor ˌsem.i.kənˈdʌk|.təʳ, US -tɚ, -aɪ- **-tors** -təz, US -tɚz **-ting** -tɪŋ
semiconscious ˌsem.iˈkɒn.*t*ʃəs, US -ˈkɑːn-, -aɪˈ- **-ness** -nəs, -nɪs
semidesert ˌsem.iˈdez.ət, US -iˈdez.ɚt, -aɪˈ- **-s** -s
semidetached ˌsem.i.dɪˈtætʃt, US ˌsem.i-, ˌ-aɪ-
semifinal ˌsem.iˈfaɪ.nᵊl, US -iˈ-, -aɪˈ- **-s** -z
semifinalist ˌsem.iˈfaɪ.nᵊl.ɪst, US -iˈ-, -aɪˈ- **-s** -s
semiformal ˌsem.iˈfɔː.mᵊl, US -iˈfɔːr-, -aɪˈ-
Sémillon ˌseɪ.miːˈjɔ̃ːŋ, US -ˈjõʊn, ˌsem.iːˈ-
seminal ˈsem.ɪ.nᵊl, ˈsiː.mɪ-, -mə-, US ˈsem.ə- **-ly** -i
seminar ˈsem.ɪ.nɑːʳ, ˈ-ə-, US -ə.nɑːr **-s** -z
seminarist ˈsem.ɪ.nᵊr.ɪst, US ˌsem.ɪˈner- **-s** -s
seminar|y ˈsem.ɪ.nᵊr|.i, US -ner- **-ies** -iz
seminiferous ˌsem.ɪˈnɪf.ᵊr.əs
Seminole ˈsem.ɪ.nəʊl, US -noʊl **-s** -z
semiolog|y ˌsem.iˈɒl.ə.dʒ|i, ˌsiː.miˈ-, US ˌsiː.miˈɑː.lə-, ˌsem.iˈ- **-ist/s** -ɪst/s
semiotic ˌsem.iˈɒt.ɪk, ˌsiː.miˈ-, US ˌsiː.miˈɑː.t̬ɪk, ˌsem.iˈ- **-s** -s
Semipalatinsk ˌsem.i.pælˈæt.ɪnsk, US -pəˈlɑː-
semiprecious ˌsem.iˈpreʃ.əs, US -iˈ-, -aɪˈ-
semiprofessional ˌsem.i.prəˈfeʃ.ᵊn.ᵊl, US -i.prəˈ-, ˌ-aɪ-, -proʊˈ-
semiquaver ˈsem.iˌkweɪ.vəʳ, US -iˌ-, -vɚ **-s** -z
Semiramide ˌsem.ɪˈrɑː.mɪ.deɪ, -ˈræm.ɪ-, ˈ-ə-, -di
Semiramis semˈɪr.ə.mɪs, sɪˈmɪr-, US sɪˈmɪr-
semiretired ˌsem.i.rɪˈtaɪəd, -ˈtaɪ.əd, US -taɪrd, ˌ-aɪ-
semiretirement ˌsem.i.rɪˈtaɪə.mənt, US -ˈtaɪr-, ˌ-aɪ-
semiskilled ˌsem.iˈskɪld, US -iˈ-, -aɪˈ-
semiskimmed ˌsem.iˈskɪmd, US -iˈ-, -aɪˈ-
Semite ˈsiː.maɪt, ˈsem.aɪt, US ˈsem.aɪt **-s** -s
Semitic sɪˈmɪt.ɪk, sə-, semˈɪt-, US səˈmɪt̬-
Semitism ˈsem.ɪ.tɪ.zᵊm, ˈ-ə-, US ˈ-ə-
semitone ˈsem.i.təʊn, US -toʊn, -aɪ- **-s** -z
semitrailer ˈsem.iˌtreɪ.ləʳ, US -lɚ, -aɪˌ- **-s** -z
semitropical ˌsem.iˈtrɒp.ɪ.kᵊl, US -ˈtrɑː.pɪ-, -aɪˈ-
semivowel ˈsem.iˌvaʊ.əl, -vaʊəl **-s** -z
semolina ˌsem.ᵊlˈiː.nə, US -əˈliː-
semology semˈɒl.ə.dʒi, siːˈmɒl-, US semˈɑː.lə-, siːˈmɑː-
Semon ˈsiː.mən
Sempill ˈsem.pᵊl
sempiternal ˌsem.pɪˈtɜː.nᵊl, US -ˈtɝː- **-ly** -i
Semple ˈsem.pᵊl
semplice ˈsem.plɪ.tʃeɪ
sempre ˈsem.preɪ
sempstress ˈsem*p*.strɪs, -strəs, US -strɪs **-es** -ɪz
Semtex® ˈsem.teks
sen sen
senary ˈsiː.nᵊr.i
senate, S~ ˈsen.ɪt, -ət, US -ɪt **-s** -s
senator, S~ ˈsen.ə.təʳ, ˈ-ɪ-, US -ə.t̬ɚ **-s** -z
senatorial ˌsen.əˈtɔː.ri.əl, US -ˈtɔːr.i- **-ly** -i
send send **-s** -z **-ing** -ɪŋ **sent** sent **sender/s** ˈsen.dəʳ/z, US -dɚ/z
Sendai ˈsen.daɪ
Sendak ˈsen.dæk
send-off ˈsend.ɒf, US -ɑːf **-s** -s
send-up ˈsend.ʌp **-s** -s
sene ˈseɪ.neɪ
Seneca ˈsen.ɪ.kə **-s** -z
Senegal ˌsen.ɪˈgɔːl, US ˌsen.ɪˈgɔːl, -ˈgɑːl; US ˈsen.ə.gᵊl
Senegalese ˌsen.ɪ.gəˈliːz, -gɔːˈ-, US -gəˈ-
Senegambia ˌsen.ɪˈgæm.bi.ə

S

senescen|ce sɪˈnes.ənts, sə-, senˈes-, (US) səˈnes- -t -t
seneschal ˈsen.ɪ.ʃəl, (US) ˈ-ə- -s -z
Senghenydd ˌseŋˈhen.ɪð
Senghor ˈseŋ.gɔːr; *as if French:* ˈsæ̃ŋ-, -ˈ-; (US) sæ̃ŋˈgɔːr
senhor, S~ senˈjɔːr, (US) -ˈjɔːr, seɪˈnjɔːr -s -z -es -z *stress shift:* **ˌSenhor Soˈares**
senhora, S~ senˈjɔː.rə, (US) -ˈjɔːr.ə, seɪˈnjɔːr- -s -z
senhorita, S~ ˌsen.jɔːˈriː.tə, -jəˈ-, (US) ˌsen.jəˈriː.t̬ə, ˌseɪ.njəˈ-, -njɔːˈ- -s -z
senile ˈsiː.naɪl, (US) ˈsiː-, ˈsen.aɪl
senility sɪˈnɪl.ə.ti, sə-, senˈɪl-, -ɪ.ti, (US) səˈnɪl.ə.t̬i
senior, S~ ˈsiː.ni.ər, -ˈnjər, (US) -njɚ -s -z **ˌsenior ˈcitizen**
seniorit|y ˌsiː.niˈɒr.ə.t|i, -ɪ.t|i, (US) siːˈnjɔːr.ə.t̬|i -ies -iz
Senlac ˈsen.læk
senna, S~ ˈsen.ə
Sennacherib senˈæk.ə.rɪb, sɪˈnæk-, sə-, (US) səˈnæk.ɚ.ɪb
sennet ˈsen.ɪt, -ət, (US) -ɪt
sennight ˈsen.aɪt, (US) -aɪt, -ɪt -s -s
señor, senor, S~ senˈjɔːr, (US) -ˈjɔːr, seɪˈnjɔːr -s -z *stress shift:* **ˌSeñor ˈLopez**
señora, senora, S~ senˈjɔː.rə, (US) -ˈjɔːr.ə, seɪˈnjɔːr- -s -z
señorita, senorita, S~ ˌsen.jɔːˈriː.tə, -jəˈ-, (US) ˌsen.jəˈriː.t̬ə, ˌseɪ.njəˈ-, -njɔːˈ- *stress shift:* **ˌSeñorita ˈLopez**
sensate ˈsen.seɪt, (US) -seɪt, -sɪt -ly -li
sensation senˈseɪ.ʃən, sən-, (US) sen- -s -z
sensational senˈseɪ.ʃən.əl, sən-, -ˈseɪʃ.nəl, (US) sen- -ly -i
sensational|ism senˈseɪ.ʃən.əl|.ɪ.zəm, sən-, -ˈseɪʃ.nəl-, (US) sen- -ist/s -ɪst/s
sensationaliz|e, -is|e ˌsenˈseɪ.ʃən.əl.aɪz -es -ɪz -ing -ɪŋ -ed -d
sens|e sents -es -ɪz -ing -ɪŋ -ed -d **ˌsense of ˈhumo(u)r**
senseless ˈsent.sləs, -slɪs -ly -li -ness -nəs, -nɪs
sensibilit|y ˌsent.səˈbɪl.ə.t|i, -sɪˈ-, -ɪ.t|i, (US) -səˈbɪl.ə.t̬|i -ies -iz
sensib|le ˈsent.sə.b|əl, -sɪ-, (US) -sə- -ly -li
sensitive ˈsent.sɪ.tɪv, -sə-, (US) -sə.t̬ɪv -s -z -ly -li -ness -nəs, -nɪs
sensitivit|y ˌsent.sɪˈtɪv.ə.t|i, -səˈ-, -ɪ.t|i, (US) -səˈtɪv.ə.t̬|i -ies -iz
sensitization, -isa- ˌsent.sɪ.taɪˈzeɪ.ʃən, -sə-, -tɪˈ-, (US) -sə.t̬əˈ-
sensitiz|e, -is|e ˈsent.sɪ.taɪz, -sə-, (US) -sə- -es -ɪz -ing -ɪŋ -ed -d
Sensodyne® ˈsent.səʊ.daɪn, (US) -soʊ-, -sə-
sensor ˈsent.sər, (US) -sɚ -s -z
sensorial sentˈsɔː.ri.əl, (US) -ˈsɔːr.i- -ly -i
sensor|y ˈsent.sər|.i -ily -əl.i, -ɪ.li
sensual ˈsent.sjʊəl, -sju.əl, -ʃʊəl, -ʃu.əl, (US) -ʃu.əl -ly -i -ness -nəs, -nɪs
sensual|ism ˈsent.sjʊə.l|ɪ.zəm, -sju.əl|.ɪ-, -ʃʊə.l|ɪ-, -ʃu.əl|.ɪ-, (US) -ʃu.ə.l|ɪ- -ist/s -ɪst/s
sensuality ˌsent.sjuˈæl.ə.ti, -ʃuˈ-, -ɪ.ti, (US) -ʃuˈæl.ə.t̬i
sensuous ˈsent.sjʊəs, -sju.əs, -ʃʊəs, -ʃu.əs, (US) -ʃu.əs -ly -li -ness -nəs, -nɪs
Sensurround® ˈsent.sə.raʊnd
sent (from **send**) sent
sentenc|e ˈsen.tənts, (US) -t̬ənts, -tənts -es -ɪz -ing -ɪŋ -ed -t
sentential senˈten.tʃəl, sən-, (US) senˈtent.ʃəl -ly -li
sententious senˈten.tʃəs, sən-, (US) senˈtent.ʃəs -ly -li -ness -nəs, -nɪs
sentience ˈsen.tʃənts, -tʃi.ənts, (US) ˈsent.ʃənts, -ʃi.ənts
sentient ˈsen.tʃənt, -tʃi.ənt, (US) ˈsent.ʃənt, -ʃi.ənt -ly -li
sentiment ˈsen.tɪ.mənt, -tə-, (US) -t̬ə- -s -s
sentimental ˌsen.tɪˈmen.təl, -təˈ-, (US) -t̬əˈmen.t̬əl -ly -i -ism -ɪ.zəm -ist/s -ɪst/s
sentimentality ˌsen.tɪ.menˈtæl.ə.ti, -tə-, -mən-, -ɪ.ti, (US) -t̬ə.menˈtæl.ə.t̬i
sentimentalization, -isa- ˌsen.tɪ.men.təl.aɪˈzeɪ.ʃən, -ˌmen-, -tə-, -ɪˈ-, (US) -t̬əˌmen.t̬əl.əˈ-
sentimentaliz|e, -is|e ˌsen.tɪˈmen.təl.aɪz, -təˈ-, (US) -t̬əˈmen.t̬ə.laɪz -es -ɪz -ing -ɪŋ -ed -d
sentinel ˈsen.tɪ.nəl, -tə-, (US) -t̬ɪ-, -tən.əl -s -z
sentr|y ˈsen.tr|i -ies -iz **ˈsentry ˌbox**
sentry-go ˈsen.tri.gəʊ, (US) -goʊ
senza ˈsent.sə
Seoul səʊl, (US) soʊl
sepal ˈsep.əl, ˈsiː.pəl, (US) ˈsiː.pəl -s -z
separability ˌsep.ər.əˈbɪl.ə.ti, -ɪ.ti, (US) -ə.t̬i
separab|le ˈsep.ər.ə.b|əl -ly -li -leness -əl.nəs, -əl.nɪs
separate adj ˈsep.ər.ət, -ɪt, ˈ-rət, -rɪt, (US) -ɚ.ɪt, ˈ-rɪt -ly -li -ness -nəs, -nɪs
separ|ate v ˈsep.ər|.eɪt, (US) -ə.r|eɪt -ates -eɪts -ating -eɪ.tɪŋ, (US) -eɪ.t̬ɪŋ -ated -eɪ.tɪd, (US) -eɪ.t̬ɪd -ator/s -eɪ.tər/z, (US) -eɪ.t̬ɚ/z
separates ˈsep.ər.əts, -ɪts, ˈ-rəts, ˈ-rɪts, (US) -ɚ.ɪts, ˈ-rɪts
separation ˌsep.ərˈeɪ.ʃən, (US) -əˈreɪ- -s -z
separat|ism ˈsep.ər.ə.t|ɪ.zəm, ˈ-rə- -ist/s -ɪst/s
Sephardi səˈfɑː.di, sefˈɑː-, (US) səˈfɑːr.di; (US) -ˌfɑːrˈdiː **Sephardim** səˈfɑː.dɪm, sefˈɑː-, (US) səˈfɑːr.dɪm; (US) -ˌfɑːrˈdiːm
Sephardic səˈfɑː.dɪk, sefˈɑː-, (US) səˈfɑːr-
sepia ˈsiː.pi.ə
sepoy ˈsiː.pɔɪ -s -z
seppuku sepˈuː.kuː
seps|is ˈsep.s|ɪs -es -iːz
Sept. (abbrev. for **September**) sepˈtem.bər, səp-, sɪp-, (US) sepˈtem.bɚ
September sepˈtem.bər, səp-, sɪp-, (US) sepˈtem.bɚ -s -z
Septembrist sepˈtem.brɪst, səp-, sɪp-, (US) sep- -s -s
septennial sepˈten.i.əl
septet, septette sepˈtet -s -s
septic ˈsep.tɪk **ˌseptic ˈtank; ˈseptic ˌtank** (US) **ˈseptic ˌtank**
septic(a)emia ˌsep.tɪˈsiː.mi.ə, (US) -təˈ-
septillion sepˈtɪl.jən -s -z
Septimus ˈsep.tɪ.məs
septuagenarian ˌsep.tʃʊə.dʒɪˈneə.ri.ən, -tjʊə-, -dʒəˈ-, (US) -tu.ə.dʒəˈner.i-, -tju- -s -z
Septuagesima ˌsep.tʃʊəˈdʒes.ɪ.mə, -tjʊəˈ-, ˈ-ə-, (US) -tu.əˈdʒes.ɪ-, -tju-, -ˈdʒeɪ.zɪ-
Septuagint ˈsep.tʃʊə.dʒɪnt, -tjʊə-, (US) -tu.ə-, -tju-
sept|um ˈsep.t|əm -ums -əmz -a -ə
septuple ˈsep.tʃʊ.pəl, ˈ-tjʊ-, ˈ-tʃə-, ˈ-tjə-, sepˈtjuː-, (US) sepˈtʌp.əl; (US) ˈtuː.pəl, -ˈtjuː-
septuplet ˈsep.tʃʊ.plət, ˈ-tjʊ-, -plɪt-, -plet, ˈ-tʃə-, ˈ-tjə-, sepˈtʃuː.plət, -ˈtjuː-, (US) -ˈtuː-, -ˈtjuː- -s -s
sepulcher ˈsep.əl.kə, (US) -kɚ -s -z
sepulchral sɪˈpʌl.krəl, sə-, sepˈʌl-, (US) səˈpʌl- -ly -i
sepulchre ˈsep.əl.kər, (US) -kɚ -s -z
sepulture ˈsep.əl.tʃər, -ˌtjʊər, (US) -tʃɚ
sequel ˈsiː.kwəl -s -z
sequel|a sɪˈkwiː.l|ə, sə-, (US) sɪˈkwiː-, -ˈkwel|.ə -ae -iː
sequenc|e ˈsiː.kwənts, (US) -kwənts, -kwents -es -ɪz -ing -ɪŋ -ed -t
sequential sɪˈkwen.tʃəl, (US) -ˈkwent.ʃəl -ly -i
sequest|er sɪˈkwes.t|ər, sə-, (US) sɪˈkwes.t|ɚ -ers -əz, (US) -ɚz -ering -ər.ɪŋ -ered -əd, (US) -ɚd
seques|trate ˈsiː.kwə.s|treɪt, sɪˈkwes|.treɪt, sə-; (US) sɪˈkwes.|treɪt, ˈsiːk-, ˈsek.wə.s|treɪt -trates -treɪts -trating -treɪ.tɪŋ, (US) -treɪ.t̬ɪŋ -trated -treɪ.tɪd, (US) -treɪ.t̬ɪd
sequestration ˌsiː.kwesˈtreɪ.ʃən, ˌsek.wesˈ-, -wəˈstreɪ-, -wɪˈ-, (US) ˌsiː.kwəˈstreɪ-, ˌsek.wəˈ-; (US) sɪˌkwesˈtreɪ- -s -z
sequin ˈsiː.kwɪn -s -z -(n)ed -d
sequoia sɪˈkwɔɪ.ə, sekˈwɔɪ.ə, (US) sɪˈkwɔɪ.ə -s -z
seraglio serˈɑː.li.əʊ, sɪˈrɑː-, sə-, -ˈɑːl.jəʊ, (US) sɪˈræl.joʊ, -ˈrɑːl- -s -z
serai serˈaɪ, səˈraɪ, (US) sɪˈreɪ.i, sə- -s -z
seraph, S~ ˈser.əf -s -s -im -ɪm
seraphic serˈæf.ɪk, sɪˈræf-, sə-, (US) səˈræf- -al -əl -ally -əl.i, -li
Serapis ˈser.ə.pɪs, səˈreɪ-
Serb sɜːb, (US) sɝːb -s -z
Serbi|a ˈsɜː.bi|.ə, (US) ˈsɝː- -an/s -ən/z

Serbo-Croat ˌsɜː.bəʊˈkrəʊ.æt, (US) ˌsɝː.boʊˈkroʊ- -s -s
Serbo-Croatian ˌsɜː.bəʊ.krəʊˈeɪ.ʃən, (US) ˌsɝː.boʊ.kroʊˈ- -s -z
sere sɪəʳ, (US) sɪr -s -z
Serena səˈriː.nə, sɪ-, -ˈreɪ-, (US) səˈriː-
serenad|e ˌser.əˈneɪd, -ɪˈ-, (US) -əˈ- -es -z -ing -ɪŋ -ed -ɪd
serenata ˌser.ɪˈnɑː.tə, -əˈ-, (US) -əˈnɑː.t̬ə -s -z
serendipit|y ˌser.ənˈdɪp.ə.t|i, -enˈ-, -ɪ.t|i, (US) -ənˈdɪp.ə.t̬|i -ous -əs
seren|e sɪˈriːn, sə-, (US) sə- -est -ɪst, -əst -ely -li
Serengeti ˌser.ənˈget.i, -əŋˈ-, -ɪnˈ-, -ɪŋˈ-, (US) -ənˈget̬-
serenity sɪˈren.ɪ.ti, sə-, -ə.ti, (US) səˈren.ə.t̬i
serf sɜːf, (US) sɝːf -s -s -dom -dəm
serg|e, S~ sɜːdʒ, (US) sɝːdʒ -es -ɪz
sergeant, S~ ˈsɑː.dʒənt, (US) ˈsɑːr- -s -s ˌ**sergeant** ˈ**major**
sergeant-at-arms, (S A) ˌsɑː.dʒənt.ətˈɑːmz, (US) ˌsɑːr.dʒənt̬.ət̬ˈɑːrmz **sergeants-at-arms** ˌsɑː.dʒənts-, (US) ˌsɑːr.dʒənts-
Sergei ˈseə.geɪ, ˈsɜː-, -ˈ-, (US) ˈser.geɪ, ˈsɝː-
serial ˈsɪə.ri.əl, (US) ˈsɪr.i- -s -z ˈ**serial** ˌ**killer;** ˈ**serial** ˌ**number**
serialization, -isa- ˌsɪə.ri.əl.aɪˈzeɪ.ʃən, -ɪˈ-, (US) ˌsɪr.i.əl.əˈ- -s -z
serializ|e, -is|e ˈsɪə.ri.əl.aɪz, (US) ˈsɪr.i.ə.laɪz -es -ɪz -ing -ɪŋ -ed -d
seriatim ˌsɪə.riˈeɪ.tɪm, ˌser.iˈ-, -ˈɑː-, (US) ˌsɪr.iˈeɪ.t̬ɪm
series ˈsɪə.riːz, -rɪz, (US) ˈsɪr.iːz, ˈsiː.riːz
serif ˈser.ɪf -s -s
Serifos ˈser.ɪ.fɒs, (US) səˈraɪ.fəs; (US) ˈser.ɪ.fɑːs
serin ˈser.ɪn -s -z
seringa sɪˈrɪŋ.gə, sə-, (US) sə- -s -z
Seringapatam səˌrɪŋ.gə.pəˈtɑːm, sɪ-, -ˈtæm
seriocomic ˌsɪə.ri.əʊˈkɒm.ɪk, (US) ˌsɪr.i.oʊˈkɑː.mɪk -ally -əl.i, -li
serious ˈsɪə.ri.əs, (US) ˈsɪr.i- -ly -li -ness -nəs, -nɪs
serjeant, S~ ˈsɑː.dʒənt, (US) ˈsɑːr- -s -s ˌ**serjeant-at-**ˈ**arms**
Serjeantson ˈsɑː.dʒənt.sən, (US) ˈsɑːr-
sermon ˈsɜː.mən, (US) ˈsɝː- -s -z
sermonette ˌsɜː.məˈnet, (US) ˌsɝː- -s -s
sermoniz|e, -is|e ˈsɜː.mə.naɪz, (US) ˈsɝː- -es -ɪz -ing -ɪŋ -ed -d
serolog|y sɪˈrɒl.ə.dʒ|i, sɪə-, (US) sɪˈrɑː.lə- -ist/s -ɪst/s
seronegative ˌsɪə.rəʊˈneg.ə.tɪv, (US) ˌsɪr.oʊˈneg.ə.t̬ɪv
seropositive ˌsɪə.rəʊˈpɒz.ɪ.tɪv, ˈ-ə-, (US) ˌsɪr.oʊˈpɑː.zə.t̬ɪv
Serota səˈrəʊ.tə, sɪ-, (US) -ˈroʊ.t̬ə
serotonin ˌser.əˈtəʊ.nɪn, ˌsɪə.rəˈ-, (US) ˌser.əˈtoʊ-, ˌsɪr-
serous ˈsɪə.rəs, (US) ˈsɪr.əs
Serpell ˈsɜː.pəl, (US) ˈsɝː-
Serpens ˈsɜː.penz, -pənz, (US) ˈsɝː-
serpent ˈsɜː.pənt, (US) ˈsɝː- -s -s
serpentine, S~ ˈsɜː.pən.taɪn, (US) ˈsɝː-
SERPS, Serps sɜːps, (US) sɝːps
serrate ˈser.ɪt, -eɪt, -ət, (US) -eɪt, -ɪt
serrated sɪˈreɪ.tɪd, sə-, serˈeɪ-, (US) ˈser.eɪ.t̬ɪd
serration sɪˈreɪ.ʃən, sə-, serˈeɪ-, (US) səˈreɪ-, serˈeɪ- -s -z
serried ˈser.id ˌ**serried** ˈ**ranks**
ser|um ˈsɪə.r|əm, (US) ˈsɪr|.əm -ums -əmz -a -ə
servant ˈsɜː.vənt, (US) ˈsɝː- -s -s
serv|e sɜːv, (US) sɝːv -es -z -ing -ɪŋ -ed -d -er/s -əʳ/z, (US) -ɚ/z
server|y ˈsɜː.vər|.i, (US) ˈsɝː- -ies -iz
servic|e, S~ ˈsɜː.vɪs, (US) ˈsɝː- -es -ɪz -ing -ɪŋ -ed -t ˈ**service** ˌ**charge;** ˈ**service** ˌ**station**
serviceability ˌsɜː.vɪ.səˈbɪl.ə.ti, -ɪ.ti, (US) ˌsɝː.vɪ.səˈbɪl.ə.t̬i
serviceab|le ˈsɜː.vɪ.sə.b|əl, (US) ˈsɝː- -ly -li -leness -əl.nəs, -əl.nɪs
service|man ˈsɜː.vɪs|.mən, -mæn, (US) ˈsɝː- -men -mən
service|woman ˈsɜː.vɪs|ˌwʊm.ən, (US) ˈsɝː- -women -wɪm.ɪn
serviette ˌsɜː.viˈet, -s, (US) ˌsɝː- -s -s
servile ˈsɜː.vaɪl, (US) ˈsɝː.vəl, -vaɪl -ly -li
servility sɜːˈvɪl.ə.ti, -ɪ.ti, (US) sɝːˈvɪl.ə.t̬i
serving ˈsɜː.vɪŋ, (US) ˈsɝː- -s -z
serving-spoon ˈsɜː.vɪŋ.spuːn, (US) ˈsɝː- -s -z
servitor ˈsɜː.vɪ.təʳ, (US) ˈsɝː.və.t̬ɚ -s -z
servitude ˈsɜː.vɪ.tʃuːd, -tjuːd, (US) ˈsɝː.və.tuːd, -tjuːd
servo ˈsɜː.vəʊ, (US) ˈsɝː.voʊ -s -z
servomechanism ˈsɜː.vəʊˌmek.ə.nɪ.zəm, ˌsɜː.vəʊˈmek-, (US) ˌsɝː.voʊˈmek- -s -z
servomotor ˈsɜː.vəʊˌməʊ.təʳ, (US) ˈsɝː.voʊˌmoʊ.t̬ɚ -s -z
sesame, S~ ˈses.ə.mi -s -z ˈ**sesame** ˌ**seed**
Sesotho sesˈuː.tuː, sɪˈsuː-, sə-, -ˈsəʊ.θəʊ, (US) sesˈuː.tuː, sɪˈsuː-, sə-, -ˈsoʊ.θoʊ
sesqui- ˈses.kwɪ
sesquicentennial ˌses.kwɪ.senˈten.i.əl, -sənˈ-, (US) -senˈ-
sesquipedalian ˌses.kwɪ.pɪˈdeɪ.li.ən, -pəˈ-, -pedˈeɪ-, (US) -pəˈdeɪ-, -ˈdeɪl.jən
sessile ˈses.aɪl, (US) -ɪl, -aɪl
session ˈseʃ.ən -s -z
sessional ˈseʃ.ən.əl -s -z
sesterc|e ˈses.tɜːs, -təs, (US) -tɝːs -es -ɪz
sesterti|um sesˈtɜː.ti|.əm, -ʃi-, (US) -ˈtɝː.ʃi-, ˈ-ʃ|əm -a -ə
sestet sesˈtet, (US) sesˈtet, ˈ-- -s -s
set set -s -s -ting -ɪŋ, (US) ˈset̬.ɪŋ ˌ**set** ˈ**book;** ˌ**set** ˈ**piece** (US) ˈ**set** ˌ**piece;** ˌ**set** ˈ**point** (US) ˈ**set** ˌ**point**
setaceous sɪˈteɪ.ʃəs, sə-, (US) sɪ- -ly -li
setback ˈset.bæk -s -s
Setchell ˈsetʃ.əl
Setebos ˈset.ɪ.bɒs, (US) ˈset̬.ə.bɑːs
Seth seθ
set-off ˈset.ɒf, (US) -ɑːf -s -s
seton, S~ ˈsiː.tən -s -z
setsquare ˈset.skweəʳ, (US) -skwer -s -z
sett set -s -s
settee setˈiː -s -z
setter, S~ ˈset.əʳ, (US) ˈset̬.ɚ -s -z
setting ˈset.ɪŋ, (US) ˈset̬.ɪŋ -s -z
settl|e, S~ ˈset.əl, (US) ˈset̬- -es -z -ing -ɪn, ˈset.lɪŋ -ed -d
settlement ˈset.əl.mənt, (US) ˈset̬- -s -s
settler ˈset.əl.əʳ, ˈ-ləʳ, (US) ˈset.lɚ, ˈset̬.əl.ɚ -s -z
set-to ˈset.tuː
Setúbal səˈtuː.bəl, setˈuː-
setup ˈset.ʌp, (US) ˈset̬- -s -s
Seurat ˈsɜː.rɑː, -ˈ-, (US) sɝːˈrɑː
Seuss sjuːs, (US) suːs
Sevastopol səˈvæst.ə.pɒl, (US) -poʊl
Seve ˈsev.i
seven ˈsev.ən -s -z -fold -fəʊld, (US) -foʊld ˌ**seven** ˈ**seas**
sevenish ˈsev.ən.ɪʃ
Sevenoaks ˈsev.ən.əʊks, (US) -oʊks
seven|pence ˈsev.ən|.pənts, -əm-, (US) -ən- -penny -pən.i
Note: See note under **penny**.
seventeen ˌsev.ənˈtiːn -s -z -th/s -tθ/s
seventh ˈsev.əntθ -s -s -ly -li ˌ**seventh** ˈ**heaven**
sevent|y ˈsev.ən.t|i, (US) -t̬|i -ies -iz -ieth/s -i.əθ/s, -i.ɪθ/s
seventy-eight, 78 ˌsev.ən.tiˈeɪt, (US) -t̬iˈ- -s -s
sev|er ˈsev|.əʳ, (US) -ɚ -ers -əz, (US) -ɚz -ering -ər.ɪŋ -ered -əd, (US) -ɚd
several ˈsev.ər.əl, ˈ-rəl -ly -i
severalty ˈsev.ər.əl.ti, ˈ-rəl-
severance ˈsev.ər.ənts ˈ**severance** ˌ**pay**
sever|e sɪˈvɪəʳ, sə-, (US) səˈvɪr -er -əʳ, (US) -ɚ -est -ɪst, -əst -ely -li -eness -nəs, -nɪs
severit|y sɪˈver.ə.t|i, sə-, -ɪ.t|i, (US) səˈver.ə.t̬|i -ies -iz
Severn ˈsev.ən, (US) -ɚn
Severus sɪˈvɪə.rəs, sə-, (US) səˈvɪr.əs
seviche səvˈiː.tʃeɪ
Sevier ˈsev.i.əʳ, (US) -ɚ; (US) səˈvɪr
Seville səˈvɪl, sɪ-, sevˈɪl; ˈsev.ɪl, -əl; *stress shift, see compound:* (US) səˈvɪl ˌ**Seville** ˈ**orange**
Sèvres ˈseɪ.vrə, -vəʳ, (US) -vrə
sew səʊ, (US) soʊ -s -z -ing -ɪŋ -ed -d -n -n
sewage ˈsuː.ɪdʒ, ˈsjuː-, (US) ˈsuː-
Sewanee səˈwɒn.i, (US) -ˈwɑː.ni, -ˈwɔː-
Seward ˈsiː.wəd, (US) ˈsuː.ɚd; (US) ˈsiː.wɚd
Sewell ˈsjuː.əl, sjʊəl, (US) ˈsuː.əl
sewer *one who sews:* ˈsəʊ.əʳ, (US)

Pronouncing the letters SH

The consonant digraph **sh** is most commonly pronounced /ʃ/, e.g.:

sheep ʃiːp

In addition

When the two letters come together as a result of the addition of a prefix, the pronunciation is /s.h/, or /s/ alone with a silent **h**, e.g.:

mishap ˈmɪs.hæp

dishonest dɪsˈɒn.ɪst US -ˈɑː.nɪst

ˈsoʊ.ɚ *drain:* sʊəʳ, sjʊəʳ, US ˈsuː.ɚ -s -z

sewerage ˈsʊə.rɪdʒ, ˈsjʊə-, US ˈsuː.ɚ.ɪdʒ

sewing ˈsəʊ.ɪŋ, US ˈsoʊ- ˈ**sewing maˌchine**

sewn (from **sew**) səʊn, US soʊn

sex seks -es -ɪz -ing -ɪŋ -ed -t ˈ**sex apˌpeal;** ˈ**sex ˌchange;** ˈ**sex ˌkitten;** ˈ**sex ˌobject**

sexagenarian ˌsek.sə.dʒɪˈneə.ri.ən, -dʒəˈ-, US -dʒɪˈner.i- -s -z

Sexagesi|ma ˌsek.səˈdʒes.ɪ|.mə, US -ˈdʒes.ɪ|.mə, -ˈdʒeɪ.zɪ-

sexagesimal ˌsek.səˈdʒes.ɪ.məl, ˈ-ə-

sex|ism ˈsek.s|ɪ.zəm -ist/s -ɪst/s

sexless ˈsek.sləs, -slɪs -ness -nəs, -nɪs

sexolog|y sekˈsɒl.ə.dʒ|i, US -ˈsɑː.lə- -ist/s -ɪst/s

sexploitation ˌsek.splɔɪˈteɪ.ʃən

sexpot ˈseks.pɒt, US -pɑːt -s -s

sext sekst -s -s -ing -ɪŋ -ed -ɪd

sextant ˈsek.stənt -s -s

sextet, sextette sekˈstet -s -s

sextillion sekˈstɪl.jən, -i.ən, US ˈ-jən -s -z

sexto ˈsek.stəʊ, US -stoʊ -s -z

sexton, S~ ˈsek.stən -s -z

sextuple ˈseks.tʃʊ.pəl, ˈsek.stjʊ-, ˈseks.tʃə-, ˈsek.stjə-; seksˈtʃuː-, sekˈstjuː-, US sekˈstuː-, -ˈstjuː-; US ˈsek.stə.pəl

sextuplet ˈseks.tʃʊ.plət, ˈsek.stjʊ-; -plɪt, -plet, seksˈtʃuː-, seksˈtjuː, US sekˈstʌp.lɪt, -ˈstuː.plɪt, -ˈstjuː-; US ˈsek.stə- -s -s

sexual ˈsek.ʃʊəl, -ʃu.əl, -sjʊəl, -sju.əl, US -ʃu.əl -ly -i ˌ**sexual** ˈ**intercourse;** ˌ**sexual reˈlations;** ˌ**sexual reproˈduction**

sexuality ˌsek.ʃuˈæl.ə.ti, -sjuˈ-, -ɪ.ti, US -ʃuˈæl.ə.t̬i

sex|y ˈsek.s|i -ier -i.əʳ, US -i.ɚ -iest -i.ɪst, -i.əst -ily -əl.i, -ɪ.li -iness -ɪ.nəs, -ɪ.nɪs

Sey seɪ

Seychelles seɪˈʃelz, ˈ--, US seɪˈʃelz, -ˈʃel

Seymour ˈsiː.mɔːʳ, ˈseɪ-, -məʳ, US -mɔːr

> Note: /ˈseɪ-/ chiefly in families of Scottish origin.

Sfax sfæks, US sfɑːks

sforzando sfɔːtˈsæn.dəʊ, US sfɔːrtˈsɑːn.doʊ

sgian-dhu ˌskiː.ənˈduː, ˌskɪənˈ-, US ˌskiː.ənˈ- -s -z

sgraffit|o sgræfˈiː.t|əʊ, US skræfˈiː.t|oʊ, zgrɑːˈfiː- -i -i

Sgt. (abbrev. for **Sergeant**) ˈsɑː.dʒənt, US ˈsɑːr-

sh, shh, ssh ʃ

> Note: Used to command silence.

Shabbat ʃəˈbæt

shabb|y ˈʃæb|.i -ier -i.əʳ, US -i.ɚ -iest -i.ɪst, -i.əst -ily -əl.i, -ɪ.li -iness -ɪ.nəs, -ɪ.nɪs

Shabuoth ˈʃæb.u.ɒt, US ˌʃɑː.vuːˈɑːt; US ʃəˈvuː.oʊt, -oʊθ

shack ʃæk -s -s

shackl|e, S~ ˈʃæk.əl -es -z -ing -ɪŋ, ˈʃæk.lɪŋ -ed -d

Shackleton ˈʃæk.əl.tən

shad ʃæd -s -z

Shadbolt ˈʃæd.bəʊlt, US -boʊlt

shaddock, S~ ˈʃæd.ək

shad|e ʃeɪd -es -z -ing -ɪŋ -ed -ɪd

shadoof ʃædˈuːf, ʃəˈduːf, US ʃɑːˈduːf -s -s

shadow ˈʃæd.əʊ, US -oʊ -s -z -ing -ɪŋ -ed -d -y -i -iness -ɪ.nəs, -ɪ.nɪs

shadowbox ˈʃæd.əʊ.bɒks, US -oʊ.bɑːks -es -ɪz -ing -ɪŋ -ed -t

shadowless ˈʃæd.əʊ.ləs, -lɪs, US -oʊ-

Shadrach, Shadrak ˈʃæd.ræk

> Note: Some Jews pronounce /-rɑːx/.

Shadwell ˈʃæd.wel, -wəl

shad|y ˈʃeɪ.d|i -ier -i.əʳ, US -i.ɚ -iest -i.ɪst, -i.əst -ily -əl.i, -ɪ.li -iness -ɪ.nəs, -ɪ.nɪs

Shaffer ˈʃæf.əʳ, US ˈʃeɪ.fɚ, ˈʃæf.ɚ

shaft ʃɑːft, US ʃæft -s -s -ing -ɪŋ -ed -ɪd

Shaftesbury ˈʃɑːfts.bər.i, US ˈʃæftsˌber-, ˈʃɑːfts-, -bɚ-

shag ʃæg -s -z -ging -ɪŋ -ged -d

shagg|y ˈʃæg|.i -ier -i.əʳ, US -i.ɚ -iest -i.ɪst, -i.əst -ily -əl.i, -ɪ.li -iness -ɪ.nəs, -ɪ.nɪs ˌ**shaggy** ˈ**dog ˌstory**

shagreen ʃægˈriːn, ʃəˈgriːn, US ʃəˈgriːn

shah, S~ ʃɑː -s -z

Shairp ʃeəp, ʃɑːp, US ʃerp, ʃɑːrp

shak|e ʃeɪk -es -s -ing -ɪŋ **shook** ʃʊk **shaken** ˈʃeɪ.kən

shakedown ˈʃeɪk.daʊn -s -z

shaken (from **shake**) ˈʃeɪ.kən

shakeout ˈʃeɪk.aʊt -s -s

shaker, S~ ˈʃeɪ.kəʳ, US -kɚ -s -z -ism -ɪ.zəm

Shakespear(e) ˈʃeɪk.spɪəʳ, US -spɪr

Shakespearean ˌʃeɪkˈspɪə.ri.ən, US -ˈspɪr.i- -s -z

Shakespeareana ʃeɪkˌspɪə.riˈɑː.nə, ˌʃeɪk-, US ˌʃeɪk.spɪr.i.æn.ə, -ˈɑː.nə

Shakespearian ʃeɪkˈspɪə.ri.ən, US -ˈspɪr.i- -s -z

Shakespeariana ʃeɪkˌspɪə.riˈɑː.nə, ˌʃeɪk.spɪə-, US ˌʃeɪk.spɪr.iˈæn.ə, -ˈɑː.nə

shake-up ˈʃeɪk.ʌp -s -s

shako ˈʃæk.əʊ, ˈʃeɪ.kəʊ, ˈʃɑː-, US ˈʃæk.oʊ, ˈʃeɪ.koʊ, ˈʃɑː- -(e)s -z

Shakur ʃəˈkʊəʳ, ʃækˈʊəʳ, US ʃəˈkʊr, ʃækˈʊr

shak|y ˈʃeɪ.k|i -ier -i.əʳ, US -i.ɚ -iest -i.ɪst, -i.əst -ily -əl.i, -ɪ.li -iness -ɪ.nəs, -ɪ.nɪs

shale ʃeɪl

shall *strong form:* ʃæl; *weak form:* ʃəl
Note: Weak-form word. The strong form is used for strong insistence or prediction (e.g. 'You **shall** go to the ball, Cinderella'), and in final position (e.g. 'And so you **shall**'). The weak form is used elsewhere (e.g. 'What shall we do today?' /ˌwɒt.ʃəl.wiˌduː.təˈdeɪ/ US /ˌwɑːt-/). American English uses 'shall' much less frequently than British English.

shallop ˈʃæl.əp -s -s

shallot, S~ ʃəˈlɒt, US -ˈlɑːt; US ˈʃæl.ət -s -s

shallow, S~ ˈʃæl.əʊ, US -oʊ -s -z -er -əʳ, US -ɚ -est -ɪst, -əst -ly -li -ness -nəs, -nɪs

shalom ʃælˈɒm, ʃəˈlɒm, -ˈləʊm, US ʃɑːˈloʊm, ʃə-

shalt (from **shall**) *strong form:* ʃælt; *weak form:* ʃəlt

shall|y ˈʃeɪ.l|i -iness -ɪ.nəs, -ɪ.nɪs

sham ʃæm -s -z -ming -ɪŋ -med -d -mer/s -əʳ/z, US -ɚ/z

shaman ˈʃeɪm.ən, ˈʃæ.mən, ˈʃɑː-, US ˈʃɑː.mən, ˈʃeɪ-, ˈʃæm.ən -s -z -ist/s -ɪst/s -ism -ɪ.zəm

shamateur ˌʃæm.əˈtɜːʳ, US -ˈtɝː -s -z -ism -ɪ.zəm

shambl|e ˈʃæm.bəl -es -z -ing -ɪŋ, ˈ-blɪŋ -ed -d

shambles **n** ˈʃæm.bəlz

shambolic ʃæmˈbɒl.ɪk, US -ˈbɑː.lɪk

sham|e ʃeɪm -es -z -ing -ɪŋ -ed -d

shamefaced ˌʃeɪmˈfeɪst, US ˈ-- *stress shift, British only:* ˌ**shamefaced** ˈ**person**

shamefaced|ness ˌʃeɪmˈfeɪst|.nəs, -ˈfeɪ.sɪd-, -nɪs, US ˈʃeɪm.feɪst-; US ˌʃeɪmˈfeɪ.sɪd- -ly -li

shameful ˈʃeɪm.fəl, -fʊl **-ly** -i **-ness** -nəs, -nɪs
shameless ˈʃeɪm.ləs, -lɪs **-ly** -li **-ness** -nəs, -nɪs **ˌshameless ˈhussy**
Shamir ʃæmˈɪəʳ, ʃəˈmɪəʳ, (US) ʃəˈmɪr, ʃæmˈɪr
shamm|y ˈʃæm.i **-ies** -iz
shampoo ʃæmˈpuː **-(e)s** -z **-ing** -ɪŋ **-ed** -d
shamrock, S~ ˈʃæm.rɒk, (US) -rɑːk
Shan ʃɑːn, (US) ʃɑːn, ʃæn
Shana ˈʃɑː.nə, (US) ˈʃeɪ-, ˈʃɑː-
shand|y, S~ ˈʃæn.d|i **-ies** -iz
Shane ʃɑːn, ʃɔːn, ʃeɪn, (US) ʃeɪn
shanghai v ˌʃæŋˈhaɪ, (US) ˈʃæŋ.haɪ, -ˈ- **-s** -z **-ing** -ɪŋ **-ed** -d *stress shift, British only:* **ˌShanghai ˈtrader**
Shanghai ˌʃæŋˈhaɪ, (US) ˌʃæŋ-, ˌʃɑːŋ-, ˈ--
Shangri-la ˌʃæŋ.griˈlɑː
shank ʃæŋk **-s** -s **ˌshank's ˈpony; ˌshanks's ˈpony**
Shankill ˈʃæŋ.kɪl
Shanklin ˈʃæŋ.klɪn
Shanks ʃæŋks
Shanna ˈʃæn.ə
Shannon ˈʃæn.ən
shan't (= **shall not**) ʃɑːnt, (US) ʃænt
shantung *silk material:* ˌʃænˈtʌŋ
Shantung ˌʃænˈdʌŋ, -tʌŋ, -dʊŋ, -tʊŋ, (US) ˌʃænˈ-, ˌʃɑːnˈ-
shan't've (= **shall not have**) ˈʃɑːnt.əv, (US) ˈʃænt.əv
shant|y ˈʃæn.t|i, (US) -ţ|i **-ies** -iz
shantytown ˈʃæn.ti.taʊn, (US) -ţi- **-s** -z
shap|e ʃeɪp **-es** -s **-ing** -ɪŋ **-ed** -t
SHAPE ʃeɪp
shapeless ˈʃeɪp.ləs, -lɪs **-ly** -li **-ness** -nəs, -nɪs
shapel|y ˈʃeɪ.pl|i **-ier** -i.əʳ, (US) -i.ɚ **-iest** -i.ɪst, -i.əst **-iness** -ɪ.nəs, -ɪ.nɪs
Shapiro ʃəˈpɪə.rəʊ, (US) -ˈpɪr.oʊ
Shaq ʃæk
Sharapova ˌʃær.əˈpəʊ.və, (US) -ˈpoʊ-
shard ʃɑːd, (US) ʃɑːrd **-s** -z
shar|e ʃeəʳ, (US) ʃer **-es** -z **-ing** -ɪŋ **-ed** -d
sharecropp|er ˈʃeəˌkrɒp|.əʳ, (US) ˈʃerˌkrɑː.p|ɚ **-ers** -əz, (US) -ɚz **-ing** -ɪŋ
sharehold|er ˈʃeəˌhəʊl.d|əʳ, (US) ˈʃerˌhoʊl.d|ɚ **-ers** -əz, (US) -ɚz **-ing/s** -ɪŋ/z
share-out ˈʃeəʳ.aʊt, (US) ˈʃer- **-s** -s
shareware ˈʃeə.weəʳ, (US) ˈʃer.wer
sharia(h) ʃəˈriː.ə
Sharif ʃəˈriːf, ʃɑː-, ʃærˈiːf
Sharjah ˈʃɑː.dʒɑː, -ʒɑː, -dʒə, (US) ˈʃɑːr.dʒɑː
shark ʃɑːk, (US) ʃɑːrk **-s** -s
sharkskin ˈʃɑːk.skɪn, (US) ˈʃɑːrk-
Sharman ˈʃɑː.mən, (US) ˈʃɑːr-
Sharon *female name & fruit:* ˈʃær.ən, ˈʃɑː.rən, ˈʃeə-, -rɒn, (US) ˈʃer.ən, ˈʃær- *Israeli politician:* ʃəˈrɒn, -ˈrəʊn, (US) -ˈroʊn
sharp, S~ ʃɑːp, (US) ʃɑːrp **-s** -s **-er** -əʳ, (US) -ɚ **-est** -ɪst, -əst **-ly** -li **-ness** -nəs, -nɪs **ˌsharp ˈend; ˈsharp ˌend; ˌsharp ˈpractice**
Sharpe ʃɑːp, (US) ʃɑːrp
sharpen ˈʃɑː.pən, (US) ˈʃɑːr- **-s** -z **-ing** -ɪŋ, -ɪŋ **-ed** -d
sharpener ˈʃɑː.pən.əʳ, (US) ˈʃɑːr.pən.ɚ **-s** -z
sharper ˈʃɑː.pəʳ, (US) ˈʃɑːr.pɚ **-s** -z
Sharpeville ˈʃɑːp.vɪl, (US) ˈʃɑːrp-
sharp-eyed ˌʃɑːpˈaɪd, (US) ˌʃɑːrp-
sharpish ˈʃɑː.pɪʃ, (US) ˈʃɑːr-
Sharples ˈʃɑː.pəlz, (US) ˈʃɑːr-
sharp-set ˌʃɑːpˈset, (US) ˈʃɑːrp.set *stress shift, British only:* **ˌsharp-set ˈfeatures**
sharpshooter ˈʃɑːpˌʃuː.təʳ, (US) ˈʃɑːrpˌʃuː.ţɚ **-s** -z
sharp-sighted ˌʃɑːpˈsaɪ.tɪd, (US) ˈʃɑːrpˌsaɪ.ţɪd *stress shift, British only:* **ˌsharp-sighted ˈperson**
Sharpton ˈʃɑːp.tən, (US) ˈʃɑːrp-
sharp-witted ˌʃɑːpˈwɪt.ɪd, (US) ˈʃɑːrpˌwɪţ- *stress shift, British only:* **ˌsharp-witted ˈperson**
shashlik ʃɑːʃˈlɪk, ʃæʃ-, ˈ--, (US) ˈʃɑːʃ- **-s** -s
Shasta ˈʃæs.tə
Shastri ˈʃæs.tri, (US) ˈʃɑː.stri
shat (from **shit**) ʃæt

> Note: This past-tense form is rarely used in American English.

Shatner ˈʃæt.nəʳ, (US) -nɚ
Shatt-al-Arab ˌʃæt.ælˈær.əb, (US) -əlˈer-, -ˈær-
shatt|er ˈʃæt|.əʳ, (US) ˈʃæţ|.ɚ **-ers** -əz, (US) -ɚz **-ering** -ər.ɪŋ **-ered** -əd, (US) -ɚd
shatterproof ˈʃæt.ə.pruːf, (US) ˈʃæţ.ɚ-
Shaughnessy ˈʃɔː.nə.si, (US) ˈʃɑː-, ˈʃɔː-
Shaula ˈʃəʊ.lə, (US) ˈʃoʊ-, ˈʃɔː-
Shaun ʃɔːn, (US) ʃɑːn, ʃɔːn
Shauna ˈʃɔː.nə, (US) ˈʃɑː-, ˈʃɔː-
shav|e ʃeɪv **-es** -z **-ing** -ɪŋ **-ed** -d **ˈshaving ˌbrush; ˈshaving ˌcream; ˈshaving ˌfoam**
shaven ˈʃeɪ.vən
shaver ˈʃeɪ.vəʳ, (US) -vɚ **-s** -z
Shavian ˈʃeɪ.vi.ən
shaving ˈʃeɪ.vɪŋ **-s** -z
shaw, S~ ʃɔː, (US) ʃɑː, ʃɔː **-s** -z
shawl ʃɔːl, (US) ʃɑːl, ʃɔːl **-s** -z
shawm ʃɔːm, (US) ʃɑːm, ʃɔːm **-s** -z
Shawn ʃɔːn, (US) ʃɑːn, ʃɔːn
Shawna ˈʃɔː.nə, (US) ˈʃɑː-, ˈʃɔː-
Shawnee ʃɔːˈniː, (US) ʃɑː-, ʃɔː- **-s** -z
shay ʃeɪ **-s** -z
Shayler ˈʃeɪ.lə, -lɚ
she *normal form:* ʃiː; *freq. weak form:* ʃi
Note: Weak-form word. The strong form, /ʃiː/ is used mainly contrastively (e.g. 'I wouldn't go, so **she** went') or emphatically (e.g. 'What does **she** want?'). The weak form is /ʃi/ (e.g. 'off she went', /ˌɒf.ʃiˈwent/ (US) /ˌɑːf-/).
shea ʃɪə, ˈʃiː.ə, ʃiː, (US) ʃiː, ʃeɪ **-s** -z
Shea ʃeɪ
shea|f ʃiː|f **-ves** -vz
Sheaffer ˈʃeɪ.fəʳ, (US) -fɚ
shear ʃɪəʳ, (US) ʃɪr **-s** -z **-ing** -ɪŋ **-ed** -d **shorn** ʃɔːn, (US) ʃɔːrn
Sheard ʃeəd, ʃɪəd, ʃɜːd, (US) ʃerd, ʃɪrd, ʃɝːd
shearer, S~ ˈʃɪə.rəʳ, (US) ˈʃɪr.ɚ **-s** -z
Shearman ˈʃɪə.mən, ˈʃɜː.mən, (US) ˈʃɪr-, ˈʃɝː-
Shearn ʃɪən, ʃɜːn, (US) ʃɪrn, ʃɝːn
shears, S~ ʃɪəz, (US) ʃɪrz
Shearson ˈʃɪə.sən, (US) ˈʃɪr-
shearwater ˈʃɪəˌwɔː.təʳ, (US) ˈʃɪrˌwɑː.ţɚ, -ˌwɔː- **-s** -z
shea|th ʃiː|θ **-ths** -ðz, -θs
sheath|e ʃiːð **-es** -z **-ing** -ɪŋ **-ed** -d
sheaves (plural of **sheaf**) ʃiːvz
Sheba ˈʃiː.bə
shebang ʃɪˈbæŋ, ʃə-
she-bear ˈʃiː.beəʳ, (US) -ber **-s** -z
shebeen ʃɪˈbiːn, ʃə-, ʃebˈiːn, (US) ʃɪˈbiːn **-s** -z
she-cat ˈʃiː.kæt **-s** -s
Shechem ˈʃiː.kem, ˈʃek.em; *as if Jewish:* ʃəˈxem; (US) ˈʃiː.kəm, ˈʃek.əm
shed ʃed **-s** -z **-ding** -ɪŋ
she'd (= **she would** or **she had**) *strong form:* ʃiːd; *weak form:* ʃid
Note: The use of the strong form /ʃiːd/ and the weak form /ʃid/ is parallel to the two forms of **she**.
she-devil ˈʃiːˌdev.əl **-s** -z
shedload ˈʃed.ləʊd, (US) -loʊd **-s** -z
she'd've (= **she would have**) *strong form:* ˈʃiːd.əv; *weak form:* ʃid.əv
Note: The use of the strong form /ˈʃiːd.əv/ and the weak form /ʃid.əv/ is parallel to the two forms of **she**.
Shee ʃiː
sheen, S~ ʃiːn
Sheena ˈʃiː.nə
sheen|y ˈʃiː.n|i **-ies** -iz
sheep ʃiːp **ˈsheep's ˌeyes; ˌseparate the ˌsheep from the ˈgoats**
sheep-dip ˈʃiːp.dɪp
sheepdog ˈʃiːp.dɒg, (US) -dɑːg, -dɔːg **-s** -z
sheepfold ˈʃiːp.fəʊld, (US) -foʊld **-s** -z
sheepish ˈʃiː.pɪʃ **-ly** -li **-ness** -nəs, -nɪs
sheepshank ˈʃiːp.ʃæŋk **-s** -s
Sheepshanks ˈʃiːp.ʃæŋks
sheepshear|ing ˈʃiːpˌʃɪə.r|ɪŋ, (US) -ˌʃɪr|.ɪŋ **-er/s** -əʳ/z, (US) -ɚ/z
sheepskin ˈʃiːp.skɪn **-s** -z
sheer ʃɪəʳ, (US) ʃɪr **-s** -z **-ing** -ɪŋ **-ed** -d
Sheerness ˌʃɪəˈnes, (US) ˈʃɪr.nes
sheet ʃiːt **-s** -s **-ing** -ɪŋ, (US) ˈʃiː.ţɪŋ **ˈsheet ˌanchor; ˌsheet ˈlightning** (US) **ˈsheet ˌlightning; ˌsheet ˈmetal; ˈsheet ˌmusic; ˌwhite as a ˈsheet**
Sheffield ˈʃef.iːld; *locally:* -ɪld, (US) -iːld
Shefford ˈʃef.əd, (US) -ɚd
she-goat ˈʃiː.gəʊt, (US) -goʊt **-s** -s
sheik(h) ʃeɪk, ʃiːk, ʃek, ʃex, (US) ʃiːk, ʃeɪk **-s** -s **-dom/s** -dəm/z
sheila, S~ ˈʃiː.lə **-s** -z
shekel ˈʃek.əl **-s** -z

Shekinah ʃek'aɪ.nə, ʃɪ'kaɪ-, (US) ʃə'kiː-, -'kaɪ-
Shelagh 'ʃiː.lə
Shelby 'ʃel.bi
Sheldon 'ʃel.dᵊn
Sheldonian ʃel'dəʊ.ni.ən, (US) -'doʊ-
sheldrake 'ʃel.dreɪk **-s** -s
Sheldrick 'ʃel.drɪk
shelduck 'ʃel.dʌk **-s** -s
shel|f ʃel|f **-ves** -vz
Shelfield 'ʃel.fiːld
shelf-life 'ʃelf.laɪf **-lives** -laɪvz
Shelford 'ʃel.fəd, (US) -fɚd
shell, S~ ʃel **-s** -z **-ing** -ɪŋ **-ed** -d **'shell ˌshock; 'shell ˌsuit**
she'll (= **she will** or **she shall**) *strong form:* ʃiːl; *weak form:* ʃil
Note: The use of the strong form /ʃiːl/ and the weak form /ʃil/ is parallel to the two forms of **she**.
shellac ʃə'læk, ʃel'æk; 'ʃel.æk, (US) ʃə'læk **-s** -s **-king** -ɪŋ **-ked** -t
Shelley 'ʃel.i
shellfish 'ʃel.fɪʃ
Shelta 'ʃel.tə
shelt|er 'ʃel.t|əʳ, (US) -t|ɚ **-ers** -əz, (US) -ɚz **-ering** -ᵊr.ɪŋ **-ered** -əd, (US) -ɚd
shelt|ie, shelt|y 'ʃel.t|i **-ies** -iz
Shelton 'ʃel.tən, (US) -tᵊn
shelv|e ʃelv **-es** -z **-ing** -ɪŋ **-ed** -d
Shem ʃem
shemozzle ʃɪ'mɒz.ᵊl, ʃə-, (US) -'mɑː.zᵊl **-s** -z
Shenandoah ˌʃen.ən'dəʊ.ə, -'dəʊə, (US) -'doʊ.ə
shenanigan ʃɪ'næn.ɪ.gən, ʃə- **-s** -z
Shennan 'ʃen.ən
Shenstone 'ʃen.stən
Shenyang ˌʃen'jæŋ, (US) ˌʃʌn'jɑːŋ
Shepard 'ʃep.əd, (US) -ɚd
shepherd, S~ 'ʃep.əd, (US) -ɚd **-s** -z **-ing** -ɪŋ **-ed** -ɪd **ˌshepherd's 'pie**
shepherdess ˌʃep.ə'des; '---, -dɪs, (US) 'ʃep.ɚ.dɪs **-es** -ɪz
Sheppard 'ʃep.əd, (US) -ɚd
Shepperton 'ʃep.ə.tᵊn, (US) -ɚ.t̬ən
Sheppey 'ʃep.i
Shepreth 'ʃep.rəθ
Shepshed 'ʃep.ʃed
Shepton Mallet ˌʃep.tən'mæl.ɪt
Sheraton 'ʃer.ə.tᵊn, (US) -t̬ən, -tᵊn
sherbet, sherbert 'ʃɜː.bət, (US) 'ʃɝː-, -bɚt

> Note: Both pronunciations are possible for both variants in American English, even though only one is spelt with an **r**.

Sherborne 'ʃɜː.bən, -bɔːn, (US) 'ʃɝː.bɔːrn, -bɚn
Sherbrooke 'ʃɜː.brʊk, (US) 'ʃɝː-
sherd ʃɜːd, (US) ʃɝːd **-s** -z
Shere ʃɪəʳ, (US) ʃɪr
Shergar 'ʃɜː.gɑːʳ, 'ʃeə-, (US) 'ʃɝː.gɑːr, 'ʃer-
Sheridan 'ʃer.ɪ.dᵊn
sheriff, S~ 'ʃer.ɪf **-s** -s
Sheringham 'ʃer.ɪŋ.əm
sherlock, S~ 'ʃɜː.lɒk, (US) 'ʃɝː.lɑːk
Sherman 'ʃɜː.mən, (US) 'ʃɝː-
Sherpa 'ʃɜː.pə, (US) 'ʃɝː- **-s** -z
Sherrin 'ʃer.ɪn
sherr|y, S~ 'ʃer|.i **-ies** -iz
Sherwood 'ʃɜː.wʊd, (US) 'ʃɝː- **ˌSherwood 'Forest**
she's (= **she is** or **she has**) *strong form:* ʃiːz; *weak form:* ʃiz
Note: The use of the strong form /ʃiːz/ and the weak form /ʃiz/ is parallel to the two forms of **she**.
Shetland 'ʃet.lənd **-s** -z **-er/s** -əʳ/z, (US) -ɚ/z **'Shetland ˌIslands; ˌShetland 'pony**
Shevardnadze ˌʃev.əd'nɑːd.zeɪ, -zə, (US) -ɚd'nɑːd.ziː
Shevington 'ʃev.ɪŋ.tən
shew ʃəʊ, (US) ʃoʊ **-s** -z **-ing** -ɪŋ **-ed** -d **-n** -n
shewbread 'ʃəʊ.bred, (US) 'ʃoʊ-
Shewell ʃʊəl, 'ʃuː.əl, (US) 'ʃuː.əl
shewn (from **shew**) ʃəʊn, (US) ʃoʊn
she-wol|f 'ʃiː.wʊl|f **-ves** -vz
shh, sh, ssh ʃ

> Note: Used to command silence.

Shia(h) 'ʃiː.ə **ˌShia 'Muslim**
shiatsu ʃi'æt.su, (US) -'ɑːt-
shibboleth, S~ 'ʃɪb.ᵊl.eθ, -əθ, -ɪθ, (US) -ə.leθ, -ləθ **-s** -s
shickered 'ʃɪk.əd, (US) -ɚd
shield, S~ ʃiːld **-s** -z **-ing** -ɪŋ **-ed** -ɪd
shieling 'ʃiː.lɪŋ **-s** -z
Shiels ʃiːlz
Shifnal 'ʃɪf.nᵊl
shift ʃɪft **-s** -s **-ing** -ɪŋ **-ed** -ɪd **'shift ˌstick**
shiftless 'ʃɪft.ləs, -lɪs **-ly** -li **-ness** -nəs, -nɪs
shiftwork 'ʃɪft.wɜːk, (US) -wɝːk **-er/s** -əʳ/z, (US) -ɚ/z
shift|y 'ʃɪf.t|i **-ier** -i.əʳ, (US) -i.ɚ **-iest** -i.ɪst, -i.əst **-ily** -ᵊl.i, -ɪ.li **-iness** -ɪ.nəs, -ɪ.nɪs
Shiism 'ʃiː.ɪ.zᵊm
Shiite 'ʃiː.aɪt **-s** -s
shikari ʃɪ'kɑː.ri, -'kær.i, (US) -'kɑːr.i **-s** -z
Shikoku ʃɪ'kəʊ.kuː, (US) -'kɑː-, ʃiː-, -'kɔː-
shiksa 'ʃɪk.sə **-s** -z
shikse 'ʃɪk.sə **-s** -z
Shildon 'ʃɪl.dᵊn
Shillan ʃɪ'læn
shillela(g)h, S~ ʃɪ'leɪ.lə, -li, (US) -li, -lə **-s** -z
shilling 'ʃɪl.ɪŋ **-s** -z
shilly-shall|y 'ʃɪl.iˌʃæl|.i, ˌʃɪl.i'ʃæl-, (US) 'ʃɪl.iˌʃæl- **-ies** -iz **-ying** -i.ɪŋ **-ied** -id
Shiloh 'ʃaɪ.ləʊ, (US) -loʊ
Shilton 'ʃɪl.tᵊn
shimm|er 'ʃɪm|.əʳ, (US) -ɚ **-ers** -əz, (US) -ɚz **-ering** -ᵊr.ɪŋ **-ered** -əd, (US) -ɚd
shimm|y 'ʃɪm|.i **-ies** -iz **-ying** -i.ɪŋ **-ied** -id
shin ʃɪn **-s** -z **-ning** -ɪŋ **-ned** -d
shinbone 'ʃɪn.bəʊn, 'ʃɪm-, (US) 'ʃɪn.boʊn **-s** -z
shindig 'ʃɪn.dɪg **-s** -z
shind|y 'ʃɪn.d|i **-ies** -iz
shin|e ʃaɪn **-es** -z **-ing** -ɪŋ **-ed** -d
shone ʃɒn, (US) ʃoʊn, ʃɑːn
shiner 'ʃaɪ.nəʳ, (US) -nɚ **-s** -z
shingle 'ʃɪŋ.gᵊl **-s** -z
shingly 'ʃɪŋ.gli, -gᵊl.i
shinn|y 'ʃɪn|.i **-ies** -iz **-ying** -i.ɪŋ **-ied** -id
shinsplints 'ʃɪn.splɪnts
Shinto 'ʃɪn.təʊ, (US) -toʊ **-ism** -ɪ.zᵊm **-ist/s** -ɪst/s
Shinwell 'ʃɪn.wəl, -wel
shin|y 'ʃaɪ.n|i **-ier** -i.əʳ, (US) -i.ɚ **-iest** -i.ɪst, -i.əst **-iness** -ɪ.nəs, -ɪ.nɪs
ship ʃɪp **-s** -s **-ping** -ɪŋ **-ped** -t **-per/s** -əʳ/z, (US) -ɚ/z
-ship ʃɪp
Note: Suffix. Normally unstressed, e.g. **kinship** /'kɪn.ʃɪp/.
shipboard 'ʃɪp.bɔːd, (US) -bɔːrd
shipbroker 'ʃɪpˌbrəʊ.kəʳ, (US) -ˌbroʊ.kɚ **-s** -z
shipbuild|er 'ʃɪpˌbɪl.d|əʳ, (US) -d|ɚ **-ers** -əz, (US) -ɚz **-ing** -ɪŋ
Shiplake 'ʃɪp.leɪk
Shipley 'ʃɪp.li
shipload 'ʃɪp.ləʊd, (US) -loʊd **-s** -z
Shipman 'ʃɪp.mən
shipmaster 'ʃɪpˌmɑː.stəʳ, (US) -ˌmæs.tɚ **-s** -z
shipmate 'ʃɪp.meɪt **-s** -s
shipment 'ʃɪp.mənt **-s** -s
Shipp ʃɪp
shipping 'ʃɪp.ɪŋ **'shipping ˌclerk**
shipshape 'ʃɪp.ʃeɪp
Shipston 'ʃɪp.stən
Shipton 'ʃɪp.tən
shipway 'ʃɪp.weɪ **-s** -z
shipwreck 'ʃɪp.rek **-s** -s **-ing** -ɪŋ **-ed** -t
shipwright, S~ 'ʃɪp.raɪt **-s** -s
shipyard 'ʃɪp.jɑːd, (US) -jɑːrd **-s** -z
Shiraz ʃɪə'rɑːz, ʃɪ-, -'ræz, (US) ʃiː-
shire ʃaɪəʳ, 'ʃaɪ.əʳ, (US) 'ʃaɪ.ɚ **-s** -z **'shire ˌhorse**
-shire ʃəʳ, ʃɪəʳ, (US) ʃɚ, ʃɪr
Note: Suffix. Does not normally change the stress pattern of the stem to which it is added, e.g. **Lincoln** /'lɪŋ.kən/, **Lincolnshire** /'lɪŋ.kən.ʃəʳ/ (US) /-ʃɚ/.
Shirebrook 'ʃaɪə.brʊk, 'ʃaɪ.ə-, (US) 'ʃaɪ.ɚ-
Shiremoor 'ʃaɪə.mɔːʳ, -mʊəʳ, (US) 'ʃaɪ.ɚ.mɔːr, -mʊr
shirk ʃɜːk, (US) ʃɝːk **-s** -s **-ing** -ɪŋ **-ed** -t **-er/s** -əʳ/z, (US) -ɚ/z
Shirley 'ʃɜː.li, (US) 'ʃɝː-
shirr ʃɜːʳ, (US) ʃɝː **-s** -z **-ing** -ɪŋ **-ed** -d
shirt, S~ ʃɜːt, (US) ʃɝːt **-s** -s
shirtdress 'ʃɜːt.dres, (US) 'ʃɝːt- **-es** -ɪz
shirt-front 'ʃɜːt.frʌnt, (US) 'ʃɝːt- **-s** -s
shirting 'ʃɜː.tɪŋ, (US) 'ʃɝː.t̬ɪŋ
shirt-sleev|es 'ʃɜːt.sliːv|z, -'-, (US) 'ʃɝːt- **-ed** -d
shirt-tail 'ʃɜːt.teɪl, (US) 'ʃɝːt- **-s** -z
shirtwaist 'ʃɜːt.weɪst, (US) 'ʃɝːt- **-s** -s

shirtwaister ˈʃɜːtˌweɪ.stəʳ, ˌ-ˈ--, (US) ˈʃɝːtˌweɪ.stɚ **-s** -z
shirt|y ˈʃɜː.t|i, (US) ˈʃɝː.ţ|i **-ier** -i.əʳ, (US) -i.ɚ **-iest** -i.ɪst, -i.əst **-iness** -ɪ.nəs, -ɪ.nɪs
Shishak ˈʃaɪ.ʃæk, -ʃək; *rarely:* ˈʃɪʃ.æk, -ək, (US) ˈʃaɪ.ʃɑːk, -ʃæk
shish kebab ˈʃiːʃ.kɪˌbæb, -kəˌ-, ˌ--ˈ-, (US) ˈʃɪʃ.kəˌbɑːb **-s** -z
shit ʃɪt **-s** -s **-ting** -ɪŋ, (US) ˈʃɪţ.ɪŋ **shat** ʃæt

> Note: The past-tense form **shat** is rarely used in American English, the normal past tense being **shit**.

shite ʃaɪt **-s** -s
shitfaced ˈʃɪt.feɪst
shithouse ˈʃɪt.haʊs
shitless ˈʃɪt.ləs, -lɪs
shitload ˈʃɪt.ləʊd, (US) -loʊd **-s** -z
shitt|y ˈʃɪt|.i, (US) ˈʃɪţ|.i **-ier** -i.əʳ, (US) -i.ɚ **-iest** -i.ɪst, -i.əst **-iness** -ɪ.nəs, -ɪ.nɪs
Shiva ˈʃiː.və, ˈʃɪv.ə, (US) ˈʃiː.və
shiv|er ˈʃɪv|.əʳ, (US) -ɚ **-ers** -əz, (US) -ɚz **-ering/ly** -ᵊr.ɪŋ/li **-ered** -əd, (US) -ɚd
shiver|y ˈʃɪv.ᵊr|.i **-iness** -ɪ.nəs, -ɪ.nɪs
shlemiel ʃləˈmiːl **-s** -z
shlep ʃlep **-s** -s **-ping** -ɪŋ **-ped** -t
shlock ʃlɒk, (US) ʃlɑːk **-s** -s
shlockmeister ˈʃlɒkˌmaɪ.stəʳ, (US) ˈʃlɑːkˌmaɪ.stɚ **-s** -z
Shloer® ʃlɜːʳ, (US) ʃlɝː
shmal(t)z ʃmɔːlts, ʃmɒlts, ʃmælts, (US) ʃmɑːlts, ʃmɔːlts **-y** -i **-ier** -i.əʳ, (US) -i.ɚ **-iest** -i.ɪst, -i.əst
shmooz|e ʃmuːz **-es** -ɪz **-ing** -ɪŋ **-ed** -d **-er/s** -əʳ/z, (US) -ə/z
shmuck ʃmʌk **-s** -s
shoal ʃəʊl, (US) ʃoʊl **-s** -z
shock ʃɒk, (US) ʃɑːk **-s** -s **-ing** -ɪŋ **-ed** -t **-er/s** -əʳ/z, (US) -ɚ/z ˈ**shock abˌsorber;** ˈ**shock ˌtreatment;** ˈ**shock ˌwave**
shocking ˈʃɒk.ɪŋ, (US) ˈʃɑː.kɪŋ **-ly** -li
shockproof ˈʃɒk.pruːf, (US) ˈʃɑːk-
shodd|y ˈʃɒd|.i, (US) ˈʃɑː.d|i **-ier** -i.əʳ, (US) -i.ɚ **-iest** -i.ɪst, -i.əst **-ily** -ᵊl.i, -ɪ.li **-iness** -ɪ.nəs, -ɪ.nɪs
shoe ʃuː **-s** -z **-ing** -ɪŋ **shod** ʃɒd, (US) ʃɑːd ˈ**shoe ˌleather**
shoeblack ˈʃuː.blæk **-s** -s
Shoeburyness ˌʃuː.bᵊr.iˈnes
shoehorn ˈʃuː.hɔːn, (US) -hɔːrn **-s** -z **-ing** -ɪŋ **-ed** -d
shoelac|e ˈʃuː.leɪs **-es** -ɪz
shoeless ˈʃuː.ləs, -lɪs
shoemaker, S~ ˈʃuːˌmeɪ.kəʳ, (US) -kɚ **-s** -z
shoeshine ˈʃuː.ʃaɪn **-s** -z
shoestring ˈʃuː.strɪŋ **-s** -z
shoetree ˈʃuː.triː **-s** -z
shogun ˈʃəʊ.gʌn, -guːn, -gən, (US) ˈʃoʊ.gʌn, -gʊn, -guːn **-s** -z
Sholokhov ˈʃɒl.ə.kɒf, (US) ˈʃɔː.lə.kɔːf
Shona *female name:* ˈʃəʊ.nə, (US) ˈʃoʊ- *African language & people:* ˈʃɒ.nə, ˈʃɔː-, ˈʃəʊ-, (US) ˈʃoʊ-

shone (from **shine**) ʃɒn, (US) ʃoʊn
shonk|y ˈʃɒŋ.ki, (US) ˈʃɑːŋ- **-ier** -i.əʳ, (US) -i.ɚ **-iest** -i.ɪst, -i.əst
shoo ʃuː **-s** -z **-ing** -ɪŋ **-ed** -d
shoofl|y ˈʃuː.fl|aɪ **-ies** -aɪz
shoo-in ˈʃuː.ɪn **-s** -z
shook (from **shake**) ʃʊk
shook-up ˌʃʊkˈʌp
shoot ʃuːt **-s** -s **-ing** -ɪŋ, (US) ˈʃuː.ţɪŋ **shot** ʃɒt, (US) ʃɑːt ˌ**shoot the** ˈ**breeze**
shooter, S~ ˈʃuː.təʳ, (US) -ţɚ **-s** -z
shooting ˈʃuː.tɪŋ, (US) -ţɪŋ **-s** -z ˈ**shooting ˌgallery;** ˌ**shooting** ˈ**star;** ˈ**shooting ˌstar** (US) ˌ**shooting** ˈ**star;** ˈ**shooting ˌstick**
shoot-out ˈʃuːt.aʊt **-s** -s
shop ʃɒp, (US) ʃɑːp **-s** -s **-ping** -ɪŋ **-ped** -t **-per/s** -əʳ/z, (US) -ɚ/z ˈ**shop asˌsistant;** ˌ**shop** ˈ**steward** (US) ˈ**shop ˌsteward;** ˌ**shop** ˈ**window**
shopaholic ˌʃɒp.əˈhɒl.ɪk, (US) ˌʃɑː.pəˈhɑː.lɪk **-s** -s
shopfloor ˌʃɒpˈflɔːʳ, (US) ˌʃɑːpˈflɔːr
shopfront ˌʃɒpˈfrʌnt, ˈ--, (US) ˈʃɑːp.frʌnt **-s** -s
shopgirl ˈʃɒp.gɜːl, (US) ˈʃɑːp.gɝːl **-s** -z
shopkeeper ˈʃɒpˌkiː.pəʳ, (US) ˈʃɑːpˌkiː.pɚ **-s** -z
shoplift ˈʃɒp.lɪft, (US) ˈʃɑːp- **-s** -s **-ing** -ɪŋ **-ed** -ɪd
shop-lifter ˈʃɒpˌlɪf.təʳ, (US) ˈʃɑːpˌlɪf.tɚ **-s** -z
shopping ˈʃɒp.ɪŋ ˈ**shopping ˌcentre/ˌcenter;** ˈ**shopping ˌlist;** ˈ**shopping ˌmall**
shop-soiled ˈʃɒp.sɔɪld, (US) ˈʃɑːpˌsɔɪld
shoptalk ˈʃɒp.tɔːk, (US) ˈʃɑːp.tɑːk, -tɔːk
shopwalker ˈʃɒpˌwɔː.kəʳ, (US) ˈʃɑːpˌwɔː.kɚ, -ˌwɑː- **-s** -z
shopworn ˈʃɒp.wɔːn, (US) ˈʃɑːp.wɔːrn
shor|e ʃɔːʳ, (US) ʃɔːr **-es** -z **-ing** -ɪŋ **-ed** -d
Shoreditch ˈʃɔː.dɪtʃ, (US) ˈʃɔːr-
Shoreham ˈʃɔː.rəm, (US) ˈʃɔːr.əm
shoreline ˈʃɔː.laɪn, (US) ˈʃɔːr-
shoreward ˈʃɔː.wəd, (US) ˈʃɔːr.wɚd
shorn (from **shear**) ʃɔːn, (US) ʃɔːrn
Shorncliffe ˈʃɔːn.klɪf, (US) ˈʃɔːrn-
short, S~ ʃɔːt, (US) ʃɔːrt **-s** -s **-er** -əʳ, (US) ˈʃɔːr.ţɚ **-est** -ɪst, -əst, (US) ˈʃɔːr.ţɪst, -ţəst **-ly** -li **-ness** -nəs, -nɪs **-ing** -ɪŋ **-ed** -ɪd ˌ**short** ˌ**back and** ˈ**sides;** ˌ**short** ˈ**shrift;** ˌ**short** ˈ**story; the** ˌ**long and the** ˈ**short of it; the** ˌ**short** ˌ**end of the** ˈ**stick**
shortag|e ˈʃɔː.tɪdʒ, (US) ˈʃɔːr.ţɪdʒ **-es** -ɪz
shortbread ˈʃɔːt.bred, (US) ˈʃɔːrt- **-s** -z
shortcake ˈʃɔːt.keɪk, (US) ˈʃɔːrt- **-s** -s
short-chang|e ˌʃɔːtˈtʃeɪndʒ, (US) ˌʃɔːrt- **-es** -ɪz **-ing** -ɪŋ **-ed** -d
short-cir|cuit ˌʃɔːtˈsɜː|.kɪt, (US) ˌʃɔːrtˈsɝː- **-cuits** -kɪts **-cuiting** -kɪ.tɪŋ, (US) -kɪ.ţɪŋ **-cuited** -kɪ.tɪd, (US) -kɪ.ţɪd

shortcoming ˈʃɔːtˌkʌm.ɪŋ, ˌ-ˈ--, (US) ˈʃɔːrtˌkʌm- **-s** -z
shortcrust ˈʃɔːt.krʌst, (US) ˈʃɔːrt- **-s** -s ˌ**shortcrust** ˈ**pastry**
shortcut ˈʃɔːt.kʌt, (US) ˈʃɔːrt- **-s** -s
short-dated ˌʃɔːtˈdeɪ.tɪd, (US) ˌʃɔːrtˈdeɪ.ţɪd
short-eared ˌʃɔːtˈɪəd, (US) ˈʃɔːrt.ɪrd *stress shift, British only:* ˌ**short-eared** ˈ**rabbit**
shorten ˈʃɔː.tᵊn, (US) ˈʃɔːr- **-s** -z **-ing** -ɪŋ, ˈʃɔːt.nɪŋ, (US) ˈʃɔːr.tᵊn.ɪŋ, ˈʃɔːrt.nɪŋ **-ed** -d
shortening ˈʃɔːt.nɪŋ; ˈʃɔː.tᵊn.ɪŋ, (US) ˈʃɔːrt.nɪŋ; (US) ˈʃɔːr.tᵊn.ɪŋ
shortfall ˈʃɔːt.fɔːl, (US) ˈʃɔːrt-, -fɑːl **-s** -z
shorthand ˈʃɔːt.hænd, (US) ˈʃɔːrt- ˌ**shorthand** ˈ**typist**
short-handed ˌʃɔːtˈhæn.dɪd, (US) ˌʃɔːrt- *stress shift:* ˌ**short-handed** ˈ**vessel**
short-haul ˈʃɔːt.hɔːl, ˌ-ˈ-, (US) ˈʃɔːrt.hɑːl, -hɔːl, ˌ-ˈ-
shorthorn ˈʃɔːt.hɔːn, (US) ˈʃɔːrt.hɔːrn **-s** -z
shortlist ˈʃɔːt.lɪst, (US) ˈʃɔːrt- **-s** -s **-ing** -ɪŋ **-ed** -ɪd
short-lived ˌʃɔːtˈlɪvd, (US) ˌʃɔːrtˈlɪvd, -ˈlaɪvd *stress shift, British only:* ˌ**short-lived** ˈ**glory**
short-order ˈʃɔːtˌɔː.dəʳ, ˌ-ˈ--, (US) ˈʃɔːrtˌɔːr.dɚ
short-range ˌʃɔːtˈreɪndʒ, (US) ˌʃɔːrt- *stress shift:* ˌ**short-range** ˈ**missile**
shortsighted ˌʃɔːtˈsaɪ.tɪd, (US) ˈʃɔːrtˌsaɪ.ţɪd **-ly** -li **-ness** -nəs, -nɪs *stress shift, British only:* ˌ**short-sighted** ˈ**person**
short-staffed ˌʃɔːtˈstɑːft, (US) ˌʃɔːrtˈstæft *stress shift:* ˌ**short-staffed** ˈ**bar**
shortstop ˈʃɔːt.stɒp, (US) ˈʃɔːrt.stɑːp **-s** -s
short-tempered ˌʃɔːtˈtem.pəd, (US) ˌʃɔːrtˈtem.pɚd *stress shift:* ˌ**short-tempered** ˈ**person**
short-term ˌʃɔːtˈtɜːm, (US) ˈʃɔːrt.tɝːm **-ism** -ɪ.zᵊm *stress shift, British only:* ˌ**short-term** ˈ**plans**
shortwave ˈʃɔːt.weɪv, (US) ˈʃɔːrt- **-s** -z
short-winded ˌʃɔːtˈwɪn.dɪd, (US) ˈʃɔːrtˌwɪn-, ˌ-ˈ-- *stress shift, British only:* ˌ**short-winded** ˈ**story**
short|y ˈʃɔː.t|i, (US) ˈʃɔːr.ţ|i **-ies** -iz
Shostakovich ˌʃɒs.təˈkəʊ.vɪtʃ, (US) ˌʃɑː.stəˈkoʊ-
shot ʃɒt, (US) ʃɑːt **-s** -s ˈ**shot** ˌ**put;** ˈ**shot** ˌ**putter**
shotgun ˈʃɒt.gʌn, (US) ˈʃɑːt- **-s** -z ˌ**shotgun** ˈ**wedding**
Shotton ˈʃɒt.ᵊn, (US) ˈʃɑː.tᵊn
Shotts ʃɒts, (US) ʃɑːts
should *strong form:* ʃʊd; *weak forms:* ʃəd, ʃd, ʃt
Note: Weak-form word. The strong form is used for emphatic pronunciation (e.g. 'He **should** have asked first'), or for contrast (e.g. 'Don't tell me what I should or shouldn't do'). It is also used in final position

(e.g. 'We both should'). The most usual weak form is /ʃəd/, as in 'When should it arrive?' /ˌwen.ʃəd.ɪt.əˈraɪv/, but in rapid speech we also find /ʃd/ before voiced sounds (e.g. 'I should go now' /ˌaɪ.ʃdˈɡəʊ.naʊ/ US /-ˈɡoʊ-/) and /ʃt/ before voiceless sounds (e.g. 'You should try to finish' /ju.ʃtˌtraɪ.təˈfɪn.ɪʃ/ US /-t̬ə-/).

shoulder ˈʃəʊl.d|əʳ, US ˈʃoʊl.d|ɚ -ers -əz, US -ɚz -ering -ᵊr.ɪŋ -ered -əd, US -ɚd **ˈshoulder ˌbag; ˈshoulder ˌblade; ˈshoulder ˌpad; ˈshoulder ˌstrap; a ˈshoulder to ˌcry on; a ˌshoulder to ˈcry on** US **a ˌshoulder to ˈcry on**

shoulder-length ˈʃəʊl.dəˌleŋkθ, US ˈʃoʊl.dɚ-

shouldn't (= **should not**) ˈʃʊd.ᵊnt

shouldn't've (= **should not have**) ˈʃʊd.ᵊnt.ᵊv

should've (= **should have**) ˈʃʊd.ᵊv

shout ʃaʊt -s -s -ing -ɪŋ, US ˈʃaʊ.t̬ɪŋ -ed -ɪd, US ˈʃaʊ.t̬ɪd

shov|e **n, v** ʃʌv -es -z -ing -ɪŋ -ed -d

shove-halfpenny ˌʃʌvˈheɪp.ni

shovel, S~ ˈʃʌv.ᵊl -s -z -(l)ing -ɪŋ, ˈʃʌv.lɪŋ -(l)ed -d -(l)er/s -əʳ/z, ˈʃʌv.ləʳ/z, US ˈ-ᵊl.ɚ/z, ˈ-lɚ/z -ful/s -fʊl/z

show ʃəʊ, US ʃoʊ -s -z -ing -ɪŋ -ed -d -n -n **ˈshow ˌbusiness; ˌshow ˈtrial; ˈshow ˌtrial**

showbiz ˈʃəʊ.bɪz, US ˈʃoʊ-

showboat ˈʃəʊ.bəʊt, US ˈʃoʊ.boʊt -s -s -ing -ɪŋ

showbread ˈʃəʊ.bred, US ˈʃoʊ-

showcas|e ˈʃəʊ.keɪs, US ˈʃoʊ- -es -ɪz -ing -ɪŋ -ed -t

showdown ˈʃəʊ.daʊn, US ˈʃoʊ- -s -z

shower *fall of rain etc.:* ˈʃaʊ.əʳ, ʃaʊər, US ˈʃaʊ.ɚ -s -z -ing -ɪŋ -ed -d -y -i *one who shows:* ˈʃəʊ.əʳ, US ˈʃoʊ.ɚ -s -z

shower-ba|th ˈʃaʊ.ə.bɑː|θ, ˈʃaʊə-, US ˈʃaʊ.ɚ.bæ|θ -ths -ðz

showerhead ˈʃaʊ.ə.hed, ˈʃaʊə-, US ˈʃaʊ.ɚ- -s -z

showerproof ˈʃaʊ.ə.pruːf, ˈʃaʊə-, US ˈʃaʊ.ɚ-

showgirl ˈʃəʊ.ɡɜːl, US ˈʃoʊ.ɡɝːl -s -z

showjump ˈʃəʊ.dʒʌmp, US ˈʃoʊ- -s -s -ing -ɪŋ -er/s -əʳ/z, US -ɚ/z

show|man ˈʃəʊ|.mən, US ˈʃoʊ- -men -mən, -men

showmanship ˈʃəʊ.mən.ʃɪp, US ˈʃoʊ-

shown (from **show**) ʃəʊn, US ʃoʊn

show-off ˈʃəʊ.ɒf, US ˈʃoʊ.ɑːf

showpiec|e ˈʃəʊ.piːs, US ˈʃoʊ- -es -ɪz

showplac|e ˈʃəʊ.pleɪs, US ˈʃoʊ- -es -ɪz

showroom ˈʃəʊ.rʊm, -ruːm, US ˈʃoʊ.ruːm, -rʊm -s -z

showstopp|er ˈʃəʊˌstɒp|.əʳ, US ˈʃoʊˌstɑː.p|ɚ -ers -əz, US -ɚz -ing -ɪŋ

show|y ˈʃəʊ|.i, US ˈʃoʊ- -ier -i.əʳ, US -i.ɚ -iest -i.ɪst, -i.əst -ily -ᵊl.i, -ɪ.li -iness -ɪ.nəs, -ɪ.nɪs

shoyu ˈʃɔɪ.juː, US ˈʃoʊ.juː

shrank (from **shrink**) ʃræŋk

shrapnel ˈʃræp.nᵊl

shred ʃred -s -z -ding -ɪŋ -ded -ɪd -der/s -əʳ/z, US -ɚ/z

Shredded Wheat® ˌʃred.ɪdˈ*h*wiːt -s -s

shrew ʃruː -s -z

shrewd ʃruːd -er -əʳ, US -ɚ -est -ɪst, -əst -ly -li -ness -nəs, -nɪs

shrewish ˈʃruː.ɪʃ -ly -li -ness -nəs, -nɪs

Shrewsbury *in the UK:* ˈʃrəʊz.bᵊr.i, ˈʃruːz-, ˈ-bri, US ˈʃruːzˌber.i, ˈʃroʊz-, -bɚ- *in the US:* ˈʃruːz.bᵊr.i, US -ˌber-, -bɚ-

> Note: /ˈʃrəʊz-/ is the most widely used pronunciation, but /ˈʃruːz-/ or /ˈʃuːz-/ is more usually used by many local people.

shriek ʃriːk -s -s -ing -ɪŋ -ed -t

shrift ʃrɪft

shrike ʃraɪk -s -s

shrill ʃrɪl -er -əʳ, US -ɚ -est -ɪst, -əst -y -i, -li -ness -nəs, -nɪs

shrimp ʃrɪmp -s -s -ing -ɪŋ -er/s -əʳ/z, US -ɚ/z

Shrimpton ˈʃrɪmp.tən

shrine ʃraɪn -s -z

shriner, S~ ˈʃraɪ.nəʳ, US -nɚ -s -z

shrink ʃrɪŋk -s -s -ing/ly -ɪŋ/li **shrank** ʃræŋk **shrunk** ʃrʌŋk **shrunken** ˈʃrʌŋ.kən **ˌshrinking ˈviolet**

shrinkage ˈʃrɪŋ.kɪdʒ

shrink-wrap ˈʃrɪnk.ræp, -ˈ- -s -s -ping -ɪŋ -ped -t

shriv|e, S~ ʃraɪv -es -z -ing -ɪŋ **shrove** ʃrəʊv, US ʃroʊv **shriven** ˈʃrɪv.ᵊn

shrivel ˈʃrɪv.ᵊl -s -z -(l)ing -ɪŋ, ˈʃrɪv.lɪŋ -(l)ed -d

shriven (from **shrive**) ˈʃrɪv.ᵊn

shroff ʃrɒf, US ʃrɑːf -s -s -ing -ɪŋ -ed -t

Shropshire ˈʃrɒp.ʃəʳ, -ʃɪəʳ, US ˈʃrɑːp.ʃɚ, -ʃɪr

shroud ʃraʊd -s -z -ing -ɪŋ -ed -ɪd -less -ləs, -lɪs

shrove (from **shrive**) ʃrəʊv, US ʃroʊv

Shrove ʃrəʊv, US ʃroʊv **ˌShrove ˈTuesday**

Shrovetide ˈʃrəʊv.taɪd, US ˈʃroʊv-

shrub ʃrʌb -s -z

shrubber|y ˈʃrʌb.ᵊr|.i -ies -iz

shrubby ˈʃrʌb.i

shrug ʃrʌɡ -s -z -ging -ɪŋ -ged -d

shrunk (from **shrink**) ʃrʌŋk -en -ᵊn

shtick ʃtɪk

shuck ʃʌk -s -s -ing -ɪŋ -ed -d

Shuckburgh ˈʃʌk.bᵊr.ə, US -bɚ.ə

shudd|er ˈʃʌd|.əʳ, US -ɚ -ers -əz, US -ɚz -ering -ᵊr.ɪŋ -ered -əd, US -ɚd

shuffl|e ˈʃʌf.ᵊl -es -z -ing -ɪŋ, ˈʃʌf.lɪŋ -ed -d -er/s -əʳ/z, ˈʃʌf.ləʳ/z, US ˈ-ᵊl.ɚ/z, ˈ-lɚ/z

shuffleboard ˈʃʌf.ᵊl.bɔːd, US -bɔːrd -s -z

shufti ˈʃʊf.ti, ˈʃʌf- -s -z

Shulamite ˈʃuː.lə.maɪt

shun ʃʌn -s -z -ning -ɪŋ -ned -d

shunt ʃʌnt -s -s -ing -ɪŋ, US ˈʃʌn.t̬ɪŋ -ed -ɪd, US ˈʃʌn.t̬ɪd -er/s -əʳ/z, US ˈʃʌn.t̬ɚ/z

shush ʃʊʃ, ʃʌʃ -es -ɪz -ing -ɪŋ -ed -t

shut ʃʌt -s -s -ting -ɪŋ, US ˈʃʌt̬.ɪŋ

shutdown ˈʃʌt.daʊn -s -z

Shute ʃuːt

shut-eye ˈʃʌt.aɪ, US ˈʃʌt̬-

shutout ˈʃʌt.aʊt -s -z

shutt|er ˈʃʌt|.əʳ, US ˈʃʌt̬|.ɚ -ers -əz, US -ɚz -ering -ᵊr.ɪŋ -ered -əd, US -ɚd

shuttle ˈʃʌt.ᵊl, US ˈʃʌt̬- -s -z -ling -ɪŋ -ed -d **ˌshuttle diˈplomacy**

shuttlecock ˈʃʌt.ᵊl.kɒk, US ˈʃʌt̬.ᵊl.kɑːk -s -s

Shuttleworth ˈʃʌt.ᵊl.wəθ, -wɜːθ, US ˈʃʌt̬.ᵊl.wɚθ, -wɝːθ

shwa ʃwɑː -s -z

sh|y ʃ|aɪ -ies -aɪz -yer -aɪ.əʳ, US -aɪ.ɚ -yest -aɪ.ɪst, -aɪ.əst -yly -aɪ.li -yness -aɪ.nəs, -nɪs -ying -aɪ.ɪŋ -ied -aɪd

shylock, S~ ˈʃaɪ.lɒk, US -lɑːk

shyster ˈʃaɪ.stəʳ, US -stɚ -s -z

si siː

Sialkot siˈæl.kɒt, US -ˈɑːl.koʊt

Siam saɪˈæm, ˈ--

Siamese ˌsaɪ.əˈmiːz, US -ˈmiːz, -ˈmiːs *stress shift, see compounds:* **ˌSiamese ˈcat; ˌSiamese ˈtwins**

Sian, Siân ʃɑːn

Sibbald ˈsɪb.əld

Sibelius sɪˈbeɪ.li.əs, US -li.əs, -ˈbeɪl.jəs

Siberi|a saɪˈbɪə.ri|.ə, US -ˈbɪr.i- -an/s -ən/z

sibilan|ce ˈsɪb.ɪ.lᵊn|*t*s, -ᵊl.ᵊn|*t*s, US -ᵊl.ᵊn|*t*s -t/s -t/s

sibilation ˌsɪb.ɪˈleɪ.ʃᵊn, US -ᵊlˈeɪ-, -əˈleɪ -s -z

Sibley ˈsɪb.li

sibling ˈsɪb.lɪŋ -s -z **ˌsibling ˈrivalry**

sibyl, S~ ˈsɪb.ᵊl, -ɪl, US -ᵊl -s -z

sibylline ˈsɪb.ə.laɪn, ˈ-ɪ-; sɪˈbɪl.aɪn, US ˈsɪb.ə.laɪn, -liːn, -lɪn

sic sɪk, siːk

Sichuan ˌsɪtʃˈwɑːn, US ˈ-ˌ-

Sicilian sɪˈsɪl.jən, sə-, -i.ən -s -z

Sicil|y ˈsɪs.ɪ.l|i, -ᵊl|.i, US -ᵊl|.i -ies -iz

sick sɪk -er -əʳ, US -ɚ -est -ɪst, -əst -ness -nəs, -nɪs **ˈsick bay; ˌsick ˈbuilding ˌsyndrome; ˈsick ˌleave; ˈsick ˌpay**

sickbed ˈsɪk.bed -s -z

sicken ˈsɪk.ᵊn -s -z -ing/ly -ɪŋ/li, ˈsɪk.nɪŋ/li -ed -d

Sickert ˈsɪk.ət, US -ɚt

sickie ˈsɪk.i -s -z

sickle ˈsɪk.ᵊl -s -z **ˌsickle-cell aˈn(a)emia**

sickl|y ˈsɪk.l|i -ier -i.əʳ, US -i.ɚ -iest -i.ɪst, -i.əst -iness -ɪ.nəs, -ɪ.nɪs

sickness ˈsɪk.nəs, -nɪs

S

sicko ˈsɪk.əʊ, ⓤⓢ -oʊ **-s** -z
sick-out ˈsɪk.aʊt **-s** -s
sickroom ˈsɪk.rʊm, -ruːm, ⓤⓢ -ruːm, -rʊm **-s** -z
sic transit gloria mundi ˌsɪkˌtræn.zɪtˌglɔː.ri.əˈmʊn.di, ˌsiːk-, -ˌtrænt.sɪt-, -ˌtrɑːn.zɪt-, -ˌtrɑːnt.sɪt-, ⓤⓢ ˌsɪkˌtræn.sɪtˌglɔːr.i.əˈmʌn.di
Sid sɪd
Sidcup ˈsɪd.kʌp, -kəp
Siddeley ˈsɪd.əl.i
Siddharta sɪˈdɑː.tə, ⓤⓢ -ˈdɑːr.t̬ə
Siddons ˈsɪd.ənz
sid|e saɪd **-es** -z **-ing** -ɪŋ **-ed** -ɪd **ˈside arm; ˌside by ˈside; ˈside ˌdish; ˈside ˌdrum; ˈside efˌfect; ˈside ˌissue; ˈside ˌsalad; ˈside ˌstreet; ˌknow which ˌside one's ˌbread is ˈbuttered (on); ˌknow which ˌside one's ˈbread is ˌbuttered (on); ˌlaugh on the ˌother ˌside of one's ˈface; ˌlook on the ˈbright ˌside (of things)**
sidebar ˈsaɪd.bɑːr, ⓤⓢ -bɑːr **-s** -z
sideboard ˈsaɪd.bɔːd, ⓤⓢ -bɔːrd **-s** -z
Sidebotham ˈsaɪdˌbɒt.əm, ⓤⓢ -ˌbɑː.t̬əm
Sidebottom ˈsaɪdˌbɒt.əm, ˈsiːd-, ˌsɪd.ɪ.bəˈtəʊm, ⓤⓢ ˈsaɪdˌbɑː.t̬əm, ˈsiːd-; ˌsɪd.ɪ.bəˈtoʊm
sideburn ˈsaɪd.bɜːn, ⓤⓢ -bɝːn **-s** -z
sidecar ˈsaɪd.kɑːr, ⓤⓢ -kɑːr **-s** -z
sidedish ˈsaɪd.dɪʃ **-es** -ɪz
sidekick ˈsaɪd.kɪk **-s** -s
sidelight ˈsaɪd.laɪt **-s** -s
sidelin|e ˈsaɪd.laɪn **-es** -z **-ing** -ɪŋ **-ed** -d
sidelong ˈsaɪd.lɒŋ, ⓤⓢ -lɑːŋ, -lɔːŋ
sidereal saɪˈdɪə.ri.əl, sɪ-, ⓤⓢ saɪˈdɪr.i-
siderite ˈsaɪ.dər.aɪt, ˈsɪd.ər-, ⓤⓢ ˈsɪd.ə.raɪt
Sidery ˈsaɪ.dər.i
sidesaddle ˈsaɪdˌsæd.əl **-s** -z
sideshow ˈsaɪd.ʃəʊ, ⓤⓢ -ʃoʊ **-s** -z
sideslip ˈsaɪd.slɪp **-s** -s **-ping** -ɪŋ **-ped** -t
sides|man ˈsaɪdz|.mən **-men** -mən, -men
sidespin ˈsaɪd.spɪn
sidesplitting ˈsaɪdˌsplɪt.ɪŋ, ⓤⓢ -ˌsplɪt̬-
sidestep ˈsaɪd.step **-s** -s **-ping** -ɪŋ **-ped** -t
sidestroke ˈsaɪd.strəʊk, ⓤⓢ -stroʊk **-s** -s
sideswip|e ˈsaɪd.swaɪp **-es** -s **-ing** -ɪŋ **-ed** -t
sidetrack ˈsaɪd.træk **-s** -s **-ing** -ɪŋ **-ed** -t
sidewalk ˈsaɪd.wɔːk, ⓤⓢ -wɑːk, -wɔːk **-s** -s
sideways ˈsaɪd.weɪz
sidewinder ˈsaɪdˌwaɪn.dər, ⓤⓢ -dɚ **-s** -z
Sidgwick ˈsɪdʒ.wɪk
siding ˈsaɪ.dɪŋ **-s** -z
Sidlaw ˈsɪd.lɔː, ⓤⓢ -lɑː, -lɔː
sidl|e ˈsaɪ.dəl **-es** -z **-ing** -ɪŋ, ˈsaɪd.lɪŋ **-ed** -d
Sidmouth ˈsɪd.məθ
Sidney ˈsɪd.ni
Sidon ˈsaɪ.dən, -dɒn, ⓤⓢ -dən
Sidonian saɪˈdəʊ.ni.ən, sɪ-, ⓤⓢ saɪˈdoʊ.ni.ən **-s** -z
Sidonie sɪˈdəʊ.ni, ⓤⓢ -ˈdoʊ-
SIDS sɪdz
sieg|e siːdʒ **-es** -ɪz **ˈsiege menˌtality**
Siegfried ˈsiːg.friːd; *as if German:* ˈziːg-; ⓤⓢ ˈsɪg-, ˈsiːg-
Sieg Heil ˌsiːgˈhaɪl; *as if German:* ˌziːk-
Sieglinde siːˈglɪn.də; *as if German:* ziː-; ⓤⓢ siː-, ziː-, sɪ-
Siegmund ˈsiːg.mʊnd; *as if German:* ˈziːg-; -mənd, ⓤⓢ ˈsɪg-, ˈsiːg-
Siemens ˈsiː.mənz; *as if German:* ˈziː- **ˌSiemens-ˈNixdorf®**
Siena siˈen.ə
Sienese ˌsi.enˈiːz, -əˈniːz, ⓤⓢ -əˈniːz, -ˈniːs
sienna siˈen.ə
sierra, S~ siˈer.ə, -ˈeə.rə, ⓤⓢ siˈer.ə **-s** -z
Sierra Leone siˌer.ə.liˈəʊn, -ˌeə.rə-, -ˈəʊ.ni, ⓤⓢ siˌer.ə.liˈoʊn
Sierra Madre siˌer.əˈmɑː.dreɪ, -ˌeə.rəˈ-, ⓤⓢ siˌer.əˈ-
Sierra Nevada siˌer.ə.nəˈvɑː.də, -ˈeə.rə-, ⓤⓢ siˌer.ə.nəˈvæd.ə, -ˈvɑː.də
siesta siˈes.tə **-s** -z
siev|e sɪv **-es** -z **-ing** -ɪŋ **-ed** -d
sift sɪft **-s** -s **-ing** -ɪŋ **-ed** -ɪd **-er/s** -ər/z, ⓤⓢ -ɚ/z
sigh saɪ **-s** -z **-ing** -ɪŋ **-ed** -d
sight saɪt **-s** -s **-ing/s** -ɪŋ/s, ⓤⓢ ˈsaɪ.t̬ɪŋ/s **-ed** -ɪd, ⓤⓢ ˈsaɪ.t̬ɪd **-less/ness** -ləs, -lɪs **ˌsight unˈseen**
sightl|y ˈsaɪt.l|i **-iness** -ɪ.nəs, -ɪ.nɪs
sightread *present tense:* ˈsaɪt.riːd **-s** -z **-ing** -ɪŋ *past tense:* ˈsaɪt.red
sightreader ˈsaɪtˌriː.dər, ⓤⓢ -dɚ **-s** -z
sightscreen ˈsaɪt.skriːn **-s** -z
sightsee ˈsaɪt.siː **-s** -z **-ing** -ɪŋ
sight-seeing ˈsaɪtˌsiː.ɪŋ
sightseer ˈsaɪtˌsiː.ər, ⓤⓢ -ɚ **-s** -z
Sigismond, Sigismund ˈsɪg.ɪs.mənd, ˈsɪdʒ-, -ɪz-, ⓤⓢ -ɪs-
sigma, S~ ˈsɪg.mə **-s** -z
Sigmund ˈsɪg.mənd; *as if German:* ˈzɪg-
sign saɪn **-s** -z **-ing/s** -ɪŋ/s **-ed** -d **-er/s** -ər/z, ⓤⓢ -ɚ/z **-age** -ɪdʒ **ˈsign ˌlanguage; ˌsign of the ˈtimes**
signal ˈsɪg.nəl **-s** -z **-(l)y** -i **-(l)ing** -ɪŋ **-(l)ed** -d **-(l)er/s** -ər/z, ⓤⓢ -ɚ/z **ˈsignal ˌbox**
signaliz|e, -is|e ˈsɪg.nəl.aɪz, ⓤⓢ -nə.laɪz **-es** -ɪz **-ing** -ɪŋ **-ed** -d
signal|man ˈsɪg.nəl|.mən, -mæn **-men** -mən, -men
signator|y ˈsɪg.nə.tər|.i, ⓤⓢ -tɔːr- **-ies** -iz
signature ˈsɪg.nə.tʃər, -nɪ-, ⓤⓢ -nə.tʃɚ **-s** -z **ˈsignature ˌtune**
signboard ˈsaɪn.bɔːd, ˈsaɪm-, ⓤⓢ ˈsaɪn.bɔːrd **-s** -z
signer ˈsaɪ.nər, ⓤⓢ -nɚ **-s** -z
signet ˈsɪg.nɪt, -nət **-s** -s **ˈsignet ˌring**
significance sɪgˈnɪf.ɪ.kənts, ˈ-ə-, ⓤⓢ ˈ-ə-
significant sɪgˈnɪf.ɪ.kənt, ˈ-ə-, ⓤⓢ ˈ-ə- **-ly** -li **sigˌnificant ˈother**
signification ˌsɪg.nɪ.fɪˈkeɪ.ʃən, -nə-, -fəˈ-, ⓤⓢ -nə-
significative sɪgˈnɪf.ɪ.kə.tɪv, ˈ-ə-, -keɪ-, ⓤⓢ -keɪ.t̬ɪv **-ly** -li **-ness** -nəs, -nɪs
signi|fy ˈsɪg.nɪ|.faɪ, -nə- **-fies** -faɪz **-fying** -faɪ.ɪŋ **-fied** -faɪd **-fier/s** -faɪ.ər/z, ⓤⓢ -faɪ.ɚ/z
signor, S~ ˈsiː.njɔːr, ⓤⓢ siːˈnjɔːr **-s** -z
signora, S~ siˈnjɔː.rə, siː- **-s** -z
signorina, S~ ˌsiː.njɔːˈriː.nə, -njəˈ- **-s** -z
signpost ˈsaɪn.pəʊst, ˈsaɪm-, ⓤⓢ ˈsaɪn.poʊst **-s** -s **-ing** -ɪŋ **-ed** -ɪd
Sigourney sɪˈgɔː.ni, sə-, ⓤⓢ -ˈgɔːr-
Sigurd *English first name:* ˈsiː.gɜːd, ˈsɪg.ɜːd, ⓤⓢ ˈsɪg.ɚd *Scandinavian name:* ˈsɪg.ʊəd, -ɜːd, ⓤⓢ ˈsɪg.ɚd
Sikes saɪks
Sikh siːk **-s** -s **-ism** -ɪ.zəm
Sikkim ˈsɪk.ɪm, sɪˈkɪm, ⓤⓢ ˈsɪk.ɪm
Sikorsky sɪˈkɔː.ski, ⓤⓢ -ˈkɔːr-
silage ˈsaɪ.lɪdʒ
Silas ˈsaɪ.ləs, -læs, ⓤⓢ -ləs
Silchester ˈsɪl.tʃɪ.stər, -tʃə-, -tʃes.tər, ⓤⓢ -tʃes.tɚ
Sileby ˈsaɪl.bi
silenc|e ˈsaɪ.lənts **-es** -ɪz **-ing** -ɪŋ **-ed** -t
silencer ˈsaɪ.lənt.sər, ⓤⓢ -sɚ **-s** -z
silent ˈsaɪ.lənt **-ly** -li **-ness** -nəs, -nɪs **ˌsilent maˈjority; ˌsilent ˈpartner**
Silenus saɪˈliː.nəs, sɪ-, -ˈleɪ-, ⓤⓢ saɪˈliː-
Silesi|a saɪˈliː.zi|.ə, sɪ-, -ʒi|.ə, ˈ-ʒ|ə, -si|.ə, -ʃi|.ə, ˈ-ʃ|ə, ⓤⓢ saɪˈliː.ʃ|ə, sɪ-, -ʒ|ə **-an/s** -ən/z
silex ˈsaɪ.leks
silhouett|e ˌsɪl.uˈet, ˈ---, ⓤⓢ ˌsɪl.uˈet **-es** -s **-ing** -ɪŋ **-ed** -ɪd
silica ˈsɪl.ɪ.kə **ˌsilica ˈgel** ⓤⓢ **ˈsilica ˌgel**
silicate ˈsɪl.ɪ.keɪt, ˈ-ə-, -kət, -kɪt, ⓤⓢ -ɪ.keɪt, -kɪt
silicon ˈsɪl.ɪ.kən, ˈ-ə-, ⓤⓢ ˈ-ɪ-, -kɑːn **ˌsilicon ˈchip** ⓤⓢ **ˈsilicon ˌchip; ˌSilicon ˈValley**
silicone ˈsɪl.ɪ.kəʊn, ˈ-ə-, ⓤⓢ -ɪ.koʊn
silicosis ˌsɪl.ɪˈkəʊ.sɪs, -əˈ-, ⓤⓢ -ɪˈkoʊ-
silicotic ˌsɪl.ɪˈkɒt.ɪk, -əˈ-, ⓤⓢ -ɪˈkɑː.t̬ɪk **-s** -s
silk, S~ sɪlk **-s** -s **-en** -ən
Silkin ˈsɪl.kɪn
silk-screen ˈsɪlk.skriːn **-s** -z **-ing** -ɪŋ **-ed** -d **ˌsilk-screen ˈprinting**
silkworm ˈsɪlk.wɜːm, ⓤⓢ -wɝːm **-s** -z
silk|y ˈsɪl.k|i **-ier** -i.ər, ⓤⓢ -i.ɚ **-iest** -i.ɪst, -i.əst **-iness** -ɪ.nəs, -ɪ.nɪs
sill, S~ sɪl **-s** -z
sillabub ˈsɪl.ə.bʌb, -bəb, ⓤⓢ -bʌb **-s** -z
Sillery ˈsɪl.ər.i
Sillitoe ˈsɪl.ɪ.təʊ, ⓤⓢ -toʊ
Silloth ˈsɪl.əθ

S

silly ˈsɪl|.i **-ies** -iz **-ier** -i.əʳ, (US) -i.ɚ **-iest** -i.ɪst, -i.əst **-ily** -əl.i, -ɪ.li **-iness** -ɪ.nəs, -ɪ.nɪs
silly-billy ˌsɪl.iˈbɪl|.i **-ies** -iz
silo ˈsaɪ.ləʊ, (US) -loʊ **-s** -z
Siloam saɪˈləʊ.əm, sɪ-, -æm, (US) sɪˈloʊ.əm, saɪ-
Silsden ˈsɪlz.dən
silt sɪlt **-s** -s **-ing** -ɪŋ, (US) ˈsɪl.t̬ɪŋ **-ed** -ɪd, (US) ˈsɪl.t̬ɪd **-y** -i, (US) ˈsɪl.t̬i
Silurian saɪˈlʊə.ri.ən, sɪ-, -ˈljʊə-, -ˈljɔː-, (US) sɪˈlʊr.i-, saɪ-
Silva ˈsɪl.və
silvan ˈsɪl.vən
Silvanus sɪlˈveɪ.nəs
silv|er, S~ ˈsɪl.v|əʳ, (US) -v|ɚ **-ers** -əz, (US) -ɚz **-ering** -ər.ɪŋ **-ered** -əd, (US) -ɚd **-ery** -ər.i **-eriness** -ər.ɪ.nəs, -nɪs ˌ**silver** ˈ**birch**; ˌ**silver** ˈ**foil** (US) ˈ**silver** ˌ**foil**; ˌ**silver** ˈ**lining**; ˌ**silver** ˈ**nitrate**; ˌ**silver** ˈ**paper**; ˌ**silver** ˈ**plate** (US) ˈ**silver** ˌ**plate**; ˌ**silver** ˈ**screen**; ˌ**silver** ˈ**spoon**; ˌ**silver** ˈ**wedding**
silverfish ˈsɪl.və.fɪʃ, (US) -vɚ- **-es** -ɪz
Silverman ˈsɪl.və.mən, (US) -vɚ-
Silvers ˈsɪl.vəz, (US) -vɚz
silverside ˈsɪl.və.saɪd, (US) -vɚ- **-s** -z
silversmith ˈsɪl.və.smɪθ, (US) -vɚ- **-s** -s
Silverstone ˈsɪl.və.stəʊn, -stən, (US) -vɚ.stoʊn, -stən
silver-tongued ˌsɪl.vəˈtʌŋd, -ˈtɒŋd, (US) -vɚˈtʌŋd *stress shift:* ˌ**silver-tongued** ˈ**devil**
Silvertown ˈsɪl.və.taʊn, (US) -vɚ- **-s** -z
silverware ˈsɪl.və.weəʳ, (US) -vɚ.wer
Silvester sɪlˈves.təʳ, (US) -tɚ
Silvia ˈsɪl.vi.ə
Silvikrin® ˈsɪl.vɪ.krɪn, -və-
Sim sɪm
Simca® ˈsɪm.kə **-s** -z
SIM card ˈsɪmkɑːd, (US) -kɑːrd
Simcox ˈsɪm.kɒks, (US) -kɑːks
Simenon ˈsiː.mə.nɔ̃ːŋ, ˈsɪm.ə-, -nɒn, (US) ˈsiː.mə.noʊn, -nɔ̃ːn
Simeon ˈsɪm.i.ən
simian ˈsɪm.i.ən **-s** -z
similar ˈsɪm.ɪ.ləʳ, ˈ-ə-, (US) -ə.lɚ **-ly** -li
similarit|y ˌsɪm.ɪˈlær.ə.t|i, -əˈ-, -ɪ.t|i, (US) -əˈler.ə.t̬|i, -ˈlær- **-ies** -iz
simile ˈsɪm.ɪ.li, -əl.i, (US) -ə.li **-s** -z
similitude sɪˈmɪl.ɪ.tʃuːd, ˈ-ə-, -tjuːd, (US) səˈmɪl.ə.tuːd, -tjuːd **-s** -z
Simla ˈsɪm.lə
simm|er ˈsɪm|.əʳ, (US) -ɚ **-ers** -əz, (US) -ɚz **-ering** -ər.ɪŋ **-ered** -əd, (US) -ɚd
Simmonds ˈsɪm.əndz
Simmons ˈsɪm.ənz
Simms sɪmz
simnel, S~ ˈsɪm.nəl **-s** -z ˈ**simnel** ˌ**cake**
Simon ˈsaɪ.mən
Simond ˈsaɪ.mənd, ˈsɪm.ənd
Simonds ˈsɪm.əndz
Simone sɪˈməʊn, sə-, (US) -ˈmoʊn
simoniacal ˌsaɪ.məʊˈnaɪ.ə.kəl, (US) -məˈ-, ˌsɪm.əˈ-
Simons ˈsaɪ.mənz
simony ˈsaɪ.mə.ni, ˈsɪm.ə-
simoom sɪˈmuːm, (US) sɪ-, saɪ- **-s** -z
simpatico sɪmˈpæt.ɪ.kəʊ, (US) -ˈpæt̬.ɪ.koʊ
simp|er ˈsɪm.p|əʳ, (US) -p|ɚ **-ers** -əz, (US) -ɚz **-ering/ly** -ər.ɪŋ **-ered** -əd, (US) -ɚd
Simpkin ˈsɪmp.kɪn **-s** -z **-son** -sən
simp|le ˈsɪm.p|əl **-ler** -ləʳ, (US) -lɚ **-lest** -lɪst, -ləst **-ly** -li **-leness** -əl.nəs, -nɪs
simplehearted ˌsɪm.pəlˈhɑː.tɪd, (US) -ˈhɑːr.t̬ɪd *stress shift:* ˌ**simple-hearted** ˈ**person**
simple-minded ˌsɪm.pəlˈmaɪn.dɪd *stress shift:* ˌ**simple-minded** ˈ**person**
simpleton ˈsɪm.pəl.tən, (US) -tən **-s** -z
simplex ˈsɪm.pleks **-es** -ɪz
simplicity sɪmˈplɪs.ə.ti, -ɪ.ti, (US) -ə.t̬i
simplification ˌsɪm.plɪ.fɪˈkeɪ.ʃən, -plə-, -fəˈ-, (US) -plə- **-s** -z
simpli|fy ˈsɪm.plɪ|.faɪ, -plə- **-fies** -faɪz **-fying** -faɪ.ɪŋ **-fied** -faɪd
simplistic sɪmˈplɪs.tɪk **-ally** -əl.i, -li
Simplon ˈsæ̃m.plɔ̃ːŋ, ˈsæm-, ˈsɪm-, -plən, (US) ˈsɪm.plɑːn; (US) ˈsæ̃m.plɔ̃ːn
simply ˈsɪm.pli
Simpson ˈsɪmp.sən
Sims sɪmz
Simson ˈsɪmp.sən
simulacr|um ˌsɪm.jəˈleɪ.kr|əm, -jʊˈ-, -ˈlæk.r|əm, (US) -ˈleɪ-, -ˈlæk.r|əm **-ums** -əmz **-a** -ə
simu|late ˈsɪm.jə|.leɪt, -jʊ- **-lates** -leɪts **-lating** -leɪ.tɪŋ, (US) -leɪ.t̬ɪŋ **-lated** -leɪ.tɪd, (US) -leɪ.t̬ɪd
simulation ˌsɪm.jəˈleɪ.ʃən, -jʊˈ- **-s** -z
simulator ˈsɪm.jə.leɪ.təʳ, -jʊ-, (US) -t̬ɚ **-s** -z ˈ**flight** ˌ**simulator**
simulcast ˈsɪm.əl.kɑːst, (US) ˈsaɪ.məl.kæst, ˈsɪm.əl- **-s** -s **-ing** -ɪŋ
simultaneity ˌsɪm.əl.təˈneɪ.ə.ti, ˌsaɪ.məl-, -ˈniː-, -ɪ.ti, (US) ˌsaɪ.məl.təˈniː.ə.t̬i, ˌsɪm.əl-
simultaneous ˌsɪm.əlˈteɪ.ni.əs, ˌsaɪ.məlˈ-, (US) ˌsaɪ.məlˈteɪ.njəs, ˌsɪm.əlˈ-, -ni.əs **-ly** -li **-ness** -nəs, -nɪs
sin **n, v** *do wrong:* sɪn **-s** -z **-ning** -ɪŋ **-ned** -d **-ner/s** -əʳ/z, (US) -ɚ/z ˈ**sin** ˌ**bin**
sin *in trigonometry:* saɪn
Sinai ˈsaɪ.naɪ, -ni.aɪ, -neɪ, (US) ˈsaɪ.naɪ
sinapism ˈsɪn.ə.pɪ.zəm **-s** -z
Sinatra sɪˈnɑː.trə
Sinbad ˈsɪn.bæd, ˈsɪm-, (US) ˈsɪn-
since sɪnts
sincer|e sɪnˈsɪəʳ, sən-, (US) sɪnˈsɪr **-er** -əʳ, (US) -ɚ **-est** -ɪst, -əst **-ely** -li **-eness** -nəs, -nɪs
sincerity sɪnˈser.ə.ti, sən-, -ɪ.ti, (US) sɪnˈser.ə.t̬i
Sinclair ˈsɪŋ.kleəʳ, ˈsɪn-, -kləʳ; sɪŋˈkleəʳ, sɪn-, (US) sɪnˈkler, ˈ--
Sind sɪnd
Sindbad ˈsɪnd.bæd
Sindh sɪnd
Sindhi ˈsɪn.diː, -di
Sindlesham ˈsɪn.dəl.ʃəm
Sindy® ˈsɪn.di ˈ**Sindy** ˌ**doll**
sine *maths term:* saɪn **-s** -z *Latin word:* ˈsaɪ.ni, ˈsɪn.eɪ
Sinead, Sinéad ʃɪˈneɪd, -ˈneəd, (US) -ˈneɪd
sinecure ˈsaɪ.nɪ.kjʊəʳ, ˈsɪn.ɪ-, -kjɔːʳ, (US) ˈsaɪ.nə.kjʊr, ˈsɪn.ə- **-s** -z
sine die ˌsɪn.eɪˈdiː.eɪ; ˌsaɪ.niˈdaɪ.iː, (US) ˌsaɪ.niˈdaɪ, ˌsɪn.eɪˈdiː.eɪ
Sinel ˈsɪn.əl
sine qua non ˌsɪn.i.kwɑːˈnəʊn, ˌsaɪ.ni.kweɪˈnɒn, (US) ˌsɪn.eɪ.kwɑːˈnoʊn, ˌsaɪ.ni.kweɪˈnɑːn **-s** -z
sinew ˈsɪn.juː **-s** -z **-y** -i
sinfonia sɪnˈfəʊ.ni.ə; ˌsɪn.fəʊˈniː-, (US) ˌsɪn.fəˈniː-; (US) sɪnˈfoʊ.ni- **-s** -z
sinfonia concertante sɪnˌfəʊ.ni.əˌkɒnt.ʃəˈtæn.teɪ, (US) ˌsɪn.fəˌniː.əˌkɑːnt.sɚˈtɑːn.teɪ, -ˌkɑːn.tʃɚˈ-; (US) sɪnˌfoʊ.ni-
sinfonietta ˌsɪn.fəʊ.niˈet.ə, -fɒn.iˈ-, (US) -fəˈnjet̬-, -foʊˈ- **-s** -z
sinful ˈsɪn.fəl, -fʊl **-ly** -i **-ness** -nəs, -nɪs
sing sɪŋ **-s** -z **-ing** -ɪŋ **sang** sæŋ **sung** sʌŋ **singer/s** ˈsɪŋ.əʳ/z, (US) -ɚ/z
singable ˈsɪŋ.ə.bəl
sing-along ˈsɪŋ.ə.lɒŋ, (US) -lɑːŋ **-s** -z
Singapore ˌsɪŋ.əˈpɔːʳ, -gəˈ-, ˈ---, (US) ˈsɪŋ.ə.pɔːr, -gə-
Singaporean ˌsɪŋ.ə.pɔːˈriː.ən, -gə-; -ˈpɔː.ri-, (US) ˌsɪŋ.ə.pɔːˈriː-, -gə-; (US) -ˈpɔːr.i- **-s** -z
singe sɪndʒ **-es** -ɪz **-eing** -ɪŋ **-ed** -d
Singer ˈsɪŋ.əʳ, -gəʳ, (US) -ɚ, -gɚ
Singh sɪŋ
Singhalese ˌsɪŋ.həˈliːz, -gəˈ-, (US) -gəˈliːz, -ˈliːs
sing|le, S~ ˈsɪŋ.g|əl **-les** -z **-ling** -ɪŋ, ˈsɪŋ.glɪŋ **-led** -d **-ly** -li **-leness** -əl.nəs, -nɪs ˌ**single** ˈ**bed** (US) ˈ**single** ˌ**bed**; ˌ**single** ˈ**currency**; ˌ**single** ˈ**figures**; ˌ**single** ˈ**file**
single-breasted ˌsɪŋ.gəlˈbres.tɪd *stress shift:* ˌ**single-breasted** ˈ**jacket**
single-decker ˌsɪŋ.gəlˈdek.əʳ, (US) -ɚ **-s** -z *stress shift:* ˌ**single-decker** ˈ**bus**
single-handed ˌsɪŋ.gəlˈhæn.dɪd **-ly** -li **-ness** -nəs, -nɪs *stress shift:* ˌ**single-handed** ˈ**crossing**
single-hearted ˌsɪŋ.gəlˈhɑː.tɪd, (US) ˌsɪŋ.gəlˈhɑːr.t̬ɪd **-ly** -li **-ness** -nəs, -nɪs *stress shift, British only:* ˌ**single-hearted** ˈ**love**
single-minded ˌsɪŋ.gəlˈmaɪn.dɪd, (US) ˈsɪŋ.gəlˌmaɪn- **-ly** -li **-ness** -nəs, -nɪs *stress shift, British only:* ˌ**single-minded** ˈ**person**
single-sex ˌsɪŋ.gəlˈseks *stress shift:* ˌ**single-sex** ˈ**school**
singlestick ˈsɪŋ.gəl.stɪk **-s** -s
singlet ˈsɪŋ.glɪt, -glət **-s** -s
singleton, S~ ˈsɪŋ.gəl.tən **-s** -z
singly ˈsɪŋ.gli
singsong ˈsɪŋ.sɒŋ, (US) -sɑːŋ, -sɔːŋ **-s** -z
singular ˈsɪŋ.gjə.ləʳ, -gjʊ-, (US) -lɚ **-s** -z **-ly** -li

S

singularit|y ˌsɪŋ.gjəˈlær.ə.t|i, -gjʊˈ-, -ɪ.t|i, ⓤⓢ -ˈler.ə.ţ|i, -ˈlær- **-ies** -iz
Sinhalese ˌsɪŋ.həˈliːz, ˌsɪn-, ⓤⓢ ˌsɪn.həˈliːz, -ˈliːs
Sinim ˈsɪn.ɪm, ˈsaɪ.nɪm
sinister ˈsɪn.ɪ.stəʳ, ⓤⓢ -stɚ
sinistral ˈsɪn.ɪ.strəl **-ly** -i
Sinitic saɪˈnɪt.ɪk, sɪ-, ⓤⓢ -ˈnɪţ-
sink sɪŋk **-s** -s **-ing** -ɪŋ **sank** sæŋk **sunk** sʌŋk **sunken** ˈsʌŋ.kən
sinker ˈsɪŋ.kəʳ, ⓤⓢ -kɚ **-s** -z
sinless ˈsɪn.ləs, -lɪs **-ly** -li **-ness** -nəs, -nɪs
sinner ˈsɪn.əʳ, ⓤⓢ -ɚ **-s** -z
Sinn Fein ˌʃɪnˈfeɪn **-er/s** -əʳ/z, ⓤⓢ -ɚ/z
Sino- ˈsaɪ.nəʊ, ⓤⓢ -noʊ, -nə
sinologue ˈsɪn.ə.lɒg, ˈsaɪ.nə-, -ləʊg, ⓤⓢ ˈsaɪ.nə.lɑːg, ˈsɪn.ə-, -lɔːg **-s** -z
sinolog|y saɪˈnɒl.ə.dʒ|i, sɪ-, ⓤⓢ -ˈnɑː.lə- **-ist/s** -ɪst/s
sinuosit|y ˌsɪn.juˈɒs.ə.t|i, -ɪ.t|i, ⓤⓢ -ˈɑː.sə.ţ|i **-ies** -iz
sinuous ˈsɪn.ju.əs **-ly** -li **-ness** -nəs, -nɪs
sinus ˈsaɪ.nəs **-es** -ɪz
sinusitis ˌsaɪ.nəˈsaɪ.tɪs, -təs, ⓤⓢ -ţɪs, -ţəs
sinusoid ˈsaɪ.nə.sɔɪd **-s** -z
Siobhan ʃɪˈvɔːn, ʃə-, ⓤⓢ -ˈvɑːn, -ˈvɔːn
Sion ˈsaɪ.ən, ˈzaɪ-, ⓤⓢ ˈsaɪ-
Sioux singular: suː, sjuː, ⓤⓢ suː **plural:** suːz, sjuːz, suː, sjuː, ⓤⓢ suːz, suː
sip sɪp **-s** -s **-ping** -ɪŋ **-ped** -t
siphon n, v ˈsaɪ.fən **-s** -z **-ing** -ɪŋ, ˈsaɪf.nɪŋ **-ed** -d
sir, S~ *strong forms:* sɜːʳ, ⓤⓢ sɝː; *weak forms:* səʳ, ⓤⓢ sɚ **-s** -z
Note: Weak-form word. The strong form is used in various social situations. In school, it is often used by children to address a male teacher (e.g. 'Sir, can I go now?'), and contrastively (e.g. 'Dear Sir or Madam'). Similarly, in old-fashioned speech, the strong form would be used to begin addressing someone (e.g. 'Sir, you are a scoundrel'). When it occurs utterance-finally in addressing someone, either form may be used, although the weak form is more common in military usage (e.g. 'Ready to sail, sir'). In the title of a Knight (e.g. **Sir John Roberts**), the weak form is always used.
sirdar, S~ ˈsɜː.dɑːʳ, ⓤⓢ sɚˈdɑːr; ⓤⓢ ˈsɝː.dɑːr **-s** -z
sir|e saɪəʳ, ˈsaɪ.əʳ, ⓤⓢ saɪ.ɚ **-es** -z **-ing** -ɪŋ **-ed** -d
siren ˈsaɪə.rən, -rɪn, ⓤⓢ ˈsaɪ.rən **-s** -z
Sirion ˈsɪr.i.ən
Sirius ˈsɪr.i.əs
sirloin ˈsɜː.lɔɪn, ⓤⓢ ˈsɝː- **-s** -z
sirocco sɪˈrɒk.əʊ, sə-, ⓤⓢ səˈrɑː.koʊ, ʃə- **-s** -z
Siros ˈsɪə.rɒs, ⓤⓢ ˈsiː.rɑːs
sirrah ˈsɪr.ə
sirree, siree ˌsɜːˈriː, sə-, ⓤⓢ sə-
sis sɪs
sisal ˈsaɪ.səl, ⓤⓢ ˈsaɪ-, ˈsɪs.əl
Sisal *Mexican port:* sɪˈsɑːl, ⓤⓢ ˈsiː.səl, ˈsɪs.ɑːl
Sisera ˈsɪs.ər.ə
siskin, S~ ˈsɪs.kɪn **-s** -z
Sisley ˈsɪz.li
Sissinghurst ˈsɪs.ɪŋ.hɜːst, ⓤⓢ -hɝːst
Sisson ˈsɪs.ən **-s** -z
siss|y ˈsɪs|.i **-ies** -iz
sist|er ˈsɪs.t|əʳ, ⓤⓢ -t|ɚ **-ers** -əz, ⓤⓢ -ɚz **-erly** -əl.i, ⓤⓢ -ɚ.li
sisterhood ˈsɪs.tə.hʊd, ⓤⓢ -tɚ- **-s** -z
sister-in-law ˈsɪs.tər.ɪn.lɔː, ⓤⓢ -tɚ.ɪn.lɑː, -lɔː **sisters-in-law** -təz-, ⓤⓢ -tɚz-
Sistine ˈsɪs.tiːn, -taɪn, ⓤⓢ -tiːn, -ˈ- ˌ**Sistine** ˈ**Chapel**
sistrum ˈsɪs.trəm **-s** -z
Sisulu sɪˈsuː.luː
Sisyphean, Sisyphian ˌsɪs.ɪˈfiː.ən, -əˈ-, ⓤⓢ -əˈ-
Sisyphus ˈsɪs.ɪ.fəs, ˈ-ə-, ⓤⓢ ˈ-ə-
sit sɪt **-s** -s **-ting/s** -ɪŋ/z, ⓤⓢ ˈsɪţ.ɪŋ/z **sat** sæt ˌ**sit on the** ˈ**fence**
Sita ˈsɪt.ə, ˈsiː.tə, ⓤⓢ ˈsiː.tɑː
sitar sɪˈtɑːʳ; ˈsɪt.ɑːʳ, ⓤⓢ sɪˈtɑːr
sitcom ˈsɪt.kɒm, ⓤⓢ -kɑːm **-s** -z
sit-down ˈsɪt.daʊn
sit|e saɪt **-es** -s **-ing** -ɪŋ **-ed** -ɪd
sit-in ˈsɪt.ɪn, ⓤⓢ ˈsɪţ- **-s** -z
sitter ˈsɪt.əʳ, ⓤⓢ ˈsɪţ.ɚ **-s** -z
sitting ˈsɪt.ɪŋ, ⓤⓢ ˈsɪţ- **-s** -z ˌ**Sitting** ˈ**Bull;** ˌ**sitting** ˈ**duck;** ˈ**sitting** ˌ**room;** ˌ**sitting** ˈ**target;** ˌ**sitting** ˈ**tenant**
Sittingbourne ˈsɪt.ɪŋ.bɔːn, ⓤⓢ ˈsɪţ.ɪŋ.bɔːrn
situate adj ˈsɪt.ju.eɪt, ˈsɪtʃ.u-, -ɪt, -ət, ⓤⓢ ˈsɪtʃ.u.ɪt, -eɪt
situ|ate v ˈsɪt.ju|.eɪt, ˈsɪtʃ.u-, ⓤⓢ ˈsɪtʃ.u- **-ates** -eɪts **-ating** -eɪ.tɪŋ, ⓤⓢ -eɪ.ţɪŋ **-ated** -eɪ.tɪd, ⓤⓢ -eɪ.ţɪd
situation ˌsɪt.juˈeɪ.ʃən, ˌsɪtʃ.uˈ-, ⓤⓢ ˌsɪtʃ.uˈ- **-s** -z ˌ**situation** ˈ**comedy**
sit-up ˈsɪt.ʌp **-s** -s
Sitwell ˈsɪt.wəl, -wel
Siva ˈʃiː.və, ˈsiː-, ˈsɪv.ə, ˈʃɪv-, ⓤⓢ ˈʃiː.və, ˈsiː-
Siward ˈsjuː.əd, ⓤⓢ -ɚd, ˈsuː-
six sɪks **-es** -ɪz **-fold** -fəʊld, ⓤⓢ -foʊld
sixer ˈsɪk.səʳ, ⓤⓢ -sɚ **-s** -z
sixish ˈsɪk.sɪʃ
six-pack ˈsɪks.pæk **-s** -s
six|pence ˈsɪks|.pənts **-pences** -pənt.sɪz **-penny** -pən.i
Note: See note under **penny**.
six-shooter ˈsɪksˌʃuː.təʳ, ˈsɪkʃ-, ˌ-ˈ--, ⓤⓢ ˈsɪksˌʃuː.ţɚ **-s** -z
sixte sɪkst
sixteen ˌsɪkˈstiːn **-s** -z **-th/s** -θ/s **-thly** -θ.li *stress shift, British only:* ˌ**sixteen** ˈ**days;** *stress shift, British only:* **six**ˈ**teenth** ˌ**note**
sixteenmo, 16mo sɪkˈstiːn.məʊ, ⓤⓢ -moʊ **-s** -z
sixth sɪksθ **-s** -s **-ly** -li ˈ**sixth** ˌ**form;** ˌ**sixth form** ˈ**college;** ˌ**sixth** ˈ**sense**
Sixtus ˈsɪk.stəs
sixt|y ˈsɪk.st|i **-ies** -iz **-ieth/s** -i.əθs, -i.ɪθ/s
sixty-nine, 69 ˌsɪk.stiˈnaɪn
sizar ˈsaɪ.zəʳ, ⓤⓢ -zɚ **-s** -z **-ship/s** -ʃɪp/s
siz|e saɪz **-es** -ɪz **-ing** -ɪŋ **-ed** -d
sizeab|le, sizab|le ˈsaɪ.zə.b|əl **-ly** -li **-leness** -əl.nəs, -nɪs
Sizer ˈsaɪ.zəʳ, ⓤⓢ -zɚ
Sizewell ˈsaɪz.wəl, -wel
sizzl|e ˈsɪz.əl **-es** -z **-ing** -ɪŋ, ˈsɪz.lɪŋ **-ed** -d
sizzler ˈsɪz.ləʳ, -əl.əʳ, ⓤⓢ ˈ-lɚ, -əl.ɚ **-s** -z
sjambok ˈʃæm.bɒk, -bʌk, ⓤⓢ -bɑːk, -bʌk **-s** -s **-ing** -ɪŋ **-ed** -t
ska skɑː
Skagerrak ˈskæg.ə.ræk
skanky ˈskæŋ.ki **-ier** -i.əʳ, ⓤⓢ -i.ɚ **-iest** -i.ɪst, i.əst
Skara Brae ˌskær.əˈbreɪ
skat skæt
skat|e skeɪt **-es** -s **-ing** -ɪŋ, ⓤⓢ ˈskeɪ.ţɪŋ **-ed** -ɪd, ⓤⓢ ˈskeɪ.ţɪd **-er/s** -əʳ/z, ⓤⓢ ˈskeɪ.ţɚ/z
skateboard ˈskeɪt.bɔːd, ⓤⓢ -bɔːrd **-s** -z **-er/s** -əʳ/z, ⓤⓢ -ɚ/z **-ing** -ɪŋ
skating-rink ˈskeɪ.tɪŋ.rɪŋk **-s** -s
skean dhu ˌskiː.ənˈduː, ˌskiːnˈ-, ⓤⓢ ˌskiːn-, ˌʃkiːn- **-s** -z
Skeat skiːt
skedaddl|e skɪˈdæd.əl **-es** -z **-ing** -ɪŋ, -ˈdæd.lɪŋ **-ed** -d
Skeels skiːlz
Skeggs skegz
Skegness ˌskegˈnes *stress shift:* ˌ**Skegness** ˈ**beach**
skein skeɪn **-s** -z
skeletal ˈskel.ɪ.təl, ˈ-ə-; skɪˈliː-, skə-, ⓤⓢ ˈskel.ə.ţəl **-ly** -i
skeleton ˈskel.ɪ.tən, ˈ-ə-, ⓤⓢ ˈ-ə- **-s** -z ˈ**skeleton** ˌ**key;** ˌ**skeleton in the** ˈ**cupboard;** ˌ**skeleton in the** ˈ**closet**
Skelmanthorpe ˈskel.mən.θɔːp, ⓤⓢ -θɔːrp
Skelmersdale ˈskel.məz.deɪl, ⓤⓢ -mɚz-
skelter ˈskel.təʳ, ⓤⓢ -tɚ
Skelton ˈskel.tən
skeptic ˈskep.tɪk **-s** -s **-al** -əl **-ally** -əl.i, -li
skepticism ˈskep.tɪ.sɪ.zəm, -tə-, ⓤⓢ -tə-
sketch sketʃ **-es** -ɪz **-ing** -ɪŋ **-ed** -t **-able** -ə.bəl **-er/s** -əʳ/z, ⓤⓢ -ɚ/z
sketchbook ˈsketʃ.bʊk **-s** -s
Sketchley ˈsketʃ.li
sketchpad ˈsketʃ.pæd **-s** -z
sketch|y ˈsketʃ|.i **-ier** -i.əʳ, ⓤⓢ -i.ɚ **-iest** -i.ɪst, -i.əst **-ily** -əl.i, -ɪ.li **-iness** -ɪ.nəs, -ɪ.nɪs
skew skjuː **-s** -z **-ing** -ɪŋ **-ed** -d
skewbald ˈskjuː.bɔːld, ⓤⓢ -bɑːld, -bɔːld
skewer ˈskjuː.əʳ, ⓤⓢ ˈskjuː.ɚ **-s** -z **-ing** -ɪŋ **-ed** -d
skew-whiff ˌskjuːˈhwɪf
Skey skiː
ski skiː **-s** -z **-ing** -ɪŋ **-ed** -d ˈ**ski** ˌ**lift;** ˈ**ski** ˌ**pants**

S

skibob ˈskiː.bɒb, (US) -bɑːb **-s** -z **-bing** -ɪŋ **-bed** -d
skid skɪd **-s** -z **-ding** -ɪŋ **-ded** -ɪd **-dy** -i ˌ**skid** ˈ**row**
Skiddaw ˈskɪd.ɔː; *locally:* -ə, (US) ˈskɪd.ɑː, -ɔː
Skidmore ˈskɪd.mɔːʳ, (US) -mɔːr
skidpan ˈskɪd.pæn **-s** -z
skier ˈskiː.əʳ, (US) -ɚ **-s** -z
skiff skɪf **-s** -s
skiffle ˈskɪf.əl
ski-jump ˈskiː.dʒʌmp **-s** -s **-ing** -ɪŋ **-ed** -t **-er/s** -əʳ/z, (US) -ɚ/z
skilful ˈskɪl.fəl, -fʊl **-ly** -i **-ness** -nəs, -nɪs
skill skɪl **-s** -z **-ed** -d
skillet ˈskɪl.ɪt **-s** -s
skilly ˈskɪl.i
skim skɪm **-s** -z **-ming** -ɪŋ **-med** -d **-mer/s** -əʳ/z, (US) -ɚ/z
skimp skɪmp **-s** -s **-ing/ly** -ɪŋ/li **-ed** -t
skimp|y ˈskɪm.p|i **-ier** -i.əʳ, (US) -i.ɚ **-iest** -i.ɪst, -i.əst **-ily** -əl.i, -ɪ.li **-iness** -ɪ.nəs, -ɪ.nɪs
skin skɪn **-s** -z **-ning** -ɪŋ **-ned** -d **-less** -ləs, -lɪs **by the** ˌ**skin of one's** ˈ**teeth**
skincare ˈskɪn.keəʳ, ˈskɪŋ-, (US) -ker
skin-deep ˌskɪnˈdiːp, (US) ˌskɪnˈdiːp, ˈ-- *stress shift, British only:* ˌ**skin-deep** ˈ**wound**
skin-div|ing ˈskɪnˌdaɪ.v|ɪŋ **-er/s** -əʳ/z, (US) -ɚ/z
skinflint ˈskɪn.flɪnt **-s** -s
skinful ˈskɪn.fʊl **-s** -z
skinhead ˈskɪn.hed **-s** -z
skink skɪŋk **-s** -s
skinner, S~ ˈskɪn.əʳ, (US) -ɚ **-s** -z
skinn|y ˈskɪn|.i **-ier** -i.əʳ, (US) -i.ɚ **-iest** -i.ɪst, -i.əst **-iness** -ɪ.nəs, -ɪ.nɪs
skinny-dip ˈskɪn.i.dɪp **-s** -s **-ping** -ɪŋ **-ped** -t
skint skɪnt
skintight ˈskɪn.taɪt
skip skɪp **-s** -s **-ping** -ɪŋ **-ped** -t
skipjack ˈskɪp.dʒæk **-s** -s
skipper ˈskɪp.əʳ, (US) -ɚ **-s** -z **-ing** -ɪŋ **-ed** -d
skipping-rope ˈskɪp.ɪŋ.rəʊp, (US) -roʊp **-s** -s
Skipton ˈskɪp.tən
skirl skɜːl, (US) skɝːl **-s** -z
skirmish ˈskɜː.mɪʃ, (US) ˈskɝː- **-es** -ɪz **-ing** -ɪŋ **-ed** -t **-er/s** -əʳ/z, (US) -ɚ/z
skirt skɜːt, (US) skɝːt **-s** -s **-ing/s** -ɪŋ/z, (US) ˈskɝː.t̬ɪŋ/z **-ed** -ɪd, (US) ˈskɝː.t̬ɪd
skirting ˈskɜː.tɪŋ, (US) ˈskɝː.t̬ɪŋ **-s** -z
skirting-board ˈskɜː.tɪŋ.bɔːd, (US) ˈskɝː.t̬ɪŋ.bɔːrd **-s** -z
skit skɪt **-s** -s
skitter ˈskɪt.əʳ, (US) ˈskɪt̬.ɚ **-s** -z **-ing** -ɪŋ **-ed** -d
skittish ˈskɪt.ɪʃ, (US) ˈskɪt̬- **-ly** -li **-ness** -nəs, -nɪs
skittle ˈskɪt.əl, (US) ˈskɪt̬- **-s** -z
skiv|e skaɪv **-es** -z **-ing** -ɪŋ **-ed** -d **-er/s** -əʳ/z, (US) -ɚ/z
skivv|y ˈskɪv|.i **-ies** -iz
Skoda® ˈskəʊ.də, (US) ˈskoʊ-
Skokholm ˈskɒk.həʊm; ˈskəʊ.kəm, (US) ˈskɑːk.hoʊm; ˈskoʊ.kəm
Skol® skɒl, skəʊl, (US) skoʊl, skɑːl
Skopje ˈskɔː.pjeɪ, ˈskɒp.jeɪ, (US) ˈskɔː.pjeɪ, ˈskɑː-
Skrimshire ˈskrɪm.ʃəʳ, -ʃaɪəʳ, (US) -ʃɚ, -ʃaɪɚ
Skrine skriːn
skua ˈskjuː.ə, skjʊə, (US) ˈskjuː.ə **-s** -z
skul(l)duggery skʌlˈdʌg.ər.i
skulk skʌlk **-s** -s **-ing** -ɪŋ **-ed** -t
skull skʌl **-s** -z ˌ**skull and** ˈ**cross-bones**
skullcap ˈskʌl.kæp **-s** -s
skunk skʌŋk **-s** -s
sk|y, S~® sk|aɪ **-ies** -aɪz **-ying** -aɪ.ɪŋ **-ied** -aɪd **-ier/s** -aɪ.əʳ/z, (US) -aɪ.ɚ/z
sky-blue ˌskaɪˈbluː *stress shift:* ˌ**sky-blue** ˈ**fabric**
skycap, S~ ˈskaɪ.kæp **-s** -s
skydiv|er ˈskaɪˌdaɪ.v|əʳ, (US) -v|ɚ **-ers** -əz, (US) -ɚz **-ing** -ɪŋ
Skye skaɪ
sky-high ˌskaɪˈhaɪ *stress shift:* ˌ**sky-high** ˈ**prices**
skyjack ˈskaɪ.dʒæk **-s** -s **-ing** -ɪŋ **-ed** -t **-er/s** -əʳ/z, (US) -ɚ/z
skylark ˈskaɪ.lɑːk, (US) -lɑːrk **-s** -s **-ing** -ɪŋ **-ed** -t **-er/s** -əʳ/z, (US) -ɚ/z
skylight ˈskaɪ.laɪt **-s** -s
skyline ˈskaɪ.laɪn **-s** -z
Skype skaɪp
skyrock|et ˈskaɪˌrɒk|.ɪt, (US) -ˌrɑː.k|ɪt **-ets** -ɪts **-eting** -ɪ.tɪŋ, (US) -ɪ.t̬ɪŋ **-eted** -ɪ.tɪd, (US) -ɪ.t̬ɪd
skyscape ˈskaɪ.skeɪp **-s** -s
skyscraper ˈskaɪˌskreɪ.pəʳ, (US) -pɚ **-s** -z
skyward ˈskaɪ.wəd, (US) -wɚd **-s** -z
skywriting ˈskaɪˌraɪ.tɪŋ, (US) -t̬ɪŋ
slab slæb **-s** -z **-bing** -ɪŋ **-bed** -d
slack slæk **-s** -s **-er** -əʳ, (US) -ɚ **-est** -ɪst, -əst **-ly** -li **-ness** -nəs, -nɪs **-ing** -ɪŋ **-ed** -t **-er/s** -əʳ/z, (US) -ɚ/z
slacken ˈslæk.ən **-s** -z **-ing** -ɪŋ, ˈslæk.nɪŋ **-ed** -d
Slade sleɪd
slag slæg **-s** -z **-ging** -ɪŋ **-ged** -d **-gy** -i
slagheap ˈslæg.hiːp **-s** -s
slain (from **slay**) sleɪn
slainte ˈslɑːn.tʃə, -tjə
Slaithwaite ˈslæθ.wət, -weɪt; *locally also:* ˈslaʊ.ɪt
slak|e sleɪk **-es** -s **-ing** -ɪŋ **-ed** -t
slalom ˈslɑː.ləm **-s** -z
slam slæm **-s** -z **-ming** -ɪŋ **-med** -d
slam-bang ˌslæmˈbæŋ *stress shift:* ˌ**slam-bang** ˈ**clatter**
slam-dunk ˌslæmˈdʌŋk, ˈ-- **-s** -s **-ing** -ɪŋ **-ed** -t
slammer ˈslæm.əʳ, (US) -ɚ **-s** -z
sland|er ˈslɑːn.d|əʳ, (US) ˈslæn.d|ɚ **-ers** -əz, (US) -ɚz **-ering** -ər.ɪŋ **-ered** -əd, (US) -ɚd **-erer/s** -ər.əʳ/z, (US) -ɚ.ɚ/z
slanderous ˈslɑːn.dər.əs, ˈ-drəs, (US) ˈslæn.dɚ.əs, ˈ-drəs **-ly** -li **-ness** -nəs, -nɪs
slang slæŋ **-s** -z **-ing** -ɪŋ **-ed** -d **-y** -i **-ier** -i.əʳ, (US) -i.ɚ **-iest** -i.ɪst, -i.əst **-ily** -əl.i, -ɪ.li **-iness** -ɪ.nəs, -ɪ.nɪs ˈ**slanging** ˌ**match**
slant slɑːnt, (US) slænt **-s** -s **-ing/ly** -ɪŋ/li, (US) ˈslæn.t̬ɪŋ/li **-ed** -ɪd, (US) ˈslæn.t̬ɪd
slantways ˈslɑːnt.weɪz, (US) ˈslænt-
slantwise ˈslɑːnt.waɪz, (US) ˈslænt-
slap slæp **-s** -s **-ping** -ɪŋ **-ped** -t ˌ**slap and** ˈ**tickle**
slap-bang ˌslæpˈbæŋ *stress shift:* ˌ**slap-bang** ˈ**central**
slapdash ˈslæp.dæʃ, ˌ-ˈ-
slaphappy ˌslæpˈhæp.i, (US) ˈ-ˌ-- *stress shift, British only:* ˌ**slaphappy** ˈ**state**
slapper ˈslæp.əʳ, (US) -ɚ **-s** -z
slapstick ˈslæp.stɪk **-s** -s
slap-up ˌslæpˈʌp, (US) ˈ-- *stress shift, British only:* ˌ**slap-up** ˈ**meal**
slash slæʃ **-es** -ɪz **-ing** -ɪŋ **-ed** -t **-er/s** -əʳ/z, (US) -ɚ/z
slash-and-burn ˌslæʃ.ənd ˈbɜːn, -əmˈ-, (US) -ənd ˈbɝːn *stress shift:* ˌ**slash-and-burn** ˈ**farming**
slat slæt **-s** -s **-ted** -ɪd
slat|e sleɪt **-es** -s **-ing** -ɪŋ, (US) ˈsleɪ.t̬ɪŋ **-ed** -ɪd, (US) ˈsleɪ.t̬ɪd **-er/s** -əʳ/z, (US) ˈsleɪ.t̬ɚ/z
Slater ˈsleɪ.təʳ, (US) -t̬ɚ
slath|er ˈslæð|.əʳ, (US) -ɚ **-ers** -əz, (US) -ɚz **-ering** -ər.ɪŋ **-ered** -əd, (US) -ɚd
Slatkin ˈslæt.kɪn
slattern ˈslæt.ən, -ɜːn, (US) ˈslæt̬.ɚn **-s** -z **-ly** -li **-liness** -lɪ.nəs, -nɪs
Slattery ˈslæt.ər.i, (US) ˈslæt̬.ɚ-
slaty ˈsleɪ.ti, (US) -t̬i
slaught|er, S~ n, v ˈslɔː.t|əʳ, (US) ˈslɑː.t̬|ɚ, ˈslɔː- **-ers** -əz, (US) -ɚz **-ering** -ər.ɪŋ **-ered** -əd, (US) -ɚd **-erer/s** -ər.əʳ/z, (US) -ɚ.ɚ/z **-erous/ly** -ər.əs/li
slaughterhou|se ˈslɔː.tə.haʊ|s, (US) ˈslɑː.t̬ɚ-, ˈslɔː- **-ses** -zɪz
Slav slɑːv, (US) slɑːv, slæv **-s** -z
slav|e sleɪv **-es** -z **-ing** -ɪŋ **-ed** -d **-er/s** -əʳ/z, (US) -ɚ/z ˈ**slave** ˌ**driver;** ˌ**slave** ˈ**labour;** ˈ**slave** ˌ**trade**
slave-owner ˈsleɪvˌəʊ.nəʳ, (US) -ˌoʊ.nɚ **-s** -z
slaver n *slave-trader:* ˈsleɪ.vəʳ, (US) -vɚ **-s** -z
slav|er n, v *slobber:* ˈslæv|.əʳ, ˈsleɪ.v|əʳ, (US) ˈslæv|.ɚ **-ers** -əz, (US) -ɚz **-ering** -ər.ɪŋ **-ered** -əd, (US) -ɚd
slavery ˈsleɪ.vər.i
slavey ˈsleɪ.vi, ˈslæv.i **-s** -z
Slavic ˈslɑː.vɪk, ˈslæv.ɪk
slavish ˈsleɪ.vɪʃ **-ly** -li **-ness** -nəs, -nɪs
Slavonic sləˈvɒn.ɪk, slævˈɒn-, (US) sləˈvɑː.nɪk
slaw slɔː, (US) slɑː, slɔː **-s** -z
slay sleɪ **-s** -z **-ing/s** -ɪŋ/z **-ed** -d **slew** sluː **slain** sleɪn **slayer/s** sleɪ.əʳ/z, (US) -ɚ/z
Slazenger® ˈslæz.ən.dʒəʳ, (US) -dʒɚ
Sleaford ˈsliː.fəd, (US) -fɚd
sleaze sliːz
sleazebag ˈsliːz.bæg **-s** -z

S

sleazeball ˈsliːz.bɔːl, (US) -bɔːl, -bɑːl -s -z
sleaz|y ˈsliː.z|i -ier -i.əʳ, (US) -i.ɚ -iest -i.ɪst, -i.əst -ily -əl.i, -ɪ.li -iness -ɪ.nəs, -ɪ.nɪs
sled sled -s -z -ding -ɪŋ -ded -ɪd
sledg|e sledʒ -es -ɪz -ing -ɪŋ -ed -d
sledgehammer ˈsledʒˌhæm.əʳ, (US) -ɚ -s -z -ing -ɪŋ -ed -d
sleek sliːk -er -əʳ, (US) -ɚ -est -ɪst, -əst -ly -li -ness -nəs, -nɪs
sleep sliːp -s -s -ing -ɪŋ slept slept ˈ**sleeping ˌbag**; ˌ**Sleeping ˈBeauty**; ˈ**sleeping ˌcar**; ˈ**sleeping ˌdraught**; ˈ**sleeping ˌpartner**; ˈ**sleeping ˌpill**; ˌ**sleeping poˈliceman**; ˈ**sleeping ˌsickness**
sleeper ˈsliː.pəʳ, (US) -pɚ -s -z
sleepless ˈsliː.pləs, -plɪs -ly -li -ness -nəs, -nɪs
sleepout ˈsliːp.aʊt -s -s
sleepover ˈsliːpˌəʊ.vəʳ, (US) -ˌoʊ.vɚ -s -z
sleepwalk|er ˈsliːpˌwɔː.k|əʳ, (US) -ˌwɑː.k|ɚ, -ˌwɔː- -ers -əz, (US) -ɚz -ing -ɪŋ
sleep|y ˈsliː.p|i -ier -i.əʳ, (US) -i.ɚ -iest -i.ɪst, -i.əst -ily -əl.i, -ɪ.li -iness -ɪ.nəs, -ɪ.nɪs
sleepyhead ˈsliː.pi.hed -s -z
sleet sliːt -s -s -ing -ɪŋ, (US) ˈsliː.t̬ɪŋ -ed -ɪd, (US) ˈsliː.t̬ɪd -y -i, (US) ˈsliː.t̬i -iness -ɪ.nəs, -ɪ.nɪs, (US) ˈsliː.t̬ɪ.nəs, -nɪs
sleeve sliːv -s -z -d -d -less -ləs, -lɪs
sleigh sleɪ -s -z -ing -ɪŋ -ed -d ˈ**sleigh ˌbells**
sleight, S~ slaɪt ˌ**sleight of ˈhand**
Sleights slaɪts
slender ˈslen.dəʳ, (US) -dɚ -er -əʳ, (US) -ɚ -est -ɪst, -əst -ly -li -ness -nəs, -nɪs
slenderiz|e ˈslen.dər.aɪz, (US) -də.raɪz -es -ɪz -ing -ɪŋ -ed -d
slept (from **sleep**) slept
sleuth sluːθ, sljuːθ, (US) sluːθ -s -s -ing -ɪŋ -ed -t
sleuthhound ˈsluːθ.haʊnd, ˈsljuːθ-, (US) ˈsluːθ- -s -z
slew sluː -s -z -ing -ɪŋ -ed -d
slic|e slaɪs -es -ɪz -ing -ɪŋ -ed -t -er/s -əʳ/z, (US) -ɚ/z ˌ**sliced ˈbread**
slick slɪk -er -əʳ, (US) -ɚ -est -ɪst, -əst -s -z -ing -ɪŋ -ly -li -ed -t -ness -nəs, -nɪs
slicker ˈslɪk.əʳ, (US) -ɚ -s -z
slid (from **slide**) slɪd
slid|e slaɪd -es -z -ing -ɪŋ slid slɪd ˈ**slide proˌjector**; ˈ**slide ˌrule**; ˈ**slide ˌvalve**; ˌ**sliding ˈdoor**; ˌ**sliding ˈscale**
slider ˈslaɪ.dəʳ, (US) -dɚ -s -z
slight slaɪt -s -s -er -əʳ, (US) ˈslaɪ.t̬ɚ -est -ɪst, -əst, (US) ˈslaɪ.t̬ɪst, -t̬əst -ly -li -ness -nəs, -nɪs -ing/ly -ɪŋ/li, (US) ˈslaɪ.t̬ɪŋ/li -ed -ɪd, (US) ˈslaɪ.t̬ɪd
Sligo ˈslaɪ.gəʊ, (US) -goʊ
slim, S~ slɪm -mer/s -əʳ/z, (US) -ɚ/z -mest -ɪst, -əst -ly -li -ness -nəs, -nɪs -s -z -ming -ɪŋ -med -d ˈ**Slim diˌsease**
Slimbridge ˈslɪm.brɪdʒ
slim|e slaɪm -es -z -ing -ɪŋ -ed -d
slimline ˈslɪm.laɪn
slim|y ˈslaɪ.m|i -ier -i.əʳ, (US) -i.ɚ -iest -i.ɪst, -i.əst -ily -əl.i, -ɪ.li -iness -ɪ.nəs, -ɪ.nɪs
sling slɪŋ -s -z -ing -ɪŋ slung slʌŋ
slingback ˈslɪŋ.bæk -s -s
slingshot ˈslɪŋ.ʃɒt, (US) -ʃɑːt -s -s
slink slɪŋk -s -s -ing -ɪŋ slunk slʌŋk
slink|y ˈslɪŋ.k|i -ier -i.əʳ, (US) -i.ɚ -iest -i.ɪst, -i.əst
slip slɪp -s -s -ping -ɪŋ -ped -t ˌ**slipped ˈdisc**; ˈ**slip ˌroad**; ˈ**slip ˌstitch**; ˌ**give someone the ˈslip**
slipcas|e ˈslɪp.keɪs -es -ɪz
slipcover ˈslɪpˌkʌv.əʳ, (US) -ɚ -s -z
slipknot ˈslɪp.nɒt, (US) -nɑːt -s -s
slip-on ˈslɪp.ɒn, (US) -ɑːn -s -z
slipover ˈslɪpˌəʊ.vəʳ, (US) -ˌoʊ.vɚ -s -z
slippag|e ˈslɪp.ɪdʒ -es -ɪz
slipper ˈslɪp.əʳ, (US) -ɚ -s -z -ing -ɪŋ -ed -d
slipper|y ˈslɪp.ər|.i -ier -i.əʳ, (US) -i.ɚ -iest -i.ɪst, -i.əst -ily -əl.i, -ɪ.li -iness -ɪ.nəs, -ɪ.nɪs ˌ**slippery ˈslope**
slipp|y ˈslɪp|.i -ier -i.əʳ, (US) -i.ɚ -iest -i.ɪst, -i.əst -iness -ɪ.nəs, -ɪ.nɪs
slipshod ˈslɪp.ʃɒd, (US) -ʃɑːd
slipstream ˈslɪp.striːm -s -z -ing -ɪŋ -ed -d
slip-up ˈslɪp.ʌp -s -s
slipway ˈslɪp.weɪ -s -z
slit slɪt -s -s -ting -ɪŋ, (US) ˈslɪt̬.ɪŋ
slith|er ˈslɪð|.əʳ, (US) -ɚ -ers -əz, (US) -ɚz -ering -ər.ɪŋ -ered -əd, (US) -ɚd -ery -ər.i
sliv|er ˈslɪv|.əʳ, (US) -ɚ -ers -əz, (US) -ɚz -ering -ər.ɪŋ -ered -əd, (US) -ɚd
slivovitz ˈslɪv.ə.vɪts, ˈsliː.və-, (US) ˈslɪv.ə-
Sloan sləʊn, (US) sloʊn
Sloan|e sləʊn, (US) sloʊn -es -z -ey -i -ier -i.əʳ, (US) -ɚ -iest -i.ɪst, -əst ˌ**Sloane ˈRanger**; ˌ**Sloane ˈSquare**
slob slɒb, (US) slɑːb -s -z -bing -ɪŋ -bed -d -bish -ɪʃ
slobb|er ˈslɒb|.əʳ, (US) ˈslɑː.b|ɚ -ers -əz, (US) -ɚz -ering -ər.ɪŋ -ered -əd, (US) -ɚd -erer/s -ə.rəʳ/z, (US) -ɚ.ɚ/z
slobber|y ˈslɒb.ər|.i, (US) ˈslɑː.bɚ- -iness -ɪ.nəs, -ɪ.nɪs
Slobodan ˈslɒb.ə.dæn, sləˈbɒd.ən, (US) ˈslɑːbə-
Slocombe ˈsləʊ.kəm, (US) ˈsloʊ-
Slocum ˈsləʊ.kəm, (US) ˈsloʊ-
sloe sləʊ, (US) sloʊ -s -z ˌ**sloe ˈgin**
slog slɒg, (US) slɑːg, slɔːg -s -z -ging -ɪŋ -ged -d -ger/s -əʳ/z, (US) -ɚ/z
slogan ˈsləʊ.gən, (US) ˈsloʊ- -s -z
sloganeer ˌsləʊ.gəˈnɪəʳ, (US) ˌsloʊ.gəˈnɪr -s -z -ing/s -ɪŋ/z -ed -d
sloganiz|e, -is|e ˈsləʊ.gə.naɪz, (US) ˈsloʊ- -es -ɪz -ing -ɪŋ -ed -d -er/s -əʳ/z, (US) -ɚ/z
sloop sluːp -s -s
slop slɒp, (US) slɑːp -s -s -ping -ɪŋ -ped -t
slop|e sləʊp, (US) sloʊp -es -s -ing/ly -ɪŋ/li -ed -t -er/s -əʳ/z, (US) -ɚ/z
Sloper ˈsləʊ.pəʳ, (US) ˈsloʊ.pɚ
slopp|y ˈslɒp|.i, (US) ˈslɑː.p|i -ier -i.əʳ, (US) -i.ɚ -iest -i.ɪst, -i.əst -ily -əl.i, -ɪ.li -iness -ɪ.nəs, -ɪ.nɪs ˌ**sloppy ˈjoe**
slosh slɒʃ, (US) slɑːʃ -es -ɪz -ing -ɪŋ -ed -t
slosh|y ˈslɒʃ|.i, (US) ˈslɑː.ʃ|i -ier -i.əʳ, (US) -i.ɚ -iest -i.ɪst, -i.əst -iness -ɪ.nəs, -ɪ.nɪs
slot slɒt, (US) slɑːt -s -s -ting -ɪŋ, (US) ˈslɑː.t̬ɪŋ -ted -ɪd, (US) ˈslɑː.t̬ɪd
sloth sləʊθ, (US) slɑːθ, slɔːθ, sloʊθ -s -s
slothful ˈsləʊθ.fəl, -fʊl, (US) ˈslɑːθ-, ˈslɔːθ-, ˈsloʊθ- -ly -i -ness -nəs, -nɪs
slot-machine ˈslɒt.məˌʃiːn, (US) ˈslɑːt- -s -z
slouch slaʊtʃ -es -ɪz -ing/ly -ɪŋ/li -ed -t
slough **n** *bog:* slaʊ, (US) sluː, slaʊ -s -z -y -i
slough **v** *skin:* slʌf -s -s -ing -ɪŋ -ed -t
Slough slaʊ
Slovak ˈsləʊ.væk, (US) ˈsloʊ.vɑːk, -væk -s -s
Slovaki|a sləʊˈvæk.i|.ə, -ˈvɑː.ki|-, (US) sloʊˈvɑː.ki|-, -ˈvæk.i|- -an/s -ən/z
sloven ˈslʌv.ən -s -z
Slovene sləʊˈviːn; ˈsləʊ.viːn, (US) ˈsloʊ.viːn -s -z
Sloveni|a sləʊˈviː.ni|.ə, ˈ-nj|ə, (US) sloʊ- -an/s -ən/z
slovenl|y ˈslʌv.ən.l|i -iness -ɪ.nəs, -ɪ.nɪs
slow sləʊ, (US) sloʊ -er -əʳ, (US) -ɚ -est -ɪst, -əst -ly -li -ness -nəs, -nɪs -s -z -ing -ɪŋ -ed -d ˌ**slow ˈmotion**
slowcoach ˈsləʊ.kəʊtʃ, (US) ˈsloʊ.koʊtʃ -es -ɪz
slowdown ˈsləʊ.daʊn, (US) ˈsloʊ- -s -z
slowpoke ˈsləʊ.pəʊk, (US) ˈsloʊ.poʊk -s -s
slow-witted ˌsləʊˈwɪt.ɪd, (US) ˌsloʊˈwɪt̬-
slowworm ˈsləʊ.wɜːm, (US) ˈsloʊ.wɝːm -s -z
slub slʌb -s -z -bing -ɪŋ -bed -d
sludg|e slʌdʒ -y -i
slu|e sluː -s -z -ing -ɪŋ -ed -d
slug slʌg -s -z -ging -ɪŋ -ged -d
slugabed ˈslʌg.ə.bed -s -z
sluggard ˈslʌg.əd, (US) -ɚd -s -z -ly -li
sluggish ˈslʌg.ɪʃ -ly -li -ness -nəs, -nɪs
sluic|e sluːs -es -ɪz -ing -ɪŋ -ed -t ˈ**sluice ˌgate**
sluiceway ˈsluːs.weɪ -s -z
slum slʌm -s -z -ming -ɪŋ -med -d -mer/s -əʳ/z, (US) -ɚ/z
slumb|er ˈslʌm.b|əʳ, (US) -b|ɚ -ers -əz, (US) -ɚz -ering -ər.ɪŋ -ered -əd, (US) -ɚd -erer/s -ər.əʳ/z, (US) -ɚ.ɚ/z ˈ**slumber ˌparty**
slumm|y ˈslʌm|.i -ier -i.əʳ, (US) -i.ɚ -iest -i.ɪst, -i.əst -iness -ɪ.nəs, -ɪ.nɪs
slump slʌmp -s -s -ing -ɪŋ -ed -t
slung (from **sling**) slʌŋ

slunk (from **slink**) slʌŋk
slur slɜːʳ, (US) slɝː -s -z -ring -ɪŋ -red -d
slurp slɜːp, (US) slɝːp -s -s -ing -ɪŋ -ed -t
slurr|y ˈslʌr|.i, (US) ˈslɝː- -ies -iz
slush slʌʃ -y -i -ier -i.əʳ, (US) -i.ɚ -iest -i.ɪst, -i.əst -iness -ɪ.nəs, -ɪ.nɪs **ˈslush ˌfund**
slut slʌt -s -s -ty -i
sluttish ˈslʌt.ɪʃ, (US) ˈslʌt̬- -ly -li -ness -nəs, -nɪs
Sluys slɔɪs
sly slaɪ -er -əʳ, (US) -ɚ -est -ɪst, -əst -ly -li -ness -nəs, -nɪs
slyboots ˈslaɪ.buːts
SM ˌesˈem
smack smæk -s -s -ing/s -ɪŋ/z -ed -t -er/s -əʳ/z, (US) -ɚ/z
smacker ˈsmæk.əʳ, (US) -ɚ -s -z
smackeroo ˌsmæk.əʳˈuː, (US) -əˈruː -s -z
Smale smeɪl
small, S~ smɔːl, (US) smɔːl, smɑːl -s -z -er -əʳ, (US) -ɚ -est -ɪst, -əst -ness -nəs, -nɪs -ish -ɪʃ **ˈsmall ˌad; ˌsmall ˈad; ˌsmall ˈarm; ˌsmall ˈbeer; ˌsmall ˈchange; ˈsmall ˌfry; ˈsmall ˌhours (US) ˌsmall ˈhours; ˌsmall poˈtatoes; ˌsmall ˈprint; ˈsmall ˌprint (US) ˌsmall ˈprint; ˌsmall ˈscreen; ˈsmall ˌtalk**
small-claims ˌsmɔːlˈkleɪmz, (US) ˌsmɔːl-, ˌsmɑːl- **ˌsmall-ˈclaims ˌcourt; ˌsmall-claims ˈcourt**
Smalley ˈsmɔː.li, (US) ˈsmɔː-, ˈsmɑː-
small-hold|er ˈsmɔːlˌhəʊl.d|əʳ, (US) -ˌhoʊl.d|ɚ, ˈsmɑːl- -ers -əz, (US) -ɚz -ing/s -ɪŋ/z
smallish ˈsmɔː.lɪʃ, (US) ˈsmɔː-, ˈsmɑː-
small-minded ˌsmɔːlˈmaɪn.dɪd, (US) ˌsmɔːl-, ˌsmɑːl- -ly -li -ness -nəs, -nɪs *stress shift:* **ˌsmall-minded ˈperson**
smallpox ˈsmɔːl.pɒks, (US) -pɑːks, ˈsmɑːl-
small-scale ˌsmɔːlˈskeɪl, (US) ˈ--, ˈsmɑːl- *stress shift, British only:* **ˌsmall-scale ˈproject**
small-tim|e ˌsmɔːlˈtaɪm, (US) ˈ--, ˈsmɑːl- -er/s -əʳ/z, (US) -ɚ/z
small-town ˈsmɔːl.taʊn, (US) ˈsmɔːl-, ˈsmɑːl-
Smallwood ˈsmɔːl.wʊd, (US) ˈsmɔːl-, ˈsmɑːl-
smalt smɔːlt, smɒlt, (US) smɔːlt, smɑːlt
smarm smɑːm, (US) smɑːrm -s -z -ing -ɪŋ -ed -d
smarm|y ˈsmɑː.m|i, (US) ˈsmɑːr- -ily -əl.i, -ɪli -iness -ɪ.nəs, -ɪ.nɪs
smart, S~ smɑːt, (US) smɑːrt -s -s -er -əʳ, (US) ˈsmɑːr.t̬ɚ -est -ɪst, -əst, (US) ˈsmɑːr.t̬ɪst, -t̬əst -ly -li -ness -nəs, -nɪs -ing -ɪŋ, (US) ˈsmɑːr.t̬ɪŋ -ed -ɪd, (US) ˈsmɑːr.t̬ɪd **ˈsmart ˌalec(k) (US) ˌsmart ˈalec(k); ˈsmart ˌcard; ˌsmart ˈmoney; ˈsmart ˌset**
smartars|e ˈsmɑːt.ɑːs, (US) ˈsmɑːrt.ɑːrs -es -ɪz
smartass ˈsmɑːt.ɑːs, -æs, (US) ˈsmɑːrt̬.æs -es -ɪz
smarten ˈsmɑː.tᵊn, (US) ˈsmɑːr- -s -z -ing -ɪŋ, ˈsmɑːt.nɪŋ, (US) ˈsmɑːrt- -ed -d
Smarties® ˈsmɑː.tiz, (US) ˈsmɑːr.t̬iz
smartish ˈsmɑː.tɪʃ, (US) ˈsmɑːr.t̬ɪʃ
Smartphone® ˈsmɑːt.fəʊn, (US) ˈsmɑːrt.foʊn -s -z
smarty-pants ˈsmɑː.ti.pænts, (US) ˈsmɑːr.t̬i-
smash smæʃ -es -ɪz -ing -ɪŋ -ed -t -er/s -əʳ/z, (US) -ɚ/z **ˌsmash ˈhit**
smash-and-grab ˌsmæʃ.ənd̩ˈgræb, -əŋˈ-, (US) -ənd̩ˈ- -s -z *stress shift:* **ˌsmash-and-grab ˈraid**
smattering ˈsmæt.əʳ.ɪŋ, (US) ˈsmæt̬- -s -z
smear smɪəʳ, (US) smɪr -s -z -ing -ɪŋ -ed -d -y -i -iness -ɪ.nəs, -ɪ.nɪs **ˈsmear camˌpaign; ˈsmear ˌtest**
Smeaton ˈsmiː.tᵊn
Smedley ˈsmed.li
Smeeth smiːð, smiːθ
smegma ˈsmeg.mə
smell smel -s -z -ing -ɪŋ -ed -d, -t **smelt** smelt **ˈsmelling ˌsalts**
smell|y ˈsmel|.i -ier -i.əʳ, (US) -i.ɚ -iest -i.ɪst, -i.əst -iness -ɪ.nəs, -ɪ.nɪs
smelt smelt -s -s -ing -ɪŋ, (US) ˈsmel.t̬ɪŋ -ed -ɪd, (US) ˈsmel.t̬ɪd -er/s -əʳ/z, (US) -ɚ/z
Smetana ˈsmet.ᵊn.ə
Smethwick ˈsmeð.ɪk
smew smjuː -s -z
smidgen, smidgin, smidgeon ˈsmɪdʒ.ᵊn, -ɪn -s -z
Smieton ˈsmiː.tᵊn
Smike smaɪk
smilax ˈsmaɪ.læks -es -ɪz
smil|e smaɪl -es -z -ing/ly -ɪŋ/li -ed -d
Smiles smaɪlz
smil|ey, S~ ˈsmaɪ.l|i -eys -iz -ier -i.əʳ, (US) -i.ɚ -iest -i.ɪst, -i.əst
Smillie ˈsmaɪ.li
smirch smɜːtʃ, (US) smɝːtʃ -es -ɪz -ing -ɪŋ -ed -t
smirk smɜːk, (US) smɝːk -s -s -ing -ɪŋ -ed -t -er/s -əʳ/z, (US) -ɚ/z
Smirke smɜːk, (US) smɝːk
Smirnoff® ˈsmɜː.nɒf, (US) ˈsmɝː.nɔːf, ˈsmɪr-, -nɑːf
smit (from **smite**) smɪt
smit|e smaɪt -es -s -ing -ɪŋ, (US) ˈsmaɪ.t̬ɪŋ **smote** sməʊt, (US) smoʊt **smit** smɪt **smitten** ˈsmɪt.ᵊn
smith, S~ smɪθ -s -s
Smithells ˈsmɪð.ᵊlz
smithereens ˌsmɪð.əʳˈiːnz, (US) -əˈriːnz
Smithers ˈsmɪð.əz, (US) -ɚz
Smithfield ˈsmɪθ.fiːld
Smithson ˈsmɪθ.sᵊn
Smithsonian smɪθˈsəʊ.ni.ən, (US) -ˈsoʊ-
smith|y ˈsmɪð|.i, ˈsmɪθ-, (US) ˈsmɪθ-, ˈsmɪð- -ies -iz
smitten (from **smite**) ˈsmɪt.ᵊn
smock smɒk, (US) smɑːk -s -s -ing -ɪŋ -ed -t
smog smɒg, (US) smɑːg, smɔːg
smogg|y ˈsmɒg|.i, (US) ˈsmɑː.g|i, ˈsmɔː- -ier -i.əʳ, (US) -i.ɚ -iest -i.ɪst, -i.əst
smok|e sməʊk, (US) smoʊk -es -s -ing -ɪŋ -ed -t -er/s -əʳ/z, (US) -ɚ/z **ˈsmoke aˌlarm; ˌsmoke and ˈmirrors; ˈsmoke ˌscreen; ˈsmoking comˌpartment; ˈsmoking ˌjacket; ˈsmoking ˌroom; ˌgo up in ˈsmoke; there's ˌno ˌsmoke without ˈfire**
smokehou|se ˈsməʊk.haʊ|s, (US) ˈsmoʊk- -ses -zɪz
smokeless ˈsməʊk.ləs, -lɪs, (US) ˈsmoʊk-
smokestack ˈsməʊk.stæk, (US) ˈsmoʊk- -s -s **ˈsmokestack ˌindustry**
Smokies ˈsməʊ.kiz, (US) ˈsmoʊ-
smoko ˈsməʊ.kəʊ, (US) ˈsmoʊ.koʊ -s -z
smok|y ˈsməʊ.k|i, (US) ˈsmoʊ- -ier -i.əʳ, (US) -i.ɚ -iest -i.ɪst, -i.əst -ily -əl.i, -ɪ.li -iness -ɪ.nəs, -ɪ.nɪs
smold|er ˈsməʊl.d|əʳ, (US) ˈsmoʊl.d|ɚ -ers -əz, (US) -ɚz -ering -əʳ.ɪŋ -ered -əd, (US) -ɚd
Smollett ˈsmɒl.ɪt, (US) ˈsmɑː.lɪt
smolt sməʊlt, (US) smoʊlt
smooch smuːtʃ -es -ɪz -ing -ɪŋ -ed -t -y -i
smooth adj smuːð -er -əʳ, (US) -ɚ -est -ɪst, -əst -ly -li -ness -nəs, -nɪs
smooth|(e) v smuːð -(e)s -z -ing -ɪŋ -ed -d
smoothbore ˈsmuːð.bɔːʳ, (US) -bɔːr -s -z
smooth|ie, smooth|y ˈsmuː.ð|i -ies -iz
smorgasbord ˈsmɔː.gəs.bɔːd, (US) ˈsmɔːr.gəs.bɔːrd -s -z
smote (from **smite**) sməʊt, (US) smoʊt
smoth|er ˈsmʌð|.əʳ, (US) -ɚ -ers -əz, (US) -ɚz -ering -əʳ.ɪŋ -ered -əd, (US) -ɚd
smould|er ˈsməʊl.d|əʳ, (US) ˈsmoʊl.d|ɚ -ers -əz, (US) -ɚz -ering -əʳ.ɪŋ -ered -əd, (US) -ɚd
SMS ˌes.emˈes
smudg|e smʌdʒ -es -ɪz -ing -ɪŋ -ed -d -y -i -ier -i.əʳ, (US) -i.ɚ -iest -i.ɪst, -i.əst -ily -əl.i, -ɪ.li -iness -ɪ.nəs, -ɪ.nɪs
smug smʌg -ly -li -ness -nəs, -nɪs -ger -əʳ, (US) -gɚ -gest -ɪst, -gəst
smuggl|e ˈsmʌg|.əl -es -z -ing -ɪŋ, ˈsmʌg.lɪŋ -ed -d
smuggler ˈsmʌg.ləʳ, ˈ-əl.əʳ, (US) ˈ-lɚ, ˈ-əl.ɚ -s -z
smut smʌt -s -s -ty -i, (US) ˈsmʌt̬.i -tier -i.əʳ, (US) ˈsmʌt̬.i.ɚ -tiest -i.ɪst, -i.əst, (US) ˈsmʌt̬.i.ɪst, -i.əst -tily -ɪ.li, -əl.i, (US) ˈsmʌt̬.ɪ.li, -əl.i -tiness -ɪ.nəs, -ɪ.nɪs, (US) ˈsmʌt̬.ɪ.nəs, -ɪ.nɪs
Smylie ˈsmaɪ.li
Smyrna ˈsmɜː.nə, (US) ˈsmɝː-
Smyth smɪθ, smaɪθ
Smythe smaɪð, smaɪθ

S

snack snæk **-s** -s **-ing** -ɪŋ **-ed** -d ˈ**snack** ˌ**bar**
Snaefell ˌsneɪˈfel
snaffl|e ˈsnæf.əl **-es** -z **-ing** -ɪŋ, ˈsnæf.lɪŋ **-ed** -d
snafu snæfˈuː, (US) snæfˈuː, ˈ-- **-es** -z **-ing** -ɪŋ **-ed** -d
snag snæg **-s** -z **-ging** -ɪŋ **-ged** -d
Snagge snæg
snail sneɪl **-s** -z **-like** -laɪk ˈ**snail's** ˌ**pace**
snak|e sneɪk **-es** -s **-ing** -ɪŋ **-ed** -t ˈ**snake** ˌ**charmer;** ˌ**snake in the** ˈ**grass** (US) ˈ**snake in the** ˌ**grass;** ˌ**snakes and** ˈ**ladders**
snakebite ˈsneɪk.baɪt **-s** -s
snakeskin ˈsneɪk.skɪn
snak|y ˈsneɪ.k|i **-iness** -ɪ.nəs, -ɪ.nɪs
snap snæp **-s** -s **-ping** -ɪŋ **-ped** -t ˈ**snap** ˌ**fastener**
snapdragon ˈsnæpˌdræg.ən **-s** -z
Snape sneɪp
snapper ˈsnæp.əʳ, (US) -ɚ **-s** -z
snappish ˈsnæp.ɪʃ **-ly** -li **-ness** -nəs, -nɪs
Snapple® ˈsnæp.əl
snapp|y ˈsnæp|.i **-ier** -i.əʳ, (US) -i.ɚ **-iest** -i.ɪst, -i.əst **-ily** -əl.i, -ɪ.li **-iness** -ɪ.nəs, -ɪ.nɪs
snapshot ˈsnæp|.ʃɒt, (US) -ʃɑːt **-s** -s
snar|e sneəʳ, (US) sner **-es** -z **-ing** -ɪŋ **-ed** -d ˈ**snare** ˌ**drum**
snark snɑːk, (US) snɑːrk **-s** -s
snarky ˈsnɑː.ki, (US) ˈsnɑːr.ki
snarl snɑːl, (US) snɑːrl **-s** -z **-ing** -ɪŋ **-ed** -d
snarl-up ˈsnɑːl.ʌp, (US) ˈsnɑːrl- **-s** -s
snatch snætʃ **-es** -ɪz **-ing** -ɪŋ **-ed** -t **-er/s** -əʳ/z, (US) -ɚ/z
snatch|y ˈsnætʃ|.i **-ier** -i.əʳ, (US) -i.ɚ **-iest** -i.ɪst, -i.əst **-ily** -əl.i, -ɪ.li
snazz|y ˈsnæz|.i **-ier** -i.əʳ, (US) -i.ɚ **-iest** -i.ɪst, -i.əst **-ily** -əl.i, -ɪ.li **-iness** -ɪ.nəs, -ɪ.nɪs
sneak sniːk **-s** -s **-ing/ly** -ɪŋ/li **-ed** -t **-y** -i **-ier** -i.əʳ, (US) -i.ɚ **-iest** -i.ɪst, -i.əst **-ily** -əl.i, -ɪ.li **-iness** -ɪ.nəs, -ɪ.nɪs ˌ**sneak** ˈ**preview;** ˈ**sneak** ˌ**thief;** ˌ**sneak** ˈ**thief** (US) ˈ**sneak** ˌ**thief**
sneaker ˈsniː.kəʳ, (US) -kɚ **-s** -z
sneakers ˈsniː.kəz, (US) -kɚz
sneaky ˈsniː.ki **-ier** -i.əʳ, (US) -i.ɚ **-iest** -i.ɪst, -i.əst **-iness** -ɪ.nəs, -ɪ.nɪs
Snedden ˈsned.ən
sneer snɪəʳ, (US) snɪr **-s** -z **-ing/ly** -ɪŋ/li **-ed** -d
sneez|e sniːz **-es** -ɪz **-ing** -ɪŋ **-ed** -d
Snelgrove ˈsnel.grəʊv, (US) -groʊv
snell, S~ snel **-s** -z
Sneyd sniːd
snib snɪb **-s** -z
snick snɪk **-s** -s **-ing** -ɪŋ **-ed** -t
snick|er ˈsnɪk|.əʳ, (US) -ɚ **-ers** -əz, (US) -ɚz **-ering** -ər.ɪŋ **-ered** -əd, (US) -ɚd
Snickers® ˈsnɪk.əz, (US) -ɚz
snickersnee ˌsnɪk.əˈsniː, ˈ---, (US) ˈsnɪk.ɚ.sniː **-s** -z
snide snaɪd **-ly** -li **-ness** -nəs, -nɪs
sniff snɪf **-s** -s **-ing** -ɪŋ **-ed** -t **-y** -i **-ier** -i.əʳ, (US) -i.ɚ **-iest** -i.ɪst, -i.əst **-ily** -əl.i, -ɪ.li **-iness** -ɪ.nəs, -ɪ.nɪs
sniffer ˈsnɪf.əʳ, (US) -ɚ **-s** -z ˈ**sniffer** ˌ**dog**
sniffl|e ˈsnɪf.əl **-es** -z **-ing** -ɪŋ, ˈsnɪf.lɪŋ **-ed** -d
snifter ˈsnɪf.təʳ, (US) -tɚ **-s** -z
snigg|er ˈsnɪg|.əʳ, (US) -ɚ **-ers** -əz, (US) -ɚz **-ering** -ər.ɪŋ **-ered** -əd, (US) -ɚd **-erer/s** -ə.rəʳ/z, (US) -ɚ.ɚ/z
snip snɪp **-s** -s **-ping** -ɪŋ **-ped** -t **-per/s** -əʳ/z, (US) -ɚ/z
snip|e snaɪp **-es** -s **-ing** -ɪŋ **-ed** -t **-er/s** -əʳ/z, (US) -ɚ/z
snipp|et ˈsnɪp|.ɪt **-ets** -ɪts **-ety** -ɪ.ti, (US) -ɪ.t̬i
snit snɪt **-s** -s
snitch snɪtʃ **-es** -ɪz **-ing** -ɪŋ **-ed** -t
snivel ˈsnɪv.əl **-s** -z **-(l)ing** -ɪŋ, ˈsnɪv.lɪŋ **-(l)ed** -d **-(l)er/s** -əʳ/z, ˈsnɪv.ləʳ/z, (US) ˈ-əl.ɚ/z, ˈ-lɚ/z
snob snɒb, (US) snɑːb **-s** -z **-bism** -ɪ.zəm
snobbery ˈsnɒb.ər.i, (US) ˈsnɑː.bɚ-
snobbish ˈsnɒb.ɪʃ, (US) ˈsnɑː.bɪʃ **-ly** -li **-ness** -nəs, -nɪs
snobb|y ˈsnɒb|.i, (US) ˈsnɑː.b|i **-ier** -i.əʳ, (US) -i.ɚ **-iest** -i.ɪst, -i.əst
SNOBOL ˈsnəʊ.bɒl, (US) ˈsnoʊ.bɔːl, -bɑːl
Snodgrass ˈsnɒd.grɑːs, (US) ˈsnɑːd.græs
Snodland ˈsnɒd.lənd, (US) ˈsnɑːd-
snoek snʊk, snuːk **-s** -s
snog snɒg, (US) snɑːg, snɔːg **-s** -z **-ging** -ɪŋ **-ged** -d
snood snuːd, snʊd, (US) snuːd **-s** -z **-ed** -ɪd
Snoody ˈsnuː.di
snook snuːk, (US) snʊk, snuːk **-s** -s
snooker ˈsnuː.kəʳ, (US) ˈsnʊk.ɚ **-s** -z **-ing** -ɪŋ **-ed** -d
snoop snuːp **-s** -s **-ing** -ɪŋ **-ed** -t **-er/s** -əʳ/z, (US) -ɚ/z
Snoopy® ˈsnuː.pi
snoot snuːt **-s** -s
snoot|y ˈsnuː.t|i, (US) -t̬|i **-ily** -əl.i, -ɪ.li **-iness** -ɪ.nəs, -ɪ.nɪs **-ier** -i.əʳ, (US) -i.ɚ **-iest** -i.ɪst, -i.əst
snooz|e snuːz **-es** -ɪz **-ing** -ɪŋ **-ed** -d **-er/s** -əʳ/z, (US) -ɚ/z
snor|e snɔːʳ, (US) snɔːr **-es** -z **-ing** -ɪŋ **-ed** -d **-er/s** -əʳ/z, (US) -ɚ/z
snorkel ˈsnɔː.kəl, (US) ˈsnɔːr- **-s** -z **-(l)ing** -ɪŋ **-(l)ed** -d **-(l)er/s** -əʳ/z, (US) -ɚ/z
snort snɔːt, (US) snɔːrt **-s** -s **-ing** -ɪŋ, (US) ˈsnɔːr.t̬ɪŋ **-ed** -ɪd, (US) ˈsnɔːr.t̬ɪd
snorter ˈsnɔː.təʳ, (US) ˈsnɔːr.t̬ɚ **-s** -z
snort|y ˈsnɔː.t|i, (US) ˈsnɔːr.t̬|i **-ier** -i.əʳ, (US) -i.ɚ **-iest** -i.ɪst, -i.əst **-ily** -əl.i, -ɪ.li **-iness** -ɪ.nəs, -ɪ.nɪs
snot snɒt, (US) snɑːt **-ty** -i, (US) ˈsnɑː.t̬i
snout, S~ snaʊt **-s** -s
snow, S~ snəʊ, (US) snoʊ **-s** -z **-ing** -ɪŋ **-ed** -d **-er/s** -əʳ/z, (US) -ɚ/z ˈ**snow** ˌ**blindness;** ˈ**snow** ˌ**goose;** ˌ**Snow** ˈ**White**
snowball ˈsnəʊ.bɔːl, (US) ˈsnoʊ.bɔːl, -bɑːl **-s** -z **-ing** -ɪŋ **-ed** -d
snowberr|y ˈsnəʊ.bər|.i, -br|i, (US) ˈsnoʊˌber|.i **-ies** -iz
snow-blind ˈsnəʊ.blaɪnd, (US) ˈsnoʊ-
snowblower ˈsnəʊˌbləʊ.əʳ, (US) ˈsnoʊˌbloʊ.ɚ **-s** -z
snowboard ˈsnəʊ.bɔːd, (US) ˈsnoʊ.bɔːrd **-s** -z **-ing** -ɪŋ **-ed** -ɪd **-er/s** -əʳ/z, (US) -ɚ/z
snowbound ˈsnəʊ.baʊnd, (US) ˈsnoʊ-
snowcap ˈsnəʊ.kæp, (US) ˈsnoʊ- **-s** -s **-ped** -t
Snowden, Snowdon ˈsnəʊ.dən, (US) ˈsnoʊ-
Snowdonia snəʊˈdəʊ.ni.ə, (US) snoʊˈdoʊ-
snowdrift ˈsnəʊ.drɪft, (US) ˈsnoʊ- **-s** -s
snowdrop ˈsnəʊ.drɒp, (US) ˈsnoʊ.drɑːp **-s** -s
snowfall ˈsnəʊ.fɔːl, (US) ˈsnoʊ-, -fɑːl **-s** -z
snowfield ˈsnəʊ.fiːld, (US) ˈsnoʊ- **-s** -z
snowflake ˈsnəʊ.fleɪk, (US) ˈsnoʊ- **-s** -s
snow|man ˈsnəʊ|.mæn, (US) ˈsnoʊ- **-men** -men
snowmobile ˈsnəʊ.məˌbiːl, (US) ˈsnoʊ.moʊˌ- **-s** -z
snowplough, snowplow ˈsnəʊ.plaʊ, (US) ˈsnoʊ- **-s** -z **-ing** -ɪŋ **-ed** -d
snowshoe ˈsnəʊ.ʃuː, (US) ˈsnoʊ- **-s** -z
snowstorm ˈsnəʊ.stɔːm, (US) ˈsnoʊ.stɔːrm **-s** -z
snowsuit ˈsnəʊ.suːt, -sjuːt, (US) ˈsnoʊ.suːt **-s** -s
snow-white ˌsnəʊˈhwaɪt, (US) ˌsnoʊ- *stress shift:* ˌ**snow-white** ˈ**hair**
snow|y ˈsnəʊ|.i, (US) ˈsnoʊ- **-ier** -i.əʳ, (US) -i.ɚ **-iest** -i.ɪst, -i.əst **-ily** -əl.i, -ɪ.li **-iness** -ɪ.nəs, -ɪ.nɪs ˌ**snowy** ˈ**owl**
SNP ˌes.enˈpiː, -emˈ-, (US) -enˈ-
snr, S~ (abbrev. for **senior**) ˈsiː.ni.əʳ, -njəʳ, (US) -njɚ
snub snʌb **-s** -z **-bing** -ɪŋ **-bed** -d
snub-nosed ˌsnʌbˈnəʊzd, (US) ˈsnʌb.noʊzd *stress shift, British only:* ˌ**snub-nosed** ˈ**bullet**
snuck snʌk
snuff snʌf **-s** -s **-ing** -ɪŋ **-ed** -t **-er/s** -əʳ/z, (US) -ɚ/z ˈ**snuff** ˌ**box**
snuffl|e ˈsnʌf.əl **-es** -z **-ing** -ɪŋ, ˈsnʌf.lɪŋ **-ed** -d **-er/s** -əʳ/z, ˈsnʌf.ləʳ/z, (US) ˈ-əl.ɚ/z, ˈ-lɚ/z **-y** -i
snug snʌg **-ger** -əʳ, (US) -ɚ **-gest** -ɪst, -əst **-ly** -li **-ness** -nəs, -nɪs
snugger|y ˈsnʌg.ər|.i **-ies** -iz
snuggl|e ˈsnʌg.əl **-es** -z **-ing** -ɪŋ, ˈsnʌg.lɪŋ **-ed** -d
Snyder ˈsnaɪ.dəʳ, (US) -dɚ
so *normal forms:* səʊ, (US) soʊ; *occasional weak form:* sə ˌ**so** ˈ**long** (US) ˈ**so** ˌ**long**
Note: Weak-form word. The weak form is used only rarely, and only in casual speech before adjectives and adverbs (e.g. 'Not so bad' /ˌnɒt.səˈbæd/ (US) /ˌnɑːt-/, 'Don't go

so fast' /ˌdəʊnt.gəʊ.səˈfɑːst/ (US) /ˌdoʊnt.goʊ.səˈfæst/).
oak səʊk, (US) soʊk -s -s -ing -ɪŋ -ed -t
oakaway ˈsəʊk.əˌweɪ, (US) ˈsoʊk- -s -z
Soames səʊmz, (US) soʊmz
so-and-so ˈsəʊ.ənd.səʊ, (US) ˈsoʊ.ənd.soʊ -(')s -z
Soane səʊn, (US) soʊn -s -z
soap səʊp, (US) soʊp -s -s -ing -ɪŋ -ed -t -y -i -ier -i.əʳ, (US) -i.ɚ -iest -i.ɪst, -i.əst -ily -əl.i, -ɪ.li -iness -ɪ.nəs, -ɪ.nɪs
soapbox ˈsəʊp.bɒks, (US) ˈsoʊp.bɑːks -es -ɪz
soap opera ˈsəʊpˌɒp.ər.ə, ˌ-rə, (US) ˈsoʊpˌɑː.pɚ.ə, ˌ-prə -s -z
soapstone ˈsəʊp.stəʊn, (US) ˈsoʊp.stoʊn
soapsuds ˈsəʊp.sʌdz, (US) ˈsoʊp-
soar, S~ sɔːʳ, (US) sɔːr -s -z -ing -ɪŋ -ed -d
soaraway ˈsɔː.rə.weɪ, (US) ˈsɔːr.ə-
Soares səʊˈɑː.rɪz, (US) soʊˈɑːr.ɪz
sob sɒb, (US) sɑːb -s -z -bing -ɪŋ -bed -d ˈsob ˌstory
SOB ˌes.əʊˈbiː, (US) -oʊˈ-
Sobel ˈsəʊ.bel, (US) ˈsoʊ-
sob|er ˈsəʊ.b|əʳ, (US) ˈsoʊ.b|ɚ -erer -ər.əʳ, (US) -ɚ.ɚ -erest -ər.ɪst, -ər.əst -erly -əl.i, (US) -ɚ.li -erness -ə.nəs, -ə.nɪs, (US) -ɚ.nəs, -ɚ.nɪs -ers -əz, (US) -ɚz -ering/ly -ər.ɪŋ/li -ered -əd, (US) -ɚd
Sobers ˈsəʊ.bəz, (US) ˈsoʊ.bɚz
sobersides ˈsəʊ.bə.saɪdz, (US) ˈsoʊ.bɚ-
sobriety səʊˈbraɪ.ɪ.ti, ˈ-ə-, (US) səˈbraɪ.ə.t̬i, soʊ-
sobriquet ˈsəʊ.brɪ.keɪ, (US) ˈsoʊ-, -ket, ˌ--ˈ- -s -z
soc(c)age ˈsɒk.ɪdʒ, (US) ˈsɑː.kɪdʒ
so-called ˌsəʊˈkɔːld, (US) ˌsoʊˈkɑːld, -ˈkɔːld *stress shift:* ˌ**so-called** ˈ**friend**
soccer ˈsɒk.əʳ, (US) ˈsɑː.kɚ
sociability ˌsəʊ.ʃəˈbɪl.ə.ti, -ɪ.ti, (US) ˌsoʊ.ʃəˈbɪl.ə.t̬i
sociab|le ˈsəʊ.ʃə.b|əl, (US) ˈsoʊ- -ly -li -leness -əl.nəs, -nɪs
social ˈsəʊ.ʃəl, (US) ˈsoʊ- -s -z -ly -i **ˌsocial ˈclimber** (US) **ˈsocial ˌclimber; ˌsocial deˈmocracy; ˌsocial ˈdemocrat; ˈsocial ˌlife; ˌsocial ˈscience** (US) **ˈsocial ˌscience; ˌsocial ˈsecretary; ˌsocial seˈcurity; ˌsocial ˈservice** (US) **ˈsocial ˌservice; ˈsocial ˌwork**
social|ism ˈsəʊ.ʃəl|.ɪ.zəm, (US) ˈsoʊ- -ist/s -ɪst/s
socialistic ˌsəʊ.ʃəlˈɪs.tɪk, (US) ˌsoʊ.ʃəˈlɪs-
socialite ˈsəʊ.ʃəl.aɪt, (US) ˈsoʊ.ʃə.laɪt -s -s
socialization, -isa- ˌsəʊ.ʃəl.aɪˈzeɪ.ʃən, -ɪˈ-, (US) ˌsoʊ.ʃəl.əˈ-
socializ|e, -is|e ˈsəʊ.ʃəl.aɪz, (US) ˈsoʊ.ʃə.laɪz -es -ɪz -ing -ɪŋ -ed -d
societal səˈsaɪ.ə.təl, (US) -t̬əl
societ|y, S~ səˈsaɪ.ə.t|i, (US) -t̬|i -ies -iz

Socinian səʊˈsɪn.i.ən, (US) soʊ- -s -z
Socinus səʊˈsaɪ.nəs, (US) soʊ-
socio- ˈsəʊ.ʃi.əʊ, ˈ-si-; ˌsəʊ.ʃiˈɒ, -siˈ-, (US) ˈsoʊ.si.oʊ, ˈ-ʃi-, -ə; (US) ˌsoʊ.siˈɑː, -ʃiˈ-
Note: Prefix. Normally either takes primary or secondary stress on the first syllable, e.g. **sociopath** /ˈsəʊ.ʃi.əʊ.pæθ/ (US) /ˈsoʊ.si.ə-/, **sociopolitical** /ˌsəʊ.ʃi.əʊ.pəˈlɪt.ɪ.kəl/ (US) /ˌsoʊ.si.oʊ.pəˈlɪt̬-/, or secondary stress on the first syllable and primary stress on the third syllable, e.g. **sociology** /ˌsəʊ.ʃiˈɒl.ə.dʒi/ (US) /ˌsoʊ.siˈɑː.lə-/.
sociobiolog|y ˌsəʊ.ʃi.əʊ.baɪˈɒl.ə.dʒ|i, -si-, (US) ˌsoʊ.si.oʊ.baɪˈɑː.lə-, -ʃi- -ist/s -ɪst/s
sociocultural ˌsəʊ.ʃi.əʊˈkʌl.tʃər.əl, -si-, (US) ˌsoʊ.si.oʊ-, -ʃi- -ly -i
socioeconomic ˌsəʊ.ʃi.əʊˌiː.kəˈnɒm.ɪk, -si-, -ˌek.əˈ-, (US) ˌsoʊ.si.oʊˌek.əˈnɑː.mɪk, -ʃi-, -ˌiː.kəˈ-
sociolinguist ˌsəʊ.ʃi.əʊˈlɪŋ.gwɪst, -si-, (US) ˌsoʊ.si.oʊˈ-, -ʃi- -s -s
sociolinguistic ˌsəʊ.ʃi.əʊ.lɪŋˈgwɪs.tɪk, -si-, (US) ˌsoʊ.si.oʊ-, -ʃi- -s -s
sociologic|al ˌsəʊ.ʃi.əˈlɒdʒ.ɪ.k|əl, -si-, (US) ˌsoʊ.si.əˈlɑː.dʒɪ-, -ʃi- -ally -əl.i, -li
sociologist ˌsəʊ.ʃiˈɒl.ə.dʒ|ɪst, -siˈ-, (US) ˌsoʊ.siˈɑː.lə-, -ʃiˈ- -s -s
sociolog|y ˌsəʊ.ʃiˈɒl.ə.dʒ|i, -siˈ-, (US) ˌsoʊ.siˈɑː.lə-, -ʃiˈ- -ist/s -ɪst/s
sociopath ˈsəʊ.ʃi.əʊ.pæθ, -si-, (US) ˈsoʊ.si.ə-, -ʃi- -s -s
sociopolitical ˌsəʊ.ʃi.əʊ.pəlˈɪt.ɪ.kəl, -si-, (US) ˌsoʊ.si.oʊ.pəˈlɪt̬-, -ʃi-
socioreligious ˌsəʊ.ʃi.əʊ.rɪˈlɪdʒ.əs, -si-, -rəˈ-, (US) ˌsoʊ.si.oʊ-, -ʃi-
sock sɒk, (US) sɑːk -s -s -ing -ɪŋ -ed -t
sockdolager, sockdologer sɒkˈdɒl.ə.dʒəʳ, (US) sɑːkˈdɑː.lə.dʒɚ -s -z
sock|et ˈsɒk|.ɪt, (US) ˈsɑː.k|ɪt -ets -ɪts -eted -ɪ.tɪd, (US) -ɪ.t̬ɪd
Socotra səʊˈkəʊ.trə, sɒkˈəʊ-, (US) soʊˈkoʊ-
Socrates ˈsɒk.rə.tiːz, (US) ˈsɑː.krə-
socratic, S~ sɒkˈræt.ɪk, səʊˈkræt-, (US) səˈkræt̬-, soʊ- -ally -əl.i, -li
sod sɒd, (US) sɑːd -s -z -ding -ɪŋ -ded -ɪd **ˌsod's ˈlaw; ˈsod's ˌlaw**
soda ˈsəʊ.də, (US) ˈsoʊ- -s -z **ˈsoda ˌbiscuit; ˈsoda ˌbread; ˈsoda ˌcracker; ˈsoda ˌfountain; ˈsoda ˌpop; ˈsoda ˌsiphon; ˈsoda ˌwater**
sodalit|y səʊˈdæl.ə.t|i, -ɪ.t|i, (US) soʊˈdæl.ə.t̬|i -ies -iz
sodden ˈsɒd.ən, (US) ˈsɑː.dən -ness -nəs, -nɪs -s -z -ing -ɪŋ -ed -d
sodding ˈsɒd.ɪŋ, (US) ˈsɑː.dɪŋ
sodium ˈsəʊ.di.əm, (US) ˈsoʊ-
Sodom ˈsɒd.əm, (US) ˈsɑː.dəm
sodomiz|e, -is|e ˈsɒd.ə.maɪz, (US) ˈsɑː.də- -es -ɪz -ing -ɪŋ -ed -d
sodom|y ˈsɒd.ə.m|i, (US) ˈsɑː.də- -ite/s -aɪt/s

Sodor ˈsəʊ.dəʳ, (US) ˈsoʊ.dɚ
Soeharto suˈhɑː.təʊ, (US) -ˈhɑːr.t̬oʊ
soever səʊˈev.əʳ, (US) soʊˈev.ɚ
sofa ˈsəʊ.fə, (US) ˈsoʊ- -s -z
sofabed ˈsəʊ.fə.bed, (US) ˈsoʊ- -s -z
Sofala səʊˈfɑː.lə, (US) soʊ-, sə-
soffit ˈsɒf.ɪt, (US) ˈsɑː.fɪt -s -s
Sofia ˈsɒf.i.ə, ˈsəʊ.fi-, (US) ˈsoʊ.fi-; (US) soʊˈfiː-
soft sɒft, (US) sɑːft -s -s -er -əʳ, (US) -ɚ -est -ɪst, -əst -ly -li -ness -nəs, -nɪs **ˌsoft ˈcopy; ˌsoft ˈdrink** (US) **ˈsoft ˌdrink; ˌsoft ˈfruit; ˌsoft ˈfurnishings; ˌsoft ˈlanding; ˌsoft ˈoption; ˌsoft ˈsell; ˈsoft ˌspot; ˌsoft ˈspot** (US) **ˈsoft ˌspot; ˌsoft ˈtarget; ˈsoft ˌtouch; ˌsoft ˈtouch**
softback ˈsɒft.bæk, (US) ˈsɑːft- -s -s
softball ˈsɒft.bɔːl, (US) ˈsɑːft-, -bɑːl
soft-boil ˌsɒftˈbɔɪl, (US) ˌsɑːft- -s -z -ing -ɪŋ -ed -d
soft-centred ˌsɒftˈsen.təd, (US) ˌsɑːftˈsen.tɚd
soft-core ˈsɒft.kɔːʳ, (US) ˈsɑːft.kɔːr
softcover ˌsɒftˈkʌv.əʳ, (US) ˈsɑːft.kʌv.ɚ -s -z
soften ˈsɒf.ən, (US) ˈsɑː.fən -s -z -ing -ɪŋ, ˈsɒf.nɪŋ, (US) ˈsɑːf- -ed -d
softener ˈsɒf.ən.əʳ, ˈ-nəʳ, (US) ˈsɑː.fən.ɚ, ˈsɑːf.nɚ -s -z
softhearted ˌsɒftˈhɑː.tɪd, (US) ˈsɑːftˌhɑːr.t̬ɪd -ly -li -ness -nəs, -nɪs *stress shift, British only:* ˌ**softhearted** ˈ**person**
soft|ie ˈsɒf.t|i, (US) ˈsɑːf- -ies -iz
softish ˈsɒf.tɪʃ, (US) ˈsɑːf-
softly-softly ˌsɒft.liˈsɒft.li, (US) ˌsɑːft.liˈsɑːft-
soft-pedal ˌsɒftˈped.əl, (US) ˌsɑːft- -s -z -(l)ing -ɪŋ, -ˈped.lɪŋ -(l)ed -d
soft-soap ˌsɒftˈsəʊp, (US) ˌsɑːftˈsoʊp -s -s -ing -ɪŋ -ed -t
soft-spoken ˌsɒftˈspəʊ.kən, (US) ˌsɑːftˈspoʊ- *stress shift:* ˌ**soft-spoken** ˈ**person**
software ˈsɒft.weəʳ, (US) ˈsɑːft.wer
softwood ˈsɒft.wʊd, (US) ˈsɑːft- -s -z
soft|y ˈsɒf.t|i, (US) ˈsɑːf- -ies -iz
SOGAT ˈsəʊ.gæt, (US) ˈsoʊ-
sogg|y ˈsɒg|.i, (US) ˈsɑː.g|i -ily -əl.i, -ɪ.li -ier -i.əʳ, (US) -i.ɚ -iest -i.ɪst, -i.əst -iness -ɪ.nəs, -ɪ.nɪs
soh səʊ, (US) soʊ -s -z
Soham ˈsəʊ.əm, (US) ˈsoʊ-
Soho ˈsəʊ.həʊ, (US) ˈsoʊ.hoʊ
soi-disant ˌswɑː.diːˈzɑ̃ːŋ, ˌ-ˈ--, (US) ˌswɑː.diːˈzɑ̃ːn
soigné(e) ˈswɑː.njeɪ, -ˈ-, (US) swɑːˈnjeɪ
soil sɔɪl -s -z -ing -ɪŋ -ed -d **ˈsoil ˌpipe**
soirée, soiree ˈswɑː.reɪ, ˈswɒr.eɪ, -ˈ-, (US) swɑːˈreɪ -s -z
soixante-neuf ˌswæs.ɑ̃ːntˈnɜːf, ˌswʌs-, (US) ˌswɑː.sɑ̃ːntˈnɜːf
sojourn ˈsɒdʒ.ɜːn, ˈsʌdʒ-, -ən, (US) ˈsoʊ.dʒɝːn, -ˈ- -s -z -ing -ɪŋ -ed -d -er/s -əʳ/z, (US) -ɚ/z
Sokoto ˈsəʊ.kə.təʊ, ˌ--ˈ-, (US) ˈsoʊ.koʊ.toʊ, ˌ--ˈ-; (US) səˈkoʊ-
sol, S~ sɒl, (US) soʊl, sɑːl -s -z

sola ˈsəʊ.lə, (US) ˈsoʊ-
solac|e ˈsɒl.əs, -ɪs, (US) ˈsɑː.lɪs **-es** -ɪz **-ing** -ɪŋ **-ed** -t
solanum səʊˈleɪ.nəm, -ˈlɑː-, (US) soʊˈleɪ-
solar ˈsəʊ.ləʳ, (US) ˈsoʊ.lɚ ˌ**solar ˈenergy;** ˌ**solar ˈpanel;** ˌ**solar ˈplexus;** ˈ**solar ˌsystem**
solari|um səʊˈleə.ri.əm, (US) soʊˈler.i-, sə- **-ums** -z **-a** -ə
solati|um səʊˈleɪ.ʃi|.əm, (US) soʊ- **-ums** -əmz **-a** -ə
sold (from **sell**) səʊld, (US) soʊld
sold|er ˈsəʊl.d|əʳ, ˈsɒl-, (US) ˈsɑː.d|ɚ **-ers** -əz, (US) -ɚz **-ering** -ər.ɪŋ **-ered** -əd, (US) -ɚd ˈ**soldering ˌiron**
soldi|er ˈsəʊl.dʒ|əʳ, (US) ˈsoʊl.dʒ|ɚ **-ers** -əz, (US) -ɚz **-ering** -ər.ɪŋ **-ered** -əd, (US) -ɚd ˌ**soldier of ˈfortune**
soldierly ˈsəʊl.dʒəl.i, (US) ˈsoʊl.dʒɚ.li
soldiery ˈsəʊl.dʒər.i, (US) ˈsoʊl-
sol|e, S~ səʊl, (US) soʊl **-es** -z **-ely** -li **-ing** -ɪŋ **-ed** -d
solecism ˈsɒl.ɪ.sɪ.zəm, ˈ-ə-, -es.ɪ-, (US) ˈsɑː.lə- **-s** -z
solemn ˈsɒl.əm, (US) ˈsɑː.ləm **-ly** -li **-ness** -nəs, -nɪs
solemnif|y səˈlem.nɪ.f|aɪ, sɒlˈem-, (US) səˈlem.nɪ-, ˈ-nə- **-ies** -z **-ying** -ɪŋ **-ied** -d
solemnit|y səˈlem.nə.t|i, sɒlˈem-, -nɪ-, (US) səˈlem.nə.ţ|i **-ies** -z
solemnization, -isa- ˌsɒl.əm.naɪˈzeɪ.ʃən, -nɪˈ-, (US) ˌsɑː.ləm.nəˈ- **-s** -z
solemniz|e, -is|e ˈsɒl.əm.naɪz, (US) ˈsɑː.ləm- **-es** -ɪz **-ing** -ɪŋ **-ed** -d
solenoid ˈsəʊ.lə.nɔɪd, ˈsɒl.ə-, ˈ-ɪ-, (US) ˈsoʊ.lə-, ˈsɑː- **-s** -z
Solent ˈsəʊ.lənt, (US) ˈsoʊ-
sol-fa, S~ ˌsɒlˈfɑː, ˈ--, (US) ˌsoʊl-
solfegg|io sɒlˈfedʒ|.i.əʊ, (US) soʊlˈfedʒ|.i.oʊ; (US) sɑːlˈfedʒ|.oʊ **-i** -iː
solferino, S~ ˌsɒl.fərˈiː.nəʊ, (US) ˌsoʊl.fəˈriː.noʊ, ˌsɑːl-
solic|it səˈlɪs|.ɪt **-its** -ɪts **-iting** -ɪ.tɪŋ, (US) -ɪ.ţɪŋ **-ited** -ɪ.tɪd, (US) -ɪ.ţɪd
solicitation səˌlɪs.ɪˈteɪ.ʃən **-s** -z
solicitor səˈlɪs.ɪ.təʳ, ˈ-ə-, (US) -ţɚ **-s** -z **soˌlicitor ˈgeneral**
solicitous səˈlɪs.ɪ.təs, (US) -ţəs **-ly** -li **-ness** -nəs, -nɪs
solicitude səˈlɪs.ɪ.tʃuːd, -tjuːd, (US) -tuːd, -tjuːd
solid ˈsɒl.ɪd, (US) ˈsɑː.lɪd **-s** -z **-est** -ɪst, -əst **-ly** -li **-ness** -nəs, -nɪs
solidarity, S~ ˌsɒl.ɪˈdær.ə.ti, -ɪ.ti, (US) ˌsɑː.ləˈder.ə.ţi, -ˈdær-
solidifiable səˈlɪd.ɪ.faɪ.ə.bəl, sɒlˈɪd-, (US) səˈlɪd-
solidification səˌlɪd.ɪ.fɪˈkeɪ.ʃən, -fəˈ-, sɒlˌɪd-, (US) səˌlɪd.ə-
solidi|fy səˈlɪd.ɪ.|faɪ, ˈ-ə-, sɒlˈɪd-, (US) səˈlɪd.ɪ-, ˈ-ə- **-fies** -faɪz **-fying** -faɪ.ɪŋ **-fied** -faɪd
solidity səˈlɪd.ə.ti, sɒlˈɪd-, -ɪ.ti, (US) səˈlɪd.ə.ţi
solid-state ˌsɒl.ɪdˈsteɪt, (US) ˌsɑː.lɪdˈ- *stress shift, see compound:* ˌ**solid-state ˈphysics**
solid|us ˈsɒl.ɪ.d|əs, (US) ˈsɑː.lɪ- **-i** -aɪ, -iː
Solihull ˌsəʊ.lɪˈhʌl, ˌsɒl.ɪˈ-, (US) ˌsoʊ.lɪˈ- *stress shift:* ˌ**Solihull ˈresidents**
soliloquiz|e, -is|e səˈlɪl.ə.kwaɪz, sɒlˈɪl-, (US) səˈlɪl- **-es** -ɪz **-ing** -ɪŋ **-ed** -d
soliloqu|y səˈlɪl.ə.kw|i, sɒlˈɪl-, (US) səˈlɪl- **-ies** -iz
solipsism ˈsɒl.ɪp.sɪ.zəm, ˈsəʊ.lɪp-, (US) ˈsɑː.lɪp-, ˈsoʊ- **-s** -z
solipsist ˈsɒl.ɪp.sɪst, (US) ˈsɑː.lɪp- **-s** -s **-ic** -ɪk
solitaire ˌsɒl.ɪˈteəʳ, ˈ---, (US) ˈsɑː.lə.ter **-s** -z
solitar|y ˈsɒl.ɪ.tər|.i, ˈ-ə-, -tr|i, (US) ˈsɑː.lə.ter|.i **-ies** -iz **-ily** -əl.i, -ɪ.li **-iness** -ɪ.nəs, -ɪ.nɪs ˌ**solitary conˈfinement**
solitude ˈsɒl.ɪ.tʃuːd, ˈ-ə-, -tjuːd, (US) ˈsɑː.lə.tuːd, -tjuːd **-s** -z
Solloway ˈsɒl.ə.weɪ, (US) ˈsɑː.lə-
solo ˈsəʊ.ləʊ, (US) ˈsoʊ.loʊ **-s** -z
soloist ˈsəʊ.ləʊ.ɪst, (US) ˈsoʊ.loʊ- **-s** -s
Solomon ˈsɒl.ə.mən, (US) ˈsɑː.lə- ˈ**Solomon ˌIslands**
Solon ˈsəʊ.lɒn, -lən, (US) ˈsoʊ.lən, -lɑːn
so-long ˌsəʊˈlɒŋ; sə-, (US) ˌsoʊˈlɑːŋ, sə-, -ˈlɔːŋ
solstic|e ˈsɒl.stɪs, (US) ˈsɑːl- **-es** -ɪz
Solti ˈʃɒl.ti, (US) ˈsoʊlˌtiː
solubility ˌsɒl.jəˈbɪl.ə.ti, -jʊˈ-, -ɪ.ti, (US) ˌsɑːl.jəˈbɪl.ə.ţi, -jʊˈ-
soluble ˈsɒl.jə.bəl, -jʊ-, (US) ˈsɑːl-
solus ˈsəʊ.ləs, (US) ˈsoʊ-
solution səˈluː.ʃən, -ˈljuː-, (US) -ˈluː- **-s** -z
solvability ˌsɒl.vəˈbɪl.ə.ti, -ɪ.ti, (US) ˌsɑːl.vəˈbɪl.ə.ţi
solv|e sɒlv, (US) sɑːlv **-es** -z **-ing** -ɪŋ **-ed** -d **-able** -ə.bəl
solvency ˈsɒl.vənt.si, (US) ˈsɑːl-
solvent ˈsɒl.vənt, (US) ˈsɑːl- ˈ**solvent aˌbuse**
Solway ˈsɒl.weɪ, (US) ˈsɑːl-
Solzhenitsyn ˌsɒl.ʒəˈnɪt.sɪn, (US) ˌsoʊl.ʒəˈniːt-
som|a ˈsəʊ.m|ə, (US) ˈsoʊ- **-ata** -ə.tə, (US) -ə.ţə
Somali səˈmɑː.li, (US) soʊ-, sə- **-s** -z
Somali|a səˈmɑː.li|.ə, (US) soʊ-, sə- **-an/s** -ən/z
somatic səʊˈmæt.ɪk, (US) soʊˈmæţ-
somatostatin ˌsəʊ.mə.təˈstæt.ɪn, (US) səˌmæţ.əˈstæt.ən; (US) ˌsoʊ.mə.ţəˈ-
somatotropin səʊˌmæt.əˈtrəʊ.pɪn; ˌsəʊ.mə.təˈ-, (US) səˌmæţ.əˈtroʊ.pən; (US) ˌsoʊ.mə.ţəˈ-
somb|er ˈsɒm.b|əʳ, (US) ˈsɑːm.b|ɚ **-erest** -ər.ɪst, -ər.əst **-erly** -ə.li, (US) -ɚ.li **-erness** -ə.nəs, -ə.nɪs, (US) -ɚ.nəs, -ɚ.nɪs
sombr|e ˈsɒm.b|əʳ, (US) ˈsɑːm.b|ɚ **-est** -ər.ɪst, -ər.əst **-ely** -ə.li (US) -ɚ.li **-eness** -ə.nəs, -ə.nɪs, (US) -ɚ.nəs, -ɚ.nɪs
sombrero sɒmˈbreə.rəʊ, (US) sɑːmˈbrer.oʊ, səm- **-s** -z
some *strong form:* sʌm; *weak form:* səm

Note: Weak-form word. There are two grammatical functions for this word, one being the determiner, as in 'some apples, some bananas', etc., where a weak form is used, the other being a quantifier, as in 'some were tired and some were hungry', where the strong form is usual. In final position, the strong form is used (e.g. 'I want some').

-some səm

Note: Suffix. Does not normally change the stress pattern of the word to which it is added, e.g. **trouble** /ˈtrʌb.əl/, **troublesome** /ˈtrʌb.əl.səm/.

somebody ˈsʌm.bə.di, -ˌbɒd.i, (US) -ˌbɑː.di, -ˌbʌd.i, -bə.di
someday ˈsʌm.deɪ
somehow ˈsʌm.haʊ
someone ˈsʌm.wʌn
someplace ˈsʌm.pleɪs
Somerfield® ˈsʌm.ə.fiːld, (US) -ɚ-
Somers ˈsʌm.əz, (US) -ɚz
somersault ˈsʌm.ə.sɔːlt, -sɒlt, (US) -ɚ.sɑːlt, -sɔːlt **-s** -s **-ing** -ɪŋ **-ed** -ɪd
Somerset ˈsʌm.ə.set, -sɪt, (US) ˈ-ɚ- **-shire** -ʃəʳ, -ʃɪəʳ, (US) -ʃɚ, -ʃɪr
Somerton ˈsʌm.ə.tən, (US) -ɚ.ţən
Somervell ˈsʌm.ə.vɪl, -vel, (US) ˈ-ɚ-
Somerville ˈsʌm.ə.vɪl, (US) ˈ-ɚ-
something ˈsʌm*p*.θɪŋ
sometime ˈsʌm.taɪm
sometimes ˈsʌm.taɪmz
someway ˈsʌm.weɪ
somewhat ˈsʌm.*h*wɒt, (US) -*h*wɑːt, -*h*wʌt, -*h*wət
somewhere ˈsʌm.*h*weəʳ, (US) -*h*wer
Somme sɒm, (US) sʌm
sommelier sɒmˈel.i.eɪ, sʌm-, -əʳ; ˈsʌm.əl.jeɪ, ˈsɒm-, (US) ˌsʌm.əlˈjeɪ **-s** -z
somnambul|ism sɒmˈnæm.bjə.l|ɪ.zəm, -bjʊ-, (US) sɑːmˈnæm- **-ist/s** -ɪst/s
somniferous sɒmˈnɪf.ər.əs, (US) sɑːm-
somnolen|ce ˈsɒm.nəl.ən|*t*s, (US) ˈsɑːm- **-t/ly** -t/li
Sompting ˈsɒm*p*.tɪŋ, ˈsʌm*p*-, (US) ˈsɑːm*p*-
son, S~ sʌn **-s** -z ˌ**son of a ˈbitch;** ˌ**son of a ˈgun**
sonagram ˈsəʊ.nə.græm, ˈsɒn.ə-, (US) ˈsɑː.nə-, ˈsoʊ- **-s** -z
sonagraph, S~® ˈsəʊ.nə.grɑːf, ˈsɒn.ə-, -græf, (US) ˈsɑː.nə.græf, ˈsoʊ- **-s** -s
sonant ˈsəʊ.nənt, (US) ˈsoʊ- **-s** -s
sonar ˈsəʊ.nɑːʳ, (US) ˈsoʊ.nɑːr
sonata səˈnɑː.tə, (US) -ţə **-s** -z
sonatina ˌsɒn.əˈtiː.nə, (US) ˌsɑː.nəˈ- **-s** -z
Sondheim ˈsɒnd.haɪm, (US) ˈsɑːnd-
son et lumière ˌsɒn.eɪ.luːˈmjeəʳ, ˌsɔːn-, -ˈluː.mjeəʳ, (US) ˌsɑːn.eɪˈluː.mjer, ˌsɔːn-

song sɒŋ, (US) sɑːŋ, sɔːŋ -s -z ˌ**song and ˈdance;** ˈ**song ˌthrush**
songbird ˈsɒŋ.bɜːd, (US) ˈsɑːŋ.bɝːd, ˈsɔːŋ- -s -z
songbook ˈsɒŋ.bʊk, (US) ˈsɑːŋ-, ˈsɔːŋ- -s -s
songfest ˈsɒŋ.fest, (US) ˈsɑːŋ-, ˈsɔːŋ- -s -s
songster ˈsɒŋk.stəʳ, (US) ˈsɑːŋk.stɚ, ˈsɔːŋk- -s -z
songstress ˈsɒŋ.strəs, -strɪs, (US) ˈsɑː-, ˈsɔː- -es -ɪz
songwrit|er ˈsɒŋˌraɪ.t|əʳ, (US) ˈsɑːŋˌraɪ.ţ|ɚ, ˈsɔːŋ- -ers -əz, (US) -ɚz -ing -ɪŋ
Sonia ˈsɒn.jə, ˈsəʊ.njə, (US) ˈsɑː.njə, ˈsoʊ-
sonic ˈsɒn.ɪk, (US) ˈsɑː.nɪk ˌ**sonic ˈboom**
son-in-law ˈsʌn.ɪn.lɔː, (US) -lɑː, -lɔː **sons-in-law** ˈsʌnz-
sonnet ˈsɒn.ɪt, (US) ˈsɑː.nɪt -s -s
sonneteer ˌsɒn.ɪˈtɪəʳ, -əˈ-, (US) ˌsɑː.nəˈtɪr -s -z
Sonning ˈsɒn.ɪŋ, ˈsʌn-, (US) ˈsɑː.nɪŋ, ˈsʌn.ɪŋ
sonn|y ˈsʌn|.i -ies -iz
sonogram ˈsəʊ.nə.græm, ˈsɒn.ə-, (US) ˈsɑː.nə-, ˈsoʊ- -s -z
sonograph ˈsəʊ.nə.grɑːf, ˈsɒn.ə-, -græf, (US) ˈsɑː.nə.græf, ˈsoʊ- -s -s
sonometer səʊˈnɒm.ɪ.təʳ, ˈ-ə-, (US) səˈnɑː.mə.ţɚ, soʊ- -s -z
Sonora səˈnɔː.rə, (US) -ˈnɔːr.ə
sonorant ˈsɒn.ər.ənt, ˈsəʊ.nər-, (US) ˈsɑː.nɚ-, ˈsoʊ-; (US) səˈnɔːr-, soʊ- -s -s
sonorit|y səʊˈnɒr.ə.t|i, -ɪ.t|i, (US) səˈnɔːr.ə.ţ|i, soʊ- -ies -iz
sonorous ˈsɒn.ər.əs; səˈnɔː.rəs, (US) səˈnɔːr.əs, soʊ-; (US) ˈsɑː.nɚ-, ˈsoʊ- -ly -li
sonsie, sonsy ˈsɒnt.si, (US) ˈsɑːnt-
Sontag ˈsɒn.tæg, (US) ˈsɑːn-
Sony® ˈsəʊ.ni, ˈsɒn.i, (US) ˈsoʊ.ni
Sonya ˈsɒn.jə, ˈsəʊ.njə, (US) ˈsɑː.njə, ˈsoʊ-
soon suːn -er -əʳ, (US) -ɚ -est -ɪst, -əst ˌ**sooner or ˈlater**
Sooners ˈsuː.nəz, (US) -nɚz
soot sʊt, (US) sʊt, suːt
sooth suːθ
sooth|e suːð -es -z -ing/ly -ɪŋ/li -ed -d
soothsayer ˈsuːθˌseɪ.əʳ, (US) -ɚ -s -z
soot|y, S~ ˈsʊt|.i, (US) ˈsʊţ-, ˈsuː.ţ|i -ier -i.əʳ, (US) -i.ɚ -iest -i.ɪst, -i.əst -iness -ɪ.nəs, -ɪ.nɪs
sop sɒp, (US) sɑːp -s -s -ping -ɪŋ -ped -t
Sophia səʊˈfiː.ə, -ˈfaɪ-, (US) soʊ-
Sophie ˈsəʊ.fi, (US) ˈsoʊ-
soph|ism ˈsɒf|.ɪ.zəm, (US) ˈsɑː.f|ɪ- -isms -ɪ.zəmz -ist/s -ɪst/s
sophister ˈsɒf.ɪ.stəʳ, (US) ˈsɑː.fɪ.stɚ -s -z
sophistic səʊˈfɪs.tɪk, (US) sə- -al -əl -ally -əl.i, -li
sophisticate n səˈfɪs.tɪ.kət, -kɪt, -keɪt, (US) -tə.kɪt -s -s
sophisti|cate v səˈfɪs.tɪ|.keɪt, (US) -tə- -cates -keɪts -cating -keɪ.tɪŋ, (US) -keɪ.ţɪŋ -cated -keɪ.tɪd, (US) -keɪ.ţɪd
sophistication səˌfɪs.tɪˈkeɪ.ʃən, -təˈ-, (US) -təˈ-
sophistr|y ˈsɒf.ɪ.str|i, (US) ˈsɑː.fɪ- -ies -iz
Sophoclean ˌsɒf.əˈkliː.ən, (US) ˌsɑː.fəˈ-
Sophocles ˈsɒf.ə.kliːz, (US) ˈsɑː.fə-
sophomore ˈsɒf.ə.mɔːʳ, (US) ˈsɑː.fə.mɔːr -s -z
sophomoric ˌsɒf.əˈmɒr.ɪk, (US) ˌsɑː.fəˈmɔːr-
Sophy ˈsəʊ.fi, (US) ˈsoʊ-
soporific ˌsɒp.ərˈɪf.ɪk, ˌsəʊ.pərˈ-, (US) ˌsɑː.pəˈrɪf-, ˌsoʊ- -ally -əl.i, -li
sopping ˈsɒp.ɪŋ, (US) ˈsɑː.pɪŋ ˌ**sopping ˈwet**
sopp|y ˈsɒp|.i, (US) ˈsɑː.p|i -ier -i.əʳ, (US) -i.ɚ -iest -i.ɪst, -i.əst -iness -ɪ.nəs, -ɪ.nɪs -ily -əl.i, -ɪ.li
sopranino ˌsɒp.rəˈniː.nəʊ, (US) ˌsoʊ.prəˈniː.noʊ -s -z
sopran|o səˈprɑː.n|əʊ, (US) -ˈpræn|.oʊ, -ˈprɑː.n|oʊ -os -əʊz, (US) -oʊz -i -iː
Sopwith ˈsɒp.wɪθ, (US) ˈsɑːp- -s -s
sorbet ˈsɔː.beɪ, (US) ˈsɔːr.beɪ; (US) sɔːrˈbət -s -s
sorbic ˈsɔː.bɪk, (US) ˈsɔːr- ˌ**sorbic ˈacid**
sorbitol ˈsɔː.bɪ.tɒl, (US) ˈsɔːr.bɪ.tɑːl, -tɔːl, -toʊl
Sorbonne sɔːˈbɒn, (US) sɔːrˈbɑːn, -ˈbʌn
sorcer|y ˈsɔː.sər|.i, (US) ˈsɔːr- -ies -iz -er/s -əʳ/z, (US) -ɚ/z -ess/es -ɪs/ɪz, -es/ɪz
Sorcha ˈsɔː.ʃə, -kə, -xə (US) sɔr-, -tʃə
Sordello sɔːˈdel.əʊ, (US) sɔːrˈdel.oʊ
sordid ˈsɔː.dɪd, (US) ˈsɔːr- -ly -li -ness -nəs, -nɪs
sordin|o sɔːˈdiː.n|əʊ, (US) sɔːrˈdiː.n|oʊ -i -iː
sor|e sɔːʳ, (US) sɔːr -es -z -er -əʳ, (US) -ɚ -est -ɪst, -əst -ely -li -eness -nəs, -nɪs
sorehead ˈsɔː.hed, (US) ˈsɔːr- -s -z
sorghum ˈsɔː.gəm, (US) ˈsɔːr-
Soroptimist səˈrɒp.tɪ.mɪst, -tə-, (US) -ˈrɑːp.tɪ- -s -s
sororit|y səˈrɒr.ə.t|i, sɒrˈɒr-, -ɪ.t|i, (US) səˈrɔːr.ə.ţ|i -ies -iz
sorrel ˈsɒr.əl, (US) ˈsɔːr-
Sorrento səˈren.təʊ, (US) -toʊ
sorrow ˈsɒr.əʊ, (US) ˈsɑːr.oʊ -s -z -ing/ly -ɪŋ/li -ed -d -er/s -əʳ/z, (US) -ɚ/z
sorrow|ful ˈsɒr.əʊ|.fəl, -fʊl, (US) ˈsɑːr.ə- -fully -fəl.i, -fli, -fʊl.i -fulness -fəl.nəs, -fʊl.nəs, -nɪs
sorr|y ˈsɒr|.i, (US) ˈsɑːr- -ier -i.əʳ, (US) -i.ɚ -iest -i.ɪst, -i.əst -ily -əl.i, -ɪ.li -iness -ɪ.nəs, -ɪ.nɪs
sort sɔːt, (US) sɔːrt -s -s -ing -ɪŋ, (US) ˈsɔːr.ţɪŋ -ed -ɪd, (US) ˈsɔːr.ţɪd -er/s -əʳ/z, (US) ˈsɔːr.ţɚ/z
sortie ˈsɔː.ti, (US) ˈsɔːr.tiː, ˌ-ˈ- -s -z
sortilege ˈsɔː.tɪ.lɪdʒ, (US) ˈsɔːr.ţəl.ɪdʒ, -edʒ
sort-out ˈsɔː.t.aʊt, (US) ˈsɔːrţ-
SOS ˌes.əʊˈes, (US) -oʊˈ-
so-so ˈsəʊ.səʊ, ˌ-ˈ-, (US) ˌsoʊˈsoʊ
sostenuto ˌsɒs.təˈnuː.təʊ, -tɪˈ-, -ˈnjuː-, (US) ˌsɑː.stəˈnuː.ţoʊ, ˌsoʊ-
sot sɒt, (US) sɑːt -s -s
Sotheby ˈsʌð.ə.bi -'s -z
Sothern ˈsʌð.ən, (US) -ɚn
Sotho ˈsuː.tuː, ˈsəʊ.təʊ, (US) ˈsoʊ.toʊ -s -z
sottish ˈsɒt.ɪʃ, (US) ˈsɑː.ţɪʃ -ly -li -ness -nəs, -nɪs
sotto voce ˌsɒt.əʊˈvəʊ.tʃeɪ, (US) ˌsɑː.ţoʊˈvoʊ-
sou suː -s -z
soubise suːˈbiːz
soubrette suːˈbret, sʊ-, (US) suː- -s -s
soubriquet ˈsuː.brɪ.keɪ, ˈsoʊ-, -brə-, (US) ˈsuː.brə-, -ket -s -z
souchong ˌsuːˈtʃɒŋ, ˈ--, (US) ˈsuː.tʃɑːŋ, -ʃɑːŋ
souffle ˈsuː.fəl -s -z
soufflé ˈsuː.fleɪ, (US) suːˈfleɪ, ˈ-- -s -z -ed -d
sough saʊ, sʌf -s saʊz, sʌfs -ing ˈsaʊ.ɪŋ, ˈsʌf.ɪŋ -ed saʊd, sʌft
sought (from **seek**) sɔːt, (US) sɑːt, sɔːt
sought-after ˈsɔːtˌɑːf.təʳ, (US) ˈsɑːtˌæf.tɚ, ˈsɔːt-
souk suːk -s -s
soul səʊl, (US) soʊl -s -z ˈ**soul ˌfood;** ˈ**soul ˌmate**
Soulbury ˈsəʊl.bər.i, (US) ˈsoʊl-, -ber.i
soul-destroying ˈsəʊl.dɪˌstrɔɪ.ɪŋ, (US) ˈsoʊl-
soulful ˈsəʊl.fəl, -fʊl, (US) ˈsoʊl- -ly -i -ness -nəs, -nɪs
soulless ˈsəʊl.ləs, -lɪs, (US) ˈsoʊl- -ly -li -ness -nəs, -nɪs
soulmate ˈsəʊl.meɪt, (US) ˈsoʊl- -s -s
soul-searching ˈsəʊlˌsɜː.tʃɪŋ, (US) ˈsoʊlˌsɝː-
sound saʊnd -s -z -er -əʳ, (US) -ɚ -est -ɪst, -əst -ly -li -ness -nəs, -nɪs -ing/s -ɪŋ/z -ed -ɪd ˈ**sound ˌbarrier;** ˈ**sound ˌbox;** ˈ**sound efˌfect**
soundbite ˈsaʊnd.baɪt, ˈsaʊm-, (US) ˈsaʊnd- -s -s
soundboard ˈsaʊnd.bɔːd, ˈsaʊm-, (US) ˈsaʊnd.bɔːrd -s -z
soundless ˈsaʊnd.ləs, -lɪs -ly -li
soundproof ˈsaʊnd.pruːf, ˈsaʊm-, (US) ˈsaʊnd- -s -s -ing -ɪŋ -ed -t
soundtrack ˈsaʊnd.træk -s -s
soundwave ˈsaʊnd.weɪv -s -z
soup suːp -s -s -y -i -ed -t ˈ**soup ˌkitchen;** ˌ**souped ˈup**
soupçon ˈsuːp.sɔ̃ːŋ, -sɒŋ, -sɒn, (US) suːpˈsõʊn, suː-, -ˈsɑːn, ˈ-- -s -z
soupspoon ˈsuːp.spuːn -s -z
sour ˈsaʊ.əʳ, saʊəʳ, (US) ˈsaʊ.ɚ -er -əʳ, (US) -ɚ -est -ɪst, -əst -ly -li -ness -nəs, -nɪs -s -z -ing -ɪŋ -ed -d ˌ**sour ˈcream;** ˌ**sour ˈgrapes**
sourc|e sɔːs, (US) sɔːrs -es -ɪz -ing -ɪŋ -ed -t
sourdine sʊəˈdiːn, (US) sʊr- -s -z
sourdough ˈsaʊ.ə.dəʊ, ˈsaʊə-, (US) ˈsaʊ.ɚ.doʊ

S

sourpuss ˈsaʊ.ə.pʊs, ˈsaʊə-, (US) ˈsaʊ.ɚ- **-es** -ɪz
Sousa ˈsuː.zə, (US) -zə, -sə
sousaphone ˈsuː.zə.fəʊn, (US) -zə.foʊn, -sə- **-s** -z
sous-chef ˈsuː.ʃef **-s** -s
sous|e saʊs **-es** -ɪz **-ing** -ɪŋ **-ed** -t
Sousse suːs
soutane suːˈtɑːn, (US) -ˈtæn, -ˈtɑːn **-s** -z
Souter ˈsuː.təʳ, (US) -t̬ɚ
south, S~ saʊθ ˌ**South ˈAfrica;** ˌ**South Aˈmerica;** ˌ**South Caroˈlina;** ˌ**South Daˈkota;** ˌ**South ˈIsland** (US) ˈ**South ˌIsland;** ˌ**South Koˈrea;** ˌ**south ˈpole;** ˌ**South ˈSeas**
Southall *place in London:* ˈsaʊ.θɔːl, -ðɔːl, (US) -θɔːl, -θɑːl, -ðɔːl, -ðɑːl *surname:* ˈsʌð.ɔːl, -əl, (US) -ɔːl, -ɑːl, -əl
Southam ˈsaʊ.θəm
Southampton saʊˈθæmp.tən, saʊθˈhæmp-
southbound ˈsaʊθ.baʊnd
Southbourne ˈsaʊθ.bɔːn, (US) -bɔːrn
Southdown ˈsaʊθ.daʊn
southeast, S~ ˌsaʊθˈiːst; *in nautical usage also:* ˌsaʊ- **-wards** -wədz, (US) -wɚdz *stress shift:* ˌ**southeast ˈwind**
south-easter ˌsaʊθˈiː.stəʳ, (US) -stɚ; *in nautical usage also:* ˌsaʊ- **-s** -z
southeasterl|y ˌsaʊθˈiː.stəl.i, (US) -stɚ.li; *in nautical usage also:* ˌsaʊ- **-ies** -iz
southeastern, S~ ˌsaʊθˈiː.stən, (US) -stɚn; *in nautical usage also:* ˌsaʊ- **-er/s** -əʳ/z, (US) -ɚ/z *stress shift:* ˌ**southeastern ˈwind**
southeastward ˌsaʊθˈiːst.wəd, (US) -wɚd **-s** -z
Southend ˌsaʊθˈend *stress shift:* ˌ**Southend ˈpier**
southerl|y ˈsʌð.əl|.i, (US) -ɚ.l|i **-ies** -iz
southern, S~ ˈsʌð.ən, (US) -ɚn **-most** -ən.məʊst, -əm.məʊst, (US) -ɚn.moʊst ˌ**Southern ˈCross**
southerner, S~ ˈsʌð.ən.əʳ, (US) -ɚ.nɚ **-s** -z
southernwood ˈsʌð.ən.wʊd, (US) -ɚn-
Southey ˈsaʊ.ði, ˈsʌð.i
Southgate ˈsaʊθ.geɪt, -gɪt
Southon ˈsaʊ.ðən
southpaw ˈsaʊθ.pɔː, (US) -pɑː, -pɔː **-s** -z
Southport ˈsaʊθ.pɔːt, (US) -pɔːrt
southron, S~ ˈsʌð.rən **-s** -z
Southsea ˈsaʊθ.siː, -si
south-southeast ˌsaʊθ.saʊθˈiːst; *in nautical usage also:* ˌsaʊ.saʊˈ-
south-southwest ˌsaʊθ.saʊθˈwest; *in nautical usage also:* ˌsaʊ.saʊˈ-
southward ˈsaʊθ.wəd, (US) -wɚd **-s** -z **-ly** -li
Southwark ˈsʌð.ək, (US) -ɚk
Southwell *surname:* ˈsaʊθ.wəl, -wel; ˈsʌð.əl *town in Nottinghamshire:* ˈsaʊθ.wəl; *locally:* ˈsʌð.əl

> Note: Viscount Southwell is /ˈsʌð.əl/.

southwest, S~ ˌsaʊθˈwest; *in nautical usage also:* ˌsaʊ- **-wards** -wədz, (US) -wɚdz *stress shift:* ˌ**southwest ˈwind**
south-wester ˌsaʊθˈwes.təʳ, (US) -tɚ; *in nautical usage also:* ˌsaʊ- **-s** -z
south-westerl|y ˌsaʊθˈwes.təl|.i, (US) -tɚ.l|i; *in nautical usage also:* ˌsaʊ- **-ies** -iz
southwestern, S~ ˌsaʊθˈwes.tən, (US) -tɚn; *in nautical usage also:* ˌsaʊ- **-er/s** -əʳ/z, (US) -ɚ/z *stress shift:* ˌ**southwestern ˈwind**
south-westward ˌsaʊθˈwest.wəd, (US) -wɚd; *in nautical usage also:* ˌsaʊ- **-s** -z
Southwick *in West Sussex:* ˈsaʊθ.wɪk *in Northamptonshire:* ˈsʌð.ɪk *in Hampshire:* ˈsʌð.ɪk, ˈsaʊθ.wɪk
Southwold ˈsaʊθ.wəʊld, (US) -woʊld
Soutter ˈsuː.təʳ, (US) -t̬ɚ
souvenir ˌsuː.vənˈɪəʳ, -vɪˈnɪəʳ, ˈ---, (US) ˌsuː.vəˈnɪr, ˈ--- **-s** -z
sou'wester saʊˈwes.təʳ, (US) -tɚ **-s** -z
Souza ˈsuː.zə
sovereign ˈsɒv.ər.ɪn, ˈ-rɪn, (US) ˈsɑːv.rən, -ɚ.ən **-s** -z **-ly** -li
sovereignty ˈsɒv.rən.ti, -rɪn-, (US) ˈsɑːv.rən.t̬i, -ɚ.ən-
soviet, S~ ˈsəʊ.vi.ət, ˈsɒv.i-, (US) ˈsoʊ.vi.et, -ɪt; (US) ˌ--ˈ- **-s** -s **-ism** -ɪ.zəm ˌ**Soviet ˈUnion**
sovran ˈsɒv.rən, (US) ˈsɑːv- **-s** -z
sow n *pig, metal, channel for metal:* saʊ **-s** -z
sow v *plant seed:* səʊ, (US) soʊ **-s** -z **-ing** -ɪŋ **-ed** -d **-n** -n **-er/s** -əʳ/z, (US) -ɚ/z
Sowerby *in North Yorkshire:* ˈsaʊ.ə.bi, (US) ˈsaʊ.ɚ- *in West Yorkshire, surname:* ˈsəʊ.ə.bi, ˈsaʊ.ə-, (US) ˈsoʊ.ɚ-, ˈsaʊ.ɚ-
Soweto səˈwet.əʊ, -ˈweɪ.təʊ, (US) -ˈwet̬.oʊ, -ˈweɪ.t̬oʊ
sox sɒks, (US) sɑːks
soy sɔɪ ˌ**soy ˈsauce** (US) ˈ**soy ˌsauce**
soya ˈsɔɪ.ə ˈ**soya ˌbean**
soybean ˈsɔɪ.biːn **-s** -z
Soyinka sɔɪˈɪŋ.kə
Soyuz sɔːˈjʊz, səˈjuːz, (US) ˈsɑː.juːz, ˈsɔɪ.jʊz
sozzled ˈsɒz.əld, (US) ˈsɑː.zəld
spa, S~ spɑː **-s** -z
spac|e speɪs **-es** -ɪz **-ing** -ɪŋ **-ed** -t ˈ**space ˌage;** ˈ**space ˌbar;** ˈ**space ˌshuttle;** ˈ**space ˌstation;** ˈ**space ˌsuit;** ˈ**space ˌwalk**
spacecraft ˈspeɪs.krɑːft, (US) -kræft **-s** -s
spaced-out ˌspeɪstˈaʊt *stress shift:* ˌ**spaced-out ˈperson**
spacelab ˈspeɪs.læb **-s** -z
space|man ˈspeɪs|.mæn, -mən **-men** -men, -mən
space-saving ˈspeɪsˌseɪ.vɪŋ
spaceship ˈspeɪs.ʃɪp, ˈspeɪʃ-, (US) ˈspeɪs- **-s** -s
space-time ˌspeɪsˈtaɪm *stress shift:* ˌ**space-time conˈtinuum**
spacewalk ˈspeɪs.wɔːk, (US) -wɔːk, -wɑːk **-s** -s **-ing** -ɪŋ **-ed** -t **-er/s** -əʳ/z, (US) -ɚ/z
spac|ey ˈspeɪ.s|i **-ier** -i.əʳ, (US) -i.ɚ **-iest** -i.ɪst, -i.əst **-iness** -ɪ.nəs, -ɪ.nɪs
spacious ˈspeɪ.ʃəs **-ly** -li **-ness** -nəs, -nɪs
spade speɪd **-s** -z **-ful/s** -fʊl/z ˌ**call a ˌspade a ˈspade**
spadework ˈspeɪd.wɜːk, (US) -wɝːk
spaghetti spəˈget.i, (US) -ˈget̬- **spaˌghetti bologˈnese**
spahi ˈspɑː.hiː, -iː, (US) -hiː **-s** -z
Spain speɪn
spake (archaic past tense of **speak**) speɪk
Spalding ˈspɔːl.dɪŋ, ˈspɒl-, (US) ˈspɔːl-, ˈspɑːl-
spall spɔːl, (US) spɔːl, spɑːl **-s** -z **-ing** -ɪŋ **-ed** -d
spam, S~ spæm **-s** -z **-ming** -ɪŋ **-med** -d **-er/s** -əʳ/z, (US) -mɚ/z
span spæn **-s** -z **-ning** -ɪŋ **-ned** -d
Spandau ˈspæn.daʊ
spandex ˈspæn.deks
spandrel ˈspæn.drəl **-s** -z
spangl|e ˈspæŋ.gəl **-es** -z **-ing** -ɪŋ, ˈspæŋ.glɪŋ **-ed** -d
spangly ˈspæŋ.gli, -gəl.i
Spaniard ˈspæn.jəd, (US) -jɚd **-s** -z
spaniel ˈspæn.jəl **-s** -z
Spanish ˈspæn.ɪʃ ˌ**Spanish ˈfly;** ˌ**Spanish ˈomelette;** ˌ**Spanish ˈonion;** ˌ**Spanish Saˈhara**
spank spæŋk **-s** -s **-ing** -ɪŋ **-ed** -t **-er/s** -əʳ/z, (US) -ɚ/z
spanking ˈspæŋ.kɪŋ **-s** -z
spanner ˈspæn.əʳ, (US) -ɚ **-s** -z
spar spɑːʳ, (US) spɑːr **-s** -z **-ring** -ɪŋ **-red** -d ˈ**sparring ˌmatch;** ˈ**sparring ˌpartner**
spar|e speəʳ, (US) sper **-ely** -li **-eness** -nəs, -nɪs **-es** -z **-ing/ly** -ɪŋ/li **-ed** -d ˌ**spare ˈpart;** ˌ**spare ˈrib;** ˌ**spare ˈtyre**
sparing ˈspeə.rɪŋ, (US) ˈsper.ɪŋ **-ly** -li
spark, S~ spɑːk, (US) spɑːrk **-s** -s **-ing** -ɪŋ **-ed** -t ˈ**spark ˌplug;** ˈ**sparking ˌplug**
Sparkes spɑːks, (US) spɑːrks
sparkl|e ˈspɑː.kəl, (US) ˈspɑːr- **-es** -z **-ing** -ɪŋ, ˈspɑː.klɪŋ, (US) ˈspɑːr- **-ed** -d **-y** -i, ˈspɑː.kli, (US) ˈspɑːr- ˌ**sparkling ˈwine**
sparkler ˈspɑː.kləʳ, (US) ˈspɑːr.klɚ **-s** -z
spark|y ˈspɑː.k|i, (US) ˈspɑːr.k|i **-ier** -i.əʳ, (US) -i.ɚ **-iest** -i.ɪst, -i.əst **-iness** -ɪ.nəs, -ɪ.nɪs **-ily** -əl.i, -ɪ.li
sparrow, S~ ˈspær.əʊ, (US) ˈsper.oʊ, ˈspær- **-s** -z
sparrowhawk ˈspær.əʊ.hɔːk, (US) ˈsper.oʊ.hɑːk, ˈspær-, -hɔːk **-s** -s
spars|e spɑːs, (US) spɑːrs **-er** -əʳ, (US)

-ə -est -ɪst, -əst -ely -li -eness -nəs, -nɪs -ity -ə.ti, -ɪ.ti, (US) -ə.ţi
Spar|ta ˈspɑː|.tə, (US) ˈspɑːr|.ţə -tan/s -tən/z
Spartacus ˈspɑː.tə.kəs, (US) ˈspɑːr.ţə-
spartan ˈspɑː.tən, (US) ˈspɑːr-
spasm ˈspæz.əm -s -z
spasmodic spæzˈmɒd.ɪk, (US) -ˈmɑː.dɪk -ally -əl.i, -li
spastic ˈspæs.tɪk -s -s
spasticity spæsˈtɪs.ə.ti, -ɪ.ti, (US) -ə.ţi
spat spæt -s -s -ting -ɪŋ -ted -ɪd
spatchcock ˈspætʃ.kɒk, (US) -kɑːk -s -s -ing -ɪŋ -ed -t
spate speɪt -s -s
spatial ˈspeɪ.ʃəl -ly -i
spatt|er ˈspæt|.əʳ, (US) ˈspæţ|.ɚ -ers -əz, (US) -ɚz -ering -ər.ɪŋ -ered -əd, (US) -ɚd
spatul|a ˈspætʃ.ə.l|ə, ˈ-ʊ-, ˈspæt.jə-, ˈspæt.jʊ-, (US) ˈspætʃ.ə- -ae -iː -as -əz
spatulate ˈspætʃ.ə.lət, ˈ-ʊ-, ˈspæt.jə-, ˈ-jʊ-, -lɪt, -leɪt, (US) ˈspætʃ.ə.lɪt, -leɪt
spavin ˈspæv.ɪn -ed -d
spawn spɔːn, (US) spɑːn, spɔːn -s -z -ing -ɪŋ -ed -d
spay speɪ -s -z -ing -ɪŋ -ed -d
Speaight speɪt
speak spiːk -s -s -ing -ɪŋ spoke spəʊk, (US) spoʊk spoken ˈspəʊ.kən, (US) ˈspoʊ- speaker/s ˈspiː.kəʳ/z, (US) -kɚ/z
speakeas|y ˈspiːkˌiː.z|i -ies -iz
speakerphone ˈspiː.kə.fəʊn, (US) -kɚ.foʊn -s -z
Spean spɪən, ˈspiː.ən, (US) ˈspiː.ən
spear spɪəʳ, (US) spɪr -s -z -ing -ɪŋ -ed -d
spearhead ˈspɪə.hed, (US) ˈspɪr- -s -z -ing -ɪŋ -ed -ɪd
spear|man, S~ ˈspɪə|.mən, (US) ˈspɪr- -men -mən, -men
spearmint ˈspɪə.mɪnt, (US) ˈspɪr-
spec spek
speci|al ˈspeʃ|.əl -als -əlz -ally -əl.i, -li -alness -əl.nəs, -əl.nɪs **ˈSpecial ˌBranch; ˌspecial deˈlivery; ˌspecial efˈfects**
speciali|ism ˈspeʃ.əl.ɪ|.zəm, ˈ-lɪ-, (US) ˈ-əl.ɪ- -s -z
specialist ˈspeʃ.əl.ɪst -s -s
specialit|y ˌspeʃ.iˈæl.ə.t|i, -ɪ.t|i, (US) -ə.ţ|i -ies -iz
specialization, -isa- ˌspeʃ.əl.aɪˈzeɪ.ʃən, -ɪˈ-, (US) -əˈ-
specializ|e, -is|e ˈspeʃ.əl.aɪz, (US) -ə.laɪz -es -ɪz -ing -ɪŋ -ed -d
specialt|y ˈspeʃ.əl.t|i -ies -iz
specie ˈspiː.ʃiː, -ʃi, (US) -ʃiː, -siː
species ˈspiː.ʃiːz, -ʃɪz, -siːz, -sɪz, (US) -ʃiːz, -siːz -ism -ɪ.zəm
specific spəˈsɪf.ɪk, spɪ-, (US) spə- -s -s -ally -əl.i, -li **speˌcific ˈgravity**
specification ˌspes.ɪ.fɪˈkeɪ.ʃən, ˌ-ə-, -fəˈ-, (US) ˌ-ə- -s -z
specificity ˌspes.ɪˈfɪs.ə.ti, -ɪ.ti, (US) -əˈfɪs.ə.ţi
speci|fy ˈspes.ɪ|.faɪ, ˈ-ə- -fies -faɪz -fying -faɪ.ɪŋ -fied -faɪd -fiable -faɪ.ə.bəl
specimen ˈspes.ə.mɪn, ˈ-ɪ-, -mən, (US) -ə.mən -s -z
specious ˈspiː.ʃəs -ly -li -ness -nəs, -nɪs
speck spek -s -s -ed -t
speckle ˈspek.əl -s -z -d -d
speckless ˈspek.ləs, -lɪs
specs speks
spectacle ˈspek.tə.kəl, -tɪ- -s -z -d -d
spectacular spekˈtæk.jə.ləʳ, -jʊ-, (US) -lɚ -ly -li
spectat|e spekˈteɪt -es -s -ing -ɪŋ -ed -ɪd
spectator, S~ spekˈteɪ.təʳ, (US) -ţɚ -s -z **specˌtator ˈsport; specˈtator ˌsport**
specter ˈspek.təʳ, (US) -tɚ -s -z
Spector ˈspek.təʳ, (US) -tɚ
spectral ˈspek.trəl
spectre ˈspek.təʳ, (US) -tɚ -s -z
spectrogram ˈspek.trəʊ.græm, (US) -trə- -s -z
spectrograph ˈspek.trəʊ.grɑːf, -græf, (US) -trə.græf -s -s
spectrographic ˌspek.trəʊˈgræf.ɪk, (US) -trəˈ- *stress shift:* **ˌspectrographic ˈsection**
spectrography spekˈtrɒg.rə.fi, (US) -ˈtrɑː.grə-
spectrometer spekˈtrɒm.ɪ.təʳ, ˈ-ə-, (US) -ˈtrɑː.mə.ţɚ -s -z
spectroscope ˈspek.trə.skəʊp, (US) -trə.skoʊp -s -s
spectroscopic ˌspek.trəˈskɒp.ɪk, (US) -ˈskɑː.pɪk -al -əl -ally -əl.i, -li *stress shift:* **ˌspectroscopic ˈpicture**
spectroscop|ist spekˈtrɒs.kə.p|ɪst, (US) -ˈtrɑː.skə- -ists -ɪsts -y -i
spectr|um ˈspek.tr|əm -a -ə -ums -əmz
specu|late ˈspek.jə|.leɪt, -jʊ- -lates -leɪts -lating -leɪ.tɪŋ, (US) -leɪ.ţɪŋ -lated -leɪ.tɪd, (US) -leɪ.ţɪd -lator/s -leɪ.təʳ/z, (US) -leɪ.ţɚ/z
speculation ˌspek.jəˈleɪ.ʃən, -jʊˈ- -s -z
speculative ˈspek.jə.lə.tɪv, -jʊ-, -leɪ-, (US) -leɪ.ţɪv, -lə- -ly -li -ness -nəs, -nɪs
specul|um ˈspek.jə.l|əm, -jʊ- -a -ə -ar -əʳ, (US) -ɚ
sped (from **speed**) sped
speech spiːtʃ -es -ɪz **ˈspeech ˌday; ˈspeech imˌpediment; ˌspeech ˈsynthesiser**
speechification ˌspiː.tʃɪ.fɪˈkeɪ.ʃən, -tʃə-, -fəˈ-, (US) -tʃə- -s -z
speechi|fy ˈspiː.tʃɪ|.faɪ, -tʃə- -fies -faɪz -fying -faɪ.ɪŋ -fied -faɪd -fier/s -faɪ.əʳ/z, (US) -faɪ.ɚ/z
speechless ˈspiːtʃ.ləs, -lɪs -ly -li -ness -nəs, -nɪs
speed, S~ spiːd -s -z -ing -ɪŋ -ed -ɪd sped sped **ˈspeed ˌbump; ˈspeed ˌlimit; ˈspeed ˌtrap**
speedboat ˈspiːd.bəʊt, (US) -boʊt -s -s
speed-cop ˈspiːd.kɒp, (US) -kɑːp -s -s
speedo ˈspiː.dəʊ, (US) -doʊ -s -z
speedometer spiːˈdɒm.ɪ.təʳ, spɪ-, -mə-, (US) -ˈdɑː.mə.ţɚ -s -z
speed-read ˈspiːd.riːd -s -z -ing -ɪŋ *past tense:* ˈspiːd.red
speed|skate ˈspiːd|.skeɪt -skating -ˌskeɪ.tɪŋ, (US) -ţɪŋ -skater/s -ˌskeɪ.təʳ/z, (US) -ţɚ/z
speedway ˈspiːd.weɪ -s -z
speedwell, S~ ˈspiːd.wel, -wəl -s -z
Speedwriting® ˈspiːdˌraɪ.tɪŋ, (US) -ţɪŋ
speed|y ˈspiː.d|i -ier -i.əʳ, (US) -i.ɚ -iest -i.ɪst, -i.əst -ily -əl.i, -ɪ.li -iness -ɪ.nəs, -ɪ.nɪs
Speen spiːn
Speer speəʳ, spɪəʳ; *as if German:* ʃpeəʳ; (US) spɪr; *as if German:* (US) ʃper
Speight speɪt
Speirs spɪəz, (US) spɪrz
speiss spaɪs
Speke spiːk
speleological ˌspiː.li.əˈlɒdʒ.ɪ.kəl, ˌspel.i-, (US) -ˈlɑː.dʒɪ-
speleolog|y ˌspiː.liˈɒl.ə.dʒ|i, ˌspel.iˈ-, (US) ˌspiː.liˈɑː.lə- -ist/s -ɪst/s
spell spel -s -z -ing/s -ɪŋ/z -ed -d, -t spelt spelt speller/s ˈspel.əʳ/z, (US) -ɚ/z **ˈspelling ˌbee**
spell|bind ˈspel|.baɪnd -binds -baɪndz -binding -baɪn.dɪŋ -bound -baʊnd -binder/s -ˌbaɪn.dəʳ/z, (US) -ˌbaɪn.dɚ/z
spellbound ˈspel.baʊnd
spellchecker ˈspelˌtʃek.əʳ, (US) -ɚ -s -z
spelt spelt
spelt|er ˈspel.t|əʳ, (US) -t|ɚ -ers -əz, (US) -ɚz -ering -ər.ɪŋ -ered -əd, (US) -ɚd
spelunk|er spəˈlʌŋ.k|əʳ, (US) -k|ɚ; (US) ˈspiː.lʌŋ- -er/s -ər.əʳ/z, (US) -ɚ.ɚ/z -ing -ɪŋ
spenc|e, S~ spents -es -ɪz
spencer, S~ ˈspent.səʳ, (US) -sɚ -s -z
spend spend -s -z -ing -ɪŋ spent -t spender/s ˈspen.dəʳ/z, (US) -dɚ/z
Spender ˈspen.dəʳ, (US) -dɚ
spendthrift ˈspend.θrɪft -s -s
Spengler ˈspeŋ.gləʳ, (US) -glɚ
Spenlow ˈspen.ləʊ, (US) -loʊ
Spennymoor ˈspen.i.mɔːʳ, -mʊəʳ, (US) -mɔːr, -mʊr
Spens spenz
Spenser ˈspent.səʳ, (US) -sɚ
Spenserian spenˈsɪə.ri.ən, (US) -ˈsɪr.i-
spent (from **spend**) spent
sperm spɜːm, (US) spɝːm -s -z **ˈsperm ˌbank; ˈsperm ˌwhale**
spermaceti ˌspɜː.məˈset.i, -ˈsiː.ti, (US) ˌspɝː.məˈsiː.ti, -ˈset.i
spermatozo|on ˌspɜː.mə.təʊˈzəʊ|.ɒn, -ən, (US) ˌspɝː.mə.ţəˈzoʊ|.ɑːn, -ən -a -ə
spermicidal ˌspɜː.mɪˈsaɪ.dəl, (US) ˌspɝː.mə-
spermicide ˈspɜː.mɪ.saɪd, (US) ˈspɝː.mə- -s -z
Sperrin ˈsper.ɪn
spew spjuː -s -z -ing -ɪŋ -ed -d

S

Spey speɪ

Spezia ˈspet.si.ə, ˈsped.zi-, US ˈspet.si.ɑː

sphagnum ˈsfæg.nəm ˌ**sphagnum** ˈ**moss**

sphene sfiːn **-s** -z

sphere sfɪəʳ, US sfɪr **-s** -z

spheric ˈsfer.ɪk, US ˈsfɪr-, ˈsfer- **-s** -s **-al** -əl **-ally** -əl.i, -li

spheroid ˈsfɪə.rɔɪd, US ˈsfɪr.ɔɪd, ˈsfer- **-s** -z

spheroidal sfɪəˈrɔɪ.dəl, sferˈɔɪ-, US sfɪˈrɔɪ-, sferˈɔɪ-

spherometer sfɪəˈrɒm.ɪ.təʳ, sferˈɒm-, ˈ-ə-, US sfɪˈrɑː.mə.tɚ, sferˈɑː- **-s** -z

sphincter ˈsfɪŋk.təʳ, US -tɚ **-s** -z

sphinx sfɪŋks **-es** -ɪz

sphragistics sfrəˈdʒɪs.tɪks

sphygmomanometer ˌsfɪg.məʊ.məˈnɒm.ɪ.təʳ, ˈ-ə-, US -moʊ.məˈnɑː.mə.t̬ɚ **-s** -z

spic spɪk **-s** -s

spi|ca, S~ ˈspaɪ|.kə **-cae** -siː **-cas** -kəz

spiccato spɪˈkɑː.təʊ, US -t̬oʊ

spic|e, S~ spaɪs **-es** -ɪz **-ing** -ɪŋ **-ed** -t

spiceberr|y ˈspaɪs.bər|.i, -br|i, US -ˌber|.i **-ies** -iz

Spicer ˈspaɪ.səʳ, US -sɚ

spick spɪk ˌ**spick and** ˈ**span**

spicule ˈspɪk.juːl, ˈspaɪ.kjuːl, US ˈspɪk.juːl **-s** -z

spic|y ˈspaɪ.s|i **-ier** -i.əʳ, US -i.ɚ **-iest** -i.ɪst, -i.əst **-ily** -əl.i, -ɪ.li **-iness** -ɪ.nəs, -ɪ.nɪs

spid|er ˈspaɪ.d|əʳ, US -d|ɚ **-ers** -əz, US -ɚz **-ery** -ər.i ˈ**spider** ˌ**monkey**; ˈ**spider** ˌ**plant**

spidergram ˈspaɪ.də.græm, US -dɚ- **-s** -z

spiderweb ˈspaɪ.də.web, US -dɚ- **-s** -z

spiel ʃpiːl, spiːl, US spiːl, ʃpiːl

Spielberg ˈspiːl.bɜːg, US -bɝːg

spiffing ˈspɪf.ɪŋ **-ly** -li

spiff|y ˈspɪf|.i **-ier** -i.əʳ, US -i.ɚ **-iest** -i.ɪst, -i.əst

spigot ˈspɪg.ət **-s** -s

spik spɪk **-s** -s

spik|e spaɪk **-es** -s **-ing** -ɪŋ **-ed** -t

spikenard ˈspaɪk.nɑːd, ˈspaɪ.kə-, US ˈspaɪk.nɑːrd, -nɚd

Spikins ˈspaɪ.kɪnz

spik|y ˈspaɪ.k|i **-ier** -i.əʳ, US -i.ɚ **-iest** -i.ɪst, -i.əst **-iness** -ɪ.nəs, -ɪ.nɪs

spill spɪl **-s** -z **-ing** -ɪŋ **-ed** -d **spilt** -t

spillag|e ˈspɪl.ɪdʒ **-es** -ɪz

spiller, S~ ˈspɪl.əʳ, US -ɚ **-s** -z

spillikin ˈspɪl.ɪ.kɪn **-s** -z

Spilling ˈspɪl.ɪŋ

spillover ˈspɪl.əʊ.vəʳ, US -oʊ.vɚ **-s** -z

spilt (from **spill**) spɪlt

spin spɪn **-s** -z **-ning** -ɪŋ **span** spæn **spun** spʌn **spinner/s** ˈspɪn.əʳ/z, US -ɚ/z ˌ**spin** ˈ**bowling** US ˈ**spin** ˌ**bowling**; ˈ**spin** ˌ**doctor**; ˈ**spinning** ˌ**wheel**

spina bifida ˌspaɪ.nəˈbɪf.ɪ.də, -ˈbaɪ.fɪ-, US -ˈbɪf.ɪ-

spinach ˈspɪn.ɪtʃ, -ɪdʒ, US -ɪtʃ

spinal ˈspaɪ.nəl ˈ**spinal** ˌ**cord**; ˌ**spinal** ˈ**cord** US ˈ**spinal** ˌ**cord**

spindl|e ˈspɪn.dəl **-es** -z **-y** -i, ˈspɪnd.li

spindle-legged ˌspɪn.dəlˈlegd, US ˈspɪn.dəl.legd, -ˌleg.ɪd *stress shift, British only:* ˌ**spindle-legged** ˈ**chair**

spindrift ˈspɪn.drɪft

spin-dr|y ˌspɪnˈdr|aɪ, ˈ-–, US ˈspɪn.dr|aɪ **-ies** -aɪz **-ying** -aɪ.ɪŋ **-ied** -aɪd **-ier/s** -aɪ.əʳ/z, US -aɪ.ɚ/z

spine spaɪn **-s** -z **-d** -d

spine-chill|ing ˈspaɪnˌtʃɪl|.ɪŋ **-ingly** -ɪŋ.li **-er/s** -əʳ/z, US -ɚ/z

spinel spɪˈnel, US spɪˈnel; US ˈspɪn.əl

spineless ˈspaɪn.ləs, -lɪs **-ly** -li **-ness** -nəs, -nɪs

spinet spɪˈnet; ˈspɪn.et, -ɪt, US ˈspɪn.ɪt **-s** -s

spinifex ˈspɪn.ɪ.feks, ˈ-ə-

Spink spɪŋk **-s** -s

spinnaker ˈspɪn.ə.kəʳ, ˈ-ɪ-, US -ə.kɚ **-s** -z

spinney ˈspɪn.i **-s** -z

spinoff ˈspɪn.ɒf, US -ɑːf **-s** -s

spinose ˈspaɪ.nəʊs, -ˈ-, US ˈspaɪ.noʊs

spinous ˈspaɪ.nəs

Spinoza spɪˈnəʊ.zə, US -ˈnoʊ-

spinster ˈspɪnt.stəʳ, US -stɚ **-s** -z **-hood** -hʊd **-ish** -ɪʃ

spin|y ˈspaɪ.n|i **-iness** -ɪ.nəs, -ɪ.nɪs

Spion Kop ˌspaɪ.ənˈkɒp, -əŋˈ-, US -ənˈkɑːp

spiraea spaɪˈriː.ə, -ˈrɪə, US -ˈriː.ə **-s** -z

spiral ˈspaɪə.rəl, US ˈspaɪ- **-s** -z **-ly** -i **-(l)ing** -ɪŋ **-(l)ed** -d ˌ**spiral** ˈ**staircase**

spirant ˈspaɪə.rənt, US ˈspaɪ- **-s** -s

spire spaɪəʳ, US spaɪɚ **-s** -z **-d** -d

spirea spaɪˈrɪə, -ˈriː.ə, US -ˈriː.ə **-s** -z

spiri|t ˈspɪr.ɪ|t, -ə|t **-ts** -ts **-ting** -tɪŋ, US -t̬ɪŋ **-ted/ly** -tɪd/li, US -t̬ɪd/li ˈ**spirit** ˌ**lamp**; ˈ**spirit** ˌ**level**

spiritism ˈspɪr.ɪ.tɪ.zəm, US -t̬ɪ-

spiritless ˈspɪr.ɪt.ləs, -lɪs **-ly** -li **-ness** -nəs, -nɪs

spiritual ˈspɪr.ɪ.tʃu.əl, ˈ-ə-, -tju-, US -tʃu- **-s** -z **-ly** -i

spiritual|ism ˈspɪr.ɪ.tʃu.əl|.ɪ.zəm, ˈ-ə-, -tju-, US -tʃu- **-ist/s** -ɪst/s

spiritualistic ˌspɪr.ɪ.tʃu.əlˈɪs.tɪk, ˌ-ə-, -tju-, US -tʃu-

spiritualit|y ˌspɪr.ɪ.tʃuˈæl.ə.t|i, ˌ-ə-, -tjuˈ-, -ɪ.t|i, US -tʃuˈæl.ə.t̬|i **-ies** -iz

spirituous ˈspɪr.ɪ.tʃu.əs, -tju.əs, US -tʃu-

spiritus ˈspɪr.ɪ.təs, ˈ-ə-, US -t̬əs

spirogyra ˌspaɪə.rəʊˈdʒaɪə.rə, US ˌspaɪ.roʊˈdʒaɪ-

spirt spɜːt, US spɝːt **-s** -s **-ing** -ɪŋ, US ˈspɝː.t̬ɪŋ **-ed** -ɪd, US ˈspɝː.t̬ɪd

spit n, v spɪt **-s** -s **-ting** -ɪŋ, US ˈspɪt̬.ɪŋ **-ted** -ɪd, US ˈspɪt̬.ɪd **spat** spæt ˌ**spitting** ˈ**image**; ˌ**spit and** ˈ**polish**

Spitalfields ˈspɪt.əl.fiːldz, US ˈspɪt̬-

spitball ˈspɪt.bɔːl, US -bɔːl, -bɑːl **-s** -z

spit|e spaɪt **-es** -s **-ing** -ɪŋ, US ˈspaɪ.t̬ɪŋ **-ed** -ɪd, US ˈspaɪ.t̬ɪd

spiteful ˈspaɪt.fəl, -fʊl **-ly** -i **-ness** -nəs, -nɪs

spitfire, S~ ˈspɪt.faɪəʳ, -faɪ.əʳ, US -faɪ.ɚ **-s** -z

Spithead ˌspɪtˈhed *stress shift:* ˌ**Spithead** ˈ**coastline**

Spitsbergen ˈspɪtsˌbɜː.gən, ˌ-ˈ--, US ˈspɪtsˌbɝː-

spittle ˈspɪt.əl, US ˈspɪt̬-

spittoon spɪˈtuːn **-s** -z

Spitz spɪts

Spitzer ˈspɪt.səʳ, US -sɚ

spiv spɪv **-s** -z **-vy** -i

splash splæʃ **-es** -ɪz **-ing** -ɪŋ **-ed** -t **-er/s** -əʳ/z, US -ɚ/z ˈ**splash** ˌ**guard**

splashback ˈsplæʃ.bæk **-s** -s

splashboard ˈsplæʃ.bɔːd, US -bɔːrd **-s** -z

splashdown ˈsplæʃ.daʊn **-s** -z

splash|y ˈsplæʃ|.i **-iness** -ɪ.nəs, -ɪ.nɪs

splat splæt **-s** -s **-ting** -ɪŋ **-ted** -ɪd

splatt|er ˈsplæt|.əʳ, US ˈsplæt̬|.ɚ **-ers** -əz, US -ɚz **-ering** -ər.ɪŋ **-ered** -əd, US -ɚd

splay spleɪ **-s** -z **-ing** -ɪŋ **-ed** -d

splayfooted ˌspleɪˈfʊt.ɪd, US ˈspleɪˌfʊt̬- *stress shift, British only:* ˌ**splayfooted** ˈ**walk**

spleen spliːn **-s** -z **-ful** -fəl, -fʊl **-fully** -fəl.i, -fʊ.li

splendid ˈsplen.dɪd **-ly** -li **-ness** -nəs, -nɪs

splendiferous splenˈdɪf.ər.əs **-ly** -li **-ness** -nəs, -nɪs

splendo(u)r ˈsplen.dəʳ, US -dɚ **-s** -z

splenetic spləˈnet.ɪk, splɪ-, US splɪˈnet̬- **-s** -s **-ally** -əl.i, -li

splic|e splaɪs **-es** -ɪz **-ing** -ɪŋ **-ed** -t

spliff splɪf **-s** -s

splint splɪnt **-s** -s **-ing** -ɪŋ, US ˈsplɪn.t̬ɪŋ **-ed** -ɪd, US ˈsplɪn.t̬ɪd

splint|er ˈsplɪn.t|əʳ, US -t̬|ɚ **-ers** -əz, US -ɚz **-ering** -ər.ɪŋ **-ered** -əd, US -ɚd **-ery** -ər.i ˈ**splinter** ˌ**group**

split, S~ splɪt **-s** -s **-ting** -ɪŋ, US ˈsplɪt̬.ɪŋ **-ter/s** -əʳ/z, US ˈsplɪt̬.ɚ/z ˌ**split deˈcision**; ˌ**split** ˈ**ends**; ˌ**split** ˈ**hairs**; ˌ**split inˈfinitive**; ˌ**split** ˈ**pea**; ˌ**split persoˈnality**; ˌ**split** ˈ**screen** *stress shift:* ˌ**split screen** ˈ**picture** ˌ**split** ˈ**second** *stress shift:* ˌ**split second** ˈ**timing**

split-level ˌsplɪtˈlev.əl *stress shift:* ˌ**split-level** ˈ**flat**

splodg|e splɒdʒ, US splɑːdʒ **-es** -ɪz

splodg|y ˈsplɒdʒ|.i, US ˈsplɑː.dʒ|i **-ier** -i.əʳ, US -i.ɚ **-iest** -i.ɪst, -i.əst **-iness** -ɪ.nəs, -ɪ.nɪs

splosh splɒʃ, US splɑːʃ **-es** -ɪz **-ing** -ɪŋ **-ed** -t

splotch splɒtʃ, US splɑːtʃ **-es** -ɪz **-y** -i

splurg|e splɜːdʒ, US splɝːdʒ **-es** -ɪz **-ing** -ɪŋ **-ed** -d

splutt|er ˈsplʌt|.əʳ, US ˈsplʌt̬|.ɚ **-ers** -əz, US -ɚz **-ering** -ər.ɪŋ **-ered** -əd, US -ɚd

Spock spɒk, US spɑːk

spod spɒd, US spɑːd -s -z
Spode spəʊd, US spoʊd
Spofforth ˈspɒf.əθ, US ˈspɑː.fɚθ
Spohr spɔːʳ; *as if German:* ʃpɔːʳ; US spɔːr; *as if German:* US ʃpɔːr
spoil spɔɪl -s -z -ing -ɪŋ -ed -d, -t -t -er/s -əʳ/z, US -ɚ/z -age -ɪdʒ
spoilsport ˈspɔɪl.spɔːt, US -spɔːrt -s -s
Spokane spəʊˈkæn, US spoʊ-
spoke *of wheel:* spəʊk, US spoʊk -s -s
spok|e (from **speak**) spəʊk, US spoʊk -en -ən
spokes|man ˈspəʊks|.mən, US ˈspoʊks- -men -mən
spokes|person ˈspəʊks|ˌpɜː.sən, US ˈspoʊks|ˌpɝː- -persons -ˌpɜː.sənz, US -ˌpɝː- -people -ˌpiː.pəl
spokes|woman ˈspəʊks|ˌwʊm.ən, US ˈspoʊks- -women -ˌwɪm.ɪn
spoliation ˌspəʊ.liˈeɪ.ʃən, US ˌspoʊ-
spondee ˈspɒn.diː, -di, US ˈspɑːn- -s -z
spondulicks spɒnˈduː.lɪks, US spɑːnˈduː-
spondylitis ˌspɒn.dɪˈlaɪ.tɪs, -dəˈ-, -təs, US ˌspɑːn.dəˈlaɪ.t̬ɪs, -t̬əs
spong|e spʌndʒ -es -ɪz -(e)ing -ɪŋ -ed -d -er/s -əʳ/z, US -ɚ/z **ˈsponge ˌbag**; **ˈsponge ˌcake**; **ˌsponge ˈfinger**
spongiform ˈspʌn.dʒɪ.fɔːm, US -fɔːrm
spong|y ˈspʌn.dʒ|i -ier -i.əʳ, US -i.ɚ -iest -i.ɪst, -i.əst -iness -ɪ.nəs, -ɪ.nɪs
sponson ˈspɒnt.sən, US ˈspɑːnt- -s -z
spons|or ˈspɒnt.s|əʳ, US ˈspɑːnt.s|ɚ -ors -əz, US -ɚz -oring -ər.ɪŋ -ored -əd, US -ɚd -orship -ə.ʃɪp, US -ɚ.ʃɪp
spontaneity ˌspɒn.təˈneɪ.ə.ti, -ˈniː.ə.ti, -ɪ.ti, US ˌspɑːn.tənˈeɪ.ə.t̬i, -ˈiː-
spontaneous spɒnˈteɪ.ni.əs, spən-, US spɑːn- -ly -li -ness -nəs, -nɪs **sponˌtaneous comˈbustion**
spoof spuːf -s -s -ing -ɪŋ -ed -t
spook spuːk -s -s -ing -ɪŋ -ed -t -ish -ɪʃ
spook|y ˈspuː.k|i -ier -i.əʳ, US -i.ɚ -iest -i.ɪst, -i.əst -ily -əl.i, -ɪ.li -iness -ɪ.nəs, -ɪ.nɪs
spool spuːl -s -z -ing -ɪŋ -ed -d
spoon spuːn -s -z -ing -ɪŋ -ed -d
spoonbill ˈspuːn.bɪl, ˈspuːm-, US ˈspuːn- -s -z -ed -d
Spooner ˈspuː.nəʳ, US -nɚ
spoonerism ˈspuː.nər.ɪ.zəm -s -z
spoon|-feed ˈspuːn|.fiːd -feeds -fiːdz -feeding -ˌfiː.dɪŋ -fed -fed
spoonful ˈspuːn.fʊl -s -z **spoonsful** ˈspuːnz-
spoon|y ˈspuː.n|i -ier -i.əʳ, US -i.ɚ -iest -i.ɪst, -i.əst -ily -əl.i, -ɪ.li -iness -ɪ.nəs, -ɪ.nɪs
spoor spɔːʳ, spʊəʳ, US spʊr -s -z -ing -ɪŋ -ed -d
Sporades ˈspɒr.ə.diːz, US ˈspɔːr-
sporadic spəˈræd.ɪk, spɒrˈæd-, US spəˈræd-, spɔː- -ally -əl.i, -li
sporangi|um spəˈræn.dʒi|.əm, US spə-, spoʊ- -a -ə
spore spɔːʳ, US spɔːr -s -z
sporran ˈspɒr.ən, US ˈspɔːr-, ˈspɑːr- -s -z
sport spɔːt, US spɔːrt -s -s -ing -ɪŋ, US ˈspɔːr.t̬ɪŋ -ed -ɪd, US ˈspɔːr.t̬ɪd **ˈsports ˌcar**; **ˈsports ˌday**; **ˈsports ˌjacket**
sportive ˈspɔː.tɪv, US ˈspɔːr.t̬ɪv -ly -li -ness -nəs, -nɪs
sportscast ˈspɔːts.kɑːst, US ˈspɔːrts.kæst -s -s -ing -ɪŋ -er/s -əʳ/z, US -ɚ/z
sports|man ˈspɔːts|.mən, US ˈspɔːrts- -men -mən
sportsman|like ˈspɔːts.mən|.laɪk, US ˈspɔːrts- -ship -ʃɪp
sports|person ˈspɔːts|ˌpɜː.sən, US ˈspɔːrts|ˌpɝː- -persons -ˌpɜː.sənz, US -ˌpɝː- -people -ˌpiː.pəl
sportswear ˈspɔːts.weəʳ, US ˈspɔːrts.wer
sports|woman ˈspɔːts|ˌwʊm.ən, US ˈspɔːrts- -women -ˌwɪm.ɪn
sport|y ˈspɔː.t|i, US ˈspɔːr.t̬|i -ier -i.əʳ, US -i.ɚ -iest -i.ɪst, -i.əst -ily -əl.i, -ɪ.li -iness -ɪ.nəs, -ɪ.nɪs
spot spɒt, US spɑːt -s -s -ting -ɪŋ, US ˈspɑː.t̬ɪŋ -ted -ɪd, US ˈspɑː.t̬ɪd **spotted ˈdick**; **ˌknock (the) ˈspots off**
spot-check ˌspɒtˈtʃek, ˈ--, US ˈspɑːt.tʃek -s -s -ing -ɪŋ -ed -t
spotless ˈspɒt.ləs, -lɪs, US ˈspɑːt- -ly -li -ness -nəs, -nɪs
spotlight ˈspɒt.laɪt, US ˈspɑːt- -s -s -ing -ɪŋ -ed -ɪd **spotlit** -lɪt
spot-on ˌspɒtˈɒn, US spɑːt̬ˈɑːn
Spottiswoode ˈspɒt.ɪs.wʊd, -ɪz-; ˈspɒt.swʊd, US ˈspɑː.tɪs.wʊd, ˈspɑːt.swʊd
spott|y ˈspɒt|.i, US ˈspɑː.t̬|i -ier -i.əʳ, US -i.ɚ -iest -i.ɪst, -i.əst -iness -ɪ.nəs, -ɪ.nɪs
spous|e spaʊs -es -ɪz
spout spaʊt -s -s -ing -ɪŋ, US ˈspaʊ.t̬ɪŋ -ed -ɪd, US ˈspaʊ.t̬ɪd -er/s -əʳ/z, US ˈspaʊ.t̬ɚ/z
Spragge spræg
Sprague spreɪg
sprain spreɪn -s -z -ing -ɪŋ -ed -d
sprang (from **spring**) spræŋ
Sprangle ˈspræŋ.gəl
sprat, S~ spræt -s -s
Spratt spræt
sprawl sprɔːl, US sprɑːl, sprɔːl -s -z -ing -ɪŋ -ed -d -er/s -əʳ/z, US -ɚ/z
spray spreɪ -s -z -ing -ɪŋ -ed -d -er/s -əʳ/z, US -ɚ/z **ˈspray ˌgun**
spraycan ˈspreɪ.kæn -s -z
spread spred -s -z -ing -ɪŋ -er/s -əʳ/z, US -ɚ/z
spread-eagl|e ˌspredˈiː.gəl, US ˈspredˌiː- -es -z -ing -ɪŋ, -ˈiː.glɪŋ, US -ˌiː.glɪŋ -ed -d
spreadsheet ˈspred.ʃiːt -s -s
sprechgesang, S~ ˈʃprek.gə.sæŋ; *as if German:* ˈʃprex.gə.zæŋ; US ˈʃprek.gə.sɑːŋ
spree spriː -s -z
sprig sprɪg -s -z
Sprigg sprɪg -s -z
sprightl|y ˈspraɪt.l|i -ier -i.əʳ, US -i.ɚ -iest -i.ɪst, -i.əst -iness -ɪ.nəs, -ɪ.nɪs
spring, S~ sprɪŋ -s -z -ing -ɪŋ **sprang** spræŋ **sprung** sprʌŋ **springer/s** ˈsprɪŋ.əʳ/z, US -ɚ/z **ˌspring ˈbalance**; **ˈspring ˌbalance** US **ˈspring ˌbalance**; **ˌspring ˈchicken**; **ˌspring ˈfever**; **ˌspring ˈgreens**; **ˌspring ˈonion**; **ˌspring ˈroll** US **ˈspring ˌroll**
springboard ˈsprɪŋ.bɔːd, US -bɔːrd -s -z
springbok, S~ ˈsprɪŋ.bɒk, US -bɑːk -s -s
spring-clean ˌsprɪŋˈkliːn -s -z -ing -ɪŋ -ed -d
spring|e sprɪndʒ -es -ɪz
springer, S~ ˈsprɪŋ.əʳ, US -ɚ **ˌspringer ˈspaniel**
Springfield ˈsprɪŋ.fiːld
springlike ˈsprɪŋ.laɪk
Springsteen ˈsprɪŋ.stiːn
springtime ˈsprɪŋ.taɪm
spring|y ˈsprɪŋ|.i -ier -i.əʳ, US -i.ɚ -iest -i.ɪst, -i.əst -ily -əl.i, -ɪ.li -iness -ɪ.nəs, -ɪ.nɪs
sprinkl|e ˈsprɪŋ.kəl -es -z -ing -ɪŋ, ˈsprɪŋ.klɪŋ -ed -d -er/s -əʳ/z, ˈsprɪŋ.kləʳ/z, US ˈ-kəl.ɚ/z, ˈ-klɚ/z
sprinkling ˈsprɪŋ.klɪŋ, ˈ-kəl.ɪŋ -s -z
sprint sprɪnt -s -s -ing -ɪŋ, US ˈsprɪn.t̬ɪŋ -ed -ɪd, US ˈsprɪn.t̬ɪd -er/s -əʳ/z, US ˈsprɪn.t̬ɚ/z
sprit sprɪt -s -s
sprite spraɪt -s -s
spritsail ˈsprɪt.səl, -seɪl, US -seɪl, -səl -s -z
spritz sprɪts -es -ɪz -ing -ɪŋ -ed -t
spritzer ˈsprɪt.səʳ, US -sɚ -s -z
sprocket ˈsprɒk.ɪt, US ˈsprɑː.kɪt -s -s
sprog sprɒg, US sprɑːg, sprɔːg -s -z -ging -ɪŋ -ged -d
Sproule sprəʊl, US spraʊl, sproʊl
sprout spraʊt -s -s -ing -ɪŋ, US ˈspraʊ.t̬ɪŋ -ed -ɪd, US ˈspraʊ.t̬ɪd
spruc|e spruːs -es -ɪz -er -əʳ, US -ɚ -est -ɪst, -əst -ely -li -eness -nəs, -nɪs -ing -ɪŋ -ed -t
sprue spruː -s -z
sprung (from **spring**) sprʌŋ
spry, S~ spraɪ -er -əʳ, US -ɚ -est -ɪst, -əst -ness -nəs, -nɪs
spud spʌd -s -z
spu|e spjuː -es -z -ing -ɪŋ -ed -d
spum|e spjuːm -es -z -ing -ɪŋ -ed -d -y -i
spun (from **spin**) spʌn
spunk spʌŋk -y -i -ier -i.əʳ, US -i.ɚ -iest -i.ɪst, -i.əst -iness -ɪ.nəs, -ɪ.nɪs
spur spɜːʳ, US spɝː -s -z -ring -ɪŋ -red -d **on the ˌspur of the ˈmoment**
spurg|e spɜːdʒ, US spɝːdʒ -es -ɪz
Spurgeon ˈspɜː.dʒən, US ˈspɝː-

spurious ˈspjʊə.ri.əs, ˈspjɔː-, (US) ˈspjʊr.i- **-ly** -li **-ness** -nəs, -nɪs

spurn, S~ spɜːn, (US) spɝːn **-s** -z **-ing** -ɪŋ **-ed** -d

Spurr spɜːʳ, (US) spɝː

Spurrier ˈspʌr.i.əʳ, (US) ˈspɝː.i.ɚ

spurt spɜːt, (US) spɝːt **-s** -s **-ing** -ɪŋ, (US) ˈspɝː.t̬ɪŋ **-ed** -ɪd, (US) ˈspɝː.t̬ɪd

sputnik, S~ ˈspʌt.nɪk, ˈspʊt-

sputt|er ˈspʌt|.əʳ, (US) ˈspʌt̬|.ɚ **-ers** -əz, (US) -ɚz **-ering** -ᵊr.ɪŋ **-ered** -əd, (US) -ɚd **-erer/s** -ᵊr.əʳ/z, (US) -ɚ.ɚ/z

sput|um ˈspjuː|.təm, (US) -t̬əm **-a** -ə

sp|y sp|aɪ **-ies** -aɪz **-ying** -aɪ.ɪŋ **-ied** -aɪd

spyglass ˈspaɪ.glɑːs, (US) -glæs **-es** -ɪz

spyhole ˈspaɪ.həʊl, (US) -hoʊl **-s** -z

spymaster ˈspaɪˌmɑː.stəʳ, (US) -ˌmæs.tɚ **-s** -z

sq (abbrev. for **square**) skweəʳ, (US) skwer

squab skwɒb, (US) skwɑːb **-s** -z ˌ**squab** ˈ**pie**

squabbl|e ˈskwɒb.ᵊl, (US) ˈskwɑː.bᵊl **-es** -z **-ing** -ɪŋ, ˈskwɒb.lɪŋ, (US) ˈskwɑː.blɪŋ **-ed** -d **-er/s** -əʳ/z, ˈskwɒb.ləʳ/z, (US) ˈskwɑː.bᵊl.ɚ/z, ˈ-blɚ/z

squad skwɒd, (US) skwɑːd **-s** -z ˈ**squad** ˌ**car**

squadd|y, squadd|ie ˈskwɒd|.i, (US) ˈskwɑː.d|i **-ies** -iz

squadron ˈskwɒd.rᵊn, (US) ˈskwɑː.drən **-s** -z

squalid ˈskwɒl.ɪd, (US) ˈskwɑː.lɪd **-est** -ɪst, -əst **-ly** -li **-ness** -nəs, -nɪs

squall skwɔːl, (US) skwɔːl, skwɑːl **-s** -z **-ing** -ɪŋ **-ed** -d **-y** -i

squalor ˈskwɒl.əʳ, (US) ˈskwɑː.lɚ

squam|a ˈskweɪ.m|ə, ˈskwɑː- **-ae** -iː

squam|ose ˈskweɪ.m|əʊs, ˈskwɑː-, (US) -m|oʊs **-ous/ness** -əs/nəs, -nɪs

squand|er ˈskwɒn.d|əʳ, (US) ˈskwɑːn.d|ɚ **-ers** -əz, (US) -ɚz **-ering** -ᵊr.ɪŋ **-ered** -əd, (US) -ɚd **-erer/s** -ᵊr.əʳ/z, (US) -ɚ.ɚ/z

squar|e skweəʳ, (US) skwer **-es** -z **-er** -əʳ, (US) -ɚ **-est** -ɪst, -əst **-ely** -li **-eness** -nəs, -nɪs **-ing** -ɪŋ **-ed** -d ˈ**square** ˌ**dance**; ˌ**square** ˈ**deal**; ˌ**square** ˈ**foot**; ˌ**square** ˈ**leg**; ˌ**square** ˈ**meal**; ˌ**Square** ˈ**Mile**; ˌ**square** ˈ**one**; ˌ**square** ˈ**root**

squarish ˈskweə.rɪʃ, (US) ˈskwer.ɪʃ

squash skwɒʃ, (US) skwɑːʃ **-es** -ɪz **-ing** -ɪŋ **-ed** -t

squash|y ˈskwɒʃ|.i, (US) ˈskwɑː.ʃ|i **-ier** -i.əʳ, (US) -i.ɚ **-iest** -i.ɪst, -i.əst **-iness** -ɪ.nəs, -ɪ.nɪs

squat skwɒt, (US) skwɑːt **-ly** -li **-ness** -nəs, -nɪs **-s** -s **-ting** -ɪŋ, (US) ˈskwɑː.t̬ɪŋ **-ted** -ɪd, (US) ˈskwɑː.t̬ɪd **-ter/s** -əʳ/z, (US) ˈskwɑː.t̬ɚ/z

squaw skwɔː, (US) skwɑː, skwɔː **-s** -z

squawk skwɔːk, (US) skwɑːk, skwɔːk **-s** -s **-ing** -ɪŋ **-ed** -t

squeak skwiːk **-s** -s **-ing** -ɪŋ **-ed** -t **-er/s** -əʳ/z, (US) -ɚ/z

squeak|y ˈskwiː.k|i **-ier** -i.əʳ, (US) -i.ɚ **-iest** -i.ɪst, -i.əst **-ily** -ᵊl.i, -ɪ.li **-iness** -ɪ.nəs, -ɪ.nɪs

squeaky-clean ˌskwiː.kiˈkliːn

squeal skwiːl **-s** -z **-ing** -ɪŋ **-ed** -d **-er/s** -əʳ/z, (US) -ɚ/z

squeamish ˈskwiː.mɪʃ **-ly** -li **-ness** -nəs, -nɪs

squeegee ˈskwiː.dʒiː, ˌ-ˈ-, (US) ˈskwiː.dʒiː **-s** -z **-ing** -ɪŋ **-d** -d

Squeers skwɪəz, (US) skwɪrz

squeez|e skwiːz **-es** -ɪz **-ing** -ɪŋ **-ed** -d **-er/s** -əʳ/z, (US) -ɚ/z **-able** -ə.bᵊl **-y** -i

squeeze-box ˈskwiːz.bɒks, (US) -bɑːks **-es** -ɪz

squelch skweltʃ **-es** -ɪz **-ing** -ɪŋ **-ed** -t **-y** -i

squib skwɪb **-s** -z

squid skwɪd **-s** -z

squidg|y ˈskwɪdʒ|.i **-ier** -i.əʳ, (US) -i.ɚ **-iest** -i.ɪst, -i.əst **-iness** -ɪ.nəs, -ɪ.nɪs

squiff|y ˈskwɪf|.i **-ed** -t **-ier** -i.əʳ, (US) -i.ɚ **-iest** -i.ɪst, -i.əst **-iness** -ɪ.nəs, -ɪ.nɪs

squiggl|e ˈskwɪg|.ᵊl **-es** -z **-ing** -ɪŋ, ˈskwɪg.lɪŋ **-ed** -d **-y** -i

squill skwɪl **-s** -z

squinch skwɪntʃ **-es** -ɪz **-ing** -ɪŋ **-ed** -t

squint skwɪnt **-s** -s **-ing** -ɪŋ, (US) ˈskwɪn.t̬ɪŋ **-ed** -ɪd, (US) ˈskwɪn.t̬ɪd **-y** -i

squirarch|y ˈskwaɪə.rɑː.k|i, (US) ˈskwaɪɚ.ɑːr- **-ies** -iz

squir|e, S~ skwaɪəʳ, ˈskwaɪ.əʳ, (US) ˈskwaɪ.ɚ **-es** -z **-ing** -ɪŋ **-ed** -d

squirearch|y ˈskwaɪə.rɑː.k|i, (US) ˈskwaɪ.ɚ.ɑːr- **-ies** -iz

Squires skwaɪəz, ˈskwaɪ.əz, (US) ˈskwaɪ.ɚz

squirm skwɜːm, (US) skwɝːm **-s** -z **-ing** -ɪŋ **-ed** -d **-y** -i

squirrel ˈskwɪr.ᵊl, (US) ˈskwɝː- **-s** -z **-(l)ing** -ɪŋ **-(l)ed** -d

squirt skwɜːt, (US) skwɝːt **-s** -s **-ing** -ɪŋ, (US) ˈskwɝː.t̬ɪŋ **-ed** -ɪd, (US) ˈskwɝː.t̬ɪd **-er/s** -əʳ/z, (US) -ɚ/z

squish skwɪʃ **-es** -ɪz **-ing** -ɪŋ **-ed** -t **-y** -i

sr, Sr (abbrev. for **senior**) ˈsiː.ni.əʳ, -njəʳ, (US) -njɚ

Srebrenica ˌsreb.rəˈniːt.sə, ʃreb-, -tʃə

Sri Lank|a ˌsriːˈlæŋ.k|ə, ˌsrɪ-, ˌʃriː-, (US) -ˈlɑːŋ- **-an/s** -ən/z

Srinagar srɪˈnʌg.əʳ, sriː-, ʃrɪ-, ʃriː-, -ˈnɑː.gəʳ, (US) ˌsriːˈnʌg.ɚ

SS *Nazi unit:* ˌesˈes *stress shift:* ˌ**SS** ˈ**officer**

SS (abbrev. for **steamship**) ˌesˈes *stress shift:* ˌ**SS Great** ˈ**Britain**

SSE (abbrev. for **south-southeast**) ˌsaʊθ.saʊθˈiːst; *in nautical usage also:* ˌsaʊ.saʊ-

ssh, sh, shh ʃ

> Note: Used to command silence

SSW (abbrev. for **south-southwest**) ˌsaʊθ.saʊθˈwest; *in nautical usage also:* ˌsaʊ.saʊ-

st (abbrev. for **stone**) stəʊn, (US) stoʊn

St. (abbrev. for **Street**) striːt

St. (abbrev. for **Saint**) sᵊnt, sɪnt, seɪnt, (US) seɪnt

Note: See panel information at **Saint**.

stab stæb **-s** -z **-bing/s** -ɪŋ/z **-bed** -d

Stabat Mater ˌstɑː.bætˈmɑː.təʳ, -bətˈ-, (US) -bɑːtˈmɑː.tɚ **-s** -z

St. Abb's sᵊntˈæbz, sɪnt-, (US) seɪnt-

stability stəˈbɪl.ə.ti, -ɪ.ti, (US) -ə.t̬i

stabilization, -isa- ˌsteɪ.bᵊl.aɪˈzeɪ.ʃᵊn, -bɪ.laɪ-, -lɪˈ-, (US) -bᵊl.əˈ-

stabiliz|e, -is|e ˈsteɪ.bᵊl.aɪz, -bɪ.laɪz, (US) -bə.laɪz **-es** -ɪz **-ing** -ɪŋ **-ed** -d **-er/s** -əʳ/z, (US) -ɚ/z

stabl|e ˈsteɪ.bᵊl **-es** -z **-y** -i, ˈsteɪ.bli **-eness** -nəs, -nɪs **-ing** -ɪŋ, ˈsteɪ.blɪŋ **-ed** -d ˌ**stable** ˈ**door**; ˈ**stable** ˌ**lad**

stablemate ˈsteɪ.bᵊl.meɪt **-s** -s

stabling ˈsteɪ.bᵊl.ɪŋ, ˈ-blɪŋ

stablish ˈstæb.lɪʃ **-es** -ɪz **-ing** -ɪŋ **-ed** -t

staccato stəˈkɑː.təʊ, (US) -t̬oʊ **-s** -z

Stacey, Stacie ˈsteɪ.si

stack stæk **-s** -s **-ing** -ɪŋ **-ed** -t

Stacpoole ˈstæk.puːl

Stacy ˈsteɪ.si

stadi|um ˈsteɪ.di|.əm **-ums** -əmz **-a** -ə

staff stɑːf, (US) stæf **-s** -s **-ing** -ɪŋ **-ed** -t ˈ**staff** ˌ**nurse**; ˈ**staff** ˌ**sergeant**

Staffa ˈstæf.ə

staffer ˈstɑː.fəʳ, (US) ˈstæf.ɚ **-s** -z

Stafford ˈstæf.əd, (US) -ɚd **-shire** -ʃəʳ, -ʃɪəʳ, (US) -ʃɚ, -ʃɪr

staffroom ˈstɑːf.rʊm, -ruːm, (US) ˈstæf.ruːm, -rʊm **-s** -z

Staffs. (abbrev. for **Staffordshire**) stæfs

stag stæg **-s** -z ˈ**stag** ˌ**night**

stag|e steɪdʒ **-es** -ɪz **-ing** -ɪŋ **-ed** -d ˌ**stage** ˈ**door**; ˈ**stage** ˌ**fright**

stagecoach ˈsteɪdʒ.kəʊtʃ, (US) -koʊtʃ **-es** -ɪz

stagecraft ˈsteɪdʒ.krɑːft, (US) -kræft

stagehand ˈsteɪdʒ.hænd **-s** -z

stage-manag|e ˌsteɪdʒˈmæn.ɪdʒ, ˈ-ˌ--, (US) ˈsteɪdʒˌmæn- **-es** -ɪz **-ing** -ɪŋ **-ed** -d **-ment** -mənt

stage-manager ˌsteɪdʒˈmæn.ə.dʒəʳ, ˈ-ɪ-, (US) ˈsteɪdʒˌmæn.ə.dʒɚ

stager ˈsteɪ.dʒəʳ, (US) -dʒɚ **-s** -z

stage-struck ˈsteɪdʒ.strʌk

stag|ey ˈsteɪ.dʒ|i **-ier** -i.əʳ, (US) -i.ɚ **-iest** -i.ɪst, -i.əst **-iness** -ɪ.nəs, -ɪ.nɪs

stagflation ˌstægˈfleɪ.ʃᵊn

stagg|er ˈstæg|.əʳ, (US) -ɚ **-ers** -əz, (US) -ɚz **-ering/ly** -ᵊr.ɪŋ/li **-ered** -əd, (US) -ɚd **-erer/s** -ᵊr.əʳ/z, (US) -ɚ.ɚ/z

staghound ˈstæg.haʊnd **-s** -z

staging ˈsteɪ.dʒɪŋ **-s** -z

Stagirite ˈstædʒ.ɪ.raɪt, (US) ˈ-ə- **-s** -s

stagnancy ˈstæg.nənt.si

stagnant ˈstæg.nənt **-ly** -li

stagna|te stægˈneɪ|t, ˈ--, (US)

'stæg.neɪ|t -tes -ts -ting -tɪŋ, (US) -t̬ɪŋ -ted -tɪd, (US) -t̬ɪd

tagnation stæg'neɪ.ʃᵊn

t. Agnes sᵊnt'æg.nɪs, sɪnt-, seɪnt-, (US) seɪnt-

tag|y 'steɪ.dʒ|i -ier -i.əʳ, (US) -i.ɚ -iest -i.ɪst, -i.əst -ily -ᵊl.i, -ɪ.li -iness -ɪ.nəs, -ɪ.nɪs

taid steɪd -ly -li -ness -nəs, -nɪs

tain steɪn -s -z -ing -ɪŋ -ed -d -er/s -əʳ/z, (US) -ɚ/z **ˌstained 'glass**

tainer *English name:* 'steɪ.nəʳ, (US) -nɚ *German name:* 'staɪ.nəʳ; *as if German:* 'ʃtaɪ-; (US) -nɚ

taines steɪnz

Stainforth 'steɪn.fəθ, (US) -fɚθ

stainless 'steɪn.ləs, -lɪs -ly -li -ness -nəs, -nɪs **ˌstainless 'steel**

stair steəʳ, (US) ster -s -z

staircas|e 'steə.keɪs, (US) 'ster- -es -ɪz

stair-rod 'steə.rɒd, (US) 'ster.rɑːd -s -z

stairway 'steə.weɪ, (US) 'ster- -s -z

stairwell 'steə.wel, (US) 'ster- -s -z

Staithes steɪðz

stak|e steɪk -es -s -ing -ɪŋ -ed -t

stakeholder 'steɪkˌhəʊl.dəʳ, (US) -ˌhoʊl.dɚ -s -z

stakeout 'steɪk.aʊt -s -s

Stakhanov|ite stæk'æn.ə.v|aɪt, (US) stə'kɑː.nə- -ites -aɪts -ism -ɪ.zᵊm

Stakis 'stæk.ɪs

stalactite 'stæl.ək.taɪt, (US) stə'læk-; (US) 'stæl.ək- -s -s

stalag 'stæl.æg, (US) 'stɑː.lɑːg, 'stæl.æg -s -z

stalagmite 'stæl.əg.maɪt, (US) stə'læg-; (US) 'stæl.əg- -s -s

St. Albans sᵊnt'ɔːl.bənz, sɪnt-, -'ɒl-, (US) seɪnt'ɔːl-, -'ɑːl-

Stalbridge 'stɔːl.brɪdʒ, (US) 'stɑːl-

St. Aldate's sᵊnt'ɔːl.deɪts, sɪnt-, -'ɒl-, -dɪts; *old-fashioned:* -'əʊldz, (US) seɪnt'ɔːl.deɪts, -'ɑːl-

stal|e steɪl -er -əʳ, (US) -ɚ -est -ɪst, -əst -ely -li -eness -nəs, -nɪs

stale|mate 'steɪl|.meɪt -mates -meɪts -mating -meɪ.tɪŋ, (US) -meɪ.t̬ɪŋ -mated -meɪ.tɪd, (US) -meɪ.t̬ɪd

Stalin 'stɑː.lɪn, 'stæl.ɪn -ism -ɪ.zᵊm

Stalingrad 'stɑː.lɪn.græd, 'stæl.ɪn-, -grɑːd, (US) 'stɑː.lɪn.græd, 'stæl.ɪn-

stalin|ism, S~ 'stɑː.lɪ.n|ɪ.zᵊm, 'stæl.ɪ-, (US) 'stɑː.lɪ- -ist/s -ɪst/s

stalk stɔːk, (US) stɔːk, stɑːk -s -s -ing -ɪŋ -ed -t -er/s -əʳ/z, (US) -ɚ/z

stalking-hors|e 'stɔː.kɪŋ.hɔːs, (US) -hɔːrs, 'stɑː- -es -ɪz

Stalky 'stɔː.ki, (US) 'stɔː-, 'stɑː-

stall stɔːl, (US) stɔːl, stɑːl -s -z -ing -ɪŋ -ed -d

stallage 'stɔː.lɪdʒ

stallholder 'stɔːlˌhəʊl.dəʳ, (US) 'stɔːlˌhoʊl.dɚ, 'stɑːl- -s -z

stallion 'stæl.jən, -i.ən, (US) '-jən -s -z

Stallone stə'ləʊn, stæl'əʊn, (US) stə'loʊn

stalwart 'stɔːl.wət, 'stɒl-, (US) 'stɔːl.wɚt, 'stɑːl- -s -s -ly -li -ness -nəs, -nɪs

Stalybridge 'steɪ.lɪ.brɪdʒ

Stamboul stæm'buːl, (US) stɑːm-

St. Ambrose sᵊnt'æm.brəʊz, sɪnt-, -brəʊs, (US) seɪnt'æm.broʊz, -broʊs

stamen 'steɪ.men, -mən -s -z

Stamford 'stæm*p*.fəd, (US) -fɚd

stamina 'stæm.ɪ.nə, '-ə-, (US) '-ə-

stamm|er 'stæm|.əʳ, (US) -ɚ -ers -əz, (US) -ɚz -ering -ᵊr.ɪŋ -ered -əd, (US) -ɚd -erer/s -ᵊr.əʳ/z, (US) -ɚ.ɚ/z

stamp, S~ stæmp -s -s -ing -ɪŋ -ed -t -er/s -əʳ/z, (US) -ɚ/z **'stamp ˌalbum; 'stamp colˌlector; 'stamp ˌduty; 'stamping ˌground**

stamped|e stæm'piːd -es -z -ing -ɪŋ -ed -ɪd

Stan stæn

Stanbury 'stæn.bᵊr.i, 'stæm-, '-bri, (US) 'stæn.ber.i, -bɚ-

stanc|e stæn*t*s, stɑːn*t*s, (US) stæn*t*s -es -ɪz

stanch stɑːn*t*ʃ, (US) stɑːntʃ, stɔːntʃ, stæntʃ -es -ɪz -ing -ɪŋ -ed -t

stanchion 'stɑːn.*t*ʃᵊn, 'stæn-, (US) 'stæn- -s -z -ing -ɪŋ -ed -d

stand stænd -s -z -ing -ɪŋ stood stʊd

stand-alone 'stænd.əˌləʊn, -ᵊlˌəʊn, (US) -əˌloʊn

standard 'stæn.dəd, (US) -dɚd -s -z **ˌstandard deviˈation; 'standard ˌlamp; ˌstandard of 'living; 'standard ˌtime**

standard-bearer 'stæn.dədˌbeə.rəʳ, (US) -dɚdˌber.ɚ -s -z

standardization, -isa- ˌstæn.də.daɪ'zeɪ.ʃᵊn, -dɪ'-, (US) -dɚ.də'-

standardiz|e, -is|e 'stæn.də.daɪz, (US) -dɚ- -es -ɪz -ing -ɪŋ -ed -d

standby 'stæn*d*.baɪ, 'stæm-, (US) 'stænd- -s -z

stand-in 'stænd.ɪn -s -z

standing 'stæn.dɪŋ -s -z **ˌstanding 'joke; ˌstanding 'order; 'standing ˌroom**

standish, S~ 'stæn.dɪʃ -es -ɪz

standoff 'stænd.ɒf, (US) -ɑːf -s -s

standoffish ˌstænd'ɒf.ɪʃ, (US) -'ɑː.fɪʃ -ly -li -ness -nəs, -nɪs

standout 'stænd.aʊt -s -s

standpipe 'stæn*d*.paɪp, 'stæm-, (US) 'stæn*d*- -s -s

standpoint 'stæn*d*.pɔɪnt, 'stæm-, (US) 'stæn*d*- -s -s

St. Andrew sᵊnt'æn.druː, sɪnt-, (US) seɪnt- -(')s -z **St. ˌAndrew's 'cross**

standstill 'stæn*d*.stɪl -s -z

stand-up 'stænd.ʌp

Staneydale 'steɪ.ni.deɪl

Stanfield 'stæn.fiːld

Stanford 'stæn.fəd, (US) -fɚd

Stanford-Binet ˌstæn.fəd'biː.neɪ, ˌstæm-; -bɪ'neɪ, (US) ˌstæn.fɚd.bɪ'neɪ

Stanford le Hope ˌstæn.fəd.lɪ'həʊp, (US) -fɚd.lɪ'hoʊp

stanhope, S~ 'stæn.əp, -həʊp, (US) -hoʊp, -əp -s -s

Stanis|las 'stæn.ɪ.s|læs, '-ə-, -s|ləs, -s|lɑːs, (US) -s|lɑːs -laus -s|lɔːs

Stanislavski ˌstæn.ɪ'slæv.ski, -'slæf-, (US) -ə'slɑːv-, -'slɑːf- **Staniˈslavski ˌmethod**

stank (from **stink**) stæŋk

Stanley 'stæn.li **'Stanley ˌknife**

Stanmore 'stæn.mɔːʳ, 'stæm-, (US) 'stæn.mɔːr

Stannard 'stæn.əd, (US) -ɚd

stannar|y 'stæn.ᵊr|.i -ies -iz

St. Anne sᵊnt'æn, sɪnt-, (US) seɪnt- -'s -z

stann|ic 'stæn|.ɪk -ous -əs

Stansfield 'stænz.fiːld, 'stæn*t*s-

Stansted 'stæn*t*.sted, -stɪd, -stəd **ˌStansted 'Airport**

Stansted Mountfitchet ˌstæn*t*.sted.maʊnt'fɪtʃ.ɪt, -stɪd-, -stəd

St. Anthony sᵊnt'æn.tə.ni, sɪnt-, (US) seɪnt'æn.tᵊn.i, -θə.ni

Stanton 'stæn.tən, 'stɑːn-, (US) 'stæn.tᵊn

stanza 'stæn.zə -s -z

stapes 'steɪ.piːz

staphylo|coccus ˌstæf.ɪ.ləʊ|'kɒk.əs, -ᵊl.əʊ'-, (US) -ə.loʊ|'kɑː.kəs -cocci -'kɒk.saɪ, -aɪ, -iː, (US) -'kɑːk.saɪ, -aɪ -coccal -'kɒk.ᵊl, (US) -'kɑː.kᵊl -coccic -'kɒk.ɪk, (US) -'kɑː.kɪk

stapl|e, S~ 'steɪ.pᵊl -es -z -ing -ɪŋ, 'steɪ.plɪŋ -ed -d

Stapleford 'steɪ.pᵊl.fəd, (US) -fɚd

staple-gun 'steɪ.pᵊl.gʌn -s -z

stapler 'steɪ.pləʳ, (US) -plɚ -s -z

Stapleton 'steɪ.pᵊl.tən

Stapley 'stæp.li, 'steɪ.pli

star stɑːʳ, (US) stɑːr -s -z -ring -ɪŋ -red -d **ˌStars and 'Bars; ˌstar 'chamber; ˌStar of 'David; 'star ˌsign; ˌStars and 'Stripes; 'star ˌwars**

starboard 'stɑː.bəd, -bɔːd, (US) 'stɑːr.bɚd, -bɔːrd

> Note: The nautical pronunciation is /'stɑː.bəd/ (US) /'stɑːrbɚd/.

Starbuck 'stɑː.bʌk, (US) 'stɑːr- -s -s

starch stɑːtʃ, (US) stɑːrtʃ -es -ɪz -ing -ɪŋ -ed -t -y -i -ier -i.əʳ, (US) -i.ɚ -iest -i.ɪst, -i.əst -iness -ɪ.nəs, -ɪ.nɪs -ily -ᵊl.i, -ɪ.li

starch-reduced ˌstɑːtʃ.rɪ'dʒuːst, -rə'-, -'djuːst, '--ˌ-, (US) 'stɑːrtʃ.rɪˌduːst, -ˌdjuːst

star-crossed 'stɑː.krɒst, (US) 'stɑːr.krɑːst **ˌstar-crossed 'lovers**

stardom 'stɑː.dəm, (US) 'stɑːr-

stardust 'stɑː.dʌst, (US) 'stɑːr-

star|e steəʳ, (US) ster -es -z -ing/ly -ɪŋ/li -ed -d -er/s -əʳ/z, (US) -ɚ/z

starfish 'stɑː.fɪʃ, (US) 'stɑːr- -es -ɪz

stargaz|e 'stɑː.geɪz, (US) 'stɑːr- -es -ɪz -ing -ɪŋ -er/s -əʳ/z, (US) -ɚ/z

stark, S~ stɑːk, (US) stɑːrk -ly -li -ness -nəs, -nɪs **ˌstark 'naked; ˌstark ˌraving 'mad**

starkers ˈstɑː.kəz, US ˈstɑːr.kɚz
Starks stɑːks, US stɑːrks
star|less ˈstɑː|.ləs, -lɪs, US ˈstɑːr-
starlet ˈstɑː.lət, -lɪt, US ˈstɑːr- **-s** -s
starlight ˈstɑː.laɪt, US ˈstɑːr-
starling, S~ ˈstɑː.lɪŋ, US ˈstɑːr- **-s** -z
starlit ˈstɑː.lɪt, US ˈstɑːr-
Starr stɑːʳ, US stɑːr
starr|y ˈstɑː.r|i, US ˈstɑːr|.i **-iness** -ɪ.nəs, -ɪ.nɪs
starry-eyed ˌstɑː.riˈaɪd, US ˈstɑːr.i.aɪd *stress shift, British only:* ˌ**starry-eyed** ˈ**fan**
star-spangled ˈstɑːˌspæŋ.gəld, US ˈstɑːr- ˌ**star-**ˌ**spangled** ˈ**banner**
starstruck ˈstɑː.strʌk, US ˈstɑːr-
star-studded ˈstɑːˌstʌd.ɪd, US ˈstɑːr-
start, S~ stɑːt, US stɑːrt **-s** -s **-ing** -ɪŋ, US ˈstɑːr.t̬ɪŋ **-ed** -ɪd, US ˈstɑːr.t̬ɪd **-er/s** -əʳ/z, US ˈstɑːr.t̬ɚ/z ˈ**starting** ˌ**block;** ˈ**starting** ˌ**point**
startl|e ˈstɑː.təl, US ˈstɑːr.t̬əl **-es** -z **-ing/ly** -ɪŋ/li, ˈstɑːt.lɪŋ/li, US ˈstɑːrt- **-ed** -d **-er/s** -əʳ/z, ˈstɑːt.ləʳ/z, US ˈstɑːr.t̬əl.ɚ/z, ˈstɑːrt.lɚ/z
Start-rite® ˈstɑːt.raɪt, US ˈstɑːrt-
start-up ˈstɑːt.ʌp, US ˈstɑːrt- **-s** -s
starvation stɑːˈveɪ.ʃən, US stɑːr- **star**ˌ**vation** ˈ**wages**
starv|e stɑːv, US stɑːrv **-es** -z **-ing** -ɪŋ **-ed** -d
starveling ˈstɑːv.lɪŋ, US ˈstɑːrv- **-s** -z
St. Asaph səntˈæs.əf, sɪnt-, US seɪnt-
stash stæʃ **-es** -ɪz **-ing** -ɪŋ **-ed** -t
Stasi ˈstɑː.zi; *as if German:* ˈʃtɑː-
stas|is ˈsteɪ.s|ɪs, US ˈsteɪ-, ˈstæs|.ɪs **-es** -iːz
stat|e steɪt **-es** -s **-ing** -ɪŋ, US ˈsteɪ.t̬ɪŋ **-ed/ly** -ɪd/li, US ˈsteɪ.t̬ɪd/li ˈ**State** ˌ**Department;** ˌ**state of** **e**ˈ**mergency;** ˈ**state** ˌ**school;** ˌ**state** ˈ**trooper**
statecraft ˈsteɪt.krɑːft, US -kræft
statehood ˈsteɪt.hʊd
stateless ˈsteɪt.ləs, -lɪs **-ness** -nəs, -nɪs
statel|y ˈsteɪt.l|i **-ier** -i.əʳ, US -i.ɚ **-iest** -i.ɪst, -i.əst **-iness** -ɪ.nəs, -ɪ.nɪs ˌ**stately** ˈ**home**
statement ˈsteɪt.mənt **-s** -s
Staten Island ˌstæt.ənˈaɪ.lənd
state-of-the-art ˌsteɪt.əv.ðiˈɑːt, US -ˈɑːrt *stress shift:* ˌ**state-of-the-art** ˈ**gadget**
state-owned ˌsteɪtˈəʊnd, US -ˈoʊnd *stress shift:* ˌ**state-owned** ˈ**business**
stateroom ˈsteɪt.rʊm, -ruːm, US -ruːm, -rʊm **-s** -z
States steɪts
stateside ˈsteɪt.saɪd
states|man ˈsteɪts|.mən **-men** -mən
statesman|like ˈsteɪts.mən|.laɪk **-ly** -li **-ship** -ʃɪp
states|woman ˈsteɪts|ˌwʊm.ən **-women** -ˌwɪm.ɪn
statewide ˈsteɪt.waɪd
Statham ˈsteɪ.θəm, -ðəm, US -ðəm, -θəm, -t̬əm; US ˈstæt̬.əm
St. Athan sənˈtæθ.ən, sɪnt-, US seɪnt-
static ˈstæt.ɪk, US ˈstæt̬- **-s** -s **-al** -əl **-ally** -əl.i, -li
static|e ˈstæt.ɪs, -ɪ.s|i, US ˈstæt̬.ə.s|i, ˈ-ɪs **-es** -ɪz, -iz
statin ˈstæt.ɪn, US ˈstæt.ən **-s** -z
station ˈsteɪ.ʃən **-s** -z **-ing** -ɪŋ, ˈsteɪʃ.nɪŋ **-ed** -d ˈ**station** ˌ**wagon;** ˌ**stations of the** ˈ**cross**
stationar|y ˈsteɪ.ʃən.ər|.i, ˈsteɪʃ.nər-, US ˈsteɪ.ʃə.ner- **-ily** -əl.i, -ɪ.li **-iness** -ɪ.nəs, -ɪ.nɪs
stationer ˈsteɪ.ʃən.əʳ, ˈsteɪʃ.nəʳ, US -ʃən.ɚ, ˈsteɪʃ.nɚ **-s** -z
stationery ˈsteɪ.ʃən.ər.i, ˈsteɪʃ.nər-, US ˈsteɪ.ʃə.ner-
stationmaster ˈsteɪ.ʃənˌmɑː.stəʳ, US -ˌmæs.tɚ **-s** -z
stat|ism ˈsteɪ.t|ɪ.zəm, US -t̬|ɪ- **-ist/s** -ɪst/s
statistic stəˈtɪs.tɪk, stætˈɪs-, US stəˈtɪs- **-s** -s **-al** -əl **-ally** -əl.i, -li
statistician ˌstæt.ɪˈstɪʃ.ən, -əˈ-, US -ɪˈ- **-s** -z
Statius ˈsteɪ.ʃəs
stative ˈsteɪ.tɪv, US -t̬ɪv
stator ˈsteɪ.təʳ, US -t̬ɚ **-s** -z
stats stæts
statuary ˈstætʃ.u.ər.i, ˈstæt.ju-, US ˈstætʃ.u.er-
statue ˈstætʃ.uː, ˈstæt.juː, US ˈstætʃ.uː **-s** -z
statuesque ˌstæt.juˈesk, ˌstætʃ.uˈ-, US ˌstætʃ.uˈ-
statuette ˌstæt.juˈet, ˌstætʃ.uˈ-, US ˌstætʃ.uˈ- **-s** -s
stature ˈstætʃ.əʳ, ˈstæt.jəʳ, US ˈstætʃ.ɚ **-s** -z
status ˈsteɪ.təs, US stæ.t̬əs **-es** -ɪz ˈ**status** ˌ**symbol**
status quo ˌsteɪ.təsˈkwəʊ, ˌstæt.əsˈ-, US ˌstæt̬.əsˈkwoʊ, ˌsteɪ.t̬əsˈ-
statute ˈstæt.juːt, ˈstætʃ.uːt, US ˈstætʃ.uːt **-s** -s ˈ**statute** ˌ**book**
statutory ˈstæt.jə.tər.i, -jʊ-, ˈstætʃ.ə-, ˈ-ʊ-, US ˈstætʃ.ə.tɔːr-, ˈ-ʊ- ˌ**statutory** ˈ**rape**
St. Augustine sənt.ɔːˈgʌs.tɪn, sɪnt-, ˌsent-, ˌseɪnt-, -əˈ-, US seɪntˈɔː.gə.stiːn, -ˈɑː-
staunch stɔːntʃ, US stɔːntʃ, stɑːntʃ **-er** -əʳ, US -ɚ **-est** -ɪst, -əst **-ly** -li **-ness** -nəs, -nɪs **-es** -ɪz **-ing** -ɪŋ **-ed** -t
Staunton *English surname:* ˈstɔːn.tən, US ˈstɑːn.tən, ˈstɔːn- *towns in US:* ˈstæn.tən, US -tən
St. Austell sənˈtɔː.stəl, sɪnt-; *locally:* -ˈɔː.səl, US seɪntˈɑː.stəl, -ˈɔː-
Stavanger stəˈvæŋ.əʳ, stævˈæŋ-, US stəˈvɑː.ŋ.ɚ, stɑː-
stav|e steɪv **-es** -z **-ing** -ɪŋ **-ed** -d **stove** stəʊv, US stoʊv
Staveley ˈsteɪv.li
stay steɪ **-s** -z **-ing** -ɪŋ **-ed** -d **-er/s** -əʳ/z, US -ɚ/z
stay-at-home ˈsteɪ.ət.həʊm, US -hoʊm
staycation ˌsteɪˈkeɪ.ʃən **-s** -z **-ing** -ɪŋ **-ed** -d **-er/s** -əʳ/z, US -ɚ/z
staysail ˈsteɪ.seɪl; *nautical pronunciation:* -səl **-s** -z
St. Bartholomew sənt.bɑːˈθɒl.ə.mjuː, sɪnt-, -bəˈ-, US ˌseɪnt.bɑːrˈθɑː.lə- **-'s** -z
St. Bees səntˈbiːz, sɪnt-, US seɪnt-
St. Bernard səntˈbɜː.nəd, sɪnt-, US ˌseɪnt.bɚˈnɑːrd **-s** -z
St. Blaize səntˈbleɪz, sɪnt-, US seɪnt-
St. Blazey səntˈbleɪ.zi, sɪnt-, US seɪnt-
St. Bride's səntˈbraɪdz, sɪnt-, US seɪnt-
St. Bruno səntˈbruː.nəʊ, sɪnt-, US seɪntˈbruː.noʊ
St. Catherine, St. Catharine səntˈkæθ.ər.ɪn, sɪnt-, səŋˈ-, ˈ-rɪn, US seɪnt- **-'s** -z
St. Cecilia sənt.sɪˈsɪl.i.ə, sɪnt-, -ˈsiː.li.ə, ˈ-ljə, US ˌseɪnt.sɪˈsiːl.jə
St. Christopher səntˈkrɪs.tə.fəʳ, sɪnt-, səŋ-, US seɪntˈkrɪs.tə.fɚ **-s** -z
St. Clair *surname:* ˈsɪŋ.kleəʳ, ˈsɪn-, US seɪntˈkler *place in US:* səntˈkleəʳ, sɪnt-, səŋ-, US seɪntˈkler *name of saint:* səntˈkleəʳ, səŋ-, sɪnt-, US seɪntˈkler
St. Columb səntˈkɒl.əm, sɪnt-, US seɪntˈkɑː.ləm
STD ˌes.tiːˈdiː **ST**ˈ**D** ˌ**code**
St. David səntˈdeɪ.vɪd, sɪnt-, US seɪnt- **-'s** -z
stead, S~ sted
steadfast ˈsted.fɑːst, -fəst, US -fæst, -fəst **-ly** -li **-ness** -nəs, -nɪs
steading ˈsted.ɪŋ **-s** -z
Steadman ˈsted.mən
stead|y ˈsted|.i **-ier** -i.əʳ, US -i.ɚ **-iest** -i.ɪst, -i.əst **-ily** -əl.i, -ɪ.li **-iness** -ɪ.nəs, -ɪ.nɪs **-ies** -iz **-ying** -i.ɪŋ **-ied** -id ˌ**steady** ˈ**state;** ˌ**steady** ˈ**state** ˌ**theory**
steak steɪk **-s** -s ˌ**steak tar**ˈ**tare;** ˌ**steak and** ˌ**kidney** ˈ**pie**
steakhou|se ˈsteɪk.haʊ|s **-ses** -zɪz
steal stiːl **-s** -z **-ing** -ɪŋ **stole** stəʊl, US stoʊl **stolen** ˈstəʊ.lən, US ˈstoʊ- **stealer/s** ˈstiː.ləʳ/z, US -lɚ/z
stealth stelθ
stealth|y ˈstel.θ|i **-ier** -i.əʳ, US -i.ɚ **-iest** -i.ɪst, -i.əst **-ily** -əl.i, -ɪ.li **-iness** -ɪ.nəs, -ɪ.nɪs
steam stiːm **-s** -z **-ing** -ɪŋ **-ed** -d **-er/s** -əʳ/z, US -ɚ/z ˈ**steam** ˌ**engine;** ˈ**steam** ˌ**iron;** ˈ**steam** ˌ**power**
steamboat ˈstiːm.bəʊt, US -boʊt **-s** -s
steam-hammer ˈstiːmˌhæm.əʳ, US -ɚ **-s** -z
steamroll ˈstiːm.rəʊl, US -roʊl **-s** -z **-ing** -ɪŋ **-ed** -d
steamroll|er ˈstiːmˌrəʊ.l|əʳ, US -ˌroʊ.l|ɚ **-ers** -əz, US -ɚz **-ering** -ər.ɪŋ **-ered** -əd, US -ɚd
steamship ˈstiːm.ʃɪp **-s** -s

S

steam|y ˈstiː.m|i **-ier** -i.əʳ, (US) -i.ɚ **-iest** -i.ɪst, -i.əst **-iness** -ɪ.nəs, -ɪ.nɪs
stearic stiˈær.ɪk, (US) stiˈær-; (US) ˈstɪr-
stearin ˈstɪə.rɪn, (US) ˈstiː.ɚ.ɪn; (US) ˈstɪr-
Stearn(e) stɜːn, (US) stɝːn **-s** -z
steatite ˈstɪə.taɪt, (US) ˈstiː.ə-
steatolysis stɪəˈtɒl.ə.sɪs, ˈ-ɪ-, (US) ˌstiː.əˈtɑː.lə-
steatopygia ˌstɪə.təʊˈpɪdʒ.i.ə, -ˈpaɪ.dʒi-, ˈ-dʒə, (US) ˌstiː.æt.əˈpaɪ.dʒi.ə, -ˈpɪdʒ.i-
steatopygous ˌstɪə.təʊˈpaɪ.gəs; stɪəˈtɒp.ɪ-, (US) ˌstiː.æt.əˈpaɪ-
Stedman ˈsted.mən
St. Edmunds sᵊntˈed.məndz, sɪnt-, (US) seɪnt-
steed stiːd **-s** -z
steel, S~ stiːl **-s** -z **-ing** -ɪŋ **-ed** -d ˌ**steel** ˈ**wool**
Steele stiːl
Steelers ˈstiː.ləz, (US) -ɚz
steel-plated ˌstiːlˈpleɪ.tɪd, (US) ˈ-ˌ-- *stress shift, British only:* ˌ**steel-plated** ˈ**hull**
steelworker ˈstiːlˌwɜː.kəʳ, (US) -ˌwɝː.kɚ **-s** -z
steelworks ˈstiːl.wɜːks, (US) -wɝːks
steel|y ˈstiː.l|i **-ier** -i.əʳ, (US) -i.ɚ **-iest** -i.ɪst, -i.əst **-iness** -ɪ.nəs, -ɪ.nɪs
steelyard ˈstiːl.jɑːd, ˈstɪl.jəd, (US) ˈstiːl.jɑːrd, ˈstɪl.jɚd **-s** -z
steenbok ˈstiːn.bɒk, ˈsteɪn-, (US) -bɑːk **-s** -s
Steenson ˈstiːnt.sən
steep stiːp **-s** -s **-er** -əʳ, (US) -ɚ **-est** -ɪst, -əst **-ly** -li **-ness** -nəs, -nɪs **-ing** -ɪŋ **-ed** -t
steepen ˈstiː.pᵊn **-s** -z **-ing** -ɪŋ, ˈstiːp.nɪŋ **-ed** -d
steeple ˈstiː.pᵊl **-s** -z **-d** -d
steeplechas|e ˈstiː.pᵊl.tʃeɪs **-es** -ɪz **-ing** -ɪŋ **-er/s** -əʳ/z, (US) -ɚ/z
steeplejack ˈstiː.pᵊl.dʒæk **-s** -s
steer stɪəʳ, (US) stɪr **-s** -z **-ing** -ɪŋ **-ed** -d **-er/s** -əʳ/z, (US) -ɚ/z ˈ**steering** **comˌmittee**; ˈ**steering** ˌ**gear**; ˈ**steering** ˌ**wheel**
steerage ˈstɪə.rɪdʒ, (US) ˈstɪr.ɪdʒ
steers|man ˈstɪəz|.mən, (US) ˈstɪrz- **-men** -mən
steev|e stiːv **-es** -z **-ing** -ɪŋ **-ed** -d
Steevens ˈstiː.vᵊnz
Stefanie ˈstef.ᵊn.i
Steiger ˈstaɪ.gəʳ, (US) -gɚ
stein *beer mug:* staɪn; *as if German:* ʃtaɪn **-s** -z
Stein *surname:* staɪn, stiːn; *as if German:* ʃtaɪn
Steinbeck ˈstaɪn.bek, ˈstaɪm-, (US) ˈstaɪn-
steinbock ˈstaɪn.bɒk, ˈstaɪm-, (US) ˈstaɪn.bɑːk **-s** -s
Steinbrenner ˈstaɪnˌbren.əʳ, ˈstaɪm-, (US) ˈstaɪnˌbren.ɚ
Steinem ˈstaɪ.nəm
Steiner ˈstaɪ.nəʳ, (US) -nɚ
Steinway® ˈstaɪn.weɪ **-s** -z
stel|e *monument:* ˈstiː.l|i; stiːl, (US) ˈstiː.l|i *in architecture or botany:* ˈstiː.l|i; stiːl, (US) stiːl; (US) ˈstiː.l|i **-ae** -iː **-es** ˈstiː.liz; stiːlz, (US) stiːlz; (US) ˈstiː.liz
St. Elian sᵊntˈiː.li.ən, sɪnt-, (US) seɪnt-
St. Elias sᵊnt.ɪˈlaɪ.əs, sɪnt-, -æs, (US) ˌseɪnt.ɪˈlaɪ.əs
Stella ˈstel.ə *TM:* ˌ**Stella** ˈ**Artois**; *as if French:* ˌ**Stella** **Arˈtois**
stellar ˈstel.əʳ, (US) -ɚ
St. Elmo sᵊntˈel.məʊ, sɪnt-, (US) seɪntˈel.moʊ **-'s** -z **St.** ˌ**Elmo's** ˈ**fire**
stem stem **-s** -z **-ming** -ɪŋ **-med** -d
stem-cell ˈstem.sel
stemple ˈstem.pᵊl **-s** -z
Sten sten ˈ**Sten** ˌ**gun**
stench stentʃ, (US) stentʃ **-es** -ɪz
stencil ˈstent.sᵊl, -ɪl, (US) -sᵊl **-s** -z **-(l)ing** -ɪŋ **-(l)ed** -d
Stendhal ˈstɑ̃ːn.dɑːl, -ˈ-, (US) ˈsten-, ˈstæn-
Stenhouse ˈsten.haʊs
Stenhousemuir ˌsten.haʊsˈmjʊəʳ, -əsˈ-, -ˈmjɔːʳ, (US) -ˈmjʊɚ
Stenness ˈsten.əs
steno ˈsten.əʊ, (US) -oʊ **-s** -z
stenograph ˈsten.əʊ.grɑːf, -græf, (US) -ə.græf **-s** -s
stenograph|er stəˈnɒg.rə.f|əʳ, stenˈɒg-, (US) stəˈnɑː.grə.f|ɚ **-ers** -əz, (US) -ɚz **-y** -i
stenotyp|e ˈsten.əʊ.taɪp, (US) ˈ-ə- **-ing** -ɪŋ **-ist/s** -ɪst/s
stentorian stenˈtɔː.ri.ən, (US) -ˈtɔːr.i-
step step **-s** -s **-ping** -ɪŋ **-ped** -t **-per/s** -əʳ/z, (US) -ɚ/z ˌ**step ae**ˈ**robics**; ˈ**step** ˌ**dance**; ˌ**step by** ˈ**step**
stepbrother ˈstepˌbrʌð.əʳ, (US) -ðɚ **-s** -z
step|child ˈstep|.tʃaɪld **-children** -ˌtʃɪl.drᵊn
stepdad ˈstep.dæd **-s** -z
stepdaughter ˈstepˌdɔː.təʳ, (US) -ˌdɑː.t̬ɚ, -ˌdɔː- **-s** -z
stepfather ˈstepˌfɑː.ðəʳ, (US) -ðɚ **-s** -z
Stephanie ˈstef.ᵊn.i
Stephano ˈstef.ᵊn.əʊ, (US) -ə.noʊ
stephanotis ˌstef.əˈnəʊ.tɪs, (US) -ˈnoʊ.t̬ɪs
Stephen ˈstiː.vᵊn **-s** -z
Stephenson ˈstiː.vᵊn.sᵊn
stepladder ˈstepˌlæd.əʳ, (US) -ɚ **-s** -z
stepmother ˈstepˌmʌð.əʳ, (US) -ɚ **-s** -z
stepmum ˈstep.mʌm **-s** -z
Stepney ˈstep.ni
stepparent ˈstepˌpeə.rᵊnt, (US) -ˌper.ᵊnt, -ˌpær- **-s** -s
steppe step **-s** -s
Steppenwolf ˈstep.ᵊn.wʊlf
stepping-stone ˈstep.ɪŋ.stəʊn, (US) -stoʊn **-s** -z
stepsister ˈstepˌsɪs.təʳ, (US) -tɚ **-s** -z
stepson ˈstep.sʌn **-s** -z
Steptoe ˈstep.təʊ, (US) -toʊ
-ster stəʳ, (US) stɚ
Note: Suffix. Does not normally change the stress pattern of the word to which it is added, e.g. **prank** /præŋk/, **prankster** /ˈpræŋk.stəʳ/ (US) /-stɚ/.
stereo ˈster.i.əʊ, ˈstɪə.ri-, (US) ˈster.i.oʊ, ˈstɪr- **-s** -z

> Note: The pronunciation /ˈstɪə-/ should be regarded as old-fashioned.

stereo- ˈster.i.əʊ, ˈstɪə.ri-; ˌster.iˈɒ, ˌstɪə.riˈ-, (US) ˈster.i.oʊ, ˈstɪr-, -ə; (US) ˌster.iˈɑː, ˌstɪr-
Note: Prefix. Normally either takes primary or secondary stress on the first syllable, e.g. **stereoscope** /ˈster.i.əʊ.skəʊp/ (US) /-ə.skoʊp/, **stereophonic** /ˌster.i.əʊˈfɒn.ɪk/ (US) /-əˈfɑː.nɪk/, or secondary stress on the first syllable and primary stresson the third syllable, e.g. **stereophony** /ˌster.iˈɒf.ᵊn.i/ (US) /-ˈɑː.fᵊn-/.
stereophonic ˌster.i.əʊˈfɒn.ɪk, ˌstɪə.ri-, (US) ˌster.i.əˈfɑː.nɪk, ˌstɪr-
stereophony ˌster.iˈɒf.ᵊn.i, ˌstɪə.riˈ-, (US) ˌster.iˈɑː.fᵊn-, ˌstɪr-
stereopticon ˌster.iˈɒp.tɪ.kən, ˌstɪə.riˈ-, (US) ˌster.iˈɑːp-, ˌstɪr-, -kɑːn **-s** -z
stereoscope ˈster.i.ə.skəʊp, ˈstɪə.ri-, (US) ˈster.i.ə.skoʊp, ˈstɪr- **-s** -s
stereoscopic ˌster.i.əˈskɒp.ɪk, ˌstɪə.ri-, (US) ˌster.i.əˈskɑː.pɪk, ˌstɪr- **-al** -ᵊl **-ally** -ᵊl.i, -li
stereoscopy ˌster.iˈɒs.kə.pi, ˌstɪə.riˈ-, (US) ˌster.iˈɑː.skə-, ˌstɪr-
stereotyp|e ˈster.i.əʊ.taɪp, ˈstɪə.ri-, (US) ˈster.i.ə-, ˈstɪr- **-es** -s **-ing** -ɪŋ **-ed** -t
stereotypic|al ˌster.i.əʊˈtɪp.ɪ.k|ᵊl, ˌstɪə.ri-, (US) ˌster.i.əˈ-, ˌstɪr- **-ally** -ᵊl.i, -li
sterile ˈster.aɪl, (US) -ᵊl
sterility stəˈrɪl.ə.ti, sterˈɪl-, -ɪ.ti, (US) stəˈrɪl.ə.t̬i
sterilization, -isa- ˌster.ᵊl.aɪˈzeɪ.ʃᵊn, -ɪ.laɪˈ-, -lɪˈ-, (US) -ᵊl.əˈ- **-s** -z
sterilız|e, -is|e ˈster.ᵊl.aɪz, -ɪ.laɪz, (US) -ə.laɪz **-es** -ɪz **-ing** -ɪŋ **-ed** -d **-er/s** -əʳ/z, (US) -ɚ/z
sterling, S~ ˈstɜː.lɪŋ, (US) ˈstɝː-
stern, S~ **adj** stɜːn, (US) stɝːn **-er** -əʳ, (US) -ɚ **-est** -ɪst, -əst **-ly** -li **-ness** -nəs, -nɪs
Sterne stɜːn, (US) stɝːn
stern|um ˈstɜː.n|əm, (US) ˈstɝː- **-ums** -əmz **-a** -ə
steroid ˈster.ɔɪd, ˈstɪə.rɔɪd, (US) ˈster-, ˈstɪr- **-s** -z
stertorous ˈstɜː.tᵊr.əs, (US) ˈstɝː.t̬ɚ- **-ly** -li **-ness** -nəs, -nɪs
stet stet **-s** -s **-ting** -ɪŋ, (US) ˈstet̬.ɪŋ **-ted** -ɪd, (US) ˈstet̬.ɪd
stethoscope ˈsteθ.ə.skəʊp, (US) -skoʊp **-s** -s
stethoscopic ˌsteθ.əˈskɒp.ɪk, (US) -ˈskɑː.pɪk **-al** -ᵊl **-ally** -ᵊl.i, -li
stethoscopy steθˈɒs.kə.pi, (US) -ˈɑː.skə-

Stetson® ˈstet.sᵊn
Steve stiːv
stevedore ˈstiː.və.dɔːʳ, -vɪ-, (US) -və.dɔːr -s -z
Steven ˈstiː.vᵊn -s -z
Stevenage ˈstiː.vᵊn.ɪdʒ
Stevenson ˈstiː.vᵊn.sᵊn
Stevenston ˈstiː.vᵊn.stᵊn
Stevie ˈstiː.vi
stew stjuː, stʃuː, (US) stuː, stjuː -s -z -ing -ɪŋ -ed -d
steward, S~ ˈstjuː.əd, ˈstʃuː.əd, (US) ˈstuː.ɚd, ˈstjuː- -s -z -ing -ɪŋ -ed -ɪd
stewardess ˈstjuː.ə.dɪs, ˈstʃuː.ə-, -dəs, -des; ˌstjuː.əˈdes, ˌstʃuː-, (US) ˈstuː.ɚ.dɪs, ˈstjuː- -es -ɪz
stewardship ˈstjuː.əd.ʃɪp, ˈstʃuː.əd-, (US) ˈstuː.ɚd-, ˈstjuː-
Stewart stjʊət, stʃʊət, ˈstʃuː.ət, ˈstjuː-, (US) ˈstuː.ɚt, ˈstjuː-, stʊrt
Stewarton ˈstjʊə.tᵊn, ˈstʃʊə-, ˈstjuː.ə-, ˈstʃuː-, (US) ˈstuː.ɚ-, ˈstjuː-, stʊr.tᵊn
Steyn staɪn
Steyne stiːn
Steyning ˈsten.ɪŋ
St. Fagans sᵊn*t*ˈfæg.ᵊnz, sɪn*t*-, (US) seɪntˈfæg-, -ˈfeɪ.gᵊnz
St. Francis sᵊn*t*ˈfrɑːn*t*.sɪs, sɪn*t*-, (US) seɪntˈfræn*t*-
stg. (abbrev. for **sterling**) ˈstɜː.lɪŋ, (US) ˈstɝː-
St. Gall sᵊn*t*ˈgæl, sɪn*t*-, -gɑːl, -gɔːl, (US) seɪnt-
St. Gallen sᵊn*t*ˈgæl.ən, sɪn*t*-, (US) seɪntˈgɑː.lən
St. George sᵊn*t*ˈdʒɔːdʒ, sɪn*t*-, (US) seɪntˈdʒɔːrdʒ -'s -ɪz
St. Giles sᵊn*t*ˈdʒaɪlz, sɪn*t*-, (US) seɪnt- -'s -ɪz
St. Godric sᵊn*t*ˈgɒd.rɪk, sɪn*t*-, (US) seɪntˈgɑː.drɪk
St. Gotthard sᵊn*t*ˈgɒt.əd, sɪn*t*-, -ɑːd, (US) seɪntˈgɑː.t̬ɚd
St. Helen sᵊntˈhel.ən, sɪnt-, -ɪn, (US) seɪntˈhel.ən -s -z
St. Helena *Saint:* sᵊntˈhel.ə.nə, sɪnt-, ˈ-ɪ-, (US) ˌseɪnt.həˈliː-; (US) seɪntˈhel.ə- *island:* ˌsent.*h*ɪˈliː.nə, ˌsɪnt-, sᵊnt-, -*h*əˈ-, (US) ˌseɪnt.həˈ-; (US) seɪntˈhel.ə-
St. Helier sᵊntˈhel.i.əʳ, sɪnt-, (US) seɪntˈhel.jɚ -s -z
Stich stɪx; *as if German:* ʃtiːx
stichomythia ˌstɪk.əʊˈmɪθ.i.ə, (US) -əˈ-, -oʊˈ- -s -z
stick stɪk -s -s -ing -ɪŋ **stuck** stʌk **ˈstick ˌinsect**; **ˈsticking ˌplaster**; **ˈstick ˌshift**; **get (ˌhold of) the ˌwrong ˌend of the ˈstick**
sticker ˈstɪk.əʳ, (US) -ɚ -s -z
stick-in-the-mud ˈstɪk.ɪn.ðəˌmʌd -s -z
stickjaw ˈstɪk.dʒɔː, (US) -dʒɑː, -dʒɔː -s -z
stickleback ˈstɪk.ᵊl.bæk -s -s
stickler ˈstɪk.ləʳ, -ᵊl.əʳ, (US) ˈ-lɚ, -ᵊl.ɚ -s -z
stick-on ˈstɪk.ɒn, (US) -ɑːn
stickpin ˈstɪk.pɪn
stick-up ˈstɪk.ʌp -s -s
stick|y ˈstɪk|.i -ier -i.əʳ, (US) -i.ɚ -iest -i.ɪst, -i.əst -ily -ᵊl.i, -ɪ.li -iness -ɪ.nəs, -ɪ.nɪs
stickybeak ˈstɪk.i.biːk -s -s
stiff stɪf -er -əʳ, (US) -ɚ -est -ɪst, -əst -ing -ɪŋ -ed -t -ly -li -ness -nəs, -nɪs **ˌstiff ˌupper ˈlip**
stiffen ˈstɪf.ᵊn -s -z -ing -ɪŋ, ˈstɪf.nɪŋ -ed -d
Stiffkey ˈstɪf.ki; *traditional local pronunciation:* ˈstjuː.ki, ˈstuː-
stiff-necked ˌstɪfˈnekt, (US) ˈstɪf.nekt *stress shift:* **ˌstiff-necked ˈpride**
stiff|y ˈstɪf|.i -ies -iz
stifl|e ˈstaɪ.fᵊl -es -z -ing/ly -ɪŋ/li, ˈstaɪ.flɪŋ/li -ed -d
Stiggins ˈstɪg.ɪnz
stigma ˈstɪg.mə -s -z -tism -tɪ.zᵊm
stigmata (alternative plural of **stigma**) stɪgˈmɑː.tə, (US) -t̬ə, -ˈmæt̬.ə
stigmatic stɪgˈmæt.ɪk, (US) -ˈmæt̬-
stigmatization, -isa- ˌstɪg.mə.taɪˈzeɪ.ʃᵊn, -tɪˈ-, (US) -t̬əˈ-
stigmatiz|e, -is|e ˈstɪg.mə.taɪz -es -ɪz -ing -ɪŋ -ed -d
stilbene ˈstɪl.biːn
stilbestrol stɪlˈbiː.strəl, -strɒl, -ˈbes.trəl, -trɒl, (US) -ˈbes.trɔːl, -troʊl
stile staɪl -s -z
stiletto stɪˈlet.əʊ, (US) -ˈlet̬.oʊ -(e)s -z
still, S~ stɪl -s -z -er -əʳ, (US) -ɚ -est -ɪst, -əst -ness -nəs, -nɪs -ing -ɪŋ -ed -d **ˌstill ˈlife** *stress shift:* **ˌstill life ˈpainting**
stillbirth ˈstɪl.bɜːθ, (US) -bɝːθ -s -s
stillborn ˈstɪl.bɔːn, (US) ˈstɪl.bɔːrn
Stillson ˈstɪl.sᵊn **ˈStillson ˌwrench**®
stilly ˈstɪl.i
stilt stɪlt -s -s
stilted ˈstɪl.tɪd -ly -li -ness -nəs, -nɪs
Stilton ˈstɪl.tᵊn -s -z
Stimpson ˈstɪmp.sᵊn
Stimson ˈstɪm*p*.sᵊn
stimulant ˈstɪm.jə.lənt, -jʊ- -s -s
stimu|late ˈstɪm.jə|.leɪt, -jʊ- -lates -leɪts -lating -leɪ.tɪŋ, (US) -leɪ.t̬ɪŋ -lated -leɪ.tɪd, (US) -leɪ.t̬ɪd -lator/s -leɪ.təʳ/z, (US) -leɪ.t̬ɚ/z
stimulation ˌstɪm.jəˈleɪ.ʃᵊn, -jʊˈ- -s -z
stimulative ˈstɪm.jə.lə.tɪv, -jʊ-, -leɪ-, (US) -leɪ.t̬ɪv
stimul|us ˈstɪm.jə.l|əs, -jʊ- -i -aɪ, -iː
stim|y ˈstaɪ.m|i -ies -iz -ying -i.ɪŋ -ied -id
sting stɪŋ -s -z -ing -ɪŋ **stung** stʌŋ **stinger/s** ˈstɪŋ.əʳ/z, (US) -ɚ/z **ˈstinging ˌnettle**
stingo ˈstɪŋ.gəʊ, (US) -goʊ -s -z
stingray ˈstɪŋ.reɪ -s -z
sting|y ˈstɪn.dʒ|i -ier -i.əʳ, (US) -i.ɚ -iest -i.ɪst, -i.əst -ily -ᵊl.i, -ɪ.li -iness -ɪ.nəs, -ɪ.nɪs
stink stɪŋk -s -s -ing -ɪŋ **stank** stæŋk **stunk** stʌŋk
stink-bomb ˈstɪŋk.bɒm, (US) -bɑːm -s -z
stinker ˈstɪŋ.kəʳ, (US) -kɚ -s -z
stinkpot ˈstɪŋk.pɒt, (US) -pɑːt -s -s
stint stɪnt -s -s -ing -ɪŋ, (US) ˈstɪn.t̬ɪŋ -ed -ɪd, (US) ˈstɪn.t̬ɪd
stipend ˈstaɪ.pend, -pənd -s -z
stipendiar|y staɪˈpen.di.əʳ|.i, stɪ-, (US) staɪˈpen.di.er- -ies -iz
stippl|e ˈstɪp.ᵊl -es -z -ing -ɪŋ, ˈstɪp.lɪŋ -ed -d -er/s -əʳ/z, (US) -ɚ/z
stipu|late ˈstɪp.jə|.leɪt, -jʊ- -lates -leɪts -lating -leɪ.tɪŋ, (US) -leɪ.t̬ɪŋ -lated -leɪ.tɪd, (US) -leɪ.t̬ɪd
stipulation ˌstɪp.jəˈleɪ.ʃᵊn, -jʊˈ- -s -z
stipule ˈstɪp.juːl -s -z
stir stɜːʳ, (US) stɝː -s -z -ring/ly -ɪŋ/li -red -d -rer/s -əʳ/z, (US) -ɚ/z
stir-crazy ˈstɜːˌkreɪ.zi, ˌ-ˈ--, (US) ˈstɝːˌ-, ˌ-ˈ--
stir|-fry ˈstɜː|ˌfraɪ, (US) ˈstɝː- -fries -ˌfraɪz, (US) -ˌfraɪz -frying -ˌfraɪ.ɪŋ, (US) -ˌfraɪ.ɪŋ -fried -ˌfraɪd, (US) -ˌfraɪd
Stirling ˈstɜː.lɪŋ, (US) ˈstɝː- -shire -ʃəʳ, -ʃɪəʳ, (US) -ʃɚ, -ʃɪr
stirp|s stɜːp|s, (US) stɝːp|s -es -iːz, -eɪz
stirrup ˈstɪr.əp, (US) ˈstɝː-, ˈstɪr- -s -s **ˈstirrup ˌpump**
stitch stɪtʃ -es -ɪz -ing -ɪŋ -ed -t
St. Ivel sᵊntˈaɪ.vᵊl, sɪnt-, (US) seɪnt-
St. Ives sᵊntˈaɪvz, sɪnt-, (US) seɪnt-
St. James sᵊn*t*ˈdʒeɪmz, sɪn*t*-, (US) seɪnt- -'s -ɪz
St. Joan sᵊn*t*ˈdʒəʊn, sɪn*t*-, (US) seɪntˈdʒoʊn
St. John *Saint, place:* sᵊn*t*ˈdʒɒn, sɪn*t*-, (US) seɪntˈdʒɑːn *surname:* ˈsɪn.dʒᵊn, (US) seɪntˈdʒɑːn -'s -z
St. Joseph sᵊn*t*ˈdʒəʊ.zɪf, sɪn*t*-, -zəf, (US) seɪntˈdʒoʊ.zəf, -səf
St. Kilda sᵊn*t*ˈkɪl.də, sɪn*t*-, (US) seɪnt-
St. Kitts sᵊn*t*ˈkɪts, sɪn*t*-, (US) seɪnt-
St. Kitts and Nevis sᵊn*t*ˌkɪts.ᵊn*d*ˈniː.vɪs, sɪn*t*-, (US) seɪnt-
St. Laurent *Yves:* ˌsæ̃n.lɔːˈrɑ̃ːŋ, -ləˈ-, (US) -lɔːˈrɑːn *place in Canada:* ˌsæn.lɔːˈrɑ̃ːŋ, -ləˈ-, -ˈrɑːnt, (US) ˌsæ̃n.lɔːˈrɑːn, ˌsæn.lɔːˈrent
St. Lawrence sᵊn*t*ˈlɒr.ᵊn*t*s, sɪn*t*-, (US) seɪntˈlɔːr- **St. ˌLawrence ˈSeaway**
St. Leger *surname:* sᵊn*t*ˈledʒ.əʳ, sɪnt-; ˈsel.ɪn.dʒəʳ, (US) seɪntˈledʒ.ɚ; (US) ˈsel.ɪn.dʒɚ *race:* sᵊn*t*ˈledʒ.əʳ, sɪnt-, (US) seɪntˈledʒ.ɚ

> Note: Most people bearing this name (including Irish families) pronounce /sᵊntˈledʒ.əʳ/ (US) /seɪnt-/. Some English families pronounce the name /ˈsel.ɪn.dʒəʳ/ (US) /-dʒɚ/.

St. Leonards sᵊn*t*ˈlen.ədz, sɪnt-, (US) seɪntˈlen.ədz *city in Quebec:* sænˈleɪ.əʊ.nɑːʳ, -oʊ.nɑːr
St. Levan sᵊn*t*ˈlev.ən, sɪnt-, (US) seɪnt-
St. Louis *city in US:* sᵊn*t*ˈluː.ɪs, sɪnt-, (US) seɪnt-, -i; *sometimes locally:* (US) sænt- *places in Canada:* sᵊn*t*ˈluː.i, sɪn*t*-, -ɪs, (US) seɪnt-

St. Lucia sᵊntˈluː.ʃə, sɪnt-, -ʃi.ə, -si.ə, (US) seɪntˈluː.ʃi.ə, -si-, ˈ-ʃə
St. Ludger sᵊntˈluː.dʒəʳ, sɪnt-, (US) seɪntˈluː.dʒɚ
St. Luke sᵊntˈluːk, sɪnt-, (US) seɪnt-
St. Malo sᵊntˈmɑː.ləʊ, sɪnt-, sæ̃n-; *as if French:* ˌsæ̃n.mɑːˈləʊ; (US) ˌsæn.mɑːˈloʊ
St. Margaret sᵊntˈmɑː.gᵊr.ɪt, sɪnt-, ˈ-grɪt, (US) seɪntˈmɑːr.grət **-'s** -s
St. Mark sᵊntˈmɑːk, sɪnt-, (US) seɪntˈmɑːrk **-'s** -s
St. Martin sᵊntˈmɑː.tɪn, sɪnt-, (US) seɪntˈmɑːr.tᵊn **-'s** -z
St. Mary sᵊntˈmeə.ri, sɪnt-, (US) seɪntˈmer.i **-'s** -z
St. Mary Axe sᵊntˌmeə.riˈæks, sɪnt-, (US) seɪntˌmer.iˈ-

> Note: The old form /ˌsɪm.ᵊr.iˈæks/ is used in Gilbert and Sullivan's opera 'The Sorcerer'.

St. Marylebone sᵊntˈmær.ᵊl.ə.bən, sɪnt-, -ɪ.lə-, (US) seɪntˈmer.ᵊl.ə.boʊn
St. Mary-le-Bow sᵊntˌmeə.ri.ləˈbəʊ, sɪnt-, (US) seɪntˌmer.i.ləˈboʊ
St. Matthew sᵊntˈmæθ.juː, sɪnt-, (US) seɪnt-
St. Mawes sᵊntˈmɔːz, sɪnt-, (US) seɪntˈmɑːz, -ˈmɔːz
St. Michael sᵊntˈmaɪ.kᵊl, sɪnt-, (US) seɪnt- **-'s** -z
St. Moritz ˌsæn.mᵊrˈɪts, ˌsæm-; sᵊntˈmɒr.ɪts, sɪnt-, (US) ˌsæn.məˈrɪts, ˌseɪnt-, -mɔːˈ-
St. Neots sᵊntˈniː.əts, sɪnt-, -niːts, (US) seɪnt-
St. Nicholas sᵊntˈnɪk.ᵊl.əs, sɪnt-, ˈ-ləs, (US) seɪnt-
stoat stəʊt, (US) stoʊt **-s** -s
Stobart ˈstəʊ.bɑːt, (US) ˈstoʊ.bɑːrt
stochastic stɒkˈæs.tɪk, stəˈkæs-, (US) stoʊˈkæs-, stə-
stock stɒk, (US) stɑːk **-s** -s **-ing** -ɪŋ **-ed** -t **ˈstock ˌcar; ˈstock ˌcube; ˈstock exˌchange; ˈstock ˌmarket**
stockad|e stɒkˈeɪd, (US) stɑːˈkeɪd **-es** -z **-ing** -ɪŋ **-ed** -ɪd
stockbreed|er ˈstɒkˌbriː.d|əʳ, (US) ˈstɑːkˌbriː.d|ɚ **-ers** -əz, (US) -ɚz **-ing** -ɪŋ
Stockbridge ˈstɒk.brɪdʒ, (US) ˈstɑːk-
stockbrok|er ˈstɒkˌbrəʊ.k|əʳ, (US) ˈstɑːkˌbroʊ.k|ɚ **-ers** -əʳz, (US) -ɚz **-ing** -ɪŋ **ˈstockbroker ˌbelt**
stockfish ˈstɒk.fɪʃ, (US) ˈstɑːk-
Stockhausen ˈstɒkˌhaʊ.zᵊn; *as if German:* ˈʃtɒk-; (US) ˈstɑːk-
stockholder ˈstɒkˌhəʊl.dəʳ, (US) ˈstɑːkˌhoʊl.dɚ **-s** -z
Stockholm ˈstɒk.həʊm, (US) ˈstɑːk.hoʊlm, -hoʊm
stockinet(te) ˌstɒk.ɪˈnet, (US) ˌstɑː.kɪˈ-
stocking ˈstɒk.ɪŋ, (US) ˈstɑː.kɪŋ **-s** -z **-ed** -d **ˈstocking ˌcap; ˈstocking ˌfiller; ˈstocking ˌstitch; in one's ˌstocking/ed ˈfeet**
stock-in-trade ˌstɒk.ɪnˈtreɪd, (US) ˌstɑːk-
stockist ˈstɒk.ɪst, (US) ˈstɑː.kɪst **-s** -s
stockjobb|er ˈstɒkˌdʒɒb|.əʳ, (US) ˈstɑːkˌdʒɑː.b|ɚ **-ers** -əz, (US) -ɚz **-ing** -ɪŋ
stock|man, S~ ˈstɒk.mən, (US) ˈstɑːk- **-men** -men, -mən
stockpil|e ˈstɒk.paɪl, (US) ˈstɑːk- **-es** -z **-ing** -ɪŋ **-ed** -d
Stockport ˈstɒk.pɔːt, (US) ˈstɑːk.pɔːrt
stockpot ˈstɒk.pɒt, (US) ˈstɑːk.pɑːt **-s** -s
stockroom ˈstɒk.rʊm, -ruːm, (US) ˈstɑːk.ruːm, -rʊm **-s** -z
Stocksbridge ˈstɒks.brɪdʒ, (US) ˈstɑːks-
stock-still ˌstɒkˈstɪl, (US) ˌstɑːk-
stocktaking ˈstɒkˌteɪ.kɪŋ, (US) ˈstɑːk-
Stockton ˈstɒk.tən, (US) ˈstɑːk-
Stockton-on-Tees ˌstɒk.tən.ɒnˈtiːz, (US) ˌstɑːk.tən.ɑːnˈ-
Stockwell ˈstɒk.wel, -wəl, (US) ˈstɑːk-
stock|y ˈstɒk|.i, (US) ˈstɑː.k|i **-ier** -i.əʳ, (US) -i.ɚ **-iest** -i.ɪst, -i.əst **-iness** -ɪ.nəs, -ɪ.nɪs **-ily** -ᵊl.i, -ɪ.li
stockyard ˈstɒk.jɑːd, (US) ˈstɑːk.jɑːrd **-s** -z
Stoddard ˈstɒd.əd, -ɑːd, (US) ˈstɑː.dɚd
Stoddart ˈstɒd.ət, -ɑːt, (US) ˈstɑː.dɚt
stodg|e stɒdʒ, (US) stɑːdʒ **-es** -ɪz **-ing** -ɪŋ **-ed** -d **-y** -i **-ier** -i.əʳ, (US) -i.ɚ **-iest** -i.ɪst, -i.əst **-iness** -ɪ.nəs, -ɪ.nɪs
stoep stuːp **-s** -s
Stogumber *in Somerset:* stəʊˈgʌm.bəʳ; ˈstɒg.əm-, (US) stoʊˈgʌm.bɚ; (US) ˈstɑː.gəm- *character in Shaw's 'Saint Joan':* ˈstɒg.əm.bəʳ, (US) ˈstɑː.gəm.bɚ, ˈstɔː-
Stogursey stəʊˈgɜː.zi, (US) stoʊˈgɝː-
stoic, S~ ˈstəʊ.ɪk, (US) ˈstoʊ- **-s** -s **-al** -ᵊl **-ally** -ᵊl.i, -li
stoicism, S~ ˈstəʊ.ɪ.sɪ.zᵊm, ˈ-ə-, (US) ˈstoʊ.ɪ-
stok|e, S~ stəʊk, (US) stoʊk **-es** -s **-ing** -ɪŋ **-ed** -t **-er/s** -əʳ/z, (US) -ɚ/z
Stoke Courcy stəʊˈgɜː.zi, (US) stoʊˈgɝː-
Stoke d'Abernon ˌstəʊkˈdæb.ᵊn.ən, (US) ˌstoʊkˈdæb.ɚ.nən
stokehold ˈstəʊk.həʊld, (US) ˈstoʊk.hoʊld **-s** -z
stokehole ˈstəʊk.həʊl, (US) ˈstoʊk.hoʊl **-s** -z
Stoke Mandeville ˌstəʊkˈmæn.də.vɪl, ˈ-dɪ-, (US) ˌstoʊk-
Stoke on Trent ˌstəʊk.ɒnˈtrent, (US) ˌstoʊk.ɑːnˈ-
Stoke Poges ˌstəʊkˈpəʊ.dʒɪz, (US) ˌstoʊkˈpoʊ-
stoker, S~ ˈstəʊ.kəʳ, (US) ˈstoʊ.kɚ **-s** -z
STOL stɒl, ˈes.tɒl, (US) stɑːl, ˈes.tɑːl
St. Olaves, St. Olave's sᵊntˈɒl.ɪvz, sɪnt-, -əvz, (US) seɪntˈɑː.lɪvz, -ləvz
stole, S~ stəʊl, (US) stoʊl **-s** -z
stol|e (from **steal**) stəʊl, (US) stoʊl **-en** -ən
stolid ˈstɒl.ɪd, (US) ˈstɑː.lɪd **-est** -ɪst, -əst **-ly** -li
stolidity stɒlˈɪd.ə.ti, stəˈlɪd-, -ɪ.ti, (US) stəˈlɪd.ə.t̬i
Stoll stəʊl, stɒl, (US) stoʊl, stɑːl
stollen ˈstɒl.ən; *as if German:* ˈʃtɒl-; (US) ˈstoʊ.lən; *as if German:* (US) ˈʃtoʊ- **-s** -z
stolon ˈstəʊ.lɒn, -lən, (US) ˈstoʊ.lɑːn, -lən **-s** -z
stoma ˈstəʊ.mə, (US) ˈstoʊ- **-s** -z **-ta** -tə
stomach ˈstʌm.ək **-s** -s **-ing** -ɪŋ **-ed** -t **ˈstomach ˌpump**
stomachache ˈstʌm.ək.eɪk **-s** -s
stomacher ˈstʌm.ə.kəʳ, (US) -kɚ **-s** -z
stomachic stəʊˈmæk.ɪk, stɒmˈæk-; ˈstʌm.ə.kɪk, (US) stəˈmæk.ɪk
stomati|tis ˌstəʊ.məˈtaɪ|.tɪs, ˌstɒm.əˈ-, -təs, (US) ˌstoʊ.məˈtaɪ|.t̬ɪs, ˌstɑː-, -t̬əs **-tides** -tɪ.diːz **-tises** -tɪ.siːz, -tɪ.ziːz
stomatoscope stəʊˈmæt.ə.skəʊp, stɒmˈæt-, (US) stoʊˈmæt̬.ə.skoʊp, stɑː- **-s** -s
stomp stɒmp, (US) stɑːmp **-s** -s **-ing** -ɪŋ **-ed** -t
ston|e, S~ stəʊn, (US) stoʊn **-es** -z **-ing** -ɪŋ **-ed** -d **-y** -i **ˈStone ˌAge; kill ˌtwo ˌbirds with ˌone ˈstone; leave ˌno ˌstone unˈturned; a ˈstone's ˌthrow; a ˌstone's ˈthrow**
stone-blind ˌstəʊnˈblaɪnd, ˌstəʊm-, (US) ˌstoʊn- **-ness** -nəs, -nɪs
stonechat ˈstəʊn.tʃæt, (US) ˈstoʊn- **-s** -s
stone-cold ˌstəʊnˈkəʊld, ˌstəʊŋ-, (US) ˌstoʊnˈkoʊld *stress shift, see compound:* **ˌstone-cold ˈsober**
stonecrop ˈstəʊn.krɒp, ˈstəʊŋ-, (US) ˈstoʊn.krɑːp **-s** -s
stonecutter ˈstəʊnˌkʌt.əʳ, ˈstəʊŋ-, (US) ˈstoʊnˌkʌt̬.ɚ **-s** -z
stone-dead ˌstəʊnˈded, (US) ˌstoʊn-
stone-deaf ˌstəʊnˈdef, (US) ˌstoʊn- **-ness** -nəs, -nɪs
stonefish ˈstəʊn.fɪʃ, (US) ˈstoʊn- **-es** -ɪz
stoneground ˌstəʊnˈgraʊnd, ˌstəʊŋ-, (US) ˌstoʊn-
Stonehaven ˈstəʊnˌheɪ.vᵊn, (US) ˈstoʊn-
Stonehenge ˌstəʊnˈhendʒ, (US) ˈstoʊn.hendʒ
Stonehouse ˈstəʊn.haʊs, (US) ˈstoʊn-
stonemason ˈstəʊnˌmeɪ.sᵊn, ˈstəʊm-, (US) ˈstoʊn- **-s** -z
stonewall, S~ ˌstəʊnˈwɔːl, (US) ˈstoʊn- **-s** -z **-ing** -ɪŋ **-ed** -d **-er/s** -əʳ/z, (US) -ɚ/z
stoneware ˈstəʊn.weəʳ, (US) ˈstoʊn.wer
stone-washed ˌstəʊnˈwɒʃt, (US) ˌstoʊnˈwɑːʃt *stress shift, British only:* **ˌstonewashed ˈjeans**
stonework ˈstəʊn.wɜːk, (US) ˈstoʊn.wɝːk

S

Stoney ˈstəʊ.ni, (US) ˈstoʊ-
stonkered ˈstɒŋ.kəd, (US) ˈstɑːŋ.kɚd
stonking ˈstɒŋ.kɪŋ, (US) ˈstɑːŋ- **-ly** -li
Stonor ˈstəʊ.nəʳ, ˈstɒn.əʳ, (US) ˈstoʊ.nɚ, ˈstɑː.nɚ
ston|y ˈstəʊ.n|i, (US) ˈstoʊ- **-ier** -i.əʳ, (US) -i.ɚ **-iest** -i.ɪst, -i.əst **-ily** -ᵊl.i, -ɪ.li **-iness** -ɪ.nəs, -ɪ.nɪs ˌ**stony** ˈ**broke**
stony-hearted ˌstəʊ.niˈhɑː.tɪd, (US) ˈstoʊ.niˌhɑːr.t̬ɪd **-ness** -nəs, -nɪs
Stony Stratford ˌstəʊ.niˈstræt.fəd, (US) ˌstoʊ.niˈstræt.fɚd
stood (from **stand**) stʊd
stoog|e stuːdʒ **-es** -ɪz **-ing** -ɪŋ **-ed** -d
stook stuːk, stʊk **-s** -s
stool stuːl **-s** -z ˈ**stool** ˌ**pigeon**; ˌ**fall be**ˌ**tween two** ˈ**stools**
stoop stuːp **-s** -s **-ing** -ɪŋ **-ed** -t **-er/s** -əʳ/z, (US) -ɚ/z
stop stɒp, (US) stɑːp **-s** -s **-ping** -ɪŋ **-ped** -t **-per/s** -əʳ/z, (US) -ɚ/z ˈ**stop** ˌ**volley**
stop-and-go ˌstɒp.ənˈgəʊ, (US) ˌstɑːp.ənˈgoʊ
stopcock ˈstɒp.kɒk, (US) ˈstɑːp.kɑːk **-s** -s
Stopes stəʊps, (US) stoʊps
Stopford ˈstɒp.fəd, (US) ˈstɑːp.fɚd
stopgap ˈstɒp.gæp, (US) ˈstɑːp- **-s** -s
stop-go ˌstɒpˈgəʊ, (US) ˌstɑːpˈgoʊ
stoplight ˈstɒp.laɪt, (US) ˈstɑːp- **-s** -s
stopover ˈstɒpˌəʊ.vəʳ, (US) ˈstɑːpˌoʊ.vɚ **-s** -z
stoppag|e ˈstɒp.ɪdʒ, (US) ˈstɑː.pɪdʒ **-es** -ɪz
Stoppard ˈstɒp.ɑːd, -əd, (US) ˈstɑː.pɚd
stopper ˈstɒp.əʳ, (US) ˈstɑː.pɚ **-s** -z **-ing** -ɪŋ **-ed** -d
stop-press ˌstɒpˈpres, (US) ˌstɑːp-
stopwatch ˈstɒp.wɒtʃ, (US) ˈstɑːp.wɑːtʃ, -wɔːtʃ **-es** -ɪz
storage ˈstɔː.rɪdʒ, (US) ˈstɔːr.ɪdʒ ˈ**storage** ˌ**heater**
stor|e stɔːʳ, (US) stɔːr **-es** -z **-ing** -ɪŋ **-ed** -d **-able** -ə.bᵊl ˈ**store** ˌ**brand**; ˈ**store de**ˌ**tective**; ˌ**store de**ˈ**tective**
store-bought ˈstɔː.bɔːt, (US) ˈstɔːr.bɑːt
storefront ˈstɔː.frʌnt, (US) ˈstɔːr- **-s** -s
storehou|se ˈstɔː.haʊ|s, (US) ˈstɔːr- **-ses** -zɪz
storekeep|er ˈstɔːˌkiː.p|əʳ, (US) ˈstɔːrˌkiː.p|ɚ **-ers** -əz, (US) -ɚz **-ing** -ɪŋ
storeroom ˈstɔː.rʊm, -ruːm, (US) ˈstɔːr.ruːm, -rʊm **-s** -z
storey, S~ ˈstɔː.ri, (US) ˈstɔːr.i **-s** -z **-ed** -d
storiated ˈstɔː.ri.eɪ.tɪd, (US) ˈstɔːr.i.eɪ.t̬ɪd
stork stɔːk, (US) stɔːrk **-s** -s
storm, S~ stɔːm, (US) stɔːrm **-s** -z **-ing** -ɪŋ **-ed** -d ˈ**storm** ˌ**cloud**; ˈ**storm** ˌ**lantern**; ˈ**storm** ˌ**petrel**; ˈ**storm** ˌ**trooper**; ˈ**storm** ˌ**window**; **a** ˌ**storm in a** ˈ**teacup**
stormbound ˈstɔːm.baʊnd, (US) ˈstɔːrm-
Stormont ˈstɔː.mɒnt, -mənt, (US) ˈstɔːr.mɑːnt, -mənt
Stormonth ˈstɔː.mənθ, -mʌnθ, (US) ˈstɔːr-
stormproof ˈstɔːm.pruːf, (US) ˈstɔːrm-
storm|y ˈstɔː.m|i, (US) ˈstɔːr- **-ier** -i.əʳ, (US) -i.ɚ **-iest** -i.ɪst, -i.əst **-ily** -ᵊl.i, -ɪ.li **-iness** -ɪ.nəs, -ɪ.nɪs
Stornoway ˈstɔː.nə.weɪ, (US) ˈstɔːr-
Storr stɔːʳ, (US) stɔːr **-s** -z
Storrington ˈstɒr.ɪŋ.tən, (US) ˈstɔːr-
Stort stɔːt, (US) stɔːrt
Stortford ˈstɔː.t.fəd, ˈstɔː-, (US) ˈstɔːrt.fɚd, ˈstɔːr-
Storthing ˈstɔː.tɪŋ, (US) ˈstɔːr.t̬ɪŋ
stor|y, S~ ˈstɔː.r|i, (US) ˈstɔːr|.i **-ies** -iz **-ied** -id
storyboard ˈstɔː.ri.bɔːd, (US) ˈstɔːr.i.bɔːrd **-s** -z
storybook ˈstɔː.ri.bʊk, (US) ˈstɔːr.i- **-s** -s
storyline ˈstɔː.ri.laɪn, (US) ˈstɔːr.i- **-s** -z
storytell|er ˈstɔː.riˌtel|.əʳ, (US) ˈstɔːr.iˌtel|.ɚ **-ers** -əʳz, (US) -ɚz **-ing** -ɪŋ
St. Osyth sᵊntˈəʊ.zɪθ, sɪnt-, -sɪθ, (US) seɪntˈoʊ-
Stotfold ˈstɒt.fəʊld, (US) ˈstɑːt.foʊld
Stothard ˈstɒð.əd, (US) ˈstɑː.ðɚd
Stoughton *in West Sussex, Leicestershire and US:* ˈstəʊ.tᵊn, (US) ˈstoʊ- *in Somerset:* ˈstɔː.tᵊn, (US) ˈstɔː-, ˈstɑː- *in Surrey:* ˈstaʊ.tᵊn *surname:* ˈstɔː.tᵊn, ˈstaʊ-, ˈstəʊ-, (US) ˈstɔː-, ˈstɑː-, ˈstaʊ-, ˈstoʊ-

> Note: /ˈstəʊ.tᵊn/ (US) /ˈstoʊ-/ in **Hodder & Stoughton**, the publishers.

stoup stuːp **-s** -s
Stour *in Suffolk, Essex:* stʊəʳ, (US) stʊr *in Kent:* stʊəʳ, ˈstaʊ.əʳ, (US) stʊr, ˈstaʊ.ɚ *in Hampshire:* ˈstaʊ.əʳ, stʊəʳ, (US) ˈstaʊ.ɚ, stʊr *in Warwickshire, Hereford & Worcestershire, and Oxfordshire:* ˈstaʊ.əʳ, ˈstəʊ.əʳ, (US) ˈstaʊ.ɚ, ˈstoʊ.ɚ *in Dorset:* ˈstaʊ.əʳ, (US) ˈstaʊ.ɚ
Stourbridge *in West Midlands:* ˈstaʊ.ə.brɪdʒ, ˈstəʊ.ə-, (US) ˈstaʊ.ɚ-, ˈstoʊ.ɚ- *Common in Cambridge:* ˈstaʊ.ə.brɪdʒ, (US) ˈstaʊ.ɚ-
Stourhead ˈstɔː.hed, ˈstaʊ.ə-, (US) ˈstɔːr-, ˈstaʊ.ɚ-
Stourminster ˈstaʊ.əˌmɪnt.stəʳ, ˈstɜː-, ˈstʊə-, (US) ˈstaʊr.mɪn.stɚ-, ˈstɝː-, ˈstʊr-
Stourmouth ˈstaʊ.ə.maʊθ, ˈstʊə-, (US) ˈstaʊ.ɚ-, ˈstʊr-
Stourport ˈstaʊ.ə.pɔːt, ˈstʊə-, (US) ˈstaʊ.ɚ.pɔːrt, ˈstʊr-
Stourton *surname:* ˈstɜː.tᵊn, (US) ˈstɝː- *in Hereford & Worcestershire:* ˈstɔː.tᵊn, (US) ˈstɔːr- *in Wiltshire:* ˈstɜː.tᵊn, ˈstɔː-, (US) ˈstɝː-, ˈstɔːr-
stout, S~ staʊt **-s** -s **-er** -əʳ, (US) ˈstaʊ.t̬ɚ **-est** -ɪst, -əst, (US) ˈstaʊ.t̬ɪst, -t̬əst **-ly** -li **-ness** -nəs, -nɪs
stout-hearted ˌstaʊtˈhɑː.tɪd, (US) -ˈhɑːr.t̬ɪd **-ly** -li **-ness** -nəs, -nɪs
stoutish ˈstaʊ.tɪʃ, (US) -t̬ɪʃ
stove stəʊv, (US) stoʊv **-s** -z
stovepipe ˈstəʊv.paɪp, (US) ˈstoʊv- **-s** -s
stovetop ˈstəʊv.tɒp, (US) ˈstoʊv.tɑːp **-s** -s
stow, S~ stəʊ, (US) stoʊ **-s** -z **-ing** -ɪŋ **-ed** -d **-age** -ɪdʒ
stowaway ˈstəʊ.əˌweɪ, (US) ˈstoʊ- **-s** -z
Stowe stəʊ, (US) stoʊ
Stowers staʊ.əz, (US) staʊ.ɚz
Stowey ˈstəʊ.i, (US) ˈstoʊ-
Stowmarket ˈstəʊˌmɑː.kɪt, (US) ˈstoʊˌmɑːr-
Stow-on-the-Wold ˌstəʊ.ɒn.ðəˈwəʊld, (US) ˌstoʊ.ɑːn.ðəˈwoʊld
St. Pancras sᵊntˈpæŋ.krəs, sɪnt-, sᵊm-, (US) seɪnt-, -ˈpæn-
St. Patrick sᵊntˈpæt.rɪk, sɪnt-, sᵊm-, (US) seɪnt- **St.** ˈ**Patrick's** ˌ**Day**
St. Paul sᵊntˈpɔːl, sɪnt-, sᵊm-, (US) seɪntˈpɑːl, -ˈpɔːl **-'s** -z
St. Peter sᵊntˈpiː.təʳ, sɪnt-, sᵊm-, (US) seɪntˈpiː.t̬ɚ **-'s** -z
St. Petersburg sᵊntˈpiː.təz.bɜːg, sɪnt-, sᵊm-, (US) seɪntˈpiː.t̬ɚz.bɝːg
Strabane strəˈbæn
strabismus strəˈbɪz.məs, stræbˈɪz-, (US) strəˈbɪz-
Strabo ˈstreɪ.bəʊ, (US) -boʊ
Strabolgi strəˈbəʊ.gi, (US) -ˈboʊ-
Strachan strɔːn; ˈstræk.ən, (US) strɑːn, strɔːn; (US) ˈstræk.ən
Strachey ˈstreɪ.tʃi, (US) -ki, -tʃi
Strad stræd **-s** -z
Strada® ˈstrɑː.də **-s** -z
straddl|e ˈstræd.ᵊl **-es** -z **-ing** -ɪŋ, ˈstræd.lɪŋ **-ed** -d
Stradivari ˌstræd.ɪˈvɑː.ri, -əˈ-, (US) ˌstrɑː.diˈvɑːr.i **-s** -z
Stradivarius ˌstræd.ɪˈveə.ri.əs, -əˈ-, -ˈvɑː-, (US) -əˈver.i- **-es** -ɪz
straf|e streɪf, strɑːf, (US) streɪf **-es** -s **-ing/s** -ɪŋ/z **-ed** -t
Strafford ˈstræf.əd, (US) -ɚd
straggl|e ˈstræg.ᵊl **-es** -z **-ing** -ɪŋ, ˈstræg.lɪŋ **-ed** -d **-er/s** -əʳ/z, ˈstræg.ləʳ/z, ˈ-ᵊl.ɚ/z, (US) ˈ-lɚ/z
straggl|y ˈstræg.ᵊl|.i, ˈ-l|i **-iness** -ɪ.nəs, -ɪ.nɪs
Strahan strɔːn, strɑːn
straight streɪt **-er** -əʳ, (US) ˈstreɪ.t̬ɚ **-est** -ɪst, -əst, (US) ˈstreɪ.t̬ɪst, -t̬əst **-ness** -nəs, -nɪs ˌ**straight** ˈ**face**; ˌ**straight and** ˈ**narrow**
straightaway adv ˌstreɪt.əˈweɪ, (US) ˌstreɪt̬-
straightaway n ˈstreɪt.ə.weɪ, (US) ˈstreɪt̬- **-s** -z
straightedg|e ˈstreɪt.edʒ, (US) ˈstreɪt̬- **-es** -ɪz
straighten ˈstreɪ.tᵊn **-s** -z **-ing** -ɪŋ, ˈstreɪt.nɪŋ **-ed** -d
straight-|faced ˌstreɪtˈfeɪst

-facedly -ˈfeɪ.sɪd.li *stress shift:* **ˌstraight-faced ˈspeaker**
straightforward ˌstreɪtˈfɔː.wəd, (US) -ˈfɔːr.wɚd **-ly** -li **-ness** -nəs, -nɪs
straightjacket ˈstreɪtˌdʒæk.ɪt **-s** -s **-ing** -ɪŋ **-ed** -ɪd
straightlaced ˌstreɪtˈleɪst, (US) ˈ-- **-ly** -ˈleɪ.sɪd.li **-ness** -nəs, -nɪs *stress shift, British only:* **ˌstraightlaced ˈteacher**
straightway ˈstreɪt.weɪ
strain, S~ streɪn **-s** -z **-ing** -ɪŋ **-ed** -d **-er/s** -əʳ/z, (US) -ɚ/z
strait, S~ streɪt **-s** -s **-ened** -ənd
straitjacket ˈstreɪtˌdʒæk.ɪt **-s** -s **-ing** -ɪŋ **-ed** -ɪd
straitlaced ˌstreɪtˈleɪst, (US) ˈ-- **-ly** -ˈleɪ.sɪd.li **-ness** -nəs, -nɪs *stress shift, British only:* **ˌstraitlaced ˈteacher**
Straker ˈstreɪ.kəʳ, (US) -kɚ
strand, S~ strænd **-s** -z **-ing** -ɪŋ **-ed** -ɪd
Strang stræŋ
strang|e, S~ streɪndʒ **-er** -əʳ, (US) -ɚ **-est** -ɪst, -əst **-ely** -li **-eness** -nəs, -nɪs
stranger ˈstreɪn.dʒəʳ, (US) -dʒɚ **-s** -z
Strangeways ˈstreɪndʒ.weɪz
Strangford ˈstræŋ.fəd, (US) -fɚd
strangl|e ˈstræŋ.gəl **-es** -z **-ing** -ɪŋ, ˈstræŋ.glɪŋ **-ed** -d **-er/s** -əʳ/z, (US) -ɚ/z
stranglehold ˈstræŋ.gəl.həʊld, (US) -hoʊld **-s** -z
strangu|late ˈstræŋ.gjə|.leɪt, -gjʊ- **-lates** -leɪts **-lating** -leɪ.tɪŋ, (US) -leɪ.t̬ɪŋ **-lated** -leɪ.tɪd, (US) -leɪ.t̬ɪd
strangulation ˌstræŋ.gjəˈleɪ.ʃən, -gjʊˈ- **-s** -z
Strangways ˈstræŋ.weɪz
Stranraer strænˈrɑːʳ, strən-, (US) -ˈrɑːr
strap stræp **-s** -s **-ping** -ɪŋ **-ped** -t **-per/s** -əʳ/z, (US) -ɚ/z **-py** -i
strap|hang ˈstræp|.hæŋ **-hangs** -hæŋz **-hanging** -ˌhæŋ.ɪŋ **-hung** -hʌŋ **-hanger/s** -ˌhæŋ.əʳ/z, (US) -ɚ/z
strapless ˈstræp.ləs, -lɪs
Strasb(o)urg ˈstræz.bɜːg, -bʊəg, -bɔːg, (US) ˈstrɑːs.bʊrg, ˈstrɑːz-; (US) ˈstræs.bɝːg
strata (plural of **stratum**) ˈstrɑː.tə, ˈstreɪ-, (US) ˈstreɪ.t̬ə, ˈstræt̬.ə
stratagem ˈstræt.ə.dʒəm, ˈ-ɪ-, -dʒɪm, -dʒem, (US) ˈstræt̬.ə.dʒəm **-s** -z
strategic strəˈtiː.dʒɪk, strætˈiː-, (US) strəˈtiː- **-al** -əl **-ally** -əl.i, -li **Straˌtegic Deˈfence Iˌnitiative**
strategist ˈstræt.ə.dʒɪst, ˈ-ɪ-, (US) ˈstræt̬.ə- **-s** -s
strateg|y ˈstræt.ə.dʒ|i, ˈ-ɪ-, (US) ˈstræt̬.ə- **-ies** -iz
Stratford ˈstræt.fəd, (US) -fɚd
Stratford-atte-Bowe ˌstræt.fəd.æt.ɪˈbəʊ, -ˈbəʊ.i; -ˌæt.əˈbəʊ.ə, (US) -fɚdˌæt̬.əˈboʊ
Stratford-upon-Avon ˌstræt.fəd.əˌpɒnˈeɪ.vən, (US) -fɚd.ə.pɑːnˈ-, -vɑːn
strath stræθ **-s** -s
Strathaven ˈstreɪ.vən
Strathavon stræθˈɑːn
Strathclyde stræθˈklaɪd *stress shift:* **ˌStrathclyde ˈcampus**
Strathcona stræθˈkəʊ.nə, (US) -ˈkoʊ-
Strathearn stræθˈɜːn, (US) -ˈɝːn
Strathmore stræθˈmɔːʳ, (US) -ˈmɔːr
strathspey, S~ stræθˈspeɪ **-s** -z
stratification ˌstræt.ɪ.fɪˈkeɪ.ʃən, ˌ-ə-, -fəˈ-, (US) ˌstræt̬.ə-
strati|fy ˈstræt.ɪ|.faɪ, ˈ-ə-, (US) ˈstræt̬.ɪ-, ˈ-ə- **-fies** -faɪz **-fying** -faɪ.ɪŋ **-fied** -faɪd
stratocruiser ˈstræt.əˌkruː.zəʳ, (US) ˈstræt̬.əˌkruː.zɚ **-s** -z
Straton ˈstræt.ən
stratosphere ˈstræt.əʊˌsfɪəʳ, (US) ˈstræt̬.ə.sfɪr **-s** -z
stratospheric ˌstræt.əʊˈsfer.ɪk, (US) ˌstræt̬.əˈsfɪr-, -ˈsfer-
Stratton ˈstræt.ən
strat|um ˈstrɑː.t|əm, ˈstreɪ-, (US) ˈstreɪ.t̬|əm, ˈstræt̬|.əm **-a** -ə
stratus ˈstreɪ.təs, ˈstrɑː-, (US) ˈstreɪ.t̬əs, ˈstræt̬.əs
Straus(s) straʊs; *as if German:* ʃtraʊs
Stravinsky strəˈvɪnt.ski
straw, S~ strɔː, (US) strɑː, strɔː **-s** -z **-y** -i **ˌstraw ˈpoll** (US) **ˈstraw ˌpoll; ˌstraw ˈvote** (US) **ˈstraw ˌvote; ˌclutch at ˈstraws; the ˌstraw that ˌbreaks the ˌcamel's ˈback**
strawberr|y ˈstrɔː.bər|.i, -br|i, (US) ˈstrɑːˌber|.i, ˈstrɔː- **-ies** -iz **ˌstrawberry ˈblonde; ˈstrawberry ˌmark**
strawboard ˈstrɔː.bɔːd, (US) ˈstrɑː.bɔːrd, ˈstrɔː-
stray, S~ streɪ **-s** -z **-ing** -ɪŋ **-ed** -d
streak striːk **-s** -s **-ing** -ɪŋ **-ed** -t
streak|y ˈstriː.k|i **-ier** -i.əʳ, (US) -i.ɚ **-iest** -i.ɪst, -i.əst **-iness** -ɪ.nəs, -ɪ.nɪs **ˌstreaky ˈbacon**
stream striːm **-s** -z **-ing** -ɪŋ **-ed** -d
streamer ˈstriː.məʳ, (US) -mɚ **-s** -z
streamlet ˈstriːm.lət, -lɪt, (US) -lɪt **-s** -s
streamlin|e ˈstriːm.laɪn **-es** -z **-ing** -ɪŋ **-ed** -d
stream-of-consciousness ˌstriːm.əvˈkɒn.tʃəs.nəs, -nɪs, (US) -ˈkɑːnt.ʃəs-
Streatham ˈstret.əm, (US) ˈstret̬-
Streatley ˈstriːt.li
Streep striːp
street, S~ striːt **-s** -s **ˈstreet ˌcred; ˌstreet crediˈbility** (US) **ˈstreet crediˌbility; ˌstreet ˈtheatre/ ˈtheater** (US) **ˈstreet ˌtheatre/ ˌtheater; ˈstreet ˌvalue**
streetcar ˈstriːt.kɑːʳ, (US) -kɑːr **-s** -z
streetlight ˈstriːt.laɪt **-s** -s
streetwalk|er ˈstriːtˌwɔː.k|əʳ, (US) -ˌwɑː.k|ɚ, -ˌwɔː- **-ers** -əz, (US) -ɚz **-ing** -ɪŋ
streetwise ˈstriːt.waɪz
St. Regis səntˈriː.dʒɪs, sɪnt-, (US) seɪnt-
Streisand ˈstraɪ.zænd, -sənd, -sænd
strength streŋ*k*θ **-s** -s
strengthen ˈstreŋ*k*.θən **-s** -z **-ing** -ɪŋ, ˈstreŋ*k*θ.nɪŋ **-ed** -d **-er/s** -əʳ/z, ˈstreŋ*k*θ.nəʳ/z, (US) ˈstreŋ*k*.θən.ɚ/z, ˈstreŋ*k*θ.nɚ/z
strenuous ˈstren.ju.əs **-ly** -li **-ness** -nəs, -nɪs
strep strep **ˌstrep ˈthroat**
strepto|coccus ˌstrep.təʊ|ˈkɒk.əs, (US) -tə|ˈkɑː.kəs **-cocci** -ˈkɒk.saɪ, -aɪ, -iː, (US) -ˈkɑːk.saɪ, -aɪ **-coccal** -ˈkɒk.əl, (US) -ˈkɑː.kəl **-coccic** -ˈkɒk.ɪk, (US) -ˈkɑː.kɪk
streptomycin ˌstrep.təʊˈmaɪ.sɪn, (US) -təˈ-
stress stres **-es** -ɪz **-ing** -ɪŋ **-ed** -t
stressful ˈstres.fʊl, -fəl **-ly** -i **-ness** -nəs, -nɪs
stressless ˈstres.ləs, -lɪs **-ness** -nəs, -nɪs
stretch stretʃ **-es** -ɪz **-ing** -ɪŋ **-ed** -t **ˌstretch(ed) ˈlimo**
stretcher ˈstretʃ.əʳ, (US) -ɚ **-s** -z **-ing** -ɪŋ **-ed** -d
stretcher-bearer ˈstretʃ.əˌbeə.rəʳ, (US) -ɚˌber.ɚ **-s** -z
stretchmark ˈstretʃ.mɑːk, (US) -mɑːrk **-s** -s
stretch|y ˈstretʃ|.i **-ier** -i.əʳ, (US) -i.ɚ **-iest** -i.ɪst, -i.əst
Stretford ˈstret.fəd, (US) -fɚd
Strevens ˈstrev.ənz
strew struː **-s** -z **-ing** -ɪŋ **-ed** -d **-n** -n
strewth struːθ
stri|a ˈstraɪ|.ə **-ae** -iː
stri|ate v ˈstri|.eɪt **-ates** -eɪts **-ating** -eɪ.tɪŋ, (US) -eɪ.t̬ɪŋ **-ated** -eɪ.tɪd, (US) -eɪ.t̬ɪd **striˌated ˈmuscle**
striation straɪˈeɪ.ʃən **-s** -z
stricken (from **strike**) ˈstrɪk.ən
Strickland ˈstrɪk.lənd
strict strɪkt **-er** -əʳ, (US) -ɚ **-est** -ɪst, -əst **-ly** -li **-ness** -nəs, -nɪs
stricture ˈstrɪk.tʃəʳ, (US) -tʃɚ **-s** -z
strid|e straɪd **-es** -z **-ing** -ɪŋ **strode** strəʊd, (US) stroʊd **stridden** ˈstrɪd.ən
stridency ˈstraɪ.dənt.si
strident ˈstraɪ.dənt **-ly** -li
StrideRite® ˈstraɪd.raɪt
stridu|late ˈstrɪd.jə|.leɪt, -jʊ-, (US) ˈstrɪdʒ.ə-, ˈ-ʊ- **-lates** -leɪts **-lating** -leɪ.tɪŋ, (US) -leɪ.t̬ɪŋ **-lated** -leɪ.tɪd, (US) -leɪ.t̬ɪd **-lation/s** ˌ--ˈleɪ.ʃən/z
strife straɪf
strigil ˈstrɪdʒ.ɪl **-s** -z
strik|e straɪk **-es** -s **-ing/ly** -ɪŋ/li **struck** strʌk **stricken** ˈstrɪk.ən **striker/s** ˈstraɪ.kəʳ/z, (US) -kɚ/z **ˈstrike ˌpay; ˌstrike while the ˌiron's ˈhot**
strikebound ˈstraɪk.baʊnd
strikebreak|er ˈstraɪkˌbreɪ.k|əʳ, (US) -k|ɚ **-ers** -əz, (US) -ɚz **-ing** -ɪŋ
strikeout ˈstraɪ.kaʊt **-s** -s
strike-pay ˈstraɪk.peɪ
strim strɪm **-s** -z **-ming** -ɪŋ **-med** -d
Strimmer® ˈstrɪm.əʳ, (US) -ɚ

Strindberg ˈstrɪnd.bɜːg, ˈstrɪm-, (US) ˈstrɪnd.bɝːg

string strɪŋ **-s** -z **-ing** -ɪŋ **-ed** -d **strung** strʌŋ **stringer/s** ˈstrɪŋ.əʳ/z, (US) -ɚ/z ˌ**string** ˈ**bean**; ˌ**string quar**ˈ**tet**

stringency ˈstrɪn.dʒənt.si

stringendo strɪnˈdʒen.dəʊ, (US) -doʊ

stringent ˈstrɪn.dʒənt **-ly** -li

stringer, S~ ˈstrɪŋ.əʳ, (US) -ɚ

Stringfellow ˈstrɪŋˌfel.əʊ, (US) -oʊ

string-pull|ing ˈstrɪŋˌpʊl|.ɪŋ **-er/s** -əʳ/z, (US) -ɚ/z

string|y ˈstrɪŋ|.i **-ier** -i.əʳ, (US) -i.ɚ **-iest** -i.ɪst, -i.əst **-iness** -ɪ.nəs, -ɪ.nɪs

strip strɪp **-s** -s **-ping** -ɪŋ **-ped** -t **-per/s** -əʳ/z, (US) -ɚ/z ˌ**strip car**ˈ**toon**; ˈ**strip** ˌ**club**; ˈ**strip** ˌ**light**; ˌ**strip** ˈ**poker**

strip|e straɪp **-es** -s **-ing** -ɪŋ **-ed** -t **-(e)y** -i **-iness** -ɪ.nəs, -ɪ.nɪs

striplight ˈstrɪp.laɪt **-s** -s **-ing** -ɪŋ

stripling ˈstrɪp.lɪŋ **-s** -z

strippagram ˈstrɪp.ə.græm **-s** -z

strip-search ˌstrɪpˈsɜːtʃ, ˈ--, (US) ˈstrɪp.sɝːtʃ **-es** -ɪz **-ing** -ɪŋ **-ed** -t

striptease|e ˈstrɪp.tiːz, ˌ-ˈ- **-er/s** -əʳ/z, (US) -ɚ/z

striv|e straɪv **-es** -z **-ing/s** -ɪŋ/z **-ed** -d **strove** strəʊv, (US) stroʊv **striven** ˈstrɪv.ən **striver/s** ˈstraɪ.vəʳ/z, (US) -vɚ/z

strobe strəʊb, (US) stroʊb **-s** -z ˈ**strobe** ˌ**light**

stroboscope ˈstrəʊ.bə.skəʊp, ˈstrɒb.ə-, (US) ˈstroʊ.bə.skoʊp, ˈstrɑː- **-s** -s

stroboscopic ˌstrəʊ.bəˈskɒp.ɪk, ˌstrɒb.əˈ-, (US) ˌstroʊ.bəˈskɑː.pɪk, ˌstrɑː-

stroboscopy strəʊˈbɒs.kə.pi, strɒbˈɒs-, (US) strəˈbɑː.skə-

strode (from **stride**) strəʊd, (US) stroʊd

stroganoff ˈstrɒg.ə.nɒf, (US) ˈstrɔː.gə.nɔːf, ˈstroʊ- **-s** -s

strok|e strəʊk, (US) stroʊk **-es** -s **-ing** -ɪŋ **-ed** -t

strokeplay ˈstrəʊk.pleɪ, (US) ˈstroʊk-

stroll strəʊl, (US) stroʊl **-s** -z **-ing** -ɪŋ **-ed** -d **-er/s** -əʳ/z, (US) -ɚ/z

Stromberg ˈstrɒm.bɜːg, (US) ˈstrɑːm.bɝːg

Stromboli ˈstrɒm.bəl.i, -bʊ.li, -bəʊ-; strɒmˈbəʊ.li, (US) ˈstrɑːm.bə-, -ˈboʊ.li

Stromness ˈstrɒm.nes, ˈstrʌm-, (US) ˈstrɑːm-, ˈstrʌm-

St. Ronan səntˈrəʊ.nən, sɪnt-, (US) seɪntˈroʊ-

strong, S~ strɒŋ, (US) strɑːŋ, strɔːŋ **-er** -gəʳ, (US) -gɚ **-est** -gɪst, -gəst **-ly** -li **-ish** -ɪʃ ˌ**strong** ˈ**language**; ˈ**strong** ˌ**point**; ˈ**strong** ˌ**room**

strong-arm ˈstrɒŋ.ɑːm, (US) ˈstrɑːŋ.ɑːrm, ˈstrɔːŋ- **-s** -z **-ing** -ɪŋ **-ed** -d

strongbox ˈstrɒŋ.bɒks, (US) ˈstrɑːŋ.bɑːks, ˈstrɔːŋ- **-es** -ɪz

stronghold ˈstrɒŋ.həʊld, (US) ˈstrɑːŋ.hoʊld, ˈstrɔːŋ- **-s** -z

strong|man ˈstrɒŋ|.mæn, (US) ˈstrɑːŋ- **-men** -men

strong-minded ˌstrɒŋˈmaɪn.dɪd, (US) ˈstrɑːŋ-, ˈstrɔːŋ- **-ly** -li **-ness** -nəs, -nɪs *stress shift:* ˌ**strong-minded** ˈ**person**

strong-willed ˌstrɒŋˈwɪld **-ness** -nəs, -nɪs *stress shift:* ˌ**strong-willed** ˈ**child**

stronti|a ˈstrɒn.ti|.ə, -tʃi-, ˈ-tʃ|ə, -tj|ə, (US) ˈstrɑːnt.ʃi.|ə, ˈ-ʃ|ə **-an** -ən **-um** -əm

Strood struːd

strop strɒp, (US) strɑːp **-s** -s **-ping** -ɪŋ **-ped** -t

strophe ˈstrəʊ.fi, ˈstrɒf.i, (US) ˈstroʊ.fi **-s** -z

strophic ˈstrɒf.ɪk, ˈstrəʊ.fɪk, (US) ˈstrɑː.fɪk, ˈstroʊ-

stropp|y ˈstrɒp|.i, (US) ˈstrɑː.p|i **-ier** -i.əʳ, (US) -i.ɚ **-iest** -i.ɪst, -i.əst **-iness** -ɪ.nəs, -ɪ.nɪs

Stroud straʊd

> Note: As a surname, the pronunciation /struːd/ is sometimes heard.

strove (from **strive**) strəʊv, (US) stroʊv

strow strəʊ, (US) stroʊ **-s** -z **-ing** -ɪŋ **-ed** -d **-n** -n

struck (from **strike**) strʌk

structural ˈstrʌk.tʃər.əl **-ly** -i ˌ**structural engi**ˈ**neer**

structural|ism ˈstrʌk.tʃər.əl|.ɪ.zəm **-ist/s** -ɪst/s

structur|e ˈstrʌk.tʃəʳ, (US) -tʃɚ **-es** -z **-ing** -ɪŋ **-ed** -d

strudel ˈstruː.dəl; *as if German:* ˈʃtruː- **-s** -z

struggl|e ˈstrʌg.əl **-es** -z **-ing** -ɪŋ, ˈstrʌg.lɪŋ **-ed** -d **-er/s** -əʳ/z, ˈstrʌg.ləʳ/z, (US) ˈ-əl.ɚ/z, ˈ-lɚ/z

strum strʌm **-s** -z **-ming** -ɪŋ **-med** -d **-mer/s** -əʳ/z, (US) -ɚ/z

strumpet ˈstrʌm.pɪt **-s** -s

strung (from **string**) strʌŋ ˌ**strung** ˈ**out**

strung-up ˌstrʌŋˈʌp

strut strʌt **-s** -s **-ting** -ɪŋ, (US) ˈstrʌt̬.ɪŋ **-ted** -ɪd, (US) ˈstrʌt̬.ɪd

struth struːθ

Struthers ˈstrʌð.əz, (US) -ɚz

Strutt strʌt

Struwwelpeter ˌstruː.əlˈpiː.təʳ, ˈstruː.əlˌpiː-; ˌstruːlˈpiː-, ˈ-ˌ--, (US) ˈstruː.əlˌpiː.t̬ɚ

strychnine ˈstrɪk.niːn, -nɪn, (US) -naɪn, -nɪn, -niːn

St. Salvator's səntˌsælˈveɪ.təz, sɪnt-, (US) seɪntˈsæl.və.tɔːrz

St. Simon səntˈsaɪ.mən, sɪnt-, (US) seɪnt-

St. Swithin səntˈswɪð.ɪn, sɪnt-, (US) seɪnt-

St. Thomas səntˈtɒm.əs, sɪnt-, (US) seɪntˈtɑː.məs **-'s** -ɪz

St. Trinian's səntˈtrɪn.i.ənz

St. Tropez ˌsæn.trəʊˈpeɪ, (US) ˌsæn.trɔːˈpeɪ, -troʊˈ-

Stuart stʃʊət, stjʊət, ˈstʃuː.ət, ˈstjuː.ət, (US) ˈstuː.ɚt, ˈstjuː-, stʊrt **-s** -s

stub stʌb **-s** -z **-bing** -ɪŋ **-bed** -d

Stubbings ˈstʌb.ɪŋz

Stubbington ˈstʌb.ɪŋ.tən

stubbl|e ˈstʌb.əl **-y** -i, ˈstʌb.li

stubborn ˈstʌb.ən, (US) -ɚn **-er** -əʳ, (US) -ɚ **-est** -ɪst, -əst **-ly** -li **-ness** -nəs, -nɪs

Stubbs stʌbz

stubb|y ˈstʌb|.i **-ier** -i.əʳ, (US) -i.ɚ **-iest** -i.ɪst, -i.əst **-iness** -ɪ.nəs, -ɪ.nɪs **-ies** -iz

stucco ˈstʌk.əʊ, (US) -oʊ **-(e)s** -z **-ing** -ɪŋ **-ed** -d

stuck (from **stick**) stʌk

stuck-up ˌstʌkˈʌp

Stucley ˈstʃuː.kli, ˈstjuː-, (US) ˈstuː-, ˈstjuː-

stud stʌd **-s** -z **-ding** -ɪŋ **-ded** -ɪd ˌ**stud** ˈ**poker**

studding-sail ˈstʌd.ɪŋ.seɪl; *nautical pronunciation:* ˈstʌnt.səl **-s** -z

Studebaker ˈstjuː.dɪˌbeɪ.kəʳ, ˈstʃuː-, (US) ˈstuː.dəˌbeɪ.kɚ, ˈstjuː-

student ˈstjuː.dənt, ˈstʃuː-, (US) ˈstuː-, ˈstjuː- **-s** -s ˌ**student** ˈ**grant**; ˌ**student** ˈ**loan**; ˌ**student** ˈ**teacher**; ˌ**student** ˈ**union**

studentship ˈstjuː.dənt.ʃɪp, ˈstʃuː-, (US) ˈstuː-, ˈstjuː- **-s** -s

studio ˈstjuː.di.əʊ, ˈstʃuː-, (US) ˈstuː.di.oʊ, ˈstjuː- **-s** -z ˌ**studio** ˈ**flat** (US) ˈ**studio** ˌ**flat**

studious ˈstjuː.di.əs, ˈstʃuː-, (US) ˈstuː-, ˈstjuː- **-ly** -li **-ness** -nəs, -nɪs

Studley ˈstʌd.li

stud|y ˈstʌd|.i **-ies** -iz **-ying** -i.ɪŋ **-ied** -id

stuff stʌf **-s** -s **-ing** -ɪŋ **-ed** -t ˌ**stuffed** ˈ**shirt**

stuffing ˈstʌf.ɪŋ **-s** -z

stuff|y ˈstʌf|.i **-ier** -i.əʳ, (US) -i.ɚ **-iest** -i.ɪst, -i.əst **-iness** -ɪ.nəs, -ɪ.nɪs **-ily** -əl.i, -ɪ.li

stultification ˌstʌl.tɪ.fɪˈkeɪ.ʃən, -tə-, -fəˈ-, (US) -tə-

stulti|fy ˈstʌl.tɪ|.faɪ, -tə- **-fies** -faɪz **-fying** -ˌfaɪ.ɪŋ **-fied** -faɪd

stum stʌm

stumbl|e ˈstʌm.bəl **-es** -z **-ing** -ɪŋ, ˈstʌm.blɪŋ **-ed** -d **-er/s** -əʳ/z, ˈstʌm.bləʳ/z, (US) ˈ-bəl.ɚ/z, ˈ-blɚ/z ˈ**stumbling** ˌ**block**

stumm ʃtʊm

stump stʌmp **-s** -s **-ing** -ɪŋ **-ed** -t **-y** -i **-ier** -i.əʳ, (US) -i.ɚ **-iest** -i.ɪst, -i.st **-iness** -ɪ.nəs, -ɪ.nɪs

stun stʌn **-s** -z **-ning/ly** -ɪŋ/li **-ned** -d ˈ**stun** ˌ**gun**

stung (from **sting**) stʌŋ

stunk (from **stink**) stʌŋk

stunner ˈstʌn.əʳ, (US) -ɚ **-s** -z

stunt stʌnt **-s** -s **-ing** -ɪŋ, (US) ˈstʌn.t̬ɪŋ **-ed** -ɪd, (US) ˈstʌn.t̬ɪd

stunt|man ˈstʌnt|.mæn **-men** -men

stunt|woman ˈstʌnt|ˌwʊm.ən **-women** -ˌwɪm.ɪn

tupa ˈstuː.pə -s -z
tupe stjuːp, stʃuːp, (US) stuːp, stjuːp -s -s
tupefaction ˌstjuː.pɪˈfæk.ʃᵊn, ˌstʃuː-, (US) ˌstuː.pəˈ-, ˌstjuː-
tupe|fy ˈstjuː.pɪ|.faɪ, ˈstʃuː-, (US) ˈstuː.pə-, ˈstjuː- -fies -faɪz -fying/ly -ˌfaɪ.ɪŋ/li -fied -faɪd
tupendous stjuːˈpen.dəs, stʃuː-, (US) stuː-, stjuː- -ly -li -ness -nəs, -nɪs
tupid ˈstjuː.pɪd, ˈstʃuː-, (US) ˈstuː-, ˈstjuː- -er -əʳ, (US) -ɚ -est -ɪst, -əst -ly -li -ness -nəs, -nɪs
tupidit|y stjuːˈpɪd.ə.t|i, stʃuː-, -ɪ.t|i, (US) stuːˈpɪd.ə.ţ|i, stjuː- -ies -iz
tupor ˈstjuː.pəʳ, ˈstʃuː-, (US) ˈstuː.pɚ, ˈstjuː-
sturd|y ˈstɜː.d|i, (US) ˈstɝː- -ier -i.əʳ, (US) -i.ɚ -iest -i.ɪst, -i.əst -ily -ᵊl.i, -ɪ.li -iness -ɪ.nəs, -ɪ.nɪs
sturgeon, S~ ˈstɜː.dʒᵊn, (US) ˈstɝː- -s -z
Sturminster ˈstɜː.mɪnt.stəʳ, (US) ˈstɝː.mɪnt.stɚ
Sturm und Drang ˌʃtʊəm.ʊntˈdræŋ, ˌstʊərm-, (US) ˌʃtʊrm.ʊntˈdrɑːŋ
Sturtevant ˈstɜː.tɪ.vənt, -tə-, -vænt, (US) ˈstɝː.ţə-
stutt|er ˈstʌt|.əʳ, (US) ˈstʌţ|.ɚ -ers -əz, (US) -ɚz -ering -ᵊr.ɪŋ -ered -əd, (US) -ɚd -erer/s -ᵊr.əʳ/z, (US) -ɚ.ɚ/z
Stuttgart ˈʃtʊt.gɑːt, ˈstʊt-, (US) ˈstʌt.gɑːrt, ˈstʊt-, ˈʃtʊt-
Stuyvesant ˈstaɪ.vɪ.sənt, -və-, (US) -və-
St. Valentine sᵊntˈvæl.ᵊn.taɪn, (US) seɪnt- **St. ˈValentine's ˌDay**
St. Vincent sᵊntˈvɪnt.sᵊnt, sɪnt-, (US) seɪnt-
St. Vitus sᵊntˈvaɪ.təs, sɪnt-, (US) seɪntˈvaɪ.ţəs -'s -ɪz **St. ˌVitus's ˈdance** (US) **St. ˈVitus's ˌdance**
st|y st|aɪ -ies -aɪz
Styal ˈstaɪ.əl
stye staɪ -s -z
stygian, S~ ˈstɪdʒ.i.ən, (US) -i.ən, ˈ-ən
styl|e staɪl -es -z -ing -ɪŋ -ed -d
styleless ˈstaɪl.ləs, -lɪs -ly -li -ness -nəs, -nɪs
Styles staɪlz
stylet ˈstaɪ.lət, -lɪt, (US) -lɪt -s -s
stylish ˈstaɪ.lɪʃ -ly -li -ness -nəs, -nɪs
stylist ˈstaɪ.lɪst -s -s
stylistic staɪˈlɪs.tɪk -s -s -ally -ᵊl.i, -li
stylite ˈstaɪ.laɪt -s -s
Stylites staɪˈlaɪ.tiːz, (US) -ţiːz
stylization, -isa- ˌstaɪ.laɪˈzeɪ.ʃᵊn, -lɪˈ-, (US) -ləˈ-
styliz|e, -is|e ˈstaɪ.laɪz -es -ɪz -ing -ɪŋ -ed -d
stylograph ˈstaɪ.ləʊ.grɑːf, -græf, (US) -lə.græf -s -s
stylographic ˌstaɪ.ləʊˈgræf.ɪk, (US) -ləˈ-
styl|us ˈstaɪ.l|əs -uses -ə.sɪz -i -aɪ
stym|ie ˈstaɪ.m|i -ies -iz -ying -i.ɪŋ -ied -id
styptic ˈstɪp.tɪk **ˌstyptic ˈpencil**
styrax ˈstaɪə.ræks, (US) ˈstaɪ- -es -ɪz
Styrofoam® ˈstaɪə.rəʊ.fəʊm, (US) -rə.foʊm
Styron ˈstaɪə.rən
Styx stɪks
suable ˈsuː.ə.bᵊl, ˈsjuː-, (US) ˈsuː-
Suak|im ˈsuː.ɑː.k|ɪm, ˈswɑː.k|ɪm, (US) ˈswɑː.k|ɪm -in -ɪn
suasion ˈsweɪ.ʒᵊn
sua sponte ˌsuː.ɑːˈspɒn.teɪ, (US) ˌswɑːˈspɑːn.teɪ
suav|e swɑːv -er -əʳ, (US) -ɚ -est -ɪst, -əst -ely -li -eness -nəs, -nɪs
suavity ˈswɑː.və.ti, ˈsweɪ-, ˈswæv.ə-, -ɪ.ti, (US) ˈswɑː.və.ţi, ˈswæv.ə-
sub sʌb -s -z -bing -ɪŋ -bed -d
sub- sʌb
subacid sʌbˈæs.ɪd, ˌsʌb-
subacute ˌsʌb.əˈkjuːt
subalpine sʌbˈæl.paɪn, ˌsʌb-, (US) -paɪn, -pɪn
subaltern ˈsʌb.ᵊl.tən, (US) səbˈɔːl.tɚn, -ˈɑːl- -s -z
subaqua sʌbˈæk.wə, ˌsʌb-, (US) -ˈɑː.kwə, -ˈæk.wə
subarctic sʌbˈɑːk.tɪk, ˌsʌb-, (US) -ˈɑːrk-
Subaru® ˌsuː.bᵊrˈuː, ˈ---, (US) ˈsuː.bə.ruː -s -z
subatomic ˌsʌb.əˈtɒm.ɪk, (US) -ˈtɑː.mɪk **subatomic ˈparticles**
sub-bass ˌsʌbˈbeɪs, (US) ˈ-- -es -ɪz
Subbuteo® səˈbjuː.ti.əʊ, sʌbˈjuː-, -ˈuː-, (US) sʌbˈjuː.ţi.oʊ
subclass ˈsʌb.klɑːs, (US) -klæs -es -ɪz
subclassification sʌbˌklæs.ɪ.fɪˈkeɪ.ʃᵊn, ˌsʌb.klæs-, -ə-, -fəˈ-, (US) ˌsʌb.klæs- -s -z
subclassi|fy sʌbˈklæs.ɪ|.faɪ, ˌsʌb-, ˈ-ə- -fies -faɪz -fying -faɪ.ɪŋ -fied -faɪd
subclinical sʌbˈklɪn.ɪ.kᵊl, ˌsʌb-
subcommittee ˈsʌb.kəˌmɪt.i, ˌsʌb.kəˈmɪt.i, (US) -ˌmɪţ- -s -z
subcompact ˌsʌbˈkɒm.pækt, (US) -ˈkɑːm- -s -s
subconscious sʌbˈkɒn.tʃəs, ˌsʌb-, (US) -ˈkɑːnt.ʃəs -ly -li -ness -nəs, -nɪs
subcontinent sʌbˈkɒn.tɪ.nənt, ˌsʌb-, (US) ˈsʌbˌkɑːn.tᵊn.ənt, ˌsʌbˈkɑːn- -s -s
subcontinental ˌsʌb.kɒn.tɪˈnen.tᵊl, -təˈ-, (US) -kɑːn.tᵊnˈen.ţᵊl -ly -i
subcontract v ˌsʌb.kənˈtrækt, (US) sʌbˈkɑːn.trækt -s -s -ing -ɪŋ -ed -ɪd -or/s -əʳ/z, (US) -ɚ/z
subcontract n ˈsʌbˌkɒn.trækt, (US) -ˌkɑːn-, -ˈkɑːn- -s -s
subculture ˈsʌbˌkʌl.tʃəʳ, (US) -tʃɚ -s -z
subcutaneous ˌsʌb.kjuːˈteɪ.ni.əs
subdean sʌbˈdiːn, ˌsʌb- -s -z
subdivid|e ˌsʌb.dɪˈvaɪd, -dəˈ-, ˈ--ˌ- -es -z -ing -ɪŋ -ed -ɪd
subdivision ˌsʌb.dɪˈvɪʒ.ᵊn, -dəˈ-, ˈsʌb.dɪˌvɪʒ-, -dəˌ-, (US) ˌsʌb.dɪˈvɪʒ.ᵊn, ˈsʌb.dɪˌvɪʒ- -s -z
subdominant sʌbˈdɒm.ɪ.nənt, ˌsʌb-, (US) -ˈdɑː.mə- -s -s
subdu|e səbˈdʒuː, -ˈdjuː-, (US) -ˈduː, -ˈdjuː -es -z -ing -ɪŋ -ed -d -er/s -əʳ/z, (US) -ɚ/z -able -ə.bᵊl
subed|it sʌbˈed|.ɪt, ˌsʌb- -its -ɪts -iting -ɪ.tɪŋ, (US) -ɪ.ţɪŋ -ited -ɪ.tɪd, (US) -ɪ.ţɪd
subeditor sʌbˈed.ɪ.təʳ, ˈsʌbˌed-, (US) sʌbˈed.ɪ.ţɚ -s -z -ship/s -ʃɪp/s
subentr|y ˈsʌbˌen.tr|i, ˌ-ˈ-- -ies -iz
subfamil|y ˈsʌbˌfæm.ᵊl|.i, -ɪ.l|i, (US) -ᵊl|.i -ies -iz
subfusc ˈsʌb.fʌsk, -ˈ-
subglottal sʌbˈglɒt.ᵊl, (US) -ˈglɑː.ţᵊl
subgroup ˈsʌb.gruːp -s -s
subhead sʌbˈhed, ˌsʌb-, (US) ˈsʌb.hed -s -z
subheading ˈsʌbˌhed.ɪŋ, -ˈ--, (US) ˈsʌbˌhed- -s -z
subhuman sʌbˈhjuː.mən, ˌsʌb- -s -z
subito ˈsuː.bɪ.təʊ, ˈsʊb.ɪ-, (US) -ţoʊ
subjacency sʌbˈdʒeɪ.sᵊnt.si, səb-, (US) sʌb-
subjacent sʌbˈdʒeɪ.sᵊnt, səb-, (US) sʌb-
subject n, adj ˈsʌb.dʒɪkt, -dʒekt -s -s **ˈsubject ˌmatter**
subject v səbˈdʒekt, sʌb-; ˈsʌb.dʒekt, -dʒɪkt, (US) səbˈdʒekt -s -s -ing -ɪŋ -ed -ɪd
subjection səbˈdʒek.ʃᵊn
subjective səbˈdʒek.tɪv, sʌb-, (US) səb- -ly -li -ness -nəs, -nɪs
subjectivism səbˈdʒek.tɪ.vɪ.zᵊm, sʌb-, (US) səb-
subjectivity ˌsʌb.dʒekˈtɪv.ə.ti, -dʒɪk-, -ɪ.ti, (US) -ə.ţi
subjoin sʌbˈdʒɔɪn, ˌsʌb-, (US) səb- -s -z -ing -ɪŋ -ed -d
sub judice ˌsʌbˈdʒuː.dɪ.si, ˌsʊb-, -də-, -seɪ, (US) ˌsʌbˈdʒuː.də.si
subju|gate ˈsʌb.dʒə|.geɪt, -dʒʊ- -gates -geɪts -gating -geɪ.tɪŋ, (US) -geɪ.ţɪŋ -gated -geɪ.tɪd, (US) -geɪ.ţɪd -gator/s -geɪ.təʳ/z, (US) -geɪ.ţɚ/s
subjugation ˌsʌb.dʒəˈgeɪ.ʃᵊn, -dʒʊˈ-
subjunct ˈsʌb.dʒʌŋkt -s -s
subjunctive səbˈdʒʌŋk.tɪv -s -z
subleas|e n ˈsʌb.liːs -es -ɪz
subleas|e v sʌbˈliːs, ˌsʌb- -es -ɪz -ing -ɪŋ -ed -t
sublessee ˌsʌb.lesˈiː -s -z
sublessor ˌsʌb.lesˈɔːʳ, (US) -ˈɔːr; (US) sʌbˈles.ɔːr -s -z
suble|t sʌbˈle|t, ˌsʌb-, (US) sʌbˈle|t, ˌsʌb-, ˈ-- -ts -ts -tting -tɪŋ, (US) -ţɪŋ
sublieutenanc|y ˌsʌb.lefˈten.ənt.s|i, -ləf-, (US) -luː- -ies -iz
sublieutenant ˌsʌb.lefˈten.ənt, -ləfˈ-, (US) -luːˈ- -s -s
sublimate n ˈsʌb.lɪ.mət, -lə-, -mɪt, -meɪt, (US) -meɪt, -mɪt -s -s
subli|mate v ˈsʌb.lɪ|.meɪt, -lə- -mates -meɪts -mating -meɪ.tɪŋ, (US) -meɪ.ţɪŋ -mated -meɪ.tɪd, (US) -meɪ.ţɪd

S

sublimation ˌsʌb.lɪˈmeɪ.ʃᵊn, -ləˈ-

sublim|e səˈblaɪm **-ely** -li **-eness** -nəs, -nɪs **-es** -z **-ing** -ɪŋ **-ed** -d

subliminal sʌbˈlɪm.ɪ.nᵊl, səˈblɪm-, -ᵊn.ᵊl, ⓊⓈ sʌbˈlɪm.ᵊn- **-ly** -i

sublimity səˈblɪm.ə.ti, -ɪ.ti, ⓊⓈ -ə.t̬i

submachine gun ˌsʌb.məˈʃiːnˌɡʌn, -ˈʃiːŋˌ-, ⓊⓈ -ˈʃiːnˌ- **-s** -z

submarin|e ˌsʌb.mᵊrˈiːn, ˈ---, ⓊⓈ ˈsʌb.mə.riːn, ˌ--ˈ- **-es** -z **-ing** -ɪŋ **-ed** -d

submariner sʌbˈmær.ɪ.nəʳ, ˌsʌb-, -ᵊn.əʳ, ⓊⓈ ˌsʌb.məˈriː.nɚ, ˈsʌb.məˌriː-; ⓊⓈ sʌbˈmer.ᵊn.ɚ, -ˈmær- **-s** -z

submerg|e səbˈmɜːdʒ, sʌb-, ⓊⓈ -ˈmɝːdʒ **-es** -ɪz **-ing** -ɪŋ **-ed** -d **-ence** -ᵊnts

submers|e səbˈmɜːs, sʌbˈ-, ⓊⓈ səbˈmɝːs **-es** -ɪz **-ing** -ɪŋ **-ed** -t

submersible səbˈmɜː.sə.bᵊl, sʌb-, -sɪ-, ⓊⓈ -ˈmɝː.sə- **-s** -z

submersion səbˈmɜː.ʃᵊn, sʌb-, ⓊⓈ -ˈmɝː.ʒᵊn, -ʃᵊn **-s** -z

submission səbˈmɪʃ.ᵊn **-s** -z

submissive səbˈmɪs.ɪv **-ly** -li **-ness** -nəs, -nɪs

sub|mit səb|ˈmɪt **-mits** -ˈmɪts **-mitting** -ˈmɪt.ɪŋ, ⓊⓈ -ˈmɪt̬.ɪŋ **-mitted** -ˈmɪt.ɪd, ⓊⓈ -ˈmɪt̬.ɪd

submultiple sʌbˈmʌl.tɪ.pᵊl, ˌsʌb-, ⓊⓈ -tə- **-s** -z

subnormal sʌbˈnɔː.mᵊl, ˌsʌb-, ⓊⓈ -ˈnɔːr- **-ly** -i

subnormality ˌsʌb.nɔːˈmæl.ə.ti, -ɪ.ti, ⓊⓈ -nɔːrˈmæl.ə.t̬i

subnuclear sʌbˈnjuː.kli.əʳ, ˌsʌb-, ⓊⓈ -ˈnuː.kli.ɚ, -ˈnjuː-

suboctave ˈsʌbˌɒk.tɪv, ⓊⓈ -ˌɑːk- **-s** -z

suborbital sʌbˈɔː.bɪ.tᵊl, ˌsʌb-, ⓊⓈ -ˈɔːr.bə.t̬ᵊl

subordinate n, adj səˈbɔː.dᵊn.ət, -dɪ.nət, -ˈbɔːd.nət, -nɪt, ⓊⓈ -ˈbɔːr.dᵊn.ɪt **-s** -s **-ly** -li

subordin|ate v səˈbɔː.dɪ.n|eɪt, ⓊⓈ -ˈbɔːr.dᵊn|.eɪt **-ates** -eɪts **-ating** -eɪ.tɪŋ, ⓊⓈ -eɪ.t̬ɪŋ **-ated** -eɪ.tɪd, ⓊⓈ -eɪ.t̬ɪd

subordination səˌbɔː.dɪˈneɪ.ʃᵊn, ⓊⓈ -ˌbɔːr.dᵊnˈeɪ-

subordinative səˈbɔː.dɪ.nə.tɪv, -dᵊn.ə-, ⓊⓈ -ˈbɔːr.dᵊn.eɪ.t̬ɪv, -dɪ.nə-

suborn səˈbɔːn, sʌbˈɔːn, ⓊⓈ səˈbɔːrn **-s** -z **-ing** -ɪŋ **-ed** -d **-er/s** -əʳ/z, ⓊⓈ -ɚ/z

subornation ˌsʌb.ɔːˈneɪ.ʃᵊn, ⓊⓈ -ɔːrˈ-

Subotica suˈbɒt.ɪt.sə, ⓊⓈ suːˈbɔː.tiːt.sə, -bə-

subplot ˈsʌb.plɒt, ⓊⓈ -plɑːt **-s** -s

subpoena səˈpiː.nə, sʌb-, ⓊⓈ sə- **-s** -z **-ing** -ɪŋ **-ed** -d

subpostmaster ˌsʌbˈpəʊstˌmɑː.stəʳ, ⓊⓈ -ˈpoʊstˌmæs.tɚ **-s** -z

subpostmistress ˌsʌbˈpəʊstˌmɪs.trəs, -trɪs, ⓊⓈ -ˈpoʊst- **-es** -ɪz

subpostoffice ˌsʌbˈpəʊstˌɒf.ɪs, ⓊⓈ -ˈpoʊstˌɑː.fɪs **-s** -ɪz

subprefect sʌbˈpriː.fekt, ˌsʌb- **-s** -s

subprime ˌsʌbˈpraɪm *stress shift:* **ˌsubprime ˈmortgage**

subprogram ˌsʌbˈprəʊ.ɡræm, ⓊⓈ ˈsʌbˌproʊ-, -ɡrəm **-s** -z

subrogation ˌsʌb.rəʊˈɡeɪ.ʃᵊn, ⓊⓈ -roʊˈ-, -rəˈ-

sub rosa ˌsʌbˈrəʊ.zə, -zɑː, ⓊⓈ -ˈroʊ.zə

subroutine ˈsʌb.ruːˌtiːn **-s** -z

subscrib|e səbˈskraɪb **-es** -z **-ing** -ɪŋ **-ed** -d **-er/s** -əʳ/z, ⓊⓈ -ɚ/z

subscript ˈsʌb.skrɪpt

subscription səbˈskrɪp.ʃᵊn **-s** -z

subsection ˈsʌbˌsek.ʃᵊn **-s** -z

subsequent ˈsʌb.sɪ.kwənt, -sə-, ⓊⓈ -sɪ- **-ly** -li

subserv|e səbˈsɜːv, sʌb-, ⓊⓈ səbˈsɝːv **-es** -z **-ing** -ɪŋ **-ed** -d

subservien|ce səbˈsɜː.vi.ən*t*|s, sʌb-, ⓊⓈ səbˈsɝː- **-cy** -si

subservient səbˈsɜː.vi.ənt, sʌb-, ⓊⓈ səbˈsɝː- **-ly** -li

subset ˈsʌb.set **-s** -s

subsid|e səbˈsaɪd **-es** -z **-ing** -ɪŋ **-ed** -ɪd

subsidence səbˈsaɪ.dᵊn*t*s; ˈsʌb.sɪ.dᵊn*t*s, -sə- **-s** -ɪz

subsidiarity səbˌsɪd.iˈær.ə.ti, -ɪ.ti, ⓊⓈ -ˈer.ə.t̬i, -ˈær-

subsidiar|y səbˈsɪd.i.ᵊr|.i, ⓊⓈ -er-, -ɚ- **-ies** -iz **-ily** -ᵊl.i, -ɪ.li

subsidization ˌsʌb.sɪ.daɪˈzeɪ.ʃᵊn, -dɪˈ-, -sə-, ⓊⓈ -dəˈ- **-s** -z

subsidiz|e, -is|e ˈsʌb.sɪ.daɪz, -sə-, ⓊⓈ -sə- **-es** -ɪz **-ing** -ɪŋ **-ed** -d

subsid|y ˈsʌb.sɪ.d|i, -sə-, ⓊⓈ -sə- **-ies** -iz

sub silentio ˌsʌb.sɪˈlen.ti.əʊ, ⓊⓈ ˌsʌb.sɪˈlen.ti.oʊ, -ˈlen*t*.ʃi-

subsist səbˈsɪst **-s** -s **-ing** -ɪŋ **-ed** -ɪd

subsistence səbˈsɪs.tᵊn*t*s **subˈsistence ˌlevel**

subsoil ˈsʌb.sɔɪl **-s** -z

subsonic sʌbˈsɒn.ɪk, ˌsʌb-, ⓊⓈ -ˈsɑː.nɪk

subspecies ˈsʌbˌspiː.ʃiːz, -ʃɪz, -siːz, -sɪz, ⓊⓈ -ʃiːz, -siːz

substanc|e ˈsʌb.stᵊn*t*s **-es** -ɪz **-less** -ləs, -lɪs

substandard sʌbˈstæn.dəd, ˌsʌb-, ⓊⓈ -dɚd

substantial səbˈstæn.*t*ʃᵊl, -ˈstɑːn-, ⓊⓈ -ˈstæn*t*.ʃᵊl **-ly** -i **-ness** -nəs, -nɪs

substantiality səbˌstæn.*t*ʃiˈæl.ə.ti, -ˌstɑːn-, -ɪ.ti, ⓊⓈ -ˌstæn*t*.ʃiˈæl.ə.t̬i

substanti|ate səbˈstæn.*t*ʃi|.eɪt, -ˈstɑːn-; -ˈstæn*t*.si-, -ˈstɑːn*t*-, ⓊⓈ -ˈstæn*t*.ʃi- **-ates** -eɪts **-ating** -eɪ.tɪŋ, ⓊⓈ -eɪ.t̬ɪŋ **-ated** -eɪ.tɪd, ⓊⓈ -eɪ.t̬ɪd

substantiation səbˌstæn.*t*ʃiˈeɪ.ʃᵊn, -ˌstɑːn-, -ˌstæn*t*.siˈ-, -ˌstɑːn*t*-, ⓊⓈ -ˌstæn*t*.ʃiˈ-

substantival ˌsʌb.stᵊnˈtaɪ.vᵊl

substantive n ˈsʌb.stᵊn.tɪv, ⓊⓈ -t̬ɪv **-s** -z

substantive adj ˈsʌb.stᵊn.tɪv; səbˈstæn-, ⓊⓈ -t̬ɪv **-s** -z **-ly** -li **-ness** -nəs, -nɪs

> Note: In British English, generally /səbˈstæn.tɪv/ when applied to rank, pay, etc.

substation ˈsʌbˌsteɪ.ʃᵊn **-s** -z

substitutable ˈsʌb.stɪ.tʃuː.tə.bᵊl, -tjuː-, ˌsʌb.stɪˈtʃuː-, -ˈtjuː-, ⓊⓈ ˈsʌb.stə.tuː.t̬ə-, -tjuː-

substitu|te ˈsʌb.stɪ.tʃuː|t, -tjuːt, ⓊⓈ -stə.tuː|t, -tjuː|t **-tes** -ts **-ting** -tɪŋ, ⓊⓈ -t̬ɪŋ **-ted** -tɪd, ⓊⓈ -t̬ɪd

substitution ˌsʌb.stɪˈtʃuː.ʃᵊn, -ˈtjuː-, ⓊⓈ -stəˈtuː-, -ˈtjuː- **-s** -z

substitutional ˌsʌb.stɪˈtʃuː.ʃᵊn.ᵊl, -ˈtʃuːʃ.nᵊl, -ˈtjuː-, ⓊⓈ -stəˈtuː.ʃᵊn.ᵊl, -ˈtjuː- **-ly** -i

substitutive ˈsʌb.stɪ.tʃuː.tɪv, -tjuː-, ⓊⓈ -stə.tuː.t̬ɪv, -tjuː-

substrate ˈsʌb.streɪt **-s** -s

substratosphere sʌbˈstræt.əʊˌsfɪəʳ, -ˈstrɑː.təʊ-, ⓊⓈ -ˈstræt.ə.sfɪr **-s** -z

substrat|um sʌbˈstrɑː.t|əm, -ˈstreɪ-, ˈ-ˌ--, ⓊⓈ ˈsʌbˌstreɪ.t̬|əm, -ˌstræt̬|.əm **-a** -ə

substructure ˈsʌbˌstrʌk.tʃəʳ, ⓊⓈ -tʃɚ **-s** -z

subsum|e səbˈsjuːm, ⓊⓈ -ˈsuːm **-es** -z **-ing** -ɪŋ **-ed** -d

subsystem ˈsʌbˌsɪs.təm, -tɪm, ⓊⓈ -təm **-s** -z

subtangent sʌbˈtæn.dʒᵊnt, ˌsʌb- **-s** -s

subtenancy sʌbˈten.ən*t*.si, ˌsʌb-, ˈsʌbˌten-, ⓊⓈ sʌbˈten-, ˌsʌb-

subtenant sʌbˈten.ᵊnt, ˌsʌb-, ˈ-ˌ--, ⓊⓈ ˈsʌbˌten- **-s** -s

subtend səbˈtend, sʌb- **-s** -z **-ing** -ɪŋ **-ed** -ɪd

subterfug|e ˈsʌb.tə.fjuː*d*ʒ, ⓊⓈ -tɚ- **-es** -ɪz

subterrane|an ˌsʌb.tᵊrˈeɪ.ni|.ən, ⓊⓈ -təˈreɪ- **-ous** -əs

subtext ˈsʌb.tekst **-s** -s

subtil(e) ˈsʌt.ᵊl, ⓊⓈ ˈsʌt̬.ᵊl; ⓊⓈ ˈsʌb.tɪl

subtility sʌbˈtɪl.ə.ti, -ɪ.ti, ⓊⓈ -ə.t̬i

subtiliz|e, -is|e ˈsʌt.ᵊl.aɪz, -ɪ.laɪz, ⓊⓈ ˈsʌt̬.ᵊl.aɪz, ˈsʌb.tɪ.laɪz **-es** -ɪz **-ing** -ɪŋ **-ed** -d

subtilty ˈsʌt.ᵊl.ti, -ɪl-, ⓊⓈ ˈ-ᵊl.ti, ˈsʌb.tɪl-

subtitl|e ˈsʌbˌtaɪ.tᵊl, -ˈ--, ⓊⓈ ˈsʌbˌtaɪ.t̬ᵊl **-es** -z **-ing** -ɪŋ **-ed** -d

subtl|e ˈsʌt.ᵊl, ⓊⓈ ˈsʌt̬- **-er** -əʳ, ˈsʌt.ləʳ, ⓊⓈ ˈsʌt̬.ᵊl.ɚ, ˈsʌt.lɚ **-est** -ɪst -əst, ˈsʌt.lɪst, -ləst, ⓊⓈ ˈsʌt̬.ᵊl.ɪst, -əst, ˈsʌt.lɪst, -ləst **-y** -i **-eness** -nəs -nɪs

subtlet|y ˈsʌt.ᵊl.t|i, ⓊⓈ ˈsʌt̬.ᵊl.t|i **-ies** -iz

subtopia sʌbˈtəʊ.pi.ə, ⓊⓈ -ˈtoʊ-

subtotal ˈsʌbˌtəʊ.tᵊl, -ˈ--, ˌ-ˈ--, ⓊⓈ ˈsʌbˌtoʊ.t̬ᵊl **-s** -s **-(l)ing** -ɪŋ **-(l)ed** -d

subtract səbˈtrækt **-s** -s **-ing** -ɪŋ **-ed** -ɪd

subtraction səbˈtræk.ʃᵊn **-s** -z

S

subtrahend ˈsʌb.trə.hend -s -z
subtropic sʌbˈtrɒp.ɪk, (US) -ˈtrɑː.pɪk -s -s
subtropical sʌbˈtrɒp.ɪ.kəl, ˌsʌb-, (US) -ˈtrɑː.pɪ-
suburb ˈsʌb.ɜːb, (US) -ɝːb -s -z
suburban səˈbɜː.bən, (US) -ˈbɝː-
suburbanite səˈbɜː.bən.aɪt, (US) -ˈbɝː- -s -s
suburbanization, -isa- səˌbɜː.bən.aɪˈzeɪ.ʃən, -ɪˈ-, (US) -ˌbɝː.bən.əˈ-
suburbaniz|e, -is|e səˈbɜː.bən.aɪz, (US) -ˈbɝː- -es -ɪz -ing -ɪŋ -ed -d
suburbia səˈbɜː.bi.ə, (US) -ˈbɝː-
subvariet|y ˈsʌb.vərˌaɪ.ə.t|i, (US) -vəˌraɪ.ə.ţ|i -ies -iz
subvention səbˈven.tʃən, sʌb-, (US) -ˈvent.ʃən -s -z
subversion səbˈvɜː.ʃən, sʌb-, -ʒən, (US) -ˈvɝː.ʒən, -ʃən
subversive səbˈvɜː.sɪv, sʌb-, (US) -ˈvɝː- -ly -li -ness -nəs, -nɪs
sub|vert sʌb|ˈvɜːt, səb-, (US) -ˈvɝːt -verts -ˈvɜːts, (US) -ˈvɝːts -verting -ˈvɜː.tɪŋ, (US) -ˈvɝː.ţɪŋ -verted -ˈvɜː.tɪd, (US) -ˈvɝː.ţɪd
subway ˈsʌb.weɪ -s -z
subzero sʌbˈzɪə.rəʊ, ˌsʌb-, (US) -ˈzɪr.oʊ, -ˈziː.roʊ
succeed səkˈsiːd -s -z -ing -ɪŋ -ed -ɪd
succès de scandale sjuːkˌseɪ.dəˌskɑ̃ːnˈdɑːl; *as if French:* sʊk-
success səkˈses -es -ɪz **sucˈcess ˌstory**
successful səkˈses.fəl, -fʊl -ly -li -ness -nəs, -nɪs
succession səkˈseʃ.ən -s -z
successive səkˈses.ɪv -ly -li
successor səkˈses.ər, (US) -ɚ -s -z
succinct səkˈsɪŋkt, sʌk- -ly -li -ness -nəs, -nɪs
succ|or ˈsʌk|.ər, (US) -ɚ -ors -əz, (US) -ɚz -oring -ər.ɪŋ -ored -əd, (US) -ɚd
succory ˈsʌk.ər.i
succotash ˈsʌk.ə.tæʃ
Succoth ˈsʌk.əs, ˈsʊk-; sʊˈkɒt, (US) ˈsʊk.əs; (US) ˈsuː.kɔːt
succ|our ˈsʌk|.ər, (US) -ɚ -ours -əz, (US) -ɚz -ouring -ər.ɪŋ -oured -əd, (US) -ɚd
succub|a ˈsʌk.jə.b|ə, -jʊ- -ae -iː
succub|us ˈsʌk.jə.b|əs, -jʊ- -i -aɪ
succulence ˈsʌk.jə.lənts, -jʊ-
succulent ˈsʌk.jə.lənt, -jʊ- -ly -li
succumb səˈkʌm -s -z -ing -ɪŋ -ed -d
such *usual form:* sʌtʃ; *occasional weak form:* sətʃ
such-and-such ˈsʌtʃ.ən.sʌtʃ
Suchard® ˈsuː.ʃɑːd, -ʃɑː, (US) -ʃɑːrd
suchlike ˈsʌtʃ.laɪk
suck sʌk -s -s -ing -ɪŋ -ed -t **ˈsucking ˌpig**
sucker ˈsʌk.ər, (US) -ɚ -s -z
suckl|e ˈsʌk.əl -es -z -ing -ɪŋ, ˈsʌk.lɪŋ -ed -d
suckling, S~ ˈsʌk.lɪŋ, ˈ-əl.ɪŋ -s -z
sucre, S~ *currency:* ˈsuː.kreɪ -s -z
sucrose ˈsuː.krəʊs, ˈsjuː-, -krəʊz, (US) ˈsuː.kroʊs
suction ˈsʌk.ʃən **ˈsuction ˌpad; ˈsuction ˌpump**
Sudan suːˈdɑːn, sʊ-, -ˈdæn, (US) suːˈdæn
Sudanese ˌsuː.dənˈiːz
Sudanic suːˈdæn.ɪk, sʊ-, (US) suː-
sudarium sjuːˈdeə.ri.əm, suː-, (US) suːˈder.i- -s -z
sudatory ˈsjuː.də.tər.i, ˈsuː-, (US) ˈsuː.də.tɔːr-
Sudbury ˈsʌd.bər.i, ˈsʌb-, (US) ˈsʌd.ber-, -bɚ-
sudd sʌd
sudden ˈsʌd.ən -est -ɪst, -əst -ly -li -ness -nəs, -nɪs **ˌsudden ˈdeath**
Sudetenland sʊˈdeɪ.tən.lænd, (US) suː-
sudoku suˈdəʊ.ku, suːˈdɒk.uː, sə-, (US) suˈdoʊ-
sudorific ˌsjuː.dərˈɪf.ɪk, ˌsuː-, -dɒrˈ-, (US) ˌsuː.dəˈrɪf- -s -s
suds sʌdz
suds|y ˈsʌd.z|i -ier -i.ər, (US) -i.ɚ -iest -i.ɪst, -i.əst -iness -ɪ.nəs, -ɪ.nɪs
su|e, S~ suː, sjuː, (US) suː -es -z -ing -ɪŋ -ed -d
suede sweɪd
su|et ˈsuː|.ɪt, ˈsjuː-, (US) ˈsuː- -ety -ɪ.ti, (US) -ɪ.ţi **ˌsuet ˈpudding**
Suetonius swɪˈtəʊ.ni.əs, swiː-; ˌsjuː.ɪˈ-, ˌsuː-, -iːˈ-, (US) swiːˈtoʊ-, swɪ-
Suez ˈsuː.ɪz, ˈsjuː-, (US) suːˈez, ˈ-- **ˌSuez Caˈnal**
suff|er ˈsʌf|.ər, (US) -ɚ -ers -əz, (US) -ɚz -ering/s -ər.ɪŋ/z -ered -əd, (US) -ɚd -erer/s -ər.ər/z, (US) -ɚ.ɚ/z -erable -ər.ə.bəl -erance -ər.ənts
suffic|e səˈfaɪs -es -ɪz -ing -ɪŋ -ed -t
sufficiency səˈfɪʃ.ənt.si
sufficient səˈfɪʃ.ənt -ly -li
suffix v ˈsʌf.ɪks; səˈfɪks, sʌfˈɪks, (US) ˈsʌf.ɪks; (US) səˈfɪks -es -ɪz -ing -ɪŋ -ed -t
suffix n ˈsʌf.ɪks -es -ɪz
suffo|cate ˈsʌf.ə|.keɪt -cates -keɪts -cating/ly -keɪ.tɪŋ/li, (US) -keɪ.ţɪŋ/li -cated -keɪ.tɪd, (US) -keɪ.ţɪd
suffocation ˌsʌf.əˈkeɪ.ʃən
Suffolk ˈsʌf.ək
suffragan ˈsʌf.rə.gən -s -z
suffrag|e ˈsʌf.rɪdʒ -es -ɪz
suffragette ˌsʌf.rəˈdʒet -s -s
suffragist ˈsʌf.rə.dʒɪst -s -s
suffus|e səˈfjuːz, sʌfˈjuːz, (US) səˈfjuːz -es -ɪz -ing -ɪŋ -ed -d
suffusion səˈfjuː.ʒən, sʌfˈjuː-, (US) səˈfjuː- -s -z
Suf|i ˈsuː.f|i -is -iz -ism -ɪ.zəm -ic -ɪk
sug|ar ˈʃʊg|.ər, (US) -ɚ -ars -əz, (US) -ɚz -aring -ər.ɪŋ -ared -əd, (US) -ɚd **ˈsugar ˌbeet; ˈsugar ˌdaddy**
sugarcane ˈʃʊg.ə.keɪn, (US) ˈ-ɚ- -s -z
sugarloa|f ˈʃʊg.ə.ləʊ|f, (US) -ɚ.loʊ|f -ves -vz **ˌSugarloaf ˈMountain**
sugarplum ˈʃʊg.ə.plʌm, (US) ˈ-ɚ- -s -z
sugar|y ˈʃʊg.ər|.i -iest -i.ɪst, -i.əst -iness -ɪ.nəs, -ɪ.nɪs
suggest səˈdʒest, (US) səg- -s -s -ing -ɪŋ -ed -ɪd
suggestibility səˌdʒes.təˈbɪl.ə.ti, -tɪˈ-, -ɪ.ti, (US) səgˌdʒes.təˈbɪl.ə.ţi
suggestible səˈdʒes.tə.bəl, -tɪ-, (US) səgˈdʒes.tə-
suggestion səˈdʒes.tʃən, -ˈdʒeʃ-, (US) səgˈdʒes- -s -z
suggestive səˈdʒes.tɪv, (US) səgˈdʒes- -ly -li -ness -nəs, -nɪs
Suharto sʊˈhɑː.təʊ, (US) -ˈhɑːr.ţoʊ
suicidal ˌsuː.ɪˈsaɪ.dəl, ˌsjuː-, (US) ˌsuː.əˈ- -ly -i
suicide ˈsuː.ɪ.saɪd, ˈsjuː-, (US) ˈsuː.ə- -s -z
sui generis ˌsjuː.iːˈdʒen.ər.ɪs, ˌsuː-, -aɪˈ-, -ˈgen-, (US) ˌsuː.iːˈdʒen-, -aɪˈ-
sui juris ˌsjuː.iːˈdʒʊə.rɪs, ˌsuː-, -aɪˈ-, -ˈdʒɔː-, (US) ˌsuː.iːˈdʒʊr.ɪs, -aɪˈ-
suit suːt, sjuːt, (US) suːt -s -s -ing/s -ɪŋ/z, (US) ˈsuː.ţɪŋ/z -ed -ɪd, (US) ˈsuː.ţɪd
suitability ˌsuː.təˈbɪl.ə.ti, ˌsjuː-, -ɪ.ti, (US) ˌsuː.ţəˈbɪl.ə.ţi
suitab|le ˈsuː.tə.b|əl, ˈsjuː-, (US) ˈsuː.ţə- -ly -li -leness -əl.nɪs, -nəs
suitcas|e ˈsuːt.keɪs, ˈsjuːt-, (US) ˈsuːt- -es -ɪz
suite swiːt -s -s
suitor ˈsuː.tər, ˈsjuː-, (US) ˈsuː.ţɚ -s -z
sukiyaki ˌsuː.kiˈjæk.i, (US) -ˈjɑː.ki, ˌsʊk.iˈ-
Sukkot(h) ˈsʊk.ɒt, (US) -ɑːt
Sukkur ˈsʊk.ʊə, (US) ˈsʊk.ʊr, -ɚ
Sulawesi ˌsuː.ləˈweɪ.si, -læˈ-, (US) -lɑːˈ-
sulcal ˈsʌl.kəl
sulcalization, -isa- ˌsʌl.kəl.aɪˈzeɪ.ʃən, -ɪˈ-, (US) -əˈ-
sulcaliz|e, -is|e ˈsʌl.kəl.aɪz -es -ɪz -ing -ɪŋ -ed -d
sulcate ˈsʌl.keɪt, -kɪt, -kət, (US) -keɪt
Suleiman ˌsʊl.eɪˈmɑːn, ˌsuː.leɪˈ-, -lɪˈ-, ˈ---, (US) ˈsuː.leɪ.mɑːn, -lə-
sulfanilamide ˌsʌl.fəˈnɪl.ə.maɪd, (US) -maɪd, -mɪd
sulfate ˈsʌl.feɪt, -fɪt, -fət, (US) -feɪt -s -s
sulf|ide ˈsʌl.f|aɪd -ides -aɪdz -ite/s -aɪt/s
sulfonamide sʌlˈfɒn.ə.maɪd, (US) -ˈfɑː.nə-, -mɪd -s -z
sulfur ˈsʌl.fər, (US) -fɚ
sulfureous sʌlˈfjʊə.ri.əs, -ˈfjɔː-, (US) -ˈfjʊr.i-
sulfuretted ˈsʌl.fjʊ.ret.ɪd, -fjʊə-, -fə-, (US) -fjə.reţ-, -fə-, -fjʊ-
sulfuric sʌlˈfjʊə.rɪk, -ˈfjɔː-, (US) -ˈfjʊr.ɪk **sulˌfuric ˈacid**
sulfurous ˈsʌl.fər.əs, -fjʊ.rəs, (US) -fɚ-; (US) sʌlˈfjʊr.əs
sulfury ˈsʌl.fər.i
Suliman ˌsʊl.ɪˈmɑːn, ˈ---, (US) ˈsuː.leɪ.mɑːn, -lə-
sulk sʌlk -s -s -ing -ɪŋ -ed -t -y -i -ier -i.ər, (US) -i.ɚ -iest -i.ɪst, -i.əst -ily -əl.i, -ɪ.li -iness -ɪ.nəs, -ɪ.nɪs
Sulla ˈsʌl.ə, ˈsʊl-, (US) ˈsʌl-
sullen ˈsʌl.ən -est -ɪst, -əst -ly -li -ness -nəs, -nɪs
Sullivan ˈsʌl.ɪ.vən

S

Sullom Voe ˌsuː.ləmˈvəʊ, ˌsʌl.əmˈ-, (US) -ˈvoʊ
sull|y, S~ ˈsʌl|.i **-ies** -iz **-ying** -i.ɪŋ **-ied** -id
sulphanilamide ˌsʌl.fəˈnɪl.ə.maɪd, (US) -maɪd, -mɪd
sulphate ˈsʌl.feɪt, -fɪt, -fət, (US) -feɪt **-s** -s
sulph|ide ˈsʌl.f|aɪd **-ides** -aɪdz **-ite/s** -aɪt/s
sulphonamide sʌlˈfɒn.ə.maɪd, (US) -ˈfɑː.nə-, -mɪd **-s** -z
sulphur ˈsʌl.fəʳ, (US) -fɚ
sulphureous sʌlˈfjʊə.ri.əs, -ˈfjɔː-, (US) -ˈfjʊr.i-
sulphuretted ˈsʌl.fjʊ.ret.ɪd, -fjʊə-, -fə-, (US) -fjə.reṭ-, -fə-, -fjʊ-
sulphuric sʌlˈfjʊə.rɪk, -ˈfjɔː-, (US) -ˈfjʊr.ɪk **sulˌphuric ˈacid**
sulphurous ˈsʌl.fᵊr.əs, -fjʊ.rəs, (US) -fɚ.əs; (US) sʌlˈfjʊr.əs
sulphury ˈsʌl.fᵊr.i
sultan, S~ ˈsʌl.tᵊn **-s** -z
sultana *kind of raisin:* sᵊlˈtɑː.nə, sʌl-, (US) sʌlˈtæn.ə, -ˈtɑː.nə *sultan's wife, mother, etc.:* sʌlˈtɑː.nə, sʊl-, (US) sʌlˈtæn.ə, -ˈtɑː.nə **-s** -z
sultanate ˈsʌl.tə.nət, -neɪt, -nɪt, (US) -tᵊn.ɪt, -eɪt **-s** -s
sultr|y ˈsʌl.tr|i **-ier** -i.əʳ, (US) -i.ɚ **-iest** -i.ɪst, -i.əst **-ily** -ᵊl.i, -ɪ.li **-iness** -ɪ.nəs, -ɪ.nɪs
Sulu ˈsuː.luː
sum sʌm **-s** -z **-ming** -ɪŋ **-med** -d **ˌsum ˈtotal**
sumac(h) ˈsuː.mæk, ˈsjuː-, ˈʃuː-, (US) ˈsuː.mæk, ˈʃʊm.æk **-s** -s
Sumatr|a sʊˈmɑː.tr|ə, sjʊ-, (US) suː- **-an/s** -ən/z
Sumburgh ˈsʌm.bᵊr.ə, (US) -bɚ.ə
Sumerian sʊˈmɪə.ri.ən, suː-, sjʊ-, sjuː-, -ˈmeə-, (US) suːˈmɪr.i-, -ˈmer-
summa cum laude ˌsʊm.ɑː.kʊmˈlaʊ.deɪ, (US) -əˌ-, -di; (US) ˌsʌm.əˌkʌmˈlɔː.di
summariz|e, -is|e ˈsʌm.ᵊr.aɪz, (US) -ə.raɪz **-es** -ɪz **-ing** -ɪŋ **-ed** -d
summar|y ˈsʌm.ᵊr|.i **-ies** -iz **-ily** -ᵊl.i, -ɪ.li **-iness** -ɪ.nəs, -ɪ.nɪs
summat ˈsʌm.ət
summation sʌmˈeɪ.ʃᵊn, səˈmeɪ-, (US) səˈmeɪ- **-s** -z
summer, S~ ˈsʌm.əʳ, (US) -ɚ **-s** -z **-ing** -ɪŋ **-ed** -d **-like** -laɪk **ˌsummer ˈpudding; ˈsummer ˌschool; ˈSummer ˌTime**
Summerfield ˈsʌm.ə.fiːld, (US) ˈ-ɚ-
-s -z
summerhou|se ˈsʌm.ə.haʊ|s, (US) ˈ-ɚ- **-ses** -zɪz
Summers ˈsʌm.əz, (US) -ɚz
summertime ˈsʌm.ə.taɪm, (US) ˈ-ɚ-
Summerville ˈsʌm.ə.vɪl, (US) ˈ-ɚ-
summery ˈsʌm.ᵊr.i
summing-up ˌsʌm.ɪŋˈʌp **summings-up** ˌsʌm.ɪŋzˈ-
summit ˈsʌm.ɪt **-s** -s
summiteer ˌsʌm.ɪˈtɪəʳ, (US) -ˈtɪɚ **-s** -z
summon ˈsʌm.ən **-s** -z **-ing** -ɪŋ **-ed** -d **-er/s** -əʳ/z, (US) -ɚ/z
summons ˈsʌm.ənz **-es** -ɪz **-ing** -ɪŋ **-ed** -d
Sumner ˈsʌm.nəʳ, (US) -nɚ
sumo ˈsuː.məʊ, (US) -moʊ **ˈsumo ˌwrestler; ˌsumo ˈwrestler; ˌsumo ˈwrestling; ˈsumo ˌwrestling**
sump sʌmp **-s** -s
sumpter, S~ ˈsʌmp.təʳ, (US) -tɚ **-s** -z
sumptuary ˈsʌmp.tʃʊə.ri, -tjʊə-, -tʃʊ-, -tjʊ-, (US) -tʃu.er.i
sumptuous ˈsʌmp.tʃu.əs, -tju-, (US) -tʃu- **-ly** -li **-ness** -nəs, -nɪs
sun, S~ sʌn **-s** -z **-ning** -ɪŋ **-ned** -d **ˌSun ˈCity; ˈsun ˌdeck; ˈsun ˌhat; ˈsun ˌlounge**
Sun. (abbrev. for **Sunday**) ˈsʌn.deɪ, -di
sunbaked ˈsʌn.beɪkt, ˈsʌm-, (US) ˈsʌn-
sunba|th ˈsʌn.bɑː|θ, ˈsʌm-, (US) ˈsʌn.bæ|θ **-ths** -ðz
sunbath|e ˈsʌn.beɪð, ˈsʌm-, (US) ˈsʌn- **-es** -z **-ing** -ɪŋ **-ed** -d **-er/s** -əʳ/z, (US) -ɚ/z
sunbeam, S~ ˈsʌn.biːm, ˈsʌm-, (US) ˈsʌn- **-s** -z
sunbed ˈsʌn.bed, ˈsʌm-, (US) ˈsʌn- **-s** -z
sun-belt ˈsʌn.belt, ˈsʌm- **-s** -s
sunblind ˈsʌn.blaɪnd, ˈsʌm-, (US) ˈsʌn- **-s** -z
sunblock ˈsʌn.blɒk, ˈsʌm-, (US) ˈsʌn.blɑːk **-s** -s
sun-bonnet ˈsʌnˌbɒn.ɪt, ˈsʌm-, (US) ˈsʌnˌbɑː.nɪt **-s** -s
sunburn ˈsʌn.bɜːn, ˈsʌm-, (US) ˈsʌn.bɝːn **-s** -z **-ed** -d **-t** -t
sunburst ˈsʌn.bɜːst, ˈsʌm-, (US) ˈsʌn.bɝːst **-s** -s
Sunbury ˈsʌn.bᵊr.i, ˈsʌm-, (US) ˈsʌn-, -beri
Sunda ˈsʌn.də
sundae ˈsʌn.deɪ, (US) -di, -deɪ **-s** -z
Sundanese ˌsʌn.dəˈniːz
Sunday ˈsʌn.deɪ, -di **-s** -z **ˌSunday ˈbest; ˈSunday ˌschool; ˌin a ˌmonth of ˈSundays**
sund|er ˈsʌn.d|əʳ, (US) -d|ɚ **-ers** -əz, (US) -ɚz **-ering** -ᵊr.ɪŋ **-ered** -əd, (US) -ɚd
Sunderland ˈsʌn.dᵊl.ənd, (US) -dɚ.lənd
sundial ˈsʌn.daɪl **-s** -z
sundown ˈsʌn.daʊn
sundowner ˈsʌnˌdaʊ.nəʳ, (US) -nɚ **-s** -z
sundrenched ˈsʌn.drentʃt
sundress ˈsʌn.dres **-es** -ɪz
sun-dried ˈsʌn.draɪd
sundr|y ˈsʌn.dr|i **-ies** -iz
sunfish ˈsʌn.fɪʃ
sunflower ˈsʌn.flaʊəʳ, -flaʊ.əʳ, (US) -flaʊ.ɚ **-s** -z **ˈsunflower ˌseed**
sung (from **sing**) sʌŋ
Sung sʊŋ, sʌŋ, (US) sʊŋ
sunglasses ˈsʌnˌglɑː.sɪz, ˈsʌŋ-, (US) ˈsʌnˌglæs.ɪs
sunk (from **sink**) sʌŋk
sunken (from **sink**) ˈsʌŋ.kən
sunkissed ˈsʌn.kɪst, ˈsʌŋ-
sunlamp ˈsʌn.læmp **-s** -s
sunless ˈsʌn.ləs, -lɪs
sun|light ˈsʌn|.laɪt **-lit** -lɪt
sunlounger ˈsʌnˌlaʊn.dʒəʳ, (US) -dʒɚ **-s** -z
Sunn|i ˈsʊn|.i, ˈsʌn-, (US) ˈsʊn- **-ite/s** -aɪt/s **-ism** -ɪ.zᵊm **ˌSunni ˈMuslim**
Sunningdale ˈsʌn.ɪŋ.deɪl
sunn|y ˈsʌn|.i **-ier** -i.əʳ, (US) -i.ɚ **-iest** -i.ɪst, -i.əst **-iness** -ɪ.nəs, -ɪ.nɪs **ˌsunny-side ˈup**
Sunnyside ˈsʌn.i.saɪd
sunproof ˈsʌn.pruːf, ˈsʌm-, (US) ˈsʌn-
sunray ˈsʌn.reɪ **-s** -z
sunris|e ˈsʌn.raɪz **-es** -ɪz
sunroo|f ˈsʌn.ruː|f, (US) -ruː|f, -rʊ|f **-fs** -fs **-ves** -vz
sunscreen ˈsʌn.skriːn **-s** -z **-ing** -ɪŋ
sunset ˈsʌn.set **-s** -s
sunshade ˈsʌn.ʃeɪd **-s** -z
sunshin|e ˈsʌn.ʃaɪn **-y** -i
sunspot ˈsʌn.spɒt, (US) -spɑːt **-s** -s
sunstroke ˈsʌn.strəʊk, (US) -stroʊk **-s** -s
suntan ˈsʌn.tæn **-s** -z **-ned** -d
Sun-Times ˈsʌn.taɪmz
suntrap ˈsʌn.træp **-s** -s
sunup ˈsʌn.ʌp **-s** -s
sun-worship ˈsʌnˌwɜː.ʃɪp, (US) -ˌwɝː- **-per/s** -əʳ/z, (US) -ɚ/z
suo nomine ˌsuː.əʊˈnəʊ.mɪ.neɪ, ˌsjuː-, -ˈnɒm.ɪ-, (US) ˌsuː.oʊˈnoʊ.mɪ-, -ˈnɑː-
sup sʌp **-s** -s **-ping** -ɪŋ **-ped** -t
super ˈsuː.pəʳ, ˈsjuː-, (US) ˈsuː.pɚ **-s** -z
super- ˈsuː.pəʳ, ˈsjuː-, (US) ˈsuː.pɚ
superab|le ˈsuː.pᵊr.ə.b|ᵊl, ˈsjuː-, (US) ˈsuː.pɚ- **-ly** -li **-leness** -ᵊl.nəs, -nɪs
superabundan|ce ˌsuː.pᵊr.əˈbʌn.dən|ts, ˌsjuː-, (US) ˌsuː- **-t/ly** -t/li
superannu|ate ˌsuː.pᵊrˈæn.ju|.eɪt, ˌsjuː-, (US) ˌsuː- **-ates** -eɪts **-ating** -eɪ.tɪŋ, (US) -eɪ.ṭɪŋ **-ated** -eɪ.tɪd, (US) -eɪ.ṭɪd
superannuation ˌsuː.pᵊrˌæn.juˈeɪ.ʃᵊn, ˌsjuː-, (US) ˌsuː- **-s** -z
superb suːˈpɜːb, sjuː-, sʊ-, sjʊ-, (US) səˈpɝːb, sʊ-, suː- **-ly** -li **-ness** -nəs, -nɪs
Superbowl ˈsuː.pə.bəʊl, ˈsjuː-, (US) ˈsuː.pɚ.boʊl
superbug ˈsuː.pə.bʌg, ˈsjuː-, (US) ˈsuː.pɚ- **-s** -z
supercargo ˈsuː.pəˌkɑː.gəʊ, ˈsjuː-, (US) ˈsuː.pɚˌkɑːr.goʊ **-es** -z
supercharg|e ˈsuː.pə.tʃɑːdʒ, ˈsjuː-, (US) ˈsuː.pɚ.tʃɑːrdʒ **-es** -ɪz **-ing** -ɪŋ **-ed** -d
supercharger ˈsuː.pəˌtʃɑː.dʒəʳ, ˈsjuː-, (US) ˈsuː.pɚˌtʃɑːr.dʒɚ **-s** -z
superchip ˈsuː.pə.tʃɪp, ˈsjuː-, (US) ˈsuː.pɚ- **-s** -s
supercilious ˌsuː.pəˈsɪl.i.əs, ˌsjuː-, (US) ˌsuː.pɚˈ- **-ly** -li **-ness** -nəs, -nɪs
supercomputer ˈsuː.pə.kəmˌpjuː.təʳ, ˈsjuː-, (US) ˈsuː.pɚ.kəmˌpjuː.ṭɚ **-s** -z
superconductivity ˌsuː.pəˌkɒn.dʌkˈtɪv.ə.ti, ˌsjuː-,

-dʌkˈ-, -ɪ.ti, US ˌsuː.pɚˌkɑːn.dʌkˈtɪv.ə.t̬i
superconductor ˈsuː.pə.kənˌdʌk.t|əʳ, ˈsjuː-, US ˈsuː.pɚ.kənˌdʌk.t|ɚ **-ors** -əz, US -ɚz **-ing** -ɪŋ
supercool ˌsuː.pəˈkuːl, ˌsjuː-, US ˌsuː.pɚˈ- **-s** -z **-ing** -ɪŋ **-ed** -d
superdelegate ˈsuː.pəˌdel.ɪ.gət, ˈsjuː-, ˈ-ə-, -geɪt, -gɪt, US ˈsuː.pɚˌdel.ɪ.gɪt, -geɪt **-s** -s
Superdrug® ˈsuː.pə.drʌg, ˈsjuː-, US ˈsuː.pɚ-
super-duper ˌsuː.pəˈduː.pəʳ, ˌsjuː-, US ˌsuː.pɚˈduː.pɚ
superego ˌsuː.pəʳˈiː.gəʊ, ˌsjuː-, -ˈeg.əʊ, US ˌsuː.pɚˈiː.goʊ **-s** -z
supererogation ˌsuː.pəʳˌer.əʊˈgeɪ.ʃən, ˌsjuː-, US ˌsuː.pɚˌer.əˈ-
supererogatory ˌsuː.pəʳ.erˈɒg.ə.tər.i, ˌsjuː-, -ɪˈrɒg-, US ˌsuː.pɚ.ɪˈrɑː.gə.tɔːr-
superficial ˌsuː.pəˈfɪʃ|.əl, ˌsjuː-, US ˌsuː.pɚˈ- **-ally** -əl.i **-alness** -əl.nəs, -nɪs
superficiality ˌsuː.pəˌfɪʃ.iˈæl.ə.t|i, ˌsjuː-, -ɪ.t|i, US ˌsuː.pɚˌfɪʃ.iˈæl.ə.t̬|i **-ies** -iz
superficies ˌsuː.pəˈfɪʃ.iːz, ˌsjuː-, -i.iːz, US ˌsuː.pɚˈfɪʃ.i.iːz, ˈ-iːz
superfine ˌsuː.pəˈfaɪn, ˌsjuː-, ˈ---, US ˈsuː.pɚ.faɪn, ˌ--ˈ-
superfix ˈsuː.pə.fɪks, ˈsjuː-, US ˈsuː.pɚ-
superfluity ˌsuː.pəˈfluː.ə.t|i, ˌsjuː-, -ɪ.t|i, US ˌsuː.pɚˈfluː.ə.t̬|i **-ies** -iz
superfluous suːˈpɜː.flu.əs, sjuː-, su-, sju-, US -ˈpɝː- **-ly** -li **-ness** -nəs, -nɪs
Superglue® ˈsuː.pə.gluː, ˈsjuː-, US ˈsuː.pɚ-
supergrass ˈsuː.pə.grɑːs, ˈsjuː-, US ˈsuː.pɚ.græs **-es** -ɪz
supergravity ˌsuː.pəˈgræv.ə.ti, ˌsjuː-, -ɪ.ti, US ˌsuː.pɚˈgræv.ə.t̬i
supergroup ˈsuː.pə.gruːp, ˈsjuː-, US ˈsuːpɚ- **-s** -s
supergun ˈsuː.pə.gʌn, ˈsjuː-, US ˈsuː.pɚ- **-s** -z
superhead ˈsuː.pə.hed, ˈsjuː-, US ˈsuː.pɚ- **-s** -z
superheat v ˌsuː.pəˈhiːt, ˌsjuː-, US ˌsuː.pɚˈ- **-s** -s **-ing** -ɪŋ **-ed** -ɪd
superheat n ˈsuː.pə.hiːt, ˈsjuː-, US ˈsuː.pɚ-
superhero ˈsuː.pəˌhɪə.rəʊ, ˈsjuː-, ˌsuː.pəˈhɪə.rəʊ, US ˈsuː.pɚ- **-es** -z
superheterodyne ˌsuː.pəˈhet.ər.əʊ.daɪn, ˌsjuː-, US ˌsuː.pɚˈhet̬.ə.roʊ.daɪn, -rə.daɪn **-s** -z
superhighway ˌsuː.pəˈhaɪ.weɪ, ˌsjuː-, ˈsuː.pəˌhaɪ.weɪ, US ˈsuː.pɚ- **-s** -z ˌ**information** ˈ**super**ˌ**highway;** ˌ**information** ˌ**super**ˈ**highway**
superhuman ˌsuː.pəˈhjuː.mən, ˌsjuː-, US ˌsuː.pɚˈhjuː- **-ly** -li **-ness** -nəs, -nɪs
superimpose ˌsuː.pər.ɪmˈpəʊz, ˌsjuː-, US ˌsuː.pɚ.ɪmˈpoʊz **-es** -ɪz **-ing** -ɪŋ **-ed** -d
superintend ˌsuː.pər.ɪnˈtend, ˌsjuː-, US ˌsuː.pɚ- **-s** -z **-ing** -ɪŋ **-ed** -ɪd **-ence** -ənts
superintendency ˌsuː.pər.ɪnˈten.dənt.s|i, ˌsjuː-, US ˌsuː.pɚ- **-ies** -iz
superintendent ˌsuː.pər.ɪnˈten.dənt, ˌsjuː-, US ˌsuː.pɚ- **-s** -s
superior, S~ suːˈpɪə.ri.əʳ, sjuː-, su-, sju-, sə-, US səˈpɪr.i.ɚ, su- **-s** -z
superiority suːˌpɪə.riˈɒr.ə.t|i, sjuː-, su-, sju-, sə-, -ɪ.t|i, US səˌpɪr.iˈɔːr.ə.t̬|i, su- **-ies** -iz
superlative suːˈpɜː.lə.tɪv, sjuː-, su-, sju-, US səˈpɝː.lə.t̬ɪv, su-, suː- **-s** -z **-ly** -li **-ness** -nəs, -nɪs
Superleague ˈsuː.pə.liːg, ˈsjuː-, US ˈsuː.pɚ- **-s** -z
superman, S~ ˈsuː.pə|.mæn, ˈsjuː-, US ˈsuː.pɚ- **-men** -men
supermarket ˈsuː.pəˌmɑː.kɪt, ˈsjuː-, US ˈsuː.pɚˌmɑːr- **-s** -s
supermodel ˈsuː.pəˌmɒd.əl, ˈsjuː-, US ˈsuː.pɚˌmɑː.dəl **-s** -z
supernal suːˈpɜː.nəl, sjuː-, su-, sju-, US səˈpɝː-, su-, suː-
supernatural ˌsuː.pəˈnætʃ.ər.əl, ˌsjuː-, -ʊ.rəl, US ˌsuː.pɚˈnæt.ʃɚ.əl **-ly** -i **-ness** -nəs, -nɪs
supernormal ˌsuː.pəˈnɔː.məl, ˌsjuː-, US ˌsuː.pɚˈnɔːr-
supernova ˌsuː.pəˈnəʊ.v|ə, ˌsjuː-, US ˌsuː.pɚˈnoʊ- **-ae** -iː **-as** -əz
supernumerary ˌsuː.pəˈnjuː.mər.ər|.i, ˌsjuː-, US ˌsuː.pɚˈnuː.mə.rer|.i, -ˈnjuː- **-ies** -iz
superoctave ˈsuː.pərˌɒk.tɪv, ˈsjuː-, US ˈsuː.pɚˌɑːk- **-s** -z
superordinate ˌsuː.pərˈɔː.dən.ət, ˌsjuː-, -dɪ.nət, -nɪt, -neɪt, US ˌsuː.pɚˈɔːr.dən.ɪt **-s** -s
superpose ˌsuː.pəˈpəʊz, ˌsjuː-, US ˌsuː.pɚˈpoʊz **-es** -ɪz **-ing** -ɪŋ **-ed** -d
superposition ˌsuː.pə.pəˈzɪʃ.ən, ˌsjuː-, US ˌsuː.pɚ- **-s** -z
superpower ˈsuː.pəˌpaʊ.əʳ, -ˌpaʊəʳ, ˈsjuː-, US ˈsuː.pɚˌpaʊ.ɚ **-s** -z
superpriority ˌsuː.pə.praɪˈɒr.ə.t|i, ˌsjuː-, -ɪ.t|i, US ˌsuː.pɚ.praɪˈɔːr.ə.t̬|i **-ies** -iz
supersaver ˈsuː.pəˌseɪ.vəʳ, ˈsjuː-, US ˈsuː.pɚˌseɪ.vɚ **-s** -z
superscribe ˌsuː.pəˈskraɪb, ˌsjuː-, ˈ---, US ˈsuː.pɚ.skraɪb **-es** -z **-ing** -ɪŋ **-ed** -d
superscript ˈsuː.pə.skrɪpt, ˈsjuː-, US ˈsuː.pɚ-
superscription ˌsuː.pəˈskrɪp.ʃən, ˌsjuː-, US ˌsuː.pɚˈ- **-s** -z
supersede ˌsuː.pəˈsiːd, ˌsjuː-, US ˌsuː.pɚˈ- **-es** -z **-ing** -ɪŋ **-ed** -ɪd
supersession ˌsuː.pəˈseʃ.ən, ˌsjuː-, US ˌsuː.pɚˈ-
supersize ˈsuː.pə.saɪz, US -pɚ- **-es** -ɪz **-ing** -ɪŋ **-ed** -d
supersonic ˌsuː.pəˈsɒn.ɪk, ˌsjuː-, US ˌsuː.pɚˈsɑː.nɪk **-s** -z **-ally** -əl.i, -li
superstar ˈsuː.pə.stɑːʳ, ˈsjuː-, US ˈsuː.pɚ.stɑːr **-s** -z **-dom** -dəm
superstate ˈsuː.pə.steɪt, ˈsjuː-, US ˈsuː.pɚ- **-s** -s
superstition ˌsuː.pəˈstɪʃ.ən, ˌsjuː-, US ˌsuː.pɚˈ- **-s** -z
superstitious ˌsuː.pəˈstɪʃ.əs, ˌsjuː-, US ˌsuː.pɚˈ- **-ly** -li **-ness** -nəs, -nɪs
superstore ˈsuː.pə.stɔːʳ, ˈsjuː-, US ˈsuː.pɚ.stɔːr **-s** -z
superstring ˈsuː.pə.strɪŋ, ˈsjuː-, US ˈsuː.pɚ- **-s** -z
superstructure ˈsuː.pəˌstrʌk.tʃəʳ, ˈsjuː-, US ˈsuː.pɚˌstrʌk.tʃɚ **-s** -z
supertanker ˈsuː.pəˌtæŋ.kəʳ, ˈsjuː-, US ˈsuː.pɚˌtæŋ.kɚ **-s** -z
supertax ˈsuː.pə.tæks, ˈsjuː-, ˌ--ˈ-, US ˈsuː.pɚ.tæks **-es** -ɪz
supertitle ˈsuː.pəˌtaɪ.təl, ˈsjuː-, US ˈsuː.pɚ- **-s** -z
supertonic ˌsuː.pəˈtɒn.ɪk, ˌsjuː-, US ˌsuː.pɚˈtɑː.nɪk **-s** -s
superuser ˈsuː.pəˌjuː.zəʳ, ˈsjuː-, US -pɚˌjuː.zɚ **-s** -z
supervene ˌsuː.pəˈviːn, ˌsjuː-, US ˌsuː.pɚˈ- **-es** -z **-ing** -ɪŋ **-ed** -d
supervise ˈsuː.pə.vaɪz, ˈsjuː-, US ˈsuː.pɚ- **-es** -ɪz **-ing** -ɪŋ **-ed** -d
supervision ˌsuː.pəˈvɪʒ.ən, ˌsjuː-, US ˌsuː.pɚˈ- **-s** -z
supervisor ˈsuː.pə.vaɪ.zəʳ, ˈsjuː-, US ˈsuː.pɚ.vaɪ.zɚ **-s** -z
supervisory ˌsuː.pəˈvaɪ.zər.i, ˌsjuː-, ˈsuː.pə.vaɪ-, ˈsjuː-, US ˌsuː.pɚˈvaɪ.zɚ-
superwoman ˈsuː.pə|ˌwʊm.ən, ˈsjuː-, US ˈsuː.pɚˌ- **-women** -ˌwɪm.ɪn
supine n ˈsuː.paɪn, ˈsjuː-, US ˈsuː- **-s** -z
supine adj ˈsuː.paɪn, ˈsjuː-, -ˈ-, US suːˈpaɪn, ˈ-- **-ly** -li **-ness** -nəs, -nɪs
supper ˈsʌp.əʳ, US -ɚ **-s** -z **-less** -ləs, -lɪs
supplant sə|ˈplɑːnt, US -ˈplænt **-plants** -ˈplɑːnts, US -ˈplænts **-planting** -ˈplɑːn.tɪŋ, US -ˈplæn.t̬ɪŋ **-planted** -ˈplɑːn.tɪd, US -ˈplæn.t̬ɪd **-planter/s** -ˈplɑːn.təʳ/z, US -ˈplæn.t̬ɚ/z
supple ˈsʌp|.əl **-leness** -əl.nəs, -nɪs **-ly** -li, -əl.i
supplement n ˈsʌp.lɪ.mənt, -lə-, US -lə- **-s** -s
supplement v ˈsʌp.lɪ|.ment, -lə-, ˌ--ˈ-, US ˈsʌp.lə- **-ments** -ments **-menting** -men.tɪŋ, US -men.t̬ɪŋ **-mented** -men.tɪd, US -men.t̬ɪd
supplemental ˌsʌp.lɪˈmen.təl, -ləˈ-, US -ləˈmen.t̬əl
supplementary ˌsʌp.lɪˈmen.tər.i, -ləˈ-, ˈ-tri, US -ləˈmen.t̬ɚ.i *stress shift, see compound:* ˌ**supplementary** ˈ**benefit**
supplementation ˌsʌp.lɪ.menˈteɪ.ʃən, -lə-, US -lə-
suppliant ˈsʌp.li.ənt **-s** -s **-ly** -li
supplicant ˈsʌp.lɪ.kənt, -lə-, US -lə- **-s** -s
supplicate ˈsʌp.lɪ|.keɪt, -lə-, US -lə- **-cates** -keɪts **-cating/ly** -keɪ.tɪŋ/li,

S

ⓤⓢ -keɪ.t̬ɪŋ/li **-cated** -keɪ.tɪd, ⓤⓢ -keɪ.t̬ɪd

supplication ˌsʌp.lɪˈkeɪ.ʃən, -ləˈ-, ⓤⓢ -ləˈ- **-s** -z

supplicatory ˈsʌp.lɪ.kə.tər.i, -lə-, -keɪ-, ⓤⓢ -lə.kə.tɔːr-

supplier səˈplaɪ.əʳ, ⓤⓢ -ɚ **-s** -z

suppl|y səˈpl|aɪ **-ies** -aɪz **-ying** -aɪ.ɪŋ **-ied** -aɪd **supˌply and deˈmand; supˈply ˌteacher**

supply-sid|e səˈplaɪ.saɪd **-er/s** -əʳ/z, ⓤⓢ -ɚ/z

sup|port sə|ˈpɔːt, ⓤⓢ -ˈpɔːrt **-ports** -ˈpɔːts, ⓤⓢ -ˈpɔːrts **-porting** -ˈpɔː.tɪŋ, ⓤⓢ -ˈpɔːr.t̬ɪŋ **-ported** -ˈpɔː.tɪd, ⓤⓢ -ˈpɔːr.t̬ɪd **-porter/s** -ˈpɔː.təʳ/z, ⓤⓢ -ˈpɔːr.t̬ɚ/z

supportab|le səˈpɔː.tə.b|əl, ⓤⓢ -ˈpɔːr.t̬ə- **-ly** -li

supportive səˈpɔː.tɪv, ⓤⓢ -ˈpɔːr.t̬ɪv

suppos|e səˈpəʊz, ⓤⓢ -ˈpoʊz **-es** -ɪz **-ing** -ɪŋ **-ed** -d

supposedly səˈpəʊ.zɪd.li, ⓤⓢ -ˈpoʊ-

supposition ˌsʌp.əˈzɪʃ.ən **-s** -z

suppositional ˌsʌp.əˈzɪʃ.ən.əl, ˈ-nəl **-ly** -i

supposititious səˌpɒz.ɪˈtɪʃ.əs, -əˈ-, ⓤⓢ -ˌpɑː.zəˈ- **-ly** -li **-ness** -nəs, -nɪs

suppositor|y səˈpɒz.ɪ.tər|.i, ˈ-ə-, -tr|i, ⓤⓢ -ˈpɑː.zə.tɔːr|.i **-ies** -iz

suppress səˈpres **-es** -ɪz **-ing** -ɪŋ **-ed** -t **-or/s** -əʳ/z, ⓤⓢ -ɚ/z **-ible** -ə.bəl, -ɪ.bəl

suppressant səˈpres.ənt **-s** -s

suppression səˈpreʃ.ən **-s** -z

suppu|rate ˈsʌp.jə|.reɪt, -jʊ- **-rates** -reɪts **-rating** -reɪ.tɪŋ, ⓤⓢ -reɪ.t̬ɪŋ **-rated** -reɪ.tɪd, ⓤⓢ -reɪ.t̬ɪd

suppuration ˌsʌp.jərˈeɪ.ʃən, -jʊˈreɪ-, ⓤⓢ -jəˈreɪ-, -jʊˈ- **-s** -z

supra- ˈsuː.prə, ˈsjuː-, ⓤⓢ ˈsuː.prə

supradental ˌsuː.prəˈden.təl, ˌsjuː-, ⓤⓢ ˌsuː.prəˈden.t̬əl

suprafix ˈsuː.prə.fɪks, ˈsjuː-, ⓤⓢ ˈsuː-

supraglottal ˌsuː.prəˈglɒt.əl, ˌsjuː-, ⓤⓢ -ˈglɑː.t̬əl

supranational ˌsuː.prəˈnæʃ.ən.əl, ˌsjuː-, ˈ-nəl, ⓤⓢ ˌsuː- **-ly** -li

suprarenal ˌsuː.prəˈriː.nəl, ˌsjuː-, ˈsuː.prəˌriː-, ˈsjuː-, ⓤⓢ ˌsuː.prəˈriː-

suprasegmental ˌsuː.prə.segˈmen.təl, ˌsjuː-, ⓤⓢ ˌsuː.prə.segˈmen.t̬əl

supremacist suːˈprem.ə.sɪst, sjuː-, sʊ-, sjʊ-, ⓤⓢ səˈ-, sʊ-, suː- **-s** -s

supremac|y suːˈprem.ə.s|i, sjuː-, sʊ-, sjʊ-, ⓤⓢ sə-, sʊ-, suː- **-ies** -iz

supreme suːˈpriːm, sjuː-, sʊ-, sjʊ-, ⓤⓢ sə-, sʊ-, suː- **-ly** -li **-ness** -nəs, -nɪs **Suˌpreme ˈCourt; Suˌpreme ˈSoviet**

supremo suːˈpriː.məʊ, sjuː-, sʊ-, sjʊ-, ⓤⓢ suːˈpriː.moʊ, sʊ-, sə- **-s** -z

supt, S~ (abbrev. for **superintendent**) ˌsuː.pər.ɪnˈten.dənt, ˌsjuː-, ⓤⓢ ˌsuː.pɚ-

sura ˈsʊə.rə, ⓤⓢ ˈsʊr.ə **-s** -z

surah ˈsjʊə.rə, ⓤⓢ ˈsʊr.ə

surat sʊˈræt, sjuː-, ⓤⓢ ˈsʊr.æt

Surat ˈsʊə.rət, ˈsuː-; sʊˈrɑːt, -ˈræt, ⓤⓢ ˈsʊr.ət; ⓤⓢ səˈræt

Surbiton ˈsɜː.bɪ.tən, ⓤⓢ ˈsɝː.bɪ.t̬ən

surceas|e v sɜːˈsiːs, ⓤⓢ sɝː- **-es** -ɪz **-ing** -ɪŋ **-ed** -t

surceas|e n sɜːˈsiːs, ⓤⓢ sɝː-, ˈ-- **-es** -ɪz

surcharg|e n ˈsɜː.tʃɑːdʒ, ˌ-ˈ-, ⓤⓢ ˈsɝː.tʃɑːrdʒ **-es** -ɪz

surcharg|e v ˈsɜː.tʃɑːdʒ, ˌ-ˈ-, ⓤⓢ ˈsɝː.tʃɑːrdʒ, -ˈ- **-es** -ɪz **-ing** -ɪŋ **-ed** -d

surcingle ˈsɜː.sɪŋ.gəl, ⓤⓢ ˈsɝː- **-s** -z

surcoat ˈsɜː.kəʊt, ⓤⓢ ˈsɝː.koʊt **-s** -s

surd sɜːd, ⓤⓢ sɝːd **-s** -z **-ity** -ə.ti, -ɪ.ti, ⓤⓢ -ə.t̬i

sur|e ʃɔːʳ, ʃʊəʳ, ⓤⓢ ʃʊr **-er** -əʳ, ⓤⓢ -ɚ **-est** -ɪst, -əst **-ness** -nəs, -nɪs

surefire ˈʃɔː.faɪəʳ, ˈʃʊə-, -ˌfaɪ.əʳ, ˌ-ˈ-, ⓤⓢ ˈʃʊr.faɪ.ɚ

surefooted ˌʃɔːˈfʊt.ɪd, ˌʃʊə-, ⓤⓢ ˈʃʊrˌfʊt̬.ɪd **-ly** -li **-ness** -nəs, -nɪs

surely ˈʃɔː.li, ˈʃʊə-, ⓤⓢ ˈʃʊr-

suret|y ˈʃɔː.rə.t|i, ˈʃʊə-, ⓤⓢ ˈʃʊr.ə.t̬|i, ˈ-t̬|i **-ies** -iz **-yship/s** -i.ʃɪp/s

surf sɜːf, ⓤⓢ sɝːf **-s** -s **-ing** -ɪŋ **-ed** -t

surfac|e ˈsɜː.fɪs, -fəs, ⓤⓢ ˈsɝː- **-es** -ɪz **-ing** -ɪŋ **-ed** -t **ˈsurface ˌmail; ˈsurface ˌstructure; ˌsurface ˈtension** ⓤⓢ **ˈsurface ˌtension**

surface-to-air ˌsɜː.fɪs.tuˈeəʳ, ⓤⓢ ˌsɝː.fɪs.tuˈer **ˌsurface-to-air ˈmissile**

surface-to-surface ˌsɜː.fɪs.təˈsɜː.fɪs, ⓤⓢ ˌsɝː.fɪs.təˈsɝːr- *stress shift:* **ˌsurface-to-surface ˈmissile**

surfactant sɜːˈfæk.tənt, ⓤⓢ sɝː- **-s** -s

surfboard ˈsɜːf.bɔːd, ⓤⓢ ˈsɝːf.bɔːrd **-s** -z **-er/s** -əʳ/z, ⓤⓢ -ɚ/z

surfboat ˈsɜːf.bəʊt, ⓤⓢ ˈsɝːf.boʊt **-s** -s

surfei|t ˈsɜː.fɪ|t, -ə|t, ⓤⓢ ˈsɝː.fɪ|t **-ts** -ts **-ting** -tɪŋ, ⓤⓢ -t̬ɪŋ **-ted** -tɪd, ⓤⓢ -t̬ɪd

surfer ˈsɜː.fəʳ, ⓤⓢ ˈsɝː.fɚ **-s** -z

surfing ˈsɜː.fɪŋ, ⓤⓢ ˈsɝː-

surg|e sɜːdʒ, ⓤⓢ sɝːdʒ **-es** -ɪz **-ing** -ɪŋ **-ed** -d

surgeon ˈsɜː.dʒən, ⓤⓢ ˈsɝː- **-s** -z

surger|y ˈsɜː.dʒər|.i, ⓤⓢ ˈsɝː- **-ies** -iz

surgic|al ˈsɜː.dʒɪ.k|əl, ⓤⓢ ˈsɝː- **-ally** -əl.i, -li **ˌsurgical ˈspirit**

Suriname, Surinam ˌsʊə.rɪˈnæm, ˌsjʊə-, ˈ---, ⓤⓢ ˌsʊr.ɪˈnɑːm; ⓤⓢ ˈsʊr.ɪ.næm

Surinamese ˌsʊə.rɪ.næmˈiːz, ˌsjʊə-

surl|y ˈsɜː.l|i, ⓤⓢ ˈsɝː- **-ier** -i.əʳ, ⓤⓢ -i.ɚ **-iest** -i.ɪst, -i.əst **-ily** -əl.i, -ɪ.li **-iness** -ɪ.nəs, -ɪ.nɪs

surmis|e n ˈsɜː.maɪz; ˌ-ˈ-, sə-, ⓤⓢ sɚˈmaɪz; ⓤⓢ ˈsɝːr.maɪz **-es** -ɪz

surmis|e v sɜːˈmaɪz, sə-; ˈsɜː.maɪz, ⓤⓢ sɚˈmaɪz **-es** -ɪz **-ing** -ɪŋ **-ed** -d

sur|mount sə|ˈmaʊnt, sɜː-, ⓤⓢ sɚ- **-mounts** -ˈmaʊnts **-mounting** -ˈmaʊn.tɪŋ, ⓤⓢ -ˈmaʊn.t̬ɪŋ **-mounted** -ˈmaʊn.tɪd, ⓤⓢ -ˈmaʊn.t̬ɪd **-mountable** -ˈmaʊn.tə.bəl, ⓤⓢ -ˈmaʊn.t̬ə.bəl

surnam|e ˈsɜː.neɪm, ⓤⓢ ˈsɝː- **-es** -z **-ing** -ɪŋ **-ed** -d

surpass səˈpɑːs, sɜː-, ⓤⓢ sɚˈpæs **-es** -ɪz **-ing/ly** -ɪŋ/li **-ed** -t **-able** -ə.bəl

surplic|e ˈsɜː.plɪs, -pləs, ⓤⓢ ˈsɝː- **-es** -ɪz **-ed** -t

surplus ˈsɜː.pləs, ⓤⓢ ˈsɝː-, -plʌs **-es** -ɪz **-age** -ɪdʒ

surpris|e səˈpraɪz, ⓤⓢ sɚ- **-es** -ɪz **-ing/ly** -ɪŋ/li **-ed/ly** -ɪd/li, -d/li

surreal səˈrɪəl, ⓤⓢ səˈriː.əl, -ˈriːl

surreal|ism səˈrɪə.lɪ|.zəm, ⓤⓢ -ˈriː.ə-, -ˈriː.lɪ- **-ist/s** -ɪst/s

surrealistic səˌrɪəˈlɪs.tɪk, ⓤⓢ -ˌriː.əˈ-, -ˌriːˈ-

surrend|er sərˈen.d|əʳ, ⓤⓢ səˈren.d|ɚ **-ers** -əz, ⓤⓢ -ɚz **-ering** -ər.ɪŋ **-ered** -əd, ⓤⓢ -ɚd

surreptitious ˌsʌr.əpˈtɪʃ.əs, -ɪpˈ-, -epˈ-, ⓤⓢ ˌsɝː.əpˈ- **-ly** -li **-ness** -nəs, -nɪs

Surrey, surrey ˈsʌr.i, ⓤⓢ ˈsɝː-

surrogac|y ˈsʌr.ə.gə.s|i **-ies** -iz

surrogate ˈsʌr.ə.gɪt, -gət, -geɪt, ⓤⓢ ˈsɝː.ə.gɪt, -geɪt **-s** -s **ˌsurrogate ˈmother**

surround səˈraʊnd **-s** -z **-ing/s** -ɪŋ/z **-ed** -ɪd **surˌround ˈsound**

sursum corda ˌsɜː.səmˈkɔː.də, -sʊmˈ-, ⓤⓢ ˌsɝː.səmˈkɔːr-, -sʊmˈ-

surtax ˈsɜː.tæks, ⓤⓢ ˈsɝː- **-es** -ɪz

Surtees ˈsɜː.tiːz, ⓤⓢ ˈsɝː-

surtit|le ˈsɜːˌtaɪ.təl, ⓤⓢ ˈsɝːˌtaɪ.t̬əl **-es** -z **-ing** -ɪŋ, -ˌtaɪt.lɪŋ **-ed** -d

Surtsey ˈsɜːt.si, -seɪ, ⓤⓢ ˈsɝːt-

surveil səˈveɪ **-s** -z **-ing** -ɪŋ **-led** -d **-lant/s** -ənt/s

surveillance sɜːˈveɪ.lənts, sə-, ⓤⓢ sɚ-, -ˈveɪl.ənts

survey n ˈsɜː.veɪ; ˌ-ˈ-, sə-, ⓤⓢ ˈsɝː.veɪ **-s** -z

survey v səˈveɪ, sɜː-; ˈsɜː.veɪ, ⓤⓢ sɚˈveɪ; ⓤⓢ ˈsɝː.veɪ **-s** -z **-ing** -ɪŋ **-ed** -d

surveyor səˈveɪ.əʳ, ⓤⓢ sɚˈveɪ.ɚ **-s** -z

survival səˈvaɪ.vəl, ⓤⓢ sɚ- **-s** -z **surˌvival of the ˈfittest**

survivalist səˈvaɪ.vəl.ɪst, ⓤⓢ sɚ- **-s** -s

surviv|e səˈvaɪv, ⓤⓢ sɚ- **-es** -z **-ing** -ɪŋ **-ed** -d **-able** -ə.bəl

survivor səˈvaɪ.vəʳ, ⓤⓢ sɚˈvaɪ.vɚ **-s** -z

Susan ˈsuː.zən

Susanna(h) suːˈzæn.ə, sʊ-

susceptibilit|y səˌsep.təˈbɪl.ə.t|i, -tɪˈ-, -ɪ.t|i, ⓤⓢ -təˈbɪl.ə.t̬|i **-ies** -iz

susceptib|le səˈsep.tə.b|əl, -tɪ-, ⓤⓢ -tə- **-ly** -li

susceptive səˈsep.tɪv

sushi ˈsuː.ʃi

Susie ˈsuː.zi

suspect n, adj ˈsʌs.pekt **-s** -s

suspect v səˈspekt **-s** -s **-ing** -ɪŋ **-ed** -ɪd

suspend səˈspend **-s** -z **-ing** -ɪŋ **-ed** -ɪd

suspender səˈspen.dəʳ, ⓤⓢ -dɚ **-s** -z **suˈspender ˌbelt**

suspens|e səˈspents **-ible** -ə.bəl, -ɪ.bəl

suspensibility səˌspent.səˈbɪl.ə.ti, -sɪˈ-, -ɪ.ti, ⓤⓢ -səˈbɪl.ə.t̬i

suspension səˈspen.tʃən, Ⓤⓢ -ˈspent.ʃən **-s** -z **suˈspension ˌbridge**
suspens|ive səˈspent.s|ɪv **-ory** -ər.i
suspicion səˈspɪʃ.ən **-s** -z
suspicious səˈspɪʃ.əs **-ly** -li **-ness** -nəs, -nɪs
suss sʌs **-es** -ɪz **-ing** -ɪŋ **-ed** -t
Sussex ˈsʌs.ɪks
Susskind ˈsʊs.kɪnd, Ⓤⓢ ˈsʌs-
sustain səˈsteɪn **-s** -z **-ing** -ɪŋ **-ed** -d **-er/s** -ər/z, Ⓤⓢ -ɚ/z **-able** -ə.bəl
sustainability səˌsteɪ.nəˈbɪl.ə.ti, -ɪ.ti, Ⓤⓢ -ə.ţi
sustenance ˈsʌs.tɪ.nənts, -tən.ənts, Ⓤⓢ -tən.ənts
sustentation ˌsʌs.tenˈteɪ.ʃən, -tənˈ-
susurr|ate ˈsuː.sər|.eɪt, ˈsjuː-, Ⓤⓢ suːˈsɝː|.eɪt, sʊ-, sə- **-ates** -eɪts **-ating** -eɪ.tɪŋ, Ⓤⓢ -eɪ.ţɪŋ **-ated** -eɪ.tɪd, Ⓤⓢ -eɪ.ţɪd
susurration ˌsuː.sərˈeɪ.ʃən, ˌsjuː-, Ⓤⓢ ˌsuː.səˈreɪ- **-s** -z
Sutcliffe ˈsʌt.klɪf
Sutherland ˈsʌð.əl.ənd, Ⓤⓢ -ɚ.lənd
Sutlej ˈsʌt.lɪdʒ, -ledʒ, Ⓤⓢ -ledʒ
sutler ˈsʌt.lər, Ⓤⓢ -lɚ **-s** -z
Sutro ˈsuː.trəʊ, Ⓤⓢ -troʊ
suttee ˈsʌt.iː, -ˈ-, Ⓤⓢ səˈtiː; Ⓤⓢ ˈsʌt.iː **-s** -z
Sutton ˈsʌt.ən
Sutton Coldfield ˌsʌt.ənˈkəʊld.fiːld, Ⓤⓢ -ˈkoʊld-
Sutton Hoo ˌsʌt.ənˈhuː
sutur|e ˈsuː.tʃər, ˈsjuː-, -tjər, Ⓤⓢ ˈsuː.tʃɚ **-es** -z **-ing** -ɪŋ **-ed** -d
SUV ˌes.juːˈviː **-s** -z
Suva ˈsuː.və
Suzanne suːˈzæn, sʊ-
suzerain ˈsuː.zər.eɪn, ˈsjuː-, Ⓤⓢ ˈsuː.zɚ.ɪn, -zə.raɪn **-s** -z
suzeraint|y ˈsuː.zər.eɪn.t|i, ˈsjuː-, -ən-, Ⓤⓢ ˈsuː.zɚ.ɪn-, -zə.raɪn- **-ies** -iz
Suzuki® səˈzuː.ki, sʊ- **-s** -z
Suzy ˈsuː.zi
svarabhakti ˌsvʌr.əˈbʌk.ti, ˌsvɑː.rəˈ-, -ˈbæk-, -tiː, Ⓤⓢ ˌsvɑːr.ɑːˈbɑːk-
svelt|e svelt, sfelt **-ely** -li **-eness** -nəs, -nɪs
Svengali sveŋˈgɑː.li, sfeŋ-, Ⓤⓢ sven-, sfen- **-s** -z
Sverdlovsk sveədˈlɒvsk, -ˈlɒfsk; ˈ--, -ləvsk, -ləfsk, Ⓤⓢ sverdˈlɔːfsk
SW (abbrev. for **southwest**) saʊθˈwest
swab swɒb, Ⓤⓢ swɑːb **-s** -z **-bing** -ɪŋ **-bed** -d **-ber/s** -ər/z, Ⓤⓢ -ɚ/z
Swabi|a ˈsweɪ.bi|.ə **-an/s** -ən/z
swaddl|e ˈswɒd.əl, Ⓤⓢ ˈswɑː.dəl **-es** -z **-ing** -ɪŋ, ˈswɒd.lɪŋ, Ⓤⓢ ˈswɑːd- **-ed** -d **ˈswaddling ˌclothes**
Swadlincoat ˈswɒd.lɪn.kəʊt, -lɪŋ-, Ⓤⓢ ˈswɑːd.lɪn.koʊt
Swadling ˈswɒd.lɪŋ, Ⓤⓢ ˈswɑːd-
Swaffer ˈswɒf.ər, Ⓤⓢ ˈswɑː.fɚ
Swaffham ˈswɒf.əm, Ⓤⓢ ˈswɑː.fəm
swag swæg
swag|e sweɪdʒ **-es** -ɪz **-ing** -ɪŋ **-ed** -d
Swaggart ˈswæg.ət, Ⓤⓢ -ɚt
swagg|er ˈswæg|.ər, Ⓤⓢ -ɚ **-ers** -əz, Ⓤⓢ -ɚz **-ering/ly** -ər.ɪŋ/li **-ered** -əd, Ⓤⓢ -ɚd **-erer/s** -ər.ər/z, Ⓤⓢ -ɚ.ɚ/z **ˈswagger ˌstick**
swag|man ˈswæg|.mæn, -mən **-men** -men, -mən
Swahili swɑːˈhiː.li, swə-, Ⓤⓢ swɑː- **-s** -z
swain, S~ sweɪn **-s** -z
swale, S~ sweɪl
Swaledale ˈsweɪl.deɪl
SWALK swɔːlk, Ⓤⓢ swɑːk, swɔːk
swallow ˈswɒl.əʊ, Ⓤⓢ ˈswɑː.loʊ **-s** -z **-ing** -ɪŋ **-ed** -d
swallowtail ˈswɒl.əʊ.teɪl, Ⓤⓢ ˈswɑː.loʊ- **-s** -z **-ed** -d
swam (from **swim**) swæm
swami ˈswɑː.mi **-(e)s** -z
swamp swɒmp, Ⓤⓢ swɑːmp, swɔːmp **-s** -s **-ing** -ɪŋ **-ed** -t **-y** -i **-ier** -i.ər, Ⓤⓢ -i.ɚ **-iest** -i.ɪst, -i.əst **-iness** -ɪ.nəs, -ɪ.nɪs
swampland ˈswɒmp.lænd, Ⓤⓢ ˈswɑːmp- **-s** -z
swan, S~ swɒn, Ⓤⓢ swɑːn **-s** -z **-ning** -ɪŋ **-ned** -d **ˈswan ˌsong**
Swanage ˈswɒn.ɪdʒ, Ⓤⓢ ˈswɑː.nɪdʒ
Swanee ˈswɒn.i, Ⓤⓢ ˈswɑː.ni
swank swæŋk **-y** -i **-ier** -i.ər, Ⓤⓢ -i.ɚ **-iest** -i.ɪst, -i.əst **-ily** -əl.i, -ɪ.li **-iness** -ɪ.nəs, -ɪ.nɪs
Swanley ˈswɒn.li, Ⓤⓢ ˈswɑːn-
Swann swɒn, Ⓤⓢ swɑːn
swanner|y ˈswɒn.ər|.i, Ⓤⓢ ˈswɑː.nɚ- **-ies** -iz
Swanscombe ˈswɒnz.kəm, Ⓤⓢ ˈswɑːnz-
swansdown ˈswɒnz.daʊn, Ⓤⓢ ˈswɑːnz-
Swansea *in Wales:* ˈswɒn.zi, Ⓤⓢ ˈswɑːn- *in Tasmania:* ˈswɒnt.si, -siː, Ⓤⓢ ˈswɑːnt-
Swanson ˈswɒnt.sən, Ⓤⓢ ˈswɑːnt-
swan-upp|ing ˈswɒnˌʌp|.ɪŋ, ˌ-ˈ--, Ⓤⓢ ˈswɑːn- **-er/s** -ər/z, Ⓤⓢ -ɚ/z
Swanwick ˈswɒn.ɪk, Ⓤⓢ ˈswɑː.nɪk
swap swɒp, Ⓤⓢ swɑːp **-s** -s **-ping** -ɪŋ **-ped** -t **ˈswap ˌshop**
Swapo, SWAPO ˈswɑː.pəʊ, ˈswɒp.əʊ, Ⓤⓢ ˈswɑː.poʊ
sward swɔːd, Ⓤⓢ swɔːrd **-s** -z
swarf swɔːf, Ⓤⓢ swɔːrf
Swarfega® swɔːˈfiː.gə, Ⓤⓢ swɔːr-
swarm swɔːm, Ⓤⓢ swɔːrm **-s** -z **-ing** -ɪŋ **-ed** -d
swart swɔːt, Ⓤⓢ swɔːrt
swarth|y ˈswɔː.ð|i, Ⓤⓢ ˈswɔːr-, -θ|i **-ier** -i.ər, Ⓤⓢ -i.ɚ **-iest** -i.ɪst, -i.əst **-ily** -əl.i, -ɪ.li **-iness** -ɪ.nəs, -ɪ.nɪs
swash swɒʃ, Ⓤⓢ swɑːʃ **-es** -ɪz **-ing** -ɪŋ **-ed** -t
swashbuckl|er ˈswɒʃˌbʌk.əl|.ər, ˌ-l|ər, Ⓤⓢ ˈswɑːʃˌbʌk.əl|.ɚ, ˌ-l|ɚ **-ers** -əz, Ⓤⓢ -ɚz **-ing** -ɪŋ
swastika ˈswɒs.tɪ.kə, Ⓤⓢ ˈswɑː.stɪ- **-s** -z
swat swɒt, Ⓤⓢ swɑːt **-s** -s **-ting** -ɪŋ, Ⓤⓢ ˈswɑː.ţɪŋ **-ted** -ɪd, Ⓤⓢ ˈswɑː.ţɪd **-ter/s** -ər/z, Ⓤⓢ ˈswɑː.ţɚ/s
swatch, S~® swɒtʃ, Ⓤⓢ swɑːtʃ **-es** -ɪz
swa|th swɒ|θ, swɔː|θ, Ⓤⓢ swɑː|θ, swɔː|θ **-ths** -θs, -ðz
swath|e sweɪð **-es** -z **-ing** -ɪŋ **-ed** -d
sway sweɪ **-s** -z **-ing** -ɪŋ **-ed** -d
Swazi ˈswɑː.zi **-s** -z
Swaziland ˈswɑː.zi.lænd
swear sweər, Ⓤⓢ swer **-s** -z **-ing** -ɪŋ **swore** swɔːr, Ⓤⓢ swɔːr **sworn** swɔːn, Ⓤⓢ swɔːrn
swearword ˈsweə.wɜːd, Ⓤⓢ ˈswer.wɝːd **-s** -z
sweat swet **-s** -s **-ing** -ɪŋ, Ⓤⓢ ˈsweţ.ɪŋ **-ed** -ɪd, Ⓤⓢ ˈsweţ.ɪd
sweatband ˈswet.bænd **-s** -z
sweater ˈswet.ər, Ⓤⓢ ˈsweţ.ɚ **-s** -z
sweatpants ˈswet.pænts
sweatshirt ˈswet.ʃɜːt, Ⓤⓢ -ʃɝːt **-s** -s
sweatshop ˈswet.ʃɒp, Ⓤⓢ -ʃɑːp **-s** -s
sweat|y ˈswet|.i, Ⓤⓢ ˈsweţ- **-ier** -i.ər, Ⓤⓢ -i.ɚ **-iest** -i.ɪst, -i.əst **-iness** -ɪ.nəs, -ɪ.nɪs
swede, S~ swiːd **-s** -z
Sweden ˈswiː.dən
Swedenborg ˈswiː.dən.bɔːg, -dəm-, Ⓤⓢ -dən.bɔːrg
Swedenborgian ˌswiː.dənˈbɔː.dʒən, -dəmˈ-, -dʒi.ən, -gən, -gi.ən, Ⓤⓢ -dənˈbɔːr.dʒi.ən, -gi- **-s** -z
Swedish ˈswiː.dɪʃ **ˌSwedish ˈmassage** Ⓤⓢ **ˌSwedish masˈsage**
Sweeney ˈswiː.ni
sweep swiːp **-s** -s **-ing/s** -ɪŋ/z **swept** swept **sweeper/s** ˈswiː.pər/z, Ⓤⓢ -pɚ/z
sweepstake ˈswiːp.steɪk **-s** -s
sweet, S~ swiːt **-s** -s **-er** -ər, Ⓤⓢ ˈswiː.ţɚ **-est** -ɪst, -əst, Ⓤⓢ ˈswiː.ţɪst, -ţəst **-ly** -li **-ness** -nəs, -nɪs **ˌsweet ˈnothings; ˌsweet ˈpea; ˌsweet poˈtato** Ⓤⓢ **ˈsweet poˌtato; ˌsweet ˈtooth** Ⓤⓢ **ˈsweet ˌtooth; ˌsweet ˈWilliam; ˌsweetness and ˈlight**
sweet-and-sour ˌswiːt.ənˈsaʊ.ər, -ˈsaʊər, Ⓤⓢ -ˈsaʊ.ɚ
sweetbread ˈswiːt.bred **-s** -z
sweetbrier ˈswiːt.braɪ.ər, -braɪ.ər, Ⓤⓢ -braɪ.ɚ **-s** -z
sweetcorn ˈswiːt.kɔːn, Ⓤⓢ -kɔːrn
sweeten ˈswiː.tən **-s** -z **-ing** -ɪŋ, ˈswiːt.nɪŋ **-ed** -d **-er/s** -ər/z, ˈswiːt.nər/z, Ⓤⓢ ˈswiː.tən.ɚ/z, ˈswiːt.nɚ/z
Sweetex® ˈswiː.teks
sweetheart ˈswiːt.hɑːt, Ⓤⓢ -hɑːrt **-s** -s
sweetie ˈswiː.ti, Ⓤⓢ -ţi **-s** -z
sweeting, S~ ˈswiː.tɪŋ, Ⓤⓢ -ţɪŋ **-s** -z
sweetish ˈswiː.tɪʃ, Ⓤⓢ -ţɪʃ
sweetmeal ˈswiːt.miːl
sweetmeat ˈswiːt.miːt **-s** -s
sweet-talk ˈswiːt.tɔːk, Ⓤⓢ -tɑːk, -tɔːk **-s** -s **-ing** -ɪŋ **-ed** -t
sweet|y ˈswiː.t|i, Ⓤⓢ -ţ|i **-ies** -iz
swell swel **-s** -z **-ing/s** -ɪŋ/z **-ed** -d **swollen** ˈswəʊ.lən, Ⓤⓢ ˈswoʊ- **ˌswelled ˈhead**
swelt|er ˈswel.t|ər, Ⓤⓢ -t|ɚ **-ers** -əz, Ⓤⓢ -ɚz **-ering/ly** -ər.ɪŋ/li **-ered** -əd, Ⓤⓢ -ɚd
swept (from **sweep**) swept

S

swerv|e swɜːv, (US) swɝːv **-es** -z **-ing** -ɪŋ **-ed** -d
Swettenham ˈswet.ᵊn.əm
swift, S~ swɪft **-s** -s **-er** -əʳ, (US) -ɚ **-est** -ɪst, -əst **-ly** -li **-ness** -nəs, -nɪs
Swiftsure ˈswɪft.ʃɔːʳ, -ʃʊəʳ, (US) -ʃʊr
swig swɪɡ **-s** -z **-ging** -ɪŋ **-ged** -d
swill swɪl **-s** -z **-ing** -ɪŋ **-ed** -d **-er/s** -əʳ/z, (US) -ɚ/z
swim swɪm **-s** -z **-ming/ly** -ɪŋ/li **swam** swæm **swum** swʌm **swimmer/s** ˈswɪm.əʳ/z, (US) -ɚ/z ˈ**swimming** ˌ**bath(s);** ˈ**swimming** ˌ**costume;** ˈ**swimming** ˌ**pool**
swimsuit ˈswɪm.suːt, -sjuːt, (US) -suːt **-s** -s
swimwear ˈswɪm.weəʳ, (US) -wer
Swinbourne ˈswɪn.bɔːn, ˈswɪm-, (US) ˈswɪn.bɔːrn
Swinburne ˈswɪn.bɜːn, ˈswɪm-, -bən, (US) ˈswɪn.bɝːn, -bɚn
swindl|e ˈswɪn.dᵊl **-es** -z **-ing** -ɪŋ, ˈswɪnd.lɪŋ **-ed** -d **-er/s** -əʳ/z, ˈswɪnd.ləʳ/z, (US) ˈswɪn.dᵊl.ɚ/z, ˈswɪnd.lɚ/z
Swindon ˈswɪn.dən
swine swaɪn **-s** -z
swineherd ˈswaɪn.hɜːd, (US) -hɝːd **-s** -z
swing swɪŋ **-s** -z **-ing** -ɪŋ **swung** swʌŋ **swinger/s** ˈswɪŋ.əʳ/z, (US) -ɚ/z ˌ**swing** ˈ**door;** ˌ**swings and** ˈ**roundabouts**
swingbridge ˈswɪŋ.brɪdʒ **-s** -ɪz
swingeing ˈswɪn.dʒɪŋ
swingl|e ˈswɪŋ.ɡᵊl **-es** -z **-ing** -ɪŋ, ˈswɪŋ.ɡlɪŋ **-ed** -d
swingometer swɪŋˈɒm.ɪ.təʳ, -ə.təʳ, (US) -ˈɑː.mə.t̬ɚ **-s** -z
swing-wing ˌswɪŋˈwɪŋ, (US) ˈ-- *stress shift:* ˌ**swing-wing** ˈ**plane**
swinish ˈswaɪ.nɪʃ **-ly** -li **-ness** -nəs, -nɪs
Swinton ˈswɪn.tən, (US) -tᵊn
swip|e swaɪp **-es** -s **-ing** -ɪŋ **-ed** -t **-er/s** -əʳ/z, (US) -ɚ/z
swirl swɜːl, (US) swɝːl **-s** -z **-ing** -ɪŋ **-ed** -d **-y** -i
swish swɪʃ **-es** -ɪz **-ing** -ɪŋ **-ed** -t
swish|y ˈswɪʃ|.i **-ier** -i.əʳ, (US) -i.ɚ **-iest** -i.ɪst, -i.əst
Swiss swɪs ˌ**Swiss** ˈ**cheese;** ˌ**Swiss** ˈ**cheese** ˌ**plant;** ˌ**Swiss** ˈ**roll**
Swissair® swɪsˈeəʳ, (US) -ˈer
switch, S~® swɪtʃ **-es** -ɪz **-ing** -ɪŋ **-ed** -t
switchback ˈswɪtʃ.bæk **-s** -s
switchblade ˈswɪtʃ.bleɪd **-s** -z
switchboard ˈswɪtʃ.bɔːd, (US) -bɔːrd **-s** -z
switchgear ˈswɪtʃ.ɡɪəʳ, (US) -ɡɪr
Swithin ˈswɪð.ɪn, ˈswɪθ-
Switzerland ˈswɪt.sᵊl.ənd, (US) -sɚ.lənd
swivel ˈswɪv.ᵊl **-s** -z **-(l)ing** -ɪŋ, ˈswɪv.lɪŋ **-(l)ed** -d ˌ**swivel** ˈ**chair**
swiz(z) swɪz **-es** -ɪz
swizzl|e ˈswɪz.ᵊl **-es** -z **-ing** -ɪŋ, ˈswɪz.lɪŋ **-ed** -d **-er/s** -əʳ/z, ˈswɪz.ləʳ/z, (US) ˈ-ᵊl.ɚ/z, ˈ-lɚ/z ˈ**swizzle** ˌ**stick**
swollen (from **swell**) ˈswəʊ.lən, (US) ˈswoʊ- ˌ**swollen** ˈ**head**
swoon swuːn **-s** -z **-ing** -ɪŋ **-ed** -d
swoop swuːp **-s** -s **-ing** -ɪŋ **-ed** -t
swoosh swuːʃ, swʊʃ **-es** -ɪz **-ing** -ɪŋ **-ed** -t
swop swɒp, (US) swɑːp **-s** -s **-ping** -ɪŋ **-ped** -t
sword sɔːd, (US) sɔːrd **-s** -z ˈ**sword** ˌ**dance**
Sworder ˈsɔː.dəʳ, (US) ˈsɔːr.dɚ
swordfish ˈsɔːd.fɪʃ, (US) ˈsɔːrd-
swordplay ˈsɔːd.pleɪ, (US) ˈsɔːrd-
swords|man ˈsɔːdz|.mən, (US) ˈsɔːrdz- **-men** -mən **-manship** -mən.ʃɪp
swordstick ˈsɔːd.stɪk, (US) ˈsɔːrd- **-s** -s
sword-swallower ˈsɔːdˌswɒl.əʊ.əʳ, (US) ˈsɔːrdˌswɑː.loʊ.ɚ **-s** -z
swore (from **swear**) swɔːʳ, (US) swɔːr
sworn (from **swear**) swɔːn, (US) swɔːrn
swot swɒt, (US) swɑːt **-s** -s **-ting** -ɪŋ, (US) ˈswɑː.t̬ɪŋ **-ted** -ɪd, (US) ˈswɑː.t̬ɪd **-ter/s** -əʳ/z, (US) ˈswɑː.t̬ɚ/z
swum (from **swim**) swʌm
swung (from **swing**) swʌŋ
Sybaris ˈsɪb.ᵊr.ɪs; sɪˈbɑːr-, (US) ˈsɪb.ɚ.ɪs
sybarite ˈsɪb.ᵊr.aɪt, (US) -ə.raɪt **-s** -s
sybaritic ˌsɪb.ᵊrˈɪt.ɪk, (US) -əˈrɪt̬- **-ally** -ᵊl.i, -li
Sybil ˈsɪb.ɪl, -ᵊl, (US) -ᵊl

> Note: As a feminine name, /ˈsɪb.ᵊl/ is more common in British English; the /-ɪl/ ending is more usual for the soothsayer.

sycamore, S~ ˈsɪk.ə.mɔːʳ, (US) -mɔːr **-s** -z
syc|e saɪs **-es** -ɪz
sycophancy ˈsɪk.ə.fᵊnt.si, ˈsaɪ.kə-, -ˈfænt-, (US) -fᵊnt-
sycophant ˈsɪk.ə.fænt, ˈsaɪ.kə-, -fənt, (US) -fᵊnt **-s** -s
sycophantic ˌsɪk.əʊˈfæn.tɪk, ˌsaɪ.kəˈ-, (US) -oʊˈfæn.t̬ɪk
Sydenham ˈsɪd.ᵊn.əm, ˈ-nəm
Sydney ˈsɪd.ni
Sydneysider ˈsɪd.niˌsaɪ.dəʳ, (US) -dɚ
syenite ˈsaɪ.ə.naɪt, ˈ-ɪ-, (US) ˈ-ə-
Sykes saɪks
syllabar|y ˈsɪl.ə.bᵊr|.i, (US) -ber- **-ies** -iz
syllabic sɪˈlæb.ɪk, sə-, (US) sɪ- **-ally** -ᵊl.i, -li
syllabi|cate sɪˈlæb.ɪ|.keɪt, sə-, ˈ-ə-, (US) sɪˈlæb.ə- **-cates** -keɪts **-cating** -keɪ.tɪŋ, (US) -keɪ.t̬ɪŋ **-cated** -keɪ.tɪd, (US) -keɪ.t̬ɪd
syllabication sɪˌlæb.ɪˈkeɪ.ʃᵊn, sə-, -əˈ-, (US) sɪˌlæb.əˈ-
syllabicity ˌsɪl.əˈbɪs.ə.ti, -ɪ.ti, (US) -ə.t̬i
syllabification sɪˌlæb.ɪ.fɪˈkeɪ.ʃᵊn, sə-, ˌ-ə-, -fəˈ-, (US) sɪˌlæb.ə-
syllabi|fy sɪˈlæb.ɪ|.faɪ, sə-, ˈ-ə-, (US) sɪˈlæb.ɪ-, ˈ-ə- **-fies** -faɪz **-fying** -faɪ.ɪŋ **-fied** -faɪd
syllabism ˈsɪl.ə.bɪ.zᵊm
syllable ˈsɪl.ə.bᵊl **-s** -z
syllabub ˈsɪl.ə.bʌb
syllab|us ˈsɪl.ə.b|əs **-uses** -əs.ɪz **-i** -aɪ
syllep|sis sɪˈlep|.sɪs, sə-, (US) sɪ- **-tic** -tɪk
syllogism ˈsɪl.ə.dʒɪ.zᵊm **-s** -z
syllogistic ˌsɪl.əˈdʒɪs.tɪk **-ally** -ᵊl.i, -li
syllogiz|e, -is|e ˈsɪl.ə.dʒaɪz **-es** -ɪz **-ing** -ɪŋ **-ed** -d
sylph sɪlf **-s** -s
sylphlike ˈsɪlf.laɪk
sylvan ˈsɪl.vən
Sylvester sɪlˈves.təʳ, (US) -tɚ
Sylvia ˈsɪl.vi.ə
symbiont ˈsɪm.baɪ.ɒnt, -bi-, (US) -bi.ɑːnt, -baɪ- **-s** -s
symbiosis ˌsɪm.baɪˈəʊ.sɪs, -biˈ-, (US) -biˈoʊ-, -baɪ-
symbiotic ˌsɪm.baɪˈɒt.ɪk, -biˈ-, (US) -bi-, -baɪˈɑː.t̬ɪk
symbol ˈsɪm.bᵊl **-s** -z
symbolic sɪmˈbɒl.ɪk, (US) -ˈbɑː.lɪk **-al** -ᵊl **-ally** -ᵊl.i, -li
symbolism ˈsɪm.bᵊl.ɪ.zᵊm
symbolist ˈsɪm.bᵊl.ɪst **-s** -s
symbolization, -isa- ˌsɪm.bᵊl.aɪˈzeɪ.ʃᵊn, -ɪˈ-, (US) -əˈ-
symboliz|e, -is|e ˈsɪm.bᵊl.aɪz, (US) -bə.laɪz **-es** -ɪz **-ing** -ɪŋ **-ed** -d
Syme saɪm
Symington ˈsaɪ.mɪŋ.tən, ˈsɪm.ɪŋ-
symmetric sɪˈmet.rɪk, sə-, (US) sɪ- **-al** -ᵊl **-ally** -ᵊl.i, -li **-alness** -ᵊl.nəs, -nɪs
symmetry ˈsɪm.ə.tri, ˈ-ɪ-, (US) ˈ-ə-
Symond ˈsaɪ.mənd
Symonds ˈsaɪ.məndz, ˈsɪm.əndz
Symonds Yat ˌsɪm.əndzˈjæt
Symons ˈsaɪ.mənz, ˈsɪm.ənz
sympathetic ˌsɪm.pəˈθet.ɪk, (US) -ˈθet̬- **-al** -ᵊl **-ally** -ᵊl.i, -li
sympathiz|e, -is|e ˈsɪm.pə.θaɪz **-es** -ɪz **-ing** -ɪŋ **-ed** -d **-er/s** -əʳ/z, (US) -ɚ/z
sympath|y ˈsɪm.pə.θ|i **-ies** -iz
symphonic sɪmˈfɒn.ɪk, (US) -ˈfɑː.nɪk
symphon|y ˈsɪmp.fə.n|i **-ies** -iz ˈ**symphony** ˌ**orchestra** (US) ˌ**symphony** ˈ**orchestra**
symposi|um sɪmˈpəʊ.zi|.əm, (US) -ˈpoʊ- **-ums** -əmz **-a** -ə
symptom ˈsɪmp.təm **-s** -z
symptomatic ˌsɪmp.təˈmæt.ɪk, (US) -ˈmæt̬- **-ally** -ᵊl.i, -li
synaesthesia ˌsɪn.ɪsˈθiː.zi.ə, -iːsˈ-, -əsˈ-, -ʒə, -ʒi.ə, (US) -ɪsˈθiː.ʒə, -ʒi.ə, -zi-
synagogue ˈsɪn.ə.ɡɒɡ, (US) -ɡɑːɡ, -ɡɔːɡ **-s** -z
synaloepha ˌsɪn.ᵊlˈiː.fə, (US) -əˈliː-
synapse ˈsaɪ.næps, ˈsɪn.æps; sɪˈnæps, (US) ˈsɪn.æps; (US) sɪˈnæps
synap|sis sɪˈnæp|.sɪs **-ses** -siːz **-tic/ally** -tɪk/.ᵊl.i, -tɪk/.li
sync(h) sɪŋk **-s** -s **-ing** -ɪŋ **-ed** -t
synchromesh ˈsɪŋ.krəʊ.meʃ, ˈsɪn-,

S

ˌ--ˈ-, US ˈsɪŋ.krə-, ˈsɪn-, -kroʊ- -es -ɪz

ynchronic sɪŋˈkrɒn.ɪk, sɪn-, US sɪnˈkrɑː.nɪk, sɪŋ-

ynchronicity ˌsɪŋ.krəˈnɪs.ə.ti, ˌsɪn-, -krɒnˈɪs-, -ɪ.ti, US -krəˈnɪs.ə.t̬i

ynchronism ˈsɪŋ.krə.nɪ.zəm, ˈsɪn-

ynchronistic ˌsɪŋ.krəˈnɪs.tɪk, ˌsɪn-

ynchronization, -isa- ˌsɪŋ.krə.naɪˈzeɪ.ʃən, ˌsɪn-, -nɪˈ-, US -nəˈ- -s -z

ynchroniz|e, -is|e ˈsɪŋ.krə.naɪz, ˈsɪn- -es -ɪz -ing -ɪŋ -ed -d ˌ**synchronized ˈswimming**

ynchronous ˈsɪŋ.krə.nəs, ˈsɪn- -ly -li -ness -nəs, -nɪs

ynchrony ˈsɪŋ.krə.ni, ˈsɪn-

ynchrotron ˈsɪŋ.krəʊ.trɒn, ˈsɪn-, US -krə.trɑːn -s -z

ynco|pate ˈsɪŋ.kə|.peɪt, US ˈsɪŋ-, ˈsɪn- -pates -peɪts -pating -peɪ.tɪŋ, US -peɪ.t̬ɪŋ -pated -peɪ.tɪd, US -peɪ.t̬ɪd

yncopation ˌsɪn.kəˈpeɪ.ʃən, ˌsɪŋ-, US ˌsɪŋ-, ˌsɪn- -s -z

yncope ˈsɪŋ.kə.pi, ˈsɪn-

yncretic sɪŋˈkriː.tɪk, sɪn-, -ˈkret.ɪk, US -ˈkret̬.ɪk

yncretism ˈsɪŋ.krɪ.tɪ.zəm, ˈsɪn-, US -krə-

yndesis sɪnˈdiː.sɪs, US ˈsɪn.də-; US sɪnˈdiː-

yndetic sɪnˈdet.ɪk, US -ˈdet̬-

yndic ˈsɪn.dɪk -s -s

yndical|ism ˈsɪn.dɪ.kəl|.ɪ.zəm -ist/s -ɪst/s

yndicate n ˈsɪn.dɪ.kət, -kɪt, US -də.kɪt -s -s

yndi|cate v ˈsɪn.dɪ|.keɪt, US -də- -cates -keɪts -cating -keɪ.tɪŋ, US -keɪ.t̬ɪŋ -cated -keɪ.tɪd, US -keɪ.t̬ɪd

yndication ˌsɪn.dɪˈkeɪ.ʃən, -dəˈ-, US -dəˈ-

syndrome ˈsɪn.drəʊm, US -droʊm -s -z

syne saɪn

synecdoche sɪˈnek.də.ki

syneres|is sɪˈnɪə.rə.s|ɪs, -rɪ-, US -ˈner.ə- -es -iːz

synergism ˈsɪn.ə.dʒɪ.zəm, US ˈ-ɚ-

synerg|y ˈsɪn.ə.dʒ|i, US ˈ-ɚ- -ies -iz

synesthesia ˌsɪn.ɪsˈθiː.zi.ə, -iːsˈ-, -əsˈ-, -ʒə, -ʒi.ə, US -ɪsˈθiː.ʒə, -ʒi.ə, -zi-

Synge sɪŋ

synod ˈsɪn.əd, -ɒd, US -əd -s -z -al -əl

synodic sɪˈnɒd.ɪk, US -ˈnɑː.dɪk -al -əl -ally -əl.i, -li

synonym ˈsɪn.ə.nɪm -s -z

synonymous sɪˈnɒn.ɪ.məs, ˈ-ə-, US -ˈnɑː.nə- -ly -li

synonymy sɪˈnɒn.ɪ.mi, ˈ-ə-, US -ˈnɑː.nə-

synops|is sɪˈnɒp.s|ɪs, US -ˈnɑːp- -es -iːz

synoptic sɪˈnɒp.tɪk, US -ˈnɑːp- -s -s -al -əl -ally -əl.i, -li

synovi|a saɪˈnəʊ.vi|.ə, sɪ-, US sɪˈnoʊ- -al -əl

synovitis ˌsaɪ.nəʊˈvaɪ.tɪs, ˌsɪn.əʊˈ-, -təs, US ˌsaɪ.nəˈvaɪ.t̬ɪs, ˌsɪn.əˈ-, -t̬əs

syntactic sɪnˈtæk.tɪk -al -əl -ally -əl.i, -li

syntagm ˈsɪn.tæm -s -z

syntagmatic ˌsɪn.tægˈmæt.ɪk, US -ˈmæt̬-

syntax ˈsɪn.tæks -es -ɪz

synthes|is ˈsɪnt.θə.s|ɪs, -θɪ-, US -θə- -es -iːz

synthesiz|e, -is|e ˈsɪnt.θə.saɪz, -θɪ-, US -θə- -es -ɪz -ing -ɪŋ -ed -d -er/s -ər/z, US -ɚ/z

synthespian sɪnˈθes.pi.ən -s -z

synthetic sɪnˈθet.ɪk, US -ˈθet̬- -s -s -ally -əl.i, -li

syphilis ˈsɪf.ɪ.lɪs, -əl.ɪs, US -əl.ɪs

syphilitic ˌsɪf.ɪˈlɪt.ɪk, -əlˈɪt-, US -əˈlɪt̬-

syphon ˈsaɪ.fən -s -z -ing -ɪŋ -ed -d

Syracusan ˌsaɪə.rəˈkjuː.zən, ˌsɪr.əˈ-, US ˌsɪr.əˈ-

Syracuse *in classical history:* ˈsaɪə.rə.kjuːz, US ˈsɪr.ə- *modern town in Sicily:* ˈsaɪə.rə.kjuːz, ˈsɪr.ə-, US ˈsɪr.ə- *town in US:* ˈsɪr.ə.kjuːs, -kjuːz

Syri|a ˈsɪr.i|.ə -an/s -ən/z

Syriac ˈsɪr.i.æk

syringa sɪˈrɪŋ.gə -s -z

syring|e sɪˈrɪndʒ, sə-; ˈsɪr.ɪndʒ, US səˈrɪndʒ; US ˈsɪr.ɪndʒ -es -ɪz -ing -ɪŋ -ed -d

syrinx ˈsɪr.ɪŋks -es -ɪz

syrophoenician ˌsaɪə.rəʊ.fɪˈnɪʃ.ən, -fiːˈ-, -ʃi.ən, -si.ən, US ˌsaɪ.roʊ.fiːˈnɪʃ.ən, -fɪˈ-

syr|tis, S~ ˈsɜː|.tɪs, US ˈsɝː|.t̬ɪs -tes -tiːz

syrup ˈsɪr.əp, US ˈsɪr-, ˈsɝː- -s -s -y -i

systaltic sɪˈstæl.tɪk, US -ˈstɑːl.tɪk, -ˈstæl-

system ˈsɪs.təm, -tɪm, US -təm -s -z ˌ**systems ˈanalyst**

systematic ˌsɪs.təˈmæt.ɪk, -tɪˈ-, US -təˈmæt̬- -ally -əl.i, -li

systematization, -isa- ˌsɪs.tə.mə.taɪˈzeɪ.ʃən, -tɪ-, -tɪˈ-, US -tə.mə.t̬əˈ-

systematiz|e, -is|e ˈsɪs.tə.mə.taɪz, -tɪ-, US -tə- -es -ɪz -ing -ɪŋ -ed -d -er/s -ər/z, US -ɚ/z

systemic sɪˈstem.ɪk, -ˈstiː.mɪk, US -ˈstem.ɪk

systemiz|e ˈsɪs.tə.maɪz, -tɪ-, US -tə- -es -ɪz -ing -ɪŋ -ed -d

systole ˈsɪs.təl.i

systolic sɪˈstɒl.ɪk, US sɪsˈtɑː.lɪk

syzyg|y ˈsɪz.ɪ.dʒ|i, ˈ-ə-, US ˈ-ə- -ies -iz

Szczecin ˈʃtʃet.ʃiːn

Szeged ˈseg.ed

S

T

Pronouncing the letter T

→ *See also* **TH, TZ**

The consonant letter **t** has several possible realizations.

In word initial and final position, it is most often realized as /t/, e.g.:

tap	tæp
get	get

However, in consonant clusters /t/ may be elided, and it is silent in some words borrowed from French, e.g.:

castle	ˈkɑː.sl̩ (US) ˈkæ-
depot	ˈdep.əʊ (US) ˈdiː.poʊ

In US English, **t** is often pronounced as a voiced consonant in certain environments. The **t** must be at the end of a stressed syllable, preceded either by one of /n/, /r/, or a vowel, and followed by an unstressed syllable, either beginning with a vowel or containing a syllabic consonant other than /n/. Such a pronunciation is shown in EPD as /t̬/.

When appearing between two vowels, **t** is most likely to be pronounced as a tap or flap, e.g.:

butter	ˈbʌt.əʳ (US) ˈbʌt̬.ɚ

Before a syllabic consonant, and following /n/ or /l/, **t** is pronounced as a brief voiced plosive rather than a tap or flap, e.g.:

little	ˈlɪt.əl (US) ˈlɪt̬-
canter	ˈkæn.təʳ (US) -t̬ɚ

In careful speech, these words may be pronounced with a voiceless /t/, as in British English.

Another common pronunciation for **t** is /ʃ/ where it is followed by a suffix which begins with the letter **i**, e.g.:

negotiate	nɪˈgəʊ.ʃi.eɪt (US) -ˈgoʊ-
affection	əˈfek.ʃən

In addition

t can be pronounced as a GLOTTAL STOP either word-finally or between two vowels.

t is also sometimes realized as tʃ, e.g.:

adventure	ədˈven.tʃəʳ (US) -tʃɚ
picture	ˈpɪk.tʃəʳ (US) -tʃɚ

Due to coalescence between /t/ and /j/ in British English and omission of /j/ in US English, syllables beginning with **tu** do not always sound the same, e.g.:

Tuesday	ˈtʃuːz.deɪ (US) ˈtuːz-

t, T tiː -ˈs -z
ta *Tonic Sol-fa name for diminished seventh from the tonic:* tɔː, (US) tɑː **-s** -z
ta *syllable used in Tonic Sol-fa for counting time:* tɑː
ta *thank you:* tɑː

> Note: This form is used in casual British English.

Taal tɑːl
tab tæb **-s** -z **-bing** -ɪŋ **-bed** -d
tabard ˈtæb.ɑːd, -əd, (US) -ɚd **-s** -z
Tabasco® təˈbæs.kəʊ, (US) -koʊ
Tabatha ˈtæb.ə.θə
tabbouleh təˈbuː.leɪ, ˈtæb.u.leɪ, -li
tabb|y ˈtæb|.i **-ies** -iz
tabernacle ˈtæb.əˌnæk.əl, (US) -ɚˌ- **-s** -z
Taberner təˈbɜː.nəʳ; ˈtæb.ən.əʳ, (US) təˈbɝː.nɚ; (US) ˈtæb.ɚ.nɚ
tabes ˈteɪ.biːz
Tabitha ˈtæb.ɪ.θə, ˈ-ə-
tabla ˈtæb.lə, (US) ˈtɑː.blə, -blɑː **-s** -z
tablature ˈtæb.lə.tʃəʳ, -lɪ-, -tjʊəʳ, (US) -lə.tʃɚ **-s** -z
tabl|e, T~ ˈteɪ.bəl **-es** -z **-ing** -ɪŋ, ˈteɪ.blɪŋ **-ed** -d ˈ**table** ˌ**linen;** ˈ**table** ˌ**manners;** ˈ**table** ˌ**tennis;** ˌ**table** ˈ**tennis;** ˈ**table** ˌ**wine;** ˌ**drink someone** ˌ**under the** ˈ**table;** ˌ**turn the** ˈ**tables on** ˌ**someone**
tableau ˈtæb.ləʊ, (US) -loʊ, -ˈ- **-s** -z
tableaux (alternative plural of **tableau**) ˈtæb.ləʊ, -ləʊz, (US) -loʊ, -loʊz, -ˈ-
table|cloth ˈteɪ.bəl|.klɒθ, (US) -klɑːθ **-cloths** -klɒθs, -klɒðz, (US) -klɑːθs, -klɑːðz
table d'hôte ˌtɑː.bləˈdəʊt, -bləˈ-, (US) -bləˈdoʊt, ˌtæb.əlˈ-
table-hop ˈteɪ.bəl.hɒp, (US) -hɑːp **-s** -s **-ping** -ɪŋ **-ped** -t **-per/s** -əʳ/z, (US) -ɚ/z
tableland ˈteɪ.bəl.lænd **-s** -z
tablemat ˈteɪ.bəl.mæt **-s** -s
tablespoon ˈteɪ.bəl.spuːn **-s** -z
tablespoonful ˈteɪ.bəlˌspuːn.fʊl **-s** -z
tablespoonsful (alternative plural of **tablespoonful**) ˈteɪ.bəlˌspuːnz.fʊl
tablet ˈtæb.lət, -lɪt, (US) -lɪt **-s** -s ˌ**tablets of** ˈ**stone**
table-turning ˈteɪ.bəlˌtɜː.nɪŋ, (US) -ˌtɝː-
tableware ˈteɪ.bəl.weəʳ, (US) -wer
tabloid ˈtæb.lɔɪd **-s** -z
taboo təˈbuː, tæbˈuː **-s** -z **-ing** -ɪŋ **-ed** -d
tabor ˈteɪ.bəʳ, -bɔːʳ, (US) -bɚ **-s** -z
Tabor ˈteɪ.bɔːʳ, -bəʳ, (US) -bɚ
tabo(u)ret ˈtæb.ər.ɪt, -et, (US) ˌtæb.əˈret, ˈ--- **-s** -s
Tabriz tæbˈriːz, (US) tɑːˈbriːz, tə-
tabular ˈtæb.jə.ləʳ, -jʊ-, (US) -lɚ
tabula rasa ˌtæb.jə.ləˈrɑː.sə, -jʊ-, -zə **tabulae rasae** ˌtæb.jə.liːˈrɑː.siː, -jʊ-, -ziː
tabu|late ˈtæb.jə|.leɪt, -jʊ- **-lates** -leɪts **-lating** -leɪ.tɪŋ, (US) -leɪ.t̬ɪŋ **-lated** -leɪ.tɪd, (US) -leɪ.t̬ɪd **-lator/s** -leɪ.təʳ/z, (US) -leɪ.t̬ɚ/z
tabulation ˌtæb.jəˈleɪ.ʃən, -jʊˈ- **-s** -z
tacet ˈteɪ.set, ˈtæs.et, -ɪt, (US) ˈteɪ.set, ˈtæs.et; (US) ˈtɑː.ket
tach|e tɑːʃ, tæʃ, (US) tætʃ **-es** -ɪz
tach|ism, T~ ˈtæʃ|.ɪ.zəm **-ist/s** -ɪst/s **-iste/s** -ˈiːst/s
tachograph ˈtæk.əʊ.grɑːf, -græf, (US) -ə.græf **-s** -s
tachometer tækˈɒm.ɪ.təʳ, ˈ-ə-, (US) tækˈɑː.mə.t̬ɚ, təˈkɑː- **-s** -z
tachycardia ˌtæk.ɪˈkɑː.di.ə, (US) -ˈkɑːr-
tachygraph ˈtæk.ɪ.grɑːf, -græf, (US) -græf **-s** -s
tachygraph|y tækˈɪ.grə.f|i, təˈkɪg- **-er/s** -əʳ/z, (US) -ɚ/z
tacit ˈtæs.ɪt **-ly** -li **-ness** -nəs, -nɪs
taciturn ˈtæs.ɪ.tɜːn, (US) -ə.tɝːn **-ly** -li
taciturnity ˌtæs.ɪˈtɜː.nə.ti, -nɪ-, (US) -əˈtɝː.nə.t̬i
Tacitus ˈtæs.ɪ.təs, (US) -t̬əs
tack tæk **-s** -s **-ing** -ɪŋ **-ed** -t
tackl|e ˈtæk.əl; *nautical often:* ˈteɪ.kəl **-es** -z **-ing** -ɪŋ, ˈtæk.lɪŋ, ˈteɪ.klɪŋ **-ed** -d **-er/s** -əʳ/z, ˈtæk.ləʳ/z, ˈteɪ.kləʳ/z, (US) ˈtæk.əl.ɚ/z, ˈteɪ.kəl.ɚ/z, ˈtæk.lɚ/z, ˈteɪ.klɚ/z

tack|y ˈtæk|.i **-ier** -i.əʳ, (US) -i.ɚ **-iest** -i.ɪst, -i.əst **-ily** -əl.i, -ɪ.li **-iness** -ɪ.nəs, -ɪ.nɪs

taco ˈtæk.əʊ, ˈtɑː.kəʊ, (US) ˈtɑː.koʊ **-s** -z

Tacoma təˈkəʊ.mə, (US) -ˈkoʊ-

tact tækt

tactful ˈtækt.fəl, -fʊl **-ly** -i **-ness** -nəs, -nɪs

tactic ˈtæk.tɪk **-s** -s **-al** -əl **-ally** -əl.i, -li

tactician tækˈtɪʃ.ən **-s** -z

tactile ˈtæk.taɪl, (US) -təl

tactless ˈtækt.ləs, -lɪs **-ly** -li **-ness** -nəs, -nɪs

tactual ˈtæk.tʃu.əl, -tju-, (US) -tʃu- **-ly** -i

tad tæd **-s** -z

Tadcaster ˈtædˌkæs.təʳ, -kə.stəʳ, (US) -ˌkæs.tɚ

Tadema ˈtæd.ɪ.mə, ˈ-ə-

Tadley ˈtæd.li

tadpole ˈtæd.pəʊl, (US) -poʊl **-s** -z

Tadworth ˈtæd.wəθ, -wɜːθ, (US) -wɚθ, -wɜːθ

Tadzhik ˈtɑː.dʒiːk, -ˈ-, ˈtædʒ.ɪk, (US) ˌtɑːˈdʒɪk, -ˈdʒiːk

Tadzhikistan tɑːˌdʒɪk.ɪˈstɑːn, -ˌdʒiː.kɪˈ-, tædʒ.ɪk.ɪˈstæn, (US) -ˈdʒɪk.ɪ.stæn, -ˈdʒiː.kɪ-, -stɑːn

Taegu ˌteɪˈguː, (US) ˈtaɪ.guː, -ˈ-

Tae Kwon Do ˌtaɪˈkwɒn.dəʊ, ˌteɪ-, ˌ--ˈ-, (US) ˌtaɪ.kwɑːnˈdoʊ, ˌ-ˈ--

tael teɪl **-s** -z

ta'en (dialectal for **taken**) teɪn

Taff tæf

taffeta ˈtæf.ɪ.tə, ˈ-ə-, (US) -ɪ.t̬ə

taffrail ˈtæf.reɪl, -rɪl, -rəl, (US) -reɪl **-s** -z

taffy *US for toffee:* ˈtæf.i

Taff|y *Brit slang for Welsh:* ˈtæf|.i **-ies** -iz

Taft *surname:* tæft, tɑːft, (US) tæft *town in Iran:* tɑːft

tag tæg **-s** -z **-ging** -ɪŋ **-ged** -d **-ger/s** -əʳ/z, (US) -ɚ/z ˈ**tag** ˌ**question**

Tagalog təˈgɑː.lɒg, -ləg, (US) -lɑːg, -ləg

tagetes tædʒˈiː.tiːz

Taggart ˈtæg.ət, (US) -ɚt

tagliatelle ˌtæl.jəˈtel.i, (US) ˌtɑːl.jəˈ-

tagmeme ˈtæg.miːm **-s** -z

tagmemic tægˈmiː.mɪk **-s** -s

Tagore təˈgɔːʳ, (US) -ˈgɔːr

Tagus ˈteɪ.gəs

tahini tɑːˈhiː.ni, tə-, (US) tə-, tɑː-

Tahi|ti tɑːˈhiː|.ti, tə-, (US) təˈhiː|.t̬i **-tian/s** -ʃən/z, (US) -ʃən/z, -t̬i.ənz

Tahoe ˈtɑː.həʊ, (US) -hoʊ

t'ai chi, tai chi ˌtaɪˈtʃiː, -ˈdʒiː, (US) -ˈdʒiː, -ˈtʃiː

Taichung, T'ai-chung ˌtaɪˈtʃʊŋ

Taig taɪk, taɪx **-s** -s

taiga ˈtaɪ.gə, -gɑː, (US) -gə

tail teɪl **-s** -z **-ing** -ɪŋ **-ed** -d **-less** -ləs, -lɪs ˌ**tail** ˈ**end;** **make** ˌ**head or** ˈ**tail of;** **with one's** ˌ**tail between one's** ˈ**legs**

tailback ˈteɪl.bæk **-s** -s

tailboard ˈteɪl.bɔːd, (US) -bɔːrd **-s** -z

tailbone ˈteɪl.bəʊn, (US) -boʊn **-s** -z

tailcoat ˈteɪl.kəʊt, -ˈ-, (US) ˈteɪl.koʊt **-s** -s

tail|gate ˈteɪl|.geɪt **-gates** -geɪts **-gating** -geɪ.tɪŋ, (US) -geɪ.t̬ɪŋ **-gated** -geɪ.tɪd, (US) -geɪ.t̬ɪd **-gater/s** -ˌgeɪ.təʳ/z, (US) -ˌgeɪ.t̬ɚ/z

taille taɪ, (US) teɪl

tail|or ˈteɪ.l|əʳ, (US) -l|ɚ **-ors** -əz, (US) -ɚz **-oring** -ər.ɪŋ **-ored** -əd, (US) -ɚd

tailor-made ˌteɪ.ləˈmeɪd, (US) ˈteɪ.lɚ- **-s** -z *stress shift:* ˌ**tailor-made** ˈ**suit**

tailpiec|e ˈteɪl.piːs **-es** -ɪz

tailpipe ˈteɪl.paɪp **-s** -s

tail-rhyme ˈteɪl.raɪm

tailspin ˈteɪl.spɪn **-s** -z

tailwind ˈteɪl.wɪnd **-s** -z

Taine teɪn

taint teɪnt **-s** -s **-ing** -ɪŋ, (US) ˈteɪn.t̬ɪŋ **-ed** -ɪd, (US) ˈteɪn.t̬ɪd **-less** -ləs, -lɪs

taipan ˈtaɪ.pæn, (US) ˈ--, -ˈ- **-s** -z

Taipei ˌtaɪˈpeɪ

Taiping ˌtaɪˈpɪŋ

Tait teɪt

Taiwan ˌtaɪˈwɑːn, -ˈwæn, (US) -ˈwɑːn

Taiwanese ˌtaɪ.wəˈniːz, -wɑːˈ-, (US) -wəˈniːz, -ˈniːs

Ta'izz tɑːˈiːz, tæ-, (US) tæˈɪz

Tajik tɑːˈdʒiːk; ˈtɑː.dʒɪk **-s** -s

Tajikistan tɑːˌdʒɪk.ɪˈstɑːn, -ˌdʒiː.kɪˈ-, tædʒ.ɪk.ɪˈstæn, (US) -ˈdʒɪk.ɪ.stæn, -ˈdʒiː.kɪ-, -stɑːn

Taj Mahal ˌtɑːdʒ.məˈhɑːl

taka ˈtɑː.kɑː

tak|e teɪk **-es** -s **-ing** -ɪŋ **took** tʊk **taken** ˈteɪ.kən **taker/s** ˈteɪ.kəʳ/z, (US) -kɚ/z ˌ**take a** ˈ**hike;** ˌ**take a** ˈ**walk**

takeaway ˈteɪk.ə.weɪ **-s** -z

take-home pay ˌteɪk.həʊmˈpeɪ, ˈ--ˌ-, (US) ˈteɪk.hoʊmˌpeɪ

take-it-or-leave-it ˌteɪk.ɪt.ɔːˈliːv.ɪt, -əˈ-, (US) -ɔːrˈ-, -ɚˈ-

take-off ˈteɪk.ɒf, (US) -ɑːf **-s** -s

takeout ˈteɪk.aʊt **-s** -s

takeover ˈteɪkˌəʊ.vəʳ, (US) -ˌoʊ.vɚ **-s** -z ˈ**takeover** ˌ**bid**

take-up ˈteɪk.ʌp **-s** -s

taking ˈteɪ.kɪŋ **-s** -z **-ly** -li **-ness** -nəs, -nɪs

tala ˈtɑː.lɑː

Talbot ˈtɔːl.bət, ˈtɒl-, (US) ˈtɔːl-, ˈtæl-

> Note: Both pronunciations are current for **Port Talbot** in Wales.

talc tælk **-s** -s

Talcahuano ˌtæl.kəˈwɑː.nəʊ, (US) ˌtɑːl.kɑːˈwɑː.noʊ, ˌtæl.kəˈ-

talcum powder ˈtæl.kəmˌpaʊ.dəʳ, (US) -dɚ **-s** -z

tale teɪl **-s** -z

Taleban ˈtæl.ɪ.bæn, ˈtɑː.lɪ-, -lə-, -bɑːn, ˌ--ˈ-, (US) ˈtæl.ə.bæn, -bɑːn, ˈtɑːl-, -i-

talebearer ˈteɪlˌbeə.rəʳ, (US) -ˌber.ɚ **-s** -z

tal|ent ˈtæl|.ənt **-ents** -ənts **-ented** -ən.tɪd, (US) -ən.t̬ɪd **-entless** -ənt.ləs, -lɪs ˈ**talent** ˌ**contest;** ˈ**talent** ˌ**scout**

talent|-spot ˈtæl.ənt|.spɒt, (US) -spɑːt **-spots** -spɒts, (US) -spɑːts **-spotting** -ˌspɒt.ɪŋ, (US) -ˌspɑː.t̬ɪŋ **-spotted** -ˌspɒt.ɪd, (US) -ˌspɑː.t̬ɪd **-spotter/s** -ˌspɒt.əʳ/z, (US) -ˌspɑː.t̬ɚ/z

tales *law:* ˈteɪ.liːz, (US) ˈteɪ.liːz; (US) teɪlz

tales|man ˈteɪ.liːz|.mən, ˈteɪlz-, -mæn, (US) ˈteɪlz-, ˈteɪl.iːz- **-men** -mən, -men

taletell|er ˈteɪlˌtel|.əʳ, (US) -ɚ **-er/s** -əʳ/z, (US) -ɚ/z **-ing** -ɪŋ

Talfourd ˈtæl.fəd, (US) -fɚd

Taliban ˈtæl.ɪ.bæn, ˈtɑː.lɪ-, -lə-, -bɑːn, ˌ--ˈ-, (US) ˈtæl.ə.bæn, -bɑːn, ˈtɑːl-, -i-

Taliesin ˌtæl.iˈes.ɪn, ˌ-ˈjes-, (US) -iˈes.ɪn

talisman ˈtæl.ɪz.mən, -ɪs- **-s** -z

talismanic ˌtæl.ɪzˈmæn.ɪk, -ɪsˈ- **-ally** -əl.i, -li

talk tɔːk, (US) tɔːk, tɑːk **-s** -s **-ing** -ɪŋ **-ed** -t **-er/s** -əʳ/z, (US) -ɚ/z ˌ**talking** ˈ**head;** ˈ**talking** ˌ**point;** ˈ**talk** ˌ**show;** **(to)** ˌ**talk** ˈ**shop**

talkathon ˈtɔː.kə.θɒn, (US) -θɑːn, ˈtɑː- **-s** -z

talkative ˈtɔː.kə.tɪv, (US) -t̬ɪv, ˈtɑː- **-ly** -li **-ness** -nəs, -nɪs

talkback ˈtɔːk.bæk, (US) ˈtɔːk-, ˈtɑːk- **-s** -s

talkie ˈtɔː.ki, (US) ˈtɔː-, ˈtɑː- **-s** -z

talking-to ˈtɔː.kɪŋ.tuː, (US) ˈtɔː-, ˈtɑː- **-s** -z

tall tɔːl **-er** -əʳ, (US) -ɚ **-est** -ɪst, -əst **-ness** -nəs, -nɪs ˌ**tall** ˈ**story**

tallage ˈtæl.ɪdʒ

Tallahassee ˌtæl.əˈhæs.i

tallboy ˈtɔːl.bɔɪ **-s** -z

Talleyrand ˈtæl.i.rænd

Tallin(n) ˈtæl.ɪn, -ˈ-, -ˈiːn, (US) ˈtɑː.lɪn, ˈtæl.ɪn

Tallis ˈtæl.ɪs

tallish ˈtɔː.lɪʃ

tallow ˈtæl.əʊ, (US) -oʊ **-y** -i

Tallulah təˈluː.lə

tall|y ˈtæl|.i **-ies** -iz **-ying** -i.ɪŋ **-ied** -id

tally-ho ˌtæl.iˈhəʊ, (US) -ˈhoʊ **-s** -z

tally|man ˈtæl.i|.mən **-men** -mən, -men

Talman ˈtɔːl.mən

Talmud ˈtæl.mʊd, -məd, -mʌd, (US) ˈtɑːl.mʊd, ˈtæl-, -məd

talmudic, T~ tælˈmʊd.ɪk, -ˈmʌd-, -ˈmjuː.dɪk, (US) tɑːlˈmʊd.ɪk, tæl- **-al** -əl

talmud|ism, T~ ˈtæl.mʊd|.ɪ.zəm, -məd-, -mʌd- **-ist/s** -ɪst/s

talon ˈtæl.ən **-s** -z

Tal-y-llyn ˌtæl.iˈhlɪn, -əˈ-, -ˈθlɪn

tamable ˈteɪ.mə.bəl

Tamagotchi® ˌtæm.əˈgɒtʃ.i, (US) ˌtɑː.məˈgɑːtʃ.i **-s** -z

tamale *Mexican dish:* təˈmɑː.li, -leɪ

Tamale *in Ghana:* təˈmɑː.leɪ

Tamaqua təˈmɑː.kwə

Tamar *river in W. of England:* ˈteɪ.məʳ,

-mɑːʳ, ⓤⓢ -mɚ, -mɑːr *biblical name:* ˈteɪ.mɑːʳ, -məʳ, ⓤⓢ -mɑːr, -mɚ
Tamara təˈmɑː.rə, -ˈmær.ə; ˈtæm.ᵊr.ə, ⓤⓢ təˈmɑːr.ə, -ˈmær-, -ˈmer-
tamarillo ˌtæm.ᵊrˈɪl.əʊ, ⓤⓢ -əˈrɪl.oʊ -s -z
tamarin ˈtæm.ᵊr.ɪn, ⓤⓢ -ɚ.ɪn, -ə.ræn -s -z
tamarind ˈtæm.ᵊr.ɪnd -s -z
tamarisk ˈtæm.ᵊr.ɪsk -s -s
tambala tæmˈbɑː.lə, ⓤⓢ tɑːmˈbɑː.lɑː -s -z
tamber ˈtæm.bəʳ, ⓤⓢ -bɚ -s -z
Tambo ˈtæm.bəʊ, ⓤⓢ -boʊ
tambour ˈtæm.bʊəʳ, -bɔːʳ, -bəʳ, ⓤⓢ -bʊr -s -z
tamboura tæmˈbʊə.rə, -ˈbɔː-, ⓤⓢ tɑːmˈbʊr.ə -s -z
tambourine ˌtæm.bᵊrˈiːn, ⓤⓢ -bəˈriːn -s -z
Tamburlaine ˈtæm.bə.leɪn, ⓤⓢ -bɚ-
tam|e teɪm **-er/s** -əʳ/z, ⓤⓢ -ɚ/z **-est** -ɪst, -əst **-ely** -li **-eness** -nəs, -nɪs **-es** -z **-ing** -ɪŋ **-ed** -d
tameable ˈteɪ.mə.bᵊl
Tamerlane ˈtæm.ə.leɪn, ⓤⓢ ˈ-ɚ-
Tameside ˈteɪm.saɪd
Tamil ˈtæm.ɪl, -ᵊl, ⓤⓢ -ᵊl, ˈtɑː.mᵊl, ˈtʊm.ᵊl -s -z
Tamil Nadu ˌtæm.ɪlˈnɑː.duː, -ᵊl-, ⓤⓢ -ᵊlˈnɑː.duː, ˌtɑː.mᵊlˈ-, ˌtʊm.ᵊlˈ-, -nɑːˈduː
Tammany ˈtæm.ᵊn.i
Tammerfors ˈtæm.ə.fɔːz, ⓤⓢ -ɚ.fɔːrz
Tammuz ˈtæm.uːz, -ʊz, ⓤⓢ ˈtɑː.mʊz
Tammy ˈtæm.i
Tamora ˈtæm.ᵊr.ə
tam-o'-shanter ˌtæm.əˈʃæn.təʳ, ⓤⓢ ˈtæm.əˌʃæn.t̬ɚ -s -z
tamoxifen təˈmɒk.sɪ.fen, tæmˈɒk-, -sə-, ⓤⓢ təˈmɑːk-, tæmˈɑːk-
tamp tæmp -s -s **-ing** -ɪŋ **-ed** -t **-er/s** -əʳ/z, ⓤⓢ -ɚ/z
Tampa ˈtæm.pə
Tampax® ˈtæm.pæks
tamp|er ˈtæm.p|əʳ, ⓤⓢ -p|ɚ **-ers** -əz, ⓤⓢ -ɚz **-ering** -ᵊr.ɪŋ **-ered** -əd, ⓤⓢ -ɚd **-erer/s** -ə.rəʳ/z, ⓤⓢ -ɚ.ɚ/z
Tampere ˈtæm.pᵊr.eɪ, ⓤⓢ ˈtɑːm.pə.reɪ
tamper-evident ˌtæm.pᵊrˈev.ɪ.dᵊnt, ⓤⓢ -pɚˈ-
tamper-proof ˈtæm.pə.pruːf, ⓤⓢ -pɚ-
Tampico tæmˈpiː.kəʊ, ⓤⓢ -koʊ, tɑːm-
tampon ˈtæm.pɒn, ⓤⓢ -pɑːn -s -z
Tamsin ˈtæm.zɪn, -sɪn
Tamworth ˈtæm.wəθ, -wɜːθ, ⓤⓢ -wɚθ, -wɝːθ
tan tæn -s -z **-ning** -ɪŋ **-ned** -d **-ner/s** -əʳ/z, ⓤⓢ -ɚ/z
Tancred ˈtæŋ.kred, -krɪd, ⓤⓢ -krɪd
tandem ˈtæn.dəm, -dem, ⓤⓢ -dəm -s -z
tandoori tænˈdʊə.ri, -ˈdɔː-, ⓤⓢ tɑːnˈdʊr.i
Tandy ˈtæn.di
Tanfield ˈtæn.fiːld
tang tæŋ -s -z -y -i
Tang tæŋ, ⓤⓢ tɑːŋ
Tanga ˈtæŋ.gə
Tanganyika ˌtæŋ.gəˈnjiː.kə, -gænˈjiː-, ⓤⓢ -gəˈnjiː-
tangenc|y ˈtæn.dʒənt.s|i **-ies** -iz
tangent ˈtæn.dʒᵊnt -s -s
tangential tænˈdʒen.tʃᵊl, ⓤⓢ -ˈdʒent.ʃᵊl **-ly** -i **-ness** -nəs, -nɪs
tangerine ˌtæn.dʒᵊrˈiːn, ˈ---, ⓤⓢ ˌtæn.dʒəˈriːn, ˈ--- -s -z
tangibility ˌtæn.dʒəˈbɪl.ə.ti, -dʒɪˈ-, -ɪ.ti, ⓤⓢ -dʒəˈbɪl.ə.t̬i
tangib|le ˈtæn.dʒə.b|ᵊl, -dʒɪ-, ⓤⓢ -dʒə- **-ly** -li **-leness** -ᵊl.nəs, -nɪs
Tangier tænˈdʒɪəʳ, ˈ--, ⓤⓢ tænˈdʒɪr -s -z
tangl|e ˈtæŋ.gᵊl **-es** -z **-ing** -ɪŋ, ˈtæŋ.glɪŋ **-ed** -d
Tanglewood ˈtæŋ.gᵊl.wʊd
tangly ˈtæŋ.gli, ˈ-gᵊl.i
tango ˈtæŋ.gəʊ, ⓤⓢ -goʊ -s -z **-ing** -ɪŋ **-ed** -d
tang|y ˈtæŋ|.i **-ier** -i.əʳ, ⓤⓢ -i.ɚ **-iest** -i.ɪst, -i.əst **-iness** -ɪ.nəs, -ɪ.nɪs
Tangye ˈtæŋ.gi
tanh θæn, tæntʃ
tank tæŋk -s -s **-age** -ɪdʒ **-er/s** -əʳ/z, ⓤⓢ -ɚ/z **ˈtank ˌtop; ˌtanked ˈup**
tankard ˈtæŋ.kəd, ⓤⓢ -kɚd -s -z
tankful ˈtæŋk.fʊl -s -z
tankini tæŋˈkiː.ni -s -z
tanner, T~ ˈtæn.əʳ, ⓤⓢ -ɚ -s -z
tanner|y ˈtæn.ᵊr|.i **-ies** -iz
Tannhäuser ˈtænˌhɔɪ.zəʳ, ⓤⓢ ˈtɑːnˌhɔɪ.zɚ, ˈtæn-
tann|ic ˈtæn|.ɪk **-in** -ɪn **ˌtannic ˈacid**
tannin ˈtæn.ɪn -s -z
Tannoy® ˈtæn.ɔɪ
Tanqueray ˈtæŋ.kᵊr.i, -eɪ, ⓤⓢ -kə.reɪ, -kɚ.i
tansy, T~ ˈtæn.zi
tantalization, -isa- ˌtæn.tᵊl.aɪˈzeɪ.ʃᵊn, -ɪˈ-, ⓤⓢ -t̬ᵊl.əˈ- -s -z
tantaliz|e, -is|e ˈtæn.tᵊl.aɪz, ⓤⓢ -t̬ə.laɪz **-es** -ɪz **-ing/ly** -ɪŋ/li **-ed** -d **-er/s** -əʳ/z, ⓤⓢ -ɚ/z
tantalum ˈtæn.tᵊl.əm, ⓤⓢ -t̬ᵊl- -s -z
tantalus, T~ ˈtæn.tᵊl.əs, ⓤⓢ -t̬ᵊl- **-es** -ɪz
tantamount ˈtæn.tə.maʊnt, ⓤⓢ -t̬ə-
tantiv|y tænˈtɪv|.i **-ies** -iz
tanto ˈtæn.təʊ, ⓤⓢ -toʊ
tantr|a, T~ ˈtæn.tr|ə, ˈtʌn-, ⓤⓢ ˈtʌn-, ˈtɑːn-, ˈtæn- **-ic** -ɪk
tantrum ˈtæn.trəm -s -z
Tanya ˈtæn.jə, ˈtɑː.njə, ⓤⓢ ˈtɑː.njə, ˈtæn.jə
Tanzani|a ˌtæn.zəˈniː|.ə; tænˈzeɪ.ni|-, ⓤⓢ ˌtæn.zəˈniː|- **-an/s** -ən/z
Tao taʊ, ⓤⓢ daʊ, taʊ
Taoiseach ˈtiː.ʃək, -ʃəx, ⓤⓢ -ʃək
Tao|ism ˈtaʊ|.ɪ.zᵊm, ˈteɪ.əʊ-, ⓤⓢ ˈdaʊ|.ɪ-, ˈtaʊ- **-ist/s** -ɪst/s
tap tæp -s -s **-ping** -ɪŋ **-ped** -t **-per/s** -əʳ/z, ⓤⓢ -ɚ/z
tapas ˈtæp.æs, -əs **ˈtapas ˌbar**
tap-danc|e ˈtæpˌdɑːnts, ⓤⓢ -ˌdænts **-es** -ɪz **-ing** -ɪŋ **-ed** -t **-er/s** -əʳ/z, ⓤⓢ -ɚ/z
tap|e, T~ teɪp **-es** -s **-ing** -ɪŋ **-ed** -t **ˈtape ˌdeck; ˈtape ˌmeasure; ˈtape reˌcorder**
tap|er ˈteɪ.p|əʳ, ⓤⓢ -p|ɚ **-ers** -əz, ⓤⓢ -ɚz **-ering** -ᵊr.ɪŋ **-ered** -əd, ⓤⓢ -ɚd
tapestr|y ˈtæp.ɪ.str|i, ˈ-ə-, ⓤⓢ ˈ-ə- **-ies** -iz
tapeworm ˈteɪp.wɜːm, ⓤⓢ -wɝːm -s -z
tapioca ˌtæp.iˈəʊ.kə, ⓤⓢ -ˈoʊ-
tapir ˈteɪ.pəʳ, -pɪəʳ, ⓤⓢ -pɚ -s -z
tapis ˈtæp.iː, -pi, ⓤⓢ -i, -ɪs; ⓤⓢ tæpˈiː
tappet ˈtæp.ɪt -s -s
taproom ˈtæp.rʊm, -ruːm, ⓤⓢ -ruːm, -rʊm -s -z
tap-root ˈtæp.ruːt -s -s
tapster ˈtæp.stəʳ, ⓤⓢ -stɚ -s -z
tar tɑːʳ, ⓤⓢ tɑːr -s -z **-ring** -ɪŋ **-red** -d
Tara *literary location, place in Ireland:* ˈtɑː.rə, ⓤⓢ ˈter.ə, ˈtær- *female name:* ˈtɑː.rə, ⓤⓢ ˈtɑːr.ə
taradiddle ˈtær.əˌdɪd.ᵊl, ⓤⓢ ˈter-, ˈtær- -s -z
taramasalata, taramosalata ˌtær.ə.mə.səˈlɑː.tə, ⓤⓢ ˌter.ə.mɑː.səˈlɑː.t̬ə
Taransay ˈtær.ən.seɪ
tarantella ˌtær.ᵊnˈtel.ə, ⓤⓢ ˌter-, ˌtær- -s -z
Tarantino ˌtær.ᵊnˈtiː.nəʊ, ⓤⓢ ˌter.ᵊnˈtiː.noʊ, ˌtær-
Taranto təˈræn.təʊ, ⓤⓢ -toʊ; ⓤⓢ ˈtɑːr.ɑːn-
tarantula təˈræn.tʃə.lə, -tʃʊ-, -tjə-, -tjʊ-, ⓤⓢ -tʃə-, -tʃʊ-, -tjʊ-, -t̬ə- -s -z
Tarawa təˈrɑː.wə, ⓤⓢ təˈrɑː-; ⓤⓢ ˈtɑːr.ə-
taraxacum təˈræk.sə.kəm
Tarbuck ˈtɑː.bʌk, ⓤⓢ ˈtɑːr-
Tardis ˈtɑː.dɪs, ⓤⓢ ˈtɑːr- **-es** -ɪz
tard|y ˈtɑː.d|i, ⓤⓢ ˈtɑːr- **-ier** -i.əʳ, ⓤⓢ -i.ɚ **-iest** -i.ɪst, -i.əst **-ily** -ᵊl.i, -ɪ.li **-iness** -ɪ.nəs, -ɪ.nɪs
tare teəʳ, ⓤⓢ ter -s -z
tar|get ˈtɑː|.gɪt, ⓤⓢ ˈtɑːr- **-gets** -gɪts **-geting** -gɪ.tɪŋ, ⓤⓢ -gɪ.t̬ɪŋ **-geted** -gɪ.tɪd, ⓤⓢ -gɪ.t̬ɪd **ˈtarget ˌpractice**
tariff ˈtær.ɪf, ⓤⓢ ˈter-, ˈtær- -s -s
Tariq ˈtær.ɪk, ˈtɑː.rɪk, ⓤⓢ ˈtɑːr.ɪk
Tarka ˈtɑː.kə, ⓤⓢ ˈtɑːr-
Tarkington ˈtɑː.kɪŋ.tən, ⓤⓢ ˈtɑːr-
Tarleton ˈtɑːl.tən, ˈtɑː.lə-, ⓤⓢ ˈtɑːrl.tən, ˈtɑːr.lə-
tarmac, T~® ˈtɑː.mæk, ⓤⓢ ˈtɑːr- -s -s **-king** -ɪŋ **-ked** -t
tarmacadam ˌtɑː.məˈkæd.əm, ⓤⓢ ˌtɑːr-
tarn tɑːn, ⓤⓢ tɑːrn -s -z
tarnation tɑːˈneɪ.ʃᵊn, ⓤⓢ tɑːr-
tarnish ˈtɑː.nɪʃ, ⓤⓢ ˈtɑːr- **-es** -ɪz **-ing** -ɪŋ **-ed** -t
taro ˈtær.əʊ, ˈtɑː.rəʊ, ⓤⓢ ˈtɑːr.oʊ, ˈter-
tarot ˈtær.əʊ, ⓤⓢ -oʊ, -ət, ˈter-; ⓤⓢ təˈroʊ -s -z **ˈtarot ˌcard** ⓤⓢ **ˈtarot ˌcard taˈrot ˌcard**
tarp tɑːp, ⓤⓢ tɑːrp -s -s

tarpaulin tɑːˈpɔː.lɪn, ⓊⓈ tɑːrˈpɑː-, -ˈpɔː-; ⓊⓈ ˈtɑːr.pə- **-s** -z
Tarpeian tɑːˈpiː.ən, ⓊⓈ tɑːr-
tarpon ˈtɑː.pɒn, ⓊⓈ ˈtɑːr.pən, -pɑːn **-s** -z
Tarquin ˈtɑː.kwɪn, ⓊⓈ ˈtɑːr- **-s** -z
Tarquini|us tɑːˈkwɪn.i|.əs, ⓊⓈ tɑːr- **-i** -aɪ, -iː
tarradiddle ˈtær.əˌdɪd.əl, ⓊⓈ ˈter-, ˈtær- **-s** -z
tarragon ˈtær.ə.gən, ⓊⓈ ˈter.ə.gɑːn, ˈtær-
Tarragona ˌtær.əˈgəʊ.nə, ⓊⓈ ˌter.əˈgoʊ-, ˌtær-, ˌtɑːr.ɑːˈ-
tarrah təˈrɑː; trɑː
Tarrant ˈtær.ənt, ⓊⓈ ˈter-, ˈtær-
Tarring ˈtær.ɪŋ, ⓊⓈ ˈter-, ˈtær-
tarrock ˈtær.ək, ⓊⓈ ˈter-, ˈtær- **-s** -s
tarry adj *tarred, like tar:* ˈtɑː.ri, ⓊⓈ ˈtɑːr.i
tarr|y v *wait:* ˈtær|.i, ⓊⓈ ˈter-, ˈtær- **-ies** -iz **-ying** -i.ɪŋ **-ied** -id **-ier/s** -i.əʳ/z, ⓊⓈ -i.ɚ/z
Tarshish ˈtɑː.ʃɪʃ, ⓊⓈ ˈtɑːr-
tars|us, T~ ˈtɑː.s|əs, ⓊⓈ ˈtɑːr- **-i** -aɪ
tart tɑːt, ⓊⓈ tɑːrt **-s** -s **-ly** -li **-ness** -nəs, -nɪs
tartan ˈtɑː.tən, ⓊⓈ ˈtɑːr- **-s** -z
tartar, tartare, T~ ˈtɑː.təʳ, ⓊⓈ ˈtɑːr.t̬ɚ **-s** -z **ˌtartar ˈsauce** ⓊⓈ **ˈtartar ˌsauce**
tartaric tɑːˈtær.ɪk, ⓊⓈ tɑːr-, -ˈter-, -ˈtɑːr- **tarˌtaric ˈacid**
Tartar|us ˈtɑː.tər|.əs, ⓊⓈ ˈtɑːr.t̬ɚ- **-y** -i
tartlet ˈtɑːt.lət, -lɪt, ⓊⓈ ˈtɑːrt.lət, -lɪt **-s** -s
tartrazine ˈtɑː.trə.ziːn, -zɪn, ⓊⓈ ˈtɑːr-
Tartu ˈtɑː.tu, ⓊⓈ ˈtɑːr-
Tartuffe tɑːˈtʊf, -ˈtuːf, ⓊⓈ tɑːr-
tart|y ˈtɑː.t|i, ⓊⓈ ˈtɑːr.t̬|i **-ier** -i.əʳ, ⓊⓈ -i.ɚ **-iest** -i.ɪst, -i.əst **-ily** -əl.i, -ɪ.li **-iness** -ɪ.nəs, -ɪ.nɪs
Tarzan ˈtɑː.zən, -zæn, ⓊⓈ ˈtɑːr-
Tasha ˈtæʃ.ə
Tashkent tæʃˈkent, ⓊⓈ tæʃ-, tɑːʃ-
task tɑːsk, ⓊⓈ tæsk **-s** -s **-ing** -ɪŋ **-ed** -t **ˈtask ˌforce**
taskbar ˈtɑːsk.bɑːʳ, ⓊⓈ ˈtæsk.bɑːr **-s** -z
Tasker ˈtæs.kəʳ, ⓊⓈ -kɚ
taskmaster ˈtɑːskˌmɑː.stəʳ, ⓊⓈ ˈtæskˌmæs.tɚ **-s** -z
taskmistress ˈtɑːskˌmɪs.trəs, -trɪs, ⓊⓈ ˈtæskˌmɪs.trɪs **-es** -ɪz
Tasman ˈtæz.mən
Tasmani|a tæzˈmeɪ.ni|.ə **-an/s** -ən/z
Tass, TASS tæs
tassel ˈtæs.əl **-s** -z **-(l)ed** -d
tassie, T~ ˈtæs.i
Tasso ˈtæs.əʊ, ⓊⓈ -oʊ
tast|e teɪst **-es** -s **-ing** -ɪŋ **-ed** -ɪd **-er/s** -əʳ/z, ⓊⓈ -ɚ/z **give someone a ˌtaste of their own ˈmedicine**
tastebud ˈteɪst.bʌd **-s** -z
tasteful ˈteɪst.fəl, -fʊl **-ly** -i **-ness** -nəs, -nɪs
tasteless ˈteɪst.ləs, -lɪs **-ly** -li **-ness** -nəs, -nɪs
tast|y ˈteɪ.st|i **-ier** -i.əʳ, ⓊⓈ -i.ɚ **-iest** -i.ɪst, -i.əst **-ily** -əl.i, -ɪ.li **-iness** -ɪ.nəs, -ɪ.nɪs
tat tæt **-s** -s **-ting** -ɪŋ, ⓊⓈ ˈtæt̬.ɪŋ **-ted** -ɪd, ⓊⓈ ˈtæt̬.ɪd
ta-ta təˈtɑː, tætˈɑː, ⓊⓈ tɑːˈtɑː
tatami təˈtɑː.mi, tɑː-, tætˈɑː-, ⓊⓈ təˈtɑː- **-s** -z
Tatar ˈtɑː.təʳ, ⓊⓈ -t̬ɚ **-s** -z
Tatchell ˈtætʃ.əl
Tate teɪt **ˌTate ˈGallery**
Tatham ˈteɪ.θəm, -ðəm; ˈtæt.əm
Tati ˈtæt.i, -ˈ-, ⓊⓈ tɑːˈtiː
Tatiana ˌtæt.iˈɑː.nə, ⓊⓈ ˌ-ˈjɑː.nə
tatler, T~® ˈtæt.ləʳ, ⓊⓈ -lɚ **-s** -z
Tatra ˈtɑː.trə, ˈtæt.rə, ⓊⓈ ˈtɑː.trə
tatter ˈtæt.əʳ, ⓊⓈ ˈtæt̬.ɚ **-s** -z **-ed** -d
tatterdemalion ˌtæt.ə.dəˈmeɪ.li.ən, -dɪˈ-, -ˈmæl.i-, ⓊⓈ ˌtæt̬.ɚ-
tattersall, T~ ˈtæt.ə.sɔːl, -səl, ⓊⓈ ˈtæt̬.ɚ.sɔːl, -sɑːl **-s** -z
tattl|e ˈtæt.əl, ⓊⓈ ˈtæt̬- **-es** -z **-ing** -ɪŋ, ˈtæt.lɪŋ **-ed** -d **-er/s** -əʳ/z, ˈtæt.ləʳ/z, ⓊⓈ ˈ-əl.ɚ/z, ˈ-lɚ/z
tattletale ˈtæt.əl.teɪl, ⓊⓈ ˈtæt̬- **-s** -z
Tatton ˈtæt.ən
tattoo tætˈuː, təˈtuː, ⓊⓈ tætˈuː **-s** -z **-ing** -ɪŋ **-ed** -d **-er/s** -əʳ/z, ⓊⓈ -ɚ/z
tattooist tætˈuː.ɪst, təˈtuː-, ⓊⓈ tætˈuː- **-s** -s
tatt|y ˈtæt|.i, ⓊⓈ ˈtæt̬- **-ier** -i.əʳ, ⓊⓈ -i.ɚ **-iest** -i.ɪst, -i.əst **-ily** -əl.i, -ɪ.li **-iness** -ɪ.nəs, -ɪ.nɪs
Tatum ˈteɪ.təm, ⓊⓈ -t̬əm
tau taʊ, tɔː, ⓊⓈ taʊ, tɔː, tɑː
Tauchnitz ˈtaʊk.nɪts; *as if German:* ˈtaʊx-
taught (from **teach**) tɔːt, ⓊⓈ tɑːt, tɔːt
taun|t tɔːn|t, ⓊⓈ tɑːn|t, tɔːn|t **-ts** -ts **-ting/ly** -tɪŋ/li, ⓊⓈ -t̬ɪŋ/li **-ted** -tɪd, ⓊⓈ -t̬ɪd **-ter/s** -təʳ/z, ⓊⓈ -t̬ɚ/z
Taunton ˈtɔːn.tən; *locally:* ˈtɑːn-, ⓊⓈ ˈtɑːn.tən, ˈtɔːn-
taupe təʊp, ⓊⓈ toʊp
Taupo ˈtaʊ.pəʊ, ⓊⓈ ˈtoʊ.poʊ
Taurean ˈtɔː.ri.ən; tɔːˈriː-, ⓊⓈ ˈtɔːr.i- **-s** -z
Taurus ˈtɔː.rəs, ⓊⓈ ˈtɔːr.əs
taut tɔːt, ⓊⓈ tɑːt, tɔːt **-er** -əʳ, ⓊⓈ -ɚ **-est** -ɪst, -əst **-ly** -li **-ness** -nəs, -nɪs
tauten ˈtɔː.tən, ⓊⓈ ˈtɑː- **-s** -z **-ing** -ɪŋ **-ed** -d
tautologic ˌtɔː.təˈlɒdʒ.ɪk, ⓊⓈ ˌtɑː.t̬əˈlɑː.dʒɪ-, ˌtɔː- **-al** -əl **-ally** -əl.i, -li
tautologic|al ˌtɔː.təˈlɒdʒ.ɪk|.əl, ⓊⓈ ˌtɑː.t̬əˈlɑː.dʒɪk-, ˌtɔː- **-ally** -əl.i, -li
tautologism tɔːˈtɒl.ə.dʒɪ.zəm, ⓊⓈ tɑːˈtɑː.lə-, tɔːˈ- **-s** -z
tautologiz|e, -is|e tɔːˈtɒl.ə.dʒaɪz, ⓊⓈ tɑːˈtɑː.lə-, tɔː- **-es** -ɪz **-ing** -ɪŋ **-ed** -d
tautologous tɔːˈtɒl.ə.gəs, ⓊⓈ tɑːˈtɑː.lə-, tɔː-
tautolog|y tɔːˈtɒl.ə.dʒ|i, ⓊⓈ tɑːˈtɑː.lə-, tɔː- **-ies** -iz
Tavener ˈtæv.ən.əʳ, -nəʳ, ⓊⓈ -ən.ɚ, -nɚ
Taverham ˈteɪ.vər.əm
tavern ˈtæv.ən, ⓊⓈ -ɚn **-s** -z **-er/s** -əʳ/z, ⓊⓈ -ɚ/z
taverna təˈvɜː.nə, ˌtævˈɜː-, ⓊⓈ tɑːˈvɜː-, tə- **-s** -z
Tavistock ˈtæv.ɪ.stɒk, ˈ-ə-, ⓊⓈ -ə.stɑːk
taw tɔː, ⓊⓈ tɑː, tɔː **-s** -z **-ing** -ɪŋ **-ed** -d
tawdr|y ˈtɔː.dr|i, ⓊⓈ ˈtɑː-, ˈtɔː- **-ier** -i.əʳ, ⓊⓈ -i.ɚ **-iest** -i.ɪst, -i.əst **-ily** -əl.i, -ɪ.li **-iness** -ɪ.nəs, -ɪ.nɪs
Tawe ˈtaʊ.i, -eɪ
Tawell tɔːl; ˈtɔː.əl, ⓊⓈ tɑːl, tɔːl, ˈtɑː.əl, ˈtɔː-
tawn|y ˈtɔː.n|i, ⓊⓈ ˈtɑː-, ˈtɔː- **-ier** -i.əʳ, ⓊⓈ -i.ɚ **-iest** -i.ɪst, -i.əst **-iness** -ɪ.nəs, -ɪ.nɪs **ˌtawny ˈowl; ˈtawny ˌowl**
tax tæks **-es** -ɪz **-ing/ly** -ɪŋ/li **-ed** -t **-er/s** -əʳ/z, ⓊⓈ -ɚ/z **ˈtax eˌvasion; ˈtax ˌexile; ˈtax ˌhaven; ˈtax inˌspector; ˈtax ˌoffice; ˈtax reˌturn; ˈtax ˌyear**
taxability ˌtæk.səˈbɪl.ə.ti, -ɪ.ti, ⓊⓈ -ə.t̬i
taxable ˈtæk.sə.bəl **-ness** -nəs, -nɪs
taxation tækˈseɪ.ʃən **-s** -z
tax-deductible ˌtæks.dɪˈdʌk.tə.bəl, -dəˈ- *stress shift:* **ˌtax-deductible ˈearnings**
tax-deferred ˌtæks.dɪˈfɜːd, ⓊⓈ -ˈfɝːd *stress shift:* **ˌtax-deferred ˈearnings**
taxeme ˈtæk.siːm
taxemic tækˈsiː.mɪk
tax-exempt ˌtæks.ɪgˈzempt, -egˈ-; -ɪkˈsempt, -ekˈ-, ⓊⓈ -ɪgˈzempt, -egˈ- *stress shift:* **ˌtax-exempt ˈearnings**
tax-free ˌtæksˈfriː *stress shift:* **ˌtax-free ˈbonus**
tax|i ˈtæk.s|i **-i(e)s** -iz **-ying** -i.ɪŋ **-iing** -i.ɪŋ **-ied** -id **ˈtaxi ˌrank; ˈtaxi ˌstand**
taxicab ˈtæk.si.kæb **-s** -z
taxidermic ˌtæk.sɪˈdɜː.mɪk, ⓊⓈ -ˈdɝː-
taxidermist ˈtæk.sɪ.dɜː.mɪst, ˌtæk.sɪˈdɜː-; tækˈsɪd.ə-, ⓊⓈ ˈtæk.sɪ.dɝː- **-s** -s
taxidermy ˈtæk.sɪ.dɜː.mi, ⓊⓈ -dɝː-
taximeter ˈtæk.siˌmiː.təʳ, ⓊⓈ -t̬ɚ **-s** -z
tax|is, T~ ˈtæk.s|ɪs **-es** -iːz
taxiway ˈtæk.si.weɪ **-s** -z
taxman ˈtæks.mæn **-men** -men
taxonomic ˌtæk.səˈnɒm.ɪk, ⓊⓈ -ˈnɑː.mɪk **-ally** -əl.i, -li
taxonom|y tækˈsɒn.ə.m|i, ⓊⓈ -ˈsɑː.nə- **-ist/s** -ɪst/s
taxpayer ˈtæksˌpeɪ.əʳ, ⓊⓈ -ɚ **-s** -z
tay *syllable used in Tonic Sol-fa in counting time:* teɪ, te

> Note: In the sequence 'tay fe' this may be pronounced /te/.

Tay teɪ
tayberr|y ˈteɪ.bər|.i, ˈ-br|i, -ˌber|.i, ⓊⓈ -ˌber|.i **-ies** -iz
Taylor ˈteɪ.ləʳ, ⓊⓈ -lɚ
Taylorian teɪˈlɔː.ri.ən, ⓊⓈ -ˈlɔːr.i-

T

Taymouth ˈteɪ.maʊθ, -məθ
Tay-Sachs ˌteɪˈsæks, (US) ˌ-ˈ-, ˈ-- ˌ**Tay-ˈSachs diˌsease**
Tayside ˈteɪ.saɪd
TB ˌtiːˈbiː
T-bar ˈtiː.bɑːʳ, (US) -bɑːr **-s** -z
Tbilisi tə.bɪˈliː.si; təˈbɪl.ɪ-, (US) təˌbɪl.iˈsiː; (US) ˌtʌb.ɪˈliː.si; (US) təˈbɪl.i-
T-bone ˈtiː.bəʊn, (US) -boʊn **-s** -z ˌ**T-bone ˈsteak**
tbs., tbsp. (abbrev. for **tablespoon, tablespoonful**) ˈteɪ.bəl.spuːn, ˈteɪ.bəlˌspuːn.fʊl
T-cell ˈtiː.sel **-s** -z
Tchad tʃæd
Tchaikovsky tʃaɪˈkɒf.ski, -ˈkɒv-, (US) -ˈkɔːf-, -ˈkɑːv-
Tcherkasy tʃɜːˈkæs.i, (US) tʃɝː-
TCP® ˌtiː.siːˈpiː
te *Tonic Sol-fa name for leading note:* tiː **-s** -z
tea tiː **-s** -z ˈ**tea ˌbag;** ˈ**tea ˌbreak;** ˈ**tea ˌchest;** ˈ**tea ˌcosy;** ˈ**tea ˌdance;** ˈ**tea ˌlady;** ˈ**tea ˌleaf;** ˈ**tea ˌparty;** ˈ**tea ˌset;** ˈ**tea ˌshop;** ˈ**tea ˌtowel;** ˈ**tea ˌtray;** ˈ**tea ˌtrolley;** ˈ**tea ˌwagon; not for ˌall the ˌtea in ˈChina**
teabread ˈtiː.bred
tea-cadd|y ˈtiːˌkæd|.i **-ies** -iz
teacake ˈtiː.keɪk **-s** -s
teach tiːtʃ **-es** -ɪz **-ing/s** -ɪŋ/z **taught** tɔːt, (US) tɑːt, tɔːt ˈ**teaching ˌpractice**
teachability ˌtiː.tʃəˈbɪl.ə.ti, -ɪ.ti, (US) -ə.t̬i
teachable ˈtiː.tʃə.bəl **-ness** -nəs, -nɪs
teacher ˈtiː.tʃəʳ, (US) -tʃɚ **-s** -z ˌ**teacher(s') ˈtraining ˌcollege**
teach-in ˈtiːtʃ.ɪn **-s** -z
tea|cloth ˈtiː|.klɒθ, (US) -klɑːθ **-cloths** -klɒθs, -klɒðz, (US) -klɑːθs, -klɑːðz
teacup ˈtiː.kʌp **-s** -s **-ful/s** -fʊl/z
Teague tiːg **-s** -z
teahou|se ˈtiː.haʊ|s **-ses** -zɪz
teak tiːk
teakettle ˈtiːˌket.əl, (US) -ˌket̬- **-s** -z
teal tiːl **-s** -z
team tiːm **-s** -z **-ing** -ɪŋ **-ed** -d ˌ**team ˈspirit;** ˈ**team ˌspirit**
teammate ˈtiːm.meɪt **-s** -s
teamster, T~ ˈtiːmp.stəʳ, (US) -stɚ **-s** -z ˌ**Teamsters' ˈUnion** (US) ˈ**Teamsters' ˌUnion**
teamwork ˈtiːm.wɜːk, (US) -wɝːk
teapot ˈtiː.pɒt, (US) -pɑːt **-s** -s
teapoy ˈtiː.pɔɪ **-s** -z
tear n *fluid from the eye:* tɪəʳ, (US) tɪr **-s** -z ˈ**tear ˌgas**
tear n, v *pull apart, rush, a rent etc.:* teəʳ, (US) ter **-s** -z **-ing** -ɪŋ **tore** tɔːʳ, (US) tɔːr **torn** tɔːn, (US) tɔːrn
tearaway ˈteə.rə.weɪ, (US) ˈter.ə- **-s** -z
teardrop ˈtɪə.drɒp, (US) ˈtɪr.drɑːp **-s** -s
tearful ˈtɪə.fəl, -fʊl, (US) ˈtɪr- **-ly** -i **-ness** -nəs, -nɪs
teargas ˈtɪə.gæs, (US) ˈtɪr- **-es** -ɪz **-sing** -ɪŋ **-sed** -t
tearjerker ˈtɪəˌdʒɜː.kəʳ, (US) ˈtɪrˌdʒɝː.kɚ **-s** -z
tearless ˈtɪə.ləs, -lɪs, (US) ˈtɪr- **-ly** -li **-ness** -nəs, -nɪs
tearoom ˈtiː.rʊm, -ruːm, (US) -ruːm, -rʊm **-s** -z
tearstained ˈtɪə.steɪnd, (US) ˈtɪr-
tear|y ˈtɪə.r|i, (US) ˈtɪr|.i **-ily** -əl.i, -ɪ.li
teas|e tiːz **-es** -ɪz **-ing/ly** -ɪŋ/li **-ed** -d **-er/s** -əʳ/z, (US) -ɚ/z
teasel ˈtiː.zəl **-s** -z **-(l)ing** -ɪŋ, ˈtiːz.lɪŋ **-(l)ed** -d
Teasmade® ˈtiːz.meɪd
teaspoon ˈtiː.spuːn **-s** -z
teaspoonful ˈtiː.spuːn.fʊl **-s** -z
teaspoonsful (alternative plural of **teaspoonful**) ˈtiː.spuːnz.fʊl
tea-strainer ˈtiːˌstreɪ.nəʳ, (US) -nɚ **-s** -z
teat tiːt **-s** -s
tea-table ˈtiːˌteɪ.bəl **-s** -z
teatime ˈtiː.taɪm
tea-tree ˈtiː.triː **-s** -z ˈ**tea-tree ˌoil**
tea-urn ˈtiː.ɜːn, (US) -ɝːn **-s** -z
teazel ˈtiː.zəl **-s** -z
teazle, T~ ˈtiː.zəl **-s** -z
Tebay ˈtiː.beɪ; *locally:* -bi
Tebbitt ˈteb.ɪt
tec tek **-s** -s
tech tek **-s** -s
techie ˈtek.i **-s** -z
technetium tekˈniː.ʃi.əm, -si-, ˈ-ʃəm, (US) -ʃi.əm, ˈ-ʃəm
technic|al ˈtek.nɪ.k|əl **-ally** -əl.i, -li **-alness** -əl.nəs, -nɪs ˈ**technical ˌcollege**
technicalit|y ˌtek.nɪˈkæl.ə.t|i, -nəˈ-, -ɪ.t|i, (US) -nəˈkæl.ə.t̬|i **-ies** -iz
technician tekˈnɪʃ.ən **-s** -z
Technicolor® ˈtek.nɪˌkʌl.əʳ, (US) -ɚ
technicolo(u)r ˈtek.nɪˌkʌl.əʳ, (US) -ɚ **-ed** -d
technics, T~® ˈtek.nɪks
technique tekˈniːk **-s** -s
techno ˈtek.nəʊ, (US) -noʊ
techno- ˈtek.nəʊ; tekˈnɒ, (US) ˈtek.noʊ, -nə; (US) tekˈnɑː
Note: Prefix. This may carry primary or secondary stress on the first syllable, e.g. **technophobe** /ˈtek.nəʊ.fəʊb/ (US) /-foʊb/, **technophobia** /ˌtek.nəʊˈfəʊ.bi.ə/ (US) /-ˈfoʊ-/, or on the second syllable, e.g. **technology** /tekˈnɒl.ə.dʒi/ (US) /tekˈnɑː-/.
technocrat ˈtek.nəʊ.kræt, (US) -nə- **-s** -s
technocratic ˌtek.nəʊˈkræt.ɪk, (US) -nəˈkræt̬-
technofix ˈtek.nəʊ.fɪks, (US) -noʊ-, -nə- **-es** -ɪz
technologic|al ˌtek.nəˈlɒdʒ.ɪ.k|əl, (US) -ˈlɑː.dʒɪ- **-ly** -əl.i, -li
technolog|y tekˈnɒl.ə.dʒ|i, (US) -ˈnɑː.lə- **-ist/s** -ɪst/s **-ies** -iz
technophobe ˈtek.nəʊ.fəʊb, (US) -nə.foʊb **-s** -z
technophob|ia ˌtek.nəʊˈfəʊ.b|i.ə, (US) -nəˈfoʊ- **-ic** -ɪk
tech|y ˈtetʃ|.i **-ier** -i.əʳ, (US) -i.ɚ **-iest** -i.ɪst, -i.əst **-ily** -əl.i, -ɪ.li **-iness** -ɪ.nəs, -ɪ.nɪs
Teck tek
tectonic tekˈtɒn.ɪk, (US) -ˈtɑː.nɪk **-s** -s **tecˌtonic ˈplates**
ted, T~ ted **-s** -z **-ding** -ɪŋ **-ded** -ɪd **-der/s** -əʳ/z, (US) -ɚ/z
Teddington ˈted.ɪŋ.tən
tedd|y, T~ ˈted|.i **-ies** -iz ˈ**teddy ˌbear;** ˌ**Teddy Bear's ˈPicnic;** ˈ**teddy ˌboy**
Te Deum ˌteɪˈdeɪ.ʊm, ˌtiːˈdiː.əm **-s** -z
tedious ˈtiː.di.əs, (US) -di.əs, -dʒəs **-ly** -li **-ness** -nəs, -nɪs
tedium ˈtiː.di.əm
tee tiː **-s** -z **-ing** -ɪŋ **-d** -d
tee-hee ˌtiːˈhiː **-s** -z
teem tiːm **-s** -z **-ing** -ɪŋ **-ed** -d
teen tiːn **-s** -z
teenage ˈtiːn.eɪdʒ **-d** -d
teenager ˈtiːnˌeɪ.dʒəʳ, (US) -dʒɚ **-s** -z
teens|y ˈtiːn.z|i **-ier** -i.əʳ, (US) -i.ɚ **-iest** -i.ɪst, -i.əst
teensy-weensy ˌtiːn.ziˈwiːn.zi, ˌtiːnt.siˈwiːnt.si *stress shift:* ˌ**teensy-weensy ˈhouse**
teen|y ˈtiː.n|i **-iest** -i.ɪst, -i.əst
teenybopper ˈtiː.niˌbɒp.əʳ, (US) -ˌbɑː.pɚ **-s** -z
teeny-weeny ˌtiː.niˈwiː.ni *stress shift:* ˌ**teeny-weeny ˈhouse**
teepee ˈtiː.piː **-s** -z
Tees tiːz
Teesdale ˈtiːz.deɪl
teeshirt ˈtiː.ʃɜːt, (US) -ʃɝːt **-s** -s
tee-square ˈtiː.skweəʳ, ˌ-ˈ-, (US) ˈtiː.skwer **-s** -z
Teesside ˈtiː.saɪd, ˈtiːz-
teet|er ˈtiː.t|əʳ, (US) -t̬|ɚ **-ers** -əz, (US) -ɚz **-ering** -ər.ɪŋ **-ered** -əd, (US) -ɚd
teeter-totter ˌtiː.təˈtɒt|.əʳ, (US) -t̬ɚˈtɑː.t̬|ɚ **-ers** -əz, (US) -ɚz **-ering** -ər.ɪŋ **-ered** -əd, (US) -ɚd
teeth (plural of **tooth**) tiːθ ˌ**grit one's ˈteeth;** ˌ**set someone's ˈteeth on ˌedge**
teeth|e tiːð **-es** -z **-ing** -ɪŋ **-ed** -d ˈ**teething ˌring;** ˈ**teething ˌtroubles**
teetotal ˌtiːˈtəʊ.təl, (US) -ˈtoʊ.t̬əl, ˈ-ˌ-- **-ism** -ɪ.zəm
teetotal(l)er ˌtiːˈtəʊ.təl.əʳ, -ˈtəʊt.ləʳ, (US) -ˈtoʊ.t̬əl.ɚ, -ˈtoʊt.lɚ, ˈtiːˌtoʊ.t̬əl.ɚ, -ˌtoʊt.lɚ **-s** -z
teetotum ˌtiːˈtəʊ.təm, ˈ---; ˌtiː.təʊˈtʌm, (US) ˌtiːˈtoʊt̬.əm **-s** -z
TEFL ˈtef.əl
Teflon® ˈtef.lɒn, (US) -lɑːn
Tegucigalpa tegˌuː.sɪˈgæl.pə, (US) -səˈgæl.pɑː, -ˈgɑːl-
tegument ˈteg.jʊ.mənt, -jə- **-s** -s
Tehran, Teheran teəˈrɑːn, -ˈræn; ˌte.hərˈɑːn, ˌteɪ.ərˈ-, -ˈæn, (US) terˈɑːn, təˈrɑːn, teə-, -ˈræn
Tehuantepec təˈwɑːn.tə.pek, (US) -t̬ə-
Teifi ˈtaɪ.vi
Teign tɪn, tiːn

Teignbridge ˈtɪn.brɪdʒ, ˈtiːn-, ˈtɪm-, ˈtiːm-, (US) ˈtɪn-, ˈtiːn-
Teignmouth ˈtɪn.məθ, ˈtiːn-, ˈtɪm-, ˈtiːm-; *locally also:* ˈtɪŋ-, (US) ˈtɪn-, ˈtiːn-
Teignton ˈteɪn.tən, (US) -tᵊn
Teiresias taɪəˈriː.si.əs, (US) taɪ-
Te Kanawa teɪˈkɑː.nə.wə, tɪ-
tel. (abbrev. for **telephone**) ˈtel.ɪ.fəʊn, (US) -ə.foʊn
telaesthesia ˌtel.əsˈθiː.zi.ə, -ɪsˈ-, -iːsˈ-, -ʒi-, ˈ-ʒə, (US) ˌtel.əsˈθiː.ʒə
telaesthetic ˌtel.əsˈθet.ɪk, -ɪsˈ-, -iːsˈ-, (US) -ˈθet̬- **-s** -s **-ally** -ᵊl.i, -li
telamon, T~ ˈtel.ə.mən, -mɒn, (US) -mən, -mɑːn **-s** -z
Tel Aviv ˌtel.əˈviːv, -ævˈiːv, -ˈɪv, (US) -əˈviːv, -ɑːˈ-
Telco® ˈtel.kəʊ, (US) -koʊ
tele ˈtel.i **-s** -z
tele- ˈtel.ɪ; tɪˈle, tə-, (US) ˈtel.ə; (US) tɪˈle, tə-, ˈtel.ɪ
Note: Prefix. This may carry primary or secondary stress on the first syllable, e.g. **telephone** /ˈtel.ɪ.fəʊn/ (US) /ˈtel.ə.foʊn/, **telegraphic** /ˌtel.ɪˈgræf.ɪk/ (US) /-əˈ-/, or on the second syllable, e.g. **telephony** /təˈlef.ə.ni/.
telebanking ˈtel.ɪˌbæŋ.kɪŋ
telecamera ˈtel.ɪˌkæm.ᵊr.ə, ˌ-rə **-s** -z
telecast ˈtel.ɪ.kɑːst, (US) -kæst **-s** -s **-ing** -ɪŋ **-ed** -ɪd **-er/s** -əʳ/z, (US) -ɚ/z
tele-cine ˌtel.ɪˈsɪn.i
telecom ˈtel.ɪ.kɒm, (US) -kɑːm **-s** -z
telecommunications ˌtel.ɪ.kəˌmjuː.nɪˈkeɪ.ʃᵊnz, -nəˈ-
telecom|mute ˌtel.ɪ.kə|ˈmjuːt, (US) ˈ---- **-mutes** -ˈmjuːts **-muting** -ˈmjuː.tɪŋ, (US) -mjuː.t̬ɪŋ **-muted** -ˈmjuː.tɪd, (US) -mjuː.t̬ɪd **-muter/s** -ˈmjuː.təʳ/z, (US) -mjuː.t̬ɚ/z
teleconferenc|e ˌtel.ɪˈkɒn.fᵊr.ᵊnts, (US) ˈtel.ɪˌkɑːn- **-es** -ɪz
teleconferencing ˌtel.ɪˈkɒn.fᵊr.ᵊnt.sɪŋ, (US) -ˈkɑːn-
telecottag|e ˈtel.ɪˌkɒt.ɪdʒ, (US) -ˌkɑː.t̬ɪdʒ **-ing** -ɪŋ
telefilm ˈtel.ɪ.fɪlm, (US) ˈ-ə- **-s** -z
telegenic ˌtel.ɪˈdʒen.ɪk, (US) -əˈ-
telegram ˈtel.ɪ.græm **-s** -z **-ming** -ɪŋ **-med** -d
telegramese ˌtel.ɪ.græmˈiːz
telegraph ˈtel.ɪ.grɑːf, -græf, (US) -græf **-s** -s **-ing** -ɪŋ **-ed** -t ˈ**telegraph** ˌ**pole**; ˈ**telegraph** ˌ**wire**
telegrapher tɪˈleg.rə.fəʳ, telˈeg-, təˈleg-, (US) təˈleg.rə.fɚ **-s** -z
telegraphese ˌtel.ɪ.grɑːˈfiːz, -græfˈiːz, -grəˈfiːz, (US) -græfˈiːz, -grəˈfiːz
telegraphic ˌtel.ɪˈgræf.ɪk, (US) -əˈ- **-ally** -ᵊl.i, -li
telegraph|y tɪˈleg.rə.f|i, telˈeg-, təˈleg-, (US) təˈleg- **-ist/s** -ɪst/s
teleki|nesis ˌtel.ɪ.kɪ|ˈniː.sɪs, -ə-, -kaɪˈ-, (US) -kɪˈ- **-netic** -ˈnet.ɪk, (US) -ˈnet̬-
Telemachus tɪˈlem.ə.kəs, telˈem-, təˈlem-, (US) təˈlem-
Telemann ˈteɪ.lə.mæn, (US) -mɑːn
telemark ˈtel.ɪ.mɑːk, ˈ-ə-, (US) -ə.mɑːrk **-s** -s **-ing** -ɪŋ **-ed** -t
telemarketing ˌtel.ɪˈmɑː.kɪ.tɪŋ, -kə-, ˈtel.ɪˌmɑː-, (US) ˈtel.əˌmɑːr.kə.t̬ɪŋ
Telemessag|e® ˈtel.ɪˌmes.ɪdʒ **-es** -ɪz
telemet|er təˈlem.ɪ.t|əʳ, ˈ-ə-; ˈtel.ɪˌmiː-, (US) ˈtel.əˌmiː.t̬|ɚ; (US) təˈlem.ə- **-ers** -əz, (US) -ɚz **-ering** -ᵊr.ɪŋ **-ered** -əd, (US) -ɚd
telemetric ˌtel.ɪˈmet.rɪk, (US) -əˈ- **-ally** -ᵊl.i, -li
telemetry tɪˈlem.ə.tri, tə-, ˈ-ɪ-, (US) təˈlem.ə-
teleological ˌtel.i.əˈlɒdʒ.ɪ.kᵊl, ˌtiː.li-, (US) ˌtiː.li.əˈlɑː.dʒɪ-, ˌtel.i-
teleolog|y ˌtel.iˈɒl.ə.dʒ|i, ˌtiː.liˈ-, (US) ˌtiː.liˈɑː.lə-, ˌtel.iˈ- **-ist/s** -ɪst/s
telepathic ˌtel.ɪˈpæθ.ɪk, (US) -əˈ- **-ally** -ᵊl.i, -li
telepathiz|e, -is|e tɪˈlep.ə.θaɪz, telˈep-, təˈlep-, (US) təˈlep- **-es** -ɪz **-ing** -ɪŋ **-ed** -d
telepath|y tɪˈlep.ə.θ|i, telˈep-, təˈlep-, (US) təˈlep- **-ist/s** -ɪst/s
telephon|e ˈtel.ɪ.fəʊn, (US) -ə.foʊn **-es** -z **-ing** -ɪŋ **-ed** -d **-er/s** -əʳ/z, (US) -ɚ/z ˈ**telephone** ˌ**book**; ˈ**telephone** ˌ**booth**; ˈ**telephone** ˌ**box**; ˈ**telephone** ˌ**call**; ˈ**telephone** **di**ˌ**rectory**; ˈ**telephone** ˌ**number**; ˈ**telephone** ˌ**pole**
telephonic ˌtel.ɪˈfɒn.ɪk, -əˈ-, (US) -əˈfɑː.nɪk **-ally** -ᵊl.i, -li
telephonist tɪˈlef.ᵊn.ɪst, telˈef-, təˈlef-, (US) təˈlef- **-s** -s
telephony tɪˈlef.ᵊn.i, telˈef-, təˈlef-, (US) təˈlef-
telephoto ˌtel.ɪˈfəʊ.təʊ, (US) ˈtel.ə.foʊ.t̬oʊ **-s** -z *stress shift, see compound:* ˌ**telephoto** ˈ**lens**
telephotography ˌtel.ɪ.fəˈtɒg.rə.fi, (US) -ə.fəˈtɑː.grə-
tele|port ˈtel.ɪ|.pɔːt, (US) -ə|.pɔːrt **-ports** -pɔːts, (US) -pɔːrts **-porting** -pɔː.tɪŋ, (US) -pɔːr.t̬ɪŋ **-ported** -pɔː.tɪd, (US) -pɔːr.t̬ɪd
teleprinter ˈtel.ɪˌprɪn.təʳ, (US) -əˌprɪn.t̬ɚ **-s** -z
teleprompter ˈtel.ɪˌprɒmp.təʳ, (US) -əˌprɑːmp.tɚ **-s** -z
telerecord n ˈtel.ɪˌrek.ɔːd, (US) -ɚd **-s** -z
telerecord v ˈtel.ɪ.rɪˌkɔːd, -rəˌ-, ˌtel.ɪ.rɪˈkɔːd, -rəˈ-, (US) ˈtel.ɪ.rɪˌkɔːrd, -rə-, ˌtel.ɪ.rɪˈkɔːrd, -rəˈ- **-s** -z **-ing/s** -ɪŋ/z **-ed** -ɪd
telesales ˈtel.ɪ.seɪlz
telescop|e ˈtel.ɪ.skəʊp, (US) -ə.skoʊp **-es** -s **-ing** -ɪŋ **-ed** -t
telescopic ˌtel.ɪˈskɒp.ɪk, (US) -əˈskɑː.pɪk **-ally** -ᵊl.i, -li
telescreen ˈtel.ɪ.skriːn **-s** -z
teleshopping ˈtel.ɪˌʃɒp.ɪŋ, ˌtel.ɪˈʃɒp-, (US) ˈtel.əˌʃɑː.pɪŋ
telesthesia ˌtel.əsˈθiː.zi.ə, -ɪsˈ-, -iːsˈ-, -ʒi-, ˈ-ʒə-, (US) ˌtel.əsˈθiː.ʒə
telesthetic ˌtel.əsˈθet.ɪk, -ɪsˈ-, -iːsˈ-, (US) -ˈθet̬- **-s** -s **-ally** -ᵊl.i, -li
Teletex® ˈtel.ɪ.teks
teletext ˈtel.ɪ.tekst, (US) ˈ-ə- **-s** -s
telethon ˈtel.ɪ.θɒn, (US) -ə.θɑːn **-s** -z
Teletype® ˈtel.ɪ.taɪp, (US) ˈ-ə- **-s** -s
televangel|ism ˌtel.ɪˈvæn.dʒə.l|ɪ.zᵊm, -dʒɪ- **-ist/s** -ɪst/s
teleview ˈtel.ɪ.vjuː, (US) ˈ-ə- **-s** -z **-ing** -ɪŋ **-ed** -d **-er/s** -əʳ/z, (US) -ɚ/z
televis|e ˈtel.ɪ.vaɪz, (US) ˈ-ə- **-es** -ɪz **-ing** -ɪŋ **-ed** -d
television ˈtel.ɪ.vɪʒ.ᵊn, ˌtel.ɪˈvɪʒ-, (US) ˈtel.ə.vɪʒ- **-s** -z ˈ**television** ˌ**set**; **tele**ˈ**vision** ˌ**set**
televisor ˈtel.ɪ.vaɪ.zəʳ, (US) -ə.vaɪ.zɚ **-s** -z
televisual ˌtel.ɪˈvɪʒ.u.əl, -ˈvɪz.ju-, (US) -əˈvɪʒ.u- **-ly** -i
telework|ing ˈtel.ɪˌwɜː.k|ɪŋ, (US) -ˌwɜː- **-er/s** -əʳ/z, (US) -ɚ/z
telex ˈtel.eks **-es** -ɪz **-ing** -ɪŋ **-ed** -t
Telfer ˈtel.fəʳ, (US) -fɚ
Telford ˈtel.fəd, (US) -fɚd
telic ˈtel.ɪk, (US) ˈtiː.lɪk, ˈtel.ɪk
tell, T~ tel **-s** -z **-ing/ly** -ɪŋ/li **told** təʊld, (US) toʊld
teller, T~ ˈtel.əʳ, (US) -ɚ **-s** -z
telling-off ˌtel.ɪŋˈɒf, (US) -ˈɑːf **tellings-off** ˌtel.ɪŋzˈɒf, (US) -ˈɑːf
telltale ˈtel.teɪl **-s** -z
tellurian telˈʊə.ri.ən, təˈlʊə-, tɪ-, -ˈljʊə-, (US) telˈʊr.i-, təˈlʊr- **-s** -z
telluric telˈʊə.rɪk, təˈlʊə-, tɪ-, -ˈljʊə-, (US) telˈʊr.ɪk, təˈlʊr-
tellurium telˈʊə.ri.əm, təˈlʊə-, tɪ-, -ˈljʊə-, (US) telˈʊr.i-, təˈlʊr-
tell|y ˈtel|.i **-ies** -iz
Telstar® ˈtel.stɑːʳ, (US) -stɑːr
Telugu ˈtel.ə.guː, ˈ-ʊ-, (US) ˈ-ə-
temerity tɪˈmer.ə.ti, tə-, temˈer-, -ɪ.ti, (US) təˈmer.ə.t̬i
temp temp **-s** -s **-ing** -ɪŋ **-ed** -t
Tempe ˈtem.pi
tempeh ˈtem.peɪ **-s** -z
temp|er ˈtem.p|əʳ, (US) -p|ɚ **-ers** -əz, (US) -ɚz **-ering** -ᵊr.ɪŋ **-ered** -əd, (US) -ɚd **-erer/s** -ᵊr.əʳ/z, (US) -ɚ.ɚ/z
tempera ˈtem.pᵊr.ə
temperament ˈtem.pᵊr.ə.mənt, -prə.mənt **-s** -s
temperamental ˌtem.pᵊr.əˈmen.tᵊl, -prəˈ-, (US) -t̬ᵊl **-ly** -i
temperance ˈtem.pᵊr.ᵊnts, ˈ-prənts
temperate ˈtem.pᵊr.ət, ˈ-prət, -prɪt **-ly** -li **-ness** -nəs, -nɪs
temperature ˈtem.prə.tʃəʳ, -prɪ-, -pᵊr.ə-, -ɪ-, (US) -pɚ.ə.tʃɚ, ˈ-prə-, -pɚ-, -pə- **-s** -z
-tempered ˈtem.pəd, (US) -pɚd **-ly** -li
Temperley ˈtem.pᵊl.i, (US) -pɚ.li
tempest ˈtem.pɪst, -pəst **-s** -s
tempestuous temˈpes.tʃu.əs, -tju-, (US) -tʃu- **-ly** -li **-ness** -nəs, -nɪs
Templar ˈtem.pləʳ, -plɑːʳ, (US) -plɚ **-s** -z
template ˈtem.pleɪt, -plɪt, (US) -plɪt **-s** -s
temple, T~ ˈtem.pᵊl **-s** -z

T

templet ˈtem.plɪt, -plət, (US) -plɪt **-s** -s
Templeton ˈtem.pəl.tən
temp|o ˈtem.p|əʊ, (US) -p|oʊ **-os** -əʊz, (US) -oʊz **-i** -iː
temporal ˈtem.pər.əl **-ly** -i
temporality ˌtem.pərˈæl.ə.ti, -ɪ.ti, (US) -pəˈræl.ə.t̬i
temporar|y ˈtem.pər.ər|.i, -prər-, (US) -pə.rer|.i **-ies** -iz **-ily** -əl.i, -ɪ.li **-iness** -ɪ.nəs, -ɪ.nɪs
temporization, -isa- ˌtem.pər.aɪˈzeɪ.ʃən, -ɪˈ-, (US) -əˈ-
temporiz|e, -is|e ˈtem.pər.aɪz, (US) -pə.raɪz **-es** -ɪz **-ing/ly** -ɪŋ/li **-ed** -d **-er/s** -ər/z, (US) -ɚ/z
tempt tempt **-s** -s **-ing** -ɪŋ **-ed** -ɪd **-er/s** -ər/z, (US) -ɚ/z
temptation tempˈteɪ.ʃən **-s** -z
tempting ˈtemp.tɪŋ **-ly** -li **-ness** -nəs, -nɪs
temptress ˈtemp.trəs, -trɪs, (US) -trɪs **-es** -ɪz
tempura ˈtem.pər.ə; temˈpʊə.rə, (US) ˈtem.pʊ.rɑː; (US) temˈpʊr.ə
tempus fugit ˌtem.pəsˈfjuː.dʒɪt, -pʊsˈ-, -gɪt, (US) -pəsˈfjuː.dʒɪt
ten ten **-s** -z ˌ**Ten Comˈmandments**
tenability ˌten.əˈbɪl.ə.ti, -ɪ.ti, (US) -ə.t̬i
tenable ˈten.ə.bəl **-ness** -nəs, -nɪs
tenacious tɪˈneɪ.ʃəs, tə-, tenˈeɪ-, (US) təˈneɪ- **-ly** -li **-ness** -nəs, -nɪs
tenacity tɪˈnæs.ə.ti, tə-, tenˈæs-, -ɪ.ti, (US) təˈnæs.ə.t̬i
tenanc|y ˈten.ənt.s|i **-ies** -iz
tenant ˈten.ənt **-s** -s **-ing** -ɪŋ **-ed** -ɪd
tenantry ˈten.ən.tri
Tenbury ˈten.bər.i, ˈtem-, (US) ˈten.ber-, -bɚ-
Tenby ˈten.bi, ˈtem-, (US) ˈten-
tench tentʃ
tend tend **-s** -z **-ing** -ɪŋ **-ed** -ɪd
tendencious tenˈden.tʃəs, (US) -ˈdent.ʃəs **-ly** -li **-ness** -nəs, -nɪs
tendenc|y ˈten.dənt.s|i **-ies** -iz
tendentious tenˈden.tʃəs, (US) -ˈdent.ʃəs **-ly** -li **-ness** -nəs, -nɪs
tend|er ˈten.d|ər, (US) -d|ɚ **-ers** -əz, (US) -ɚz **-erer** -ər.ər, (US) -ɚ.ɚ **-erest** -ər.ɪst, -əst **-erly** -əl.i, (US) -ɚ.li **-erness** -ə.nəs, -nɪs, (US) -ɚ.nəs, -nɪs **-ering** -ər.ɪŋ **-ered** -əd, (US) -ɚd
tender|foot ˈten.də|.fʊt, (US) -dɚ- **-foots** -s **-feet** -fiːt
tender-hearted ˌten.dəˈhɑː.tɪd, ˈten.dəˌhɑː-, (US) ˈten.dɚˌhɑːr.t̬ɪd, ˌten.dɚˈhɑːr- **-ly** -li **-ness** -nəs, -nɪs *stress shift, British only:* ˌ**tender-hearted** ˈ**person**
tenderization, -isa- ˌten.dər.aɪˈzeɪ.ʃən, -ɪˈ-, (US) -əˈ-
tenderiz|e, -is|e ˈten.dər.aɪz, (US) -də.raɪz **-es** -ɪz **-ing** -ɪŋ **-ed** -d **-er/s** -ər/z, (US) -ɚ/z
tenderloin ˈten.dəl.ɔɪn, (US) -dɚ.lɔɪn **-s** -z
tendinitis ˌten.dɪˈnaɪ.tɪs, -dəˈ-, -təs, (US) -t̬ɪs, -t̬əs
tendon ˈten.dən **-s** -z
tendonitis ˌten.dəˈnaɪ.tɪs, -təs, (US) -t̬ɪs, -t̬əs
tendril ˈten.drəl, -drɪl, (US) -drəl **-s** -z
Tenebrae ˈten.ɪ.briː, ˈ-ə-, -breɪ, -braɪ, (US) -ə.breɪ, -briː
tenebrous ˈten.ɪ.brəs, ˈ-ə-, (US) ˈ-ə-
tenement ˈten.ə.mənt, ˈ-ɪ-, (US) ˈ-ə- **-s** -s
Tenerif(f)e ˌten.ərˈiːf, (US) -əˈriːf
tenet ˈten.ɪt **-s** -s
tenfold ˈten.fəʊld, (US) -foʊld
ten-four ˌtenˈfɔːr, (US) -ˈfɔːr
ten-gallon hat ˌtenˌgæl.ənˈhæt, ˌteŋ-, (US) ˌten- **-s** -s
Tengu ˈteŋ.gu **-s** -z
Teniers ˈten.i.əz, ˈ-jəz, (US) -i.ɚz, ˈ-jɚz; (US) təˈnɪrz
Tenison ˈten.ɪ.sən
Tenko ˈteŋ.kəʊ, (US) -koʊ
Tenn. (abbrev. for **Tennessee**) ˌten.əˈsiː, -ɪˈ-, (US) ˌten.ɪˈsiː; *regionally:* ˈten.ɪ.si, -ə-
Tennant ˈten.ənt
tenner ˈten.ər, (US) -ɚ **-s** -z
Tennessee ˌten.əˈsiː, -ɪˈ-, (US) ˌten.ɪˈsiː; *regionally:* ˈten.ɪ.si, -ə-
Tenniel ˈten.i.əl, ˈ-jəl
tennis ˈten.ɪs ˈ**tennis** ˌ**ball**; ˈ**tennis** ˌ**court**; ˌ**tennis** ˈ**elbow**; ˈ**tennis** ˌ**racket**
Tennyson ˈten.ɪ.sən
tenon ˈten.ən **-s** -z
tenor ˈten.ər, (US) -ɚ **-s** -z
tenour ˈten.ər, (US) -ɚ
ten|pence ˈten|.pənts, ˈtem-, (US) ˈten- **-penny** -pən.i
tenpin ˈten.pɪn, ˈtem-, (US) ˈten- **-s** -z ˌ**tenpin** ˈ**bowling**
tenpins ˈten.pɪnz, ˈtem-, (US) ˈten-
tens|e tents **-es** -ɪz **-er** -ər, (US) -ɚ **-est** -ɪst, -əst **-ing** -ɪŋ **-ed** -t **-ely** -li **-eness** -nəs, -nɪs
tensile ˈtent.saɪl, (US) -sɪl, -saɪl
tension ˈten.tʃən, (US) ˈtent.ʃən **-s** -z
tensity ˈtent.sə.ti, -sɪ-, (US) -sə.t̬i
tensor ˈtent.sər, (US) -sɚ **-s** -z
tent tent **-s** -s **-ing** -ɪŋ, (US) ˈten.t̬ɪŋ **-ed** -ɪd, (US) ˈten.t̬ɪd
tentacle ˈten.tə.kəl, -tɪ-, (US) -t̬ə- **-s** -z
tentacular tenˈtæk.jə.lər, -jʊ-, (US) -lɚ
tentative ˈten.tə.tɪv, (US) -t̬ə.t̬ɪv **-s** -z **-ly** -li
tenter ˈten.tər, (US) -t̬ɚ **-s** -z
Tenterden ˈten.tə.dən, (US) -t̬ɚ-
tenterhook ˈten.tə.hʊk, (US) -t̬ɚ- **-s** -s
tenth tentθ **-s** -s **-ly** -li
tenu|is ˈten.ju|.ɪs **-es** -iːz, -eɪz
tenuity tenˈjuː.ə.ti, təˈnjuː-, tɪ-, -ɪ.ti, (US) təˈnuː.ə.t̬i, -ˈnjuː-
tenuous ˈten.ju.əs **-ly** -li **-ness** -nəs, -nɪs
tenur|e ˈten.jər, -jʊər, (US) -jɚ, -jʊr **-es** -z **-ed** -d
tepal ˈtiː.pəl, ˈtep.əl
tepee ˈtiː.piː **-s** -z
tepid ˈtep.ɪd **-est** -ɪst, -əst **-ly** -li **-ness** -nəs, -nɪs
tepidity tepˈɪd.ə.ti, -ɪ.ti, (US) təˈpɪd.ə.t̬i
tequila təˈkiː.lə, tɪ-, (US) tə- **-s** -z **te**ˌ**quila** ˈ**sunrise**
ter *three times:* tɜːr, (US) tɝː, ter
Ter *river in Essex:* tɑːr, (US) tɑːr
tera- ˈter.ə
teraph ˈter.əf **-im** -ɪm
terbium ˈtɜː.bi.əm, (US) ˈtɝː-
tercel *hawk:* ˈtɜː.səl, (US) ˈtɝː- **-s** -z
Tercel *car:* ˈtɜː.sel, (US) tɚˈsel
tercentenar|y ˌtɜː.senˈtiː.nər|.i, -ˈten.ər-; tɜːˈsen.tɪ.nər-, (US) tɚˈsen.tən.er-; (US) ˌtɝː.senˈten.ɚ- **-ies** -iz
tercentennial ˌtɜː.senˈten.i.əl, (US) ˌtɝː-
tercet ˈtɜː.sɪt, -set, (US) ˈtɝː.sɪt; (US) tɚˈset **-s** -s
terebene ˈter.ə.biːn, ˈ-ɪ-, (US) ˈ-ə-
terebinth ˈter.ə.bɪntθ, ˈ-ɪ-, (US) ˈ-ə- **-s** -s
Terence ˈter.ənts
Teresa təˈriː.zə, tɪ-, -ˈreɪ-, terˈiː-, (US) təˈriː.sə, -zə, -ˈreɪ-
tergiver|sate ˈtɜː.dʒɪ.vɜː|.seɪt, -və-, (US) ˈtɝː.dʒɪ.vɚ- **-sates** -seɪts **-sating** -seɪ.tɪŋ, (US) -seɪ.t̬ɪŋ **-sated** -seɪ.tɪd, (US) -seɪ.t̬ɪd
tergiversation ˌtɜː.dʒɪ.vɜːˈseɪ.ʃən, -vəˈ-, (US) ˌtɝː.dʒɪ.vɚ-
teriyaki ˌter.iˈæk.i, (US) -ˈjɑː.ki
Terling ˈtɑː.lɪŋ, ˈtɜː-, (US) ˈtɑːr-, ˈtɝː-
term tɜːm, (US) tɝːm **-s** -z **-ing** -ɪŋ **-ed** -d **-ly** -li
termagant, T~ ˈtɜː.mə.gənt, (US) ˈtɝː- **-s** -s **-ly** -li
terminab|le ˈtɜː.mɪ.nə.b|əl, -mə-, (US) ˈtɝː- **-ly** -li **-leness** -əl.nəs, -nɪs
terminal ˈtɜː.mɪ.nəl, -mə-, (US) ˈtɝː- **-s** -z **-ly** -i
termi|nate ˈtɜː.mɪ|.neɪt, -mə-, (US) ˈtɝː- **-nates** -neɪts **-nating** -neɪ.tɪŋ, (US) -neɪ.t̬ɪŋ **-nated** -neɪ.tɪd, (US) -neɪ.t̬ɪd **-nator/s** -neɪ.tər/z, (US) -neɪ.t̬ɚ/z
termination ˌtɜː.mɪˈneɪ.ʃən, -məˈ-, (US) ˌtɝː- **-s** -z
terminative ˈtɜː.mɪ.nə.tɪv, -mə-, -neɪ-, (US) ˈtɝː.mɪ.neɪ.t̬ɪv, -mə- **-ly** -li
terminer ˈtɜː.mɪ.nər, -mə-, (US) ˈtɝː.mɪ.nɚ, -mə-
terminologic|al ˌtɜː.mɪ.nəˈlɒdʒ.ɪ.k|əl, -mə-, (US) ˌtɝː.mɪ.nəˈlɑː.dʒɪ-, -mə- **-ally** -əl.i, -li
terminolog|y ˌtɜː.mɪˈnɒl.ə.dʒ|i, -məˈ-, (US) ˌtɝː.mɪˈnɑː.lə-, -məˈ- **-ies** -iz
termin|us ˈtɜː.mɪ.n|əs, -mə-, (US) ˈtɝː- **-i** -aɪ **-uses** -ə.sɪz
termite ˈtɜː.maɪt, (US) ˈtɝː- **-s** -s
termtime ˈtɜːm.taɪm, (US) ˈtɝːm-
tern tɜːn, (US) tɝːn **-s** -z
ternary ˈtɜː.nər.i, (US) ˈtɝː-
Ternate tɜːˈnɑː.ti, (US) tɝːˈnɑː.teɪ
Terpsichore tɜːpˈsɪk.ər.i, (US) tɚp-
terpsichorean ˌtɜːp.sɪ.kərˈiː.ən, -kɒrˈ-, (US) ˌtɝːp.sɪ.kəˈriː-; (US) ˌtɝːp.sɪˈkɔːr.i-
terra ˈter.ə
terrac|e ˈter.ɪs, -əs **-es** -ɪz **-ing** -ɪŋ **-ed** -t

erracotta ˌter.əˈkɒt.ə, (US) -ˈkɑː.t̬ə
erra firma ˌter.əˈfɜː.mə, (US) -ˈfɝː-
errain təˈreɪn, tɪ-, terˈeɪn; ˈter.eɪn, (US) terˈeɪn, təˈreɪn; (US) ˈter.eɪn -s -z
erra incognita ˌter.ə.ɪŋˈkɒg.nɪ.tə, -ɪnˈ-; -kɒgˈniː.tə, (US) -ɪnˈkɑːg.nɪ.t̬ə
terrae incognitae ˌter.aɪ.ɪŋˈkɒg.nɪ.taɪ, ˌter.iː.ɪŋˈkɒg.nɪ.tiː, -ɪnˈ-; -kɒgˈniː.taɪ, (US) -ɪnˈkɑːg.nɪ.t̬aɪ, -t̬iː
Terramycin® ˌter.əˈmaɪ.sɪn
Terrance ˈter.ənts
errapin ˈter.ə.pɪn -s -z
errari|um təˈreə.ri|.əm, terˈeə-, tɪˈreə-, (US) təˈrer.i- -ums -əmz -a -ə
errazzo terˈæt.səʊ, təˈræt-, tɪ-, (US) təˈrɑːt.soʊ, terˈɑːt-; (US) təˈræz.oʊ -s -z
Terrell ˈter.əl
Terrence ˈter.ənts
errestrial təˈres.tri.əl, terˈes-, tɪˈres-, (US) təˈres- -s -z -ly -i -ness -nəs, -nɪs
terret ˈter.ɪt -s -s
Terri ˈter.i
terrib|le ˈter.ə.b|əl, ˈ-ɪ-, (US) ˈ-ə- -ly -li -leness -əl.nəs, -nɪs
terrier ˈter.i.əʳ, (US) -ɚ -s -z
terrific təˈrɪf.ɪk, tɪ-, (US) tə- -ally -əl.i, -li
terri|fy ˈter.ə|.faɪ, ˈ-ɪ- -fies -faɪz -fying/ly -faɪ.ɪŋ/li -fied -faɪd
terrine terˈiːn, təˈriːn; ˈter.iːn, (US) terˈiːn -s -z
territorial ˌter.ɪˈtɔː.ri.əl, -əˈ-, (US) -əˈtɔːr.i- -s -z -ly -i *stress shift, see compounds:* ˌ**Territorial** ˈ**Army**; **Terri**ˌ**torial** ˈ**Army**; **terri**ˌ**torial** ˈ**waters**
territorializ|e, -is|e ˌter.ɪˈtɔː.ri.əl.aɪz, -əˈ-, (US) -əˈtɔːr.i- -es -ɪz -ing -ɪŋ -ed -d
territor|y ˈter.ɪ.tər|.i, ˈ-ə-, -tr|i, (US) -ə.tɔːr|.i -ies -iz
terror ˈter.əʳ, (US) -ɚ -s -z
terror|ism ˈter.ər|.ɪ.zəm -ist/s -ɪst/s
terrorization, -isa- ˌter.ər.aɪˈzeɪ.ʃən, -ɪˈ-, (US) -əˈ-
terroriz|e, -is|e ˈter.ər.aɪz, (US) -ə.raɪz -es -ɪz -ing -ɪŋ -ed -d -er/s -əʳ/z, (US) -ɚ/z
terror-stricken ˈter.əˌstrɪk.ən, (US) -ɚˌ-
terror-struck ˈter.ə.strʌk, (US) ˈ-ɚ-
terr|y, T~ ˈter|.i -ies -iz ˌ**terry** ˈ**nappy**; ˌ**terry** ˈ**towelling**
ters|e tɜːs, (US) tɝːs -er -əʳ, (US) -ɚ -est -ɪst, -əst -ely -li -eness -nəs, -nɪs
tertian ˈtɜː.ʃən, -ʃi.ən, (US) ˈtɝː.ʃən
tertiary ˈtɜː.ʃər.i, -ʃi.ər-, (US) ˈtɝː.ʃi.er-, -ʃɚ.i ˌ**tertiary edu**ˈ**cation**
tertium quid ˌtɜː.ti.əmˈkwɪd, ˌ-ʃəmˈ-, -ʃi.əmˈ-, (US) ˌtɝː.ʃi.əmˈ-; (US) ˌter.ti.ʊmˈ-
Tertius ˈtɜː.ʃəs, -ʃi.əs, -ti-
Tertullian tɜːˈtʌl.i.ən, ˈ-jən, (US) tɚ-
terylene, T~® ˈter.ə.liːn, ˈ-ɪ-, (US) ˈ-ɪ-
terza rima ˌteət.səˈriː.mə, ˌtɜːt-, (US) ˌtert-
Tesco® ˈtes.kəʊ, (US) -koʊ -'s -z

TESL ˈtes.əl
tesla, T~ ˈtes.lə
TESOL ˈtiː.sɒl, (US) -sɑːl; (US) ˈtes.əl
Tess tes
Tessa, TESSA ˈtes.ə
tesse(l)l|ate ˈtes.əl|.eɪt, -ɪ.l|eɪt, (US) -ə.l|eɪt -ates -eɪts -ating -eɪ.tɪŋ, (US) -eɪ.t̬ɪŋ -ated -eɪ.tɪd, (US) -eɪ.t̬ɪd
tessellation ˌtes.əlˈeɪ.ʃən, -ɪˈleɪ-, (US) -əˈleɪ- -s -z
tessitura ˌtes.ɪˈtʊə.rə, -əˈ-, -ˈtjʊə-, -ˈtɔː-, -ˈtjɔː-, (US) -ɪˈtʊr.ə
test, T~ test -s -s -ing -ɪŋ -ed -ɪd -able -ə.bəl -er/s -əʳ/z, (US) -ɚ/z ˈ**test** ˌ**card**; ˈ**test** ˌ**case**; ˈ**test** ˌ**match**
testace|an tesˈteɪ.ʃ|ən, -ʃi|.ən, (US) ˈ-ʃ|ən -ous -əs
testacy ˈtes.tə.si
testament, T~ ˈtes.tə.mənt -s -s
testament|ary ˌtes.təˈmen.t|ər.i, (US) -t̬|ɚ- -al -əl
testate ˈtes.teɪt, -tɪt, (US) -teɪt -s -s
testator tesˈteɪ.təʳ, (US) ˈtes.teɪ.t̬ɚ, -ˈ-- -s -z
testatri|x tesˈteɪ.trɪ|ks -ces -siːz
test-bed ˈtest.bed -s -z
test-|drive ˈtest|.draɪv -drives -draɪvz -driving -ˌdraɪ.vɪŋ -drove -drəʊv, (US) -droʊv -driven -ˌdrɪv.ən
testes (plural of **testis**) ˈtes.tiːz
testicle ˈtes.tɪ.kəl, -tə- -s -z
testicular tesˈtɪk.jə.ləʳ, -jʊ-, (US) -lɚ
testification ˌtes.tɪ.fɪˈkeɪ.ʃən, -tə-, -fəˈ- -s -z
testi|fy ˈtes.tɪ|.faɪ, -tə- -fies -faɪz -fying -faɪ.ɪŋ -fied -faɪd -fier/s -faɪ.əʳ/z, (US) -faɪ.ɚ/z
testimonial ˌtes.tɪˈməʊ.ni.əl, -təˈ-, (US) -ˈmoʊ- -s -z
testimonializ|e, -is|e ˌtes.tɪˈməʊ.ni.əl.aɪz, -təˈ-, (US) -ˈmoʊ.ni.ə.laɪz -es -ɪz -ing -ɪŋ -ed -d
testimon|y ˈtes.tɪ.mə.n|.i, -tə-, (US) -moʊ.n|i -ies -iz
test|is ˈtes.t|ɪs -es -iːz
Teston ˈtiː.sən
testosterone tesˈtɒs.tər.əʊn, (US) -ˈtɑː.stə.roʊn
test-tube ˈtest.tʃuːb, -tjuːb, (US) -tuːb, -tjuːb -s -z ˌ**test-tube** ˈ**baby** (US) ˈ**test-tube** ˌ**baby**
testud|o tesˈtjuː.d|əʊ, -ˈtuː-, (US) -ˈtuː.d|oʊ, -ˈtjuː- -os -əʊz, (US) -oʊz -ines -dɪ.niːz, -neɪz, (US) -dɪ.niːz
test|y ˈtes.t|i -ier -i.əʳ, (US) -i.ɚ -iest -i.ɪst, -i.əst -ily -əl.i, -ɪ.li -iness -ɪ.nəs, -ɪ.nɪs
tetanus ˈtet.ən.əs
Tetbury ˈtet.bər.i, (US) -ber-, -bɚ-
tetch|y ˈtetʃ|.i -ier -i.əʳ, (US) -i.ɚ -iest -i.ɪst, -i.əst -ily -əl.i, -ɪ.li -iness -ɪ.nəs, -ɪ.nɪs
tête-à-tête ˌteɪt.ɑːˈteɪt, ˌtet.əˈtet, (US) ˌteɪt.əˈteɪt, ˌtet.əˈtet -s -s
teth|er ˈteð|.əʳ, (US) -ɚ -ers -əz, (US) -ɚz -ering -ər.ɪŋ -ered -əd, (US) -ɚd
Tetley ˈtet.li
Tétouan tetˈwɑːn, (US) tetˈwɑːn; (US) ˈteɪ.twɑːn

Tetovo ˈtet.əʊ.vəʊ, (US) -oʊ.voʊ
tetrachord ˈtet.rə.kɔːd, (US) -kɔːrd -s -z
tetrad ˈtet.ræd, -rəd, (US) -ræd -s -z
tetragon ˈtet.rə.gən, (US) -gɑːn -s -z
tetrahedr|on ˌtet.rəˈhiː.dr|ən, -ˈhed.r|ən, (US) -ˈhiː- -ons -ənz -a -ə -al -əl
tetralog|y tetˈræl.ə.dʒ|i, təˈtræl-, (US) tetˈrɑː.lə- -ies -iz
tetrameter tetˈræm.ɪ.təʳ, ˈ-ə-, (US) -ə.t̬ɚ -s -z
tetrarch ˈtet.rɑːk, (US) -rɑːrk -s -s -y -i -ies -iz
tetrasyllabic ˌtet.rə.sɪˈlæb.ɪk, -səˈ-, (US) -sɪˈ-
tetrasyllable ˈtet.rəˌsɪl.ə.bəl, ˌtet.rəˈsɪl- -s -z
tetrathlon tetˈræθ.lɒn, tɪˈtræθ-, tə-, -lən, (US) tetˈræθ.lɑːn
Tettenhall ˈtet.ən.hɔːl
tetter ˈtet.əʳ, (US) ˈtet̬.ɚ
Teucer ˈtʃuː.səʳ, ˈtjuː-, (US) ˈtuː.sɚ, ˈtjuː-
Teuton ˈtʃuː.tən, ˈtjuː-, (US) ˈtuː-, ˈtjuː- -s -z
Teutonic tʃuːˈtɒn.ɪk, tjuː-, (US) tuːˈtɑː.nɪk, tjuː-
teutonization, -isa- ˌtʃuː.tən.aɪˈzeɪ.ʃən, ˌtjuː-, -ɪˈ-, (US) ˌtuː.tən.əˈ-, ˌtjuː-
teutoniz|e, -is|e ˈtʃuː.tən.aɪz, ˈtjuː-, (US) ˈtuː-, ˈtjuː- -es -ɪz -ing -ɪŋ -ed -d
Teviot *river:* ˈtiː.vi.ət *Lord:* ˈtev.i.ət
Teviotdale ˈtiː.vi.ət.deɪl
Tewfik ˈtʃuː.fɪk, ˈtjuː-, (US) ˈtuː-, ˈtjuː-
Tewkesbury ˈtʃuːks.bər.i, ˈtjuː-, (US) ˈtuːks.ber-, ˈtjuːks-, -bɚ-
Tex. (abbrev. for **Texas**) ˈtek.səs
Texaco® ˈtek.sə.kəʊ, (US) -sɪ.koʊ, -sə-
Texan ˈtek.sən -s -z
Texas ˈtek.səs
Texel ˈtek.səl
Tex-Mex ˌteksˈmeks *stress shift:* ˌ**Tex-Mex** ˈ**food**
text tekst -s -s -ing -ɪŋ -ed -ɪd

> Note: Now in frequent use as a verb meaning 'to send a text message', the final consonant cluster is often simplified when word-final by elision of the final /t/, thus /teks/.

textbook ˈtekst.bʊk -s -s
textile ˈtek.staɪl, (US) -staɪl, -stɪl -s -z
textual ˈteks.tʃu.əl, (US) -tju- -ly -i
textural ˈteks.tʃər.əl
textur|e ˈteks.tʃəʳ, (US) -tʃɚ -es -z -ing -ɪŋ -ed -d
Tey teɪ
Teynham ˈten.əm, ˈteɪ.nəm

> Note: The former is the pronunciation for Baron Teynham.

-th θ
Note: Suffix. Not a syllable in itself, and does not affect the word stress, e.g. **tenth** /tentθ/.

T

Pronouncing the letters TH

The consonant digraph **th** is most commonly pronounced /θ/ or /ð/. In initial position, /ð/ occurs mostly in function or grammar words like determiners and conjunctions, e.g.:

the	ðə
that	ðæt, ðət

In content words like nouns and main verbs, /θ/ most usually appears in initial position, e.g.:

theme	θiːm
think	θɪŋk

At the ends of words, it is more difficult to predict which realization will occur. However, /ð/ is more common here than /θ/, and is highly likely in verbs. For example, before **e** or the grammatical inflection *-ing*, the pronunciation is usually /ð/, e.g.:

loathe	ləʊð ⓊⓈ loʊð
loath	ləʊθ, ləʊð
bathe	beɪð
bath	bɑːθ ⓊⓈ bæθ

Note that the verb *bathe* and *bath* when used as a verb both have the same spelling for the present participle, *bathing*, but different pronunciations.

In addition

In some names and a few other words, **th** is pronounced as /t/, e.g.:

Thames	temz
thyme	taɪm

The suffix *-th* when applied to numbers is always pronounced /θ/, e.g.:

eighth	eɪtθ
sixteenth	sɪkˈstiːnθ

When the two letters come together due to the addition of a prefix, the pronunciation is /t.h/, e.g.:

lighthouse	ˈlaɪt.haʊs
sweetheart	ˈswiːt.hɑːt ⓊⓈ -hɑːrt

Occasionally, **th** may be silent, e.g.:

asthma	ˈæsθ.mə, ˈæs- ⓊⓈ ˈæz-

Thacker ˈθæk.əʳ, ⓊⓈ -ɚ
Thackeray ˈθæk.əʳ.i, ˈ-ri
Thackley ˈθæk.li
Thaddeus ˈθæd.i.əs; θædˈiː-
Thai taɪ -s -z
Thailand ˈtaɪ.lænd, -lənd
Thake θeɪk
thalam|us ˈθæl.ə.m|əs -i -aɪ, -iː
thalassotherapy θəˌlæs.əʊˈθer.ə.pi, θælˌæs-, ⓊⓈ -əˈ-
Thalben ˈθæl.bən, ˈθɔːl-
thaler ˈtɑː.ləʳ, ⓊⓈ -lɚ -s -z
Thales ˈθeɪ.liːz
Thali|a θəˈlaɪ|.ə, ˈθæl.i.|ə, ˈθɑː.li-, ˈθɑːl.j|ə, ⓊⓈ θəˈlaɪ|.ə, ˈθeɪ.li.|ə, ˈθɑːl.j|ə -an -ən
thalidomide θəˈlɪd.ə.maɪd, θælˈɪd-, ⓊⓈ θəˈlɪd-
thallium ˈθæl.i.əm
Thame teɪm
Thames *in England, Canada, New Zealand:* temz *in Connecticut:* θeɪmz, teɪmz, temz
Thamesmead ˈtemz.miːd
than *strong form:* ðæn; *weak forms:* ðᵊn, ðən, ðn̩
Note: Weak-form word. The strong form /ðæn/ is rarely used; it is sometimes found in emphatic utterances such as 'The Queen, than whom no one is richer...', but it normally has the weak pronunciation /ðən/, e.g. 'faster than sound', /ˌfɑː.stə.ðənˈsaʊnd/ ⓊⓈ /-stɚ-/, or in rapid speech /ðn̩/, e.g. 'better than ever', /ˌbet.ə.ðn̩ˈev.ə/ ⓊⓈ /ˌbeţ.ɚ.ðn̩ˈev.ɚ/.
Thanatos ˈθæn.ə.tɒs, ⓊⓈ -tɑːs
thane, T~ θeɪn -s -z
Thanet ˈθæn.ɪt
thank θæŋk -s -s -ing -ɪŋ -ed -t -er/s -əʳ/z, ⓊⓈ -ɚ/z
thankful ˈθæŋk.fᵊl, -fʊl -ly -i -ness -nəs, -nɪs
thankless ˈθæŋ.kləs, -klɪs -ly -li -ness -nəs, -nɪs
thanksgiving, T~ ˌθæŋksˈgɪv.ɪŋ, ⓊⓈ ˌ-ˈ--, ˈ-ˌ-- -s -z **Thanksˈgiving ˌDay** ⓊⓈ **Thanksˈgiving ˌDay** **ˈThanksgiving ˌDay**
thank-you ˈθæŋk.ju -s -z **ˈthank-you ˌletter**

> Note: Although the most common abbreviation for 'thank you' is 'thanks', the pronunciation /kjuː/ is also heard in British English, usually with high pitch, in casual speech.

Thant θænt
that adj, demonstr. pron, adv ðæt
Note: Weak-form word. When used demonstratively it is always pronounced with its strong form /ðæt/, e.g. 'that's final', 'I like **that** one'.
that relative pron *strong form:* ðæt; *weak form:* ðət; *weak form:* ðt
Note: The strong form is seldom used, except in very deliberate speech or when the word is said in isolation.
that conj *strong form:* ðæt; *weak form:* ðət
Note: The strong form is rarely used.
thataway ˈðæt.əˌweɪ, ⓊⓈ ˈðæţ-
thatch θætʃ -es -ɪz -ing -ɪŋ -ed -t -er/s -əʳ/z, ⓊⓈ -ɚ/z
Thatcham ˈθætʃ.əm
Thatch|er ˈθætʃ|.əʳ, ⓊⓈ -ɚ -erism -ᵊr.ɪ.zᵊm -erite/s -ᵊr.aɪt/s, ⓊⓈ -ə.raɪt/s
thaumaturg|e ˈθɔː.mə.tɜːdʒ, ⓊⓈ -tɝːdʒ, ˈθɑː- -es -ɪz
thaumaturgic ˌθɔː.məˈtɜː.dʒɪk, ⓊⓈ -ˈtɝː-, ˌθɑː-
thaumaturg|y ˈθɔː.mə.tɜː.dʒ|i, ⓊⓈ -tɝː-, ˈθɑː- -ist/s -ɪst/s
thaw, T~ θɔː, ⓊⓈ θɑː, θɔː -s -z -ing -ɪŋ -ed -d
the *strong form:* ðiː; *weak form before vowels:* ði; *weak form before consonants:* ðə
Note: Weak-form word. The strong form /ðiː/ is used for emphasis, e.g. 'This is **the** place to eat' or contrast, e.g. 'It's not **a** solution, but **the** solution'. Weak forms are /ðə/ before consonants, e.g 'the cat' /ðəˈkæt/ and /ði/ before vowels, e.g. 'the apple' /ðiˈæp.ᵊl/.
Thea θɪə, ˈθiː.ə, ⓊⓈ ˈθiː.ə
Theakston ˈθiːk.stən -'s -z
theatre, theater ˈθɪə.təʳ, ˈθiː.ə-; θiˈet.əʳ, ⓊⓈ ˈθiː.ə.ţɚ -s -z
theatregoer, theatergoer ˈθɪə.təˌgəʊ.əʳ, ˈθiː.ə-; θiˈet.əˌ-, ⓊⓈ ˈθiː.ə.ţɚˌgoʊ.ɚ -s -z
theatreland, theaterland ˈθɪə.tə.lænd, ˈθiː.ə-; θiˈet.ə-, ⓊⓈ ˈθiː.ə.ţɚ-
theatric|al θiˈæt.rɪ.k|ᵊl -als -ᵊlz -ally -ᵊl.i, -li -alness -ᵊl.nəs, -nɪs -alism -ᵊl.ɪ.zᵊm
theatricality θiˌæt.rɪˈkæl.ə.ti, -ɪ.ti, ⓊⓈ -ə.ţi
theatrics θiˈæt.rɪks
Thebaid ˈθiː.beɪ.ɪd, -bi-
Theban ˈθiː.bən -s -z
thebe ˈtiː.beɪ
Thebes θiːbz
thee *normal form:* ðiː; *occasional weak form:* ði
theft θeft -s -s
thegn θeɪn -s -z
their *normal form:* ðeəʳ, ⓊⓈ ðer;

occasional weak form when a vowel follows: ðəʳr, (US) ðɚ
Note: The weak form is sometimes found in commonly used phrases such as 'on their own' /ˌɒn.ðəʳr'əʊn/ (US) /ˌɑːn.ðɚ'oʊn/.

theirs ðeəz, (US) ðerz

the|ism 'θiː|.ɪ.zəm **-ist/s** -ɪst/s

theistic θiː'ɪs.tɪk **-al** -əl

Thelma 'θel.mə

Thelwall 'θel.wɔːl

Thelwell 'θel.wəl, -wel

them *strong form:* ðem; *weak forms:* ðəm, ðm; *occasional weak forms:* əm, əm
Note: Weak-form word. The strong form /ðem/ is used for contrast, e.g. 'them and us' or for emphasis, e.g. 'look at **them**'. The weak form is usually /ðəm/, e.g. 'leave them alone' /ˌliːv.ðəm.ə'ləʊn/ (US) /-'loʊn/, or in rapid, casual speech /ðm/, e.g. 'run them out', /ˌrʌn.ðm'aʊt/.

thematic θɪ'mæt.ɪk, θiː-, (US) θiː'mæt̬- **-ally** -əl.i, -li

them|e θiːm **-es** -z **-ing** -ɪŋ **-ed** -d
'**theme** ˌ**park**

Themistocles θɪ'mɪs.tə.kliːz, θem'ɪs-, θə'mɪs-, (US) θə'mɪs-

themselves ðəm'selvz, (US) ðəm-, ðem-

then ðen

thence ðents

thenceforth ˌðents'fɔːθ, (US) -'fɔːrθ

thenceforward ˌðents'fɔː.wəd, (US) -'fɔːr.wɚd

Theo 'θiː.əʊ, (US) -oʊ

theo- 'θiː.əʊ, 'θɪə; θi'ɒ, (US) 'θi.oʊ, -ə, θi'ɑː
Note: Prefix. Normally stressed on the second syllable, e.g. **theology** /θi'ɒl.ə.dʒi/ (US) /θi'ɑː-/, but may also carry secondary stress on the first syllable with primary stress on the third syllable, e.g. **theological** /ˌθiː.ə'lɒdʒ.ɪ.kəl/ (US) /-'lɑːdʒ-/. This prefix is not present in 'theory' and related words.

Theobald 'θiː.ə.bɔːld, 'θɪə-; *formerly:* 'θɪb.əld, 'tɪb-, (US) 'θiː.ə.bɔːld, -bɑːld; (US) 'tɪb.əld

Theobalds *in Hertfordshire:* 'θiː.ə.bɔːldz, 'θɪə-, (US) 'θiː.ə-, -bɑːldz *road in London:* 'θiː.ə.bɔːldz, 'θɪə-; *formerly:* 'tɪb.əldz, (US) 'θiː.ə.bɔːldz, -bɑːldz; (US) 'tɪb.əldz

theocrac|y θi'ɒk.rə.s|i, (US) -'ɑː.krə- **-ies** -iz

theocratic ˌθiː.əʊ'kræt.ɪk, ˌθɪə'-, (US) ˌθiː.ə'kræt̬- **-al** -əl

Theocritus θi'ɒk.rɪ.təs, (US) -'ɑː.krə.t̬əs

theodicy θi'ɒd.ɪ.si, '-ə-, (US) -'ɑː.də-

theodolite θi'ɒd.əl.aɪt, (US) -'ɑː.də.laɪt **-s** -s

Theodora ˌθiː.ə'dɔː.rə, ˌθɪə'-, (US) ˌθiː.ə'dɔːr.ə

Theodore 'θiː.ə.dɔːʳ, 'θɪə-, (US) 'θiː.ə.dɔːr

Theodoric θi'ɒd.əʳr.ɪk, (US) -'ɑː.dɚ-

Theodosi|a ˌθiː.ə'dəʊ.si|.ə, ˌθɪə'-, (US) ˌθiː.oʊ'doʊ.ʃi|.ə, -ə'-, '-ʃ|ə **-us** -əs

theologian ˌθiː.ə'ləʊ.dʒən, ˌθɪə'-, -dʒi.ən, (US) ˌθiː.ə'loʊ.dʒən, -dʒi.ən **-s** -z

theologic ˌθiː.ə'lɒdʒ.ɪk, ˌθɪə'-, (US) ˌθiː.ə'lɑː.dʒɪk

theologi|cal ˌθiː.ə'lɒdʒ.ɪ|.kəl, ˌθɪə'-, (US) ˌθiː.ə'lɑː.dʒɪ- **-cally** -kəl.i, -kli

theologiz|e, -is|e θi'ɒl.ə.dʒaɪz, (US) -'ɑː.lə- **-es** -ɪz **-ing** -ɪŋ **-ed** -d

theolog|y θi'ɒl.ə.dʒ|i, (US) -'ɑː.lə- **-ist/s** -ɪst/s

Theophilus θi'ɒf.ɪ.ləs, -əl.əs, (US) -'ɑː.fəl.əs

Theophrastus ˌθiː.əʊ'fræs.təs, ˌθɪə'-, (US) ˌθiː.oʊ'-, -ə'-

theorbo θi'ɔː.bəʊ, (US) -'ɔːr.boʊ **-s** -z

theorem 'θɪə.rəm, 'θiː.ə-, -rem, -rɪm, (US) 'θiː.rəm, 'θiː.ɚ.əm, -em **-s** -z

theoretic θɪə'ret.ɪk, ˌθiː.ə'-, (US) ˌθiː.ə'ret̬-

theoreti|cal θɪə'ret.ɪ|.kəl, ˌθiː.ə'-, (US) ˌθiː.ə'ret̬- **-cally** -kəl.i, -kli

theoretician ˌθɪə.rə'tɪʃ.ən, ˌθiː.ə-, -rɪ'-, -ret'ɪʃ-, (US) ˌθiː.ə.rə'tɪʃ-, ˌθɪr.ə'- **-s** -z

theorist 'θɪə.rɪst, 'θiː.ə-, (US) 'θiː.ɚ.ɪst, 'θɪr.ɪst **-s** -s

theoriz|e, -is|e 'θɪə.raɪz, 'θiː.ə-, (US) 'θiː.ə-, 'θɪr.aɪz **-es** -ɪz **-ing** -ɪŋ **-ed** -d **-er/s** -əʳ/z, (US) -ɚ/z

theor|y 'θɪə.r|i, 'θiː.ə-, (US) 'θiː.ə-, 'θɪr|.i **-ies** -iz

theosophic ˌθiː.ə'sɒf.ɪk, ˌθɪə'-, (US) ˌθiː.ə'sɑː.fɪk **-al** -əl **-ally** -əl.i, -li

theosophiz|e, -is|e θi'ɒs.ə.faɪz, (US) -'ɑː.sə- **-es** -ɪz **-ing** -ɪŋ **-ed** -d

theosoph|y θi'ɒs.ə.f|i, (US) -'ɑː.sə- **-ist/s** -ɪst/s **-ism** -ɪ.zəm

Thera 'θɪə.rə, (US) 'θɪr.ə

therapeutic ˌθer.ə'pjuː.tɪk, (US) -t̬ɪk **-s** -s **-ally** -əl.i, -li

therapeutist ˌθer.ə'pjuː.tɪst, (US) -t̬ɪst **-s** -s

therap|y 'θer.ə.p|i **-ies** -iz **-ist/s** -ɪst/s

Theravada ˌθer.ə'vɑː.də

there *strong form:* ðeəʳ, (US) ðer; *weak form:* ðəʳ, (US) ðɚ; *alternative weak form before vowels:* ðəʳr, (US) ðɚ
Note: Weak-form word. The weak forms occur only when **there** is used existentially as in 'there is', 'there are', 'there was', 'there won't be', etc. The strong form /ðeəʳ/ (US) /ðer/ is also used in such expressions, and is the normal pronunciation for **there** as a place adverbial, e.g. 'there it is'.

thereabout 'ðeə.rə.baʊt, ˌ--'-, (US) 'ðer.ə.baʊt, ˌ--'- **-s** -s

> Note: The form /ˌðeəʳ.ə'baʊts/ (US) /ˌðer-/ is always used in the expression 'there or thereabouts'.

thereafter ˌðeə'rɑːf.təʳ, (US) ˌðer'æf.tɚ

thereat ˌðeə'ræt, (US) ˌðer'æt

thereby ˌðeə'baɪ, (US) ˌðer-

there'd ðeəd, (US) ðerd

therefor ˌðeə'fɔːʳ, (US) ˌðer'fɔːr

therefore 'ðeə.fɔːʳ, (US) 'ðer.fɔːr

therefrom ˌðeə'frɒm, (US) ˌðer'frʌm, -'frɑːm

therein ˌðeə'rɪn, (US) ˌðer'ɪn

thereinafter ˌðeə.rɪn'ɑːf.təʳ, (US) ˌðer.ɪn'æf.tɚ

thereinto ˌðeə'rɪn.tuː, (US) ˌðer'ɪn-

there'll ðeəl; *weak form:* ðəl, ðəl, (US) ðerl
Note: See note for 'there'.

thereof ˌðeə'rɒv, (US) ˌðer'ɑːv, -'ʌv

thereon ˌðeə'rɒn, (US) ˌðer'ɑːn

there's (**= there is, there has**) *strong form:* ðeəz, (US) ðerz; *weak form:* ðəz, (US) ðɚz
Note: See note for 'there'.

Theresa tɪ'riː.zə, tə-, (US) tə'riː.sə, -zə

thereto ˌðeə'tuː, (US) ˌðer-

theretofore ˌðeə.tuː'fɔːʳ, (US) ˌðer.t̬ə'fɔːr, '---

thereunder ˌðeə'rʌn.dəʳ, (US) ˌðer'ʌn.dɚ

thereunto ˌðeə'rʌn.tuː, ˌ--'-, (US) ˌðer'ʌn.tuː, ˌ--'-

thereupon ˌðeə.rə'pɒn, '---, (US) ˌðer.ə'pɑːn, '---

there've *strong forms:* 'ðeəʳ.əv, (US) 'ðer-; *weak forms:* ðəʳ.əv, ðəv, (US) ðɚ.əv

therewith ˌðeə'wɪð, -'wɪθ, (US) ˌðer-

therewithal ˌðeə.wɪð'ɔːl, -wɪθ'-; *when used as a noun:* '---, (US) ˌðer-, '---

therm θɜːm, (US) θɝːm **-s** -z

thermal 'θɜː.məl, (US) 'θɝː- **-ly** -i

thermic 'θɜː.mɪk, (US) 'θɝː- **-ally** -əl.i, -li

Thermidor 'θɜː.mɪ.dɔːʳ, (US) 'θɝː.mə.dɔːr

thermion 'θɜː.mi.ən, (US) 'θɝː- **-s** -z

thermionic ˌθɜː.mi'ɒn.ɪk, (US) ˌθɝː.mi'ɑː.nɪk **-s** -s

thermistor θɜː'mɪs.təʳ, (US) 'θɝː.mɪ.stɚ, θɚ'mɪs.tɚ **-s** -z

Thermit® 'θɜː.mɪt, (US) 'θɝː-

thermite 'θɜː.maɪt, (US) 'θɝː-

thermo- 'θɜː.məʊ; θə'mɒ, (US) 'θɝː.moʊ, -mə, θɚ'mɑː
Note: Prefix. There may be primary or secondary stress on the first syllable, e.g. **thermocouple** /'θɜː.məʊˌkʌp.əl/ (US) /'θɝːr.moʊ-/, **thermometric** /ˌθɜː.məʊ'met.rɪk/ (US) /ˌθɝːr.moʊ'-/, or on the second syllable, e.g. **thermometer** /θə'mɒm.ɪ.tə/ (US) /θɚ'mɑː.mə.t̬ɚ/.

thermocouple 'θɜː.məʊˌkʌp.əl, (US) 'θɝː.moʊ-, -mə- **-s** -z

thermodynamic ˌθɜː.məʊ.daɪ'næm.ɪk, -dɪ'-, (US) ˌθɝː.moʊ.daɪ'-, -mə- **-s** -s **-ally** -əl.i, -li

thermoelectric ˌθɜː.məʊ.ɪ'lek.trɪk, -ə'-, (US) ˌθɝː.moʊ- **-ally** -əl.i, -li

thermoelectricity ˌθɜː.məʊ.ɪˌlek'trɪs.ə.ti, -əˌ-, -ˌiː.lek'-,

-ˌel.ɪkˈ-, -ˈtrɪz-, -ɪ.ti, (US) ˌθɝː.moʊˌiː.lekˈtrɪs.ə.t̬i

thermograph ˈθɜː.məʊ.grɑːf, -græf, (US) ˈθɝː.moʊ.græf, -mə- **-s** -s

thermometer θəˈmɒm.ɪ.təʳ, ˈ-ə-, (US) θɚˈmɑː.mə.t̬ɚ **-s** -z

thermometric ˌθɜː.məʊˈmet.rɪk, (US) ˌθɝː.moʊˈ-, -məˈ- **-al** -ᵊl **-ally** -ᵊl.i, -li

thermonuclear ˌθɜː.məʊˈnjuː.kli.əʳ, (US) ˌθɝː.moʊˈnuː.kli.ɚ, -məˈ-, -ˈnjuː-

thermopile ˈθɜː.məʊ.paɪl, (US) ˈθɝː.moʊ-, -mə- **-s** -z

thermoplastic ˌθɜː.məʊˈplæs.tɪk, -ˈplɑː.stɪk, (US) ˌθɝː.moʊˈplæs.tɪk, -məˈ- **-s** -s

Thermopylae θɜːˈmɒp.ɪ.liː, θə-, -ᵊl.iː, -i, -aɪ, (US) θɚˈmɑː.pə.liː

Thermos® ˈθɜː.mɒs, -məs, (US) ˈθɝː.məs **-es** -ɪz **ˈThermos ˌflask**

thermosetting ˈθɜː.məʊˌset.ɪŋ, (US) ˈθɝː.moʊˌset̬-, -məˌ-

thermostat ˈθɜː.mə.stæt, (US) ˈθɝː.mə- **-s** -s **-(t)ing** -ɪŋ **-(t)ed** -ɪd

thermostatic ˌθɜː.məˈstæt.ɪk, (US) ˌθɝː.məˈstæt̬-

Theron θeəˈrɒn, (US) ˈθer.ən, ˌθerˈɑːn

Theroux θəˈruː

Thersites θɜːˈsaɪ.tiːz, θə-, (US) θɚˈsaɪ-

thesaur|us θɪˈsɔː.r|əs, θiː-, θə-, (US) θɪˈsɔːr|.əs **-i** -aɪ **-uses** -ə.sɪz

these (plural of **this**) ðiːz

Theseus *in Greek legend:* ˈθiː.sjuːs, -sjəs, -si.əs, (US) -si.əs, -sjuːs *Shakespearian character, and as name of ship:* ˈθiː.sjəs, -si.əs

Thesiger ˈθes.ɪ.dʒəʳ, (US) -dʒɚ

thes|is *dissertation:* ˈθiː.s|ɪs *metrical term:* ˈθes.ɪs, ˈθiː.sɪs, (US) ˈθiː.sɪs **-es** -iːz

thespian, T~ ˈθes.pi.ən **-s** -z

Thespis ˈθes.pɪs

Thessalonian ˌθes.ᵊlˈəʊ.ni.ən, (US) -əˈloʊ- **-s** -z

Thessalonika ˌθes.ᵊlˈɒn.ɪ.kə, (US) -əˈlɑː.nɪ-

Thessaly ˈθes.ᵊl.i

theta ˈθiː.tə, (US) ˈθeɪ.t̬ə, ˈθiː- **-s** -z

Thetford ˈθet.fəd, (US) -fɚd

Thetis *Greek:* ˈθet.ɪs, (US) ˈθet̬- *otherwise:* ˈθiː.tɪs, (US) -t̬ɪs

thews θjuːz

they ðeɪ

they'd (= **they would** or **they had**) ðeɪd

Theydon Bois ˌθeɪ.dᵊnˈbɔɪz

they'd've (= **they would have**) ˈðeɪ.dᵊv

they'll (= **they will** or **they shall**) ðeɪl

they're (= **they are**) ðeəʳ, (US) ðer

they've ðeɪv

thiamin(e) ˈθaɪ.ə.miːn, -mɪn, (US) -mɪn, -miːn

thick θɪk **-er** -əʳ, (US) -ɚ **-est** -ɪst, -əst **-ly** -li **-ness/es** -nəs/ɪz, -nɪs/ɪz **as ˌthick as ˈthieves; as ˌthick as ˌtwo ˌshort ˈplanks; ˌgive someone a ˌthick ˈear; through ˌthick and ˈthin**

thicken ˈθɪk.ən **-s** -z **-ing** -ɪŋ, ˈθɪk.nɪŋ **-ed** -d **-er/s** -əʳ/z, (US) -ɚ/z

thicket ˈθɪk.ɪt **-s** -s

thickhead ˈθɪk.hed **-s** -z

thickheaded ˌθɪkˈhed.ɪd, (US) ˈ-ˌ--, ˌ-ˈ-- **-ness** -nəs, -nɪs *stress shift, British only:* **ˌthickheaded ˈfool**

thickish ˈθɪk.ɪʃ

thicko ˈθɪk.əʊ, (US) -oʊ **-s** -z

thickset ˌθɪkˈset, (US) ˈ-ˌ-, ˌ-ˈ- *stress shift, British only:* **ˌthickset ˈman**

thick-skinned ˌθɪkˈskɪnd, (US) ˈ--, ˌ-ˈ- *stress shift, British only:* **ˌthick-skinned ˈman**

thick-skulled ˌθɪkˈskʌld, (US) ˈ--, ˌ-ˈ- *stress shift, British only:* **ˌthick-skulled ˈidiot**

thick-witted ˌθɪkˈwɪt.ɪd, (US) ˈθɪkˌwɪt̬.ɪd, ˌ-ˈ-- *stress shift, British only:* **ˌthick-witted ˈfool**

thie|f θiː|f **-ves** -vz

Thiès tjez, (US) tjes

thiev|e θiːv **-es** -z **-ing** -ɪŋ **-ed** -d **-ery** -ᵊr.i

thievish ˈθiː.vɪʃ **-ly** -li **-ness** -nəs, -nɪs

thigh θaɪ **-s** -z

thighbone ˈθaɪ.bəʊn, (US) -boʊn **-s** -z

thill θɪl **-s** -z

thimble ˈθɪm.bᵊl **-s** -z **-ful/s** -fʊl/z

thimblerig ˈθɪm.bᵊl.rɪg **-s** -z **-ging** -ɪŋ **-ged** -d

Thimbu ˈθɪm.buː

Thimphu ˈθɪm*p*.fuː

thin θɪn **-ner** -əʳ, (US) -ɚ **-nest** -ɪst, -əst **-ly** -li **-ness** -nəs, -nɪs **-s** -z **-ning** -ɪŋ **-ned** -d **into ˌthin ˈair**

thine ðaɪn

thing θɪŋ **-s** -z

thingamabob ˈθɪŋ.ə.məˌbɒb, (US) -ˌbɑːb **-s** -z

thingamajig ˈθɪŋ.ə.məˌdʒɪg **-s** -z

thingam|y ˈθɪŋ.ə.m|i **-ies** -iz

thingie ˈθɪŋ.i **-s** -z

thingumabob ˈθɪŋ.ə.məˌbɒb, (US) -ˌbɑːb **-s** -z

thingumajig ˈθɪŋ.ə.məˌdʒɪg **-s** -z

thingumm|y ˈθɪŋ.ə.m|i **-ies** -iz

thing|y ˈθɪŋ|.i **-ies** -z

think θɪŋk **-s** -s **-ing/ly** -ɪŋ/li **thought** θɔːt, (US) θɑːt, θɔːt **thinker/s** ˈθɪŋ.kəʳ/z, (US) -kɚ/z **ˈthink ˌtank**

thinkable ˈθɪŋ.kə.bᵊl

Thinn θɪn

thinnish ˈθɪn.ɪʃ

thin-skinned ˌθɪnˈskɪnd, (US) ˈ-- *stress shift, British only:* **ˌthin-skinned ˈperson**

third θɜːd, (US) θɝːd **-s** -z **-ly** -li **ˌthird ˈclass; ˌthird diˈmension; ˌthird ˈparty; ˌthird ˈperson; ˌThird ˈWorld; ˌgive someone the ˌthird deˈgree**

third-degree ˌθɜːd.dɪˈgriː, -dəˈ-, (US) ˌθɝːd- *stress shift, see compound:* **ˌthird-degree ˈburn**

thirdhand ˌθɜːdˈhænd, (US) ˌθɝːd- *stress shift:* **ˌthirdhand ˈgossip**

third-ra|te ˌθɜːdˈreɪ|t, (US) ˌθɝːd- **-ter/s** -təʳ/z, (US) -t̬ɚ/z *stress shift:* **ˌthird-rate ˈdrama**

Thirsk θɜːsk, (US) θɝːsk

thirst θɜːst, (US) θɝːst **-s** -s **-ing** -ɪŋ **-ed** -ɪd

thirst|y ˈθɜː.st|i, (US) ˈθɝː- **-ier** -i.əʳ, (US) -i.ɚ **-iest** -i.ɪst, -i.əst **-ily** -ᵊl.i, -ɪ.li **-iness** -ɪ.nəs, -ɪ.nɪs

thirteen θɜːˈtiːn, (US) θɝː- **-s** -z *stress shift:* **ˌthirteen ˈpounds**

thirteenth θɜːˈtiːn*t*θ, (US) θɝː- **-s** -s *stress shift:* **ˌthirteenth ˈplace**

thirtieth ˈθɜː.ti.əθ, (US) ˈθɝː.t̬i- **-s** -s

thirt|y ˈθɜː.t|i, (US) ˈθɝː.t̬|i **-ies** -iz **ˈthirty ˌsomething; ˌThirty ˌYears' ˈWar**

thirtyfold ˈθɜː.ti.fəʊld, (US) ˈθɝː.t̬i.foʊld

this ðɪs; *occasional weak form:* ðəs **ˌthis, ˌthat, and the ˈother**
Note: Some speakers use a weak form /ðəs/ in 'this morning, afternoon, evening'.

Thisbe ˈθɪz.bi

Thiselton ˈθɪs.ᵊl.tən

thistle ˈθɪs.ᵊl **-s** -z

thistledown ˈθɪs.ᵊl.daʊn

thistly ˈθɪs.ᵊl.i, ˈ-li

thither ˈðɪð.əʳ, (US) ˈθɪð.ɚ, ˈðɪð- **-ward/s** -wəd/z, (US) -wɚd/z

tho' ðəʊ, (US) ðoʊ

Thoday ˈθəʊ.deɪ, (US) ˈθoʊ-

thole θəʊl, (US) θoʊl **-s** -z

Thom tɒm, (US) tɑːm

Thomas ˈtɒm.əs, (US) ˈtɑː.məs

Thomasin ˈtɒm.ə.sɪn, (US) ˈtɑː.mə-

Thomond ˈθəʊ.mənd, (US) ˈθoʊ-

Thompson ˈtɒm*p*.sᵊn, (US) ˈtɑːm*p*-

Thompstone ˈtɒm*p*.stəʊn, (US) ˈtɑːm*p*.stoʊn

Thomson ˈtɒm*p*.sᵊn, (US) ˈtɑːm*p*-

thong θɒŋ, (US) θɑːŋ, θɔːŋ **-s** -z

Thor θɔːʳ, (US) θɔːr

Thora ˈθɔː.rə, (US) ˈθɔːr.ə

thoraces (alternative plural of **thorax**) ˈθɔː.rə.siːz

thoracic θɔːˈræs.ɪk, θɒrˈæs-, θəˈræs-, (US) θɔːˈræs-, θə-

thorax ˈθɔː.ræks, (US) ˈθɔːr.æks **-es** -ɪz

Thorburn ˈθɔː.bɜːn, (US) ˈθɔːr.bɚn

Thoreau θɔːˈrəʊ, θə-; ˈθɔː.rəʊ, (US) θəˈroʊ, θɔː-; ˈθɔːr.oʊ

thorium ˈθɔː.ri.əm, (US) ˈθɔːr.i-

thorn, T~ θɔːn, (US) θɔːrn **-s** -z **a ˌthorn in one's ˈflesh/side**

Thornaby ˈθɔː.nə.bi, (US) ˈθɔːr-

Thornbury ˈθɔːn.bᵊr.i, ˈθɔːm-, (US) ˈθɔːrn.ber-, -bɚ-

thornbush ˈθɔːn.bʊʃ, ˈθɔːm-, (US) ˈθɔːrn- **-es** -ɪz

Thorndike ˈθɔːn.daɪk, (US) ˈθɔːrn-

Thorne θɔːn, (US) θɔːrn

Thorneycroft ˈθɔː.nɪ.krɒft, (US) ˈθɔːr.nɪ.krɑːft

Thornhill ˈθɔːn.hɪl, (US) ˈθɔːrn-

thornless ˈθɔːn.ləs, -lɪs, (US) ˈθɔːrn-

Thornton ˈθɔːn.tən, (US) ˈθɔːrn.tᵊn

thorn|y ˈθɔː.n|i, US ˈθɔːr- **-ier** -i.əʳ, US -i.ɚ **-iest** -i.ɪst, -i.əst **-ily** -əl.i, -ɪ.li **-iness** -ɪ.nəs, -ɪ.nɪs
Thorold ˈθɒr.əld, ˈθʌr-, US ˈθɔːr-, ˈθɝː-
thorough ˈθʌr.ə, US ˈθɝː.oʊ, -ə **-ly** -li **-ness** -nəs, -nɪs
thoroughbass ˈθʌr.ə.beɪs, US ˈθɝː.oʊ-, ˈ-ə-
thoroughbred ˈθʌr.ə.bred, US ˈθɝː.oʊ-, ˈ-ə- **-s** -z
thoroughfare ˈθʌr.ə.feəʳ, US ˈθɝː.oʊ.fer, ˈ-ə- **-s** -z
thoroughgoing ˌθʌr.əˈgəʊ.ɪŋ, US ˌθɝː.oʊˈgoʊ-, -əˈ-
thorough-paced ˌθʌr.əˈpeɪst, US ˈθɝː.oʊ.peɪst, ˈ-ə-
Thorowgood ˈθʌr.ə.gʊd, US ˈθɝː.oʊ-
Thorpe θɔːp, US θɔːrp
those (plural of **that**) ðəʊz, US ðoʊz
Thoth θəʊθ, təʊt, θɒθ, US θoʊθ, toʊt
thou *you:* ðaʊ
thou (abbrev. for **thousand**) θaʊ
though ðəʊ, US ðoʊ
thought θɔːt, US θɑːt, θɔːt **-s** -s
thoughtful ˈθɔːt.fəl, -fʊl, US ˈθɑːt-, ˈθɔːt- **-ly** -i **-ness** -nəs, -nɪs
thoughtless ˈθɔːt.ləs, -lɪs, US ˈθɑːt-, ˈθɔːt- **-ly** -li **-ness** -nəs, -nɪs
thought-out ˌθɔːtˈaʊt, US ˌθɑːţ-, ˌθɔːţ-
thought-provoking ˈθɔːt.prəˌvəʊ.kɪŋ, US ˈθɑːt.prəˌvoʊ-, ˈθɔːt-
Thouless ˈθaʊ.les, -lɪs
thous|and ˈθaʊ.z|ənd **-ands** -əndz **ˌThousand ˌIsland ˈdressing**
thousandfold ˈθaʊ.zənd.fəʊld, US -foʊld
thousandth ˈθaʊ.zəndθ **-s** -s
Thrace θreɪs
Thracian ˈθreɪ.ʃən, -ʃi.ən, US ˈ-ʃən **-s** -z
thral(l)dom ˈθrɔːl.dəm, US ˈθrɔːl-, ˈθrɑːl-
thrall θrɔːl, US θrɔːl, θrɑːl **-s** -z **-ing** -ɪŋ **-ed** -d
thrash θræʃ **-es** -ɪz **-ing** -ɪŋ **-ed** -t **-er/s** -əʳ/z, US -ɚ/z
thread θred **-s** -z **-ing** -ɪŋ **-ed** -ɪd
threadbare ˈθred.beəʳ, US -ber
Threadneedle θredˈniː.dəl, ˈ-ˌ--
thread|y ˈθred|.i **-iness** -ɪ.nəs, -ɪ.nɪs
threat θret **-s** -s
threaten ˈθret.ən **-s** -z **-ing/ly** -ɪŋ/li, ˈθret.nɪŋ/li **-ed** -d
three θriː **-s** -z
three-cornered ˌθriːˈkɔː.nəd, US -ˈkɔːr- *stress shift:* **ˌthree-cornered ˈhat**
three-D, 3-D ˌθriːˈdiː *stress shift:* **ˌthree-D ˈglasses**
three-day ˌθriːˈdeɪ **ˌthree-day eˈvent; ˌthree-day ˈweek**
three-decker ˌθriːˈdek.əʳ, US ˈθriːˌdek.ɚ **-s** -z
three-dimensional ˌθriː.dɪˈmen.tʃən.əl, -daɪˈ-, -ˈmentʃ.nəl, US -dəˈment.ʃən.əl
threefold ˈθriː.fəʊld, US -foʊld
threeish ˈθriː.ɪʃ
three-legged ˌθriːˈlegd, -ˈleg.ɪd, US ˈθriː.legd, -ˌleg.ɪd *stress shift:* **ˌthree-legged ˈstool ˌthree-ˈlegged ˌrace**
three-line ˌθriːˈlaɪn *stress shift, see compound:* **ˌthree-line ˈwhip**
three|pence ˈθre|p.ənts, ˈθrɪ|p-, ˈθrʌ|p-, ˈθrʊ|p- **-pences** -pənt.sɪz **-penny** -pən.i, -p.ni
Note: See note for **penny**.
three-piece ˌθriːˈpiːs *stress shift, see compound:* **ˌthree-piece ˈsuite**
three-ply ˈθriː.plaɪ, ˌ-ˈ-
three-point ˌθriːˈpɔɪnt *stress shift, see compound:* **ˌthree-point ˈturn**
three-quarter ˌθriːˈkwɔː.təʳ, US -ˈkwɔːr.ţɚ **-s** -z *stress shift:* **ˌthree-quarter ˈlength**
three-ring ˌθriːˈrɪŋ *stress shift, see compound:* **ˌthree-ring ˈcircus**
three R's ˌθriːˈɑːz, US -ˈɑːrz
threescore ˌθriːˈskɔːʳ, US ˈθriː.skɔːr *stress shift:* **ˌthreescore ˈyears ˌthreescore ˌyears and ˈten**
threesome ˈθriː.səm **-s** -z
three-star ˌθriːˈstɑːʳ, US -ˈstɑːr *stress shift:* **ˌthree-star hoˈtel**
threnod|y ˈθren.ə.d|i, ˈθriː.nə-, US ˈθren.ə- **-ies** -iz
thresh θreʃ **-es** -ɪz **-ing** -ɪŋ **-ed** -t **-er/s** -əʳ/z, US -ɚ/z **ˈthreshing maˌchine**
thresher, T~® ˈθreʃ.əʳ, US -ɚ **-s** -z
threshold ˈθreʃ.həʊld, US -hoʊld **-s** -z
threw (from **throw**) θruː
thrice θraɪs
thrift θrɪft **ˈthrift ˌshop**
thriftless ˈθrɪft.ləs, -lɪs **-ly** -li **-ness** -nəs, -nɪs
thrift|y ˈθrɪf.t|i **-ier** -i.əʳ, US -i.ɚ **-iest** -i.ɪst, -i.əst **-ily** -əl.i, -ɪ.li **-iness** -ɪ.nəs, -ɪ.nɪs
thrill θrɪl **-s** -z **-ing/ly** -ɪŋ/li **-ed** -d **-er/s** -əʳ/z, US -ɚ/z
Thring θrɪŋ
thrip θrɪp **-s** -s
thriv|e θraɪv **-es** -z **-ing** -ɪŋ **-ed** -d **throve** θrəʊv, US θroʊv **thriven** ˈθrɪv.ən
thro' θruː
throat θrəʊt, US θroʊt **-s** -s **-ed** -ɪd, US ˈθroʊ.ţɪd
throat|y ˈθrəʊ.t|i, US ˈθroʊ.ţ|i **-ier** -i.əʳ, US -i.ɚ **-iest** -i.ɪst, -i.əst **-ily** -əl.i, -ɪ.li **-iness** -ɪ.nəs, -ɪ.nɪs
throb θrɒb, US θrɑːb **-s** -z **-bing/ly** -ɪŋ/li **-bed** -d
throes θrəʊz, US θroʊz
Throgmorton θrɒgˈmɔː.tən, ˈ---, US θrɑːgˈmɔːr-, θrɔːg-, ˈ---
thrombin ˈθrɒm.bɪn, US ˈθrɑːm-
thrombos|is θrɒmˈbəʊ.s|ɪs, US θrɑːmˈboʊ- **-es** -iːz
thromb|us ˈθrɒm.b|əs, US ˈθrɑːm- **-i** -aɪ
thron|e θrəʊn, US θroʊn **-es** -z **-ing** -ɪŋ **-ed** -d
throng θrɒŋ, US θrɑːŋ, θrɔːŋ **-s** -z **-ing** -ɪŋ **-ed** -d
throstle ˈθrɒs.əl, US ˈθrɑː.səl **-s** -z
throttl|e ˈθrɒt.əl, US ˈθrɑː.ţəl **-es** -z **-ing** -ɪŋ, ˈθrɒt.lɪŋ, US ˈθrɑːt- **-ed** -d
through θruː **ˌthrough and ˈthrough**
throughout θruˈaʊt
throughput ˈθruː.pʊt **-s** -s
throughway ˈθruː.weɪ **-s** -z
throve (from **thrive**) θrəʊv, US θroʊv
throw θrəʊ, US θroʊ **-s** -z **-ing** -ɪŋ **threw** θruː **thrown** θrəʊn, US θroʊn **thrower/s** ˈθrəʊ.əʳ/z, US ˈθroʊ.ɚ/z
throwaway ˈθrəʊ.ə.weɪ, US ˈθroʊ-
throwback ˈθrəʊ.bæk, US ˈθroʊ- **-s** -s
thru θruː
thrum θrʌm **-s** -z **-ming** -ɪŋ **-med** -d
thrush θrʌʃ **-es** -ɪz
thrust θrʌst **-s** -s **-ing** -ɪŋ
thruway ˈθruː.weɪ **-s** -z
Thucydides θjuːˈsɪd.ɪ.diːz, θjʊ-, ˈ-ə-, US θuːˈsɪd.ə-
thud θʌd **-s** -z **-ding** -ɪŋ **-ded** -ɪd
thug θʌg **-s** -z
thuggery ˈθʌg.ər.i
thuggish ˈθʌg.ɪʃ **-ly** -li **-ness** -nəs, -nɪs
thuja ˈθuː.jə, US ˈθuː-, ˈθjuː- **-s** -z
Thule *Northernmost region of the world:* ˈθjuː.liː, ˈθuː-, -li; θuːl, US ˈθuː.li, ˈθjuː-, ˈtuː-, ˈtjuː- *Eskimo settlement:* ˈtuː.li, US ˈθuː-, ˈθjuː-
thulium ˈθuː.li.əm, US ˈθuː-, ˈθjuː-
thumb θʌm **-s** -z **-ing** -ɪŋ **-ed** -d **ˌthumb ˈindex**
thumbnail ˈθʌm.neɪl **-s** -z **ˌthumbnail ˈsketch**
thumbprint ˈθʌm.prɪnt **-s** -s
thumbscrew ˈθʌm.skruː **-s** -z
thumbs-down ˌθʌmzˈdaʊn
thumbs-up ˌθʌmzˈʌp
thumbtack ˈθʌm.tæk **-s** -s
Thummim ˈθʌm.ɪm; *in Jewish usage also:* ˈθʊm-, ˈtʊm-
thump θʌmp **-s** -s **-ing** -ɪŋ **-ed** -t **-er/s** -əʳ/z, US -ɚ/z
Thun tuːn
thund|er ˈθʌn.d|əʳ, US -d|ɚ **-ers** -əz, US -ɚz **-ering/ly** -ər.ɪŋ/li **-ered** -əd, US -ɚd **-erer/s** -ər.əʳ/z, US -ɚ.ɚ/z
Thunderball ˈθʌn.də.bɔːl, US -dɚ-, -bɑːl
thunderbird, T~ ˈθʌn.də.bɜːd, US -dɚ.bɝːd **-s** -z
thunderbolt ˈθʌn.də.bəʊlt, US -dɚ.boʊlt **-s** -s
thunderclap ˈθʌn.də.klæp, US -dɚ- **-s** -s
thundercloud ˈθʌn.də.klaʊd, US -dɚ- **-s** -z
thunderfl|y ˈθʌn.də.fl|aɪ, US -dɚ- **-ies** -aɪz
thunderhead ˈθʌn.də.hed, US -dɚ- **-s** -z
thunderous ˈθʌn.dər.əs **-ly** -li
thunderstorm ˈθʌn.də.stɔːm, US -dɚ.stɔːrm **-s** -z

T

thunderstruck ˈθʌn.də.strʌk, ⓊⓈ -dɚ-

thunder|y ˈθʌn.dər|.i **-iness** -ɪ.nəs, -ɪ.nɪs

Thur. (abbrev. for **Thursday**) ˈθɜː.z.deɪ, -di, ⓊⓈ ˈθɝːz-

Thurber ˈθɜː.bər, ⓊⓈ ˈθɝː.bɚ

Thurcroft ˈθɜː.krɒft, ⓊⓈ ˈθɝː.krɑːft

thurible ˈθjʊə.rɪ.bəl, ˈθjɔː-, -rə-, ⓊⓈ ˈθɝː.ə-, ˈθʊr-, ˈθjʊr- **-s** -z

Thuringi|a θjʊəˈrɪn.dʒi|.ə, tʊə-, -ˈrɪŋ.gi|.ə, ⓊⓈ θʊˈrɪn.dʒi|.ə, θjʊ-, ˈ-dʒ|ə **-an/s** -ən/z

Thurloe, Thurlow ˈθɜː.ləʊ, ⓊⓈ ˈθɝː.loʊ

Thurman ˈθɜː.mən, ⓊⓈ θɝː-

Thuron tʊəˈrɒn, tə-, ⓊⓈ -ˈrɑːn

Thurs. (abbrev. for **Thursday**) ˈθɜː.z.deɪ, -di, ⓊⓈ ˈθɝːz-
Note: This abbreviation may also be pronounced /θɜːz/ in British English.

Thursday ˈθɜː.z.deɪ, -di, ⓊⓈ ˈθɝːz- **-s** -z

Thurso ˈθɜː.səʊ, -zəʊ, ⓊⓈ ˈθɝː.soʊ, -zoʊ

Thurston ˈθɜː.stən, ⓊⓈ ˈθɝː-

thus ðʌs

thwack θwæk **-s** -s **-ing** -ɪŋ **-ed** -t

Thwackum ˈθwæk.əm

thwaite, T~ θweɪt **-s** -s

thwart n *of a boat:* θwɔːt, ⓊⓈ θwɔːrt; *in nautical usage also:* θɔːt, ⓊⓈ θɔːrt **-s** -s

thwart v θwɔːt, ⓊⓈ θwɔːrt **-s** -s **-ing** -ɪŋ, ⓊⓈ ˈθwɔːr.t̬ɪŋ **-ed** -ɪd, ⓊⓈ ˈθwɔːr.t̬ɪd

thy ðaɪ

thyme taɪm **-s** -z

thymine ˈθaɪ.miːn, ⓊⓈ -miːn, -mɪn

thymol ˈθaɪ.mɒl, ⓊⓈ -mɔːl, -moʊl

thymus ˈθaɪ.məs **-es** -ɪz

Thynne θɪn

thyroid ˈθaɪ.rɔɪd **-s** -z ˈ**thyroid** ˌ**gland**

thyroxin θaɪˈrɒk.siːn, -sɪn, ⓊⓈ -ˈrɑːk-

Thyrsis ˈθɜː.sɪs, ⓊⓈ ˈθɝː-

thyself ðaɪˈself

Tia Maria® ˌtiː.ə.məˈriː.ə

Tiananmen Square tiˌæn.ən.mɪnˈskweər, -menˈ-, ⓊⓈ ˌtjen.ə.mɪnˈskwer; ⓊⓈ tiˌæn.ən-

Tianjin ˌtjenˈdʒɪn

tiara tiˈɑː.rə, ⓊⓈ -ˈer.ə, -ˈær-, -ˈɑːr- **-s** -z **-ed** -d

Tibbitts ˈtɪb.ɪts

Tibbs tɪbz

Tiber ˈtaɪ.bər, ⓊⓈ -bɚ

Tiberias taɪˈbɪə.ri.æs, -əs, ⓊⓈ -ˈbɪr.i.əs

Tiberius taɪˈbɪə.ri.əs, ⓊⓈ -ˈbɪr.i-

Tibet tɪˈbet

Tibetan tɪˈbet.ən **-s** -s

tibi|a ˈtɪb.i|.ə, ˈtaɪ.bi-, ⓊⓈ ˈtɪb.i- **-ae** -iː **-as** -əz

Tibullus tɪˈbʌl.əs, -ˈbʊl-

tic tɪk **-s** -s

tic douloureux ˌtɪk.duː.lərˈɜː, ⓊⓈ -lʊˈruː

tic|e taɪs **-es** -ɪz **-ing** -ɪŋ **-ed** -t

Ticehurst ˈtaɪs.hɜːst, ⓊⓈ -hɝːst

Tichborne ˈtɪtʃ.bɔːn, -bən, ⓊⓈ -bɔːrn, -bɚn

Ticino tɪˈtʃiː.nəʊ, ⓊⓈ -noʊ

tick tɪk **-s** -s **-ing** -ɪŋ **-ed** -t **-er/s** -ər/z, ⓊⓈ -ɚ/z ˌ**ticking** ˈ**off**

ticker tape ˈtɪk.ə.teɪp, ⓊⓈ ˈ-ɚ- ˌ**ticker tape reˈception;** ˈ**ticker tape** ˌ**parade**

tick|et ˈtɪk|.ɪt **-ets** -ɪts **-eting** -ɪ.tɪŋ, ⓊⓈ -ɪ.t̬ɪŋ **-eted** -ɪ.tɪd, ⓊⓈ -ɪ.t̬ɪd ˈ**ticket** ˌ**office**

tickety-boo ˌtɪk.ɪ.tiˈbuː, ˌ-ə-, ⓊⓈ -ə.t̬iˈ-

ticking ˈtɪk.ɪŋ **-s** -z

ticking-off ˌtɪk.ɪŋˈɒf, ⓊⓈ -ˈɑːf **tickings-off** ˌtɪk.ɪŋzˈɒf, ⓊⓈ -ˈɑːf

tickl|e ˈtɪk.əl **-es** -z **-ing** -ɪŋ, ˈtɪk.lɪŋ **-ed** -d **-er/s** -ər/z, ˈtɪk.lər/z, ⓊⓈ ˈ-əl.ɚ/z, ˈ-lɚ/z

Tickler ˈtɪk.lər, ⓊⓈ -lɚ

ticklish ˈtɪk.lɪʃ, ˈ-əl.ɪʃ **-ly** -li **-ness** -nəs, -nɪs

tickl|y ˈtɪk.əl|.i, ˈ-l|i **-ier** -i.ər, ⓊⓈ -i.ɚ **-iest** -i.ɪst, -i.əst **-iness** -ɪ.nəs, -ɪ.nɪs

ticktacktoe ˌtɪkˌtækˈtəʊ, ⓊⓈ -ˈtoʊ

ticktock ˈtɪk.tɒk, ⓊⓈ -tɑːk **-s** -s

tic-tac-toe ˌtɪkˌtækˈtəʊ, ⓊⓈ -ˈtoʊ

tidal ˈtaɪ.dəl ˈ**tidal** ˌ**wave;** ˌ**tidal** ˈ**wave**

tidbit ˈtɪd.bɪt **-s** -s

tiddledywink ˈtɪd.əl.di.wɪŋk **-s** -s

tiddler ˈtɪd.əl.ər, ˈ-lər, ⓊⓈ ˈ-lɚ, ˈ-əl.ɚ **-s** -z

Tiddles ˈtɪd.əlz

tiddl|y ˈtɪd.l|i, ˈ-əl|.i **-ier** -i.ər, ⓊⓈ -i.ɚ **-iest** -i.ɪst, -i.əst **-iness** -ɪ.nəs, -ɪ.nɪs

tiddlywink ˈtɪd.əl.i.wɪŋk, ˈ-li-, ⓊⓈ ˈ-li-, ˈ-əl.i- **-s** -s

tid|e taɪd **-es** -z **-ing** -ɪŋ **-ed** -ɪd

tideland ˈtaɪd.lænd **-s** -z

tidemark ˈtaɪd.mɑːk, ⓊⓈ -mɑːrk **-s** -s

tidewater ˈtaɪdˌwɔː.tər, ⓊⓈ -ˌwɑː.t̬ɚ, -ˌwɔː-

tideway ˈtaɪd.weɪ

tidings ˈtaɪ.dɪŋz

Tidworth ˈtɪd.wəθ, -wɜːθ, ⓊⓈ -wɚθ, -wɝːθ

tid|y ˈtaɪ.d|i **-ies** -iz **-ier** -i.ər, ⓊⓈ -i.ɚ **-iest** -i.ɪst, -i.əst **-ily** -əl.i, -ɪ.li **-iness** -ɪ.nəs, -ɪ.nɪs **-ying** -i.ɪŋ **-ied** -id

tie taɪ **-s** -z **tying** ˈtaɪ.ɪŋ **tieing** ˈtaɪ.ɪŋ **tied** taɪd ˌ**tied** ˈ**house**

tie-break ˈtaɪ.breɪk **-s** -s **-er/s** -ər/z, ⓊⓈ -ɚ/z

tie-dy|e ˈtaɪ.daɪ **-es** -z **-ing** -ɪŋ **-ed** -d

tie-in ˈtaɪ.ɪn **-s** -z

Tientsin ˌtjentˈsɪn

tiepin ˈtaɪ.pɪn **-s** -z

Tiepolo tiˈep.əl.əʊ, ⓊⓈ -ə.loʊ

tier *one who ties:* ˈtaɪ.ər, ⓊⓈ -ɚ **-s** -z *set of seats in theatre, etc.:* tɪər, ⓊⓈ tɪr **-s** -z **-ed** -d

tierc|e *in music, fencing, cash:* tɪəs, ⓊⓈ tɪrs **-es** -ɪz *in cards:* tɜːs, tɪəs, ⓊⓈ tɪrs **-es** -ɪz

tiercel ˈtɜː.səl, ˈtɪə-, ⓊⓈ ˈtɪr- **-s** -z

Tierra del Fuego tiˌer.ə.del-ˈfweɪ.gəʊ, ˌtjer.ə-, -fuˈeɪ-, ⓊⓈ tiˌer.ə.delˈfweɪ.goʊ

tiff tɪf **-s** -s **-ing** -ɪŋ **-ed** -t

tiffany, T~ ˈtɪf.ən.i

tiffin, T~ ˈtɪf.ɪn **-s** -z

Tiflis ˈtɪf.lɪs

tig tɪg **-s** -z

tig|e tiːʒ **-es** -ɪz

tiger ˈtaɪ.gər, ⓊⓈ -gɚ **-s** -z ˈ**tiger** ˌ**lily;** ˈ**tiger** ˌ**moth**

tigerish ˈtaɪ.gər.ɪʃ **-ly** -li **-ness** -nəs, -nɪs

Tigger ˈtɪg.ər, ⓊⓈ -ɚ

Tiggy-Winkle ˈtɪg.iˌwɪŋ.kəl

Tighe taɪ

tight taɪt **-er** -ər, ⓊⓈ ˈtaɪ.t̬ɚ **-est** -ɪst, -əst, ⓊⓈ ˈtaɪ.t̬ɪst, -t̬əst **-ly** -li **-ness** -nəs, -nɪs

tighten ˈtaɪ.tən **-s** -z **-ing** -ɪŋ, ˈtaɪt.nɪŋ **-ed** -d **-er/s** -ər/z, ˈtaɪt.nər/z, ⓊⓈ ˈtaɪ.tən.ɚ/z, ˈtaɪt.nɚ/z

tightfisted ˌtaɪtˈfɪs.tɪd, ⓊⓈ ˈ-ˌ--, ˌ-ˈ-- **-ly** -li **-ness** -nəs, -nɪs *stress shift, British only:* ˌ**tightfisted** ˈ**miser**

tightknit ˌtaɪtˈnɪt, ⓊⓈ ˈ--, ˌ-ˈ- *stress shift, British only:* ˌ**tightknit** ˈ**group**

tight-lipped ˌtaɪtˈlɪpt, ⓊⓈ ˈ--, ˌ-ˈ- *stress shift, British only:* ˌ**tight-lipped** ˈ**speaker**

tightrope ˈtaɪt.rəʊp, ⓊⓈ -roʊp ˈ**tightrope** ˌ**walker**

tights taɪts

tightwad ˈtaɪt.wɒd, ⓊⓈ -wɑːd **-s** -z

Tiglath-pileser ˌtɪg.læθ.paɪˈliː.zər, -pɪˈ-, -pəˈ-, ⓊⓈ -zɚ

tigon ˈtaɪ.gən **-s** -z

Tigré ˈtiː.greɪ

tigress ˈtaɪ.gres, -grɪs, ⓊⓈ -grɪs **-es** -ɪz

Tigris ˈtaɪ.grɪs

Tijuana tɪˈhwɑː.nə, ˌtiː.əˈ-, ⓊⓈ ˌtiː.əˈwɑː-, tiːˈhwɑː-

tike taɪk **-s** -s

tikka ˈtɪk.ə, ˈtiː.kə

tilbur|y, T~ ˈtɪl.bər|.i, ⓊⓈ -ber-, -bɚ- **-ies** -iz

tilde ˈtɪl.də, -di, -deɪ; tɪld, ⓊⓈ ˈtɪl.də **-s** -z

til|e taɪl **-es** -z **-ing** -ɪŋ **-ed** -d **-er/s** -ər/z, ⓊⓈ -ɚ/z

Tilehurst ˈtaɪl.hɜːst, ⓊⓈ -hɝːst

till, T~ tɪl **-s** -z **-ing** -ɪŋ **-ed** -d **-er/s** -ər/z, ⓊⓈ -ɚ/z **-able** -ə.bəl **-age** -ɪdʒ

tiller ˈtɪl.ər, ⓊⓈ -ɚ **-s** -z

Tilley ˈtɪl.i

Tillicoultry ˌtɪl.ɪˈkuː.tri, -əˈ-

Tilling ˈtɪl.ɪŋ **-s** -z

Tillotson ˈtɪl.ət.sən

Tilly ˈtɪl.i

tilt tɪlt **-s** -s **-ing** -ɪŋ, ⓊⓈ ˈtɪl.tɪŋ **-ed** -ɪd, ⓊⓈ ˈtɪl.tɪd **-er/s** -ər/z, ⓊⓈ ˈtɪl.tɚ/z

tilth tɪlθ

tilt-yard ˈtɪlt.jɑːd, ⓊⓈ -jɑːrd **-s** -z

Tim tɪm

Timaeus taɪˈmiː.əs, tɪ-, ⓊⓈ taɪˈ-

timbal ˈtɪm.bəl **-s** -z

timbale tæmˈbɑːl; tɪmˈ-, ˈtɪm.bəl,

tɪm'bɑːl, (US) 'tɪm.bᵊl; (US) tɪm'bɑːl, tæm- **-s** -z

timb|er 'tɪm.b|əʳ, (US) -b|ɚ **-ers** -əz, (US) -ɚz **-ering** -ᵊr.ɪŋ **-ered** -əd, (US) -ɚd

Timberlake 'tɪm.bə.leɪk, (US) -bɚ-

timberland, T~® 'tɪm.bə.lænd, (US) -bɚ- **-s** -z

timberline 'tɪm.bə.laɪn, (US) -bɚ-

timbre 'tæ̃m.brə, 'tæm-, -bəʳ; 'tɪm.bəʳ, (US) 'tæm.bɚ, 'tɪm- **-s** -z

timbrel 'tɪm.brᵊl **-s** -z

Timbuktu, Timbuctoo ˌtɪm.bʌk'tuː, -bək'-, (US) -bʌk'-

tim|e taɪm **-es** -z **-ing** -ɪŋ **-ed** -d **-er/s** -əʳ/z, (US) -ɚ/z **ˌtime and a 'half; ˌtime and 'motion; ˌtime after 'time; since ˌtime imme'morial; 'time ˌbomb; 'time ˌcapsule; ˌtime 'off; 'time ˌswitch; 'time ˌwarp; 'time ˌzone; ˌfall on ˌhard 'times**

time-consuming 'taɪm.kənˌsjuː.mɪŋ, -ˌsuː-, (US) -ˌsuː-

time-hono(u)red 'taɪmˌɒn.əd, ˌ-'--, (US) 'taɪmˌɑː.nɚd

timekeep|er 'taɪmˌkiː.p|əʳ, (US) -p|ɚ **-ers** -əz, (US) -ɚz **-ing** -ɪŋ

time-lapse 'taɪm.læps **-s** -ɪz **ˌtime-lapse pho'tography**

timeless 'taɪm.ləs, -lɪs **-ly** -li **-ness** -nəs, -nɪs

timeline 'taɪm.laɪn **-s** -z

time-lock 'taɪm.lɒk, (US) -lɑːk **-s** -s

timel|y 'taɪm.l|i **-ier** -i.əʳ, (US) -i.ɚ **-iest** -i.ɪst, -i.əst **-iness** -ɪ.nəs, -ɪ.nɪs

timeous 'taɪ.məs

time-out ˌtaɪm'aʊt, '-- **time-outs** ˌtaɪm'aʊts, '-- **times-out** ˌtaɪmz'aʊt, '--

timepiec|e 'taɪm.piːs **-es** -ɪz

time-saving 'taɪmˌseɪ.vɪŋ

timescale 'taɪm.skeɪl **-s** -z

timeserv|er 'taɪmˌsɜː.v|əʳ, (US) -ˌsɝː.v|ɚ **-ers** -əz, (US) -ɚz **-ing** -ɪŋ

timeshar|e 'taɪm.ʃeəʳ, (US) -ʃer **-es** -z **-er/s** -əʳ/z, (US) -ɚ/z **-ing** -ɪŋ

timesheet 'taɪm.ʃiːt **-s** -s

time-switch 'taɪm.swɪtʃ **-es** -ɪz

timetabl|e 'taɪmˌteɪ.bᵊl **-es** -z **-ing** -ɪŋ, -ˌteɪ.blɪŋ **-ed** -d

timework 'taɪm.wɜːk, (US) -wɝːk **-er/s** -əʳ/z, (US) -ɚ/z

timeworn 'taɪm.wɔːn, (US) -wɔːrn

Timex® 'taɪ.meks

timid 'tɪm.ɪd **-est** -ɪst, -əst **-ly** -li **-ness** -nəs, -nɪs

timidity tɪ'mɪd.ə.ti, -ɪ.ti, (US) -ə.t̬i

Timisoara ˌtɪm.ɪ'ʃwɑː.rə, (US) ˌtiː.miː'ʃwɑːr.ə

Timmins 'tɪm.ɪnz

Timms tɪmz

Timon 'taɪ.mən, -mɒn, (US) -mən

Timor 'tiː.mɔːʳ, 'taɪ-, (US) -mɔːr; (US) tiː'mɔːr

timorous 'tɪm.ᵊr.əs **-ly** -li **-ness** -nəs, -nɪs

Timotheus tɪ'məʊ.θi.əs, (US) -'moʊ-, taɪ-, -'mɑː-

Timothy 'tɪm.ə.θi

timpan|i, timpan|y 'tɪm.pə.n|i **-ist/s** -ɪst/s

Timpson 'tɪmp.sᵊn

tin tɪn **-s** -z **-ning** -ɪŋ **-ned** -d **ˌtin 'can; ˌtin 'god; 'tin ˌopener; ˌtin ˌpan 'alley**

Tina 'tiː.nə

tinctorial tɪŋk'tɔː.ri.əl, (US) -'tɔːr.i-

tinct|ure 'tɪŋk.tʃ|əʳ, (US) -tʃ|ɚ **-ures** -əz, (US) -ɚz **-uring** -ᵊr.ɪŋ **-ured** -əd, (US) -ɚd

Tindal(l), Tindale 'tɪn.dᵊl

tinder 'tɪn.dəʳ, (US) -dɚ

tinderbox 'tɪn.də.bɒks, (US) -dɚ.bɑːks **-es** -ɪz

tine taɪn **-s** -z

tinfoil 'tɪn.fɔɪl, ˌ-'-, (US) 'tɪn.fɔɪl

ting tɪŋ

ting|e tɪndʒ **-es** -ɪz **-(e)ing** -ɪŋ **-ed** -d

Tingey 'tɪŋ.gi

tingl|e 'tɪŋ.gᵊl **-es** -z **-ing** -ɪŋ, 'tɪŋ.glɪŋ **-ed** -d

tingly 'tɪŋ.gli, '-gᵊl.i

tink|er 'tɪŋ.k|əʳ, (US) -k|ɚ **-ers** -əz, (US) -ɚz **-ering** -ᵊr.ɪŋ **-ered** -əd, (US) -ɚd **ˌtinker's 'cuss; ˌtinker's 'damn**

Tinkerbell 'tɪŋ.kə.bel, (US) -kɚ-

Tinkertoy® 'tɪŋ.kə.tɔɪ, (US) -kɚ-

tinkl|e 'tɪŋ.kᵊl **-es** -z **-ing/s** -ɪŋ/z, 'tɪŋ.klɪŋ/z **-ed** -d

Tinnevelly tɪ'nev.ᵊl.i; ˌtɪn.ɪ'vel.i

tinnitus 'tɪn.ɪ.təs, '-ə-, (US) tɪ'naɪ.t̬əs; (US) 'tɪn.ɪ-

tinn|y 'tɪn|.i **-ies** -iz **-ier** -i.əʳ, (US) -i.ɚ **-iest** -i.ɪst, -i.əst **-ily** -ᵊl.i, -ɪ.li **-iness** -ɪ.nəs, -ɪ.nɪs

Tinos 'tiː.nɒs, (US) -nɑːs

tinplate 'tɪn.pleɪt, 'tɪm-, ˌ-'-, (US) 'tɪn.pleɪt **-d** -ɪd

tin-pot 'tɪn.pɒt, 'tɪm-, (US) 'tɪn.pɑːt **ˌtin-pot dic'tator**

tinsel 'tɪnt.sᵊl **-ly** -i **'tinsel ˌtown**

Tinseltown 'tɪnt.sᵊl.taʊn

tint tɪnt **-s** -s **-ing** -ɪŋ, (US) 'tɪn.t̬ɪŋ **-ed** -ɪd, (US) 'tɪn.t̬ɪd **-er/s** -əʳ/z, (US) 'tɪn.t̬ɚ/z

Tintagel tɪn'tædʒ.əl

Tintern 'tɪn.tən, -tɜːn, (US) -tɚn, -tɝːn

Tintin 'tin.tɪn

tintinnabulation ˌtɪn.tɪˌnæb.jə'leɪ.ʃᵊn, -jʊ'- **-s** -z

tintinnabul|um ˌtɪn.tɪ'næb.jə.l|əm, -jʊ- **-a** -ə **-ar** -əʳ, (US) -ɚ **-ary** -ᵊr.i **-ous** -əs

Tintoretto ˌtɪn.tᵊr'et.əʊ, -tɒr'-, (US) -tə'ret̬.oʊ **-s** -z

tin|y 'taɪ.n|i **-ier** -i.əʳ, (US) -i.ɚ **-iest** -i.ɪst, -i.əst **-iness** -ɪ.nəs, -ɪ.nɪs

-tion ʃᵊn

Note: Suffix. Words containing **-tion** are normally stressed on the penultimate syllable, e.g. **fruition** /fru'ɪʃ.ᵊn/.

Tio Pepe® ˌtiː.əʊ'pep.eɪ, -i, (US) -oʊ'-

-tious ʃəs

Note: Suffix. Words containing **-tious** are normally stressed on the penultimate syllable, e.g. **propitious** /prə'pɪʃ.əs/.

tip tɪp **-s** -s **-ping** -ɪŋ **-ped** -t **-per/s** -əʳ/z, (US) -ɚ/z

tipcat 'tɪp.kæt

tipi 'tiː.piː **-s** -z

Tipo® 'tiː.pəʊ, (US) -poʊ

tip-off 'tɪp.ɒf, (US) -ɑːf **-s** -s

Tipperary ˌtɪp.ᵊr'eə.ri, (US) -ə'rer.i

tippet 'tɪp.ɪt **-s** -s

Tippett 'tɪp.ɪt

Tippex® 'tɪp.eks **-es** -ɪz **-ing** -ɪŋ **-ed** -t

tippl|e 'tɪp.ᵊl **-es** -z **-ing** -ɪŋ, 'tɪp.lɪŋ **-ed** -d **-er/s** -əʳ/z, 'tɪp.ləʳ/z, (US) '-ᵊl.ɚ/z, '-lɚ/z

tip|staff 'tɪp|.stɑːf, (US) -stæf **-staves** -steɪvz

tipster 'tɪp.stəʳ, (US) -stɚ **-s** -z

tips|y 'tɪp.s|i **-ier** -i.əʳ, (US) -i.ɚ **-iest** -i.ɪst, -i.əst **-ily** -ᵊl.i, -ɪ.li **-iness** -ɪ.nəs, -ɪ.nɪs

tipto|e 'tɪp.təʊ, (US) -toʊ **-es** -z **-(e)ing** -ɪŋ **-ed** -d

Tipton 'tɪp.tᵊn

tiptop ˌtɪp'tɒp, (US) 'tɪp.tɑːp *stress shift:* **ˌtiptop 'shape**

Tiptree 'tɪp.triː

tirade taɪ'reɪd, tɪ-, -'rɑːd, (US) 'taɪ.reɪd, -'- **-s** -z

tiramisu ˌtɪr.ə.mɪ'suː, (US) -'miː.suː

Tirana, Tiranë tɪ'rɑː.nə, (US) tɪ-, tiː-

tirass|e tɪ'ræs **-es** -ɪz

tir|e taɪəʳ, 'taɪ.əʳ, (US) taɪ.ɚ **-es** -z **-ing** -ɪŋ **-ed** -d

tired taɪəd, 'taɪ.əd, (US) 'taɪ.ɚd **-ly** -li **-ness** -nəs, -nɪs

Tiree taɪ'riː

tireless 'taɪə.ləs, 'taɪ.ə-, -lɪs, (US) 'taɪ.ɚ- **-ly** -li **-ness** -nəs, -nɪs

Tiresias taɪə'riː.si.æs, -'res.i-, -əs, '-sjəs, (US) taɪ'riː.si.əs

tiresome 'taɪə.səm, 'taɪ.ə-, (US) 'taɪ.ɚ- **-ly** -li **-ness** -nəs, -nɪs

tiro 'taɪə.rəʊ, (US) 'taɪ.roʊ **-s** -z

Tirol tɪ'rəʊl; 'tɪr.əʊl, (US) tɪ'roʊl, -'rɑːl; (US) 'tɪr.oʊl, 'taɪ.roʊl, -rɑːl

Tirolean ˌtɪr.əʊ'liː.ən, (US) tɪ'roʊ.li-, taɪ-; (US) ˌtɪr.ə'liː-

Tirolese ˌtɪr.əʊ'liːz, (US) -ə'liːz, -'liːs

'tis tɪz

tisane tɪ'zæn, tiː-, -'sæn, (US) tɪ'zæn **-s** -z

Tishbite 'tɪʃ.baɪt **-s** -s

Tissot 'tiː.səʊ, (US) tiː'soʊ

tissue 'tɪʃ.uː, 'tɪs.juː, (US) 'tɪʃ.uː **-s** -z **'tissue ˌpaper**

tit tɪt **-s** -s **ˌtit for 'tat**

titan, T~ 'taɪ.tᵊn **-s** -z

Titania tɪ'tɑː.njə, taɪ-, -'teɪ-, -ni.ə, (US) tɪ'teɪ.ni.ə, taɪ-, -'tɑː-

titanic, T~ taɪ'tæn.ɪk, tɪ- **-ally** -ᵊl.i, -li

titanium tɪ'teɪ.ni.əm, taɪ-, (US) taɪ-, tɪ-

titbit 'tɪt.bɪt **-s** -s

titch tɪtʃ

Titchmarsh 'tɪtʃ.mɑːʃ, (US) -mɑːrʃ

titch|y 'tɪtʃ|.i **-ier** -i.əʳ, (US) -i.ɚ **-iest** -i.ɪst, -i.əst

tith|e taɪð **-es** -z **-ing** -ɪŋ **-ed** -d

tithing 'taɪ.ðɪŋ **-s** -z

Tithonus tɪ'θəʊ.nəs, taɪ-, (US) -'θoʊ-

T

Titian ˈtɪʃ.ən, -i.ən, US -ən -s -z
Titicaca ˌtɪt.ɪˈkɑː.kɑː, -kə, US ˌtɪt.ɪ-, ˌtiː.tɪˈ-
titill|ate ˈtɪt.ɪ.l|eɪt, -əl|.eɪt, US -əl|.eɪt -ates -eɪts -ating -eɪ.tɪŋ, US -eɪ.t̬ɪŋ -ated -eɪ.tɪd, US -eɪ.t̬ɪd
titillation ˌtɪt.ɪˈleɪ.ʃən, -əlˈeɪ-, US -əlˈeɪ- -s -z
titi|vate ˈtɪt.ɪ|.veɪt, ˈ-ə-, US ˈtɪt̬.ə- -vates -veɪts -vating -veɪ.tɪŋ, US -veɪ.t̬ɪŋ -vated -veɪ.tɪd, US -veɪ.t̬ɪd
titivation ˌtɪt.ɪˈveɪ.ʃən, -əˈ-, US ˌtɪt̬.əˈ- -s -z
title ˈtaɪ.təl, US -t̬əl -s -z -ing -ɪŋ -d -d -less -ləs, -lɪs ˈ**title** ˌ**deed**
titleholder ˈtaɪ.təlˌhəʊl.dəʳ, US -ˌhoʊl.dɚ -s -z
Titmarsh ˈtɪt.mɑːʃ, US -mɑːrʃ
tit|mouse ˈtɪt|.maʊs -mice -maɪs
Tito ˈtiː.təʊ, US -t̬oʊ, -toʊ
Titograd ˈtiː.təʊ.græd, US -t̬oʊ-, -grɑːd
titration taɪˈtreɪ.ʃən, tɪ-, US taɪ-
titt|er ˈtɪt|.əʳ, US ˈtɪt̬|.ɚ -ers -əz, US -ɚz -ering -ər.ɪŋ -ered -əd, US -ɚd -erer/s -ər.əʳ/z, US -ɚ.ɚ/z
tittle ˈtɪt.əl, US ˈtɪt̬- -s -z
tittle-tattle ˈtɪt.əlˌtæt.əl, US ˈtɪt̬.əlˌtæt̬-
titular ˈtɪtʃ.ə.ləʳ, ˈ-ʊ-, ˈtɪt.jə-, ˈtɪt.jʊ, US ˈtɪtʃ.ə.lɚ, ˈ-ʊ-, ˈtɪt.jə-, -jʊ- -s -z -ly -li
titular|y ˈtɪtʃ.ə.lər|.i, ˈ-ʊ-, ˈtɪt.jə-, ˈtɪt.jʊ-, US ˈtɪtʃ.ə.ler-, ˈ-ʊ-, ˈtɪt.jə-, -jʊ- -ies -iz
Titus ˈtaɪ.təs, US -t̬əs
Tiverton ˈtɪv.ə.tən, US -ɚ.t̬ən
Tivoli ˈtɪv.əl.i
Tivy ˈtaɪ.vi
Tizard ˈtɪz.əd, US -ɚd
Tizer® ˈtaɪ.zəʳ, US -zɚ
tizz tɪz -es -ɪz
tizz|y ˈtɪz|.i -ies -iz
T-junction ˈtiːˌdʒʌŋk.ʃən -s -z
Tlaxcala tləˈskɑː.lə, tlæsˈkɑː-, US tlɑːˈskɑː.lə
Tlemcen tlemˈsen
TM ˌtiːˈem
tmesis ˈtmiː.sɪs, ˈmiː-; təˈmiː-, US təˈmiː-, ˈmiː-
TN (abbrev. for **Tennessee**) ten.əˈsiː, -ɪˈ-, US ˈten.ə.siː; *regionally:* ˈten.ɪ.si, -ə-
TNT ˌtiː.enˈtiː
to adv tuː
Note: This form of **to** is found in expressions such as 'to and fro'.
to prep *strong form:* tuː; *weak forms:* tʊ, tu, tə, US tə, t̬ə, tu
Note: Weak-form word. The strong form /tuː/ is used contrastively, e.g. 'the letter was **to** him, not **from** him', and sometimes in final position, e.g. 'I don't want to', though the /u/ vowel is more often used in this context. The weak form /tə/ is used before consonants, e.g. 'to cut' /təˈkʌt/, while the pronunciation /tu/ is used before vowels in British English, e.g. 'to eat' /tuˈiːt/. In American English, the schwa form is usual before both vowels and consonants, so the latter is /təˈiːt/.
toad təʊd, US toʊd -s -z
toadflax ˈtəʊd.flæks, US ˈtoʊd-
toad-in-the-hole ˌtəʊd.ɪn.ðəˈhəʊl, US ˌtoʊd.ɪn.ðəˈhoʊl
toadstool ˈtəʊd.stuːl, US ˈtoʊd- -s -z
toad|y ˈtəʊ.d|i, US ˈtoʊ- -ies -iz -ying -i.ɪŋ -ied -id
Toal təʊl, US toʊl
to-and-fro ˌtuː.ənd̮ˈfrəʊ, US -ˈfroʊ
toast təʊst, US toʊst -s -s -ing -ɪŋ -ed -ɪd -er/s -əʳ/z, US -ɚ/z -y -i ˈ**toasting** ˌ**fork**; ˈ**toast** ˌ**rack**
toastmaster ˈtəʊstˌmɑː.stəʳ, US ˈtoʊstˌmæs.tɚ -s -z
tobacco təˈbæk.əʊ, US -oʊ -s -z
tobacconist təˈbæk.ən.ɪst -s -s
Tobagan təʊˈbeɪ.gən, US tə- -s -z
Tobago təʊˈbeɪ.gəʊ, US toʊˈbeɪ.goʊ, tə-
Tobagonian ˌtəʊ.bəˈgəʊ.ni.ən, US ˌtoʊ.bəˈgoʊ- -s -z
to-be təˈbiː
Tobermory ˌtəʊ.bəˈmɔː.ri, US ˌtoʊ.bɚˈmɔːr.i
Tobias təʊˈbaɪ.əs, US toʊ-, tə-
Tobin ˈtəʊ.bɪn, US ˈtoʊ-
Tobit ˈtəʊ.bɪt, US ˈtoʊ-
Toblerone® ˈtəʊ.blə.rəʊn, US ˈtoʊ.blə.roʊn
toboggan təˈbɒg.ən, US -ˈbɑː.gən -s -z -ing -ɪŋ -ed -d -er/s -əʳ/z, US -ɚ/z
Tobruk təˈbrʊk, US tə-, toʊ-
tob|y, T~ ˈtəʊ.b|i, US ˈtoʊ- -ies -iz ˈ**toby** ˌ**jug**
toccata təˈkɑː.tə, tɒkˈɑː-, US təˈkɑː.t̬ə -s -z
Toc H ˌtɒkˈeɪtʃ, US ˌtɑːk-
Tocharian tɒkˈeə.ri.ən, təʊˈkeə-, -ˈkɑː-, US toʊˈker.i-, -ˈkær-, -ˈkɑːr-
tocopherol təˈkɒf.ə.rɒl, tɒkˈɒf-, US təˈkɑː.fə.rɑːl, tɑː-
Tocqueville ˈtɒk.vɪl, ˈtəʊk-, US ˈtoʊk-, ˈtɑːk-
tocsin ˈtɒk.sɪn, US ˈtɑːk- -s -z
tod, T~ tɒd, US tɑːd -s -z
today təˈdeɪ, tʊ-, US tə-, tʊ-, tu-
Todd tɒd, US tɑːd
toddl|e ˈtɒd.əl, US ˈtɑː.dəl -es -z -ing -ɪŋ, ˈtɒd.lɪŋ, US ˈtɑːd- -ed -d -er/s -əʳ/z, ˈtɒd.ləʳ/z, ˈtɑːd.əl.ɚ/z, US ˈ-lɚ/z
todd|y ˈtɒd|.i, US ˈtɑː.d|i -ies -iz
Todhunter ˈtɒdˌhʌn.təʳ, -hən.təʳ, US ˈtɑːdˌhʌn.t̬ɚ, -hən.t̬ɚ
Todmorden ˈtɒd.mə.dən, -ˌmɔː.dən, US ˈtɑːd.mɚ.dən, -ˌmɔːr.dən
to-do təˈduː, tʊ- -s -z
toe təʊ, US toʊ -s -z -ing -ɪŋ -d -d ˈ**toe** ˌ**cap**; ˌ**toe the** ˈ**line**; ˌ**tread on someone's** ˈ**toes**
toea ˈtəʊ.jɑː, US ˈtoʊ-
toe-curling ˈtəʊˌkɜː.lɪŋ, US ˈtoʊˌkɝː-
TOEFL ˈtəʊ.fəl, US ˈtoʊ-
toehold ˈtəʊ.həʊld, US ˈtoʊ.hoʊld -s -z
toenail ˈtəʊ.neɪl, US ˈtoʊ- -s -z
toerag ˈtəʊ.ræg, US ˈtoʊ- -s -z
toff tɒf, US tɑːf -s -s
toffee ˈtɒf.i, US ˈtɑː.fi -s -z ˈ**toffee** ˌ**apple**; ˌ**toffee** ˈ**apple**
toffee-nosed ˈtɒf.i.nəʊzd, US ˈtɑː.fi.noʊzd
toff|y ˈtɒf|.i, US ˈtɑː.f|i -ies -iz
Tofts tɒfts, US tɑːfts
tofu ˈtəʊ.fuː, US ˈtoʊ-
tog tɒg, US tɑːg, tɔːg -s -z -ging -ɪŋ -ged -d
toga ˈtəʊ.gə, US ˈtoʊ- -s -z -ed -d
together təˈgeð.əʳ, US -ɚ -ness -nəs, -nɪs
toggery ˈtɒg.ər.i, US ˈtɑː.gɚ-, ˈtɔː-
toggl|e ˈtɒg.əl, US ˈtɑː.gəl, ˈtɔː- -es -z -ing -ɪŋ -ed -d
Togo ˈtəʊ.gəʊ, US ˈtoʊ.goʊ -land -lænd
Togolese ˌtəʊ.gəʊˈliːz, US ˌtoʊ.goʊˈ-, -ˈliːs *stress shift:* ˌ**Togolese** ˈ**people**
Toibin təʊˈbiːn, US ˈtɔɪ.bɪn
toil tɔɪl -s -z -ing -ɪŋ -ed -d -er/s -əʳ/z, US -ɚ/z
toile twɑːl, twɔːl, US twɑːl -s -z
toilet ˈtɔɪ.lət -s -s ˈ**toilet** ˌ**bag**; ˈ**toilet** ˌ**paper**; ˈ**toilet** ˌ**roll**; ˈ**toilet** ˌ**training**; ˈ**toilet** ˌ**water**
toiletr|y ˈtɔɪ.lə.tr|i, -lɪ- -ies -iz
toilette twɑːˈlet -s -s
toilsome ˈtɔɪl.səm -ly -li -ness -nəs, -nɪs
toilworn ˈtɔɪl.wɔːn, US -wɔːrn
to-ing and fro-ing ˌtuː.ɪŋ.ənd̮ˈfrəʊ.ɪŋ, US -ˈfroʊ- **to-ings and fro-ings** ˌtuː.ɪŋz.ənd̮ˈfrəʊ.ɪŋz, US -ˈfroʊ-
tokay, T~ təʊˈkeɪ, -ˈkaɪ, ˈ--; tɒkˈaɪ, -ˈeɪ, US toʊˈkeɪ
Tokelau ˈtəʊ.kə.laʊ, ˈtɒk.ə-, US ˈtoʊ.kə-
token ˈtəʊ.kən, US ˈtoʊ- -s -z -ism -ɪ.zəm
Tokharian tɒkˈeə.ri.ən, təʊˈkeə-, -ˈkɑː-, US toʊˈker.i-, -ˈkær-
Toklas ˈtɒk.ləs, ˈtəʊk-, -læs, US ˈtoʊk.ləs
Tokley ˈtəʊ.kli, US ˈtoʊ-
Tokyo ˈtəʊ.ki.əʊ, US ˈtoʊ.ki.oʊ
Toland ˈtəʊ.lənd, US ˈtoʊ-
told (from **tell**) təʊld, US toʊld
toledo *blade:* təˈliː.dəʊ, tɒlˈiː-, US təˈliː.doʊ -s -z
Toledo *in Spain:* tɒlˈeɪ.dəʊ, təˈleɪ-, -ˈliː-, US təˈliː.doʊ, -ˈleɪ- *in US:* təˈliː.dəʊ, US -doʊ
tolerability ˌtɒl.ər.əˈbɪl.ə.ti, -ɪ.ti, US ˌtɑː.lɚ.əˈbɪl.ə.t̬i
tolerabl|e ˈtɒl.ər.ə.b|əl, US ˈtɑː.lɚ- -ly -li -leness -əl.nəs, -nɪs
tolerance ˈtɒl.ər.ənts, US ˈtɑː.lɚ-
tolerant ˈtɒl.ər.ənt, US ˈtɑː.lɚ- -ly -li
toler|ate ˈtɒl.ər|.eɪt, US ˈtɑː.lə.r|eɪt -ates -eɪts -ating -eɪ.tɪŋ, US -eɪ.t̬ɪŋ -ated -eɪ.tɪd, US -eɪ.t̬ɪd
toleration ˌtɒl.ərˈeɪ.ʃən, US ˌtɑː.ləˈreɪ-
Tolkien ˈtɒl.kiːn, -ˈ-, US ˈtoʊl.kiːn, ˈtɑːl-

oll təʊl, US toʊl -s -z -ing -ɪŋ -ed -d -er/s -əʳ/z, US -ɚ/z ˈ**toll ˌbridge**; ˈ**toll ˌcall**
ollbooth ˈtɒl|.buːθ, ˈtəʊl-, -buːð, US ˈtoʊl- -booths -buːθs, -buːðz
ollemache ˈtɒl.mæʃ, -mɑːʃ, US ˈtɑːl-
ollesbury ˈtəʊlz.bᵊr.i, US ˈtoʊlz.ber-, -bɚ-
olleshunt ˈtəʊlz.hʌnt, US ˈtoʊlz-
olley ˈtɒl.i, US ˈtɑː.li
oll-free ˌtəʊlˈfriː, ˌtoʊl- *stress shift:* ˌ**toll-free** ˈ**call**
ollgate ˈtəʊl.geɪt, US ˈtoʊl- -s -s
ollhou|se ˈtəʊl.haʊ|s, US ˈtoʊl- -ses -zɪz
Tolpuddle ˈtɒlˌpʌd.ᵊl; *locally also:* -ˌpɪd-, US ˈtɑːl-
Tolstoy ˈtɒl.stɔɪ, US ˈtɑːl-, ˈtoʊl-
Toltec ˈtɒl.tek, US ˈtɑːl-, ˈtoʊl- -s -s
tolu, T~ tɒlˈuː, təʊˈluː, -ˈljuː, US toʊˈluː
toluene ˈtɒl.ju.iːn, US ˈtɑːl-
Tolworth ˈtɒl.wəθ, -wɜːθ, US ˈtɑːl.wɚθ, -wɝːθ
tom, T~ tɒm, US tɑːm -s -z ˌ**Tom** ˈ**Collins**; ˌ**Tom**, ˌ**Dick and** ˈ**Harry**; ˌ**Tom and** ˈ**Jerry**; ˌ**Tom** ˈ**Thumb**
tomahawk ˈtɒm.ə.hɔːk, US ˈtɑː.mə.hɑːk, -hɔːk -s -s -ing -ɪŋ -ed -t
Tomalin ˈtɒm.ᵊl.ɪn, US ˈtɑː.mᵊl-
toman təʊˈmɑːn, US toʊ-, tə- -s -z
tomato təˈmɑː.təʊ, US -ˈmeɪ.t̬oʊ -es -z
tomb tuːm -s -z
tombola tɒmˈbəʊ.lə, US tɑːmˈboʊ-, ˈtɑːm.bᵊl.ə -s -z
tomboy ˈtɒm.bɔɪ, US ˈtɑːm- -s -z
tombstone, T~ ˈtuːm.stəʊn, US -stoʊn -s -z
tomcat ˈtɒm.kæt, US ˈtɑːm- -s -s
tome təʊm, US toʊm -s -z
Tomelty ˈtʌm.ᵊl.ti
tomfool ˌtɒmˈfuːl, US ˌtɑːm- -s -z -ery -ᵊr.i, US -ɚ.i
Tomintoul ˌtɒm.ɪnˈtaʊl, -ənˈ-, US ˌtɑːm-
Tomkins ˈtɒmp.kɪnz, US ˈtɑːmp-
Tomlinson ˈtɒm.lɪn.sən, US ˈtɑːm-
tomm|y, tomm|ie, T~ ˈtɒm|.i, US ˈtɑː.m|i -ies -iz ˈ**tommy ˌgun**
tommyrot ˈtɒm.i.rɒt, ˌ--ˈ-, US ˈtɑː.mi.rɑːt
tomogram ˈtəʊ.mə.græm, ˈtɒm.ə-, US ˈtoʊ.mə- -s -z
tomography təˈmɒg.rə.fi, US toʊˈmɑː.grə-, təˈ-
tomorrow təˈmɒr.əʊ, tʊ-, US -ˈmɑːr.oʊ -s -z **toˌmorrow after**ˈ**noon**; **toˌmorrow** ˈ**evening**; **toˌmorrow** ˈ**morning**; **toˌmorrow** ˈ**night**
Tompion ˈtɒm.pi.ən, US ˈtɑːm-
Tompkins ˈtɒmp.kɪnz, US ˈtɑːmp-
Tomsk tɒmpsk, US tɑːmpsk
tomtit ˈtɒm.tɪt, ˌ-ˈ-, US ˌtɑːmˈtɪt, ˈ-- -s -s
tom-tom ˈtɒm.tɒm, US ˈtɑːm.tɑːm -s -z
ton *weight:* tʌn -s -z *fashion:* tɔ̃ːŋ, US tõʊn
tonal ˈtəʊ.nᵊl, US ˈtoʊ-
tonalit|y təʊˈnæl.ə.t|i, -ɪ.t|i, US toʊˈnæl.ə.t̬|i, tə- -ies -iz
Tonbridge ˈtʌn.brɪdʒ, ˈtʌm-, US ˈtʌn-
ton|e təʊn, US toʊn -es -z -ing -ɪŋ -ed -d
tone-deaf ˌtəʊnˈdef, US ˈtoʊn-, ˌ-ˈ- -ness -nəs, -nɪs *stress shift, British only:* ˌ**tone-deaf** ˈ**person**
toneless ˈtəʊn.ləs, -lɪs, US ˈtoʊn- -ly -li -ness -nəs, -nɪs
tonematic ˌtəʊ.nɪˈmæt.ɪk, US ˌtoʊ.nɪˈmæt̬.ɪk -s -s
toneme ˈtəʊ.niːm, US ˈtoʊ- -s -z
tonemic təʊˈniː.mɪk, US toʊ-, tə- -s -s
toner, T~ ˈtəʊ.nəʳ, US ˈtoʊ.nɚ -s -z
tonetic təʊˈnet.ɪk, US toʊˈnet̬-, tə- -s -s
ton|ey ˈtəʊ.n|i, US ˈtoʊ- -ier -i.əʳ, US -i.ɚ -iest -i.ɪst, -i.əst
tonga *cart, medicinal bark:* ˈtɒŋ.gə, US ˈtɑːŋ-, ˈtɔːŋ- -s -z
Tong|a *Pacific islands:* ˈtɒŋ|.ə, -g|ə, US ˈtɑːŋ-, ˈtɔːŋ- -an/s -ən/z *East Africa:* ˈtɒŋ.g|ə, US ˈtɑːŋ-, ˈtɔːŋ- -as -əz -an -ən
Tongking ˌtɒŋˈkɪŋ, US ˌtɑːŋ-, ˌtɔːŋ-
tongs tɒŋz, US tɑːŋz, tɔːŋz
tongu|e tʌŋ -es -z -ing -ɪŋ -ed -d -eless -ləs, -lɪs ˌ**tongue and** ˈ**groove**; ˈ**tongue ˌtwister**; ˌ**bite one's** ˈ**tongue**
tongue-in-cheek ˌtʌŋ.ɪnˈtʃiːk, ˌtɒŋ-, US ˌtʌŋ- *stress shift:* ˌ**tongue-in-cheek** ˈ**article**
tongue-lashing ˈtʌŋˌlæʃ.ɪŋ, ˈtɒŋ-, US ˈtʌŋ- -s -z
tongue-tied ˈtʌŋ.taɪd, ˈtɒŋ-, US ˈtʌŋ-
Toni ˈtəʊ.ni, US ˈtoʊ-
tonic ˈtɒn.ɪk, US ˈtɑː.nɪk -s -s -ally -ᵊl.i, -li
tonicity təʊˈnɪs.ə.ti, -ɪ.ti, US toʊˈnɪs.ə.t̬i, tə-
tonic-solfa, (T S) ˌtɒn.ɪk.sɒlˈfɑː, US ˌtɑː.nɪk.soʊlˈfɑː, -sɑːlˈ-
tonight təˈnaɪt
tonka bean ˈtɒŋ.kə.biːn, US ˈtɑːŋ-, ˈtɔːŋ- -s -z
Tonks tɒŋks, US tɑːŋks, tɔːŋks
tonnag|e ˈtʌn.ɪdʒ -es -ɪz
tonne tʌn -s -z
tonsil ˈtɒnt.sᵊl, -sɪl, US ˈtɑːnt.sᵊl -s -z
tonsil(l)itis ˌtɒnt.sᵊlˈaɪ.tɪs, -sɪˈlaɪ-, -təs, US ˌtɑːnt.səˈlaɪ.t̬ɪs, -t̬əs
tonsillectom|y ˌtɒnt.sᵊlˈek.tə.m|i, -sɪˈlek-, US ˌtɑːnt.səˈlek- -ies -iz
tonsorial tɒnˈsɔː.ri.əl, US tɑːnˈsɔːr.i-
tonsure ˈtɒn.tʃəʳ, ˈtɒnt.ʃʊəʳ, -ˌsjʊəʳ, US ˈtɑːnt.ʃɚ -s -z -d -d
tontine ˈtɒn.tiːn, -taɪn; tɒnˈtiːn, US ˈtɑːn.tiːn, -ˈ-
Tonto ˈtɒn.təʊ, US ˈtɑːn.t̬oʊ
ton-up ˌtʌnˈʌp *stress shift:* ˌ**ton-up** ˈ**bike**
ton|y, T~ ˈtəʊ.n|i, US ˈtoʊ- -ier -i.əʳ, US -i.ɚ -iest -i.ɪst, -i.əst ˈ**Tony Aˌward**
Tonya ˈtɒn.jə, US ˈtɑːn-
Tonypandy ˌtɒn.iˈpæn.di, US ˌtɑː.niˈ-
Tonyrefail ˌtɒn.iˈrev.aɪl, US ˌtɑː.niˈ-
too tuː
toodle-oo ˌtuː.dᵊlˈuː
toodle-pip ˌtuː.dᵊlˈpɪp
took (from **take**) tʊk
Tooke tʊk
tool tuːl -s -z -ing -ɪŋ -ed -d
toolbar ˈtuːl.bɑːʳ, US -bɑːr -s -z
toolbox ˈtuːl.bɒks, US -bɑːks -es -ɪz
Toole tuːl
Tooley ˈtuː.li
toolmaker ˈtuːlˌmeɪ.kəʳ, US -kɚ -s -z
tooltip ˈtuːl.tɪp -s -s
toonie ˈtuː.ni -s -z
toot tuːt -s -s -ing -ɪŋ, US ˈtuː.t̬ɪŋ -ed -ɪd, US ˈtuː.t̬ɪd -er/s -əʳ/z, US ˈtuː.t̬ɚ/z
tooth tuːθ -s -s -ing -ɪŋ -ed -t **teeth** tiːθ ˈ**tooth ˌfairy**; ˈ**tooth ˌpowder**; ˌ**long in the** ˈ**tooth**; ˌ**tooth and** ˈ**nail**
toothache ˈtuːθ.eɪk
toothbrush ˈtuːθ.brʌʃ -es -ɪz -ing -ɪŋ
toothless ˈtuːθ.ləs, -lɪs -ly -li -ness -nəs, -nɪs
toothpaste ˈtuːθ.peɪst -s -s
toothpick ˈtuːθ.pɪk -s -s
toothsome ˈtuːθ.səm -ly -li -ness -nəs, -nɪs
tooth|y ˈtuː.θ|i -ier -i.əʳ, US -i.ɚ -iest -i.ɪst, -i.əst -ily -ᵊl.i, -ɪ.li -iness -ɪ.nəs, -ɪ.nɪs
Tooting ˈtuː.tɪŋ, US -t̬ɪŋ
tootl|e ˈtuː.tᵊl, US -t̬ᵊl -es -z -ing -ɪŋ, ˈtuːt.lɪŋ -ed -d
toots|y, toots|ie ˈtʊt.s|i, ˈtuːt-, US ˈtʊt- -ies -iz
Toowoomba təˈwʊm.bə, tʊ-
top tɒp, US tɑːp -s -s -ping -ɪŋ -ped -t ˌ**top** ˈ**brass**; ˌ**top** ˈ**dog**; ˌ**top** ˈ**drawer**; ˌ**top** ˈ**gear**; ˌ**top** ˈ**hat** US ˈ**top ˌhat**; ˌ**top** ˈ**secret**; **at the ˌtop of one's** ˈ**voice**; ˌ**off the ˌtop of one's** ˈ**head**; **on ˌtop of the** ˈ**world**
topaz ˈtəʊ.pæz, US ˈtoʊ- -es -ɪz
top-class ˌtɒpˈklɑːs, US ˌtɑːpˈklæs *stress shift:* ˌ**top-class** ˈ**model**
topcoat ˈtɒp.kəʊt, US ˈtɑːp.koʊt -s -s
top-down ˌtɒpˈdaʊn, US ˌtɑːp- *stress shift:* ˌ**top-down** ˈ**processing**
top-dress ˌtɒpˈdres, ˈ--, US ˈtɑːp.dres -es -ɪz -ing -ɪŋ -ed -t
top|e təʊp, US toʊp -es -s -ing -ɪŋ -ed -t -er/s -əʳ/z, US -ɚ/z
topee ˈtəʊ.piː, -pi; toʊˈpiː, US toʊˈpiː, ˈ-- -s -z
Topeka təʊˈpiː.kə, US tə-
top-flight ˌtɒpˈflaɪt, US ˈtɑːp.flaɪt, ˌ-ˈ- *stress shift:* ˌ**top-flight** ˈ**surgeon**
topgallant ˌtɒpˈgæl.ᵊnt, US ˌtɑːp-; *nautical pronunciation:* təˈgæl-
Topham ˈtɒp.əm, US ˈtɑː.pəm
top-heav|y ˌtɒpˈhev|.i, US

ˈtɑːpˌhev- **-iness** -ɪ.nəs, -ɪ.nɪs *stress shift:* ˌ**top-heavy** ˈ**cargo**
Tophet(h) ˈtəʊ.fet, (US) ˈtoʊ-
top-hole ˌtɒpˈhəʊl, (US) ˌtɑːpˈhoʊl
topi ˈtəʊ.piː, -pi; toʊˈpiː, (US) toʊˈpiː, ˈ-- **-s** -z
topiary ˈtəʊ.pjər.i, -pi.ər-, (US) ˈtoʊ.pi.er-
topic ˈtɒp.ɪk, (US) ˈtɑː.pɪk **-s** -s **-al** -əl **-ally** -əl.i, -li
topicalit|y ˌtɒp.ɪˈkæl.ə.t|i, -ɪ.t|i, (US) ˌtɑː.pɪˈkæl.ə.ţ|i **-ies** -iz
topknot ˈtɒp.nɒt, (US) ˈtɑːp.nɑːt **-s** -s
Toplady ˈtɒpˌleɪ.di, (US) ˈtɑːp-
topless ˈtɒp.ləs, -lɪs, (US) ˈtɑːp- **-ness** -nəs, -nɪs
top-level ˌtɒpˈlev.əl, (US) ˈtɑːpˌlev- *stress shift, British only:* ˌ**top-level** ˈ**leak**
topmast ˈtɒp.mɑːst, (US) ˈtɑːp.mæst; *nautical pronunciation:* -məst **-s** -s
topmost ˈtɒp.məʊst, (US) ˈtɑːp-
top-notch ˌtɒpˈnɒtʃ, (US) ˌtɑːpˈnɑːtʃ, ˌ-ˈ- *stress shift:* ˌ**top-notch** ˈ**person**
topographic ˌtɒp.əʊˈgræf.ɪk, (US) ˌtɑː.pəˈ- **-al** -əl **-ally** -əl.i, -li
topograph|y tɒpˈɒg.rə.f|i, təˈpɒg-, (US) təˈpɑː.grə- **-er/s** -ər/z, (US) -ɚ/z
topologic|al ˌtɒp.əlˈɒdʒ.ɪ.k|əl, (US) ˌtɑː.pəˈlɑː.dʒɪ- **-ally** -əl.i, -li
topolog|y tɒpˈɒl.ə.dʒ|i, təˈpɒl-, (US) təˈpɑː.lə- **-ies** -iz **-ist/s** -ɪst/s
toponymy tɒpˈɒn.ɪ.mi, təˈpɒn-, ˈ-ə-, (US) təˈpɑː.nə-, toʊ-
top|os ˈtɒp|.ɒs, (US) ˈtoʊ.p|oʊs, -ɑːs **-oi** -ɔɪ
topper ˈtɒp.ər, (US) ˈtɑː.pɚ **-s** -z
topping, T~ ˈtɒp.ɪŋ, (US) ˈtɑː.pɪŋ **-s** -z **-ly** -li
toppl|e ˈtɒp.əl, (US) ˈtɑː.pəl **-es** -z **-ing** -ɪŋ, ˈtɒp.lɪŋ, (US) ˈtɑː.plɪŋ **-ed** -d
top-ranking ˌtɒpˈræŋ.kɪŋ, (US) ˌtɑːp- *stress shift:* ˌ**top-ranking** ˈ**amateur**
topsail ˈtɒp.seɪl, (US) ˈtɑːp-; *nautical pronunciation:* -səl **-s** -z
Topsham ˈtɒp.səm, (US) ˈtɑːp-
Topshop® ˈtɒp.ʃɒp, (US) ˈtɑːp.ʃɑːp
topside ˈtɒp.saɪd, (US) ˈtɑːp-
topsoil ˈtɒp.sɔɪl, (US) ˈtɑːp- **-s** -z
topspin ˈtɒp.spɪn, (US) ˈtɑːp-
topsy-turv|y ˌtɒp.siˈtɜː.v|i, (US) ˌtɑːp.siˈtɝː- **-ily** -əl.i, -ɪ.li **-iness** -ɪ.nəs, -nɪs **-ydom** -ɪ.dəm
top-up ˈtɒp.ʌp, ˌ-ˈ-, (US) ˈtɑːp.ʌp, ˌ-ˈ- **-s** -s
toque təʊk, (US) toʊk **-s** -s
tor tɔːr, (US) tɔːr **-s** -z
Torah ˈtɔː.rə; *with some Jews:* ˈtəʊ.rɑː, ˌ-ˈ-, ˌtɔː-, (US) ˈtɔːr.ə; (US) tɔːˈrɑː; (US) ˈtoʊ.rə
Torbay ˌtɔːˈbeɪ, (US) ˌtɔːr- *stress shift:* ˌ**Torbay** ˈ**guesthouse**
torch tɔːtʃ, (US) tɔːrtʃ **-es** -ɪz **-ing** -ɪŋ **-ed** -t ˈ**torch** ˌ**song**
torchlight ˈtɔːtʃ.laɪt, (US) ˈtɔːrtʃ-
torchon ˈtɔː.ʃən, -ʃɒn, (US) ˈtɔːr.ʃɑːn
tore (from **tear**) tɔːr, (US) tɔːr
toreador ˈtɒr.i.ə.dɔːr, (US) ˈtɔːr.i.ə.dɔːr **-s** -z
Torfaen ˌtɔːˈvaɪn, (US) ˌtɔːr-
torment n ˈtɔː.ment, (US) ˈtɔːr- **-s** -s
tormen|t v tɔːˈmen|t, (US) tɔːr-, ˈ-- **-ts** -ts **-ting/ly** -tɪŋ/li, (US) -ţɪŋ/li **-ted** -tɪd, (US) -ţɪd
tormentor, tormenter tɔːˈmen.tər, (US) tɔːrˈmen.ţɚ, ˈ--- **-s** -z
torn (from **tear**) tɔːn, (US) tɔːrn
tornado tɔːˈneɪ.dəʊ, (US) tɔːrˈneɪ.doʊ **-(e)s** -z
Toronto təˈrɒn.təʊ, (US) -ˈrɑːn.ţoʊ
torpedo tɔːˈpiː.dəʊ, (US) tɔːrˈpiː.doʊ **-es** -z **-ing** -ɪŋ **-ed** -d
Torpenhow ˈtɔː.pən.haʊ, trɪˈpen.ə; *locally:* trə-, (US) ˈtɔːr.pen.haʊ
torpid ˈtɔː.pɪd, (US) ˈtɔːr- **-s** -z **-ly** -li **-ness** -nəs, -nɪs
torpidity tɔːˈpɪd.ə.ti, -ɪ.ti, (US) tɔːrˈpɪd.ə.ţi
Torpoint ˌtɔːˈpɔɪnt, (US) ˌtɔːr-
torpor ˈtɔː.pər, (US) ˈtɔːr.pɚ
Torquay ˌtɔːˈkiː, (US) ˌtɔːr- *stress shift:* ˌ**Torquay** ˈ**guesthouse**
torque tɔːk, (US) tɔːrk **-s** -s
Torquemada ˌtɔː.kɪˈmɑː.də, -kemˈɑː-, -kwɪˈmɑː-, -kwemˈɑː-, (US) ˌtɔːr.kəˈmɑː-, -kwəˈ-
torr tɔːr, (US) tɔːr
Torrance ˈtɒr.ənts, (US) ˈtɔːr-
torrefaction ˌtɒr.ɪˈfæk.ʃən, -əˈ-, (US) ˌtɔːr.əˈ-
torre|fy ˈtɒr.ɪ|.faɪ, ˈ-ə-, (US) ˈtɔːr.ə- **-fies** -faɪz **-fying** -faɪ.ɪŋ **-fied** -faɪd
Torremolinos ˌtɒr.ɪ.məˈliː.nɒs, ˌ-ə-, (US) ˌtɔːr.ə.məˈliː.nɑːs, -əs
Torrens ˈtɒr.ənz, (US) ˈtɔːr-
torrent ˈtɒr.ənt, (US) ˈtɔːr- **-s** -s
torrential təˈren.tʃəl, tɒrˈen-, (US) tɔːˈrent.ʃəl, tə- **-ly** -i
Torres ˈtɒr.ɪs, ˈtɔː.rɪs, -rɪz, (US) ˈtɔːr.ɪz, -ɪs
Torricelli ˌtɒr.ɪˈtʃel.i, (US) ˌtɔːr.əˈ- **-an** -ən
torrid ˈtɒr.ɪd, (US) ˈtɔːr.ɪd **-ly** -li **-ness** -nəs, -nɪs
Torridge ˈtɒr.ɪdʒ, (US) ˈtɔːr-
Torrington ˈtɒr.ɪŋ.tən, (US) ˈtɔːr-
torsion ˈtɔː.ʃən, (US) ˈtɔːr-
torso ˈtɔː.səʊ, (US) ˈtɔːr.soʊ **-s** -z
tort tɔːt, (US) tɔːrt **-s** -s
torte ˈtɔː.tə; tɔːt, (US) tɔːrt; ˈtɔːr.tə **-s** -z
Tortelier tɔːˈtel.i.eɪ, (US) tɔːr-
tortellini ˌtɔː.təlˈiː.ni, (US) ˌtɔːr.ţəˈliː-
tortelloni ˌtɔː.təlˈəʊ.ni, (US) ˌtɔːr.ţəˈloʊ-
tortfeasor ˌtɔːtˈfiː.zər, (US) ˌtɔːrtˈfiː.zɚ **-s** -z
tortilla tɔːˈtiː.ə, -jə; -ˈtɪl.ə, (US) tɔːrˈtiː.jə **torˈtilla** ˌ**chip**
tortious ˈtɔː.ʃəs, (US) ˈtɔːr- **-ly** -li
tortois|e ˈtɔː.təs, (US) ˈtɔːr.ţəs **-es** -ɪz
tortoiseshell ˈtɔː.təʃ.ʃel, -tə.ʃel, (US) ˈtɔːr.ţəs.ʃel
tortuosity ˌtɔː.tʃuˈɒs.ə.ti, -tjuˈ-, -ɪ.ti, (US) ˌtɔːr.tʃuˈɑː.sə.ţi
tortuous ˈtɔː.tʃu.əs, -tju-, (US) ˈtɔːr.tʃu- **-ly** -li **-ness** -nəs, -nɪs
tort|ure ˈtɔː.tʃ|ər, (US) ˈtɔːr.tʃ|ɚ **-ures** -əz, (US) -ɚz **-uring/ly** -ər.ɪŋ/li **-ured** -əd, (US) -ɚd **-urer/s** -ər.ər/z, (US) -ɚ.ɚ/z ˈ**torture** ˌ**chamber**
torturous ˈtɔː.tʃər.əs, (US) ˈtɔːr- **-ly** -li **-ness** -nəs, -nɪs
tor|us ˈtɔː.r|əs, (US) ˈtɔːr|.əs **-i** -aɪ
Torvill ˈtɔː.vɪl, (US) ˈtɔːr-
tor|y, T~ ˈtɔː.r|i, (US) ˈtɔːr|.i **-ies** -iz **-yism** -i.ɪ.zəm ˈ**Tory** ˌ**party**
Tosca ˈtɒs.kə, (US) ˈtɑː.skə
Toscanini ˌtɒs.kəˈniː.ni, (US) ˌtɑː.skəˈ-
tosh tɒʃ, (US) tɑːʃ
Toshiba® təˈʃiː.bə, tɒʃˈiː-, (US) toʊˈʃiː.bə, tə-
toss tɒs, (US) tɑːs **-es** -ɪz **-ing** -ɪŋ **-ed** -t **-er/s** -ər/z, (US) -ɚ/z ˌ**argue the** ˈ**toss**
tosspot ˈtɒs.pɒt, (US) ˈtɑːs.pɑːt **-s** -s
toss-up ˈtɒs.ʌp, (US) ˈtɑːs- **-s** -s
tostad|a tɒsˈtɑː.d|ə, (US) toʊˈstɑː- **-as** -əz **-o** -əʊ, (US) -oʊ **-os** -əʊz, (US) -oʊz
tot tɒt, (US) tɑːt **-s** -s **-ting** -ɪŋ, (US) ˈtɑː.ţɪŋ **-ted** -ɪd, (US) ˈtɑː.ţɪd
total, T~ ˈtəʊ.təl, (US) ˈtoʊ.ţəl **-s** -z **-ly** -i **-(l)ing** -ɪŋ, -ɪŋ **-(l)ed** -d ˌ**total** ˈ**recall**; ˌ**total reˈcall**
totalitarian təʊˌtæl.ɪˈteə.ri.ən, -əˈ-; ˌtəʊ.tæl-, (US) toʊˌtæl.əˈter.i-, ˌtoʊ.tæl- **-ism** -ɪ.zəm
totalit|y təʊˈtæl.ə.t|i, -ɪ.t|i, (US) toʊˈtæl.ə.ţ|i **-ies** -iz
totalizator, -isa- ˈtəʊ.təl.aɪ.zeɪ.tər, -ɪ-, (US) ˈtoʊ.ţəl.ɪ.zeɪ.ţɚ **-s** -z
totaliz|e, -is|e ˈtəʊ.təl.aɪz, (US) ˈtoʊ.ţə.laɪz **-es** -ɪz **-ing** -ɪŋ **-ed** -d **-er/s** -ər/z, (US) -ɚ/z
tot|e təʊt, (US) toʊt **-es** -s **-ing** -ɪŋ **-ed** -ɪd ˈ**tote** ˌ**bag**
totem ˈtəʊ.təm, (US) ˈtoʊ.ţəm **-s** -z **-ism** -ɪ.zəm ˈ**totem** ˌ**pole**
totemic təʊˈtem.ɪk, (US) toʊ- **-ally** -əl.i, -li
t'other, tother ˈtʌð.ər, (US) -ɚ
Tothill ˈtɒt.hɪl, (US) ˈtɑː.tɪl, ˈtɑːt.hɪl
Totnes ˈtɒt.nɪs, -nəs, (US) ˈtɑːt-
Totten ˈtɒt.ən, (US) ˈtɑː.tən
Tottenham ˈtɒt.ən.əm, ˈ-nəm, (US) ˈtɑː.tən.əm ˌ**Tottenham Court** ˈ**Road**; ˌ**Tottenham** ˈ**Hotspur**
tott|er ˈtɒt|.ər, (US) ˈtɑː.ţ|ɚ **-ers** -əz, (US) -ɚz **-ering/ly** -ər.ɪŋ/li **-ered** -əd, (US) -ɚd **-erer/s** -ər.ər/z, (US) -ɚ.ɚ/z **-ery** -ər.i
Totteridge ˈtɒt.ər.ɪdʒ, (US) ˈtɑː.ţɚ-
Tottington ˈtɒt.ɪŋ.tən, (US) ˈtɑː.ţɪŋ-
Totton ˈtɒt.ən, (US) ˈtɑː.tən
totty ˈtɒt.i, (US) ˈtɑː.ţi
toucan ˈtuː.kæn, -kən, (US) -kæn, -kɑːn, -kən; (US) tuːˈkæn, -ˈkɑːn **-s** -z
touch tʌtʃ **-es** -ɪz **-ing** -ɪŋ **-ed** -t ˌ**touch and** ˈ**go**
touchable ˈtʌtʃ.ə.bəl
touchdown ˈtʌtʃ.daʊn **-s** -z
touché tuːˈʃeɪ, ˈ--, (US) tuːˈʃeɪ
touching ˈtʌtʃ.ɪŋ **-ly** -li **-ness** -nəs, -nɪs
touchline ˈtʌtʃ.laɪn **-s** -z
touchpaper ˈtʌtʃˌpeɪ.pər, (US) -pɚ
touchscreen ˈtʌtʃ.skriːn **-s** -z
touchstone, T~ ˈtʌtʃ.stəʊn, (US) -stoʊn **-s** -z
touch-tone ˈtʌtʃ.təʊn, (US) -toʊn

T

touch-typ|e ˈtʌtʃ.taɪp **-es** -s **-ing** -ɪŋ **-ed** -t **-ist/s** -ɪst/s
touchwood ˈtʌtʃ.wʊd
touch|y ˈtʌtʃ|.i **-ier** -i.əʳ, Ⓤⓢ -i.ɚ **-iest** -i.ɪst, -i.əst **-ily** -əl.i, -ɪ.li **-iness** -ɪ.nəs, -ɪ.nɪs
touchy-feely ˌtʌtʃ.iˈfiː.li *stress shift:* **ˌtouchy-feely ˈmethod**
tough tʌf **-s** -s **-er** -əʳ, Ⓤⓢ -ɚ **-est** -ɪst, -əst **-ly** -li **-ness** -nəs, -nɪs
toughen ˈtʌf.ən **-s** -z **-ing** -ɪŋ, ˈtʌf.nɪŋ **-ed** -d
tough|ie, tough|y ˈtʌf|.i **-ies** -z
Toulon tuːˈlɔ̃ːŋ, Ⓤⓢ -ˈlõʊn, -ˈlɑːn
Toulouse tuːˈluːz
Toulouse-Lautrec ˌtuː.luːz.ləʊˈtrek, tuːˌluːz-, Ⓤⓢ tuːˌluːz.loʊˈ-, -ˌluːs-, -ləˈ-
toupée, toupee ˈtuː.peɪ, -ˈ-, Ⓤⓢ tuːˈpeɪ **-s** -z
tour tʊəʳ, tɔːʳ, Ⓤⓢ tʊr **-s** -z **-ing** -ɪŋ **-ed** -d **-er/s** -əʳ/z, Ⓤⓢ -ɚ/z **ˈtour ˌoperator**
Touraine tʊˈreɪn, Ⓤⓢ -ˈreɪn, -ˈren
tourbillion tʊəˈbɪl.i.ən, ˈ-jən, Ⓤⓢ tʊrˈbɪl.jən **-s** -z
tour de force ˌtʊə.dəˈfɔːs, ˌtɔː-, Ⓤⓢ ˌtʊr.dəˈfɔːrs **tours de force** ˌtʊəz-, ˌtɔːz-, Ⓤⓢ ˌtʊrz-
Tour de France ˌtʊə.dəˈfrɑːnts, ˌtɔː-, Ⓤⓢ ˌtʊr-
Tourette syndrome tʊəˈretˌsɪn.drəʊm, tɔː-, Ⓤⓢ tʊˈretˌsɪn.droʊm
tourism ˈtʊə.rɪ.zəm, ˈtɔː-, Ⓤⓢ ˈtʊr.ɪ-
tourist ˈtʊə.rɪst, ˈtɔː-, Ⓤⓢ ˈtʊr.ɪst **-s** -s **ˈtourist atˌtraction; ˈtourist ˌclass; ˌtourist inforˈmation office**
touristic tʊəˈrɪs.tɪk, tɔː-, Ⓤⓢ tʊˈrɪs- **-ally** -əl.i, -li
touristy ˈtʊə.rɪ.sti, ˈtɔː-, Ⓤⓢ ˈtʊr.ɪ-
tourmaline ˈtʊə.mə.liːn, ˈtɜː-, ˈtɔː-, -lɪn, Ⓤⓢ ˈtʊr.mə.lɪn, -liːn
Tournai ˈtʊə.neɪ, -ˈ-, Ⓤⓢ tʊrˈneɪ
tournament ˈtʊə.nə.mənt, ˈtɔː-, ˈtɜː-, Ⓤⓢ ˈtɝː-, ˈtʊr- **-s** -s
tournedos (sing.) ˈtʊə.nə.dəʊ, ˈtɔː-, ˈtɜː-, Ⓤⓢ ˈtʊr.nə.doʊ, ˌ--ˈ-(plural) -z
Tourneur ˈtɜː.nəʳ, Ⓤⓢ ˈtɝː.nɚ
tourney ˈtʊə.ni, ˈtɔː-, Ⓤⓢ ˈtɝː-, ˈtʊr- **-s** -z
tourniquet ˈtʊə.nɪ.keɪ, ˈtɔː-, ˈtɜː-, Ⓤⓢ ˈtɝː.nɪ.kɪt, ˈtʊr-, -ket **-s** -z
tournure ˈtʊə.njʊəʳ, ˈtɔː-, -ˈ-, Ⓤⓢ ˈtɝː.njʊr **-s** -z
Tours *French town:* tʊəʳ, Ⓤⓢ tʊr *English musical composer:* tʊəz, tɔːz, Ⓤⓢ tʊrz
tousl|e ˈtaʊ.zəl **-es** -z **-ing** -ɪŋ, ˈtaʊz.lɪŋ **-ed** -d
tout taʊt **-s** -s **-ing** -ɪŋ, Ⓤⓢ ˈtaʊ.t̬ɪŋ **-ed** -ɪd, Ⓤⓢ ˈtaʊ.t̬ɪd
Tout *in* **Belle Tout** *in East Sussex:* tuːt *surname:* taʊt
tout court ˌtuːˈkʊəʳ, -ˈkɔːʳ, Ⓤⓢ -ˈkʊr
tout de suite ˌtuːtˈswiːt
Tovey ˈtəʊ.vi, ˈtʌv.i, Ⓤⓢ ˈtoʊ.vi, ˈtʌv.i
tow, T~ təʊ, Ⓤⓢ toʊ **-s** -z **-ing** -ɪŋ **-ed** -d
towage ˈtəʊ.ɪdʒ, Ⓤⓢ ˈtoʊ-
toward adj ˈtəʊ.əd; tɔːd, Ⓤⓢ tɔːrd; Ⓤⓢ ˈtoʊ.ɚd **-ly** -li **-ness** -nəs, -nɪs
toward prep təˈwɔːd, tʊ-; twɔːd, tɔːd, Ⓤⓢ tɔːrd, twɔːrd; Ⓤⓢ ˈtoʊ.ɚd; Ⓤⓢ təˈwɔːrd **-s** -z
towaway ˈtəʊ.ə.weɪ, Ⓤⓢ ˈtoʊ- **-s** -z
towbar ˈtəʊ.bɑːʳ, Ⓤⓢ ˈtoʊ.bɑːr **-s** -z
Towcester ˈtəʊ.stəʳ, Ⓤⓢ ˈtoʊ.stɚ
towel ˈtaʊ.əl, taʊəl **-s** -z **-(l)ing** -ɪŋ **-(l)ed** -d **ˌthrow in the ˈtowel**
towelette ˌtaʊ.əˈlet, ˌtaʊəˈ-, Ⓤⓢ ˌtaʊə- **-s** -s
tower, T~ ˈtaʊ.əʳ, taʊəʳ, Ⓤⓢ ˈtaʊ.ɚ **-s** -z **-ing/ly** -ɪŋ/li **-ed** -d **ˈtower ˌblock; ˌTower ˈHamlets; ˌTower of ˈLondon; ˌtower of ˈstrength**
towhead ˈtəʊ.hed, Ⓤⓢ ˈtoʊ- **-s** -z **-ed** -ɪd
Towle təʊl, Ⓤⓢ toʊl
Towler ˈtaʊ.ləʳ, Ⓤⓢ -lɚ
town taʊn **-s** -z **ˌtown ˈcentre; ˌtown ˈcrier; ˌtown ˈhall; ˈtown ˌhouse; ˌtown ˈplanning; ˌpaint the ˌtown ˈred**
Towne taʊn **-s** -z
townee taʊˈniː, ˈ-- **-s** -z
townie ˈtaʊ.ni **-s** -z
townscape ˈtaʊn.skeɪp **-s** -s
Townsend ˈtaʊn.zend
townsfolk ˈtaʊnz.fəʊk, Ⓤⓢ -foʊk
Townshend ˈtaʊn.zend
township ˈtaʊn.ʃɪp **-s** -s
towns|man ˈtaʊnz|.mən **-men** -mən, -men
townspeople ˈtaʊnzˌpiː.pəl
Townsville ˈtaʊnz.vɪl
towns|woman ˈtaʊnz|ˌwʊm.ən **-women** -ˌwɪm.ɪn
town|y ˈtaʊ.n|i **-ies** -iz
towpa|th ˈtəʊ.pɑː|θ, Ⓤⓢ ˈtoʊ.pæ|θ **-ths** -ðz, Ⓤⓢ -θs, -ðz
towrope ˈtəʊ.rəʊp, Ⓤⓢ ˈtoʊ.roʊp **-s** -z
Towton ˈtaʊ.tən
Towy ˈtaʊ.i
Towyn ˈtaʊ.ɪn
tox(a)emia tɒkˈsiː.mi.ə, Ⓤⓢ tɑːk-
toxic ˈtɒk.sɪk, Ⓤⓢ ˈtɑːk- **-al** -əl **-ally** -əl.i, -li **ˌtoxic ˈshock ˌsyndrome; ˌtoxic ˈwaste**
toxicity tɒkˈsɪs.ə.ti, -ɪ.ti, Ⓤⓢ tɑːkˈsɪs.ə.t̬i
toxicological ˌtɒk.sɪ.kəlˈɒdʒ.ɪ.kəl, Ⓤⓢ ˌtɑːk.sɪ.kəˈlɑː.dʒɪ-
toxicolog|y ˌtɒk.sɪˈkɒl.ə.dʒ|i, Ⓤⓢ ˌtɑːk.sɪˈkɑː.lə- **-ist/s** -ɪst/s
toxin ˈtɒk.sɪn, Ⓤⓢ ˈtɑːk- **-s** -z
toxophilite tɒkˈsɒf.ɪ.laɪt, -əl.aɪt, Ⓤⓢ tɑːkˈsɑː.fə.laɪt **-s** -s
toxoplasmosis ˌtɒk.səʊ.plæzˈməʊ.sɪs, Ⓤⓢ ˌtɑːk.soʊ.plæzˈmoʊ-
Toxteth ˈtɒk.steθ, -stəθ, Ⓤⓢ ˈtɑːk-
toy tɔɪ **-s** -z **-ing** -ɪŋ **-ed** -d
Toya(h) ˈtɔɪ.ə
toyboy ˈtɔɪ.bɔɪ **-s** -z
Toye tɔɪ
Toynbee ˈtɔɪn.biː, ˈtɔɪm-, Ⓤⓢ ˈtɔɪn-
Toyota® tɔɪˈəʊ.tə, tɔːˈjəʊ-, Ⓤⓢ tɔɪˈjoʊ.t̬ə, -ˈoʊ-
toyshop ˈtɔɪ.ʃɒp, Ⓤⓢ -ʃɑːp **-s** -s
Tozer ˈtəʊ.zəʳ, Ⓤⓢ ˈtoʊ.zɚ
trac|e treɪs **-es** -ɪz **-ing** -ɪŋ **-ed** -t **-er/s** -əʳ/z, Ⓤⓢ -ɚ/z **ˈtrace ˌelement; ˈtracing ˌpaper**
traceab|le ˈtreɪ.sə.b|əl **-ly** -li **-leness** -əl.nəs, -nɪs
tracer|y ˈtreɪ.sər|.i **-ies** -iz
Tracey ˈtreɪ.si
trache|a trəˈkiː|.ə; ˈtreɪ.ki-, Ⓤⓢ ˈtreɪ.ki- **-as** -əz **-ae** -iː
tracheal trəˈkiː.əl; ˈtreɪ.ki-, Ⓤⓢ ˈtreɪ.ki-
tracheostom|y ˌtræk.iˈɒst.ə.m|i, ˌtreɪ.ki-, Ⓤⓢ ˌtreɪ.kiˈɑː.stə- **-ies** -iz
tracheotom|y ˌtræk.iˈɒt.ə.mi, ˌtreɪ.ki-, Ⓤⓢ ˌtreɪ.kiˈɑː.t̬ə- **-ies** -ɪz
trachoma trəˈkəʊ.mə, trækˈəʊ-, Ⓤⓢ trəˈkoʊ-
Traci ˈtreɪ.si
tracing ˈtreɪ.sɪŋ **-s** -z
track træk **-s** -s **-ing** -ɪŋ **-ed** -t **-er/s** -əʳ/z, Ⓤⓢ -ɚ/z **ˌtrack and ˈfield; ˈtrack eˌvent; ˈtrack ˌrecord; ˌtrack ˈrecord** Ⓤⓢ **ˈtrack ˌrecord; keep ˈtrack of ˌsomeone/someˈthing; ˌoff the ˌbeaten ˈtrack**
trackball ˈtræk.bɔːl, Ⓤⓢ -bɔːl, -bɑːl
trackless ˈtræk.ləs, -lɪs
trackpad ˈtræk.pæd **-s** -z
tracksuit ˈtræk.suːt, -sjuːt, Ⓤⓢ -suːt **-s** -s **-ed** -ɪd
tract trækt **-s** -s
tractability ˌtræk.təˈbɪl.ə.ti, -ɪ.ti, Ⓤⓢ -ə.t̬i
tractab|le ˈtræk.tə.b|əl **-ly** -li **-leness** -əl.nəs, -nɪs
Tractarian trækˈteə.ri.ən, Ⓤⓢ -ˈter.i- **-s** -z **-ism** -ɪ.zəm
tractate ˈtræk.teɪt **-s** -s
tractile ˈtræk.taɪl, Ⓤⓢ -tɪl, -taɪl
traction ˈtræk.ʃən **ˈtraction ˌengine**
tractor ˈtræk.təʳ, Ⓤⓢ -tɚ **-s** -z
Tracy ˈtreɪ.si
trad træd **ˌtrad ˈjazz**
trad|e treɪd **-es** -z **-ing** -ɪŋ **-ed** -ɪd **-er/s** -əʳ/z, Ⓤⓢ -ɚ/z **ˈtrade ˌbook; Trades Desˈcription ˌAct; ˈtrading eˌstate; ˈtrade ˌfair; ˈtrade ˌgap; ˈtrade ˌname; ˈtrading ˌpost; ˈtrade ˌprice; ˈtrade ˌroute; ˌtrade ˈsecret; ˌtrade(s) ˈunion** Ⓤⓢ **ˈtrade(s) ˌunion; ˈtrade ˌwind**
trade-in ˈtreɪd.ɪn **-s** -z
trademark ˈtreɪd.mɑːk, Ⓤⓢ -mɑːrk **-s** -s **-ing** -ɪŋ **-ed** -t
trade-off ˈtreɪd.ɒf, Ⓤⓢ -ɑːf **-s** -s
Tradescant trəˈdes.kənt
tradescantia ˌtræd.ɪˈskæn.ti.ə, ˌtreɪ.dɪˈ-, -desˈkæn-, -dəˈskæn-, Ⓤⓢ ˌtræd.esˈkænt.ʃi.ə, ˈ-ʃə **-s** -z
tradesfolk ˈtreɪdz.fəʊk, Ⓤⓢ -foʊk
trades|man ˈtreɪdz|.mən **-men** -mən
tradespeople ˈtreɪdzˌpiː.pəl
tradition trəˈdɪʃ.ən **-s** -z
traditional trəˈdɪʃ.ən.əl, -ˈdɪʃ.nəl **-ly** -i
traditional|ism trəˈdɪʃ.ən.əl|.ɪ.zəm, ˈ-nəl- **-ist/s** -ɪst/s

T

traduc|e trəˈdʒuːs, -ˈdjuːs, (US) -ˈduːs, -ˈdjuːs -es -ɪz -ing -ɪŋ -ed -t -er/s -əʳ/z, (US) -ɚ/z -ement -mənt

Trafalgar *in Spain:* trəˈfæl.gəʳ; *archaic and poetical:* ˌtræf.əlˈgɑːʳ, (US) trəˈfæl.gɚ *Square:* trəˈfæl.gəʳ, (US) -gɚ *Viscount:* trəˈfæl.gəʳ, (US) -gɚ *House near Salisbury:* ˌtræf.əlˈgɑːʳ; trəˈfæl.gəʳ, (US) ˌtræf.əlˈgɑːr; (US) trəˈfæl.gɚ

> Note: The present Lord Nelson pronounces the family name as /trəˈfæl.gəʳ/ (US) /-gɚ/. Previous holders of the title pronounced /ˌtræf.əlˈgɑːʳ/ (US) /-ˈgɑːr/.

traffic ˈtræf.ɪk -s -s -king -ɪŋ -ked -t -ker/s -əʳ/z, (US) -ɚ/z **ˈtraffic ˌcalming; ˈtraffic ˌcircle; ˈtraffic ˌjam; ˈtraffic ˌlight; ˈtraffic ˌwarden**

trafficator ˈtræf.ɪ.keɪ.təʳ, (US) -t̬ɚ -s -z

Trafford ˈtræf.əd, (US) -ɚd

tragacanth ˈtræg.ə.kæntθ, ˈtrædʒ-, -sæntθ, (US) -kæntθ

tragedian trəˈdʒiː.di.ən -s -z

traged|y ˈtrædʒ.ə.d|i, ˈ-ɪ-, (US) ˈ-ə- -ies -iz

Trager ˈtreɪ.gəʳ, (US) -gɚ

tragic ˈtrædʒ.ɪk -al -əl -ally -əl.i, -li

tragicomed|y ˌtrædʒ.ɪˈkɒm.ə.d|i, ˈ-ɪ-, (US) -ˈkɑː.mə- -ies -iz

tragicomic ˌtrædʒ.ɪˈkɒm.ɪk, (US) -ˈkɑː.mɪk -al -əl -ally -əl.i, -li

tra|gus ˈtreɪ|.gəs -gi -gaɪ, -dʒaɪ, (US) -dʒaɪ

Traherne trəˈhɜːn, (US) -ˈhɝːn

trail treɪl -s -z -ing -ɪŋ -ed -d -er/s -əʳ/z, (US) -ɚ/z

trailblaz|er ˈtreɪlˌbleɪ.z|əʳ, (US) -z|ɚ -er/s -ə/z, (US) -ɚ/z -ing -ɪŋ

trailhead ˈtreɪl.hed -s -z

train treɪn -s -z -ing/s -ɪŋ/z -ed -d -er/s -əʳ/z, (US) -ɚ/z **ˈtraining ˌcollege; ˈtraining ˌcourse; ˈtrain ˌset; ˈtraining ˌshoe; ˈtrain ˌspotter**

trainbearer ˈtreɪnˌbeə.rəʳ, ˈtreɪm-, (US) ˈtreɪnˌber.ɚ -s -z

trainee ˌtreɪˈniː -s -z -ship/s -ʃɪp/s

Trainor ˈtreɪ.nəʳ, (US) -nɚ

traips|e treɪps -es -ɪz -ing -ɪŋ -ed -t

trait treɪt, treɪ, (US) treɪt **traits** treɪz, treɪts, (US) treɪts

traitor ˈtreɪ.təʳ, (US) -t̬ɚ -s -z

traitoress ˈtreɪ.tər.ɪs, -əs, (US) -t̬ɚ- -es -ɪz

traitorous ˈtreɪ.tər.əs, (US) -t̬ɚ- -ly -li -ness -nəs, -nɪs

traitress ˈtreɪ.trəs, -trɪs, (US) -trɪs -es -ɪz

Trajan ˈtreɪ.dʒən

trajector|y trəˈdʒek.tər|.i, ˈ-tr|i, (US) -tɚ|.i -ies -iz

Tralee trəˈliː

tram træm -s -z

tramcar ˈtræm.kɑːʳ, (US) -kɑːr -s -z

tramline ˈtræm.laɪn -s -z

trammel ˈtræm.əl -s -z -(l)ing -ɪŋ -(l)ed -d

tramontane ˌtræm.ɒnˈteɪn, (US) ˈtrɑː.moʊn.teɪn; (US) træmˈɑːn-; (US) ˌtræm.ɑːnˈteɪn

tramp træmp -s -s -ing -ɪŋ -ed -t -er/s -əʳ/z, (US) -ɚ/z

trampl|e ˈtræm.pəl -es -z -ing -ɪŋ, ˈtræm.plɪŋ -ed -d -er/s -əʳ/z, ˈtræm.pləʳ/z, (US) ˈ-pəl.ɚ/z, ˈ-plɚ/z

trampolin|e ˈtræm.pəl.iːn, -ɪn; ˌtræm.pəlˈiːn, (US) ˌtræm.pəˈliːn, -pəl.ɪn; (US) ˈtræm.pə.liːn -es -z -ing -ɪŋ -ist/s -ɪst/s

tramway ˈtræm.weɪ -s -z

tranc|e trɑːnts, (US) trænts -es -ɪz

tranch|e trɑːntʃ, trɔːntʃ, træntʃ, (US) trɑːntʃ -es -ɪz

Tranent trəˈnent

Tranmere ˈtræn.mɪəʳ, (US) -mɪr

trann|y, trann|ie ˈtræn|.i -ies -iz

tranquil ˈtræŋ.kwɪl, (US) ˈtræŋ-, ˈtræn- -ly -i -ness -nəs, -nɪs

tranquil(l)ity træŋˈkwɪl.ə.ti, -ɪ.ti, (US) -ə.t̬i, træn-

tranquil(l)ization, -isa- ˌtræŋ.kwɪ.laɪˈzeɪ.ʃən, -kwə-, -lɪˈ-, (US) -kwə.ləˈ-, ˌtræn-

tranquil(l)iz|e, -is|e ˈtræŋ.kwɪ.laɪz, -kwə-, (US) ˈtræŋ-, ˈtræn- -es -ɪz -ing/ly -ɪŋ/li -ed -d -er/s -əʳ/z, (US) -ɚ/z

trans- trænts, trɑːnts, trænz, trɑːnz, (US) trænts, trænz
Note: Prefix. May carry primary or secondary stress, or be unstressed; see individual entries.

transact trænˈzækt, trɑːn-, træntˈsækt, trɑːntˈsækt, (US) trænˈzækt, træntˈsækt -s -s -ing -ɪŋ -ed -ɪd -or/s -əʳ/z, (US) -ɚ/z

transaction trænˈzæk.ʃən, trɑːn-, træntˈsæk-, trɑːntˈsæk-, (US) trænˈzæk.ʃən, træntˈsæk- -s -z

transalpine trænˈzæl.paɪn, trɑːn-, træntˈsæl-, trɑːntˈsæl-, (US) trænˈzæl-, træntˈsæl-

transatlantic ˌtræn.zətˈlæn.tɪk, ˌtrɑːn-, ˌtrænt.sət-, ˌtrɑːnt.sət-, (US) ˌtræn.zətˈlæn.t̬ɪk, -sətˈ- *stress shift:* **ˌtransatlantic ˈyacht**

transcend træntˈsend, trɑːnt-, (US) træntˈsend -s -z -ing -ɪŋ -ed -ɪd

transcenden|ce træntˈsen.dənt|s, trɑːnt-, (US) trænt- -cy -si

transcendent træntˈsen.dənt, trɑːntˈ-, (US) træntˈ- -ly -li

transcendental ˌtrænt.senˈden.təl, ˌtrɑːnt-, -sənˈ-, (US) ˌtrænt.senˈden.t̬əl -ly -i **ˌtranscendental mediˈtation**

transcendental|ism ˌtrænt.senˈden.təl|.ɪ.zəm, ˌtrɑːnt-, -sənˈ-, (US) ˌtrænt.senˈden.t̬əl- -ist/s -ɪst/s

transcontinental ˌtræntˌskɒn.tɪˈnen.təl, ˌtrɑːnt-, -təˈ-, (US) ˌtræntˌskɑːn.tənˈen-

transcrib|e træntˈskraɪb, trɑːnt-, (US) træntˈskraɪb -es -z -ing -ɪŋ -ed -d -er/s -əʳ/z, (US) -ɚ/z

transcript ˈtrænt.skrɪpt, ˈtrɑːnt-, (US) ˈtrænt- -s -s

transcription træntˈskrɪp.ʃən, trɑːnt-, (US) trænt- -s -z

transducer trænzˈdʒuː.səʳ, -ˈdjuː-, trɑːnz-, træntsˈ-, trɑːntsˈ-, (US) træntsˈduː.sɚ, trænz-, -ˈdjuː- -s -z

transept ˈtrænt.sept, ˈtrɑːnt-, (US) ˈtrænt- -s -s

transexual træntˈsek.ʃʊəl, trɑːnt-, -ʃu.əl, -sjʊəl, -sju.əl, (US) træntˈsek.ʃu.əl -s -z -ism -ɪ.zəm

transexuality træntˌsek.ʃuˈæl.ɪ.ti, -sjuˈ-, -ə.ti, (US) -ʃuˈæl.ə.t̬i

transfer n ˈtrænt.sfɜːʳ, ˈtrɑːnt-, (US) ˈtrænt.sfɝː -s -z

transfer v træntˈsfɜːʳ, trɑːnt-, (US) træntˈsfɝː, ˈ-- -s -z -ring -ɪŋ -red -d -rer/s -əʳ/z, (US) -ɚ/z

transferability ˌtrænt.sfər.əˈbɪl.ə.ti, ˌtrɑːnt-, -ɪ.ti; træntˌsfɜː.rəˈ-, trɑːnt-, (US) træntˌsfɝː.əˈbɪl.ə.t̬i

transferable træntˈsfɜː.rə.bəl, trɑːntˈ-; ˈtrænt.sfər.ə-, ˈtrɑːnt-, (US) træntˈsfɝː.ə-

transferee ˌtrænt.sfɜːˈriː, ˌtrɑːnt-, -fəˈ-, (US) ˌtrænt.sfəˈriː -s -z

transferenc|e træntˈsfɜː.rənts, trɑːnt-; ˈtrænt.sfər.ənts, ˈtrɑːnt-, (US) træntˈsfɝː-; (US) ˈtrænt.sfɚ- -es -ɪz

transfiguration, T~ ˌtrænt.sfɪ.gərˈeɪ.ʃən, ˌtrɑːnt-, -fɪg.jərˈeɪ-; træntˌsfɪg.ərˈ-, trɑːnt-, -jərˈ-, (US) ˌtrænt.sfɪg.jəˈreɪ-, træntˌsfɪg-, -jʊˈ- -s -z

transfig|ure træntˈsfɪg|.əʳ, trɑːnt-, (US) træntˈsfɪg.j|ɚ -ures -əz, (US) -ɚz -uring -ər.ɪŋ -ured -əd, (US) -ɚd -urement/s -ə.mənt/s, (US) -ɚ.mənt/s

transfinite træntˈsfaɪ.naɪt, trɑːnt-, (US) trænt-

transfix træntˈsfɪks, trɑːnt-, (US) trænt- -es -ɪz -ing -ɪŋ -ed -t

transfixion træntˈsfɪk.ʃən, trɑːnt-, (US) trænt- -s -z

transform træntˈsfɔːm, trɑːnt-, (US) træntˈsfɔːrm -s -z -ing -ɪŋ -ed -d -er/s -əʳ/z, (US) -ɚ/z -able -ə.bəl

transformation ˌtrænt.sfəˈmeɪ.ʃən, ˌtrɑːnt-, -fɔːˈ-, (US) ˌtrænt.sfɚˈ-, -fɔːrˈ- -s -z

transformational ˌtrænt.sfəˈmeɪ.ʃən.əl, ˌtrɑːnt-, -ˈmeɪʃ.nəl, (US) ˌtrænt.sfɚˈ-, -fɔːrˈ- *stress shift, see compound:* **ˌtransformational ˈgrammar**

transfusable træntsˈfjuː.zə.bəl, trɑːnts-, (US) trænts-

transfus|e træntsˈfjuːz, trɑːnts-, (US) trænts- -es -ɪz -ing -ɪŋ -ed -d -er/s -əʳ/z, (US) -ɚ/z

transfusible træntsˈfjuː.zə.bəl, trɑːnts-, -zɪ-, (US) trænts-

transfusion træntsˈfjuː.ʒən, trɑːnts-, (US) trænts- -s -z

transgender ˌtrænzˈdʒen.dəʳ, ˌtrɑːnz-, ˌtræntsˈ-, ˌtrɑːntsˈ-, (US) ˌtrænz.ˈdʒen.dɚ, ˌtrænts.-

transgenic trænzˈdʒen.ɪk, trɑːnzˈ-,

trænts'-, trɑːnts'-, (US) trænz'-, trænts'-

transgress trænz'gres, trɑːnz-, trænts-, trɑːnts-, (US) trænz-, trænts- **-es** -ɪz **-ing** -ɪŋ **-ed** -t **-or/s** -əʳ/z, (US) -ɚ/z

transgression trænz'greʃ.ən, trɑːnz-, trænts-, trɑːnts-, (US) trænts-, trænz- **-s** -z

tranship trænts'ʃɪp, trɑːnts-, træn-, trɑːn-, (US) trænts-, træn- **-s** -s **-ping** -ɪŋ **-ped** -t **-ment/s** -mənt/s

transhuman|ce trænts'hjuː.mən|ts, trɑːnts-, (US) trænts'- **-t** -t

transien|ce 'træn.zi.ənt|s, 'trɑːn-; 'trænt.si-, 'trɑːnt.si-, (US) 'trænt.ʃənt|s, -si.ənt|s; (US) 'træn.ʒənt|s, -zi.ənt|s **-cy** -si

transient 'træn.zi.ənt, 'trɑːn-; 'trænt.si.ənt, 'trɑːnt-, (US) 'trænt.ʃənt, -si.ənt; (US) 'træn.ʒənt, -zi.ənt **-ly** -li **-ness** -nəs, -nɪs

transilient træn'zɪl.i.ənt, trɑːn-, trænt'sɪl-, trɑːnt'sɪl-, (US) træn'zɪl-, '-jənt, trænt'sɪl-

transistor træn'zɪs.təʳ, trɑːn-, trænt'sɪs-, trɑːnt'sɪs-, (US) træn'zɪs.tɚ, trænt'sɪs- **-s** -z **tran,sistor 'radio; ,transistor 'radio**

transistoriz|e, -is|e træn'zɪs.tər.aɪz, trɑːn-, trænt'sɪs-, trɑːnt'sɪs-, (US) træn'zɪs.tə.raɪz, trænt'sɪs- **-es** -ɪz **-ing** -ɪŋ **-ed** -d

transit 'træn.zɪt, 'trɑːn-, 'trænt.sɪt, 'trɑːnt-; (US) 'træn.zɪt, 'trænt.sɪt **-s** -s **'transit ,lounge**

transition træn'zɪʃ.ən, trɑːn'-, trən'-, trænt'sɪʃ-, trɑːnt'sɪʃ-, -'sɪʒ-, (US) træn'zɪʃ-, -'sɪʃ-, -'sɪʒ- **-s** -z

transitional træn'zɪʃ.ən.əl, trɑːn'-, trən'-, trænt'sɪʃ-, trɑːnt'-, -'sɪʒ-, '-nəl, (US) træn'zɪʃ-, trænt'sɪʃ-, -'sɪʃ-, -'sɪʒ- **-li** -i

transitive 'trænt.sə.tɪv, 'trɑːnt-, -sɪ-; 'træn.zə-, 'trɑːn-, -zɪ-, (US) 'trænt.sə.t̬ɪv; (US) 'træn.zə- **-ly** -li **-ness** -nəs, -nɪs

transitivity ,trænt.sə'tɪv.ɪ.ti, ,trɑːnt-, -sɪ'-; ,træn.zə'-, ,trɑːn-, -zɪ'-, (US) ,trænt.sə'tɪv.ə.t̬i; (US) ,træn.zə'-

transitor|y 'trænt.sɪ.tər|.i, 'trɑːnt-, -sə-; 'træn.zɪ-, 'trɑːn-, -zə-, (US) 'trænt.sə.tɔːr-; (US) 'træn.zə- **-ily** -əl.i, -ɪ.li **-iness** -ɪ.nəs, -ɪ.nɪs

Transkei ,trænt'skaɪ, ,trɑːnt-; ,trænz'kaɪ, ,trɑːnz-, (US) træn'skeɪ, -'skaɪ

transla|te trænz'leɪ|t, trɑːnz-; trænt'sleɪ|t, trɑːnt-, (US) træn'sleɪ|t, '--; (US) trænz'leɪ|t, '-- **-tes** -ts **-ting** -tɪŋ, (US) -t̬ɪŋ **-ted** -tɪd, (US) -t̬ɪd **-tor/s** -təʳ/z, (US) -t̬ɚ/z **-table** -tə.bəl, (US) -t̬ə.bəl

translation trænz'leɪ.ʃən, trɑːnz'-; trænt'sleɪ-, trɑːnt'-, (US) træn'sleɪ-; (US) trænz'leɪ- **-s** -z

translative trænz'leɪ.tɪv, trɑːnz-; trænt'sleɪ-, trɑːnt-, (US) træn'sleɪ.t̬ɪv; trænz'leɪ-

translatory trænz'leɪ.tər.i, trɑːnz-; trænt'sleɪ-, trɑːnt'-, (US) træn'sleɪ.t̬ɚ-; (US) trænz'leɪ-

transliter|ate trænz'lɪt.ər|.eɪt, trɑːnz-; trænt'slɪt-, trɑːnt-, (US) træn'slɪt̬.ə.r|eɪt; (US) trænz'lɪt̬- **-ates** -eɪts **-ating** -eɪ.tɪŋ, (US) -eɪ.t̬ɪŋ **-ated** -eɪ.tɪd, (US) -eɪ.t̬ɪd **-ator/s** -eɪ.təʳ/z, (US) -eɪ.t̬ɚ/z

transliteration ,trænz.lɪ.tər'eɪ.ʃən, ,trɑːnz-; trænz,lɪt.ər'-, trɑːnz,-; ,trænt.slɪ.tər-, ,trɑːnt-; træn,slɪt.ər'-, trɑːn,-, (US) træn,slɪt̬.ə'reɪ-; (US) trænz,lɪt̬- **-s** -z

translocation ,trænz.ləʊ'keɪ.ʃən, ,trɑːnz-, ,trænt.sləʊ'-, ,trɑːnt.sləʊ'-, (US) ,trænz.loʊ-

translucenc|e trænz'luː.sənts, trɑːnz-, -'ljuː-; trænt'sluː-, trɑːnt'-; trænz'ljuː-, trɑːnz'-, (US) træn'sluː-; (US) trænz'luː- **-y** -i

translucent trænz'luː.sənt, trɑːnz'-, -'ljuː-; trænt'sluː-, trɑːnt-; trænz'ljuː-, trɑːnz-, (US) træn'sluː-; (US) trænz'luː- **-ly** -li

transmigra|te ,trænz.maɪ'greɪ|t, ,trɑːnz-; ,trænt.smaɪ'-, ,trɑːnt-, (US) ,trænt'smaɪ.greɪ|t; (US) ,trænz'maɪ- **-tes** -ts **-ting** -tɪŋ, (US) -t̬ɪŋ **-ted** -tɪd, (US) -t̬ɪd **-tor/s** -təʳ/z, (US) -t̬ɚ/z

transmigration ,trænz.maɪ'greɪ.ʃən, ,trɑːnz-; ,trænt.smaɪ'-, ,trɑːnt-, (US) ,trænt.smaɪ'-; (US) ,trænz.maɪ'- **-s** -z

transmigratory trænz'maɪ.grə.tər.i, trɑːnz'-; trænt'smaɪ-, trɑːnt'-, (US) træn'smaɪ.grə.tɔːr-; (US) trænz'maɪ-

transmissibility trænz,mɪs.ə'bɪl.ə.ti, trɑːnz,-, -ɪ'-, -ɪ.ti; trænt,smɪs-, trɑːnt-; ,trænz.mɪ.sə'-, ,trɑːnz-, -sɪ'-; ,trænt.smɪ-, ,trɑːnt-, (US) ,trænt.smɪs.ə'bɪl.ə.t̬i; (US) ,trænz.mɪs-

transmissible trænz'mɪs.ə.bəl, trɑːnz'-, '-ɪ-; trænt'smɪs-, trɑːnt'-, (US) træn'smɪs-; (US) trænz'mɪs-

transmission trænz'mɪʃ.ən, trɑːnz-; trænt'smɪʃ-, trɑːnt-, (US) træn'smɪʃ-; (US) trænz'mɪʃ- **-s** -z

transmi|t trænz'mɪ|t, trɑːnz-; trænt'smɪ|t, trɑːnt-, (US) træn'smɪ|t; (US) trænz'mɪ|t **-ts** -ts **-tting** -tɪŋ, (US) -t̬ɪŋ **-tted** -tɪd, (US) -t̬ɪd **-tter/s** -təʳ/z, (US) -t̬ɚ/z

transmittal trænz'mɪt.əl, trɑːnz'-; trænt'smɪt-, trɑːnt'-, (US) træn'smɪt̬-; (US) trænz'mɪt̬- **-s** -z

transmittanc|e trænz'mɪt.ənts, trɑːnz-; trænt'smɪt-, trɑːnt-, (US) træn'smɪt̬-; (US) trænz'mɪt̬- **-es** -ɪz

transmogrification ,trænz.mɒg.rɪ.fɪ'keɪ.ʃən, ,trɑːnz-, trænz,mɒg-, trɑːnz-, -rə-, -fə'-; ,trænt.smɒg-, ,trɑːnt-, trænt,smɒg-, trɑːnt-, (US) trænt,smɑː.grə-; (US) trænz,mɑːg-

transmogri|fy trænz'mɒg.rɪ|.faɪ, trɑːnz-, -rə-; trænt'smɒg-, trɑːnt-, (US) træn'smɑː.grɪ-, '-grə-; (US) trænz'mɑː- **-fies** -faɪz **-fying** -faɪ.ɪŋ **-fied** -faɪd

transmutability trænz,mjuː.tə'bɪl.ə.ti, trɑːnz-, trænts-, trɑːnts-, ,trænz.mjuː-, ,trɑːnz-, ,trænts-, ,trɑːnts-, -ɪ.ti, (US) ,trænts.mjuː.t̬ə'bɪl.ə.t̬i, ,trænz-

transmutation ,trænz.mjuː'teɪ.ʃən, ,trɑːnz-, ,trænts-, ,trɑːnts-, -mjʊ'-, (US) ,trænts-, ,trænz- **-s** -z

trans|mute trænz|'mjuːt, trɑːnz-, trænts-, trɑːnts-, (US) trænts-, trænz- **-mutes** -'mjuːts **-muting** -'mjuː.tɪŋ, (US) -'mjuː.t̬ɪŋ **-muted** -'mjuː.tɪd, (US) -'mjuː.t̬ɪd **-muter/s** -'mjuː.təʳ/z, (US) -'mjuː.t̬ɚ/z **-mutable** -'mjuː.tə.bəl, (US) -'mjuː.t̬ə.bəl

transnational trænz'næʃ.ən.əl, trɑːnz-, '-nəl; trænt'snæʃ-, trɑːnt'-, (US) trænt'snæʃ-; (US) trænz'næʃ-

transoceanic ,træn.zəʊ.ʃi'æn.ɪk, ,trɑːn-, -si'-; ,trænt.səʊ-, ,trɑːnt.səʊ-, (US) ,trænt.soʊ.ʃi'-; (US) ,træn.zoʊ-

transom 'trænt.səm **-s** -z

transpacific ,trænt.spə'sɪf.ɪk, ,trɑːnts-; ,trænz.pə'-, ,trɑːnz-, (US) ,trænt.spə-, ,trænz-

transparenc|y træn'spær.ənt.s|i, trɑːn-, trən-, -'speə.rənt-; trænz'pær.ənt-, trɑːnz-, trənz-, -'peə.rənt-, (US) træn'sper.ənt-, -'spær- **-ies** -iz

transparen|t trænt'spær.ən|t, trɑːnt-, trənt-, -speə.rən|t; trænz'pær.ən|t, trɑːnz-, trənz-, -'peə.rən|t, (US) træn'sper.ən|t, -'spær- **-tly** -t.li **-tness** -t.nəs, -t.nɪs **-ce** -ts

transpiration ,trænt.spɪ'reɪ.ʃən, ,trɑːnt-, -spə'-, (US) ,trænt-

transpir|e træn'spaɪəʳ, -'spaɪ.əʳ, trɑːn-, (US) træn'spaɪ.ɚ **-es** -z **-ing** -ɪŋ **-ed** -d

transplant n 'trænt.splɑːnt, 'trɑːn-, (US) 'trænt.splænt **-s** -s

transplan|t v trænts'plɑːn|t, trɑːnts-, (US) trænts'plæn|t; (US) 'trænts.plæn|t **-ts** -ts **-ting** -tɪŋ, (US) -t̬ɪŋ **-ted** -tɪd, (US) -t̬ɪd **-table** -tə.bəl, (US) -t̬ə.bəl

transplantation ,trænt.splɑːn'teɪ.ʃən, ,trɑːnt-, (US) ,trænt.splæn'- **-s** -z

transponder træn'spɒn.dəʳ, trɑːnt'-, (US) træn'spɑːn.dɚ **-s** -z

transpontine trænt'spɒn.taɪn, trɑːnt-; trænz'pɒn-, trɑːnz-, (US) træn'spɑːn.taɪn, -tɪn, -tiːn

transport n 'trænt.spɔːt, 'trɑːnt-, (US) 'trænt.spɔːrt **-s** -s **'transport ,cafe**

transpor|t v trænt'spɔː|t, trɑːnt-, (US) trænt'spɔːr|t, '-- **-ts** -ts **-ting** -tɪŋ, (US) -t̬ɪŋ **-ted** -tɪd, (US) -t̬ɪd **-table** -tə.bəl, (US) -t̬ə.bəl

transportability ,trænt.spɔː.tə'bɪl.ə.ti, ,trɑːnt-,

trænt͵spɔː-, trɑːnt͵-, -ɪ.ti, (US) trænt͵spɔːr.t̬əˈbɪl.ə.t̬i
transportation ͵trænt.spɔːˈteɪ.ʃᵊn, ͵trɑːnt-, -spəˈ-, (US) ͵trænt.spɚˈ- **-s** -z
transporter træntˈspɔː.təʳ, trɑːnt-, (US) træntˈspɔːr.t̬ɚ **-s** -z
transpos|e træntˈspəʊz, trɑːnt-, (US) træntˈspoʊz **-es** -ɪz **-ing** -ɪŋ **-ed** -d **-er/s** -əʳ/z, (US) -ɚ/z **-able** -ə.bᵊl **-al/s** -ᵊl/z
transposition ͵trænt.spəˈzɪʃ.ᵊn, ͵trɑːnt-, (US) ͵trænt- **-s** -z
transputer træntˈspjuː.təʳ, trɑːnt-; trænzˈpjuː-, trɑːnz-, (US) træntˈspjuː.t̬ɚ **-s** -z
transsexual træntˈsek.ʃu.əl, trɑːntˈ-, træntsˈ-, trɑːntsˈ-, -ʃʊəl, -sjʊəl, -sju.əl, (US) træntˈsek.ʃu.əl, træntsˈ- **-s** -z **-ism** -ɪ.zᵊm
transsexuality trænt͵sek.ʃuˈæl.ɪ.ti, trɑːnt-, trænts͵-, trɑːnts͵-, -sju-, -ə.ti, (US) trænt͵sek.ʃuˈæl.ə.t̬i, trænts͵sek.ʃuˈæl.ə.t̬i
transship træntsˈʃɪp, trɑːnts-, trænˈ-, trɑːnˈ-, (US) træntsˈʃɪp, trænˈʃɪp **-s** -s **-ping** -ɪŋ **-ped** -t **-ment/s** -mənt/s
Trans-Siberian ͵trænts.saɪˈbɪə.ri.ən, ͵trɑːnts-, ͵trænz-, ͵trɑːnz-, (US) ͵trænts.saɪˈbɪr.i-, ͵trænz-
transubstanti|ate ͵trænt.səbˈstæn.tʃi|.eɪt, ͵trɑːnt-, -ˈstɑːn-; -ˈstænt.si-, -ˈstɑːnt-, (US) ͵trænt.səbˈstænt.ʃi- **-ates** -eɪts **-ating** -eɪ.tɪŋ, (US) -eɪ.t̬ɪŋ **-ated** -eɪ.tɪd, (US) -eɪ.t̬ɪd
transubstantiation ͵trænt.səb͵stænt.ʃiˈeɪ.ʃᵊn, ͵trɑːnt-, -͵stɑːn-; -͵stænts.i-, -͵stɑːnts.i-, (US) ͵trænt.səb͵stænt.ʃiˈ- **-s** -z
Transvaal ͵trænzˈvɑːl, ͵trɑːnzˈ-, ͵træntsˈ-, ͵trɑːntsˈ-, ˈ--, (US) ͵træntsˈvɑːl, ͵trænz-
Transvaaler ͵trænzˈvɑː.ləʳ, ͵trɑːnzˈ-, ͵træntsˈ-, ͵trɑːntsˈ-, ˈ-͵--, (US) ͵træntsˈvɑː.lɚ, ͵trænz- **-s** -z
transversal trænzˈvɜː.sᵊl, trɑːnz-, trænts-, trɑːnts-, (US) træntsˈvɝː-, trænz- **-s** -z
transverse adj trænzˈvɜːs, trɑːnz-, trænts-, trɑːnts-, (US) træntsˈvɝːs, trænz- **-ly** -li *stress shift:* **͵transverse ˈengine**
transverse n ˈtrænz.vɜːs, ˈtrɑːnz-, ˈtrænts-, ˈtrɑːnts-, ͵-ˈ-, (US) ˈtrænts-, ˈtrænz-
transvestism trænzˈves.tɪ.zᵊm, trɑːnz-, trænts-, trɑːnts-, (US) trænts-, trænz-
transvestite trænzˈves.taɪt, trɑːnz-, trænts-, trɑːnts-, (US) trænts-, trænz- **-s** -s
Transylvani|a ͵trænt.sɪlˈveɪ.ni|.ə, ͵trɑːnt-, -sᵊlˈ-, ˈ-nj|ə, (US) ͵trænt- **-an/s** -ən
tranter, T~ ˈtræn.təʳ, (US) -t̬ɚ **-s** -z
trap træp **-s** -s **-ping/s** -ɪŋ/z **-ped** -t **-per/s** -əʳ/z, (US) -ɚ/z
trapdoor ͵træpˈdɔːʳ, (US) ˈtræp.dɔːr, ͵-ˈ- **-s** -z *stress shift, British only:* **͵trapdoor ˈspider**
trapes treɪps **-es** -ɪz **-ing** -ɪŋ **-ed** -t
trapez|e trəˈpiːz, (US) træpˈiːz, trəˈpiːz **-es** -ɪz
trapezi|um trəˈpiː.zi|.əm **-ums** -əmz **-a** -ə
trapezoid ˈtræp.ɪ.zɔɪd **-s** -z
Trapp træp
trappings ˈtræp.ɪŋz
Trappist ˈtræp.ɪst **-s** -s
trapshoot|ing ˈtræp͵ʃuː.t|ɪŋ **-er/s** -əʳ/z, (US) -ɚ/z
Traquair trəˈkweəʳ, (US) -ˈkwer
trash træʃ **-es** -ɪz **-ing** -ɪŋ **-ed** -t
trashcan ˈtræʃ.kæn **-s** -z
trash|man ˈtræʃ|.mæn, -mən **-men** -men, -mən
trash|y ˈtræʃ|.i **-ier** -i.əʳ, (US) -i.ɚ **-iest** -i.ɪst, -i.əst **-iness** -ɪ.nəs, -ɪ.nɪs
Trasimene ˈtræz.ɪ.miːn, ˈ-ə-, (US) ˈtrɑː.zɪ.miːn, -zə-
trattoria ͵træt.ᵊrˈiː.ə, (US) ͵trɑː.t̬əˈriː.ə, -tɔːˈ-; (US) trɑːˈtɔːr.i- **-s** -z
traum|a ˈtrɔː.m|ə, ˈtraʊ-, (US) ˈtrɑː-, ˈtrɔː-, ˈtraʊ- **-as** -əz **-ata** -ə.tə, (US) -ə.t̬ə
traumatic trɔːˈmæt.ɪk, traʊ-, (US) trɑːˈmæt̬-, trɔː-, traʊ- **-ally** -ᵊl.i, -li
traumatism ˈtrɔː.mə.tɪ.zᵊm, (US) ˈtrɑː-, ˈtrɔː- **-s** -z
traumatization, -isa- ͵trɔː.mə.taɪˈzeɪ.ʃᵊn, ͵traʊ-, -tɪˈ-, (US) ͵trɑː.mə.t̬əˈ-, ͵trɔː-, ͵traʊ-
traumatiz|e, -is|e ˈtrɔː.mə.taɪz, ˈtraʊ-, (US) ˈtrɑː-, ˈtrɔː-, ˈtraʊ- **-es** -ɪz **-ing** -ɪŋ **-ed** -d
travail ˈtræv.eɪl; trəˈveɪl, (US) trəˈveɪl; (US) ˈtræv.eɪl **-s** -z **-ing** -ɪŋ **-ed** -d
Travancore ͵træv.ᵊŋˈkɔːʳ, (US) -ˈkɔːr
travel ˈtræv.ᵊl **-s** -z **-(l)ing** -ɪŋ, ˈtræv.lɪŋ **-(l)ed** -d **ˈtravel ͵agency; ˈtravel ͵agent; ˈtravelling ex͵penses; ͵travelling ˈsalesman; ˈtravel ͵sickness**
travelator ˈtræv.ᵊl.eɪ.təʳ, (US) -ə.leɪ.t̬ɚ **-s** -z
Travelcard ˈtræv.ᵊl.kɑːd, (US) -kɑːrd
travel(l)er ˈtræv.ᵊl.əʳ, ˈ-ləʳ, (US) ˈ-ᵊl.ɚ, ˈ-lɚ **-s** -z **ˈtravel(l)er's ͵cheque**
travelogue, travelog ˈtræv.ᵊl.ɒg, (US) -ə.lɑːg, -lɔːg **-s** -z
Travers ˈtræv.əz, (US) -ɚz
travers|e n, adj ˈtræv.əs, -ɜːs; trəˈvɜːs, trævˈɜːs, (US) ˈtræv.ɚs, -ɝːs; (US) trəˈvɝːs, trævˈɝːs **-es** -ɪz
travers|e v trəˈvɜːs, trævˈɜːs; ˈtræv.ɜːs, (US) trəˈvɝːs, trævˈɝːs; (US) ˈtræv.ɚs **-es** -ɪz **-ing** -ɪŋ **-ed** -t
travest|y ˈtræv.ə.st|i, ˈ-ɪ-, (US) ˈ-ɪ- **-ies** -iz **-ying** -i.ɪŋ **-ied** -id **͵travesty of ˈjustice**
Traviata ͵træv.iˈɑː.tə, (US) ͵trɑː.viˈɑː.t̬ə
Travis ˈtræv.ɪs
travolator ˈtræv.ᵊl.eɪ.təʳ, (US) -t̬ɚ **-s** -z
Travolta trəˈvəʊl.tə, -ˈvɒl-, (US) -ˈvoʊl.tə
trawl trɔːl, (US) trɑːl, trɔːl **-s** -z **-ing** -ɪŋ **-ed** -d
trawler ˈtrɔː.ləʳ, (US) ˈtrɑː.lɚ, ˈtrɔː- **-s** -z
trawler|man ˈtrɔː.lə|.mən, (US) ˈtrɑː.lɚ-, ˈtrɔː- **-men** -mən
tray treɪ **-s** -z
Traynor ˈtreɪ.nəʳ, (US) -nɚ
treacherous ˈtretʃ.ᵊr.əs **-ly** -li **-ness** -nəs, -nɪs
treacher|y ˈtretʃ.ᵊr|.i **-ies** -iz
treacle ˈtriː.kᵊl **-s** -z **͵treacle ˈtart**
treacl|y ˈtriː.kᵊl|.i, ˈ-kl|i **-iness** -ɪ.nəs, -ɪ.nɪs
tread tred **-s** -z **-ing** -ɪŋ **trod** trɒd, (US) trɑːd **trodden** ˈtrɒd.ᵊn, (US) ˈtrɑː.dᵊn **treader/s** ˈtred.əʳ/z, (US) -ɚ/z **͵tread on someone's ˈtoes**
treadle ˈtred.ᵊl **-s** -z
treadmill ˈtred.mɪl **-s** -z
Treadwell ˈtred.wel
treason ˈtriː.zᵊn **-s** -z
treasonab|le ˈtriː.zᵊn.ə.b|ᵊl, ˈtriːz.nə- **-ly** -li **-leness** -ᵊl.nəs, -nɪs
treasonous ˈtriː.zᵊn.əs, ˈtriːz.nəs
treas|ure ˈtreʒ|.əʳ, (US) -ɚ **-ures** -əz, (US) -ɚz **-uring** -ᵊr.ɪŋ **-ured** -əd, (US) -ɚd **ˈtreasure ͵hunt; ˈtreasure ͵trove**
treasure-hou|se ˈtreʒ.ə.haʊ|s, (US) ˈ-ɚ- **-ses** -zɪz
treasurer ˈtreʒ.ᵊr.əʳ, (US) -ɚ **-s** -z
treasurership ˈtreʒ.ᵊr.ə.ʃɪp, (US) -ɚ- **-s** -s
treasure-trove ˈtreʒ.ə.trəʊv, (US) ˈ-ɚ.troʊv
treasur|y, T~ ˈtreʒ.ᵊr|.i **-ies** -iz
treat triːt **-s** -s **-ing** -ɪŋ, (US) ˈtriː.t̬ɪŋ **-ed** -ɪd, (US) ˈtriː.t̬ɪd
treatable ˈtriː.tə.bᵊl, (US) -t̬ə-
treatis|e ˈtriː.tɪz, -tɪs, (US) -t̬ɪs **-es** -ɪz
treatment ˈtriːt.mənt **-s** -s
treat|y ˈtriː.t|i, (US) -t̬|i **-ies** -iz
Trebizond ˈtreb.ɪ.zɒnd, (US) -zɑːnd
trebl|e ˈtreb.ᵊl **-es** -z **-y** -i, ˈtreb.li **-ing** -ɪŋ, ˈtreb.lɪŋ **-ed** -d
Treblinka trəˈblɪŋ.kə, trebˈlɪŋ-, (US) trəˈblɪŋ-; (US) trebˈliːŋ-
Trebor ˈtriː.bɔːʳ, (US) -bɔːr
trebuchet ˈtreb.ʊ.ʃeɪ, -jʊ-, -uː-, -ʃet, (US) ˈtreb.ʊ.ʃeɪ, -ʃet, -ˈʃeɪ **-s** -z
Tredegar trɪˈdiː.gəʳ, trə-, (US) -gɚ
tree, T~ triː **-s** -z **-ing** -ɪŋ **-d** -d **ˈtree ͵frog; ͵Tree of ˈKnowledge; ˈtree ͵surgeon; ͵bark up the ͵wrong ˈtree**
treecreeper ˈtriː͵kriː.pəʳ, (US) -pɚ **-s** -z
treeless ˈtriː.ləs, -lɪs
treeline ˈtriː.laɪn
tree-lined ˈtriː.laɪnd
treetop ˈtriː.tɒp, (US) -tɑːp **-s** -z
trefoil ˈtref.ɔɪl, ˈtriː.fɔɪl, ˈtrɪf.ɔɪl, (US) ˈtriː.fɔɪl, ˈtref.ɔɪl **-s** -z
Trefor ˈtrev.əʳ, (US) -ɚ
Trefusis trɪˈfjuː.sɪs, trə-
Tregear trɪˈgɪəʳ, trə-, (US) -ˈgɪr
Treharne trɪˈhɑːn, trə-, -ˈhɜːn, (US) -ˈhɑːrn, -ˈhɝːn
Treharris trɪˈhær.ɪs, trə-, (US) -ˈher-, -ˈhær-

Treherne trɪˈhɜːn, trə-, (US) -ˈhɝːn
trek trek **-s** -s **-king** -ɪŋ **-ked** -t **-ker/s** -əʳ/z, (US) -ɚ/z
Trekkie ˈtrek.i **-s** -z
Trelawn(e)y trɪˈlɔː.ni, trə-, (US) -ˈlɑː-, -ˈlɔː-
Treleaven trɪˈlev.ən, trə-
trellis ˈtrel.ɪs **-es** -ɪz **-ed** -t
trelliswork ˈtrel.ɪs.wɜːk, (US) -wɝːk
Tremadoc trɪˈmæd.ək, trə-
Tremain, Tremayne trɪˈmeɪn, trə-
trembl|e ˈtrem.bəl **-es** -z **-ing/ly** -ɪŋ/li, ˈtrem.blɪŋ/li **-ed** -d **-er/s** -əʳ/z, ˈtrem.bləʳ/z, (US) ˈ-əl.ɚ/z, ˈ-lɚ/z
trembl|y ˈtrem.bl|i, ˈ-bəl|.i **-ier** -i.əʳ, (US) -i.ɚ **-iest** -i.ɪst, -i.əst **-iness** -ɪ.nəs, -ɪ.nɪs
tremendous trɪˈmen.dəs, trə- **-ly** -li **-ness** -nəs, -nɪs
tremolo ˈtrem.əl.əʊ, (US) -ə.loʊ **-s** -z
tremor ˈtrem.əʳ, (US) -ɚ **-s** -z
tremulant ˈtrem.jə.lənt, -jʊ- **-s** -s
tremulous ˈtrem.jə.ləs, -jʊ- **-ly** -li **-ness** -nəs, -nɪs
trench, T~ trentʃ **-es** -ɪz **-ing** -ɪŋ **-ed** -t **-er/s** -əʳ/z, (US) -ɚ/z ˈ**trench coat;** ˌ**trench** ˈ**foot;** ˌ**trench** ˈ**warfare**
trenchancy ˈtren.*t*ʃənt.si
trenchant ˈtren.*t*ʃənt **-ly** -li
Trenchard ˈtren.*t*ʃɑːd, -*t*ʃəd, (US) -*t*ʃɑːrd, -*t*ʃɚd
trencher|man ˈtren.*t*ʃə|.mən, (US) -*t*ʃɚ- **-men** -mən
trend trend **-s** -z **-ing** -ɪŋ **-ed** -ɪd
trendsett|er ˈtrendˌset|.əʳ, (US) -ˌseţ|.ɚ **-er/s** -əʳ/z, (US) -ɚ/z **-ing** -ɪŋ
trendspotter ˈtrendˌspɒt.əʳ, (US) -ˌspɑː.ţɚ **-s** -z
trend|y ˈtren.d|i **-ies** -iz **-ier** -i.əʳ, (US) -i.ɚ **-iest** -i.ɪst, -i.əst **-ily** -əl.i, -ɪ.li **-iness** -ɪ.nəs, -ɪ.nɪs
Trent trent
Trentham ˈtren.təm
Trenton ˈtren.tən, (US) -tən
trepan trɪˈpæn, trə- **-s** -z **-ning** -ɪŋ **-ned** -d
trepang trɪˈpæŋ, trə- **-s** -z
trephin|e trɪˈfiːn, trefˈiːn, trəˈfiːn, -ˈfaɪn, (US) trɪˈfaɪn, triː-, -ˈfiːn **-es** -z **-ing** -ɪŋ **-ed** -d
trepidation ˌtrep.ɪˈdeɪ.ʃən, -əˈ-
Tresilian trɪˈsɪl.i.ən, trə-, ˈ-jən
trespass v ˈtres.pəs, (US) -pæs, -pəs **-es** -ɪz **-ing** -ɪŋ **-ed** -t **-er/s** -əʳ/z, (US) -ɚ/z
trespass n ˈtres.pəs **-es** -ɪz
tress tres **-es** -ɪz **-ed** -t
trestle ˈtres.əl **-s** -z ˌ**trestle** ˈ**table;** ˈ**trestle** ˌ**table**
Trethowan trɪˈθəʊ.ən, trə-, -ˈθaʊ.ən, -ˈθɔː.ən, (US) -ˈθoʊ.ən, -ˈθaʊ.ən, -ˈθɑː.ən, -ˈθɔː-
Trevelyan *in Cornwall:* trɪˈvɪl.jən, trə-, (US) trɪˈvel-, -ˈvɪl- *in Northumbria:* trɪˈvel.jən, trə-
Treves triːvz
Trevethick trɪˈveθ.ɪk, trə-
Trevisa trɪˈviː.sə, trə-
Treviso trɪˈviː.səʊ, -zəʊ, (US) -soʊ
Trevithick ˈtrev.ɪ.θɪk, (US) -ə-
Trevor ˈtrev.əʳ, (US) -ɚ
Trevor-Roper ˌtrev.əˈrəʊ.pəʳ, (US) -ɚˈroʊ.pɚ
Trewin trɪˈwɪn, trə-
trews truːz
trey treɪ **-s** -z
tri- traɪ, trɪ, triː
Note: Prefix. See individual entries for pronunciation and stressing.
triable ˈtraɪ.ə.bəl **-ness** -nəs, -nɪs
triad, T~ ˈtraɪ.æd, -əd **-s** -z
triage ˈtriː.ɑːʒ; ˈtraɪ.ɪdʒ, (US) ˈtriː.ɑːʒ
trial ˈtraɪ.əl **-s** -z **-(l)ing** -ɪŋ **-(l)ed** -d ˌ**trial and** ˈ**error;** ˌ**trials and tribu**ˈ**lations;** ˌ**trial** ˈ**run**
trialogue ˈtraɪ.ə.lɒg, (US) -lɑːg, -lɔːg **-s** -z
triangle ˈtraɪ.æŋ.gəl **-s** -z **-d** -d
triangular traɪˈæŋ.gjə.ləʳ, -gjʊ-, (US) -lɚ **-ly** -li
triangularity traɪˌæŋ.gjəˈlær.ə.ti, ˌtraɪ.æŋ-, -jʊˈ-, -ɪ.ti, (US) traɪˌæŋ.gjəˈler.ə.ţi, -gjʊˈ-, -ˈlær-
triangu|late traɪˈæŋ.gjə|.leɪt, -gjʊ- **-lates** -leɪts **-lating** -leɪ.tɪŋ, (US) -leɪ.ţɪŋ **-lated** -leɪ.tɪd, (US) -leɪ.ţɪd
triangulation traɪˌæŋ.gjəˈleɪ.ʃən, ˌtraɪ.æŋ-, -gjʊˈ-, (US) traɪˌæŋ-
Triangulum traɪˈæŋ.gjə.ləm, -gjʊ-
Triassic traɪˈæs.ɪk
triathlete traɪˈæθ.liːt **-s** -s
triathlon traɪˈæθ.lɒn, -lən, (US) -lɑːn, -lən **-s** -z
triatomic ˌtraɪ.əˈtɒm.ɪk, (US) -ˈtɑː.mɪk
tribadism ˈtrɪb.ə.dɪ.zəm, ˈtraɪ.bə-
tribal ˈtraɪ.bəl **-ly** -i **-ism** -ɪ.zəm
tribalistic ˌtraɪ.bəlˈɪs.tɪk, (US) -bəˈlɪs-
tribasic traɪˈbeɪ.sɪk
tribe traɪb **-s** -z
tribes|man ˈtraɪbz|.mən **-men** -mən, -men **-woman** -ˌwʊm.ən **-women** -ˌwɪm.ɪn
tribespeople ˈtraɪbzˌpiː.pəl
tribrach ˈtraɪ.bræk, ˈtrɪb.ræk **-s** -s
tribrachic traɪˈbræk.ɪk, trɪ-
tribulation ˌtrɪb.jəˈleɪ.ʃən, -jʊˈ- **-s** -z
tribunal traɪˈbjuː.nəl, trɪ- **-s** -z
tribunate ˈtrɪb.jə.neɪt, -jʊ-, -nɪt, -nət, (US) -nɪt, -neɪt **-s** -s
tribune, T~ ˈtrɪb.juːn **-s** -z
tributar|y ˈtrɪb.jə.tər|.i, -jʊ-, -tr|i, (US) -ter|.i **-ies** -iz
tribute ˈtrɪb.juːt **-s** -s
trice traɪs
Tricel® ˈtraɪ.sel
triceps ˈtraɪ.seps **-es** -ɪz
trichin|a trɪˈkaɪ.n|ə, trə- **-ae** -iː **-as** -əz
Trichinopoly ˌtrɪtʃ.ɪˈnɒp.əl.i, -əˈ-, (US) -ˈnɑː.pəl-
trichinosis ˌtrɪk.ɪˈnəʊ.sɪs, -əˈ-, (US) -ɪˈnoʊ-
trichloride traɪˈklɔː.raɪd, (US) -ˈklɔːr.aɪd **-s** -z
trichology trɪˈkɒl.ə.dʒ|i, trə-, (US) -ˈkɑː.lə- **-ist/s** -ɪst/s
trichord ˈtraɪ.kɔːd, (US) -kɔːrd **-s** -z
trichosis trɪˈkəʊ.sɪs, trə-, (US) -ˈkoʊ-
trichotomy trɪˈkɒt.ə.mi, trə-, (US) -ˈkɑː.ţə-
Tricia ˈtrɪʃ.ə
Tricity® ˈtrɪs.ə.ti, -ɪ.ti, (US) -ə.ţi
trick trɪk **-s** -s **-ing** -ɪŋ **-ed** -t **-er/s** -əʳ/z, (US) -ɚ/z ˌ**trick** ˈ**cyclist;** ˌ**trick or** ˈ**treat**
tricker|y ˈtrɪk.ər|.i **-ies** -iz
trickl|e ˈtrɪk.əl **-es** -z **-ing** -ɪŋ, ˈtrɪk.lɪŋ **-ed** -d ˈ**trickle** ˌ**charger**
trickledown ˈtrɪk.əl.daʊn
trickly ˈtrɪk.əl.i, ˈ-li
trickster ˈtrɪk.stəʳ, (US) -stɚ **-s** -z
tricks|y ˈtrɪk.s|i **-ier** -i.əʳ, (US) -i.ɚ **-iest** -i.ɪst, -i.əst **-iness** -ɪ.nəs, -ɪ.nɪs
trick|y ˈtrɪk|.i **-ier** -i.əʳ, (US) -i.ɚ **-iest** -i.ɪst, -i.əst **-ily** -əl.i, -ɪ.li **-iness** -ɪ.nəs, -ɪ.nɪs
tricolo(u)r ˈtrɪk.əl.əʳ; ˈtraɪˌkʌl.əʳ, (US) ˈtraɪˌkʌl.ɚ **-s** -z
tricorn(e) ˈtraɪ.kɔːn, (US) -kɔːrn
tricot ˈtriː.kəʊ, ˈtrɪk.əʊ, (US) ˈtriː.koʊ **-s** -z
tricycl|e ˈtraɪ.sɪ.kəl, -sə- **-es** -z **-ing** -ɪŋ, -klɪŋ **-ed** -d
trident, T~ ˈtraɪ.dənt **-s** -s
Tridentine traɪˈden.taɪn, trɪ-, trə-, -tiːn, (US) traɪˈden.taɪn, -tiːn, -tɪn
tried (from **try**) traɪd
triennial traɪˈen.i.əl, ˈ-jəl **-ly** -i
trier ˈtraɪ.əʳ, (US) -ɚ **-s** -z
Trier trɪəʳ, (US) trɪr
trierarch ˈtraɪ.ər.ɑːk, (US) -ə.rɑːrk **-s** -s **-y** -i **-ies** -iz
tries (from **try**) traɪz
Trieste triˈest; -ˈes.teɪ
triffid, T~ ˈtrɪf.ɪd **-s** -z
trifid ˈtraɪ.fɪd
trifl|e ˈtraɪ.fəl **-es** -z **-ing/ly** -ɪŋ/li, ˈtraɪ.flɪŋ/li **-ed** -d **-er/s** -əʳ/z, ˈtraɪ.fləʳ/z, (US) ˈ-fəl.ɚ/z, ˈ-flɚ/z
trifolium traɪˈfəʊ.li.əm, (US) -ˈfoʊ- **-s** -z
trifori|um traɪˈfɔː.ri|.əm, (US) -ˈfɔːr.i- **-a** -ə
trig trɪg **-s** -z **-ging** -ɪŋ **-ged** -d
Trigg trɪg
trigg|er ˈtrɪg|.əʳ, (US) -ɚ **-ers** -əz, (US) -ɚz **-ering** -ər.ɪŋ **-ered** -əd, (US) -ɚd
trigger-happy ˈtrɪg.əˌhæp.i, (US) -ɚˌ-
triglyph ˈtraɪ.glɪf, ˈtrɪg.lɪf, (US) ˈtraɪ.glɪf **-s** -s
trigon ˈtraɪ.gən, -gɒn, (US) -gɑːn **-s** -z
trigonometric ˌtrɪg.ə.nəʊˈmet.rɪk, (US) -nəˈ- **-al** -əl **-ally** -əl.i, -li
trigonometr|y ˌtrɪg.əˈnɒm.ə.tr|i, ˈ-ɪ-, (US) -ˈnɑː.mə- **-ies** -iz
trigraph ˈtraɪ.grɑːf, -græf, (US) -græf **-s** -s
trihedral traɪˈhiː.drəl
trike traɪk **-s** -s
trilateral traɪˈlæt.ər.əl, ˈ-rəl, (US) -ˈlæţ.ɚ.əl, -ˈlæt.rəl **-ly** -i **-ness** -nəs, -nɪs
trilb|y, T~ ˈtrɪl.b|i **-ies** -iz
trilingual traɪˈlɪŋ.gwəl **-ly** -i
triliteral traɪˈlɪt.ər.əl, ˈ-rəl, (US) -ˈlɪţ.ɚ.əl, -ˈlɪt.rəl
trill trɪl **-s** -z **-ing** -ɪŋ **-ed** -d

T

Trilling ˈtrɪl.ɪŋ
trillion ˈtrɪl.jən, -i.ən, (US) ˈ-jən **-s** -z **-th/s** -t.θ/s
trilobite ˈtraɪ.ləʊ.baɪt, (US) -loʊ-, -lə- **-s** -s
trilog|y ˈtrɪl.ə.dʒ|i **-ies** -iz
trim, T~ trɪm **-mer/s** -əʳ/z, (US) -ɚ/z **-mest** -ɪst, -əst **-ly** -li **-ness** -nəs, -nɪs **-s** -z **-ming/s** -ɪŋ/z **-med** -d
trimaran ˈtraɪ.məʳr.æn, ˌ--ˈ-, (US) ˈtraɪ.mə.ræn **-s** -z
Trimble ˈtrɪm.bəl
trimester trɪˈmes.təʳ, traɪ-, (US) traɪˈmes.tɚ, ˈ--- **-s** -z
trimestral trɪˈmes.trəl, traɪ-, (US) traɪ-, ˈ---
trimestrial trɪˈmes.tri.əl, traɪ-, (US) traɪ-
trimeter ˈtrɪm.ɪ.təʳ, ˈ-ə-, (US) -ə.t̬ɚ **-s** -z
Trincomalee ˌtrɪŋ.kəʊ.məlˈiː, (US) -koʊ.məˈliː
Trinculo ˈtrɪŋ.kjə.ləʊ, -kjʊ-, (US) -loʊ
Trinder ˈtrɪn.dəʳ, (US) -dɚ
trine, T~ traɪn **-s** -z
Tring trɪŋ
Trinidad ˈtrɪn.ɪ.dæd, ˈ-ə-, ˌ--ˈ-, (US) ˈtrɪn.ɪ.dæd **ˌTrinidad and Toˈbago**
Trinidadian ˌtrɪn.ɪˈdæd.i.ən, -əˈ-, -ˈdeɪ.di-, (US) -ɪˈdæd.i- **-s** -z
Trinitarian ˌtrɪn.ɪˈteə.ri.ən, -əˈ-, (US) -ɪˈter.i- **-s** -z **-ism** -ɪ.zəm
trinitroglycerin(e) ˌtraɪ.naɪ.trəʊˈglɪs.əʳr.ɪn, traɪˌnaɪ-, -iːn, (US) ˌtraɪ.naɪ.troʊˈglɪs.ɚ.ɪn
trinitrotoluene ˌtraɪ.naɪ.trəʊˈtɒl.ju.iːn, traɪˌnaɪ-, (US) traɪˌnaɪ.troʊˈtɑːl-
trinit|y, T~ ˈtrɪn.ə.t|i, -ɪ.t|i, (US) -ə.t̬|i **-ies** -iz
trinket ˈtrɪŋ.kɪt, -kət **-s** -s
trinomial traɪˈnəʊ.mi.əl, (US) -ˈnoʊ- **-s** -z
trio ˈtriː.əʊ, (US) -oʊ **-s** -z
triode ˈtraɪ.əʊd, (US) -oʊd **-s** -z
triolet ˈtriː.əʊ.let, ˈtraɪ-, ˈtrɪə.let, -lɪt, -lət, (US) ˈtriː.ə-, ˈtraɪ- **-s** -s
trioxide traɪˈɒk.saɪd, (US) -ˈɑːk- **-s** -z
trip trɪp **-s** -s **-ping/ly** -ɪŋ/li **-ped** -t **-per/s** -əʳ/z, (US) -ɚ/z **ˈtrip ˌwire**
tripartite ˌtraɪˈpɑː.taɪt, (US) -ˈpɑːr- **-ly** -li *stress shift:* **ˌtripartite ˈtalks**
tripe traɪp
triphthong ˈtrɪf.θɒŋ, ˈtrɪp-, (US) -θɑːŋ, -θɔːŋ **-s** -z
triphthongal trɪfˈθɒŋ.gəl, trɪp-, (US) -ˈθɑːŋ-, -ˈθɔːŋ- **-ly** -i
triplane ˈtraɪ.pleɪn **-s** -z
tripl|e ˈtrɪp.əl **-y** -i **-es** -z **-ing** -ɪŋ, ˈtrɪp.lɪŋ **-ed** -d **ˈtriple ˌjump; ˌtriple ˈjump**
triplet ˈtrɪp.lət, -lɪt **-s** -s
triplex, T~® ˈtrɪp.leks **-es** -ɪz
triplicate **adj** ˈtrɪp.lɪ.kət, -lə-, -kɪt, (US) -kɪt
tripli|cate **v** ˈtrɪp.lɪ|.keɪt, -lə- **-cates** -keɪts **-cating** -keɪ.tɪŋ, (US) -keɪ.t̬ɪŋ **-cated** -keɪ.tɪd, (US) -keɪ.t̬ɪd
triploid ˈtrɪp.lɔɪd **-s** -z **-y** -i
tripod ˈtraɪ.pɒd, (US) -pɑːd **-s** -z
Tripoli, tripoli ˈtrɪp.əl.i
Tripolitania ˌtrɪp.əl.ɪˈteɪ.ni.ə, -ɒl-; trɪˌpɒl-, (US) ˌtrɪp.əl.əˈ-; (US) trɪˌpɑː.ləˈ-
tripos ˈtraɪ.pɒs, (US) -pɑːs **-es** -ɪz
Tripp trɪp
triptych ˈtrɪp.tɪk **-s** -s
tripwire ˈtrɪp.waɪəʳ, -waɪ.əʳ, (US) -waɪ.ɚ **-s** -z
trireme ˈtraɪ.riːm **-s** -z
trisect traɪˈsekt **-s** -s **-ing** -ɪŋ **-ed** -ɪd **-or/s** -əʳ/z, (US) -ɚ/z
trisection traɪˈsek.ʃən **-s** -z
Trisha ˈtrɪʃ.ə
Tristan ˈtrɪs.tən, -tæn, (US) -tən, -tæn, -tɑːn
Tristan da Cunha ˌtrɪs.tən.dəˈkuː.nə, -njə
Tristram ˈtrɪs.trəm, -træm, (US) -trəm
trisyllabic ˌtraɪ.sɪˈlæb.ɪk, -səˈ-, (US) -sɪˈ- **-al** -əl **-ally** -əl.i, -li
trisyllable traɪˈsɪl.ə.bəl **-s** -z
trit|e traɪt **-er** -əʳ, (US) ˈtraɪ.t̬ɚ **-est** -ɪst, -əst, (US) ˈtraɪ.t̬ɪst, -t̬əst **-ely** -li **-eness** -nəs, -nɪs
tritium ˈtrɪt.i.əm, ˈ-jəm, (US) ˈtrɪt̬.i.əm, ˈtrɪʃ-
triton, T~ *sea god, mollusc:* ˈtraɪ.tɒn, -tən, (US) -tən *physics:* ˈtraɪ.tɒn, -tən, (US) -tɑːn **-s** -z
tritone ˈtraɪ.təʊn, (US) -toʊn **-s** -z
triumph, T~® ˈtraɪ.əmpf, -ʌmpf **-s** -s **-ing** -ɪŋ **-ed** -t
triumphal traɪˈʌmp.fəl **-ism** -ɪ.zəm **-ist/s** -ɪst/s
triumphant traɪˈʌmp.fənt **-ly** -li
triumv|ir traɪˈʌm.v|əʳ, tri-, -ˈʊm-, -v|ɪəʳ, -v|ɜːʳ; ˈtraɪ.ʌm-, -əm-, (US) traɪˈʌm.v|ɪr, -v|ɚ **-irs** -əz, -ɪəz, -ɜːz, (US) -ɪrz, -ɚz **-iri** -ɪˌriː, -əʳr.iː, -aɪ, (US) -ɪ.raɪ
triumvirate traɪˈʌm.vɪ.rət, tri-, -vəʳr.ət, -ɪt, (US) traɪˈʌm.vɪ.rɪt, -vɚ.ɪt **-s** -s
triumviri traɪˈʌm.vɪˌriː, tri-, -vəʳr.iː, -aɪ, ˈtraɪ.ʌm-, -əm-, (US) traɪˈʌm.vɪˌraɪ, -və-
triune, T~ ˈtraɪ.uːn, (US) -juːn
trivalent traɪˈveɪ.lənt; ˈtrɪv.əl.ənt, (US) traɪˈveɪ.lənt, ˌtraɪ-, ˈ---
trivet ˈtrɪv.ɪt **-s** -s
trivia ˈtrɪv.i.ə
trivial ˈtrɪv.i.əl **-ly** -i **-ness** -nəs, -nɪs **ˌTrivial Purˈsuit**
trivialit|y ˌtrɪv.iˈæl.ə.t|i, -ɪ.t|i, (US) -ə.t̬|i **-ies** -iz
trivializ|e, -is|e ˈtrɪv.i.əl.aɪz, ˈ-jəl-, (US) -i.əl- **-es** -ɪz **-ing** -ɪŋ **-ed** -d
trivi|um ˈtrɪv.i|.əm **-a** -ə
Trixie ˈtrɪk.si
trizonal traɪˈzəʊ.nəl, (US) -ˈzoʊ-
Trizone ˈtraɪ.zəʊn, (US) -zoʊn
Troad ˈtrəʊ.æd, (US) ˈtroʊ-
Troas ˈtrəʊ.æs, (US) ˈtroʊ-
Trocadero ˌtrɒk.əˈdɪə.rəʊ, (US) ˌtrɑː.kəˈder.oʊ, ˌtroʊ-
trochaic trəʊˈkeɪ.ɪk, trɒkˈeɪ-, (US) troʊˈkeɪ-
troch|e trəʊʃ, ˈtroʊ.ki **-es** -ɪz
trochee ˈtrəʊ.kiː, -ki, (US) ˈtroʊ- **-s** -z
trod (from **tread**) trɒd, (US) trɑːd **-den** -ən
Troed-y-rhiw ˌtrɔɪd.ə.riˈuː
trog trɒg, (US) trɑːg, trɔːg **-s** -z **-ging** -ɪŋ **-ged** -d
troglodyte ˈtrɒg.ləʊ.daɪt, (US) ˈtrɑː.glə- **-s** -s
troika ˈtrɔɪ.kə **-s** -z
troilism ˈtrɔɪ.lɪ.zəm
Troilus ˈtrɔɪ.ləs, ˈtrəʊ.ɪ.ləs, (US) ˈtrɔɪ.ləs, ˈtroʊ.ə-
Trojan ˈtrəʊ.dʒən, (US) ˈtroʊ- **-s** -z **ˌTrojan ˈhorse; ˌTrojan ˈWar**
troll trəʊl, trɒl, (US) troʊl **-s** -z **-ing** -ɪŋ **-ed** -d
trolley ˈtrɒl.i, (US) ˈtrɑː.li **-s** -z
trolleybus ˈtrɒl.i.bʌs, (US) ˈtrɑː.li- **-es** -ɪz
trolleyed ˈtrɒl.id, (US) ˈtrɑː.lid
trollop ˈtrɒl.əp, (US) ˈtrɑː.ləp **-s** -s
Trollope ˈtrɒl.əp, (US) ˈtrɑː.ləp
Tromans ˈtrəʊ.mənz, (US) ˈtroʊ-
trombone trɒmˈbəʊn, (US) trɑːmˈboʊn, trəm-; (US) ˈtrɑːm.boʊn **-s** -z
trombonist trɒmˈbəʊ.nɪst, (US) trɑːmˈboʊ-, ˈ--- **-s** -s
tromp trɒmp, (US) trɑːmp, trɔːmp **-s** -s **-ing** -ɪŋ **-ed** -d
trompe l'oeil ˌtrɒmpˈlɔɪ; *as if French:* ˌtrɔ̃ːmpˈlɜː.i; (US) ˌtrɔːmpˈlɔɪ **-s** -z
Trondheim ˈtrɒnd.haɪm, (US) ˈtrɑːn.heɪm
Troon truːn
troop truːp **-s** -s **-ing** -ɪŋ **-ed** -t **-er/s** -əʳ/z, (US) -ɚ/z **ˈtroop ˌcarrier**
troopship ˈtruːp.ʃɪp **-s** -s
trope trəʊp, (US) troʊp **-s** -s
trophic ˈtrɒf.ɪk, (US) ˈtrɑː.fɪk
troph|y ˈtrəʊ.f|i, (US) ˈtroʊ- **-ies** -iz
tropic ˈtrɒp.ɪk, (US) ˈtrɑː.pɪk **-s** -s **-al** -əl **-ally** -əl.i, -li **ˌtropic of ˈCancer; ˌtropic of ˈCapricorn**
tropism ˈtrəʊ.pɪ.zəm, (US) ˈtroʊ- **-s** -z
tropistic trəʊˈpɪs.tɪk, (US) troʊ-
troppo ˈtrɒp.əʊ, (US) ˈtrɑː.poʊ
Trossachs ˈtrɒs.əks, -æks, -əxs, (US) ˈtrɑː.səks, -sæks
trot, T~ trɒt, (US) trɑːt **-s** -s **-ting** -ɪŋ, (US) ˈtrɑː.t̬ɪŋ **-ted** -ɪd, (US) ˈtrɑː.t̬ɪd
troth trəʊθ, trɒθ, (US) trɑːθ, trɔːθ, troʊθ
Trotsky ˈtrɒt.ski, (US) ˈtrɑːt- **-ist/s** -ɪst/s **-ite/s** -aɪt/s **-ism** -ɪ.zəm
Trotskyite ˈtrɒt.ski.aɪt, (US) ˈtrɑːt- **-s** -s
Trott trɒt, (US) trɑːt
trotter, T~ ˈtrɒt.əʳ, (US) ˈtrɑː.t̬ɚ **-s** -z
Trottiscliffe ˈtrɒz.li, ˈtrɒs-, (US) ˈtrɑːz-, ˈtrɑːs-
troubadour ˈtruː.bə.dɔːʳ, -dʊəʳ, (US) -dɔːr **-s** -z
troubl|e ˈtrʌb.əl **-es** -z **-ing/ly** -ɪŋ/li, ˈtrʌb.lɪŋ/li **-ed** -d **-er/s** -əʳ/z, ˈtrʌb.ləʳ/z, (US) ˈ-əl.ɚ/z, ˈ-lɚ/z **ˌtrouble and ˈstrife; ˈtrouble ˌspot**
trouble-free ˌtrʌb.əlˈfriː *stress shift:* **ˌtrouble-free ˈjourney**

roublemaker ˈtrʌb.əlˌmeɪ.kəʳ, (US) -kɚ -s -z
roubleshoot|er ˈtrʌb.əlˌʃuː.t|əʳ, (US) -t̬|ɚ -ers -əz, (US) -ɚz -ing -ɪŋ
roublesome ˈtrʌb.əl.səm -ly -li -ness -nəs, -nɪs
roublous ˈtrʌb.ləs -ly -li -ness -nəs, -nɪs
roubridge ˈtruː.brɪdʒ
rough trɒf, (US) trɑːf, trɔːf -s -s

Note: Some bakers pronounce /traʊ/.

Troughton ˈtraʊ.tən, ˈtrɔː-
rounc|e traʊnts -es -ɪz -ing/s -ɪŋ/z -ed -t
Troup truːp
troup|e truːp -es -s -er/s -əʳ/z, (US) -ɚ/z
trouper ˈtruː.pəʳ, (US) -pɚ -s -z
trouser ˈtraʊ.zəʳ, (US) -zɚ ˈtrouser ˌpress; ˈtrouser ˌsuit
trousers ˈtraʊ.zəz, (US) -zɚz
trousseau ˈtruː.səʊ, -ˈ-, (US) ˈtruː.soʊ, -ˈ- -s -z -x -z
trout traʊt -s -s
trove trəʊv, (US) troʊv
trover ˈtrəʊ.vəʳ, (US) ˈtroʊ.vɚ
trow trəʊ, traʊ, (US) troʊ
Trowbridge ˈtrəʊ.brɪdʒ, (US) ˈtroʊ-
trowel ˈtraʊ.əl -s -z -(l)ing -ɪŋ -(l)ed -d
Trowell ˈtrəʊ.əl, ˈtraʊ.əl, (US) ˈtroʊ.əl, ˈtraʊ.əl
troy, T~ trɔɪ
truancy ˈtruː.ənt.si
truant ˈtruː.ənt -s -s -ing -ɪŋ -ed -ɪd
Trübner ˈtruːb.nəʳ, (US) -nɚ
truc|e truːs -es -ɪz
trucial, T~ ˈtruː.ʃəl, (US) ˈ-ʃəl
truck trʌk -s -s -ing -ɪŋ -ed -t -age -ɪdʒ -er/s -əʳ/z, (US) -ɚ/z ˈtruck ˌstop
truckl|e ˈtrʌk.əl -es -z -ing -ɪŋ, ˈtrʌk.lɪŋ -ed -d ˈtruckle ˌbed
truckload ˈtrʌk.ləʊd, (US) -loʊd -s -z
truculen|ce ˈtrʌk.jə.lənt|s, -jʊ- -cy -si
truculent ˈtrʌk.jə.lənt, -jʊ- -ly -li
Trudeau ˈtruː.dəʊ, (US) truːˈdoʊ, ˈ--
trudg|e trʌdʒ -es -ɪz -ing -ɪŋ -ed -d -er/s -əʳ/z, (US) -ɚ/z
trudgen, T~ ˈtrʌdʒ.ən
Trudgill ˈtrʌd.gɪl
Trudy, Trudi ˈtruː.di
tru|e, T~ truː -er -əʳ, (US) -ɚ -est -ɪst, -əst -ly -li -eness -nəs, -nɪs
true-blue ˌtruːˈbluː -s -z *stress shift:* ˌ**true-blue** ˈ**Tory**
trueborn ˈtruː.bɔːn, (US) -bɔːrn
Truefitt ˈtruː.fɪt
truehearted ˌtruːˈhɑː.tɪd, (US) ˈtruːˌhɑːr.t̬ɪd -ness -nəs, -nɪs *stress shift, British only:* ˌ**truehearted** ˈ**person**
true-life ˌtruːˈlaɪf *stress shift:* ˌ**true-life** ˈ**story**
truelove ˈtruː.lʌv
Trueman ˈtruː.mən
Truffaut ˈtruː.fəʊ, ˈtrʊf.əʊ, (US) truːˈfoʊ
truffle ˈtrʌf.əl -s -z -d -d
trug trʌg -s -z
truism ˈtruː.ɪ.zəm -s -z
Trujillo trʊˈhiː.jəʊ, (US) truːˈhiː.joʊ
Truk trʌk, trʊk
truly ˈtruː.li
Truman ˈtruː.mən
Trumbull ˈtrʌm.bʊl, (US) -bʊl, -bəl
trump, T~ trʌmp -s -s -ing -ɪŋ -ed -t ˈ**trump** ˌ**card**; ˌ**trump** ˈ**card**
trumped-up ˌtrʌmptˈʌp *stress shift:* ˌ**trumped-up** ˈ**charges**
Trumper ˈtrʌm.pəʳ, (US) -pɚ
trumpery ˈtrʌm.pər.i
trum|pet ˈtrʌm|.pɪt, (US) -pət -pets -pɪts, (US) -pəts -peting/s -pɪ.tɪŋ/z, (US) -pə.t̬ɪŋ/z -peted -pɪ.tɪd, (US) -pə.t̬ɪd -peter/s -pɪ.təʳ/z, (US) -pə.t̬ɚ/z ˌ**blow one's** ˌ**own** ˈ**trumpet**
trunca|te trʌŋˈkeɪ|t, ˈ--, (US) ˈtrʌŋ.keɪ|t, ˈtrʌn- -tes -ts -ting -tɪŋ, (US) -t̬ɪŋ -ted -tɪd, (US) -t̬ɪd
truncation trʌŋˈkeɪ.ʃən, (US) trʌŋ-, trʌn- -s -z
truncheon ˈtrʌn.tʃən, (US) ˈtrʌnt.ʃən -s -z -ing -ɪŋ -ed -d
trundl|e ˈtrʌn.dəl -es -z -ing -ɪŋ, ˈtrʌnd.lɪŋ -ed -d -er/s -əʳ/z, (US) -ɚ/z
trunk trʌŋk -s -s -ful/s -fʊl/z ˈ**trunk** ˌ**call**; ˈ**trunk** ˌ**road**
trunnion ˈtrʌn.i.ən, ˈ-jən, (US) ˈ-jən -s -z -ed -d
Truro ˈtrʊə.rəʊ, (US) ˈtrʊr.oʊ
Truscott ˈtrʌs.kət, (US) -kət, -kɑːt
Truslove ˈtrʌs.lʌv
truss trʌs -es -ɪz -ing -ɪŋ -ed -t
trust trʌst -s -s -ing/ly -ɪŋ/li -ed -ɪd ˈ**trust** ˌ**fund**
trustee trʌsˈtiː -s -z
trusteeship trʌsˈtiː.ʃɪp -s -s
trustful ˈtrʌst.fəl, -fʊl -ly -i -ness -nəs, -nɪs
Trusthouse Forte® ˌtrʌst.haʊsˈfɔː.teɪ, (US) -ˈfɔːr-
trustworth|y ˈtrʌstˌwɜː.ð|i, (US) -ˌwɝː- -iness -ɪ.nəs, -ɪ.nɪs
trust|y ˈtrʌs.t|i -ier -i.əʳ, (US) -i.ɚ -iest -i.ɪst, -i.əst -ily -əl.i, -ɪ.li -iness -ɪ.nəs, -ɪ.nɪs
tru|th truː|θ -ths -ðz, -θs ˈ**truth** ˌ**drug**
truthful ˈtruːθ.fəl, -fʊl -ly -i -ness -nəs, -nɪs
tr|y tr|aɪ -ies -aɪz -ying/ly -aɪ.ɪŋ/li -ied -aɪd -ier/s -aɪ.əʳ/z, (US) -aɪ.ɚ/z
try-on ˈtraɪ.ɒn, (US) -ɑːn -s -z
Tryon traɪ.ən
tryout ˈtraɪ.aʊt -s -s
trypanosome ˈtrɪp.ə.nəʊ.səʊm; trɪˈpæn.ə-, (US) trɪˈpæn.ə.soʊm; (US) ˈtrɪp.ə.noʊ- -s -z
trypanosomiasis ˌtrɪp.ə.nəʊ.səʊˈmaɪ.ə.sɪs; trɪˌpæn.əʊ-, (US) trɪˌpæn.ə.soʊˈ-; (US) ˌtrɪp.ə.noʊ-
trypsin ˈtrɪp.sɪn
trypsinogen trɪpˈsɪn.ə.dʒən, (US) ˈ-oʊ-
tryst trɪst -s -s -ing -ɪŋ -ed -ɪd
Trystan ˈtrɪs.tæn, -tən
tsar, T~ zɑːʳ, tsɑːʳ, (US) zɑːr, tsɑːr -s -z
tsarevitch, tsarevich, T~ ˈzɑː.rə.vɪtʃ, ˈtsɑː-, -rɪ-, (US) ˈzɑːr.ə-, ˈtsɑːr- -es -ɪz
tsarina, T~ zɑːˈriː.nə, tsɑː- -s -z
tsarism ˈzɑː.rɪ.zəm, ˈtsɑː-, (US) ˈzɑːr.ɪ-, ˈtsɑːr-
tsarist ˈzɑː.rɪst, ˈtsɑː-, (US) ˈzɑːr.ɪst, ˈtsɑːr- -s -s
TSB® ˌtiː.esˈbiː
tsetse ˈtet.si, ˈtset-, (US) ˈtset-, ˈtsiːt-, ˈtet-, ˈtiːt- -s -z ˈ**tsetse** ˌ**fly**
T-shirt ˈtiː.ʃɜːt, (US) -ʃɝːt -s -s
tsk **interj** tɪsk

Note: This spelling represents the tongue click used (usually repeated) to indicate disapproval; it may be described as a voiceless affricated alveolar click, symbolized as [!ˢ]. The pronunciation given above is only used in mock disapproval. See also **tut.**

tsp (abbrev. for **teaspoon, teaspoonful**) ˈtiː.spuːn, ˈtiː.spuːn.fʊl
T-square ˈtiː.skweəʳ, (US) -skwer -s -z
tsunam|i tsʊˈnɑː.m|i, sʊ-, -ˈnæm|.i, (US) tsuːˈnɑː.m|i -is -iz -ic -ɪk
Tsvangirai ˈtʃæŋ.gɪ.raɪ, -gə-, (US) ˈtʃæŋ.gɚ.aɪ, ˈtʃɑːŋ.gɚ.eɪ; ˌ--ˈ-
Tswana ˈtswɑː.nə, ˈswɑː- -s -z
TT ˌtiːˈtiː ˌ**T**ˈ**T** ˌ**races**
Tuamotu ˌtuː.əˈməʊ.tuː, (US) -ˈmoʊ-
Tuareg ˈtwɑː.reg, (US) ˈtwɑːr.eg -s -z
tub tʌb -s -z -bing -ɪŋ -bed -d
tuba ˈtʃuː.bə, ˈtjuː-, (US) ˈtuː-, ˈtjuː- -s -z
tubb|y ˈtʌb|.i -ier -i.əʳ, (US) -i.ɚ -iest -i.ɪst, -i.əst -iness -ɪ.nəs, -ɪ.nɪs
tube tʃuːb, tjuːb, (US) tuːb, tjuːb -s -z
tubeless ˈtʃuː.bləs, ˈtjuː-, -blɪs, (US) ˈtuː-, ˈtjuː-
tuber ˈtʃuː.bəʳ, ˈtjuː-, (US) ˈtuː.bɚ, ˈtjuː- -s -z
tubercle ˈtʃuː.bə.kəl, ˈtjuː-, -bɜː-, (US) ˈtuː.bɚ-, ˈtjuː- -s -z
tubercular tʃuːˈbɜː.kjə.ləʳ, tjuː-, tʃʊ-, tjʊ-, -kjʊ-, (US) tuːˈbɝː.kjə.lɚ, tjuː-, tə-, -kjʊ-
tuberculin tʃuːˈbɜː.kjə.lɪn, tjuː-, tʃʊ-, tjʊ-, -kjʊ-, (US) tuːˈbɝː-, tjuː-, tə-
tuberculization, -isa- tʃuːˌbɜː.kjə.laɪˈzeɪ.ʃən, tjuː-, tʃʊ-, tjʊ-, -kjʊ-, -lɪˈ-, (US) tuːˌbɝː.kjə.ləˈ-, tjuː-, tə-, -kjʊ-
tuberculiz|e, -is|e tʃuːˈbɜː.kjə.laɪz, tjuː-, tʃʊ-, tjʊ-, -kjʊ-, (US) tuːˈbɝː-, tjuː-, tə- -es -ɪz -ing -ɪŋ -ed -d
tuberculoid tʃuːˈbɜː.kjə.lɔɪd, tjuː-, tʃʊ-, tjʊ-, -kjʊ-, (US) tuːˈbɝː-, tjuː-, tə-
tuberculosis tʃuːˌbɜː.kjəˈləʊ.sɪs,

tjuː-, tʃʊ-, tjʊ-, -kjʊ-, (US) tuːˌbɝː.kjəˈloʊ-, tjuː-, tə-, -kjʊ-

tuberculous tʃʊˈbɜː.kjə.ləs, tju-, -kjʊ-, (US) tuˈbɝː-, tju-, tə-

tuberose n ˈtʃuː.bər.əʊz, ˈtjuː-, -brəʊz, (US) ˈtuːb.roʊz, ˈtjuːb-, -ə.roʊz

tuberose adj ˈtʃuː.bər.əʊs, ˈtjuː-, (US) ˈtuː.bə.roʊs, ˈtjuː-

tuberous ˈtʃuː.bər.əs, ˈtjuː-, (US) ˈtuː-, ˈtjuː-

tubful ˈtʌb.fʊl -s -z

tubiform ˈtjuː.bɪ.fɔːm, ˈtʃuː-, (US) ˈtuː.bɪ.fɔːrm, ˈtjuː-

tubing ˈtʃuː.bɪŋ, ˈtjuː-, (US) ˈtuː-, ˈtjuː- -s -z

Tübingen ˈtjuː.bɪŋ.ən, ˈtuː-, (US) ˈtuː-

tub-thump|ing ˈtʌbˌθʌm.p|ɪŋ -er/s -ər/z, (US) -ɚ/z

Tubuai ˌtuː.buˈaɪ

tubular ˈtʃuː.bjə.lər, ˈtjuː-, -bjʊ-, (US) ˈtuː.bjə.lɚ, ˈtjuː-, -bjʊ-

tubule ˈtʃuː.bjuːl, ˈtjuː-, (US) ˈtuː-, ˈtjuː- -s -z

TUC ˌtiː.juːˈsiː

tuck, T~ tʌk -s -s -ing -ɪŋ -ed -t

tucker, T~ ˈtʌk.ər, (US) -ɚ -s -z

tuck-shop ˈtʌk.ʃɒp, (US) -ʃɑːp -s -s

Tucson ˈtuː.sɒn, (US) ˈtuː.sɑːn

Tudjman ˈtʊdʒ.mən, ˈtʊdz-, ˈtʌdʒ-

Tudor ˈtjuː.dər, ˈtʃuː-, (US) ˈtuː.dɚ, ˈtjuː- -s -z

Tue. (abbrev. for **Tuesday**) ˈtʃuːz.deɪ, ˈtjuːz-, -di, (US) ˈtuːz-, ˈtjuːz-

Tues. (abbrev. for **Tuesday**) ˈtʃuːz.deɪ, ˈtjuːz-, -di, (US) ˈtuːz-, ˈtjuːz-
Note: This abbreviation may also be pronounced /tʃuːz/ in British English.

Tuesday ˈtʃuːz.deɪ, ˈtjuːz-, -di, (US) ˈtuːz-, ˈtjuːz- -s -z

tufa ˈtjuː.fə, (US) ˈtuː-, ˈtjuː-

tuffet ˈtʌf.ɪt, -ət -s -s

Tufnell ˈtʌf.nəl ˌ**Tufnell** ˈ**Park**

tuft tʌft -s -s -ing -ɪŋ -ed -ɪd

tuft|y ˈtʌf.t|i -ier -i.ər, (US) -i.ɚ -iest -i.ɪst, -i.əst -iness -ɪ.nəs, -ɪ.nɪs

tug tʌg -s -z -ging -ɪŋ -ged -d -ger/s -ər/z, (US) -ɚ/z

tugboat ˈtʌg.bəʊt, (US) -boʊt -s -s

tug-of-love ˌtʌg.əvˈlʌv

tug-of-war ˌtʌg.əvˈwɔːr, (US) -ˈwɔːr -s -z **tugs-of-war** ˌtʌgz.əvˈwɔːr, (US) -ˈwɔːr

tugrik ˈtuː.griːk -s -s

Tuileries ˈtwiː.lər.iː, -i, (US) -iː, -i, -iz

tuition tʃuˈɪʃ.ən, tjuˈ-, (US) tu-, tju- -s -z -al -əl

Tuke tʃuːk, tjuːk, (US) tuːk, tjuːk

tulip ˈtʃuː.lɪp, ˈtjuː-, (US) ˈtuː-, ˈtjuː- -s -s

Tull tʌl

tulle tjuːl, (US) tuːl -s -z

Tulloch ˈtʌl.ək, -əx, (US) -ək

Tully ˈtʌl.i

Tulsa ˈtʌl.sə

Tulse tʌls

tum tʌm -s -z

tumb|le ˈtʌm.bəl -es -z -ing -ɪŋ, -blɪŋ -ed -d -er/s -ər/z, (US) -ɚ/z

tumbledown, T~ ˈtʌm.bəl.daʊn

tumble-drier, tumble-dryer ˌtʌm.bəlˈdraɪ.ər, ˈtʌm.bəlˌdraɪ-, (US) -ɚ -s -z

tumble-dr|y ˌtʌm.bəlˈdr|aɪ, ˈ--- -ies -aɪz -ying -aɪ.ɪŋ -ied -aɪd

tumbler ˈtʌm.blər, ˈ-bəl.ər, (US) ˈ-blɚ, ˈ-bəl.ɚ -s -z -ful/s -fʊl/z

tumbleweed ˈtʌm.bəl.wiːd

tumbrel ˈtʌm.brəl -s -z

tumbril ˈtʌm.brɪl, -brəl -s -z

tumefaction ˌtʃuː.mɪˈfæk.ʃən, ˌtjuː-, -məˈ-, (US) ˌtuː.məˈ-, ˌtjuː-

tume|fy ˈtʃuː.mɪ|.faɪ, ˈtjuː-, -mə-, (US) ˈtuː.mə-, ˈtjuː- -fies -faɪz -fying -faɪ.ɪŋ -fied -faɪd

tumescen|t tʃuːˈmes.ən|t, tjuːˈ-, tʃʊ-, tjʊ-, (US) tuː-, tjuː- -ce -ts

tumid ˈtʃuː.mɪd, ˈtjuː-, (US) ˈtuː-, ˈtjuː- -ly -li

tumidity tʃuːˈmɪd.ə.ti, tjuːˈ-, tʃʊ-, tjʊ-, -ɪ.ti, (US) tuːˈmɪd.ə.t̬i, tjuː-

Tummel ˈtʌm.əl

tumm|y ˈtʌm|.i -ies -iz ˈ**tummy** ˌ**ache**; ˈ**tummy** ˌ**button**

tumo(u)r ˈtʃuː.mər, ˈtjuː-, (US) ˈtuː.mɚ, ˈtjuː- -s -z

tumo(u)rous ˈtʃuː.mər.əs, ˈtjuː-, (US) ˈtuː-, ˈtjuː-

tumult ˈtʃuː.mʌlt, ˈtjuː-, -məlt, (US) ˈtuː-, ˈtjuː- -s -s

tumultuous tʃuːˈmʌl.tju.əs, tjuːˈ-, tʃʊ-, tjʊ-, (US) tuːˈmʌl.tʃuː.əs, tjuː-, tə-, -tʃə.wəs -ly -li -ness -nəs, -nɪs

tumul|us ˈtʃuː.mjə.l|əs, ˈtjuː-, -mju-, (US) ˈtuː-, ˈtjuː- -i -aɪ

tun tʌn -s -z

tuna ˈtʃuː.nə, ˈtjuː-, (US) ˈtuː-, ˈtjuː- -s -z ˈ**tuna** ˌ**fish**

Tunbridge ˈtʌn.brɪdʒ, ˈtʌm-, (US) ˈtʌn- ˌ**Tunbridge** ˈ**Wells**

tundra ˈtʌn.drə -s -z

tun|e tʃuːn, tjuːn, (US) tuːn, tjuːn -es -z -ing -ɪŋ -ed -d -er/s -ər/z, (US) -ɚ/z ˈ**tuning** ˌ**fork**; ˈ**tuning** ˌ**peg**; ˌ**change one's** ˈ**tune**

tuneful ˈtʃuːn.fəl, ˈtjuːn-, -fʊl, (US) ˈtuːn-, ˈtjuːn- -ly -i -ness -nəs, -nɪs

tuneless ˈtʃuːn.ləs, ˈtjuːn-, -lɪs, (US) ˈtuːn-, ˈtjuːn- -ly -li -ness -nəs, -nɪs

tunesmith ˈtʃuːn.smɪθ, ˈtjuːn-, (US) ˈtuːn-, ˈtjuːn- -s -s

tungsten ˈtʌŋk.stən

tunic ˈtʃuː.nɪk, ˈtjuː-, (US) ˈtuː-, ˈtjuː- -s -s

tunicle ˈtʃuː.nɪ.kəl, ˈtjuː-, (US) ˈtuː-, ˈtjuː- -s -z

Tunis ˈtʃuː.nɪs, ˈtjuː-, (US) ˈtuː-, ˈtjuː-

Tunisi|a tʃuːˈnɪz.i|.ə, tjuː-, tʃʊ-, tjʊ-, -ˈnɪs-, (US) tuːˈniː.ʒ|ə, tjuː-, -ˈnɪʒ|.ə, -ˈnɪʃ|.ə -an/s -ən/z

Tunnard ˈtʌn.əd, (US) -ɚd

tunnel ˈtʌn.əl -s -z -(l)ing -ɪŋ -(l)ed -d -(l)er/s -ər/z, (US) -ɚ/z ˌ**tunnel** ˈ**vision**; ˌ**light at the** ˌ**end of the** ˈ**tunnel**

Tunnicliff(e) ˈtʌn.ɪ.klɪf

tunn|y ˈtʌn|.i -ies -iz

Tunstall ˈtʌnt.stəl, -stɔːl

Tuoh(e)y ˈtuː.i, -hi

Tupman ˈtʌp.mən

tuppenc|e ˈtʌp.ənts, -əmps -es -ɪz

tuppenny ˈtʌp.ən.i, ˈ-ni

tuppeny ˈtʌp.ən.i, ˈ-ni

Tupperware® ˈtʌp.ə.weər, (US) -ɚ.wer

tuque tjuːk, (US) tuːk, tjuːk -s -s

tu quoque ˌtuːˈkwəʊ.kwi, -ˈkwɒk.weɪ, (US) ˌtuːˈkwoʊ.kwi, ˌtjuː-, -kweɪ -s -z

Turandot ˈtʊə.rən.dɒt, ˈtjʊə-, -dəʊ, (US) ˈtʊr.ən.dɑːt, -doʊ

Turani|a tjʊəˈreɪ.ni|.ə, (US) tʊˈreɪ-, tjʊ-, -ˈrɑː- -an/s -ən/z

turban ˈtɜː.bən, (US) ˈtɝː- -s -z -(n)ed -d

turbid ˈtɜː.bɪd, (US) ˈtɝː- -ly -li -ness -nəs, -nɪs

turbidity tɜːˈbɪd.ə.ti, -ɪ.ti, (US) tɝːˈbɪd.ə.t̬i

turbine ˈtɜː.baɪn, -bɪn, (US) ˈtɝː.bɪn, -baɪn -s -z

turbo ˈtɜː.bəʊ, (US) ˈtɝː.boʊ -s -z

turbocharg|e ˈtɜː.bəʊ.tʃɑːdʒ, (US) ˈtɝː.boʊ.tʃɑːrdʒ -es -ɪz -ing -ɪŋ -ed -d -er/s -ər/z, (US) -ɚ/z

turbofan ˈtɜː.bəʊ.fæn, (US) ˈtɝː.boʊ- -s -z

turbo-jet ˈtɜː.bəʊ.dʒet, ˌ--ˈ-, (US) ˈtɝː.boʊ.dʒet -s -s

turbo-prop ˈtɜː.bəʊ.prɒp, ˌ--ˈ-, (US) ˈtɝː.boʊ.prɑːp -s -s

turbot ˈtɜː.bət, (US) ˈtɝː- -s -s

turbulence ˈtɜː.bjə.lənts, -jʊ-, (US) ˈtɝː-

turbulent ˈtɜː.bjə.lənt, -bjʊ-, (US) ˈtɝː- -ly -li

Turco- ˈtɜː.kəʊ, (US) ˈtɝː.koʊ, -kə

Turcoman ˈtɜː.kəʊ.mən, -mæn, -mɑːn, (US) ˈtɝː.koʊ.mən, -kə- -s -z

turd tɜːd, (US) tɝːd -s -z

tureen tʃʊˈriːn, tjʊˈ-, tʃə-, tjə-, tə-, tʊ-, (US) tʊ-, tjʊ- -s -z

turf v tɜːf, (US) tɝːf -s -s -ing -ɪŋ -ed -t

tur|f n tɜː|f, (US) tɝː|f -fs -fs -ves -vz -fing -fɪŋ -fed -ft ˈ**turf ac**ˌ**countant**

Turgenev tɜːˈgeɪ.njev, tʊə-, -ˈgen.jev, -jef, -jɪf, -ev, -əv, (US) tʊrˈgeɪ.nəf, tɝː-, -gen-, -njef, -njev

turgescen|ce tɜːˈdʒes.ən|ts, (US) tɝːˈ- -t -t

turgid ˈtɜː.dʒɪd, (US) ˈtɝː- -ly -li -ness -nəs, -nɪs

turgidity tɜːˈdʒɪd.ə.ti, -ɪ.ti, (US) tɝːˈdʒɪd.ə.t̬i

turgor ˈtɜː.gər, (US) ˈtɝː.gɚ

Turin tjʊəˈrɪn, (US) tʊ-, tjʊ- *stress shift, see compound:* ˌ**Turin** ˈ**Shroud**

Turing ˈtjʊə.rɪŋ, (US) ˈtʊr.ɪŋ, ˈtjʊr-

Turk tɜːk, (US) tɝːk -s -s

Turkestan ˌtɜː.kɪˈstɑːn, -kəˈ-, -stæn, (US) ˈtɝː.kɪ.stæn, -stɑːn

turkey, T~ ˈtɜː.ki, (US) ˈtɝː- -s -z

turkey-cock ˈtɜː.ki.kɒk, (US) ˈtɝː.ki.kɑːk -s -s

Turki ˈtɜː.kiː, -ki, (US) ˈtɝː-

Turkic ˈtɜː.kɪk, (US) ˈtɝː-

Turkington ˈtɜː.kɪŋ.tən, (US) ˈtɝː-

Turkish ˈtɜː.kɪʃ, (US) ˈtɝː- ˌ**Turkish** ˈ**bath**; ˌ**Turkish de**ˈ**light**

Turkmenia tɜːkˈmiː.ni.ə, (US) tɝːk-

Turkmenistan tɜːkˌmen.ɪˈstɑːn, -ˈstæn, (US) tɝːkˈmen.ɪ.stæn, -stɑːn
Turko- ˈtɜː.kəʊ, (US) ˈtɝː.koʊ, -kə
Turkoman ˈtɜːk.əʊ.mən, -mæn, -mɑːn, (US) ˈtɝː.koʊ.mən, -kə- **-s** -z
Turku ˈtʊə.kuː, ˈtɜː-, (US) ˈtʊr-
Turley ˈtɜː.li, (US) ˈtɝː-
turmeric ˈtɜː.mᵊr.ɪk, (US) ˈtɝː-
turmoil ˈtɜː.mɔɪl, (US) ˈtɝː-
turn tɜːn, (US) tɝːn **-s** -z **-ing** -ɪŋ **-ed** -d **-er/s** -əʳ/z, (US) -ɚ/z **ˈturning ˌpoint; ˌturn of ˈphrase**
turnabout ˈtɜːn.əˌbaʊt, (US) ˈtɝːn- **-s** -s
Turnage ˈtɜː.nɪdʒ, (US) ˈtɝː-
turnaround ˈtɜːn.əʳˈaʊnd, (US) ˈtɝːn.ɚ- **-s** -z
Turnbull ˈtɜːn.bʊl, ˈtɜːm-, (US) ˈtɝːn-, -bᵊl
turncoat ˈtɜːn.kəʊt, ˈtɜːŋ-, (US) ˈtɝːn.koʊt **-s** -s
turned-on ˌtɜːndˈɒn, (US) ˌtɝːndˈɑːn
turner, T~ ˈtɜː.nəʳ, (US) ˈtɝː.nɚ **-s** -z
turnery ˈtɜː.nᵊr.i, (US) ˈtɝː-
Turnham ˈtɜː.nəm, (US) ˈtɝː-
Turnhouse ˈtɜːn.haʊs, (US) ˈtɝːn-
turning ˈtɜː.nɪŋ, (US) ˈtɝː- **-s** -z
turning-point ˈtɜː.nɪŋ.pɔɪnt, (US) ˈtɝː- **-s** -s
turnip ˈtɜː.nɪp, (US) ˈtɝː- **-s** -s
turnkey ˈtɜːn.kiː, ˈtɜːŋ-, (US) ˈtɝːn- **-s** -z
turn-off ˈtɜːn.ɒf, (US) ˈtɝːn.ɑːf **-s** -s
turn-on ˈtɜːn.ɒn, (US) ˈtɝːn.ɑːn **-s** -z
turnout ˈtɜːn.aʊt, (US) ˈtɝːn- **-s** -s
turnover ˈtɜːnˌəʊ.vəʳ, (US) ˈtɝːnˌoʊ.vɚ **-s** -z
turnpike ˈtɜːn.paɪk, ˈtɜːm-, (US) ˈtɝːn- **-s** -s
turnround ˈtɜːn.raʊnd, (US) ˈtɝːn- **-s** -z
turnstile ˈtɜːn.staɪl, (US) ˈtɝːn- **-s** -z
turnstone ˈtɜːn.stəʊn, (US) ˈtɝːn.stoʊn **-s** -z
turntable ˈtɜːnˌteɪ.bᵊl, (US) ˈtɝːn- **-s** -z
turn-up ˈtɜːn.ʌp, (US) ˈtɝːn- **-s** -s
turpentine ˈtɜː.pᵊn.taɪn, -pᵊm-, (US) ˈtɝː.pᵊn-
Turpin ˈtɜː.pɪn, (US) ˈtɝː-
turpitude ˈtɜː.pɪ.tʃuːd, -tjuːd, (US) ˈtɝː.pɪ.tuːd, -tjuːd
turps tɜːps, (US) tɝːps
turquois|e ˈtɜː.kwɑːz, -kwɔɪz, (US) ˈtɝː.kwɔɪz, -kɔɪz **-es** -ɪz
turre|t ˈtʌr.ɪ|t, -ə|t, (US) ˈtɝː.ɪ|t **-ts** -ts **-ted** -tɪd, (US) -ţɪd
turtle ˈtɜː.tᵊl, (US) ˈtɝː.ţᵊl **-s** -z
turtledove ˈtɜː.tᵊl.dʌv, (US) ˈtɝː.ţᵊl- **-s** -z
turtleneck ˈtɜː.tᵊl.nek, (US) ˈtɝː.ţᵊl- **-s** -s
Turton ˈtɜː.tᵊn, (US) ˈtɝː-
turves (plural of **turf**) tɜːvz, (US) tɝːvz
Tuscan ˈtʌs.kən **-s** -z
Tuscany ˈtʌs.kə.ni
tush interj tʌʃ
tush *tooth:* tʌʃ *buttocks:* tʊʃ **-es** -ɪz
tusk tʌsk **-s** -s **-ed** -t
tusker ˈtʌs.kəʳ, (US) -kɚ **-s** -z
tussah ˈtʌs.ə
Tussaud *surname:* ˈtuː.səʊ, (US) tuːˈsoʊ
Tussaud's *exhibition:* tʊˈsɔːdz, tjʊ-, tə-, -ˈsəʊdz, -ˈsəʊz, (US) tʊˈsoʊz, tə-, -ˈsɑːd, -ˈsɔːd; (US) ˈtuː.soʊz
Tusser ˈtʌs.əʳ, (US) -ɚ
tussl|e ˈtʌs.ᵊl **-es** -z **-ing** -ɪŋ, ˈtʌs.lɪŋ **-ed** -d **-er/s** -əʳ/z, (US) -ɚ/z
tussock ˈtʌs.ək **-s** -s **-y** -i
tussore ˈtʌs.əʳ, -ɔːʳ, (US) -ɚ
tut v tʌt **-s** -s **-ting** -ɪŋ, (US) ˈtʌţ.ɪŋ **-ted** -ɪd, (US) ˈtʌţ.ɪd
tut interj tʌt

> Note: This spelling represents the tongue click used (usually repeated – see **tut-tut**) to indicate disapproval; it may be described as a voiceless affricated alveolar click, symbolized as [ǃs].

Tutankhamen, Tutankhamon ˌtuː.tᵊnˈkɑː.mən, -təŋ-, -tæŋ-, -tɑːŋ-, -kɑːˈmuːn
Tutbury ˈtʌt.bᵊr.i, (US) -ber-, -bɚ-
tutee ˌtʃuːˈtiː, ˌtjuː-, (US) ˌtuː-, ˌtjuː- **-s** -z
tutelage ˈtʃuː.tɪ.lɪdʒ, ˈtjuː-, -tᵊl.ɪdʒ, (US) ˈtuː.ţᵊl.ɪdʒ, ˈtjuː-
tutelar ˈtʃuː.tᵊl.əʳ, ˈtjuː-, (US) ˈtuː.ţᵊl.ɚ, ˈtjuː-
tutelary ˈtʃuː.tᵊl.ᵊr.i, ˈtjuː-, (US) ˈtuː.ţᵊl.er.i, ˈtjuː-
Tutin ˈtjuː.tɪn, (US) ˈtuː-, ˈtjuː-
tut|or ˈtʃuː.t|əʳ, ˈtjuː-, (US) ˈtuː.ţ|ɚ, ˈtjuː- **-ors** -əz, (US) -ɚz **-oring** -ᵊr.ɪŋ **-ored** -əd, (US) -ɚd **-orage** -ᵊr.ɪdʒ
tutorial tʃuːˈtɔː.ri.əl, tʃʊ-, tjuː-, tjʊ-, (US) tuːˈtɔːr.i-, tjuː- **-s** -z **-ly** -i
tutorship ˈtʃuː.tə.ʃɪp, ˈtjuː-, (US) ˈtuː.ţɚ-, ˈtjuː- **-s** -s
Tutsi ˈtʊt.si **-s** -z
tutti ˈtʊt.i, ˈtuː.ti, -tiː, (US) ˈtuː.ţi **-s** -z
tutti-frutti ˌtuː.tiˈfruː.ti, ˌtʊt.iˈ-, -ˈfrʊt.i, (US) ˌtuː.ţiˈfruː.ţi **-s** -z
Tuttle ˈtʌt.ᵊl, (US) ˈtʌţ-
tut|-tut tʌt|ˈtʌt **-tuts** -ˈtʌts **-tutting** -ˈtʌt.ɪŋ, (US) -ˈtʌţ.ɪŋ **-tutted** -ˈtʌt.ɪd, (US) -ˈtʌţ.ɪd
tutu, T~ ˈtuː.tuː **-s** -z
Tuvalu tuːˈvɑː.luː; ˈtuː.və-, (US) ˌtuː.vəˈluː; (US) tuːˈvɑː.luː
tu-whit tu-whoo tʊˌhwɪt.tʊˈhwuː, tə-, -təˈ-
tux tʌks **-es** -ɪz
tuxedo, T~ tʌkˈsiː.dəʊ, (US) -doʊ **-(e)s** -z
Tuxford ˈtʌks.fəd, (US) -fɚd
Tuzla ˈtʊz.lə, ˈtuːz-, (US) ˈtuːz.lɑː
TV ˌtiːˈviː **-s** -z **ˌTV ˈdinner; ˌTˈV ˌprogram(me)**
Twaddell ˈtwɒd.ᵊl; twɒdˈel, (US) twɑːˈdel; (US) ˈtwɑː.dᵊl
twaddl|e ˈtwɒd.ᵊl, (US) ˈtwɑː.dᵊl **-es** -z **-ing** -ɪŋ, ˈtwɒd.lɪŋ, (US) ˈtwɑːd- **-ed** -d **-er/s** -əʳ/z, ˈtwɒd.ləʳ/z, (US) ˈtwɑː.dᵊl.ɚ/z, ˈtwɑːd.lɚ/z **-y** -i, ˈtwɒd.li, (US) ˈtwɑː.dᵊl.i, ˈtwɑːd.li
twain, T~ tweɪn
twang twæŋ **-s** -z **-ing** -ɪŋ **-ed** -d **-y** -i
Twank(e)y ˈtwæŋ.ki
'twas *strong form:* twɒz, (US) twɑːz; *weak form:* twəz
twat twæt, twɒt, (US) twɑːt **-s** -s
tweak twiːk **-s** -s **-ing** -ɪŋ **-ed** -t
twee twiː
tweed, T~ twiːd **-s** -z
Tweeddale ˈtwiːd.deɪl
Tweedie ˈtwiː.di
tweedl|e ˈtwiː.dᵊl **-es** -z **-ing** -ɪŋ, ˈtwiːd.lɪŋ **-ed** -d
Tweedledee ˌtwiː.dᵊlˈdiː
Tweedledum ˌtwiː.dᵊlˈdʌm
Tweedmouth ˈtwiːd.məθ, -maʊθ
Tweedsmuir ˈtwiːdz.mjʊəʳ, -mjɔːʳ, (US) -mjʊr, -mjʊɚ
tweed|y ˈtwiː.d|i **-ier** -i.əʳ, (US) -i.ɚ **-iest** -i.ɪst, -i.əst **-iness** -ɪ.nəs, -ɪ.nɪs
'tween twiːn
tweenager ˈtwiːnˌeɪ.dʒəʳ, (US) -dʒɚ **-s** -z
tween|y ˈtwiː.n|i **-ies** -iz
tweet twiːt **-s** -s **-ing** -ɪŋ, (US) ˈtwiː.ţɪŋ **-ed** -ɪd, (US) ˈtwiː.ţɪd **-er/s** -əʳ/z, (US) ˈtwiː.ţɚ/z
tweezers ˈtwiː.zəz, (US) -zɚz
twelfth twelfθ **-s** -s **-ly** -li **ˌTwelfth ˈNight** (US) **ˈTwelfth ˌNight**
twelve twelv **-s** -z
twelvemonth ˈtwelv.mʌn*t*θ **-s** -s
twelvish ˈtwel.vɪʃ
twentieth ˈtwen.ti.ɪθ, -əθ, (US) -ţi- **-s** -s
twent|y ˈtwen.t|i, (US) -ţ|i **-ies** -iz **ˌtwenty-ˌtwenty ˈvision**
twenty-first ˌtwen.tiˈfɜːst, (US) -ţiˈfɝːst *stress shift:* **ˌtwenty-first ˈbirthday**
twentyfold ˈtwen.ti.fəʊld, (US) -ţi.foʊld
Twentyman ˈtwen.ti.mən, (US) -ţi-
twenty-one ˌtwen.tiˈwʌn, (US) -ţiˈ- *stress shift:* **ˌtwenty-one ˈyears**
'twere *strong form:* twɜːʳ, (US) twɝː; *weak form:* twəʳ, (US) twɚ
twerp twɜːp, (US) twɝːp **-s** -s
Twi twiː
twice twaɪs
twice-told twaɪsˈtəʊld, (US) -ˈtoʊld *stress shift:* **ˌtwice-told ˈtale**
Twickenham ˈtwɪk.ᵊn.əm, ˈ-nəm
twiddl|e ˈtwɪd.ᵊl **-es** -z **-ing** -ɪŋ, ˈtwɪd.lɪŋ **-ed** -d **ˌtwiddle your ˈthumbs**
twiddl|y ˈtwɪd.l|i, -ᵊl|.i **-ier** -i.əʳ, (US) -i.ɚ **-iest** -i.ɪst, -i.əst
twig twɪg **-s** -z **-ging** -ɪŋ **-ged** -d
Twigg twɪg
twiggy, T~ ˈtwɪg.i
twilight ˈtwaɪ.laɪt **-s** -s **ˈtwilight ˌzone**
twilit ˈtwaɪ.lɪt
twill twɪl **-s** -z **-ing** -ɪŋ **-ed** -d **-y** -i
'twill *normal form:* twɪl; *occasional weak form:* twᵊl

Pronouncing the letters TZ

The consonant digraph **tz** is most commonly pronounced /ts/, e.g.:

chintz	tʃɪnts
quartz	kwɔːts US kwɔːrts

However, the /t/ is sometimes optional in British English, e.g.:

waltz	wɒlts, wɔːlts US wɑːlts, wɔːlts

twin twɪn **-s** -z **-ning** -ɪŋ **-ned** -d ˌ**twin** ˈ**bed**
twin|e twaɪn **-es** -z **-ing/ly** -ɪŋ/li **-ed** -d **-er/s** -əʳ/z, US -ɚ/z
twing|e twɪndʒ **-es** -ɪz **-(e)ing** -ɪŋ **-ed** -d
Twingo ˈtwɪŋ.gəʊ, US -goʊ
Twining ˈtwaɪ.nɪŋ
Twinkie® ˈtwɪŋ.ki **-s** -z
twinkl|e ˈtwɪŋ.kᵊl **-es** -z **-ing** -ɪŋ, ˈtwɪŋ.klɪŋ **-ed** -d **-er/s** -əʳ/z, ˈtwɪŋ.kləʳ/z, US ˈ-kl.ɚ/z, ˈ-klɚ/z
Twinn twɪn
twinset ˈtwɪn.set **-s** -s
twin-track ˌtwɪnˈtræk *stress shift:* ˌ**twin-track** ˈ**railway**
twin-tub ˈtwɪn.tʌb **-s** -z
twirl twɜːl, US twɝːl **-s** -z **-ing** -ɪŋ **-ed** -d **-y** -i
twirler ˈtwɜː.ləʳ, US ˈtwɝː.lɚ **-s** -z
twirp twɜːp, US twɝːp **-s** -s
twist, T~ twɪst **-s** -s **-ing** -ɪŋ **-ed** -ɪd **-er/s** -əʳ/z, US -ɚ/z
Twistington ˈtwɪs.tɪŋ.tən
twist-tie ˈtwɪst.taɪ **-s** -z
twist|y ˈtwɪs.t|i **-ier** -i.əʳ, US -i.ɚ **-iest** -i.ɪst, -i.əst **-iness** -ɪ.nəs, -ɪ.nɪs
twit twɪt **-s** -s **-ting/ly** -ɪŋ/li, US ˈtwɪţ.ɪŋ/li **-ted** -ɪd, US ˈtwɪţ.ɪd
twitch twɪtʃ **-es** -ɪz **-ing/s** -ɪŋ/z **-ed** -t **-er/s** -əʳ/z, US -ɚ/z
twitch|y ˈtwɪtʃ|.i **-ier** -i.əʳ, US -i.ɚ **-iest** -i.ɪst, -i.əst
twite twaɪt **-s** -s
twitt|er, T~ ˈtwɪt|.əʳ, US ˈtwɪţ|.ɚ **-ers** -əz, US -ɚz **-ering** -ᵊr.ɪŋ, US -ɚ.ɪŋ **-ered** -əd, US -ɚd **-ery** -ᵊr.i, US -ɚ.i
'twixt twɪkst
two tuː **-s** -z **put** ˌ**two and** ˌ**two to**ˈ**gether**
two-bit tuːˈbɪt, US ˈ-- *stress shift, British only:* ˌ**two-bit** ˈ**liar**
two-by-four ˌtuː.baɪˈfɔːʳ, -bəˈ-, -bɪˈ-, US ˈtuː.baɪ.fɔːr, -bə-
two-dimensional ˌtuː.dɪˈmen.tʃᵊn.ᵊl, -daɪˈ-, -ˈmentʃ.nᵊl, US -dəˈ-, -dɪˈ-, -daɪˈ-
two-edged ˌtuːˈedʒd *stress shift:* ˌ**two-edged** ˈ**sword**
two-|faced ˌtuː|ˈfeɪst, US ˈ-- **-facedly** -ˈfeɪ.sɪd.li; -ˈfeɪst.li, US -feɪ.sɪd.li, -feɪst.li **-facedness** -ˈfeɪ.sɪd.nəs, -nɪs; -ˈfeɪst.nəs, -nɪs, US -feɪ.sɪd.nəs, -nɪs; US -feɪst.nəs, -nɪs *stress shift, British only:* ˌ**two-faced** ˈ**liar**
twofold ˈtuː.fəʊld, US -foʊld
two-handed ˌtuːˈhæn.dɪd *stress shift:* ˌ**two-handed** ˈ**grip**
two-hander ˌtuːˈhæn.dəʳ, US -dɚ **-s** -z
two-ish ˈtuː.ɪʃ
two-legged ˌtuːˈlegd; -ˈleg.ɪd, US ˈtuː.legd; US -ˌleg.ɪd *stress shift, British only:* ˌ**two-legged** ˈ**creature**
twopenc|e ˈtʌp.ᵊnts, -ᵊmps **-es** -ɪz

> Note: The British English pronunciations of **twopenny, twopence,** etc., date from the period before the introduction of decimal coinage in 1971.

twopenny ˈtʌp.ᵊn.i, ˈ-ni
twopenny-halfpenny ˌtʌp.niˈheɪp.ni, ˌtʌp.ᵊn.iˈheɪ.pᵊn.i
twopennyworth ˌtuːˈpen.i.wɜːθ, ˈ-əθ; ˈtʌp.ᵊn.i.wɜːθ, ˈ-ni-, -wəθ, US -wɝːθ, -wɚθ **-s** -s
two-piece ˈtuː.piːs
two-ply ˈtuː.plaɪ
two-seater ˌtuːˈsiː.təʳ, US -ţɚ, ˈ-ˌ-- **-s** -z *stress shift:* ˌ**two-seater** ˈ**sports-car**
twosome ˈtuː.səm **-s** -z
two-step ˈtuː.step **-s** -s
two-stroke ˈtuː.strəʊk, US -stroʊk
two-time ˌtuːˈtaɪm, ˈ--, US ˈ-- **-s** -z **-ing** -ɪŋ **-ed** -d **-er/s** -əʳ/z, US -ɚ/z
two-tone ˌtuːˈtəʊn, ˈ--, US ˈtuː.toʊn **-d** -d
two-way ˌtuːˈweɪ, US ˈ-- *stress shift, British only:* ˌ**two-way** ˈ**mirror**
Twyford ˈtwaɪ.fəd, US -fɚd
TX (abbrev. for **Texas**) ˈtek.səs
Tybalt ˈtɪb.ᵊlt
Tyburn ˈtaɪ.bɜːn, US -bɝːn
Tycho ˈtaɪ.kəʊ, US -koʊ
tycoon taɪˈkuːn **-s** -z
Tydeus ˈtaɪ.djuːs, -djəs, -di.əs, US ˈtaɪ.di.əs, ˈ-djəs
Tydfil ˈtɪd.vɪl
tyger ˈtaɪ.gəʳ, US -gɚ
tying (from **tie**) ˈtaɪ.ɪŋ
tyke taɪk **-s** -s
Tyldesley ˈtɪldz.li
Tylenol ˈtaɪ.lə.nɒl, US -nɑːl, -nɔːl
Tyler ˈtaɪ.ləʳ, US -lɚ
tympan|i ˈtɪm.pə.n|i **-ist/s** -ɪst/s
tympanic tɪmˈpæn.ɪk
tympan|um ˈtɪm.pᵊn|.əm **-ums** -əmz **-a** -ə
tympan|y ˈtɪm.pᵊn|.i **-ies** -iz
Tynan ˈtaɪ.nən
Tyndale, Tyndall ˈtɪn.dᵊl
Tyndrum ˈtaɪn.drʌm
Tyne taɪn ˌ**Tyne and** ˈ**Wear**
Tynecastle ˈtaɪnˌkɑː.sᵊl, US -ˌkæs.ᵊl
Tynemouth ˈtaɪn.maʊθ, ˈtaɪm-, -məθ; ˈtɪn.məθ, ˈtɪm-, US ˈtaɪn-
Tynesid|e ˈtaɪn.saɪd **-er/s** -əʳ/z, US -ɚ/z
Tynwald ˈtɪn.wəld
typ|e taɪp **-es** -s **-ing** -ɪŋ **-ed** -t ˈ**typing** ˌ**pool**
typecast ˈtaɪp.kɑːst, US -kæst **-s** -s **-ing** -ɪŋ
Typee ˌtaɪˈpiː
typefac|e ˈtaɪp.feɪs **-es** -ɪz
typefounder ˈtaɪpˌfaʊn.dəʳ, US -dɚ **-s** -z
typefoundr|y ˈtaɪpˌfaʊn.dr|i **-ies** -iz
typescript ˈtaɪp.skrɪpt **-s** -s
type|set ˈtaɪp|.set **-sets** -sets **-setting** -ˌset.ɪŋ, US -ˌseţ.ɪŋ **-setter/s** -ˌset.əʳ/z, US -ˌseţ.ɚ/z
typesetter ˈtaɪpˌset.əʳ, US -ˌseţ.ɚ **-s** -z
type|write ˈtaɪp|.raɪt **-writes** -raɪts **-writing** -ˌraɪ.tɪŋ, US -ˌraɪ.ţɪŋ **-wrote** -rəʊt, US -roʊt **-written** -ˌrɪt.ᵊn
typewriter ˈtaɪpˌraɪ.təʳ, US -ţɚ **-s** -z
typhoid ˈtaɪ.fɔɪd
typhonic taɪˈfɒn.ɪk, US -ˈfɑː.nɪk
Typhoo® taɪˈfuː
typhoon taɪˈfuːn **-s** -z
typh|us ˈtaɪ.f|əs **-ous** -əs
typic|al ˈtɪp.ɪ.k|ᵊl **-ally** -ᵊl.i, -li **-alness** -ᵊl.nəs, -nɪs
typicality ˌtɪp.ɪˈkæl.ə.ti, -ɪ.ti, US -ə.ţi
typi|fy ˈtɪp.ɪ|.faɪ, ˈ-ə- **-fies** -faɪz **-fying** -faɪ.ɪŋ **-fied** -faɪd
typist ˈtaɪ.pɪst **-s** -s
typo ˈtaɪ.pəʊ, US -poʊ **-s** -z
typographic ˌtaɪ.pəʊˈgræf.ɪk, US -pəˈ-, -poʊˈ- **-al** -ᵊl **-ally** -ᵊl.i, -li
typograph|y taɪˈpɒg.rə.f|i, US -ˈpɑː.grə- **-er/s** -əʳ/z, US -ɚ/z
typolog|y taɪˈpɒl.ə.dʒ|i, US -ˈpɑː.lə- **-ies** -iz
tyrannic|al tɪˈræn.ɪ.k|ᵊl, tə-, taɪ-, US tə-, tɪ-, taɪ- **-ally** -ᵊl.i, -li **-alness** -ᵊl.nəs, -nɪs
tyrannicide tɪˈræn.ɪ.saɪd, tə-, taɪ-, US tə-, tɪ-, taɪ- **-s** -z
tyranniz|e, -is|e ˈtɪr.ᵊn.aɪz **-es** -ɪz **-ing** -ɪŋ **-ed** -d
tyrannosaur tɪˈræn.ə.sɔːʳ, tə-, taɪ-, US təˈræn.ə.sɔːr, tɪ-, taɪ- **-s** -z
tyrannosaurus tɪˌræn.əˈsɔː.rəs, tə-, taɪ-, US təˌræn.əˈsɔːr.əs, tɪ-, taɪ- **-es** -ɪz **ty**ˌ**ranno**ˌ**saurus** ˈ**rex**
tyrannous ˈtɪr.ᵊn.əs **-ly** -li
tyrann|y ˈtɪr.ᵊn|.i **-ies** -iz
tyrant ˈtaɪə.rənt, US ˈtaɪ- **-s** -s
tyre, T~ taɪəʳ, ˈtaɪ.əʳ, US ˈtaɪ.ɚ **-s** -z
Tyrian ˈtɪr.i.ən **-s** -z
tyro ˈtaɪə.rəʊ, US ˈtaɪ.roʊ **-s** -z
Tyrol tɪˈrəʊl, tə-; ˈtɪr.ᵊl, US tɪˈroʊl, taɪ-; US ˈtɪr.oʊl, -ɑːl
Tyrolean ˌtɪr.əʊˈliː.ən; tɪˈrəʊ.li-, tə-, US tɪˈroʊ.li-, taɪ-; US ˌtɪr.əˈliː-
Tyrolese ˌtɪr.əʊˈliːz, US -əˈliːz, -ˈliːs

Tyrolienne tɪˌrəʊ.liˈen, tə-; ˌtɪr.əʊ-, (US) tɪˈroʊ.li.ən; (US) ˌtɪr.əˈliː-, ˌtaɪ.rəˈ- -s -z

Tyrone *in Ireland:* tɪˈrəʊn, tə-, (US) -ˈroʊn *person's name:* ˈtaɪə.rəʊn; taɪˈrəʊn, tɪ-, tə-, (US) ˈtaɪ.roʊn, ˌ-ˈ-

Tyrrell ˈtɪr.əl

Tyrrhenian tɪˈriː.ni.ən, tə-, (US) tɪ-

Tyrtaeus tɜːˈtiː.əs, (US) tɝː-

Tyrwhitt ˈtɪr.ɪt

Tyser ˈtaɪ.zəʳ, (US) -zɚ

Tyson ˈtaɪ.sən

Tytler ˈtaɪt.ləʳ, (US) -lɚ

Tyzack ˈtaɪ.zæk, ˈtɪz.æk, -ək

tzar, T~ zɑːʳ, tsɑːʳ, (US) zɑːr, tsɑːr -s -z

tzarina, T~ zɑːˈriː.nə, tsɑː- -s -z

tzar|ism ˈzɑː.r|ɪ.zəm, ˈtsɑː-, (US) ˈzɑːr|.ɪ-, ˈtsɑːr|- -ist/s -ɪst/s

tzetze ˈtet.si, ˈtset-, (US) ˈtset-, ˈtsiːt-, ˈtet-, ˈtiːt- -s -z **ˈtzetze ˌfly**

U

Pronouncing the letter U

→ *See also* **UE, UI, UOU, UY**

The vowel letter **u** has several strong pronunciations linked to spelling. 'Short' pronunciations include /ʌ/ and /ʊ/, and 'long' pronunciations include /uː/ and /juː/. In 'short' pronunciations pronounced /ʌ/, the **u** is generally followed by a consonant letter which ends the word, or a double consonant before another vowel. Words containing /ʊ/ which end with a consonant sound often have two consonant letters finally, a notable exception being *put* /pʊt/, e.g.:

tub	tʌb
tubby	ˈtʌb.i
bull	bʊl
bully	ˈbʊl.i

The 'long' pronunciations usually mean the **u** is followed by a single consonant letter and then a vowel, e.g.:

tube	tʃuːb (US) tuːb
tubing	ˈtʃuː.bɪŋ (US) ˈtuː-
supervise	ˈsuː.pə.vaɪz (US) -pɚ-

In word-initial position, the 'long' pronunciation is almost always pronounced /juː/, e.g.:

unique	juːˈniːk
useful	ˈjuːs.fəl

However, there are exceptions to these guidelines, e.g.:

study	ˈstʌd.i
sugar	ˈʃʊg.əʳ (US) -ɚ
truth	truːθ

When **u** is followed by **r**, the strong pronunciation is one of several possibilities: /jʊə, jɔː/ (US) /jʊr/, /ʊə, ɔː/ (US) /ʊr/, /ɜː/ (US) /ɝː/, or /ʌ/ (US) /ɝː/, e.g.:

cure	kjʊəʳ, kjɔːʳ (US) kjʊr
plural	ˈplʊə.rəl, ˈplɔː- (US) ˈplʊr.əl
burn	bɜːn (US) bɝːn
hurry	ˈhʌr.i (US) ˈhɝː.i

An exceptional case is /e/ in bury /ˈber.i/.

In weak syllables

The vowel letter **u** is realized as one of /jə/, /jʊ/, /ə/, or /ʊ/ in weak syllables, e.g.:

failure	ˈfeɪ.ljəʳ (US) ˈfeɪl.jɚ
accurate	ˈæk.jə.rət, -jʊ- (US) -jɚ.ət, -jʊ.rət
status	ˈsteɪ.təs (US) ˈstæ.t̬əs
July	dʒʊˈlaɪ

It may also result in a syllabic consonant, e.g.:

hopeful	ˈhəʊp.fəl, -fʊl (US) ˈhoʊp-

u, U juː **-'s** -z
UAE ˌjuː.eɪˈiː
UB40 ˌjuː.biːˈfɔː.ti, (US) -ˈfɔːr.t̬i **-s** -z
Ubbelohde ˈʌb.əl.əʊd, (US) -oʊd
U-bend ˈjuː.bend **-s** -z
über- ˈuː.bəʳ, (US) -bɚ
Übermensch ˈuː.bə.mentʃ, (US) -bɚ- **-en** -ən
ubiquitarian, U~ juːˌbɪk.wɪˈteə.ri.ən, ˌjuː.bɪ.kwɪˈ-, (US) juːˌbɪk.wəˈter.i- **-s** -z
ubiquitous juːˈbɪk.wɪ.təs, (US) -wə.t̬əs **-ly** -li **-ness** -nəs, -nɪs
ubiquity juːˈbɪk.wə.ti, -wɪ-, (US) -wə.t̬i
U-boat ˈjuː.bəʊt, (US) -boʊt **-s** -s
Ubu Roi ˌuː.buːˈrwɑː
UCAS, Ucas ˈjuː.kæs
UCATT ˈʌk.ət, ˈjuː.kæt
UCCA ˈʌk.ə
Uccello uːˈtʃel.əʊ, (US) -oʊ
Uckfield ˈʌk.fiːld
UCLA ˌjuː.siː.elˈeɪ
UDA ˌjuː.diːˈeɪ
Udall ˈjuː.dəl, (US) -dɔːl, -dɑːl, -dəl
udder ˈʌd.əʳ, (US) -ɚ **-s** -z
Uddin ˈʌd.ɪn
Uddingston ˈʌd.ɪŋ.stən
UDI ˌjuː.diːˈaɪ
Udolpho uːˈdɒl.fəʊ, juː-, (US) -ˈdɑːl.foʊ
UDR ˌjuː.diːˈɑːʳ, (US) -ˈɑːr
UEFA, Uefa juːˈeɪ.fə, -ˈiː-
Uffizi juːˈfɪt.si, uː-, -ˈfiːt-
UFO ˌjuː.efˈəʊ, (US) -ˈoʊ **-(')s** -z
ufolog|y juːˈfɒl.ə.dʒ|i, (US) -ˈfɑː.lə- **-ist/s** -ɪst/s
Ugand|a juːˈgæn.d|ə, jʊ-, (US) juː-, uː- **-an/s** -ən/z
Ugaritic ˌuː.gəˈrɪt.ɪk, ˌjuː-, (US) -gəˈrɪt̬-
ugh ʌx, ɜːh, ʌg

> Note: Used to indicate disgust. Many other pronunciations are possible, including [ɯːx], [ɯh], [uɸ].

ugli ˈʌg.li **-s** -z ˈ**ugli** ˌ**fruit**
uglification ˌʌg.lɪ.fɪˈkeɪ.ʃən, -lə-, -fəˈ-
ugli|fy ˈʌg.lɪ|.faɪ, ˈ-lə- **-fies** -faɪz **-fying** -faɪ.ɪŋ **-fied** -faɪd
ugl|y ˈʌg.l|i **-ier** -i.əʳ, (US) -i.ɚ **-iest** -i.ɪst, -i.əst **-iness** -ɪ.nəs, -ɪ.nɪs ˌ**ugly** ˈ**duckling**
Ugrian ˈuː.gri.ən, ˈjuː- **-s** -z
Ugric ˈuː.grɪk, ˈjuː-
UHF ˌjuː.eɪtʃˈef
uh-huh ʌˈhʌ, ˈʌ.hʌ
uhlan ˈuː.lɑːn, ˈjuː-, -lən; uːˈlɑːn, juː- **-s** -z
Uhland ˈuː.lənd, -lænd, -lɑːnd, (US) -lɑːnt, -lɑːnd
uh-oh ˈʌʔ.əʊ, (US) -oʊ
UHT ˌjuː.eɪtʃˈtiː *stress shift, see compound:* ˌ**UHT** ˈ**milk**
Uhu® ˈjuː.huː, ˈuː-
uh-uh ˈʌʔˌʌʔ, (US) ˈʌ̃ʔˌʌ̃

> Note: Pronounced with falling pitch, this has the meaning 'no'.

uhuru, U~ uːˈhuː.ruː, -ˈhʊə-
Uig ˈuː.ɪg, ˈjuː-
Uighur ˈwiː.gʊəʳ, -gəʳ, (US) -gʊr, -gɚ **-s** -z
Uist ˈjuː.ɪst
uitlander, U~ ˈeɪtˌlæn.dəʳ, ˈɔɪt-, (US) ˈɔɪtˌlæn.dɚ, ˈeɪt-, ˈaɪt- **-s** -z
UK ˌjuːˈkeɪ *stress shift:* ˌ**UK** ˈ**citizen**
ukas|e juːˈkeɪz, -ˈkeɪs, (US) juːˈkeɪz, -ˈkeɪs, ˈ-- **-es** -ɪz
uke juːk **-s** -s
ukelele ˌjuː.kəlˈeɪ.li, (US) -kəˈleɪ- **-s** -z
UKIP ˈjuː.kɪp
Ukrain|e juːˈkreɪn, (US) -ˈkreɪn, ˈjuː.kreɪn **-ian/s** -iən/z
ukulele ˌjuː.kəlˈeɪ.li, (US) -kəˈleɪ- **-s** -z
ulan ˈuː.lɑːn, ˈjuː-, -lən; uːˈlɑːn, juː- **-s** -z
Ulan Bator uːˌlɑːnˈbɑː.tɔːʳ, (US) ˌuː.lɑːnˈbɑː.tɔːr
Ulan-Ude uːˌlɑːn.uːˈdeɪ, (US) uːˌlɑːn.uːˈdeɪ, uːˈlɑːn.uːˌdeɪ

Pronouncing the letters UE

The vowel digraph **ue** is most commonly pronounced as /juː/ or /uː/. The /j/ sound is not always present in US English where it is found in British English. In general, the /j/ is dropped in US English where it appears in British English following an alveolar consonant such as /t/, /d/, or /n/, e.g.:

cue	kjuː
due	dʒuː (US) duː

Another possible pronunciation is /juː.ə/ or /jʊə/, e.g.:

duel	ˈdʒuː.əl, dʒʊəl (US) ˈduː.əl

In addition

Other sounds are associated with the digraph **ue**, e.g.:

weɪ	suede /sweɪd/
e	guess /ges/
uː.ɪ	suet, bluest /ˈsuː.ɪt/, /ˈbluː.ɪst/
silent	league /liːg/

ulcer ˈʌl.səʳ, (US) -sɚ **-s** -z
ulcer|ate ˈʌl.sᵊr|.eɪt, (US) -sə.r|eɪt **-ates** -eɪts **-ating** -eɪ.tɪŋ, (US) -eɪ.t̬ɪŋ **-ated** -eɪ.tɪd, (US) -eɪ.t̬ɪd
ulceration ˌʌl.sᵊrˈeɪ.ʃᵊn, (US) -səˈreɪ- **-s** -z
ulcerative ˈʌl.sᵊr.ə.tɪv, -eɪ-, (US) -sə.reɪ.t̬ɪv, -sɚ.ə-
ulcerous ˈʌl.sᵊr.əs
ulema ˈuː.lɪ.mə, -lə-, -mɑː; ˌuː.lɪˈmɑː, -ləˈ-, (US) ˌuː.ləˈmɑː, ˈ--- **-s** -z
Ulfilas ˈʊl.fɪ.læs, -fə-, -ləs, (US) ˈʌl.fɪ.ləs
ullage ˈʌl.ɪdʒ
Ullah ˈʌl.ə
Ullapool ˈʌl.ə.puːl
Ullman(n) ˈʊl.mən, ˈʌl-, (US) ˈʌl-, ˈʊl-
Ullswater ˈʌlzˌwɔː.təʳ, (US) -ˌwɑː.t̬ɚ, -ˌwɔː-
Ulm ʊlm
uln|a ˈʌl.n|ə **-as** -əz **-ae** -iː **-ar** -əʳ, (US) -ɚ
Ulrica ˈʊl.rɪkə, ˈʌl-
Ulrich ˈʊl.rɪk; *as if German:* -rɪx; (US) ˈʌl-, ˈʊl-
Ulrika ʊlˈriː.kə
Ulster, ulster ˈʌl.stəʳ, (US) -stɚ **-s** -z
Ulster|man ˈʌl.stə|.mən, (US) -stɚ- **-men** -mən
Ulster|woman ˈʌl.stə|ˌwʊm.ən, (US) -stɚ- **-women** -ˌwɪm.ɪn
ulterior ʌlˈtɪə.ri.əʳ, (US) -ˈtɪr.i.ɚ **-ly** -li ulˌterior ˈmotive
ultima ˈʌl.tɪ.mə, -tə-, (US) -tɪ- ˌultima ˈThule
ultimate ˈʌl.tɪ.mət, -tə- **-ly** -li
ultimat|um ˌʌl.tɪˈmeɪ.t|əm, (US) -təˈmeɪ.t̬|əm **-ums** -əmz **-a** -ə
ultimo ˈʌl.tɪ.məʊ, -tə-, (US) -tə.moʊ
ultra ˈʌl.trə **-s** -z
ultra- ˈʌl.trə
Note: Prefix. Normally takes primary or secondary stress on the first syllable, e.g. **ultrasound** /ˈʌl.trə.saʊnd/, **ultrasonic** /ˌʌl.trəˈsɒn.ɪk/ (US) /-ˈsɑː.nɪk/.
ultra-high frequenc|y ˌʌl.trəˌhaɪˈfriː.kwənt.s|i **-ies** -iz
ultramarine ˌʌl.trə.məˈriːn *stress shift:* ˌultramarine ˈblue
ultramodern ˌʌl.trəˈmɒd.ən, (US) -ˈmɑː.dɚn **-ist/s** -ɪst/s *stress shift:* ˌultramodern ˈstyling
ultramontane ˌʌl.trəˈmɒn.teɪn, -mɒnˈteɪn, (US) -ˈmɑːn.teɪn, -mɑːnˈteɪn
ultramontanism, U~ ˌʌl.trəˈmɒn.tə.nɪ.zᵊm, -tɪ-, -teɪ-, (US) -ˈmɑːn.tə-
ultrasonic ˌʌl.trəˈsɒn.ɪk, (US) -ˈsɑː.nɪk **-s** -s **-ally** -ᵊl.i, -li *stress shift:* ˌultrasonic ˈscanner
ultrasound ˈʌl.trə.saʊnd
ultraviolet ˌʌl.trəˈvaɪə.lət, -lɪt, (US) -lɪt *stress shift, see compound:* ˌultraviolet ˈlight
ultra vires ˌʌl.trəˈvaɪə.riːz, ˌʊl.trɑːˈvɪə.reɪz, (US) ˌʌl.trəˈvaɪ.riːz
ululant ˈjuː.ljə.lənt, ˈʌl.jə-, -jʊ-, (US) ˈjuːl.jə.lənt, ˈʌl-, -jə-
ulu|late ˈjuː.ljə|.leɪt, ˈʌl.jə-, -jʊ-, (US) ˈjuːl.jə-, ˈʌl-, -jə- **-lates** -leɪts **-lating** -leɪ.tɪŋ, (US) -leɪ.t̬ɪŋ **-lated** -leɪ.tɪd, (US) -leɪ.t̬ɪd
ululation ˌjuː.ljəˈleɪ.ʃᵊn, ˌʌl.jəˈ-, -jʊˈ-, (US) ˌjuːl.jəˈ-, ˌʌl-, -jəˈ- **-s** -z
Uluru uːˈluː.ruː; ˌʊl.əˈruː
Ulverston ˈʌl.və.stən, (US) -vɚ-
Ulyanovsk ʊlˈjɑː.nɒfsk, (US) uːlˈjɑː.nɔːfsk
Ulysses ˈjuː.lɪ.siːz; juːˈlɪs.iːz, (US) juːˈlɪs-
umami uːˈmɑː.mi
umbel ˈʌm.bəl, -bel **-s** -z
umbellifer ʌmˈbel.ɪ.fəʳ, (US) -fɚ
umbelliferae ˌʌm.bᵊlˈɪf.ᵊr.iː, -belˈ-, (US) -bəˈlɪf.ə.riː
umbelliferous ˌʌm.bᵊlˈɪf.ᵊr.əs, -belˈ-, (US) -bəˈlɪf-
umber ˈʌm.bəʳ, (US) -bɚ **-s** -z
Umberto ʊmˈbeə.təʊ, -ˈbɜː-, (US) -ˈber.toʊ
umbilical ʌmˈbɪl.ɪ.kᵊl; ˌʌm.bɪˈlaɪ-, -bəˈ-, (US) ʌmˈbɪl.ɪ-, ˈ-ə- umˌbilical ˈcord; ˌumbiˌlical ˈcord (US) umˈbilical ˌcord
umbilic|us ʌmˈbɪl.ɪ.k|əs, ˈ-ə-; ˌʌm.bɪˈlaɪ-, -bəˈ- **-uses** -ə.sɪz **-i** -aɪ
umbles ˈʌm.bᵊlz
um|bo ˈʌm|.bəʊ, (US) -boʊ **-bos** -bəʊz, (US) -boʊz **-bones** -ˈbəʊ.neɪz, (US) -ˈboʊ-
umbr|a ˈʌm.br|ə **-as** -əz **-ae** -iː **-al** -ᵊl
umbrage ˈʌm.brɪdʒ
umbrageous ʌmˈbreɪ.dʒəs **-ly** -li **-ness** -nəs, -nɪs
umbrella ʌmˈbrel.ə **-s** -z
Umbri|a ˈʌm.bri|.ə **-an/s** -ən/z
Umbro® ˈʌm.brəʊ, (US) -broʊ
umiak ˈuː.mi.æk, -mjæk **-s** -s
umlaut ˈʊm.laʊt **-s** -s
umpirag|e ˈʌm.paɪə.rɪdʒ **-es** -ɪz
umpir|e ˈʌm.paɪəʳ, -paɪ.əʳ, (US) -paɪ.ɚ **-es** -z **-ing** -ɪŋ **-ed** -d
umpteen ʌmpˈtiːn **-th** -θ *stress shift:* ˌumpteen ˈtimes
UN ˌjuːˈen
un- ʌn
Note: Prefix. It may be unstressed, usually when a stressed syllable follows it and it is a frequently used word, e.g. **unable** /ʌnˈeɪ.bᵊl/. Otherwise it will have secondary stress, e.g. **unadvisable** /ˌʌn.ədˈvaɪ.zə.bᵊl/. This syllable frequently becomes the main stress in the word through stress shift, e.g. **unattended** /ˌʌn.əˈten.dɪd/, **unattended parking** /ˌʌn.ə.ten.dɪdˈpɑː.kɪŋ/ (US) /-ˈpɑːr-/. There are so many such cases that individual examples are not given for each word.
'un ən **-s** -z

Note: Old-fashioned colloquial form for 'one', as in 'little 'un'.

Una ˈjuː.nə, ˈuː-
unabash|ed ˌʌn.əˈbæʃ|t **-edly** -ɪd.li
unabated ˌʌn.əˈbeɪ.tɪd, (US) -t̬ɪd **-ly** -li
unable ʌnˈeɪ.bᵊl, ˌʌn-
Unabomber ˈjuː.nəˌbɒm.əʳ, (US) -ˌbɑː.mɚ
unabridged ˌʌn.əˈbrɪdʒd
unaccented ˌʌn.əkˈsen.tɪd, -ækˈ-, (US) ʌnˈæk.sen.t̬ɪd
unacceptability ˌʌn.ək.sep.təˈbɪl.ə.ti, -ɪ.ti, (US) -ə.t̬i
unaccepta|ble ˌʌn.əkˈsep.tə|.bᵊl, -ækˈ- **-bly** -bli
unaccompanied ˌʌn.əˈkʌm.pə.nid, -ˈkʌmp.nid
unaccountability ˌʌn.əˌkaʊn.təˈbɪl.ɪ.ti, -ə.ti, (US) -t̬əˈbɪl.ə.t̬i
unaccountab|le ˌʌn.əˈkaʊn.tə.b|ᵊl, (US) -t̬ə- **-ly** -li **-leness** -ᵊl.nəs, -nɪs
unaccounted ˌʌn.əˈkaʊn.tɪd, (US) -t̬ɪd ˌunacˈcounted ˌfor
unaccustomed ˌʌn.əˈkʌs.təmd **-ly** -li

Pronouncing the letters UI

There are several pronunciation possibilities for the vowel digraph **ui**. The most common is likely to be /uː/, e.g.:

fruit   fruːt

A similar pronunciation is /juː/ in British English, realized as /uː/ in US English, e.g.:

nuisance   ˈnjuː.sᵊnts (US) ˈnuː-
suit   sjuːt, suːt (US) suːt

In addition

Other vowel sounds are associated with the digraph **ui**, e.g.:

wiː   suite /swiːt/
wɪ   linguist /ˈlɪŋ.gwɪst/
ɪ   build /bɪld/
aɪ   guide /gaɪd/
u.ɪ   fruition /fruˈɪʃ.ᵊn/
uː.ɪ   ruin /ˈruː.ɪn/

It should also be noted that **ui** may follow **q**, producing the sound /kwɪ/ or /kwaɪ/.

unacknowledged ˌʌn.əkˈnɒl.ɪdʒd, (US) -ˈnɑː.lɪdʒd
unacquainted ˌʌn.əˈkweɪn.tɪd, (US) -t̬ɪd
unadaptable ˌʌn.əˈdæp.tə.bᵊl
unaddressed ˌʌn.əˈdrest
unadopted ˌʌn.əˈdɒp.tɪd, (US) -ˈdɑːp-
unadorned ˌʌn.əˈdɔːnd, (US) -ˈdɔːrnd
unadulterated ˌʌn.əˈdʌl.tᵊr.eɪ.tɪd, (US) -tə.reɪ.t̬ɪd
unadvised ˌʌn.ədˈvaɪzd
unadvisedly ˌʌn.ədˈvaɪ.zɪd.li
unaffected ˌʌn.əˈfek.tɪd **-ly** -li **-ness** -nəs, -nɪs
unaffectionate ˌʌn.əˈfek.ʃᵊn.ət **-ly** -li
unafraid ˌʌn.əˈfreɪd
unaided ʌnˈeɪ.dɪd, ˌʌn-
unalienab|le ʌnˈeɪ.li.ə.nə.b|ᵊl, ˌʌn-, ˈ-ljə-, (US) -li.ə-, -ˈeɪl.jə- **-ly** -li
unaligned ˌʌn.əˈlaɪnd
unalloyed ˌʌn.əˈlɔɪd
unalterability ˌʌn.ɔːl.tᵊr.əˈbɪl.ɪ.ti, ʌnˌɔːl--, -ə.ti, (US) ˌʌn.ɑːl.tɚ.əˈbɪl.ə.t̬i, -ɔːl-
unalterab|le ʌnˈɔːl.tᵊr.ə.b|ᵊl, ˌʌn-, (US) -ˈɔːl.tɚ-, -ˈɑːl- **-ly** -li **-leness** -ᵊl.nəs, (US) -nɪs
unaltered ʌnˈɔːl.təd, ˌʌn-, (US) -tɚd, -ˈɑːl-
unambiguous ˌʌn.æmˈbɪg.ju.əs **-ly** -li **-ness** -nəs, -nɪs
unambivalent ˌʌn.æmˈbɪv.ᵊl.ənt **-ly** -li
un-American ˌʌn.əˈmer.ɪ.kən
unanalysab|le ˌʌn.æn.ᵊlˈaɪ.zə.b|ᵊl, ʌnˌæn-, -ˈæn.ᵊl.aɪ-, (US) ˌʌn.æn.əˈlaɪ-, -ˈæn.ə.laɪ- **-ly** -li **-leness** -ᵊl.nəs, -nɪs
unanimity ˌjuː.nəˈnɪm.ə.ti, -nænˈɪm-, -ɪ.ti, (US) -nəˈnɪm.ə.t̬i
unanimous juːˈnæn.ɪ.məs, ˈ-ə-, (US) ˈ-ə- **-ly** -li **-ness** -nəs, -nɪs, -nəs
unannounced ˌʌn.əˈnaʊntst
unanswerability ˌʌn.ɑːnt.sᵊr.əˈbɪl.ɪ.ti, ʌnˌɑnt.-, -ə.ti, (US) ˌʌn.ænt.sɚ.əˈbɪl.ə.t̬i
unanswerab|le ʌnˈɑːnt.sᵊr.ə.b|ᵊl, ˌʌn-, (US) -ˈænt- **-ly** -li
unanswered ʌnˈɑːnt.səd, ˌʌn-, (US) -ˈænt.sɚd
unappealing ˌʌn.əˈpiː.lɪŋ **-ly** -li
unappeasable ˌʌn.əˈpiː.zə.bᵊl
unappeased ˌʌn.əˈpiːzd
unappetizing, -ising ʌnˈæp.ɪ.taɪ.zɪŋ, ˌʌn-, ˈ-ə-, (US) ˈ-ə- **-ly** -li
unapplied ˌʌn.əˈplaɪd
unappreciated ˌʌn.əˈpriː.ʃi.eɪ.tɪd, (US) -t̬ɪd
unappreciative ˌʌn.əˈpriː.ʃi.ə.tɪv, (US) -t̬ɪv **-ly** -li
unapproachability ˌʌn.əˌprəʊ.tʃəˈbɪl.ɪ.ti, -ə.ti, (US) -ˌproʊ.tʃəˈbɪl.ə.t̬i
unapproachab|le ˌʌn.əˈprəʊ.tʃə.b|ᵊl, (US) -ˈproʊ- **-ly** -bli **-leness** -bᵊl.nəs, -nɪs
unappropriate ˌʌn.əˈprəʊ.pri.ət, (US) -ˈproʊ- **-ly** -li **-ness** -nəs, -nɪs
unappropriated ˌʌn.əˈprəʊ.pri.eɪ.tɪd, (US) -ˈproʊ.pri.eɪ.t̬ɪd
unapproved ˌʌn.əˈpruːvd
unapt ʌnˈæpt **-ly** -li **-ness** -nəs, -nɪs
unarguab|le ʌnˈɑː.gju.ə.b|ᵊl, (US) -ˈɑːr- **-ly** -li **-leness** -ᵊl.nəs, -nɪs
unarm ʌnˈɑːm, ˌʌn-, (US) -ˈɑːrm **-s** -z **-ing** -ɪŋ **-ed** -d ˌ**unarmed** ˈ**combat**
unarticulated ˌʌn.ɑːˈtɪk.jə.leɪ.tɪd, -jʊ-, (US) -ɑːrˈtɪk.jə.leɪ.t̬ɪd
unary ˈjuː.nᵊr.i
unasha|med ˌʌn.əˈʃeɪ|md **-medly** -mɪd.li **-medness** -mɪd.nəs, -nɪs
unasked ʌnˈɑːskt, ˌʌn-, (US) -ˈæskt
unaspirated ʌnˈæs.pᵊr.eɪ.tɪd, ˌʌn-, (US) -pə.reɪ.t̬ɪd
unassailability ˌʌn.əˌseɪ.ləˈbɪl.ɪ.ti, -ə.ti, (US) -ə.t̬i
unassailab|le ˌʌn.əˈseɪ.lə.b|ᵊl **-ly** -li **-leness** -ᵊl.nəs, -nɪs
unassertive ˌʌn.əˈsɜː.tɪv, (US) -ˈsɝː.t̬ɪv **-ly** -li **-ness** -nəs, -nɪs
unassigned ˌʌn.əˈsaɪnd
unassimilated ˌʌn.əˈsɪm.ᵊl.eɪ.tɪd, -ɪ.leɪ-, (US) -t̬ɪd
unassisted ˌʌn.əˈsɪs.tɪd
unassuageable ˌʌn.əˈsweɪ.dʒə.bᵊl
unassuming ˌʌn.əˈsjuː.mɪŋ, -ˈsuː-, (US) -ˈsuː- **-ly** -li **-ness** -nəs, -nɪs
unattached ˌʌn.əˈtætʃt
unattainab|le ˌʌn.əˈteɪ.nə.b|ᵊl **-ly** -li **-ness** -nəs, -nɪs
unattended ˌʌn.əˈten.dɪd
unattested ˌʌn.əˈtes.tɪd
unattractive ˌʌn.əˈtræk.tɪv **-ly** -li **-ness** -nəs, -nɪs
unauthenticated ˌʌn.ɔːˈθen.tɪ.keɪ.tɪd, (US) -ɑːˈθen.t̬ɪ.keɪ.t̬ɪd, -ɔːˈ-
unauthorized, -ised ʌnˈɔː.θᵊr.aɪzd, ˌʌn-, (US) -ˈɑː.θə.raɪzd, -ˈɔː-
unavailability ˌʌn.əˌveɪ.ləˈbɪl.ɪ.ti, -ə.ti, (US) -ə.t̬i
unavailable ˌʌn.əˈveɪ.lə.bᵊl
unavailing ˌʌn.əˈveɪ.lɪŋ **-ly** -li **-ness** -nəs, -nɪs
unavenged ˌʌn.əˈvendʒd
unavoidab|le ˌʌn.əˈvɔɪ.də.b|ᵊl **-ly** -li
unaware ˌʌn.əˈweəʳ, (US) -ˈwer **-s** -z **-ly** -li **-ness** -nəs, -nɪs
unbalanc|e ʌnˈbæl.ənts, ˌʌn-, ʌm-, ˌʌm-, (US) ʌn-, ˌʌn- **-es** -ɪz **-ing** -ɪŋ **-ed** -t
unbaptized ˌʌn.bæpˈtaɪzd, ˌʌm-, (US) ʌnˈbæp.taɪzd
unbar ʌnˈbɑːʳ, ˌʌn-, ʌm-, ˌʌm-, (US) ʌnˈbɑːr, ˌʌn- **-s** -z **-ring** -ɪŋ **-red** -d
unbearab|le ʌnˈbeə.rə.b|ᵊl, ˌʌn-, ʌm-, ˌʌm-, (US) ʌnˈber.ə-, ˌʌn- **-ly** -li **-leness** -ᵊl.nəs, -nɪs
unbeatab|le ʌnˈbiː.tə.b|ᵊl, ˌʌn-, ʌm-, ˌʌm-, (US) ʌnˈbiː.t̬ə-, ˌʌn- **-ly** -li
unbeaten ʌnˈbiː.tᵊn, ˌʌn-, ʌm-, ˌʌm-, (US) ʌn-, ˌʌn-
unbecoming ˌʌn.bɪˈkʌm.ɪŋ, ˌʌm-, -bəˈ-, (US) ˌʌn- **-ly** -li **-ness** -nəs, -nɪs
unbegotten ˌʌn.bɪˈgɒt.ᵊn, ˌʌm-, -bəˈ-, (US) ˌʌn.bɪˈgɑː.tᵊn, -bəˈ-
unbeknown ˌʌn.bɪˈnəʊn, ˌʌm-, -bəˈ-, (US) ˌʌn.bɪˈnoʊn, -bəˈ- **-st** -tst
unbelief ˌʌn.bɪˈliːf, ˌʌm-, -bəˈ-, (US) ˌʌn-
unbelievab|le ˌʌn.bɪˈliː.və.b|ᵊl, ˌʌm-, -bəˈ-, (US) ˌʌn- **-ly** -li
unbeliever ˌʌn.bɪˈliː.vəʳ, ˌʌm-, -bəˈ-, (US) ˌʌn.bɪˈliː.vɚ, -bəˈ- **-s** -z
unbelieving ˌʌn.bɪˈliː.vɪŋ, ˌʌm-, -bəˈ-, (US) ˌʌn- **-ly** -li
un|bend ʌnˈbend, ˌʌn-, ʌm-, ˌʌm-, (US) ʌn-, ˌʌn- **-bends** -ˈbendz **-bending** -ˈben.dɪŋ **-bended** -ˈben.dɪd **-bent** -ˈbent
unbeneficed ʌnˈben.ɪ.fɪst, ˌʌn-, ʌm-, ˌʌm-, (US) ʌn-, ˌʌn-
unbias(s)ed ʌnˈbaɪ.əst, ˌʌn-, ʌm-, ˌʌm-, (US) ʌn-, ˌʌn- **-ness** -nəs, -nɪs

nbidden ʌnˈbɪd.ən, ˌʌn-, ʌm-, ˌʌm-, ⓊⓈ ʌn-, ˌʌn-
n|bind ʌn|ˈbaɪnd, ˌʌn-, ʌm-, ˌʌm-, ⓊⓈ ʌn-, ˌʌn- **-binds** -ˈbaɪndz **-binding** -ˈbaɪn.dɪŋ **-bound** -ˈbaʊnd
nbleached ʌnˈbliːtʃt, ˌʌn-, ʌm-, ˌʌm-, ⓊⓈ ʌn-, ˌʌn-
nblemished ʌnˈblem.ɪʃt, ˌʌn-, ʌm-, ˌʌm-, ⓊⓈ ʌn-, ˌʌn-
nblinking ʌnˈblɪŋ.kɪŋ, ʌm-, ⓊⓈ ʌn- **-ly** -li **-ness** -nəs, -nɪs
nblock ʌnˈblɒk, ʌm-, ⓊⓈ ʌnˈblɑːk **-s** -s **-ing** -ɪŋ **-ed** -t **-er/s** -əʳ/z, ⓊⓈ -ɚ/z
nblushing ʌnˈblʌʃ.ɪŋ, ˌʌn-, ʌm-, ˌʌm-, ⓊⓈ ʌn-, ˌʌn- **-ly** -li
n|bolt ʌn|ˈbəʊlt, ˌʌn-, ʌm-, ˌʌm-, ⓊⓈ ʌn|ˈboʊlt, ˌʌn- **-bolts** -ˈbəʊlts, ⓊⓈ -ˈboʊlts **-bolting** -ˈbəʊl.tɪŋ, ⓊⓈ -ˈboʊl.tɪŋ **-bolted** -ˈbəʊl.tɪd, ⓊⓈ -ˈboʊl.tɪd
unborn ʌnˈbɔːn, ˈʌn-, ʌm-, ˌʌm-, ⓊⓈ ʌnˈbɔːrn, ˌʌn- ˌ**unborn ˈchild**
unbosom ʌnˈbʊz.əm, ˌʌn-, ʌm-, ˌʌm-, ⓊⓈ ʌn-, ˌʌn- **-s** -z **-ing** -ɪŋ **-ed** -d
unbound ʌnˈbaʊnd, ˌʌn-, ʌm-, ˌʌm-, ⓊⓈ ʌn-, ˌʌn-
unbounded ʌnˈbaʊn.dɪd, ˌʌn-, ʌm-, ˌʌm-, ⓊⓈ ʌn-, ˌʌn- **-ness** -nəs, -nɪs
unbowed ʌnˈbaʊd, ˌʌn-, ʌm-, ˌʌm-, ⓊⓈ ʌn-, ˌʌn-
unbreakable ʌnˈbreɪ.kə.bəl
unbridled ʌnˈbraɪ.dəld, ˌʌn-, ʌm-, ˌʌm-, ⓊⓈ ʌn-, ˌʌn-
unbroken ʌnˈbrəʊ.kən, ˌʌn-, ʌm-, ˌʌm-, ⓊⓈ ʌnˈbroʊ-, ˌʌn-
unbuckl|e ʌnˈbʌk.əl, ˌʌn-, ʌm-, ˌʌm-, ⓊⓈ ʌn-, ˌʌn- **-es** -z **-ing** -ɪŋ, -ˈbʌk.lɪŋ **-ed** -d
unbuilt ʌnˈbɪlt, ʌm-, ⓊⓈ ʌn-
unburden ʌnˈbɜː.dən, ˌʌn-, ʌm-, ˌʌm-, ⓊⓈ ʌnˈbɝː-, ˌʌn- **-s** -z **-ing** -ɪŋ **-ed** -d
unburied ʌnˈber.id, ˌʌn-, ʌm-, ˌʌm-, ⓊⓈ ʌn-, ˌʌn-
unbusiness-like ʌnˈbɪz.nɪs.laɪk, -nəs-, ˌʌn-, ʌm-, ˌʌm-, ⓊⓈ ʌn-, ˌʌn-
unbutton ʌnˈbʌt.ən, ˌʌn-, ʌm-, ˌʌm-, ⓊⓈ ʌn-, ˌʌn- **-s** -z **-ing** -ɪŋ, -ˈbʌt.nɪŋ **-ed** -d
uncalculat|ed ʌnˈkæl.kjə.leɪ.t|ɪd, ʌŋ-, -kjʊ-, ⓊⓈ ʌnˈkæl.kjə.leɪ.ţ|ɪd **-ing** -ɪŋ
uncalled-for ʌnˈkɔːld.fɔːʳ, ˌʌn-, ʌŋ-, ˌʌŋ-, ⓊⓈ ʌnˈkɔːld.fɔːr, ˌʌn-, -ˈkɑːld-
uncann|y ʌnˈkæn|.i, ˌʌn-, ʌŋ-, ˌʌŋ-, ⓊⓈ ʌn-, ˌʌn- **-ier** -i.əʳ, ⓊⓈ -i.ɚ **-iest** -i.ɪst, -i.əst **-ily** -əl.i, -ɪ.li **-iness** -ɪ.nəs, -ɪ.nɪs
uncanonical ˌʌn.kəˈnɒn.ɪ.kəl, ˌʌŋ-, ⓊⓈ ˌʌn.kəˈnɑː.nɪ-
uncap ʌnˈkæp, ˌʌn-, ʌŋ-, ˌʌŋ-, ⓊⓈ ʌn-, ˌʌn- **-s** -s **-ping** -ɪŋ **-ped** -t
uncared-for ʌnˈkeəd.fɔːʳ, ˌʌn-, ʌŋ-, ˌʌŋ-, ⓊⓈ ʌnˈkerd.fɔːr, ˌʌn-
uncaring ʌnˈkeə.rɪŋ, ʌŋ-, ⓊⓈ ʌn- **-ly** -li **-ness** -nəs, -nɪs
Uncas ˈʌŋ.kəs
uncatalog(u)ed ʌnˈkæt.əl.ɒgd, ˌʌn-, ʌŋ-, ˌʌŋ-, ⓊⓈ ʌnˈkæţ.əl.ɑːgd, ˌʌn-, -ɔːgd
unceasing ʌnˈsiː.sɪŋ, ˌʌn- **-ly** -li **-ness** -nəs, -nɪs
uncensored ʌnˈsent.səd, ˌʌn-, ⓊⓈ -sɚd
unceremonious ˌʌn.ser.ɪˈməʊ.ni.əs, ʌnˈser-, -əˈ-, ⓊⓈ -ˈmoʊ- **-ly** -li **-ness** -nəs, -nɪs
uncertain ʌnˈsɜː.tən, ˌʌn-, ⓊⓈ -ˈsɝː- **-ly** -li
uncertaint|y ʌnˈsɜː.tən.t|i, ˌʌn-, ⓊⓈ -ˈsɝː.tən.ţ|i **-ies** -iz
unchain ʌnˈtʃeɪn, ˌʌn- **-s** -z **-ing** -ɪŋ **-ed** -d
unchallenged ʌnˈtʃæl.ɪndʒd, ˌʌn-, -əndʒd
unchangeability ˌʌn.tʃeɪn.dʒəˈbɪl.ɪ.ti, ʌnˌtʃeɪn-, -ə.ti, ⓊⓈ -ə.ţi
unchangeab|le ʌnˈtʃeɪn.dʒə.b|əl, ˌʌn- **-ly** -li **-leness** -əl.nəs, -nɪs
unchanged ʌnˈtʃeɪndʒd, ˌʌn-
unchanging ʌnˈtʃeɪn.dʒɪŋ, ˌʌn-
uncharacteristic ˌʌn.kær.ək.təˈrɪs.tɪk, ʌnˈkær-, ˌʌŋ-, ⓊⓈ ˌʌn.ker.ɪk.təˈrɪs.tɪk, -kær- **-ally** -əl.i, -li
uncharged ʌnˈtʃɑːdʒd, ˌʌn-, ⓊⓈ -ˈtʃɑːrdʒd
uncharitab|le ʌnˈtʃær.ɪ.tə.b|əl, ˌʌn-, ˈ-ə-, ⓊⓈ -ˈtʃer.ə.ţə-, -ˈtʃær- **-ly** -li **-leness** -əl.nəs, -nɪs
uncharted ʌnˈtʃɑː.tɪd, ˌʌn-, ⓊⓈ -ˈtʃɑːr.ţɪd **unˌcharted ˈwaters**; ˌ**uncharted ˈwaters**
unchartered ʌnˈtʃɑː.təd, ˌʌn-, ⓊⓈ -ˈtʃɑːr.ţɚd
unchaste ʌnˈtʃeɪst, ⓊⓈ ˌʌn- **-ly** -li
unchastened ʌnˈtʃeɪ.sənd, ˌʌn-
unchecked ʌnˈtʃekt, ˌʌn-
unchivalrous ʌnˈʃɪv.əl.rəs **-ly** -li **-ness** -nəs, -nɪs
unchristian ʌnˈkrɪs.tʃən, ˌʌn-, ʌŋ-, ˌʌŋ-, -ˈkrɪʃ-, -ti.ən, ⓊⓈ ʌnˈkrɪs-, ˌʌn-
uncial ˈʌnt.si.əl, ⓊⓈ -ʃi-, ˈ-ʃəl **-s** -z
unciform ˈʌnt.sɪ.fɔːm, ⓊⓈ -fɔːrm
uncinate ˈʌn.sɪ.nət, -nɪt, -neɪt
uncircumcised ʌnˈsɜː.kəm.saɪzd, ˌʌn-, ⓊⓈ -ˈsɝː-
uncircumcision ˌʌn.sɜː.kəmˈsɪʒ.ən, ʌnˈsɜː-, ⓊⓈ -sɝː-
uncivil ʌnˈsɪv.əl, -ɪl, ˌʌn- **-ly** -i
uncivilized, -ised ʌnˈsɪv.əl.aɪzd, ˌʌn-, -ɪ.laɪzd
unclaimed ʌnˈkleɪmd, ˌʌn-, ʌŋ-, ˌʌŋ-, ⓊⓈ ʌn-, ˌʌn-
unclamp ʌnˈklæmp, ʌŋ-, ⓊⓈ ʌn- **-s** -s **-ing** -ɪŋ **-ed** -t
unclasp ʌnˈklɑːsp, ˌʌn-, ʌŋ-, ˌʌŋ-, ⓊⓈ ʌnˈklæsp, ˌʌn- **-s** -s **-ing** -ɪŋ **-ed** -t
unclassified ʌnˈklæs.ɪ.faɪd, ˌʌn-, ʌŋ-, ˌʌŋ-, ⓊⓈ ʌn-, ˌʌn-
uncle ˈʌŋ.kəl **-s** -z ˌ**Uncle ˈSam**; ˌ**Uncle ˈTom**
unclean ʌnˈkliːn, ˌʌn-, ʌŋ-, ˌʌŋ-, ⓊⓈ ʌn-, ˌʌn- **-ly** -li **-ness** -nəs, -nɪs
uncleanl|y ʌnˈklen.l|i, ˌʌn-, ʌŋ-, ˌʌŋ-, ⓊⓈ ʌn-, ˌʌn- **-iness** -ɪ.nəs, -ɪ.nɪs
unclear ʌnˈklɪəʳ, ˌʌn-, ʌŋ-, ˌʌŋ-, ⓊⓈ ʌnˈklɪr, ˌʌn-
unclench ʌnˈklentʃ, ˌʌn-, ʌŋ-, ˌʌŋ-, ⓊⓈ ʌnˈklentʃ, ˌʌn- **-es** -ɪz **-ing** -ɪŋ **-ed** -t
unclog ʌnˈklɒg, ʌŋ-, ⓊⓈ ʌnˈklɑːg, -ˈklɔːg **-s** -z **-ging** -ɪŋ **-ged** -d
unclos|e ʌnˈkləʊz, ˌʌn-, ʌŋ-, ˌʌŋ-, ⓊⓈ ʌnˈkloʊz, ˌʌn- **-es** -ɪz **-ing** -ɪŋ **-ed** -d
unclothed ʌnˈkləʊðd, ˌʌn-, ʌŋ-, ˌʌŋ-, ⓊⓈ ʌnˈkloʊðd, ˌʌn-
unclouded ʌnˈklaʊ.dɪd, ˌʌn-, ʌŋ-, ˌʌŋ-, ⓊⓈ ʌn-, ˌʌn-
uncluttered ʌnˈklʌt.əd, ˌʌn-, ʌŋ-, ˌʌŋ-, ⓊⓈ ʌnˈklʌţ.ɚd, ˌʌn-
uncoil ʌnˈkɔɪl, ˌʌn-, ʌŋ-, ˌʌŋ-, ⓊⓈ ʌn-, ˌʌn- **-s** -z **-ing** -ɪŋ **-ed** -d
uncollected ˌʌn.kəˈlek.tɪd, ˌʌŋ-, ⓊⓈ ˌʌn-
uncolo(u)red ʌnˈkʌl.əd, ˌʌn-, ʌŋ-, ˌʌŋ-, ⓊⓈ ʌnˈkʌl.ɚd, ˌʌn-
uncomfortab|le ʌnˈkʌmpf.tə.b|əl, ˌʌn-, ʌŋ-, ˌʌŋ-, -ˈkʌmp.fə.tə-, ⓊⓈ ʌnˈkʌmp.fɚ.ţə-, ˌʌn-, -ˈkʌmpf.tə- **-ly** -li **-leness** -əl.nəs, -nɪs
uncommercial ˌʌn.kəˈmɜː.ʃəl, ˌʌŋ-, ⓊⓈ ˌʌn.kəˈmɝː-
uncommercialized, -ised ˌʌn.kəˈmɜː.ʃəl.aɪzd, ˌʌŋ-, ⓊⓈ ˌʌn.kəˈmɝː-
uncommitted ˌʌn.kəˈmɪt.ɪd, ˌʌŋ-, ⓊⓈ ˌʌn.kəˈmɪţ-
uncommon ʌnˈkɒm.ən, ˌʌn-, ʌŋ-, ˌʌŋ-, ⓊⓈ ʌnˈkɑː.mən, ˌʌn- **-ly** -li **-ness** -nəs, -nɪs
uncommunicable ˌʌn.kəˈmjuː.nɪ.kə.bəl, ˌʌŋ-, -nə-, ⓊⓈ ˌʌn-
uncommunicated ˌʌn.kəˈmjuː.nɪ.keɪ.tɪd, ˌʌŋ-, -nə-, ⓊⓈ ˌʌn.kəˈmjuː.nɪ.keɪ.ţɪd, -nə-
uncommunicative ˌʌn.kəˈmjuː.nɪ.kə.tɪv, ˌʌŋ-, -nə-, -keɪ-, ⓊⓈ ˌʌn.kəˈmjuː.nɪ.kə.ţɪv, -nə-, -keɪ- **-ness** -nəs, -nɪs
uncompetitive ˌʌn.kəmˈpet.ɪ.tɪv, ˌʌŋ-, ˈ-ə-, ⓊⓈ ˌʌn.kəmˈpeţ.ə.ţɪv **-ly** -li **-ness** -nəs, -nɪs
uncomplaining ˌʌn.kəmˈpleɪ.nɪŋ, ˌʌŋ-, ⓊⓈ ˌʌn- **-ly** -li
uncompleted ˌʌn.kəmˈpliː.tɪd, ˌʌŋ-, ⓊⓈ ˌʌn.kəmˈpliː.ţɪd
uncomplicated ˌʌnˈkɒm.plɪ.keɪ.tɪd, ˌʌŋ-, ⓊⓈ ʌnˈkɑːm.plɪ.keɪ.ţɪd
uncomplimentary ˌʌn.kɒm.plɪˈmen.tər.i, ʌnˌkɒm-, ˌʌŋ-, ʌŋˌ-, -pləˈ-, ⓊⓈ ˌʌn.kɑːm.pləˈmen.ţɚ-, ʌnˌkɑːm-
uncompounded ˌʌn.kəmˈpaʊn.dɪd, ˌʌŋ-, ⓊⓈ ˌʌn-
uncomprehending ˌʌn.kɒm.prɪˈhen.dɪŋ, ˌʌŋ-, ⓊⓈ ˌʌn.kɑːm- **-ly** -li
uncompromising ʌnˈkɒm.prə.maɪ.zɪŋ, ˌʌn-, ʌŋ-, ˌʌŋ-, ⓊⓈ ʌnˈkɑːm-, ˌʌn- **-ly** -li **-ness** -nəs, -nɪs

U

unconcealed ˌʌn.kənˈsiːld, ˌʌŋ-, (US) ˌʌn-
unconcern ˌʌn.kənˈsɜːn, ˌʌŋ-, (US) ˌʌn.kənˈsɝːn **-ed** -d **-edly** -d.li, -ɪd.li **-edness** -d.nəs, -nɪs, -ɪd.nəs, -nɪs
unconditional ˌʌn.kənˈdɪʃ.ən.əl, ˌʌŋ-, ˈ-nəl, (US) ˌʌn- **-ly** -i ˌ**uncondiˌtional ˈoffer**
unconditioned ˌʌn.kənˈdɪʃ.ənd, ˌʌŋ-, (US) ˌʌn-
unconfined ˌʌn.kənˈfaɪnd, ˌʌŋ-, (US) ˌʌn-
unconfirmed ˌʌn.kənˈfɜːmd, ˌʌŋ-, (US) ˌʌn.kənˈfɝːmd
unconformit|y ˌʌn.kənˈfɔː.mə.t|i, ˌʌŋ-, -mɪ.t|i, (US) ˌʌn.kənˈfɔːr.mə.ţ|i **-ies** -iz
uncongenial ˌʌn.kənˈdʒiː.ni.əl, ˌʌŋ-, (US) ˌʌn-, -jəl
uncongeniality ˌʌn.kənˌdʒiː.niˈæl.ɪ.ti, ˌʌŋ-, -ə.ti, (US) ˌʌn.kənˌdʒiː.niˈæl.ə.ţi
unconnected ˌʌn.kəˈnek.tɪd, ˌʌŋ-, (US) ˌʌn- **-ness** -nəs, -nɪs
unconquerab|le ʌnˈkɒŋ.kər.ə.b|əl, ˌʌn-, ʌŋ-, ˌʌŋ-, (US) ʌnˈkɑːŋ-, ˌʌn- **-ly** -li
unconquered ʌnˈkɒŋ.kəd, ˌʌn-, ʌŋ-, ˌʌŋ-, (US) ʌnˈkɑːŋ.kɚd, ˌʌn-
unconscionab|le ʌnˈkɒn.tʃən.ə.b|əl, ˌʌn-, ʌŋ-, ˌʌŋ-, (US) ʌnˈkɑːn-, ˌʌn- **-ly** -li **-leness** -əl.nəs, -nɪs
unconscious ʌnˈkɒn.tʃəs, ˌʌn-, ʌŋ-, ˌʌŋ-, (US) ʌnˈkɑːn-, ˌʌn- **-ly** -li **-ness** -nəs, -nɪs
unconsecrated ʌnˈkɒnt.sɪ.kreɪ.tɪd, ˌʌn-, ʌŋ-, ˌʌŋ-, -sə-, (US) ʌnˈkɑːnt.sə.kreɪ.ţɪd, ˌʌn-
unconsidered ˌʌn.kənˈsɪd.əd, ˌʌŋ-, (US) ˌʌn.kənˈsɪd.ɚd
unconstitutional ˌʌn.kɒnt.stɪˈtʃuː.ʃən.əl, ʌnˌkɒn-, ʌŋ-, ˌʌŋ-, -stəˈ-, -ˈtjuː-, -ˈtʃuːʃ.nəl, -ˈtjuːʃ-, (US) ˌʌn.kɑːnt.stəˈtuː-, ʌnˌkɑːn-, -ˈtjuː- **-ly** -i
unconstrain|ed ˌʌn.kənˈstreɪn|d, ˌʌŋ-, (US) ˌʌn- **-edly** -d.li, -ɪd.li
uncontaminated ˌʌn.kənˈtæm.ɪ.neɪ.tɪd, ˌʌŋ-, ˈ-ə-, (US) ˌʌn.kənˈtæm.ɪ.neɪ.ţɪd, ˈ-ə-
uncontestable ˌʌn.kənˈtes.tə.bəl, ˌʌŋ-, (US) ˌʌn-
uncontested ˌʌn.kənˈtes.tɪd, ˌʌŋ-, (US) ˌʌn-
uncontradicted ˌʌn.kɒn.trəˈdɪk.tɪd, ʌnˌkɒn-, ˌʌŋ-, ʌŋ-, (US) ˌʌn.kɑːn-, ʌnˌkɑːn-
uncontrollab|le ˌʌn.kənˈtrəʊ.lə.b|əl, ˌʌŋ-, (US) ˌʌn.kənˈtroʊ- **-ly** -li **-leness** -əl.nəs, -nɪs
uncontrolled ˌʌn.kənˈtrəʊld, ˌʌŋ-, (US) ˌʌn.kənˈtroʊld
unconvention|al ˌʌn.kənˈven.tʃən|.əl, ˌʌŋ-, -ˈventʃ.n|əl, (US) ˌʌn.kənˈvent.ʃən|.əl, -ˈventʃ.n|əl **-ally** -əl.i
unconventionalit|y ˌʌn.kənˌven.tʃənˈæl.ə.t|i, ˌʌŋ-, -ɪ.t|i, (US) ˌʌn.kənˌven.tʃənˈæl.ə.ţ|i **-ies** -iz
unconverted ˌʌn.kənˈvɜː.tɪd, ˌʌŋ-, (US) ˌʌn.kənˈvɝː.ţɪd
unconvertible ˌʌn.kənˈvɜː.tə.bəl, ˌʌŋ-, -tɪ-, (US) ˌʌn.kənˈvɝː.ţə-
unconvinced ˌʌn.kənˈvɪntst, ˌʌŋ-, (US) ˌʌn-
unconvincing ˌʌn.kənˈvɪnt.sɪŋ, ˌʌŋ-, (US) ˌʌn- **-ly** -li
uncooked ʌnˈkʊkt, ˌʌn-, ʌŋ-, ˌʌŋ-, (US) ʌn-, ˌʌn-
uncool ʌnˈkuːl, ˌʌn-, ʌŋ-, (US) ʌn-, ˌʌn- **-ly** -li **-ness** -nəs, -nɪs
uncooperative ˌʌn.kəʊˈɒp.ər.ə.tɪv, ˌʌŋ-, ˈ-rə-, (US) ˌʌn.koʊˈɑː.pɚ.ə.ţɪv, ˈ-prə- **-ly** -li **-ness** -nəs, -nɪs
uncoordinated ˌʌn.kəʊˈɔː.dɪ.neɪ.tɪd, ˌʌŋ-, (US) ˌʌn.koʊˈɔːr.dən.eɪ.ţɪd
uncork ʌnˈkɔːk, ˌʌn-, ʌŋ-, ˌʌŋ-, (US) ʌnˈkɔːrk, ˌʌn- **-s** -s **-ing** -ɪŋ **-ed** -t
uncorrected ˌʌn.kərˈek.tɪd, ˌʌŋ-, (US) ˌʌn.kəˈrek-
uncorroborated ˌʌn.kərˈɒb.ər.eɪ.tɪd, ˌʌŋ-, (US) ˌʌn.kəˈrɑː.bə.reɪ.ţɪd
uncorrupt ˌʌn.kərˈʌpt, ˌʌŋ-, (US) ˌʌn.kəˈrʌpt **-ness** -nəs, -nɪs
uncorrupted ˌʌn.kərˈʌp.tɪd, ˌʌŋ-, (US) ˌʌn.kəˈrʌp-
uncountable ʌnˈkaʊn.tə.bəl, ˌʌn-, ʌŋ-, ˌʌŋ-, (US) ʌnˈkaʊn.ţə-, ˌʌn- **unˌcountable ˈnoun**
uncounted ʌnˈkaʊn.tɪd, ˌʌn-, ʌŋ-, ˌʌŋ-, (US) ʌnˈkaʊn.ţɪd, ˌʌn-
uncoupl|e ʌnˈkʌp.əl, ˌʌn-, ʌŋ-, ˌʌŋ-, (US) ʌn-, ˌʌn- **-es** -z **-ing** -ɪŋ, -ˈkʌp.lɪŋ **-ed** -d
uncouth ʌnˈkuːθ, ˌʌn-, ʌŋ-, ˌʌŋ-, (US) ʌn-, ˌʌn- **-ly** -li **-ness** -nəs, -nɪs
uncov|er ʌnˈkʌv|.əʳ, ˌʌn-, ʌŋ-, ˌʌŋ-, (US) ʌnˈkʌv|.ɚ, ˌʌn- **-ers** -əz, (US) -ɚz **-ering** -ər.ɪŋ **-ered** -əd, (US) -ɚd
uncritic|al ʌnˈkrɪt.ɪ.k|əl, ˌʌn-, ʌŋ-, ˌʌŋ-, (US) ʌnˈkrɪţ.ɪ-, ˌʌn- **-ally** -əl.i, -li
uncrossed ʌnˈkrɒst, ˌʌn-, ʌŋ-, ˌʌŋ-, (US) ʌnˈkrɑːst, ˌʌn-
uncrowned ʌnˈkraʊnd, ˌʌn-, ʌŋ-, ˌʌŋ-, (US) ʌn-, ˌʌn- *stress shift, see compounds:* ˌ**uncrowned ˈking;** ˌ**uncrowned ˈqueen**
uncrushable ʌnˈkrʌʃ.ə.bəl, ˌʌn-, ʌŋ-, ˌʌŋ-, (US) ʌn-, ˌʌn-
unction ˈʌŋk.ʃən **-s** -z
unctuosity ˌʌŋk.tʃuˈɒs.ə.ti, -tjuˈ-, -ɪ.ti, (US) -tʃuˈɑː.sə.ţi
unctuous ˈʌŋk.tʃu.əs, -tju-, (US) -tʃu-, ˈ-tʃəs **-ly** -li **-ness** -nəs, -nɪs
uncultivated ʌnˈkʌl.tɪ.veɪ.tɪd, ˌʌn-, ʌŋ-, ˌʌŋ-, -tə-, (US) ʌnˈkʌl.tə.veɪ.ţɪd, ˌʌn-
uncultured ʌnˈkʌl.tʃəd, ˌʌn-, ʌŋ-, ˌʌŋ-, (US) ʌnˈkʌl.tʃɚd, ˌʌn-
uncurbed ʌnˈkɜːbd, ˌʌn-, ʌŋ-, ˌʌŋ-, (US) ʌnˈkɝːbd, ˌʌn-
uncurl ʌnˈkɜːl, ˌʌn-, ʌŋ-, ˌʌŋ-, (US) ʌnˈkɝːl, ˌʌn- **-s** -z **-ing** -ɪŋ **-ed** -d
uncut ʌnˈkʌt, ˌʌn-, ʌŋ-, ˌʌŋ-, (US) ʌn-, ˌʌn-
undamaged ʌnˈdæm.ɪdʒd, ˌʌn-
undated *wavy:* ˈʌn.deɪ.tɪd, (US) -ţɪd *not dated:* ʌnˈdeɪ.tɪd, ˌʌn-, (US) -ţɪd
undaunted ʌnˈdɔːn.tɪd, ˌʌn-, (US) -ˈdɑːn.ţɪd, -ˈdɔːn- **-ly** -li **-ness** -nəs, -nɪs
undebated ˌʌn.dɪˈbeɪ.tɪd, -dəˈ-, (US) -ţɪd
undeceiv|e ˌʌn.dɪˈsiːv, -dəˈ- **-es** -z **-ing** -ɪŋ **-ed** -d
undecided ˌʌn.dɪˈsaɪ.dɪd, -dəˈ- **-ly** -li **-ness** -nəs, -nɪs
undecipherab|le ˌʌn.dɪˈsaɪ.fər.ə.b|əl, -dəˈ- **-ly** -li
undecisive ˌʌn.dɪˈsaɪ.sɪv, -dəˈ-, -zɪv, (US) -sɪv **-ly** -li **-ness** -nəs, -nɪs
undeclared ˌʌn.dɪˈkleəd, -dəˈ-, (US) -ˈklerd
undefeated ˌʌn.dɪˈfiː.tɪd, -dəˈ-, (US) -dɪˈfiː.ţɪd
undefended ˌʌn.dɪˈfen.dɪd, -dəˈ-
undefiled ˌʌn.dɪˈfaɪld, -dəˈ-
undefinab|le ˌʌn.dɪˈfaɪ.nə.b|əl, -dəˈ- **-ly** -li
undefined ˌʌn.dɪˈfaɪnd, -dəˈ-
unde|lete ˌʌn.dɪ|ˈliːt, -dəˈ-, (US) -dɪˈ- **-letes** -ˈliːts **-leting** -ˈliː.tɪŋ, (US) -ˈliː.ţɪŋ **-leted** -ˈliː.tɪd, (US) -ˈliː.ţɪd
undelivered ˌʌn.dɪˈlɪv.əd, -dəˈ-, (US) -ɚd
undemanding ˌʌn.dɪˈmɑːn.dɪŋ, -dəˈ-, (US) -dɪˈmæn-
undemocratic ˌʌn.dem.əˈkræt.ɪk, (US) -ˈkræţ- **-ally** -əl.i, -li
undemonstrative ˌʌn.dɪˈmɒnt.strə.tɪv, -dəˈ-, (US) -ˈmɑːnt.strə.ţɪv **-ly** -li **-ness** -nəs, -nɪs
undeniab|le ˌʌn.dɪˈnaɪ.ə.b|əl, -dəˈ- **-ly** -li
undenominational ˌʌn.dɪˌnɒm.ɪˈneɪ.ʃən.əl, -dəˌ-, -əˈ-, -ˈneɪʃ.nəl, (US) -ˌnɑː.mɪˈ-, -məˈ- **-ism** -ɪ.zəm
under ˈʌn.dəʳ, (US) -dɚ **-s** -z ˌ**under ˈway**
under- ˈʌn.dəʳ, (US) ˈʌn.dɚ
Note: Prefix. May receive primary stress, e.g. **undercarriage** /ˈʌn.dəˌkær.ɪdʒ/ (US) /ˈʌn.dɚ.ker-/, or secondary stress, e.g. **understand** /ˌʌn.dəˈstænd/ (US) /-dɚˈ-/. Such secondary-stressed syllables may come to carry the strongest stress in the word through stress shift, e.g. **understand** /ˌʌn.dəˈstænd/ (US) /ˌʌn.dɚ-/, **understand problems** /ˌʌn.də.stændˈprɒb.ləmz/ (US) /ˌʌn.dɚ.stændˈprɑː.bləmz/. Although /r/ is normally assigned to a following strong syllable in American English, when /ɚ/ is perceived to be morphemically linked to the preceding unit /r/ is retained as /ɚ/.
underachiev|e ˌʌn.dər.əˈtʃiːv, (US) -dɚ- **-es** -z **-ing** -ɪŋ **-ed** -d **-er/s** -əʳ/z, (US) -ɚ/z **-ment/s** -mənt/s
underact ˌʌn.dərˈækt, (US) -dɚˈ- **-s** -s **-ing** -ɪŋ **-ed** -ɪd

under-age ˌʌn.dᵊrˈeɪdʒ, (US) -dɚˈ- *stress shift:* ˌ**under-age** ˈ**drinking**
underarm ˈʌn.dᵊr.ɑːm, (US) -dɚ.ɑːrm
underbell|y ˈʌn.dəˌbel|.i, (US) -dɚˌ- **-ies** -iz
underbid ˌʌn.dəˈbɪd, (US) -dɚˈ- **-s** -z **-ding** -ɪŋ **-der/s** -əʳ/z, (US) -ɚ/z
underbred ˌʌn.dəˈbred, (US) -dɚˈ- *stress shift:* ˌ**underbred** ˈ**stock**
underbrush ˈʌn.də.brʌʃ, (US) -dɚ-
underbudgeted ˌʌn.dəˈbʌdʒ.ɪ.tɪd, ˈ-ə-, (US) -dɚˈbʌdʒ.ɪ.t̬ɪd
under|buy ˌʌn.də|ˈbaɪ, (US) -dɚˈ- **-buys** -ˈbaɪz **-buying** -ˈbaɪ.ɪŋ **-bought** -ˈbɔːt, (US) -ˈbɑːt, -ˈbɔːt
undercapitaliz|e, -is|e ˌʌn.dəˈkæp.ɪ.tᵊl.aɪz, (US) -dɚˈ- **-es** -ɪz **-ing** -ɪŋ **-ed** -d
undercard ˈʌn.də.kɑːd, (US) -dɚ.kɑːrd **-s** -z
undercarriag|e ˈʌn.dəˌkær.ɪdʒ, (US) -dɚˌker-, -ˌkær- **-es** -ɪz
undercharg|e n ˈʌn.dəˌtʃɑːdʒ, ˌ--ˈ-, (US) ˈʌn.dɚ.tʃɑːrdʒ **-es** -ɪz
undercharg|e v ˌʌn.dəˈtʃɑːdʒ, (US) -dɚˈtʃɑːrdʒ **-es** -ɪz **-ing** -ɪŋ **-ed** -d
underclass ˈʌn.də.klɑːs, (US) -dɚ.klæs **-es** -ɪz
under-clerk ˈʌn.də.klɑːk, (US) -dɚ.klɝːk **-s** -s
underclothes ˈʌn.də.kləʊðz, (US) -dɚ.kloʊðz, -kloʊz
underclothing ˈʌn.dəˌkləʊ.ðɪŋ, (US) -dɚˌkloʊ-
undercoat ˈʌn.də.kəʊt, (US) -dɚ.koʊt **-s** -s **-ing** -ɪŋ
undercook ˌʌn.dəˈkʊk, (US) -dɚˈ- **-s** -s **-ing** -ɪŋ **-ed** -t
undercover ˌʌn.dəˈkʌv.əʳ, (US) -dɚˈkʌv.ɚ *stress shift:* ˌ**undercover** ˈ**agent**
undercroft ˈʌn.də.krɒft, (US) -dɚ.krɑːft **-s** -s
undercurrent ˈʌn.dəˌkʌr.ᵊnt, (US) -dɚˌkɝː- **-s** -s
undercut n ˈʌn.də.kʌt, (US) -dɚ- **-s** -s
under|cut adj, v ˌʌn.də|ˈkʌt, (US) -dɚˈ- **-cuts** -ˈkʌts **-cutting** -ˈkʌt.ɪŋ, (US) -ˈkʌt̬.ɪŋ
underdevelop|ed ˌʌn.də.dɪˈvel.əp|t, -dəˈ-, (US) -dɚ- **-ment** -mənt *stress shift:* ˌ**under-developed** ˈ**brain**
under|do ˌʌn.də|ˈduː, (US) -dɚˈ- **-does** -ˈdʌz **-doing** -ˈduːɪŋ **-did** -ˈdɪd **-done** -ˈdʌn
underdog ˈʌn.də.dɒg, (US) -dɚ.dɑːg, -dɔːg **-s** -z
underdone ˌʌn.dəˈdʌn, (US) -dɚˈ- *stress shift:* ˌ**underdone** ˈ**beef**
underdress ˌʌn.dəˈdres, (US) -dɚˈ- **-es** -ɪz **-ing** -ɪŋ **-ed** -t
undereducated ˌʌn.dᵊrˈedʒ.ʊ.keɪ.tɪd, -ˈed.jʊ-, (US) -dɚˈedʒ.ʊ.keɪ.t̬ɪd, ˈ-ə-
undereducation ˌʌn.dᵊrˌedʒ.ʊˈkeɪ.ʃᵊn, -ˌed.jʊ-, (US) -dɚˌedʒ.ʊ-, -əˈ-
underemployed ˌʌn.dᵊr.ɪmˈplɔɪd, -emˈ-, (US) -dɚ- *stress shift:* ˌ**under-employed** ˈ**workforce**
underemployment ˌʌn.dᵊr.ɪmˈplɔɪ.mənt, (US) -dɚ-
underestimate n ˌʌn.dᵊrˈes.tɪ.mət, -tə-, -mɪt, -meɪt, (US) -dɚˈes.tə.mɪt, -mət **-s** -s
underesti|mate v ˌʌn.dᵊrˈes.tɪ|.meɪt, -tə-, (US) -dɚˈes.tə- **-mates** -meɪts **-mating** -meɪ.tɪŋ, (US) -meɪ.t̬ɪŋ **-mated** -meɪ.tɪd, (US) -meɪ.t̬ɪd
underestimation ˌʌn.dᵊrˌes.tɪˈmeɪ.ʃᵊn, -təˈ-, (US) -dɚˌes.təˈ- **-s** -z
under-expos|e ˌʌn.dᵊr.ɪkˈspəʊz, -ekˈ-, (US) -dɚ.ɪkˈspoʊz, -ekˈ- **-es** -ɪz **-ing** -ɪŋ **-ed** -d
underexposure ˌʌn.dᵊr.ɪkˈspəʊ.ʒəʳ, -ekˈ-, (US) -dɚ.ɪkˈspoʊ.ʒɚ, -ekˈ- **-s** -z
under-eye ˈʌn.dᵊr.aɪ
under|feed ˌʌn.də|ˈfiːd, (US) -dɚˈ- **-feeds** -ˈfiːdz **-feeding** -ˈfiː.dɪŋ **-fed** -ˈfed *stress shift:* ˌ**underfed** ˈ**chickens**
underfelt ˈʌn.də.felt, (US) -dɚ- **-s** -s
underfinanced ˌʌn.dəˈfaɪ.næntst, (US) -dɚˈ-
underfloor ˌʌn.dəˈflɔːʳ, (US) -dɚˈflɔːr *stress shift:* ˌ**underfloor** ˈ**heating**
underfoot ˌʌn.dəˈfʊt, (US) -dɚˈ-
underfund ˌʌn.dəˈfʌnd, (US) -dɚˈ- **-s** -z **-ing** -ɪŋ **-ed** -ɪd
undergarment ˈʌn.dəˌgɑː.mənt, (US) -dɚˌgɑːr- **-s** -s
under|go ˌʌn.də|ˈgəʊ, (US) -dɚ|ˈgoʊ **-goes** -ˈgəʊz, (US) -ˈgoʊz **-going** -ˈgəʊ.ɪŋ, (US) -ˈgoʊ.ɪŋ **-went** -ˈwent **-gone** -ˈgɒn, (US) -ˈgɑːn *stress shift:* ˌ**undergo** ˈ**treatment**
undergrad ˈʌn.də.græd, (US) -dɚ- **-s** -z
undergraduate ˌʌn.dəˈgrædʒ.u.ət, -ˈgræd.ju-, -ɪt, (US) -dɚˈgrædʒ.u.ət, -ə.wət **-s** -s *stress shift:* ˌ**undergraduate** ˈ**humour**
underground, U~ n, adj ˈʌn.də.graʊnd, (US) -dɚ- **-er/s** -əʳ/z, (US) -ɚ/z
underground adv ˌʌn.dəˈgraʊnd, (US) -dɚˈ-
undergrown ˌʌn.dəˈgrəʊn, (US) -dɚˈgroʊn *stress shift:* ˌ**undergrown** ˈ**trees**
undergrowth ˈʌn.də.grəʊθ, (US) -dɚ.groʊθ
underhand ˌʌn.dəˈhænd, (US) -dɚˈ- **-ed/ly** -ɪd/li **-edness** -ɪd.nəs, -nɪs *stress shift:* ˌ**underhand** ˈ**trick**
Underhill ˈʌn.də.hɪl, (US) -dɚ-
underhung ˌʌn.dəˈhʌŋ, (US) -dɚˈ- *stress shift:* ˌ**underhung** ˈ**axle**
underinsured ˌʌn.dᵊr.ɪnˈʃʊəd, -ˈʃɔːd, (US) -dɚ.ɪnˈʃʊrd
underlay n ˈʌn.dᵊl.eɪ, (US) -dɚ.leɪ **-s** -z
under|lay v ˌʌn.də|ˈleɪ, (US) -dɚˈ- **-lays** -ˈleɪz **-laying** -ˈleɪ.ɪŋ **-laid** -ˈleɪd
under|let ˌʌn.də|ˈlet, (US) -dɚˈ- **-lets** -ˈlets **-letting** -ˈlet.ɪŋ, (US) -ˈlet̬.ɪŋ
under|lie ˌʌn.də|ˈlaɪ, (US) -dɚˈ- **-lies** -ˈlaɪz **-lying** -ˈlaɪ.ɪŋ **-lay** -ˈleɪ **-lain** -ˈleɪn
underline n ˈʌn.dᵊl.aɪn, (US) ˈʌn.dɚ.laɪn **-s** -z
underlin|e v ˌʌn.dəˈlaɪn, (US) -dɚˈ-, ˈ--- **-es** -z **-ing** -ɪŋ **-ed** -d
underling ˈʌn.dᵊl.ɪŋ, (US) -dɚ.lɪŋ **-s** -z
underlip ˈʌn.dᵊl.ɪp, (US) -dɚ.lɪp **-s** -s
underlying ˌʌn.dəˈlaɪ.ɪŋ, (US) -dɚˈ-, ˈʌn.dɚˌlaɪ.ɪŋ *stress shift, British only:* ˌ**underlying** ˈ**cause**
underman ˌʌn.dəˈmæn, (US) -dɚˈ- **-s** -z **-ning** -ɪŋ **-ned** -d *stress shift:* ˌ**undermanned** ˈ**industry**
undermentioned ˌʌn.dəˈmen.tʃᵊnd, (US) -dɚˈ- *stress shift:* ˌ**undermentioned** ˈ**clause**
undermin|e ˌʌn.dəˈmaɪn, (US) -dɚˈ-, ˈ--- **-es** -z **-ing** -ɪŋ **-ed** -d **-er/s** -əʳ/z, (US) -ɚ/z *stress shift, British only:* ˌ**undermine** ˈ**confidence**
undermost ˈʌn.də.məʊst, (US) -dɚ.moʊst
underneath ˌʌn.dəˈniːθ, (US) -dɚˈ- *stress shift:* ˌ**underneath** ˈ**every-thing**
undernourish ˌʌn.dəˈnʌr.ɪʃ, (US) -dɚˈnɝː- **-es** -ɪz **-ing** -ɪŋ **-ed** -t **-ment** -mənt
underpants ˈʌn.də.pænts, (US) -dɚ-
underpass ˈʌn.də.pɑːs, (US) -dɚ.pæs **-es** -ɪz
under|pay ˌʌn.də|ˈpeɪ, (US) -dɚˈ- **-pays** -ˈpeɪz **-paying** -ˈpeɪ.ɪŋ **-paid** -ˈpeɪd *stress shift:* ˌ**underpaid** ˈ**staff**
underpayment ˌʌn.dəˈpeɪ.mənt, (US) -dɚˈ- **-s** -s
underperform ˌʌn.də.pəˈfɔːm, (US) -dɚ.pɚˈfɔːrm **-s** -z **-ing** -ɪŋ **-ed** -d **-er/s** -əʳ/z, (US) -ɚ/z *stress shift:* ˌ**underperforming** ˈ**worker**
underpin ˌʌn.dəˈpɪn, (US) -dɚˈ-, ˈ--- **-s** -z **-ning** -ɪŋ **-ned** -d
underpinning ˈʌn.dəˌpɪn.ɪŋ, (US) -dɚˌ- **-s** -z
underplay ˌʌn.dəˈpleɪ, (US) -dɚˈ-, ˈ--- **-s** -z **-ing** -ɪŋ **-ed** -d
underpopulated ˌʌn.dəˈpɒp.jə.leɪ.tɪd, -ˈpɒ.pjʊ-, (US) -dɚˈpɑː.pjə.leɪ.t̬ɪd, ˈ-pjʊ-
underpri|ce ˌʌn.dəˈpraɪ|s, (US) -dɚˈ- **-ces** -sɪz **-ced** -st **-cing** -sɪŋ
underprivileged ˌʌn.dəˈprɪv.ᵊl.ɪdʒd, -vɪ.lɪdʒd, (US) -dɚˈprɪv.ᵊl.ɪdʒd, ˈ-lɪdʒd
underproduc|e ˌʌn.də.prəˈdʒuːs, -ˈdjuːs, (US) -dɚ.prəˈduːs, -ˈdjuːs **-es** -ɪz **-ing** -ɪŋ **-ed** -t
underproduction ˌʌn.də.prəˈdʌk.ʃᵊn, (US) -dɚ-
underprop ˌʌn.dəˈprɒp, (US) -dɚˈprɑːp **-s** -s **-ping** -ɪŋ **-ped** -t
under|rate ˌʌn.də|ˈreɪt, (US) -dɚˈ- **-rates** -ˈreɪts **-rating** -ˈreɪ.tɪŋ, (US) -ˈreɪ.t̬ɪŋ **-rated** -ˈreɪ.tɪd, (US) -ˈreɪ.t̬ɪd

U

underrepresentation ˌʌn.dəˌrep.rɪ.zenˈteɪ.ʃən, (US) -dɚˌrep- **-s** -z

underrepresented ˌʌn.dəˌrep.rɪˈzen.tɪd, -rəˈ-, (US) -dɚˌrep.rɪˈzen.t̬ɪd

underripe ˌʌn.dəˈraɪp, (US) -dɚˈ- *stress shift:* ˌ**underripe** ˈ**fruit**

under|run ˌʌn.də|ˈrʌn, (US) -dɚˈ- **-runs** -ˈrʌnz **-running** -ˈrʌn.ɪŋ **-ran** -ˈræn

underscore **n** ˈʌn.də.skɔːʳ, (US) -dɚ.skɔːr **-s** -z

underscor|e **v** ˌʌn.dəˈskɔːʳ, (US) -dɚˈskɔːr, ˈ--- **-es** -z **-ing** -ɪŋ **-ed** -d

undersea ˌʌn.dəˈsiː, (US) -dɚˈ- **-s** -z *stress shift:* ˌ**undersea** ˈ**cable**

underseal ˈʌn.də.siːl, (US) -dɚ- **-s** -z **-ing** -ɪŋ **-ed** -d

undersecretar|y ˌʌn.dəˈsek.rə.tər|.i, -rɪ-, -tr|i, (US) -dɚˈsek.rə.ter|- **-ies** -iz **-yship/s** -i.ʃɪp/s

under|sell ˌʌn.də|ˈsel, (US) -dɚˈ- **-sells** -ˈselz **-selling** -ˈsel.ɪŋ **-sold** -ˈsəʊld, (US) -ˈsoʊld

undersexed ˌʌn.dəˈsekst, (US) -dɚˈ-

Undershaft ˈʌn.də.ʃɑːft, (US) -dɚ.ʃæft

undersheriff ˈʌn.dəˌʃer.ɪf, (US) -dɚˌ- **-s** -s

undershirt ˈʌn.də.ʃɜːt, (US) -dɚ.ʃɝːt **-s** -s

undershoot **n** ˈʌn.də.ʃuːt, ˌ--ˈ-, (US) ˈʌn.dɚ.ʃuːt, ˌ--ˈ- **-s** -s

under|shoot **v** ˌʌn.də|ˈʃuːt, (US) -dɚˈ- **-shoots** -ˈʃuːts **-shooting** -ˈʃuː.tɪŋ, (US) -ˈʃuː.t̬ɪŋ **-shot** -ˈʃɒt, (US) -ˈʃɑːt

undershorts ˈʌn.də.ʃɔːts, (US) -dɚˈʃɔːrts

undershot **adj** ˌʌn.dəˈʃɒt, (US) -dɚˈʃɑːt *stress shift:* ˌ**undershot** ˈ**wheel**

undershot (from **undershoot**) ˌʌn.dəˈʃɒt, (US) -dɚˈʃɑːt

underside ˈʌn.də.saɪd, (US) -dɚ- **-s** -z

undersigned ˈʌn.də.saɪnd, ˌ--ˈ-, (US) ˈʌn.dɚ.saɪnd

undersized ˌʌn.dəˈsaɪzd, (US) ˈʌn.dɚ.saɪzd *stress shift, British only:* ˌ**undersized** ˈ**belt**

underskirt ˈʌn.də.skɜːt, (US) -dɚ.skɝːt **-s** -s

underspend ˌʌn.dəˈspend, (US) -dɚˈ- **-s** -z **-ing** -ɪŋ **underspent** ˌʌn.dəˈspent, (US) -dɚˈ-

understaffed ˌʌn.dəˈstɑːft, (US) -dɚˈstæft *stress shift:* ˌ**understaffed** ˈ**school**

under|stand ˌʌn.də|ˈstænd, (US) -dɚˈ- **-stands** -ˈstændz **-standing** -ˈstæn.dɪŋ **-stood** -ˈstʊd

understandab|le ˌʌn.dəˈstæn.də.b|əl, (US) -dɚˈ- **-ly** -li

under|state ˌʌn.də|ˈsteɪt, (US) -dɚˈ- **-states** -ˈsteɪts **-stating** -ˈsteɪ.tɪŋ, (US) -ˈsteɪ.t̬ɪŋ **-stated** -ˈsteɪ.tɪd, (US) -ˈsteɪ.t̬ɪd

understatement ˌʌn.dəˈsteɪt.mənt, ˈʌn.dəˌsteɪt-, (US) ˌʌn.dɚˈsteɪt-, ˈʌn.dɚˌsteɪt- **-s** -s

understocked ˌʌn.dəˈstɒkt, (US) -dɚˈstɑːkt *stress shift:* ˌ**understocked** ˈ**shelves**

understood (from **understand**) ˌʌn.dəˈstʊd, (US) -dɚˈ- *stress shift:* ˌ**understood** ˈ**plan**

understrapper ˈʌn.dəˌstræp.əʳ, (US) -dɚˌstræp.ɚ **-s** -z

understud|y ˈʌn.dəˌstʌd|.i, (US) -dɚˌ- **-ies** -iz **-ying** -i.ɪŋ **-ied** -id

undersubscrib|e ˌʌn.də.səbˈskraɪb, (US) -dɚ- **-es** -z **-ing** -ɪŋ **-ed** -d

under|take ˌʌn.də|ˈteɪk, (US) -dɚˈ- **-takes** -ˈteɪks **-taking** -ˈteɪ.kɪŋ **-took** -ˈtʊk **-taken** -ˈteɪ.kən, -kəŋ, (US) -kən

undertaker *person who agrees to do something:* ˌʌn.dəˈteɪ.kəʳ, (US) -dɚˈteɪ.kɚ *person who arranges funerals:* ˈʌn.dəˌteɪ.kəʳ, (US) -dɚˌteɪ.kɚ **-s** -z

undertaking *enterprise, promise:* ˌʌn.dəˈteɪ.kɪŋ, ˈʌn.dəˌteɪ-, (US) ˌʌn.dɚˈteɪ-, ˈʌn.dɚˌteɪ- **-s** -z *arranging funerals:* ˈʌn.dəˌteɪ.kɪŋ, (US) -dɚˌ-

under-the-counter ˌʌn.də.ðəˈkaʊn.təʳ, (US) -dɚ.ðəˈkaʊn.t̬ɚ *stress shift:* ˌ**under-the-counter** ˈ**deal**

underthings ˈʌn.də.θɪŋz, (US) -dɚ-

undertint ˈʌn.də.tɪnt, (US) -dɚ- **-s** -s

undertone ˈʌn.də.təʊn, (US) -dɚ.toʊn **-s** -z

undertook (from **undertake**) ˌʌn.dəˈtʊk, (US) -dɚˈ-

undertow ˈʌn.də.təʊ, (US) -dɚ.toʊ **-s** -z

underused ˌʌn.dəˈjuːzd, (US) -dɚˈ- *stress shift:* ˌ**underused** ˈ**path**

underutiliz|e, -is|e ˌʌn.dəˈjuː.tɪ.laɪz, -təl.aɪz, (US) -dɚˈjuː.t̬əl.aɪz **-es** -ɪz **-ing** -ɪŋ **-ed** -d

undervaluation ˌʌn.dəˌvæl.juˈeɪ.ʃən, (US) -dɚˌ- **-s** -z

underval|ue ˌʌn.dəˈvæl|.juː, (US) -dɚˈ- **-ues** -juːz **-uing** -juː.ɪŋ **-ued** -juːd *stress shift:* ˌ**undervalued** ˈ**shares**

underwater ˌʌn.dəˈwɔː.təʳ, (US) -dɚˈwɑː.t̬ɚ, -ˈwɔː- *stress shift:* ˌ**underwater** ˈ**camera**

underway ˌʌn.dəˈweɪ, (US) -dɚˈ-

underwear ˈʌn.də.weəʳ, (US) -dɚ.wer

underweight ˌʌn.dəˈweɪt, (US) -dɚˈ-, ˈ--- *stress shift:* ˌ**underweight** ˈ**baggage**

underwent (from **undergo**) ˌʌn.dəˈwent, (US) -dɚˈ- *stress shift:* ˌ**underwent** ˈ**surgery**

underwhelm ˌʌn.dəˈhwelm, (US) -dɚˈ- **-s** -z **-ing** -ɪŋ **-ed** -d

underwing ˈʌn.də.wɪŋ, (US) -dɚ- **-s** -z

underwired ˌʌn.dəˈwaɪ.əd, -ˈwaɪəd, (US) -dɚˈwaɪ.ɚd, ˈ--- *stress shift:* ˌ**underwired** ˈ**bra**

underwood, U~ ˈʌn.də.wʊd, (US) -dɚ- **-s** -z

underworld, U~ ˈʌn.də.wɜːld, (US) -dɚ.wɝːld

underwri|te ˌʌn.dərˈaɪ|t, ˈ---, (US) ˈʌn.dɚ.raɪ|t **-tes** -ts **-ting** -tɪŋ, (US) -t̬ɪŋ **underwrote** ˌʌn.dərˈəʊt, ˈ---, (US) ˈʌn.dɚ.roʊt **underwritten** ˌʌn.dərˈɪt.ən, ˈʌn.dərˌɪt-, (US) ˈʌn.dɚˌrɪt.ən

underwriter ˈʌn.dərˌaɪ.təʳ, (US) -dɚˌraɪ.t̬ɚ **-s** -z

undescended ˌʌn.dɪˈsen.dɪd

undescribab|le ˌʌn.dɪˈskraɪ.bə.b|əl, -dəˈ- **-ly** -li

undeserv|ed ˌʌn.dɪˈzɜːv|d, -dəˈ-, (US) -ˈzɝːv|d **-edly** -ɪd.li **-edness** -ɪd.nəs, -nɪs

undeserving ˌʌn.dɪˈzɜː.vɪŋ, -dəˈ-, (US) -ˈzɝː- **-ly** -li

undesigning ˌʌn.dɪˈzaɪ.nɪŋ

undesirability ˌʌn.dɪˌzaɪə.rəˈbɪl.ə.ti, -dəˌ-, -ɪ.ti, (US) -ˌzaɪ.rəˈbɪl.ə.t̬i

undesirab|le ˌʌn.dɪˈzaɪə.rə.b|əl, -dəˈ-, (US) -ˈzaɪ- **-ly** -li **-leness** -əl.nəs, -nɪs

undetected ˌʌn.dɪˈtek.tɪd, -dəˈ-

undeterminable ˌʌn.dɪˈtɜː.mɪ.nə.bəl, -dəˈ-, -mə-, (US) -ˈtɝː-

undeterminate ˌʌn.dɪˈtɜː.mɪ.nət, -dəˈ-, -mə-, -nɪt, (US) -ˈtɝː- **-ly** -li **-ness** -nəs, -nɪs

undetermination ˌʌn.dɪˌtɜː.mɪˈneɪ.ʃən, -də-, -məˈ-, (US) -ˌtɝː-

undetermined ˌʌn.dɪˈtɜː.mɪnd, -dəˈ-, (US) -ˈtɝː-

undeterred ˌʌn.dɪˈtɜːd, -dəˈ-, (US) -ˈtɝːd

undeveloped ˌʌn.dɪˈvel.əpt, -dəˈ-

undeviating ʌnˈdiː.vi.eɪ.tɪŋ, ˌʌn-, (US) -t̬ɪŋ **-ly** -li

undid (from **undo**) ʌnˈdɪd, ˌʌn-

undies ˈʌn.diz

undigested ˌʌn.daɪˈdʒes.tɪd, -dɪˈ-, -dəˈ-

undignified ʌnˈdɪg.nɪ.faɪd, ˌʌn-, -nə-

undiluted ˌʌn.daɪˈluː.tɪd, -dɪˈ-, -ˈljuː-, (US) -ˈluː.t̬ɪd

undiminished ˌʌn.dɪˈmɪn.ɪʃt, -dəˈ-

undimmed ʌnˈdɪmd, ˌʌn-

undine, U~ ˈʌn.diːn; ʌnˈdiːn, ʊn-, (US) ʌnˈdiːn; (US) ˈʌn.diːn, -daɪn **-s** -z

undiplomatic ˌʌn.dɪp.ləˈmæt.ɪk, (US) -ˈmæt̬- **-ally** -əl.i, -li

undiscerning ˌʌn.dɪˈsɜː.nɪŋ, -dəˈ-, -ˈzɜː-, (US) -ˈsɝː-, -ˈzɝː-

undischarged ˌʌn.dɪsˈtʃɑːdʒd, (US) -ˈtʃɑːrdʒd

undisciplined ʌnˈdɪs.ɪ.plɪnd, ˌʌn-, ˈ-ə-

undisclosed ˌʌn.dɪsˈkləʊzd, (US) -ˈkloʊzd

undiscouraged ˌʌn.dɪˈskʌr.ɪdʒd, (US) -ˈskɝː-

undiscovered ˌʌn.dɪˈskʌv.əd, (US) -ɚd

undiscussed ˌʌn.dɪˈskʌst

undisguised ˌʌn.dɪsˈgaɪzd, -dɪzˈ-
undismayed ˌʌn.dɪˈsmeɪd, -dəˈ-
undisputed ˌʌn.dɪˈspjuː.tɪd, -dəˈ-, US -t̬ɪd
undissolved ˌʌn.dɪˈzɒlvd, -ˈsɒlvd, US -ˈzɑːlvd
undistinguishab|le ˌʌn.dɪˈstɪŋ.gwɪ.ʃə.b|əl, -dəˈ- **-ly** -li **-leness** -əl.nəs, -nɪs
undistinguished ˌʌn.dɪˈstɪŋ.gwɪʃt, -dəˈ-
undistracted ˌʌn.dɪˈstræk.tɪd, -dəˈ-
undisturbed ˌʌn.dɪˈstɜːbd, -dəˈ-, US -ˈstɝːbd
undivided ˌʌn.dɪˈvaɪ.dɪd, -dəˈ- **-ly** -li **-ness** -nəs, -nɪs
un|do ʌn|ˈduː, ˌʌn- **-does** -ˈdʌz **-doing** -ˈduː.ɪŋ **-did** -ˈdɪd **-done** -ˈdʌn **-doer/s** -ˈduː.əʳ/z, US -ˈduː.ɚ/z
undock ʌnˈdɒk, ˌʌn-, US -ˈdɑːk **-s** -s **-ing** -ɪŋ **-ed** -t
undocumented ʌnˈdɒk.jə.men.tɪd, -jʊ-, US -ˈdɑː.kjə.men.t̬ɪd, -kjʊ-
undomesticated ˌʌn.dəˈmes.tɪ.keɪ.tɪd, US -t̬ɪd
undone (from **undo**) ʌnˈdʌn, ˌʌn-
undoubted ʌnˈdaʊ.tɪd, ˌʌn-, US -t̬ɪd **-ly** -li
undreamed, undreamt ʌnˈdriːmd, ʌnˈdrempt **unˈdreamed ˌof**
undress ʌnˈdres, ˌʌn- **-es** -ɪz **-ing** -ɪŋ **-ed** -t
undrinkable ʌnˈdrɪŋ.kə.bəl, ˌʌn-
undrunk ʌnˈdrʌŋk
undue ʌnˈdʒuː, -ˈdjuː-, ˌʌn-, US -ˈduː, -ˈdjuː
undulant ˈʌn.dʒə.lənt, -dʒʊ.lənt, -djə.lənt, -djʊ.lənt, US -dʒə.lənt, -djə-
undu|late ˈʌn.dʒə|.leɪt, -dʒʊ-, -djə-, -djʊ-, US -dʒə-, -djə- **-lates** -leɪts **-lating/ly** -leɪ.tɪŋ/li, US -leɪ.t̬ɪŋ/li **-lated** -leɪ.tɪd, US -leɪ.t̬ɪd
undulation ˌʌn.dʒəˈleɪ.ʃən, -dʒʊˈ-, -djəˈ-, -djʊˈ-, US -dʒəˈ-, -djəˈ-, -dəˈ- **-s** -z
undulatory ˈʌn.dʒəl.ə.tər.i, -dʒʊ.lə-, -djəl.ə-, -djʊ.lə-, -tri; ˌʌn.djəˈleɪ.tər-, -djʊˈ-, US ˈʌn.dʒəl.ə.tɔːr.i, -djəl-, -dəl-
unduly ʌnˈdʒuː.li, ˌʌn-, -ˈdjuː-, US -ˈduː-, -ˈdjuː-
undutiful ʌnˈdʒuː.tɪ.fəl, ˌʌn-, -ˈdjuː-, -fʊl, US -ˈduː.t̬ɪ-, -ˈdjuː- **-ly** -i **-ness** -nəs, -nɪs
undying ʌnˈdaɪ.ɪŋ, ˌʌn- **-ly** -li
unearned ʌnˈɜːnd, ˌʌn-, US -ˈɝːnd
unearth ʌnˈɜːθ, ˌʌn-, US -ˈɝːθ **-s** -s **-ing** -ɪŋ **-ed** -t
unearthl|y ʌnˈɜːθ.l|i, ˌʌn-, US -ˈɝːθ- **-iness** -ɪ.nəs, -ɪ.nɪs
unease ʌnˈiːz, ˌʌn-
uneas|y ʌnˈiː.z|i, ˌʌn- **-ier** -i.əʳ, US -i.ɚ **-iest** -i.ɪst, -i.əst **-ily** -əl.i, -ɪ.li **-iness** -ɪ.nəs, -ɪ.nɪs
uneatable ʌnˈiː.tə.bəl, ˌʌn-, US -t̬ə- **-ness** -nəs, -nɪs
uneaten ʌnˈiː.tən, ˌʌn-
uneconomic ˌʌn.iː.kəˈnɒm.ɪk, ʌnˌiː-, -ek.əˈ-, US ˌʌn.ek.əˈnɑː.mɪk, -iː.kəˈ- **-al** -əl **-ally** -əl.i, -li
unedifying ʌnˈed.ɪ.faɪ.ɪŋ, ˌʌn-
unedited ʌnˈed.ɪ.tɪd, US -t̬ɪd
uneducated ʌnˈedʒ.ʊ.keɪ.tɪd, ˌʌn-, ˈ-ə-, -ˈed.jʊ-, -jə-, US -ˈedʒ.ʊ.keɪ.t̬ɪd, ˈ-ə-
unelected ˌʌn.ɪˈlek.tɪd
unembarrassed ˌʌn.ɪmˈbær.əst, -emˈ-, US -emˈber-, -ɪmˈ-, -ˈbær-
unemotional ˌʌn.ɪˈməʊ.ʃən.əl, US -ˈmoʊ- **-ly** -i
unemphatic ˌʌn.ɪmˈfæt.ɪk, -emˈ-, US -ˈfæt̬- **-ally** -əl.i, -li
unemployability ˌʌn.ɪmˌplɔɪ.əˈbɪl.ɪ.ti, -emˌ-, -ə.ti, US -ə.t̬i
unemployable ˌʌn.ɪmˈplɔɪ.ə.bəl, -emˈ-
unemployed ˌʌn.ɪmˈplɔɪd, -emˈ-
unemployment ˌʌn.ɪmˈplɔɪ.mənt, -emˈ- **unemˈployment ˌbenefit; ˌunemployment ˈbenefit** US **unemˈployment ˌbenefit**
unenclosed ˌʌn.ɪnˈkləʊzd, -ɪŋˈ-, -enˈ-, -eŋˈ-, US -ɪnˈkloʊzd, -enˈ-
unencumbered ˌʌn.ɪŋˈkʌm.bəd, -ɪnˈ-, -eŋˈ-, -enˈ-, US -ɪnˈkʌm.bɚd, -enˈ-
unending ʌnˈen.dɪŋ, ˌʌn- **-ly** -li
unendowed ˌʌn.ɪnˈdaʊd, -enˈ-
unendurab|le ˌʌn.ɪnˈdʒʊə.rə.b|əl, -ˈdjʊə-, -enˈ-, -ˈdʒɔː-, -ˈdjɔː-, US -ˈdʊr.ə-, -ˈdjʊr-, -ˈdɝː- **-ly** -li **-leness** -əl.nəs, -nɪs
unenforceable ˌʌn.ɪnˈfɔː.sə.bəl, US -ˈfɔːr-
unengaged ˌʌn.ɪŋˈgeɪdʒd, -ɪnˈ-, -eŋˈ-, -enˈ-, US -ɪnˈ-, -enˈ-
un-English ˌʌnˈɪŋ.glɪʃ **-ness** -nəs, -nɪs
unenlightened ˌʌn.ɪnˈlaɪ.tənd, -enˈ-
unenterprising ʌnˈen.tə.praɪ.zɪŋ, ˌʌn-, US -t̬ɚ- **-ly** -li
unenthusiastic ˌʌn.ɪnˌθjuː.ziˈæs.tɪk, -enˌ-, US -ˌθuː-, -ˌθjuː- **-ally** -əl.i, -li
unenviab|le ʌnˈen.vi.ə.b|əl, ˌʌn- **-ly** -li
unequal ʌnˈiː.kwəl, ˌʌn- **-s** -z **-ly** -i **-ness** -nəs, -nɪs **-(l)ed** -d
unequitab|le ʌnˈek.wɪ.tə.b|əl, ˌʌn-, -wə-, US -t̬ə- **-ly** -li
unequivoc|al ˌʌn.ɪˈkwɪv.ə.k|əl **-ally** -əl.i, -li **-alness** -əl.nəs, -nɪs
unerring ʌnˈɜː.rɪŋ, ˌʌn-, US -ˈɝː.ɪŋ, -ˈer- **-ly** -li **-ness** -nəs, -nɪs
unescapable ˌʌn.ɪˈskeɪ.pə.bəl
UNESCO, Unesco juːˈnes.kəʊ, US -koʊ
unessential ˌʌn.ɪˈsen.tʃəl
unethic|al ʌnˈeθ.ɪ.k|əl **-ly** -əl.i, -li **-ness** -nəs, -nɪs
uneven ʌnˈiː.vən, ˌʌn- **-ly** -li **-ness** -nəs, -nɪs
uneventful ˌʌn.ɪˈvent.fəl, -fʊl **-ly** -i **-ness** -nəs, -nɪs
unexampled ˌʌn.ɪgˈzɑːm.pəld, -egˈ-, -ɪkˈsɑːm-, -ekˈ-, US -ɪgˈzæm-, -egˈ-
unexceptionab|le ˌʌn.ɪkˈsep.ʃən.ə.b|əl, -ekˈ-, -ˈsepʃ.nə- **-ly** -li **-leness** -əl.nəs, US -nɪs
unexceptional ˌʌn.ɪkˈsep.ʃən.əl, -ekˈ-, -ˈsepʃ.nəl **-ly** -i
unexhausted ˌʌn.ɪgˈzɔː.stɪd, -egˈ-, -ɪkˈsɔː-, -ekˈ-, US -ɪgˈzɑː-, -egˈ-, -ˈzɔː-
unexpected ˌʌn.ɪkˈspek.tɪd, -ekˈ- **-ly** -li **-ness** -nəs, -nɪs
unexpired ˌʌn.ɪkˈspaɪ.əd, -ekˈ-, US -ˈspaɪ.ɚd
unexplained ˌʌn.ɪkˈspleɪnd, -ekˈ-
unexplored ˌʌn.ɪkˈsplɔːd, -ekˈ-, US -ˈsplɔːrd
unexposed ˌʌn.ɪkˈspəʊzd, -ekˈ-, US -ˈspoʊzd
unexpressib|le ˌʌn.ɪkˈspres.ə.b|əl, -ekˈ-, ˈ-ɪ- **-ly** -li
unexpressive ˌʌn.ɪkˈspres.ɪv, -ekˈ-
unexpurgated ʌnˈek.spə.geɪ.tɪd, ˌʌn-, -spɜː-, US -spɚ.geɪ.t̬ɪd
unfading ʌnˈfeɪ.dɪŋ, ˌʌn- **-ly** -li
unfailing ʌnˈfeɪ.lɪŋ, ˌʌn- **-ly** -li **-ness** -nəs, -nɪs
unfair ʌnˈfeəʳ, ˌʌn-, US -ˈfer **-ly** -li **-ness** -nəs, -nɪs **ˌunfair disˈmissal**
unfaithful ʌnˈfeɪθ.fəl, ˌʌn-, -fʊl **-ly** -i **-ness** -nəs, -nɪs
unfaltering ʌnˈfɔːl.tər.ɪŋ, ˌʌn-, -ˈfɒl-, US -ˈfɑːl.tɚ-, -ˈfɔːl- **-ly** -li
unfamiliar ˌʌn.fəˈmɪl.jəʳ, ˈ-i.əʳ, US ˈ-jɚ **-ly** -li
unfamiliarity ˌʌn.fəˌmɪl.iˈær.ə.ti, -ɪ.ti, US -ˈer.ə.t̬i, -ˈær-
unfashionab|le ʌnˈfæʃ.ən.ə.b|əl, ˌʌn-, ˈ-nə- **-ly** -li
unfasten ʌnˈfɑː.sən, ˌʌn-, US -ˈfæs.ən **-s** -z **-ing** -ɪŋ, -ˈfɑːs.nɪŋ, US -ˈfæs.nɪŋ **-ed** -d
unfathomab|le ʌnˈfæð.ə.mə.b|əl, ˌʌn- **-ly** -li **-leness** -əl.nəs, -nɪs
unfathomed ʌnˈfæð.əmd, ˌʌn-
unfavo(u)rab|le ʌnˈfeɪ.vər.ə.b|əl, ˌʌn-, -ˈfeɪv.rə- **-ly** -li **-leness** -əl.nəs, -nɪs
unfavo(u)rite ʌnˈfeɪ.vər.ɪt, ˌʌn-, -ˈfeɪv.rɪt
unfazed ʌnˈfeɪzd
unfed ʌnˈfed, ˌʌn-
unfeeling ʌnˈfiː.lɪŋ, ˌʌn- **-ly** -li **-ness** -nəs, -nɪs
unfeigned ʌnˈfeɪnd, ˌʌn-
unfeigned|ly ʌnˈfeɪ.nɪd|.li, ˌʌn- **-ness** -nəs, -nɪs
unfelt ʌnˈfelt, ˌʌn-
unfermented ˌʌn.fəˈmen.tɪd, -fɜːˈ-, US -fɚˈmen.t̬ɪd
unfertilized, -ised ʌnˈfɜː.təl.aɪzd, ˌʌn-, -tɪ.laɪzd, US -ˈfɝː.t̬əl.aɪzd
unfett|er ʌnˈfet|.əʳ, ˌʌn-, US -ˈfet̬|.ɚ **-ers** -əz, US -ɚz **-ering** -ər.ɪŋ **-ed** -əd, US -ɚd
unfettered ʌnˈfet.əd, US -ˈfet̬.ɚd
unfilial ʌnˈfɪl.i.əl, ˌʌn- **-ly** -i
unfinished ʌnˈfɪn.ɪʃt, ˌʌn- **ˌunfinished ˈbusiness; unˌfinished ˈbusiness**

U

unfit adj ʌnˈfɪt -ly -li -ness -nəs, -nɪs

un|fit v ʌn|ˈfɪt, ˌʌn- -fits -ˈfɪts -fitting/ly -ˈfɪt.ɪŋ/li, US -ˈfɪt̬.ɪŋ/li -fitted -ˈfɪt.ɪd, US -ˈfɪt̬.ɪd

unfix ʌnˈfɪks, ˌʌn- -es -ɪz -ing -ɪŋ -ed -t

unflagging ʌnˈflæɡ.ɪŋ, ˌʌn- -ly -li

unflappab|le ʌnˈflæp.ə.b|^{ə}l, ˌʌn- -ly -li

unflattering ʌnˈflæt.^{ə}r.ɪŋ, ˌʌn-, US -ˈflæt̬- -ly -li

unfledged ʌnˈfledʒd, ˌʌn-

unflinching ʌnˈflɪn.tʃɪŋ, ˌʌn- -ly -li -ness -nəs, -nɪs

unfold ʌnˈfəʊld, ˌʌn-, US -ˈfoʊld -s -z -ing -ɪŋ -ed -ɪd

unforeseeable ˌʌn.fɔːˈsiː.ə.b^{ə}l, -fəˈ-, US -fɔːrˈ-, -fɚˈ-

unforeseen ˌʌn.fɔːˈsiːn, -fəˈ-, US -fɔːrˈ-, -fɚˈ- **ˌunforeseen ˈcircumstances**

unforgettab|le ˌʌn.fəˈɡet.ə.b|^{ə}l, US -fɚˈɡet̬- -ly -li

unforgivable ˌʌn.fəˈɡɪv.ə.b^{ə}l, US -fɚˈ-

unforgiven ˌʌn.fəˈɡɪv.ən, US -fɚˈ-

unforgiving ˌʌn.fəˈɡɪv.ɪŋ, US -fɚˈ- -ly -li -ness -nəs, -nɪs

unforgotten ˌʌn.fəˈɡɒt.^{ə}n, US -fɚˈɡɑː.t^{ə}n

unformatted ʌnˈfɔː.mæt.ɪd, US -ˈfɔːr.mæt̬-

unformed ʌnˈfɔːmd, ˌʌn-, US -ˈfɔːrmd

unforthcoming ˌʌn.fɔːθˈkʌm.ɪŋ, US -fɔːrθ-

unfortified ʌnˈfɔː.tɪ.faɪd, ˌʌn-, US -ˈfɔːr.t̬ɪ-

unfortunate ʌnˈfɔː.tʃ^{ə}n.ət, ˌʌn-, -ɪt, US -ˈfɔːr- -ly -li -ness -nəs, -nɪs

unfounded ʌnˈfaʊn.dɪd, ˌʌn-

unframed ʌnˈfreɪmd, ˌʌn-

un|freeze ʌn|ˈfriːz, US ˌʌn- -freezes -ˈfriː.zɪz -froze -ˈfrəʊz, US -ˈfroʊz -frozen -ˈfrəʊ.z^{ə}n, US -ˈfroʊ.z^{ə}n

unfrequented ˌʌn.frɪˈkwen.tɪd, US ʌnˈfriː.kwen.t̬ɪd, ˌʌn-

unfriend ˌʌnˈfrend, ʌn- -s -z -ing -ɪŋ -ed -ɪd

unfriend|ly ʌnˈfrend|.li, ˌʌn- -liness -lɪ.nəs, -lɪ.nɪs

unfrock ʌnˈfrɒk, ˌʌn-, US -ˈfrɑːk -s -s -ing -ɪŋ -ed -t

unfruitful ʌnˈfruːt.f^{ə}l, ˌʌn-, -fʊl -ly -i -ness -nəs, -nɪs

unfulfilled ˌʌn.fʊlˈfɪld

unfunny ʌnˈfʌn.i, ˌʌn-

unfurl ʌnˈfɜːl, ˌʌn-, US -ˈfɝːl -s -z -ing -ɪŋ -ed -d

unfurnished ʌnˈfɜː.nɪʃt, ˌʌn-, US -ˈfɝː-

ungainl|y ʌnˈɡeɪn.l|i, ˌʌn-, ʌŋ-, ˌʌŋ-, US ʌn-, ˌʌn- -iest -i.ɪst, -i.əst -iness -ɪ.nəs, -ɪ.nɪs

ungallant ʌnˈɡæl.ənt, ˌʌn.ɡəˈlænt, ʌŋ-, ˌʌŋ-, US ʌnˈɡæl.ənt, ˌʌn.ɡəˈlænt, -ˈlɑːnt -ly -li

ungenerous ʌnˈdʒen.^{ə}r.əs, ˌʌn- -ly -li

ungentlemanl|y ʌnˈdʒent.^{ə}l.mən.l|i, ˌʌn- -iness -ɪ.nəs, -ɪ.nɪs

un-get-at-able ˌʌn.ɡetˈæt.ə.b^{ə}l, ˌʌŋ-, US ˌʌn.ɡet̬ˈæt̬-

ungird ʌnˈɡɜːd, ˌʌn-, ʌŋ-, ˌʌŋ-, US ʌnˈɡɝːd, ˌʌn- -s -z -ing -ɪŋ -ed -ɪd

unglazed ʌnˈɡleɪzd, ˌʌn-, ʌŋ-, ˌʌŋ-, US ʌn-, ˌʌn-

ungloved ʌnˈɡlʌvd, ˌʌn-, ʌŋ-, ˌʌŋ-, US ʌn-, ˌʌn-

unglu|e ʌnˈɡluː, ˌʌn-, ʌŋ-, ˌʌŋ-, US ʌn-, ˌʌn- -es -z -ing -ɪŋ -ed -d

ungodl|y ʌnˈɡɒd.l|i, ˌʌn-, ʌŋ-, ˌʌŋ-, US ʌnˈɡɑːd.l|i, ˌʌn- -ier -i.ə^{r}, US -i.ɚ -iest -i.ɪst, -i.əst -iness -ɪ.nəs, -ɪ.nɪs

Ungoed ˈʌŋ.ɡɔɪd

ungotten ʌnˈɡɒt.^{ə}n, ˌʌn-, ʌŋ-, ˌʌŋ-, US ʌnˈɡɑː.t^{ə}n, ˌʌn-

ungovernab|le ʌnˈɡʌv.^{ə}n.ə.b|^{ə}l, ˌʌn-, ʌŋ-, ˌʌŋ-, ˈ-nə-, US ʌnˈɡʌv.ɚ.nə-, ˌʌn- -ly -li -leness -^{ə}l.nəs, US -nɪs

ungoverned ʌnˈɡʌv.^{ə}nd, ˌʌn-, ʌŋ-, ˌʌŋ-, US ʌnˈɡʌv.ɚnd, ˌʌn-

ungraceful ʌnˈɡreɪs.f^{ə}l, ˌʌn-, ʌŋ-, ˌʌŋ-, -fʊl, US ʌn-, ˌʌn- -ly -i -ness -nəs, -nɪs

ungracious ʌnˈɡreɪ.ʃəs, ˌʌn-, ʌŋ-, ˌʌŋ-, US ʌn-, ˌʌn- -ly -li -ness -nəs, -nɪs

ungrammatic|al ˌʌn.ɡrəˈmæt.ɪ.k|^{ə}l, ˌʌŋ-, US ˌʌn.ɡrəˈmæt̬- -ally -^{ə}l.i, -li

ungrateful ʌnˈɡreɪt.f^{ə}l, ˌʌn-, ʌŋ-, ˌʌŋ-, -fʊl, US ʌn-, ˌʌn- -ly -li -ness -nəs, -nɪs

ungrounded ʌnˈɡraʊn.dɪd, ˌʌn-, ʌŋ-, ˌʌŋ-, US ʌn-, ˌʌn-

ungrudging ʌnˈɡrʌdʒ.ɪŋ, ˌʌn-, ʌŋ-, ˌʌŋ-, US ʌn-, ˌʌn- -ly -li

unguarded ʌnˈɡɑː.dɪd, ˌʌn-, ʌŋ-, ˌʌŋ-, US ʌnˈɡɑːr-, ˌʌn- -ly -li -ness -nəs, -nɪs

unguent ˈʌŋ.ɡwənt, -ɡju.ənt, US -ɡwənt -s -s

unguided ʌnˈɡaɪ.dɪd, ˌʌn-, ʌŋ-, ˌʌŋ-, US ʌn-, ˌʌn-

ungul|a ˈʌŋ.ɡjə.l|ə, -ɡjʊ- -ae -iː

ungulate ˈʌŋ.ɡjə.leɪt, -ɡjʊ-, -lət, -lɪt, US -lɪt, -leɪt -s -s

unhallowed ʌnˈhæl.əʊd, ˌʌn-, US -oʊd

unhampered ʌnˈhæm.pəd, ˌʌn-, US -pɚd

unhand ʌnˈhænd, ˌʌn- -s -z -ing -ɪŋ -ed -ɪd

unhandy ʌnˈhæn.di, ˌʌn-

unhapp|y ʌnˈhæp|.i, ˌʌn- -ier -i.ə^{r}, US -i.ɚ -iest -i.ɪst, -i.əst -ily -^{ə}l.i, -ɪ.li -iness -ɪ.nɪs, -ɪ.nəs

unharmed ʌnˈhɑːmd, ˌʌn-, US -ˈhɑːrmd

unharness ʌnˈhɑː.nɪs, ˌʌn-, US -ˈhɑːr- -es -ɪz -ing -ɪŋ -ed -t

unhatched ʌnˈhætʃt, ˌʌn-

unhealth|y ʌnˈhel.θ|i, ˌʌn- -ier -i.ə^{r}, US -i.ɚ -iest -i.ɪst, -i.əst -ily -^{ə}l.i, -ɪ.li -iness -ɪ.nəs, -ɪ.nɪs

unheard ʌnˈhɜːd, ˌʌn-, US -ˈhɝːd

unheard-of ʌnˈhɜːd ˌɒv, US -ˈhɝːd ˌɑːv, -əv

unheeded ʌnˈhiː.dɪd, ˌʌn-

unheeding ʌnˈhiː.dɪŋ -ly -li

unhelpful ʌnˈhelp.f^{ə}l, -fʊl -ly -i -ness -nəs, -nɪs

unheralded ʌnˈher.əl.dɪd

unhesitating ʌnˈhez.ɪ.teɪ.tɪŋ, ˌʌn-, ˈ-ə-, US -t̬ɪŋ -ly -li

unhing|e ʌnˈhɪndʒ, ˌʌn- -es -ɪz -ing -ɪŋ -ed -d

unhistoric ˌʌn.hɪˈstɒr.ɪk, -ɪˈ-, US -hɪˈstɔːr- -al -^{ə}l

unhitch ʌnˈhɪtʃ, ˌʌn- -es -ɪz -ing -ɪŋ -ed -t

unhol|y ʌnˈhəʊ.l|i, ˌʌn-, US -ˈhoʊ- -iness -ɪ.nəs, -ɪ.nɪs **unˌholy alˈliance**

unhook ʌnˈhʊk, ˌʌn- -s -s -ing -ɪŋ -ed -t

unhoped-for ʌnˈhəʊpt ˌfɔː^{r}, US -ˈhoʊpt ˌfɔːr

unhors|e ʌnˈhɔːs, ˌʌn-, US -ˈhɔːrs -es -ɪz -ing -ɪŋ -ed -t

unhous|e ʌnˈhaʊz, ˌʌn- -es -ɪz -ing -ɪŋ -ed -d

unhuman ʌnˈhjuː.mən, ˌʌn-

unhung ʌnˈhʌŋ, ˌʌn-

unhurried ʌnˈhʌr.ɪd, ˌʌn-, US -ˈhɝː- -ly -li -ness -nəs, -nɪs

unhurt ʌnˈhɜːt, ˌʌn-, US -ˈhɝːt

uni ˈjuː.ni -s -z

uni- juː.nɪ, -ni

Note: Prefix. Normally takes primary or secondary stress on the first syllable, e.g. **unify** /ˈjuː.nɪ.faɪ/ US /-nə-/, **unification** /ˌjuː.nɪ.fɪˈkeɪ.ʃ^{ə}n/ US /-nə-/.

Uniate ˈjuː.ni.ət, -ɪt, -eɪt, US -ɪt, -eɪt -s -s

unicameral ˌjuː.nɪˈkæm.^{ə}r.^{ə}l

UNICEF, Unicef ˈjuː.nɪ.sef

unicellular ˌjuː.nɪˈsel.jə.lə^{r}, -jʊ-, US -jə.lɚ

unicorn ˈjuː.nɪ.kɔːn, US -kɔːrn -s -z

unicycl|e ˈjuː.nɪˌsaɪ.k^{ə}l, US -nə- -es -z -ist/s -ɪst/s

unidentified ˌʌn.aɪˈden.tɪ.faɪd, US -t̬ə- **ˌunidentified ˌflying ˈobject**

unidimensional ˌjuː.nɪ.daɪˈmen.tʃ^{ə}n.^{ə}l, -dɪˈ-, -dəˈ-, US -nə.dəˈment.ʃə-, -dɪˈ-, -daɪ-

unidiomatic ˌʌn.ɪd.i.əʊˈmæt.ɪk, ʌnˌɪd-, US -əˈmæt̬- -ally -^{ə}l.i, -li

unifiable ˈjuː.nɪ.faɪ.ə.b^{ə}l, US -nə-

unification ˌjuː.nɪ.fɪˈkeɪ.ʃ^{ə}n, -nə-, -fəˈ-, US -nə- -s -z

uniform ˈjuː.nɪ.fɔːm, -nə-, US -nə.fɔːrm -s -z -ed -d -ly -li -ness -nəs, -nɪs

uniformity ˌjuː.nɪˈfɔː.mə.ti, -nəˈ-, -mɪ-, US -nəˈfɔːr.mə.t̬i

uni|fy ˈjuː.nɪ|.faɪ, -nə- -fies -faɪz -fying -faɪ.ɪŋ -fied -faɪd -fier/s -faɪ.ə^{r}/z, US -faɪ.ɚ/z

Unigate® ˈjuː.nɪ.ɡeɪt, -nə-, US -nə-

unilateral ˌjuː.nɪˈlæt.^{ə}r.^{ə}l, US -nəˈlæt̬- -ly -i -ism -ɪ.z^{ə}m -ist/s -ɪst/s

Unilever® ˈjuː.nɪ.liː.və^{r}, US -nə.liː.vɚ

unimaginab|le ˌʌn.ɪˈmædʒ.ɪ.nə.b|əl, -ən.ə- **-ly** -li **-leness** -əl.nəs, -nɪs
unimaginative ˌʌn.ɪˈmædʒ.ɪ.nə.tɪv, -ən.ə-, (US) -t̬ɪv **-ly** -li **-ness** -nəs, -nɪs
unimagined ˌʌn.ɪˈmædʒ.ɪnd, -ənd
unimpaired ˌʌn.ɪmˈpeəd, (US) -ˈperd
unimpassioned ˌʌn.ɪmˈpæʃ.ənd
unimpeachab|le ˌʌn.ɪmˈpiː.tʃə.b|əl **-ly** -li **-leness** -əl.nəs, -nɪs
unimpeded ˌʌn.ɪmˈpiː.dɪd
unimportance ˌʌn.ɪmˈpɔː.tənts, (US) -ˈpɔːr-
unimportant ˌʌn.ɪmˈpɔː.tənt, (US) -ˈpɔːr- **-ly** -li
unimpressed ˌʌn.ɪmˈprest
unimpressive ˌʌn.ɪmˈpres.ɪv **-ly** -li
unimproved ˌʌn.ɪmˈpruːvd
uninflated ˌʌn.ɪnˈfleɪ.tɪd, (US) -t̬ɪd
uninflected ˌʌn.ɪnˈflek.tɪd
uninfluenced ʌnˈɪn.flu.əntst, ˌʌn-, -fluəntst, (US) -flu.əntst
uninformative ˌʌn.ɪnˈfɔː.mə.tɪv, (US) -ˈfɔːr.mə.t̬ɪv **-ly** -li
uninformed ˌʌn.ɪnˈfɔːmd, (US) -ˈfɔːrmd
uninhabitable ˌʌn.ɪnˈhæb.ɪ.tə.bəl, ˈ-ə-, (US) -t̬ə- **-ness** -nəs, -nɪs
uninhabited ˌʌn.ɪnˈhæb.ɪ.tɪd, ˈ-ə-, (US) -t̬ɪd
uninhibited ˌʌn.ɪnˈhɪb.ɪ.tɪd, ˈ-ə-, (US) -t̬ɪd **-ly** -li **-ness** -nəs, -nɪs
uninitiated ˌʌn.ɪˈnɪʃ.i.eɪ.tɪd, (US) -t̬ɪd
uninjured ʌnˈɪn.dʒəd, ˌʌn-, (US) -dʒɚd
uninspired ˌʌn.ɪnˈspaɪ.əd, (US) -ˈspaɪ.ɚd
uninspiring ˌʌn.ɪnˈspaɪ.ə.rɪŋ, -ˈspaɪə-, (US) -ˈspaɪ- **-ly** -li
uninstall ˌʌn.ɪnˈstɔːl, (US) -ˈstɔːl, -ˈstɑːl **-s** -z **-ing** -ɪŋ **-ed** -d
uninstructed ˌʌn.ɪnˈstrʌk.tɪd
uninsured ˌʌn.ɪnˈʃʊəd, -ˈʃɔːd, (US) -ˈʃʊrd
unintelligent ˌʌn.ɪnˈtel.ɪ.dʒənt, ˈ-ə- **-ly** -li
unintelligibility ˌʌn.ɪnˌtel.ɪ.dʒəˈbɪl.ə.ti, ˌ-ə-, -dʒɪˈ-, -ɪ.ti, (US) -ə.t̬i
unintelligib|le ˌʌn.ɪnˈtel.ɪ.dʒə.b|əl, ˈ-ə-, -dʒɪ- **-ly** -li
unintended ˌʌn.ɪnˈten.dɪd *stress shift:* ˌ**unintended** ˈ**pun**
unintentional ˌʌn.ɪnˈten.*t*ʃən.əl, -ˈtentʃ.nəl **-ly** -i
uninterest|ed ʌnˈɪn.trə.st|ɪd, ˌʌn-, -trɪ-, -tres.t|ɪd, -tər.ə.st|ɪd, -ɪ-, -es.t|ɪd, (US) -trɪ.st|ɪd, -trə-, -tres.t|ɪd, -tɚ.es-, -ə.st|ɪd **-ing** -ɪŋ
uninterrupted ˌʌn.ɪn.tərˈʌp.tɪd, ʌnˌɪn-, (US) -təˈrʌp- **-ly** -li
uninvited ˌʌn.ɪnˈvaɪ.tɪd, (US) -t̬ɪd
uninviting ˌʌn.ɪnˈvaɪ.tɪŋ, (US) -t̬ɪŋ **-ly** -li **-ness** -nəs, -nɪs
union, U~ ˈjuː.njən, -ni.ən, (US) ˈ-njən **-s** -z ˌ**Union** ˈ**Jack**
union|ism, U~ ˈjuː.njə.n|ɪ.zəm, ˈ-ni.ə-, (US) ˈ-njə- **-ist/s** -ɪst/s
unionization, -isa- juː.njə.naɪˈzeɪ.ʃən, -ni.ə-, -ɪˈ-, (US) -njə.nə-
unioniz|e, -is|e ˈjuː.njə.naɪz, -ni.ə-, (US) -ˈnjə- **-es** -ɪz **-ing** -ɪŋ **-ed** -d
unipartite ˌjuː.nɪˈpɑː.taɪt, (US) -ˈpɑːr-
unique juːˈniːk **-ly** -li **-ness** -nəs, -nɪs
Uniroyal® ˈjuː.nɪ.rɔɪ.əl
unisex ˈjuː.nɪ.seks, (US) -nə-
unisexual ˌjuː.nɪˈsek.ʃʊəl, -sjʊəl, (US) -nəˈsek.ʃu.əl
unison ˈjuː.nɪ.sən, -nə-, -zən, (US) -nə- **-s** -z
unissued ʌnˈɪʃ.uːd, ˌʌn-, -ˈɪs.juːd, (US) -ˈɪʃ.uːd
unit ˈjuː.nɪt **-s** -s ˌ**unit** ˈ**trust**
UNITA, Unita juːˈniː.tə, (US) -t̬ə
unitable juːˈnaɪ.tə.bəl, (US) -t̬ə-
unitarian, U~ ˌjuː.nɪˈteə.ri.ən, (US) -ˈter.i- **-s** -z **-ism** -ɪ.zəm
unitary ˈjuː.nɪ.tər.i, -tri, (US) -ter.i
u|nite juː|ˈnaɪt, jʊ- **-nites** -ˈnaɪts **-niting** -ˈnaɪ.tɪŋ, (US) -ˈnaɪ.t̬ɪŋ **-nited/ly** -ˈnaɪ.tɪd/li, (US) -ˈnaɪ.t̬ɪd/li **-niter/s** -ˈnaɪ.tər/z, (US) -ˈnaɪ.t̬ɚ/z
United Arab Emirates juːˌnaɪ.tɪdˌær.əbˈem.ɪ.rəts, jʊ-, -ər.əts, -ɪts, -eɪts, (US) -t̬ɪdˌer.əbˈem.ɚ.əts, -ˌær-; (US) -ɪˈmɪr-
United Kingdom juːˌnaɪ.tɪdˈkɪŋ.dəm, jʊ-, (US) -t̬ɪdˈ-
United Nations juːˌnaɪ.tɪdˈneɪ.ʃənz, jʊ-, (US) -t̬ɪdˈ-
United Reformed Church juːˌnaɪ.tɪd.rɪˈfɔːmdˌtʃɜːtʃ, jʊ-, (US) -t̬ɪd.rɪˈfɔːrmdˌtʃɝːtʃ
United States juːˌnaɪ.tɪdˈsteɪts, jʊ-, (US) -t̬ɪdˈ- **U**ˌ**nited** ˌ**States of A**ˈ**merica**
unit|y, U~ ˈjuː.nə.t|i, -nɪ-, (US) -nə.t̬|i **-ies** -iz
univalen|t ˌjuː.nɪˈveɪ.lən|t, (US) -nəˈ-; (US) juːˈnɪv.əl.ən|t **-ce** -*t*s
univalve ˈjuː.nɪ.vælv, (US) -nə- **-s** -z
universal ˌjuː.nɪˈvɜː.səl, -nəˈ-, (US) -nəˈvɝː- **-s** -z **-ly** -i **-ness** -nəs, -nɪs **-ism** -ɪ.zəm **-ist/s** -ɪst/s *stress shift:* ˌ**universal** ˈ**joint**
universality ˌjuː.nɪ.vɜːˈsæl.ə.ti, -nə-, -ɪ.ti, (US) -nə.vɝːˈsæl.ə.t̬i
universaliz|e, -is|e juː.nɪˈvɜː.səl.aɪz, -nəˈ-, (US) -nəˈvɝː.sə.laɪz **-es** -ɪz **-ing** -ɪŋ **-ed** -d
univers|e ˈjuː.nɪ.vɜːs, -nə-, (US) -nə.vɝːs **-es** -ɪz
universit|y ˌjuː.nɪˈvɜː.sə.t|i, -nəˈ-, -sɪ-, (US) -nəˈvɝː.sə.t̬|i **-ies** -iz *stress shift:* ˌ**university** ˈ**grant**
univocal ˌjuː.nɪˈvəʊ.kəl, (US) -ˈnɪv.ə- **-s** -z
Unix® ˈjuː.nɪks
unjust ʌnˈdʒʌst, ˌʌn- **-ly** -li **-ness** -nəs, -nɪs
unjustifiab|le ˌʌn.dʒʌs.tɪˈfaɪ.ə.b|əl, ʌnˌdʒʌs-, -təˈ-, (US) ˌʌn.dʒʌs.tɪˈfaɪ.ə.b|əl, ʌnˌdʒʌs-, -təˈ-, -ˈdʒʌs.tɪ.faɪ-, -tə- **-ly** -li **-leness** -əl.nəs, -nɪs
unjustified ʌnˈdʒʌs.tɪ.faɪd, ˌʌn-, -tə- **-ly** -li
unkempt ʌnˈkempt, ˌʌn-, ʌŋ-, ˌʌŋ-, (US) ʌn-, ˌʌn-
unkept ʌnˈkept, ˌʌn-, ʌŋ-, ˌʌŋ-, (US) ʌn-, ˌʌn-
unkin|d ʌnˈkaɪn|d, ˌʌn-, ʌŋ-, ˌʌŋ-, (US) ʌn-, ˌʌn- **-der** -dər, (US) -dɚ **-dest** -dɪst, -dəst **-dly** -d.li **-dness** -*d*.nɪs, -nəs
un|knot ʌn|ˈnɒt, ˌʌn-, (US) -ˈnɑːt **-knots** -ˈnɒts, (US) -ˈnɑːts **-knotting** -ˈnɒt.ɪŋ, (US) -ˈnɑː.t̬ɪŋ **-knotted** -ˈnɒt.ɪd, (US) -ˈnɑː.t̬ɪd
unknowable ʌnˈnəʊ.ə.bəl, ˌʌn-, (US) -ˈnoʊ-
unknowing ʌnˈnəʊ.ɪŋ, ˌʌn-, (US) -ˈnoʊ- **-ly** -li **-ness** -nəs, -nɪs
unknown ʌnˈnəʊn, ˌʌn-, (US) -ˈnoʊn **-s** -z ˌ**unknown** ˈ**quantity;** ˌ**Unknown** ˈ**Soldier**
unlac|e ʌnˈleɪs, ˌʌn- **-es** -ɪz **-ing** -ɪŋ **-ed** -t
unlad|e ʌnˈleɪd, (US) ˌʌn- **-es** -z **-ing** -ɪŋ **-ed** -ɪd **-en** -ən
unladylike ʌnˈleɪ.di.laɪk, ˌʌn-
unlamented ˌʌn.ləˈmen.tɪd, (US) -t̬ɪd
unlash ʌnˈlæʃ, (US) ˌʌn- **-es** -ɪz **-ing** -ɪŋ **-ed** -t
unlatch ʌnˈlætʃ, (US) ˌʌn- **-es** -ɪz **-ing** -ɪŋ **-ed** -t
unlawful ʌnˈlɔː.fəl, ˌʌn-, -fʊl, (US) -ˈlɑː-, -ˈlɔː- **-ly** -i **-ness** -nəs, -nɪs
unleaded ʌnˈled.ɪd, ˌʌn- ˌ**unleaded** ˈ**petrol;** **un**ˌ**leaded** ˈ**petrol**
unlearn ʌnˈlɜːn, ˌʌn-, (US) -ˈlɝːn **-s** -z **-ing** -ɪŋ **-ed** -t, -d **-t** -t
unlearned ʌnˈlɜː.nɪd, ˌʌn-, (US) -ˈlɝː- **-ly** -li **-ness** -nəs, -nɪs
unleash ʌnˈliːʃ, ˌʌn- **-es** -ɪz **-ing** -ɪŋ **-ed** -t
unleavened ʌnˈlev.ənd, ˌʌn- ˌ**unleavened** ˈ**bread;** **un**ˌ**leavened** ˈ**bread**
unled ʌnˈled, ˌʌn-
unless ənˈles, ʌn-
unlettered ʌnˈlet.əd, ˌʌn-, (US) -ˈlet̬.ɚd
unliberated ʌnˈlɪb.ər.eɪ.tɪd, ˌʌn-, (US) -ə.reɪ.t̬ɪd
unlicensed ʌnˈlaɪ.sən*t*st, ˌʌn-
unlike ʌnˈlaɪk, ˌʌn-
unlikel|y ʌnˈlaɪ.kl|i, ˌʌn- **-ier** -i.ər, (US) -i.ɚ **-iest** -i.ɪst, -i.əst **-ihood** -ɪ.hʊd **-iness** -ɪ.nəs, -ɪ.nɪs
unlikeness ʌnˈlaɪk.nəs, ˌʌn-, -nɪs
unlimb|er ʌnˈlɪm.b|ər, ˌʌn-, (US) -b|ɚ **-ers** -əz, (US) -ɚz **-ering** -ər.ɪŋ **-ered** -əd, (US) -ɚd
unlimited ʌnˈlɪm.ɪ.tɪd, ˌʌn-, (US) -t̬ɪd
unlink ʌnˈlɪŋk, (US) ˌʌn- **-s** -s **-ing** -ɪŋ **-ed** -t
unliquidated ʌnˈlɪk.wɪ.deɪ.tɪd, ˌʌn-, -wə-, (US) -wə.deɪ.t̬ɪd
unlisted ʌnˈlɪs.tɪd
unlit ʌnˈlɪt, ˌʌn-
unload ʌnˈləʊd, ˌʌn-, (US) -ˈloʊd **-s** -z **-ing** -ɪŋ **-ed** -ɪd **-er/s** -ər/z, (US) -ɚ/z

U

unlock ʌnˈlɒk, ˌʌn-, ⓊⓈ -ˈlɑːk **-s** -s **-ing** -ɪŋ **-ed** -t
unlooked-for ʌnˈlʊkt ˌfɔːʳ, ˌʌn-, ⓊⓈ -ˌfɔːr
unloos|e ʌnˈluːs, ˌʌn- **-es** -ɪz **-ing** -ɪŋ **-ed** -t
unloosen ʌnˈluː.sᵊn, ˌʌn- **-s** -z **-ing** -ɪŋ, -ˈluːs.nɪŋ **-ed** -d
unloved ʌnˈlʌvd, ˌʌn- *stress shift:* ˌ**unloved ˈdaughter**
unlovel|y ʌnˈlʌv.l|i, ˌʌn- **-iness** -ɪ.nəs, -ɪ.nɪs
unloving ʌnˈlʌv.ɪŋ, ˌʌn-
unluck|y ʌnˈlʌk|.i, ˌʌn- **-ier** -i.əʳ, ⓊⓈ -i.ɚ **-iest** -i.ɪst, -i.əst **-ily** -ᵊl.i, -ɪ.li **-iness** -ɪ.nəs, -ɪ.nɪs
unmade ʌnˈmeɪd, ˌʌn-
un|make ʌn|ˈmeɪk, ˌʌn- **-makes** -ˈmeɪks **-making** -ˈmeɪ.kɪŋ **-made** -ˈmeɪd
unman ʌnˈmæn, ˌʌn- **-s** -z **-ning** -ɪŋ **-ned** -d
unmanageab|le ʌnˈmæn.ɪ.dʒə.b|ᵊl, ˌʌn-, ˈ-ə- **-ly** -li **-leness** -ᵊl.nəs, -nɪs
unmanl|y ʌnˈmæn.l|i, ˌʌn- **-iness** -ɪ.nəs, -ɪ.nɪs
unmannered ʌnˈmæn.əd, ⓊⓈ -ɚd **-ly** -li
unmannerl|y ʌnˈmæn.ᵊl|.i, ˌʌn-, ⓊⓈ -ɚ.l|i **-iness** -ɪ.nəs, -ɪ.nɪs
unmarked ʌnˈmɑːkt, ˌʌn-, ⓊⓈ -ˈmɑːrkt
unmarriageable ʌnˈmær.ɪ.dʒə.bᵊl, ˌʌn-, ⓊⓈ -ˈmer-, -ˈmær-
unmarried ʌnˈmær.ɪd, ˌʌn-, ⓊⓈ -ˈmer-, -ˈmær-
unmask ʌnˈmɑːsk, ˌʌn-, ⓊⓈ -ˈmæsk **-s** -s **-ing** -ɪŋ **-ed** -t
unmatched ʌnˈmætʃt, ˌʌn-
unmeaning ʌnˈmiː.nɪŋ, ˌʌn-
unmeasurable ʌnˈmeʒ.ᵊr.ə.bᵊl, ˌʌn-
unmeasured ʌnˈmeʒ.əd, ˌʌn-, ⓊⓈ -ɚd
unmentionable ʌnˈmen.*t*ʃᵊn.ə.bᵊl, ˌʌn-, -ˈmen*t*ʃ.nə-, ⓊⓈ -ˈment.ʃᵊn.ə-, -ˈmen*t*ʃ.nə- **-s** -z **-ness** -nəs, -nɪs
unmentioned ʌnˈmen.*t*ʃᵊnd, ˌʌn-, ⓊⓈ -ˈment.ʃᵊnd
unmerciful ʌnˈmɜː.sɪ.fᵊl, ˌʌn-, -sə-, -fʊl, ⓊⓈ -ˈmɝː- **-ly** -i **-ness** -nəs, -nɪs
unmerited ʌnˈmer.ɪ.tɪd, ˌʌn-, ⓊⓈ -t̬ɪd
unmethodic|al ˌʌn.məˈθɒd.ɪ.k|ᵊl, -mɪˈ-, -meθˈɒd-, ⓊⓈ -məˈθɑː.dɪ- **-ally** -ᵊl.i, -li
unmetred, unmetered ʌnˈmiː.təd, ⓊⓈ -t̬ɚd
unmindful ʌnˈmaɪn*d*.fᵊl, ˌʌn-, -fʊl **-ly** -i **-ness** -nəs, -nɪs
unmissable ʌnˈmɪs.ə.bᵊl
unmistakab|le ˌʌn.mɪˈsteɪ.kə.b|ᵊl **-ly** -li **-leness** -ᵊl.nəs, -nɪs
unmitigated ʌnˈmɪt.ɪ.geɪ.tɪd, ˌʌn-, ˈ-ə-, ⓊⓈ -ˈmɪt̬.ə.geɪ.t̬ɪd
unmixed ʌnˈmɪkst, ˌʌn-
unmodifiable ʌnˈmɒd.ɪ.faɪ.ə.bᵊl, ˌʌn-, ⓊⓈ -ˈmɑː.dɪ-
unmodified ʌnˈmɒd.ɪ.faɪd, ˌʌn-, ⓊⓈ -ˈmɑː.dɪ-
unmolested ˌʌn.məʊˈles.tɪd, ⓊⓈ -məˈ-
unmounted ʌnˈmaʊn.tɪd, ˌʌn-, ⓊⓈ -t̬ɪd
unmourned ʌnˈmɔːnd, ˌʌn-, ⓊⓈ -ˈmɔːrnd
unmov(e)able ʌnˈmuː.və.bᵊl, ˌʌn-
unmoved ʌnˈmuːvd, ˌʌn-
unmuffl|e ʌnˈmʌf.ᵊl, ˌʌn- **-es** -z **-ing** -ɪŋ, -ˈmʌf.lɪŋ **-ed** -d
unmusic|al ʌnˈmjuː.zɪ.k|ᵊl, ˌʌn- **-ally** -ᵊl.i, -li
unmuzzl|e ʌnˈmʌz.ᵊl, ˌʌn- **-es** -z **-ing** -ˈmʌz.lɪŋ **-ed** -d
unnamed ʌnˈneɪmd, ˌʌn-
unnatural ʌnˈnætʃ.ᵊr.ᵊl, ˌʌn-, -ʊ.rᵊl, ⓊⓈ -ɚ.əl, ˈ-rᵊl **-ly** -i **-ness** -nəs, -nɪs
unnavigable ʌnˈnæv.ɪ.gə.bᵊl, ˌʌn-
unnecessarily ʌnˈnes.ə.sᵊr.ᵊl.i, ˌʌn-, ˈ-ɪ-, -ɪ.li; -ˌnes.əˈser-, -ɪˈ-, ⓊⓈ -ˌnes.əˈser-; ⓊⓈ -ˈnes.ə.ser-
unnecessary ʌnˈnes.ə.sᵊr.i, ˌʌn-, ˈ-ɪ-, -ser-, ⓊⓈ -ser-
unneighbo(u)rl|y ʌnˈneɪ.bᵊl|.i, ˌʌn-, ⓊⓈ -bɚ.l|i **-iness** -ɪ.nəs, -ɪ.nɪs
unnerv|e ʌnˈnɜːv, ˌʌn-, ⓊⓈ -ˈnɝːv **-es** -z **-ing/ly** -ɪŋ/li **-ed** -d
unnoticeab|le ʌnˈnəʊ.tɪ.sə.b|ᵊl, ˌʌn-, -tə-, ⓊⓈ -ˈnoʊ.t̬ə- **-ly** -li
unnoticed ʌnˈnəʊ.tɪst, ˌʌn-, ⓊⓈ -ˈnoʊ.t̬ɪst
unnumbered ʌnˈnʌm.bəd, ˌʌn-, ⓊⓈ -bɚd
uno, U~ ˈuː.nəʊ, ˈjuː-, ⓊⓈ -noʊ ˌ**Fiat ˈUno®**
UNO ˈjuː.nəʊ, ⓊⓈ -noʊ
unobjectionab|le ˌʌn.əbˈdʒek.ʃᵊn.ə.b|ᵊl, -ˈdʒekʃ.nə- **-ly** -li
unobliging ˌʌn.əˈblaɪ.dʒɪŋ **-ly** -li
unobliterated ˌʌn.əˈblɪt.ᵊr.eɪ.tɪd, ⓊⓈ -ˈblɪt̬.ə.reɪ.t̬ɪd
unobservant ˌʌn.əbˈzɜː.vᵊnt, ⓊⓈ -ˈzɝː- **-ly** -li
unobserv|ed ˌʌn.əbˈzɜːv|d, ⓊⓈ -ˈzɝːv|d **-edly** -ɪd.li
unobstructed ˌʌn.əbˈstrʌk.tɪd
unobtainable ˌʌn.əbˈteɪ.nə.bᵊl
unobtrusive ˌʌn.əbˈtruː.sɪv, ⓊⓈ -əbˈ- **-ly** -li **-ness** -nəs, -nɪs
unoccupied ʌnˈɒk.jə.paɪd, ˌʌn-, -jʊ-, ⓊⓈ -ˈɑː.kjə-
unoffending ˌʌn.əˈfen.dɪŋ
unoffensive ˌʌn.əˈfen*t*.sɪv
unofficial ˌʌn.əˈfɪʃ.ᵊl **-ly** -li
unopened ʌnˈəʊ.pᵊnd, ʌn-, ⓊⓈ -ˈoʊ-
unopposed ˌʌn.əˈpəʊzd, ⓊⓈ -ˈpoʊzd
unordained ˌʌn.ɔːˈdeɪnd, ⓊⓈ -ɔːrˈ-
unordered ʌnˈɔː.dəd, ˌʌn-, ⓊⓈ -ˈɔːr.dɚd
unorganized, -ised ʌnˈɔː.gᵊn.aɪzd, ˌʌn-, ⓊⓈ -ˈɔːr-
unorthodox ʌnˈɔː.θə.dɒks, ˌʌn-, ⓊⓈ -ˈɔːr.θə.dɑːks **-ly** -li
unorthodoxy ʌnˈɔː.θə.dɒk.si, ˌʌn-, ⓊⓈ -ˈɔːr.θə.dɑːk-
unostentatious ˌʌn.ɒs.tenˈteɪ.ʃəs, ʌnˌɒs-, -tənˈ-, ⓊⓈ -ˌɑː.stənˈ- **-ly** -li **-ness** -nəs, -nɪs
unowned ʌnˈəʊnd, ˌʌn-, ⓊⓈ -ˈoʊnd
unpack ʌnˈpæk, ˌʌn-, ʌm-, ˌʌm-, ⓊⓈ ʌn-, ˌʌn- **-s** -s **-ing** -ɪŋ **-ed** -t **-er/s** -əʳ/z, ⓊⓈ -ɚ/z
unpaid ʌnˈpeɪd, ˌʌn-, ʌm-, ˌʌm-, ⓊⓈ ʌn-, ˌʌn-
unpaired ʌnˈpeəd, ˌʌn-, ʌm-, ˌʌm-, ⓊⓈ ʌnˈperd, ˌʌn-
unpalatability ˌʌn.pæl.ə.təˈbɪl.ɪ.ti, ʌnˌpæl-, ˌʌm-, ʌmˌ-, ˌ-ɪ-, -ə.ti, ⓊⓈ ˌʌn.pæl.ə.t̬əˈbɪl.ə.t̬i, ʌnˌpæl-
unpalatab|le ʌnˈpæl.ə.tə.b|ᵊl, ˌʌn-, ʌm-, ˌʌm-, ˈ-ɪ-, ⓊⓈ ʌnˈpæl.ə.t̬ə-, ˌʌn- **-leness** -ᵊl.nəs, -nɪs
unparalleled ʌnˈpær.ᵊl.eld, ˌʌn-, ʌm-, ˌʌm-, ⓊⓈ ʌnˈper-, ˌʌn-, -ˈpær-
unpardonab|le ʌnˈpɑː.dᵊn.ə.b|ᵊl, ˌʌn-, ʌm-, ˌʌm-, -ˈpɑːd.nə-, ⓊⓈ ʌnˈpɑːr.dᵊn.ə-, ˌʌn-, -ˈpɑːrd.nə- **-leness** -ᵊl.nəs, -nɪs
unpardonab|ly ʌnˈpɑː.dᵊn.ə.b|li, ˌʌn-, ʌm-, ˌʌm-, -ˈpɑːd.nə-, ⓊⓈ ʌnˈpɑːr.dᵊn.ə-, ˌʌn-, -ˈpɑːrd.nə-
unparliamentary ˌʌn.pɑː.ləˈmen.tᵊr.i, ʌnˌpɑː-, ˌʌm-, ʌmˌ-, -lɪˈ-, -li.əˈ-, ⓊⓈ ˌʌn.pɑːr.ləˈmen.t̬ɚ-, ʌnˌpɑːr-, ˈ-tri
unpasteurized, -ised ʌnˈpæs.tʃᵊr.aɪzd, ˌʌn-, ʌm-, ˌʌm-, -ˈpɑːs-, -tjᵊr-, -tᵊr-, ⓊⓈ ʌnˈpæs.tʃə.raɪzd, ˌʌn-, -tə-
unpatriotic ˌʌn.pæt.riˈɒt.ɪk, ʌn-, ʌm-, ˌʌm-, -ˌpeɪ.triˈ-, ⓊⓈ ˌʌn.peɪ.triˈɑː.t̬ɪk, ʌn- **-ally** -ᵊl.i, -li
unpaved ʌnˈpeɪvd, ˌʌn-, ʌm-, ˌʌm-, ⓊⓈ ʌn-, ˌʌn-
unpeeled ʌnˈpiːld, ˌʌn-, ʌm-, ˌʌm-, ⓊⓈ ʌn-, ˌʌn-
unperceiv|able ˌʌn.pəˈsiː.v|ə.bᵊl, ˌʌm-, ⓊⓈ ˌʌn.pɚˈ- **-ed** -d
unperforated ʌnˈpɜː.fᵊr.eɪ.tɪd, ˌʌn-, ʌm-, ˌʌm-, ⓊⓈ ʌnˈpɝː.fə.reɪ.t̬ɪd, ˌʌn-
unperformed ˌʌn.pəˈfɔːmd, ˌʌm-, ⓊⓈ ˌʌn.pɚˈfɔːrmd
unpersuadable ˌʌn.pəˈsweɪ.də.bᵊl, ˌʌm-, ⓊⓈ ˌʌn.pɚˈ-
unpersuaded ˌʌn.pəˈsweɪ.dɪd, ˌʌm-, ⓊⓈ ˌʌn.pɚˈ-
unpersuasive ˌʌn.pəˈsweɪ.sɪv, ˌʌm-, -zɪv, ⓊⓈ ˌʌn.pɚˈ-
unperturbable ˌʌn.pəˈtɜː.bə.bᵊl, ˌʌm-, ⓊⓈ ˌʌn.pɚˈtɝː-
unperturbed ˌʌn.pəˈtɜːbd, ˌʌm-, ⓊⓈ ˌʌn.pɚˈtɝːbd
unphilosophic|al ˌʌn.fɪl.əˈsɒf.ɪ.k|ᵊl, ⓊⓈ -ˈsɑː.fɪ- **-ally** -ᵊl.i, -li **-alness** -ᵊl.nəs, -nɪs
unpick ʌnˈpɪk, ˌʌn-, ʌm-, ˌʌm-, ⓊⓈ ʌn-, ˌʌn- **-s** -s **-ing** -ɪŋ **-ed** -t
unpiloted ʌnˈpaɪ.lə.tɪd, ˌʌn-, ʌm-, ˌʌm-, ⓊⓈ ʌnˈpaɪ.lə.t̬ɪd, ˌʌn-
unpin ʌnˈpɪn, ˌʌn-, ʌm-, ˌʌm-, ⓊⓈ ʌn-, ˌʌn- **-s** -z **-ning** -ɪŋ **-ned** -d
unpitying ʌnˈpɪt.i.ɪŋ, ˌʌn-, ʌm-, ˌʌm-, ⓊⓈ ʌnˈpɪt̬.i-, ˌʌn- **-ly** -li
unplaced ʌnˈpleɪst, ˌʌn-, ʌm-, ˌʌm-, ⓊⓈ ʌn-, ˌʌn-

nplanned ʌnˈplænd, ˌʌn-, ʌm-, ˌʌm-, (US) ʌn-, ˌʌn-
nplayable ʌnˈpleɪ.ə.bəl, ˌʌn-, ʌm-, ˌʌm-, (US) ʌn-, ˌʌn-
npleasant ʌnˈplez.ənt, ˌʌn-, ʌm-, ˌʌm-, (US) ʌn-, ˌʌn- **-ly** -li **-ness** -nəs, -nɪs
npleasing ʌnˈpliː.zɪŋ, ˌʌn-, ʌm-, ˌʌm-, (US) ʌn-, ˌʌn- **-ly** -li **-ness** -nəs, -nɪs
nplug ʌnˈplʌg, ˌʌn-, ʌm-, ˌʌm-, (US) ʌn-, ˌʌn- **-s** -z **-ging** -ɪŋ **-ged** -d
nplumbed ʌnˈplʌmd, ˌʌn-, ʌm-, ˌʌm-, (US) ʌn-, ˌʌm-
npoetic|al ˌʌn.pəʊˈet.ɪ.k|əl, ˌʌm-, (US) ˌʌn.poʊˈet̬- **-ally** -əl.i, -li **-alness** -əl.nəs, -nɪs
npolished ʌnˈpɒl.ɪʃt, ˌʌn-, ʌm-, ˌʌm-, (US) ʌnˈpɑː.lɪʃt, ˌʌn-
npolitical ˌʌn.pəˈlɪt.ɪ.kəl, ˌʌm-, (US) ˌʌn.pəˈlɪt̬-
unpolluted ˌʌn.pəˈluː.tɪd, ˌʌm-, -ˈljuː-, (US) ˌʌn.pəˈluː.t̬ɪd
unpopular ʌnˈpɒp.jə.ləʳ, ˌʌn-, ʌm-, ˌʌm-, -jʊ-, (US) ʌnˈpɑː.pjə.lɚ, ˌʌn-
unpopularity ˌʌn.pɒp.jəˈlær.ə.ti, ʌnˌpɒp-, ˌʌm-, ʌm-, -jʊˈ-, -ɪ.ti, (US) ˌʌn.pɑː.pjəˈler.ə.t̬i, ʌnˌpɑː-, -pjʊˈ-, -ˈlær-
unpractic|al ʌnˈpræk.tɪ.k|əl, ˌʌn-, ʌm-, ˌʌm-, (US) ʌn-, ˌʌn- **-ally** -əl.i, -li
unpracticality ˌʌn.præk.tɪˈkæl.ə.ti, ʌnˌpræk-, ˌʌm-, ʌm-, -təˈ-, -ɪ.ti, (US) ˌʌn.præk.təˈkæl.ə.t̬i, ʌnˌpræk-
unpractised, -iced ʌnˈpræk.tɪst, ˌʌn-, ʌm-, ˌʌm-, (US) ʌn-, ˌʌn-
unprecedented ʌnˈpres.ɪ.dən.tɪd, ˌʌn-, ʌm-, ˌʌm-, -ˈpriː.sɪ-, -den-, (US) ʌnˈpres.ə.den.t̬ɪd, ˌʌn-
unpredictability ˌʌn.prɪˌdɪk.təˈbɪl.ɪ.ti, ˌʌm-, -prə-, -ɪ.ti, (US) ˌʌn.prɪˌdɪk.təˈbɪl.ə.t̬i, -ˌpriː-
unpredictab|le ˌʌn.prɪˈdɪk.tə.b|əl, ˌʌm-, -prəˈ-, (US) ˌʌn.prɪˈ-, -priːˈ- **-ly** -li
unprejudiced ʌnˈpredʒ.ə.dɪst, ˌʌn-, ʌm-, ˌʌm-, ˈ-ʊ-, (US) ʌnˈpredʒ.ə-, ˌʌn-
unpremeditated ˌʌn.priːˈmed.ɪ.teɪ.tɪd, ˌʌm-, -prɪˈ-, ˈ-ə-, (US) ˌʌn.priːˈmed.ɪ.teɪ.t̬ɪd
unpre|pared ˌʌn.prɪ|ˈpeəd, ˌʌm-, -prəˈ-, (US) ˌʌn.prɪ|ˈperd, -priːˈ- **-paredly** -ˈpeə.rɪd.li, -ˈpeəd.li, (US) -ˈper.ɪd.li, -ˈperd.li **-paredness** -ˈpeə.rɪd.nəs, -ˈpeəd.nəs, -nɪs, (US) -ˈper.ɪd.nəs, -ˈperd.nəs, -nɪs
unprepossessing ˌʌn.priː.pəˈzes.ɪŋ, ʌnˌpriː-, ˌʌm-, ʌmˌ-, (US) ˌʌn-, ʌnˌ- **-ly** -li
unpresentable ˌʌn.prɪˈzen.tə.bəl, ˌʌm-, -prəˈ-, (US) ˌʌn.prɪˈzen.t̬ə-, -priːˈ-
unpresuming ˌʌn.prɪˈzjuː.mɪŋ, ˌʌm-, -prəˈ-, -ˈzuː-, (US) ˌʌn.prɪˈzuː-, -priːˈ-, -ˈzjuː-
unpretending ˌʌn.prɪˈten.dɪŋ, ˌʌm-, -prəˈ-, (US) ˌʌn.prɪˈten.dɪŋ, -priːˈ- **-ly** -li
unpretentious ˌʌn.prɪˈten.tʃəs, ˌʌm-, -prəˈ-, (US) ˌʌn.prɪˈ-, -priːˈ- **-ly** -li **-ness** -nəs, -nɪs
unpreventable ˌʌn.prɪˈven.tə.bəl, ˌʌm-, -prəˈ-, (US) ˌʌn.prɪˈven.t̬ə-, -priːˈ-
unpriced ʌnˈpraɪst, ˌʌn-, ʌm-, ˌʌm-, (US) ʌn-, ˌʌn-
unprincipled ʌnˈprɪnt.sə.pəld, ˌʌn-, ʌm-, ˌʌm-, -sɪ-, (US) ʌn-, ˌʌn-
unprintable ʌnˈprɪn.tə.bəl, ˌʌn-, ʌm-, ˌʌm-, (US) ʌnˈprɪn.t̬ə-, ˌʌn-
unprinted ʌnˈprɪn.tɪd, ˌʌn-, ʌm-, ˌʌm-, (US) ʌnˈprɪn.t̬ɪd, ˌʌn-
unproclaimed ˌʌn.prəʊˈkleɪmd, ˌʌm-, (US) ˌʌn.proʊˈ-, -prəˈ-
unprocurable ˌʌn.prəˈkjʊə.rə.bəl, ˌʌm-, -ˈkjɔː-, (US) ˌʌn.prəˈkjʊr.ə-, -proʊˈ-
unproductive ˌʌn.prəˈdʌk.tɪv, ˌʌm-, (US) ˌʌn- **-ly** -li **-ness** -nəs, -nɪs
unprofessional ˌʌn.prəˈfeʃ.ən.əl, ˌʌm-, -ˈfeʃ.nəl, (US) ˌʌn- **-ly** -i **-ness** -nəs, -nɪs
unprofitab|le ʌnˈprɒf.ɪ.tə.b|əl, ˌʌn-, ʌm-, ˌʌm-, ˈ-ə-, (US) ʌnˈprɑː.fɪ.t̬ə-, ˌʌn- **-ly** -li **-leness** -əl.nəs, -nɪs
Unprofor ˈʌn.prə.fɔːʳ, ˈʌm-, (US) ˈʌn.prə.fɔːr
unprohibited ˌʌn.prəʊˈhɪb.ɪ.tɪd, ˌʌm-, ˈ-ə-, (US) ˌʌn.proʊˈhɪb.ə.t̬ɪd, -prəˈ-
unpromising ʌnˈprɒm.ɪ.sɪŋ, ˌʌn-, ʌm-, ˌʌm-, ˈ-ə-, (US) ʌnˈprɑː.mə-, ˌʌn- **-ly** -li
unprompted ʌnˈprɒmp.tɪd, ˌʌn-, ʌm-, ˌʌm-, (US) ʌnˈprɑːmp-, ˌʌn-
unpronounceable ˌʌn.prəˈnaʊnt.sə.bəl, ˌʌm-, (US) ˌʌn-
unprop ʌnˈprɒp, ˌʌn-, ʌm-, ˌʌn-, (US) ʌnˈprɑːp, ˌʌn- **-s** -s **-ping** -ɪŋ **-ped** -t
unpropitious ˌʌn.prəˈpɪʃ.əs, ˌʌm-, (US) ˌʌn.prəˈ-, -proʊˈ- **-ly** -li **-ness** -nəs, -nɪs
unprotected ˌʌn.prəˈtek.tɪd, ˌʌm-, (US) ˌʌn-
unproved ʌnˈpruːvd, ˌʌn-, ʌm-, ˌʌm-, (US) ʌn-, ˌʌn-
unproven ʌnˈpruː.vən, ˌʌn-, ʌm-, ˌʌm-, -ˈprəʊ-, (US) ʌnˈpruː-, ˌʌn-
unprovided ˌʌn.prəˈvaɪ.dɪd, ˌʌm-, (US) ˌʌn-
unprovok|ed ˌʌn.prəˈvəʊk|t, ˌʌm-, (US) ˌʌn.prəˈvoʊk|t **-edly** -ɪd.li, -t.li
unpublished ʌnˈpʌb.lɪʃt, ˌʌn-, ʌm-, ˌʌm-, (US) ʌn-, ˌʌn-
unpunctual ʌnˈpʌŋk.tʃu.əl, ˌʌn-, ʌm-, ˌʌm-, -tʃʊəl, -tju.əl, -tjʊəl, (US) ʌnˈpʌŋk.tʃu.əl, ˌʌn- **-ly** -i
unpunctuality ˌʌn.pʌŋk.tʃuˈæl.ə.ti, ʌnˌpʌŋk-, ˌʌm-, ʌmˌ-, -tjuˈ-, -ɪ.ti, (US) ˌʌn.pʌŋk.tʃuˈæl.ə.t̬i, ʌnˌpʌŋk-
unpunished ʌnˈpʌn.ɪʃt, ˌʌn-, ʌm-, ˌʌm-, (US) ʌn-, ˌʌn-
unputdownable ˌʌn.pʊtˈdaʊ.nə.bəl, ˌʌm-, (US) ˌʌn-
unqualified ʌnˈkwɒl.ɪ.faɪd, ˌʌn-, ʌŋ-, ˌʌŋ-, ˈ-ə-, (US) ʌnˈkwɑː.lə-, ˌʌn-
unquenchable ʌnˈkwen.tʃə.bəl, ˌʌn-, ʌŋ-, ˌʌŋ-, (US) ʌn-, ˌʌn-
unquestionab|le ʌnˈkwes.tʃə.nə.b|əl, ˈ-tjə-, ˌʌn-, ʌŋ-, ˌʌŋ-, -ˈkweʃ-, (US) ʌnˈkwes.tʃə-, ˌʌn-, -tjə- **-ly** -li **-leness** -əl.nəs, -nɪs
unquestioned ʌnˈkwes.tʃənd, ˈ-tjənd, ˌʌn-, ʌŋ-, ˌʌŋ-, -ˈkweʃ-, (US) ʌnˈkwes.tʃənd, ˌʌn-, -tjənd
unquestioning ʌnˈkwes.tʃə.nɪŋ, ˈ-tjə-, ˌʌn-, ʌŋ-, ˌʌŋ-, -ˈkweʃ-, (US) ʌnˈkwes.tʃə-, ˌʌn-, -tjə- **-ly** -li
unquiet ʌnˈkwaɪət, -ˈkwaɪ.ət, (US) -ˈkwaɪ.ət, ʌŋ- **-ly** -li **-ness** -nəs, -nɪs
unquote ʌnˈkwəʊt, ˌʌn-, ʌŋ-, ˌʌŋ-, (US) ʌnˈkwoʊt, ˌʌn-
unravel ʌnˈræv.əl, ˌʌn- **-s** -z **-(l)ing** -ɪŋ, -ˈræv.lɪŋ **-(l)ed** -d **-(l)er/s** -əʳ/z, -ɚ/z, (US) -ˈræv.ləʳ/z, -lɚ/z
unread ʌnˈred, ˌʌn-
unreadable ʌnˈriː.də.bəl, ˌʌn- **-ness** -nəs, -nɪs
unread|y ʌnˈred|.i, ˌʌn- **-ily** -əl.i, -ɪ.li **-iness** -ɪ.nəs, -ɪ.nɪs
unreal ʌnˈrɪəl, ˌʌn-, (US) -ˈriːl, -ˈriː.əl
unrealistic ˌʌn.rɪəˈlɪs.tɪk, (US) -ri.əˈ- **-ally** -əl.i, -li
unrealit|y ˌʌn.riˈæl.ə.t|i, -ɪ.t|i, (US) -ə.t̬|i **-ies** -iz
unreason ʌnˈriː.zən, ˌʌn-
unreasonab|le ʌnˈriː.zən.ə.b|əl, ˌʌn-, -ˈriːz.nə- **-ly** -li **-leness** -əl.nəs, -nɪs
unreasoning ʌnˈriː.zən.ɪŋ, ˌʌn-, -ˈriːz.nɪŋ
unreceived ˌʌn.rɪˈsiːvd, -rəˈ-, (US) -rɪˈ-
unreciprocated ˌʌn.rɪˈsɪp.rə.keɪ.tɪd, -rəˈ-, (US) -rɪˈsɪp.rə.keɪ.t̬ɪd
unreclaimed ˌʌn.rɪˈkleɪmd
unrecognizable, -isa- ʌnˈrek.əg.naɪ.zə.bəl, ˌʌn-, ˌʌn.rek.əgˈnaɪ-, (US) ˌʌn.rek.əgˈnaɪ-, ʌnˈrek.əg.naɪ-, ˌʌn-
unrecognized, -ised ʌnˈrek.əg.naɪzd, ˌʌn-
unreconcilable ˌʌn.rek.ənˈsaɪ.lə.bəl, ʌnˈrek.ən.saɪ-
unreconciled ʌnˈrek.ən.saɪld, ˌʌn-
unreconstructed ˌʌn.riː.kənˈstrʌk.tɪd
unrecorded ˌʌn.rɪˈkɔː.dɪd, -rəˈ-, (US) -rɪˈkɔːr-
unrecounted ˌʌn.rɪˈkaʊn.tɪd, -rəˈ-, (US) -rɪˈkaʊn.t̬ɪd
unredeemable ˌʌn.rɪˈdiː.mə.bəl, -rəˈ-, (US) -rɪˈ-
unredeemed ˌʌn.rɪˈdiːmd, -rəˈ-, (US) -rɪˈ-
unrefined ˌʌn.rɪˈfaɪnd, -rəˈ-, (US) -rɪˈ-
unreflecting ˌʌn.rɪˈflek.tɪŋ, -rəˈ-, (US) -rɪˈ-
unreformed ˌʌn.rɪˈfɔːmd, -rəˈ-, (US) -rɪˈfɔːrmd
unrefuted ˌʌn.rɪˈfjuː.tɪd, -rəˈ-, (US) -rɪˈfjuː.t̬ɪd
unregenerate ˌʌn.rɪˈdʒen.ər.ət, -rəˈ-, -ɪt, (US) -rəˈdʒen.ɚ.ɪt
unregistered ʌnˈredʒ.ɪ.stəd, ˌʌn-, (US) -stɚd

U

unregulated ʌnˈreg.jə.leɪ.tɪd, -jʊ-, Ⓤⓢ -t̬ɪd
unrehearsed ˌʌn.rɪˈhɜːst, -rəˈ-, Ⓤⓢ -rɪˈhɝːst
unrelated ˌʌn.rɪˈleɪ.tɪd, -rəˈ-, Ⓤⓢ -rɪˈleɪ.t̬ɪd
unrelaxed ˌʌn.rɪˈlækst, -rəˈ-, Ⓤⓢ -rɪˈ-
unrelenting ˌʌn.rɪˈlen.tɪŋ, -rəˈ-, Ⓤⓢ -rɪˈlen.t̬ɪŋ **-ly** -li **-ness** -nəs, -nɪs
unreliability ˌʌn.rɪ.laɪ.əˈbɪl.ɪ.ti, -rə-, -ə.ti, Ⓤⓢ -rɪ.laɪ.əˈbɪl.ə.t̬i
unreliab|le ˌʌn.rɪˈlaɪ.ə.b|əl, -rəˈ-, Ⓤⓢ -rɪˈ- **-ly** -li **-leness** -əl.nəs, -nɪs
unreliev|ed ˌʌn.rɪˈliːv|d, -rəˈ-, Ⓤⓢ -rɪˈ- **-edly** -ɪd.li
unremarkable ˌʌn.rɪˈmɑː.kə.bəl, -rəˈ-, Ⓤⓢ -ˈmɑːr-
unremembered ˌʌn.rɪˈmem.bəd, -rəˈ-, Ⓤⓢ -rɪˈmem.bɚd
unremitting ˌʌn.rɪˈmɪt.ɪŋ, -rəˈ-, Ⓤⓢ -rɪˈmɪt̬- **-ly** -li **-ness** -nəs, -nɪs
unremovable ˌʌn.rɪˈmuː.və.bəl, -rəˈ-, Ⓤⓢ -rɪˈ-
unremunerative ˌʌn.rɪˈmjuː.nər.ə.tɪv, -rəˈ-, Ⓤⓢ -rɪˈmjuː.nɚ.ə.t̬ɪv, -nə.reɪ-
unrepaired ˌʌn.rɪˈpeəd, Ⓤⓢ -ˈperd
unrepeatable ˌʌn.rɪˈpiː.tə.bəl, -rəˈ-, Ⓤⓢ -rɪˈpiː.t̬ə-
unrepentant ˌʌn.rɪˈpen.tənt, -rəˈ-, Ⓤⓢ -rɪˈpen.tənt
unreplaceable ˌʌn.rɪˈpleɪs.ə.bəl
unreported ˌʌn.rɪˈpɔː.tɪd, -rəˈ-, Ⓤⓢ -rɪˈpɔːr.t̬ɪd
unrepresentative ˌʌn.rep.rɪˈzen.tə.tɪv, Ⓤⓢ -t̬ə.t̬ɪv
unrepresented ˌʌn.rep.rɪˈzen.tɪd, Ⓤⓢ -t̬ɪd
unrequested ˌʌn.rɪˈkwes.tɪd, -rəˈ-, Ⓤⓢ -rɪˈ-
unrequited ˌʌn.rɪˈkwaɪ.tɪd, -rəˈ-, Ⓤⓢ -rɪˈkwaɪ.t̬ɪd ˌ**unrequited** ˈ**love**
unreserv|ed ˌʌn.rɪˈzɜːv|d, -rəˈ-, Ⓤⓢ -rɪˈzɝːv|d **-edly** -ɪd.li **-edness** -ɪd.nəs, -nɪs
unresisting ˌʌn.rɪˈzɪs.tɪŋ, -rəˈ-, Ⓤⓢ -rɪˈ- **-ly** -li
unresolved ˌʌn.rɪˈzɒlvd, -rəˈ-, Ⓤⓢ -rɪˈzɑːlvd
unresponsive ˌʌn.rɪˈspɒnt.sɪv, -rəˈ-, Ⓤⓢ -rɪˈspɑːnt- **-ly** -li **-ness** -nəs, -nɪs
unrest ʌnˈrest, ˌʌn-, Ⓤⓢ ʌnˈrest, ˌʌn-, ˈ--
unrestful ʌnˈrest.fəl, ˌʌn-, -fʊl **-ly** -i **-ness** -nəs, -nɪs
unresting ʌnˈres.tɪŋ, ˌʌn-
unrestored ˌʌn.rɪˈstɔːd, -rəˈ-, Ⓤⓢ -rɪˈstɔːrd
unrestrain|ed ˌʌn.rɪˈstreɪn|d, -rəˈ-, Ⓤⓢ -rɪˈ- **-edly** -ɪd.li
unrestraint ˌʌn.rɪˈstreɪnt
unrestricted ˌʌn.rɪˈstrɪk.tɪd, -rəˈ-, Ⓤⓢ -rɪˈ-
unretentive ˌʌn.rɪˈten.tɪv, -rəˈ-, Ⓤⓢ -rɪˈten.t̬ɪv
unreveal|ed ˌʌn.rɪˈviːl|d, -rəˈ-, Ⓤⓢ -rɪˈ- **-ing** -ɪŋ
unrevoked ˌʌn.rɪˈvəʊkt, -rəˈ-, Ⓤⓢ -rɪˈvoʊkt
unrewarded ˌʌn.rɪˈwɔː.dɪd, -rəˈ-, Ⓤⓢ -rɪˈwɔːr-
unriddl|e ʌnˈrɪd.əl **-es** -z **-ing** -ɪŋ **-ed** -d
unrighteous ʌnˈraɪ.tʃəs, -ti.əs, Ⓤⓢ -tʃəs **-ly** -li **-ness** -nəs, -nɪs
unrightful ʌnˈraɪt.fəl, ˌʌn-, -fʊl **-ly** -i **-ness** -nəs, -nɪs
unripe ʌnˈraɪp, ˌʌn- **-ness** -nəs, -nɪs
unrival(l)ed ʌnˈraɪ.vəld, ˌʌn-
unrob|e ʌnˈrəʊb, ˌʌn-, Ⓤⓢ -ˈroʊb **-es** -z **-ing** -ɪŋ **-ed** -d
unroll ʌnˈrəʊl, ˌʌn-, Ⓤⓢ -ˈroʊl **-s** -z **-ing** -ɪŋ **-ed** -d
unromantic ˌʌn.rəʊˈmæn.tɪk, Ⓤⓢ -roʊˈmæn.t̬ɪk, -rəˈ- **-ally** -əl.i, -li
unrounded ʌnˈraʊn.dɪd, ˌʌn-
unruffled ʌnˈrʌf.əld, ˌʌn-
unrul|y ʌnˈruː.l|i, ˌʌn- **-ier** -i.əʳ, Ⓤⓢ -i.ɚ **-iest** -i.ɪst, -i.əst **-iness** -ɪ.nəs, -ɪ.nɪs
unsaddl|e ʌnˈsæd.əl, ˌʌn- **-es** -z **-ing** -ɪŋ, -ˈsæd.lɪŋ **-ed** -d
unsafe ʌnˈseɪf, ˌʌn- **-ly** -li **-ness** -nəs, -nɪs
unsaid ʌnˈsed, ˌʌn-
unsal(e)able ʌnˈseɪ.lə.bəl, ˌʌn-
unsalted ʌnˈsɔːl.tɪd, ˌʌn-, -ˈsɒl-, Ⓤⓢ -ˈsɔːl.tɪd, -sɑː-
unsanctified ʌnˈsæŋk.tɪ.faɪd, ˌʌn-
unsanitary ʌnˈsæn.ɪ.tər.i, ˌʌn-, ˈ-ə-, -tri, Ⓤⓢ -ˈsæn.ə.ter.i
unsatisfactor|y ˌʌn.sæt.ɪsˈfæk.tər|.i, ʌnˌsæt-, Ⓤⓢ ˌʌn.sæt̬-, ʌnˌsæt̬- **-ily** -əl.i, -ɪ.li **-iness** -ɪ.nəs, -ɪ.nɪs
unsatisf|ied ʌnˈsæt.ɪs.f|aɪd, ˌʌn-, Ⓤⓢ -ˈsæt̬- **-ying** -aɪ.ɪŋ
unsaturated ʌnˈsætʃ.ər.eɪ.tɪd, ˌʌn-, -tʃʊ.reɪ-, -tjər.eɪ, -tjʊ.reɪ-, Ⓤⓢ -ˈsætʃ.ə.reɪ.t̬ɪd **un**ˌ**saturated** ˈ**fat**
unsavo(u)r|y ʌnˈseɪ.vər|.i, ˌʌn- **-iness** -ɪ.nəs, -ɪ.nɪs
un|say ʌn|ˈseɪ, ˌʌn- **-says** -ˈsez **-saying** -ˈseɪ.ɪŋ **-said** -ˈsed **-sayable** -ˈseɪ.ə.bəl
unscathed ʌnˈskeɪðd, ˌʌn-
unscented ʌnˈsen.tɪd, ˌʌn-, Ⓤⓢ -t̬ɪd
unscheduled ʌnˈʃed.juːld, ˌʌn-, -ˈʃedʒ.uːld, -ˈsked.juːld, -ˈskedʒ.uːld, -əld, Ⓤⓢ -ˈskedʒ.ʊld, -uːld, -u.əld
unscholarly ʌnˈskɒl.ə.li, ˌʌn-, Ⓤⓢ -ˈskɑː.lɚ-
unschooled ʌnˈskuːld, ˌʌn-
unscientific ˌʌn.saɪ.ənˈtɪf.ɪk **-ally** -əl.i, -li
Unscom ˈʌn.skɒm, Ⓤⓢ -skɑːm
unscrambl|e ʌnˈskræm.bəl, ˌʌn- **-es** -z **-ing** -ɪŋ, -ˈskræm.blɪŋ **-ed** -d
unscrew ʌnˈskruː, ˌʌn- **-s** -z **-ing** -ɪŋ **-ed** -d
unscripted ʌnˈskrɪp.tɪd, ˌʌn-
unscriptural ʌnˈskrɪp.tʃər.əl, ˌʌn-, -tʃʊ.rəl, Ⓤⓢ -tʃɚ.əl **-ly** -i
unscrupulous ʌnˈskruː.pjə.ləs, ˌʌn-, -pjʊ-, Ⓤⓢ -pjə-, -pjʊ- **-ly** -li **-ness** -nəs, -nɪs
unseal ʌnˈsiːl, ˌʌn- **-s** -z **-ing** -ɪŋ **-ed** -d
unseasonab|le ʌnˈsiː.zən.ə.b|əl, ˌʌn-, -ˈsiːz.nə- **-ly** -li **-leness** -əl.nəs -nɪs
unseasoned ʌnˈsiː.zənd, ˌʌn-
un|seat ʌn|ˈsiːt, ˌʌn- **-seats** -ˈsiːts **-seating** -ˈsiː.tɪŋ, Ⓤⓢ -ˈsiː.t̬ɪŋ **-seated** -ˈsiː.tɪd, Ⓤⓢ -ˈsiː.t̬ɪd
unseaworth|y ʌnˈsiːˌwɜː.ð|i, ˌʌn-, Ⓤⓢ -ˌwɝː- **-iness** -ɪ.nəs, -ɪ.nɪs
unsectarian ˌʌn.sekˈteə.ri.ən, Ⓤⓢ -ˈter.i-
unsecured ˌʌn.sɪˈkjʊəd, -səˈ-, -ˈkjɔːd, Ⓤⓢ -ˈkjʊrd
unseeded ʌnˈsiː.dɪd, ˌʌn-
unseeing ʌnˈsiː.ɪŋ, ˌʌn- **-ly** -li
unseeml|y ʌnˈsiːm.l|i, Ⓤⓢ ˌʌn- **-iness** -ɪ.nəs, -ɪ.nɪs
unseen ʌnˈsiːn, ˌʌn-
unselfconscious ˌʌn.selfˈkɒn.tʃəs, Ⓤⓢ -ˈkɑːn- **-ly** -li **-ness** -nəs, -nɪs
unselfish ʌnˈsel.fɪʃ, ˌʌn- **-ly** -li **-ness** -nəs, -nɪs
unsensational ˌʌn.senˈseɪ.ʃən.əl, -sənˈ-, -ˈseɪʃ.nəl
unsensitive ʌnˈsent.sə.tɪv, ˌʌn-, -sɪ-, Ⓤⓢ -sə.t̬ɪv **-ly** -li **-ness** -nəs, -nɪs
unsentimental ˌʌn.sen.tɪˈmen.təl, Ⓤⓢ -t̬əl **-ly** -i
unserviceable ʌnˈsɜː.vɪ.sə.bəl, ˌʌn-, Ⓤⓢ -ˈsɝː-
unsettl|e ʌnˈset.əl, ˌʌn-, Ⓤⓢ -ˈset̬- **-es** -z **-ing/ly** -ɪŋ/li, -ˈset.lɪŋ/li
unsettled ʌnˈset.əld, Ⓤⓢ -ˈset̬-
unsevered ʌnˈsev.əd, ˌʌn-, Ⓤⓢ -ɚd
unshackl|e ʌnˈʃæk.əl, ˌʌn- **-es** -z **-ing** -ɪŋ, -ˈʃæk.lɪŋ **-ed** -d
unshak(e)able ʌnˈʃeɪ.kə.bəl, ˌʌn-
unshaken ʌnˈʃeɪ.kən, ˌʌn-
unshapely ʌnˈʃeɪ.pli, ˌʌn-
unshaven ʌnˈʃeɪ.vən, ˌʌn-
unsheath|e ʌnˈʃiːð, ˌʌn- **-es** -z **-ing** -ɪŋ **-ed** -d
unship ʌnˈʃɪp, ˌʌn- **-s** -s **-ping** -ɪŋ **-ped** -t
unshockable ʌnˈʃɒk.ə.bəl, ˌʌn-, Ⓤⓢ -ˈʃɑː.kə-
unshod ʌnˈʃɒd, ˌʌn-, Ⓤⓢ -ˈʃɑːd
unshorn ʌnˈʃɔːn, ˌʌn-, Ⓤⓢ -ˈʃɔːrn
unshrinkable ʌnˈʃrɪŋ.kə.bəl, ˌʌn-
unshrinking ʌnˈʃrɪŋ.kɪŋ, ˌʌn- **-ly** -li
unsighted ʌnˈsaɪ.tɪd, ˌʌn-, Ⓤⓢ -t̬ɪd
unsightl|y ʌnˈsaɪt.l|i, ˌʌn- **-ier** -i.əʳ, Ⓤⓢ -i.ɚ **-iest** -i.ɪst, -i.əst **-iness** -ɪ.nəs, -ɪ.nɪs
unsigned ʌnˈsaɪnd, ˌʌn-
unskilful ʌnˈskɪl.fəl, ˌʌn-, -fʊl **-ly** -i
unskilled ʌnˈskɪld, ˌʌn- ˌ**unskilled** ˈ**worker**
unslaked ʌnˈsleɪkt, ˌʌn-
unsliced ʌnˈslaɪst
unsociability ˌʌn.səʊ.ʃəˈbɪl.ɪ.ti, -ˌsəʊ-, -ə.ti, Ⓤⓢ -soʊ.ʃəˈbɪl.ə.t̬i, -ˌsoʊ-
unsociab|le ʌnˈsəʊ.ʃə.b|əl, ˌʌn-, Ⓤⓢ -ˈsoʊ- **-ly** -li **-leness** -əl.nəs, -nɪs
unsocial ʌnˈsəʊ.ʃəl, ˌʌn-, Ⓤⓢ -ˈsoʊ- **-ly** -i ˌ**unsocial** ˈ**hours;** **un**ˌ**social** ˈ**hours**
unsold ʌnˈsəʊld, ˌʌn-, Ⓤⓢ -ˈsoʊld
unsold|er ʌnˈsəʊl.d|əʳ, ˌʌn-, -ˈsɒl-,

U

Ⓤⓢ -ˈsɑː.d|ɚ, -ˈsɑːl- **-ers** -əz, Ⓤⓢ -ɚz **-ering** -ər.ɪŋ **-ered** -əd, Ⓤⓢ -ɚd
unsolicited ˌʌn.səˈlɪs.ɪ.tɪd, Ⓤⓢ -t̬ɪd
unsolved ʌnˈsɒlvd, ˌʌn-, Ⓤⓢ -ˈsɑːlvd, -ˈsɔːlvd
unsophisticated ˌʌn.səˈfɪs.tɪ.keɪ.tɪd, -tə-, Ⓤⓢ -tə.keɪ.t̬ɪd **-ly** -li **-ness** -nəs, -nɪs
unsophistication ˌʌn.səˌfɪs.tɪˈkeɪ.ʃən, -təˈ-
unsorted ʌnˈsɔː.tɪd, ˌʌn-, Ⓤⓢ -ˈsɔːr.t̬ɪd
unsought ʌnˈsɔːt, ˌʌn-, Ⓤⓢ -ˈsɑːt, -ˈsɔːt
unsound ʌnˈsaʊnd, ˌʌn- **-ly** -li **-ness** -nəs, -nɪs
unsparing ʌnˈspeə.rɪŋ, ˌʌn-, Ⓤⓢ -ˈsper.ɪŋ **-ly** -li **-ness** -nəs, -nɪs
unspeakab|le ʌnˈspiː.kə.b|əl, ˌʌn- **-ly** -li
unspecified ʌnˈspes.ɪ.faɪd, ˌʌn-, -ˈə-
unspent ʌnˈspent, ˌʌn-
unspoiled ʌnˈspɔɪlt, ˌʌn-, -ˈspɔɪld, Ⓤⓢ -ˈspɔɪld
unspoilt ʌnˈspɔɪlt, ˌʌn-
unspoken ʌnˈspəʊ.kən, ˌʌn-, Ⓤⓢ -ˈspoʊ-
unsporting ʌnˈspɔː.tɪŋ, ˌʌn-, Ⓤⓢ -ˈspɔːr.t̬ɪŋ **-ly** -li **-ness** -nəs, -nɪs
unsportsmanlike ʌnˈspɔːts.mən.laɪk, ˌʌn-, Ⓤⓢ -ˈspɔːrts-
unspotted ʌnˈspɒt.ɪd, ˌʌn-, Ⓤⓢ -ˈspɑː.t̬ɪd
Unst ʌntst
unstable ʌnˈsteɪ.bəl, ˌʌn- **-ness** -nəs, -nɪs
unstack ʌnˈstæk, ˌʌn- **-s** -s **-ing** -ɪŋ **-ed** -t
unstamped ʌnˈstæmpt, ˌʌn-
unstarched ʌnˈstɑːtʃt, ˌʌn-, Ⓤⓢ -ˈstɑːrtʃt
unstated ʌnˈsteɪ.tɪd, Ⓤⓢ -t̬ɪd
unstatesmanlike ʌnˈsteɪts.mən.laɪk, ˌʌn-
unstead|y ʌnˈsted|.i, ˌʌn- **-ier** -i.ər, Ⓤⓢ -i.ɚ **-iest** -i.ɪst, -i.əst **-ily** -əl.i, -ɪ.li **-iness** -ɪ.nəs, -ɪ.nɪs
unstick ʌnˈstɪk, ˌʌn- **-s** -s **-ing** -ɪŋ
unstuck ʌnˈstʌk, ˌʌn-
unstinted ʌnˈstɪn.tɪd, ˌʌn-, Ⓤⓢ -t̬ɪd
unstinting ʌnˈstɪn.tɪŋ, ˌʌn-, Ⓤⓢ -t̬ɪŋ **-ly** -li
unstitch ʌnˈstɪtʃ, ˌʌn- **-es** -ɪz **-ing** -ɪŋ **-ed** -t
unstop ʌnˈstɒp, ˌʌn-, Ⓤⓢ -ˈstɑːp **-s** -s **-ping** -ɪŋ **-ped** -t
unstoppab|le ʌnˈstɒp.ə.b|əl, ˌʌn-, Ⓤⓢ -ˈstɑː.pə- **-ly** -li
unstrap ʌnˈstræp, ˌʌn- **-s** -s **-ping** -ɪŋ **-ped** -t
unstressed ʌnˈstrest, ˌʌn-
unstructured ʌnˈstrʌk.tʃəd, Ⓤⓢ -tʃɚd
unstrung ʌnˈstrʌŋ, ˌʌn-
unstuck (from **unstick**) ʌnˈstʌk, ˌʌn- **ˌcome unˈstuck**
unstudied ʌnˈstʌd.ɪd, ˌʌn-
unstylish ʌnˈstaɪ.lɪʃ, ˌʌn- **-ly** -li
unsubmissive ˌʌn.səbˈmɪs.ɪv **-ly** -li **-ness** -nəs, -nɪs
unsubscribe ˌʌn.səbˈskraɪb **-es** -z **-ing** -ɪŋ **-ed** -d
unsubstantial ˌʌn.səbˈstæn.tʃəl, -ˈstɑːn-, Ⓤⓢ -ˈstænt.ʃəl **-ly** -i
unsubstantiated ˌʌn.səbˈstæn.tʃi.eɪ.tɪd, -ˈstɑːn-, Ⓤⓢ -ˈstænt.ʃi.eɪ.t̬ɪd
unsuccess ˌʌn.səkˈses, ˈ---, Ⓤⓢ ˌʌn.səkˈses
unsuccessful ˌʌn.səkˈses.fəl, -fʊl **-ly** -i **-ness** -nəs, -nɪs
unsuitability ˌʌn.suː.təˈbɪl.ə.ti, -sjuː-, ʌnˌsuː-, -ˌsjuː-, -ɪ.ti, Ⓤⓢ ˌʌn.suː.t̬əˈbɪl.ə.t̬i, ʌnˌsuː-
unsuitab|le ʌnˈsuː.tə.b|əl, ˌʌn-, -ˈsjuː-, Ⓤⓢ -ˈsuː.t̬ə- **-ly** -li **-leness** -əl.nəs, -nɪs
unsuited ʌnˈsuː.tɪd, ˌʌn-, -ˈsjuː-, Ⓤⓢ -ˈsuː.t̬ɪd
unsullied ʌnˈsʌl.ɪd, ˌʌn-
unsung ʌnˈsʌŋ, ˌʌn-
unsupportab|le ˌʌn.səˈpɔː.tə.b|əl, Ⓤⓢ -ˈpɔːr.t̬ə- **-ly** -li **-leness** -əl.nəs, -nɪs
unsupported ˌʌn.səˈpɔː.tɪd, Ⓤⓢ -ˈpɔːr.t̬ɪd
unsure ʌnˈʃɔːr, ˌʌn-, -ʃʊər, Ⓤⓢ -ˈʃʊr
unsurmountab|le ˌʌn.səˈmaʊn.tə.b|əl, Ⓤⓢ -sɚˈmaʊn.t̬ə- **-ly** -li
unsurpassable ˌʌn.səˈpɑː.sə.bəl, Ⓤⓢ -sɚˈpæs.ə-
unsurpassed ˌʌn.səˈpɑːst, Ⓤⓢ -sɚˈpæst
unsurprising ˌʌn.səˈpraɪ.zɪŋ, Ⓤⓢ -sɚ- **-ly** -li
unsusceptible ˌʌn.səˈsep.tə.bəl, -tɪ-
unsuspected ˌʌn.səˈspek.tɪd
unsuspecting ˌʌn.səˈspek.tɪŋ **-ly** -li **-ness** -nəs, -nɪs
unsuspicious ˌʌn.səˈspɪʃ.əs **-ly** -li **-ness** -nəs, -nɪs
unsustainable ˌʌn.səˈsteɪ.nə.bəl
unsweetened ʌnˈswiː.tənd, ˌʌn-
unswerving ʌnˈswɜː.vɪŋ, ˌʌn-, Ⓤⓢ -ˈswɝː- **-ly** -li
Unsworth ˈʌnz.wəθ, -wɜːθ, Ⓤⓢ -wɚθ, -wɝːθ
unsymmetric ˌʌn.sɪˈmet.rɪk, -səˈ- **-al** -əl **-ally** -əl.i, -li
unsymmetry ʌnˈsɪm.ə.tri, ˌʌn-, ˈ-ɪ-
unsympathetic ˌʌn.sɪm.pəˈθet.ɪk, -ˌsɪm-, Ⓤⓢ -ˈθet̬- **-ally** -əl.i, -li
unsystematic ˌʌn.sɪ.stəˈmæt.ɪk, -ˌsɪs.təˈ-, -tɪˈ-, Ⓤⓢ -stəˈmæt̬- **-al** -əl **-ally** -əl.i, -li
untainted ʌnˈteɪn.tɪd, ˌʌn-, Ⓤⓢ -t̬ɪd
untamable, untameable ʌnˈteɪ.mə.bəl, ˌʌn-
untangl|e ʌnˈtæŋ.gəl, ˌʌn- **-es** -z **-ing** -ɪŋ, -ˈtæŋ.glɪŋ **-ed** -d
untapped ʌnˈtæpt, ˌʌn-
untarnished ʌnˈtɑː.nɪʃt, ˌʌn-, Ⓤⓢ -ˈtɑːr-
untaught ʌnˈtɔːt, ˌʌn-, Ⓤⓢ -ˈtɑːt, -ˈtɔːt
untaxed ʌnˈtækst, ˌʌn-
unteachable ʌnˈtiː.tʃə.bəl, ˌʌn-
untempered ʌnˈtem.pəd, ˌʌn-, Ⓤⓢ -pɚd
untenability ˌʌn.ten.əˈbɪl.ɪ.ti, -ˌten-, -ə.ti, Ⓤⓢ -ə.t̬i
untenable ʌnˈten.ə.bəl, ˌʌn-
untenanted ʌnˈten.ən.tɪd, ˌʌn-, Ⓤⓢ -t̬ɪd
unthankful ʌnˈθæŋk.fəl, ˌʌn-, -fʊl **-ly** -i **-ness** -nəs, -nɪs
unthinka|ble ʌnˈθɪŋ.kə|.bəl, ˌʌn- **-bly** -bli
unthinking ʌnˈθɪŋ.kɪŋ, ˌʌn- **-ly** -li
unthought ʌnˈθɔːt, Ⓤⓢ -ˈθɑːt, -ˈθɔːt **unˈthought of**
unthread ʌnˈθred, ˌʌn- **-s** -z **-ing** -ɪŋ **-ed** -ɪd
untid|y ʌnˈtaɪ.d|i, ˌʌn- **-ier** -i.ər, Ⓤⓢ -i.ɚ **-iest** -i.ɪst, -i.əst **-ily** -əl.i, -ɪ.li **-iness** -ɪ.nəs, -ɪ.nɪs **-ies** -iz **-ying** -i.ɪŋ **-ied** -id
un|tie ʌn|ˈtaɪ, ˌʌn- **-ties** -ˈtaɪz **-tying** -ˈtaɪ.ɪŋ **-tied** -ˈtaɪd
until ənˈtɪl, ʌnˈtɪl
Note: There is an occasional form /ˈʌn.tɪl, -təl/ in stress-shift environments (e.g. ˌ**until** ˈ**death**), but this is rare.
untimel|y ʌnˈtaɪm.l|i, ˌʌn- **-iness** -ɪ.nəs, -ɪ.nɪs
untinged ʌnˈtɪndʒd, ˌʌn-
untiring ʌnˈtaɪə.rɪŋ, ˌʌn-, Ⓤⓢ -ˈtaɪ- **-ly** -li **-ness** -nəs, -nɪs
untitled ʌnˈtaɪ.təld, ˌʌn-, Ⓤⓢ -t̬əld
unto ˈʌn.tuː, -tu, -tə, Ⓤⓢ -tuː, -t̬ə, -tu
untold ʌnˈtəʊld, ˌʌn-, Ⓤⓢ -ˈtoʊld
untouchability ˌʌn.tʌtʃ.əˈbɪl.ə.ti, ʌnˌtʌtʃ-, -ɪ.ti, Ⓤⓢ -ə.t̬i
untouchable ʌnˈtʌtʃ.ə.bəl, ˌʌn- **-s** -z
untouched ʌnˈtʌtʃt, ˌʌn-
untoward ˌʌn.təˈwɔːd, -tʊˈ-; -ˈtəʊəd, Ⓤⓢ -ˈtɔːrd, -təˈwɔːrd **-ly** -li **-ness** -nəs, -nɪs
untraceable ʌnˈtreɪ.sə.bəl, ˌʌn-
untrained ʌnˈtreɪnd, ˌʌn-
untrammel(l)ed ʌnˈtræm.əld, ˌʌn-
untransferable ˌʌn.træntsˈfɜː.rə.bəl, -trɑːntsˈ-, ʌnˈtrænts.fɜː-, -ˈtrɑːnts-, Ⓤⓢ ˌʌn.træntsˈfɝː.ə-, ʌnˈtrænts.fɚ-
untranslat|able ˌʌn.træntˈsleɪ.t|ə.bəl, -trɑːntˈ-, -trənˈ-; -trænzˈleɪ-, -trɑːnzˈ-, -trənzˈ-, Ⓤⓢ -trænˈsleɪ.t̬|ə-, -trænzˈleɪ- **-ed** -ɪd
untried ʌnˈtraɪd, ˌʌn-
untrimmed ʌnˈtrɪmd, ˌʌn-
untrodden ʌnˈtrɒd.ən, ˌʌn-, Ⓤⓢ -ˈtrɑː.dən
untroubled ʌnˈtrʌb.əld, ˌʌn-
untrue ʌnˈtruː, ˌʌn- **-ness** -nəs, -nɪs
untruly ʌnˈtruː.li, ˌʌn-
untrustworth|y ʌnˈtrʌstˌwɜː.ð|i, ˌʌn-, Ⓤⓢ -ˌwɝː- **-ily** -əl.i, -ɪ.li **-iness** -ɪ.nəs, -ɪ.nɪs
untru|th ʌnˈtruː|θ, ˌʌn- **-ths** -ðz, -θs
untruthful ʌnˈtruːθ.fəl, ˌʌn-, -fʊl **-ly** -i **-ness** -nəs, -nɪs
untuck ʌnˈtʌk, ˌʌn- **-s** -s **-ing** -ɪŋ **-ed** -t
unturned ʌnˈtɜːnd, ˌʌn-, Ⓤⓢ -ˈtɝːnd

U

Pronouncing the letters UOU

The vowel letter combination **uou** has only one possible pronunciation: /ju.ə/, e.g.:

ambiguous æmˈbɪg.ju.əs

ˌ**leave no ˌstone unˈturned; leave ˌno ˌstone unˈturned**

untutored ʌnˈtʃuː.təd, -ˈtjuː-, ˌʌn-, ⓊⓈ -ˈtuː.t̬ɚd, -ˈtjuː-

untwist ʌnˈtwɪst, ˌʌn- **-s** -s **-ing** -ɪŋ **-ed** -ɪd

untypic|al ʌnˈtɪp.ɪ.k|əl **-ly** -əl.i, -li

unused *not made use of:* ʌnˈjuːzd, ˌʌn- *not accustomed:* ʌnˈjuːst, ˌʌn-

unusual ʌnˈjuː.ʒəl, ˌʌn-, -ʒu.əl, ⓊⓈ -ʒu.əl, -ˈjuː.ʒ.wəl **-ly** -i **-ness** -nəs, -nɪs

unutterab|le ʌnˈʌt.ər.ə.b|əl, ˌʌn-, ⓊⓈ -ˈʌt̬- **-ly** -li **-leness** -əl.nəs, -nɪs

unvaried ʌnˈveə.rid, ˌʌn-, ⓊⓈ -ˈver.id, -ˈvær-

unvarnished ʌnˈvɑː.nɪʃt, ˌʌn-, ⓊⓈ -ˈvɑːr-

unvarying ʌnˈveə.ri.ɪŋ, ˌʌn-, ⓊⓈ -ˈver.i-, -ˈvær.i-

unveil ʌnˈveɪl, ˌʌn- **-s** -z **-ing** -ɪŋ **-ed** -d

unventilated ʌnˈven.tɪ.leɪ.tɪd, ˌʌn-, -tə-, ⓊⓈ -t̬ə.leɪ.t̬ɪd

unversed ʌnˈvɜːst, ˌʌn-, ⓊⓈ -ˈvɝːst

unvoiced ʌnˈvɔɪst, ˌʌn-

unwaged ʌnˈweɪdʒd, ˌʌn-

unwanted ʌnˈwɒn.tɪd, ˌʌn-, ⓊⓈ -ˈwɑːn.t̬ɪd

unwarlike ʌnˈwɔː.laɪk, ˌʌn-, ⓊⓈ -ˈwɔːr-

unwarned ʌnˈwɔːnd, ˌʌn-, ⓊⓈ -ˈwɔːrnd

unwarrantab|le ʌnˈwɒr.ən.tə.b|əl, ˌʌn-, ⓊⓈ -ˈwɔːr.ən.t̬ə-, -ˈwɑːr- **-ly** -li **-leness** -əl.nəs, -nɪs

unwarranted ʌnˈwɒr.ən.tɪd, ˌʌn-, ⓊⓈ -ˈwɔːr.ən.t̬ɪd, -ˈwɑːr-

unwar|y ʌnˈweə.r|i, ˌʌn-, ⓊⓈ -ˈwer|.i **-ily** -əl.i, -ɪ.li **-iness** -ɪ.nəs, -ɪ.nɪs

unwashed ʌnˈwɒʃt, ˌʌn-, ⓊⓈ -ˈwɑːʃt, -ˈwɔːʃt

unwavering ʌnˈweɪ.vər.ɪŋ, ˌʌn- **-ly** -li

unwearable ʌnˈweə.rə.bəl, ˌʌn-, ⓊⓈ -ˈwer.ə-

unwearied ʌnˈwɪə.rid, ˌʌn-, ⓊⓈ -ˈwɪr.id

unwearying ʌnˈwɪə.ri.ɪŋ, ˌʌn-, ⓊⓈ -ˈwɪr.i-

unwed ʌnˈwed, ˌʌn-

unwelcome ʌnˈwel.kəm, ˌʌn-

unwell ʌnˈwel, ˌʌn-

unwholesome ʌnˈhəʊl.səm, ˌʌn-, ⓊⓈ -ˈhoʊl- **-ly** -li **-ness** -nəs, -nɪs

unwield|y ʌnˈwiːl.d|i, ˌʌn- **-ier** -i.ər, ⓊⓈ -i.ɚ **-iest** -i.ɪst, -i.əst **-ily** -əl.i, -ɪ.li **-iness** -ɪ.nəs, -ɪ.nɪs

unwilling ʌnˈwɪl.ɪŋ, ˌʌn- **-ly** -li **-ness** -nəs, -nɪs

Unwin ˈʌn.wɪn

unwind ʌnˈwaɪnd, ˌʌn- **-s** -z **-ing** -ɪŋ **unwound** ʌnˈwaʊnd, ˌʌn-

unwise ʌnˈwaɪz, ˌʌn- **-ly** -li

unwish ʌnˈwɪʃ **-es** -ɪz **-ing** -ɪŋ **-ed** -t **unˈwished ˌfor**

unwitting ʌnˈwɪt.ɪŋ, ˌʌn-, ⓊⓈ -ˈwɪt̬- **-ly** -li

unwomanl|y ʌnˈwʊm.ən.l|i, ˌʌn- **-iness** -ɪ.nəs, -ɪ.nɪs

unwonted ʌnˈwəʊn.tɪd, ˌʌn-, ⓊⓈ -ˈwɔːn.t̬ɪd, -ˈwoʊn-, -ˈwɑːn-, -ˈwʌn- **-ly** -li **-ness** -nəs, -nɪs

unworkable ʌnˈwɜː.kə.bəl, ˌʌn-, ⓊⓈ -ˈwɝː-

unworkmanlike ʌnˈwɜːk.mən.laɪk, ˌʌn-, ⓊⓈ -ˈwɝːk-

unworldl|y ʌnˈwɜːld.l|i, ˌʌn-, ⓊⓈ -ˈwɝːld- **-iness** -ɪ.nəs, -ɪ.nɪs

unworn ʌnˈwɔːn, ˌʌn-, ⓊⓈ -ˈwɔːrn

unworth|y ʌnˈwɜː.ð|i, ˌʌn-, ⓊⓈ -ˈwɝː- **-ily** -əl.i, -ɪ.li **-iness** -ɪ.nəs, -ɪ.nɪs

unwound (from **unwind**) ʌnˈwaʊnd, ˌʌn-

unwounded ʌnˈwuːn.dɪd, ˌʌn-

unwrap ʌnˈræp, ˌʌn- **-s** -s **-ping** -ɪŋ **-ped** -t

unwritten ʌnˈrɪt.ən, ˌʌn- ˌ**unwritten ˌconstiˈtution; ˌunwritten ˈlaw; ˌunwritten ˈrule**

unwrought ʌnˈrɔːt, ˌʌn-, ⓊⓈ -ˈrɑːt, -ˈrɔːt

unyielding ʌnˈjiːl.dɪŋ, ˌʌn- **-ly** -li **-ness** -nəs, -nɪs

unyok|e ʌnˈjəʊk, ˌʌn-, ⓊⓈ -ˈjoʊk **-es** -s **-ing** -ɪŋ **-ed** -t

unzip ʌnˈzɪp, ˌʌn- **-s** -s **-ping** -ɪŋ **-ped** -t

up ʌp **-s** -s **-ping** -ɪŋ **-ped** -t

up- ʌp

Note: Prefix. It is normally unstressed or receives secondary stress. It may carry the strongest stress in stress-shift cases.

up-and-coming ˌʌp.əŋˈkʌm.ɪŋ, -əndˈ-, ⓊⓈ -əndˈ- *stress shift:* ˌ**up-and-coming ˈleader**

up-and-down ˌʌp.əndˈdaʊn *stress shift:* ˌ**up-and-down ˈmotion**

up-and-up ˌʌp.əndˈʌp

Upanishad ʊˈpʌn.ɪ.ʃəd, jʊ-, -ˈpæn-, -ʃæd, ⓊⓈ uːˈpæn.ɪ.ʃæd, juː-, -ˈpɑː.nɪ-, -ʃɑːd **-s** -z

upas ˈjuː.pəs **-es** -ɪz

upbeat adj ʌpˈbiːt, ⓊⓈ ˈ-- *stress shift, British only:* ˌ**upbeat ˈending**

upbeat n ˈʌp.biːt **-s** -s

upbraid ʌpˈbreɪd, ˌʌp- **-s** -z **-ing** -ɪŋ **-ed** -ɪd

upbringing ˈʌpˌbrɪŋ.ɪŋ

upcast ˈʌp.kɑːst, ⓊⓈ -kæst **-s** -s

upchuck ˈʌp.tʃʌk **-s** -s **-ing** -ɪŋ **-ed** -t

upcoming ˈʌpˌkʌm.ɪŋ, -ˈ--, ⓊⓈ ˈʌpˌkʌm-

Upcott ˈʌp.kət, -kɒt, ⓊⓈ -kət, -kɑːt

up-country adv ʌpˈkʌn.tri

up-countr|y n, adj ˌʌpˈkʌn.tr|i, ⓊⓈ ˈ--- **-ies** -iz *stress shift, British only:* ˌ**up-country ˈfarm**

update n ˈʌp.deɪt **-s** -s

up|date v ʌp|ˈdeɪt, ˌʌp- **-dates** -ˈdeɪts **-dating** -ˈdeɪ.tɪŋ, ⓊⓈ -ˈdeɪ.t̬ɪŋ **-dated** -ˈdeɪ.tɪd, ⓊⓈ -ˈdeɪ.t̬ɪd

Updike ˈʌp.daɪk

upend ʌpˈend, ˌʌp- **-s** -z **-ing** -ɪŋ **-ed** -ɪd

up-front ʌpˈfrʌnt, ˌʌp- *stress shift:* ˌ**up-front ˈpayment**

upgrade n ˈʌp.greɪd **-s** -z

upgrad|e v ʌpˈgreɪd, ˌʌp- **-es** -z **-ing** -ɪŋ **-ed** -ɪd

Upham ˈʌp.əm

upheaval ʌpˈhiː.vəl **-s** -z

upheav|e ʌpˈhiːv **-es** -z **-ing** -ɪŋ **-ed** -d

upheld (from **uphold**) ʌpˈheld

uphill ʌpˈhɪl, ˌʌp- *stress shift:* ˌ**uphill ˈstruggle**

up|hold ʌp|ˈhəʊld, ⓊⓈ -ˈhoʊld **-holds** -ˈhəʊldz, ⓊⓈ -ˈhoʊldz **-holding** -ˈhəʊl.dɪŋ, ⓊⓈ -ˈhoʊl.dɪŋ **-held** -ˈheld **-holder/s** -ˈhəʊl.dər/z, ⓊⓈ -ˈhoʊl.dɚ/z

upholst|er ʌpˈhəʊl.st|ər, əp-, ⓊⓈ ʌpˈhoʊl.st|ɚ **-ers** -əz, ⓊⓈ -ɚz **-ering** -ər.ɪŋ **-ered** -əd, ⓊⓈ -ɚd **-erer/s** -ər.ər/z, ⓊⓈ -ɚ.ɚ/z **-ery** -ər.i

Upjohn ˈʌp.dʒɒn, ⓊⓈ -dʒɑːn

upkeep ˈʌp.kiːp

upland ˈʌp.lənd, ⓊⓈ -lənd, -lænd **-s** -z **-er/s** -ər/z, ⓊⓈ -ɚ/z

uplift n ˈʌp.lɪft

uplift v ʌpˈlɪft, ˌʌp- **-s** -s **-ing** -ɪŋ **-ed** -ɪd

uplifting ʌpˈlɪf.tɪŋ, ˌʌp- *stress shift:* ˌ**uplifting ˈday**

uplighter ˈʌpˌlaɪ.tər, ⓊⓈ -t̬ɚ **-s** -z

upload v ʌpˈləʊd, ⓊⓈ -ˈloʊd **-s** -z **-ing** -ɪŋ **-ed** -ɪd

upload n ˈʌp.ləʊd, ⓊⓈ -loʊd **-s** -z

up-market ʌpˈmɑː.kɪt, ⓊⓈ ˈʌpˌmɑːr- *stress shift, British only:* ˌ**up-market ˈshop**

Upminster ˈʌpˌmɪnt.stər, ⓊⓈ -stɚ

upmost ˈʌp.məʊst, ⓊⓈ -moʊst

upon *strong form:* əˈpɒn, ⓊⓈ -ˈpɑːn; *occasional weak form:* ə.pən

upper ˈʌp.ər, ⓊⓈ -ɚ **-s** -z ˌ**upper ˈclass; ˌupper ˈcrust; ˌUpper ˈHouse; ˌstiff upper ˈlip; have the ˌupper ˈhand**

upper-case ˌʌp.əˈkeɪs, ⓊⓈ -ɚˈ- *stress shift, see compound:* ˌ**upper-case ˈletters**

uppercut ˈʌp.ə.kʌt, ⓊⓈ ˈ-ɚ- **-s** -s

Uppermill ˈʌp.ə.mɪl, ⓊⓈ ˈ-ɚ-

uppermost ˈʌp.ə.məʊst, ⓊⓈ -ɚ.moʊst

Uppingham ˈʌp.ɪŋ.əm

uppish ˈʌp.ɪʃ **-ly** -li **-ness** -nəs, -nɪs

uppity ˈʌp.ɪ.ti, ⓊⓈ -t̬i **-ness** -nəs, -nɪs

Uppsala ʊpˈsɑː.lə, ʌp-, ˈ---; ˈʌp.səl.ə, ˈʊp-, -sɑː.lɑː, ⓊⓈ ʌpˈsɑː.lɑː, ʊp-; ⓊⓈ ˈʌp.səl.ə

uprais|e ʌpˈreɪz, ˌʌp- **-es** -ɪz **-ing** -ɪŋ **-ed** -d

uprear ʌpˈrɪəʳ, ˌʌp-, (US) -ˈrɪr **-s** -z **-ing** -ɪŋ **-ed** -d

Uprichard juːˈprɪtʃ.ɑːd, -əd; ʌpˈrɪtʃ.əd, (US) juːˈprɪtʃ.ɑːrd, -ɚd; (US) ʌpˈrɪtʃ.ɚd

upright ˈʌp.raɪt **-s** -s **-ly** -li **-ness** -nəs, -nɪs

uprising ˈʌpˌraɪ.zɪŋ, -ˈ--, ˌ-ˈ--, (US) ˈʌpˌraɪ- **-s** -z

upriver ˌʌpˈrɪv.əʳ, (US) -ɚ

uproar ˈʌp.rɔːʳ, (US) -rɔːr **-s** -z

uproarious ʌpˈrɔː.ri.əs, (US) -ˈrɔːr.i- **-ly** -li **-ness** -nəs, -nɪs

up|root ʌp|ˈruːt, ˌʌp- **-roots** -ˈruːts **-rooting** -ˈruː.tɪŋ, (US) -ˈruː.t̬ɪŋ **-rooted** -ˈruː.tɪd, (US) -ˈruː.t̬ɪd **-rooter/s** -ˈruː.təʳ/z, (US) -ˈruː.t̬ɚ/z

upsadaisy ˌʌps.əˈdeɪ.zi, ˌʊps-

Upsala ʊpˈsɑː.lə, ʌp-, ˈ---; ˈʌp.sᵊl.ə, ˈʊp-, -sɑː.lɑː, (US) ʌpˈsɑː.lɑː, ʊp-; (US) ˈʌp.sᵊl.ə

upscale ˌʌpˈskeɪl

up|set v ʌp|ˈset, ˌʌp- **-sets** -ˈsets **-setting** -ˈset.ɪŋ, (US) -ˈset̬.ɪŋ

upset n ˈʌp.set **-s** -s

upset adj ʌpˈset, ˌʌp- *stress shift, see compound:* **ˌupset ˈstomach**

upshot ˈʌp.ʃɒt, (US) -ʃɑːt

upside ˈʌp.saɪd **-s** -z **ˌupside ˈdown**

upsilon juːpˈsaɪ.lən, ʊp-, ʌp-, -lɒn; ˈjuːp.sɪl.ən, ˈʌp-, -ɒn, (US) ˈʌp.sə.lɑːn, ˈuːp- **-s** -z

upstage adj, adv ʌpˈsteɪdʒ, ˌʌp-, (US) ˈʌp.steɪdʒ *stress shift, British only:* **ˌupstage ˈspeech**

upstag|e v ʌpˈsteɪdʒ, ˌʌp- **-es** -ɪz **-ing** -ɪŋ **-ed** -d

upstairs ʌpˈsteəz, ˌʌp-, (US) -ˈsterz *stress shift:* **ˌupstairs ˈwindow**

upstanding ʌpˈstæn.dɪŋ, ˌʌp- **-ness** -nəs, -nɪs *stress shift:* **ˌupstanding ˈsoldier**

upstart ˈʌp.stɑːt, (US) -stɑːrt **-s** -s

upstate ˌʌpˈsteɪt, (US) ˈʌp-, -ˈ- *stress shift, British only:* **ˌupstate ˈtown**

upstream ʌpˈstriːm, ˌʌp- *stress shift:* **ˌupstream ˈjourney**

upstretched ʌpˈstretʃt, ˌʌp- *stress shift:* **ˌupstretched ˈhands**

upstroke ˈʌp.strəʊk, (US) -stroʊk **-s** -s

upsurg|e ˈʌp.sɜːdʒ, (US) -sɝːdʒ **-es** -ɪz

upswept ʌpˈswept, ˌʌp- *stress shift:* **ˌupswept ˈwings**

upswing n ˈʌp.swɪŋ **-s** -z

upswing v ʌpˈswɪŋ, ˌʌp- **-s** -z **-ing** -ɪŋ **upswung** ʌpˈswʌŋ, ˌʌp-

uptake ˈʌp.teɪk **-s** -s

up-tempo ˌʌpˈtem.pəʊ, (US) -poʊ

upthrust ˈʌp.θrʌst **-s** -s

uptight ʌpˈtaɪt, ˌʌp- **-ness** -nəs, -nɪs *stress shift:* **ˌuptight ˈperson**

up|tilt ʌp|ˈtɪlt, ˌʌp- **-tilts** -ˈtɪlts **-tilting** -ˈtɪl.tɪŋ, (US) -ˈtɪl.t̬ɪŋ **-tilted** -ˈtɪl.tɪd, (US) -ˈtɪl.t̬ɪd

up-to-date ˌʌp.təˈdeɪt **-ness** -nəs, -nɪs *stress shift:* **ˌup-to-date ˈmethod**

Upton ˈʌp.tən

up-to-the-minute ˌʌp.tə.ðəˈmɪn.ɪt, -tʊ- *stress shift:* **ˌup-to-the-minute ˈstyling**

uptown ʌpˈtaʊn, ˌʌp-, (US) ˈʌp.taʊn, ˌ-ˈ- *stress shift, British only:* **ˌuptown ˈhouse**

upturn v ʌpˈtɜːn, (US) -ˈtɝːn **-s** -z **-ing** -ɪŋ **-ed** -d

upturn n ˈʌp.tɜːn, (US) -tɝːn **-s** -z

upturned ʌpˈtɜːnd, ˌʌp-, (US) -ˈtɝːnd *stress shift:* **ˌupturned ˈboat**

upward ˈʌp.wəd, (US) -wɚd **-ly** -li **-s** -z **ˌupwardly ˈmobile**

upwind ʌpˈwɪnd

Ur ɜːʳ, ʊəʳ, (US) ɝː, ʊr

uraemia jʊəˈriː.mi.ə, jə-, jɔː-, (US) juːˈriː-, jʊ-

Ural ˈjʊə.rᵊl, ˈjɔː-, (US) ˈjʊr.ᵊl **-s** -z **ˌUral ˈMountains**

uralite ˈjʊə.rᵊl.aɪt, ˈjɔː-, (US) ˈjʊr.ə.laɪt

Urani|a jʊəˈreɪ.ni|.ə, jə-, jɔː-, (US) jʊ- **-an** -ən

uranium jʊəˈreɪ.ni.əm, jə-, jɔː-, (US) jʊ-, jə-

Uranus ˈjʊə.rᵊn.əs, ˈjɔː-; jʊəˈreɪ.nəs, jə-, (US) ˈjʊr.ᵊn.əs; juːˈreɪ.nəs

> Note: The pronunciation /jʊəˈreɪ.nəs/ has virtually disappeared from use, after many years of bad jokes based on the fact that it is homophonous with 'your anus'.

urate ˈjʊə.reɪt, ˈjɔː-, -rɪt, (US) ˈjʊr.eɪt **-s** -s

urban, U~ ˈɜː.bᵊn **urban** (US) ˈɝː- **-ite/s** -aɪt/s **ˌurban guerˈrilla**

Urbana ɜːˈbæn.ə, -ˈbɑː.nə, (US) ɝːˈbæn.ə

urbane ɜːˈbeɪn, (US) ɝː- **-ly** -li **-ness** -nəs, -nɪs

urban|ism ˈɜː.bᵊn|.ɪ.zᵊm, (US) ˈɝː- **-ist/s** -ɪst/s

urbanistic ˌɜː.bᵊnˈɪs.tɪk, (US) ˌɝː- **-ally** -ᵊl.i, -li

urbanity ɜːˈbæn.ə.ti, -ɪ.ti, (US) ɝːˈbæn.ə.t̬i

urbanization, -isa- ˌɜː.bᵊn.aɪˈzeɪ.ʃᵊn, -ɪˈ-, (US) ˌɝː.bᵊn.əˈ-

urbaniz|e, -is|e ˈɜː.bᵊn.aɪz, (US) ˈɝː- **-es** -ɪz **-ing** -ɪŋ **-ed** -d

Urbervilles ˈɜː.bə.vɪlz, (US) ˈɝː-

urchin ˈɜː.tʃɪn, (US) ˈɝː- **-s** -z

Urdu ˈʊə.duː, ˈɜː-, ˌ-ˈ-, (US) ˈʊr.duː, ˈɝː-

Ure jʊəʳ, (US) jʊr

-ure əʳ, (US) ɚ

Note: Suffix. In words containing **-ure** where the stem is free, **-ure** does not normally affect the stress pattern of the word, e.g. **proceed** /prəʊˈsiːd/ (US) /prə-/, **procedure** /prəʊˈsiː.dʒəʳ/ (US) /prəˈsiː.dʒɚ/. Where the stem is bound, the word is normally stressed on the penultimate or antepenultimate syllable, e.g. **furniture** /ˈfɜː.nɪ.tʃəʳ/ (US) /ˈfɝː.nɪ.tʃɚ/. Exceptions exist; see individual entries.

ure|a jʊəˈriː|.ə; ˈjʊə.ri-, ˈjɔː-, (US) jʊˈriː-; (US) ˈjʊr.i- **-al** -ᵊl

ureter jʊəˈriː.təʳ; ˈjʊə.rɪ-, -rə-, (US) jʊˈriː.t̬ɚ **-s** -z

ureth|ra jʊəˈriː.θ|rə, (US) jʊ- **-rae** -riː **-ras** -rəz

urethritis ˌjʊə.rəˈθraɪ.tɪs, ˌjɔː-, -rɪˈ-, -təs, (US) ˌjʊr.əˈθraɪ.t̬ɪs, -t̬əs

urg|e ɜːdʒ, (US) ɝːdʒ **-es** -ɪz **-ing** -ɪŋ **-ed** -d **-er/s** -əʳ/z, (US) -ɚ/z

urgency ˈɜː.dʒᵊnt.si, (US) ˈɝː-

urgent ˈɜː.dʒᵊnt, (US) ˈɝː- **-ly** -li

Uriah jʊəˈraɪ.ə, jə-, (US) jʊ-

Uribe uˈriː.beɪ

uric ˈjʊə.rɪk, ˈjɔː-, (US) ˈjʊr.ɪk

Uriel ˈjʊə.ri.əl, ˈjɔː-, (US) ˈjʊr.i-

Urim ˈjʊə.rɪm, ˈjɔː-, ˈʊə-, (US) ˈjʊr.ɪm

urinal jʊəˈraɪ.nᵊl, jə-; ˈjʊə.rɪ.nᵊl, ˈjɔː-, -rᵊn.ᵊl, (US) ˈjʊr.ᵊn.ᵊl **-s** -z

urinary ˈjʊə.rɪ.nᵊr.i, ˈjɔː-, -rᵊn.ᵊr-, (US) ˈjʊr.ə.ner.i

urin|ate ˈjʊə.rɪ.n|eɪt, ˈjɔː-, -rᵊn|.eɪt, (US) ˈjʊr.ə.n|eɪt **-ates** -eɪts **-ating** -eɪ.tɪŋ, (US) -eɪ.t̬ɪŋ **-ated** -eɪ.tɪd, (US) -eɪ.t̬ɪd

urination ˌjʊə.rɪˈneɪ.ʃᵊn, ˌjɔː-, -rᵊnˈeɪ-, (US) ˌjʊr.əˈneɪ-

urine ˈjʊə.rɪn, ˈjɔː-, (US) ˈjʊr.ɪn **-s** -z

uriniferous ˌjʊə.rɪˈnɪf.ᵊr.əs, ˌjɔː-, -rᵊnˈɪf-, (US) ˌjʊr.əˈnɪf-

urinogenital ˌjʊə.rɪ.nəʊˈdʒen.ɪ.tᵊl, ˌjɔː-, ˈ-ə-, (US) ˌjʊr.ə.noʊˈdʒen.ə.t̬ᵊl

URL ˌjuː.ɑːʳˈel, (US) -ɑːrˈ- **-s** -z

Urmia ˈɜː.mi.ə, ˈʊə-, (US) ˈʊr-

Urmston ˈɜːm.stᵊn, (US) ˈɝːm-

urn ɜːn, (US) ɝːn **-s** -z

uro- ˈjʊə.rəʊ, ˈjɔː-, (US) ˈjʊr.oʊ, ˈ-ə

urolog|y jʊəˈrɒl.ə.dʒ|i, (US) jʊˈrɑː- **-ist/s** -ɪst/s

Urquhart ˈɜː.kət, (US) ˈɝː.kɚt, -kɑːrt

Ursa ˈɜː.sə, (US) ˈɝː- **ˌUrsa ˈMajor; ˌUrsa ˈMinor**

ursine ˈɜː.saɪn, (US) ˈɝː-, -sɪn

Ursula ˈɜː.sjə.lə, -sjʊ-, -ʃə-, -ʃʊ-, (US) ˈɝː.sə.lə

Ursuline ˈɜː.sjə.laɪn, -sjʊ-, -ʃə-, -ʃʊ-, -lɪn, (US) ˈɝː.sə.lɪn, -laɪn **-s** -z

urticaria ˌɜː.tɪˈkeə.ri.ə, (US) ˌɝː.t̬ɪˈker.i-

Uruguay ˈjʊə.rə.gwaɪ, ˈʊr.ə-, ˈ-ʊ-, -gweɪ, (US) ˈjʊr.ə.gweɪ, ˈʊr-, ˈuː.ruː-, -gwaɪ

Uruguayan ˌjʊə.rəˈgwaɪ.ən, ˌʊr.əˈ-, -ʊˈ-, -ˈgweɪ-, (US) ˌjʊr.əˈgweɪ-, ˌʊr-, ˌuː.ruː-, -ˈgwaɪ- **-s** -z

urus ˈjʊə.rəs, ˈjɔː-, (US) ˈjʊr.əs

us *strong form:* ʌs; *weak forms:* əs, s

Note: Weak-form word. The strong form is used mainly for contrast, e.g. 'a them and us attitude', or for emphasis, e.g. 'This land belongs to **us**'. The weak form is used when unstressed, and can occur in final position, e.g. 'They joined us' /ðeɪˈdʒɔɪnd.əs/.

US juːˈes

USA ˌjuː.esˈeɪ

usability ˌjuː.zəˈbɪl.ə.ti, -ɪ.ti, (US) -ə.t̬i

usable ˈjuː.zə.bᵊl

USAF ˌjuː.es.eɪˈef

Pronouncing the letters UY

The vowel digraph **uy** has two possible pronunciations: /aɪ/ and, at the end of words where it is usually preceded by the letter **q**, /wi/, e.g.:

buy	baɪ
soliloquy	səˈlɪl.ə.kwi

An exceptional case is the word *Gruyère*, borrowed from French.

Gruyère	ˈgruː.jeəʳ, gruˈjeəʳ ⓊⓈ gruˈjer

usag|e ˈjuː.sɪdʒ, -zɪdʒ **-es** -ɪz
usanc|e ˈjuː.zᵊnts **-es** -ɪz
USC ˌjuː.esˈsiː
USDAW ˈʌs.dɔː, ˈʌz-, ⓊⓈ -dɑː, -dɔː
use n juːs **uses** ˈjuː.sɪz
us|e v *make use of:* juːz **-es** -ɪz **-ing** -ɪŋ **-ed** -d **-er/s** -əʳ/z, ⓊⓈ -ɚ/z
useab|le ˈjuː.zə.b|ᵊl **-ly** -li **-leness** -ᵊl.nəs, -nɪs
used (from **use** v.) juːzd
used adj *accustomed:* juːst, juːzd
used v *was or were accustomed; when followed by* **to***:* juːst; *when not followed by* **to***:* juːst, juːzd
usedn't *when followed by* **to***:* ˈjuː.sᵊnt; *when not followed by* **to***:* ˈjuː.sᵊnt
Note: This form is rare in present-day English, especially in American English.
useful ˈjuːs.fᵊl, -fʊl **-ly** -i **-ness** -nəs, -nɪs
useless ˈjuː.sləs, -slɪs **-ly** -li **-ness** -nəs, -nɪs
usen't *when followed by* **to***:* ˈjuː.sᵊnt; *when not followed by* **to***:* ˈjuː.sᵊnt
Note: See note for 'usedn't'.
user-friendl|y ˌjuː.zəˈfrend.l|i, ⓊⓈ -zɚˈ- **-iness** -ɪ.nəs, -ɪ.nɪs *stress shift:* ˌ**user-friendly** ˈ**product**
username ˈjuː.zə.neɪm, ⓊⓈ -zɚ- **-s** -z
uses (plural of **use** n.) ˈjuː.sɪz
uses (from **use** v.) ˈjuː.zɪz
Ushant ˈʌʃ.ᵊnt
Ushaw ˈʌʃ.ə, -ɔː, ⓊⓈ -ə, -ɑː, -ɔː
ush|er, U~ ˈʌʃ|.əʳ, ⓊⓈ -ɚ **-ers** -əz, ⓊⓈ -ɚz **-ering** -ᵊr.ɪŋ **-ered** -əd, ⓊⓈ -ɚd
usherette ˌʌʃ.ᵊrˈet **-s** -s
Usk ʌsk
USN ˌjuː.esˈen
usquebaugh ˈʌs.kwɪ.bɔː, -kwə-, ⓊⓈ -bɑː, -bɔː **-s** -z
Ussher ˈʌʃ.əʳ, ⓊⓈ -ɚ
USSR ˌjuː.es.esˈɑːʳ, ⓊⓈ -ˈɑːr
Ustinov ˈjuː.stɪ.nɒf, ˈuː-, -stə-, -nɒv, ⓊⓈ -nɑːf, -nɔːf, -nɑːv
usu. (abbrev. for **usual/ly**) ˈjuː.ʒᵊl/i, -ʒu.əl-, ⓊⓈ -ʒu.əl.i, ˈjuːʒ.wəl.i
usual ˈjuː.ʒᵊl, -ʒu.əl, ⓊⓈ -ʒu.əl, ˈjuːʒ.wəl **-ly** -i **-ness** -nəs, -nɪs
usufruct ˈjuː.sjʊ.frʌkt, -zjʊ-, ⓊⓈ -zʊ-, -sʊ-, -zə-, -sə- **-s** -s
usurer ˈjuː.ʒᵊr.əʳ, ⓊⓈ -ɚ **-s** -z
usurious juːˈzjʊə.ri.əs, -ˈʒʊə-, -ˈzjɔː-, ⓊⓈ juːˈʒʊr.i- **-ly** -li **-ness** -nəs, -nɪs
usurp juːˈzɜːp, -ˈsɜːp, ⓊⓈ -ˈsɝːp, -ˈzɝːp **-s** -s **-ing** -ɪŋ **-ed** -t **-er/s** -əʳ/z, ⓊⓈ -ɚ/z
usurpation ˌjuː.zɜːˈpeɪ.ʃᵊn, -sɜːˈ-, ⓊⓈ -sɚˈ-, -zɚˈ- **-s** -z
usury ˈjuː.ʒᵊr.i, ⓊⓈ -ʒɚ.i
Ut. (abbrev. for **Utah**) ˈjuː.tɑː, ⓊⓈ -tɔː, -tɑː
Utah ˈjuː.tɑː, ⓊⓈ -tɔː, -tɑː
Utd. (abbrev. for **United**) juːˈnaɪ.tɪd, jʊ-, ⓊⓈ -ˈnaɪ.t̬ɪd
Ute juːt **-s** -s
utensil juːˈtent.sᵊl, -sɪl, ⓊⓈ -sᵊl **-s** -z
uteri (alternative plural of **uterus**) ˈjuː.tᵊr.aɪ, ⓊⓈ -t̬ə.raɪ
uterine ˈjuː.tᵊr.aɪn, ⓊⓈ -t̬ɚ.ɪn, -t̬ə.raɪn
uterus ˈjuː.tᵊr.əs, ⓊⓈ -t̬ɚ- **-es** -ɪz
Uther ˈjuː.θəʳ, ⓊⓈ -θɚ
Utica ˈjuː.tɪ.kə, ⓊⓈ -t̬ɪ-
utilitarian ˌjuː.tɪ.lɪˈteə.ri.ən, -ləˈ-; juːˌtɪl.ɪˈ-, -əˈ-, ⓊⓈ juːˌtɪl.əˈter.i- **-s** -z **-ism** -ɪ.zᵊm
utilit|y juːˈtɪl.ə.t|i, -ɪ.t|i, ⓊⓈ -ə.t̬|i **-ies** -iz **uˈtility ˌroom**
utilization, -isa- ˌjuː.tᵊl.aɪˈzeɪ.ʃᵊn, -tɪ.laɪˈ-, -lɪˈ-, ⓊⓈ -t̬ᵊl.əˈ-
utiliz|e, -is|e ˈjuː.tɪ.laɪz, -tᵊl.aɪz, ⓊⓈ -t̬ᵊl.aɪz **-es** -ɪz **-ing** -ɪŋ **-ed** -d **-er/s** -əʳ/z, ⓊⓈ -ɚ/z **-able** -ə.bᵊl
utmost ˈʌt.məʊst, -məst, ⓊⓈ -moʊst
utopi|a, U~ juːˈtəʊ.pi|.ə, ⓊⓈ -ˈtoʊ- **-an/s** -ən/z
utopianism, U~ juːˈtəʊ.pi.ə.nɪ.zᵊm, ⓊⓈ -ˈtoʊ-
Utrecht ˈjuː.trekt, -trext, -ˈ-, ⓊⓈ ˈjuː.trekt
utricle ˈjuː.trɪ.kᵊl **-s** -z
Utrillo juːˈtrɪl.əʊ, uː-, ⓊⓈ -oʊ
Utsira uːtˈsɪə.rə, ⓊⓈ -ˈsɪr.ə
Uttar Pradesh ˌʊt.ə.prəˈdeʃ, -ˈdeɪʃ, ⓊⓈ ˌuː.t̬ɚ-
utt|er ˈʌt|.əʳ, ⓊⓈ ˈʌt̬|.ɚ **-erly** -ᵊl.i, ⓊⓈ -ɚ.li **-erness** -ə.nəs, -ə.nɪs, ⓊⓈ -ɚ- **-ers** -əz, ⓊⓈ -ɚz **-ering** -ᵊr.ɪŋ **-ered** -əd, ⓊⓈ -ɚd **-erer/s** -ᵊr.əʳ/z, ⓊⓈ -ɚ.ɚ/z **-erable** -ᵊr.ə.bᵊl
utteranc|e ˈʌt.ᵊr.ᵊnts, ⓊⓈ ˈʌt̬- **-es** -ɪz
uttermost ˈʌt.ə.məʊst, ⓊⓈ ˈʌt̬.ɚ.moʊst
Uttley ˈʌt.li
Uttoxeter juːˈtɒk.sɪ.təʳ, ʌtˈɒk-, ˈʌk.sɪ-, ⓊⓈ juːˈtɑːk.sɪ.t̬ɚ, ʌt̬ˈɑːk-, ˈʌk.sɪ-

> Note: The common pronunciation is /juːˈtɒk.sɪ.təʳ/ ⓊⓈ /-ˈtɑːk.sɪ.t̬ɚ/ or /ʌtˈɒk.sɪ.təʳ/ ⓊⓈ /-ˈɑːk.sɪ.t̬ɚ/. The former is more frequent, and is the pronunciation of most outsiders.

U-turn ˈjuː.tɜːn, juːˈtɜːn, ⓊⓈ ˈjuː.tɝːn, ˌ-ˈ- **-s** -z
UV ˌjuːˈviː *stress shift, see compound:* ˌ**UV** ˈ**light**
uvul|a ˈjuː.vjə.l|ə, -vjʊ- **-as** -z **-ae** -i
uvular ˈjuː.vjə.ləʳ, -vjʊ-, ⓊⓈ -lɚ
Uxbridge ˈʌks.brɪdʒ
uxorial ʌkˈsɔː.ri.əl, ⓊⓈ -ˈsɔːr.i-; ⓊⓈ ʌgˈzɔːr-
uxorious ʌkˈsɔː.ri.əs, ⓊⓈ -ˈsɔːr.i-; ⓊⓈ ʌgˈzɔːr- **-ly** -li **-ness** -nəs, -nɪs
Uyghur ˈwiː.gʊəʳ, -gəʳ, ⓊⓈ -gʊr, -gɚ **-s** -z
Uzbek ˈʊz.bek, ˈʌz- **-s** -s
Uzbekistan ʊzˌbek.ɪˈstɑːn, ʌz-, ⓊⓈ -ˈstæn, -ˈstɑːn **-i/s** -i/z
Uzi® ˈuː.zi

V

Pronouncing the letter V

The consonant letter **v** is always realized as /v/ in English words, e.g.:

van	væn
love	lʌv

However, in words borrowed from German and Slavic languages, the pronunciation may be /f/, e.g.:

Volkswagen	ˈfɒlksˌvɑː.ɡən, ˈvɒlks- ⓊⓈ ˈfoʊlks-, ˈvoʊlks-
Gorbachev	ˈɡɔː.bə.tʃɒf ⓊⓈ ˈɡɔːr.bə.tʃɑːf

v, V viː -'s -z ˈ**v** ˌ**sign**
v. *versus:* viː, ˈvɜː.səs, ⓊⓈ viː, ˈvɝː- *vide:* viː.diː, ˈviːd.eɪ, ˈvaɪ.di, ⓊⓈ ˈviː.deɪ
Va. (abbrev. for **Virginia**) vəˈdʒɪn.jə, vɜː-, -i.ə; ˌviːˈeɪ, ⓊⓈ vɚˈdʒɪn.jə; ⓊⓈ ˌviːˈeɪ
Vaal vɑːl
vac væk -s -s
vacanc|y ˈveɪ.kənt.s|i -ies -iz
vacant ˈveɪ.kənt -ly -li ˌ**vacant** ˈ**lot**
vaca|te vəˈkeɪ|t, veɪ-, ⓊⓈ ˈveɪ.keɪ|t, -ˈ- -tes -ts -ting -tɪŋ, ⓊⓈ -t̬ɪŋ -ted -tɪd, ⓊⓈ -t̬ɪd
vacation vəˈkeɪ.ʃən, ⓊⓈ veɪ-, və- -s -z -ing -ɪŋ -ed -d -er/s -əʳ/z, ⓊⓈ -ɚ/z -ist/s -ɪst/s
vaccin|ate ˈvæk.sɪ.n|eɪt, -sən|.eɪt, ⓊⓈ -sə.n|eɪt -ates -eɪts -ating -eɪ.tɪŋ, ⓊⓈ -eɪ.t̬ɪŋ -ated -eɪ.tɪd, ⓊⓈ -eɪ.t̬ɪd -ator/s -eɪ.təʳ/z, ⓊⓈ -eɪ.t̬ɚ/z
vaccination ˌvæk.sɪˈneɪ.ʃən, -sənˈeɪ-, ⓊⓈ -səˈneɪ- -s -z
vaccine ˈvæk.siːn, -sɪn, ⓊⓈ vækˈsiːn, ˈ-- -s -z
Vachel(l) ˈveɪ.tʃəl
Vacher ˈvæʃ.əʳ, ˈveɪ.tʃəʳ, ⓊⓈ ˈvæʃ.ɚ, ˈveɪ.tʃɚ
vacill|ate ˈvæs.əl|.eɪt, -sɪ.l|eɪt, ⓊⓈ -ə.l|eɪt -ates -eɪts -ating/ly -eɪ.tɪŋ/li, ⓊⓈ -eɪ.t̬ɪŋ/li -ated -eɪ.tɪd, ⓊⓈ -eɪ.t̬ɪd -ator/s -eɪ.təʳ/z, ⓊⓈ -eɪ.t̬ɚ/z
vacillation ˌvæs.əlˈeɪ.ʃən, -ɪˈleɪ-, ⓊⓈ -əˈleɪ- -s -z
Václav ˈvæt.slæv, ⓊⓈ ˈvɑːt.slɑːf
vacuity vækˈjuː.ə.ti, vəˈkjuː-, -ɪ.ti, ⓊⓈ -ə.t̬i
vacuolar ˌvæk.juˈəʊ.ləʳ, ⓊⓈ ˈvæk.ju.wə.lɚ; ⓊⓈ ˌvæk.juˈoʊ-, -lɑːr
vacuole ˈvæk.ju.əʊl, ⓊⓈ -oʊl -s -z
vacuous ˈvæk.ju.əs -ly -li -ness -nəs, -nɪs
vacuum ˈvæk.juːm, -jʊm, -juəm, ⓊⓈ -juːm, -ju.əm, -jʊm, -jəm -s -z -ing -ɪŋ -ed -d ˈ**vacuum** ˌ**cleaner**; ˈ**vacuum** ˌ**flask**; ˈ**vacuum** ˌ**pump**
vacuum-packed ˌvæk.juːmˈpækt, -jʊmˈ-, -juəmˈ-, ⓊⓈ -ju.əmˈ-, -juːmˈ-, -jʊmˈ-, -jəmˈ-, ˈ---
vade-mecum ˌvɑː.deɪˈmeɪ.kəm, -kʊm; ˌveɪ.diˈmiː.kəm, -kʌm, ⓊⓈ ˌveɪ.diˈmiː.kəm, ˌvɑː-, -ˈmeɪ- -s -z
Vaduz vɑːˈduːts
vagabond ˈvæɡ.ə.bɒnd, -bənd, ⓊⓈ -bɑːnd -s -z -ish -ɪʃ -ism -ɪ.zəm
vagabondage ˈvæɡ.əˌbɒn.dɪdʒ, ⓊⓈ -ˌbɑːn-
vagar|y ˈveɪ.ɡər|.i; vəˈɡeə.r|i, ⓊⓈ ˈveɪ.ɡɚ.|i; ⓊⓈ vəˈɡer|.i -ies -iz
vagina vəˈdʒaɪ.nə -s -z
vaginal vəˈdʒaɪ.nəl; ˈvædʒ.ɪ-, -ən.əl, ⓊⓈ ˈvædʒ.ən.əl -ly -i
vaginismus ˌvædʒ.ɪˈnɪz.məs, -əˈ-, -ˈnɪs-, ⓊⓈ -əˈnɪz-
vagrancy ˈveɪ.ɡrənt.si
vagrant ˈveɪ.ɡrənt -s -s
vagu|e veɪɡ -er -əʳ, ⓊⓈ -ɚ -est -ɪst, -əst -ely -li -eness -nəs, -nɪs
vail, V~ veɪl -s -z -ing -ɪŋ -ed -d
Vaile veɪl
vain veɪn -er -əʳ, ⓊⓈ -ɚ -est -ɪst, -əst -ly -li -ness -nəs, -nɪs
vainglorious ˌveɪnˈɡlɔː.ri.əs, ˌveɪŋˈ-, ⓊⓈ ˌveɪnˈɡlɔːr.i- -ly -li -ness -nəs, -nɪs
vainglory ˌveɪnˈɡlɔː.ri, ˌveɪŋ-, ⓊⓈ ˈveɪnˌɡlɔːr.i, ˌ-ˈ--
Vaishnav|a ˈveʃ.nə.v|ɑː -ism -ɪ.zəm
Val væl
Valais ˈvæl.eɪ
valanc|e ˈvæl.ənts, ⓊⓈ ˈvæl-, ˈveɪ.lənts -es -ɪz -ed -t
Valdez vælˈdiːz
vale, V~ *valley:* veɪl -s -z
vale *latin word meaning "goodbye":* ˈvɑː.leɪ, ˈveɪ.li, ˈvæl.eɪ, ⓊⓈ ˈveɪ.li, ˈvɑː.leɪ
valediction ˌvæl.ɪˈdɪk.ʃən, -əˈ-, ⓊⓈ ˌvæl.əˈdɪk.ʃən -s -z
valedictorian ˌvæl.ɪ.dɪkˈtɔː.ri.ən, ˌ-ə-, ⓊⓈ ˌvæl.ə.dɪkˈtɔːr.i- -s -z
valedictor|y ˌvæl.ɪˈdɪk.tər|.i, -əˈ-, ⓊⓈ ˌvæl.əˈdɪk.tɚ- -ies -iz
valence ˈveɪ.lənts
Valencia vəˈlent.si.ə
Valenciennes ˌvæl.ən.siˈen, -ɑ̃ːn-, -ɑːnt-, -ˈsjen, ⓊⓈ -siˈenz, -ˈsjenz; ⓊⓈ vəˌlent.siˈenz, -ˌlɑːnt-
valenc|y ˈveɪ.lənt.s|i -ies -iz
valentine, V~ *person or card:* ˈvæl.ən.taɪn -s -z ˈ**Valentine's** ˌ**card**; ˈ**Valentine's** ˌ**Day**
Valentine *first name/surname:* ˈvæl.ən.taɪn, -tɪn, ⓊⓈ -taɪn
Valentinian ˌvæl.ənˈtɪn.i.ən
Valentino ˌvæl.ənˈtiː.nəʊ, ⓊⓈ -noʊ
valerian, V~ vəˈlɪə.ri.ən, -ˈleə-, ⓊⓈ -ˈlɪr.i- -s -z
Valerie, Valery ˈvæl.ər.i
Valerius vəˈlɪə.ri.əs, -ˈleə-, ⓊⓈ -ˈlɪr.i-
Valéry ˈvæl.eə.riː, ˌvæl.eəˈriː, ⓊⓈ ˌvæl.əˈriː, ˌvɑː.lerˈiː
valet ˈvæl.eɪ, -ɪt, -ət, -i, ⓊⓈ ˈvæl.ɪt; ⓊⓈ vəˈleɪ, vælˈeɪ; ⓊⓈ ˈvæl.eɪ **valets** ˈvæl.eɪz, -ɪts, -əts, -iz, ⓊⓈ ˈvæl.ɪts; ⓊⓈ vəˈleɪz, vælˈeɪz; ⓊⓈ ˈvæl.eɪz **valeting** ˈvæl.eɪ.ɪŋ, -ɪ.tɪŋ, -ə.tɪŋ, -i.ɪŋ, ⓊⓈ ˈvæl.ɪ.t̬ɪŋ; ⓊⓈ vəˈleɪ.ɪŋ, vælˈeɪ.ɪŋ; ⓊⓈ ˈvæl.eɪ.ɪŋ **valeted** ˈvæl.eɪd, -ɪ.tɪd, -ə.tɪd, ˈ-id, ⓊⓈ ˈvæl.ɪ.t̬ɪd; ⓊⓈ vəˈleɪd, vælˈeɪd; ⓊⓈ ˈvæl.eɪd ˈ**valet** ˌ**parking**
valetudinarian ˌvæl.ɪ.tʃuː.dɪˈneə.ri.ən, ˌ-ə-, -tjuː-, ⓊⓈ -əˌtuː.dəˈner.i-, -ˌtjuː- -s -z -ism -ɪ.zəm
Valhalla vælˈhæl.ə, ⓊⓈ vælˈhæl-, vɑːlˈhɑː.lə
valiant ˈvæl.i.ənt, ˈ-jənt, ⓊⓈ ˈ-jənt -ly -li -ness -nəs, -nɪs
valid ˈvæl.ɪd -ly -li -ness -nəs, -nɪs
vali|date ˈvæl.ɪ|.deɪt, ˈ-ə-, ⓊⓈ ˈ-ə- -dates -deɪts -dating -deɪ.tɪŋ, ⓊⓈ -deɪ.t̬ɪŋ -dated -deɪ.tɪd, ⓊⓈ -deɪ.t̬ɪd
validation ˌvæl.ɪˈdeɪ.ʃən, -əˈ-, ⓊⓈ -əˈ- -s -z
validit|y vəˈlɪd.ə.t|i, vælˈɪd-, -ɪ.t|i, ⓊⓈ vəˈlɪd.ə.t̬|i -ies -iz
valis|e vəˈliːz, vælˈiːz, -ˈiːs, ⓊⓈ vəˈliːs, -ˈliːz -es -ɪz
Valium® ˈvæl.i.əm, ⓊⓈ ˈ-i.əm, ˈ-jəm -s -z

Valkyrie vælˈkɪə.ri, ˈvæl.kər.i, -kɪ.ri, ⓊⓈ vælˈkɪr.i, ˈvæl.kɚ.i, -kɪ.ri -s -z
Valladolid ˌvæl.ə.dəʊˈlɪd, -dɒlˈɪd; *as if Spanish:* ˌvaɪ.ɑː.dɒlˈiːd; ⓊⓈ -doʊˈlɪd
Vallance ˈvæl.ənts
Valletta vəˈlet.ə, ⓊⓈ vɑːˈlet.ɑː
valley ˈvæl.i -s -z
Vallone vəˈləʊn, ⓊⓈ -ˈloʊn
Valois ˈvæl.wɑː, ⓊⓈ vɑːlˈwɑː; ⓊⓈ ˈvæl.wɑː
valor ˈvæl.əʳ, ⓊⓈ -ɚ
valorization, -isa- ˌvæl.ər.aɪˈzeɪ.ʃən, -ɪˈ-, ⓊⓈ -əˈ- -s -z
valoriz|e, -is|e ˈvæl.ər.aɪz, ⓊⓈ -ə.raɪz -es -ɪz -ing -ɪŋ -ed -d
valorous ˈvæl.ər.əs -ly -li -ness -nəs, -nɪs
valour ˈvæl.əʳ, ⓊⓈ -ɚ

Valparaiso ˌvæl.pᵊrˈaɪ.zəʊ, -ˈeɪ-, (US) -pəˈraɪ.zoʊ, -ˈreɪ-

Valpolicella ˌvæl.pɒl.ɪˈtʃel.ə, (US) ˌvɑːl.poʊ.lɪ-

vals|e vɑːls, væls, vɔːls, (US) vɑːls, vʌls **-es** -ɪz

valuab|le ˈvæl.jʊ.b|ᵊl, -jə.b|ᵊl, -ju.ə- **-les** -ᵊlz **-ly** -li **-leness** -ᵊl.nəs, -nɪs

valuat|e ˈvæl.ju.eɪt **-es** -s **-ing** -ɪŋ **-ed** -ɪd

valuation ˌvæl.juˈeɪ.ʃᵊn **-s** -z

valu|e ˈvæl.juː **-es** -z **-ing** -ɪŋ **-ed** -d **-er/s** -əʳ/z, (US) -ɚ/z **ˈvalue ˌjudgment; ˌfamily ˈvalues**

value-added ˌvæl.juːˈæd.ɪd **ˌvalue-ˌadded ˈtax; ˌvalue-ˈadded ˌtax**

valueless ˈvæl.juː.ləs, -jʊ-, -lɪs

valve vælv **-s** -z

valvular ˈvæl.vjə.ləʳ, -vjʊ-, (US) -vjə.lɚ

valvule ˈvæl.vjuːl **-s** -z

vamoos|e vəˈmuːs, væmˈuːs, (US) væmˈuːs, vəˈmuːs **-es** -ɪz **-ing** -ɪŋ **-ed** -t

vamp væmp **-s** -s **-ing** -ɪŋ **-ed** -t

vampire ˈvæm.paɪəʳ, -paɪ.əʳ, (US) -paɪ.ɚ **-s** -z **ˈvampire ˌbat**

vampirism ˈvæm.paɪə.rɪ.zᵊm, (US) -paɪ-, -pɪ-

vampish ˈvæm.pɪʃ **-ly** -li **-ness** -nəs, -nɪs

van, V~ væn **-s** -z

vanadium vəˈneɪ.di.əm

Van Allen vænˈæl.ən **Van ˌAllen ˈbelt** (US) **Van ˈAllen ˌbelt**

Vanbrugh ˈvæn.brə, ˈvæm-, (US) ˈvæn.bruː

> Note: **Sir John Vanbrugh**, the seventeenth-century dramatist and architect, is also sometimes referred to as /ˈvæn.bruː/ in British English.

Vance vænts, vɑːnts, (US) vænts

Vancouver vænˈkuː.vəʳ, væŋ-, (US) vænˈkuː.vɚ

V and A, V & A (abbrev. for **Victoria and Albert Museum**) ˌviː.əndˈeɪ

vandal, V~ ˈvæn.dᵊl **-s** -z

vandalism ˈvæn.dᵊl.ɪ.zᵊm

vandaliz|e, -is|e ˈvæn.dᵊl.aɪz **-es** -ɪz **-ing** -ɪŋ **-ed** -d

Van de Graaff generator ˌvæn.dəˌgrɑːfˈdʒen.ᵊ.reɪ.təʳ, (US) -t̬ɚ, -ˌgræf- **-s** -z

Vanderbilt ˈvæn.də.bɪlt, (US) -dɚ-

Vanderbyl ˈvæn.də.bɪl, (US) -dɚ-

Vandermeer ˌvæn.dəˈmɪəʳ, (US) -dɚˈmɪr

van der Post ˌvæn.dəˈpɒst, (US) -dɚˈpɑːst

Van Diemen vænˈdiː.mən

Vandyke, Van Dyck vænˈdaɪk *stress shift, see compounds:* **ˌVandyke ˈbrown; ˌVandyke ˈcollar**

vane, V~ veɪn **-s** -z **-d** -d

Vanessa vəˈnes.ə

Van Eyck vænˈaɪk **-s** -s

Vange vændʒ

Van Gogh vænˈgɒf, væŋ-, -ˈgɒk, -ˈgɒx, (US) vænˈgoʊ, -ˈgɔːx

vanguard ˈvæn.gɑːd, ˈvæŋ-, (US) ˈvæn.gɑːrd **-s** -z

Van Helsing vænˈhel.sɪŋ, (US) væn-, vɑːn-

vanilla vəˈnɪl.ə **vaˈnilla ˌpod**

vanish ˈvæn.ɪʃ **-es** -ɪz **-ing** -ɪŋ **-ed** -t **ˈvanishing ˌcream; ˈvanishing ˌpoint**

Vanitory® ˈvæn.ɪ.tᵊr.i **ˈVanitory ˌunit**

vanit|y ˈvæn.ə.t|i, -ɪ.t|i, (US) -ə.t̬|i **-ies** -iz **ˈvanity ˌcase; ˌVanity ˈFair; ˈvanity ˌplates; ˈvanity ˌtable**

vanquish ˈvæŋ.kwɪʃ, (US) ˈvæŋ-, ˈvæn- **-es** -ɪz **-ing** -ɪŋ **-ed** -t **-er/s** -əʳ/z, (US) -ɚ/z **-able** -ə.bᵊl

van Rompuy vænˈrɒm.pɜː.i, -pu.i, -pwi, (US) –ˈrɑːm-

Vansittart vænˈsɪt.ət, -ɑːt, (US) -ˈsɪt̬.ɚt

van Straubenzee ˌvæn.strɔːˈben.zi, (US) -strɑːˈ-, -strɔːˈ-

vantag|e ˈvɑːn.tɪdʒ, (US) ˈvæn.t̬ɪdʒ **-es** -ɪz **ˈvantage ˌpoint**

Vanuatu ˌvæn.uˈɑː.tuː, -ˈæt.uː, (US) vænˈwɑː.tuː

Vanunu vəˈnuː.nuː

Van Vechten vænˈvek.tən

Vanya ˈvɑː.njə, ˈvæn.jə, (US) ˈvɑː.njə

vapid ˈvæp.ɪd **-ly** -li **-ness** -nəs, -nɪs

vapidity væpˈɪd.ə.ti, vəˈpɪd-, -ɪ.ti, (US) væpˈɪd.ə.t̬i

vap|or ˈveɪ.p|əʳ, (US) -p|ɚ **-ors** -əz, (US) -ɚz **-ory** -ᵊr.i **ˈvapor ˌtrail**

vaporett|o ˌvæp.ᵊrˈet|.əʊ, (US) -əˈret̬|.oʊ **-os** -əʊz, (US) -oʊz **-i** -i

vaporization, -isa- ˌveɪ.pᵊr.aɪˈzeɪ.ʃᵊn, -ɪˈ-, (US) -əˈ- **-s** -z

vaporiz|e, -is|e ˈveɪ.pᵊr.aɪz, (US) -pə.raɪz **-es** -ɪz **-ing** -ɪŋ **-ed** -d **-er/s** -əʳ/z, (US) -ɚ/z

vaporous ˈveɪ.pᵊr.əs **-ly** -li **-ness** -nəs, -nɪs

vap|our ˈveɪ.p|əʳ, (US) -p|ɚ **-ours** -əz, (US) -ɚz **-oury** -ᵊr.i **ˈvapour ˌtrail**

vapourware ˈveɪ.pə.weəʳ, (US) -pɚ.wer

Varah ˈvɑː.rə, (US) ˈvɑːr.ə

Varden ˈvɑː.dᵊn, (US) ˈvɑːr-

varec ˈvær.ek, -ɪk, (US) ˈver-, ˈvær-

variability ˌveə.ri.əˈbɪl.ə.ti, -ɪ.ti, (US) ˌver.i.əˈbɪl.ə.t̬i, ˌvær-

variab|le ˈveə.ri.ə.b|ᵊl, (US) ˈver.i-, ˈvær- **-les** -ᵊlz **-ly** -li **-leness** -ᵊl.nəs, -nɪs

variance ˈveə.ri.ənts, (US) ˈver.i-, ˈvær-

variant ˈveə.ri.ənt, (US) ˈver.i-, ˈvær- **-s** -s

variate ˈveə.ri.ət, -ɪt, (US) ˈver.i.ɪt, ˈvær- **-s** -s

variation ˌveə.riˈeɪ.ʃᵊn, (US) ˌver.iˈ-, ˌvær- **-s** -z

varicella ˌvær.ɪˈsel.ə, (US) ˌver-, ˌvær-, -ə-

varices (plural of **varix**) ˈvær.ɪ.siːz, ˈveə.rɪ-, (US) ˈver.ə.siːz, ˈvær-

varicose ˈvær.ɪ.kəʊs, (US) ˈver.ə.koʊs, ˈvær- **ˌvaricose ˈveins**

varicosity ˌvær.ɪˈkɒs.ə.ti, -ɪ.ti, (US) ˌver.ɪˈkɑː.sə.t̬i, ˌvær-

varied ˈveə.rɪd, (US) ˈver.ɪd, ˈvær- **-ly** -li

varie|gate ˈveə.rɪ|.geɪt, -ri|.ə-, (US) ˈver.i|.ə-, ˈvær- **-gates** -geɪts **-gating** -geɪ.tɪŋ, (US) -geɪ.t̬ɪŋ **-gated** -geɪ.tɪd, (US) -geɪ.t̬ɪd **-gator/s** -geɪ.təʳ/z, (US) -geɪ.t̬ɚ/z

variegation ˌveə.rɪˈgeɪ.ʃᵊn, -ri.əˈ-, (US) ˌver.i.əˈ-, ˌvær- **-s** -z

varietal vəˈraɪ.ə.tᵊl, (US) -t̬ᵊl

variet|y vəˈraɪ.ə.t|i, (US) -t̬|i **-ies** -iz **vaˈriety ˌshow; vaˈriety ˌstore**

variform ˈveə.rɪ.fɔːm, (US) ˈver.ə.fɔːrm, ˈvær-

Varig® ˈvær.ɪg, (US) ˈver-, ˈvær-

variola vəˈraɪ.ə.lə

variole ˈveə.ri.əʊl, (US) ˈver.i.oʊl, ˈvær- **-s** -z

variorum ˌveə.riˈɔː.rəm, ˌvær-, (US) ˌver.iˈɔːr.əm, ˌvær-

various ˈveə.ri.əs, (US) ˈver.i-, ˈvær- **-ly** -li **-ness** -nəs, -nɪs

variphone ˈveə.rɪ.fəʊn, (US) ˈver.ɪ.foʊn, ˈvær- **-s** -z

varix ˈveə.rɪks, (US) ˈver.ɪks, ˈvær- **varices** ˈvær.ɪ.siːz, ˈveə.rɪ-, (US) ˈvær.ə-, ˈver-

varlet ˈvɑː.lət, -lɪt, (US) ˈvɑːr- **-s** -s

Varley ˈvɑː.li, (US) ˈvɑːr-

varmint ˈvɑː.mɪnt, (US) ˈvɑːr- **-s** -s

Varna ˈvɑː.nə, (US) ˈvɑːr-

Varney ˈvɑː.ni, (US) ˈvɑːr-

varnish ˈvɑː.nɪʃ, (US) ˈvɑːr- **-es** -ɪz **-ing** -ɪŋ **-ed** -t **-er/s** -əʳ/z, (US) -ɚ/z

Varro ˈvær.əʊ, (US) -oʊ, ˈver-

varsit|y ˈvɑː.sə.t|i, -ɪ.t|i, (US) ˈvɑːr.sə.t̬|i **-ies** -iz

Varuna værˈuː.nə, (US) vʌr-, vɑːˈruː-

var|y ˈveə.r|i, (US) ˈver|.i, ˈvær- **-ies** -iz **-ying/ly** -i.ɪŋ/li **-ied** -id

Vasari vəˈsɑː.ri, (US) vɑːˈsɑːr.i

Vasco da Gama ˌvæs.kəʊ.dəˈgɑː.mə, -dɑːˈ-, (US) ˌvɑː.skoʊ-, -ˈgæm.ə

vascular ˈvæs.kjə.ləʳ, -kjʊ-, (US) -kjə.lɚ

vascularity ˌvæs.kjəˈlær.ə.ti, -kjʊˈ-, -ɪ.ti, (US) -kjəˈler.ə.t̬i, -ˈlær-

vascul|um ˈvæs.kjə.l|əm, -kjʊ-, (US) -kjə- **-a** -ə

vas deferens ˌvæsˈdef.ə.renz, ˌvæz-, (US) ˌvæsˈdef.ə.renz

vas|e vɑːz, (US) veɪs, veɪz, vɑːz **-es** -ɪz

vasectom|y vəˈsek.tə.m|i, væsˈek- **-ies** -iz

Vaseline® ˈvæs.ᵊl.iːn, -ɪ.liːn, ˌ--ˈ-, (US) ˈvæs.ə.liːn, ˌ--ˈ-

Vashti ˈvæʃ.ti, (US) ˈvɑːʃ.ti, -taɪ

vasoconstriction ˌveɪ.zəʊ.kənˈstrɪk.ʃᵊn, ˌvæs.əʊ-, (US) ˌvæs.oʊ-, ˌveɪ.zoʊ-

vasoconstrictor ˌveɪ.zəʊ.kənˈstrɪk.təʳ, ˌvæs.əʊ-, (US) ˌvæs.oʊ-, ˌveɪ.zoʊ- **-s** -z

vasodilation ˌveɪ.zəʊ.daɪˈleɪ.ʃᵊn, ˌvæs.əʊ-, (US) ˌvæs.oʊ-, ˌveɪ.zoʊ-

vasodilator ˌveɪ.zəʊ.daɪˈleɪ.təʳ,

ˌvæs.əʊ-, US ˌvæs.oʊˈdaɪ.leɪ.t̬ɚ, ˌveɪ.zoʊ-, -dəˈ-; US -daɪˈleɪ- -s -z
vasomotor ˌveɪ.zəʊˈməʊ.təʳ, ˌvæs.əʊ-, US ˌvæs.oʊˈmoʊ.t̬ɚ, ˌveɪ.zoʊˈ-
vassal ˈvæs.əl -s -z
vassalage ˈvæs.əl.ɪdʒ
Vassar ˈvæs.əʳ, US -ɚ
vast vɑːst, US væst -er -əʳ, US -ɚ -est -ɪst, -əst -ly -li -ness/es -nəs/ɪz, -nɪs/ɪz
Västerås ˌves.təˈrɔːs
vat væt -s -s -ting -ɪŋ, US ˈvæt̬.ɪŋ -ted -ɪd, US ˈvæt̬.ɪd
VAT ˌviː.eɪˈtiː, væt -able ˈvæt.ə.bəl
Vathek ˈvæθ.ek, ˈvɑː.θek
vatic ˈvæt.ɪk, US ˈvæt̬-
Vatican ˈvæt.ɪ.kən, US ˈvæt̬- ˌ**Vatican** ˈ**City**
vaticinate vəˈtɪs.ɪ|.neɪt, vætˈɪs-, US ˈ-ə- -nates -neɪts -nating -neɪ.tɪŋ, US -neɪ.t̬ɪŋ -nated -neɪ.tɪd, US -neɪ.t̬ɪd
vaticination ˌvæt.ɪ.sɪˈneɪ.ʃən, ˌ-ə-; vəˌtɪs.ɪˈ-, vætˌɪs-, US ˌvæt̬.ə.səˈ-; US vəˌtɪs-, vætˌɪs- -s -z
vatu ˈvɑː.tuː -s -z
Vaucluse vəʊˈkluːz, US voʊ-
Vaud vəʊ, US voʊ
vaudeville ˈvɔː.də.vɪl, ˈvəʊ-; ˈvɔːd.vɪl, -vəl, US ˈvɑːd.vɪl, ˈvɔːd-, ˈvoʊd-, ˈvɑː.də-, ˈvɔː-, ˈvoʊ- -s -z
vaudevillian ˌvɔː.dəˈvɪl.i.ən, ˌvəʊ-, ˌvɔːdˈvɪl-, US ˌvɑːdˈvɪl-, ˌvɔːd-, ˌvoʊd-, ˌvɑː.dəˈ-, ˌvɔː-, ˌvoʊ- -s -z
Vaudin ˈvəʊ.dɪn, US ˈvoʊ-
Vaudois sing ˈvəʊ.dwɑː, -ˈ-, -dwɔː, US voʊˈdwɑː **plur** -z
Vaughan vɔːn, US vɑːn, vɔːn
Vaughan Williams ˌvɔːnˈwɪl.jəmz, -i.əmz, US ˌvɑːnˈ-, ˌvɔːnˈ-
Vaughn vɔːn, US vɑːn, vɔːn
vault vɔːlt, vɒlt, US vɑːlt, vɔːlt -s -s -ing/s -ɪŋ/z, US ˈvɑːl.tɪŋz, ˈvɔːl- -ed -ɪd, US ˈvɑːl.tɪd, ˈvɔːl- -er/s -əʳ/z, US ˈvɑːl.tɚ/z, ˈvɔːl- ˈ**vaulting** ˌ**horse**
vaunt vɔːnt, US vɑːnt, vɔːnt -s -s -ing/ly -ɪŋ/li, US ˈvɑːn.t̬ɪŋ/li, ˈvɔːn- -ed -ɪd, US ˈvɑːn.t̬ɪd, ˈvɔːn- -er/s -əʳ/z, US ˈvɑːn.t̬ɚ/z, ˈvɔːn-
Vaux *English surname:* vɔːz, vɒks, vɔːks, vəʊks, US vɔːks, vɑːks *in* **de Vaux**: vəʊ, US voʊ

> Note: **Brougham and Vaux** is /ˌbrʊm.ənˈvɔːks/

Vauxhall® ˈvɒk.sɔːl, ˈvɒks.hɔːl, -ˈ-, US ˈvɑːks.hɔːl, ˈvɔːks-
vavaso(u)r, V~ ˈvæv.ə.sʊəʳ, -sɔːʳ, US -sɔːr -s -z
VAX® væks
Vaz væz
VC ˌviːˈsiː -s -z
VCR ˌviː.siːˈɑːʳ, US -ˈɑːr -s -z
VD ˌviːˈdiː
VDT ˌviː.diːˈtiː -s -z
VDU, vdu ˌviː.diːˈjuː -s -z
-'ve (= **have**) v, əv
veal viːl -y -i
Veblen ˈveb.lən
vector n ˈvek.təʳ, -tɔːʳ, US -tɚ -s -z
vect|or v ˈvek.t|əʳ, US -t|ɚ -ors -əz, US -ɚz -oring -ər.ɪŋ -ored -əd, US -ɚd
vectorial vekˈtɔː.ri.əl, US -ˈtɔːr.i-
Veda ˈveɪ.də, ˈviː- -s -z
Vedanta vedˈɑːn.tə, vɪˈdɑːn-, və-, -ˈdæn-, US vɪˈdɑːn-, -ˈdæn-
V-E Day ˌviːˈiː.deɪ
vedette vɪˈdet, və-, vedˈet, US və- -s -s
Vedic ˈveɪ.dɪk, ˈviː-
veep, V~ viːp
veer vɪəʳ, US vɪr -s -z -ing/ly -ɪŋ/li -ed -d
veg vedʒ ˌ**meat and two** ˈ**veg**
Vega *star:* ˈviː.gə, US ˈviː-, ˈveɪ- *Spanish dramatist:* ˈveɪ.gə
vegan ˈviː.gən -s -z -ism -ɪzəm
Vegas ˈveɪ.gəs
vegeburger ˈvedʒ.iˌbɜː.gəʳ, US -ˌbɝː.gɚ -s -z
Vegemite® ˈvedʒ.i.maɪt, ˈ-ə-
vegetable ˈvedʒ.tə.bəl, ˈ-ə.tə-, ˈ-ɪ-, US ˈvedʒ.tə-, -ə.t̬ə- -s -z
vegetal ˈvedʒ.ɪ.təl, ˈ-ə-, US ˈ-ə-
vegetarian ˌvedʒ.ɪˈteə.ri.ən, -əˈ-, US -əˈter.i- -s -z -ism -ɪ.zəm
vege|tate ˈvedʒ.ɪ|.teɪt, ˈ-ə-, US ˈ-ə- -tates -teɪts -tating -teɪ.tɪŋ, US -teɪ.t̬ɪŋ -tated -teɪ.tɪd, US -teɪ.t̬ɪd
vegetation ˌvedʒ.ɪˈteɪ.ʃən, -əˈ-, US -əˈ- -s -z
vegetative ˈvedʒ.ɪ.tə.tɪv, ˈ-ə-, -teɪ-, US -ə.teɪ.t̬ɪv -ly -li
veggie ˈvedʒ.i -s -z
veggieburger ˈvedʒ.iˌbɜː.gəʳ, US ˌbɝː.gɚ -s -z
vegg|y ˈvedʒ|.i -ies -iz
vehemence ˈviː.ə.mənts, ˈ-ɪ-, -hɪ-, -hə-, ˈvɪə.mənts, US ˈviː.ə-, -hə-
vehement ˈviː.ə.mənt, ˈ-ɪ-, -hɪ-, -hə-, ˈvɪə.mənt, US ˈviː.ə-, -hə- -ly -li
vehicle ˈvɪə.kəl, ˈviː.ɪ-, US ˈviː.ə-, -hɪ- -s -z
vehicular viˈɪk.jə.ləʳ, vɪˈhɪk-, və-, -jʊ-, US viːˈhɪk.jə.lɚ, -jʊ-
veil veɪl -s -z -ing/s -ɪŋ/z -ed -d
Veil viːl, US veɪ, viːl
vein veɪn -s -z -ed -d -less -ləs, -lɪs
vein|y ˈveɪ.n|i -ier -i.əʳ, US -i.ɚ -iest -i.ɪst, -i.əst
Veitch viːtʃ
velar ˈviː.ləʳ, US -lɚ -s -z
velaric viːˈlær.ɪk, vɪ-, US -ˈler-, -ˈlær-
velarization, -isa- ˌviː.lər.aɪˈzeɪ.ʃən, -ɪˈ-, US -əˈ- -s -z
velariz|e, -is|e ˈviː.lər.aɪz, US -lə.raɪz -es -ɪz -ing -ɪŋ -ed -d
Velasquez, Velazquez vɪˈlæs.kwɪz, velˈæs-, -kɪz, -kez, -kwɪθ, US vəˈlɑː.skes, -ˈlæs.kes, -kwez
Velcro® ˈvel.krəʊ, US -kroʊ
veldt, veld, V~ velt, US velt, felt -s -z
velic ˈviː.lɪk
velleity velˈiː.ə.ti, vəˈliː-, -ɪ.ti, US vəˈliː-
vellum ˈvel.əm -s -z
veloce vɪˈləʊ.tʃeɪ, velˈəʊ-, vəˈləʊ-, US verˈloʊ.tʃeɪ
velocipede vɪˈlɒs.ɪ.piːd, və-, ˈ-ə-, US vəˈlɑː.sə- -s -z
velocit|y vɪˈlɒs.ə.t|i, və-, -ɪ.t|i, US vəˈlɑː.sə.t̬|i -ies -iz
velodrome ˈvel.ə.drəʊm, ˈviː.ləʊ-, US ˈvel.ə.droʊm -s -z
velour vəˈlʊəʳ, US -ˈlʊr -s -z
velouté vəˈluː.teɪ -s -z
vel|um ˈviː.l|əm -a -ə
velvet ˈvel.vɪt, -vət -s -s
velveteen ˌvel.vɪˈtiːn, -vəˈ-, ˈ--- -s -z
velvet|y ˈvel.vɪ.t|i, -və-, US -və.t̬|i -iness -ɪ.nəs, -nɪs
Venables ˈven.ə.bəlz
vena cava ˌviː.nəˈkeɪ.və, -ˈkɑː-, US -ˈkeɪ- **venae cavae** -niːˈkeɪ.viː, -ˈkɑː-, US -ˈkeɪ-
venal ˈviː.nəl -ly US -i
venality viːˈnæl.ə.ti, vɪ-, -ɪ.ti, US vɪˈnæl.ə.t̬i
venation viːˈneɪ.ʃən
vend vend -s -z -ing -ɪŋ -ed -ɪd -er/s -əʳ/z, US -ɚ/z ˈ**vending ma**ˌ**chine**
Venda ˈven.də
vendee venˈdiː -s -z
vendetta venˈdet.ə, US -ˈdet̬- -s -z
vendor ˈven.dɔːʳ, -dəʳ, US -dɚ, -dɔːr -s -z
veneer vəˈnɪəʳ, vɪ-, US -ˈnɪr -s -z -ing -ɪŋ -ed -d
venerab|le ˈven.ər.ə.b|əl -ly -li -ness -əl.nəs, -nɪs
vener|ate ˈven.ər|.eɪt, US -ə.r|eɪt -ates -eɪts -ating -eɪ.tɪŋ, US -eɪ.t̬ɪŋ -ated -eɪ.tɪd, US -eɪ.t̬ɪd -ator/s -eɪ.təʳ/z, US -eɪ.t̬ɚ/z
veneration ˌven.ərˈeɪ.ʃən, US -əˈreɪ-
venereal vəˈnɪə.ri.əl, vɪ-, US vəˈnɪr.i- **ve**ˈ**nereal di**ˌ**sease**
venereology vəˌnɪə.ri.ˈɒl.ə.dʒi, vɪ-, US -ˌnɪr.iˈɑː.lə-
venery ˈven.ər.i
Venetia vəˈniː.ʃi.ə, vɪ-, ˈ-ʃə
Venetian, venetian vəˈniː.ʃən, vɪ-, US ˈ-ʃən -s -z **ve**ˌ**netian** ˈ**blind**
Venezuel|a ˌven.ɪˈzweɪ.l|ə, -ezˈweɪ-, -əˈzweɪ-, US -əˈzweɪ-, -ˈzwiː- -an/s -ən/z
veng|e vendʒ -es -ɪz -ing -ɪŋ -ed -d
vengeance ˈven.dʒənts
vengeful ˈvendʒ.fəl, -fʊl -ly -i -ness -nəs, US -nɪs
Vengerov ˈveŋ.gə.rɒf, US -gɚ.ɑːf
veni, vidi, vici ˌveɪ.niːˌviː.diːˈviː.kiː, ˌweɪ.niːˌwiː.diːˈwiː.kiː
venial ˈviː.ni.əl, ˈ-njəl -ly -i -ness -nəs, -nɪs ˌ**venial** ˈ**sin**
veniality ˌviː.niˈæl.ə.ti, -ɪ.ti, US -ə.t̬i
Venice ˈven.ɪs
venire vəˈnɪə.riː, US -ˈnaɪ-, -ˈnɪr.iː
venison ˈven.ɪ.sən, ˈ-ə-, -zən
Venite vɪˈnaɪ.ti, venˈaɪ-, -ˈniː-, US vəˈniː- -s -z
Venn ven ˈ**Venn** ˌ**diagram**; ˌ**Venn** ˈ**diagram**

V

Venner ˈven.əʳ, (US) -ɚ
venom ˈven.əm **-s** -z **-ed** -d
venomous ˈven.ə.məs **-ly** -li **-ness** -nəs, -nɪs
venous ˈviː.nəs **-ly** -li
vent vent **-s** -s **-ing** -ɪŋ, (US) ˈven.t̬ɪŋ **-ed** -ɪd, (US) ˈven.t̬ɪd
Vent-Axia® ˌventˈæk.si.ə
ventil|ate ˈven.tɪ.l|eɪt, -tᵊl|.eɪt, (US) -t̬ə.l|eɪt **-ates** -eɪts **-ating** -eɪ.tɪŋ, (US) -eɪ.t̬ɪŋ **-ated** -eɪ.tɪd, (US) -eɪ.t̬ɪd
ventilation ˌven.tɪˈleɪ.ʃᵊn, -tᵊlˈeɪ-, (US) -t̬əˈleɪ-
ventilator ˈven.tɪ.leɪ.təʳ, -tᵊl.eɪ-, (US) -t̬ə.leɪ.t̬ɚ **-s** -z
Ventnor ˈvent.nəʳ, (US) -nɚ
Ventolin® ˈven.təʊ.lɪn, -tᵊl.ɪn, (US) -t̬ᵊl.ɪn, -toʊ.lɪn
ventral ˈven.trᵊl **-ly** -i
ventricle ˈven.trɪ.kᵊl **-s** -z
ventricular venˈtrɪk.jə.ləʳ, -jʊ-, (US) -jə.lɚ
ventriloquial ˌven.trɪˈləʊ.kwi.əl, -trəˈ-, (US) -trəˈloʊ- **-ly** -i
ventriloquism venˈtrɪl.ə.kwɪ.zᵊm
ventriloquist venˈtrɪl.ə.kwɪst **-s** -s
ventriloquiz|e, -is|e venˈtrɪl.ə.kwaɪz **-es** -ɪz **-ing** -ɪŋ **-ed** -d
ventriloquy venˈtrɪl.ə.kwi
vent|ure ˈven.tʃ|əʳ, (US) -tʃ|ɚ **-ures** -əz, (US) -ɚz **-uring** -ᵊr.ɪŋ **-ured** -əd, (US) -ɚd **-urer/s** -ᵊr.əʳ/z, (US) -ɚ.ɚ/z **ˌventure ˈcapital** (US) **ˈventure ˌcapital; ˈVenture ˌScout**
venturesome ˈven.tʃə.səm, (US) -tʃɚ- **-ly** -li **-ness** -nəs, -nɪs
venturi venˈtʃʊə.ri, -ˈtjʊə-, (US) -ˈtʊr.i **-s** -z
venturous ˈven.tʃᵊr.əs **-ly** -li **-ness** -nəs, -nɪs
venue ˈven.juː **-s** -z
venul|ar ˈven.jʊ.l|əʳ, -jə-, (US) -juː.l|ɚ, ˈviː.njuː-, -njə- **-ose** -əʊs, (US) -oʊs
venule ˈven.juːl, (US) ˈven.juːl, ˈviː.njuːl **-s** -z
Venus ˈviː.nəs **-es** -ɪz **ˌVenus' ˈflytrap**
Venusian vɪˈnjuː.si.ən, və-, -zi.ən, (US) vɪˈnuː.ʃᵊn, -ʒᵊn, -zi.ən **-s** -z
Vera ˈvɪə.rə, (US) ˈvɪr.ə
veracious vəˈreɪ.ʃəs, vɪ-, verˈeɪ-, (US) vəˈreɪ- **-ly** -li **-ness** -nəs, -nɪs
veracity vəˈræs.ə.ti, vɪ-, verˈæs-, -ɪ.ti, (US) vəˈræs.ə.t̬i
Veracruz ˌvɪə.rəˈkruːz, ˌver.əˈ-, ˌveə.rəˈ-, (US) ˌver.əˈ-
veranda(h) vəˈræn.də **-s** -z
verb vɜːb, (US) vɝːb **-s** -z
verbal ˈvɜː.bᵊl, (US) ˈvɝː- **-ly** -i
verbal|ism ˈvɜː.bᵊl|.ɪ.zᵊm, (US) ˈvɝː- **-ist/s** -ɪst/s
verbalization ˌvɜː.bᵊl.aɪˈzeɪ.ʃᵊn, -ɪˈ-, (US) ˌvɝː.bᵊl.əˈ-
verbaliz|e, -is|e ˈvɜː.bᵊl.aɪz, (US) ˈvɝː.bə.laɪz **-es** -ɪz **-ing** -ɪŋ **-ed** -d
verbatim vɜːˈbeɪ.tɪm, və-, (US) vɚˈbeɪ.t̬ɪm, -t̬əm
verbena vɜːˈbiː.nə, və-, (US) vɚ- **-s** -z
verbiage ˈvɜː.bi.ɪdʒ, (US) ˈvɝː-
Verbier ˈveə.bi.eɪ, (US) ˈver-
verbose vɜːˈbəʊs, və-, (US) vɚˈboʊs **-ly** -li **-ness** -nəs, -nɪs
verbosity vɜːˈbɒs.ə.ti, və-, -ɪ.ti, (US) vɚˈbɑː.sə.t̬i
verboten vɜːˈbəʊ.tᵊn; *as if German:* fəˈ-; (US) vɚˈboʊ-
Vercingetorix ˌvɜː.sɪnˈdʒet.ə.rɪks, -sᵊnˈ-, -ˈget-, (US) ˌvɝː.sɪnˈdʒet̬.ɚ.ɪks, -ˈget̬-
verdancy ˈvɜː.dᵊnt.si, (US) ˈvɝː-
verdant ˈvɜː.dᵊnt, (US) ˈvɝː- **-ly** -li
Verde vɜːd, (US) vɝːd
Verdi ˈveə.diː, -di, (US) ˈver- **-an** -ən
verdict ˈvɜː.dɪkt, (US) ˈvɝː- **-s** -s
verdigris ˈvɜː.dɪ.griːs, -griː, (US) ˈvɝː.dɪ.griːs, -grɪs, -griː
Verdun vɜːˈdʌn, ˈ--, (US) verˈdʌn, ˌvɝː-
verdure ˈvɜː.dʒəʳ, -djəʳ, -djʊəʳ, (US) ˈvɝː.dʒɚ
Vere vɪəʳ, (US) vɪr
verg|e vɜːdʒ, (US) vɝːdʒ **-es** -ɪz **-ing** -ɪŋ **-ed** -d
verger ˈvɜː.dʒəʳ, (US) ˈvɝː.dʒɚ **-s** -z
Vergil ˈvɜː.dʒɪl, (US) ˈvɝː- **-s** -z
Vergilian vɜːˈdʒɪl.i.ən, və-, (US) vɝː-, ˈ-jən
verifiable ˈver.ɪ.faɪ.ə.bᵊl, ˈ-ə-, ˌver.ɪˈfaɪ-, -əˈ-, (US) ˌver.əˈfaɪ-
verification ˌver.ɪ.fɪˈkeɪ.ʃᵊn, ˌ-ə-, -fəˈ-, (US) ˌ-ə- **-s** -z
veri|fy ˈver.ɪ|.faɪ, ˈ-ə- **-fies** -faɪz **-fying** -faɪ.ɪŋ **-fied** -faɪd **-fier/s** -faɪ.əʳ/z, (US) -faɪ.ɚ/z
verily ˈver.ᵊl.i, -ɪ.li
verisimilitude ˌver.ɪ.sɪˈmɪl.ɪ.tʃuːd, -tjuːd, ˌ-ə-, -səˈ-, (US) -ə.səˈmɪl.ə.tuːd, -tjuːd
verismo vəˈrɪz.moʊ
veritab|le ˈver.ɪ.tə.b|ᵊl, (US) -ə.t̬ə- **-ly** -li
verit|y, V~ ˈver.ə.t|i, -ɪ.t|i, (US) -ə.t̬|i **-ies** -iz
Verizon® vəˈraɪ.zᵊn, (US) vɚ-
verjuice ˈvɜː.dʒuːs, (US) ˈvɝː-
Verlaine veəˈlen, vɜː-, (US) vɚˈleɪn, -ˈlen
Vermeer vəˈmɪəʳ, vɜː-, -ˈmeəʳ, (US) vɚˈmɪr **-s** -z
vermeil ˈvɜː.meɪl, -mɪl, (US) ˈvɝː.mɪl; (US) vɚˈmeɪl
vermicelli ˌvɜː.mɪˈtʃel.i, -ˈsel-, (US) ˌvɝː.məˈtʃel-, -ˈsel-
vermicide ˈvɜː.mɪ.saɪd, (US) ˈvɝː.mə- **-s** -z
vermicular vɜːˈmɪk.jə.ləʳ, -jʊ-, (US) vɚˈmɪk.jə.lɚ
vermiform ˈvɜː.mɪ.fɔːm, (US) ˈvɝː.mə.fɔːrm **ˌvermiform apˈpendix**
vermil(l)ion vəˈmɪl.jən, vɜː-, -i.ən, (US) vɚˈmɪl.jən **-s** -z
vermin ˈvɜː.mɪn, (US) ˈvɝː- **-ous** -əs
Vermont vəˈmɒnt, vɜː-, (US) vɚˈmɑːnt
vermouth ˈvɜː.məθ, -muːθ; vɜːˈmuːθ, və-, (US) vɚˈmuːθ **-s** -s
vernacular vəˈnæk.jə.ləʳ, vɜː-, -jʊ-, (US) vɚˈnæk.jə.lɚ **-s** -z **-ly** -li
vernal ˈvɜː.nᵊl, (US) ˈvɝː- **-ly** -i **ˌvernal ˈequinox**
Verne vɜːn, veən, (US) vɝːn
Verner *English surname:* ˈvɜː.nəʳ, (US) ˈvɝː.nɚ *Danish grammarian:* ˈvɜː.nəʳ, ˈveə-, (US) ˈvɝː.nɚ, ˈver-
Verney ˈvɜː.ni, (US) ˈvɝː-
vernier ˈvɜː.ni.əʳ, (US) ˈvɝː.ni.ɚ **-s** -z
Vernon ˈvɜː.nən, (US) ˈvɝː-
Verona vəˈrəʊ.nə, vɪ-, verˈəʊ-, (US) vəˈroʊ-
Veronal® ˈver.ə.nᵊl
Veronese *artist:* ˌver.əʊˈneɪ.zeɪ, (US) -əˈneɪ.si, -zi *(person) from Verona:* ˌver.əˈniːz, -əʊˈ-, (US) -əˈniːz
veronica, V~ vəˈrɒn.ɪ.kə, vɪ-, verˈɒn-, (US) vəˈrɑː.ni- **-s** -z
Verrazano ˌver.əˈzɑː.nəʊ, (US) -noʊ *stress shift, see compound:* **ˌVerrazano ˈNarrows**
verru|ca vəˈruː|.kə, vɪ-, verˈuː-, (US) vəˈruː- **-cas** -kəz **-cae** -kiː, -kaɪ
Versace vəˈsɑː.tʃi, vɜː-, (US) vɚ-
Versailles *in France:* veəˈsaɪ, vɜː-, (US) vɝːˈsaɪ, ver- *in US:* vɜːˈseɪlz, (US) vɝː-
versant ˈvɜː.sᵊnt, (US) ˈvɝː- **-s** -s
versatile ˈvɜː.sə.taɪl, (US) ˈvɝː.sə.t̬ᵊl **-ly** -li **-ness** -nəs, -nɪs
versatility ˌvɜː.səˈtɪl.ə.ti, -ɪ.ti, (US) ˌvɝː.səˈtɪl.ə.t̬i
vers de société ˌveə.dəˌsɒs.jeɪˈteɪ, (US) ˌver.dɪ.soʊˈsiː.eɪ.teɪ; (US) -dəˌsɑː.sjeɪˈteɪ
vers|e vɜːs, (US) vɝːs **-es** -ɪz **-ed** -t
versicle ˈvɜː.sɪ.kᵊl, (US) ˈvɝː- **-s** -z
versification ˌvɜː.sɪ.fɪˈkeɪ.ʃᵊn, -sə-, -fəˈ-, (US) ˌvɝː.sə-
versificator ˈvɜː.sɪ.fɪ.keɪ.təʳ, -sə-, (US) ˈvɝː.sə.fɪ.keɪ.t̬ɚ **-s** -z
versi|fy ˈvɜː.sɪ|.faɪ, -sə-, (US) ˈvɝː.sɪ-, ˈ-sə- **-fies** -faɪz **-fying** -faɪ.ɪŋ **-fied** -faɪd **-fier/s** -faɪ.əʳ/z, (US) -faɪ.ɚ/z
version ˈvɜː.ʃᵊn, -ʒᵊn, (US) ˈvɝː.ʒᵊn, -ʃᵊn **-s** -z
verso ˈvɜː.səʊ, (US) ˈvɝː.soʊ **-s** -z
versus ˈvɜː.səs, (US) ˈvɝː-
vert, V~ vɜːt, (US) vɝːt **-s** -s
vertebr|a ˈvɜː.tɪ.br|ə, -tə-, (US) ˈvɝː.t̬ə- **-ae** -iː, -aɪ, -eɪ **-as** -əz
vertebral ˈvɜː.tɪ.brᵊl, -tə-, (US) ˈvɝː.t̬ə- **-ly** -i **ˌvertebral ˈcolumn**
vertebrata ˌvɜː.tɪˈbrɑː.tə, -təˈ-, -ˈbreɪ-, (US) -ˈbreɪ.t̬ə, -ˈbrɑː-
vertebrate ˈvɜː.tɪ.breɪt, -tə-, -brət, -brɪt, (US) ˈvɝː.tə.brɪt, -breɪt **-s** -s
ver|tex ˈvɜː|.teks, (US) ˈvɝː- **-tices** -tɪ.siːz, (US) -t̬ɪ- **-texes** -tek.sɪz
vertic|al ˈvɜː.tɪ.k|ᵊl, (US) ˈvɝː.t̬ə- **-ally** -ᵊl.i, -li **-alness** -ᵊl.nəs, -nɪs
vertiginous vɜːˈtɪdʒ.ɪ.nəs, ˈ-ə-, (US) vɚˈtɪdʒ.ə- **-ly** -li
vertigo ˈvɜː.tɪ.gəʊ, -tə-, (US) ˈvɝː.t̬ə.goʊ
Verulam ˈver.ʊ.ləm, (US) -juː-
Verulamium ˌver.ʊˈleɪ.mi.əm, (US) -juːˈ-
vervain ˈvɜː.veɪn, (US) ˈvɝː-
verve vɜːv, (US) vɝːv
Verwoerd fəˈvʊət, feə-, -ˈvɔːt, (US) fɚˈvɔːrt, -ˈvʊrt
Verwood ˈvɜː.wʊd, (US) ˈvɝː-

V

very **adj, adv** ˈver.i
Very *surname:* ˈvɪə.ri, ˈver.i, (US) ˈvɪr.i, ˈver-
Vesalius vesˈeɪ.li.əs
Vesey ˈviː.zi
vesi|ca ˈves.ɪ|.kə; vɪˈsaɪ|.kə, və-, (US) vɪˈsaɪ-, -ˈsiː- **-cae** -kiː
vesicle ˈves.ɪ.kəl **-s** -z
vesicular vɪˈsɪk.jə.ləʳ, vəˈ-, (US) -lɚ
Vespa® ˈves.pə
Vespasian vesˈpeɪ.zi.ən, -ʒi-, ˈ-ʒən, (US) ˈ-ʒən, -ʒi.ən
vesper, V~ ˈves.pəʳ, (US) -pɚ **-s** -z
vespertine ˈves.pə.taɪn, (US) -pɚ.tɪn, -taɪn
Vespucci vesˈpuː.tʃi
vessel ˈves.əl **-s** -z
vest vest **-s** -s **-ing** -ɪŋ **-ed** -ɪd ˌ**vested** ˈ**interest**
vesta, V~ ˈves.tə **-s** -z
vestal ˈves.təl **-s** -z ˌ**vestal** ˈ**virgin**
vestibular vesˈtɪb.jə.ləʳ, -jʊ-, (US) -jə.lɚ
vestibule ˈves.tɪ.bjuːl, (US) -tə- **-s** -z **-d** -d
vestig|e ˈves.tɪdʒ **-es** -ɪz
vestigial vesˈtɪdʒ.i.əl, ˈ-əl **-ly** -i
vestment ˈvest.mənt **-s** -s
vest-pocket ˌvestˈpɒk.ɪt, (US) -ˈpɑː.kɪt, ˈ-ˌ--
Vestris ˈves.trɪs
vestr|y ˈves.tr|i **-ies** -iz
vesture ˈves.tʃəʳ, -tjəʳ, (US) -tʃɚ **-s** -z
vesuvian, V~ vɪˈsuː.vi.ən, və-, -ˈsjuː-, (US) vəˈsuː- **-s** -z **-ite** -aɪt
Vesuvius vɪˈsuː.vi.əs, və-, -ˈsjuː-, (US) vəˈsuː-
vet vet **-s** -s **-ting** -ɪŋ, (US) ˈveṭ.ɪŋ **-ted** -ɪd, (US) ˈveṭ.ɪd
vetch vetʃ **-es** -ɪz
veteran ˈvet.ər.ən, -rən, (US) ˈveṭ.ɚ.ən; (US) ˈvet.rən **-s** -z ˈ**Veterans** ˌ**Day**
veterinarian ˌvet.ər.ɪˈneə.ri.ən, -rəˈ-, (US) -ˈner.i- **-s** -z
veterinar|y ˈvet.ər.ɪ.nər|.i, ˈ-rə.nər-, (US) -ner- **-ies** -iz ˈ**veterinary** ˌ**surgeon**
veto ˈviː.təʊ, (US) -ṭoʊ **-es** -z **-ing** -ɪŋ **-ed** -d **-er/s** -əʳ/z, (US) -ɚ/z
Vevey ˈvev.eɪ, -i, (US) vəˈveɪ
vex veks **-es** -ɪz **-ing** -ɪŋ **-ed** -t ˌ**vexed** ˈ**question**
vexation vekˈseɪ.ʃən **-s** -z
vexatious vekˈseɪ.ʃəs **-ly** -li **-ness** -nəs, -nɪs
vgc ˌviː.dʒiːˈsiː
VHF ˌviː.eɪtʃˈef
via ˈvaɪ.ə, (US) ˈvaɪ.ə, ˈviː.ə
viability ˌvaɪ.əˈbɪl.ə.ti, -ɪ.ti, (US) -ə.ṭi
viab|le ˈvaɪ.ə.b|əl **-ly** -li
Viacom® ˈvaɪ.ə.kɒm, (US) -kɑːm
via dolorosa ˌviː.əˌdɒl.əˈrəʊ.sə, (US) -ˌdɑː.ləˈroʊ-, -ˌdoʊ-
viaduct ˈvaɪ.ə.dʌkt **-s** -s
Viagra vaɪˈæg.rə, vi-
vial vaɪəl, (US) ˈvaɪ.əl; (US) vaɪl **-s** -z
Vialli viˈɑː.li
viand ˈvaɪ.ənd **-s** -z
viatic|um vaɪˈæt.ɪ.k|əm, vi-, (US) vaɪˈæṭ- **-ums** -əmz **-a** -ə

vibe vaɪb **-s** -z
vibrancy ˈvaɪ.brənt.si
vibrant ˈvaɪ.brənt **-ly** -li
vibraphone ˈvaɪ.brə.fəʊn, (US) -foʊn **-s** -z
vibra|te vaɪˈbreɪ|t, (US) ˈ-- **-tes** -ts **-ting** -tɪŋ, (US) -ṭɪŋ **-ted** -tɪd, (US) -ṭɪd
vibration vaɪˈbreɪ.ʃən **-s** -z
vibrational vaɪˈbreɪ.ʃən.əl, -ˈbreɪʃ.nəl
vibrative vaɪˈbreɪ.tɪv, (US) ˈvaɪ.brə.ṭɪv
vibrato vɪˈbrɑː.təʊ, (US) -ṭoʊ **-s** -z
vibrator vaɪˈbreɪ.təʳ, (US) ˈvaɪ.breɪ.ṭɚ **-s** -z
vibratory ˈvaɪ.brə.tər.i; vaɪˈbreɪ-, (US) ˈvaɪ.brə.tɔːr-
viburnum vaɪˈbɜː.nəm, (US) -ˈbɝː- **-s** -z
vic, V~ vɪk **-s** -s
vicar ˈvɪk.əʳ, (US) -ɚ **-s** -z
vicarag|e ˈvɪk.ər.ɪdʒ **-es** -ɪz
vicarial vɪˈkeə.ri.əl, vaɪ-, və-, (US) -ˈker.i-, -ˈkær-
vicarious vɪˈkeə.ri.əs, vaɪ-, və-, (US) -ˈker.i-, -ˈkær- **-ly** -li **-ness** -nəs, -nɪs
vic|e **n** vaɪs **-es** -ɪz ˈ**vice** ˌ**squad**
vice **prep** ˈvaɪ.si, -sə, (US) -sə, -si
vice- ˌvaɪs
Note: Prefix. This usually receives secondary stress. It may carry the strongest stress in the word in stress-shift cases.
vice-admiral ˌvaɪsˈæd.mər.əl, -mɪ.rəl **-s** -z *stress shift:* ˌ**vice-admiral's** ˈ**flag**
vice-chair|man ˌvaɪsˈtʃeə|.mən, (US) -ˈtʃer- **-men** -mən *stress shift:* ˌ**vice-chairman's** ˈ**privilege**
vice-chancellor ˌvaɪsˈtʃɑːnt.səl.əʳ, (US) -ˈtʃænt- **-s** -z *stress shift:* ˌ**vice-chancellor's** ˈ**secretary**
vice-consul ˌvaɪsˈkɒnt.səl, (US) -ˈkɑːnt- **-s** -z *stress shift:* ˌ**vice-consul's** ˈ**post**
vice-consulate ˌvaɪsˈkɒnt.sjə.lət, -sjʊ-, -lɪt, (US) -ˈkɑːnt.sə.lət **-s** -s
vicegerent ˌvaɪsˈdʒer.ənt, -ˈdʒɪə.rənt, (US) -ˈdʒɪr.ənt **-s** -s
vice-like ˈvaɪs.laɪk
vice-presidenc|y ˌvaɪsˈprez.ɪ.dənt.s|i **-ies** -iz
vice-president ˌvaɪsˈprez.ɪ.dənt **-s** -s *stress shift:* ˌ**vice-president's** ˈ**vote**
vice-presidential ˌvaɪs.prez.ɪˈdent.ʃəl
vice-principal ˌvaɪsˈprɪnt.sə.pəl, -sɪ.pəl **-s** -z *stress shift:* ˌ**vice-principal's** ˈ**office**
viceregal ˌvaɪsˈriː.gəl *stress shift:* ˌ**viceregal** ˈ**privilege**
vicereine ˌvaɪsˈreɪn, ˈ--, (US) ˈvaɪs.reɪn **-s** -z
viceroy ˈvaɪs.rɔɪ **-s** -z
viceroyalt|y ˌvaɪsˈrɔɪ.əl.t|i, (US) -ṭ|i **-ies** -iz
viceroyship ˈvaɪs.rɔɪ.ʃɪp **-s** -s

vice versa ˌvaɪ.siˈvɜː.sə, -səˈ-, ˌvaɪsˈ-, (US) ˌvaɪ.səˈvɝː-, ˌvaɪsˈ-
Vichy ˈviː.ʃiː, -ʃi, ˈvɪʃ.iː, -i
vichyssoise ˌviː.ʃiˈswɑːz, ˌvɪʃ.iˈ-
vicinage ˈvɪs.ɪ.nɪdʒ, ˈ-ə-, (US) ˈ-ə-
vicinity vɪˈsɪn.ə.ti, və-, vaɪ-, -ɪ.ti, (US) vəˈsɪn.ə.ṭi
vicious ˈvɪʃ.əs **-ly** -li **-ness** -nəs, -nɪs ˌ**vicious** ˈ**circle**
vicissitude vɪˈsɪs.ɪ.tʃuːd, -tjuːd, və-, vaɪs-, ˈ-ə-, (US) vɪˈsɪs.ə.tuːd, -tjuːd **-s** -z
Vick® vɪk
Vickers ˈvɪk.əz, (US) -ɚz
Vickery ˈvɪk.ər.i
Vicki, Vicky ˈvɪk.i
victim ˈvɪk.tɪm, -təm **-s** -z **-less** -ləs, -lɪs
victimization, -isa- ˌvɪk.tɪ.maɪˈzeɪ.ʃən, -tə-, -məˈ-, (US) -tə.mɪˈ-
victimiz|e, -is|e ˈvɪk.tɪ.maɪz, -tə-, (US) -tə- **-es** -ɪz **-ing** -ɪŋ **-ed** -d **-er/s** -əʳ/z, (US) -ɚ/z
victor, V~ ˈvɪk.təʳ, (US) -tɚ **-s** -z
Victoria, victoria vɪkˈtɔː.ri.ə, (US) -ˈtɔːr.i- **-s** -z **Vic**ˌ**toria** ˈ**Cross**; **Vic**ˈ**toria** ˌ**Day**; **Vic**ˌ**toria** ˈ**Falls**; **Vic**ˌ**toria** ˈ**sandwich**
Victorian, victorian vɪkˈtɔː.ri.ən, (US) -ˈtɔːr.i- **-s** -z **Vic**ˌ**torian** ˈ**values**
Victoriana ˌvɪk.tɔː.riˈɑː.nə, vɪkˌtɔː-, (US) vɪkˌtɔːr.iˈæn.ə
victorious vɪkˈtɔː.ri.əs, (US) -ˈtɔːr.i- **-ly** -li **-ness** -nəs, -nɪs
victor ludorum ˌvɪk.təˌluːˈdɔː.rəm, (US) -tɚ.luːˈdɔːr.əm **victores ludorum** vɪkˌtɔː.reɪsˌ-, (US) -ˌtɔːr.eɪs-
victor|y ˈvɪk.tər|.i, ˈ-tr|i **-ies** -iz
victual ˈvɪt.əl, (US) ˈvɪṭ- **-s** -z **-(l)ing** -ɪŋ **-(l)ed** -d **-(l)er/s** -əʳ/z, (US) -ɚ/z

Note: Although this word has been pronounced without a /k/ for many centuries, the spelling pronunciation /ˈvɪk.tʃu.əl/ is now becoming widespread.

vicuña, vicuna vɪˈkjuː.nə, vaɪ-, və-, -ˈkuː-, -ˈkuː.njə, (US) vaɪˈkjuː.nə, vɪ-, -ˈkuː-, -ˈkuː.njə
Vidal vɪˈdɑːl, və-, -ˈdæl; ˈvaɪ.dəl, (US) vɪˈdæl, -ˈdɑːl

Note: The author Gore Vidal is normally /vɪˈdɑːl/; Vidal Sassoon is normally /vɪˈdæl/.

vide ˈvaɪ.diː, -di; ˈvɪd.eɪ, (US) ˈvaɪ.diː, -di; (US) ˈviː.deɪ, ˈwiː-
videlicet vɪˈdiː.lɪ.set, vaɪ-, və-; -ˈdeɪ.lɪ.ket, (US) vɪˈdel.ə.sɪt, wɪ-
video ˈvɪd.i.əʊ, (US) -oʊ **-s** -z **-ing** -ɪŋ **-ed** -d ˈ**video ar**ˌ**cade**; ˈ**video** ˌ**camera**; ˈ**video** ˌ**game**; ˌ**video** ˈ**nasty**; ˈ**video rec**ˌ**order**
videocassette ˌvɪd.i.əʊ.kəˈset, -kæsˈet, (US) -oʊ.kəˈset **-s** -s ˌ**video-cas**ˈ**sette rec**ˌ**order**

videoconferenc|e ˌvɪd.i.əʊˈkɒn.fər.əntsˌ Ⓤⓢ ˈvɪd.i.oʊˌkɑːn.fɚ-, -frəns **-es** -ɪz **-ing** -ɪŋ
videodisc ˈvɪd.i.əʊ.dɪsk, Ⓤⓢ -oʊ- **-s** -s
videofit ˈvɪd.i.əʊ.fɪt, Ⓤⓢ -oʊ- **-s** -s
video-link ˈvɪd.i.əʊ.lɪŋk, Ⓤⓢ -oʊ- **-s** -s **-ing** -ɪŋ **-ed** -t
Videophone® ˈvɪd.i.əʊ.fəʊn, Ⓤⓢ -oʊ.foʊn
videorecorder ˈvɪd.i.əʊ.rɪˌkɔː.dər, Ⓤⓢ -oʊ.rɪˌkɔːr.dɚ **-s** -z
videorecording ˈvɪd.i.əʊ.rɪˌkɔː.dɪŋ, -rəˌ-, Ⓤⓢ -oʊ.rɪˌkɔːr-, -rəˌ- **-s** -z
videotap|e ˈvɪd.i.əʊ.teɪp, Ⓤⓢ -oʊ- **-es** -s **-ing** -ɪŋ **-ed** -t
videotext ˈvɪd.i.əʊ.tekst, Ⓤⓢ -oʊ- **-s** -s
vie vaɪ **vies** vaɪz **vying** ˈvaɪ.ɪŋ **vied** vaɪd
Vienna viˈen.ə
Viennese ˌvɪəˈniːz, Ⓤⓢ ˌviː.əˈ-
Vientiane ˌvjenˈtjɑːn
Vietcong, Viet Cong ˌvjetˈkɒŋ, Ⓤⓢ ˌviː.etˈkɑːŋ, -ˈkɔːŋ; Ⓤⓢ viˌetˈ-; Ⓤⓢ ˌvjetˈ- *stress shift:* **ˌVietcong ˈfighters**
Vietminh ˌvjetˈmɪn, Ⓤⓢ ˌviː.etˈ-; Ⓤⓢ viˌetˈ-; Ⓤⓢ ˌvjetˈ-
Vietnam, Viet Nam ˌvjetˈnæm, -ˈnɑːm, Ⓤⓢ ˌviː.etˈnɑːm, -ətˈ-, -ˈnæm; Ⓤⓢ vɪˌetˈ-; Ⓤⓢ ˌvjetˈ- *stress shift:* **ˌVietnam ˈwar**
Vietnamese ˌvjet.nəˈmiːz, Ⓤⓢ viˌet-; Ⓤⓢ ˌvjet-, ˌviː.ət- *stress shift:* **ˌVietnamese ˈpeople**
view vjuː **-s** -z **-ing** -ɪŋ **-ed** -d **-er/s** -ər/z, Ⓤⓢ -ɚ/z **-able** -ə.bəl **-less** -ləs, -lɪs
viewfinder ˈvjuːˌfaɪn.dər, Ⓤⓢ -dɚ **-s** -z
Viewpark ˈvjuː.pɑːk, Ⓤⓢ -pɑːrk
viewpoint ˈvjuː.pɔɪnt **-s** -s
Vigar ˈvaɪ.gər, Ⓤⓢ -gɚ
Vigers ˈvaɪ.gəz, Ⓤⓢ -gɚz
vigil ˈvɪdʒ.ɪl, -əl, Ⓤⓢ -əl **-s** -z
vigilance ˈvɪdʒ.ɪ.ləns, -əl.ənts
vigilant ˈvɪdʒ.ɪ.lənt, -əl.ənt **-ly** -li
vigilant|e ˌvɪdʒ.ɪˈlæn.t|i, -əˈ-, Ⓤⓢ -ţ|i **-es** -iz **-ism** -ɪ.zəm
vig|nette vɪ|ˈnjet, -ˈnet, Ⓤⓢ -ˈnjet **-nettes** -ˈnjets, -ˈnets, Ⓤⓢ -ˈnjets **-netting** -ˈnjet.ɪŋ, -ˈnet-, Ⓤⓢ -ˈnjeţ.ɪŋ **-netted** -ˈnjet.ɪd, -ˈnet-, Ⓤⓢ -ˈnjeţ.ɪd **-nettist/s** -ˈnjet.ɪst/s, Ⓤⓢ -ˈnjeţ.ɪst/s
Vignoles ˈviː.njəʊlz, ˈvɪn.jəʊlz, -jəʊl, -jɒlz; vɪˈnjɒlz, -ˈnjəʊlz, Ⓤⓢ viːˈnjoʊl, -ˈnjoʊlz, ˈ--
Vigo ˈviː.gəʊ, ˈvaɪ-, Ⓤⓢ ˈviː.goʊ
vigor ˈvɪg.ər, Ⓤⓢ -ɚ
vigorous ˈvɪg.ər.əs **-ly** -li **-ness** -nəs, -nɪs
Vigotsky vɪˈgɒt.ski, Ⓤⓢ -ˈgɑːt-
vigour ˈvɪg.ər, Ⓤⓢ -ɚ
viking, V~ ˈvaɪ.kɪŋ **-s** -z
Vila ˈviː.lə
vil|e vaɪl **-er** -ər, Ⓤⓢ -ɚ **-est** -ɪst, -əst **-ely** -li **-eness** -nəs, -nɪs
vilification ˌvɪl.ɪ.fɪˈkeɪ.ʃən, ˌ-ə-, -fəˈ-, Ⓤⓢ ˌ-ə-
vili|fy ˈvɪl.ɪ|.faɪ, ˈ-ə- **-fies** -faɪz **-fying** -faɪ.ɪŋ **-fied** -faɪd **-fier/s** -faɪ.ər/z, Ⓤⓢ -faɪ.ɚ/z
villa, V~ *house:* ˈvɪl.ə **-s** -z
Villa *foreign name:* ˈviː.ə
villag|e ˈvɪl.ɪdʒ **-es** -ɪz
villager ˈvɪl.ɪ.dʒər, ˈ-ə-, Ⓤⓢ -ə.dʒɚ **-s** -z
villain ˈvɪl.ən; *in historical sense also:* -ɪn, -eɪn, Ⓤⓢ -ən **-s** -z
villainess ˌvɪl.əˈnes **-es** -ɪz
villainous ˈvɪl.ə.nəs **-ly** -li **-ness** -nəs, -nɪs
villain|y ˈvɪl.ə.n|i **-ies** -iz
Villa-Lobos ˌviː.ləˈləʊ.bɒs, Ⓤⓢ ˌviː.ləˈloʊ.bəs, -boʊs
villanelle ˌvɪl.əˈnel **-s** -z
-ville vɪl, viːl, Ⓤⓢ vɪl, vəl
villein ˈvɪl.ɪn, -eɪn, Ⓤⓢ -ən **-s** -z **-age** -ɪdʒ
Villeneuve ˈviːl.nɜːv, Ⓤⓢ vɪl.əˈnɜːv
Villette vɪˈlet
Villiers ˈvɪl.əz, -jəz, -i.əz, Ⓤⓢ ˈ-ɚz, -jɚz
Villon ˈvɪl.ən; *as if French:* viːˈjɔ̃ːŋ; Ⓤⓢ viːˈjoʊn
vill|us ˈvɪl|.əs **-i** -aɪ
Vilna ˈvɪl.nə
Vilnius ˈvɪl.ni.əs, Ⓤⓢ -ʊs, -əs
vim, V~® vɪm
Vimto® ˈvɪmp.təʊ, Ⓤⓢ -toʊ
vin(s) væ̃ŋ, væn
Viña del Mar ˌviː.njə.delˈmɑːr, Ⓤⓢ -ˈmɑːr
vinaigrette ˌvɪn.ɪˈgret, -eɪˈ-, Ⓤⓢ -əˈ- **-s** -s
Vince vɪnts
Vincennes *in France:* væ̃nˈsen, væn-, Ⓤⓢ væn- *in Indiana:* vɪnˈsenz
Vincent ˈvɪnt.sənt
Vinci ˈvɪn.tʃiː, -tʃi
vincul|um ˈvɪŋ.kjə.l|əm, -kjʊ-, Ⓤⓢ -kjə- **-a** -ə **-ums** -əmz
vindaloo ˌvɪn.dəlˈuː, Ⓤⓢ -dəˈluː **-s** -z
vin(s) de pays ˌvæ̃n.də.peɪˈiː, ˌvæn-
vindicable ˈvɪn.dɪ.kə.bəl
vindi|cate ˈvɪn.dɪ|.keɪt, Ⓤⓢ -də- **-cates** -keɪts **-cating** -keɪ.tɪŋ, Ⓤⓢ -keɪ.ţɪŋ **-cated** -keɪ.tɪd, Ⓤⓢ -keɪ.ţɪd **-cator/s** -keɪ.tər/z, Ⓤⓢ -keɪ.ţɚ/z
vindication ˌvɪn.dɪˈkeɪ.ʃən, -dəˈ-, Ⓤⓢ -dəˈ-
vindicative ˈvɪn.dɪ.kə.tɪv, -keɪ-; vɪnˈdɪk.ə-, Ⓤⓢ vɪnˈdɪk.ə.ţɪv; Ⓤⓢ ˈvɪn.dɪ.keɪ-
vindictive vɪnˈdɪk.tɪv **-ly** -li **-ness** -nəs, -nɪs
vine vaɪn **-s** -z
vineg|ar ˈvɪn.ɪ.g|ər, ˈ-ə-, Ⓤⓢ -ə.g|ɚ **-ars** -əz, Ⓤⓢ -ɚz **-ary** -ər.i
viner|y ˈvaɪ.nər|.i **-ies** -iz
Viney ˈvaɪ.ni
vineyard ˈvɪn.jəd, -jɑːd, Ⓤⓢ -jɚd **-s** -z
vingt-et-un ˌvæ̃n.teɪˈɜ̃ːŋ, -ˈɜːn, Ⓤⓢ ˌvæn.teɪˈɜːn
viniculture ˈvɪn.ɪˌkʌl.tʃər, ˌvɪn.ɪˈkʌl-, Ⓤⓢ ˈvɪn.ɪˌkʌl.tʃɚ
viniculturist ˌvɪn.ɪˈkʌl.tʃər.ɪst, ˈvɪn.ɪˌkʌl-, Ⓤⓢ ˌvɪn.ɪˈkʌl- **-s** -s
vino ˈviː.nəʊ, Ⓤⓢ -noʊ
vin(s) ordinaire(s) ˌvæ̃n.ɔː.dɪˈneər, ˌvæn-, Ⓤⓢ ˌvæ̃n.ɔːr.dənˈer
vinous ˈvaɪ.nəs
vintag|e ˈvɪn.tɪdʒ, Ⓤⓢ -ţɪdʒ **-es** -ɪz **ˌvintage ˈyear**
Vinter ˈvɪn.tər, Ⓤⓢ -ţɚ
vintner ˈvɪnt.nər, Ⓤⓢ -nɚ **-s** -z
viny ˈvaɪ.ni
vinyl ˈvaɪ.nəl, -nɪl, Ⓤⓢ -nəl
viol ˈvaɪ.əl, vaɪl, vɪəl, Ⓤⓢ ˈvaɪ.əl **-s** -z
viola *flower:* ˈvaɪə.lə, ˈvaɪ.əʊ-, ˈviː.ə-, -əʊ-; vaɪˈəʊ-, viˈ-, Ⓤⓢ ˈviː.ə.lə; Ⓤⓢ vaɪˈoʊ- *musical instrument:* viˈəʊ.lə, Ⓤⓢ viˈoʊ- **-s** -z
viola *musical instrument:* viˈəʊ.lə, Ⓤⓢ viˈoʊ- **-s** -z
Viola *female name:* ˈvaɪ.ə.lə, ˈvaɪ.əʊ-, ˈviː.ə.lə; viˈəʊ-, vaɪ-, Ⓤⓢ vaɪˈoʊ.lə, vi-; Ⓤⓢ viː.ə-
violable ˈvaɪ.ə.lə.bəl
viola da gamba viˌəʊ.lə.dəˈgæm.bə, Ⓤⓢ -ˌoʊ.lə.dəˈgɑːm- **-s** -z **viole da gamba** viˌəʊ.leɪ-, Ⓤⓢ -ˌoʊ-
viola d'amore viˌəʊ.lə.dæmˈɔː.reɪ, Ⓤⓢ -ˌoʊ.lə.dɑːˈmɔːr.eɪ, -ˌoʊ- **viole d'amore** viˌəʊ.leɪ-
violate **adj** ˈvaɪ.ə.lɪt, ˈvaɪ.əʊ-, Ⓤⓢ ˈvaɪ.ə-
vio|late **v** ˈvaɪ.ə|.leɪt, ˈvaɪ.əʊ-, Ⓤⓢ ˈvaɪ.ə- **-lates** -leɪts **-lating** -leɪ.tɪŋ, Ⓤⓢ -leɪ.ţɪŋ **-lated** -leɪ.tɪd, Ⓤⓢ -leɪ.ţɪd **-lator/s** -leɪ.tər/z, Ⓤⓢ -leɪ.ţɚ/z
violation ˌvaɪ.əˈleɪ.ʃən, ˌvaɪ.əʊˈ-, Ⓤⓢ ˌvaɪ.əˈ- **-s** -z
violence ˈvaɪ.ə.lənts
violent ˈvaɪ.ə.lənt **-ly** -li
violet, V~ ˈvaɪə.lət, ˈvaɪ.ə-, -lɪt, Ⓤⓢ -lɪt **-s** -s
violin ˌvaɪ.əˈlɪn **-s** -z
violinist vaɪ.əˈlɪn.ɪst, ˌvaɪ.ə- **-s** -s
violist *viola player:* viˈəʊ.lɪst, Ⓤⓢ -ˈoʊ- *viol player:* ˈvaɪ.ə.lɪst **-s** -s
violoncellist ˌvaɪ.ə.lənˈtʃel.ɪst, ˌvɪə.lənˈ-, -lɪnˈ-, Ⓤⓢ ˌviː.ə.lɑːnˈ-, ˌvaɪ.ə.lɑːnˈ- **-s** -s
violoncello ˌvaɪ.ə.lənˈtʃel.əʊ, ˌvɪə.lənˈ-, -lɪnˈ-, Ⓤⓢ ˌviː.ə.lɑːnˈtʃel.oʊ, ˌvaɪ.ə.lɑːnˈ- **-s** -z
violone ˈvaɪ.ə.ləʊn, ˈvɪə-, ˌvɪəˈləʊ.neɪ, Ⓤⓢ ˌviː.əˈloʊn **-s** -z
VIP ˌviː.aɪˈpiː **-s** -z
vip|er ˈvaɪ.p|ər, Ⓤⓢ -p|ɚ **-ers** -əz, Ⓤⓢ -ɚz **-erish** -ər.ɪʃ **-erous** -ər.əs
virago, V~ vɪˈrɑː.gəʊ, -ˈreɪ-, Ⓤⓢ vəˈrɑː.goʊ, -ˈreɪ-; Ⓤⓢ ˈvɪr.ə- **-(e)s** -z
viral ˈvaɪə.rəl, Ⓤⓢ ˈvaɪ-
vires ˈvaɪə.riːz, Ⓤⓢ ˈvaɪ-
Virgil ˈvɜː.dʒɪl, Ⓤⓢ ˈvɝː.dʒəl **-s** -z
Virgilian vɜːˈdʒɪl.i.ən, və-, Ⓤⓢ vɝː-, ˈ-jən
virgin, V~® ˈvɜː.dʒɪn, Ⓤⓢ ˈvɝː- **-s** -z **ˌvirgin ˈbirth; ˈVirgin ˌIslands** Ⓤⓢ **ˌVirgin ˈIslands; ˌVirgin ˈMary**
virginal ˈvɜː.dʒɪ.nəl, -dʒən.əl, Ⓤⓢ ˈvɝː- **-s** -z **-ly** -li
Virgini|a, virgini|a vəˈdʒɪn.j|ə,

vɜː-, -i|.ə, (US) vɚ- **-as** -əz **-an/s** -ən/z **virˌginia ˈcreeper**

virginity vəˈdʒɪn.ə.ti, vɜː-, -ɪ.ti, (US) vɚˈdʒɪn.ə.t̬i

Virgo ˈvɜː.gəʊ, ˈvɪə-, (US) ˈvɝː.goʊ **-s** -z

Virgoan vɜːˈgəʊ.ən, (US) vɝːˈgoʊ- **-s** -z

virgule ˈvɜː.gjuːl, (US) ˈvɝː- **-s** -z

viridescen|t ˌvɪr.ɪˈdes.ᵊn|t, (US) -əˈ- **-ce** -ts

viridian vɪˈrɪd.i.ən, və-, (US) və-

virile ˈvɪr.aɪl, (US) -ᵊl, -aɪl

virility vɪˈrɪl.ə.ti, və-, -ɪ.ti, (US) vəˈrɪl.ə.t̬i

virolog|y vaɪəˈrɒl.ə.dʒ|i, (US) vaɪˈrɑː.lə- **-ist/s** -ɪst/s

virtu vɜːˈtuː, (US) vɚ-; (US) ˈvɝː.tuː

virtual ˈvɜː.tʃu.əl, -tju-, ˈ-tʃʊəl, -tjʊəl, (US) ˈvɝː.tʃu- **-ly** -i **ˌvirtual reˈality**

virtue ˈvɜː.tʃuː, -tjuː, (US) ˈvɝː.tʃuː **-s** -z

virtuosity ˌvɜː.tʃuˈɒs.ə.ti, -tjuˈ-, -ɪ.ti, (US) ˌvɝː.tʃuˈɑː.sə.t̬i

virtuos|o ˌvɜː.tʃuˈəʊ.s|əʊ, -tjuˈ-, -z|əʊ, (US) ˌvɝː.tʃuˈoʊ.s|oʊ **-os** -əʊz, (US) -oʊz **-i** -i

virtuous ˈvɜː.tʃu.əs, -tju-, (US) ˈvɝː.tʃu- **-ly** -li **-ness** -nəs, -nɪs

virulence ˈvɪr.ʊ.lənts, ˈ-ə-, -jʊ-, -jə-, (US) -jə-, ˈ-ə-, -jʊ-

virulent ˈvɪr.ʊ.lᵊnt, ˈ-ə-, -jʊ-, -jə-, (US) -jə-, ˈ-ə-, -jʊ- **-ly** -li

virus ˈvaɪə.rəs, (US) ˈvaɪ- **-es** -ɪz

vis vɪs

visa, V~® ˈviː.zə, (US) -zə, -sə **-s** -z **-ing** -ɪŋ **-ed** -d

visag|e ˈvɪz.ɪdʒ **-es** -ɪz

visagiste ˌvɪz.ɑːˈʒiːst **-s** -s

vis-à-vis ˌviː.zəˈviː, ˌvɪz-, -ɑːˈ-, -æˈ-, (US) ˌviː.zəˈviː

viscera ˈvɪs.ᵊr|.ə

visceral ˈvɪs.ᵊr.ᵊl **-ly** -i

viscid ˈvɪs.ɪd

viscidity vɪˈsɪd.ə.ti, -ɪ.ti, (US) -ə.t̬i

Visconti vɪˈskɒn.ti, (US) -ˈskɑːn-

viscose ˈvɪs.kəʊs, -kəʊz, (US) -koʊs, -koʊz

viscosity vɪˈskɒs.ə.ti, -ɪ.ti, (US) -ˈskɑː.sə.t̬i

vis|count ˈvaɪ|.kaʊnt **-counts** -kaʊnts **-county** -kaʊn.ti, (US) -kaʊn.t̬i **-counties** -kaʊn.tiz, (US) -kaʊn.t̬iz

viscountc|y ˈvaɪ.kaʊnt.s|i **-ies** -iz

viscountess ˌvaɪ.kaʊnˈtes; ˈvaɪ.kaʊn.tɪs, -təs, (US) ˈvaɪ.kaʊn.t̬ɪs **-es** -ɪz

viscous ˈvɪs.kəs **-ness** -nəs, -nɪs

vis|e vaɪs **-es** -ɪz **-ing** -ɪŋ **-ed** -t

visé ˈviː.zeɪ, (US) ˈviː.zeɪ, -ˈ- **-s** -z **-ing** -ɪŋ **-d** -d

Vishnu ˈvɪʃ.nuː

visibility ˌvɪz.əˈbɪl.ə.ti, -ɪˈ-, -ɪ.ti, (US) -əˈbɪl.ə.t̬i

visib|le ˈvɪz.ə.b|ᵊl, ˈ-ɪ-, (US) ˈ-ə- **-ly** -li **-leness** -ᵊl.nəs, -nɪs

Visigoth ˈvɪz.ɪ.gɒθ, ˈvɪs-, (US) -ə.gɑːθ **-s** -s

Visigothic ˌvɪz.ɪˈgɒθ.ɪk, ˌvɪs-, (US) -əˈgɑː.θɪk

vision ˈvɪʒ.ᵊn **-s** -z

visional ˈvɪʒ.ᵊn.ᵊl, ˈ-nᵊl, (US) ˈvɪʒ.ᵊn.ᵊl **-ly** -i

visionar|y ˈvɪʒ.ᵊn.ᵊr|.i, -ᵊn.r|i, (US) -ᵊn.er|.i **-ies** -iz

vis|it ˈvɪz|.ɪt **-its** -ɪts **-iting** -ɪ.tɪŋ, (US) -ɪ.t̬ɪŋ **-ited** -ɪ.tɪd, (US) -ɪ.t̬ɪd **ˈvisiting card; ˌvisiting proˈfessor**

visitant ˈvɪz.ɪ.tᵊnt, (US) -t̬ᵊnt **-s** -s

visitation ˌvɪz.ɪˈteɪ.ʃᵊn, (US) -əˈ- **-s** -z

visitor ˈvɪz.ɪ.təʳ, (US) -t̬ɚ **-s** -z **ˈvisitors' ˌbook**

vis major ˌvɪsˈmeɪ.dʒəʳ, (US) -dʒɚ

visor ˈvaɪ.zəʳ, (US) -zɚ **-s** -z

vista ˈvɪs.tə **-s** -z

Vistula ˈvɪs.tjʊ.lə, ˈ-tʃə-, (US) -tʃuː-

visual ˈvɪʒ.u.əl, ˈvɪz.ju-, (US) ˈvɪʒ.u- **-s** -z **-ly** -i **ˌvisual ˈaid; ˌvisual diˈsplay ˌunit**

visualization, -isa- ˌvɪʒ.u.ᵊl.aɪˈzeɪ.ʃᵊn, ˌvɪz.ju-, -ɪˈ-, (US) ˌvɪʒ.u.ᵊl.əˈ-

visualiz|e, -is|e ˈvɪʒ.u.ᵊl.aɪz, ˈvɪz.ju-, (US) ˈvɪʒ.u.ə.laɪz **-es** -ɪz **-ing** -ɪŋ **-ed** -d **-er/s** -əʳ/z, (US) -ɚ/z

vita *glass:* ˈvaɪ.tə, (US) -t̬ə *aqua:* ˈviː.tə, (US) -t̬ə

Vita ˈviː.tə, (US) -t̬ə

vitae *curriculum:* ˈviː.taɪ, ˈvaɪ.tiː, (US) ˈvaɪ.t̬iː, ˈviː-, -taɪ

vital ˈvaɪ.tᵊl, (US) -t̬ᵊl **-ly** -i **ˌvital ˈsigns** (US) **ˈvital ˌsigns; ˌvital staˈtistics**

Vitalite® ˈvaɪ.tə.laɪt

vitality vaɪˈtæl.ə.ti, -ɪ.ti, (US) -ə.t̬i

vitalization, -isa- ˌvaɪ.tᵊl.aɪˈzeɪ.ʃᵊn, -ɪˈ-, (US) -tᵊl.əˈ-

vitaliz|e, -is|e ˈvaɪ.tᵊl.aɪz, (US) -t̬ə.laɪz **-es** -ɪz **-ing** -ɪŋ **-ed** -d

vitals ˈvaɪ.tᵊlz, (US) -t̬ᵊlz

vitamin ˈvɪt.ə.mɪn, ˈvaɪ-, (US) ˈvaɪ.t̬ə- **-s** -z **ˌvitamin ˈC**

VitBe® ˈvɪt.biː

vitellus vɪˈtel.əs, (US) vɪ-, vaɪ-

Vitez ˈviː.tez

viti|ate ˈvɪʃ.i|.eɪt **-ates** -eɪts **-ating** -eɪ.tɪŋ, (US) -eɪ.t̬ɪŋ **-ated** -eɪ.tɪd, (US) -eɪ.t̬ɪd **-ator/s** -eɪ.təʳ/z, (US) -eɪ.t̬ɚ/z

vitiation ˌvɪʃ.iˈeɪ.ʃᵊn

viticulture ˈvɪt.ɪ.kʌl.tʃəʳ, ˈvaɪ-, (US) -t̬ə.kʌl.tʃɚ

vitiligo ˌvɪt.ɪˈlaɪ.gəʊ, (US) ˌvɪt̬.ɪˈlaɪ.goʊ

vitreous ˈvɪt.ri.əs **-ness** -nəs, -nɪs

vitric ˈvɪt.rɪk

vitrifaction ˌvɪt.rɪˈfæk.ʃᵊn, (US) -rəˈ-

vitrification ˌvɪt.rɪ.fɪˈkeɪ.ʃᵊn, -rə-, -fəˈ-, (US) -rə-

vitri|fy ˈvɪt.rɪ|.faɪ, ˈvɪ.trə- **-fies** -faɪz **-fying** -faɪ.ɪŋ **-fied** -faɪd **-fiable** -faɪ.ə.bᵊl

vitriol ˈvɪt.ri.əl, -ɒl, (US) -əl, -ɔːl

vitriolic ˌvɪt.riˈɒl.ɪk, (US) -ˈɑː.lɪk **-ally** -ᵊl.i, -li

vitro ˈviː.trəʊ, (US) -troʊ

Vitruvius vɪˈtruː.vi.əs

Vitter ˈvɪt.əʳ, (US) ˈvɪt̬.ɚ

vittles ˈvɪt.ᵊlz, (US) ˈvɪt̬-

Vittoria vɪˈtɔː.ri.ə, (US) -ˈtɔːr.i-

vituper|ate vɪˈtʃuː.pᵊr|.eɪt, -ˈtjuː-, vaɪ-, (US) vaɪˈtuː.pɚ|.eɪt, vɪ-, -ˈtjuː- **-ates** -eɪts **-ating** -eɪ.tɪŋ, (US) -eɪ.t̬ɪŋ **-ated** -eɪ.tɪd, (US) -eɪ.t̬ɪd **-ator/s** -eɪ.təʳ/z, (US) -eɪ.t̬ɚ/z

vituperation vɪˌtʃuː.pᵊrˈeɪ.ʃᵊn, -ˌtjuː-, vaɪ-, (US) vaɪˌtuː.pəˈreɪ-, vɪ-, -ˌtjuː- **-s** -z

vituperative vɪˈtʃuː.pᵊr.ə.tɪv, -ˈtjuː-, vaɪ-, -eɪ-, (US) vaɪˈtuː.pɚ.ə.t̬ɪv, vɪ-, -ˈtjuː-, -pə.reɪ- **-ly** -li

vituperatory vɪˈtʃuː.pᵊr.ə.tᵊr.i, -ˈtjuː-, vaɪ-, (US) vaɪˈtuː.pɚ.ə.tɔːr-, -tjuː-, -prə.tɔːr-

Vitus ˈvaɪ.təs, (US) -t̬əs

viva exclamation *long live:* ˈviː.və

viva n *examination:* ˈvaɪ.və, (US) ˈvaɪ.və, ˈviː- **-s** -z **ˌviva ˈvoce**

Viva® ˈviː.və

vivace vɪˈvɑː.tʃeɪ, (US) -tʃeɪ **-s** -z

vivacious vɪˈveɪ.ʃəs, vaɪ- **-ly** -li **-ness** -nəs, -nɪs

vivacity vɪˈvæs.ə.ti, vaɪ-, -ɪ.ti, (US) -ə.t̬i

Vivaldi vɪˈvæl.di, (US) -ˈvɑːl-

vivari|um vaɪˈveə.ri|.əm, vɪ-, (US) vaɪˈver.i- **-ums** -əmz **-a** -ə

vivat ˈvaɪ.væt, ˈviː-

vive viːv

Vivendi® vɪˈven.di

Vivian ˈvɪv.i.ən

vivid ˈvɪv.ɪd **-ly** -li **-ness** -nəs, -nɪs

Vivien ˈvɪv.i.ən

Vivienne ˈvɪv.i.ən, ˌvɪv.iˈen

vivification ˌvɪv.ɪ.fɪˈkeɪ.ʃᵊn, -fəˈ-, (US) ˌ-ə-

vivi|fy ˈvɪv.ɪ|.faɪ, ˈ-ə- **-fies** -faɪz **-fying** -faɪ.ɪŋ **-fied** -faɪd

viviparity ˌvɪv.ɪˈpær.ə.ti, -ɪ.ti, (US) -əˈper.ə.t̬i, -ˈpær-

viviparous vɪˈvɪp.ᵊr.əs, vaɪ-, (US) vaɪ- **-ly** -li **-ness** -nəs, -nɪs

vivisect ˌvɪv.ɪˈsekt, ˈ---, (US) ˈvɪv.ə.sekt **-s** -s **-ing** -ɪŋ **-ed** -ɪd **-or/s** -əʳ/z, (US) -ɚ/z

vivisection ˌvɪv.ɪˈsek.ʃᵊn, (US) -əˈ-, ˈvɪv.ə.sek-

vivisectionist ˌvɪv.ɪˈsek.ʃᵊn.ɪst, (US) -əˈ- **-s** -s

vixen ˈvɪk.sᵊn **-s** -z

vixenish ˈvɪk.sᵊn.ɪʃ

Viyella® vaɪˈel.ə

viz. vɪz; vɪˈdiː.lɪ.set, vaɪ-; vɪˈdeɪ.lɪ.ket, (US) vɪz; (US) vɪˈdel.ɪ.set, wɪ-

> Note: Many people in reading aloud substitute **namely** (/ˈneɪm.li/) for this word.

Vizetelly ˌvɪz.ɪˈtel.i

vizier vɪˈzɪəʳ, ˈvɪz.ɪəʳ, (US) vɪˈzɪr; (US) ˈvɪz.jɚ **-s** -z

vizor ˈvaɪ.zəʳ, (US) -zɚ **-s** -z

VJ-Day ˌviːˈdʒeɪ.deɪ

Vladimir ˈvlæd.ɪ.mɪəʳ, -məʳ, vlædˈiː.mɪəʳ, (US) -ə.mɪr

Vladivostok ˌvlæd.ɪˈvɒs.tɒk, (US) -ˈvɑː.stɑːk

V-neck ˈviː.nek, (US) ˌ-ˈ- **-s** -s **-ed** -t

vocab ˈvəʊ.kæb, (US) ˈvoʊ-

vocable ˈvəʊ.kə.bəl, ⓊⓈ ˈvoʊ- -s -z
vocabular|y vəʊˈkæb.jə.lər|.i, -jʊ-, ⓊⓈ voʊˈkæb.jə.ler-, -jʊ- -ies -iz
vocal ˈvəʊ.kəl, ⓊⓈ ˈvoʊ- -s -z -ly -i ˌ**vocal** ˈ**cords** ⓊⓈ ˈ**vocal** ˌ**cords**
vocalic vəʊˈkæl.ɪk, ⓊⓈ voʊ-
vocalism ˈvəʊ.kəl.ɪ.zəm, ⓊⓈ ˈvoʊ-
vocalist ˈvəʊ.kəl.ɪst, ⓊⓈ ˈvoʊ- -s -s
vocality vəʊˈkæl.ə.ti, -ɪ.ti, ⓊⓈ voʊˈkæl.ə.t̬i
vocalization, -isa- ˌvəʊ.kəl.aɪˈzeɪ.ʃən, -ɪˈ-, ⓊⓈ ˌvoʊ.kəl.əˈ- -s -z
vocaliz|e, -is|e ˈvəʊ.kəl.aɪz, ⓊⓈ ˈvoʊ.kə.laɪz -es -ɪz -ing -ɪŋ -ed -d -er/s -ər/z, ⓊⓈ -ɚ/z
vocation vəʊˈkeɪ.ʃən, ⓊⓈ voʊ- -s -z
vocational vəʊˈkeɪ.ʃən.əl, -ˈkeɪʃ.nəl, ⓊⓈ voʊ- -ly -i
vocational|ism vəʊˈkeɪ.ʃən.əl|.ɪ.zəm, -ˈkeɪʃ.nəl-, ⓊⓈ voʊ- -ist/s -ɪst/s
vocative ˈvɒk.ə.tɪv, ⓊⓈ ˈvɑː.kə.t̬ɪv -s -z
voce (in **viva voce**) ˈvəʊ.si, -tʃi, -tʃeɪ, ⓊⓈ ˈvoʊ.siː (in **sotto voce**) ˈvəʊ.tʃi, ⓊⓈ ˈvoʊ.tʃi, -tʃeɪ
vocifer|ate vəʊˈsɪf.ər|.eɪt, ⓊⓈ voʊˈsɪf.ə.r|eɪt -ates -eɪts -ating -eɪ.tɪŋ, ⓊⓈ -eɪ.t̬ɪŋ -ated -eɪ.tɪd, ⓊⓈ -eɪ.t̬ɪd -ator/s -eɪ.tər/z, ⓊⓈ -eɪ.t̬ɚ/z
vociferation vəʊˌsɪf.əˈreɪ.ʃən, ⓊⓈ voʊ- -s -z
vociferous vəʊˈsɪf.ər.əs, ⓊⓈ voʊ- -ly -li -ness -nəs, -nɪs
vocoid ˈvəʊ.kɔɪd, ⓊⓈ ˈvoʊ- -s -z
Vodafone®, Vodaphone ˈvəʊ.də.fəʊn, ⓊⓈ ˈvoʊ.də.foʊn
vodcast ˈvɒd.kɑːst, ⓊⓈ ˈvɑːd.kæst -s -s -ing -ɪŋ
vodka ˈvɒd.kə, ⓊⓈ ˈvɑːd- -s -z
Vogt vəʊkt, ⓊⓈ voʊkt
vogue, V~® vəʊg, ⓊⓈ voʊg
voic|e vɔɪs -es -ɪz -ing -ɪŋ -ed -t ˌ**Voice of Aˈmerica**; ˈ**voice** ˌ**box**
voiceless ˈvɔɪ.sləs, -slɪs -ly -li -ness -nəs, -nɪs
voicemail ˈvɔɪs.meɪl
voice-over ˈvɔɪsˌəʊ.vər, ⓊⓈ -ˌoʊ.vɚ -s -z
voiceprint ˈvɔɪs.prɪnt -s -s
void vɔɪd -s -z -ing -ɪŋ -ed -ɪd -able -ə.bəl -ance -ənts -ness -nəs, -nɪs
voilà vwælˈɑː, vwɒl-, vwɑːˈlɑː, ⓊⓈ vwɑːˈlɑː
voile vɔɪl
voir dire ˌvwɑːˈdɪər, ⓊⓈ ˌvwɑːrˈdɪr
vol vɒl, ⓊⓈ vɑːl
volant ˈvəʊ.lənt, ⓊⓈ ˈvoʊ-
Volapük ˈvɒl.ə.puːk, ˈvəʊl-, -pʊk, ˌ--ˈ-, ⓊⓈ ˈvoʊ.lɑː-, ˈvɑː-
volatile adj ˈvɒl.ə.taɪl, ⓊⓈ ˈvɑː.lə.t̬əl -ness -nəs, -nɪs
volatile (in **sal volatile**) vəʊˈlæt.ə.li, vɒlˈæt-, ⓊⓈ voʊˈlæt.li
volatility ˌvɒl.əˈtɪl.ə.ti, -ɪ.ti, ⓊⓈ ˌvɑː.ləˈtɪl.ə.t̬i
volatilization, -isa- vɒlˌæt.ɪ.laɪˈzeɪ.ʃən, vəʊˌlæt-, -əl.aɪˈ-, -ɪˈ-; ˌvɒl.ə.tɪ.laɪˈ-, -təl.aɪˈ-, -ɪˈ-, ⓊⓈ ˌvɑː.lə.təl.əˈ-
volatiliz|e, -is|e vɒlˈæt.ɪ.laɪz, vəʊˈlæt-, -əl.aɪz; ˈvɒl.ə.tɪ.laɪz, -təl.aɪz, ⓊⓈ ˈvɑː.lə.tə.laɪz -es -ɪz -ing -ɪŋ -ed -d
vol-au-vent ˈvɒl.əʊ.vɑ̃ːŋ, ˌ--ˈ-, ⓊⓈ ˌvɔː.loʊˈvɑ̃ːn, ˌvoʊ- -s -z
volcanic vɒlˈkæn.ɪk, ⓊⓈ vɑːl- -ally -əl.i, -li
volcanicity ˌvɒl.kəˈnɪs.ə.ti, -ɪ.ti, ⓊⓈ ˌvɑːl.kəˈnɪs.ə.t̬i
volcanism ˈvɒl.kə.nɪ.zəm, ⓊⓈ ˈvɑːl-
volcano vɒlˈkeɪ.nəʊ, ⓊⓈ vɑːlˈkeɪ.noʊ -(e)s -z
volcanology ˌvɒl.kəˈnɒl.ə.dʒi, ⓊⓈ ˌvɑːl.kəˈnɑː.lə-
vole vəʊl, ⓊⓈ voʊl -s -z
volenti non fit injuria vɒlˌen.tiːˌnəʊn.fɪt.ɪnˈjʊə.ri.ə, -ˈjɔː-, ⓊⓈ voʊˌlen.ti.nɑːnˌfɪt.ɪnˈdʒʊr.i.ə
volet ˈvɒl.eɪ, ⓊⓈ ˈvoʊ.leɪ, -ˈ- -s -z
Volga ˈvɒl.gə, ⓊⓈ ˈvɑːl-, ˈvoʊl-
Volgograd ˈvɒl.gəʊ.græd, ⓊⓈ ˈvɑːl.gə-, ˈvoʊl-
volition vəʊˈlɪʃ.ən, ⓊⓈ voʊ-, və- -al -əl
volitive ˈvɒl.ɪ.tɪv, ˈ-ə-, ⓊⓈ ˈvɑː.lə.t̬ɪv
volks|lied ˈfɒlks|.liːd, ˈvɒlks-; *as if German:* -liːt; ⓊⓈ ˈfɔːlks|.liːt -lieder -ˌliː.dər, ⓊⓈ -ˌliː.dɚ
volkstaat ˈfɒlk.ʃtɑːt, ⓊⓈ ˈfɔːlk- -s -s
Volkswagen® ˈfɒlksˌvɑː.gən, ˈvɒlks-, ⓊⓈ ˈfɔːlks-, ˈvɔːlks-, ˈvoʊks-, -ˌwɑː-, -ˌwæg.ən -s -z
volley ˈvɒl.i, ⓊⓈ ˈvɑː.li -s -z -ing -ɪŋ -ed -d -er/s -ər/z, ⓊⓈ -ɚ/z
volleyball ˈvɒl.i.bɔːl, ⓊⓈ ˈvɑː.li-
Volos ˈvɒl.ɒs, ⓊⓈ ˈvɔː.lɑːs
volplan|e ˈvɒl.pleɪn, ⓊⓈ ˈvɑːl- -es -z -ing -ɪŋ -ed -d
Volpone vɒlˈpəʊ.neɪ, -ni, ⓊⓈ vɑːlˈpoʊ-
Volsci ˈvɒl.skiː, -saɪ, ⓊⓈ ˈvɑːl.saɪ, -skiː
Volscian ˈvɒl.ski.ən, -ʃi-, -si-, ⓊⓈ ˈvɑːl.ʃən, -ski.ən
Volstead ˈvɒl.sted, ⓊⓈ ˈvɑːl-
volt *electric unit:* vəʊlt, vɒlt, ⓊⓈ voʊlt -s -s *movement of horse, movement in fencing:* vɒlt, ⓊⓈ voʊlt, vɑːlt, vɔːlt -s -s
volta *dance:* ˈvɒl.tə, ⓊⓈ ˈvɑːl- -s -z
Volta *physicist:* ˈvɒl.tə, ˈvəʊl-, ⓊⓈ ˈvoʊl.tə *lake and river:* ˈvɒl.tə, ⓊⓈ ˈvɑːl.tə, ˈvɔːl-, ˈvoʊl-
voltag|e ˈvəʊl.tɪdʒ, ˈvɒl-, ⓊⓈ ˈvoʊl.tɪdʒ -es -ɪz
voltaic vɒlˈteɪ.ɪk, ⓊⓈ vɑːl-, voʊl-
Voltaire vɒlˈteər, ˈ--, ⓊⓈ voʊlˈter, vɑːl-
voltameter vɒlˈtæm.ɪ.tər, vəʊl-, ˈ-ə-, ⓊⓈ voʊlˈtæm.ə.t̬ɚ, vɑːl- -s -z
volte ˈvɒl.teɪ, -ti, ⓊⓈ vɑːlt, voʊlt -s -z
volte-fac|e ˌvɒltˈfæs, ⓊⓈ ˌvɑːltˈfɑːs -es -ɪz
voltmeter ˈvəʊltˌmiː.tər, ˈvɒlt-, ⓊⓈ ˈvoʊltˌmiː.t̬ɚ -s -z
volubility ˌvɒl.jəˈbɪl.ə.ti, -jʊˈ-, -ɪ.ti, ⓊⓈ ˌvɑːl.jəˈbɪl.ə.t̬i, -jʊˈ-
volub|le ˈvɒl.jə.b|əl, -jʊ-, ⓊⓈ ˈvɑːl- -ly -li -leness -əl.nəs, -nɪs
volume ˈvɒl.juːm, -jʊm, -jəm, ⓊⓈ ˈvɑːl.juːm, -jəm -s -z
volumeter vɒlˈjuː.mɪ.tər, vəˈljuː-, -ˈluː-, -mə-, ⓊⓈ ˈvɑːl.jʊˌmiː.t̬ɚ -s -z
volumetric ˌvɒl.jəˈmet.rɪk, -jʊˈ-, ⓊⓈ ˌvɑːl- -al -əl -ally -əl.i, -li
voluminous vəˈluː.mɪ.nəs, vɒlˈuː-, -ˈjuː-, -mə-, ⓊⓈ vəˈluː.mə- -ly -li -ness -nəs, -nɪs
voluntar|y ˈvɒl.ən.tər|.i, -tr|i, ⓊⓈ ˈvɑː.lən.ter|.i -ies -iz -ily -əl.i, -ɪ.li, ˌvɒl.ənˈteə.rəl.i, -ˈtær-, -ɪ.li -iness -ɪ.nəs, -ɪ.nɪs
volunteer ˌvɒl.ənˈtɪər, ⓊⓈ ˌvɑː.lənˈtɪr -s -z -ing -ɪŋ -ed -d
voluptuar|y vəˈlʌp.tʃʊə.r|i, -tjʊə-, ⓊⓈ -tʃu.er|.i -ies -iz
voluptuous vəˈlʌp.tʃu.əs, -tju.əs, ⓊⓈ -tʃu- -ly -li -ness -nəs, -nɪs
volu|te vəʊˈluː|t, vɒlˈuː|t, -ˈjuː|t, ⓊⓈ vəˈluː|t -tes -ts -ted -tɪd, ⓊⓈ -t̬ɪd
volution vəʊˈluː.ʃən, vɒlˈuː-, -ˈjuː-, ⓊⓈ vəˈluː- -s -z
Volvo® ˈvɒl.vəʊ, ⓊⓈ ˈvɑːl.voʊ -s -z
vom|it ˈvɒm|.ɪt, ⓊⓈ ˈvɑː.m|ɪt -its -ɪts -iting -ɪ.tɪŋ, ⓊⓈ -ɪ.t̬ɪŋ -ited -ɪ.tɪd, ⓊⓈ -ɪ.t̬ɪd
vomitor|y ˈvɒm.ɪ.tər|.i, -tr|i, ⓊⓈ ˈvɑː.mə.tɔːr|.i -ies -iz
von, V~ vɒn, fɒn, ⓊⓈ vɑːn, fɑːn
Vonnegut ˈvɒn.ɪ.gət, ⓊⓈ ˈvɑː.nə-
voodoo ˈvuː.duː -s -z -ing -ɪŋ -ed -d -ist/s -ɪst/s -ism -ɪ.zəm
Vooght vuːt
voracious vəˈreɪ.ʃəs, vɔː-, vɒrˈeɪ-, ⓊⓈ vɔːˈreɪ-, və- -ly -li -ness -nəs, -nɪs
voracity vəˈræs.ə.ti, vɔː-, vɒrˈæs-, -ɪ.ti, ⓊⓈ vɔːˈræs.ə.t̬i, və-
Vorderman ˈvɔː.də.mən, ⓊⓈ ˈvɔːr.dɚ-
Vorster ˈfɔː.stər, ⓊⓈ ˈfɔːr.stɚ
vort|ex ˈvɔː.t|eks, ⓊⓈ ˈvɔːr- -ices -ɪ.siːz -exes -ek.sɪz
vortic|al ˈvɔː.tɪ.k|əl, ⓊⓈ ˈvɔːr.t̬ɪ- -ally -əl.i, -li
vortices (plural of **vortex**) ˈvɔː.tɪ.siːz, ⓊⓈ ˈvɔːr.t̬ɪ-
vortic|ism, V~ ˈvɔː.tɪ.s|ɪ.zəm, ⓊⓈ ˈvɔːr.t̬ɪ- -ist/s -ɪst/s
Vortigern ˈvɔː.tɪ.gɜːn, -gən, ⓊⓈ ˈvɔːr.t̬ɪ.gɝːn
Vosges vəʊʒ, ⓊⓈ voʊʒ
Voss vɒs, ⓊⓈ vɑːs
votaress ˈvəʊ.tər.es, -ɪs, ⓊⓈ ˈvoʊ.t̬ɚ.əs, ˈ-trəs -es -ɪz
votar|y ˈvəʊ.tər|.i, ⓊⓈ ˈvoʊ.t̬ɚ- -ies -iz -ist/s -ɪst/s
vot|e vəʊt, ⓊⓈ voʊt -es -s -ing -ɪŋ, ⓊⓈ ˈvoʊ.t̬ɪŋ -ed -ɪd, ⓊⓈ ˈvoʊ.t̬ɪd -er/s -ər/z, ⓊⓈ ˈvoʊ.t̬ɚ/z ˌ**vote of (**ˌ**no) ˈconfidence**; ˌ**vote of ˈthanks**; ˌ**vote with one's ˈfeet**
voteless ˈvəʊt.ləs, -lɪs, ⓊⓈ ˈvoʊt-
votive ˈvəʊ.tɪv, ⓊⓈ ˈvoʊ.t̬ɪv -ly -li -ness -nəs, -nɪs
vouch vaʊtʃ -es -ɪz -ing -ɪŋ -ed -t
voucher ˈvaʊ.tʃər, ⓊⓈ -tʃɚ -s -z ˈ**voucher** ˌ**system**
vouchsaf|e ˌvaʊtʃˈseɪf, ˈ-- -es -s -ing -ɪŋ -ed -t

V

Vouvray ˈvuː.vreɪ, (US) -ˈ-
vow vaʊ **-s** -z **-ing** -ɪŋ **-ed** -d
vowel ˈvaʊ.əl, vaʊəl **-s** -z **-(l)ing** -ɪŋ **-(l)ed** -d
Vowles vəʊlz, vaʊlz, (US) voʊlz, vaʊlz
vox, V~ vɒks, (US) vɑːks
vox humana ˌvɒks.hjuːˈmɑː.nə, (US) ˌvɑːks-, -ˈmeɪ- **-s** -z
vox pop ˌvɒksˈpɒp, (US) ˌvɑːksˈpɑːp
vox populi ˌvɒksˈpɒp.jʊ.liː, -jə-, (US) ˌvɑːksˈpɑː.pjuː.laɪ, -liː
voyag|e ˈvɔɪ.ɪdʒ **-es** -ɪz **-ing** -ɪŋ **-ed** -d
voyager ˈvɔɪ.ɪ.dʒəʳ, ˈvɔɪ.ə-, (US) ˈvɔɪ.ɪ.dʒɚ **-s** -z
voyeur vwɑːˈjɜːʳ, vɔɪˈɜːʳ, (US) vɔɪˈjɝː, vwɑː- **-s** -z
voyeurism vwɑːˈjɜː.rɪ.zᵊm, vɔɪˈɜː-, ˈvwɑː.jɜː-, ˈvɔɪ.ɜː-, (US) vɔɪˈjɝː.ɪ-, vwɑː-; (US) ˈvɔɪ.jɚ.ɪ-
voyeuristic ˌvɔɪ.əˈrɪ.stɪk, ˌvwɑː.jɜːˈ-, (US) ˌvɔɪ.jəˈ-, ˌvwɑː- **-ally** -ᵊl.i, li
VP ˌviːˈpiː **-s** -z
vroom vruːm, vrʊm
vs. ˈvɜː.səs, (US) ˈvɝː-
VSO ˌviː.esˈəʊ, (US) -ˈoʊ
V/STOL ˈviːˌstɒl, (US) -ˌstɑːl
Vt. (abbrev. for **Vermont**) vəˈmɒnt, vɜː-, (US) vɚˈmɑːnt
VTOL ˈviː.tɒl, (US) -tɑːl
Vuillard ˈvuː.jɑː, -ˈ-
Vuitton® ˈvjuː.ɪ.tɔ̃ːŋ, ˈvwiː.tɒn, (US) vwiːˈtɔ̃ːn
Vukovar ˈvʊk.ə.vəʳ, -vɑːʳ, (US) -vɚ
Vulcan ˈvʌl.kən **-s** -z
vulcanite ˈvʌl.kə.naɪt
vulcanization, -isa- ˌvʌl.kə.naɪˈzeɪ.ʃᵊn, -nɪˈ-, (US) -nəˈ-
vulcaniz|e, -is|e ˈvʌl.kə.naɪz **-es** -ɪz **-ing** -ɪŋ **-ed** -d
vulgar, V~ ˈvʌl.gəʳ, (US) -gɚ **-ly** -li
ˌ**Vulgar** ˈ**Latin**
vulgarian vʌlˈgeə.ri.ən, (US) -ˈger.i- **-s** -z
vulgarism ˈvʌl.gᵊr.ɪ.zᵊm **-s** -z
vulgarit|y vʌlˈgær.ə.t|i, -ɪ.t|i, (US) -ˈger.ə.ţ|i, -ˈgær- **-ies** -iz
vulgarization, -isa- ˌvʌl.gᵊr.aɪˈzeɪ.ʃᵊn, -ɪˈ-, (US) -əˈ-
vulgariz|e, -is|e ˈvʌl.gᵊr.aɪz, (US) -gə.raɪz **-es** -ɪz **-ing** -ɪŋ **-ed** -d **-er/s** -əʳ/z, (US) -ɚ/z
vulgate, V~ ˈvʌl.geɪt, -gɪt, -gət, (US) -geɪt, -gɪt
Vulliamy ˈvʌl.jə.mi
vulnerability ˌvʌl.nᵊr.əˈbɪl.ə.ti, ˌvʌn.ᵊr-, ˌvʌn.rəˈ-, -ɪ.ti, (US) ˌvʌl.nɚ.əˈbɪl.ə.ţi
vulnerab|le ˈvʌl.nᵊr.ə.b|ᵊl, ˈvʌn.ᵊr-, ˈvʌn.rə.b|ᵊl, (US) ˈvʌl.nɚ.ə- **-ly** -li **-leness** -ᵊl.nəs, -nɪs
Vulpecula vʌlˈpek.jə.lə, -jʊ-
vulpine ˈvʌl.paɪn, (US) -paɪn, -pɪn
vulture ˈvʌl.tʃəʳ, (US) -tʃɚ **-s** -z
vulturous ˈvʌl.tʃᵊr.əs, -tʃʊ.rəs, -tjᵊr.əs, -tjʊ.rəs, (US) -tʃɚ.əs
vulv|a ˈvʌl.v|ə **-as** -əz **-ae** -iː
vuvuzela ˌvuː.vuːˈzeɪ.lə, -ˈzel.ə
VW ˌviːˈdʌb.ᵊl.ju, -juː, (US) -juː, -jə **-s** -z
Vye vaɪ
vying (from **vie**) ˈvaɪ.ɪŋ

W

Pronouncing the letter W

→ *See also* **WH**

The consonant letter **w** is most often realized as /w/, e.g.:

wet	wet
swing	swɪŋ

In addition

w can be silent. There are four conditions under which this can occur. In the spelling combination **wr**, **w** is not pronounced and the realization is /r/. In some instances of **tw** when at the beginning of a word, the pronunciation is /t/. Some word-medial **sw** spellings are pronounced /s/. Finally, in (mostly) British place names ending *–wich*, **w** is not normally pronounced, although exceptions do exist. E.g.:

write	raɪt
two	tuː
answer	ˈɑːnt.səʳ (US) ˈæn .sɚ
Greenwich	ˈgren.ɪdʒ

The examples given above are for **w** in word or syllable-initial position. The letter **w** can also appear at the end of a word or syllable. These instances of **w** are covered at the panels for **aw** and **ow**.

In words borrowed from German, **w** may be pronounced /v/. Words borrowed from Slavic may have /v/ or /f/. E.g.:

Wagner	ˈvɑːg.nəʳ (US) -nɚ
Krakow	ˈkræk.ɒv, -ɒf (US) ˈkrɑː.kuf

w, W ˈdʌb.əl.juː, -ju, (US) -juː, -jə **-'s** -z
W (abbrev. for **west**) west
Waaf, WAAF wæf **-s** -s
Wabash ˈwɔː.bæʃ, (US) ˈwɔː-, ˈwɑː-
Wace weɪs
Wachovia wəˈkəʊ.vi.ə, (US) -koʊ-
wacko ˈwæk.əʊ, (US) -oʊ **-s** -z
wack|y ˈwæk|.i **-ier** -i.əʳ, (US) -i.ɚ **-iest** -i.ɪst, -i.əst **-ily** -əl.i, -ɪ.li **-iness** -ɪ.nəs, -ɪ.nɪs
Waco ˈweɪ.kəʊ, (US) -koʊ
wad wɒd, (US) wɑːd **-s** -z **-ding** -ɪŋ **-ded** -ɪd
Waddell wɒdˈel, ˈwɒd.əl, (US) wɑːˈdel, ˈwɑː.dəl
wadding ˈwɒd.ɪŋ, (US) ˈwɑː.dɪŋ
Waddington ˈwɒd.ɪŋ.tən, (US) ˈwɑː.dɪŋ-
waddl|e ˈwɒd.əl, (US) ˈwɑː.dəl **-es** -z **-ing** -ɪŋ, ˈwɒd.lɪŋ, (US) ˈwɑːd- **-ed** -d **-er/s** -əʳ/z, ˈwɒd.ləʳ/z, (US) ˈwɑː.dəl.ɚ/z, ˈwɑːd.lɚ/z
wadd|y, W~ ˈwɒd|.i, (US) ˈwɑː.d|i **-ies** -iz
wad|e, W~ weɪd **-es** -z **-ing** -ɪŋ **-ed** -ɪd
Wadebridge ˈweɪd.brɪdʒ
Wade-Giles ˌweɪdˈdʒaɪlz
wader ˈweɪ.dəʳ, (US) -dɚ **-s** -z
Wadey ˈweɪ.di
wadg|e wɒdʒ, (US) wɑːdʒ **-es** -ɪz
Wadham ˈwɒd.əm, (US) ˈwɑː.dəm
Wadhurst ˈwɒd.hɜːst, (US) ˈwɑːd.hɝːst
wadi ˈwɒd.i, ˈwæd-, ˈwɑː.di, (US) ˈwɑː.di **-s** -z
Wadi Halfa ˌwɒd.iˈhæl.fə, ˌwæd-, ˌwɑː.diˈ-, (US) ˌwɑː.diˈhɑːl.fə
Wadman ˈwɒd.mən, (US) ˈwɑːd-
Wad Medani ˌwɑːd.məˈdɑː.ni
Wadsworth ˈwɒdz.wəθ, -wɜːθ, (US) ˈwɑːdz.wɚθ, -wɝːθ
WAF, Waf wæf **-s** -s
Wafd wɒft, wæft, wɑːft, (US) wɑːft
waf|er ˈweɪ.f|əʳ, (US) -f|ɚ **-ers** -əz, (US) -ɚz **-ery** -əʳ.i
wafer-thin ˌweɪ.fəˈθɪn, (US) -fɚˈ- *stress shift:* **ˌwafer-thin ˈmints**
waffl|e ˈwɒf.əl, (US) ˈwɑː.fəl **-es** -z **-ing** -ɪŋ, ˈwɒf.lɪŋ, (US) ˈwɑːf- **-ed** -d **-er/s** -əʳ/z, ˈwɒf.ləʳ/z, (US) ˈwɑː.fəl.ɚ/z, ˈwɑːf.lɚ/z **-y** -i, ˈwɒf.li, (US) ˈwɑː.fəl.i, ˈwɑːf.li
waffle-iron ˈwɒf.əl.aɪən, -ˌaɪ.ən, (US) ˈwɑː.fəlˌaɪ.ɚn **-s** -z
waft wɒft, wɑːft, (US) wɑːft, wæft **-s** -s **-ing** -ɪŋ **-ed** -ɪd
wag wæg **-s** -z **-ging** -ɪŋ **-ged** -d
wag|e weɪdʒ **-es** -ɪz **-ing** -ɪŋ **-ed** -d **ˈwage ˌpacket**
wage-earner ˈweɪdʒˌɜː.nəʳ, (US) -ˌɝː.nɚ **-s** -z
wag|er ˈweɪ.dʒ|əʳ, (US) -dʒ|ɚ **-ers** -əz, (US) -ɚz **-ering** -əʳ.ɪŋ **-ered** -əd, (US) -ɚd **-erer/s** -əʳ.əʳ/z, (US) -ɚ.ɚ/z
wageworker ˈweɪdʒˌwɜː.kəʳ, (US) -ˌwɝː.kɚ **-s** -z
waggish ˈwæg.ɪʃ **-ly** -li **-ness** -nəs, -nɪs
waggl|e ˈwæg.əl **-es** -z **-ing** -ɪŋ, ˈwæg.lɪŋ **-ed** -d
waggon ˈwæg.ən **-s** -z
waggoner ˈwæg.ən.əʳ, (US) -ɚ **-s** -z
waggonette ˌwæg.əˈnet **-s** -s
Waghorn ˈwæg.hɔːn, (US) -hɔːrn
Wagnall ˈwæg.nəl
Wagner *English name:* ˈwæg.nəʳ, (US) -nɚ *German composer:* ˈvɑːg.nəʳ, (US) -nɚ
Wagnerian vɑːgˈnɪə.ri.ən, (US) -ˈnɪr.i-, -ˈner- **-s** -z
wagon ˈwæg.ən **-s** -z
wagoner ˈwæg.ə.nəʳ, (US) -nɚ **-s** -z
wagonette ˌwæg.əˈnet **-s** -s
wagon-lit ˌvæg.ɔ̃ːnˈliː, ˌvɑːg-, -gɒnˈ-, ˈ---, (US) ˌvɑː.gɔ̃ːnˈliː **-s** -z
Wagstaff ˈwæg.stɑːf, (US) -stæf
wagtail ˈwæg.teɪl **-s** -z
Wah(h)abi wəˈhɑː.bi, wɑː- **-s** -z
Wahlberg ˈwɑːl.bɜːg, (US) -bɝːg
waif weɪf **-s** -s
waif-like ˈweɪf.laɪk
Waikiki ˌwaɪ.kiˈkiː, ˈ---
wail weɪl **-s** -z **-ing/ly** -ɪŋ/li **-ed** -d
wain, W~ weɪn **-s** -z
Wain(e) weɪn
Wainfleet ˈweɪn.fliːt
wainsco|t ˈweɪn.skə|t, ˈwen-, -skɒ|t, (US) ˈweɪn.skə|t, -skɑː|t, -skoʊ|t **-ts** -ts **-t(t)ing** -tɪŋ, (US) -t̬ɪŋ **-t(t)ed** -tɪd, (US) -t̬ɪd
Wainwright ˈweɪn.raɪt
waist weɪst **-s** -s **-ed** -ɪd
waistband ˈweɪst.bænd **-s** -z
waistcoat ˈweɪst.kəʊt; *old-fashioned:* ˈwes.kət, -kɪt, (US) ˈwes.kət, ˈweɪst.koʊt **-s** -s

> Note: In British English the change from the traditional pronunciation /ˈwes.kɪt/ to present-day /ˈweɪst.kəʊt/ is often cited as an example of spelling pronunciation.

waist-deep ˌweɪstˈdiːp *stress shift:* **ˌwaist-deep ˈwater**
waist-high ˌweɪstˈhaɪ *stress shift:* **ˌwaist-high ˈwater**
waistline ˈweɪst.laɪn **-s** -z
wait weɪt **-s** -s **-ing** -ɪŋ, (US) ˈweɪ.t̬ɪŋ **-ed** -ɪd, (US) ˈweɪ.t̬ɪd **ˈwaiting ˌlist**
Waite weɪt
waiter ˈweɪ.təʳ, (US) -t̬ɚ **-s** -z
waiting-room ˈweɪ.tɪŋ.rʊm, -ruːm, (US) -t̬ɪŋ.ruːm, -rʊm **-s** -z
wait|person ˈweɪt|ˌpɜː.sən, (US) -ˌpɝː- **-people** -ˌpiː.pəl
waitress ˈweɪ.trəs, -trɪs, (US) -trɪs **-es** -ɪz
Waitrose® ˈweɪ.trəʊz, (US) -troʊz
waiv|e weɪv **-es** -z **-ing** -ɪŋ **-ed** -d
waiver ˈweɪ.vəʳ, (US) -vɚ **-s** -z

Wajda ˈvaɪ.də
wak|e weɪk **-es** -s **-ing** -ɪŋ **-ed** -t
woke wəʊk, (US) woʊk **woken** ˈwəʊ.kᵊn, (US) ˈwoʊ-
Wakefield ˈweɪk.fiːld
wakeful ˈweɪk.fᵊl, -fʊl **-ly** -i **-ness** -nəs, -nɪs
Wakeham ˈweɪ.kəm
Wakehurst ˈweɪk.hɜːst, (US) -hɝːst
Wakeling ˈweɪ.klɪŋ
Wakeman ˈweɪk.mən
waken ˈweɪ.kᵊn **-s** -z **-ing** -ɪŋ, ˈweɪk.nɪŋ **-ed** -d
wakey wakey ˌweɪ.kiˈweɪ.ki
Wakley ˈweɪ.kli
Wakonda wəˈkɒn.də, (US) wɑːˈkɑːn-
Wal wɒl, wɔːl, (US) wɑːl
Walachi|a wɒlˈeɪ.ki|.ə, wəˈleɪ-, (US) wɑːˈleɪ-, wə- **-an/s** -ən/z
Walberswick ˈwɔːl.bəz.wɪk, ˈwɒl-, (US) ˈwɔːl.bɚz-, ˈwɑːl-
Walbrook ˈwɔːl.brʊk, ˈwɒl-, (US) ˈwɔːl-, ˈwɑːl-
Walcott ˈwɔːl.kət, ˈwɒl-, -kɒt, (US) ˈwɔːl.kət, ˈwɑːl-, -kɑːt
Waldeck ˈwɔːl.dek, ˈwɒl-, (US) ˈwɔːl-, ˈvɑːl-
Waldegrave ˈwɔːl.greɪv, ˈwɒl-, -də.greɪv, (US) ˈwɔːl-, ˈwɑːl-

Note: Earl Waldegrave is /ˈwɔːl.greɪv, ˈwɒl-/ (US) /ˈwɔːl-, ˈwɑːl-/; the politician William (now Lord) Waldegrave is /ˈwɔːl.də.greɪv, ˈwɒl-/ (US) /ˈwɔːl-, ˈwɑːl-/.

Waldemar ˈvæl.də.mɑːʳ, ˈvɑːl-, ˈwɔːl-, -dɪ-, (US) ˈvɑːl.də.mɑːr
Walden ˈwɔːl.dᵊn, ˈwɒl-, (US) ˈwɔːl-, ˈwɑːl-
Waldheim ˈvɑːld.haɪm; *as if German:* ˈvælt-; (US) ˈwɑːld-; *as if German:* (US) ˈvɑːlt-
Waldo ˈwɔːl.dəʊ, ˈwɒl-, (US) ˈwɔːl.doʊ, ˈwɑːl-
Waldock ˈwɔːl.dɒk, ˈwɒl-, (US) ˈwɔːl.dɑːk, ˈwɑːl-
Waldorf ˈwɔːl.dɔːf, ˈwɒl-, (US) ˈwɔːl.dɔːrf, ˈwɑːl- **ˌWaldorf ˈsalad**
Waldron ˈwɔːl.drən, ˈwɒl-, (US) ˈwɔːl-, ˈwɑːl-
Waldstein *American name:* ˈwɔːld.staɪn, ˈwɒld-, (US) ˈwɔːld-, ˈwɑːld- *German name, Beethoven sonata:* ˈvæld.staɪn, ˈvɑːld-, ˈvɔːld-, ˈvɒld-, ˈwɔːld-, ˈwɒld-, -ʃtaɪn, (US) ˈvɑːlt.ʃtaɪn, ˈvɑːld-
wale weɪl **-s** -z
waler, W~ ˈweɪ.ləʳ, (US) -lɚ **-s** -z
Waleran *buildings in Borough High Street, London:* ˈwɒl.ᵊr.ən, (US) ˈwɑː.lɚ-, ˈwɔː- *Baron:* ˈwɔːl.rən, ˈwɒl-, (US) ˈwɔːl-, ˈwɑːl-
Wales weɪlz
Walesa vɑːˈwent.sə, væˈ-, (US) wɑːˈlent.sə; (US) vɑːˈwent.sɑː
Waley ˈweɪ.li
Walfish ˈwɔːl.fɪʃ, ˈwɒl-, (US) ˈwɔːl-, ˈwɑːl-
Walford ˈwɔːl.fəd, ˈwɒl-, (US) ˈwɔːl.fɚd, ˈwɑːl-
Walhalla vælˈhæl.ə, (US) wɑːlˈhɑː.lə; (US) wælˈhæl.ə, væl-
Walham ˈwɒl.əm, (US) ˈwɑː.ləm
walk wɔːk, (US) wɑːk, wɔːk **-s** -s **-ing** -ɪŋ **-ed** -t **-er/s** -əʳ/z, (US) -ɚ/z **ˈwalking ˌstick**
walkabout ˈwɔː.kəˌbaʊt, (US) ˈwɑː-, ˈwɔː- **-s** -s
walkaway ˈwɔː.kə.weɪ, (US) ˈwɑː-, ˈwɔː-
Walkden ˈwɔːk.dən, (US) ˈwɑːk-, ˈwɔːk-
Walker ˈwɔː.kəʳ, (US) ˈwɑː.kɚ, ˈwɔː-
Walkern ˈwɔːl.kən, -kɜːn, (US) ˈwɔːl.kɚn, ˈwɑːl-, -kɝːn
walkies ˈwɔː.kiz, (US) ˈwɑː-, ˈwɔː-
walkie-talkie ˌwɔː.kiˈtɔː.ki, (US) ˌwɑː.kiˈtɑː-, ˌwɔː-, -ˈtɔː- **-s** -z
walk-in ˈwɔːk.ɪn, (US) ˈwɑːk-, ˈwɔːk-
Walkman® ˈwɔːk.mən, (US) ˈwɑːk-, ˈwɔːk- **-s** -z
walk-on ˈwɔːk.ɒn, (US) ˈwɑːk.ɑːn, ˈwɔːk- **-s** -z
walkout ˈwɔːk.aʊt, (US) ˈwɑːk-, ˈwɔːk- **-s** -s
walkover ˈwɔːkˌəʊ.vəʳ, (US) ˈwɑːkˌoʊ.vɚ, ˈwɔːk- **-s** -z
walk-up ˈwɔːk.ʌp, (US) ˈwɑːk- **-s** -s
walkway ˈwɔːk.weɪ, (US) ˈwɑːk-, ˈwɔːk- **-s** -z
Walkyrie vælˈkɪə.ri; ˈvæl.kᵊr.i, -kɪ.ri, (US) wɑːlˈkɪr.i; (US) ˈwɑːl.kɚ-, ˈvɑːl- **-s** -z
walky-talk|y ˌwɔː.kiˈtɔː.k|i, (US) ˌwɑː.kiˈtɑː-, ˌwɔː-, -ˈtɔː- **-ies** -iz
wall, W~ wɔːl, (US) wɔːl, wɑːl **-s** -z **-ing** -ɪŋ **-ed** -d **ˈWall ˌStreet; ˌWall Street ˈJournal; ˌbang one's ˌhead against a ˌbrick ˈwall**
walla(h) ˈwɒl.ə, (US) ˈwɑː.lɑː **-s** -z
wallab|y, W~ ˈwɒl.ə.b|i, (US) ˈwɑː.lə- **-ies** -iz
Wallace ˈwɒl.ɪs, -əs, (US) ˈwɑː.lɪs, -ləs
Wallach ˈwɒl.ək, (US) ˈwɑː.lək **-s** -s
Wallachi|a wɒlˈeɪ.ki|.ə, wəˈleɪ-, (US) wɑːˈleɪ- **-an/s** -ən/z
Wallasey ˈwɒl.ə.si, (US) ˈwɑː.lə-
wallboard ˈwɔːl.bɔːd, (US) ˈwɔːl.bɔːrd, ˈwɑːl-
wallchart ˈwɔːl.tʃɑːt, (US) -tʃɑːrt, ˈwɑːl- **-s** -s
Waller ˈwɒl.əʳ, (US) ˈwɑː.lɚ
wallet ˈwɒl.ɪt, (US) ˈwɑː.lɪt **-s** -s
wall-eye ˈwɔːl.aɪ, (US) ˈwɔːl-, ˈwɑːl- **-s** -z **-d** -d
wallflower ˈwɔːl.flaʊəʳ, -flaʊ.əʳ, (US) -flaʊ.ɚ, ˈwɑːl- **-s** -z
Wallingford ˈwɒl.ɪŋ.fəd, (US) ˈwɑː.lɪŋ.fɚd
Wallington ˈwɒl.ɪŋ.tən, (US) ˈwɑː.lɪŋ-
Wallis ˈwɒl.ɪs, (US) ˈwɑː.lɪs
Wallonia wəˈləʊ.ni.ə, (US) wɑːˈloʊ-
Walloon wɒlˈuːn, wəˈluːn, (US) wɑːˈluːn **-s** -z
wallop ˈwɒl.əp, (US) ˈwɑː.ləp **-s** -s **-ing/s** -ɪŋ/z **-ed** -t
wallow ˈwɒl.əʊ, (US) ˈwɑː.loʊ **-s** -z **-ing** -ɪŋ **-ed** -d **-er/s** -əʳ/z, (US) -ɚ/z
wallpap|er ˈwɔːlˌpeɪ.p|əʳ, (US) -p|ɚ, ˈwɑːl- **-ers** -əz, (US) -ɚz **-ering** -ᵊr.ɪŋ **-ered** -əd, (US) -ɚd
Wallsend ˈwɔːl.zend, (US) ˈwɔːl-, ˈwɑːl-
wall-to-wall ˌwɔːl.təˈwɔːl, -tuˈ-, (US) -təˈ-, ˌwɑːl-, -ˈwɑːl *stress-shift:* **ˌwall-to-wall ˈcarpeting**
Wallwork ˈwɔːl.wɜːk, ˈwɒl-, (US) ˈwɔːl.wɝːk, ˈwɑːl-
wall|y, W~ ˈwɒl|.i, (US) ˈwɑː.l|i **-ies** -iz
Wal-Mart® ˈwɒl.mɑːt, (US) ˈwɔːl.mɑːrt, ˈwɑːl-
Walmer ˈwɔːl.məʳ, ˈwɒl-, (US) ˈwɔːl.mɚ, ˈwɑːl-
Walmisley ˈwɔːmz.li, (US) ˈwɑːmz-, ˈwɔːmz-
Walm(e)sley ˈwɔːmz.li, (US) ˈwɑːmz-, ˈwɔːmz-
Walney ˈwɔːl.ni, ˈwɒl-, (US) ˈwɔːl-, ˈwɑːl-
walnut ˈwɔːl.nʌt, -nət, (US) ˈwɔːl-, ˈwɑːl- **-s** -s
Walpole ˈwɔːl.pəʊl, ˈwɒl-, (US) ˈwɔːl.poʊl, ˈwɑːl-
Walpurgis vælˈpʊə.gɪs, vɑːl-, -ˈpɜː-, (US) vɑːlˈpʊr.gɪs
walrus ˈwɔːl.rəs, ˈwɒl-, -rʌs, (US) ˈwɔːl.rəs, ˈwɑːl- **-es** -ɪz
Walsall ˈwɔːl.sɔːl, ˈwɒl-, -sᵊl, (US) ˈwɔːl.sɔːl, ˈwɑːl-, -sɑːl
Walsh wɒlʃ, wɔːlʃ, (US) wɔːlʃ, wɑːlʃ
Walsham ˈwɔːl.ʃəm; *locally:* -səm, (US) ˈwɔːl-, ˈwɑːl-
Walsingham *surname:* ˈwɔːl.sɪŋ.əm, ˈwɒl-, (US) ˈwɔːl-, ˈwɑːl- *place:* ˈwɔːl.zɪŋ.əm, ˈwɒl-, -sɪŋ-, (US) ˈwɔːl-, ˈwɑːl-
Walt wɒlt, wɔːlt, (US) wɔːlt, wɑːlt
Walter *English name:* ˈwɒl.təʳ, ˈwɔːl-, (US) ˈwɔːl.tɚ, ˈwɑːl- *German name:* ˈvɑːl.təʳ, (US) -tɚ
Walter Mitty ˌwɒl.təˈmɪt.i, ˌwɔːl-, (US) ˌwɔːl.tɚˈmɪţ-, ˌwɑːl-
Walters ˈwɒl.təz, ˈwɔːl-, (US) ˈwɔːl.tɚz, ˈwɑːl-
Waltham Great *and* **Little**, *in Essex:* ˈwɔːl.təm, ˈwɒl-, (US) ˈwɔːl-, ˈwɑːl- *other places:* ˈwɔːl.θəm, ˈwɒl-, (US) ˈwɔːl-, ˈwɑːl- **ˌWaltham ˈForest**

Note: Some new residents pronounce /-θəm/.

Walthamstow ˈwɒl.θəm.stəʊ, ˈwɔːl-, (US) ˈwɔːl.θəm.stoʊ, ˈwɑːl-
Walther ˈvɑːl.təʳ, (US) -tɚ
Walton ˈwɒl.tᵊn, ˈwɔːl-, (US) ˈwɔːl-, ˈwɑːl-
Walton-on-the-Naze ˌwɒl.tᵊn.ɒn.ðəˈneɪz, ˌwɔːl-, (US) ˌwɔːl.tᵊnˌɑːn-, ˌwɑːl-
waltz wɒls, wɔːls, wɒlts, wɔːlts, (US) wɔːlts, wɑːlts **-es** -ɪz **-ing** -ɪŋ **-ed** -t **-er/s** -əʳ/z, (US) -ɚ/z
Walworth ˈwɒl.wəθ, ˈwɔːl-, -wɜːθ, (US) ˈwɔːl.wɝːθ, ˈwɑːl-, -wɚθ
wampum ˈwɒm.pəm, (US) ˈwɑːm-, ˈwɔːm- **-s** -z
wan wɒn, (US) wɑːn **-ner** -əʳ, (US) -ɚ

-nest -ɪst, -əst -ly -li -ness -nəs, -nɪs
WAN wæn
Wanamaker ˈwɒn.ə.meɪ.kəʳ, US ˈwɑː.nə.meɪ.kɚ
wand, W~ wɒnd, US wɑːnd -s -z
Wanda ˈwɒn.də, US ˈwɑːn-
wand|er ˈwɒn.d|əʳ, US ˈwɑːn.d|ɚ -ers -əz, US -ɚz -ering/s -ᵊr.ɪŋ/z -ered -əd, US -ɚd -erer/s -ᵊr.əʳ/z, US -ɚ.ɚ/z
wanderlust ˈwɒn.də.lʌst, ˈvɑːn.də.lʊst, US ˈwɑːn.dɚ.lʌst
Wandle ˈwɒn.dᵊl, US ˈwɑːn-
Wandsworth ˈwɒndz.wəθ, US ˈwɑːndz.wɚθ
wan|e weɪn -es -z -ing -ɪŋ -ed -d
Wang® wæŋ
Wanganui ˌwɑːŋ.əˈnuː.i, ˌwɒŋ.ə-
wangl|e ˈwæŋ.gᵊl -es -z -ing -ɪŋ, US ˈwæŋ.glɪŋ -ed -d
wank wæŋk -s -s -ing -ɪŋ -ed -t
wanker ˈwæŋ.kəʳ, US -kɚ -s -z
Wann wɒn, US wɑːn
wanna ˈwɒn.ə, US ˈwɑː.nə
wannabe(e) ˈwɒn.ə.bi, -biː, US ˈwɑː.nə- -s -z
Wansbeck ˈwɒnz.bek, US ˈwɑːnz-
Wanstall ˈwɒn.stɔːl, US ˈwɑːn.stɑːl, -stɔːl
Wanstead ˈwɒnt.sted, -stɪd, US ˈwɑːnt-
wan|t wɒn|t, US wɑːn|t, wɔːn|t, wʌn|t -ts -ts -ting -tɪŋ, US -t̬ɪŋ -ted -tɪd, US -t̬ɪd
Wantage ˈwɒn.tɪdʒ, US ˈwɑːn.t̬ɪdʒ
wanton ˈwɒn.tən, US ˈwɑːn.tᵊn -ly -li -ness -nəs, -nɪs
WAP, Wap wæp, wɒp, US wɑːp, wæp
wapentake ˈwæp.ən.teɪk, ˈwɒp-, US ˈwɑː.pən-, ˈwæp.ən- -s -s
wapiti ˈwɒp.ɪ.ti, US ˈwɑː.pə.t̬i -s -z
Wapping ˈwɒp.ɪŋ, US ˈwɑː.pɪŋ
Wappinger ˈwɒp.ɪn.dʒəʳ, US ˈwɑː.pɪn.dʒɚ
war wɔːʳ, US wɔːr -s -z -ring -ɪŋ -red -d ˈwar ˌcrime; ˈwar ˌdance; ˈwar ˌgame; ˈwar meˌmorial; ˌwar of ˈnerves; ˈwar ˌpaint; ˈwar ˌwidow
Warbeck ˈwɔː.bek, US ˈwɔːr-
warbl|e ˈwɔː.bᵊl, US ˈwɔːr- -es -z -ing -ɪŋ, ˈ-blɪŋ, US ˈwɔːr.bᵊl.ɪŋ, ˈ-blɪŋ -ed -d
warbler ˈwɔː.bləʳ, -bᵊl.əʳ, US ˈwɔːr.blɚ, -bᵊl.ɚ -s -z
Warburg ˈwɔː.bɜːg, US ˈwɔːr.bɝːg
Warburton ˈwɔː.bə.tᵊn, -bɜː-, US ˈwɔːr.bɚ-, -bɝː-
war-cr|y ˈwɔː.kr|aɪ, US ˈwɔːr- -ies -aɪz
ward, W~ wɔːd, US wɔːrd -s -z -ing -ɪŋ -ed -ɪd
-ward wəd, US wɚd
Note: Suffix. Normally unstressed, e.g. **homeward** /ˈhəʊm.wəd/ US /ˈhoʊm.wɚd/.
warden, W~ ˈwɔː.dᵊn, US ˈwɔːr- -s -z
warder, W~ ˈwɔː.dəʳ, US ˈwɔːr.dɚ -s -z
Wardlaw ˈwɔːd.lɔː, US ˈwɔːrd.lɑː, -lɔː
Wardle ˈwɔː.dᵊl, US ˈwɔːr-
Wardour ˈwɔː.dəʳ, US ˈwɔːr.dɚ
wardress ˈwɔː.drɪs, -drəs, US ˈwɔːr.drɪs -es -ɪz
wardrobe ˈwɔː.drəʊb, US ˈwɔːr.droʊb -s -z
wardroom ˈwɔːd.rʊm, -ruːm, US ˈwɔːrd.ruːm, -rʊm -s -z
-wards wədz, US wɚdz
Note: See note for **-ward**.
wardship ˈwɔːd.ʃɪp, US ˈwɔːrd- -s -s
ware, W~ weəʳ, US wer -s -z
-ware weəʳ, US wer
Note: Suffix. Normally unstressed, e.g. **tableware** /ˈteɪ.bᵊl.weəʳ/ US /-wer/.
Wareham ˈweə.rəm, US ˈwer.əm
warehou|se **n** ˈweə.haʊ|s, US ˈwer- -ses -zɪz
warehou|se **v** ˈweə.haʊ|z, -haʊ|s, US ˈwer- -ses -zɪz, -sɪz -sing -zɪŋ, -sɪŋ -sed -zd, -st
warehouse|man ˈweə.haʊs|.mən, US ˈwer- -men -mən
warfare ˈwɔː.feəʳ, US ˈwɔːr.fer
warfarin ˈwɔː.fᵊr.ɪn, US ˈwɔːr-
Wargrave ˈwɔː.greɪv, US ˈwɔːr-
Warham ˈwɔː.rəm, US ˈwɔːr.əm
warhead ˈwɔː.hed, US ˈwɔːr- -s -z
Warhol ˈwɔː.həʊl, US ˈwɔːr.hɔːl, -hoʊl
warhors|e ˈwɔː.hɔːs, US ˈwɔːr.hɔːrs -es -ɪz
Waring ˈweə.rɪŋ, US ˈwer.ɪŋ
warlike ˈwɔː.laɪk, US ˈwɔːr-
Warlingham ˈwɔː.lɪŋ.əm, US ˈwɔːr-
warlock, W~ ˈwɔː.lɒk, US ˈwɔːr.lɑːk -s -s
warlord ˈwɔː.lɔːd, US ˈwɔːr.lɔːrd -s -z
warm wɔːm, US wɔːrm -er -əʳ, US -ɚ -est -ɪst, -əst -ly -li -ness -nəs, -nɪs -s -z -ing -ɪŋ -ed -d
warm-blooded ˌwɔːmˈblʌd.ɪd, US ˌwɔːrm- -ness -nəs, -nɪs *stress shift:* ˌ**warm-blooded** ˈ**animal**
warmer ˈwɔː.məʳ, US ˈwɔːr.mɚ -s -z
warm-hearted ˌwɔːmˈhɑː.tɪd, US ˌwɔːrmˈhɑːr.t̬ɪd -ly -li -ness -nəs, -nɪs *stress shift:* ˌ**warm-hearted** ˈ**person**
warming-pan ˈwɔː.mɪŋ.pæn, US ˈwɔːr- -s -z
Warmington ˈwɔː.mɪŋ.tən, US ˈwɔːr-
Warminster ˈwɔː.mɪnt.stəʳ, US ˈwɔːr.mɪnt.stɚ
warmong|er ˈwɔːˌmʌŋ.g|əʳ, US ˈwɑːrˌmʌŋ.g|ɚ, ˈwɔːr-, -ˌmɑːŋ- -ers -əz, US -ɚz -ering -ᵊr.ɪŋ
warmth wɔːmpθ, US wɔːrmpθ
warn wɔːn, US wɔːrn -s -z -ing/ly -ɪŋ/li -ed -d
Warne wɔːn, US wɔːrn
Warner ˈwɔː.nəʳ, US ˈwɔːr.nɚ
warning ˈwɔː.nɪŋ, US ˈwɔːr- -s -z
Warnock ˈwɔː.nɒk, US ˈwɔːr.nɑːk
warp wɔːp, US wɔːrp -s -s -ing -ɪŋ -ed -t
warpath ˈwɔː.pɑːθ, US ˈwɔːr.pæθ
warr|ant ˈwɒr|.ᵊnt, US ˈwɔːr-, ˈwɑːr- -ants -ᵊnts -anting -ᵊn.tɪŋ, US -ᵊn.t̬ɪŋ -anted -ᵊn.tɪd, US -ᵊn.t̬ɪd -anter/s -ᵊn.təʳ/z, US -ᵊn.t̬ɚ/z
ˈ**warrant** ˌ**officer**
warrantab|le ˈwɒr.ᵊn.tə.b|ᵊl, US ˈwɔːr.ᵊn.t̬ə-, ˈwɑːr- -ly -li -leness -ᵊl.nəs, -nɪs
warrantee ˌwɒr.ᵊnˈtiː, US ˌwɔːr-, ˌwɑːr- -s -z
warrantor ˈwɒr.ᵊn.tɔːʳ, -təʳ, ˌwɒr.ᵊnˈtɔːʳ, US ˈwɔːr.ᵊn.tɔːr, ˈwɑːr-, -t̬ɚ -s -z
warrant|y ˈwɒr.ᵊn.t|i, US ˈwɔːr.ᵊn.t̬|i, ˈwɑːr- -ies -iz
Warre wɔːʳ, US wɔːr
warren, W~ ˈwɒr.ᵊn, -ɪn, US ˈwɔːr.ᵊn, ˈwɑːr- -s -z
Warrender ˈwɒr.ən.dəʳ, -ɪn-, US ˈwɔːr.ən.dɚ, ˈwɑːr-, -ɪn-
Warrenpoint ˈwɒr.ən.pɔɪnt, -əm-, US ˈwɔːr.ən-, ˈwɑːr-
Warrington ˈwɒr.ɪŋ.tən, US ˈwɔːr-, ˈwɑːr-
warrior, W~ ˈwɒr.i.əʳ, US ˈwɔːr.jɚ, ˈwɑːr-, -i.ɚ -s -z
Warrnambool ˈwɔː.nəm.buːl, US ˈwɔːr-
Warsaw ˈwɔː.sɔː, US ˈwɔːr.sɑː, -sɔː
ˌ**Warsaw** ˈ**Pact**
warship ˈwɔː.ʃɪp, US ˈwɔːr- -s -s
Warsop ˈwɔː.səp, US ˈwɔːr-
Warspite ˈwɔː.spaɪt, US ˈwɔːr-
wart wɔːt, US wɔːrt -s -s -y -i, US ˈwɔːr.t̬i
warthog ˈwɔːt.hɒg, US ˈwɔːrt.hɑːg, -hɔːg -s -z
wartime ˈwɔː.taɪm, US ˈwɔːr-
Warton ˈwɔː.tᵊn, US ˈwɔːr-
war-torn ˈwɔː.tɔːn, US ˈwɔːr.tɔːrn
war-weary ˈwɔːˌwɪə.ri, US ˈwɔːrˌwɪr.i
Warwick *in Britain:* ˈwɒr.ɪk, US ˈwɔːr.ɪk, ˈwɑːr- -shire -ʃəʳ, -ʃɪəʳ, US -ʃɚ, -ʃɪr *in US:* ˈwɔː.wɪk, US ˈwɔːr-
war-worn ˈwɔː.wɔːn, US ˈwɔːr.wɔːrn
war|y ˈweə.r|i, US ˈwer|.i -ier -i.əʳ, US -i.ɚ -iest -i.ɪst, -i.əst -ily -ᵊl.i, -ɪ.li -iness -ɪ.nəs, -ɪ.nɪs
was (from **be**) *strong forms:* wɒz, US wɑːz, wʌz; *weak forms:* wəz, wz
Note: Weak-form word. The strong forms are used in contrastive contexts (e.g. 'I don't know whether it **was** or it **wasn't**), and for emphasis (e.g. 'I **was** right!'). The strong form is also usual in final position (e.g. 'That's where it was'). The weak forms are used elsewhere; the form /wz/ is found only in rapid, casual speech.
wasabi ˈwæs.æb.i, wəˈsɑː.bi, US ˈwɑː.sə.bi, wəˈsɑː.bi
Wasbrough ˈwɒz.brə, US ˈwɑːz-
wash, W~ wɒʃ, US wɑːʃ, wɔːʃ -es -ɪz -ing -ɪŋ -ed -t -able -ə.bᵊl ˌ**wash and** ˈ**wear**

Wash. (abbrev. for **Washington**) ˈwɒʃ.ɪŋ.tən, ⓊⓈ ˈwɑː.ʃɪŋ-, ˈwɔː-
washbasin ˈwɒʃˌbeɪ.sən, ⓊⓈ ˈwɑːʃ-, ˈwɔːʃ- **-s** -z
washboard ˈwɒʃ.bɔːd, ⓊⓈ ˈwɑːʃ.bɔːrd, ˈwɔːʃ- **-s** -z
washbowl ˈwɒʃ.bəʊl, ⓊⓈ ˈwɑːʃ.boʊl, ˈwɔːʃ- **-s** -z
wash|cloth ˈwɒʃ|.klɒθ, ⓊⓈ ˈwɑːʃ|.klɑːθ, ˈwɔːʃ- **-cloths** -klɒθs, -klɒðz, ⓊⓈ -klɑːθs, -klɑːðz
washday ˈwɒʃ.deɪ, ⓊⓈ ˈwɑːʃ-, ˈwɔːʃ- **-s** -z
washed-out ˌwɒʃtˈaʊt, ⓊⓈ ˌwɑːʃt-, ˌwɔːʃt- *stress shift:* **ˌwashed-out ˈcolour**
washed-up ˌwɒʃtˈʌp, ⓊⓈ ˌwɑːʃt-, ˌwɔːʃt- *stress shift:* **ˌwashed-up ˈwriter**
washer ˈwɒʃ.əʳ, ⓊⓈ ˈwɑː.ʃɚ, ˈwɔː- **-s** -z
washer-dryer ˌwɒʃ.əˈdraɪ.əʳ, ⓊⓈ ˌwɑː.ʃɚˈdraɪ.ɚ, ˌwɔː- **-s** -z
washer-up ˌwɒʃ.əʳˈʌp, ⓊⓈ ˌwɑː.ʃɚ-, ˌwɔː- **washers-up** ˌwɒʃ.əzˈ-, ⓊⓈ ˌwɑː.ʃɚzˈ-, ˌwɔː-
washer|woman ˈwɒʃ.ə|ˌwʊm.ən, ⓊⓈ ˈwɑː.ʃɚ-, ˈwɔː- **-women** -ˌwɪm.ɪn
wash-hou|se ˈwɒʃ.haʊ|s, ⓊⓈ ˈwɑːʃ-, ˈwɔːʃ- **-ses** -zɪz
washing ˈwɒʃ.ɪŋ, ⓊⓈ ˈwɑː.ʃɪŋ, ˈwɔː- **ˈwashing maˌchine; ˈwashing ˌpowder**
Washingborough ˈwɒʃ.ɪŋˌbʌr.ə, ⓊⓈ ˈwɑː.ʃɪŋ.bɚ.oʊ, ˈwɔː-
Washington ˈwɒʃ.ɪŋ.tən, ⓊⓈ ˈwɑː.ʃɪŋ-, ˈwɔː- **ˌWashington ˌDˈC; ˌWashington ˈState**
Washingtonian ˌwɒʃ.ɪŋˈtəʊ.ni.ən, ⓊⓈ ˌwɑː.ʃɪŋˈtoʊ-, ˌwɔː- **-s** -z
washing-up ˌwɒʃ.ɪŋˈʌp, ⓊⓈ ˌwɑː.ʃɪŋˈ-, ˌwɔː-
washout ˈwɒʃ.aʊt, ⓊⓈ ˈwɑːʃ-, ˈwɔːʃ- **-s** -s
washrag ˈwɒʃ.ræg, ⓊⓈ ˈwɑːʃ-, ˈwɔːʃ- **-s** -z
washroom ˈwɒʃ.rʊm, -ruːm, ⓊⓈ ˈwɑːʃ.ruːm, ˈwɔːʃ-, -rʊm **-s** -z
washstand ˈwɒʃ.stænd, ⓊⓈ ˈwɑːʃ-, ˈwɔːʃ- **-s** -z
wash-tub ˈwɒʃ.tʌb, ⓊⓈ ˈwɑːʃ-, ˈwɔːʃ- **-s** -z
wash|y ˈwɒʃ|.i, ⓊⓈ ˈwɑː.ʃ|i, ˈwɔː- **-ier** -i.əʳ, ⓊⓈ -i.ɚ **-iest** -i.ɪst, -i.əst **-iness** -ɪ.nəs, -ɪ.nɪs
Wasilla wɑːˈsɪl.ə, wəˈ-
wasn't ˈwɒz.ənt, ⓊⓈ ˈwɑː.zənt, ˈwʌz-
wasp, WASP, W~ wɒsp, ⓊⓈ wɑːsp **-s** -s
waspish ˈwɒs.pɪʃ, ⓊⓈ ˈwɑː.spɪʃ **-ly** -li **-ness** -nəs, -nɪs
wassail ˈwɒs.eɪl, ˈwæs-, -əl, ⓊⓈ ˈwɑː.səl, ˈwæs.əl, -eɪl; ⓊⓈ wɑːˈseɪl **-s** -z
wassailing ˈwɒs.əl.ɪŋ, ˈwæs-, -eɪ.lɪŋ, ⓊⓈ ˈwɑː.səl.ɪŋ, ˈwæs.əl-, -eɪ.lɪŋ; ⓊⓈ wɑːˈseɪ.lɪŋ
Wassell ˈwæs.əl
Wasson ˈwɒs.ən, ⓊⓈ ˈwɑː.sən
wast (from **be**) *strong forms:* wɒst, ⓊⓈ wɑːst; *weak form:* wəst
Wast wɒst, ⓊⓈ wɑːst
wast|e weɪst **-es** -s **-ing** -ɪŋ **-ed** -ɪd **-er/s** -əʳ/z, ⓊⓈ -ɚ/z **-age** -ɪdʒ **ˈwaste ˌproduct; ˌwaste ˈproduct**
wastebasket ˈweɪstˌbɑː.skɪt, ⓊⓈ -ˌbæs.kət **-s** -s
wasteful ˈweɪst.fəl, -fʊl **-ly** -i **-ness** -nəs, -nɪs
wasteland ˈweɪst.lænd **-s** -z
wastepaper ˌweɪstˈpeɪ.pəʳ, ˈ-ˌ--, ⓊⓈ ˈweɪstˌpeɪ.pɚ **wasteˈpaper ˌbasket; ˈwastepaper ˌbasket; wasteˈpaper ˌbin**
wastepipe ˈweɪst.paɪp **-s** -s
wastrel ˈweɪ.strəl **-s** -z
Wastwater ˈwɒstˌwɔː.təʳ, ⓊⓈ ˈwɑːstˌwɑː.t̬ɚ, -ˌwɔː-
Wat wɒt, ⓊⓈ wɑːt
watch wɒtʃ, ⓊⓈ wɑːtʃ, wɔːtʃ **-es** -ɪz **-ing** -ɪŋ **-ed** -t **-er/s** -əʳ/z, ⓊⓈ -ɚ/z
watchable ˈwɒtʃ.ə.bəl, ⓊⓈ ˈwɑː.tʃə-, ˈwɔː-
watchamacallit ˈwɒtʃ.ə.məˌkɔːl.ɪt, ⓊⓈ ˈwɑː.tʃə-, ˈwɔː-, -ˌkɑːl- **-s** -s
watch-cas|e ˈwɒtʃ.keɪs, ⓊⓈ ˈwɑːtʃ-, ˈwɔːtʃ- **-es** -ɪz
watchdog ˈwɒtʃ.dɒg, ⓊⓈ ˈwɑːtʃ.dɑːg, ˈwɔːtʃ-, -dɔːg **-s** -z
Watchet ˈwɒtʃ.ɪt, ⓊⓈ ˈwɑː.tʃɪt, ˈwɔː-
watchful ˈwɒtʃ.fəl, -fʊl, ⓊⓈ ˈwɑːtʃ-, ˈwɔːtʃ- **-ly** -i **-ness** -nəs, -nɪs
watchmak|er ˈwɒtʃˌmeɪ.k|əʳ, ⓊⓈ ˈwɑːtʃˌmeɪ.k|ɚ, ˈwɔːtʃ- **-ers** -əz, ⓊⓈ -ɚz **-ing** -ɪŋ
watch|man ˈwɒtʃ|.mən, ⓊⓈ ˈwɑːtʃ-, ˈwɔːtʃ- **-men** -mən, -men
watchstrap ˈwɒtʃ.stræp, ⓊⓈ ˈwɑːtʃ-, ˈwɔːtʃ- **-s** -s
watchtower, W~ ˈwɒtʃ.taʊ.əʳ, -taʊəʳ, ⓊⓈ ˈwɑːtʃ.taʊ.ɚ, ˈwɔːtʃ- **-s** -z
watchword ˈwɒtʃ.wɜːd, ⓊⓈ ˈwɑːtʃ.wɝːd, ˈwɔːtʃ- **-s** -z
wat|er ˈwɔː.t|əʳ, ⓊⓈ ˈwɑː.t̬|ɚ, ˈwɔː- **-ers** -əz, ⓊⓈ -ɚz **-ering** -ər.ɪŋ **-ered** -əd, ⓊⓈ -ɚd **ˈwater ˌbed; ˈwater ˌbeetle; ˈwater ˌbottle; ˈwater ˌbuffalo; ˌwater ˈbuffalo** ⓊⓈ **ˈwater ˌbuffalo; ˈwater ˌcannon; ˌwater ˈchestnut** ⓊⓈ **ˈwater ˌchestnut; ˈwater ˌcloset; ˈwater ˌice; ˈwater ˌmain; ˈwater ˌmeadow; ˈwater ˌmill; ˈwater supˌply; ˈwater ˌtable; ˈwater ˌtower; ˌkeep one's ˌhead above ˈwater; ˌpour cold ˈwater on; like ˌwater off a ˌduck's ˈback** ⓊⓈ **like ˌwater off a ˈduck's ˌback; ˌwater ˌunder the ˈbridge**
water-borne ˈwɔː.tə.bɔːn, ⓊⓈ ˈwɑː.t̬ɚ.bɔːrn, ˈwɔː-
waterbuck ˈwɔː.tə.bʌk, ⓊⓈ ˈwɑː.t̬ɚ-, ˈwɔː-
Waterbur|y ˈwɔː.tə.bər|.i, ⓊⓈ ˈwɑː.t̬ɚˌber-, ˈwɔː-, -bɚ- **-ies** -iz
water-chute ˈwɔː.tə.ʃuːt, ⓊⓈ ˈwɑː.t̬ɚ-, ˈwɔː- **-s** -s
watercolo(u)r ˈwɔː.təˌkʌl.əʳ, ⓊⓈ ˈwɑː.t̬ɚˌkʌl.ɚ, ˈwɔː- **-s** -z
watercolo(u)rist ˈwɔː.təˌkʌl.ər.ɪst, ⓊⓈ ˈwɑː.t̬ɚ-, ˈwɔː- **-s** -s
water-cooled ˌwɔː.təˈkuːld, ⓊⓈ ˈwɑː.t̬ɚ.kuːld, ˈwɔː- *stress shift, British only:* **ˌwater-cooled ˈengines**
watercours|e ˈwɔː.tə.kɔːs, ⓊⓈ ˈwɑː.t̬ɚ.kɔːrs, ˈwɔː- **-es** -ɪz
watercress ˈwɔː.tə.kres, ⓊⓈ ˈwɑː.t̬ɚ-, ˈwɔː-
water-divin|ing ˈwɔː.tə.dɪˌvaɪ.n|ɪŋ, -dəˌ-, ⓊⓈ ˈwɑː.t̬ɚ-, ˈwɔː- **-er/s** -əʳ/z, ⓊⓈ -ɚ/z
watered-down ˌwɔː.tədˈdaʊn, ⓊⓈ ˌwɑː.t̬ɚdˈ-, ˌwɔː- *stress shift:* **ˌwatered-down ˈrum**
waterfall ˈwɔː.tə.fɔːl, ⓊⓈ ˈwɑː.t̬ɚ.fɔːl, ˈwɔː-, -fɑːl **-s** -z
water-finder ˈwɔː.təˌfaɪn.dəʳ, ⓊⓈ ˈwɑː.t̬ɚˌfaɪn.dɚ, ˈwɔː- **-s** -z
Waterford ˈwɔː.tə.fəd, ⓊⓈ ˈwɑː.t̬ɚ.fɚd, ˈwɔː-
waterfowl ˈwɔː.tə.faʊl, ⓊⓈ ˈwɑː.t̬ɚ-, ˈwɔː- **-s** -z **-er/s** -əʳ/z, ⓊⓈ -ɚ/z
waterfront ˈwɔː.tə.frʌnt, ⓊⓈ ˈwɑː.t̬ɚ-, ˈwɔː- **-s** -s
Watergate ˈwɔː.tə.geɪt, ⓊⓈ ˈwɑː.t̬ɚ-, ˈwɔː-
waterhole ˈwɔː.tə.həʊl, ⓊⓈ ˈwɑː.t̬ɚ.hoʊl, ˈwɔː- **-s** -z
Waterhouse ˈwɔː.tə.haʊs, ⓊⓈ ˈwɑː.t̬ɚ-, ˈwɔː-
wateriness ˈwɔː.tər.ɪ.nəs, -nɪs, ⓊⓈ ˈwɑː.t̬ɚ-, ˈwɔː-
watering-can ˈwɔː.tər.ɪŋ.kæn, ⓊⓈ ˈwɑː.t̬ɚ-, ˈwɔː- **-s** -z
watering-hole ˈwɔː.tər.ɪŋ.həʊl, ⓊⓈ ˈwɑː.t̬ɚ.ɪŋ.hoʊl, ˈwɔː- **-s** -z
watering-plac|e ˈwɔː.tər.ɪŋ.pleɪs, ⓊⓈ ˈwɑː.t̬ɚ-, ˈwɔː- **-es** -ɪz
waterless ˈwɔː.təl.əs, -lɪs, ⓊⓈ ˈwɑː.t̬ɚ.ləs, ˈwɔː-
water-level ˈwɔː.təˌlev.əl, ⓊⓈ ˈwɑː.t̬ɚ-, ˈwɔː- **-s** -z
water-lil|y ˈwɔː.təˌlɪl|.i, ⓊⓈ ˈwɑː.t̬ɚ-, ˈwɔː- **-ies** -iz
water-line ˈwɔː.tə.laɪn, ⓊⓈ ˈwɑː.t̬ɚ-, ˈwɔː- **-s** -z
waterlog ˈwɔː.tə.lɒg, ⓊⓈ ˈwɑː.t̬ɚ.lɑːg, ˈwɔː-, -lɔːg **-s** -z **-ging** -ɪŋ **-ged** -d
waterlogged ˈwɔː.tə.lɒgd, ⓊⓈ ˈwɑː.t̬ɚ.lɑːgd, ˈwɔː-, -lɔːgd
waterloo, W~ ˌwɔː.təˈluː, ⓊⓈ ˈwɑː.t̬ɚ-, ˈwɔː-, ˌ--ˈ- **-s** -z *stress shift, British only:* **ˌWaterloo ˈBridge**
Waterlooville ˌwɔː.təˈluː.vɪl, ˌwɔː.təl.uːˈvɪl, ⓊⓈ ˈwɑː.t̬ɚˌluː.vɪl, ˈwɔː-
water|man, W~ ˈwɔː.tə|.mən, ⓊⓈ ˈwɑː.t̬ɚ-, ˈwɔː- **-men** -mən, -men
watermark ˈwɔː.tə.mɑːk, ⓊⓈ ˈwɑː.t̬ɚ.mɑːrk, ˈwɔː- **-s** -s **-ing** -ɪŋ **-ed** -t
watermelon ˈwɔː.təˌmel.ən, ⓊⓈ ˈwɑː.t̬ɚ-, ˈwɔː- **-s** -z
watermill ˈwɔː.tə.mɪl, ⓊⓈ ˈwɑː.t̬ɚ-, ˈwɔː- **-s** -z
water-nymph ˈwɔː.tə.nɪmpf, ⓊⓈ ˈwɑː.t̬ɚ-, ˈwɔː- **-s** -s

W

waterpolo ˈwɔː.təˌpəʊ.ləʊ, (US) ˈwɑː.t̬ɚˌpoʊ.loʊ, ˈwɔː-
waterproof ˈwɔː.tə.pruːf, (US) ˈwɑː.t̬ɚ-, ˈwɔː- **-s** -s **-ing** -ɪŋ **-ed** -t
water-resistant ˈwɔː.tə.rɪˌzɪs.tənt, -rə-, (US) ˈwɑː.t̬ɚ-, ˈwɔː-
Waters ˈwɔː.təz, (US) ˈwɑː.t̬ɚz, ˈwɔː-
watershed ˈwɔː.tə.ʃed, (US) ˈwɑː.t̬ɚ-, ˈwɔː- **-s** -z
Watership ˈwɔː.tə.ʃɪp, (US) ˈwɑː.tɚ-, ˈwɔː-
watersid|e ˈwɔː.tə.saɪd, (US) ˈwɑː.t̬ɚ-, ˈwɔː- **-er/s** -əʳ/z, (US) -ɚ/z
water-ski ˈwɔː.tə.skiː, (US) ˈwɑː.t̬ɚ-, ˈwɔː- **-s** -z **-ing** -ɪŋ **-ed** -d **-er/s** -əʳ/z, (US) -ɚ/z
watersport ˈwɔː.tə.spɔːt, (US) ˈwɑː.t̬ɚ.spɔːrt, ˈwɔː- **-s** -s
waterspout ˈwɔː.tə.spaʊt, (US) ˈwɑː.t̬ɚ-, ˈwɔː- **-s** -s
Waterstone ˈwɔː.tə.stəʊn, (US) ˈwɑː.t̬ɚ.stoʊn, ˈwɔː-, -stən **'s** -z
watertight ˈwɔː.tə.taɪt, (US) ˈwɑː.t̬ɚ-, ˈwɔː-
waterway ˈwɔː.tə.weɪ, (US) ˈwɑː.t̬ɚ-, ˈwɔː- **-s** -z
waterwheel ˈwɔː.tə.*h*wiːl, (US) ˈwɑː.t̬ɚ-, ˈwɔː- **-s** -z
waterwings ˈwɔː.tə.wɪŋz, (US) ˈwɑː.t̬ɚ-, ˈwɔː-
waterworks ˈwɔː.tə.wɜːks, (US) ˈwɑː.t̬ɚ.wɝːks, ˈwɔː-
water|y ˈwɔː.tᵊr|.i, -tr|i, (US) ˈwɑː.t̬ɚ|.i, ˈwɔː- **-iness** -ɪ.nəs, -ɪ.nɪs
Watford ˈwɒt.fəd, (US) ˈwɑːt.fɚd
Wath upon Dearne ˌwɒθ.əˌpɒnˈdɜːn, ˌwæθ-, (US) ˌwɑːθ.əˌpɑːnˈdɝːn, ˌwæθ-
Watkin ˈwɒt.kɪn, (US) ˈwɑːt- **-s** -z
Watling ˈwɒt.lɪŋ, (US) ˈwɑːt-
Watson ˈwɒt.sᵊn, (US) ˈwɑːt-
watt, W~ wɒt, (US) wɑːt **-s** -s
wattag|e ˈwɒt.ɪdʒ, (US) ˈwɑː.t̬ɪdʒ **-es** -ɪz
Watteau ˈwɒt.əʊ, (US) wɑːˈtoʊ
Watters ˈwɔː.təz, ˈwɒt.əz, (US) ˈwɑː.t̬ɚz, ˈwɔː-
Watterson ˈwɔː.tə.sᵊn, ˈwɒt.ə-, (US) ˈwɑː.t̬ɚ-, ˈwɔː-
wattle ˈwɒt.ᵊl, (US) ˈwɑː.t̬ᵊl **-s** -z **-d** -d
wattmeter ˈwɒtˌmiː.təʳ, (US) ˈwɑːtˌmiː.t̬ɚ **-s** -z
Watton ˈwɒt.ᵊn, (US) ˈwɑː.tᵊn
Wauchope ˈwɔː.kəp, ˈwɒx.əp, (US) ˈwɑː.kəp, ˈwɔː-
Waugh wɔː, wɒx, wɒf, wɑːf, (US) wɑː, wɔː

> Note: /wɔː/ (US) /wɑː, wɔː/ are the appropriate pronunciations for authors Auberon and Evelyn Waugh.

wav|e weɪv **-es** -z **-ing** -ɪŋ **-ed** -d **-eless** -ləs, -lɪs
waveband ˈweɪv.bænd **-s** -z
waveform ˈweɪv.fɔːm, (US) -fɔːrm **-s** -z
wavelength ˈweɪv.leŋ*k*θ **-s** -s
wavelet ˈweɪv.lət, -lɪt **-s** -s
Wavell ˈweɪ.vᵊl
Waveney ˈweɪv.ni
wav|er ˈweɪ.v|əʳ, (US) -v|ɚ **-ers** -əz, (US) -ɚz **-ering/ly** -ᵊr.ɪŋ/li **-ered** -əd, (US) -ɚd **-erer/s** -ᵊr.əʳ/z, (US) -ɚ.ɚ/z
Waverley ˈweɪ.vᵊl.i, (US) -vɚ.li
wav|y ˈweɪ.v|i **-ier** -i.əʳ, (US) -i.ɚ **-iest** -i.ɪst, -i.əst **-ily** -ᵊl.i, -ɪ.li **-iness** -ɪ.nəs, -ɪ.nɪs
wax wæks **-es** -ɪz **-ing** -ɪŋ **-ed** -t **-en** -ᵊn
waxhead ˈwæks.hed **-s** -z
Waxman ˈwæks.mən
waxwing ˈwæks.wɪŋ **-s** -z
waxwork ˈwæks.wɜːk, (US) -wɝːk **-s** -s
wax|y ˈwæk.s|i **-ier** -i.əʳ, (US) -i.ɚ **-iest** -i.ɪst, -i.əst **-iness** -ɪ.nəs, -ɪ.nɪs
way, W~ weɪ **-s** -z ˌ**right of** ˈ**way** (US) ˈ**right of** ˌ**way;** ˌ**ways and** ˈ**means**
waybill ˈweɪ.bɪl **-s** -z
wayfar|er ˈweɪˌfeə.r|əʳ, (US) -ˌfer|.ɚ **-ers** -əz, (US) -ɚz **-ing** -ɪŋ
Wayland ˈweɪ.lənd
way|lay ˌweɪ|ˈleɪ, (US) ˈweɪ|.leɪ, -ˈ- **-lays** -ˈleɪz, (US) -leɪz, -ˈleɪz **-laying** -ˈleɪ.ɪŋ, (US) -ˌleɪ.ɪŋ, -ˈleɪ.ɪŋ **-laid** -ˈleɪd, (US) -leɪd, -ˈleɪd **-layer/s** -ˈleɪ.əʳ/z, (US) -ˌleɪ.ɚ/z, -ˈleɪ.ɚ/z
Wayman ˈweɪ.mən
Wayne weɪn
Waynflete ˈweɪn.fliːt
way out *exit:* ˌweɪˈaʊt
way-out *unusual and daring:* ˌweɪˈaʊt *stress shift:* ˌ**way-out** ˈ**clothes**
-ways weɪz, wɪz
Note: Suffix. Normally unstressed, e.g. **lengthways** /ˈleŋ*k*θ.weɪz/.
wayside ˈweɪ.saɪd ˌ**fall by the** ˈ**wayside**
wayward ˈweɪ.wəd, (US) -wɚd **-ly** -li **-ness** -nəs, -nɪs
wazoo wæzˈuː, wəˈzuː, (US) wɑːˈzuː **-s** -z
wazzock ˈwæz.ək **-s** -s
WC ˌdʌb.ᵊl.juːˈsiː, -jʊ-, (US) -juːˈ-, -jəˈ- **-s** -z
we *strong form:* wiː; *weak form:* wi
Note: Weak-form word. The strong form is used contrastively (e.g. 'We, not they, will win it') or for emphasis (e.g. '**We** are the winners'). It is also used in final position (e.g. 'So are we'). The weak form is used elsewhere.
weak wiːk **-er** -əʳ, (US) -ɚ **-est** -ɪst, -əst **-ly** -li ˌ**weak at the** ˈ**knees**
weaken ˈwiː.kᵊn **-s** -z **-ing** -ɪŋ, ˈwiːk.nɪŋ **-ed** -d
weak-kneed ˌwiːkˈniːd, (US) ˈwiːk.niːd *stress shift, British only:* ˌ**weak-kneed** ˈ**coward**
weakling ˈwiː.klɪŋ **-s** -z
weak-minded ˌwiːkˈmaɪn.dɪd **-ness** -nəs, -nɪs *stress shift:* ˌ**weak-minded** ˈ**person**
weakness ˈwiːk.nəs, -nɪs **-es** -ɪz
weal wiːl **-s** -z
weald, W~ wiːld **-s** -z
wealden, W~ ˈwiːl.dᵊn
Wealdstone ˈwiːld.stəʊn, (US) -stoʊn
wealth welθ
wealth|y ˈwel.θ|i **-ier** -i.əʳ, (US) -i.ɚ **-iest** -i.ɪst, -i.əst **-ily** -ᵊl.i, -ɪ.li **-iness** -ɪ.nəs, -ɪ.nɪs
wean n *child or baby:* weɪn **-s** -z
wean v *withdraw mother's milk:* wiːn **-s** -z **-ing** -ɪŋ **-ed** -d
weaner ˈwiː.nəʳ, (US) -nɚ **-s** -z
weanling ˈwiːn.lɪŋ **-s** -z
weapon ˈwep.ən **-s** -z **-less** -ləs, -lɪs **-ry** -ri
weaponiz|e ˈwep.ə.naɪz **-es** -ɪz **-ing** -ɪŋ **-d** -d
weapons-grade ˈwep.ənzˌgreɪd
wear weəʳ, (US) wer **-s** -z **-ing** -ɪŋ **wore** wɔːʳ, (US) wɔːr **worn** wɔːn, (US) wɔːrn **wearer/s** ˈweə.rəʳ/z, (US) ˈwer.ɚ/z ˌ**wear and** ˈ**tear**
Wear *river:* wɪəʳ, (US) wɪr
wearability ˌweə.rəˈbɪl.ə.ti, -ɪ.ti, (US) ˌwer.əˈbɪl.ə.t̬i
wearable ˈweə.rə.bᵊl, (US) ˈwer.ə-
Wearing ˈweə.rɪŋ, (US) ˈwer.ɪŋ
wearisome ˈwɪə.rɪ.sᵊm, (US) ˈwɪr.ɪ- **-ly** -li **-ness** -nəs, -nɪs
Wearmouth ˈwɪə.məθ, -maʊθ, (US) ˈwɪr-
Wearn wɜːn, (US) wɝːn
wear|y ˈwɪə.r|i, (US) ˈwɪr|.i **-ier** -i.əʳ, (US) -i.ɚ **-iest** -i.ɪst, -i.əst **-ily** -ᵊl.i, -ɪ.li **-iness** -ɪ.nəs, -ɪ.nɪs **-ies** -iz **-ying** -i.ɪŋ **-ied** -id
weasel ˈwiː.zᵊl **-s** -z
weaselly ˈwiː.zᵊl.i, ˈwiːz.li
weath|er ˈweð|.əʳ, (US) -ɚ **-ers** -əz, (US) -ɚz **-ering** -ᵊr.ɪŋ **-ered** -əd, (US) -ɚd ˈ**weather** ˌ**forecast;** ˌ**make** ˌ**heavy** ˈ**weather of** ˌ**something**
weather-beaten ˈweð.əˌbiː.tᵊn, (US) -ɚˌ-
weatherboard ˈweð.ə.bɔːd, (US) -ɚ.bɔːrd **-s** -z **-ing** -ɪŋ
weather-bound ˈweð.ə.baʊnd, (US) ˈ-ɚ-
weathercock ˈweð.ə.kɒk, (US) -ɚ.kɑːk **-s** -s
weather-eye ˈweð.əʳ.aɪ, ˌ--ˈ-, (US) ˈweð.ɚ.aɪ **-s** -z ˌ**keep a** ˈ**weather-eye open for something**
weather-glass ˈweð.ə.glɑːs, (US) -ɚ.glæs **-es** -ɪz
Weatherhead ˈweð.ə.hed, (US) ˈ-ɚ-
weatherly, W~ ˈweð.ᵊl.i, (US) -ɚ.li
weather|man ˈweð.ə|.mæn, (US) ˈ-ɚ- **-men** -men
weatherproof ˈweð.ə.pruːf, (US) ˈ-ɚ-
weathervane ˈweð.ə.veɪn, (US) ˈ-ɚ- **-s** -z
weather-wise ˈweð.ə.waɪz, (US) ˈ-ɚ-
weather-worn ˈweð.ə.wɔːn, (US) -ɚ.wɔːrn
weav|e wiːv **-es** -z **-ing** -ɪŋ **-ed** -d **wove** wəʊv, (US) woʊv **woven** ˈwəʊ.vᵊn, (US) ˈwoʊ-

weaver, W~ ˈwiː.vəʳ, ⓤⓢ -vɚ -s -z
Weaverham ˈwiː.vəʳr.əm, ⓤⓢ -vɚ.hæm, -əm
web web -s -z
Webb(e) web
web-based ˈweb.beɪst
webbed webd ˌwebbed ˈfeet
Webber ˈweb.əʳ, ⓤⓢ -ɚ
webb|ing ˈweb|.ɪŋ -y -i
webcam ˈweb.kæm -s -z
webcast ˈweb.kɑːst, ⓤⓢ -kæst -s -s -ing -ɪŋ
Weber *English name:* ˈweb.əʳ, ˈweɪ.bəʳ, ˈwiː-, ⓤⓢ ˈweb.ɚ, ˈweɪ.bɚ, ˈwiː- *German composer:* ˈveɪ.bəʳ, ⓤⓢ -bɚ
Webern ˈveɪ.bɜːn, ⓤⓢ -bɚn
webfooted ˌwebˈfʊt.ɪd, ˈwebˌfʊt̬.ɪd *stress shift, British only:* ˌ**webfooted** ˈ**bird**
webinar ˈweb.ɪ.nɑːʳ, ˈ-ə-, ⓤⓢ -ə.nɑːr -s -z
weblog ˈweb.lɒg, ⓤⓢ -lɑːg, -lɔːg -s -z
webmaster ˈwebˌmɑː.stəʳ, ⓤⓢ -ˌmæs.tɚ -s -z
webpag|e ˈweb.peɪdʒ -es -ɪz
website ˈweb.saɪt -s -s
Webster ˈweb.stəʳ, ⓤⓢ -stɚ -s -z
wed wed -s -z -ding -ɪŋ -ded -ɪd
Wed. (abbrev. for **Wednesday**) ˈwenz.deɪ, ˈwed.ənz-, -di, ⓤⓢ ˈwenz.deɪ, -di
we'd (= **we had, we would**) *strong form:* wiːd; *weak form:* wid
Note: see note for **we**
Weddell *surname:* wəˈdel, ˈwed.əl *Sea:* ˈwed.əl
Wedderburn ˈwed.ə.bɜːn, ⓤⓢ -ɚ.bɝːn
wedding ˈwed.ɪŋ -s -z ˈ**wedding** ˌ**breakfast**; ˈ**wedding** ˌ**cake**; ˈ**wedding** ˌ**day**; ˈ**wedding** ˌ**dress**; ˈ**wedding** ˌ**march**; ˈ**wedding** ˌ**ring**
Wedekind ˈveɪ.də.kɪnd, -kɪnt, ⓤⓢ -kɪnt, -kɪnd
wedg|e wedʒ -es -ɪz -ing -ɪŋ -ed -d -ewise -waɪz
wedge-shaped ˈwedʒ.ʃeɪpt
Wedg(e)wood ˈwedʒ.wʊd
wedlock ˈwed.lɒk, ⓤⓢ -lɑːk
Wednesbury ˈwenz.bəʳr.i; *locally also:* ˈwedʒ-, ⓤⓢ ˈwenz.bɚ-
Wednesday ˈwenz.deɪ, ˈwed.nz-, -di, ⓤⓢ ˈwenz.deɪ, -di -s -z
Wednesfield ˈwenz.fiːld; *locally also:* ˈwedʒ-, ⓤⓢ ˈwenz-
Weds. (abbrev. for **Wednesday**) ˈwenz.deɪ, ˈwed.nz-, -di, ⓤⓢ ˈwenz.deɪ, -di
we'd've *strong form:* ˈwiː.d.əv; *weak form:* wid.əv
Note: see note for **we**
wee wiː
weed wiːd -s -z -ing -ɪŋ -ed -ɪd
weedkiller ˈwiːdˌkɪl.əʳ, ⓤⓢ -ɚ -s -z
Weedon ˈwiː.dən
weed|y ˈwiː.d|i -ier -i.əʳ, ⓤⓢ -i.ɚ -iest -i.ɪst, -i.əst -iness -ɪ.nəs, -ɪ.nɪs
week wiːk -s -s
weekday ˈwiːk.deɪ -s -z
weekend ˌwiːkˈend, ˈ--, ⓤⓢ ˈwiːk.end -s -z *stress shift, British only:* ˌ**weekend** ˈ**traffic**
weekender ˌwiːkˈen.dəʳ, ⓤⓢ ˈwiːk.ˌen.dɚ -s -z
Weekes wiːks
weekl|y ˈwiː.kl|i -ies -iz
Weekl(e)y ˈwiː.kli
weeknight ˈwiːk.naɪt -s -s
Weeks wiːks
Weelkes wiːlks
ween wiːn -s -z -ing -ɪŋ -ed -d
ween|y ˈwiː.n|i -ies -iz -ier -i.əʳ, ⓤⓢ -i.ɚ -iest -i.ɪst, -i.əst
weenybopper ˈwiː.niˌbɒp.əʳ, ⓤⓢ -ˌbɑː.pɚ -s -z
weep wiːp -s -s -ing -ɪŋ **wept** wept
weeper ˈwiː.pəʳ, ⓤⓢ -pɚ -s -z
weepie ˈwiː.pi -s -z
weep|y ˈwiː.p|i -ier -i.əʳ, ⓤⓢ -i.ɚ -iest -i.ɪst, -i.əst -ily -əl.i, -ɪ.li -iness -ɪ.nəs, -ɪ.nɪs
Weetabix® ˈwiː.tə.bɪks
weever ˈwiː.vəʳ, ⓤⓢ -vɚ -s -z
weevil ˈwiː.vəl, -vɪl, ⓤⓢ -vəl -s -z
wee-wee ˈwiː.wiː -s -z -ing -ɪŋ -d -d
weft weft
Weidenfeld ˈvaɪ.dən.felt, ˈwaɪ-
Weigall ˈwaɪ.gɔːl
weigela waɪˈdʒiː.lə, -ˈgiː-, ⓤⓢ waɪˈgiː-, -ˈjiː-; ⓤⓢ ˈwaɪ.gə- -s -z
weigelia waɪˈdʒiː.li.ə, -ˈgiː-, ⓤⓢ waɪˈgiː- -s -z
weigh weɪ -s -z -ing -ɪŋ -ed -d -able -ə.bəl
weighbridg|e ˈweɪ.brɪdʒ -es -ɪz
weight weɪt -s -s -ing -ɪŋ, ⓤⓢ ˈweɪ.t̬ɪŋ -ed -ɪd, ⓤⓢ ˈweɪ.t̬ɪd ˈ**weight** ˌ**training**
weightless ˈweɪt.ləs, -lɪs -ly -li -ness -nəs, -nɪs
weightlift|ing ˈweɪtˌlɪf.t|ɪŋ -er/s -əʳ/z, ⓤⓢ -ɚ/z
Weighton *in* **Market Weighton**, *Humberside:* ˈwiː.tən
WeightWatchers® ˈweɪtˌwɒtʃ.əz, ⓤⓢ -ˌwɑː.tʃɚz
weightwatch|ing ˈweɪtˌwɒtʃ|.ɪŋ, ⓤⓢ -ˌwɑː.tʃ|ɪŋ -er/s -əʳ/z, ⓤⓢ -ɚ/z
weight|y ˈweɪ.t|i, ⓤⓢ -t̬|i -ier -i.əʳ, ⓤⓢ -i.ɚ -iest -i.ɪst, -i.əst -ily -əl.i, -ɪ.li -iness -ɪ.nəs, -ɪ.nɪs
Weill *English surname:* wiːl, vaɪl *German composer:* vaɪl
Weimar ˈvaɪ.mɑːʳ, ⓤⓢ -mɑːr
Weinberger ˈwaɪnˌbɜː.gəʳ, ˈwaɪm-, ⓤⓢ ˈwaɪnˌbɝː.gɚ
Weinstein ˈwaɪn.stiːn
weir, W~ wɪəʳ **weir** ⓤⓢ wɪr -s -z
weird wɪəd, ⓤⓢ wɪrd -er -əʳ, ⓤⓢ -ɚ -est -ɪst, -əst -ly -li -ness -nəs, -nɪs
weirdo ˈwɪə.dəʊ, ⓤⓢ ˈwɪr.doʊ -s -z
Weiss vaɪs
Weisshorn ˈvaɪs.hɔːn, ⓤⓢ -hɔːrn
Weissmuller ˈvaɪsˌmʊl.əʳ, ˈwaɪs-, ⓤⓢ ˈwaɪsˌmʌl.ɚ
Weland ˈweɪ.lənd, ˈwiː-
Welbeck ˈwel.bek
Welby ˈwel.bi
welch, W~ v, adj weltʃ -es -ɪz -ing -ɪŋ -ed -t -er/s -əʳ/z, ⓤⓢ -ɚ/z
Welcombe ˈwel.kəm
welcom|e ˈwel.kəm -es -z -ing -ɪŋ -ed -d
weld weld -s -z -ing -ɪŋ -ed -ɪd -er/s -əʳ/z, ⓤⓢ -ɚ/z
Weldon ˈwel.dən
welfare ˈwel.feəʳ, ⓤⓢ -fer ˌ**welfare** ˈ**state** ⓤⓢ ˈ**welfare** ˌ**state**
Welford ˈwel.fəd, ⓤⓢ -fɚd
welkin ˈwel.kɪn
well wel -s -z -ing -ɪŋ -ed -d -ness -nəs, -nɪs
we'll (= **we will** or **we shall**) *strong form:* wiːl; *weak form:* wil
Note: see note for **we**
well-advised ˌwel.ədˈvaɪzd *stress shift:* ˌ**well-advised** ˈ**action**
Welland ˈwel.ənd
well-appointed ˌwel.əˈpɔɪn.tɪd, ⓤⓢ -t̬ɪd *stress shift:* ˌ**well-appointed** ˈ**office**
well-balanced ˌwelˈbæl.əntst *stress shift:* ˌ**well-balanced** ˈ**diet**
well-behaved ˌwel.bɪˈheɪvd, -bəˈ- *stress shift:* ˌ**well-behaved** ˈ**dog**
well-being ˌwelˈbiː.ɪŋ, ˈ-ˌ--
well-born ˌwelˈbɔːn, ⓤⓢ -ˈbɔːrn *stress shift:* ˌ**well-born** ˈ**lady**
well-bred ˌwelˈbred *stress shift:* ˌ**well-bred** ˈ**child**
well-built ˌwelˈbɪlt *stress shift:* ˌ**well-built** ˈ**person**
Wellby ˈwel.bi
well-chosen ˌwelˈtʃəʊ.zən, ⓤⓢ -ˈtʃoʊ- *stress shift:* ˌ**well-chosen** ˈ**words**
Wellcome ˈwel.kəm
well-conducted ˌwel.kənˈdʌk.tɪd *stress shift:* ˌ**well-conducted** ˈ**scheme**
well-connected ˌwel.kəˈnek.tɪd *stress shift:* ˌ**well-connected** ˈ**person**
well-cooked ˌwelˈkʊkt *stress shift:* ˌ**well-cooked** ˈ**food**
well-disposed ˌwel.dɪˈspəʊzd, ⓤⓢ -ˈspoʊzd *stress shift:* ˌ**well-disposed** ˈ**manner**

well-do|er ˈwelˌduː|.əʳ, ˌ-ˈ--, ⓤⓢ ˈwelˌduː|.ɚ -ers -əz, ⓤⓢ -ɚz -ing -ɪŋ
Welldon ˈwel.dən
well-done ˌwelˈdʌn *stress shift:* ˌ**well-done** ˈ**food**
well-earned ˌwelˈɜːnd, ⓤⓢ -ˈɝːnd *stress shift:* ˌ**well-earned** ˈ**rest**
Weller ˈwel.əʳ, ⓤⓢ -ɚ
Welles welz
Wellesley ˈwelz.li
well-fed ˌwelˈfed *stress shift:* ˌ**well-fed** ˈ**cat**
well-formed ˌwelˈfɔːmd, ⓤⓢ -ˈfɔːrmd *stress shift:* ˌ**well-formed** ˈ**sentence**
well-found ˌwelˈfaʊnd *stress shift:* ˌ**well-found** ˈ**ship**

well-groomed ˌwelˈgruːmd *stress shift:* ˌ**well-groomed** ˈ**man**
well-grounded ˌwelˈgraʊn.dɪd *stress shift:* ˌ**well-grounded** ˈ**argument**
well-heeled ˌwelˈhiːld *stress shift:* ˌ**well-heeled** ˈ**owner**
wellie ˈwel.i **-s** -z
well-informed ˌwel.ɪnˈfɔːmd, (US) -ˈfɔːrmd *stress shift:* ˌ**well-informed** ˈ**journalist**
Welling ˈwel.ɪŋ
Wellingborough ˈwel.ɪŋ.bᵊr.ə, (US) -bɚ.oʊ
wellington, W~ ˈwel.ɪŋ.tən **-s** -z ˌ**wellington** ˈ**boot** (US) ˈ**wellington** ˌ**boot**
wellingtonia ˌwel.ɪŋˈtəʊ.ni.ə, (US) -ˈtoʊ- **-s** -z
well-intentioned ˌwel.ɪnˈten.tʃᵊnd *stress shift:* ˌ**well-intentioned** ˈ**action**
well-judged ˌwelˈdʒʌdʒd *stress shift:* ˌ**well-judged** ˈ**shot**
well-known ˌwelˈnəʊn, (US) -ˈnoʊn *stress shift:* ˌ**well-known** ˈ**writer**
well-made ˌwelˈmeɪd *stress shift:* ˌ**well-made** ˈ**product**
well-meaning ˌwelˈmiː.nɪŋ *stress shift:* ˌ**well-meaning** ˈ**action**
well-meant ˌwelˈment *stress shift:* ˌ**well-meant** ˈ**gesture**
well-nigh ˌwelˈnaɪ *stress shift:* ˌ**well-nigh im**ˈ**possible**
well-off ˌwelˈɒf, (US) -ˈɑːf *stress shift:* ˌ**well-off** ˈ**person**
well-ordered ˌwelˈɔː.dəd, (US) -ˈɔːr.dɚd *stress shift:* ˌ**well-ordered** ˈ**household**
well-proportioned ˌwel.prəˈpɔː.ʃᵊnd, (US) -ˈpɔːr- *stress shift:* ˌ**well-proportioned** ˈ**room**
well-read ˌwelˈred *stress shift:* ˌ**well-read** ˈ**person**
well-rounded ˌwelˈraʊn.dɪd *stress shift:* ˌ**well-rounded** ˈ**character**
Wells welz
well-spoken ˌwelˈspəʊ.kᵊn, (US) -ˈspoʊ- *stress shift:* ˌ**well-spoken** ˈ**person**
wellspring ˈwel.sprɪŋ **-s** -z
well-thumbed ˌwelˈθʌmd *stress shift:* ˌ**well-thumbed** ˈ**book**
well-timed ˌwelˈtaɪmd *stress shift:* ˌ**well-timed** ˈ**action**
well-to-do ˌwel.təˈduː *stress shift:* ˌ**well-to-do** ˈ**person**
well-versed ˌwelˈvɜːst, (US) -ˈvɝːst *stress shift:* ˌ**well-versed** ˈ**teacher**
well-wisher ˈwelˌwɪʃ.əʳ, ˌ-ˈ--, (US) ˈwelˌwɪʃ.ɚ **-s** -z
well-worn ˌwelˈwɔːn, (US) -ˈwɔːrn *stress shift:* ˌ**well-worn** ˈ**phrase**
well|y ˈwel|.i **-ies** -iz
Welsch weltʃ
welsh, W~ welʃ **-es** -ɪz **-ing** -ɪŋ **-ed** -t **-er/s** -əʳ/z, (US) -ɚ/z ˌ**Welsh** ˈ**dresser**; ˌ**Welsh** ˈ**Nationalists**; ˌ**Welsh** ˈ**rarebit**
Welsh|man ˈwelʃ|.mən **-men** -mən
Welshpool ˈwelʃ.puːl, ˌ-ˈ-

Welsh|woman ˈwelʃ|ˌwʊm.ən **-women** -ˌwɪm.ɪn
welt welt **-s** -s **-ing** -ɪŋ, (US) ˈwel.tɪŋ **-ed** -ɪd, (US) ˈwel.tɪd
weltanschauung, W~ ˈvelt.ænˌʃaʊ.ʊŋ, (US) -ɑːnˌ-
welt|er ˈwel.t|əʳ, (US) -t|ɚ **-ers** -əz, (US) -ɚz **-ering** -ᵊr.ɪŋ **-ered** -əd, (US) -ɚd
welterweight ˈwel.tə.weɪt, (US) -tɚ- **-s** -s
weltschmerz, W~ ˈvelt.ʃmeəts, (US) -ʃmerts
Welty ˈwel.ti, (US) -ti
Welwyn ˈwel.ɪn ˌ**Welwyn** ˌ**Garden** ˈ**City**
Wembley ˈwem.bli
Wemyss wiːmz
wen wen **-s** -z
Wenceslas ˈwen.sɪ.sləs, -sə-, -slæs, (US) -sɪ.slɑːs, -slɔːs
wench wentʃ **-es** -ɪz
wend wend **-s** -z **-ing** -ɪŋ **-ed** -ɪd
Wend wend, vend **-s** -z **-ic** -ɪk **-ish** -ɪʃ
Wendell ˈwen.dᵊl
Wenders ˈwen.dəz, (US) ˈven.dɚz
Wendover ˈwen.dəʊ.vəʳ, (US) -doʊ.vɚ
Wendy ˈwen.di ˈ**Wendy** ˌ**house**
Wengen ˈveŋ.ən
Wenger ˈveŋ.gəʳ, (US) -gɚ
Wengern Alp ˌveŋ.ənˈælp, (US) -ɚnˈ-
Wenham ˈwen.əm
Wenlock ˈwen.lɒk, (US) -lɑːk ˌ**Wenlock** ˈ**Edge**
Wensleydale ˈwenz.li.deɪl
went (from **go**) went
Wentworth ˈwent.wəθ, -wɜːθ, (US) -wɚθ, -wɝːθ
wept (from **weep**) wept
were (from **be**) *strong forms:* wɜːʳ, (US) wɝː; *weak forms:* wəʳ, (US) wɚ
Note: Weak-form word. The strong form is used for emphasis (e.g. 'You **were** a long time') and for contrast (e.g. 'what they were and what they might have been'). The strong form is also usual in final position (e.g. 'We didn't know where we were'). The weak form is used elsewhere.
we're (= **we are**) wɪəʳ, (US) wɪr
weren't wɜːnt, (US) wɝːnt
werewol|f ˈweə.wʊl|f, ˈwɪə-, ˈwɜː-, (US) ˈwer-, ˈwɪr-, ˈwɝː- **-ves** -vz
Werner ˈwɜː.nəʳ; *as if German:* ˈveə-; (US) ˈwɝː.nɚ; *as if German:* (US) ˈvɝː-
wert (from **be**) *strong forms:* wɜːt, (US) wɝːt; *weak forms:* wət, (US) wɚt
Note: Archaic form; see information at **were**.
Weser ˈveɪ.zəʳ, (US) -zɚ

> Note: /ˈwiː.zəʳ/ (US) /-zɚ/ is necessary for rhyme in Browning's 'Pied Piper', but this pronunciation is exceptional.

Wesker ˈwes.kəʳ, (US) -kɚ

Wesley ˈwez.li, ˈwes-, (US) ˈwes-, ˈwez-

> Note: Most people bearing the name **Wesley** pronounce /ˈwes.li/.

Wesleyan ˈwez.li.ən, ˈwes-, (US) ˈwes-, ˈwez- **-s** -z **-ism** -ɪ.zᵊm

> Note: /ˈwes-/ appears to be the more usual pronunciation among Wesleyans; with those who are not Wesleyans /ˈwez-/ is probably the commoner form in British English. There exists also an old-fashioned pronunciation /wesˈliː.ən/.

Wessex ˈwes.ɪks
west, W~ west ˌ**West** ˈ**Bank** *stress shift:* ˌ**West Bank** ˈ**settlement** ˌ**West** ˈ**Coast** *stress shift:* ˌ**West Coast** ˈ**singer** ˈ**West** ˌ**Country**; ˌ**West** ˈ**End** *stress shift:* ˌ**West End** ˈ**play** ˌ**West** ˈ**Indian**; ˌ**West** ˈ**Indies**; ˌ**West** ˈ**Point** (US) ˈ**West** ˌ**Point**; ˌ**West** ˌ**Side** ˈ**Story** (US) ˈ**West Side** ˌ**Story**; ˌ**West Vir**ˈ**ginia**
westbound ˈwest.baʊnd
Westbourne ˈwest.bɔːn, -bən, (US) -bɔːrn, -bɚn
West Bridgford ˌwestˈbrɪdʒ.fəd, (US) -fɚd
Westbrook ˈwest.brʊk
Westbury ˈwest.bᵊr.i
Westchester ˈwestˌtʃes.təʳ, (US) -tɚ
Westcott ˈwest.kət
Westergate ˈwes.tə.geɪt, (US) -tɚ-
Westerham ˈwes.tᵊr.əm
westering ˈwes.tᵊr.ɪŋ
westerl|y ˈwes.tᵊl|.i, (US) -tɚ.l|i **-ies** -iz
western, W~ ˈwes.tən, (US) -tɚn **-s** -z **-er/s** -əʳ/z, (US) -ɚ/z **-most** -məʊst, (US) -moʊst ˌ**Western Aus**ˈ**tralia**; ˈ**Western** ˌ**Isles**; ˌ**Western** ˈ**Isles**
westernization, -isa- ˌwes.tᵊn.aɪˈzeɪ.ʃᵊn, -ɪˈ-, (US) -tɚ.nəˈ-
westerniz|e, -is|e ˈwes.tən.aɪz, (US) -tɚ.naɪz **-es** -ɪz **-ing** -ɪŋ **-ed** -d
Westfield ˈwest.fiːld
Westgate ˈwest.geɪt, -gɪt
Westhill ˈwest.hɪl
Westhoughton ˌwestˈhɔː.tᵊn, (US) -ˈhɑː-, -ˈhɔː-
Westinghouse ˈwes.tɪŋ.haʊs
Westlake ˈwest.leɪk
Westland® ˈwest.lənd
Westlife ˈwest.laɪf
Westly ˈwest.li
Westmeath ˌwestˈmiːð
West Mersea ˌwestˈmɜː.zi, (US) -ˈmɝː-
Westminster westˈmɪnt.stəʳ, ˈ---, (US) westˈmɪnt.stɚ, ˈ--- ˌ**Westminster** ˈ**Abbey**
Westmor(e)land ˈwest.mᵊl.ənd, (US) -mɔːr.lənd
west-northwest ˌwest.nɔːθˈwest, (US) -nɔːrθˈ-; *nautical pronunciation:* -nɔːˈ-, (US) -nɔːrˈ-

W

Pronouncing the letters **WH**

The consonant digraph **wh** is found in word or morpheme-initial position in English, and usually pronounced as /w/ in British English and /hw/ in US English. The phonemic symbols /hw/ together represent a voiceless version of /w/, for which the phonetic symbol is /ʍ/. The realization /hw/ also occurs amongst some speakers of British English. In this dictionary, the transcription /*h*w/ is used to cover both variants, e.g.:

when	*h*wen
where	*h*weəʳ (US) *h*wer

Another realization of the consonant digraph **wh** is /h/, e.g.:

who	huː
wholesome	ˈhəʊl.səm (US) ˈhoʊl-

Weston ˈwes.tən
Weston-super-Mare ˌwes.tənˌsuː.pəˈmeəʳ, -ˌsjuː-; -ˈsuː.pə.meəʳ, -ˈsjuː-, (US) -ˌsuː.pɚˈmer, -ˈsuː.pɚ.mer
Westphali|a ˌwest*ˈ*feɪ.li|.ə, ˈ-lj|ə, (US) ˈ-li|.ə, -ˈfeɪl.j|ə **-an/s** -ən/z
Westray ˈwes.treɪ
Westside ˈwest.saɪd
west-southwest ˌwest.saʊθˈwest; *nautical pronunciation:* -saʊˈ-
westward ˈwest.wəd, (US) -wɚd **-s** -z **-ly** -li
Westward Ho! ˌwest.wədˈhəʊ, (US) -wɚdˈhoʊ
Westwood ˈwest.wʊd
wet wet **-ter** -əʳ, (US) ˈwet̬.ɚ **-test** -ɪst, -əst, (US) ˈwet̬.ɪst, -əst **-s** -s **-ting** -ɪŋ, (US) ˈwet̬.ɪŋ **-ted** -ɪd, (US) ˈwet̬.ɪd **-ly** -li **-ness** -nəs, -nɪs ˌ**wet** ˈ**blanket;** ˈ**wet** ˌ**suit; (still)** ˌ**wet behind the** ˈ**ears**
wetback ˈwet.bæk **-s** -s
wether ˈweð.əʳ, (US) -ɚ **-s** -z
Wetherby ˈweð.ə.bi, (US) ˈ-ɚ-
wetland ˈwet.lənd, (US) -lænd **-s** -z
wet-look ˈwet.lʊk
wet nurs|e ˈwet.nɜːs, (US) -nɝːs **-es** -ɪz
wetsuit ˈwet.suːt, -sjuːt, (US) -suːt **-s** -s
we've (= **we have**) *strong form:* wiːv; *weak form:* wiv
Note: Weak-form word. The weak form is usually found when the word is unstressed, but the strong form may also be used in this situation.
Wexford ˈweks.fəd, (US) -fɚd
Wey weɪ
Weybridge ˈweɪ.brɪdʒ
Weyman ˈweɪ.mən
Weymouth ˈweɪ.məθ
whack *h*wæk **-s** -s **-ing/s** -ɪŋ/z **-ed** -t **-er/s** -əʳ/z, (US) -ɚ/z
whacko ˈ*h*wæk.əʊ, (US) -oʊ
whack|y ˈ*h*wæk|.i **-ier** -i.əʳ, (US) -i.ɚ **-iest** -i.ɪst, -i.əst **-ily** -əl.i, -ɪ.li
whal|e, W~ *h*weɪl **-es** -z **-ing** -ɪŋ **-er/s** -əʳ/z, (US) -ɚ/z ˌ**have a** ˈ**whale of a** ˌ**time**
whalebone ˈ*h*weɪl.bəʊn, (US) -boʊn
whale-oil ˈ*h*weɪl.ɔɪl
Whaley ˈ*h*weɪ.li
Whalley *surname:* ˈ*h*weɪ.li, ˈ*h*wɔː-, ˈ*h*wɒl.i, (US) ˈ*h*weɪ.li, ˈ*h*wɑː.li *abbey near Blackburn:* ˈ*h*wɔː.li, (US) ˈ*h*wɑː-
wham *h*wæm **-s** -z **-ming** -ɪŋ **-med** -d
whammo ˈ*h*wæm.əʊ, (US) -oʊ
whamm|y ˈ*h*wæm|.i **-ies** -iz
whamo ˈ*h*wæm.əʊ, (US) -oʊ
whang *h*wæŋ **-s** -z **-ing** -ɪŋ **-ed** -d
whangee ˌ*h*wæŋˈgiː, -ˈiː, (US) -ˈgiː
whar|f *h*wɔː|f, (US) *h*wɔːr|f **-ves** -vz **-fs** -fs
wharfage ˈ*h*wɔː.fɪdʒ, (US) ˈ*h*wɔːr-
Wharfedale ˈ*h*wɔːf.deɪl, (US) ˈ*h*wɔːrf-
wharfinger ˈ*h*wɔː.fɪn.dʒəʳ, (US) ˈ*h*wɔːr.fɪn.dʒɚ **-s** -z
Wharton ˈ*h*wɔː.tən, (US) ˈ*h*wɔːr-
what *h*wɒt, (US) *h*wʌt, *h*wɑːt
whatchamacallit ˈ*h*wɒtʃ.ə.məˌkɔː.lɪt, (US) ˈ*h*wʌtʃ-
what-d'you-call-it ˈ*h*wɒt.dʒəˌkɔː.lɪt, -djəˌ-, -dʒuˌ-, -djuˌ-, (US) ˈ*h*wʌt̬.i.jəˌkɔː-, ˈ*h*wʌtʃ.əˌ-, -ˌkɑː-
what-d'you-ma-call-it ˈ*h*wɒt.dʒə.məˌkɔː.lɪt, -djə-, -dʒu-, -dju-, (US) ˈ*h*wʌt̬.i.jə.məˌkɔː-, -*h*wʌtʃ.ə-, -kɑː-
whate'er *h*wɒtˈeəʳ, (US) *h*wʌtˈer, *h*wɑːt-
Whateley ˈ*h*weɪt.li
whatever *h*wɒtˈev.əʳ, (US) *h*wʌtˈev.ɚ, *h*wɑːt-
Whatley ˈ*h*wɒt.li, (US) ˈ*h*wɑːt-
Whatman ˈ*h*wɒt.mən, (US) ˈ*h*wɑːt-
Whatmough ˈ*h*wɒt.məʊ, (US) ˈ*h*wɑːt.moʊ
whatnot ˈ*h*wɒt.nɒt, (US) ˈ*h*wʌt.nɑːt, ˈ*h*wɑːt- **-s** -s
what's-her-name ˈ*h*wɒt.sən.eɪm, (US) ˈ*h*wʌt.sɚ.neɪm, ˈ*h*wɑːt-
what's-his-name ˈ*h*wɒt.sɪz.neɪm, (US) ˈ*h*wʌt-, ˈ*h*wɑːt-
whatsit ˈ*h*wɒt.sɪt, (US) ˈ*h*wʌt- **-s** -s
whatsoe'er ˌ*h*wɒt.səʊˈeəʳ, (US) ˌ*h*wʌt.soʊˈer, ˌ*h*wɑːt-
whatsoever ˌ*h*wɒt.səʊˈev.əʳ, (US) ˌ*h*wʌt.soʊˈev.ɚ, ˌ*h*wɑːt-
wheal *h*wiːl **-s** -z
wheat *h*wiːt **-en** -ən
wheatgerm ˈ*h*wiːt.dʒɜːm, (US) -dʒɝːm
Wheathampstead ˈ*h*wiː.təmp.sted, ˈ*h*wet.əmp-
Wheatley ˈ*h*wiːt.li
wheatmeal ˈ*h*wiːt.miːl
Wheaton ˈ*h*wiː.tən
Wheatstone ˈ*h*wiːt.stən, -stəʊn, (US) -stoʊn, -stən
wheedl|e ˈ*h*wiː.dəl **-es** -z **-ing** -ɪŋ, ˈ*h*wiːd.lɪŋ **-ed** -d **-er/s** -əʳ/z, ˈ*h*wiːd.ləʳ/z, (US) ˈ*h*wiː.dəl.əʳ/z, ˈ*h*wiːd.lɚ/z
wheel *h*wiːl **-s** -z **-ing** -ɪŋ **-ed** -d ˈ**wheel** ˌ**clamp**
wheelbarrow ˈ*h*wiːlˌbær.əʊ, (US) -ˌber.oʊ, -ˌbær- **-s** -z
wheelbas|e ˈ*h*wiːl.beɪs **-es** -ɪz
wheelchair ˈ*h*wiːl.tʃeəʳ, (US) -tʃer **-s** -z
wheeler, W~ ˈ*h*wiː.ləʳ, (US) -lɚ **-s** -z
wheeler-dealer ˌ*h*wiː.ləˈdiː.ləʳ, (US) -lɚˈdiː.lɚ **-s** -z
wheelhou|se ˈ*h*wiːl.haʊ|s **-ses** -zɪz
wheelie ˈ*h*wiː.li **-s** -z ˈ**wheelie** ˌ**bin**
Wheelock ˈ*h*wiː.lək
wheelwright, wheelright, W~ ˈ*h*wiːl.raɪt **-s** -s
Wheen ˈ*h*wiːn
wheez|e *h*wiːz **-es** -ɪz **-ing** -ɪŋ **-ed** -d **-y** -i **-ier** -i.əʳ, (US) -i.ɚ **-iest** -i.ɪst, -i.əst **-iness** -ɪ.nəs, -ɪ.nɪs
Whelan ˈ*h*wiː.lən
whelk welk, (US) *h*welk **-s** -s
whelm *h*welm **-s** -z **-ing** -ɪŋ **-ed** -d
whelp *h*welp **-s** -s **-ing** -ɪŋ **-ed** -t
when *h*wen
whence *h*wents
whene'er *h*wenˈeəʳ, (US) -ˈer
whenever *h*wenˈev.əʳ, *h*wənˈ-, (US) -ɚ
whensoever ˌ*h*wen.səʊˈev.əʳ, (US) -soʊˈev.ɚ
where *h*weəʳ, (US) *h*wer
whereabout ˌ*h*weə.rəˈbaʊt, (US) ˈ*h*wer.əˌ-
whereabouts n ˈ*h*weə.rə.baʊts, (US) ˈ*h*wer.ə-
whereabouts adv *interrogation:* ˌ*h*weə.rəˈbaʊts, (US) ˌ*h*wer.əˈ-
whereas *h*weəˈræz, *h*wər-, (US) *h*werˈæz, *h*wɚ-
whereat *h*weəˈræt, *h*wər-, (US) *h*werˈæt, *h*wɚ-
whereby *h*weəˈbaɪ, (US) *h*wer-
where'er *h*weəˈreəʳ, *h*wə-, (US) *h*werˈer, *h*wɚ-
wherefore ˈ*h*weə.fɔːʳ, (US) ˈ*h*wer.fɔːr **-s** -z
wherein *h*weəˈrɪn, (US) *h*werˈɪn
whereof *h*weəˈrɒv, (US) *h*werˈɑːv
whereon *h*weəˈrɒn, (US) *h*werˈɑːn
wheresoe'er ˌ*h*weə.səʊˈeəʳ, (US) ˌ*h*wer.soʊˈer
wheresoever ˌ*h*weə.səʊˈev.əʳ, (US) ˌ*h*wer.soʊˈev.ɚ
whereto *h*weəˈtuː, (US) *h*wer-
whereunder *h*weəˈrʌn.dəʳ, (US) *h*werˈʌn.dɚ
whereunto ˌ*h*weə.rʌnˈtuː, (US) ˌ*h*wer.ʌnˈ-

whereupon ˌhweə.rəˈpɒn, ˈ--ˌ-, US ˈhwer.əˌpɑːn
wherever hweəˈrev.əʳ, hwər-, US hwerˈev.ɚ, hwɚ-
wherewith hweəˈwɪθ, -ˈwɪð, US hwer-
wherewithal n ˈhweə.wɪ.ðɔːl, US ˈhwer-, -θɔːl, -ðɑːl, -θɑːl
wherewithal adv ˌhweə.wɪˈðɔːl, ˈ---, US ˈhwer.wɪ.ðɔːl, -θɔːl, -ðɑːl, -θɑːl
Whernside ˈhwɜːn.saɪd, US ˈhwɝːn-
wherr|y ˈhwer|.i **-ies** -iz
whet hwet **-s** -s **-ting** -ɪŋ, US ˈhwet̬.ɪŋ **-ted** -ɪd, US ˈhwet̬.ɪd
whether ˈhweð.əʳ, US -ɚ
whetstone, W~ ˈhwet.stəʊn, US -stoʊn **-s** -z
whew ʍ̥, fjuː

> Note: This is an attempt at a symbolic representation of an interjection used to indicate that the speaker is either surprised, or suffering from the heat. The sound is related to a whistle (falling or rising-falling pitch), but in speech is more usually a whispered sound. The pronunciation /fjuː/ is an alternative based on the spelling.

Whewell ˈhjuː.əl, -el, -ɪl; hjʊəl, US ˈhjuː.əl
whey hweɪ
which hwɪtʃ
whichever hwɪˈtʃev.əʳ, US -ɚ
whick|er, W~ ˈhwɪk|.əʳ, US -ɚ **-ers** -əz, US -ɚz **-ering** -ᵊr.ɪŋ **-ered** -əd, US -ɚd
Whickham ˈhwɪk.əm
whiff hwɪf **-s** -s **-ing** -ɪŋ **-ed** -t
Whiffen ˈhwɪf.ɪn, -ən
Whig hwɪg **-s** -z
Whigg|ery ˈhwɪg|.ᵊr.i **-ism** -ɪ.zᵊm
Whiggish ˈhwɪg.ɪʃ
Whigham ˈhwɪg.əm
whil|e ˈhwaɪl **-es** -z **-ing** -ɪŋ **-ed** -d
whilst hwaɪlst
whim hwɪm **-s** -z
whimbrel ˈhwɪm.brᵊl **-s** -z

whimp|er ˈhwɪm.p|əʳ, US -p|ɚ **-ers** -əz, US -ɚz **-ering/ly** -ᵊr.ɪŋ/li **-ered** -əd, US -ɚd
whimsic|al ˈhwɪm.zɪ.k|ᵊl, -sɪ-, US -zɪ- **-ally** -ᵊl.i, -li **-alness** -ᵊl.nəs, -nɪs
whimsicality ˌhwɪm.zɪˈkæl.ə.ti, -sɪˈ-, -ɪ.ti, US -zɪˈkæl.ə.t̬i
whims|y ˈhwɪm.z|i **-ies** -iz
whin hwɪn **-s** -z
whinchat ˈhwɪn.tʃæt **-s** -s
whin|e hwaɪn **-es** -z **-ing/ly** -ɪŋ/li **-ed** -d **-er/s** -əʳ/z, US -ɚ/z
whing|e hwɪndʒ **-es** -ɪz **-(e)ing** -ɪŋ **-ed** -d **-er/s** -əʳ/z, US -ɚ/z
whinn|y ˈhwɪn|.i **-ies** -iz **-ying** -i.ɪŋ **-ied** -id
whin|y ˈhwaɪ.n|i **-ier** -i.əʳ, US -i.ɚ **-iest** -i.ɪst, -i.əst **-iness** -ɪ.nəs, -ɪ.nɪs
whip hwɪp **-s** -s **-ping/s** -ɪŋ/z **-ped** -t **have the ˌwhip ˈhand**
whipcord ˈhwɪp.kɔːd, US -kɔːrd
whiplash ˈhwɪp.læʃ
whipp|er-in ˌhwɪp|.əʳˈɪn, US -ɚˈ- **-ers-in** -əzˈɪn, US -ɚzˈ-
whippersnapper ˈhwɪp.əˌsnæp.əʳ, US -ɚˌsnæp.ɚ **-s** -z
whippet ˈhwɪp.ɪt **-s** -s
whipping-boy ˈhwɪp.ɪŋ.bɔɪ **-s** -z
Whippingham ˈhwɪp.ɪŋ.əm
Whipple ˈhwɪp.ᵊl
whippoorwill ˈhwɪp.ə.wɪl, -ʊə-, -pʊə-, -pɔː-, US ˈ-ɚ- **-s** -z
whip-round ˈhwɪp.raʊnd **-s** -z
whipsaw ˈhwɪp.sɔː, US -sɑː, -sɔː **-s** -z
Whipsnade ˈhwɪp.sneɪd
whir hwɜːʳ, US hwɝː **-s** -z **-ring/s** -ɪŋ/z **-red** -d
whirl hwɜːl, US hwɝːl **-s** -z **-ing** -ɪŋ **-ed** -d
whirligig ˈhwɜː.lɪ.gɪg, US ˈhwɝː- **-s** -z
whirlpool ˈhwɜːl.puːl, US ˈhwɝːl- **-s** -z
whirlwind ˈhwɜːl.wɪnd, US ˈhwɝːl- **-s** -z
whirlybird ˈhwɜː.lɪ.bɜːd, US ˈhwɝː.lɪ.bɝːd **-s** -z
whirr hwɜːʳ, US hwɝː **-s** -z **-ing/s** -ɪŋ/z **-ed** -d
whisk hwɪsk **-s** -s **-ing** -ɪŋ **-ed** -t
Whiskas® ˈhwɪs.kəz
whisker ˈhwɪs.kəʳ, US -kɚ **-s** -z **-ed** -d
whiskey ˈhwɪs.ki **-s** -z
whisk|y ˈhwɪs.k|i **-ies** -iz
whisp|er ˈhwɪs.p|əʳ, US -p|ɚ **-ers** -əz, US -ɚz **-ering/s** -ᵊr.ɪŋ/z **-ered** -əd, US -ɚd **-erer/s** -ᵊr.əʳ/z, US -ɚ.ɚ/z
whist hwɪst ˈ**whist** ˌ**drive**
whistl|e ˈhwɪs.ᵊl **-es** -z **-ing** -ɪŋ, ˈhwɪs.lɪŋ **-ed** -d ˌ**blow the** ˈ**whistle** ˌ**on**
whistle-blower ˈhwɪs.ᵊlˌbləʊ.əʳ, US -ˌbloʊ.ɚ **-s** -z
whistler, W~ ˈhwɪs.ləʳ, -ᵊl.əʳ, US ˈ-lɚ, -ᵊl.ɚ **-s** -z
whistle-stop ˈhwɪs.ᵊl.stɒp, US -stɑːp **-s** -s **-ping** -ɪŋ **-ped** -t ˌ**whistle-stop** ˈ**tour**
whit, W~ hwɪt
Whitaker ˈhwɪt.ə.kəʳ, ˈ-ɪ-, US hwɪt̬.ə.kɚ
Whitbread ˈhwɪt.bred
Whitburn ˈhwɪt.bɜːn, US -bɝːn
Whitby ˈhwɪt.bi
Whitchurch ˈhwɪt.tʃɜːtʃ, US -tʃɝːtʃ
Whitcombe ˈhwɪt.kəm
Whitcut ˈhwɪt.kʌt
whit|e, W~ hwaɪt **-es** -s **-er** -əʳ, US ˈhwaɪ.t̬ɚ **-est** -ɪst, -əst, US ˈhwaɪ.t̬ɪst, -t̬əst **-ely** -li **-eness** -nəs, -nɪs **-ing** -ɪŋ, US ˈhwaɪ.t̬ɪŋ **-ed** -ɪd, US ˈhwaɪ.t̬ɪd ˌ**white** ˈ**elephant;** ˌ**white** ˈ**flag;** ˈ**white** ˌ**goods;** ˈ**White** ˌ**House;** ˌ**white** ˈ**knight;** ˌ**white** ˈ**lie;** ˈ**white** ˌ**man;** ˌ**white** ˈ**paper** US ˈ**white** ˌ**paper;** ˌ**white** ˈ**sauce** US ˈ**white** ˌ**sauce;** ˌ**white** ˈ**trash;** ˌ**white** ˈ**wedding;** ˌ**white as a** ˈ**sheet**
whitebait ˈhwaɪt.beɪt
whitebeard ˈhwaɪt.bɪəd, US -bɪrd **-s** -z **-ed** -ɪd
whiteboard ˈhwaɪt.bɔːd, US -bɔːrd **-s** -z
whitecap ˈhwaɪt.kæp **-s** -s
Whitechapel ˈhwaɪtˌtʃæp.ᵊl
white-collar ˌhwaɪtˈkɒl.əʳ, US -ˈkɑː.lɚ *stress shift:* ˌ**white-collar** ˈ**worker**
Whitefield ˈhwaɪt.fiːld, ˈhwɪt-
whitefl|y ˈhwaɪt.fl|aɪ **-ies** -aɪz
Whitefriars ˈhwaɪt.fraɪəz, -fraɪ.əz, ˌ-ˈ-, US ˈhwaɪt.fraɪ.ɚz, ˌ-ˈ-
Whitehall ˈhwaɪt.hɔːl, ˌ-ˈ-, US ˈhwaɪt.hɔːl, -hɑːl
Whitehaven ˈhwaɪtˌheɪ.vᵊn
whitehead, W~ ˈhwaɪt.hed **-s** -z
Whitehorn ˈhwaɪt.hɔːn, US -hɔːrn
Whitehorse ˈhwaɪt.hɔːs, US -hɔːrs
white-hot ˌhwaɪtˈhɒt, US -ˈhɑːt *stress shift:* ˌ**white-hot** ˈ**metal**
Whitehouse ˈhwaɪt.haʊs
Whitelaw ˈhwaɪt.lɔː, US -lɑː, -lɔː
Whiteley ˈhwaɪt.li
white-livered ˈhwaɪtˌlɪv.əd, ˌ-ˈ--, US -ɚd
whiten ˈhwaɪ.tᵊn **-s** -z **-ing** -ɪŋ, ˈhwaɪt.nɪŋ **-ed** -d
whitener ˈhwaɪt.nəʳ, ˈhwaɪ.tᵊn.əʳ, US ˈhwaɪt.nɚ, ˈhwaɪ.tᵊn.ɚ **-s** -z
whiteout ˈhwaɪt.aʊt **-s** -s
Whiteread ˈhwaɪt.riːd
Whiteside ˈhwaɪt.saɪd
whitethorn ˈhwaɪt.θɔːn, US -θɔːrn **-s** -z
whitethroat ˈhwaɪt.θrəʊt, US -θroʊt **-s** -s
whitewash ˈhwaɪt.wɒʃ, US -wɑːʃ **-es** -ɪz **-ing** -ɪŋ **-ed** -t **-er/s** -əʳ/z, US -ɚ/z
whitewater, W~ ˈhwaɪt.wɔː.təʳ, US -wɑː.t̬ɚ, -wɔː- ˌ**whitewater** ˈ**rafting**
whitewood ˈhwaɪt.wʊd
whitey ˈhwaɪ.ti, US -t̬i
Whitfield ˈhwɪt.fiːld
Whitgift ˈhwɪt.gɪft
whither ˈhwɪð.əʳ, US -ɚ
whithersoever ˌhwɪð.ə.səʊˈev.əʳ, US -ɚ.soʊˈev.ɚ
whiting, W~ ˈhwaɪ.tɪŋ, US -t̬ɪŋ **-s** -z
whitish ˈhwaɪ.tɪʃ, US -t̬ɪʃ
Whitlam ˈhwɪt.ləm
Whitley ˈhwɪt.li
whitlow ˈhwɪt.ləʊ, US -loʊ **-s** -z
Whitman ˈhwɪt.mən
Whitmarsh ˈhwɪt.mɑːʃ, US -mɑːrʃ
Whitmore ˈhwɪt.mɔːʳ, US -mɔːr
Whitney ˈhwɪt.ni
Whitstable ˈhwɪt.stə.bᵊl
Whitstone ˈhwɪt.stəʊn, -stᵊn, US -stoʊn, -stᵊn
Whitsun ˈhwɪt.sᵊn
Whitsunday ˌhwɪtˈsʌn.deɪ, -di; -sᵊnˈdeɪ **-s** -z
Whitsuntide ˈhwɪt.sᵊn.taɪd **-s** -z

Whittaker ˈhwɪt.ə.kəʳ, ˈ-ɪ-, US ˈhwɪt̬.ə.kɚ
Whittall ˈhwɪt.əl, -ɔːl, US ˈhwɪt̬-
Whittier ˈhwɪt.i.əʳ, US ˈhwɪt̬.i.ɚ
Whittingeham(e) ˈhwɪt.ɪn.dʒəm, US ˈhwɪt̬-
Whittington ˈhwɪt.ɪŋ.tən, US ˈhwɪt̬-
whittl|e, W~ ˈhwɪt.əl, US ˈhwɪt̬- **-es** -z **-ing** -ɪŋ, ˈhwɪt.lɪŋ **-ed** -d
Whittlesey ˈhwɪt.əl.si, US ˈhwɪt̬-
Whitworth ˈhwɪt.wəθ, -wɜːθ, US -wɚθ, -wɜːθ
whit|y ˈhwaɪ.t|i, US -t̬|i **-iness** -ɪ.nəs, -ɪ.nɪs
whiz, whizz hwɪz **-zes** -ɪz **-zing** -ɪŋ **-zed** -d ˌ**gee** ˈ**whiz(z)**; ˈ**whiz(z)** ˌ**kid**
whiz(z)-bang ˈhwɪz.bæŋ **-s** -z
who *strong form:* huː; *weak form:* hu ˌ**Who's** ˈ**Who**
Note: Weak-form word. The weak form is only found in unstressed syllables, and the /h/ is frequently not pronounced. The strong form is also found in unstressed syllables.
WHO ˌdʌb.əl.juːˌeɪtʃˈəʊ, US ˌdʌb.əl.juːˌeɪtʃˈoʊ, -jəˌ-
whoa hwəʊ, US hwoʊ
who'd huːd
whodun(n)it ˌhuːˈdʌn.ɪt **-s** -s
whoe'er huːˈeəʳ, hu-, US -ˈer
whoever huːˈev.əʳ, hu-, US -ɚ
whole həʊl, US hoʊl **-ness** -nəs, -nɪs **go the** ˌ**whole** ˈ**hog**
wholefood ˈhəʊl.fuːd, US ˈhoʊl- **-s** -z
wholegrain ˈhəʊl.greɪn, US ˈhoʊl-
whole-hearted ˌhəʊlˈhɑː.tɪd, US ˌhoʊlˈhɑːr.t̬ɪd **-ly** -li **-ness** -nəs, -nɪs *stress shift:* ˌ**whole-hearted** ˈ**effort**
wholemeal ˈhəʊl.miːl, US ˈhoʊl-
wholesale ˈhəʊl.seɪl, US ˈhoʊl-
wholesaler ˈhəʊlˌseɪ.ləʳ, US ˈhoʊlˌseɪ.lɚ **-s** -z
wholesom|e ˈhəʊl.səm, US ˈhoʊl- **-est** -ɪst, -əst **-ely** -li **-eness** -nəs, -nɪs
wholewheat ˈhəʊl.hwiːt, US ˌhoʊlˈhwiːt
wholism ˈhəʊ.lɪ.zəm, US ˈhoʊ-
wholistic həʊˈlɪs.tɪk, US hoʊ-
who'll huːl
wholly ˈhəʊl.li, ˈhəʊ-, US ˈhoʊl.li, ˈhoʊ-
whom huːm
whomever ˌhuːˈmev.əʳ, hʊˈ-
whomsoever ˌhuːm.səʊˈev.əʳ, ˌhʊm-, US -soʊˈev.ɚ
whoop hwuːp, huːp **-s** -s **-ing** -ɪŋ **-ed** -t
whoop-de-doo ˌwʊp.dɪˈduː, US -diˈ-, ˌwuːp-
whoopee n ˈhwʊp.i, US ˈhwuː.pi ˈ**whoopee** ˌ**cushion interj** hwʊˈpiː
Whoopi ˈhwʊp.i, US ˈhwʊp.i, ˈhwuː.pi
whooping-cough ˈhuː.pɪŋ.kɒf, US -kɑːf, ˈhʊp.ɪŋ-, ˈwuː.pɪŋ-, ˈwʊp.ɪŋ-
whoops hwʊps, US hwʊps, hwuːps
whoops-a-daisy ˈhwʊps.əˌdeɪ.zi, US ˈhwʊps-, ˈhwuːps-
whoosh hwʊʃ, US hwʊʃ, hwuːʃ **-es** -ɪz **-ing** -ɪŋ **-ed** -t
whop hwɒp, US hwɑːp **-s** -s **-ping/s** -ɪŋ/z **-ped** -t
whopper ˈhwɒp.əʳ, US ˈhwɑː.pɚ **-s** -z
whopping ˈhwɒp.ɪŋ, US ˈhwɑː.pɪŋ
whor|e hɔːʳ, US hɔːr **-es** -z **-ing** -ɪŋ **-ed** -d
who're ˈhuː.əʳ, hʊəʳ, hu.əʳ, US ˈhuː.ɚ, hʊɚ, hu.ɚ
whoredom ˈhɔː.dəm, US ˈhɔːr-
whorehou|se ˈhɔː.haʊ|s, US ˈhɔːr- **-ses** -zɪz
whoreson ˈhɔː.sən, US ˈhɔːr- **-s** -z
Whorf hwɔːf, US hwɔːrf
whorish ˈhɔː.rɪʃ, US ˈhɔːr.ɪʃ
whorl hwɜːl, US hwɜːl, hwɔːrl **-s** -z **-ed** -d
whortle ˈhwɜː.təl, US ˈhwɜː.t̬əl **-s** -z
whortleberr|y ˈhwɜː.təlˌber|.i, -bər-, US ˈhwɜː.t̬əlˌber- **-ies** -iz
who's huːz
whose huːz
whoso ˈhuː.səʊ, US -soʊ
whosoever ˌhuː.səʊˈev.əʳ, US -soʊˈev.ɚ
who've huːv
why hwaɪ **-s** -z
Whybrow ˈhwaɪ.braʊ
why'll hwaɪl
Whymper ˈhwɪm.pəʳ, US -pɚ
why're ˈhwaɪ.əʳ, US -ɚ
why's hwaɪz
Whyte hwaɪt
why've hwaɪv, ˈhwaɪ.əv
WI ˌdʌb.əl.juːˈaɪ
Wichita ˈwɪtʃ.ɪ.tɔː, ˈ-ə-, US -ə.tɔː, -tɑː
wick, W~ wɪk **-s** -s
wicked ˈwɪk.ɪd **-est** -ɪst, -əst **-ly** -li **-ness/es** -nəs/ɪz, -nɪs/ɪz
Wicken ˈwɪk.ən
Wickens ˈwɪk.ɪnz
wicker, W~ ˈwɪk.əʳ, US -ɚ
wickerwork ˈwɪk.ə.wɜːk, US -ɚ.wɜːk
wicket ˈwɪk.ɪt **-s** -s ˈ**wicket** ˌ**gate**
wicket-keeper ˈwɪk.ɪtˌkiː.pəʳ, US -pɚ **-s** -z
Wickford ˈwɪk.fəd, US -fɚd
Wickham ˈwɪk.əm
Wickliffe ˈwɪk.lɪf
Wicklow ˈwɪk.ləʊ, US -loʊ
Widdecombe, Widdicombe ˈwɪd.ɪ.kəm
Widdowson ˈwɪd.əʊ.sən, US -oʊ-, ˈ-ə-
wid|e waɪd **-es** -z **-er** -əʳ, US -ɚ **-est** -ɪst, -əst **-ely** -li **-eness** -nəs, -nɪs ˈ**wide** ˌ**boy**
wide-angle ˌwaɪdˈæŋ.gəl *stress shift:* ˌ**wide-angle** ˈ**lens**
wide-awake adj ˌwaɪd.əˈweɪk
Widecombe ˈwɪd.ɪ.kəm
wide-eyed ˌwaɪdˈaɪd, US ˈ-- *stress shift, British only:* ˌ**wide-eyed** ˈ**stare**
Widemouth ˈwɪd.məθ
widen ˈwaɪ.dən **-s** -z **-ing** -ɪŋ, ˈwaɪd.nɪŋ **-ed** -d
Wideopen ˈwaɪdˌəʊ.pən, US -ˌoʊ-
wide-ranging ˌwaɪdˈreɪn.dʒɪŋ *stress shift:* ˌ**wide-ranging** ˈ**interests**
widescreen ˈwaɪd.skriːn
widespread ˈwaɪd.spred
widgeon ˈwɪdʒ.ən, -ɪn **-s** -z
widget ˈwɪdʒ.ɪt **-s** -s
widish ˈwaɪ.dɪʃ
Widmerpool ˈwɪd.mə.puːl, US -mɚ-
Widnes ˈwɪd.nəs, -nɪs
widow ˈwɪd.əʊ, US -oʊ **-s** -z **-ed** -d
widower ˈwɪd.əʊ.əʳ, US -oʊ.ɚ **-s** -z
widowhood ˈwɪd.əʊ.hʊd, US -oʊ-
Widsith ˈwɪd.sɪθ
width wɪtθ, wɪdθ **-s** -s
wield wiːld **-s** -z **-ing** -ɪŋ **-ed** -ɪd
Wiener schnitzel ˌviː.nəˈʃnɪt.səl, US ˈviː.nəˌʃnɪt- **-s** -z
Wiesbaden ˈviːsˌbɑː.dən, ˈviːz-, ˌ-ˈ--, US ˈviːsˌbɑː-
Wiesenthal ˈwiː.zən.tɑːl, ˈviː-, US ˈwiː.zən.tɑːl, ˈviː-, -θɔːl
wi|fe waɪ|f **-ves** -vz
wife|hood ˈwaɪf|.hʊd **-less** -ləs, -lɪs
wifelike ˈwaɪf.laɪk
wifely ˈwaɪ.fli
wife-swapping ˈwaɪfˌswɒp.ɪŋ, US -ˌswɑː.pɪŋ
Wiffen ˈwɪf.ɪn
Wiffle ball® ˈwɪf.əlˌbɔːl, US -ˌbɑːl, -ˌbɔːl
wi-fi ˈwaɪ.faɪ
wig wɪg **-s** -z **-ging** -ɪŋ **-ged** -d
Wigan ˈwɪg.ən
wigeon ˈwɪdʒ.ən, -ɪn **-s** -z
Wiggin ˈwɪg.ɪn **-s** -z
wigging ˈwɪg.ɪŋ **-s** -z
wiggl|e ˈwɪg.əl **-es** -z **-ing** -ɪŋ, ˈwɪg.lɪŋ **-ed** -d
Wigglesworth ˈwɪg.əlz.wəθ, -wɜːθ, US -wɚθ, -wɜːθ
wiggly ˈwɪg.əl.i, ˈwɪg.li
wight, W~ waɪt **-s** -s
Wigley ˈwɪg.li
Wigmore ˈwɪg.mɔːʳ, US -mɔːr
Wigram ˈwɪg.rəm
Wigston ˈwɪg.stən
Wigton ˈwɪg.tən

Wigtown ˈwɪg.taʊn, -tən
Wigtownshire ˈwɪg.tən.ʃəʳ, -ʃɪəʳ, US -ʃɚ, -ʃɪr
wigwam ˈwɪg.wæm, US -wɑːm **-s** -z
Wii wiː **-s** -z
wiki ˈwɪ.ki **-s** -z
Wikileaks ˈwɪk.iˌliːks
Wikipedia ˌwɪk.ɪˈpiː.di.ə
Wilberforce ˈwɪl.bə.fɔːs, US -bɚ.fɔːrs
Wilbraham *surname:* ˈwɪl.brə.hæm, ˈ-brəm, ˈ-bri.əm, US ˈ-brə.hæm, ˈ-brəm **Great** *and* **Little** *in Cambridgeshire:* ˈwɪl.brəm, -brə.hæm
Wilbur ˈwɪl.bəʳ, US -bɚ
Wilbye ˈwɪl.bi
wilco ˈwɪl.kəʊ, US -koʊ

Wilcox ˈwɪl.kɒks, (US) -kɑːks
wild, W~ waɪld **-s** -z **-er** -əʳ, (US) -ɚ **-est** -ɪst, -əst **-ly** -li **-ness** -nəs, -nɪs **ˈwild ˌcard; ˈwild ˌchild; ˌWild ˈWest; ˌsow one's ˌwild ˈoats**
wild|cat ˈwaɪld|.kæt **-cats** -kæts **-catting** -ˌkæt.ɪŋ, (US) -ˌkæţ.ɪŋ **-catted** -ˌkæt.ɪd, (US) -ˌkæţ.ɪd **-catter/s** -ˌkæt.əʳ/z, (US) -ˌkæţ.ɚ/z **ˌwildcat ˈstrike**
Wilde waɪld
wildebeest ˈwɪl.dɪ.biːst, ˈvɪl-, -də-, (US) -də- **-s** -s
Wilder ˈwaɪl.dəʳ, (US) -dɚ
wilderness ˈwɪl.də.nəs, -nɪs, (US) -dɚ- **-es** -ɪz
Wilderspin ˈwɪl.də.spɪn, (US) -dɚ-
Wildfell ˈwaɪld.fel
wildfire ˈwaɪld.faɪəʳ, -faɪ.əʳ, (US) -faɪ.ɚ
wildfowl ˈwaɪld.faʊl **-ing** -ɪŋ **-er/s** -əʳ/z, (US) -ɚ/z
wild-goose chase ˌwaɪldˈguːsˌtʃeɪs
wilding, W~ ˈwaɪl.dɪŋ **-s** -z
wildlife ˈwaɪld.laɪf **ˈwildlife ˌpark**
wil|e, W~ waɪl **-es** -z **-ing** -ɪŋ **-ed** -d
Wiley ˈwaɪ.li
Wilfred, Wilfrid ˈwɪl.frɪd, -frəd, (US) ˈwɪl-
wilful ˈwɪl.fəl, -fʊl **-ly** -i **-ness** -nəs, -nɪs
Wilhelmina ˌwɪl.helˈmiː.nə, -əˈ-
Wilkerson ˈwɪl.kə.sən, (US) -kɚ-
Wilkes wɪlks
Wilkie ˈwɪl.ki
Wilkin ˈwɪl.kɪn
Wilkins ˈwɪl.kɪnz
Wilkinson ˈwɪl.kɪn.sən
Wilks wɪlks
will, W~ n wɪl **-s** -z
will transitive v wɪl **-s** -z **-ing** -ɪŋ **-ed** -d
will auxil. v *strong form:* wɪl; *weak forms:* wəl, əl
Note: Weak-form word. The strong form is used for emphasis (e.g. 'I **will** do it') and contrast (e.g. 'I don't know if I will or not'). It is also the usual form of **will** in final position (e.g. 'I think they both will'). Elsewhere the weak form (often spelt in contracted form as **'ll**) is used.

Willard ˈwɪl.ɑːd, -əd, (US) -ɚd
Willcocks, -cox ˈwɪl.kɒks, (US) -kɑːks
Willenhall ˈwɪl.ən.hɔːl
Willes wɪlz
Willesden ˈwɪlz.dən
Willett ˈwɪl.ɪt **-s** -s
willful ˈwɪl.fəl, -fʊl **-ly** -i **-ness** -nəs, -nɪs
William ˈwɪl.jəm, -i.əm, (US) ˈ-jəm **-s** -z **-son** -sən
willie, W~ ˈwɪl.i **-s** -z
willing, W~ ˈwɪl.ɪŋ **-ly** -li **-ness** -nəs, -nɪs
Willingdon ˈwɪl.ɪŋ.dən
Willington ˈwɪl.ɪŋ.tən
Willis ˈwɪl.ɪs
Willmott ˈwɪl.mɒt, -mət, (US) -mɑːt, -mət
will-o'-the-wisp ˌwɪl.ə.ðəˈwɪsp, ˈwɪl.ə.ðə.wɪsp, (US) ˌwɪl.ə.ðəˈwɪsp **-s** -s
Willoughby ˈwɪl.ə.bi
willow ˈwɪl.əʊ, (US) -oʊ **-s** -z **-ing** -ɪŋ **-ed** -d
willowherb ˈwɪl.əʊ.hɜːb, (US) -oʊ.hɝːb
willow-pattern ˈwɪl.əʊˌpæt.ən, (US) -oʊˌpæţ.ɚn
willowy ˈwɪl.əʊ.i, (US) -oʊ-
willpower ˈwɪl.paʊ.əʳ, -paʊəʳ, (US) -paʊ.ɚ **-s** -z
Wills wɪlz
Willson ˈwɪl.sən
will've (= **will have**) ˈwɪl.əv
will|y, W~ ˈwɪl|.i **-ies** -iz
willy-nilly ˌwɪl.iˈnɪl.i
Wilma ˈwɪl.mə
Wilmcote ˈwɪlm.kəʊt, (US) -koʊt, -kət
Wilmington ˈwɪl.mɪŋ.tən
Wilmot(t) ˈwɪl.mɒt, -mət, (US) -mɑːt, -mət
Wilmslow ˈwɪlmz.ləʊ; *locally:* ˈwɪmz.ləʊ, (US) ˈwɪlmz.loʊ
Wilna ˈvɪl.nə
Wilno ˈwɪl.nəʊ, (US) -noʊ
Wilsden ˈwɪlz.dən
Wilshire ˈwɪl.ʃəʳ, -ʃɪəʳ, (US) -ʃɚ, -ʃɪr
Wilson ˈwɪl.sən
wilt (from **will,** auxil. v.) *normal form:* wɪlt; *occasional weak form:* əlt
Note: This archaic form is rarely used.
wilt wɪlt **-s** -s **-ing** -ɪŋ, (US) ˈwɪl.tɪŋ **-ed** -ɪd, (US) ˈwɪl.tɪd
Wilton ˈwɪl.tən, (US) -tən, -tən **-s** -z
Wilts. (abbrev. for **Wiltshire**) wɪlts
Wiltshire ˈwɪlt.ʃəʳ, -ʃɪəʳ, (US) -ʃɚ, -ʃɪr
wil|y ˈwaɪ.l|i **-ier** -i.əʳ, (US) -i.ɚ **-iest** -i.ɪst, -i.əst **-iness** -ɪ.nəs, -ɪ.nɪs
wimble ˈwɪm.bəl **-s** -z
Wimbledon ˈwɪm.bəl.dən **ˌWimbledon ˈCommon**
Wimborne ˈwɪm.bɔːn, (US) -bɔːrn
Wimms wɪmz
wimp wɪmp **-s** -s **-y** -i
WIMP wɪmp
Wimpey ˈwɪm.pi
wimpish ˈwɪm.pɪʃ **-ly** -li **-ness** -nəs, -nɪs
wimple ˈwɪm.pəl **-s** -z
Wimpole ˈwɪm.pəʊl, (US) -poʊl
Wimpy® ˈwɪm.pi **-bar/s** -bɑːʳ/z, (US) -bɑːr/z
Wimsey ˈwɪm.zi
win wɪn **-s** -z **-ning** -ɪŋ **won** wʌn **winner/s** ˈwɪn.əʳ/z, (US) -ɚ/z
Winalot® ˈwɪn.ə.lɒt, (US) -lɑːt
Wincanton wɪŋˈkæn.tən, wɪn-, (US) wɪnˈkæn.tən
winc|e wɪnts **-es** -ɪz **-ing** -ɪŋ **-ed** -t
wincey ˈwɪnt.si
winceyette ˌwɪnt.siˈet
winch wɪntʃ **-es** -ɪz **-ing** -ɪŋ **-ed** -t
Winchelsea ˈwɪn.tʃəl.si
Winchester ˈwɪn.tʃɪ.stəʳ, -tʃə-, (US) -tʃes.tɚ, -tʃə.stɚ
Winchfield ˈwɪntʃ.fiːld
Winchilsea ˈwɪn.tʃəl.si
Winchmore ˈwɪntʃ.mɔːʳ, (US) -mɔːr
wind n *air blowing:* wɪnd **-s** -z **ˈwind ˌtunnel; take the ˌwind out of someone's ˈsails**
wind v *go round, roll round:* waɪnd **-s** -z **-ing** -ɪŋ **wound** waʊnd **-er/s** -əʳ/z, (US) -ɚ/z *blow horn:* waɪnd, (US) waɪnd, wɪnd **-s** -z **-ing** -ɪŋ **-ed** -ɪd *detect by scent, make unable to breathe:* wɪnd **-s** -z **-ing** -ɪŋ **-ed** -ɪd
windage ˈwɪn.dɪdʒ
windbag ˈwɪnd.bæg **-s** -z
windblown ˈwɪnd.bləʊn, (US) -bloʊn
windbreak ˈwɪnd.breɪk **-s** -s **-er/s** -əʳ/z, (US) -ɚ/z
windburn ˈwɪnd.bɜːn, (US) -bɝːn **-ed** -t, -d **-t** -t
windcheater ˈwɪndˌtʃiː.təʳ, (US) -ţɚ **-s** -z
wind-chest ˈwɪnd.tʃest **-s** -s
windchill ˈwɪnd.tʃɪl
wind-cone ˈwɪnd.kəʊn, (US) -koʊn **-s** -z
Windermere ˈwɪn.də.mɪəʳ, (US) -dɚ.mɪr
windfall ˈwɪnd.fɔːl, (US) -fɔːl, -fɑːl **-s** -z
Windham ˈwɪn.dəm
Windhoek ˈwɪnd.hʊk, ˈwɪnt-, ˈvɪnt-, (US) ˈvɪnt-
windhover ˈwɪndˌhɒv.əʳ, (US) -ˌhʌv.ɚ, -ˌhɑː.vɚ **-s** -z
winding n *in furnaces:* ˈwɪn.dɪŋ
winding n, adj ˈwaɪn.dɪŋ **-s** -z **-ly** -li
winding-sheet ˈwaɪn.dɪŋ.ʃiːt **-s** -s
winding-up ˌwaɪn.dɪŋˈʌp
wind-instrument ˈwɪndˌɪn.strə.mənt, -strʊ- **-s** -s
windjammer ˈwɪndˌdʒæm.əʳ, (US) -ɚ **-s** -z
windlass ˈwɪnd.ləs **-es** -ɪz
Windley ˈwɪnd.li
windmill ˈwɪnd.mɪl **-s** -z
Windolene® ˈwɪn.dəʊ.liːn, (US) -doʊ-, -də-
window ˈwɪn.dəʊ, (US) -doʊ **-s** -z **ˈwindow ˌbox; ˈwindow ˌcleaner; ˈwindow ˌdressing; ˈwindow ˌseat**
windowpane ˈwɪn.dəʊ.peɪn, (US) -doʊ- **-s** -z
window-shop ˈwɪn.dəʊ.ʃɒp, (US) -doʊ.ʃɑːp **-s** -s **-ping** -ɪŋ **-ped** -t
windowsill ˈwɪn.dəʊ.sɪl, (US) -doʊ- **-s** -z
windpipe ˈwɪnd.paɪp **-s** -s
windproof ˈwɪnd.pruːf
windrow ˈwɪn.drəʊ, (US) -droʊ **-s** -z
Windrush ˈwɪn.drʌʃ
Windscale ˈwɪnd.skeɪl
windscreen ˈwɪnd.skriːn **-s** -z **ˈwindscreen ˌwiper**
windshield ˈwɪnd.ʃiːld **-s** -z **ˈwindshield ˌwiper**
windsock ˈwɪnd.sɒk, (US) -sɑːk **-s** -s
Windsor ˈwɪnd.zəʳ, (US) -zɚ

Windsor ˈCastle; ˌDuke of ˈWindsor; ˌDuchess of ˈWindsor
windstorm ˈwɪnd.stɔːm, (US) -stɔːrm **-s** -z
windsurf ˈwɪnd.sɜːf, (US) -sɝːf **-s** -s **-ing** -ɪŋ **-ed** -t **-er/s** -əʳ/z, (US) -ɚ/z
windswept ˈwɪnd.swept
wind-up ˈwaɪnd.ʌp **-s** -s
Windus ˈwɪn.dəs
windward, W~ ˈwɪnd.wəd, (US) -wɚd
wind|y ˈwɪn.d|i **-ier** -i.əʳ, (US) -i.ɚ **-iest** -i.ɪst, -i.əst **-ily** -əl.i, -ɪ.li **-iness** -ɪ.nəs, -ɪ.nɪs **ˌWindy ˈCity**
win|e waɪn **-es** -z **-ing** -ɪŋ **-ed** -d **ˈwine ˌbar; ˈwine ˌbottle; ˈwine ˌcellar; ˌwine ˈvinegar**
winebibber ˈwaɪnˌbɪb.əʳ, (US) -ɚ **-s** -z
wineglass ˈwaɪn.glɑːs, (US) -glæs **-es** -ɪz
Winehouse ˈwaɪn.haʊs
winemaker ˈwaɪnˌmeɪ.kəʳ, ˈwaɪm-, (US) ˈwaɪnˌmeɪ.kɚ **-s** -z
winer|y ˈwaɪ.nər|.i **-ies** -iz
winey ˈwaɪ.ni
Winfrey ˈwɪn.fri
wing, W~ wɪŋ **-s** -z **-ing** -ɪŋ **-ed** -d **ˈwing ˌnut; ˌclip someone's ˈwings**
Wingate ˈwɪn.geɪt, ˈwɪŋ-, -gɪt, (US) ˈwɪn-
wing-commander ˌwɪŋ.kəˈmɑːn.dəʳ, (US) ˈwɪŋ.kəˌmæn.dɚ **-s** -z *stress shift, British only:* **ˌwing-commander ˈSmith**
winged wɪŋd
winger ˈwɪŋ.əʳ, (US) -ɚ **-s** -z
-winger ˈwɪŋ.əʳ, (US) -ɚ **-s** -z
Note: Suffix. Normally carries primary stress as shown, e.g. **left-winger** /ˌleftˈwɪŋ.əʳ/ (US) /-ɚ/.
Wingerworth ˈwɪŋ.ə.wəθ, -wɜːθ, (US) -ɚ.wɚθ, -wɝːθ
Wingfield ˈwɪŋ.fiːld
wingspan ˈwɪŋ.spæn
Winifred ˈwɪn.ɪ.frɪd, (US) ˈ-ə-
wink, W~ wɪŋk **-s** -s **-ing** -ɪŋ **-ed** -t **-er/s** -əʳ/z, (US) -ɚ/z
Winkfield ˈwɪŋk.fiːld
Winkie ˈwɪŋ.ki
winkle, W~ ˈwɪŋ.kəl **-s** -z
winkle-picker ˈwɪŋ.kəlˌpɪk.əʳ, (US) -ɚ **-s** -z
winnable ˈwɪn.ə.bəl
Winnebago® ˌwɪn.ɪˈbeɪ.gəʊ, -əˈ-, (US) -əˈbeɪ.goʊ **-s** -z
winner ˈwɪn.əʳ, (US) -ɚ **-s** -z
Winnie ˈwɪn.i
Winnie-the-Pooh ˌwɪn.i.ðəˈpuː
winning, W~ ˈwɪn.ɪŋ **-s** -z **-ly** -li
winning-post ˈwɪn.ɪŋ.pəʊst, (US) -poʊst **-s** -s
Winnipeg ˈwɪn.ɪ.peg
winnow ˈwɪn.əʊ, (US) -oʊ **-s** -z **-ing** -ɪŋ **-ed** -d **-er/s** -əʳ/z, (US) -ɚ/z
wino ˈwaɪ.nəʊ, (US) -noʊ **-s** -z
Winona wɪˈnəʊ.nə, (US) -ˈnoʊ-
Winsford ˈwɪnz.fəd, ˈwɪns-, (US) -fɚd
Winslet ˈwɪndz.lɪt, -lət
Winslow ˈwɪnz.ləʊ, (US) -loʊ
winsome ˈwɪn.səm **-ly** -li **-ness** -nəs, -nɪs
Winstanley *in Greater Manchester:* ˈwɪnt.stən.li; wɪnˈstæn- *surname:* wɪnˈstæn.li; ˈwɪnt.stən-
Winston ˈwɪnt.stən
Winstone ˈwɪnt.stəʊn, -stən, (US) -stoʊn, -stən
wint|er, W~ ˈwɪn.t|əʳ, (US) -t̬|ɚ **-ers** -əz, (US) -ɚz **-ering** -ər.ɪŋ **-ered** -əd, (US) -ɚd **ˌwinter ˈsports; ˌWinter Oˈlympics**
Winterbottom ˈwɪn.təˌbɒt.əm, (US) -t̬ɚˌbɑː.t̬əm
Winterbourne ˈwɪn.tə.bɔːn, (US) -t̬ɚ.bɔːrn
Winters ˈwɪn.təz, (US) -t̬ɚz
Winterson ˈwɪn.tə.sən, (US) -t̬ɚ-
Winterthur ˈvɪn.tə.tʊəʳ, (US) -t̬ɚ.tʊr
wintertime ˈwɪn.tə.taɪm, (US) -t̬ɚ-
Winterton ˈwɪn.tə.tən, (US) -t̬ɚ.tən
Winthrop ˈwɪn.θrɒp, ˈwɪnt.θrəp, (US) ˈwɪnt.θrəp
Winton ˈwɪn.tən, (US) -tən
Wintour ˈwɪn.təʳ, (US) -t̬ɚ
wintr|y ˈwɪn.tr|i **-iness** -ɪ.nəs, -ɪ.nɪs
Winwick ˈwɪn.ɪk
Winwood ˈwɪn.wʊd
winy ˈwaɪ.ni
wip|e waɪp **-es** -s **-ing** -ɪŋ **-ed** -t **-er/s** -əʳ/z, (US) -ɚ/z **ˌwiped ˈout**
wipeout ˈwaɪp.aʊt **-s** -s
wir|e waɪəʳ, ˈwaɪ.əʳ, (US) ˈwaɪ.ɚ **-es** -z **-ing** -ɪŋ **-ed** -d
wire-cutter ˈwaɪəˌkʌt.əʳ, ˈwaɪ.ə-, (US) ˈwaɪ.ɚˌkʌt̬.ɚ **-s** -z
wire|draw ˈwaɪə|.drɔː, ˈwaɪ.ə-, (US) ˈwaɪ.ɚ|.drɑː, -drɔː **-draws** -drɔːz, (US) -drɑːz, -drɔːz **-drawing** -ˌdrɔː.ɪŋ, (US) -ˌdrɑː.ɪŋ, -ˌdrɔː- **-drew** -druː **-drawn** -drɔːn, (US) -drɑːn, -drɔːn **-drawer/s** -ˌdrɔː.əʳ/z, (US) -ˌdrɑː.ɚ/z, -ˌdrɔː-
wire-haired ˈwaɪə.heəd, ˈwaɪ.ə-, (US) ˈwaɪ.ɚ.herd
wireless ˈwaɪə.ləs, ˈwaɪ.ə-, -lɪs, (US) ˈwaɪ.ɚ- **-es** -ɪz
wiretap ˈwaɪə.tæp, ˈwaɪ.ə-, (US) ˈwaɪ.ɚ- **-s** -s **-ping** -ɪŋ **-ped** -t
wireworm ˈwaɪə.wɜːm, ˈwaɪ.ə-, (US) ˈwaɪ.ɚ.wɝːm **-s** -z
wiring ˈwaɪə.rɪŋ, (US) ˈwaɪ.ɚ.ɪŋ
Wirksworth ˈwɜːk.swəθ, -swɜːθ, (US) ˈwɝːk.swɚθ, -swɝːθ
Wirral ˈwɪr.əl
wir|y ˈwaɪə.r|i, (US) ˈwaɪ.ɚ|.i **-ier** -i.əʳ, (US) -i.ɚ **-iest** -i.ɪst, -i.əst **-iness** -ɪ.nəs, -ɪ.nɪs
Wis. (abbrev. for **Wisconsin**) wɪˈskɒnt.sɪn, (US) -ˈskɑːnt.sən
Wisbech ˈwɪz.biːtʃ; *locally:* -bɪtʃ
Wisbey ˈwɪz.bi
Wisconsin wɪˈskɒnt.sɪn, (US) -ˈskɑːnt.sən
Wisden ˈwɪz.dən
wisdom ˈwɪz.dəm **ˈwisdom ˌtooth**
wis|e, W~ waɪz **-er** -əʳ, (US) -ɚ **-est** -ɪst, -əst **-ely** -li **-eness** -nəs, -nɪs **ˈwise ˌguy; ˌthree ˌwise ˈmen**
wiseacre ˈwaɪzˌeɪ.kəʳ, (US) -kɚ **-s** -z
wisecrack ˈwaɪz.kræk **-s** -s
Wiseman ˈwaɪz.mən
wish wɪʃ **-es** -ɪz **-ing** -ɪŋ **-ed** -t **-er/s** -əʳ/z, (US) -ɚ/z
Wishart ˈwɪʃ.ət, (US) -ɚt
Wishaw ˈwɪʃ.ɔː, (US) -ɑː, -ɔː
wishbone ˈwɪʃ.bəʊn, (US) -boʊn **-s** -z
wishful ˈwɪʃ.fəl, -fʊl **-ly** -i **-ness** -nəs, -nɪs **ˌwishful ˈthinking**
wish-fulfillment ˈwɪʃ.fʊlˌfɪl.mənt
wishing-well ˈwɪʃ.ɪŋ.wel **-s** -z
wish-wash ˈwɪʃ.wɒʃ, (US) -wɑːʃ, -wɔːʃ
wishy-washy ˈwɪʃ.iˌwɒʃ.i, ˌwɪʃ.iˈwɒʃ-, (US) ˈwɪʃ.iˌwɑː.ʃi, -ˌwɔː-
wisp wɪsp **-s** -s
wisp|y ˈwɪs.p|i **-ier** -i.əʳ, (US) -i.ɚ **-iest** -i.ɪst, -i.əst **-ily** -əl.i, -ɪ.li **-iness** -ɪ.nəs, -ɪ.nɪs
wist wɪst
Wistar ˈwɪs.təʳ, (US) -tɚ
wistaria wɪˈsteə.ri.ə, -ˈstɪə-, (US) -ˈster.i-, -ˈstɪr- **-s** -z
Wister ˈwɪs.təʳ, (US) -tɚ
wisteria wɪˈstɪə.ri.ə, -ˈsteə-, (US) -ˈstɪr.i-, -ˈster- **-s** -z
wistful ˈwɪst.fəl, -fʊl **-ly** -i **-ness** -nəs, -nɪs
wit wɪt **-s** -s
witch wɪtʃ **-es** -ɪz **-ing/ly** -ɪŋ/li **-ed** -t
witchcraft ˈwɪtʃ.krɑːft, (US) -kræft
witchdoctor ˈwɪtʃˌdɒk.təʳ, (US) -ˌdɑːk.tɚ **-s** -z
witcher|y ˈwɪtʃ.ər|.i **-ies** -iz
witch-hazel ˈwɪtʃˌheɪ.zəl, ˌ-ˈ--, (US) ˈwɪtʃˌheɪ- **-s** -z
witch-hunt ˈwɪtʃ.hʌnt **-s** -s **-er/s** -əʳ/z, (US) -ɚ/z
witching ˈwɪtʃ.ɪŋ **ˈwitching ˌhour**
witenagemot(e) ˈwɪt.ɪ.nə.gɪˌməʊt, -ən.ə-, -gəˈ-, (US) ˈwɪt.ən.ə.gəˌmoʊt
Wite-Out® ˈwaɪt.aʊt, (US) ˈwaɪt̬-
with wɪð, wɪθ
Note: The pronunciation /wɪθ/ is most frequently found when followed by a voiceless consonant (e.g. 'with care' /wɪθˈkeə/ (US) /-ˈker/).
withal wɪˈðɔːl, (US) wɪˈðɔːl, -ˈðɑːl
Witham ˈwɪð.əm *town in Essex:* ˈwɪt.əm, (US) ˈwɪt̬-
withdraw wɪðˈdrɔː, wɪθ-, (US) -ˈdrɑː, -ˈdrɔː **-s** -z **-ing** -ɪŋ **withdrew** wɪðˈdruː, wɪθ- **withdrawn** wɪðˈdrɔːn, wɪθ-, (US) -ˈdrɑːn, -ˈdrɔːn
withdrawal wɪðˈdrɔː.əl, wɪθ-, (US) -ˈdrɑː-, -ˈdrɔː- **-s** -z **withˈdrawal ˌmethod; withˈdrawal ˌsymptoms**
wi|the wɪ|θ, wɪ|ð, waɪ|ð **-s** -θs, -ðz
with|er, W~ ˈwɪð|.əʳ, (US) -ɚ **-ers** -əz, (US) -ɚz **-ering/ly** -ər.ɪŋ/li **-ered** -əd, (US) -ɚd
Withernsea ˈwɪð.ən.siː, (US) -ɚn-
withers, W~ n ˈwɪð.əz, (US) -ɚz
Witherspoon ˈwɪð.ə.spuːn, (US) ˈ-ɚ-
with|hold wɪθ|ˈhəʊld, wɪð-, (US) -ˈhoʊld **-holds** -ˈhəʊldz, (US)

-ˈhoʊldz **-holding** -ˈhəʊl.dɪŋ, (US) -ˈhoʊl.dɪŋ **-held** -ˈheld **-holden** -ˈhəʊl.dᵊn, (US) -ˈhoʊl.dᵊn **-holder/s** -ˈhəʊl.dəʳ/z, (US) -ˈhoʊl.dɚ/z

within wɪˈðɪn; ˈwɪð.ɪn, (US) wɪˈðɪn, -ˈθɪn

with-it ˈwɪð.ɪt, (US) ˈwɪð-, ˈwɪθ-

withless ˈwɪt.ləs, -lɪs **-ly** -li **-ness** -nəs, -nɪs

without wɪˈðaʊt; ˈwɪð.aʊt, (US) wɪˈðaʊt, -ˈθaʊt

withstand wɪðˈstænd, wɪθ-, (US) wɪθ-, wɪð- **-s** -z **-ing** -ɪŋ **withstood** wɪðˈstʊd, wɪθ-, (US) wɪθ-, wɪð-

with|y ˈwɪð|.i, (US) ˈwɪð-, ˈwɪθ- **-ies** -iz

witless ˈwɪt.ləs, -lɪs **-ly** -li **-ness** -nəs, -nɪs

Witley ˈwɪt.li

witness n, v ˈwɪt.nəs, -nɪs **-es** -ɪz **-ing** -ɪŋ **-ed** -t ˈ**witness** ˌ**box**

witney, W~ ˈwɪt.ni

-witted ˈwɪt.ɪd, (US) ˌwɪţ.ɪd

Note: Suffix. May take either primary or secondary stress in British English, unless it is used attributively, in which case it always takes secondary stress, e.g. **quick-witted** /ˌkwɪkˈwɪt.ɪd/, ˌ**quick-witted** ˈ**fox**. Normally takes only secondary stress in American English.

Wittenberg ˈvɪt.ᵊn.bɜːg, -beəg; *old-fashioned:* ˈwɪt.ᵊn.bɜːg, (US) ˈwɪt.ᵊn.bɝːg, ˈvɪt-

witter ˈwɪt.əʳ, (US) ˈwɪţ.ɚ **-s** -z **-ing** -ɪŋ **-ed** -d **-er/s** -əʳ/z, (US) -ɚ/z

Wittgenstein ˈvɪt.gən.ʃtaɪn, -staɪn

witticism ˈwɪt.ɪ.sɪ.zᵊm, (US) ˈwɪţ.ə- **-s** -z

wittingly ˈwɪt.ɪŋ.li, (US) ˈwɪţ-

witt|y ˈwɪt|.i, (US) ˈwɪţ- **-ier** -i.əʳ, (US) -i.ɚ **-iest** -i.ɪst, -i.əst **-ily** -ᵊl.i, -ɪ.li **-iness** -ɪ.nəs, -ɪ.nɪs

Witwatersrand wɪtˈwɔː.təz.rænd, -rɑːnd, -rɑːnt; ˈwɪtˌwɔː-, ˈvɪtˌvɑː.təz.rɒnt, (US) wɪtˈwɔː.ţɚz.rænd, -ˈwɑː-

Wiveliscombe ˈwɪv.ᵊl.ɪ.skəm, ˌwɪv.əˈlɪs.kəm; *locally also:* ˈwɪl.skəm

Wivelsfield ˈwɪv.ᵊlz.fiːld

Wivenhoe ˈwɪv.ᵊn.həʊ, (US) -hoʊ

wives (plural of **wife**) waɪvz

wizard ˈwɪz.əd, (US) -ɚd **-s** -z **-ry** -ri

wizen ˈwɪz.ᵊn **-ed** -d

wk (abbrev. for **week**) wiːk

WNW (abbrev. for **west-northwest**) ˌwest.nɔːθˈwest, (US) -nɔːrθˈ-; *nautical pronunciation:* -nɔːˈ-, (US) -nɔːrˈ-

wo wəʊ, (US) woʊ

woad wəʊd, (US) woʊd

wobbl|e ˈwɒb.ᵊl, (US) ˈwɑː.bᵊl **-es** -z **-ing** -ɪŋ, ˈwɒb.lɪŋ, (US) ˈwɑː.blɪŋ **-ed** -d **-er/s** -əʳ/z, (US) ˈwɒb.ləʳ/z, ˈwɑː.bᵊl.əʳ/z, ˈwɑː.blɚ/z

wobbl|y ˈwɒb.ᵊl|.i, ˈ-l|i, (US) ˈwɑː.bᵊl|.i, ˈ-bl|i **-iness** -ɪ.nəs, -ɪ.nɪs

Wobegon ˈwəʊ.bɪ.gɒn, (US) ˈwoʊ.bɪ.gɑːn

Woburn *Abbey:* ˈwuː.bɜːn, -bən, (US) -bɝːn, -bɚn *street and square in London:* ˈwəʊ.bən, -bɜːn, (US) ˈwoʊ.bɚn, -bɝːn *village:* ˈwəʊ.bən, ˈwuː-, (US) ˈwoʊ.bɚn, ˈwuː-

Wodehouse ˈwʊd.haʊs

Woden ˈwəʊ.dᵊn, (US) ˈwoʊ-

wodge wɒdʒ, (US) wɑːdʒ **-s** -ɪz

woe wəʊ, (US) woʊ **-s** -z

woebegone ˈwəʊ.bɪ.gɒn, (US) ˈwoʊ.bɪ.gɑːn

woeful ˈwəʊ.fᵊl, -fʊl, (US) ˈwoʊ- **-ly** -i **-ness** -nəs, -nɪs

Woffington ˈwɒf.ɪŋ.tən, (US) ˈwɑː.fɪŋ-

wog wɒg, (US) wɑːg, wɔːg **-s** -z

Wogan ˈwəʊ.gən, (US) ˈwoʊ-

wok wɒk, (US) wɑːk **-s** -s

woke (from **wake**) wəʊk, (US) woʊk

woken (from **wake**) ˈwəʊ.kᵊn, (US) ˈwoʊ-

Woking ˈwəʊ.kɪŋ, (US) ˈwoʊ-

Wokingham ˈwəʊ.kɪŋ.əm, (US) ˈwoʊ-

Wolborough ˈwɒl.bᵊr.ə, (US) ˈwɑːl.bɚ.oʊ

Wolcot(t) ˈwʊl.kət, (US) ˈwʊl-, ˈwɔːl-

wold wəʊld, (US) woʊld **-s** -z

Woldingham ˈwəʊl.dɪŋ.əm, (US) ˈwoʊl-

Woledge ˈwʊl.ɪdʒ

wolf v wʊlf **-s** -s **-ing** -ɪŋ **-ed** -t

wol|f, W~ n wʊl|f **-ves** -vz **a** ˌ**wolf in** ˌ**sheep's** ˈ**clothing; keep the** ˌ**wolf from**ˌ**the** ˈ**door; keep the** ˈ**wolf from the** ˌ**door**

wolf-cub ˈwʊlf.kʌb **-s** -z

Wolfe wʊlf

Wolfenden ˈwʊl.fᵊn.dən

Wolff wʊlf, vɒlf, (US) wʊlf, vɔːlf

Wolfgang ˈwʊlf.gæŋ

wolfhound ˈwʊlf.haʊnd **-s** -z

wolfish ˈwʊl.fɪʃ **-ly** -li **-ness** -nəs, -nɪs

wolfram, W~ ˈwʊl.frəm **-ite** -aɪt

Wolfson ˈwʊlf.sᵊn

wolf-whistl|e ˈwʊlfˌ*h*wɪs.ᵊl **-es** -z **-ing** -ɪŋ, -ˌ*h*wɪs.lɪŋ **-ed** -d

Wollard ˈwʊl.ɑːd, (US) -ɑːrd, -ɚd

Wollaston ˈwʊl.ə.stᵊn

Wollaton ˈwʊl.ə.tᵊn, (US) -tᵊn

Wollongong ˈwʊl.ən.gɒŋ, -əŋ-, (US) -ən.gɑːŋ

Wollstonecraft ˈwʊl.stən.krɑːft, (US) -kræft, -krɑːft

Wolmer ˈwʊl.məʳ, (US) -mɚ

Wolseley® ˈwʊlz.li

Wolsey ˈwʊl.zi

Wolsingham ˈwɒl.sɪŋ.əm, (US) ˈwɑːl-

Wolstenholme ˈwʊl.stᵊn.həʊm, (US) -hoʊm

Wolverhampton ˌwʊl.vəˈhæm*p*.tən, ˈwʊl.vəˌhæm*p*-, (US) ˈwʊl.vɚˌhæm*p*-

wolverine ˈwʊl.vᵊr.iːn, (US) ˌwʊl.vəˈriːn, ˈ--- **-s** -z

Wolverton ˈwʊl.və.tᵊn, (US) -vɚ-

wolves (plural of **wolf**) wʊlvz

Womad ˈwəʊ.mæd, (US) ˈwoʊ-

woman ˈwʊm.ən **women** ˈwɪm.ɪn ˌ**woman of the** ˈ**world**

woman-hat|er ˈwʊm.ənˌheɪ.t|əʳ, (US) -ţ|ɚ **-ers** -əz, (US) -ɚz **-ing** -ɪŋ

womanhood ˈwʊm.ən.hʊd

womanish ˈwʊm.ə.nɪʃ **-ly** -li **-ness** -nəs, -nɪs

womanist ˈwʊm.ə.nɪst **-s** -s

womaniz|e, -is|e ˈwʊm.ə.naɪz **-es** -ɪz **-ing** -ɪŋ **-ed** -d **-er/s** -əʳ/z, (US) -ɚ/z

womankind ˌwʊm.ənˈkaɪnd, -əŋˈ-, ˈ---, (US) ˈwʊm.ən.kaɪnd

womanlike ˈwʊm.ən.laɪk

womanl|y ˈwʊm.ən.l|i **-iness** -ɪ.nəs, -ɪ.nɪs

womb wuːm **-s** -z

wombat ˈwɒm.bæt, (US) ˈwɑːm- **-s** -s

Womble ˈwɒm.bᵊl, ˈwʌm-, (US) ˈwɑː.m-

Wombourne ˈwɒm.bɔːn, (US) ˈwɑːm.bɔːrn

Wombwell *place in South Yorkshire:* ˈwʊm.wel, -wəl *surname:* ˈwʊm.wəl, ˈwʌm-, ˈwɒm-, (US) ˈwʊm-, ˈwʌm-, ˈwɑːm-

women (plural of **woman**) ˈwɪm.ɪn ˌ**Women's** ˈ**Institute;** ˌ**women's** ˈ**lib;** ˈ**women's** ˌ**movement;** ˈ**women's** ˌ**room**

womenfolk ˈwɪm.ɪn.fəʊk, (US) -foʊk

womenkind ˌwɪm.ɪnˈkaɪnd, -ɪŋˈ-, ˈ---, (US) ˈwɪm.ɪn.kaɪnd

womenswear ˈwɪm.ɪnz.weəʳ, (US) -wer

won (from **win**) wʌn

won *Korean money:* wɒn, (US) wɑːn

wond|er, W~ ˈwʌn.d|əʳ, (US) -d|ɚ **-ers** -əz, (US) -ɚz **-ering/ly** -ᵊr.ɪŋ/li **-ered** -əd, (US) -ɚd **-erer/s** -ᵊr.əʳ/z, (US) -ɚ.ɚ/z

wonder|ful ˈwʌn.də|.fᵊl, -fʊl, (US) -dɚ- **-fully** -fᵊl.i, -fʊl-, -fli **-fulness** -fᵊl.nəs, -fʊl-, -nɪs

wonderland, W~ ˈwʌn.dᵊl.ænd, (US) -dɚ.lænd ˌ**Alice in** ˈ**Wonderland**

wonderment ˈwʌn.də.mənt, (US) -dɚ-

wondrous ˈwʌn.drəs **-ly** -li **-ness** -nəs, -nɪs

wonga ˈwɒŋ.gə, (US) ˈwɑːŋ-, ˈwɔːŋ-

wonk ˈwɒŋk, (US) ˈwɑːŋk **-s** -s

wonk|y ˈwɒŋ.k|i, (US) ˈwɑːŋ-, ˈwɔːŋ- **-ier** -i.əʳ, (US) -i.ɚ **-iest** -i.ɪst, -i.əst **-ily** -ᵊl.i, -ɪ.li **-iness** -ɪ.nəs, -ɪ.nɪs

Wonsan ˌwɒnˈsæn, (US) ˌwɑːnˈsɑːn, ˌwʌn-

won|t n, adj wəʊn|t, (US) wɔːn|t, wɑːn|t, woʊn|t, wʌn|t **-ted** -tɪd, (US) -ţɪd

won't (= **will not**) wəʊnt, (US) woʊnt

wonton ˌwɒnˈtɒn, (US) ˈwɑːn.tɑːn

won't've (= **will not have**) ˈwəʊnt.ᵊv, (US) ˈwoʊnt.ᵊv

woo wuː **-s** -z **-ing** -ɪŋ **-ed** -d **-er/s** -əʳ/z, (US) -ɚ/z

wood, W~ wʊd **-s** -z **-ed** -ɪd **not see the** ˌ**wood for the** ˈ**trees**

Woodall ˈwʊd.ɔːl, (US) -ɔːl, -ɑːl

Woodard ˈwʊd.ɑːd, (US) -ɚd

woodbine, W~ ˈwʊd.baɪn **-s** -z

woodblock ˈwʊd.blɒk, (US) -blɑːk -s -s
Woodbridge ˈwʊd.brɪdʒ
Woodbury ˈwʊd.bᵊr.i, (US) -ber-, -bɚ-
wood-carv|er ˈwʊdˌkɑː.v|əʳ, (US) -ˌkɑːr.v|ɚ -ers -əz, (US) -ɚz -ing/s -ɪŋ/z
woodchuck ˈwʊd.tʃʌk -s -s
woodcock, W~ ˈwʊd.kɒk, (US) -kɑːk -s -s
woodcut ˈwʊd.kʌt -s -s
woodcutter ˈwʊdˌkʌt.əʳ, (US) -ˌkʌţ.ɚ -s -z
wooden ˈwʊd.ᵊn -ly -li -ness -nəs, -nɪs
wooden-headed ˌwʊd.ᵊnˈhed.ɪd *stress shift:* **ˌwooden-headed ˈperson**
Woodfield ˈwʊd.fiːld
Woodford(e) ˈwʊd.fəd, (US) -fɚd
Woodgate ˈwʊd.geɪt, ˈwʊg-, (US) ˈwʊd-
Woodhead ˈwʊd.hed
Woodhouse ˈwʊd.haʊs
woodland ˈwʊd.lənd -s -z
Woodley ˈwʊd.li
wood|louse ˈwʊd|.laʊs -lice -laɪs
wood|man, W~ ˈwʊd|.mən -men -mən
wood-nymph ˈwʊd.nɪmpf -s -s
woodpecker ˈwʊdˌpek.əʳ, (US) -ɚ -s -z
wood-pigeon ˈwʊdˌpɪdʒ.ən, -ɪn -s -z
Woodroffe ˈwʊd.rɒf, -rʌf, (US) -rɑːf, -rʌf
Woodrow ˈwʊd.rəʊ, (US) -roʊ
woodruff, W~ ˈwʊd.rʌf -s -s
Woods wʊdz
woodshed ˈwʊd.ʃed -s -z -ing -ɪŋ -ed -ɪd
Woodside ˌwʊdˈsaɪd, ˈ--, (US) ˈwʊd.saɪd
woodsman ˈwʊdz.mən
Woodstock ˈwʊd.stɒk, (US) -stɑːk
Woodward ˈwʊd.wəd, (US) -wɚd
woodwind ˈwʊd.wɪnd -s -z
woodwork ˈwʊd.wɜːk, (US) -wɝːk -ing -ɪŋ
woodworm ˈwʊd.wɜːm, (US) -wɝːm
wood|y, W~ ˈwʊd|.i -ier -i.əʳ, (US) -i.ɚ -iest -i.ɪst, -i.əst -iness -ɪ.nəs, -ɪ.nɪs
woof *weaving:* wuːf, (US) wuːf, wʊf *dog's bark:* wʊf -s -s
Woof *surname:* wʊf
woofer ˈwʊf.əʳ, (US) -ɚ -s -z
woofter ˈwʊf.təʳ, (US) -tɚ -s -z
Wookey ˈwʊk.i
wool wʊl -s -z
Woolacombe ˈwʊl.ə.kəm
Wooldridge ˈwʊl.drɪdʒ
woolen ˈwʊl.ən -s -z
Wooler ˈwʊl.əʳ, (US) -ɚ
Woolf wʊlf
Woolfardisworthy *near Bideford, Devon:* ˈwʊl.zᵊr.i, ˈwʊl.fɑː.dɪˌswɜː.ði, (US) ˈwʊl.zɚ.i, ˈwʊl.fɑːr.dɪ.swɝː.ði *near Crediton, Devon:* ˈwʊl.fɑː.dɪˌswɜː.ði, (US) -fɑːr.dɪˌswɝː-
Woolford ˈwʊl.fəd, (US) -fɚd
wool-gathering ˈwʊlˌgæð.ᵊr.ɪŋ
Woollard ˈwʊl.ɑːd, (US) -ɚd
woollen ˈwʊl.ən -s -z
Woolley ˈwʊl.i
wooll|y ˈwʊl|.i -ies -iz -ier -i.əʳ, (US) -i.ɚ -iest -i.ɪst, -i.əst -iness -ɪ.nəs, -ɪ.nɪs
woolly-headed ˌwʊl.iˈhed.ɪd, (US) ˈwʊl.iˌhed- *stress shift, British only:* **ˌwoolly-headed ˈperson**
Woolner ˈwʊl.nəʳ, (US) -nɚ
Woolnough ˈwʊl.nəʊ, (US) -noʊ
woolpack ˈwʊl.pæk -s -s
woolsack ˈwʊl.sæk -s -s
Woolsey ˈwʊl.zi
Woolwich ˈwʊl.ɪdʒ, -ɪtʃ
Woolworth ˈwʊl.wəθ, -wɜːθ, (US) -wɚθ, -wɝːθ -'s -s
wooll|y ˈwʊl|.i -ier -i.əʳ, (US) -i.ɚ -iest -i.ɪst, -i.əst -iness -ɪ.nəs, -ɪ.nɪs
Woomera ˈwʊm.ᵊr.ə, ˈwuː.mᵊr-
Woorstead ˈwʊs.tɪd, -təd, (US) ˈwʊs-, ˈwɝː-
Woosley ˈwuːz.li
Woosnam ˈwuːz.nəm
Wooster ˈwʊs.təʳ, (US) -tɚ
woot wuːt
Woot(t)on ˈwʊt.ᵊn
wooz|y ˈwuː.z|i -ier -i.əʳ, (US) -i.ɚ -iest -i.ɪst, -i.əst -ily -ᵊl.i, -ɪ.li -iness -ɪ.nəs, -ɪ.nɪs
wop wɒp, (US) wɑːp -s -s
Worboys ˈwɔː.bɔɪz, (US) ˈwɔːr-
Worcester ˈwʊs.təʳ, (US) -tɚ -shire -ʃəʳ, -ʃɪəʳ, (US) -ʃɚ, -ʃɪr **ˌWorcester ˈsauce**
Worcs. (abbrev. for **Worcestershire**) ˈwʊs.tə.ʃəʳ, -ʃɪəʳ, (US) -tɚ.ʃɚ, -ʃɪr
word wɜːd, (US) wɝːd -s -z -ing/s -ɪŋ/z -ed -ɪd -less -ləs, -lɪs **ˈword ˌorder; ˈword ˌprocessor; ˌword ˈprocessor; ˌeat one's ˈwords; get a ˌword in ˈedgewise; put ˌwords in(to) someone's ˈmouth** (US) **put ˈwords in(to) someone's ˌmouth**
wordbook ˈwɜːd.bʊk, (US) ˈwɝːd- -s -s
Worde wɔːd, (US) wɔːrd
word-formation ˈwɜːd.fɔːˌmeɪ.ʃᵊn, (US) ˈwɝːd.fɔːr.-
word-for-word ˌwɜːd.fəˈwɜːd, (US) ˌwɝːd.fɚˈwɝːrd
wordless ˈwɜːd.ləs, -lɪs, (US) ˈwɝːd- -ly -li -ness -nəs, -nɪs
word-of-mouth ˌwɜːd.əvˈmaʊθ, (US) ˌwɝːd-
word-perfect ˌwɜːdˈpɜː.fɪkt, -fekt, (US) ˌwɝːdˈpɝːr.fɪkt
wordplay ˈwɜːd.pleɪ, (US) ˈwɝːd- -s -z
word processing ˈwɜːdˌprəʊ.ses.ɪŋ, -ˌ-ˈ---, (US) ˈwɝːdˌprɑː-, -ˌproʊ-
wordsmith ˈwɜːd.smɪθ, (US) ˈwɝːd- -s -s
Wordsworth ˈwɜːdz.wəθ, -wɜːθ, (US) ˈwɝːdz.wɚθ, -wɝːθ
Wordsworthian ˌwɜːdzˈwɜː.θi.ən, (US) ˌwɝːdzˈwɝːr-
word|y ˈwɜː.d|i, (US) ˈwɝː- -ier -i.əʳ, (US) -i.ɚ -iest -i.ɪst, -i.əst -ily -ᵊl.i, -ɪ.li -iness -ɪ.nəs, -ɪ.nɪs
wore (from **wear**) wɔːʳ, (US) wɔːr
work wɜːk, (US) wɝːk -s -s -ing/s -ɪŋ/z -ed -t -er/s -əʳ/z, (US) -ɚ/z **ˌworking ˈday** (US) **ˈworking ˌday; ˌworking ˈknowledge** (US) **ˈworking ˌknowledge; ˌwork of ˈart; ˌworking ˈorder** (US) **ˈworking ˌorder**
workable ˈwɜː.kə.bᵊl, (US) ˈwɝː- -ness -nəs, -nɪs
workaday ˈwɜː.kə.deɪ, (US) ˈwɝː-
workaholic ˌwɜː.kəˈhɒl.ɪk, (US) ˌwɝː.kəˈhɑː.lɪk -s -s
workaholism ˈwɜː.kə.hɒl.ɪ.zᵊm, (US) ˈwɝː.kə.hɑː.lɪ-
workbag ˈwɜːk.bæg, (US) ˈwɝːk- -s -z
workbasket ˈwɜːkˌbɑː.skɪt, (US) ˈwɝːkˌbæs.kɪt -s -s
workbench ˈwɜːk.bentʃ, (US) ˈwɝːk- -es -ɪz
workbook ˈwɜːk.bʊk, (US) ˈwɝːk- -s -s
workbox ˈwɜːk.bɒks, (US) ˈwɝːk.bɑːks -es -ɪz
workday ˈwɜːk.deɪ, (US) ˈwɝːk- -s -z
worker ˈwɜː.kəʳ, (US) ˈwɝː.kɚ -s -z
workfare ˈwɜːk.feəʳ, (US) ˈwɝːk.fer
workforc|e ˈwɜːk.fɔːs, (US) ˈwɝːk.fɔːrs -es -ɪz
workhors|e ˈwɜːk.hɔːs, (US) ˈwɝːk.hɔːrs -es -ɪz
workhou|se ˈwɜːk.haʊ|s, (US) ˈwɝːk- -ses -zɪz
working class n ˌwɜː.kɪŋˈklɑːs, (US) ˈwɝː.kɪŋˌklæs -es -ɪz
working-class adj ˌwɜː.kɪŋˈklɑːs, (US) ˈwɝː.kɪŋˌklæs *stress shift, British only:* **ˌworking-class ˈorigins**
Workington ˈwɜː.kɪŋ.tən, (US) ˈwɝː-
workload ˈwɜːk.ləʊd, (US) ˈwɝːk.loʊd -s -z
work|man, W~ ˈwɜːk|.mən, (US) ˈwɝːk- -men -mən
workman|like ˈwɜːk.mən|.laɪk, (US) ˈwɝːk- -ly -li
workmanship ˈwɜːk.mən.ʃɪp, (US) ˈwɝːk-
workmate ˈwɜːk.meɪt, (US) ˈwɝːk- -s -s
workout ˈwɜːk.aʊt, (US) ˈwɝːk- -s -s
workpeople ˈwɜːkˌpiː.pᵊl, (US) ˈwɝːk-
workplac|e ˈwɜːk.pleɪs, (US) ˈwɝːk- -es -ɪz
workroom ˈwɜːk.rʊm, -ruːm, (US) ˈwɝːk.ruːm, -rʊm -s -z
worksheet ˈwɜːk.ʃiːt, (US) ˈwɝːk- -s -s
workshop ˈwɜːk.ʃɒp, (US) ˈwɝːk.ʃɑːp -s -s
work-shy ˈwɜːk.ʃaɪ, (US) ˈwɝːk-
Worksop ˈwɜːk.sɒp, -səp, (US) ˈwɝːk.sɑːp, -səp

W

workstation ˈwɜːkˌsteɪ.ʃᵊn, ⓤⓢ ˈwɝːk- **-s** -s
worktable ˈwɜːkˌteɪ.bᵊl, ⓤⓢ ˈwɝːk- **-s** -z
worktop ˈwɜːk.tɒp, ⓤⓢ ˈwɝːk.tɑːp **-s** -s
work-to-rule ˌwɜːk.təˈruːl, ⓤⓢ ˌwɝːk- **-s** -z
world wɜːld, ⓤⓢ wɝːld **-s** -z **ˌWorld ˈCup; ˌWorld ˈSeries; ˌWorld ˈService; ˌworld ˈwar; ˌWorld ˌWar ˈI; ˌWorld ˌWar ˈII; ˌWorld Wide ˈWeb; ˌout of this ˈworld**
world-class ˌwɜːldˈklɑːs, ⓤⓢ ˈwɝːld.klæs, ˌ-ˈ- *stress shift, British only:* **ˌworld-class ˈsportsman**
world-famous ˌwɜːldˈfeɪ.məs, ⓤⓢ ˈwɝːldˌfeɪ-, ˌ-ˈ-- *stress shift, British only:* **ˌworld-famous ˈactor**
worldling ˈwɜːld.lɪŋ, ⓤⓢ ˈwɝːld- **-s** -z
worldl|y ˈwɜːld.l|i, ⓤⓢ ˈwɝːld- **-ier** -i.əʳ, ⓤⓢ -i.ɚ **-iest** -i.ɪst, -i.əst **-iness** -ɪ.nəs, -ɪ.nɪs
worldly-wise ˌwɜːld.liˈwaɪz, ⓤⓢ ˈwɝːld.liˌwaɪz, ˌ--ˈ- *stress shift, British only:* **ˌworldly-wise ˈperson**
worldview ˈwɜːld.vjuː, ˌ-ˈ-, ⓤⓢ ˈwɝːld- **-s** -z
world-wear|y ˌwɜːldˈwɪə.r|i, ˈ-ˌ--, ⓤⓢ ˈwɝːldˌwɪr|.i **-ier** -i.əʳ, ⓤⓢ -i.ɚ **-iest** -i.ɪst, -i.əst **-ily** -ᵊl.i, -ɪ.li **-iness** -ɪ.nəs, -ɪ.nɪs *stress shift, British only:* **ˌworld-weary ˈattitude**
worldwide ˌwɜːldˈwaɪd, ⓤⓢ ˈwɝːld.waɪd, ˌ-ˈ- *stress shift, British only:* **ˌworldwide ˈcoverage**
worm wɜːm, ⓤⓢ wɝːm **-s** -z **-ing** -ɪŋ **-ed** -d
WORM wɜːm, ⓤⓢ wɝːm
wormcast ˈwɜːm.kɑːst, ⓤⓢ ˈwɝːm.kæst **-s** -s
worm-eaten ˈwɜːmˌiː.tᵊn, ⓤⓢ ˈwɝːm-
wormhole ˈwɜːm.həʊl, ⓤⓢ ˈwɝːm.hoʊl **-s** -z
Worms vɔːmz, wɜːmz, ⓤⓢ wɝːmz, vɔːrmz
wormwood, W~ ˈwɜːm.wʊd **ˌWormwood ˈScrubs**
worm|y ˈwɜː.m|i, ⓤⓢ ˈwɝː- **-iness** -ɪ.nəs, -ɪ.nɪs
worn (from **wear**) wɔːn, ⓤⓢ wɔːrn
worn-out ˌwɔːnˈaʊt, ⓤⓢ ˌwɔːrn- *stress shift:* **ˌworn-out ˈshoes**
Worple ˈwɔː.pᵊl, ⓤⓢ ˈwɔːr-
Worplesdon ˈwɔː.pᵊlz.dən, ⓤⓢ ˈwɔːr-
Worrall ˈwʌr.ᵊl, ˈwɒr-, ⓤⓢ ˈwɔːr-, ˈwɝː-
worrisome ˈwʌr.ɪ.səm, ⓤⓢ ˈwɝː.i- **-ly** -li
worr|y ˈwʌr|.i, ⓤⓢ ˈwɝː- **-ies** -iz **-ying/ly** -i.ɪŋ/li **-ied** -id **-ier/s** -i.əʳ/z, ⓤⓢ -i.ɚ/z **ˈworry ˌbeads**
worrywart ˈwʌr.i.wɔːt, ⓤⓢ ˈwɝː.i.wɔːrt **-s** -s
Worsborough ˈwɜːz.bᵊr.ə, ⓤⓢ ˈwɝːz.bɚ.oʊ, -ə
worse wɜːs, ⓤⓢ wɝːs
worsen ˈwɜː.sᵊn, ⓤⓢ ˈwɝː- **-s** -z **-ing** -ɪŋ, ˈwɜːs.nɪŋ, ⓤⓢ ˈwɝːs- **-ed** -d
worse-off ˌwɜːsˈɒf, ⓤⓢ ˌwɝːsˈɑːf *stress shift:* **ˌworse-off ˈcircumstances**
Worsfold ˈwɜːs.fəʊld, ˈwɔːz-, ⓤⓢ ˈwɝːs.foʊld, ˈwɔːrz-
worship, W~ ˈwɜː.ʃɪp, ⓤⓢ ˈwɝː- **-s** -s **-(p)ing** -ɪŋ **-(p)ed** -t **-(p)er/s** -əʳ/z, ⓤⓢ -ɚ/z
worshipful ˈwɜː.ʃɪp.fᵊl, -fʊl, ⓤⓢ ˈwɝː- **-ly** -i **-ness** -nəs, -nɪs
Worsley *surname:* ˈwɜː.sli, ˈwɜːz.li, ⓤⓢ ˈwɝː.sli, ˈwɝːz.li *place near Manchester:* ˈwɜː.sli, ⓤⓢ ˈwɝː-
worst wɜːst, ⓤⓢ wɝːst **-s** -s **-ing** -ɪŋ **-ed** -ɪd
worst-case ˌwɜːstˈkeɪs, ⓤⓢ ˌwɝːst- *stress shift:* **ˌworst-case sceˈnario**
Worstead ˈwʊs.tɪd, -təd, ⓤⓢ ˈwʊs-, ˈwɝː.stɪd, -stəd
worsted *yarn, cloth:* ˈwʊs.tɪd, -təd, ⓤⓢ ˈwʊs-, ˈwɝː.stɪd, -stəd
worsted (from **worst**) ˈwɜː.stɪd, ⓤⓢ ˈwɝː-
Worsthorne ˈwɜːs.θɔːn, ⓤⓢ ˈwɝːs.θɔːrn
Worswick ˈwɜː.sɪk, ⓤⓢ ˈwɝː-
wort wɜːt, ⓤⓢ wɝːt, wɔːrt **-s** -s
worth, W~ wɜːθ, ⓤⓢ wɝːθ
Worthing ˈwɜː.ðɪŋ, ⓤⓢ ˈwɝː- **-ton** -tən
worthless ˈwɜːθ.ləs, -lɪs, ⓤⓢ ˈwɝːθ- **-ly** -li **-ness** -nəs, -nɪs
worthwhile ˌwɜːθˈhwaɪl, ⓤⓢ ˌwɝːθ- *stress shift:* **ˌworthwhile ˈprogress**
worth|y ˈwɜː.ð|i, ⓤⓢ ˈwɝː- **-ies** -iz **-ier** -i.əʳ, ⓤⓢ -i.ɚ **-iest** -i.ɪst, -i.əst **-ily** ⓤⓢ -ᵊl.i, -ɪ.li **-iness** -ɪ.nəs, -ɪ.nɪs
Wortley ˈwɜːt.li, ⓤⓢ ˈwɝːt-
wot wɒt, ⓤⓢ wɑːt
Wotan ˈwəʊ.tæn, ˈvəʊ-, ⓤⓢ ˈvoʊ.tɑːn
wotcha ˈwɒtʃ.ə, ⓤⓢ ˈwɑː.tʃə
wotcher ˈwɒt.ʃəʳ, ⓤⓢ ˈwɑː.tʃɚ
Wotherspoon ˈwɒð.ə.spuːn, ⓤⓢ ˈwɑː.ðɚ-
Wotton ˈwɒt.ᵊn, ˈwʊt-, ⓤⓢ ˈwɑː.tᵊn, ˈwʊt.ᵊn

> Note: The place in Buckinghamshire is pronounced /ˈwʊt.ᵊn/.

would (from **will**) *strong form:* wʊd; *weak forms:* wəd, əd, d
Note: Weak-form word. The strong form is used contrastively (e.g. 'I don't know if he would or he wouldn't') and emphatically (e.g. 'I certainly **would**'). The strong form is always used in final position, even when unstressed (e.g. 'I **knew** she would'). The weak forms are used elsewhere. The forms /əd/ and /d/ are usually represented in spelling as **'d** (e.g 'John'd do it' /ˈdʒɒn.ədˌduː.ɪt/ ⓤⓢ /ˈdʒɑːn-/; 'I'd do it' /ˈaɪdˌduː.ɪt/).
would-be ˈwʊd.bi
wouldn't (= **would not**) ˈwʊd.ᵊnt
wouldn't've = **would not have** ˈwʊd.ᵊnt.ᵊv
wouldst wʊdst
would've would have ˈwʊd.ᵊv
wound n, v wuːnd **-s** -z **-ing** -ɪŋ **-ed** -ɪd
wound (from **wind,** v.) waʊnd
wov|e (from **weave**) wəʊv, ⓤⓢ woʊv **-en** -ᵊn
wow waʊ **-s** -z **-ing** -ɪŋ **-ed** -d
wowser ˈwaʊ.zəʳ, ⓤⓢ -zɚ **-s** -z
Wozzeck ˈvɒt.sek, ⓤⓢ ˈvɑːt.sek
WP ˌdʌb.ᵊl.juːˈpiː
WPC ˌdʌb.ᵊl.juːˌpiːˈsiː, -jʊˌ-, ⓤⓢ -juːˌ-, -jəˌ- **-s** -z *stress shift:* **ˌWPC ˈSmith**
WRAC ræk, ˌdʌb.ᵊl.juːˌɑːʳeɪˈsiː, -ju-, ⓤⓢ ræk, -juːˌɑːr-, -jəˌ-
wrack ræk **-s** -s **-ing** -ɪŋ **-ed** -t
WRAF ræf; ˌdʌb.ᵊl.juːˌɑːʳ.eɪˈef, ⓤⓢ ræf; ˌdʌb.ᵊl.juːˌɑːr.eɪˈef
Wragg ræg
wraith reɪθ **-s** -s
wrangl|e ˈræŋ.gᵊl **-es** -z **-ing** -ɪŋ, ˈ-glɪŋ **-ed** -d **-er/s** -əʳ/z, ˈ-gləʳ/z, ⓤⓢ ˈ-gᵊl.ɚ/z, ˈ-glɚ/z
wrangler, W~® ˈræŋ.gləʳ, ⓤⓢ -glɚ **-s** -z
wrap ræp **-s** -s **-ping/s** -ɪŋ/z **-ped** -t
wraparound ˈræp.ə.raʊnd **-s** -z
wrapper ˈræp.əʳ, ⓤⓢ -ɚ **-s** -z
wrapround ˈræp.raʊnd
wrass|e ræs **-es** -ɪz
wrath rɒθ, rɔːθ, ⓤⓢ ræθ, rɑːθ
Wrath *Cape:* rɔːθ, rɑːθ, ræθ, ⓤⓢ ræθ, rɑːθ
wrathful ˈrɒθ.fᵊl, ˈrɔːθ-, -fʊl, ⓤⓢ ˈræθ-, ˈrɑːθ- **-ly** -i **-ness** -nəs, -nɪs
Wraxall ˈræk.sɔːl
Wray reɪ
wreak riːk **-s** -s **-ing** -ɪŋ **-ed** -t
wrea|th riː|θ **-ths** -ðz, -θs
wreath|e riːð **-es** -z **-ing** -ɪŋ **-ed** -d
Wreay reɪ; *locally:* rɪə
wreck rek **-s** -s **-ing** -ɪŋ **-ed** -t **-er/s** -əʳ/z, ⓤⓢ -ɚ/z
wreckag|e ˈrek.ɪdʒ **-es** -ɪz
Wrekin ˈriː.kɪn
wren, W~ ren **-s** -z
wrench rentʃ **-es** -ɪz **-ing** -ɪŋ **-ed** -t
Wrenn ren
wrest rest **-s** -s **-ing** -ɪŋ **-ed** -ɪd
wrestl|e ˈres.ᵊl **-es** -z **-ing** -ɪŋ, ˈres.lɪŋ **-ed** -d **-er/s** -əʳ/z, ˈres.ləʳ/z, ⓤⓢ ˈres.ᵊl.ɚ/z, ˈres.lɚ/z
wretch retʃ **-es** -ɪz
wretched ˈretʃ.ɪd **-ly** -li **-ness** -nəs, -nɪs
Wrexham ˈrek.səm
wriggl|e ˈrɪg.ᵊl **-es** -z **-ing** -ɪŋ, ˈrɪg.lɪŋ **-ed** -d **-er/s** -əʳ/z, ˈrɪg.ləʳ/z, ⓤⓢ ˈrɪg.ᵊl.ɚ/z, ˈrɪg.lɚ/z
wright, W~ raɪt **-s** -s
Wrigley ˈrɪg.li
wring rɪŋ **-s** -z **-ing** -ɪŋ **-er/s** -əʳ/z, ⓤⓢ -ɚ/z **wrung** rʌŋ
wrinkl|e ˈrɪŋ.kᵊl **-es** -z **-ing** -ɪŋ, ˈrɪŋ.klɪŋ **-ed** -d
wrinkl|y ˈrɪŋ.kl|i **-ies** -iz
Wriothesley ˈraɪ.əθ.sli
wrist rɪst **-s** -s

W

wristband ˈrɪst.bænd **-s** -z
wristlet ˈrɪst.lɪt, -lət **-s** -s
wristwatch ˈrɪst.wɒtʃ, ⓊⓈ -wɑːtʃ **-es** -ɪz
wristy ˈrɪs.ti
writ rɪt **-s** -s
writ (= **written**) rɪt
writ|e raɪt **-es** -s **-ing/s** -ɪŋ/z, ⓊⓈ ˈraɪ.t̬ɪŋ/z **wrote** rəʊt, ⓊⓈ roʊt **written** ˈrɪt.ən **writer/s** ˈraɪ.təʳ/z, ⓊⓈ ˈraɪ.t̬ɚ/z ˌ**writer's** ˈ**cramp**
writh|e raɪð **-es** -z **-ing** -ɪŋ **-ed** -d
writing ˈraɪ.tɪŋ, ⓊⓈ -t̬ɪŋ **-s** -z **see the** ˌ**writing on the** ˈ**wall**
writing-cas|e ˈraɪ.tɪŋ.keɪs, ⓊⓈ -t̬ɪŋ- **-es** -ɪz
writing-paper ˈraɪ.tɪŋˌpeɪ.pəʳ, ⓊⓈ -t̬ɪŋˌpeɪ.pɚ
written-off ˌrɪt.ənˈɒf, ⓊⓈ -ˈɑːf
Writtle ˈrɪt.əl, ⓊⓈ ˈrɪt̬-
WRNS (abbrev. for **Women's Royal Navy Service**) renz; ˌdʌb.əl.juːˌɑːʳ.enˈes, ⓊⓈ renz; ˌdʌb.əl.juːˌɑːr.enˈes
Wroclaw ˈvrɒt.slɑːf, -slæf, -swɑːf, ⓊⓈ ˈvrɑːt.slɑːf
wrong, W~ rɒŋ, ⓊⓈ rɑːŋ, rɔːŋ **-s** -z **-ly** -li **-ness** -nəs, -nɪs **-ing** -ɪŋ **-ed** -d
wrong-doer ˈrɒŋˌduː.əʳ, ˌ-ˈ--, ⓊⓈ ˈrɑːŋˌduː.ɚ, ˈrɔːŋ- **-s** -z
wrong-doing ˈrɒŋˌduː.ɪŋ, ˌ-ˈ--, ⓊⓈ ˈrɑːŋˌduː-, ˈrɔːŋ-
wrong|-foot ˌrɒŋ|ˈfʊt, ⓊⓈ ˌrɑːŋ-, ˌrɔːŋ- **-foots** -ˈfʊts **-footing** -ˈfʊt.ɪŋ, ⓊⓈ -ˈfʊt̬.ɪŋ **-footed** -ˈfʊt.ɪd, ⓊⓈ -ˈfʊt̬.ɪd
wrongful ˈrɒŋ.fəl, -fʊl, ⓊⓈ ˈrɑːŋ-, ˈrɔːŋ- **-ly** -i **-ness** -nəs, -nɪs
wrongheaded ˌrɒŋˈhed.ɪd, ⓊⓈ ˌrɑːŋ-, ˌrɔːŋ-, ˈ-ˌ-- **-ly** -li **-ness** -nəs, -nɪs
wrote (from **write**) rəʊt, ⓊⓈ roʊt
wroth rəʊθ, rɔːθ, rɒθ, ⓊⓈ rɔːθ, rɑːθ
Wrotham ˈruː.təm, ⓊⓈ -t̬əm
Wrottesley ˈrɒt.sli, ⓊⓈ ˈrɑːt-
wrought rɔːt, ⓊⓈ rɑːt, rɔːt
wrought-iron ˌrɔːtˈaɪən, ⓊⓈ -ˈaɪ.ən, ˌrɑːt̬ˈaɪ.ɚn, ˌrɔːt- *stress shift:* ˌ**wrought-iron** ˈ**gate**
Wroughton ˈrɔː.tən, ⓊⓈ ˈrɑː-, ˈrɔː-
Wroxham ˈrɒk.səm, ⓊⓈ ˈrɑːk-
wrung (from **wring**) rʌŋ
W.R.V.S. ˌdʌb.əl.juːˌɑːˌviːˈes, -jʊˌ-, ⓊⓈ -juːˌɑːrˌ-, -jəˌ-
wry raɪ **wrier, wryer** ˈraɪ.əʳ, ⓊⓈ -ɚ **wriest, wryest** ˈraɪ.ɪst, -əst **wryly** ˈraɪ.li **wryness** ˈraɪ.nəs, -nɪs
wryneck ˈraɪ.nek **-s** -s
Wrythe raɪð
WSW (abbrev. for **west southwest**) ˌwest.saʊθˈwest; *nautical pronunciation:* -saʊˈ-
wt (abbrev. for **weight**) weɪt
Wuhan ˌwuːˈhæn, ⓊⓈ -ˈhɑːn
Wulf wʊlf
Wulfstan ˈwʊlf.stən, ⓊⓈ -stæn, -stɑːn
wunder|kind ˈwʊn.də|.kɪnd, ˈvʊn-, ⓊⓈ -dɚ|.kɪnt, ˈwʌn- **-kinder** -ˌkɪn.dəʳ, ⓊⓈ -ˌkɪn.dɚ
Wuornos ˈwɜː.nɒs, ⓊⓈ ˈwɝː.noʊz
Wurlitzer ˈwɜː.lɪt.səʳ, -lət-, ⓊⓈ ˈwɝː.lət.sɚ **-s** -z
Württemberg ˈvɜː.təm.beəg; ˈwɜː.təm.bɜːg, ⓊⓈ ˈwɝː.t̬əm.bɝːrg; ⓊⓈ ˈvɝː.təm.berk
Würzburg ˈvɜːts.beəg; ˈwɜːts.bɜːg, ⓊⓈ ˈwɝːts.bɝːrg; ⓊⓈ ˈvɝːts.burk
wuss wʊs **-es** -ɪz
Wuthering ˈwʌð.ər.ɪŋ ˌ**Wuthering** ˈ**Heights**
W.Va. (abbrev. for **West Virginia**) ˌwest.vəˈdʒɪn.jə, -vɜːˈ-, ˈ-i.ə, ⓊⓈ -vɚˈ-
WVS ˌdʌb.əl.juːˌviːˈes, -jʊˌ-, ⓊⓈ -juːˌ-, -jəˌ-
Wyandotte ˈwaɪ.ən.dɒt, ⓊⓈ -dɑːt **-s** -s
Wyat(t) waɪ.ət
Wych waɪtʃ, wɪtʃ
Wycherley ˈwɪtʃ.əl.i, ⓊⓈ -ɚ.li
wych-hazel ˈwɪtʃˌheɪ.zəl, ˌ-ˈ--, ⓊⓈ ˈwɪtʃˌheɪ- **-s** -z
Wycliffe, Wyclif ˈwɪk.lɪf
Wycliffite ˈwɪk.lɪ.faɪt **-s** -s
Wycombe ˈwɪk.əm
Wye waɪ
Wygram ˈwaɪ.grəm
Wykeham ˈwɪk.əm **-ist/s** -ɪst/s
Wyld(e) waɪld
Wyl(l)ie ˈwaɪ.li
Wyman ˈwaɪ.mən
Wymondham *in Norfolk:* ˈwɪm.ən.dəm; *locally:* ˈwɪn.dəm *in Leicestershire:* ˈwaɪ.mən.dəm
Wyndham ˈwɪn.dəm
Wynn(e) wɪn
Wynyard ˈwɪn.jəd, -jɑːd, ⓊⓈ -jɚd, -jɑːrd
Wyo. (abbrev. for **Wyoming**) waɪˈəʊ.mɪŋ, ⓊⓈ -ˈoʊ-
Wyoming waɪˈəʊ.mɪŋ, ⓊⓈ -ˈoʊ-
WYSIWYG ˈwɪz.i.wɪg
Wyss waɪs
Wystan ˈwɪs.tən
Wytch Farm ˌwɪtʃˈfɑːm, ⓊⓈ -ˈfɑːrm
Wytham ˈwaɪ.təm, ⓊⓈ -t̬əm
Wythenshawe ˈwɪð.ən.ʃɔː, ⓊⓈ -ʃɑː, -ʃɔː
wyvern, W~ ˈwaɪ.vən, ⓊⓈ -vɚn, -vɝːn **wyvern** -vɜːn **-s** -z

Pronouncing the letter X

→ *See also* **XC**

The consonant letter **x**, which rarely occurs at the beginning of a word, has three main pronunciations: /ks/, /gz/, and /kʃ/, e.g.:

box	bɒks (US) bɑːks
examine	ɪgˈzæm.ɪn, ɪkˈsæm- (US) ɪgˈzæm-
noxious	ˈnɒk.ʃəs (US) ˈnɑːk-

When **x** does appear at the beginning of a word, it is almost always pronounced /z/, e.g.:

z	xylophone /ˈzaɪ.lə.fəʊn/ (US) /-foʊn/

Another pronunciation associated with **x** is /eks/, e.g.:

eks	X-ray /ˈeks.reɪ/ (US) /ˈek.sreɪ/

Pronouncing the letters XC

The consonant digraph **xc** has two pronunciations: /ks/ and /ksk/.

Before the vowel letters **i** or **e**, it is pronounced as /ks/, e.g.:

exceed	ɪkˈsiːd

In other situations, **xc** is pronounced as /ksk/, e.g.:

exclaim	ɪksˈkleɪm

x, X eks -'s -ɪz

Xanadu ˈzæn.ə.duː, ˌ--ˈ-, (US) ˈzæn.ə.duː, -djuː, ˌ--ˈ-

Xanthe ˈzæn*t*.θi

Xanthipp|e zæn*t*ˈθɪp|.i, zænˈtɪp-, (US) zænˈtɪp- **-us** -əs

Xanthus ˈzæn*t*.θəs

Xantia® ˈzæn.ti.ə, (US) zænˈtiː-

Xavier ˈzæv.i.əʳ, -eɪ, ˈzeɪ.vi.əʳ, ˈ-vjəʳ, (US) ˈzeɪ.vjɚ, ˈzæv.jɚ, -i.ɚ

Xbox® ˈeks.bɒks, (US) -bɑːks **-es** -ɪz

X-certificate ˌeks.səˈtɪf.ɪ.kət, -sɜːˈ-, ˈ-ə-, -kɪt, (US) -sɚˈ- **-s** -s

xebec ˈziː.bek **-s** -s

Xenia ˈzen.i.ə, ˈksen-, ˈziː.ni-, ˈksiː-, ˈ-njə, (US) ˈziː.njə, ˈ-ni.ə

xeno- ˈzen.ə*ʊ*, ˈziː.nə*ʊ*; zɪˈnɒ, (US) ˈzen.oʊ, ˈziː.noʊ, ˈnə; (US) zɪˈnɑː
Note: Prefix. Normally either takes primary or secondary stress on the first syllable, e.g. **xenophobe** /ˈzen.ə*ʊ*.fəʊb/ (US) /-ə.foʊb/, **xenophobia** /ˌzen.ə*ʊ*ˈfəʊ.bi.ə/ (US) /-əˈfoʊ-/, or primary stress on the second syllable, e.g. **xenogamy** /zɪˈnɒg.ə.mi/ (US) /-ˈnɑː.gə-/.

xenogamy zɪˈnɒg.ə.mi, (US) -ˈnɑː.gə-

xenon ˈziː.nɒn, (US) -nɑːn, ˈzen.ɑːn

xenophobe ˈzen.ə*ʊ*.fəʊb, (US) -ə.foʊb, ˈziː.nə- **-s** -z

xenophobia ˌzen.ə*ʊ*ˈfəʊ.bi.ə, (US) -əˈfoʊ-, ˌziː.nəˈ-, -noʊˈ-

xenophobic ˌzen.ə*ʊ*ˈfəʊ.bɪk, (US) -əˈfoʊ-, ˌziː.nə-, -noʊ- *stress shift:* **ˌxenophobic ˈsentiment**

Xenophon ˈzen.ə.fᵊn, (US) -fən, -fɑːn

xerography zɪəˈrɒg.rə.fi, zerˈɒg-, (US) zɪˈrɑː.grə-

xerox, X~® **n, v** ˈzɪə.rɒks, (US) ˈzɪr.ɑːks, ˈziː.rɑːks **-es** -ɪz **-ing** -ɪŋ **-ed** -t

Xerxes ˈzɜːk.siːz, (US) ˈzɝːk-

Xhosa ˈkɔː.sə, ˈkəʊ-, -zə, (US) ˈkoʊ.sɑː, -zɑː

xi saɪ, ksaɪ, (US) zaɪ, saɪ **-'s** -z

Xiaoping ˌʃaʊˈpɪŋ

Xinhua ˌʃɪnˈhwɑː *stress shift:* **ˌXinhua ˈNews Agency**

Xmas ˈkrɪs*t*.məs, ˈeks.məs, (US) ˈkrɪs-

XML ˌeks.emˈel

X-rated ˈeksˌreɪ.tɪd, (US) -t̬ɪd

X-ray ˈeks.reɪ, ˌ-ˈ-, (US) ˈek.sreɪ **-s** -z **-ing** -ɪŋ **-ed** -d

xu suː

xylem ˈzaɪ.ləm, -lem

xylene ˈzaɪ.liːn

xylograph ˈzaɪ.lə*ʊ*.grɑːf, -græf, (US) -loʊ.græf, -lə- **-s** -s

xylograph|y zaɪˈlɒg.rə.f|i, (US) -ˈlɑː.grə- **-er/s** -əʳ/z, (US) -ɚ/z

xylonite ˈzaɪ.lə.naɪt

xylophone ˈzaɪ.lə.fəʊn, (US) -foʊn **-s** -z

xylose ˈzaɪ.ləʊs, -ləʊz, (US) -loʊs

xyster ˈzɪs.təʳ, (US) -tɚ

Pronouncing the letter Y

The consonant letter **y** is special in that it can act as both vowel and consonant. At the beginning of a word, it most often behaves as a consonant and, when doing so, is pronounced as /j/, e.g.:

yes	jes
youth	juːθ

When acting as a vowel, the letter **y** has two main strong pronunciations: a 'short' pronunciation /ɪ/ and a 'long' pronunciation /aɪ/. There are no definite rules for when either of these pronunciations will occur, e.g.:

myth	mɪθ
cycle	ˈsaɪ.kl̩

At the end of a word, in adjectives and adverbs ending with a letter **y**, a short /i/ is usually used. However, for other types of word, either /i/ or /aɪ/ may occur, e.g.:

happy	ˈhæp.i
happily	ˈhæp.ɪ.li
study	ˈstʌd.i
apply	əˈplaɪ

When **y** is followed by **r**, the strong pronunciation is one of the following possibilities: /aɪə/ (US) /aɪ.ɚ/, /aɪə.r/ (US) /aɪ.r/ or /ɪ/ when followed by a single consonant and then a vowel, otherwise /ɜː/ (US) /ɝː/, e.g.:

tyre	taɪəʳ (US) taɪ.ɚ
gyrate (v.)	dʒaɪəˈreɪt (US) ˈdʒaɪ.reɪt
lyric	ˈlɪr.ɪk
myrrh	mɜːʳ (US) mɝː

In addition

When acting as a vowel, **y** can also be realized as /iː/ or /ɪ/ in a small number of words, usually proper nouns, e.g.:

Yves	iːv

In weak syllables

When acting as a vowel, the letter **y** is realized with the vowels /ɪ/ and, occasionally, /ə/ and /i/ in word-medial weak syllables, e.g.:

oxygen	ˈɒk.sɪ.dʒən, -sə- (US) ˈɑːk.sɪ-
anybody	ˈen.iˌbɒd.i (US) -ˌbɑː.di

y, Y waɪ **-'s** -z
yacht jɒt, (US) jɑːt **-s** -s **-ing** -ɪŋ, (US) ˈjɑː.t̬ɪŋ **-ed** -ɪd, (US) ˈjɑː.t̬ɪd
yachts|man ˈjɒts|.mən, (US) ˈjɑːts- **-men** -mən **-woman** -ˌwʊm.ən **-women** -ˌwɪm.ɪn
yack jæk **-s** -s **-ing** -ɪŋ **-ed** -t
yah jɑː
yahoo, Y~ interj jəˈhuː, jɑː- **-s** -z **n** ˈjɑː.huː, (US) ˈjɑː-, ˈjeɪ-

> Note: The pronunciation for the noun is also suitable for the characters in Swift's **Gulliver's Travels**. The name of **Yahoo!**, the provider of Internet services, may be pronounced with any of the above pronunciations.

Yahveh ˈjɑː.veɪ, -və, jɑːˈveɪ, (US) ˈjɑː.veɪ
Yahweh ˈjɑː.weɪ
yak jæk **-s** -s
yakka ˈjæk.ə
Yakutsk jækˈʊtsk, jɑːˈkʊtsk, jə-, (US) jɑːˈkʊtsk
yakuza ˈjæk.ʊ.zɑː, (US) ˈjɑː.kʊ- **-s** -z
Yalding *surname:* ˈjæl.dɪŋ *place name:* ˈjɔːl.dɪŋ, (US) ˈjɑːl-, ˈjɔːl-
Yale jeɪl
y'all jɔːl, (US) jɑːl
Yalta ˈjæl.tə, ˈjɔːl-, ˈjɒl-, (US) ˈjɑːl.tə, ˈjɔːl-, -tə
yam jæm **-s** -z
Yamaha ˈjæm.ə.hɑː, -hə, (US) ˈjɑː.mə-
Yamamoto jæm.əˈməʊ.təʊ, (US) ˌjɑː.məˈmoʊ.t̬oʊ, -toʊ
yamm|er ˈjæm|.əʳ, (US) -ɚ **-ers** -əz, (US) -ɚz **-ering** -ᵊr.ɪŋ **-ed** -əd, (US) -ɚd
yang jæŋ, (US) jæŋ, jɑːŋ
Yangtze, Yangtse, Yangzi ˈjæŋkt.si, (US) ˈjæŋkt-, ˈjɑːŋkt-
yank, Y~ jæŋk **-s** -s **-ing** -ɪŋ **-ed** -t
Yankee ˈjæŋ.ki **-s** -z
Yaoundé ˌjɑː.ʊnˈdeɪ, -ˈuːn-, (US) ˌjɑː.ʊnˈdeɪ
yap jæp **-s** -s **-ping** -ɪŋ **-ped** -t
Yap jæp, (US) jɑːp, jæp
yard jɑːd, (US) jɑːrd **-s** -z ˈ**yard** ˌ**sale**
yardage ˈjɑː.dɪdʒ, (US) ˈjɑːr- **-s** -ɪz
yardarm ˈjɑːd.ɑːm, (US) ˈjɑːrd.ɑːrm **-s** -z
yardbird ˈjɑːd.bɜːd, (US) ˈjɑːrd.bɝːd **-s** -z
Yardie ˈjɑː.di, (US) ˈjɑːr- **-s** -z
Yardley ˈjɑːd.li, (US) ˈjɑːrd-
yardstick ˈjɑːd.stɪk, (US) ˈjɑːrd- **-s** -s
Yare *in Norfolk:* jeəʳ, (US) jer *in the Isle of Wight:* jɑːʳ, (US) jɑːr
Yarm jɑːm, (US) jɑːrm
yarmelke ˈjʌm.ʊl.kə, ˈjɑː.mʊl-, -mᵊl-, (US) ˈjɑːr.məl-, ˈjɑː- **-s** -z
Yarmouth ˈjɑː.məθ, (US) ˈjɑːr-
yarmulke, yarmulka ˈjʌm.ʊl.kə, ˈjɑː.mʊl-, -mᵊl-, (US) ˈjɑːr.məl-, ˈjɑː- **-s** -z
yarn jɑːn, (US) jɑːrn **-s** -z **-ing** -ɪŋ **-ed** -d
Yaroslavl ˌjær.əʊˈslɑː.vᵊl, (US) ˌjɑːr.oʊˈslɑː.vᵊl, -əˈ-
yarrow, Y~ ˈjær.əʊ, (US) ˈjer.oʊ, ˈjær-
yashmak ˈjæʃ.mæk, (US) ˈjɑːʃ.mɑːk, ˈjæʃ.mæk **-s** -s
Yasmin ˈjæz.mɪn
Yasser ˈjæs.əʳ, (US) -ɚ, ˈjɑː.sɚ
yataghan ˈjæt.ə.gən, (US) -gæn, -gən **-s** -z
Yate jeɪt **-s** -s
Yately ˈjeɪt.li
Yatman ˈjæt.mən
Yatton ˈjæt.ᵊn
yaw jɔː, (US) jɑː, jɔː **-s** -z **-ing** -ɪŋ **-ed** -d
Yaweh ˈjɑː.weɪ
yawl jɔːl, (US) jɑːl, jɔːl **-s** -z
yawn jɔːn, (US) jɑːn, jɔːn **-s** -z **-ing/ly** -ɪŋ/li **-ed** -d
yaws jɔːz, (US) jɑːz, jɔːz
Yaxley ˈjæk.sli
yclept ɪˈklept, (US) i-
yd (abbrev. for **yard**) *singular:* jɑːd, (US) jɑːrd; *plural:* jɑːdz, (US) jɑːrdz
ye *you. Normal form:* jiː; *occasional weak form:* ji
Note: The weak form is rarely used, and only in imitation of archaic or dialect sayings such as 'Sit ye down' /ˌsɪt.jiˈdaʊn/.
ye *the:* jiː

> Note: As a pronunciation of the definite article, this is rarely used except in joking. It is a mistake resulting from reading the Old English letter 'thorn' (which represented 'th' sounds) as a 'y', which it resembles.

yea jeɪ

Yeading ˈjed.ɪŋ
Yeadon ˈjiː.dᵊn
yeah jeə, ⓊⓈ jeə, jæə

> Note: Aside from the examples given for American English, there are many possibilities here, another being /jɑː/.

Yeames jiːmz
yean jiːn **-s** -z **-ing** -ɪŋ **-ed** -d
year jɪəʳ, jɜːʳ, ⓊⓈ jɪr **-s** -z **-ly** -li ˌ**year in (and)** ˌ**year** ˈ**out**
yearbook ˈjɪə.bʊk, ˈjɜː-, ⓊⓈ ˈjɪr- **-s** -s
yearling ˈjɪə.lɪŋ, ˈjɜː-, ⓊⓈ ˈjɪr- **-s** -z
yearlong ˌjɪəˈlɒŋ, ˌjɜː-, ⓊⓈ ˈjɪr.lɑːŋ, -lɔːŋ, ˌ-ˈ- *stress shift, British only:* ˌ**yearlong** ˈ**truce**
yearn jɜːn, ⓊⓈ jɝːn **-s** -z **-ing/s** -ɪŋ/z **-ed** -d
yeast jiːst **-y** -i **-iness** -ɪ.nəs, -ɪ.nɪs
Yeates jeɪts
Yeatman ˈjiːt.mən, ˈjeɪt-, ˈjet-
Yeats jeɪts
Yeddo ˈjed.əʊ, ⓊⓈ -oʊ
Yehudi jeˈhuː.di, jɪ-, jə-
yell, Y~ jel **-s** -z **-ing** -ɪŋ **-ed** -d
Yelland ˈjel.ənd
yellow ˈjel.əʊ, ⓊⓈ -oʊ **-s** -z **-ing** -ɪŋ **-ed** -d **-y** -i ˌ**yellow** ˈ**fever;** ˌ**yellow** ˌ**brick** ˈ**road;** ˌ**yellow** ˈ**line;** ˌ**Yellow** ˈ**Pages** ⓊⓈ ˈ**Yellow** ˌ**Pages;** ˌ**yellow** ˈ**peril**
yellowhammer ˈjel.əʊˌhæm.əʳ, ⓊⓈ -oʊˌhæm.ɚ **-s** -z
yellowish ˈjel.əʊ.ɪʃ, ⓊⓈ -oʊ- **-ness** -nəs, -nɪs
yellowjacket ˈjel.əʊˌdʒæk.ɪt, ⓊⓈ -oʊ- **-s** -s
Yellowknife ˈjel.əʊ.naɪf, ⓊⓈ -oʊ-
yellowness ˈjel.əʊ.nəs, -nɪs, ⓊⓈ -oʊ-
Yellowstone ˈjel.əʊ.stəʊn, -stən, ⓊⓈ -oʊ.stoʊn
yellowtail ˈjel.əʊ.teɪl, ⓊⓈ -oʊ- **-s** -z
yelp jelp **-s** -s **-ing** -ɪŋ **-ed** -t
Yeltsin ˈjelt.sɪn
Yemen ˈjem.ən, -en, ⓊⓈ -ən, ˈjeɪ.mən **-i** -i **-is** -iz
Yemenite ˈjem.ən.aɪt, ⓊⓈ ˈjem-, ˈjeɪ.mən- **-s** -s
yen jen **-s** -z
Yentob ˈjen.tɒb, ⓊⓈ -tɑːb
Yeo jəʊ, ⓊⓈ joʊ
Yeoburgh ˈjɑː.bᵊr.ə, -bɚ.ə
yeo|man ˈjəʊ|.mən, ⓊⓈ ˈjoʊ- **-men** -mən **-manly** -mən.li
yeomanry ˈjəʊ.mən.ri, ⓊⓈ ˈjoʊ-
Yeomans ˈjəʊ.mənz, ⓊⓈ ˈjoʊ-
Yeovil ˈjəʊ.vɪl, ⓊⓈ ˈjoʊ-
yep jep
yer *informal pronunciation of 'you' (not normally used before vowels):* jə *informal pronunciation of 'your' or 'you're' :* jəʳ, ⓊⓈ jɚ
Yerby ˈjɜː.bi, ⓊⓈ ˈjɝː-
Yerevan ˌjer.əˈvɑːn, ˈjer.ə.væn
Yerkes ˈjɜː.kiːz, ⓊⓈ ˈjɝː-
yes jes
yes|man ˈjes|.mæn **-men** -men

yesterday ˈjes.tə.deɪ, ˌ--ˈ-, -di, ⓊⓈ -tɚ-
yesteryear ˈjes.tə.jɪəʳ, ˌ--ˈ-, ⓊⓈ -tɚ.jɪr
yet jet
Yetholm ˈjet.əm, ⓊⓈ ˈjeţ-
yeti ˈjet.i, ⓊⓈ ˈjeţ- **-s** -z
Yevtushenko ˌjev.tʊˈʃeŋ.kəʊ, -tuːˈ-, ⓊⓈ -koʊ
yew juː **-s** -z
Y-Front® ˈwaɪ.frʌnt **-s** -s
Yg(g)drasil ˈɪg.drə.sɪl, ɪgˈdræs.ᵊl, ⓊⓈ ˈɪg.drə.sɪl
yid jɪd **-s** -z
Yiddish ˈjɪd.ɪʃ
yield jiːld **-s** -z **-ing/ly** -ɪŋ/li **-ed** -ɪd
yin jɪn
yippee jɪˈpiː, ⓊⓈ ˈjɪp.iː
Yitzhak ˈjɪt.sɑːk, -sæk
ylang-ylang ˌiː.læŋˈiː.læŋ, ⓊⓈ -lɑːŋˈiː.lɑːŋ
YMCA ˌwaɪ.em.siːˈeɪ
Ynys Mon ˌʌn.ɪsˈmɔːn
yo jəʊ, ⓊⓈ joʊ
yob jɒb, ⓊⓈ jɑːb **-s** -z
yobbish ˈjɒb.ɪʃ, ⓊⓈ ˈjɑː.bɪʃ **-ly** -li **-ness** -nəs, -nɪs
yobbo ˈjɒb.əʊ, ⓊⓈ ˈjɑː.boʊ **-s** -z
yod jɒd, ⓊⓈ jɑːd **-s** -z
yodel ˈjəʊ.dᵊl, ⓊⓈ ˈjoʊ- **-s** -z **-(l)ing** -ɪŋ, ˈjəʊd.lɪŋ, ⓊⓈ ˈjoʊd- **-(l)ed** -d **-(l)er/s** -əʳ/z, ⓊⓈ -ɚ/z
yog|a ˈjəʊ.g|ə, ⓊⓈ ˈjoʊ- **-ic** -ɪk
yogh(o)urt ˈjɒg.ət, ˈjəʊ.gət, -gɜːt, ⓊⓈ ˈjoʊ.gɚt **-s** -s
yog|i ˈjəʊ.g|i, ⓊⓈ ˈjoʊ- **-is** -iz **-ism** -ɪ.zᵊm ˌ**Yogi** ˈ**Bear,** ˈ**Yogi** ˌ**Bear**
yogic ˈjəʊ.gɪk, ⓊⓈ ˈjoʊ-
yogurt ˈjɒg.ət, ˈjəʊ.gət, -gɜːt, ⓊⓈ ˈjoʊ.gɚt **-s** -s
Yohji ˈjəʊ.dʒi, ˈjɒdʒ.i, ⓊⓈ ˈjoʊ.dʒi
yoicks jɔɪks
yok|e jəʊk, ⓊⓈ joʊk **-es** -s **-ing** -ɪŋ **-ed** -t
yokel ˈjəʊ.kᵊl, ⓊⓈ ˈjoʊ- **-s** -z
Yokohama ˌjəʊ.kəʊˈhɑː.mə, ⓊⓈ ˌjoʊ.kəˈ-
Yolanda, Yolande jəʊˈlæn.də, ⓊⓈ joʊˈlɑːn-, -ˈlæn-
yolk jəʊk, ⓊⓈ joʊk **-s** -s **-y** -i
Yom Kippur ˌjɒm.kɪˈpʊəʳ; -ˈkɪp.əʳ, ⓊⓈ ˌjɑːm.kɪpˈʊr, ˌjɔːm-; ⓊⓈ -ˈkɪp.ɚ
yomp jɒmp, ⓊⓈ jɑːmp **-s** -s **-ing** -ɪŋ **-ed** -t **-er/s** -əʳ/z, ⓊⓈ -ɚ/z
yon jɒn, ⓊⓈ jɑːn
yond jɒnd, ⓊⓈ jɑːnd
yonder ˈjɒn.dəʳ, ⓊⓈ ˈjɑːn.dɚ
Yonge jʌŋ
Yonkers ˈjɒŋ.kəz, ⓊⓈ ˈjɑːŋ.kɚz, ˈjɔːŋ-
yonks jɒŋks, ⓊⓈ jɑːŋks, jɔːŋks
yoof juːf
Yorba Linda ˌjɔː.bəˈlɪn.də, ⓊⓈ ˌjɔːr-
yore jɔːʳ, ⓊⓈ jɔːr
Yorick ˈjɒr.ɪk, ⓊⓈ ˈjɔːr-
York jɔːk, ⓊⓈ jɔːrk
Yorke jɔːk, ⓊⓈ jɔːrk
yorker ˈjɔː.kəʳ, ⓊⓈ ˈjɔːr.kɚ **-s** -z
Yorkist ˈjɔː.kɪst, ⓊⓈ ˈjɔːr- **-s** -s
Yorks. (abbrev. for **Yorkshire**) jɔːks, ⓊⓈ jɔːrks

Yorkshire ˈjɔːk.ʃəʳ, -ʃɪəʳ, ⓊⓈ ˈjɔːrk.ʃɚ, -ʃɪr ˌ**Yorkshire** ˈ**pudding;** ˌ**Yorkshire** ˈ**terrier**
Yorkshire|man ˈjɔːk.ʃə.|mən, ⓊⓈ ˈjɔːrk.ʃɚ- **-men** -mən, -men **-woman** -ˌwʊm.ən **-women** -ˌwɪm.ɪn
Yorktown ˈjɔːk.taʊn, ⓊⓈ ˈjɔːrk-
Yoruba ˈjɒr.ʊ.bə, ˈjəʊ.rʊ-, ⓊⓈ ˈjɔːr.ʊ.bə, ˈjoʊ.rə-, -ruː-, -bɑː
Yosemite jəʊˈsem.ɪ.ti, ⓊⓈ joʊˈsem.ə.ţi **Yo**ˌ**semite** ˌ**National** ˈ**Park;** **Yo**ˌ**semite** ˈ**Sam**
Yossarian jɒsˈeə.ri.ən, ⓊⓈ joʊˈser.i-, -ˈsɑːr-
Yost jəʊst, ⓊⓈ joʊst **-s** -s
you *strong form:* juː; *weak forms:* ju, jə
Note: Weak-form word. The strong form is used contrastively (e.g. 'Will it be **you**, or **me**?') or emphatically (e.g. 'It was **you** that broke it'). Elsewhere the weak forms are used: in British English, /ju/ is the form found before vowels and in final position (e.g. 'You ought' /juˈɔːt/ ⓊⓈ /-ɑːt/; 'Thank you' /ˈθæŋk.ju/), while /jə/ is only used before consonants (e.g. 'if you can' /ɪf.jəˈkæn/); in American English, /jə/ is more common in both unstressed environments. The strong form is also found in unstressed syllables. Sometimes when 'you' is weakly stressed and is preceded by a word normally ending in /d/, the two words are joined closely together as if they formed a single word with the affricate sound /dʒ/ linking the two parts. Thus 'did you' is often pronounced /ˈdɪdʒ.u/, and 'behind you' /bɪˈhaɪn.dʒu/. Similarly when the preceding word normally ends in /t/ (e.g. 'hurt you') it is sometimes pronounced /ˈhɜː.tʃu/ ⓊⓈ /ˈhɝː-/ and 'don't you know' as /ˌdəʊn.tʃəˈnəʊ/ ⓊⓈ /ˌdoʊn.tʃəˈnoʊ/.
you-all juˈɔːl, ⓊⓈ juˈɔːl, jɔːl, jɑːl
you'd (= **you would** or **you had**) *strong form:* juːd; *weak forms:* jud, jəd
Note: The use of strong and weak forms follows that of **you**.
you'd've (= **you would have**) *strong form:* ˈjuːd.ᵊv; *weak forms:* jud-, jəd-
Note: The use of strong and weak forms follows that of **you**.
Youens ˈjuː.ɪnz
Youghal *near Cork:* jɔːl *on Lake Derg:* ˈjɒk.ᵊl, ˈjɒx-, ⓊⓈ ˈjɑː.kᵊl
you'll (= **you will**) *strong form:* juːl; *weak forms:* jul, jəl
Note: The use of strong and weak forms follows that of **you**.
Youmans ˈjuː.mənz
young, Y~ jʌŋ **-er** -gəʳ, ⓊⓈ -gɚ **-est** -gɪst, -gəst
Younger ˈjʌŋ.əʳ, -gəʳ, ⓊⓈ -gɚ, -ɚ
Younghusband ˈjʌŋˌhʌz.bənd
youngish ˈjʌŋ.ɪʃ, -gɪʃ

Youngman ˈjʌŋ.mən
youngster ˈjʌŋk.stəʳ, (US) -stɚ **-s** -z
younker ˈjʌŋ.kəʳ, (US) -kɚ **-s** -z
your *normal forms:* jɔːʳ, jʊəʳ, (US) jʊr, jɔːr; *occasional weak forms:* jəʳ, (US) jɚ
Note: Weak-form word. The strong form /jʊə/(US)/jʊr/ or /jɔː/(US)/jɔːr/ is usually used for emphasis (e.g. 'It's **your** fault') or contrast (e.g. 'with **your** looks and **my** brains'). This pronunciation is quite common also in weakly stressed positions in careful speech. In British English, the weak form is /jə/ before consonants (e.g. 'take your time' /ˌteɪk.jəˈtaɪm/) and /jər/ before vowels (e.g. 'on your own' /ɒn.jərˈəʊn/); in American English, /jɚ/ is used in both cases.
you're (= **you are**) *strong forms:* jɔːʳ, jʊəʳ, (US) jʊr, jɔːr; *weak forms:* jəʳ, (US) jɚ
Note: The use of strong and weak forms follows that of **you**.
yours jɔːz, jʊəz, (US) jʊrz, jɔːrz
yourse|lf jɔːˈsel|f, jʊə-, jə-, (US) jʊr-, jɔːr-, jɚ- **-ves** -vz
you|th juː|θ **-ths** -ðz ˈ**youth** ˌ**club**; ˈ**youth** ˌ**hostel**; ˌ**youth** ˈ**training** ˌ**scheme**
youthful ˈjuːθ.fəl, -fʊl **-ly** -i **-ness** -nəs, -nɪs
YouTube® ˈjuːˌtʃuːb, -tjuːb, (US) -tuːb, -tjuːb
you've (= **you have**) *strong form:* juːv; *weak forms:* jʊv, jəv
Note: The use of strong and weak forms follows that of **you**.
yowl jaʊl **-s** -z **-ing** -ɪŋ **-ed** -d
yo-yo ˈjəʊ.jəʊ, (US) ˈjoʊ.joʊ **-s** -z **-ing** -ɪŋ **-ed** -d
Ypres *in Belgium:* ˈiː.prə, ˈiː.pəz; *sometimes facetiously:* ˈwaɪ.pəz, (US) ˈiː.prə *tower at Rye:* ˈiː.prə, ˈiː.preɪ, ˈwaɪ.pəz, (US) ˈiː.prə
Yser ˈiː.zəʳ, (US) -zɚ, -zer
Ysolde ɪˈzɒl.də, (US) -ˈzoʊl-
Ystradgynlais ˌʌs.trædˈgʌn.laɪs, -trədˈ-
Ystwyth ˈʌs.twɪθ
Ythan ˈaɪ.θən
YTS ˌwaɪ.tiːˈes
ytterbium ɪˈtɜː.bi.əm, (US) -ˈtɝː-
yttrium ˈɪt.ri.əm
Yucatan ˌjuː.kəˈtɑːn, ˌjʊk.əˈ-, -ˈtæn, (US) ˌjuː.kəˈtæn, -ˈtɑːn
yucca ˈjʌk.ə **-s** -z
yuck jʌk **-y** -i **-ier** -i.əʳ, (US) -i.ɚ **-iest** -i.ist, -i.əst
Yugoslav ˈjuː.gəʊ.slɑːv, ˌ--ˈ-, (US) ˈjuː.goʊ.slɑːv, -gə- **-s** -z
Yugoslavi|a ˌjuː.gəʊˈslɑː.vi|.ə, (US) -goʊˈ- **-an** -ən
Yuill ˈjuː.ɪl
yuk jʌk **-ky** -i
Yukon ˈjuː.kɒn, (US) -kɑːn
yule, Y~ juːl ˈ**yule** ˌ**log**
yuletide, Y~ ˈjuːl.taɪd
yumm|y ˈjʌm|.i **-ier** -i.əʳ, (US) -i.ɚ **-iest** -i.ɪst, -i.əst
Yum-Yum ˌjʌmˈjʌm
Yunnan jʊˈnæn
yuppie ˈjʌp.i **-s** -z
yuppif|y ˈjʌp.ɪ.f|aɪ, ˈ-ə- **-ies** -aɪz **-ying** -aɪ.ɪŋ **-ied** -aɪd
yupp|y, yupp|ie ˈjʌp|.i **-ies** -iz
yurt jɜːt, jʊət, (US) jʊrt, jɝːt **-s** -s
Yussuf ˈjʊs.ʊf, -əf
Yves iːv
Yvette ɪˈvet, iːˈ-, (US) iː-
Yvonne ɪˈvɒn, iːˈ-, (US) iːˈvɑːn
Ywain ɪˈweɪn, iːˈ-
YWCA ˌwaɪˌdʌb.əl.juː.siːˈeɪ, -ju-, (US) -juː-, -jə-

Z

Pronouncing the letter Z

The consonant letter **z** is most often realized as /z/, e.g.:

zest	zest
gaze	geɪz

It can also be pronounced /ʒ/ in words where it is followed by the letter **u**, e.g.:

seizure	ˈsiː.ʒəʳ Ⓤⓢ -ʒɚ

In addition

In the word rendezvous, **z** is silent, e.g.:

rendezvous	ˈrɒn.dɪ.vuː Ⓤⓢ ˈrɑːn.deɪ-

This is an exceptional case; the word is a borrowing from French.

z, Z zed, Ⓤⓢ ziː **-'s** -z
zabaglione ˌzæb.əlˈjəʊ.ni, -neɪ, -ælˈ-, Ⓤⓢ ˌzɑː.bəlˈjoʊ-, -bɑːlˈ-, -neɪ
Zacchaeus zækˈiː.əs, zəˈkiː-
Zachariah ˌzæk.əˈraɪ.ə, Ⓤⓢ -əˈraɪ-
Zacharias ˌzæk.əˈraɪ.əs, -æs, Ⓤⓢ -əˈraɪ-
Zachary ˈzæk.ər.i
Zadar ˈzæd.ɑːʳ, Ⓤⓢ ˈzɑː.dɑːr
Zadok ˈzeɪ.dɒk, Ⓤⓢ -dɑːk
Zagreb ˈzɑː.greb, ˈzæg.reb; zɑːˈgreb, Ⓤⓢ ˈzɑː.greb
zaire zaɪˈɪəʳ, zɑː-, Ⓤⓢ -ˈɪr
Zaïr|e, Zair|e zaɪˈɪəʳ, zɑː-, Ⓤⓢ -ˈɪr **-ean** -i.ən
Zambezi, Zambesi zæmˈbiː.zi
Zambi|a ˈzæm.bi|.ə **-an** -ən
Zamboni® zæmˈbəʊ.ni, Ⓤⓢ -ˈboʊ-
Zamenhof ˈzɑː.mən.hɒf, Ⓤⓢ -hɑːf
Zangwill ˈzæŋ.gwɪl, Ⓤⓢ -gwɪl, -wɪl
Zanu ˈzæn.uː, ˈzɑː.nuː
zan|y ˈzeɪ.n|i **-ies** -iz **-ier** -i.əʳ, Ⓤⓢ -i.ɚ **-iest** -i.ɪst, -i.əst
Zanzibar ˈzæn.zɪ.bɑːʳ, ˌ--ˈ-, Ⓤⓢ -zə.bɑːr
zap zæp **-s** -s **-ping** -ɪŋ **-ped** -t **-per/s** -əʳ/z, Ⓤⓢ -ɚ/z
Zapata zəˈpɑː.tə, zæpˈɑː-, Ⓤⓢ -t̬ə
Zapatero ˌzæp.əˈteə.rəʊ, -ˈter.əʊ, Ⓤⓢ -ˈter.oʊ
Zapatista ˌzæp.əˈtɪs.tə **-s** -z
Zaporozhye ˌzæp.əˈrəʊ.ʒeɪ, -ɔːˈ-, Ⓤⓢ ˌzɑː.pəˈroʊ.ʒə
Zapotek ˈzæp.ə.tek, ˈzɑː.pə-, ˌ--ˈ-, Ⓤⓢ ˈzɑː.pə.tek, ˈsɑː- **-s** -s
Zappa ˈzæp.ə
zapp|y ˈzæp|.i **-ier** -i.əʳ, Ⓤⓢ -i.ɚ **-iest** -i.ɪst, -əst
Zara ˈzɑː.rə, Ⓤⓢ ˈzɑː.rə, ˈzær.ə
Zaragoza ˌsær.əˈgɒs.ə; *as if Spanish:* ˌθær.əˈgɒθ.ə; Ⓤⓢ ˌzær.əˈgoʊ.zə, ˌzer-
Zarathustra ˌzær.əˈθuː.strə, ˌzɑː.rəˈ-, Ⓤⓢ ˌzer.əˈ-, ˌzær-
zareba zəˈriː.bə **-s** -z
Zaria ˈzɑː.ri.ə, Ⓤⓢ ˈzɑːr.i-
Zarqa ˈzɑː.kə, Ⓤⓢ ˈzɑːr-
Zatopek ˈzæt.ə.pek, Ⓤⓢ ˈzæt̬-
zeal ziːl
Zealand ˈziː.lənd **-er/s** -əʳ/z, Ⓤⓢ -ɚ/z
zealot ˈzel.ət **-s** -s **-ry** -ri
zealous ˈzel.əs **-ly** -li **-ness** -nəs, -nɪs
Zebedee ˈzeb.ɪ.diː, ˈ-ə-, Ⓤⓢ ˈ-ə-
zebra ˈzeb.rə, ˈziː.brə, Ⓤⓢ ˈziː.brə **-s** -z ˌ**zebra** ˈ**crossing**
zebu ˈziː.buː, -bjuː, Ⓤⓢ -bjuː, -buː **-s** -z
Zebulon, Zebulun ˈzeb.jʊ.lən; zebˈjuː-, zəˈbjuː-, Ⓤⓢ ˈzeb.jʊ-, -lɑːn
Zechariah ˌzek.əˈraɪ.ə
zed zed **-s** -z
Zedekiah ˌzed.ɪˈkaɪ.ə, -əˈ-, Ⓤⓢ -əˈ-
Zeebrugge ziːˈbrʊg.ə, zeɪ-, ˈ---, Ⓤⓢ ˈziː.brʊg-
Zeeland ˈziː.lənd, ˈzeɪ-, Ⓤⓢ ˈziː-
Zeffirelli ˌzef.əˈrel.i, -ɪˈ-
Zeiss zaɪs; *as German:* tsaɪs **-es** -ɪz
zeitgeist ˈzaɪt.gaɪst, ˈtsaɪt-
Zelazny zelˈæz.ni, Ⓤⓢ zəˈlɑːz.ni
Zelda ˈzel.də
Zeller ˈzel.əʳ, Ⓤⓢ -ɚ
Zellweger ˈzelˌweg.əʳ, Ⓤⓢ -ɚ
Zelotes ziːˈləʊ.tiːz, zɪ-, zə-, Ⓤⓢ -ˈloʊ-
zemindar ˈzem.ɪn.dɑːʳ, Ⓤⓢ -dɑːr; Ⓤⓢ zəˈmiːn- **-s** -z
zemstvo ˈzemst.vəʊ, Ⓤⓢ -voʊ **-s** -z
Zen zen
Zena ˈziː.nə
zenana zenˈɑː.nə, zɪˈnɑː-, Ⓤⓢ zenˈɑː- **-s** -z
Zenawi zenˈɑː.wi
Zend zend
Zenda ˈzen.də
Zeneca® ˈzen.ɪ.kə, -ə-
zenica ˈzen.ɪ.kə, ˈzen.ɪt.sə
zenith ˈzen.ɪθ, Ⓤⓢ ˈziː.nɪθ **-s** -s
Zeno ˈziː.nəʊ, Ⓤⓢ -noʊ
Zenobia zɪˈnəʊ.bi.ə, zenˈəʊ-, Ⓤⓢ zəˈnoʊ-
Zenocrate ˈzen.əʊ.kræt, Ⓤⓢ -oʊ-
Zepa ˈʒep.ə
Zephaniah ˌzef.əˈnaɪ.ə
zephyr, Z~ ˈzef.əʳ, Ⓤⓢ -ɚ **-s** -z
Zephyrus ˈzef.ər.əs
zeppelin, Z~ ˈzep.əl.ɪn, Ⓤⓢ ˈ-lɪn, ˈzep.ə.lɪn **-s** -z
Zermatt ˈzɜː.mæt, Ⓤⓢ ˈzɝː.mɑːt, -ˈ-
zero ˈzɪə.rəʊ, Ⓤⓢ ˈzɪr.oʊ, ˈziː.roʊ **-(e)s** -z ˈ**zero** ˌ**hour**
Zerubbabel zɪˈrʌb.ə.bəl, zə-; *in Jewish usage also:* zɪˈruːˌbɑː-, zə-, Ⓤⓢ zəˈrʌb.ə-
zest zest **-ful/ly** fəl/i, fʊl/i
zest|y ˈzes.t|i **-ier** -i.əʳ, Ⓤⓢ -i.ɚ **-iest** -i.ɪst, -i.əst
zeta ˈziː.tə, Ⓤⓢ ˈzeɪ.t̬ə, ˈziː- **-s** -z
Zetland ˈzet.lənd
zeugma ˈzjuːg.mə, ˈzuːg-, Ⓤⓢ ˈzuːg- **-s** -z
Zeus zjuːs, Ⓤⓢ zuːs
Zhirinovsky ˌʒɪr.ɪˈnɒf.ski, Ⓤⓢ -ˈnɑːf-
Zhivago ʒɪˈvɑː.gəʊ, ʒə-, Ⓤⓢ -goʊ
Zhou ʒuː, Ⓤⓢ dʒoʊ
ziggurat ˈzɪg.ə.ræt, ˈ-ʊ- **-s** -s
zigzag ˈzɪg.zæg **-s** -z **-ging** -ɪŋ **-ged** -d
zilch zɪltʃ
zillion ˈzɪl.jən, -i.ən, Ⓤⓢ ˈ-jən **-s** -z
Zimbabwe zɪmˈbɑːb.weɪ, -ˈbæb-, -wi, Ⓤⓢ -ˈbɑːb-
Zimbabwean zɪmˈbɑːb.wi.ən, -ˈbæb-, -weɪ-, Ⓤⓢ -ˈbɑːb- **-s** -z
Zimmer® ˈzɪm.əʳ, Ⓤⓢ -ɚ ˈ**Zimmer** **frame**
Zimmerman ˈzɪm.ə.mən, Ⓤⓢ ˈ-ɚ-
zinc zɪŋk **-s** -s **-king** -ɪŋ **-ked** -t **-ky** -i
zinco ˈzɪŋ.kəʊ, Ⓤⓢ -koʊ **-s** -z
zine ziːn **-s** -z
zinfandel, Z~ ˈzɪn.fən.del, ˌ--ˈ-, Ⓤⓢ ˈzɪn.fən.del
zing zɪŋ **-s** -z **-ing** -ɪŋ **-ed** -d **-y** -i
zingar|o, Z~ ˈzɪŋ.gər|.əʊ, Ⓤⓢ -gə.r|oʊ **-i** -iː
zinnia ˈzɪn.i.ə **-s** -z
Zion ˈzaɪ.ən **-ism** -ɪ.zəm **-ist/s** -ɪst/s
zip zɪp **-s** -s **-ping** -ɪŋ **-ped** -t ˈ**zip** ˌ**code;** ˌ**zip** ˈ**fastener**
zipper ˈzɪp.əʳ, Ⓤⓢ -ɚ **-s** -z
Zipporah zɪˈpɔː.rə, ˈzɪp.ər.ə, Ⓤⓢ ˈzɪp.ɚ.ə
zipp|y ˈzɪp|.i **-ier** -i.əʳ, Ⓤⓢ -i.ɚ **-iest** -i.ɪst, -i.əst
zircon ˈzɜː.kɒn, Ⓤⓢ ˈzɝː.kɑːn
zirconia zɜːˈkəʊ.ni.ə, zə-, Ⓤⓢ zɚˈkoʊ-
zirconium zɜːˈkəʊ.ni.əm, zə-, Ⓤⓢ zɚˈkoʊ-
zit zɪt **-s** -s
zither ˈzɪð.əʳ, ˈzɪθ-, Ⓤⓢ ˈzɪð.ɚ, ˈzɪθ- **-s** -z
zloty ˈzlɒt.i; *as if Polish:* ˈzwɒt-; Ⓤⓢ ˈzlɔː.t̬i, ˈzlɑː- **-s** -z
Zoar ˈzəʊ.ɑːʳ, ˈzəʊ.əʳ, Ⓤⓢ ˈzoʊ.ɑːr, ˈzoʊ.ɚ
zodiac ˈzəʊ.di.æk, Ⓤⓢ ˈzoʊ-

zodiacal zəʊˈdaɪ.ə.kəl, (US) zoʊ-
Zoe, Zoë ˈzəʊ.i, (US) ˈzoʊ-
Zog zɒg, (US) zɔːg, zɑːg
-zoic ˈzəʊ.ɪk, (US) ˈzoʊ.ɪk
Zola ˈzəʊ.lə, (US) ˈzoʊ-; (US) zoʊˈlɑː
zollverein ˈtsɒl.fər.aɪn, ˈzɒl.vər-, (US) ˈtsɔːl.fə.raɪn **-s** -z
zombie ˈzɒm.bi, (US) ˈzɑːm- **-s** -z
zonal ˈzəʊ.nəl, (US) ˈzoʊ- **-ly** -i
zon|e zəʊn, (US) zoʊn **-es** -z **-ing** -ɪŋ **-ed** -d **-eless** -ləs, -lɪs
zonked zɒŋkt, (US) zɑːŋkt, zɔːŋkt
zoo zuː **-s** -z
zoo- ˈzuː.əʊ, ˈzəʊ.əʊ; zuˈɒ, zəʊˈɒ, (US) ˈzoʊ.oʊ, ˈzuː.oʊ, -ə; (US) zoʊˈɑː, zuˈɑː
Note: Prefix. Normally either takes primary or secondary stress on the first syllable, e.g. **zoophyte** /ˈzuː.ə.faɪt/ (US) /ˈzoʊ-/, **zoomorphic** /ˌzəʊ.əˈmɔː.fɪk/ (US) /ˌzoʊ.əˈmɔːr-/, or primary stress on the second syllable, e.g. **zoology** /zuˈɒl.ə.dʒi/ (US) /zoʊˈɑː.lə-/.
zoochemi|stry ˌzuː.əʊˈkem.ɪ|.stri, ˌzəʊ-, (US) ˌzoʊ.əˈ- **-cal** -kəl
zoograph|er zuːˈɒg.rə.f|ər, zəʊ-, (US) zoʊˈɑː.grə.f|ɚ **-ers** -əz, (US) -ɚz **-y** -i
zookeeper ˈzuːˌkiː.pər, (US) ˈzuːˌkiː.pɚ **-s** -z
zooks zuːks, (US) zuːks, zʊks
zoolite ˈzuː.əʊ.laɪt, ˈzəʊ-, (US) ˈzoʊ.oʊ.laɪt, ˈ-ə- **-s** -s
zoologic|al ˌzuː.əʊˈlɒdʒ.ɪ.k|əl, ˌzəʊ.əˈ-, (US) ˌzoʊ.əˈlɑː.dʒɪ- **-ally** -əl.i, -li **zooˌlogical ˈgardens**
zoologist zuˈɒl.ə.dʒ|ɪst, zəʊ-, (US) zoʊˈɑː.lə-, zu- **-s** -s
zoolog|y zuˈɒl.ə.dʒ|i, zəʊ-, (US) zoʊˈɑː.lə-, zu- **-ist/s** -ɪst/s
zoom zuːm **-s** -z **-ing** -ɪŋ **-ed** -d **ˈzoom ˌlens**
zoomorphic ˌzuː.əˈmɔː.fɪk, ˌzəʊ-, (US) ˌzoʊ.əˈmɔːr-
-zo|on ˈzəʊ|.ɒn, (US) ˈzoʊ|.ɑːn, -ən **-a** -ə
Note: Suffix. Normally carries primary stress as shown, e.g. **protozoon** /ˌprəʊ.təʊˈzəʊ.ɒn/ (US) /ˌproʊ.t̬oʊˈzoʊ.ɑːn/.
zoophyte ˈzuː.ə.faɪt, ˈzəʊ-, (US) ˈzoʊ.ə- **-s** -s
zooplankton ˌzuː.əʊˈplæŋk.tən, ˌzəʊ-, -tɒn, (US) ˌzoʊ.əˈplæŋk.tən **-s** -z
zoot zuːt **-s** -s **ˈzoot ˌsuit**
zorbing ˈzɔː.bɪŋ, (US) ˈzɔːr-
zoril ˈzɒr.ɪl, (US) ˈzɔːr- **-s** -z
Zoroaster ˌzɒr.əʊˈæs.tər, ˈzɒr.əʊ.æs-, (US) ˈzɔːr.oʊ.æs.tɚ
Zoroastrian ˌzɒr.əʊˈæs.tri.ən, (US) ˌzɔːr.oʊˈ- **-s** -z **-ism** -ɪ.zəm
Zorro ˈzɒr.əʊ, (US) ˈzɔːr.oʊ
zouave, Z~ zuˈɑːv; zwɑːv; ˈzuː.ɑːv, (US) zuˈɑːv, zwɑːv **-s** -z
Zouch(e) zuːʃ
zounds zuːndz, zaʊndz, (US) zaʊndz
Zsa Zsa ˈʒɑː.ʒɑː
zucchini zʊˈkiː.ni, (US) zuː- **-s** -z
Zugspitze ˈzʊg.ʃpɪt.sə; *as if German:* ˈtsuːk-
Zuider Zee ˌzaɪ.dəˈziː, -ˈzeɪ, (US) -dɚˈziː
Zuleika zuːˈleɪ.kə, zʊ-, -ˈlaɪ-
Zulu ˈzuː.luː **-s** -z
Zululand ˈzuː.luː.lænd
Zuma ˈzuː.mə
Zuñi, Zuni ˈzʊn.ji, (US) ˈzuː.ni, -nji
zuppa inglese ˌzʊp.ɑː.ɪŋˈgleɪ.zeɪ, -zi, (US) ˌzuː.pə.ɪnˈgleɪ.zeɪ, ˌtsuː-, -ɪŋˈ-
Zürich ˈzjʊə.rɪk, ˈzʊə-; *as if German:* ˈtsjʊə-; (US) ˈzʊr.ɪk
Zutphen ˈzʌt.fən
Zwelithini ˌzwel.ɪˈθiː.ni
zwieback ˈzwiː.bæk, -bɑːk, (US) ˈzwaɪ.bæk, ˈzwiː-, ˈswiː-, ˈswaɪ-, -bɑːk **-s** -s
zygoma zaɪˈgəʊ.mə, zɪ-, (US) -ˈgoʊ- **-ta** -tə, (US) -t̬ə
zygote ˈzaɪ.gəʊt, ˈzɪg.əʊt, (US) ˈzaɪ.goʊt, ˈzɪg.oʊt **-s** -s
zymosis zaɪˈməʊ.sɪs, zɪ-, (US) -ˈmoʊ-
zymotic zaɪˈmɒt.ɪk, zɪ-, (US) -ˈmɑː.t̬ɪk
Zyuganov ʒʊˈgɑː.nɒf, (US) -nɑːf
zzz zː

> Note: This is rarely pronounced, but is used in comic strips to represent sleeping, or, more specifically, snoring. The suggested pronunciation derives from the spelling.

Z

Glossary

abbreviations

The pronunciation of individual abbreviations is not predictable and must be treated on a word-by-word basis.

Examples

Some good examples of abbreviations which are spoken in full are to be found in titles used for people, e.g.:

Mr /ˈmɪs.təʳ/ (US) /-tɚ/
Mrs /ˈmɪs.ɪz/
Dr /ˈdɒk.təʳ/ (US) /ˈdɑːk.tɚ/
Esq /ɪˈskwaɪəʳ/ (US) /ˈes.kwaɪ.ɚ/

However, in some cases, an abbreviation may be pronounced the way it is written, e.g.:

Bros. (*Brothers*) /ˈbrʌð.əz/, /brɒs/ (US) /ˈbrʌð.ɚz/
des res (*desirable residence*) /ˌdezˈrez/

Some words or phrases are abbreviated to initial letters. In this case, the item may be pronounced as the initial letters, or in full. This is not the same as an ACRONYM, in which the letters are pronounced as a word (see, for example, *NATO*), e.g.:

MS (*multiple sclerosis; manuscript*) /ˌemˈes/
NBA (*National Basketball Association*) /ˌen.biːˈeɪ/
UCLA (*University of California Los Angeles*) /ˌjuː.siː.elˈeɪ/

Abbreviations derived from Latin words and phrases are common, but do not all follow the same pattern, some being pronounced in full, some as letters, and some as they are spelt, e.g.:

e.g. (*exempli gratia*) /ˌiːˈdʒiː/
et al (*et alia*) /etˈæl/ (US) /-ˈɑːl/
etc. (*et cetera*) /ɪtˈset.ər.ə/ (US) /-ˈset̬.ɚ-/
i.e. (*id est*) /ˌaɪˈiː/

accent

Accent may refer to prominence given to a syllable (see STRESS), or to a particular way of pronouncing. This entry concentrates on the latter definition.

Examples for English

Speakers may share the same grammar and vocabulary, but pronounce what they say with different accents. In Britain, for example, there are accents such as Scots, Cockney (in London), and Scouse (in Liverpool), and in the United States the New York accent differs considerably from that commonly heard in Texas. There are also different world standard English accents, such as British, American, Australian, Indian, or Singaporean.

Major differences between British and US English include the vowel in words such as *glass*, the use of a flapped /t/ in words like *butter*, and the fact that US English is RHOTIC while British English is non-rhotic, that is, an *r* in the spelling is always pronounced in US English, but only where a vowel follows in British English, e.g.:

glass /glɑːs/ (US) /glæs/
butter /ˈbʌt.əʳ/ (US) /ˈbʌt̬.ɚ/
car /kɑːʳ/ (US) /kɑːr/

More information on the accents chosen to represent British and American English is given in the Introduction.

acronyms

Acronyms are words or phrases written in an abbreviated form, usually with their initial letters, and pronounced as if they were words, usually with the most obvious pronunciation. However, it is best to treat them on a word-by-word basis, since there are exceptions.

Examples

Many organizations, particularly those to do with government, charities, and trade unions, use acronyms. Phrases can also be reduced to acronym form. Acronyms are usually written using capital letters, although there are exceptions. Where there is a letter *E* at the end of an acronym, it is usually pronounced /iː/, e.g.:

► NATFHE (*National Association of Teachers in Further and Higher Education*) /ˈnæt.fiː/
► NATO (*North Atlantic Treaty Organization*) /ˈneɪ.təʊ/ (US) /-t̬oʊ/
► snafu (*situation normal, all fouled up*) /snæfˈuː/
► Tardis (*time and relative dimensions in space*) /ˈtɑː.dɪs/ (US) /ˈtɑːr-/

Some words or phrases are abbreviated to initial letters but do not become acronyms. See ABBREVIATIONS.

affricate

A type of consonant consisting of a PLOSIVE followed by a FRICATIVE with the same place of ARTICULATION.

Examples for English

Examples are the /tʃ/ and /dʒ/ sounds (sometimes symbolized /č/ and /ǰ/ by American writers) at the beginning and end of the words *church* and *judge*, where the first of these sounds is voiceless and the second voiced (see VOICING), e.g.:

church /tʃɜːtʃ/ (US) /tʃɝːtʃ/
judge /dʒʌdʒ/

It is often difficult to decide whether any particular combination of a plosive plus a fricative should be classed as a single affricate sound or as two separate sounds, and the question depends on whether these are to be regarded as separate PHONEMES or not. It is usual to regard /tʃ/ and /dʒ/ as affricate phonemes in English; /ts dz tr dr/ also occur in English but are not usually regarded as affricate phonemes, but are treated as clusters. The two phrases *why choose* and *white shoes* are said to show the difference between the /tʃ/ affricate (in the first example) and separate /t/ and /ʃ/ (in the second), e.g.:

why choose /*h*waɪ tʃuːz/
white shoes /*h*waɪt ʃuːz/

llophone
variant of a phoneme.

xamples for English
entral to the concept of the PHONEME is the idea that may be pronounced in many different ways. In nglish we take it for granted that the /r/ sounds in y and *tray* are 'the same sound' (i.e. the same honeme), but in reality the two sounds are very fferent – the /r/ in *ray* is voiced and non-fricative, hile the /r/ sound in *tray* is voiceless and FRICATIVE. phonemic transcription we use the same symbol / for both (the slant brackets indicate that phoneic symbols are being used), but we know that the lophones of /r/ include the voiced non-fricative und and the voiceless fricative one. Using the uare brackets that indicate PHONETIC (allophonic) mbols, the former is [ɹ] and the latter [ɹ̥], e.g.:

y /reɪ/ [ɹeɪ]
ay /treɪ/ [tɹ̥eɪ]

theory, a phoneme can have an infinite number of lophones, but in practice for descriptive purposes tend to concentrate on the ones that occur most gularly and recognizably.

lveolar
veolar sounds are made with a place of articulation hind the upper front teeth, against the hard, bony dge called the alveolar ridge; the skin covering it is rrugated with transverse wrinkles.

xamples for English
e tongue comes into contact with the alveolar ridge some of the consonants of English and many other nguages; sounds such as [t], [d], [s], [z], [n], [l] are nsonants with alveolar place of articulation. Some amples for English follow, e.g.:

 /tɪp/
p /zɪp/
p /dɪp/
p /nɪp/
p /sɪp/
 /lɪp/

though /r/ is described as alveolar or post-alveolar British English, in US English it is in fact nearer to TROFLEX, e.g.:

 /rɪp/ [ɹɪʔp] (US) [ɻɪʔp]

pproximant
phonetic term of comparatively recent origin, used denote a consonant which makes very little struction to the airflow.

xamples for English
aditionally approximants have been divided into o groups. Sounds in the first group are known as emivowels' such as the /w/ and /j/, which are very milar to 'close vowels' such as [u] and [i] but are oduced as a rapid glide, e.g.:

et /wet/
t /jet/

iquids' are sounds which have an identifiable constriction of the airflow but not one that is sufficiently obstructive to produce fricative noise, compression, or the diversion of airflow through another part of the vocal tract as in nasals. This category includes laterals such as /l/ and non-fricative /r/ (phonetically [ɹ] in British English and [ɻ] in US English), e.g.:

lead /liːd/
read /riːd/

Approximants therefore are never fricative and never contain interruptions to the flow of air.

articulation
The movement of the vocal organs to produce speech sounds. The vocal organs are often referred to as 'articulators', and these include the tongue, the lips, the hard palate, the soft palate, the teeth, the pharynx, and the larynx. In classifying CONSONANTS, phoneticians note the 'place of articulation' (the point in the vocal tract where the obstruction to the airflow is made) and the 'manner of articulation' (the type of obstruction made by the articulators). Thus the sound [s] is classified as ALVEOLAR (because the place of articulation is at the alveolar ridge, just behind the upper front teeth) and FRICATIVE (because the obstruction is one which allows air to escape with difficulty, creating a hissing noise).

aspiration
Noise made when the constriction of a plosive consonant is released and air is allowed to escape relatively freely.

Examples for English
English /p t k/ at the beginning of a syllable are aspirated in most accents. In words like *pea*, *tea*, *key*, there is a silent period during which the compressed air is prevented from escaping by the articulatory closure; this is followed by a sound similar to /h/ before the VOICING of the vowel begins, the result of the vocal folds being widely parted at the time of the articulatory release. Aspiration is an important factor in whether we perceive a sound to be /p t k/ or /b d g/ in syllable-initial position.

/p t k/ are aspirated at the beginning of a syllable containing a full vowel, e.g.:

pin /pɪn/ [pʰĩn]
tick /tɪk/ [tʰɪʔk]
kin /kɪn/ [kʰĩn]
appease /əˈpiːz/ [əˈpʰiːz̥]
attain /əˈteɪn/ [əˈtʰeĩn]
accord /əˈkɔːd/ [əˈkʰɔːd̥] (US) /əˈkɔːrd/ [əˈkʰɔːɻd̥]

When followed by /l r w/ or /j/ in initial consonant clusters, the release of the PLOSIVE gives the following sound a voiceless quality, e.g.:

play /pleɪ/ [pl̥eɪ]
tree /triː/ [tɹ̥iː]
queue /kjuː/ [kj̊ʉː]
twice /twaɪs/ [tw̥aɪs]

It is noticeable that when /p t k/ are preceded by /s/ at the beginning of a syllable they are not aspirated. This makes them very similar to /b d g/, and is an example of NEUTRALIZATION – the distinctive difference between /p t k/ and /b d g/ is lost when there is a preceding /s/, e.g.:

spin /spɪn/ [spĩn] (compare pɪn [p^{h}ĩn])
stick /stɪk/ [stɪʔk] (compare tɪk [t^{h}ɪʔk])
skin /skɪn/ [skĩn] (compare kɪn [k^{h}ĩn])

Word final /p t k/ may be aspirated or not, for stylistic reasons.

assimilation

Assimilation is what happens to a sound when it is influenced by one of its neighbours; essentially it becomes more similar to a neighbour.

Examples for English

Assimilation is said to be 'progressive' when a sound influences a following sound, or 'regressive' when a sound influences one which precedes it. The most familiar case of regressive assimilation in English is that of ALVEOLAR consonants (e.g. /t d s z n/) which are followed by non-alveolar consonants: assimilation results in a change of place of articulation from alveolar to a different place. For example, the word *this* has the sound /s/ at the end if it is pronounced on its own, but when followed by post-alveolar /ʃ/ in a word such as *shop* it often changes in rapid speech (through assimilation) to /ʃ/, giving the pronunciation /ðɪʃʃɒp/. The following examples occur especially in British English:

batman /ˈbæt.mæn/ → [ˈbæp.mæn]
fruitcake /ˈfruːt.keɪk/ → [ˈfruːk.keɪk]
handbag /ˈhæn*d*.bæg/ → [ˈhæm*b*.bæg]

Progressive assimilation is exemplified by the behaviour of the 's' plural ending in English, which is pronounced with a voiced /z/ after a voiced consonant but with a voiceless /s/ after a voiceless consonant, e.g.:

dog /dɒg/ (US) /dɑːg/ + plural → /dɒgz/ (US) /dɑːgz/
cat /kæt/ + plural → /kæts/

bilabial

Bilabial articulations involve both of the lips.

Examples for English

In English, /p b m/ are examples of bilabial sounds. These are all made with a complete closure of the lips. /w/ is also sometimes referred to as bilabial, but, as it has tongue movement towards the velum in addition to lip rounding, it is more accurately described as 'labial-velar'. E.g.:

pan /pæn/
ban /bæn/
man /mæn/

The plosives /p/ and /b/ are one of the pairs which are said to be distinguished by being FORTIS and LENIS respectively, rather than voiceless and voiced.

cardinal vowel

One of the vowels of the standard classification system used in phonetics.

Description

Phoneticians have always needed some way o classifying vowels which is independent of the vowe system of a particular language. With most conso nants it is quite easy to observe how their articulatio is organized, and to specify the place and manner o the constriction formed; vowels, however, are muc less easy to observe.

Early in the 20th century, the English phonetici Daniel Jones worked out a set of 'cardinal vowels' tha students learning phonetics could be taught to mak and which would serve as reference points that othe vowels could be related to. The vowels are located o the four-sided figure shown below:

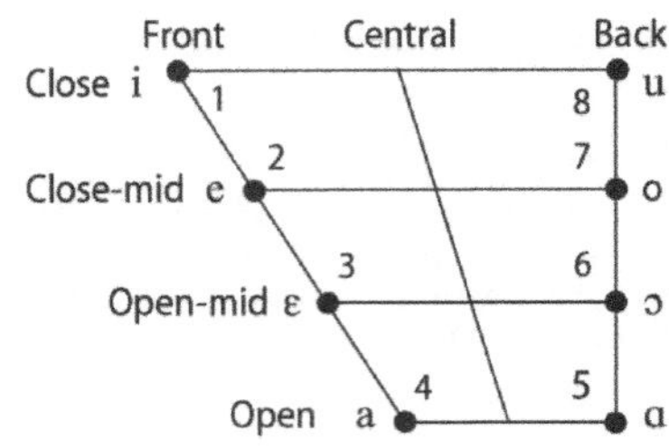

The cardinal vowel figure is used to specify th qualities of the English vowels and diphthongs in th Introduction to this dictionary.

The cardinal vowel diagram is used both for rounde and unrounded vowels, and Jones proposed tha there should be a primary set of cardinal vowels and secondary set. The primary includes the fron unrounded vowels [i e ɛ a], the back unrounde vowel [ɑ], and the rounded back vowels [ɔ o u], whil the secondary set comprises the front rounded vowe [y ø œ ɶ], the back rounded [ɒ], and the bac unrounded [ʌ ɤ ɯ].

Phonetic 'ear-training' makes much use of th cardinal vowel system, and students can learn t identify and discriminate a very large number c different vowels in relation to the cardinal vowels.

clear l

A type of LATERAL sound in which the air escapes pas the sides of the tongue, found normally only befor vowels. Usually contrasted with DARK L.

Examples for English

In the case of an alveolar lateral (e.g. English /l/) th blade of the tongue (the part further back than th tip) is in contact with the alveolar ridge, but the rest o the tongue is free to take up different shapes. On possibility is for the front of the tongue (the par behind the blade) to be raised in the same shape a that for a close front vowel [i]. This gives the /l/ an [i like sound, and the result is a 'clear l'. It is found i BBC pronunciation only before vowels, but in som other accents, notably Irish and Welsh ones, it i found in all positions. However, the variant mos often found in all positions is 'DARK L', e.g.:

pill /pɪl/ [p^{h}ɪɫ]

cluster

Two or more CONSONANT PHONEMES in sequence, with no vowel sound between them.

Examples for English

English can allow up to three consonants in a cluster syllable initially in the ONSET, and four finally in the CODA. For example, the word *stray* /streɪ/ begins with three consonants, and *sixths* /sɪksθs/ ends with four.

Some types of grammatical information are shown by adding certain consonants at the ends of words in English, giving rise to consonant clusters, e.g.:

likes /laɪks/
lives /lɪvz/
liked /laɪkt/
lived /lɪvd/
Mark's /mɑːks/ (US) /mɑːrks/
John's /dʒɒnz/ (US) /dʒɑːnz/
cats /kæts/
dogs /dɒgz/ (US) /dɑːgz/

coalescence

A kind of ASSIMILATION in which a fusion of neighbouring sounds takes place during rapid or CONNECTED SPEECH.

Examples for English

The most frequently observed situation in which coalescence occurs in English is when ALVEOLAR consonants /t d s z/ are followed by /j/, e.g.:

won't you /wəʊnt ju/ (US) /woʊnt ju/ → /ˈwəʊntʃu/ (US) /ˈwoʊntʃu/
would you /wʊd ju/ → /ˈwʊdʒu/

In the case of coalescence with /s z/, there will usually be extra length to the resulting fricative sounds, e.g.:

miss you /mɪs ju/ → /ˈmɪʃʃu/
lose you /luːz ju/ → /ˈluːʒʒu/

A common very much reduced example of coalescence is *do you* being pronounced as /dʒə/.

coarticulation

The influence of phonetic context on the articulation of speech sounds.

Examples for English

Phonetics studies coarticulation as a way of finding out how the brain controls the production of speech. When we speak, many muscles are active at the same time and sometimes the brain tries to make them do things that they are not capable of. For example, in the word *mum* the vowel phoneme is one that is normally pronounced with the soft palate raised to prevent the escape of air through the nose, while the two /m/ phonemes must have the soft palate lowered. The soft palate cannot be raised very quickly, so the vowel is likely to be pronounced with the soft palate still lowered, giving a nasalized quality to the vowel, e.g.:

mum /mʌm/ [mɐ̃m]

Another example is the lip rounding of a consonant in the environment of rounded vowels: in the phrase 'you too', the /t/ occurs between two rounded vowels, and there is not enough time in normal speech for the lips to move from rounded to unrounded and back again in a few hundredths of a second; consequently the /t/ is pronounced with lip rounding, e.g.:

you too /juː tuː/ [jʉːtʷʉː]

Coarticulation is a phenomenon closely related to ASSIMILATION. The major difference is that assimilation is used as a name for the process whereby one sound becomes like another neighbouring sound, while coarticulation, though it refers to a similar process, is concerned with articulatory explanations for why the assimilation occurs, and considers cases where the changes may occur over a number of segments.

coda

The end of a syllable, which is said to be made up of an ONSET, a peak, and a coda. The peak and the coda constitute the RHYME (or RIME) of the syllable.

Examples for English

English allows up to four consonants to occur in the coda, so the total number of possible codas in English is very large – several hundred in fact, e.g.:

sick /sɪk/
six /sɪks/
sixth /sɪksθ/
sixths /sɪksθs/

The central part of a syllable is almost always a vowel, and if the syllable contains nothing after the vowel it is said to have no coda ('zero coda'), e.g.:

bough /baʊ/
buy /baɪ/

compounds

Compounds are words made up of two other words which can exist independently in English. They are written in a variety of ways: closed, e.g. *armchair*, *sunflower*; hyphenated, e.g. *front-runner, she-devil*; open, e.g. *side salad*, *bank manager*. Sometimes it is possible for the same compounds to be written in different ways, e.g. *shoulder blade* or *shoulderblade*.

There are some rules for compound word stress in English, but they are not completely reliable. In addition, British and US English differ. The rules which follow are therefore guidelines, but exceptions exist.

Examples

Words that combine two nouns usually have primary stress on the first element, e.g.:

coffee pot /ˈkɒf.i.pɒt/ (US) /ˈkɑː.fi.pɑːt/
suitcase /ˈsuːt.keɪs/

In US English it is more frequently the case that compound nouns have first-element stress, and this tendency is appearing among some British English speakers. For example, *ice cream* can have first- or second-element stress in British English, but tends to be stressed on the first element in US English.

Other types of compound are usually stressed on the

second element. These include words ending in *-ed* which are used as adjectives, words with a number as a first element, and words functioning as adverbs or verbs, e.g.:

kind-hearted /ˌkaɪndˈhɑː.tɪd/ (US) /-ˈhɑːr.t̬ɪd/
three-piece /ˌθriːˈpiːs/
southeast /ˌsaʊθˈiːst/

These words are subject to stress shift when a stressed syllable follows closely (e.g. *a ˌkind-hearted ˈman*).

connected speech phenomena

The processes which result in words being pronounced differently from their dictionary form when they occur in close contact with other words.

Examples for English

In natural speech we rarely leave gaps between words, and we can observe many processes that result in differences between isolated words and the same words occurring in connected speech: examples are ASSIMILATION and ELISION, e.g.:

assimilation

one boy /wʌn bɔɪ/ → /wʌm bɔɪ/

elision

last time /lɑːst taɪm/ (US) /læst taɪm/ → /lɑːs taɪm/ (US) /læs taɪm/

The study of connected speech also involves looking at the process of VOWEL REDUCTION in weak syllables (see also WEAK FORM), at RHYTHM and at prosodic phenomena such as INTONATION and STRESS.

consonant

A speech sound which obstructs the flow of air though the vocal tract or a letter of the alphabet representing such a vowel.

Examples for English

There are many types of consonant, but what all have in common is that they obstruct the flow of air through the vocal tract. Some do this a lot, some not very much: those which make the maximum obstruction (i.e. PLOSIVES, which form a complete stoppage of the airstream) are the most consonantal, e.g.:

bat /bæt/
keep /kiːp/

NASAL consonants result in complete stoppage of the oral cavity but are less obstructive than plosives since air is allowed to escape through the nose, e.g.:

man /mæn/
name /neɪm/

FRICATIVES make a considerable obstruction to the flow of air, but not a total closure, e.g.:

sheaf /ʃiːf/
south /saʊθ/

The class of sounds called APPROXIMANTS comprises sounds which make very little obstruction to the flow of air. The post-alveolar approximant that is the usual pronunciation of /r/ in BBC pronunciation involves no contact between the tongue and the palate, e.g.:

red /red/ [ɹed]
arrive /əˈraɪv/ [əˈɹaɪv]

LATERAL approximants obstruct the flow of air only in the centre of the mouth, not at the sides, so obstruction is slight, e.g.:

lull /lʌl/

Other sounds classed as approximants make so little obstruction to the flow of air that they could almost be thought to be vowels if they were in a different context. These are sometimes referred to as 'semi vowels', e.g.:

you /juː/
woo /wuː/

Finally, AFFRICATES begin as plosives and are released as fricatives, with no intervening gap, e.g.:

church /tʃɜːtʃ/ (US) /tʃɝːtʃ/
judge /dʒʌdʒ/

The above explanation is based on phonetic criteria. An alternative approach is to look at the *phonological* characteristics of consonants: for example, consonants are typically found at the beginning and end of syllables while vowels are typically found in the middle.

dark l

A type of LATERAL sound, recognizably different from CLEAR L.

Examples for English

If, when pronouncing the sound /l/, the back of the tongue is raised as for an [u] vowel, the quality is [u]-like and 'dark'; this effect is even more noticeable if the lips are rounded at the same time. This sound is typically found when /l/ occurs before a consonant or before a pause, e.g.:

help /help/ [he̜ɫp]
hill /hɪl/ [hɪɫ]

In several accents of English, particularly those close to London, the dark l has given way to a [w] sound, so that *help* and *hill* might be transcribed /hewp/ and /hɪw/; this process is known as 'l vocalization'.

In other languages

The process of l vocalization took place in Polish some time ago, and the sound represented in Polish writing by the letter ł is almost always pronounced as [w], though foreigners usually try to pronounce it as [l].

dental

A sound in which there is contact between the tongue and the front teeth.

Examples for English

In English, the dentals usually referred to are the FRICATIVES /θ/ and /ð/, of which /θ/ is voiceless and /ð/ is voiced. In a careful production of these sounds the tongue tip may be protruded between the upper and lower teeth; the sounds are sometimes referred to as 'interdental' for this reason, e.g.:

thigh /θaɪ/
ether /ˈiː.θəʳ/ (US) /-θɚ/
breath /breθ/
thy /ðaɪ/
either /ˈaɪ.ðəʳ/ (US) /ˈiː.ðɚ/
breathe /briːð/

devoicing

A process affecting a sound which we would normally expect to be voiced but which is pronounced without VOICING in a particular context.

Examples for English

In English, the /l/ in *blade* /bleɪd/ [bleɪd̥] is usually voiced, but in *played* /pleɪd/ [pl̥eɪd̥] the /l/ is usually voiceless because of the preceding voiceless plosive. Note also that the /d/ at the end of the word in each case is devoiced if it is followed by a voiceless consonant or a pause.

The notion of devoicing leads to a rather confusing use of phonetic symbols in cases where there are separate symbols for voiced and voiceless pairs of sounds: a devoiced /d/ can be symbolized by adding a diacritic that indicates lack of voice – [d̥], but one is then left in doubt as to what the difference is between this sound and [t]. The usual reason for doing this is to leave the symbol looking like the phoneme it represents.

diphthong

A sound in which there is a glide from one vowel quality to another.

Examples for English

BBC English and US English contain a large number of diphthongs: in both accents, there are three ending in [ɪ] (/eɪ aɪ ɔɪ/), sometimes referred to as 'front-closing', and two ending in [ʊ] (/aʊ əʊ/), sometimes referred to as 'back-closing'. In US English, the preferred transcription of the BBC vowel /əʊ/ is /oʊ/, which indicates a rounded initial vowel.

BBC English also has three diphthongs ending in [ə] (/ɪə eə ʊə/), which are sometimes known as 'centring'. The /ʊə/ diphthong is now less commonly used than /ɔː/. These diphthongs usually appear in US English with an /r/ final (/ɪr er ʊr/), as words containing them generally end with an *r* in the spelling, e.g.:

bay /beɪ/
buy /baɪ/
boy /bɔɪ/
go /gəʊ/ (US) /goʊ/
cow /kaʊ/
pier /pɪə/ (US) /pɪr/
pear /peə/ (US) /per/
poor /pʊə/ (more often /pɔː/) (US) /pʊr/

Opinions differ as to whether diphthongs should be treated as phonemes in their own right, or as combinations of two phonemes.

elision

The omission of sounds which are normally present if words are pronounced slowly and clearly but appear not to be pronounced when the same words are produced in a rapid, colloquial style, or when the words occur in a different context. These missing sounds are said to have been 'elided'. See also CONNECTED SPEECH PHENOMENA.

Examples for English

It is easy to find examples of elision, but very difficult to state rules that govern which sounds may be elided and which may not. Elision of vowels in English usually happens when a short, unstressed vowel occurs between voiceless consonants, e.g. in the first syllable of *perhaps*, *potato*, the second syllable of *bicycle*, or the third syllable of *philosophy*. Elision also occurs when a weak vowel occurs between a PLOSIVE or FRICATIVE consonant and a consonant such as a NASAL or a LATERAL: this process leads to SYLLABIC CONSONANTS, e.g.:

sudden /ˈsʌd.ən/ → /ˈsʌd.n̩/
awful /ˈɔː.fʊl/ (US) /ˈɑː-/ → /ˈɔː.fl̩/ (US) /ˈɑː-/

Elision of consonants in English happens most commonly when a speaker 'simplifies' a complex consonant cluster, e.g.:

acts /ækts/ → /æks/
twelfth night /ˌtwelfθˈnaɪt/ → /ˌtwelθˈnaɪt/ or /ˌtwelfˈnaɪt/

In *twelfth night* above, it seems much less likely that any of the other consonants could be left out: the /l/ and the /n/ seem to be unelidable.

It is very important to note that sounds do not simply 'disappear' like a light being switched off. A transcription such as /æks/ for *acts* implies that the /t/ phoneme has dropped out altogether, but detailed examination of speech shows that such effects are more gradual: in slow speech the /t/ may be fully pronounced, with an audible transition from the preceding /k/ and to the following /s/, while in a more rapid style it may be articulated but not given any audible realization, and in very rapid speech it may be observable, if at all, only as a rather early movement of the tongue blade towards the /s/ position. Much more research in this area is needed (not only on English) for us to understand what processes are involved when speech is 'reduced' in rapid articulation.

flap

A type of consonant sound that is closely similar to the TAP. It is usually voiced, and is produced by slightly curling back the tip of the tongue, then throwing it forward and allowing it to strike the alveolar ridge as it descends. The phonetic symbol for the sound is [ɽ]

Examples in English

This sound, although occurring in some accents of English, is not a PHONEME, and is uncommon in British English. It appears, however, in US English, where it is sometimes heard in words like *party* and *birdie*, where the /r/ consonant causes retroflexion of the tongue and the stress pattern favours a flap-like articulation. In this dictionary we represent the former as /t̬/, e.g.:

party /ˈpɑː.ti/ (US) /ˈpɑːr.t̬i/ [ˈpʰɑːɻ.ɾi]
birdie /ˈbɜː.di/ (US) /ˈbɝː.di/ [ˈb̥ɝː.ɾi]

In other languages

A flap is most commonly heard in languages which have other RETROFLEX consonants, such as languages of the Indian subcontinent; it is also heard in the English of native speakers of such languages, often as a realization of /r/.

fortis

Fortis sounds are said to be made with a relatively high degree of effort.

Examples for English

It is claimed that in some languages (including English) there are pairs of consonants whose members can be distinguished from each other in terms of whether they are 'strong' (fortis) or 'weak' (LENIS). These terms refer to the amount of energy used in their production, and are similar to the terms TENSE and LAX more usually used in relation to vowels. It is argued that English /b d g v ð z ʒ/ often have little or no voicing in normal speech, and it is therefore a misnomer to call them voiced. Since they seem to be more weakly articulated than /p t k f θ s ʃ/ it would be appropriate to use the term lenis instead, e.g.:

pin /pɪn/ [pʰĩn]
bin /bɪn/ [b̥ĩn]
fine /faɪn/ [faĩn]
vine /vaɪn/ [v̥aĩn]

French words and phrases

French has provided a substantial proportion of English vocabulary since the Norman Conquest in 1066, with new words being incorporated all the time. The longest-established and the most commonly used words are usually the most completely anglicized, and the most noticeable changes from the French original are found where English phonology does not easily accommodate them. Often there are many possible anglicized pronunciations: see for example the many listed for *restaurant*.

Examples

Word-final /r/: this is not usually pronounced in British English unless followed by a vowel in a following word. However, it is pronounced in US English, e.g.:

savoir faire /ˌsæv.wɑːˈfeəʳ/ (US) /-wɑːrˈfer, -wɑːˈ-/

Nasalized vowels: although some English speakers who have a good command of French may attempt to produce the French nasalized vowels /ɛ̃/, /ɑ̃/, /ɔ̃/, and even occasionally /œ̃/, these are pronounced by many people with a following /ŋ/.

Croissant is given the pronunciation /ˈkwæs.ɑ̃ːŋ/ for British English, indicating that the vowel in the last syllable will be pronounced with a nasalized vowel but possibly also a velar nasal consonant. In US English, however, a velar nasal is not usually produced following a nasalized vowel, and *croissant* is pronounced /kwɑːˈsɑ̃ː/. (It should be noted that in both cases other pronunciations exist.) This example also shows the simplification of the initial consonant cluster /krw/, which occurs in French but not in English.

Word-final stress: many French words and names with final stress are modified by British English speakers to have the stress at the beginning of the word. In US English, this occurs in some words, but not in others, e.g.:

ballet /ˈbæl.eɪ/ (US) /bælˈeɪ, ˈ- -/
Paris /ˈpær.ɪs/ (US) /ˈper-, ˈpær-/
restaurant /ˈres.tᵊr.ɔ̃ːŋ/ (US) /-tə.rɑːnt/

The phoneme /ʒ/: while this phoneme occurs frequently in the middle of words, it is rare at the beginning and end. Many such cases are in words of French origin. English speakers sometimes substitute /dʒ/ for this sound, e.g.:

gigolo /ˈdʒɪg.ə.ləʊ, ˈʒɪg-/ (US) /-loʊ/
garage /ˈgær.ɑːʒ, -ɪdʒ, -ɑːdʒ/ (US) /gəˈrɑːʒ, -ˈrɑːdʒ/

fricative

A type of consonant made by forcing air through a narrow gap so that a hissing noise is generated. This may be accompanied by VOICING, in which case the sound is a voiced fricative, such as [z], or it may be voiceless, such as [s].

Examples for English

British and US English have nine fricative phonemes: /f θ s ʃ h/ (voiceless) and /v ð z ʒ/ (voiced).

All except /h/ are permitted to occur in all positions in English, but /ʒ/ as in 'measure' /ˈmeʒə/ is of rather low frequency compared to the other eight sounds. /h/ may not end a syllable. The quality and intensity of fricative sounds varies greatly, but all are acoustically composed of energy at relatively high frequency – an indication of this is that much of the fricative sound is too high to be transmitted over a phone (which usually cuts out the highest and lowest frequencies in order to reduce the cost), giving rise to the confusions that often arise over sets of words like English *fin*, *thin*, *sin*, and *shin*. In order for the sound quality to be produced accurately, the size and direction of the jet of air has to be very precisely controlled. A distinction is sometimes made between 'sibilant' or 'strident' fricatives (such as [s] and [ʃ]), which are strong and clearly audible, and others which are weak and less audible (such as [θ] and [f]).

glottalization

The addition of a glottal stop before a consonant.

Examples for English

Adding a glottal stop before certain consonants has the effect of making the preceding vowel somewhat shorter. In English this usually happens before a voiceless PLOSIVE or AFFRICATE consonant if there is not a vowel immediately following (e.g. in *captive*, *catkin*, *arctic*; a similar case is that of /tʃ/ when following a stressed vowel or when syllable final, as in *butcher*).

This addition of a glottal stop is sometimes called 'glottal reinforcement', e.g.:

back /bæk/ [b̥æʔk]
captive /ˈkæp.tɪv/ [ˈkʰæʔp̚.tɪv̥]
catkin /ˈkæt.kɪn/ [ˈkʰæʔk̚.kɪ̃n]
arctic /ˈɑːk.tɪk/ [ˈɑˑʔk̚.tɪk] ⓊⓈ /ˈɑːrk.tɪk/ [ˈɑˑɻʔk̚.tɪk]
butcher /ˈbʊtʃ.ər/ [ˈbʊʔ.t͡ʃ ə] ⓊⓈ /ˈbʊtʃ.ɚ/ [ˈbʊʔ.t͡ʃɚ]

This feature of English is an important one for perception. As the difference in voicing between /p t k tʃ/ and /b d g dʒ/ in syllable-final position is negligible, it is the length of the vowel rather than the voicing of the final consonant which contributes strongly to a native speaker's decision of whether a speaker has produced e.g. *back* or *bag*.

glottal stop

A consonant made by closure of the vocal folds. The phonetic symbol for a glottal stop is [ʔ].

Examples for English

In some British accents, a glottal stop can actually replace the voiceless alveolar plosive [t] as the realization of the /t/ phoneme when it follows a stressed vowel, e.g.:

getting better /ˌget.ɪŋˈbet.əʳ/ → [ˌgẹʔ.ɪ̃ŋˈbẹʔ.ə]

This type of pronunciation is found in many urban accents, notably London (Cockney), Leeds, Glasgow, Edinburgh, and others, and is increasingly accepted among educated young people. Sometimes a glottal stop is pronounced in front of a /p/, /t/, or /k/ if there is not a vowel immediately following (see GLOTTALIZATION).

In a true glottal stop there is complete obstruction to the passage of air, and the result is a period of silence. In casual speech it often happens that a speaker aims to produce a complete glottal stop but instead makes a low-pitched creak-like sound.

homographs

When two lexical items have the same form in spelling, these are known as homographs. Homographs can be pronounced the same as or different from each other.

Examples

Here are some examples of homographs with the same pronunciation:

- bank /bæŋk/ (*e.g. financial institution; area of ground by a river*)
- well /wel/ (*e.g. source of water; healthy; adv.*)

Other homographs differ in their pronunciation, but usually only in the vowel sound used, e.g.:

- bow
  — (*e.g. knot; device for shooting arrows*) /bəʊ/ ⓊⓈ /boʊ/
  — (*e.g. incline the head or trunk; submit*) /baʊ/
- dove
  — (*pigeon*) /dʌv/
  — (*past tense of* dive) /dəʊv/ ⓊⓈ /doʊv/

Homographs also appear in noun/verb, noun/adjective, and verb/adjective pairs. The difference in pronunciation indicates which part of speech is being used, e.g.:

insert (*n.*) /ˈɪn.sɜːt/ ⓊⓈ /-sɝːt/
(*v.*) /ɪnˈsɜːt/ ⓊⓈ /-ˈsɝːt/
deliberate (*adj.*) /dɪˈlɪb.ᵊr.ət/
(*v.*) /dɪˈlɪb.ᵊr.eɪt/ ⓊⓈ /-ə.reɪt/
arithmetic (*n.*) /əˈrɪθ.mə.tɪk/
(*adj.*) /ˌær.ɪθˈmet.ɪk/ ⓊⓈ /ˌer.ɪθˈmeţ-/

Pronunciation tip

In most cases it is necessary to check the pronunciation of a word individually, as the correct realization is not obvious from the form of the word. However, some rules are available. For example, the pronunciation of word pairs ending with *-ate* is predictable depending on the part of speech. In two-syllable words where the stress moves to show the difference between a noun and a verb (e.g. *insert*, *export*), the noun is almost always stressed on the first syllable and the verb on the second.

intonation

The use of the pitch of the voice to convey linguistic information. The word is used with two rather different meanings. In a restricted sense, it is the variations in the pitch of a speaker's voice used to convey or alter meaning. In a broader and more popular sense, intonation is equivalent to 'prosody', where variations in such things as voice quality, tempo, and loudness are included.

Examples for English

Intonation is said to convey emotions and attitudes. Other linguistic functions have also been claimed: interesting relationships exist in English between intonation and grammar, for example. In a few extreme cases a perceived difference in grammatical meaning may depend on the pitch movement, e.g.:

- she didn't go because of her ˇ<u>time</u>table (meaning 'she did go, but it was not because of her timetable')
- she didn't go because of her ˋ<u>time</u>table (meaning 'she didn't go, the reason being her timetable').

Other 'meanings' of intonation include things like the difference between statement and question, e.g.:

- it was ˋcold (meaning 'it was cold')
- it was ˊcold (meaning 'was it cold?')

the contrast between 'open' and 'closed' lists, e.g.:

- would you like ˊ<u>wine</u>, ˊ<u>sher</u>ry or ˊ<u>beer</u> ('open', implying other things are also on offer)
- would you like ˊ<u>wine</u>, ˊ<u>sher</u>ry or ˋ<u>beer</u> ('closed', implying no further choices are available)

and the indication of whether a relative clause is restrictive or non-restrictive, e.g.:

- the students who were ˇ<u>ner</u>vous ˋ<u>failed</u> (restrictive relative clause: only students who were nervous failed)

- ▶ the ˇstudents, who were ˇnervous, ˋfailed (non-restrictive relative clause: all students were nervous and all failed)

Another approach to intonation is to concentrate on its role in conversational discourse: this involves such aspects as indicating whether the particular thing being said constitutes new information or old, the regulation of turn-taking in conversation, the establishment of dominance, and the elicitation of co-operative responses. As with the signalling of attitudes, it seems that though analysts concentrate on pitch movements, there are many other prosodic factors being used to create these effects.

labiodental

A consonant articulated with contact between the lips and the teeth.

Examples for English

By far the most common type of labiodental articulation is one where the inner surface of the lower lip touches the upper front teeth, as in the fricatives [f] (voiceless) and [v] (voiced); these two occur in English, e.g.:

fine /faɪn/
safe /seɪf/
vine /vaɪn/
save /seɪv/

The fricative noise made by /f/ and /v/ is very weak. In final position, as /f/ is FORTIS and /v/ is LENIS, 'pre-fortis clipping' of the vowel occurs. This has the effect of shortening the vowel in *safe*, making it much shorter than the one in *save*.

larynx

The larynx is located in the throat and its main biological function is to act as a valve that can stop air entering or escaping from the lungs and also (usually) prevents food and other solids from entering the lungs. It consists of a rigid framework or box made of cartilage and, inside, the vocal folds, which are two small lumps of muscular tissue like a very small pair of lips with the division between them (the 'glottis') running from front to back of the throat. There is a complex set of muscles inside the larynx that can open and close the vocal folds as well as changing their length and tension.

In speech the larynx has many important functions including the following:

i) the distinction between voiced and voiceless sounds

ii) the control of pitch

iii) the production of the glottal fricative [h] and the glottal stop [ʔ]

iv) producing variation in voice quality.

lateral

A lateral consonant is one where there is obstruction to the passage of air in the centre (mid-line) of the air passage and the air flows to the side of the obstruction.

Examples for English

In English the /l/ phoneme is lateral both in its 'clear' and its 'dark' allophones (see CLEAR L and DARK L): the blade of the tongue is in contact with the alveolar ridge as for /t d n/ but the sides of the tongue are lowered to allow the passage of air, e.g.:

lip /lɪp/
pill /pɪl/

When an alveolar plosive precedes a lateral consonant in English it is usual for it to have a 'lateral release'. This means that to go from /t/ or /d/ to /l/ we simply lower the sides of the tongue to release the compressed air, rather than lowering and then raising the tongue blade. A syllabic /l/ is the usual result of this in word final position (see SYLLABIC CONSONANT), e.g.:

bottle /ˈbɒt.l̩/
puddle /ˈpʌd.l̩/

Most laterals are produced with the air passage to both sides of the obstruction (they are 'bilateral'), but sometimes we find air passing to one side only ('unilateral').

In other languages

Other lateral consonants are found in other languages: the Welsh *ll* sound is a voiceless lateral fricative [ɬ], and Xhosa and Zulu have a voiced lateral fricative [ɮ]. Several Southern African languages have lateral clicks (where the plosive occlusion is released laterally) and at least one language (of Papua New Guinea) has a contrast between alveolar and velar lateral.

Latin words and phrases

Words, names, and phrases from Latin have entered the English language at many different times. Some words and names are in relatively common use and have been completely anglicized, while others are used in particular types of discourse which to some extent determine their pronunciation. The pronunciation used by academic scholars of Latin has tended to be based on a reconstruction of what was supposed to be the pronunciation in Roman times. Ecclesiastical Latin, previously used in the Roman Catholic church and closely similar to the pronunciation of Italian, has largely disappeared, but phrases such as *Gloria in excelsis* or *Humanae Vitae* are still heard. Legal Latin is also now much less widely used than it used to be, but some phrases survive, such as *habeas corpus, ultra vires* (usual pronunciation /ˌheɪ.bi.əsˈkɔː.pəs, US /-ˈkɔːr-/ and /ˌʌl.trəˈvaɪə.riːz, ˌʊl.trɑːˈvɪə.reɪz/ US /ˌʌl.trəˈvaɪ.riːz/). Most of the Latin words, phrases, and names in this dictionary are ones that have been fully anglicized, but there is no set of rules to determine exactly how this is done.

Examples

Words, e.g.:

accidia /ækˈsɪd.i.ə/
flamen /ˈfleɪ.men/
vale /ˈvɑː.leɪ, ˈveɪ.li, ˈvæl.eɪ/ US /ˈveɪ.li, ˈvɑː.leɪ/

Names, e.g.:

Aeneas /iːˈniː.əs, ɪˈniː-, -æs/
Flaminius /fləˈmɪn.i.əs, flæmˈɪn-/ US /fləˈmɪn-/

hrases, e.g.:

l hoc /ˌædˈhɒk, -ˈhəʊk/ (US) /-ˈhɑːk, -ˈhoʊk/
x voto /ˌeksˈvəʊ.təʊ/ (US) /-ˈvoʊ.toʊ/
agrante delicto /fləˌgræn.teɪ.dɪˈlɪk.təʊ/, /flægˌræn-, -ti-, -dəˈ-, -deɪˈ-/ (US) /fləˌgræn.ti.diːˈlɪk.t̬oʊ/

ax

lax sound is produced with relatively little articu-tory energy. Since there is no established standard r measuring articulatory energy, this concept only as meaning if it is used relative to some other unds that are felt to be articulated with a mparatively greater amount of energy (i.e. TENSE).

xamples for English

is mainly American phonologists who use the terms x and tense in describing English vowels; the short owels /ɪ e æ ʌ ʊ ə/ are classed as lax, while what are ferred to in our description of BBC pronunciation as e long vowels and the diphthongs are tense. The rms can also be used of consonants as equivalent to RTIS (tense) and LENIS (lax), though this is not mmonly done in present-day descriptions.

ength

term used in phonetics to refer to a subjective npression of how much time a sound takes; it is stinct from physically measurable 'duration'. sually, however, the term is used as synonymous th duration.

xamples for English

ength is important in many ways in speech: in nglish and most other languages, stressed syllables nd to be longer than unstressed (see RHYTHM, STRESS nd WEAK FORM). Some languages have phonemic fferences between long and short sounds, and BBC nglish is claimed by some writers to be of this type, ntrasting short vowels /ɪ e æ ʌ ɒ ʊ ə/ with long owels /iː ɜː ɑː ɔː uː/ (though other, equally valid alyses have been put forward). However, the ntext in which these sounds occur must be taken to account. For example, the vowel /iː/ is said to be nger than /ɪ/ as well as having a different quality, it the vowel in *beat* is unlikely to be longer than the owel in *bid* as the phonetic environment in *beat* uses the vowel to be shorter.

other languages

hen languages have long/short consonant differ-nces, as does Arabic, for example, it is usual to treat e long consonants as geminate; it is odd that this is ot done equally regularly in the case of vowels. erhaps the most interesting example of length fferences comes from Estonian, which has tradi-onally been said to have a threeway distinction etween short, long, and extra-long consonants and owels.

lenis

A lenis sound is weakly articulated (the word comes from Latin, where it means 'smooth, gentle'). The opposite term is FORTIS.

Examples for English

In general, the term lenis is used of voiced consonants (which are supposed to be less strongly articulated than their corresponding voiceless ones), and is resorted to for languages such as German, Russian, and English where voiced PHONEMES like /b d g/ are not always voiced. (See the entry at FORTIS for examples.) However, it is claimed that the language which most clearly shows a distinction between fortis and lenis consonants is Korean.

liaison

The linking or joining together of sounds.

Examples for English

In English the best-known case of liaison is the 'linking r': there are many words in English (e.g. *car*, *here*, *tyre*) which in a RHOTIC accent such as US English or Scots would be pronounced with a final /r/, but which in BBC pronunciation end in a vowel when they are pronounced before a pause or before a consonant. When they are followed by a vowel, British English speakers pronounce /r/ at the end, e.g.:

the car stopped /ðə kɑː stɒpt/ (US) /ðə kɑːr stɑːpt/
the car is blue /ðə kɑːr ɪz bluː/ (US) /ðə kɑːr ɪz bluː/

In BBC English there is also 'intrusive r' – an /r/ inserted between two vowels at word boundaries where there is none in the spelling. This does not occur after close vowels (/iː uː/), or diphthongs which end with a close element (/eɪ aɪ ɔɪ aʊ əʊ/), e.g.:

China and Japan /tʃaɪnə r ən dʒəˈpæn/ (US) /tʃaɪnə ən dʒəˈpæn/
law and order /lɔː r ən ˈɔː.də/ (US) /lɑː ən ˈɔːr.dɚ/

It has been argued that this elision has the purpose of avoiding bringing two vowels into contact with each other, but since many languages do run vowels together with no apparent difficulty for speakers, the argument should be treated with caution.

Another aspect of liaison in English is the movement of a single consonant at the end of an unstressed word to the beginning of the next if that is strongly stressed. A well known example in British English is *none at all*, where the /t/ of *at* becomes initial (and therefore strongly aspirated) in the final syllable for many speakers.

monophthong

A single vowel. The term is used only in contrast with the word DIPHTHONG, which originally meant a 'double sound'.

Examples for English

British English has 12 vowel monophthongs /ɪ e æ ʌ ɒ ʊ ə iː ɑː ɔː ɜː uː/, and US English has 11, or 12 if r-coloured SCHWA /ɚ/ is taken into account. In British English these are traditionally divided into short and long, with a length mark [ː] used to show that there is a difference in length as well as vowel quality. This convention is extended in this dictionary to US English vowels. Long vowels are permitted to appear in a stressed syllable without a CODA, whereas short vowels are not. It should be noted that the schwa vowel, /ə/, never appears in stressed syllables and has a different distribution from the other short vowels.

names of people and places

It can be difficult to work out the pronunciation of some English words, and something like between ten to thirty percent of words in any text will have irregular spellings. Proper nouns for people and places can have really unexpected pronunciations. Here, we look at a few of the most interesting ones.

Examples

Family names are well known for having interesting realizations. This can be because some letters are not pronounced, but, in some cases, the way a word is written looks almost entirely different from the pronunciation, e.g.:

Cholmondeley /ˈtʃʌm.li/
Colquhoun /kəˈhuːn/
Dalziel /diːˈel; ˈdæl.ziːl/
Featherstonehawe /ˈfeð.ə.stən.hɔː; ˈfæn.ʃɔː/
Ⓤⓢ /ˈfeð.ɚ.stən.hɑː; ˈfæn.ʃɑː/
Quesnel /ˈkeɪ.nᵊl/

It is a similar situation for place names, e.g.:

Alnwick /ˈæn.ɪk/
Cirencester /ˈsaɪə.rᵊn.ses.təʳ; ˈsɪs.ɪ.təʳ/
Ⓤⓢ /ˈsaɪ.rᵊn.ses.tɚ/
Lympne /lɪm/
Woolfardisworthy /ˈwʊl.zᵊr.i; wʊlˈfɑː.dɪˌswɜː.ði/
Ⓤⓢ /ˈwʊl.zɚ.i; wʊlˈfɑːr.dɪˌswɝː.ði/
Worcester /ˈwʊs.təʳ/ Ⓤⓢ /-ɚ/

Welsh place names can be very difficult to decipher for people who do not know the rules that govern the spelling of Welsh. Although Welsh is written using the same alphabet as English, the values of the letters are frequently different, e.g.:

Llanrwst /ɬænˈruːst/
Penmaenmawr /ˌpen.mənˈmaʊ.əʳ, -ˈmɔːʳ/
Ⓤⓢ /-ˈmaʊ.ɚ, -ˈmɔːr/

There is some regularity amongst suffixes in some place names. The suffix *-ham* in British place names, for example, is usually pronounced /-əm/, as in *Birmingham*. However, in the North American place name *Birmingham*, *-ham* is pronounced /-hæm/. Another common suffix in British place names, *-cester*, is usually pronounced /-stəʳ/ Ⓤⓢ /-stɚ/, e.g. as in *Worcester* above (although note also *Cirencester*, in which one possible realization is /-ses.təʳ/ Ⓤⓢ /-ses.tɚ/). Finally, the suffix *-wick* in e.g. *Warwick* is usually pronounced /-ɪk/ in British place names, although there are exceptions.

nasal consonant

A consonant in which the air escapes only through the nose. For this to happen, two articulatory actions are necessary: firstly, the 'soft palate' (or 'velum') must be lowered to allow air to escape past it and, secondly, a closure must be made in the oral cavity to prevent air from escaping through it. The closure may be at any place of articulation from BILABIAL at the front of the oral cavity to 'uvular' at the back (in the latter case there is contact between the tip of the lowered soft palate and the raised back of the tongue).

Examples for English

English has three commonly found nasal consonants: bilabial, alveolar, and velar, for which the symbols /m n ŋ/ are used. /ŋ/ cannot occur at the beginning of a syllable, e.g.:

map /mæp/
nap /næp/
sang /sæŋ/

There is disagreement over the phonemic status of the velar nasal: some claim that it must be a phoneme since it can be placed in contrastive contexts like *sum/sun/sung*, while others state that the velar nasal is an ALLOPHONE of /n/ which occurs before /k/ and /g/.

In English we find 'nasal release' of PLOSIVE consonants: when a plosive is followed by a nasal consonant the usual articulation is to release the compressed air by lowering the soft palate. This is particularly noticeable when the plosive and the nasal are 'homorganic' (share the same place of articulation), as for example in *topmost*, *Putney*. The result is that no plosive release is heard from the speaker's mouth before the nasal consonant, e.g.:

topmost /ˈtɒp.məʊst/ Ⓤⓢ /ˈtɑːp.moʊst/
Putney /ˈpʌt.ni/

Nasal release can also result in a SYLLABIC CONSONANT, e.g.:

button /ˈbʌtn̩/

nasalization

The addition of nasal escape of air to a sound which would not normally have it.

Examples for English

The best-known examples of nasalization in English are nasalized vowels. In most vowels the airflow escapes entirely through the mouth, but often, in a vowel preceding or following a nasal consonant, we find air escaping also through the nose.

This is a kind of coarticulation, e.g.:

pin /pɪn/ [pʰɪ̃n]
man /mæn/ [mæ̃n]
sing /sɪŋ/ [sɪ̃ŋ]

Nasalized vowels are not phonemically contrastive in English.

In other languages

Nasalized vowels are phonemically contrastive in a number of languages, such as French, which has pairs of words such as *beau – bon* /bo – bõ/ and *mais – main* /mɛ – mɛ̃/.

neutral

A term used to describe lip configuration in speech sounds, in which the lips are neither rounded nor spread (see ROUNDING and SPREADING). The term 'unrounded' is also commonly used but can apply equally to spread lips.

Examples for English

The English vowels /ə/ and /ɜː/ are thought of as having a neutral lip configuration.

neutralization

The loss of contrast between PHONEMES.

Examples for English

In its simple form, the theory of the phoneme implies that two sounds that are in opposition to each other (e.g. /t/ and /d/ in English) are in this relationship in all contexts throughout the language. Closer study of phonemes has, however, shown that there are some contexts where the opposition no longer functions: for example, in a word like *still* /stɪl/, the /t/ is in a position (following /s/ and preceding a vowel) where voiced (LENIS) PLOSIVES do not occur. There is no possibility in English of the existence of a pair of words such as /stɪl/ and */sdɪl/, so in this context the opposition between /t/ and /d/ is 'neutralized'. One consequence of this is that one could equally well claim that the plosive in this word is a /d/, not a /t/. (See also ASPIRATION.)

onset

In the analysis of syllable structure (and occasionally in other areas), the first part of a syllable.

Examples for English

In English the onset may be zero (when no consonant precedes the vowel in a syllable), one consonant, or two, or three, e.g.:

in /ɪn/
spin /spɪn/
pin /pɪn/
spring /sprɪŋ/

There are many restrictions on what clusters of consonants may occur in onsets: for example, if an English syllable has a three-consonant onset, the first consonant must be /s/ and the last one must be one of /l r j w/.

palatal

A palatal consonant is one in which the tongue makes contact with or approaches the highest part of the hard palate. The hard palate is mainly composed of a thin layer of bone and is dome-shaped, as you can feel by exploring it with the tip of your tongue.

Examples for English

In English, the only phoneme described as palatal is /j/, e.g.:

yes /jes/
beautiful /ˈbjuː.tɪ.fəl/ (US) /-t̬ə-/

However, phonetically a voiceless palatal fricative [ç] can also occur for the consonants in the sequence /hjuː/, e.g.:

huge /hjuːdʒ/ [çʉːd̥ʒ̊]
Hugh, Huw /hjuː/ [çʉː]

palato-alveolar

Palato-alveolar sounds are made between the upper teeth and the front part of the palate. In the description of English, this term has been largely replaced by POST-ALVEOLAR.

In other languages

It has been proposed that there is a difference between palato-alveolar and 'alveolo-patatal' that can be reliably distinguished, though others argue that factors other than place of articulation are usually involved. The latter sounds are placed further forward in the mouth than the former: an example of an alveolo-palatal consonant is that of Polish /ɕ/ in *Kasia* (compare /ʃ/ in *kasza*).

pharyngeal

Descriptive of a sound made by constricting the muscles of the pharynx (and usually also some of the LARYNX muscles) to create an obstruction to the airflow from the lungs.

Examples for English

English does not have any pharyngeal phonemes.

In other languages

The best known language that has pharyngeal consonants is Arabic, most dialects of which have voiced and voiceless fricatives.

phone

A unit at the phonetic level in the study of speech. The term PHONEME is very widely used for a contrastive unit of sound in language. However, a term is also needed for a unit at the phonetic level, since there is not always a one-to-one correspondence between units at the two levels.

Examples for English

The English word *can't* is phonemically /kɑːnt/ in British English and /kænt/ in US English (four phonemic units), but may be pronounced [kɑ̃ːt] or [kæ̃t] with the nasal consonant phoneme absorbed into the preceding vowel as NASALIZATION (three phonetic units).

phoneme

A fundamental unit of phonology, usually said to be the smallest unit of speech. It has been defined and used in many different ways.

Examples for English

Virtually all theories of phonology hold that spoken language can be broken down into a string of sound units (phonemes), and that each language has a small, relatively fixed set of these phonemes. Most phonemes can be put into groups; for example, in English we can identify a group of PLOSIVE phonemes /p t k b d g/, a group of voiceless FRICATIVES /f θ s ʃ h/, and so on. An important question in phoneme theory is how the analyst can establish what the phonemes of a language are.

The most widely accepted view is that phonemes are 'contrastive' and one must find cases where the difference between two words is dependent on the difference between two phonemes. For example, we can prove that the difference between *pin* and *pan* depends on the vowel, and that /ɪ/ and /æ/ are different phonemes.

Pairs of words that differ in just one phoneme are known as 'minimal pairs'. We can establish the same fact about /p/ and /b/ by citing *pin* and *bin*.

Tests like these are called 'commutation tests' and can only be carried out when a provisional list of possible phonemes has been established, so some basic phonetic analysis must precede this stage.

phonetics

The scientific study of speech. It has a long history, going back certainly to well over two thousand years ago. The central concerns in phonetics are the discovery of how speech sounds are produced, how they are used in spoken language, how we can record speech sounds with written symbols and how we hear and recognize different sounds.

In the first of these areas, when we study the production of speech sounds we can observe what speakers do ('articulatory' observation) and we can try to feel what is going on inside our vocal tract ('kinaesthetic' observation). The second area is where phonetics overlaps with PHONOLOGY: usually in phonetics we are only interested in sounds that are used in meaningful speech, and phoneticians are interested in discovering the range and variety of sounds used in this way in all the known languages of the world. This is sometimes known as 'linguistic phonetics'. Thirdly, there has always been a need for agreed conventions for using phonetic symbols that represent speech sounds; the International Phonetic Association has played a very important role in this. Finally, the 'auditory' aspect of speech is very important. The ear is capable of making fine discrimination between different sounds, and sometimes it is not possible to define in articulatory terms precisely what the difference is. A good example of this is in vowel classification. While it is important to know the position and shape of the tongue and lips, it is often very important to have been trained in an agreed set of standard auditory qualities that vowels can be reliably related to (see CARDINAL VOWEL). Another important area is acoustic phonetics which studies the physical properties of speech sounds.

phonology

The study of the sound systems of languages.

The most basic activity in phonology is 'phonemic analysis', in which the objective is to establish what the PHONEMES are and arrive at the 'phonemic inventory' of the language. Very few phonologists have ever believed that this would be an adequate analysis of the sound system of a language: it is necessary to go beyond this. One can look at 'suprasegmental' phonology – the study of STRESS, RHYTHM, and INTONATION. One can go beyond the phoneme and look into the detailed characteristics of each unit in terms of 'distinctive features'. The way in which sounds can combine in a language is studied in 'phonotactics' and in the analysis of syllable structure.

For some phonologists the most important area is the relationships between the different phonemes – how they form groups, the nature of the contrasts between them and how those oppositions may be neutralized (see NEUTRALIZATION). For others, the most important activity is to discover the rules which affect the phonemes of the language and the way they are produced, and to express these rules as economically as possible.

pitch

An auditory sensation which places sounds on a scale from low to high.

When we hear a regularly vibrating sound such as a note played on a musical instrument, or a vowel produced by the human voice, we hear a high pitch if the rate of vibration is high and a low pitch if the rate of vibration is low. Many speech sounds are voiceless (e.g. [s]), and cannot give rise to a sensation of pitch in this way. The pitch sensation that we receive from a voiced sound corresponds quite closely to the frequency of vibration of the vocal folds. However we usually refer to this vibration frequency as 'fundamental frequency' (which we can measure) in order to distinguish it from the subjective impression of pitch.

Pitch is used in many languages as an essential component of the pronunciation of a word, so that a change of pitch may cause a change in meaning; these are called 'tone languages'. In most languages (whether or not they are tone languages) pitch plays a central role in INTONATION.

plosive

A sound produced by forming a complete obstruction to the flow of air out of the mouth and nose. Normally this results in a build-up of compressed air inside the chamber formed by the closure. When the closure is released, there is a small explosion that causes a sharp noise.

Examples for English

British English and US English have six plosive consonants, /p t k/ (voiceless) and /b d g/ (voiced).

In syllable-initial position, sounds in the voiceless group /p t k/ are strongly aspirated (see ASPIRATION) and in final position GLOTTALIZATION of these sounds causes a shortening of the preceding vowel. Sounds in the voiced group /b d g/ tend to be 'devoiced' at the beginning and ends of words. At the ends of words the pairs of sounds /p b/, /t d/, and /k g/ can sound very similar due to this, and one must listen to the length of the vowel to work out which consonant is being produced.

The basic plosive consonant type can be of many different forms: plosives may have any place of articulation, may be voiced or voiceless and may have an 'egressive' (breathing out) or 'ingressive' (breathing in) airflow. The airflow may be from the lungs ('pulmonic'), from the larynx ('glottalic') or generated in the mouth ('velaric'). We find great variation in the release of the plosive.

postalveolar

Descriptive of sounds made between the upper teeth and the front part of the palate.

Examples for English

British and US English have two sets of sounds referred to postalveolar, the fricatives /ʃ ʒ/ and the affricates /tʃ dʒ/. These are also referred to as PALATO-ALVEOLAR, e.g.:

pressure /ˈpreʃ.əʳ/ ⓊⓈ /-ɚ/
pleasure /ˈpleʒ.əʳ/ ⓊⓈ /-ɚ/
church /tʃɜːtʃ/ ⓊⓈ /tʃɝːtʃ/
judge /dʒʌdʒ/

prefixes

A prefix is an element placed at the beginning of a word to modify or alter its meaning. In general, prefixes do not alter the original pronunciation of the word stem on to which they are affixed, though they may attract secondary stress.

A narrow definition of *prefix* would apply only in the case of words where removal of the prefix would leave a freestanding word (for example, 'unfit' is 'un' + 'fit'), but many treatments of English word stress also treat as prefixes such elements as 'con' in 'contain' or 'in' in 'insert', where 'tain' and 'sert' do not exist independently as words.

Examples

Some examples of words containing unstressed prefixes follow, e.g.:

admire /ədˈmaɪəʳ/ ⓊⓈ /-ˈmaɪ.ɚ/
contain /kənˈteɪn/
desist /dɪˈsɪst/
undo /ʌnˈduː/

A prefix may attract secondary stress if it is affixed to a word beginning with an unstressed syllable (e.g. another prefix), e.g.:

undivided /ˌʌn.dɪˈvaɪ.dɪd/
unforseen /ˌʌn.fɔːˈsiːn/ ⓊⓈ /-fɔːrˈ-/

A prefix may be stressed to avoid a clash of two stressed syllables in stress-shift situations, e.g.:

unfair dismissal /ˌʌn.feə dɪˈsmɪs.əl/ ⓊⓈ /-fer-/

In homographic noun/verb pairs containing prefixes, the prefix is usually stressed in the nominal form and unstressed in the verbal form (see HOMOGRAPHS), e.g.:

insert (*n.*) /ˈɪn.sɜːt/ ⓊⓈ /-sɝːt/
(*v.*) /ɪnˈsɜːt/ ⓊⓈ /-ˈsɝːt/
record (*n.*) /ˈrek.ɔːd/ ⓊⓈ /-ɚd/
(*v.*) /rɪˈkɔːd/ ⓊⓈ /-ˈkɔːrd/

retroflex

In a retroflex articulation the tip of the tongue is curled upward and backward.

Examples for English

The /r/ sound of some British and American accents is sometimes described as being retroflex, though in BBC pronunciation the degree of retroflexion is relatively small.

In US English and some accents of southwest England it is common for vowels preceding /r/ (e.g. /ɑː/ in *car*, or /ɜː/ in *bird*) to be affected by the consonant so that they have a retroflex quality for most of their duration. This 'r-colouring' is most common in back or central vowels where the forward part of the tongue is relatively free to change shape.

In other languages

Other languages have retroflex consonants with a more noticeable auditory quality, the best known examples being the great majority of the languages of the Indian subcontinent. The sound of retroflex consonants is fairly familiar to English listeners, since first-generation immigrants from India and Pakistan tend to carry the retroflex quality into their pronunciation of English consonants which are alveolar in BBC pronunciation.

rhotic

In rhotic varieties of English pronunciation the /r/ PHONEME is found in all phonological contexts.

Examples for English

In BBC pronunciation, /r/ is only found before vowels, and never before consonants or before a pause (see also LIAISON), e.g.:

red /red/
around /əˈraʊnd/
there is /ðər ɪz/

In US English and other rhotic accents, on the other hand, /r/ may occur before consonants and before a pause, e.g.:

cart /kɑːt/ ⓊⓈ /kɑːrt/
car /kɑːʳ/ ⓊⓈ /kɑːr/

While the BBC accent is non-rhotic, many accents of the British Isles are rhotic, including most of the south and west of England, much of Wales and all of Scotland and Ireland. Most speakers of American English speak with a rhotic accent, but there are non-rhotic areas including the Boston area, lower-class New York and the Deep South.

rhyme/rime

In the phonological analysis of the syllable, this is a way of referring to the vowel in the middle of the syllable forming its 'peak' plus any sounds following the peak within the syllable (the CODA).

Examples for English

In the word *spoon* the rhyme (or rime) is /uːn/, in *tea* it is /iː/ and in *strengths* it is /eŋθs/ or /eŋkθs/.

Note

The spelling 'rhyme' also refers to a pair of lines that end with the same sequence of sounds in verse. If we examine the sound sequences that must match each other, we find that these consist of the vowel and any final consonants of the last syllable: thus *moon* and *June* rhyme, and the initial consonants of these two words are not important (of course, we do find longer-running rhymes than this in verse, e.g. *ability* rhyming with *senility*).

rhythm

The way events in speech are distributed in time.

Examples for English

Obvious examples of vocal rhythms are chanting as part of games or physical activities. In conversational speech the rhythms are vastly more complicated, but it is clear that the timing of speech is not random. An extreme view (though a quite common one) is that English speech has a rhythm that allows us to divide it up into more or less equal intervals of time called 'feet', each of which begins with a stressed syllable: this is called the 'stress-timed rhythm hypothesis', e.g.:

London	ˈlondon
a return to London	a re | ˈturn to | ˈlondon
a day return to London	a | ˈday re | ˈturn to | ˈlondon

Languages where the length of each syllable remains more or less the same as that of its neighbours whether or not it is stressed are called 'syllable-timed'.

Most evidence from the study of real speech suggests that such rhythms only exist in very careful, controlled speaking, but it appears from psychological research that listeners' brains tend to hear timing regularities even where there is little or no physical regularity.

rounding

A term used to describe lip configuration in speech sounds.

Examples for English

Practically any vowel or consonant may be produced with different amounts of lip rounding. The lips are rounded by muscles that act rather like a drawstring round the neck of a bag, bringing the edges of the lips towards each other. Except in unusual cases, this results not only in the mouth opening adopting a round shape, but also in a protrusion or 'pushing forward' of the lips. In theory, any vowel position (defined in terms of height and frontness/backness) may be produced rounded or unrounded, though we do not necessarily find all possible vowels in natural languages. BBC English has four rounded vowel monophthongs, while US English has three:

pot	/pɒt/ ⓊⓈ /pɑːt/ (unrounded)
put	/pʊt/
core	/kɔːʳ/ ⓊⓈ /kɔːr/
coo	/kuː/

Consonants, too, may have rounded lips (in [w], the basic consonantal articulation itself consists of lip rounding): this lip rounding in consonants is regarded as a 'secondary articulation', and it is usual to refer to it as 'labialization'. In British English, it is common to find /ʃ/, /tʃ/, and /r/ with lip rounding.

In other languages

Swedish is described as having a rounded vowel without lip protrusion.

schwa

An unstressed central vowel.

Examples for English

One of the most noticeable features of English pronunciation is the phonetic difference between stressed and unstressed syllables. In most languages, any of the vowels of the language can occur in any syllable whether that syllable is stressed or not. In English, however, a syllable which bears no stress is more likely to have one of a small number of weak vowels. The most common weak vowel is one which never occurs in a stressed syllable, the schwa vowel (symbolized ə), which is generally described as being unrounded, central (i.e. between front and back), and mid (i.e. between close and open), e.g.:

appease	/əˈpiːz/
syllable	/ˈsɪl.ə.bᵊl/
China	/ˈtʃaɪ.nə/
mother	/ˈmʌð.əʳ/ ⓊⓈ /ˈmʌð.ɚ/

Statistically, schwa is reported to be the most frequently occurring vowel of English (over 10% of all vowels).

soft palate

The rear part of the roof of the mouth.

Most of the roof of the mouth consists of 'hard palate', which has bone beneath the skin. Towards the back of the mouth, the layer of bone comes to an end but the layer of soft tissue continues for some distance, ending eventually in a loose appendage that can easily be seen by looking in a mirror. This dangling object is the 'uvula', and the layer of soft tissue attached to it is called the soft palate (it is also sometimes known as the 'velum'). In normal breathing the velum is allowed to hang down so that air may pass above it and escape through the nose, but for most speech sounds it is lifted up and pressed against the upper back wall of the throat so that no air can escape through the nose. This is necessary for a PLOSIVE, for example, so that air may be compressed within the vocal tract. However, for NASAL consonants (e.g. [m], [n]) the soft palate must be lowered since air should escape only through the nose in these sounds.

In nasalized vowels (such vowels are found in considerable numbers in French, for example) the soft palate is lowered and air escapes through the mouth and the nose together.

spelling pronunciation

It is well known that English spelling is a poor guide to the pronunciation of a word. In some cases the spelling represents the pronunciation that was current several centuries ago, and in others the spelling has been changed by self-appointed authorities to fit with their views on the origins of a word. Sometimes a 'spelling pronunciation' arises when speakers pronounce a word in a way that is closer to what is suggested by the spelling. One reason for such a change is found where a word which has had a widespread pronunciation that was very different from the spelling becomes less frequently used. When 'waistcoat' referred to a garment that most men wore, it was /ˈweskɪt/; now that waistcoats are much less often worn, the pronunciation /ˈweɪst.kəʊt/ predominates/. We can see the process in operation in the gradual loss of the traditional pronunciations of many nautical terms as the number of people working in boats diminishes, leaving only amateur sailors to continute the tradition: nowadays 'leeward' is more often /ˈliː.wəd/ than /ˈluː.əd/, 'rowlocks' are /ˈrəʊ.lɒks/ rather than /ˈrɒl.əks/, and you are more likely to hear directions such as 'northeast', 'southwest' pronounced as /nɔːθˈiːst/, /saʊθˈwest/ than as /nɔːrˈiːst/, /saʊˈwest/. Not all cases of spelling pronunciation can be explained in this way. The word 'conduit' was pronounced /ˈkɒndɪt/ for centuries, but is now usually /ˈkɒndjuɪt/, despite the fact that it remains quite a well-known word, and it is hard to see a reason for the change from /t/ to /θ/ in the pronunciation of the name 'Anthony'.

spreading

A term used to describe lip positions in speech, produced by pulling the corners of the mouth away from each other, as in a smile.

Phonetics books tend to be rather inconsistent about this, sometimes implying that any sound that is not rounded has spread lips, but elsewhere treating lip spreading as being different from NEUTRAL lip shape. Vowels with spreading are often referred to as 'unrounded'.

Examples for English

The English vowel /iː/ is thought of as having strong lip spreading, while /ɪ/ has spreading to a lesser degree.

stress

A property of syllables which makes them stand out as more noticeable than others.

Examples for English

Stress is a large topic, which cannot be covered in its entirety here. However, some examples follow.

The position of stress can change the meaning or word class of a word, and so forms part of the phonological composition of the word, e.g.:

import (n) /ˈɪm.pɔːt/ (US) /-pɔːrt/
import (v) /ɪmˈpɔːt/ (US) /-ˈpɔːrt/
record (n) /ˈrek.ɔːd/ (US) /-ɚd/
record (v) /rɪˈkɔːd/ (US) /-ˈkɔːrd/

It is necessary to consider what factors make a syllable count as stressed. It seems likely that stressed syllables are produced with greater effort than unstressed, and that this effort is manifested in the air pressure generated in the lungs for producing the syllable and also in the articulatory movements in the vocal tract. These effects of stress produce in turn various audible results: one is 'pitch prominence', in which the stressed syllable stands out from its context (for example, being higher if its unstressed neighbours are low in PITCH, or lower if those neighbours are high; often a pitch glide such as a fall or rise is used to give greater pitch prominence). Another effect of stress is that stressed syllables tend to be longer – this is very noticeable in English, less so in some other languages. Also, stressed syllables tend to be louder than unstressed, though experiments have shown that differences in loudness alone are not very noticeable to most listeners. It has been suggested by many writers that the term 'accent' should be used to refer to some of the manifestations of stress (particularly pitch prominence), but the word, though widely used, has never acquired a distinct meaning of its own.

One of the areas in which there is little agreement is that of 'levels' of stress. Some descriptions of languages manage with just two levels (stressed and unstressed), while others use more. In English, one can argue that if one takes the word *indicator* as an example, the first syllable is the most strongly stressed, the third syllable is the next most strongly stressed and the second and fourth syllables are weakly stressed, or unstressed. This gives us three levels: it is possible to argue for more, though this rarely seems to give any practical benefit.

stress shift

A change in the position of the stress in a word when that word is combined with others in a phrase.

Examples for English

The RHYTHM of English prefers patterns in which two stressed syllables do not come together. In order to avoid this, stress in some polysyllabic words may move to an earlier syllable when combined with another in a phrase, e.g.:

Heathrow /hiːθˈrəʊ/ (US) /-ˈroʊ/
Heathrow Airport /ˌhiːθ.rəʊ ˈeə.pɔːt/ (US) /-roʊ ˈer.pɔːrt/
academic /ˌæk.əˈdem.ɪk/
academic dress /ˌæk.ə.dem.ɪk ˈdres/

In this dictionary, words which change their stress in this way are shown with an example demonstrating the stress shift.

suffixes

A suffix is an element placed at the end of a word to modify or alter its meaning. Unlike PREFIXES, it is possible for suffixes to alter the original pronunciation of the word stem on to which they are affixed. This depends on whether the suffix is stress-neutral, pre-stressed or stress-attracting.

Examples

Some suffixes do not change the pronunciation of the word stem. These are known as 'stress-neutral' suffixes. Some words containing stress-neutral suffixes follow:

eleventh /ɪˈlev.ən*t*θ/
dramatize /ˈdræm.ə.taɪz/ (US) /ˈdrɑː.mə-/
fatherhood /ˈfɑː.ðə.hʊd/ (US) /-ðɚ-/
happily /ˈhæp.ɪ.li/

A suffix which attracts stress is known as 'stress-attracting'.

Some words containing stress-attracting suffixes follow:

engineer /ˌen.dʒɪˈnɪə^{r}/ (US) /-ˈnɪr/
Japanese /ˌdʒæp.əˈniːz/
nineteen /ˌnaɪnˈtiːn/

A 'pre-stressed' suffix is one in which the affixation of the suffix causes stress to be assigned to a syllable before it. There are a number of different types of pre-stressed suffixes. Here is an example where the stress falls on the syllable immediately before the suffix:

despotic /dɪˈspɒt.ɪk/ (US) /desˈpɑː.t̬ɪk/

In other words, the stress falls two syllables ahead of the suffix:

insecticide /ɪnˈsek.tɪ.saɪd/

There are also 'mixed' pre-stressed suffixes where the stress may fall either one or two syllables before the suffix.

The suffix *-ation* is actually a combination of the stress-neutral *-ate* and the pre-stressed suffix *-ion*. In words containing *-ation*, the strongest stress is always on the penultimate syllable, e.g.:

condemnation /ˌkɒn.demˈneɪ.ʃᵊn/ (US) /ˌkɑːn-/

syllabic consonant

A consonant which can stand alone as a syllable.

Examples for English

The great majority of syllables in all languages have a vowel at their centre, and may have one or more consonants preceding and following the vowel (though languages differ greatly in the possible occurrences of consonants in syllables). However, in a few cases we find syllables which contain nothing that could conventionally be classed as a vowel. In English, syllabic consonants appear to arise as a consequence of a weak vowel becoming lost, and some appear to have become obligatory in present-day speech, e.g.:

bottle /ˈbɒt.l̩/ (US) /ˈbɑː.t̬l̩/

In many other cases in English it appears to be possible either to pronounce /m n ŋ l r/ as syllabic consonants or to pronounce them with a preceding vowel, e.g.:

button /ˈbʌt.n̩/
orderly /ˈɔː.dl̩.i, -də.li/ (US) /ˈɔːr.dɚ.li/
history /ˈhɪs.tr̩.i, -tə.ri/ (US) /-tr̩.i, -tɚ-/

In this dictionary, the use of a superscript schwa (ᵊ) indicates the possibility of a syllabic consonant.

The matter is more confusing because of the fact that speakers do not agree in their intuitions about whether a consonant (particularly /l/) is syllabic or not: while most would agree that, for example, *cuddle* and *cycle* are disyllabic (i.e. contain two syllables), *cuddly* and *cycling* are disyllabic for some people (and therefore do not contain a syllabic consonant) while for others they are trisyllabic.

In other languages

For syllables not to contain a vowel is a normal state of affairs in some languages (consider the first syllables of the Czech names *Brno* and *Vltava*). In Japanese some consonants appear to be able to stand as syllables by themselves, according to the intuitions of native speakers who are asked to divide speech up into rhythmical beats.

syllable

A fundamentally important unit – the most basic unit in speech. Here we are concerned with the phonological notion of the syllable.

Examples for English

Phonologists are interested in the structure of the syllable, since there appear to be interesting observations to be made about which phonemes may occur at the beginning, in the middle, and at the end of syllables. In English, it is possible to have from zero to up to three consonants in the ONSET of a syllable, and from zero to up to four in the CODA.

The study of sequences of phonemes is called 'phonotactics', and it seems that the phonotactic possibilities of a language are determined by syllabic structure. This means that any sequence of sounds that a native speaker produces can be broken down into syllables without any segments being left over. For example, in *Their strengths triumphed frequently*, we find the rather daunting sequences of consonant phonemes /ŋθstr/ and /mftfr/, but using what we know of English phonotactics we can split these clusters into one part that belongs to the end of one syllable and another part that belongs to the beginning of another. Thus the first one can only be divided /ŋθ | str/ or /ŋθs | tr/ and the second can only be /mft | fr/. Phonological treatments of syllable structure usually call the first part of a syllable the ONSET, the middle part the 'peak' and the end part the CODA. The combination of peak and coda is called the RHYME. Syllable breaks, however, may be problematic when approximants occur at syllable boundaries.

tap

A sound which resembles [t] or [d], being made by a complete closure between the tongue and the alveolar region, but which is very brief and is produced by a sharp upward throw of the tongue blade. As soon as contact is made, the effects of gravity and air pressure cause the tongue to fall again.

Examples for English

The tap sound (for which the phonetic symbol is [ɾ]) is noticeable in Scottish accents as the realization of /r/, and in US English it is often heard as a (voiced) realization of /t/ when it occurs after a stressed vowel and before an unstressed one, e.g.:

getting better (US) /ˈget̬.ɪŋ ˈbet̬.ɚ/ [g̊eɾɪŋb̥eɾɚ]

In British English it used to be quite common to hear a tap for /r/ in careful or emphatic speech (e.g. *very* [veɾɪ]), though this is less often heard now. It is increasingly common to hear the American-style tapped /t/ in England.

Several varieties of tap are possible: they may be voiced or voiceless. For instance, Scottish pre-pausal /r/ is often realized as a voiceless tap, as in *here* [hiɾ̥]. Taps may also be produced with the SOFT PALATE lowered, resulting in a nasalized tap which is sometimes heard in the US English pronunciation of words like *mental* [mẽɾ̃əɫ]. A closely related sound is the FLAP, and the TRILL also has some similar characteristics.

ense

ɛe LAX.

one

n identifiable movement or level of PITCH that is ɛed in a linguistically contrastive way.

xamples for English

English, tone forms the central part of INTONATION, ıd the difference between, for example, a rising and falling tone on a particular word may cause a fferent interpretation of the sentence in which it :curs, e.g.:

it was `cold
(meaning 'it was cold')
it was ˇcold
(meaning 'was it cold?')

ıere are often recognized as being at least five tones English: a fall, a rise, a fall-rise, a rise-fall, and a vel tone.

eanings are frequently ascribed to each tone; the ope of this glossary does not allow us to discuss this rther. In intonation, tone may be spread over many llables, e.g., in:

his ˇcar could have broken down
(in which the pitch movement falls on *car* and rises on *down*)

other languages

some languages (known as 'tone languages') the ıguistic function of tone is to change the meaning a word: in Mandarin Chinese, for example, [ma] id on a high pitch means *mother* while [ma] said on low rising tone means *hemp*. It is usual to identify nes as being a property of individual syllables.

one unit

unit of speech consisting of one or more syllables or et.

xamples for English

tone unit must contain a tonic syllable, that is, a llable on which a pitch movement begins. Only one nic syllable is allowed in an English tone unit. The ne unit may also contain a 'head' (from the first ressed syllable up to the tonic syllable), a 'pre-head' ny unstressed syllables preceding the head), and a ail' (all syllables after the tonic syllable). The tonic llable is underlined in each of the examples which llow:

`yes
tonic
ˈJoe said `yes
head + tonic
and then ˈJoe said `yes
pre-head + head + tonic
and then ˈJoe said `yes to me
pre-head + head + tonic + tail

s each of the non-tonic elements is optional, it is ɔssible to have any combination together with the nic syllable, e.g.:

- ▶ was it ˇyou
  pre-head + tonic
- ▶ it was ˇyesterday
  pre-head + tonic + tail
- ▶ ˇnow I understand
  tonic + tail

In the study of INTONATION it is usual to divide speech into larger units than syllables. If one studies only short sentences said in isolation it may be sufficient to make no subdivision of the utterance, but in longer utterances there must be some points at which the analyst marks a break between the end of one pattern and the beginning of the next. These breaks divide speech into 'tone units', and are called 'tone-unit boundaries', e.g.:

| the ˇlast time I saw her | was `yesterday |

If the study of intonation is part of phonology, these boundaries should be identifiable with reference to their effect on pronunciation rather than to grammatical information about word and clause boundaries; statistically, however, we find that in most cases tone-unit boundaries do fall at obvious syntactic boundaries, and it would be rather odd to divide two tone units in the middle of a phrase. The most obvious factor to look for in trying to establish boundaries is the presence of a pause, and in slow careful speech (e.g. in lectures, sermons, and political speeches) this may be done quite regularly. However, it seems that we detect tone-unit boundaries even when the speaker does not make a pause, if there is an identifiable break or discontinuity in the rhythm or in the intonation pattern.

There is evidence that we use a larger number of shorter tone units in informal conversational speech, and fewer, longer tone units in formal styles.

trill

A speech sound produced by the rapid vibration of one of the vocal organs.

Examples

The parts of the body that are used in speaking (the 'vocal apparatus') include some 'wobbly bits' that can be made to vibrate. When this type of vibration is made as a speech sound, it is called a trill. The possibilities include a BILABIAL trill, where the lips vibrate (used as a mild insult, this is sometimes called 'blowing a raspberry', or, in the US, a 'Bronx cheer'), a tongue-tip trill which is produced in many languages for a sound represented alphabetically as r, and a uvular trill, which is a rather dramatic way of pronouncing a 'uvular r' as found in French, German, and many other European languages, most commonly used in acting and singing.

In British English, the trill most likely to occur is the ALVEOLAR trill, which is (perhaps confusingly) represented by the symbol [r], and is an allophone of the English phoneme /r/. However, it most frequently occurs in restricted contexts, such as singing.

triphthong
A vowel glide within a word that has three distinguishable vowel qualities.

Examples for English
In British English there are five triphthongs, formed by combining the diphthongs /eɪ aɪ ɔɪ aʊ əʊ/ with /ə/. It is not always easy to decide if they form one syllable or two. The following examples are given without syllable divisions:

layer /leɪəʳ/ ⓊⓈ /ˈleɪɚ/
liar /laɪəʳ/ ⓊⓈ /ˈlaɪɚ/
loyal /lɔɪəl/ ⓊⓈ /ˈlɔɪəl/
power /paʊəʳ/ ⓊⓈ /paʊɚ/
mower /məʊəʳ/ ⓊⓈ /ˈmoʊɚ/

Other combinations of three vowel qualities, such as /eɪɒ/ in *play-off* /ˈpleɪɒf/ (ⓊⓈ /eɪɑː/ in /ˈpleɪɑːf/), or /iːəʊ/ in *reopen* /ˌriːˈəʊpən/ (ⓊⓈ /iːoʊ/ in *reopen* /ˌriːˈoʊpən/) do not seem to form such tightly knit units, though from the strictly phonetic point of view they are triphthongs.

Syllable division
For General American it can be assumed that these triphthongs have two syllables, and the above examples can be written with syllable divisions: /ˈleɪ.ɚ/, /ˈlaɪ.ɚ/, /ˈlɔɪ.əl/, /paʊ.ɚ/, /ˈmoʊ.ɚ/. In British English, however, it is not always possible to decide whether a triphthong is monosyllabic or disyllabic. In some northern accents the division into two syllables is so clear that a transcription with /j/ or /w/ would be suitable (e.g. 'fire' /ˈfa.jəʳ/, 'power' /ˈpa.wəʳ/, but in BBC pronunciation some words seem to be monosyllabic, though not all speakers. Thus 'fire' is often a single syllable /faɪəʳ/ with a very weak /ɪ/ in the middle, though some speakers pronounce it as two syllables /ˈfaɪ.əʳ/. Where both possible pronunciations exist, they are both shown in this dictionary.

uvular
A consonant sound made between the back of the tongue and a lump of soft tissue (uvula) which is in the back of the mouth, dangling from the end of the soft palate.

Examples for English
English does not have any examples of uvular sounds as phonemes, but sounds with this place of articulation are widely found in other languages.

In other languages
The voiceless uvular PLOSIVE [q] is found as the phoneme /q/ in many dialects of Arabic. Uvular FRICATIVES [χ ʁ] are found quite commonly: German, Hebrew, Dutch, and Spanish, for example, have voiceless ones, and French, Arabic, and Danish have voiced ones. The uvular NASAL [ɴ] is found in some Inuit languages. The uvula itself is active only when it vibrates in a uvular TRILL, [ʀ].

velar
Velar consonant sounds are produced between the tongue and the SOFT PALATE, or 'velum'.

Examples for English
Velar sounds occurring as English phonemes are /k/, /g/, and /ŋ/. The first two are PLOSIVES, and the last, NASAL. Although /k/ and /g/ can occur syllable initially and finally, /ŋ/ is restricted to syllable-final position only in English, e.g.:

cap /kæp/
gap /gæp/
sack /sæk/
sag /sæg/
sang /sæŋ/

/k/ and /g/ are one of the pairs of consonants said to be distinguished from each other by being FORTIS or LENIS rather than voiced or voiceless.

velarization
A type of secondary articulation in which a constriction in the vocal tract is added to the primary constriction which gives a consonant its place of articulation.

Examples for English
In the case of English DARK L, the /l/ phoneme is articulated with its usual primary constriction in the alveolar region, while the back of the tongue is raised as for an [u] vowel creating a secondary constriction (see DARK L).

In other languages
Arabic has a number of consonant phonemes that are velarized, and are known as 'emphatic' consonants.

vocal folds
An essential part of the larynx, performing a number of important linguistic functions. The term 'vocal cords' is also used.

The vocal folds may be firmly closed to produce what is sometimes called a GLOTTAL STOP, and while they are closed the larynx may be moved up or down to move air out of or into the vocal tract; this is done in the production of 'ejective' and 'implosive' consonants. When brought into light contact with each other the vocal folds tend to vibrate if air is forced through them, producing VOICING, also called 'phonation'. This vibration can be made to vary in many ways, resulting in differences in such things as PITCH, loudness, and voice quality. If a narrow opening is made between the vocal folds, friction noise can result, and this is found in whispering and in the glottal fricative [h]. A more widely open glottis is found in most voiceless consonants.

voice onset time
A measure of the timing of the start of voicing.

All languages distinguish between voiced and voiceless consonants, and PLOSIVES are the most common consonants to be distinguished in this way. However this is not a simple matter of a plosive being either completely voiced or completely voiceless: the timing of the voicing in relation to the consonant articulation is very important. In one particular case this is so noticeable that it has for a long time been given its own name: ASPIRATION, in which the beginning of full voicing does not happen until some time after the release of the plosive (usually voiceless). This delay, or 'lag', has been the subject of much experimental investigation which has led to the development of a scientific measure of voice timing called voice onset time or V.O.T. The onset of voicing in a plosive may lag behind the plosive release, or it may precede ('lead') it, resulting in a fully or partially voiced plosive. Both can be represented on the V.O.T. scale, one case having positive values and the other negative values.

voicing

A term used to refer to the vibration of the VOCAL FOLDS.

A sound made with this vibration is called *voiced*, and one without vibration is called *voiceless*. Most vowels in most languages are voiced, though voiceless vowels are found in some languages. Among consonants, it is very common to find pairs that are distinguished from each other by the presence or absence of voicing, but in English we find that consonants such as /b d g v ð z ʒ/, though frequently described as voiced (in contrast with the corresponding voiceless consonants /p t k f θ s ʃ/) often have little or no voicing. See FORTIS, LENIS, VOICE ONSET TIME. Whispering is speech that is entirely voiceless.

In other languages

Many pairs of consonants distinguished by the voiced/voiceless contrast are found in different languages. Welsh has voiced and voiceless LATERAL consonants, while Burmese has voiced and voiceless NASAL consonants.

vowel

The class of sound which makes the least obstruction to the flow of air. They are almost always found at the centre of a syllable, and it is rare to find any sound other than a vowel which is able to stand alone as a whole syllable.

Examples for English

Here we examine the vowel monophthongs of English.

In phonetic terms, each vowel has a number of properties that distinguish it from other vowels. These include the shape of the lips, which may be rounded (as for an [u] vowel), NEUTRAL (as for [ə]) or spread (as in a smile, or an [i] vowel – photographers traditionally ask their subjects to say *cheese* /tʃiːz/ so that they will seem to be smiling):

Unrounded	Rounded	Ⓤⓢ Unrounded	Rounded
iː	uː	iː	uː
ɪ	u	ɪ	ʊ
e	ɔː	e	ɔː
æ	ɒ	æ	
ʌ		ʌ	
ɑː		ɑː	
ɜː		ɜ˞ː	
ə		ə ɚ	

Secondly, the front, the middle, or the back of the tongue may be raised, giving different vowel qualities: the BBC English /æ/ vowel (*cat*) is a front vowel, while the /ɑː/ of *cart* is a back vowel:

Front	Central	Back	Ⓤⓢ Front	Central	Back
iː	ʌ	uː	iː	ʌ	uː
ɪ	ɜː	ʊ	ɪ	ɜ˞ː	ʊ
e	ə	ɔː	e	ə ɚ	ɔː
æ		ɒ	æ		ɑː
		ɑː			

The tongue (and the lower jaw) may be raised close to the roof of the mouth, or the tongue may be left low in the mouth with the jaw comparatively open. In British phonetics we talk about 'close' and 'open' vowels, whereas American phoneticians more often talk about 'high' and 'low' vowels. The meaning is clear in either case, e.g.:

Close	Mid	Open	Ⓤⓢ High	Mid	Low
iː	e	ʌ	iː	e	ʌ
ɪ	ɜː	ɒ	ɪ	ɜ˞ː	ɑː
uː	ə	ɑː	uː	ə ɚ	æ
ʊ	ɔː	æ	ʊ	ɔː	

Vowels also differ in other ways: they may be 'nasalized' (see NASALIZATION) by being pronounced with the soft palate lowered as for [m], [n], or [ŋ]. Vowels may be voiced, as the great majority are, or voiceless: in English the first vowel in *perhaps* or *potato* is often voiceless. It is claimed that in some languages (including English) there is a distinction to be made between TENSE and LAX vowels, the former being made with greater force than the latter.

In other languages

Nasalization is phonemically contrastive in French, where we find 'minimal pairs' such as *très* /trɛ/ (*very*) and *train* /trɛ̃/ (*train*), where the [~] diacritic indicates nasality. Concerning voiceless vowels: in Portuguese, for example, unstressed vowels in the last syllable of a word are often voiceless. Less usual is the case of stressed voiceless vowels, but these are found in French: close vowels, particularly /i/ but also the close front rounded /y/, become voiceless for some speakers when they are word-final before a pause (for example *oui* [wi̊], *midi* [midi̊], and also *entendu* [ɑ̃tɑ̃dẙ]).

vowel reduction

The process by which an unstressed vowel may change to become like the mid central vowel 'schwa' /ə/. In the words 'photograph', 'photographic', and 'photography', the vowels in the first three syllables alternate between full vowels and /ə/ according to the position of stress, e.g.:

photograph /ˈfəʊ.tə.grɑːf/
photographic /ˌfəʊ.təˈgræf.ɪk/
photography /fəˈtɒg.rə.fi/

Although the word 'man' is pronounced /mæn/, the reduced form can be seen in 'postman' /ˈpəʊst.mən/, 'chairman' /ˈtʃeə.mən/, etc.

Another example of vowel reduction is found in the alternation between /e/ and /ɪ/ in, for example, the first syllables of 'exhibition' /ˌek.sɪˈbɪʃ.ən/ and /ɪgˈzɪb.ɪt/.

weak form

A variant form of a word, used when it is unstressed.

Examples for English

A very important aspect of the dynamics of English pronunciation is that many very common words have not only a 'strong' or 'full' pronunciation (which is used when the word is said in isolation), but also one or more weak forms which are used when the word occurs in certain contexts. Words which have weak forms are, for the most part, function words such as conjunctions (e.g. *and*, *but*), articles (e.g. *a*, *the*), pronouns (e.g. *she*, *he*, *her*), prepositions (e.g. *for*, *to*) and some auxiliary and modal verbs (e.g. *do*, *must*). Generally the strong form of such words is used when the word is being quoted (e.g. the word *and* is given its strong form in the sentence 'We use the word <u>and</u> to join clauses'), when it is being contrasted (e.g. *for* in 'There are arguments for and against'), and when it is at the end of a sentence (e.g. *from* in 'Where did you get it from?'). Often the pronunciation of a weak-form word is so different from its strong form that if it were heard in isolation it would be impossible to recognize it: for example, *and* can become /n̩/ in *us and them*, *fish and chips*, and *of* can become /f/ or /v/ in *of course*. The reason for this is that to someone who knows the language well these words are usually highly predictable in their normal context.